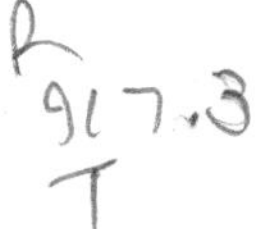

Toll-Free Phone Book USA

A Directory of Toll-Free Telephone Numbers for Businesses and Organizations Nationwide

2017

21st Edition

Containing Toll-Free Numbers, Telephone Numbers, and Mailing Addresses for Leading U.S. Businesses, Organizations, Agencies, and Institutions, Including Companies, Associations, Educational Institutions, Media, Political Organizations, Societies, Travel Providers, and U.S. Government Agencies. Arranged Alphabetically by Name of Organization and in a Classified Section by Type of Business.

Omnigraphics

Omnigraphics
A Part of Relevant Information

Pearline Jaikumar, *Editor*
Karthikeyan Ponnambalam, *Research Manager*

* * *

Keith Jones,
Managing Editor

ISBN 978-0-7808-1504-9

ISSN 1092-0085

Printed in the United States of America

Relevant Information
615 Griswold, Ste. 901, Detroit, MI 48226
Phone Orders: 800-234-1340 • Fax Orders: 800-875-1340
Mail Orders: P.O. Box 8002 • Aston, PA 19014-8002
www.omnigraphics.com

Table of Contents

Abbreviations Used in *Toll-Free Phone Book USA* .... Inside Front Cover

HOW TO USE THIS DIRECTORY 4

CHARTS AND TABLES

Area Codes in Numerical Order 6

Area Codes in State Order 7

Toll-Free Phone Book USA

Alphabetical Section 11

Classified Section 465

INDEX TO CLASSIFIED HEADINGS 947

Sample Entry .... Inside Back Cover

How To Use This Directory

Toll-Free Phone Book USA provides toll-free numbers, along with other key contact information, for some of the largest and most important corporations, organizations, and institutions in the United States. This 21st edition contains **more than 43,000** individual listings, presented alphabetically by company or organization name as well as in a classified subject arrangement according to business or organization type. The directory is intended as a convenient resource for toll-free calling nationwide, with supplemental contact data provided as an aid to follow-up correspondence or additional research.

What's Included in Toll-Free Phone Book USA?

Toll-free phone numbers, addresses, and local telephone numbers are provided for major businesses and industries located throughout the United States, as well as for organizations that serve as important information resources for businesses. Included also are listings for top Canadian companies and organizations.

Types of businesses listed in *Toll-Free Phone Book USA* include:

- manufacturing, retail, and wholesale companies;
- construction, mining, transportation, and utilities industries;
- agricultural interests;
- media and communications;
- and a full range of service industries.

Examples of other types of organizations listed include:

- associations;
- colleges and universities;
- libraries;
- research centers; and
- US Government agencies and offices.

How Do I Find What I'm Looking For?

Toll-Free Phone Book USA is organized in two main sections: an **Alphabetical Section,** in which listings are presented alphabetically according to company or organization name; and a **Classified Section**, where listings are organized under subject headings and subheadings according to business or organization type. All of the 43,000 plus entries are listed in each section.

- **Alphabetizing in *Toll-Free Phone Book USA***

  Alphabetizing throughout *Toll-Free Phone Book USA* is on a word-by-word, rather than letter-by-letter, basis. No distinction is made between upper and lower case letters, and articles, conjunctions, and most prepositions are ignored for sorting purposes. Names that begin with symbols or numerals rather than letters file first. Symbols that may accompany numerals (e.g., a pound sign [#] or dollar sign [$]) are ignored for alphabetical sorting.

  The following example illustrates these alphabetizing rules:

  1 on 1 Computing
  $1 Sunglasses Ltd
  3M Co
  All Weather Vacuuming
  C & S Inc
  Calido Hotels
  Cambridge Fire Insurance
  Damon Corp
  DAS Co
  Data Generation Inc
  La Quinta Motor Inns
  Laacke Co

- **Index to Classified Headings**

  All of the subject headings under which listings are organized in the Classified Section of *Toll-Free Phone*

Book USA are identified in the Index to Classified Headings located at the back of the directory. Page numbers given for each index citation refer to the page on which a particular subject category begins, rather than to a specific company or organization name. "See" and "See also" references are included to help guide users to appropriate subject categories.

Content of Individual Listings

Each listing in *Toll-Free Phone Book USA* provides the official name of the company, organization, or institution; street or other mailing address; city, state, and zip code; tollfree telephone number; and local telephone number (with area code). For publicly traded companies, stock exchange information is provided as well.

Classification Codes

In addition to these items of contact information, each listing in *Toll-Free Phone Book USA* contains a **classification code.** Classification codes are numbers that appear to the left of subject headings in the Classified Section and in a "Class" column to the right of listings in the Alphabetical Section, thus providing a common element that links the two sections. Users can determine a company's business activity by matching a number in a "Class" column to the corresponding subject heading number in the Classified Section.

Some listings in the Classified Section may be organized under a second level of subheadings within the broader category named in a heading. In situations where there are two levels of headings, two levels of classification codes are given as well. For instance, if a heading numbered as 200 is followed by a series of subheadings, the first subheading would be numbered 200-1, the second would be 200-2, and so on. Headings that have been created only to provide a reference to another heading category—i.e., "See" and "See also" references—are ***not*** numbered.

- **Company Names**

  As a general rule, complete official names are given for companies and organizations listed in *Toll-Free Phone Book USA*. In the case of listings for companies that are clearly named after individuals, information usually is presented both by the person's first name and by the last name. For example, LL Bean Inc would also be listed as Bean LL Inc.

  Companies that are well-known by an acronym or initialism — for example, IBM — usually are listed both by acronym and by full name (i.e., "IBM" and "International Business Machines Corp").

- **Addresses**

  Most of the addresses provided in this directory are street addresses, unless mail cannot be accepted at a particular location, in which case a post office box or other mailing address is provided. All listings include the city, state, and zip code as well.

- **Toll-Free Numbers**

  All ten digits, including the area code (800, 855, 866, 877, or 888), are given for each listing's toll-free number. If the toll-free number is intended for a specific use (e.g., customer service, human resources, or technical support) rather than for general calling, an asterisk is printed to the right of the toll-free number and an explanatory note (e.g., *Cust Svc) is printed on the line below the name/address data.

- **Telephone Numbers**

  Local telephone numbers given in *Toll-Free Phone Book USA* are usually for the main switchboard of a company or organization, and area codes are included with all phone numbers listed.

- **Stock Exchange Information**

  Trading symbols and corresponding stock exchanges for publicly traded companies are provided below the company's name and address.

Comments Welcome

Comments from readers concerning this publication, including suggestions for additions and improvements, are welcome. Please send to:

Editor — *Toll-Free Phone Book USA*
Relevant Information Inc.
615 Griswold, Ste. 901
Detroit, MI 48226
editorial@omnigraphics.com

Area Codes in Numerical Order

201 ... New Jersey
202 ... District of Columbia
203 ... Connecticut
204 ... Manitoba
205 ... Alabama
206 ... Washington
207 ... Maine
208 ... Idaho
209 ... California
210 ... Texas
212 ... New York
213 ... California
214 ... Texas
215 ... Pennsylvania
216 ... Ohio
217 ... Illinois
218 ... Minnesota
219 ... Indiana
224 ... Illinois
225 ... Louisiana
226 ... Ontario
228 ... Mississippi
229 ... Georgia
231 ... Michigan
234 ... Ohio
239 ... Florida
240 ... Maryland
242 ... Bahamas
246 ... Barbados
248 ... Michigan
250 ... British Columbia
251 ... Alabama
252 ... North Carolina
253 ... Washington
254 ... Texas
256 ... Alabama
260 ... Indiana
262 ... Wisconsin
264 ... Anguilla
267 ... Pennsylvania
268 ... Antigua and Barbuda
269 ... Michigan
270 ... Kentucky
276 ... Virginia
281 ... Texas
284 ... British Virgin Islands
289 ... Ontario
301 ... Maryland
302 ... Delaware
303 ... Colorado
304 ... West Virginia
305 ... Florida
306 ... Saskatchewan
307 ... Wyoming
308 ... Nebraska
309 ... Illinois
310 ... California
312 ... Illinois
313 ... Michigan
314 ... Missouri
315 ... New York
316 ... Kansas
317 ... Indiana
318 ... Louisiana
319 ... Iowa
320 ... Minnesota
321 ... Florida
323 ... California
325 ... Texas
330 ... Ohio
331 ... Illinois
334 ... Alabama
336 ... North Carolina
337 ... Louisiana
339 ... Massachusetts
340 ... US Virgin Islands
345 ... Cayman Islands
347 ... New York
351 ... Massachusetts
352 ... Florida
360 ... Washington
361 ... Texas
385 ... Utah
386 ... Florida
401 ... Rhode Island
402 ... Nebraska
403 ... Alberta
404 ... Georgia
405 ... Oklahoma
406 ... Montana
407 ... Florida
408 ... California
409 ... Texas
410 ... Maryland
412 ... Pennsylvania
413 ... Massachusetts
414 ... Wisconsin
415 ... California
416 ... Ontario
417 ... Missouri
418 ... Quebec
419 ... Ohio
423 ... Tennessee
424 ... California
425 ... Washington
430 ... Texas
432 ... Texas
434 ... Virginia
435 ... Utah
438 ... Quebec
440 ... Ohio
441 ... Bermuda
442 ... California
443 ... Maryland
450 ... Quebec
458 ... Oregon
469 ... Texas
470 ... Georgia
473 ... Grenada
475 ... Connecticut
478 ... Georgia
479 ... Arkansas
480 ... Arizona
484 ... Pennyslvania
501 ... Arkansas
502 ... Kentucky
503 ... Oregon
504 ... Louisiana
505 ... New Mexico
506 ... New Brunswick
507 ... Minnesota
508 ... Massachusetts
509 ... Washington
510 ... California
512 ... Texas
513 ... Ohio
514 ... Quebec
515 ... Iowa
516 ... New York
517 ... Michigan
518 ... New York
519 ... Ontario
520 ... Arizona
530 ... California
534 ... Wisconsin
540 ... Virginia
541 ... Oregon
551 ... New Jersey
559 ... California
561 ... Florida
562 ... California
563 ... Iowa
567 ... Ohio
570 ... Pennsylvania
571 ... Virginia
573 ... Missouri
574 ... Indiana
575 ... New Mexico
580 ... Oklahoma
581 ... Quebec
585 ... New York
586 ... Michigan
587 ... Alberta
601 ... Mississippi
602 ... Arizona
603 ... New Hampshire
604 ... British Columbia
605 ... South Dakota
606 ... Kentucky
607 ... New York
608 ... Wisconsin
609 ... New Jersey
610 ... Pennsylvania
612 ... Minnesota
613 ... Ontario
614 ... Ohio
615 ... Tennessee
616 ... Michigan
617 ... Massachusetts
618 ... Illinois
619 ... California
620 ... Kansas
623 ... Arizona
626 ... California
630 ... Illinois
631 ... New York
636 ... Missouri
641 ... Iowa
646 ... New York
647 ... Ontario
649 ... Turks and Caicos
650 ... California
651 ... Minnesota
657 ... California
660 ... Missouri
661 ... California
662 ... Mississippi
664 ... Montserrat
671 ... Guam
678 ... Georgia
681 ... West Virginia
682 ... Texas
684 ... American Samoa
689 ... Florida
701 ... North Dakota
702 ... Nevada
703 ... Virginia
704 ... North Carolina
705 ... Ontario
706 ... Georgia
707 ... California
708 ... Illinois
709 ... Newfoundland
712 ... Iowa
713 ... Texas
714 ... California
715 ... Wisconsin
716 ... New York
717 ... Pennsylvania
718 ... New York
719 ... Colorado
720 ... Colorado
724 ... Pennsylvania
727 ... Florida
731 ... Tennessee
732 ... New Jersey
734 ... Michigan
740 ... Ohio
747 ... California
754 ... Florida
757 ... Virginia
758 ... Saint Lucia
760 ... California
762 ... Georgia
763 ... Minnesota
765 ... Indiana
767 ... Dominica
769 ... Mississippi
770 ... Georgia
772 ... Florida
773 ... Illinois
774 ... Massachusetts
775 ... Nevada
778 ... British Columbia
779 ... Illinois
780 ... Alberta
781 ... Massachusetts
784 ... Saint Vincent & the Grenadines
785 ... Kansas
786 ... Florida
787 ... Puerto Rico
800 ... Toll-free; all states
801 ... Utah
802 ... Vermont
803 ... South Carolina
804 ... Virginia
805 ... California
806 ... Texas
807 ... Ontario
808 ... Hawaii
809 ... Dominican Republic
810 ... Michigan
812 ... Indiana
813 ... Florida
814 ... Pennsylvania
815 ... Illinois
816 ... Missouri
817 ... Texas
818 ... California
819 ... Quebec
828 ... North Carolina
829 ... Dominican Republic
830 ... Texas
831 ... California
832 ... Texas
843 ... South Carolina
845 ... New York
847 ... Illinois
848 ... New Jersey
850 ... Florida
855 ... Toll-free; all states
856 ... New Jersey
857 ... Massachusetts
858 ... California
859 ... Kentucky
860 ... Connecticut
862 ... New Jersey
863 ... Florida
864 ... South Carolina
865 ... Tennessee
866 ... Toll-free; all states
867 ... NorthWest Territories
868 ... Trinidad and Tobago
869 ... Saint Kitts and Nevis
870 ... Arkansas
876 ... Jamaica
877 ... Toll-free; all states
878 ... Pennsylvania
880 ... Toll Calls: From Canada & The Caribbean
881 ... Toll Calls: From Canada & The Caribbean
888 ... Toll-free; all states
901 ... Tennessee
902 ... Nova Scotia
903 ... Texas
904 ... Florida
905 ... Ontario
906 ... Michigan
907 ... Alaska
908 ... New Jersey
909 ... California
910 ... North Carolina
912 ... Georgia
913 ... Kansas
914 ... New York
915 ... Texas
916 ... California
917 ... New York
918 ... Oklahoma
919 ... North Carolina
920 ... Wisconsin
925 ... California
928 ... Arizona
931 ... Tennessee
936 ... Texas
937 ... Ohio
939 ... Puerto Rico
940 ... Texas
941 ... Florida
947 ... Michigan
949 ... California
951 ... California
952 ... Minnesota
954 ... Florida
956 ... Texas
959 ... Connecticut
970 ... Colorado
971 ... Oregon
972 ... Texas
973 ... New Jersey
978 ... Massachusetts
979 ... Texas
980 ... North Carolina
985 ... Louisiana
989 ... Michigan

Area Codes in State Order

Alabama
205 Birmingham & Tuscaloosa
251 Southwest
256 North & East Central
334 South

Alaska
907 All locations

American Samoa
684 All locations

Arizona
480 East of Phoenix including Tempe & Scottsdale
520 Southeast
602 Phoenix
623 West of Phoenix including Glendale
928 Most of State except South Central & Southeast areas

Arkansas
479 West Central & Northwest
501 Little Rock & surrounding areas
870 East & South

California
209 Central
213 Los Angeles
310 Long Beach/West
323 Los Angeles
408 West Central
415 San Francisco
424 Long Beach/West
442 Southeast except San Diego Area
510 Oakland
530 North
559 Central
562 Long Beach
619 San Diego & surrounding area (except North)
626 Pasadena/East
650 South of San Francisco
657 Northern Orange County
661 Bakersfield & Northern La County
707 Northwest
714 Northern Orange County
747 Burbank & Glendale Area
760 Southeast except San Diego Area
805 South
818 Burbank & Glendale Area
831 West Central
858 San Diego/North
909 San Bernardino & surrounding area
916 Sacramento & surrounding area
925 East of Oakland
949 Southern Orange County
951 Riverside & surrounding area (except North)

Canada
204 All locations in Manitoba
226 Southern Ontario
250 Outside Vancouver Area including Vancouver Island
289 North of Toronto
306 All locations in Saskatchewan
403 Southern Alberta
416 Toronto
418 Eastern Quebec
438 Montreal Metro Area
450 Outside Montreal Metro Area
506 All locations in New Brunswick
514 Montreal Metro Area
519 Southern Ontario
581 Eastern Quebec
587 All locations in Alberta
604 Vancouver Area
613 Northeast of Toronto
647 Toronto
705 Eastern Ontario
709 All locations in Newfoundland
778 Vancouver Area
780 Central & Northern Alberta
807 Western Ontario
819 Western Quebec
867 All locations in Yukon & Northwest Territories
902 All locations in Nova Scotia & Prince Edward Island
905 North of Toronto

Caribbean, Bahamas & Bermuda
242 Bahamas
246 Barbados
264 Anguilla
268 Antigua & Barbuda
284 British Virgin Islands
340 US Virgin Islands
345 Cayman Islands
441 Bermuda
473 Grenada
649 Turks & Caicos
664 Montserrat
758 Saint Lucia
767 Dominica
784 Saint Vincent & Grenadines
787 Puerto Rico
809 Dominican Republic
829 Dominican Republic
868 Trinidad & Tobago
869 Saint Kitts & Nevis
876 Jamaica
939 Puerto Rico

Colorado
303 Denver
719 South & East
720 Denver
970 West & North

Connecticut
203 Southwest
475 Southwest
860 Except Southwest
959 Except Southwest

Delaware
302 All locations

District of Columbia
202 All locations

Florida
239 Southwest (Lee, Collier & part of Monroe Counties)
305 Southeast
321 Central & East Central
352 Gainesville, Ocala & surrounding areas
386 Northeast except Jacksonville, St. Augustine & surrounding areas
407 Central
561 Palm Beach County
689 Central & East Central
727 Saint Petersburg/Clearwater
754 Fort Lauderdale & surrounding area
772 Martin, St. Lucie, Indian River & part of Brevard Counties
786 Southeast
813 Tampa
850 Northwest
863 South Central
904 Jacksonville, St. Augustine & surrounding areas
941 Southwest (Sarasota, Char Lotte & Manatee Counties)
954 Fort Lauderdale & surrounding area

Georgia
229 Southwest
404 Atlanta
470 Atlanta & surrounding area
478 Central
678 Atlanta Area
706 North except Atlanta Area
762 North except Atlanta Area
770 Atlanta suburbs
912 Southeast

Guam
671 All locations

Hawaii
808 All locations

Idaho
208 All locations

Illinois
217 Central
224 Suburban Chicago
309 West
312 Chicago
331 Northeast
618 South
630 Northeast
708 Northeast
773 Chicago (outside central commercial area)
779 North
815 North
847 Suburban Chicago

Indiana
219 North West
260 Northeast
317 Indianapolis Metro Area
574 North Central
765 Central except Indianapolis Metro Area
812 South

Iowa
319 East Central
515 Central including Des Moines & Ames
563 East
641 South central & East Central
712 West

Kansas
316 Wichita & surrounding area
620 South except Wichita & surrounding area
785 North except Kansas City
913 Kansas City

Kentucky
270 West & Central
502 North including Louisville
606 East
859 North Central

Louisiana
225 East Central
318 North & West
337 West Central & Southwest
504 New Orleans Area
985 Southeast except New Orleans Area

Maine
207 All locations

Maryland
240 West
301 West
410 East
443 East

Massachusetts
339 Outside Metro Boston
351 North
413 West
508 Southeast
617 Boston Metro Area
774 Southeast
781 Outside Metro Boston
857 Boston Metro Area
978 North

Michigan
231 Northwest
248 East (Oakland County)
269 Southwest
313 Detroit & inner suburbs
517 South Central
586 East (Macomb County)
616 West/Southwest
734 West of Detroit
810 East (except Oakland & Macomb Counties)
906 North
947 East (Oakland County)
989 Central

Minnesota
218 North
320 Central except Minneapolis/Saint Paul Metro Area
507 South
612 Minneapolis
651 Saint Paul & East Central
763 Suburbs North & Northwest of Minneapolis
952 Suburbs South & Southwest of Minneapolis

Mississippi
228 Gulfport/Biloxi & surrounding area
601 South except Gulfport/Biloxi & surrounding area
662 North
769 South except Gulfport/Biloxi & surrounding area

Missouri
314 Saint Louis
417 Southwest
573 East except Saint Louis Metro Area
636 East (outside Saint Louis)
660 North except Kansas City & Saint Joseph
816 Kansas City & Saint Joseph

Montana
406 All locations

Nebraska
308 West
402 East

Nevada
702 Las Vegas Area
775 All locations except Las Vegas

New Hampshire
603 All locations

New Jersey
201 Northeast
551 Northeast
609 Southeast
732 East Central
848 East Central
856 Southwest
862 Northwest
908 West Central
973 Northwest

Area Codes in State Order (continued)

New Mexico

505 Northwest
575 Entire State except Northwest

New York

212 New York City
315 North Central
347 New York City
516 Nassau County
518 Northeast
585 West-Central
607 South Central
631 Suffolk County
646 New York City
716 West
718 New York City
845 North & West of Westchester County
914 Westchester County
917 New York City

North Carolina

252 East
336 Greensboro & Winston-Salem areas
704 Southwest
828 West
910 South Central
919 North Central
980 Southwest

North Dakota

701 All locations

Ohio

216 Cleveland Metro Area
234 Northeast except Cleveland
330 Northeast except Cleveland
419 Northwest
440 North Central except Cleveland Metro Area
513 Southwest
567 Northwest
614 Columbus Area
740 East & Central except Columbus Area
937 Southwest except Cincinnati Area

Oklahoma

405 Central
580 South & West
918 Northeast

Oregon

458 Outside Portland Area
503 Portland Area
541 Outside Portland Area
971 Portland Area

Pennsylvania

215 Philadelphia
267 Philadelphia
412 Pittsburgh Metro Area
484 Southeast
570 Northeast
610 Southeast
717 Southeast
724 Outside Pittsburgh Metro Area
814 West
878 Pittsburgh & surrounding area

Rhode Island

401 All locations

South Carolina

803 Central
843 East
864 Northwest

South Dakota

605 All locations

Tennessee

423 Northeast & Southeast
615 North Central
731 West except Shelby, Fayette & Tipton Counties
865 Knoxville & surrounding area
901 Southwest (Shelby, Fayette & Tipton Counties)
931 Nashville & North Central

Texas

210 San Antonio Metro Area
214 Dallas
254 North Central
281 Houston
325 Central
361 Corpus Christi & surrounding Area
409 East of Houston Area
430 Northeast
432 West Central
469 Dallas
512 Austin & surrounding area
682 Fort Worth Metro Area & Arlington
713 Houston
806 Northwest
817 Fort Worth Metro Area & Arlington
830 South Central
832 Houston
903 Northeast
915 West (including El Paso)
936 North of Houston Area
940 North
956 South
972 Dallas
979 West of Houston Area

Toll Calls: From Canada & The Caribbean

880
881

Toll-Free; All States

800
855
866
877
888

Utah

385 Salt Lake City, Ogden & Provo Metro areas
435 All locations except Salt Lake City/Ogden/Provo Metro areas
801 Salt Lake City, Ogden & Provo Metro areas

Vermont

802 All locations

Virginia

276 Southwest
434 South & Central
540 North
571 Northeast
703 Northeast
757 Norfolk & surrounding area
804 East

Washington

206 Seattle Area
253 Tacoma Area
360 West except Seattle, Tacoma & Everett areas
425 East of Seattle between Everett & Kent
509 East

West Virginia

304 All locations
681 All locations

Wisconsin

262 Southeast except Milwaukee
414 Milwaukee
534 North
608 Southwest
715 North
920 Southeast except Milwaukee & surrounding area (South)

Wyoming

307 All locations

Toll-Free Phone Book USA

Alphabetical Section

Listings here are presented in alphabetical order by company or organization name. Alphabetizing is on a word-by-word rather than letter-by-letter basis. For a detailed explanation of the scope and arrangement of listings in this directory, please refer to "How To Use This Directory" at the beginning of this book. An explanation of individual page elements is also provided under the "Sample Entry" on the back inside cover of the book.

SYMBOLS & NUMERALS

Company / Address	City	State	ZIP	Toll-Free	Phone	Class
1 Biotechnology PO Box 758	Oneco	FL	34264	**800-951-4246**	941-355-8451	415
100 Fountain Spa at the Pillar & Post Inn 48 John St PO Box 48	Niagara-on-the-Lake	ON	L0S1J0	**888-669-5566**	905-468-2123	705
102.7Jack FM 711 W 40th St	Baltimore	MD	21211	**888-410-1027**	410-366-7600	642-11
105.9 KGBX 1856 S Glenstone Ave	Springfield	MO	65804	**800-445-1059**	417-890-5555	642-118
106.1 Kiss Fm 645 Elliott Ave W Ste 400	Seattle	WA	98119	**888-343-1061**	206-494-2000	642-111
107.9 The Link 1 Julian Price Pl	Charlotte	NC	28208	**844-258-8477**	704-570-1079	642-27
1&1 Internet Inc 701 Lee Rd Ste 300	Chesterbrook	PA	19087	**877-461-2631**		688
1-800 Postcards Inc 121 Varick St	New York	NY	10013	**800-767-8227**		626
1-800-Flowers.com Inc 1 Old Country Rd Ste 500 *NASDAQ: FLWS*	Carle Place	NY	11514	**800-356-9377**	516-237-6000	294
1-800-Got-Junk 887 Great Northern Way	Vancouver	BC	V5T4T5	**800-468-5865**		311
1-800-Water Damage 1167 Mercer St	Seattle	WA	98109	**800-928-3732**	206-381-3041	311
180s Inc 700 S Caroline St	Baltimore	MD	21231	**877-725-4386**	410-534-6320	154-8
1886 Crescent Hotel & Spa 75 Prospect Ave	Eureka Springs	AR	72632	**877-342-9766**	479-253-9766	379
1888 Mills LLC 1520 Kensington Rd Ste 115	Oak Brook	IL	60523	**800-346-3660**		743
1928 Jewelry Co 3000 W Empire Ave	Burbank	CA	91504	**800-227-1928**	818-841-1928	408
1932 & 1980 Lake Placid Winter Olympic Museum Olympic Ctr 2634 Main St	Lake Placid	NY	12946	**800-462-6236**	518-523-1655	521
1MAGE Software Inc 384 Inverness Pkwy Ste 206	Englewood	CO	80112	**800-844-1468**		180-1
1secureaudit LLC 1600 Tysons Blvd Fl 8	Mc Lean	VA	22102	**800-321-0706**	424-220-8940	196
1st Choice Facilities Services Corp 1941 Whitfield Park Loop	Sarasota	FL	34243	**866-241-0070**		188
1st Colonial Bancorp Inc 1040 Haddon Ave *OTC: FCOB*	Collingswood	NJ	08108	**800-500-1044**	856-858-1100	69
1st Discount Brokerage Inc 8927 Hypoluxo Rd Ste A-5	Lake Worth	FL	33467	**888-642-2811**	561-515-3200	688
1st Mechanical 1295 Bluegrass Lakes Pkwy	Alpharetta	GA	30004	**888-346-0792**	770-346-0792	609
1st Source Bank 100 N Michigan St	South Bend	IN	46601	**800-513-2360**	574-235-2254	69
1stWEST Financial Corp 1536 Cole Blvd Ste 333	Lakewood	CO	80401	**866-670-3443**		465
2 Checkoutcom Inc 1785 O'Brien Rd	Columbus	OH	43228	**877-294-0273**	614-921-2450	458
2 Places At 1 Time Inc 270 Peachtree St 20th Fl	Atlanta	GA	30303	**877-275-2237**		462
2020 Exhibits Inc 10550 S Sam Huston Pkwy W	Houston	TX	77071	**800-856-6659**	713-354-0900	198
21st Century Christian Inc PO Box 40526	Nashville	TN	37204	**800-251-2477**	615-383-3842	94
21st Mortgage Corp 620 Market St Ste 100	Knoxville	TN	37902	**800-955-0021**	865-292-2120	508
220 Marketing 3405 Kenyon St Ste 501	San Diego	CA	92110	**877-220-6584**		197
24 Asset Management Corp 2020 Camino del Rio N Ste 900	San Diego	CA	92108	**855-414-2424**		393
24hourtek LLC 268 Bush St	San Francisco	CA	94104	**855-378-0787**	415-294-4449	177
29 Prime Inc 9701 Jeronimo Rd	Irvine	CA	92618	**888-513-7746**		5
32 Degrees Capital 650 635-8th Ave S W	Calgary	AB	T2P3M3	**866-695-1069**	403-695-1074	527
320 Guest Ranch Inc 205 Buffalo Horn Creek Rd	Gallatin Gateway	MT	59730	**800-243-0320**	406-995-4283	241
33Across Inc 229 W 28th St 12th Fl	New York	NY	10001	**888-297-4094**		387
360 Solutions LLC 2114 Austin Ave	Waco	TX	76701	**800-374-2879**	254-755-7000	196
360 Technologies Inc 15401 Debba Dr	Austin	TX	78734	**888-883-0360**	512-266-7360	462
390th Memorial Museum 6000 E Valencia Rd	Tucson	AZ	85706	**800-639-4992**	520-574-0287	519
3balls.com 319 Manley St Ste 1	West Bridgewater	MA	02379	**888-289-0300**		709
3D Exhibits Inc 2900 Lively Blvd	Elk Grove Village	IL	60007	**800-471-9617**	847-250-9000	234
3D Internet 633 W Fifth St US Bank Twr Fl 28	Los Angeles	CA	90071	**800-442-5299**		5
3D Systems Inc 333 Three D Systems Cir	Rock Hill	SC	29730	**800-793-3669**	803-326-3900	180-8
3Dlabs Inc Ltd 1901 McCarthy Blvd	Milpitas	CA	95035	**800-464-3348**	408-530-4700	624
3M Canada Co 300 Tartan Dr	London	ON	N5V4M9	**888-364-3577**		729
3M Co 3M Ctr Bldg 225-3S-06 *NYSE: MMM*	Saint Paul	MN	55144	**800-364-3577**	651-733-1110	187
3M Digital Signage 600 Ericksen Ave NE Ste 200	Bainbridge Island	WA	98110	**888-464-7239**	206-855-2000	613
3M Electronic Handling & Protection Div 6801 River Pl Blvd	Austin	TX	78726	**800-328-1368**		255
3M ESPE Dental Products Div 3M Ctr Bldg 0275-02-SE-03	Saint Paul	MN	55144	**800-634-2249**	651-575-5144	230
3M Interconnect Solutions Div 6801 River Pl Blvd	Austin	TX	78726	**800-225-5373**	512-984-1800	255
3M Telecommunications Div 6801 River Pl Blvd	Austin	TX	78726	**800-426-8688**		250
3M Touch Systems 501 Griffin Brook Dr	Methuen	MA	01844	**866-407-6666**	978-659-9000	175-2
3M Unitek 2724 Peck Rd	Monrovia	CA	91016	**800-634-5300**		230
3rd Federal Bank 3 Penns Trail	Newtown	PA	18940	**800-822-3321**	215-579-4600	69
411 Local Search Corp Inc 1200 Eglinton Ave E Ste 300 N York	Toronto	ON	M3C1H9	**866-411-4411**	416-849-1432	387
4checks.com 8245 N Union Blvd	Colorado Springs	CO	80920	**800-995-9925**		141
4D Inc 3031 Tisch Way Ste 900	San Jose	CA	95128	**800-785-3303**	408-557-4600	180-1
4Life Research 9850 South 300 West *Sales	Sandy	UT	84070	**888-454-3374***	801-256-3102	366
4over Inc 5900 San Fernando Rd	Glendale	CA	91202	**877-782-2737**		626
4Rivers Equipment 3763 Monarch St	Frederick	CO	80516	**800-490-6162**	303-833-5900	358
4Sight Group LLC 4001 Kennett Pk Ste 134-233	Wilmington	DE	19807	**800-490-2131**		182
4-Star Trailers Inc 10000 NW Tenth St	Oklahoma City	OK	73127	**800-848-3095**	405-324-7827	777
4th Source Inc 2400 Veterans Blvd Ste 480	Kenner	LA	70062	**855-875-4700**		179
5 Alarm Fire & Safety Equipment LLC 350 Austin Cir	Delafield	WI	53018	**800-615-6789**	262-646-5911	691
5.11 Inc 4300 Spyres Way	Modesto	CA	95356	**866-451-1726**	209-527-4511	156-5
5th Business 5100 Orbitor Dr Ste 100	Mississauga	ON	L4W4Z4	**866-875-2220**	905-275-2220	197
600 WREC 2650 Thousand Oaks Blvd Ste 4100	Memphis	TN	38118	**800-474-9732**	901-259-1300	642-74
63 Ranch PO Box 979	Livingston	MT	59047	**888-395-5151**		241
66 Federal Credit Union PO Box 1358	Bartlesville	OK	74005	**800-897-6991**	918-336-7662	221
6s Marketing 1120 Hamilton St	Vancouver	BC	V6B2S2	**888-642-6765**	604-642-6765	197
7 D Ranch 7D Ranch PO Box 100	Cody	WY	82414	**888-587-9885**	307-587-9885	241
70 Park Avenue Hotel 70 Pk Ave at 38th St	New York	NY	10016	**877-707-2752**	212-973-2400	379
7-Eleven Inc 1722 Routh Ste 100	Dallas	TX	75221	**800-255-0711**	703-255-1800	206
7-sigma Inc 2843 26th Ave S	Minneapolis	MN	55406	**888-722-8396**	612-722-5358	607
7strategy LLC 117 N Cooper St	Olathe	KS	66061	**888-231-3062**	913-638-2130	182
7Summits LLC 1110 Old World Third St Ste 500	Milwaukee	WI	53203	**866-705-6372**		197
82 Queen 82 Queen St	Charleston	SC	29401	**800-849-0082**	843-723-7591	669
84 Lumber Co 1019 Rt 519	Eighty Four	PA	15330	**800-664-1984**	724-228-8820	193-3

Name	Address	City	State	ZIP	Toll-Free	Phone	Class
89.1 WBOI	3204 Clairmont Ct; *General	Fort Wayne	IN	46808	**800-471-9264***	260-452-1189	642-46
8x8 Inc	810 W Maude Ave; *NASDAQ: EGHT*	Sunnyvale	CA	94085	**888-898-8733**	408-727-1885	694
911 Restoration Enterprises Inc	7721 Densmore Ave	Van Nuys	CA	91406	**888-243-6653**		665
92.5 FM WVNN	1717 Hwy 72 E	Athens	AL	35611	**866-494-9866**	256-830-8300	643
92.5 WESC-FM	101 N Main St PO Box 100	Greenville	SC	29601	**800-248-0863**	864-242-4660	642-52
930 AM The Answer	9601 McAllister Fwy Ste 1200	San Antonio	TX	78216	**866-308-8867**	210-344-8481	642-104
96.5 FM KISS Country	600 Old Marion Rd NE	Cedar Rapids	IA	52402	**800-258-0096**	319-395-0530	642-23
97.3 Kiss Fm	245 Alfred St	Savannah	GA	31408	**800-543-3548**	912-964-7794	642-109
98.5 KFOX	201 Third St Ste 1200	San Francisco	CA	94103	**877-410-5369**		642-107
99 Cents Only Stores	4000 Union Pacific Ave	Commerce	CA	90023	**888-582-5999**	323-980-8145	789
99.5 The River	1203 Troy-Schenectady Rd Riverhill Ctr	Latham	NY	12110	**800-995-9783**	518-452-4800	643
99.5 WMAG	2-B PAI Pk	Greensboro	NC	27409	**866-415-4158**	336-822-2000	643
@Comm Corp	150 Dow St	Manchester	NH	03101	**800-641-5400**	650-375-8188	180-7

A

Name	Address	City	State	ZIP	Toll-Free	Phone	Class
A & A Express Inc	PO Box 707	Brandon	SD	57005	**800-658-3549**	605-582-2402	778
A & A Global Industries Inc	17 Stenersen Ln	Cockeysville	MD	21030	**800-638-6000**	410-252-1020	482
A & A Maintenance Enterprise Inc	965 Midland Ave	Yonkers	NY	10704	**800-280-0601**	914-969-0009	194
A & B Aluminum & Brass Foundry	11165 Denton Dr	Dallas	TX	75229	**800-743-4995**	972-247-3579	491
A & B Freight Line Inc	4805 Sandy Hollow Rd	Rockford	IL	61125	**800-231-2235**	815-874-4700	315
A & K Railroad Materials Inc	1505 S Redwood Rd; *Sales	Salt Lake City	UT	84104	**800-453-8812***	801-974-5484	768
A & N Trailer Parts	6028 S 118th E Ave	Tulsa	OK	74146	**800-272-1898**	918-461-8404	119
A & S Services Group LLC	310 N Zarfoss Dr	York	PA	17404	**800-227-6782**	717-759-3017	312
A & Z Hayward Co	655 Waterman Ave	East Providence	RI	02914	**800-556-7462**	401-438-0550	408
A 1 Auto Recyclers	7804 S Hwy 79	Rapid City	SD	57701	**800-456-0715**	605-348-8442	53
A 1 Termite & Pest Control Inc	2686 Morganton Blvd Sw	Lenoir	NC	28645	**800-532-7378**	828-758-4312	576
A A Blueprint Company Inc	2757 Gilchrist Rd	Akron	OH	44305	**800-821-3700**	330-794-8803	779
A All Languages Ltd	421 Bloor St E Ste 306	Toronto	ON	M4W3T1	**800-567-8100**	416-975-5000	318
A Better Chance Inc	253 W 35th St 6th Fl	New York	NY	10001	**800-562-7865**	646-346-1310	47-11
A Betterway Rent-a-car Inc	1110 Northchase Pkwy SE	Marietta	GA	30067	**800-527-0700**	770-240-3305	125
A C e International Company Inc	85 Independence Dr	Taunton	MA	02780	**800-223-4685**	508-884-9600	196
A C Nelson Rv World	11818 L St	Omaha	NE	68137	**888-655-2332**	402-333-1122	56
A Colonial Moving & Storage Co	17 Mercer St	Hackensack	NJ	07601	**877-549-7783**	201-343-5777	518
A Contemporary Theatre (ACT)	700 Union St Kreielsheimer Pl	Seattle	WA	98101	**888-584-4849**	206-292-7660	571
A Daigger & Company Inc	620 Lakeview Pkwy	Vernon Hills	IL	60061	**800-621-7193**	847-816-5060	602
A Duchini Inc	2550 McKinley Ave	Erie	PA	16503	**800-937-7317**	814-456-7027	185
A Duie Pyle Inc	650 Westtown Rd	West Chester	PA	19381	**800-523-5020**	610-696-5800	448
A Finkl & Sons Co	2011 N Southport Ave	Chicago	IL	60614	**800-343-2562**	773-975-2510	721
A H Belo Corp	508 Young St PO Box 224866; *NYSE: AHC*	Dallas	TX	75202	**800-230-1074**	214-977-8200	579
A Matter of Fax	105 Harrison Ave	Harrison	NJ	07029	**800-433-3329**	973-482-3700	181
A Partner in Technology	105 Dresden Ave	Gardiner	ME	04345	**877-582-0888**	207-582-0888	182
A Plus Benefits Inc	395 West 600 North	Lindon	UT	84042	**800-748-5102**	801-443-1090	390
A Plus International Inc	5138 Eucalyptus Ave	Chino	CA	91710	**800-762-1123**	909-591-5168	474
A Rifkin Co	1400 Sans Souci Pkwy; *Cust Svc	Wilkes-Barre	PA	18706	**800-458-7300***	570-825-9551	66
A Schulman Inc	3550 W Market St; *NASDAQ: SHLM*	Akron	OH	44333	**800-547-3746**	330-666-3751	604-2
A Stucki Co	2600 Neville Rd	Pittsburgh	PA	15225	**888-266-6630**	412-771-7300	648
A Web That Works	2733 Concession Rd 7	Bowmanville	ON	L1C3K6	**800-579-9253**	905-263-2666	4
A Yankee Line	370 W First St	Boston	MA	02127	**800-942-8890**	617-268-8890	106
A'Gaci LLC	12460 Network Blvd Ste 106	San Antonio	TX	78249	**866-265-3036**		156-6
A'viands LLC	1751 County Rd B W Ste 300	Roseville	MN	55113	**888-872-3788**	651-631-0940	300
A+ School Apparel	401 Knoss Ave	Star City	AR	71667	**800-227-3215**		154-18
A. M. Ortega Construction Inc	10125 Ch Rd	Lakeside	CA	92040	**800-909-1988**	619-390-1988	191-4
A.G. Ferrari Foods	2000 N Loop Rd	Alameda	CA	94502	**877-878-2783**	510-346-2100	345
A.R. Sandri Inc	400 Chapman St	Greenfield	MA	01301	**800-628-1900**	413-772-2121	578
A.R.M. Solutions Inc	PO Box 2929	Camarillo	CA	93011	**888-772-6468**		159
A.T. Still University of Health Sciences	800 W Jefferson St	Kirksville	MO	63501	**866-626-2878**	660-626-2121	161
A/G (Assemblies of God)	1445 N Boonville Ave	Springfield	MO	65802	**800-641-4310**	417-862-2781	47-20
A123 Systems Inc	200 W St	Waltham	MA	02451	**800-224-7654**	617-778-5700	73
AA Importing Co Inc	7700 Hall St; *Cust Svc	Saint Louis	MO	63147	**800-325-0602***	314-383-8800	361
Aa Temps Inc	7002 little river tpke	Annandale	VA	22003	**800-901-8367**	703-642-9050	5
AA Wheel & Truck Supply Inc	717 E 16th Ave	Kansas City	MO	64116	**800-486-4335**	816-221-9556	60
AAA (American Academy of Audiology)	11730 Plz America Dr Ste 300	Reston	VA	20190	**800-222-2336**	703-790-8466	48-8
AAA (American Angus Assn)	3201 Frederick Ave	Saint Joseph	MO	64506	**800-821-5478**	816-383-5100	47-2
AAA (American Arbitration Assn Inc)	1633 Broadway 10th Fl	New York	NY	10019	**800-778-7879**	212-716-5800	40
AAA (American Ambulance Assn)	8400 Wpark Dr Fl 2	McLean	VA	22102	**800-523-4447**	703-610-9018	48-21
AAA Allied Group Inc	15 W Central Pkwy	Cincinnati	OH	45202	**800-543-2345**	513-762-3100	52
AAA Carolinas	6600 AAA Dr	Charlotte	NC	28212	**800-477-4222**	704-569-3600	52
AAA Chicago Motor Club	975 Meridian Lake Dr	Aurora	IL	60504	**866-968-7222**		52
AAA Collections Inc	3500 S First Ave Cir	Sioux Falls	SD	57105	**800-611-7371**	605-339-1333	159
AAA Colorado	4100 E Arkansas Ave	Denver	CO	80222	**866-625-3601**	303-753-8800	52
AAA Cooper Transportation	1751 Kinsey Rd	Dothan	AL	36303	**800-633-7571**	334-793-2284	778
AAA East Penn	1020 W Hamilton St	Allentown	PA	18101	**800-222-4357**		52
AAA Financial Corp	4613 N University Dr	Coral Springs	FL	33065	**800-881-2530**	954-344-2530	508
Aaa Flag & Banner Manufacturing Co	8955 National Blvd	Los Angeles	CA	90034	**800-266-4222**		289
AAA Hawaii	1130 N Nimitz Hwy Ste A-170	Honolulu	HI	96817	**800-736-2886**	808-593-2221	52
AAA Massillon Auto Club	1972 Wales Rd NE	Massillon	OH	44646	**800-222-4357**	330-833-1084	52
AAA Michigan	1 Auto Club Dr	Dearborn	MI	48126	**800-222-6424**		52
AAA Minnesota/Iowa	600 W Travelers Trl	Burnsville	MN	55337	**800-222-1333**	952-707-4500	52
AAA Missouri	12901 N Forty Dr	Saint Louis	MO	63141	**800-222-4357**	314-523-7350	52
AAA MountainWest	2100 11th Ave	Helena	MT	59601	**800-332-6119**	406-447-8100	52
Aaa Moving & Storage Inc	747 E Ship Creek Ave	Anchorage	AK	99501	**866-641-4446**	888-927-3330	778
AAA Nebraska	910 N 96th St	Omaha	NE	68114	**800-222-6327**	402-390-1000	52
AAA North Penn	1035 N Washington Ave	Scranton	PA	18509	**800-222-4357**	570-348-2511	52
AAA Northern New England	68 Marginal Way	Portland	ME	04104	**800-222-4357**	207-780-6800	52
AAA Northway	112 Railroad St	Schenectady	NY	12305	**866-222-7283**	518-374-4696	52
AAA Northwest Ohio	7150 W Central Ave	Toledo	OH	43617	**800-428-0060**	419-843-1200	52
AAA Ohio Auto Club	90 E Wilson Bridge Rd	Worthington	OH	43085	**888-222-6446**	614-431-7901	52
AAA Oklahoma	2121 E 15th St	Tulsa	OK	74104	**800-222-2582**	918-748-1000	52
AAA Southern New England	110 Royal Little Dr	Providence	RI	02904	**800-222-7448**	401-868-2000	52
AAA Southern Pennsylvania	2840 Eastern Blvd	York	PA	17402	**800-222-1469**	717-600-8700	52
AAA Washington-Inland	1745 114th Ave SE	Bellevue	WA	98004	**800-222-4357**	425-646-2058	52
AAA Western & Central New York	100 International Dr	Williamsville	NY	14221	**800-836-2582**	716-633-9860	52
AAA Wisconsin	8401 Excelsior Dr	Madison	WI	53717	**800-236-1300**	608-828-2495	52
AAAAI (American Academy of Allergy Asthma & Immunology)	555 E Wells St Ste 1100	Milwaukee	WI	53202	**800-654-2452**	414-272-6071	48-8
AAAASF (American Assn for Accreditation of Ambulatory Surgery Facilities Inc)	5101 Washington St Ste 2F PO Box 9500	Gurnee	IL	60031	**888-545-5222**	847-775-1985	47-1
AAACCVB (Annapolis & Anne Arundel County Conference & Visitors Bureau)	26 W St	Annapolis	MD	21401	**888-302-2852**	410-280-0445	208
AAAE (American Assn of Airport Executives)	601 Madison St Ste 400	Alexandria	VA	22314	**800-609-7374**	703-824-0500	48-21
AAAOM (American Assn of Acupunture & Oriental Medicine)	PO Box 162340	Sacramento	CA	95816	**866-455-7999**	916-443-4770	47-17
AAB (American Assn of Bioanalysts)	906 Olive St Ste 1200	Saint Louis	MO	63101	**800-457-3332**	314-241-1445	48-8
AABBA (Anchorage Alaska Bed & Breakfast Assn)	PO Box 242623	Anchorage	AK	99524	**888-584-5147**	907-272-5909	376

Name / Address	Toll-Free	Phone	Class
AABBN (Alexandria & Arlington Bed & Breakfast Networks)			
4938 Hampden Ln Ste 164 Bethesda MD 20814	888-549-3415	703-549-3415	376
AABP (American Assn of Bovine Practitioners)			
3320 Skyway Dr Ste 802			
PO Box 3610 Auburn AL 36831	800-269-2227	334-821-0442	47-2
AACAP (American Academy of Child & Adolescent Psychiatry)			
3615 Wisconsin Ave NW Washington DC 20016	800-333-7636	202-966-7300	48-15
AACC (Asset Acceptance Capital Corp)			
28405 Van Dyke Ave Warren MI 48093	800-545-9931	586-939-9600	159
NASDAQ: AACC			
AACC (American Assn for Clinical Chemistry Inc)			
1850 K St NW Ste 625 Washington DC 20006	800-892-1400*	202-857-0717	48-19
*Cust Svc			
AACC (American Assn of Cereal Chemists Inc)			
3340 Pilot Knob Rd Saint Paul MN 55121	800-328-7560	651-454-7250	48-6
AACD (American Academy of Cosmetic Dentistry)			
402 W Wilson St Madison WI 53703	800-543-9220	608-222-8583	48-8
AACE (American Assn of Clinical Endocrinologists)			
245 Riverside Ave Ste 2000 Jacksonville FL 32202	800-435-7352	904-353-7878	48-8
AACE (Association for the Advancement of Computing in Education)			
PO Box 1545 Chesapeake VA 23327	800-352-5397	757-366-5606	48-5
AACE International - Assn for the Advancement of Cost Engineering			
209 Prairie Ave Ste 100 Morgantown WV 26501	800-858-2678	304-296-8444	48-1
AACN (American Assn of Critical-Care Nurses)			
101 Columbia Aliso Viejo CA 92656	800-809-2273	949-362-2000	48-8
AACOM (American Assn of Colleges of Osteopathic Medicine)			
5550 Friendship Blvd			
Ste 310 Chevy Chase MD 20815	800-356-7836	301-968-4100	48-8
Aacom Inc			
201 Stuyvesant Ave Lyndhurst NJ 07071	800-273-3719	201-438-2244	198
AACR (American Assn for Cancer Research)			
615 Chestnut St 17th Fl Philadelphia PA 19106	866-423-3965	215-440-9300	48-8
AACRAO (American Assn of Collegiate Registrars & Admissions Officers)			
1 Dupont Cir NW Ste 520 Washington DC 20036	800-222-4922	202-293-9161	48-5
AAD (American Academy of Dermatology)			
930 E Woodfield Rd Schaumburg IL 60173	800-868-2472	847-330-0230	48-8
AADEP (American Academy of Disability Evaluating Physicians)			
223 W Jackson Blvd Ste 1104 Chicago IL 60606	800-456-6095	312-663-1171	48-8
AADMM (American Assn of Daily Money Managers)			
174 Crestview Dr Bellefonte PA 16823	877-326-5991		48-2
AADP (American Assn of Drugless Practitioners)			
2200 Market St Ste 803 Galveston TX 77550	888-764-2237	409-621-2600	47-17
AAE (American Assn of Endodontists)			
211 E Chicago Ave Ste 1100 Chicago IL 60611	800-872-3636	312-266-7255	48-8
AAEP (American Assn of Equine Practitioners)			
4075 Iron Works Pkwy Lexington KY 40511	800-443-0177	859-233-0147	47-3
AAES (American Assn of Engineering Societies)			
1620 'I' St NW Ste 210 Washington DC 20006	888-400-2237*	202-296-2237	48-19
*Orders			
AAF (American Adv Federation)			
1101 Vermont Ave NW Ste 500 Washington DC 20005	800-999-2231	202-898-0089	48-18
AAF International Corp			
10300 Ormsby Pk Pl Ste 600 Louisville KY 40223	888-223-2003	502-637-0011	18
AAFA (American Apparel & Footwear Assn)			
1601 N Kent St Ste 1200 Arlington VA 22209	800-520-2262	703-524-1864	48-4
AAFA (Asthma & Allergy Foundation of America)			
8201 Corporate Dr Ste 1000 Landover MD 20785	800-727-8462	202-466-7643	47-17
AAFCS (American Assn of Family & Consumer Sciences)			
400 N Columbus St Ste 202 Alexandria VA 22314	800-424-8080	703-706-4600	48-5
AAFD (American Assn of Franchisees & Dealers)			
PO Box 10158 Palm Desert CA 92255	800-733-9858	619-209-3775	48-18
AAFP (American Academy of Family Physicians)			
11400 Tomahawk Creek Pkwy Leawood KS 66211	800-274-2237	913-906-6000	48-8
AAG (Association of American Geographers)			
1710 16th St NW Washington DC 20009	800-696-7353	202-234-1450	48-19
AAGL (American Assn of Gynecological Laparoscopists)			
6757 Katella Ave Cypress CA 90630	800-554-2245	714-503-6200	48-8
AAHA (American Animal Hospital Assn)			
12575 W Bayaud Ave Lakewood CO 80228	800-252-2242	303-986-2800	47-3
AAH-PERD (American Alliance for Health Physical Education Recreation & Dance)			
1900 Assn Dr Reston VA 20191	800-213-7193	703-476-3400	47-22
AAI (American Assn of Immunologists)			
9650 Rockville Pike Bethesda MD 20814	888-503-1050	301-634-7178	48-8
AAI (American Athletic Inc)			
200 American Ave Jefferson IA 50129	800-247-3978	515-386-3125	346
AAIA (Automotive Aftermarket Industry Assn)			
7101 Wisconsin Ave Bethesda MD 20814	800-936-8906	301-654-6664	48-21
AAIDD (American Assn on Intellectual & Developmental Disabilities)			
444 N Capitol St NW Ste 846 Washington DC 20001	800-424-3688	202-387-1968	47-17
AAIHDS (American Assn of Integrated Healthcare Delivery Systems Inc)			
4435 Waterfront Dr Ste 101 Glen Allen VA 23060	888-491-8833	804-747-5823	48-8
AAII (American Assn of Individual Investors)			
625 N Michigan Ave Ste 1900 Chicago IL 60611	800-428-2244	312-280-0170	48-2
AAIS (American Assn of Insurance Services)			
1745 S Naperville Rd Wheaton IL 60189	800-564-2247	630-681-8347	48-9
AAJ (American Assn for Justice)			
777 Sixth St NW Ste 200 Washington DC 20001	800-424-2725	202-965-3500	48-10
AALDEF (Asian American Legal Defense & Education Fund)			
99 Hudson St 12th Fl New York NY 10013	800-966-5946	212-966-5932	47-8
AALU (Association for Advanced Life Underwriting)			
11921 Freedom Dr Ste 1100 Reston VA 20190	888-275-0092	703-641-9400	48-9
AAM (American Assn of Museums)			
1575 Eye St NW Ste 400 Washington DC 20005	866-226-2150	202-289-1818	47-4
AAMA (American Amusement Machine Assn)			
450 E Higgins Rd			
Ste 201 Elk Grove Village IL 60007	866-372-5190	847-290-9088	47-23
AAMA (American Assn of Medical Assistants)			
20 N Wacker Dr Ste 1575 Chicago IL 60606	800-228-2262	312-899-1500	48-8
AAMC (Association of American Medical Colleges)			
2450 N St NW Washington DC 20037	800-273-8255	202-828-0400	48-5
A-American Self Storage Management Co Inc			
11560 Tennessee Ave Los Angeles CA 90064	888-333-6479	310-914-4022	801-3
AAMGA (American Assn of Managing General Agents)			
610 Freedom Business Ctr			
Ste 110 King of Prussia PA 19406	800-467-8725	610-225-1999	48-9
AAMI (Association for the Advancement of Medical Instrumentation)			
4301 N Fairfax Dr Ste 301 Arlington VA 22203	800-332-2264	703-525-4890	48-8
AAMRO (American Assn of Medical Review Officers)			
PO Box 12873 Research Triangle Park NC 27709	800-489-1839	919-489-5407	48-8
AAN (Association of Alternative Newsweeklies)			
115615th St NW Washington DC 20005	866-415-0704	202-289-8484	48-14
AAN (American Academy of Neurology)			
1080 Montreal Ave Saint Paul MN 55116	800-879-1960	651-695-1940	48-8
AANA (Arthroscopy Assn of North America)			
9400 W Higgins Rd Ste 200 Rosemont IL 60018	877-924-0305	847-292-2262	48-8
AANA (American Assn of Nurse Anesthetists)			
222 S Prospect Ave Park Ridge IL 60068	855-526-2262	847-692-7050	48-8
AANAPAC (American Assn of Nurse Anesthetists PAC)			
222 S Prospect Ave Park Ridge IL 60068	855-526-2262	847-692-7050	614
AANEM (American Assn of Neuromuscular & Electrodiagnostic Medicine)			
2621 Superior Dr NW Rochester MN 55901	844-347-3277	507-288-0100	48-8
AANN (American Assn of Neuroscience Nurses)			
4700 W Lk Ave Glenview IL 60025	888-557-2266	847-375-4733	48-8
AANP (American Assn of Naturopathic Physicians)			
818 18th St Ste 250 Washington DC 20006	866-538-2267	202-237-8150	47-17
AANS (American Assn of Neurological Surgeons)			
5550 Meadowbrook Dr Rolling Meadows IL 60008	888-566-2267	847-378-0500	48-8
AAO (American Academy of Optometry)			
6110 Executive Blvd Ste 506 Rockville MD 20852	800-368-6263	301-984-1441	48-8
AAO-HNS (American Academy of Otolaryngology-Head & Neck Surgery)			
1650 Diagonal Rd Alexandria VA 22314	877-722-6467	703-836-4444	48-8
AAOMS (American Assn of Oral & Maxillofacial Surgeons)			
9700 W Bryn Mawr Ave Rosemont IL 60018	800-822-6637	847-678-6200	48-8
AAOP (American Academy of Orthotists & Prosthetists)			
526 King St Ste 201 Alexandria VA 22314	800-669-6024	703-836-0788	48-8
AAOS (American Academy of Orthopaedic Surgeons)			
6300 N River Rd Rosemont IL 60018	800-346-2267	847-823-7186	48-8
AAP (American Academy of Pediatrics)			
141 NW Pt Blvd Elk Grove Village IL 60007	800-433-9016	847-434-4000	48-8
AAP (American Academy of Periodontology)			
737 N Michigan Ave Ste 800 Chicago IL 60611	800-282-4867	312-787-5518	48-8
AAP (Association of American Publishers Inc)			
71 Fifth Ave New York NY 10003	866-271-4968	212-255-0200	48-16
AAPAR (American Assn for Physical Activity & Recreation)			
1900 Assn Dr Reston VA 20191	800-213-7193	703-476-3400	47-23
AAPB (Association for Applied Psychophysiology & Biofeedback)			
10200 W 44th Ave Ste 304 Wheat Ridge CO 80033	800-477-8892	303-422-8436	48-8
AAPCC (American Assn of Poison Control Centers)			
3201 New Mexico Ave Ste 310 Washington DC 20016	800-222-1222		48-8
AAPD (American Academy of Pediatric Dentistry)			
211 E Chicago Ave Ste 1600 Chicago IL 60611	800-974-3084	312-337-2169	48-8
AAPG (American Assn of Petroleum Geologists)			
1444 S Boulder Ave PO Box 979 Tulsa OK 74119	800-364-2274	918-584-2555	47-12
AAPG Explorer Magazine			
1444 S Boulder Ave Tulsa OK 74119	800-364-2274	918-584-2555	456-21
AAPL (American Academy of Psychiatry & the Law)			
1 Regency Dr PO Box 30 Bloomfield CT 06002	800-331-1389	860-242-5450	48-15
AAPL (American Assn of Professional Landmen)			
4100 Fossil Creek Blvd Fort Worth TX 76137	888-566-2275	817-847-7700	47-12
AAPM (American Academy of Pain Management)			
13947 Mono Way Ste A Sonora CA 95370	888-519-9901	209-533-9744	48-8
AAPS (American Assn of Pharmaceutical Scientists)			
2107 Wilson Blvd Ste 700 Arlington VA 22201	877-998-2277	703-243-2800	48-19
AAR (American Academy of Religion)			
825 Houston Mill Rd NE Ste 300 Atlanta GA 30329	800-282-6632	404-727-3049	47-20
AAR (Alliance for Aging Research)			
750 17th St NW Ste 1100 Washington DC 20006	866-840-6283	202-293-2856	47-17
AAR Aircraft Component Services			
747 Zeckendorf Blvd Garden City NY 11530	800-422-2213	516-222-9000	24
AAR Aircraft Turbine Ctr			
1100 N Wood Dale Rd 1 AAR Pl Wood Dale IL 60191	800-422-2213*	630-227-2000	768
*General			
AAR Composites			
14201 Myerlake Cir Clearwater FL 33760	800-422-2213	727-539-8585	22
AAR Corp			
1100 N Wood Dale Rd 1 AAR Pl Wood Dale IL 60191	800-422-2213	630-227-2000	21
NYSE: AIR			
AAR Defense Systems & Logistics			
1100 N Wood Dale Rd 1 AAR Pl Wood Dale IL 60191	877-227-9200	630-227-2000	768
AAR Distribution			
1100 N Wood Dale Rd 1 AAR Pl Wood Dale IL 60191	800-422-2213	630-227-2000	768
AAR Landing Gear Services			
9371 NW 100th St Miami FL 33178	800-422-2213	305-887-4027	24
Aarch Caster & Equipment			
314 Axminister Dr Fenton MO 63026	888-349-0220	636-349-0220	351
AARDA (American Autoimmune Related Disease Assn)			
22100 Gratiot Ave Eastpointe MI 48021	800-598-4668	586-776-3900	47-17
Aaron & Company Inc			
PO Box 8310 Piscataway NJ 08855	800-734-4822	732-752-8200	611
Aaron Diamond AIDS Research Ctr			
455 First Ave 7th Fl New York NY 10016	800-782-2737	212-448-5000	666
AaronEquipment Company Inc			
735 E Green St PO Box 80 Bensenville IL 60106	800-492-2766	630-350-2200	385
AARP 601 E St NW Washington DC 20049	888-687-2277	202-434-2277	47-6
AARP Grandparent Information Ctr			
601 E St NW Washington DC 20049	888-687-2277	202-434-3525	47-6
AARP Health Care Options			
PO Box 1017 Montgomeryville PA 18936	800-523-5800		391-3
AARP Motoring Plan			
601 E St NW Washington DC 20049	888-687-2277	800-555-1121	52
AARP Public Policy Institute			
601 E St NW Washington DC 20049	888-687-2277	202-434-2277	631
AARP the Magazine			
601 E St NW Washington DC 20049	888-687-2277	202-434-3525	456-10
AASA (American Assn of School Administrators)			
801 N Quincy St Ste 700 Arlington VA 22203	800-771-1162	703-528-0700	48-5
AASCU (American Assn of State Colleges & Universities)			
1307 New York Ave NW 5th Fl Washington DC 20005	800-558-3417	202-293-7070	48-5
AASHTO (American Assn of State Highway & Transportation Officials)			
444 N Capitol St NW Ste 249 Washington DC 20001	800-880-4117	202-624-5800	48-7
AASL (American Assn of School Librarians)			
50 E Huron St Chicago IL 60611	800-545-2433	312-280-4386	48-11
Aasys Group			
11301 N US Hwy 301 Ste 106 Thonotosassa FL 33592	800-852-7091	813-246-4757	182
AATBS (Association for Advanced Training in the Behavioral Sciences)			
5126 Ralston St Ventura CA 93003	800-472-1931	805-676-3030	48-5

Name / Address	City	State	ZIP	Toll-Free	Phone	Class
AATG (American Assn of Teachers of German) 112 Haddontowne Ct Ste 104	Cherry Hill	NJ	08034	**800-835-6770**	856-795-5553	48-5
AATH (Association for Applied & Therapeutic Humor) 65 Enterprise	Aliso Viejo	CA	92656	**888-747-2284**	815-708-6587	47-17
AATS (American Assn for Thoracic Surgery) 900 Cummings Ctr Ste 221-U	Beverly	MA	01915	**800-424-5249**	978-927-8330	48-8
AATSP (American Assn of Teachers of Spanish & Portuguese) 900 Ladd Rd	Walled Lake	MI	48390	**877-832-2457**	248-960-2180	48-5
AAU (Amateur Athletic Union of the US) 1910 Hotel Plaza Blvd	Lake Buena Vista	FL	32830	**800-228-4872**	407-934-7200	47-22
AAUP (American Assn of University Professors) 1133 Nineteenth St Ste 200	Washington	DC	20036	**800-424-2973**	202-737-5900	48-5
AAUW (American Assn of University Women) 1111 16th St NW	Washington	DC	20036	**800-326-2289**	202-785-7700	48-5
AAUW Outlook Magazine 1111 16th St NW	Washington	DC	20036	**800-326-2289**	202-785-7700	456-10
Aava Whistler Hotel Ltd 4005 Whistler Way	Whistler	BC	V0N1B4	**800-663-5644**	604-932-2522	378
Aavid Thermalloy LLC 70 Commercial St Ste 200	Concord	NH	03301	**855-322-2843**	603-224-9988	255
AAVSO (American Assn of Variable Star Observers) 49 Bay State Rd	Cambridge	MA	02138	**888-802-7827**	617-354-0484	48-19
AB (AllianceBernstein Holding LP) 1345 Ave of the Americas *NYSE: AB* ■ *Cust Svc	New York	NY	10105	**800-221-5672***	212-486-5800	401
Ab Ovo Inc 2320-H Walsh Ave	Santa Clara	CA	95051	**866-549-0782**	408-567-9090	198
A&B Process Systems Corp 201 S Wisconsin Ave	Stratford	WI	54484	**888-258-2789**	715-687-4332	491
AB Watley Direct Inc 50 Broad St Ste 1614	New York	NY	10004	**877-993-4886**	646-753-9301	688
A&B Wiper Supply Inc 5601 Paschall Ave	Philadelphia	PA	19143	**800-333-7247**	215-482-6100	507
AB Young Cos Inc 15305 Stony Creek Way	Noblesville	IN	46060	**800-886-7001**	317-565-5000	611
ABA (American Bicycle Assn) 1645 W Sunrise Blvd	Gilbert	AZ	85233	**866-650-4867**	480-961-1903	47-22
ABA (American Bankers Assn) 1120 Connecticut Ave NW *Cust Svc	Washington	DC	20036	**800-226-5377***	202-663-5000	48-2
ABA (American Baptist Assn) 4605 N State Line Ave	Texarkana	TX	75503	**800-264-2482**	903-792-2783	47-20
ABA (American Bar Assn) 321 N Clark St	Chicago	IL	60610	**800-285-2221**	312-988-5000	48-10
ABA (American Booksellers Assn) 200 White Plains Rd Ste 600	Tarrytown	NY	10591	**800-637-0037**	914-591-2665	48-18
ABA Commission on Domestic Violence 321 N Clark St 9th Fl	Chicago	IL	60654	**800-799-7233**	312-988-5000	48-10
ABA Marketing Network 1120 Connecticut Ave NW	Washington	DC	20036	**800-226-5377**	202-663-5000	48-2
Abacus Technology Corp 5454 Wisconsin Ave Ste 1100	Chevy Chase	MD	20815	**800-225-2135**	301-907-8500	182
Abalon Precision Mfg Corp 1040 Home St	Bronx	NY	10459	**800-888-2225**	718-589-5682	695
ABAPAC (American Bankers Assn PAC) 1120 Connecticut Ave NW	Washington	DC	20036	**800-226-5377**		614
Abatement Technologies 605 Satellite Blvd Ste 300	Suwanee	GA	30024	**800-634-9091**	678-889-4200	36
Abatix Corp 2400 Skyline Dr Ste 400	Mesquite	TX	75149	**800-426-3983**	214-381-0322	385
Abaxis Inc 3240 Whipple Rd *NASDAQ: ABAX*	Union City	CA	94587	**800-822-2947**	510-675-6500	419
ABB Inc 501 Merritt 7 *Prod Info	Norwalk	CT	06851	**800-626-4999***	203-750-2200	386
ABB SSAC 8242 Loop Rd *Tech Supp	Baldwinsville	NY	13027	**800-377-7722***	315-638-1300	205
Abba Technologies Inc 1501 San Pedro Dr NE	Albuquerque	NM	87110	**888-222-2832**	505-889-3337	196
Abbco Inc 2401 American Ln	Elkgrove Vlg	IL	60007	**866-986-6546**	630-595-7115	454
Abbey Delray 2000 Lowson Blvd	Delray Beach	FL	33445	**888-791-9363**	561-454-2000	670
Abbey Resort & Fontana Spa 269 Fontana Blvd	Fontana	WI	53125	**800-709-1323**	262-275-9000	667
Abbi Home Care Inc 6453 SW Blvd	Benbrook	TX	76132	**877-383-2224**	817-377-0889	363
Abbot & Abbot Box Corp 37-11 Tenth St	Long Island	NY	11101	**888-525-7186**		202
Abbott Ambulance Inc 2500 Abbott Pl	Saint Louis	MO	63143	**888-974-7035**	314-768-1000	30
Abbott Interfast Corp 190 Abbott Dr	Wheeling	IL	60090	**800-877-0789**	847-459-6200	620
Abbott Laboratories Abbott Diagnostics Div 100 Abbott Pk Rd	Abbott Park	IL	60064	**800-387-8378**	847-937-6100	233
Abbott Laboratories Animal Health Div 1401 Sheridan Rd	North Chicago	IL	60064	**888-299-7416**	847-937-6100	581
Abbott Laboratories Pharmaceutical Products Div 100 Research Dr Bioresearch Ctr	Worcester	MA	01605	**866-427-8477**	224-667-6100	582
Abbott Laboratories Ross Products Div 625 Cleveland Ave *PR	Columbus	OH	43215	**800-227-5767***	614-624-7485	297-10
Abbott Northwestern Hospital 800 E 28th St	Minneapolis	MN	55407	**800-582-5175**	612-863-4000	374-3
Abbott Vascular 26531 Ynez Rd	Temecula	CA	92591	**800-227-9902**		110
Abbozzo Gallery 401 Richmond Stt W Ste 128	Toronto	ON	M5V3A8	**866-844-4481**	416-260-2220	41
Abbyland Foods Inc 502 E Linden St PO Box 69	Abbotsford	WI	54405	**800-732-5483**	715-223-6386	472
ABC (America's Blood Centers) 725 15th St NW Ste 700	Washington	DC	20005	**888-872-5663**	202-393-5725	48-8
ABC (Associated Builders & Contractors Inc) 4250 Fairfax Dr	Arlington	VA	22203	**877-889-5627**	703-812-2000	48-3
ABC (Audit Bureau of Circulations) 48 W Seegers Rd	Arlington Heights	IL	60005	**800-759-6397**	224-366-6939	48-18

Name / Address	City	State	ZIP	Toll-Free	Phone	Class
ABC American Bio-clinical 2730 N Main St Ste 101	Los Angeles	CA	90031	**800-262-1688**		418
ABC Appliance Inc 1 Silverdome Industrial Pk	Pontiac	MI	48343	**800-981-3866**	248-335-4222	34
ABC Compounding Company Inc & Acme Wholesale 6970 Jonesboro Rd	Morrow	GA	30260	**800-795-9222**	770-968-9222	150
ABC Global Services 6400 Shafer Ct Ste 310	Rosemont	IL	60018	**800-722-5179**		769
ABC Home Medical Supply Inc 15 E Uwchlan Ave Ste 430	Exton	PA	19341	**866-897-8588**		474
ABC Industrie PO Box 77	Warsaw	IN	46581	**800-426-0921**	574-267-5166	370
ABC Metals Inc 500 W Clinton St	Logansport	IN	46947	**800-238-8470**		491
A-B-C Packaging Machine Corp 811 Live Oak St	Tarpon Springs	FL	34689	**800-237-5975**	727-937-5144	546
ABC Seamless 3001 Fiechtner Dr	Fargo	ND	58103	**800-732-6577**	701-293-5952	193-4
ABC Supply Company Inc 1 ABC Pkwy	Beloit	WI	53511	**800-738-7477**	608-362-7777	193-4
ABC-CLIO Inc 130 Cremona Dr	Goleta	CA	93117	**800-368-6868**	805-968-1911	634-2
Abco Cleaning Products 6800 NW 36th Ave	Miami	FL	33147	**888-694-2226**	305-694-2226	507
Abco Distribution Inc 6282 Proprietors Rd	Worthington	OH	43085	**800-821-9435**		627
Abco Inc 1621 Wall St	Dallas	TX	75215	**800-969-2226**	214-565-1191	85
Abco Laboratories Inc 2450 S Watney Way	Fairfield	CA	94533	**800-678-2226**	707-432-2200	297-37
Abco Office Furniture 4121 Rushton St	Florence	AL	35630	**800-336-0070**	256-767-4100	320-1
ABCT (Association for Behavioral & Cognitive Therapies) 305 Seventh Ave 16th Fl	New York	NY	10001	**800-685-2228**	212-647-1890	48-15
Abel Automatics Inc 165 Aviador St	Camarillo	CA	93010	**866-511-7444**	805-484-8789	708
Abel Reel, The 165 Aviador St	Camarillo	CA	93010	**866-511-7444**	805-484-8789	754
Abell Corp 2500 Sterlington Rd	Monroe	LA	71203	**800-325-7204**		282
Abell-Howe Crane Inc 2143 Internationale Pkwy Ste 400	Woodridge	IL	60517	**800-366-0068**		469
ABELSoft Inc 3310 S Service Rd	Burlington	ON	L7N3M6	**800-267-2235**		462
Aberdeen & Rockfish Railroad Co 101 E Main St	Aberdeen	NC	28315	**800-849-8985**	910-944-2341	646
Aberdeen American News 124 S Second St	Aberdeen	SD	57402	**800-925-4100**	605-225-4100	531-2
Aberdeen Area Chamber of Commerce 516 S Main St	Aberdeen	SD	57401	**800-874-9038**	605-225-2860	138
Aberdeen Convention & Visitors Bureau 10 Railroad Ave SW PO Box 78	Aberdeen	SD	57401	**800-645-3851**	605-225-2414	208
Aberdeen Group Inc 451 D St Ste 710	Boston	MA	02210	**800-577-7891**	617-854-5200	465
Aberdeen LLC 9130 Norwalk Blvd	Santa Fe Springs	CA	90670	**800-500-9526**	562-699-6998	175-1
ABF Freight Systems Inc 3801 Old Greenwood Rd	Fort Smith	AR	72903	**800-610-5544**	479-785-8913	778
ABHES (Accrediting Bureau of Health Education Schools) 7777 Leesburg Pike Ste 314 N	Falls Church	VA	22043	**800-228-9290**	703-917-9503	47-1
ABI (Advanced Biotechnologies Inc) 9108 Guilford Rd	Columbia	MD	21046	**800-426-0764**	410-792-9779	233
ABI (Atkinson-Baker Inc) 500 N Brand Blvd 3rd Fl	Glendale	CA	91203	**800-288-3376**	818-551-7300	444
ABI (American Biltrite Inc Tape Products Div) 105 Whittendale Dr	Moorestown	NJ	08057	**888-224-6325**	856-778-0700	729
Abilene Christian University Brown Library (ACU) 760 Library Ct	Abilene	TX	79699	**800-460-6228**	325-674-2000	434-6
Abilene Convention & Visitors Bureau 201 NW Second St	Abilene	KS	67410	**800-569-5915**	785-263-2231	208
Abilene Machine Inc PO Box 129	Abilene	KS	67410	**800-255-0337**	785-655-9455	276
Abilene Reporter-News 101 Cypress St	Abilene	TX	79601	**866-604-2020**	325-673-4271	531-2
Ability Center of Greater Toledo Inc 5605 Monroe St	Sylvania	OH	43560	**866-885-5733**	419-885-5733	670
ABIM (American Board of Internal Medicine) 510 Walnut St Ste 1700	Philadelphia	PA	19106	**800-441-2246**	215-446-3500	47-1
Abingdon Convention & Visitors Bureau 335 Cummings St	Abingdon	VA	24210	**800-435-3440**	276-676-2282	208
ABIOMED Inc 22 Cherry Hill Dr *NASDAQ: ABMD*	Danvers	MA	01923	**800-422-8666**	978-777-5410	252
Abipa Canada Inc 2000, Blvd Dagenais ouest	Laval	QC	H7L5W2	**877-963-6888**	450-963-6888	21
Abita Brewing Co 21084 Hwy 36	Covington	LA	70433	**800-737-2311**	985-893-3143	101
Abitec Corp Inc PO Box 569 *Sales	Columbus	OH	43215	**800-555-1255***	614-429-6464	297-29
ABL (American Beverage Licensees) 5101 River Rd Ste 108	Bethesda	MD	20816	**800-656-3241**	301-656-1494	48-6
Able 2 Products Company Inc PO Box 543	Cassville	MO	65625	**800-641-4098**	417-847-4791	438
Able Services 868 Folsom St	San Francisco	CA	94107	**800-461-9577**	415-546-6534	258
Able Steel Equipment Co Inc 50-02 23rd St	Long Island	NY	11101	**800-428-8722**	718-361-9240	288
ABMA (American Boiler Manufacturers Assn) 8221 Old Courthouse Rd Ste 207	Vienna	VA	22182	**800-227-1966**	703-356-7172	48-13
ABMC (American Bio Medica Corp) 122 Smith Rd *OTC: ABMC* ■ *General	Kinderhook	NY	12106	**800-227-1243***	518-758-8158	84
ABMP (Associated Bodywork & Massage Professionals) 25188 Genesee Trl Rd Ste 200	Golden	CO	80401	**800-458-2267**	303-674-8478	47-17

Name / Address	City	State	ZIP	Toll-Free	Phone	Class
Above Security Inc 955 Michele-Bohec Blvd Ste 244	Blainville	QC	J7C5J6	**866-430-8166**	450-430-8166	364
Abraham Baldwin Agricultural College 2802 Moore Hwy ABAC 3	Tifton	GA	31793	**800-733-3653**	229-391-5001	161
Abraham Lincoln Presidential Library & Museum 112 N Sixth St	Springfield	IL	62701	**800-610-2094**	217-557-6250	434-2
Abresist Corp PO Box 38	Urbana	IN	46990	**800-348-0717**	260-774-3327	185
Abrisa Technologies 200 S Hallock Dr	Santa Paula	CA	93060	**877-622-7472**		332
ABRY Partners LLC 111 Huntington Ave 29th Fl	Boston	MA	02199	**800-777-3674**	617-859-2959	405
ABS Global Inc 1525 River Rd PO Box 459 *Cust Svc	DeForest	WI	53532	**800-356-5331***	608-846-3721	11-2
Absocold Corp PO Box 1545	Richmond	IN	47375	**800-843-3714**	765-935-7501	609
Absolut Aire Inc 5496 N Riverview Dr	Kalamazoo	MI	49004	**800-804-4000**	269-382-1875	14
Absopure Water Co 8845 General Dr	Plymouth	MI	48170	**800-422-7678**	765-449-4892	803
Abt Foam LLC 259 Murdock Rd	Troutman	NC	28166	**800-438-6057**	704-528-9806	491
ABT Internet Inc 175 E Shore Rd	Great Neck	NY	11023	**800-367-3414**	516-829-5484	398
ABTA (American Brain Tumor Assn) 2720 River Rd	Des Plaines	IL	60018	**800-886-2282**	847-827-9910	47-17
ABWA (American Business Women's Assn) 11050 Roe Ave Ste 200	Overland Park	KS	66211	**800-228-0007**		48-12
ABX Air Inc 145 Hunter Dr	Wilmington	OH	45177	**800-736-3973**	937-382-5591	12
Abx Engineering 880 Hinckley Rd	Burlingame	CA	94010	**800-366-4588**	650-552-2322	258
AC & T Company Inc 11535 Hopewell Rd	Hagerstown	MD	21740	**800-458-3835**	301-582-2700	317
AC Central Reservations Inc 201 Tilton Rd London Sq Mall Ste 17B	Northfield	NJ	08225	**888-227-6667**	609-383-8880	376
Ac Coin & Slot 201 W Decatur Ave	Pleasantville	NJ	08232	**800-284-7568**	609-641-7811	323
AC Corp 301 Creek Ridge Rd	Greensboro	NC	27406	**800-422-7378**	336-273-4472	191-10
AC Doctor LLC 2151 W Hillsboro Blvd Ste 400	Deerfield Beach	FL	33442	**866-264-1479**		789
AC Moore Arts & Crafts Inc 130 AC Moore Dr *NASDAQ: ACMR*	Berlin	NJ	08009	**888-226-6673**		44
AC Nutrition 158 N Main St	Winters	TX	79567	**800-588-3333**	325-754-4546	446
ACA (American Council on Alcoholism) 1000 E Indian School Rd	Phoenix	AZ	85014	**800-527-5344**		47-17
ACA (Auto Club of America Corp) 9411 N Georgia St	Oklahoma City	OK	73120	**800-411-2007**	405-751-4430	52
ACA (American Camp Assn) 5000 State Rd 67 N	Martinsville	IN	46151	**800-428-2267**	765-342-8456	47-23
ACA (American Canoe Assn) 503 Sophia St Ste 100	Fredericksburg	VA	22401	**888-229-3792**	540-907-4460	47-22
ACA (American Chiropractic Assn) 1701 Clarendon Blvd 2nd Fl	Arlington	VA	22209	**800-986-4636**	703-276-8800	48-8
ACA (American Correctional Assn) 206 N Washington St Ste 200	Alexandria	VA	22314	**800-222-5646**	703-224-0000	48-7
ACA (American Counseling Assn) 5999 Stevenson Ave	Alexandria	VA	22304	**800-347-6647**	703-823-9800	48-15
ACA (American AgCredit) PO Box 1120	Santa Rosa	CA	95402	**800-800-4865**	707-545-1200	218
ACA International - Assn of Credit & Collection Professionals 4040 W 70th St PO Box 390106	Minneapolis	MN	55439	**800-844-5654**	952-926-6547	48-2
ACAAI (American College of Allergy Asthma & Immunology) 85 W Algonquin Rd Ste 550	Arlington Heights	IL	60005	**800-466-3649**	847-427-1200	48-8
Acacia Life Insurance Co 7315 Wisconsin Ave	Bethesda	MD	20814	**800-444-1889**	301-280-1000	391-2
Academe Magazine 1133 19th St NW Ste 200	Washington	DC	20036	**800-424-2973**	202-737-5900	456-8
Academic Apparel 20644 Superior St	Chatsworth	CA	91311	**800-626-5000**	818-886-8697	154-13
Academy Bus LLC 111 Paterson Ave	Hoboken	NJ	07030	**800-442-7272**	201-420-7000	758
Academy for Guided Imagery Inc 10780 Santa Monica Blvd Ste 290	Los Angeles	CA	90025	**800-726-2070**		764
Academy Hotel Colorado Springs, The 8110 N Academy Blvd	Colorado Springs	CO	80920	**800-766-8524**	719-598-5770	379
Academy of Art University 79 New Montgomery St	San Francisco	CA	94105	**800-544-2787**	415-274-2200	167
Academy of Court Reporting *Clawson* 1055 W Maple Rd	Clawson	MI	48017	**888-314-7780**		798
Academy of Court Reporting Cleveland 2044 Euclid Ave	Cleveland	OH	44115	**888-314-7780**		798
Academy of Court Reporting Columbus 150 E Gay St	Columbus	OH	43215	**866-865-8067**	614-221-7770	798
Academy of General Dentistry (AGD) 211 E Chicago Ave Ste 900	Chicago	IL	60611	**888-243-3368**	312-440-4300	48-8
Academy of Managed Care Pharmacy (AMCP) 100 N Pitt St Ste 400	Alexandria	VA	22314	**800-827-2627**	703-683-8416	48-8
Academy of Management (AOM) 235 Elm Rd PO Box 3020	Briarcliff Manor	NY	10510	**800-633-4931**	914-923-2607	48-12
Academy of Model Aeronautics (AMA) 5161 E Memorial Dr	Muncie	IN	47302	**800-435-9262**	765-287-1256	47-18
Academy of Osseointegration 85 W Algonquin Rd Ste 550	Arlington Heights	IL	60005	**800-656-7736**	847-439-1919	48-8
Academy of Pharmacy Practice & Management American Pharmacists Assn 1100 15th St NW Ste 400	Washington	DC	20005	**800-237-2742**	202-628-4410	48-8
Academy of Students of Pharmacy American Pharmacists Assn 1100 15th St NW Ste 400	Washington	DC	20005	**800-237-2742**	202-628-4410	48-8
Academy Sports & Outdoors 1800 N Mason Rd	Katy	TX	77449	**888-922-2336**	281-646-5200	709
Acadia Divinity College 38 Highland Ave	Wolfville	NS	B4P2R6	**866-875-8975**	902-585-2210	168-3
Acadia Inn 98 Eden St	Bar Harbor	ME	04609	**800-638-3636**	207-288-3500	379
Acadia University 15 University Ave	Wolfville	NS	B4P2R6	**877-585-1121**	902-542-2201	783
Acadian Ambulance Service Inc 300 Hopkins St	Lafayette	LA	70501	**800-259-3333**		30
Acadiana Symphony Orchestra 412 Travis St	Lafayette	LA	70503	**800-826-4919**	337-232-4277	572-3
ACAOM (Accreditation Commission for Acupuncture & Oriental Medicine) 7501 Greenway Ctr Dr Ste 760	Greenbelt	MD	20770	**800-735-2968**	301-313-0855	47-1
ACA-PAC (American Chiropractic Assn PAC) 1701 Clarendon Blvd	Arlington	VA	22209	**800-986-4636**	703-276-8800	614
Acapulco Hotel & Resort 2505 S Atlantic Ave	Daytona Beach Shores	FL	32118	**855-922-3224**	386-761-2210	379
ACAT (Accreditation Council for Accountancy & Taxation) 1010 N Fairfax St	Alexandria	VA	22314	**888-289-7763**	703-549-2228	47-1
ACB (American Council of the Blind) 1155 15th St NW Ste 1004	Washington	DC	20005	**800-424-8666**	202-467-5081	47-17
ACB (America's Community Bankers) 1120 Connecticut Ave NW	Washington	DC	20036	**800-226-5377**		48-2
ACBL (American Contract Bridge League) 6575 Windchase Blvd *Sales	Horn Lake	MS	38637	**800-264-2743***	662-253-3100	47-18
ACC (Alpena Community College) 665 Johnson St	Alpena	MI	49707	**888-468-6222**	989-356-9021	161
ACC (American College of Cardiology) 2400 N St NW *Cust Svc	Washington	DC	20037	**800-253-4636***	202-375-6000	48-8
ACC (Association of Corporate Counsel) 1025 Connecticut Ave NW Ste 200	Washington	DC	20036	**877-647-3411**	202-293-4103	48-10
ACC (Austin Community College) 5930 Middle Fiskville Rd	Austin	TX	78752	**877-442-3522**	512-223-7000	161
Acc Technical Services Inc 106 Dwight Park Cir	Syracuse	NY	13209	**855-484-4500**	315-484-4500	462
ACCE (American Chamber of Commerce Executives) 4875 Eisenhower Ave Ste 250	Alexandria	VA	22304	**800-394-2223**	703-998-0072	48-12
Accede Mold & Tool Company Inc 1125 Lexington Ave	Rochester	NY	14606	**888-236-2427**	585-254-6490	695
Accel Aviation Accessories LLC 11900 Lacy Ln	Fort Myers	FL	33966	**877-999-2391**		359
Accel Networks LLC 4905 34th StS #227	St. Petersburg	FL	33711	**877-406-8585**		226
Accelerated Genetics E 10890 Penny Ln	Baraboo	WI	53913	**800-451-9275**	608-356-8357	11-2
Accelrys Inc 10188 Telesis Ct Ste 100 *NASDAQ: ACCL*	San Diego	CA	92121	**888-249-2284**	858-799-5000	180-5
Accent 7171 Mercy Rd Ste 200	Omaha	NE	68106	**800-397-7243**	402-397-9920	393
Accent Health 60 E 42nd St Ste 1543	New York	NY	10165	**800-235-4930**		736
Accent Inns Vancouver Airport 10551 St Edwards Dr	Richmond	BC	V6X3L8	**800-663-0298**	604-273-3311	379
Accent Inns Vancouver-Burnaby 3777 Henning Dr	Burnaby	BC	V5C6N5	**800-663-0298**	604-473-5000	379
Access America 2805 N Parham Rd	Richmond	VA	23294	**800-284-8300**		391-7
Access Business Group 7575 Fulton St E *Cust Svc	Ada	MI	49355	**800-253-6500***	616-787-6000	448
Access Communications Co-operative Ltd 2250 Park St	Regina	SK	S4N7K7	**866-211-6334**	306-569-2225	115
Access Energy Co-op 1800 W Washington St	Mount Pleasant	IA	52641	**866-242-4232**	319-385-1577	247
Access Innovations Inc 4725 Indian School Rd NE Ste 100	Albuquerque	NM	87110	**800-926-8328**	505-265-3591	179
Access Intelligence LLC 4 Choke Cherry Rd 2nd Fl	Rockville	MD	20850	**800-777-5006**	301-354-2000	634-9
Access Magazine 444 N Michigan Ave Ste 3400	Chicago	IL	60611	**800-243-2342**	312-440-8900	456-16
Access National Corp 1800 Robert Fulton Dr Ste 310 *NASDAQ: ANCX*	Reston	VA	20191	**800-931-0370**	703-871-2100	360-2
Access Point Inc 1100 Crescent Green	Cary	NC	27518	**877-419-4274**	919-851-4838	733
Access Securities Inc 30 Buxton Farm Rd	Stamford	CT	06905	**800-331-6171**	203-322-3377	688
Access Specialties International LLC 15230 Carrousel Way	Rosemount	MN	55068	**800-332-1013**	651-453-1283	176
Access To Media 432 Front St	Chicopee	MA	01013	**866-612-0034**		7
Access US 712 N Second St Ste 300	Saint Louis	MO	63102	**800-638-6373**	314-655-7700	398
Access Worldwide Inc 5192 Southridge Pkwy Ste 112	Atlanta	GA	30349	**877-564-8581**	404-675-0633	5
AccessPoint LLC 28800 Orchard Lake Rd	Farmington Hills	MI	48334	**866-513-3861**		731
Accident Fund Co 232 S Capitol Ave PO Box 40790 *Mktg	Lansing	MI	48901	**888-276-0327***	517-342-4200	391-4
ACCO Engineered Systems 6265 San Fernando Rd *Cust Svc	Glendale	CA	91201	**800-998-2226***	818-243-1727	191-10
Accompass 1052 Yonge St	Toronto	ON	M4W2L1	**866-969-8588**	416-969-8588	462
Accord Carton 6155 W 115th St	Alsip	IL	60803	**800-648-6780**		44
Accord Creditor Services LLC PO Box 10005	Newnan	GA	30271	**800-373-0760**		393

Name / Address	City	State	ZIP	Toll-Free	Phone	Class
Accord Industries						
4001 Forsyth Rd	Winter Park	FL	32792	**800-876-6989***	407-671-6989	185
*General						
Accordant Company LLC						
365 S St Ste 100	Morristown	NJ	07960	**800-363-1002**	973-887-8900	181
Accounting Principals						
10151 Deerwood Park Blvd						
Ste 400	Jacksonville	FL	32256	**800-981-3849**		719
AccountingWEB Inc						
PO Box 2252	Westerville	OH	43086	**866-688-1678**		529
Accounts Payable Chexs Inc						
1829 Ranchlands Blvd Nw	Calgary	AB	T3G2A7	**888-437-0624**	403-247-8913	2
Accoutrements						
10915 47th Ave W	Mukilteo	WA	98275	**800-886-2221**	425-349-3838	329
ACCP (American College of Chest Physicians)						
3300 Dundee Rd	Northbrook	IL	60062	**800-343-2227**	847-498-1400	48-8
Accram Inc						
2901 W Clarendon Ave	Phoenix	AZ	85017	**800-786-0288**		177
Accreditation Commission for Acupuncture & Oriental Medicine (ACAOM)						
7501 Greenway Ctr Dr Ste 760	Greenbelt	MD	20770	**800-735-2968**	301-313-0855	47-1
Accreditation Council for Accountancy & Taxation (ACAT)						
1010 N Fairfax St	Alexandria	VA	22314	**888-289-7763**	703-549-2228	47-1
Accrediting Bureau of Health Education Schools (ABHES)						
7777 Leesburg Pike						
Ste 314 N	Falls Church	VA	22043	**800-228-9290**	703-917-9503	47-1
Accrediting Council for Independent Colleges & Schools (ACICS)						
750 First St NE Ste 980	Washington	DC	20002	**800-258-3826**	202-336-6780	47-1
Accredo Health Group Inc						
1640 Century Ctr Pkwy	Memphis	TN	38134	**877-222-7336**	901-385-3600	586
ACCT (Association of Community College Trustees)						
1101 17th St NW Ste 300	Washington	DC	20036	**866-895-2228**	202-775-4667	48-5
Accu Therm Inc						
PO Box 249	Monroe City	MO	63456	**888-925-4332**	573-735-1060	386
Accucaps Industries Ltd						
2125 Ambassador Dr	Windsor	ON	N9C3R5	**800-665-7210**	519-969-5404	582
AccuCode Inc						
6886 S Yosemite St Ste 100	Centennial	CO	80112	**866-705-9879**	303-639-6111	179
AccuConference						
6300 Ridglea Pl Ste 318	Ft Worth	TX	76116	**800-977-4607**		318
Accufax PO Box 35563	Tulsa	OK	74153	**800-256-8898**		632
Accugenix Inc						
223 Lake Dr	Newark	DE	19702	**877-274-8371**	302-292-8888	418
Accu-Label Inc						
2021 Research Dr	Fort Wayne	IN	46808	**888-482-5223**	260-482-5223	626
Acculink						
1055 Greenville Blvd Sw	Greenville	NC	27834	**800-948-4110**	252-321-5805	626
Accumedic Computer Systems Inc						
11 Grace Ave Ste 401	Great Neck	NY	11021	**800-765-9300**	516-466-6800	179
Accuplan Benefits Services						
515 East 4500 South						
Ste G200	Salt Lake City	UT	84107	**800-454-2649**	801-266-9900	48-2
Accuracy in Media Inc (AIM)						
4350 EW Hwy Ste 555	Bethesda	MD	20814	**800-787-4567**	202-364-4401	48-14
Accurate Air Engineering Inc						
16207 Carmennita Rd	Cerritos	CA	90703	**800-438-5577**	562-484-6370	385
Accurate Alloys Inc						
5455 Irwindale Ave	Irwindale	CA	91706	**800-842-2222**	626-338-4012	491
Accurate Bushing Company Inc						
443 N Ave	Garwood	NJ	07027	**800-932-0076***	908-789-1121	74
*Sales						
Accurate Chemical & Scientific Corp						
300 Shames Dr	Westbury	NY	11590	**800-645-6264**	516-333-2221	233
Accurate Dial & Nameplate Inc						
329 Mira Loma Ave	Glendale	CA	91204	**800-400-4455**	323-245-9181	413
Accurate Mailings Inc						
215 O'Neill Ave	Belmont	CA	94002	**800-732-3290**	650-508-8885	5
Accurate Perforating Co						
3636 S Kedzie Ave	Chicago	IL	60632	**800-621-0273**	773-254-3232	487
Accurate Surgical & Scientific Instruments Corp						
300 Shames Dr	Westbury	NY	11590	**800-645-3569**	516-333-2570	475
Accuray Inc						
1310 Chesapeake Terr	Sunnyvale	CA	94089	**888-522-3740**	408-716-4600	475
NASDAQ: ARAY						
Accuride Corp						
7140 Office Cir	Evansville	IN	47715	**800-823-8332***	812-962-5000	59
NYSE: ACW ■ *Cust Svc						
Accuristix						
2844 Bristol Cir	Oakville	ON	L6H6G4	**866-356-6830**	905-829-9927	360-2
Accu-Sort Systems Inc						
511 School House Rd	Telford	PA	18969	**800-227-2633**	215-723-0981	175-7
Accusource Inc						
1240 E Ontario Ave Ste 102-140	Corona	CA	92881	**888-649-6272**	951-734-8882	740
Accu-time Systems Inc						
420 Somers Rd	Ellington	CT	06029	**800-355-4648**	860-870-5000	55
Accutron Inc						
1733 Parkside Ln	Phoenix	AZ	85027	**800-531-2221**	623-780-2020	230
Accuvant Inc						
1125 17th St Ste 1700	Denver	CO	80202	**800-574-0896**	303-298-0600	691
AccuWeather Inc						
385 Science Pk Rd	State College	PA	16803	**800-566-6606***	814-235-8650	529
*Sales						
Accuzip						
3216 El Camino Real	Atascadero	CA	93422	**800-233-0555**	805-461-7300	179
ACDI/VOCA						
50 F St NW Ste 1075	Washington	DC	20001	**800-929-8622**	202-638-4661	47-5
ACE (American Council on Exercise)						
4851 Paramount Dr	San Diego	CA	92123	**800-825-3636**	858-576-6500	47-17
ACE (Altamont Commuter Express)						
949 E Ch St	Stockton	CA	95202	**800-411-7245**		467
ACE Cash Express						
1231 Greenway Dr Ste 600	Irving	TX	75038	**800-817-5106**	972-550-5000	140
Ace Doran Hauling & Rigging Co Inc						
1601 Blue Rock St	Cincinnati	OH	45223	**800-829-0929**	513-681-7900	778
Ace Forms of Kansas Inc						
2900 N Rotary Terr	Pittsburg	KS	66762	**800-223-9287**		109
Ace Glass Inc						
1430 NW Blvd PO Box 688	Vineland	NJ	08360	**800-223-4524**	856-692-3333	333
Ace ImageWear						
4120 Truman Rd	Kansas City	MO	64127	**800-366-0564**	816-231-5737	442

Name / Address	City	State	ZIP	Toll-Free	Phone	Class
Ace Mart - Downtown San Antonio						
1220 S St Mary's	San Antonio	TX	78210	**888-898-8079**	210-224-0082	113
Ace Medical Inc						
94-910 Moloalo St	Waipahu	HI	96797	**866-678-3601**	808-678-3600	474
Ace Parking Management Inc						
645 Ash St	San Diego	CA	92101	**855-223-7275***	619-233-6624	561
*General						
Ace Products Management G						
12801 W Silver Spring Rd	Butler	WI	53007	**800-294-9007**	262-754-1289	462
Ace Relocation Systems Inc						
5608 Eastgate Dr	San Diego	CA	92121	**800-453-0964**	858-677-5500	778
ACE Rent A Car						
4529 W 96th St	Indianapolis	IN	46268	**888-261-7368**	317-248-5686	125
Ace Tool Co						
7337 Bryan Dairy Rd	Largo	FL	33777	**800-777-5910**	727-544-4331	60
ACE USA						
436 Walnut St PO Box 1000	Philadelphia	PA	19106	**866-357-3797**	215-640-1000	391-4
Ace Wire & Cable Co Inc						
7201 51st Ave	Woodside	NY	11377	**800-225-2354**	718-458-9200	811
Ace World Wide Moving						
1900 E College Ave	Cudahy	WI	53110	**800-558-3980**	414-764-1000	518
ACEC (Allamakee-Clayton Electric Co-op)						
229 Hwy 51 PO Box 715	Postville	IA	52162	**888-788-1551**	563-864-7611	247
Aceco 4419 Federal Way	Boise	ID	83716	**800-359-7012**	208-343-7712	350
ACEI (Association for Childhood Education International)						
1101 16th St NW Ste 300	Washington	DC	20036	**800-423-3563**	202-372-9986	48-5
ACEP (American College of Emergency Physicians)						
1125 Executive Cir PO Box 619911	Dallas	TX	75261	**800-798-1822**	972-550-0911	48-8
Acer America Corp						
333 W San Carlos St Ste 1500	San Jose	CA	95110	**800-103-3311**	408-533-7700	175-1
ACerS (American Ceramic Society)						
600 N Cleveland Ave # 210	Westerville	OH	43082	**866-721-3322**	614-890-4700	47-4
Ace-Tex Enterprises						
7601 Central St	Detroit	MI	48210	**800-444-3800**	313-834-4000	442
ACF (Association of Consulting Foresters of America)						
312 Montgomery St Ste 208	Alexandria	VA	22314	**888-540-8733**	703-548-0990	47-2
ACF (American Culinary Federation Inc)						
180 Ctr Pl Way	Saint Augustine	FL	32095	**800-624-9458**	904-824-4468	48-6
ACF Components & Fasteners Inc						
31012 Huntwood Ave	Hayward	CA	94544	**800-227-2901***	510-487-2100	248
*Cust Svc						
ACFA (Alameda County Fair Assn)						
4501 Pleasanton Ave	Pleasanton	CA	94566	**800-874-9253**	925-426-7600	639
ACFAS (American College of Foot & Ankle Surgeons)						
8725 W Higgins Rd Ste 555	Chicago	IL	60631	**800-421-2237**	773-693-9300	48-8
ACFC (American Coalition for Fathers & Children)						
1718 M St NW Ste 1187	Washington	DC	20036	**800-978-3237**		47-6
ACFC (Atlantic Coast Bank)						
505 Haines Ave	Waycross	GA	31501	**800-342-2824**	912-283-4711	360-2
NASDAQ: ACFC						
ACFE (Association of Certified Fraud Examiners)						
716 W Ave	Austin	TX	78701	**800-245-3321**	512-478-9000	48-1
ACFEI (American College of Forensic Examiners International)						
2750 E Sunshine St	Springfield	MO	65804	**800-423-9737**	417-881-3818	48-8
ACG (American Cotton Growers Textile Div)						
PO Box 2827	Lubbock	TX	79408	**800-333-8011**	806-763-8011	742-1
ACG (Association for Corporate Growth)						
125 S. Wacker Dr Ste 3100	Chicago	IL	60606	**877-358-2220**	312-957-4260	48-12
ACG Advisory Services Inc						
1640 Huguenot Rd	Midlothian	VA	23113	**800-231-6409**	804-323-1886	527
Acg Inc						
7007 Corporate Way	Dayton	OH	45459	**800-890-5023**	937-433-8122	182
ACH Foam Technologies LLC						
5250 Sherman St	Denver	CO	80216	**800-525-8697**	303-297-3844	600
ACH Food Cos Inc						
7171 Goodlet Farms Pkwy	Cordova	TN	38016	**800-691-1106**	901-381-3000	297-30
ACHE (Association for Continuing Higher Education)						
1700 Asp Ave	Norman	OK	73072	**800-807-2243**		48-5
Achieva Inc						
197 Funder Dr PO Box 729	Mocksville	NC	27028	**800-788-7213**	336-751-7104	320-3
AchieveGlobal Inc						
8875 Hidden River Pkwy Ste 400	Tampa	FL	33637	**800-566-0630**		763
Achievement Incentives & Meetings						
64 River Rd	East Hanover	NJ	07936	**800-454-1424**	973-386-9500	196
Achilles Guard Inc						
4201 Spring Vly Rd Ste 1400	Dallas	TX	75244	**866-525-8680**		182
ACI (Arkansas Correctional Industries)						
6841 W. 13th St	Pine Bluff	AR	71602	**877-635-7213**	870-730-0385	629
ACI (Axis Communications Inc)						
100 Apollo Dr	Chelmsford	MA	01824	**800-444-2947**	978-614-2000	178
ACI (AREBA Casriel Inc)						
500 W 57th St	New York	NY	10019	**800-724-4444**	212-293-3000	724
ACI Worldwide						
4965 Preston Pk Blvd Ste 800	Plano	TX	75093	**877-238-3095**	972-599-5600	180-1
Acic Fine Chemicals Inc						
81 St Claire Blvd	Brantford	ON	N3S7X6	**800-265-6727**	519-751-3668	478
ACICS (Accrediting Council for Independent Colleges & Schools)						
750 First St NE Ste 980	Washington	DC	20002	**800-258-3826**	202-336-6780	47-1
Acier Picard Inc						
3000 Rue De L' Etchemin	Levis	QC	G6W7X6	**888-834-0646**	418-834-8300	491
ACIL (American Council of Independent Laboratories)						
1875 I St NW Ste 500	Washington	DC	20006	**800-368-1131**	202-887-5872	48-19
ACIPCO (American Cast Iron Pipe Co)						
1501 31st Ave N	Birmingham	AL	35207	**800-442-2347**	205-325-7701	308
ACIST Medical Systems Inc						
7905 Fuller Rd	Eden Prairie	MN	55344	**888-667-6648**	952-941-3507	475
Ackermann Public Relations & Marketing						
1111 Northshore Dr Ste N-400	Knoxville	TN	37919	**877-325-9453***	865-584-0550	633
*General						
ACL (Atlantic Container Line)						
50 Cardinal Dr	Westfield	NJ	07090	**800-225-1235**	908-518-5300	314
ACLU (American Civil Liberties Union)						
125 Broad St 18th Fl	New York	NY	10004	**877-867-1025**	212-549-2500	47-8
ACM (Association for Computing Machinery)						
2 Penn Plz Ste 701	New York	NY	10121	**800-342-6626**	212-626-0500	47-9
ACMA Computers Inc						
1565 Reliance Way	Fremont	CA	94539	**800-800-6328***	510-651-8886	175-1
*Sales						

	Toll-Free	Phone	Class
ACMC (Ashtabula County Medical Ctr) 2420 Lake Ave ... Ashtabula OH 44004	866-213-2262	440-997-2262	374-3
ACMC (Affiliated Community Medical Centers) 101 Willmar Ave SW ... Willmar MN 56201	888-225-6580	320-231-5000	374-3
ACMCM (American College of Managed Care Medicine) 4435 Waterfront Dr Ste 101 ... Glen Allen VA 23060	888-491-8833	804-527-1905	48-8
ACME (Association for Couples in Marriage Enrichment) PO Box 21374 ... Winston-Salem NC 27120	800-634-8325	336-724-1526	47-6
Acme Analytical Laboratories Ltd 1020 Cordova St E ... Vancouver BC V6A4A3	800-990-2263	604-253-3158	740
Acme Brick Co 3024 Acme Brick Plaza ... Fort Worth TX 76109	866-430-2263	817-332-4101	149
Acme Cryogenics Inc 2801 Mitchell Ave ... Allentown PA 18103	800-422-2790	610-966-4488	453
Acme Distribution Centers Inc 18101 E Colfax Ave ... Aurora CO 80011	800-444-3614	303-340-2100	801-1
Acme Dynamics Inc 3608 Sydney Rd PO Box 1780 ... Plant City FL 33566	800-622-9355	813-752-3137	638
Acme Electric N85 W12545 Westbrook Crossing ... Menomonee Falls WI 53051	800-334-5214	910-738-1121	386
Acme Engineering & Manufacturing Corp PO Box 978 ... Muskogee OK 74402	800-382-2263	918-682-7791	18
Acme Food Sales Inc 5940 1st Ave S ... Seattle WA 98108	800-777-2263	206-762-5150	298-8
Acme Industrial Co 441 Maple Ave ... Carpentersville IL 60110	800-323-5582	847-428-3911	492
Acme Markets Inc 75 Valley Stream Pkwy ... Malvern PA 19355	877-932-7948	610-889-4000	345
Acme Paper & Supply Company Inc 8229 Sandy Ct PO Box 422 ... Savage MD 20763	800-462-5812	410-792-2333	547
Acme Spirally Wound Paper Products Inc 4810 W 139th St PO Box 35320 ... Cleveland OH 44135	800-274-2797	216-267-2950	124
Acme Truck Line Inc 1180 Destrehan Ave ... Harvey LA 70058	800-825-6246	504-368-2510	778
Acme United Corp 60 Round Hill Rd ... Fairfield CT 06824 *NYSE: ACU*	800-835-2263	203-254-6060	475
Acme Wire Products Co 7 Broadway Ave ... Mystic CT 06355	800-723-7015	860-572-0511	448
ACOFP (American College of Osteopathic Family Physicians) 330 E Algonquin Rd Ste 1 ... Arlington Heights IL 60005	800-323-0794	847-952-5100	48-8
ACOM Solutions Inc 2850 E 29th St ... Long Beach CA 90806	800-347-3638	562-424-7899	180-1
Acor Orthopaedic Inc 18530 S Miles Pkwy ... Cleveland OH 44128	800-237-2267	216-662-4500	302
ACORD (Association for Co-op Operations Research & Development) 1 Blue Hill Plz PO Box 1529 ... Pearl River NY 10965	800-444-3341	845-620-1700	48-9
Acorn Deck House Co 852 Main St ... Acton MA 01720	800-727-3325	978-263-6800	105
Acorn Engineering Co 15125 Proctor Ave PO Box 3527 ... City of Industry CA 91744	800-488-8999	626-336-4561	608
Acorn Gencon Plastics Inc 15125 Proctor Ave ... City of Industry CA 91746	800-782-7706	626-968-6681	386
Acorn Manufacturing Company Inc 457 School St ... Mansfield MA 02048	800-835-0121		350
Acorn Wire & Iron Works Inc 2035 S Racine Ave ... Chicago IL 60608	800-552-2676	773-585-0600	281
Acousti Engineering Co of Florida Inc 4656 34th St SW ... Orlando FL 32811	800-434-3467	407-425-3467	191-9
Acoustic Neuroma Assn (ANA) 600 Peachtree Pkwy Ste 108 ... Cumming GA 30041	877-200-8211	770-205-8211	47-17
ACP (American College of Physicians) 190 N Independence Mall W ... Philadelphia PA 19106	800-523-1546	215-351-2400	48-8
ACPA (American Chronic Pain Assn) PO Box 850 ... Rocklin CA 95677	800-533-3231	916-632-0922	47-17
ACPE (American College of Physician Executives) 400 N Ashley Dr Ste 400 ... Tampa FL 33602	800-562-8088	813-287-2000	48-8
ACPHS (Albany College of Pharmacy) 106 New Scotland Ave ... Albany NY 12208 *General	888-203-8010*	518-694-7221	167
Acqua Hotel 555 Redwood Hwy ... Mill Valley CA 94941	888-662-9555	415-380-0400	379
Acqualina 17875 Collins Ave ... Sunny Isles Beach FL 33160	877-312-9742	305-918-8000	379
Acquizition.biz Inc 1100 Rene-Levesque Blvd W 24th Fl ... Montreal QC H3B4X9	866-499-0334	514-499-0334	387
ACR (American College of Radiology) 1892 Preston White Dr ... Reston VA 20191	800-227-5463	703-648-8900	48-8
ACR (Association for Conflict Resolution) 12100 Sunset Hills Rd Ste 130 ... Reston VA 20190	800-880-7303	703-234-4141	48-10
ACR Electronics Inc 5757 Anglers Ave ... Fort Lauderdale FL 33312	800-432-0227	954-981-3333	676
Acranet 521 W Maxwell Ave Ste 209 ... Spokane WA 99201	800-304-1249		182
ACRL (Association of College & Research Libraries) 50 E Huron St ... Chicago IL 60611	800-545-2433	312-280-2519	48-11
Acro Labels Inc 2530 Wyandotte Rd ... Willow Grove PA 19090	800-355-2235	215-657-5366	413
Acro Media Inc 2303 Leckie Rd Ste 103 ... Kelowna BC V1X6Y5	877-763-8844	250-763-8884	807
Acromag Inc 30765 S Wixom Rd ... Wixom MI 48393	877-295-7092	248-624-1541	624
Acroprint Time Recorder Co 5640 Departure Dr ... Raleigh NC 27616	800-334-7190	919-872-5800	533
ACRP (Association of Clinical Research Professionals) 500 Montgomery St Ste 800 ... Alexandria VA 22314	888-508-5731	703-254-8100	48-8
ACRT Inc 1333 Home Ave ... Akron OH 44310	800-622-2562	330-945-7500	195
Acrylic Design Assoc 6050 Nathan Ln N ... Plymouth MN 55442	800-445-2167	763-559-8395	235
Acrylic Plastic Products Company Inc 4815 Hwy 80 W ... Jackson MS 39209	800-331-8819	601-922-2651	607
Acryline USA Inc 2015 Becancour ... Lyster QC G0S1V0	800-567-0920		350
ACS (American Cancer Society) 250 William St NW ... Atlanta GA 30303	800-227-2345	404-320-3333	47-17
ACS (American Chemical Society) 1155 16th St NW ... Washington DC 20036	800-227-5558	202-872-4600	48-19
ACS (American College of Surgeons) 633 N St Clair St ... Chicago IL 60611	800-621-4111	312-202-5000	48-8
ACS Group 1100 E Woodfield Rd Ste 588 ... Schaumburg IL 60173	800-783-7835	847-273-7700	14
ACS Industries Inc 1 New England Way ... Lincoln RI 02865	866-783-4838	401-769-4700	686
ACSA (Association of Collegiate Schools of Architecture) 1735 New York Ave NW 3rd Fl ... Washington DC 20006	877-426-6323	202-785-2324	48-5
ACSH (American Council on Science & Health) 110 E 42nd St Ste 1300 ... New York NY 10017	866-905-2694	212-362-7044	48-19
ACSI (Association of Christian Schools International) 731 Chapel Hills Dr ... Colorado Springs CO 80920 *Cust Svc	800-367-0798*	719-528-6906	48-5
ACT (A Contemporary Theatre) 700 Union St Kreielsheimer Pl ... Seattle WA 98101	888-584-4849	206-292-7660	571
ACT Conferencing 1526 Cole Blvd Bldg 3 Ste 300 ... Lakewood CO 80401	800-433-2900	303-233-3500	733
Act2 Retirement Consulting LLC 5120 Watchwood Path ... Columbia MD 21044	866-992-9256		462
ACTE (Association for Career & Technical Education) 1410 King St ... Alexandria VA 22314	800-826-9972	703-683-3111	48-5
Actel Corp 2061 Stierlin Ct ... Mountain View CA 94043	800-262-1060	650-318-4200	694
ACTFL (American Council on the Teaching of Foreign Languages) 1001 N Fairfax St Ste 200 ... Alexandria VA 22314	844-685-4373	703-894-2900	48-5
Actify LLC 7635 Interactive Way Ste 200 ... Indianapolis IN 46278	800-467-0830		248
Action Against Hunger 247 W 37th St 10th Fl ... New York NY 10018	877-777-1420	212-967-7800	47-5
Action Aircraft Lp 10570 Olympic Dr ... Dallas TX 75220	800-909-7616	214-351-1284	21
Action Bolt & Tool Co (WURTH) 2051 E Blue Heron Blvd ... Riviera Beach FL 33404	800-423-0700	561-845-8800	351
Action Capital Corp 230 Peachtree St Ste 910 ... Atlanta GA 30343	800-525-7767	404-524-3181	274
Action Co 1425 N Tennessee St ... McKinney TX 75069 *Sales	800-937-3700*	972-542-8700	431
Action Mailing Corp 3165 W Heartland Dr ... Liberty MO 64068	866-990-9001	816-415-9000	5
Action Security Inc 243 E Fifth Ave ... Anchorage AK 99501	800-478-3785	907-279-7050	691
Action Sports Systems Inc 617 Carbon City Rd PO Box 1442 ... Morganton NC 28655	800-631-1091	828-584-8000	154-18
Action Stainless & Alloys Inc 1505 Halsey Way ... Carrollton TX 75007	800-749-2523	972-466-1500	491
ActionCOACH 5781 S Ft Apache Rd ... Las Vegas NV 89148	888-483-2828	702-795-3188	763
ActionTec Electronics Inc 760 N Mary Ave ... Sunnyvale CA 94085 *Tech Supp	888-436-0657*	408-752-7700	175-3
Activation Laboratories Ltd 1336 Sandhill Dr ... Ancaster ON L9G4V5	888-228-5227	905-648-9611	740
Active Aero Group 2068 E St ... Belleville MI 48111 *Cust Svc	800-872-5387*	734-547-7200	13
Active Captive Management 16485 Laguna Canyon Rd Ste 200 ... Irvine CA 92618	800-921-0155	949-727-0155	2
Active Day/Senior Care Inc 400 Redland Ct Ste 114 ... Owings Mills MD 21117	877-435-3372	866-724-9599	450
Active Network 10182 Telesis Ct Ste 100 ... San Diego CA 92121	888-543-7223	858-964-3800	7
Active Organics Inc 1097 Yates St ... Lewisville TX 75057	800-541-1478	972-221-7500	298-8
Active Parenting Publishers 1955 Vaughn Rd Ste 108 ... Kennesaw GA 30144	800-825-0060	770-429-0565	512
Active Power Inc 2128 W Breaker Ln ... Austin TX 78758 *NASDAQ: ACPW*	800-625-1731	512-836-6464	765
Active Professionals Inc 9647b Folsom Blvd ... Sacramento CA 95827	888-838-5086		731
Activeforevercom 10799 N 90th St ... Scottsdale AZ 85260	800-377-8033	480-459-3202	322
activePDF Inc 27405 Puerta Real Ste 100 ... Mission Viejo CA 92691	866-468-6733	949-582-9002	180-12
Acton Institute for the Study of Religion & Liberty 161 Ottawa Ave NW Ste 301 ... Grand Rapids MI 49503	800-345-2286	616-454-3080	631
Actors Theatre of Louisville 316 W Main St ... Louisville KY 40202	800-428-5849	502-584-1205	746
Actsoft Inc 8910 N Dale Mabry Hwy ... Tampa FL 33614	888-732-6638	813-936-2331	179
Actuarial Systems Corp 15840 Monte St Ste 108 ... Sylmar CA 91342	800-950-2082		390
Actuate Corp 2207 Bridgepointe Pkwy Ste 500 ... San Mateo CA 94404 *NASDAQ: OTEX* ■ *Sales	800-914-2259*	650-645-3000	180-1
ACU (Abilene Christian University Brown Library) 760 Library Ct ... Abilene TX 79699	800-460-6228	325-674-2000	434-6
ACU Serve Corp 2020 Front St Ste 205 ... Cuyahoga Fls OH 44221	800-887-8965	330-923-5258	2
Acumen Capital Finance Partners Ltd 404 Sixth Ave S W Ste 700 ... Calgary AB T2P0R9	888-422-8636	403-571-0300	401
Acumenex Com 2201 Brant St ... Burlington ON L7P3N8	877-788-5028		396
Acushnet Co 333 Bridge St ... Fairhaven MA 02719	800-225-8500	508-979-2000	708
AcuSport Corp 1 Hunter Pl ... Bellefontaine OH 43311	800-543-3150	937-593-7010	708
Acxiom Corp 601 E Third St ... Little Rock AR 72201 *NASDAQ: ACXM*	888-337-7699	501-342-7799	5

Alphabetical Section

Company / Address	City	State	Zip	Toll-Free	Phone	Class
Ad Art Co						
3260 E 26th St	Los Angeles	CA	90058	**800-266-7522**	323-981-8941	699
ADA (American Diabetes Assn)						
1701 N Beauregard St	Alexandria	VA	22311	**800-232-3472**	703-549-1500	47-17
ADA (Americans for Democratic Action)						
1625 K St NW Ste 210	Washington	DC	20006	**855-712-8441**	202-785-5980	47-7
ADA Technologies Inc						
8100 Shaffer Pkwy Ste 130	Littleton	CO	80127	**800-232-0296**	303-792-5615	666
Ada/Cascade/Forest Hills Advance						
PO Box 9	Jenison	MI	49429	**800-439-0960**	616-669-2700	531-4
ADAA (Anxiety Disorders Assn of America)						
8730 Georgia Ave Ste 600	Silver Spring	MD	20910	**800-922-8947**	240-485-1001	47-17
ADAA (American Dental Assistants Assn)						
140 N Bloomingdale Rd	Bloomingdale	IL	60108	**877-874-3785**	312-541-1550	48-8
ADA-ES Inc						
9135 S Ridgeline Blvd Ste 200	Highlands Ranch	CO	80129	**888-822-8617**	303-734-1727	144
NASDAQ: ADES						
Adair Printing Technologies						
7850 Second St	Dexter	MI	48130	**800-637-5025**	734-426-2822	625
Adam Broderick Salon & Spa						
89 Danbury Rd	Ridgefield	CT	06877	**800-438-3834**	203-431-3994	76
Adams Air & Hydraulics Inc						
7209 E Adamo Dr	Tampa	FL	33619	**800-282-4165**	813-626-4128	358
Adams Construction Co						
523 Rutherford Ave NE	Roanoke	VA	24016	**800-237-6060**	540-982-2366	190-4
Adams County Travel & Visitors Bureau						
509 E Main St	West Union	OH	45693	**877-232-6764**	937-544-5639	138
Adams County Winery						
251 Peach Tree Rd	Orrtanna	PA	17353	**877-601-7936**	717-334-4631	49-6
Adams Electric Co-op						
700 Eastwood St PO Box 247	Camp Point	IL	62320	**800-232-4797**	217-593-7701	247
Adams Electric Co-op Inc						
1338 Biglerville Rd PO Box 1055	Gettysburg	PA	17325	**888-232-6732**	717-334-2171	247
Adams Elevator Equipment Co						
6310 W Howard St	Niles	IL	60714	**800-929-9247**	847-581-2900	676
Adams Express Co						
500 E Pratt St Ste 1300	Baltimore	MD	21202	**800-638-2479**	410-752-5900	405
NYSE: ADX						
Adams Keegan Inc						
6055 Primacy Pkwy Ste 300	Memphis	TN	38119	**800-621-1308**	901-683-5353	630
Adams Oceanfront Resort						
4 Read St	Dewey Beach	DE	19971	**800-448-8080**	302-227-3030	379
Adams Products Co						
5701 McCrimmon Pkwy PO Box 189	Morrisville	NC	27560	**800-672-3131**	919-467-2218	185
Adams Remco Inc						
PO Box 3968	South Bend	IN	46619	**800-627-2113**	574-288-2113	111
Adams Rite Manufacturing Co						
10027 S 51st St Ste 102	Phoenix	AZ	85044	**800-872-3267**	909-632-2300	350
Adams Rural Electric Co-op Inc						
4800 SR 125	West Union	OH	45693	**800-283-1846**	937-544-2305	247
Adams State College						
208 Edgemont Blvd	Alamosa	CO	81102	**800-824-6494**	719-587-7712	167
Adams USA Inc						
610 S Jefferson Ave	Cookeville	TN	38501	**800-426-9784**		708
Adams-Burch Inc						
1901 Stanford Ct	Landover	MD	20785	**800-347-8093***	301-276-2000	301
*Cust Svc						
Adams-Columbia Electric Co-op						
401 E Lake St	Friendship	WI	53934	**800-831-8629**	608-339-3346	247
Adamson Global Technology Corp						
13101 N Eron Church Rd	Chester	VA	23836	**800-525-7703**		90
Adaptive Micro Systems Inc						
7840 N 86th St	Milwaukee	WI	53224	**800-558-4187**	414-357-2020	180-7
ADB (American Drill Bushings Co)						
5740 Hunt Rd	Valdosta	GA	31606	**800-423-4425**	229-253-8928	492
AdCare Hospital of Worcester						
107 Lincoln St	Worcester	MA	01605	**800-252-6465**	508-799-9000	724
Adco Inc PO Box 815382	Dallas	TX	75381	**800-486-4583**	972-484-6177	42
Adco Manufacturing Inc						
2170 Academy Ave	Sanger	CA	93657	**888-608-5946**	559-875-5563	385
ADDCO LLC						
240 Arlington Ave E	Saint Paul	MN	55117	**800-616-4408**	651-488-8600	698
Adden Furniture Inc						
710 Chelmsford St	Lowell	MA	01851	**800-625-3876**	978-454-7848	320-3
Addison Biological Laboratory Inc						
507 N Cleveland Ave	Fayette	MO	65248	**800-331-2530**	660-248-2215	581
Addison House Interiors Inc						
5201 Nw 77th Ave Ste 400	Doral	FL	33166	**800-426-2988**	305-640-2400	322
Addison Insurance Co						
118 Second Ave SE PO Box 73909	Cedar Rapids	IA	52401	**800-332-7977**	319-399-5700	391-4
Adducent Technology Inc						
230 Parque Margarita	Rohnert Park	CA	94928	**800-648-0656**	707-478-8136	528
Addus HealthCare Inc						
2401 S Plum Grove Rd	Palatine	IL	60067	**888-233-8746**	847-303-5300	353
NASDAQ: ADUS						
ADEA (American Dental Education Assn)						
1400 K St NW Ste 1100	Washington	DC	20005	**800-353-2237**	202-289-7201	48-5
A-dec Inc						
2601 Crestview Dr	Newberg	OR	97132	**800-547-1883***	503-538-7478	230
*Cust Svc						
Adec Industries						
2700 Industrial Pkwy	Elkhart	IN	46516	**866-730-3111**	574-295-3167	87
Adecco Inc						
175 Broad Hollow Rd	Melville	NY	11747	**800-978-3729***	631-844-7650	719
*General						
Adell Plastics Inc						
4530 Annapolis Rd	Baltimore	MD	21227	**800-638-5218**	410-789-7780	742-2
Adelman Travel Group						
6980 N Port Washington Rd	Milwaukee	WI	53217	**800-248-5562***	414-352-7600	769
*Cust Svc						
Adelphi University						
PO Box 701	Garden City	NY	11530	**800-233-5744**	516-877-3050	167
Manhattan Ctr						
75 Varick St 2nd Fl	New York	NY	10013	**800-233-5744**	212-965-8340	167
Adelphia Steel Equipment Co						
7372 State Rd	Philadelphia	PA	19136	**800-865-8211**	215-333-6300	320-1
Adept Corp						
4601 N Susquehanna Trl	York	PA	17406	**800-451-2254**	717-266-3606	358
Adept Technology Inc						
5960 Inglewood Dr	Pleasanton	CA	94588	**800-292-3378**	925-245-3400	386
NASDAQ: ADEP						
Aderans Hair Goods Inc						
Simplicity Hair Extensions						
9135 Independence Ave	Chatsworth	CA	91311	**877-413-5225***		348
*Sales						
ADESA Inc						
13085 Hamilton Crossing Blvd	Carmel	IN	46032	**800-923-3725**	317-815-1100	50
Adexa Inc						
5933 W Century Blvd 12th Fl	Los Angeles	CA	90045	**888-300-7692**	310-642-2100	180-1
Adfirmative LLC						
11416 Hollister Dr Ste	Austin	TX	78739	**866-966-9968**		197
ADG Promotional Products						
2300 Main St	Hugo	MN	55038	**800-852-5208**		9
ADHA (American Dental Hygienists' Assn)						
444 N Michigan Ave Ste 3400	Chicago	IL	60611	**800-243-2342**	312-440-8900	48-8
Adhesive Packaging Specialties Inc						
PO Box 31	Peabody	MA	01960	**800-222-1117**	978-531-3300	547
Adhesives Research Inc						
400 Seaks Run Rd PO Box 100	Glen Rock	PA	17327	**800-445-6240**	717-235-7979	3
AdHub LLC, The						
146 Alexander St	Rochester	NY	14607	**866-712-2986**	585-442-2585	393
Adi American Distributors Inc						
2 Emery Ave	Randolph	NJ	07869	**800-877-0510**	973-328-1181	248
Adirondack Community College						
640 Bay Rd	Queensbury	NY	12804	**888-786-9235**	518-743-2200	161
Adirondack Council						
103 Hand Ave Ste 3 Ste 3	Elizabethtown	NY	12932	**877-873-2240**	518-873-2240	47-13
Adirondack Direct						
3040 48th Ave	Long Island	NY	11101	**800-221-2444**	718-204-4500	321
Adirondack Mountain Club						
814 Goggins Rd	Lake George	NY	12845	**800-395-8080***	518-668-4447	47-23
*Orders						
Adirondack Trailways						
499 Hurley Ave	Hurley	NY	12443	**800-858-8555**	845-339-4230	107
ADL (Anti-Defamation League)						
605 Third Ave	New York	NY	10158	**866-386-3235**	212-885-7700	47-8
Adleta Co						
1645 Diplomat Dr Ste 200	Carrollton	TX	75006	**800-423-5382**	972-620-5600	361
ADM (Archer Daniels Midland Co)						
4666 E Faries Pkwy	Decatur	IL	62526	**800-637-5843**	217-424-5200	187
NYSE: ADM						
ADM (ADM Milling Co)						
8000 W 110th St	Overland Park	KS	66210	**800-422-1688**	913-491-9400	297-23
ADM Alliance Nutrition Inc						
1000 N 30th St	Quincy	IL	62301	**800-292-3333**	217-222-7100	446
ADM Cocoa Div						
77 W Wacker Dr	Chicago	IL	60601	**800-637-5843**	217-424-5200	297-8
ADM Corn Processing						
4666 Faries Pkwy	Decatur	IL	62526	**866-574-9690**	217-424-5200	277
ADM Corn Processing Div						
4666 E Faries Pkwy	Decatur	IL	62526	**800-637-5843**	217-424-5200	297-23
ADM Corp						
100 Lincoln Blvd	Middlesex	NJ	08846	**800-327-0718**	732-469-0900	265
ADM Milling Co (ADM)						
8000 W 110th St	Overland Park	KS	66210	**800-422-1688**	913-491-9400	297-23
ADM Natural Health & Nutrition						
Archer Daniels Midland Co						
4666 Faries Pkwy	Decatur	IL	62526	**800-637-5843**	217-451-7231	797
ADM Specialty Food Ingredients Div						
4666 E Faries Pkwy	Decatur	IL	62526	**800-637-5843**	217-424-5200	297-17
AdMail Express Inc						
31640 Hayman St	Hayward	CA	94544	**800-273-6245**		626
Admar Supply Co Inc						
1950 Brighton Henriett	Rochester	NY	14623	**800-836-2367**	585-272-9390	358
Admarc Southwest Ltd						
10 Desta Dr Ste 170LL	Midland	TX	79705	**888-823-6272**	432-687-1127	633
Administrative-Maximum US Penitentiary						
Florence PO Box 8500	Florence	CO	81226	**877-623-8426**	719-784-9464	214
Admiral Craft Equipment Corp						
940 S Oyster Bay Rd	Hicksville	NY	11801	**800-223-7750**	516-433-3535	487
Admiral Fell Inn						
888 S Broadway Historic Fell's Pt	Baltimore	MD	21231	**866-583-4162**	410-522-7377	379
Admiral Inc						
10 Taylor Ave	Annapolis	MD	21401	**800-864-4429**	410-267-8381	426
Admiral on Baltimore						
2 Baltimore Ave	Rehoboth Beach	DE	19971	**888-882-4188**	302-227-1300	379
Admiral Packaging Inc						
10 Admiral St	Providence	RI	02908	**800-556-6454**	401-274-7000	547
Admiralty Room						
666 Wisconsin Ave	Madison	WI	53703	**800-922-5512**	608-256-9071	669
AdMobilize LLC						
1680 Michigan Ave Ste 736	Miami	FL	33139	**855-236-6245**		387
ADMS (American Donkey & Mule Society)						
1346 Morningside Ave	Lewisville	TX	75057	**877-752-4068**	972-219-0781	47-3
Adobe Systems Inc						
345 Pk Ave	San Jose	CA	95110	**800-833-6687**	408-536-6000	180-8
NASDAQ: ADBE						
Adobe Ventures LP						
345 Pk Ave	San Jose	CA	95110	**877-722-7088**	408-536-6000	790
Adolphus, The						
1321 Commerce St	Dallas	TX	75202	**800-221-9083**	214-742-8200	379
Adoption ARC Inc						
4701 Pine St Ste J-7	Philadelphia	PA	19143	**800-884-4004**	215-748-1441	47-6
Adoptive Families Magazine						
108 West 39th St Ste 805	New York	NY	10018	**800-372-3300**	646-366-0830	456-10
Adorama Camera Inc						
42 W 18th St	New York	NY	10011	**800-223-2500**	212-741-0052	118
ADP (Association of Directory Publishers)						
PO Box 209	Traverse City	MI	49685	**800-267-9002**	231-486-2182	48-16
ADP (Automatic Data Processing Inc)						
1 ADP Blvd	Roseland	NJ	07068	**800-225-5237**		227
NASDAQ: ADP						

Company / Address	City	State	ZIP	Toll-Free	Phone	Class
Adp Media Group LLC 7700 Camp Bowie W Blvd Ste B	Fort Worth	TX	76116	**800-925-5700**	817-244-2740	626
ADP TotalSource Co 10200 Sunset Dr	Miami	FL	33173	**800-447-3237**	305-630-1000	630
ADRA (Adventist Development & Relief Agency International) 12501 Old Columbia Pk	Silver Spring	MD	20904	**800-424-2372**	301-680-6380	47-5
Adrenalin Inc 54 W 11th Ave	Denver	CO	80204	**888-757-5646**	303-454-8888	344
Adrian College 110 S Madison St *Admissions	Adrian	MI	49221	**800-877-2246***	517-265-5161	167
Adrienne Arsht Ctr for the Performing Arts of Miami-Dade County Inc 1300 Biscayne Blvd	Miami	FL	33132	**877-949-6722**	786-468-2000	571
Adroit Medical Systems Inc 1146 CaRding Machine Rd	Loudon	TN	37774	**800-267-6077**		476
ADS Environmental Services 4940 Research Dr	Huntsville	AL	35805	**800-633-7246**	256-430-3366	203
ADS Security LP 3001 Armory Dr Ste 100	Nashville	TN	37204	**800-448-8652**		690
ADS Tactical Inc Lynnwood Plz 621 Lynnhaven Pkwy Ste 400	Virginia Beach	VA	23452	**800-948-9433**	757-481-7758	448
ADS/Transicoil 9 Iron Bridge Dr	Collegeville	PA	19426	**800-323-7115**	484-902-1100	517
ADSA (American Dairy Science Assn) 1111 N Dunlap Ave	Savoy	IL	61874	**888-670-2250**	217-356-5146	47-2
ADT Security Services Inc 14200 E Exposition Ave	Aurora	CO	80012	**800-238-2455**		690
Ad-tech Medical Instrument Inc 1901 William St	Racine	WI	53404	**800-776-1555**	262-634-1555	475
ADTRAN Inc 901 Explorer Blvd *NASDAQ: ADTN*	Huntsville	AL	35806	**800-923-8726**	256-963-8000	732
ADTRAV Travel Management 4555 S Lake Pkwy	Birmingham	AL	35244	**800-476-2952**	205-444-4800	769
Advance America Cash Advance Centers Inc 135 N Church St *NYSE: AEA*	Spartanburg	SC	29306	**800-538-1579**	864-342-5600	140
Advance Auto Parts Inc 5008 Airport Rd *NYSE: AAP*	Roanoke	VA	24012	**877-238-2623**		53
Advance Bag & Packaging Technologies 5720 Williams Lk Rd	Waterford	MI	48329	**800-475-2247**	248-674-3126	599
Advance Carbon Products Inc 2036 National Ave	Hayward	CA	94545	**800-283-1249**	510-293-5930	126
Advance Corp Braille-Tac Div 8200 97th St S	Cottage Grove	MN	55016	**800-328-9451**	651-771-9297	699
Advance Energy Technologies Inc 1 Solar Dr	Clifton Park	NY	12065	**800-724-0198**	518-371-2140	662
Advance Engineering Co 7505 Baron Dr	Canton	MI	48187	**800-497-6388**	313-537-3500	488
Advance Food Company Inc 9987 Carver Rd Ste 500	Cincinnati	OH	45242	**800-969-2747**		300
Advance Insurance Company of Kansas 1133 SW Topeka Blvd	Topeka	KS	66629	**800-530-5989**	785-273-9804	391-2
Advance Lifts Inc 701 Kirk Rd	Saint Charles	IL	60174	**800-843-3625**	630-584-9881	469
Advance Reservations Inn Arizona PO Box 950	Tempe	AZ	85280	**800-456-0682**	480-990-0682	376
Advance Scale of MD LLC 2400 Egg Harbor Rd	Lindenwold	NJ	08021	**888-447-2253**	856-627-0700	682
Advance Tabco 200 Heartland Blvd	Edgewood	NY	11717	**800-645-3166**	631-242-4800	301
Advance Transportation Systems Inc 1125 Glendale Milford Rd	Cincinnati	OH	45215	**800-878-4849**	513-771-4848	312
Advanced Alarm Systems Inc 101 Lindsey St	Fall River	MA	02720	**800-442-5276**	508-675-1937	691
Advanced Bionics LLC 28515 Westinghouse Pl	Valencia	CA	91355	**877-829-0026**	661-362-1400	255
Advanced Biotechnologies Inc (ABI) 9108 Guilford Rd	Columbia	MD	21046	**800-426-0764**	410-792-9779	233
Advanced Cell Diagnostics Inc 3960 Point Eden Way	Hayward	CA	94545	**877-576-3636**	510-576-8800	666
Advanced Chemistry Development Inc 110 Yonge St 14th Fl	Toronto	ON	M5C1T4	**800-304-3988**	416-368-3435	179
Advanced Circuits Inc 21101 E 32nd Pkwy	Aurora	CO	80011	**800-979-4722**	303-576-6610	624
Advanced Digital Data Inc 6 Laurel Dr	Flanders	NJ	07836	**800-922-0972**	973-584-4026	179
Advanced Drainage Systems Inc 4640 Trueman Blvd	Hilliard	OH	43026	**800-821-6710**		595
Advanced Electronics 2601 Manhattan Beach Blvd	Redondo Beach	CA	90278	**800-750-7234**	310-725-0410	196
Advanced Energy Corp 909 Capability Dr Ste 2100	Raleigh	NC	27606	**800-869-8001**	919-857-9000	196
Advanced Energy Industries Inc 1625 Sharp Pt Dr *NASDAQ: AEIS*	Fort Collins	CO	80525	**800-446-9167**	970-221-4670	693
Advanced Hydraulics Inc 13568 Vintage Pl	Chino	CA	91710	**888-581-8079**	909-590-7644	455
Advanced Image Direct 1415 S Acacia Ave	Fullerton	CA	92831	**800-540-3848**	714-502-3900	458
Advanced Industrial Services Inc 3250 Susquehanna Trial	York	PA	17406	**800-544-5080**	717-764-9811	188
Advanced Information Systems Group Inc 11315 Corporate Blvd Ste 210	Orlando	FL	32817	**800-593-8359**	407-581-2929	182
Advanced Lighting Technologies Inc 7905 Cochran Rd Ste 300	Glenwillow	OH	44139	**888-440-2358**	440-519-0500	437
Advanced Looseleaf Technologies Inc 1424 Somerset Ave	Dighton	MA	02715	**800-339-6354**	508-669-6354	85
Advanced Machine & Engineering Co 2500 Latham St	Rockford	IL	61103	**800-225-4263**	815-962-6076	492
Advanced Micro Devices Inc (AMD) 1 AMD Pl PO Box 3453 *NYSE: AMD*	Sunnyvale	CA	94088	**800-538-8450**	408-749-4000	694
Advanced MP Technology 1010 Calle Sombra	San Clemente	CA	92673	**800-492-3113**	949-492-3113	248
Advanced Orthomolecular Research Inc 3900 - 12 St Ne	Calgary	AB	T2E8H9	**800-387-0177**	403-250-9997	345
Advanced Photographic Solutions 1525 Hardeman Ln	Cleveland	TN	37312	**800-241-9234**	423-479-5481	587
Advanced Poly Packaging Inc 1331 Emmitt Rd	Akron	OH	44306	**800-754-4403**	330-785-4000	556
Advanced Probing Systems Inc 2300 Central Ave	Boulder	CO	80301	**800-631-0005**	303-939-9384	593
Advanced Sterilization Products (ASP) 33 Technology Dr	Irvine	CA	92618	**888-783-7723**		476
Advanced Support Products Inc 24227 Fm 2978 Rd	Tomball	TX	77375	**800-941-5737**	281-357-1277	491
Advanced Technology Co 2858 E Walnut St	Pasadena	CA	91107	**800-447-2442**	626-449-2696	22
Advancement LLC 32200 Solon Rd	Solon	OH	44139	**866-364-3370**	440-248-8550	196
Advantage Credit Inc 32065 Castle Ct Ste 300	Evergreen	CO	80439	**800-670-7993**	303-670-7993	220
Advantage Electronic Product Development 34 Garden Ctr	Broomfield	CO	80020	**866-841-5581**	303-410-0292	694
Advantage Engineering Inc 525 E S- 18 Rd	Greenwood	IN	46142	**800-669-1282**	317-887-0729	14
Advantage Funding Corp 1000 Parkwood Cir SE	Atlanta	GA	30339	**800-241-2274**	770-955-2274	274
Advantage Home Health Care Inc 4008 N Wheeling Ave	Muncie	IN	47304	**800-884-5088**	765-284-1211	363
Advantage Metals Recycling LLC 3005 Manchester Trfy	Kansas City	MO	64129	**866-527-4733**	816-861-2700	684
Advantage Mktg Inc 14 W Main St	Ashland	OH	44805	**800-670-7479**	419-281-4762	94
Advantage Payroll Services Inc 126 Merrow Rd PO Box 1330 *Cust Svc	Auburn	ME	04211	**800-876-0178***	207-784-0178	569
Advantage Performance Group Inc 700 Larkspur Landing Cir	Larkspur	CA	94939	**800-494-6646**	415-925-6832	196
Advantage Rent-A-Car 1288 Old Bayshore Hwy *Cust Svc	Burlingame	CA	94010	**800-777-5500***		125
Advantage Resourcing 220 Norwood Pk S	Norwood	MA	02062	**800-343-4314**	781-251-8000	719
Advantage RN LLC 8892 Beckett Rd	West Chester	OH	45069	**866-301-4045**	513-874-8717	262
Advantage Truck Accessories Inc 6535 Jacson Rd	Ann Arbor	MI	48103	**800-773-3110**		60
Advantec MFS Inc 6723 Sierra Ct Ste A	Dublin	CA	94568	**800-334-7132**	925-479-0625	18
Advantech International Inc PO Box 6739	Somerset	NJ	08875	**800-322-6150**		60
AdVantis Hospitality Alliance LLC 615 N Highland Ste 2A	Murfreesboro	TN	37130	**866-218-4782**	615-904-6133	705
Advantix Solutions Group 1202 Richardson Dr Ste 200	Richardson	TX	75080	**866-238-2684**		387
Advantor Systems Corp 12612 Challenger Pkwy Ste 300	Orlando	FL	32809	**800-238-2686**	407-859-3350	690
Advent Capital Management LLC 1065 Ave of the Americas 31st Fl	New York	NY	10018	**888-523-8368**	212-482-1600	401
Advent Software Inc 600 Townsend St Ste 500 5th Fl *NASDAQ: ADVS*	San Francisco	CA	94103	**800-727-0605**	415-543-7696	180-1
Adventist Behavioral Health 14901 Broschart Rd	Rockville	MD	20850	**800-204-8600**	301-251-4500	374-5
Adventist Community Services 12501 Old Columbia Pk	Silver Spring	MD	20904	**877-227-2702**	301-680-6438	47-5
Adventist Development & Relief Agency International (ADRA) 12501 Old Columbia Pk	Silver Spring	MD	20904	**800-424-2372**	301-680-6380	47-5
Adventist Health 2100 Douglas Blvd	Roseville	CA	95661	**877-336-3566**	916-781-2000	353
Adventure Alaska Tours Inc PO Box 64	Hope	AK	99605	**800-365-7057**	907-782-3730	758
Adventure Aquarium 1 Riverside Dr	Camden	NJ	08103	**800-616-5297**	856-365-3300	39
Adventure Connection PO Box 475	Coloma	CA	95613	**800-556-6060**	530-626-7385	758
Adventure Cycling Assn 150 E Pine St PO Box 8308	Missoula	MT	59807	**800-755-2453**	406-721-1776	47-22
Adventure Life South America 1655 S Third St W Ste 1	Missoula	MT	59801	**800-344-6118**	406-541-2677	758
Ad-venture Promotions LLC 2625 Regency Rd	Lexington	KY	40503	**800-218-5488**	859-263-4299	128
Adventuredome 2880 Las Vegas Blvd S	Las Vegas	NV	89109	**866-456-8894**	702-691-5861	32
Adventureland Inn 305 34th Ave NW	Altoona	IA	50009	**800-910-5382**	515-265-7321	379
Adventureland Park 305 34th Ave NW	Altoona	IA	50009	**800-532-1286**	515-266-2121	32
Adventures Out West 1680 S 21st St	Colorado Springs	CO	80904	**800-755-0935**		758
Advertising Council Inc 815 Second Ave 9th Fl	New York	NY	10016	**888-200-4005**	212-922-1500	48-18
Advertising Specialties Institute 4800 St Rd	Trevose	PA	19053	**800-546-1350**	215-942-8600	634-9
Advice Media LLC PO Box 982064	Park City	UT	84098	**800-260-9497**		630
Advion BioSciences Inc 19 Brown Rd	Ithaca	NY	14850	**877-523-8466**	607-266-0665	666
Advisor & Source Newspapers 48075 Van Dyke Ave	Shelby Township	MI	48317	**800-252-7345**	586-731-1000	531-4
Advisor Today 2901 Telestar Ct	Falls Church	VA	22042	**800-247-4074**		456-5
Advisors Excel LLC 1300 SW Arrowhead Rd Ste 200	Topeka	KS	66604	**866-363-9595**		197
Advocacy Center for Persons With Disabilities 2728 Centerview Dr Ste 102	Tallahassee	FL	32301	**800-342-0823**	850-488-9071	428
Advocare International Lp 2801 Summit Ave	Plano	TX	75074	**800-542-4800**	972-665-5800	366

Name / Address	City	State	ZIP	Toll-Free	Phone	Class
Advocate Sherman Hospital 1425 N Randall Rd	Elgin	IL	60123	800-397-9000	847-742-9800	374-3
Advocate, The 22 N First St	Newark	OH	43055	877-424-0208	740-345-4053	531-2
Advocates for Highway & Auto Safety 750 First St NE Ste 901	Washington	DC	20002	877-366-0711	202-408-1711	47-10
Advocates for Self-Government 1010 N Tennessee St Ste 215	Cartersville	GA	30120	800-932-1776	770-386-8372	47-7
Adwerx Inc 307 W Main St	Durham	NC	27701	888-746-5678		5
Adxstudio Inc 200 - 1445 Park St	Regina	SK	S4N4C5	800-508-7811	306-569-6500	227
Adzzup LLC 8240 S Kyrene Rd Ste 101	Tempe	AZ	85284	888-723-9987		5
AE Petsche Company Inc 2112 W Div St	Arlington	TX	76012	844-237-7600	817-461-9473	248
AEA Advocate Magazine 345 E Palm Ln	Phoenix	AZ	85004	800-352-5411	602-264-1774	456-8
Aearo Co 5457 W 79th St	Indianapolis	IN	46268	877-327-4332	317-692-6666	575
AEB (American Egg Board) 1460 Renaissance Dr Ste 301	Park Ridge	IL	60068	888-549-2140	847-296-7043	47-2
AEB (American Exchange Bank) 510 W Main St PO Box 818	Henryetta	OK	74437	888-652-3321	918-652-3321	69
AEC (Applied Energy Company Inc) 1205 Venture Ct Ste 100	Carrollton	TX	75006	800-580-1171	214-355-4200	637
AED (Associated Equipment Distributors) 650 E Algonquin Rd Ste 305	Schaumburg	IL	60173	800-388-0650	630-574-0650	48-18
AEE (Association of Energy Engineers) 4025 Pleasantdale Rd Ste 420	Atlanta	GA	30340	877-407-0784	770-447-5083	47-12
Aegis Assisted Living 17602 NE Union Hill Rd	Redmond	WA	98052	888-252-3447	425-861-9993	450
Aegis Security Inc PO Box 3153	Harrisburg	PA	17105	800-233-2160	717-657-9671	391-4
Aehr Test Systems 400 Kato Terr *NASDAQ: AEHR*	Fremont	CA	94539	800-962-4284	510-623-9400	693
AEI (American Enterprise Institute for Public Policy Research) 1150 17th St NW	Washington	DC	20036	800-862-5801	202-862-5800	631
AEI Speakers Bureau 214 Lincoln St Ste 113	Allston	MA	02134	800-447-7325	617-782-3111	706
AELE (Americans for Effective Law Enforcement) 841 W Touhy Ave	Park Ridge	IL	60068	800-763-2802	847-685-0700	47-8
AELI (Agape English Language Institute) 610 Pickens St PO Box 12504	Columbia	SC	29201	877-476-2354	803-799-3452	423
AEM (Association of Equipment Manufacturers) 6737 W Washington St Ste 2400	Milwaukee	WI	53214	866-236-0442	414-272-0943	48-13
AEP Industries Inc 125 Phillips Ave *NASDAQ: AEPI*	South Hackensack	NJ	07606	800-999-2374	201-641-6600	599
AEP River Operations 16150 Main Cir Dr Ste 400	Chesterfield	MO	63017	800-621-3362	636-530-2100	464
AEPhi (Alpha Epsilon Phi Sorority) 11 Lake Ave Ext Ste 1-A	Danbury	CT	06811	888-668-4293	203-748-0029	47-16
Aer Lingus Airlines Gold Cir Club 300 Jericho Quad Ste 130	Jericho	NY	11753	800-474-7424		26
Aer Mfg Inc PO Box 979	Carrollton	TX	75011	800-753-5237	972-417-2582	59
AERA (American Educational Research Assn) 1430 K St NW Ste 1200	Washington	DC	20005	800-893-7950	202-238-3200	48-5
AERA (Automotive Engine Rebuilders Assn) 500 Coventry Ln Ste 180	Crystal Lake	IL	60014	888-326-2372	847-541-6550	48-21
Aerco International Inc 159 Paris Ave	Northvale	NJ	07647	800-526-0288	201-768-2400	357
Aerial Innovations Inc 3703 W Azeele St	Tampa	FL	33609	800-223-1701	813-254-7339	198
Aermotor Pumps Inc 293 Wright St	Delavan	WI	53115	800-230-1816		638
Aero Air LLC 2050 NE 25th Ave	Hillsboro	OR	97124	800-448-2376	503-640-3711	13
Aero ALL-GAS Company Inc, The 3150 Main St	Hartford	CT	06120	800-255-4277	860-278-2376	317
Aero Industries Inc 4243 W Bradbury Ave *Sales	Indianapolis	IN	46241	800-535-9545*	317-244-2433	730
Aero Plastics Inc 91 Citation Dr	Concord	ON	L4K2Y8	877-660-2376	905-738-9010	600
Aero Rubber Company Inc 8100 W 185th St	Tinley Park	IL	60487	800-662-1009	708-430-4900	370
Aero Tec Labs Inc 45 Spear Rd Industrial Pk	Ramsey	NJ	07446	800-526-5330	201-825-1400	674
Aero Tech Designs Cycling Apparel 1132 Fourth Ave	Coraopolis	PA	15108	800-783-8326	412-262-3255	709
Aerobics & Fitness Assn of America (AFAA) 15250 Ventura Blvd Ste 200	Sherman Oaks	CA	91403	877-968-7263	818-905-0040	47-22
Aerodyne Alloys LLC 350 Pleasant Vly Rd	South Windsor	CT	06074	800-243-4344	860-289-6011	486
Aerofin Corp 4621 Murray Pl PO Box 10819	Lynchburg	VA	24506	800-237-6346	434-845-7081	90
Aeroflex 35 South Service Rd PO Box 6022	Plainview	NY	11803	800-843-1553	913-764-2452	250
Aeroflex Inc 35 S Service Rd PO Box 6022 *TSE: ARX*	Plainview	NY	11803	800-843-1553	516-694-6700	694
Aeroflot Russian International Airlines 10 Rockefeller Plaza Ste 1015	New York	NY	10020	866-879-7647	212-944-2300	25
Aeroflow Inc 3165 Sweeten Creek Rd	Asheville	NC	28803	888-345-1780		474
Aeroglide Corp 100 Aeroglide Dr	Cary	NC	27511	800-722-7483	919-851-2000	386
Aeromedixcom LLC Po Box 14730	Jackson	WY	83002	888-362-7123	307-732-2642	458
Aeronet Worldwide 42 Corporate Pk	Irvine	CA	92606	800-552-3869	949-474-3000	12
Aeroshade Inc 433 Oakland Ave	Waukesha	WI	53186	800-331-7179	262-547-2101	86
Aerosoles Inc 201 Meadow Rd	Edison	NJ	08817	800-798-9478	732-985-6900	302
Aerospace America Inc 900 Harry Truman Pkwy	Bay City	MI	48706	800-237-6414	989-684-2121	479
Aerospace America Magazine 1801 Alexander Bell Dr Ste 500	Reston	VA	20191	800-639-2422	703-264-7500	456-21
Aerospace Industries Assn of America (AIA) 1000 Wilson Blvd Ste 1700	Arlington	VA	22209	877-229-7555	703-358-1000	48-21
Aerospace Products International (API) 3778 Distriplex Dr N	Memphis	TN	38118	888-274-2497	901-365-3470	22
Aero-Space Southwest Inc 21450 N Third Ave	Phoenix	AZ	85027	800-289-2779	623-582-2779	351
Aerospec Inc 505 E Alamo Dr	Chandler	AZ	85225	888-854-2376	480-892-7195	258
Aerotek Inc 7301 Pkwy Dr	Hanover	MD	21076	800-237-6835	410-694-5100	719
AeroVironment Inc 181 W Huntington Dr Ste 202 *NASDAQ: AVAV*	Monrovia	CA	91016	888-833-2148	626-357-9983	20
Aervoe Industries Inc PO Box 485	Gardnerville	NV	89410	800-227-0196	775-783-3100	549
AES (American Epilepsy Society) 342 N Main St	West Hartford	CT	06117	888-233-2334	860-586-7505	47-17
AES Electrophoresis Society 1202 Ann St	Madison	WI	53713	800-242-4363	608-258-1565	48-19
AESC (Association of Energy Service Cos) 14531 Fm 529 Ste 250	Houston	TX	77095	800-692-0771	713-781-0758	47-12
Aesco Electronics Inc 2230 Picton Pkwy	Akron	OH	44312	877-442-6987	330-245-2630	248
AESCULAP Inc 3773 Corporate Pkwy	Center Valley	PA	18034	800-282-9000		475
AESP Inc 16295 NW 13th Ave	Miami	FL	33169	800-446-2377	305-944-7710	255
AESU Travel Inc 3922 Hickory Ave	Baltimore	MD	21211	800-638-7640	410-366-5494	769
AETEA Information Technology Inc 1445 Research Blvd Ste 300	Rockville	MD	20850	888-772-3832	301-721-4200	182
AETEK UV Systems 1229 Lakeview Ct	Romeoville	IL	60446	800-333-2304	630-226-4200	437
AETN (Arkansas Educational Television Network) 350 S Donaghey Ave	Conway	AR	72034	800-662-2386	501-682-2386	629
Aetna Felt Corp 2401 W Emaus Ave	Allentown	PA	18103	800-526-4451	610-791-0900	742-6
Aetna Inc 151 Farmington Ave *NYSE: AET*	Hartford	CT	06156	800-872-3862	860-273-0123	391-3
Aetna Plastics Corp 1702 St Clair Ave	Cleveland	OH	44114	800-634-3074	216-781-4421	602
Aetna US Healthcare Inc 980 Jolly Rd	Blue Bell	PA	19422	800-872-3862	215-775-4800	391-3
Aexcel Corp 7373 Production Dr	Mentor	OH	44060	800-854-0782	440-974-3800	549
AFA (American Fence Assn) 800 Roosevelt Rd Bldg C-312	Glen Ellyn	IL	60137	800-822-4342	630-942-6598	48-3
AFA (American Federation of Astrologers) 6535 S Rural Rd	Tempe	AZ	85283	888-301-7630	480-838-1751	47-18
AFA (American Finance Assn) 350 Main St	Malden	MA	02148	800-835-6770	781-388-8599	48-2
AFA (Air Force Assn) 1501 Lee Hwy 4th Fl	Arlington	VA	22209	800-727-3337	703-247-5800	47-19
AFAA (Aerobics & Fitness Assn of America) 15250 Ventura Blvd Ste 200	Sherman Oaks	CA	91403	877-968-7263	818-905-0040	47-22
AFAR (American Federation for Aging Research) 55 W 39th St 16th Fl	New York	NY	10018	888-582-2327	212-703-9977	48-8
AFB (American Foundation for the Blind) 2 Penn Plaza	New York	NY	10001	800-232-5463	212-502-7600	47-17
AFC (AMPAC Fine Chemicals) MS 1007 PO Box 1718	Rancho Cordova	CA	95741	800-311-9668	916-357-6880	144
AFC (Automotive Finance Corp) 13085 Hamilton Crossing Blvd	Carmel	IN	46032	888-335-6675	865-384-8250	218
AFC Cable Systems Inc 272 Duchaine Blvd	New Bedford	MA	02745	800-757-6996	508-998-1131	811
AFC Industries Inc 13-16 133rd Pl	College Point	NY	11356	800-663-3412	718-747-0237	196
AFCA (American Football Coaches Assn) 100 Legends Ln	Waco	TX	76706	877-557-5338	254-754-9900	47-22
AFCEA (Armed Forces Communications & Electronics Assn) 4400 Fair Lakes Ct	Fairfax	VA	22033	800-336-4583	703-631-6100	47-19
AFCI (Association of Film Commissioners International) 109 E 17th St	Cheyenne	WY	82001	888-765-5777	307-637-4422	47-4
AFCO (Alex C Fergusson LLC) 5000 Letterkenny Rd	Chambersburg	PA	17201	800-345-1329		144
AFCO Credit Corp 14 Wall St	New York	NY	10005	800-288-6901	212-401-4400	218
Afco Industries Inc 3400 Roy St	Alexandria	LA	71302	800-551-6576		481
AFCU (Andrews Federal Credit Union) 5711 Allentown Rd	Suitland	MD	20746	800-487-5500	301-702-5500	221
Affiliated Car Rental 105 Hwy 36	Eatontown	NJ	07724	800-367-5159		125
Affiliated Chamber of Commerce of Greater Springfield 1441 Main St	Springfield	MA	01103	888-283-3757	413-787-1555	138
Affiliated Community Medical Centers (ACMC) 101 Willmar Ave SW	Willmar	MN	56201	888-225-6580	320-231-5000	374-3
Affiliated Control Equipment Inc 640 Wheat Ln	Wood Dale	IL	60191	800-942-8753	630-595-4680	54
Affiliated Foods Inc 1401 W Farmers Ave	Amarillo	TX	79118	800-234-3661	806-372-3851	298-8
Affiliated Power Purchasers International LLC 224 Phillip Morris Dr Ste 402	Salisbury	MD	21804	800-520-6685		196
Affina Dumont 150 E 34th St	New York	NY	10016	866-233-4642	212-481-7600	379
Affinia 50 155 E 50th St	New York	NY	10022	866-246-2203	212-751-5710	379
Affinia Chicago 155 E 50th St	New York	NY	10022	866-246-2203	212-751-5710	379
Affinia Gardens 215 E 64th St	New York	NY	10065	866-233-4642	212-355-1230	379

Name / Address	City	State	Zip	Toll-Free	Phone	Class
Affinia Manhattan 371 Seventh Ave	New York	NY	10001	**866-246-2203**	212-563-1800	379
Affinigent Inc 4 Kent Rd Ste 200	York	PA	17402	**800-932-3380**	717-600-0033	227
Affinion Group Inc 6 High Ridge Pk	Stamford	CT	06905	**800-251-2148**	203-956-1000	390
Affinitas Corp 1015 N 98th St Ste 100	Omaha	NE	68114	**800-369-6495**	402-505-5000	196
Affinity Federal Credit Union 73 Mountain View Blvd PO Box 621	Basking Ridge	NJ	07920	**800-325-0808**		221
Affinity Medical Ctr 875 Eigth St NE	Massillon	OH	44646	**800-999-6673**	330-832-8761	374-3
Affinity Wealth Management Inc 1702 Lovering Ave	Wilmington	DE	19806	**800-825-8399**	302-652-6767	196
Affordable Car Rental LC 105 Hwy 36	Eatontown	NJ	07724	**800-367-5159**	732-380-0888	125
Affordable Housing Update 8204 Fenton St	Silver Spring	MD	20910	**800-666-6380**	301-588-6380	530-8
Affymetrix Inc 3420 Central Expy *NASDAQ: AFFX*	Santa Clara	CA	95051	**888-362-2447**	408-731-5000	252
Afghanistan Embassy 2341 Wyoming Ave NW	Washington	DC	20008	**866-323-8609**	202-483-6410	259
AFI (American Film Institute) 2021 N Western Ave	Los Angeles	CA	90027	**866-234-3378**	323-856-7600	47-4
AFI (Armed Forces Insurance Exchange) PO Box G	Fort Leavenworth	KS	66027	**800-255-0187**	800-255-6792	391-4
AFI Fest 2021 N Western Ave	Los Angeles	CA	90027	**866-234-3378**	323-856-7600	284
Afinety Inc 1956 Cotner Ave	Los Angeles	CA	90025	**877-423-4638**	310-996-2700	322
AFLAC (American Family Life Assurance Company of Columbus) 1932 Wynnton Rd *Cust Svc	Columbus	GA	31999	**800-992-3522***	706-323-3431	391-2
AFLAC Inc 1932 Wynnton Rd *NYSE: AFL*	Columbus	GA	31999	**800-992-3522**	706-323-3431	360-4
AFLAC PAC (American Family Life Assurance Co PAC) 1932 Wynnton Rd Ste 300 *NYSE: AFL* ■ *Cust Svc	Columbus	GA	31999	**800-992-3522***	706-323-3431	614
AFL-CIO (American Federation of Labor & Congress of Industrial Organizations) 815 16th St NW	Washington	DC	20006	**877-850-4959**	202-637-5000	414
AFL-CIO Committee on Political Education 815 16th St NW	Washington	DC	20006	**855-712-8441**		614
AFM (American Federation of Musicians of the US & Canada) 1501 Broadway Ste 600	New York	NY	10036	**800-762-3444**	212-869-1330	414
AFMR (American Federation for Medical Research) 900 Cummings Ctr Ste 221-U	Beverly	MA	01915	**888-737-9477**	978-927-8330	48-8
AFOP (Association of Farmworker Opportunity Programs) 1120 20th St NW Ste 300	Washington	DC	20036	**866-487-9243**	202-828-6006	47-2
AFP (Association of Fundraising Professionals) 4300 Wilson Blvd Ste 300	Arlington	VA	22203	**800-666-3863**	703-684-0410	48-12
AFP Transformers Inc 206 Talmedge Rd	Edison	NJ	08817	**800-843-1215**	732-248-0305	765
AF&PA (American Forest & Paper Assn) 1111 19th St NW Ste 800	Washington	DC	20036	**800-878-8878**	202-463-2700	47-2
Africa Adventure Co, The 5353 N Federal Hwy Ste 300	Fort Lauderdale	FL	33308	**800-882-9453**	954-491-8877	758
African Lion Safari & Game Farm RR 1 Ste 1	Cambridge	ON	N1R5S2	**800-461-9453**	519-623-2620	821
African Safari Wildlife Park 267 S Lightner Rd	Port Clinton	OH	43452	**800-521-2660**	419-732-3606	821
African Travel Inc 330 N Brand Blvd Ste 950	Glendale	CA	91203	**800-421-8907**	818-507-7893	758
African Wildlife Foundation (AWF) 1400 16th St NW Ste 120	Washington	DC	20036	**888-494-5354**	202-939-3333	47-3
AFRL (Air Force Research Laboratory) AFRL/PA 1864 Fourth St Bldg 15 Rm 225	Wright-Patterson AFB	OH	45433	**800-222-0336**		666
Afro-American Newspapers Co 2519 N Charles St	Baltimore	MD	21218	**800-237-6892**	410-554-8200	634-8
AFS (American Folklore Society) 1501 Neil Ave 1501 Neil Ave	Columbus	OH	43201	**866-311-1200**	614-292-4715	47-14
AFS (American Foundry Society) 1695 N Penny Ln	Schaumburg	IL	60173	**800-537-4237**	847-824-0181	48-13
AFSA (American Foreign Service Assn) 2101 E St NW	Washington	DC	20037	**800-704-2372**	202-338-4045	48-7
AFSP (American Foundation for Suicide Prevention) 120 Wall St 22nd Fl	New York	NY	10005	**888-333-2377**	212-363-3500	47-17
AFT (American Farmland Trust) 1200 18th St	Washington	DC	20036	**800-431-1499**	202-331-7300	47-2
AFT (American Federation of Teachers) 555 New Jersey Ave NW	Washington	DC	20001	**800-238-1133**	202-879-4400	414
AFT Healthcare 555 New Jersey Ave NW	Washington	DC	20001	**800-238-1133**	202-879-4491	414
After Six 118 W 20th St	New York	NY	10011	**800-444-8304**	646-638-9600	154-11
Afton State Park 6959 Peller Ave S	Hastings	MN	55033	**800-366-8917**	651-436-5391	564
AG Partners Inc 512 S Eigth St PO Box 467	Lake City	MN	55041	**800-772-2990**	651-345-3328	446
Ag Processing Inc 12700 W Dodge Rd PO Box 2047	Omaha	NE	68103	**800-247-1345**	402-496-7809	297-29
Ag West Supply Inc 9055 Rickreall Rd	Rickreall	OR	97371	**800-842-2224**	503-363-2332	276
AGA (American Gastroenterological Assn) 4930 Del Ray Ave	Bethesda	MD	20814	**800-227-7888**	301-654-2055	48-8
AGA (American Galvanizers Assn) 6881 S Holly Cir Ste 108	Centennial	CO	80112	**800-468-7732**	720-554-0900	48-13
AGA (Association of Government Accountants) 2208 Mt Vernon Ave	Alexandria	VA	22301	**800-242-7211**	703-684-6931	48-1
Aga Khan Foundation USA (AKF) 1825 K St NW Ste 901	Washington	DC	20006	**800-267-2532**	202-293-2537	47-5
Agape English Language Institute (AELI) 610 Pickens St PO Box 12504	Columbia	SC	29201	**877-476-2354**	803-799-3452	423
Agati Inc 1219 W Lake St	Chicago	IL	60607	**866-418-8710**	312-829-1977	322
AGB (Association of Governing Boards of Universities & Colleges) 1133 20th St NW Ste 300	Washington	DC	20036	**800-356-6317**	202-296-8400	48-5
AGC (Associated General Contractors of America) 2300 Wilson Blvd Ste 400	Arlington	VA	22201	**800-242-1766**	703-548-3118	48-3
AGC Flat Galss North America Inc 11175 Cicero Dr Ste 400	Alpharetta	GA	30022	**800-251-0441**	404-446-4200	330
Agcall Inc 251 Midpark Blvd SE	Calgary	AB	T2X1S3	**877-273-4333**	403-256-1229	196
AGCO (AGCO Corp) 4205 River Green Pkwy *NYSE: AGCO*	Duluth	GA	30096	**877-525-4384**	770-813-9200	275
AGCO Corp (AGCO) 4205 River Green Pkwy *NYSE: AGCO*	Duluth	GA	30096	**877-525-4384**	770-813-9200	275
AGD (Academy of General Dentistry) 211 E Chicago Ave Ste 900	Chicago	IL	60611	**888-243-3368**	312-440-4300	48-8
Ageatia Technology Consultancy Services Inc 850 E Higgins Rd Ste 125	Schaumburg	IL	60173	**855-243-4842**	847-517-8415	196
Agency for Healthcare Research & Quality 540 Gaither Rd	Rockville	MD	20850	**800-358-9295**	301-427-1200	340-8
Agency for Toxic Substances & Disease Registry 4770 Buford Hwy NE	Atlanta	GA	30341	**800-232-4636**		340-8
Agency Mabu 1003 Gateway Ave	Bismarck	ND	58503	**800-568-9346**	701-250-0728	7
Agency Revolution 698 NW	Bend	OR	97701	**800-606-0477**		5
Agency Software Inc 215 W Commerce Dr	Hayden Lake	ID	83835	**800-342-7327**	208-762-7188	390
Aget Manufacturing Co 1408 E Church St	Adrian	MI	49221	**800-832-2438**	517-263-5781	18
AGF Management Ltd 66 Wellington St W 31st Fl	Toronto	ON	M5K1E9	**800-268-8583**	905-214-8203	401
Agfa Corp 611 River Dr	Elmwood Park	NJ	07407	**888-274-8626**	201-440-2500	590
AGFA HealthCare Corp 10 S Academy St	Greenville	SC	29601	**877-777-2432**	864-421-1600	180-10
Agfinity 260 Factory Rd	Eaton	CO	80615	**800-433-4688**	970-454-4000	278
AGI (American Geological Institute) 4220 King St	Alexandria	VA	22302	**800-334-2564**	703-379-2480	48-19
AGI (Audio General Inc) 1680 Republic Rd	Huntingdon Valley	PA	19006	**866-866-2600**	267-288-0300	513
AGI (Alan Guttmacher Institute) 125 Maiden Ln 7th Fl	New York	NY	10038	**800-355-0244**	212-248-1111	47-5
Agilith Capital Inc Victory Bldg 80 Richmond St W Ste 203	Toronto	ON	M5H2A4	**866-345-1231**	416-915-0284	527
AgilQuest Corp 9407 Hull St Rd	Richmond	VA	23236	**888-745-7455**	804-745-0467	180-1
Agilysys NV LLC 28925 Fountain Pkwy	Solon	OH	44139	**800-241-8768**	770-810-7800	179
Aging News Alert 8204 Fenton St	Silver Spring	MD	20910	**800-666-6380**	301-588-6385	530-8
Agissar Corp 526 Benton St	Stratford	CT	06615	**800-627-8256**	203-375-8662	110
AGL Corp 2202 N Redmond Rd PO Box 189	Jacksonville	AR	72076	**800-643-9696**	501-982-4433	425
AGL Resources Inc 10 Peachtree Pl PO Box 4569 *NYSE: GAS* ■ *Cust Svc	Atlanta	GA	30309	**866-977-4278***	404-584-4000	785
AGM Container Controls Inc 3526 E Ft Lowell Rd	Tucson	AZ	85716	**800-995-5590**	520-881-2130	350
AGM Industries Inc 16 Jonathan Dr	Brockton	MA	02301	**800-225-9990**	508-587-3900	809
AGMA (American Guild of Musical Artists) 1430 Broadway 14th Fl	New York	NY	10018	**800-543-2462**	212-265-3687	47-4
AGN International-North America 2851 S Parker Rd Ste 850	Aurora	CO	80014	**800-782-2272**	303-743-7880	48-1
Agnes Scott College 141 E College Ave	Decatur	GA	30030	**800-868-8602**	404-471-6000	167
Agnico-Eagle Mines Ltd 145 King St E Ste 500 *NYSE: AEM*	Toronto	ON	M5C2Y7	**888-822-6714**	416-947-1212	501
AGO (American Guild of Organists) 475 Riverside Dr Ste 1260	New York	NY	10115	**855-631-0759**	212-870-2310	47-4
AGPA (American Group Psychotherapy Assn) 25 E 21st St 6th Fl	New York	NY	10010	**877-668-2472**	212-477-2677	48-15
Agracel Inc 2201 Willenborg Ave	Effingham	IL	62401	**800-600-8085**	217-342-4443	273
Agralite Electric Co-op 320 Hwy 12 SE	Benson	MN	56215	**800-950-8375**	320-843-4150	247
Agrex Inc 10975 Grandview Dr St Ste 200	Overland Park	KS	66210	**800-523-8181**	913-851-6300	10-3
Agri Beef Co 1555 Shoreline Dr Ste 320	Boise	ID	83702	**800-657-6305**	208-338-2500	10-1
agriCAREERS Inc 613 Main St PO Box 140	Massena	IA	50853	**800-633-8387**		262
Agricultural Retailers Assn (ARA) 1156 15th St NW Ste 500	Washington	DC	20005	**800-535-6272**	202-457-0825	47-2
Agricultural Workers Mutual Auto Insurance Co PO Box 88	Fort Worth	TX	76101	**800-772-7424**	817-831-9900	391-4
AgriGold Hybrids 5381 Akin Rd	Saint Francisville	IL	62460	**800-262-7333**	618-943-5776	692
Agri-King Inc 18246 Waller Rd	Fulton	IL	61252	**800-435-9560**	815-589-2525	446
Agri-Service 300 Agri-Service Way	Kimberly	ID	83341	**800-388-3599**	208-734-7772	276
Agrium Inc 13131 Lk Fraser Dr SE *NYSE: AGU*	Calgary	AB	T2J7E8	**877-247-4861**	403-225-7000	282
AGS (American Gem Society) 8881 W Sahara Ave	Las Vegas	NV	89117	**866-805-6500**	702-255-6500	48-4
AGS (Augusta Regional Airport - Bush Field) 1501 Aviation Way	Augusta	GA	30906	**866-289-9673**	706-798-3236	27
AGSI 3343 Peachtree Rd NE Ste 510	Atlanta	GA	30326	**800-768-2474**	404-816-7577	182

Alphabetical Section

Name / Address	City	State	ZIP	Toll-Free	Phone	Class
AGTA (American Gem Trade Assn) 3030 LBJ Fwy Ste 840	Dallas	TX	75234	**800-972-1162**	214-742-4367	48-4
AGU (American Geophysical Union) 2000 Florida Ave NW	Washington	DC	20009	**800-966-2481**	202-462-6900	48-19
Agua Caliente Casino Resort Spa 32-250 Bob Hope Dr	Rancho Mirage	CA	92270	**888-999-1995**	760-321-2000	132
AGVA (American Guild of Variety Artists) 363 Seventh Ave 17th Fl	New York	NY	10001	**800-331-0890**	212-675-1003	47-4
AgVantage FS Inc 1600 Eigth St SW	Waverly	IA	50677	**800-346-0058**	319-483-4900	278
AH Harris & Son Inc 367 Alumni Rd	Newington	CT	06111	**800-382-6555**	860-665-9494	266-3
A&h Lithoprint Inc 2540 S 27th Ave	Broadview	IL	60155	**855-305-7628**	708-345-1196	626
AHA (American Heart Assn) 7272 Greenville Ave	Dallas	TX	75231	**800-242-8721**	214-373-6300	47-17
AHA (American Historical Assn) 400 A St SE	Washington	DC	20003	**888-444-6664**	202-544-2422	48-5
AHA (American Hospital Assn) 155 N Wacker Dr	Chicago	IL	60606	**800-424-4301**	312-422-3000	48-8
AHA (American Humane Assn) 63 Inverness Dr E	Englewood	CO	80112	**800-227-4645**	303-792-9900	47-6
AHAM (Association of Home Appliance Manufacturers) 1111 19th St NW Ste 402	Washington	DC	20036	**888-258-3247**	202-872-5955	48-4
AHAPAC (American Hospital Assn PAC) 325 Seventh St NW	Washington	DC	20004	**800-424-4301**	202-638-1100	614
AHAVA North America 330 7th Avenue	New York	NY	10001	**800-366-7254**		217
AHC Media LLC 3525 Piedmont Rd NE Bldg 6 Ste 400 *Cust Svc	Atlanta	GA	30305	**800-688-2421***	404-262-5476	634-9
AHCA (American Health Care Assn) 1201 L St NW	Washington	DC	20005	**800-321-0343**	202-842-4444	48-8
AHDI (Association for Healthcare Documentation Integrity) 4230 Kiernan Ave Ste 130	Modesto	CA	95356	**800-982-2182**	209-527-9620	48-8
Ahead Hum Res Inc/Prosoft LLC 2209 Heather Ln	Louisville	KY	40218	**888-749-1000**	502-485-1000	179
Ahead LLC 270 Samuel Barnet Blvd	New Bedford	MA	02745	**800-282-2246**	508-985-9898	154-8
AheadTek Inc 6410 Via Del Oro	San Jose	CA	95119	**800-971-9191**	408-226-9991	645
Ahearn & Soper Inc 100 Woodbine Downs Blvd	Rexdale	ON	M9W5S6	**800-263-4258**	416-675-3999	176
AHEPA (American Hellenic Educational Progressive Assn) 1909 Q St NW Ste 500	Washington	DC	20009	**855-473-3512**	202-232-6300	47-14
Ahern Adcock Devlin LLP 1650 Iowa Ave Ste 200	Riverside	CA	92507	**888-226-9449**	951-683-0672	2
Ahern Rentals Inc 4241 Arville St	Las Vegas	NV	89103	**800-589-6797**	702-362-0623	266-3
AHI International Corp 8550 W Bryn Mawr Ave Ste 600	Chicago	IL	60631	**800-323-7373**		758
AHI Supply Inc PO Box 884	Friendswood	TX	77549	**800-873-5794**	281-331-0088	193-1
AHIA (Association of Healthcare Internal Auditors) 10200 W 44th Ave Ste 304	Wheat Ridge	CO	80033	**888-275-2442**	303-327-7546	48-1
AHIMA (American Health Information Management Assn) 233 N Michigan Ave Ste 2100	Chicago	IL	60601	**800-335-5535**	312-233-1100	48-8
AHLA (Alberta Hotel & Lodging Assn) 2707 Ellwood Dr	Edmonton	AB	T6X0P7	**888-436-6112**	780-436-6112	47-23
Ahmad, Zavitsanos, Anaipakos, Alavi & Mensing PC 1 Houston Ctr 1221 McKinney St Ste 3460	Houston	TX	77010	**800-856-8153**	713-655-1101	428
AHNA (American Holistic Nurses' Assn) 323 N San Francisco St Ste 201	Flagstaff	AZ	86001	**800-278-2462**	928-526-2196	47-17
Ahola Corp, The 6820 W Snowville Rd	Brecksville	OH	44141	**800-727-2849**	440-717-7620	2
AHRA (American Healthcare Radiology Administrators) 490-B Boston Post Rd Ste 200	Sudbury	MA	01776	**800-334-2472**	978-443-7591	48-8
Ahrberg Milling Co 200 S Depot St PO Box 968	Cushing	OK	74023	**800-324-0267**	918-225-0267	446
AHS (American Hiking Society) 1422 Fenwick Ln	Silver Spring	MD	20910	**800-972-8608**	301-565-6704	47-23
AHS (American Horticultural Society) 7931 E Blvd Dr	Alexandria	VA	22308	**800-777-7931**	703-768-5700	47-18
AHS (American Helicopter Society International) 217 N Washington St	Alexandria	VA	22314	**855-247-4685**	703-684-6777	48-21
AI Friedman Company Inc 44 W 18th St	New York	NY	10011	**800-204-6352**	212-243-9000	44
AIA (Aerospace Industries Assn of America) 1000 Wilson Blvd Ste 1700	Arlington	VA	22209	**877-229-7555**	703-358-1000	48-21
AIA (American Institute of Architects) 1735 New York Ave NW *Orders	Washington	DC	20006	**800-242-3837***	202-626-7300	47-4
AIA (Archaeological Institute of America) 656 Beacon St 4th Fl	Boston	MA	02215	**877-524-6300**	617-353-9361	47-11
AIAA (American Institute of Aeronautics & Astronautics Inc) 1801 Alexander Bell Dr Ste 500	Reston	VA	20191	**800-639-2422**	703-264-7500	48-19
AIADA (American International Automobile Dealers Assn) 500 Montgomery St Ste 800	Alexandria	VA	22314	**800-462-4232**	703-519-7800	48-18
AIAG (Automotive Industry Action Group) 26200 Lahser Rd Ste 200	Southfield	MI	48033	**877-275-2424**	248-358-3570	48-21
AIB (Art Institute of Boston at Lesley) 29 Everett St	Cambridge	MA	22138	**800-773-0494**	617-585-6600	163
AIB College of Business 2500 Fleur Dr	Des Moines	IA	50321	**800-444-1921**	515-244-4221	798
AIBS (American Institute of Biological Sciences) 1444 'I' St NW Ste 200	Washington	DC	20005	**800-992-2427**	202-628-1500	48-19
AIC (American Institute of Chemists) 315 Chestnut St	Philadelphia	PA	19106	**800-829-0115**	215-873-8224	48-19
AICA (American-International Charolais Assn) 11700 NW Plaza Cir	Kansas City	MO	64153	**800-270-7711**	816-464-5977	47-2
AIChE (American Institute of Chemical Engineers) 120 Wall St Fl 23 *Cust Svc	New York	NY	10005	**800-242-4363***	203-702-7660	48-19
AICPA (American Institute of Certified Public Accountants) 1211 Ave of the Americas	New York	NY	10036	**888-777-7077**	212-596-6200	48-1
AICPCU/IIA (American Institute for CPCU & Insurance Institute of America) 720 Providence Rd Ste 100	Malvern	PA	19355	**800-644-2101**	610-644-2100	48-9
AICR Newsletter 1759 R St NW	Washington	DC	20009	**800-843-8114**	202-328-7744	530-8
Aid Maintenance Co 300 Roosevelt Ave	Pawtucket	RI	02860	**800-886-6627**	401-722-6627	103
Aidells Sausage Co 1625 Alvarado St	San Leandro	CA	94577	**877-243-3557**	510-614-5450	297-26
AIDS Foundation of Chicago 200 W Jackson Blvd Ste 2200	Chicago	IL	60606	**866-895-2437**	312-922-2322	306
AIDS Library 1233 Locust St 2nd Fl	Philadelphia	PA	19107	**877-613-4533**	215-985-4851	434-4
AIDSinfo PO Box 6303	Rockville	MD	20849	**800-448-0440**	301-519-0459	340-8
AIFD (American Institute of Floral Designers) 720 Light St	Baltimore	MD	21230	**877-865-5320**	410-752-3318	48-4
AIFP (American International Forest Products LLC) 5560 SW 107th Ave	Beaverton	OR	97005	**800-366-1611**	503-641-1611	193-3
AIG SunAmerica Inc 21650 Oxnard St	Woodland Hills	CA	91367	**800-445-7862**		360-4
AIGA (American Institute of Graphic Arts) 164 Fifth Ave	New York	NY	10010	**800-548-1634**	212-807-1990	47-4
Aigner Index Inc 23 Mac Arthur Ave	New Windsor	NY	12553	**800-242-3919**	845-562-4510	607
Aiken County 828 Richland Ave W	Aiken	SC	29801	**866-876-7074**	803-642-2012	338
Aiken Electric Co-op Inc 2790 Wagener Rd *Tech Supp	Aiken	SC	29802	**877-264-5368***	803-649-6245	247
Aiken Regional Medical Centers 302 University Pkwy	Aiken	SC	29801	**800-245-3679**	803-641-5000	374-3
Aiken State Natural Area 1145 State Pk Rd	Windsor	SC	29856	**866-345-7275**	803-649-2857	564
AIL (American Income Life Insurance Co) 1200 Wooded Acres	Waco	TX	76710	**800-433-3405**	254-761-6400	391-2
AIM (Accuracy in Media Inc) 4350 EW Hwy Ste 555	Bethesda	MD	20814	**800-787-4567**	202-364-4401	48-14
Aim 2 Berkeley St Ste 403	Toronto	ON	M5A4J5	**866-645-2224**	416-594-9393	181
Aim Engineering & Surveying Inc 5300 Lee Blvd	Lehigh Acres	FL	33971	**800-226-4569**	239-332-4569	263
AIM Supply Co 7337 Bryan Dairy Rd	Largo	FL	33777	**800-999-0125**	727-544-6211	385
Aimco 10000 SE Pine St	Portland	OR	97216	**800-852-1368**		385
AIME (American Institute of Mining Metallurgical & Petroleum Engineers) 12999 E Adam Aircraft Cir	Englewood	CO	80112	**888-702-0049**	303-325-5185	47-12
Aims Community College 5401 W 20th St	Greeley	CO	80634	**800-301-5388**	970-330-8008	161
AIMS Inc 235 Desiard St	Monroe	LA	71201	**800-729-2467**	318-323-2467	180-10
AIN Plastics Inc 1750 E Heights Dr *Cust Svc	Madison Heights	MI	48071	**877-246-7700***	248-356-4000	602
AIPB (American Institute of Professional Bookkeepers) 6001 Montrose Rd Ste 500	Rockville	MD	20852	**800-622-0121**		48-1
Air & Waste Management Assn (A&WMA) 420 Fort Duquesne Blvd 1 Gateway Ctr 3rd Fl	Pittsburgh	PA	15222	**800-270-3444**	412-232-3444	47-12
Air Center Inc 2175 Stephenson Hwy	Troy	MI	48083	**800-247-2959**	248-619-7800	358
Air Charter Team 4151 N Mulberry Dr Ste 250	Kansas City	MO	64116	**800-205-6610**	816-283-3280	13
Air Chek Inc 1936 Butler Bridge Rd	Mills River	NC	28759	**800-247-2435**	828-684-0893	198
Air Cleaning Technologies Inc 1300 W Detroit	Broken Arrow	OK	74012	**800-351-1858**	918-251-8000	34
Air Comfort Corp 2550 Braga Dr	Broadview	IL	60155	**800-466-3779**	708-345-1900	191-10
Air Compressor Solutions 3001 Kermit Hwy	Odessa	TX	79764	**800-527-4137**	432-335-5900	318
Air Conditioning Heating & Refrigeration News 2401 W Big Beaver Rd Ste 700	Troy	MI	48084	**800-837-8337**	248-362-3700	456-21
Air Contact Transport Inc PO Box 570	Budd Lake	NJ	07828	**800-765-2769**		189
Air Creebec Inc 101 Fecteau St	Val-d'or	QC	J9P0G4	**800-567-6567**	819-825-8375	12
Air Cycle Corp 2200 Ogden Ave Ste 100	Lisle	IL	60532	**800-909-9709**		296
Air Force Assn (AFA) 1501 Lee Hwy 4th Fl	Arlington	VA	22209	**800-727-3337**	703-247-5800	47-19
Air Force Federal Credit Union 1560 Cable Ranch Rd Ste 200	San Antonio	TX	78245	**800-227-5328**	210-673-5610	221
Air Force Magazine 1501 Lee Hwy	Arlington	VA	22209	**800-727-3337**	703-247-5800	456-12
Air Force Research Laboratory (AFRL) AFRL/PA 1864 Fourth St Bldg 15 Rm 225	Wright-Patterson AFB	OH	45433	**800-222-0336**		666
Air Force Times Magazine 6883 Commercial Dr	Springfield	VA	22159	**800-368-5718**	703-750-7400	456-12
Air India 570 Lexington Ave 15th Fl	New York	NY	10022	**800-223-7776**		25
Air Lift Co 2727 Snow Rd	Lansing	MI	48917	**800-248-0892**	517-322-2144	53
Air Line Pilots Assn 535 Herndon Pkwy	Herndon	VA	20170	**877-331-1223**	703-689-2270	414
Air Liquide America LP 2700 Post Oak Blvd Ste 1800	Houston	TX	77056	**877-855-9533**		142
Air Logistics Inc 4605 Industrial Dr	New Iberia	LA	70560	**800-365-6771**	337-365-6771	359
Air Monitor Corp 1050 Hopper Ave	Santa Rosa	CA	95403	**800-247-3569**	707-544-2706	611
Air North Charter & Training Ltd 150 Condor Rd	Whitehorse	YT	Y1A6E6	**800-661-0407**	867-668-2228	12
Air Palm Springs 145 S Gene Autry Trl Ste 14	Palm Springs	CA	92262	**800-760-7774**	760-322-1104	13

Name / Address	City	State	Zip	Toll-Free	Phone	Class
Air Products & Chemicals Inc 7201 Hamilton Blvd; NYSE: APD *Prod Info	Allentown	PA	18195	**800-345-3148***	610-481-4911	142
Air Quality Engineering Inc 7140 Northland Dr N	Brooklyn Park	MN	55428	**888-883-3273**	763-531-9823	18
Air Sunshine Inc PO Box 22237	Fort Lauderdale	FL	33335	**800-435-8900**	954-434-8900	25
Air Systems International Inc 829 Juniper Crescent	Chesapeake	VA	23320	**800-866-8100**	757-424-3967	638
Air Tahiti Nui 1990 E Grand Ave; *Cust Svc	El Segundo	CA	90245	**877-824-4846***	310-662-1860	25
Air Technical Industries 7501 Clover Ave	Mentor	OH	44060	**800-321-9680**	440-951-5191	469
Air Techniques Inc 1295 Walt Whitman Rd	Melville	NY	11747	**888-247-8481**	516-433-7676	230
Air Traffic Control Assn (ATCA) 1101 King St Ste 300	Alexandria	VA	22314	**866-953-2189**	703-299-2430	48-21
Air Van Moving Group 2340 130th Ave NE Ste 201	Bellevue	WA	98005	**800-989-8905**	425-629-4101	518
Air Vent Inc 4117 Pinnacle Pnt Dr Ste 400	Dallas	TX	75211	**800-247-8368**		695
Air Zoo, The 6151 Portage Rd	Portage	MI	49002	**866-524-7966**	269-382-6555	519
Airbiquity Inc 1011 Western Ave Ste 600	Seattle	WA	98104	**888-334-7741**	206-219-2700	645
AirBoss of America Corp Rubber Compounding 101 Glasgow St	Kitchener	ON	N2G4X8	**800-294-5723**	519-576-5565	604-3
Airbrush Action Inc PO Box 438	Allenwood	NJ	08720	**800-876-2472**	732-223-7878	5
Airbus Helicopters Canada 1100 Gilmore Rd PO Box 250	Fort Erie	ON	L2A5M9	**800-267-4999**	905-871-7772	13
Airbus Helicopters Inc 2701 Forum Dr	Grand Prairie	TX	75052	**800-873-0001**	972-641-0000	20
Airbus North America Holdings 198 Van Buren St Ste 300	Herndon	VA	20170	**888-340-2375**	703-834-3400	196
AirClic Inc 900 Northbrook Dr Ste 100	Trevose	PA	19053	**800-419-8495**	215-504-0560	175-7
Aircom Mfg Inc 6205 E 30th St	Indianapolis	IN	46219	**800-925-2426**	317-545-5383	695
Aircraft Owners & Pilots Assn (AOPA) 421 Aviation Way	Frederick	MD	21701	**800-872-2672**	301-695-2000	48-21
Aircraft Technical Publishers 101 S Hill Dr	Brisbane	CA	94005	**800-227-4610**	415-330-9500	634-11
Aire Serv Heating & Air Conditioning Inc 1020 N University Parks Dr Ste 101	Waco	TX	76707	**855-259-2280**	254-523-3600	191-10
Airefco Inc 18755 SW Teton Ave PO Box 1349	Tualatin	OR	97062	**800-869-1349**	503-692-3210	15
Aire-Master of America Inc 1821 N State Hwy Cc	Nixa	MO	65714	**800-525-0957**	417-725-2691	311
Airespring Inc 6060 Sepulveda Blvd Ste 220	Van Nuys	CA	91411	**888-389-2899**	818-786-8990	387
AirFlite Inc 3250 AirFlite Way	Long Beach	CA	90807	**800-241-3548**	562-490-6200	13
Airfloat LLC 2230 Brush College Rd	Decatur	IL	62526	**800-888-0018**	217-423-6001	209
Airflow Systems Inc 11221 Pagemill Rd	Dallas	TX	75243	**800-818-6185**	214-503-8008	18
Airgas Inc 259 N Radnor-Chester Rd Ste 100; NYSE: ARG	Radnor	PA	19087	**800-255-2165**	610-687-5253	145
Airgas Specialty Products 2530 Sever Rd Ste 300	Lawrenceville	GA	30043	**800-295-2225**		282
Airguard Industries Inc 100 River Ridge Cir	Jeffersonville	IN	47130	**800-999-3458**	866-247-4827	18
AirIQ Inc 1845 Sandstone Manor Ste 10	Pickering	ON	L1W3W9	**888-606-6444**	905-831-6444	733
Airlie Conference Ctr 6809 Airlie Rd	Warrenton	VA	20187	**800-288-9573**	540-347-1300	377
Airmate Co Inc 16280 County Rd D	Bryan	OH	43506	**800-544-3614**	419-636-3184	9
Airosol Company Inc 1206 Illinois St	Neodesha	KS	66757	**800-633-9576**	620-325-2666	144
AirPair Inc 875 Howard St	San Francisco	CA	94103	**800-487-0668**		387
Airparts Company Inc 2310 NW 55th Ct	Fort Lauderdale	FL	33309	**800-392-4999**	954-739-3575	768
Airport Settle Inn 2620 S Packerland Dr	Green Bay	WI	54313	**800-688-9052**	920-499-1900	379
AIR-serv Group LLC 1370 Mendota Heights Rd	Mendota Heights	MN	55120	**800-247-8363**	651-454-0465	54
AirTek Indoor Air Solutions Inc 9424 Chesapeake Dr	San Diego	CA	92123	**877-858-6213**		194
Airtel Plaza Hotel 7277 Valjean Ave	Van Nuys	CA	91406	**877-939-9268**	818-997-7676	379
Airtex Consumer Products a Div of Federal Foam Technologies 150 Industrial Pk Blvd	Cokato	MN	55321	**800-851-8887**		742-6
Airtex Products 407 W Main St	Fairfield	IL	62837	**800-880-3056**	618-842-2111	59
Airvoice Wireless LLC 2425 Franklin Rd	Bloomfield Hills	MI	48302	**888-944-2355**		733
Air-Way Manufacturing Co 586 N Main St; *Cust Svc	Olivet	MI	49076	**800-253-1036***	269-749-2161	788
Airways Freight Corp 3849 W Wedington Dr	Fayetteville	AR	72704	**800-643-3525**	479-442-6301	312
AIS (AmSouth Investment Services Inc) 250 Riverchase Pkwy E 4th Fl	Birmingham	AL	35244	**866-512-3479**		401
AIS RealTime 4440 Bowen Blvd SE	Grand Rapids	MI	49508	**877-314-1100**		197
AISES (American Indian Science & Engineering Society) 2305 Renard SE Ste 200	Albuquerque	NM	87106	**800-759-5219**	505-765-1052	48-19
AIT (Avante International Technology Inc) 70 Washington Rd	Princeton Junction	NJ	08550	**800-735-5040**	609-799-9388	799
AITDomains.com 421 Maiden Ln	Fayetteville	NC	28301	**877-549-2881**		396
AIUM (American Institute of Ultrasound in Medicine) 14750 Sweitzer Ln Ste 100	Laurel	MD	20707	**800-638-5352**	301-498-4100	48-8
AIUSA (Amnesty International USA) 5 Penn Plaza 16th Fl	New York	NY	10001	**866-273-4466**	212-807-8400	47-5
AJ Desmond & Sons Funeral Directors 2600 Crooks Rd	Troy	MI	48084	**800-210-7135**	248-362-2500	509
Aj Ross Creative Media 1149 NY 17M	Chester	NY	10918	**800-723-4644**	845-783-5770	4
Ajax Paving Industries Inc 1957 Crooks Rd Ste A	Troy	MI	48084	**888-468-5489**	248-244-3300	190-4
Ajax Tocco Magnethermic Corp 1745 Overland Ave NE	Warren	OH	44483	**800-547-1527**	330-372-8511	319
Ajilon Communications 970 Peachtree Industrial Blvd Ste 200	Suwanee	GA	30024	**800-843-6910**	678-482-5103	198
AJLI (Association of Junior Leagues International Inc) 80 Maiden Ln Ste 305	New York	NY	10038	**800-955-3248**	212-951-8300	47-15
AJS (American Judicature Society) 2700 University Ave	Des Moines	IA	50311	**800-626-4089**	515-271-2281	48-10
AJWS (American Jewish World Service) 45 W 36th St	New York	NY	10018	**800-889-7146**	212-792-2900	47-5
AK Draft Seal Ltd 7470 Buller Ave	Burnaby	BC	V5J4S5	**888-520-9009**	604-451-1080	236
AK Steel Corp 9227 Centre Pt Dr; NYSE: AKS	West Chester	OH	45069	**800-331-5050**	513-425-5000	721
AK Tube LLC 30400 E Broadway	Walbridge	OH	43465	**800-955-8031**	419-661-4150	489
Aka Printing & Mailing Inc 44 Joseph Mills Dr	Fredericksburg	VA	22408	**800-232-1515**	540-373-1111	626
Akal Security Inc 7 Infinity Loop	Espanola	NM	87532	**888-325-2527**	505-692-6600	690
Akamai Technologies Inc 150 Broadway; NASDAQ: AKAM	Cambridge	MA	02142	**877-425-2624**	617-444-3000	180-7
Akcros Chemicals America 500 Jersey Ave; *Cust Svc	New Brunswick	NJ	08901	**800-500-7890***	732-220-6882	604-2
Akdo Intertrade Inc 1435 State St	Bridgeport	CT	06605	**800-811-2536**	203-336-5199	722
AKF (American Kidney Fund) 6110 Executive Blvd Ste 1010	Rockville	MD	20852	**800-638-8299**		47-17
AKF (Aga Khan Foundation USA) 1825 K St NW Ste 901	Washington	DC	20006	**800-267-2532**	202-293-2537	47-5
Akhurst Machinery Ltd 1669 Foster's Way (Annacis Island)	Delta	BC	V3M6S7	**888-265-4336**	604-540-1430	358
Akorn Inc 1925 W Field Ct; NASDAQ: AKRX	Lake Forest	IL	60045	**800-932-5676**	847-279-6100	233
AKRF Inc 440 Pk Ave S	New York	NY	10016	**800-899-2573**	212-696-0670	263
Akrochem Corp 255 Fountain St	Akron	OH	44304	**800-321-2260**	330-535-2100	604-3
Akro-Mils Inc 1293 S Main St	Akron	OH	44301	**800-253-2467**		201
Akron Auto Auction Inc 2471 Ley Dr	Akron	OH	44319	**800-773-0033**	330-773-8245	50
Akron Gasket & Packing Enterprises Inc 445 NE Ave	Tallmadge	OH	44278	**800-888-2088**	330-633-3742	327
Akron General Medical Ctr 400 Wabash Ave	Akron	OH	44307	**800-221-4601**	330-344-6000	374-3
Akron Paint & Varnish Inc 1390 Firestone Pkwy	Akron	OH	44301	**800-772-3452**	330-773-8911	549
Akron Porcelain & Plastics Co 2739 Cory Ave PO Box 15157	Akron	OH	44314	**800-737-9664**	330-745-2159	603
Akron Rubber Development Laboratory Inc 2887 Gilchrist Rd	Akron	OH	44305	**866-778-2735**	330-794-6600	740
Akron Steel Treating Co 336 Morgan Ave	Akron	OH	44311	**800-364-2782**	330-773-8211	483
Akron/Summit County Convention & Visitors Bureau 77 E Mill St	Akron	OH	44308	**800-245-4254**	330-374-8900	208
Akron-Canton Airport 5400 Lauby Rd NW	North Canton	OH	44720	**888-434-2359**	330-499-4221	27
AKSM (American Kidney Stone Management Ltd) 797 Thomas Ln	Columbus	OH	43214	**800-637-5188**	614-447-0281	353
AKT Enterprises 6424 Forest City Rd	Orlando	FL	32810	**877-306-3651**		5
Aktina Medical Physics Corp 360 N Route 9W	Congers	NY	10920	**888-433-3380**	845-268-0101	474
Akzo Nobel Chemicals Inc 10 Finderne Ave	Bridgewater	NJ	08807	**888-331-6212**		144
AkzoNobel Surface Chemistry LLC 525 W Van Buren St; *Cust Svc	Chicago	IL	60607	**800-937-5449***	312-544-7000	142
Al Betz & Assoc Inc 125 Airport Dr Ste 30	Westminster	MD	21157	**877-402-3376**	410-875-3376	444
Al Copeland Investments Inc 1001 Harimaw Ct S	Metairie	LA	70001	**800-401-0401**	504-830-1000	668
Al Hirschfeld Theatre 302 W 45th St	New York	NY	10036	**800-432-7780**	212-239-6262	744
Al Hoffer's Pest Protection Inc 12329 NW 35 St	Coral Springs	FL	33065	**866-549-7987**		576
Al Neyer Inc 302 W Third St Ste 800	Cincinnati	OH	45202	**877-271-6400**	513-271-6400	651
ALA (Alliance for Lupus Research) 28 W 44th St Ste 501	New York	NY	10036	**800-867-1743**	212-218-2840	47-17
ALA (American Library Assn) 50 E Huron St	Chicago	IL	60611	**800-545-2433**	312-944-6780	48-11
ALA (American Logistics Assn) 1133 15th St NW Ste 640	Washington	DC	20005	**800-791-7146**	202-466-2520	47-19
ALA (American Lung Assn) 14 Wall St	New York	NY	10005	**800-586-4872**	212-315-8700	47-17
ALA (Legal Management: Journal of the Assn of Legal Administrators) 75 Tri State International Ste 222	Lincolnshire	IL	60069	**877-675-5571**	847-267-1252	456-15
ALA (Association of Legal Administrators) 75 Tri-State International Ste 222	Lincolnshire	IL	60069	**877-675-5571**	847-267-1252	48-10

	City	State	ZIP	Toll-Free	Phone	Class
ALA (American Lighting Assn) 2050 Stemmons Fwy Ste 10046	Dallas	TX	75207	**800-605-4448**	214-698-9898	48-4
Ala Moana Hotel 410 Atkinson Dr	Honolulu	HI	96814	**800-367-6025**	808-955-4811	379
Alabama						
Administrative Office of Alabama Courts 300 Dexter Ave	Montgomery	AL	36104	**866-954-9411**	334-954-5000	339-1
Conservation & Natural Resources Dept 64 N Union St PO Box 301450	Montgomery	AL	36130	**800-262-3151**	334-242-3486	339-1
Crime Victims Compensation Commission 5845 Carmichael Rd	Montgomery	AL	36117	**800-541-9388**	334-290-4420	339-1
Emergency Management Agency 5898 County Rd 41 PO Box 2160	Clanton	AL	35046	**800-843-0699**	205-280-2200	339-1
Mental Health & Mental Retardation Dept 100 N Union St PO Box 301410	Montgomery	AL	36130	**800-367-0955**	334-242-3454	339-1
Public Health Dept 201 Monroe St	Montgomery	AL	36104	**800-252-1818**	334-206-5300	339-1
Public Service Commission 100 N Union St RSA Union PO Box 304260	Montgomery	AL	36130	**800-392-8050**	334-242-5218	339-1
Rehabilitation Services Dept 602 S Lawrence St	Montgomery	AL	36104	**800-441-7607**	334-293-7500	339-1
Securities Commission 770 Washington Ave Ste 570	Montgomery	AL	36130	**800-222-1253**	334-242-2984	339-1
State Parks Div 64 N Union St	Montgomery	AL	36130	**800-252-7275**		339-1
Tourism Department 401 Adams Ave PO Box 4927	Montgomery	AL	36104	**800-252-2262**	334-242-4169	339-1
Alabama Agricultural & Mechanical University 4900 Meridian St PO Box 1087	Huntsville	AL	35810	**800-553-0816**	256-372-5000	167
Alabama Art Supply Inc 1006 23rd St S *Cust Svc	Birmingham	AL	35205	**800-749-4741***	205-322-4741	44
Alabama Assn of Realtors 522 Washington Ave PO Box 4070	Montgomery	AL	36104	**800-446-3808**	334-262-3808	654
Alabama Card Systems Inc 500 Gene Reed Dr Ste 102	Birmingham	AL	35215	**800-985-7507**	205-833-1116	759
Alabama Constitution Village 109 Gates Ave	Huntsville	AL	35801	**800-678-1819**	256-564-8100	519
Alabama Correctional Industries 1400 Lloyd St	Montgomery	AL	36107	**800-224-7007**	334-261-3600	629
Alabama Crown Distributing 421 Industrial Ln	Birmingham	AL	35211	**800-548-1869**	205-941-1155	80-3
Alabama Educational Television Commission 2112 11th Ave S Ste 400	Birmingham	AL	35205	**800-239-5233**	205-328-8756	629
Alabama Eye Bank 500 Robert Jemison Rd	Birmingham	AL	35209	**800-423-7811**		271
Alabama Farmers Co-op Inc PO Box 2227	Decatur	AL	35601	**888-255-2667**	256-353-6843	282
Alabama Gas Corp (Alagasco) 605 Richard Arrington Jr Blvd N	Birmingham	AL	35203	**800-292-4005**	205-326-8100	785
Alabama Graphics & Engineering Supply Inc 2801 Fifth Ave S	Birmingham	AL	35233	**800-292-3806**	205-252-8505	258
Alabama Gulf Coast Convention & Visitors Bureau 3150 Gulf Shores Pkwy PO Box 457	Gulf Shores	AL	36547	**800-745-7263**	251-968-7511	208
Alabama Lawyer Magazine 415 Dexter Ave	Montgomery	AL	36104	**800-354-6154**	334-269-1515	456-15
Alabama Medical Assn 19 S Jackson St	Montgomery	AL	36104	**800-239-6272**		473
Alabama Metal Industries Corp (AMICO) 3245 Fayette Ave	Birmingham	AL	35208	**800-366-2642**	205-787-2611	490
Alabama Motor Express Inc 10720 E US Hwy 84 E	Ashford	AL	36312	**800-633-7590**		778
Alabama Outdoors Inc 3054 Independence Dr	Birmingham	AL	35209	**800-870-0011**	205-870-1919	709
Alabama Pharmacy Assn 1211 Carmichael Way *General	Montgomery	AL	36106	**877-877-3962***	334-271-4222	584
Alabama Prepaid Affordable College Tuition (PACT) Program 100 N Union St Ste 660	Montgomery	AL	36130	**800-252-7228**	334-242-7514	723
Alabama Public Television (APT) 2112 11th Ave S Ste 400	Birmingham	AL	35205	**800-239-5233**	205-328-8756	629
Alabama Republican Party 3505 Lorna Rd Ste 219	Birmingham	AL	35216	**800-274-8683**	205-212-5900	615-2
Alabama School Journal 422 Dexter Ave	Montgomery	AL	36104	**800-392-5839**	334-834-9790	456-8
Alabama Shakespeare Festival 1 Festival Dr	Montgomery	AL	36117	**800-841-4273**	334-271-5300	746
Alabama Southern Community College 2800 S Alabama Ave	Monroeville	AL	36461	**866-901-1117**	251-575-3156	161
Alabama Specialty Products Inc 152 Metal Samples Rd PO Box 8	Munford	AL	36268	**888-388-1006**	256-358-5200	319
Alabama State Bar 415 Dexter Ave	Montgomery	AL	36104	**800-392-5660**	334-269-1515	71
Alabama State Legislature State House 11 S Union St	Montgomery	AL	36130	**800-499-3051**	334-242-7600	433
Alabama State Nurses Assn (ASNA) 360 N Hull St	Montgomery	AL	36104	**800-270-2762**	334-262-8321	532
Alabama State University 915 S Jackson St *Admissions	Montgomery	AL	36104	**800-253-5037***	334-229-4100	167
Alabama Theatre 4750 Hwy 17 S	North Myrtle Beach	SC	29582	**800-342-2262**	843-272-1111	571
Alacare Home Health & Hospice 2400 John Hawkins Pkwy	Birmingham	AL	35244	**800-852-4724**	205-981-8000	363
Alachua County Library District 401 E University Ave	Gainesville	FL	32601	**866-341-2730**	352-334-3900	434-3
Alachua County Visitors & Convention Bureau 30 E University Ave	Gainesville	FL	32601	**866-778-5002**	352-374-5260	208
ALACO Ladder Co 5167 G St	Chino	CA	91710	**888-310-7040**	909-591-7561	421
Aladdin Steel Inc PO Box 89	Gillespie	IL	62033	**800-637-4455**	217-839-2121	491
Alagasco (Alabama Gas Corp) 605 Richard Arrington Jr Blvd N	Birmingham	AL	35203	**800-292-4005**	205-326-8100	785
Alaglass Swimming Pools 165 Sweet Bay Rd	Saint Matthews	SC	29135	**877-655-7179**		375
Alaka'i Mechanical Corp 2655 Waiwai Loop	Honolulu	HI	96819	**800-600-1085**	808-834-1085	191-10
Alamance Community College PO Box 8000	Graham	NC	27253	**877-667-7533**	336-578-2002	161
Alamance-Burlington School District 1712 Vaughn Rd	Burlington	NC	27217	**888-764-7001**	336-570-6060	683
Alamar Resort Inn 311 16th St	Virginia Beach	VA	23451	**800-346-5681**	757-428-7582	667
Alameda County Fair Assn (ACFA) 4501 Pleasanton Ave	Pleasanton	CA	94566	**800-874-9253**	925-426-7600	639
Alameda County Library 2450 Stevenson Blvd	Fremont	CA	94538	**888-663-0660**	510-745-1500	434-3
Alameda County Water District 43885 S Grimmer Blvd	Fremont	CA	94537	**866-275-3772**	510-668-4200	785
Alameda Times-Star 7677 Oakport St Ste 950	Oakland	CA	94604	**866-225-5277**	510-208-6300	634-8
Alameda-Contra Costa Transit District 1600 Franklin St 10th Fl	Oakland	CA	94612	**877-878-8883**	510-891-4777	467
Alamo Group Inc 1627 E Walnut *NYSE: ALG* ■ *Cust Svc	Seguin	TX	78155	**800-788-6066***	830-379-1480	275
Alamo Industrial Inc 1502 East Walnut St	Seguin	TX	78155	**800-356-6286**		296
Alamo Iron Works Inc 943 AT&T Ctr Pkwy	San Antonio	TX	78219	**800-292-7817**	210-223-6161	385
Alamo Lumber Co 10800 Sentinel Dr	San Antonio	TX	78217	**855-828-9792**	210-352-1300	193-3
Alamo Music Ctr 425 N Main Ave	San Antonio	TX	78205	**800-822-5010**	210-224-1010	525
Alamo Tee's & Advertising 12814 Cogburn	San Antonio	TX	78249	**888-562-3800**	210-699-3800	7
Alamo Tissue Service Ltd 5844 Rocky Point Dr	San Antonio	TX	78249	**800-226-9091**	210-738-2663	544
Alamo Travel Group Inc 8930 Wurzbach Rd	San Antonio	TX	78240	**800-692-5266**	210-593-0084	769
Alamodome 100 Montana St	San Antonio	TX	78203	**800-884-3663**	210-207-3663	718
Alamogordo Chamber of Commerce 1301 N White Sands Blvd	Alamogordo	NM	88310	**800-826-0294**	575-437-6120	138
Alan b Harris Attorney at Law 409 N Texas Ave	Odessa	TX	79761	**800-887-1676**	432-580-3118	428
Alan Guttmacher Institute (AGI) 125 Maiden Ln 7th Fl	New York	NY	10038	**800-355-0244**	212-248-1111	47-5
Alan Ritchey Inc 740 S I-35 E Frontage Rd	Valley View	TX	76272	**800-877-0273**	940-726-3276	778
Al-Anon Family Group Inc 1600 Corporate Landing Pkwy	Virginia Beach	VA	23454	**888-425-2666**	757-563-1600	47-21
Alaska						
Banking Securities & Corporations Div 333 Willoughby Ave Fl 9 PO Box 110807	Juneau	AK	99801	**888-925-2521**	907-465-2521	339-2
Enterprise Technology Services Div PO Box 110206	Juneau	AK	99811	**888-565-8680**		339-2
Housing Finance Corp 4300 Boniface Pkwy 99504 PO Box 101020	Anchorage	AK	99504	**800-478-2432**	907-338-6100	339-2
Military & Veterans Affairs Dept (DMVA) PO Box 5800	Fort Richardson	AK	99505	**888-248-3682**	907-428-6896	339-2
Postsecondary Education Commission 3030 Vintage Blvd PO Box 110510	Juneau	AK	99801	**800-441-2962**	907-465-2962	339-2
Vocational Rehabilitation Div 801 W Tenth St Ste 200	Juneau	AK	99801	**800-478-2815**	907-465-2814	339-2
Alaska Assn of Realtors 4205 Minnesota Dr	Anchorage	AK	99503	**800-478-3763**	907-563-7133	654
Alaska Bar Assn 550 W Seventh Ave Ste 1900 PO Box 100279	Anchorage	AK	99501	**800-478-4372**	907-272-7469	71
Alaska Bible College 248 E Elmwood Ave	Palmer	AK	99645	**800-478-7884**	907-822-3201	160
Alaska Business Monthly 501 W Northern Lights Blvd Ste 100	Anchorage	AK	99503	**800-770-4373**	907-276-4373	456-5
Alaska Commercial Co 550 W 64th Ave Ste 200	Anchorage	AK	99518	**800-563-0002**	907-273-4600	345
Alaska Commission on Postsecondary Education PO Box 110510	Juneau	AK	99811	**800-441-2962**	907-465-2962	723
Alaska Communications Systems Group Inc 600 Telephone Ave *NASDAQ: ALSK*	Anchorage	AK	99503	**800-808-8083**	907-563-8000	733
Alaska Computer Brokers 551 W Dimond Blvd	Anchorage	AK	99515	**866-261-4225**	907-267-4200	182
Alaska Industrial Hardware Inc 2192 Viking Dr	Anchorage	AK	99501	**800-478-7201**	907-276-7201	364
Alaska Magazine 301 Arctic Slope Ave Ste 300	Anchorage	AK	99518	**800-288-5892**	386-246-0444	456-22
Alaska Marine Highway System 6858 Glacier Hwy PO Box 112505	Juneau	AK	99801	**800-642-0066**	907-465-3941	467
Alaska Marine Lines Inc 5615 W Marginal Way SW *Cust Svc	Seattle	WA	98106	**800-326-8346***	206-763-4244	313
Alaska Municipal League Joint Insurance Association 807 G St Ste 356	Anchorage	AK	99501	**800-337-3682**	907-258-2625	532
Alaska Native Heritage Ctr 8800 Heritage Ctr Dr	Anchorage	AK	99504	**800-315-6608**	907-330-8000	519
Alaska Native Medical Ctr (ANMC) 4315 Diplomacy Dr *Admitting	Anchorage	AK	99508	**800-478-6661***	907-563-2662	374-3
Alaska Pacific University 4101 University Dr	Anchorage	AK	99508	**800-252-7528**	907-564-8248	167
Alaska Pharmacist's Assn 203 W 15th Ave Ste 100	Anchorage	AK	99501	**800-228-9290**	907-563-8880	584
Alaska Power & Telephone Co 193 Otto St PO Box 3222 *OTC: APTL* ■ *Cust Svc	Port Townsend	WA	98368	**800-982-0136***	360-385-1733	785
Alaska State Medical Assn 4107 Laurel St	Anchorage	AK	99508	**800-951-8712**	907-562-0304	473

Name / Address	City	State	ZIP	Toll-Free	Phone	Class
Alaska State Museum 395 Whittier St	Juneau	AK	99801	**800-440-2919**	907-465-2901	519
Alaska Stock Images 2505 Fairbanks St	Anchorage	AK	99503	**800-487-4285**	907-276-1343	592
Alaska Tour & Travel 9170 Jewel Lk Rd Ste 202 PO Box 221011	Anchorage	AK	99502	**800-208-0200**	907-245-0200	769
Alaska Travel Adventures Inc 9085 Glacier Hwy Ste 301	Juneau	AK	99801	**800-323-5757**	907-789-0052	769
Alaska USA Federal Credit Union 4000 Credit Union Dr PO Box 196613	Anchorage	AK	99503	**800-525-9094**	907-563-4567	221
Alaskan Copper & Brass Co 3223 Sixth Ave S	Seattle	WA	98134	**800-552-7661**	206-623-5800	491
Alban Tractor Co 8531 Pulaski Hwy	Baltimore	MD	21237	**800-492-6994**	410-686-7777	358
Albany Area Chamber of Commerce 225 W Broad Ave	Albany	GA	31701	**800-475-8700**	229-434-8700	138
Albany College of Pharmacy (ACPHS) 106 New Scotland Ave *General	Albany	NY	12208	**888-203-8010***	518-694-7221	167
Albany County Convention & Visitors Bureau 25 Quackenbush Sq	Albany	NY	12207	**800-258-3582**	518-434-1217	208
Albany Democrat-Herald 600 Lyons St SW PO Box 130	Albany	OR	97321	**877-634-2867**	541-926-2211	531-2
Albany Herald Publishing Company Inc 126 N Washington St	Albany	GA	31702	**800-234-3725**	229-888-9300	634-8
Albany Industries Inc 504 N Glenfield Rd	New Albany	MS	38652	**877-534-9804**	662-534-9800	320-2
Albany International Corp 1373 Broadway PO Box 1907 *NYSE: AIN*	Albany	NY	12204	**888-797-6735**	518-445-2200	742-3
Albany International Research Co 216 Airport Dr	Rochester	NH	03867	**888-797-6735**	603-330-5850	666
Albany Law School of Union University (ALS) 80 New Scotland Ave	Albany	NY	12208	**800-448-3500**	518-445-2311	168-1
Albany Steel Inc 566 Broadway	Albany	NY	12204	**800-342-9317**	518-436-4851	191-14
Albany Visitors Assn 300 Second Ave SW	Albany	OR	97321	**800-526-2256**	541-928-0911	208
Albemarle Electric Membership Corp PO Box 69	Hertford	NC	27944	**800-215-9915**	252-426-5735	247
Alberic Colon Auto Sales Inc Ave John F Kennedy Carr Ste 2 KM 3.4	San Juan	PR	00920	**877-292-4610**		56
Albert at Bay Suite Hotel 435 Albert St	Ottawa	ON	K1R7X4	**800-267-6644**	613-238-8858	379
Albert College 160 Dundas St W	Belleville	ON	K8P1A6	**800-952-5237**	613-968-5726	621
Albert E. Sleeper State Park 6573 State Pk Rd	Caseville	MI	48725	**800-447-2757**	989-856-4411	564
Albert Einstein Healthcare Network 5501 Old York Rd	Philadelphia	PA	19141	**800-346-7834**	215-456-7890	353
Albert Einstein Medical Ctr 5501 Old York Rd	Philadelphia	PA	19141	**800-346-7834**		374-3
Albert Guarnieri Co 1133 E Market St	Warren	OH	44483	**800-686-2639**	330-394-5636	298-8
Albert H Notini & Sons Inc 225 Aiken St	Lowell	MA	01854	**800-366-8464**	978-459-7151	754
Albert Lea Seed House 1414 W Main St	Albert Lea	MN	56007	**800-352-5247**	507-373-3161	692
Albert Lea Tribune, The 808 W Front St	Albert Lea	MN	56007	**800-657-4996**	507-373-1411	634-8
Albert's Organics Inc 3268 E Vernon Ave	Vernon	CA	90058	**800-899-5944**		298-7
Alberta Bair Theater for the Performing Arts 2722 Third Ave N Ste 200 PO Box 1556	Billings	MT	59103	**877-321-2074**	406-256-8915	571
Alberta Blue Cross 10009 108th St NW	Edmonton	AB	T5J3C5	**800-661-6995**	780-498-8100	391-3
Alberta Chambers of Commerce 10025 - 102A Ave Edmonton Ctr Ste 1808	Edmonton	AB	T5J2Z2	**800-272-8854**	780-425-4180	137
Alberta College of Art & Design 1407 14th Ave NW	Calgary	AB	T2N4R3	**800-251-8290**	403-284-7600	783
Alberta Hotel & Lodging Assn (AHLA) 2707 Ellwood Dr	Edmonton	AB	T6X0P7	**888-436-6112**	780-436-6112	47-23
Alberta Oil Tool 9530 60th Ave	Edmonton	AB	T6E0C1	**877-432-3404**	780-434-8566	536
Alberta Soccer 9023 111 Ave Nw	Edmonton	AB	T5B0C3	**866-250-2200**	780-474-2200	136
Alberta-Pacific Forest Industries Inc PO Box 8000	Boyle	AB	T0A0M0	**800-661-5210**	780-525-8000	635
Albertus Magnus College 700 Prospect St *Admissions	New Haven	CT	06511	**800-578-9160***	203-773-8550	167
Albertville Quality Foods Inc 130 Quality Dr	Albertville	AL	35950	**800-353-2806**	256-840-9923	297-26
Albion College 611 E Porter St	Albion	MI	49224	**800-858-6770**	517-629-1000	167
Albion Hotel 1650 James Ave *General	Miami Beach	FL	33139	**877-782-3557***	305-913-1000	379
Albion Industries Inc 800 N Clark St	Albion	MI	49224	**800-835-8911**	517-629-9441	350
Albion Laboratories Inc 101 N Main St	Clearfield	UT	84015	**800-453-2406**	801-773-4631	446
Albright College 1621 N 13th St	Reading	PA	19604	**800-252-1856**	610-921-2381	167
Albuquerque Convention & Visitors Bureau 20 First Plz Ste 601	Albuquerque	NM	87102	**800-733-9918**	505-842-9918	208
Albuquerque Journal 7777 Jefferson St NE	Albuquerque	NM	87109	**800-990-5765**	505-823-7777	531-2
Albuquerque Public Schools (APS) 6400 Uptown Blvd NE	Albuquerque	NM	87110	**866-563-9297**	505-880-3700	683
Alcazar Networks Inc 419 State Ave Ste 3	Emmaus	PA	18049	**800-349-6192**	484-664-2800	462
ALCO Inc 6925 - 104 St	Edmonton	AB	T6H2L5	**800-563-1498**	780-435-3502	403
ALCO Sales & Service Co 6851 High Grove Blvd	Burr Ridge	IL	60527	**800-323-4282**	630-655-1900	196
Alcoa Inc 390 Park Ave	New York	NY	10022	**800-523-9596**	412-553-4545	484
Alcoa Primary Metals 900 S Gay St Riverview Twr Ste 1100	Knoxville	TN	37902	**800-852-0238**	865-594-4700	484
Alcoa Wheel Products International 1600 Harvard Ave	Cleveland	OH	44105	**800-242-9898**	216-641-3600	482
Alcohol & Tobacco Tax & Trade Bureau 1310 G St NW Ste 300	Washington	DC	20220	**877-882-3277**	202-453-2000	340-16
Alcoholic Beverage Control PO Box 27491	Richmond	VA	23261	**800-552-3200**	804-213-4565	530-7
Alcon Laboratories Inc 6201 S Fwy	Fort Worth	TX	76134	**800-862-5266**	817-293-0450	271
Alcop Adhesive Label Co 826 Perkins Ln	Beverly	NJ	08010	**888-313-3017**	609-871-4400	413
Alcopro Inc 2547 Sutherland Ave	Knoxville	TN	37919	**800-227-9890**	865-525-4900	415
Alcorn County Electric Power Assn 1909 S Tate St	Corinth	MS	38834	**866-448-3046**	662-287-4402	247
Alcott Group 71 Executive Blvd	Farmingdale	NY	11735	**888-425-2688**	631-420-0100	630
ALCTS (Association for Library Collections & Technical Services) 50 E Huron St	Chicago	IL	60611	**800-545-2433**	312-280-5038	48-11
Aldebaran Capital LLC 10293 N Meridian St Ste 100	Indianapolis	IN	46290	**888-742-7827**	317-818-7827	401
Aldelo LP 4641 Spyres Way Ste 4	Modesto	CA	95356	**800-801-6036**	209-338-5488	255
Alderbrook Resort & Spa 7101 E SR-106	Union	WA	98592	**800-622-9370**	360-898-2200	667
Alderfer Inc 382 Main St PO Box 2 *Sales	Harleysville	PA	19438	**800-222-2319***		297-26
Alderson Reporting Co 1155 Connecticut Ave NW Ste 200	Washington	DC	20036	**800-367-3376**	202-289-2260	444
Alderson-Broaddus College 101 College Hill Rd *Admissions	Philippi	WV	26416	**800-263-1549***	304-457-1700	167
ALDI Inc 1200 N Kirk Rd	Batavia	IL	60510	**800-366-2324**	630-879-8100	345
Aldila Inc 14145 Danielson St Ste B *OTC: ALDA*	Poway	CA	92064	**800-854-2786**	858-513-1801	708
Aldo Shoes 2300 Emile Belanger	Montreal	QC	H4R3J4	**888-818-2536**	514-747-2536	302
Alebra Technologies Inc 3810 Pheasant Ridge Dr NE Ste 100	Minneapolis	MN	55449	**888-340-2727**	651-366-6140	179
Alego Health 24651 Center Ridge Rd., Ste 400	Westlake	OH	44145	**855-918-4570**	440-918-4570	196
Alembic Inc 3005 Wiljan Ct	Santa Rosa	CA	95407	**800-322-5893**	707-523-2611	526
Alemite LLC 1057-521 Corporate Ctr Dr Ste 100	Fort Mill	SC	29715	**800-267-8022**	803-802-0001	386
ALerCHEK Inc 15 Oak St Ste 302	Springvale	ME	04083	**877-282-9542**	207-490-2266	233
Alere Inc 51 Sawyer Rd Ste 200	Waltham	MA	02453	**877-441-7440**	781-647-3900	233
Alere San Diego Inc 9975 Summers Ridge Rd	San Diego	CA	92121	**866-284-3684**	781-647-3900	233
Aleris International Inc 25825 Science Pk Dr Ste 400	Beachwood	OH	44122	**866-266-2586**	216-910-3400	721
AlertOne Services Inc 1000 Commerce Park Dr Ste 300 *Cust Svc	Williamsport	PA	17701	**866-581-4540***		574
Alerus Retirement Solutions 2 Pine Tree Dr Ste 400	Arden Hills	MN	55112	**800-795-2697**		527
Alesco Data Group LLC 5276 Summerlin Commons Way	Fort Myers	FL	33907	**800-701-6531**	239-275-5006	4
Aleutians East Borough 3380 C St Ste 205	Anchorage	AK	99503	**888-383-2699**	907-274-7555	338
Alex C Fergusson LLC (AFCO) 5000 Letterkenny Rd	Chambersburg	PA	17201	**800-345-1329**		144
Alexander & Baldwin Inc 822 Bishop St *NYSE: ALEX*	Honolulu	HI	96813	**866-442-6551**	808-525-6611	187
Alexander Communications Group Inc 712 Main St Ste 187-B	Boonton	NJ	07005	**800-232-4317**	973-265-2300	634-9
Alexander Mfg Co 12978 Tesson Ferry Rd *General	Sappington	MO	63128	**800-258-2743***	314-842-3344	9
Alexander Open Systems Inc 12851 Foster St	Overland Park	KS	66213	**800-473-1110**	913-307-2300	176
Alexandria & Arlington Bed & Breakfast Networks (AABBN) 4938 Hampden Ln Ste 164	Bethesda	MD	20814	**888-549-3415**	703-549-3415	376
Alexandria Archaeology Museum 105 N Union St Ste 327	Alexandria	VA	22314	**800-367-7623**	703-746-4399	519
Alexandria Black History Museum 902 Wythe St	Alexandria	VA	22314	**800-367-7623**	703-838-4356	519
Alexandria Convention & Visitors Assn 221 King St	Alexandria	VA	22314	**800-388-9119**	703-746-3301	208
Alexandria Daily Town Talk PO Box 7558	Alexandria	LA	71306	**800-523-8391**	318-487-6397	531-2
Alexandria Extrusion Co 401 County Rd 22 NW	Alexandria	MN	56308	**800-568-6601**	320-763-6537	486
Alexandria Lakes Area Chamber of Commerce 206 Broadway	Alexandria	MN	56308	**800-235-9441**	320-763-3161	138
Alexandria Moulding 20352 Powerdam Rd	Alexandria	ON	K0C1A0	**866-377-2539**	613-525-2784	310
Alexandria National Cemetery 209 E Shamrock St	Pineville	LA	71360	**800-827-1000**	318-449-1793	135

Alphabetical Section

Name / Address	City	State	ZIP	Toll-Free	Phone	Class
Alexandria Real Estate Equities Inc 385 E Colorado Blvd Ste 299 *NYSE: ARE*	Pasadena	CA	91101	800-776-9437	626-578-0777	653
Alexandria Veterans Affairs Medical Ctr 2495 Shreveport Hwy 71 N	Pineville	LA	71360	800-375-8387	318-473-0010	374-8
Alexandria/Pineville Area Convention & Visitors Bureau (APACVB) 707 Main St PO Box 1070	Alexandria	LA	71301	800-551-9546	318-442-9546	208
Alexian Bros Medical Ctr 800 Biesterfield Rd	Elk Grove Village	IL	60007	800-432-5005	847-437-5500	374-3
Alexis Hotel 1007 First Ave	Seattle	WA	98104	866-356-8894	206-624-4844	379
Alexis Park Resort 375 E Harmon Ave	Las Vegas	NV	89169	800-582-2228	702-796-3300	667
ALF (American Liver Foundation) 39 Broadway	New York	NY	10006	800-465-4837	212-668-1000	47-17
Alfa Aesar Co 26 Parkridge Rd	Ward Hill	MA	01835	800-343-0660	978-521-6300	144
Alfa Corp 2108 E S Blvd	Montgomery	AL	36116	800-964-2532	334-288-0375	456-1
Alfalfa Electric Co-op Inc 121 E Main St	Cherokee	OK	73728	888-736-3837	580-596-3333	247
Alfiniti Inc 1152 rue Manic	Chicoutimi	QC	G7K1A2	800-334-8731	418-696-2545	491
Alforex Seeds 38001 County Rd 27	Woodland	CA	95695	877-560-5181	530-666-3331	278
Alfred A. Loeb State Park 725 Summer St NE Ste C	Salem	OR	97301	800-551-6949	503-986-0707	564
Alfred Angelo Inc 1301 Virginia Dr	Fort Washington	PA	19034	888-218-0044	215-659-5300	154-20
Alfred Hitchcock Mystery Magazine 44 Wall St Ste 904	New York	NY	10005	800-220-7443		456-11
Alfred Nickles Bakery Inc 26 N Main St	Navarre	OH	44662	800-597-9096	330-879-5635	297-1
Alger Family of Funds PO Box 8480	Boston	MA	02266	800-992-3863		527
Alger Mfg Company Inc 724 S Bon View Ave	Ontario	CA	91761	800-854-9833	909-986-4591	620
Algo Communication Products Ltd 4500 Beedie St	Burnaby	BC	V5J5L2	800-226-7722	604-438-3333	248
Algoa Correctional Ctr 8501 No More Victims Rd	Jefferson City	MO	65102	800-392-1111	573-751-3911	215
Algoma Hardwoods Inc 1001 Perry St	Algoma	WI	54201	800-678-8910	920-487-5221	238
Algoma University College 1520 Queen St E	Sault Sainte Marie	ON	P6A2G4	888-254-6628	705-949-2301	354
Algy Team Collection 440 NE First Ave	Hallandale	FL	33009	800-458-2549	954-457-8100	154-18
ALI (American Law Institute) 4025 Chestnut St	Philadelphia	PA	19104	800-253-6397	215-243-1600	48-10
ALI's Database Consultants 1151 Williams Dr	Aiken	SC	29803	866-257-8970	803-648-5931	182
Alice Lloyd College 100 Purpose Rd *Admissions	Pippa Passes	KY	41844	888-280-4252*	606-368-6000	167
Alice Travel Luxury Cruises & Tour 277 Fairfield Rd Ste 218	Fairfield	NJ	07004	800-229-2542		770
Alidade Technology Inc 111 Knoll Dr	Collegeville	PA	19426	877-265-1581		198
Alien Technology Corp 18220 Butterfield Blvd	Morgan Hill	CA	95037	866-734-3669	408-782-3900	645
Aliments Asta Inc 511 Ave De La Gare	St Alexandre-De-Kamouraska	QC	G0L2G0	800-463-1355	418-495-2728	297-26
ALine Inc 2206 E Gladwick St	Rancho Dominguez	CA	90220	877-707-8575		740
Alion Science & Technology 1750 Tysons Blvd Ste 1300	McLean	VA	22102	877-439-9227	703-918-4480	263
Alisal Guest Ranch & Resort 1054 Alisal Rd	Solvang	CA	93463	800-425-4725	805-688-6411	667
Alisal Union Elementary School District 1205 E Market St	Salinas	CA	93905	800-782-7463	831-753-5700	683
ALISE (Association for Library & Information Science Education) 2150 N 107th St Ste 205	Seattle	WA	98133	877-275-7547	206-209-5267	48-11
Alishaev Bros Inc 20 W 47th St Ste 203	New York	NY	10036	877-859-6020		411
Alive Hospice Inc 1718 Patterson St	Nashville	TN	37203	800-327-1085	615-327-1085	371
Aljira Ctr for Contemporary Arts 591 Broad St	Newark	NJ	07102	800-852-7699	973-622-1600	519
Alk - Abello Pharmaceuticals Inc 35-151 Brunel Rd	Mississauga	ON	L4Z2H6	800-663-0972	905-290-9952	233
Alken Inc 40 Hercules Dr	Colchester	VT	05446	800-357-4777	802-655-3159	690
Alkermes Inc 852 Winter St *NASDAQ: ALKS*	Waltham	MA	02451	800-848-4876	781-609-6000	84
Alkinco PO Box 278	New York	NY	10116	800-424-7118	212-719-3070	348
All Aboard Benefits 6162 E Mockingird Ln Ste 104	Dallas	TX	75214	800-462-2322	214-821-6677	391-7
All Aboard Cruises Inc 11114 SW 127th Ct	Miami	FL	33186	800-883-8657	305-385-8657	769
All Aboard Travel PO Box 90074	Chattanooga	TN	37412	800-499-9877	423-499-9977	758
All American Grating Inc 3001 Grand Ave	Pittsburgh	PA	15225	800-962-9692	412-771-6970	491
All American Moving Group LLC PO Box 271277	Memphis	TN	38167	800-467-2900	901-353-3900	778
All American Ticket Service 2616 Philadelphia Pike Ste E	Claymont	DE	19703	800-669-0571		748
All Classical Portland 211 SE Caruthers St Ste 200	Portland	OR	97214	888-306-5277	503-943-5828	642-93
All Cruise Travel 1723 Hamilton Ave	San Jose	CA	95125	800-227-8473	408-295-1200	769
All Direct Travel Services Inc 19000 Macarthur Blvd Ste 625	Irvine	CA	92612	800-862-1516	949-474-8100	770
All Foils Inc 16100 Imperial Pkwy	Strongsville	OH	44149	800-521-0054	440-572-3645	491
All Graphic Supplies 6691 Edwards Blvd	Mississauga	ON	L5T2H8	800-501-4451	905-795-2610	789
All in One Poster Co 8521 Whitaker St	Buena Park	CA	90621	800-273-0307	714-521-7720	44
All Inc 185 Plato Blvd W	Saint Paul	MN	55107	800-829-2127	651-227-6331	37
All Makes Office Equipment Co 2558 Farnam St	Omaha	NE	68131	800-341-2413	402-341-2413	322
All Metals Industries Inc PO Box 807	Belmont	NH	03220	800-654-6043	603-267-7023	491
All New Stamping Co 10801 Lower Azusa Rd	El Monte	CA	91731	800-877-7775		487
All Nippon Airways Company Ltd 2050 W 190th St Ste 100	Torrance	CA	90504	800-235-9262		25
All Source Security Container Mfg Corp 40 Mills Rd	Barrie	ON	L4N6H4	866-526-4579	705-726-6460	801-1
All Star Glass Co Inc 1845 Morena Blvd	San Diego	CA	92110	800-225-4184	619-275-3343	61-2
All States Inc 602 N 12th St *Cust Svc	Saint Charles	IL	60174	800-621-5837*	773-728-0525	607
All Tile Inc 1201 Chase Ave	Elk Grove Village	IL	60007	877-255-8453	847-979-2500	193-1
All Tune & Lube Brakes & More Inc 8334 Veteran's Hwy	Millersville	MD	21108	877-978-1758	410-987-1011	61-5
All Tune & Lube International Inc *ATL International Inc* 8334 Veterans Hwy *Cust Svc	Millersville	MD	21108	877-978-1758*	410-987-1011	61-5
All Weather Inc 1165 National Dr	Sacramento	CA	95834	800-824-5873	916-928-1000	471
All West Coach Lines 7701 Wilbur Way	Sacramento	CA	95828	800-843-2121	916-423-4000	106
All West Communications Inc 50 West 100 North	Kamas	UT	84036	866-255-9378	435-783-4361	115
All West Select Sires 450 N Hill Blvd	Burlington	WA	98233	800-426-2697		445
All World Travel Inc 314 Gilmer St	Sulphur Springs	TX	75482	866-298-6067	903-885-0896	773
Alladin Plastics Inc 140 Industrial Dr	Surgoinsville	TN	37873	877-536-4693	423-345-2351	603
Allamakee-Clayton Electric Co-op (ACEC) 229 Hwy 51 PO Box 715	Postville	IA	52162	888-788-1551	563-864-7611	247
All-American Co-op PO Box 125	Stewartville	MN	55976	888-354-4058	507-533-4222	275
Allamon Tool Company Inc 18935 Freeport Dr	Montgomery	TX	77356	877-449-5433		538
Allan A Myers Inc 1805 Berks Rd PO Box 1340	Worcester	PA	19490	800-596-6118	610-222-8800	190-4
Allan Hancock College 800 S College Dr	Santa Maria	CA	93454	866-342-5242	805-922-6966	161
Allan Window Technologies Ltd 131 Caldari Rd	Concord	ON	L4K3Z9	800-760-5665	905-738-8600	236
Allana Buick & Bers Inc 990 Commercial St	Palo Alto	CA	94303	800-378-3405	650-543-5600	258
Allant Group Inc, The 2056 Westings Ave Ste 500	Naperville	IL	60563	800-367-7311		196
Allcare Medical Inc 125 Newtown Rd Ste 300	Plainview	NY	11803	800-244-4660		363
All-Clad Metalcrafters LLC 424 Morganza Rd *Cust Svc	Canonsburg	PA	15317	800-255-2523*	724-745-8300	485
Allegacy Federal Credit Union 1691 Westbrook Plaza Dr	Winston-Salem	NC	27103	800-782-4670	336-774-3400	221
Allegan County Tourist & Recreational Council 3255 122nd Ave Ste 103	Allegan	MI	49010	888-425-5342	269-686-9088	208
Allegany College of Maryland 12401 Willowbrook Rd SE	Cumberland	MD	21502	800-974-0203	301-784-5000	161
Allegheny College 520 N Main St	Meadville	PA	16335	800-521-5293	814-332-4351	167
Allegheny Design Management Inc 1154 Parks Industrial Dr	Vandergrift	PA	15690	800-927-2611	724-845-7336	778
Allegheny Institute for Public Policy 305 Mt Lebanon Blvd Ste 208	Pittsburgh	PA	15234	800-242-2184	412-440-0079	631
Allegheny Petroleum Products Co 999 Airbrake Ave	Wilmerding	PA	15148	800-600-2900	412-829-1990	579
Allegheny Power 800 Cabin Hill Dr *Cust Svc	Greensburg	PA	15601	800-255-3443*	724-837-3000	785
Allegheny Technologies Inc 1000 Six PPG Pl *NYSE: ATI* ■ *Sales	Pittsburgh	PA	15222	800-258-3586*	412-394-2800	721
Allegheny Valley Bank 5137 Butler St *OTC: AVLY*	Pittsburgh	PA	15201	888-397-3742	412-781-1464	360-2
Allegheny Wesleyan College 2161 Woodsdale Rd	Salem	OH	44460	800-292-3153	330-337-6403	160
Allegiance Health 205 NE Ave	Jackson	MI	49201	800-872-6480	517-788-4800	374-3
Allegiance Security Group LLC 2900 Arendell St Ste 18	Morehead City	NC	28557	866-747-2748	252-247-1138	691
Allegiant International LLC 1710 N Main St	Auburn	IN	46706	866-841-3671		262
Allegis Group Inc 7301 Pkwy Dr	Hanover	MD	21076	800-927-8090	410-579-3000	719
Allegra Network LLC 47585 Galleon Dr *General	Plymouth	MI	48170	800-726-9050*	248-596-8600	112
Allegro Coffee Co 12799 Claude Ct	Thornton	CO	80241	800-530-3995	303-444-4844	297-7
Allegro Corp 20048 NE San Rafael St	Portland	OR	97230	800-288-2007	503-491-8480	522
Allen & Co Inc 1401 South Florida Avenue	Lakeland	FL	33803	800-950-2526	863-688-9000	688
Allen Bros Inc 3737 S Halsted St	Chicago	IL	60609	800-548-7777	773-890-5100	472
Allen Co 712 E Main St	Blanchester	OH	45107	800-329-2491	937-783-2491	9

Name	Address	City	State	ZIP	Toll-Free	Phone	Class
Allen Communication Learning Services	55 West 900 South	Salt Lake City	UT	84101	**866-310-7800**	801-537-7800	180-3
Allen Company Inc	525 Burbank St	Broomfield	CO	80020	**800-876-8600**	303-469-1857	190-4
Allen County	1 N Washington St	Iola	KS	66749	**866-444-1407**	620-365-1407	338
Allen County Community College	1801 N Cottonwood St	Iola	KS	66749	**800-444-0535**	620-365-5116	161
Allen County Public Library	900 Library Plaza	Fort Wayne	IN	46802	**800-448-6160**	260-421-1200	434-3
Allen County War Memorial Coliseum	4000 Parnell Ave	Fort Wayne	IN	46805	**800-745-3000**	260-482-9502	718
Allen Industries Inc	6434 Burnt Poplar Rd	Greensboro	NC	27409	**800-967-2553**	336-668-2791	699
Allen Lumber Company Inc	502 N Main St	Barre	VT	05641	**800-696-2666**	802-476-4156	114
Allen Lund Company Inc	4529 Angeles Crest Hwy Ste 300	La Canada	CA	91011	**800-777-6142**		312
Allen Memorial Hospital	1825 Logan Ave	Waterloo	IA	50703	**888-343-4165**	319-235-3941	374-3
Allen Parish	PO Box 1280	Oberlin	LA	70655	**888-639-4868**	337-639-4868	338
Allen Press Inc	810 E Tenth St PO Box 1897	Lawrence	KS	66044	**800-627-0932**	785-843-1235	46
Allen Systems Group Inc (ASG)	1333 Third Ave S	Naples	FL	34102	**800-932-5536**	239-435-2200	180-12
Allen University	1530 Harden St	Columbia	SC	29204	**877-625-5368**	803-376-5700	167
Allen Ventures Inc	517 State Farm Rd	Deerfield	WI	53531	**877-423-9800**	608-423-9800	659
Allenberry Resort	1559 Boiling Springs Rd	Boiling Springs	PA	17007	**800-430-5468**	717-258-3211	667
Allen-Edmonds Shoe Corp	201 E Seven Hills Rd *Cust Svc	Port Washington	WI	53074	**800-235-2348***	262-235-6512	302
Allentown Equipment	1733 90th St	Sturtevant	WI	53177	**800-553-3414**		386
Allentown School District (ASD)	31 S Penn St	Allentown	PA	18105	**877-262-1492**	484-765-4000	683
Allen-Vanguard Corp	2400 St Laurent Blvd	Ottawa	ON	K1G5B4	**800-644-9078**	613-739-9646	575
Allerair Industries Inc	9600 Rte Transcanadienne	Saint-laurent	QC	H4S1V9	**888-852-8247**		40
Allergan	2525 Dupont Dr PO Box 19534	Irvine	CA	92612	**800-347-4500**	714-246-4500	476
Allergan Inc	2525 Dupont Dr *NYSE: AGN*	Irvine	CA	92612	**800-347-4500**	714-246-4500	582
Allergychoices Inc	2800 National Dr Ste 100	Onalaska	WI	54650	**866-793-1680**	608-793-1580	239
Allermed Laboratories Inc	7203 Convoy Ct	San Diego	CA	92111	**800-221-2748**		233
ALLETE Inc	30 W Superior St *NYSE: ALE*	Duluth	MN	55802	**800-228-4966**	218-279-5000	360-5
Allevity HR & Payroll	870 Manzanita Ct Ste A	Chico	CA	95926	**800-447-8233**	530-345-2486	630
All-Fab Building Components Inc	1755 Dugald Rd	Winnipeg	MB	R2J0H3	**800-665-0335**	204-661-8880	44
Alliance Abroad Group LP	1221 S Mo Pac Expy Ste 250	Austin	TX	78746	**866-622-7623**	512-457-8062	40
Alliance Corp	2395 Meadowpine Blvd	Mississauga	ON	L5N7W6	**888-821-4797**	905-821-4797	491
Alliance Credit Counseling Inc	15720 Brixham Hill Ave Ste 575	Charlotte	NC	28277	**888-995-7856**	704-341-1010	40
Alliance for Aging Research (AAR)	750 17th St NW Ste 1100	Washington	DC	20006	**866-840-6283**	202-293-2856	47-17
Alliance for Children & Families Inc	11700 W Lk Pk Dr	Milwaukee	WI	53224	**800-221-3726**	414-359-1040	47-6
Alliance For Employee Growth & Development Inc, The	80 Cottontail Ln Ste 320	Somerset	NJ	08873	**800-323-3436**		195
Alliance for International Educational & Cultural Exchange	1776 Massachusetts Ave NW Ste 620	Washington	DC	20036	**888-304-9023**	202-293-6141	47-11
Alliance for Lupus Research (ALR)	28 W 44th St Ste 501	New York	NY	10036	**800-867-1743**	212-218-2840	47-17
Alliance for Retired Americans	815 16th St NW 4th Fl	Washington	DC	20006	**888-373-6497**	202-637-5399	47-6
Alliance for Telecommunications Industry Solutions (ATIS)	1200 G St NW Ste 500	Washington	DC	20005	**800-649-1202**	202-628-6380	48-20
Alliance Grain Co	1306 W Eigth St	Gibson City	IL	60936	**800-222-2451**	217-784-4284	277
Alliance Imaging Inc	100 Bayview Cir Ste 400	Newport Beach	CA	92660	**800-544-3215**	949-242-5300	383
Alliance Limousine Inc	14553 Delano St Ste 210	Van Nuys	CA	91411	**800-954-5466**		441
Alliance One International Inc	8001 Aerial Ctr Pkwy PO Box 2009 *NYSE: AOI*	Morrisville	NC	27560	**800-937-5449**	919-379-4300	754
Alliance Reservations Network	21640 N 19th Ave Ste C102 *Cust Svc	Phoenix	AZ	85027	**800-419-1545***	602-444-9993	376
Alliance Rubber Co	210 Carpenter Dam Rd	Hot Springs	AR	71901	**800-626-5940**		674
Alliance to Save Energy (ASE)	1850 M St NW Ste 600	Washington	DC	20036	**800-862-2086**	202-857-0666	47-12
Alliance Wood Group Engineering LP	330 Barker Cypress Rd	Houston	TX	77094	**866-313-0052**	281-828-6000	193-2
Alliance Worldwide Investigative Group Inc	4 Executive Park Dr	Clifton Park	NY	12065	**800-579-2911**	518-514-2944	390
Alliance, The	810 Tate St	Corinth	MS	38834	**877-347-0545**	662-287-5269	138
AllianceBernstein Holding LP (AB)	1345 Ave of the Americas *NYSE: AB* ■ *Cust Svc	New York	NY	10105	**800-221-5672***	212-486-5800	401
AllianceOne Inc	4850 E St Rd Ste 300	Trevose	PA	19053	**866-405-7241**	215-354-5511	159
Alliant Energy Corp	4902 N Biltmore Ln Ste 1000 *NYSE: LNT*	Madison	WI	53718	**800-255-4268**		785
Alliant International University	10455 Pomerado Rd	San Diego	CA	92131	**866-825-5426**	858-635-4772	167
Alliant Powder	2299 Snake River Ave	Lewiston	ID	83501	**800-276-9337**	800-379-1732	270
Allianz Life Insurance Company of North America	PO Box 1344	Minneapolis	MN	55416	**800-950-5872**		391-2
Allied Aerofoam Products LLC	216 Kelsey Ln	Tampa	FL	33619	**800-338-9140**	813-626-0090	600
Allied Air Enterprises	215 Metropolitan Dr	West Columbia	SC	29170	**800-448-5872**		15
Allied Automotive Group	2302 ParkLake Dr Bldg 15 Ste 600	Atlanta	GA	30345	**800-476-2058**		778
Allied Bldg Products Corp	15 E Union Ave	East Rutherford	NJ	07073	**800-541-2198**	201-507-8400	193-3
Allied Body Works Inc	625 S 96th St *General	Seattle	WA	98108	**800-733-7450***	206-763-7811	515
Allied Construction Products LLC	3900 Kelley Ave *Cust Svc	Cleveland	OH	44114	**800-321-1046***	216-431-2600	192
Allied Construction Services & Color Inc	2122 Fleur Dr PO Box 937	Des Moines	IA	50304	**800-365-4855**	515-288-4855	191-9
Allied Container Systems Inc	201 N Civic Dr Ste 180	Walnut Creek	CA	94596	**800-943-6510**		548
Allied Controls Inc	150 E Aurora St	Waterbury	CT	06708	**800-788-0955**	203-757-4200	205
Allied Corrosion Industries Inc	1550 Cobb Industrial Dr	Marietta	GA	30066	**800-241-0809**	770-425-1355	258
Allied Court Reporters Inc	115 Phenix Ave	Cranston	RI	02920	**888-443-3767**	401-946-5500	444
Allied Electronics Inc	7151 Jack Newell Blvd S	Fort Worth	TX	76118	**866-433-5722**	817-595-3500	248
Allied Employer Group	4400 Buffalo Gap Rd Ste 4500	Abilene	TX	79606	**800-495-3836**	325-695-5822	630
Allied Erecting & Dismantling Company Inc	2100 Poland Ave	Youngstown	OH	44502	**800-624-2867**	330-744-0808	191-16
Allied Fastener & Tool Inc	1130 Ng St	Lake Worth	FL	33460	**877-353-3731**	561-585-2113	350
Allied Fire & Security Inc	425 W Second Ave *Acctg	Spokane	WA	99201	**888-333-2632***	509-321-8778	690
Allied Fire Protection LP	PO Box 2842	Pearland	TX	77588	**800-604-2600**	281-485-6803	191-10
ALLIED Group Inc	1100 Locust St	Des Moines	IA	50391	**800-532-1436**	515-508-4211	391-4
Allied Group Inc, The	25 Amflex Dr	Cranston	RI	02921	**800-556-6310**	401-946-6100	176
Allied Health Group LLC	145 Technology Pkwy NW	Norcross	GA	30092	**800-355-6150**	800-741-4674	719
Allied Healthcare Products Inc	1720 Sublette Ave *NASDAQ: AHPI*	Saint Louis	MO	63110	**800-444-3954**	314-771-2400	476
Allied Infosecurity Inc	1009 W 9th Ave Ste B	King Of Prussia	PA	19406	**866-240-0094**		396
Allied Insurance	1100 Locust St	Des Moines	CA	50391	**800-532-1436**		391-4
Allied International	13207 Bradley Ave *General	Sylmar	CA	91342	**800-533-8333***	818-364-2333	351
Allied International Credit Corp	16635 Young St Unit 26	Newmarket	ON	L3X1V6	**877-451-2594**		159
Allied International NA Inc	700 Oakmont Ln	Westmont	IL	60559	**800-444-6787**	630-570-3500	518
Allied Machine & Engineering Corp	120 Deeds Dr	Dover	OH	44622	**800-321-5537**	330-343-4283	492
Allied Mechanical Services Inc	145 N Plains Industrial Rd	Wallingford	CT	06492	**888-237-3017**	269-344-0191	191-10
Allied Motion Technologies Inc	495 Commerce Dr Ste 3 *NASDAQ: AMOT*	Amherst	NY	14228	**888-392-5543**	716-242-8634	250
Allied Moulded Products Inc	222 N Union St	Bryan	OH	43506	**800-722-2679**	419-636-4217	814
Allied Oil & Supply Inc	2209 S 24th St	Omaha	NE	68108	**800-333-3717**	402-344-4343	578
Allied Oilfield Machine and Pump LLC	202 Hulon Moreland Rd	Levelland	TX	79336	**855-378-4787**		537
Allied Photocopy Inc	1821 University Dr NW	Huntsville	AL	35801	**877-539-2973**	256-539-2973	626
Allied Plastics Company Inc	2001 Walnut St *Cust Svc	Jacksonville	FL	32206	**800-999-0386***	904-359-0386	320-1
Allied Power Group LLC	10131 Mills Rd	Houston	TX	77070	**888-830-3535**	281-444-3535	263
Allied Printing Services Inc	1 Allied Way	Manchester	CT	06045	**800-225-8777**	860-643-1101	626
Allied Services Rehabilitation Hospital	475 Morgan Hwy	Scranton	PA	18508	**888-734-2272**	570-348-1300	374-6
Allied Sinterings Inc	29 Briar Ridge Rd	Danbury	CT	06810	**877-875-0464**		491
Allied Steel Construction Co Inc	2211 NW First Terr	Oklahoma City	OK	73107	**800-522-4658**	405-232-7531	266-3
Allied Supply Company Inc	1100 E Monument Ave	Dayton	OH	45402	**800-589-5690**	937-224-9833	663
Allied Systems Co	21433 SW Oregon St	Sherwood	OR	97140	**800-285-7000**	503-625-2560	275
Allied Telesyn International Corp	19800 N Creek Pkwy Ste 100	Bothell	WA	98011	**800-424-4284**	425-481-3895	178
Allied Tool Products	9334 N 107th St	Milwaukee	WI	53224	**800-558-5147**	414-355-8280	454
Allied Toyotalift	1640 Island Home Ave	Knoxville	TN	37920	**866-538-0667**	865-573-0995	56
Allied Vaughn	7600 Parklawn Ste 300	Minneapolis	MN	55435	**800-323-0281**	952-832-3100	656

Company / Address	City	State	ZIP	Toll-Free	Phone	Class
AlliedBarton Security Services 150 S Warner Rd	King of Prussia	PA	19406	**866-703-7666**	484-654-3800	691
Allied-Horizontal Wireline Services LLC 15995 N Barker's Landing Ste 140	Houston	TX	77079	**888-494-9580**	713-343-7280	535
Allied-Locke Industries 1088 Corregidor Rd	Dixon	IL	61021	**800-435-7752**	815-288-1471	619
Alligator Records & Artist Management Inc PO Box 60234	Chicago	IL	60660	**800-344-5609**	773-973-7736	655
All-Inclusive Vacations Inc 1595 Iris St	Lakewood	CO	80215	**866-980-6483**	303-980-6483	769
Allison Payment Systems LLC 2200 Production Dr	Indianapolis	IN	46241	**800-755-2440**		109
Allmar Inc 287 Riverton Ave	Winnipeg	MB	R2L0N2	**800-230-5516**	204-668-1000	238
AllMed Healthcare Management Inc 621 SW Alder St Ste 740	Portland	OR	97205	**888-289-6015**	503-274-9916	462
AllMeds Inc 151 Lafayette Dr Ste 401	Oak Ridge	TN	37830	**888-343-6337**	865-482-1999	38
Allomatic Products Co 102 Jericho Tpke Ste 104 Floral Pk	Floral Park	NY	11001	**800-568-0330**	516-775-0330	60
Allor Manufacturing Inc 12534 Emerson Dr	Brighton	MI	48116	**888-382-6300**	248-486-4500	209
AlloSource 6278 S Troy Cir	Centennial	CO	80111	**888-873-8330**	720-873-0213	544
Allot Communications 300 Tradecenter Ste 4680	Woburn	MA	01801	**877-255-6826**	781-939-9300	180-10
Alloy Engineering & Casting Co 1700 W Washington St	Champaign	IL	61821	**800-348-2880**	217-398-3200	308
Alloy Stainless Products Co 611 Union Blvd	Totowa	NJ	07512	**800-631-8372**	973-256-1616	594
All-Pro Fasteners Inc 1916 Peyco Dr N	Arlington	TX	76001	**800-361-6627**	817-467-5700	351
Allscripts Healthcare Solutions 222 Merchandise Mart Plz Ste 2024 *NASDAQ: MDRX*	Chicago	IL	60654	**800-654-0889**		180-10
All-Search & Inspection Inc 1108 E S Union Ave	Midvale	UT	84047	**800-227-3152**	801-984-8160	632
All-South Subcontractors Inc 2678 Queenstown Rd	Birmingham	AL	35210	**800-873-8110**	205-836-8111	191-12
Allstar Fire Equipment Inc 12328 Lower Azusa Rd	Arcadia	CA	91006	**800-425-5787**	626-652-0900	677
Allstar Magnetics LLC 6205 NE 63rd St	Vancouver	WA	98661	**800-356-5977**	360-693-0213	248
All-Star Recruiting LLC 6119 Lyons Rd	Coconut Creek	FL	33073	**800-928-0229**		262
Allstate Corp 2775 Sanders Rd *NYSE: ALL*	Northbrook	IL	60062	**800-255-7828**	847-402-5000	360-4
Allstate Floral & Craft Inc 14038 Park Pl	Cerritos	CA	90703	**800-433-4056**	562-926-2302	295
Allstate Leasing Inc 1 Olympic Pl	Towson	MD	21204	**800-223-4885**		291
Allstate Life Insurance Co 3100 Sanders Rd Allstate W Plz *Cust Svc	Northbrook	IL	60062	**800-366-1411***	847-402-5000	391-2
Allsteel Inc 2210 Second Ave *Cust Svc	Muscatine	IA	52761	**888-255-7833***	563-272-4800	320-1
Allstream Corp 200 Wellington St W *Cust Svc	Toronto	ON	M5V3G2	**888-288-2273***	416-345-2000	733
Allsup Inc 300 Allsup Pl	Belleville	IL	62223	**800-854-1418**		196
Alltech Inc 3031 Catnip Hill Pike	Nicholasville	KY	40356	**800-289-8324**	859-885-9613	581
All-Temp Refrigeration Services Inc 271 Hwy 1085	Madisonville	LA	70447	**888-626-1277**		609
ALL-TEST Pro LLC 123 Spencer Plain Rd	Old Saybrook	CT	06475	**800-952-8776**	860-399-4222	203
Allvac Inc 2020 Ashcraft Ave PO Box 5030	Monroe	NC	28110	**800-841-5491**	704-289-4511	484
Allview Networks LLC 8303 Arlington Dr Ste 210	Fairfax	VA	22031	**888-982-8489**		5
Allway Tools Inc 1255 Seabury Ave	Bronx	NY	10462	**800-422-5592**	718-792-3636	756
All-Ways Adv Co 1442 Broad St	Bloomfield	NJ	07003	**800-255-9291**	973-338-0700	4
Allwire Inc 16395 Ave 24 1/2 PO Box 1000	Chowchilla	CA	93610	**800-255-3828**	559-665-4893	811
Ally Plm Solutions Inc 9155 Governors Way	Cincinnati	OH	45249	**800-631-5961**	513-984-0480	258
ALM (American Lawyer Media Inc) 120 Broadway 5th Fl	New York	NY	10271	**877-256-2472**	212-457-9400	634-9
Alma College 614 W Superior St	Alma	MI	48801	**800-321-2562**	989-463-7139	167
Alma Products Co 2000 Michigan Ave	Alma	MI	48801	**877-427-2624**	989-463-1151	59
Almanac, The 2600 Boyce Plz Rd Ste 142	Pittsburgh	PA	15241	**800-222-6397**	724-941-7725	531-4
Almatis Inc 501 W Pk Rd	Leetsdale	PA	15056	**800-643-8771**	412-630-2800	142
Almo Corp 2709 Commerce Way	Philadelphia	PA	19154	**800-345-2566**	215-698-4000	37
Almost Family Inc 9510 Ormsby Stn Rd Ste 300 *NASDAQ: AFAM*	Louisville	KY	40223	**800-828-9769**	502-891-1000	363
Alnylam Pharmaceuticals Inc 300 Third St 3rd Fl *NASDAQ: ALNY*	Cambridge	MA	02142	**866-330-0326**	617-551-8200	84
ALOA (Associated Locksmiths of America) 3500 Easy St	Dallas	TX	75247	**800-532-2562**	214-819-9733	48-3
Aloft Broomfield Denver 8300 Arista Pl	Broomfield	CO	80021	**866-716-8143**	303-635-2000	705
Aloft Chicago O'hare 9700 Balmoral Ave	Rosemont	IL	60018	**866-716-8143**	847-671-4444	705

Company / Address	City	State	ZIP	Toll-Free	Phone	Class
Aloha Medicinals Inc 2300 Arrowhead Dr	Carson City	NV	89706	**877-835-6091**	775-886-6300	233
Aloha Petroleum Ltd 1132 Bishop St Ste 1700	Honolulu	HI	96813	**800-621-4654**	808-522-9700	112
Alostar Bank 3680 Grandview Pkwy Ste 200	Birmingham	AL	35243	**877-738-6391**	205-298-6391	69
ALP Industries Inc 1229 W Lincoln Hwy	Coatesville	PA	19320	**800-220-2571**	610-384-1300	676
Alpena Area Chamber of Commerce 235 W Chisholm St	Alpena	MI	49707	**800-425-7362**	989-354-4181	138
Alpena Area Convention & Visitors Bureau 235 W Chisholm St	Alpena	MI	49707	**800-425-7362**	989-354-4181	208
Alpena Community College (ACC) 665 Johnson St	Alpena	MI	49707	**888-468-6222**	989-356-9021	161
Alpena County George N Fletcher Public Library 211 N First Ave	Alpena	MI	49707	**877-737-4106**	989-356-6188	434-3
Alpena Oil Co Inc 235 Water St	Alpena	MI	49707	**800-968-1098**	989-356-1098	325
Alpena Regional Medical Ctr 1501 W Chisholm St	Alpena	MI	49707	**800-556-8842**	989-356-7000	374-3
Alpenhof Lodge 3255 W Village Dr	Teton Village	WY	83025	**800-732-3244**	307-733-3242	379
Alpha & Omega Financial Management Consultants Inc 8580 La Mesa Blvd Ste 100	La Mesa	CA	91942	**800-755-5060**		196
Alpha 1 Induction Service Ctr Inc 1525 Old Alum Creek Dr	Columbus	OH	43209	**800-991-2599**	614-253-8900	319
Alpha Assoc Inc 145 Lehigh Ave	Lakewood	NJ	08701	**800-631-5399**	732-634-5700	742-2
Alpha Card Services Inc 475 Veit Rd	Huntingdon Valley	PA	19006	**866-253-2227**		253
Alpha Chi Omega 5939 Castle Creek Pkwy N Dr	Indianapolis	IN	46250	**800-328-0522**	317-579-5050	47-16
Alpha Chi Sigma 2141 N Franklin Rd	Indianapolis	IN	46219	**800-252-4369**	317-357-5944	47-16
Alpha Energy Solutions Inc 7200 Distribution Dr	Louisville	KY	40258	**888-212-6324**	502-968-0121	609
Alpha Epsilon Phi Sorority (AEPhi) 11 Lake Ave Ext Ste 1-A	Danbury	CT	06811	**888-668-4293**	203-748-0029	47-16
Alpha Epsilon Pi Fraternity Inc 8815 Wesleyan Rd	Indianapolis	IN	46268	**800-684-3608**	317-876-1913	47-16
Alpha Gamma Rho 10101 NW Ambassador Dr	Kansas City	MO	64153	**888-241-4546**	816-891-9200	47-16
Alpha Group, The 3767 Alpha Way	Bellingham	WA	98226	**800-322-5742**	360-647-2360	255
Alpha Imaging Inc 4455 Glenbrook Rd	Willoughby	OH	44094	**800-331-7327**	440-953-3800	474
Alpha Industries Inc 14200 Pk Meadow Dr Ste 110S *General	Chantilly	VA	20151	**866-631-0719***	703-378-1420	154-5
Alpha Natural Resources Inc 1 Alpha Pl PO Box 16429 *OTC: ANR*	Bristol	VA	24209	**866-322-5742**	276-619-4410	500
Alpha Omega International Dental Fraternity 50 W Edmonston Dr	Rockville	MD	20852	**877-368-6326**	301-738-6400	47-16
Alpha Omicron Pi International 5390 Virginia Way	Brentwood	TN	37027	**855-230-1183**	615-370-0920	47-16
Alpha Packaging 1555 Page Industrial Blvd	Saint Louis	MO	63132	**800-421-4772**	314-427-4300	97
Alpha Pro Tech Ltd 60 Centurian Dr	Markham	ON	L3R9R2	**800-749-1363**	905-479-0654	230
Alpha Rae Personnel Inc 347 W Berry St Ste 700	Fort Wayne	IN	46802	**800-837-8940**	260-426-8227	262
Alpha Sigma Phi National Fraternity 710 Adams St	Carmel	IN	46032	**866-515-4747**	317-843-1911	47-16
Alpha Tau Omega Fraternity (ATO) 1 N Pennsylvania St 12th Fl	Indianapolis	IN	46204	**800-798-9286**	317-684-1865	47-16
Alpha Technologies Services LLC 3030 Gilchrist Rd	Akron	OH	44305	**800-356-9886**	330-745-1641	203
Alpha Wire Co 711 Lidgerwood Ave	Elizabeth	NJ	07207	**800-522-5742**	908-925-8000	812
AlphaGraphics Inc 215 S State St Ste 320	Salt Lake City	UT	84111	**800-955-6246**	801-595-7270	626
AlphaKOR Group Inc 7800 Twin Oaks Dr	Windsor	ON	N8N5B6	**877-944-6009**	519-944-6009	182
Alphanumeric Systems Inc 3801 Wake Forest Rd	Raleigh	NC	27609	**800-638-6556**	919-781-7575	112
AlphaStaff Inc 800 Corporate Dr Ste 600	Fort Lauderdale	FL	33334	**888-335-9545**	954-267-1760	630
Alpina Manufacturing LLC 3418 N Knox Ave	Chicago	IL	60641	**800-915-2828**	773-202-8887	44
Alpine Adventure Trails Tours Inc 7495 Lower Thomaston Rd	Macon	GA	31220	**888-478-4004**		758
Alpine Bank of Colorado 2200 Grand Ave	Glenwood Springs	CO	81601	**888-425-7463**	970-945-2424	360-2
Alpine Electronics of America 19145 Gramercy Pl	Torrance	CA	90501	**800-257-4631**	310-326-8000	51
Alpine Engineered Products Inc 1100 Pk Central Blvd S Ste 2400 & 3800 *General	Pompano Beach	FL	33064	**800-786-6086***	954-781-3333	815
Alpine Fresh Inc 9300 NW 58th St Ste 201	Miami	FL	33178	**800-292-8777**	305-594-9117	298-7
Alpine Helen/White County Convention & Visitors Bureau 726 Bruckenstrasse PO Box 730	Helen	GA	30545	**800-858-8027**	706-878-2181	208
Alpine Innovations 275 North 950 East	Lehi	UT	84043	**866-489-6788**	801-766-4994	196
Alpine Lodge 434 Indian Creek Cir	Branson	MO	65616	**888-563-4388**	417-338-2514	705
Alpine Lumber Co 1120 W 122nd Ave Ste 301	Denver	CO	80234	**800-499-1634**	303-451-8001	193-3
Alpine Meats 9850 Lowr Sacramento Rd	Stockton	CA	95210	**800-399-6328**	209-477-2691	472
Alpine Power Systems Inc 24355 Capitol	Redford	MI	48239	**877-769-3762**	313-531-6600	757
Alpine Solutions Inc 3222 Corte Malpaso Ste 204	Camarillo	CA	93012	**855-388-1883**	805-388-1699	382

Name / Address	City	State	ZIP	Toll-Free	Phone	Class
Alpine Testing Inc 51 W Ctr St	Orem	UT	84057	**844-625-7463**		246
Alro Steel Corp 3100 E High St	Jackson	MI	49204	**800-877-2576**	517-787-5500	491
ALS (Albany Law School of Union University) 80 New Scotland Ave	Albany	NY	12208	**800-448-3500**	518-445-2311	168-1
ALS (American Littoral Society) 18 Hartshorne Dr Ste 1	Highlands	NJ	07732	**800-424-8802**	732-291-0055	47-13
ALSAC (American Lebanese Syrian Associated Charities) 262 Danny Thomas Pl	Memphis	TN	38105	**800-822-6344**	901-578-2000	47-5
Alsay Inc 6615 Gant St	Houston	TX	77066	**800-833-5969**	281-444-6960	191-15
ALSC (Association for Library Service to Children) 50 E Huron St	Chicago	IL	60611	**800-545-2433**	312-280-2163	48-11
Alsco Inc 505 East South Temple	Salt Lake City	UT	84102	**800-408-0208**	801-328-8831	785
Alsea Bay Historic Interpretive Ctr 725 Summer St NE Ste C	Salem	OR	97301	**800-551-6949**		564
ALTA (American Land Title Assn) 1828 L St NW Ste 705	Washington	DC	20036	**800-787-2582**	202-296-3671	48-10
Alta California N8350 High Rd	Watertown	WI	53094	**800-932-2855**	920-261-5065	11-2
Alta Dena Dairy 17851 E Railrd	City of Industry	CA	91748	**800-535-1369***		297-27
*Orders						
Alta Equipment Co 28775 Beck Rd	Wixom	MI	48393	**800-261-9642**	248-449-6700	358
Alta Lodge PO Box 8040	Alta	UT	84092	**800-707-2582***	801-742-3500	667
*Cust Svc						
Alta Resources 120 N Commercial St	Neenah	WI	54956	**877-464-2582**		734
Alta Via Consulting LLC 127 ConKinnon Dr	Lenoir City	TN	37772	**877-258-2842**		179
Alta-Fab Structures Ltd 504-13 Ave	Nisku	AB	T9E7P6	**800-252-7990**	780-955-7733	777
ALTAFF (Association for Library Trustees, Advocates, Friends & Foundations) 50 E Huron St	Chicago	IL	60611	**800-545-2433**		48-11
Altair Customer Intelligence 341 Cool Springs Blvd Ste 450	Franklin	TN	37067	**800-241-6631**	615-468-6800	196
Altair Engineering Inc 1820 E Big Beaver Rd	Troy	MI	48083	**888-222-7822**	248-614-2400	196
Altamaha Electric Membership Corp 611 W Liberty Ave PO Box 346	Lyons	GA	30436	**800-822-4563**	912-526-8181	247
Altamed Health Services Corp 500 Citadel Dr Ste 490	Los Angeles	CA	90040	**877-462-2582**	323-725-8751	363
Altametrics Inc 3191 Red Hill Ave Ste 100	Costa Mesa	CA	92626	**800-676-1281**		176
Altamont Commuter Express (ACE) 949 E Ch St	Stockton	CA	95202	**800-411-7245**		467
Altech LLC 242 America Pl	Jeffersonville	IN	47130	**800-264-8256**	812-282-8256	484
Altech Services Inc 1160 Parsippany Blvd Ste 202	Parsippany	NJ	07054	**888-725-8324**		179
Alter Trading Corp 700 Office Pkwy	Saint Louis	MO	63141	**888-337-2727**	314-872-2400	684
Altera Corp 101 Innovation Dr	San Jose	CA	95134	**800-767-3753***	408-544-7000	694
NASDAQ: ALTR ■ *Cust Svc						
Altera Payroll Inc 2400 Northside Crossing	Macon	GA	31210	**877-474-6060**	478-477-6060	2
Althoff Industries Inc 8001 S Rt 31	Crystal Lake	IL	60014	**800-225-2443**	815-455-7000	191-10
AltiGen Communications Inc 410 E Plumeria Dr	San Jose	CA	95134	**888-258-4436**	408-597-9000	732
OTC: ATGN						
Altimate Medical Inc 262 W First St	Morton	MN	56270	**800-342-8968**	507-697-6393	475
Altium Inc 2175 Salk Ave Ste 100	Carlsbad	CA	92008	**800-544-4186***	760-231-0760	180-5
*Sales						
Altman Lighting Inc 57 Alexander St	Yonkers	NY	10701	**800-425-8626**	914-476-7987	439
Altman Specialty Plants Inc 3742 Blue BiRd Canyon Rd	Vista	CA	92084	**800-773-7667**	760-744-8191	369
Altman Weil Inc PO Box 625	Newtown Square	PA	19073	**866-886-3600**	610-359-9900	196
Altmas Products 1201 Francisco St	Torrance	CA	90502	**800-678-6463**	310-559-4093	611
Altmeyer Home Stores Inc 6515 Rt 22	Delmont	PA	15626	**800-394-6628**	724-468-3434	362
Alton Memorial Hospital 1 Memorial Dr	Alton	IL	62002	**800-994-6610**	618-463-7311	374-3
Alton National Cemetery 600 Pearl St	Alton	IL	62003	**800-535-1117**	314-845-8320	135
Alton Regional Convention & Visitors Bureau (ARCVB) 200 Piasa St	Alton	IL	62002	**800-258-6645**	618-465-6676	208
Altoona Mirror 301 Cayuga Ave	Altoona	PA	16602	**800-222-1962**	814-946-7411	531-2
Altoona Regional Health System Altoona Hospital 620 Howard Ave	Altoona	PA	16601	**877-855-8152**	814-889-2011	374-3
Altoona VA Medical Ctr 2907 Pleasant Vly Blvd	Altoona	PA	16602	**877-626-2500**		374-8
Altoros Systems 830 Stewart Dr Ste 119	Sunnyvale	CA	94085	**855-258-6767**	650-395-7002	196
Alto-Shaam Inc W 164 N 9221 Water St PO Box 450	Menomonee Falls	WI	53052	**800-329-8744**	262-251-3800	299
Altran Solutions USA 2525 Rt 130 S	Cranbury	NJ	08512	**855-425-8726**	609-409-9790	740
ALTRES Inc 967 Kapiolani Blvd	Honolulu	HI	96814	**888-425-8737**	808-591-4940	719
Altru Hospital 1200 S Columbia Rd	Grand Forks	ND	58201	**800-732-4277**	701-780-5000	374-3
Alturas Analytics Inc 1324 Alturas Dr	Moscow	ID	83843	**877-344-1279**	208-883-3400	740
AlturnaMATS Inc 701 E Spring St Mailbox #9	Titusville	PA	16354	**800-438-9336**	814-827-8884	297
Altus Consulting Corp 38699 Old Wheatland Rd	Waterford	VA	20197	**800-300-4505**	703-929-4000	462
Aluchem Inc 1 Landy Ln	Cincinnati	OH	45215	**800-336-8519**	513-733-8519	486
Alumaweld Boats Inc 1601 Ave F	White City	OR	97503	**800-401-2628**	541-826-7171	89
Alumicor Ltd 290 Humberline Dr	Toronto	ON	M9W5S2	**877-258-6426**	416-745-4222	480
Aluminum & Stainless Inc PO Box 3484	Lafayette	LA	70502	**800-252-9074**	337-837-4381	491
Aluminum Distributing 2930 Sw Second Ave	Fort Lauderdale	FL	33315	**866-825-9271**	954-523-6474	491
Aluminum Ladder Co 1430 W Darlington St	Florence	SC	29501	**800-752-2526**	843-662-2595	486
Aluminum Line Products Co 24460 Sperry Cir	Westlake	OH	44145	**800-321-3154**	440-835-8880	695
Aluminum Precision Products Inc 3333 W Warner St	Santa Ana	CA	92704	**800-411-8983**	714-546-8125	482
Alumni Center, The 1241 University Dr N	Fargo	ND	58102	**800-279-8971**	701-231-6800	669
Alutiiq LLC 3909 Arctic Blvd Ste 400	Anchorage	AK	99503	**800-829-8547**	907-222-9500	360-3
Alva-Amco Pharmacal Cos Inc 7711 Merrimac Ave	Niles	IL	60714	**800-792-2582**	847-663-0700	582
Alvah Bushnell Co 519 E Chelten Ave	Philadelphia	PA	19144	**800-255-7434**	215-842-9520	559
Alvarado Hospital Medical Ctr 6655 Alvarado Rd	San Diego	CA	92120	**800-258-2723**	619-287-3270	374-3
Alvarado Mfg Company Inc 12660 Colony St	Chino	CA	91710	**800-423-4143**	909-591-8431	490
Alvernia College 540 Upland Ave	Reading	PA	19611	**888-258-3764**	610-796-8200	167
Alverno College PO Box 343922	Milwaukee	WI	53234	**800-933-3401**	414-382-6100	167
Alvin & Company Inc 1335 Blue Hills Ave	Bloomfield	CT	06002	**800-444-2584**	860-243-8991	42
Alvin C York Medical Ctr 3400 Lebanon Pike	Murfreesboro	TN	37129	**800-228-4973**	615-867-6000	374-8
Alvin Hollis & Co 1 Hollis St	South Weymouth	MA	02190	**800-649-5090**	781-335-2100	317
Alvin-Manvel Area Chamber of Commerce 105 W Willis St	Alvin	TX	77511	**888-755-6864**	281-331-3944	138
Alyeska Prince Hotel & Resort 1000 Arlberg Ave PO Box 249	Girdwood	AK	99587	**800-880-3880**	907-754-1111	667
Alzheimer's Assn 225 N Michigan Ave Fl 17	Chicago	IL	60601	**800-272-3900**	312-335-8700	47-17
Alzheimer's Disease Education & Referral Ctr PO Box 8250	Silver Spring	MD	20907	**800-438-4380**	301-495-1080	199
AM 570 LA Sports 3400 W Olive Ave Ste 550	Burbank	CA	91505	**866-987-2570**	818-559-2252	643
AM Best Co Ambest Rd	Oldwick	NJ	08858	**800-424-2378**	908-439-2200	634-10
AM Kinney 150 E Fourth St	Cincinnati	OH	45202	**800-265-3682**	513-421-2265	263
A&M Supply Corp 6701 90th Ave N	Pinellas Park	FL	33782	**800-877-8551**	727-541-6631	818
AMA (American Marketing Assn) 311 S Wacker Dr Ste 5800	Chicago	IL	60606	**800-262-1150**	312-542-9000	48-18
AMA (American Medical Assn) 515 N State St	Chicago	IL	60610	**800-621-8335**	312-464-5000	48-8
AMA (American Motorcyclist Assn) 13515 Yarmouth Dr	Pickerington	OH	43147	**800-262-5646**	614-856-1900	47-22
AMA (Academy of Model Aeronautics) 5161 E Memorial Dr	Muncie	IN	47302	**800-435-9262**	765-287-1256	47-18
AMACO (American Art Clay Co) 6060 Guion Rd	Indianapolis	IN	46254	**800-374-1600**	317-244-6871	42
Amada America Inc 7025 Firestone Blvd	Buena Park	CA	90621	**800-626-6612**	714-739-2111	455
Amadeus North America Inc 3470 NW 82nd Ave Ste 1000	Miami	FL	33122	**888-262-3387**	305-499-6000	335
Amador County Chamber of Commerce 115 Main St PO Box 596	Jackson	CA	95642	**800-822-9466***	209-223-0350	138
*General						
AMAG Technology Inc 20701 Manhattan Pl	Torrance	CA	90501	**800-889-9138**	310-518-2380	690
Amalgamated Bank of New York 275 Seventh Ave	New York	NY	10001	**800-662-0860**		69
Amalgamated Transit Union (ATU) 10000 New Hampshire Ave	Silver Spring	MD	20903	**888-240-1196**	202-537-1645	414
Amana Appliances Inc 2800 220th Trl	Amana	IA	52204	**800-843-0304***	319-622-5511	15
*Cust Svc						
Amana Colonies 622 46th Ave	Amana	IA	52203	**800-579-2294**	319-622-7622	10-3
Amana Colonies Convention & Visitors Bureau 622 46th Ave	Amana	IA	52203	**800-579-2294**	319-622-7622	208
Amangani Resort 1535 NE Butte Rd	Jackson	WY	83001	**877-734-7333**	307-734-7333	667
Amano Cincinnati Inc 140 Harrison Ave	Roseland	NJ	07068	**800-526-2559**	973-403-1900	110
Amarillo Convention & Visitor Council 1000 S Polk St	Amarillo	TX	79101	**800-692-1338**	806-374-1497	208
Amarillo Economic Development Corp 801 S Fillmore Ste 205	Amarillo	TX	79101	**800-333-7892**	806-379-6411	462
Amarillo National Bank 410 S Taylor St Plaza 1	Amarillo	TX	79101	**800-253-1031**	806-378-8000	69
Amarillo Wind Machine Co 20513 Ave 256	Exeter	CA	93221	**800-311-4498**	559-592-4256	275
Amateur Athletic Union of the US (AAU) 1910 Hotel Plaza Blvd	Lake Buena Vista	FL	32830	**800-228-4872**	407-934-7200	47-22
Amateur Trapshooting Assn (ATA) 601 W National Rd	Vandalia	OH	45377	**800-671-8042**	937-898-4638	47-22
Amatex Corp 1032 Stambridge St	Norristown	PA	19404	**800-441-9680**	610-277-6100	742-3
AmaWaterways 26010 Mureau Rd	Calabasas	CA	91302	**800-626-0126**		758
Amax Engineering Corp 1565 Reliance Way	Fremont	CA	94539	**800-889-2629***	510-651-8886	175-1
*Cust Svc						

Company	Address	City	State	ZIP	Toll-Free	Phone	Class
Amax Nutrasource Inc	14291 E Don Julian Rd	City Of Industry	CA	91746	**800-893-5306**	626-961-6600	345
Amazing Mail-print Center	2130 S 7th Ave Ste 170	Phoenix	AZ	85007	**888-681-1214**		5
Amazing Recycled Products Inc	PO Box 312	Denver	CO	80201	**800-241-2174**	303-699-7693	659
Amazon.com Inc (*NASDAQ: AMZN* ■ *Cust Svc)	1200 12th Ave S Ste 1200	Seattle	WA	98144	**800-201-7575***	206-266-1000	95
AMB Financial Corp (*OTC: AMFC*)	8230 Hohman Ave	Munster	IN	46321	**800-436-5113**	219-836-5870	360-2
AMBAC Assurance Corp	1 State St Plaza 15th Fl	New York	NY	10004	**800-221-1854**	212-658-7470	391-5
AMBAC Financial Group Inc (*OTC: ABKFQ*)	1 State St Plz 15th Fl	New York	NY	10004	**800-221-1854**	212-668-0340	360-4
AMBAC International Inc	910 Spears Creek Ct	Elgin	SC	29045	**800-628-6894**	803-735-1400	59
Ambassador Hotel	2308 W Wisconsin Ave	Milwaukee	WI	53233	**888-322-3326**	414-345-5000	379
Amber Diagnostics Inc	2180 Premier Row	Orlando	FL	32809	**866-919-2959**	407-438-7847	474
Amber Lotus Publishing	PO Box 11329	Portland	OR	97211	**800-326-2375**	503-284-6400	129
AMBEST Inc	5115 Maryland Way	Brentwood	TN	37027	**800-910-7220**	615-371-5187	325
Ambient Healthcare Inc	15851 SW 41st St Ste 600	Davie	FL	33331	**877-342-9352**	954-796-3338	240
Ambit Energy LP	1801 N Lamar St Ste 200	Dallas	TX	75202	**877-282-6248**		785
Amboy Bancorp	3590 US Hwy 9 S	Old Bridge	NJ	08857	**800-942-6269**	732-591-8700	360-2
Amboy National Bank	3590 US Hwy 9 S	Old Bridge	NJ	08857	**800-942-6269**	732-591-8700	69
Ambriola Company Inc	7 Patton Dr	West Caldwell	NJ	07006	**800-962-8224**		298-4
Ambrosia House Tropical Lodging	622 Fleming St	Key West	FL	33040	**800-535-9838**	305-296-9838	379
AMBUCS (National AMBUCS Inc)	4285 Regency Ct PO Box 5127	High Point	NC	27265	**800-838-1845**	336-852-0052	47-5
AMC (Augusta Medical Ctr)	78 Medical Ctr Dr PO Box 1000	Fishersville	VA	22939	**800-932-0262**	540-932-4000	374-3
AMC (Appalachian Mountain Club) (*Orders)	5 Joy St	Boston	MA	02108	**800-262-4455***	617-523-0655	47-13
AMC Star Theatres	25333 W 12-Mile Rd	Southfield	MI	48034	**888-262-4386**	248-368-1802	745
AMC Theatres	920 Main St	Kansas City	MO	64105	**877-341-6397**	816-221-4000	745
Amcest Nationwide Monitoring	1017 Walnut St	Roselle	NJ	07203	**800-631-7370**		198
AmChel Communications Inc	2800 Capital St	Wylie	TX	75098	**866-388-6959**	972-442-1030	479
AMCI	4755 Alla Rd Ste 1000	Marina Del Rey	CA	90292	**855-486-5527**		7
AMCOL International Corp (*NYSE: ACO* ■ *General)	2870 Forbs Ave	Hoffman Estates	IL	60192	**800-962-8586***	847-851-1500	502-2
Amcom Software Inc	10400 Yellow Cir Dr	Eden Prairie	MN	55343	**800-852-8935**	952-230-5200	180-7
Amcon Block & Precast Inc	2211 Hwy 10 S	Saint Cloud	MN	56304	**888-251-6030**	320-251-6030	362
AMCON Distributing Co (*NYSE: DIT*)	7405 Irvington Rd	Omaha	NE	68122	**888-201-5997**	402-331-3727	754
AMCP (Academy of Managed Care Pharmacy)	100 N Pitt St Ste 400	Alexandria	VA	22314	**800-827-2627**	703-683-8416	48-8
AMD (Advanced Micro Devices Inc) (*NYSE: AMD*)	1 AMD Pl PO Box 3453	Sunnyvale	CA	94088	**800-538-8450**	408-749-4000	694
AMD Industries Inc	4620 W 19th St	Cicero	IL	60804	**800-367-9999**	708-863-8900	235
AMDA (American Medical Directors Assn)	11000 Broken Land Pkwy Ste 400	Columbia	MD	21044	**800-876-2632**	410-740-9743	48-8
Amdocs Ltd (*NYSE: DOX*)	1390 Timberlake Manor Pkwy	Chesterfield	MO	63017	**866-426-8003**	314-212-7000	180-10
AME Inc	2467 Coltharp Rd PO Box 909	Fort Mill	SC	29716	**800-849-7766**	803-548-7766	190-6
AME Label Corp	25155 W Ave Stanford	Valencia	CA	91355	**866-278-9268**	661-257-2200	413
Amedica Corp	1885 West 2100 South	Salt Lake City	UT	84119	**855-839-3500**		252
Amedisys Hospice	209 10th Ave S Ste 512	Nashville	TN	37203	**800-659-2633**	423-587-9484	371
Amedisys Inc (*NASDAQ: AMED*)	5959 S Sherwood Forest Blvd Ste 300	Baton Rouge	LA	70816	**800-464-0020**	225-292-2031	352
Amegy Bank of Texas	4400 Post Oak Pkwy	Houston	TX	77027	**800-287-0301**	713-235-8800	69
Amelia Island Plantation	39 Beach Lagoon Rd	Amelia Island	FL	32034	**800-834-4900**	904-261-6161	667
Amendia Inc	1755 W Oak Pkwy	Marietta	GA	30062	**877-755-3329**	678-445-3784	474
AmerAssist Inc	8415 Pulsar Pl	Columbus	OH	43240	**877-294-9707**		462
AmerCable Inc	350 Bailey Rd	El Dorado	AR	71730	**800-643-1516**	870-862-4919	811
Ameren Corp (*NYSE: AEE*)	1901 Chouteau Ave	Saint Louis	MO	63103	**800-552-7583**	314-621-3222	360-5
Ameresco Canada Inc	90 Sheppard Ave E	North York	ON	M2N3A1	**888-483-7267**	416-512-7700	465
Ameresco Inc	111 Speen St Ste 410	Framingham	MA	01701	**866-263-7372**	508-661-2200	194
Ameriana Bancorp (*NASDAQ: ASBI*)	2118 Bundy Ave	New Castle	IN	47362	**866-844-7584**	765-529-2230	360-2
America First Credit Union	1344 West 4675 South	Ogden	UT	84405	**800-999-3961**	801-627-0900	221
America II Electronics Inc	2600 118th Ave N	Saint Petersburg	FL	33716	**800-767-2637**	727-573-0900	248
America Outdoors	5816 Kingston Pk	Knoxville	TN	37919	**800-524-4814**	865-558-3595	47-23
America's Best Franchising Inc (*America's Best Inns & Suites*)	50 Glen Lake Pkwy NE Ste 350	Atlanta	GA	30328	**800-237-8466**	770-393-2662	379
America's Blood Centers (ABC)	725 15th St NW Ste 700	Washington	DC	20005	**888-872-5663**	202-393-5725	48-8
America's Call Center Inc	7901 Baymeadows Way Ste 14	Jacksonville	FL	32256	**800-598-2580**	904-224-2000	734
America's Community Bankers (ACB)	1120 Connecticut Ave NW	Washington	DC	20036	**800-226-5377**		48-2
America's Ctr Convention Ctr	701 Convention Plz Ste 300	Saint Louis	MO	63101	**800-325-7962**	314-342-5036	207
America's Second Harvest	35 E Wacker Dr Ste 2000	Chicago	IL	60601	**800-771-2303**	312-263-2303	47-5
Americall	1502 Tacoma Ave S	Tacoma	WA	98402	**800-964-3556**	253-272-4111	40
American Academy McAllister Institute of Funeral Service	619 W 54th St 2nd Fl	New York	NY	10019	**866-932-2264**	212-757-1190	798
American Academy of Actuaries	1100 17th St NW 7th Fl	Washington	DC	20036	**888-888-1778**	202-223-8196	48-9
American Academy of Allergy Asthma & Immunology (AAAAI)	555 E Wells St Ste 1100	Milwaukee	WI	53202	**800-654-2452**	414-272-6071	48-8
American Academy of Art	332 S Michigan Ave 3rd Fl	Chicago	IL	60604	**888-461-0600**	312-461-0600	163
American Academy of Arts & Sciences	136 Irving St	Cambridge	MA	02138	**800-666-2211**	617-576-5000	47-4
American Academy of Audiology (AAA)	11730 Plz America Dr Ste 300	Reston	VA	20190	**800-222-2336**	703-790-8466	48-8
American Academy of Child & Adolescent Psychiatry (AACAP)	3615 Wisconsin Ave NW	Washington	DC	20016	**800-333-7636**	202-966-7300	48-15
American Academy of Cosmetic Dentistry (AACD)	402 W Wilson St	Madison	WI	53703	**800-543-9220**	608-222-8583	48-8
American Academy of Dermatology (AAD)	930 E Woodfield Rd	Schaumburg	IL	60173	**800-868-2472**	847-330-0230	48-8
American Academy of Disability Evaluating Physicians (AADEP)	223 W Jackson Blvd Ste 1104	Chicago	IL	60606	**800-456-6095**	312-663-1171	48-8
American Academy of Dramatic Arts	120 Madison Ave	New York	NY	10016	**800-463-8990**	212-686-9244	163
American Academy of Family Physicians (AAFP)	11400 Tomahawk Creek Pkwy	Leawood	KS	66211	**800-274-2237**	913-906-6000	48-8
American Academy of Neurology (AAN)	1080 Montreal Ave	Saint Paul	MN	55116	**800-879-1960**	651-695-1940	48-8
American Academy of Ophthalmology	655 Beach St	San Francisco	CA	94109	**866-561-8558**	415-561-8500	48-8
American Academy of Ophthalmology PAC	Governmental Affairs Div 20 F St NW Ste 400	Washington	DC	20001	**866-561-8558**	202-737-6662	614
American Academy of Optometry (AAO)	6110 Executive Blvd Ste 506	Rockville	MD	20852	**800-368-6263**	301-984-1441	48-8
American Academy of Orthopaedic Surgeons (AAOS)	6300 N River Rd	Rosemont	IL	60018	**800-346-2267**	847-823-7186	48-8
American Academy of Orthotists & Prosthetists (AAOP)	526 King St Ste 201	Alexandria	VA	22314	**800-669-6024**	703-836-0788	48-8
American Academy of Otolaryngology-Head & Neck Surgery (AAO-HNS)	1650 Diagonal Rd	Alexandria	VA	22314	**877-722-6467**	703-836-4444	48-8
American Academy of Pain Management (AAPM)	13947 Mono Way Ste A	Sonora	CA	95370	**888-519-9901**	209-533-9744	48-8
American Academy of Pediatric Dentistry (AAPD)	211 E Chicago Ave Ste 1600	Chicago	IL	60611	**800-974-3084**	312-337-2169	48-8
American Academy of Pediatrics (AAP)	141 NW Pt Blvd	Elk Grove Village	IL	60007	**800-433-9016**	847-434-4000	48-8
American Academy of Periodontology (AAP)	737 N Michigan Ave Ste 800	Chicago	IL	60611	**800-282-4867**	312-787-5518	48-8
American Academy of Psychiatry & the Law (AAPL)	1 Regency Dr PO Box 30	Bloomfield	CT	06002	**800-331-1389**	860-242-5450	48-15
American Academy of Religion (AAR)	825 Houston Mill Rd NE Ste 300	Atlanta	GA	30329	**800-282-6632**	404-727-3049	47-20
American Accounts & Advisors	PO Box 250	Cottage Grove	MN	55016	**866-714-0489**	651-287-6100	159
American Achievement Corp	7211 Cir S Rd	Austin	TX	78745	**800-531-5055**	512-444-0571	409
American Adv Federation (AAF)	1101 Vermont Ave NW Ste 500	Washington	DC	20005	**800-999-2231**	202-898-0089	48-18
American Aerospace Controls Inc	570 Smith St	Farmingdale	NY	11735	**888-873-8559**	631-694-5100	258
American AgCredit (ACA)	PO Box 1120	Santa Rosa	CA	95402	**800-800-4865**	707-545-1200	218
American Agriculturist	5227-B Baltimore Pike	Littlestown	PA	17340	**800-441-1410**	717-359-0150	456-1
American Air Charter Inc	577 Bell Ave	Chesterfield	MO	63005	**888-532-2710**	636-532-2707	13
American Airlines CR Smith Museum	4601 Hwy 360 at FAA Rd	Fort Worth	TX	76155	**877-277-6484**	817-967-1560	519
American Airlines Ctr	2500 Victory Ave	Dallas	TX	75219	**800-745-3000**	214-222-3687	718
American Airlines Employees Federal Credit Union	4151 Amon Carter Blvd PO Box 155489	Fort Worth	TX	76155	**800-533-0035**	817-952-4500	221
American Airlines Inc	4333 Amon Carter Blvd	Fort Worth	TX	76155	**800-433-7300**	817-963-1234	25
American Alliance for Health Physical Education Recreation & Dance (AAH-PERD)	1900 Assn Dr	Reston	VA	20191	**800-213-7193**	703-476-3400	47-22
American Aluminum Extrusion Company LLC	1 Saint Lawrence Ave	Beloit	WI	53511	**877-896-2236**	608-361-1800	491
American Ambulance Assn (AAA)	8400 Wpark Dr Fl 2	McLean	VA	22102	**800-523-4447**	703-610-9018	48-21
American Amicable Life Insurance Co	PO Box 2549	Waco	TX	76702	**800-736-7311**	254-297-2777	391-2

Name / Address	City	State	ZIP	Toll-Free	Phone	Class
American Amusement Machine Assn (AAMA)						
450 E Higgins Rd						
Ste 201	Elk Grove Village	IL	60007	866-372-5190	847-290-9088	47-23
American Angus Assn (AAA)						
3201 Frederick Ave	Saint Joseph	MO	64506	800-821-5478	816-383-5100	47-2
American Animal Hospital Assn (AAHA)						
12575 W Bayaud Ave	Lakewood	CO	80228	800-252-2242	303-986-2800	47-3
American Anti-Slavery Group, The						
198 Tremont St	Boston	MA	02116	800-884-0719	617-426-8161	47-5
American Apparel & Footwear Assn (AAFA)						
1601 N Kent St Ste 1200	Arlington	VA	22209	800-520-2262	703-524-1864	48-4
American Apparel & Footwear Assn PAC						
1601 N Kent St Ste 1200	Arlington	VA	22209	800-520-2262	703-524-1864	614
American Apparel LLC						
747 Warehouse St	Los Angeles	CA	90021	888-747-0070	213-488-0226	154-11
American Arbitration Assn Inc (AAA)						
1633 Broadway 10th Fl	New York	NY	10019	800-778-7879	212-716-5800	40
American Art Clay Co (AMACO)						
6060 Guion Rd	Indianapolis	IN	46254	800-374-1600	317-244-6871	42
American Artstone Co						
2025 N Broadway St	New Ulm	MN	56073	800-967-2076	507-233-3700	185
American Assn for Accreditation of Ambulatory Surgery Facilities Inc (AAAASF)						
5101 Washington St Ste 2F						
PO Box 9500	Gurnee	IL	60031	888-545-5222	847-775-1985	47-1
American Assn for Cancer Research (AACR)						
615 Chestnut St 17th Fl	Philadelphia	PA	19106	866-423-3965	215-440-9300	48-8
American Assn for Clinical Chemistry Inc (AACC)						
1850 K St NW Ste 625	Washington	DC	20006	800-892-1400*	202-857-0717	48-19
*Cust Svc						
American Assn for Justice (AAJ)						
777 Sixth St NW Ste 200	Washington	DC	20001	800-424-2725	202-965-3500	48-10
American Assn for Physical Activity & Recreation (AAPAR)						
1900 Assn Dr	Reston	VA	20191	800-213-7193	703-476-3400	47-23
American Assn for Thoracic Surgery (AATS)						
900 Cummings Ctr Ste 221-U	Beverly	MA	01915	800-424-5249	978-927-8330	48-8
American Assn of Acupunture & Oriental Medicine (AAAOM)						
PO Box 162340	Sacramento	CA	95816	866-455-7999	916-443-4770	47-17
American Assn of Airport Executives (AAAE)						
601 Madison St Ste 400	Alexandria	VA	22314	800-609-7374	703-824-0500	48-21
American Assn of Bioanalysts (AAB)						
906 Olive St Ste 1200	Saint Louis	MO	63101	800-457-3332	314-241-1445	48-8
American Assn of Bovine Practitioners (AABP)						
3320 Skyway Dr Ste 802						
PO Box 3610	Auburn	AL	36831	800-269-2227	334-821-0442	47-2
American Assn of Cereal Chemists Inc (AACC)						
3340 Pilot Knob Rd	Saint Paul	MN	55121	800-328-7560	651-454-7250	48-6
American Assn of Clinical Endocrinologists (AACE)						
245 Riverside Ave Ste 2000	Jacksonville	FL	32202	800-435-7352	904-353-7878	48-8
American Assn of Colleges of Osteopathic Medicine (AACOM)						
5550 Friendship Blvd						
Ste 310	Chevy Chase	MD	20815	800-356-7836	301-968-4100	48-8
American Assn of Collegiate Registrars & Admissions Officers (AACRAO)						
1 Dupont Cir NW Ste 520	Washington	DC	20036	800-222-4922	202-293-9161	48-5
American Assn of Critical-Care Nurses (AACN)						
101 Columbia	Aliso Viejo	CA	92656	800-809-2273	949-362-2000	48-8
American Assn of Daily Money Managers (AADMM)						
174 Crestview Dr	Bellefonte	PA	16823	877-326-5991		48-2
American Assn of Drugless Practitioners (AADP)						
2200 Market St Ste 803	Galveston	TX	77550	888-764-2237	409-621-2600	47-17
American Assn of Endodontists (AAE)						
211 E Chicago Ave Ste 1100	Chicago	IL	60611	800-872-3636	312-266-7255	48-8
American Assn of Engineering Societies (AAES)						
1620 'I' St NW Ste 210	Washington	DC	20006	888-400-2237*	202-296-2237	48-19
*Orders						
American Assn of Equine Practitioners (AAEP)						
4075 Iron Works Pkwy	Lexington	KY	40511	800-443-0177	859-233-0147	47-3
American Assn of Family & Consumer Sciences (AAFCS)						
400 N Columbus St Ste 202	Alexandria	VA	22314	800-424-8080	703-706-4600	48-5
American Assn of Franchisees & Dealers (AAFD)						
PO Box 10158	Palm Desert	CA	92255	800-733-9858	619-209-3775	48-18
American Assn of Gynecological Laparoscopists (AAGL)						
6757 Katella Ave	Cypress	CA	90630	800-554-2245	714-503-6200	48-8
American Assn of Immunologists (AAI)						
9650 Rockville Pike	Bethesda	MD	20814	888-503-1050	301-634-7178	48-8
American Assn of Individual Investors (AAII)						
625 N Michigan Ave Ste 1900	Chicago	IL	60611	800-428-2244	312-280-0170	48-2
American Assn of Insurance Services (AAIS)						
1745 S Naperville Rd	Wheaton	IL	60189	800-564-2247	630-681-8347	48-9
American Assn of Integrated Healthcare Delivery Systems Inc (AAIHDS)						
4435 Waterfront Dr Ste 101	Glen Allen	VA	23060	888-491-8833	804-747-5823	48-8
American Assn of Managing General Agents (AAMGA)						
610 Freedom Business Ctr						
Ste 110	King of Prussia	PA	19406	800-467-8725	610-225-1999	48-9
American Assn of Medical Assistants (AAMA)						
20 N Wacker Dr Ste 1575	Chicago	IL	60606	800-228-2262	312-899-1500	48-8
American Assn of Medical Review Officers (AAMRO)						
PO Box 12873	Research Triangle Park	NC	27709	800-489-1839	919-489-5407	48-8
American Assn of Museums (AAM)						
1575 Eye St NW Ste 400	Washington	DC	20005	866-226-2150	202-289-1818	47-4
American Assn of Naturopathic Physicians (AANP)						
818 18th St Ste 250	Washington	DC	20006	866-538-2267	202-237-8150	47-17
American Assn of Neurological Surgeons (AANS)						
5550 Meadowbrook Dr	Rolling Meadows	IL	60008	888-566-2267	847-378-0500	48-8
American Assn of Neuromuscular & Electrodiagnostic Medicine (AANEM)						
2621 Superior Dr NW	Rochester	MN	55901	844-347-3277	507-288-0100	48-8
American Assn of Neuroscience Nurses (AANN)						
4700 W Lk Ave	Glenview	IL	60025	888-557-2266	847-375-4733	48-8
American Assn of Nurse Anesthetists (AANA)						
222 S Prospect Ave	Park Ridge	IL	60068	855-526-2262	847-692-7050	48-8
American Assn of Nurse Anesthetists PAC (AANAPAC)						
222 S Prospect Ave	Park Ridge	IL	60068	855-526-2262	847-692-7050	614
American Assn of Oral & Maxillofacial Surgeons (AAOMS)						
9700 W Bryn Mawr Ave	Rosemont	IL	60018	800-822-6637	847-678-6200	48-8
American Assn of Orthodontists PAC						
401 N Lindbergh Blvd	Saint Louis	MO	63141	800-424-2841	314-993-1700	614
American Assn of Petroleum Geologists (AAPG)						
1444 S Boulder Ave PO Box 979	Tulsa	OK	74119	800-364-2274	918-584-2555	47-12
American Assn of Pharmaceutical Scientists (AAPS)						
2107 Wilson Blvd Ste 700	Arlington	VA	22201	877-998-2277	703-243-2800	48-19
American Assn of Poison Control Centers (AAPCC)						
3201 New Mexico Ave Ste 310	Washington	DC	20016	800-222-1222		48-8
American Assn of Professional Landmen (AAPL)						
4100 Fossil Creek Blvd	Fort Worth	TX	76137	888-566-2275	817-847-7700	47-12
American Assn of School Administrators (AASA)						
801 N Quincy St Ste 700	Arlington	VA	22203	800-771-1162	703-528-0700	48-5
American Assn of School Librarians (AASL)						
50 E Huron St	Chicago	IL	60611	800-545-2433	312-280-4386	48-11
American Assn of State Colleges & Universities (AASCU)						
1307 New York Ave NW 5th Fl	Washington	DC	20005	800-558-3417	202-293-7070	48-5
American Assn of State Highway & Transportation Officials (AASHTO)						
444 N Capitol St NW Ste 249	Washington	DC	20001	800-880-4117	202-624-5800	48-7
American Assn of Teachers of German (AATG)						
112 Haddontowne Ct Ste 104	Cherry Hill	NJ	08034	800-835-6770	856-795-5553	48-5
American Assn of Teachers of Spanish & Portuguese (AATSP)						
900 Ladd Rd	Walled Lake	MI	48390	877-832-2457	248-960-2180	48-5
American Assn of University Professors (AAUP)						
1133 Nineteenth St Ste 200	Washington	DC	20036	800-424-2973	202-737-5900	48-5
American Assn of University Women (AAUW)						
1111 16th St NW	Washington	DC	20036	800-326-2289	202-785-7700	48-5
American Assn of Variable Star Observers (AAVSO)						
49 Bay State Rd	Cambridge	MA	02138	888-802-7827	617-354-0484	48-19
American Assn on Intellectual & Developmental Disabilities (AAIDD)						
444 N Capitol St NW Ste 846	Washington	DC	20001	800-424-3688	202-387-1968	47-17
American Association for Justice						
777 6th St NW Ste 200	Washington	DC	20001	800-424-2727	202-965-3500	530-7
American Athletic Inc (AAI)						
200 American Ave	Jefferson	IA	50129	800-247-3978	515-386-3125	346
American Auction Co						
951 W Watkins	Phoenix	AZ	85007	800-801-8880		50
American Augers Inc						
135 US Rt 42	West Salem	OH	44287	800-324-4930	419-869-7107	56
American Autoimmune Related Disease Assn (AARDA)						
22100 Gratiot Ave	Eastpointe	MI	48021	800-598-4668	586-776-3900	47-17
American Automobile Association, Inc.						
321 Whittington Pkwy	Louisville	KY	40222	800-727-2552	502-582-3311	52
American Avionics						
7023 Perimeter Rd S	Seattle	WA	98108	800-518-5858*	206-763-8530	24
*Sales						
American Backflow Specialties						
3940 Home Ave	San Diego	CA	92105	800-662-5356	619-527-2525	611
American Baler Co						
800 E Centre St	Bellevue	OH	44811	800-843-7512	419-483-5790	386
American Bank of Texas NA						
200 N Austin St	Seguin	TX	78155	800-567-1817	830-379-5236	69
American Banker Magazine						
1 State St Plaza 27th Fl	New York	NY	10004	800-221-1809	212-803-8200	456-5
American Bankers Assn (ABA)						
1120 Connecticut Ave NW	Washington	DC	20036	800-226-5377*	202-663-5000	48-2
*Cust Svc						
American Bankers Assn PAC (ABAPAC)						
1120 Connecticut Ave NW	Washington	DC	20036	800-226-5377		614
American Baptist Assn (ABA)						
4605 N State Line Ave	Texarkana	TX	75503	800-264-2482	903-792-2783	47-20
American Baptist Churches USA						
PO Box 851	Valley Forge	PA	19482	800-222-3872	610-768-2000	47-20
American Baptist News Service						
PO Box 851	Valley Forge	PA	19482	800-222-3872	610-768-2000	529
American Baptist Seminary of the West						
2606 Dwight Way	Berkeley	CA	94704	800-799-7233	510-841-1905	168-3
American Bar Assn (ABA)						
321 N Clark St	Chicago	IL	60610	800-285-2221	312-988-5000	48-10
American Behavioral Benefits Managers						
2204 Lakeshore Dr Ste 135	Birmingham	AL	35209	800-925-5327	205-871-7814	461
American Benefits Council						
1501 M St NW Ste 600	Washington	DC	20005	877-829-5500	202-289-6700	48-2
American Beverage Licensees (ABL)						
5101 River Rd Ste 108	Bethesda	MD	20816	800-656-3241	301-656-1494	48-6
American Bible Society						
1865 Broadway	New York	NY	10023	800-322-4253	212-408-1200	634-3
American Bicycle Assn (ABA)						
1645 W Sunrise Blvd	Gilbert	AZ	85233	866-650-4867	480-961-1903	47-22
American Biltrite Inc Tape Products Div (ABI)						
105 Whittendale Dr	Moorestown	NJ	08057	888-224-6325	856-778-0700	729
American Bio Medica Corp (ABMC)						
122 Smith Rd	Kinderhook	NY	12106	800-227-1243*	518-758-8158	84
OTC: ABMC ■ *General						
American Biologics						
1180 Walnut Ave	Chula Vista	CA	91911	800-227-4473	619-429-8200	419
American BOA Inc						
1420 Redi Rd	Cumming	GA	30040	800-856-4580	770-889-9400	479
American Board of Internal Medicine (ABIM)						
510 Walnut St Ste 1700	Philadelphia	PA	19106	800-441-2246	215-446-3500	47-1
American Boiler Manufacturers Assn (ABMA)						
8221 Old Courthouse Rd Ste 207	Vienna	VA	22182	800-227-1966	703-356-7172	48-13
American Bolt & Screw Manufacturing Corp						
601 Kettering Dr	Ontario	CA	91761	800-325-0844	909-390-0522	350
American Booksellers Assn (ABA)						
200 White Plains Rd Ste 600	Tarrytown	NY	10591	800-637-0037	914-591-2665	48-18
American Borate Corp						
5700 Cleveland St						
Ste 350	Virginia Beach	VA	23462	800-486-1072	757-490-2242	502-1
American Botanical Council						
6200 Manor Rd PO Box 144345	Austin	TX	78723	800-373-7105	512-926-4900	47-17
American Boychoir School						
19 Lambert Dr	Princeton	NJ	08540	800-627-7468	609-924-5858	621
American Brain Tumor Assn (ABTA)						
2720 River Rd	Des Plaines	IL	60018	800-886-2282	847-827-9910	47-17
American Brass Manufacturing Co						
5000 Superior Ave	Cleveland	OH	44103	800-431-6440	216-431-6565	608
American Buildings Co						
1150 State Docks Rd	Eufaula	AL	36027	888-307-4338	334-687-2032	104
American Bullion Inc						
12301 Wilshire Blvd Ste 650	Los Angeles	CA	90025	800-326-9598	310-689-7720	790
American Business Systems Inc						
315 Littleton Rd	Chelmsford	MA	01824	800-356-4034		180-1
American Business Women's Assn (ABWA)						
11050 Roe Ave Ste 200	Overland Park	KS	66211	800-228-0007		48-12

Name / Address	Toll-Free	Phone	Class
American Camp Assn (ACA) 5000 State Rd 67 N, Martinsville IN 46151	**800-428-2267**	765-342-8456	47-23
American Cancer Society (ACS) 250 William St NW, Atlanta GA 30303	**800-227-2345**	404-320-3333	47-17
American Cancer Society Hope Lodge of Baltimore 636 W Lexington St, Baltimore MD 21201	**888-227-6333**	410-547-2522	372
American Cancer Society Hope Lodge of Charleston 269 Calhoun St, Charleston SC 29401	**800-227-2345**	843-958-0930	372
American Cancer Society Hope Lodge Worcester 7 Oak St, Worcester MA 01609	**800-227-2345**	508-792-2985	372
American Cancer Society Joe Lee Griffin Hope Lodge 1104 Ireland Way, Birmingham AL 35205	**800-227-2345**	205-558-7860	372
American Cancer Society Winn-Dixie Hope Lodge 250 Williams St NW, Atlanta GA 30303	**800-227-2345**	404-327-9200	372
American Canoe Assn (ACA) 503 Sophia St Ste 100, Fredericksburg VA 22401	**888-229-3792**	540-907-4460	47-22
American Capital Group Inc 100 Spectrum Ctr Dr Ste 750, Irvine CA 92618	**877-814-6871**	949-485-3005	790
American Capital Partners LLC 205 Oser Ave, Hauppauge NY 11788	**800-393-0493**	631-851-0918	401
American Career College Inc 151 Innovation Dr, Irvine CA 92617	**877-832-0790**	949-783-4800	167
American Caresource Holdings Inc 222 W. LAS COLINAS BLVD Ste 500N, IRVING TX 75039 *NASDAQ: ANCI*	**800-370-5994**		353
American Carrier Equipment Trailer Sales LLC 2285 E Date Ave, Fresno CA 93706	**800-344-2174**	559-442-1500	777
American Cast Iron Pipe Co (ACIPCO) 1501 31st Ave N, Birmingham AL 35207	**800-442-2347**	205-325-7701	308
American Casting & Manufacturing Corp 51 Commercial St, Plainview NY 11803	**800-342-0333**	516-349-7010	327
American Century Investments Inc 4500 Main St PO Box 419200, Kansas City MO 64111	**800-345-2021**	816-531-5575	401
American Century Proprietary Holdings Inc PO Box 419200, Kansas City MO 64141	**800-345-2021**	816-531-5575	527
American Ceramic Society (ACerS) 600 N Cleveland Ave # 210, Westerville OH 43082	**866-721-3322**	614-890-4700	47-4
American Chamber of Commerce Executives (ACCE) 4875 Eisenhower Ave Ste 250, Alexandria VA 22304	**800-394-2223**	703-998-0072	48-12
American Chemical Society (ACS) 1155 16th St NW, Washington DC 20036	**800-227-5558**	202-872-4600	48-19
American Chiropractic Assn (ACA) 1701 Clarendon Blvd 2nd Fl, Arlington VA 22209	**800-986-4636**	703-276-8800	48-8
American Chiropractic Assn PAC (ACA-PAC) 1701 Clarendon Blvd, Arlington VA 22209	**800-986-4636**	703-276-8800	614
American Chiropractor, The 8619 NW 68Th St, Miami FL 33166	**888-369-1396**		529
American Chrome Co 518 W Crossroads Pkwy, Bolingbrook IL 60440	**800-562-4488**	630-685-2200	491
American Chronic Pain Assn (ACPA) PO Box 850, Rocklin CA 95677	**800-533-3231**	916-632-0922	47-17
American Cinematographer Magazine 1782 N Orange Dr, Los Angeles CA 90028	**800-448-0145**	323-969-4333	456-9
American Civil Liberties Union (ACLU) 125 Broad St 18th Fl, New York NY 10004	**877-867-1025**	212-549-2500	47-8
American Clay Enterprises LLC 2418 Second St SW, Albuquerque NM 87102	**866-404-1634**	505-243-5300	502-6
American Cleaning Solutions 39-30 Review Ave, Long Island NY 11101	**888-929-7587**	718-392-8080	150
American Club, The 419 Highland Dr, Kohler WI 53044	**800-344-2838**	920-457-8000	667
American Coach Limousine 1100 Jorie Blvd Ste 314, Oak Brook IL 60523	**888-709-5466**	630-629-0001	441
American Coalition for Fathers & Children (ACFC) 1718 M St NW Ste 1187, Washington DC 20036	**800-978-3237**		47-6
American College 270 S Bryn Mawr Ave, Bryn Mawr PA 19010	**888-263-7265**	610-526-1000	798
American College of Allergy Asthma & Immunology (ACAAI) 85 W Algonquin Rd Ste 550, Arlington Heights IL 60005	**800-466-3649**	847-427-1200	48-8
American College of Cardiology (ACC) 2400 N St NW, Washington DC 20037 *Cust Svc	**800-253-4636***	202-375-6000	48-8
American College of Chest Physicians (ACCP) 3300 Dundee Rd, Northbrook IL 60062	**800-343-2227**	847-498-1400	48-8
American College of Emergency Physicians (ACEP) 1125 Executive Cir PO Box 619911, Dallas TX 75261	**800-798-1822**	972-550-0911	48-8
American College of Foot & Ankle Surgeons (ACFAS) 8725 W Higgins Rd Ste 555, Chicago IL 60631	**800-421-2237**	773-693-9300	48-8
American College of Forensic Examiners International (ACFEI) 2750 E Sunshine St, Springfield MO 65804	**800-423-9737**	417-881-3818	48-8
American College of Managed Care Medicine (ACMCM) 4435 Waterfront Dr Ste 101, Glen Allen VA 23060	**888-491-8833**	804-527-1905	48-8
American College of Osteopathic Family Physicians (ACOFP) 330 E Algonquin Rd Ste 1, Arlington Heights IL 60005	**800-323-0794**	847-952-5100	48-8
American College of Physician Executives (ACPE) 400 N Ashley Dr Ste 400, Tampa FL 33602	**800-562-8088**	813-287-2000	48-8
American College of Physicians (ACP) 190 N Independence Mall W, Philadelphia PA 19106	**800-523-1546**	215-351-2400	48-8
American College of Radiology (ACR) 1892 Preston White Dr, Reston VA 20191	**800-227-5463**	703-648-8900	48-8
American College of Surgeons (ACS) 633 N St Clair St, Chicago IL 60611	**800-621-4111**	312-202-5000	48-8
American Commerce Insurance Co 3590 Twin Creeks Dr, Columbus OH 43204	**800-848-2945**	614-308-3366	391-4
American Commercial Barge Lines Inc 1701 E Market St, Jeffersonville IN 47130	**800-457-6377**		315
American Contract Bridge League (ACBL) 6575 Windchase Blvd, Horn Lake MS 38637 *Sales	**800-264-2743***	662-253-3100	47-18
American Coolair Corp 3604 Mayflower St, Jacksonville FL 32205	**877-250-2822**	904-389-3646	14
American Correctional Assn (ACA) 206 N Washington St Ste 200, Alexandria VA 22314	**800-222-5646**	703-224-0000	48-7
American Corrugated Products Inc 4700 Alkire Rd, Columbus OH 43228	**800-248-6840**	614-870-2000	99
American Cotton Growers Textile Div (ACG) PO Box 2827, Lubbock TX 79408	**800-333-8011**	806-763-8011	742-1
American Council of Independent Laboratories (ACIL) 1875 I St NW Ste 500, Washington DC 20006	**800-368-1131**	202-887-5872	48-19
American Council of the Blind (ACB) 1155 15th St NW Ste 1004, Washington DC 20005	**800-424-8666**	202-467-5081	47-17
American Council on Alcoholism (ACA) 1000 E Indian School Rd, Phoenix AZ 85014	**800-527-5344**		47-17
American Council on Exercise (ACE) 4851 Paramount Dr, San Diego CA 92123	**800-825-3636**	858-576-6500	47-17
American Council on Science & Health (ACSH) 110 E 42nd St Ste 1300, New York NY 10017	**866-905-2694**	212-362-7044	48-19
American Council on the Teaching of Foreign Languages (ACTFL) 1001 N Fairfax St Ste 200, Alexandria VA 22314	**844-685-4373**	703-894-2900	48-5
American Counseling Assn (ACA) 5999 Stevenson Ave, Alexandria VA 22304	**800-347-6647**	703-823-9800	48-15
American Craft Council 72 Spring St 6th Fl, New York NY 10012	**800-836-3470**	212-274-0630	47-4
American Crane & Equipment Corp 531 Old Swede Rd, Douglassville PA 19518	**877-877-6778**	610-385-6061	469
American Cruise Lines 741 Boston Post Rd Ste 200, Guilford CT 06437	**800-814-6880**	203-453-6800	223
American Culinary Federation Inc (ACF) 180 Ctr Pl Way, Saint Augustine FL 32095	**800-624-9458**	904-824-4468	48-6
American Dairy Science Assn (ADSA) 1111 N Dunlap Ave, Savoy IL 61874	**888-670-2250**	217-356-5146	47-2
American Dehydrated Foods Inc 3801 E Sunshine, Springfield MO 65809	**800-456-3447**	417-881-7755	618
American Dental Assistants Assn (ADAA) 140 N Bloomingdale Rd, Bloomingdale IL 60108	**877-874-3785**	312-541-1550	48-8
American Dental Assn 1111 14th St NW Ste 1100, Washington DC 20005	**800-353-2237**	202-898-2424	614
American Dental Education Assn (ADEA) 1400 K St NW Ste 1100, Washington DC 20005	**800-353-2237**	202-289-7201	48-5
American Dental Hygienists' Assn (ADHA) 444 N Michigan Ave Ste 3400, Chicago IL 60611	**800-243-2342**	312-440-8900	48-8
American Dental Partners Inc 401 Edgewater Pl Ste 430, Wakefield MA 01880 *NASDAQ: ADPI*	**800-838-6563**	781-213-6500	462
American Desk 1302 Industrial Blvd, Temple TX 76504	**800-433-3142**		320-3
American Diabetes Assn (ADA) 1701 N Beauregard St, Alexandria VA 22311	**800-232-3472**	703-549-1500	47-17
American Donkey & Mule Society (ADMS) 1346 Morningside Ave, Lewisville TX 75057	**877-752-4068**	972-219-0781	47-3
American Douglas Metals Inc 783 Thorpe Rd, Orlando FL 32824	**800-428-0023**	407-855-6590	491
American Drill Bushings Co (ADB) 5740 Hunt Rd, Valdosta GA 31606	**800-423-4425**	229-253-8928	492
American Driving Records Inc 2860 Gold Tailings Ct PO Box 1970, Rancho Cordova CA 95670	**800-766-6877**	916-456-3200	632
American Eagle Federal Credit Union 417 Main St, East Hartford CT 06118	**800-842-0145**	860-568-2020	221
American Eagle Outfitters Inc 77 Hot Metal St, Pittsburgh PA 15203 *NYSE: AEO* ■ *Cust Svc	**888-232-4535***	412-432-3300	156-4
American Ecotech LLC 100 Elm St Factory D, Warren RI 02885	**877-247-0403**		198
American Educational Products Inc 401 Hickory St PO Box 2121, Fort Collins CO 80522	**800-289-9299**	970-484-7445	245
American Educational Research Assn (AERA) 1430 K St NW Ste 1200, Washington DC 20005	**800-893-7950**	202-238-3200	48-5
American Educator Magazine 555 New Jersey Ave NW, Washington DC 20001	**800-238-1133**	202-879-4400	456-8
American Egg Board (AEB) 1460 Renaissance Dr Ste 301, Park Ridge IL 60068	**888-549-2140**	847-296-7043	47-2
American Electric Power Company Inc 1 Riverside Plz, Columbus OH 43215 *NYSE: AEP* ■ *Cust Svc	**800-277-2177***	614-716-1000	360-5
American Electronic Components 1101 Lafayette St, Elkhart IN 46516	**888-847-6552**	574-295-6330	249
American Engineering Testing Inc 550 Cleveland Ave N, Saint Paul MN 55114	**800-972-6364**	651-659-9001	263
American Enterprise Institute for Public Policy Research (AEI) 1150 17th St NW, Washington DC 20036	**800-862-5801**	202-862-5800	631
American Environmental Container Corp 2302 Lasso Ln, Lakeland FL 33801	**800-535-7946**	863-666-3020	99
American Epilepsy Society (AES) 342 N Main St, West Hartford CT 06117	**888-233-2334**	860-586-7505	47-17
American Equity Investment Life Insurance Co 6000 Westown Pkwy, West Des Moines IA 50266	**888-221-1234**	515-221-0002	391-2
American Excelsior Co 850 Ave H E, Arlington TX 76011	**800-777-7645**		600
American Exchange Bank (AEB) 510 W Main St PO Box 818, Henryetta OK 74437	**888-652-3321**	918-652-3321	69
American Express Company Inc World Financial Ctr 200 Vesey St, New York NY 10285 *NYSE: AXP*	**800-528-4800**	212-640-2000	219
American Exteriors LLC 1169 W Littleton Blvd, Littleton CO 80120	**800-794-6369**	303-794-6369	237
American Family Association PO Box 2440, Tupelo MS 38803	**800-326-4543**	662-844-5036	641
American Family Care 3700 Cahaba Beach Rd, Birmingham AL 35242	**800-258-7535**	205-403-8902	352
American Family Life Assurance Co PAC (AFLAC PAC) 1932 Wynnton Rd Ste 300, Columbus GA 31999 *NYSE: AFL* ■ *Cust Svc	**800-992-3522***	706-323-3431	614
American Family Life Assurance Company of Columbus (AFLAC) 1932 Wynnton Rd, Columbus GA 31999 *Cust Svc	**800-992-3522***	706-323-3431	391-2
American Family Life Insurance Co 6000 American Pkwy, Madison WI 53783	**800-692-6326**	608-249-2111	391-2
American Family Mutual Insurance Co 6000 American Pkwy, Madison WI 53783 *Cust Svc	**800-374-0008***	608-249-2111	391-2
American Fan Company Inc 2933 Symmes Rd, Fairfield OH 45014	**866-771-6266**	513-874-2400	18

Name / Address	Toll-Free	Phone	Class
American Farmland Trust (AFT)			
1200 18th St, Washington DC 20036	800-431-1499	202-331-7300	47-2
American Faucet & Coating Corp			
3280 Corporate Vw, Vista CA 92081	800-621-8383	760-598-5895	611
American Federation for Aging Research (AFAR)			
55 W 39th St 16th Fl, New York NY 10018	888-582-2327	212-703-9977	48-8
American Federation for Medical Research (AFMR)			
900 Cummings Ctr Ste 221-U, Beverly MA 01915	888-737-9477	978-927-8330	48-8
American Federation of Astrologers (AFA)			
6535 S Rural Rd, Tempe AZ 85283	888-301-7630	480-838-1751	47-18
American Federation of Government Employees			
80 F St NW, Washington DC 20001	888-844-2343	202-737-8700	414
American Federation of Labor & Congress of Industrial Organizations (AFL-CIO)			
815 16th St NW, Washington DC 20006	877-850-4959	202-637-5000	414
American Federation of Musicians of the US & Canada (AFM)			
1501 Broadway Ste 600, New York NY 10036	800-762-3444	212-869-1330	414
American Federation of Police & Concerned Citizens			
6350 Horizon Dr, Titusville FL 32780	800-435-7352	321-264-0911	48-7
American Federation of Teachers (AFT)			
555 New Jersey Ave NW, Washington DC 20001	800-238-1133	202-879-4400	414
American Fence Assn (AFA)			
800 Roosevelt Rd Bldg C-312, Glen Ellyn IL 60137	800-822-4342	630-942-6598	48-3
American Fence Inc			
2502 N 27th Ave, Phoenix AZ 85009	888-691-4565	602-272-2333	193-2
American Fidelity Assurance Co			
2000 N Classen Blvd, Oklahoma City OK 73106	800-654-8489	405-523-2000	360-4
American Film Institute (AFI)			
2021 N Western Ave, Los Angeles CA 90027	866-234-3378	323-856-7600	47-4
American Finance Assn (AFA)			
350 Main St, Malden MA 02148	800-835-6770	781-388-8599	48-2
American Fitness Magazine			
15250 Ventura Blvd Ste 200, Sherman Oaks CA 91403	800-446-2322	818-905-0040	456-13
American Floor Products Company Inc			
7977 Cessna Ave, Gaithersburg MD 20879	800-342-0424		293
American Fluorescent Corp			
2345 Ernie Krueger Cir, Waukegan IL 60087	800-873-2326	847-249-5970	439
American Folklore Society (AFS)			
1501 Neil Ave 1501 Neil Ave, Columbus OH 43201	866-311-1200	614-292-4715	47-14
American Food & Vending Corp			
124 Metropolitan Pk Dr, Syracuse NY 13088	800-466-9261	315-457-9950	300
American Foods Group Inc			
544 Acme St, Green Bay WI 54302	800-345-0293	920-437-6330	472
American Football Coaches Assn (AFCA)			
100 Legends Ln, Waco TX 76706	877-557-5338	254-754-9900	47-22
American Foreign Service Assn (AFSA)			
2101 E St NW, Washington DC 20037	800-704-2372	202-338-4045	48-7
American Forest & Paper Assn (AF&PA)			
1111 19th St NW Ste 800, Washington DC 20036	800-878-8878	202-463-2700	47-2
American Forests			
1220 L St NW Ste 750, Washington DC 20005	800-368-5748	202-737-1944	47-13
American Foundation for Suicide Prevention (AFSP)			
120 Wall St 22nd Fl, New York NY 10005	888-333-2377	212-363-3500	47-17
American Foundation for the Blind (AFB)			
2 Penn Plaza, New York NY 10001	800-232-5463	212-502-7600	47-17
American Foundry Society (AFS)			
1695 N Penny Ln, Schaumburg IL 60173	800-537-4237	847-824-0181	48-13
American Furniture Warehouse Co			
8501 Grant St, Thornton CO 80229	888-615-9415	303-289-3300	322
American Galvanizers Assn (AGA)			
6881 S Holly Cir Ste 108, Centennial CO 80112	800-468-7732	720-554-0900	48-13
American Gaming & Electronics			
9500 W 55th St Ste A, Countryside IL 60525	800-336-6630	708-290-2100	323
American Gastroenterological Assn (AGA)			
4930 Del Ray Ave, Bethesda MD 20814	800-227-7888	301-654-2055	48-8
American Gelbvieh Assn			
10900 Dover St, Westminster CO 80021	800-529-0900	303-465-2333	47-2
American Gem Society (AGS)			
8881 W Sahara Ave, Las Vegas NV 89117	866-805-6500	702-255-6500	48-4
American Gem Trade Assn (AGTA)			
3030 LBJ Fwy Ste 840, Dallas TX 75234	800-972-1162	214-742-4367	48-4
American Geological Institute (AGI)			
4220 King St, Alexandria VA 22302	800-334-2564	703-379-2480	48-19
American Geophysical Union (AGU)			
2000 Florida Ave NW, Washington DC 20009	800-966-2481	202-462-6900	48-19
American Girl Inc			
8400 Fairway Pl, Middleton WI 53562	800-845-0005*	608-836-4848	760
*Orders			
American Glass Distributors			
3901 Airline Dr, Houston TX 77022	800-570-3303	713-692-8522	53
American Golf Corp			
2951 28th St, Santa Monica CA 90405	800-238-7267	310-664-4000	653
American Gramaphone LLC			
9130 Mormon Bridge Rd, Omaha NE 68152	800-348-3434	402-457-4341	655
American Granby Inc			
7652 Morgan Rd, Liverpool NY 13090	800-776-2266	315-451-1100	611
American Greetings Corp			
1 American Rd, Cleveland OH 44144	800-777-4891*	216-252-7300	129
NYSE: AM ■ *Sales			
American Grinding & Machine Co			
2000 N Mango Ave, Chicago IL 60639	877-988-4343	773-889-4343	453
American Group Psychotherapy Assn (AGPA)			
25 E 21st St 6th Fl, New York NY 10010	877-668-2472	212-477-2677	48-15
American Guild of Musical Artists (AGMA)			
1430 Broadway 14th Fl, New York NY 10018	800-543-2462	212-265-3687	47-4
American Guild of Organists (AGO)			
475 Riverside Dr Ste 1260, New York NY 10115	855-631-0759	212-870-2310	47-4
American Guild of Variety Artists (AGVA)			
363 Seventh Ave 17th Fl, New York NY 10001	800-331-0890	212-675-1003	47-4
American Gypsum Co			
3811 Turtle Creek Blvd Ste 1200, Dallas TX 75219	866-439-5800	214-530-5500	347
American Health Associates			
671 Ohio Pk Ste K, Cincinnati IN 45245	800-522-7556		415
American Health Care Assn (AHCA)			
1201 L St NW, Washington DC 20005	800-321-0343	202-842-4444	48-8
American Health Information Management Assn (AHIMA)			
233 N Michigan Ave Ste 2100, Chicago IL 60601	800-335-5535	312-233-1100	48-8
American Healthcare Radiology Administrators (AHRA)			
490-B Boston Post Rd Ste 200, Sudbury MA 01776	800-334-2472	978-443-7591	48-8

Name / Address	Toll-Free	Phone	Class
American Healthcare Services LLC			
1000 John R Ste 250, Troy MI 48083	866-227-9998	248-588-9700	719
American Heart Assn (AHA)			
7272 Greenville Ave, Dallas TX 75231	800-242-8721	214-373-6300	47-17
American Helicopter Society International (AHS)			
217 N Washington St, Alexandria VA 22314	855-247-4685	703-684-6777	48-21
American Hellenic Educational Progressive Assn (AHEPA)			
1909 Q St NW Ste 500, Washington DC 20009	855-473-3512	202-232-6300	47-14
American Hiking Society (AHS)			
1422 Fenwick Ln, Silver Spring MD 20910	800-972-8608	301-565-6704	47-23
American Historical Assn (AHA)			
400 A St SE, Washington DC 20003	888-444-6664	202-544-2422	48-5
American Holistic Nurses' Assn (AHNA)			
323 N San Francisco St			
Ste 201, Flagstaff AZ 86001	800-278-2462	928-526-2196	47-17
American Home Base			
428 Childers St, Pensacola FL 32534	800-549-0595*	850-857-0860	734
*General			
American Home Furnishings			
3535 Menaul Blvd NE, Albuquerque NM 87107	800-854-6755	505-883-2211	322
American Home Shield			
889 Ridge Lake Blvd PO Box 851, Memphis TN 38120	800-776-4663	901-537-8000	367
American HomePatient Inc			
5200 Maryland Way Ste 400, Brentwood TN 37027	800-890-7271	615-221-8884	363
American Homestar Corp			
2450 S Shore Blvd Ste 300, League City TX 77573	800-313-5570	281-334-9700	504
American Honda Motor Company Inc			
1919 Torrance Blvd, Torrance CA 90501	800-999-1009	310-783-3170	58
American Horticultural Society (AHS)			
7931 E Blvd Dr, Alexandria VA 22308	800-777-7931	703-768-5700	47-18
American Hose & Rubber Co			
3645 E 44th St, Tucson AZ 85713	800-272-7537	520-514-1666	370
American Hospital Assn (AHA)			
155 N Wacker Dr, Chicago IL 60606	800-424-4301	312-422-3000	48-8
American Hospital Assn PAC (AHAPAC)			
325 Seventh St NW, Washington DC 20004	800-424-4301	202-638-1100	614
American Hotel Register Co			
100 S Milwaukee Ave, Vernon Hills IL 60061	800-323-5686	847-743-3000	558
American Humane Assn (AHA)			
63 Inverness Dr E, Englewood CO 80112	800-227-4645	303-792-9900	47-6
American Income Life Insurance Co (AIL)			
1200 Wooded Acres, Waco TX 76710	800-433-3405	254-761-6400	391-2
American Indian College Fund			
8333 Greenwood Blvd, Denver CO 80221	800-776-3863	303-426-8900	47-11
American Indian College of the Assemblies of God			
10020 N 15th Ave, Phoenix AZ 85021	800-621-7440	602-944-3335	167
American Indian Science & Engineering Society (AISES)			
2305 Renard SE Ste 200, Albuquerque NM 87106	800-759-5219	505-765-1052	48-19
American Institute for Cancer Research			
1759 R St NW, Washington DC 20009	800-843-8114	202-328-7744	666
American Institute for CPCU & Insurance Institute of America (AICPCU/IIA)			
720 Providence Rd Ste 100, Malvern PA 19355	800-644-2101	610-644-2100	48-9
American Institute of Aeronautics & Astronautics Inc (AIAA)			
1801 Alexander Bell Dr Ste 500, Reston VA 20191	800-639-2422	703-264-7500	48-19
American Institute of Architects (AIA)			
1735 New York Ave NW, Washington DC 20006	800-242-3837*	202-626-7300	47-4
*Orders			
American Institute of Biological Sciences (AIBS)			
1444 'I' St NW Ste 200, Washington DC 20005	800-992-2427	202-628-1500	48-19
American Institute of Certified Public Accountants (AICPA)			
1211 Ave of the Americas, New York NY 10036	888-777-7077	212-596-6200	48-1
American Institute of Chemical Engineers (AIChE)			
120 Wall St Fl 23, New York NY 10005	800-242-4363*	203-702-7660	48-19
*Cust Svc			
American Institute of Chemists (AIC)			
315 Chestnut St, Philadelphia PA 19106	800-829-0115	215-873-8224	48-19
American Institute of Floral Designers (AIFD)			
720 Light St, Baltimore MD 21230	877-865-5320	410-752-3318	48-4
American Institute of Graphic Arts (AIGA)			
164 Fifth Ave, New York NY 10010	800-548-1634	212-807-1990	47-4
American Institute of Mining Metallurgical & Petroleum Engineers (AIME)			
12999 E Adam Aircraft Cir, Englewood CO 80112	888-702-0049	303-325-5185	47-12
American Institute of Professional Bookkeepers (AIPB)			
6001 Montrose Rd Ste 500, Rockville MD 20852	800-622-0121		48-1
American Institute of Ultrasound in Medicine (AIUM)			
14750 Sweitzer Ln Ste 100, Laurel MD 20707	800-638-5352	301-498-4100	48-8
American Institutes for Research			
1000 Thomas Jefferson St NW, Washington DC 20007	877-334-3499	202-403-5000	666
American InterContinental University			
Atlanta			
6600 Peachtree Dunwoody Rd			
500 Embassy Row NE, Atlanta GA 30328	800-491-0182	404-965-6500	167
Dunwoody			
6600 Peachtree-Dunwoody Rd			
500 Embassy Row, Atlanta GA 30328	855-377-1888	404-965-6500	167
American InterContinental University Los Angeles			
231 N Martingale Rd 6th Fl, Schaumburg IL 60173	877-701-3800		167
American Intercontinental University South Florida			
2250 N Commerce Pkwy, Weston FL 33326	855-377-1888	954-446-6100	167
American International Automobile Dealers Assn (AIADA)			
500 Montgomery St Ste 800, Alexandria VA 22314	800-462-4232	703-519-7800	48-18
American International College			
1000 State St, Springfield MA 01109	800-242-3142*	413-205-3201	167
*Admissions			
American International Forest Products LLC (AIFP)			
5560 SW 107th Ave, Beaverton OR 97005	800-366-1611	503-641-1611	193-3
American International Inc			
1040 Avendia Acaso, Camarillo CA 93012	800-336-6500	805-388-6800	255
American Iron Magazine			
1010 Summer St, Stamford CT 06905	877-693-3572*	203-425-8777	456-3
*Cust Svc			
American Jazz Museum			
1616 E 18th St, Kansas City MO 64108	800-734-3447	816-474-8463	519
American Jewish World Service (AJWS)			
45 W 36th St, New York NY 10018	800-889-7146	212-792-2900	47-5
American Journal of Psychiatry			
1000 Wilson Blvd Ste 1825, Arlington VA 22209	800-368-5777	703-907-7300	456-16
American Judicature Society (AJS)			
2700 University Ave, Des Moines IA 50311	800-626-4089	515-271-2281	48-10

Name / Address	City	State	ZIP	Toll-Free	Phone	Class
American Kidney Fund (AKF) 6110 Executive Blvd Ste 1010	Rockville	MD	20852	**800-638-8299**		47-17
American Kidney Stone Management Ltd (AKSM) 797 Thomas Ln	Columbus	OH	43214	**800-637-5188**	614-447-0281	353
American Land Title Assn (ALTA) 1828 L St NW Ste 705	Washington	DC	20036	**800-787-2582**	202-296-3671	48-10
American Law Institute (ALI) 4025 Chestnut St	Philadelphia	PA	19104	**800-253-6397**	215-243-1600	48-10
American Lawyer Media Inc (ALM) 120 Broadway 5th Fl	New York	NY	10271	**877-256-2472**	212-457-9400	634-9
American Lebanese Syrian Associated Charities (ALSAC) 262 Danny Thomas Pl	Memphis	TN	38105	**800-822-6344**	901-578-2000	47-5
American Lecithin Company Inc 115 Hurley Rd Unit 2B	Oxford	CT	06478	**800-364-4416**	203-262-7100	297-29
American Legion, The 700 N Pennsylvania St *Cust Svc	Indianapolis	IN	46204	**800-433-3318***	317-630-1200	47-19
American Library Assn (ALA) 50 E Huron St	Chicago	IL	60611	**800-545-2433**	312-944-6780	48-11
American Lighting Assn (ALA) 2050 Stemmons Fwy Ste 10046	Dallas	TX	75207	**800-605-4448**	214-698-9898	48-4
American Limousines Inc 4401 E Fairmount Ave	Baltimore	MD	21224	**800-787-1690**	410-522-0400	441
American Littoral Society (ALS) 18 Hartshorne Dr Ste 1	Highlands	NJ	07732	**800-424-8802**	732-291-0055	47-13
American Liver Foundation (ALF) 39 Broadway	New York	NY	10006	**800-465-4837**	212-668-1000	47-17
American Locker Group Inc 815 S Main St *OTC: ALGI*	Grapevine	TX	76051	**800-828-9118**	817-329-1600	690
American Locker Security Systems Inc 608 Allen St *Sales	Jamestown	NY	14701	**800-828-9118***		690
American Logistics Assn (ALA) 1133 15th St NW Ste 640	Washington	DC	20005	**800-791-7146**	202-466-2520	47-19
American Louver Co 7700 N Austin Ave	Skokie	IL	60077	**800-772-0355**	847-470-3300	439
American Lubrication Equipment Corp 11212A McCormick Rd PO Box 1350	Hunt Valley	MD	21030	**888-252-9300**		540
American Lung Assn (ALA) 14 Wall St	New York	NY	10005	**800-586-4872**	212-315-8700	47-17
American Machine & Tool Company Inc 400 Spring St	Royersford	PA	19468	**888-268-7867**	610-948-3800	638
American Marazzi Tile Inc 359 Clay Rd	Sunnyvale	TX	75182	**800-289-8453**	972-232-3801	749
American Marketing Assn (AMA) 311 S Wacker Dr Ste 5800	Chicago	IL	60606	**800-262-1150**	312-542-9000	48-18
American Marking Systems Inc 1015 Paulison Ave PO Box 1677	Clifton	NJ	07011	**800-782-6766**	973-478-5600	466
American Massage Therapy Assn (AMTA) 500 Davis St Ste 900	Evanston	IL	60201	**877-905-2700**	847-864-0123	47-17
American Mathematical Society (AMS) 201 Charles St *Cust Svc	Providence	RI	02904	**800-321-4267***	401-455-4000	48-19
American Medical Assn (AMA) 515 N State St	Chicago	IL	60610	**800-621-8335**	312-464-5000	48-8
American Medical Directors Assn (AMDA) 11000 Broken Land Pkwy Ste 400	Columbia	MD	21044	**800-876-2632**	410-740-9743	48-8
American Medical ID 949 Wakefield Ste 100	Houston	TX	77018	**800-363-5985**		474
American Medical Rehabilitation Providers Assn (AMRPA) 1710 N St NW	Washington	DC	20036	**888-346-4624**	202-223-1920	48-8
American Medical Response (AMR) 6200 S Syracuse Way Ste 200	Greenwood Village	CO	80111	**877-244-4890**	303-495-1200	30
American Medical Student Assn (AMSA) 1902 Assn Dr	Reston	VA	20191	**800-767-2266**	703-620-6600	48-5
American Medical Technologists (AMT) 10700 W Higgins Rd Ste 150	Rosemont	IL	60018	**800-275-1268**	847-823-5169	48-8
American Megatrends Inc (AMI) 5555 Oakbrook Pkwy Bldg 200	Norcross	GA	30093	**800-828-9264**	770-246-8600	178
American Mensa Ltd 1229 Corporate Dr W	Arlington	TX	76006	**800-666-3672**	817-607-0060	47-15
American Mental Health Counselors Assn (AMHCA) 801 N Fairfax St Ste 304	Alexandria	VA	22314	**800-326-2642**	703-548-6002	48-15
American Metal & Plastics Inc 450 32nd St SW	Grand Rapids	MI	49548	**800-382-0067**	616-452-6061	488
American Metal Bearing Co 7191 Acacia Ave	Garden Grove	CA	92841	**800-888-3048**	714-892-5527	619
American Metalcraft Inc 2074 George St	Melrose Park	IL	60160	**800-333-9133**	708-345-1177	487
American Meteorological Society (AMS) 45 Beacon St	Boston	MA	02108	**800-824-0405**	617-227-2425	48-19
American Modern Home Insurance Co PO Box 5323	Cincinnati	OH	45201	**800-543-2644**	513-943-7200	391-4
American Moistening Company Inc 10402 Rodney St	Pineville	NC	28134	**800-948-5540**	704-889-7281	609
American Morgan Horse Assn (AMHA) 4066 Shelburne Rd Ste 5	Shelburne	VT	05482	**888-436-3700**	802-985-4944	47-3
American Motel Management 2200 Northlake Pkwy Ste 277	Tucker	GA	30084	**800-580-8258**	770-939-1801	653
American Motorcyclist Assn (AMA) 13515 Yarmouth Dr	Pickerington	OH	43147	**800-262-5646**	614-856-1900	47-22
American Moving & Storage Assn (AMSA) 1611 Duke St	Alexandria	VA	22314	**888-849-2672**	703-683-7410	48-21
American Moving & Storage Assn PAC 1611 Duke St	Alexandria	VA	22314	**888-849-2672**	703-683-7410	614
American Muscle 7 Lee Blvd	Malvern	PA	19355	**888-332-7930**	610-251-2397	789
American Museum of Fly Fishing 4104 Main Rd	Manchester	VT	05254	**800-333-1550**	802-362-3300	521
American Musical Supply PO Box 152	Spicer	MN	56288	**800-458-4076**	320-796-2088	525
American Musicological Society (AMS) 6010 College Stn	Brunswick	ME	04011	**888-421-1442**	207-798-4243	47-4
American National Bank 628 Main St *NASDAQ: AMNB*	Danville	VA	24541	**800-240-8190**	434-792-5111	360-2
American National Property & Casualty Co 1949 E Sunshine St	Springfield	MO	65899	**800-333-2860**	417-887-0220	391-4
American National Rubber Co Main & High St *Cust Svc	Ceredo	WV	25507	**800-624-3410***	304-453-1311	675
American National Standards Institute (ANSI) 25 W 43rd St 4th fl	New York	NY	10036	**800-374-3818**	212-642-4900	47-1
American Nephrology Nurses Assn (ANNA) 200 E Holly Ave	Sewell	NJ	08080	**888-600-2662**	856-256-2320	48-8
American Nickeloid Co 2900 Main St	Peru	IL	61354	**800-645-5643**	815-223-0373	480
American Nuclear Society (ANS) 555 N Kensington Ave	La Grange Park	IL	60526	**800-323-3044**	708-352-6611	48-19
American Nurses Assn (ANA) 8515 Georgia Ave Ste 400	Silver Spring	MD	20910	**800-274-4262**	301-628-5000	48-8
American Nurses Assn PAC (ANA PAC) 8515 Georgia Ave Ste 400	Silver Spring	MD	20910	**800-274-4262**	301-628-5000	614
American Occupational Therapy Assn Inc (AOTA) 4720 Montgomery Ln PO Box 31220	Bethesda	MD	20824	**800-877-1383**	301-652-2682	48-8
American Oil Chemists Society (AOCS) 2710 S Boulder PO Box 17190	Urbana	IL	61802	**866-535-2730**	217-359-2344	47-12
American Orthodontics Corp 1714 Cambridge Ave	Sheboygan	WI	53081	**800-558-7687**	920-457-5051	230
American Orthopaedic Society for Sports Medicine (AOSSM) 6300 N River Rd Ste 500	Rosemont	IL	60018	**877-321-3500**	847-292-4900	48-8
American Osteopathic Assn (AOA) 142 E Ontario St	Chicago	IL	60611	**800-621-1773**	312-202-8000	48-8
American Outdoor Products Inc 6350 Gunpark Dr	Boulder	CO	80301	**800-641-0500**	303-581-0518	297-37
American Outfitters Ltd 3700 Sunset Ave	Waukegan	IL	60087	**800-397-6081**	847-623-3959	709
American Packaging Corp 777 Driving Pk Ave	Rochester	NY	14613	**800-551-8801**	585-254-9500	547
American Packaging Corp Extrusion Div 777 Driving Pk Ave	Rochester	NY	14613	**800-551-8801**	585-254-9500	547
American Packing & Gasket Co (APG) 6039 Armour Dr PO Box 213	Houston	TX	77020	**800-888-5223**	713-675-5271	327
American Pain Society (APS) 4700 W Lake Ave	Glenview	IL	60025	**877-752-4754**	847-375-4715	47-17
American Panel Corp 5800 SE 78th St	Ocala	FL	34472	**800-327-3015**	352-245-7055	662
American Paper & Twine Co 7400 Cockrill Bend Blvd	Nashville	TN	37209	**800-251-2437**	615-350-9000	558
American Paper Recycling Corp 87 Central St *Cust Svc	Mansfield	MA	02048	**800-762-6790***		658
American Park & Recreation Society (APRS) 22377 Belmont Ridge Rd	Ashburn	VA	20148	**800-765-3110**	703-858-0784	47-23
American Parkinson Disease Assn (APDA) 135 Parkinson Ave	Staten Island	NY	10305	**800-223-2732**	718-981-8001	47-17
American Pavilion 1706 Warrington Ave	Danville	IL	61832	**800-424-9699**	217-443-0800	730
American Permanent Ware Inc 729 Third Ave	Dallas	TX	75226	**800-527-2100**	214-421-7366	299
American Pet Products Manufacturers Assn (APPMA) 255 Glenville Rd	Greenwich	CT	06831	**800-452-1225**	203-532-0000	48-4
American Pharmacists Assn PAC 2215 Constitution Ave NW	Washington	DC	20037	**800-237-2742**	202-628-4410	614
American Photo Magazine 1633 Broadway 43rd Fl	New York	NY	10019	**800-274-4514**	212-767-6000	456-14
American Physical Society (APS) 1 Physics Ellipse	College Park	MD	20740	**866-918-1164**	301-209-3200	48-19
American Physical Therapy Assn (APTA) 1111 N Fairfax St	Alexandria	VA	22314	**800-999-2782**	703-684-2782	48-8
American Phytopathological Society, The (APS) 3340 Pilot Knob Rd	Saint Paul	MN	55121	**800-328-7560**	651-454-7250	48-19
American Plastic Toys Inc 799 Ladd Rd	Walled Lake	MI	48390	**800-521-7080**	248-624-4881	760
American Playground Corp 2328 Jefferson St	Anderson	IN	46016	**800-541-1602**	765-642-0288	346
American Pneumatic Tool Inc 9949 Tabor Pl	Santa Fe Springs	CA	90670	**800-532-7402**	562-204-1555	757
American Podiatric Medical Assn (APMA) 9312 Old Georgetown Rd	Bethesda	MD	20814	**800-275-2762**	301-581-9200	48-8
American Polarizers Inc 141 S Seventh St	Reading	PA	19602	**800-736-9031**	610-373-5177	543
American Polywater Corp 11222 60th St N	Stillwater	MN	55082	**800-328-9384**	651-430-2270	144
American Portwell Technology Inc 44200 Christy St	Fremont	CA	94538	**877-278-8899**	510-403-3399	176
American Power Conversion Corp (APC) 132 Fairgrounds Rd *Cust Svc	West Kingston	RI	02892	**800-788-2208***	401-789-5735	255
American Power Pull Corp 550 W Linfoot St PO Box 109	Wauseon	OH	43567	**800-808-5922**	419-335-7050	469
American Press 4900 Hwy 90 E *News Rm	Lake Charles	LA	70615	**800-442-2511***	337-494-4080	531-2
American Printing House for the Blind 1839 Frankfort Ave PO Box 6085	Louisville	KY	40206	**800-223-1839**	502-895-2405	634-10
American Product Distributors Inc (APD) 8350 Arrowridge Blvd	Charlotte	NC	28273	**800-849-5842**	704-522-9411	533
American Products LLC 597 Evergreen Rd	Strafford	MO	65757	**855-736-2135**	417-736-2135	487
American Psychiatric Assn (APA) 1000 Wilson Blvd Ste 1825	Arlington	VA	22209	**888-357-7924**	703-907-7300	48-15
American Psychiatric Nurses Assn (APNA) 1555 Wilson Blvd Ste 530	Arlington	VA	22209	**866-243-2443**	703-243-2443	48-8
American Psychiatric Publishing Inc 1000 Wilson Blvd Ste 1825	Arlington	VA	22209	**800-368-5777**	703-907-7322	634-9
American Psychological Assn (APA) 750 First St NE	Washington	DC	20002	**800-374-2721**	202-336-5500	48-15
American Public Communications Council Inc (APCC) 625 Slaters Ln Ste 104	Alexandria	VA	22314	**800-868-2722**	703-739-1322	48-20
American Public Gas Assn (APGA) 201 Massachusetts Ave NE Ste C-4	Washington	DC	20002	**800-927-4204**	202-464-2742	47-12

Name / Address	Toll-Free	Phone	Class
American Public Life Insurance Co 2305 Lakeland Dr PO Box 925 .... Jackson MS 39205	**800-256-8606**	601-936-6600	391-5
American Public Power Assn (APPA) 1875 Connecticut Ave Ste 1200 .... Washington DC 20009	**800-369-6220**	202-467-2900	47-12
American Public University System (AMU) 111 W Congress St .... Charles Town WV 25414	**877-777-9081**	304-724-3700	168
American Public Works Assn (APWA) 2345 Grand Blvd Ste 700 .... Kansas City MO 64108	**800-848-2792**	816-472-6100	48-7
American Quarter Horse Assn (AQHA) 1600 Quarter Horse Dr .... Amarillo TX 79104	**800-291-7323**	806-376-4811	47-3
American Radio Relay League (ARRL) 225 Main St .... Newington CT 06111	**888-277-5289**	860-594-0200	48-14
American Radiolabeled Chemicals Inc (ARC) 101 ARC Dr .... Saint Louis MO 63146	**800-331-6661**	314-991-4545	144
American Railcar Industries Inc 100 Clark St .... Saint Charles MO 63301 *NASDAQ: ARII*	**800-489-9888**	636-940-6000	648
American Realty Investors Inc 1800 Vly View Ln Ste 300 .... Dallas TX 75234 *NYSE: ARL*	**800-400-6407**	469-522-4200	653
American Recycled Plastic Inc 773 N. Union Grove Rd .... Friendsville TN 37737	**866-417-5821**	865-738-3439	659
American Red Ball International 9750 Third Ave NE Ste 200 .... Seattle WA 98115	**800-669-6424**	206-526-1730	518
American Red Ball Transit Company Inc PO Box 1127 .... Indianapolis IN 46206	**800-733-8139**		518
American Red Cross 2025 E St NW .... Washington DC 20006	**800-257-7575**	202-303-4498	47-5
American Red Cross In Greater New York (Inc) 520 W 49th St .... New York NY 10019	**877-733-2767**		352
American Reeling Devices Inc 15 Airpark Vista Blvd .... Dayton NV 89403 *Sales	**800-354-7335***		116
American Refugee Committee (ARC) 430 Oak Grove St Ste 204 .... Minneapolis MN 55403	**800-875-7060**	612-872-7060	47-5
American Registry of Diagnostic Medical Sonographers (ARDMS) 1401 Rockville Pike Ste 600 .... Rockville MD 20852	**800-541-9754**	301-738-8401	48-8
American Religious Town Hall Meeting Inc PO Box 180118 .... Dallas TX 75218	**800-783-9828**	214-328-9828	450
American Renal Assoc Inc 66 Cherry Hill Dr .... Beverly MA 01915	**877-997-3625**	978-922-3080	353
American Rental Assn (ARA) 1900 19th St .... Moline IL 61265	**800-334-2177**	309-764-2475	48-4
American Republic Insurance Co 601 Sixth Ave .... Des Moines IA 50309 *Cust Svc	**800-247-2190***		391-2
American Residential Services LLC 9010 Maier Rd Ste 105 .... Laurel MD 20723	**866-399-2885**	901-271-9700	191-10
American Rifleman Magazine 11250 Waples Mill Rd .... Fairfax VA 22030	**800-672-3888**		456-20
American River Bankshares 3100 Zinfandel Dr Ste 450 .... Rancho Cordova CA 95670 *NASDAQ: AMRB*	**800-544-0545**		360-2
American Rivers 1101 14th St NW Ste 1400 .... Washington DC 20005	**877-347-7550**	202-347-7550	47-13
American Road & Transportation Builders Assn (ARTBA) 1219 28th St NW .... Washington DC 20007	**800-636-2377**	202-289-4434	48-3
American Roentgen Ray Society (ARRS) 44211 Slatestone Ct .... Leesburg VA 20176	**800-438-2777**	703-729-3353	48-8
American Rose Society (ARS) 8877 Jefferson Paige Rd .... Shreveport LA 71119	**800-637-6534**	318-938-5402	47-18
American Royal Assn 1701 American Royal Ct .... Kansas City MO 64102	**866-844-2295**	816-221-9800	47-2
American Running Assn 4405 E W Hwy Ste 405 .... Bethesda MD 20814	**800-776-2732**	301-913-9517	47-22
American Saddlebred Museum 4083 Iron Works Pkwy .... Lexington KY 40511	**800-829-4438**	859-259-2746	519
American Safety Technologies Inc 565 Eagle Rock Ave .... Roseland NJ 07068	**800-631-7841**	973-403-2600	549
American Salon Magazine 757 Third Ave 5th Fl .... New York NY 10017	**866-871-0656**	323-966-4662	456-21
American Savings Bank FSB 1001 Bishop St PO Box 2300 .... Honolulu HI 96813	**800-272-2566**	808-627-6900	69
American School Counselor Assn (ASCA) 1101 King St Ste 625 .... Alexandria VA 22314	**800-306-4722**	703-683-2722	48-5
American Science & Engineering Inc 829 Middlesex Tpke .... Billerica MA 01821 *NASDAQ: ASEI*	**800-225-1608**	978-262-8700	690
American Scientist Magazine 3106 E NC Hwy 54 PO Box 13975 .... Research Triangle Park NC 27709	**800-243-6534**	919-549-4691	456-19
American Seating Co 401 American Seating Ctr NW .... Grand Rapids MI 49504 *Cust Svc	**800-748-0268***	616-732-6600	320-3
American Seed Trade Assn (ASTA) 1701 Duke St Ste 275 .... Alexandria VA 22304	**888-890-7333**	703-837-8140	47-2
American Seminar Leaders Assn (ASLA) 2405 E Washington Blvd .... Pasadena CA 91104	**800-801-1886**	626-791-1211	48-12
American Services Inc 1300 Rutherford Rd .... Greenville SC 29609	**877-292-7450**	864-292-7450	691
American Shared Hospital Services 4 Embarcadero Ctr Ste 3700 .... San Francisco CA 94111 *NYSE: AMS*	**800-735-0641**	415-788-5300	266-4
American Shore & Beach Preservation Assn (ASBPA) 5460 Beaujolais Ln .... Fort Myers FL 33919	**800-331-1600**	239-489-2616	47-13
American Shorthorn Assn 8288 Hascall St .... Omaha NE 68124	**877-272-0686**	402-393-7200	47-3
American Sleep Apnea Assn (ASAA) 6856 Eastern Ave NW #203 .... Washington DC 20012	**888-293-3650**	202-293-3650	47-17
American Social Health Assn (ASHA) PO Box 13827 .... Research Triangle Park NC 27709	**800-552-4375**	919-361-8400	47-17
American Society for Aesthetic Plastic Surgery, The (ASAPS) 11262 Monarch St .... Garden Grove CA 92841	**800-364-2147**	562-799-2356	48-8
American Society for Clinical Pathology (ASCP) 33 W Monroe St Ste 1600 .... Chicago IL 60603 *Cust Svc	**800-621-4142***	312-541-4999	48-8
American Society for Colposcopy & Cervical Pathology (ASCCP) 152 W Washington St .... Hagerstown MD 21740	**800-787-7227**	301-733-3640	48-8
American Society for Gastrointestinal Endoscopy (ASGE) 1520 Kensington Rd Ste 202 .... Oak Brook IL 60523	**866-353-2743**	630-573-0600	48-8
American Society for Horticultural Science (ASHS) 1018 Duke St .... Alexandria VA 22314	**800-331-1600**	703-836-4606	47-2
American Society for Laser Medicine & Surgery Inc (ASLMS) 2100 Stewart Ave Ste 240 .... Wausau WI 54401	**877-258-6028**	715-845-9283	48-8
American Society for Nondestructive Testing Inc (ASNT) 1711 Arlingate Ln PO Box 28518 ...... Columbus OH 43228 *Orders	**800-222-2768***	614-274-6003	48-19
American Society for Nutrition (ASNS) 9211 Corporate Blvd Ste 300 .... Rockville MD 20850	**800-627-8723**	301-634-7050	48-6
American Society for Parenteral & Enteral Nutrition (ASPEN) 8630 Fenton St Ste 412 .... Silver Spring MD 20910	**800-727-4567**	301-587-6315	48-8
American Society for Quality (ASQ) 600 N Plankinton Ave .... Milwaukee WI 53203	**800-248-1946**	414-272-8575	48-13
American Society for Therapeutic Radiology & Oncology (ASTRO) 8280 Willow Oaks Corporate Dr Ste 500 .... Fairfax VA 22031	**800-962-7876**	703-502-1550	48-8
American Society of Agronomy (ASA) 5585 Guilford Rd .... Madison WI 53711	**866-359-9161**	608-273-8080	47-2
American Society of Anesthesiologists (ASA) 520 N NW Hwy .... Park Ridge IL 60068	**800-331-1600**	847-825-5586	48-8
American Society of Appraisers (ASA) 555 Herndon Pkwy Ste 125 .... Herndon VA 20170	**800-272-8258**	703-478-2228	48-17
American Society of Assn Executives (ASAE) 1575 'I' St NW .... Washington DC 20005	**888-950-2723**	202-626-2723	48-12
American Society of Cataract & Refractive Surgery (ASCRS) 4000 Legato Rd Ste 700 .... Fairfax VA 22033	**877-996-4464**	703-591-2220	48-8
American Society of Cinematographers (ASC) 1782 N Orange Dr .... Hollywood CA 90028	**800-448-0145**	323-969-4333	47-4
American Society of Civil Engineers (ASCE) 1801 Alexander Bell Dr .... Reston VA 20191	**800-548-2723**	703-295-6300	456-21
American Society of Clinical Oncology (ASCO) 2318 Mill Rd Ste 800 .... Alexandria VA 22314	**888-282-2552**	571-483-1300	48-8
American Society of Consultant Pharmacists (ASCP) 1321 Duke St .... Alexandria VA 22314	**800-355-2727**	703-739-1300	48-8
American Society of Dermatopathology, The 111 Deer Lake Rd Ste 100 .... Deerfield IL 60015	**800-445-8667**	847-686-2231	48-8
American Society of Health-System Pharmacists (ASHP) 7272 Wisconsin Ave .... Bethesda MD 20814	**866-279-0681**	301-664-8700	48-8
American Society of Heating Refrigerating & Air-Conditioning Engineers Inc (ASHRAE) 1791 Tullie Cir NE .... Atlanta GA 30329 *Cust Svc	**800-527-4723***	404-636-8400	48-3
American Society of Home Inspectors (ASHI) 932 Lee St Ste 101 .... Des Plaines IL 60016	**800-743-2744**	847-759-2820	48-3
American Society of Human Genetics (ASHG) 9650 Rockville Pike .... Bethesda MD 20814	**800-720-4363**	301-634-7300	48-19
American Society of Landscape Architects (ASLA) 636 'I' St NW .... Washington DC 20001	**888-999-2752**	202-898-2444	47-2
American Society of Limnology & Oceanography (ASLO) 5400 Bosque Blvd Ste 680 .... Waco TX 76710	**800-929-2756**	254-399-9635	48-19
American Society of Military Comptrollers (ASMC) 415 N Alfred St .... Alexandria VA 22314	**800-462-5637**	703-549-0360	47-19
American Society of PeriAnesthesia Nurses (ASPAN) 90 Frontage Rd .... Cherry Hill NJ 08034	**877-737-9696**	856-616-9600	48-8
American Society of Plastic Surgeons (ASPS) 444 E Algonquin Rd .... Arlington Heights IL 60005	**888-475-2784**	847-228-9900	48-8
American Society of Professional Estimators (ASPE) 2525 Perimeter Pl Dr Ste 103 .... Nashville TN 37214	**888-378-6283**	615-316-9200	48-3
American Society of Radiologic Technologists (ASRT) 15000 Central Ave SE .... Albuquerque NM 87123	**800-444-2778**	505-298-4500	48-8
American Society of Regional Anesthesia & Pain Medicine (ASRA) 239 Fourth Ave Ste 1714 .... Pittsburgh PA 15222	**855-795-2772**	412-471-2718	48-8
American Society of Travel Agents (ASTA) 1101 King St Ste 200 .... Alexandria VA 22314	**800-275-2782**	703-739-2782	47-23
American Society of Travel Agents PAC 1101 King St Ste 490 .... Alexandria VA 22314	**800-275-2782**	703-739-2782	614
American Society on Aging (ASA) 575 Market St Ste 2100 .... San Francisco CA 94105	**800-537-9728**	415-974-9600	47-6
American Sociological Assn (ASA) 1307 New York Ave .... Washington DC 20005	**800-524-9400**	202-383-9005	48-5
American Software Inc 470 E Paces Ferry Rd .... Atlanta GA 30305 *NASDAQ: AMSWA*	**800-726-2946**	404-261-4381	180-1
American Solutions for Business 31 E Minnesota Ave PO Box 218 ...... Glenwood MN 56334	**800-862-3690**		533
American Southern Insurance Co 3715 Northside Pkwy NW Bldg 400 Ste 800 .... Atlanta GA 30327	**800-241-1172**	404-266-9599	391-4
American Soybean Assn (ASA) 12125 Woodcrest Executive Dr Ste 100 .... Saint Louis MO 63141	**800-688-7692**	314-576-1770	47-2
American Specialty Health Plans 10221 Wateridge Cir .... San Diego CA 92121	**800-848-3555**		391-3
American Spectator Magazine 933 N. Kenmore St Ste 405 .... Arlington VA 22201	**800-524-3469**	703-807-2011	456-17
American Spectrum Realty Inc 2401 Fountain View 7th Fl .... Houston TX 77057 *NYSE: AQQ*	**888-315-2776**	713-706-6200	653
American Speech-Language-Hearing Assn (ASHA) 2200 Research Blvd .... Rockville MD 20850	**800-498-2071**	301-296-5700	48-8
American Spoon Foods Inc 1668 Clarion Ave .... Petoskey MI 49770	**800-222-5886**	231-347-9030	297-20
American Sports 74 Albe Dr Ste 1 .... Newark DE 19702	**866-207-3179**	302-369-9480	708
American Staffing Assn (ASA) 277 S Washington St Ste 200 .... Alexandria VA 22314	**800-456-4324**	703-253-2020	48-12
American Stage 163 Third St N .... Saint Petersburg FL 33731	**800-435-7352**	727-823-1600	571
American Stair Corp Inc 642 Forestwood Dr .... Romeoville IL 60446	**800-872-7824**		490
American Standard Cos Inc 1 Centennial Ave .... Piscataway NJ 08855	**800-442-1902**		360-3

Name / Address	City	State	ZIP	Toll-Free	Phone	Class
American Standard Cos Inc Bath & Kitchen Products Div 1 Centennial Ave PO Box 6820	Piscataway	NJ	08855	**800-442-1902**		610
American Standard Insurance Company of Wisconsin 6000 American Pkwy	Madison	WI	53783	**800-692-6326**	608-249-2111	391-2
American State Bank 1401 Ave Q	Lubbock	TX	79401	**800-531-1401**	806-767-7000	360-2
American States Water Co 630 E Foothill Blvd *NYSE: AWR*	San Dimas	CA	91773	**800-999-4033**	909-394-3600	360-5
American Statistical Assn (ASA) 732 N Washington St	Alexandria	VA	22314	**888-231-3473**	703-684-1221	48-19
American String Teachers Assn (ASTA) 4155 Chain Bridge Rd	Fairfax	VA	22030	**800-821-7303**	703-279-2113	48-5
American Strip Steel Inc 901 Coopertown Rd	Delanco	NJ	08075	**800-526-1216**		491
American Studies Assn (ASA) 1120 19th St NW Ste 301	Washington	DC	20036	**800-468-3571**	202-467-4783	48-5
American Subcontractors Assn Inc (ASA) 1004 Duke St	Alexandria	VA	22314	**866-378-8866**	703-684-3450	48-3
American Surplus Inc 1 Noyes Ave Bldg B	Rumford	RI	02916	**800-876-3736**	401-434-4355	322
American Systems Corp 14151 Pk Meadow Dr Ste 500	Chantilly	VA	20151	**800-733-2721**	703-968-6300	182
American Tank & Fabricating Co (AT&F) 12314 Elmwood Ave	Cleveland	OH	44111	**800-544-5316**	216-252-1500	721
American Teacher Magazine 555 New Jersey Ave NW	Washington	DC	20001	**800-238-1133**	202-879-4400	456-8
American Technology Network Corp 1341 San Mateo Ave	South San Francisco	CA	94080	**800-910-2862**	650-875-0130	543
American Textile Co 10 N Linden St *Cust Svc	Duquesne	PA	15110	**800-289-2826***	412-948-1020	743
American Theological Library Assn (ATLA) 300 S Wacker Dr Ste 2100	Chicago	IL	60606	**888-665-2852**	312-454-5100	47-20
American Therapeutic Recreation Assn (ATRA) 629 N Main St	Hattiesburg	MS	39401	**800-433-5255**	601-450-2872	47-17
American Thermoplastic Co (ATC) 106 Gamma Dr	Pittsburgh	PA	15238	**800-245-6600**		85
American Thoracic Society (ATS) 61 Broadway 4th Fl	New York	NY	10006	**866-316-2673**	212-315-8600	48-8
American Tinnitus Assn (ATA) 522 SW Fifth Ave Ste 825	Portland	OR	97204	**800-634-8978**	503-248-9985	47-17
American Tire Depot 1123 W Commonwealth Ave	Fullerton	CA	92833	**855-333-2823**	714-525-2306	753
American Tort Reform Assn (ATRA) 1101 Connecticut Ave NW Ste 400	Washington	DC	20036	**877-333-2227**	202-682-1163	48-10
American Tower Corp 116 Huntington Ave 11th Fl *NYSE: AMT*	Boston	MA	02116	**877-282-7483**	617-375-7500	172
American Traffic Safety Services Assn (ATSSA) 15 Riverside Pkwy Ste 100	Fredericksburg	VA	22406	**800-272-8772**	540-368-1701	48-21
American Trails PO Box 491797	Redding	CA	96049	**866-363-7226**	530-547-2060	47-23
American Trails West (ATW) 92 Middle Neck Rd	Great Neck	NY	11021	**800-645-6260**	516-487-2800	758
American Translators Assn (ATA) 225 Reinekers Ln Ste 590	Alexandria	VA	22314	**800-253-2252**	703-683-6100	48-5
American Trucking Assn (ATA) 950 N Glebe Rd Ste 210	Arlington	VA	22203	**800-282-5463**	703-838-1700	48-21
American Type Culture Collection (ATCC) 10801 University Blvd PO Box 1549 *Cust Svc	Manassas	VA	20108	**800-638-6597***	703-365-2700	666
American Ultraviolet Co 40 Morristown Rd	Bernardsville	NJ	07924	**800-288-9288**	908-696-1130	809
American United Life Insurance Co 1 American Sq 510A PO Box 368	Indianapolis	IN	46206	**800-537-6442**	317-285-1877	391-2
American University 4400 Massachusetts Ave NW	Washington	DC	20016	**800-829-1040**	202-885-1000	167
American University Washington College of Law 4801 Massachusetts Ave NW	Washington	DC	20016	**800-995-6423**	202-274-4101	168-1
American Urban Radio Networks 960 Penn Ave 4th Fl	Pittsburgh	PA	15222	**800-456-4211**	412-456-4000	644
American Urological Assn (AUA) 1000 Corporate Blvd	Linthicum	MD	21090	**866-746-4282**	410-689-3700	48-8
American Utility Management Inc 2211 S York Rd Ste 320	Oak Brook	IL	60523	**866-520-1245**		462
American Vending Sales Inc 750 Morse Ave	Elk Grove Village	IL	60007	**800-441-0009**	847-439-9400	54
American Veterinary Medical Assn (AVMA) 1931 N Meacham Rd Ste 100	Schaumburg	IL	60173	**800-248-2862**	847-925-8070	48-8
American Veterinary Medical Assn PAC (AVMA) 1910 Sunderland Pl NW	Washington	DC	20036	**800-321-1473**	202-789-0007	614
American Volkssport Assn (AVA) 1001 Pat Booker Rd Ste 101	Universal City	TX	78148	**855-999-5200**	210-659-2112	47-22
American Watchmakers-Clockmakers Institute (AWI) 701 Enterprise Dr	Harrison	OH	45030	**866-367-2924**	513-367-9800	48-4
American Water Works Assn (AWWA) 6666 W Quincy Ave	Denver	CO	80235	**800-926-7337**	303-794-7711	47-12
American Water Works Co Inc 1025 Laurel Oak Rd *NYSE: AWK*	Voorhees	NJ	08043	**888-282-6816**	856-346-8200	360-5
American Welding & Tank Co 4718 Old Gettysburg Rd Ste 300	Mechanicsburg	PA	17055	**800-345-2495**	717-763-5080	90
American Welding Society (AWS) 550 NW 42nd Ave	Miami	FL	33126	**800-443-9353**	305-443-9353	48-3
American Whitewater (AW) PO Box 1540	Cullowhee	NC	28723	**866-262-8429**	828-586-1930	47-23
American Window & Glass Inc 2715 Lynch Rd	Evansville	IN	47711	**877-671-6943**	812-464-9400	607
American Youth Soccer Organization (AYSO) 19750 S Vermont Ave Ste 200	Torrance	CA	90502	**800-872-2976**		47-22
Americana Tickets NY 1535 Broadway	New York	NY	10036	**800-833-3121**	212-581-6660	748
AmericanChurch Inc 525 McClurg Rd PO Box 3120	Youngstown	OH	44513	**800-446-3035**	330-758-4545	265
American-International Charolais Assn (AICA) 11700 NW Plaza Cir	Kansas City	MO	64153	**800-270-7711**	816-464-5977	47-2
Americanna Co 29 Aldrin Rd *Cust Svc	Plymouth	MA	02360	**888-747-5550***	508-747-5550	9
Americans for Democratic Action (ADA) 1625 K St NW Ste 210	Washington	DC	20006	**855-712-8441**	202-785-5980	47-7
Americans for Effective Law Enforcement (AELE) 841 W Touhy Ave	Park Ridge	IL	60068	**800-763-2802**	847-685-0700	47-8
Americans for Peace Now (APN) 1101 14th St NW 6th Fl	Washington	DC	20005	**877-429-0678**	202-728-1893	47-7
Americans for the Arts 1000 Vermont Ave NW 6th Fl	Washington	DC	20005	**866-471-2787**	202-371-2830	47-4
Americans United for Separation of Church & State 518 C St NE	Washington	DC	20002	**800-875-3707**	202-466-3234	47-7
AmericanStyle Magazine 3000 Chestnut Ave Ste 304	Baltimore	MD	21211	**800-642-4314**	410-889-3093	456-2
AmeriCares Foundation 88 Hamilton Ave	Stamford	CT	06902	**800-486-4357**	203-658-9500	47-5
Americas Styrenics LLC 24 Waterway Ave Ste 1200	Woodlands	TX	77380	**844-512-1212**		145
AmericasMart 240 Peachtree St NW Ste 2200	Atlanta	GA	30303	**800-285-6278**	404-220-3000	207
Americhem Inc 2000 Americhem Way	Cuyahoga Falls	OH	44221	**800-228-3476**	330-929-4213	142
AmericInn International LLC 250 Lake Dr E *Resv	Chanhassen	MN	55317	**800-634-3444***	952-294-5000	379
Americo Financial Life & Annuity Insurance Co PO Box 410288	Kansas City	MO	64141	**800-231-0801**		391-2
Americo Life Inc 300 W 11th St *General	Kansas City	MO	64105	**800-231-0801***	816-391-2000	360-4
AmeriCom Inc PO Box 2146	Sandy	UT	84091	**800-820-6296**	801-571-2446	733
Americomm 804 Greenbrier Cir	Chesapeake	VA	23320	**800-527-6757**	757-622-2724	5
Ameridial Inc 4535 Strausser St NW	North Canton	OH	44720	**800-445-7128**		734
Ameridrives Couplings 1802 Pittsburgh Ave PO Box 4000	Erie	PA	16502	**800-352-0141**	814-480-5000	619
AmeriDrives International 1802 Pittsburgh Ave	Erie	PA	16502	**800-352-0141**	814-480-5000	619
AmeriFactors 215 Celebration Pl Ste 340	Celebration	FL	34747	**800-884-3863**	407-566-1150	274
Ameri-Fax Corp 6520 W 20th Ave Unit 2	Hialeah	FL	33016	**800-262-8214**		553
Ameriflight Inc 4700 Empire Ave Hngr 1	Burbank	CA	91505	**800-800-4538**	818-847-0000	12
AmeriGas Partners LP 460 N Gulph Rd *NYSE: APU*	King of Prussia	PA	19406	**800-427-4968**	610-337-7000	317
AMERIGROUP Corp 4425 Corporation Ln *NYSE: AGP*	Virginia Beach	VA	23462	**800-600-4441**	757-490-6900	391-3
AmeriHealth Mercy Health Plan 8040 Carlson Rd Ste 500	Harrisburg	PA	17112	**888-991-7200**	717-651-3540	352
Ameril-Co Carriers Inc 1702 E Overland	Scottsbluff	NE	69361	**800-445-5400**	308-635-3157	778
Amerijet International Inc 2800 S Andrews Ave	Fort Lauderdale	FL	33316	**800-927-6059**	954-320-5300	12
Amerilist Inc 978 Route 45 Ste L2	Pomona	NY	10970	**800-457-2899**	845-362-6737	318
Amerimade Technology Inc 449 Mtn Vista Pkwy	Livermore	CA	94551	**800-938-3824**	925-243-9090	607
Amerimax Home Products Inc 450 Richardson Dr	Lancaster	PA	17603	**800-347-2586**	717-299-3711	479
Ameripack Inc 107 N Gold Dr	Robbinsville	NJ	08691	**800-456-7963**	609-259-7004	5
AmeriPride Services Inc 10801 Wayzata Blvd *Cust Svc	Minnetonka	MN	55305	**800-750-4628***	952-738-4200	442
Ameriprise Brokerage 70400 Ameriprise Financial Ctr	Minneapolis	MN	55474	**800-535-2001**		688
Ameriprise Financial Inc 834 Ameriprise Financial Ctr *NYSE: AMP*	Minneapolis	MN	55474	**866-673-3673**	612-671-3131	401
Ameriprise Financial Services Inc 70100 Ameriprise Financial Ctr	Minneapolis	MN	55474	**866-483-8434**		401
Ameris Bank 24 Second Ave SE PO Box 3668	Moultrie	GA	31768	**866-616-6020**		188
AMERISAFE Inc 2301 Hwy 190 W *NASDAQ: AMSF*	DeRidder	LA	70634	**800-256-9052**	337-463-9052	391-4
Ameriserv Financial 216 Franklin St PO Box 520 *NASDAQ: ASRV*	Johnstown	PA	15907	**800-837-2265**	814-533-5300	69
AmerisourceBergen Corp 1300 Morris Dr Ste 100 PO Box 959 *NYSE: ABC*	Chesterbrook	PA	19087	**800-829-3132**	610-727-7000	240
Amerispa 90 Rue de Stanstead St Ste 101	Bromont	QC	J2L1K6	**866-263-7477**	450-534-2717	704
AmeriSpan Unlimited 1334 Walnut St 6 Fl	Philadelphia	PA	19107	**800-879-6640**	215-751-1100	423
AmeriSpec Inc 3839 Forest Hill Irene Rd	Memphis	TN	38125	**877-769-5217**	901-820-8500	365
Ameristar Casino & Hotel 3200 N Ameristar Dr	Kansas City	MO	64161	**888-777-8700**	816-414-7000	379
Ameristar Casino Hotel Council Bluffs 2200 River Rd	Council Bluffs	IA	51501	**866-667-3386**	712-328-8888	132

Name / Address	City	State	Zip	Toll-Free	Phone	Class
Ameristar Casinos Inc 3773 Howard Hughes Pkwy Ste 490-S *NASDAQ: ASCA*	Las Vegas	NV	89169	**888-708-5699**	702-567-7000	131
Ameristar Fence Products Inc 1555 N Mingo Rd	Tulsa	OK	74116	**888-333-3422**	918-835-0898	490
Amerisure Insurance Co 26777 Halsted Rd Ste 200	Farmington Hills	MI	48331	**800-257-1900**	248-615-9000	391-4
Ameritas Direct 5900 'O' St	Lincoln	NE	68510	**800-555-4655**		391-2
Ameritas Life Insurance Corp 5900 'O' St	Lincoln	NE	68510	**800-745-1112**	402-467-1122	391-2
Ameritel Inn Boise Towne Square 7965 W Emerald St	Boise	ID	83704	**800-600-6001**	208-378-7000	379
Ameritel Inn Pocatello 1440 Pocatello Bench Rd	Pocatello	ID	83201	**800-600-6001**	208-234-7500	379
Ameriwood Industries Inc 410 E S First St *General	Wright City	MO	63390	**800-489-3351***	636-745-3351	320-2
Amery Regional Medical Ctr 265 Griffin St E	Amery	WI	54001	**800-424-5273**	715-268-8000	353
Ames Chamber of Commerce 1601 Golden Aspen Dr Ste 110	Ames	IA	50010	**800-288-7470**	515-232-2310	138
Ames Community School District 415 Stanton Ave	Ames	IA	50014	**800-262-3867**	515-268-6600	683
Ames Taping Tools Inc 3350 Breckinridge Blvd Ste 100	Duluth	GA	30096	**800-408-2801**	800-303-1827	756
Ames True Temper Inc 465 Railroad Ave	Camp Hill	PA	17011	**800-393-1846**		756
AMETEK Automation & Process Technologies 1080 N Crooks	Clawson	MI	48017	**800-635-0289**	248-435-0700	203
Ametek HDR Power Systems Inc 3563 Interchange Rd	Columbus	OH	43204	**888-797-2685**	614-308-5500	255
AMETEK Inc 1100 Cassatt Rd PO Box 1764 *NYSE: AME*	Berwyn	PA	19312	**800-473-1286**	610-647-2121	360-3
AMETEK Inc Chemical Products Div 455 Corporate Blvd *Orders	Newark	DE	19702	**800-441-7777***	302-456-4400	742-3
AMETEK Inc Dixson Div 287 27 Rd	Grand Junction	CO	81503	**888-302-0639**	970-242-8863	494
AMETEK Inc Test & Calibration Instruments Div 8600 Somerset Dr	Largo	FL	33773	**800-733-5427**	727-538-6132	471
AMETEK National Controls Corp 1725 Western Dr	West Chicago	IL	60185	**800-323-2593**	630-231-5900	205
AMETEK Sensor Technology Drexelbrook Div 205 Keith Valley Rd *Cust Svc	Horsham	PA	19044	**800-553-9092***	215-674-1234	494
AMETEK Solidstate Controls 875 Dearborn Dr	Columbus	OH	43085	**800-635-7300**	614-846-7500	255
AMETEK US Gauge 820 Pennsylvania Blvd	Feasterville	PA	19053	**888-631-5454**	215-355-6900	471
AMF Bakery Systems 2115 W Laburnum Ave	Richmond	VA	23227	**800-225-3771**	804-355-7961	209
AMF Bowling Worldwide Inc 7313 Bell Creek Rd	Mechanicsville	VA	23111	**800-342-5263**		98
Amfed Cos LLC 576 Highland Colony Pkwy	Ridgeland	MS	39157	**800-264-8085**	601-853-4949	390
AMFM Inc 240 Capitol St Ste 500	Charleston	WV	25301	**800-348-1623**	304-344-1623	462
AMG Medical Inc 8505 Dalton	Montreal	QC	H4T1V5	**800-363-2381**	514-737-5251	476
AMG Resources Corp 2 Robinson Plaza # 350	Pittsburgh	PA	15205	**877-395-8338**	412-777-7300	684
Am-Gard Security Inc 600 Main St	Pittsburgh	PA	15215	**800-554-0412**	412-781-5800	691
Amgen Canada Inc 6775 Financial Dr Ste 100	Mississauga	ON	L5N0A4	**800-665-4273**	905-285-3000	84
Amgen Inc 1 Amgen Ctr Dr	Thousand Oaks	CA	91320	**800-563-9798**	805-447-1000	84
Amgraf Inc 1501 Oak St	Kansas City	MO	64108	**800-304-4797**	816-474-4797	182
AMHA (American Morgan Horse Assn) 4066 Shelburne Rd Ste 5	Shelburne	VT	05482	**888-436-3700**	802-985-4944	47-3
AMHCA (American Mental Health Counselors Assn) 801 N Fairfax St Ste 304	Alexandria	VA	22314	**800-326-2642**	703-548-6002	48-15
Amherst College 220 S Pleasant St	Amherst	MA	01002	**866-542-4438**	413-542-2000	167
AMI (American Megatrends Inc) 5555 Oakbrook Pkwy Bldg 200	Norcross	GA	30093	**800-828-9264**	770-246-8600	178
Ami Adini & Assoc Inc 4609 Russell Ave	Los Angeles	CA	90027	**888-400-4260**	323-913-4073	196
AMI Metals Inc 1738 General George Patton Dr	Brentwood	TN	37027	**800-727-1903**	615-377-0400	491
Amica Mutual Insurance Co 100 Amica Way	Lincoln	RI	02865	**800-652-6422**		391-4
Amicalola Electric Membership Corp 544 Hwy 515 S	Jasper	GA	30143	**800-282-7411**	706-253-5200	247
Amick Farms Inc 2079 Batesburg Hwy	Batesburg	SC	29006	**800-926-4257**	803-532-1400	10-7
AMICO (Alabama Metal Industries Corp) 3245 Fayette Ave	Birmingham	AL	35208	**800-366-2642**	205-787-2611	490
Amico Corp 85 Fulton Way	Richmond Hill	ON	L4B2N4	**877-462-6426**	905-764-0800	638
Amidon Graphics 1966 Benson Ave	Saint Paul	MN	55116	**800-328-6502**	651-690-2401	626
Amigos de las Americas 1800 West Loop S Ste 1325	Houston	TX	77027	**800-231-7796**	713-782-5290	47-5
Amigos Library Services 14400 Midway Rd	Dallas	TX	75244	**800-843-8482**	972-851-8000	387
Aminian Business Services Inc 50 Tesla	Irvine	CA	92618	**888-800-5207**	949-724-1155	112
Amino Transport Inc 223 NE Loop 820 Ste 101	Hurst	TX	76053	**800-304-3360**		196
Amity Foundation of California 2260 Watson Way	Vista	CA	92083	**888-508-9269**		306
Amivest Capital Management 703 Market St 18th Fl	San Francisco	CA	94103	**800-541-7774**		401
AMJ Campbell International 1445 Courtneypark Dr E	Mississauga	ON	L5T2E3	**800-363-6683**	905-670-6683	315
AML Partners LLC 4 Grand Cove Way	Edgewater	NJ	07020	**866-790-5095**	201-484-8835	465
Ammeraal Beltech USA 7501 N St Louis Ave *Cust Svc	Skokie	IL	60076	**800-323-4170***	847-673-6720	370
AMN Healthcare Services Inc 12400 High Bluff Dr Ste 100 *NYSE: AHS*	San Diego	CA	92130	**866-871-8519**		719
Amneal Pharmaceuticals LLC 75 Adams Ave *NYSE: IPAH*	Hauppauge	NY	11788	**866-525-7270**	631-952-0214	582
Amnesty International USA (AIUSA) 5 Penn Plaza 16th Fl	New York	NY	10001	**866-273-4466**	212-807-8400	47-5
AMOA (Amusement & Music Operators Assn) 600 Spring Hill Ring Rd Ste 111	West Dundee	IL	60118	**800-937-2662**	847-428-7699	47-23
AMOA-National Dart Assn (NDA) 9100 PuRdue Rd Ste 200	Indianapolis	IN	46268	**800-808-9884**	317-387-1299	47-22
Amoco Federal Credit Union PO Box 889	Texas City	TX	77592	**800-231-6053**	409-948-8541	221
Amon Carter Museum 3501 Camp Bowie Blvd	Fort Worth	TX	76107	**800-573-1933**	817-738-1933	519
Amoray Dive Resort Inc 104250 Overseas Hwy	Key Largo	FL	33037	**800-426-6729**	305-451-3595	705
Amos Press Inc 911 S Vandemark Rd	Sidney	OH	45365	**866-468-1622**	937-498-2111	634-9
AMPAC Fine Chemicals (AFC) MS 1007 PO Box 1718	Rancho Cordova	CA	95741	**800-311-9668**	916-357-6880	144
Ampac Packaging LLC 12025 Tricon Rd	Cincinnati	OH	45246	**800-543-7030**	513-671-1777	65
Ampac Seed Co 32727 Hwy 99 E	Tangent	OR	97389	**800-547-3230**	541-928-1651	692
Ampacet Corp 660 White Plains Rd *Cust Svc	Tarrytown	NY	10591	**800-888-4267***	914-631-6600	142
Ampco Manufacturers Inc 9 Burbidge St Ste 101	Coquitlam	BC	V3K7B2	**800-663-5482**	604-472-3800	626
Ampco Metal Inc 1117 E Algonquin Rd	Arlington Heights	IL	60005	**800-844-6008**	847-437-6000	484
Ampco Pumps Company Inc 2045 W Mill Rd	Glendale	WI	53209	**800-737-8671**	414-643-1852	638
Ampersand Art Supply 1235 S Loop 4 Ste 400	Buda	TX	78610	**800-822-1939**	512-322-0278	42
Ampersand Capital Partners 55 William St Ste 240	Wellesley	MA	02481	**800-477-6834**	781-239-0700	790
Ampex Corp 500 Broadway	Redwood City	CA	94063	**800-835-5095**	650-367-2011	656
Amphastar Pharmaceuticals Inc 11570 Sixth St	Rancho Cucamonga	CA	91730	**800-423-4136**	909-980-9484	582
Amphenol Aerospace 40-60 Delaware Ave	Sidney	NY	13838	**800-678-0141**	607-563-5011	255
Amphenol Corp 358 Hall Ave *NYSE: APH*	Wallingford	CT	06492	**877-267-4366**	203-265-8900	813
Amphenol Optimize Manufacturing Co 528 N Mariposa Rd Bldg. A	Nogales	AZ	85621	**800-288-4746**	520-397-7015	465
Amphenol RF 4 Old Newtown Rd	Danbury	CT	06810	**800-627-7100**	203-743-9272	255
Amphenol Spectra-Strip 720 Sherman Ave	Hamden	CT	06514	**800-846-6400**	203-281-3200	255
Amphenol-Tuchel Electronics 6900 Haggerty Rd Ste 200	Canton	MI	48187	**800-380-8052**	734-451-6400	255
AMPI 315 N Broadway	New Ulm	MN	56073	**800-533-3580**	507-354-8295	298-4
Amplicon Express Inc 2345 Ne Hopkins Ct	Pullman	WA	99163	**877-332-8080**	509-332-8080	740
AmpliPhi Biosciences Corp 3579 Valley Centre Dr Ste 100 *OTC: APHB*	San Diego	CA	92130	**877-795-3647**	804-205-5069	84
AmpliVox Sound Systems LLC 3995 Commercial Ave	Northbrook	IL	60062	**800-267-5486**	847-498-9000	51
Ampronix Inc 15 Whatney	Irvine	CA	92618	**800-400-7972**	949-273-8000	474
AMR (American Medical Response) 6200 S Syracuse Way Ste 200	Greenwood Village	CO	80111	**877-244-4890**	303-495-1200	30
AmRad Engineering Inc 32 Hargrove Grade	Palm Coast	FL	32137	**800-445-6033**	386-445-6000	255
AmRent 250 E BRd St 21st Fl	Columbus	OH	43215	**800-324-4595**	713-266-1870	632
Amresco Inc 6681 Cochran Rd	Solon	OH	44139	**800-448-4442**	440-349-1313	233
Amridge University 1200 Taylor Rd	Montgomery	AL	36117	**888-790-8080**	334-387-3877	167
Amro Music Stores 2918 Poplar Ave *General	Memphis	TN	38111	**800-626-2676***	901-323-8888	525
AMRPA (American Medical Rehabilitation Providers Assn) 1710 N St NW	Washington	DC	20036	**888-346-4624**	202-223-1920	48-8
AMS (American Musicological Society) 6010 College Stn	Brunswick	ME	04011	**888-421-1442**	207-798-4243	47-4
AMS (American Mathematical Society) 201 Charles St *Cust Svc	Providence	RI	02904	**800-321-4267***	401-455-4000	48-19
AMS (American Meteorological Society) 45 Beacon St	Boston	MA	02108	**800-824-0405**	617-227-2425	48-19
AMS Filling Systems 2500 Chestnut Tree Rd	Honey Brook	PA	19344	**800-647-5390**	610-942-4200	546
AMS Health Sciences Inc 4000 N Lindsay	Oklahoma City	OK	73105	**800-426-4267**	405-842-0131	297-11
Ams Mechanical Systems Inc 140 E Tower Dr	Burr Ridge	IL	60527	**800-794-5033**	630-887-7700	263
AMSA (American Medical Student Assn) 1902 Assn Dr	Reston	VA	20191	**800-767-2266**	703-620-6600	48-5
AMSA (American Moving & Storage Assn) 1611 Duke St	Alexandria	VA	22314	**888-849-2672**	703-683-7410	48-21

Name / Address	City	State	Zip	Toll-Free	Phone	Class
Amscan Inc 80 Grasslands Rd	Elmsford	NY	10523	**800-444-8887**	914-345-2020	565
Amsco Windows Inc 1880 S 1045 W	Salt Lake City	UT	84104	**800-748-4661**	801-978-5000	236
Amset Technical Consulting 1864 S Elmhurst Rd	Mount Prospect	IL	60056	**888-982-6783**	847-229-1155	263
Amsoil Inc 925 Tower Ave *Sales	Superior	WI	54880	**800-777-7094***	715-392-7101	540
AmSouth Investment Services Inc (AIS) 250 Riverchase Pkwy E 4th Fl	Birmingham	AL	35244	**866-512-3479**		401
Amstan Logistics 101 Knightsbridge Dr	Hamilton	OH	45011	**800-322-5546**	513-863-4627	778
Amstek Metal LLC 2408 W Mcdonough	Joliet	IL	60436	**800-551-9473**	815-725-2520	491
Amsterdam Printing & Litho Corp 166 Wallins Corners Rd *Cust Svc	Amsterdam	NY	12010	**800-833-6231***	518-842-6000	9
Amster-Kirtz Co 2830 Cleveland Ave NW	Canton	OH	44709	**800-257-9338**	330-535-6021	298-8
AmSurg Corp 1A Burton Hills Blvd *NASDAQ: AMSG*	Nashville	TN	37215	**800-945-2301**	615-665-1283	352
AMSUS (Association of Military Surgeons of the United States) 9320 Old Georgetown Rd	Bethesda	MD	20814	**800-761-9320**	301-897-8800	48-8
AMT (American Medical Technologists) 10700 W Higgins Rd Ste 150	Rosemont	IL	60018	**800-275-1268**	847-823-5169	48-8
AMT (Association for Mfg Technology) 7901 Westpark Dr	McLean	VA	22102	**800-524-0475**	703-893-2900	48-12
AMT Datasouth Corp 803 Camarillo Springs Rd Ste D	Camarillo	CA	93012	**800-215-9192**	805-388-5799	175-6
AMT Machine Systems Ltd 868 Fwy Dr N	Columbus	OH	43229	**866-204-0660**	614-635-8050	258
AMTA (American Massage Therapy Assn) 500 Davis St Ste 900	Evanston	IL	60201	**877-905-2700**	847-864-0123	47-17
Amtelco 4800 Curtin Dr	McFarland	WI	53558	**800-356-9148**	608-838-4194	732
Amtote International Inc 11200 Pepper Rd	Hunt Valley	MD	21031	**800-345-1566**	410-771-8700	323
Am-Touch Dental 28703 Industry Dr	Valencia	CA	91355	**800-350-4568**	661-294-1213	230
AmTrust Bank 1801 E Ninth St	Cleveland	OH	44114	**888-696-4444**	216-736-3480	69
AMU (American Public University System) 111 W Congress St	Charles Town	WV	25414	**877-777-9081**	304-724-3700	168
Amusement & Music Operators Assn (AMOA) 600 Spring Hill Ring Rd Ste 111	West Dundee	IL	60118	**800-937-2662**	847-428-7699	47-23
Amvac Chemical Corp 4100 E Washington Blvd	Los Angeles	CA	90023	**800-424-9300**	323-264-3910	282
AMVETS 4647 Forbes Blvd	Lanham	MD	20706	**877-726-8387**	301-459-9600	47-19
Amvic Inc 501 McNicoll Ave	Toronto	ON	M2H2E2	**877-470-9991**	416-410-5674	185
Amway Corp 7575 Fulton St E	Ada	MI	49355	**800-253-6500**	616-787-4000	366
Amway Grand Plaza Hotel 187 Monroe Ave NW	Grand Rapids	MI	49503	**800-253-3590**	616-774-2000	379
AMX Corp 3000 Research Dr	Richardson	TX	75082	**855-269-8585**	469-624-8585	205
AN Deringer Inc 64 N Main St	Saint Albans	VT	05478	**800-448-8108**	802-524-8110	448
ANA (Acoustic Neuroma Assn) 600 Peachtree Pkwy Ste 108	Cumming	GA	30041	**877-200-8211**	770-205-8211	47-17
ANA (American Nurses Assn) 8515 Georgia Ave Ste 400	Silver Spring	MD	20910	**800-274-4262**	301-628-5000	48-8
ANA PAC (American Nurses Assn PAC) 8515 Georgia Ave Ste 400	Silver Spring	MD	20910	**800-274-4262**	301-628-5000	614
ANAC (Association of Nurses in AIDS Care) 3538 Ridgewood Rd	Akron	OH	44333	**800-260-6780**	330-670-0101	48-8
Anacom General Corp 1240 S Claudina St	Anaheim	CA	92805	**800-955-9540**	714-774-8484	392
Anadarko Petroleum Corp 1201 Lk Robbins Dr *NYSE: APC*	Spring	TX	77380	**800-800-1101**	832-636-1000	535
Anaheim Automation 910 E Orangefair Ln *Sales	Anaheim	CA	92801	**800-345-9401***	714-992-6990	205
Anaheim Custom Extruders 4640 E La Palma Ave *Cust Svc	Anaheim	CA	92807	**800-229-2760***	714-693-8508	599
Anaheim Ducks 2695 E Katella Ave	Anaheim	CA	92806	**877-945-3946**		714
Anaheim Extrusion Company Inc 1330 N Kraemer Blvd PO Box 6380	Anaheim	CA	92806	**800-660-3318**	714-630-3111	484
Anaheim Marriott 700 W Convention Way	Anaheim	CA	92802	**800-845-5279**	714-750-8000	669
Anaheim Mfg Co 2680 Orbiter St PO Box 4146 *Cust Svc	Brea	CA	92821	**800-854-3229***	310-542-5259	35
Anaheim Plaza Hotel & Suites 1700 S Harbor Blvd	Anaheim	CA	92802	**800-631-4144**	714-772-5900	379
Anaheim University 1240 S State College Blvd Rm 110	Anaheim	CA	92806	**800-955-6040**	714-772-3330	164
Anaheim/Orange County Visitor & Convention Bureau 800 W Katella Ave	Anaheim	CA	92802	**855-405-5020**	714-765-8888	208
Analog Devices Inc 3 Technology Way *NASDAQ: ADI*	Norwood	MA	02062	**800-262-5643**	781-329-4700	694
Analysts Inc 22750 Hawthorne Blvd Ste 220	Torrance	CA	90505	**800-336-3637**		740
Analytic Investors LLC 555 W Fifth St 50th Fl	Los Angeles	CA	90013	**800-618-1872**	213-688-3015	401
Analytical Graphics Inc 220 Vly Creek Blvd	Exton	PA	19341	**800-220-4785**	610-981-8000	179
Analytics Corp 10329 Stony Run Ln	Ashland	VA	23005	**800-888-8061**	804-365-3000	740
Anaqua Grill 555 S Alamo St	San Antonio	TX	78205	**800-845-5279**	210-229-1000	669
Anaren Microwave Inc 6635 Kirkville Rd *NASDAQ: ANEN*	East Syracuse	NY	13057	**800-544-2414**	315-432-8909	255
AnaSpec Inc 34801 Campus Dr	Fremont	CA	94555	**800-452-5530**	510-791-9560	233
Ancestry 360 W 4800 N	Provo	UT	84604	**800-262-3787**	801-705-7000	397
Ancestry.com 360 W 4800 N *Cust Svc	Provo	UT	84604	**800-262-3787***	801-705-7000	397
Anchor BanCorp Wisconsin Inc 25 W Main St *NYSE: ABCW*	Madison	WI	53707	**800-252-6246**	608-252-8700	360-2
Anchor Bank 1055 Wayzata Blvd E	Wayzata	MN	55391	**800-425-5150**	952-473-4606	69
Anchor Bay School District 5201 County Line Rd Ste 100	Casco Township	MI	48064	**800-285-4460**	586-725-2861	683
Anchor Benefit Consulting Inc 2400 Maitland Ctr Pkwy Ste 111	Maitland	FL	32751	**800-845-7629**	407-667-8766	196
Anchor Computer Inc 1900 New Hwy	Farmingdale	NY	11735	**800-728-6262**	631-293-6100	180-10
Anchor Fabrication Ltd 1200 Lawson Rd	Fort Worth	TX	76131	**800-635-0386**	817-498-2521	479
Anchor Hocking Co 519 Pierce Ave	Lancaster	OH	43130	**800-562-7511**	740-681-6478	334
Anchor Hospital 5454 Yorktowne Dr	Atlanta	GA	30349	**866-667-8797**	770-991-6044	724
Anchor Industries Inc 1100 Burch Dr	Evansville	IN	47725	**800-544-4445**	812-867-2421	730
Anchor Paper Company Inc 480 Broadway St	Saint Paul	MN	55101	**800-652-9755**	651-298-1311	552
Anchor Tampa Inc 3907 W Osborne Ave	Tampa	FL	33614	**800-879-8685**	813-879-8685	188
Anchor Tool & Die Co 12200 Brookpark Rd	Cleveland	OH	44130	**888-341-8910**	216-362-1850	755
Anchorage Alaska Bed & Breakfast Assn (AABBA) PO Box 242623	Anchorage	AK	99524	**888-584-5147**	907-272-5909	376
Anchorage Convention & Visitors Bureau 524 W Fourth Ave	Anchorage	AK	99501	**800-478-6657**	907-276-4118	208
Anchorage Daily News 1001 Northway Dr	Anchorage	AK	99508	**800-478-4200**	907-257-4200	531-2
Anchorage Film Festival 1231 W Northern Lights Blvd Ste 844	Anchorage	AK	99503	**800-544-0786**	907-338-3761	284
AnchorBank 25 W Main St PO Box 7933	Madison	WI	53703	**800-252-6246**	608-252-8827	69
Anchor-Harvey Components LLC 600 W Lamm Rd	Freeport	IL	61032	**888-367-4464**	815-233-3833	482
Ancient Cedars Spa at the Wickaninnish Inn 500 Osprey Ln PO Box 250	Tofino	BC	V0R2Z0	**800-333-4604**	250-725-3113	705
Ancira Winton Chevrolet 6111 Bandera Rd *General	San Antonio	TX	78238	**800-299-5286***	210-762-4545	56
ANCO Insurance 1111 Briarcrest Dr PO Box 3889	Bryan	TX	77802	**800-749-1733**	979-776-2626	390
Anco Products Inc (API) 2500 S 17th St	Elkhart	IN	46517	**800-837-2626**	574-293-5574	389
Ancra International LLC 4880 W Rosecrans Ave	Hawthorne	CA	90250	**800-973-5092**	310-973-5000	676
Andaz San Diego 600 F St	San Diego	CA	92101	**877-489-4489**	619-849-1234	379
Anderol Inc 215 Merry Ln	East Hanover	NJ	07936	**888-263-3765**	973-887-7410	540
Andersen Corp 100 Fourth Ave N	Bayport	MN	55003	**888-888-7020**	651-264-5150	238
Andersen Manufacturing Inc 3125 N Yellowstone Hwy	Idaho Falls	ID	83401	**800-635-6106**	208-523-6460	645
Anderson Area Chamber of Commerce 907 N Main St Ste 200	Anderson	SC	29621	**800-922-1150**	864-226-3454	138
Anderson Brass Co 1629 W Bobo Newsome Hwy	Hartsville	SC	29550	**800-476-9876**	843-332-4111	787
Anderson Chemical Co 325 S Davis	Litchfield	MN	55355	**800-366-2477**	320-693-2477	144
Anderson Coach & Travel 1 Anderson Plz	Greenville	PA	16125	**800-345-3435**	724-588-8310	758
Anderson Copper & Brass Co 7231 W Laraway Rd	Frankfort	IL	60423	**800-323-5284**	708-535-9030	608
Anderson Equipment Co 1000 Washington Pk	Bridgeville	PA	15017	**800-414-4554**	412-343-2300	358
Anderson Erickson Dairy Co 2420 E University Ave	Des Moines	IA	50317	**800-234-7257**	515-265-2521	297-27
Anderson Forest Products Inc 1267 Old Edmonton Rd	Tompkinsville	KY	42167	**800-489-6778**	270-487-6778	550
Anderson Independent-Mail PO Box 2507	Anderson	SC	29622	**800-859-6397**	864-224-4321	531-2
Anderson International Corp 6200 Harvard Ave	Cleveland	OH	44105	**800-336-4730**	216-641-1112	299
Anderson Ranch Arts Ctr 5263 Owl Creek Rd PO Box 5598	Snowmass Village	CO	81615	**800-525-6363**	970-923-3181	49-1
Anderson Trucking Service Inc 725 Opportunity St PO Box 1377	Saint Cloud	MN	56301	**800-328-2316**	320-255-7400	778
Anderson Tube Company Inc 1400 Fairgrounds Rd	Hatfield	PA	19440	**800-523-2258**	215-855-0118	611
Anderson University 1100 E Fifth St *Admissions	Anderson	IN	46012	**800-428-6414***	765-649-9071	167
Anderson/Madison County Visitors & Convention Bureau 6335 S Scatterfield Rd	Anderson	IN	46013	**800-533-6569**	765-643-5633	208
Andersons Inc 480 W Dussel Dr *NASDAQ: ANDE*	Maumee	OH	43537	**800-537-3370**	419-893-5050	187
Andex Industries Inc 1911 Fourth Ave N	Escanaba	MI	49829	**800-338-9882**		87
Andis Co 1800 County Rd H	Sturtevant	WI	53177	**800-558-9441**	262-884-2600	36

Name / Address	City	State	ZIP	Toll-Free	Phone	Class
Andover College 265 Western Ave	South Portland	ME	04106	**800-639-3110**	207-774-6126	798
Andover Healthcare Inc 9 Fanaras Dr	Salisbury	MA	01952	**800-432-6686**	978-465-0044	475
Andover Newton Theological School 210 Herrick Rd	Newton Center	MA	02459	**800-964-2687**	617-964-1100	168-3
Andreas Furniture Company Inc 114 Dover Rd Ne	Sugarcreek	OH	44681	**800-846-7448**	330-852-2494	322
Andreini & Co 220 W 20th Ave	San Mateo	CA	94403	**800-969-2522**	650-573-1111	390
Andrew College 501 College St	Cuthbert	GA	39840	**800-664-9250**		161
Andrew G Gordon Inc 306 Washington St	Norwell	MA	02061	**866-243-2259**	781-659-2262	390
Andrew Technologies LLC 1421 Edinger Ave Ste D	Tustin	CA	92780	**888-959-7674**		474
Andrews & Hamilton Company Inc 3829 S Miami Blvd	Durham	NC	27703	**800-443-6866**	919-787-4100	358
Andrews Federal Credit Union (AFCU) 5711 Allentown Rd	Suitland	MD	20746	**800-487-5500**	301-702-5500	221
Andrews Hooper Pavlik Plc 5300 Gratiot Rd	Saginaw	MI	48638	**888-754-8478**	989-497-5300	2
Andrews Hotel 624 Post St	San Francisco	CA	94109	**800-926-3739**	415-563-6877	379
Andrews Logistics Inc 2445 E Southlake Blvd	Southlake	TX	76092	**866-536-1234**	817-527-2770	196
Andrews University 3976 Rose Dr	Berrien Springs	MI	49103	**800-253-2874**	269-471-7771	167
Andrews University James White Library 4190 Admin Dr	Berrien Springs	MI	49104	**800-253-2874**	269-471-3264	434-6
Andrews University Seventh-day Adventist Theological Seminary 4145 E Campus Cir Dr Andrews University	Berrien Springs	MI	49104	**800-253-2874**	269-471-3537	168-3
Andrews Van Lines Inc 310 S Seventh St *Cust Svc	Norfolk	NE	68701	**800-228-8146***	402-371-5440	518
Andrie Inc 561 E Western Ave	Muskegon	MI	49442	**800-722-2421**	231-728-2226	315
Androscoggin Home Health Services Inc PO Box 819	Lewiston	ME	04243	**800-482-7412**	207-777-7740	363
Andrus Transportation Services LLC 3185 East Deseret Dr North	Saint George	UT	84790	**800-888-5838**	435-673-1566	360-2
Andy Frain Services Inc 761 Shoreline Dr	Aurora	IL	60504	**877-707-4771**	630-820-3820	691
Andy Williams Moon River Theatre 2500 Hwy 76	Branson	MO	65616	**800-666-6094**	417-334-1800	571
Anemostat 1220 Watsoncenter Rd PO Box 4938	Carson	CA	90745	**877-423-7426**	310-835-7500	236
Anesthesia Service Inc 1821 N Classen Blvd	Oklahoma City	OK	73106	**800-336-3356**	405-525-3588	474
ANEXIO Technology Services Inc 1 Bank of America Plz 421 Fayetteville St	Raleigh	NC	27601	**844-208-6512**	941-556-3410	198
ANG Federal Credit Union PO Box 170204	Birmingham	AL	35217	**800-237-6211**	205-841-4525	221
Angel Fire Resort PO Box 130	Angel Fire	NM	87710	**800-633-7463**	575-377-6401	667
Angel Stadium 2000 Gene Autry Way	Anaheim	CA	92806	**866-800-1275**	714-940-2000	718
Angela Hospice Home Care 14100 Newburgh Rd *General	Livonia	MI	48154	**866-464-7810***	734-464-7810	371
Angell & Phelps Chocolate Factory 154 S Beach St	Daytona Beach	FL	32114	**800-969-2634**	386-252-6531	669
Angelo State University 2601 W Ave N ASU Stn 11014	San Angelo	TX	76909	**800-946-8627**	325-942-2041	167
Angelo State University Henderson Library 2025 S Johnson St	San Angelo	TX	76909	**800-946-8627**	325-942-2051	434-6
Angie's Cantina 11 E Buchanan St	Duluth	MN	55802	**800-706-7672**	218-727-6117	669
Angler's Inn 265 N Millward	Jackson	WY	83001	**800-867-4667**	307-733-3682	379
Angola Wire Products Inc 803 Wohlert St	Angola	IN	46703	**800-800-7225**	260-665-9447	288
Angstrom Graphics 2025 McKinley St	Hollywood	FL	33020	**800-634-1262**	954-920-7300	626
Angstrom Graphics Inc 4437 E 49th St	Cleveland	OH	44125	**800-634-1262**	216-271-5300	626
Angstrom Technologies Inc 7880 Foundation Dr *Cust Svc	Florence	KY	41042	**800-543-7358***	859-282-0020	144
Anguil Environmental Systems Inc 8855 N 55th St	Milwaukee	WI	53223	**800-488-0230**	414-365-6400	18
Anguilla Tourist Marketing Office 246 Central Ave	White Plains	NY	10606	**800-553-4939**	914-287-2400	773
Angus Barn 9401 Glenwood Ave	Raleigh	NC	27617	**800-277-2270**	919-781-2444	669
Anheuser-Busch Cos Inc 1 Busch Pl	Saint Louis	MO	63118	**800-342-5283**	314-577-2000	79-1
Animal Ark Wildlife Sanctuary & Nature Ctr 1265 Deerlodge Rd	Reno	NV	89508	**866-366-5771**	775-970-3111	821
Animal Supply Company LLC 32001 32nd Ave S Ste 420	Federal Way	WA	98001	**800-323-2963**	253-237-0400	298-8
Animas Corp 200 Lawrence Dr	West Chester	PA	19380	**877-937-7867**	610-644-8990	476
Animation Mentor 1400 65th St Ste 250	Emeryville	CA	94608	**877-326-4628**		762
Anixter Inc 2301 Patriot Blvd	Glenview	IL	60026	**800-492-1212**	224-521-8000	191-4
Anixter International Inc 2301 Patriot Blvd *NYSE: AXE*	Glenview	IL	60025	**800-492-1212**	224-521-8000	248
ANL (Argonne National Laboratory) 9700 S Cass Ave	Argonne	IL	60439	**800-632-8990**	630-252-2000	666
Anlin Industries 1665 Tollhouse Rd	Clovis	CA	93611	**800-287-7996**	559-322-1531	498
ANMC (Alaska Native Medical Ctr) 4315 Diplomacy Dr *Admitting	Anchorage	AK	99508	**800-478-6661***	907-563-2662	374-3
Ann & Hope Inc 1 Ann & Hope Way	Cumberland	RI	02864	**877-228-7824**		231
Ann Arbor Area Convention & Visitors Bureau 120 W Huron St	Ann Arbor	MI	48104	**800-888-9487**	734-995-7281	208
Ann Inc 7 Times Sq *NYSE: ANN*	New York	NY	10036	**800-677-6788**	212-541-3300	156-6
Ann Sacks Tile & Stone Inc 8120 NE 33rd Dr	Portland	OR	97211	**800-278-8453**	503-281-7751	749
ANNA (American Nephrology Nurses Assn) 200 E Holly Ave	Sewell	NJ	08080	**888-600-2662**	856-256-2320	48-8
Anna Griffin Inc 99 Armour Dr	Atlanta	GA	30324	**888-817-8170**	404-817-8170	551-2
Anna Maria College 50 Sunset Ln	Paxton	MA	01612	**800-344-4586**		167
Anna's Linens Inc 3550 Hyland Ave	Costa Mesa	CA	92626	**866-266-2728**	714-850-0504	362
Annals of Internal Medicine Magazine 190 N Independence Mall W	Philadelphia	PA	19106	**800-523-1546**	215-351-2400	456-16
Annan & Bird Lithographers Ltd 1060 Tristar Dr	Mississauga	ON	L5T1H9	**800-565-5618**	905-670-0604	626
Annapolis & Anne Arundel County Conference & Visitors Bureau (AAACCVB) 26 W St	Annapolis	MD	21401	**888-302-2852**	410-280-0445	208
Annapolis Bancorp Inc 1000 Bestgate Rd *NASDAQ: ANNB*	Annapolis	MD	21401	**800-555-5455**	410-224-4455	360-2
Annenberg Media 1301 Pennsylvania Ave NW ste302	Washington	DC	20004	**800-532-7637**		629
Annex Brands Inc 7580 Metropolitan Dr Ste 200	San Diego	CA	92108	**877-722-5236**	619-563-4800	112
Annex Pro Inc 49 Dunlevy Ave Ste 220	Vancouver	BC	V6A3A3	**800-682-6639**	604-682-6639	525
Annie E Casey Foundation 701 St Paul St	Baltimore	MD	21202	**800-222-1099**	410-547-6600	306
Annie Penn Hospital 618 S Main St	Reidsville	NC	27320	**866-391-2734**	336-951-4000	374-3
Annin & Co 105 Eisenhower Pkwy	Roseland	NJ	07068	**888-252-4569**	973-228-9400	289
Anniston Sportswear Corp PO Box 189	Anniston	AL	36201	**866-814-9253**	256-236-1551	154-11
Anniston Star 4305 McClellan Blvd PO Box 189	Anniston	AL	36202	**866-814-9253**	256-236-1551	531-2
AnnTaylor Inc 7 Times Sq	New York	NY	10036	**800-342-5266**	212-541-3300	156-6
Annual Reviews 4139 El Camino Way	Palo Alto	CA	94303	**800-523-8635**	650-493-4400	634-9
Annuvia Inc 1725 Clay St Ste 100	San Francisco	CA	94109	**866-364-7940**		40
Anoka Technical College 1355 W Hwy 10	Anoka	MN	55303	**800-627-3529**	763-433-1100	798
Anoka-Hennepin Independent School District 11 2727 N Ferry St	Anoka	MN	55303	**800-729-6164**	763-506-1000	683
Anoka-Ramsey Community College 11200 Mississippi Blvd NW	Coon Rapids	MN	55433	**800-627-3529**	763-433-1100	161
Anonymizer Inc 6755 Mira Mesa Blvd Ste 123-164	San Diego	CA	92121	**888-270-0141**		524
ANR Pipeline Co 717 Texas St	Houston	TX	77002	**800-827-5267**	832-320-5230	326
Anresco Inc 1375 Van Dyke Ave	San Francisco	CA	94124	**800-359-0920**	415-822-1100	40
Anritsu Co 490 Jarvis Dr	Morgan Hill	CA	95037	**800-267-4878**	408-778-2000	250
ANS (American Nuclear Society) 555 N Kensington Ave	La Grange Park	IL	60526	**800-323-3044**	708-352-6611	48-19
Ansar Group Inc, The 240 S Eigth St	Philadelphia	PA	19107	**888-883-7804**	215-922-6088	474
Ansell Healthcare Inc 111 S Wood Ave Ste 210	Iselin	NJ	08830	**800-365-2282**	732-345-5400	575
ANSI (American National Standards Institute) 25 W 43rd St 4th fl	New York	NY	10036	**800-374-3818**	212-642-4900	47-1
Answer One Inc 2216 Young Dr Ste 3	Lexington	KY	40505	**800-517-7395**	859-269-3482	181
AnswerDash Inc 4000 Mason Rd New Ventures Facility Fluke Hall	Seattle	WA	98195	**800-311-5786**		387
Answers Corp 237 W 35th St Ste 1101	New York	NY	10001	**888-885-5008**	646-502-4778	180-7
ANSYS Inc 275 Technology Dr *NASDAQ: ANSS*	Canonsburg	PA	15317	**800-937-3321**	724-746-3304	180-5
Antea Group 5910 Rice Creek Pkwy Ste 100	Saint Paul	MN	55126	**800-477-7411**	651-639-9449	665
Antec Inc 47900 Fremont Blvd	Fremont	CA	94538	**800-222-6832**	510-770-1200	255
Antelope Valley Press 37404 Sierra Hwy	Palmdale	CA	93550	**888-874-2527**	661-273-2700	531-2
Anthelio Healthcare Solutions Inc 5400 LBJ Fwy Ste 200	Dallas	TX	75240	**855-268-4354**	214-257-7000	363
Anthem Blue Cross & Blue Shield 2015 Staples Mill Rd	Richmond	VA	23230	**800-451-1527**	804-354-7000	391-3
Anthem Blue Cross & Blue Shield Maine 2 Gannett Dr *Cust Svc	South Portland	ME	04106	**800-482-0966***	207-822-7000	391-3
Anthem Blue Cross & Blue Shield of Connecticut 370 Bassett Rd	North Haven	CT	06473	**800-922-1742**	800-922-4670	391-3
Anthem Blue Cross & Blue Shield of Nevada 9133 W Russell Rd	Las Vegas	NV	89148	**800-332-3842**	702-228-2583	391-3
Anthem Blue Cross Blue Shield Colorado 700 Broadway	Denver	CO	80273	**800-654-9338**	303-831-2131	391-3
Anthem Inc 120 Monument Cir	Indianapolis	IN	46204	**800-999-7222**	317-488-6000	461
Anthem Insurance Cos Inc 120 Monument Cir Ste 200	Indianapolis	IN	46204	**800-331-1476**	317-488-6000	360-4
Anthem Life Insurance Co 6740 N High St Ste 200	Worthington	OH	43085	**800-551-7265**	614-436-0688	391-2

Name / Address	City	State	Zip	Toll-Free	Phone	Class
Anthony & Sylvan Pools Corp 3739 Easton Rd Rt 611	Doylestown	PA	18901	**800-366-7958**	215-489-5600	726
Anthony Forest Products Co 309 N Washington Ave	El Dorado	AR	71730	**800-221-2326**	870-862-3414	681
Anthony International 12391 Montera Ave	Sylmar	CA	91342	**800-772-0900**	818-365-9451	330
Anthony-Thomas Candy Co 1777 Arlingate Ln	Columbus	OH	43228	**877-226-3921**	614-274-8405	297-8
Anthro Corp 10450 SW Manhasset Dr	Tualatin	OR	97062	**800-325-3841**	503-691-2556	320-1
Antibodies Inc PO Box 1560	Davis	CA	95617	**800-824-8540**		84
AntiCancer Inc 7917 Ostrow St	San Diego	CA	92111	**800-511-2555**	858-654-2555	233
Anti-Defamation League (ADL) 605 Third Ave	New York	NY	10158	**866-386-3235**	212-885-7700	47-8
Antigua & Barbuda *Embassy* 3216 New Mexico Ave NW	Washington	DC	20016	**866-978-7299**	202-362-5122	259
Antigua & Barbuda Dept of Tourism & Trade 305 E 47th St 6th Fl	New York	NY	10017	**888-268-4227**	212-541-4117	773
Antigua Sportswear Inc 16651 N 84 Ave	Peoria	AZ	85382	**800-528-3133**	623-523-6000	154-11
Antillean Marine Shipping Corp 3038 NW N River Dr	Miami	FL	33142	**888-633-6361**	305-633-6361	314
Antioch University 2326 Sixth Ave	Seattle	WA	98121	**888-268-4477**	206-441-5352	167
Antiochian Orthodox Christian Archdiocese of North America 358 Mountain Rd	Englewood	NJ	07631	**888-421-1442**	201-871-1355	47-20
Antique Car Museum/Grovewood Gallery 111 Grovewood Rd	Asheville	NC	28804	**877-622-7238**	828-253-7651	519
Antique Collectors Club 116 Pleasant St	EastHampton	MA	01027	**800-254-4100**	413-529-0861	634-2
Antique Mall 1251 S Virginia St	Reno	NV	89502	**888-316-6255**	775-324-4141	459
Antique Trader 700 E State St	Iola	WI	54990	**800-258-0929**	715-445-2214	456-14
Antitrust & Trade Regulation Daily 1801 S Bell St	Arlington	VA	22202	**800-372-1033**		530-2
Antler Inn 43 W Pearl St PO Box 575	Jackson	WY	83001	**800-483-8667**	307-733-2535	379
Anton/Bauer Inc 14 Progress Dr	Shelton	CT	06484	**800-422-3473**	203-929-1100	590
Antonelli Institute 300 Montgomery Ave	Erdenheim	PA	19038	**800-722-7871**	215-836-2222	163
Anvil Cases 15730 Salt Lake Ave	City of Industry	CA	91745	**800-359-2684**	626-968-4100	452
Anxiety Disorders Assn of America (ADAA) 8730 Georgia Ave Ste 600	Silver Spring	MD	20910	**800-922-8947**	240-485-1001	47-17
AnyDoc Software Inc 5404 Cypress Ctr Dr Ste 140	Tampa	FL	33609	**888-495-2638**		180-7
Anza ElectricCo-op Inc 58470 Hwy 371 PO Box 391909	Anza	CA	92539	**844-311-7201**	951-763-4333	247
AO Smith Corp 11270 W Pk Pl Ste 170 PO Box 245008 *NYSE: AOS*	Milwaukee	WI	53224	**800-359-4065**	414-359-4000	517
AO Smith Electrical Products Co 531 N Fourth St	Tipp City	OH	45371	**800-543-9450**	937-667-2431	517
AO Smith Water Products Co 500 Tennessee Waltz Pkwy	Ashland City	TN	37015	**800-527-1953**		35
AOA (American Osteopathic Assn) 142 E Ontario St	Chicago	IL	60611	**800-621-1773**	312-202-8000	48-8
AOAC International 481 N Frederick Ave Ste 500	Gaithersburg	MD	20877	**800-379-2622**	301-924-7077	48-19
AOAExcel Inc 243 N Lindbergh Blvd Fl 1	St. Louis	MO	63141	**800-365-2219**		387
AOC (Association of Old Crows) 1000 N Payne St Ste 300	Alexandria	VA	22314	**800-247-5626**	703-549-1600	47-19
AOCA (Automotive Oil Change Assn) 330 N. Wabash Ave Ste 2000	Chicago	IL	60611	**800-230-0702**	312-321-5132	48-21
AOCS (American Oil Chemists Society) 2710 S Boulder PO Box 17190	Urbana	IL	61802	**866-535-2730**	217-359-2344	47-12
AODME (Association of Osteopathic Directors & Medical Educators) 142 E Ontario St	Chicago	IL	60611	**800-621-1773**	312-202-8211	48-8
AOL Canada Inc 99 Spadina Ave Ste 200	Toronto	ON	M5V3P8	**888-265-6306**	416-263-8100	226
AOM (Academy of Management) 235 Elm Rd PO Box 3020	Briarcliff Manor	NY	10510	**800-633-4931**	914-923-2607	48-12
Aon Corp 200 E Randolph St	Chicago	IL	60601	**877-384-4276**	312-381-1000	360-4
Aon Risk Services Inc 200 E Randolph St	Chicago	IL	60601	**877-384-4276**	312-381-1000	390
AOPA (Aircraft Owners & Pilots Assn) 421 Aviation Way	Frederick	MD	21701	**800-872-2672**	301-695-2000	48-21
AOPA Pilot Magazine 421 Aviation Way	Frederick	MD	21701	**800-872-2672**	301-695-2000	456-14
AORN Inc 2170 S Parker Rd Ste 300	Denver	CO	80231	**800-755-2676**	303-755-6300	48-8
Aos Thermal Compounds LLC 22 Meridian Rd Ste 6	Eatontown	NJ	07724	**888-662-7337**	732-389-5514	578
AOSSM (American Orthopaedic Society for Sports Medicine) 6300 N River Rd Ste 500	Rosemont	IL	60018	**877-321-3500**	847-292-4900	48-8
AOTA (American Occupational Therapy Assn Inc) 4720 Montgomery Ln PO Box 31220	Bethesda	MD	20824	**800-877-1383**	301-652-2682	48-8
AP Exhaust Technologies Inc 300 Dixie Trial	Goldsboro	NC	27530	**800-277-2787**	919-580-2000	59
ap Services LLC, The 562 Watertown Ave Ste 3	Waterbury	CT	06708	**866-843-7270**		40
APA (American Psychiatric Assn) 1000 Wilson Blvd Ste 1825	Arlington	VA	22209	**888-357-7924**	703-907-7300	48-15
APA (American Psychological Assn) 750 First St NE	Washington	DC	20002	**800-374-2721**	202-336-5500	48-15
APA Services 4150 International Plz Tower I Ste 510	Fort Worth	TX	76109	**877-425-5023**		731
Apache Corp 2000 Post Oak Blvd Ste 100 *NYSE: APA*	Houston	TX	77056	**800-272-2434**	713-296-6000	535
Apache Greyhound Park 3801 E Washington	Phoenix	AZ	85034	**800-772-0852**	480-982-2371	132
Apache Hose & Belting Co Inc 4805 Bowling St SW *Sales	Cedar Rapids	IA	52404	**800-553-5455***	319-365-0471	370
Apache Stainless Equipment Corp 200 W Industrial Dr PO Box 538	Beaver Dam	WI	53916	**800-444-0398**	920-356-9900	386
APACVB (Alexandria/Pineville Area Convention & Visitors Bureau) 707 Main St PO Box 1070	Alexandria	LA	71301	**800-551-9546**	318-442-9546	208
Apalachicola Bay Chamber of Commerce 122 Commerce St	Apalachicola	FL	32320	**866-269-3022**	850-653-9419	138
Aparaa Corp 14900 Landmark Blvd Ste 630	Dallas	TX	75254	**888-441-2535**		179
Apartment Investment & Management Co 4582 S Ulster St Pkwy Ste 1100 *NYSE: AIV* ■ *General	Denver	CO	80237	**888-789-8600***	303-691-4350	653
APC (American Power Conversion Corp) 132 Fairgrounds Rd *Cust Svc	West Kingston	RI	02892	**800-788-2208***	401-789-5735	255
APC Integrated Services Inc 770 SPIRIT OF SAINT LOUIS Blvd	CHESTERFIELD	MO	63005	**888-294-7886**		318
APCC (American Public Communications Council Inc) 625 Slaters Ln Ste 104	Alexandria	VA	22314	**800-868-2722**	703-739-1322	48-20
APCO Bulletin 351 N Williamson Blvd	Daytona Beach	FL	32114	**888-272-6911**	386-322-2500	530-8
APCO Employees Credit Union 750 17th St N	Birmingham	AL	35203	**800-249-2726**	205-257-3601	221
Apco Extruders Inc 180 National Rd *Orders	Edison	NJ	08817	**800-942-8725***	732-287-3000	547
APCO Graphics Inc 388 Grant St SE	Atlanta	GA	30312	**877-988-2726**	404-688-9000	699
APCON Inc 9255 SW Pioneer Ct	Wilsonville	OR	97070	**800-624-6808**	503-682-4050	176
APD (American Product Distributors Inc) 8350 Arrowridge Blvd	Charlotte	NC	28273	**800-849-5842**	704-522-9411	533
APDA (American Parkinson Disease Assn) 135 Parkinson Ave	Staten Island	NY	10305	**800-223-2732**	718-981-8001	47-17
Apetito Canada Ltd 12 Indell Ln	Brampton	ON	L6T3Y3	**800-268-8199**	905-799-1022	298-8
Apex Asset Management LLC 2501 Oregon Pike Ste 201	Lancaster	PA	17601	**888-592-2149**	717-519-1780	197
Apex Color 200 N Lee St	Jacksonville	FL	32204	**800-367-6790**		109
Apex Digital Imaging Inc 16057 Tampa Palms Blvd W	Tampa	FL	33647	**866-973-3034**	813-973-3034	699
Apex Geoscience Inc 2120 Brandon Dr	Tyler	TX	75703	**800-755-8461**	903-581-8080	258
Apex Homes Inc 7172 Rt 522	Middleburg	PA	17842	**800-326-9524**	570-837-2333	188
Apex Industries Inc 100 Millennium Blvd	Moncton	NB	E1E2G8	**800-268-3331**	506-857-1620	479
Apex Mills Corp 168 Doughty Blvd	Inwood	NY	11096	**800-989-2739**	516-239-4400	742-4
Apex Packing & Rubbr Co 1855 New Hwy Ste D	Farmingdale	NY	11735	**800-645-9110**	631-420-8150	358
Apex Paper Box Co 5601 Walworth Ave *Cust Svc	Cleveland	OH	44102	**800-438-2269***	216-416-9475	100
Apex Piping Systems Inc 302 Falco Dr	Wilmington	DE	19804	**888-995-2739**	302-995-6136	609
APEX Systems Inc 4400 Cox Rd Ste 100	Glen Allen	VA	23060	**800-452-7391**	804-254-2600	719
Apex Voice Communications Inc 21700 Oxnard St Ste 1060	Woodland Hills	CA	91367	**800-727-3970**	818-379-8400	180-7
APG (Automation Products Group Inc) 1025 West 1700 North	Logan	UT	84321	**888-525-7300**	435-753-7300	203
APG (American Packing & Gasket Co) 6039 Armour Dr PO Box 213	Houston	TX	77020	**800-888-5223**	713-675-5271	327
APGA (American Public Gas Assn) 201 Massachusetts Ave NE Ste C-4	Washington	DC	20002	**800-927-4204**	202-464-2742	47-12
ApHC (Appaloosa Horse Club) 2720 W Pullman Rd	Moscow	ID	83843	**888-304-7768**	208-882-5578	47-3
APHL (Association of Public Health Laboratories) 8515 Georgia Ave Ste 700	Silver Spring	MD	20910	**800-899-2278**	240-485-2745	48-7
API (Anco Products Inc) 2500 S 17th St	Elkhart	IN	46517	**800-837-2626**	574-293-5574	389
API (Aerospace Products International) 3778 Distriplex Dr N	Memphis	TN	38118	**888-274-2497**	901-365-3470	22
API Construction Co 1100 Old Hwy 8 NW	New Brighton	MN	55112	**800-223-4922**	651-636-4320	191-9
APi Group Inc 1100 Old Hwy 8 NW	New Brighton	MN	55112	**800-223-4922**		187
API Heat Transfer Inc 2777 Walden Ave	Buffalo	NY	14225	**877-274-4328**	716-684-6700	90
APi Systems Group Inc 10575 Vista Park Rd *General	Dallas	TX	75238	**877-828-1200***	214-291-1200	690
APIC (Association for Professionals in Infection Control & Epidemiology Inc) 1275 K St NW Ste 1000	Washington	DC	20005	**800-650-9883**	202-789-1890	48-8
Apio Inc PO Box 727 *Sales	Guadalupe	CA	93434	**800-454-1355***	805-343-2835	297-21
APL Access & Security Inc 115 S William Dillard Dr	Gilbert	AZ	85233	**866-873-2288**	480-497-9471	691
APL Logistics Inc 16220 N Scottsdale Rd Ste 300	Scottsdale	AZ	85254	**866-896-2005**		448
Aplus.net Internet Services 3680 Victoria St N	Shoreview	MN	55126	**877-275-8763**	858-410-6929	398
APM Hexseal Corp 44 Honeck St	Englewood	NJ	07631	**800-498-9034**	201-569-5700	327
APMA (American Podiatric Medical Assn) 9312 Old Georgetown Rd	Bethesda	MD	20814	**800-275-2762**	301-581-9200	48-8

Name / Address	City	State	ZIP	Toll-Free	Phone	Class
Apmetrix Inc 5414 Oberlin Dr Ste 200	San Diego	CA	92121	**800-490-3184**		387
APN (Americans for Peace Now) 1101 14th St NW 6th Fl	Washington	DC	20005	**877-429-0678**	202-728-1893	47-7
APN Media LLC PO Box 20113	New York	NY	10023	**800-470-7599**	212-581-3380	634-9
APNA (American Psychiatric Nurses Assn) 1555 Wilson Blvd Ste 530	Arlington	VA	22209	**866-243-2443**	703-243-2443	48-8
Apogee Enterprises Inc 4400 W 78th St Ste 520 *NASDAQ: APOG*	Minneapolis	MN	55435	**877-752-3432**	952-835-1874	330
Apollo Design Technology Inc 4130 Fourier Dr	Fort Wayne	IN	46818	**800-288-4626**	260-497-9191	720
Apollo Group Inc 4025 E Elwood St *NASDAQ: APOL*	Phoenix	AZ	85040	**800-990-2765**		244
Apollo Oil LLC 1175 Early Dr	Winchester	KY	40391	**800-473-5823**	859-744-5444	317
Apollo Professional Svc 29 Stiles Rd Ste 302	Salem	NH	03079	**866-277-3343**		263
Apotex Corp 2400 N Commerce Pkwy Ste 400	Weston	FL	33326	**877-427-6839**		583
Apotex Inc 150 Signet Dr	Toronto	ON	M9L1T9	**800-268-4623**	416-749-9300	582
Apothecary Products 11750 12th Ave S Burnsville	Burnsville	MN	55337	**800-328-2742**		217
APPA (American Public Power Assn) 1875 Connecticut Ave Ste 1200	Washington	DC	20009	**800-369-6220**	202-467-2900	47-12
Appalachian Mountain Club (AMC) 5 Joy St *Orders	Boston	MA	02108	**800-262-4455***	617-523-0655	47-13
Appalachian Regional Healthcare Service (ARH) 80 Hospital Dr PO Box 8086	Barbourville	KY	40906	**888-654-0015**	859-226-2440	353
Appalachian School of Law 1169 Edgewater Dr	Grundy	VA	24614	**800-895-7411**	276-935-4349	168-1
Appalachian State University *Belk Library* 218 College St PO Box 32026	Boone	NC	28608	**877-423-0086**	828-262-2300	434-6
Appalachian Trail Conservancy (ATC) 799 Washington St PO Box 807 *Sales	Harpers Ferry	WV	25425	**888-287-8673***	304-535-6331	47-23
Appaloosa Horse Club (ApHC) 2720 W Pullman Rd	Moscow	ID	83843	**888-304-7768**	208-882-5578	47-3
Apparelmaster 123 Harrison Ave	Harrison	OH	45030	**877-543-1678**	513-202-1600	442
Appeal-Democrat 1530 Ellis Lk Dr PO Box 431	Marysville	CA	95901	**800-831-2345**	530-741-2345	531-2
Appian Analytics Inc 2000 Crow Canyon Pl Ste 300	San Ramon	CA	94583	**877-757-7646**		623
Apple & Eve Inc 2 Seaview Blvd	Port Washington	NY	11050	**866-487-2365**	516-621-1122	297-20
Apple Bank for Savings 122 E 42nd St 9th Fl	New York	NY	10168	**800-824-0710**	914-902-2775	69
Apple Creek Banc Corp 3 W Main St PO Box 237	Apple Creek	OH	44606	**888-327-7533**	330-698-2631	69
Apple Discount Drugs 404 N Fruitland Blvd	Salisbury	MD	21801	**800-424-8401**	410-749-8401	23
Apple Farm Bakery 2015 Monterey St	San Luis Obispo	CA	93401	**800-255-2040**	805-544-6100	378
Apple Inc 1 Infinite Loop *NASDAQ: AAPL* ■ *Cust Svc	Cupertino	CA	95014	**800-275-2273***	408-996-1010	175-1
Apple Rubber Products Inc 310 Erie St *Cust Svc	Lancaster	NY	14086	**800-828-7745***	716-684-6560	327
Apple Saddlery 1875 Innes Rd	Ottawa	ON	K1B4C6	**800-867-8225**	613-744-4040	709
Apple Tree Inn 9508 N Div St	Spokane	WA	99218	**800-323-5796**	509-466-3020	379
Apple Vacations Inc 101 NW Pt Blvd	Elk Grove Village	IL	60007	**800-517-2000**		769
Apple Valley Chamber of Commerce 14800 Galaxie Ave Ste 101	Apple Valley	MN	55124	**800-301-9435**	952-432-8422	138
Applegate Insulation Manufacturing Inc 1000 Highview Dr	Webberville	MI	48892	**800-627-7536**	517-521-3545	389
AppleOne Employment Services Inc 327 W Broadway	Glendale	CA	91204	**800-872-2677**	310-750-3400	719
Appleton Group Wealth Management LLC 100 W Lawrence St 3/F Apple.	Wisconsin	WI	54911	**866-993-7727**	920-993-7727	401
Appleton Medical Ctr 1818 N Meade St	Appleton	WI	54911	**800-236-4101**	920-731-4101	374-3
Appleton Papers Inc 825 E Wisconsin Ave PO Box 359	Appleton	WI	54912	**888-593-9546**	920-734-9841	551-1
Appleton Partners Inc 1 Post Office Sq 6th Fl	Boston	MA	02109	**800-338-0745**	617-338-0700	401
Applewood Books Inc 1 River Rd *General	Carlisle	MA	01741	**800-277-5312***	978-369-4172	634-2
Applewood Manor Inn 62 Cumberland Cir	Asheville	NC	28801	**800-442-2197**	828-254-2244	379
Appliance Recycling Centers of America Inc 7400 Excelsior Blvd *NASDAQ: ARCI*	Minneapolis	MN	55426	**800-452-8680**	952-930-9000	658
Applicant Insight Ltd 5396 School Rd PO Box 458	New Port Richey	FL	34652	**800-771-7703**		632
Applied Business Software 2847 Gundry Ave	Signal Hill	CA	90755	**800-833-3343**	562-426-2188	179
Applied Card Systems 50 Applied Card Way	Glen Mills	PA	19342	**866-227-5627**		219
Applied Diagnostics Inc 1140 Business Center Dr Ste 370	Houston	TX	77043	**855-239-8378**	713-271-4133	415
Applied Dynamics International Inc 3800 Stone School Rd	Ann Arbor	MI	48108	**888-465-4329**	734-973-1300	180-2
Applied Energy Company Inc (AEC) 1205 Venture Ct Ste 100	Carrollton	TX	75006	**800-580-1171**	214-355-4200	637
Applied Energy Solutions LLC 1 Technology Pl	Caledonia	NY	14423	**800-836-2132**	585-538-4421	73
Applied Fiber Inc PO Box 1339	Leesburg	GA	31763	**800-226-5394**	229-759-8301	543
Applied Laser Technologies 8404 Venture Cir	Schofield	WI	54476	**888-359-3002**	715-359-3002	491
Applied Materials Inc 3050 Bowers Ave PO Box 58039 *NASDAQ: AMAT*	Santa Clara	CA	95054	**877-356-9175**	408-727-5555	693
Applied Materials/Semitool 655 W Reserve Dr	Kalispell	MT	59901	**877-356-9175**	406-752-2107	693
Applied Mechanical Systems Inc 5598 Wolf Creek Pk	Dayton	OH	45426	**888-854-3073**	937-854-3073	609
Applied Membranes Inc 2325 Cousteau Ct	Vista	CA	92081	**800-321-9321**	760-727-3711	611
Applied Microstructures Inc 2381 Bering Dr	San Jose	CA	95131	**877-683-2678**	408-907-2885	203
Applied Process Cooling Corp 555 Price Ave	Redwood City	CA	94063	**877-231-6406**	650-595-0665	662
Applied Research & Technology 215 Tremont St	Rochester	NY	14608	**800-775-2427**	585-436-2720	51
Applied Software Inc 3919 National Dr Ste 200	Burtonsville	MD	20866	**888-624-8439**		179
Applied Systems Inc 200 Applied Pkwy *Sales	University Park	IL	60466	**800-999-5368***	708-534-5575	180-11
Applied Technology & Management Inc 5550 NW 111th Blvd	Gainesville	FL	32653	**800-275-6488**		263
Applied Thermal Systems 8401 73rd Ave N Ste 74	Brooklyn Park	MN	55428	**800-479-4783**	763-535-5545	611
Appling County Board of Education 249 Blackshear Hwy	Baxley	GA	31513	**866-632-9992**	912-367-8600	683
APPMA (American Pet Products Manufacturers Assn) 255 Glenville Rd	Greenwich	CT	06831	**800-452-1225**	203-532-0000	48-4
Appraisal Institute 550 W Van Buren St Ste 1000	Chicago	IL	60607	**888-756-4624**	312-335-4100	48-17
Appraisal Journal 200 W Madison Ste 1500	Chicago	IL	60606	**888-756-4624**		456-5
Appro International Inc 901 Fifth Ave Ste 1000	Seattle	WA	98164	**800-950-2729**	206-701-2000	175-8
AppsHosting Inc 13772 Goldenwest St Ste 321	Westminster	CA	92683	**877-625-6610**		387
AppTech Corp 2011 Palomar Airport Rd Ste 102	Carlsbad	CA	92011	**877-720-0022**		179
Apptis Inc 4800 Westfields Blvd	Chantilly	VA	20151	**888-277-8478**	703-279-3000	180-4
APPX Software Inc 11363 San Jose Blvd Ste 301	Jacksonville	FL	32223	**800-879-2779**	904-880-5560	180-1
APQC 123 N Post Oak Ln Ste 300	Houston	TX	77024	**800-776-9676**	713-681-4020	48-12
APRA (Automotive Parts Remanufacturers Assn) 4215 Lafayette Ctr Dr Ste 3	Chantilly	VA	20151	**877-734-4827**	703-968-2772	48-21
Apria Healthcare Group Inc 26220 Enterprise Ct	Lake Forest	CA	92630	**800-277-4288**	949-639-2000	363
Apricorn Inc 12191 Kirkham Rd	Poway	CA	92064	**800-458-5448**	858-513-2000	175-8
Apriva Inc 8501 N Scottsdale Rd Ste 110	Scottsdale	AZ	85253	**877-277-0728**	480-421-1210	179
APRO (Association of Progressive Rental Organizations) 1504 Robin Hood Trl	Austin	TX	78703	**800-204-2776**	512-794-0095	48-18
APRS (American Park & Recreation Society) 22377 Belmont Ridge Rd	Ashburn	VA	20148	**800-765-3110**	703-858-0784	47-23
APS (American Pain Society) 4700 W Lake Ave	Glenview	IL	60025	**877-752-4754**	847-375-4715	47-17
APS (Albuquerque Public Schools) 6400 Uptown Blvd NE	Albuquerque	NM	87110	**866-563-9297**	505-880-3700	683
APS (American Physical Society) 1 Physics Ellipse	College Park	MD	20740	**866-918-1164**	301-209-3200	48-19
APS (American Phytopathological Society, The) 3340 Pilot Knob Rd	Saint Paul	MN	55121	**800-328-7560**	651-454-7250	48-19
APS (Arizona Public Service Co) 400 N Fifth St PO Box 53999	Phoenix	AZ	85004	**800-253-9405**	602-371-7171	785
APS Healthcare Inc 44 S Broadway Ste 1200	White Plains	NY	10601	**800-305-3720**		461
Apscreen Inc PO Box 80639	Rancho Santa Margarita	CA	92688	**800-277-2733**	949-646-4003	632
APSP (Association of Pool & Spa Professionals) 2111 Eisenhower Ave Ste 500	Alexandria	VA	22314	**800-323-3996**	703-838-0083	48-4
APT (Alabama Public Television) 2112 11th Ave S Ste 400	Birmingham	AL	35205	**800-239-5233**	205-328-8756	629
APT Foundation 1 Long Wharf Dr Ste 321	New Haven	CT	06511	**855-378-4373**	203-781-4600	724
APTA (American Physical Therapy Assn) 1111 N Fairfax St	Alexandria	VA	22314	**800-999-2782**	703-684-2782	48-8
Aptech Computer Systems Inc 135 Delta Dr	Pittsburgh	PA	15238	**800-245-0720**	412-963-7440	180-11
APWA (American Public Works Assn) 2345 Grand Blvd Ste 700	Kansas City	MO	64108	**800-848-2792**	816-472-6100	48-7
AQA International LLC 501 Commerce Dr, NE	Columbia	SC	29223	**800-281-4384**		465
AQHA (American Quarter Horse Assn) 1600 Quarter Horse Dr	Amarillo	TX	79104	**800-291-7323**	806-376-4811	47-3
Aqua America Inc 762 W Lancaster Ave *NYSE: WTR*	Bryn Mawr	PA	19010	**877-987-2782**		785
Aqua Bamboo 2425 Kuhio Ave	Honolulu	HI	96815	**855-747-0754**	808-922-7777	379
Aqua Bath Company Inc 921 Cherokee Ave	Nashville	TN	37207	**800-232-2284**	615-227-0017	609
Aqua Data Inc 95 Fifth Ave	Pincourt	QC	J7V5K8	**800-567-9003**	514-425-1010	244
Aqua Hospitality Corp 445 Seaside Ave	Honolulu	HI	96815	**855-747-0755**	808-923-2345	379
Aqua Waikiki Wave 2299 Kuhio Ave	Honolulu	HI	96815	**855-747-0754**	808-922-1262	379

Name	Address	City	State	ZIP	Toll-Free	Phone	Class
Aqua-Aerobic Systems Inc	6306 N Alpine Rd	Loves Park	IL	61111	800-940-5008	815-654-2501	804
Aquae Sulis Spa at the JW Marriott Resort Las Vegas	221 N Rampart Blvd	Las Vegas	NV	89144	877-869-8777	702-869-7807	705
Aqua-Leisure Industries Inc	PO Box 239	Avon	MA	02322	866-807-3998		708
Aqualung America Inc	2340 Cousteau Ct	Vista	CA	92083	800-446-2671	760-597-5000	708
Aquarion Co	835 Main St	Bridgeport	CT	06604	800-732-9678	203-336-7662	785
Aquarius Casino Resort	1900 S Casino Dr	Laughlin	NV	89029	888-662-5825	702-298-5111	132
Aquaterra Spa at the Surf & Sand Resort	1555 S Coast Hwy	Laguna Beach	CA	92651	877-741-5908	949-376-2772	705
Aquatherm Industries Inc	1940 Rutgers University Blvd	Lakewood	NJ	08701	800-535-6307		357
Aquatic Informatics Inc	570 Granville St Ste 1100	Vancouver	BC	V6C3P1	877-870-2782	604-873-2782	145
Aqueduct Medical Inc	665 Third St Ste 20	San Francisco	CA	94107	877-365-4325		474
Aquent LLC	711 Boylston St	Boston	MA	02116	855-767-6333	617-535-5000	719
Aquila Group of Funds	380 Madison Ave Ste 2300	New York	NY	10017	800-437-1020	212-697-6666	527
Aquinas College	4210 HaRding Rd *Admissions	Nashville	TN	37205	800-649-9956*	615-297-7545	167
Aquinas Institute of Theology	23 S Spring Ave	Saint Louis	MO	63108	800-977-3869	314-256-8800	168-3
A-r Editions Inc	1600 Aspen Cmns Ste 100	Middleton	WI	53562	800-736-0070	608-836-9000	522
AR Thomson Group	7930 130th St	Surrey	BC	V3W0H7	800-410-9116	604-507-6050	327
AR Wilfley & Sons Inc	7350 E Progress Pl Ste 200	Englewood	CO	80111	800-525-9930	303-779-1777	638
ARA (American Rental Assn)	1900 19th St	Moline	IL	61265	800-334-2177	309-764-2475	48-4
ARA (Agricultural Retailers Assn)	1156 15th St NW Ste 500	Washington	DC	20005	800-535-6272	202-457-0825	47-2
ARA (Awards and Personalization Association)	8735 W Higgins Rd Ste 300	Chicago	IL	60631	800-344-2148	847-375-4800	48-4
ARA (Automotive Recyclers Assn)	3975 Fair Ridge Dr Ste 20N	Fairfax	VA	22033	888-385-1005	703-385-1001	48-21
Arabel Inc	16301 NW 49th Ave *Sales	Hialeah	FL	33014	800-759-5959*	305-623-8302	193-2
Arabian Horse World Magazine	1316 Tamson Dr Ste 101	Cambria	CA	93428	800-955-9423	805-771-2300	456-14
Arachnid Inc	6212 Material Ave	Loves Park	IL	61111	800-435-8319	815-654-0212	323
Arakansas Ethics Commission	PO Box 1917	Little Rock	AR	72203	800-422-7773	501-324-9600	267
ARAMARK Corp	1101 Market St	Philadelphia	PA	19107	800-388-3300	937-660-4708	187
Aramark Parks & Destinations	27655 Hwy 26 & 287	Moran	WY	83013	866-278-4245	307-543-2847	667
ARAMARK Uniform & Career Apparel LLC	2860 Rudder Rd	Memphis	TN	38118	800-272-6275		273
Aramco Services Co	9009 W Loop S	Houston	TX	77096	866-287-3592	713-432-4000	535
Aramsco Inc	1480 Grandview Ave	Paulsboro	NJ	08086	800-767-6933	856-686-7700	145
Arandell Inc	N 82 W 13118 Leon Rd	Menomonee Falls	WI	53051	800-558-8724	262-255-4400	626
Arapahoe Community College	5900 S Santa Fe Dr	Littleton	CO	80160	888-800-9198	303-797-0100	161
Arbella Mutual Insurance Co	1100 Crown Colony Dr	Quincy	MA	02169	800-972-5348	617-328-2800	391-4
Arbill	PO Box 820542	Philadelphia	PA	19154	800-523-5367		677
Arbitration Forums Inc	3350 Buschwood Pk Dr Ste 295 *Cust Svc	Tampa	FL	33618	800-967-8889*	813-931-4004	40
Arbitron Inc	9705 Patuxent Woods Dr *NYSE: ARB*	Columbia	MD	21046	800-543-7300	410-312-8000	465
Arbor Acres	1240 Arbor Rd	Winston-Salem	NC	27104	866-658-2724	336-724-7921	670
Arbor Centers for Eyecare	2640 W 183rd St	Homewood	IL	60430	866-798-6633	708-798-6633	239
Arbor Hospice & Home Care	2366 Oak Vly Dr	Ann Arbor	MI	48103	888-992-2273	734-662-5999	371
Arbor Realty Trust Inc	333 Earle Ovington Blvd Ste 900 *NYSE: ABR*	Uniondale	NY	11553	800-272-6710		652
Arbor Tree Surgery Inc	802 Paso Robles St	Paso Robles	CA	93446	800-247-8733	805-239-1239	774
Arboretum, The	Arboretum Rd University of Guelph	Guelph	ON	N1G2W1	877-674-1610	519-824-4120	96
Arbutus Software Inc	6450 Roberts St	Burnaby	BC	V5G4E1	877-333-6336	604-437-7873	181
ARC (Austin Ribbon & Computer Supplies Inc)	9211 Waterford Centre Blvd Ste 202	Austin	TX	78758	800-783-7459	512-452-0651	196
ARC (American Radiolabeled Chemicals Inc)	101 ARC Dr	Saint Louis	MO	63146	800-331-6661	314-991-4545	144
ARC (American Refugee Committee)	430 Oak Grove St Ste 204	Minneapolis	MN	55403	800-875-7060	612-872-7060	47-5
ARC Industries Inc	2879 Johnstown Rd	Columbus	OH	43219	800-734-7007		719
Arc of Stanly County, The	350 Pee Dee Ave Ste A	Albemarle	NC	28001	800-230-7525	704-986-1500	48-15
Arc of the US	1010 Wayne Ave Ste 650	Silver Spring	MD	20910	800-433-5255	301-565-3842	47-17
ARC Resources Ltd	308 Fourth Ave SW Ste 1200 *TSE: ARX*	Calgary	AB	T2P0H7	888-272-4900	403-503-8600	673
ARC the Hotel Ottawa	140 Slater St	Ottawa	ON	K1P5H6	800-699-2516	613-238-2888	379
Arcadia University	450 S Easton Rd	Glenside	PA	19038	877-272-2342	215-572-2900	167
Arcane Technologies Inc	918 Monticello Ave	Charlottesville	VA	22902	844-977-4890		182
Arcet Equipment Company Inc	1700 Chamberlayne Ave	Richmond	VA	23222	800-388-0302		203
Arch Chemicals Inc	1200 Old Lower River Rd PO Box 800 *NYSE: ARJ*	Charleston	TN	37310	800-638-8174	423-780-2724	144
Arch Crown Tags Inc	460 Hillside Ave	Hillside	NJ	07205	800-526-8353	973-731-6300	413
Arch Insurance Group Inc	1 Liberty Plz 53rd Fl	New York	NY	10006	866-993-9978	212-651-6500	391-2
Archadeck	2924 Emerywood Pkwy Ste 101	Richmond	VA	23294	800-722-4668	804-353-6999	191-2
Archaeological Institute of America (AIA)	656 Beacon St 4th Fl	Boston	MA	02215	877-524-6300	617-353-9361	47-11
Archaeology Magazine	36-36 33rd St	Long Island	NY	11106	877-275-9782	718-472-3050	456-19
Archbold Container Corp	800 W Barre Rd PO Box 10	Archbold	OH	43502	800-446-2520	419-445-8865	235
Archdiocese of Saint Paul & Minneapolis	226 Summit Ave	Saint Paul	MN	55102	877-290-1605	651-291-4411	47-20
Archer Daniels Midland Co (ADM)	4666 E Faries Pkwy *NYSE: ADM*	Decatur	IL	62526	800-637-5843	217-424-5200	187
Architectural & Transportation Barriers Compliance Board	1331 F St NW Ste 1000	Washington	DC	20004	800-872-2253	202-272-0080	340-18
Architectural Bronze Aluminum Corp	655 Deerfield Rd Ste 100	Deerfield	IL	60015	800-339-6581		775
Architectural Digest	4 Times Sq 18th Fl	New York	NY	10036	800-365-8032		456-2
Architectural Floor Systems Inc	595 Supreme Dr	Bensenville	IL	60106	877-437-3567		130
Architectural Record Magazine	2 Penn Plaza 9th Fl	New York	NY	10121	800-393-6343	646-849-7100	456-2
Architectural Woodwork Institute (AWI)	46179 Westlake Dr Ste 120	Potomac Falls	VA	20165	866-877-6933	571-323-3636	48-3
Architel Inc	8350 N Central Expy Ste 250	Dallas	TX	75206	866-649-7571	214-550-2000	182
Architex International	3333 Commercial Ave	Northbrook	IL	60062	800-621-0827	847-205-1333	361
Archive-cd LLC	910 Beverly Way	Jacksonville	OR	97530	800-323-1868	541-899-5704	179
Archway Marketing Services Inc	19850 S Diamond Lake Rd	Rogers	MN	55374	866-779-9855	763-428-3300	462
ARCO Coffee Company	2206 Winter St	Superior	WI	54880	800-283-2726	715-392-4771	297-7
Arco Electric Products Corp	2325 E Michigan Rd	Shelbyville	IN	46176	800-428-4370	317-398-9713	517
Arcos Industries	1 Arcos Dr	Mount Carmel	PA	17851	800-233-8460	570-339-5200	809
Arctic Glacier Holdings Inc	625 Henry Ave	Winnipeg	MB	R3A0V1	888-573-9237	204-772-2473	577
Arctic Industries Inc	9731 NW 114th Way	Miami	FL	33178	800-325-0123	305-883-5581	14
Arctic Slope Regional Corp	1230 Agvik St PO Box 129	Barrow	AK	99723	800-770-2772	907-852-8633	537
Arctic Star Refrigeration Mfg Company Inc	3540 W Pioneer Pkwy	Arlington	TX	76013	800-229-6562	817-274-1396	662
Arctic Storm Management Group LLC	2727 Alaskan Way Pier 69	Seattle	WA	98121	800-929-0908	206-547-6557	287
Arctic Wolf Networks Inc	440 Wolfe Rd Mail Stop 147	Sunnyvale	CA	94085	888-272-8429		198
ArcticDx Inc	MaRS Centre S Tower 101 College St Ste 200	Toronto	ON	M5G1L7	866-964-5182		416
Arcturus Advisors	1643 Plantation Oaks Ln	Fernandina Beach	FL	32034	866-593-2207		40
ARCVB (Alton Regional Convention & Visitors Bureau)	200 Piasa St	Alton	IL	62002	800-258-6645	618-465-6676	208
Arcweb Technologies LLC	234 Market St 5th Fl	Philadelphia	PA	19106	800-846-7980		462
Arden Cos	30400 Telegraph Rd Ste 200	Bingham Farms	MI	48025	800-876-7336	248-415-8500	743
Ardenwood Historic Farm	34600 Ardenwood Blvd	Fremont	CA	94555	888-327-2757	510-544-2797	519
ARDMS (American Registry of Diagnostic Medical Sonographers)	1401 Rockville Pike Ste 600	Rockville	MD	20852	800-541-9754	301-738-8401	48-8
Ards Trucking Company Inc	4190 Alligator Rd	Timmonsville	SC	29161	877-273-7297	843-393-5101	778
ARE (Association for Research & Enlightenment)	215 67th St	Virginia Beach	VA	23451	800-333-4499	757-428-3588	47-17
ARE (Association for Retail Environment)	4651 Sheridan St Ste 470	Hollywood	FL	33021	800-421-3483	954-893-7300	48-3
Area 51 Esg Inc	51 Post	Irvine	CA	92618	877-476-8751	949-387-0051	248
Area Agency On Aging	9549 Koger Blvd Gadsden Bldg Ste 100	St Petersburg	FL	33702	800-963-5337	727-570-9696	449
Area Agency On Aging 10b Inc	1550 Corporate Woods Pkwy	Uniontown	OH	44685	800-421-7277	330-896-9172	449
Area Development Magazine	400 Post Ave Ste 304	Westbury	NY	11590	800-735-2732	516-338-0900	456-5
Area Development Partnership	1 Convention Ctr Plz	Hattiesburg	MS	39401	800-238-4288	601-296-7500	138
Area Temps Inc	1228 Euclid Ave	Cleveland	OH	44115	866-995-5627	440-646-1333	719
AREBA Casriel Inc (ACI)	500 W 57th St	New York	NY	10019	800-724-4444	212-293-3000	724
Arends & Sons Inc	715 S Sangamon Ave	Gibson City	IL	60936	800-637-6052	217-784-4241	276
Arends Bros Inc	1190 E 1200N Rd	Melvin	IL	60952	800-356-6811	217-388-7717	276

Name / Address	City	State	ZIP	Toll-Free	Phone	Class
Ares Sportswear Ltd						
3704 Lacon Rd	Hilliard	OH	43026	**800-439-8614**	614-767-1950	685
ARG Trucking Corp						
369 Bostwick Rd	Phelps	NY	14532	**800-334-1314**	315-789-8871	778
Argenia LLC						
11524 Fairview Rd	Little Rock	AR	72212	**800-482-5968**	501-227-9670	390
ARGI Investment Services LLC						
1914 Stanley Gault Pkwy	Louisville	KY	40223	**866-568-9719**	502-753-0609	401
Argo International Corp						
160 Chubb Ave	Lyndhurst	NJ	07071	**877-274-6468**	201-561-7010	248
ARGO Systems LLC						
1362 Mellon Rd Ste 100	Hanover	MD	21076	**877-994-2746**	410-768-2444	263
Argo Translation Inc						
2420 Ravine Way Ste 200	Glenview	IL	60025	**888-961-9291**	847-901-4075	766
Argonaut Hotel						
495 Jefferson St	San Francisco	CA	94109	**866-415-0704**	415-563-0800	379
Argonne National Laboratory (ANL)						
9700 S Cass Ave	Argonne	IL	60439	**800-632-8990**	630-252-2000	666
Argosy University						
1515 Central Pkwy	Eagan	MN	55121	**888-844-2004**	651-846-2882	167
Argosy University Hawaii						
400 ASB Tower 1001 Bishop St	Honolulu	HI	96813	**888-323-2777**	808-536-5555	798
Argosy's Alton Belle Casino						
1 Piasa St	Alton	IL	62002	**800-711-4263**		132
Argus Interactive Agency Inc						
217 N Main St Ste 200	Santa Ana	CA	92701	**866-595-9597**		529
Argus Leader						
200 S Minnesota Ave	Sioux Falls	SD	57104	**800-530-6397**	605-331-2200	531-2
Argus Machine Company Ltd						
5820 97th St NW	Edmonton	AB	T6E3J1	**888-434-9451**	780-434-9451	538
ARH (Appalachian Regional Healthcare Service)						
80 Hospital Dr PO Box 8086	Barbourville	KY	40906	**888-654-0015**	859-226-2440	353
ARHP (Association of Reproductive Health Professionals)						
1901 L St NW Ste 300	Washington	DC	20036	**877-311-8972**	202-466-3825	48-8
ARI (Autism Research Institute)						
4182 Adams Ave	San Diego	CA	92116	**866-366-3361**	619-281-7165	47-17
ARi Industries Inc						
381 Ari Ct	Addison	IL	60101	**800-237-6725**	630-953-9100	203
ARI Network Services Inc						
10850 W Pk Pl Ste 1200	Milwaukee	WI	53224	**877-805-0803**	414-973-4300	180-10
Aria Communications Corp						
717 W Saint Germain St	St. Cloud	MN	56301	**800-955-9924**		734
Aria Spa & Club at the Vail Cascade Resort						
1300 Westhaven Dr	Vail	CO	81657	**888-824-5772**	970-479-5942	705
Ariba Inc						
807 11th Ave	Sunnyvale	CA	94089	**866-772-7422**	650-390-1000	38
NASDAQ: ARBA						
Aribex Inc						
744 South 400 East	Orem	UT	84097	**866-340-5522**	801-226-5522	230
Ariel Technologies						
1980 E Lohman Ave	Las Cruces	NM	88001	**877-524-6860**		177
ARINC Inc						
2551 Riva Rd	Annapolis	MD	21401	**866-321-6060**	410-266-4000	679
Ariosa Diagnostics Inc						
5945 Optical Ct	San Jose	CA	95138	**855-927-4672**		418
Aris Horticulture Inc						
115 Third St SE	Barberton	OH	44203	**800-232-9557**		369
Aristatek Inc						
710 E Garfield St Ste 220	Laramie	WY	82070	**877-912-2200**	307-721-2126	179
Aristocrat Technologies						
7230 Amigo St	Las Vegas	NV	89119	**800-748-4156**	702-270-1000	323
Aristotle Capital Management LLC						
11100 Santa Monica Blvd Ste 1700	Los Angeles	CA	90025	**877-478-4722**	310-478-4005	401
Aristotle Inc						
205 Pennsylvania Ave SE	Washington	DC	20003	**800-296-2747***	202-543-8345	180-11
*Sales						
Arizona						
Attorney General						
1275 W Washington St	Phoenix	AZ	85007	**888-377-6108**	602-542-5025	339-3
Children Youth & Families Div						
1789 W Jefferson St	Phoenix	AZ	85007	**866-229-5553**	602-542-0419	339-3
Historic Preservation Office						
1300 W Washington St	Phoenix	AZ	85007	**800-285-3703**	602-542-4174	339-3
Legislature						
Capitol Complex 1700 W Washington St	Phoenix	AZ	85007	**800-352-8404**	602-926-3559	339-3
Motor Vehicle Div						
PO Box 2100	Phoenix	AZ	85001	**800-251-5866**	602-255-0072	339-3
Rehabilitation Services Admin						
1789 W Jefferson St 2nd Fl NW	Phoenix	AZ	85007	**800-563-1221**	602-542-3332	339-3
Tourism Office						
1110 W Washington St Ste 155	Phoenix	AZ	85007	**888-520-3434**	602-364-3700	339-3
Treasurer						
1700 W Washington St 1st Fl	Phoenix	AZ	85007	**877-365-8310**	602-542-7800	339-3
Weights & Measures Dept						
4425 W Olive Ave Ste 134	Glendale	AZ	85302	**800-277-6675**	602-771-4920	339-3
Arizona Art Supply						
4025 N 16th St	Phoenix	AZ	85016	**877-264-9514**	602-264-9514	44
Arizona Assn of Realtors						
255 E Osborne Rd Ste 200	Phoenix	AZ	85012	**800-426-7274**	602-248-7787	654
Arizona Attorney Magazine						
4201 N 24th St Ste 200	Phoenix	AZ	85016	**866-482-9227**	602-252-4804	456-15
Arizona Automobile Dealers Association						
4701 N 24th St Ste B3	Phoenix	AZ	85016	**800-678-3875**	602-468-0888	136
Arizona Biltmore Resort & Spa						
2400 E Missouri	Phoenix	AZ	85016	**800-950-0086**	602-955-6600	667
Arizona Cardinals						
8701 S Hardy Dr	Tempe	AZ	85284	**800-999-1402**	602-379-0101	713-3
Arizona Chamber of Commerce & Industry						
3200 N Central Ave Ste 1125	Phoenix	AZ	85012	**866-275-5816**	602-248-9172	139
Arizona Charlie's Boulder Casino & Hotel						
4575 Boulder Hwy	Las Vegas	NV	89121	**888-236-9066**	702-951-5800	379
Arizona Charlie's Decatur Casino & Hotel						
740 S Decatur Blvd	Las Vegas	NV	89107	**888-236-8645**	702-258-5200	132
Arizona Community Foundation						
2201 E Camelback Rd Ste 405B	Phoenix	AZ	85016	**800-222-8221**	602-381-1400	304
Arizona Culinary Institute						
10585 N 114th St Ste 401	Scottsdale	AZ	85259	**866-294-2433**	480-603-1066	162
Arizona Daily Star						
4850 S Pk Ave	Tucson	AZ	85714	**800-695-4492**	520-573-4343	531-2
Arizona Dental Assn						
3193 N Drinkwater Blvd	Scottsdale	AZ	85251	**800-866-2732**	480-344-5777	229
Arizona Federal Credit Union						
PO Box 60070	Phoenix	AZ	85082	**800-523-4603**	602-683-1000	221
Arizona Golf Resort & Conference Ctr						
425 S Power Rd	Mesa	AZ	85206	**800-528-8282**	480-832-3202	667
Arizona Grand Resort						
8000 S Arizona Grand Pkwy	Phoenix	AZ	85044	**866-267-1321**	602-438-9000	667
Arizona Highways Magazine						
2039 W Lewis Ave	Phoenix	AZ	85009	**800-543-5432**		456-22
Arizona Inn						
2200 E Elm St	Tucson	AZ	85719	**800-933-1093**		379
Arizona Leather Company Inc						
4235 Schaefer Ave	Chino	CA	91710	**888-669-5328**	909-993-5101	322
Arizona Limousines Inc						
8900 N Central Ave Ste 101	Phoenix	AZ	85020	**800-678-0033**	602-267-7097	441
Arizona Medical Assn, The (ArMA)						
810 W Bethany Home Rd	Phoenix	AZ	85013	**800-482-3480**	602-246-8901	473
Arizona Mills						
5000 Arizona Mills Cir	Tempe	AZ	85282	**877-746-6642**	480-491-7300	459
Arizona Osteopathic Medical Association						
5150 N 16th St Ste A122	Phoenix	AZ	85016	**888-266-6699**	602-266-6699	532
Arizona Partsmaster Inc						
7125 W Sherman St PO Box 23169	Phoenix	AZ	85043	**888-924-7278**	602-233-3580	611
Arizona Precision Sheet Metal						
2140 W Pinnacle Peak Rd	Phoenix	AZ	85027	**800-443-7039**	623-516-3700	695
Arizona Public Service Co (APS)						
400 N Fifth St PO Box 53999	Phoenix	AZ	85004	**800-253-9405**	602-371-7171	785
Arizona Publishing Cos						
PO Box 1950	Phoenix	AZ	85001	**800-331-9303**	602-444-8000	634-8
Arizona Republic						
200 E Van Buren St	Phoenix	AZ	85004	**800-331-9303**	602-444-8000	531-2
Arizona State Capitol Museum						
1700 W Washington St	Phoenix	AZ	85007	**800-228-4710**	602-542-4675	519
Arizona State Hospital						
2500 E Van Buren St	Phoenix	AZ	85008	**877-588-5163**	602-244-1331	374-5
Arizona State Prison Complex-Eyman						
4374 E Butte Ave PO Box 3500	Florence	AZ	85132	**866-333-2039**	520-868-0201	215
Arizona State University						
Sandra Day O'Connor College of Law						
PO Box 877906	Tempe	AZ	85287	**855-278-5080**	480-965-6181	168-1
West PO Box 37100	Phoenix	AZ	85069	**855-278-5080**	602-543-5500	167
Arizona State University Art Museum						
10th St & Mill Ave Nelson Fine Arts Ctr Arizona State University	Tempe	AZ	85287	**855-278-5080**	480-965-2787	519
Arizona Western College						
2020 S Ave 8 E	Yuma	AZ	85366	**888-293-0392**	928-317-6000	161
Arizona Wholesale Supply Co						
2020 E University Dr	Phoenix	AZ	85034	**866-977-6849**	602-258-7901	611
Arjobex America Mill						
10901 Westlake Dr	Charlotte	NC	28273	**800-765-9278**		556
ARK Diagnostics Inc						
48089 Fremont Blvd	Fremont	CA	94538	**877-869-2320**	510-270-6270	363
Ark TeleServices						
2 E Merrick Rd	Valley Stream	NY	11580	**800-898-5367**		393
Ark Valley Electric Co-op Assn						
10 E Tenth St	South Hutchinson	KS	67504	**888-297-9212**	620-662-6661	247
Arkadin Inc						
5 Concourse Pkwy Ste 1600	Atlanta	GA	30328	**866-551-1432**		387
Arkansas						
Attorney General						
323 Ctr St Ste 200	Little Rock	AR	72201	**800-482-8982***	501-682-2007	339-4
*Consumer Info						
Child Support Enforcement Office						
1509 W Seventh St	Little Rock	AR	72201	**800-264-2445**	501-682-8398	339-4
Crime Victims Reparations Board						
323 Ctr St Ste 200	Little Rock	AR	72201	**800-448-3014**	501-682-1020	339-4
Game & Fish Commission						
2 Natural Resource Dr	Little Rock	AR	72205	**800-364-4263**	501-223-6300	339-4
Highway & Transportation Dept						
10324 I- 30	Little Rock	AR	72209	**800-245-1672**	501-569-2000	339-4
Insurance Dept						
1200 W Third St	Little Rock	AR	72201	**800-282-9134**	501-371-2600	339-4
Parks & Tourism Dept						
1 Capitol Mall	Little Rock	AR	72201	**800-628-8725**	501-682-7777	339-4
Rehabilitation Services						
525 W Capitol Ave	Little Rock	AR	72201	**800-330-0632**	501-296-1600	339-4
Securities Dept						
201 E Markham St Rm 300	Little Rock	AR	72201	**800-981-4429**	501-324-9260	339-4
Vital Records Div						
4815 W Markham St Slot 44	Little Rock	AR	72205	**800-637-9314**	501-661-2336	339-4
Worker's Compensation Commission						
324 S Spring St	Little Rock	AR	72203	**800-622-4472**	501-682-3930	339-4
Arkansas Anatomic Pathology Services pa						
411 E Matthews Ave	Jonesboro	AR	72401	**800-764-0447**	870-930-3518	418
Arkansas Arts Ctr						
501 E Ninth St	Little Rock	AR	72202	**800-264-2787**	501-372-4000	519
Arkansas Baptist Foundation						
10 Remington Dr	Little Rock	AR	72204	**800-838-2272**	501-376-0732	47-20
Arkansas Blue Cross Blue Shield						
PO Box 2181	Little Rock	AR	72203	**800-238-8379**	501-712-1114	391-3
Arkansas Business LP						
122 E Second St	Little Rock	AR	72201	**888-322-6397**	501-372-1443	456-5
Arkansas Capital Corp Group						
200 S Commerce St Ste 400	Little Rock	AR	72201	**800-216-7237**	501-374-9247	218
Arkansas Correctional Industries (ACI)						
6841 W. 13th St	Pine Bluff	AR	71602	**877-635-7213**	870-730-0385	629
Arkansas Democrat-Gazette						
121 E Capital St	Little Rock	AR	72203	**800-482-1121***	501-378-3400	531-2
*Cust Svc						
Arkansas Dept of Corrections Maximum Security Unit						
2501 State Farm Rd	Tucker	AR	72168	**866-801-3435**	501-842-3800	215
Arkansas Dept of Corrections Tucker Unit						
2400 State Farm Rd PO Box 240	Tucker	AR	72168	**800-682-7377**	501-842-2519	215
Arkansas Distributing Company LLC						
800 E Barton Ave	West Memphis	AR	72301	**877-735-3506**	870-735-3506	80-1

Name / Address	City	State	ZIP	Toll-Free	Phone	Class
Arkansas Educational Television Network (AETN) 350 S Donaghey Ave	Conway	AR	72034	**800-662-2386**	501-682-2386	629
Arkansas Educator Magazine 1500 W Fourth St	Little Rock	AR	72201	**800-632-0624**	501-375-4611	456-8
Arkansas Financial Aid Office 114 Silas Hunt Hall	Fayetteville	AR	72701	**800-547-8839**	479-575-3806	723
Arkansas Graphics Inc 800 S Gaines St	Little Rock	AR	72201	**877-918-4847**	501-376-8436	626
Arkansas Hospice 14 Parkstone Cir	North Little Rock	AR	72116	**877-257-3400**	501-748-3333	371
Arkansas Juvenile Access & Treatment Ctr 425 W Capitol Ste 1620	Little Rock	AR	72201	**877-727-3468**	501-324-8900	412
Arkansas Lawyer Magazine 2224 Cottondale Ln	Little Rock	AR	72202	**800-609-5668**	501-375-4606	456-15
Arkansas Museum of Natural Resources 3853 Smackover Hwy	Smackover	AR	71762	**888-287-2757**	870-725-2877	564
Arkansas Realtors Assn 11224 Executive Ctr Dr	Little Rock	AR	72211	**888-333-2206**	501-225-2020	654
Arkansas Repertory Theatre 601 Main St PO Box 110	Little Rock	AR	72201	**866-684-3737**	501-378-0445	572-4
Arkansas State Chamber of Commerce 1200 W Capitol Ave PO Box 3645	Little Rock	AR	72203	**800-482-1127**	501-372-2222	139
Arkansas State Dental Assn 7480 Hwy 107	Sherwood	AR	72120	**800-501-2732**	501-834-7650	229
Arkansas State Library 900 W Capitol Ste 100	Little Rock	AR	72201	**866-801-3435**	501-682-2053	434-5
Arkansas State University PO Box 1630	State University	AR	72467	**800-382-3030**	870-972-3024	167
Arkansas State University Museum PO Box 490	State University	AR	72467	**800-342-2923**	870-972-2074	519
Arkansas State University Newport 7648 Victory Blvd	Newport	AR	72112	**800-976-1676**	870-512-7800	161
Arkansas Trailer Manufacturing Co 3200 S Elm St	Little Rock	AR	72204	**800-666-5417**	501-666-5417	777
Arkansas Valley Electric Co-op Corp 1811 W Commercial St PO Box 47	Ozark	AR	72949	**800-468-2176**	479-667-2176	247
Arkansas Valley Regional Medical Ctr (AVRMC) 1100 Carson Ave	La Junta	CO	81050	**877-696-6775**	719-384-5412	374-3
Arkwin Industries Inc 686 Main St	Westbury	NY	11590	**800-284-2551**	516-333-2640	788
Arlington Capital Management Inc 21 S Evergreen Ave Ste 210	Arlington Heights	IL	60005	**855-471-5796**	847-670-4030	196
Arlington Central School District 144 Todd Hill Rd	LaGrangeville	NY	12540	**800-993-8982**	845-486-4460	683
Arlington Coal & Lumber Company Inc 41 Pk Ave	Arlington	MA	02476	**800-649-8101**	781-643-8100	364
Arlington Computer Products Inc 851 Commerce Ct *Orders	Buffalo Grove	IL	60089	**800-548-5105***	847-541-6333	182
Arlington Convention & Visitors Bureau 1905 E Randol Mill Rd	Arlington	TX	76011	**800-433-5374**	817-265-7721	208
Arlington Industries Inc 1616 Lakeside Dr	Waukegan	IL	60085	**800-323-4147**	847-689-2754	533
Arlington Public Library 101 E Abram St	Arlington	TX	76010	**888-227-7669**	817-459-6900	434-3
Arlington Resort Hotel & Spa 239 Central Ave	Hot Springs	AR	71901	**800-643-1502**	501-623-7771	667
Arlington School District 315 N French Ave	Arlington	WA	98223	**888-535-0747**	360-618-6200	683
Arlo G. Lott Trucking Inc 257 S 100 E	Jerome	ID	83338	**800-443-5688**	208-324-5053	778
Arlon Graphics 2811 S Harbor Blvd	Santa Ana	CA	92704	**800-232-7161**	714-540-2811	3
ARM (Associated Risk Managers) 2 Pierce Pl	Itasca	IL	60143	**800-735-5441**	630-285-4324	48-9
ArMA (Arizona Medical Assn, The) 810 W Bethany Home Rd	Phoenix	AZ	85013	**800-482-3480**	602-246-8901	473
ARMA (Asphalt Roofing Manufacturers Assn) 529 14th St NW Ste 750	Washington	DC	20045	**800-247-6637**	202-207-0917	48-3
ARMA International 11880 College Blvd Ste 450	Overland Park	KS	66210	**800-422-2762**	913-341-3808	48-12
Armada Group Inc, The 325 Soquel Ave Ste A	Santa Cruz	CA	95062	**800-408-2120**		344
Armand Manufacturing Inc 2399 Silver Wolf Dr	Henderson	NV	89011	**800-669-9811**	702-565-7500	65
Armani Exchange 568 Broadway	New York	NY	10012	**800-717-2929**	212-431-6000	279
Armanino Foods of Distinction Inc 30588 San Antonio St *OTC: AMNF*	Hayward	CA	94544	**800-255-5855**	510-441-9300	297-36
Armatron International Inc 15 Highland Ave	Malden	MA	02148	**800-343-3280**	781-321-2300	429
Armature Dns 2000 Inc 11001 Jean Meunier	Montreal	QC	H1G4S7	**800-363-7996**	514-324-1141	789
Armed Forces Communications & Electronics Assn (AFCEA) 4400 Fair Lakes Ct	Fairfax	VA	22033	**800-336-4583**	703-631-6100	47-19
Armed Forces Insurance Exchange (AFI) PO Box G	Fort Leavenworth	KS	66027	**800-255-0187**	800-255-6792	391-4
Armed Forces Retirement Home - Gulfport 1800 Beach Dr	Gulfport	MS	39507	**800-422-9988**		670
Armed Forces Retirement Home - Washington 3700 N Capitol St NW *Admissions	Washington	DC	20011	**800-422-9988***		449
Armed Services Mutual Benefit Assn (ASMBA) PO Box 160384	Nashville	TN	37216	**800-251-8434**	615-851-0800	47-19
Armellini Express Lines Inc 3446 SW Armellini Ave	Palm City	FL	34990	**800-327-7887**	772-287-0575	778
Armen Computing Ltd 286 Bethany Ct	Inman	SC	29349	**800-372-6078**		807
Armentor Glenn Law Corp 300 Stewart St	Lafayette	LA	70501	**800-960-5551**	337-233-1471	428
Armistead Mechanical Inc 168 Hopper Ave	Waldwick	NJ	07463	**800-587-5267**	201-447-6740	191-10
Armor Group Inc, The 4600 N Mason-Montgomery Rd	Mason	OH	45040	**800-255-0393**		319
Armor Protective Packaging 951 Jones St	Howell	MI	48843	**800-365-1117**	517-546-1117	556
Armour Transportation Systems Inc 689 Edinburgh Dr	Moncton	NB	E1E2L4	**800-561-7987**	506-857-0205	23
Arms Acres 75 Seminary Hill Rd	Carmel	NY	10512	**800-989-2676**	845-225-3400	724
Armstrong Atlantic State University 11935 Abercorn St	Savannah	GA	31419	**800-633-2349**		167
Armstrong County Tourist Bureau 125 Market St Ste 2	Kittanning	PA	16201	**888-265-9954**	724-543-4003	208
Armstrong International Inc 2081 SE Ocean Blvd 4th Fl	Stuart	FL	34996	**866-738-5125**	772-286-7175	787
Armstrong Lumber Co Inc 2709 Auburn Way N	Auburn	WA	98002	**800-868-9066**	253-833-6666	815
Armstrong Medical Industries Inc 575 Knightsbridge Pkwy *Cust Svc	Lincolnshire	IL	60069	**800-323-4220***	847-913-0101	476
Armstrong Mfg Co 2700 SE Tacoma St	Portland	OR	97202	**800-426-6226**	503-228-8381	493
Armstrong School District 410 Main St	Ford City	PA	16226	**888-573-5733**	724-763-5200	683
Armstrong World Industries Inc 2500 Columbia Ave *NYSE: AWI* ■ *Cust Svc	Lancaster	PA	17603	**800-233-3823***	717-397-0611	293
Army & Navy Academy 2605 Carlsbad Blvd PO Box 3000	Carlsbad	CA	92018	**888-762-2338**	760-729-2385	621
Army Distaff Foundation 6200 Oregon Ave NW	Washington	DC	20015	**800-541-4255**	202-541-0149	47-19
ARMY Magazine 2425 Wilson Blvd	Arlington	VA	22201	**800-336-4570**	703-841-4300	456-12
Army Residence Community 7400 Crestway	San Antonio	TX	78239	**800-725-0083**	210-646-5316	670
ARN (Association of Rehabilitation Nurses) 4700 W Lk Ave	Glenview	IL	60025	**800-229-7530**	847-375-4710	48-8
Arnaud's 813 Bienville St	New Orleans	LA	70112	**866-230-8895**	504-523-5433	669
Arneg Canada Inc 18 Rue Richelieu	Lacolle	QC	J0J1J0	**800-363-3439**	450-246-3837	609
Arneg LLC 750 Old Hargrave Rd	Lexington	NC	27295	**800-276-3487**	336-956-5300	609
Arnoff Moving & Storage Inc 1282 Dutchess Tpke	Poughkeepsie	NY	12603	**800-633-6683**	845-471-1504	518
Arnold & Assoc 14275 Midway Rd Ste 170	Addison	TX	75001	**800-535-6329**	972-991-1144	258
Arnold & Itkin LLP 6009 Memorial Dr	Houston	TX	77007	**888-493-1629**	713-222-3800	428
Arnold Lumber Co 251 Fairgrounds Rd	West Kingston	RI	02892	**800-339-0116**	401-783-2266	193-3
Arnold Machinery Co 2975 West 2100 South *Cust Svc	Salt Lake City	UT	84119	**800-821-0548***	801-972-4000	358
Arnold Palmer Hospital for Children & Women 92 W Miller St	Orlando	FL	32806	**800-648-3818**	407-649-9111	374-1
Arnold Refrigeration Inc 1122 N Cherry	San Antonio	TX	78202	**800-441-1170**	210-225-5493	191-10
Arnold Transportation Services Inc 9523 Florida Mining Blvd	Jacksonville	FL	32257	**800-846-4321**	972-986-3154	778
Arns Law Firm, The 515 Folsom St Fl 3	San Francisco	CA	94105	**800-495-7800**	415-495-7800	428
Aromaland Inc 1326 Rufina Cir	Santa Fe	NM	87507	**800-933-5267**	505-438-0402	76
Aroostook Home Health Services 658 Main St Ste 2	Caribou	ME	04736	**877-688-9977**	207-492-8290	363
AroundWire.Com LLC 18107 Sherman Way Ste 206	Reseda	CA	91335	**888-382-3793**		387
ARPAC Group 9511 W River St	Schiller Park	IL	60176	**800-496-7210**	847-678-9034	546
ArQule Inc 19 Presidential Way *NASDAQ: ARQL*	Woburn	MA	01801	**800-373-7827**	781-994-0300	84
Array BioPharma Inc 3200 Walnut St *NASDAQ: ARRY*	Boulder	CO	80301	**877-633-2436**	303-381-6600	84
Array Marketing 45 Progress Ave	Toronto	ON	M1P2Y6	**800-295-4120**	416-299-4865	235
Arris 60 Decibel Rd	State College	PA	16801	**800-233-2267**	814-238-2461	645
Arris Group Inc 3871 Lakefield Dr *NASDAQ: ARRS*	Suwanee	GA	30024	**866-362-7747**	678-473-2000	645
ARRL (American Radio Relay League) 225 Main St	Newington	CT	06111	**888-277-5289**	860-594-0200	48-14
Arrow Electric Company Inc 317 Wabasso Ave	Louisville	KY	40209	**888-999-5591**	502-367-0141	191-4
Arrow Engine Co 2301 E Independence St	Tulsa	OK	74110	**800-331-3662**	918-583-5711	264
Arrow Fastener Co Inc 271 Mayhill St	Saddle Brook	NJ	07663	**800-776-2228**	201-843-6900	756
Arrow Financial Corp 250 Glen St *NASDAQ: AROW*	Glens Falls	NY	12801	**800-937-5449**	518-415-4307	360-2
Arrow Florist & Park Avenue Greenhouses Inc 757 Pk Ave	Cranston	RI	02910	**800-556-7097**	401-785-1900	294
Arrow Freight Management Inc 1001 Berryville st	El Paso	TX	79928	**888-598-9891**		312
Arrow Lock Co 100 Arrow Dr	New Haven	CT	06511	**800-839-3157**		350
Arrow Stage Lines 720 E Norfolk Ave	Norfolk	NE	68701	**800-672-8302**	402-371-3850	106
Arrow Tank & Engineering Co 650 N Emerson St	Cambridge	MN	55008	**888-892-7769**	763-689-3360	90
Arrow Truck Sales Inc 3200 Manchester Trfy	Kansas City	MO	64129	**800-311-7144**	816-923-5000	56
Arrow Tru-Line Inc 2211 S Defiance St	Archbold	OH	43502	**877-285-7253**	419-446-2785	487
Arrow Uniform Rental Inc 6400 Monroe Blvd	Taylor	MI	48180	**888-332-7769**	313-299-5000	442
Arrow Value Recovery 9101 Burnet Rd Ste 203	Austin	TX	78758	**800-393-7627**		658

Company / Address	City	State	ZIP	Toll-Free	Phone	Class
Arrowhead Containers Inc						
4330 Clary Blvd	Kansas City	MO	64130	888-861-9225	816-861-8050	99
Arrowhead Electric Co-op Inc						
5401 W Hwy 61 PO Box 39	Lutsen	MN	55612	800-864-3744	218-663-7239	247
Arrowhead Library System						
210 Dodge St	Janesville	WI	53548	855-352-9003	608-758-6690	434-3
Arrowhead Regional Medical Ctr						
400 N Pepper Ave	Colton	CA	92324	855-422-8029	909-580-1000	374-3
Arrow-Magnolia International						
2646 Rodney Ln	Dallas	TX	75229	800-527-2101	972-247-7111	150
Arrowpoint Capital						
Whitehall Corporate Ctr Ste 3						
3600 Arco Corporate Dr	Charlotte	NC	28273	866-236-7750	704-522-2000	391-4
Arrowwood Resort & Conference Ctr						
2100 Arrowwood Ln NW	Alexandria	MN	56308	866-386-5263*	320-762-1124	667
*Resv						
ARRS (American Roentgen Ray Society)						
44211 Slatestone Ct	Leesburg	VA	20176	800-438-2777	703-729-3353	48-8
ARS (American Rose Society)						
8877 Jefferson Paige Rd	Shreveport	LA	71119	800-637-6534	318-938-5402	47-18
ARS National Services Inc						
201 W Grand Ave	Escondido	CA	92025	800-456-5053		393
Art Academy of Cincinnati						
1212 Jackson St	Cincinnati	OH	45202	800-323-5692	513-562-6262	163
Art Brands LLC						
225 Business Ctr Dr	Blacklick	OH	43004	877-755-4278	614-755-4278	685
Art Craft Display Inc						
500 Business Centre Dr	Lansing	MI	48917	800-878-0710	517-485-2221	228
Art Gallery of Ontario						
317 Dundas St W	Toronto	ON	M5T1G4	877-225-4246	416-979-6660	306
Art in America Magazine						
575 Broadway	New York	NY	10012	800-925-8059*	212-941-2800	456-2
*Cust Svc						
Art Institute of Atlanta						
6600 Peachtree Dunwoody Rd NE						
100 Embassy Row	Atlanta	GA	30328	800-275-4242	770-394-8300	163
Art Institute of Boston at Lesley (AIB)						
29 Everett St	Cambridge	MA	22138	800-773-0494	617-585-6600	163
Art Institute of California						
Inland Empire						
674 E Brier Dr	San Bernardino	CA	92408	800-353-0812	909-915-2100	163
Los Angeles						
2900 31st St	Santa Monica	CA	90405	888-646-4610	310-752-4700	163
San Diego						
7650 Mission Valley Rd	San Diego	CA	92108	888-624-0300	858-598-1200	163
San Francisco						
1170 Market St	San Francisco	CA	94102	888-493-3261	415-865-0198	163
Art Institute of Charlotte						
3 Lake Pointe Plz						
3 LakePointe Plz	Charlotte	NC	28217	800-872-4417	704-357-8020	163
Art Institute of Colorado						
1200 Lincoln St	Denver	CO	80203	800-275-2420	303-837-0825	163
Art Institute of Dallas						
8080 Pk Ln Ste 100	Dallas	TX	75231	800-275-4243	214-692-8080	163
Art Institute of Fort Lauderdale						
1799 SE 17th St	Fort Lauderdale	FL	33316	800-275-7603	954-463-3000	163
Art Institute of Houston						
1900 Yorktown St	Houston	TX	77056	800-275-4244	713-623-2040	163
Art Institute of Indianapolis						
3500 Depauw Blvd	Indianapolis	IN	46268	866-441-9031	317-613-4800	163
Art Institute of Las Vegas						
2350 Corporate Cir	Henderson	NV	89074	800-833-2678	702-369-9944	163
Art Institute of Ohio						
Cincinnati						
8845 Governor's Hill Dr						
Ste 100	Cincinnati	OH	45249	866-613-5184	513-833-2400	163
Art Institute of Philadelphia						
1622 Chestnut St	Philadelphia	PA	19103	800-275-2474	215-567-7080	163
Art Institute of Pittsburgh						
420 Blvd of the Allies	Pittsburgh	PA	15219	800-275-2470	412-263-6600	163
Art Institute of Portland						
1122 NW Davis St	Portland	OR	97209	888-228-6528	503-228-6528	163
Art Institute of Seattle						
2323 Elliott Ave	Seattle	WA	98121	800-275-2471	206-448-0900	163
Art Institute of Tampa						
4401 N Himes Ave Ste 150	Tampa	FL	33614	866-703-3277	813-873-2112	163
Art Institute of Washington						
1820 N Ft Myer Dr	Arlington	VA	22209	877-303-3771	703-358-9550	163
Art Institutes , The						
15 S Ninth St	Minneapolis	MN	55402	800-777-3643	612-332-3361	163
Art Iron Inc						
860 Curtis St	Toledo	OH	43609	800-472-1113	419-241-1261	491
Art Material Services Inc						
625 Joyce Kilmer Ave	New Brunswick	NJ	08901	888-522-5526	732-545-8888	362
Art Moehn						
2200 Seymour Rd	Jackson	MI	49201	866-495-5942		515
Art Morrison Enterprises Inc						
5301 Eighth St E	Fife	WA	98424	888-640-0516	253-922-7188	56
Art Partners LLC						
284 S Sharon Amity Rd	Charlotte	NC	28211	888-472-6866		542
Art Resource Inc						
536 Broadway 5th Fl	New York	NY	10012	888-505-8666	212-505-8700	623
ART Studio Clay Co						
9320 Michigan Ave	Sturtevant	WI	53177	800-323-0212	262-884-4278	42
Art Supply Warehouse						
6672 Westminster Blvd	Westminster	CA	92683	800-854-6467	714-891-3626	44
ARTBA (American Road & Transportation Builders Assn)						
1219 28th St NW	Washington	DC	20007	800-636-2377	202-289-4434	48-3
Artco-Bell Corp						
1302 Industrial Blvd	Temple	TX	76504	877-778-1811	254-778-1811	320-3
Artcraft Company Inc, The						
200 John L Dietsch Blvd						
	North Attleboro	MA	02763	800-659-4042	508-695-4042	429
Art-Craft Optical Company Inc						
57 Goodway Dr S	Rochester	NY	14623	800-828-8288	585-546-6640	541
Artech Information Systems LLC						
240 Cedar Knolls Rd						
Ste 100	Cedar Knolls	NJ	07927	800-950-9496	973-998-2500	719
Artel 25 Bradley Dr	Westbrook	ME	04092	888-406-3463	207-854-0860	252
Artel Video Systems Corp						
5B Lyberty Way	Westford	MA	01886	800-225-0228	978-263-5775	645
Artesian Resources Corp						
664 Churchmans Rd	Newark	DE	19702	800-332-5114	302-453-6900	360-5
NASDAQ: ARTNA						
Artforum International Magazine						
350 Seventh Ave 19th Fl	New York	NY	10001	800-966-2783	212-475-4000	456-2
Arthrex Inc						
1370 Creekside Blvd	Naples	FL	34108	800-934-4404	239-643-5553	476
Arthritis Foundation						
1330 W Peachtree St Ste 100	Atlanta	GA	30309	800-283-7800	404-872-7100	47-17
Arthroscopy Assn of North America (AANA)						
9400 W Higgins Rd Ste 200	Rosemont	IL	60018	877-924-0305	847-292-2262	48-8
Arthur Blank & Co Inc						
225 Rivermoor St	Boston	MA	02132	800-776-7333	617-325-9600	9
Arthur G James Cancer Hospital & Richard J Solove Research Institute						
Bone Marrow Transplant Program						
300 W Tenth Ave Ste 519	Columbus	OH	43210	800-293-5066		767
Arthur J Gallagher & Co						
2 Pierce Pl	Itasca	IL	60143	888-285-5106	630-773-3800	390
NYSE: AJG						
Arthur J. Glatfelter Agency Inc						
PO Box 2726	York	PA	17405	800-233-1957	717-741-0911	390
Arthur Rutenberg Homes Inc						
13922 58th St N	Clearwater	FL	33760	800-274-6637	727-536-5900	189
Arthur State Bank						
100 E Main St PO Box 769	Union	SC	29379	877-226-5246	864-427-1213	69
Arthur Vining Davis Foundations						
225 Water St	Jacksonville	FL	32202	888-427-4313	904-359-0670	306
Artifex Technology Consulting Inc						
614 George Washington Hwy	Lincoln	RI	02865	888-278-4339	401-723-6644	196
Artisan Funds						
PO Box 8412	Boston	MA	02266	800-344-1770*		527
*Cust Svc						
Artisan Laboratories Inc						
2532 Se Hawthorne Blvd	Portland	OR	97214	800-222-6721	503-238-6006	475
Artisan's Bank						
2961 Centerville Rd	Wilmington	DE	19808	800-282-8255	302-658-6881	69
Artisans Inc						
W4146 Second St PO Box 278	Glen Flora	WI	54526	800-311-8756	715-322-5285	130
Artist Brand Canvas						
2448 Loma Ave	South El Monte	CA	91733	888-579-2704*	626-579-2740	42
*Orders						
Artist's Magazine, The						
4700 E Galbraith Rd	Cincinnati	OH	45236	800-422-2550	513-531-2222	456-2
Artistic Carton Co						
1975 Big Timber Rd	Elgin	IL	60123	800-735-7225	847-741-0247	99
Artistic Checks Inc						
1809 Fashion Ct PO Box 1000	Conyers	GA	30012	800-243-2577	800-824-3255	141
ARTnews Magazine						
48 W 38th St 9th Fl	New York	NY	10018	800-284-4625	212-398-1690	456-2
Artpark						
450 S Fourth St	Lewiston	NY	14092	877-325-5787	716-754-9000	571
Art-Phyl Creations						
16250 NW 48th Ave	Hialeah	FL	33014	800-327-8318	305-624-2333	235
Arts Ctr of Coastal Carolina						
14 Shelter Cove Ln	Hilton Head Island	SC	29928	888-860-2787	843-686-3945	571
Arts-Way Mfg Co Inc						
5556 Hwy 9 PO Box 288	Armstrong	IA	50514	800-535-4517	712-864-3131	275
NASDAQ: ARTW						
Aruba Networks Inc						
1344 Crossman Ave	Sunnyvale	CA	94089	800-943-4526	408-227-4500	179
NASDAQ: ARUN						
Aruba Tourism Authority						
1750 Powder Springs St Ste 190	Marietta	GA	30064	800-862-7822	404-892-7822	773
Arvato Digital Services LLC						
29011 Commerce Ctr Dr	Valencia	CA	91355	800-223-1478		393
Arvco Container Corp						
845 Gibson St	Kalamazoo	MI	49001	800-968-9127	269-381-0900	99
Arvinyl Metal Laminates Corp						
233 N Sherman Ave	Corona	CA	92882	800-278-4695		484
ARVO (Association for Research in Vision & Ophthalmology)						
12300 Twinbrook Pkwy Ste 250	Rockville	MD	20852	888-503-1050	240-221-2900	48-8
Arx Networks LLC						
581 Foster City Blvd						
Ste 210	Foster City	CA	94404	800-972-2175	650-403-4279	182
Arzel Zoning Technology Inc						
4801 Commerce Pkwy	Cleveland	OH	44128	800-611-8312	216-831-6068	203
ASA (Autism Society of America)						
4340 EW Hwy Ste 350	Bethesda	MD	20814	800-328-8476	301-657-0881	47-17
ASA (American Studies Assn)						
1120 19th St NW Ste 301	Washington	DC	20036	800-468-3571	202-467-4783	48-5
ASA (American Society of Agronomy)						
5585 Guilford Rd	Madison	WI	53711	866-359-9161	608-273-8080	47-2
ASA (American Society of Anesthesiologists)						
520 N NW Hwy	Park Ridge	IL	60068	800-331-1600	847-825-5586	48-8
ASA (American Society of Appraisers)						
555 Herndon Pkwy Ste 125	Herndon	VA	20170	800-272-8258	703-478-2228	48-17
ASA (American Society on Aging)						
575 Market St Ste 2100	San Francisco	CA	94105	800-537-9728	415-974-9600	47-6
ASA (American Sociological Assn)						
1307 New York Ave	Washington	DC	20005	800-524-9400	202-383-9005	48-5
ASA (American Soybean Assn)						
12125 Woodcrest Executive Dr						
Ste 100	Saint Louis	MO	63141	800-688-7692	314-576-1770	47-2
ASA (American Statistical Assn)						
732 N Washington St	Alexandria	VA	22314	888-231-3473	703-684-1221	48-19
ASA (American Subcontractors Assn Inc)						
1004 Duke St	Alexandria	VA	22314	866-378-8866	703-684-3450	48-3
ASA (Automotive Service Assn)						
1901 Airport Fwy	Bedford	TX	76021	800-272-7467*		48-21
*Cust Svc						
ASA (American Staffing Assn)						
277 S Washington St Ste 200	Alexandria	VA	22314	800-456-4324	703-253-2020	48-12
ASA Alloys Inc						
81 Steinway Blvd	Etobicoke	ON	M9W6H6	800-387-9166	416-213-0000	491
ASA Computers Inc						
645 National Ave	Mountain View	CA	94043	800-732-5727	650-230-8000	178

Name	Address	City	State	Zip	Toll-Free	Phone	Class
ASA Tire Systems Inc	651 S Stratford Dr	Meridian	ID	83642	**800-241-8472**	208-855-0781	176
ASAA (American Sleep Apnea Assn)	6856 Eastern Ave NW #203	Washington	DC	20012	**888-293-3650**	202-293-3650	47-17
ASAE (American Society of Assn Executives)	1575 'I' St NW	Washington	DC	20005	**888-950-2723**	202-626-2723	48-12
Asahi Kasei Plastics North America Inc	900 E Van Riper Rd *Cust Svc	Fowlerville	MI	48836	**800-993-5382***	517-223-2000	604-2
ASAPS (American Society for Aesthetic Plastic Surgery, The)	11262 Monarch St	Garden Grove	CA	92841	**800-364-2147**	562-799-2356	48-8
ASBO (Association of School Business Officials International)	11401 N Shore Dr	Reston	VA	20190	**866-682-2729**		48-5
ASBPA (American Shore & Beach Preservation Assn)	5460 Beaujolais Ln	Fort Myers	FL	33919	**800-331-1600**	239-489-2616	47-13
Asbury College	1 Macklem Dr *Admissions	Wilmore	KY	40390	**800-888-1818***	859-858-3511	167
Asbury Methodist Village	201 Russell Ave	Gaithersburg	MD	20877	**800-327-2879**	301-216-4100	670
Asbury Park Press	3601 Hwy 66 PO Box 1550	Neptune	NJ	07754	**800-883-7737**	732-922-6000	531-2
Asbury Theological Seminary	204 N Lexington Ave	Wilmore	KY	40390	**800-227-2879**	859-858-3581	168-3
ASC (American Society of Cinematographers)	1782 N Orange Dr	Hollywood	CA	90028	**800-448-0145**	323-969-4333	47-4
ASC Profiles Inc	2110 Enterprise Blvd *Cust Svc	West Sacramento	CA	95691	**800-360-2477***	916-372-0933	695
ASCA (American School Counselor Assn)	1101 King St Ste 625	Alexandria	VA	22314	**800-306-4722**	703-683-2722	48-5
ASCCP (American Society for Colposcopy & Cervical Pathology)	152 W Washington St	Hagerstown	MD	21740	**800-787-7227**	301-733-3640	48-8
ASCD (Association for Supervision & Curriculum Development)	1703 N Beauregard St	Alexandria	VA	22311	**800-933-2723**	703-578-9600	48-5
ASCE (American Society of Civil Engineers)	1801 Alexander Bell Dr	Reston	VA	20191	**800-548-2723**	703-295-6300	456-21
Ascend Federal Credit Union	520 Airpark Dr PO Box 1210	Tullahoma	TN	37388	**800-342-3086**	931-455-5441	221
Ascend Therapeutics Inc	607 Herndon Pkwy Ste 110	Herndon	VA	20170	**888-412-5751**	703-471-4744	233
Ascendant Advisors LLC	4 Oaks Pl 1330 Post Oak Blvd Ste 1550	Houston	TX	77056	**800-552-6010**		527
Ascenta Health Ltd	4-15 Garland Ave	Dartmouth	NS	B3B0A6	**866-224-1775**	902-435-7329	345
Ascentium Capital LLC	23970 Hwy 59 N	Kingwood	TX	77339	**866-722-8500**		508
Ascentra Credit Union	1710 Grant St	Bettendorf	IA	52722	**800-426-5241**	563-355-0152	221
ASCLA (Association of Specialized & Co-op Library Agencies)	50 E Huron St	Chicago	IL	60611	**800-545-2433**	312-280-4395	48-11
ASCO (Association of Schools & Colleges of Optometry)	6110 Executive Blvd Ste 420	Rockville	MD	20852	**800-397-2424**	301-231-5944	48-8
ASCO (American Society of Clinical Oncology)	2318 Mill Rd Ste 800	Alexandria	VA	22314	**888-282-2552**	571-483-1300	48-8
ASCP (American Society of Consultant Pharmacists)	1321 Duke St	Alexandria	VA	22314	**800-355-2727**	703-739-1300	48-8
ASCP (American Society for Clinical Pathology)	33 W Monroe St Ste 1600 *Cust Svc	Chicago	IL	60603	**800-621-4142***	312-541-4999	48-8
ASCRS (American Society of Cataract & Refractive Surgery)	4000 Legato Rd Ste 700	Fairfax	VA	22033	**877-996-4464**	703-591-2220	48-8
ASD (Allentown School District)	31 S Penn St	Allentown	PA	18105	**877-262-1492**	484-765-4000	683
ASD	6255 Sunset Blvd 19th Fl	Los Angeles	CA	90028	**800-421-4511**	323-817-2200	186
ASD Data Services LLC	PO Box 1184	Manchester	TN	37349	**877-742-7297**		634-6
ASE (Alliance to Save Energy)	1850 M St NW Ste 600	Washington	DC	20036	**800-862-2086**	202-857-0666	47-12
Asel Art Supply	2701 Cedar Springs	Dallas	TX	75201	**888-273-5278**	214-871-2425	44
AseraCare Hospice of Austin	14205 Burnet Rd	Austin	TX	78728	**800-332-3982**	512-218-9890	371
AseraCare Hospice of Milwaukee	7160 Dallas Pkwy Ste 400	Plano	TX	75024	**800-598-5132**	262-785-1356	371
ASF (Atlantic Salmon Federation)	PO Box 5200	Saint Andrews	NB	E5B3S8	**800-565-5666**	506-529-1033	47-3
ASG (Allen Systems Group Inc)	1333 Third Ave S	Naples	FL	34102	**800-932-5536**	239-435-2200	180-12
ASG Renaissance	22226 Garrison St	Dearborn	MI	48124	**800-238-0890**	313-565-4700	263
ASGE (American Society for Gastrointestinal Endoscopy)	1520 Kensington Rd Ste 202	Oak Brook	IL	60523	**866-353-2743**	630-573-0600	48-8
Ash Grove Cement Co	8900 Indian Creek Pkwy *OTC: ASHG*	Overland Park	KS	66210	**800-545-1882**	913-451-8900	134
ASHA (American Social Health Assn)	PO Box 13827	Research Triangle Park	NC	27709	**800-552-4375**	919-361-8400	47-17
ASHA (American Speech-Language-Hearing Assn)	2200 Research Blvd	Rockville	MD	20850	**800-498-2071**	301-296-5700	48-8
Ashaway Line & Twine Manufacturing Co	24 Laurel St	Ashaway	RI	02804	**800-556-7260**	401-377-2221	210
Ashbrook Ctr	401 College Ave Ashland University	Ashland	OH	44805	**877-289-5411**	419-289-5411	631
Ashe County Chamber of Commerce	1 N Jefferson Ave Ste C PO Box 31	West Jefferson	NC	28694	**888-343-2743**	336-846-9550	338
Asher's Chocolates	80 Wambold Rd	Souderton	PA	18964	**800-223-4420**	215-721-3000	297-8
Asheville Area Chamber of Commerce	36 Montford Ave	Asheville	NC	28802	**888-314-1041**	828-258-6101	138
Asheville Chevrolet Inc	205 Smokey Pk Hwy	Asheville	NC	28806	**866-921-1073**	828-665-4444	56
Asheville Citizen Times	14 O'Henry Ave	Asheville	NC	28801	**800-800-4204**	828-252-5622	531-2
Asheville Civic Ctr	87 Haywood St	Asheville	NC	28801	**888-464-4218**	828-259-5743	207
Asheville Regional Airport	61 Terminal Dr Ste 1	Fletcher	NC	28732	**866-719-3910**	828-684-2226	27
Asheville Savings Bank S S B	PO Box 652	Asheville	NC	28802	**800-222-3230**	828-254-7411	69
Ashford University	400 N Bluff Blvd	Clinton	IA	52732	**800-242-4153**	563-242-4023	167
ASHG (American Society of Human Genetics)	9650 Rockville Pike	Bethesda	MD	20814	**800-720-4363**	301-634-7300	48-19
ASHI (American Society of Home Inspectors)	932 Lee St Ste 101	Des Plaines	IL	60016	**800-743-2744**	847-759-2820	48-3
Ashland Alliance Chamber of Commerce	1733 Winchester Ave	Ashland	KY	41101	**800-233-3826**	606-324-5111	138
Ashland Community & Technical College	1400 College Dr	Ashland	KY	41101	**800-928-4256**	606-326-2000	161
Ashland Inc	50 E River Ctr Blvd PO Box 391 *NYSE: ASH*	Covington	KY	41012	**877-546-2782**	859-815-3333	187
Ashland Independent School District	PO Box 3000	Ashland	KY	41105	**800-752-6200**	606-327-2706	683
Ashland Springs Hotel	212 E Main St	Ashland	OR	97520	**888-795-4545**	541-488-1700	379
Ashland University	401 College Ave	Ashland	OH	44805	**800-882-1548**	419-289-4142	167
Ashland University Library	509 College Ave	Ashland	OH	44805	**866-434-5222**	419-289-5400	434-6
Ashland-The Henry Clay Estate	120 Sycamore Rd	Lexington	KY	40502	**800-735-5251**	859-266-8581	49-2
Ashlar Inc	9600 Great Hills Trl Ste 150W-1625	Austin	TX	78759	**800-877-2745**	512-250-2186	180-5
Ashley Furniture Industries Inc	1 Ashley Way	Arcadia	WI	54612	**800-477-2222**	608-323-6225	320-2
Ashley Madison Agency, The	2300 Yonge St	Toronto	ON	M4P1E4	**866-742-2218**		228
Ashley-Chicot Electric Co-op Inc	307 E Jefferson St	Hamburg	AR	71646	**800-281-5212**	870-853-5212	247
ASHP (American Society of Health-System Pharmacists)	7272 Wisconsin Ave	Bethesda	MD	20814	**866-279-0681**	301-664-8700	48-8
ASHRAE (American Society of Heating Refrigerating & Air-Conditioning Engineers Inc)	1791 Tullie Cir NE *Cust Svc	Atlanta	GA	30329	**800-527-4723***	404-636-8400	48-3
ASHS (American Society for Horticultural Science)	1018 Duke St	Alexandria	VA	22314	**800-331-1600**	703-836-4606	47-2
Ashta Chemicals Inc	3509 Middle Rd *Cust Svc	Ashtabula	OH	44004	**800-492-5082***	440-997-5221	142
Ashtabula County Medical Ctr (ACMC)	2420 Lake Ave	Ashtabula	OH	44004	**866-213-2262**	440-997-2262	374-3
Ashtead Technology Inc	19407 Pk Row Ste 170	Houston	TX	77084	**800-242-3910**	281-398-9533	195
ASI Corp	48289 Fremont Blvd	Fremont	CA	94538	**800-200-0274**	510-226-8000	176
ASI DataMyte Inc	2800 Campus Dr Ste 60	Plymouth	MN	55441	**800-207-5631**	763-553-1040	180-10
Asi Networks Inc	19331 E Walnut Dr N	City Of Industry	CA	91748	**800-251-1336**		182
Asi System Integration Inc	48 W 37th St	New York	NY	10018	**866-308-3920**		112
Asi Technologies Inc	5848 N 95th Ct	Milwaukee	WI	53225	**800-558-7068**	414-464-6200	236
Asian American Legal Defense & Education Fund (AALDEF)	99 Hudson St 12th Fl	New York	NY	10013	**800-966-5946**	212-966-5932	47-8
Asics America Corp	29 Parker Ste 100	Irvine	CA	92618	**800-333-8404**	949-453-8888	302
Ask Associates Inc	1201 Wakarusa Ste C-1	Lawrence	KS	66049	**800-315-4333**	785-841-8194	735
ASK Services Inc	42180 Ford Rd Ste 101	Canton	MI	48187	**888-416-1313**	734-983-9040	400
Aski Financial Inc	419 Notre Dame Ave	Winnipeg	MB	R3B1R3	**866-987-7180**	204-987-7180	136
ASKO Appliances Inc	PO Box 44848	Madison	WI	53744	**800-898-1879**		35
ASKO Inc	501 W Seventh Ave	Homestead	PA	15120	**800-321-1310**	412-461-4110	492
ASL Services	3700 Commerce Blvd Ste 216	Kissimmee	FL	34741	**888-744-6275**	407-518-7900	699
ASLA (American Seminar Leaders Assn)	2405 E Washington Blvd	Pasadena	CA	91104	**800-801-1886**	626-791-1211	48-12
ASLA (American Society of Landscape Architects)	636 'I' St NW	Washington	DC	20001	**888-999-2752**	202-898-2444	47-2
ASLMS (American Society for Laser Medicine & Surgery Inc)	2100 Stewart Ave Ste 240	Wausau	WI	54401	**877-258-6028**	715-845-9283	48-8
ASLO (American Society of Limnology & Oceanography)	5400 Bosque Blvd Ste 680	Waco	TX	76710	**800-929-2756**	254-399-9635	48-19
ASM Industries Inc Pacer Pumps Div	41 Industrial Cir *Cust Svc	Lancaster	PA	17601	**800-233-3861***	717-656-2161	638
ASM International	9639 Kinsman Rd	Materials Park	OH	44073	**800-336-5152**	440-338-5151	48-13
ASMBA (Armed Services Mutual Benefit Assn)	PO Box 160384	Nashville	TN	37216	**800-251-8434**	615-851-0800	47-19
ASMC (American Society of Military Comptrollers)	415 N Alfred St	Alexandria	VA	22314	**800-462-5637**	703-549-0360	47-19
ASNA (Alabama State Nurses Assn)	360 N Hull St	Montgomery	AL	36104	**800-270-2762**	334-262-8321	532
ASNS (American Society for Nutrition)	9211 Corporate Blvd Ste 300	Rockville	MD	20850	**800-627-8723**	301-634-7050	48-6
ASNT (American Society for Nondestructive Testing Inc)	1711 Arlingate Ln PO Box 28518 *Orders	Columbus	OH	43228	**800-222-2768***	614-274-6003	48-19
Asnuntuck Community College	170 Elm St	Enfield	CT	06082	**800-501-3967**	860-253-3000	161
Asolo Repertory Theatre	5555 N Tamiami Tr	Sarasota	FL	34243	**800-361-8388**	941-351-9010	746
ASP (Advanced Sterilization Products)	33 Technology Dr	Irvine	CA	92618	**888-783-7723**		476

Name	Address	City	State	ZIP	Toll-Free	Phone	Class
ASP Inc	460 Brant St Ste 212	Burlington	ON	L7R4B6	**877-552-5535**	905-333-4242	691
ASPAN (American Society of PeriAnesthesia Nurses)	90 Frontage Rd	Cherry Hill	NJ	08034	**877-737-9696**	856-616-9600	48-8
ASPCA Animal Poison Control Ctr	424 E 92nd St	New York	NY	10128	**888-426-4435**	212-876-7700	47-3
ASPE (American Society of Professional Estimators)	2525 Perimeter Pl Dr Ste 103	Nashville	TN	37214	**888-378-6283**	615-316-9200	48-3
ASPE Inc	114 Edinburgh S Dr Ste 200	Cary	NC	27511	**877-800-5221**		762
ASPEN (American Society for Parenteral & Enteral Nutrition)	8630 Fenton St Ste 412	Silver Spring	MD	20910	**800-727-4567**	301-587-6315	48-8
Aspen Chamber Resort Assn	425 Rio Grande Pl	Aspen	CO	81611	**800-670-0792**	970-925-1940	138
Aspen Grove Lifestyle Ctr	7301 S Santa Fe Dr	Littleton	CO	80120	**877-225-5337**		459
Aspen Marketing Services	1240 N Ave	West Chicago	IL	60185	**800-848-0212**	630-293-9600	4
Aspen Meadows Resort	845 Meadows Rd	Aspen	CO	81611	**800-452-4240**	970-925-4240	667
Aspen Medical Products	6481 Oak Cyn	Irvine	CA	92618	**800-295-2776**	949-681-0200	475
Aspen Santa Fe Ballet	0245 Sage Way	Aspen	CO	81611	**866-449-0464**	970-925-7175	572-1
Aspen Ski & Board Co	1170 E Powell Rd	Lewis Center	OH	43035	**877-861-0777**	614-848-6600	709
Aspen Skiing Co	117 ABC	Aspen	CO	81611	**855-754-2863**	970-925-1220	667
Aspen Surgical	6945 Southbelt Dr SE	Caledonia	MI	49316	**888-364-7004**	616-698-7100	476
Aspen Technology Inc	200 Wheeler Rd *NASDAQ: AZPN*	Burlington	MA	01803	**888-996-7100**	781-221-6400	180-5
Asphalt Roofing Manufacturers Assn (ARMA)	529 14th St NW Ste 750	Washington	DC	20045	**800-247-6637**	202-207-0917	48-3
Aspirus Wausau Hospital	333 Pine Ridge Blvd	Wausau	WI	54401	**800-283-2881**	715-847-2121	374-3
Asplundh Tree Expert Co	708 Blair Mill Rd	Willow Grove	PA	19090	**800-248-8733**	215-784-4200	774
Asponte Technology Inc	11523 Palmbrush Trl Ste 137	Lakewood Ranch	FL	34202	**888-926-9434**		182
ASPR (Association of Staff Physician Recruiters)	1000 Westgate Dr Ste 252	Saint Paul	MN	55114	**800-830-2777**		48-8
ASPS (American Society of Plastic Surgeons)	444 E Algonquin Rd	Arlington Heights	IL	60005	**888-475-2784**	847-228-9900	48-8
Aspyra Inc	4360 Pk Terr Dr Ste 100 *OTC: APYI*	Westlake Village	CA	91361	**800-437-9000**		180-10
ASQ (American Society for Quality)	600 N Plankinton Ave	Milwaukee	WI	53203	**800-248-1946**	414-272-8575	48-13
ASRA (American Society of Regional Anesthesia & Pain Medicine)	239 Fourth Ave Ste 1714	Pittsburgh	PA	15222	**855-795-2772**	412-471-2718	48-8
ASRT (American Society of Radiologic Technologists)	15000 Central Ave SE	Albuquerque	NM	87123	**800-444-2778**	505-298-4500	48-8
ASSA ABLOY	110 Sargent Dr	New Haven	CT	06511	**800-377-3948**		236
Assa Abloy of Canada Ltd	160 Four Vly Dr	Vaughan	ON	L4K4T9	**800-461-3007**	905-738-2466	350
ASSA Inc	110 Sargent Dr	New Haven	CT	06511	**800-235-7482**	203-624-5225	350
Assateague State Park	7307 Stephen Decatur Hwy	Berlin	MD	21811	**888-432-2267**	410-641-2120	564
Assay Technology Inc	1382 Stealth St	Livermore	CA	94551	**800-833-1258**	925-461-8880	636
Assemblies of God (A/G)	1445 N Boonville Ave	Springfield	MO	65802	**800-641-4310**	417-862-2781	47-20
Assemblies of God Theological Seminary	1435 N Glenstone Ave	Springfield	MO	65802	**800-467-2487**	417-268-1000	168-3
Assembly of Turkish American Assn (ATAA)	1526 18th St NW	Washington	DC	20036	**800-627-7692**	202-483-9090	47-14
Assent Consulting Inc	2 Grand Central Twr 140 E 45th St	New York	NY	10017	**866-627-4473**		630
Assessment Technology Inc	6700 E Speedway Blvd	Tucson	AZ	85710	**800-367-4762**	520-323-9033	227
Asset Acceptance Capital Corp (AACC)	28405 Van Dyke Ave *NASDAQ: AACC*	Warren	MI	48093	**800-545-9931**	586-939-9600	159
Asset Marketing Systems Insurance Services LLC	15050 Ave of Science	San Diego	CA	92128	**888-303-8755**		367
Asset Strategy Consultants LLC	6 N Park Dr Ste 208	Hunt Valley	MD	21030	**866-344-8282**	410-528-8282	401
AssetMark Inc	1655 Grant St 10th Fl	Concord	CA	94520	**800-664-5345**		401
Assiniboine Park Zoo	55 Pavilion Crescent	Winnipeg	MB	R3P2N6	**877-927-6006**	204-927-8080	821
Assist Cornerstone Technologies Inc	150 West Civic Ctr Dr Ste 601	Sandy	UT	84070	**800-732-0136**		179
Assist-2-Sell Inc	1610 Meadow Wood Ln	Reno	NV	89502	**800-528-7816**	775-688-6060	650
Associated Bag Co	400 W Boden St	Milwaukee	WI	53207	**800-926-6100**		65
Associated Banc-Corp	1200 Hansen Rd *NYSE: ASB* ■ *PR	Green Bay	WI	54304	**800-236-2722***	920-491-7000	360-2
Associated Bank	2870 Holmgren Way	Green Bay	WI	54304	**800-728-3501**	262-879-0133	69
Associated Bank Green Bay NA	200 N Adams St	Green Bay	WI	54301	**800-728-3501**	920-433-3200	69
Associated Bank Illinois NA	612 N Main St	Rockford	IL	61103	**800-236-8866**	815-987-3500	69
Associated Bank Milwaukee	401 E Kilbourn Ave	Milwaukee	WI	53202	**800-236-8866**	414-271-1786	69
Associated Bank North	303 S First Ave	Wausau	WI	54401	**800-236-8866**	715-848-4793	69
Associated Behavioral Health Care Inc	4700 42nd Ave SW Ste 470	Seattle	WA	98116	**800-858-6702**	206-935-1282	461

Name	Address	City	State	ZIP	Toll-Free	Phone	Class
Associated Bodywork & Massage Professionals (ABMP)	25188 Genesee Trl Rd Ste 200	Golden	CO	80401	**800-458-2267**	303-674-8478	47-17
Associated Builders & Contractors Inc (ABC)	4250 Fairfax Dr	Arlington	VA	22203	**877-889-5627**	703-812-2000	48-3
Associated Distributors LLC	401 Woodlake Dr	Chesapeake	VA	23320	**800-308-2600**	757-424-6300	80-1
Associated Equipment Corp	5043 Farlan Ave	Saint Louis	MO	63115	**800-949-1472**	314-385-5178	250
Associated Equipment Distributors (AED)	650 E Algonquin Rd Ste 305	Schaumburg	IL	60173	**800-388-0650**	630-574-0650	48-18
Associated Fabrics Corp	15-01 Pollitt Dr Unit 7	Fair Lawn	NJ	07410	**800-232-4077**		593
Associated Floors	32 Morris Ave	Springfield	NJ	07081	**800-800-4320**		191-2
Associated Food Stores Inc	1850 West 2100 South *Cust Svc	Salt Lake City	UT	84119	**888-574-7100***	801-973-4400	298-8
Associated General Contractors of America (AGC)	2300 Wilson Blvd Ste 400	Arlington	VA	22201	**800-242-1766**	703-548-3118	48-3
Associated General Contractors PAC	2300 Wilson Blvd Ste 400	Arlington	VA	22201	**800-242-1767**	703-548-3118	614
Associated Global Systems Inc	3333 New Hyde Pk Rd *Cust Svc	New Hyde Park	NY	11042	**800-645-8300***	516-627-8910	448
Associated Grocers Inc	8600 Anselmo Ln	Baton Rouge	LA	70810	**800-637-2021**	225-444-1000	298-8
Associated Grocers of New England Inc	11 Co-op Way	Pembroke	NH	03275	**800-242-2248**	603-223-6710	298-8
Associated Grocers of the South	3600 Vanderbilt Rd	Birmingham	AL	35217	**800-695-6051**	205-841-6781	298-8
Associated Hygienic Products LLC	3400 River Green Ct Ste 600 *General	Duluth	GA	30096	**800-757-0927***	770-497-9800	557
Associated Industries Of Massachusetts Mutual Insurance Com	PO Box 4070	Burlington	MA	01803	**866-270-3354**	781-221-1600	391-4
Associated Locksmiths of America (ALOA)	3500 Easy St	Dallas	TX	75247	**800-532-2562**	214-819-9733	48-3
Associated Materials Inc	3773 State Rd	Cuyahoga Falls	OH	44223	**800-257-4335**	330-929-1811	695
Associated Materials Inc Alside Div	PO Box 2010 *Cust Svc	Akron	OH	44309	**800-922-6009***		237
Associated Mennonite Biblical Seminary	3003 Benham Ave	Elkhart	IN	46517	**800-964-2627**	574-295-3726	168-3
Associated Petroleum Carriers Inc	PO Box 2808 *Cust Svc	Spartanburg	SC	29304	**800-573-9301***	864-573-9301	778
Associated Press	1100 13th St NW Ste 700	Washington	DC	20005	**800-824-5498**	202-641-9000	644
Associated Risk Managers (ARM)	2 Pierce Pl	Itasca	IL	60143	**800-735-5441**	630-285-4324	48-9
Associated Steel Corp	18200 Miles Rd	Cleveland	OH	44128	**800-321-9300**		351
Associated Wholesalers Inc	PO Box 67	Robesonia	PA	19551	**800-927-7771**	610-693-3161	298-8
Association for Advanced Life Underwriting (AALU)	11921 Freedom Dr Ste 1100	Reston	VA	20190	**888-275-0092**	703-641-9400	48-9
Association for Advanced Training in the Behavioral Sciences (AATBS)	5126 Ralston St	Ventura	CA	93003	**800-472-1931**	805-676-3030	48-5
Association for Applied & Therapeutic Humor (AATH)	65 Enterprise	Aliso Viejo	CA	92656	**888-747-2284**	815-708-6587	47-17
Association for Applied Psychophysiology & Biofeedback (AAPB)	10200 W 44th Ave Ste 304	Wheat Ridge	CO	80033	**800-477-8892**	303-422-8436	48-8
Association for Assessment & Accreditation of Laboratory Animal Care International	5283 Corporate Dr Ste 203	Frederick	MD	21703	**800-926-0066**	301-696-9626	47-1
Association for Behavioral & Cognitive Therapies (ABCT)	305 Seventh Ave 16th Fl	New York	NY	10001	**800-685-2228**	212-647-1890	48-15
Association for Career & Technical Education (ACTE)	1410 King St	Alexandria	VA	22314	**800-826-9972**	703-683-3111	48-5
Association for Childhood Education International (ACEI)	1101 16th St NW Ste 300	Washington	DC	20036	**800-423-3563**	202-372-9986	48-5
Association for Computing Machinery (ACM)	2 Penn Plz Ste 701	New York	NY	10121	**800-342-6626**	212-626-0500	47-9
Association for Conflict Resolution (ACR)	12100 Sunset Hills Rd Ste 130	Reston	VA	20190	**800-880-7303**	703-234-4141	48-10
Association for Continuing Higher Education (ACHE)	1700 Asp Ave	Norman	OK	73072	**800-807-2243**		48-5
Association for Co-op Operations Research & Development (ACORD)	1 Blue Hill Plz PO Box 1529	Pearl River	NY	10965	**800-444-3341**	845-620-1700	48-9
Association for Corporate Growth (ACG)	125 S. Wacker Dr Ste 3100	Chicago	IL	60606	**877-358-2220**	312-957-4260	48-12
Association for Couples in Marriage Enrichment (ACME)	PO Box 21374	Winston-Salem	NC	27120	**800-634-8325**	336-724-1526	47-6
Association for Healthcare Documentation Integrity (AHDI)	4230 Kiernan Ave Ste 130	Modesto	CA	95356	**800-982-2182**	209-527-9620	48-8
Association for Library & Information Science Education (ALISE)	2150 N 107th St Ste 205	Seattle	WA	98133	**877-275-7547**	206-209-5267	48-11
Association for Library Collections & Technical Services (ALCTS)	50 E Huron St	Chicago	IL	60611	**800-545-2433**	312-280-5038	48-11
Association for Library Service to Children (ALSC)	50 E Huron St	Chicago	IL	60611	**800-545-2433**	312-280-2163	48-11
Association for Library Trustees, Advocates, Friends & Foundations (ALTAFF)	50 E Huron St	Chicago	IL	60611	**800-545-2433**		48-11
Association for Linen Management	2161 Lexington Rd Ste 2	Richmond	KY	40475	**800-669-0863**	859-624-0177	48-4
Association for Mfg Technology (AMT)	7901 Westpark Dr	McLean	VA	22102	**800-524-0475**	703-893-2900	48-12
Association for Professionals in Infection Control & Epidemiology Inc (APIC)	1275 K St NW Ste 1000	Washington	DC	20005	**800-650-9883**	202-789-1890	48-8
Association for Research & Enlightenment (ARE)	215 67th St	Virginia Beach	VA	23451	**800-333-4499**	757-428-3588	47-17
Association for Research in Vision & Ophthalmology (ARVO)	12300 Twinbrook Pkwy Ste 250	Rockville	MD	20852	**888-503-1050**	240-221-2900	48-8
Association for Retail Environment (ARE)	4651 Sheridan St Ste 470	Hollywood	FL	33021	**800-421-3483**	954-893-7300	48-3
Association for Supervision & Curriculum Development (ASCD)	1703 N Beauregard St	Alexandria	VA	22311	**800-933-2723**	703-578-9600	48-5

Name / Address	City	State	ZIP	Toll-Free	Phone	Class
Association for the Advancement of Computing in Education (AACE) PO Box 1545	Chesapeake	VA	23327	**800-352-5397**	757-366-5606	48-5
Association for the Advancement of Medical Instrumentation (AAMI) 4301 N Fairfax Dr Ste 301	Arlington	VA	22203	**800-332-2264**	703-525-4890	48-8
Association for Vascular Access (AVA) 5526 West 13400 South Ste 229	Herriman	UT	84096	**888-576-2826**	801-792-9079	48-8
Association for Women in Science Inc (AWIS) 1321 Duke St Ste 210	Alexandria	VA	22314	**866-736-7343**	703-894-4490	48-19
Association Management Magazine 1575 'I' St NW	Washington	DC	20005	**888-950-2723**	202-371-0940	456-5
Association of Alternative Newsweeklies (AAN) 115615th St NW	Washington	DC	20005	**866-415-0704**	202-289-8484	48-14
Association of American Chambers of Commerce in Latin America 1615 H St NW 3rd Fl	Washington	DC	20062	**800-638-6582**	202-463-5485	136
Association of American Geographers (AAG) 1710 16th St NW	Washington	DC	20009	**800-696-7353**	202-234-1450	48-19
Association of American Medical Colleges (AAMC) 2450 N St NW	Washington	DC	20037	**800-273-8255**	202-828-0400	48-5
Association of American Publishers Inc (AAP) 71 Fifth Ave	New York	NY	10003	**866-271-4968**	212-255-0200	48-16
Association of Certified Fraud Examiners (ACFE) 716 W Ave	Austin	TX	78701	**800-245-3321**	512-478-9000	48-1
Association of Christian Schools International (ACSI) 731 Chapel Hills Dr	Colorado Springs	CO	80920	**800-367-0798***	719-528-6906	48-5
*Cust Svc						
Association of Clinical Research Professionals (ACRP) 500 Montgomery St Ste 800	Alexandria	VA	22314	**888-508-5731**	703-254-8100	48-8
Association of College & Research Libraries (ACRL) 50 E Huron St	Chicago	IL	60611	**800-545-2433**	312-280-2519	48-11
Association of Collegiate Schools of Architecture (ACSA) 1735 New York Ave NW 3rd Fl	Washington	DC	20006	**877-426-6323**	202-785-2324	48-5
Association of Community College Trustees (ACCT) 1101 17th St NW Ste 300	Washington	DC	20036	**866-895-2228**	202-775-4667	48-5
Association of Consulting Foresters of America (ACF) 312 Montgomery St Ste 208	Alexandria	VA	22314	**888-540-8733**	703-548-0990	47-2
Association of Corporate Counsel (ACC) 1025 Connecticut Ave NW Ste 200	Washington	DC	20036	**877-647-3411**	202-293-4103	48-10
Association of Directory Publishers (ADP) PO Box 209	Traverse City	MI	49685	**800-267-9002**	231-486-2182	48-16
Association of Energy Engineers (AEE) 4025 Pleasantdale Rd Ste 420	Atlanta	GA	30340	**877-407-0784**	770-447-5083	47-12
Association of Energy Service Cos (AESC) 14531 Fm 529 Ste 250	Houston	TX	77095	**800-692-0771**	713-781-0758	47-12
Association of Equipment Manufacturers (AEM) 6737 W Washington St Ste 2400	Milwaukee	WI	53214	**866-236-0442**	414-272-0943	48-13
Association of Farmworker Opportunity Programs (AFOP) 1120 20th St NW Ste 300	Washington	DC	20036	**866-487-9243**	202-828-6006	47-2
Association of Film Commissioners International (AFCI) 109 E 17th St	Cheyenne	WY	82001	**888-765-5777**	307-637-4422	47-4
Association of Fundraising Professionals (AFP) 4300 Wilson Blvd Ste 300	Arlington	VA	22203	**800-666-3863**	703-684-0410	48-12
Association of Governing Boards of Universities & Colleges (AGB) 1133 20th St NW Ste 300	Washington	DC	20036	**800-356-6317**	202-296-8400	48-5
Association of Government Accountants (AGA) 2208 Mt Vernon Ave	Alexandria	VA	22301	**800-242-7211**	703-684-6931	48-1
Association of Healthcare Internal Auditors (AHIA) 10200 W 44th Ave Ste 304	Wheat Ridge	CO	80033	**888-275-2442**	303-327-7546	48-1
Association of Home Appliance Manufacturers (AHAM) 1111 19th St NW Ste 402	Washington	DC	20036	**888-258-3247**	202-872-5955	48-4
Association of Junior Leagues International Inc (AJLI) 80 Maiden Ln Ste 305	New York	NY	10038	**800-955-3248**	212-951-8300	47-15
Association of Legal Administrators (ALA) 75 Tri-State International Ste 222	Lincolnshire	IL	60069	**877-675-5571**	847-267-1252	48-10
Association of Military Surgeons of the United States (AMSUS) 9320 Old Georgetown Rd	Bethesda	MD	20814	**800-761-9320**	301-897-8800	48-8
Association of Nurses in AIDS Care (ANAC) 3538 Ridgewood Rd	Akron	OH	44333	**800-260-6780**	330-670-0101	48-8
Association of Old Crows (AOC) 1000 N Payne St Ste 300	Alexandria	VA	22314	**800-247-5626**	703-549-1600	47-19
Association of Osteopathic Directors & Medical Educators (AODME) 142 E Ontario St	Chicago	IL	60611	**800-621-1773**	312-202-8211	48-8
Association of Performing Arts Presenters 1211 Connecticut Ave NW Ste 200	Washington	DC	20036	**888-820-2787**	202-833-2787	47-4
Association of Pool & Spa Professionals (APSP) 2111 Eisenhower Ave Ste 500	Alexandria	VA	22314	**800-323-3996**	703-838-0083	48-4
Association of Professional Flight Attendants 1004 W Euless Blvd	Euless	TX	76040	**800-395-2732**	817-540-0108	414
Association of Progressive Rental Organizations (APRO) 1504 Robin Hood Trl	Austin	TX	78703	**800-204-2776**	512-794-0095	48-18
Association of Public Health Laboratories (APHL) 8515 Georgia Ave Ste 700	Silver Spring	MD	20910	**800-899-2278**	240-485-2745	48-7
Association of Public-Safety Communications Officials International Inc 351 N Williamson Blvd	Daytona Beach	FL	32114	**888-272-6911**	386-322-2500	48-7
Association of Rehabilitation Nurses (ARN) 4700 W Lk Ave	Glenview	IL	60025	**800-229-7530**	847-375-4710	48-8
Association of Reproductive Health Professionals (ARHP) 1901 L St NW Ste 300	Washington	DC	20036	**877-311-8972**	202-466-3825	48-8
Association of School Business Officials International (ASBO) 11401 N Shore Dr	Reston	VA	20190	**866-682-2729**		48-5
Association of Schools & Colleges of Optometry (ASCO) 6110 Executive Blvd Ste 420	Rockville	MD	20852	**800-397-2424**	301-231-5944	48-8
Association of Social Work Boards (ASWB) 400 S Ridge Pkwy Ste B	Culpeper	VA	22701	**800-225-6880**	540-829-6880	48-7
Association of Specialized & Co-op Library Agencies (ASCLA) 50 E Huron St	Chicago	IL	60611	**800-545-2433**	312-280-4395	48-11
Association of Staff Physician Recruiters (ASPR) 1000 Westgate Dr Ste 252	Saint Paul	MN	55114	**800-830-2777**		48-8
Association of State Wetland Managers 32 Tandberg Trail Ste 2A	Windham	ME	04062	**800-451-6027**	207-892-3399	48-7
Association of Surgical Technologists (AST) 6 W Dry Creek Cir Ste 200	Littleton	CO	80120	**800-637-7433**	303-694-9130	48-8
Association of Test Publishers 601 Pennsylvania Ave NW Ste 900	Washington	DC	20004	**866-240-7909**		48-5
Association of the US Army (AUSA) 2425 Wilson Blvd	Arlington	VA	22201	**800-336-4570**	703-841-4300	47-19
Association of Universities for Research in Astronomy (AURA) 1200 New York Ave NW Ste 350	Washington	DC	20005	**888-624-8373**	202-483-2101	48-5
Association of University Centers on Disabilities (AUCD) 1100 Wayne Avenue Ste 1000	Silver Spring	MD	20910	**888-572-2249**	301-588-8252	48-5
Association of University Programs in Health Administration (AUPHA) 2000 N 14th St Ste 780	Arlington	VA	22201	**877-275-6462**	703-894-0941	48-8
Association of Washington Business PO Box 658	Olympia	WA	98507	**800-521-9325**	360-943-1600	139
Association of Water Technologies (AWT) 9707 Key W Ave Ste 100	Rockville	MD	20850	**800-858-6683**	301-740-1421	47-2
Association of Women's Health Obstetric & Neonatal Nurses (AWHONN) 2000 L St NW Ste 740	Washington	DC	20036	**800-673-8499**	202-261-2400	48-8
Association of Zoos & Aquariums (AZA) 8403 Colesville Rd Ste 710	Silver Spring	MD	20910	**800-323-6593**	301-562-0777	47-3
Assumption College 500 Salisbury St	Worcester	MA	01609	**888-882-7786**	508-767-7000	167
Assumption Parish 4813 Hwy 1 PO Box 520	Napoleonville	LA	70390	**800-315-9513**	985-369-7435	338
AssuranceAmerica Corp 5500 I- N Pkwy Ste 600	Atlanta	GA	30328	**800-450-7857**	770-952-0200	391-4
Assurant Employee Benefits 2323 Grand Blvd	Kansas City	MO	64108	**800-733-7879**	816-474-2345	391-2
Assurant Group 11222 Quail Roost Dr	Miami	FL	33157	**800-852-2244**	305-253-2244	360-4
Assurity Life Insurance Co PO Box 82533	Lincoln	NE	68501	**800-869-0355**	402-476-6500	390
AST (Association of Surgical Technologists) 6 W Dry Creek Cir Ste 200	Littleton	CO	80120	**800-637-7433**	303-694-9130	48-8
AST Bearings 115 Main Rd	Montville	NJ	07045	**800-526-1250**	973-335-2230	74
AST Products Inc 9 Linnell Cir	Billerica	MA	01821	**877-667-4500**	978-667-4500	480
AST Sports Science Inc 120 Capitol Dr	Golden	CO	80401	**800-627-2788**	303-278-1420	797
ASTA (American Seed Trade Assn) 1701 Duke St Ste 275	Alexandria	VA	22304	**888-890-7333**	703-837-8140	47-2
ASTA (American String Teachers Assn) 4155 Chain Bridge Rd	Fairfax	VA	22030	**800-821-7303**	703-279-2113	48-5
ASTA (American Society of Travel Agents) 1101 King St Ste 200	Alexandria	VA	22314	**800-275-2782**	703-739-2782	47-23
Asta Funding Inc 210 Sylvan Ave	Englewood Cliffs	NJ	07632	**866-389-7627**	201-567-5648	274
NASDAQ: ASFI						
Astatech Inc 2525 Pearl Buck Rd	Bristol	PA	19007	**800-387-2269**	215-785-2656	198
Astea International Inc 240 Gibraltar Rd	Horsham	PA	19044	**800-878-4657**	215-682-2500	180-1
NASDAQ: ATEA						
Astellas Pharma US Inc 1 Astellas Way	Northbrook	IL	60062	**800-695-4321**		84
AstenJohnson 4399 Corporate Rd	Charleston	SC	29405	**800-529-7990**	843-747-7800	742-3
Asthma & Allergy Foundation of America (AAFA) 8201 Corporate Dr Ste 1000	Landover	MD	20785	**800-727-8462**	202-466-7643	47-17
Asticou Inn 15 Peabody Dr	Northeast Harbor	ME	04662	**800-258-3373**	207-276-3344	379
ASTM International 100 Barr Harbor Dr PO Box C700	West Conshohocken	PA	19428	**800-814-1017**	610-832-9500	48-19
Aston Funds PO Box 9765	Providence	RI	02940	**800-992-8151**	312-268-1400	527
Aston Hotel & Resorts Sunvalley 333 S Main St	Ketchum	ID	83340	**877-997-6667**	208-622-6400	667
Aston Hotels & Resorts 2155 Kalakaua Ave Ste 500	Honolulu	HI	96815	**800-775-4228**	808-931-1400	379
Astor Crowne Plaza 739 Canal St	New Orleans	LA	70130	**877-408-9661**	504-962-0500	379
Astor Hotel, The 924 E Juneau Ave	Milwaukee	WI	53202	**800-558-0200**	414-271-4220	379
Astoria Ford 710 W Marine Dr	Astoria	OR	97103	**888-760-9303**	503-325-6411	56
Astoria-Pacific Inc 15130 SE 82nd Dr	Clackamas	OR	97015	**800-536-3111**	503-657-3010	294
AstraZeneca Canada Inc 1004 Middlegate Rd	Mississauga	ON	L4Y1M4	**800-565-5877**	905-277-7111	582
AstraZeneca Pharmaceuticals LP 1800 Concord Pk PO Box 15437	Wilmington	DE	19850	**800-236-9933**		582
Astrex Inc 205 Express St	Plainview	NY	11803	**800-633-6360**	516-433-1700	248
ASTRO (American Society for Therapeutic Radiology & Oncology) 8280 Willow Oaks Corporate Dr Ste 500	Fairfax	VA	22031	**800-962-7876**	703-502-1550	48-8
Astro Chemicals Inc 126 Memorial Dr	Springfield	MA	01104	**800-223-0776**	413-781-7240	145
Astro Industries Inc 4403 Dayton-Xenia Rd	Dayton	OH	45432	**800-543-5810**	937-429-5900	811
Astro Pak Corp 270 E Baker St Ste 100	Costa Mesa	CA	92626	**888-278-7672**	866-492-7876	740
Astrodyne Corp 375 Forbes Blvd	Mansfield	MA	02048	**800-823-8082**	508-964-6300	258
Astronomical Society of the Pacific 390 Ashton Ave	San Francisco	CA	94112	**800-335-2624**	415-337-1100	47-11
Asure Softwar 110 Wild Basin Rd	Austin	TX	78746	**888-323-8835**	512-437-2700	180-7
NASDAQ: ASUR						
ASW Global LLC 3375 Gilchrist Rd	Mogadore	OH	44260	**888-826-5087**	330-733-6291	801-1
ASWB (Association of Social Work Boards) 400 S Ridge Pkwy Ste B	Culpeper	VA	22701	**800-225-6880**	540-829-6880	48-7
AT & T Inc 175 E Houston St PO Box 2933	San Antonio	TX	78299	**800-351-7221**	210-821-4105	733
NYSE: AT&T						
AT Clayton & Co Inc 300 Atlantic St	Stamford	CT	06901	**800-282-5298**	203-658-1200	552

Company / Address	City	State	ZIP	Toll-Free	Phone	Class
At Health Inc 7829 Center Blvd SE	Snoqualmie	WA	98065	**888-284-3258**	425-292-0329	356
At Last Naturals Inc 401 Columbus Ave	Valhalla	NY	10595	**800-527-8123**		217
ATA (American Tinnitus Assn) 522 SW Fifth Ave Ste 825	Portland	OR	97204	**800-634-8978**	503-248-9985	47-17
ATA (Amateur Trapshooting Assn) 601 W National Rd	Vandalia	OH	45377	**800-671-8042**	937-898-4638	47-22
ATA (American Trucking Assn) 950 N Glebe Rd Ste 210	Arlington	VA	22203	**800-282-5463**	703-838-1700	48-21
ATA (American Translators Assn) 225 Reinekers Ln Ste 590	Alexandria	VA	22314	**800-253-2252**	703-683-6100	48-5
ATAA (Assembly of Turkish American Assn) 1526 18th St NW	Washington	DC	20036	**800-627-7692**	202-483-9090	47-14
Ataco Steel Products Corp PO Box 270	Cedarburg	WI	53012	**800-536-4822**	262-377-3000	487
ATAP Inc 130 Industry way	Eastaboga	AL	36260	**800-362-2827**	256-362-2221	469
ATAS International Inc 6612 Snowdrift Rd	Allentown	PA	18106	**800-468-1441**	610-395-8445	490
Atascadero Chamber of Commerce 6904 El Camino Real	Atascadero	CA	93422	**877-204-9830**	805-466-2044	138
Atascadero State Hospital 10333 S Camino Real	Atascadero	CA	93422	**844-210-6207**	805-468-2000	374-5
ATC (American Thermoplastic Co) 106 Gamma Dr	Pittsburgh	PA	15238	**800-245-6600**		85
ATC (Appalachian Trail Conservancy) 799 Washington St PO Box 807 *Sales	Harpers Ferry	WV	25425	**888-287-8673***	304-535-6331	47-23
ATCA (Air Traffic Control Assn) 1101 King St Ste 300	Alexandria	VA	22314	**866-953-2189**	703-299-2430	48-21
ATCC (American Type Culture Collection) 10801 University Blvd PO Box 1549 *Cust Svc	Manassas	VA	20108	**800-638-6597***	703-365-2700	666
Atchison County 405 S Main St PO Box 243	Rock Port	MO	64482	**800-989-4115**	660-744-6562	338
Atchison-Holt Electric Co-op 18585 Industrial Rd PO Box 160	Rock Port	MO	64482	**888-744-5366**	660-744-5344	247
ATCO Ltd 700 909 11th Ave SW *TSE: ACO/X*	Calgary	AB	T2R1N6	**800-242-3447**	403-292-7500	785
Atco Rubber Products Inc 7101 Atco Dr	Fort Worth	TX	76118	**800-877-3828**	817-595-2894	370
ATD-American Co 135 Greenwood Ave	Wyncote	PA	19095	**866-283-9327**	215-576-1380	321
ATEL Capital Group 600 California St 6th Fl	San Francisco	CA	94108	**800-543-2835**	415-989-8800	218
Aten Technology Inc 23 Hubble	Irvine	CA	92618	**888-999-2836**	949-428-1111	175-2
AT&F (American Tank & Fabricating Co) 12314 Elmwood Ave	Cleveland	OH	44111	**800-544-5316**	216-252-1500	721
ATG Technologies Inc 2639 N Monroe St Cedars Bldg B Ste 200	Tallahassee	FL	32303	**800-775-7790**		393
Athabasca University 1 University Dr	Athabasca	AB	T9S3A3	**800-788-9041**	780-675-6111	783
Athana Inc 1624 W 240 St	Harbor City	CA	90710	**800-421-1591**	310-539-7280	656
Athea Laboratories Inc 1900 W Cornell St	Milwaukee	WI	53209	**800-743-6417**		144
Athena Controls Inc 5145 Campus Dr	Plymouth Meeting	PA	19462	**800-782-6776**	610-828-2490	203
Athena Diagnostics Inc 377 Plantation St 2nd Fl	Worcester	MA	01605	**800-394-4493**	508-756-2886	233
Athena Engineering Inc 456 E Foothill Blvd	San Dimas	CA	91773	**877-777-4778**	909-599-0947	191-4
athenahealth Inc 311 Arsenal St *NASDAQ: ATHN*	Watertown	MA	02472	**800-981-5084**	617-402-1000	180-1
Atheneum Suite Hotel & Conference Ctr 1000 Brush Ave	Detroit	MI	48226	**800-772-2323**	313-962-2323	379
Athens Area Chamber of Commerce 449 E State St Ste 1	Athens	OH	45701	**877-360-3608**	740-594-2251	138
Athens Banner-Herald 1 Press Pl	Athens	GA	30601	**800-533-4252**	706-549-0123	531-2
Athens Convention & Visitors Bureau 300 N Thomas St	Athens	GA	30601	**800-653-0603**	706-357-4430	208
Athens County Convention & Visitors Bureau 667 E State St	Athens	OH	45701	**800-878-9767**	740-592-1819	208
Athens Pastries & Frozen Foods Inc 13600 Snow Rd	Brookpark	OH	44142	**800-837-5683**	216-676-8500	297-2
Athens Services 14048 Valley Blvd	La Puente	CA	91746	**888-336-6100**	626-336-3636	802
Athens State Bank 6530 N State Rt 29	Springfield	IL	62707	**800-367-7576**	217-487-7766	69
Atherotech Inc 201 London Pkwy	Birmingham	AL	35211	**800-719-9807**		418
Atherton Baptist Homes 214 S Atlantic Blvd	Alhambra	CA	91801	**800-340-4178**	626-863-1224	670
Athletic Supply Co 16101 NE 87th St	Redmond	WA	98052	**800-732-9259**	425-882-1456	709
ATI Allegheny Ludlum Corp 100 River Rd *Sales	Brackenridge	PA	15014	**800-258-3586***	724-224-1000	721
ATI Metal Working Products 1 Teledyne Pl	La Vergne	TN	37086	**888-926-4211**	615-641-4200	492
ATIS (Alliance for Telecommunications Industry Solutions) 1200 G St NW Ste 500	Washington	DC	20005	**800-649-1202**	202-628-6380	48-20
Atiwa Computer Leasing Exchange 6950 Portwest Dr Ste 100	Houston	TX	77024	**800-428-2532**	713-467-9390	181
Atkins & Pearce Inc 1 Braid Way	Covington	KY	41017	**800-837-7477**	859-356-2001	210
Atkins Nutritionals Inc 1050 17th St Ste 1000	Denver	CO	80265	**800-628-5467**	303-633-2840	797
Atkinson Candy Co 1608 W Frank Ave	Lufkin	TX	75904	**800-231-1203**	936-639-2333	297-8
Atkinson Conway & Gagnon Inc 420 L St Ste 500	Anchorage	AK	99501	**800-478-1900**	907-276-1700	428
Atkinson County School System 98 Roberts Ave E	Pearson	GA	31642	**800-639-0850**	912-422-7373	683
Atkinson-Baker Inc (ABI) 500 N Brand Blvd 3rd Fl	Glendale	CA	91203	**800-288-3376**	818-551-7300	444
ATLA (American Theological Library Assn) 300 S Wacker Dr Ste 2100	Chicago	IL	60606	**888-665-2852**	312-454-5100	47-20
Atlanta Attachment Co Inc 362 Industrial Pk Dr	Lawrenceville	GA	30045	**877-206-5116**	770-963-7369	35
Atlanta Braves PO Box 4064	Atlanta	GA	30302	**800-326-4000**	404-522-7630	711
Atlanta Cutlery Corp 2147 Gees Mill Rd	Conyers	GA	30013	**800-883-0300**	770-922-3700	224
Atlanta Fixture & Sales Co 3185 NE Expy	Atlanta	GA	30341	**800-282-1977**	770-455-8844	301
Atlanta Hardwood Corp 5596 Riverview Rd SE	Mableton	GA	30126	**800-476-5393**	404-792-2290	364
Atlanta Hospital Hospitality House 1815 S Ponce De Leon Ave NE	Atlanta	GA	30307	**855-286-9658**	404-377-6333	372
Atlanta Motor Speedway PO Box 500	Hampton	GA	30228	**877-926-7849**	770-946-4211	514
Atlanta Petroleum Equipment Co 4732 N Royal Atlanta Dr	Tucker	GA	30084	**800-562-4060**	770-491-6644	538
Atlanta Postal Credit Union 501 Pulliam St SW Ste 350	Atlanta	GA	30312	**800-849-8431**	404-768-4126	221
Atlanta's DeKalb Convention & Visitors Bureau 1957 Lakeside Pkwy Ste 510	Tucker	GA	30084	**800-999-6055**	770-492-5000	208
Atlantech Online Inc 1010 Wayne Ave Ste 630	Silver Spring	MD	20910	**800-256-1612**	301-589-3060	227
Atlantic Bay Mortgage Group 596 Lynnhaven Pkwy Ste 102	Virginia Beach	VA	23452	**866-877-3143**	757-213-1660	216
Atlantic British Ltd Halfmoon Light Industrial Pk 6 Enterprise Ave	Clifton Park	NY	12065	**800-533-2210**	518-664-6169	56
Atlantic Bulk Carrier Corp PO Box 112	Providence Forge	VA	23140	**800-966-0030**	804-966-5459	448
Atlantic Center For The Arts Inc 1414 Art Ctr Ave	New Smyrna Beach	FL	32168	**800-393-6975**	386-427-6975	328
Atlantic City Convention & Visitors Authority 2314 Pacific Ave	Atlantic City	NJ	08401	**888-228-4748**	609-348-7100	208
Atlantic City Free Public Library 1 N Tennessee Ave	Atlantic City	NJ	08401	**800-621-3362**	609-345-2269	434-3
Atlantic Coast Bank (ACFC) 505 Haines Ave *NASDAQ: ACFC*	Waycross	GA	31501	**800-342-2824**	912-283-4711	360-2
Atlantic Concrete Products Inc 8900 Old Rt 13	Tullytown	PA	19007	**800-988-7837**	215-945-5600	185
Atlantic Construction Fabrics Inc 2831 CaRdwell Rd	Richmond	VA	23234	**800-448-3636**	804-271-2363	192
Atlantic Container Line (ACL) 50 Cardinal Dr	Westfield	NJ	07090	**800-225-1235**	908-518-5300	314
Atlantic Council of the United States 1101 15th St NW 11th Fl	Washington	DC	20005	**800-311-9410**	202-463-7226	631
Atlantic Credit & Finance Inc 2727 Franklin Rd	Roanoke	VA	24014	**800-888-9419**	540-772-7800	159
Atlantic Eyrie Lodge 6 Norman Rd	Bar Harbor	ME	04609	**800-422-2883**		379
Atlantic Gasket Corp 3908 Frankford Ave	Philadelphia	PA	19124	**800-229-8881**	215-533-6400	327
Atlantic India Rubber Co 1437 Kentucky Rt 1428	Hagerhill	KY	41222	**800-476-6638**	606-789-9115	675
Atlantic Information Services Inc 1100 17th St NW Ste 300	Washington	DC	20036	**800-521-4323**	202-775-9008	634-9
Atlantic International University 900 Ft St Mall	Honolulu	HI	96813	**800-993-0066**	808-924-9567	167
Atlantic Lift Truck Inc 2945 Whittington Ave	Baltimore	MD	21230	**800-638-4566**	410-644-7777	385
Atlantic Monthly Magazine 600 New Hampshire Ave NW *Cust Svc	Washington	DC	20037	**800-234-2411***	202-266-6000	456-11
Atlantic Oakes 119 Eden St	Bar Harbor	ME	04609	**800-356-3585**	207-288-5801	667
Atlantic Packaging Co 806 N 23rd St	Wilmington	NC	28405	**800-722-5841**	910-343-0624	552
Atlantic Paper & Twine Co Inc 85 York Ave	Pawtucket	RI	02904	**800-613-0950**	401-725-0950	558
Atlantic Personnel Search Inc 9624 Pennsylvania Ave	Upper Marlboro	MD	20772	**877-229-5254**	301-599-2108	195
Atlantic Premium Shutters 29797 Beck Rd	Wixom	MI	48393	**866-288-2726**	248-668-6408	697
Atlantic Publishing Co 315 E Washington St	Starke	FL	32091	**800-814-1132**		634-2
Atlantic Relocation Systems Inc 1314 Chattahoochee Ave NW *Cust Svc	Atlanta	GA	30318	**800-241-1140***	404-351-5311	518
Atlantic Salmon Federation (ASF) PO Box 5200	Saint Andrews	NB	E5B3S8	**800-565-5666**	506-529-1033	47-3
Atlantic Sands Hotel 101 N Boardwalk	Rehoboth Beach	DE	19971	**800-422-0600**	302-227-2511	379
Atlantic Spas & Billiards 8721 Glenwood Ave	Raleigh	NC	27617	**800-849-8827**	919-783-7447	375
Atlantic Spring PO Box 650	Flemington	NJ	08822	**877-231-6474**	908-788-5800	717
Atlantic Track & Turnout Co 270 N Broad St	Bloomfield	NJ	07003	**800-631-1274**	973-748-5885	768
Atlantic Trust 100 E Pratt St 23rd Fl	Baltimore	MD	21202	**866-644-4144**	410-539-4660	401
Atlantic Union College 338 Main St	South Lancaster	MA	01561	**800-282-2030**	978-368-2000	167
Atlantica Hotel & Marina Oak Island 36 Treasure Dr PO Box 6	Western Shore	NS	B0J3M0	**800-565-5075**	902-627-2600	667
Atlantis Casino Resort 3800 S Virginia St	Reno	NV	89502	**800-723-6500**	775-825-4700	667
Atlantis Seafood Steakhouse 3800 S Virginia St Atlantis Casino Resort	Reno	NV	89502	**800-723-6500**		669

Company	Address	City	State	ZIP	Toll-Free	Phone	Class
Atlantix Global Systems	1 Sun Ct	Norcross	GA	30092	**877-552-8526**	770-248-7700	176
Atlas Air Worldwide Holdings Inc	2000 Westchester Ave *NASDAQ: AAWW*	Purchase	NY	10577	**866-434-1617**	914-701-8000	12
Atlas Bolt & Screw Co	1628 Troy Rd	Ashland	OH	44805	**800-321-6977**	419-289-6171	280
Atlas Brown Investment Advisors Inc	333 E Main St - 400	Louisville	KY	40202	**866-871-0334**	502-271-2900	196
Atlas Carpet Mills Inc	2200 Saybrook Ave	Los Angeles	CA	90040	**800-272-8527**	323-724-9000	130
Atlas Construction Supply Inc	4640 Brinnell St	San Diego	CA	92111	**877-588-2100**	858-277-2100	193-1
Atlas Container Corp	8140 Telegraph Rd	Severn	MD	21144	**800-394-4894**	410-551-6300	99
Atlas Copco North America LLC	7 Campus Dr Ste 200	Parsippany	NJ	07054	**800-732-6762**	973-397-3432	360-3
Atlas Copco Tools & Assembly Systems	2998 Dutton Rd	Auburn Hills	MI	48326	**800-859-3746**	248-373-3000	757
Atlas Distributing Corp	44 Southbridge St	Auburn	MA	01501	**800-649-6221**	508-791-6221	80-1
Atlas Match LLC	1801 S Airport Cir	Euless	TX	76040	**800-628-2426**	817-267-1500	9
Atlas Metal Industries	1135 NW 159th Dr *Cust Svc	Miami	FL	33169	**800-762-7565***	305-625-2451	299
Atlas Minerals & Chemicals Inc	1227 Valley Rd *Cust Svc	Mertztown	PA	19539	**800-523-8269***	610-682-7171	3
Atlas Model Railroad Company Inc	378 Florence Ave *Orders	Hillside	NJ	07205	**800-872-2521***	908-687-0880	760
Atlas Oil Co	24501 Ecorse Rd	Taylor	MI	48180	**800-878-2000**	313-292-5500	578
Atlas Pacific Engineering Co	1 Atlas Ave	Pueblo	CO	81001	**800-588-5438**	719-948-3040	299
Atlas Paper Mills LLC	3301 NW 107th St	Miami	FL	33167	**800-562-2860**	305-636-5740	557
Atlas Roofing Corp	2322 Valley Rd *Cust Svc	Meridian	MS	39307	**800-478-0258***	601-483-7111	45
Atlas Roofing Falcon Foam Div	8240 Byron Ctr Rd SW	Byron Center	MI	49315	**800-917-9138**		599
Atlas Sound	1601 Jack McKay Blvd	Ennis	TX	75119	**800-876-3333**	972-875-8413	51
Atlas Steel Products Co	7990 Bavaria Rd	Twinsburg	OH	44087	**800-444-1682**	330-425-1600	491
Atlas Systems Inc	5712 Cleveland St Ste 200	Virginia Beach	VA	23462	**800-567-7401**	757-467-7872	179
Atlas Tube	1855 E 122nd St	Chicago	IL	60633	**800-733-5683**	773-646-4500	489
Atlas Van Lines Inc	1212 St George Rd	Evansville	IN	47711	**800-638-9797**	812-424-2222	518
Atlas Water Systems Inc	301 Second Ave	Waltham	MA	02451	**888-877-0561**	781-373-4700	804
Atlas World Group Inc	1212 St George Rd	Evansville	IN	47711	**800-252-8885**	812-424-2222	360-3
Atm Merchant Systems	1667 Helm Dr	Las Vegas	NV	89119	**888-878-8166**	702-837-8787	68
Atmos Energy Corp	5430 LBJ Fwy Ste 1800 *NYSE: ATO*	Dallas	TX	75240	**888-286-6700**	972-934-9227	360-5
ATO (Alpha Tau Omega Fraternity)	1 N Pennsylvania St 12th Fl	Indianapolis	IN	46204	**800-798-9286**	317-684-1865	47-16
Atomic USA	2030 Lincoln Ave	Ogden	UT	84401	**800-258-5020**		708
Atom-Jet Industries Ltd	2110 Park Ave	Brandon	MB	R7B0R9	**800-573-5048**	204-728-8590	275
ATRA (Automatic Transmission Rebuilders Assn)	2400 Latigo Ave	Oxnard	CA	93030	**866-464-2872**	805-604-2000	48-21
ATRA (American Therapeutic Recreation Assn)	629 N Main St	Hattiesburg	MS	39401	**800-433-5255**	601-450-2872	47-17
ATRA (American Tort Reform Assn)	1101 Connecticut Ave NW Ste 400	Washington	DC	20036	**877-333-2227**	202-682-1163	48-10
Atrex Inc	175 Industrial Loop S	Orange Park	FL	32073	**800-874-4505**	904-264-9086	645
AtriCure Inc	6217 Centre Pk Dr *NASDAQ: ATRC*	West Chester	OH	45069	**888-347-6403**	513-755-4100	84
Atrion Networking Corp	30 Service Ave	Warwick	RI	02886	**800-890-4526**	401-736-6400	198
Atris Inc	1151 S Trooper Rd Ste E	Norristown	PA	19403	**800-724-3384**		732
Atrium Hotel	18700 MacArthur Blvd	Irvine	CA	92612	**800-854-3012**	949-833-2770	379
Atrium Medical Corp	5 Wentworth Dr	Hudson	NH	03051	**800-528-7486**	603-880-1433	475
Atrium Medical Ctr	1 Medical Ctr Dr	Middletown	OH	45005	**800-338-4057**	513-424-2111	374-3
ATS (American Thoracic Society)	61 Broadway 4th Fl	New York	NY	10006	**866-316-2673**	212-315-8600	48-8
Ats All Tire Supply Co	6600 Long Point Rd Ste 101	Houston	TX	77055	**888-339-6665**		53
ATS Systems Inc	30222 Esperanza	Rancho Santa Margarita	CA	92688	**800-321-1833**	949-888-1744	695
Ats Systems Oregon Inc	2121 NE Jack London St	Corvallis	OR	97330	**800-564-6253**	541-758-3329	386
ATS Tours	300 Continental Blvd Ste 350	El Segundo	CA	90245	**888-410-5770**		758
ATSSA (American Traffic Safety Services Assn)	15 Riverside Pkwy Ste 100	Fredericksburg	VA	22406	**800-272-8772**	540-368-1701	48-21
AT&T Ctr	1 AT&T Ctr Pkwy *Resv	San Antonio	TX	78219	**800-745-3000***	210-444-5000	718
AttachmateWRQ	1500 Dexter Ave N *Sales	Seattle	WA	98109	**800-872-2829***	206-217-7500	180-1
Attain Capital Management LLC	1 E Wacker Dr 30th Fl	Chicago	IL	60601	**800-311-1145**	312-604-0926	401
Attendee Management Inc	15572 Ranch Rd 12 Ste 1	Wimberley	TX	78676	**877-947-5174**	512-847-5174	623
AtticSalt Greetings Inc	PO Box 5773	Topeka	KS	66605	**888-345-6005**		129
Attorney Aid Divorce & Bankruptcy Center Inc	3605 Long Beach Blvd Ste 300	Long Beach	CA	90807	**877-905-5297**	562-988-0885	428
Attorney's Title Insurance Fund Inc	6545 Corporate Ctr Blvd	Orlando	FL	32822	**800-336-3863**	407-240-3863	391-6
Attraction Inc	672 Rue du Parc	Lac-Drolet	QC	G0Y1C0	**800-567-6095**	819-549-2477	154-3
Attunity Inc	70 BlanchaRd Rd	Burlington	MA	01803	**866-288-8648**	781-730-4070	180-1
Attwood Corp	1016 N Monroe St	Lowell	MI	49331	**844-808-5704**	616-897-9241	350
ATU (Amalgamated Transit Union)	10000 New Hampshire Ave	Silver Spring	MD	20903	**888-240-1196**	202-537-1645	414
ATW (American Trails West)	92 Middle Neck Rd	Great Neck	NY	11021	**800-645-6260**	516-487-2800	758
Atwater Chamber of Commerce	1181 Third St	Atwater	CA	95301	**844-269-9688**	209-358-4251	138
Atwood Mobile Products	1120 N Main St	Elkhart	IN	46514	**800-546-8759**	574-264-2131	59
ATX Networks Corp	1-501 Clements Rd W	Ajax	ON	L1S7H4	**800-565-7488**	905-428-6068	645
Au Naturel Wellness & Medical Spa at the Brookstreet Hotel	525 Legget Dr	Ottawa	ON	K2K2W2	**888-826-2220**	613-271-1800	705
Au Sable Woodworking Co	PO Box 108	Frederic	MI	49733	**800-248-9261**	989-348-7086	775
AUA (American Urological Assn)	1000 Corporate Blvd	Linthicum	MD	21090	**866-746-4282**	410-689-3700	48-8
Auberge De La Fontaine b & b Inn	1301 Rue Rachel E	Montreal	QC	H2J2K1	**800-597-0597**	514-597-0166	705
Auberge du Soleil	180 Rutherford Hill Rd	Rutherford	CA	94573	**800-348-5406**	707-963-1211	379
Auberge du Tresor	20 Rue Sainte-Anne	Quebec	QC	G1R3X2	**800-566-1876**	418-694-1876	669
Auberge du Vieux-Port	97 Rue de la Commune E	Montreal	QC	H2Y1J1	**888-660-7678**	514-876-0081	379
Auberge et spa Le Nordik Inc	16 ch Nordik	Old Chelsea	QC	J9B2P7	**866-575-3700**	819-827-1111	354
Auberge Saint-Antoine	8 rue Saint-Antoine	Quebec	QC	G1K4C9	**888-692-2211**	418-692-2211	379
Auburn Area Chamber of Commerce	601 Lincoln Way	Auburn	CA	95603	**800-310-2355**	530-885-5616	138
Auburn City School District	PO Box 3270	Auburn	AL	36831	**866-632-9992**	334-887-2100	683
Auburn Corp	10490 164th Pl	Orland Park	IL	60467	**800-393-1826**	708-349-7676	193-3
Auburn Leather Co	125 N Caldwell St	Auburn	KY	42206	**800-635-0617**	270-542-4116	431
Auburn Manufacturing Co	29 Stack St	Middletown	CT	06457	**800-427-5387**	860-346-6677	327
Auburn Publishers Inc	25 Dill St	Auburn	NY	13021	**800-878-5311**	315-253-5311	634-8
Auburn Regional Medical Ctr	202 N Div St Plaza 1	Auburn	WA	98001	**866-268-7223**	253-833-7711	374-3
Auburn Systems LLC	8 Electronics Ave	Danvers	MA	01923	**800-255-5008**	978-777-2460	203
Auburn University	202 Mary Martin Hall *Admissions	Auburn University	AL	36849	**866-389-6770***	334-844-6425	167
Montgomery	7440 E Dr	Montgomery	AL	36117	**800-227-2649**	334-244-3000	167
Auburn-Opelika Tourism Bureau	714 E Glenn Ave	Auburn	AL	36830	**866-880-8747**	334-887-8747	208
AUCD (Association of University Centers on Disabilities)	1100 Wayne Avenue Ste 1000	Silver Spring	MD	20910	**888-572-2249**	301-588-8252	48-5
Aucoin-Hart	1525 Metairie Rd	Metairie	LA	70005	**800-992-8743**	504-834-9999	410
Audi of America	3800 Hamlin Rd	Auburn Hills	MI	48326	**888-237-2834**		58
Audible Inc	1 Washington Pk	Newark	NJ	07102	**888-283-5051**	973-820-0400	395
Audio Advisor	3427 Kraft Ave SE	Grand Rapids	MI	49512	**800-942-0220**	616-254-8870	196
Audio Authority Corp	2048 Mercer Rd	Lexington	KY	40511	**800-322-8346**	859-233-4599	387
Audio Command Systems	694 Main St	Westbury	NY	11590	**800-382-2939**	516-997-5800	51
Audio Direct	2004 E Irvington Rd Ste 264 *Cust Svc	Tucson	AZ	85714	**888-628-3467***		34
Audio Engineering Society	60 E 42nd St Rm 2520	New York	NY	10165	**800-541-7299**	212-661-8528	48-19
Audio General Inc (AGI)	1680 Republic Rd	Huntingdon Valley	PA	19006	**866-866-2600**	267-288-0300	513
Audio Video Systems Inc	14120 Sullyfield Cir	Chantilly	VA	20151	**877-287-1175**	703-263-1002	513
Audio-Digest Foundation	1577 E Chevy Chase Dr	Glendale	CA	91206	**800-423-2308**	818-240-7500	764
AudioQuest Inc	2621 White Rd	Irvine	CA	92614	**800-747-2770**	949-585-0111	255
Audiosears Corp	2 S St	Stamford	NY	12167	**800-533-7863**	607-652-7305	51
Audio-technica Us Inc	1221 Commerce Dr	Stow	OH	44224	**800-667-3745**	330-686-2600	248
Audiovox Corp	180 Marcus Blvd *NASDAQ: VOXX*	Hauppauge	NY	11788	**800-645-4994**	631-231-7750	51
Audit & Adjustment Company Inc	20700 44th Ave W Ste 100	Lynnwood	WA	98036	**800-526-1074**	425-776-9797	534

Name / Address	City	State	Zip	Toll-Free	Phone	Class
Audit Bureau of Circulations (ABC)						
48 W Seegers Rd	Arlington Heights	IL	60005	**800-759-6397**	224-366-6939	48-18
Auditorium Theatre						
50 E Congress Pkwy	Chicago	IL	60605	**800-982-2787**	312-341-2310	571
Audubon Magazine						
225 Varick St 7th Fl	New York	NY	10014	**800-274-4201***	212-979-3000	456-19
*Cust Svc						
Audubon Naturalist Society						
8940 Jones Mill Rd	Chevy Chase	MD	20815	**888-744-4723**	301-652-9188	47-13
Audubon Nature Institute						
6500 Magazine St	New Orleans	LA	70118	**800-774-7394**	504-581-4629	821
Auer Steel & Heating Supply Co						
2935 W Silver Spring Dr	Milwaukee	WI	53209	**800-242-0406**	414-463-1234	14
Auglaize & Mercer Counties Convention & Visitors Bureau						
900 Edgewater Dr	Saint Marys	OH	45885	**800-860-4726**	419-394-1294	208
Auglaize County						
209 S Blackhoof St Ste 201	Wapakoneta	OH	45895	**877-836-3206**	419-739-6710	338
Augsburg College						
2211 Riverside Ave	Minneapolis	MN	55454	**800-788-5678**	612-330-1000	167
Augsburg Fortress Publishers						
510 Marquette Ave Ste 800	Minneapolis	MN	55402	**800-426-0115**	612-330-3300	634-3
August Inc						
354 Congress Park Dr	Centerville	OH	45459	**800-318-5242**	937-434-2520	322
August Winter & Sons Inc						
2323 N Roemer Rd	Appleton	WI	54911	**800-236-8882**	920-739-8881	191-13
Augusta Chronicle						
725 Broad St	Augusta	GA	30901	**866-249-8223**	706-724-0851	531-2
Augusta Medical Ctr (AMC)						
78 Medical Ctr Dr						
PO Box 1000	Fishersville	VA	22939	**800-932-0262**	540-932-4000	374-3
Augusta Metro Chamber of Commerce						
1 10th St Ste 120	Augusta	GA	30901	**888-639-8188**	706-821-1300	138
Augusta Metropolitan Convention & Visitors Bureau						
1450 Greene St Ste 560	Augusta	GA	30901	**800-726-0243**	706-823-6600	208
Augusta Regional Airport - Bush Field (AGS)						
1501 Aviation Way	Augusta	GA	30906	**866-289-9673**	706-798-3236	27
Augusta State Airport						
75 Airport Rd	Augusta	ME	04330	**800-654-3131**	207-626-2306	27
Augusta State University						
2500 Walton Way	Augusta	GA	30904	**800-341-4373**	706-737-1632	167
Augustana College						
639 38th St	Rock Island	IL	61201	**800-798-8100**	309-794-7000	167
Augustine Casino						
84-001 Ave 54	Coachella	CA	92236	**888-752-9294**	760-391-9500	132
AUPHA (Association of University Programs in Health Administration)						
2000 N 14th St Ste 780	Arlington	VA	22201	**877-275-6462**	703-894-0941	48-8
AURA (Association of Universities for Research in Astronomy)						
1200 New York Ave NW Ste 350	Washington	DC	20005	**888-624-8373**	202-483-2101	48-5
Aura Systems Inc						
1310 E Grand Ave	El Segundo	CA	90245	**800-909-2872**	310-643-5300	517
OTC: AUSI						
Auragan LLC						
PO Box 1501	New Canaan	CT	06840	**866-644-2872**		733
Aureole						
135 W 42nd St	New York	NY	10036	**800-889-7188**	212-319-1660	669
Aurico Reports Inc						
116 W Eastman St	Arlington Heights	IL	60004	**866-255-1852**		400
Aurora Area Convention & Visitors Bureau						
43 W Galena Blvd	Aurora	IL	60506	**800-477-4369**	630-897-5581	208
Aurora Chamber of Commerce						
43 W Galena Blvd	Aurora	IL	60506	**866-947-8081**	630-256-3180	138
Aurora Contractors Inc						
100 Raynor Ave	Ronkonkoma	NY	11779	**866-423-2197**	631-981-3785	609
Aurora Co-op Elevator Co						
605 12th St PO Box 209	Aurora	NE	68818	**800-642-6795**	402-694-2106	277
Aurora Corp of America						
3500 Challenger St	Torrance	CA	90503	**800-327-8508**	310-793-5650	533
Aurora Las Encinas Hospital						
2900 E Del Mar Blvd	Pasadena	CA	91107	**800-792-2345**	626-795-9901	374-5
Aurora National Life Assurance Co						
PO Box 4490	Hartford	CT	06147	**800-265-2652**		391-2
Aurora Networks Inc						
5400 Betsy Ross Dr	Santa Clara	CA	95054	**888-287-6726**	408-235-7000	732
Aurora Pictures Inc						
5249 Chicago Ave	Minneapolis	MN	55417	**800-346-9487**	612-821-6490	513
Aurora Sentinel						
14305 E Alameda Ave Ste 200	Aurora	CO	80012	**855-269-4484**	303-750-7555	531-4
Aurora Sinai Medical Ctr						
945 N 12th St	Milwaukee	WI	53201	**888-863-5502**	414-219-2000	374-3
Aurora Textile Finishing Co						
911 N Lake St PO Box 70	Aurora	IL	60507	**800-864-0303**	630-892-7651	742-7
Aurora University						
347 S Gladstone Ave	Aurora	IL	60506	**800-742-5281**	630-844-5533	167
Aurora VNA Zilber Family Hospice						
1155 N Honey Creek Pkwy	Wauwatosa	WI	53213	**888-206-6955**	414-615-5900	371
Aurum Ceramic Dental Laboratories Ltd						
115 17 Ave SW	Calgary	AB	T2S0A1	**800-665-8815**	403-228-5120	418
AUSA (Association of the US Army)						
2425 Wilson Blvd	Arlington	VA	22201	**800-336-4570**	703-841-4300	47-19
Auspex Pharmaceuticals Inc						
3333 N Torrey Pines Court						
Ste 400	La Jolla	CA	92037	**800-487-7671**	858-558-2400	240
Austad's Golf						
2801 E 10th St	Sioux Falls	SD	57103	**800-444-1234***	605-331-4653	709
*Cust Svc						
Aus-Tex Printing & Mailing						
2431 Forbes Dr	Austin	TX	78754	**800-472-7581**	512-476-7581	626
Austin American-Statesman						
305 S Congress Ave	Austin	TX	78704	**800-445-9898**	512-445-4040	531-2
Austin Chronicle						
PO Box 49066	Austin	TX	78765	**866-271-4900**	512-454-5766	531-5
Austin College						
900 N Grand Ave	Sherman	TX	75090	**866-776-0056**	903-813-3000	167
Austin Community College (ACC)						
5930 Middle Fiskville Rd	Austin	TX	78752	**877-442-3522**	512-223-7000	161
Eastview						
3401 Webberville Rd	Austin	TX	78702	**888-626-1697**	512-223-5100	161
Northridge						
11928 Stonehollow Dr	Austin	TX	78758	**877-990-0462**	512-223-4000	161
Pinnacle						
7748 Hwy 290 W	Austin	TX	78736	**888-626-1697**	512-223-8001	161
Rio Grande						
1212 Rio Grande St	Austin	TX	78701	**877-990-0462**	512-223-3000	161
Riverside						
1020 Grove Blvd	Austin	TX	78741	**877-990-0462**	512-223-6000	161
Austin Convention & Visitors Bureau						
301 Congress Ave Ste 200	Austin	TX	78701	**800-926-2282**	512-474-5171	208
Austin Film Festival						
1801 Salina St Ste 210	Austin	TX	78702	**800-310-3378**	512-478-4795	284
Austin Graduate School of Theology						
7640 Guadalupe St	Austin	TX	78752	**866-287-4723**	512-476-2772	167
Austin Hotel & Spa						
305 Malvern Ave	Hot Springs	AR	71901	**877-623-6697**	501-623-6600	379
Austin Industrial Inc						
2801 E 13th S PO Box 87888	La Porte	TX	77571	**866-308-2592**	713-641-3400	190-9
Austin Peay State University						
601 College St	Clarksville	TN	37044	**800-844-2778***	931-221-7661	167
*Admissions						
Austin Powder Co						
25800 Science Pk Dr Ste 300	Cleveland	OH	44122	**800-321-0752**	216-464-2400	270
Austin Pump & Supply Co						
PO Box 17037	Austin	TX	78760	**800-252-9692**	512-442-2348	385
Austin Ribbon & Computer Supplies Inc (ARC)						
9211 Waterford Centre Blvd						
Ste 202	Austin	TX	78758	**800-783-7459**	512-452-0651	196
Austin State Hospital						
4110 Guadalupe St	Austin	TX	78751	**866-407-3773**	512-452-0381	374-5
Austin Symphony Orchestra						
1101 Red River St	Austin	TX	78701	**888-462-3787**	512-476-6064	572-3
AustinMohawk & Company Inc						
2175 Beechgrove Pl	Utica	NY	13501	**800-765-3110**	315-793-3000	90
Australia						
Consulate General						
1000 Bishop St PH	Honolulu	HI	96813	**866-343-3086**	808-529-8100	259
Embassy						
2005 Massachusetts Ave NW	Washington	DC	20036	**800-345-6541**	202-558-2216	259
Austria						
Consulate General						
11859 Wilshire Blvd Ste 501	Los Angeles	CA	90025	**800-255-2414**	310-444-9310	259
Embassy						
3524 International Ct NW	Washington	DC	20008	**800-255-2414**	202-895-6700	259
Authentic Pine Floors Inc						
4042 Hwy 42	Locust Grove	GA	30248	**800-283-6038**		750
Authentix Inc						
4355 Excel Pkwy Ste 100	Addison	TX	75001	**866-434-1402**	469-737-4400	690
Author House						
1663 Liberty Dr Ste 200	Bloomington	IN	47403	**888-728-8467**	812-339-6000	634-2
Authorize.Net Corp						
PO Box 8999	San Francisco	CA	94128	**877-447-3938**	801-492-6450	180-7
Autism Research Institute (ARI)						
4182 Adams Ave	San Diego	CA	92116	**866-366-3361**	619-281-7165	47-17
Autism Society of America (ASA)						
4340 EW Hwy Ste 350	Bethesda	MD	20814	**800-328-8476**	301-657-0881	47-17
Autistic Treatment Center Inc						
10503 Metric Dr	Dallas	TX	75243	**877-666-2747**	972-644-2076	147
Auto Club Ltd						
PO Box 162526	Austin	TX	78716	**866-247-3728**		52
Auto Club of America Corp (ACA)						
9411 N Georgia St	Oklahoma City	OK	73120	**800-411-2007**	405-751-4430	52
Auto Club Speedway						
9300 Cherry Ave	Fontana	CA	92335	**800-944-7223**	909-429-5000	514
Auto Crane Co						
PO Box 580697	Tulsa	OK	74158	**888-848-5445**	918-836-0463	515
Auto Data Direct Inc						
1379 Cross Creek Cir	Tallahassee	FL	32301	**866-923-3123**	850-877-8804	226
Auto Europe						
39 Commercial St	Portland	ME	04101	**800-223-5555**	207-842-2000	125
Auto Export Shipping Inc						
187 Mill Ln Ste 103	Mountainside	NJ	07092	**800-829-4933**	908-436-2150	94
Auto FX Software						
141 Village St Ste 2	Birmingham	AL	35242	**800-839-2008**	205-980-0056	180-8
Auto Lenders Liquidation Center						
104 Rt 73	Voorhees	NJ	08043	**888-305-5968**		56
Auto Meter Products Inc						
413 W Elm St	Sycamore	IL	60178	**866-248-6356**	815-895-8141	494
Auto Profit Masters						
250 E Dry Creek Rd	Littleton	CO	80122	**866-826-7911**	303-795-5838	462
Auto Truck Inc						
1420 Brewster Creek Blvd	Bartlett	IL	60103	**877-284-4440**	630-860-5600	515
Autobahn Freight Lines Ltd						
27 Automatic Rd	Brampton	ON	L6S5N8	**877-989-9994**	416-741-5454	312
Autobell Car Wash Inc						
1521 E Third St	Charlotte	NC	28204	**800-582-8096**	704-527-9274	61-1
Autobytel Inc						
18872 MacArthur Blvd	Irvine	CA	92612	**888-422-8999**	949-225-4500	57
NASDAQ: ABTL						
Autocam Corp						
4070 E Paris Ave	Kentwood	MI	49512	**800-747-6978**	616-698-0707	59
Autocrat Coffee Inc						
10 Blackstone Vly Pl	Lincoln	RI	02865	**800-288-6272**	401-333-3300	297-7
Autodesk Inc						
111 McInnis Pkwy	San Rafael	CA	94903	**800-964-6432***	415-507-5000	180-5
NASDAQ: ADSK ■ *Tech Supp						
Autofusion Corp						
6215 Ferris Sq Ste 200	San Diego	CA	92121	**800-410-7354**	858-270-9444	57
Auto-Graphics Inc						
430 N Vineyard Ave	Ontario	CA	91764	**800-776-6939**	909-595-7004	779
Autoland						
170 Rt 22 E	Springfield	NJ	07081	**877-813-7239***	973-467-2900	56
*Sales						
Automated Bldg Components Inc						
2359 Grant Rd	North Baltimore	OH	45872	**800-837-2152**	419-257-2152	815
Automated Medical Systems Inc						
2310 N Patterson St Bldg H	Valdosta	GA	31602	**800-256-3240**		181

Name / Address	City	State	Zip	Toll-Free	Phone	Class
Automated Packaging Systems Inc 10175 Phillip Pkwy *Sales	Streetsboro	OH	44241	**800-527-0733***	330-528-2000	546
Automated Quality Technologies Inc 563 Shoreview Park Rd	St Paul	MN	55126	**800-250-9297**	651-484-6544	695
Automatic Data Processing Inc (ADP) 1 ADP Blvd *NASDAQ: ADP*	Roseland	NJ	07068	**800-225-5237**		227
Automatic Fire Sprinkler Inc 7272 Mars Dr	Huntington Beach	CA	92647	**800-436-2066**	714-841-2066	609
Automatic Funds Transfer Services 151 S Landers St Ste C	Seattle	WA	98134	**800-275-2033**	206-254-0975	68
Automatic Products International Ltd 165 Bridgepoint Dr	Saint Paul	MN	55075	**800-523-8363**		54
Automatic Systems Inc 9230 E 47th St	Kansas City	MO	64133	**800-366-3488**	816-356-0660	209
Automatic Transmission Rebuilders Assn (ATRA) 2400 Latigo Ave	Oxnard	CA	93030	**866-464-2872**	805-604-2000	48-21
Automation Products Group Inc (APG) 1025 West 1700 North	Logan	UT	84321	**888-525-7300**	435-753-7300	203
Automation Service 13871 Parks Steed Dr	Earth City	MO	63045	**800-325-4808**	314-785-6600	203
Automobile Club of Southern California 2601 S Figueroa St	Los Angeles	CA	90007	**800-400-4222**	213-741-3686	52
Automobile Consumer Services Inc 6249 Stewart Rd	Cincinnati	OH	45227	**800-223-4882**	513-527-7700	57
Automobile Racing Club of America 8117 Lewis Ave	Temperance	MI	48182	**800-385-2503**	734-847-6726	56
Automotive Aftermarket Industry Assn (AAIA) 7101 Wisconsin Ave	Bethesda	MD	20814	**800-936-8906**	301-654-6664	48-21
Automotive Distribution Network 3085 Fountainside Dr Ste 210	Germantown	TN	38138	**800-727-8112**	901-682-9090	48-18
Automotive Distributors Company Inc 2981 Morse Rd	Columbus	OH	43231	**800-421-5556**		60
Automotive Engine Rebuilders Assn (AERA) 500 Coventry Ln Ste 180	Crystal Lake	IL	60014	**888-326-2372**	847-541-6550	48-21
Automotive Finance Corp (AFC) 13085 Hamilton Crossing Blvd	Carmel	IN	46032	**888-335-6675**	865-384-8250	218
Automotive Industry Action Group (AIAG) 26200 Lahser Rd Ste 200	Southfield	MI	48033	**877-275-2424**	248-358-3570	48-21
Automotive Information Ctr 18872 MacArthur Blvd	Irvine	CA	92612	**888-422-8999**		57
Automotive News Magazine 1155 Gratiot Ave	Detroit	MI	48207	**877-812-1584**	313-446-0450	456-21
Automotive Oil Change Assn (AOCA) 330 N. Wabash Ave Ste 2000	Chicago	IL	60611	**800-230-0702**	312-321-5132	48-21
Automotive Parts Headquarters 2959 Clearwater Rd	Saint Cloud	MN	56301	**800-247-0339**	320-252-5411	60
Automotive Parts Remanufacturers Assn (APRA) 4215 Lafayette Ctr Dr Ste 3	Chantilly	VA	20151	**877-734-4827**	703-968-2772	48-21
Automotive Racing Products Inc 1863 Eastman Ave	Ventura	CA	93003	**800-826-3045**	805-339-2200	350
Automotive Recyclers Assn (ARA) 3975 Fair Ridge Dr Ste 20N	Fairfax	VA	22033	**888-385-1005**	703-385-1001	48-21
Automotive Resources Inc 12775 Randolph Ridge Ln	Manassas	VA	20109	**800-562-3250**	703-359-6265	296
Automotive Service Assn (ASA) 1901 Airport Fwy *Cust Svc	Bedford	TX	76021	**800-272-7467***		48-21
Automotive Service Inc 910 Mtn Home Rd PO Box 2157	Sinking Spring	PA	19608	**800-383-3421**	610-678-3421	317
Automotive Training Center-warminster pa Campus 114 Pickering Way	Exton	PA	19341	**888-321-8992**	610-363-6716	167
Autonet Mobile Inc 3636 N Laughlin Rd Ste 150	Santa Rosa	CA	95403	**800-977-2107**	415-223-0316	642-10
Auto-Owners Insurance Co 6101 Anacapri Blvd	Lansing	MI	48917	**800-346-0346**	517-323-1200	391-4
Autoquip Corp 1058 W Industrial Rd	Guthrie	OK	73044	**888-811-9876**	405-282-5200	469
Autorama Inc 5389 Poplar Ave	Memphis	TN	38119	**888-356-7636**	901-345-6211	56
AutoRevo LTD 7920 Belt Line Rd Ste 450	Dallas	TX	75254	**888-311-7386**	972-715-8600	56
AutoStar 114 Ave of the Americas Ste 39	New York	NY	10036	**800-288-6782**	212-930-9400	652
Autostar Solutions Inc 1300 Summit Ave Ste 800	Fort Worth	TX	76102	**800-682-2215**		176
Autotrol Corp 365 E Prairie St PO Box 557	Crystal Lake	IL	60039	**800-228-6207**	815-459-3080	517
Autotruck Federal Credit Union 3611 Newburg Rd	Louisville	KY	40218	**800-459-2328**	502-459-8981	221
AutoTruckToys.com 2814 W Wood St	Paris	TN	38242	**800-544-6194**	731-642-3535	789
AutoVision Wireless Inc 360 Deerhide Crescent	Toronto	ON	M9M2Y6	**866-514-8030**	416-747-4444	227
AutoWeek Magazine 1155 Gratiot Ave *Circ	Detroit	MI	48207	**888-288-6954***	313-446-6000	456-3
AutoZone Inc 123 S Front St *NYSE: AZO*	Memphis	TN	38103	**800-288-6966**	901-495-6500	53
Autry Greer & Sons Inc 2850 W Main St	Mobile	AL	36612	**800-999-7750**	251-457-8655	345
AV Homes Inc 8601 N Scottsdale Rd Ste 225 *NASDAQ: AVHI*	Scottsdale	AR	85283	**800-284-6637**	480-214-7400	651
AVA (Association for Vascular Access) 5526 West 13400 South Ste 229	Herriman	UT	84096	**888-576-2826**	801-792-9079	48-8
AVA (American Volkssport Assn) 1001 Pat Booker Rd Ste 101	Universal City	TX	78148	**855-999-5200**	210-659-2112	47-22
AVAD Canada Ltd 205 Courtneypark Dr W	Mississauga	ON	L5W0A5	**866-523-2823**		176
Avalign Technologies Inc 272 E Deerpath Rd Ste 208	Lake Forest	IL	60045	**855-282-5446**		474
Avalon Corporate Furnished Apartments 1553 Empire Blvd	Webster	NY	14580	**800-934-9763**	585-671-4421	379
Avalon Hotel 16 W Tenth St	Erie	PA	16501	**888-295-4949**	814-459-2220	379
Avanade Inc 818 Stewart St	Seattle	WA	98101	**844-282-6233**	206-239-5600	38
Avancen MOD Corp 1156 Bowman Rd Ste 200	Mount Pleasant	SC	29464	**800-607-1230**		252
Avanquest Software USA 1333 W 120th Ave	Westminster	CO	80234	**800-011-2312**		180-7
Avant Ministries 10000 N Oak Trafficway	Kansas City	MO	64155	**800-468-1892**	816-734-8500	47-20
Avante International Technology Inc (AIT) 70 Washington Rd	Princeton Junction	NJ	08550	**800-735-5040**	609-799-9388	799
Avanti Destinations Inc 1629 SW Salmon St	Portland	OR	97205	**800-422-5053**	503-295-1100	769
Avanti Foods 109 Depot St	Walnut	IL	61376	**800-243-3739**	815-379-2155	297-36
Avanti Polar Lipids Inc 700 Industrial Pk Dr	Alabaster	AL	35007	**800-227-0651**	205-663-2494	478
Avanti Press Inc 155 W Congress St Ste 200	Detroit	MI	48226	**800-228-2684**	313-961-0022	129
Avantica Technologies 2680 Bayshore Pkwy Ste 416	Mountain View	CA	94043	**877-372-1955**	650-248-9678	198
Avantpage Translations 1138 Villaverde Ln	Davis	CA	95618	**877-269-5264**	530-750-2040	318
Avantus 15 W Strong St Ste 20A	Pensacola	FL	32501	**800-600-2510**	850-470-9336	180-10
Avatar Management Services Inc 8157 Bavaria Dr E	Macedonia	OH	44056	**800-728-2827**	330-963-3900	462
Avatier Corp 2603 Camino Ramon Ste 110	San Ramon	CA	94583	**800-609-8610**	925-217-5170	180-12
Avaya Government Solutions Inc 12730 Fair Lakes Cir	Fairfax	VA	22033	**800-492-6769**	703-653-8000	180-10
Avaya Inc 211 Mt Airy Rd	Basking Ridge	NJ	07920	**866-462-8292**	908-953-6000	178
Avcorp Industries Inc 10025 River Way	Delta	BC	V4G1M7	**866-781-3111**	604-582-6677	22
Ave Intervision LLC 1840 W State St	Alliance	OH	44601	**800-448-9126**		683
Ave Maria University 5050 Ave Maria Blvd	Naples	FL	34119	**877-283-8648**	239-280-2500	167
Aveda Corp 4000 Pheasant Ridge Dr	Blaine	MN	55449	**800-644-4831**	763-951-4000	217
Avedis Zildjian Co 22 Longwater Dr	Norwell	MA	02061	**800-229-8672**	781-871-2200	526
Avemco Insurance Co 411 Aviation Way	Frederick	MD	21701	**800-874-9125**	301-694-5700	391-4
Aventura Hospital 20900 Biscayne Blvd	Aventura	FL	33180	**800-523-5772**	305-682-7000	374-3
Avenue Inn & Spa 33 Wilmington Ave	Rehoboth Beach	DE	19971	**800-433-5870**		379
Avenue Plaza Resort 2111 St Charles Ave	New Orleans	LA	70130	**800-614-8685**	504-566-1212	379
Avenue Stores Inc 365 W Passaic St	Rochelle Park	NJ	07662	**888-843-2836**	201-845-0880	156-6
Avera Queen of Peace Hospital 525 N Foster St	Mitchell	SD	57301	**888-531-1685**	605-995-2000	374-3
Avera Saint Luke's Hospital 305 S State St	Aberdeen	SD	57401	**800-658-3535**	605-622-5000	374-3
Avere Systems Inc 5000 Mcknight Rd Ste 404	Pittsburgh	PA	15237	**888-882-8373**	412-894-2570	175-8
Averitt Express Inc 1415 Neal St	Cookeville	TN	38501	**800-283-7488**		778
Avery Dennison 950 German St	Lenoir	NC	28645	**800-444-4947**		742-5
Avery Dennison Corp 207 Goode Ave *NYSE: AVY* ■ *Cust Svc	Glendale	CA	91203	**888-567-4387***	626-304-2000	729
Avery Dennison Fastener Div 224 Industrial Rd	Fitchburg	MA	01420	**800-225-5913**		607
Avery Dennison Specialty Tapes Div 250 Chester St Bldg 5	Painesville	OH	44077	**866-462-8379**	626-304-2000	729
Avery Dennison Worldwide Graphics Div 207 Goode Ave Bldg 8	Glendale	CA	44077	**800-443-9380**	440-358-3700	551-1
Avery Dennison Worldwide Office Products Div 207 Goode Ave	Glendale	CA	91203	**800-462-8379**	626-304-2000	533
Avery Weigh-Tronix Inc 1000 Armstrong Dr	Fairmont	MN	56031	**800-458-7062**	507-238-4461	682
Aves Audio Visual Systems Inc PO Box 500	Sugar Land	TX	77487	**800-365-2837**	281-295-1300	37
Avesta Computer Services Ltd 1 Executive Dr Ste 120	Somerset	NJ	08873	**888-283-7821**	201-369-9400	198
AVG Automation 4140 Utica St	Bettendorf	IA	52722	**877-774-3279**		255
Avi Systems Inc 9675 W 76th St Ste 200	Eden Prairie	MN	55344	**800-488-4954**	952-949-3700	645
Aviagen Group 5015 Bradford Dr	Huntsville	AL	35805	**800-826-9685**	256-890-3800	10-7
Aviation Ground Equipment Corp 53 Hanse Ave	Freeport	NY	11520	**800-758-0044**	516-546-0003	56
Aviation Institute of Maintenance Houston 7651 Airport Blvd	Houston	TX	77061	**888-349-5387**	713-644-7777	798
Aviation Supplies & Academics Inc 7005 132nd Pl Se	Newcastle	WA	98059	**800-272-2359**	425-235-1500	634-2
Aviation Systems of Northwest Florida Inc 175 E Olive Rd	Pensacola	FL	32514	**800-759-0953**		21
Aviation Week & Space Technology Magazine 1200 G St NW	Washington	DC	20005	**800-525-5003**		456-19
AviationWeek 1200 G St NW Ste 900	Washington	DC	20005	**800-525-5003**		530-13
Avid Payment Solutions 950 S Old Woodward Ste 220	Birmingham	MI	48009	**888-855-8644**		257
Avid Technology Inc 65-75 Network Dri *NASDAQ: AVID*	Burlington	MA	01803	**800-949-2843**	978-640-6789	180-8
Avila University 11901 Wornall Rd	Kansas City	MO	64145	**866-943-5787**	816-501-2400	167

Name / Address	City	State	ZIP	Toll-Free	Phone	Class
Avionic Instruments Inc 1414 Randolph Ave	Avenel	NJ	07001	800-468-3571	732-388-3500	255
Avis Rent A Car System Inc 6 Sylvan Way	Parsippany	NJ	07054	800-331-1212	973-496-3500	125
Avisen Securities Inc 3620 American River Dr Ste 145	Sacramento	CA	95864	800-230-7704	916-480-2747	688
Avista Corp 1411 E Mission St *NYSE: AVA*	Spokane	WA	99202	800-936-6629	509-489-0500	785
Avista Utilities 1411 E Mission St	Spokane	WA	99252	800-227-9187		785
Avistar Communications Corp 1855 S Grant St 4th Fl *OTC: AVSR*	San Mateo	CA	94402	800-803-0153	650-525-3300	180-7
Avitus Group PO Box 81590	Billings	MT	59108	800-454-2446		731
Avjobs Inc PO Box 260830	Littleton	CO	80163	888-624-8691	303-683-2322	262
AVMA (American Veterinary Medical Assn PAC) 1910 Sunderland Pl NW	Washington	DC	20036	800-321-1473	202-789-0007	614
AVMA (American Veterinary Medical Assn) 1931 N Meacham Rd Ste 100	Schaumburg	IL	60173	800-248-2862	847-925-8070	48-8
AvMed 4300 NW 89th Blvd	Gainesville	FL	32606	800-346-0231	352-372-8400	391-3
Avnet Electronics Marketing Inc 2211 S 47th St	Phoenix	AZ	85034	888-822-8638	480-643-2000	255
Avnet Inc 2211 S 47th St *NYSE: AVT*	Phoenix	AZ	85034	888-822-8638	480-643-2000	248
Avnet Technology Solutions 8700 S Price Rd	Tempe	AZ	85284	800-409-1483	480-794-6500	176
Avocent Corp 4991 Corporate Dr	Huntsville	AL	35805	866-286-2368	256-430-4000	175-3
Avon Old Farms School 500 Old Farms Rd	Avon	CT	06001	800-464-2866	860-404-4100	621
Avon Products Inc 1345 Ave of the Americas *NYSE: AVP* ■ *Cust Svc	New York	NY	10017	800-367-2866*	212-282-7000	217
Avoyelles Journal 105 N Main St	Marksville	LA	71351	800-565-4321	318-253-5413	531-4
AVRMC (Arkansas Valley Regional Medical Ctr) 1100 Carson Ave	La Junta	CO	81050	877-696-6775	719-384-5412	374-3
AVS Inc 60 Fitchburg Rd	Ayer	MA	01432	800-772-0710	978-772-0710	319
Avstar Aviation Ltd 12 N Haven Ln	East Northport	NY	11731	800-575-2359	631-499-0048	13
AVT Inc 341 Bonnie Cir Ste 102	Corona	CA	92880	877-424-3663		182
Avtec Inc 6 Industrial Pk	Cahokia	IL	62206	800-552-8832	618-337-7800	438
Avtech Software Inc 16 Cutler St Cutler Mill	Warren	RI	02885	888-220-6700	401-847-6700	179
AW (American Whitewater) PO Box 1540	Cullowhee	NC	28723	866-262-8429	828-586-1930	47-23
AW Chesterton Co 500 Unicorn Pk Dr	Woburn	MA	01801	888-400-4872	781-438-7000	327
Award Solutions Inc 2100 Lakeside Blvd	Richardson	TX	75082	877-472-9273	972-664-0727	196
Awards and Personalization Association (ARA) 8735 W Higgins Rd Ste 300	Chicago	IL	60631	800-344-2148	847-375-4800	48-4
AWC Commercial Window Coverings Inc 825 Williamson Ave	Fullerton	CA	92832	800-252-2280	714-879-3880	191-1
AWF (African Wildlife Foundation) 1400 16th St NW Ste 120	Washington	DC	20036	888-494-5354	202-939-3333	47-3
AWHONN (Association of Women's Health Obstetric & Neonatal Nurses) 2000 L St NW Ste 740	Washington	DC	20036	800-673-8499	202-261-2400	48-8
AWI (American Watchmakers-Clockmakers Institute) 701 Enterprise Dr	Harrison	OH	45030	866-367-2924	513-367-9800	48-4
AWI (Architectural Woodwork Institute) 46179 Westlake Dr Ste 120	Potomac Falls	VA	20165	866-877-6933	571-323-3636	48-3
AWIS (Association for Women in Science Inc) 1321 Duke St Ste 210	Alexandria	VA	22314	866-736-7343	703-894-4490	48-19
A&WMA (Air & Waste Management Assn) 420 Fort Duquesne Blvd 1 Gateway Ctr 3rd Fl	Pittsburgh	PA	15222	800-270-3444	412-232-3444	47-12
AWP Inc 826 Overholt Rd	Kent	OH	44240	800-343-2650		691
Awrey Bakeries Inc 12301 Farmington Rd	Livonia	MI	48150	800-950-2253	734-522-1100	67
AWS (American Welding Society) 550 NW 42nd Ave	Miami	FL	33126	800-443-9353	305-443-9353	48-3
AWT (Association of Water Technologies) 9707 Key W Ave Ste 100	Rockville	MD	20850	800-858-6683	301-740-1421	47-2
AWWA (American Water Works Assn) 6666 W Quincy Ave	Denver	CO	80235	800-926-7337	303-794-7711	47-12
Axcera Corp 103 Freedom Dr	Lawrence	PA	15055	800-215-2614	724-873-8100	645
Axcet HR Solutions *Axet* 8325 Lenexa Dr Ste 410	Lenexa	KS	66214	800-801-7557	913-383-2999	630
Axcient Inc 1161 San Antonio Rd	Mountain View	CA	94043	800-715-2339		179
Axel Plastics Research Laboratories Inc 5820 Broadway	Woodside	NY	11377	800-332-2935	718-672-8300	540
Axeon Specialty Products LLC 750 Washington Blvd Ste 600	Stamford	CT	06901	855-378-4958		578
AXIA Consulting LLC 1391 W Fifth Ave Ste 320	Columbus	OH	43212	866-937-5550	614-675-4050	198
Axial Inc 45 E 20th St 12th Fl	New York	NY	10003	800-860-4519		689
Axiobionics 6111 Jackson Rd Ste 200	Ann Arbor	MI	48103	800-552-3539	734-327-2946	252
Axiom Memory Solutions LLC 15 Chrysler	Irvine	CA	92618	888-658-3326	949-581-1450	176
Axiom Resource Management Inc 5203 Leesburg Pk Ste 300	Falls Church	VA	22041	800-566-9305	703-208-3000	196
Axiom Software Ltd 400 Columbus Ave	Valhalla	NY	10595	800-588-8805	914-769-8800	179

B

Name / Address	City	State	ZIP	Toll-Free	Phone	Class
B & B Agency of Boston 47 Commercial Wharf Ste 3	Boston	MA	02110	800-248-9262		376
B & B Electronics Manufacturing Co PO Box 1040	Ottawa	IL	61350	800-346-3119	815-433-5100	694
B & B Media Group 109 S Main St	Corsicana	TX	75110	800-927-0517	903-872-0517	633
B & B Trade Distribution Centre 1950 Oxford St E	London	ON	N5V2Z8	800-265-0382	519-679-1770	609
B & C Transportation Inc 427 Continental Dr	Maryville	TN	37804	877-812-2287	865-983-4653	106
B & D Litho of Arizona 3820 N 38th Ave	Phoenix	AZ	85019	800-735-0375	602-269-2526	626
B & F System Inc 3920 S Walton Walker	Dallas	TX	75236	877-586-2926	214-333-2111	361
B & G Mfg Company Inc 3067 Unionville Pk	Hatfield	PA	19440	800-366-3067	215-822-1925	280
B & H Manufacturing Co 3461 Roeding Rd	Ceres	CA	95307	888-643-0444	209-556-6160	546
B & H Manufacturing Inc 141 County Rd 34 E	Jackson	MN	56143	800-240-3288	507-847-2802	275
B & H Photo-Video-Pro Audio Corp 420 Ninth Ave	New York	NY	10001	800-947-9954	212-444-6615	118
B & O Railroad Museum 901 W Pratt St	Baltimore	MD	21223	866-468-7630	410-752-2490	519
B & R Eckel's Transport Ltd 5514B - 50 Ave	Bonnyville	AB	T9N2K8	800-661-3290	780-826-3889	538
B & W Press Inc 401 E Main St	Georgetown	MA	01833	877-246-3467	978-352-6100	265
B Berger Co 1380 Highland Rd *Cust Svc	Macedonia	OH	44056	800-288-8400*	330-425-3838	593
B Braun Medical Inc 824 12th Ave	Bethlehem	PA	18018	800-523-9676	610-691-5400	475
B Carroll Reece Museum PO Box 70660	Johnson City	TN	37614	855-590-3878	423-439-4392	519
B D N Industrial Hygiene Consultants Inc 8105 Valleywood Ln	Portage	MI	49024	800-968-0123	269-329-1237	198
B E Meyers & Co Inc 9461 Willows Rd NE	Redmond	WA	98052	800-327-5648	425-881-6648	543
B Frank Joy LLC 5355 Kilmer Pl	Hyattsville	MD	20781	800-992-3569	301-779-9400	190-10
B Green Innovations Inc 750 Hwy 34	Matawan	NJ	07747	877-996-9333	732-441-7700	182
B H G Inc PO Box 309	Garrison	ND	58540	800-658-3485	701-463-2201	626
B Jcc Inspections 1000 Banks Draw	Rexford	MT	59930	877-248-6006	406-882-4825	263
B M Ross & Assoc Ltd 62 N St	Goderich	ON	N7A2T4	888-524-2641	519-524-2641	258
B Sharp Technologies Inc 23 Lesmill Rd Ste 404	Toronto	ON	M3B3P6	866-994-2499	416-445-7162	179
B'nai B'rith International 2020 K St NW 7th Fl	Washington	DC	20006	888-388-4224	202-857-6600	47-20
B'nai B'rith Klutznick National Jewish Museum 1120 20th St NW	Washington	DC	20036	888-388-4224	202-857-6600	519
B'Nai B'Rith Magazine 2020 K St NW 7th Fl	Washington	DC	20006	888-388-4224	202-857-6600	456-18
B. E. Smith Inc 9777 Ridge Dr	Lenexa	KS	66219	800-467-9117		195
B.C. Government & Service Employees' Union 4911 Canada Way	Burnaby	BC	V5G3W3	800-663-1674	604-291-9611	414
B2 Gold Corp 595 Burrard St Ste 3100 PO Box 49143	Vancouver	BC	V7X1J1	800-316-8855	604-681-8371	501
B98-FM 97.9 311 Lexington Ave	Fort Smith	AR	72901	866-503-1398	479-782-8888	642-47
BA Robinson Company Ltd 619 Berry St	Winnipeg	MB	R3H0S2	866-903-6275	204-784-0150	611
BAB Inc 500 Lk Cook Rd Ste 475 *OTC: BABB*	Deerfield	IL	60015	800-251-6101		668
Babcock & Wilcox Co 20 S Van Buren Ave	Barberton	OH	44203	800-222-2625	330-753-4511	90
Babcock Lumber Company Inc 2220 Palmer St PO Box 8348	Pittsburgh	PA	15218	800-553-4441	412-351-3515	193-3
Babcock Power Inc 6 Kimball Ln Ste 210	Lynnfield	MA	01940	800-523-0480	978-646-3300	90
Babcock State Park 486 Babcock Rd	Clifftop	WV	25831	800-225-5982	304-438-3004	564
Babcock-Davis 9300 73rd Ave N	Brooklyn Park	MN	55428	888-412-3726	763-488-9247	236
Babe Ruth League Inc 1770 Brunswick Pk PO Box 5000	Trenton	NJ	08638	800-880-3142	609-695-1434	47-22
Babe Winkelman Productions PO Box 407	Brainerd	MN	56401	800-333-0471		739
Babson College 231 Forest St *Admissions	Babson Park	MA	02457	800-488-3696*	781-235-1200	167
Baby Jogger Co 8575 Magellan Pkwy Ste 1000	Richmond	VA	23227	800-241-1848		63
Baby Trend Inc 1567 S Campus Ave *Cust Svc	Ontario	CA	91761	800-328-7363*		63
Baby's Dream Furniture Inc 411 Industrial Blvd	Buena Vista	GA	31803	800-835-2742	229-649-4404	320-2
BabyCenter LLC 163 Freelon St	San Francisco	CA	94107	866-241-2229	415-537-0900	356
BAC (International Union of Bricklayers & Allied Craftworkers) 1776 eye St NW	Washington	DC	20006	888-880-8222	202-783-3788	414
Bacara Resort & Spa 8301 Hollister Ave	Santa Barbara	CA	93117	855-968-0100	805-968-0100	667

Name / Address	City	State	ZIP	Toll-Free	Phone	Class
Baccala Concrete Corp 100 Armento St	Johnston	RI	02919	**866-705-2382**	401-231-8300	184
Baccarat New York LLC 20 W 53rd St	New York	NY	10019	**866-957-5139**	212-790-8800	705
Bacharach Inc 621 Hunt Vly Cir	New Kensington	PA	15068	**800-736-4666**	724-334-5000	203
Bachem Bioscience Inc 3132 Kashiwa St	Torrance	CA	90505	**888-422-2436**	310-539-4171	478
Bachem-Peninsula Laboratories Inc 305 Old County Rd	San Carlos	CA	94070	**800-922-1516**	650-801-6090	233
Bachman's Inc 6010 Lyndale Ave S	Minneapolis	MN	55419	**888-222-4626**	612-861-7311	294
Bachmann Industries Inc 1400 E Erie Ave *Cust Svc	Philadelphia	PA	19124	**800-356-3910***	215-533-1600	760
Back Country Horsemen of America (BCHA) PO Box 1367	Graham	WA	98338	**888-893-5161**	360-832-2461	47-23
Backcountry Gear LLC 1855 W Second Ave	Eugene	OR	97402	**800-953-5499**	541-485-4007	709
Backcountry.com 2607 South 3200 West Ste A *Orders	West Valley City	UT	84119	**800-409-4502***		458
Background Bureau Inc 2019 Alexandria Pike	Highland Heights	KY	41076	**800-854-3990**	859-781-3400	632
Background Information Services Inc 1800 30th St Ste 204	Boulder	CO	80301	**800-433-6010**	303-442-3960	632
Backroads 801 Cedar St	Berkeley	CA	94710	**800-462-2848**	510-527-1555	758
Backtrack Inc 8850 Tyler Blvd	Mentor	OH	44060	**800-991-9694**	440-205-8280	262
Backupify Inc 17 Sellers St,	Cambridge	MA	02139	**800-571-4984**		807
Bacon Veneer Co 6951 High Grove Blvd	Burr Ridge	IL	60527	**800-443-7995**	630-323-1414	612
Bacone College 2299 Old Bacone Rd *Admissions	Muskogee	OK	74403	**888-682-5514***	918-683-4581	167
Bacon-Universal Company Inc 918 Ahua St	Honolulu	HI	96819	**800-352-3508**	808-839-7202	358
BACVA (Baltimore Area Convention & Visitors Assn) 100 Light St 12th Fl	Baltimore	MD	21202	**877-225-8466**	410-659-7300	208
Bad Dog Tools 24 Broadcommon Rd	Bristol	RI	02809	**800-252-1330**	401-253-1330	350
Badge A Minit Ltd 345 N Lewis Ave	Oglesby	IL	61348	**800-223-4103**	815-883-8822	455
Badger Air Brush Co 9128 Belmont Ave	Franklin Park	IL	60131	**800-247-2787**	847-678-3104	42
Badger Bus 5501 Femrite Dr	Madison	WI	53718	**800-442-8259**	608-255-1511	106
Badger Coaches Inc 5501 Femrite Dr	Madison	WI	53718	**800-442-8259**	608-255-1511	758
Badger Express LLC 181 Quality Ct	Fall River	WI	53932	**800-972-0084**	920-484-5808	194
Badger Liquor Company Inc 850 S Morris St	Fond du Lac	WI	54936	**800-242-9708**	920-923-8160	80-3
Badger Meter Inc 4545 W Brown Deer Rd *NYSE: BMI*	Milwaukee	WI	53224	**800-876-3837**	414-355-0400	494
Badger Mining Corp 409 S Church St PO Box 328	Berlin	WI	54923	**800-932-7263**	920-361-2388	501
Badger Mutual Insurance Co 1635 W National Ave	Milwaukee	WI	53204	**800-837-7833**	414-383-1234	390
Badger Sportswear Inc 111 Badger Ln	Statesville	NC	28625	**888-871-0990**	704-871-0990	154-3
Badger State Industries (BSI) 3099 E Washington Ave PO Box 8990	Madison	WI	53708	**800-862-1086**	608-240-5200	629
Badger West Wine & Spirits LLC 5400 Old Town Hall Rd	Eau Claire	WI	54701	**800-472-6674**	715-836-8600	80-3
Badgley Phelps & Bell Inc 1420 Fifth Ave Ste 3200	Seattle	WA	98101	**800-869-7173**	206-623-6172	401
Badorf Shoe Co Inc 1958 Auction Rd	Manheim	PA	17545	**800-325-1545**	717-653-0155	302
Baer Supply Co 909 Forest Edge Dr	Vernon Hills	IL	60061	**800-944-2237**	847-913-2237	351
BAF Industries Inc 1451 Edinger Ave	Tustin	CA	92780	**800-437-9893**	714-258-8055	150
Bag Makers Inc 6606 S Union Rd	Union	IL	60180	**800-458-9031**		65
BagcraftPapercon 3900 W 43rd St	Chicago	IL	60632	**800-621-8468**	773-254-8000	553
Bagdad Roller Mills Inc 5740 Elmburg Rd	Bagdad	KY	40003	**800-928-3333**	502-747-8968	446
Baggett Transportation Co 2 S 32nd St	Birmingham	AL	35233	**800-633-8982**	888-224-4388	778
Baghouse & Industrial Sheet Metal Services Inc 1731 Pomona Rd	Corona	CA	92880	**888-224-4687**	951-272-6610	18
Bahama Breeze 8849 International Dr	Orlando	FL	32819	**877-500-9715**	407-248-2499	669
Bahama House 2001 S Atlantic Ave	Daytona Beach Shores	FL	32118	**888-687-1894**		379
Bahamas *Embassy* 2220 Massachusetts Ave NW	Washington	DC	20008	**800-883-7421**	202-319-2660	259
Bahamas Tourism Office 1200 S Pine Island Rd Ste 750	Plantation	FL	33324	**800-327-7678**	954-236-9292	773
Bahia Mar Beach Resort & Yachting Ctr 801 Seabreeze Blvd	Fort Lauderdale	FL	33316	**888-802-2442**	954-764-2233	667
Bahia Mar Resort & Conference Ctr 6300 Padre Blvd	South Padre Island	TX	78597	**800-926-6926**		667
Bahia Resort Hotel 998 W Mission Bay Dr	San Diego	CA	92109	**800-576-4229**	858-488-0551	667
Bahl & Gaynor Inc 212 E Third St Ste 200	Cincinnati	OH	45202	**800-341-1810**	513-287-6100	401
BAI (Bank Administration Institute) 115 S LaSalle St Ste 3300 *Cust Svc	Chicago	IL	60603	**800-224-9889***	312-683-2464	48-2
Baier Marine Company Inc 2920 Airway Ave	Costa Mesa	CA	92626	**800-455-3917**		350
Bailard Biehl & Kaiser Group 950 Tower Ln Ste 1900	Foster City	CA	94404	**800-224-5273**	650-571-5800	401
Bailey Farms LLC 549 Karem Dr	Marshall	WI	53559	**800-655-1705**		577
Bailey Matthews Shell Museum 3075 Sanibel-Captiva Rd PO Box 1580	Sanibel	FL	33957	**888-679-6450**	239-395-2233	519
Bailey Properties 106 Aptos Beach Dr	Aptos	CA	95003	**800-347-6830**	831-688-7009	650
Bailey's Express Inc 61 Industrial Pk Rd	Middletown	CT	06457	**800-523-3758**	860-632-0388	778
Baille Lumber Co 4002 Legion Dr PO Box 6	Hamburg	NY	14075	**800-950-2850**	716-649-2850	193-3
Baillio's Inc 5301 Menaul Blvd NE	Albuquerque	NM	87110	**800-540-7511**	505-883-7511	38
Bain Pest Control Service Inc 1320 Middlesex St	Lowell	MA	01851	**800-272-3661**	978-452-9621	576
Baird & Warner Inc 120 S LaSalle St Ste 2000	Chicago	IL	60603	**888-661-1176**	312-368-1855	650
Baird Patrick & Company Inc 305 Plz Ten	Jersey City	NJ	07311	**800-221-7747**	201-680-7300	688
Baisch & Skinner Inc 2721 Lasalle St	Saint Louis	MO	63104	**800-523-0013**	314-664-1212	294
Baja Expeditions Inc 3096 Palm St	San Diego	CA	92104	**800-843-6967**	858-581-3311	222
Baja Fresh 320 Commerce Ste 100	Irvine	CA	92602	**877-225-2373**	949-270-8900	669
Baka Communications Inc 630 The East Mall	Etobicoke	ON	M9B4B1	**866-884-3329**	416-641-2800	198
Bake'n Joy Foods Inc 351 Willow St	North Andover	MA	01845	**800-666-4937**	978-683-1414	297-16
Baker & Taylor Inc 2550 W Tyvola Rd Ste 300	Charlotte	NC	28217	**800-775-1800**		94
Baker Book House Company Inc 6030 E Fulton St *Orders	Ada	MI	49301	**800-877-2665***	616-676-9185	634-3
Baker Book House Company Inc Revell Div 6030 E Fulton St *Orders	Ada	MI	49301	**800-877-2665***	616-676-9185	634-3
Baker College						
Auburn Hills 1500 University Dr	Auburn Hills	MI	48326	**888-429-0410**	248-340-0600	167
Cadillac 9600 E 13th St	Cadillac	MI	49601	**888-313-3463**	231-876-3100	167
Clinton Township 34950 Little Mack Ave	Clinton Township	MI	48035	**888-272-2842**	586-791-6610	167
Flint 1050 W Bristol Rd	Flint	MI	48507	**800-964-4299**	810-767-7600	167
Jackson 2800 Springport Rd	Jackson	MI	49202	**888-343-3683**	517-788-7800	167
Owosso 1020 S Washington St	Owosso	MI	48867	**800-879-3797**	989-729-3350	167
Port Huron 3403 Lapeer Rd	Port Huron	MI	48060	**888-262-2442**	810-985-7000	167
Baker Communications Inc 10101 SW Fwy #630	Houston	TX	77074	**877-253-8506**	713-627-7700	763
Baker Company Inc 161 Gatehouse Rd PO Box E	Sanford	ME	04073	**800-992-2537**	207-324-8773	420
Baker Concrete Construction Inc 900 N Garver Rd	Monroe	OH	45050	**800-359-3935**	513-539-4000	191-3
Baker County Visitors & Convention Bureau 490 Campbell St	Baker City	OR	97814	**800-523-1235**	541-523-3356	208
Baker Distributing Co 14610 Breakers Dr Ste 100	Jacksonville	FL	32258	**844-289-0033**	800-217-4698	611
Baker Group 4224 Hubbell Ave	Des Moines	IA	50317	**855-262-4000**	515-262-4000	191-10
Baker Hughes Inc (BHI) 2929 Allen Pkwy Ste 1200 *NYSE: BHI*	Houston	TX	77019	**800-229-7447**	713-439-8600	538
Baker Hughes Inc Baker Petrolite Div 12645 W Airport Blvd	Sugar Land	TX	77478	**800-231-3606**	281-276-5400	144
Baker Krizner Financial Planning 2230 N Limestone St	Springfield	OH	45503	**888-390-8753**	937-390-8750	462
Baker Products 55480 Hwy 21 N PO Box 128	Ellington	MO	63638	**800-548-6914**	573-663-7711	819
Baker Rock Resources 21880 SW Farmington Rd	Beaverton	OR	97007	**800-340-7625**	503-642-2531	45
Baker Roofing Co 517 Mercury St	Raleigh	NC	27603	**800-849-4096**	919-828-2975	191-12
Baker Triangle 401 Highway 80 E	Mesquite	TX	75150	**800-458-3480**	972-289-5534	191-9
Bal Seal Engineering Company Inc 19650 Pauling	Foothill Ranch	CA	92610	**800-366-1006**	949-460-2100	327
Balance Rock Inn 21 Albert Meadow	Bar Harbor	ME	04609	**800-753-0494**	207-288-2610	379
Balasa Dinverno Foltz LLC 500 Park Blvd Ste 1400	Itasca	IL	60143	**800-840-4740**	630-875-4900	40
Balboa Park Inn 3402 Pk Blvd	San Diego	CA	92103	**800-938-8181**	619-298-0823	379
Balboa Travel Management Inc 5414 Oberlin Dr Ste 300	San Diego	CA	92121	**800-359-8773**	858-678-3300	769
Balcan Plastics Ltd 9340 Meaux St	Saint Leonard	QC	H1R3H2	**877-422-5226**	514-326-0200	600
Balchem Corp 52 Sunrise Pk Rd PO Box 600 *NASDAQ: BCPC*	New Hampton	NY	10958	**877-407-8289**	845-326-5613	478
Baldwin & Lyons Inc 111 Congressional Blvd Ste 500 *NASDAQ: BWINB*	Carmel	IN	46032	**800-644-5501**	317-636-9800	391-4
Baldwin County Electric Membership Corp 19600 Hwy 59	Summerdale	AL	36580	**800-837-3374**	251-989-6247	247
Baldwin Filters 4400 Hwy 30	Kearney	NE	68847	**800-822-5394**		59
Baldwin Hardware Corp 841 E Wyomissing Blvd	Reading	PA	19611	**800-566-1986**	610-777-7811	350

Name / Address	City	State	ZIP	Toll-Free	Phone	Class
Baldwin Richardson Foods Company Inc 20201 S La Grange Rd Ste 200 *Cust Svc	Frankfort	IL	60423	**866-644-2732***	815-464-9994	297-25
Baldwin-Wallace College 275 Eastland Rd	Berea	OH	44017	**877-292-7759**	440-826-2222	167
Balfour 7211 Cir S Rd	Austin	TX	78745	**800-225-3687**		409
Bali Steak & Seafood 2005 Kalia Rd	Honolulu	HI	96815	**800-445-8667**	808-949-4321	669
Balihoo Inc 404 S Eighth St Ste 300	Boise	ID	83702	**866-446-9914**		181
Ball Automotive Group 1935 National City Blvd	National City	CA	91950	**888-318-6492**	619-474-6431	56
Ball Beauty Supplies 416 N Fairfax Ave	Los Angeles	CA	90036	**800-588-0244**	323-655-2330	76
Ball Bounce & Sport Inc/Hedstrom Plastics 1 Hedstrom Dr	Ashland	OH	44805	**800-765-9665**	419-289-9310	760
Ball Homes LLC 3609 Walden Dr	Lexington	KY	40517	**888-268-1101**	859-268-1191	189
Ball Horticultural Co 622 Town Rd	West Chicago	IL	60185	**800-879-2255**	630-231-3600	295
Ball State University 2000 W University Ave	Muncie	IN	47306	**800-382-8540**	765-289-1241	167
Ballantyne Resort Hotel 10000 Ballantyne Commons Pkwy	Charlotte	NC	28277	**866-248-4824**	704-248-4000	667
Ballantyne Strong Inc 13710 FNB Pkwy *NYSE: BTN* ■ *General	Omaha	NE	68154	**800-424-1215***		590
Ballard's Farm Sausage Inc 7275 Right Fork Wilson Creek *General	Wayne	WV	25570	**800-346-7675***	304-272-5147	297-26
Ballet Magnificat 5406 I-55 N	Jackson	MS	39211	**866-617-3257**	601-977-1001	572-1
Ballew's Aluminum Products Inc 2 Shelter Dr	Greer	SC	29650	**800-231-6666**	864-272-4453	695
Balloons Everywhere Inc 16474 Greeno Rd	Fairhope	AL	36532	**800-239-2000**		565
Bally's Atlantic City 1900 Pacific Ave	Atlantic City	NJ	08401	**800-772-7777**	609-340-2000	667
Bally's Casino Tunica 1450 Bally's Blvd	Robinsonville	MS	38664	**866-422-5597**		132
Bally's Las Vegas 3645 Las Vegas Blvd S *Resv	Las Vegas	NV	89109	**800-522-4700***	702-967-4111	132
Ballymore Co 501 Gunnard Carlson Dr	Coatesville	PA	19365	**800-762-8327**	610-593-5062	421
Balmoral Inn 120 Balmoral Ave	Biloxi	MS	39531	**800-393-9131**	228-388-6776	379
Balnea Spa 319 chemin du Lac Gale	Bromont	QC	J2L2S5	**866-734-2110**	450-534-0604	228
BALSAMS Grand Resort Hotel, The 1000 Cold Spring Rd	Dixville Notch	NH	03576	**800-255-0800**		377
Baltimore Area Convention & Visitors Assn (BACVA) 100 Light St 12th Fl	Baltimore	MD	21202	**877-225-8466**	410-659-7300	208
Baltimore Behavioral Health (BBH) 1101 W Pratt St	Baltimore	MD	21223	**800-789-2647**	410-962-7180	724
Baltimore City Community College 2901 Liberty Heights Ave	Baltimore	MD	21215	**888-203-1261**	410-462-8000	161
Baltimore County Public Library 320 York Rd	Towson	MD	21204	**800-705-3493**	410-887-6100	434-3
Baltimore County Revenue Authority 115 Towsontown Blvd E	Baltimore	MD	21286	**888-246-5384**	410-887-3127	561
Baltimore Gas & Electric Co 110 W Fayette St PO Box 1475	Baltimore	MD	21201	**800-685-0123**	410-470-7433	785
Baltimore International College 17 Commerce St	Baltimore	MD	21202	**800-624-9926**	410-752-4710	162
Baltimore Life Cos 10075 Red Run Blvd	Owings Mills	MD	21117	**800-628-5433**	410-581-6600	391-2
Baltimore Magazine 1000 Lancaster St Ste 400 *Cust Svc	Baltimore	MD	21202	**800-935-0838***	410-752-4200	456-22
Baltimore Museum of Art 10 Art Museum Dr	Baltimore	MD	21218	**800-735-2964**	443-573-1700	519
Baltimore National Cemetery 5501 Frederick Ave	Baltimore	MD	21228	**800-535-1117**	410-644-9696	135
Baltimore Rigging Company Inc, The 6601 Tributary St	Baltimore	MD	21224	**800-626-2150**	443-696-4001	191-1
Baltimore Sun 501 N Calvert St	Baltimore	MD	21278	**800-829-8000**	410-332-6000	531-2
Baltimore Symphony Orchestra 1212 Cathedral St	Baltimore	MD	21201	**877-276-1444**	410-783-8100	572-3
Baltimore Times 2513 N Charles St	Baltimore	MD	21218	**800-944-7403**	410-366-3900	531-4
Baltimore Washington Medical Ctr 301 Hospital Dr	Glen Burnie	MD	21061	**800-994-6610**	410-787-4000	374-3
Baltimore/Washington International Thurgood Marshall Airport (BWI) PO Box 8766	Baltimore	MD	21240	**800-435-9294**	410-859-7111	27
Balzer Pacific Equipment Co 2136 SE Eigth Ave	Portland	OR	97214	**800-442-0966**	503-232-5141	358
Bamberger Polymers Inc 2 Jericho Plz Ste 109	Jericho	NY	11753	**800-888-8959**	516-622-3600	602
BAMC (Brooke Army Medical Ctr) 3551 Roger Brooke Dr	Fort Sam Houston	TX	78234	**800-443-2262**	210-916-4141	331-4
BAMC (Bay Area Medical Ctr) 3100 Shore Dr	Marinette	WI	54143	**888-788-2070**	715-735-4200	374-3
Banacol Marketing Corp 355 Alhambra Cir Ste 1510	Coral Gables	FL	33134	**877-324-7619**	305-441-9036	298-7
Bancorp Bank 409 Silverside Rd Ste 105 *NASDAQ: TBBK* ■ *Cust Svc	Wilmington	DE	19809	**866-255-9831***	302-385-5000	69
BancorpSouth Inc 2910 W Jackson St *NYSE: BXS*	Tupelo	MS	38801	**888-797-7711**	662-680-2000	360-2
Bancroft Bag Inc 425 Bancroft Blvd	West Monroe	LA	71292	**800-551-4950**	318-387-2550	64
Bandera County Convention & Visitors Bureau 126 State Hwy 16 S PO Box 171	Bandera	TX	78003	**800-364-3833**	830-796-3045	208
Bandera Electric Co-op Inc 3172 State Hwy 16 N	Bandera	TX	78003	**866-226-3372**		247
Bandimere Speedway 3051 S Rooney Rd	Morrison	CO	80465	**888-737-5253**	303-697-6001	514
Bandit Industries Inc 6750 W Millbrook Rd	Remus	MI	49340	**800-952-0178**	989-561-2270	192
Band-It-IDEX Inc 4799 Dahlia St	Denver	CO	80216	**800-525-0758**	303-320-4555	350
Bane Machinery Inc PO Box 541355	Dallas	TX	75354	**800-594-2263**	214-352-2468	358
Banff Adventures Unlimited 211 Bear St Bison Courtyard	Banff	AB	T1L1A8	**800-644-8888**	403-762-4554	758
Banff Centre, The 107 Tunnel Mtn Dr PO Box 1020	Banff	AB	T1L1H5	**800-884-7574**	403-762-6100	377
Banff National Park PO Box 900	Banff	AB	T1L1K2	**877-737-3783**	403-762-1550	562
Banfield the Pet Hospital 18101 SE 6th Way	Vancouver	WA	98683	**866-894-7927**		792
Bang Printing Inc 3323 Oak St	Brainerd	MN	56401	**800-328-0450**	218-829-2877	625
Bangor Daily News 491 Main St PO Box 1329	Bangor	ME	04402	**800-432-7964**	207-990-8000	531-2
Bangor Hydro Electric Co PO Box 932	Bangor	ME	04402	**800-499-6600**	207-945-5621	785
Bangor International Airport 287 Godfrey Blvd	Bangor	ME	04401	**866-359-2264**	207-992-4600	27
Bangor Public Library 145 Harlow St	Bangor	ME	04401	**800-442-4293**	207-947-8336	434-3
Bangor Savings Bank 99 Franklin St	Bangor	ME	04401	**877-226-4671**	207-942-5211	69
Bangor Symphony Orchestra PO Box 1441 *General	Bangor	ME	04402	**800-639-3221***	207-942-5555	572-3
Bangor Theological Seminary 159 State St	Portland	ME	04101	**800-287-6781**	207-942-6781	168-3
Bank Administration Institute (BAI) 115 S LaSalle St Ste 3300 *Cust Svc	Chicago	IL	60603	**800-224-9889***	312-683-2464	48-2
Bank Financial 6415 W 95th St	Chicago Ridge	IL	60415	**800-894-6900**		69
Bank Independent 710 S Montgomery Ave	Sheffield	AL	35660	**877-865-5050**	256-386-5000	360-2
Bank Leumi USA 579 Fifth Ave	New York	NY	10017	**800-892-5430**	917-542-2343	69
Bank Mutual Corp 4949 W Brown Deer Rd *NASDAQ: BKMU*	Milwaukee	WI	53223	**844-256-8684**	414-354-1500	360-2
Bank of Albuquerque NA 201 3rd St NW Ste 1400	Albuquerque	NM	87102	**800-583-0709**	505-855-0855	69
Bank of America Card Services 1 Commercial Pl 2nd Fl	Norfolk	VA	23510	**800-732-9194**	757-441-4770	219
Bank of Commerce Holdings 1901 Churn Creek Rd *NASDAQ: BOCH*	Redding	CA	96002	**800-421-2575**	530-224-3333	360-2
Bank of Hawaii Corp 130 Merchant St 20th Fl *NYSE: BOH*	Honolulu	HI	96813	**888-643-3888**		360-2
Bank of Louisiana 300 St Charles Ave	New Orleans	LA	70130	**866-392-9952**	504-592-0600	69
Bank of Marin 504 Tamalpais Dr *NASDAQ: BMRC*	Corte Madera	CA	94925	**800-654-5111**	415-927-2265	69
Bank of McKenney 20718 First St *OTC: BOMK*	McKenney	VA	23872	**800-528-2273**	804-478-4434	69
Bank of Montreal 3 Times Sq	New York	NY	10036	**877-225-5266**		69
Bank of Nevada 2700 W Sahara Ave	Las Vegas	NV	89102	**877-750-0010**	702-248-4200	69
Bank of North Dakota 1200 Memorial Hwy	Bismarck	ND	58504	**800-472-2166**	701-328-5600	69
Bank of Nova Scotia 1 Liberty Plaza 26th Fl *TSE: BNS*	New York	NY	10006	**800-472-6842**	212-225-5000	69
Bank of Oklahoma NA PO Box 2300	Tulsa	OK	74192	**800-234-6181**	918-588-6010	69
Bank of South Carolina Corp 256 Meeting St *NASDAQ: BKSC*	Charleston	SC	29401	**800-523-4175**	843-724-1500	360-2
Bank of Springfield 2600 Adlai Stevenson Dr	Springfield	IL	62703	**877-698-3278**	217-529-5555	69
Bank of Stanly PO Box 338	Albemarle	NC	28002	**800-438-6864**	704-983-6181	69
Bank of Stockton PO Box 1110	Stockton	CA	95201	**800-941-1494**	209-929-1600	69
Bank of Sunset & Trust Co 863 Napoleon Ave	Sunset	LA	70584	**800-264-5578**	337-662-5222	69
Bank of the Carolinas 135 Boxwood Village Dr *OTC: BCAR*	Mocksville	NC	27028	**877-751-5755**	336-751-5755	69
Bank of the Orient 233 Sansome St	San Francisco	CA	94104	**877-275-3342**	415-338-0843	188
Bank of the Ozarks 4328 Old Spanish Trail	Houston	TX	77021	**800-274-4482**	713-747-9000	69
Bank of the Ozarks Inc 12615 Chenal Pkwy PO Box 8811 *NASDAQ: OZRK*	Little Rock	AR	72211	**800-628-3552**	501-978-2265	360-2
Bank of the Sierra PO Box 1930 *Cust Svc	Porterville	CA	93258	**888-454-2265***	559-782-4900	69
Bank Of Utica 222 Genesee St *OTC: BKUT*	Utica	NY	13502	**800-442-1028**	315-797-2700	69
Bank of Virginia 11730 Hull St Rd *NASDAQ: BOVA*	Midlothian	VA	23112	**800-500-1044**	804-744-7576	69
BankAtlantic 200 W Second St	Winston-Salem	NC	27101	**800-226-5228**	888-628-3926	69
BankCard Services 3055 Wilshire Blvd 3rd Fl	Los Angeles	CA	90010	**888-339-0100**	213-365-1122	395

Alphabetical Section

Name	Address	City	State	Zip	Toll-Free	Phone	Class
Bankers Fidelity Life Insurance Co	4370 Peachtree Rd; *NASDAQ: AAME*	Atlanta	GA	30319	**866-458-7504**	404-266-5500	391-2
Bankers Life & Casualty Co	111 E Wacker Dr Ste 2100	Chicago	IL	60601	**800-231-9150**	312-396-6000	391-2
Bankers' Bank	7700 Mineral Point Rd	Madison	WI	53717	**800-388-5550**	608-833-5550	69
Bank-Fund Staff Federal Credit Union	PO Box 27755	Washington	DC	20038	**800-923-7328**	202-458-4300	221
Banking Daily	1801 S Bell St	Arlington	VA	22202	**800-372-1033**		530-1
Banking Strategies Magazine	115 S LaSalle St Ste 3300	Chicago	IL	60603	**888-224-0037**	312-553-4600	456-5
Banko Beverage Co	5001 Crackersport Rd; *General	Allentown	PA	18104	**800-322-9295***	610-434-0147	80-1
Bankruptcy Court Decisions	360 Hiatt Dr	Palm Beach Gardens	FL	33418	**800-621-5463**	561-622-6520	530-1
Bankruptcy Law Letter	610 Opperman Dr	Eagan	MN	55123	**800-937-8529**	651-687-7000	530-7
Bankruptcy Management Solutions Inc	5 Peters Canyon Rd Ste 200	Irvine	CA	92606	**800-634-7734**		462
Bankshot Sports Organization	330-U N Stonestreet Ave Ste 504	Rockville	MD	20852	**800-933-0140**	301-309-0260	708
Bankwest Corporation	2050 N California Blvd	Walnut Creek	CA	94596	**888-389-8668**	925-933-7810	69
Bankwest Inc	420 S Pierre St PO Box 998	Pierre	SD	57501	**800-253-0362**	605-224-7391	69
Bannack State Park	4200 Bannack Rd	Dillon	MT	59725	**855-922-6768**	406-834-3413	564
Banneker-Douglas Museum	84 Franklin St	Annapolis	MD	21401	**877-634-6361**	410-216-6180	519
Banner Bank	PO Box 907; *NASDAQ: BANR*	Walla Walla	WA	99362	**800-272-9933**	509-527-3636	360-2
Banner Behavioral Health Hospital	7575 E Earll Dr	Scottsdale	AZ	85251	**800-254-4357**	480-941-7500	374-5
Banner Del E Webb Memorial Hospital	14502 W Meeker Blvd	Sun City West	AZ	85375	**800-254-4357**	623-214-4000	374-3
Banner Engineering Corp	9714 Tenth Ave N	Minneapolis	MN	55441	**888-373-6767**	763-544-3164	255
Banner Health	1441 N 12th St	Phoenix	AZ	85006	**866-451-3399**	602-495-4000	353
Banner Life Insurance Co	1701 Research Blvd	Rockville	MD	20850	**800-638-8428**	301-279-4800	391-2
Banner Supply Co	7195 NW 30th St	Miami	FL	33122	**888-511-4004**	305-593-2946	193-3
Banner-Gazette	490 E State Rd 60 PO Box 38	Pekin	IN	47165	**800-889-3390**	812-967-3176	531-4
Bannister Family House	406 Dickinson St	San Diego	CA	92103	**800-926-8273**	619-543-7977	372
Bannister's Wharf	1 Bannister's Wharf	Newport	RI	02840	**800-395-1343**	401-846-4500	49-5
Banterra Corp	1404 US Rt 45 S	Eldorado	IL	62930	**877-541-2265**	618-273-9346	69
Banyan Air Service	5360 NW 20th Terr	Fort Lauderdale	FL	33309	**800-200-2031**	954-491-3170	62
Banyan International Corp	11629 49th Pl W	Mukilteo	WA	98275	**888-782-8548**	325-677-1372	474
Banyan Medical Systems Inc	4106 S 87th St	Omaha	NE	68127	**866-225-7790**	402-403-4400	182
Banyan Resort	323 Whitehead St	Key West	FL	33040	**866-371-9222**	305-296-7786	667
Banyan Water Inc	11002-B Metric Blvd	Austin	TX	78758	**800-276-1507**		462
Baptist Bible College	628 E Kearney St	Springfield	MO	65803	**800-228-5754**		160
Baptist College of Florida	5400 College Dr	Graceville	FL	32440	**800-328-2660**	850-263-3261	167
Baptist Health	1 Trillium Way	Corbin	KY	40701	**800-395-4435**	606-528-1212	374-3
Baptist Health Louisville	4000 Kresge Way	Louisville	KY	40207	**800-489-3002**	502-897-8100	374-3
Baptist Health Paducah (WBH)	2501 Kentucky Ave	Paducah	KY	42003	**877-271-4176**	270-575-2100	374-3
Baptist Health South Florida Inc	5000 University Dr	Coral Gables	FL	33146	**800-622-2838**	786-662-7000	353
Baptist Hospital of Miami	8900 SW 88th St	Miami	FL	33176	**800-994-6610**	786-596-1960	374-3
Baptist Medical Ctr	1225 N State St	Jackson	MS	39202	**800-948-6262**	601-968-1000	374-3
Baptist Memorial Health Care Corp	350 N Humphreys Blvd	Memphis	TN	38120	**800-422-7847**	901-227-5920	353
Baptist Memorial Hospital Golden Triangle	2520 Fifth St N	Columbus	MS	39703	**800-422-7847**	662-244-1000	374-3
Baptist Memorial Hospital Union City	1201 Bishop St	Union City	TN	38261	**800-344-2470**	731-885-2410	374-3
Baptist Missionary Assn Theological Seminary	1530 E Pine St	Jacksonville	TX	75766	**800-259-5673**	903-586-2501	168-3
Baptist Theological Seminary at Richmond	8040 Villa Park Dr Ste 250	Richmond	VA	23227	**888-345-2877**	804-355-8135	168-3
Baptist Trinity Home Care & Hospice	6019 Walnut Grove Rd	Memphis	TN	38120	**800-422-7847**	901-226-5000	371
Baptist University of the Americas	8019 S Pan Am Expy	San Antonio	TX	78224	**800-721-1396**	210-924-4338	160
Baptist World Alliance	405 N Washington St	Falls Church	VA	22046	**844-862-2739**	703-790-8980	47-20
Bar Harbor Bankshares	82 Main St PO Box 400; *NYSE: BHB*	Bar Harbor	ME	04609	**888-853-7100**	207-288-3314	360-2
Bar Harbor Chamber of Commerce	2 Cottage St	Bar Harbor	ME	04609	**888-540-9990**	207-288-5103	138
Bar Harbor Hotel-Bluenose Inn	90 Eden St	Bar Harbor	ME	04609	**800-445-4077**	207-288-3348	379
Bar Harbor Inn Oceanfront Resort	Newport Dr	Bar Harbor	ME	04609	**800-248-3351**	207-288-3351	667
Bar Lazy J Guest Ranch	447 County Rd 3 PO Box N	Parshall	CO	80468	**800-396-6279**	970-725-3437	241
Bar None Auction Inc	4751 Power Inn Rd	Sacramento	CA	95826	**866-372-1700**		189
Bar Productscom Inc	1990 Lake Ave SE	Largo	FL	33771	**800-256-6396**	727-584-2093	322
Barbara Ann Karmanos Cancer Institute	4100 John R St	Detroit	MI	48201	**800-527-6266**		666
Barbara B Mann Performing Arts Hall	13350 FSW Pkwy	Fort Myers	FL	33919	**800-440-7469**	239-489-3033	571
Barbershop Harmony Society	110 Seventh Ave N	Nashville	TN	37203	**800-876-7464**	615-823-3993	47-18
Barbour Welting Company Div Barbour Corp	1001 N Montello St	Brockton	MA	02301	**800-955-9649**	508-583-8200	302
Bar-B-Q Shop, The	1782 Madison Ave	Memphis	TN	38104	**877-372-8237**	901-272-1277	669
BARC Electric Co-op	84 High St PO Box 264	Millboro	VA	24460	**800-846-2272**		247
Barchart.com Inc	330 S Wells Ste 618	Chicago	IL	60606	**800-238-5814**	312-554-8122	318
Barclay College	607 N Kingman St	Haviland	KS	67059	**800-862-0226**	620-862-5252	160
Barclay Products Ltd	4000 Porett Dr Ste B	Gurnee	IL	60031	**800-446-9700**	847-244-1234	608
Barclays Capital Inc	200 Pk Ave	New York	NY	10166	**888-227-2275**	212-412-4000	688
Barco Electronic Systems Pvt Ltd	11101 Trade Ctr Dr	Rancho Cordova	CA	95670	**888-414-7226**	916-859-2500	175-4
BARCO Industries Inc	1020 MacArthur Rd; *Cust Svc	Reading	PA	19605	**800-234-8665***		756
Barco Rent a Truck	717 South 5600 West	Salt Lake City	UT	84104	**800-453-4761**	801-532-7777	776
Barco Uniforms Inc	350 W Rosecrans Ave	Gardena	CA	90248	**800-421-1874**	310-323-7315	154-18
Barcoding Inc	2220 Boston St	Baltimore	MD	21231	**888-412-7226**	410-385-8532	181
Barcontrol Systems & Services Inc	113 Edinburgh Ct	Greenville	SC	29607	**800-947-4362**	864-421-0050	179
Bard Access Systems Inc	605 North 5600 West	Salt Lake City	UT	84116	**800-443-5505**	801-522-5000	475
Bard College	PO Box 5000	Annandale-on-Hudson	NY	12504	**800-872-7423**	845-758-7472	167
Bard Inc Peripheral Vascular	1625 W Third St	Tempe	AZ	85281	**800-321-4254**	480-894-9515	475
Bard Mfg Co Inc	1914 Randolph Dr	Bryan	OH	43506	**800-563-5660**	419-636-1194	15
Barden & Robeson Corp	103 Kelly Ave	Middleport	NY	14105	**800-724-0141**	716-735-3732	105
Barden Corp	200 Pk Ave	Danbury	CT	06810	**800-243-1060**	203-744-2211	619
Bardes Plastics Inc	5225 W Clinton Ave; *Cust Svc	Milwaukee	WI	53223	**800-558-5161***		601
Barefoot Resort & Golf	4980 Barefoot Resort Bridge Rd	North Myrtle Beach	SC	29582	**866-638-4818**	843-390-3200	667
Barfield Inc	4101 NW 29th St	Miami	FL	33142	**800-321-1039**	305-894-5300	24
Bargain Supply Co	844 E Jefferson St	Louisville	KY	40206	**800-322-5226**	502-562-5000	351
Barger Packaging Inc	2901 Oakland Ave	Elkhart	IN	46517	**888-525-2845**		600
Bargreen Ellingson Inc	2925 70th Ave E	Fife	WA	98424	**866-722-2665**	253-722-2600	301
Barix Clinics	135 S Prospect St	Ypsilanti	MI	48198	**800-282-0066**	734-547-4700	808
Barker Air & Hydraulics Inc	1308 Miller Rd	Greenville	SC	29607	**800-922-3324**	864-288-3537	638
Barker Martin PS	719 Second Ave Ste 1200	Seattle	WA	98104	**888-381-9806**	360-756-9806	428
Barkman Honey	120 Santa Fe St	Hillsboro	KS	67063	**800-364-6623**		297-24
Barksdale Inc	3211 Fruitland Ave	Los Angeles	CA	90058	**800-835-1060**	323-589-6181	203
Barlow	1305 Grand Dd SE	Faucett	MO	64448	**800-688-1202**	816-238-3373	778
Barn Furniture Mart Inc	6206 N Sepulveda Blvd	Van Nuys	CA	91411	**888-302-2276**	818-780-4070	322
Barnes & Thornburg	11 S Meridian St	Indianapolis	IN	46204	**800-236-1352**	317-236-1313	428
Barnes Advertising Corp	1580 Fairview Rd	Zanesville	OH	43701	**800-458-1410**	740-453-6836	7
Barnes Distribution	1301 E Ninth St Ste 700	Cleveland	OH	44114	**800-726-9626**	216-416-7200	385
Barnes Farming Corp	7840 Old Bailey Hwy	Spring Hope	NC	27882	**800-367-2799**		10-9
Barnes International Inc	814 Chestnut St PO Box 1203	Rockford	IL	61105	**800-435-4877**	815-964-8661	454
Barnes Lodge	4520 Clayton Ave	Saint Louis	MO	63110	**800-551-3492**	314-652-4319	372
Barnes Transportation Services Inc	2309 Whitley Rd	Wilson	NC	27895	**800-898-5897**		360-2
barnesandnoble.com Inc	122 Fifth Ave	New York	NY	10011	**800-843-2665**	212-414-6000	95
Barnet Associates LLC	2 Round Lake Rd	Ridgefield	CT	06877	**888-827-7070**		318
Barnet-Dulaney Eye Ctr	4800 N 22nd St	Phoenix	AZ	85016	**866-742-6581**	602-955-1000	796
Barnett & Ramel Optical Co	7154 N 16th St	Omaha	NE	68112	**800-228-9732**		542
Barnett Inc	801 W Bay St	Jacksonville	FL	32204	**888-803-4467**	904-384-6530	611
Barney Trucking Inc	235 State Rt 24	Salina	UT	84654	**800-524-7930**		683
Barnhardt Mfg Co	1100 Hawthorne Ln	Charlotte	NC	28205	**800-277-0377**		230

Name / Address	City	State	ZIP	Toll-Free	Phone	Class
Barnhart Crane & Rigging Co 1701 Dunn Ave	Memphis	TN	38106	**800-727-0149**	901-775-3000	192
Barnhill Bolt Company Inc 2500 Princeton Dr Ne	Albuquerque	NM	87107	**800-472-3900**	505-884-1808	350
Barnsley Gardens 597 Barnsley Gardens Rd	Adairsville	GA	30103	**877-773-2447**	770-773-7480	667
Barnstead Inn 349 Bonnet St	Manchester Center	VT	05255	**800-331-1619**	802-362-1619	379
Baron Funds 767 Fifth Ave 49th Fl	New York	NY	10153	**800-992-2766**	212-583-2000	527
Baron Metal Industries Inc 101 Ashbridge Cir	Woodbridge	ON	L4L3R5	**800-263-7515**	416-749-2111	479
Baron Mfg Company LLC 1200 Capitol Dr	Addison	IL	60101	**800-368-8585**	630-628-9110	350
Baron Oilfield Supply Ltd 9515-108 St	Grande Prairie	AB	T8V5R7	**888-532-5661**	780-532-5661	358
Barona Resort & Casino 1932 Wildcat Canyon Rd	Lakeside	CA	92040	**888-722-7662**	619-443-2300	132
Baronne Plaza Hotel 201 Baronne St	New Orleans	LA	70112	**888-756-0083**	504-522-0083	379
Barr Engineering Co 4700 W 77th St	Minneapolis	MN	55435	**800-632-2277**	952-832-2600	263
Barrett Business Services Inc 8100 NE Pkwy Dr Ste 200 *NASDAQ: BBSI*	Vancouver	WA	98662	**800-494-5669**	360-828-0700	630
Barrett Carpet Mills Inc 2216 Abutment Rd	Dalton	GA	30721	**800-241-4064**		130
Barrick Gold Corp TD Canada Trust Tower 161 Bay St PO Box 212 *NYSE: ABX*	Toronto	ON	M5J2S1	**800-720-7415**	416-861-9911	501
Barrie House Coffee Company Inc 4 Warehouse ln	Elmsford	NY	10523	**800-876-2233**		298-2
Barriere Construction Co LLC 1 Galleria Blvd Ste 1650	Metairie	LA	70001	**866-645-3060**	504-581-7283	190-4
Barrington Hotel & Suites 263 Shepherd of the Hills Expy	Branson	MO	65616	**800-760-8866**	417-334-8866	379
Barris, Sott, Denn & Driker PLLC 333 W Fort St Ste 1200	Detroit	MI	48226	**877-529-8750**	313-965-9725	428
Barron Electric Co-op 1434 State Hwy 25 N	Barron	WI	54812	**800-322-1008**	715-537-3171	247
Barron's Educational Series Inc 250 Wireless Blvd	Hauppauge	NY	11788	**800-645-3476**	631-434-3311	634-2
Barry Bunker Chevrolet Inc 1307 N Wabash Ave *Sales	Marion	IN	46952	**866-603-8625***	765-664-1275	56
Barry Callebaut USA LLC 400 Industrial Pk Rd	Saint Albans	VT	05478	**866-443-0460**	802-524-9711	297-8
Barry Electric Co-op 4015 Main St PO Box 307	Cassville	MO	65625	**866-847-2333**		247
Barry University 11300 NE Second Ave	Miami Shores	FL	33161	**800-756-6000**	305-899-3000	167
Barry Memorial Library 11300 NE Second Ave	Miami Shores	FL	33161	**800-756-6000**	305-899-3000	434-6
Orlando 1650 Sandlake Rd Ste 390	Orlando	FL	32809	**800-756-6000**	407-438-4150	167
Tallahassee 325 John Knox Rd Bldg A	Tallahassee	FL	32303	**800-756-6000**	850-385-2279	167
Barry University Dwayne O Andreas School of Law 6441 E Colonial Dr	Orlando	FL	32807	**800-756-6000**	321-206-5600	168-1
Barry-owen Co Inc 5625 Smithway St	Los Angeles	CA	90040	**800-682-6682**	323-724-4800	294
Barry-Wehmiller Cos Inc 8020 Forsyth Blvd	Saint Louis	MO	63105	**800-862-8020**	314-862-8000	546
Barry-Wehmiller Cos Inc Accraply Div 3580 Holly Ln N	Plymouth	MN	55447	**800-328-3997**	763-557-1313	546
Bar-S Foods Co PO Box 29049	Phoenix	AZ	85038	**800-699-4115**		297-26
Barstow College 2700 Barstow Rd	Barstow	CA	92311	**877-823-2378**	760-252-2411	161
Bar-T-5 Covered Wagon Cook Out & Wild West Show 812 Cache Creek Dr	Jackson	WY	83001	**800-772-5386**	307-733-5386	669
Bartech Group 17199 N Laurel Pk Dr Ste 224	Livonia	MI	48152	**800-828-4410**	734-953-5050	719
Bartell Machinery Systems LLC 6321 Elmer Hill Rd	Rome	NY	13440	**800-537-8473**	315-336-7600	493
Bartender Magazine PO Box 158 *Sales	Liberty Corner	NJ	07938	**800-829-4222***	908-766-6006	456-21
Barth Electric Company Inc 1934 N Illinois St	Indianapolis	IN	46202	**800-666-6226**	317-924-6226	191-4
Barthco International Inc 5101 S Broad St *General	Philadelphia	PA	19112	**877-401-6400***	215-238-8600	312
Bartholomew County Rural Electric Membership Corp 1697 W. Deaver Rd	Columbus	IN	47201	**800-927-5672**	812-372-2546	247
Bartizan Corp 217 Riverdale Ave	Yonkers	NY	10705	**800-899-2278**	914-965-7977	533
Bartle & Gibson Company Ltd 13475 Ft Rd NW	Edmonton	AB	T5A1C6	**800-661-5615**	780-472-2850	611
Bartlett & Co 600 Vine St Ste 2100	Cincinnati	OH	45202	**800-800-4612**	513-621-4612	401
Bartlett & West Engineers Inc 1200 SW Executive Dr	Topeka	KS	66615	**888-200-6464**	785-272-2252	263
Barton Brescome Inc 69 Defco Park Rd	North Haven	CT	06473	**800-922-4840**	203-239-4901	79-3
Barton College PO Box 5000	Wilson	NC	27893	**800-345-4973**	252-399-6300	167
Barton Cotton Inc 3030 Waterview Ave	Baltimore	MD	21230	**800-638-4652**	800-348-1102	318
Barton County Community College 245 NE 30th Rd	Great Bend	KS	67530	**800-722-6842**	620-792-2701	161
Barton County Electric Co-op 91 US-160	Lamar	MO	64759	**800-286-5636**	417-682-5636	247
Barton Solvents Inc 1920 NE Broadway Ave	Des Moines	IA	50313	**800-728-6488**	515-265-7998	145
Barts Water Sports 7581 E 800 N	North Webster	IN	46555	**800-348-5016**	574-834-7666	709

Name / Address	City	State	ZIP	Toll-Free	Phone	Class
Baruch College 55 Lexington Ave at 24th St	New York	NY	10010	**800-273-8255**	646-312-1000	167
Basalite Concrete Products LLC 605 Industrial Way	Dixon	CA	95620	**800-776-6690**	707-678-1901	185
Basco Shower Enclosures 7201 Snider Rd	Mason	OH	45040	**800-543-1938**	513-573-1900	330
Bascom Palmer Eye Institute 900 NW 17th St	Miami	FL	33136	**800-329-7000**	305-326-6000	374-7
Bascom-Turner Instrument 111 Downey St	Norwood	MA	02062	**800-225-3298**	781-769-9660	611
Baseball Express Inc 5750 NW Pkwy Ste 100	San Antonio	TX	78249	**800-937-4824**	210-348-7000	709
Baseball Hall of Fame 910 S 3rd St	Minneapolis	MN	55415	**888-375-9707**	612-375-9707	521
BASF Canada 100 Milverton Dr 5th Fl *Cust Svc	Mississauga	ON	L5R4H1	**866-485-2273***	289-360-1300	142
BASF Corp 100 Campus Dr	Florham Park	NJ	07932	**800-526-1072**	973-245-6000	142
BASF Corp/Bldg Systems 889 Valley Pk Dr *Cust Svc	Shakopee	MN	55379	**800-433-9517***	952-496-6000	3
Bashas Inc 22402 S Bashas Rd	Chandler	AZ	85248	**800-755-7292**	480-895-9350	345
Basic Carbide Corp 900 Main St	Lowber	PA	15660	**800-426-4291**	724-446-1630	1
Basic Commodities Inc 863 S Orlando Ave	Winter Park	FL	32789	**800-338-7006**	407-629-2000	171
Basic Components Inc 1201 S Second Ave	Mansfield	TX	76063	**800-452-1780**	817-473-7224	193-2
Basic Metals Inc W180 Nn11819 River Ln	Germantown	WI	53022	**800-989-1996**	262-255-9034	491
Basin Disposal Inc 2021 N Commercial Ave	Pasco	WA	99301	**800-642-6447**	509-547-2476	802
Basin Harbor Club 4800 Basin Harbor Rd	Vergennes	VT	05491	**800-622-4000**	802-475-2311	667
Basin Tire & Auto Inc 2700 E Main St	Farmington	NM	87402	**800-832-9832**	505-326-2231	61-5
Basis International Ltd 5901 Jefferson St NE *Orders	Albuquerque	NM	87109	**800-423-1394***	505-345-5232	180-12
Baskin Auto Truck & Tractor Inc 1844 Hwy 51 S	Covington	TN	38019	**877-476-2626**	901-476-2626	56
Baskin-Robbins Inc 130 Royall St	Canton	MA	02021	**800-859-5339**	781-737-3000	381
Bass Performance Hall 4th & Calhoun Sts	Fort Worth	TX	76102	**877-212-4280**	817-212-4300	571
Bass Player Magazine 28 E 28th St 12th Fl *Cust Svc	New York	NY	10016	**866-246-3595***	212-378-0400	456-9
Bassett Furniture Industries Inc 3525 Fairystone Pk Hwy PO Box 626 *NASDAQ: BSET*	Bassett	VA	24055	**877-525-7070**	714-222-1010	320-2
Bassett Healthcare Network 1 Atwell Rd	Cooperstown	NY	13326	**800-227-7388**	607-547-3456	374-3
Bassett Printing Corp 3321 Fairystone Park Hwy	Bassett	VA	24055	**800-336-5102**		626
Bassmaster Magazine 3500 Blue Lake Dr Ste 330	Birmingham	FL	35243	**877-227-7872**		456-20
Bastian Material Handling LLC (BMH) 10585 N Meridian St 3rd Fl	Indianapolis	IN	46290	**800-772-0464**	317-575-9992	54
Bastian Trucking Inc 440 South Main	Aurora	UT	84620	**800-452-5126**	435-529-7453	778
Bat Conservation International (BCI) 500 N Capital of Texas Hwy	Austin	TX	78746	**800-538-2287**	512-327-9721	47-3
Batavia VA Medical Ctr 222 Richmond Ave	Batavia	NY	14020	**800-273-8255**	585-297-1000	374-8
BatchMaster Software Inc 24461 Ridge Rt Dr Ste 210	Laguna Hills	CA	92653	**800-359-0920**	949-583-1646	180-10
Bates College 2 Andrews Rd Ln Hall Rm1	Lewiston	ME	04240	**888-522-8371**	207-786-6255	167
Bates Container 6433 Davis Blvd	North Richland Hills	TX	76182	**888-541-0192**	817-498-3200	99
Bates Ford 1673 W Main St	Lebanon	TN	37087	**888-834-4671**		56
Batesville Casket Co 1 Batesville Blvd *Cust Svc	Batesville	IN	47006	**800-622-8373***	812-934-7500	133
Bath & Body Works 7 Limited Pkwy E	Reynoldsburg	OH	43068	**800-395-1001**		217
Bath County PO Box 309	Warm Springs	VA	24484	**888-823-1710**	540-839-7221	338
Bath Veterans Affairs Medical Ctr 76 Veterans Ave	Bath	NY	14810	**877-845-3247**	607-664-4000	374-8
Bathcrest Inc 265E 3900 S	Salt Lake City	UT	84107	**800-826-6790**	801-957-1400	191-11
Bath-Tec Inc PO Box 1118	Ennis	TX	75120	**800-526-3301**	972-646-5279	375
Baton Rouge Community College (BRCC) 201 Community College Dr	Baton Rouge	LA	70806	**866-217-9823**	225-216-8000	161
Baton Rouge Convention & Visitors Bureau 359 Third St	Baton Rouge	LA	70801	**800-527-6843**	225-383-1825	208
Baton Rouge Metropolitan Airport 9430 Jackie Cochran Dr Ste 300	Baton Rouge	LA	70807	**877-359-2538**	225-355-0333	27
Battelle Memorial Institute Inc 505 King Ave	Columbus	OH	43201	**800-201-2011**	614-424-6424	666
Battered Women's Justice Project 1801 Nicollet Ave S Ste 102	Minneapolis	MN	55403	**800-903-0111**	612-824-8768	48-10
Battery Wharf Hotel & Spa, The 3 Battery Wharf	Boston	MA	02109	**877-794-6218**	617-994-9000	705
Battle Creek Enquirer 155 W Van Buren St	Battle Creek	MI	49017	**800-333-4139**	269-964-7161	531-2
Battle Creek/Calhoun County Convention & Visitors Bureau 77 E Michigan Ave Ste 100	Battle Creek	MI	49017	**800-397-2240**	269-962-2240	208
Battle Ground Lake State Park 18002 NE 249th St	Battle Ground	WA	98604	**888-226-7688**	360-687-4621	564

Name / Address	City	State	Zip	Toll-Free	Phone	Class
Battlefield Farms Inc 23190 Clarks Mtn Rd	Rapidan	VA	22733	800-722-0744		369
Baublys Control Laser Corp 7101 Tpc Dr Ste 100	Orlando	FL	32822	866-612-8619	407-926-3500	425
Baudville Inc 5380 52nd St SE *Orders	Grand Rapids	MI	49512	800-728-0888*	616-698-0889	180-1
Baue Funeral Homes 620 Jefferson St	Saint Charles	MO	63301	888-724-0073	636-940-1000	509
Bauer Built Inc PO Box 248	Durand	WI	54736	800-268-5114	715-672-4295	753
Bauer Premium Fly Reels 585 Clover Ln Ste 1	Ashland	OR	97520	888-484-4165	541-488-8246	708
Bauer-Pileco Inc 100 N FM 3083 E	Conroe	TX	77303	800-474-5326	713-691-3000	386
Bauerware LLC 3886 17th St	San Francisco	CA	94114	877-864-5662	415-864-3886	362
Baum Textile Mills Inc 812 Jersey Ave	Jersey City	NJ	07310	866-842-7631	201-659-0444	593
Bauman Associates Ltd PO Box 1225	Eau Claire	WI	54702	888-952-2866	715-834-2001	2
Baumfolder Corp 1660 Campbell Rd	Sidney	OH	45365	800-543-6107	937-492-1281	555
Baumgarten's 144 Ottley Dr	Atlanta	GA	30324	800-247-5547	404-874-7675	533
Bausch & Lomb Inc 1400 N Goodman St	Rochester	NY	14609	800-553-5340	585-338-6000	541
Bausch & Lomb Pharmaceuticals Inc 8500 Hidden River Pkwy *Cust Svc	Tampa	FL	33637	800-323-0000*	800-553-5340	582
Baxter Corp 7125 Mississauga Rd	Mississauga	ON	L5N0C2	866-234-2345	905-369-6000	233
Baxter International Inc 1 Baxter Pkwy *NYSE: BAX*	Deerfield	IL	60015	800-422-9837	847-948-2000	476
Baxter Regional Medical Ctr 624 Hospital Dr	Mountain Home	AR	72653	800-695-3627	870-424-1000	374-3
BaxterBoo 7025 S Fulton St Ste 150	Centennial	CO	80112	888-887-0063		688
Bay Area Anesthesia Inc PO Box 1547	Ukiah	CA	95482	800-327-8427	707-462-9420	719
Bay Area Medical Ctr (BAMC) 3100 Shore Dr	Marinette	WI	54143	888-788-2070	715-735-4200	374-3
Bay Bank 2328 W Joppa Rd *NASDAQ: BYBK*	Lutherville	MD	21093	800-222-6566	410-494-2580	360-2
Bay City Flower Company Inc 2265 Cabrillo Hwy S *Sales	Half Moon Bay	CA	94019	800-399-5858*	650-726-5535	369
Bay City Times 311 Fifth St	Bay City	MI	48708	800-727-7661	989-895-8551	531-2
Bay Club Hotel & Marina 2131 Shelter Island Dr	San Diego	CA	92106	800-672-0800	619-224-8888	379
Bay County 515 Ctr Ave Ste 101	Bay City	MI	48708	877-229-9960	989-895-4280	338
Bay de Noc Community College 2001 N Lincoln Rd	Escanaba	MI	49829	800-221-2001	906-786-5802	161
Bay Hill Golf Club & Lodge 9000 Bay Hill Blvd	Orlando	FL	32819	888-422-9445	407-876-2429	667
Bay Houston Towing Co 2243 Milford St	Houston	TX	77253	800-324-3755	713-529-3755	464
Bay Mechanical Inc 2696 Reliance Dr Ste 200	Virginia Beach	VA	23452	888-229-6324	757-468-6700	191-10
Bay Medical Ctr 615 N Bonita Ave	Panama City	FL	32401	800-268-2435	850-769-1511	374-3
Bay Mills Community College 12214 W Lakeshore Dr	Brimley	MI	49715	800-844-2622	906-248-3354	164
Bay Park Hotel 1425 Munras Ave *Resv	Monterey	CA	93940	800-338-3564*	831-649-1020	379
Bay Path College 588 Longmeadow St	Longmeadow	MA	01106	800-782-7284		167
Bay Regional Medical Ctr (BRMC) 1900 Columbus Ave	Bay City	MI	48708	800-656-3950	989-894-3000	374-3
Bay Shore Systems Inc 14206 N Ohio St	Rathdrum	ID	83858	888-569-3745	208-687-3311	192
Bay State College 122 Commonwealth Ave	Boston	MA	02116	800-815-3276	617-217-9000	798
Bay State Milling Co 100 Congress St	Quincy	MA	02169	800-553-5687		297-23
Bay Swiss Mfg Company Inc 5 Airpark Vista Blvd	Dayton	NV	89403	800-247-3207	775-246-7100	620
Bay Technical Assoc Inc 5239 Ave A	Long Beach Industrial Park	MS	39560	800-523-2702	228-563-7334	176
Bay Valley Hotel & Resort 2470 Old Bridge Rd	Bay City	MI	48706	888-241-4653	989-686-3500	667
Bay Watch Resort & Conference Ctr 2701 S Ocean Blvd	North Myrtle Beach	SC	29582	866-270-2172	843-272-4600	667
Bayada Nurses Home Care Specialists 290 Chester Ave	Moorestown	NJ	08057	877-591-1527	856-231-1000	363
Bayco Products Inc 640 Sanden Blvd	Wylie	TX	75098	800-233-2155	469-326-9400	437
Bayer Inc 77 Belfield Rd	Toronto	ON	M9W1G6	800-622-2937	416-248-0771	582
Bayer MaterialScience LLC 100 Bayer Rd	Pittsburgh	PA	15205	800-662-2927	412-777-2000	604-2
Bayerkohler & Graff Ltd 11132 Zealand Ave N	Champlin	MN	55316	866-315-2771	763-427-2542	731
Bayfield Electric Co-op Inc 68460 District St	Iron River	WI	54847	800-278-0166	715-372-4287	247
Bayhead Products Corp 173 Crosby Rd	Dover	NH	03820	800-229-4323	603-742-3000	469
Bayhealth Medical Ctr 21 W Clarke Ave	Milford	DE	19963	877-453-7107	302-430-5738	374-3
Baylis Medical Company Inc 5959 Trans-Canada Hwy	Montreal	QC	H4T1A1	800-850-9801	514-488-9801	476
Baylor Plaza Hotel 3600 Gaston Ave	Dallas	TX	75246	800-422-9567		372
Baylor Regional Medical Ctr at Grapevine 1650 W College St	Grapevine	TX	76051	800-422-9567	817-481-1588	374-3
Baylor Trucking Inc 9269 E State Rd 48	Milan	IN	47031	800-322-9567	812-623-2020	778
Baylor University 1301 S University Parks Dr	Waco	TX	76798	800-229-5678	254-710-3718	167
Baylor University School of Law 1114 S University Parks Dr 1 Bear Pl 97288	Waco	TX	76798	800-229-5678	254-710-1911	168-1
Baymont Inn 4025 McDonald Dr	Dubuque	IA	52003	800-337-0550	563-582-3752	379
Bayou Segnette State Park 7777 Westbank Expy	Westwego	LA	70094	888-677-2296	504-736-7140	564
BayPort Credit Union Inc 3711 Huntington Ave	Newport News	VA	23607	800-928-8801	757-928-8850	221
Bays Corp PO Box 1455	Chicago	IL	60690	800-367-2297		297-1
Bayshore Medical Ctr 4000 Spencer Hwy	Pasadena	TX	77504	800-465-4837	713-359-2000	374-3
Bayshore Town Center 5800 N Bayshore Dr Ste A256	Glendale	WI	53217	800-235-4636	414-963-8780	459
Bayshore Transportation System Inc 901 Dawson Dr	Newark	DE	19713	800-523-3319	302-366-0220	778
Bayside Resort Hotel 225 Massachusetts 28	West Yarmouth	MA	02673	800-243-1114	508-775-5669	667
Bayside Solutions Inc 6160 Stoneridge Mall Rd Ste 320	Pleasanton	CA	94588	800-220-0074		262
Baystate Visiting Nurse Assn & Hospice 50 Maple St	Springfield	MA	01103	800-249-8298	413-794-6411	371
Baytex Energy Corp 2800 520 - Third Ave SW	Calgary	AB	T2P0R3	800-524-5521	587-952-3000	535
Bayview Limousine Service 15701 Nelson Pl S	Seattle	WA	98188	800-606-7880	206-824-6200	441
Bayview Press 30 Knox St PO Box 153	Thomaston	ME	04861	800-903-2346	207-354-9919	129
Bayway Lincoln-mercury Inc 12333 Gulf Fwy	Houston	TX	77034	888-262-9275		56
Bazon Cox & Associates Inc 1244 Executive Blvd	Chesapeake	VA	23320	800-769-1763	757-410-2128	182
Bazz Houston Co 12700 Western Ave	Garden Grove	CA	92841	800-385-9608	714-898-2666	487
BB & T Corp 200 W Second St *NYSE: BBT*	Winston-Salem	NC	27101	800-226-5228	336-733-1470	360-2
B&B Image Group 1712 Marshall St NE	Minneapolis	MN	55413	888-788-9461	612-788-9461	344
Bb Riverboats Inc 101 Riverboat Row	Newport	KY	41071	800-261-8586	859-261-8500	746
BBCN Bank 3731 Wilshire Blvd Ste 1000 *NASDAQ: NARA*	Los Angeles	CA	90010	888-811-6272	213-639-1700	360-2
BBH (Baltimore Behavioral Health) 1101 W Pratt St	Baltimore	MD	21223	800-789-2647	410-962-7180	724
BC Wire Rope & Rigging 2720 E Regal Park Dr	Anaheim	CA	92806	800-669-5919	714-666-8000	491
BCAA (British Columbia Automobile Assn) 4567 Canada Way	Burnaby	BC	V5G4T1	800-222-4357	604-268-5000	52
BCC (Brevard Community College) *Cocoa* 1519 Clearlake Rd	Cocoa	FL	32922	888-747-2802	321-632-1111	161
BCC Research LLC 49 Walnut Pk Bldg 2	Wellesley	MA	02481	866-285-7215	781-489-7301	634-9
BCCR (Brown College of Court Reporting & Medical Transcription) 1900 Emery St NW Ste 200	Atlanta	GA	30318	800-849-0703	404-876-1227	798
BCCVB (Bucks County Conference & Visitors Bureau) 3207 St Rd	Bensalem	PA	19020	800-836-2825	215-639-0300	208
BCF LLP 25th Fl 1100 Rene-Levesque Blvd W	Montreal	QC	H3B5C9	866-511-8501	514-397-8500	428
Bcg Attorney Search 175 S Lk Ave Unit 200	Pasadena	CA	91101	800-298-6440		262
BCHA (Back Country Horsemen of America) PO Box 1367	Graham	WA	98338	888-893-5161	360-832-2461	47-23
BCI (Bat Conservation International) 500 N Capital of Texas Hwy	Austin	TX	78746	800-538-2287	512-327-9721	47-3
BCI Burke Company Inc 660 Van Dyne Rd	Fond du Lac	WI	54937	800-356-2070	920-921-9220	346
BCLC (British Columbia Lottery Corp) 74 W Seymour St	Kamloops	BC	V2C1E2	866-815-0222	250-828-5500	451
BCM Resources Corp 1040 W Georgia St	Vancouver	BC	V6E4H1	888-646-0144	604-646-0144	501
B&CMA (Biscuit & Cracker Manufacturers Assn) 6325 Woodside Ct Ste 125	Columbia	MD	21046	877-701-8111	443-545-1645	48-6
BCN (Bliss Clearing Niagara) 1004 E State St	Hastings	MI	49058	800-642-5477	269-948-3300	455
Bcn Transportation Services 3650 W Liberty Rd	Ann Arbor	MI	48103	800-891-9911	734-994-4100	462
BCP Veterinary Pharmacy 1614 Webster St	Houston	TX	77003	800-481-1729	713-771-1144	239
BCSCVB (Bryan/College Station Convention & Visitors Bureau) 715 University Dr E	College Station	TX	77840	800-777-8292	979-260-9898	208
BCVB (Bloomington Convention & Visitors Bureau) 7900 International Dr Ste 990	Bloomington	MN	55425	800-346-4289	952-858-8500	208
BCW Diversified 514 E 31st St	Anderson	IN	46016	800-433-4229	765-644-2033	626
BCWSA (Bucks County Water & Sewer Authority) 1275 Almshouse Rd	Warrington	PA	18976	800-222-2068	215-343-2538	804
BD Biosciences 2350 Qume Dr	San Jose	CA	95131	800-223-8226	408-432-9475	419
BD Biosciences PharMingen 10975 Torreyana Rd	San Diego	CA	92121	800-848-6227	858-812-8800	84
BD Diagnostics 7 Loveton Cir	Sparks	MD	21152	800-666-6433	410-316-4000	233
B&D Industries Inc 9720 Bell Ave Se	Albuquerque	NM	87123	866-315-8349	505-299-4464	248
BD Medical 9450 S State St	Sandy	UT	84070	888-237-2762	801-565-2300	475

Company / Address	City	State	ZIP	Toll-Free	Phone	Class
BD Week 9737 Washingtonian Blvd Ste 100	Gaithersburg	MD	20878	866-777-8567	646-223-6771	530-7
BDA (Bensinger DuPont & Assoc) 134 N LaSalle St Ste 2200	Chicago	IL	60602	800-227-8620	312-726-8620	461
BDA (Bensussen Deutsch & Assoc Inc) 15525 Woodinville-Redmond Rd NE	Woodinville	WA	98072	800-451-4764	425-492-6111	465
BDB Payroll Inc 768 Bedford Ave	Brooklyn	NY	11205	800-729-7687	718-522-2000	731
Bde Computer Services LLC 399 Lakeview Ave	Clifton	NJ	07011	877-233-4877	973-772-8507	177
BDEC (Burke-Divide Electric Co-op Inc) 9549 Hwy 5 W	Columbus	ND	58727	800-472-2983	701-939-6671	247
B-D-R Transport Inc 7994 US Rt 5	Westminster	VT	05158	800-421-0126	802-463-0606	778
BE Implement Co 1645 FM 403 PO Box 752	Brownfield	TX	79316	800-725-5435	806-637-3594	276
BEA (Broadcast Education Assn) 1771 N St NW	Washington	DC	20036	888-326-1415	202-429-3935	48-5
Beach Camera 203 Rt 22 E	Green Brook	NJ	08812	800-572-3224	732-968-6400	118
Beach Colony Resort 5308 N Ocean Blvd *General	Myrtle Beach	SC	29577	800-222-2141*	843-449-4010	667
Beach Manufacturing Co PO Box 129	Donnelsville	OH	45319	800-543-5942	937-882-6372	59
Beach Properties of Hilton Head Inc 64 Arrow Rd PO Box 7408	Hilton Head Island	SC	29928	800-671-5155	843-671-5155	654
Beach Realty & Construction 4826 N Croatan Hwy	Kitty Hawk	NC	27949	800-635-1559	252-261-3815	650
Beach Terrace Motor Inn 3400 Atlantic Ave	Wildwood	NJ	08260	800-841-8416	609-522-8100	378
Beachcomber Resort Hotel & Villas 1200 S Ocean Blvd	Pompano Beach	FL	33062	800-231-2423	954-941-7830	667
Beacher's Lodge 6970 A1A S	Saint Augustine	FL	32080	800-527-8849	904-471-8849	379
Beacon Assoc Inc 900-A S Main St Ste 102	Bel Air	MD	21014	877-846-5046	410-638-7279	196
Beacon Container Corp 700 W First St	Birdsboro	PA	19508	800-422-8383	610-582-2222	99
Beacon Credit Union PO Box 627	Wabash	IN	46992	800-762-3136	260-563-7443	221
Beacon Financial Partners 25800 Science Park Dr Ste 100	Beachwood	OH	44122	866-568-3951	216-910-1850	196
Beacon Hotel 720 Ocean Dr	Miami Beach	FL	33139	877-674-8200	305-674-8200	379
Beacon Hotel & Corporate Quarters 1615 Rhode Island Ave NW	Washington	DC	20036	800-823-1700	202-296-2100	379
Beacon House 1301 N Third St	Marquette	MI	49855	800-562-9753	906-225-7100	372
Beacon Industries Inc 12300 Old Tesson Rd	Saint Louis	MO	63128	800-454-7159	314-487-7600	21
Beacon Medaes 1800 Overview Dr	Rock Hill	SC	29730	888-463-3427	803-817-5600	252
Beacon Products LLC 2041 58th Ave Cir E	Bradenton	FL	34203	800-345-4928		362
Beacon Rock State Park 34841 State Rd 14	Skamania	WA	98648	888-226-7688	509-427-8265	564
Beacon Roofing Supply Inc 1 Lakeland Pk Dr *NASDAQ: BECN*	Peabody	MA	01960	877-645-7663	978-535-7668	193-4
Beacon Trust Co 163 Madison Ave Ste 600	Morristown	NJ	07960	866-377-8090	973-377-8090	401
Beacon Wireless Solutions Inc 206 Laird Dr Ste 207	Toronto	ON	M4G3W5	866-867-7770	416-696-7555	645
Bead & Button Magazine 21027 Crossroads Cir *Cust Svc	Waukesha	WI	53186	800-533-6644*	262-796-8776	456-14
Bead Industries Inc 11 Cascade Blvd	Milford	CT	06460	800-297-4851	203-301-0270	486
Beadles Lumber Company Inc 900 Sixth St NE PO Box 3457	Moultrie	GA	31776	800-763-2400	229-985-6996	681
Beads Galore International Inc 3320 S Priest Dr Ste 3	Tempe	AZ	85282	800-424-9577	480-921-3949	709
BeadStyle Magazine 21027 Crossroads Cir *Cust Svc	Waukesha	WI	53186	800-533-6644*	262-796-8776	456-14
Beal College 99 Farm Rd	Bangor	ME	04401	800-660-7351	207-947-4591	798
Beall Corp 9200 N Ramsey Blvd	Portland	OR	97203	855-219-5686		777
Beam Industries 1700 W Second St	Webster City	IA	50595	800-369-2326	515-832-4620	786
Beam Mack Sales & Service Inc 2674 W Henrietta Rd	Rochester	NY	14623	877-650-8789	585-424-4860	778
Beamers Hells Canyon Tours & Excursions PO Box 1243	Lewiston	ID	83501	800-522-6966	509-758-4800	758
Beanstalk Data 656 michael wylie dr	Charlotte	NC	28217	800-892-3997		227
Beanstream Internet Commerce Inc 1803 Douglas St Ste 200	Victoria	BC	V8T5C3	888-472-0811	250-472-2326	227
Bear Creek Lake State Park 22 Bear Creek Lk Rd	Cumberland	VA	23040	800-933-7275	804-492-4410	564
Bear Creek Mountain Resort 101 Doe Mtn Ln	Macungie	PA	18062	866-754-2822	610-641-7101	378
Bear Mountain Golf Course 43101 Gold Mine Dr PO Box 77	Big Bear Lake	CA	92315	844-462-2327	909-866-5766	667
Bear Staffing Services Inc 47 S Broad St	Woodbury	NJ	08096	866-580-2327		262
Bearcom Inc 4009 Distribution Dr Ste 200 *Sales	Garland	TX	75041	800-527-1670*		248
Bearing Distributors Inc 8000 Hub Pkwy	Cleveland	OH	44125	888-423-4872	216-642-9100	385

Company / Address	City	State	ZIP	Toll-Free	Phone	Class
Bearing Inspection Inc 4500 Mount Pleasant NW *Cust Svc	North Canton	OH	44720	800-416-8881*	234-262-3000	74
Bearing Service Co of Pennsylvania 630 Alpha Dr RIDC Park	Pittsburgh	PA	15238	800-783-2327	412-963-7710	74
Bearskin Airlines 1475 W Walsh St	Thunder Bay	ON	P7E4X6	800-465-2327	807-577-1141	25
Beartooth Electric Co-op Inc 1306 N Broadway St PO Box 1110	Red Lodge	MT	59068	800-472-9821	406-446-2310	247
Beartown State Park HC 64 PO Box 189 *General	Hillsboro	WV	24946	800-225-5982*	304-653-4254	564
Beason & Nalley Inc 101 Monroe St Ne	Huntsville	AL	35801	800-416-1946	256-533-1720	2
Beatty Group International 9800 Beaverton Hillsdale Ste 105	Beaverton	OR	97005	800-285-6215	503-644-3340	384
Beau Rivage Resort & Casino 875 Beach Blvd	Biloxi	MS	39530	888-750-7111	228-386-7111	667
Beaufort Memorial Hospital 955 Ribaut Rd	Beaufort	SC	29902	877-532-6472	843-522-5200	374-3
Beaufort National Cemetery 1601 Boundary St	Beaufort	SC	29902	800-273-8255	843-524-3925	135
Beaufurn LLC 5269 US Hwy 158	Advance	NC	27006	888-766-7706		322
Beaulieu of America Inc 1502 Coronet Dr PO Box 1248	Dalton	GA	30722	800-227-7211		130
Beaulieu Vineyard 1960 St Helena Hwy	Rutherford	CA	94573	800-373-5896	707-967-5233	79-3
Beaumont Civic Ctr Complex 701 Main St	Beaumont	TX	77701	800-782-3081	409-838-3435	207
Beaumont Convention & Visitors Bureau 505 Willow St	Beaumont	TX	77701	800-392-4401	409-880-3749	208
Beauregard Electric Co-op Inc 1010 E First St	DeRidder	LA	70634	800-367-0275	337-463-6221	247
Beauregard Parish Library 205 S Washington Ave	DeRidder	LA	70634	800-524-6239	337-463-6217	434-3
BeautiControl Inc 2121 Midway Rd PO Box 815189	Carrollton	TX	75006	800-232-8841		217
Beauti-Vue Products Inc 8555 194th Ave	Bristol	WI	53104	800-558-9431	262-857-2306	86
Beauty Brands Inc 4600 Madison St Ste 400	Kansas City	MO	64112	877-640-2248	816-531-2266	76
Beauty Craft Supply & Equipment Co 11110 Bren Rd W	Minnetonka	MN	55343	800-328-5010	952-935-4420	76
Beaver Creek Lodge 26 Avon Dale Ln	Beaver Creek	CO	81620	800-525-7280	970-845-9800	379
Beaver Creek Nature Area 20641 SD Hwy 1806 25495 485th Ave	Fort Pierre	SD	57532	800-710-2267	605-223-7660	564
Beaver Dunes State Park Hwy 270 N	Beaver	OK	73932	800-654-8240	580-625-3373	564
Beaver Express Service LLC 4310 Oklahoma Ave PO Box 1147	Woodward	OK	73802	800-593-2328	580-256-6460	778
Beaver Run Resort & Conference Ctr 620 Village Rd	Breckenridge	CO	80424	800-525-2253	970-453-6000	667
Beaver Street Fisheries Inc 1741 W Beaver St	Jacksonville	FL	32209	800-874-6426	904-354-8533	297-13
Beavers Bend Resort Park PO Box 10	Broken Bow	OK	74728	800-435-5514	580-494-6300	564
Beaverton Foods Inc 7100 NW Century Blvd	Hillsboro	OR	97124	800-223-8076	503-646-8138	297-19
Beavertooth Oak Inc 401 S Fir St	Medford	OR	97501	800-306-1942	541-779-1942	193-3
bebe stores Inc 400 Valley Dr *NASDAQ: BEBE*	Brisbane	CA	94005	877-232-3777	415-715-3900	154-20
Becharas Bros Coffee Co Inc 14501 Hamilton Ave	Highland Park	MI	48203	800-944-9675	313-869-4700	298-2
Bechik Products Inc 1020 Discovery Rd Ste 150	Eagan	MN	55121	800-328-6569	651-698-0364	470
Becker Arena Products Inc 6611 W Hwy 13	Savage	MN	55378	800-234-5522	952-890-2690	188
Becker Capital Management Inc 1211 S W Fifth Ave Ste 2185	Portland	OR	97204	800-551-3998	503-223-1720	401
Becker College 61 Sever St	Worcester	MA	01609	877-523-2537	508-791-9241	167
Becker Electric Supply Inc 1341 E Fourth St	Dayton	OH	45402	800-762-9515	937-226-1341	248
Becker"s ASC Review 77 Wacker	Chicago	IL	60611	800-417-2035	312-750-6016	196
Beckerman & Co 430 Lake Ave	Colonia	NJ	07067	800-339-1836	732-499-9200	390
Beckett Air Inc 37850 Beckett Pkwy	North Ridgeville	OH	44039	800-831-7839	440-327-9999	18
Beckett Corp 3250 Skyway Cir N	Irving	TX	75038	888-232-5388	972-871-8000	638
Beckley-Raleigh County Chamber of Commerce 245 N Kanawha St	Beckley	WV	25801	877-987-3847	304-252-7328	138
Beckmanxmo 376 Morrison Rd	Columbus	OH	43213	800-864-2232	614-864-2232	626
Be-Cool Inc 310 Woodside Ave	Essexville	MI	48732	800-691-2667	989-895-9699	611
Becton Dickinson & Co 1 Becton Dr *NYSE: BDX* ■ *Cust Svc	Franklin Lakes	NJ	07417	888-237-2762*	201-847-6800	476
Bed & Breakfast Atlanta 790 N Ave Ste 202	Atlanta	GA	30306	800-967-3224	404-875-0525	376
Bed & Breakfast Cape Cod PO Box 2250	Mashpee	MA	02649	800-556-3815	508-255-3824	376
Bed Bath & Beyond Inc 650 Liberty Ave *NASDAQ: BBBY*	Union	NJ	07083	800-462-3966	908-688-0888	362
Bed Wood & Parts LLC 8345 Madisonville Rd	Hopkinsville	KY	42240	877-205-9663	270-424-3000	56
BedandBreakfast.com 700 Brazos St Ste B-700 *Sales	Austin	TX	78701	800-462-2632*	512-322-2700	771

Company / Address	City	State	ZIP	Toll-Free	Phone	Class
Beden-Baugh Products Inc 105 Lisbon Rd	Laurens	SC	29360	**866-598-5794**	864-682-3136	201
Bedford County Chamber of Commerce 137 E Pitt St	Bedford	PA	15522	**800-732-0999**	814-623-2233	138
Bedford County Visitors Bureau 131 S Juliana St	Bedford	PA	15522	**800-765-3331**	814-623-1771	208
Bedford Gazette 424 W Penn St	Bedford	PA	15522	**800-242-4250**	814-623-1151	531-3
Bedford Industries Inc 1659 Rowe Ave *Cust Svc	Worthington	MN	56187	**877-233-3673***	507-376-4136	547
Bedford Laboratories Inc 300 Northfield Rd	Bedford	OH	44146	**800-562-4797**	440-232-3320	478
Bedford Machine & Tool Inc 2103 John Williams Blvd	Bedford	IN	47421	**800-264-1948**	812-275-1948	490
Bedford Materials Co Inc 7676 Allegheny Rd	Manns Choice	PA	15550	**800-773-4276**		814
Bedford Public Schools 1623 W Sterns Rd	Temperance	MI	48182	**866-261-9184**	734-850-6000	683
Bedford Road Pharmacy Inc 11306 Bedford Rd Ne	Cumberland	MD	21502	**800-788-6693**	301-777-1771	240
Bedford Rural Electric Co-op Inc 8846 Lincoln Hwy	Bedford	PA	15522	**800-808-2732**	814-623-5101	247
Bedford Technology LLC 2424 Armour Rd PO Box 609	Worthington	MN	56187	**800-721-9037**	507-372-5558	659
Bedford Village Inn 2 Olde Bedford Way	Bedford	NH	03110	**800-852-1166**	603-472-2001	669
Bedrock Prime 1309 N Wilson Rd Ste A	Radcliff	KY	40160	**866-334-5914**	270-351-8043	179
Beecher Hill LLC 9991 Beecher Hill Rd	Peshastin	WA	98847	**866-414-0559**	509-548-0559	379
Beech-Nut Nutrition Corp 1 Nutritious Pl	Amsterdam	NY	12010	**800-233-2468**		297-36
Beechwood Hotel 363 Plantation St	Worcester	MA	01605	**800-344-2589**	508-754-5789	379
Beef Magazine 7900 International Dr Ste 300 *Cust Svc	Minneapolis	MN	55425	**800-722-5334***	952-851-9329	456-1
Beef O'Bradys Inc 5660 W Cypress St Ste A	Tampa	FL	33607	**800-728-8878**	813-226-2333	668
Beehive Botanicals Inc 16297 W Nursery Rd	Hayward	WI	54843	**800-233-4483**	715-634-4274	797
Beehive Specialty Co 8701 Wall St Ste 900	Austin	TX	78754	**866-898-8774**	512-912-7940	4
Beekley Corp 1 Prestige Ln	Bristol	CT	06010	**800-233-5539**	860-583-4700	475
Beelman Truck Co 1 Racehorse Dr *Sales	East Saint Louis	IL	62205	**800-541-5918***	618-646-5300	778
Beemac Trucking 2747 Litionville Rd	Ambridge	PA	15003	**800-282-8781**	724-266-8781	683
Beemer Precision Inc 230 New York Dr PO Box 3080	Fort Washington	PA	19034	**800-836-2340**	215-646-8440	619
BeenVerified Inc 307 Fifth Ave 16th Fl	New York	NY	10016	**888-579-5910**		318
Beepi 240 Third St Ste 200	Los Altos	CA	94022	**888-542-3374**		387
Beer Institute 440 First St NW Ste 350	Washington	DC	20001	**800-379-2739**	202-737-2337	48-6
Beere Precision Products Inc 4915 21st St	Racine	WI	53406	**800-348-0101**	262-632-0472	789
BEGINNINGS 156 Wind Chime Ct Ste A	Raleigh	NC	27605	**800-541-4327**	919-715-4092	47-17
Behavioral Science Technology Inc 417 Bryant Cir	Ojai	CA	93023	**800-548-5781**	805-646-0166	196
Behr Process Corp 3400 W Segerstrom Ave	Santa Ana	CA	92704	**800-854-0133**	714-545-7101	549
BEI Technologies Inc Industrial Encoder Div 7230 Hollister Ave *Sales	Goleta	CA	93117	**800-350-2727***	805-968-0782	255
Beitler-Mckee Optical Co 160 S 22nd St	Pittsburgh	PA	15203	**800-989-4700**	412-481-4700	541
Bekins Van Lines LLC 8010 Castleton Rd	Indianapolis	IN	46250	**800-456-8092**		518
Bel Aire Displays 506 W Ohio Ave	Richmond	CA	94804	**877-439-4320**	510-439-4300	626
Bel Fuse Inc 206 Van Vorst St *NASDAQ: BELFA*	Jersey City	NJ	07302	**800-235-3873**	201-432-0463	727
Belair Produce Company Inc 7226 Pkwy Dr	Hanover	MD	21076	**888-782-8008**	410-782-8000	298-7
Belaire Products Inc 763 S Broadway St	Akron	OH	44311	**800-886-3224**	330-253-3116	9
Bel-Art Products Inc 661 Rte 23 S	Wayne	NJ	07440	**800-423-5278**	973-694-0500	420
Belarus Tractor International Inc 7842 N Faulkner Rd	Milwaukee	WI	53224	**800-356-2336**		276
Belcam Inc Delagar Div 27 Montgomery St	Rouses Point	NY	12979	**800-328-3006**	518-297-3366	217
Belcan Corp 10200 Anderson Way	Cincinnati	OH	45242	**800-423-5226**	513-891-0972	263
Belco Mfg Company Inc 2303 Taylors Vly Rd	Belton	TX	76513	**800-251-8265**	254-933-9000	201
Belco Packaging Systems Inc 910 S Mountain Ave	Monrovia	CA	91016	**800-833-1833**	626-357-9566	546
Belden Inc Americas Div 2200 US Hwy 27 S PO Box 1980	Richmond	IN	47375	**800-235-3362**	765-983-5200	812
Belding Tank Technologies Inc 200 N Gooding St PO Box 160	Belding	MI	48809	**800-253-4252**	616-794-1130	609
Beldon Enterprises Inc PO Box 13380	San Antonio	TX	78213	**800-688-7663**	210-341-3100	191-12
Belfast Area Chamber of Commerce 14 Main St	Belfast	ME	04915	**877-338-9015**	207-338-5900	138
BELFOR (Canada) Inc 3300 Bridgeway St	Vancouver	BC	V5K1H9	**888-432-1123**	604-432-1123	665
Belhaven College 1500 Peachtree St PO Box 153	Jackson	MS	39202	**800-960-5940**	601-968-5940	167
Beliefnet Inc 999 Waterside Dr Ste 1900	Norfolk	VA	23150	**800-311-2458**		173
Believe In Tomorrow National Children's Foundation 6601 Frederick Rd	Baltimore	MD	21228	**800-933-5470**	410-744-1032	47-6
Bell Aliant Regional Communications 1505 Barrington St Maritime Ctr *TSE: BA*	Halifax	NS	B3J3K5	**800-555-1212**	800-267-1110	733
Bell Canada 1050 Beaver Hall Hill	Montreal	QC	H2Z1S4	**800-667-0123**		733
Bell County 101 E Central Ave PO Box 480	Belton	TX	76513	**800-460-2355**	254-933-5160	338
Bell Electrical Contractors Inc 128 Millwell Dr	Maryland Heights	MO	63043	**800-717-2355**	314-739-7744	191-4
Bell Equipment Inc 511 Fourth St	Nezperce	ID	83543	**800-343-2355**	208-937-2402	276
Bell Ford Inc 2401 W Bell Rd	Phoenix	AZ	85023	**800-688-1776**	602-866-1776	56
Bell Harbor International Conference Ctr 2211 Alaskan Way Pier 66	Seattle	WA	98121	**888-772-4422**	206-441-6666	207
Bell Helicopter Textron Inc 600 E Hurst Blvd (State Hwy 10)	Hurst	TX	76053	**888-874-5884**	817-280-2011	20
Bell Industries Inc Recreational Products Group 580 Yankee Doodle Rd	Eagan	MN	55121	**800-866-5017**	651-203-2300	60
Bell Investment Advisors 1111 Broadway Ste 1630	Oakland	CA	94607	**800-700-0089**	510-433-1066	401
Bell Lifestyle Products Inc 3164 Pepper Mill Ct	Mississauga	ON	L5L4X4	**800-333-7995**		709
Bell Lumber & Pole Co 778 First St NW PO Box 120786	New Brighton	MN	55112	**877-633-4334**	651-633-4334	816
Bell Sports Corp 6225 N St Hwy 161 Ste 300	Irving	TX	75038	**866-525-2357**	469-417-6600	575
Bell Supply Inc 7221 Rt 130	Pennsauken	NJ	08110	**888-834-2371**	856-663-3900	688
Bell Techlogix 5777 Decatur Blvd	Indianapolis	IN	46241	**866-782-2355**	317-333-7777	182
Bell Tower Hotel 300 S Thayer St	Ann Arbor	MI	48104	**800-562-3559**	734-769-3010	379
Bell Tower Inn 1235 Second St SW	Rochester	MN	55902	**800-448-7583**	507-289-2233	379
Bellagio Hotel & Casino 3600 Las Vegas Blvd S	Las Vegas	NV	89109	**888-987-7111**	702-693-7111	667
Bellarmine University 2001 Newburg Rd	Louisville	KY	40205	**800-274-4723**	502-272-8000	167
Bellasera Hotel 221 Ninth St S	Naples	FL	34102	**855-990-0301**	239-649-7333	379
Bellco First Federal Credit Union 7600 E OrchaRd Rd Ste 400N	Greenwood Village	CO	80111	**800-235-5261**	303-689-7800	221
Bellco Glass Inc 340 Edrudo Rd	Vineland	NJ	08360	**800-257-7043**	856-691-1075	333
Belle Bonfils Memorial Blood Ctr 717 Yosemite St	Denver	CO	80230	**800-365-0006**	303-341-4000	88
Belle Meade Plantation 5025 Harding Pk	Nashville	TN	37205	**800-270-3991**	615-356-0501	519
Belle of Baton Rouge Casino 103 France St	Baton Rouge	LA	70802	**800-676-4847**		132
Belle Tire Inc 1000 Enterprise Dr	Allen Park	MI	48101	**888-462-3553**	313-271-9400	61-5
Bellefonte Area School District 318 N Allegheny St	Bellefonte	PA	16823	**866-632-9992**	814-355-4814	683
Belle-Pak Packaging Inc 7465 Birchmount Rd	Markham	ON	L3R5X9	**800-565-2137**	905-475-5151	600
Belleville Chamber of Commerce 5 Moira St E	Belleville	ON	K8P2S3	**888-852-9992**	613-962-4597	137
Belleville General Hospital 265 Dundas St E	Belleville	ON	K8N5A9	**800-483-2811**	613-969-7400	374-2
Belleville News-Democrat 120 S Illinois St	Belleville	IL	62220	**800-642-3878**	618-234-1000	531-2
Belleville Wire Cloth Inc 18 Rutgers Ave	Cedar Grove	NJ	07009	**800-631-0490**	973-239-0074	686
Bellevue Arts Museum 510 Bellevue Way NE	Bellevue	WA	98004	**800-367-2648**	425-519-0770	519
Bellevue Club Hotel 11200 SE Sixth St	Bellevue	WA	98004	**800-579-1110**	425-454-4424	379
Bellevue Leader 604 Fort Crook Rd N	Bellevue	NE	68005	**800-284-6397**	402-733-7300	531-4
Bellevue University 1000 Galvin Rd S	Bellevue	NE	68005	**800-756-7920**	402-293-2000	167
Bellin College of Nursing 3201 Eaton Rd	Green Bay	WI	54311	**800-236-8707**	920-433-6699	167
Bellingham Marine Industries Inc 1001 C St	Bellingham	WA	98225	**800-733-5679**	360-676-2800	190-5
Bellingrath Gardens & Home 12401 Bellingrath Garden Rd	Theodore	AL	36582	**800-247-8420**	251-973-2217	96
Bellmoor, The 6 Christian St	Rehoboth Beach	DE	19971	**800-425-2355**	302-227-5800	379
Bellomy Research Inc 175 Sunnynoll Ct	Winston-Salem	NC	27106	**800-443-7344**		197
Bellus Health Inc 275 Armand Frappier Blvd *TSE: BLU*	Laval	QC	H7V4A7	**877-680-4500**	450-680-4500	84
Belmont Abbey College 100 Belmont-Mt Holly Rd	Belmont	NC	28012	**888-222-0110**	704-461-6748	167
Belmont University 1900 Belmont Blvd	Nashville	TN	37212	**800-563-6765**	615-460-6000	167
Beloit College 700 College St *Admissions	Beloit	WI	53511	**800-331-4943***	608-363-2500	167
Beloit Convention & Visitors Bureau 500 Public Ave	Beloit	WI	53511	**800-423-5648**	608-365-4838	208
Beloit Daily News 149 State St	Beloit	WI	53511	**800-356-3411**	608-365-8811	531-2
Beloit Health System 1969 W Hart Rd	Beloit	WI	53511	**800-637-2641**	608-363-5724	374-3
Beloit Regional Hospice 655 Third St Ste 200	Beloit	WI	53511	**877-363-7421**	608-363-7421	371

Company / Address	City	State	Zip	Toll-Free	Phone	Class
Bel-Rea Institute of Animal Technology 1681 S Dayton St	Denver	CO	80247	**800-950-8001**	303-751-8700	798
Belshaw Bros Inc 1750 22nd Ave S	Seattle	WA	98144	**800-578-2547**	206-322-5474	299
Belshire Environmental Services Inc 25971 Towne Centre Dr	Foothill Ranch	CA	92610	**800-995-8220**	949-460-5200	62
Belson Outdoors Inc 111 N River Rd	North Aurora	IL	60542	**800-323-5664**	630-897-8489	320-4
Belstra Milling Company Inc 424 15th St	Demotte	IN	46310	**800-276-2789**		446
Belt Railway Co of Chicago 6900 S Central Ave	Bedford Park	IL	60638	**877-772-5772**	708-496-4000	649
Belt Tech Industrial Inc 2574 E 700 S	Washington	IN	47501	**877-554-2358**	812-644-7623	358
Belterra Casino Resort 777 Belterra Dr	Florence	IN	47020	**888-235-8377**	812-427-7777	667
Belterra Corp 1638 Fosters Way	Delta	BC	V3M6S6	**888-860-5600**	604-540-1950	370
Belting Industries Company Inc 20 Boright Ave	Kenilworth	NJ	07033	**800-843-2358**	908-272-8591	370
Belton Industries Inc 1205 Hanby Rd PO Box 127	Belton	SC	29627	**800-845-8753**	864-338-5711	742-3
Beltone Electronics Corp 2601 Patriot Blvd	Glenview	IL	60026	**800-235-8663**	847-832-3300	476
Beltrami Electric Co-op Inc 4111 Technology Dr NW	Bemidji	MN	56601	**800-955-6083**	218-444-2540	247
Beltservice Corp 4143 Rider Trl N	Earth City	MO	63045	**800-727-2358**	314-344-8500	209
Belvac Production Machinery Inc 237 Graves Mill Rd	Lynchburg	VA	24502	**800-423-5822**	434-239-0358	493
Belvedere Hotel 319 W 48th St	New York	NY	10036	**800-492-8122**	212-245-7000	379
Belvedere Terminals Inc 138 107th Ave Ste 313	Treasure Island	FL	33706	**800-716-8515**		537
Belvedere USA Corp 1 Belvedere Blvd	Belvidere	IL	61008	**800-435-5491**	815-544-3131	75
Belwith International Ltd 3100 Broadway Ave	Grandville	MI	49418	**800-235-9484**		350
Bement School 94 Main St PO Box 8	Deerfield	MA	01342	**877-405-3949**	413-774-7061	621
Bemidji Area Chamber of Commerce 300 Bemidji Ave	Bemidji	MN	56601	**800-458-2223**	218-444-3541	138
Bemidji State University 1500 Birchmont Dr NE *Admissions	Bemidji	MN	56601	**800-475-2001***	218-755-2001	167
Bemis Co Inc Bemis Clysar Div 2451 Badger Ave	Oshkosh	WI	54903	**888-425-9727**	920-303-7800	547
Bemis Company Inc Paper Packaging Div 2445 Deer Pk Blvd	Omaha	NE	68105	**800-541-4303**		64
Bemis Manufacturing Co 300 Mill St	Sheboygan Falls	WI	53085	**800-558-7651**	920-467-4621	320-4
Ben Arnold Beverage Company LP 101 Beverage Blvd *Acctg	Ridgeway	SC	29130	**888-262-9787***	803-337-3500	80-3
Ben Bridge Jeweler Inc PO Box 1908 *Cust Svc	Seattle	WA	98111	**888-917-9171***	206-239-6811	410
Ben Lippen School 7401 Monticello Rd	Columbia	SC	29203	**800-777-2227**	803-786-7200	621
Ben Lomond Suites LLC 2510 Washington Blvd	Ogden	UT	84401	**877-627-1900**	801-627-1900	379
Ben Moss Jewellers 300-201 Portage Ave	Winnipeg	MB	R3B3K6	**888-236-6677**	204-947-6682	410
Ben Tire Distributors Ltd 203 E Madison St PO Box 158	Toledo	IL	62468	**800-252-8961**		753
Ben Venue Laboratories Inc 300 Northfield Rd *General	Bedford	OH	44146	**800-989-3320***	440-232-3320	478
Bench & Bar of Minnesota Magazine 600 Nicollet Mall Ste 380	Minneapolis	MN	55402	**800-366-4812**	612-333-1183	456-15
Benchmark Group 4053 Maple Rd	Amherst	NY	14226	**800-876-0160**	716-833-4986	652
Benchmark Technologies International Inc 411 Hackensack Ave Fl 8	Hackensack	NJ	07601	**800-265-8254**	201-996-0077	196
Benco Dental Co 295 CenterPoint Blvd	Pittston	PA	18640	**800-462-3626**		474
Benco Electric Co-op 20946 549 Ave PO Box 8	Mankato	MN	56002	**888-792-3626**	507-387-7963	247
Bend Chamber of Commerce 777 NW Wall St	Bend	OR	97701	**800-905-2363**	541-382-3221	138
Bender Engineering Inc 10037 E River St	Irvine	CA	92618	**800-255-5675**	949-458-7560	263
Bender Group 345 Parr Cir	Reno	NV	89512	**800-621-9402**	775-788-8800	448
Bendix Commercial Vehicle Systems LLC 901 Cleveland St	Elyria	OH	44035	**800-247-2725**	440-329-9000	60
BendTec Inc 366 Garfield Ave	Duluth	MN	55802	**800-236-3832**	218-722-0205	594
Benecaid Health Benefit Solutions Inc 185 The W Mall Ste 800	Toronto	ON	M9C5L5	**877-797-7448**	416-626-8786	391-3
Benedict College 1600 Harden St	Columbia	SC	29204	**800-868-6598**	803-253-5000	167
Benedictine College 1020 N Second St	Atchison	KS	66002	**800-467-5340**	913-367-5340	167
Benedictine Health System 503 E Third St Ste 400	Duluth	MN	55805	**800-833-7208**	218-786-2370	353
Benedictine University 5700 College Rd	Lisle	IL	60532	**888-829-6363**	630-829-6300	167
Benefact Consulting Group 6285 Northam Dr Ste 200	Mississauga	ON	L4V1X5	**855-829-2225**		462
Beneficial Financial Group 55 N 300 W	Salt Lake City	UT	84145	**800-233-7979**	801-933-1100	391-2
Beneficial Mutual Savings Bank 530 Walnut St	Philadelphia	PA	19106	**800-784-8490**	215-864-6000	69
Benefis HealthSystems *East Campus* 1101 26th St S	Great Falls	MT	59405	**800-648-6632**	406-455-5000	374-3
Benefit & Risk Management Services Inc 10860 Gold Ctr Dr Ste 300	Rancho Cordova	CA	95670	**888-326-2555**	916-858-2950	390
Benefit Advantage Inc 3431 Commodity Ln	Green Bay	WI	54304	**800-686-6829**	920-339-0351	462
BeneFit Cosmetics 225 Bush St *Cust Svc	San Francisco	CA	94104	**800-781-2336***	415-781-8153	217
BenefitHelp Solutions Inc 10505 SE 17th Ave	Milwaukie	OR	97222	**888-398-8057**	503-219-3679	534
BenefitMall 3450 Lakeside Dr Ste 400	Miramar	FL	33027	**877-729-6299**	954-874-4800	2
BenefitMall Inc 4851 LBJ Fwy Ste 1100	Dallas	TX	75244	**888-338-6293**	469-791-3300	180-10
Benefitvision Inc 4522 RFD	Long Grove	IL	60047	**800-810-2200**		198
Benemax Inc 7 W Mill St	Medfield	MA	02052	**800-528-1530**		196
Benesyst Inc 800 Washington Ave N 8th Fl	Minneapolis	MN	55401	**866-786-3366**	800-422-4661	258
Benetrends Inc 1180 Welsh Rd	North Wales	PA	19454	**866-423-6387**	267-498-0059	462
Benjamin Franklin Institute of Technology 41 Berkeley St	Boston	MA	02116	**877-400-2348**	617-423-4630	798
Benjamin Franklin Plumbing 50 Central Ave Ste 920	Sarasota	FL	34236	**800-471-0809**	941-366-9692	311
Benjamin Moore & Co 101 Paragon Dr	Montvale	NJ	07645	**800-344-0400**	201-573-9600	549
Benjamin N Cardozo School of Law Yeshiva University 55 Fifth Ave Brookdale Ctr	New York	NY	10003	**800-232-5463**	212-790-0200	168-1
Benjamin, The 125 E 50th St	New York	NY	10022	**866-222-2365**	212-715-2500	379
Benner-Nawman Inc 3450 Sabin Brown Rd	Wickenburg	AZ	85390	**800-992-3833**	928-684-2813	288
Bennett College 900 E Washington St *Admissions	Greensboro	NC	27401	**800-413-5323***	336-370-8624	167
Bennett Pump Co 1218 Pontaluna Rd	Spring Lake	MI	49456	**800-235-7618**	231-798-1310	636
Bennington Area Chamber of Commerce 100 Veterans Memorial Dr	Bennington	VT	05201	**800-229-0252**	802-447-3311	138
Bennington College 1 College Dr	Bennington	VT	05201	**800-833-6845**	802-442-5401	167
Bennington County 100 Veterans Memorial Dr	Bennington	VT	05201	**800-229-0252**	802-447-3311	338
Benny Hinn Ministries PO Box 162000	Irving	TX	75016	**800-433-1900**	817-722-2000	47-20
Benny Whitehead Inc 3265 S Eufaula Ave	Eufaula	AL	36027	**800-633-7617**	334-687-8055	360-2
BenQ America Corp 15375 Barranca Ste A205	Irvine	CA	92618	**866-600-2367**	949-255-9500	175-7
Bensinger DuPont & Assoc (BDA) 134 N LaSalle St Ste 2200	Chicago	IL	60602	**800-227-8620**	312-726-8620	461
Benson's Gourmet Seasonings PO Box 638	Azusa	CA	91702	**800-325-5619**	626-969-4443	297-37
Benson, The 309 SW Broadway	Portland	OR	97205	**800-663-1144**	503-228-2000	379
Bensussen Deutsch & Assoc Inc (BDA) 15525 Woodinville-Redmond Rd NE	Woodinville	WA	98072	**800-451-4764**	425-492-6111	465
Bent Gate Mountaineering 1313 Washington Ave	Golden	CO	80401	**877-236-8428**	303-271-9382	709
Bentley College 175 Forest St *Admissions	Waltham	MA	02452	**800-642-7131***	781-891-2244	167
Bentley Historical Library 1150 Beal Ave	Ann Arbor	MI	48109	**866-233-6661**	734-764-3482	434-4
Bentley Mfg Company Inc 520 Pk Industrial Dr	La Habra	CA	90631	**800-424-2425**	562-501-2955	327
Bentley Prince Street 14641 E Don Julian Rd	City of Industry	CA	91746	**800-423-4709**		130
Bentley Systems Inc 685 Stockton Dr	Exton	PA	19341	**800-236-8539**	610-458-5000	180-5
Benton Express Inc 1045 S River Industrial Blvd SE	Atlanta	GA	30315	**888-423-6866**	404-267-2200	778
Benton Rural Electric Assn (BREA) 402 Seventh St PO Box 1150	Prosser	WA	99350	**800-221-6987**	509-786-2913	247
Bentsen-Rio Grande Valley State Park 2800 S Bensen Palm Dr	Mission	TX	78572	**800-792-1112**	956-585-1107	564
Bentz Whaley Flessner 7251 Ohms Ln	Minneapolis	MN	55439	**800-921-0111**	952-921-0111	318
Benz Communications LLC 209 Mississippi St	San Francisco	CA	94107	**888-550-5251**		195
Benzel's Pretzel Bakery Inc 5200 Sixth Ave	Altoona	PA	16602	**800-344-4438**	814-942-5062	297-9
Benzie County 448 Ct Pl	Beulah	MI	49617	**800-315-3593**	231-882-9671	338
Berchtold Equipment Co Inc 330 E 19th St	Bakersfield	CA	93305	**800-691-7817**	661-323-7817	276
Berding & Weil LLP 2175 N California Blvd Ste 500	Walnut Creek	CA	94596	**800-838-2090**	925-838-2090	428
Berea College 101 Chestnut St	Berea	KY	40403	**800-326-5948**	859-985-3500	167
Berendsen Fluid Power 401 S Boston Ave Ste 1200	Tulsa	OK	74103	**800-360-2327**	918-592-3781	385
Berenson Corp 2495 Main St	Buffalo	NY	14214	**800-333-0578**	716-833-2402	350
Beretta USA Corp 17601 Beretta Dr	Accokeek	MD	20607	**800-237-3882**	301-283-2191	286
Berg Equipment Co 2700 W Veterans Pkwy	Marshfield	WI	54449	**800-494-1738**	715-384-2151	275
Berg's Ski & Snowboard Shop 367 W 13th Ave	Eugene	OR	97401	**800-800-1953**	541-683-1300	709
Bergad Inc 747 Eljer Way	Ford City	PA	16226	**888-476-8664**	724-763-2883	470

Name / Address	City	State	Zip	Toll-Free	Phone	Class
Bergamot Inc						
820 E Wisconsin St	Delavan	WI	53115	**800-922-6733***	262-728-5572	9
*Cust Svc						
Bergdorf Goodman Inc						
754 Fifth Ave	New York	NY	10019	**888-774-2424***	212-753-7300	156-4
*Cust Svc						
Bergen Community College						
400 Paramus Rd	Paramus	NJ	07652	**877-612-5381**	201-447-7200	161
Berger & Montague PC						
1622 Locust St	Philadelphia	PA	19103	**800-424-6690**	215-875-3000	428
Berger Bldg Products Inc						
805 Pennsylvania Blvd	Feasterville	PA	19053	**800-523-8852***	215-355-1200	695
*Cust Svc						
Berger Transfer & Storage Inc						
2950 Long Lk Rd	Saint Paul	MN	55113	**877-268-2101**		518
Bergey's Inc						
462 Harleysville Pike	Souderton	PA	18964	**800-237-4397**	215-723-6071	61-5
Bergmann Assoc Inc						
28 E Main St						
200 1st Federal Plaza	Rochester	NY	14614	**800-724-1168**	585-232-5135	263
Bergquist Co						
18930 W 78th St	Chanhassen	MN	55317	**800-347-4572**	952-835-2322	255
Bergstrom of Kaukauna						
2929 Lawe St	Kaukauna	WI	54130	**866-939-0130**		56
Bering Air						
1470 Sepalla Dr PO Box 1650	Nome	AK	99762	**800-478-5422**	907-443-5464	25
Berkeley Chamber of Commerce						
1834 University Ave	Berkeley	CA	94703	**800-847-4823**	510-549-7000	138
Berkeley College						
Garrett Mountain						
44 Rifle Camp Rd	Woodland Park	NJ	07424	**800-446-5400**	973-278-5400	798
Paramus						
64 E Midland Ave	Paramus	NJ	07652	**800-446-5400**	201-967-9667	798
Woodbridge						
430 Rahway Ave	Woodbridge	NJ	07095	**800-446-5400**	732-750-1800	798
Berkeley College New York City						
3 E 43rd St	New York	NY	10017	**800-446-5400**	212-986-4343	798
Berkeley College White Plains						
99 Church St	White Plains	NY	10601	**800-446-5400**	914-694-1122	798
Berkeley Communications Corp						
1321 67th St	Emeryville	CA	94608	**877-237-5266**	510-644-1599	196
Berkeley County Chamber of Commerce						
PO Box 968	Moncks Corner	SC	29461	**800-882-0337**	843-761-8238	138
Berkeley Hotel, The						
1200 E Cary St	Richmond	VA	23219	**888-780-4422**	804-780-1300	379
Berkeley Pumps						
293 Wright St	Delavan	WI	53115	**866-582-2032**	262-728-5551	638
Berkeley Repertory Theatre						
2025 Addison St	Berkeley	CA	94704	**888-427-8849**	510-647-2949	746
Berkeley Sensor & Actuator Ctr (BSAC)						
University of California						
403 Cory Hall MC Ste 1774	Berkeley	CA	94720	**800-549-1002**	510-643-6690	666
Berkeleys Northside Travel Inc						
1824 Euclid Ave	Berkeley	CA	94709	**800-575-3411**	510-843-1000	770
Berklee College of Music						
1140 Boylston St	Boston	MA	02215	**800-421-0084**	617-747-2221	167
Berklee Performance Ctr						
136 Massachusetts Ave	Boston	MA	02115	**877-237-5533**	617-747-2261	571
Berkley Risk Administrators Company LLC						
222 S Ninth St Ste 1300	Minneapolis	MN	55402	**800-449-7707**	612-766-3000	390
Berkowitz Dick Pollack & Brant LLP						
200 S Biscayne Blvd 6th Fl	Miami	FL	33131	**800-999-1272**	305-379-7000	2
Berks Packing Company Inc						
307-323 Bingaman St PO Box 5919	Reading	PA	19610	**800-882-3757**		297-26
Berks VNA						
1170 Berkshire Blvd	Wyomissing	PA	19610	**855-843-8627**		371
Berkshire Advisors Inc						
2240 Ridgewood Rd	Wyomissing	PA	19610	**800-566-4325**	610-376-6970	401
Berkshire Bank						
PO Box 1308	Pittsfield	MA	01202	**800-773-5601**	413-443-5601	69
Berkshire Eagle						
75 S Church St PO Box 1171	Pittsfield	MA	01202	**800-234-7404**	413-447-7311	531-2
Berkshire Gas Company Inc						
115 Cheshire Rd	Pittsfield	MA	01201	**800-292-5012**	413-442-1511	785
Berkshire Hathaway Group (BHG)						
3024 Harney St	Omaha	NE	68131	**800-223-2064**	402-536-3100	391-4
Berkshire Hathaway Homestates Cos (BHHC)						
PO Box 2048	Omaha	NE	68103	**888-495-8949**		391-4
Berkshire Hathaway Inc						
3555 Farnam St Ste 1440	Omaha	NE	68131	**800-223-2064**	402-346-1400	187
NYSE: BRK/A						
Berkshire Hills Bancorp Inc						
24 N St	Pittsfield	MA	01201	**800-773-5601**	413-443-5601	360-2
NYSE: BHLB						
Berkshire School						
245 N Undermountain Rd	Sheffield	MA	01257	**866-738-5500**	413-229-8511	621
Berlin Metals LLC						
3200 Sheffield Ave	Hammond	IN	46327	**800-754-8867**	219-933-0111	491
Berman Moving & Storage Inc						
23800 Corbin Dr	Cleveland	OH	44128	**800-333-0582**	216-663-8816	313
Bermuda Dept of Tourism						
675 Third Ave 20th Fl	New York	NY	10017	**800-223-6106**	212-818-9800	773
Bermuda Village						
142 Bermuda Village Dr	Advance	NC	27006	**800-843-5433***		670
*Mktg						
Bernard Food Industries Inc						
1125 Hartrey Ave	Evanston	IL	60204	**800-323-3663**	847-869-5222	297-18
Bernard L Madoff Investment Securities Co						
885 Third Ave 18th Fl	New York	NY	10022	**800-334-1343**	212-230-2424	688
Bernards Inn						
27 Mine Brook Rd	Bernardsville	NJ	07924	**888-766-0002**	908-766-0002	379
Bernardus Lodge						
415 Carmel Valley Rd	Carmel Valley	CA	93924	**800-223-2533**	831-658-3400	379
Bernatello's						
PO Box 729	Maple Lake	MN	55358	**800-622-6935**	952-831-6622	297-21
Berne Apparel Co						
2210 Summit St	New Haven	IN	46774	**800-843-7657**	260-469-3136	154-18
Berner Foods Inc						
2034 E Factory Rd	Dakota	IL	61018	**800-819-8199**	815-563-4222	297-5
Berney-Karp Inc						
3350 E 26th St	Los Angeles	CA	90058	**800-237-6395**	323-260-7122	334
Berns Co						
1250 W 17th St	Long Beach	CA	90813	**800-421-3773**	562-437-0471	469
Berry Aviation Inc						
1807 Airport Dr	San Marcos	TX	78666	**800-229-2379**	512-353-2379	13
Berry College						
2277 Martha Berry Hwy						
PO Box 490159	Mount Berry	GA	30149	**800-237-7942**	706-232-5374	167
Berry Dunn Mcneil & Parker						
100 Middle St 4th Fl	Portland	ME	04101	**800-908-4490**	207-775-2387	2
Berry Plastics Corp						
101 Oakley St	Evansville	IN	47710	**877-662-3779**	812-424-2904	201
Berryman Products Inc						
3800 E Randol Mill Rd	Arlington	TX	76011	**800-433-1704**	817-640-2376	145
Bertek Systems Inc						
133 Bryce Blvd	Fairfax	VT	05454	**800-367-0210**	802-752-3170	626
Berthel Fisher & Co						
701 Tama St Bldg B PO Box 609	Marion	IA	52302	**800-356-5234**	319-447-5700	688
Besco Electric Supply Co						
711 S 14th St	Leesburg	FL	34748	**800-541-6618**		362
Besl Transfer Co						
5700 Este Ave	Cincinnati	OH	45232	**800-456-2375**	513-242-3456	778
Besly Cutting Tools Inc						
16200 Woodmint Ln	South Beloit	IL	61080	**800-435-2965**	815-389-2231	492
Bessam-Aire Inc						
10145 Philipp Pkwy Unit B	Streetsboro	OH	44146	**800-321-5992**		662
Bessemer Area Chamber of Commerce						
321 N 18th St	Bessemer	AL	35020	**888-423-7736**	205-425-3253	138
Bessemer Trust Co						
630 Fifth Ave	New York	NY	10111	**866-271-7403**	212-708-9100	401
Besser Co						
801 Johnson St	Alpena	MI	49707	**800-530-9980**	989-354-4111	386
Bessire & Associates Inc						
7621 Little Ave Ste 106	Charlotte	NC	28226	**800-797-7355**	704-341-1423	195
Best Access Systems						
6161 E 75th St	Indianapolis	IN	46250	**855-365-2407**	317-849-2250	350
Best Bath Systems						
723 Garber St	Caldwell	ID	83605	**866-333-8657**	208-342-6823	375
Best Buy Company Inc						
7601 Penn Ave S	Minneapolis	MN	55423	**888-237-8289**	612-291-1000	34
NYSE: BBY						
Best Chevrolet Inc						
128 Derby St	Hingham	MA	02043	**866-208-7873**		56
Best Label Co						
2900 Faber St	Union City	CA	94587	**800-637-5333**	510-489-5400	413
Best Life & Health Insurance Co						
2505 McCabe Way	Irvine	CA	92614	**800-433-0088**	949-253-4080	391-2
Best Maid Products Inc						
PO Box 1809	Fort Worth	TX	76101	**800-447-3581**	817-335-5494	297-19
Best Material Handling Inc						
4754 N Chestnut St	Colorado Springs	CO	80907	**800-933-5270**	719-599-9191	322
Best Plumbing Specialties						
3039 Ventrie Ct	Myersville	MD	21773	**800-448-6710**		611
Best Provision Company Inc						
144 Avon Ave	Newark	NJ	07108	**800-631-4466**	973-242-5000	297-26
Best Registration Services Inc						
1418 S Third St	Louisville	KY	40208	**800-977-3475**	502-637-4528	396
Best Sweet Inc						
288 Mazeppa Rd	Mooresville	NC	28115	**888-211-5530**	704-664-4300	297-8
Best Telecom Inc						
262 E End Ave	Beaver	PA	15009	**888-365-2273**		387
Best Theratronics Ltd						
413 March Rd	Ottawa	ON	K2K0E4	**866-792-8598**	613-591-2100	475
Best Travel Inc						
8600 W Bryn Mawr Ave	Chicago	IL	60631	**800-927-7357**	773-380-0150	769
Best Vascular						
4350 International Blvd Ste A	Norcross	GA	30093	**800-668-6783**	770-717-0904	475
Best Way Logistics						
14004 Century Ln	Grandview	MO	64030	**877-923-7892**	816-767-8008	315
Best Western Chincoteague Island						
7105 Maddox Blvd	Chincoteague Island	VA	23336	**800-553-6117**	757-336-6557	379
Best Western Grandma's Feather Bed						
9300 Glacier Hwy	Juneau	AK	99801	**888-781-5005**	907-789-5005	669
Best Western Inn of the Ozarks						
207 W Van Buren	Eureka Springs	AR	72632	**800-552-3785**	479-253-9768	667
Best Western International Inc						
6201 N 24th Pkwy	Phoenix	AZ	85016	**800-528-1234**	602-957-4200	379
Best Western Laguna Brisas Spa Hotel						
1600 S Coast Hwy	Laguna Beach	CA	92651	**888-296-6834**	949-497-7272	379
Best Western Tuscan Inn						
425 N Point St	San Francisco	CA	94133	**800-648-4626**	415-561-1100	705
Best Western Victorian Inn						
487 Foam St	Monterey	CA	93940	**800-232-4141**	831-373-8000	379
Bestar Inc						
4220 Villeneuve St	Lac-Megantic	QC	G6B2C3	**888-823-7827**	819-583-1017	320-1
Bestforms Inc						
1135 Avenida Acaso	Camarillo	CA	93012	**800-350-0618**	805-383-6993	109
Bestolife Corp						
2777 Stemmons Fwy Ste 1800	Dallas	TX	75207	**855-243-9164**	214-583-0271	3
Best-Rite Mfg						
2885 Lorraine Ave	Temple	TX	76501	**800-749-2258**		288
Bestway Inc						
12400 Coit Rd Ste 950	Dallas	TX	75251	**800-316-4567**	214-630-6655	266-2
Bestway Tours & Safaris						
8678 Greenall Ave	Burnaby	BC	V5J3M6	**800-663-0844**	604-264-7378	758
Beta Gamma Sigma Inc (BGS)						
125 Weldon Pkwy	Maryland Heights	MO	63043	**800-337-4677**	314-432-5650	47-16
Beta LaserMike Inc						
8001 Technology Blvd	Dayton	OH	45424	**800-886-9935**	937-233-9935	471
Beta Screen Corp						
707 Commercial Ave	Carlstadt	NJ	07072	**800-272-7336**	201-939-2400	590
Beta Theta Pi						
5134 Bonham Rd	Oxford	OH	45056	**800-800-2382**		47-16
Bete Fog Nozzle Inc						
50 Greenfield St	Greenfield	MA	01301	**800-235-0049**	413-772-0846	350
Beth Israel Deaconess Medical Ctr (BIDMC)						
330 Brookline Ave	Boston	MA	02215	**800-667-5356**	617-667-7000	374-3

Name / Address	City	State	ZIP	Toll-Free	Phone	Class
Bethany Bible College						
26 Western St	Sussex	NB	E4E1E6	**888-432-4444**	506-432-4400	783
Bethany College						
31 E Campus Dr	Bethany	WV	26032	**800-922-7611**	304-829-7000	167
Bethany House Publishers						
11400 Hampshire Ave S	Bloomington	MN	55438	**800-328-6109**	616-676-9185	634-3
Bethany Lutheran College						
700 Luther Dr	Mankato	MN	56001	**800-944-3066**	507-344-7000	167
Bethany Theological Seminary						
615 National Rd W	Richmond	IN	47374	**800-287-8822**	765-983-1800	168-3
Bethea Baptist Retirement Community						
157 Home Ave	Darlington	SC	29532	**877-393-2867**	843-393-2867	670
Bethel College						
300 E 27th St	North Newton	KS	67117	**800-522-1887**	316-283-2500	167
Beth-El College of Nursing & Health Sciences						
1420 Austin Bluffs Pkwy	Colorado Springs	CO	80918	**800-990-8227**	719-255-8227	167
Bethel Inn & Country Club						
21 Broad St PO Box 49	Bethel	ME	04217	**800-654-0125**	207-824-2175	667
Bethel Seminary						
3949 Bethel Dr	Saint Paul	MN	55112	**800-255-8706**	651-638-6400	168-3
Bethel University						
3900 Bethel Dr	Saint Paul	MN	55112	**800-255-8706**	651-638-6400	167
Bethesda Hospital						
2951 Maple Ave	Zanesville	OH	43701	**800-322-4762**	740-454-4000	374-3
Bethlehem Area Public Library						
11 W Church St	Bethlehem	PA	18018	**800-732-0999**	610-867-3761	434-3
Bethpage Federal Credit Union						
899 S Oyster Bay Rd	Bethpage	NY	11714	**800-628-7070**		221
Bethpage State Park						
Bethpage Pkwy	Farmingdale	NY	11735	**800-456-2267**	516-249-0701	564
Bethune-Cookman College						
640 Dr Mary McLeod Bethune Blvd	Daytona Beach	FL	32114	**800-448-0228***	386-481-2900	167
*Admissions						
Betson Enterprises Inc						
303 Patterson Plank Rd	Carlstadt	NJ	07072	**800-524-2343**	201-438-1300	54
Betsy Hotel						
1440 Ocean Dr	Miami Beach	FL	33139	**866-792-3879**	305-531-6100	379
Bettcher Industries Inc						
PO Box 336	Vermilion	OH	44089	**800-321-8763**	440-965-4422	299
Bettendorf-Stanford						
1370 W Main St	Salem	IL	62881	**800-548-2253**	618-548-3555	361
Better Business Bureau Heartland						
11811 P St	Omaha	NE	68137	**800-649-6814**	402-391-7612	78
Better Business Bureau Inc						
1000 Broadway Ste 625	Oakland	CA	94607	**866-411-2221**	510-844-2000	78
Better Business Bureau of Ark-La-Tex						
401 Edwards St Ste 135	Shreveport	LA	71101	**800-372-4222**	318-222-7575	78
Better Business Bureau of Asheville/Western North Carolina						
112 Executive Pk	Asheville	NC	28801	**800-452-2882**	828-253-2392	78
Better Business Bureau of Canton Region/West Virginia						
1434 Cleveland Ave NW	Canton	OH	44703	**800-362-0494**	330-454-9401	78
Better Business Bureau of Central & Eastern Kentucky						
1460 Newtown Pk	Lexington	KY	40511	**800-866-6668**	859-259-1008	78
Better Business Bureau of Central East Texas						
3600 Old BullaRd Rd Bldg 1	Tyler	TX	75701	**800-443-0131**	903-581-5704	78
Better Business Bureau of Central East Texas Longview Branch						
102 Commander Ste 7	Longview	TX	75605	**800-443-0131**	903-758-3222	78
Better Business Bureau of Central Illinois						
112 Harrison St	Peoria	IL	61602	**800-763-4222**	309-688-3741	78
Better Business Bureau of Central Indiana						
151 N Delaware St	Indianapolis	IN	46204	**866-463-9222**	317-488-2222	78
Better Business Bureau of Central Louisiana & Ark-La-Tex						
5220-C Rue Verdun	Alexandria	LA	71303	**800-372-4222***	318-473-4494	78
*General						
Better Business Bureau of Central Northeast Northwest & Southwest Arizona						
4428 N 12th St	Phoenix	AZ	85014	**877-291-6222**	602-264-1721	78
Better Business Bureau of Central Ohio						
1169 Dublin Rd	Columbus	OH	43215	**800-759-2400**	614-486-6336	78
Better Business Bureau of Eastern Massachusetts Maine Rhode Island & Vermont						
290 Donald Lynch Blvd Ste 102	Marlborough	MA	01752	**800-422-2811**	508-652-4800	78
Better Business Bureau of Greater Kansas City						
8080 Ward Pkwy Ste 401	Kansas City	MO	64114	**877-606-0695**	816-421-7800	78
Better Business Bureau of Hawaii						
1132 Bishop St Ste 615	Honolulu	HI	96813	**877-222-6551**	808-536-6956	78
Better Business Bureau of Kansas Inc						
345 N Riverview St Ste 720	Wichita	KS	67203	**800-856-2417**	316-263-3146	78
Better Business Bureau of Louisville Southern Indiana & Western Kentucky						
844 S Fourth St	Louisville	KY	40203	**800-388-2222**	502-583-6546	78
Better Business Bureau of Maine						
290 Donald Lynch Blvd Ste 102	Marlborough	MA	01752	**800-422-2811**	508-652-4800	78
Better Business Bureau of Metropolitan New York						
257 Pk Ave S	New York	NY	10010	**800-684-3322**	212-533-6200	78
Better Business Bureau of New Jersey						
1700 Whitehorse-Hamilton Sq Rd Ste D-5	Trenton	NJ	08690	**888-494-4009**	609-588-0808	78
Better Business Bureau of Northeast California						
3075 Beacon Blvd	West Sacramento	CA	95691	**866-334-6272**	916-443-6843	78
Better Business Bureau of Northeast Florida & The Southeast Atlantic						
4417 Beach Blvd Ste 202	Jacksonville	FL	32207	**800-713-6661**	904-721-2288	78
Better Business Bureau of Northeast Ohio						
2800 Euclid Ave 4th Fl	Cleveland	OH	44115	**800-233-0361**	216-241-7678	78
Better Business Bureau of Northern Colorado & East Central Wyoming						
8020 S County Rd 5 Ste 100	Fort Collins	CO	80528	**800-564-0371**	970-484-1348	78
Better Business Bureau of Northern Indiana						
4011 Parnell Ave	Fort Wayne	IN	46805	**800-552-4631**	260-423-4433	78
Better Business Bureau of Northwest North Carolina						
500 W Fifth St Ste 202	Winston-Salem	NC	27101	**800-777-8348**	336-725-8348	78
Better Business Bureau of Northwest Ohio & Southeast Michigan						
7668 King's Pt Rd	Toledo	OH	43617	**800-743-4222**	419-531-3116	78
Better Business Bureau of Rockford						
330 North Wabash Ave Ste 3120	Chicago	IL	60611	**800-955-5100**	312-832-0500	78
Better Business Bureau of Saskatchewan						
980 Albert St Ste 201	Regina	SK	S4R2P7	**888-352-7601**	306-352-7601	77
Better Business Bureau of Southeast Florida & the Caribbean						
4411 Beacon Cir Ste 4	West Palm Beach	FL	33407	**866-966-7226**	561-842-1918	78
Better Business Bureau of Southeast Tennessee & Northwest Georgia						
508 N Market St	Chattanooga	TN	37405	**800-548-4456**	423-266-6144	78
Better Business Bureau of Southeast Texas						
550 Fannin St Ste 100	Beaumont	TX	77701	**800-685-7650**	409-835-5348	78
Better Business Bureau of Southwest Georgia						
PO Box 2587	Columbus	GA	31902	**800-768-4222**	706-324-0712	78
Better Business Bureau of Southwest Idaho & Eastern Oregon						
1200 N Curtis Rd PO Box 9817	Boise	ID	83706	**800-218-1001**	208-342-4649	78
Better Business Bureau of Southwest Louisiana Inc						
2309 E Prien Lk Rd	Lake Charles	LA	70601	**800-542-7085**	337-478-6253	78
Better Business Bureau of the Akron Inc						
222 W Market St	Akron	OH	44303	**800-825-8887**	330-253-4590	78
Better Business Bureau of the Bakersfield Area						
1601 H St Ste 101	Bakersfield	CA	93301	**800-675-8118**	661-322-2074	78
Better Business Bureau of the Denver-Boulder Metro Area						
1020 Cherokee St	Denver	CO	80204	**800-356-6333**	303-758-2100	78
Better Business Bureau of the Mid-South						
3693 Tyndale Dr	Memphis	TN	38125	**800-222-8754**	901-759-1300	78
Better Business Bureau of Upstate New York						
100 Bryant Woods S	Amherst	NY	14228	**800-828-5000**	716-881-5222	78
Better Business Bureau of Utah						
5673 S Redwood Rd	Salt Lake City	UT	84123	**800-456-3907**	801-892-6009	78
Better Business Bureau of Vancouver Island						
220-1175 Cook St Ste 220	Victoria	BC	V8V4A1	**877-826-4222**	250-386-6348	77
Better Business Bureau of West Florida						
2655 McCormick Dr	Clearwater	FL	33759	**800-525-1447**	727-535-5522	78
Better Business Bureau of West Georgia & East Alabama						
PO Box 2587	Columbus	GA	31902	**800-768-4222**	706-324-0712	78
Better Business Bureau of Western Massachusetts						
35 Ctr St Ste 203	Chicopee	MA	01013	**866-566-9222**		78
Better Business Bureau Online						
Council of Better Business Bureaus, The						
4200 Wilson Blvd Ste 800	Arlington	VA	22203	**800-459-8875**	703-276-0100	78
Better Business Bureau Serving Central California						
4201 W Shaw Ave Ste 107	Fresno	CA	93722	**800-675-8118**	559-222-8111	78
Better Business Bureau Serving Mainland British Columbia						
788 Beatty St Ste 404	Vancouver	BC	V6B2M1	**888-803-1222**	604-682-2711	77
Better Business Bureau Serving Western Ontario						
190 Wortley Rd Ste 206	London	ON	N6C4Y7	**877-283-9222**	519-673-3222	77
Better Business Bureau Serving Winnipeg & Manitoba						
1030B Empress St	Winnipeg	MB	R3G3H4	**800-385-3074**	204-989-9010	77
Better Hearing Institute (BHI)						
1444 I St NW Ste 700	Washington	DC	20005	**800-639-3884**	202-449-1100	47-17
Better Homes & Gardens WOOD Magazine						
1716 Locust St	Des Moines	IA	50309	**800-374-9663**		456-14
Better Investing						
PO Box 220	Royal Oak	MI	48068	**877-275-6242**	248-583-6242	48-2
Better Label & Products Inc						
3333 Empire Blvd SW	Atlanta	GA	30354	**800-448-1813**	404-763-8440	626
Better Made Snack Foods Inc						
10148 Gratiot Ave	Detroit	MI	48213	**800-332-2394**	313-925-4774	297-35
Better Management Corp (BMC)						
41738 Esterly Dr	Columbiana	OH	44408	**877-293-4300**	330-482-7070	658
Better Packages Inc						
255 Canal St PO Box 711	Shelton	CT	06484	**800-237-9151**	203-926-3722	110
Better Vision Institute, The (BVI)						
Vision Council, The						
225 Reinekers Ln Ste 700	Alexandria	VA	22314	**800-372-3937**	703-548-4560	47-17
Bettinger Farms Inc						
11602 Frankfort Rd	Swanton	OH	43558	**855-629-7661**	419-829-2771	369
Betty Dain Creations Inc						
9701 NW 112 Ave Ste 10	Miami	FL	33178	**800-327-5256***	305-769-3451	75
*General						
Beulah Heights Bible College						
892 Berne St SE PO Box 18145	Atlanta	GA	30316	**888-777-2422**	404-627-2681	160
Beutler Air Conditioning Service						
855 National Dr Ste 109	Sacramento	CA	95834	**866-559-0108**		191-10
Bevco Precision Manufacturing Co						
21320 Doral Rd	Waukesha	WI	53186	**800-864-2991**	262-798-9200	320-1
Bevco Sales International Inc						
9354 194 St	Surrey	BC	V4N4E9	**800-663-0090**	604-888-1455	358
Beverage Distributors Co						
14200 E Moncrieff Pl	Aurora	CO	80011	**888-262-9787***	303-371-3421	80-3
*General						
Beverage Marketing Corp						
850 Third Ave 18th Fl	New York	NY	10022	**800-275-4630**	212-688-7640	197
Beverage-Air Corp						
3779 Champion Blvd	Winston-Salem	NC	27105	**800-845-9800**	336-245-6400	662
Beverly Beach State Park						
198 NE 123rd St	Newport	OR	97365	**800-452-5687**		564
Beverly Chamber of Commerce						
100 Cummings Ctr Ste 107K	Beverly	MA	01915	**800-924-8167**	978-232-9559	138
Beverly Hills Hotel						
9641 Sunset Blvd	Beverly Hills	CA	90210	**800-650-1842**	310-276-2251	379
Beverly Hills Transfer & Storage Co						
15500 S Main St	Gardena	CA	90248	**800-999-7114**		518
Beverly Hills Unified School District						
255 S Lasky Dr	Beverly Hills	CA	90212	**877-220-7229**	310-551-5100	683
Beverly Hilton						
9876 Wilshire Blvd	Beverly Hills	CA	90210	**800-605-8896**	310-274-7777	379
Beverly Wilshire - A Four Seasons Hotel						
9500 Wilshire Blvd	Beverly Hills	CA	90212	**800-545-4000**	310-275-5200	379
Bevill State Community College						
2631 Temple Ave N	Fayette	AL	35555	**800-648-3271**	205-932-3221	161
Jasper						
1411 Indiana Ave	Jasper	AL	35501	**800-648-3271**	205-387-0511	161
Bexil Corp						
11 Hanover Sq	New York	NY	10005	**800-937-5449**	212-785-0400	360-4
OTC: BXLC						
Bexley City School District						
348 S Cassingham Rd	Columbus	OH	43209	**800-282-1780**	614-231-7611	683
Beyond Components						
5 Carl Thompson Rd	Westford	MA	01886	**800-971-4242**		248
Beyond Digital Imaging						
36 Apple Creek Blvd	Markham	ON	L3R4Y4	**888-689-1888**	905-415-1888	699
Beyond Pesticides						
701 E St SE Ste 200	Washington	DC	20003	**866-260-6653**	202-543-5450	47-13

Name / Address	City	State	ZIP	Toll-Free	Phone	Class
Beyond the Arc Inc 2600 Tenth St Ste 616	Berkeley	CA	94710	**877-676-3743**		462
BFC Forms Service Inc 1051 N Kirk Rd	Batavia	IL	60510	**800-774-6840**	630-879-9240	626
BFG Supply Co LLC PO Box 479	Burton	OH	44021	**800-883-0234**	440-834-1883	278
BFGoodrich Tires Inc 1 Pkwy S	Greenville	SC	29602	**877-788-8899**		753
BFMA (Business Forms Management Assn) 3800 Old Cheney Rd Ste 101-285	Lincoln	NE	68516	**888-367-3078**	402-216-0479	48-12
Bframe Data Systems Inc 3057 Peachtree Industrial Blvd Ste 200	Duluth	GA	30097	**800-833-1059**	678-387-0100	179
B&G Equipment Company Inc 135 Region S Dr	Jackson	GA	30233	**800-544-8811**	678-688-5601	296
B-G Mechanical Service Inc 12 Second Ave	Chicopee	MA	01020	**800-992-7386**	413-888-1500	191-10
BG Products Inc 740 S Wichita St	Wichita	KS	67213	**800-961-6228**	316-265-2686	540
BGA (Lincoln Botanical Garden & Arboretum) University of Nebraska 1309 N 17th St	Lincoln	NE	68588	**800-742-8800**	402-472-2679	96
BGD Cos Inc 5323 Lakeland Ave N	Minneapolis	MN	55429	**800-699-3537**	612-338-6804	320-1
BGF Industries Inc 3802 Robert Porcher Way	Greensboro	NC	27410	**800-476-4845**		742-3
BGK Finishing Systems 4131 Pheasant Ridge Dr NE	Minneapolis	MN	55449	**800-663-5498**	763-784-0466	469
BGR Inc 6392 Gano Rd	West Chester	OH	45069	**800-628-9195**	513-755-7100	558
BGS (Beta Gamma Sigma Inc) 125 Weldon Pkwy	Maryland Heights	MO	63043	**800-337-4677**	314-432-5650	47-16
BGSU (Bowling Green State University Jerome Library) 1001 E Wooster St	Bowling Green	OH	43403	**866-246-6732**	419-372-2051	434-6
B-H Transfer Co 750 Sparta Rd PO Box 151	Sandersville	GA	31082	**800-342-6462**	478-552-5119	448
BHG (Berkshire Hathaway Group) 3024 Harney St	Omaha	NE	68131	**800-223-2064**	402-536-3100	391-4
BHHC (Berkshire Hathaway Homestates Cos) PO Box 2048	Omaha	NE	68103	**888-495-8949**		391-4
BHI (Baker Hughes Inc) 2929 Allen Pkwy Ste 1200 *NYSE: BHI*	Houston	TX	77019	**800-229-7447**	713-439-8600	538
BHI (Better Hearing Institute) 1444 I St NW Ste 700	Washington	DC	20005	**800-639-3884**	202-449-1100	47-17
BHK Securities LLC 2200 Lakeshore Dr Ste 250	Birmingham	AL	35209	**888-529-2610**	205-322-2025	688
BI Inc 6400 Lookout Rd	Boulder	CO	80301	**800-241-2911**	303-218-1000	690
BIA (Brick Industry Assn) 1850 Centennial Pk Dr Ste 301	Reston	VA	20191	**866-644-1293**	703-620-0010	48-18
BIA (Bureau of Indian Affairs Regional Offices) *Alaska Region* 3601 C St Ste 1100	Anchorage	AK	99503	**800-645-8397**	907-271-1536	340-11
BIA Financial Network Inc 15120 Enterprise Ct	Chantilly	VA	20151	**800-331-5086**	703-818-2425	196
Biamp Systems Inc 9300 SW Gemini Dr	Beaverton	OR	97008	**800-826-1457**		51
Bianchi Motors Inc 8430 Peach St	Erie	PA	16509	**866-979-8132**	814-864-5809	515
Bibbero Systems Inc 1300 N McDowell Blvd	Petaluma	CA	94954	**800-242-2376**	707-778-3131	626
Bibby Financial Services 600 TownPark Ln Ste 450	Kennesaw	GA	30144	**877-882-4229**		274
Bible Broadcasting Network Inc 11530 Carmel Commons Blvd PO Box 7300	Charlotte	NC	28226	**800-888-7077**	704-523-5555	640
Bible League 3801 Eagle Nest Dr	Crete	IL	60417	**866-825-4636**	817-595-1664	47-20
Biblical Archaeology Review 4710 41st St NW	Washington	DC	20016	**800-221-4644**	202-364-3300	456-18
Biblical Theological Seminary 200 N Main St	Hatfield	PA	19440	**800-235-4021**	215-368-5000	168-3
Bickel's Snack Foods 1120 Zinns Quarry Rd	York	PA	17404	**800-233-1933**	717-843-0738	297-35
Bickford's Family Restauarants Inc 37 Oak St Ext	Brockton	MA	02301	**800-969-5653**		668
Bicon LLC 501 Arborway	Boston	MA	02130	**800-882-4266**	617-524-4443	230
Bicycle Garage of Indy Inc 4340 E 82nd St	Indianapolis	IN	46250	**800-238-7389**	317-842-4140	709
Bicycling Magazine 400 S Tenth St	Emmaus	PA	18098	**800-666-2806**		456-14
Biddeford Blankets 300 Terr Dr	Mundelein	IL	60060	**800-789-6441**		743
Biddle Precision Components Inc 701 S Main St	Sheridan	IN	46069	**800-428-4387**	317-758-4451	620
BIDMC (Beth Israel Deaconess Medical Ctr) 330 Brookline Ave	Boston	MA	02215	**800-667-5356**	617-667-7000	374-3
Bid-Well Corp PO Box 97	Canton	SD	57013	**800-843-9824**		192
Bienville House Hotel 320 Decatur St	New Orleans	LA	70130	**800-535-7836**	504-529-2345	379
Bierlein Cos Inc 2000 Bay City Rd	Midland	MI	48642	**800-336-6626**	989-496-0066	191-16
Bierschbach Equipment & Supply Co PO Box 1444	Sioux Falls	SD	57101	**800-843-3707**	605-332-4466	193-1
Biff Duncan Associates Inc 450 Shrewsbury Plz	Shrewsbury	NJ	07702	**866-335-2433**	732-876-0263	263
Big 5 Sporting Goods Corp 2525 E El Segundo Blvd *NASDAQ: BGFV*	El Segundo	CA	90245	**800-898-2994**	310-536-0611	709
Big Apple Bagels 500 Lk Cook Rd Ste 475	Deerfield	IL	60015	**800-251-6101**	847-948-7520	67
Big Apple Circus 1 Metrotech Ctr 3rd Fl	Brooklyn	NY	11201	**800-922-3772**	212-268-2500	148
Big Bang ERP Inc 105 De Louvain W	Montreal	QC	H2N1A3	**844-361-4408**	514-360-4408	198

Name / Address	City	State	ZIP	Toll-Free	Phone	Class
Big Bend Community College 7662 Chanute St	Moses Lake	WA	98837	**877-745-1212**	509-793-2222	161
Big Bend Electric Co-op 1373 N Hwy 261 PO Box 348	Ritzville	WA	99169	**866-844-2363**	509-659-1700	247
Big Bend Telephone Company Inc 808 N Fifth St	Alpine	TX	79830	**800-520-0092**	432-364-1000	115
Big C Lumber Inc 50860 Princess Way PO Box 176	Granger	IN	46530	**888-297-0010**	574-277-4550	193-3
Big Country Electric Co-op 1010 W S First St PO Box 518	Roby	TX	79543	**888-662-2232**	325-776-2244	247
Big Dogs 519 Lincoln County Pkwy	Lincolnton	NC	28092	**800-244-3647**		154-3
Big Fitness 5 Progress St	Seekonk	MA	02771	**800-383-2008**	401-885-5200	354
Big Five Tours & Expeditions 1551 SE Palm Ct	Stuart	FL	34994	**800-244-3483**	772-287-7995	758
Big Flat Electric Co-op Inc 333 S Seventh St	Malta	MT	59538	**800-242-2040**	406-654-2040	247
Big Foot Beach State Park 1452 Wells St	Lake Geneva	WI	53147	**888-936-7463**	262-248-2528	564
Big G Cereals PO Box 9452 PO Box 9452	Minneapolis	MN	55440	**800-248-7310**		297-4
Big G Express Inc PO Box 1650	Shelbyville	TN	37162	**800-955-9140**	800-684-9140	778
Big Girls Bras Etcetera Inc 3540 NW 56th St Ste 207	Lauderdale	FL	33309	**866-352-4494**	954-484-2701	156-6
Big Horn Rural Electric Co-op 208 S Fifth St PO Box 270	Basin	WY	82410	**800-564-2419**	307-568-2419	247
Big Kaiser Precision Tooling Inc 641 Fargo Ave	Elk Grove Village	IL	60007	**888-866-5776**	847-228-7660	492
Big Lots Inc (BLI) 300 Phillipi Rd *NYSE: BIG*	Columbus	OH	43228	**877-998-1697**	614-278-6800	789
Big Ridge State Park 1015 Big Ridge Rd	Maynardville	TN	37807	**800-471-5305**	865-992-5523	564
Big River Zinc Corp 2401 Mississippi Ave	Sauget	IL	62201	**800-274-4002**	618-274-5000	484
Big Rock Sports LLC 173 Hankison Dr	Newport	NC	28570	**800-334-2661**	252-808-3500	708
Big Sandy Community & Technical College 1 Bert T Combs Dr	Prestonsburg	KY	41653	**888-641-4132**	606-886-3863	161
Big Sandy Rural Electric Co-op Corp 504 11th St	Paintsville	KY	41240	**888-789-7322**	606-789-4095	247
Big Shoals State Park PO Box G	White Springs	FL	32096	**877-635-3655**	386-397-4331	564
Big Sky Resort 1 L1 Mtn Trl PO Box 160001	Big Sky	MT	59716	**800-548-4486**	406-995-5000	667
Big Sky Technologies 9325 Sky Pk Ct Ste 120	San Diego	CA	92123	**800-736-2751**	858-715-5000	180-7
Big Spring Convention & Visitor Bureau 215 W Third St PO Box 3359	Big Spring	TX	79720	**866-222-7100**	432-264-6032	208
Big Spring Independent School District 708 E 11th Pl	Big Spring	TX	79720	**866-632-9992**	432-264-3600	683
Big Stone Lake State Park 35889 Meadowbrook State Pk Rd	Ortonville	MN	56278	**888-646-6367**	320-839-3663	564
Big Y Foods Inc 2145 Roosevelt Ave *Cust Svc	Springfield	MA	01102	**800-828-2688***	413-784-0600	345
Bigbend Hospice 1723 Mahan Ctr Blvd	Tallahassee	FL	32308	**800-772-5862**	850-878-5310	371
Bigelow Tea 201 Black Rock Tpke	Fairfield	CT	06825	**888-244-3569**		297-40
Bigge Crane & Rigging Company Inc 10700 Bigge St PO Box 1657	San Leandro	CA	94577	**888-337-2444**	510-638-8100	191-1
Biggers Chevrolet 1385 E Chicago St	Elgin	IL	60120	**866-431-1555**	847-742-9000	56
Bigrentz Inc 1063 Mcgaw Ave Ste 200	Irvine	CA	92614	**855-999-5438**		23
BII (Burgess Industries Inc) 7500 Boone Ave N Ste 111	Brooklyn Park	MN	55428	**800-233-2589**	763-553-7800	628
Bike Friday Travel Systems 3364 W 11th Ave	Eugene	OR	97402	**800-777-0258**	541-687-0487	773
Bilbrey Insurance Services Inc 5701 Greendale Rd	Johnston	IA	50131	**800-383-0116**		390
Bil-Jax Inc 125 Taylor Pkwy	Archbold	OH	43502	**800-537-0540**	419-445-8915	490
Bilkays Express Co 2400 Bedle Place	Linden	NJ	07036	**800-526-4006**	908-289-2400	778
Bill & Melinda Gates Foundation PO Box 23350	Seattle	WA	98102	**800-728-3843**	206-709-3100	306
Bill Barrett Corp 1099 18th St Ste 2300 *NYSE: BBG*	Denver	CO	80202	**800-826-6762**	303-293-9100	537
Bill Collins 4220 BaRdstown Rd	Louisville	KY	40218	**888-327-9095**	502-459-9550	56
Bill Miller Bar-B-Q Inc 2750 Bill Miller Ln PO Box 839925	San Antonio	TX	78223	**800-339-3111**	210-225-4461	668
Bill Snethkamp Lansing Dodge Inc 6131 S Pennsylvania Ave	Lansing	MI	48911	**800-863-6343**	517-394-1200	56
Billings Area Chamber of Commerce 815 S 27th St	Billings	MT	59101	**855-328-9116**	406-245-4111	138
Billings C'mon Inn Hotel 2020 Overland Ave	Billings	MT	59102	**800-655-1170**	406-655-1100	379
Billings Clinic 2800 Tenth Ave N	Billings	MT	59101	**800-332-7156**	406-238-2501	374-3
Billings Convention & Visitors Bureau 815 S 27th St PO Box 31177	Billings	MT	59107	**800-735-2635**	406-245-4111	208
Billings Gazette 401 N 28th St	Billings	MT	59101	**800-543-2505**	406-657-1200	531-2
Billings Hotel & Convention Ctr 1223 Mullowney Ln	Billings	MT	59101	**800-537-7286**	406-248-7151	379
Billows Electric Supply Co 9100 State Rd	Philadelphia	PA	19136	**877-519-7302**	215-332-9700	248
Billpro Management Systems Inc 30575 Euclid Ave	Wickliffe	OH	44092	**800-736-0587**	440-516-3776	179

Name	Address	City	State	ZIP	Toll-Free	Phone	Class
Billy Graham Evangelistic Assn	1 Billy Graham Pkwy	Charlotte	NC	28201	**877-247-2426**	704-401-2432	47-20
BI-LO LLC	PO Box B	Jacksonville	SC	32203	**800-967-9105**	800-768-4438	345
Biltmore Greensboro Hotel	111 W Washington St *General	Greensboro	NC	27401	**800-332-0303***	336-272-3474	379
Biltmore Hotel & Conference Ctr of the Americas	1200 Anastasia Ave *Cust Svc	Coral Gables	FL	33134	**800-727-1926***	305-445-1926	667
Biltmore Hotel & Suites	2151 Laurelwood Rd	Santa Clara	CA	95054	**800-255-9925**	408-988-8411	379
Biltmore Hotel Oklahoma	401 S Meridian Ave	Oklahoma City	OK	73108	**800-522-6620**	405-947-7681	379
Biltmore Suites	205 W Madison St	Baltimore	MD	21201	**800-868-5064**	410-728-6550	379
Bilt-Rite Conveyors	735 Industrial Loop Rd	New London	WI	54961	**800-558-3616**	920-982-6600	209
Biltrite Corp	51 Sawyer Rd	Waltham	MA	02454	**800-877-8775**	781-647-1700	674
Bimbo Bakeries USA	PO Box 976	Horsham	PA	19044	**800-984-0989**		297-1
Bimeda-MTC Animal Health Inc	420 Beaverdale Rd	Cambridge	ON	N3C2W4	**888-524-6332**	519-654-8000	581
Bindagraphics Inc	2701 Wilmarco Ave	Baltimore	MD	21223	**800-326-0300**	410-362-7200	91
Binghamton Knitting Co Inc	11 Alice St	Binghamton	NY	13904	**877-746-3368**		154-15
Binghamton University	4400 Vestal Pkwy E	Binghamton	NY	13902	**800-782-0289**	607-777-2000	167
Binion's Gambling Hall & Hotel	128 E Fremont St	Las Vegas	NV	89101	**800-937-6537**	702-382-1600	132
Binkley & Hurst LP	133 Rothsville Stn Rd	Lititz	PA	17543	**800-414-4705**	717-626-4705	429
Binswanger Glass	965 Ridge Lk Blvd Ste 305	Memphis	TN	38120	**800-365-9922**		330
Bio Compression Systems Inc	120 W Commercial Ave	Moonachie	NJ	07074	**800-888-0908**	201-939-0716	475
Bio Medic Data Systems Inc	1 Silas Rd	Seaford	DE	19973	**800-526-2637**	302-628-4100	82
Bio Medical Innovations	814 Airport Way	Sandpoint	ID	83864	**800-201-3958**		252
Bio/Data Corp	PO Box 347	Horsham	PA	19044	**800-257-3282**	215-441-4000	419
Bioanalytical Systems Inc	2701 Kent Ave *NASDAQ: BASI*	West Lafayette	IN	47906	**800-845-4246**	765-463-4527	419
Bio-Botanica Inc	75 Commerce Dr	Hauppauge	NY	11788	**800-645-5720**	631-231-5522	478
BioCardia Inc	125 Shoreway Rd Ste B	San Carlos	CA	94070	**800-624-1179**	650-226-0120	475
Biocell Laboratories Inc	2001 University Dr	Rancho Dominguez	CA	90220	**800-222-8382**	310-537-3300	233
Biodex Medical Systems Inc	20 Ramsay Rd	Shirley	NY	11967	**800-224-6339**	631-924-9000	475
Bioethics Legal Review	1617 JFK Blvd Ste 1750	Philadelphia	PA	19103	**877-256-2472**	215-557-2300	530-7
Biofit Engineered Products	15500 Biofit Way	Bowling Green	OH	43402	**800-597-0246**	419-823-1089	320-1
Bioflex Low Intensity Laser System	411 Horner Ave	Etobicoke	ON	M8W4W3	**888-557-4004**	416-251-1055	475
BioGenex Laboratories Inc	4600 Norris Canyon Rd	San Ramon	CA	94583	**800-421-4149**	925-275-0550	233
Biohelix Corp	500 Cummings Ste 5550	Beverly	MA	01915	**866-800-5458**	978-927-5056	233
BioHorizons Inc	2300 Riverchase Ctr	Birmingham	AL	35244	**888-246-8338**	205-967-7880	476
Biola University	13800 Biola Ave *Admissions	La Mirada	CA	90639	**800-652-4652***	562-903-6000	167
Bio-Lab Inc	1725 N Brown Rd PO Box 30000	Lawrenceville	GA	30043	**800-859-7946**	678-502-4000	142
BioLase Technology Inc	4 Cromwell	Irvine	CA	92618	**800-699-9462**	888-424-6527	424
BioLegend Inc	11080 Roselle St	San Diego	CA	92121	**877-246-5343**	858-455-9588	666
bioLytical Laboratories Inc	1108 - 13351 Commerce Pkwy	Richmond	BC	V6V2X7	**866-674-6784**	604-204-6784	666
Biomarine Inc	456 Creamery Way	Exton	PA	19341	**800-378-2287**	610-524-8800	575
Biomerica Inc	1533 Monrovia Ave *OTC: BMRA* ■ *Cust Svc	Newport Beach	CA	92663	**800-854-3002***	949-645-2111	233
BioMerieux Inc	595 Anglum Rd	Hazelwood	MO	63042	**800-634-7656**	314-731-8500	475
Biomet Inc	56 E Bell Dr PO Box 587	Warsaw	IN	46582	**800-348-9500**	574-267-6639	476
Biomet Microfixation Inc	1520 Tradeport Dr	Jacksonville	FL	32218	**800-874-7711**	904-741-4400	475
BioMotiv LLC	3605 Warrensville Ctr Rd	Cleveland	OH	44122	**800-477-6307**	216-455-3200	240
Bionetics Corp, The	101 Production Dr Ste 100	Yorktown	VA	23693	**800-868-0330**	757-873-0900	263
Bioniche Life Sciences Inc.	231 Dundas St E *TSE: BNC*	Belleville	ON	K8N1E2	**800-265-5464**	613-966-8058	581
Bionostics Inc	7 Jackson Rd *General	Devens	MA	01434	**800-776-3856***	978-772-7070	233
BIOPAC Systems Inc	42 Aero Camino	Goleta	CA	93117	**877-524-6722**	805-685-0066	740
Bioquant Image Analysis Corp	5611 Ohio Ave	Nashville	TN	37209	**800-221-0549**	615-350-7866	513
Bio-Rad Laboratories	1000 Alfred Nobel Dr *NYSE: BIO*	Hercules	CA	94547	**800-424-6723**	510-724-7000	233
Bio-Recovery Corp	1863 Pond Rd Ste 4	Ronkonkoma	NY	11779	**800-556-0621**	631-676-2600	83
Bio-Reference Laboratories Inc	481 Edward H Ross Dr *NASDAQ: BRLI*	Elmwood Park	NJ	07407	**800-229-5227**		416
BioReliance Corp	14920 Broschart Rd	Rockville	MD	20850	**800-553-5372**	301-738-1000	84
Bio-Research Products Inc	323 W Cherry St	North Liberty	IA	52317	**800-326-3511**	319-626-6707	740
Biosan Laboratories Inc	1950 Tobsal Ct	Warren	MI	48091	**800-253-6800**	586-755-8970	740
Bio-Scene Recovery	13191 Meadow St NE	Alliance	OH	44601	**877-380-5500**	330-823-5500	83
BioScience	1444 'I' St NW Ste 200	Washington	DC	20005	**800-992-2427**	202-628-1500	456-19
BioScrip	1600 Bdwy Ste 950 *NASDAQ: BIOS*	Denver	CO	80202	**877-409-2301**	720-697-5200	585
Bioseal	167 W Orangethorpe Ave	Placentia	CA	92870	**800-441-7325**	714-528-4695	475
Biosense Webster Inc	3333 S Diamond Canyon Rd	Diamond Bar	CA	91765	**800-729-9010**	909-839-8500	475
Bio-Serv	3 Foster Lane Ste 201	Flemington	NJ	08822	**800-996-9908**	908-284-2155	581
BioSpace Inc	90 New Montgomery St Ste 414	San Francisco	CA	94105	**888-246-7722**	877-277-7585	397
BiosPacific Inc	5980 Horton St Ste 225	Emeryville	CA	94608	**800-344-6686**	510-652-6155	233
BioTechniques	52 Vanderbilt Ave 7th Fl	New York	NY	10017	**800-606-6246**	212-520-2777	456-19
Biotechnology Industry Organization	1201 Maryland Ave SW Ste 900	Washington	DC	20024	**866-356-5155**	202-962-9200	48-19
Biotechnology Software	140 Huguenot St 3rd Fl	New Rochelle	NY	10801	**800-654-3237**	914-740-2100	530-3
BioTek Instruments Inc	100 Tigan St PO Box 998	Winooski	VT	05404	**888-451-5171**	802-655-4740	419
bioTheranostics Inc	9640 Towne Centre Dr Ste 200	San Diego	CA	92121	**877-886-6739**	858-587-5870	740
Bio-Tissue	7000 SW 97th Ave Ste 211	Miami	FL	33173	**888-296-8858**	305-412-4430	544
Biotools Inc	17546 Bee Line Hwy	Jupiter	FL	33458	**866-286-6571**	561-625-0133	583
Biovet Inc	4375 Ave Beaudry	Saint-Hyacinthe	QC	J2S8W2	**888-824-6838**	450-771-7291	581
Biovet USA Inc	9025 Penn Ave S	Bloomington	MN	55431	**877-824-6838**	952-884-3113	581
BioZyme Inc	6010 Stockyards Expy	Saint Joseph	MO	64504	**800-821-3070**	816-238-3326	446
Birch Communications Inc	2300 Main St 6th Fl	Kansas City	MO	64108	**866-424-5100**	816-300-3000	733
Birchcraft Studios Inc	10 Railroad St	Abington	MA	02351	**800-333-0405**	781-878-5152	129
Birchwood Laboratories Inc	7900 Fuller Rd	Eden Prairie	MN	55344	**800-328-6156**	952-937-7900	144
Bird Electronic Corp	30303 Aurora Rd	Solon	OH	44139	**866-695-4569**	440-248-1200	250
Bird Precision	1 Spruce St PO Box 540569 *Cust Svc	Waltham	MA	02454	**800-454-7369***	781-894-0160	619
Bird Solutions International	1338 N Melrose Dr Ste H	Vista	CA	92083	**800-210-9514**	760-758-9747	576
Bird Studies Canada	115 Front St PO Box 160	Port Rowan	ON	N0E1M0	**888-448-2473**	519-586-3531	47-3
Bird Talk Magazine	3 Burroughs *Resv	Irvine	CA	92618	**800-695-6088***	949-855-8822	456-14
Bird Technologies Group Inc	30303 Aurora Rd	Solon	OH	44139	**866-695-4569**	440-248-1200	250
Birdair Inc	65 Lawrence Bell Dr Ste 100	Amherst	NY	14221	**800-622-2246**	716-633-9500	191-12
Birdie Golf Balls Golf Equipment	208 Margate Ct	Margate	FL	33063	**800-333-7271**	954-973-2741	709
Birds & Blooms Magazine	5400 S 60th St	Greendale	WI	53129	**888-860-8040**		456-14
BirdWatching Magazine	25 Braintree Hill Office Pk Ste 404	Braintree	MA	02184	**877-252-8141**		456-14
Birks & Mayors Inc	1240 du Sq-Phillips St	Montreal	QC	H3B3H4	**800-758-2511**		410
Birmingham Civil Rights Institute	520 16th St N	Birmingham	AL	35203	**866-328-9696**	205-328-9696	519
Birmingham International Forest Products LLC	300 Riverhills Business Pk	Birmingham	AL	35242	**800-767-2437**	205-972-1500	193-3
Birmingham News	2201 Fourth Ave N	Birmingham	AL	35203	**800-283-4001**	205-325-4444	531-2
Birmingham Race Course	1000 John Rogers Dr	Birmingham	AL	35210	**800-998-8238**	205-838-7500	132
Birmingham Rail & Locomotive Company Inc	PO Box 530157	Birmingham	AL	35253	**800-241-2260**	205-424-7245	768
Birmingham Times	115 Third Ave W	Birmingham	AL	35204	**866-456-4995**	205-251-5158	531-4
Birmingham Vending Co	540 Second Ave N	Birmingham	AL	35204	**800-288-7635**	205-324-7526	54
Birmingham-Southern College	900 Arkadelphia Rd	Birmingham	AL	35254	**800-523-5793**	205-226-4600	167
Birnbaum Interpreting Services	8730 Georgia Ave Ste 210	Silver Spring	MD	20910	**800-471-6441**	301-587-8885	766
Birner Dental Management Services Inc	1777 S Harrison St Ste 1400	Denver	CO	80210	**877-898-1083**	303-691-0680	462
Birnie Bus Service Inc	248 Otis St	Rome	NY	13441	**800-734-3950**	315-336-3950	108
Birthday Direct	120 Commerce St	Muscle Shoals	AL	35661	**888-491-9185**	256-381-0310	294
Biscayne Rod Manufacturing Inc	425 E Ninth St	Hialeah	FL	33010	**866-969-0808**	305-884-0808	708
Bischoff Insurance Agency Inc	1300 Oakridge Dr Ste 100	Fort Collins	CO	80525	**888-229-5558**	970-223-9400	390
Bisco Dental Products (Canada) Inc	2571 Smith St	Richmond	BC	V6X2J1	**800-667-8811**	604-276-8662	474

Name / Address	City	State	Zip	Toll-Free	Phone	Class
Bisco Industries Inc						
1500 N Lakeview Ave	Anaheim	CA	92807	**800-323-1232**		248
Biscom Inc						
321 Billerica Rd	Chelmsford	MA	01824	**800-477-2472**	978-250-1800	175-3
Biscuit & Cracker Manufacturers Assn (B&CMA)						
6325 Woodside Ct Ste 125	Columbia	MD	21046	**877-701-8111**	443-545-1645	48-6
Bishop Distributing Co						
5200 36th St SE	Grand Rapids	MI	49512	**800-748-0363***		361
*Cust Svc						
Bishop International Airport						
G-3425 W Bristol Rd	Flint	MI	48507	**800-433-7300**	810-235-6560	27
Bishop-Wisecarver Corp						
2104 Martin Way	Pittsburg	CA	94565	**888-580-8272**	925-439-8272	619
Bismarck Expressway Suites						
180 E Bismarck Expy	Bismarck	ND	58504	**888-774-5566**	701-222-3311	379
Bismarck State College						
1500 Edwards Ave	Bismarck	ND	58501	**800-445-5073**	701-224-5400	161
Bismarck Tribune						
707 E Front Ave	Bismarck	ND	58504	**866-476-5348**	701-223-2500	531-2
Bismarck-Mandan Convention & Visitors Bureau						
1600 Burnt Boat Dr	Bismarck	ND	58503	**800-767-3555**	701-222-4308	208
Bison Gear & Engineering Corp						
3850 Ohio Ave	Saint Charles	IL	60174	**800-282-4766**	630-377-4327	707
Bison Inc 603 L St	Lincoln	NE	68508	**800-247-7668**	402-474-3353	708
Bisque Imports						
1 Belmont Ave	Belmont	NC	28012	**888-568-5991**	704-829-9290	361
bitHeads Inc						
1309 Carling Ave	Ottawa	ON	K1Z7L3	**855-622-3232**	613-722-3232	182
Bitterman Scales LLC						
413 Radcliff Rd	Willow Street	PA	17584	**877-464-3009**	717-464-3009	362
Bituminous Insurance Cos						
320 18th St	Rock Island	IL	61201	**800-475-4477**		391-4
Bix Beiderbecke Memorial Society						
PO Box 3688	Davenport	IA	52808	**888-249-5487**	563-324-7170	47-4
Bix Produce Co						
1415 L'Orient St	Saint Paul	MN	55117	**800-642-9514**	651-487-8000	298-7
Bixel & Co						
8721 Sunset Blvd Ste 101	Los Angeles	CA	90069	**855-854-9830**	310-854-3828	186
BizLand Inc						
70 BlanchaRd Rd	Burlington	MA	01803	**800-249-5263**		38
Bizlink Technology Inc						
3400 Gateway Blvd	Fremont	CA	94538	**800-326-4193**	510-252-0786	813
BizQuest LLC						
2100 E Rt 66 Ste 200	Glendora	CA	91740	**888-280-3815**		393
BKR International						
19 Fulton St Ste 401	New York	NY	10038	**800-257-4685**	212-964-2115	48-1
BL Cos						
355 Research Pkwy	Meriden	CT	06450	**800-301-3077**	203-630-1406	263
BL Downey Company LLC						
2125 Gardner Rd	Broadview	IL	60155	**800-323-1206**	708-345-8000	480
Blach Distributing Co						
131 W Main St	Elko	NV	89801	**800-310-5099**	775-738-7111	80-1
Blachly-Lane Inc						
PO Box 70	Junction City	OR	97448	**800-446-8418**	541-688-8711	247
Black Bear Casino Resort						
1785 Hwy 210 PO Box 777	Carlton	MN	55718	**888-771-0777**	218-878-2327	132
Black Box Corp						
1000 Pk Dr	Lawrence	PA	15055	**877-877-2269**	724-746-5500	178
NASDAQ: BBOX						
Black Butte Ranch						
12930 Hawks BeaRd Rd						
PO Box 8000	Black Butte Ranch	OR	97759	**866-901-2961**	541-595-1252	667
Black Cultural Centre for Nova Scotia						
10 Cherry Brook Rd	Cherry Brook	NS	B2Z1A8	**800-465-0767**	902-434-6223	519
Black Enterprise Magazine						
130 Fifth Ave	New York	NY	10011	**800-727-7777***	212-242-8000	456-5
*Cust Svc						
Black Forest Decor LLC						
PO Box 297	Jenks	OK	74037	**800-605-0915**		789
Black Hat Inc						
1932 First Ave Ste 204	Seattle	WA	98101	**866-203-8081**	206-443-5489	690
Black Hawk College						
East						
1501 State Hwy 78	Kewanee	IL	61443	**800-233-5671**	309-852-5671	161
Quad Cities						
6600 34th Ave	Moline	IL	61265	**800-334-1311**	309-796-5000	161
Black Hills Caverns						
2600 Cavern Rd	Rapid City	SD	57702	**800-837-9358**	605-343-0542	49-4
Black Hills Corp						
625 Ninth St	Rapid City	SD	57701	**866-264-8003**	605-721-1700	360-5
NYSE: BKH						
Black Hills Electric Co-op						
25191 Co-op Way PO Box 792	Custer	SD	57730	**800-742-0085**	605-673-4461	247
Black Hills Health & Education Ctr						
PO Box 19	Hermosa	SD	57744	**866-757-0160***	605-255-4101	704
*Cust Svc						
Black Hills State University						
1200 University St Unit 9502	Spearfish	SD	57799	**800-255-2478**	605-642-6343	167
Black Mann & Graham LLP						
2905 Corporate Cir	Flower Mound	TX	75028	**888-293-0505**	972-353-4174	428
Black Mountain Ranch						
4000 Conger Mesa Rd	McCoy	CO	80463	**800-967-2401**	970-653-4226	241
Black Mountain-Swannanoa Chamber of Commerce						
201 E State St	Black Mountain	NC	28711	**800-669-2301**	828-669-2300	138
Black Photo Corp						
200 Consilium Pl Ste 1600	Toronto	ON	M1H3J3	**800-668-3826**	416-279-0007	118
Black Radio Network						
166 Madison Ave	New York	NY	10016	**866-342-6892**	212-686-6850	641
Black River Electric Co-op						
2600 Hwy 67 PO Box 31	Fredericktown	MO	63645	**800-392-4711**	573-783-3381	247
Black River State Forest						
101 S Webster St PO Box 7921	Madison	WI	53707	**888-936-7463**	608-266-2621	564
Black River Technical College						
1410 Hwy 304 E	Pocahontas	AR	72455	**866-890-6933**	870-248-4000	161
Blackbaud Inc						
2000 Daniel Island Dr	Charleston	SC	29492	**800-468-8996**	843-216-6200	180-1
NASDAQ: BLKB						
BlackBerry						
2200 University Ave E Ste 200	Waterloo	ON	N2L3X2	**877-255-2377**	519-888-7465	226
Blackboard Inc						
1899 L St NW 5th Fl	Washington	DC	20036	**800-424-9299**	202-463-4860	180-3
Blackbourn						
200 Fourth Ave N	Edgerton	MN	56128	**800-842-7550**		85
Blackburn College						
700 College Ave	Carlinville	IL	62626	**800-233-3550**	217-854-3231	167
Blackburn's Physicians Pharmacy Inc						
301 Corbet St	Tarentum	PA	15084	**800-472-2440**	724-224-9100	475
Blackfoot Inn						
5940 Blackfoot Trl SE	Calgary	AB	T2H2B5	**800-661-1151**	403-252-2253	379
Blackhawk Bank						
PO Box 719	Beloit	WI	53511	**888-769-2600**	608-364-4534	68
Blackhawk Technical College						
6004 S County Rd G	Janesville	WI	53546	**800-498-1282**	608-758-6900	798
Blackledge Furniture						
233 Sw Second St	Corvallis	OR	97333	**800-782-4851**	541-753-4851	322
Blackman Kallick						
10 S Riverside Plaza	Chicago	IL	60606	**866-939-3921**	312-207-1040	2
Blackmer						
1809 Century Ave	Grand Rapids	MI	49503	**888-363-7886**	616-241-1611	638
Blackmore Company Inc						
10800 Blackmore Ave	Belleville	MI	48111	**800-874-8660**	734-483-8661	607
BlackRock Inc						
601 Union St 56th Fl	Seattle	WA	98101	**800-441-7450**	206-613-6700	790
NYSE: BLK						
Blackstone Industries Inc						
16 Stoney Hill Rd	Bethel	CT	06801	**800-272-2885**	203-792-8622	757
Blackstone Valley Chamber of Commerce						
110 Church St	Whitinsville	MA	01588	**800-841-0919**	508-234-9090	138
Blackwell, The						
2110 Tuttle Pk Pl	Columbus	OH	43210	**866-247-4003**	614-247-4000	379
Blade						
541 N Superior St	Toledo	OH	43660	**800-245-3317**	419-724-6000	531-2
Blade Energy Partners Ltd						
2600 Network Blvd Ste 550	Frisco	TX	75034	**800-849-1545**	972-712-8407	194
Blade-Tech Industries Inc						
5530 184th St East	Puyallup	WA	98375	**877-331-5793**	253-655-8059	709
Bladon Springs State Park						
3921 Bladon Rd	Bladon Springs	AL	36919	**800-252-7275**	251-754-9207	564
Blaine County						
420 Ohio St	Chinook	MT	59523	**800-666-6124**	406-442-9830	338
Blaine Tech Services Inc						
1680 Rogers Ave	San Jose	CA	95112	**800-545-7558**	408-573-0555	196
Blaine's Art Supply						
1025 Photo Ave	Anchorage	AK	99503	**866-561-4278**	907-561-5344	44
Blair Cedar & Novelty Works Inc						
680 W US Hwy 54	Camdenton	MO	65020	**800-325-3943**	573-346-2235	329
Blair Packaging Inc						
1515 Independence St	Cape Girardeau	MO	63703	**800-624-3150**	573-334-2146	85
Blakely New York						
136 W 55th St	New York	NY	10019	**800-735-0710**	212-245-1800	379
Blanchard Compact Equipment						
1410 Ashville Hwy	Spartanburg	SC	29303	**888-799-3606**	864-582-1245	276
Blanco America Inc						
110 Mount Holly By-Pass	Lumberton	NJ	08048	**800-451-5782**		362
Blank Quilting Corp						
Blank Quilting						
49 West 37th St 14th fl	New York	NY	10018	**800-294-9495**		593
Blanks Printing & Imaging Inc						
2343 N Beckley Ave	Dallas	TX	75208	**800-325-7651**	214-741-3905	779
Blanks/USA Inc						
7700 68th Ave N #7	Minneapolis	MN	55428	**800-328-7311**		559
Blanton & Assoc Inc						
5 Lakeway Centre Ct Ste 200	Austin	TX	78734	**888-863-5881**	512-264-1095	196
Blantyre						
16 Blantyre Rd PO Box 995	Lenox	MA	01240	**844-881-0104**	413-637-3556	379
Blasingame, Burch, Garrard & Ashley PC						
440 College Ave	Athens	GA	30603	**866-354-3544**	706-354-4000	428
Blast Advanced Media						
950 Reserve Dr Ste 150	Roseville	CA	95678	**888-252-7866**	916-724-6701	182
Blast Inc						
220 Chatham Business Dr						
PO Box 818	Pittsboro	NC	27312	**800-242-5278**	919-533-0143	180-7
Blauch Bros Inc						
911 Chicago Ave	Harrisonburg	VA	22802	**888-881-3939**	540-434-2589	609
Blauer Mfg Co Inc						
20 Aberdeen St	Boston	MA	02215	**800-225-6715**	617-536-6606	154-18
Blazer Industries Inc						
PO Box 489	Aumsville	OR	97325	**877-211-3437**	503-749-1900	105
Bledsoe Telephone Co-op Corp (BTC)						
338 Cumberland Ave PO Box 609	Pikeville	TN	37367	**888-382-1222**	423-447-2121	733
Blendex Company Inc						
11208 Electron Dr	Louisville	KY	40299	**800-626-6325**	502-267-1003	297-23
Blenko Glass Co						
PO Box 67	Milton	WV	25541	**877-425-3656**	304-743-9081	334
Blessing Hospital						
Broadway at 11th St	Quincy	IL	62301	**866-460-3933**	217-223-8400	374-3
BLET (Brotherhood of Locomotive Engineers & Trainmen)						
1370 Ontario St						
Mezzanine Level	Cleveland	OH	44113	**877-772-5772**	216-241-2630	414
Bleyhl Farm Service Inc						
940 E Wine Country Rd	Grandview	WA	98930	**800-862-6806***	509-882-2248	278
*Cust Svc						
BLI (Bulk Lift International Inc)						
1013 Tamarac Dr	Carpentersville	IL	60110	**800-879-2247**	847-428-6059	66
BLI (Big Lots Inc)						
300 Phillipi Rd	Columbus	OH	43228	**877-998-1697**	614-278-6800	789
NYSE: BIG						
Blish-Mize Co						
223 S Fifth St	Atchison	KS	66002	**800-995-0525**	913-367-1250	351
Bliss Clearing Niagara (BCN)						
1004 E State St	Hastings	MI	49058	**800-642-5477**	269-948-3300	455
Bliss Communications Inc						
PO Box 5001	Janesville	WI	53547	**800-422-7128**	608-754-3311	640
Bliss Direct Media						
641 15Th Ave Ne	Saint Joseph	MN	56374	**800-578-7947**	320-271-1600	387
Blissfield Manufacturing Co						
626 Depot St	Blissfield	MI	49228	**800-626-1772***	517-486-2121	14
*Cust Svc						

Name / Address	City	State	ZIP	Toll-Free	Phone	Class
Blistex Inc 1800 Swift Dr *Cust Svc	Oak Brook	IL	60523	**800-837-1800***		582
Blitt & Gaines Pc 661 Glenn Ave	Wheeling	IL	60090	**888-920-0620**	847-403-4900	428
Blizzard Internet Marketing Inc 50629 Hwy 6	Glenwood Springs	CO	81601	**888-840-5893**	970-928-7875	227
Blodgett Supply Co Inc 100 Ave D PO Box 759	Williston	VT	05495	**888-888-3424**	802-864-9831	37
Blommer Chocolate Co 600 W Kinzie St	Chicago	IL	60610	**800-621-1606**	312-226-7700	297-8
Blonder Tongue Laboratories Inc 1 Jake Brown Rd *NYSE: BDR*	Old Bridge	NJ	08857	**877-407-8033**	732-679-4000	645
Blood Assurance Inc 705 E Fourth St	Chattanooga	TN	37403	**800-962-0628**	423-756-0966	88
Blood Bank of Delmarva 100 Hygeia Dr	Newark	DE	19713	**800-548-4009**	302-737-8405	88
Blood Bank of Hawaii 2043 Dillingham Blvd	Honolulu	HI	96819	**800-372-9966**	808-845-9966	88
Blood Bank of the Redwoods 2324 Bethards Dr	Santa Rosa	CA	95405	**888-393-4483**	707-545-1222	88
Blood Centers of the Pacific 250 Bush St Ste 136	San Francisco	CA	94104	**888-393-4483**	415-567-6400	88
Blood Ctr, The 2609 Canal St	New Orleans	LA	70112	**800-862-5663**	504-524-1322	88
Blood Donor Ctr at Presbyterian/St Luke's Medical Ctr 1719 E 19th Ave	Denver	CO	80218	**800-231-2222**	303-839-6000	767
Blood Systems Laboratories 2424 W Erie Dr	Tempe	AZ	85282	**800-288-2199**	602-343-7000	417
BloodCenter of Wisconsin 638 N 18th St	Milwaukee	WI	53233	**877-232-4376**	414-933-5000	88
Blood-Horse Magazine PO Box 911088	Lexington	KY	40591	**800-866-2361**	859-278-2361	456-14
BloodSource 1608 Q St	Sacramento	CA	95811	**800-995-4420**	916-456-1500	88
Bloomfield College 467 Franklin St	Bloomfield	NJ	07003	**800-848-4555**	973-748-9000	167
Bloomfield Township Public Library 1099 Lone Pine Rd	Bloomfield Hills	MI	48302	**800-318-2596**	248-642-5800	434-3
Bloomingdale's 1000 Third Ave	New York	NY	10022	**800-950-0047**	212-705-2000	231
Bloomington Convention & Visitors Bureau (BCVB) 7900 International Dr Ste 990	Bloomington	MN	55425	**800-346-4289**	952-858-8500	208
Bloomington/Monroe County Convention & Visitors Bureau 2855 N Walnut St	Bloomington	IN	47404	**800-800-0037**	812-334-8900	208
Bloomington-Normal Area Convention & Visitors Bureau 3201 CIRA Dr Ste 201	Bloomington	IL	61704	**800-433-8226**	309-665-0033	208
BloomNation LLC 8889 W Olympic Blvd	Beverly Hills	CA	90211	**877-702-5666**		294
BloomNet Inc 1 Old Country Rd Ste 500	Carle Place	NY	11514	**866-256-6663**		387
Bloomsburg Carpet Industries Inc 4999 Columbia Blvd	Bloomsburg	PA	17815	**800-233-8773**	570-784-9188	130
Bloomsburg University 400 E Second St	Bloomsburg	PA	17815	**888-651-6117**	570-389-3900	167
Blossman Gas Inc 809 Washington Ave	Ocean Springs	MS	39564	**800-256-7762**	888-256-7762	317
Blossom Music Ctr Tickets 1145 W Steels Corners Rd	Cuyahoga Falls	OH	44223	**800-745-3000**	330-920-8040	571
Blount County Chamber of Commerce 201 S Washington St	Maryville	TN	37804	**855-257-3964**	865-983-2241	138
Blount Memorial Hospital 907 E Lamar Alexander Pkwy	Maryville	TN	37804	**800-448-0219**	865-983-7211	374-3
Blount Seafood Corp 630 Currant Rd *Hotline	Fall River	MA	02720	**800-274-2526***	774-888-1300	297-14
Blount Small Ship Adventures 461 Water St	Warren	RI	02885	**800-556-7450**	401-247-0955	222
Blower Application Company Inc N 114 W 19125 Clinton Dr	Germantown	WI	53022	**800-959-0880**	262-255-5580	386
Blowfish Direct LLC 11130 Holder St	Cypress	CA	90630	**877-725-6934**		688
Blowing Rock Chamber of Commerce 7738 Vly Blvd	Blowing Rock	NC	28605	**800-295-7851**	828-295-7851	138
BLR (Business & Legal Reports Inc) 141 Mill Rock Rd E	Old Saybrook	CT	06475	**800-727-5257**	860-510-0100	634-9
BLT Prime 111 E 22nd St	New York	NY	10010	**800-855-2880**	212-995-8500	669
Blue & Co 12800 N Meridian St Ste 400	Carmel	IN	46032	**800-717-2583**	317-848-8920	2
Blue Box Group Inc 119 Pine St Ste 200	Seattle	WA	98101	**800-613-4305**		387
Blue Care Network of Michigan 20500 Civic Ctr Dr	Southfield	MI	48076	**800-662-6667**	248-799-6400	391-3
Blue Cat Design Mastwoods Rd	Port Hope	ON	L1A3V5	**888-258-3228**	905-753-1017	7
Blue Chip Casino Inc 777 Blue Chip Dr	Michigan City	IN	46360	**888-879-7711**	219-879-7711	132
Blue Coat Systems Inc 420 N Mary Ave *NASDAQ: BCSI*	Sunnyvale	CA	94085	**866-302-2628**	408-220-2200	178
Blue Cross & Blue Shield Assn 225 N Michigan Ave	Chicago	IL	60601	**888-630-2583**	312-297-6000	48-9
Blue Cross & Blue Shield of Alabama 450 Riverchase Pkwy E	Birmingham	AL	35244	**800-292-8868**	205-988-2200	391-3
Blue Cross & Blue Shield of Kansas City 2301 Main St	Kansas City	MO	64108	**800-892-6048**	816-395-2222	391-3
Blue Cross & Blue Shield of Michigan 600 Lafayette Blvd E	Detroit	MI	48226	**855-237-3501**	313-225-9000	391-3
Blue Cross & Blue Shield of Mississippi PO Box 1043	Jackson	MS	39215	**800-222-8046**	601-932-3704	391-3
Blue Cross & Blue Shield of Montana 560 N Pk Ave PO Box 4309	Helena	MT	59604	**800-447-7828**	406-437-5000	391-3
Blue Cross & Blue Shield of Nebraska 1919 Aksarben Dr PO Box 3248	Omaha	NE	68180	**800-422-2763**	402-982-7000	391-3
Blue Cross & Blue Shield of New Mexico PO Box 27630	Albuquerque	NM	87125	**800-835-8699**	505-291-3500	391-3
Blue Cross & Blue Shield of North Carolina 1965 Ivory Creek Blvd *Cust Svc	Durham	NC	27702	**800-446-8053***	919-489-7431	391-3
Blue Cross & Blue Shield of Oklahoma 1215 S Boulder Ave *Cust Svc	Tulsa	OK	74119	**800-942-5837***	918-560-3500	391-3
Blue Cross & Blue Shield of Rhode Island 500 Exchange St	Providence	RI	02903	**800-637-3718**	401-459-1000	391-3
Blue Cross & Blue Shield of Texas Inc 1001 E Lookout Dr	Richardson	TX	75082	**800-521-2227**	972-766-6900	391-3
Blue Cross & Blue Shield of Vermont 445 Industrial Ln *Cust Svc	Montpelier	VT	05602	**800-247-2583***	802-223-6131	391-3
Blue Cross Blue Shield of Arizona 2444 W Las Palmaritas Dr	Phoenix	AZ	85021	**800-232-2345**	602-864-4400	391-3
Blue Cross Blue Shield of Delaware PO Box 1991	Wilmington	DE	19899	**800-572-4400**	800-876-7639	391-3
Blue Cross Blue Shield of Georgia 3350 Peachtree Rd NE *Cust Svc	Atlanta	GA	30326	**800-441-2273***	404-842-8000	391-3
Blue Cross Blue Shield of Kansas 1133 SW Topeka Blvd	Topeka	KS	66629	**800-432-0216**	785-291-7000	391-3
Blue Cross Blue Shield of Louisiana 5525 Reitz Ave	Baton Rouge	LA	70898	**800-599-2583**	225-295-3307	391-3
Blue Cross Blue Shield of Massachusetts 401 Pk Dr	Boston	MA	02215	**800-262-2583**	617-246-5000	391-3
Blue Cross Blue Shield of North Dakota 4510 13th Ave S	Fargo	ND	58121	**800-342-4718**	701-282-1100	391-3
Blue Cross Blue Shield of Wyoming 4000 House Ave	Cheyenne	WY	82001	**800-851-9145**	307-634-1393	391-3
Blue Cross of California 2 Gannett Dr	South Portland	ME	04106	**800-999-3643**	800-482-0966	391-3
Blue Cross of Idaho 3000 E Pine Ave	Meridian	ID	83642	**800-274-4018**	208-345-4550	391-3
Blue Cross of Northeastern Pennsylvania 19 N Main St *Cust Svc	Wilkes-Barre	PA	18711	**800-577-3742***		391-3
Blue Generation Div of M Rubin & Sons Inc 34-01 38th Ave	Long Island	NY	11101	**888-336-4687**	718-361-2800	154-18
Blue Giant Equipment Corp 85 Heart Lk Rd South	Brampton	ON	L6W3K2	**800-668-7078**	905-457-3900	358
Blue Grass Airport 4000 Terminal Dr	Lexington	KY	40510	**800-800-4000**	859-425-3100	27
Blue Grass Energy Co-op Corp 1201 Lexington Rd	Nicholasville	KY	40356	**888-546-4243**	859-885-4191	247
Blue Grass Regional Library 104 E Sixth St	Columbia	TN	38401	**888-345-5575**	931-388-9282	434-3
Blue Grass Regional Mental Health-Mental Retardation Board Inc 1351 Newtown Pike Bldg 1	Lexington	KY	40511	**800-928-8000**	859-253-1686	47-6
Blue Grass Stockyard 375 Lisle Industrial Ave PO Box 1023	Lexington	KY	40588	**800-621-3972**	859-255-7701	445
Blue Horizon Hotel 1225 Robson St	Vancouver	BC	V6E1C3	**800-663-1333**	604-688-1411	379
Blue Lakes Charters & Tours 12154 N Saginaw Rd	Clio	MI	48420	**800-282-4287**	810-686-4287	106
Blue Lance Inc 410 Pierce St	Houston	TX	77002	**800-856-2583**	713-255-4800	180-12
Blue Licks Battlefield State Resort Park Hwy 68	Mount Olivet	KY	41064	**800-443-7008**		564
Blue Moon Hotel 944 Collins Ave	Miami Beach	FL	33139	**800-553-7739**	305-673-2262	379
Blue Mounds State Park 1410 161st St	Luverne	MN	56156	**888-646-6367**	507-283-1307	564
Blue Mountain Air Inc 707 Aldridge Rd	Vacaville	CA	95688	**800-889-2085**		609
Blue Mountain Arts Inc PO Box 4549 *Sales	Boulder	CO	80306	**800-545-8573***	303-449-0536	129
Blue Mountain College PO Box 160	Blue Mountain	MS	38610	**800-235-0136**	662-685-4771	167
Blue Mountain Community College 2411 NW Carden Ave PO Box 100	Pendleton	OR	97801	**888-441-7232**	541-276-1260	161
Blue Nile Inc 705 Fifth Ave S Ste 900 *NASDAQ: NILE*	Seattle	WA	98104	**800-242-2728**	206-336-6700	410
Blue Parrot Inn 409 Angela St	Key West	FL	33040	**800-549-4430**	305-296-0033	379
Blue Pillar Inc 9025 N River Rd Ste 150	Indianapolis	IN	46240	**888-234-3212**		194
Blue Ribbon Home Warranty Inc 95 S Wadsworth Blvd	Lakewood	CO	80226	**800-571-0475**	303-986-3900	367
Blue Ribbon Tag & Label Corp 4035 N 29th Ave	Hollywood	FL	33020	**800-433-4974**	954-922-9292	413
Blue Ribbon Travel-american 3601 W 76th St Ste 190	Minneapolis	MN	55435	**800-626-5309**	952-835-2724	773
Blue Ridge Bank & Trust Co 4240 Blue Ridge Blvd Ste 100	Kansas City	MO	64133	**800-569-4287**	816-358-5000	69
Blue Ridge Community College 1 College Ln PO Box 80	Weyers Cave	VA	24486	**888-750-2722**	540-234-9261	161
Blue Ridge Electric Membership Corp 1216 Blowing Rock Blvd	Lenoir	NC	28645	**800-451-5474**	828-758-2383	247
Blue Ridge Public Television 1215 McNeil Dr	Roanoke	VA	24015	**888-332-7788**	540-344-0991	629
Blue Ridge X-Ray Company Inc 120 Vista Blvd	Arden	NC	28704	**800-727-7290**		474
Blue Rock Technologies 800 Kirts Blvd	Troy	MI	48084	**866-390-8200**	248-786-6100	227
Blue Seal Feeds Inc 2905 US Hwy 61 N *Cust Svc	Muscatine	IA	52761	**866-647-1212***		446
Blue Sky Cycling Inc 2530 Randolph St	Huntington Park	CA	90255	**800-585-4137**	323-585-3934	709
Blue Sky Energy Inc 2598 Fortune Way Ste K	Vista	CA	92081	**800-493-7877**	760-597-1642	609

Name / Address	City	State	ZIP	Toll-Free	Phone	Class
Blue Sky Swimwear						
729 E International Speedway Blvd	Daytona Beach	FL	32118	**800-799-6445***	386-255-2590	154-16
*Orders						
Blue Water Area Chamber of Commerce						
512 McMorran Blvd	Port Huron	MI	48060	**800-361-0526**	810-985-7101	138
Blue Water Resort						
291 S Shore Dr	South Yarmouth	MA	02664	**800-367-9393**	508-398-2288	667
Blue Water Sailing Magazine						
747 Aquidneck Ave Ste 201						
Ste 201	Middletown	RI	02842	**888-800-7245**	401-847-7612	456-4
Blue Williams LLP						
3421 N Causeway Blvd Ste 900	Metairie	LA	70002	**800-326-4991**	504-831-4091	428
Blue Zebra Appointment Setting						
25 PEQUOT AVE Ste A	Port Washington	NY	11050	**800-755-0094**		7
BlueCross BlueShield of Tennessee Inc						
1 Cameron Hill Cir	Chattanooga	TN	37402	**800-848-0298**	423-755-5600	221
BlueCross BlueShield of Western New York						
257 W Genesee St	Buffalo	NY	14240	**800-888-0757**	716-887-6900	391-3
Bluefield College						
3000 College Dr	Bluefield	VA	24605	**800-872-0175**	276-326-3682	167
Bluefield Regional Medical Ctr (BRMC)						
500 Cherry St	Bluefield	WV	24701	**800-994-6610**	304-327-1100	374-3
Bluefield State College						
219 Rock St	Bluefield	WV	24701	**800-654-7798**	304-327-4000	167
Bluefly Inc						
42 W 39th St 9th Fl	New York	NY	10018	**877-258-3359***	212-944-8000	156-6
NASDAQ: BFLY ■ *Cust Svc						
Blue-Grace Logistics LLC						
2846 S Falkenburg Rd	Riverview	FL	33578	**800-697-4477**	813-641-0357	312
Bluegrass Cellular Inc						
2902 Ring Rd	Elizabethtown	KY	42701	**800-928-2355**	270-769-0339	733
Bluegrass Community & Technical College						
Cooper Campus						
470 Cooper Dr	Lexington	KY	40506	**866-774-4872**	859-246-6200	161
Bluegreen Corp						
4960 Conference Way N						
Ste 100	Boca Raton	FL	33431	**800-456-2582**	561-912-8000	751
NYSE: BXG						
Blueharbor Bank						
106 Corporate Park Dr	Mooresville	NC	28117	**877-322-8228**	704-662-7700	69
Bluelock LLC						
6325 Morenci Trl	Indianapolis	IN	46268	**888-402-2583**		182
Bluemetal Architects Inc						
44 Pleasant St	Watertown	MA	02472	**866-252-0111**		198
Bluenose Inn & Suites						
636 Bedford Hwy	Halifax	NS	B3M2L8	**800-553-5339**	800-565-2301	379
Bluepoint Leadership Development Ltd						
25 Whitney Dr	Milford	OH	45150	**888-221-8685**	513-683-4702	196
BlueSpire Strategic Marketing						
7650 Edinborough Way						
Ste 500	Minneapolis	MN	55435	**800-727-6397**		5
Bluestem Electric Co-op Inc						
614 E Hwy 24 PO Box 5	Wamego	KS	66547	**800-558-1580**	785-456-2212	247
BlueTie Inc						
2480 Browncroft Blvd Ste 2b	Rochester	NY	14625	**800-258-3843**	585-586-2000	227
Bluewater Adventures Ltd						
252 E First St Ste 3	North Vancouver	BC	V7L1B3	**888-877-1770**	604-980-3800	222
Bluewater Bay Resort						
2000 Bluewater Blvd	Niceville	FL	32578	**800-874-2128**	850-897-3613	667
Bluewater Resort						
2001 S Ocean Blvd	Myrtle Beach	SC	29577	**800-845-6994**	843-626-8345	667
Bluewater Thermal Solutions						
201 Brookfield Pwy Ste 102	Greenville	SC	29607	**877-990-0050**	864-990-0050	483
Bluffton Motor Works LLC						
410 E Spring St	Bluffton	IN	46714	**800-579-8527**	260-827-2200	517
Bluffton Today						
52 Persimmon St	Bluffton	SC	29910	**855-665-8549**	843-815-0800	531-4
Bluffton University						
1 University Dr	Bluffton	OH	45817	**800-488-3257**	419-358-3000	167
Blum Inc						
7733 Old Plank Rd	Stanley	NC	28164	**800-438-6788**	704-827-1345	350
Blumenthal Lansing Co						
30 Two Bridges Rd Ste 110	Fairfield	NJ	07004	**800-448-9749**	201-935-6220	593
Bluteau DeVenney & Company Inc						
5670 Spring Garden Rd Ste 901A	Halifax	NS	B3J1H6	**877-210-9800**	902-425-0467	40
Blytheco LLC						
23161 Mill Creek Dr	Laguna Hills	CA	92653	**800-425-9843**	949-583-9500	182
BMC (Better Management Corp)						
41738 Esterly Dr	Columbiana	OH	44408	**877-293-4300**	330-482-7070	658
BMC Software Inc						
2101 City W Blvd	Houston	TX	77042	**800-841-2031**	713-918-8800	180-1
NASDAQ: BMC						
BMDA (Building Material Dealers Assn)						
1006 SE Grand Ave Ste 301	Portland	OR	97214	**888-960-6329**	503-208-3763	48-3
BMG Aviation Inc						
984 S Kirby Rd	Bloomington	IN	47403	**888-457-3787**	812-825-7979	62
BMG Metals Inc						
950 Masonic Ln	Richmond	VA	23231	**800-552-1510**	804-226-1024	491
BMH (Bastian Material Handling LLC)						
10585 N Meridian St 3rd Fl	Indianapolis	IN	46290	**800-772-0464**	317-575-9992	54
BMH Books						
1104 Kings Hwy PO Box 544	Winona Lake	IN	46590	**800-348-2756**		634-8
BMI (Brotherhood Mutual Insurance Co)						
6400 Brotherhood Way						
PO Box 2589	Fort Wayne	IN	46825	**800-333-3735***		391-4
*Cust Svc						
BMI Educational Services						
PO Box 800	Dayton	NJ	08810	**800-222-8100**	732-329-6991	94
BMI Imaging Systems						
1115 E Arques Ave	Sunnyvale	CA	94085	**800-359-3456**	408-736-7444	495
Bmo Bankcorp Inc						
111 W Monroe St	Chicago	IL	60603	**888-340-2265**		360-2
BMO Financial Corp						
1 First Canadian Place 11th Fl	Toronto	ON	M5X1A1	**800-553-0332**	416-359-4440	218
BMO Harris Bank						
111 W Monroe St	Chicago	IL	60603	**888-340-2265**	847-238-2265	69
BMS (Broadcast Microwave Services Inc)						
12367 Crosthwaite Cir	Poway	CA	92064	**800-669-9667**	858-391-3050	226
Bms Integrated Services Inc						
1277 Georgia St E	Vancouver	BC	V6A2A9	**866-676-0136**	604-676-0136	691
BMW of Darien						
140 Ledge Rd	Darien	CT	06820	**855-349-6240**	203-656-1804	56
BMW of Manhattan Inc						
555 W 57th St	New York	NY	10019	**877-855-4607**	212-586-2269	53
BMW of North America LLC						
300 Chestnut Ridge Rd	Woodcliff Lake	NJ	07677	**800-831-1117**	201-307-4000	58
BNC National Bank						
322 E Main Ave	Bismarck	ND	58501	**800-262-2265**	701-250-3000	69
BNN (Business News Network)						
299 Queen St W	Toronto	ON	M5V2Z5	**855-326-6266**	416-384-6600	736
BNSF (Burlington Northern & Santa Fe Railway)						
2650 Lou Menk Dr	Fort Worth	TX	76131	**800-795-2673**		646
BNSF (Burlington Northern Santa Fe Corp)						
500 New Jersey Ave NW						
Ste 550	Washington	DC	20001	**800-964-9386**	202-347-8662	614
BNSF Logistics LLC						
4700 S Thompson Ste A202	Springdale	AR	72764	**888-285-4514**		227
BNX Shipping Inc						
910 E 236th St	Carson	CA	90745	**844-221-3091**	310-764-0999	312
BNZ Materials Inc						
6901 S Pierce St Ste 260	Littleton	CO	80128	**800-999-0890**	303-978-1199	660
Boa Technology Inc						
1760 Platte St	Denver	CO	80202	**844-203-1297**	303-455-5126	196
Boa-Franc Inc						
1255-98th St	Saint-georges	QC	G5Y8J5	**800-463-1303**	418-227-1181	292
Boar's Head Inn						
200 Ednam Dr	Charlottesville	VA	22903	**800-476-1988**	434-296-2181	667
Boarder to Boarder Trucking Inc						
PO Box 328	Edinburg	TX	78541	**800-678-8789**	956-316-4444	683
Boardroom Communications Inc						
Bank Of America Plaza 1776 N Pine Island Rd						
Ste 320	Fort Lauderdale	FL	33322	**877-773-4761**	954-370-8999	633
Boardroom Inc						
281 Tresser Blvd 8th Fl	Stamford	CT	06901	**800-274-5611**		634-9
Boardwalk Pipeline Partners LP						
3800 Frederica St	Owensboro	KY	42301	**866-913-2122**	270-686-3620	326
NYSE: BWP						
Boardwalk Plaza Hotel						
2 Olive Ave	Rehoboth Beach	DE	19971	**800-332-3224**	302-227-7169	379
Boart Longyear Co						
2640 W 1700 S	Salt Lake City	UT	84104	**800-453-8740**	801-972-6430	192
Boat Owners Assn of the US						
880 S Pickett St	Alexandria	VA	22304	**800-395-2628**	703-823-9550	47-22
BOB 94.9 WRBT						
600 Corporate Cir	Harrisburg	PA	17110	**800-682-3047**	717-540-8800	642-53
Bob Allen Ford						
9239 Metcalf Ave	Overland Park	KS	66212	**888-573-6364**	913-381-3000	56
Bob Barker Company Inc						
PO Box 429	Fuquay Varina	NC	27526	**800-334-9880**		593
Bob Davidson Ford Lincoln						
1845 E Joppa Rd	Baltimore	MD	21234	**877-885-7890**	410-661-6400	56
Bob Evans Farms Inc						
3776 S High St	Columbus	OH	43207	**800-939-2338**		668
NASDAQ: BOBE						
Bob Jones University						
1700 Wade Hampton Blvd	Greenville	SC	29614	**800-252-6363***	864-242-5100	167
*Admissions						
Bob Reeves Brass Mouthpieces						
25574 Rye Canyon Rd Ste D	Valencia	CA	91355	**800-837-0980**	661-775-8820	709
Bob Stall Chevrolet						
7601 Alvarado Rd	La Mesa	CA	91942	**800-295-2695**	619-460-1311	56
Bob Straub State Park						
US 101	Pacific City	OR	97112	**800-551-6949**		564
Bob Ward & Sons Inc						
3015 Paxson St	Missoula	MT	59801	**800-800-5083**	406-728-3220	709
Bob's Red Mill Natural Foods Inc						
13521 SE Pheasant Ct	Milwaukie	OR	97222	**800-553-2258**	503-654-3215	297-4
Bob's Sporting Goods						
1111 Hudson St	Longview	WA	98632	**800-292-5551**	360-425-3870	231
Bob's Stores Inc						
160 Corporate Ct	Meriden	CT	06450	**866-333-2627**	203-235-5775	156-2
Bobby Jones Retail Corp						
1034 Windward Ridge Pkwy	Alpharetta	GA	30005	**888-776-0076***		154-3
*Cust Svc						
Bobco Metals Co						
2000 S Alameda St	Los Angeles	CA	90058	**877-952-6226**		491
Bobit Business Media						
3520 Challenger St	Torrance	CA	90503	**888-239-2455**	310-533-2400	634-9
Boca Raton Museum of Art						
501 Plaza Real Mizner Pk	Boca Raton	FL	33432	**866-481-1689**	561-392-2500	519
Boca Raton Resort & Club						
501 E Camino Real	Boca Raton	FL	33432	**888-543-1224**	561-447-3000	667
Boca Resorts						
501 E Camino Real	Boca Raton	FL	33432	**888-543-1277**	561-447-3000	360-3
Bocada Inc						
5555 Lakeview Dr	Kirkland	WA	98033	**866-262-2321**	425-818-4400	387
Boccardo Law Firm Inc, The						
111 W Saint John St Ste 400	San Jose	CA	95113	**800-662-9807**		444
Bodega Bay Lodge						
103 Coast Hwy 1	Bodega Bay	CA	94923	**888-875-2250***	707-875-3525	379
*Resv						
Boden Inc						
P.O. Box 258	Helmetta	NJ	08828	**866-291-3363**		807
Bodine Co						
PO Box 460	Collierville	TN	38027	**800-223-5728**	901-853-7211	765
Bodine Electric Co						
201 Northfield Rd	Northfield	IL	60093	**800-726-3463**	773-478-3515	517
Body & Soul						
42 Pleasant St	Watertown	MA	02472	**800-999-6518**	617-449-5506	456-18
Body-Solid Inc						
1900 Des Plaines Ave	Forest Park	IL	60130	**800-833-1227**	708-427-3500	269
BoeFly LLC						
50 W 72nd St Ste C6	New York	NY	10023	**800-277-3158**		387
Boehringer Ingelheim Pharmaceuticals Inc						
900 Ridgebury Rd	Ridgefield	CT	06877	**800-243-0127**	203-798-9988	582
Boehringer Ingelheim Vetmedica Inc						
2621 N Belt Hwy	Saint Joseph	MO	64506	**800-821-7467**	816-233-2571	581

Name / Address	City	State	Zip	Toll-Free	Phone	Class
Boekel Scientific 855 Pennsylvania Blvd	Feasterville	PA	19053	**800-336-6929**	215-396-8200	420
Boelter Cos Inc N22W23685 Ridgeview Pkwy W	West Waukesha	WI	53188	**800-263-5837**	262-523-6200	301
Boenning & Scattergood Inc 200 Barr Harbor Dr Four Tower Bridge Ste 300	West Conshohocken	PA	19428	**800-883-1212**	610-832-1212	401
Boesen the Florist 3422 Beaver Ave	Des Moines	IA	50310	**800-274-4761**	515-274-4761	294
Bogdahn Group, The 4901 Vineland Rd Ste 600	Orlando	FL	32811	**866-240-7932**		401
Bogen Communications International Inc 50 Spring St *OTC: BOGN*	Ramsey	NJ	07446	**800-999-2809**	201-934-8500	51
Boh Bros Construction Co LLC 730 S Tonti St	New Orleans	LA	70119	**800-284-3377**	504-821-2400	190-4
Bohannan Huston Inc 7500 Jefferson St NE Courtyard 1	Albuquerque	NM	87109	**800-877-5332**	505-823-1000	180-5
Boheme, The 325 S Orange Ave	Orlando	FL	32801	**866-663-0024**	407-313-9000	669
Bohemian Hotel Celebration 700 Bloom St	Celebration	FL	34747	**888-249-4007**	407-566-6000	379
Bohler-Uddeholm North America 2505 Millenium Dr	Elgin	IL	60124	**800-638-2520**	630-883-3100	491
Bohrens Moving & Storage Inc 3 Applegate Dr	Robbinsville	NJ	08691	**800-326-4736**	609-208-1470	518
Boies Schiller & Flexner LLP 5301 Wisconsin Ave NW	Washington	DC	20015	**877-224-0464**	202-237-2727	428
Boiling Springs Savings Bank (BSSB) 25 Orient Way	Rutherford	NJ	07070	**888-388-7459**	201-939-5000	69
Boingo Wireless Inc 10960 Wilshire Blvd Ste 800	Los Angeles	CA	90024	**800-880-4117**	310-586-5180	179
Boise Bible College 8695 W Marigold St	Boise	ID	83714	**800-893-7755**	208-376-7731	160
Boise Convention & Visitors Bureau 250 S Fifth St Ste 300	Boise	ID	83702	**800-635-5240**	208-344-7777	208
Boise State University 1910 University Dr	Boise	ID	83725	**800-824-7017**	208-426-1156	167
Boise Valley Feeders LLC 1555 Shoreline Dr Ste 320	Boise	ID	83702	**800-657-6305**	208-338-2605	10-1
Boiseries Raymond Inc 11880, 56e Ave	Montreal	QC	H1E2L6	**800-361-6577**	514-494-1141	498
Boise-Winnemucca Stage Lines Inc 1105 S La Pt St	Boise	ID	83706	**800-448-5692**	208-336-3300	106
Boisfeuillet Jones Atlanta Civic Ctr 395 Piedmont Ave	Atlanta	GA	30308	**877-430-7596**	404-523-6275	571
Boite a Fleur De Laval Inc La 3266 Boul Sainte-Rose	Laval	QC	H7P4K8	**800-784-3495**	450-622-0341	294
Bojangles' Restaurants Inc 9432 Southern Pine Blvd	Charlotte	NC	28273	**800-366-9921**	704-335-1804	668
Boker's Inc 3104 Snelling Ave	Minneapolis	MN	55406	**800-927-4377**	612-729-9365	620
Boland 30 W Watkins Mill Rd	Gaithersburg	MD	20878	**800-552-6526**	240-306-3000	609
Bolden Lipkin PC 3993 Huntingdon Pk	Huntingdon Valley	PA	19006	**888-947-3750**	215-947-3750	2
Bolger LLC 3301 Como Ave SE	Minneapolis	MN	55414	**866-264-3287**	651-645-6311	626
Bolin Marketing & Advertising 2523 Wayzata Blvd Ste 300	Minneapolis	MN	55405	**800-876-6264**	612-374-1200	7
Bolivar County Library 104 S Leflore Ave	Cleveland	MS	38732	**888-268-8076**	662-843-2774	434-3
Bolle Inc 9200 Cody St	Overland Park	KS	66214	**800-423-3537**	913-752-3400	541
Bolthouse Farms 7200 E Brundage Ln	Bakersfield	CA	93307	**800-467-4683**		10-9
Bolton & Hay Inc 2701 Delaware Ave	Des Moines	IA	50317	**800-362-1861**	515-265-2554	301
Bolttech Mannings 501 Mosside Blvd	North Versailles	PA	15137	**888-846-8827**	724-872-4873	385
BOMA (Building Owners & Managers Assn International) 1101 15th St NW Ste 800	Washington	DC	20005	**800-426-6292**	202-408-2662	48-17
Bo-mac Contractors Ltd 1020 Lindbergh Dr	Beaumont	TX	77707	**800-526-6221**	409-842-2125	190
Bomag Americas Inc 2000 Kentville Rd	Kewanee	IL	61443	**800-782-6624**	309-853-3571	192
Bombardier Aerospace 400 Cote-Vertu Rd W *General	Dorval	QC	H4S1Y9	**866-855-5001***	514-855-5000	20
Bombardier Capital Group 261 Mountain View Dr 4th Fl	Colchester	VT	05446	**800-949-5568**	802-764-5232	218
Bombet Cashio & Assoc 11220 N Harrells Ferry Rd	Baton Rouge	LA	70816	**800-256-5333**	225-275-0796	400
Bommarito Automotive Group 15736 Manchester Rd	Ellisville	MO	63011	**800-367-2289**	636-391-7200	56
Bommer Industries Inc PO Box 187	Landrum	SC	29356	**800-334-1654**	864-457-3301	350
Bon Homme Yankton Electric Assn 134 S Lidice St	Tabor	SD	57063	**800-925-2929**	605-463-2507	247
Bon Secours Community Hospital 160 E Main St	Port Jervis	NY	12771	**866-522-4984**	845-858-7000	374-3
Bon Secours Memorial Regional Medical Ctr 8260 Atlee Rd	Mechanicsville	VA	23116	**888-455-3766**	804-764-6000	374-3
Bon Secours Saint Mary's Hospital 5801 Bremo Rd	Richmond	VA	23226	**877-342-1500**	804-285-2011	374-3
Bon Voyage Travel 1640 E River Rd Ste 115	Tucson	AZ	85718	**800-439-7963**	520-797-1110	769
Bonadio Group, The 171 Sully's Trail Ste 201	Pittsford	NY	14534	**877-917-3077**	585-381-1000	2
Bonair Daydreams PO Box 1522	Wrightsville Beach	NC	28480	**888-226-6247**	910-617-3887	129
Bonaire Government Tourist Office 80 Broad St Ste 3202 32nd Fl	New York	NY	10004	**877-267-2572**	212-956-5912	773
Bonanza Creek Country Guest Ranch 523 Bonanza Creek Rd	Martinsdale	MT	59053	**800-476-6045**	406-572-3366	241
Bonanza Press Inc 19860 141st Pl NE	Woodinville	WA	98072	**800-233-0008**	425-486-3399	626
Bonanza Trade & Supply 6853 Lankershim Blvd	North Hollywood	CA	91605	**888-965-6577**	818-765-6577	196
Bonaventure Tours 8 Boudreau Ln	Haute-Aboujagane	NB	E4P5N1	**800-561-1213**	506-532-3674	758
Bond Auto Parts 45 Summer St	Barre	VT	05641	**800-639-1982**	802-476-3108	53
Bond Place Hotel 65 Dundas St E	Toronto	ON	M5B2G8	**800-268-9390**	416-362-6061	379
Bond Pro LLC 1501 E Second Ave	Tampa	FL	33605	**888-789-4985**		391-5
Bondcote Corp PO Box 729	Pulaski	VA	24301	**800-368-2160**	540-980-2640	742-2
Bonded Concrete Inc 303 Rt 155	Watervliet	NY	12189	**800-252-8589**	518-273-5800	184
Bondhus Corp 1400 E Broadway St PO Box 660 *Cust Svc	Monticello	MN	55362	**800-328-8310***	763-295-2162	756
Bone Bank Allografts 4808 Research Dr *Sales	San Antonio	TX	78240	**800-397-0088***	210-696-7616	544
Bonfit America Inc 5741 Buckingham Pkwy Unit A	Culver City	CA	90232	**800-526-6348**	310-204-7880	567
Bonhams & Butterfields 220 San Bruno Ave	San Francisco	CA	94103	**800-223-2854**	415-861-7500	50
Bonita Pioneer Packaging Products Inc 7333 SW Bonita Rd	Portland	OR	97224	**800-677-7725**		64
Bonita Springs Area Chamber of Commerce 25071 Chamber of Commerce Dr	Bonita Springs	FL	34135	**800-226-2943**	239-992-2943	138
Bonland Industries Inc 50 Newark-Pompton Tpke	Wayne	NJ	07470	**800-232-6600**	973-694-3211	191-12
Bonneville Billing & Collection Inc 1186 East 4600 South Ste 100	Ogden	UT	84403	**800-660-6138**	801-621-7880	159
Bonnie Castle Resort 31 Holland St	Alexandria Bay	NY	13607	**800-955-4511**	315-482-4511	667
Bonnie Lure State Recreation Area 11321 SW Terwilliger Blvd	Portland	OR	97219	**800-551-6949**		564
Bonsal American Inc 8201 Arrowridge Blvd	Charlotte	NC	28273	**800-424-9300**	704-525-1621	185
Bonstone Materials Corp 707 Swan Dr	Mukwonago	WI	53149	**800-425-2214**	262-363-9877	3
Bon-Ton Stores Inc 2801 E Market St *NASDAQ: BONT*	York	PA	17402	**800-945-4438**	717-757-7660	231
Book Depot Inc 67 Front St N	Thorold	ON	L2V1X3	**888-402-7323**	905-680-7230	94
Book Exchange Inc 152 Willey St	Morgantown	WV	26505	**800-339-7691**	304-292-7354	95
Book House Inc, The 208 W Chicago St	Jonesville	MI	49250	**800-248-1146**		95
Book Marketing Update PO Box 2887	Taos	NM	87571	**888-468-7386**	575-751-3398	530-10
Book Passage 51 Tamal Vista Blvd	Corte Madera	CA	94925	**800-999-7909**	415-927-0960	95
Bookazine Company Inc 75 Hook Rd	Bayonne	NJ	07002	**800-221-8112**	201-339-7777	94
Booklist Magazine 50 E Huron St	Chicago	IL	60611	**800-545-2433**		456-11
BookPal LLC 18101 Von Karman Ave Ste 1240	Irvine	CA	92612	**866-522-6657**		95
BookPeople 603 N Lamar	Austin	TX	78703	**800-853-9757**	512-472-5050	95
Books on the Square 471 Angell St	Providence	RI	02906	**888-669-9660**	401-331-9097	95
Books-A-Million Inc 402 Industrial Ln *NASDAQ: BAMM*	Birmingham	AL	35211	**800-201-3550**	205-942-3737	95
Booksource Inc 1230 Macklind Ave	Saint Louis	MO	63110	**800-444-0435**	314-647-0600	94
Boomer Consulting 610 Humboldt St	Manhattan	KS	66502	**800-739-9998**	785-537-2358	196
Boomers & Beyond Inc 1998 Ruffin Mill Rd	Colonial Heights	VA	23834	**800-958-8324**	804-524-9888	197
Boomtown Casino & Hotel Reno 2100 Garson Rd *Resv	Verdi	NV	89439	**800-648-3790***	775-345-6000	132
Boomtown Casino Biloxi 676 Bayview Ave	Biloxi	MS	39530	**800-627-0777**	228-435-7000	132
Boomtown Inc 2100 Garson Rd	Verdi	NV	89439	**800-648-3790**	775-345-6000	131
Boomtown Internet Group Inc 111 Rosemary Ln	Glenmoore	PA	19343	**888-454-3330**		196
Boone County 601 N Main St	Belvidere	IL	61008	**877-225-7077**	815-547-4770	338
Boone County Rural Electric Membership Corp 1207 Indianapolis Ave	Lebanon	IN	46052	**800-897-7362**	765-482-2390	247
Boone Electric Co-op 1413 Rangeline St	Columbia	MO	65201	**800-225-8143**	573-449-4181	247
Boone Tavern Hotel of Berea College 100 S Main St	Berea	KY	40403	**800-366-9358**	859-985-3700	379
Boonville Correctional Ctr 1216 E Morgan St	Boonville	MO	65233	**800-392-8486**	660-882-6521	215
Boos Dental Laboratory 1000 Boone Ave N Ste 660	Golden Valley	MN	55427	**800-333-2667**	763-544-1446	415
Boost Motor Group Inc 3080 Yonge St	Toronto	ON	M4N3N1	**877-266-7841**	416-487-7000	179
Boost Rewards 811 E Fourth St Ste B	Dayton	OH	45402	**800-324-9756**		197
Boostability Inc 2600 West Executive Pkwy Ste 200	Lehi	UT	84043	**800-261-1537**		5
Booth 4900 Nautilus Ct N Ste 220	Boulder	CO	80301	**800-332-6684**	323-805-0150	5
Booth Theatre 222 W 45th St	New York	NY	10036	**800-432-7780**	212-239-6200	744
Booz Allen Hamilton Inc 8283 Greensboro Dr	McLean	VA	22102	**866-390-3908**	703-902-5000	196

Name / Address	City	State	Zip	Toll-Free	Phone	Class
BOP (Brookfield Properties Corp) 181 Bay St Ste 330 *NYSE: BPO*	Toronto	ON	M5J2T3	800-387-0825	416-369-2300	653
Boral Bricks Inc 9143 Bob Williams Pkwy	Covington	GA	30014	800-526-7255	678-625-4051	149
Border Foods Inc 4065 J St SE	Deming	NM	88030	800-323-4358		297-36
Border Gold Corp 15234 N Bluff Rd	White Rock	BC	V4B3E6	888-312-2288	604-535-3287	689
Border States Electric Supply 105 25th St N	Fargo	ND	58102	800-800-0199	701-293-5834	248
Boreal Genomics Inc 5150 El Camino Real	Los Altos	CA	94022	800-681-5644	604-822-8268	233
Boren, Oliver & Coffey LLP 59 N Jefferson St	Martinsville	IN	46151	800-403-9971	765-342-0147	428
Borgata Hotel Casino & Spa 1 Borgata Way	Atlantic City	NJ	08401	877-786-9900	609-317-1000	379
Borla Performance Industries Inc 500 Borla Dr	Johnson City	TN	37604	877-462-6752	423-979-4000	59
Born Free USA United with Animal Protection Institute 1122 S St	Sacramento	CA	95814	800-348-7387	916-447-3085	47-3
Born Into It Inc 185 New Boston St	Woburn	MA	01801	800-560-2840	781-491-0707	156-6
Borough of Manhattan Community College 199 Chambers St Rm S-300	New York	NY	10007	877-222-8387	212-220-1265	161
Borroughs Corp 3002 N Burdick St	Kalamazoo	MI	49004	800-748-0227	269-342-0161	288
Borsheim's Inc 120 Regency Pkwy	Omaha	NE	68114	800-642-4438	402-391-0400	410
Bosch Rexroth PO Box 394	Wooster	OH	44691	800-739-7684	330-263-3300	786
Bosch Rexroth Corp 5150 Prairie Stone Pkwy	Hoffman Estates	IL	60192	800-860-1055	847-645-3600	517
Bosch Rexroth Corp Piston Pump Div 8 Southchase Ct	Fountain Inn	SC	29644	877-266-7811	864-967-2777	637
Bosch Security Systems 130 Perinton Pkwy	Fairport	NY	14450	800-289-0096	585-223-4060	690
Bosch Thermotechnology 340 Mad River Pk	Waitsfield	VT	05673	800-283-3787		357
Bose Corp The Mountain *Sales	Framingham	MA	01701	800-379-2073*	508-766-1099	51
Boss Chair Inc 5353 Jillson St	Commerce	CA	90040	800-593-1888	323-262-1919	322
Bosshardt Realty Services LLC 5542 NW 43rd St	Gainesville	FL	32653	800-284-6110	352-371-6100	650
Bossier Chamber of Commerce 710 Benton Rd	Bossier City	LA	71111	800-659-2955	318-746-0252	138
Boston Academy of English 38 Chauncy St 8th Fl	Boston	MA	02111	800-704-9313		423
Boston Academy of English inc 38 Chauncy St 8th Fl	Boston	MA	02111	800-704-9313		423
Boston Advisors Inc 1 Liberty Sq 10th Fl	Boston	MA	02109	800-523-5903	617-348-3100	401
Boston Architectural College 320 Newbury St	Boston	MA	02115	877-585-0100	617-585-0100	798
Boston Baptist College 950 Metropolitan Ave	Boston	MA	02136	888-235-2014	617-364-3510	167
Boston Beer Co 1 Design Ctr Pl Ste 850 *NYSE: SAM*	Boston	MA	02210	888-661-2337	617-368-5000	101
Boston College 140 Commonwealth Ave	Chestnut Hill	MA	02467	800-360-2522	617-552-3100	167
Boston College Law School 885 Centre St	Newton	MA	02459	800-321-2211	617-552-8550	168-1
Boston Color Graphics LLC 755 Middlesex Tpke	Billerica	MA	01821	800-767-0067		779
Boston Consumers Checkbook 185 Franklin St	Boston	MA	02110	888-382-1222		95
Boston Duck Tours Ltd 4 Copley Pl Ste 310	Boston	MA	02116	800-226-7442	617-450-0065	758
Boston Family Office LLC, The 88 Broad St 2nd Fl	Boston	MA	02110	800-900-4401	617-624-0800	401
Boston Financial Data Services 2000 Crown Colony Dr	Quincy	MA	02169	888-772-2337	617-483-5000	401
Boston Globe Book Festival PO Box 55819 PO Box 2378	Boston	MA	02205	888-694-5623		283
Boston Group 400 Riverside Ave	Medford	MA	02155	800-225-1633		288
Boston Harbor Hotel 70 Rowes Wharf	Boston	MA	02110	800-752-7077	617-439-7000	379
Boston Harbor Islands National Recreation Area 408 Atlantic Ave Ste 228	Boston	MA	02110	877-874-2478	617-223-8666	563
Boston Language Institute Inc 648 Beacon St Kenmore Sq	Boston	MA	02215	877-998-3500	617-262-3500	766
Boston Market Corp 14103 Denver W Pkwy *General	Golden	CO	80401	866-977-9090*	303-278-9500	668
Boston Park Plaza Hotel & Towers 50 Pk Plz	Boston	MA	02116	800-225-2008	617-426-2000	379
Boston Pizza Restaurants LP 1501 LBJ Fwy Ste 450	Dallas	TX	75234	866-277-8721	972-484-9022	668
Boston Pops 301 Massachusetts Ave Symphony Hall	Boston	MA	02115	888-266-1200	617-266-1492	572-3
Boston Private Financial Holdings Inc 10 Post Office Sq *NASDAQ: BPFH*	Boston	MA	02109	855-738-8916	617-912-1900	360-2
Boston Sand & Gravel Company Inc 100 N Washington St *OTC: BSND*	Boston	MA	02114	800-624-2724	617-227-9000	184
Boston Scientific Corp 1 Boston Scientific Pl *NYSE: BSX*	Natick	MA	01760	888-272-1001	508-650-8000	475
Boston Symphony Hall 301 Massachusetts Ave	Boston	MA	02115	888-266-1200	617-266-1492	571
Boston Symphony Orchestra 301 Massachusetts Ave Symphony Hall	Boston	MA	02115	888-266-1200	617-266-1492	572-3
Boston University School of Law 765 Commonwealth Ave	Boston	MA	02215	800-321-2211	617-353-3100	168-1
Boston Warehouse Trading Corp 59 Davis Ave	Norwood	MA	02062	800-811-2672	781-769-8550	361
Boston Whaler Inc 100 Whaler Way	Edgewater	FL	32141	877-294-5645		89
Boston's Best Chimney Sweep 76 Bacon St *Cust Svc	Waltham	MA	02451	800-660-6708*	781-893-6611	151
Bostwick-Braun Co PO Box 912	Toledo	OH	43697	800-777-9640	419-259-3600	351
Botanical Gardens at Asheville 151 WT Weaver Blvd	Asheville	NC	28804	888-823-4622	828-252-5190	96
Botanical Laboratories Inc 1441 W Smith Rd	Ferndale	WA	98248	800-232-4005	360-384-5656	582
Bott Radio Network 10550 Barkley St Ste 100	Overland Park	KS	66212	800-875-1903	913-642-7770	640
Bottom Line/Personal 281 Tresser Blvd 8th Fl *Cust Svc	Stamford	CT	06901	800-678-5835*	800-274-5611	530-6
Bottomline Technologies 325 Corporate Dr *NASDAQ: EPAY*	Portsmouth	NH	03801	800-243-2528	603-436-0700	180-1
Bouchey Financial Group Ltd 1819 Fifth Ave	Troy	NY	12180	800-783-0339	518-720-3333	401
Boudreau-Espley-Pitre Corp 1040 Lorne St Unit 3	Sudbury	ON	P3C4R9	877-675-7720	705-675-7720	263
Boulder Adventure Lodge (A-Lodge) 91 Four Mile Canyon Rd	Boulder	CO	80302	800-556-3446	435-335-7460	379
Boulder Arts & Crafts 1421 Pearl St Mall	Boulder	CO	80302	866-656-2667	303-443-3683	459
Boulder Book Store 1107 Pearl St	Boulder	CO	80302	800-244-4651	303-447-2074	95
Boulder Convention & Visitors Bureau 2440 Pearl St	Boulder	CO	80302	800-444-0447	303-442-2911	208
Boulder Station Hotel & Casino 4111 Boulder Hwy	Las Vegas	NV	89121	800-683-7777	702-432-7777	132
Boulders Resort & Golden Door Spa 34631 N Tom Darlington Dr PO Box 2090	Carefree	AZ	85377	888-579-2631	480-488-9009	667
Bound to Stay Bound Books Inc (BTSB) 1880 W Morton Ave	Jacksonville	IL	62650	800-637-6586	217-245-5191	91
Bourbon & Boots Inc 419 Main St	North Little Rock	AR	72114	877-791-8079	855-623-3562	688
Bourbon Orleans - A Wyndham Historic Hotel 717 Orleans St	New Orleans	LA	70116	866-513-9744	504-523-2222	379
Bourns Inc 1200 Columbia Ave	Riverside	CA	92507	877-426-8767	951-781-5690	624
Boutique Spa at the Ritz-Carlton Georgetown 3100 S St NW	Washington	DC	20007	800-241-3333	202-912-4175	705
Boval Company LP 505 W Industrial Blvd	Cleburne	TX	76031	800-635-1706	817-645-1706	418
Bovie Medical Corp 734 Walt Whitman Rd Ste 207 *NYSE: BVX*	Melville	NY	11747	800-888-4999	631-421-5452	252
Bow Plastics Ltd 5700 Cote de Liesse	Montreal	QC	H4T1B1	800-852-8527	514-735-5671	606
Bowden Manufacturing Corp 4590 Beidler Rd	Willoughby	OH	44094	800-876-8970	440-946-1770	755
Bowden Oil Company Inc PO Box 145	Sylacauga	AL	35150	800-280-0393	256-245-5611	317
Bowditch Ford Inc 11291 Jefferson Ave	Newport News	VA	23601	866-399-2616	757-595-2211	53
Bowdoin College 5000 College Stn	Brunswick	ME	04011	800-829-1040	207-725-3000	167
BOWE Bell + Howell 760 S Wolf Rd	Wheeling	IL	60090	800-220-3030	847-675-7600	175-7
Bowen Workforce Solutions Inc 602 12 Ave Sw Ste 700	Calgary	AB	T2R1J3	866-692-6936	403-262-1156	262
Bowers Envelope Co 5331 N Tacoma Ave	Indianapolis	IN	46220	800-333-4321	317-253-4321	265
Bowie Industries Inc 1004 E Wise St	Bowie	TX	76230	800-433-0934	940-872-1106	275
Bowie State University 14000 Jericho Pk Rd	Bowie	MD	20715	877-772-6943	301-860-4000	167
Bowie-Cass Electric Co-op Inc 117 N St	Douglassville	TX	75560	800-794-2919	903-846-2311	247
Bowles Mattress Co Inc 1220 Watt St	Jeffersonville	IN	47130	800-223-7509	812-288-8614	470
Bowling Green Area Chamber of Commerce 710 College St	Bowling Green	KY	42101	866-330-2422	270-781-3200	138
Bowling Green State University 1001 E Wooster St	Bowling Green	OH	43403	866-246-6732	419-372-2531	167
Bowling Green State University Jerome Library (BGSU) 1001 E Wooster St	Bowling Green	OH	43403	866-246-6732	419-372-2051	434-6
Bowling Green Technical College 1845 Loop Dr	Bowling Green	KY	42101	866-590-9238	270-901-1000	798
Bowling Proprietors' Assn of America (BPAA) 621 Six Flags Dr PO Box 5802	Arlington	TX	76011	800-343-1329	817-649-5105	47-23
Bowman Hollis Manufacturing Inc 2925 Old Steele Creek Rd	Charlotte	NC	28208	888-269-2358	704-374-1500	741
Bowman Mfg Company Inc 17301 51st Ave Ne	Arlington	WA	98223	800-962-4660	360-435-5005	607
Box Elder County 01 S Main St	Brigham City	UT	84302	877-390-2326	435-734-3300	338
Boxworks Technologies Inc 2065 Pkwy Blve	Salt Lake City	UT	84119	877-495-2250	801-214-6100	182
Boyajian Inc 144 Will Dr *General	Canton	MA	02021	800-965-0665*	781-828-9966	297-41
Boyce Thompson Arboretum 37615 US Hwy 60	Superior	AZ	85273	877-763-5315	520-689-2723	96
Boyd Bros Transportation Inc 3275 Alabama 30	Clayton	AL	36016	800-700-2693	334-775-1400	778

Name / Address	City	State	Zip	Toll-Free	Phone	Class
Boyd Coffee Co						
19730 NE Sandy Blvd	Portland	OR	97230	**800-545-4077***	503-666-4545	297-7
*Cust Svc						
Boyd Gaming Corp						
3883 Howard Hughes Pkwy 9th Fl	Las Vegas	NV	89169	**800-522-4700**	702-792-7200	131
NYSE: BYD						
Boyd Group Inc, The						
3570 Portage Ave	Winnipeg	MB	R3K0Z8	**800-385-5451**	204-895-1244	61
Boyden Caverns						
5350 Moaning Cave Rd	Vallecito	CA	95251	**866-762-2837**	209-736-2708	49-4
Boyden World Corp						
50 Broadway	Hawthorne	NY	10532	**877-226-9336**	914-747-0093	268
Boyett Petroleum						
601 McHenry Ave	Modesto	CA	95350	**800-545-9212**	209-577-6000	578
Boyle Energy Services & Technology Inc						
28 Locke Rd	Concord	NH	03301	**800-428-8872**	603-227-5200	258
Boyne Country Sports						
1200 Bay View Rd	Petoskey	MI	49770	**800-462-6963**	231-439-4906	709
Boyne Highlands Resort						
600 Highlands Dr	Harbor Springs	MI	49740	**800-462-6963**	231-526-3000	667
Boyne Mountain Resort						
11521 Huffman Lake Rd	Boyne Falls	MI	49713	**800-462-6963**	231-549-6060	667
Boynton Beach Mall						
801 N Congress Ave	Boynton Beach	FL	33426	**877-746-6642**	561-736-7902	459
Boys & Girls Clubs of America						
1275 Peachtree St NE	Atlanta	GA	30309	**800-995-3579**	404-487-5700	47-15
Boys Town						
14100 Crawford St	Boys Town	NE	68010	**800-448-3000**	402-498-1300	47-6
Bozzuto Group						
7850 Walker Dr Ste 400	Greenbelt	MD	20770	**866-698-7513***	301-220-0100	189
*General						
BP Canada Energy Co						
240 Fourth Ave SW	Calgary	AB	T2P2H8	**877-833-1359**	403-233-1359	535
BP Canada Energy Resources Co						
240- Fourth Ave SW	Calgary	AB	T2P2H8	**800-255-4268**	403-233-1313	535
BP Lubricants USA Inc						
1500 Valley Rd	Wayne	NJ	07470	**800-333-3991**	973-633-2200	540
BP MotorClub						
PO Box 4441	Carol Stream	IL	60197	**800-334-3300**		52
BP PLC						
28100 Torch Pkwy	Warrenville	IL	60555	**800-333-3991**		579
NYSE: BP						
BPAA (Bowling Proprietors' Assn of America)						
621 Six Flags Dr PO Box 5802	Arlington	TX	76011	**800-343-1329**	817-649-5105	47-23
BPM Inc						
200 W Front St	Peshtigo	WI	54157	**800-826-0494**	715-582-4551	556
BPRR (Buffalo & Pittsburgh Railroad Inc)						
1200-C Scottsville Rd Ste 200	Rochester	NY	14624	**800-603-3385**	585-463-3307	646
BR 111 Exotic Hardwood Flooring						
1 NE 40th St	Miami	FL	33137	**800-525-2711**		3
BR Funsten & Co						
5200 Watt Ct Ste B	Fairfield	CA	94534	**888-261-2871**	209-825-5375	361
Brabazon Pumps & Compressor						
2484 Century Rd	Green Bay	WI	54303	**800-825-3222**	920-498-6020	174
Brackett Inc						
75115 SE Forbes Ave Bldg 451 J	Topeka	KS	66619	**800-255-3506**	785-862-2205	628
Bradbury Company Inc						
1200 E Cole	Moundridge	KS	67107	**800-397-6394**	620-345-6394	455
Braddock Hospital						
12500 Willowbrook Rd	Cumberland	MD	21502	**888-369-1122**	240-964-7000	374-3
Braden Mfg LLC						
5199 N Mingo Rd	Tulsa	OK	74117	**800-272-3360**		479
Braden Sutphin Ink Co						
3650 E 93rd St	Cleveland	OH	44105	**800-289-6872**	216-271-2300	388
Bradford Health Services						
2101 Magnolia Ave S Ste 518	Birmingham	AL	35205	**800-217-2849**	205-251-7753	724
Bradford School						
2469 Stelzer Rd	Columbus	OH	43219	**800-678-7981**	614-416-6200	798
Bradford Technologies Inc						
302 Piercy Rd	San Jose	CA	95138	**866-445-8367**	408-360-8520	179
Bradford White Corp						
725 Talamore Dr	Ambler	PA	19002	**800-523-2931**	215-641-9400	35
Bradley Caldwell Inc						
200 Kiwanis Blvd	Hazleton	PA	18202	**800-257-9100***	570-455-7511	278
*Cust Svc						
Bradley Corp						
W 142 N 9101 Fountain Blvd	Menomonee Falls	WI	53051	**800-272-3539**	262-251-6000	608
Bradley Graphic Solutions Inc						
941 Mill Rd	Bensalem	PA	19020	**800-638-8223**	215-638-8771	626
Bradley Inn						
3063 Bristol Rd	New Harbor	ME	04554	**800-942-5560**	207-677-2105	379
Bradley University						
1501 W Bradley Ave	Peoria	IL	61625	**800-447-6460***	309-676-7611	167
*Admissions						
Bradmark Technologies Inc						
4265 San Felipe St Ste 700	Houston	TX	77027	**800-621-2808**	713-621-2808	180-1
Brady Campaign to Prevent Gun Violence						
1225 'I' St NW Ste 1100	Washington	DC	20005	**800-732-0999**	202-898-0792	47-7
Brady Coated Products						
6555 W Good Hope Rd	Milwaukee	WI	53223	**800-662-1191**	414-358-6600	729
Brady Corp						
6555 W Good Hope Rd	Milwaukee	WI	53223	**800-541-1686***	414-358-6600	413
NYSE: BRC ■ *Cust Svc						
Brady Identification Solutions						
6555 W Good Hope Rd	Milwaukee	WI	53223	**800-537-8791***	414-358-6600	180-1
*Cust Svc						
Brady Industries Inc						
7055 Lindell Rd	Las Vegas	NV	89118	**800-293-4698**	702-876-3990	406
Brady Palmer Label Corp						
1791 Rt 6 Carmel PO Box 490	New York	NY	10512	**800-783-3097**		626
Braemar Inc						
1285 Corporate Ctr Dr	Eagan	MN	55121	**800-328-2719**	651-286-8620	475
Braille Institute of America Inc						
741 N Vermont Ave	Los Angeles	CA	90029	**800-272-4553**	323-663-1111	47-11
Brain Injury Assn of America						
1608 Spring Hill Rd Ste 110	Vienna	VA	22182	**800-444-6443**	703-761-0750	47-17
Brainerd Compressor Rebuilders Inc						
3034 Sandbrook St	Memphis	TN	38116	**800-228-4138**		14
Brainerd Industries Inc						
680 Precision Ct	Miamisburg	OH	45342	**800-790-0430**	937-228-0488	482
Brainerd International Raceway						
5523 Birchdale Rd	Brainerd	MN	56401	**866-444-4455**	218-824-7223	514
Brainerd Lakes Area Chamber of Commerce						
7393 State Hwy 371 PO Box 356	Brainerd	MN	56401	**800-450-2838**	218-829-2838	138
Brainerd Mfg Company Inc						
140 Business Pk Dr	Winston-Salem	NC	27107	**800-652-7277**	336-769-4077	350
BrainLAB Inc						
3 Westbrook Corp Ctr	Westchester	IL	60154	**800-784-7700**	708-409-1343	382
Brainworks Software Inc						
100 S Main St	Sayville	NY	11782	**800-755-1111**	631-563-5000	180-1
Brake Supply Company Inc						
5501 Foundation Blvd	Evansville	IN	47725	**800-457-5788**	812-467-1000	385
Brakebush Bros Inc						
N4993 Sixth Dr	Westfield	WI	53964	**800-933-2121**	608-296-2121	618
Brakeley Briscoe Inc						
322 W Bellevue Ave Ste 204	San Mateo	CA	94402	**800-416-3086**	650-344-8883	318
Brakewell Steel Fabricator Inc						
55 Leone Ln	Chester	NY	10918	**888-914-9131**	845-469-9131	481
Brakke Consulting Inc						
2735 Villa Creek Ste 140	Dallas	TX	75234	**877-399-6354**	972-243-4033	196
Brame Specialty Company Inc						
PO Box 27	Durham	NC	27702	**800-533-2041**	919-683-1331	558
Branch Banking & Trust Company of South Carolina						
301 College St	Greenville	SC	29601	**800-226-5228**		69
Brand Energy & Infrastructure Services Inc						
1325 Cobb International Dr Ste A-1	Kennesaw	GA	30152	**855-746-4477**	678-285-1400	490
Brand Protection Agency LLC						
2700 Fairmount St	Dallas	TX	75201	**866-339-5657**		197
Branded Emblem Co Inc						
7920 Foster St	Overland Park	KS	66204	**800-448-2267**	913-648-0573	260
Brandeis University						
415 S St	Waltham	MA	02454	**800-622-0622**	781-736-3500	167
BrandEquity International						
7 Great Meadow Rd	Newton	MA	02462	**800-969-3150**		344
Brandes Investment Partners LP						
11988 El Camino Real Ste 500	San Diego	CA	92130	**800-237-7119**	858-755-0239	401
Branding Brand						
2313 East Carson St	Pittsburgh	PA	15203	**888-979-5018**		387
Brandmovers Inc						
590 Means St Ste 250	Atlanta	GA	30318	**888-463-4933**		630
Brandpoint						
850 5Th St S	Hopkins	MN	55343	**877-374-5270**		5
BrandsMart USA Corp						
3200 SW 42nd St	Fort Lauderdale	FL	33312	**800-432-8579**		34
Brandt Tractor Ltd						
Hwy 1 E PO Box 3856	Regina	SK	S4P3R8	**888-227-2638**	306-791-7777	110
Brandtjen & Kluge Inc						
539 Blanding Woods Rd	Saint Croix Falls	WI	54024	**800-826-7320**	715-483-3265	628
Brandywine Capital Associates						
113 East Evans St	West Chester	PA	19380	**888-344-2920**	610-344-2910	401
Brandywine Global Investment Management LLC						
2929 Arch St 8th Fl	Philadelphia	PA	19104	**800-348-2499**	215-609-3500	401
Brandywine Investment Group Homalite Div						
11 Brookside Dr	Wilmington	DE	19804	**800-346-7802**	302-652-3686	599
Brandywine Machine Company Inc						
300 Creek Rd	Downingtown	PA	19335	**800-523-7128**		453
Brandywine Realty Trust						
555 E Lancaster Ave Ste 100	Radnor	PA	19087	**866-426-5400**	610-325-5600	653
NYSE: BDN						
Brannan Paving Coltd						
111 Elk Dr PO Box 3403	Victoria	TX	77903	**800-626-7064**	361-573-3130	188
Brannen Banks Of Florida Inc						
PO Box 1929	Inverness	FL	34451	**866-546-8273**	352-726-1221	360-2
Branson's Best Reservations						
2875 Green Mtn Dr	Branson	MO	65616	**800-335-2555**	417-339-2204	376
Branson/Lakes Area Chamber of Commerce						
PO Box 1897	Branson	MO	65615	**800-214-3661**	417-334-4084	138
Bran-Zan Holdings Inc						
1548 Barclay Blvd	Buffalo Grove	IL	60089	**866-266-9670**		300
Brasfield & Gorrie LLC						
3021 Seventh Ave S	Birmingham	AL	35233	**800-239-8017**	205-328-4000	188
Brasher Motor Company of Weimar Inc						
1700 I- 10	Weimar	TX	78962	**800-783-1746**	979-725-8515	56
Brasseler USA						
1 Brasseler Blvd	Savannah	GA	31419	**800-841-4522**		230
Brasstown Valley Resort						
6321 US Hwy 76	Young Harris	GA	30582	**800-201-3205**	706-379-9900	667
Braswell Food Co						
226 N Zetterower Ave	Statesboro	GA	30458	**800-673-9388**	912-764-6191	297-20
Brattleboro Area Chamber of Commerce						
180 Main St	Brattleboro	VT	05301	**877-254-4565**	802-254-4565	138
Brattleboro Memorial Hospital Inc						
17 Belmont Ave Ste 1	Brattleboro	VT	05301	**866-972-5266**	802-257-0341	374-3
Brauer Material Handling Systems Inc						
226 Molly Walton Dr	Hendersonville	TN	37075	**800-645-6083**		385
Braun Industries Inc						
1170 Production Dr	Van Wert	OH	45891	**877-344-9990**		58
Braun Intertec Corp						
11001 Hampshire Ave S	Bloomington	MN	55438	**800-279-6100**	952-995-2000	263
BRAVO | BRIO Restaurant Group						
777 Goodale Blvd Ste 100	Columbus	OH	43212	**888-452-7286**	614-326-7944	668
Bravo Sports Corp						
12801 Carmenita Rd	Santa Fe Springs	CA	90670	**800-234-9737***	562-484-5100	708
*Cust Svc						
Bray Real Estate						
637 N Ave	Grand Junction	CO	81501	**888-760-4251**	970-242-8450	650
Brazil						
Consulate General						
8484 Wilshire Blvd Ste 711	Beverly Hills	CA	90211	**877-782-5477**	323-651-2664	259
Consulate General						
1233 W Loop S Ste 1150	Houston	TX	77027	**800-326-2289**	713-961-3063	259

Name / Address	City	State	ZIP	Toll-Free	Phone	Class
Brazilian Court, The						
301 Australian Ave	Palm Beach	FL	33480	800-552-0335	561-655-7740	379
Brazilian Travel Service (BTS)						
16 W 46th St 2nd Fl	New York	NY	10036	800-342-5746	212-764-6161	16
Brazos Urethane Inc						
1031 Sixth St N	Texas City	TX	77590	866-527-2967	409-965-0011	191-12
Brazosport College						
500 College Dr	Lake Jackson	TX	77566	877-717-7873	979-230-3000	161
Brazosport Facts						
720 S Main St	Clute	TX	77531	800-864-8340	979-265-7411	531-2
BRB Contractors Inc						
3805 NW 25th St	Topeka	KS	66618	800-722-3145	785-232-1245	190-10
BRB Publications Inc						
PO Box 27869	Tempe	AZ	85285	800-929-3811	480-829-7475	634-2
BRCC (Baton Rouge Community College)						
201 Community College Dr	Baton Rouge	LA	70806	866-217-9823	225-216-8000	161
BREA (Benton Rural Electric Assn)						
402 Seventh St PO Box 1150	Prosser	WA	99350	800-221-6987	509-786-2913	247
Bread for the World						
425 Third St SW Ste 1200	Washington	DC	20024	800-822-7323*	202-639-9400	47-5
*Cust Svc						
Breakaway Tours						
3300 Bloor St Ste 1800	Toronto	ON	M8X2X2	800-465-4257	416-915-9880	758
Breakers at Waikiki, The						
250 Beach Walk	Honolulu	HI	96815	800-426-0494	808-923-3181	379
Breakers Hotel & Suites						
105 Second St	Rehoboth Beach	DE	19971	800-441-8009	302-227-6688	379
Breakers Resort						
3002 N Ocean Blvd	Myrtle Beach	SC	29577	800-952-4507	843-448-8082	667
Breakers Resort Inn						
16th & Oceanfront	Virginia Beach	VA	23451	800-237-7532	757-428-1821	667
Breakers, The						
1 S County Rd	Palm Beach	FL	33480	888-273-2537	561-655-6611	667
Breakthrough Management Group Inc						
1200 17th St Ste 180	Denver	CO	80202	800-467-4462	303-827-0010	196
Breakwater Inn						
1711 Glacier Ave	Juneau	AK	99801	888-586-6303		379
BREC (Butler Rural Electric Co-op Inc)						
3888 Still-Beckett Rd	Oxford	OH	45056	800-255-2732	513-867-4400	247
Breckinridge County School District						
86 Airport Rd	Hardinsburg	KY	40143	800-325-1713	270-756-2186	683
Breezy Point Resort						
9252 Breezy Pt Dr	Breezy Point	MN	56472	800-432-3777	218-562-7811	667
Breg Inc						
2885 Loker Ave E	Carlsbad	CA	92010	800-897-2734	760-599-3000	47-2
Breitburn Energy Partners LP						
515 S Flower St Ste 4800	Los Angeles	CA	90071	800-732-0330	213-225-5900	537
NASDAQ: BBEP						
Breitling Energy Corp						
Ste 12000 1910 PACIFIC Ave						
Ste 12000	Dallas	TX	75201	866-884-0224	214-716-2600	535
Bremen Castings Inc						
500 N Baltimore St	Bremen	IN	46506	800-837-2411		308
Bremer Financial Corp						
2100 Bremer Tower						
445 Minnesota St	Saint Paul	MN	55101	800-908-2265	651-227-7621	68
Bremner Biscuit Co						
4600 Joliet St	Denver	CO	80239	866-972-6879	303-371-8180	297-9
Brenau University						
500 Washington St	Gainesville	GA	30501	800-252-5119	770-534-6299	167
Brendan Vacations						
21625 Prairie St	Chatsworth	CA	91311	800-687-1002		758
Brendle Sprinkler Co Inc						
3635 S Montgomery St	Tacoma	WA	98409	800-392-8021		191-13
Brenham Wholesale Grocery Co						
602 W First St	Brenham	TX	77833	800-392-4869	979-836-7925	298-8
Brenham/Washington County Convention & Visitor Bureau						
314 S Austin St	Brenham	TX	77833	888-273-6426	979-836-3695	208
Brennan & Clark LLC						
721 E Madison Ste 200	Villa Park	IL	60181	800-858-7600	630-279-7600	159
Brenner Printing Inc						
1234 Triplett St	San Antonio	TX	78216	877-349-4024	210-349-4024	626
Brenntag Canada Inc						
35 Vulcan St	Rexdale	ON	M9W1L3	866-516-9707	416-243-9615	145
Brenntag Southwest Inc						
610 Fisher Rd	Longview	TX	75604	800-945-4528	903-759-7151	145
Brent House Hotel						
1512 Jefferson Hwy	New Orleans	LA	70121	800-535-3986	504-842-4140	379
Brentech Inc						
9340 Carmel Mtn Rd Ste C	San Diego	CA	92129	800-709-0440	858-484-7314	177
Brenton LLC						
4750 County Rd 13 NE	Alexandria	MN	56308	800-535-2730	320-852-7705	546
Brenton Productions Inc						
179 Gasoline Alley Ste 102A	Mooresville	NC	02777	800-572-7798		462
Brentwood A Behavioral Health Co						
1006 Highland Ave	Shreveport	LA	71101	877-678-7500	318-678-7500	374-5
Brescia University						
717 Frederica St	Owensboro	KY	42301	877-273-7242*	270-685-3131	167
*Admissions						
Bresser's Cross Index Directory Co						
684 W Baltimore St	Detroit	MI	48202	800-995-0570	313-874-0570	634-6
Bretford Manufacturing Inc						
11000 Seymour Ave	Franklin Park	IL	60131	800-521-9614	847-678-2545	320-3
Brethren Press						
1451 Dundee Ave	Elgin	IL	60120	800-441-3712		634-3
Bretthauer Oil Co						
453 SW Washington St	Hillsboro	OR	97123	800-359-3113	503-648-2531	578
Brevard College						
1 Brevard College Dr	Brevard	NC	28712	800-527-9090*	828-883-8292	167
*Admissions						
Brevard Community College (BCC)						
Cocoa 1519 Clearlake Rd	Cocoa	FL	32922	888-747-2802	321-632-1111	161
Melbourne						
3865 N Wickham Rd	Melbourne	FL	32935	888-747-2802	321-632-1111	161
Palm Bay						
250 Community College Pkwy	Palm Bay	FL	32909	888-747-2802	321-632-1111	161
Titusville						
1311 N US 1	Titusville	FL	32796	888-747-2802	321-632-1111	161
Brevard County Tourism Development						
430 Brevard Ave Ste 150	Cocoa Village	FL	32922	877-572-3224	321-433-4470	208
Brevard Zoo						
8225 N Wickham Rd	Melbourne	FL	32940	800-435-7352	321-254-9453	821
Brevard-Transylvania Chamber of Commerce						
175 E Main St	Brevard	NC	28712	800-648-4523	828-883-3700	138
Brewer & Pritchard						
3 Riverway Ste 1800	Houston	TX	77024	800-445-8710	713-209-2950	428
Brewer Co						
1354 US Hwy 50	Milford	OH	45150	800-394-0017	513-576-6300	45
Brewmatic Co						
20333 S Normandie Ave						
PO Box 2959	Torrance	CA	90509	800-421-6860	310-787-5444	299
Brewster Academy						
80 Academy Dr	Wolfeboro	NH	03894	800-842-9961	603-569-7200	621
Brewster Travel Canada						
100 Gopher St PO Box 1140	Banff	AB	T1L1J3	866-606-6700	403-762-6700	758
Brewton-Parker College						
201 David-Eliza Fountain Cir Hwy 280						
PO Box 197	Mount Vernon	GA	30445	800-342-1087	912-583-2241	167
BRG (Business Resource Group)						
10440 N Central Expy Ste 1150	Dallas	TX	75231	888-391-9166	214-777-5100	196
Brian Loncar & Associates P c						
1104 Travis St	Wichita Falls	TX	76301	877-239-4878		444
Briar Cliff University						
3303 Rebecca St	Sioux City	IA	51104	800-662-3303	712-279-5321	167
Briarcliffe College						
1055 Stewart Ave	Bethpage	NY	11714	855-512-5333	516-918-3600	164
Briarhurst Manor						
404 Manitou Ave	Manitou Springs	CO	80829	877-685-1448	719-685-1864	669
Briarwood College						
2279 Mt Vernon Rd	Southington	CT	06489	800-952-2444	860-628-4751	167
BRIC Engineered Systems Ltd						
1101 Wentworth St W Ste D1	Oshawa	ON	L1J8P7	800-937-5135	905-436-8867	258
Brice's Crossroads National Battlefield Site						
2680 Natchez Trace Pkwy	Tupelo	MS	38804	800-305-7417	662-680-4025	563
Brick Bodies Fitness Services Inc						
201 Old Padonia Rd	Cockeysville	MD	21030	866-952-7425	410-252-8058	354
Brick Industry Assn (BIA)						
1850 Centennial Pk Dr Ste 301	Reston	VA	20191	866-644-1293	703-620-0010	48-18
Brick Township Chamber of Commerce						
270 Chambers Bridge Rd	Brick	NJ	08723	877-539-2020	732-477-4949	138
Brickell Financial Services Motor Club Inc						
7300 Corporate Ctr Dr Ste 601	Miami	FL	33126	800-262-7262	305-392-4300	52
BrickKicker Inc						
849 N Ellsworth St	Naperville	IL	60563	800-821-1820		365
Bridal Guide Magazine						
330 Seventh Ave 10th Fl	New York	NY	10001	800-472-7744	212-838-7733	456-11
Bridal Veil Falls State Scenic Viewpoint						
E Bridal Veil Rd PO Box 100	Bridal Veil	OR	97010	800-551-6949		564
Bridge Capital Holdings						
55 Almaden Blvd Ste 200	San Jose	CA	95113	866-273-4265*	408-423-8500	360-2
NASDAQ: BBNK ■ *General						
Bridge Home Health & Hospice						
15100 Birchaven Ln	Findlay	OH	45840	800-982-3306	419-423-5351	371
Bridge Metrics LLC						
830 S Greenville Ave	Allen	TX	75002	877-801-7158		465
Bridgeline Digital						
80 BlanchaRd Rd	Burlington	MA	01803	800-603-9936	781-376-5555	182
Bridgepoint Education Inc						
13500 Evening Creek Dr N						
Ste 600	San Diego	CA	92128	866-475-0317	858-486-1710	244
NYSE: BPI						
BridgePort Brewing Co						
1318 NW Northrup St	Portland	OR	97209	888-834-7546	503-241-7179	101
Bridgeport City Hall						
999 Broad St	Bridgeport	CT	06604	800-978-2828	203-576-7201	337
Bridgeport News						
1000 Bridgeport Ave	Shelton	CT	06484	855-247-8573*	203-926-2080	531-4
*Advestisement						
Bridger Valley Extreme Access						
40014 Business Loop 1-80						
PO Box 399	Mountain View	WY	82939	800-276-3481	307-786-2800	247
Bridgestone Americas Holding Inc						
535 Marriott Dr	Nashville	TN	37214	877-201-2373*	615-937-1000	752
*Cust Svc						
Bridgestone Golf Inc						
15320 Industrial Pk Blvd NE	Covington	GA	30014	800-358-6319	770-787-7400	708
BridgeSTOR LLC						
18060 Old Coach Dr	Poway	CA	92064	800-280-8204	858-375-7076	175-8
Bridgewater College						
402 E College St	Bridgewater	VA	22812	800-759-8328	540-828-5375	167
Bridgewater Hotel						
723 First Ave	Fairbanks	AK	99701	800-528-4916		379
Bridge-world Language Center Inc, The						
110 Second St S Ste 213	Waite Park	MN	56387	800-835-6870	320-259-9239	766
Bridgford Foods Corp						
1308 N Patt St	Anaheim	CA	92801	800-854-3255	714-526-5533	297-26
NASDAQ: BRID						
Bridon Cordage LLC						
909 E 16th St	Albert Lea	MN	56007	800-533-6002	507-377-1601	210
Briefing.com Inc						
401 N Michigan Ste 2910	Chicago	IL	60611	800-752-3013*	312-670-4463	404
*General						
Brierley & Partners						
5465 Legacy Dr Ste 300	Plano	TX	75024	800-899-8700	214-760-8700	5
Briggs & Stratton Corp						
12301 W Wirth St	Milwaukee	WI	53222	800-444-7774	414-259-5333	264
NYSE: BGG						
Briggs Equipment						
10540 N Stemmons Fwy	Dallas	TX	75220	800-606-1833	214-630-0808	385
Briggs Industrial Equipment						
10550 N Stemmons Fwy	Dallas	TX	75220	800-516-9206	214-630-0808	385
Briggs Plumbing Products						
300 Eagle Rd	Goose Creek	SC	29445	800-888-4458		610
Brigham & Women's Hospital						
75 Francis St	Boston	MA	02115	800-722-5520	617-732-5500	374-7
Brigham Young University Idaho						
525 S Ctr	Rexburg	ID	83460	866-672-2984		167

	City	State	ZIP	Toll-Free	Phone	Class
Bright Chair Co						
51 Railroad Ave	Middletown	NY	10940	**888-524-5997**	845-343-2196	320-1
Bright Co-op Inc						
803 W Seale St	Nacogdoches	TX	75964	**800-562-0730**	936-564-8378	761
Bright Horizons Family Solutions LLC						
200 Talcott Ave S	Watertown	MA	02472	**800-324-4386**	617-673-8000	147
Bright Image Corp						
2830 S18th Ave	Broadview	IL	60155	**888-449-5656**		205
BrightMove Inc						
320 High Tide Dr # 201	Saint Augustine	FL	32080	**877-482-8840**		198
Brighton Ford Inc						
8240 W Grand River	Brighton	MI	48114	**888-644-9991**	810-227-1171	56
Brighton Securities Corp						
1703 Monroe Ave	Rochester	NY	14618	**800-388-1703**	585-473-3590	688
Brill Securities Inc						
152 W 57th St 16th Fl	New York	NY	10019	**800-933-0800**	212-957-5700	688
Brillacademic Publishers Inc						
2 liberty Sq 11th Fl	Boston	MA	02109	**800-337-9255**	617-263-2323	634-2
Brillio						
100 Town Sq Pl Ste 308	Jersey City	NJ	07310	**800-317-0575**		462
Brillion Iron Works Inc						
200 Pk Ave	Brillion	WI	54110	**855-320-0373**	920-756-2121	275
Brimar Industries Inc						
64 Outwater Ln	Garfield	NJ	07026	**800-274-6271**		626
Bri-Mar Mfg LLC						
1080 S Main St	Chambersburg	PA	17201	**800-732-5845**	717-263-6116	777
Brine Inc						
32125 Hollingsworth Ave	Warren	MI	48092	**800-968-7845**		708
Brinjac Engineering Inc						
114 N Second St	Harrisburg	PA	17101	**877-274-6526**	717-233-4502	263
Brink's Inc						
PO Box 619031	Dallas	TX	75261	**800-274-6575**	469-549-6000	691
Brinker International Inc						
6820 LBJ Fwy	Dallas	TX	75240	**800-983-4637**	972-980-9917	668
NYSE: EAT						
Brinkmann Corp						
4215 McEwen Rd	Dallas	TX	75244	**800-527-0717**	972-387-4939	439
Brinly-Hardy Co						
3230 Industrial Pkwy	Jeffersonville	IN	47130	**800-626-5329**	812-218-7200	429
BriskHeat Corp						
1055 Gibbard Ave	Columbus	OH	43201	**800-848-7673**	614-294-3376	319
Bristol Aluminum						
5514 Bristol Emilie Rd	Levittown	PA	19057	**800-338-5532**	215-946-3160	362
Bristol Compressors Inc						
15185 Industrial Pk Rd	Bristol	VA	24202	**855-601-0894**	276-466-4121	14
Bristol Construction Services LLC						
111 W 16th Ave Fl 3	Anchorage	AK	99501	**877-563-0013**	907-563-0013	188
Bristol Herald-Courier						
320 Bob Morrison Blvd	Bristol	VA	24201	**888-228-2098**	276-669-2181	531-2
Bristol Hotel						
1055 First Ave	San Diego	CA	92101	**800-662-4477**	619-232-6141	379
Bristol Memorial Works Inc						
797 King St	Bristol	CT	06010	**888-987-7821**	860-583-1654	722
Bristol Motor Speedway						
151 Speedway Blvd	Bristol	TN	37620	**866-415-4158**	423-989-6933	514
Bristol Products Corp						
700 Shelby St	Bristol	TN	37620	**800-336-8775***	423-968-4140	154-1
*Orders						
Bristol Public Library						
5 High St	Bristol	CT	06010	**877-603-7323**	860-584-7787	434-3
Bristol, The						
200 Boylston St	Boston	MA	02116	**800-819-5053**	617-338-4400	669
Bristol-Myers Squibb Canada Inc						
2344 Alfred-Nobel Blvd Ste 300	Montreal	QC	H4S0A4	**800-267-0005***	514-333-3200	582
*Cust Svc						
Bristol-Myers Squibb Co						
345 Pk Ave	New York	NY	10154	**800-332-2056**	212-546-4000	582
NYSE: BMY						
Bristow Alaska Inc						
1915 Donald Ave	Fairbanks	AK	99701	**800-686-4080**	907-452-1197	359
Brita Products Co						
1221 Broadway	Oakland	CA	94612	**800-242-7482**	510-271-7000	804
Britax Child Safety Inc						
4140 Pleasant Rd	Fort Mill	NC	29708	**888-427-4829**	704-409-1700	63
Brite-Line LLC						
10660 E 51st Ave	Denver	CO	80239	**888-201-6448**		729
BriteVision Media LLC						
50 First St Ste 600	San Francisco	CA	94105	**877-479-7777**		8
British Airways Executive Club						
PO Box 300743	Jamaica	NY	11430	**800-452-1201**		26
British Columbia Automobile Assn (BCAA)						
4567 Canada Way	Burnaby	BC	V5G4T1	**800-222-4357**	604-268-5000	52
British Columbia Chamber of Commerce						
750 W Pender St Ste 1201	Vancouver	BC	V6C2T8	**800-669-9655**	604-683-0700	137
British Columbia Lottery Corp (BCLC)						
74 W Seymour St	Kamloops	BC	V2C1E2	**866-815-0222**	250-828-5500	451
British Columbia's Women's Hospital & Health Centre						
4500 Oak St	Vancouver	BC	V6H3N1	**888-300-3088**	604-875-2424	374-2
British Standards Institution, The						
12110 Sunset Hills Rd Ste 200	Reston	VA	20190	**800-862-4977**	703-437-9000	456-5
Brittany Pointe Estates						
1001 S Valley Forge Rd	Lansdale	PA	19446	**800-504-2287**	215-855-4109	670
Britton Lumber Company Inc						
7 Ely Rd PO Box 389	Fairlee	VT	05045	**800-343-5300**	802-333-4388	193-3
Brivo Systems LLC						
7700 Old Georgetown Rd Ste 300	Bethesda	MD	20814	**866-692-7486***	301-664-5242	690
*Tech Supp						
Brixmor Property Group						
420 Lexington Ave 7th Fl	New York	NY	10170	**800-468-7526**	212-869-3000	653
BRK Brands Inc						
3901 Liberty St Rd	Aurora	IL	60504	**800-323-9005**	630-851-7330	285
3901 Liberty St Rd	Aurora	IL	60504	**800-323-9005**	630-851-7330	747
BRLI No 2 Acquisition Corp						
207 Perry Pkwy	Gaithersburg	MD	20877	**888-729-1206**	301-519-2100	415
BRMC (Bay Regional Medical Ctr)						
1900 Columbus Ave	Bay City	MI	48708	**800-656-3950**	989-894-3000	374-3
BRMC (Bluefield Regional Medical Ctr)						
500 Cherry St	Bluefield	WV	24701	**800-994-6610**	304-327-1100	374-3
Broad River Electric Co-op Inc						
811 Hamrick St	Gaffney	SC	29342	**866-687-2667**	864-489-5737	247
Broadband Dynamics LLC						
8757 E Via De Commercio	Scottsdale	AZ	85258	**888-801-1034**		387
Broadcast Education Assn (BEA)						
1771 N St NW	Washington	DC	20036	**888-326-1415**	202-429-3935	48-5
Broadcast Microwave Services Inc (BMS)						
12367 Crosthwaite Cir	Poway	CA	92064	**800-669-9667**	858-391-3050	226
Broadcom Corp						
1320 Ridder Park Dr	Irvine	CA	92617	**877-673-9442**	408-433-8000	694
NASDAQ: BRCM						
Broadfield Distributing Inc						
67A Glen Cove Ave	Glen Cove	NY	11542	**800-634-5178**	516-676-2378	248
Broadhurst Theatre						
235 W 44th St	New York	NY	10036	**800-447-7400**	212-239-6200	744
Broadlawns Medical Ctr						
1801 Hickman Rd	Des Moines	IA	50314	**866-904-5755**	515-282-2200	374-3
Broadleaf Services Inc						
10 Mall Rd	Burlington	MA	01803	**866-337-7733**		182
Broadman & Holman Publishers						
127 Ninth Ave N MSN 114	Nashville	TN	37234	**800-448-8032**		634-3
Broadmoor, The						
1 Lake Ave	Colorado Springs	CO	80906	**866-837-9520**	719-577-5775	667
Broadnet Teleservices LLC						
1805 Shea Ctr Dr						
Ste 160	Highlands Ranch	CO	80129	**877-579-4929**		115
Broadview Networks Holdings Inc						
800 Westchester Ave Ste N-501	Rye Brook	NY	10573	**800-260-8766**	914-922-7000	733
Broadway Ctr for the Performing Arts						
901 Broadway	Tacoma	WA	98402	**800-291-7593**	253-591-5890	571
Broadway Financial Corp						
4800 Wilshire Blvd	Los Angeles	CA	90010	**888-988-2265**	323-634-1700	360-2
NASDAQ: BYFC						
Broadway League, The						
729 Seventh Ave 5th Fl	New York	NY	10019	**866-442-9878**	212-764-1122	47-4
Broadway Mechanical						
873 81st Ave	Oakland	CA	94621	**800-862-4930**	510-746-4000	609
Broadway Plaza Hotel						
1155 Broadway	New York	NY	10001	**877-504-6835**	212-679-7665	378
Broadway.com						
729 Seventh Ave	New York	NY	10019	**800-762-3929**	212-541-8457	748
Broan-NuTone LLC						
926 W State St PO Box 140	Hartford	WI	53027	**800-558-1711***	262-673-4340	36
*Cust Svc						
Brocade Communications Systems Inc						
130 Holger Way	San Jose	CA	95134	**800-752-8061**	408-333-8000	178
NASDAQ: BRCD						
Brock & Company Inc						
257 Great Vly Pkwy	Malvern	PA	19355	**866-468-2783**	610-647-5656	668
Brock Services LLC						
1675 Spindletop Rd	Beaumont	TX	77705	**800-600-9675**	409-833-7571	191-8
Brock Solutions Inc						
86 Ardelt Ave	Kitchener	ON	N2C2C9	**877-702-7625**	519-571-1522	263
Brockman Coats Gedelian & Co						
1735 Merriman Rd	Akron	OH	44313	**800-968-6661**	330-864-6661	2
Brockville General Hospital						
75 Charles St	Brockville	ON	K6V1S8	**800-567-7415**	613-345-5645	374-2
Broco Inc						
10868 Bell Ct	Rancho Cucamonga	CA	91730	**800-845-7259**	909-483-3222	484
Broco Products Inc						
18624 Syracuse Ave	Cleveland	OH	44110	**800-321-0837**	216-531-0880	411
Brodart Co						
500 Arch St	Williamsport	PA	17701	**800-233-8467**	570-326-2461	180-10
Brody School of Medicine at East Carolina University						
600 Moye Blvd	Greenville	NC	27834	**800-722-3281**	252-744-1020	168-2
Broedell Plumbing Supply Inc						
1601 Commerce Ln	Jupiter	FL	33458	**888-328-2383**	561-743-6663	611
Broich Enterprises Inc						
6440 City W Pkwy	Eden Prairie	MN	55344	**800-853-3508**	952-941-2270	663
Brokers International Financial Services LLC						
102 Se 13th St	Panora	IA	50216	**877-886-1939**	641-755-4635	691
Brokers Worldwide						
701C Ashland Ave	Folcroft	PA	19032	**800-624-5287**	610-461-3661	458
Brolite Products Inc						
1900 S Pk Ave	Streamwood	IL	60107	**888-276-5483**	630-830-0340	297-42
Bronco Billy's Casino						
233 E Bennett Ave						
PO Box 590	Cripple Creek	CO	80813	**877-989-2142**	719-689-2142	132
Bronco Wine Co						
6342 Bystrum Rd	Ceres	CA	95307	**855-874-2394**	209-538-3131	79-3
Broniec Assoc Inc						
4855 Peachtree Industrial Blvd						
Ste 215	Norcross	GA	30092	**800-432-8348**	770-729-9664	2
Bronner Bros Inc						
2141 Powers Ferry Rd	Marietta	GA	30067	**800-241-6151**	770-988-0015	217
Bronson Methodist Hospital						
601 John St	Kalamazoo	MI	49007	**800-276-6766**	269-341-7654	374-3
Bronx Community College						
2155 University Ave	Bronx	NY	10453	**866-888-8777**	718-289-5100	161
Bronx Council on the Arts						
1738 Hone Ave	Bronx	NY	10461	**866-564-5226**	718-931-9500	459
Bronx Library Ctr						
310 E Kings Bridge Rd	Bronx	NY	10458	**800-342-3688**	718-579-4244	434-3
Bronx Psychiatric Ctr						
1500 Waters Pl	Bronx	NY	10461	**800-597-8481**	718-931-0600	374-5
Bronx Zoo						
2300 Southern Blvd	Bronx	NY	10460	**800-433-4149**	718-220-5100	821
BronxCare Family Wellness Center						
1276 Fulton Ave	Bronx	NY	10456	**877-451-9361**	718-590-1800	374-3
Bronze Craft Corp						
37 Will St	Nashua	NH	03060	**800-488-7747**	603-883-7747	350
Brook Furniture Rental Inc						
100 N Field Dr Ste 220	Lake Forest	IL	60045	**877-285-7368**	847-810-4000	266-2
Brook Mays Music Co						
8605 John Carpenter Fwy	Dallas	TX	75247	**800-637-8966***	214-631-0928	525
*Cust Svc						
Brookdale Community College						
765 Newman Springs Rd	Lincroft	NJ	07738	**866-767-9512**	732-842-1900	161

Name / Address	City	State	ZIP	Toll-Free	Phone	Class
Brookdale Senior Living Inc 111 Westwood Pl Ste 400	Brentwood	TN	37027	**866-785-9025**	615-221-2250	670
Brooke Army Medical Ctr (BAMC) 3551 Roger Brooke Dr	Fort Sam Houston	TX	78234	**800-443-2262**	210-916-4141	331-4
Brooke Chase Associates Inc 1543 Second St Ste 201	Sarasota	FL	34236	**877-374-0039**		719
Brooke Distributors Inc 16250 NW 52nd Ave	Hialeah	FL	33014	**800-275-8792**	305-624-9752	37
Brookfield Engineering Lab Inc 11 Commerce Blvd	Middleboro	MA	02346	**800-628-8139**	508-946-6200	203
Brookfield Properties Corp (BOP) 181 Bay St Ste 330 *NYSE: BPO*	Toronto	ON	M5J2T3	**800-387-0825**	416-369-2300	653
Brookfield Public Library 1900 N Calhoun Rd	Brookfield	WI	53005	**866-868-3947**	262-782-4140	434-3
Brookfield Residential Services Ltd 3190 Steeles Ave E Ste 200	Markham	ON	L3R1G9	**800-949-0274**	416-510-8700	650
Brookgreen Gardens 1931 Brookgreen Dr	Murrells Inlet	SC	29576	**800-849-1931**	843-235-6000	96
Brookhaven-Lincoln County Chamber of Commerce 230 S Whitworth Ave	Brookhaven	MS	39601	**800-613-4667**	601-833-1411	138
Brookings Institution 1775 Massachusetts Ave NW	Washington	DC	20036	**800-275-1447**	202-797-6000	631
Brookline Bank PO Box 470469 *NASDAQ: BRKL* ■ *Cust Svc	Brookline	MA	02445	**877-668-2265***	617-730-3520	360-2
Brookline College 2445 W Dunlap Ave Ste 100	Phoenix	AZ	85021	**800-793-2428**	602-242-6265	683
Brooks Automation Inc 15 Elizabeth Dr *NASDAQ: BRKS*	Chelmsford	MA	01824	**800-698-6149**	978-262-2400	693
Brooks Automation Inc Polycold Systems 3800 Lakeville Hwy	Petaluma	CA	94954	**800-698-6149**	707-769-7000	14
Brooks Equipment Company Inc 10926 David Taylor Dr Ste 300	Charlotte	NC	28269	**800-826-3473**		677
Brooks Lake Lodge & Guest Ranch 458 Brooks Lk Rd	Dubois	WY	82513	**866-213-4022**		241
Brooks Resources Corp 409 NW Franklin Ave	Bend	OR	97701	**877-475-9779**	541-382-1662	651
Brooks Sports Inc 19910 N Creek Pkwy Ste 200	Bothell	WA	98011	**800-227-6657**		302
Brooks Tropicals Inc 18400 SW 256th St PO Box 900160	Homestead	FL	33090	**800-327-4833**	305-247-3544	316-4
Brooks Utility Products Group 23847 Industrial Park Dr	Farmington Hills	MI	48335	**888-687-3008**	248-477-0250	636
Brookshire Bros Ltd 1201 Ellen Trout Dr	Lufkin	TX	75904	**855-467-7837**	936-634-8155	345
Brookshire Suites 120 E Lombard St	Baltimore	MD	21202	**855-345-5033**	410-625-1300	379
Brookside Gardens 1800 Glenallan Ave	Wheaton	MD	20902	**800-366-2012**	301-962-1400	96
Brookside Resort 463 E Pkwy	Gatlinburg	TN	37738	**800-251-9597**	865-436-5611	667
Brooks-Jeffrey Computer Store 19 Medical Plz	Mountain Home	AR	72653	**800-506-8064**	870-425-8064	177
Brookstone Inc 1 Innovation Way *Cust Svc	Merrimack	NH	03054	**800-846-3000***	603-880-9500	328
Brookstown Inn 200 Brookstown Ave	Winston-Salem	NC	27101	**800-845-4262**	336-725-1120	379
Brookstreet Hotel 525 Legget Dr	Ottawa	ON	K2K2W2	**888-826-2220**	613-271-1800	379
Brooksville Regional Hospital 17240 Cortez Blvd	Brooksville	FL	34601	**844-455-8708**	352-796-5111	374-3
Brookwood Cos Inc 25 W 45th St 11th Fl	New York	NY	10036	**800-426-5468**	212-551-0100	593
Broome Community College 901 Front St	Binghamton	NY	13905	**800-836-0689**	607-778-5000	161
Bro-Tex Inc 800 Hampden Ave	Saint Paul	MN	55114	**800-328-2282**	651-645-5721	507
Brother International Corp 100 Somerset Corporate Blvd *Cust Svc	Bridgewater	NJ	08807	**877-552-6255***	908-704-1700	110
Brotherhood Bank & Trust 756 Minnesota Ave	Kansas City	MO	66101	**855-522-6722**	913-321-4242	69
Brotherhood Mutual Insurance Co (BMI) 6400 Brotherhood Way PO Box 2589 *Cust Svc	Fort Wayne	IN	46825	**800-333-3735***		391-4
Brotherhood of Locomotive Engineers & Trainmen (BLET) 1370 Ontario St Mezzanine Level	Cleveland	OH	44113	**877-772-5772**	216-241-2630	414
Brothers Inc 1000 Sussex Blvd	Broomall	PA	19008	**866-276-7462**	610-328-0670	191-4
Broughton Foods Co 1701 Green St	Marietta	OH	45750	**800-283-2479**	740-373-4121	297-27
Broward Community College *Downtown Ctr* 111 E Las Olas Blvd	Fort Lauderdale	FL	33301	**888-654-6482**	954-201-7350	161
North 1000 Coconut Creek Blvd	Coconut Creek	FL	33066	**888-654-6482**	954-201-2240	161
Broward County Chamber of Commerce 2425 E Commercial Blvd #103	Fort Lauderdale	FL	33308	**877-653-4752**	954-565-5750	138
Broward County Historical Commission 151 SW Second St	Fort Lauderdale	FL	33301	**866-682-2258**	954-765-4670	519
Broward Ctr for the Performing Arts 201 SW Fifth Ave	Fort Lauderdale	FL	33312	**877-311-7469**	954-462-0222	571
Broward Fire Equipment & Service Inc 101 SW Sixth St	Fort Lauderdale	FL	33301	**800-866-3473**	954-467-6625	677
Brower Mechanical Inc 4060 Alvis Ct	Rocklin	CA	95677	**877-816-6649**	916-624-0808	609
Brown & Bigelow Inc 345 Plato Blvd E *Cust Svc	Saint Paul	MN	55107	**800-628-1755***	651-293-7000	9
Brown & Brown Insurance PO Box 1718	Tacoma	WA	98401	**800-562-8171**	253-396-5500	391-4
Brown & Haley PO Box 1596	Tacoma	WA	98401	**800-426-8400**		297-8
Brown & Saenger 711 W Russell St PO Box 84040	Sioux Falls	SD	57118	**800-952-3509**	605-336-1960	321
Brown Automotive Group LP 4300 S Georgia	Amarillo	TX	79110	**888-388-6728**	806-353-7211	56
Brown Bus Co 2111 E Sherman Ave	Nampa	ID	83686	**800-574-1580**	208-466-4181	108
Brown Coach Inc 50 Venner Rd	Amsterdam	NY	12010	**800-424-4700**	518-843-4700	106
Brown College 1345 Mendota Heights Rd	Mendota Heights	MN	55120	**888-247-4238**	651-905-3400	798
Brown College of Court Reporting & Medical Transcription (BCCR) 1900 Emery St NW Ste 200	Atlanta	GA	30318	**800-849-0703**	404-876-1227	798
Brown County Convention & Visitors Bureau 10 N Van Buren St PO Box 840	Nashville	IN	47448	**800-753-3255**	812-988-7303	208
Brown County Inn 51 State Rd 46	Nashville	IN	47448	**800-772-5249**	812-988-2291	379
Brown County Rural Electric Assn 24386 State Hwy 4 PO Box 529	Sleepy Eye	MN	56085	**800-658-2368**	507-794-3331	247
Brown Hotel, The 335 W Broadway St	Louisville	KY	40202	**888-888-5252**	502-583-1234	379
Brown Investment Advisory & Trust Co 901 S Bond St Ste 400	Baltimore	MD	21231	**800-645-3923**	410-537-5400	401
Brown Jordan Co 9860 Gidley St	El Monte	CA	91731	**800-743-4252**		320-4
Brown Machine LLC 330 N Ross St	Beaverton	MI	48612	**877-702-4142**	989-435-7741	145
Brown Mackie College *Fort Wayne* 3000 E Coliseum Blvd *General	Fort Wayne	IN	46805	**866-433-2289***	260-484-4400	798
Merrillville 1000 E 80th Pl Ste 205M	Merrillville	IN	46410	**800-258-3321**	219-769-3321	798
Michigan City 1001 E US Hwy 20	Michigan City	IN	46360	**800-519-2416**	219-877-3100	798
South Bend 3454 Douglas Rd	South Bend	IN	46635	**800-743-2447**	574-237-0774	798
Brown Mackie College Atlanta 4370 Peachtree Rd NE	Atlanta	GA	30319	**877-479-8419**	404-799-4500	798
Brown Mackie College Bettendorf 2119 E Kimberly Rd	Bettendorf	IA	52722	**888-420-1652**	563-344-1500	798
Brown Mackie College Findlay 1700 Fostoria Ave Ste 100	Findlay	OH	45840	**800-842-3687**	419-423-2211	798
Brown Mackie College Hopkinsville 4001 Ft Campbell Blvd	Hopkinsville	KY	42240	**800-359-4753**	270-886-1302	798
Brown Mackie College Lenexa 9705 Lenexa Dr	Lenexa	KS	66215	**800-635-9101**	913-768-1900	798
Brown Mackie College Louisville 3605 Fern Vly Rd	Louisville	KY	40219	**800-999-7387**	502-968-7191	798
Brown Mackie College Miami 3700 Lakeside Dr	Miramar	FL	33027	**866-505-0335**	305-341-6600	798
Brown Mackie College Northern Kentucky 309 Buttermilk Pk	Fort Mitchell	KY	41017	**800-888-1445**	859-341-5627	798
Brown Mackie College Salina 2106 S Ninth St	Salina	KS	67401	**800-365-0433**	785-825-5422	798
Brown Mfg Corp 6001 E Hwy 27	Ozark	AL	36360	**800-633-8909**		275
Brown Palace Hotel 321 17th St	Denver	CO	80202	**800-321-2599**	303-297-3111	379
Brown Stove Works Inc 1422 Carolina Ave *All	Cleveland	TN	37320	**800-251-7485***	423-476-6544	35
Brown &Tedstrom Inc 1700 Broadway Ste 500	Denver	CO	80290	**800-883-9361**	303-863-7231	401
Brown University Rockefeller Library 10 Prospect St	Providence	RI	02912	**877-668-4493**	401-863-2162	434-6
Brown Wood Preserving Company Inc 6201 Camp Ground Rd	Louisville	KY	40216	**800-537-1765**	502-448-2337	816
Brown Wood Products Co 7040 N Lawndale Ave	Lincolnwood	IL	60712	**800-328-5858**		818
Brown's Wharf Inn 121 Atlantic Ave	Boothbay Harbor	ME	04538	**800-334-8110**	207-633-5440	379
Browne & Co 100 Esna Pk Dr	Markham	ON	L3R1E3	**866-306-3672**	905-475-6104	301
Browne-Halco Inc 788 Morris Turnpike Ste 202	Short Hills	NJ	07078	**888-289-1005**	973-232-1065	301
Brownell World Travel 216 Summit Blvd Ste 220	Birmingham	AL	35243	**800-999-3960**	205-802-6222	769
Brown-Forman Corp 850 Dixie Hwy PO Box 1080 *NYSE: BFB*	Louisville	KY	40210	**800-831-9146**	502-585-1100	187
Brownlie & Braden LLC 2820 Ross Tower 500 N Akard	Dallas	TX	75201	**888-339-4650**	214-219-4650	196
Brownstone Real Estate Co 1840 Fishburn Rd	Hershey	PA	17033	**877-533-6222**	717-533-6222	650
Brownstown Electric Supply Company Inc 690 E State Rd 250 PO Box L	Brownstown	IN	47220	**800-742-8492**	812-358-4555	785
Brown-Strauss Steel 2495 Uravan St *Sales	Aurora	CO	80011	**800-677-2778***	303-371-2200	491
Brownsville Convention & Visitors Bureau 650 Ruben M Torres Sr Blvd	Brownsville	TX	78521	**800-626-2639**	956-546-3721	208
Brownsville Herald, The 1135 E Van Buren St	Brownsville	TX	78520	**800-488-4301**	956-542-4301	531-2
Browntrout Publishers Inc 201 Continental Blvd	El Segundo	CA	90245	**800-777-7812**	310-607-9010	634-2
Broyhill Co 1 N Market Sq	Dakota City	NE	68731	**800-228-1003**	402-987-3412	275
Broyhill Furniture Industries Inc 3483 Hickory Blvd *Cust Svc	Hudson	NC	28638	**800-225-0265***		320-2
Broyles Kight & Ricafort PC 8250 Haverstick Rd Ste 100	Indianapolis	IN	46240	**888-834-2692**	317-571-3600	428

Name / Address	City	State	Zip	Toll-Free	Phone	Class
BRP Manufacturing Co 637 N Jackson St	Lima	OH	45801	800-858-0482	419-228-4441	674
BRT Laboratories Inc 400 W Franklin St	Baltimore	MD	21201	800-765-5170	410-225-9595	417
BRT Realty Trust 60 Cutter Mill Rd Ste 303 *NYSE: BRT*	Great Neck	NY	11021	800-450-5816	516-466-3100	508
Bruce & Merrilees Electric Co 930 Cass St	New Castle	PA	16101	800-652-5560	724-652-5566	191-4
Bruce Foods Corp PO Box 1030	New Iberia	LA	70561	800-299-9082	337-365-8101	297-20
Bruel & Kjaer Instruments Inc 2815 Colonnades Ct Ste A	Norcross	GA	30071	800-332-2040	770-209-6907	250
Brueton Industries Inc 146 Hanse Ave *Cust Svc	Freeport	NY	11520	800-221-6783*	516-379-3400	320-2
Brulin & Company Inc 2920 Dr AJ Brown Ave	Indianapolis	IN	46205	800-776-7149	317-923-3211	144
Brunet-Garcia Advertising Inc 1510 Hendricks Ave	Jacksonville	FL	32207	866-346-1977	904-346-1977	7
Brunswick & The Golden Isles of Georgia Visitors Bureau 4 Glynn Ave	Brunswick	GA	31520	800-933-2627	912-265-0620	208
Brunswick Community College 50 College Rd	Bolivia	NC	28422	800-754-1050	910-755-7300	161
Brunswick Corp Mercury Marine Div W 6250 Pioneer Rd	Fond du Lac	WI	54935	866-408-6372	920-929-5040	264
Brunswick County Board of Education 35 Referendum Dr	Bolivia	NC	28422	800-662-7030	910-253-2900	683
Brunswick County Chamber of Commerce 4948 Main St	Shallotte	NC	28459	800-426-6644	910-754-6644	138
Brunswick Electric Membership Corp 795 Ocean Hwy PO Box 826	Shallotte	NC	28459	800-842-5871	910-754-4391	247
Brunswick School Inc 100 Maher Ave	Greenwich	CT	06830	800-546-9425	203-625-5800	40
Brunswick-Glynn County Regional Library 208 Gloucester St	Brunswick	GA	31520	800-222-6748	912-279-3740	434-3
Brunswick-Golden Isles Chamber of Commerce 1505 Richmond St 2nd Fl	Brunswick	GA	31520	888-453-5955	912-265-0620	138
Bruss Co 3548 N Kostner Ave	Chicago	IL	60641	800-621-3882	773-282-2900	298-9
Bry-Air Inc 10793 SR 37 W	Sunbury	OH	43074	877-427-9247	740-965-2974	14
Bryan College 721 Bryan Dr PO Box 7000	Dayton	TN	37321	800-277-9522	423-775-2041	167
Bryan LGH Medical Ctr East 1600 S 48th St	Lincoln	NE	68506	800-742-7844	402-481-7333	374-3
Bryan Systems 14020 US 20A Hwy	Montpelier	OH	43543	800-745-2796		778
Bryan/College Station Convention & Visitors Bureau (BCSCVB) 715 University Dr E	College Station	TX	77840	800-777-8292	979-260-9898	208
Bryant & Stratton College *Cleveland* 3121 Euclid Ave	Cleveland	OH	44115	866-948-0571	216-771-1700	798
Bryant & Stratton College Milwaukee 310 W Wisconsin Ave Ste 500-E	Milwaukee	WI	53203	866-948-0571	414-276-5200	798
Bryant & Stratton College Richmond 8141 Hull St Rd	Richmond	VA	23235	866-948-0571	804-745-2444	798
Bryant & Stratton College Syracuse North 8687 Carling Rd	Liverpool	NY	13090	800-836-5627	315-652-6500	798
Bryant Park Hotel 40 W 40th St	New York	NY	10018	877-640-9300	212-869-0100	379
Bryant University 1150 Douglas Pk *Admissions	Smithfield	RI	02917	800-622-7001*	401-232-6000	167
Bryce Corp 4505 Old Lamar Ave	Memphis	TN	38118	800-238-7277	901-369-4400	547
BryCoat Inc 207 Vollmer Ave	Oldsmar	FL	34677	800-989-8788	727-490-1000	549
BryLin Hospitals 1263 Delaware Ave	Buffalo	NY	14209	800-727-9546	716-886-8200	374-5
Bryn Mawr Bank Corp 801 Lancaster Ave *NASDAQ: BMTC*	Bryn Mawr	PA	19010	855-381-2631	610-525-1700	360-2
Bryn Mawr College 101 N Merion Ave *Admissions	Bryn Mawr	PA	19010	800-262-2586*	610-526-5000	167
Bryn Mawr Rehab Hospital 414 Paoli Pike	Malvern	PA	19355	888-876-8764	484-596-5400	374-6
BSAC (Berkeley Sensor & Actuator Ctr) *University of California* 403 Cory Hall MC Ste 1774	Berkeley	CA	94720	800-549-1002	510-643-6690	666
BSC America Inc 803 Bel Air Rd	Bel Air	MD	21014	800-764-7400		462
BSCAI (Building Service Contractors Assn International) 401 N Michigan Ave Ste 2200	Chicago	IL	60611	800-368-3414	312-321-5167	48-13
BSI (Badger State Industries) 3099 E Washington Ave PO Box 8990	Madison	WI	53708	800-862-1086	608-240-5200	629
BSI (Building Service Inc) W222 N630 Cheaney Rd	Waukesha	WI	53186	866-353-3600	262-955-6400	393
BSM Wireless Inc 75 International Blvd Ste 100	Toronto	ON	M9W6L9	866-768-4771	416-675-1201	690
BSN Medical Inc 5825 Carnegie Blvd	Charlotte	NC	28209	800-552-1157	704-554-9933	476
BSQUARE Corp 110 110th Ave NE *NASDAQ: BSQR*	Bellevue	WA	98004	888-820-4500	425-519-5900	180-2
BSSB (Boiling Springs Savings Bank) 25 Orient Way	Rutherford	NJ	07070	888-388-7459	201-939-5000	69
BT Americas Inc 2160 E Grand Ave	El Segundo	CA	90245	888-767-2988	408-330-2700	394
BT Conferencing Inc 150 Newport Ave. Ext, Ste 301	North Quincy	MA	02171	866-770-8777		360-3
B&t Service Station Contractors 630 S Frontage Rd	Nipomo	CA	93444	888-862-2552	805-929-8944	325
BTA (Business Technology Assn) 12411 Wornall Rd Ste 200	Kansas City	MO	64145	800-325-7219	816-941-3100	48-18
BTC (Bledsoe Telephone Co-op Corp) 338 Cumberland Ave PO Box 609	Pikeville	TN	37367	888-382-1222	423-447-2121	733
Btd Mfg Inc 1111 13th Ave SE	Detroit Lakes	MN	56501	866-562-3986		487
BTS (IEEE Broadcast Technology Society) 445 Hoes Ln	Piscataway	NJ	08854	800-678-4333	732-562-5407	48-19
BTS (Brazilian Travel Service) 16 W 46th St 2nd Fl	New York	NY	10036	800-342-5746	212-764-6161	16
BTS Asset Management Inc 420 Bedford St Ste 340	Lexington	MA	02420	800-343-3040		401
BTS USA Inc 300 Stamford Pl Ste 425	Stamford	CT	06902	800-445-7089	203-316-2740	196
BTSB (Bound to Stay Bound Books Inc) 1880 W Morton Ave	Jacksonville	IL	62650	800-637-6586	217-245-5191	91
BTU International Inc 23 Esquire Rd *NASDAQ: BTUI*	North Billerica	MA	01862	800-998-0666	978-667-4111	693
Bubba Gump Shrimp Co LLC 2501 Seawall Blvd	Galveston	TX	77550	800-552-6379	409-766-4952	668
Buchanan Automotive Group 50 Central Ave Ste 900	Sarasota	FL	34236	888-292-4883	941-364-9500	56
Buchanan Hauling & Rigging 4625 Industrial Rd	Fort Wayne	IN	46825	888-544-4285	260-471-1877	778
Buchanan Ingersoll & Rooney PC 301 Grant St 1 Oxford Ctr 20th Fl	Pittsburgh	PA	15219	800-444-6738	412-562-8800	428
Buchanan Technologies Inc 1026 Texan Trl	Grapevine	TX	76051	888-730-2774	972-869-3966	182
Bucher & Christian Consulting Inc 10 W Market St Ste 1300	Indianapolis	IN	46204	866-363-1132	317-423-8980	196
Buck & Knobby Equipment Co 6220 Sterns Rd	Ottawa Lake	MI	49267	855-213-2825	734-856-2811	266-3
Buck Chuck Co 2155 Traversefield Dr	Traverse City	MI	49686	800-228-2825		492
Buck Distributing Company Inc 15827 Commerce Ct *Cust Svc	Upper Marlboro	MD	20774	800-750-2825*	301-952-0400	80-1
Buck Knives Inc 660 S Lochsa St	Post Falls	ID	83854	800-326-2825	208-262-0500	224
Buck's Pizza Franchising Corp Inc PO Box 405	Du Bois	PA	15801	800-310-8848		668
Buck's Pocket State Park 393 County Rd 174	Grove Oak	AL	35975	800-760-4089	256-659-2000	564
Buckeye Business Products Inc 3830 Kelley Ave	Cleveland	OH	44114	800-837-4323		627
Buckeye Career Center 545 University Dr Ne	New Philadelphia	OH	44663	800-227-1665	330-339-2288	161
Buckeye Container Inc 3350 Long Rd	Wooster	OH	44691	800-968-6894	330-264-6336	99
Buckeye International Inc 2700 Wagner Pl	Maryland Heights	MO	63043	800-321-2583	314-291-1900	150
Buckeye Nissan Inc 3820 Pkwy Ln	Hilliard	OH	43026	800-686-4391	614-771-2345	56
Buckeye Nutrition 330 E Schultz Ave	Dalton	OH	44618	800-417-6460		446
Buckeye Pacific LLC 4386 SW Macadam Ave Ste 200	Portland	OR	97207	800-767-9191	503-274-2284	193-3
Buckeye Power Sales Company Inc 6850 Commerce Ct Dr PO Box 489	Blacklick	OH	43004	800-523-3587	614-861-6000	619
Buckeye Rural Electric Co-op PO Box 200	Rio Grande	OH	45674	800-231-2732	740-379-2025	247
Buckeye ShapeForm 555 Marion Rd	Columbus	OH	43207	800-728-0776	614-445-8433	256
Buckhorn Inc 55 W Techne Ctr Dr	Milford	OH	45150	800-543-4454	513-831-4402	201
Buckhorn Lake State Resort Park 4441 Kentucky Hwy 1833	Buckhorn	KY	41721	800-325-0058		564
Buckingham Browne & Nichols School 46 Belmont St	Watertown	MA	02472	800-233-6329	617-547-6100	683
Buckingham's Restaurant & Oasis 2820 W Hwy 76	Branson	MO	65616	800-725-2236	417-337-7777	669
Buckle Inc 2407 W 24th St *NYSE: BKE*	Kearney	NE	68845	800-626-1255	308-236-8491	156-4
Buckles-Smith 801 Savaker Ave	San Jose	CA	95126	800-833-7362	408-280-7777	248
Buckley Industries Inc 1850 E 53rd St N	Wichita	KS	67219	800-835-2779	316-744-7587	602
Buckley Oil Company Inc 1809 Rock Island St	Dallas	TX	75207	800-721-4147	214-421-4147	580
Buckley Powder Co 42 Inverness Dr E	Englewood	CO	80112	800-333-2266	303-790-7007	270
Bucklin Tractor & Implement Co 115 W Railroad PO Box 127	Bucklin	KS	67834	800-334-4823	620-826-3271	275
Buckman Laboratories Inc 1256 N McLean Blvd	Memphis	TN	38108	800-282-5626	901-278-0330	144
Buckner International 600 N Pearl St Ste 2000 20th Fl	Dallas	TX	75201	800-442-4800	214-758-8000	47-6
Bucks County 55 E Ct St	Doylestown	PA	18901	888-942-8257	215-348-6000	338
Bucks County Conference & Visitors Bureau (BCCVB) 3207 St Rd	Bensalem	PA	19020	800-836-2825	215-639-0300	208
Bucks County Water & Sewer Authority (BCWSA) 1275 Almshouse Rd	Warrington	PA	18976	800-222-2068	215-343-2538	804
Buddy Moore Trucking Inc PO Box 10047	Birmingham	AL	35202	866-704-1598	205-949-2260	778
Buddy Rogers Music Inc 6891 Simpson Ave	Cincinnati	OH	45239	800-536-2263	513-729-1950	525
Buddy's Home Furnishings 6608 E Adamo Dr	Tampa	FL	33619	866-779-5085		266-2
Budget Blinds Inc 1927 N Glassell St	Orange	CA	92865	800-800-9250	714-637-2100	86
Budget Finance Co 1849 Sawtelle Blvd	Los Angeles	CA	90025	800-225-6267	310-696-4050	216
Budget Host International 2307 Roosevelt Dr	Arlington	TX	76016	800-283-4678	817-861-6088	379

Name / Address	City	State	ZIP	Toll-Free	Phone	Class
Budget Rent A Car System Inc						
6 Sylvan Way	Parsippany	NJ	07054	**800-527-0700**	800-283-4382	125
Budget Suites of America						
2770 N Hwy 360	Grand Prairie	TX	75050	**866-877-2000**	972-647-2500	379
Budreck Truck Lines Inc						
8040 S Roberts Rd	Bridgeview	IL	60455	**800-621-0013**	708-496-0522	188
Buehler Ltd						
41 Waukegan Rd	Lake Bluff	IL	60044	**800-283-4537***	847-295-6500	419
*Sales						
Buehler Moving & Storage						
3899 Jackson St	Denver	CO	80205	**800-234-6683**	303-388-4000	518
Buehner Block Co						
2800 SW Temple	Salt Lake City	UT	84115	**800-999-2565**	801-467-5456	185
Buena Park Convention & Visitors Office						
6601 Beach Blvd	Buena Park	CA	90621	**800-541-3953**		208
Buena Vista Motor Inn						
1599 Lombard St	San Francisco	CA	94123	**800-835-4980**	415-923-9600	378
Buena Vista Palace Hotel & Spa						
1900 N Buena Vista Dr	Lake Buena Vista	FL	32830	**866-397-6516**		667
Buena Vista Regional Medical Ctr						
PO Box 309	Storm Lake	IA	50588	**877-401-8030**	712-732-4030	374-3
Buena Vista Suites						
8203 World Ctr Dr	Orlando	FL	32821	**800-537-7737***	407-239-8588	379
*Resv						
Buena Vista University						
610 W Fourth St	Storm Lake	IA	50588	**800-383-9600**	712-749-2253	167
Buff & Shine Manufacturing Inc						
2139 E Del Amo Blvd	Compton	CA	90220	**800-659-2833**	310-886-5111	296
Buffalo & Pittsburgh Railroad Inc (BPRR)						
1200-C Scottsville Rd Ste 200	Rochester	NY	14624	**800-603-3385**	585-463-3307	646
Buffalo Bill's Resort & Casino						
31900 Las Vegas Blvd S	Primm	NV	89019	**888-774-6668**	702-386-7867	132
Buffalo Bills						
Ralph Wilson Stadium						
1 Bills Dr	Orchard Park	NY	14127	**877-228-4257**	716-648-1800	713-3
Buffalo Crushed Stone Co Inc						
2544 Clinton St	Buffalo	NY	14224	**800-543-3860**	716-826-7310	499
Buffalo Dental Manufacturing Company Inc						
159 Lafayette Dr	Syosset	NY	11791	**800-828-0203**	516-496-7200	230
Buffalo Games Inc						
220 James E Casey Dr	Buffalo	NY	14206	**855-895-4290**		760
Buffalo General Hospital						
100 High St	Buffalo	NY	14203	**800-506-6480**	716-859-5600	374-3
Buffalo Grove Park District						
530 Bernard Dr	Buffalo Grove	IL	60089	**800-526-0844**	847-850-2100	31
Buffalo Industries Inc						
99 S Spokane St	Seattle	WA	98134	**800-683-0052**	206-682-9900	742-8
Buffalo Museum of Science						
1020 Humboldt Pkwy	Buffalo	NY	14211	**866-291-6660**	716-896-5200	519
Buffalo News						
1 News Plz PO Box 100	Buffalo	NY	14240	**800-777-8640**	716-849-4444	531-2
Buffalo Niagara Convention & Visitors Bureau						
403 Main St Ste 630	Buffalo	NY	14203	**800-283-3256**	716-852-2356	208
Buffalo Niagara Convention Ctr						
153 Franklin St						
Convention Ctr Plz	Buffalo	NY	14202	**800-995-7570**	716-855-5555	207
Buffalo Niagara International Airport						
4200 Genesee St	Cheektowaga	NY	14225	**877-359-2642**	716-630-6000	27
Buffalo Niagara Partnership						
665 Main St Ste 200	Buffalo	NY	14203	**844-308-9165**	716-852-7100	138
Buffalo Psychiatric Ctr						
400 Forest Ave	Buffalo	NY	14213	**800-597-8481**	716-885-2261	374-5
Buffalo Rock Co						
111 Oxmoor Rd	Birmingham	AL	35209	**800-822-9799**	205-942-3435	80-2
Buffalo Sabres						
HSBC Arena 1 Seymour H Knox III Plz						
	Buffalo	NY	14203	**888-467-2273**	716-855-4100	714
Buffalo Spree Magazine						
100 Corporate Pkwy Ste 220	Buffalo	NY	14226	**855-697-7733**	716-783-9119	456-22
Buffalo Supply Inc						
1650A Coal Creek Dr	Lafayette	CO	80026	**800-366-1812**		240
Buffalo Wire Works Co						
1165 Clinton St	Buffalo	NY	14206	**800-828-7028**	716-826-4666	686
Buffelen Woodworking Co						
1901 Taylor Way	Tacoma	WA	98421	**800-423-8810**	253-627-1191	498
Bugcrowd Inc						
921 Front St 1st Fl	San Francisco	CA	94111	**888-361-9734**	650-260-8443	198
Buglisi Dance Theatre						
229 W 42nd St Ste 502	New York	NY	10036	**800-754-0797**	212-719-3301	572-1
BUG-O Systems Inc						
161 Hillpointe Dr	Canonsburg	PA	15317	**800-245-3186**	412-331-1776	809
Buhler Inc						
13105 12th Ave N	Plymouth	MN	55441	**800-722-7483**	763-847-9900	203
Buhler Versatile Inc						
1260 Clarence Ave	Winnipeg	MB	R3T1T2	**888-524-1003**	204-661-8711	275
Build-A-Bear Workshop Inc						
1954 Innerbelt Business Ctr Dr						
	Saint Louis	MO	63114	**888-560-2327**	314-423-8000	759
NYSE: BBW						
Builder Magazine						
1 Thomas Cir NW Ste 600	Washington	DC	20005	**800-325-6180**	202-452-0800	456-21
Builders General Supply Co						
15 Sycamore Ave	Little Silver	NJ	07739	**800-570-7227**		193-3
Builders Hardware & Supply Company Inc						
1516 15th Ave W	Seattle	WA	98119	**800-828-1437**	206-281-3700	351
Builders Redi-Mix Inc						
30701 W 10 Mile Rd Ste 500						
PO Box 2900	Farmington Hills	MI	48333	**888-988-4400**		184
Building Design & Construction Magazine						
3030 W Salt Creek Ln						
Ste 201	Arlington Heights	IL	60005	**888-811-3288**	847-391-1000	456-21
Building Material Dealers Assn (BMDA)						
1006 SE Grand Ave Ste 301	Portland	OR	97214	**888-960-6329**	503-208-3763	48-3
Building Owners & Managers Assn International (BOMA)						
1101 15th St NW Ste 800	Washington	DC	20005	**800-426-6292**	202-408-2662	48-17
Building Performance Institute Inc						
107 Hermes Rd Ste 210	Malta	NY	12020	**877-274-1274**	518-899-2727	196
Building Products Corp						
950 Freeburg Ave	Belleville	IL	62220	**800-233-1996**	618-233-4427	184
Building Products Plus						
12317 Almeda Rd	Houston	TX	77045	**800-460-8627**		816
Building Service Contractors Assn International (BSCAI)						
401 N Michigan Ave Ste 2200	Chicago	IL	60611	**800-368-3414**	312-321-5167	48-13
Building Service Inc (BSI)						
W222 N630 Cheaney Rd	Waukesha	WI	53186	**866-353-3600**	262-955-6400	393
Bulgaria						
Embassy						
1621 22nd St NW	Washington	DC	20008	**800-961-6836**	202-387-0174	259
Bulk Lift International Inc (BLI)						
1013 Tamarac Dr	Carpentersville	IL	60110	**800-879-2247**	847-428-6059	66
Bulk Transit Corp						
7177 Industrial Pkwy	Plain City	OH	43064	**800-345-2855**	614-873-4632	778
Bulkmatic Transport Co						
2001 N Cline Ave	Griffith	IN	46319	**800-535-8505**		778
Bulk-pack Inc						
1025 N Ninth St	Monroe	LA	71201	**800-498-4215**	318-387-3260	99
Bull Moose Tube Co						
1819 Clarkson Rd Ste 100	Chesterfield	MO	63017	**800-325-4467**	636-537-2600	489
Bull Wealth Management Group Inc						
4100 Yonge St Ste 612	Toronto	ON	M2P2B5	**866-623-2053**	416-223-2053	688
Bull, Housser & Tupper LLP						
900 Howe St Ste 900	Vancouver	BC	V6Z2M4	**866-687-6575**	604-687-6575	428
Bullard Abrasives Inc						
6 Carol Dr	Lincoln	RI	02865	**800-227-4469**	401-333-3000	1
Bullard Co						
1898 Safety Way	Cynthiana	KY	41031	**800-227-0423**	859-234-6611	575
Bullards Beach State Park						
PO Box 569	Bandon	OR	97411	**800-551-6949**	541-347-2209	564
Bulldog Bag Ltd						
13631 Vulcan Way	Richmond	BC	V6V1K4	**800-665-1944**	604-273-8021	600
Bulldog Hiway Express						
3390 Buffalo Ave	Charleston	SC	29418	**800-331-9515**	843-744-1651	448
Bulldog Solutions LLC						
7600 N Capital of Texas Hwy Bldg C						
Ste 250	Austin	TX	78731	**877-402-9199**		5
Bullen Cos						
1640 Delmar Dr PO Box 37	Folcroft	PA	19032	**800-444-8900**	610-534-8900	150
Bulletin, The						
1777 SW Chandler Ave	Bend	OR	97702	**800-503-3933**	541-382-1811	531-2
Bullfrog Films Inc						
372 Dautrich Rd	Reading	PA	19606	**800-543-3764**	610-779-8226	513
Bullhead Area Chamber of Commerce						
1251 Hwy 95	Bullhead City	AZ	86429	**800-987-7457**	928-754-4121	138
Bulloch & Bulloch Inc						
309 Cash Memorial Blvd	Forest Park	GA	30297	**800-339-8177**	404-762-5063	25
Bullock Creek Public Schools						
1420 S Badour Rd	Midland	MI	48640	**877-706-2508**	989-631-9022	683
Bullseye Glass Co						
3722 SE 21st Ave	Portland	OR	97202	**888-220-3002**	503-232-8887	330
Bulova Corp						
Empire State Bldg						
350 Fifth Ave	Woodside	NY	10118	**800-228-5682**	718-204-3300	152
Bumble Bee Seafoods Inc						
PO Box 85362	San Diego	CA	92186	**800-800-8572**	858-715-4000	297-13
Bunker Hill Community College						
Charlestown						
250 New Rutherford Ave	Boston	MA	02129	**877-218-8829**	617-228-2000	161
Bunnell Inc						
436 Lawndale Dr	Salt Lake City	UT	84115	**800-800-4358**	801-467-0800	475
Bunn-O-Matic Corp						
1400 Stevenson Dr	Springfield	IL	62703	**800-637-8606**	217-529-6601	36
Bunting Bearings Corp						
1001 Holland Pk Blvd	Holland	OH	43528	**888-286-8464**	419-866-7000	309
Bunting Magnetics Co						
500 S Spencer Ave	Newton	KS	67114	**800-835-2526**	316-284-2020	484
Burch Fabrics Group						
4200 Brockton Dr SE	Grand Rapids	MI	49512	**800-841-8111**	616-698-2800	593
Burchell Nursery Inc, The						
12000 Hwy 120	Oakdale	CA	95361	**800-828-8733**	209-845-8733	294
Burchfield Group Inc, The						
1295 Northland Dr Ste 350	St Paul	MN	55120	**800-778-1359**	651-389-5640	196
Burco Molding Inc						
15015 Herriman Blvd	Noblesville	IN	46060	**888-883-6656**	317-773-5699	607
Burd & Fletcher						
3000 W Geospace Dr	Independence	MO	64056	**800-821-2776**	816-257-0291	100
Bureau of Consular Affairs						
2201 C St NW SA-29	Washington	DC	20520	**888-407-4747**	202-501-4444	340-14
Office of Children's Issues						
SA-17 9th Fl	Washington	DC	20522	**888-407-4747**	202-501-4444	340-14
Passport Services						
1111 19th St NW Ste 500	Washington	DC	20524	**888-874-7793**	877-487-2778	340-14
Bureau of Engraving & Printing						
14th & C Sts SW	Washington	DC	20228	**877-874-4114**		340-16
Bureau of Indian Affairs Regional Offices (BIA)						
Alaska Region						
3601 C St Ste 1100	Anchorage	AK	99503	**800-645-8397**	907-271-1536	340-11
Bureau of Labor Statistics						
Consumer Price Index						
2 Massachusetts Ave NE	Washington	DC	20212	**800-877-8339**	202-691-5200	340-13
Mountain-Plains Information Office						
2300 Main St Ste 1190	Kansas City	MO	64108	**800-487-9004**	816-285-7000	340-13
New York-New Jersey Information Office						
201 Varick St Rm 808	New York	NY	10014	**800-877-8339**	646-264-3600	340-13
Southeast Information Office						
61 Forsyth St	Atlanta	GA	30303	**800-347-3764**	404-893-4222	340-13
National Wild Horse & Burro Program						
1849 C St NW Rm. 5665	Washington	DC	20240	**866-468-7826**	202-208-3801	340-11
Bureau of Land Management Regional Offices						
Eastern States Office						
7450 Boston Blvd	Springfield	VA	22153	**800-370-3936**	703-440-1600	340-11
Bureau of National Affairs Inc						
1801 S Bell St	Arlington	VA	22202	**800-372-1033**	703-341-3000	634-2
Bureau of the Public Debt						
PO Box 7015	Parkersburg	WV	26106	**800-722-2678**		340-16
TreasuryDirect						
PO Box 7015	Parkersburg	WV	26106	**800-722-2678**	304-480-7711	340-16
Burger & Brown Engineering Inc						
4500 E 142nd St	Grandview	MO	64030	**800-764-3518**	816-878-6675	453

Name / Address	City	State	ZIP	Toll-Free	Phone	Class
Burger King Corp 5505 Blue Lagoon Dr	Miami	FL	33126	**866-394-2493**	305-378-3000	668
Burger's Ozark Country Cured Hams Inc 32819 hwy 87	California	MO	65018	**800-203-4424**	573-796-3134	297-26
Burgerville USA 109 W 17th St	Vancouver	WA	98660	**888-827-8369**	360-694-1521	668
Burgess Industries Inc (BII) 7500 Boone Ave N Ste 111	Brooklyn Park	MN	55428	**800-233-2589**	763-553-7800	628
Burgess Pigment Company Inc 525 Beck Blvd PO Box 349	Sandersville	GA	31082	**800-841-8999**	478-552-2544	499
Burgett Floral Inc 868 Fuller NE	Grand Rapids	MI	49503	**800-404-2999**	616-456-1999	369
Burghardt Sporting Goods 14660 W Capitol Dr	Brookfield	WI	53005	**866-790-6606**	262-790-1170	709
Burgundy Asset Management Ltd Bay Wellington Tower Brookfield Pl 181 Bay St Ste 4510	Toronto	ON	M5J2T3	**888-480-1790**	416-869-3222	688
Burke & Herbert Bank & Trust Co 100 S Fairfax St	Alexandria	VA	22314	**877-440-0800**	703-751-7701	69
Burke Inc 1800 Merriam Ln *Sales	Kansas City	KS	66106	**800-255-4147***		476
Burke International Tours Inc PO Box 890	Newton	NC	28658	**800-476-3900**	828-465-3900	758
Burke Rehabilitation Hospital 785 Mamaroneck Ave	White Plains	NY	10605	**888-992-8753**	914-597-2500	374-6
Burke-Divide Electric Co-op Inc (BDEC) 9549 Hwy 5 W	Columbus	ND	58727	**800-472-2983**	701-939-6671	247
Burkhalter Travel Agency 6501 Mineral Pt Rd	Madison	WI	53705	**800-556-9286**	608-833-5200	769
Burkhart Dental Supply Co 2502 S 78th St *Cust Svc	Tacoma	WA	98409	**800-562-8176***	253-474-7761	474
Burkholder Paving 621 Martindale Rd	Ephrata	PA	17522	**866-839-3426**	717-354-1340	45
Burkina Faso Embassy 2005 Massachusetts Ave NW	Washington	DC	20008	**800-345-6541**	202-332-5577	259
Burklund Distributors Inc 2500 N Main St Ste 3	East Peoria	IL	61611	**800-322-2876**	309-694-1900	298-3
Burks Tractor Co Inc 3140 Kimberly Rd	Twin Falls	ID	83301	**800-247-7419**	208-733-5543	276
Burleigh County 514 E Thayer Ave PO Box 1055	Bismarck	ND	58502	**877-222-6682**	701-222-6690	338
Burlington Chamber of Commerce 414 Locust St Ste 201	Burlington	ON	L7S1T7	**888-635-8687**	905-639-0174	137
Burlington Coat Factory 1830 Rt 130 N	Burlington	NJ	08016	**855-355-2875**	609-387-7800	362
Burlington College 351 N Ave	Burlington	VT	05401	**800-862-9616**		167
Burlington Drug Co Inc 91 Catamount Dr	Milton	VT	05468	**800-338-8703**	802-893-5105	233
Burlington Free Press 100 Bank St	Burlington	VT	05401	**800-427-3124**	802-863-3441	531-2
Burlington Hawk Eye Co 800 S Main St PO Box 10	Burlington	IA	52601	**800-397-1708**	319-754-8461	634-8
Burlington Mall 75 Middlesex Tpke	Burlington	MA	01803	**877-746-6642**	781-272-8667	459
Burlington Northern & Santa Fe Railway (BNSF) 2650 Lou Menk Dr	Fort Worth	TX	76131	**800-795-2673**		646
Burlington Northern Santa Fe Corp (BNSF) 500 New Jersey Ave NW Ste 550	Washington	DC	20001	**800-964-9386**	202-347-8662	614
Burlington/Alamance County Convention & Visitors Bureau 200 S Main St PO Box 519	Burlington	NC	27216	**800-637-3804**	336-570-1444	208
Burlington/West Burlington Area Chamber of Commerce 610 N Fourth St Ste 200	Burlington	IA	52601	**800-827-4837**	319-752-6365	138
Burmax Co 28 Barretts Ave	Holtsville	NY	11742	**800-645-5118**		75
Burndy LLC 47 E Industrial Park Dr	Manchester	NH	03109	**800-346-4175**		813
Burnett Dairy Co-op 11631 SR-70	Grantsburg	WI	54840	**800-854-2716**	715-689-2468	297-5
Burnham & Flower Group Inc 315 S Kalamazoo Mall	Kalamazoo	MI	49007	**888-748-7966**	269-381-1173	390
Burns & McBride Inc 240 S DuPont Hwy	New Castle	DE	19720	**800-756-5110**	302-656-5110	317
Burns Bog Conservation Society 7953 120 St	Delta	BC	V4C6P6	**888-850-6264**	604-572-0373	136
Burns Burns Walsh & Walsh pa 704 Topeka Ave	Lyndon	KS	66451	**888-528-3186**	785-828-4418	428
Burns Controls Co 13735 Beta Rd	Dallas	TX	75244	**800-442-2010**	972-233-6712	358
Burns Engineering Inc 10201 Bren Rd E	Minnetonka	MN	55343	**800-328-3871**	952-935-4400	258
Burns Motor Freight Inc 500 Seneca Trl N	Marlinton	WV	24954	**800-598-5674**	304-799-6106	778
Burns Pest Elimination Inc 2620 W Grovers Ave	Phoenix	AZ	85053	**877-971-4782**	602-971-4782	576
Burns Printing Inc 6131 Industrial Heights Dr	Knoxville	TN	37909	**866-288-5618**	865-584-2265	626
Burrell Imaging 1311 Merrillville Rd	Crown Point	IN	46307	**800-348-8732**	219-663-3210	587
BurrellesLuce 30 B Vreeland Rd PO Box 674	Florham Park	NJ	07932	**800-631-1160**	973-992-6600	387
Burris Company Inc 331 E Eigth St	Greeley	CO	80631	**888-228-7747**	970-356-1670	543
Burris Logistics 501 SE Fifth St PO Box 219	Milford	DE	19963	**800-805-8135**	302-839-5157	801-2
Burrows Paper Corp 501 W Main St	Little Falls	NY	13365	**800-272-7122**	315-823-2300	556
Burrows Paper Corp Packaging Group 2000 Commerce Ctr Dr	Franklin	OH	45005	**800-732-1933**	937-746-1933	547
Burrtec Waste Industries Inc 9890 Cherry Ave	Fontana	CA	92335	**888-287-7832**	909-429-4200	802
Bursma Electronic Distributing Inc 2851 Buchanan Ave SW	Grand Rapids	MI	49548	**800-777-2604**	616-831-0080	37
Burstek 12801 Westlinks Dr Ste 101	Fort Myers	FL	33913	**800-709-2551**	239-495-5900	176
Burt County Public Power District 613 N 13th St	Tekamah	NE	68061	**888-835-1620**	402-374-2631	247
Burton & Mayer Inc W140 N9000 Lilly Rd	Menomonee Falls	WI	53051	**800-236-1770**	262-781-0770	626
Bus Andrews Truck Equipment Inc 2828 N E Ave	Springfield	MO	65803	**800-273-0733**	417-869-1541	56
Busch Gardens Williamsburg 1 Busch Gardens Blvd	Williamsburg	VA	23185	**800-343-7946**		32
Busch Vacuum Technics Inc 1740 Lionel Bertrand	Boisbriand	QC	J7H1N7	**800-363-6360**	450-435-6899	638
Buse Timber & Sales Inc 3812 28th Pl NE	Everett	WA	98201	**800-305-2577**	425-258-2577	681
Bush Industries Inc 1 Mason Dr	Jamestown	NY	14701	**800-950-4782**	716-665-2000	320-2
Bushnell Corp 9200 Cody St	Overland Park	KS	66214	**800-423-3537**	913-752-3400	543
Bushnell Ctr for the Performing Arts 166 Capitol Ave	Hartford	CT	06106	**888-824-2874**	860-987-6000	571
Bushwacker Inc 6710 N Catlin Ave	Portland	OR	97203	**800-234-8920**	503-283-4335	59
Bushwick Metals LLC 560 N Washington Ave	Bridgeport	CT	06604	**888-399-4070**		721
Business & Legal Reports Inc (BLR) 141 Mill Rock Rd E	Old Saybrook	CT	06475	**800-727-5257**	860-510-0100	634-9
Business Council of Alabama 2 N Jackson St Ste 501	Montgomery	AL	36101	**800-665-9647**	334-834-6000	139
Business Council of New York State Inc 152 Washington Ave	Albany	NY	12210	**800-358-1202**	518-465-7511	139
Business Direct Inc 5620 Old Bullard Rd Ste 128	Tyler	TX	75703	**888-580-7799**		7
Business Facilities Magazine 44 Apple St Ste 3	Tinton Falls	NJ	07724	**800-524-0337**	732-842-7433	456-5
Business Forms Management Assn (BFMA) 3800 Old Cheney Rd Ste 101-285	Lincoln	NE	68516	**888-367-3078**	402-216-0479	48-12
Business Furniture Corp 6102 Victory Way	Indianapolis	IN	46278	**800-774-5544**	317-216-1600	321
Business Inn 180 MacLaren St	Ottawa	ON	K2P0L3	**800-363-1777**	613-232-1121	379
Business Insurance Magazine 711 Third Ave	New York	NY	10017	**877-812-1587**	212-210-0100	456-5
Business Intelligence Advisor 37 Broadway Ste 1	Arlington	MA	02474	**800-964-5118**	781-648-8700	530-3
Business Journal, The 25 E Boardman St	Youngstown	OH	44501	**800-837-6397**	330-744-5023	456-5
Business News Network (BNN) 299 Queen St W	Toronto	ON	M5V2Z5	**855-326-6266**	416-384-6600	736
Business News Publishing Co 2401 W Big Beaver Rd Ste 700	Troy	MI	48084	**800-837-7370**	248-362-3700	634-9
Business Professionals of America 5454 Cleveland Ave	Columbus	OH	43231	**800-334-2007**	614-895-7277	48-5
Business Resource Group (BRG) 10440 N Central Expy Ste 1150	Dallas	TX	75231	**888-391-9166**	214-777-5100	196
Business Stationery LLC 4944 Commerce Pkwy	Cleveland	OH	44128	**800-234-9954**	216-514-1277	533
Business Technology Assn (BTA) 12411 Wornall Rd Ste 200	Kansas City	MO	64145	**800-325-7219**	816-941-3100	48-18
Buskirk Lumber Co 319 Oak St	Freeport	MI	49325	**800-860-9663**	616-765-5103	681
Busler Enterprises Inc 2601 N St Joseph Ave	Evansville	IN	47720	**800-457-3232**	812-424-7511	325
BUSPAC 700 13th St NW Ste 575	Washington	DC	20005	**800-283-2877**	202-842-1645	614
Busse/SJI Corp 124 N Columbus St	Randolph	WI	53956	**800-882-4995**		469
Bus-tech Inc 26 Crosby Dr	Bedford	MA	01710	**800-284-3172**		205
Busy Beaver Bldg Centers 2940 Library Rd	Pittsburgh	PA	15234	**800-732-0999**	412-882-6633	364
Busy Body Home Fitness 9990 Empire St	San Diego	CA	92126	**800-466-3348**		709
Butchart Gardens, The 800 Benvenuto Ave	Brentwood Bay	BC	V8M1J8	**866-652-4422**	250-652-4422	96
Butcher Distributors Inc 101 Boyce Rd	Broussard	LA	70518	**800-960-0008**	337-837-2088	611
Butler Animal Health Supply LLC 400 Metro Pl N *PR	Dublin	OH	43017	**888-691-2724***	614-761-9095	474
Butler Area School District 110 Campus Ln	Butler	PA	16001	**888-800-5583**	724-287-8720	683
Butler County 205 W Central Ave	El Dorado	KS	67042	**800-822-6104**	316-322-4300	338
Butler County Community College 107 College Dr	Butler	PA	16002	**888-826-2829**	724-287-8711	161
Butler County Rural Electric Co-op 521 N Main PO Box 98	Allison	IA	50602	**888-267-2726**	319-267-2726	247
Butler County Rural Public Power District 1331 N Fourth St	David City	NE	68632	**800-230-0569**	402-367-3081	247
Butler Eagle 114 W Diamond St	Butler	PA	16001	**800-842-8098**	724-282-8000	531-2
Butler Home Products LLC 237 Cedar Hill St	Marlborough	MA	01752	**888-318-8521**	508-597-8000	507
Butler Motor Transit Company Inc 210 S Monroe St PO Box 1602	Butler	PA	16003	**800-222-8750**	724-282-1000	106
Butler National Corp 19920 W 161st St *OTC: BUKS*	Olathe	KS	66062	**800-690-6903**	913-780-9595	528
Butler Rural Electric Co-op Assn Inc 216 S Vine St PO Box 1242	El Dorado	KS	67042	**800-464-0060**	316-321-9600	247
Butler Rural Electric Co-op Inc (BREC) 3888 Still-Beckett Rd	Oxford	OH	45056	**800-255-2732**	513-867-4400	247
Butler Supply Inc 965 Horan Dr	Fenton	MO	63026	**800-850-9949**	636-349-9000	248
Butler Technologies Inc 231 W Wayne St	Butler	PA	16001	**800-494-6656**	724-283-6656	176
Butler Transport Inc 347 N James St	Kansas City	KS	66118	**800-345-8158**	913-321-0047	778

Name / Address	City	State	Zip	Toll-Free	Phone	Class
Butler University 4600 Sunset Ave	Indianapolis	IN	46208	800-368-6852	317-940-8100	167
Butler-Dearden Paper Service Inc PO Box 1069	Boylston	MA	01505	800-634-7070	508-869-9000	558
Butte College 3536 Butte Campus Dr *Hum Res	Oroville	CA	95965	800-933-8322*	530-895-2511	161
Butte Electric Co-op 109 Dartmouth Ave	Newell	SD	57760	800-928-8839	605-456-2494	247
Butterfly House - Faust Park, The 15193 Olive Blvd	Chesterfield	MO	63017	800-642-8842	636-530-0076	49-4
Butters-Fetting Company Inc 1669 S First St	Milwaukee	WI	53204	800-361-6154	414-645-1535	191-10
Butte-Silver Bow Chamber of Commerce 1000 George St	Butte	MT	59701	800-735-6814	406-723-3177	138
Butts Foods Inc 2596 Bransford Ave	Nashville	TN	37204	800-962-8570	731-423-3456	298-10
Buurma Farms Inc 3909 Kok Rd	Willard	OH	44890	888-428-8762	419-935-6411	10-9
Buxton Co 245 Cadwell Dr	Springfield	MA	01104	800-426-3638	413-734-5900	430
BUYandHOLD.com Securities Corp *c/o Freedom Investments, Inc* 375 Raritan Ctr Pkwy Ste D	Edison	NJ	08837	800-646-8212		688
Buyatab Online Inc 204 - 576 Seymour St	Vancouver	BC	V6B3K1	888-267-0447		226
BVI (Better Vision Institute, The) *Vision Council, The* 225 Reinekers Ln Ste 700	Alexandria	VA	22314	800-372-3937	703-548-4560	47-17
BW Container Systems 1305 Lakeview Dr	Romeoville	IL	60446	800-527-0494	630-759-6800	209
BWAY Corp 8607 Roberts Dr Ste 250	Atlanta	GA	30350	800-527-2267	770-645-4800	123
BWI (Baltimore/Washington International Thurgood Marshall Airport) PO Box 8766	Baltimore	MD	21240	800-435-9294	410-859-7111	27
bx.com Inc 1 W Exchange St	Providence	RI	02903	800-262-8138	401-274-8991	807
Byard F Brogan Inc PO Box 0369	Glenside	PA	19038	800-232-7642	215-885-3550	409
Bybee Stone Company Inc 6293 N Matthews Dr	Ellettsville	IN	47429	800-457-4530	812-876-2215	722
Byer California 66 Potrero Ave	San Francisco	CA	94103	844-628-4498	415-626-7844	154-4
Byerly Ford 4041 Dixie Hwy	Louisville	KY	40216	888-436-0819	502-448-1661	56
Byline Bank 3639 N Broadway St	Chicago	IL	60613	866-957-7700	773-244-7000	69
Byram Healthcare Centers Inc 120 Bloomingdale Rd	White Plains	NY	10605	800-354-4054	914-286-2000	474
Byram Laboratories Inc 1 Columbia Rd	Branchburg	NJ	08876	800-766-1212		248
Byrd Cookie Company Inc 6700 Waters Ave	Savannah	GA	31406	800-291-2973	912-355-1716	345
Bytespeed LLC 3131 24th Ave S	Moorhead	MN	56560	877-553-0777	218-227-0445	175-1

C

Name / Address	City	State	Zip	Toll-Free	Phone	Class
C & A Industries Inc 13609 California St	Omaha	NE	68154	800-574-9829	402-891-0009	719
C & D Technologies Inc 1400 Union Meeting Rd PO Box 3053	Blue Bell	PA	19422	800-543-8630	215-619-2700	73
C & F Enterprises Inc 819 Bluecrab Rd	Newport News	VA	23606	888-889-9868	757-310-6100	361
C & F Financial Corp 802 Main St PO Box 391 *NASDAQ: CFFI*	West Point	VA	23181	800-583-3863	804-843-4584	360-2
C & H Distributors LLC 770 S 70th St *Sales	Milwaukee	WI	53214	800-558-9966*	414-443-1700	385
C & H International 4751 Wilshire Blvd Ste 201	Los Angeles	CA	90010	800-833-8888	323-933-2288	16
C & H Sugar Co Inc 2300 Contra Costa Blvd Ste 600	Pleasant Hill	CA	94523	800-773-1803		297-38
C & J Jewelry Company Inc 100 Dupont Dr	Providence	RI	02907	888-527-4268	401-944-2200	408
C & L Supply Co PO Box 578	Vinita	OK	74301	800-256-6411		37
C & M Conveyor 4598 SR 37	Mitchell	IN	47446	800-551-3195	812-849-5647	209
C & R Mechanical 12825 Pennridge Dr	Bridgeton	MO	63044	800-524-3828	314-739-1800	191-10
C & R Research Services Inc 500 N Michigan Ave Ste 1200	Chicago	IL	60611	800-543-9393	312-828-9200	465
C & S Companies (CSCOS) 499 Col Eileen Collins Blvd	Syracuse	NY	13212	877-277-6583	315-455-2000	263
C Cowles & Co Inc 83 Water St	New Haven	CT	06511	800-624-4483	203-865-3117	488
C Cretors & Co 3243 N California Ave	Chicago	IL	60618	800-228-1885	773-588-1690	299
C D D 11603 Crosswinds Way Ste 100	San Antonio	TX	78233	888-858-8663	210-590-3033	415
C H Garmong & Son Inc 3050 Poplar St	Terre Haute	IN	47803	800-894-2962	812-234-3714	609
C m Buck & Associates Inc 6850 Guion Rd	Indianapolis	IN	46268	800-382-3961	317-293-5704	393
C M S North America 4095 Korona Ct Se	Caledonia	MI	49316	800-931-6083	616-698-9970	358
C M School Supply Inc 940 N Central Ave	Upland	CA	91786	800-464-6681	909-982-9695	534
C Myers Corp 8222 S 48th St Ste 275	Phoenix	AZ	85044	800-238-7475	602-840-0606	196
C P H & Associates 711 S Dearborn St Unit 205	Chicago	IL	60605	800-875-1911	312-987-9823	390
C Spire 1018 Highland Colony Pkwy Ste 300	Ridgeland	MS	39157	855-277-4735		387
C W I Inc 650 Three Springs Raod	Bowling Green	KY	42104	888-626-7576		709
C'mon Inn Grand Forks 3051 32nd Ave S	Grand Forks	ND	58201	800-255-2323	701-775-3320	379
C. L. Smith Co 1311 S 39th St	Saint Louis	MO	63110	800-264-1202	314-771-1202	607
C.a. Murren & Sons Co Inc 2275 Loganville Hwy	Grayson	GA	30017	866-912-8906	770-682-2940	188
C2F Inc 6600 SW 111th Ave	Beaverton	OR	97008	800-544-8825	503-643-9050	94
CA (Cocaine Anonymous World Services Inc) PO Box 492000	Los Angeles	CA	90049	800-347-8998	310-559-5833	47-21
CA Inc 1 CA Plz *NASDAQ: CA*	Islandia	NY	11749	800-225-5224	631-342-6000	180-1
Ca Lindman Inc 10401 Guilford Rd	Jessup	MD	20794	877-737-8675	301-470-4700	188
CAA (Canadian Automobile Assn) 2151 Thurston Dr	Ottawa	ON	K1G6C9	800-267-8713	613-820-1890	47-23
CAA (Council on Aviation Accreditation) *Aviation Accreditation Board International* 3410 Skyway Dr	Auburn	AL	36830	800-767-4767	334-844-2431	47-1
CAA Central Ontario 60 Commerce Vly Dr E	Thornhill	ON	L3T7P9	800-268-3750	905-771-3000	52
CAA Manitoba 870 Empress St	Winnipeg	MB	R3C2Z3	800-222-4357	204-262-6166	52
CAA Maritimes Ltd 378 Westmorland Rd	Saint John	NB	E2J2G4	800-471-1611	506-634-1400	52
Caa Niagara 155 Main St E	Grimsby	ON	L3M1P2	800-263-7272	905-945-5555	773
CAA North & East Ontario PO Box 8350	Ottawa	ON	K1G3T2	800-267-8713	613-820-1890	52
CAA Quebec 444 Bouvier St	Quebec	QC	G2J1E3	800-222-4357	418-624-8222	52
CAA Stoney Creek 163 Centennial Pkwy N	Hamilton	ON	L8E1H8	800-992-8143	905-664-8000	52
CAAHEP (Commission on Accreditation of Allied Health Education Programs) 1361 Pk St	Clearwater	FL	33756	800-228-2262	727-210-2350	47-1
Cabarrus County Convention & Visitors Bureau 3003 Dale Earnhardt Blvd	Kannapolis	NC	28083	800-848-3740	704-782-4340	208
Cabela's Inc 1 Cabela Dr *NYSE: CAB*	Sidney	NE	69160	800-237-8888	308-254-5505	709
Cabela's Outdoor Adventures Inc 610 Glover Rd Ste A	Sidney	NE	69162	800-346-8747		709
Cabell-Huntington Convention & Visitors Bureau PO Box 347	Huntington	WV	25708	800-635-6329	304-525-7333	208
Caber Sure Fit Inc 25A E Pearce St Unit 1	Richmond Hill	ON	L4B2M9	800-520-3152	905-886-5849	361
Cabinet Tronix LLC 290 Trousdale Dr Ste A	Chula Vista	CA	91910	866-876-6199		817
Cabinetry By Karman Inc 6000 Stratler St	Salt Lake City	UT	84107	800-255-3581	801-281-6400	114
CABLCF (Creditors Adjustment Bureau-LC Financial) 14226 Ventura Blvd	Sherman Oaks	CA	91423	800-800-4523	818-990-4800	159
Cable Connection, The 52 Heppner Dr	Carson City	NV	89706	800-851-2961	775-885-1443	115
Cable Markers Company Inc 13805-C Alton Pkwy	Irvine	CA	92618	800-746-7655		466
Cable One Inc 210 E Earll Drive	Phoenix	AZ	85012	877-692-2253	602-364-6000	115
Cable Public Affairs Ch (CPAC) PO Box 81099	Ottawa	ON	K1P1B1	877-287-2722		736
CableAmerica Corp 7822 E Gray Rd	Scottsdale	AZ	85260	866-871-4492		115
Cable-Dahmer Chevrolet Inc 1834 S Noland Rd	Independence	MO	64055	888-738-5260	816-521-7508	56
Cables to Go Inc 3599 Dayton Pk Dr	Dayton	OH	45414	800-826-7904	937-224-8646	812
Cabot Corp 2 Seaport Ln Ste 1300 *NYSE: CBT*	Boston	MA	02210	800-322-1236	617-345-0100	144
Cabot Creamery 193 Home Farm Way	Waitsfield	VT	05673	888-792-2268	802-229-9361	297-5
Cabot Heritage Corp 176 N St PO Box 2049	Salem	MA	01970	800-326-8826	978-745-5532	634-9
Cabot Market Letter 176 N St PO Box 2049 *Orders	Salem	MA	01970	800-326-8826*	978-745-5532	530-9
Cabot Microelectronics Corp 870 N Commons Dr *NASDAQ: CCMP*	Aurora	IL	60504	800-811-2756	630-375-6631	144
Cabot Oil & Gas Corp 840 Gessner Rd Ste 1200 *NYSE: COG*	Houston	TX	77024	800-434-3985	281-848-2799	785
Cabot Specialty Fluids Inc Waterway Plaza Two 10001 Woodlock Forest Dr Ste 275	The Woodlands	TX	77380	800-322-1236	281-298-9955	144
Cabrillo College 6500 Soquel Dr	Aptos	CA	95003	888-624-1139	831-479-6100	161
Cabrillo National Monument 1800 Cabrillo Memorial Dr	San Diego	CA	92106	800-236-7916	619-557-5450	563
Cabrini College 610 King of Prussia Rd	Radnor	PA	19087	800-848-1003	610-902-8552	167
CAC (Coating & Adhesive Corp) 1901 Popular St PO Box 1080	Leland	NC	28451	800-410-2999	910-371-3184	549
Cache County School District 2063 N 1200 E	North Logan	UT	84341	888-837-6437	435-752-3925	683
Cache Valley Electric Inc 875 N 1000 W	Logan	UT	84321	888-558-0600	435-752-6405	191-4

Name / Address	City	State	ZIP	Toll-Free	Phone	Class
CACI International Inc						
1100 N Glebe Rd	Arlington	VA	22201	**866-606-3471**	703-841-7800	182
NYSE: CACI						
Cacique Inc						
14923 Procter Ave	La Puente	CA	91746	**800-521-6987**	626-961-3399	297-5
Cactus Feeders Inc						
2209 W Seventh Ave	Amarillo	TX	79106	**877-698-7355**	806-373-2333	10-1
Cactus Flower Florists						
10822 N Scottsdale Rd	Scottsdale	AZ	85254	**800-922-2887**	480-483-9200	294
CACU (Community America Credit Union)						
9777 Ridge Dr	Lenexa	KS	66219	**800-892-7957**	913-905-7000	221
CAD & Graphic Supply Inc						
2410 Luna Rd Ste 114	Carrollton	TX	75006	**866-409-8211**	972-409-7333	177
Cad Store Inc, The						
15353 N 91st Ave	Peoria	AZ	85381	**800-576-6789**	623-931-7936	556
Cad Technology Center						
1000 Boone Ave N Ste 200	Minneapolis	MN	55427	**866-941-1181**	952-941-1181	182
CAD/CAM Consulting Services Inc (CCCS)						
996 Lawrence Dr Ste 101	Newbury Park	CA	91320	**888-375-7676**	805-375-7676	176
Cadbury Retirement Community						
2150 Rt 38	Cherry Hill	NJ	08002	**800-422-3287**	856-667-4550	670
CADCA (CPA Auto Dealer Consultants Assn)						
1801 W End Ave Ste 800	Nashville	TN	37203	**800-231-2524**	615-373-9880	48-1
CADE (Commission on Accreditation for Dietetics Education)						
120 S Riverside Plz Ste 2000	Chicago	IL	60606	**800-877-1600**	312-899-0040	47-1
Cade & Assoc Adv Inc						
1645 Metropolitan Blvd	Tallahassee	FL	32308	**800-715-2233**	850-385-0300	4
Cadeau Express Inc						
3494 E Sunset Rd	Las Vegas	NV	89120	**800-240-0301**	702-433-1333	240
Cadence Design Systems Inc						
2655 Seely Ave	San Jose	CA	95134	**800-746-6223***	408-943-1234	180-5
NASDAQ: CDNS ■ *Cust Svc						
Cadet Mfg Company Inc						
2500 W Fourth Plain Blvd	Vancouver	WA	98660	**800-442-2338**	360-693-2505	36
Cadex Electronics Inc						
22000 Fraserwood Way	Richmond	BC	V6W1J6	**800-565-5228**	604-231-7777	248
Cadillac Area Visitors Bureau						
201 N Mitchell St	Cadillac	MI	49601	**800-225-2537**	231-775-0657	208
Cadillac Coffee Co						
194 E Maple Rd	Troy	MI	48083	**800-438-6900**	248-545-2266	297-7
Cadmium Cd LLC						
19 Newport Dr Ste 101	Forest Hill	MD	21050	**877-426-6323**	410-638-9239	197
Cadre Computer Resources Co						
201 E Fifth St Ste 1800	Cincinnati	OH	45202	**866-762-6700**	513-762-7350	182
Cadwell Laboratories Inc						
909 N Kellogg St	Kennewick	WA	99336	**800-245-3001**	509-735-6481	475
CAE Inc						
8585 Cote de Liesse	Saint Laurent	QC	H4T1G6	**866-999-6223**	514-341-6780	701
NYSE: CAE						
CAEP (Canadian Assn of Emergency Physicians)						
1785 Alta Vista Dr Ste 104	Ottawa	ON	K1G3Y6	**800-463-1158**	613-523-3343	48-8
Caesar's Palace						
3570 Las Vegas Blvd S						
Caesar's Palace	Las Vegas	NV	89109	**800-634-6001**	702-731-7110	669
Caesars Atlantic City Hotel Casino						
2100 Pacific Ave	Atlantic City	NJ	08401	**800-522-4700**	609-348-4411	667
Caesars Head State Park						
8155 Geer Hwy	Cleveland	SC	29635	**866-345-7275**	864-836-6115	564
Caesars License Company LLC						
377 Riverside Dr E	Windsor	ON	N9A7H7	**800-991-7777**	519-258-7878	132
Cafe Fina						
47 Fisherman's Wharf Ste 1	Monterey	CA	93940	**800-843-3462**	831-372-5200	669
Cafe Modern						
3200 Darnell St	Fort Worth	TX	76107	**866-824-5566**	817-738-9215	669
Cafe, The						
3434 Peachtree Rd NE						
Ritz-Carlton Buckhead	Atlanta	GA	30326	**800-241-3333**	404-237-2700	669
Cafepress.com Inc						
1850 Gateway Dr Ste 300	Foster City	CA	94404	**877-809-1659**	650-655-3120	206
CAGW (Citizens Against Government Waste)						
1301 Pennsylvania Ave NW						
Ste 1075	Washington	DC	20004	**800-435-7352**	202-467-5300	47-7
Cagwin & Dorward Inc						
1565 S Novato Blvd Ste B	Novato	CA	94947	**800-891-7710**	415-892-7710	422
CAI (Community Assns Institute)						
6402 Arlington Blvd						
Ste 500	Falls Church	VA	22042	**888-224-4321**	703-970-9220	47-7
CAI (Chrysler Aviation Inc)						
7120 Hayvenhurst Ave Ste 309	Van Nuys	CA	91406	**800-995-0825**	818-989-7900	13
CAI (Computer Aid Inc)						
1390 Ridgeview Dr	Allentown	PA	18104	**877-432-7228**	610-530-5000	179
Cailor Fleming & Assoc Inc						
4610 Market St	Youngstown	OH	44512	**800-796-8495**	330-782-8068	390
Cain Millwork Inc						
1 Cain Pkwy	Rochelle	IL	61068	**800-417-3511**	815-561-9700	498
Cain's Foods Inc						
114 E Main St	Ayer	MA	01432	**800-225-0601**	978-772-0300	297-19
Cajun Constructors Inc						
15635 Airline Hwy	Baton Rouge	LA	70817	**877-401-5911**	225-753-5857	190-7
Cal Farley's Boys Ranch						
600 W 11th St PO Box 1890	Amarillo	TX	79174	**800-687-3722**	806-372-2341	47-6
Cal Spas Inc						
1462 E Ninth St	Pomona	CA	91766	**800-225-7727**	909-623-8781	375
CALAMCO (California Ammonia Co)						
1776 W March Ln Ste 420	Stockton	CA	95207	**800-624-4200**	209-982-1000	282
Calamos Asset Management Inc						
2020 Calamos Ct	Naperville	IL	60563	**800-582-6959**	630-245-7200	401
NASDAQ: CLMS						
Cal-ark Inc						
PO Box 990	Mabelvale	AR	72103	**888-422-5275**	501-455-3399	778
Cal-a-Vie Spa						
29402 Spa Havens Way	Vista	CA	92084	**866-772-4283**	760-945-2055	704
Calavo Growers Inc						
1141-A Cummings Rd	Santa Paula	CA	93060	**800-654-8758**	805-525-1245	316-4
NASDAQ: CVGW						
Calbag Metals Co						
2495 NW Nicolai St	Portland	OR	97210	**800-398-3441**	503-226-3441	684
Cal-Coast Dairy Systems Inc						
424 S Tegner Rd	Turlock	CA	95380	**800-732-6826***	209-634-9026	275
*Cust Svc						
Calculated Industries Inc						
4840 Hytech Dr	Carson City	NV	89706	**800-854-8075**	775-885-4900	117
Calder Casino & Race Course						
21001 NW 27th Ave	Miami	FL	33056	**800-522-4700**	305-625-1311	639
Caldwell Chamber of Commerce						
704 Blaine St	Caldwell	ID	83605	**877-375-7382**	208-459-7493	138
Caldwell Securities Ltd						
150 King St W Ste 1710	Toronto	ON	M5H1J9	**800-387-0859**	416-862-7755	688
Caldwell Trust Co						
1400 Ctr Rd Ste Two	Venice	FL	34292	**800-338-9476**	941-493-3600	401
Caldwell University						
120 Bloomfield Ave	Caldwell	NJ	07006	**888-864-9516***	973-618-3500	167
*Admissions						
CALEA (Commission on Accreditation for Law Enforcement Agencies)						
13575 Heathcote Blvd						
Ste 320	Gainesville	VA	20155	**877-789-6904**	703-352-4225	48-7
Calea Ltd						
2785 Skymark Ave Unit 2	Mississauga	ON	L4W4Y3	**888-909-3299**	905-238-1234	363
Caledon Laboratories Ltd						
40 Armstrong Ave	Georgetown	ON	L7G4R9	**877-225-3366**	905-877-0101	228
Caledon State Park						
11617 Caledon Rd	King George	VA	22485	**800-933-7275**	540-663-3861	564
Caledonia Haulers LLC						
420 W Lincoln St PO Box 31	Caledonia	MN	55921	**800-325-4728**	507-725-9000	467
Calex Express Inc						
58 Pittston Ave	Pittston	PA	18640	**800-292-2539**	570-603-0180	778
CALEX Manufacturing Co						
2401 Stanwell Dr	Concord	CA	94520	**800-542-3355**	925-687-4411	517
Calfrac Well Services Ltd						
411 8 Ave SW	Calgary	AB	T2P1E3	**866-770-3722**	403-266-6000	538
Calgary Economic Development						
731 First St SE	Calgary	AB	T2G2G9	**888-222-5855**	403-221-7831	342
Calgary Exhibition & Stampede Ltd						
1410 Olympic Way S E	Calgary	AB	T2G2W1	**888-883-3828**	403-261-0101	639
Calgary Herald						
215-16th St SE						
PO Box 2400 Stn M	Calgary	AB	T2E7P5	**800-372-9219**	403-235-7100	531-1
Calgary International Airport						
2000 Airport Rd NE	Calgary	AB	T2E6W5	**877-254-7427**	403-735-1200	27
Calgary Laboratory Services						
3535 Research Rd NW	Calgary	AB	T2L2K8	**800-661-3450**	403-770-3500	415
Calgary Sun						
2615 12th St NE	Calgary	AB	T2E7W9	**877-624-1463**	403-410-1010	531-1
Calgary Zoo Botanical Garden & Prehistoric Park						
1300 Zoo Rd NE	Calgary	AB	T2E7V6	**800-588-9993**	403-232-9300	821
Calgon Carbon Corp						
3000 GSK Dr	Moon Township	PA	15108	**800-422-7266***	412-787-6700	142
NYSE: CCC ■ *Cust Svc						
Calhoun Community College						
PO Box 2216	Decatur	AL	35609	**800-626-3628**	256-306-2500	161
Huntsville						
102B Wynn Dr	Huntsville	AL	35805	**800-626-3628**	256-890-4701	161
Redstone Arsenal						
6250 Hwy 31 N	Tanner	AL	35671	**800-626-3628**	256-306-2500	161
Calhoun County Electric Co-op Assn						
1015 Tonawanda St						
PO Box 312	Rockwell City	IA	50579	**800-821-4879**	712-297-7112	247
Calhoun Falls State Recreation Area						
46 Maintenance Shop Rd	Calhoun Falls	SC	29628	**866-345-7275**	864-447-8267	564
Calian Technology Ltd						
340 Legget Dr Ste 101	Ottawa	ON	K2K1Y6	**877-225-4264**	613-599-8600	719
TSE: CTY						
Calibre Systems Inc						
6354 Walker Ln						
Ste 300 Metro Pk	Alexandria	VA	22310	**888-225-4273**	703-797-8500	182
Calico Building Services Inc						
15550-C Rockfield Blvd	Irvine	CA	92618	**800-576-7313**		103
Califone International Inc						
9135 Alabama Ave Ste B	Chatsworth	CA	91311	**800-722-0500**	818-407-2400	255
California						
Arts Council						
1300 'I' St Ste 930	Sacramento	CA	95814	**800-201-6201**	916-322-6555	339-5
Child Support Services Dept						
PO Box 419064	Sacramento	CA	95741	**866-901-3212**	916-464-5000	339-5
Corporations Dept						
1515 K St Ste 200	Sacramento	CA	95814	**866-275-2677**	916-445-7205	339-5
Corrections Dept						
PO Box 942883	Sacramento	CA	94283	**877-256-6877**		339-5
Fish & Game Dept						
1416 Ninth St 12th Fl	Sacramento	CA	95814	**888-334-2258**	916-445-0411	339-5
Health Care Services Dept						
PO Box 997413 MS 8502	Sacramento	CA	95899	**800-735-2929**		339-5
Housing Finance Agency						
500 Capitol Mall Ste 1400	Sacramento	CA	95814	**877-922-5432**	916-322-3991	339-5
Parks & Recreation Dept						
PO Box 942896	Sacramento	CA	94296	**800-777-0369**	916-653-6995	339-5
Public Utilities Commission						
505 Van Ness Ave	San Francisco	CA	94102	**800-848-5580**	415-703-2782	339-5
Teacher Credentialing Commission						
1900 Capitol Ave	Sacramento	CA	95814	**888-921-2682**	916-445-7254	339-5
Veterans Affairs Dept						
1227 'O' St	Sacramento	CA	95814	**800-221-8998**	916-653-2158	339-5
Victim Compensation Program						
PO Box 3036	Sacramento	CA	95812	**800-777-9229**		339-5
California Ammonia Co (CALAMCO)						
1776 W March Ln Ste 420	Stockton	CA	95207	**800-624-4200**	209-982-1000	282
California Analytical Instruments Inc						
1312 W Grove Ave	Orange	CA	92865	**800-959-0949**	714-974-5560	419
California Bank & Trust						
11622 El Camino Real Ste 200	San Diego	CA	92130	**800-400-6080**	858-793-7400	69
California Baptist University						
8432 Magnolia Ave	Riverside	CA	92504	**877-228-8866**	951-689-5771	167
California Cartage Company Inc						
2931 Redondo Ave	Long Beach	CA	90806	**888-537-1432**		778
California Casualty Insurance Group						
1900 Alameda De Las Pulgas	San Mateo	CA	94403	**866-680-5143**	650-574-4000	391-4

Name / Address	City	State	ZIP	Toll-Free	Phone	Class
California Closet Co 610A DuBois St *General	San Rafael	CA	94901	888-336-9707*	415-256-8500	191-11
California College of the Arts *Oakland* 5212 Broadway	Oakland	CA	94618	800-447-1278	510-594-3600	163
San Francisco 1111 Eigth St	San Francisco	CA	94107	800-447-1278	415-703-9500	163
California Cryobank Inc 11915 La Grange Ave	Los Angeles	CA	90025	866-927-9622	310-443-5244	544
California Ctr for the Arts 340 N Escondido Blvd	Escondido	CA	92025	800-988-4253	760-839-4138	571
California Dental Assn 1201 K St	Sacramento	CA	95853	800-736-7071	916-443-0505	229
California Fair Political Practices Commission 428 J St Ste 620	Sacramento	CA	95814	866-275-3772	916-322-5660	267
California Flexrake Corp 9620 Gidley St	Temple City	CA	91780	800-266-4200	626-443-4026	429
California Gasket & Rubber Corp 533 W Collins Ave	Orange	CA	92867	800-635-7084	310-323-4250	327
California Grill 11999 Harbor Blvd Hyatt Regency Orange County	Garden Grove	CA	92840	800-233-1234	714-740-6047	669
California Hotel & Casino 12 E Ogden Ave	Las Vegas	NV	89101	800-634-6505	702-385-1222	132
California Institute of Technology 1200 E California Blvd	Pasadena	CA	91125	800-568-8324	626-395-6811	167
California Institute of the Arts 24700 McBean Pkwy	Valencia	CA	91355	800-545-2787	661-255-1050	163
California ISO 151 Blue Ravine Rd PO Box 639014	Folsom	CA	95630	800-220-4907	916-351-4400	785
California Lutheran University 60 W Olsen Rd	Thousand Oaks	CA	91360	877-258-3678	805-493-3135	167
California Lutheran University Pearson Library 60 W Olsen Rd	Thousand Oaks	CA	91360	877-258-3678	805-493-3250	434-6
California Maritime Academy 200 Maritime Academy Dr	Vallejo	CA	94590	800-561-1945	707-654-1330	167
California Market Ctr 110 E Ninth St	Los Angeles	CA	90079	800-225-6278	213-630-3600	207
California Neon Products Inc 4530 Mission Gorge Pl	San Diego	CA	92120	800-822-6366	619-283-2191	699
California Office Furniture 1724 Tenth St	Sacramento	CA	95811	877-442-6959	916-442-6959	321
California Pacific Medical Ctr Research Institute 475 Brannan St Ste 220	San Francisco	CA	94107	855-354-2778	415-600-1600	666
California Panel & Veneer Co 14055 Artesia Blvd	Cerritos	CA	90703	800-451-1745	562-926-5834	612
California Parlor Car Tours 500 Sutter St Ste 401	San Francisco	CA	94102	800-227-4250	415-474-7500	758
California Pharmacists Assn (CPhA) 4030 Lennane Dr	Sacramento	CA	95834	866-365-7472	916-779-1400	584
California Polytechnic State University 1 Grand Ave	San Luis Obispo	CA	93407	800-424-6723	805-756-1111	167
California Portland Cement Co 2025 E Financial Way *Cust Svc	Glendora	CA	91741	800-272-1891*	626-852-6200	134
California Products Corp 150 Dascomb Rd	Andover	MA	01810	800-225-1141	978-623-9980	549
California Public Radio 4100 Vachell Ln	San Luis Obispo	CA	93401	800-549-8855	805-549-8855	629
California Real Estate Magazine 525 S Virgil Ave	Los Angeles	CA	90020	888-811-5281	213-739-8200	456-5
California Saw & Knife Works 721 Brannan St	San Francisco	CA	94103	888-729-6533	415-861-0644	680
California State Archives 1020 'O' St	Sacramento	CA	95814	800-633-5155	916-653-7715	519
California State Automobile Assn 150 Van Ness Ave *Cust Svc	San Francisco	CA	94102	800-922-8228*		52
California State Library 900 N St	Sacramento	CA	95814	800-952-5666	916-654-0261	434-5
California State Railroad Museum 125 "I" St 111 'I' St	Sacramento	CA	95814	866-240-4655	916-323-9280	564
California State University *Chico* CSU Chico *Admissions	Chico	CA	95929	800-542-4426*	530-898-6321	167
Dominguez Hills 1000 E Victoria St	Carson	CA	90747	888-545-6512	310-243-3300	167
East Bay 25800 Carlos Bee Blvd	Hayward	CA	94542	877-829-5500	510-885-3000	167
Fresno 5241 N Maple Ave	Fresno	CA	93740	800-700-2320	559-278-4240	167
Fullerton 800 N State College Blvd	Fullerton	CA	92834	888-433-9406	714-278-2011	167
Long Beach 1250 Bellflower Blvd	Long Beach	CA	90840	800-663-1144	562-985-4111	167
Northridge 18111 Nordhoff St	Northridge	CA	91330	800-399-4529	818-677-1200	167
San Bernardino 5500 University Pkwy	San Bernardino	CA	92407	866-275-3772	909-537-5188	167
San Marcos 333 S Twin Oaks Valley Rd	San Marcos	CA	92096	888-225-5427	760-750-4000	167
Stanislaus 1 University Cir	Turlock	CA	95382	800-235-9292	209-667-3152	167
California Steel & Tube 16049 Stephens St	City of Industry	CA	91745	800-338-8823	626-968-5511	489
California Student Aid Commission PO Box 419027	Rancho Cordova	CA	95741	888-224-7268	916-526-8999	723
California Theatre of Performing Arts 562 W Fourth St	San Bernardino	CA	92401	800-745-3000	909-885-5152	571
California University of Pennsylvania 250 University Ave	California	PA	15419	888-412-0479	724-938-4000	167
California Water Service Group 1720 N First St *NYSE: CWT*	San Jose	CA	95112	800-750-8200	408-367-8200	785
California Western School of Law 225 Cedar St	San Diego	CA	92101	800-255-4252	619-239-0391	168-1
Caliper Life Sciences Inc 68 Elm St	Hopkinton	MA	01748	800-762-4000	508-435-9500	419
Calise & Sons Bakery Inc 2 Quality Dr	Lincoln	RI	02865	800-225-4737	401-334-3444	297-1
Calista Corp 301 Calista Ct Ste A	Anchorage	AK	99518	800-277-5516	907-279-5516	653
Calistoga Beverage Co 865 Silverado Trl	Calistoga	CA	94515	800-365-4446		803
Calistoga Ranch 580 Lommel Rd	Calistoga	CA	94515	800-942-4220	707-254-2800	667
Calistoga Spa Hot Springs 1006 Washington St	Calistoga	CA	94515	866-822-5772	707-942-6269	704
Calix Society, The 3881 Highland Ave Ste 201	St Paul	MN	55110	800-398-0524	651-773-3117	47-21
Call One Inc 400 Imperial Blvd PO Box 9002	Cape Canaveral	FL	32920	800-749-3160	321-783-2400	732
Callan & Woodworth Moving & Storage 900 Hwy 212	Michigan City	IN	46360	800-584-0551	269-447-1578	518
Callan Assoc Inc 101 California St Ste 3500	San Francisco	CA	94111	800-227-3288	415-974-5060	401
Callaway Cars Inc 3 High St	Old Lyme	CT	06371	866-927-9400	860-434-9002	56
Callaway Electric Co-op 1313 Co-op Dr PO Box 250	Fulton	MO	65251	888-642-4840	573-642-3326	247
Callaway Gardens 17800 Hwy 27	Pine Mountain	GA	31822	800-225-5292	706-663-2281	667
Callaway Golf Co 2180 Rutherford Rd *NYSE: ELY*	Carlsbad	CA	92008	800-588-9836	760-931-1771	708
Callbright Corp 6700 Hollister	Houston	TX	77040	877-462-2552		390
CallDirek 2200 S Dixie Hwy Ste 401	Miami	FL	33133	866-673-4735		387
Callenor Company Inc N 60 W 15725 Kohler Ln	Menomonee Falls	WI	53051	800-813-7429	262-252-3343	124
Caller-Times 820 N Lower Broadway	Corpus Christi	TX	78401	800-827-2011	361-884-2011	531-2
Calling Solutions By Phone Power Inc 2200 McCullough Ave *Cust Svc	San Antonio	TX	78212	800-683-5500*	210-801-9630	734
Callisto Integration 635 Fourth Line Ste 16	Oakville	ON	L6L5B3	800-387-0467	905-339-0059	196
Callon Petroleum Co 200 N Canal St *NYSE: CPE*	Natchez	MS	39120	800-451-1294	601-442-1601	539
Callware Technologies Inc 9100 S 500 W	Sandy	UT	84070	800-888-4226	801-988-6800	180-7
CalMet Services Inc 7202 Peterson Ln	Paramount	CA	90723	800-990-6387	562-259-1239	802
Calmont Leasing Ltd 14610 Yellowhead Trail NW	Edmonton	AB	T5L3C5	855-474-2568		776
Calmoseptine Inc 16602 Burke Ln	Huntington Beach	CA	92647	800-800-3405	714-840-3405	233
Calnet Inc 12359 Sunrise Vly Dr Ste 270 *General	Reston	VA	20191	877-322-5638*	703-547-6800	196
Calolympic Glove & Safety Company Inc 1720 Delilah St	Corona	CA	92879	800-421-6630	951-340-2229	677
Calphalon Corp PO Box 583	Toledo	OH	43697	800-809-7267		485
Calpico Inc 1387 San Mateo Ave	South San Francisco	CA	94080	800-998-9115	650-588-2241	327
Calpine Corp 717 Texas Ave Ste 1000 *NYSE: CPN*	Houston	TX	77002	800-367-5690	713-830-2000	785
Calpop Com Inc 600 W Seventh St	Los Angeles	CA	90017	866-467-8846		226
CalPortland Co 5975 E Marginal Way S PO Box 1730	Seattle	WA	98134	800-750-0123	206-764-3000	184
Cal-Royal Products Inc 6605 Flotilla St	City Of Commerce	CA	90040	800-876-9258	323-888-6601	350
Calsak Corp 1411 West 190th St Ste 400	Gardena	CA	90248	888-663-6005	310-719-9500	602
CalSurance 681 S Parker St Ste 300	Orange	CA	92868	800-762-7800	714-939-0800	390
Calton & Assoc Inc 14497 N Dale Mabry Hwy	Tampa	FL	33618	800-942-0262	813-264-0440	688
Calumet College of Saint Joseph 2400 New York Ave	Whiting	IN	46394	877-700-9100	219-473-4215	167
Calumet Diversified Meats Inc 10000 80th Ave	Pleasant Prairie	WI	53158	800-752-7427	262-947-7200	298-9
Calumet Specialty Products Partners LP 2780 Waterfront Pkwy E Dr Ste 200 *NASDAQ: CLMT*	Indianapolis	IN	46214	800-437-3188	317-328-5660	579
Cal-Van Tools 4300 Waterleaf Ct	Greensboro	NC	27410	800-537-1077		756
Calvary Bible College & Theological Seminary 15800 Calvary Rd	Kansas City	MO	64147	800-326-3960	816-322-3960	160
Calvert Investments Inc 4550 Montgomery Ave Ste 1000N	Bethesda	MD	20814	800-368-2748	301-951-4800	527
Calvert Labs 1225 Crescent Green Ste 115	Cary	NC	27518	800-300-8114	919-459-8653	418
Calvert Marine Museum 14200 Solomons Island Rd PO Box 97	Solomons	MD	20688	800-735-2258	410-326-2042	519
Calverton National Cemetery 210 Princeton Blvd	Calverton	NY	11933	800-829-1040	631-727-5410	135
Calvin College 3201 Burton St SE	Grand Rapids	MI	49546	800-688-0122	616-526-6000	167
Calvin Theological Seminary 3233 Burton St SE	Grand Rapids	MI	49546	800-388-6034	616-957-6036	168-3
Calzone Case Co 225 Black Rock Ave *Cust Svc	Bridgeport	CT	06605	800-243-5152*	203-367-5766	452
CAM Commerce Solutions Inc 17075 Newhope St Ste A	Fountain Valley	CA	92708	800-726-3282	714-241-9241	180-10

Name / Address	City	State	Zip	Toll-Free	Phone	Class
Cam Services Inc 5664 Selmaraine Dr	Culver City	CA	90230	**800-576-3050**	310-390-3552	258
Camas-Washougal Chamber of Commerce 422 NE Fourth Ave	Camas	WA	98607	**800-468-5865**	360-834-2472	138
Cambelt International Corp 2820 West 1100 South	Salt Lake City	UT	84104	**855-226-2358**	801-972-5511	209
Camber Corp 670 Discovery Dr	Huntsville	AL	35806	**800-998-7988**	256-922-0200	182
Cambex Corp 337 Tpke Rd *OTC: CBEX*	Southborough	MA	01772	**800-325-5565**	508-281-0209	178
Cambiar Investors Inc 2401 E Second Ave Ste 500	Denver	CO	80206	**888-673-9950**		401
Cambrex Corp 1 Meadowlands Plz *NYSE: CBM*	East Rutherford	NJ	07073	**866-286-9133**	201-804-3000	478
Cambria Capital LLC 488 E Winchester St Ste 200	Salt Lake City	UT	84107	**877-226-0477**		401
Cambria Pines Realty Inc 746-A Main St	Cambria	CA	93428	**800-676-8616**	805-927-8616	650
Cambria-Rowe Business College (CRBC) 221 Central Ave	Johnstown	PA	15902	**800-639-2273**	814-536-5168	798
Cambridge Chamber of Commerce 750 Hespeler Rd *General	Cambridge	ON	N3H5L8	**800-749-7560***	519-622-2221	137
Cambridge College Inc 360 Merrimack St 4th fl	Lawrence	MA	01843	**800-829-4723**	617-868-1000	798
Cambridge Engineering Inc PO Box 1010	Chesterfield	MO	63006	**800-899-1989**	636-532-2233	319
Cambridge Heart Inc 46 Jonspin Rd	Wilmington	MA	01887	**888-226-9283**	978-654-7600	475
Cambridge International 105 Goodwill Rd	Cambridge	MD	21613	**800-638-9560**	410-901-4979	209
Cambridge Isotope Laboratories Inc 3 Highwood Dr	Tewksbury	MA	01876	**800-322-1174**	978-749-8000	144
Cambridge Medical Ctr (CMC) 701 S Dellwood St	Cambridge	MN	55008	**800-252-4133**	763-689-7700	374-3
Cambridge Packing Co Inc 41-43 Foodmart Rd	Boston	MA	02118	**800-722-6726**	617-269-6700	298-9
Cambridge Public Library 244 S Birch St	Cambridge	MN	55008	**877-721-4862**	763-689-7390	434-3
Cambridge Savings Bank 1374 Massachusetts Ave	Cambridge	MA	02138	**888-418-5626**	617-441-4155	69
Cambridge Silversmith Ltd 116 Lehigh Dr	Fairfield	NJ	07004	**800-890-3366**	973-227-4400	361
Cambridge Street Metal Corp (CSM) 82 Stevens St	East Taunton	MA	02718	**800-254-7580**	508-822-2278	491
Cambridge Suites Hotel Halifax 1583 Brunswick St	Halifax	NS	B3J3P5	**800-565-1263**	902-420-0555	379
Cambridge Suites Hotel Toronto 15 Richmond St E	Toronto	ON	M5C1N2	**800-463-1990**	416-368-1990	379
Cambridge Technology Inc 25 Hartwell Ave	Lexington	MA	02421	**800-342-3757**	781-541-1600	471
Cambridgeport Air Systems 8 Fanaras Dr	Salisbury	MA	01952	**877-648-2872**	978-465-8481	609
CambridgeSoft Corp 100 CambridgePark Dr	Cambridge	MA	02140	**800-315-7300**	617-588-9100	180-5
CambridgeWorld 34 Franklin Ave	Brooklyn	NY	11205	**800-221-2253**	718-858-5002	118
Cambro Manufacturing Co 5801 Skylab Rd	Huntington Beach	CA	92647	**800-833-3003**	714-848-1555	301
Camco Chemical Co 8145 Holton Dr *Cust Svc	Florence	KY	41042	**800-354-1001***	859-727-3200	150
Camden County 520 Market St Rm 102	Camden	NJ	08102	**866-226-3362**	856-225-5300	338
Camden County Chamber of Commerce 2603 Osborne Rd Unit CC	Saint Marys	GA	31558	**888-331-8226**	912-729-5840	138
Camden County College 200 College Dr	Blackwood	NJ	08012	**888-228-2466**	856-227-7200	161
Camden County Library 203 Laurel Rd	Voorhees	NJ	08043	**877-222-3737**	856-772-1636	434-3
Camden National Corp 2 Elm St *NYSE: CAC*	Camden	ME	04843	**800-860-8821**	207-236-8821	360-2
Camden Property Trust 11 Greenway Plz Ste 2400 *NYSE: CPT*	Houston	TX	77046	**800-922-6336**	713-354-2500	653
Camden Publications 331 E Bell St	Camden	MI	49232	**800-222-6336**	517-368-0365	531-4
Camel Rock Casino 17486A Hwy 84/285	Santa Fe	NM	87506	**800-483-1040**	505-983-2667	132
Camelback Inn JW Marriott Resort Golf Club & Spa 5402 E Lincoln Dr	Scottsdale	AZ	85253	**800-242-2635**	480-948-1700	667
Camelot Carpet Mills Inc 17111 Red Hill Ave	Irvine	CA	92614	**800-854-8331**	949-474-4000	130
Camelot Community Care Inc 4910 D Creekside Dr	Clearwater	FL	33760	**800-435-7352**	727-593-0003	47-6
Camera Corner Inc PO Box 1899	Burlington	NC	27216	**800-868-2462**	336-228-0251	118
Cameron Balloons US PO Box 3672	Ann Arbor	MI	48106	**866-423-6178**	734-426-5525	28
Cameron Instruments Inc 173 Woolwich St	Guelph	ON	N1H3V4	**888-863-8010**	519-824-7111	358
Cameron Thomson Group Ltd 390 Bay St Ste 1706	Toronto	ON	M5H2Y2	**800-395-9943**	416-350-5009	401
Cameron Turbocompressor 3101 Broadway	Buffalo	NY	14225	**877-805-7911**	716-896-6603	174
Cameron University 2800 W Gore Blvd *Admissions	Lawton	OK	73505	**888-454-7600***	580-581-2289	167
Cameron, Hodges, Coleman, LaPointe & Wright PA 111 N Magnolia Ave Ste 1350	Orlando	FL	32801	**888-841-5030**	407-841-5030	428
Camesa Inc 1615 Spur 529	Rosenberg	TX	77471	**800-866-0001**	281-342-4494	255
Camex Equipment Sales & Rental Inc 1806 Second St	Nisku	AB	T9E0W8	**877-955-2770**	780-955-2770	538
Camin Cargo Control Inc 230 Marion Ave	Linden	NJ	07036	**800-756-8798**	908-862-1899	740
Camino Real Foods Inc 2638 E Vernon Ave	Vernon	CA	90058	**800-421-6201**	323-585-6599	297-36
Camp Butler National Cemetery 5063 Camp Butler Rd	Springfield	IL	62707	**877-907-8585**	217-492-4070	135
Camp Lebanon 1205 Acorn Rd	Burtrum	MN	56318	**800-816-1502**	320-573-2125	241
Camp Nelson National Cemetery 6980 Danville Rd	Nicholasville	KY	40356	**800-827-1000**	859-885-5727	135
Camp Olympia 723 Olympia Dr	Trinity	TX	75862	**800-735-6190**	936-594-2541	298-8
Campaign Legal Ctr Media Policy Program Campaign Legal Ctr	Washington	DC	20036	**877-855-5007**	202-736-2200	47-7
Campbell Alliance Group Inc 8045 Arco Corporate Dr Ste 500	Raleigh	NC	27617	**888-297-2001**	919-844-7100	191-4
Campbell County Board of Education 101 Orchard Ln	Alexandria	KY	41001	**800-942-3767**	859-635-2173	683
Campbell County Chamber of Commerce 314 S Gillette Ave	Gillette	WY	82716	**800-448-7801**	307-682-3673	138
Campbell Manufacturing Inc 127 E Spring St	Bechtelsville	PA	19505	**800-523-0224**	610-367-2107	594
Campbell Oil Company Inc 611 Erie St S	Massillon	OH	44646	**800-589-8555**	330-833-8555	578
Campbell Printing Co 2017 Cleveland Hwy	Dalton	GA	30721	**866-828-5240**	706-259-3344	626
Campbell Soup Co 1 Campbell Pl *NYSE: CPB*	Camden	NJ	08103	**800-257-8443**	856-342-4800	297-36
Campbell University 450 Leslie Campbell Ave PO Box 546	Buies Creek	NC	27506	**800-334-4111**	910-893-1290	167
Campbell University Norman Adrian Wiggins School of Law 113 Main St	Buies Creek	NC	27506	**800-334-4111**	919-865-5991	168-1
Campbell Wrapper Corp 1415 Fortune Ave	De Pere	WI	54115	**800-727-4210**	920-983-7100	546
Campbell's Resort 104 W Woodin Ave PO Box 278	Chelan	WA	98816	**800-553-8225**	509-682-2561	667
Campbellsville University 1 University Dr *Admissions	Campbellsville	KY	42718	**800-264-6014***	270-789-5000	167
Camperoo Inc 2900 Weslayan St Ste 545	Houston	TX	77027	**888-538-8809**		387
Camping Investigations 4427 N 27th Ave	Phoenix	AZ	85017	**800-862-8458**	602-864-7860	400
Camping World RV Sales 8155 Rivers Ave	Charleston	SC	29406	**888-586-5446**		789
Campion College at the University of Regina 3737 Wascana Pkwy	Regina	SK	S4S0A2	**800-667-7282**	306-586-4242	783
Campus Crusade for Christ International 100 Lk Hart Dr	Orlando	FL	32832	**888-278-7233**	407-826-2500	47-20
Campus Federal Credit Union PO Box 98036	Baton Rouge	LA	70898	**888-769-8841**	225-769-8841	221
Campus Special LLC, The 3575 Koger Blvd Ste 300	Duluth	GA	30096	**800-365-8520**		197
Campus Televideo Inc 100 First Stamford Pl	Stamford	CT	06902	**866-615-8674**	203-983-5400	115
Campus USA Credit Union PO Box 147029	Gainesville	FL	32614	**800-367-6440**	352-335-9090	221
Cam-Wal Electric Co-op Inc 404 W Scranton St PO Box 135	Selby	SD	57472	**800-269-7676**		247
Canaan Valley Resort & Conference Ctr 230 Main Lodge Rd	Davis	WV	26260	**800-622-4121**	304-866-4121	667
CANAC Inc 6505 Trans-Canada Hwy Ste 405	St Laurent	QC	H4T1S3	**800-588-4387**	514-734-4700	648
Canad Inns - Club Regent Casino Hotel 1415 Regent Ave W	Winnipeg	MB	R2C3B2	**888-332-2623**	204-667-5560	379
Canad Inns Fort Garry 1824 Pembina Hwy	Winnipeg	MB	R3T2G2	**888-332-2623**	204-261-7450	379
Canad Inns Garden City 2100 McPhillips St	Winnipeg	MB	R2V3T9	**888-332-2623**	204-633-0024	379
Canad Inns Polo Park 1405 St Matthews Ave	Winnipeg	MB	R3G0K5	**888-332-2623**	204-775-8791	379
Canada 885 Second Ave 14th Fl	New York	NY	10017	**800-267-8376**	212-848-1100	782
Consulate General 500 N Akard St Ste 2900	Dallas	TX	75201	**800-267-8376**	214-922-9806	259
Consulate General 1251 Ave of the Americas Concourse Level	New York	NY	10020	**800-267-8376**	212-596-1628	259
Embassy 501 Pennsylvania Ave NW	Washington	DC	20001	**800-567-6868**	202-682-1740	259
Canada Agriculture Museum Prince of Wales Dr PO Box 9724 Stn T	Ottawa	ON	K1G5A3	**866-442-4416**	613-991-3044	519
Canada Deposit Insurance Corp 50 O'Connor St 17th Fl	Ottawa	ON	K1P6L2	**800-461-2342**	613-996-2081	508
Canada Flowers 4073 Longhurst Ave	Niagara Falls	ON	L2E6G5	**888-705-9999**	905-354-2713	294
Canada Forgings Inc 130 Hagar St	Welland	ON	L3B5P8	**800-263-0440**	905-735-1220	540
Canada Life Assurance Co, The 330 University Ave	Toronto	ON	M5G1R8	**888-252-1847**	416-597-1456	391-4
Canada Media Fund 50 Wellington St E Ste 202	Toronto	ON	M5E1C8	**877-975-0766**	416-214-4400	393
Canada Science & Technology Museum 1867 St Laurent Blvd PO Box 9724	Ottawa	ON	K1G5A3	**866-442-4416**	613-991-3044	519
Canadian Academy of Sport Medicine (CASM) 180 Elgin St Ste 1400	Ottawa	ON	K2P2K3	**877-585-2394**	613-748-5851	48-8
Canadian Assn of Emergency Physicians (CAEP) 1785 Alta Vista Dr Ste 104	Ottawa	ON	K1G3Y6	**800-463-1158**	613-523-3343	48-8
Canadian Assn of Occupational Therapists (CAOT) 1125 Colonel By Dr	Ottawa	ON	K1S5R1	**800-434-2268**	613-523-2268	47-1
Canadian Automobile Assn (CAA) 2151 Thurston Dr	Ottawa	ON	K1G6C9	**800-267-8713**	613-820-1890	47-23
Canadian Bearings Ltd 1600 Drew Rd	Mississauga	ON	L5S1S5	**800-229-2327**	905-670-6700	385

Name / Address	City	St	Zip	Toll-Free	Phone	Class
Canadian College of Naturopathic Medicine 1255 Sheppard Ave E	Toronto	ON	M2K1E2	**866-241-2266**	416-498-1255	783
Canadian Federation of Humane Societies (CFHS) 30 Concourse Gate Ste 102	Ottawa	ON	K2E7V7	**888-678-2347**	613-224-8072	47-3
Canadian Finance & Leasing Association 15 Toronto St	Toronto	ON	M5C2E3	**877-213-7373**	416-860-1133	136
Canadian Football League 50 Wellington St E 3rd Fl	Toronto	ON	M5E1C8	**855-264-4242**	416-322-9650	713-2
Canadian Golf Hall of Fame & Museum Glen Abbey Golf Course 1333 Dorval Dr Ste 1	Oakville	ON	L6M4X7	**800-263-0009**	905-849-9700	521
Canadian Gypsum Company Inc 350 Burnhamthorpe Rd W 5th Fl	Mississauga	ON	L5B3J1	**800-565-6607**	905-803-5600	347
Canadian Hospital Specialties ULC 2810 Coventry Rd	Oakville	ON	L6H6R1	**800-461-1423**	905-825-9300	474
Canadian Imperial Bank of Commerce (CIBC) 199 Bay St Commerce Ct W *NYSE: CM*	Toronto	ON	M5L1A2	**800-465-2422**		69
Canadian Information Processing Society (CIPS) 5090 Explorer Dr Ste 801	Mississauga	ON	L4W4T9	**877-275-2477**	905-602-1370	47-1
Canadian Kennel Club (CKC) 200 Ronson Dr Ste 400	Etobicoke	ON	M9W5Z9	**800-250-8040**	416-675-5511	47-3
Canadian Livestock Insurance 480 University Ave Ste 412	Toronto	ON	M5G1V2	**800-727-1502**	416-510-8191	391-1
Canadian Living Magazine 25 Sheppard Ave W Ste 100	Toronto	ON	M2N6S7	**800-387-6332**	416-733-7600	456-11
Canadian Medical Assn (CMA) 1867 Alta Vista Dr	Ottawa	ON	K1G5W8	**800-663-7336**	613-731-9331	48-8
Canadian Medical Laboratories Ltd 6560 Kennedy Rd	Mississauga	ON	L5T2X4	**800-263-0801**		418
Canadian Memorial Chiropractic College 6100 Leslie St	Toronto	ON	M2H3J1	**800-463-2923**	416-482-2340	783
Canadian Museum of Civilization 100 Laurier St	Gatineau	QC	K1A0M8	**800-555-5621**	819-776-7000	519
Canadian Museum of Contemporary Photography 380 Sussex Dr PO Box 427 Stn A	Ottawa	ON	K1N9N4	**800-319-2787**	613-990-1985	519
Canadian Museum of Nature 240 McLeod St	Ottawa	ON	K2P2R1	**800-263-4433**	613-566-4700	519
Canadian Musician Magazine 4056 Dorchester Rd	Niagara Falls	ON	L2E6M9	**800-363-6336**	905-374-8878	456-9
Canadian National Railway Co 935 Rue de la Gauchetiere O *TSE: CNR*	Montreal	QC	H3B2M9	**888-668-4626**	888-888-5909	646
Canadian Natural Resources Ltd (CNRL) 855 Second St SW Ste 2500 *NYSE: CNQ*	Calgary	AB	T2P4J8	**888-878-3700**	403-517-6700	535
Canadian Newspaper Assn 890 Yonge St Ste 200	Toronto	ON	M4W3P4	**877-305-2262**	416-923-3567	48-16
Canadian Pacific Railway Co 401 9 Ave SW Ste 500	Calgary	AB	T2P4Z4	**888-333-6370**	403-319-7000	646
Canadian Parks & Wilderness Society (CPAWS) 250 City Ctr Ave Ste 506	Ottawa	ON	K1R6K7	**800-333-9453**	613-569-7226	47-13
Canadian Payroll Association 250 Bloor St E	Toronto	ON	M4W1E6	**800-387-4693**	416-487-3380	136
Canadian Peregrine Foundation 1450 O'Connor Dr Bldg B Ste 214	Toronto	ON	M4B2T8	**888-709-3944**	416-481-1233	47-3
Canadian Professional Sales Association 310 Front St W Ste 800	Toronto	ON	M5V3B5	**888-267-2772**	416-408-2685	198
Canadian Southern Baptist Seminary 200 Seminary View	Cochrane	AB	T4C2G1	**877-922-2727**	403-932-6622	168-3
Canadian Tire Corp Ltd 2180 Yonge St PO Box 770 Stn K *TSE: CTC*	Toronto	ON	M4P2V8	**800-387-8803**	416-480-3000	187
Canadian Tool & Die Ltd 1331 Chevrier Blvd	Winnipeg	MB	R3T1Y4	**800-204-4150**	204-453-6833	755
Canadian Valley Electric Co-op 11277 S 356 PO Box 751	Seminole	OK	74868	**877-382-3680**	405-382-3680	247
Canadian Veterinary Medical Assn (CVMA) 339 Booth St	Ottawa	ON	K1R7K1	**800-567-2862**	613-236-1162	48-8
Canadian Western Bank 10303 Jasper Ave Ste 3000 *TSE: CWB*	Edmonton	AB	T5J3X6	**866-317-0356**	780-423-8888	69
Canadian Wildlife Federation (CWF) 350 Michael Cowpland Dr	Kanata	ON	K2M2W1	**800-563-9453**	613-599-9594	47-13
Canal Insurance Co 400 E Stone Ave PO Box 7	Greenville	SC	29601	**800-452-6911**		391-4
Canal Park Lodge 250 Canal Pk Dr	Duluth	MN	55802	**800-777-8560**	218-279-6000	379
Canal Park Stadium 300 S Main St	Akron	OH	44308	**888-223-6000**	330-253-5151	718
Canal Wood LLC 2430 Main St	Conway	SC	29526	**866-587-1460**	843-488-9663	447
Canaletto 3355 Las Vegas Blvd S	Las Vegas	NV	89109	**866-659-9643**	702-414-1000	669
Canam Group Inc 11535 First Ave Bureau 500 *TSE: CAM*	Saint-Georges	QC	G5Y7H5	**877-499-6049**	418-228-8031	721
Can-am Plumbing Inc 151 Wyoming St	Pleasanton	CA	94566	**800-786-9797**	925-846-1833	609
Canamould Extrusions Inc 101a Roytec Rd	Woodbridge	ON	L4L8A9	**866-874-6762**	905-264-4436	498
Canandaigua Inn on the Lake 770 S Main St	Canandaigua	NY	14424	**800-228-2801**	585-394-7800	379
Canandaigua Wine Company Inc 235 N Bloomfield Rd	Canandaigua	NY	14424	**888-659-7900**	585-396-7600	79-3
Canary Hotel 31 W Carrillo	Santa Barbara	CA	93101	**866-999-5401**	805-884-0300	379
Canberra Corp 3610 Holland Sylvania Rd	Toledo	OH	43615	**800-832-8992**	419-841-6616	150
Canberra Industries Inc 800 Research Pkwy *Sales	Meriden	CT	06450	**800-243-3955***	203-238-2351	471
Canby School District 1130 S Ivy St	Canby	OR	97013	**800-475-7785**	503-266-7861	683
Cancap Pharmaceutical Ltd 13111 Vanier Pl Ste 180	Richmond	BC	V6V2J1	**877-998-2378**	604-278-2188	233

Name / Address	City	St	Zip	Toll-Free	Phone	Class
CanCare Health Services Inc 45 Sheppard Ave E Ste 204	Toronto	ON	M2N5W9	**877-226-6995**	416-226-6995	363
Cancer Care Inc 275 Seventh Ave 22nd Fl	New York	NY	10001	**800-813-4673**	212-712-8400	47-17
Cancer Genetics Inc Meadows Office Complex 201 Rt 17 N 2nd Fl	Rutherford	NJ	07070	**888-334-4988**	201-528-9200	233
Cancer Letter PO Box 9905	Washington	DC	20016	**800-513-7042**	202-362-1809	530-8
Candela Corp 530 Boston Post Rd *NASDAQ: CLZR*	Wayland	MA	01778	**800-733-8550**	508-358-7400	424
Candid Color Systems Inc 1300 Metropolitan Ave	Oklahoma City	OK	73108	**800-336-4550**	405-947-8747	587
Candlelighters Childhood Cancer Foundation 10920 Connecticut Ave Suuite A PO Box 498	Kensington	MD	20895	**800-366-2223**	301-962-3520	47-17
Cando Contracting Ltd 740 Rosser Ave Fl 4	Brandon	MB	R7A0K9	**866-989-5310**	204-725-2627	648
Can-do Promotions Inc 6517 Wise Ave Nw	North Canton	OH	44720	**800-325-7981**	330-494-3527	186
Candy Bouquet International Inc 510 Mclean St	Little Rock	AR	72202	**877-226-3901**	501-375-9990	122
Cane Creek Cycling Components 355 Cane Creek Rd	Fletcher	NC	28732	**800-234-2725**	828-684-3551	81
Cane Creek State Park 50 State Pk Rd	Star City	AR	71667	**888-287-2757**	870-628-4714	564
Caney Fork Electric Co-op Inc 920 Smithville Hwy PO Box 272	McMinnville	TN	37110	**888-505-3030**	931-473-3116	247
Caney Valley Electric Co-op Assn Inc, The 401 Lawrence St PO Box 308	Cedar Vale	KS	67024	**800-310-8911**	620-758-2262	247
Canfield & Tack Inc 925 Exchange St *General	Rochester	NY	14608	**800-836-0861***	585-235-7710	626
Canfield Connector Div 8510 Foxwood Ct	Youngstown	OH	44514	**800-554-5071**		203
Canfield Equipment Service 21533 Mound Rd	Warren	MI	48091	**800-637-3956**	586-757-2020	56
Cangene bioPharma Inc 1111 S Paca St	Baltimore	MD	21230	**800-441-4225**	410-843-5000	233
Cangro Industries Long Island Transmission Co 495 Smith St	Farmingdale	NY	11735	**800-422-9210**	631-454-9000	619
Canidium LLC 3801 Kirby Dr, S456	Houston	TX	77024	**877-651-1837**		198
Canimex Inc 285 Saint-Georges St	Drummondville	QC	J2C4H3	**855-777-1335**	819-477-1335	358
Canine Companions for Independence Inc (CCI) 2965 Dutton Ave PO Box 446	Santa Rosa	CA	95402	**800-572-2275**	707-577-1700	47-17
Canisius College 2001 Main St	Buffalo	NY	14208	**800-843-1517**	716-888-2200	167
Cankdeska Cikana Community College PO Box 269	Fort Totten	ND	58335	**888-783-1463**	701-766-4415	164
CAN-med Healthcare 200 Bluewater Rd	Bedford	NS	B4B1G9	**800-565-7553**	902-455-4649	474
Cannery Casino & Hotel, The *Cannery Casino Resorts LLC* 2121 E Craig Rd	North Las Vegas	NV	89030	**866-999-4899**	702-507-5700	379
Cannon Air Force Base 110 E Sextant Ave Ste 1150	Cannon AFB	NM	88103	**877-283-3858**	575-784-4131	496-1
Cannon Marketing Inc 4684 US Hwy 70 W	Kinston	NC	28504	**800-952-5913**	252-527-3361	663
Cannon Muskegon Corp 2875 Lincoln St PO Box 506	Muskegon	MI	49441	**800-253-0371**	231-755-1681	484
Canoga Perkins Corp 20600 Prairie St *Tech Supp	Chatsworth	CA	91311	**800-360-6642***	818-718-6300	175-3
Canon Business Solutions-Central 425 N Martingale Rd Ste 100	Schaumburg	IL	60173	**800-706-3303**	847-706-3400	111
Canon City Chamber of Commerce 403 Royal Gorge Blvd	Canon City	CO	81212	**800-876-7922**	719-275-2331	138
Canoochee Electric Membership Corp 342 E Brazell St	Reidsville	GA	30453	**800-342-0134**		247
Canplas Industries Ltd 500 Veterans Dr	Barrie	ON	L4M4V3	**800-461-1771**	705-726-3361	604-2
Cansec Systems Ltd 3105 Unity Dr Unit 9	Mississauga	ON	L5L4L2	**877-545-7755**	905-820-2404	691
Canteen Service Co 712 Industrial Dr	Owensboro	KY	42301	**800-467-2471**	270-683-2471	300
Canteen Vending Services *Compass Group* 2400 Yorkmont Rd	Charlotte	NC	28217	**800-357-0012**	704-328-4000	300
Canter & Assoc LLC 12975 Coral Tree Pl *Cust Svc	Los Angeles	CA	90066	**800-669-9011***	310-578-4700	764
Canterbury International 5632 W Washington Blvd	Los Angeles	CA	90016	**800-935-7111**	323-936-7111	152
Canterbury Park Holding Corp 1100 Canterbury Rd *NASDAQ: CPHC*	Shakopee	MN	55379	**800-340-6361**	952-445-7223	639
Canton Public Library 1200 S Canton Ctr Rd	Canton	MI	48188	**888-988-6300**	734-397-0999	434-3
Canton Regional Chamber of Commerce 222 Market Ave N	Canton	OH	44702	**800-533-4302**	330-456-7253	138
Canton/Stark County Convention & Visitors Bureau 222 Market Ave N	Canton	OH	44702	**800-552-6051**	330-454-1439	208
Canvas Products Co 274 S Waterman St	Detroit	MI	48209	**877-293-1669**	313-496-1000	730
Canweb Internet Services 1086 Modeland Rd	Sarnia	ON	N7S6L2	**877-422-6932**	519-332-6900	182
CanWest DHI 660 Speedvale Ave W	Guelph	ON	N1K1E5	**800-549-4373**	519-824-2320	740
Canyon Chamber of Commerce 1518 Fifth Ave	Canyon	TX	79015	**800-999-9481**	806-655-7815	138
Canyon Creek Cabinet Co 16726 Tye St SE	Monroe	WA	98272	**800-228-1830**	360-348-4973	114
Canyon Creek Travel Inc 333 W Campbell Rd Ste 440	Richardson	TX	75080	**800-952-1998**	972-238-1998	773

Name / Address	City	State	ZIP	Toll-Free	Phone	Class
Canyon Ranch 165 Kemble St (*Resv)	Lenox	MA	01240	**800-742-9000***	413-637-4100	667
Canyon Ranch SpaClub at the Venetian 3355 Las Vegas Blvd S Ste 1159	Las Vegas	NV	89109	**877-220-2688**	702-414-3606	705
Canyon Ranch Tucson 8600 E Rockcliff Rd	Tucson	AZ	85750	**800-742-9000**	520-749-9000	667
CAO Group Inc 4628 Skyhawk Dr	West Jordan	UT	84084	**877-877-9778**	801-256-9282	419
CAOT (Canadian Assn of Occupational Therapists) 1125 Colonel By Dr	Ottawa	ON	K1S5R1	**800-434-2268**	613-523-2268	47-1
CAP (College of American Pathologists) 325 Waukegan Rd	Northfield	IL	60093	**800-323-4040**	847-832-7000	48-8
CAP (Children Awaiting Parents Inc) 595 Blossom Rd Ste 306	Rochester	NY	14610	**888-835-8802**	585-232-5110	47-6
Capax Global LLC 590 Headquarters Plaza	Morristown	NJ	07960	**888-682-8900**	973-401-0660	227
Cape Air 660 Barnstable Rd	Hyannis	MA	02601	**800-227-3247**	508-771-6944	25
Cape Arago State Park Cape Arago Hwy	Coos Bay	OR	97420	**800-551-6949**	541-888-3778	564
Cape Breton University 1250 Grand Lk Rd	Sydney	NS	B1P6L2	**888-959-9995**	902-539-5300	783
Cape Cod Canal Regional Chamber of Commerce 70 Main St	Buzzards Bay	MA	02532	**888-332-2732**	508-759-6000	138
Cape Cod Chamber of Commerce 5 Shoot Flying Hill Rd	Centerville	MA	02632	**888-332-2732**	508-362-3225	138
Cape Cod Coast Guard Air Station 2300 Wilson Blvd Ste 500	Arlington	VA	20598	**877-669-8724**	202-372-4620	157
Cape Cod Community College 2240 Iyanough Rd	West Barnstable	MA	02668	**877-846-3672**	508-362-2131	161
Cape Cod Five Cents Savings Bank 19 W Rd PO Box 20	Orleans	MA	02653	**800-678-1855**	508-240-0555	69
Cape Cod Hospital 27 Pk St	Hyannis	MA	02601	**800-545-5014**	508-771-1800	374-3
Cape Cod Life Magazine 13 Steeple St Ste 204 PO Box 1439	Mashpee	MA	02649	**800-698-1717**	508-419-7381	456-22
Cape Cod Potato Chip Co 100 Breed's Hill Rd	Hyannis	MA	02601	**888-881-2447**	508-775-3358	297-35
Cape Cod Regional Transit Authority (CCRTA) 215 Iyannough Rd PO Box 1988	Hyannis	MA	02601	**800-352-7155**	508-775-8504	467
Cape Cod Times 319 Main St	Hyannis	MA	02601	**800-451-7887**	508-775-1200	531-2
Cape Codder Resort & Spa 1225 Iyanough Rd Rt 132 Bearse's Way	Hyannis	MA	02601	**888-297-2200**	508-771-3000	667
Cape Fear Coast Convention & Visitors Bureau 505 Nutt St Unit A	Wilmington	NC	28401	**877-406-2356**	910-341-4030	208
Cape Fear Community College 411 N Front St	Wilmington	NC	28401	**800-487-5553**	910-362-7000	161
Cape Girardeau Convention & Visitors Bureau 400 Broadway Ste 100	Cape Girardeau	MO	63701	**800-777-0068**	573-335-1631	208
Cape Hatteras Electric Co-op 47109 Light Plant Rd PO Box 9	Buxton	NC	27920	**800-454-5616**	252-995-5616	247
Cape Verde *Embassy* 3415 Massachusetts Ave NW	Washington	DC	20007	**800-343-2347**	202-965-6820	259
Capel Inc 831 N Main St	Troy	NC	27371	**800-334-3711**	800-382-6574	130
Capella Education Co 225 S Sixth St 9th Fl (*NASDAQ: CPLA* ■ *Cust Svc)	Minneapolis	MN	55402	**888-227-3552***	612-339-8650	244
Capezio/Ballet Makers Inc 1 Campus Rd (*Acctg)	Totowa	NJ	07512	**800-533-1887***	973-595-9000	302
CapFinancial Partners LLC 4208 Six Forks Rd Ste 1700	Raleigh	NC	27609	**800-216-0645**	919-870-6822	401
Capital Advisors Ltd LLC 20600 Chagrin Blvd	Shaker Heights	OH	44122	**888-295-7908**	216-295-7900	196
Capital Agricultural Property Services Inc 801 Warrenville Rd Ste 150	Lisle	IL	60532	**800-243-2060**	630-434-9150	316-3
Capital Analysts Inc 218 Glenside Ave	Wyncote	PA	19095	**800-242-1421**		390
Capital City Bank 2111 N Monroe St PO Box 900	Tallahassee	FL	32302	**888-671-0400**	850-402-7500	69
Capital City Bank Group Inc PO Box 900 (*NASDAQ: CCBG*)	Tallahassee	FL	32302	**888-671-0400**	850-402-7500	360-2
Capital Community College 950 Main St	Hartford	CT	06103	**800-894-6126**	860-906-5000	161
Capital Culinary Institute of Keiser College *Melbourne* 900 S Babcock St	Melbourne	FL	32901	**877-636-3618**	321-409-4800	162
Capital District Physicians' Health Plan 500 Patroon Creek Blvd	Albany	NY	12206	**888-258-0477**	518-641-3000	391-3
Capital Electric Co-op Inc 4111 State St	Bismarck	ND	58503	**888-223-1513**	701-223-1513	247
Capital Farm Credit Aca 7000 Woodway Dr	Waco	TX	76712	**877-944-5500**	254-776-7506	68
Capital Ford Inc 4900 Capital Blvd	Raleigh	NC	27616	**877-659-2496**	919-790-4600	56
Capital Grille 900 Boylston St	Boston	MA	02115	**866-518-9113**		669
Capital Group Cos Inc 333 S Hope St	Los Angeles	CA	90071	**800-421-8511**	213-615-0514	401
Capital Growth Management LP 1 International Pl	Boston	MA	02110	**800-345-4048**	617-737-3225	401
Capital Health Plan PO Box 15349	Tallahassee	FL	32317	**800-390-1434**	850-383-3333	391-3
Capital Hill Hotel & Suites 88 Albert St	Ottawa	ON	K1P5E9	**800-463-7705**	613-235-1413	379
Capital Hospice Inc 2900 Telestar Ct	Falls Church	VA	22042	**855-571-5700**	703-538-2065	371
Capital Hotel 111 W Markham St	Little Rock	AR	72201	**877-637-0037**	501-374-7474	379
Capital Investment Advisors Inc 200 Sandy Springs Pl Ne Ste 300	Atlanta	GA	30328	**888-531-0018**	404-531-0018	196
Capital Journal 333 W Dakota Ave	Pierre	SD	57501	**800-537-0025**	605-224-7301	531-2
Capital Medical Ctr 3900 Capital Mall Dr SW	Olympia	WA	98502	**888-677-9757**	360-754-5858	374-3
Capital Merchant Solutions Inc 3005 Gill St Ste 2	Bloomington	IL	61704	**877-495-2419**		253
Capital Newspapers 1901 Fish Hatchery Rd	Madison	WI	53713	**888-798-4468**	920-887-0321	634-8
Capital One Auto Finance Inc PO Box 60511	City of Industry	CA	91716	**800-946-0332**		69
Capital One Financial Corp 1680 Capital One Dr (*NYSE: COF*)	McLean	VA	22102	**800-655-2265**	800-926-1000	219
Capital Public Radio Inc 7055 Folsom Blvd	Sacramento	CA	95826	**877-480-5900**	916-278-8900	642-101
Capital Realty Advisors Inc 600 Sandtree Dr Ste 109	Palm Beach Gardens	FL	33403	**800-940-1088**	561-624-5888	462
Capital Region International Airport 4100 Capital City Blvd	Lansing	MI	48906	**866-841-4900**	517-321-6121	27
Capital Regional Medical Ctr (CRMC) 2626 Capital Medical Blvd	Tallahassee	FL	32308	**800-994-6610**	850-325-5000	374-3
Capital Research & Management Co (CRMC) 333 S Hope St	Los Angeles	CA	90071	**800-421-4225**	213-486-9200	401
Capital Research Ctr 1513 16th St NW	Washington	DC	20036	**800-459-3950**	202-483-6900	631
Capital Resource Partners 31 State St 6th Fl	Boston	MA	02109	**800-623-2880**	617-478-9600	790
Capital Times 1901 Fish Hatchery Rd	Madison	WI	53713	**800-362-8333**	608-252-6400	531-2
Capital University College & Main St	Columbus	OH	43209	**866-544-6175**	614-236-6101	167
Capital University Law School 303 E Broad St	Columbus	OH	43215	**800-362-2779**	614-236-6500	168-1
Capitol Aggregates Ltd 12625 Wetmore Rd Ste 301	San Antonio	TX	78247	**800-292-5315**	210-871-6100	45
Capitol Aluminum & Glass Corp 1276 W Main St	Bellevue	OH	44811	**800-331-8268**	419-483-7050	331
Capitol Archives & Record Storage Inc 133 Laurel St	Hartford	CT	06106	**800-381-2277**	860-951-8981	196
Capitol Broadcasting Co Inc 2619 Western Blvd	Raleigh	NC	27606	**800-234-4857**	919-890-6000	735
Capitol Chevrolet Montgomery 711 Eastern Blvd (*Sales)	Montgomery	AL	36117	**800-410-1137***	334-272-8700	56
Capitol City Bancshares Inc 562 Lee St SW	Atlanta	GA	30311	**866-758-6395**	404-752-6067	360-2
Capitol City Container Corp 8240 Zionsville Rd	Indianapolis	IN	46268	**800-233-5145**	317-875-0290	99
Capitol City Produce 16550 Commercial Ave	Baton Rouge	LA	70816	**800-349-1583**	225-272-8153	297-21
Capitol City Speakers Bureau 1620 S Fifth St	Springfield	IL	62703	**800-397-3183**	217-544-8552	706
Capitol Connection 4400 University Dr MS 1D2	Fairfax	VA	22030	**844-504-7161**	703-993-3100	115
Capitol Detective Agency 2922 N 18th Pl	Phoenix	AZ	85016	**800-346-0347**	602-265-3462	400
Capitol Distributing Inc 3500 E Commercial Ct	Meridian	ID	83642	**800-769-5659**	208-888-5112	345
Capitol Federal Financial 700 Kansas Ave (*NASDAQ: CFFN*)	Topeka	KS	66603	**888-822-7333**	785-235-1341	360-2
Capitol FSB 700 S Kansas Ave	Topeka	KS	66603	**888-822-7333**	785-235-1341	69
Capitol Indemnity Corp 1600 Aspen Commons	Middleton	WI	53562	**800-475-4450**	608-829-4200	391-4
Capitol Insurance Cos 1600 Aspen Commons PO Box 5900	Middleton	WI	53562	**800-475-4450**	608-829-4200	391-4
Capitol Lien Records & Research Inc 1010 N Dale St	Saint Paul	MN	55117	**800-845-4077**	651-488-0100	632
Capitol Plaza Hotel 415 W McCarty St	Jefferson City	MO	65101	**800-338-8088**	573-635-1234	669
Capitol Plaza Hotel & Conference Ctr 100 State St	Montpelier	VT	05602	**800-274-5252**	802-223-5252	379
Capitol Plaza Hotel Jefferson City 415 W McCarty St	Jefferson City	MO	65101	**800-338-8088**	573-635-1234	379
Capitol Plywood Inc 160 Commerce Cir	Sacramento	CA	95815	**800-326-1505**	916-922-8861	612
Capitol Reservations 1730 Rhode Island Ave NW	Washington	DC	20036	**800-619-4337**	202-452-1270	376
Capitol Services Inc 206 E 9th St Ste 1300	Austin	TX	78701	**800-345-4647**		632
Capitol Steps Productions Inc 210 N Washington St	Alexandria	VA	22314	**800-733-7837**	703-683-8330	629
Capitol Technology University 11301 Springfield Rd	Laurel	MD	20708	**800-950-1992**	301-369-2800	167
Capitol Transamerica Corp 1600 Aspen Commons	Middleton	WI	53562	**800-475-4450**	608-829-4200	360-4
Caplugs LLC 2150 Elmwood Ave (*Cust Svc)	Buffalo	NY	14207	**888-227-5847***	716-876-9855	153
CAPP/USA 201 Marple Ave	Clifton Heights	PA	19018	**800-356-8000**	610-394-1100	204
Capricorn Coffees Inc 353 Tenth St	San Francisco	CA	94103	**800-541-0758**	415-621-8500	298-2
CapRock Communications Inc 4400 S Sam Houston Pkwy E	Houston	TX	77048	**888-482-0289**	832-668-2300	679
Capsmith Inc 2240 Old Lk Mary Rd	Sanford	FL	32771	**800-228-3889**	407-328-7660	156-6
Capstead Mortgage Corp 8401 N Central Expy Ste 800 (*NYSE: CMO*)	Dallas	TX	75225	**800-358-2323**	214-874-2323	652
Capstone Therapeutics Corp 1275 W Washington St Ste 101 (*OTC: CAPS*)	Tempe	AZ	85281	**800-937-5520**	602-286-5520	476
Capstone Turbine Corp 21211 Nordhoff St (*NASDAQ: CPST*)	Chatsworth	CA	91311	**866-422-7786**	818-734-5300	264

Company / Address	City	State	ZIP	Toll-Free	Phone	Class
Capt Harrys Fishing Supply Company Inc 8501 Nw Seventh Ave	Miami	FL	33150	**800-327-4088**	305-374-4661	709
Capt Hirams Resort 1606 Indian River Dr	Sebastian	FL	32958	**888-447-2671**	772-589-4345	379
Captain D's LLC 624 Grassmere Park Dr Ste 30	Nashville	TN	37211	**800-314-4819**	615-391-5461	668
CAPTE (Commission on Accreditation in Physical Therapy Education) 1111 N Fairfax St	Alexandria	VA	22314	**800-999-2782**	703-706-3245	47-1
Captive Fastener Corp 19 Thornton Rd	Oakland	NJ	07436	**800-526-4430**	201-337-6800	280
Captive-aire Systems Inc 4641 Paragon Pk Rd	Raleigh	NC	27616	**800-334-9256**	919-882-2410	695
Car City Motor Company Inc 3100 S US Hwy 169	Saint Joseph	MO	64503	**800-525-7008**	816-233-9149	56
Car Clinic Productions 5675 N Davis Hwy	Pensacola	FL	32503	**888-227-2546**	850-478-3139	644
Car Toys Inc 20 W Galer St	Seattle	WA	98119	**800-997-3644**	206-443-0980	51
CARA Group Inc, The Drake Oak Brook Plz 2215 York Rd Ste 300	Oak Brook	IL	60523	**866-401-2272**	630-574-2272	182
Cara Operations Ltd 199 Four Valley Dr	Vaughan	ON	L4K0B8	**800-860-4082**	905-760-2244	300
Carahsoft Technology Corp 12369 Sunrise Vly Dr Ste D2	Reston	VA	20191	**888-662-2724**	703-871-8500	227
Caraustar Industries Inc 5000 Austell-Powder Springs Rd Ste 300	Austell	GA	30106	**800-858-1438**	770-948-3100	553
Caravan Facilities Management LLC 1400 Weiss St	Saginaw	MI	48602	**855-211-7450**		194
Caravelle Resort Hotel & Villas 6900 N Ocean Blvd	Myrtle Beach	SC	29572	**800-507-9145**	843-918-8000	667
Carbo Ceramics Inc 575 N. Dairy Ashford Rd. Ste 300 *NYSE: CRR*	Houston	TX	77079	**800-551-3247**	281-921-6400	536
Carboline Co 350 Hanley Industrial Ct	Saint Louis	MO	63144	**800-848-4645**	314-644-1000	549
Carbon County PO Box 1017	Rawlins	WY	82301	**800-228-3547**		338
Carbon Power & Light Inc 100 E Willow Ave PO Box 579	Saratoga	WY	82331	**800-359-0249**	307-326-5206	247
CarbonWrap Solutions LLC 2820 E Ft Lowell Rd	Tucson	AZ	85716	**866-380-1269**	520-292-3109	538
Carbro Corp 15724 Condon Ave PO Box 278	Lawndale	CA	90260	**888-738-4400**	310-643-8400	492
Carcinoid Cancer Foundation Inc 333 Mamaroneck Ave Ste 492	White Plains	NY	10605	**888-722-3132**	212-722-3132	47-17
CARCO Group Inc 5000 Corporate Ct	Holtsville	NY	11742	**800-645-4556**	631-862-9300	632
Carco International Inc 2721 Midland Blvd	Fort Smith	AR	72904	**800-824-3215**	479-441-3270	276
Carco National Lease Inc 2905 N 32nd St	Fort Smith	AR	72904	**800-643-2596**	479-441-3200	776
Card Pak Inc 29601 Solon Rd	Solon	OH	44139	**800-824-3342**	440-542-3100	87
Cardi's Furniture 1 Furniture Way	Swansea	MA	02777	**866-419-4096**	508-379-7510	322
Cardiac Science Corp 3303 Monte Villa Pkwy *Cust Svc	Bothell	WA	98021	**800-426-0337***	425-402-2000	252
CardiacAssist Inc 240 Alpha Dr	Pittsburgh	PA	15238	**800-373-1607**	412-963-7770	475
Cardica Inc 900 Saginaw Dr *NASDAQ: CRDC*	Redwood City	CA	94063	**888-544-7194**	650-364-9975	475
Cardiff Park Advisors 2257 Vista La Nisa	Carlsbad	CA	92009	**888-332-2238**	760-635-7526	198
Cardinal Aluminum Co 6910 Preston Hwy *Cust Svc	Louisville	KY	40219	**800-398-7833***	502-969-9302	484
Cardinal Detecto Scale Manufacturing Co 203 E Daugherty St	Webb City	MO	64870	**800-441-4237**	417-673-4631	682
Cardinal Financial Corp 8270 Greensboro Dr Ste 500 *NASDAQ: CFNL*	McLean	VA	22102	**800-473-3247**	703-584-3400	360-2
Cardinal Gates 79 Amlajack Way	Newnan	GA	30265	**800-318-3380**	770-252-4200	63
Cardinal Health Nuclear Pharmacy Services 7000 Cardinal Pl	Dublin	OH	43017	**800-326-6457**	614-757-5000	240
Cardinal Industries Inc 21-01 51st Ave	Long Island	NY	11101	**800-622-8339**	718-784-3000	760
Cardinal Meat Specialists Ltd 155 Hedgedale Rd	Brampton	ON	L6T5P3	**800-363-1439**	905-459-4436	298-9
Cardinal Office Products Inc 576 E Main St	Frankfort	KY	40601	**800-589-5886**	502-875-3300	533
Cardinal Stritch University 6801 N Yates Rd	Milwaukee	WI	53217	**800-347-8822**	414-410-4000	167
Cardinal Transport Inc 7180 E Reed Rd	Coal City	IL	60416	**800-435-9302**	815-634-4443	778
Cardiome Pharma Corp 6190 Agronomy Rd 6th Fl. *NASDAQ: CRME*	Vancouver	BC	V6T1Z3	**800-330-9928**	604-677-6905	84
CardioMed Supplies Inc 199 Saint David St	Lindsay	ON	K9V5K7	**800-387-9757**	705-328-2518	474
Cardiovascular Systems Inc 1225 Old H 8 NW	St Paul	MN	55112	**877-274-0360**	651-259-1600	475
CardLogix 16 Hughes Ste 100	Irvine	CA	92618	**866-392-8326**	949-380-1312	702
Cardlytics Inc 675 Ponce de Leon Ave NE Ste 6000	Atlanta	GA	30308	**888-798-5802**		5
Cardolite Corp 500 Doremus Ave	Newark	NJ	07105	**800-322-7365**		143
Cardone Industries Inc 5501 Whitaker Ave *Cust Svc	Philadelphia	PA	19124	**800-777-4780***	215-912-3000	59
CardScan Inc 25 First St Ste 107	Cambridge	MA	02141	**800-942-6739**	617-492-4200	175-7
CardSmart Retail Corp 11 Executive Ave	Edison	NJ	08817	**888-782-7050**		311
CardTrak LLC 4055 Tamiami Trail	Port Charlotte	FL	33952	**800-344-7714**		393
CARE (Coalition for Auto Repair Equality) 105 Oronoco St Ste 115	Alexandria	VA	22314	**800-229-5380**	703-519-7555	48-21
Care of Trees Inc 2371 Foster Ave	Wheeling	IL	60090	**888-661-8268**		774
Care Partners 68 Sweeten Creek Rd	Asheville	NC	28803	**800-627-1533**	828-252-2255	363
CARE USA 151 Ellis St NE	Atlanta	GA	30303	**800-521-2273**	404-681-2552	47-5
Care Zone Inc 1463 East Republican St Ste 198	Seattle	WA	98112	**888-407-7785**		387
CareCentric Inc 20 Church St 12th Fl	Hartford	CT	06103	**866-467-8263**	800-808-1902	180-10
Career Education Corp (CEC) 2895 Greenspoint Pkwy Ste 600 *NASDAQ: CECO*	Hoffman Estates	IL	60196	**877-559-9222**	847-781-3600	244
Careerpros LLC 3392 Hillcrest Rd	Dubuque	IA	52002	**800-383-7641**	563-556-3040	40
Careers The Next Generation Foundation 10470 176 St Nw	Edmonton	AB	T5S1L3	**888-757-7172**	780-426-3414	306
CareerStaff Unlimited Inc 6363 N State Hwy 161 Ste 525	Irving	TX	75038	**888-993-4599**		719
Carefree Resort & Conference Ctr 37220 Mule Train Rd	Carefree	AZ	85377	**888-692-4343**		705
Carefree Vacations Inc 11885 Carmel Mt Rd Ste 906	San Diego	CA	92128	**800-266-3476**	858-450-4060	769
CareFusion Corp 3750 Torrey View Ct *NYSE: CFN*	San Diego	CA	92130	**888-876-4287**	858-617-2000	475
Carelink Health Plans 500 Virginia St E Ste 400	Charleston	WV	25301	**800-348-2922**	304-348-2900	391-3
Caremark Rx Inc PO Box 832407	Richardson	TX	75083	**877-460-7766**		585
Carenet Healthcare Services 11845 Interstate 10 W Ste 400	San Antonio	TX	78230	**800-809-7000**		393
CarePartners Mountain Area Hospice PO Box 5779	Asheville	NC	28813	**800-627-1533**	828-255-0231	371
Carepoint Inc 215 E Bay St Ste 304	Charleston	SC	29401	**800-296-1825**	843-853-6999	239
Carepro Health Services 1014 Fifth Ave SE	Cedar Rapids	IA	52403	**800-575-8810**		196
CareSource 230 N Main St	Dayton	OH	45402	**800-488-0134**	937-224-3300	352
Caresource Health Plan 740 SE Seventh St	Grants Pass	OR	97526	**888-460-0185**	541-471-4106	363
Carestar Inc 5566 Cheviot Rd	Cincinnati	OH	45247	**866-834-4712**	513-618-8300	363
Care-Tech Laboratories Inc 3224 S KingsHwy Blvd	Saint Louis	MO	63139	**800-325-9681**	314-772-4610	582
Carey Digital 1718 Central Pkwy	Cincinnati	OH	45214	**800-767-6071**	513-241-5210	779
Carey Executive Limousine 245 University Ave	Atlanta	GA	30315	**800-241-3943**	404-223-2000	441
Carey International Inc 4530 Wisconsin Ave NW	Washington	DC	20016	**800-336-4646**	202-895-1200	441
Carey Theological College 5920 Iona Dr	Vancouver	BC	V6T1J6	**844-862-2739**	604-224-4308	168-3
CARF (Commission on Accreditation of Rehabilitation Facilities International) 6951 E Southpoint Rd	Tucson	AZ	85756	**888-281-6531**	520-325-1044	47-1
CARF-CCAC (Continuing Care Accreditation Commission) 1730 Rhode Island Ave NW Ste 209	Washington	DC	20036	**866-888-1122**	202-587-5001	47-1
Cargill Assoc Inc 4701 Altamesa Blvd	Fort Worth	TX	76133	**800-433-2233**	817-292-9374	318
Cargill Energy PO Box 9300	Minneapolis	MN	55440	**800-227-4455**	952-742-7575	578
Cargill Foundation 15407 McGinty Rd W Ste 46	Wayzata	MN	55391	**800-227-4455**	877-765-8867	305
Cargill Inc 15407 McGinty Rd W	Wayzata	MN	55391	**800-227-4455**	952-742-7575	277
Cargill Ltd 300-240 Graham Ave PO Box 5900	Winnipeg	MB	R3C4C5	**888-855-8558**	204-947-0141	277
Cargill Salt Inc PO Box 5621	Minneapolis	MN	55440	**888-385-7258**		678
Cargo Equipment Corp 640 Church Rd	Elgin	IL	60123	**888-557-8727**	847-741-7272	768
Cargo Management Systems Llc 827 E Main St	Richmond	KY	40475	**855-484-9235**		197
Carhartt Inc 5750 Mercury Dr	Dearborn	MI	48126	**800-833-3118**	313-271-8460	154-18
Caribbean Gardens 1590 Goodlette-Frank Rd	Naples	FL	34102	**888-520-3756**	239-262-5409	821
Caribbean Products Ltd 3624 Falls Rd	Baltimore	MD	21211	**888-689-5068**		297-26
Caribbean Resort & Villas 3000 N Ocean Blvd	Myrtle Beach	SC	29577	**800-552-8509**		667
Caribbean Travel & Life Magazine 460 N Orlando Ave Ste 200 *Sales	Winter Park	FL	32789	**800-289-9399***	407-628-4802	456-22
Caribe Royale Orlando All-Suites Hotel & Convention Ctr 8101 World Ctr Dr *Resv	Orlando	FL	32821	**800-823-8300***	407-238-8000	379
Caribou Coffee Company Inc 3900 Lakebreeze Ave N *NASDAQ: CBOU* ■ *Cust Svc	Minneapolis	MN	55429	**888-227-4268***	763-592-2200	158
Caribou County 159 S Main	Soda Springs	ID	83276	**800-972-7660**	208-547-4324	338
Caribou Highlands Lodge 371 Ski Hill Rd PO Box 99	Lutsen	MN	55612	**800-642-6036**	218-663-7241	667
Carilion New River Valley Medical Ctr 2900 Lamb Cir	Christiansburg	VA	24073	**800-432-7874**	540-731-2000	374-3
Carina Technology Inc 1300 Meridian St Ste A-13	Huntsville	AL	35806	**866-915-5464**	256-704-0422	179

Company / Address	City	State	ZIP	Toll-Free	Phone	Class
Carithers Wallace Courtenay Co 4343 NE Expy	Atlanta	GA	30340	**800-292-8220**	770-493-8200	321
Carl Buddig & Co 950 175th St	Homewood	IL	60430	**888-633-5684**	708-798-0900	297-26
Carl Fischer Inc 48 Wall St 28th Fl	New York	NY	10005	**800-762-2328**	212-777-0900	634-7
Carl Nelson Insurance Agency I 1519 N 11th Ave	Hanford	CA	93230	**800-582-4264**	559-584-4495	390
Carl R Bieber Tourways Inc 320 Fair St PO Box 180	Kutztown	PA	19530	**800-243-2374**	610-683-7333	106
Carl Sandburg College 2400 Tom L Wilson Blvd	Galesburg	IL	61401	**877-236-1862**	309-344-2518	161
Carl Sandburg Home National Historic Site 81 Carl Sadburg Ln	Flat Rock	NC	28731	**877-642-4743**	828-693-4178	563
Carl Vinson Veterans Affairs Medical Ctr 1826 Veterans Blvd	Dublin	GA	31021	**800-595-5229**	478-272-1210	374-8
Carl Zeiss Industrial Metrology 6250 Sycamore Ln N	Maple Grove	MN	55369	**800-327-9735**	763-744-2400	492
Carl's Golfland Inc 1976 S Telegraph Rd	Bloomfield Hills	MI	48302	**877-412-2757**	248-335-8095	709
Carle Hospice 611 W Park St	Urbana	IL	61801	**800-239-3620**	217-383-3311	371
Carleton College 100 S College St *Admissions	Northfield	MN	55057	**800-995-2275***	507-646-4000	167
Carleton University 1125 Colonel By Dr	Ottawa	ON	K1S5B6	**888-354-4414**	613-520-7400	783
Carley State Park 19041 Hwy 74	Altura	MN	55910	**888-646-6367**	507-932-3007	564
Carling Technologies Inc 60 Johnson Ave	Plainville	CT	06062	**800-243-8556**	860-793-9281	813
Carlisle Cos Inc 13925 Ballantyne Corporate Pl Ste 400 *NYSE: CSL*	Charlotte	NC	28277	**800-248-5995**	704-501-1100	59
Carlisle FoodService Products Inc 4711 E Hefner Rd	Oklahoma City	OK	73131	**800-654-8210**	405-475-5600	301
Carlisle Industrial Brake 1031 E Hillside Dr	Bloomington	IN	47401	**800-873-6361**	812-336-3811	59
Carlisle Sanitary Maintenance Products 402 S Black River St	Sparta	WI	54656	**800-654-8210**	608-269-2151	102
Carlisle SynTec 1285 Ritner Hwy PO Box 7000	Carlisle	PA	17013	**800-479-6832**	717-245-7000	193-4
Carlo Gavazzi Inc 750 Hastings Ln	Buffalo Grove	IL	60089	**800-222-2659**	847-465-6100	263
Carlow University 3333 Fifth Ave	Pittsburgh	PA	15213	**800-333-2275**	412-578-6000	167
Carlsbad Convention & Visitors Bureau 400 Carlsbad Village Dr	Carlsbad	CA	92008	**800-227-5722**	760-434-6093	208
Carlsbad State Beach c/o San Diego Coast District Office 4477 Pacific Hwy	San Diego	CA	92110	**800-777-0369**	760-438-3143	564
Carlson *Radisson Hotels & Resorts* 701 Carlson Pkwy	Minnetonka	MN	55305	**800-333-3333**	763-212-5000	379
Carlson Craft Inc 1750 Tower Blvd	North Mankato	MN	56003	**800-774-6848**		626
Carlson Hotels Worldwide *Country Inns & Suites by Carlson* 11340 Blondo St Ste 100	Omaha	NE	68164	**800-600-7275**		379
Carlson Restaurants 4201 Marsh Ln	Carrollton	TX	75007	**800-374-3297**	972-662-5400	668
Carlson Tool & Manufacturing Corp W57 N14386 Doerr Way PO Box 85	Cedarburg	WI	53012	**800-532-2252**	262-377-2020	755
Carlson Wagonlit Travel Inc 701 Carlson Pkwy	Minnetonka	MN	55305	**800-213-7295**		770
Carlstar Group LLC, The 725 Cool Springs Blvd Ste 500	Franklin	TN	37067	**866-773-2926**	615-503-0220	370
Carlton Bates Co 3600 W 69th St	Little Rock	AR	72209	**866-600-6040**	501-562-9100	248
Carlton Foods Corp 880 Texas 46	New Braunfels	TX	78130	**800-628-9849**	830-625-7583	297-26
Carlton Group Inc 120 Landmark Dr	Greensboro	NC	27409	**800-722-7824**	336-668-7677	361
Carlton on Madison Ave 88 Madison Ave *Resv	New York	NY	10016	**800-601-8500***	212-532-4100	379
Carlyle Hotel, The 1731 New Hampshire Ave NW	Washington	DC	20009	**877-301-0019**	202-234-3200	379
Carlyle Johnson Machine Co (CJM) 291 Boston Tpke	Bolton	CT	06043	**888-629-4867**	860-643-1531	619
CarMax Inc 12800 Tuckahoe Creek Pkwy *NYSE: KMX*	Richmond	VA	23238	**888-722-7629**	804-747-0422	56
Carmel Clay Public Library 55 Fourth Ave SE	Carmel	IN	46032	**800-908-4490**	317-844-3361	434-3
Carmel River Inn 26600 Oliver Rd	Carmel	CA	93923	**800-882-8142**	831-624-1575	379
Carmel Valley Manor 8545 Carmel Vly Rd	Carmel	CA	93923	**800-544-5546**	831-624-1281	670
Carmel Valley Ranch Resort 1 Old Ranch Rd	Carmel	CA	93923	**866-405-5037**	831-625-9500	667
Carmeuse North America 11 Stanwix St 11th Fl	Pittsburgh	PA	15222	**866-243-0965**	412-995-5500	440
Carnations Home Fashions Inc 53 Jeanne Dr	Newburgh	NY	12550	**800-866-8949**	212-679-6017	361
Carnegie Body Co 9500 Brookpark Rd	Cleveland	OH	44129	**800-362-1989**	216-749-5000	515
Carnegie Corp of New York 437 Madison Ave	New York	NY	10022	**800-336-7323**	212-371-3200	306
Carnegie East House For Seniors 1844 Second Ave	New York	NY	10128	**888-410-0033**	212-410-0033	198
Carnegie Endowment for International Peace 1779 Massachusetts Ave NW	Washington	DC	20036	**877-866-3070**	202-483-7600	631
Carnegie Hall 881 Seventh Ave	New York	NY	10019	**800-728-3843**	212-247-7800	571
Carnegie Hotel 1216 W State of Franklin Rd	Johnson City	TN	37604	**866-757-8277**	423-979-6400	379
Carnegie Learning Inc 437 Grant St	Pittsburgh	PA	15219	**888-851-7094**	412-690-6284	179
Carnegie Mellon University 5000 Forbes Ave	Pittsburgh	PA	15213	**844-625-4600**	412-268-2000	167
Carnegie Regional Library 49 W Seventh St	Grafton	ND	58237	**800-568-5964**	701-352-2754	434-3
Carneros Inn, The 4048 Sonoma Hwy	Napa	CA	94559	**888-400-9000**	707-299-4900	705
Carney, Sandoe & Associates, Limited Partnersh 44 Bromfield St	Boston	MA	02108	**800-225-7986**	617-542-0260	244
Carnival Cruise Lines 3655 NW 87th Ave	Miami	FL	33178	**800-764-7419**	305-599-2600	222
Carnow Conibear & Assoc Ltd 600 W Van Buren Ste 500	Chicago	IL	60607	**800-860-4486**	312-782-4486	195
Caro Ctr 2000 Chambers Rd	Caro	MI	48723	**888-556-0490**	989-673-3191	374-5
Caro Foods Inc 2324 Bayou Blue Rd	Houma	LA	70364	**800-395-2276**	985-872-1483	298-7
Carol Stream Public Library 616 Hiawatha Dr	Carol Stream	IL	60188	**800-829-1040**	630-653-0755	434-3
Carol Woods Retirement Community 750 Weaver Dairy Rd	Chapel Hill	NC	27514	**800-518-9333**	919-968-4511	670
Carole Fabrics Inc PO Box 1436	Augusta	GA	30903	**800-241-0920**	706-863-4742	743
Carole Joy Creations Inc 1087 Federal Rd Unit 8 *Sales	Brookfield	CT	06804	**800-223-6945***	203-740-4490	129
Carolina Advanced Digital Inc 133 Triangle Trade Dr	Cary	NC	27513	**800-435-2212**	919-663-2211	462
Carolina Bank Holdings Inc 101 N Spring St *NASDAQ: CLBH*	Greensboro	NC	27401	**800-472-3272**	336-288-1898	360-2
Carolina Biological Supply Co 2700 York Rd	Burlington	NC	27215	**800-334-5551**	336-584-0381	245
Carolina Business Furniture LLC 535 Archdale Blvd	Archdale	NC	27263	**800-763-0212**	336-431-9400	320-1
Carolina Carports Inc 187 Cardinal Ridge Trl	Dobson	NC	27017	**800-670-4262**		486
Carolina Casualty Insurance Co 5011 Gate Pkwy Ste 200	Jacksonville	FL	32256	**800-874-8053**	904-363-0900	391-4
Carolina Container Co 909 Prospect St	High Point	NC	27260	**800-627-0825**	336-883-7146	99
Carolina Designs Realty Inc 1197 Duck Rd	Kitty Hawk	NC	27949	**800-368-3825**	252-261-3934	654
Carolina Dragway 302 Dragstrip Rd	Jackson	SC	29803	**877-471-7223**	803-471-2285	514
Carolina Farms Real Estate 547 S Main St	King	NC	27021	**800-559-2113**	336-983-5263	650
Carolina Filters Inc 109 E Newberry Ave	Sumter	SC	29150	**800-849-5646**	803-773-6842	804
Carolina Glove Co 116 Mclin Creek Rd PO Box 999	Conover	NC	28613	**800-335-1918**	828-464-1132	154-7
Carolina Hurricanes RBC Ctr 1400 EdwaRds Mill Rd	Raleigh	NC	27607	**800-521-7521**	919-467-7825	714
Carolina Inn 211 Pittsboro St	Chapel Hill	NC	27516	**800-962-8519**	919-933-2001	379
Carolina International Trucks Inc 1619 Bluff Rd	Columbia	SC	29201	**800-868-4923**	803-799-4923	56
Carolina Material Handling Services Inc PO Box 6	Columbia	SC	29202	**800-922-6709**	803-695-0149	385
Carolina Meadows 100 Carolina Meadows	Chapel Hill	NC	27517	**800-458-6756**	919-942-4014	670
Carolina Medical Lab 1815 Back Creek Dr	Charlotte	NC	28213	**800-963-3522**	704-598-8818	415
Carolina Mfg 7025 Augusta Rd	Greenville	SC	29605	**800-845-2744**	864-299-0600	154-12
Carolina Opry 8901 Hwy 17 N	Myrtle Beach	SC	29572	**800-843-6779**		571
Carolina Packers Inc 2999 S Bright Leaf Blvd	Smithfield	NC	27577	**800-682-7675**	919-934-2181	472
Carolina Panthers Bank of America Stadium 800 S Mint St	Charlotte	NC	28202	**888-297-8673**	704-358-7000	713-3
Carolina Rim & Wheel Co 1308 Upper Asbury Ave	Charlotte	NC	28206	**800-247-4337**	704-334-7276	60
Carolina Skiff Inc 3231 Fulford Rd	Waycross	GA	31503	**800-422-7282**	912-287-0547	89
Carolina Trust Bank 901 E Main St *NASDAQ: CART*	Lincolnton	NC	28092	**877-983-5537**	704-735-1104	69
Carolinas Auto Supply House Inc 2135 Tipton Dr	Charlotte	NC	28206	**800-438-4070**	704-334-4646	60
Carolinas Constructions Solutions Inc 6712 Old Pineville Rd	Charlotte	NC	28217	**866-521-5624**	704-578-1567	262
Carolinas Investment Consulting LLC 5605 Carnegie Blvd Ste 400	Charlotte	NC	28209	**800-255-2904**	704-643-2455	401
Carolinas Medical Center-NorthEast 920 Church St N	Concord	NC	28025	**800-575-1275**	704-403-1275	374-3
Carolinas Medical Center-University 8800 N Tryon St	Charlotte	NC	28262	**800-821-1535**	704-863-6000	374-3
Carolinas Medical Ctr Mercy 2001 Vail Ave	Charlotte	NC	28207	**800-821-1535**		374-3
Caroline County Public Library 100 Market St	Denton	MD	21629	**800-832-3277**	410-479-1343	434-3
Carollo Engineers 2700 Ygnacio Vly Rd Ste 300	Walnut Creek	CA	94598	**800-523-5826**	925-932-1710	263
Carolyn Scott Rainbow House 7815 Harney St	Omaha	NE	68114	**800-642-8822**	402-955-7815	372
Caron Compactor Co 1204 Ullrey Ave	Escalon	CA	95320	**800-542-2766**	209-838-2062	192
Caroplast Inc PO Box 668405	Charlotte	NC	28266	**800-327-5797**	704-394-4191	611
Carousel Beachfront Hotel & Suites 11700 Coastal Hwy	Ocean City	MD	21842	**800-641-0011**	410-524-1000	379

Company	Address	City	State	ZIP	Toll-Free	Phone	Class
Carousel Industries of North America Inc	659 S County Trl	Exeter	RI	02822	**800-401-0760**		226
Carousel Inn & Suites	1530 S Harbor Blvd	Anaheim	CA	92802	**800-854-6767**	714-758-0444	379
Carpedia International Ltd	75 Navy St	Oakville	ON	L6J2Z1	**877-445-8288**		462
Carpenter Co	5016 Monument Ave	Richmond	VA	23230	**800-288-3830**	804-359-0800	600
Carpenter Contractors of America Inc	3900 Ave D NW	Winter Haven	FL	33880	**800-959-8806**	863-294-6449	191-2
Carpenter Powder Products	600 Mayer St	Bridgeville	PA	15017	**866-790-9092**	412-257-5102	594
Carpenter Specialty Alloys Operations	101 W Bern St	Reading	PA	19601	**800-654-6543**	610-208-2000	721
Carpenter Technology Corp	PO Box 14662 *NYSE: CRS*	Reading	PA	19612	**800-654-6543**	610-208-2000	721
Carquest Corp	2635 E Millbrook Rd	Raleigh	NC	27604	**800-876-1291**	919-573-3000	60
Carr Business Systems Inc	130 Spagnoli Rd	Melville	NY	11747	**800-720-2277**	631-249-9880	111
Carr Concrete Corp	Waverly Rd	Waverly	WV	26184	**800-837-8918**	304-464-4013	185
Carr Corp	1547 11th St	Santa Monica	CA	90401	**800-952-2398**	310-587-1113	590
Carriage House Cos Inc, The	196 Newton St	Fredonia	NY	14063	**800-828-8915**	716-673-1000	297-20
Carriage Services Inc	3040 Post Oak Blvd Ste 300 *NYSE: CSV*	Houston	TX	77056	**866-332-8400**	713-332-8400	509
Carrico Implement Company Inc	3160 US 24 Hwy	Beloit	KS	67420	**877-542-4099**	785-738-5744	276
Carrier Clinic	252 County Rd 601	Belle Mead	NJ	08502	**800-933-3579**	908-281-1000	374-5
Carrier Corp	1 Carrier Pl	Farmington	CT	06034	**800-227-7437**	860-674-3000	14
Carrier Services of Tennessee Inc	2534 N Mount Juliet Rd	Mount Juliet	TN	37122	**800-825-7508**	615-758-9757	477
Carrier Vibrating Equipment Inc	3400 Fern Vly Rd	Louisville	KY	40213	**800-547-7278**	502-969-3171	209
Carrillo Business Technologies Inc	750 The City Dr S Ste 225	Orange	CA	92868	**888-241-7585**		181
Carrington Convention & Visitors Bureau	City Hall 103 10th Ave N PO Box 501	Carrington	ND	58421	**800-641-9668**	701-652-2524	208
Carroll & Co	425 N Canon Dr	Beverly Hills	CA	90210	**800-238-9400**	310-273-9060	156-3
Carroll Co	2900 W Kingsley Rd	Garland	TX	75041	**800-527-5722**	972-278-1304	150
Carroll College	1601 N Benton Ave	Helena	MT	59625	**800-992-3648**	406-447-4300	167
Carroll Community College	1601 Washington Rd	Westminster	MD	21157	**888-221-9748**	410-386-8000	161
Carroll County	8215 Black Oak Rd	Mount Carroll	IL	61053	**800-485-0145**	815-244-2035	338
Carroll County Chamber of Commerce & Economic Development	61 N Lisbon St PO Box 277	Carrollton	OH	44615	**800-956-4684**	330-627-4811	138
Carroll Electric Co-op Corp	920 Hwy 62 Spur	Berryville	AR	72616	**800-432-9720**	870-423-2161	247
Carroll Electric Co-op Inc	350 Canton Rd NW	Carrollton	OH	44615	**800-232-7697**	330-627-2116	247
Carroll Lutheran Village	300 St Luke Cir	Westminster	MD	21158	**877-848-0095**	410-848-0090	670
Carroll Publishing Co	4701 Sangamore Rd Ste S-155	Bethesda	MD	20816	**800-336-4240**	301-263-9800	634-2
Carroll Seating Company Inc	10 Lincoln St	Kansas City	KS	66103	**800-972-3779**	816-471-2929	321
Carroll University	100 NE Ave	Waukesha	WI	53186	**800-227-7655**	262-547-1211	167
Carroll Valley Golf Resort	78 Country Club Trail	Carroll Valley	PA	17320	**855-784-0330**	717-642-8282	667
Carrollton Public Library	4220 N Josey Ln	Carrollton	TX	75010	**888-727-2978**	972-466-4800	434-3
Carrom	218 E Dowland St	Ludington	MI	49431	**800-223-6047**	231-845-1263	320-2
Carron Net Company Inc	1623 17th St PO Box 177	Two Rivers	WI	54241	**800-558-7768**	920-793-2217	210
Carrot Medical LLC	22122 20th Ave SE Ste H-166	Bothell	WA	98021	**866-492-3533**	425-318-8089	740
Cars.com	175 W Jackson Blvd Ste 800	Chicago	IL	60604	**888-246-6298**	312-601-5000	57
CarsDirect.com Inc	909 N Sepulveda Blvd 11th Fl *Cust Svc	El Segundo	CA	90245	**888-227-7347***		57
Carson	3125 NW 35th Ave	Portland	OR	97210	**800-998-7767**	503-224-8500	578
Carson City Nugget	507 N Carson St	Carson City	NV	89701	**800-426-5239**	775-882-1626	132
Carson Helicopters	952 Blooming Glen Rd	Perkasie	PA	18944	**800-523-2335**	215-249-3535	359
Carson Hot Springs	1500 Hot Springs Rd	Carson City	NV	89706	**888-917-3711**	775-885-8844	49-4
Carson Valley Chamber of Commerce & Visitors Authority	1477 Hwy 395 N Ste A	Gardnerville	NV	89410	**800-727-7677**	775-782-8144	138
Carson Valley Inn Inc	1627 US Hwy 395 N	Minden	NV	89423	**866-284-7766**	775-782-9711	120
Carson-Dellosa Publishing Company Inc	7027 Albert Pick Rd	Greensboro	NC	27409	**800-321-0943**	336-632-0084	245
Carsonite Composites LLC	19845 US Hwy 76	Newberry	SC	29108	**800-648-7916**	803-321-1185	676
Carson-Newman College	1646 Russell Ave	Jefferson City	TN	37760	**800-678-9061**	865-471-2000	167
CARSTAR Quality Collision Service	8400 W 110th St Ste 200 *Cust Svc	Overland Park	KS	66210	**800-227-7827***	913-451-1294	61-4
Carswell Distributing Co	3750 N Liberty St	Winston-Salem	NC	27105	**800-929-1948**	336-767-7700	429
Cartec International Inc	106 Powder Mill Rd	Canton	CT	06019	**800-821-4434**	860-693-9395	604-2
Carter BloodCare	2205 Hwy 121	Bedford	TX	76021	**800-366-2834**	817-412-5000	88
Carter Bros LLC	3015 RN Martin St	East Point	GA	30344	**888-818-0152**		690
Carter County	101 1St Ave SW	Ardmore	OK	73401	**800-231-8668**	580-223-8162	338
Carter Ctr	1 Copenhill Ave 453 Freedom Pkwy	Atlanta	GA	30307	**800-550-3560**	404-420-5100	631
Carter Express Inc	4020 W 73rd St	Anderson	IN	46011	**800-738-7705**		196
Carter Healthcare	3105 S Meridian Ave	Oklahoma City	OK	73119	**888-951-1112**	405-947-7700	363
Carteret County Chamber of Commerce	801 Arendell St Ste 1	Morehead City	NC	28557	**800-622-6278**	252-726-6350	138
Carteret-Craven Electric Co-op (CCEC)	1300 Hwy 24 W PO Box 1490	Newport	NC	28570	**800-682-2217**	252-247-3107	247
Carter-Lee ProBuild	1717 W Washington St	Indianapolis	IN	46222	**800-344-9242**	317-639-5431	498
Carthage College	2001 Alford Pk Dr *Admissions	Kenosha	WI	53140	**800-351-4058***	262-551-8500	167
Carthage Mills	4243 Hunt Rd *Sales	Cincinnati	OH	45242	**800-543-4430***	513-794-1600	742-3
Cartier Place Suite Hotel	180 Cooper St	Ottawa	ON	K2P2L5	**800-236-8399**	613-236-5000	379
Carton Service Inc	First Quality Dr PO Box 702 *General	Shelby	OH	44875	**800-533-7744***	419-342-5010	100
Cartwright Cos, The	11901 Cartwright Ave	Grandview	MO	64030	**800-821-2334**		518
CartwrightDownes Inc	950 Lee St Ste 110	Des Plaines	IL	60016	**800-323-2049**	847-685-2700	196
Carus Corp	315 Fifth St	Peru	IL	61354	**800-435-6856**	815-223-1500	142
Caruso Inc	3465 Hauck Rd	Cincinnati	OH	45241	**800-759-7659**	513-860-9200	10-9
Carvel Express	200 Glenridge Pt Pkwy Ste 200	Atlanta	GA	30342	**800-322-4848**		381
Carvin Corp	12340 World Trade Dr	San Diego	CA	92128	**800-854-2235**	858-487-8700	526
Cary Oil Company Inc	110 Mackenan Dr	Cary	NC	27511	**800-227-9645**	919-462-1100	580
Carylon Corp	2500 W Arthington St	Chicago	IL	60612	**800-621-4342**	312-666-7700	665
CAS (Chemical Abstracts Service)	2540 Olentangy River Rd	Columbus	OH	43202	**800-848-6538**	614-447-3600	387
CAS Inc	PO Box 11190	Huntsville	AL	35814	**800-729-8686**	256-971-6126	263
CAS Medical Systems Inc	44 E Industrial Rd *NASDAQ: CASM*	Branford	CT	06405	**800-227-4414**	203-488-6056	475
CASA (National Court Appointed Special Advocate Assn)	100 W Harrison St N Twr Ste 500	Seattle	WA	98119	**800-628-3233**	206-270-0072	47-6
Casa Colina Ctr for Rehabilitation	255 E Bonita Ave	Pomona	CA	91769	**800-926-5462**	909-596-7733	449
Casa Esperanza	1005 Yale NE	Albuquerque	NM	87106	**866-654-1338**	505-246-2700	372
Casa Grande Ruins National Monument	1100 W Ruins Dr	Coolidge	AZ	85128	**877-642-4743**	520-723-3172	563
Casa Grande Valley Newspaper Inc	PO Box 15002	Casa Grande	AZ	85130	**800-352-3796**	520-836-7461	634-8
Casa Herrerra Inc	2655 N Pine St	Pomona	CA	91767	**800-624-3916**	909-392-3930	299
Casa Madrona Hotel	801 Bridgeway *General	Sausalito	CA	94965	**800-288-0502***	415-332-0502	379
Casa Monica Hotel	95 Cordova St *Help Line	Saint Augustine	FL	32084	**800-648-1888***	904-827-1888	379
Casa Munras Hotel	700 Munras Ave	Monterey	CA	93940	**800-222-2446**	831-375-2411	379
Casa Palmero	1518 Cypress Dr	Pebble Beach	CA	93953	**800-654-9300**	831-622-6650	667
Casa Ybel Resort	2255 W Gulf Dr	Sanibel Island	FL	33957	**800-276-4753**	239-472-3145	667
Casablanca Fan Co	761 Corporate Ctr Dr	Pomona	CA	91768	**888-227-2178**	909-689-1477	36
Casablanca Hotel	147 W 43rd St	New York	NY	10036	**888-922-7225**	212-869-1212	379
Casablanca Resort	950 W Mesquite Blvd	Mesquite	NV	89027	**800-459-7529**	702-346-7529	667
Cascade Bancorp	1100 NW Wall St *NASDAQ: CACB* ■ *Cust Svc	Bend	OR	97701	**877-617-3400***	541-385-6205	360-2
Cascade Corp	2201 NE 201st Ave *NYSE: CASC*	Fairview	OR	97024	**800-227-2233**	503-669-6300	469
Cascade Designs Inc	4000 First Ave S *Cust Svc	Seattle	WA	98134	**800-531-9531***	206-505-9500	708
Cascade Federal Credit Union	18020 80th Ave S	Kent	WA	98032	**800-562-2853**	425-251-8888	218
Cascade Financial Management Inc	950 17th St Ste 950	Denver	CO	80202	**800-353-0008**		196
Cascade Lodge	3719 W Hwy 61	Lutsen	MN	55612	**800-322-9543**	218-387-1112	667
Cascade Machinery & Electric Inc	4600 E Marginal Way S	Seattle	WA	98134	**800-289-0500**	206-762-0500	385
Cascade Microtech Inc	2430 NW 206th Ave *NASDAQ: CSCD*	Beaverton	OR	97006	**800-854-8400**	503-601-1000	250
Cascade Natural Gas Corp (CNGC)	8113 W Grandridge Blvd	Kennewick	WA	99336	**888-522-1130**	206-624-3900	785
Cascade Receivables Management LLC	101 Second St Ste 100	Petaluma	CA	94952	**888-417-1531**		393

Name	Address	City	State	ZIP	Toll-Free	Phone	Class
Cascade Regional Blood Services	220 S 'I' St	Tacoma	WA	98405	**877-242-5663**	253-383-2553	88
Cascade Steel Rolling Mills Inc (CSRM)	3200 N Hwy 99 W PO Box 687	McMinnville	OR	97128	**800-283-2776**	503-472-4181	721
Cascade Wholesale Hardware Inc	5650 NW *General	Hillsboro	OR	97124	**800-877-9987***	503-614-2600	351
Cascade Wood Products Inc	PO Box 2429	White City	OR	97503	**800-423-3311**	541-826-2911	498
Cascades Inc	404 Marie-Victorin Blvd *TSE: CAS*	Kingsey Falls	QC	J0A1B0	**800-361-4070**	819-363-5100	560
Cascades Inn	3226 Shepherd of the Hills Expy	Branson	MO	65616	**800-588-8424**	417-335-8424	379
Cascio Interstate Music	13819 W National Ave	New Berlin	WI	53151	**800-462-2263**	262-789-7600	525
CASE (Council of Administrators of Special Education)	Osigian Office Centre 101 Katelyn Cir Ste E	Warner Robins	GA	31088	**800-585-1753**	478-333-6892	48-5
CASE (Council for Advancement & Support of Education)	1307 New York Ave NW Ste 1000 *Orders	Washington	DC	20005	**800-554-8536***	202-328-5900	48-5
Case Design Corp	333 School Ln	Telford	PA	18969	**800-847-4176**	215-703-0130	201
Case Foundation Co	1325 W Lake St	Roselle	IL	60172	**800-999-4087**	630-529-2911	190-2
Case Logic Inc	6303 Dry Creek Pkwy	Longmont	CO	80503	**800-925-8111**	303-652-1000	533
Case Management Society of America (CMSA)	6301 Ranch Dr	Little Rock	AR	72223	**800-216-2672**	501-225-2229	48-8
Case Paper Company Inc	500 Mamaroneck Ave	Harrison	NY	10528	**800-222-2922**	914-899-3500	553
Case Western Reserve University	2061 Cornell Rd	Cleveland	OH	44106	**800-967-8898**	216-368-2000	167
Case Western Reserve University School of Law	11075 E Blvd	Cleveland	OH	44106	**800-756-0036**	216-368-3600	168-1
Casella Waste Systems Inc	25 Greens Hill Ln *NASDAQ: CWST*	Rutland	VT	05701	**800-227-3552**	802-775-0325	802
Casepro Inc	21738 Hardy Oak Blvd	San Antonio	TX	78258	**888-999-2594**	210-496-8050	363
Casey Research LLC	55 NE Fifth Ave	Delray Beach	FL	33483	**888-512-2739**	602-445-2736	401
Casey State Bank	305-307 N Central Ave	Casey	IL	62420	**866-666-2754**	217-932-2136	69
Casgrain & Company Ltd	1200 Mcgill College Ave 21st Fl.	Montreal	QC	H3B4G7	**800-361-8738**	514-871-8080	401
Cash Acme Inc	2727 Paces Ferry Rd SE Ste 1800	Atlanta	GA	30339	**877-700-4242**		787
Cash Flow Solutions Inc	5166 College Corner Pk	Oxford	OH	45056	**800-736-5123**		198
Cashtown Inn Restaurant	1325 Old Rt 30 PO Box 103	Cashtown	PA	17310	**800-367-1797**	717-334-9722	669
Cash-Wa Distributing Co	401 W Fourth St	Kearney	NE	68845	**800-652-0010**	308-237-3151	298-8
CASI (Computer Analytical Systems Inc)	1418 S Third St	Louisville	KY	40208	**800-977-3475**	502-635-2019	182
Casiano Communications Inc	1700 Fernandez Juncos Ave	San Juan	PR	00909	**844-723-2351**	787-728-3000	634-8
Casino Arizona at Salt River	524 N 92nd St *General	Scottsdale	AZ	85256	**866-877-9897***	480-850-7777	132
Casino Aztar	421 NW Riverside Dr	Evansville	IN	47708	**800-342-5386**	812-433-4000	132
Casino New Brunswick LP	21 Casino Dr	Moncton	NB	E1G0R7	**877-859-7775**	506-859-7770	132
Casino Niagara	5705 Falls Ave	Niagara Falls	ON	L2E6T3	**888-325-5788**		132
Casino Nova Scotia	1983 Upper Water St	Halifax	NS	B3J3Y5	**888-642-6376**	902-425-7777	132
Casino Queen	200 S Front St	East Saint Louis	IL	62201	**800-777-0777**	618-874-5000	132
Casino Royale Hotel	3411 Las Vegas Blvd S	Las Vegas	NV	89109	**800-854-7666**	702-737-3500	379
Casio Inc	570 Mt Pleasant Ave *Cust Svc	Dover	NJ	07801	**800-634-1895***	973-361-5400	590
Cask 'n' Cleaver	8689 Ninth St	Rancho Cucamonga	CA	91730	**800-995-4452**	909-981-5771	668
CASLPA (Speech-Language and Audiology Canada)	1 Nicholas St Ste 1000	Ottawa	ON	K1N7B7	**800-259-8519**	613-567-9968	47-1
CASM (Canadian Academy of Sport Medicine)	180 Elgin St Ste 1400	Ottawa	ON	K2P2K3	**877-585-2394**	613-748-5851	48-8
Casper Area Chamber of Commerce	500 N Ctr St	Casper	WY	82601	**866-234-5311**	307-234-5311	138
Casper Area Convention & Visitors Bureau	992 N Poplar St	Casper	WY	82601	**800-852-1889**	307-234-5362	208
Casper College	125 College Dr	Casper	WY	82601	**800-442-2963**	307-268-2100	161
Casper Events Ctr	1 Events Dr	Casper	WY	82601	**800-442-2256**	307-235-8441	207
Cass Cable Tv Inc	100 Redbud Rd	Virginia	IL	62691	**800-252-1799**	217-452-7725	115
Cass County Electric Co-op Inc	4100 32nd Ave SW	Fargo	ND	58104	**800-248-3292**	701-356-4400	247
Cass Tours	2621 Green River Rd Ste 105-222	Corona	CA	92882	**800-593-6510**	951-371-3511	769
Casselman River Bridge State Park	580 Taylor Ave Tawes State Ofc Bldg	Annapolis	MD	21401	**877-620-8367**		564
Casswood Insurance Agency Ltd	5 Executive Pk Dr	Clifton Park	NY	12065	**800-972-2242**	518-373-8700	390
Castalloy Inc	1701 Industrial Ln PO Box 827	Waukesha	WI	53189	**800-211-0900**	262-547-0070	308
Cast-Crete Corp	6324 County Rd 579	Seffner	FL	33584	**800-999-4641**	813-621-4641	185

Name	Address	City	State	ZIP	Toll-Free	Phone	Class
Caster Technology Corp	11552 Markon Dr	Garden Grove	CA	92841	**866-547-8090**	714-893-6886	351
Castine Moving & Storage	1235 Chestnut St	Athol	MA	01331	**800-225-8068**	978-249-9105	518
Castle Brands Inc	122 E 42nd St Ste 4700 *NYSE: ROX*	New York	NY	10168	**800-882-8140**	646-356-0200	80-3
Castle Hill Inn & Resort	590 Ocean Dr	Newport	RI	02840	**888-466-1355**	401-849-3800	667
Castle in the Sand Hotel	3701 Atlantic Ave	Ocean City	MD	21842	**800-552-7263**	410-289-6846	379
Castle Inn & Suites	1734 S Harbor Blvd	Anaheim	CA	92802	**800-227-8530**	714-774-8111	379
Castle on the Hudson	400 Benedict Ave	Tarrytown	NY	10591	**800-616-4487**	914-631-1980	379
Castle Worldwide Inc	900 Perimeter Pk Rd Ste G	Morrisville	NC	27560	**800-655-4845**	919-572-6880	246
Castlegarde Inc	4911 S W Shore Blvd	Tampa	FL	33611	**866-751-3203**	813-872-4844	691
Castleton State College	86 Seminary St	Castleton	VT	05735	**800-639-8521**	802-468-5611	167
Casto Technical Services Inc	540 Leon Sullivan Way	Charleston	WV	25301	**800-232-2221**	304-346-0549	609
Casto Travel Inc	2560 N First St Ste 150	San Jose	CA	95131	**800-832-3445**	408-984-7000	769
Castrol Industrial North America Inc	150 W Warrenville Rd	Naperville	IL	60563	**877-641-1600**		540
Casual Designs Furniture Inc	36523 Lighthouse Rd	Selbyville	DE	19975	**888-629-1717**	302-436-8224	322
Cat Fancy Magazine	3 Burroughs *Cust Svc	Irvine	CA	92618	**800-546-7730***	949-855-8822	456-14
Catalina Express	Berth 95	San Pedro	CA	90731	**800-481-3470**	310-519-7971	467
Catalina Graphic Films Inc	27001 Agoura Rd Ste 100	Calabasas Hills	CA	91301	**800-333-3136**	818-880-8060	599
Catalina Island Visitors Bureau	1 Green Pier PO Box 217	Avalon	CA	90704	**877-854-1125**	310-510-1520	208
Catalina Marketing Corp	200 Carillon Pkwy	Saint Petersburg	FL	33716	**888-322-3814**	727-579-5000	5
Catalog.com Inc	14000 Quail Springs Pkwy Ste 3600	Oklahoma City	OK	73134	**888-932-4376**	405-753-9300	806
Catalyst Awareness Inc	355 Elmira Rd N Ste 127	Guelph	ON	N1K1S5	**866-749-3697**		262
Catapult Systems Inc	1221 S MoPac Expwy Ste 350	Austin	TX	78746	**800-528-6248**	512-328-8181	182
Catawba College	2300 W Innes St	Salisbury	NC	28144	**800-228-2922**	704-637-4111	167
Catawba Hospital	5525 Catawba Hospital Dr	Catawba	VA	24070	**800-451-5544**	540-375-4200	374-5
Catawba Valley Community College	2550 US Hwy 70 SE	Hickory	NC	28602	**800-433-3243**	828-327-7000	161
Catchpole Corp, The	10 High St Ste 502	Boston	MA	02110	**866-431-2666**	781-431-2666	462
Catfish Bend Casinos II LLC	3001 Winegard Dr	Burlington	IA	52601	**866-792-9948**	319-753-2946	451
Cathay General Bancorp Inc	777 N Broadway *NASDAQ: CATY*	Los Angeles	CA	90012	**800-922-8429**	213-625-4700	360-2
Cathay Pacific Cargo	6040 Avion Dr Ste 338	Los Angeles	CA	90045	**800-628-6960**	310-417-0052	12
Cathedral Caverns State Park	637 Cave Rd	Woodville	AL	35776	**800-252-7275**	256-728-8193	564
Cathedral Corp	632 Ellsworth Rd Griffis Technology Park	Rome	NY	13441	**800-698-0299**	315-338-0021	626
Cathedral of Our Lady of the Angels	555 W Temple St	Los Angeles	CA	90012	**800-838-1356**	213-680-5200	49
Cathedral Press Inc	600 NE Sixth St *Cust Svc	Long Prairie	MN	56347	**800-874-8332***	320-732-6143	634-10
Cathedral State Park	Rt 1 12 Cathedral Way	Aurora	WV	26705	**800-225-5982**	304-735-3771	564
Catholic Church Extension Society of the USA	150 S Wacker Dr 20th Fl.	Chicago	IL	60606	**800-842-7804**		47-20
Catholic Digest	PO Box 6015	New London	CT	06320	**800-678-2836**	860-437-3012	456-18
Catholic Healthcare Partners	615 Elsinore Pl	Cincinnati	OH	45202	**877-700-4647**	513-639-2800	353
Catholic Medical Ctr (CMC)	100 McGregor St	Manchester	NH	03102	**800-437-9666**	603-668-3545	374-3
Catholic Medical Mission Board (CMMB)	10 W 17th St	New York	NY	10011	**800-678-5659**	212-242-7757	47-5
Catholic Mutual Group	10843 Old Mill Rd	Omaha	NE	68154	**800-228-6108**	402-551-8765	391-5
Catholic Order of Foresters	355 Shuman Blvd	Naperville	IL	60563	**800-617-4176**	630-983-4900	391-2
Catholic Press Assn (CPA)	205 W Monroe St Ste 470	Chicago	IL	60606	**800-777-7432**	312-380-6789	48-14
Catholic Relief Services (CRS)	228 W Lexington St	Baltimore	MD	21201	**800-235-2772**	410-625-2220	47-5
Catholic Supply of st Louis Inc	6759 Chippewa St	Saint Louis	MO	63109	**800-325-9026**	314-644-0643	47-20
Catholic Transcript Inc, The	467 Bloomfield Ave	Bloomfield	CT	06002	**800-726-2381**	860-286-2828	47-20
Catholic University of America Press	620 Michigan Ave NE 240 Leahy Hall	Washington	DC	20064	**800-537-5487**	202-319-5052	634-4
CatholicMatch LLC	211 E Grandview Ave	Zelienople	PA	16063	**888-605-3977**		387
Cato Corp, The	8100 Denmark Rd	Charlotte	NC	28273	**800-526-9169**	704-554-8510	156-6
Catskill Area Hospice & Palliative Care Inc	1 Birchwood Dr	Oneonta	NY	13820	**800-306-3870**	607-432-6773	371
Catskill Regional Medical Ctr	68 Harris-Bushville Rd PO Box 800	Harris	NY	12742	**888-846-5945**	845-794-3300	374-3

Name / Address	City	State	Zip	Toll-Free	Phone	Class
Cattaneo Bros Inc 769 Caudill St	San Luis Obispo	CA	93401	**800-243-8537**	805-543-7188	297-26
CattleLog 10305 102nd Terrace	Sebastian	FL	32958	**866-239-2665**		465
Cauthorne Paper Co 12124 S Washington Hwy	Ashland	VA	23005	**800-552-3011**	804-798-6999	556
Cavalier Homes Inc 32 Wilson Blvd PO Box 300	Addison	AL	35540	**800-743-2284**		504
Cavalier Telephone LLC 2134 W Laburnum Ave	Richmond	VA	23227	**800-683-3944**	800-442-2410	733
Cavanagh Law Firm, The 1850 N Central Ave	Phoenix	AZ	85004	**888-824-3476**	602-322-4000	428
Cavco Industries Inc 1001 N Central Ave 8th Fl *NASDAQ: CVCO*	Phoenix	AZ	85004	**800-790-9111**	602-256-6263	504
Cayenta Canada Corp 4200 N Fraser Way Ste 201	Burnaby	BC	V5J5K7	**866-229-3682**	604-570-4300	38
Cayman Airways Cargo Services 6103 NW 72nd Ave	Miami	FL	33166	**800-252-2746**	305-526-3190	12
Cayman Airways Ltd 91 Owen Roberts Dr	Grand Cayman	KY	10092	**800-422-9626**	345-949-8200	25
Cayman Islands Dept of Tourism 350 Fifth Ave	New York	NY	10118	**800-235-5888**	212-889-9009	773
Cayman Technologies Inc 12954 Stonecreek Dr Ste E	Pickerington	OH	43147	**877-370-9470**	614-759-9461	182
Cayuga Community College 197 Franklin St	Auburn	NY	13021	**866-598-8883**	315-255-1743	161
Cazenovia College 8 Sullivan St	Cazenovia	NY	13035	**800-654-3210**	315-655-7208	167
CB Fleet Co Inc 4615 Murray Pl	Lynchburg	VA	24502	**866-255-6960**	434-528-4000	582
CBAN (Community Banking Advisory Network) 1801 W End Ave Ste 800	Nashville	TN	37203	**800-231-2524**	615-373-9880	48-2
CBB (Citizens Business Bank) 701 N Haven Ave *Cust Svc	Ontario	CA	91764	**888-222-5432***	909-980-4030	69
CBD (Cincinnati Bell Directory) 312 Plum St Ste 600	Cincinnati	OH	45202	**800-877-0475**		634-6
CBE Companies Inc 1309 Technology Pkwy	Cedar Falls	IA	50613	**800-925-6686**		393
CBI Laboratories 4201 Diplomacy Rd	Fort Worth	TX	76155	**800-822-7546**	972-241-7546	217
CBI Research Inc 600 Unicorn Park Dr	Woburn	MA	01801	**800-817-8601**	339-298-2100	196
CBI Services Inc 14105 S Route 59	Plainfield	IL	60544	**866-235-5687**	302-325-8400	191-14
CBIZ Benefits & Insurance Services of Maryland Inc 44 Baltimore St *Cust Svc	Cumberland	MD	21502	**800-615-8418***	301-777-1500	390
CBIZ Tofias PC 500 Boylston St	Boston	MA	02116	**888-761-8835**	617-761-0600	2
CBM (Christian Blind Mission) 450 E Pk Ave	Greenville	SC	29601	**800-937-2264**	864-239-0065	47-5
CBM of America Inc 1455 W Newport Ctr Dr	Deerfield Beach	FL	33442	**800-881-8202**	954-698-9104	182
CBMC (Connecting Businessmen to Christ) 5746 Marlin Rd Ste 602 Osborne Ctr	Chattanooga	TN	37411	**800-566-2262**	423-698-4444	47-20
CBMR (Crested Butte Mountain Resort) 12 Snowmass Rd PO Box 5700	Crested Butte	CO	81225	**877-547-5143**		667
CBN (Christian Broadcasting Network) 977 Centerville Tpke	Virginia Beach	VA	23463	**800-759-0700**	757-226-7000	736
CBOE (Chicago Board Options Exchange) 400 S La Salle St	Chicago	IL	60605	**800-678-4667**	312-786-5600	689
CBRL Group Inc PO Box 787	Lebanon	TN	37088	**800-333-9566**		360-3
CBV Collections 1200-100 Sheppard Ave E	Toronto	ON	M2N6N5	**866-877-9323**	416-482-9323	159
CBVE-FM 104.7 (CBC) PO Box 3220 Station C	Ottawa	ON	K1Y1E4	**866-306-4636**		642-94
CBV-FM 106.3 (CBC) PO Box 500 Stn A	Toronto	ON	M5W1E6	**866-306-4636**		643
Cbw Automation 3939 automation way	Fort collins	CO	80525	**800-229-9500**	970-229-9500	755
Cc Columbia Collectors Inc 1104 Main St Ste 311	Vancouver	WA	98660	**800-694-7585**	360-694-7585	159
C&C Fabrication Company Inc 30 Fabrication Dr	Lacey's Spring	AL	35754	**888-485-5130**	256-881-7300	200
Cc Pollen Co 3627 E Indian School Rd Ste 209	Phoenix	AZ	85018	**800-875-0096**		797
CCA (Coastal Conservation Assn) 6919 Portwest Dr Ste 100	Houston	TX	77024	**800-201-3474**	713-626-4234	47-13
CCA Global Partners 4301 Earth City Expy	Earth City	MO	63045	**800-466-6984**	314-506-0000	361
CCA Industries Inc 200 Murray Hill Pkwy *NYSE: CAW* ■ *Cust Svc	East Rutherford	NJ	07073	**800-524-2720***	201-935-3232	217
Cca Medical Inc 6 Southridge Ct	Greenville	SC	29607	**800-775-2556**	864-233-2700	182
CCC (Copyright Clearance Ctr Inc) 222 Rosewood Dr	Danvers	MA	01923	**855-239-3415**	978-750-8400	48-16
CCC (Consolidated Container Co) 3101 Towercreek Pkwy Ste 300 *Sales	Atlanta	GA	30339	**888-831-2184***	678-742-4600	547
CCC (Clovis Community College) 417 Schepps Blvd	Clovis	NM	88101	**800-769-1409**	575-769-2811	161
CCC Information Services Inc 222 Merchandise Mart Plz	Chicago	IL	60654	**800-621-8070**		227
CCCC (Conference on College Composition & Communication) 1111 W Kenyon Rd	Urbana	IL	61801	**877-369-6283**	217-328-3870	48-5
CCCS (CAD/CAM Consulting Services Inc) 996 Lawrence Dr Ste 101	Newbury Park	CA	91320	**888-375-7676**	805-375-7676	176
CCCVB (Clermont County Convention & Visitors Bureau) 410 E Main St PO Box 100	Batavia	OH	45103	**800-796-4282**	513-732-3600	208
CCDNCVB (Crescent City-Del Norte County Chamber of Commerce) 1001 Front St	Crescent City	CA	95531	**800-343-8300**	707-464-3174	208
CCEC (Carteret-Craven Electric Co-op) 1300 Hwy 24 W PO Box 1490	Newport	NC	28570	**800-682-2217**	252-247-3107	247

Name / Address	City	State	Zip	Toll-Free	Phone	Class
CCFA (Crohn's & Colitis Foundation of America) 386 Pk Ave S 17th Fl	New York	NY	10016	**800-932-2423**	212-685-3440	47-17
CCH Small Firm Services 225 Chastain Meadows Ct NW Ste 200 *Sales	Kennesaw	GA	30144	**866-345-4171***		180-10
CCH Washington Service Bureau Inc 1015 15th St NW 10th Fl	Washington	DC	20005	**800-955-5219**	202-312-6600	632
CCI (Canine Companions for Independence Inc) 2965 Dutton Ave PO Box 446	Santa Rosa	CA	95402	**800-572-2275**	707-577-1700	47-17
CCI (Charlestown Retirement Community) 715 Maiden Choice Ln	Catonsville	MD	21228	**800-917-8649**	410-242-2880	670
CCI Thermal Technologies Inc 5918 Roper Rd *Cust Svc	Edmonton	AB	T6B3E1	**800-661-8529***	780-466-3178	319
CCIM Institute 430 N Michigan Ave Ste 800	Chicago	IL	60611	**800-621-7027**	312-321-4460	48-17
CCL Label Inc 161 Worcester Rd Ste 502	Framingham	MA	01701	**877-240-9772**	508-872-4511	413
CCM (Comprehensive Care Management Corp) 1250 Waters Pl Tower 1 Ste 602	Bronx	NY	10461	**877-226-8500**		449
CCMG (Clark Capital Management Group Inc) 1650 Market St 1 Liberty Pl 53rd Fl	Philadelphia	PA	19103	**800-766-2264**	215-569-2224	401
CCON (Columbia College of Nursing) 4425 N Port Washington Rd	Glendale	WI	53212	**800-221-5573**	414-326-2330	167
CCPS (Center for Chemical Process Safety) 120 Wall St	New York	NY	10005	**800-242-4363**	646-495-1371	48-19
CCRKBA (Citizens Committee for the Right to Keep & Bear Arms) 12500 NE Tenth Pl	Bellevue	WA	98005	**800-426-4302**	425-454-4911	47-7
CCRTA (Cape Cod Regional Transit Authority) 215 Iyannough Rd PO Box 1988	Hyannis	MA	02601	**800-352-7155**	508-775-8504	467
CCS (Credit Control Services Inc) 2 Wells Ave Ste 1	Newton	MA	02459	**800-526-0532**	617-965-2000	159
CCS (Custom Computer Specialists Inc) 70 Suffolk Ct	Hauppauge	NY	11788	**800-598-8989**	631-864-6699	182
CCS (Check Cashing Store) 6340 NW Fifth Way	Fort Lauderdale	FL	33309	**800-361-1407**		140
CCS Medical Inc 1505 LBJ Fwy Ste 600	Farmers Branch	TX	75234	**800-726-9811**	800-260-8193	474
CCSAA (Cross Country Ski Areas Assn) 259 Bolton Rd	Winchester	NH	03470	**877-779-2754**	603-239-4341	47-22
CCSD (Charleston County School District) 75 Calhoun St	Charleston	SC	29401	**800-255-7688**	843-937-6300	683
CCSD (Clark County School District) 5100 W Sahara Ave	Las Vegas	NV	89146	**866-799-8997**	702-799-5000	683
CCSNH (Community College System of New Hampshire) 26 College Dr	Concord	NH	03301	**866-945-2255**	603-271-2722	161
CCT (Chesapeake Conventions & Tourism Bureau) 860 Greenbrier Cir Ste 101	Chesapeake	VA	23320	**888-889-5551**	757-502-4898	208
CCTF Corp 5407 - 53 Ave NW	Edmonton	AB	T6B3G2	**800-661-3633**	780-463-8700	110
CCUSD (Culver City Unified School District) 4034 Irving Pl	Culver City	CA	90232	**855-446-2673**	310-842-4220	683
CD Ford & Sons Inc PO Box 300	Geneseo	IL	61254	**800-383-4661**	309-944-4661	369
CD Publications 8204 Fenton St	Silver Spring	MD	20910	**800-666-6380**	301-588-6380	530-2
C&D Technologies 11 Cabot Blvd	Mansfield	MA	02048	**800-233-2765**	508-339-3000	255
CD Universe 101 N Plains Industrial Rd	Wallingford	CT	06492	**800-231-7937**	203-294-1648	524
CD Warehouse 900 N Broadway	Oklahoma City	OK	73102	**800-641-9394**	919-577-6000	524
CDA (Chemically Dependent Anonymous) PO Box 423	Severna Park	MD	21146	**888-232-4673**		47-21
CDC Distributors 10511 Medallion Dr	Cincinnati	OH	45241	**800-678-2321**	513-771-3100	361
CDC Small Business Finance Corp 2448 Historic Decatur Rd Ste 200	San Diego	CA	92106	**800-611-5170**	619-291-3594	218
CDC Trade Beam Inc 2 Waters Pk Dr Ste 100	San Mateo	CA	94403	**888-311-1415**	650-653-4800	180-1
CDF (Children's Defense Fund) 25 E St NW	Washington	DC	20001	**800-233-1200**	202-628-8787	47-6
CDGRA (Colorado Dude & Guest Ranch Assn) PO Box D	Shawnee	CO	80475	**866-942-3472**		47-23
CDI (Consolidated Devices Inc) 19220 San Jose Ave	City of Industry	CA	91748	**800-525-6319**	626-965-0668	756
CDI Corporation 1717 Arch St 35th Fl	Philadelphia	PA	19103	**866-472-2203**	215-569-2200	263
CDI Credit Inc 6160 Peachtree Dunwoody Rd NE Ste B-210	Atlanta	GA	30328	**800-633-3961**	770-350-5070	632
CdLS (Cornelia de Lange Syndrome Foundation Inc) 302 W Main St Ste 100	Avon	CT	06001	**800-753-2357**	860-676-8166	47-17
CDMA (Chain Drug Marketing Assn) 43157 W Nine-Mile Rd PO Box 995	Novi	MI	48376	**800-935-2362**	248-449-9300	48-18
CDMS Inc 550 Sherbrooke W West Tower Ste 250	Montreal	QC	H3A1B9	**866-337-2367**	514-286-2367	182
Cdo Technologies Inc 5200 Sprngfeld St Ste 320	Dayton	OH	45431	**866-307-6616**	937-258-0022	448
Cdr Assessment Group Inc 1644 S Denver Ave	Tulsa	OK	74119	**888-406-0100**	918-488-0722	197
CDS Analytical Inc 465 Limestone Rd PO Box 277	Oxford	PA	19363	**800-541-6593**	610-932-3636	419
CDS Logistics Management Inc 1225 Bengies Rd Ste A	Baltimore	MD	21220	**866-649-9559**	410-314-8000	312
CDS-John Blue Co 290 Pinehurst Dr	Huntsville	AL	35806	**800-253-2583**	256-721-9090	638
Cdspi 155 Lesmill Rd	Toronto	ON	M3B2T8	**800-561-9401**	416-296-9401	391-3
CDT (Center for Democracy & Technology) 1634 'I' St NW 11th Fl	Washington	DC	20006	**800-869-4499**	202-637-9800	47-7
CDW Corp 200 N Milwaukee Ave	Vernon Hills	IL	60061	**800-800-4239**	847-465-6000	181
CE Conover & Company Inc 4106 Blanche Rd	Bensalem	PA	19020	**800-266-6837**	215-639-6666	327

Name / Address	City	State	ZIP	Toll-Free	Phone	Class
CE Niehoff & Co 2021 Lee St *Tech Supp	Evanston	IL	60202	**800-643-4633***	847-866-6030	249
CE Resource Inc 1482 Stone Point Dr Ste 100	Roseville	CA	95661	**800-707-5644**		462
CE Rogers Co 1895 Frontage Rd	Mora	MN	55051	**800-279-8081**	320-679-2172	299
CE Thurston & Sons Inc 3335 Croft St	Norfolk	VA	23513	**800-444-7713**	757-855-7700	191-9
CEA (Cultural Experiences Abroad) 2999 N 44th St Ste 200	Phoenix	AZ	85018	**800-266-4441**	480-557-7900	758
CEC (Career Education Corp) 2895 Greenspoint Pkwy Ste 600 *NASDAQ: CECO*	Hoffman Estates	IL	60196	**877-559-9222**	847-781-3600	244
Cec Controls Co Inc 14555 Barber Ave	Warren	MI	48088	**877-924-0303**	586-779-0222	203
CEC Entertainment Inc 3903 W Airport Frwy *NYSE: CEC*	Irving	TX	75062	**888-778-7193**	972-258-8507	668
CEC Industries Ltd 599 Bond St	Lincolnshire	IL	60069	**800-572-4168**	847-821-1199	53
Cecil Community College 1 Seahawk Dr	North East	MD	21901	**866-966-1001**	410-287-6060	161
CECO (Compressor Engineering Corp) 5440 Alder Dr	Houston	TX	77081	**800-879-2326**	713-664-7333	174
CED (Committee for Economic Development) 2000 L St NW Ste 700	Washington	DC	20036	**800-676-7353**	202-296-5860	631
Cedar Breaks National Monument 2390 W Hwy 56 Ste 11	Cedar City	UT	84720	**877-642-4743**	435-586-9451	563
Cedar City-Brian Head Tourism & Convention Bureau 581 N Main St	Cedar City	UT	84721	**800-354-4849**	435-586-5124	208
Cedar Crest College 100 College Dr *Admissions	Allentown	PA	18104	**800-360-1222***	610-437-4471	167
Cedar Crest Specialties Inc 7269 Hwy 60 PO Box 260 *Hotline	Cedarburg	WI	53012	**800-877-8341***	262-377-7252	297-25
Cedar Fair Parks 14523 Carowinds Blvd	Charlotte	NC	28273	**800-888-4386**	704-588-2600	32
Cedar Farms 2100 Hornig Rd	Philadelphia	PA	19116	**800-220-2217**	215-934-7100	298-6
Cedar Grove Composting Inc 7343 E Marginal Way S	Seattle	WA	98108	**888-832-3008**	206-832-3000	188
Cedar Rapids Area Convention & Visitors Bureau 87 16th Ave Ste 200	Cedar Rapids	IA	52404	**800-735-5557**	319-398-5009	208
Cedar Rapids Truck Ctr Inc 9201 Sixth St SW	Cedar Rapids	IA	52404	**866-602-1597**	319-848-6230	778
Cedar Springs Behavioral Health System 2135 Southgate Rd	Colorado Springs	CO	80906	**800-888-1088**	719-633-4114	374-5
Cedar Springs Post 36 E Maple PO Box 370	Cedar Springs	MI	49319	**888-937-4514**	616-696-3655	531-4
Cedar Valley Hospice 2101 Kimball Ave Ste 401	Waterloo	IA	50702	**800-617-1972**	319-272-2002	371
Cedara Software Corp 6303 Airport Rd Ste 500	Mississauga	ON	L4V1R8	**800-724-5970**	905-364-8000	180-10
Cedarlane Laboratories Inc 4410 Paletta Ct	Burlington	ON	L7L5R2	**800-268-5058**	905-878-8891	233
Cedars of Lebanon State Park 328 Cedar Forest Rd	Lebanon	TN	37090	**800-250-8615**	615-443-2769	564
Cedars-Sinai Medical Ctr (CSMC) 8700 Beverly Blvd	Los Angeles	CA	90048	**800-233-2771**	310-423-3277	374-3
Cedarstore.com 5410 Rt 8	Gibsonia	PA	15044	**888-885-3806**	724-444-5300	105
Cedarville University 251 N Main St	Cedarville	OH	45314	**800-233-2784**	937-766-7700	167
CEDIA (Custom Electronic Design & Installation Assn) 7150 Winton Dr Ste 300	Indianapolis	IN	46268	**800-669-5329**	317-328-4336	48-19
Ceeva Inc 643 First Ave Ste 300	Pittsburgh	PA	15219	**866-233-8248**	412-690-2300	196
CEF Industries Inc 320 S Church St	Addison	IL	60101	**800-888-6419**	630-628-2299	22
CEI (Culbertson Enterprises Inc) 600A Snyder Ave	West Chester	PA	19382	**800-382-2685**	610-436-6400	191-7
CEI Enterprises Inc 245 WoodwaRd Rd SE	Albuquerque	NM	87102	**800-545-4034**		14
Ceilings & Interior Systems Construction Assn (CISCA) 1010 Jorie Blvd Ste 30	Oak Brook	IL	60523	**866-560-8537**	630-584-1919	48-3
Ceiva Logic Inc 214 E Magnolia Blvd *Tech Supp	Burbank	CA	91502	**877-693-7263***	818-562-1495	590
Cejka Search Inc 4 Cityplace Dr Ste 300	Saint Louis	MO	63141	**800-678-7858**	314-726-1603	719
Celadon Trucking Services Inc 9503 E 33rd St	Indianapolis	IN	46235	**800-235-2366**	317-972-7000	778
Celebritees Inc 1014 Atlantic Ave	Savannah	GA	31401	**877-831-1005**	912-233-9941	186
Celerity Consulting Group Inc 2 Gough St Ste 300	San Francisco	CA	94103	**866-224-4333**	415-986-8850	198
Celesco Transducer Products Inc 20630 Plummer St	Chatsworth	CA	91311	**800-423-5483**	818-701-2750	203
Celestial Seasonings Inc 4600 Sleepytime Dr	Boulder	CO	80301	**800-351-8175**	303-530-5300	297-40
Celestica Inc 844 Don Mills Rd *NYSE: CLS*	Toronto	ON	M3C1V7	**888-899-9998**	416-448-5800	255
Celgene Corp 86 Morris Ave *NASDAQ: CELG*	Summit	NJ	07901	**888-771-0141**	908-673-9000	84
Cell Response Formulation LLC 4115 S Pub Pl	Jackson	WY	83002	**888-364-7839**	307-734-7839	298-9
Cell Signaling Technology Inc 3 Trask Ln	Danvers	MA	01923	**877-678-8324**	978-867-2300	418
Cell Therapeutics Inc (CTI) 501 Elliott Ave W Ste 400 *NASDAQ: CTIC*	Seattle	WA	98119	**800-215-2355**	206-282-7100	84
Cell-con Inc 305 Commerce Dr Ste 300	Exton	PA	19341	**800-771-7139**	610-280-7630	73
Cellhire USA LLC 3520 W Miller Rd Ste 100	Garland	TX	75041	**877-244-7242**	214-355-5200	733
Cellino & Barnes PC 2500 Main Pl Tower 350 Main St	Buffalo	NY	14202	**800-888-8888**	716-854-2020	428
Cello Professional Products 1354 Old Post Rd	Havre de Grace	MD	21078	**800-638-4850**	410-939-1234	150
Cellofoam North America Inc 1917 Rockdale Industrial Blvd	Conyers	GA	30012	**800-241-3634**	770-929-3688	600
Cellotape Inc 47623 Fremont Blvd	Fremont	CA	94538	**800-231-0608**	510-651-5551	413
Cell-Tel Government Systems Inc 8226-B Phillips Hwy Ste 290	Jacksonville	FL	32256	**800-737-7545**	904-363-1111	248
CEL-SCI Corp 8229 Boone Blvd Ste 802 *NYSE: CVM*	Vienna	VA	22182	**800-422-6237**	703-506-9460	84
Celsion Corp 10220-L Old Columbia Rd *NASDAQ: CLSN*	Columbia	MD	21046	**888-504-7965**	410-290-5390	475
Celtic Healthcare 150 Scharberry Ln	Mars	PA	16046	**800-355-8894**		371
CEM Corp 3100 Smith Farm Rd	Matthews	NC	28104	**800-726-3331**	704-821-7015	419
CEMCO 263 N Covina Ln	City Of Industry	CA	91744	**800-775-2362**		104
Cemen Tech Inc 1700 N 14th St	Indianola	IA	50125	**800-247-2464**	515-961-7407	192
Cement Industries Inc 2925 Hanson St PO Box 823	Fort Myers	FL	33902	**800-332-1440**	239-332-1440	185
Cemex USA 840 Gessner Ste 1400 *NYSE: CX*	Houston	TX	77024	**888-292-0070**	713-650-6200	134
Cemline Corp PO Box 55	Cheswick	PA	15024	**800-245-6268**	724-274-5430	35
Cemstone Products Co 2025 Centre Pt Blvd Ste 300	Mendota Heights	MN	55120	**800-236-7866**	651-688-9292	184
Cenergistic Inc 5950 Sherry Ln Ste 900	Dallas	TX	75225	**888-782-7937**	214-346-5950	196
Cengage Learning PO Box 6904	Florence	KY	41022	**800-354-9706**		634-2
Centegra Memorial Medical Ctr 3701 Doty Rd	Woodstock	IL	60098	**877-236-8347**	815-338-2500	374-3
Centenary College 400 Jefferson St *Admissions	Hackettstown	NJ	07840	**800-236-8679***	908-852-1400	167
Centenary College of Louisiana 2911 Centenary Blvd *Admissions	Shreveport	LA	71104	**800-234-4448***	318-869-5131	167
Centenary State Historic Site 3522 College St	Jackson	LA	70748	**888-677-2364**	225-634-7925	564
Centene Corp 7700 Forsyth Blvd *NYSE: CNC* ■ *General	Saint Louis	MO	63105	**800-293-0056***	314-725-4477	391-3
Centennial Hall Convention Ctr 101 Egan Dr	Juneau	AK	99801	**800-478-4176**	907-586-5283	207
Centennial Travelers 311 S College Ave	Fort Collins	CO	80524	**800-223-0675**	970-484-4988	758
Center Court Historic Inn & Cottages 1075 Duval St C-19	Key West	FL	33040	**800-797-8787**	305-296-9292	379
Center Enterprises Inc 30 Shield St *Orders	West Hartford	CT	06110	**800-542-2214***	860-953-4423	245
Center for Animals & Public Policy Tufts Univ School of Veterinary Medicine 200 Westboro Rd	North Grafton	MA	01536	**888-748-8387**	508-839-7920	631
Center for Assn Growth 1926 Waukegan Rd Ste 1	Glenview	IL	60025	**800-492-6462**	847-657-6700	46
Center for Assn Resources Inc 1901 N Roselle Rd Ste 920	Schaumburg	IL	60195	**888-705-1434**		46
Center for Automation Research University of Maryland AV Williams Bldg 115 Rm 4413	College Park	MD	20742	**800-868-0094**	301-405-4526	666
Center for Chemical Process Safety (CCPS) 120 Wall St	New York	NY	10005	**800-242-4363**	646-495-1371	48-19
Center for Civic Education 5145 Douglas Fir Rd	Calabasas	CA	91302	**800-350-4223**	818-591-9321	196
Center for Cognitive Liberty & Ethics PO Box 73481	Davis	CA	95617	**888-950-6463**	530-750-7912	631
Center for Creative Photography 1030 N Olive Rd	Tucson	AZ	85721	**888-472-4732**	520-621-7968	519
Center for Cultural Interchange 746 N La Salle Dr	Chicago	IL	60654	**866-224-0061**	312-944-2544	196
Center for Democracy & Technology (CDT) 1634 'I' St NW 11th Fl	Washington	DC	20006	**800-869-4499**	202-637-9800	47-7
Center for Diagnostic Imaging 5775 Wayzata Blvd Ste 190	Saint Louis Park	MN	55416	**800-537-0005**	952-541-1840	383
Center for Genetic Testing at Saint Francis 6465 S Yale Ave	Tulsa	OK	74136	**877-789-6001**	918-502-1720	417
Center for Grain & Animal Health Research 1515 College Ave	Manhattan	KS	66502	**800-627-0388**		666
Center for Hospice Care Inc 111 Sunnybrook Ct	South Bend	IN	46637	**800-413-9083**	574-243-3100	371
Center for Individual Rights (CIR) 1233 20th St NW Ste 300	Washington	DC	20036	**877-426-2665**	202-833-8400	47-8
Center for Lasik Ophthalmology Consultants, The 5800 Colonial Dr Ste 103	Margate	FL	33063	**800-448-8770**	954-969-0090	796
Center for Law & Social Policy (CLASP) 1015 15th St NW Ste 400	Washington	DC	20005	**800-821-4367**	202-906-8000	631
Center for Nutrition Policy & Promotion (CNPP) 3101 Pk Ctr Dr 10th Fl	Alexandria	VA	22302	**888-779-7264**	703-305-7600	340-1
Center for Organ Recovery & Education (CORE) 204 Sigma Dr RIDC Pk	Pittsburgh	PA	15238	**800-366-6777**	412-963-3550	271
Center for Policy Research Syracuse University 426 Eggers Hall	Syracuse	NY	13244	**800-325-3535**	315-443-3114	631
Center for Practical Bioethics 1111 Main St Ste 500	Kansas City	MO	64105	**800-344-3829**	816-221-1100	47-17

Name / Address	City	State	Zip	Toll-Free	Phone	Class
Center for Puppetry Arts						
1404 Spring St NW	Atlanta	GA	30309	**800-642-3629**	404-873-3089	49-1
Center for Research in Mathematics & Science Education						
San Diego State University						
6475 Alvarado Rd Ste 206	San Diego	CA	92120	**800-573-8804**	619-594-5090	666
Center for Space Plasma & Aeronomic Research						
University of Alabama Huntsville						
	Huntsville	AL	35899	**800-824-2255**	256-961-7403	666
Center for the Arts						
103 Ctr for the Arts	Buffalo	NY	14260	**800-745-3000**	716-645-2787	571
Center for Western Studies						
2101 S Summit Ave						
Augustana College	Sioux Falls	SD	57197	**800-727-2844**	605-274-4007	519
Center of Vocational Alternative For Men						
3770 N High St	Columbus	OH	43214	**877-521-2682**	614-294-7117	244
Center on Education & Training for Employment						
Ohio State University						
1900 Kenny Rd	Columbus	OH	43210	**800-848-4815**	614-292-6869	666
Center on Human Development & Disability						
University of Washington 1701 NE Columbia Rd						
PO Box 357920	Seattle	WA	98195	**800-636-1089**	206-543-2832	666
Centerplate						
2187 Atlantic St	Stamford	CT	06902	**800-698-6992**	203-975-5900	300
CenterPoint Energy Inc						
1111 Louisiana St	Houston	TX	77002	**800-495-9880***	713-207-1111	360-5
NYSE: CNP ■ *Cust Svc						
Centers for Disease Control & Prevention						
National Center for Chronic Disease Prevention & Health Promotion (NCCDHPP)						
4770 Buford Hwy NE	Atlanta	GA	30341	**800-232-4636**		340-8
National Center for Emerging & Zoonotic Infectious Diseases						
1600 Clifton Rd	Atlanta	GA	30333	**800-232-4636**	404-639-3311	340-8
National Center for Environmental Health						
4770 Buford Hwy Bldg 101	Atlanta	GA	30341	**800-232-4636**	404-639-3311	340-8
National Center for Health Marketing						
1600 Clifton Rd NE	Atlanta	GA	30333	**800-311-3435**	404-639-3311	340-8
National Center for HIV/AIDS Viral Hepatitis STD & TB Prevention						
1600 Clifton Rd	Atlanta	GA	30333	**800-232-4636**		340-8
National Center for Immunization & Respiratory Diseases						
1600 Clifton Rd NE MS E-05	Atlanta	GA	30333	**800-232-4636**		340-8
National Center for Injury Prevention & Control (NCIPC)						
4770 Buford Hwy NE	Atlanta	GA	30341	**800-232-4636**		340-8
National Center for Public Health Informatics						
1600 Clifton Rd NE	Atlanta	GA	30333	**800-232-4636**		340-8
National Center on Birth Defects & Developmental Disabilities						
1600 Clifton Rd	Atlanta	GA	30329	**800-232-4636**	404-639-3311	340-8
National Institute for Occupational Safety & Health						
200 Independence Ave SW	Washington	DC	20201	**800-356-4674**	404-639-3286	340-8
National Office of Public Health Genomics						
4770 Buford Hwy MS K-89	Atlanta	GA	30341	**877-442-9719**	770-488-8510	340-8
Travelers Health						
1600 Clifton Rd NE	Atlanta	GA	30333	**800-232-4636**		340-8
Centers for Medicare & Medicaid Services						
Medicare Hotline						
7500 Security Blvd	Baltimore	MD	21244	**800-633-4227**		340-8
Centerstate Banks Inc						
42725 Us Hwy 27	Davenport	FL	33837	**855-863-2265**		69
CenTex House Leveling						
1120 E 52nd St	Austin	TX	78723	**888-425-5438**	512-444-5438	188
Centimark Corp						
12 Grandview Cir	Canonsburg	PA	15317	**800-558-4100**		191-12
Centon Electronics Inc						
27412 Aliso Viejo Pkwy	Aliso Viejo	CA	92656	**800-234-9292**	949-855-9111	624
Centra Health Inc						
1920 Atherholt Rd	Lynchburg	VA	24501	**800-947-5442**	434-947-3000	353
Central Alabama Community College						
1675 Cherokee Rd	Alexander City	AL	35010	**800-643-2657**	256-234-6346	161
Central Alabama Electric Co-op						
1802 Hwy 31 N	Prattville	AL	36067	**800-545-5735**	334-365-6762	247
Central Arizona College						
8470 N Overfield Rd	Coolidge	AZ	85228	**800-237-9814**	520-494-5444	161
Central Arizona Supply						
208 S Country Club Dr	Mesa	AZ	85210	**800-416-6490**	480-834-5817	611
Central BanCo						
238 Madison St	Jefferson City	MO	65101	**877-554-5535**	573-634-1155	69
Central Baptist College						
1501 College Ave	Conway	AR	72034	**800-205-6872**	501-329-6872	167
Central Baptist Theological Seminary						
6601 Monticello Rd	Shawnee	KS	66226	**800-677-2287**	913-667-5700	168-3
Central Boston Elder Services Inc						
2315 Washington St	Boston	MA	02119	**800-922-2275**	617-277-7416	449
Central Brass Mfg Company Inc						
2950 E 55th St	Cleveland	OH	44127	**800-321-8630**	216-883-0220	608
Central Builders Supply Company Inc						
125 Bridge Ave PO Box 152	Sunbury	PA	17801	**800-326-9361**	570-286-6461	184
Central Carolina Community College						
1105 Kelly Dr	Sanford	NC	27330	**800-682-8353**	919-775-5401	161
Central Carolina Hospital						
1135 Carthage St	Sanford	NC	27330	**800-292-2262**	919-774-2100	374-3
Central Christian College						
PO Box 1403	McPherson	KS	67460	**800-835-0078**	620-241-0723	167
Central Christian College of the Bible						
911 E Urbandale Dr	Moberly	MO	65270	**888-263-3900**	660-263-3900	160
Central College						
812 University St	Pella	IA	50219	**877-462-3687**	641-628-5285	167
Central Community College						
Grand Island						
3134 W Hwy 34 PO Box 4903	Grand Island	NE	68802	**877-222-0780**	308-398-4222	161
Central Concrete Supply Company Inc						
755 Stockton Ave	San Jose	CA	95126	**866-404-1000**	408-293-6272	184
Central Connecticut Co-op Farmers Assn						
10 Apel Pl PO Box 8500	Manchester	CT	06042	**800-640-4523**	860-649-4523	277
Central Crude Inc						
4187 Hwy 3059 PO Box 1863	Lake Charles	LA	70602	**800-245-8408**	337-436-1000	580
Central DuPage Hospital						
25 N Winfield Rd	Winfield	IL	60190	**800-223-9776**	630-933-1600	374-3
Central Electric Membership Corp						
128 Wilson Rd	Sanford	NC	27331	**800-446-7752**	919-774-4900	247
Central Electric Power Assn						
104 E Main St	Carthage	MS	39051	**866-846-5671**	601-267-5671	247
Central Federal Corp						
601 Main St	Wellsville	OH	14895	**866-668-4606**	330-666-7979	360-2
NASDAQ: CFBK						
Central Florida Electric Co-op Inc						
1124 N Young Blvd	Chiefland	FL	32644	**800-227-1302**	352-493-2511	247
Central Florida Visitors & Convention Bureau						
101 Adventure Ct	Davenport	FL	33837	**800-828-7655**	863-420-2586	208
Central Florida Zoological Park						
3755 NW Hwy 17-92 & I-4						
PO Box 470309	Lake Monroe	FL	32747	**800-435-7352**	407-323-4450	821
Central Flying Service Inc						
1501 Bond St	Little Rock	AR	72202	**800-888-5387**	501-375-3245	62
Central Freight Lines Inc						
PO Box 2638	Waco	TX	76702	**800-782-5036**		778
Central Georgia Electric Membership Corp						
923 S Mulberry St	Jackson	GA	30233	**800-222-4877**	770-775-7857	247
Central Georgia Technical College						
3300 Macon Tech Dr	Macon	GA	31206	**866-430-0135**	478-757-3400	798
Central Hudson Gas & Electric Corp						
284 S Ave	Poughkeepsie	NY	12601	**800-527-2714**	845-452-2700	785
Central Illinois Community Blood Ctr						
1134 S Seventh St	Springfield	IL	62703	**800-448-3253***	217-753-1530	88
*Help Line						
Central Industries Inc						
11438 Cronridge Dr Ste W	Owings Mills	MD	21117	**800-304-8484**		538
Central Ink Corp						
1100 Harvester Rd	West Chicago	IL	60185	**800-345-2541**	630-231-6500	388
Central Insulation Systems Inc						
300 Murray Rd	Cincinnati	OH	45217	**800-544-7502**	513-242-0600	665
Central Insurance Cos						
800 S Washington St	Van Wert	OH	45891	**800-736-7000**	419-238-1010	391-4
Central Iowa Co-op						
2829 Westown Pkwy						
Ste 350	West Des Moines	IA	50266	**800-513-3938**	515-225-1334	277
Central Jersey Blood Ctr						
494 Sycamore Ave	Shrewsbury	NJ	07702	**888-712-5663**	732-842-5750	88
Central Kentucky Blood Ctr						
3121 Beaumont Centre Cir	Lexington	KY	40513	**800-775-2522**	859-276-2534	88
Central Lakes College						
Brainerd						
501 W College Dr	Brainerd	MN	56401	**800-933-0346**	218-855-8199	161
Staples						
1830 Airport Rd	Staples	MN	56479	**800-247-6836**	218-894-5100	161
Central Louisiana State Hospital						
242 W Shamrock St	Pineville	LA	71360	**866-666-8335**	318-484-6200	374-5
Central Maine Community College						
1250 Turner St	Auburn	ME	04210	**800-891-2002***	207-755-5100	798
*Admissions						
Central Maine Power Co						
83 Edison Dr	Augusta	ME	04336	**800-565-0121**	207-623-3521	785
Central Maintenance & Welding Inc (CMW)						
2620 E Keysville Rd	Lithia	FL	33547	**877-704-7411**	813-737-1402	191-14
Central Methodist University						
411 Central Methodist Sq	Fayette	MO	65248	**877-268-1854**	660-248-3391	167
Central Michigan University						
102 Warriner Hall	Mount Pleasant	MI	48859	**888-292-5366***	989-774-4000	167
*Admissions						
Central Mine Equipment Company Inc						
4215 Rider Trl N	Earth City	MO	63045	**800-325-8827**	314-291-7700	192
Central Minnesota Fabricating Inc						
2725 W Gorton Ave	Willmar	MN	56201	**800-839-8857**	320-235-4181	479
Central Missouri ElectricCo-op Inc						
22702 Hwy 65 PO Box 939	Sedalia	MO	65302	**855-875-7165**	660-826-2900	247
Central Nebraska Packing Inc						
2800 E Eigth St	North Platte	NE	69103	**800-445-2881***	308-532-1250	472
*Cust Svc						
Central New Mexico Community College						
10549 Universe Blvd NW	Albuquerque	NM	87114	**888-453-1304**	505-224-3000	798
Central New York Business Journal, The						
269 W Jefferson St	Syracuse	NY	13202	**800-836-3539**	315-579-3919	456-5
Central Ontario Healthcare Procurement Alliance						
95 Mural St	Richmond Hill	ON	L4B3G2	**866-897-8812**	905-886-5319	318
Central Oregon Visitors Association						
57100 Beaver Dr Bldg 6 Ste 130	Sunriver	OR	97707	**800-800-8334**		208
Central Pacific Financial Corp						
PO Box 3590	Honolulu	HI	96811	**800-342-8422**	808-544-0500	360-2
NYSE: CPF						
Central Paper Products Co Inc						
350 Gay St						
Brown Ave Industrial Pk	Manchester	NH	03103	**800-339-4065**	603-624-4065	558
Central Pennsylvania Blood Bank						
8167 Adams Dr	Hummelstown	PA	17036	**800-771-0059**	717-566-6161	88
Central Pennsylvania College						
600 Valley Rd PO Box 309	Summerdale	PA	17093	**800-759-2727**	717-732-0702	798
Central Petroleum Transport Inc (CPT)						
6115 Mitchell St	Sioux City	IA	51111	**800-798-6357**	712-258-6357	778
Central Piedmont Community College						
1201 Elizabeth Ave	Charlotte	NC	28204	**877-530-8815**	704-330-2722	161
Central Pipe Supply Inc						
101 Ware Rd PO Box 5470	Pearl	MS	39288	**800-844-7700**	601-939-3322	594
Central Puget Sound Regional Transit Authority						
401 S Jackson St	Seattle	WA	98104	**800-201-4900**	206-398-5000	467
Central Refrigerated Service Inc						
5175 W 2100 S	West Valley City	UT	84120	**800-777-0069**	801-924-7000	778
Central Rural Electric Co-op						
3304 S Boomer Rd PO Box 1809	Stillwater	OK	74076	**800-375-2884**	405-372-2884	247
Central Securities Corp						
630 Fifth Ave Ste 820	New York	NY	10111	**866-593-2507**	212-698-2020	405
NYSE: CET						
Central Service Assn						
93 S Coley Rd	Tupelo	MS	38801	**877-842-5962**	662-842-5962	227
Central Signaling						
2033 Hamilton Rd	Columbus	GA	31904	**800-554-1101**	706-322-3756	690
Central Specialties Ltd						
220 Exchange Dr	Crystal Lake	IL	60014	**800-873-4370**	815-459-6000	63
Central State University						
1400 Brush Row Rd						
PO Box 1004	Wilberforce	OH	45384	**800-388-2781**	937-376-6011	167

Name / Address	City	State	ZIP	Toll-Free	Phone	Class
Central States Business Forms Inc						
2500 Industrial Pkwy	Dewey	OK	74029	**800-331-0920**		109
Central States Coach Repairs						
3426 Gilbert Rd	Grand Prairie	TX	75050	**800-533-1939**	972-399-1059	106
Central States Health & Life Company of Omaha						
1212 N 96th St	Omaha	NE	68114	**800-826-6587**	402-397-1111	391-2
Central Street Health Ctr						
26 Central St	Somerville	MA	02143	**800-909-2677**	617-591-6033	724
Central Texas College						
PO Box 1800	Killeen	TX	76540	**800-792-3348**	254-526-7161	161
Central Texas Electric Co-op Inc (CTEC)						
386 Friendship Ln						
PO Box 553	Fredericksburg	TX	78624	**800-900-2832***	830-997-2126	247
*General						
Central Texas Medical Ctr (CTMC)						
1301 Wonder World Dr	San Marcos	TX	78666	**800-927-9004**	512-353-8979	374-3
Central Texas Veterans Health Care System						
1901 Veterans Memorial Dr	Temple	TX	76504	**800-423-2111**	254-778-4811	374-8
Central Transportation Systems Inc						
4105 Rio Bravo Ste 100	El Paso	TX	79902	**800-283-3106**		448
Central Valley Community Bancorp						
7100 N Financial Dr Ste 101	Fresno	CA	93720	**866-294-9588**	559-298-1775	360-2
NASDAQ: CVCY						
Central Valley Co-op						
900 30th Pl NW	Owatonna	MN	55060	**800-270-2339**	507-451-1230	278
Central Vermont Chamber of Commerce						
33 Stewart Rd	Berlin	VT	05602	**877-887-3678**	802-229-5711	138
Central Vermont Home Health & Hospice						
600 Granger Rd	Barre	VT	05641	**800-286-1219**	802-223-1878	363
Central Vermont Public Service Corp						
2154 Post Rd	Rutland	VT	05701	**800-649-2877**	888-835-4672	785
Central Virginia Electric Co-op						
800 Co-op Way PO Box 247	Lovingston	VA	22949	**800-367-2832**	434-263-8336	247
Central Washington Hospital						
1201 S Miller St	Wenatchee	WA	98801	**800-365-6428**	509-662-1511	374-5
Central Washington University						
400 E University Way	Ellensburg	WA	98926	**866-298-4968***	509-963-1111	167
*Admissions						
Central Woodwork Inc						
870 Keough Rd	Collierville	TN	38017	**800-788-3775**	901-363-4141	498
Central Wyoming College						
2660 Peck Ave	Riverton	WY	82501	**800-735-8418**	307-855-2000	161
Centralia-Chehalis Chamber of Commerce						
500 NW Chamber of Commerce Way						
	Chehalis	WA	98532	**800-525-3323**	360-748-8885	138
CentralVac International						
23455 Hellman Ave PO Box 259	Dollar Bay	MI	49922	**800-666-3133**		786
Centrav Inc						
511 E Travelers Trl	Burnsville	MN	55337	**800-874-2033**	952-886-7650	16
Centre College						
600 W Walnut St	Danville	KY	40422	**800-423-6236**	859-238-5350	167
Centre County Convention & Visitors Bureau						
800 E Pk Ave	State College	PA	16803	**800-358-5466**	814-231-1400	208
Centre Daily Times						
3400 E College Ave	State College	PA	16801	**800-327-5500**	814-238-5000	531-2
Centre for Addiction & Mental Health Foundation						
901 King St W Ste 502	Toronto	ON	M5V3H5	**800-414-0471**	416-979-6909	306
Centre for Well-Being at the Phoenician						
6000 E Camelback Rd	Scottsdale	AZ	85251	**800-843-2392**		705
Centre Hospitalier Le Gardeur						
911 Montee des Pionniers	Terrebonne	QC	J6V2H2	**888-654-7525**	450-654-7525	374-2
Centre Hospitalier Pierre Boucher						
1333 Boul Jacques-Cartier E	Longueuil	QC	J4M2A5	**866-277-3553**	450-468-8111	374-2
Centre in the Square						
101 Queen St N	Kitchener	ON	N2H6P7	**800-265-8977**	519-578-1570	571
CENTRIA						
1005 Beaver Grade Rd	Moon Township	PA	15108	**800-759-7474**	412-299-8000	479
Centrix Inc						
770 River Rd	Shelton	CT	06484	**800-235-5862**	203-929-5582	230
Centron Data Services Inc						
1175 Devin Dr	Norton Shores	MI	49441	**800-732-8787***		5
*Cust Svc						
Centrus Energy Corp						
6903 Rockledge Dr Ste 800	Bethesda	MD	20817	**800-273-7754**	301-564-3200	142
NYSE: USU						
Centurion Industries Inc						
1107 N Taylor Rd	Garrett	IN	46738	**888-832-4466**	260-357-6665	192
Centurion Medical Products						
100 Centurion Way	Williamston	MI	48895	**800-248-4058**	517-546-5400	476
Century Bancorp Inc						
400 Mystic Ave	Medford	MA	02155	**866-823-6887**	781-393-4160	360-2
NASDAQ: CNBKA						
Century Casinos Inc						
2860 S Cir Dr Ste 350	Colorado Springs	CO	80906	**888-966-2257**	719-527-8300	131
NASDAQ: CNTY						
Century City Chamber of Commerce						
2029 Century Pk E						
Concourse Level	Los Angeles	CA	90067	**800-462-7899**	310-553-2222	138
Century College						
3300 Century Ave N	White Bear Lake	MN	55115	**800-228-1978**	651-779-3300	161
Century Fasteners Corp						
50-20 Ireland St	Elmhurst	NY	11373	**800-221-0769**	718-446-5000	248
Century Furniture LLC						
401 11th St NW	Hickory	NC	28601	**800-852-5552**	828-328-1851	320-2
Century Graphics & Metals Inc						
550 S N Lake Blvd						
Ste 1000	Altamonte Springs	FL	32701	**800-327-5664**		699
Century Group Inc, The						
1106 W Napoleon St PO Box 228	Sulphur	LA	70664	**800-527-5232**	337-527-5266	185
Century Health Solutions Inc						
2951 SW Woodside Dr	Topeka	KS	66614	**800-227-0089**	785-233-1816	196
Century Hotel South Beach						
140 Ocean Dr	Miami Beach	FL	33139	**877-659-8855**	305-674-8855	379
Century Insurance Group						
465 Cleveland Ave	Westerville	OH	43082	**877-855-8462**	614-895-2000	391-5
Century Interactive LLC						
1505 Federal St Ste 200	Dallas	TX	75201	**877-921-7992**	817-713-2329	733
Century Marketing Solutions LLC						
3000 Cameron St	Monroe	LA	71201	**800-256-6000**		626
Century Martial Art Supply Inc						
1000 Century Blvd	Oklahoma City	OK	73110	**800-626-2787***	405-732-2226	709
*Sales						
Century National Bank						
14 S Fifth St	Zanesville	OH	43701	**800-548-3557***	740-454-2521	69
*Cust Svc						
Century Plaza Hotel & Spa						
1015 Burrard St	Vancouver	BC	V6Z1Y5	**800-663-1818**	604-687-0575	379
Century Ready-Mix Corp						
3250 Armand St PO Box 4420	Monroe	LA	71211	**800-732-3969**	318-322-4444	184
Century Roof Tile						
23135 Saklan Rd	Hayward	CA	94545	**888-233-7548**	510-780-9489	193-1
Century Sports Inc						
1995 Rutgers University Blvd	Lakewood	NJ	08701	**800-526-7548***	732-905-4422	708
*Sales						
Century Spring Corp						
222 E 16th St	Los Angeles	CA	90015	**800-237-5225**	213-749-1466	717
Century Steel Erectors Co						
210 Washington Ave	Dravosburg	PA	15034	**888-601-8801**	412-469-8800	191-14
Century Suites Hotel						
300 SR-446	Bloomington	IN	47401	**800-766-5446**	812-336-7777	379
Century Tile Supply Co						
747 E Roosevelt Rd	Lombard	IL	60148	**888-845-3968**	630-495-2300	292
Century Tool & Mfg						
90 McMillen Rd	Antioch	IL	60002	**800-635-3831**		708
Century Wealth Management LLC						
1770 Kirby Pkwy Ste 117	Memphis	TN	38138	**855-850-5532**	901-850-5532	401
Century-National Insurance Co						
12200 Sylvan St						
PO Box 3999	North Hollywood	CA	91606	**800-894-8384***	818-760-0880	391-4
*Cust Svc						
CenturyTel Inc						
100 Centurylink Dr PO Box 4065	Monroe	LA	71211	**877-290-5458**	318-388-9000	360-3
NYSE: CTL						
CEPA Le Baluchon Inc						
3550 chemin des Trembles	Saint-Paulin	QC	J0K3G0	**800-789-5968**	819-268-2555	705
Cepheid						
904 E Caribbean Dr	Sunnyvale	CA	94089	**888-838-3222**	408-541-4191	419
NASDAQ: CPHD						
Cepia LLC						
121 Hunter Ave	Saint Louis	MO	63124	**800-225-9319**	314-725-4900	760
Cequent Towing Products						
47774 Anchor Ct W	Plymouth	MI	48170	**800-521-0510**		761
Cequent Trailer Products						
1050 Indianhead Dr	Mosinee	WI	54455	**800-604-9466**	715-693-1700	761
Ceramics Monthly						
600 N Cleveland Ave Ste 210	Westerville	OH	43082	**800-342-3594**	614-794-5867	456-14
Ceramo Company Inc						
681 Kasten Dr	Jackson	MO	63755	**800-325-8303**	573-243-3138	334
CERC (Columbia Environmental Research Ctr)						
4200 New Haven Rd	Columbia	MO	65201	**888-283-7626**	573-875-5399	666
Ceres Solutions LLP						
2112 Indianapolis Rd						
PO Box 432	Crawfordsville	IN	47933	**800-878-0952***	765-362-6700	277
*General						
Cerex Advanced Fabrics Inc						
610 Chemstrand Rd	Cantonment	FL	32533	**800-572-3739**	850-968-0100	742-6
Cermetek Microelectronics Inc						
374 Turquoise St	Milpitas	CA	95035	**800-882-6271**	408-752-5000	175-3
Cernan Earth & Space Ctr						
2000 N Fifth Ave						
Triton College	River Grove	IL	60171	**800-972-7000**	708-456-0300	597
Cerner Corp						
2800 Rockcreek Pkwy	North Kansas City	MO	64117	**888-827-7220**	816-221-1024	180-11
NASDAQ: CERN						
Ceros Financial Services Inc						
1445 Research Blvd Ste 530	Rockville	MD	20850	**866-842-3356**		688
Cerritos Civic Ctr						
18025 Bloomfield Ave	Cerritos	CA	90703	**866-402-7433**	562-916-1350	434-3
Cerritos Ctr for the Performing Arts						
12700 Ctr Ct Dr	Cerritos	CA	90703	**800-300-4345**	562-916-8501	571
Cerro Coso Community College						
Bishop 4090 W Line St	Bishop	CA	93514	**888-537-6932**	760-872-1565	161
Indian Wells Valley						
3000 College Heights Blvd	Ridgecrest	CA	93555	**888-537-6932**	760-384-6100	161
Kern River Valley						
5520 Lk Isabella Blvd	Lake Isabella	CA	93240	**888-537-6932**	760-379-5501	161
Mammoth						
101 College Pkwy						
PO Box 1865	Mammoth Lakes	CA	93546	**888-537-6932**	760-934-2875	161
South Kern						
140 Methusa Ave	Edwards AFB	CA	93524	**888-537-6932**	661-258-8644	161
Cerro Flow Products Inc						
PO Box 66800	Saint Louis	MO	63166	**888-237-7611**	618-337-6000	489
Cerro Wire & Cable Company Inc						
1099 Thompson Rd SE	Hartselle	AL	35640	**800-523-3869**	256-773-2522	811
CertainTeed Corp						
750 E Swedesford Rd	Valley Forge	PA	19482	**800-782-8777***	610-341-7000	389
*Prod Info						
CertainTeed Gypsum						
2424 Lakeshore Rd W	Mississauga	ON	L5J1K4	**800-233-8990**	905-823-9881	347
CertaPro Painters Ltd						
150 Green Tree Rd Ste 1003	Oaks	PA	19456	**800-689-7271**		191-8
Certicom Corp						
4701 Tahoe Blvd Bldg A	Mississauga	ON	L4W0B5	**800-561-6100**	905-507-4220	180-12
Certified Financial Planner Board of Standards Inc						
1425 K St NW Ste 500	Washington	DC	20005	**800-487-1497**	202-379-2200	48-2
Certified Horsemanship Assn (CHA)						
1795 Alysheba Way Ste 7102	Lexington	KY	40509	**800-399-0138**	859-259-3399	47-3
Certified Power Inc						
970 Campus Dr	Mundelein	IL	60060	**888-905-7411**	847-573-3800	619
Certified Restoration DryCleaning Network LLC						
2060 Coolidge Hwy	Berkley	MI	48072	**800-963-2736**		311
Certipay						
199 Ave B NW Ste 270	Winter Haven	FL	33881	**800-422-3782**	863-299-2400	2
Certis USA LLC						
9145 Guilford Rd Ste 175	Columbia	MD	21046	**800-250-5024**		282

Name / Address	City	State	ZIP	Toll-Free	Phone	Class
Cerus Corp 2550 Stanwell Dr *NASDAQ: CERS*	Concord	CA	94520	**800-401-1957**	925-288-6000	84
CES (IEEE Consumer Electronics Society) 445 Hoes Ln	Piscataway	NJ	08854	**800-678-4333**	732-981-0060	48-19
Cesium Telecom Inc 5798 Ferrier	Montreal	QC	H4P1M7	**877-798-8686**	514-798-8686	733
Cessco Fabrication & Engineering Ltd 7310-99 St	Edmonton	AB	T6E3R8	**800-272-9698**	780-433-9531	479
Cetac Technologies Inc 14306 Industrial Rd	Omaha	NE	68144	**800-369-2822**	402-733-2829	419
CETCO (Colloid Environmental Technologies Co) 2870 Forbs Ave	Hoffman Estates	IL	60192	**800-527-9948**	847-851-1899	3
Cetera Financial Group Inc 200 N Sepulveda Blvd Ste 1200	El Segundo	CA	90245	**866-489-3100**		688
Cev Multimedia Ltd 1020 SE Loop 289	Lubbock	TX	79404	**877-610-5017**	806-745-8820	513
CF Martin & Company Inc 510 Sycamore St PO Box 329	Nazareth	PA	18064	**888-433-9177**	610-759-2837	526
CFA (Consumer Federation of America) 1620 I St NW Ste 200	Washington	DC	20006	**877-382-4357**	202-387-6121	47-10
CFA Institute 915 E High St PO Box 3668	Charlottesville	VA	22903	**800-247-8132**	434-951-5499	48-2
CFC Farm & Home Ctr 15172 Brandy Rd PO Box 2002	Culpeper	VA	22701	**800-284-2667**	540-825-2200	282
CFC International Inc 500 State St	Chicago Heights	IL	60411	**800-393-4505**	708-891-3456	3
CFCA (Christian Foundation for Children & Aging) 1 Elmwood Ave	Kansas City	KS	66103	**800-875-6564**	913-384-6500	47-6
CFCU Community Credit Union 1030 Craft Rd	Ithaca	NY	14850	**800-428-8340**	607-257-8500	221
CFG (Creative Financial Group) 16 Campus Blvd	Newtown Square	PA	19073	**800-893-4824**	610-325-6100	401
CFG Community Bank 1422 Clarkview Rd	Baltimore	MD	21209	**866-619-1417**	410-823-0500	69
CFHS (Canadian Federation of Humane Societies) 30 Concourse Gate Ste 102	Ottawa	ON	K2E7V7	**888-678-2347**	613-224-8072	47-3
CFMA (Construction Financial Management Assn) 100 Village Blvd Ste 200A	Princeton	NJ	08540	**877-462-7827**	609-452-8000	48-1
CFO Magazine 253 Summer St	Boston	MA	02210	**800-772-1119**	617-345-9700	456-5
CFRA-AM 580 (N/T) 87 George St	Ottawa	ON	K1N9H7	**800-580-2372**	613-789-2486	642-86
CFS Bancorp Inc 707 Ridge Rd *NASDAQ: CITZ*	Munster	IN	46321	**866-622-1370**	219-513-5123	360-2
CFS the School at Church Farm PO Box 2000	Paoli	PA	19301	**800-439-4745**	610-363-7500	621
CG Schmidt Inc 11777 W Lake Pk Dr	Milwaukee	WI	53224	**800-248-1254**	414-577-1177	188
CGH (Coral Gables Hospital Inc) 3100 Douglas Rd	Coral Gables	FL	33134	**866-728-3677**	305-445-8461	374-3
CGH Medical Ctr (CGHMC) 100 E LeFevre Rd	Sterling	IL	61081	**800-625-4790**	815-625-0400	374-3
CGHMC (CGH Medical Ctr) 100 E LeFevre Rd	Sterling	IL	61081	**800-625-4790**	815-625-0400	374-3
CGI Communications Inc 130 E Main St	Rochester	NY	14604	**800-398-3029**	585-427-0020	513
CGI Group Inc 1130 Sherbrooke St W 7th Fl *TSE: GIB/A*	Montreal	QC	H3A2M8	**800-828-8377**	514-841-3200	182
CGM Funds 38 Newbury St Ste 8	Boston	MA	02116	**800-345-4048**	617-859-7714	527
CGM Inc 1445 Ford Rd	Bensalem	PA	19020	**800-523-6570**	215-638-4400	134
Cgn & Assoc Inc 415 SW Washington St	Peoria	IL	61602	**888-746-4246**	309-495-2100	196
CGNAD (Compass Group North American Div) 2400 Yorkmont Rd	Charlotte	NC	28217	**800-357-0012**	704-328-4000	300
CGR Products Inc 4655 US Hwy 29 N	Greensboro	NC	27405	**877-313-6785**	336-621-4568	327
CH (Clarion Hospital) 1 Hospital Dr	Clarion	PA	16214	**800-522-0505**	814-226-9500	374-3
CH Ellis Co Inc 2432 SE Ave *Sales	Indianapolis	IN	46201	**800-466-3351***	317-636-3351	452
CH Energy Group Inc 284 S Ave *NYSE: CHG*	Poughkeepsie	NY	12601	**800-527-2714**	845-452-2000	360-5
CH Hanson Co 2000 N Aurora Rd	Naperville	IL	60563	**800-827-3398**	630-848-2000	466
CH Robinson Worldwide Inc 14701 Charlson Rd *NASDAQ: CHRW* ■ *Cust Svc	Eden Prairie	MN	55347	**855-229-6128***	952-683-3950	448
CHA (Certified Horsemanship Assn) 1795 Alysheba Way Ste 7102	Lexington	KY	40509	**800-399-0138**	859-259-3399	47-3
CHA (Craft & Hobby Assn) 319 E 54th St	Elmwood Park	NJ	07407	**800-822-0494**	201-835-1200	47-18
CHA (Community Hospital Anderson) 1515 N Madison Ave	Anderson	IN	46011	**800-777-7775**	765-298-4242	374-3
Chabot Space & Science Ctr 10000 Skyline Blvd	Oakland	CA	94619	**800-704-9804**	510-336-7300	519
ChaCha Search Inc 14550 Clay Terr Blvd Ste 130	Carmel	IN	46032	**800-224-2242**	317-660-6680	196
Chaco Culture National Historical Park PO Box 220	Nageezi	NM	87037	**877-642-4743**	505-786-7014	563
Chad Therapeutics Inc 2975 Horseshoe Dr S Ste 600 *OTC: CHADQ*	Naples	FL	34104	**800-423-8870**	239-687-1285	475
CHADD (Children & Adults with Attention-Deficit/Hyperactivity Disorder) 8181 Professional Pl Ste 150	Landover	MD	20785	**800-233-4050**	301-306-7070	47-17
Chadderton Trucking Inc 40 Stewart Way	Sharon	PA	16146	**800-327-6868**	724-981-5050	778
Chadron State College 1000 Main St	Chadron	NE	69337	**800-242-3766**	308-432-6000	167
Chadwick's of Boston 500 Bic Dr Bldg 4	Milford	CT	06461	**877-330-3393**		458
Chain Drug Marketing Assn (CDMA) 43157 W Nine-Mile Rd PO Box 995	Novi	MI	48376	**800-935-2362**	248-449-9300	48-18
Chain Store Guide 10117 Princess Palm Ave Ste 375	Tampa	FL	33610	**800-927-9292**		634-6
Chalk & Vermilion Fine Arts Inc 55 Old Post Rd Ste 2	Greenwich	CT	06830	**800-877-2250**	203-869-9500	634-10
Challenge Printing Co, The 2 Bridewell Pl	Clifton	NJ	07014	**800-654-1234**	973-471-4700	626
Challenge Publications Inc 9509 Vassar Ave Ste A	Chatsworth	CA	91311	**800-562-9182**	818-700-6868	634-9
Challenger Ctr for Space Science Education 422 First St SE 3rd Fl *General	Washington	DC	20003	**800-969-5747***	202-827-1580	47-11
Challenger Gray & Christmas Inc 150 S Wacker Dr Ste 2800	Chicago	IL	60606	**855-242-3424**	312-332-5790	195
Challenger Learning Ctr (CLC) 316 Washington Ave Wheeling Jesuit University	Wheeling	WV	26003	**800-624-6992**	304-243-2279	519
Chally Group Worldwide Inc 3123 Research Blvd	Dayton	OH	45420	**800-254-5995**	937-259-1200	462
Chalmers & Kubeck Inc 150 Commerce Dr	Aston	PA	19014	**800-242-5637**	610-494-4300	453
Chamber Music America (CMA) 305 Seventh Ave 5th Fl	New York	NY	10001	**888-221-9836**	212-242-2022	47-4
Chamber of Business & Industry of Centre County 200 Innovation Blvd Ste 150	State College	PA	16803	**877-234-5050**	814-234-1829	138
Chamber of Commerce serving Middletown Monroe & Trenton 1500 Central Ave	Middletown	OH	45044	**800-837-3200**	513-422-4551	138
Chamber Orchestra of Philadelphia 1520 Locust St Ste 500	Philadelphia	PA	19102	**800-732-0999**	215-545-5451	572-3
Chamber South 6410 SW 80th St	South Miami	FL	33143	**800-206-3715**	305-661-1621	138
Chamberlain College of Nursing 11830 Westline Industrial Ste 106	Saint Louis	MO	63146	**888-556-8226**	314-991-6200	167
Chamberlain West Hollywood 1000 Westmount Dr	West Hollywood	CA	90069	**877-686-2082**	310-657-7400	379
Chambers of Commerce / Tourism 106 E Jefferson St	Tallahassee	FL	32301	**800-628-2866**	850-606-2305	208
Chameleon Consulting Inc 89 Falmouth Rd W	Arlington	MA	02474	**866-903-7912**	781-646-2272	182
Chaminade 1 Chaminade Ln	Santa Cruz	CA	95065	**800-283-6569**	831-475-5600	377
Chaminade College Preparatory School 425 S Lindbergh Blvd	Saint Louis	MO	63131	**877-378-6847**	314-993-4400	621
Chaminade University 3140 Waialae Ave	Honolulu	HI	96816	**800-735-3733**	808-735-4711	167
Chamizal National Memorial 800 S San Marcial St	El Paso	TX	79905	**877-642-4743**	915-532-7273	563
Champaign County Chamber of Commerce 1817 S Neil St Ste 201	Champaign	IL	61820	**800-328-1627**	217-359-1791	138
Champaign County Convention & Visitors Bureau 108 S Neil St	Champaign	IL	61820	**800-369-6151**	217-351-4133	208
Champion Bus Inc 331 Graham Rd	Imlay City	MI	48444	**800-776-4943**	810-724-6474	515
Champion Chemical Co 8319 S Greenleaf Ave	Whittier	CA	90602	**800-424-9300**		150
Champion College Services Inc 7776 S Pointe Pkwy W Ste 250	Tempe	AZ	85044	**800-761-7376**	480-947-7375	196
Champion Industries Inc PO Box 2968 PO Box 2968 *OTC: CHMP*	Huntington	WV	25728	**800-624-3431**	304-528-2791	626
Champion Mfg Industries Inc 6021 N Galena Rd	Peoria	IL	61614	**800-452-7473**	309-685-1031	594
Champion Photochemistry 7895 Tranmere Dr	Mississauga	ON	L5S1V9	**800-387-3430**	905-670-7900	590
Champion Power Equipment Inc 10006 Santa Fe Springs Rd	Santa Fe Springs	CA	90670	**877-338-0999**	562-236-9422	60
Champion Shuffleboard Ltd 7216 Burns St	Richland Hills	TX	76118	**800-826-7856**	817-284-3499	708
Champion Solutions Group 791 Pk of Commerce Blvd Ste 200	Boca Raton	FL	33487	**800-771-7000**	561-997-2900	176
Champion Window Mfg Inc 12121 Champion Way	Cincinnati	OH	45241	**877-424-2674**	513-346-4600	237
Champion-Arrowhead LLC 5147 Alhambra Ave	Los Angeles	CA	90032	**800-332-4267**	323-221-9137	608
Champions Way Enterprises Inc 980 1st St W	North Vancouver	BC	V7P3N4	**877-774-5425**		807
Champlain Cable Corp 175 Hercules Dr	Colchester	VT	05446	**800-451-5162**		812
Champlain College 163 S Willard St	Burlington	VT	05401	**800-570-5858**	802-860-2700	167
Champs Sports 311 Manatee Ave W	Bradenton	FL	34205	**800-991-6813**	941-748-0577	709
Chancellor Hotel on Union Square 433 Powell St	San Francisco	CA	94102	**800-428-4748**	415-362-2004	379
Chandler Asset Management Inc 6225 Lusk Blvd	San Diego	CA	92121	**800-317-4747**	858-546-3737	527
Chandler Chamber of Commerce 25 S Arizona Pl Ste 201	Chandler	AZ	85225	**800-963-4571**	480-963-4571	138
Chandler Hall Hospice 99 Barclay St	Newtown	PA	18940	**888-603-1973**	215-860-4000	371
Chandler Inn 26 Chandler St	Boston	MA	02116	**800-842-3450**	617-482-3450	379
Chandler Regional Hospital 475 S Dobson Rd	Chandler	AZ	85224	**877-728-5414**	480-728-3000	374-3
Chanel Inc 15 E 57th St	New York	NY	10022	**800-550-0005**	212-355-5050	573
Chaney Enterprises 12480 Mattawoman Dr PO Box 548	Waldorf	MD	20604	**888-244-0411**	301-932-5000	185
Change Companies, The 5221 Sigstrom Dr	Carson City	NV	89706	**888-889-8866**	775-885-2610	198
Channel Solutions LLC 3145 E Chandler Blvd Ste 110	Phoenix	AZ	85048	**866-501-9690**		198

Name / Address	City	State	ZIP	Toll-Free	Phone	Class
Channellock Inc 1306 S Main St	Meadville	PA	16335	**800-724-3018***		756
*Cust Svc						
Channing Bete Co 1 Community Pl	South Deerfield	MA	01373	**800-477-4776**	413-665-7611	634-10
Chant Engineering 59 Industrial Dr	New Britain	PA	18901	**888-567-0983**	215-230-4260	453
Chanticleer Inn 1458 E Dollar Lk Rd	Eagle River	WI	54521	**800-752-9193**	715-479-4486	667
CHAP (Community Health Accreditation Program Inc) 1275 K St NW Ste 800	Washington	DC	20005	**800-656-9656**	202-862-3413	47-1
Chaparral Energy Inc 701 Cedar Lake Blvd	Oklahoma City	OK	73114	**866-478-8770**	405-478-8770	537
Chaparral Suites Resort & Conference Ctr 5001 N Scottsdale Rd	Scottsdale	AZ	85250	**866-534-1797**	480-949-1414	667
Chapel Hill/Orange County Visitors Bureau 501 W Franklin St	Chapel Hill	NC	27516	**888-968-2060**		208
Chapel Hill-Carrboro Chamber of Commerce 104 S Estes Dr	Chapel Hill	NC	27515	**800-694-9784**	919-967-7075	138
Chapel Steel Co 590 N Bethlehem Pk PO Box 1000	Lower Gwynedd	PA	19002	**800-570-7674**	215-793-0899	453
Chapman University 1 University Dr	Orange	CA	92866	**888-282-7759**	714-997-6815	167
Chapman/Leonard Studio Equipment Inc 12950 Raymer St	North Hollywood	CA	91605	**888-883-6559**	818-764-6726	720
Chapters Health System 12973 Telecom Pkwy Ste 100	Temple Terrace	FL	33637	**866-204-8611**	813-871-8111	371
Char-Broil 1442 Belfast Ave	Columbus	GA	31902	**866-239-6777***	706-324-0421	35
*Cust Svc						
Charisma Magazine 600 Rinehart Rd	Lake Mary	FL	32746	**800-749-6500**	407-333-0600	456-18
Chariton Valley Electric Co-op 2090 Hwy 5 PO Box 486	Albia	IA	52531	**800-475-1702**	641-932-7126	247
CharityUSA.com LLC 600 University St Ste 1000 One Union Square	Seattle	WA	98101	**888-811-5271**	206-268-5400	387
Charles & Colvard Ltd 170 Southport Dr	Morrisville	NC	27560	**877-202-5467**		411
NASDAQ: CTHR						
Charles A. Lindbergh State Park 1615 Lindbergh Dr S PO Box 364	Little Falls	MN	56345	**888-646-6367**	320-616-2525	564
Charles C Thomas Publisher 2600 S First St	Springfield	IL	62704	**800-258-8980***	217-789-8980	634-2
*Sales						
Charles C. Parks Co 500 Belvedere Dr	Gallatin	TN	37066	**800-873-2406**	615-452-2406	298-11
Charles County Chamber of Commerce 101 Centennial St Ste A	La Plata	MD	20646	**800-992-3194**	301-932-6500	138
Charles Craft Inc 21381 Charles Craft Ln	Laurinburg	NC	28352	**800-275-4117**	910-844-3521	742-9
Charles d Hankey Law Office PC 434 E New York St	Indianapolis	IN	46202	**800-520-3633**	317-634-8565	428
Charles E Egeler Correctional Facility 3855 Cooper St	Jackson	MI	49201	**855-444-3911**	517-780-5600	215
Charles Gabus Ford Inc 4545 Merle Hay Rd	Des Moines	IA	50310	**800-934-2287***	515-270-0707	56
*Sales						
Charles GG Schmidt & Company Inc 301 W Grand Ave	Montvale	NJ	07645	**800-724-6438**	201-391-5300	756
Charles Hotel Harvard Square 1 Bennett St	Cambridge	MA	02138	**800-882-1818**	617-864-1200	379
Charles Industries Ltd 5600 Apollo Dr	Rolling Meadows	IL	60008	**800-458-4747**	847-806-6300	732
Charles Jones LLC PO Box 8488	Trenton	NJ	08650	**800-792-8888**		632
Charles Leonard Inc 145 Kennedy Dr	Hauppauge	NY	11788	**800-999-7202**	631-273-6700	350
Charles Machine Works Inc PO Box 66	Perry	OK	73077	**800-654-6481***	580-336-4402	192
*Cust Svc						
Charles Mix Electric Assn Inc 440 Lake St	Lake Andes	SD	57356	**800-208-8587**	605-487-7321	247
Charles River Analytics Inc 625 Mt Auburn St Ste 3	Cambridge	MA	02138	**877-547-4600**	617-491-3474	179
Charles River Laboratories Inc 251 Ballardvale St	Wilmington	MA	01887	**800-772-3271**	781-222-6000	666
NYSE: CRL						
Charles Ross & Son Co 710 Old Willets Path	Hauppauge	NY	11788	**800-243-7677**	631-234-0500	386
Charles Ryan Assoc Inc 601 Morris St Ste 301	Charleston	WV	25301	**877-342-0161**		633
Charles Schwab & Co Inc 211 Main St	San Francisco	CA	94105	**800-648-5300***	415-667-1009	688
*Cust Svc						
Charles Towne Landing State Historic Site 1500 Old Towne Rd	Charleston	SC	29407	**866-345-7275**	843-852-4200	564
Charleston Area Convention & Visitors Bureau 423 King St	Charleston	SC	29403	**800-868-8118**	843-853-8000	208
Charleston County School District (CCSD) 75 Calhoun St	Charleston	SC	29401	**800-255-7688**	843-937-6300	683
Charleston Gazette 1001 Virginia St E	Charleston	WV	25301	**800-982-6397**	304-348-5140	531-2
Charleston Newspapers Ltd 1001 Virginia St E	Charleston	WV	25301	**800-982-6397**	304-348-4848	531-3
Charleston Place 205 Meeting St	Charleston	SC	29401	**888-635-2350**	843-722-4900	379
Charleston Regional Chamber of Commerce 1116 Smith St	Charleston	WV	25301	**800-792-4326**	304-340-4253	138
Charleston Southern University 9200 University Blvd	Charleston	SC	29423	**800-947-7474**	843-863-7050	167
Charlestown Retirement Community (CCI) 715 Maiden Choice Ln	Catonsville	MD	21228	**800-917-8649**	410-242-2880	670
Charlevoix County 203 Antrim St	Charlevoix	MI	49720	**800-548-9157**	231-547-7200	338
Charley's Grilled Subs 2500 Farmers Dr Ste 140	Columbus	OH	43235	**800-437-8325**	614-923-4700	668
Charlie Palmer Steak 101 Constitution Ave NW	Washington	DC	20001	**877-632-7800**	202-547-8100	669
Charlotte Anodizing Products Inc 591 E Packard Hwy	Charlotte	MI	48813	**800-818-6945**	517-543-1911	480
Charlotte Appliances Inc 3200 Lake Ave	Rochester	NY	14612	**800-244-0405**	585-663-5050	322
Charlotte Convention & Visitors Bureau 500 S College St Ste 300	Charlotte	NC	28202	**800-722-1994**	704-334-2282	208
Charlotte Institute of Rehabilitation 1100 Blythe Blvd	Charlotte	NC	28203	**800-634-2256**	704-355-4300	374-6
Charlotte Motor Speedway 5555 Concord Pkwy S	Concord	NC	28027	**800-455-3267**	704-455-3200	639
Charlotte Nature Museum 1658 Sterling Rd	Charlotte	NC	28209	**800-935-0553**	704-372-6261	519
Charlotte Observer, The 600 S Tryon St	Charlotte	NC	28202	**800-332-0686**	704-358-5000	531-2
Charlotte Pipe & Foundry Co 2109 Randolph Rd	Charlotte	NC	28207	**800-438-6091**	704-372-5030	489
Charlotte Russe Inc 5910 Pacific Center Blvd	San Diego	CA	92121	**888-211-7271**		156-6
Charlotte-Mecklenburg Schools 701 E ML King Jr Blvd	Charlotte	NC	28202	**800-244-6224**	980-343-3000	683
Charm Sciences Inc 659 Andover St	Lawrence	MA	01843	**800-343-2170**	978-687-9200	478
Charmer Sunbelt Group, The 60 E 42nd St Ste 1915	New York	NY	10165	**888-262-9787**	212-699-7000	80-3
Charms Co 7401 S Cicero Ave	Chicago	IL	60629	**800-267-0037**	773-838-3400	297-8
Charter at Beaver Creek 120 Offerson Rd PO Box 5310	Avon	CO	81620	**800-525-6660**	970-949-6660	379
Charter Communications Inc 12405 Powerscourt Dr Ste 100	Saint Louis	MO	63131	**888-438-2427**	314-965-0555	115
NASDAQ: CHTR						
Charter Films Inc 1901 Winter St PO Box 277	Superior	WI	54880	**877-411-3456**	715-395-8258	547
Charter Flight Inc 1928 S Blvd	Charlotte	NC	28208	**800-521-3148**	704-359-9124	13
Charter Wire 3700 W Milwaukee Rd	Milwaukee	WI	53208	**800-436-9074**	414-390-3000	811
CharterBank 1233 OG Skinner Dr	West Point	GA	31833	**800-763-4444**	706-645-1391	69
Chartered Business Valuators 277 Wellington St W Ste 710	Toronto	ON	M5V3H2	**866-770-7315**	416-977-1117	770
Chartis Group LLC 220 W Kinzie St 5th Fl	Chicago	IL	60654	**877-667-4700**		462
Chartist Newsletter PO Box 758	Seal Beach	CA	90740	**800-942-4278**	562-596-2385	530-9
Chartpak Inc 1 River Rd	Leeds	MA	01053	**800-628-1910**	413-584-5446	42
Chartway Federal Credit Union 160 Newtown Rd	Virginia Beach	VA	23462	**800-678-8765**	757-552-1000	221
Chase & Sons Inc 295 University Ave	Westwood	MA	02090	**800-323-4182**	781-332-0700	814
Chase Bank 1 Chase Manhattan Plz	New York	NY	10005	**800-935-9935**		69
Chase Brass & Copper Co 14212 Selwyn Dr	Montpelier	OH	43543	**800-537-4291**	419-485-3193	484
Chase Hotel at Palm Springs 200 W Arenas Rd	Palm Springs	CA	92262	**877-532-4273**	760-320-8866	379
Chase Industries Inc 10021 Commerce Park Dr	Cincinnati	OH	45246	**800-543-4455**	513-860-5565	479
Chase Park Plaza 212 N KingsHwy Blvd	Saint Louis	MO	63108	**877-587-2427***	314-633-3000	379
*Resv						
Chase Paymentech Solutions LLC 14221 Dallas Pkwy	Dallas	TX	75254	**800-708-3740***		257
*Cust Svc						
Chase Plastic Services Inc 6467 Waldon Ctr Dr	Clarkston	MI	48346	**800-232-4273**	248-620-2120	688
Chateau Elan Resort & Conference Ctr 100 Rue Charlemagne	Braselton	GA	30517	**800-233-9463**	678-425-0900	377
Chateau Elan Winery 100 Tour de France	Braselton	GA	30517	**800-233-9463**	678-425-0900	49-6
Chateau Grille 415 N State Hwy 265	Branson	MO	65616	**888-333-5253**	417-334-1161	669
Chateau Louis Hotel & Conference Centre 11727 Kingsway	Edmonton	AB	T5G3A1	**800-661-9843**	780-452-7770	379
Chateau Morrisette Winery 287 Winery Rd SW	Floyd	VA	24091	**866-695-2001**	540-593-2865	49-6
Chateau on the Lake 415 N State Hwy 265	Branson	MO	65616	**888-333-5253**	417-334-1161	379
Chateau Resort & Conference Center, The 300 Camelback Rd	Tannersville	PA	18372	**800-245-5900**	570-629-5900	705
Chateau Rouge 1505 S Broadway Ave	Red Lodge	MT	59068	**800-926-1601**	406-446-1601	705
Chateau Ste Michelle Winery 14111 NE 145th St	Woodinville	WA	98072	**800-267-6793**	425-415-3300	49-6
Chateau Vaudreuil Suites Hotel 21700 Rt Transcanada Hwy	Vaudreuil-Dorion	QC	J7V8P3	**800-363-7896**	450-455-0955	379
Chateau Versailles 1659 Sherbrooke St W	Montreal	QC	H3H1E3	**888-933-8111**	514-933-3611	379
Chatham Bars Inn 297 Shore Rd	Chatham	MA	02633	**800-527-4884**	508-945-0096	667
Chatham Hall 800 Chatham Hall Cir	Chatham	VA	24531	**877-644-2941**	434-432-2941	621
Chatham Steel Corp 501 W Boundary St	Savannah	GA	31401	**800-800-1337**	912-233-5751	491
Chatham University 1 Woodland Rd	Pittsburgh	PA	15232	**800-837-1290**	412-365-1100	167
Chatr Wireless 333 Bloor St E 8th Fl	Toronto	ON	M4W1G9	**800-485-9745**		226
Chatsworth Data Corp 9735 Lurline Ave	Chatsworth	CA	91311	**877-380-6855**	818-350-5072	250
Chatsworth Products Inc 31425 Agoura Rd	Westlake Village	CA	91361	**800-834-4969**	818-735-6100	178

Name / Address	City	State	Zip	Toll-Free	Phone	Class
Chatsworth-Murray County Chamber of Commerce PO Box 516	Chatsworth	GA	30705	800-969-9490	706-695-2834	138
Chattahoochee River National Recreation Area 1978 Island Ford Pkwy	Atlanta	GA	30350	877-874-2478	678-538-1200	563
Chattanooga Area Chamber of Commerce 811 Broad St	Chattanooga	TN	37402	877-756-1684	423-756-2121	138
Chattanooga Area Convention & Visitors Bureau 215 Broad St	Chattanooga	TN	37402	800-322-3344	423-756-8687	208
Chattanooga Convention Ctr 1150 Carter St PO Box 6008	Chattanooga	TN	37402	800-962-5213	423-756-0001	207
Chattanooga Group 4717 Adams Rd	Hixson	TN	37343	800-592-7329	423-870-2281	476
Chattanooga National Cemetery 1200 Bailey Ave	Chattanooga	TN	37404	877-907-8585	423-855-6590	135
Chattanooga State Technical Community College 4501 Amnicola Hwy	Chattanooga	TN	37406	866-547-3733	423-697-4400	161
Chattanoogan, The 1201 Broad St	Chattanooga	TN	37402	877-756-1684	423-756-3400	377
Chautauqua County Visitors Bureau Chautauqua Main Gate Rt 394 PO Box 1441	Chautauqua	NY	14722	800-242-4569	716-357-4569	208
Cheaha Resort State Park 19644 Hwy 281	Delta	AL	36258	800-610-5801	256-488-5111	564
Cheap Joe's Art Stuff Inc 374 Industrial Park Dr	Boone	NC	28607	800-227-2788	828-263-5472	521
Check Cashing Store (CCS) 6340 NW Fifth Way	Fort Lauderdale	FL	33309	800-361-1407		140
Check Point Software Technologies Ltd 800 Bridge Pkwy *NASDAQ: CHKP*	Redwood City	CA	94065	800-429-4391	650-628-2000	180-12
Check Printers Inc 1530 Antioch Pike	Antioch	TN	37013	800-766-1217		141
Checkered Flag Motor Car Corp 5225 Virginia Beach Blvd	Virginia Beach	VA	23462	866-414-7820	757-687-3486	56
Checkers Drive-In Restaurants Inc 4300 W Cypress St Ste 600	Tampa	FL	33607	800-800-8072	813-283-7000	668
CheckPoint HR 2035 Lincoln Hwy Ste 1080	Edison	NJ	08817	800-385-0331	732-287-8270	569
Checkpoint Systems Inc 101 Wolf Dr *NYSE: CKP*	Thorofare	NJ	08086	800-257-5540	856-848-1800	690
Checks In The Mail Inc 2435 Goodwin Ln	New Braunfels	TX	78135	800-733-4443		141
Checks Unlimited 8245 N Union Blvd	Colorado Springs	CO	80920	800-210-0468	719-531-3900	141
Cheeca Lodge & Spa 81801 Overseas Hwy Mile Marker 82	Islamorada	FL	33036	800-327-2888	305-664-4651	705
Cheekwood Museum of Art & Botanical Garden 1200 Forrest Pk Dr	Nashville	TN	37205	877-356-8150	615-356-8000	96
Cheevers & Company Inc 440 S LaSalle St Ste 710	Chicago	IL	60605	866-928-7643	312-224-7922	688
Chella Professional Skin Care 507 Calle San Pablo	Camarillo	CA	93012	877-424-3552	805-383-7711	76
Chelsea Bldg Products 565 Cedar Way	Oakmont	PA	15139	800-424-3573		237
Chelsea Lumber Co 1 Old Barn Cir	Chelsea	MI	48118	800-875-9126	734-475-9126	193-3
Chelsea Milling Co 201 W N St PO Box 460	Chelsea	MI	48118	800-727-2460	734-475-1361	297-23
Chelsea Savoy Hotel 204 W 23rd St	New York	NY	10011	866-929-9353	212-929-9353	379
Chem Processing Inc 3910 Linden Oaks Dr	Rockford	IL	61109	800-262-2119	815-874-8118	480
Chem USA Corp 38507 Cherry St	Newark	CA	94560	800-866-2436	510-608-8818	175-1
Chemart Co 15 New England Way	Lincoln	RI	02865	800-521-5001	401-333-9200	480
Chematics Inc PO Box 293	North Webster	IN	46555	800-348-5174	574-834-2406	233
Chembio Diagnostics Inc 3661 Horseblock Rd *NASDAQ: CEMI*	Medford	NY	11763	844-243-6246	631-924-1135	582
Chemed Corp 255 E Fifth St Ste 2600 *NYSE: CHE* ■ *General	Cincinnati	OH	45202	800-982-7650*	513-762-6900	187
Chemetal 39 O'Neil St	EastHampton	MA	01027	800-807-7341	413-529-0718	296
Chemical Abstracts Service (CAS) 2540 Olentangy River Rd	Columbus	OH	43202	800-848-6538	614-447-3600	387
Chemical Financial Corp 333 E Main St *NASDAQ: CHFC*	Midland	MI	48640	800-867-9757	989-839-5350	360-2
Chemical Processing Magazine 1501 E. Woodfield Rd Ste 400N	Schaumburg	IL	60173	800-343-4048	630-467-1300	456-21
Chemical Products Corp 102 Old Mill Rd *Cust Svc	Cartersville	GA	30120	877-210-9814*	770-382-2144	142
Chemical Regulation Reporter 1801 S Bell St	Arlington	VA	22202	800-372-1033		530-5
Chemical Safety Corp 5901 Christie Ave Ste 502	Emeryville	CA	94608	888-594-1100	510-594-1000	38
Chemical Specialties Manufacturing Corp 901 N Newkirk St *Sales	Baltimore	MD	21205	800-638-7370*	410-675-4800	150
Chemical Waste Management Inc 1001 Fannin St Ste 4000	Houston	TX	77002	800-633-7871	713-512-6200	665
Chemical Week Magazine 140 E 45th St 2 Grand Central Tower,40th Fl *Cust Svc	New York	NY	10017	866-501-7540*	212-884-9528	456-21
Chemically Dependent Anonymous (CDA) PO Box 423	Severna Park	MD	21146	888-232-4673		47-21
Chemin-A-Haut State Park 14656 State Pk Rd	Bastrop	LA	71220	888-677-2436	318-283-0812	564
Chemineer Inc 5870 Poe Ave	Dayton	OH	45414	800-643-0641	937-454-3200	386
Chem-pak Inc 242 Corning Way	Martinsburg	WV	25405	800-336-9828	304-262-1880	296
Chemprene Inc 483 Fishkill Ave	Beacon	NY	12508	800-431-9981	845-831-2800	370
Chemstar Products Co 3915 Hiawatha Ave	Minneapolis	MN	55406	800-328-5037	612-722-0079	143
Chem-Tainer Industries Inc 361 Neptune Ave	West Babylon	NY	11704	800-275-2436	631-661-8300	201
Chem-Trend LP 1445 McPherson Pk Dr	Howell	MI	48843	800-727-7730	517-546-4520	540
Chemtrol Div NIBCO Inc 1516 Middlebury St	Elkhart	IN	46516	800-234-0227	574-295-3000	595
Chemtronics Inc 8125 Cobb Centre Dr	Kennesaw	GA	30152	800-645-5244	770-424-4888	144
Chemung County Chamber of Commerce 400 E Church St *General	Elmira	NY	14901	800-627-5892*	607-734-5137	138
Chemung Supply Corp PO Box 527	Elmira	NY	14903	800-733-5508	607-733-5506	193-2
Chen Instrument Design Inc 4845 NW Camas Meadows Dr	Camas	WA	98607	800-767-0119	360-833-8835	636
Cheney Lime & Cement 478 Graystone Rd PO Box 160	Allgood	AL	35013	800-752-8282	205-625-3031	440
Cheniere Energy Inc 700 Milam St Ste 800 *NYSE: LNG*	Houston	TX	77002	877-375-5002	713-375-5000	326
CHEP USA 8517 S Pk Cir *Cust Svc	Orlando	FL	32819	866-855-2437*	407-370-2437	646
Cheraw State Park 100 State Pk Rd	Cheraw	SC	29520	800-868-9630	843-537-9656	564
Cher-Make Sausage Co 2915 Calumet Ave	Manitowoc	WI	54220	800-242-7679	920-683-5980	297-26
Cherokee Brick & Tile Co Inc 3250 Waterville Rd	Macon	GA	31206	800-277-2745	478-781-6800	149
Cherokee County 165 E Sixth St Ste 203 Ste 203	Rusk	TX	75785	800-541-2524	903-683-6540	338
Cherokee Electric Co-op 1550 Clarence Chestnut Bypass PO Box 0	Centre	AL	35960	800-952-2667	256-927-5524	247
Cherokee Heritage Ctr & National Museum 21192 S Keeler Dr	Park Hill	OK	74451	888-999-6007	918-456-6007	519
Cherokee Park Ranch 436 Cherokee Hills Dr	Livermore	CO	80536	800-628-0949	970-493-6522	241
Cherokee State Park N 4475 Rd	Langley	OK	74350	866-602-4653	918-435-8066	564
Cherokee Steel Supply 196 Leroy Anderson Dr	Monroe	GA	30655	800-729-0334	770-207-4621	491
Cherokee Tribal Travel & Promotions 498 Tsali Blvd	Cherokee	NC	28719	877-440-9990	828-359-6492	208
Cherry Corp 11200 88th Ave	Pleasant Prairie	WI	53158	800-510-1689	262-942-6500	813
Cherry Creek Dodge 2727 S Havana St *Sales	Denver	CO	80014	888-891-7522*	303-751-1104	56
Cherry Creek State Park 4201 S Parker Rd	Aurora	CO	80014	866-265-6447	303-699-3860	564
Cherry Demolition 6131 Selinsky Rd	Houston	TX	77048	800-444-1123	713-987-0000	191-16
Cherry Hill Photo Enterprises Inc 4 East Stow Rd	Marlton	NJ	08053	800-969-2440		589
Cherry Tree Design 320 Pronghorn Trl	Bozeman	MT	59718	800-634-3268	406-582-8800	281
Cherry's Industrial Equipment 600 Morse Ave	Elk Grove Village	IL	60007	800-350-0011		358
Cherrydale Farms Fundraising 707 N Vly Forge Rd	Lansdale	PA	19446	877-619-4822		297-8
Cherryland Electric Co-op 5930 US 31 S PO Box 298	Grawn	MI	49637	800-442-8616	231-486-9200	247
Cherryroad Technologies Inc 301 Gibraltar Dr Ste 2C	Morris Plains	NJ	07950	877-402-7804	973-402-7802	179
Cherry-Todd Electric Co-op Inc 625 W Second St	Mission	SD	57555	800-856-4417	605-856-4416	247
Cheryl & Co 646 McCorkle Blvd	Westerville	OH	43082	800-443-8124		67
Chesapeake Bay Magazine 1819 Bay Ridge Ave Ste 180	Annapolis	MD	21403	800-283-2883	410-263-2662	456-22
Chesapeake Conventions & Tourism Bureau (CCT) 860 Greenbrier Cir Ste 101	Chesapeake	VA	23320	888-889-5551	757-502-4898	208
Chesapeake Lodging Trust (CLT) 1997 Annapolis Exchange Pkwy Ste 410 *NYSE: CHSP*	Annapolis	MD	21401	800-698-2820		652
Chesapeake Regional Medical Ctr 736 Battlefield Blvd N	Chesapeake	VA	23320	800-456-8121	757-312-8121	374-3
Cheshire Marketing Inc 3209 Guess Rd Ste 108	Durham	NC	27705	800-495-4633	919-479-2008	197
Chess Life Magazine PO Box 3967 *Sales	Crossville	TN	38557	800-903-8723*	931-787-1234	456-14
Chester County 313 W Market St Ste 6202 PO Box 2748	West Chester	PA	19380	800-692-1100	610-344-6100	338
Chester Fritz Auditorium 3475 University Ave	Grand Forks	ND	58202	800-375-4068	701-777-3076	571
Chester Mental Health Ctr 1315 Lehman Dr	Chester	IL	62233	800-843-6154	618-826-4571	374-5
Chester State Park 759 State Pk Dr	Chester	SC	29706	866-345-7275	803-385-2680	564
Chester Water Authority PO Box 467	Chester	PA	19016	800-793-2323	610-876-8185	803
Chester's International LLC 3500 Colonnade Pkwy Ste 325	Birmingham	AL	35243	800-554-4537	205-949-4690	311
Chesterfield Chamber of Commerce 101 Chesterfield Business Pkwy	Chesterfield	MO	63005	888-242-4262	636-532-3399	138
Chesterfield Hotel 363 Cocoanut Row	Palm Beach	FL	33480	800-243-7871	561-659-5800	379

Name / Address	City	State	ZIP	Toll-Free	Phone	Class
Chester-Jensen Company Inc PO Box 908	Chester	PA	19016	**800-685-3750**	610-876-6276	299
Chestnut Hill College 9601 Germantown Ave	Philadelphia	PA	19118	**800-248-0052**	215-248-7001	167
Chestnut Hill Hotel 8229 Germantown Ave	Philadelphia	PA	19118	**800-628-9744**	215-242-5905	379
Chestnut Mountain Resort 8700 Chestnut Dr	Galena	IL	61036	**800-397-1320**		378
Chevron Canada Ltd 1200 - 1050 W Pender St	Vancouver	BC	V6E3T4	**800-663-1650**	604-668-5300	579
Chevron Corp 6001 Bollinger Canyon Rd *NYSE: CVX* ■ *Cust Svc	San Ramon	CA	94583	**800-368-8357***	925-842-1000	535
Chevron Phillips Chemical Company LP 10001 Six Pines Dr	The Woodlands	TX	77380	**800-231-1212**	832-813-4100	143
Chevron Phillips Chemical Company Performance Pipe Div 5085 W Pk Blvd Ste 500	Plano	TX	75093	**800-527-0662**	972-599-6600	595
Chevron Pipe Line Co 4800 Fournace Pl	Bellaire	TX	77401	**877-596-2800**	713-432-6000	596
Chevron Texaco Credit Card Ctr PO Box P	Concord	CA	94524	**800-243-8766**		219
Chewacla State Park 124 Shell Toomer Pkwy	Auburn	AL	36830	**800-252-7275**	334-887-5621	564
Cheyenne Area Convention & Visitors Bureau 121 W 15th St Ste 202	Cheyenne	WY	82001	**800-426-5009**	307-778-3133	208
Cheyenne City Hall 2101 O'Neil Ave	Cheyenne	WY	82001	**855-491-1859**	307-637-6200	337
Cheyenne Civic Ctr 510 W 20th St	Cheyenne	WY	82001	**877-691-2787**	307-637-6364	571
Cheyenne Depot Museum 121 W 15th St Ste 300	Cheyenne	WY	82001	**800-544-2151**	307-632-3905	519
Cheyenne Mountain Conference Resort 3225 Broadmoor Vly Rd	Colorado Springs	CO	80906	**800-428-8886**	719-538-4000	377
Cheyenne Newspaper Inc 702 W Lincolnway	Cheyenne	WY	82001	**800-561-6268**	307-634-3361	634-8
Cheyney University of Pennsylvania 1837 University Cir PO Box 200	Cheyney	PA	19319	**800-243-9639**	610-399-2275	167
CHF Industries Inc 1 Pk Ave 9th Fl *Cust Svc	New York	NY	10016	**800-243-7090***	212-951-7800	743
Chi Alpha Campus Ministries USA 1445 Booneville Ave	Springfield	MO	65802	**855-700-2457**	417-862-2781	47-16
Chi Phi Fraternity 1160 Satellite Blvd	Suwanee	GA	30024	**800-849-1824**	404-231-1824	47-16
Chicago Board Options Exchange (CBOE) 400 S La Salle St	Chicago	IL	60605	**800-678-4667**	312-786-5600	689
Chicago Boiler Co 1300 NW Ave *Cust Svc	Gurnee	IL	60031	**800-522-7343***	847-662-4000	90
Chicago Botanic Garden 1000 Lake Cook Rd	Glencoe	IL	60022	**877-829-5500**	847-835-5440	96
Chicago Bridge & Iron Co 6001 Rogerdale Rd *NYSE: CBI* ■ *General	Houston	TX	77072	**866-235-5687***	713-485-1000	191-14
Chicago Display Marketing Corp 2021 W St	River Grove	IL	60171	**800-681-4340**	708-842-0001	235
Chicago Dowel Company Inc 4700 W Grand Ave	Chicago	IL	60639	**800-333-6935**	773-622-2000	818
Chicago Extruded Metals Co (CXM) 1601 S 54th Ave *Cust Svc	Cicero	IL	60804	**800-323-8102***		484
Chicago Faucets A Geberit Co 2100 S Clearwater Dr	Des Plaines	IL	60018	**800-323-5060**	847-803-5000	608
Chicago Fire 7000 S Harlem Ave	Bridgeview	IL	60455	**888-657-3473**	708-594-7200	715
Chicago Gasket Co 1285 W N Ave	Chicago	IL	60622	**800-833-5666**	773-486-3060	327
Chicago International Film Festival Cinema Chicago 30 E Adams St Ste 800	Chicago	IL	60603	**800-982-2787**	312-683-0121	284
Chicago Lakeshore Hospital 4840 N Marine Dr *Cust Svc	Chicago	IL	60640	**800-888-0560***	773-878-9700	374-5
Chicago Lumber Company of Omaha, The 1324 Pierce St PO Box 3487	Omaha	NE	68103	**800-642-8210**	402-342-0840	193-3
Chicago Magazine 435 N Michigan Ave Ste 1100	Chicago	IL	60611	**800-999-0879**	312-222-8999	456-22
Chicago Meat Authority Inc (CMA) 1120 W 47th Pl	Chicago	IL	60609	**800-383-3811**	773-254-3811	297-26
Chicago Metal Fabricators Inc 3724 S Rockwell St	Chicago	IL	60632	**877-400-5995**	773-523-5755	481
Chicago Midway Airport 5700 S Cicero Ave	Chicago	IL	60638	**800-832-6352**	773-838-0600	27
Chicago Nannies Inc 101 N Marion St Ste 300	Oak Park	IL	60301	**866-900-9605**	708-524-2101	262
Chicago Nut & Bolt Inc 150 Covington Dr	Bloomingdale	IL	60108	**888-529-8600**	630-529-8600	350
Chicago Office of Tourism & Culture 78 E Washington St 4th Fl	Chicago	IL	60602	**888-871-5311**	312-744-2400	208
Chicago Pneumatic Tool Co 1800 Overview Dr	Rock Hill	SC	29730	**800-624-4735**	803-817-7000	757
Chicago Reader 11 E Illinois St	Chicago	IL	60611	**888-473-5362**	312-828-0350	531-5
Chicago Sky 20 W Kinzie St Ste 1000	Chicago	IL	60610	**877-329-9622**	312-828-9550	712-2
Chicago Southland Convention & Visitors Bureau 2304 173rd St	Lansing	IL	60438	**888-895-8233**	708-895-8200	208
Chicago Southshore & South Bend Railroad 505 N Carroll Ave	Michigan City	IN	46360	**800-356-2079**	219-874-9000	646
Chicago Symphony Orchestra 220 S Michigan Ave	Chicago	IL	60604	**800-223-7114**	312-294-3000	572-3
Chicago Title & Trust Co 171 N Clark St	Chicago	IL	60601	**800-621-1919**	312-223-2000	391-6
Chicago Tribune 435 N Michigan Ave	Chicago	IL	60611	**800-874-2863**	312-222-3232	531-2
Chicago Tube & Iron Co 1 Chicago Tube Dr *Cust Svc	Romeoville	IL	60446	**800-972-0217***	815-834-2500	491

Name / Address	City	State	ZIP	Toll-Free	Phone	Class
Chicagoland Speedway 500 Speedway Blvd	Joliet	IL	60433	**888-629-7223**	815-722-5500	514
Chicago-Wilcox Mfg Co 16928 State St PO Box 126	South Holland	IL	60473	**800-323-5282**		327
Chick Master Incubator Co 945 Lafayette Rd PO Box 704	Medina	OH	44258	**800-727-8726**	330-722-5591	275
Chick's 18011 S Dupont Hwy	Harrington	DE	19952	**800-444-2441**	302-398-4630	709
Chickasaw Electric Co-op 17970 US Hwy 64 E PO Box 459	Somerville	TN	38068	**866-465-3591**	901-465-3591	247
Chickasaw Nation, The 520 Arlington St PO Box 1548	Ada	OK	74821	**866-466-1481**	580-436-2603	47-11
Chickasaw State Park 26955 US Hwy 43	Gallion	AL	36742	**800-760-4089**	334-295-8230	564
Chico Chamber of Commerce 441 Main St	Chico	CA	95928	**800-852-8570**	530-891-5556	138
Chico Enterprise Record 400 E Pk Ave PO Box 9	Chico	CA	95927	**877-229-8655**	530-891-1234	531-2
Chico News & Review 353 E Second St	Chico	CA	95928	**866-703-3873**	530-894-2300	531-5
Chico's FAS Inc 11215 Metro Pkwy *NYSE: CHS*	Fort Myers	FL	33966	**800-690-6903**	888-855-4986	156-6
Chicopee Provision Co Inc 19 Sitarz St	Chicopee	MA	01013	**800-924-6328**	413-594-4765	297-26
Chicot State Park 3469 Chicot Pk Rd	Ville Platte	LA	70586	**888-677-2442**	337-363-2403	564
Chief Automotive Systems Inc 1924 E Fourth St	Grand Island	NE	68802	**800-445-9262**	308-384-9747	386
Chignecto-central Regional 60 Lorne St	Truro	NS	B2N3K3	**800-770-0008**	902-897-8923	683
Child Development Assoc Inc 678 Third Ave Ste 201	Chula Vista	CA	91910	**888-755-2445**	619-427-4411	147
Child Evangelism Fellowship Inc 17482 Hwy M	Warrenton	MO	63383	**800-748-7710**	636-456-4321	47-20
Child Find Canada 212-2211 McPhillips St	Winnipeg	MB	R2V3M5	**800-387-7962**	204-339-5584	47-6
Child Lures Prevention 5166 Shelburne Rd	Shelburne	VT	05482	**800-552-2197**	802-985-8458	47-6
Child Welfare Information Gateway 1250 Maryland Ave SW 8th Fl	Washington	DC	20024	**800-394-3366**	703-385-7565	340-8
Childcare Network Inc 3025 University Ave Ste B-2	Columbus	GA	31907	**866-521-5437**	706-562-8600	147
Childcraft Education Corp 1156 Four Star Dr	Mount Joy	PA	17552	**800-631-5652**		458
Childhelp USA 4350 E Camelback Rd Bldg F250	Phoenix	AZ	85018	**800-422-4453**	480-922-8212	47-6
Children & Adults with Attention-Deficit/Hyperactivity Disorder (CHADD) 8181 Professional Pl Ste 150	Landover	MD	20785	**800-233-4050**	301-306-7070	47-17
Children & Youth Funding Report 8204 Fenton St	Silver Spring	MD	20910	**800-666-6380**	301-588-6380	530-8
Children Awaiting Parents Inc (CAP) 595 Blossom Rd Ste 306	Rochester	NY	14610	**888-835-8802**	585-232-5110	47-6
Children First Home Healthcare Service 4448 Edgewater Dr	Orlando	FL	32804	**800-207-0802**	407-513-3000	262
Children Inc 4205 Dover Rd	Richmond	VA	23221	**800-538-5381**	804-359-4562	47-6
Children International 2000 E Red Bridge Rd	Kansas City	MO	64131	**800-888-3089**	816-942-2000	47-5
Children of Lesbians & Gays Everywhere (COLAGE) 3815 S Othello St Ste 100	Seattle	WA	98118	**800-657-3717**	415-861-5437	47-21
Children of the Night 14530 Sylvan St	Van Nuys	CA	91411	**800-551-1300**	818-908-4474	47-6
Children's Bureau of Southern California 1910 Magnolia Ave	Los Angeles	CA	90004	**800-730-3933**	213-342-0100	352
Children's Defense Fund (CDF) 25 E St NW	Washington	DC	20001	**800-233-1200**	202-628-8787	47-6
Children's Healthcare of Atlanta at Egleston 1405 Clifton Rd NE	Atlanta	GA	30322	**888-785-7778**	404-785-6000	374-1
Children's Healthcare of Atlanta at Scottish Rite 1001 Johnson Ferry Rd NE	Atlanta	GA	30342	**888-785-7778**	404-785-5252	374-1
Children's Hope House 7922 W Jefferson Blvd	Fort Wayne	IN	46804	**800-706-9941**	260-459-8550	372
Children's Hospital 200 Henry Clay Ave	New Orleans	LA	70118	**800-299-9511**	504-899-9511	374-1
Children's Hospital Medical Ctr of Akron 1 Perkins Sq	Akron	OH	44308	**800-262-0333**	330-543-1000	374-1
Children's Hospital of Eastern Ontario 401 Smyth Rd	Ottawa	ON	K1H8L1	**866-797-0007**	613-737-7600	374-2
Children's Hospital of New York-Presbyterian *Pediatric Blood & Marrow Transplantation Program* 3959 Broadway	New York	NY	10032	**866-463-2778**	212-305-5593	767
Children's Hospital of Orange County Blood & Donor Services 505 S Main St	Orange	CA	92868	**800-228-5234**	714-509-8339	767
Children's Hospital of Philadelphia Stem Cell Transplant Program 3401 Civic Ctr Blvd	Philadelphia	PA	19104	**800-879-2467**		767
Children's Hospitals & Clinics Minneapolis 2525 Chicago Ave	Minneapolis	MN	55404	**866-225-3251**	612-813-6000	374-1
Children's House at Johns Hopkins 1915 McElderry St	Baltimore	MD	21205	**800-933-5470**	410-614-2560	372
Children's Institute of Pittsburgh 1405 Shady Ave	Pittsburgh	PA	15217	**877-433-1109**	412-420-2400	374-1
Children's Medical Ctr 1 Children's Plaza	Dayton	OH	45404	**800-228-4055**	937-641-3000	374-1
Children's Mercy Hospital & Clinics 2401 Gillham Rd	Kansas City	MO	64108	**866-512-2168**	816-234-3000	374-1
Children's Museum of Indianapolis 3000 N Meridian St	Indianapolis	IN	46208	**800-820-6214**	317-334-3322	519
Children's Museum of Oak Ridge 461 W Outer Dr	Oak Ridge	TN	37830	**877-524-1223**	865-482-1074	520
Children's Museum of Richmond 2626 W Broad St	Richmond	VA	23220	**866-737-5965**	804-474-7000	520
Children's National Medical Ctr (CNMC) 111 Michigan Ave NW	Washington	DC	20010	**800-884-5433**	202-476-5000	374-1
Children's Organ Transplant Assn (COTA) 2501 W Cota Dr	Bloomington	IN	47403	**800-366-2682**	812-336-8872	47-17

Name / Address	City	State	ZIP	Toll-Free	Phone	Class
Children's Place Retail Stores Inc 500 Plz Dr *NASDAQ: PLCE*	Secaucus	NJ	07094	**877-752-2387**	201-558-2400	156-1
Children's Research Institute Children's National Medical Ctr 111 Michigan Ave NW Research Fl 5	Washington	DC	20010	**888-884-2327**		666
Children's Specialized Hospital 150 New Providence Rd	Mountainside	NJ	07092	**888-244-5373**	908-233-3720	374-1
Children's Tumor Foundation 95 Pine St 16th Fl	New York	NY	10005	**800-323-7938**	212-344-6633	47-17
Children's Wish Foundation International 8615 Roswell Rd	Atlanta	GA	30350	**800-323-9474**	770-393-9474	47-17
Childrens Plus Inc 1387 Dutch American Way	Beecher	IL	60401	**800-230-1279**		95
Chile *Embassy* 1732 Massachusetts Ave NW	Washington	DC	20036	**855-310-8471**	202-785-1746	259
Chillicothe Correctional Ctr 3151 Litton Rd	Chillicothe	MO	64601	**800-392-8486**	660-646-4032	215
Chillicothe Gazette 50 W Main St	Chillicothe	OH	45601	**877-424-0215**	740-773-2111	531-2
Chiltern Inn 11 Cromwell Harbor Rd	Bar Harbor	ME	04609	**800-709-0114**	207-288-3371	379
Chime Master Systems PO Box 936	Lancaster	OH	43130	**800-344-7464**		526
Chimney Rock Park 431 Main St	Chimney Rock	NC	28720	**800-277-9611**	828-625-9611	96
Chimney Rock Public Power District 805 W Eigth St PO Box 608	Bayard	NE	69334	**877-773-6300**	308-586-1824	247
Chimo Hotel 1199 Joseph Cyr St	Ottawa	ON	K1J7T4	**800-387-9779**	613-744-1060	379
China Airlines Cargo Sales & Service 11201 Aviation Blvd	Los Angeles	CA	90045	**800-778-4838**	310-646-4293	12
China Ocean Shipping Co Americas Inc (COSCO) 100 Lighting Way	Secaucus	NJ	07094	**800-242-7354**	201-422-0500	222
China Travel Service Chicago Inc 2145b S China Pl	Chicago	IL	60616	**800-793-8856**	312-328-0688	773
Chinatrust Bank USA 801 S Figueroa St Ste 2300	Los Angeles	CA	90017	**888-839-9000**	310-791-2828	69
Chinese Chamber of Commerce of Hawaii 8 S King St	Honolulu	HI	96817	**877-533-2444**	808-533-3181	136
Chinese Chamber of Commerce of Los Angeles 977 N Broadway Ground Fl Ste E	Los Angeles	CA	90012	**800-400-7115**	213-617-0396	136
Chinese Laundry Shoes 3485 S La Cienega Blvd	Los Angeles	CA	90016	**888-935-8825**	310-838-2103	302
Chino Valley Ranchers 5611 Peck Rd	Arcadia	CA	91006	**800-354-4503**		298-10
Chinois on Main 2709 Main St	Santa Monica	CA	90405	**888-646-3387**	310-392-9025	669
Chinook Winds Casino Resort 1777 NW 44th St	Lincoln City	OR	97367	**888-244-6665**	541-996-5825	451
Chippendales USA LLC 4 ExpressWay Plz Ste 218	Roslyn Heights	NY	11577	**866-244-7999**	516-454-0981	148
Chippewa Falls Area Chamber of Commerce 10 S Bridge St	Chippewa Falls	WI	54729	**888-723-0024**	715-723-0331	138
Chippewa Trucking 510 E S Ave	Chippewa Falls	WI	54729	**866-777-1399**	715-726-2457	106
Chippewa Valley Electric Co-op 317 S Eigth St	Cornell	WI	54732	**800-300-6800**	715-239-6800	247
Chippewa Valley Technical College 620 W Clairemont Ave	Eau Claire	WI	54701	**800-547-2882**	715-833-6200	798
Chipton-ross Inc 343 Main St	El Segundo	CA	90245	**800-927-9318**	310-414-7800	630
Chiricahua National Monument 12856 E Rhyolite Creek Rd	Willcox	AZ	85643	**877-444-6777**	520-824-3560	563
Chiropractic Health Plan of California PO Box 190	Clayton	CA	94517	**800-995-2442**	310-210-5400	391-3
Chisago County 313 N Main St	Center City	MN	55012	**888-234-1246**	651-257-1300	338
Chisesi Bros Meat Packing Co 5221 Jefferson Hwy	New Orleans	LA	70123	**800-966-3550**	504-822-3550	472
Chisholm Fleming & Assoc 317 Renfrew Dr Ste 301	Markham	ON	L3R9S8	**888-241-4149**	905-474-1458	258
CHN (Coalition on Human Needs) 1120 Connecticut Ave NW	Washington	DC	20036	**800-822-7323**	202-223-2532	47-5
Chocolates a la Carte Inc 28455 Livingston Ave *Cust Svc	Valencia	CA	91355	**800-818-2462***		297-8
Choctaw Casino Resorts 3735 Choctaw Rd	Durant	OK	74701	**888-652-4628**	580-920-0160	451
Choctaw Electric Co-op Inc 1033 N 4250 Rd	Hugo	OK	74743	**800-780-6486**	580-326-6486	247
Choctawhatchee Electric Co-op Inc 1350 W Baldwin Ave	DeFuniak Springs	FL	32435	**800-342-0990**	850-892-2111	247
Choi Bros Inc 3401 W Div St	Chicago	IL	60651	**800-524-2464**	773-489-2800	154-1
Choice Books LLC 2387 Grace Chapel Rd	Harrisonburg	VA	22801	**800-224-5006**	540-434-1827	94
Choice Hotels International Inc 10750 Columbia Pk *NYSE: CHH*	Silver Spring	MD	20901	**800-424-6423**	301-592-5000	379
Choice Hotels International, Inc. 997 New Loudon Rd	Latham	NY	12110	**800-424-6423**	518-785-0931	379
Choice Hotelsÿ 3050 University Pkwy	Winston-Salem	NC	27105	**877-424-6423**		379
Cholestech Corp 9975 Summers Ridge Rd	San Diego	CA	92121	**866-284-3684**	510-732-7200	233
CHOMP (Community Hospital of the Monterey Peninsula) 23625 Holman Hwy	Monterey	CA	93940	**888-452-4667**	831-624-5311	374-3
Chopra Ctr at La Costa Resort & Spa 2013 Costa del Mar Rd	Carlsbad	CA	92009	**888-424-6772**	760-494-1600	671
Choptank Electric Co-op Inc 24820 Meeting House Rd PO Box 430	Denton	MD	21629	**877-892-0001**		247
Choristers Guild 2834 W Kingsley Rd	Garland	TX	75041	**800-246-7478**	972-271-1521	47-4
Chowan University 1 University Pl *Admissions	Murfreesboro	NC	27855	**888-424-6926***	252-398-6439	167
CHP International Inc 1040 N Blvd Ste 220	Oak Park	IL	60301	**800-449-2614**	708-848-9650	198
Chris Alston Chassisworks Inc 8661 Younger Creek Dr	Sacramento	CA	95828	**800-722-2269**	916-388-0288	53
Chrisad Inc 11 Professional Ctr Pkwy	San Rafael	CA	94903	**800-505-4150**	415-924-8575	7
Chris-Craft Boats 8161 15th St E	Sarasota	FL	34243	**800-845-5255**	941-351-4900	89
Christ Hospital 2139 Auburn Ave	Cincinnati	OH	45219	**800-527-8919**	513-585-2000	374-3
Christ in Youth Inc PO Box B	Joplin	MO	64801	**855-999-7238**	417-781-2273	47-20
Christ School 500 Christ School Rd	Arden	NC	28704	**800-422-3212**	828-684-6232	621
Christchurch School 49 Seahorse Ln	Christchurch	VA	23031	**800-296-2306**	804-758-2306	621
Christel DeHaan Fine Arts Ctr 1400 E Hanna Ave University of Indianapolis	Indianapolis	IN	46227	**800-232-8634**	317-788-3566	571
Christendom College 134 Christendom Dr	Front Royal	VA	22630	**800-877-5456**	540-636-2900	167
Christenson Transportation Inc 2001 W Old Rt 66	Strafford	MO	65757	**800-980-2493**	417-866-5993	778
Christian & Missionary Alliance 8595 Explorer Dr	Colorado Springs	CO	80920	**800-700-2651**	719-599-5999	47-20
Christian & Timbers 25825 Science Pk Dr	Cleveland	OH	44122	**800-299-9630**	216-464-8710	268
Christian Appalachian Project 6550 S KY Rt 321 PO Box 459	Hagerhill	KY	41222	**800-755-5322**		47-5
Christian Blind Mission (CBM) 450 E Pk Ave	Greenville	SC	29601	**800-937-2264**	864-239-0065	47-5
Christian Broadcasting Network (CBN) 977 Centerville Tpke	Virginia Beach	VA	23463	**800-759-0700**	757-226-7000	736
Christian Bros University 650 E Pkwy S *Admissions	Memphis	TN	38104	**800-288-7576***	901-321-3000	167
Christian Coalition of America PO Box 37030	Washington	DC	20013	**888-999-6778**	202-479-6900	47-7
Christian County Public Schools 200 Glass Ave PO Box 609	Hopkinsville	KY	42240	**800-274-7374**	270-887-7000	683
Christian Dior 712 Fifth Ave 37th Fl	New York	NY	10019	**800-929-3467**	212-582-0500	279
Christian Foundation for Children & Aging (CFCA) 1 Elmwood Ave	Kansas City	KS	66103	**800-875-6564**	913-384-6500	47-6
Christian Homes Inc 200 N Postville Dr	Lincoln	IL	62656	**800-535-8717**	217-732-9651	363
Christian Leadership Alliance (CLA) 635 Camino De Los Mares Ste 216	San Clemente	CA	92673	**800-263-6317**	949-487-0900	48-12
Christian Medical & Dental Assn (CMDA) 2604 Hwy 421 PO Box 7500	Bristol	TN	37620	**888-231-2637**	423-844-1000	48-8
Christian Reformed Church in North America (CRC) 2850 Kalamazoo Ave SE	Grand Rapids	MI	49560	**800-272-5125**	616-241-1691	47-20
Christian Reformed World Relief Committee (CRWRC) 2850 Kalamazoo Ave SE	Grand Rapids	MI	49560	**800-552-7972**	616-241-1691	47-5
Christian Schools International (CSI) 3350 E Paris Ave SE	Grand Rapids	MI	49512	**800-635-8288**	616-957-1070	48-5
Christian Science Monitor 210 Massachusetts Ave	Boston	MA	02115	**800-453-3432**	617-450-2000	531-3
Christian Science Publishing Society 210 Massachusetts Ave P02-15	Boston	MA	02115	**800-456-2220**	617-450-2300	634-8
Christian Television Network Inc (CTN) 6922 142nd Ave N	Largo	FL	33771	**800-716-7729**	727-535-5622	735
Christian Theological Seminary 1000 W 42nd St	Indianapolis	IN	46208	**800-585-0108**	317-924-1331	168-3
Christiana Care Health System 501 W 14th St	Wilmington	DE	19801	**855-250-9594**	302-366-1929	353
Christianity Today 465 Gundersen Dr *Cust Svc	Carol Stream	IL	60188	**800-222-1840***	630-260-6200	456-11
Christianity Today Magazine 465 Gundersen Dr	Carol Stream	IL	60188	**800-999-1704**	630-260-6200	456-18
Christianson Systems Inc 20421 15th St SE PO Box 138	Blomkest	MN	56216	**800-328-8896**	320-995-6141	209
Christie Cookie Co 1205 Third Ave N	Nashville	TN	37208	**800-458-2447**	615-242-3817	297-9
Christie Lodge PO Box 1196	Avon	CO	81620	**888-325-6343**	970-845-4504	378
Christopher Enterprises 155 West 2050 North	Spanish Fork	UT	84660	**800-453-1406**		355
Christopher Newport University 1 University Pl *Admissions	Newport News	VA	23606	**800-333-4268***	757-594-7015	167
Christopher Ranch 305 Bloomfield Ave	Gilroy	CA	95020	**800-779-1156**	408-847-1100	10-9
Christopher Reeve Foundation 636 Morris Tpke Ste 3A	Short Hills	NJ	07078	**800-225-0292**	973-379-2690	47-17
Christophers, The 5 Hanover Sq 11th Fl	New York	NY	10004	**888-298-4050**	212-759-4050	47-20
CHRISTUS Hospital - St Elizabeth 2830 Calder St	Beaumont	TX	77702	**866-683-3627**	409-892-7171	374-3
CHRISTUS Saint Mary Hospital 3600 Gates Blvd PO Box 3696	Port Arthur	TX	77642	**866-683-3627**	409-985-7431	374-3
CHRISTUS Schumpert Health System 1 St Mary Pl	Shreveport	LA	71101	**844-444-8440**	318-681-4500	353
CHRISTUS Schumpert Highland 1453 E Bert Kouns	Shreveport	LA	71105	**888-681-4138**	318-681-4500	374-3
CHRISTUS Spohn Health System 1702 Santa Fe St	Corpus Christi	TX	78404	**800-247-6574**	361-881-3000	353
CHRISTUS Spohn Hospice 6200 Saratoga Blvd Bldg B Ste 104	Corpus Christi	TX	78414	**844-444-8440**	361-994-3400	371
Christy Capital Management Inc 2939 Mcmanus Rd	Macon	GA	31220	**866-331-7749**	478-314-2160	763
Chrom Tech Inc 5995 149th St W Ste 102	Apple Valley	MN	55124	**800-822-5242**	952-431-6000	419

Name / Address	City	State	ZIP	Toll-Free	Phone	Class
ChromaGen Vision LLC						
326 W Cedar St Ste 1	Kennett Square	PA	19348	**855-473-2323**		543
Chromaline Corp						
4832 Grand Ave	Duluth	MN	55807	**800-328-4261**	218-628-2217	627
Chromaprobe Inc						
378 Fee Fee Rd	Maryland Heights	MO	63043	**888-964-1400**	314-738-0001	233
Chromium Corp						
14911 Quorum Dr Ste 600	Dallas	TX	75254	**888-346-4747**	216-271-4910	264
Chronicle Books						
680 Second St	San Francisco	CA	94107	**800-722-6657**	415-537-4200	634-2
Chronicle Herald, The						
PO Box 610	Halifax	NS	B3J2T2	**800-563-1187**	902-426-2811	531-1
Chronicle Independent						
909 W Dekalb St	Camden	SC	29020	**800-922-5431***	803-432-6157	531-4
*General						
Chronicle of Higher Education, The						
1255 23rd St NW Ste 700	Washington	DC	20037	**800-728-2803**	202-466-1000	456-8
Chronicle-Telegram						
225 E Ave	Elyria	OH	44035	**800-848-6397**	440-329-7000	531-2
Chronicle-Tribune						
610 S Adams St	Marion	IN	46953	**800-955-7888**	765-664-5111	531-2
Chrysalis Inn & Spa						
804 Tenth St	Bellingham	WA	98225	**888-808-0005**	360-756-1005	379
Chrysler Aviation Inc (CAI)						
7120 Hayvenhurst Ave Ste 309	Van Nuys	CA	91406	**800-995-0825**	818-989-7900	13
Chrysler Group LLC						
1000 Chrysler Dr	Auburn Hills	MI	48326	**800-423-6343***		58
*Cust Svc						
CHS Inc						
5500 Cenex Dr	Inver Grove Heights	MN	55077	**800-232-3639**	651-355-6000	278
NASDAQ: CHSCP						
CHSI (Comprehensive Health Services Inc)						
10701 Parkridge Blvd Ste 200	Reston	VA	20191	**800-638-8083**	703-760-0700	391-3
CHU Sainte-Justine						
3175 Ch de la Cote-Sainte-Catherine	Montreal	QC	H3T1C5	**888-235-3667**	514-345-4931	374-2
Chubb & Son						
15 Mountain View Rd	Warren	NJ	07059	**800-252-4670**	908-903-2000	391-4
Chubb Corp						
15 Mountain View Rd	Warren	NJ	07059	**800-252-4670**	908-903-2000	360-4
NYSE: CB						
Chubb Security Systems Inc						
7700 Gulf Fwy	Houston	TX	77017	**800-513-3576**		691
Chubb Specialty Insurance						
82 Hopmeadow St	Simsbury	CT	06070	**800-252-4670**	860-408-2000	391-5
Chugach Electric Assn Inc						
5601 Electron Dr	Anchorage	AK	99518	**800-478-7494**	907-563-7494	247
Chugach State Park						
18620 Seward Highway	Anchorage	AK	99516	**800-478-6196**	907-345-5014	564
Chukchansi Gold Resort & Casino						
711 Lucky Ln	Coarsegold	CA	93614	**866-794-6946**		378
Chula Vista Resort						
2501 River Rd	Wisconsin Dells	WI	53965	**800-388-4782**	608-254-8366	667
Chumash Casino Resort						
3400 E Hwy 246	Santa Ynez	CA	93460	**800-248-6274**	805-686-0855	451
Church & Chapel Metal Arts Inc						
2616 W Grand Ave	Chicago	IL	60612	**800-992-1234**		509
Church Metal Spinning Co						
5050 N 124th St	Milwaukee	WI	53225	**877-461-6460**	414-461-6460	755
Church Mutual Insurance Co						
3000 Schuster Ln	Merrill	WI	54452	**800-554-2642**	715-536-5577	391-4
Church of God in Christ Inc						
930 Mason St	Memphis	TN	38126	**877-746-8578**	901-947-9300	47-20
Church of God Ministries						
1201 E Fifth St	Anderson	IN	46012	**800-848-2464**	765-642-0256	47-20
Church of God World Missions (COGWM)						
2490 Keith St PO Box 8016	Cleveland	TN	37320	**800-345-7492**	423-478-7190	47-20
Church of the Brethren						
1451 Dundee Ave	Elgin	IL	60120	**800-323-8039**	847-742-5100	47-20
Church Women United (CWU)						
475 Riverside Dr Ste 243	New York	NY	10115	**800-298-5551**	212-870-2347	47-20
Church World Service						
28606 Phillips St PO Box 968	Elkhart	IN	46515	**800-297-1516**	574-264-3102	47-5
Church World Service Emergency Response Program						
475 Riverside Dr Ste 700	New York	NY	10115	**888-297-2767**	212-870-2061	47-5
Churchill Cabinet Co						
4616 W 19th St	Cicero	IL	60804	**800-379-9776***	708-780-0070	288
*Sales						
Churchill Corporate Services						
56 Utter Ave	Hawthorne	NJ	07506	**800-941-7458**	973-636-9400	212
Churchill County School District						
545 E Richards St	Fallon	NV	89406	**800-232-6382**	775-423-5184	683
Churchill Downs Inc						
700 Central Ave	Louisville	KY	40208	**800-994-9909**	502-636-4400	639
NASDAQ: CHDN						
Churchill Hotel						
1914 Connecticut Ave NW	Washington	DC	20009	**800-424-2464**	202-797-2000	379
Churchill Nature Tours						
PO Box 429	Erickson	MB	R0J0P0	**877-636-2968**	204-636-2968	758
Churchwell Co						
814 S Edgewood Ave	Jacksonville	FL	32205	**877-537-6166**	904-356-5721	9
CI (Conservation International)						
2011 Crystal Dr Ste 500	Arlington	VA	22202	**800-406-2306**	703-341-2400	47-13
Ci Radar LLC						
4046 Wetherburn Way Ste 1	Norcross	GA	30092	**888-421-0617**	678-680-2103	393
Cianbro Corp						
335 Hunnewell Ave	Pittsfield	ME	04967	**866-242-6276**		190-4
CIBA Vision Corp						
11460 Johns Creek Pkwy	Duluth	GA	30097	**800-875-3001**	678-415-3937	541
CIBC (Canadian Imperial Bank of Commerce)						
199 Bay St Commerce Ct W	Toronto	ON	M5L1A2	**800-465-2422**		69
NYSE: CM						
CIBC Mellon Global Securities Services Co						
320 Bay St PO Box 1	Toronto	ON	M5H4A6	**888-439-2457**	416-643-5000	527
CIBC Wood Gundy Capital						
425 Lexington Ave	New York	NY	10017	**800-999-6726**	212-856-4000	790
CIBER Inc						
6363 S Fiddler's Green Cir Ste 1400	Greenwood Village	CO	80111	**800-242-3799**	303-220-0100	182
NYSE: CBR						
CICA-TV Ch 19 (Ind)						
2180 Yonge St Stn Q PO Box 200	Toronto	ON	M4T2T1	**800-613-0513**	416-484-2600	738-90
Cicero Inc						
8000 Regency Pkwy Ste 542	Cary	NC	27518	**866-538-3588**	919-380-5000	180-1
CID Performance Tooling Inc						
6 Willey Rd	Saco	ME	04072	**800-964-2331**	207-286-3319	695
CiDRA Corp						
50 Barnes Pk N	Wallingford	CT	06492	**877-243-7277**	203-265-0035	732
CIEE (Council on International Educational Exchange)						
300 Fore St 2nd Fl	Portland	ME	04101	**888-268-6245***	207-553-4000	48-5
*Cust Svc						
CIENA Corp						
1201 Winterson Rd	Linthicum	MD	21090	**800-921-1144**	410-694-5700	732
NASDAQ: CIEN						
Cigar.com Inc						
1911 Spillman Dr	Bethlehem	PA	18015	**800-357-9800**		754
CIGNA						
900 Cottage Grove Rd	Hartford	CT	06002	**800-244-6224**	860-226-6000	391-2
CIGNA Behavioral Health Inc						
11095 Viking Dr Ste 350	Eden Prairie	MN	55344	**800-753-0540**	703-907-7730	461
CIGNA Foundation						
900 Cottage Grove Rd	Bloomfield	CT	06002	**866-438-2446**		305
NYSE: CI						
CIGNA Healthcare						
900 Cottage Grove Rd	Hartford	CT	06152	**800-433-5768**	860-226-6000	391-3
CIGNA Healthcare of North Carolina Inc						
701 Corporate Ctr Dr	Raleigh	NC	27607	**800-942-1654**	919-854-7000	391-3
Cimarron Electric Co-op						
PO Box 299	Kingfisher	OK	73750	**800-375-4121**	405-375-4121	247
CIMCO Refrigeration						
65 Villiers St	Toronto	ON	M5A3S1	**800-267-1418**	416-465-7581	662
Cimmaron Field Services Inc						
303 W Wall St Bank of America Tower Ste 600	Midland	TX	79701	**877-944-2705**		535
Cinch Connectors Inc						
1700 Findley Rd	Lombard	IL	60148	**800-323-9612**	630-705-6000	813
Cincinnati Art Museum						
953 Eden Pk Dr	Cincinnati	OH	45202	**877-472-4226**	513-721-2787	519
Cincinnati Bell Directory (CBD)						
312 Plum St Ste 600	Cincinnati	OH	45202	**800-877-0475**		634-6
Cincinnati Bell Inc						
221 E Fourth St	Cincinnati	OH	45202	**800-387-3638**	513-397-9900	733
NYSE: CBB						
Cincinnati Bengals						
1 Paul Brown Stadium	Cincinnati	OH	45202	**866-621-8383**	513-621-3550	713-3
Cincinnati Children's Hospital Medical Ctr						
3333 Burnet Ave	Cincinnati	OH	45229	**800-344-2462**	513-636-4200	374-1
Cincinnati Christian University						
2700 Glenway Ave	Cincinnati	OH	45204	**800-949-4228**	513-244-8100	160
Cincinnati College of Mortuary Science						
645 W N Bend Rd	Cincinnati	OH	45224	**888-377-8433**	513-761-2020	798
Cincinnati Enquirer						
312 Elm St	Cincinnati	OH	45202	**800-876-4500**	513-721-2700	531-2
Cincinnati Floor Company Inc						
5162 Broerman Ave	Cincinnati	OH	45217	**800-886-4501**	513-641-4500	191-2
Cincinnati History Museum						
1301 Western Ave Cincinnati Museum Ctr	Cincinnati	OH	45203	**800-733-2077**	513-287-7000	519
Cincinnati Playhouse in the Park						
962 Mt Adams Cir	Cincinnati	OH	45202	**800-582-3208**	513-345-2242	571
Cincinnati Preserving Company Inc						
3015 E Kemper Rd	Cincinnati	OH	45241	**800-222-9966***	513-771-2000	297-20
*Cust Svc						
Cincinnati Reds						
100 Joe Nuxhall Way	Cincinnati	OH	45202	**877-647-7337**	513-381-7337	711
Cincinnati State Technical & Community College						
3520 Central Pkwy	Cincinnati	OH	45223	**877-569-0115**	513-569-1500	161
Cincinnati Test Systems Inc						
5555 Dry Fork Rd	Cleves	OH	45002	**800-850-3189**	513-367-6699	203
Cincinnati Zoo & Botanical Garden						
3400 Vine St	Cincinnati	OH	45220	**800-944-4776**	513-281-4700	821
Cincinnatian Hotel						
601 Vine St	Cincinnati	OH	45202	**800-942-9000**	513-381-3000	379
Cincom Systems Inc						
55 Merchant St	Cincinnati	OH	45246	**800-224-6266**	513-612-2300	180-1
Cindus Corp						
515 Stn Ave	Cincinnati	OH	45215	**800-543-4691**		553
Cine Magnetics Inc						
100 Business Pk Dr	Armonk	NY	10504	**800-431-1102**	914-273-7500	656
Cinemark USA Inc						
3900 Dallas Pkwy Ste 500	Plano	TX	75093	**800-246-3627**	972-665-1000	745
Cineplex Digital Networks						
369 York St Ste 2C	London	ON	N6B3R4	**866-353-8324**	519-438-0111	8
Cineplex Entertainment LP						
1303 Yonge St	Toronto	ON	M4T2Y9	**800-333-0061**	416-323-6600	745
Cinergy Children's Museum						
1301 Western Ave Cincinnati Museum Ctr	Cincinnati	OH	45203	**800-733-2077**	513-287-7000	520
Cinmar LLC						
5566 W Chester Rd	West Chester	OH	45069	**888-263-9850**		458
Cintas Corp						
PO Box 625737	Cincinnati	OH	45262	**800-786-4367**	513-459-1200	442
NASDAQ: CTAS						
Cintrex Audio Visual						
656 Axminister Dr	Fenton	MO	63026	**800-325-9541**	636-343-0178	513
Cipher Systems LLC						
2661 Riva Rd Ste 1000	Annapolis	MD	21401	**888-899-1523**	410-412-3326	196
Ciplex						
475 Washington Blvd Ste A	Marina Del Rey	CA	90292	**866-406-8258**	310-461-0330	5
CIPS (Canadian Information Processing Society)						
5090 Explorer Dr Ste 801	Mississauga	ON	L4W4T9	**877-275-2477**	905-602-1370	47-1
CIR (Center for Individual Rights)						
1233 20th St NW Ste 300	Washington	DC	20036	**877-426-2665**	202-833-8400	47-8

Name / Address	City	State	ZIP	Toll-Free	Phone	Class
CIR Law Offices LLP 8665 Gibbs Dr Ste 150	San Diego	CA	92123	**800-496-8909**		40
Circa Inc 415 Madison Ave 19th Fl	New York	NY	10017	**877-876-5493**	212-486-6013	411
Circadian Technologies Inc 2 Main St Ste 310	Stoneham	MA	02180	**800-284-5001**	781-439-6300	196
Circle Bolt & Nut Company Inc 158 Pringle St	Kingston	PA	18704	**800-548-2658**	570-718-6001	350
Circle City Bar & Grille 350 W Maryland St	Indianapolis	IN	46225	**877-640-7666**	317-405-6100	669
Circle J Trailers 312 W Simplot Blvd	Caldwell	ID	83605	**800-247-2535**	208-459-0842	777
Circle Media Inc 5817 Old Leeds Rd	Irondale	AL	35210	**800-356-9916**		531-3
Circle Seal Controls Inc 2301 Wardlow Cir	Corona	CA	92880	**800-991-2726**	951-270-6200	787
Circle Z Ranch PO Box 194	Patagonia	AZ	85624	**888-854-2525**		241
Circleville City School District 388 Clark Dr	Circleville	OH	43113	**800-418-6423**	740-474-4340	683
Circuit Express Inc 229 S Clark Dr	Tempe	AZ	85281	**800-979-4722**		624
Circuit Playhouse, The 51 S Cooper St	Memphis	TN	38104	**888-648-8154**	901-725-0776	571
Circular Technologies 3275 Prairie Ave	Boulder	CO	80301	**800-215-1831**	303-443-8512	818
Circus Circus Hotel & Casino Reno 500 N Sierra St	Reno	NV	89503	**800-648-5010**	775-329-0711	132
Circus Circus Hotel Casino & Theme Park Las Vegas 2880 Las Vegas Blvd S *Resv	Las Vegas	NV	89109	**800-634-3450***	702-734-0410	132
Circus World Museum 550 Water St	Baraboo	WI	53913	**866-693-1500**	608-356-8341	519
Cirque Corp 2463 South 3850 West	Salt Lake City	UT	84120	**800-454-3375**	801-467-1100	175-2
Cirque du Soleil Inc 8400 Second Ave	Montreal	QC	H1Z4M6	**800-678-2119**	514-722-2324	148
Cirrascale Corp 12140 Community Rd	Poway	CA	92064	**888-942-3800**	858-874-3800	175-8
Cirro Energy Services Inc 2745 Dallas Pkwy Ste 200	Plano	TX	75093	**866-791-1911**		462
Cirrus Logic Inc 2901 Via Fortuna *NASDAQ: CRUS*	Austin	TX	78746	**800-888-5016**	512-851-4000	694
Cirrus9 Inc 15 Market Sq	Saint John	NB	E2L1E8	**855-643-6691**		226
CISCA (Ceilings & Interior Systems Construction Assn) 1010 Jorie Blvd Ste 30	Oak Brook	IL	60523	**866-560-8537**	630-584-1919	48-3
Cisco Systems Inc 170 W Tasman Dr *NASDAQ: CSCO*	San Jose	CA	95134	**800-553-6387**	408-526-4000	178
Cisco-Eagle 2120 Valley View Ln	Dallas	TX	75234	**888-877-3861**	972-406-9330	385
Cision Inc 12051 Indian Creek Ct *NASDAQ: VOCS*	Beltsville	MD	20705	**866-639-5087**	301-459-2590	38
Cisys Inc 8386 Six Forks Rd	Raleigh	NC	27615	**844-494-9236**		179
Citadel Federal Credit Union 520 Eagleview Blvd	Exton	PA	19341	**800-666-0191**	610-380-6000	221
Citadel, The 171 Moultrie St	Charleston	SC	29409	**800-868-1842**	843-953-5230	167
Citation Communications Inc 1855 Indian Rd Ste 207	West Palm Beach	FL	33409	**800-286-5109**	561-688-0330	387
CITGO Petroleum Corp 1293 Eldridge Pkwy	Houston	TX	77077	**800-424-9300**	832-486-4700	579
Citi Performing Arts Ctr Wang Theatre 270 Tremont St	Boston	MA	02116	**800-982-2787**		571
Citibank (Delaware) 4500 New Linden Hill Rd	Wilmington	DE	19808	**800-374-9700**	302-323-3600	69
Citibank NA 399 Pk Ave	New York	NY	10022	**800-627-3999**		69
Citibank (South Dakota) NA 701 E 60th St N	Sioux Falls	SD	57104	**800-627-3999**	605-331-2626	69
Cities of Gold Casino 10-B Cities of Gold Rd	Santa Fe	NM	87506	**800-455-3313**	505-455-3313	132
CitiMortgage Inc 1000 Technology Dr *Cust Svc	O'Fallon	MO	63368	**800-283-7918***		508
CitiusTech Inc 2 Research Way	Princeton	NJ	08540	**877-248-4871**		227
Citizant Inc 5180 Parkstone Dr Ste 100	Chantilly	VA	20151	**877-248-4926**	703-667-9420	179
Citizen Auto Stage Co 3594 E Lincoln St	Tucson	AZ	85714	**800-276-1528**	520-622-8811	106
Citizen National Bank Of Bluffton, The 102 S Main St PO Box 88	Bluffton	OH	45817	**800-262-4663**	419-358-8040	69
Citizen Systems America Corp 363 Van Ness Way Ste 404	Torrance	CA	90501	**800-421-6516**	310-781-1460	175-6
Citizen Tribune 1609 W First N St PO Box 625	Morristown	TN	37815	**800-624-0281**	423-581-5630	531-2
Citizen Watch Co of America Inc 1000 W 190th St	Torrance	CA	90502	**800-321-1023**		152
Citizens Against Government Waste (CAGW) 1301 Pennsylvania Ave NW Ste 1075	Washington	DC	20004	**800-435-7352**	202-467-5300	47-7
Citizens Bank of Clovis 420 Wheeler	Texico	NM	88135	**844-657-3553**	575-482-3381	69
Citizens Bank of Massachusetts 28 State St	Boston	MA	02109	**800-610-7300**		69
Citizens Bank of Mukwonago 301 N Rochester St PO Box 223	Mukwonago	WI	53149	**877-546-5868**	262-363-6500	69
Citizens Bank of Rhode Island 1 Citizens Plz *Cust Svc	Providence	RI	02903	**800-922-9999***	401-456-7000	69
Citizens Business Bank (CBB) 701 N Haven Ave *Cust Svc	Ontario	CA	91764	**888-222-5432***	909-980-4030	69
Citizens Committee for the Right to Keep & Bear Arms (CCRKBA) 12500 NE Tenth Pl	Bellevue	WA	98005	**800-426-4302**	425-454-4911	47-7
Citizens Equity First Credit Union 5401 W Dirksen Pkwy *Cust Svc	Peoria	IL	61607	**800-633-7077***	309-633-7000	221
Citizens Federal Savings & Loan Assn 110 N Main St PO Box 9	Bellefontaine	OH	43311	**800-436-5177**	937-593-0015	68
Citizens Financial Corp 12910 Shelbyville Rd Ste 300 *OTC: CFIN*	Louisville	KY	40243	**800-843-7752**	502-244-2420	360-4
Citizens Financial Group Inc 1 Citizens Dr	Riverside	RI	02915	**800-922-9999**	401-456-7000	360-2
Citizens Financial Services 707 Ridge Rd	Munster	IN	46321	**866-622-1370**	219-836-5500	69
Citizens for Tax Justice (CTJ) 1616 P St NW Ste 200-B	Washington	DC	20036	**888-626-2622**	202-299-1066	47-7
Citizens Gas & Coke Utility 2020 N Meridian St	Indianapolis	IN	46202	**800-427-4217**	317-924-3311	785
Citizens Insurance Company of America 400 E Anderson Ln	Austin	TX	78752	**800-880-5044**	512-837-7100	391-2
Citizens Security Life Insurance Co 12910 Shelbyville Rd Ste 300	Louisville	KY	40243	**800-843-7752**	502-244-2420	391-2
Citizens Telephone Co-op PO Box 137	Floyd	VA	24091	**800-941-0426**	540-745-2111	733
Citizens Trust Bank 1700 3rd Ave N	Birmingham	AL	35203	**888-214-3099**	205-328-2041	69
Citizens' Electric Co 1775 Industrial Blvd PO Box 551	Lewisburg	PA	17837	**877-487-9384**	570-524-2231	247
Citrix Systems Inc 851 W Cypress Creek Rd *NASDAQ: CTXS*	Fort Lauderdale	FL	33309	**800-393-1888**	954-267-3000	180-12
Citterio USA Corp 2008 SR 940	Freeland	PA	18224	**800-435-8888**	570-636-3171	297-26
City Auto Glass Inc 116 S Concord Exchange	South Saint Paul	MN	55075	**888-552-4272**	651-552-1000	61-2
City College of New York 138th St & Convent Ave *Admissions	New York	NY	10031	**800-286-9937***	212-650-6448	167
City College of San Francisco 50 Phelan Ave	San Francisco	CA	94112	**800-433-3243**	415-239-3000	161
City Colleges of Chicago 226 W Jackson	Chicago	IL	60606	**866-908-7582**	312-553-2500	161
City Electric Supply Inc 315 E Prentiss St	Iowa City	IA	52240	**800-272-6111**	319-338-7561	255
City Escape Holidays 13470 Washington Blvd Ste 101	Marina del Rey	CA	90292	**800-222-0022**		769
City Furniture Inc 6701 N Hiatus Rd	Tamarac	FL	33321	**888-882-5436**	954-597-2200	322
City Hospital 2500 Hospital Dr	Martinsburg	WV	25401	**888-988-1362**	304-264-1000	374-3
City National Bank 400 N Roxbury Dr *Cust Svc	Beverly Hills	CA	90210	**800-773-7100***	310-888-6000	69
City National Bank of Florida 450 E Las Olas Blvd	Fort Lauderdale	FL	33301	**800-762-2489**	954-467-6667	69
City National Bank of New Jersey (CNB) 900 Broad St	Newark	NJ	07102	**877-350-3524**	973-624-0865	69
City National Bank of West Virginia 3601 McCorckle Ave	Charleston	WV	25304	**888-816-8064**	304-926-3324	69
City of Carlsbad Library 1250 Carlsbad Village Dr	Carlsbad	CA	92008	**866-230-2273**	760-434-2870	434-3
City of Chula Vista 276 Fourth Ave	Chula Vista	CA	91910	**877-478-5478**	619-691-5047	51
City of Clarksville 199 10th St	Clarksville	TN	37040	**800-342-1003**	931-645-7464	258
City of Com, The 1559 S Brownlee Blvd	Corpus Christi	TX	78404	**888-785-0500**		7
City of Hope National Medical Ctr Hematology & Hematopoietic Cell Transplantation Div 1500 E Duarte Rd	Duarte	CA	91010	**800-826-4673**	626-256-4673	767
City of Palm Springs 300 S Sunrise Way	Palm Springs	CA	92262	**800-611-1911**	760-322-7323	434-3
City of Pendleton 500 SW Dorion Ave	Pendleton	OR	97801	**800-238-5355**	541-966-0201	207
City of Thomasville Tourism Authority 144 E Jackson St	Thomasville	GA	31792	**800-533-4587**	229-226-3424	208
City Pipe & Supply Corp PO Box 2112	Odessa	TX	79760	**844-307-4044**	432-332-1541	491
City Plumbing & Electric Supply Co 730 EE Butler Pkwy	Gainesville	GA	30501	**800-260-2024**	770-532-4123	611
City Public Service Board PO Box 1771	San Antonio	TX	78296	**800-870-1006**	210-353-2222	785
City Savings Bank & Trust 301 N Pine St	Deridder	LA	70634	**800-920-8661**	337-463-8661	69
City Securities Corp 30 S Meridian St Ste 600	Indianapolis	IN	46204	**800-800-2489**	317-634-4400	688
City Supply Corp 2326 Bell Ave	Des Moines	IA	50321	**800-400-2377**	515-288-3211	611
City University 11900 NE First St *Admissions	Bellevue	WA	98005	**800-426-5596***	425-637-1010	167
City University of New York (CUNY) 535 E 80th St	New York	NY	10075	**877-769-7441**	212-794-5555	784
CITY-TV Ch 57 (Ind) 33 Dundas St E	Toronto	ON	M5B1B8	**888-336-9978**	416-764-3003	738-90
Civacon 4304 N Mattox Rd *Sales	Kansas City	MO	64150	**888-526-5657***	816-741-6600	788
Civic Resource Group LLC 915 Wilshire Blvd Ste 1680	Los Angeles	CA	90017	**800-771-0026**	213-225-1170	198
Civil & Environmental Consultants Inc 333 Baldwin Rd	Pittsburgh	PA	15205	**800-365-2324**	412-429-2324	263
Civil Engineering Magazine 1801 Alexander Bell Dr	Reston	VA	20191	**800-548-2723**	703-295-6300	456-21
Civil Service Employees Insurance Co 2121 N California Blvd Ste 989	Walnut Creek	CA	94596	**800-282-6848**		391-4

Name / Address	City	State	ZIP	Toll-Free	Phone	Class
Civil War Preservation Trust (CWPT) 1331 H St NW Ste 1001	Washington	DC	20005	**888-606-1400**	202-367-1861	47-13
Civista Bank 100 E Water St	Sandusky	OH	44870	**888-645-4121**	419-625-4121	68
Civitan International PO Box 130744	Birmingham	AL	35213	**800-248-4826**	205-591-8910	47-15
CJK 3962 Virginia Ave	Cincinnati	OH	45227	**800-598-7808**	513-271-6035	625
CJM (Carlyle Johnson Machine Co) 291 Boston Tpke	Bolton	CT	06043	**888-629-4867**	860-643-1531	619
CJT Koolcarb Inc 494 Mission St	Carol Stream	IL	60188	**800-323-2299**	630-690-5933	492
CJW Medical Ctr 7101 Jahnke Rd	Richmond	VA	23225	**800-468-6620**	804-320-3911	374-3
CK Worldwide Inc 3501 C St NE	Auburn	WA	98002	**800-426-0877**	253-854-5820	809
CKC (Canadian Kennel Club) 200 Ronson Dr Ste 400	Etobicoke	ON	M9W5Z9	**800-250-8040**	416-675-5511	47-3
CKHS (Crozer-Keystone Health System) 190 W Sproul Rd	Springfield	PA	19064	**800-254-3258**	610-328-8700	353
CKLW-AM 800 (N/T) 1640 Ouellette Ave	Windsor	ON	N8X1L1	**800-263-2559**	519-258-8888	643
CKVR-TV Ch 3 (Ind) 299 Queen St W	Toronto	ON	M5V2Z5	**866-690-6179**	416-384-5000	
CLA (Christian Leadership Alliance) 635 Camino De Los Mares Ste 216	San Clemente	CA	92673	**800-263-6317**	949-487-0900	48-12
CLA (Coin Laundry Assn) 1s660 Midwest Rd Ste 205	Oakbrook Terrace	IL	60181	**800-570-5629**	630-953-7920	48-4
Claflin University 400 Magnolia St	Orangeburg	SC	29115	**800-922-1276**	803-535-5000	167
Claiborne County Chamber of Commerce 1732 Main St Ste 1	Tazewell	TN	37879	**800-332-8164**	423-626-4149	138
Claims Verification Inc 6700 N Andrews Ave Ste 200	Ft. Lauderdale	FL	33309	**888-284-2000**		400
Claimsnet.com Inc 14860 Montfort Dr Ste 250	Dallas	TX	75254	**800-356-1511**	972-458-1701	227
Claire Manufacturing Co 1005 S Westgate Ave *Sales	Addison	IL	60101	**800-252-4731***	630-543-7600	144
Claire's Accessories 2400 W Central Rd	Hoffman Estates	IL	60192	**800-252-4737**	847-765-1100	156-6
Claitor's Law Books & Publishing PO Box 261333	Baton Rouge	LA	70826	**800-274-1403**	225-344-0476	625
Clamp Swing Pricing Company Inc 8386 Capwell Dr	Oakland	CA	94621	**800-227-7615**	510-567-1600	413
Clamshell Structures Inc 1101 Maulhardt Ave	Oxnard	CA	93030	**800-360-8853**	805-988-1340	730
Clarcor Inc 840 Crescent Ctr Dr Ste 600 *NYSE: CLC*	Franklin	TN	37067	**800-252-7267**	615-771-3100	18
Clare Inc 78 Cherry Hill Dr	Beverly	MA	01915	**800-272-5273**	978-524-6700	694
Claremont Companies Inc 1 Lakeshore Center	Bridgewater	MA	02324	**800-848-9077**	508-279-4300	527
Claremont Resort & Spa 41 Tunnel Rd	Berkeley	CA	94705	**800-551-7266**	510-843-3000	667
Claremont Sales Corp 35 Winsome Dr PO Box 430	Durham	CT	06422	**800-222-4448**	860-349-4499	389
Claremont School of Theology 1325 N College Ave	Claremont	CA	91711	**800-733-5181**	909-447-2500	168-3
Clarendon College 1122 College Dr PO Box 968	Clarendon	TX	79226	**800-687-9737**	806-874-3571	161
Claricent Inc 22 Preserve way	Sturbridge	MA	01566	**888-325-6496**		179
Claridge Products & Equipment Inc 601 Hwy 62 65	Harrison	AR	72601	**800-434-4610**	870-743-2200	245
Clarion Corp of America 6200 Gateway Dr	Cypress	CA	90630	**800-347-8667**	310-327-9100	51
Clarion Hospital (CH) 1 Hospital Dr	Clarion	PA	16214	**800-522-0505**	814-226-9500	374-3
Clarion University of Pennsylvania 840 Wood St	Clarion	PA	16214	**800-672-7171**	814-393-2306	167
Venango 1801 W First St	Oil City	PA	16301	**800-672-7171**	814-676-6591	167
Clarion-Ledger, The 201 S Congress St	Jackson	MS	39201	**877-850-5343**	601-961-7000	531-2
Clarity Innovations Inc 1001 SE Water Ave Ste 400	Portland	OR	97214	**877-683-3187**	503-248-4300	258
Clark Atlanta University 223 James P Brawley Dr SW *Admissions	Atlanta	GA	30314	**800-688-3228***	404-880-8000	167
Clark Capital Management Group Inc (CCMG) 1650 Market St 1 Liberty Pl 53rd Fl	Philadelphia	PA	19103	**800-766-2264**	215-569-2224	401
Clark Construction Group LLC 7500 Old Georgetown Rd	Bethesda	MD	20814	**800-655-1330**	301-272-8100	188
Clark Cos NA 156 Oak St *Cust Svc	Newton Upper Falls	MA	02464	**800-211-5461***	617-964-1222	302
Clark County REMC 7810 State Rd 60 PO Box 411	Sellersburg	IN	47172	**800-462-6988**	812-246-3316	247
Clark County School District (CCSD) 5100 W Sahara Ave	Las Vegas	NV	89146	**866-799-8997**	702-799-5000	683
Clark Electric Co-op 124 N Main St PO Box 190	Greenwood	WI	54437	**800-272-6188**	715-267-6188	247
Clark Energy Co-op Inc 2640 Ironworks Rd	Winchester	KY	40391	**800-992-3269**	859-744-4251	247
Clark Engineering Corp 621 Lilac Dr N	Minneapolis	MN	55422	**877-246-9196**	763-545-9196	263
Clark Foam Products Corp 655 Remington Blvd	Bolingbrook	IL	60440	**888-284-2290**	630-226-5900	600
Clark Insurance PO Box 3543	Portland	ME	04104	**800-773-4300**	207-774-6257	390
Clark Material Handling Co 700 Enterprise Dr	Lexington	KY	40510	**866-252-5275**	859-422-6400	469
Clark Nuber PS 10900 NE Fourth St Ste 1700 *General	Bellevue	WA	98004	**800-504-8747***	425-454-4919	2
Clark Transfer Inc 800A Paxton St	Harrisburg	PA	17104	**800-488-7585**	717-238-0801	188
Clark University 950 Main St	Worcester	MA	01610	**800-462-5275**	508-793-7711	167
Clark, Gagliardi & Miller PC 99 Court St	White Plains	NY	10601	**800-734-5694**		428
Clark-Dunbar Flooring Superstore 3232 Empire Dr	Alexandria	LA	71301	**800-256-1467**	318-445-0262	292
Clarke College 1550 Clarke Dr	Dubuque	IA	52001	**888-825-2753**	563-588-6300	167
Clarke County 100 Church St PO Box 689	Quitman	MS	39355	**877-462-3222**	601-776-5701	338
Clark-Floyd Counties Convention & Tourism Bureau 315 Southern Indiana Ave	Jeffersonville	IN	47130	**800-552-3842**	812-282-6654	208
Clark-Lindsey Village 101 W Windsor Rd	Urbana	IL	61802	**800-998-2581**	217-344-2144	670
Clark-Reliance Corp 16633 Foltz Pkwy	Strongsville	OH	44149	**800-238-4027**	440-572-1500	494
Clarksburg Exponent Telegram 324 Hewes Ave	Clarksburg	WV	26301	**800-982-6034**	304-626-1400	531-2
Clarksdale Municipal School District 101 McGuire St PO Box 1088	Clarksdale	MS	38614	**877-820-7831**	662-627-8500	188
Clarksdale-Coahoma County Chamber of Commerce & Industrial Foundation 1540 DeSoto Ave	Clarksdale	MS	38614	**800-626-3764**	662-627-7337	138
Clarkson College 101 S 42nd St	Omaha	NE	68131	**800-647-5500**	402-552-3100	167
Clarkson University 10 Clarkson Ave *Admissions	Potsdam	NY	13699	**800-527-6577***	315-268-6480	167
Clarkston Consulting 2655 Meridian Pkwy Ste 400	Durham	NC	27713	**800-652-4274**	919-484-4400	182
Clarksville Area Chamber of Commerce 25 Jefferson St Ste 300	Clarksville	TN	37040	**800-530-2487**	931-647-2331	138
Clarksville Montgomery County Public Library 350 Pageant Ln	Clarksville	TN	37040	**877-239-6635**	931-648-8826	434-3
Clarksville/Montgomery County Tourist Commission 25 Jefferson St Ste 300	Clarksville	TN	37040	**800-530-2487**	931-647-2331	208
Clary Corp 150 E Huntington Dr	Monrovia	CA	91016	**800-551-6111**	626-359-4486	255
CLASP (Center for Law & Social Policy) 1015 15th St NW Ste 400	Washington	DC	20005	**800-821-4367**	202-906-8000	631
Class Act Federal Credit Union 3620 Fern Vly Rd	Louisville	KY	40219	**800-292-2960**	502-964-7575	221
Class Action Litigation Report 1801 S Bell St	Arlington	VA	22202	**800-372-1033**		530-7
Classic Brass Inc 2051 Stoneman Cir	Lakewood	NY	14750	**800-869-3173**	716-763-1400	350
Classic Custom Vacations 5893 Rue Ferrari	San Jose	CA	95138	**800-635-1333**		769
CLASSIC HOSTESS INC 2 Skillman St Ste 313	Brooklyn	NY	11205	**888-280-6539**		393
Classic Medallics Inc 520 S Fulton Ave	Mount Vernon	NY	10550	**800-221-1348**	914-530-6259	775
Classic Party Rentals 901 W. Hillcrest Blvd	Inglewood	CA	90301	**800-678-3854**	310-535-3660	266-2
Classic Sleep Products Inc 8214 Wellmoor Ct	Jessup	MD	20794	**877-707-7533**	410-904-0006	470
Classic Student Tours 75 Rhoads Ctr Dr	Dayton	OH	45458	**800-860-0246**	937-439-0032	758
Classic Trains Magazine 21027 Crossroads Cir PO Box 1612	Waukesha	WI	53186	**800-533-6644**	262-796-8776	456-14
Classic Transportation Group 1600 Locust Ave	Bohemia	NY	11716	**800-291-8090**	631-567-5100	441
Classic Travel Inc 4767 Okemos Rd	Okemos	MI	48864	**800-643-3449**	517-349-6200	770
Classic Tube 80 Rotech Dr	Lancaster	NY	14086	**800-882-3711**	716-759-1800	594
Classical Marketing LLC 150 N Martingale Rd Ste 800	Schaumburg	IL	60173	**800-613-3489**	847-969-1696	197
Clatsop Community College 1653 Jerome Ave	Astoria	OR	97103	**855-252-8767**	503-325-0910	161
Claverack Rural Electric Co-op Inc 32750 W US 6	Wysox	PA	18854	**800-326-9799**	570-265-2167	247
Clawson Tank Co 4701 White Lake Rd	Clarkston	MI	48346	**800-272-1367**	248-625-8700	90
Claxton Poultry Farms 8816 Hway 301 PO Box 428	Claxton	GA	30417	**888-739-3181**	912-739-3181	618
Claxton-Hepburn Medical Ctr 214 King St	Ogdensburg	NY	13669	**888-220-0042**	315-393-3600	374-3
Clay County Chamber of Commerce 1734 Kingsley Ave	Orange Park	FL	32073	**800-435-7352**	904-264-2651	138
Clay County Electric Co-op Corp 300 N Missouri Ave	Corning	AR	72422	**800-521-2450**	870-857-3521	247
Clay Electric Co-op Inc 7450 State Rd 100	Keystone Heights	FL	32656	**800-224-4917**	352-473-8000	247
Clay Lacy Aviation 7435 Valjean Ave	Van Nuys	CA	91406	**800-423-2904**	818-989-2900	13
Clay Today 3513 US Hwy 17	Fleming Island	FL	32003	**888-434-9844**	904-264-3200	531-4
Claybar Constracting Inc 424 Macnab St	Dundas	ON	L9H2L3	**866-801-9305**	905-627-8000	609
Claymore C Sieck Wholesale Florist 311 E Chase St	Baltimore	MD	21202	**800-624-7134**	410-685-4660	295
Clayton Block Co PO Box 3015	Lakewood	NJ	08701	**800-662-3044**		185
Clayton Corp 866 Horan Dr *Cust Svc	Fenton	MO	63026	**800-729-8220***	636-349-5333	600
Clayton Cos, The PO Box 3015	Lakewood	NJ	08701	**800-662-3044**		185
Clayton County Chamber of Commerce 2270 Mt Zion Rd	Jonesboro	GA	30236	**877-790-1831**	678-610-4021	138

Name / Address	City	State	ZIP	Toll-Free	Phone	Class
Clayton Holdings LLC 100 BeaRd Sawmill Rd Ste 200	Shelton	CT	06484	**877-291-5301**	203-926-5600	360-3
Clayton Industries 17477 Hurley St	City of Industry	CA	91744	**800-423-4585**	626-435-1200	471
Clayton L Scroggins Associates Inc 200 Northland Blvd	Cincinnati	OH	45246	**800-359-3970**	513-771-7070	462
Clayton Metals Inc 546 Clayton Ct	Wood Dale	IL	60191	**800-323-7628**		491
Clay-Union Electric Corp 1410 E Cherry St PO Box 317	Vermillion	SD	57069	**800-696-2832**	605-624-2673	247
CLC (Challenger Learning Ctr) 316 Washington Ave Wheeling Jesuit University	Wheeling	WV	26003	**800-624-6992**	304-243-2279	519
Clean Air Report 1919 S Eads St Ste 201	Arlington	VA	22202	**800-424-9068**	703-416-8505	530-5
Clean Air Technology Inc 41105 Capital Dr	Canton	MI	48187	**800-459-6320**		448
Clean Diesel Technologies Inc 4567 Telephone Rd Ste 206 *NASDAQ: CDTI*	Ventura	CA	93003	**800-661-9963**	805-639-9458	386
Clean Earth of North Jersey Inc 115 Jacobus Ave	South Kearny	NJ	07032	**877-445-3478**	973-344-4004	658
Clean Harbors Inc 42 Longwater Dr PO Box 9149 *NYSE: CLH*	Norwell	MA	02061	**800-282-0058**	781-792-5000	665
Clean Ones Corp PO Box 40008	Portland	OR	97204	**800-367-4587**	503-224-5211	258
Clean Power LLC 124 N 121st St	Milwaukee	WI	53226	**888-566-1717**	414-302-3000	151
Clean Venture/Cycle Chem Inc 201 S First St	Elizabeth	NJ	07206	**800-347-7672**	908-355-5800	665
Clean Water Action 4455 Connecticut Ave NW	Washington	DC	20008	**800-657-3864**	202-895-0420	47-13
Cleaning Authority 7230 Lee DeForest Dr	Columbia	MD	21046	**888-658-0659**	410-740-1900	311
CleanNet USA 9861 Brokenland Pkwy Ste 208	Columbia	MD	21046	**800-735-8838**	410-720-6444	151
Cleanroom Systems 7000 Performance Dr	North Syracuse	NY	13212	**800-825-3268**	315-452-7400	18
Cleantech Open, The 336 Portage Rd	Palo Alto	CA	94306	**888-989-6736**		462
Cleanwise Inc 1100 E Woodfield Rd Ste 200	Schaumburg	IL	60173	**877-255-5230**		393
Clear Brook Manor 1100 E Northampton St	Laurel Run	PA	18706	**800-582-6241**		724
Clear Creek Baptist Bible College 300 Clear Creek Rd	Pineville	KY	40977	**866-340-3196**	606-337-3196	160
Clear Edge Technical Fabrics 7160 Northland Cir N	Minneapolis	MN	55428	**800-328-3036**	763-535-3220	742-3
Clear Lake Area Chamber of Commerce 1201 NASA Pkwy	Houston	TX	77058	**800-877-8339**	281-488-7676	138
Clear Lake Convention & Visitors Bureau 205 Main Ave PO Box 188	Clear Lake	IA	50428	**800-285-5338**	641-357-2159	208
Clear View Bag Co 5 Burdick Dr	Albany	NY	12205	**800-458-7153**	518-458-7153	65
Clearbridge Technology Group 6 Fortune Dr	Billerica	MA	01821	**877-808-2284**	781-916-2284	262
Clearfield Bank & Trust Co 11 N Second St PO Box 171	Clearfield	PA	16830	**888-765-7551**	814-765-7551	69
Clearfield Hospital 809 Tpke Ave PO Box 992	Clearfield	PA	16830	**800-281-8000**	814-765-5341	374-3
ClearOne Communications Inc 5225 Wiley Post Way	Salt Lake City	UT	84116	**800-945-7730**	801-975-7200	732
ClearSail Communications LLC 3950 Braxton	Houston	TX	77063	**888-905-0888**	713-230-2800	398
ClearStream Energy Services LP 2112 Premier Way	Sherwood Park	AB	T8H2G4	**855-410-9835**	780-410-9835	535
Clearwater Power Co 4230 Hatwai Rd PO Box 997	Lewiston	ID	83501	**888-743-1501**	208-743-1501	247
Clearwater Public Library 100 N Osceola Ave	Clearwater	FL	33755	**800-342-8060**	727-562-4970	434-3
Clearwater Regional Chamber of Commerce 401 Cleveland St	Clearwater	FL	33755	**877-447-7356**	727-461-0011	138
Clearwater-Polk Electric Co-op 315 Main Ave N	Bagley	MN	56621	**888-694-3833**	218-694-6241	247
Cleary Millwork Company Inc 235 Dividend Rd	Rocky Hill	CT	06067	**800-486-7600**	860-721-0520	193-3
Cleary University 3601 Plymouth Rd	Ann Arbor	MI	48105	**800-686-1883**	734-332-4477	798
Livingston 3750 Cleary Dr	Howell	MI	48843	**800-686-1883**	517-548-3670	798
Cleaver Brooks Thomasville 221 Law St	Thomasville	GA	31792	**800-250-5883**	229-226-3024	90
Cleco Corp 2030 Donahue Ferry Rd *Cust Svc	Pineville	LA	71361	**800-622-6537***	318-484-7400	785
Cleft Palate Foundation (CPF) 1504 E Franklin St Ste 102	Chapel Hill	NC	27514	**800-242-5338**	919-933-9044	47-17
Cleftstone Manor 92 Eden St	Bar Harbor	ME	04609	**888-288-4951**	207-288-8086	379
Clement Communications Inc 3 Creek Pkwy	Upper Chichester	PA	19061	**800-253-6368**	610-459-4200	634-10
Clement Industries Inc PO Box 914 *Cust Svc	Minden	LA	71058	**800-562-5948***	318-377-2776	777
Clements National Co 6650 S Narragansett Ave	Chicago	IL	60638	**800-966-0016**	708-594-5890	18
Clemson University 105 Sikes Hall	Clemson	SC	29634	**800-640-2657**	864-656-3311	167
Clermont County Convention & Visitors Bureau (CCCVB) 410 E Main St PO Box 100	Batavia	OH	45103	**800-796-4282**	513-732-3600	208
Clermont State Historic Site 1 Clermont Ave	Germantown	NY	12526	**800-456-2267**	518-537-4240	564
Cleveland Bros Equipment Company Inc 5300 Paxton St	Harrisburg	PA	17111	**866-551-4602**	717-564-2121	358
Cleveland Cavaliers Quicken Loans Arena 1 Ctr Ct	Cleveland	OH	44115	**800-332-2287**	216-420-2000	712-1
Cleveland Clinic 9500 Euclid Ave	Cleveland	OH	44195	**800-223-2273**	216-444-2200	374-3
Cleveland Clinic Bone Marrow Transplantation Program 9500 Euclid Ave	Cleveland	OH	44195	**800-223-2273**	216-444-0261	767
Cleveland Clinic Hospital 2950 Cleveland Clinic Blvd	Weston	FL	33331	**866-293-7866**	954-689-5000	374-3
Cleveland Corp 42810 N Green Bay Rd	Zion	IL	60099	**800-281-3464**	847-872-7200	684
Cleveland Foundation 1422 Euclid Ave Ste 1300	Cleveland	OH	44115	**877-554-5054**	216-861-3810	304
Cleveland Gear Co 3249 E 80th St	Cleveland	OH	44104	**800-423-3169**	216-641-9000	707
Cleveland Golf Co 5601 Skylab Rd *Cust Svc	Huntington Beach	CA	92647	**800-999-6263***		708
Cleveland HeartLab Inc 6701 Carnegie Ave Ste 500	Cleveland	OH	44103	**866-358-9828**		415
Cleveland Institute of Art 11141 E Blvd	Cleveland	OH	44106	**800-223-4700**		163
Cleveland Institute of Electronics 1776 E 17th St	Cleveland	OH	44114	**800-243-6446**	216-781-9400	798
Cleveland Magazine 1422 Euclid Ave Ste 730	Cleveland	OH	44115	**800-210-7293**	216-771-2833	456-22
Cleveland Motion Controls Inc 7550 Hub Pkwy	Cleveland	OH	44125	**800-321-8072**	216-524-8800	205
Cleveland Museum of Art 11150 E Blvd *Sales	Cleveland	OH	44106	**800-469-4449***	216-421-7340	519
Cleveland Museum of Natural History 1 Wade Oval Dr	Cleveland	OH	44106	**800-317-9155**	216-231-4600	519
Cleveland Orchestra, The 11001 Euclid Ave Severance Hall	Cleveland	OH	44106	**800-686-1141**	216-231-1111	572-3
Cleveland Plant & Flower Co 12920 Corporate Dr	Cleveland	OH	44130	**888-231-7569**	216-898-3500	295
Cleveland Plumbing Supply Company Inc 143 E Washington St	Chagrin Falls	OH	44022	**800-331-1078**	440-247-2555	611
Cleveland Punch & Die Co 666 Pratt St PO Box 769	Ravenna	OH	44266	**888-451-4342**		755
Cleveland Range Co 1333 E 179th St	Cleveland	OH	44110	**800-338-2204**	216-481-4900	299
Cleveland State Community College 3535 Adkisson Dr	Cleveland	TN	37312	**800-604-2722**	423-472-7141	161
Cleveland State University 2121 Euclid Ave	Cleveland	OH	44115	**888-278-6446**	216-687-2000	167
Cleveland State University Cleveland-Marshall College of Law 1801 Euclid Ave LB 138	Cleveland	OH	44115	**866-687-2304**	216-687-2344	168-1
Cleveland Wire Cloth & Manufacturing Co 3573 E 78th St	Cleveland	OH	44105	**800-321-3234**	216-341-1832	686
Cleveland/Bradley Chamber of Commerce 225 Keith St	Cleveland	TN	37311	**800-533-9930**	423-472-6587	138
Clever Devices Ltd 300 Crossways Pk Dr	Woodbury	NY	11797	**800-872-6129**	516-433-6100	182
Clevest Solutions Inc 13911 Wireless Way Ste 100	Richmond	BC	V6V3B9	**866-915-0088**	604-214-9700	226
CLIA (Cruise Lines International Assn) 1201 F St NW Ste 250	Washington	DC	20004	**855-444-2542**	754-224-2200	47-23
Click2mail 3103 10th St N Ste 201	Arlington	VA	22201	**866-665-2787**	703-521-9029	626
ClickSafety.com Inc 2185 N California Blvd Ste 425	Walnut Creek	CA	94596	**800-971-1080**		763
ClickSoftware Inc 35 Corporate Dr Ste 400 *NASDAQ: CKSW*	Burlington	MA	01803	**888-438-3308**	781-272-5903	180-7
Clients First Business Solutions LLC 670 N Beers St Bldg 4	Holmdel	NJ	07733	**866-677-6290**		179
Cliff Castle Casino 555 W Middle Verde Rd	Camp Verde	AZ	86322	**800-381-7568**	928-567-7999	451
Cliff House at Pikes Peak 306 Canyon Ave	Manitou Springs	CO	80829	**888-212-7000**		379
Cliff Spa at Snowbird Hwy 210 PO Box 929000	Snowbird	UT	84092	**800-453-3000**	801-933-2225	705
Cliff Viessman Inc 215 First Ave PO Box 175	Gary	SD	57237	**800-328-2408**	605-272-5241	467
Cliff Weil Inc 8043 Industrial Pk Rd	Mechanicsville	VA	23116	**800-446-9345**	804-746-1321	542
Clifford & Rano Insurance Agency Inc 57 Cedar St	Worcester	MA	01609	**800-660-8284**	508-752-8284	390
Clifton Savings Bancorp Inc 1433 Van Houten Ave *NASDAQ: CSBK*	Clifton	NJ	07013	**888-562-6727**	973-473-2200	360-2
Clifton Springs Hospital & Clinic 2 Coulter Rd	Clifton Springs	NY	14432	**888-786-4347**	315-462-9561	374-3
Clifton T Perkins Hospital Ctr 8450 Dorsey Run Rd	Jessup	MD	20794	**877-463-3464**	410-724-3000	374-5
CliftonLarsonAllen - CLA 301 SW Adams St Ste 1000	Peoria	IL	61602	**800-354-5849**	309-671-4500	2
Climate Design Air ConditioningIn 12530 47th Way N	Clearwater	FL	33762	**888-572-7245**		191-10
Climate Registry, The 523 W Sixth St Ste 445	Los Angeles	CA	90014	**866-523-0764**		194
ClimateMaster Inc 7300 SW 44th St	Oklahoma City	OK	73179	**800-299-9747**	405-745-6000	14
Climax Manufacturing Co 7840 SR 26	Lowville	NY	13367	**800-225-4629**	315-376-8000	556
Climax Packaging Inc 4515 Easton Rd	Saint Joseph	MO	64503	**800-225-4629**	816-233-3181	100
Climbing Magazine 5720 Flatiron Pkwy	Boulder	CO	80301	**800-829-5895**		456-20
Clinch-Tite Corp 5264 Lake St PO Box 456 *General	Sandy Lake	PA	16145	**800-241-0900***	724-376-7315	550
Cline Falls State Scenic Viewpoint 62976 OB Riley Rd	Redmond	OR	97756	**800-551-6949**		564
C-Line Products Inc 1100 E Business Ctr Dr	Mount Prospect	IL	60056	**800-323-6084**	847-827-6661	533
Cline Tool & Service Co PO Box 866	Newton	IA	50208	**866-561-3022**	641-792-7081	492

Name / Address	City	State	ZIP	Toll-Free	Phone	Class
Clinic Service Corp 3464 S Willow St	Denver	CO	80231	800-929-5395	303-755-2900	2
CliniComp International 9655 Towne Ctr Dr	San Diego	CA	92121	800-350-8202	858-546-8202	180-10
Clinique Laboratories Inc 767 Fifth Ave 37th Fl	New York	NY	10153	800-419-4041	212-572-3983	217
Clinton Community College 1000 Lincoln Blvd	Clinton	IA	52732	877-495-3320	563-244-7001	161
Clinton County 137 Margaret St Ste 208	Plattsburgh	NY	12901	877-873-7283	518-565-4600	338
Clinton County Economic Partnership 212 N Jay St	Lock Haven	PA	17745	888-388-6991	570-748-5782	138
Clinton County Electric Co-op Inc 475 N Main St PO Box 40	Breese	IL	62230	800-526-7282	618-526-7282	247
Clinton Electronics Corp 6701 Clinton Rd	Loves Park	IL	61111	800-549-6393	815-633-1444	255
Clinton Inn Hotel 145 Dean Dr	Tenafly	NJ	07670	800-275-4411	201-871-3200	379
Clinton Junior College 1029 Crawford Rd	Rock Hill	SC	29730	877-837-9645	803-327-7402	161
Clinton Memorial Hospital (CMH) 610 W Main St PO Box 600	Wilmington	OH	45177	800-803-9648	937-382-6611	374-3
Clippard Instrument Lab 7390 Colerain Ave	Cincinnati	OH	45239	877-245-6247	513-521-4261	225
Clipper Exxpress Inc 9014 Heritage Pkwy Ste 300	Woodridge	IL	60517	800-678-2547	630-739-0700	448
Clipper Fund 2949 E Elvira Rd Ste 101	Tucson	AZ	85756	800-432-2504		527
Clipper Navigation Inc 2701 Alaskan Way Pier 69	Seattle	WA	98121	800-888-2535	206-443-2560	769
CLLA (Commercial Law League of America) 70 E Lake St Ste 630	Chicago	IL	60601	800-978-2552	312-781-2000	48-10
Clm Equipment Company Inc 3135 Hwy 90 E	Broussard	LA	70518	800-256-0490	337-837-6693	192
Clock Mobility 6700 Clay Ave	Grand Rapids	MI	49548	800-732-5625	616-698-9400	61-7
Clofine Dairy Products Inc 1407 New Rd	Linwood	NJ	08221	800-441-1001	609-653-1000	298-4
Cloisters Museum Fort Tryon Pk	New York	NY	10040	800-662-3397	212-923-3700	519
Clopay Bldg Products Inc 8585 Duke Blvd	Mason	OH	45040	800-225-6729		236
Clopay Plastic Products Co 8585 Duke Blvd	Mason	OH	45040	800-282-2260	513-770-4800	599
Cloquet Area Chamber of Commerce 225 Sunnyside Dr	Cloquet	MN	55720	800-554-4350	218-879-1551	138
Clorox Co 1221 Broadway *NYSE: CLX* ■ *Cust Svc	Oakland	CA	94612	800-424-9300*	510-271-7000	187
Clos du Bois 19410 Geyserville Ave *Sales	Geyserville	CA	95441	800-222-3189*	707-857-1651	79-3
Close Up Foundation 1330 Braddock Pl Ste 400	Alexandria	VA	22314	800-256-7387	703-706-3300	47-7
Closet Factory 12800 S Broadway	Los Angeles	CA	90061	800-838-7995	310-516-7000	191-11
Cloud 9 Living 4999 Pearl E Cir Ste 102	Boulder	CO	80301	866-525-6839		198
Cloud County Community College 2221 Campus Dr	Concordia	KS	66901	800-729-5101	785-243-1435	161
Cloud Peak Energy Inc (RTEA) 505 S Gillette Ave PO Box 3009	Gillette	WY	82717	866-470-4300	307-687-6000	500
Cloud-rider Designs Ltd 1260 Eighth Ave	Regina	SK	S4R1C9	800-632-1255	306-761-2119	350
CloudSway LLC 711 Pacific Ave	Tacoma	WA	98402	855-212-5683		387
Clougherty Packing Co 3049 E Vernon Ave *Sales	Los Angeles	CA	90058	800-846-7635*		472
Clover Farms Dairy PO Box 14627	Reading	PA	19612	800-323-0123	610-921-9111	297-27
Clover Global Group 2431 W Irving Park Rd	Chicago	IL	60618	888-256-8370	773-267-6767	462
Cloverdale Equipment Co 13133 Cloverdale St	Oak Park	MI	48237	888-388-9182	248-399-6600	266-3
Cloverdale Foods Co 3015 34th St NW	Mandan	ND	58554	800-669-9511		297-26
Cloverland Green Spring Dairy Inc 2701 Loch Raven Rd *Orders	Baltimore	MD	21218	800-492-0094*	410-235-4477	297-27
Clover-Stornetta Farms Inc PO Box 750369	Petaluma	CA	94975	800-237-3315	707-769-3235	298-4
Clovis Community College (CCC) 417 Schepps Blvd	Clovis	NM	88101	800-769-1409	575-769-2811	161
Clovis Unified School District 1450 Herndon Ave	Clovis	CA	93611	800-498-9055	559-327-9000	683
Clovis/Curry County Chamber of Commerce 105 E Third St	Clovis	NM	88101	800-261-7656	575-763-3435	138
Clow Valve Co 902 S Second St	Oskaloosa	IA	52577	800-829-2569	641-673-8611	787
Clowns of America International (COAI) PO Box 122	Eustis	FL	32727	877-816-6941	352-357-1676	47-4
CLS Investments LLC 17605 Wright St	Omaha	NE	68130	888-455-4244	402-493-3313	688
CLT (Chesapeake Lodging Trust) 1997 Annapolis Exchange Pkwy Ste 410 *NYSE: CHSP*	Annapolis	MD	21401	800-698-2820		652
Club Cal Neva Hotel Casino, The 38 E Second St PO Box 2071	Reno	NV	89501	877-777-7303	775-323-1046	667
Club Europa 802 W Oregon St	Urbana	IL	61801	800-331-1882	217-344-5863	758
Club Managers Assn of America (CMAA) 1733 King St	Alexandria	VA	22314	800-409-7755	703-739-9500	48-12
Club Med Sandpiper 4500 SE Pine Vly St	Port Saint Lucie	FL	34952	888-932-2582	772-398-5100	667
ClubCorp Inc 3030 Lyndon B Johnson Fwy Ste 600	Dallas	TX	75234	800-433-5079	972-243-6191	653
Clubfurniture.com 11535 Carmel Commons Blvd Ste 202	Charlotte	NC	28226	888-378-8383		789
ClubHouse Hotel & Suites Sioux Falls 2320 S Louise Ave	Sioux Falls	SD	57106	866-534-8700	605-361-8700	379
ClubLink Corp 15675 Dufferin St	King City	ON	L7B1K5	800-661-1818	905-841-3730	653
Clyde Peeling's Reptiland 18628 US Rt 15	Allenwood	PA	17810	800-737-8452		821
CLYDE UNION Pumps 4600 W Dickman Rd	Battle Creek	MI	49037	800-877-7867	269-966-4600	638
Clyde's Transfer Inc 8015 Industrial Pk Rd	Mechanicsville	VA	23116	800-342-8758	804-746-1135	683
CM Almy Inc 1 Ruth Rd	Pittsfield	ME	04967	800-225-2569	207-487-3232	154-13
CM Paula Co 6049 Hi-Tek Ct	Mason	OH	45040	800-543-4464		328
CM Ranch 167 Fish Hatchery Rd PO Box 217	Dubois	WY	82513	800-455-0721	307-455-2331	241
CM Services Inc 800 Roosevelt Rd Bldg C Ste 312	Glen Ellyn	IL	60137	800-613-6672	630-858-7337	46
CM Trailers Inc 200 County Rd PO Box 680	Madill	OK	73446	888-268-7577	580-795-5536	777
CMA (Chicago Meat Authority Inc) 1120 W 47th Pl	Chicago	IL	60609	800-383-3811	773-254-3811	297-26
CMA (Chamber Music America) 305 Seventh Ave 5th Fl	New York	NY	10001	888-221-9836	212-242-2022	47-4
CMA (Canadian Medical Assn) 1867 Alta Vista Dr	Ottawa	ON	K1G5W8	800-663-7336	613-731-9331	48-8
CMA (Country Music Assn Inc) 1 Music Cir S	Nashville	TN	37203	800-788-3045	615-244-2840	47-4
CMA (Crystal Meth Anonymous General Service Organization) 4470 W Sunset Blvd Ste 107 PO Box 555	Los Angeles	CA	90027	877-262-6691		47-21
CMA Consulting Services Inc 700 Troy Schenectady Rd	Latham	NY	12110	800-276-6101	518-783-9003	179
CMA Dishmachines 12700 Knott St	Garden Grove	CA	92841	800-854-6417	714-898-8781	386
CMAA (Crane Manufacturers Assn of America) 8720 Red Oak Blvd Ste 201	Charlotte	NC	28217	800-345-1815	704-676-1190	48-13
CMAA (Club Managers Assn of America) 1733 King St	Alexandria	VA	22314	800-409-7755	703-739-9500	48-12
CMC (Catholic Medical Ctr) 100 McGregor St	Manchester	NH	03102	800-437-9666	603-668-3545	374-3
CMC (Communications Manufacturing Co) 2234 Colby Ave *Orders	Los Angeles	CA	90064	800-462-5532*	310-828-3200	250
CMC (Community Medical Ctr) 99 Hwy 37 W	Toms River	NJ	08755	888-724-7123	732-557-8000	374-3
CMC (Cambridge Medical Ctr) 701 S Dellwood St	Cambridge	MN	55008	800-252-4133	763-689-7700	374-3
CMC Alamo Steel Co 2784 Old Dallas Rd	Waco	TX	76705	800-500-0333	254-799-2471	479
CMC Capitol City Steel 14501 S IH 35	Buda	TX	78610	888-682-7337	512-282-8820	479
CMC Construction Services 9103 E Almeda Rd	Houston	TX	77054	877-297-9111	713-799-1150	385
CMC Rebar Georgia 251 Hosea Rd	Lawrenceville	GA	30045	888-682-7337	770-963-6251	479
CMD Products 1410 Flightline Dr Ste D	Lincoln	CA	95648	800-210-9949	916-434-0228	429
CMDA (Christian Medical & Dental Assn) 2604 Hwy 421 PO Box 7500	Bristol	TN	37620	888-231-2637	423-844-1000	48-8
Cme Assoc Inc 32 Crabtree Ln	Woodstock	CT	06281	888-291-3227	860-928-7848	258
CME Group Inc 20 S Wacker Dr *NASDAQ: CME*	Chicago	IL	60606	866-716-7274	312-930-1000	689
CMH (Clinton Memorial Hospital) 610 W Main St PO Box 600	Wilmington	OH	45177	800-803-9648	937-382-6611	374-3
Cmi 6704 Guada Coma Dr	Schertz	TX	78154	800-840-1070	210-967-6169	418
CMI EFCO Inc 435 W Wilson St	Salem	OH	44460	877-225-2674	330-332-4661	319
CMI Inc 316 E Ninth St	Owensboro	KY	42303	866-835-0690	270-685-6545	528
CMI Plastics Inc 222 Pepsi Way	Ayden	NC	28513	877-395-1920	252-746-2171	607
Cml Healthcare Inc Unit 1 60 Courtneypark Dr W	Mississauga	ON	L5W0B3	800-263-0801	905-565-0043	418
CMMB (Catholic Medical Mission Board) 10 W 17th St	New York	NY	10011	800-678-5659	212-242-7757	47-5
Cmrg Business Solutions 2401 Trinity Ln	Mckinney	TX	75070	888-828-8097		228
CMS (College Music Society) 312 E Pine St	Missoula	MT	59802	800-729-0235	406-721-9616	48-5
Cms Communications Inc 722 Goddard Ave	Chesterfield	MO	63005	800-755-9169		248
CMS Electric Co-op Inc 509 E Carthage St	Meade	KS	67864	800-794-2353	620-873-2184	247
CMS Energy Corp 1 Energy Plz *NYSE: CMS*	Jackson	MI	49201	800-477-5050	517-788-0550	360-5
CMS Mid-Atlantic Inc 295 Totowa Rd	Totowa	NJ	07512	800-267-1981		393
CMS Peripherals Inc 12 Mauchly Unit E	Irvine	CA	92618	800-327-5773	714-424-5520	175-8
CMSA (Case Management Society of America) 6301 Ranch Dr	Little Rock	AR	72223	800-216-2672	501-225-2229	48-8
CMW (Central Maintenance & Welding Inc) 2620 E Keysville Rd	Lithia	FL	33547	877-704-7411	813-737-1402	191-14
CNA Corp 4825 Mark Ctr Dr	Alexandria	VA	22311	800-344-0007	703-824-2000	666
CNA Financial Corp 333 S Wabash Ave *NYSE: CNA*	Chicago	IL	60604	800-262-4357	312-822-5000	360-4

Name / Address	City	State	ZIP	Toll-Free	Phone	Class
CNA Surety Corp						
333 S Wabash Ave	Chicago	IL	60604	877-672-6115	312-822-5000	391-5
NYSE: L						
CNB (City National Bank of New Jersey)						
900 Broad St	Newark	NJ	07102	877-350-3524	973-624-0865	69
CNB Financial Corp						
1 S Second St PO Box 42	Clearfield	PA	16830	800-492-3221	814-765-9621	360-2
NASDAQ: CCNE						
CNBS Inc						
7200 W 132nd St Ste 240	Overland Park	KS	66213	800-222-0978		688
CNC Industries Ltd						
9331 39 Ave	Edmonton	AB	T6E5T3	877-262-2343	780-469-2346	453
CNC Software Inc						
671 Old Post Rd	Tolland	CT	06084	800-228-2877	860-875-5006	227
CNGC (Cascade Natural Gas Corp)						
8113 W Grandridge Blvd	Kennewick	WA	99336	888-522-1130	206-624-3900	785
CNMC (Children's National Medical Ctr)						
111 Michigan Ave NW	Washington	DC	20010	800-884-5433	202-476-5000	374-1
CNPP (Center for Nutrition Policy & Promotion)						
3101 Pk Ctr Dr 10th Fl	Alexandria	VA	22302	888-779-7264	703-305-7600	340-1
CNRL (Canadian Natural Resources Ltd)						
855 Second St SW Ste 2500	Calgary	AB	T2P4J8	888-878-3700	403-517-6700	535
NYSE: CNQ						
CNS Response Inc						
85 Enterprise Ste 410	Aliso Viejo	CA	92656	888-545-2677	949-420-4400	252
COA (Council on Accreditation)						
45 Broadway 29th Fl	New York	NY	10006	866-262-8088	212-797-3000	47-1
Coach & Equipment Manufacturing Corp						
130 Horizon Pk Dr PO Box 36	Penn Yan	NY	14527	800-724-8464		515
Coach Canada's Health Informatics Association						
250 Consumers Rd	North York	ON	M2J4V6	888-253-8554	416-494-9324	136
Coach House Inc						
3480 Technology Dr	Nokomis	FL	34275	800-235-0984	941-485-0984	119
Coach Inc						
516 W 34th St	New York	NY	10001	800-444-3611	212-594-1850	430
NYSE: COH						
Coach Tours Ltd						
475 Federal Rd	Brookfield	CT	06804	800-822-6224	203-740-1118	758
Coact Associates Ltd						
2748 Centennial Rd	Toledo	OH	43617	866-646-4400		198
Co-Advantage Resources						
3350 Buschwood Park Dr Ste 200	Tampa	FL	33618	800-868-1016	813-935-2000	630
COAI (Clowns of America International)						
PO Box 122	Eustis	FL	32727	877-816-6941	352-357-1676	47-4
Coal Outlook						
1200 G St NW Ste 1100	Washington	DC	20005	800-752-8878	212-904-3070	530-5
Coalition Against Insurance Fraud						
1012 14th St NW Ste 200	Washington	DC	20005	800-835-6422	202-393-7330	48-9
Coalition for Auto Repair Equality (CARE)						
105 Oronoco St Ste 115	Alexandria	VA	22314	800-229-5380	703-519-7555	48-21
Coalition on Human Needs (CHN)						
1120 Connecticut Ave NW	Washington	DC	20036	800-822-7323	202-223-2532	47-5
Co-Alliance LLP						
5250 E US Hwy 36 Bldg 1000	Avon	IN	46123	800-525-0272	317-745-4491	277
Co-Anon Family Groups						
PO Box 12722	Tucson	AZ	85732	800-898-9985	520-513-5028	47-21
Coast Capital Savings						
645 Tyee Rd Ste 400	Victoria	BC	V9A6X5	888-517-7000	250-483-7000	69
Coast Central Credit Union Inc						
2650 Harrison Ave	Eureka	CA	95501	800-974-9727	707-445-8801	221
Coast Dental Services Inc						
4010 W Boy Scout Blvd Ste 1100	Tampa	FL	33607	800-327-6453	813-288-1999	462
Coast Distribution System						
350 Woodview Ave	Morgan Hill	CA	95037	800-495-5858	408-782-6686	60
NYSE: CRV						
Coast Edmonton House Suite Hotel						
1090 W Georgia S Ste 900	Vancouver	BC	V6E3V7	800-716-6199	604-682-7982	379
Coast Electric Power Assn						
18020 Hwy Ste 603	Kiln	MS	39556	800-624-3348*	228-363-7000	247
*Cust Svc						
Coast Guard Exchange System						
510 Independence Pkwy						
Ste 500	Chesapeake	VA	23320	800-572-0230		789
Coast Plaza Hotel						
1316 33 St Ne	Calgary	AB	T2A6B6	800-661-1464	403-248-8888	379
Coast to Coast Business Equipment Inc						
8 Vanderbilt	Irvine	CA	92619	877-382-4357	949-457-7300	588
Coast to Coast Corporate Housing						
10773 Los Alamitos Blvd	Los Alamitos	CA	90720	800-451-9466	562-795-0250	212
Coast to Coast Moving & Storage Co						
136 41st St	Brooklyn	NY	11232	800-872-6683	718-443-5800	518
Coast Tool Co						
2099 edison ave	San leandro	CA	94577	888-675-3737	510-569-1945	350
Coast2Coast Diagnostics Inc						
600 N Tustin Ave Ste 110	Santa Ana	CA	92705	800-730-9263		415
Coastal Administrative Services Inc						
103 E Holly Ste 214	Bellingham	WA	98225	800-870-1831		262
Coastal Agrobusiness Inc						
3702 Evans St PO Box 856	Greenville	NC	27835	800-758-1828	252-756-1126	282
Coastal Bend Blood Ctr						
209 N Padre Island Dr	Corpus Christi	TX	78406	800-299-4943	361-855-4943	88
Coastal Bend College						
Beeville						
3800 Charco Rd	Beeville	TX	78102	866-722-2838	361-358-2838	161
Coastal Carolina University						
PO Box 261954	Conway	SC	29528	800-277-7000	843-349-2170	167
Coastal Conservation Assn (CCA)						
6919 Portwest Dr Ste 100	Houston	TX	77024	800-201-3474	713-626-4234	47-13
Coastal Corrosion Control Surveys LLC						
10172 Mammoth Ave	Baton Rouge	LA	70814	800-894-2120	225-275-6131	491
Coastal Electric Co-op						
1265 S Coastal Hwy PO Box 109	Midway	GA	31320	800-421-2343	912-884-3311	247
Coastal Electric Co-op Inc						
2269 Jefferies Hwy	Walterboro	SC	29488	855-880-2743	843-538-5700	247
Coastal Federal Credit Union						
1000 St Albans Dr	Raleigh	NC	27609	800-868-4262	919-420-8000	221
Coastal Helicopters Inc						
8995 Yandukin Dr	Juneau	AK	99801	800-789-5610	907-789-5600	359

Name / Address	City	State	ZIP	Toll-Free	Phone	Class
Coastal Hospice & Palliative Care						
2604 Old Ocean City Rd						
PO Box 1733	Salisbury	MD	21804	800-780-7886	410-742-8732	371
Coastal Inn Concorde						
379 Windmill Rd	Dartmouth	NS	B3A1J6	800-565-1565	902-465-7777	379
Coastal Inns Inc						
111 Warwick St Box 280	Digby	NS	B0V1A0	800-665-7829	800-401-1155	379
Coastal Journal						
97 Commercial St	Bath	ME	04530	800-649-6241	207-443-6241	531-4
Coastal Mechanical Services LLC						
394 E Dr	Melbourne	FL	32904	866-584-9528	321-725-3061	191-10
Coastal Pacific Food Distributors Inc (CPFD)						
1015 Performance Dr	Stockton	CA	95206	800-500-2611	209-983-2454	298-8
Coastal Palms Hotel						
120th St Coastal Hwy	Ocean City	MD	21842	800-641-0011		379
Coastal Training Technologies Corp						
500 Studio Dr	Virginia Beach	VA	23452	866-333-6888	757-498-9014	512
Coastal Transport Co Inc						
1603 Ackerman Rd	San Antonio	TX	78219	800-523-8612	210-661-4287	778
Coastal Transportation Inc						
4025 13th Ave W	Seattle	WA	98119	800-544-2580	206-282-9979	313
Coastline Community College						
11460 Warner Ave	Fountain Valley	CA	92708	866-422-2645	714-546-7600	161
Coating & Adhesive Corp (CAC)						
1901 Popular St PO Box 1080	Leland	NC	28451	800-410-2999	910-371-3184	549
Coats North America						
3430 Toringdon Way Ste 301	Charlotte	NC	28277	800-631-0965	704-329-5800	742-9
Coaxial Dynamics						
6800 Lake Abrams Dr	Middleburg Heights	OH	44130	800-262-9425	440-243-1100	645
COBA/Select Sires Inc						
1224 Alton Darby Creek Rd	Columbus	OH	43228	800-837-2621	614-878-5333	11-2
Cobalt Boats LLC						
1715 N Eigth St	Neodesha	KS	66757	800-468-5764	620-325-2653	89
Cobalt Digital Inc						
2506 Galen Dr	Urbana	IL	61802	800-669-1691	217-344-1243	645
Cobalt Pharmaceuticals Inc						
6500 Kitimat Rd	Mississauga	ON	L5N2B8	866-254-6111	905-814-1820	233
Cobb Chamber of Commerce						
240 I- N Pkwy	Atlanta	GA	30339	800-228-2545	770-980-2000	138
Cobb Travel & Tourism						
1 Galleria Pkwy	Atlanta	GA	30339	800-451-3480	678-303-2622	208
Cobblestone Capital Advisors LLC						
140 Allens Creek Rd	Rochester	NY	14618	800-264-2769	585-473-3333	688
Cobb-Vantress Inc						
PO Box 1030	Siloam Springs	AR	72761	800-748-9719	479-524-3166	11-2
Cober Evolving Solutions						
1351 Strasburg Rd	Kitchener	ON	N2R1H2	800-263-7136	519-745-7136	626
Cobon Plastics Corporation						
90 S St	Newark	NJ	07114	800-360-1324	973-344-6330	370
Cobra Mfg Co Inc						
7909 E 148th St S	Bixby	OK	74008	800-352-6272	918-366-7484	708
Coburn Co, The						
834 E Milwaukee St	Whitewater	WI	53190	800-776-7042	262-473-2822	599
Coburn Supply Company Inc						
390 Pk St Ste 100	Beaumont	TX	77701	800-832-8492	409-838-6363	611
Coca-Cola Bottling Co Consolidated						
4100 Coca-Cola Plaza	Charlotte	NC	28211	800-777-2653	704-557-4000	80-2
NASDAQ: COKE						
Coca-Cola Co						
1 Coca-Cola Plz PO Box 1734	Atlanta	GA	30313	800-438-2653	404-676-2121	79-2
NYSE: KO						
Coca-Cola Foundation Inc						
PO Box 1734	Atlanta	GA	30301	800-438-2653		305
Coca-Cola Nonpartisan Committee for Good Government						
PO Box 1734	Atlanta	GA	30301	800-438-2653		614
Cocaine Anonymous World Services Inc (CA)						
PO Box 492000	Los Angeles	CA	90049	800-347-8998	310-559-5833	47-21
Cocca's Inn & Suites						
Corner of Wolf Rd & Central Ave	Albany	NY	12205	888-426-2227	518-459-2240	379
Cocciardi & Associates Inc						
4 Kacey Ct	Mechanicsburg	PA	17055	800-377-3024	717-766-4500	428
Cochise College						
4190 W Hwy 80	Douglas	AZ	85607	800-966-7943	520-364-7943	161
Sierra Vista						
901 N Colombo Ave	Sierra Vista	AZ	85635	800-966-7943	520-515-0500	161
Cochran Firm LLC						
111 E Main St	Dothan	AL	36301	800-843-3476	334-793-1555	428
Cochrane Technologies Inc						
PO Box 81276	Lafayette	LA	70598	800-346-3745	337-837-3334	725
Coconino Community College						
Lonetree						
2800 S Lone Tree Rd	Flagstaff	AZ	86001	800-350-7122	928-527-1222	161
Coconino County						
219 E Cherry Ave	Flagstaff	AZ	86001	800-559-9289	928-774-5011	338
Coconut Malorie Resort						
200 59th St	Ocean City	MD	21842	855-826-6361	410-723-6100	667
CODA (Co-Dependents Anonymous Inc)						
PO Box 33577	Phoenix	AZ	85067	888-444-2359	602-277-7991	47-21
Codale Electric Supply Inc						
5225 West 2400 South						
PO Box 702070	Salt Lake City	UT	84120	800-300-6634	801-975-7300	248
Code Hennessy & Simmons Inc						
10 S Wacker Dr Ste 3175	Chicago	IL	60606	888-603-5847	312-876-1840	790
Co-Dependents Anonymous Inc (CODA)						
PO Box 33577	Phoenix	AZ	85067	888-444-2359	602-277-7991	47-21
Codington-Clark Electric Co-op						
3520 Ninth Ave SW PO Box 880	Watertown	SD	57201	800-463-8938	605-886-5848	247
Coe College						
1220 First Ave NE	Cedar Rapids	IA	52402	877-225-5263	319-399-8500	167
COECO Office Systems Co						
2521 N Church St	Rocky Mount	NC	27804	800-682-6844	252-977-1121	321
Coeur d'Alene Area Chamber of Commerce						
105 N First St Ste 100	Coeur d'Alene	ID	83814	877-782-9232	208-664-3194	138
Coeur d'Alene Resort						
115 S Second St	Coeur d'Alene	ID	83814	800-688-5253	208-765-4000	667
Coface Services North America Inc						
50 Millstone Rd	East Windsor	NJ	08520	877-626-3223	609-469-0400	220

Name / Address	City	State	ZIP	Toll-Free	Phone	Class
Coffee Bean International						
9120 NE Alderwood Rd	Portland	OR	97220	**800-877-0474**	503-227-4490	298-2
Coffee Beanery Ltd, The						
3429 Pierson Pl	Flushing	MI	48433	**800-441-2255**		158
Coffee Exchange						
207 Wickenden St	Providence	RI	02903	**877-263-3334**	401-273-1198	379
Coffee Holding Company Inc						
3475 Victory Blvd	Staten Island	NY	10314	**800-458-2233**	718-832-0800	297-7
NASDAQ: JVA						
Coffee Masters Inc						
7606 Industrial Ct	Spring Grove	IL	60081	**800-334-6485**	815-675-0088	298-2
Coffeyville Regional Medical Ctr						
1400 W Fourth St	Coffeyville	KS	67337	**800-540-2762**	620-251-1200	374-3
Coffin Turbo Pump Inc						
326 S Dean St	Englewood	NJ	07631	**800-568-9798**	201-568-2826	638
Coffman Truck Sales						
1149 W Lake St Rt 31	Aurora	IL	60506	**800-255-7641**	630-892-7093	56
Cogeco Cable Inc						
5 Pl Ville-Marie Ste 915	Montreal	QC	H3B4M7	**800-855-0511**	514-874-2600	115
Cogent Communications Group Inc						
1015 31st St NW	Washington	DC	20007	**877-875-4432**	202-295-4200	394
NASDAQ: CCOI						
Coghlan's Ltd						
121 Irene St	Winnipeg	MB	R3T4C7	**877-264-4526**	204-284-9550	709
Cognify						
PO Box 69337	Oro Valley	AZ	85737	**888-444-7992**	888-264-6439	226
Cognizant Technology Solutions Corp						
500 Frank W Burr Blvd	Teaneck	NJ	07666	**888-937-3277**	201-801-0233	182
NASDAQ: CTSH						
Cogswell Polytechnical College						
1175 Bordeaux Dr	Sunnyvale	CA	94089	**800-264-7955**	408-541-0100	167
COGWM (Church of God World Missions)						
2490 Keith St PO Box 8016	Cleveland	TN	37320	**800-345-7492**	423-478-7190	47-20
Cohber Press						
PO Box 93100	Rochester	NY	14692	**800-724-3032**	585-475-9100	779
Cohen & Steers Inc						
280 Pk Ave 10th Fl	New York	NY	10017	**800-330-7348**	212-832-3232	401
NYSE: CNS						
Cohen Highley LLP						
255 Queens Ave	London	ON	N6A5R8	**800-563-1020**	519-672-9330	428
Coherent Inc						
5100 Patrick Henry Dr	Santa Clara	CA	95054	**800-527-3786***	408-764-4000	425
NASDAQ: COHR ■ *Sales						
Cohu Inc						
12367 Crosthwaite Cir	Poway	CA	92064	**800-685-5050**	858-848-8100	250
NASDAQ: COHU						
Coilcraft Inc						
1102 Silver Lk Rd	Cary	IL	60013	**800-322-2645**	847-639-2361	255
Coilhose Pneumatics Inc						
19 Kimberly Rd	East Brunswick	NJ	08816	**800-424-9300**	732-390-8480	370
Coin Acceptors Inc						
300 Hunter Ave	Saint Louis	MO	63124	**800-325-2646**	314-725-0100	54
Coin Laundry Assn (CLA)						
1s660 Midwest Rd						
Ste 205	Oakbrook Terrace	IL	60181	**800-570-5629**	630-953-7920	48-4
Coin World Magazine						
911 S Vandemark Rd	Sidney	OH	45365	**866-519-7298**	937-498-0800	456-14
CoinLab Inc						
811 1st Ave Ste 480	Seattle	WA	98104	**855-522-2646**		393
Coinmach Service Corp						
303 Sunnyside Blvd Ste 70	Plainview	NY	11803	**877-264-6622**	516-349-8555	426
Coinstar Inc						
1800 114th Ave SE	Bellevue	WA	98004	**800-928-2274**	425-943-8000	54
Coker College						
300 E College Ave	Hartsville	SC	29550	**800-950-1908**	843-383-8000	167
Coker Consulting						
2400 Lakeview Pkwy Ste 400	Alpharetta	GA	30009	**800-345-5829**		462
Cokesbury Village						
726 Loveville Rd	Hockessin	DE	19707	**800-530-2377**	302-235-6000	670
COLA						
9881 Broken Land Pkwy Ste 200	Columbia	MD	21046	**800-981-9883**	410-381-6581	48-8
Colad Group						
801 Exchange St	Buffalo	NY	14210	**800-950-1755**	716-961-1776	554
COLAGE (Children of Lesbians & Gays Everywhere)						
3815 S Othello St Ste 100	Seattle	WA	98118	**800-657-3717**	415-861-5437	47-21
Colbert County Tourism & Convention Bureau						
719 Hwy 72 W PO Box 740425	Tuscumbia	AL	35674	**800-344-0783**	256-383-0783	208
Colby Attorneys Service Company Inc						
111 Washington Ave Ste 703	Albany	NY	12210	**800-832-1220**		632
Colby College						
4800 Mayflower Hill	Waterville	ME	04901	**800-723-3032***	207-859-4800	167
*Admissions						
Colby Community College						
1255 S Range Ave	Colby	KS	67701	**888-634-9350**	785-462-3984	161
Colby Convention & Visitors Bureau						
350 S Range Ste 10	Colby	KS	67701	**800-611-8835**	785-460-7643	208
Colby Equipment Company Inc						
3048 Ridgeview Dr	Indianapolis	IN	46226	**800-443-2981**	317-545-4221	358
Colby Hill Inn						
33 The Oaks PO Box 779	Henniker	NH	03242	**800-531-0330**	603-428-3281	379
Colby-Sawyer College						
541 Main St	New London	NH	03257	**800-272-1015***	603-526-3700	167
*Admissions						
Colchester Regional Hospital						
207 Willow St	Truro	NS	B2N5A1	**800-460-2110**	902-893-4321	374-2
Cold Shot Chillers						
14020 InterDr W	Houston	TX	77032	**800-473-9178**	281-227-8400	14
Cold Spring Granite Inc						
17482 Granite W Rd	Cold Spring	MN	56320	**800-328-5040**	320-685-3621	722
Cold Star Freight Systems Inc						
1015 Henry Eng Pl	Victoria	BC	V9B6B2	**800-201-1277**	250-381-3399	312
Cold Stone Creamery Inc						
9311 E Via De Ventura	Scottsdale	AZ	85258	**866-452-4252***	480-362-4800	381
*Cust Svc						
Coldspring						
17482 Granite W Rd	Cold Spring	MN	56320	**800-328-5040**		722
Coldwell Banker Gundaker						
2458 Old Dorsett Rd						
Ste 300	Maryland Heights	MO	63043	**800-325-1978**	314-298-5000	650
Coldwell Banker Residential Brokerage						
600 Grant St Ste 925	Denver	CO	80203	**800-552-6787***	303-409-1500	650
*All						
Coldwell Banker Residential Real Estate						
5951 Cattleridge Ave	Sarasota	FL	34232	**888-937-6426**	941-487-1400	650
Cole Hersee Co						
20 Old Colony Ave	Boston	MA	02127	**800-365-2653**	617-268-2100	813
Cole Industrial Inc						
5924 203rd St SW	Lynnwood	WA	98036	**800-627-2653**	425-774-6602	609
Cole Information Services						
3401 NW 39th St	Lincoln	NE	68524	**800-800-3271**	402-555-5678	634-6
Cole Papers Inc						
1300 N 38th St	Fargo	ND	58102	**800-800-8090**	701-282-5311	552
Cole Sport Inc						
1615 Park Ave	Park City	UT	84060	**800-345-2938**	435-649-4800	709
Cole Tool & Die Co						
241 Ashland Rd	Mansfield	OH	44905	**800-837-2653**	419-522-1272	755
Cole-Haan						
8701 Keystone Crossing	Indianapolis	IN	46240	**800-695-8945**	317-810-0160	302
Coleman American Moving Services Inc						
PO Box 960	Midland City	AL	36350	**877-693-7060**	866-929-1482	778
Coleman Co						
1100 Stearns Dr	Sauk Rapids	MN	56379	**800-835-3278**	320-252-1642	708
Coleman College						
8888 Balboa Ave	San Diego	CA	92123	**800-430-2030**	858-499-0202	167
Coleman Company Inc						
3600 N Hydraulic	Wichita	KS	67219	**800-835-3278***		708
*Cust Svc						
Coleman County Electric Co-op Inc						
3300 N Hwy 84 PO Box 860	Coleman	TX	76834	**800-560-2128**	325-625-2128	247
Coleman Dairy Inc						
6901 I-30	Little Rock	AR	72209	**800-365-1551**	501-748-1700	297-27
Coleman E Adler & Sons Inc						
722 Canal St	New Orleans	LA	70130	**800-925-7912**	504-523-5292	410
Coleman Instrument Co						
11575 Goldcoast Dr	Cincinnati	OH	45249	**800-899-5745**	513-489-5745	358
Coleman Professional Services 24 7 Emergency C						
3920 Lovers Ln	Ravenna	OH	44266	**800-673-1347**	330-296-3555	724
Cole-Parmer Instrument Co						
625 E Bunker Ct	Vernon Hills	IL	60061	**800-323-4340**	847-549-7600	420
Colgate Rochester Crozer Divinity School						
1100 S Goodman St	Rochester	NY	14620	**888-937-3732**	585-271-1320	168-3
Colite International Ltd						
5 Technology Cir	Columbia	SC	29203	**800-760-7926**	803-926-7926	609
CollabNet Inc						
8000 Marina Blvd Ste 600	Brisbane	CA	94005	**888-532-6823**	650-228-2500	179
Collaborative Consulting LLC						
70 BlanchaRd Rd Ste 500	Burlington	MA	01803	**877-376-9900**	781-565-2600	195
Collage Dance Theatre						
2934 1/2 Beverly Glen Cir	Los Angeles	CA	90077	**866-300-4287**	818-784-8669	572-1
Collectcents Inc						
1450 Meyerside Dr 2nd Fl	Mississauga	ON	L5T2N5	**800-256-8964**	905-670-7575	159
Collective Technologies LLC						
9433 Bee Caves Rd	Austin	TX	78733	**800-994-1640**	512-263-5500	227
Collectors Universe Inc						
PO Box 6280	Newport Beach	CA	92658	**800-325-1121**	949-567-1234	50
NASDAQ: CLCT						
College & University Professional Assn for Hum Res (CUPA-HR)						
1811 Commons Pt Dr	Knoxville	TN	37932	**877-287-2474**	865-637-7673	48-5
College Board						
45 Columbus Ave	New York	NY	10023	**800-927-4302**	212-713-8000	246
College Health Services LLC						
144 Turnpike Rd Ste 240	Southborough	MA	01772	**866-636-8336**		179
College Hospital						
10802 College Pl	Cerritos	CA	90703	**800-352-3301**	562-924-9581	374-5
College Hospital Costa Mesa						
301 Victoria St	Costa Mesa	CA	92627	**800-773-8001**	949-642-2734	374-5
College Merici						
755 Ch St-Louis	Quebec	QC	G1S1C1	**800-208-1463**	418-683-1591	161
College Music Society (CMS)						
312 E Pine St	Missoula	MT	59802	**800-729-0235**	406-721-9616	48-5
College of American Pathologists (CAP)						
325 Waukegan Rd	Northfield	IL	60093	**800-323-4040**	847-832-7000	48-8
College of American Pathologists PAC						
1350 I St NW Ste 590	Washington	DC	20005	**800-392-9994**	202-354-7100	614
College of Biblical Studies-Houston						
7000 Regency Sq Blvd Ste 110	Houston	TX	77036	**844-227-9673**	713-785-5995	160
College of Charleston						
66 George St	Charleston	SC	29424	**866-327-2400**	843-805-5507	167
College of Court Reporting Inc						
111 W Tenth St Ste 111	Hobart	IN	46342	**866-294-3974**	219-942-1459	798
College of Eastern Utah						
451 E 400 N	Price	UT	84501	**800-336-2381**	435-613-5000	161
San Juan						
639 West 100 South	Blanding	UT	84511	**800-395-2969**	435-678-2201	161
College of Idaho						
2112 Cleveland Blvd	Caldwell	ID	83605	**800-224-3246***	208-459-5011	167
*Admissions						
College of Menominee Nation						
PO Box 1179	Keshena	WI	54135	**800-567-2344**	715-799-5600	164
College of Mount Saint Joseph						
5701 Delhi Rd	Cincinnati	OH	45233	**800-654-9314**	513-244-4200	167
College of Mount Saint Vincent						
6301 Riverdale Ave	Riverdale	NY	10471	**800-722-4867**	718-405-3304	167
College of New Jersey						
2000 Pennington Rd PO Box 7718	Ewing	NJ	08628	**800-644-3562**	609-771-1855	167
College of New Rochelle						
29 Castle Pl	New Rochelle	NY	10805	**800-933-5923**	914-654-5000	167
College of Notre Dame of Maryland						
4701 N Charles St	Baltimore	MD	21210	**800-753-3757***	410-435-0100	167
*Admissions						
College of Nurses of Ontario						
101 Davenport Rd	Toronto	ON	M5R3P1	**800-387-5526**	416-928-0900	161
College of Saint Catherine						
2004 Randolph Ave	Saint Paul	MN	55105	**800-945-4599**	651-690-6000	167
Minneapolis						
601 25th Ave S	Minneapolis	MN	55454	**800-945-4599**	651-690-7700	167

				Toll-Free	Phone	Class
College of Saint Elizabeth						
2 Convent Rd	Morristown	NJ	07960	800-210-7900*	973-290-4700	167
*Admissions						
College of Saint Joseph in Vermont						
71 Clement Rd	Rutland	VT	05701	877-270-9998*	802-773-5900	167
*Admissions						
College of Saint Mary						
7000 Mercy Rd	Omaha	NE	68106	800-926-5534	402-399-2400	167
College of Saint Rose						
432 Western Ave	Albany	NY	12203	800-637-8556	518-454-5150	167
College of Saint Scholastica						
1200 Kenwood Ave	Duluth	MN	55811	800-447-5444	218-723-6046	167
College of Santa Fe						
1600 St Michaels Dr	Santa Fe	NM	87505	800-862-7759	505-473-6011	167
College of Southern Idaho						
PO Box 1238	Twin Falls	ID	83303	800-680-0274	208-733-9554	161
College of Southern Maryland						
Leonardtown						
22950 Hollywood Rd	Leonardtown	MD	20650	800-933-9177	240-725-5300	161
Prince Frederick						
115 J W Williams Rd	Prince Frederick	MD	20678	800-933-9177	443-550-6000	161
College of Staten Island						
2800 Victory Blvd	Staten Island	NY	10314	888-442-4551	718-982-2000	167
College of the Albemarle						
PO Box 2327	Elizabeth City	NC	27906	800-335-9050	252-335-0821	161
College of the Atlantic						
105 Eden St	Bar Harbor	ME	04609	800-528-0025*	207-288-5015	167
*Admissions						
College of the Holy Cross						
1 College St	Worcester	MA	01610	800-442-2421	508-793-2011	167
College of the Holy Cross Dinand Library						
1 College St	Worcester	MA	01610	877-433-1843	508-793-2642	434-6
College of the Ozarks						
1 Industrial Dr PO Box 17	Point Lookout	MO	65726	800-222-0525*	417-334-6411	167
*Admissions						
College of the Redwoods						
7351 Tompkins Hill Rd	Eureka	CA	95501	800-641-0400	707-476-4100	161
Del Norte						
883 W Washington Blvd	Crescent City	CA	95531	800-641-0400	707-465-2300	161
Mendocino Coast						
440 Alger St	Fort Bragg	CA	95437	800-641-0400	707-962-2600	161
College of the Siskiyous						
800 College Ave	Weed	CA	96094	888-397-4339	530-938-4461	161
College of the Southwest						
6610 N Lovington Hwy	Hobbs	NM	88240	800-530-4400	575-392-6561	167
College of Westchester (CW)						
325 Central Ave	White Plains	NY	10606	800-660-7093		798
College of William & Mary Swem Library						
PO Box 8794	Williamsburg	VA	23187	800-462-3683	757-221-3072	434-6
College of Wooster						
1189 Beall Ave	Wooster	OH	44691	800-877-9905	330-263-2000	167
College Outlook & Career Opportunities Magazine						
20 E Gregory Blvd	Kansas City	MO	64114	800-274-8867	816-361-0616	456-11
College Parents of America (CPA)						
2200 Wilson Blvd Ste 102-396	Arlington	VA	22201	888-761-6702		47-11
College Savings Bank						
PO Box 3769	Princeton	NJ	08543	800-888-2723		69
College Station Ford						
1351 Earl Rudder Fwy S	College Station	TX	77845	888-508-0241	979-694-2022	56
Colligo Networks Inc						
400-1152 Mainland St	Vancouver	BC	V6B4X2	866-685-7962	604-685-7962	181
Collin County						
200 S McDonald St Ste 120	McKinney	TX	75069	800-336-5996	972-548-4100	338
Collin Street Bakery Inc						
401 W Seventh Ave	Corsicana	TX	75151	800-267-4657*		67
*Sales						
Collington Episcopal Community						
10450 Lottsford Rd	Mitchellville	MD	20721	888-257-9468		670
Collins & Lacy PC						
1330 Lady St 6th Fl	Columbia	SC	29201	888-648-0526	803-256-2660	428
Collins Bowling Centers Inc						
750 E New Cir Rd	Lexington	KY	40505	866-252-2695	859-252-3429	98
Collins Bus Corp						
PO Box 2946	Hutchinson	KS	67504	800-533-1850	620-662-9000	58
Collins Cos						
1618 SW First Ave Ste 500	Portland	OR	97201	800-329-1219		681
Collins Electric Co Inc						
53 Second Ave	Chicopee	MA	01020	877-553-2810	413-592-9221	191-4
Collins Manufacturing Co						
2000 Bowser Rd	Cookeville	TN	38506	800-292-6450	931-528-5151	75
Colloid Environmental Technologies Co (CETCO)						
2870 Forbs Ave	Hoffman Estates	IL	60192	800-527-9948	847-851-1899	3
Colmac Coil Manufacturing Inc						
370 N Lincoln St PO Box 571	Colville	WA	99114	800-845-6778	509-684-2595	14
Colmac Industries Inc						
PO Box 72	Colville	WA	99114	800-926-5622	509-684-4505	427
Colmery-O'Neil Veterans Affairs Medical Ctr						
2200 SW Gage Blvd	Topeka	KS	66622	800-574-8387	785-350-3111	374-8
Coloma Frozen Foods Inc						
4145 Coloma Rd	Coloma	MI	49038	800-642-2723	269-849-0500	297-21
Colonial Bag Co						
1 Ocean Pond Ave PO Box 929	Lake Park	GA	31636	800-392-4875	229-559-8484	64
Colonial Bag Corp						
205 E Fullerton Ave	Carol Stream	IL	60188	800-445-7496	630-690-3999	65
Colonial Bronze Co						
511 Winsted Rd	Torrington	CT	06790	800-355-7903*	860-489-9233	350
*All						
Colonial Downs						
10515 Colonial Downs Pkwy	New Kent	VA	23124	888-482-8722	804-966-7223	639
Colonial Engineering Inc						
6400 Corporate Ave	Portage	MI	49002	800-374-0234	269-323-2495	594
Colonial Farm Credit Aca						
7104 Mechanicsville Tpke						
PO Box 727	Mechanicsville	VA	23111	800-777-8908	804-746-4581	218
Colonial Freight Systems Inc						
10924 McBride Ln	Knoxville	TN	37932	800-826-1402	865-966-9711	778
Colonial House Inn						
277 Main St Rt 6A	Yarmouth Port	MA	02675	800-999-3416	508-362-4348	669
Colonial Life & Accident Insurance Co						
1200 Colonial Life Blvd	Columbia	SC	29210	800-325-4368		391-2
Colonial National Historical Park						
PO Box 210	Yorktown	VA	23690	866-945-7920	757-898-3400	563
Colonial Parking Inc						
1050 Thomas Jefferson St NW						
Ste 100	Washington	DC	20007	877-777-4778	202-295-8100	561
Colonial Penn Life Insurance Co						
399 Market St	Philadelphia	PA	19181	800-523-9100	215-928-8000	391-2
Colonial Pipeline Co						
1185 Sanctuary Pkwy Ste 100	Alpharetta	GA	30009	800-275-3004	678-762-2200	596
Colonial Properties Trust						
6584 Poplar Ave	Memphis	TN	38138	866-620-1130		653
NYSE: CLP						
Colonial Truck Co						
1833 Commerce Rd	Richmond	VA	23224	800-234-8782	804-232-3492	778
Colonial Williamsburg Foundation						
PO Box 1776	Williamsburg	VA	23187	800-447-8679	757-229-1000	306
Colonial Williamsburg Reservation Ctr						
PO Box 1776	Williamsburg	VA	23187	800-447-8679	757-229-1000	376
ColonialWebb Contractors Co						
2820 Ackley Ave	Richmond	VA	23228	877-208-3894	804-916-1400	191-10
Colonna's Shipyard Inc						
400 E Indian River Rd	Norfolk	VA	23523	800-265-6627	757-545-2414	696
Colonnade Hotel						
120 Huntington Ave	Boston	MA	02116	800-962-3030	617-424-7000	379
Colony Hotel						
140 Ocean Ave	Kennebunkport	ME	04046	800-552-2363	207-967-3331	667
Colony Inc						
2500 Galvin Dr	Elgin	IL	60123	800-735-1300	847-426-5300	235
Colony Palms Hotel						
572 N Indian Canyon Dr	Palm Springs	CA	92262	800-557-2187	760-969-1800	131
Color Ad Inc						
19627 S Santa Fe Ave	Rancho Dominguez	CA	90221	888-264-6991		626
Color Communication Inc						
4000 W Fillmore St	Chicago	IL	60624	800-458-5743		779
Color House Graphics Inc						
3505 Eastern Ave SE	Grand Rapids	MI	49508	800-454-1916	616-241-1916	779
Color Imaging Inc						
4350 Peachtree Industrial Blvd						
Ste 100	Norcross	GA	30071	800-783-1090	770-840-1090	627
Color Me Beautiful						
7000 Infantry Ridge Rd Ste 200	Manassas	VA	20109	800-265-6763		366
Color Resolutions International						
575 Quality Blvd	Fairfield	OH	45014	800-346-8570	513-552-7200	388
Color Spot Nurseries Inc						
2575 Olive Hill Rd	Fallbrook	CA	92028	800-554-4065	760-695-1480	369
Color Wheel Paint Mfg Co Inc						
2814 Silver Star Rd	Orlando	FL	32808	855-862-6639	407-293-6810	549
Colorado						
Aging & Adult Services Div						
1575 Sherman St Ground Fl	Denver	CO	80203	800-773-1366	303-866-2636	339-6
Housing & Finance Authority						
1981 Blake St	Denver	CO	80202	800-877-2432	303-297-2432	339-6
Natural Resources Dept						
1313 Sherman St Rm 718	Denver	CO	80203	800-536-5308	303-866-3311	339-6
Parks & Outdoor Recreation Div						
1313 Sherman St Rm 618	Denver	CO	80203	800-678-2267*	303-866-3437	339-6
*Campground Resv						
Public Health & Environment Dept (CDPHE)						
4300 Cherry Creek Dr S	Denver	CO	80246	800-886-7689	303-692-2000	339-6
Public Utilities Commission						
1560 Broadway Ste 250	Denver	CO	80203	800-888-0170	303-894-2000	339-6
Regulatory Agencies Dept						
1560 Broadway Ste 1550	Denver	CO	80202	800-886-7675	303-894-7855	339-6
State Court Administrator						
1301 Pennsylvania St Ste 300	Denver	CO	80203	800-888-0001	303-837-3668	339-6
Supreme Court						
1560 Broadway Ste 1800	Denver	CO	80202	877-888-1370	303-866-6400	339-6
Victims Programs Office						
700 Kipling St Ste 1000	Lakewood	CO	80215	888-282-1080	303-239-5719	339-6
Vocational Rehabilitation Div						
1575 Sherman St 4th Fl	Denver	CO	80203	866-870-4595	303-866-4150	339-6
Workers Compensation Div						
633 17th St Ste 400	Denver	CO	80202	888-390-7936	303-318-8700	339-6
Colorado Assn of Realtors						
309 Inverness Way S	Englewood	CO	80112	800-944-6550	303-790-7099	654
Colorado Belle Hotel & Casino						
2100 S Casino Dr	Laughlin	NV	89029	877-460-0777*	702-298-4000	132
*Resv						
Colorado Business Bank						
821 17th St	Denver	CO	80202	800-574-4714	303-293-2265	360-2
Colorado Charter Lines						
4960 Locust St	Commerce	CO	80022	800-821-7491	303-287-0239	106
Colorado Christian University						
8787 W Alameda Ave	Lakewood	CO	80226	800-443-2484	303-963-3200	167
Loveland						
3553 Clydesdale Pkwy Ste 300	Loveland	CO	80538	800-443-2484	970-669-8700	167
Colorado College						
14 E Cache La Poudre St						
	Colorado Springs	CO	80903	800-542-7214	719-389-6344	167
Colorado CollegeInvest						
1560 Broadway Ste 1700	Denver	CO	80202	800-448-2424	303-376-8800	723
Colorado Correctional Industries						
4999 Oakland St	Denver	CO	80239	800-685-7891*	719-226-4206	213
*Cust Svc						
Colorado Dental Assn						
8301 E Prentice Ave						
Ste 400	Greenwood Village	CO	80111	866-777-4771	303-740-6900	229
Colorado Dude & Guest Ranch Assn (CDGRA)						
PO Box D	Shawnee	CO	80475	866-942-3472		47-23
Colorado Farm Bureau Mutual Insurance Co						
PO Box 5647	Denver	CO	80217	800-315-5998	303-749-7500	391-4
Colorado Fsb						
8400 E Prentice Ave						
Ste 545	Greenwood Village	CO	80111	877-484-2372	303-793-3555	69
Colorado Labor & Employment Dept						
633 17th St Ste 201	Denver	CO	80203	800-390-7936	303-318-8000	261

Name / Address	City	State	ZIP	Toll-Free	Phone	Class
Colorado Lawyer Magazine						
1900 Grant St 9th Fl	Denver	CO	80203	**800-332-6736**	303-860-1115	456-15
Colorado Lottery						
212 W Third St Ste 210	Pueblo	CO	81003	**800-999-2959**	719-546-2400	451
Colorado Medical Society						
7351 Lowry Blvd	Denver	CO	80230	**800-654-5653**	720-859-1001	473
Colorado Mountain College						
Alpine						
1330 Bob Adams Dr	Steamboat Springs	CO	80487	**800-621-8559**	970-870-4444	161
Aspen 0255 Sage Way	Aspen	CO	81611	**800-621-8559**	970-925-7740	161
Roaring Fork-Spring Valley						
3000 County Rd 114	Glenwood Springs	CO	81601	**800-621-8559**	970-945-7481	161
Colorado National Monument						
1750 Rim Rock Dr	Fruita	CO	81521	**866-945-7920**	970-858-3617	563
Colorado Northwestern Community College						
500 Kennedy Dr	Rangely	CO	81648	**800-562-1105**	970-675-3335	161
Craig 50 College Dr	Craig	CO	81625	**800-562-1105**		161
Colorado Passport Agency						
Colorado Agency						
3151 S Vaughn Way Ste 600	Aurora	CO	80014	**888-874-7793**	877-487-2778	340-14
Colorado Prime Foods						
500 Bi-County Blvd Ste 400	Farmingdale	NY	11735	**800-365-2404**	631-694-1111	366
Colorado Railroad Museum						
17155 W 44th Ave	Golden	CO	80403	**800-365-6263**	303-279-4591	519
Colorado School Journal						
101 W. Colfax Ave Ste 800	Denver	CO	80202	**800-336-7678**	303-837-1500	456-8
Colorado School of English						
331 14th St	Denver	CO	80202	**877-234-0654**	720-932-8900	423
Colorado School of Mines						
1600 Maple St	Golden	CO	80401	**800-446-9488**	303-273-3000	167
Colorado Serum Co						
4950 York St PO Box 16428	Denver	CO	80216	**800-525-2065***	303-295-7527	84
*Orders						
Colorado Springs Regional Business Alliance						
102 S Tejon St Ste 430	Colorado Springs	CO	80903	**866-804-8763**	719-471-8183	138
Colorado Springs City Auditorium						
221 E Kiowa St	Colorado Springs	CO	80903	**800-888-4748**	719-385-5969	207
Colorado Springs Convention & Visitors Bureau						
515 S Cascade Ave	Colorado Springs	CO	80903	**800-888-4748**	719-635-7506	208
Colorado Springs School District #11						
1115 N El Paso St	Colorado Springs	CO	80903	**800-273-8255**	719-520-2000	683
Colorado Springs Utilities						
111 S Cascade Ave						
PO Box 1103	Colorado Springs	CO	80903	**800-238-5434**	719-448-4800	785
Colorado State University						
Pueblo						
2200 Bonforte Blvd	Pueblo	CO	81001	**877-307-5678**	719-549-2100	167
Colorado Symphony Orchestra						
1000 14th St Unit 15	Denver	CO	80202	**877-292-7979**	303-623-7876	572-3
Colorado Technical University						
4435 N Chestnut St	Colorado Springs	CO	80907	**855-230-0555**	719-598-0200	167
Colorado Technical University Denver						
1865 W 121st Ave						
Bldg C Ste 100	Westminster	CO	80234	**877-250-9372**	303-362-2900	798
Colorado Time Systems						
1551 E 11th St	Loveland	CO	80537	**800-279-0111**	970-667-1000	699
Colorado Trails Ranch						
12161 County Rd 240	Durango	CO	81301	**800-323-3833**	970-247-5055	241
Colorado Trust						
1600 Sherman St	Denver	CO	80203	**888-847-9140**	303-837-1200	304
Colorado Valley Transit Inc						
108 Cardinal Ln PO Box 940	Columbus	TX	78934	**800-548-1068**	979-732-6281	107
Colorado Veterinary Medical Assn						
191 Yuma St	Denver	CO	80223	**800-228-5429**	303-318-0447	793
Colorado West Investments Inc						
1731 E Niagara Rd	Montrose	CO	81401	**888-249-9882**	970-249-9882	688
Coloradoan, The						
1300 Riverside Ave	Fort Collins	CO	80524	**877-424-0063**	970-493-6397	531-2
Colorfx Inc						
10776 Aurora Ave	Des Moines	IA	50322	**800-348-9044**		176
Color-Glo International						
7111 Ohms Ln	Minneapolis	MN	55439	**800-333-8523**	952-835-1338	61-1
Colorid LLC						
20480 Chartwls Ctr Dr	Cornelius	NC	28031	**888-682-6567**	704-987-2238	358
Colors By Design						
7723 Densmore Ave	Van Nuys	CA	91406	**800-832-8436**		129
Colors on Parade						
125 Daytona St PO Box 50940	Conway	SC	29526	**866-756-4207***	843-347-8818	61-4
*Cust Svc						
Colosseum Online Inc						
800 Petrolia Rd	Toronto	ON	M3J3K4	**877-739-7873**	416-739-7873	227
Colquitt Regional Medical Ctr (CRMC)						
3131 S Main St PO Box 40	Moultrie	GA	31768	**888-262-2762**	229-985-3420	374-3
Colt's Plastics Co						
969 N Main St PO Box 429	Dayville	CT	06241	**800-222-2658**	860-774-2301	97
Coltene/Whaledent Inc						
235 Ascot Pkwy	Cuyahoga Falls	OH	44223	**800-221-3046**	330-916-8800	230
Columbia Air Services						
175 Tower Ave						
Groton-New London Airport	Groton	CT	06340	**800-787-5001**	860-449-1400	62
Columbia Bank						
1301 A St Ste 800	Tacoma	WA	98402	**800-305-1905**	253-305-1900	360-2
NASDAQ: COLB						
Columbia Bank, The						
7168 Columbia Gateway Dr	Columbia	MD	21046	**888-822-2265**		69
Columbia Bible College						
2940 Clearbrook Rd	Abbotsford	BC	V2T2Z8	**800-283-0881**	604-853-3358	783
Columbia Cascade Co						
1300 SW Sixth Ave Ste 310	Portland	OR	97201	**800-547-1940**	503-223-1157	346
Columbia College						
600 S Michigan Ave 3rd Fl	Chicago	IL	60605	**866-705-0200**	312-663-1600	167
Columbia College Hollywood						
18618 Oxnard St	Tarzana	CA	91356	**800-785-0585**	818-345-8414	167
Columbia College Jefferson City						
3314 Emerald Ln	Jefferson City	MO	65109	**800-231-2391**	573-634-3250	167
Columbia College Lake of the Ozarks						
900 College Blvd	Osage Beach	MO	65065	**800-231-2391**	573-348-6463	167
Columbia College of Nursing (CCON)						
4425 N Port Washington Rd	Glendale	WI	53212	**800-221-5573**	414-326-2330	167
Columbia College Orlando						
2600 Technology Dr Ste 100	Orlando	FL	32804	**800-231-2391**	407-293-9911	167
Columbia Convention & Visitors Bureau						
300 S Providence Rd	Columbia	MO	65203	**800-652-0987**	573-875-1231	208
Columbia Crest Winery						
178810 State Rt 221 PO Box 231	Paterson	WA	99345	**888-309-9463**	509-875-4227	79-3
Columbia Daily Tribune						
101 N Fourth St	Columbia	MO	65201	**800-333-6799**	573-815-1700	531-2
Columbia Data Products Inc						
925 Sunshine Ln						
Ste 1080	Altamonte Springs	FL	32714	**800-613-6288***	407-869-6700	180-12
*Sales						
Columbia Distributing Co						
6840 N Cutter Cir	Portland	OR	97217	**888-417-5001**	503-289-9600	80-1
Columbia Elevator Products Company Inc						
380 Horace St	Bridgeport	NY	06610	**888-858-1558**		191-1
Columbia Environmental Research Ctr (CERC)						
4200 New Haven Rd	Columbia	MO	65201	**888-283-7626**	573-875-5399	666
Columbia Forest Products Inc Columbia Plywood Div						
7900 Triad Ctr Dr Ste 200	Greensboro	NC	27409	**800-637-1609**		612
Columbia Gas of Ohio Inc						
200 Civic Ctr Dr	Columbus	OH	43215	**800-807-9781**	614-460-6000	785
Columbia Gas of Virginia Inc						
1809 Coyote Dr	Chester	VA	23836	**800-543-8911***		785
*Cust Svc						
Columbia Gear Corp						
530 County Rd 50	Avon	MN	56310	**800-323-9838**	320-356-7301	707
Columbia Gorge Hotel						
4000 Westcliff Dr	Hood River	OR	97031	**800-345-1921**	541-386-5566	379
Columbia Industries Inc						
PO Box 746	Hopkinsville	KY	42240	**800-531-5920**	270-881-1200	708
Columbia International University						
7435 Monticello Rd	Columbia	SC	29203	**800-777-2227**	803-754-4100	160
Columbia Magazine						
1 Columbus Plaza	New Haven	CT	06510	**800-380-9995**	203-752-4000	456-10
Columbia Memorial Hospital						
71 Prospect Ave	Hudson	NY	12534	**866-539-1370**	518-828-7601	374-3
Columbia Metropolitan Convention & Visitors Bureau						
1101 Lincoln St PO Box 15	Columbia	SC	29202	**800-264-4884**	803-545-0000	208
Columbia Mfg Corp						
14400 S San Pedro St	Gardena	CA	90248	**800-729-3667**	310-327-9300	236
Columbia Missourian						
221 S Eigth St	Columbia	MO	65201	**855-270-6572**	573-882-5700	531-2
Columbia ParCar Corp						
1115 Commercial Ave	Reedsburg	WI	53959	**800-222-4653**	608-524-8888	515
Columbia Pipe & Supply Co						
1120 W Pershing Rd	Chicago	IL	60609	**888-429-4635**	773-927-6600	491
Columbia Room Inc						
1108 E Marina Way	Hood River	OR	97031	**800-828-7873**	541-386-2200	705
Columbia Rural Electric Assn Inc						
115 E Main St	Dayton	WA	99328	**800-642-1231**	509-382-2578	247
Columbia Saint Mary's Hospital Ozaukee						
13111 N Port Washington Rd	Mequon	WI	53097	**800-457-6004**	262-243-7300	374-3
Columbia Savings Bank						
19-01 Rt 208	Fair Lawn	NJ	07410	**800-747-4428***	800-522-4167	69
*Cust Svc						
Columbia Sportswear Co						
14375 NW Science Pk Dr	Portland	OR	97229	**800-622-6953**	503-985-4125	154-1
NASDAQ: COLM						
Columbia State Bank						
PO Box 2156	Tacoma	WA	98401	**800-305-1905**	253-305-1900	69
Columbia Steel Casting Co Inc						
10425 N Bloss Ave	Portland	OR	97203	**800-547-9471**	503-286-0685	308
Columbia Theological Seminary						
701 S Columbia Dr	Decatur	GA	30030	**888-601-8916**	404-378-8821	168-3
Columbia Threadneedle Investments						
1 Financial Ctr	Boston	MA	02111	**800-426-3750**		401
Columbia TriStar Motion Picture Group						
10202 W Washington Blvd	Culver City	CA	90232	**855-327-7669**	310-244-4000	513
Columbia Ultimate Business Systems Inc						
4400 NE 77th Ave Ste 100	Vancouver	WA	98662	**800-488-4420**	360-256-7358	176
Columbia University Press						
61 W 62nd St 3rd Fl	New York	NY	10023	**800-944-8648**	212-459-0600	634-4
Columbia Winery						
14030 NE 145th St						
PO Box 1248	Woodinville	WA	98072	**800-488-2347**	425-488-2776	49-6
Columbia-Greene Community College						
4400 Rt 23	Hudson	NY	12534	**888-668-4293**	518-828-4181	161
Columbia-Montour Visitors Bureau						
121 Papermill Rd	Bloomsburg	PA	17815	**800-847-4810**	570-784-8279	208
Columbian						
701 W Eigth St PO Box 180	Vancouver	WA	98660	**800-743-3391**	360-694-3391	531-2
Columbian Chemicals Co						
1800 W Oak Commons Ct	Marietta	GA	30062	**800-235-4003**	770-792-9400	144
Columbian Park Zoo						
1915 Scott St	Lafayette	IN	47904	**800-438-9926**	765-807-1540	821
Columbus Area Visitors Ctr						
506 Fifth St	Columbus	IN	47201	**800-468-6564**	812-378-2622	208
Columbus Bank & Trust Co						
1148 Broadway	Columbus	GA	31901	**800-334-9007**	706-649-4900	69
Columbus Business First						
303 W Nationwide Blvd	Columbus	OH	43215	**800-486-3289**	614-461-4040	456-5
Columbus Chamber of Commerce						
150 S Front St Ste 200	Columbus	OH	43215	**877-771-5202**	614-221-1321	138
Columbus Civic Ctr						
400 Fourth St	Columbus	GA	31901	**800-745-3000**	706-653-4482	718
Columbus College of Art & Design						
60 Cleveland Ave	Columbus	OH	43215	**877-997-2223**	614-224-9101	163
Columbus Convention & Visitors Bureau						
PO Box 789	Columbus	MS	39703	**800-327-2686**	662-329-1191	208
Columbus Dispatch						
34 S Third St	Columbus	OH	43215	**800-942-2745**	614-461-5000	531-2
Columbus Electric Co-op Inc						
900 N Gold St PO Box 631	Deming	NM	88031	**800-950-2667**	505-546-8838	247
Columbus Industries Inc						
2938 SR-752	Ashville	OH	43103	**800-766-2552**	740-983-2552	18
Columbus Ledger-Enquirer						
17 W 12th St	Columbus	GA	31901	**800-282-7859**	706-324-5526	531-2

Name / Address	City	State	ZIP	Toll-Free	Phone	Class
Columbus Life Insurance Co 400 E Fourth St PO Box 5737	Cincinnati	OH	45201	**800-677-9595**	800-677-9696	391-2
Columbus Marble Works Corp 2415 Hwy 45 N *Cust Svc	Columbus	MS	39705	**800-647-1055***	662-328-1477	722
Columbus McKinnon Corp 140 John James Audubon Pkwy *NASDAQ: CMCO*	Amherst	NY	14228	**800-888-0985**	716-689-5400	469
Columbus Public Library 3000 Macon Rd	Columbus	GA	31906	**800-652-0782**	706-243-2669	434-3
Columbus Regional Hospital 2400 E 17th St	Columbus	IN	47201	**800-841-4938**	812-379-4441	374-3
Columbus State Community College 550 E Spring St	Columbus	OH	43215	**800-621-6407**	614-287-2400	161
Columbus State University 4225 University Ave	Columbus	GA	31907	**866-264-2035**	706-507-8800	167
Columbus Symphony Orchestra 55 E State St	Columbus	OH	43215	**800-745-3000**	614-228-9600	572-3
Columbus Zoo & Aquarium 4850 W Powell Rd	Powell	OH	43065	**800-666-5397**	614-645-3400	821
Column Technologies Inc 1400 Opus Pl Ste 110	Downers Grove	IL	60515	**866-265-8665**	630-515-6660	176
Columns, The 3811 St Charles Ave	New Orleans	LA	70115	**800-445-9308**	504-899-9308	379
Comag Marketing Group LLC 155 Village Blvd 3rd Fl	Princeton	NJ	08540	**866-790-9353**	609-524-1800	94
Comal County 199 Main Plaza	New Braunfels	TX	78130	**877-724-9475**	830-221-1100	338
Comanche Electric Co-op Assn 201 W Wrights Ave	Comanche	TX	76442	**800-915-2533**	325-356-2533	247
Comar Inc 1 Comar Pl	Buena	NJ	08310	**800-962-6627**	856-692-6100	201
Comar LLC 141 N Fifth St	Saddle Brook	NJ	07663	**800-962-6627**	201-909-3400	97
COMARK Communications 104 Feeding Hills Rd	Southwick	MA	01077	**800-288-8364**	413-998-1100	645
Comark Corp 93 W St	Medfield	MA	02052	**800-280-8522**	508-359-8161	175-1
Comark Direct 507 S Main St	Ft. Worth	TX	76104	**888-742-0405**		5
Combe Inc 1101 Westchester Ave	White Plains	NY	10604	**800-431-2610**	914-694-5454	217
CombiMatrix Corp 300 Goddard Ste 100 *NASDAQ: CBMX*	Irvine	CA	92618	**800-710-0624**	949-753-0624	84
Combined Express Inc 3685 Marshall Ln	Bensalem	PA	19020	**800-777-0458**	215-633-1535	312
Combined Technologies Inc 13970 W Polo Trl Dr	Lake Forest	IL	60045	**877-968-4855**	847-968-4855	560
Combined Transport Inc 5656 Crater Lake Ave	Central Point	OR	97502	**800-547-2870**	541-734-7418	778
Comcar Industries Inc 502 E Bridgers Ave *Cust Svc	Auburndale	FL	33823	**800-524-1101***	863-967-1101	778
Comcast Corp 1701 JFK Blvd *NASDAQ: CMCSA*	Philadelphia	PA	19103	**800-266-2278**	215-665-1700	360-3
Comco Inc 2151 N Lincoln St	Burbank	CA	91504	**800-796-6626**	818-841-5500	1
Comdata Corp 5301 Maryland Way	Brentwood	TN	37027	**800-266-3282**	615-370-7000	68
Comdel Inc 11 Kondelin Rd	Gloucester	MA	01930	**800-468-3144**	978-282-0620	255
Comer Packing 1000 Poplar St PO Box 33	Aberdeen	MS	39730	**800-748-8916**	662-369-9325	472
Comerica Bank 411 W Lafayette	Detroit	MI	48226	**800-643-4418**	313-222-3344	69
Comerica Bank-California 333 W Santa Clara St	San Jose	CA	95113	**800-522-2265**	408-556-5300	69
Comerica Bank-Texas 1717 Main St	Dallas	TX	75201	**800-925-2160**		69
Cometic Gasket Inc 8090 Auburn Rd	Concord	OH	44077	**800-752-9850**	440-354-0777	327
Com-Fab Inc 4657 Price HilliaRds Rd	Plain City	OH	43064	**866-522-1794**	740-857-1107	761
ComForcare Senior Services Inc 2520 Telegraph Rd Ste 100	Bloomfield Hills	MI	48302	**800-886-4044**	248-745-9700	311
Comfort Inn & Suites Milwaukee 916 E State St	Milwaukee	WI	53202	**800-424-6423**	414-276-8800	379
Comfort Systems USA Inc 675 Bering Ste 400 *NYSE: FIX*	Houston	TX	77057	**800-723-8431**	713-830-9600	191-10
Comfortex Inc 1680 Wilkie Dr	Winona	MN	55987	**800-445-4007**	507-454-6579	470
Comfortex Window Fashions Inc 21 Elm St *Cust Svc	Maplewood	NY	12189	**800-843-4151***	518-273-3333	86
Command Alkon Inc 1800 International Pk Dr Ste 400	Birmingham	AL	35243	**800-624-1872**	205-879-3282	180-10
Command Ctr Inc 3609 S Wadsworth Blvd Ste 250 *OTC: CCNI*	Lakewood	ID	80235	**866-464-5844**		719
Command Plastic Corp 124 W Ave	Tallmadge	OH	44278	**800-321-8001**	330-434-3497	547
Command Spanish Inc PO Box 1091	Petal	MS	39465	**800-250-8637**	601-582-8378	94
Commander Hotel 1401 Atlantic Ave	Ocean City	MD	21842	**888-289-6166**		379
CommCare Corp 601 Poydras St 2755 Pan American Life Center	New Orleans	LA	70130	**877-792-5434**	504-324-8950	371
Commemorative Brands Inc 7211 Cir S Rd	Austin	TX	78745	**800-225-3687**		634-2
Commenco Inc 4901 Bristol Ave	Kansas City	MO	64129	**800-292-9725**	816-753-2166	733
Commentary Magazine 561 7th Ave 16th Fl	New York	NY	10018	**800-829-6270**	212-891-1400	456-10
Commerce Bank & Trust Co 386 Main St	Worcester	MA	01608	**800-698-2265**	508-797-6842	69

Name / Address	City	State	ZIP	Toll-Free	Phone	Class
Commerce Corp 7603 Energy Pkwy	Baltimore	MD	21226	**800-883-0234**	410-255-3500	429
Commerce Insurance Co 211 Main St	Webster	MA	01570	**800-221-1605**	508-943-9000	391-4
Commercial & Architectural Products Inc PO Box 250	Dover	OH	44622	**800-377-1221**	330-343-6621	498
Commercial Appeal 495 Union Ave	Memphis	TN	38103	**800-444-6397**	901-529-2345	531-2
Commercial Bank 301 N State St PO Box 638 *OTC: CEFC*	Alma	MI	48801	**800-547-8531**	989-463-2185	69
Commercial Driver Training 600 Patton Ave	West Babylon	NY	11704	**800-649-7447**	631-249-1330	798
Commercial Law League of America (CLLA) 70 E Lake St Ste 630	Chicago	IL	60601	**800-978-2552**	312-781-2000	48-10
Commercial Lending Litigation News 360 Hiatt Dr	Palm Beach Gardens	FL	33418	**800-621-5463**	561-622-6520	530-1
Commercial Lighting Industries 81161 Indio Blvd	Indio	CA	92201	**800-755-0155**	760-343-2704	439
Commercial Lumber & Pallet Co 135 Long Ln	City Of Industry	CA	91746	**800-252-4968**		202
Commercial Mailing Accessories Inc 28220 Playmor Beach Rd	Rocky Mount	MO	65072	**800-325-7303**		4
Commercial National Financial Corp 900 Ligonier St *OTC: CNAF*	Latrobe	PA	15650	**800-803-2265**	724-539-3501	360-2
Commercial Programming Systems Inc 4400 Coldwater Canyon Ave	Studio City	CA	91604	**888-277-4562**	323-851-2681	179
Commercial Properties Realty Trust 402 N Fourth St	Baton Rouge	LA	70802	**800-648-9064**	225-924-7206	652
Commercial Siding & Maintenance Co, The 8059 Crile Rd	Painesville	OH	44077	**800-229-4276**	440-352-7800	191-12
Commercial-News 17 W N St	Danville	IL	61832	**877-732-8258**	217-446-1000	531-2
Commission Junction Inc 530 E Montecito St	Santa Barbara	CA	93103	**800-761-1072**	805-730-8000	7
Commission on Accreditation for Dietetics Education (CADE) 120 S Riverside Plz Ste 2000	Chicago	IL	60606	**800-877-1600**	312-899-0040	47-1
Commission on Accreditation for Law Enforcement Agencies (CALEA) 13575 Heathcote Blvd Ste 320	Gainesville	VA	20155	**877-789-6904**	703-352-4225	48-7
Commission on Accreditation in Physical Therapy Education (CAPTE) 1111 N Fairfax St	Alexandria	VA	22314	**800-999-2782**	703-706-3245	47-1
Commission on Accreditation of Allied Health Education Programs (CAAHEP) 1361 Pk St	Clearwater	FL	33756	**800-228-2262**	727-210-2350	47-1
Commission on Accreditation of Rehabilitation Facilities International (CARF) 6951 E Southpoint Rd	Tucson	AZ	85756	**888-281-6531**	520-325-1044	47-1
Commission on Collegiate Nursing Education 1 Dupont Cir NW Ste 530	Washington	DC	20036	**800-441-1414**	202-887-6791	47-1
Commission on Dental Accreditation of Canada 1815 Alta Vista Dr	Ottawa	ON	K1G3Y6	**866-521-2322**	613-523-7114	47-1
Committee for Economic Development (CED) 2000 L St NW Ste 700	Washington	DC	20036	**800-676-7353**	202-296-5860	631
Commodity Futures Trading Commission 1155 21 St NW 1155 21 St NW	Washington	DC	20581	**866-366-2382**	202-418-5000	340-18
Commodity Information Systems Inc 3030 NW Expy Ste 725	Oklahoma City	OK	73112	**800-231-0477**	405-604-8726	634-9
Commodity Research Bureau 330 S Wells St Ste 612	Chicago	IL	60606	**800-621-5271**	312-554-8456	530-9
Commons at Orlando Lutheran Towers, The 300 E Church St	Orlando	FL	32801	**800-859-1033**	407-872-7088	47-20
Commonwealth Biotechnologies Inc 601 Biotech Dr	Richmond	VA	23235	**800-735-9224**	804-648-3820	417
Commonwealth Canvas Inc 5 Perkins Way	Newburyport	MA	01950	**877-922-6827**	978-499-3900	730
Commonwealth Club of California 595 Market St 2nd Fl	San Francisco	CA	94105	**800-933-7548**	415-597-6700	629
Commonwealth Credit Union PO Box 978	Frankfort	KY	40602	**800-228-6420**	502-564-4775	221
Commonwealth Financial Network 29 Sawyer Rd	Waltham	MA	02453	**800-237-0081**	781-736-0700	401
Commonwealth Health Corporation Inc 800 Park St	Bowling Green	KY	42101	**800-786-1581**	270-745-1500	363
Commonwealth Laminating & Coating Inc 345 Beaver Creek Dr *General	Martinsville	VA	24112	**888-321-5111***	276-632-4991	697
Commonwealth Land Title Insurance Co 601 Riverside Ave	Jacksonville	FL	32204	**888-866-3684**		391-6
Commonwealth Park Suites Hotel 901 Bank St	Richmond	VA	23219	**888-343-7301**	804-343-7300	379
Commonwealth Telephone Co 1 Newbury St Ste 103	Peabody	MA	01960	**800-439-7170**	978-536-9500	733
CommScope Inc 1100 Commscope Pl SE PO Box 339	Hickory	NC	28603	**800-982-1708**	828-324-2200	812
Communca Inc 31 N Erie St	Toledo	OH	43604	**800-800-7890**		513
Communibiz Inc Po Box 30062	Billings	MT	59107	**877-266-0979**	406-259-1252	462
Communication Data Services 1901 Bell Ave	Des Moines	IA	50315	**866-897-7987**	515-246-6837	227
Communication Technologies Inc 14151 Newbrook Dr Ste 400	Chantilly	VA	20151	**888-266-8358**	703-961-9080	732
Communications & Power Industries LLC 607 Hansen Way	Palo Alto	CA	94303	**800-231-4818**	650-846-2900	255
Communications Daily 2115 Ward Ct NW	Washington	DC	20037	**800-771-9202**	202-872-9200	530-11
Communications Manufacturing Co (CMC) 2234 Colby Ave *Orders	Los Angeles	CA	90064	**800-462-5532***	310-828-3200	250
Communications News PO Box 866	Osprey	FL	34229	**800-827-9715**	941-539-7579	456-5
Communications Supply Corp (CSC) 200 E Lies Rd	Carol Stream	IL	60188	**800-468-2121**	630-221-6400	248
Communications Supply Service Assn (CSSA) 5700 Murray St	Little Rock	AR	72209	**800-252-2772**	501-562-7666	48-20
Communications Test Design Inc 1339 Enterprise Dr	West Chester	PA	19380	**800-223-3910**	610-436-5203	732

Name / Address	City	State	ZIP	Toll-Free	Phone	Class
CommuniGate Systems Inc						
655 Redwood Hwy Ste 275	Mill Valley	CA	94941	**800-262-4722**	415-383-7164	180-12
Communispond Inc						
12 Barns Ln	East Hampton	NY	11937	**800-529-5925**	631-907-8010	196
Community America Credit Union (CACU)						
9777 Ridge Dr	Lenexa	KS	66219	**800-892-7957**	913-905-7000	221
Community Assns Institute (CAI)						
6402 Arlington Blvd Ste 500	Falls Church	VA	22042	**888-224-4321**	703-970-9220	47-7
Community Bank						
505 E Colorado Blvd	Pasadena	CA	91101	**800-788-9999**		68
Community Bank of Raymore						
PO Box 200	Raymore	MO	64083	**800-322-6772**	816-322-2100	69
Community Bank Shares of Indiana Inc						
101 W Spring St *NASDAQ: YCB*	New Albany	IN	47150	**866-944-2004**	812-944-2224	360-2
Community Bank System Inc						
5790 Widewaters Pkwy *NYSE: CBU*	Syracuse	NY	13214	**800-847-2911**	315-445-2282	360-2
Community Banking Advisory Network (CBAN)						
1801 W End Ave Ste 800	Nashville	TN	37203	**800-231-2524**	615-373-9880	48-2
Community Blood Bank of Northwest Pennsylvania						
2646 Peach St	Erie	PA	16508	**877-842-0631**	814-456-4206	88
Community Blood Ctr						
349 S Main St	Dayton	OH	45402	**800-388-4483**	937-461-3450	88
Blue Springs Ctr 4040 Main St	Kansas City	MO	64111	**888-647-4040**	816-753-4040	88
Gladstone Ctr 7265 N Oak Trafficway	Gladstone	MO	64118	**877-468-6844**	816-468-9813	88
Community Blood Ctr Inc						
4406 W Spencer St	Appleton	WI	54914	**800-280-4102**	920-738-3131	88
Community Blood Ctr of the Ozarks						
220 W Plainview Rd	Springfield	MO	65810	**800-280-5337**	417-227-5000	88
Community Blood Services						
970 Linwood Ave W PO Box 39	Paramus	NJ	07653	**866-228-1500**	201-444-3900	88
Community Blood Services of Illinois						
1408 W University Ave	Urbana	IL	61801	**800-217-4483**	217-367-2202	88
Community Care						
218 W Sixth St	Tulsa	OK	74119	**800-278-7563**	918-594-5200	391-3
Community Care Inc						
1555 S Layton Blvd	Milwaukee	WI	53215	**866-992-6600**	414-385-6600	196
Community Coffee Co						
PO Box 2311	Baton Rouge	LA	70821	**800-688-0990**	800-884-5282	297-7
Community College of Aurora						
16000 E Centretech Pkwy	Aurora	CO	80011	**844-493-8255**	303-360-4700	161
Community College of Baltimore County						
Essex 7201 Rossville Blvd	Baltimore	MD	21237	**877-557-2575**	410-682-6000	161
Community College of Beaver County						
1 Campus Dr	Monaca	PA	15061	**800-335-0222**	724-775-8561	161
Community College of Southern Nevada Planetarium & Observatory						
3200 E Cheyenne Ave	North Las Vegas	NV	89030	**800-630-7563**	702-651-4759	597
Community College of Vermont						
Bennington 324 Main St	Bennington	VT	05201	**800-431-0025**	802-447-2361	161
Brattleboro 70 Landmark Hill Ste 101	Brattleboro	VT	05301	**800-431-0025**	802-254-6370	161
Middlebury 10 Merchants Row Ste 223	Middlebury	VT	05753	**800-431-0025**	802-388-3032	161
Montpelier PO Box 489	Montpelier	VT	05602	**800-228-6686**	802-828-4060	161
Morrisville 197 Harrell St Ste 2	Morrisville	VT	05661	**800-431-0025**	802-888-4258	161
Newport 100 Main St Ste 150	Newport	VT	05855	**800-431-0025**	802-334-3387	161
Rutland 60 W St	Rutland	VT	05701	**800-228-6686**	802-786-6996	161
Upper Valley 145 Billings Farm Rd	White River Junction	VT	05001	**800-431-0025**	802-295-8822	161
Community College System of New Hampshire (CCSNH)						
26 College Dr	Concord	NH	03301	**866-945-2255**	603-271-2722	161
Community Development Digest						
8204 Fenton St	Silver Spring	MD	20910	**800-666-6380**	301-588-6380	530-7
Community Development Partnership						
256 W Beacon Str 256 W Beacon	Philadelphia	MS	39350	**877-752-2643**	601-656-1000	138
Community Electric Co-op						
52 W Windsor Blvd	Windsor	VA	23487	**855-700-2667**	757-242-6181	247
Community Food Bank of New Jersey Inc						
31 Evans Terminal	Hillside	NJ	07205	**866-527-1087**	908-355-3663	47-5
Community Foundation for Greater New Haven						
70 Audubon St	New Haven	CT	06510	**877-829-5500**	203-777-2386	304
Community Health Accreditation Program Inc (CHAP)						
1275 K St NW Ste 800	Washington	DC	20005	**800-656-9656**	202-862-3413	47-1
Community Health Charities						
200 N Glebe Rd Ste 801	Arlington	VA	22203	**800-654-0845**	703-528-1007	47-5
Community Health Funding Week						
8204 Fenton St	Silver Spring	MD	20910	**800-666-6380**	301-588-6380	530-7
Community Health Systems Inc						
4000 Meridian Blvd *NYSE: CYH*	Franklin	TN	37067	**888-373-9600**	615-465-7000	353
Community Hospice						
1480 Carter Ave	Ashland	KY	41101	**800-926-6184**	606-329-1890	371
Community Hospice Inc						
4368 Spyres Way	Modesto	CA	95356	**866-645-4567**	209-578-6300	371
Community Hospice of Northeast Florida						
4266 Sunbeam Rd	Jacksonville	FL	32257	**866-274-6614**	904-268-5200	371
Community Hospice of Texas						
6100 Western Pl Ste 150	Fort Worth	TX	76107	**800-226-0373**	817-870-2795	371
Community Hospital Anderson (CHA)						
1515 N Madison Ave	Anderson	IN	46011	**800-777-7775**	765-298-4242	374-3
Community Hospital of Long Beach						
1720 Termino Ave	Long Beach	CA	90804	**800-994-6610**	562-498-1000	374-3
Community Hospital of the Monterey Peninsula (CHOMP)						
23625 Holman Hwy	Monterey	CA	93940	**888-452-4667**	831-624-5311	374-3
Community Investors Bancorp Inc						
119 S Sandusky Ave *OTC: CIBN*	Bucyrus	OH	44820	**800-222-4955**	419-562-7055	360-2

Name / Address	City	State	ZIP	Toll-Free	Phone	Class
Community Medical Ctr (CMC)						
99 Hwy 37 W	Toms River	NJ	08755	**888-724-7123**	732-557-8000	374-3
Community Newspaper Co Inc						
72 Cherry Hill Dr	Beverly	MA	01915	**800-281-6498**	978-739-1300	634-8
Community of Christ						
1001 W Walnut St	Independence	MO	64050	**800-825-2806**	816-833-1000	47-20
Community Oriented Policing Services (COPS)						
1100 Vermont Ave NW 10th Fl	Washington	DC	20530	**800-421-6770**	202-514-5328	340-12
Community Pharmacies LP						
16 Commerce Dr Ste 1	Augusta	ME	04332	**800-730-4840**		239
Community Professional Loudspeakers						
333 E Fifth St	Chester	PA	19013	**800-523-4934**	610-876-3400	51
Community Resource Federal Credit Union						
20 Wade Rd	Latham	NY	12110	**888-783-2211**	518-783-2211	221
Community Services Group (CSG)						
320 Highland Dr PO Box 597	Mountville	PA	17554	**877-907-7970**	717-285-7121	353
Community Shores Bank Corp						
1030 W Norton Ave *OTC: CSHB*	Muskegon	MI	49441	**888-853-6633**	231-780-1800	360-2
Community Surgical Supply Inc						
1390 Rt 37 W	Toms River	NJ	08755	**800-349-2990**	732-349-2990	476
Community Theater						
100 S St	Morristown	NJ	07960	**888-278-7769**	973-455-1607	745
Community Tissue Services						
3573 Bristol Pike Ste 201	Bensalem	PA	19020	**800-684-7783**	215-245-4506	544
Community Title & Escrow Ltd						
2600 State St Bldg D	Alton	IL	62002	**800-854-4049**	618-466-7755	391-6
Community Transportation Assn of America (CTAA)						
1341 G St NW 10th Fl	Washington	DC	20005	**800-891-0590**	202-628-1480	48-21
Community Trust Bank NA						
346 N Mayo Trl PO Box 2947	Pikeville	KY	41501	**800-422-1090**	606-432-1414	69
Community VNA						
10 Emory St	Attleboro	MA	02703	**800-220-0110**	508-222-0118	371
Comm-Works Holdings LLC						
1405 Xenium Ln N Ste 120	Minneapolis	MN	55441	**800-853-8090**	763-258-5800	254
ComNet Marketing Group Inc						
1214 Stowe Ave	Medford	OR	97501	**877-581-2565**		197
Com-Net Services Inc						
7786 S Commerce Ave	Baton Rouge	LA	70815	**800-676-2137**	225-928-1231	226
Co-Mo Electric Co-op Inc						
29868 Hwy 5 PO Box 220	Tipton	MO	65081	**800-781-0157**	660-433-5521	247
Comox Valley Chamber of Commerce						
2040 Cliffe Ave	Courtenay	BC	V9N2L3	**888-357-4471**	250-334-3234	137
Compaction Technologies Inc						
1171 Northland Dr Ste 121	Mendota Heights	MN	55120	**877-860-6900**		194
Compak Asset Management						
1801 Dove St	Newport Beach	CA	92660	**800-388-9700**		401
Companion Life Insurance Co						
7909 Parklane Rd Ste 200	Columbia	SC	29223	**800-753-0404**	803-735-1251	391-2
Companion Pets Inc (CPI)						
2001 N Black Canyon Hwy	Phoenix	AZ	85009	**800-646-3611**	602-255-0166	577
Companion Professional Services LLC						
1301 Gervais St Ste 1700	Columbia	SC	29201	**800-780-1170**	803-765-1310	179
Companions & Homemakers Inc						
613 New Britain Ave	Farmington	CT	06032	**800-348-4663**	860-677-4948	808
Compass Bancshares Inc						
15 S 20th St	Birmingham	AL	35233	**800-266-7277**	205-297-3584	360-2
Compass Collective						
2150 Button Gwinnett Dr	Atlanta	GA	30340	**800-492-3402**	404-875-6543	8
Compass Cove Ocean Resort						
2311 S Ocean Blvd	Myrtle Beach	SC	29577	**800-331-0934**	843-448-8373	667
Compass Group North American Div (CGNAD)						
2400 Yorkmont Rd	Charlotte	NC	28217	**800-357-0012**	704-328-4000	300
Compass Minerals International						
9900 W 109th St Ste 100 *NYSE: CMP* ■ *Cust Svc	Overland Park	KS	66210	**866-755-1743***	913-344-9200	678
Compassion & Choices						
PO Box 101810	Denver	CO	80250	**800-247-7421**	303-639-1202	47-17
Compassion Canada						
985 Adelaide St S	London	ON	N6E4A3	**800-563-5437**	519-668-0224	47-20
Compassion International						
12290 Voyager Pkwy	Colorado Springs	CO	80921	**800-336-7676**	719-487-7000	47-5
Compassionate Care Hospice						
3331 St Rd Ste 410	Bensalem	PA	19020	**800-584-8165**	215-245-3525	371
Compassionate Care Hospice of Delaware						
702 Wilmington Ave *General	Wilmington	DE	19805	**800-219-0092***	302-993-9090	371
Compassionate Friends						
PO Box 3696	Oak Brook	IL	60522	**877-969-0010**	630-990-0010	47-21
CompassLearning Inc						
203 Colorado St	Austin	TX	78701	**800-232-9556**	512-478-9600	180-3
Compatico Inc						
4710 44th St SE	Grand Rapids	MI	49512	**800-336-1772**	616-940-1772	351
CompBenefits Corp						
100 Mansell Ct E Ste 400	Roswell	GA	30076	**800-633-1262**	770-552-7101	391-3
Compensation Resources Inc						
310 Rt 17 N	Upper Saddle River	NJ	07458	**877-934-0505**	201-934-0505	196
Competition Cams Inc						
3406 Democrat Rd	Memphis	TN	38118	**800-999-0853**	901-795-2400	59
Competitor Magazine						
9477 Waples St Ste 150	San Diego	CA	92121	**800-311-1255**		456-20
Compex Inc						
7918 Jones Branch Dr	Mclean	VA	22102	**800-279-8891**	503-873-0188	178
Compex Legal Services Inc						
325 S Maple Ave *Cust Svc	Torrance	CA	90503	**800-426-6739***		444
CompHealth Inc						
6440 S Millrock Dr Ste 175 Ste 175	Salt Lake City	UT	84121	**800-453-3030**	801-930-3000	719
Complemar Partners						
500 Lee Rd Ste 200	Rochester	NY	14606	**800-388-7254**	585-647-5800	554
Complete Payroll Processing Inc						
7488 SR- 39 Po Box 190	Perry	NY	14530	**888-237-5800**	585-237-5800	2
Complete Pharmacy Care Inc						
4206 Dalrock Rd	Rowlett	TX	75088	**866-804-6937**	972-675-3300	240
CompleteCampaigns.com Inc						
3635 Ruffin Rd 3rd Fl	San Diego	CA	92123	**888-217-9600**		387

Name / Address	City	State	Zip	Toll-Free	Phone	Class
Complex Steel & Wire Corp 36254 Annapolis St	Wayne	MI	48184	800-521-0666	734-326-1600	308
Compmanagement Inc PO Box 884	Dublin	OH	43017	800-825-6755	614-376-5300	462
Component Enterprises Co Inc 235 E Penn St PO Box 189	Norristown	PA	19401	877-232-7253		813
Component Hardware Group Inc 1890 Swarthmore Ave	Lakewood	NJ	08701	800-526-3694	732-363-4700	350
ComponentOne LLC 201 S Highland Ave Third Fl 3rd Fl	Pittsburgh	PA	15206	800-858-2739	412-681-4343	180-12
Components Distributors Inc 2601 Blake St Ste 200	Denver	CO	80205	800-777-7334		248
Comporium Communications 332 E Main St	Rock Hill	SC	29730	866-922-5922	888-403-2667	733
Composite Panel Assn 19465 Deerfield Ave Ste 306	Leesburg	VA	20176	866-426-6767	703-724-1128	48-3
Composition Materials Company Inc 249 Pepes Farm Rd	Milford	CT	06460	800-262-7763	203-874-6500	1
Comprehensive Care Management Corp (CCM) 1250 Waters Pl Tower 1 Ste 602	Bronx	NY	10461	877-226-8500		449
Comprehensive EAP 4 Mt Royal Ave	Marlborough	MA	01752	800-344-1011		461
Comprehensive Financial Planning Inc 1075 Main Ave Ste 216	Durango	CO	81301	877-901-5227	970-385-5227	196
Comprehensive Health Services Inc (CHSI) 10701 Parkridge Blvd Ste 200	Reston	VA	20191	800-638-8083	703-760-0700	391-3
Comprehensive Pharmacy Services Inc (CPS) 6409 N Quail Hollow Rd	Memphis	TN	38120	800-968-6962	901-748-0470	196
Comprehensive Tissue Ctr 11402 University Ave Rm 7415	Edmonton	AB	T6G2J3	866-407-1970	780-407-7510	544
Compressed Air Systems Inc 9303 Stannum St	Tampa	FL	33619	800-626-8177	813-626-8177	174
Compressor Engineering Corp (CECO) 5440 Alder Dr	Houston	TX	77081	800-879-2326	713-664-7333	174
Compressor Products International 4410 Greenbriar Dr	Stafford	TX	77477	800-675-6646	281-207-4600	127
ComPsych Corp 455 N City Front Plaza Dr NBC Tower 13th Fl	Chicago	IL	60611	800-851-1714	312-595-4000	461
Comptroller of the Currency 250 E St SW *Cust Svc	Washington	DC	20219	800-613-6743*	202-874-5000	340-16
CompuCom Systems Inc 7171 Forest Ln *Cust Svc	Dallas	TX	75230	800-597-0555*	972-856-3600	178
Compu-data International LLC 431 Nursery Rd Ste A300	Spring	TX	77380	866-936-6069	281-292-1333	179
Compugen Inc 100 Via Renzo Dr	Richmond Hill	ON	L4S0B8	800-387-5045	905-707-2000	395
Compulink Inc 1205 Gandy Blvd N	Saint Petersburg	FL	33702	800-231-6685	727-579-1500	812
CompuMed Inc 5777 W Century Blvd Ste 360	Los Angeles	CA	90045	800-421-3395	310-258-5000	419
Compunetix Inc 2420 Mosside Blvd	Monroeville	PA	15146	800-879-4266	412-373-8110	732
Compunnel Software Group Inc 103 Morgan Ln Ste 102	Plainsboro	NJ	08536	800-696-8128		719
CompuOne Corp 9888 Carroll Centre Rd Ste 201	San Diego	CA	92126	888-226-6781	858-404-7000	198
Compusearch Software Systems Inc 21251 Ridgetop Cir	Dulles	VA	20166	855-817-2720	571-449-4000	179
Computer Aid Inc (CAI) 1390 Ridgeview Dr	Allentown	PA	18104	877-432-7228	610-530-5000	179
Computer Aided Technology Inc 165 N Arlington Heights Rd Ste 101	Buffalo Grove	IL	60089	888-308-2284		176
Computer Analytical Systems Inc (CASI) 1418 S Third St	Louisville	KY	40208	800-977-3475	502-635-2019	182
Computer Arts Inc 320 SW Fifth Ave	Meridian	ID	83642	800-365-9335	208-385-9335	179
Computer Credit Inc 470 W Hanes Mill Rd Ste 200	Winston-Salem	NC	27105	800-942-2995	336-761-1524	159
Computer Dynamics Inc 3030 Whitehall Pk Dr	Charlotte	NC	28273	866-599-6512		176
Computer Economics Report, The 2082 Business Ctr Dr Ste 240	Irvine	CA	92612	800-326-8100	949-831-8700	530-3
Computer Explorers 12715 Telge Rd	Cypress	TX	77429	800-531-5053		147
Computer Guidance Corp 15035 N 75th St	Scottsdale	AZ	85260	888-361-4551	480-444-7000	179
Computer Magazine 10662 Los Vaqueros Cir *Orders	Los Alamitos	CA	90720	800-272-6657*	714-821-8380	456-7
Computer Power Solutions Inc 4644 Katella Ave	Los Alamitos	CA	90720	800-444-1938	562-493-4487	182
Computer Pundits Corp 6515 Cecilia Cir	Bloomington	MN	55439	888-786-3487	952-854-2422	182
Computer Sciences Corp 2100 E Grand Ave *NYSE: CSC*	El Segundo	CA	90245	866-310-0950	310-615-0311	182
Computer Services Inc 3901 Technology Dr *OTC: CSVI*	Paducah	KY	42001	800-545-4274	270-442-7361	227
Computer Task Group Inc (CTG) 800 Delaware Ave *OTC: CTG*	Buffalo	NY	14209	800-992-5350	716-882-8000	182
Computer Technology Law Report 1801 S Bell St	Arlington	VA	22202	800-372-1033		530-7
Computer Troubleshooters USA 755 Commerce Dr Ste 605	Decatur	GA	30030	877-704-1702	800-877-0020	311
Computer Workshop Inc, The 5131 Post Rd Ste 102	Dublin	OH	43017	800-639-3535	614-798-9505	762
ComputerJobs.com Inc 1995 N Pk Pl SE	Atlanta	GA	30339	800-850-0045	770-850-0045	262
ComputerPlus Sales & Service Inc 5 Northway Ct	Greer	SC	29651	800-849-4426		177
Computers in Libraries Magazine 143 Old Marlton Pk	Medford	NJ	08055	800-300-9868	609-654-6266	456-7
Computers Unlimited 2407 Montana Ave	Billings	MT	59101	800-763-0308	406-255-9500	180-10
Computerwise Inc 302 N Winchester Ln	Olathe	KS	66062	800-255-3739	913-829-0600	175-7
Computerworks of Chicago Inc 5153 N Clark St	Chicago	IL	60640	800-977-8212	773-275-4437	179
Computerworld Magazine 1 Speen St	Framingham	MA	01701	800-343-6474	508-879-0700	456-7
Computrition Inc 19808 Nordhoff Pl	Chatsworth	CA	91311	800-222-4488		179
Compuware Corp 1 Campus Martius St *NASDAQ: CPWR*	Detroit	MI	48226	800-292-7432	313-227-7300	180-1
comScore Inc 11950 Democracy Dr # 600	Reston	VA	20190	866-276-6972	703-438-2000	465
Comstar Enterprises Inc PO Box 6698	Springdale	AR	72766	800-533-2343	479-361-2111	47-11
ComStar Networks LLC 1820 NE Jensen Beach Blvd Ste 564	Jensen Beach	FL	34957	800-516-1595		197
Comstock Resources Inc 5300 Town & Country Blvd Ste 500 *NYSE: CRK*	Frisco	TX	75034	800-929-4884	972-668-8800	535
Comstor Inc 14850 Conference Ctr Dr Ste 200	Chantilly	VA	20151	800-955-9590	703-345-5100	176
Comstor Productivity Ctr Inc 441 W Sharp Ave	Spokane	WA	99201	800-776-2451	509-534-5080	495
ComTech21 1 Barnes Park S	Wallingford	CT	06492	877-312-5564		387
Comtel Corp 39810 Grand River Ave Ste 180	Novi	MI	48375	800-335-2505	248-888-4730	248
Comtrol Corp 100 Fifth Ave NW	Maple Grove	MN	55112	800-926-6876	763-494-4100	178
Comware Technical Services Inc 17922 Sky Park Cir Ste E	Irvine	CA	92614	800-460-1970	949-851-9600	177
Comwave Networks Inc 61 Wildcat Rd	Toronto	ON	M3J2P5	877-474-6638	416-663-9700	387
Con Cast Pipe LP 299 Brock Rd S RR#3	Guelph	ON	N1H6H9	800-668-7473		185
Con Forms 777 Maritime Dr	Port Washington	WI	53074	800-223-3676	262-284-7800	185
ConAgra Foods Foodservice Co 5 ConAgra Dr	Omaha	NE	68102	800-357-6543		298-6
ConAgra Foods Inc 1 ConAgra Dr *NYSE: CAG*	Omaha	NE	68102	877-266-2472	402-240-4000	360-3
ConAgra Foods Retail Products Co Deli Foods Group 215 W Field Rd	Naperville	IL	60563	877-266-2472	630-857-1000	472
Conair Corp 1 Cummings Pt Rd *OTC: CNGA*	Stamford	CT	06902	800-326-6247	203-351-9000	36
Conant Auto Retail Group 18900 Studebaker Rd	Cerritos	CA	90703	888-318-5001		56
Conax Buffalo Technologies LLC 2300 Walden Ave	Buffalo	NY	14225	800-223-2389	716-684-4500	203
Concentra Inc 5080 Spectrum Dr Ste 1200 W	Addison	TX	75001	866-944-6046		462
Concentrix Corp 3750 Monroe Ave	Pittsford	NY	14534	800-747-0583	585-218-5300	112
Concept Boats Corp 2410 NW 147th St	Opa Locka	FL	33054	888-635-8712	305-635-8712	89
Concepts Av Integration 3712 S 132nd St	Omaha	NE	68144	877-422-3933	402-298-5011	609
Concepts In Data Management Inc 205 Oxford St E	London	ON	N6A5G6	800-668-8768		181
Concepts NREC 217 Billings Farm Rd	White River Junction	VT	05001	888-299-8057	802-296-2321	263
ConceptShare Inc 130 Slater St	Ottawa	ON	K1P6E2	844-227-7848	613-903-4431	387
Conceptual Financial Planning Inc 3962 N Richmond St Ste B	Appleton	WI	54913	800-300-9500	920-731-9500	688
Concern America 2015 N Broadway	Santa Ana	CA	92706	800-266-2376	714-953-8575	47-5
Concerned United Birthparents Inc (CUB) PO Box 503475	San Diego	CA	92150	800-822-2777		47-21
Concerns of Police Survivors Inc (COPS) 846 Old S 5 PO Box 3199	Camdenton	MO	65020	800-784-2677	573-346-4911	47-21
Concerto Marketing Group Inc 128 Hastings St W	Vancouver	BC	V6B1G8	877-873-2738	604-684-8933	7
Conch House Heritage Inn 625 Truman Ave	Key West	FL	33040	800-207-5806	305-293-0020	379
Conch House Marina Resort 57 Comares Ave	Saint Augustine	FL	32080	800-940-6256	904-829-8646	379
Concierge Communications LLC 4801 S Lkshore Dr Ste 106	Tempe	AZ	85282	888-624-2643		115
Concord Academy 166 Main St	Concord	MA	01742	800-768-2983	978-402-2200	621
Concord Coalition 1011 Arlington Blvd Ste 300	Arlington	VA	22209	888-333-4248	703-894-6222	47-7
Concord Confections Ltd 345 Courtland Ave	Concord	ON	L4K5A6	800-267-0037	905-660-8989	297-6
Concord Group Insurance Cos 4 Bouton St	Concord	NH	03301	800-852-3380		391-4
Concord Litho Group 92 Old Tpke Rd	Concord	NH	03301	800-258-3662	603-225-3328	626
Concord Regional Visiting Nurse Assoc Hospice Program 30 Pillsbury St	Concord	NH	03301	800-924-8620	603-224-4093	371
Concord Road Equipment Manufacturing Inc 348 Chester St	Painesville	OH	44077	800-942-7623	440-357-5344	56
Concord Servicing Corp 4150 N Drinkwater Blvd	Scottsdale	AZ	85251	866-493-6393		318
Concord University PO Box 1000	Athens	WV	24712	800-344-6679	304-384-3115	167
Concorde Career Colleges 5800 Foxridge Dr Ste 500	Mission	KS	66202	800-693-7010	913-831-9977	798

	City	State	ZIP	Toll-Free	Phone	Class
Concorde Career Colleges Inc						
San Bernardino						
201 E Airport Dr	San Bernardino	CA	92408	**800-852-8434**	909-884-8891	798
San Diego						
4393 Imperial Ave Ste 100	San Diego	CA	92113	**800-693-7010**	619-688-0800	798
Concorde Career Colleges inc Miramar						
10933 Marks Way	Miramar	FL	33025	**800-693-7010**	954-731-8880	798
Concordia College						
901 Eigth St S	Moorhead	MN	56562	**800-699-9897**	218-299-4000	167
Concordia College New York						
171 White Plains Rd	Bronxville	NY	10708	**800-937-2655***	914-337-9300	167
*Admissions						
Concordia Electric Co-op Inc						
1865 Hwy 84 W PO Box 98	Jonesville	LA	71343	**800-617-6282**	318-339-7969	247
Concordia Hospital						
1095 Concordia Ave	Winnipeg	MB	R2K3S8	**888-315-9257**	204-667-1560	374-2
Concordia Language Villages						
8659 Thorsonveien Rd	Bemidji	MN	56601	**800-450-2214**	218-586-8600	241
Concordia Publishing House Inc						
3558 S Jefferson Ave	Saint Louis	MO	63118	**800-325-3040***	314-268-1000	634-3
*Cust Svc						
Concordia Seminary						
801 Seminary Pl	Saint Louis	MO	63105	**800-822-9545**	314-505-7000	168-3
Concordia Theological Seminary						
6600 N Clinton St	Fort Wayne	IN	46825	**800-481-2155**	260-452-2100	168-3
Concordia University						
1455 de Maisonneuve Blvd W	Montreal	QC	H3G1M8	**866-333-2271**	514-848-2424	783
Concordia University Ann Arbor						
4090 Geddes Rd	Ann Arbor	MI	48105	**888-282-2338**	734-995-7322	167
Concordia University Austin						
3400 IH-35 N	Austin	TX	78705	**800-865-4282**	512-486-2000	167
Concordia University Chicago						
7400 Augusta St	River Forest	IL	60305	**888-258-6773**	708-771-8300	167
Concordia University College of Alberta						
7128 Ada Blvd NW	Edmonton	AB	T5B4E4	**866-479-5200**	780-479-9220	783
Concordia University Irvine						
1530 Concordia W	Irvine	CA	92612	**800-229-1200**	949-854-8002	167
Concordia University Nebraska						
800 N Columbia Ave	Seward	NE	68434	**800-535-5494**	402-643-3651	167
Concordia University Portland						
2811 NE Holman St	Portland	OR	97211	**800-321-9371**	503-288-9371	167
Concordia University Wisconsin						
12800 N Lake Shore Dr	Mequon	WI	53097	**888-628-9472***	262-243-5700	167
*Admissions						
Concurrent						
4375 River Green Pkwy Ste 100	Duluth	GA	30096	**877-978-7363**	678-258-4000	180-8
NASDAQ: CCUR						
Conde Group Inc						
4141 Jutland Dr Ste 130	San Diego	CA	92117	**800-838-0819**		198
Conder Flag Co						
4705 Dwight Evans Rd	Charlotte	NC	28217	**800-868-3524**		556
Condo Control Central						
10 St Mary St Ste 200	Toronto	ON	M5X1C7	**888-762-6636**		226
Condon Oil Co						
126 E Jackson St	Ripon	WI	54971	**800-452-1212**	920-748-3186	578
Condor Earth Technologies Inc						
21663 Brian Ln	Sonora	CA	95370	**800-800-0490**	209-532-0361	196
Condor Outdoor Products						
5268 Rivergrade Rd	Irwindale	CA	91706	**800-552-2554**		709
Conductix 10102 F St	Omaha	NE	68127	**800-521-4888**	402-339-9300	116
Conduit Pipe Products Co						
1501 W Main St	West Jefferson	OH	43162	**800-848-6125**	614-879-9114	814
Condusiv Technologies						
7590 N Glenoaks Blvd	Burbank	CA	91504	**800-829-6468***	818-771-1600	180-12
*Sales						
Condustrial Inc						
105 East N St	Greenville	SC	29601	**888-794-7798**	864-235-3619	262
Cone Drive Operations Inc - A Textron Co						
240 E 12th St	Traverse City	MI	49685	**888-994-2663***	231-946-8410	707
*Sales						
Conestoga Capital Advisors LLC						
259 N Radnor Chester Rd Radnor Ct						
Ste 120	Radnor	PA	19087	**800-320-7790**	484-654-1380	401
Conestoga Valley School District						
2110 Horseshoe Rd	Lancaster	PA	17601	**800-732-0025**	717-397-2421	683
Conestoga Wood Specialties Inc						
245 Reading Rd	East Earl	PA	17519	**800-964-3667**		114
CoNetrix LLC						
5214 68th St Ste 200	Lubbock	TX	79424	**800-356-6568**	806-687-8600	179
Conexant Systems Inc						
1901 Main St Ste 300	Irvine	CA	92614	**888-855-4562**	949-483-4600	694
Confer Plastics Inc (CPI)						
97 Witmer Rd	North Tonawanda	NY	14120	**800-635-3213**	716-693-2056	603
Conference & Travel						
5655 Coventry Ln	Fort Wayne	IN	46804	**800-346-9807**	260-434-6600	186
Conference & Visitors Bureau of Montgomery County MD Inc						
111 Rockville Pk Ste 800	Rockville	MD	20850	**877-789-6904**	240-777-2060	208
Conference Ctr at NorthPointe						
100 Green Meadows Dr S	Lewis Center	OH	43035	**866-233-9393**	614-880-4300	377
Conference of State Bank Supervisors (CSBS)						
1129 20th St NW 5th Fl	Washington	DC	20036	**800-886-2727**	202-296-2840	48-7
Conference on College Composition & Communication (CCCC)						
1111 W Kenyon Rd	Urbana	IL	61801	**877-369-6283**	217-328-3870	48-5
Confident Care Corp						
3 University Plz Dr Ste 340	Hackensack	NJ	07601	**866-839-2273**	201-498-9400	363
Confluence Watersports Co						
575 Mauldin Rd Ste 200	Greenville	SC	29607	**800-595-2925**		708
Confluent Translations LLC						
340 Mansfield Ave	Pittsburgh	PA	15220	**888-539-9077**	412-539-1410	7
Conforma Laboratories Inc						
4705 Colley Ave	Norfolk	VA	23508	**800-426-1700**	757-321-0200	541
Conglom Inc						
2600 Marie-Curie Ave	Saint-Laurent	QC	H4S2C3	**877-333-0098**	514-333-6666	600
Congoleum Corp						
3500 Quakerridge Rd						
PO Box 3127	Mercerville	NJ	08619	**800-274-3266**	609-584-3000	293
Congress Watch						
215 Pennsylvania Ave SE	Washington	DC	20003	**800-289-3787**	202-546-4996	47-7

	City	State	ZIP	Toll-Free	Phone	Class
Conifer Park						
79 Glenridge Rd	Schenectady	NY	12302	**800-989-6446**	518-399-6446	724
Conifex Timber Inc						
980 700 W Georgia St						
PO Box 10070	Vancouver	BC	V7Y1B6	**866-301-2949**	604-216-2949	281
Conine Clubhouse						
1005 Joe DiMaggio Dr	Hollywood	FL	33021	**866-532-4362**	954-265-5324	372
CONIX Systems Inc						
7252 Main St	Manchester Center	VT	05255	**800-332-1899**		179
Conjur Inc						
460 Totten Pond Rd	Waltham	MA	02451	**855-648-5919**		387
Conklin Company Inc						
551 Valley Pk Dr	Shakopee	MN	55379	**800-888-8838**	952-445-6010	366
Conlin Travel Inc						
3270 Washtenaw Ave	Ann Arbor	MI	48104	**800-426-6546**	734-677-0900	769
Conmed Corp						
525 French Rd	Utica	NY	13502	**800-448-6506**	315-797-8375	475
NASDAQ: CNMD						
ConMed Endoscopic Technologie						
525 French Rd	Utica	NY	13502	**800-225-1332**	315-797-8375	475
CONMED Linvatec						
11311 Concept Blvd	Largo	FL	33773	**800-448-6506***	727-392-6464	475
*Cust Svc						
Conn's Inc						
3295 College St	Beaumont	TX	77701	**800-511-5750***	409-832-1696	34
NASDAQ: CONN ■ *Cust Svc						
Conneaut Savings Bank						
305 Main St PO Box 740	Conneaut	OH	44030	**888-453-2311**	440-599-8121	69
Connect America LLC						
2193 W Chester Pk	Broomall	PA	19008	**800-654-6100**		474
Connect PR						
1 Market St 36th Fl	San Francisco	CA	94105	**800-455-8855**	415-222-9691	633
Connect Tech Inc						
42 Arrow Rd	Guelph	ON	N1K1S6	**800-426-8979**	519-836-1291	182
Connected Nation Inc						
444 N Capitol St, NW	Washington	DC	20001	**877-846-7710**		465
ConnectiCare Inc						
175 Scott Swamp Rd	Farmington	CT	06032	**800-251-7722***	860-674-5700	391-3
*Cust Svc						
Connecticut						
Banking Dept						
260 Constitution Plaza	Hartford	CT	06103	**800-831-7225**	860-240-8299	339-7
Chief Medical Examiner						
11 Shuttle Rd	Farmington	CT	06032	**800-842-1508**	860-679-3980	339-7
Consumer Protection Dept						
165 Capitol Ave	Hartford	CT	06106	**800-842-2649**	860-713-6100	339-7
Emergency Management and Homeland Security Div						
25 Sigourney St 6th Fl	Hartford	CT	06106	**800-397-8876**	860-256-0800	339-7
Higher Education Dept						
61 Woodland St	Hartford	CT	06105	**800-842-0229**	860-947-1800	339-7
Public Utility Control Dept						
10 Franklin Sq	New Britain	CT	06051	**800-382-4586**	860-827-2935	339-7
Rehabilitation Services Bureau						
25 Sigourney St 11th Fl	Hartford	CT	06106	**800-537-2549**	860-424-4844	339-7
State Parks Div						
79 Elm St	Hartford	CT	06106	**866-287-2757**	860-424-3000	339-7
Veterans Affairs Dept						
287 W St	Rocky Hill	CT	06067	**800-447-0961**	860-721-5891	339-7
Victim Services Office						
225 Spring St 4th Fl	Wethersfield	CT	06109	**800-822-8428**		339-7
Workers' Compensation Commission						
21 Oak St 4th Fl	Hartford	CT	06106	**800-223-9675**	860-493-1500	339-7
Connecticut Assn of Realtors						
111 Founders Plz Ste 1101	East Hartford	CT	06108	**800-335-4862**	860-290-6601	654
Connecticut College						
270 Mohegan Ave	New London	CT	06320	**800-892-3363**	860-439-2000	167
Connecticut Innovations Inc						
865 Brook St 3rd Fl	Rocky Hill	CT	06067	**800-733-4763**	860-563-5851	790
Connecticut Laminating Company Inc						
162 James St	New Haven	CT	06513	**800-753-9119**	203-787-2184	598
Connecticut Light & Power Co						
107 Selden St	Berlin	CT	06037	**800-286-2000***	860-665-5000	785
*Cust Svc						
Connecticut Magazine						
35 Nutmeg Dr	Trumbull	CT	06611	**800-645-4328**	203-380-6600	456-22
Connecticut Medicine Magazine						
160 St Ronan St	New Haven	CT	06511	**800-842-8440**	203-865-0587	456-16
Connecticut Public Broadcasting Inc (CPBI)						
1049 Asylum Ave	Hartford	CT	06105	**800-683-2112**	860-278-5310	629
Connecticut Real Estate & Professional Trades Div						
Dept of Consumer Protection						
165 Capitol Ave	Hartford	CT	06106	**800-842-2649**	860-713-6100	339-7
Connecticut State Library						
231 Capitol Ave	Hartford	CT	06106	**866-886-4478**	860-757-6510	434-5
Connecticut State Medical Society						
160 St Ronan St	New Haven	CT	06511	**800-406-1527**	203-865-0587	473
Connecticut Valley Arms (CVA)						
1685 Boggs Rd Ste 300	Duluth	GA	30096	**800-320-8767**	770-449-4687	286
Connecticut Valley Railroad State Park						
1 Railroad Ave PO Box 452	Essex	CT	06426	**866-526-2014**	860-767-0103	564
Connecticut Water Service Inc						
93 W Main St	Clinton	CT	06413	**800-286-5700**	860-669-8636	360-5
NASDAQ: CTWS						
Connecticut Weights & Measures Div						
Dept of Consumer Protection						
165 Capitol Ave	Hartford	CT	06106	**800-842-2649**	860-713-6100	339-7
Connecting Businessmen to Christ (CBMC)						
5746 Marlin Rd						
Ste 602 Osborne Ctr	Chattanooga	TN	37411	**800-566-2262**	423-698-4444	47-20
Connecting Generations						
100 W Tenth St Ste 1115	Wilmington	DE	19801	**877-202-9050**	302-656-2122	47-6
Connection, The						
11351 Rupp Dr	Burnsville	MN	55337	**800-883-5777***	952-948-5488	734
*Sales						
Connectria Hosting						
10845 Olive Blvd Ste 300	Saint Louis	MO	63141	**800-781-7820**	314-587-7000	38
ConnectWise Inc						
4110 George Rd Ste 200	Tampa	FL	33634	**800-671-6898**	813-463-4700	181

Alphabetical Section

Name	Address	City	State	ZIP	Toll-Free	Phone	Class
Connell Bros Co Ltd	345 California St 27th Fl	San Francisco	CA	94104	**800-210-9839**	415-772-4000	145
Connell's Map Lee Flowers & Gifts	2408 E Main St	Bexley	OH	43209	**800-790-8980**	614-237-8653	294
Conner Ash PC	12101 Woodcrest Exec Dr 300	Saint Louis	MO	63141	**877-366-1690**	314-205-2510	2
Conner Prairie Living History Museum	13400 Allisonville Rd	Fishers	IN	46038	**800-966-1836**	317-776-6000	519
Connexus Energy Co-op	14601 Ramsey Blvd	Ramsey	MN	55303	**877-382-4357**	763-323-2650	247
Connors Investor Services Inc	1210 Broadcasting Rd Ste 200	Wyomissing	PA	19610	**877-376-7418**	610-376-7418	401
Connors State College	700 College Rd	Warner	OK	74469	**888-594-5171**	918-463-2931	161
Conolog Corp	5 Columbia Rd; *OTC: CNLG*	Somerville	NJ	08876	**800-526-3984**	908-722-8081	645
Conoptics International Sales Corp	19 Eagle Rd	Danbury	CT	06810	**800-748-3349**	203-743-3349	543
Conrac Inc	5124 Commerce Dr	Baldwin Park	CA	91706	**800-451-5288**	626-480-0095	175-4
Conrad Forest Products	68765 Wildwood Dr	North Bend	OR	97459	**800-356-7146**		816
Conrad Schmitt Studios Inc	2405 S 162nd St	New Berlin	WI	53151	**800-969-3033**	262-786-3030	188
Conrad-American Inc	PO Box 2000; *General	Houghton	IA	52631	**800-553-1791***		275
Conroe Regional Medical Ctr	504 Medical Ctr Blvd	Conroe	TX	77304	**888-633-2687**	936-539-1111	374-3
Conseco Annuity Assurance Co	11825 N Pennsylvania St	Carmel	IN	46032	**866-595-2255**		391-2
Conseco Inc	11825 N Pennsylvania St; *NYSE: CNO*	Carmel	IN	46032	**866-595-2255**		360-4
Conseco Senior Health Insurance Co	11825 N Pennsylvania St	Carmel	IN	46032	**866-595-2255**		391-2
Consensus Orthopedics Inc	1115 Windfield Way Ste 100	El Dorado Hills	CA	95762	**800-638-2041**	916-355-7100	476
Conservation Fund	1655 N Fort Myer Dr Ste 1300	Arlington	VA	22209	**877-347-7550**	703-525-6300	47-13
Conservation International (CI)	2011 Crystal Dr Ste 500	Arlington	VA	22202	**800-406-2306**	703-341-2400	47-13
CONSOL Energy Inc	1000 Consol Energy Dr; *NYSE: CNX*	Canonsburg	PA	15317	**800-544-8024**	724-485-4000	360-3
Consolidated Bottle Corp	77 Union St	Toronto	ON	M6N3N2	**800-561-1354**	416-656-7777	453
Consolidated Casting Corp	1501 S I-45	Hutchins	TX	75141	**800-649-5289**	972-225-7305	307
Consolidated Catfish Cos LLC	299 S St PO Box 271	Isola	MS	38754	**800-228-3474**	662-962-3101	297-14
Consolidated Container Co (CCC)	3101 Towercreek Pkwy Ste 300; *Sales	Atlanta	GA	30339	**888-831-2184***	678-742-4600	547
Consolidated Devices Inc (CDI)	19220 San Jose Ave	City of Industry	CA	91748	**800-525-6319**	626-965-0668	756
Consolidated Disposal Services Inc	12949 Telegraph Rd	Santa Fe Springs	CA	90670	**800-299-4898**		802
Consolidated Edison Inc	4 Irving Pl; *NYSE: ED*	New York	NY	10003	**800-752-6633**	212-460-4600	360-5
Consolidated Electric Co-op	3940 E Liberty St	Mexico	MO	65265	**800-621-0091**	573-581-3630	247
Consolidated Electronic Wire & Cable Co	11044 King St	Franklin Park	IL	60131	**800-621-4278**	847-455-8830	812
Consolidated Energy Co	910 Main St	Jesup	IA	50648	**800-338-3021**	319-827-1211	578
Consolidated Fibers	8100 S Blvd	Charlotte	NC	28273	**800-243-8621**		604-1
Consolidated Metco Inc	13940 N Rivergate Blvd; *Sales	Portland	OR	97203	**800-547-9473***		59
Consolidated Publishing Co	PO Box 189	Anniston	AL	36202	**866-814-9253**	256-236-1551	634-8
Consolidated Rail Corp	1717 Arch St Ste 3210	Philadelphia	PA	19103	**800-272-0911**	215-209-2000	646
Consolidated Shoe Company Inc	22290 Timberlake Rd	Lynchburg	VA	24502	**800-368-7463**	434-239-0391	302
Consolidated Steel Services Inc	632 Glendale Vly Blvd	Fallentimber	PA	16639	**800-237-8783**	814-944-5890	491
Consolidated Storage Cos	225 Main St; *Cust Svc	Tatamy	PA	18085	**800-323-0801***	610-253-2775	288
Consolidated Supply Co	7337 SW Kable Ln	Tigard	OR	97224	**800-929-5810**	503-620-7050	611
Consortium for School Networking (CoSN)	1025 Vermont Ave NW Ste 1010	Washington	DC	20005	**866-267-8747**	202-861-2676	47-9
Constantine's Wood Ctr	1040 E Oakland Pk Blvd	Fort Lauderdale	FL	33334	**800-443-9667**	954-561-1716	612
Constellation Brands Inc	207 High Pt Dr Bldg 100; *NYSE: STZ*	Victor	NY	14564	**888-724-2169**		80-3
Constellation Technology Corp	7887 Bryan Dairy Rd Ste 100	Largo	FL	33777	**800-335-7355**	727-547-0600	220
Constitutional Rights Foundation	601 S Kingsley Dr	Los Angeles	CA	90005	**800-488-4273**	213-487-5590	47-7
Construction Claims Monthly	2222 Sedwick Rd	Durham	NC	27713	**800-223-8720**		530-13
Construction Financial Management Assn (CFMA)	100 Village Blvd Ste 200A	Princeton	NJ	08540	**877-462-7827**	609-452-8000	48-1
Construction Labor Report	1801 S Bell St	Arlington	VA	22202	**800-372-1033**		530-13
Construction Metals LLC	13169 B Slover Ave	Fontana	CA	92337	**800-576-9810**	909-390-9880	238
Construction Products Inc	1631 Ashport Rd	Jackson	TN	38305	**800-238-8226**	731-668-7305	185
Construction Software Technologies Inc	4500 W Lake Forest Drive Ste 502	Cincinnati	OH	45242	**800-364-2059**	513-645-8004	180-10
Construction Specialties Inc	3 Werner Way	Lebanon	NJ	08833	**800-972-7214**	908-236-0800	490
Construction Systems Software Inc	494 Covered Bridge	Schertz	TX	78154	**800-531-1035**	210-979-6494	180-10
Constructors Association of Western Pennsylvania	1201 Banksville Rd	Pittsburgh	PA	15216	**877-343-2297**	412-343-8000	136
Construx Software	11820 Northup Way Ste E-200	Bellevue	WA	98005	**866-296-6300**	425-636-0100	179
Consult Usa Inc	634 Alpha Dr	Pittsburgh	PA	15238	**866-963-8621**	412-963-8621	179
Consultnet LLC	10813 S River Front Pkwy Ste 150	South Jordan	UT	84095	**888-215-9675**	801-208-3700	719
Consumer Bankruptcy News	360 Hiatt Dr	Palm Beach Gardens	FL	33418	**800-621-5463**	561-622-6520	530-1
Consumer Federation of America (CFA)	1620 I St NW Ste 200	Washington	DC	20006	**877-382-4357**	202-387-6121	47-10
Consumer Financial Services Law Report	360 Hiatt Dr	Palm Beach Gardens	FL	33418	**800-621-5463**	561-622-6520	530-7
Consumer Product Safety Commission (CPSC)	4340 E W Hwy Ste 502	Bethesda	MD	20814	**800-638-2772**	301-504-7923	340-18
Consumer Reports Magazine	101 Truman Ave; *Orders	Yonkers	NY	10703	**800-333-0663***	914-378-2000	456-11
Consumer Reports On Health	101 Truman Ave	Yonkers	NY	10703	**800-234-1645**	914-378-2000	530-8
Consumers Energy	2074 242nd St	Marshalltown	IA	50158	**800-696-6552**	641-752-1593	247
Consumers Energy Co	1 Energy Plz; *Cust Svc	Jackson	MI	49201	**800-477-5050***	517-788-0550	785
Consumers Pipe & Supply Co	5832 E 61st St	Los Angeles	CA	90040	**800-338-7473**	323-685-6870	491
Consumers Power Inc (CPI)	6990 W Hills Rd PO Box 1180	Philomath	OR	97370	**800-872-9036**	541-929-3124	247
Consumers Union of US Inc	101 Truman Ave	Yonkers	NY	10703	**800-927-4357**	914-378-2000	634-9
Consumers' Research Council of America (CRCA)	2020 Pennsylvania Ave NW Ste 300-A	Washington	DC	20006	**877-774-6337**	202-835-9698	47-10
Contact 101 Inc	777 N Rainbow Blvd Ste 250	Las Vegas	NV	89107	**888-731-2397**		465
Contact Industries Inc	9200 SE Sunnybrook Blvd Ste 200	Clackamas	OR	97015	**800-547-1038**	503-228-7361	498
Contact Lens Manufacturers Assn	PO Box 29398	Lincoln	NE	68529	**800-344-9060**	402-465-4122	48-4
Contactpointe of Pittsburgh	2593 Wexford Bayne Rd Ste 200	Sewickley	PA	15143	**877-255-4916**	412-788-0680	379
Container Research Corp (CRC)	1 Hollow Hill Rd	Glen Riddle	PA	19037	**844-220-9574**	610-459-2160	200
Container Store, The	500 Freeport Pkwy	Coppell	TX	75019	**800-733-3532**	972-538-6000	362
ContainerWorld Forwarding Services Inc	16133 Blundell Rd	Richmond	BC	V6W0A3	**877-838-8880**	604-276-1300	312
Contech Construction Products Inc	9025 Centre Pt Dr Ste 400	West Chester	OH	45069	**800-338-1122**	513-645-7000	695
Con-Tech Lighting	2783 Shermer Rd	Northbrook	IL	60062	**800-728-0312**	847-559-5500	439
Contemar Silo Systems Inc	30 Pennsylvania Ave Unit 8	Concord	ON	L4K4A5	**800-567-2741**	905-669-3604	297
Contemporary Arts Ctr	900 Camp St	New Orleans	LA	70130	**800-568-6968**	504-528-3805	571
Contemporary Tours	1400 Old Country Rd Ste 100	Westbury	NY	11590	**800-627-8873**	516-484-5032	758
Content Management Corp	37900 Central Ct	Newark	CA	94560	**877-495-3720**	510-505-1100	626
Conterra Ultra Broadband LLC	2101 Rexford Rd Ste 200E	Charlotte	NC	28211	**800-634-1374**	704-936-1800	650
Contiki Holidays	801 E Katella Ave 3rd Fl	Anaheim	CA	92805	**800-944-5708**	714-935-0808	758
Continental Airlines Inc	900 Grand Plz Dr	Houston	TX	77067	**800-621-7467**	713-952-1630	26
Continental Assurance Co	333 S Wabash Ave	Chicago	IL	60604	**800-251-2148**	312-822-5000	391-2
Continental Battery Corp	4919 Woodall St	Dallas	TX	75247	**800-442-0081**	214-631-5701	73
Continental Binder & Specialty Corp	407 W Compton Blvd	Gardena	CA	90248	**800-872-2897**	310-324-8227	85
Continental Cast Stone Manufacturing Inc	22001 W 83rd St	Shawnee	KS	66227	**800-989-7866**		722
Continental Casualty Co	333 S Wabash Ave	Chicago	IL	60685	**800-262-2000**	312-822-5000	391-4
Continental Cement Company LLC	14755 N Outer 40 Ste 514	Chesterfield	MO	63017	**800-625-1144**	636-532-7440	134
Continental Coin Corp	5627 Sepulveda Blvd	Van Nuys	CA	91411	**800-552-6467**	818-781-4232	411
Continental Concession Supplies Inc	575 Jericho Turnpike Ste 300	Jericho	NY	11753	**800-516-0090**	516-739-8777	298-3
Continental Electric Motors Inc	23 Sebago St	Clifton	NJ	07013	**800-335-6718**		517
Continental Electronics Corp	4212 S Buckner Blvd	Dallas	TX	75227	**800-733-5011**	214-381-7161	645
Continental Fire Sprinkler Co	4518 S 133rd St	Omaha	NE	68137	**800-543-5170**	402-330-5170	609
Continental Graphics Corp	4060 N Lakewood Blvd Bldg 801 5th Fl	Long Beach	CA	90808	**800-862-5691**	714-503-4200	227
Continental Linen Services	4200 Manchester Rd	Kalamazoo	MI	49001	**800-878-4357**		442
Continental Loose Leaf Inc	1122 16th Ave	Minneapolis	MN	55414	**888-719-5013**	612-378-4800	85
Continental Manufacturing Co	305 Rock Industrial Pk Dr	Bridgeton	MO	63044	**800-325-1051**	314-656-4301	507
Continental Maritime of San Diego Inc	1995 Bay Front St	San Diego	CA	92113	**877-631-0020**	619-234-8851	696

Name / Address	City	State	ZIP	Toll-Free	Phone	Class
Continental Motors Inc 2039 Broad St	Mobile	AL	36615	**800-718-3411**	251-438-3411	21
Continental Resources Inc 175 Middlesex Tpke	Bedford	MA	01730	**800-937-4688**	781-275-0850	178
Continental Safety Equipment 2935 Waters Rd Ste 140	Eagan	MN	55121	**800-844-7003**	651-454-7233	677
Continental Service Group Inc 200 Cross Keys Office Pk	Fairport	NY	14450	**800-724-7500**	585-421-1000	159
Continental Studwelding Ltd 35 Devon Rd	Brampton	ON	L6T5B6	**800-848-9442**	905-792-3650	480
Continental Tire North America Inc 1800 Continental Blvd	Charlotte	NC	28273	**877-235-0102**	704-583-3900	752
Continental Traffic Service Inc (CTSI) 5100 Poplar Ave 15th Fl	Memphis	TN	38137	**888-836-5135**	901-766-1500	312
Continental Western Group 11201 Douglas Ave	Urbandale	IA	50322	**800-235-2942**	515-473-3000	391-4
Contingent Workforce Solutions Inc 2430 Meadowpine Blvd Ste 101	Mississauga	ON	L5N6S2	**866-837-8630**		2
Continucare Corp 7200 Corporate Ctr Dr Ste 600	Miami	FL	33126	**866-312-7154**	305-500-2000	363
Continuing Care Accreditation Commission (CARF-CCAC) 1730 Rhode Island Ave NW Ste 209	Washington	DC	20036	**866-888-1122**	202-587-5001	47-1
Continuum 3150 Central Expy	Santa Clara	CA	95051	**888-532-1064**	408-727-3240	425
Contour Saws Inc 900 Graceland Ave	Des Plaines	IL	60016	**800-259-6834**		680
Contours Express Inc 156 Imperial Way	Nicholasville	KY	40356	**855-589-9662**		354
Contra Costa County Library 75 Santa Barbara Rd	Pleasant Hill	CA	94523	**800-984-4636**	925-646-6423	434-3
Contra Costa Health Services 2500 Alhambra Ave	Martinez	CA	94553	**877-661-6230**	925-370-5000	374-3
Contract Design Magazine 770 Broadway	New York	NY	10004	**800-697-8859**		456-5
Contract Land Staff LLC 2245 Texas Dr Ste 200	Sugar Land	TX	77479	**800-874-4519**	281-240-3370	196
Contractors Register Inc 800 E Main St PO Box 500	Jefferson Valley	NY	10535	**800-431-2584**		634-6
Contractors Steel Co 36555 Amrhein Rd	Livonia	MI	48150	**800-521-3946**	734-464-4000	491
Contrex Inc 8900 Zachary Ln N	Maple Grove	MN	55369	**800-342-4411**	763-424-7800	205
Control Flow Inc 9201 Fairbanks N Houston Rd	Houston	TX	77064	**800-231-9922**	281-890-8300	788
Control Line Equipment Inc 14750 Industrial Pkwy	Cleveland	OH	44135	**888-895-1440**	216-433-7766	225
Controlled Access Inc 1515 W 130th St	Hinckley	OH	44233	**800-942-0829**	330-273-6185	636
Controlled Contamination Services LLC 4182 Sorrento Valley Blvd	San Diego	CA	92121	**888-263-9886**	858-457-7598	258
Controlled Power Co 1955 Stephenson Hwy	Troy	MI	48083	**800-521-4792**	248-528-3700	765
Controls Southeast Inc PO Box 7500	Charlotte	NC	28241	**877-788-3030**	704-588-3030	594
Convention & Visitors Bureau of Marion County 1000 Cole St Ste A	Fairmont	WV	26554	**800-834-7365**	304-368-1123	208
Convention & Visitors Bureau-Village of Pinehurst Southern Pines Aberdeen Area 10677 Hwy 15-501	Southern Pines	NC	28387	**800-346-5362**	910-692-3330	208
Conventus Orthopaedics Inc 10200 73rd Ave N Ste 122	Maple Grove	MN	55369	**855-418-6466**	763-515-5000	476
Convergent Wealth Advisors LLC 12505 Park Potomac Ave Ste 400	Potomac	MD	20854	**888-444-6347**	301-770-6300	689
ConvergeOne LLC 3344 Hwy 149	Eagan	MN	55121	**888-321-6227**		387
Convergex Holdings LLC 1633 Broadway 48th Fl	New York	NY	10019	**800-367-8998**	212-468-7713	688
Convergys Corp 201 E Fourth St *NYSE: CVG*	Cincinnati	OH	45202	**888-284-9900**	513-723-7000	734
Converse College 580 E Main St *Admissions	Spartanburg	SC	29302	**800-766-1125***	864-596-9000	167
Conveyco Technologies Inc PO Box 1000	Bristol	CT	06011	**800-229-8215**	860-589-8215	385
Conveyer & Caster Corp 3501 Detroit Ave	Cleveland	OH	44113	**800-777-0600**	216-631-4448	351
Conveyor Components Co 130 Seltzer Rd *Cust Svc	Croswell	MI	48422	**800-233-3233***	810-679-4211	209
Conway Cemetery State Park 140 Boat Dock Cove Rd 1 Capitol Mall	Bull Shoals	AR	72169	**888-287-2757**		564
Con-Way Freight 2211 Old Earhart Rd	Ann Arbor	MI	48105	**800-755-2728**	734-994-6600	778
Conway Import Co Inc 11051 W Addison St	Franklin Park	IL	60131	**800-323-8801**	847-455-5600	297-19
Conway Marketing Communications 6400 Baum Dr	Knoxville	TN	37919	**800-882-7875**	865-588-5731	7
Conway Regional Hospital 2302 College Ave	Conway	AR	72032	**800-245-3314**	501-329-3831	374-3
Cook Aviation Inc 970 S Kirby Rd	Bloomington	IN	47403	**800-880-3499**	812-825-2392	62
Cook Biotech Inc 1425 Innovation Pl	West Lafayette	IN	47906	**888-299-4224**	765-497-3355	84
Cook Communications Ministries 4050 Lee Vance View	Colorado Springs	CO	80918	**800-708-5550**	719-536-0100	634-9
Cook Hotel & Conference Ctr 3848 W Lakeshore Dr	Baton Rouge	LA	70808	**866-610-2665**	225-383-2665	377
Cook Inc PO Box 4195	Bloomington	IN	47402	**800-457-4500**	812-339-2235	475
Cook Medical Inc 1186 Montgomery Ln *General	Vandergrift	PA	15690	**800-457-4500***	724-845-8621	475
Cook Moving Systems Inc 1845 Dale Rd	Buffalo	NY	14225	**800-828-7144**		518
Cook Truck Equipment & Tools 3701 Harlee Ave	Charlotte	NC	28208	**800-241-4210**	704-392-4138	56
Cook Urological Inc PO Box 4195	Bloomington	IN	47402	**800-457-4500**	812-339-2235	475
Cook's Ham Inc 200 S Second St	Lincoln	NE	68508	**800-332-8400**	402-475-6700	297-26
Cook's Illustrated Magazine PO Box 470739 *Circ	Brookline	MA	02447	**800-526-8442***	617-232-1000	456-11
Cookbook Publishers Inc 9825 Widmer Rd	Lenexa	KS	66215	**800-227-7282**	913-492-5900	625
Cooke County Electric Co-op 11799 W US Hwy 82 PO Box 530	Muenster	TX	76252	**800-962-0296**	940-759-2211	247
Cooke Trucking Co Inc 1759 S Andy Griffith Pkwy	Mount Airy	NC	27030	**800-888-9502**	336-786-5181	778
Cookeville Area-Putnam County Chamber of Commerce 1 W First St	Cookeville	TN	38501	**800-264-5541**	931-526-2211	138
Cookies By Design Inc 1865 Summit Ave Ste 605	Plano	TX	75074	**800-945-2665**	972-398-9536	311
Cookies The Kids Department Store 510 Fulton St	Brooklyn	NY	11201	**877-942-6654**	718-797-3300	231
Cooking & Hospitality Institute of Chicago 361 W Chestnut St *Admissions	Chicago	IL	60610	**877-828-7772***	312-944-0882	162
Cooking Light Magazine 2100 Lakeshore Dr	Birmingham	AL	35209	**800-366-4712**	205-445-6000	456-13
Cookshack 2304 N Ash St	Ponca City	OK	74601	**800-423-0698**	580-765-3669	361
Cookson Co 2417 S 50th Ave	Phoenix	AZ	85043	**800-294-4358**	602-272-4244	236
Cookson Hills Electric Co-op Inc 1002 E Main St	Stigler	OK	74462	**800-328-2368**	918-967-4614	247
CookTek LLC 156 N Jefferson St Ste 300	Chicago	IL	60661	**888-266-5835**	312-563-9600	35
Cool Gear International LLC 10 Cordage Park Cir	Plymouth	MA	02360	**855-393-2665**		361
Cool Polymers Inc 51 Circuit Dr	North Kingstown	RI	02852	**888-811-3787**	401-739-7602	607
Coolant Control Inc 5353 Spring Grove Ave	Cincinnati	OH	45217	**800-535-3885**	513-471-8770	145
Cooley Godward Kronish LLP 3000 El Camino Real	Palo Alto	CA	94306	**888-654-2411**	650-843-5000	428
Cooley Group 50 Esten Ave *Cust Svc	Pawtucket	RI	02860	**800-992-0072***	401-724-9000	742-2
Cooley Motors Corp 401 N Greenbush Rd	Rensselaer	NY	12144	**888-518-0245**	518-283-2902	56
Coon Brent & Associates Law Firm Pc 215 Orleans St	Beaumont	TX	77701	**866-335-2666**	409-835-2666	428
Coontail Corner 5466 Park St	Boulder Junction	WI	54512	**888-874-0885**	715-385-2582	709
Co-op America 1612 K St NW Ste 600	Washington	DC	20006	**800-584-7336**	202-872-5307	47-13
Co-op Communciations Inc 412 Washington Ave	Belleville	NJ	07079	**800-833-2700**		733
Co-op Elevator Co 7211 E Michigan Ave	Pigeon	MI	48755	**800-968-0601**	989-453-4500	277
Co-op Feed Dealers Inc 380 Broome Corporate Pkwy PO Box 670 *Cust Svc	Conklin	NY	13748	**800-333-0895***	607-651-9078	278
Co-op Finance Assn Inc, The 10100 N Ambassador Dr Ste 315 PO Box 901532	Kansas City	MO	64153	**877-835-5232**	816-214-4200	218
CO-OP Financial Services Inc 9692 Haven Ave	Rancho Cucamonga	CA	91730	**800-782-9042**		393
Cooper Atkins Corp 33 Reeds Gap Rd *Sales	Middlefield	CT	06455	**800-835-5011***	860-349-3473	203
Cooper B-Line Inc 509 W Monroe St	Highland	IL	62249	**800-851-7415**	618-654-2184	814
Cooper Bussmann Inc 114 Old State Rd	Ellisville	MO	63021	**855-287-7626**	636-394-2877	813
Cooper Cos Inc 6140 Stoneridge Mall Rd Ste 590 *NYSE: COO*	Pleasanton	CA	94588	**888-822-2660**	925-460-3600	541
Cooper Crouse-Hinds 1201 Wolf St	Syracuse	NY	13208	**866-764-5454**	315-477-5531	813
Cooper Farms 22348 County Rd 140 PO Box 547	Oakwood	OH	45873	**800-423-2765**	419-594-3325	10-7
Cooper Hotel & Conference Ctr 12230 Preston Rd	Dallas	TX	75230	**800-444-5187**	972-386-0306	379
Cooper Industries 600 Travis St Ste 5400 *NYSE: ETN*	Houston	TX	77002	**866-853-4293**	713-209-8400	813
Cooper Legal Services Dwayne e Cooper Atty at Law 8411 Tuskin Way	Indianapolis	IN	46278	**800-959-1825**	317-873-3600	428
Cooper Motors Inc 985 York St	Hanover	PA	17331	**866-414-2809**		56
Cooper Tire & Rubber Co 701 Lima Ave *NYSE: CTB*	Findlay	OH	45840	**800-854-6288**	419-423-1321	752
Cooper Union for the Advancement of Science & Art 30 Cooper Sq	New York	NY	10003	**800-872-2777**	212-353-4100	167
Cooper University Hospital 3 Cooper Plz	Camden	NJ	08103	**800-826-6737**	856-342-2000	374-3
Cooper Wellness Program 12230 Preston Rd	Dallas	TX	75230	**800-444-5192**	972-386-4777	704
Cooper Wiring Devices Inc 203 Cooper Cir *Cust Svc	Peachtree City	GA	30269	**866-853-4293***	770-631-2100	813
Coopers Rock State Forest 61 County Line Dr	Bruceton Mills	WV	26525	**800-225-5982**	304-594-1561	564
Cooper-smith Adv LLC 4444 Bennett Rd	Toledo	OH	43612	**800-215-8812**	419-470-5900	4
CooperSurgical Inc 95 Corporate Dr	Trumbull	CT	06611	**800-645-3760**	203-929-6321	475

Name / Address	City	State	Zip	Toll-Free	Phone	Class
CooperVision Inc 209 High Point Dr Ste 200	Victor	NY	14564	**800-538-7850**	585-385-6810	541
Coordinating Research Council Inc (CRC) 3650 Mansell Rd Ste 140	Alpharetta	GA	30022	**800-445-8667**	678-795-0506	48-19
Coors Credit Union 816 Washington Ave	Golden	CO	80401	**800-770-6414**	303-279-6414	221
CoorsTek Inc 600 Ninth St	Golden	CO	80401	**800-821-6110**	303-278-4000	251
Coos Bay-North Bend Visitor & Convention Bureau 50 Central Ave	Coos Bay	OR	97420	**800-824-8486**	541-269-0215	208
Coosa Pines Federal Credit Union 17591 Plant Rd	Childersburg	AL	35044	**800-237-9789**	256-378-5559	221
COPE Inc 1120 G St NW Ste 550	Washington	DC	20005	**800-247-3054**	202-628-5100	461
Cope Plastics Inc 4441 Industrial Dr	Godfrey	IL	62002	**800-851-5510**	618-466-0221	602
Copesan Services Inc W175 N5711 Technology Dr	Menomonee Falls	WI	53051	**800-267-3726**		576
Copia International Ltd 1220 Iroquois Dr Ste 180 *Sales	Naperville	IL	60563	**800-689-8898***	630-778-8898	175-3
Copic Insurance Co 7351 Lowry Blvd	Denver	CO	80230	**800-421-1834**	720-858-6000	391-5
Copiers Northwest Inc 601 Dexter Ave N	Seattle	WA	98109	**866-692-0700**	206-282-1200	111
Copley Hospital Inc 528 Washington Hwy	Morrisville	VT	05661	**888-833-8329**	802-888-8888	374-3
Copley Place 100 Huntington Ave Ste 100	Boston	MA	02116	**877-746-6642**	617-262-6600	459
Copley Square Hotel 47 Huntington Ave	Boston	MA	02116	**800-225-7062**	617-536-9000	379
Copper Development Assn Inc 260 Madison Ave 16th Fl	New York	NY	10016	**800-232-3282**	212-251-7200	48-13
Copper Hills Youth Ctr 5899 Rivendell Dr	West Jordan	UT	84081	**800-776-7116**		374-1
Copper Mountain College 6162 Rotary Way	Joshua Tree	CA	92252	**866-366-3791**	760-366-3791	161
Copper Mountain Resort 209 Ten Mile Cir PO Box 3001	Copper Mountain	CO	80443	**888-219-2441**	970-968-2882	667
Copper Valley Electric Assn Inc (CVEA) Mile 187 Glenn Hwy PO Box 45	Glennallen	AK	99588	**866-835-2832**	907-822-3211	247
Copperas Cove Independent School District 703 W Ave D	Copperas Cove	TX	76522	**866-632-9992**	254-547-1227	683
CopperWynd Resort & Club 13225 N Eagle Ridge Dr	Fountain Hills	AZ	85268	**877-707-7760**	480-333-1900	667
Coppin State University 2500 W N Ave *Admissions	Baltimore	MD	21216	**800-635-3674***	410-951-3600	167
Copple, Rockey, Mckeever & Schlecht PC LLO 2425 Taylor Ave	Norfolk	NE	68701	**888-860-2425**	402-371-4300	428
COPS (Community Oriented Policing Services) 1100 Vermont Ave NW 10th Fl	Washington	DC	20530	**800-421-6770**	202-514-5328	340-12
COPS (Concerns of Police Survivors Inc) 846 Old S 5 PO Box 3199	Camdenton	MO	65020	**800-784-2677**	573-346-4911	47-21
Copy Cat Printing 365 N Broadwell Ave	Grand Island	NE	68803	**800-400-8520**	308-384-8520	626
Copyright Clearance Ctr Inc (CCC) 222 Rosewood Dr	Danvers	MA	01923	**855-239-3415**	978-750-8400	48-16
Coquille Myrtle Grove State Natural Site PO Box 569	Myrtle Point	OR	97458	**800-551-6949**		564
Coral Beach Resort & Suites 1105 S Ocean Blvd	Myrtle Beach	SC	29577	**800-843-2684**	800-556-1754	667
Coral Chemical Co 1915 Industrial Ave	Zion	IL	60099	**800-228-4646**	847-246-6666	144
Coral Color Process Ltd 50 Mall Dr	Commack	NY	11725	**800-564-7303**	631-543-5200	626
Coral Gables Hospital Inc (CGH) 3100 Douglas Rd	Coral Gables	FL	33134	**866-728-3677**	305-445-8461	374-3
Coral Kay Resort 2300 Caravelle Cir	Kissimmee	FL	34746	**866-357-3682**	407-787-0718	705
Coral Reef Restaurant 1701 Atlantic Ave	Ocean City	MD	21842	**866-627-8483**	410-289-2612	669
Coral Springs Auto Mall 9400 W Atlantic Blvd	Coral Springs	FL	33071	**800-353-8660**	954-369-1016	56
Coram Healthcare Corp 555 17th St Ste 1500	Denver	CO	80202	**800-267-2642**		363
Corban College 5000 Deer Pk Dr SE	Salem	OR	97317	**800-845-3005**	503-581-8600	167
Corbett Lighting Inc 14508 Nelson Ave	City of Industry	CA	91744	**800-533-8769**	626-336-4511	439
Corbin 2360 Technology Pkwy	Hollister	CA	95023	**800-538-7035**	831-634-1100	516
Corbin Russwin Inc 225 Episcopal Rd	Berlin	CT	06037	**800-438-1951**	860-225-7411	350
Corbin Turf & Ornamental Supply 1105 Old Buncombe Rd	Greenville	SC	29617	**800-476-4504**	864-233-2113	366
Corbis Corp 710 Second Ave Ste 200	Seattle	WA	98104	**800-260-0444**	646-613-4000	592
Corby Industries Inc 1501 E Pennsylvania St *Sales	Allentown	PA	18109	**800-652-6729***	610-433-1412	690
Corcoran Group Inc, The 660 Madison Ave	New York	NY	10021	**800-544-4055**	212-355-3550	650
Cord Sets Inc 1015 Fifth St N	Minneapolis	MN	55411	**800-752-0580**	612-337-9700	813
Cordis Corp 14201 NW 60th Ave	Miami Lakes	FL	33014	**800-327-7714**	800-447-7585	475
CORE (Center for Organ Recovery & Education) 204 Sigma Dr RIDC Pk	Pittsburgh	PA	15238	**800-366-6777**	412-963-3550	271
Core Bts Inc 201 W 103rd St Ste 240	Indianapolis	IN	46290	**855-267-3287**		112
Core Management Resources Group Inc 515 Mulberry St	Macon	GA	31201	**888-741-2673**	478-741-3521	198
Core Medical Imaging Inc 6161 Ne 175th St Ste 201	Kenmore	WA	98028	**800-809-9729**	425-485-4330	474
Core Vision IT Solutions 1266 NW Hwy	Palatine	IL	60067	**855-788-5835**		198
Corel Corp 1600 Carling Ave *Orders	Ottawa	ON	K1Z8R7	**800-772-6735***	613-728-8200	180-8
CoreLogic SafeRent 7300 Westmore Rd Ste 3	Rockville	MD	20850	**866-873-3651**		632
CoreNet Global Inc 260 Peachtree St NW Ste 1500	Atlanta	GA	30303	**800-726-8111**	404-589-3200	48-17
CoreSource Inc 400 Field Dr	Lake Forest	IL	60045	**800-832-3332**	847-604-9200	585
CoreTech 550 American Ave Ste 301	King of Prussia	PA	19406	**800-220-3337**		196
Corey Steel Co 2800 S 61st Ct	Cicero	IL	60804	**800-323-2750**	708-735-8000	721
Coriell Institute for Medical Research 403 Haddon Ave	Camden	NJ	08103	**800-752-3805**	856-966-7377	666
Corinth Area Convention & Visitors Bureau 215 N Fillmore St	Corinth	MS	38834	**800-748-9048**	662-287-8300	208
Corinth National Cemetery 1551 Horton St	Corinth	MS	38834	**800-273-8255**	901-386-8311	135
Corinthian Colleges Inc 6 Hutton Centre Dr Ste 400 *NASDAQ: COCO*	Santa Ana	CA	92707	**888-370-7589**	916-431-6959	244
Corinthian Partners LLC 850 Third Ave Ste 16C	New York	NY	10022	**800-899-8950**	212-287-1500	688
Corizon 105 Westpark Dr Ste 200	Brentwood	TN	37027	**800-729-0069**		462
Corken Inc 3805 NW 36th St	Oklahoma City	OK	73112	**800-631-4929**	405-946-5576	638
Corn Belt Energy Corp 1 Energy Way	Bloomington	IL	61705	**800-879-0339**	309-662-5330	247
Corn Palace 604 N Main St	Mitchell	SD	57301	**800-289-7469**	605-995-8430	49-2
Corn Stock Theatre 1700 Pk Rd	Peoria	IL	61604	**800-220-1185**	309-676-2196	572-4
Cornelia de Lange Syndrome Foundation Inc (CdLS) 302 W Main St Ste 100	Avon	CT	06001	**800-753-2357**	860-676-8166	47-17
Cornelius Seed Corn Co 14760 317th Ave	Bellevue	IA	52031	**800-218-1862**	563-672-3463	297-20
Cornell College 600 First St SW *Admissions	Mount Vernon	IA	52314	**800-747-1112***	319-895-4215	167
Cornell Iron Works Inc 24 Elmwood Rd	Mountain Top	PA	18707	**800-233-8366**	570-474-6773	236
Cornell Plantations 1 Plantations Rd	Ithaca	NY	14850	**800-269-8368**	607-255-2400	96
Cornell University Press 750 Cascadilla St PO Box 6525 *Sales	Ithaca	NY	14850	**800-666-2211***	607-277-2338	634-4
Corner Bakery Cafe 12700 Pk Central Dr Ste 1300 *General	Dallas	TX	75251	**800-309-4642***	972-619-4100	67
CornerCap Investment Counsel Inc 1355 Peachtree St NE The Peachtree Ste 1700	Atlanta	GA	30309	**800-728-0670**	404-870-0700	527
Cornerstone Advisors Asset Management Inc 74 W Broad St Ste 340	Bethlehem	PA	18018	**800-923-0900**	610-694-0900	401
Cornerstone Group 2100 Hollywood Blvd	Hollywood	FL	33020	**800-809-4099**	305-443-8288	651
Cornerstone Medical Arts Ctr Hospital 159-05 Union Tpke	Fresh Meadows	NY	11366	**800-233-9999**	718-906-6700	724
Cornerstone Systems Inc 3250 Players Club Pkwy	Memphis	TN	38125	**800-278-7677**	901-842-0660	196
Cornerstone University 1001 E Beltline Ave NE *Admissions	Grand Rapids	MI	49525	**800-787-9778***	616-222-1426	167
Cornhusker Bank 1101 Cornhusker Hwy	Lincoln	NE	68521	**877-837-4481**	402-434-2265	69
Cornhusker Casualty Co PO Box 2048	Omaha	NE	68103	**888-495-8949**		391-4
Cornhusker Hotel, The 333 S 13th St	Lincoln	NE	68508	**866-706-7706**	402-474-7474	379
Cornhusker Public Power District 23169 235th Ave PO Box 9	Columbus	NE	68602	**800-955-2773**	402-564-2821	247
Cornhusker State Industries 800 Pioneers Blvd	Lincoln	NE	68502	**800-348-7537**	402-471-4597	629
Corning Area Chamber of Commerce 1 W Market St Ste 302	Corning	NY	14830	**866-463-6264**	607-936-4686	138
Corning Cable Systems 800 17th St NW	Hickory	NC	28603	**800-743-2671**	828-901-5000	812
Corning Hospital 176 Denison Pkwy E	Corning	NY	14830	**877-750-2042**	607-937-7200	374-3
Corning Inc Life Sciences Div 836 N St Bldg 300 Ste 3401	Tewksbury	MA	01876	**800-492-1110**	978-442-2200	419
Corning Museum of Glass 1 Museum Way *Cust Svc	Corning	NY	14830	**800-732-6845***	607-937-5371	519
Cornish College of the Arts 710 E Roy St	Seattle	WA	98121	**800-726-2787**	206-323-1400	163
Cornucopia Tool & Plastics Inc 448 Sherwood Rd PO Box 1915	Paso Robles	CA	93447	**800-235-4144**	805-369-0030	255
Cornwall Community Hospital 840 McConnell Ave	Cornwall	ON	K6H5S5	**866-263-1560**	613-938-4240	374-2
Cornwall Manor 1 Boyd St	Cornwall	PA	17016	**800-222-2476**	717-273-2647	670
Cornwell Data Services Inc 352 Evelyn St	Paramus	NJ	07652	**866-981-1050**	201-261-1050	227
Cornwell Quality Tools 667 Seville Rd	Wadsworth	OH	44281	**800-321-8356**	330-336-3506	756
Corona Brushes Inc 5065 Savarese Cir	Tampa	FL	33634	**800-458-3483**	813-885-2525	102
Corona Clipper Inc 22440 Tomasco Canyon Rd	Corona	CA	92883	**800-234-2547**	951-737-6515	429
Corotec Corp 145 Hyde Rd	Farmington	CT	06032	**800-423-0348**	860-678-0038	386

	Toll-Free	Phone	Class
Corp for National & Community Service			
AmeriCorps USA 1201 New York Ave NW .... Washington DC 20525	800-833-3722	202-606-5000	340-18
Learn & Serve America 1201 New York Ave NW .... Washington DC 20525	800-833-3722	202-606-5000	340-18
Senior Corps 1201 New York Ave NW .... Washington DC 20525	800-833-3722	202-606-5000	340-18
Corpak Medsystems Inc 1001 Asbury Dr .... Buffalo Grove IL 60089	800-323-6305	847-403-3400	475
CorpCare Assoc Inc 7000 Peachtree Dunwoody Rd Bldg 4 Ste 300 .... Atlanta GA 30328	800-728-9444		461
Corporate Accountability International 10 Milk St Ste 610 .... Boston MA 02108	800-688-8797	617-695-2525	47-8
Corporate Air LLC 15 Allegheny County Airport .... West Mifflin PA 15122	888-429-5377	412-469-6800	62
Corporate Business Solutions LLC 600 S Tower 225 Peachtree St NE .... Atlanta GA 30303	800-239-8182	404-521-6030	569
Corporate Compliance & Regulatory 1617 JFK Blvd Ste 1750 .... Philadelphia PA 19103	877-256-2472	215-557-2300	530-7
Corporate Disk Co 4610 Crime Pkwy .... McHenry IL 60050	800-634-3475		242
Corporate Executive Board Co 1919 N Lynn St .... Arlington VA 22209 *NYSE: CEB*	866-913-2632	571-303-3000	196
Corporate Fitness Works Inc 1200 16th St N .... St Petersburg FL 33705	855-417-9697	301-417-9697	354
Corporate Helicopters of San Diego 3753 John J Montgomery Dr Ste 2 .... San Diego CA 92123	800-345-6737	858-505-5650	359
Corporate It Solutions Inc 661 Pleasant St .... Norwood MA 02062	888-521-2487		198
Corporate Telephone Services 184 W Second St .... Boston MA 02127	800-274-1211	617-625-1200	248
Corporate Travel Management Group 450 E 22nd St .... Lombard IL 60148	866-545-6789	630-691-8000	769
Corporate Writer & Editor 111 E Wacker Dr Ste 500 .... Chicago IL 60601	800-878-5331	312-960-4140	530-2
Corporation for Public Broadcasting (CPB) 401 Ninth St NW .... Washington DC 20004	800-272-2190	202-879-9600	306
Corporation Service Co 2711 Centerville Rd Ste 400 .... Wilmington DE 19808	866-403-5272	302-636-5400	112
Corps Network, The 1275 K St NW Ste 1050 .... Washington DC 20005	800-245-5627	202-737-6272	47-6
Corptax LLC 1751 Lk Cook Rd Ste 100 .... Deerfield IL 60015	800-966-1639		179
Corpus Christi Convention & Visitors Bureau 101 N Shoreline Blvd Ste 430 .... Corpus Christi TX 78401	800-678-6232	361-881-1888	208
Corpus Christi Gasket & Fastener Inc PO Box 4074 .... Corpus Christi TX 78469	800-460-6366	361-884-6366	327
Corpus Christi Symphony Orchestra 555 N Carancahua St Tower II Ste 410 Ste 410 .... Corpus Christi TX 78401	877-286-6683	361-883-6683	572-3
Corradino Group 200 s Fifth st .... Louisville KY 40202	800-880-8241	502-587-7221	258
Correct Craft Inc 14700 Aerospace Pkwy .... Orlando FL 32809	800-346-2092	407-855-4141	89
Correctional Enterprises of Connecticut 24 Wolcott Hill Rd .... Wethersfield CT 06109	800-842-1146	860-263-6839	629
Corrections Corp of America 10 Burton Hills Blvd .... Nashville TN 37215 *NYSE: CXW*	800-624-2931	615-263-3000	213
Corrective Education Company LLC 2825 Cottonwood Pkwy Ste 500 .... Salt Lake City UT 84121	877-318-0983		393
Correlated Products Inc 5616 Progress Rd .... Indianapolis IN 46242	800-428-3266	317-243-3248	150
Corridor Resources Inc 5475 Spring Garden Rd .... Halifax NS B3J3T2	888-429-4511	902-429-4511	535
Corrigan Moving Systems 23923 Research Dr .... Farmington Hills MI 48335	800-267-7442		518
Corrpro Canada Inc 10848 - 214 St .... Edmonton AB T5S2A7	800-661-8390	780-447-4565	258
Corrpro Cos Inc 1055 W Smith Rd .... Medina OH 44256	800-443-3516	330-723-5082	263
Corsair Memory Inc 46221 Landing Pkwy .... Fremont CA 94538	888-222-4346	510-657-8747	175-5
Corsicana Area Chamber of Commerce 120 N 12th St .... Corsicana TX 75110	866-222-7100	903-874-4731	138
Corsicana Bedding Inc PO Box 1050 .... Corsicana TX 75151	800-323-4349	903-872-2591	470
Corsicana Public Library 100 N 12th St .... Corsicana TX 75110	877-648-2836	903-654-4810	434-3
Cortec Corp 4119 White Bear Pkwy .... Saint Paul MN 55110	800-426-7832	651-429-1100	144
Cortelco Inc 1703 Sawyer Rd .... Corinth MS 38834	800-288-3132	662-287-5281	248
Cortex Consultants Inc 1218 Langley St .... Victoria BC V8W1W2	866-931-1192	250-360-1492	462
Corunna Public School District 124 N Shiawassee St .... Corunna MI 48817	866-632-9992	989-743-6338	683
Corvallis Tourism 420 NW Second St .... Corvallis OR 97330	800-334-8118	541-757-1544	208
CorVel Corp 2010 Main St Ste 600 .... Irvine CA 92614 *NASDAQ: CRVL*	888-726-7835	949-851-1473	462
Corvirtus LLC 1011 N Weber St .... Colorado Springs CO 80903	800-322-5329		462
Corwin Press Inc 2455 Teller Rd .... Thousand Oaks CA 91320 *Orders	800-233-9936*	805-499-9734	634-2
Cosanti Originals Inc 6433 Doubletree Ranch Rd .... Paradise Valley AZ 85253	800-752-3187	480-948-6145	49-2
COSCO (China Ocean Shipping Co Americas Inc) 100 Lighting Way .... Secaucus NJ 07094	800-242-7354	201-422-0500	222
Cosco Fire Protection Inc 1075 W Lambert Rd Bldg D .... Brea CA 92821	800-485-3795	714-989-1800	191-13
Cosco Industries Inc 7220 W Wilson Ave .... Harwood Heights IL 60706	800-296-8970	708-867-5800	466
CoServ Electric 7701 S Stemmons Fwy .... Corinth TX 76210	800-274-4014	940-321-7800	247
COSI Columbus 333 W Broad St .... Columbus OH 43215	888-819-2674	614-228-2674	519
Cosmopolitan Hotel Toronto 8 Colborne St .... Toronto ON M5E1E1	800-958-3488	416-350-2000	379
Cosmopolitan International 7341 W 80th St PO Box 4588 .... Lancaster PA 17604	800-648-4331	913-648-4330	47-15
Cosmopolitan Magazine 300 W 57th St .... New York NY 10019	866-879-6636	212-649-2000	456-11
Cosmos Communications Inc 11-05 44th Dr .... Long Island NY 11101	800-223-5751	718-482-1800	626
CoSN (Consortium for School Networking) 1025 Vermont Ave NW Ste 1010 ..... Washington DC 20005	866-267-8747	202-861-2676	47-9
Cossatot River State Park-Natural Area 1980 Hwy 278 W .... Wickes AR 71973	877-665-6343	870-385-2201	564
Cost Control Associates Inc 310 Bay Rd .... Queensbury NY 12804	800-836-3787	518-798-4437	198
Cost Plus Inc 200 Fourth St .... Oakland CA 94607 *NASDAQ: CPWM*	877-967-5362	510-893-7300	362
Costa Cruise Lines 200 S Pk Rd Ste 200 .... Hollywood FL 33021	800-462-6782	954-266-5600	222
Costa Del Mar 2361 Mason Ave Ste 100 .... Daytona Beach FL 32117	800-447-3700	386-274-4000	541
Costa Fruit & Produce 18 Bunker Hill Industrial Pk PO Box 290754 .... Boston MA 02129	800-322-1374	617-241-8007	298-7
Costa Nursery Farms Inc 21800 SW 162nd Ave .... Miami FL 33170	800-327-7074		369
Costanoa Coastal Lodge & Camp 2001 Rossi Rd .... Pescadero CA 94060	877-262-7848	650-879-1100	667
CoStar Group Inc 2 Bethesda Metro Ctr 10th Fl .... Bethesda MD 20814 *NASDAQ: CSGP*	800-613-1303	301-215-8300	180-10
Costco Wholesale Corp 999 Lake Dr .... Issaquah WA 98027 *NASDAQ: COST* ■ *Cust Svc	800-774-2678*	425-313-8100	810
Costume Gallery 4451 Rt 130 .... Burlington NJ 08016	800-222-8125	609-386-6601	154-6
Costume Specialists Inc 211 N Fifth St .... Columbus OH 43215	800-596-9357	614-464-2115	154-6
COTA (Children's Organ Transplant Assn) 2501 W Cota Dr .... Bloomington IN 47403	800-366-2682	812-336-8872	47-17
Cothern Computer Systems Inc 1640 Lelia Dr Ste 200 .... Jackson MS 39216	800-844-1155	601-969-1155	180-7
Cott Corp 6525 Viscount Rd .... Mississauga ON L4V1H6 *NYSE: COT*	866-732-8683	905-672-1900	79-2
Cotterman Co 130 Seltzer Rd .... Croswell MI 48422	800-552-3337	810-679-4400	421
Cottey College 1000 W Austin Blvd .... Nevada MO 64772	888-526-8839	417-667-8181	161
Cotton & Co 633 SE Fifth St .... Stuart FL 34994	800-266-9076	772-287-6612	4
Cotton Belt Inc 401 E Sater St .... Pinetops NC 27864	800-849-4192	252-827-4192	470
Cotton Electric Co-op Inc 226 N Broadway .... Walters OK 73572	800-522-3520	580-875-3351	247
Cotton Inc 6399 Weston Pkwy .... Cary NC 27513	800-334-5868	919-678-2220	47-2
Cotton's Week 7193 Goodlett Farms Pkwy .... Cordova TN 38016	888-232-1738	901-274-9030	530-13
Cottonimages.Com Inc 10481 Nw 28th St .... Miami FL 33172	888-642-7999	305-251-2560	344
Cottrell Inc 2125 Candler Rd .... Gainesville GA 30507 *Sales	800-827-0132*	770-532-7251	777
Cottrell Paper Company Inc 1135 Rock City Rd PO Box 35 .... Rock City Falls NY 12863	800-948-3559	518-885-1702	814
Couch & Philippi Inc 10680 Fern Ave PO Box A .... Stanton CA 90680 *Orders	800-854-3360*	714-527-2261	699
Coulter Lake Guest Ranch 80 County Rd 273 .... Rifle CO 81650	800-858-3046	970-625-1473	241
Council Bluffs Area Chamber of Commerce 149 W Bdwy .... Council Bluffs IA 51503	800-228-6878	712-325-1000	138
Council for Advancement & Support of Education (CASE) 1307 New York Ave NW Ste 1000 .... Washington DC 20005 *Orders	800-554-8536*	202-328-5900	48-5
Council for Professional Recognition 2460 16th St NW .... Washington DC 20009	800-424-4310	202-265-9090	48-5
Council for Responsible Genetics (CRG) 5 Upland Rd Ste 3 .... Cambridge MA 02140	888-591-3911	617-868-0870	48-19
Council of Administrators of Special Education (CASE) Osigian Office Centre 101 Katelyn Cir Ste E .... Warner Robins GA 31088	800-585-1753	478-333-6892	48-5
Council of Better Business Bureaus Inc			
Dispute Resolution Services & Mediation Training 4200 Wilson Blvd Ste 800 .... Arlington VA 22203	855-748-4600	703-276-0100	40
Council of Canadians 170 Laurier Ave W Ste 700 .... Ottawa ON K1P5V5	800-387-7177	613-233-2773	47-7
Council of Insurance Agents & Brokers 701 Pennsylvania Ave NW Ste 750 .... Washington DC 20004	877-267-9855	202-783-4400	48-9
Council of Real Estate Brokerage Managers (CRB) 430 N Michigan Ave .... Chicago IL 60611	800-621-8738		48-17
Council of Residential Specialists 430 N Michigan Ave Ste 300 .... Chicago IL 60611	800-462-8841	312-321-4400	48-17
Council of State & Territorial Epidemiologists (CSTE) 2872 Woodcock Blvd Ste 303 .... Atlanta GA 30341	866-577-9956	770-458-3811	48-7

Name / Address	City	State	ZIP	Toll-Free	Phone	Class
Council of State Governments (CSG) 2760 Research Pk Dr *Sales	Lexington	KY	40511	**800-800-1910***	859-244-8000	48-7
Council of the Great City Schools 1301 Pennsylvania Ave NW Ste 702	Washington	DC	20004	**888-280-7903**	202-393-2427	48-5
Council of the Section of Legal Education & Admissions to the Bar 321 N Clark St 21st Fl	Chicago	IL	60654	**800-238-2667**	312-988-6738	47-1
Council on Academic Accreditation in Audiology & Speech-Language Pathology 2200 Research Blvd	Rockville	MD	20850	**800-498-2071**	301-296-5700	47-1
Council on Accreditation (COA) 45 Broadway 29th Fl	New York	NY	10006	**866-262-8088**	212-797-3000	47-1
Council on Accreditation of Nurse Anesthesia Educational Programs 222 S Prospect Ave	Park Ridge	IL	60068	**855-526-2262**	847-692-7050	47-1
Council on Aviation Accreditation (CAA) *Aviation Accreditation Board International* 3410 Skyway Dr	Auburn	AL	36830	**800-767-4767**	334-844-2431	47-1
Council on Chiropractic Education Commission on Accreditation 8049 N 85th Way	Scottsdale	AZ	85258	**888-443-3506**	480-443-8877	47-1
Council on Foundations 2121 Crystal Dr Ste 700	Arlington	VA	22202	**800-673-9036**	703-879-0600	47-5
Council on International Educational Exchange (CIEE) 300 Fore St 2nd Fl *Cust Svc	Portland	ME	04101	**888-268-6245***	207-553-4000	48-5
Council on Occupational Education 7840 Roswell Rd Bldg 300 Ste 325	Atlanta	GA	30350	**800-917-2081**	770-396-3898	47-1
Council on Social Work Education (CSWE) 1701 Duke St	Alexandria	VA	22314	**866-573-4235**	703-683-8080	48-5
Counsel Corp 1211 Ave of the Americas Ste 2902 *NYSE: CXS*	New York	NY	10036	**866-296-3743**	212-696-0100	405
Count Me In LLC 1530 E Dundee Ste 150	Palatine	IL	60074	**866-514-5888**		82
Counter Pro Inc 210 Lincoln St	Manchester	NH	03103	**800-899-2444**	603-647-2444	193-3
Counterforce Inc 2740 Matheson Blvd E Unit 2A	Mississauga	ON	L4W4X3	**800-591-7374**	905-282-6200	691
Country Bank for Savings 75 Main St	Ware	MA	01082	**800-322-8233**	413-967-6221	69
Country Cablevision Inc 9449 State Hwy 197 S	Burnsville	NC	28714	**800-722-4074**	828-682-4074	115
Country Curtains PO Box 955	Stockbridge	MA	01262	**800-937-1237**	413-243-1474	156-5
Country Hearth Inn Inc 50 Glenlake Pkwy NE Ste 350	Atlanta	GA	30328	**888-443-2784**	770-393-2662	378
Country Inn at the Mall 936 Stillwater Ave *Resv	Bangor	ME	04401	**800-244-3961***	207-941-0200	379
Country Inn Lake Resort 1332 Airport Rd	Hot Springs	AR	71913	**800-822-7402**	501-767-3535	379
COUNTRY Insurance & Financial Services 1705 Towanda Ave	Bloomington	IL	61701	**888-211-2555**	866-268-6879	391-2
Country Lane Flower Shop 729 S Michigan Ave	Howell	MI	48843	**800-764-7673**	517-546-1111	294
Country Magazine 1610 North 2nd St Ste 102	Milwaukee	WI	53212	**888-861-1265**	414-423-0100	456-11
Country Mark Co-op 1200 Refinery Rd	Mount Vernon	IN	47620	**800-832-5490**		596
Country Music Assn Inc (CMA) 1 Music Cir S	Nashville	TN	37203	**800-788-3045**	615-244-2840	47-4
Country Music Hall of Fame & Museum 222 Fifth Ave S	Nashville	TN	37203	**800-852-6437**	615-416-2001	519
Country Mutual Insurance Co 1701 Towanda Ave *Cust Svc	Bloomington	IL	61701	**888-211-2555***	309-821-3000	391-4
Country Pride Co-op (CPC) 201 S Monroe PO Box 529	Winner	SD	57580	**888-325-7743**	605-842-2711	10-4
Country Springs Hotel & Conference Ctr 2810 Golf Rd	Pewaukee	WI	53072	**800-247-6640**	262-547-0201	377
Country's Barbecue 2016 12th Ave *General	Columbus	GA	31901	**800-285-4267***	706-327-7702	669
Countryside Co-op 514 E Main St	Durand	WI	54736	**800-236-7585**	715-672-8947	278
CountryTyme Inc 3451 Cincinnati-Zanesville Rd SW	Lancaster	OH	43130	**800-213-8365**	740-475-6001	651
County College of Morris 214 Ctr Grove Rd	Randolph	NJ	07869	**888-726-3260**	973-328-5000	161
County of Greene 93 E High St	Waynesburg	PA	15370	**888-852-5399**	724-852-5210	338
Courier Graphics Corp 2621 S 37th St	Phoenix	AZ	85034	**800-454-6381**	602-437-9700	626
Courier Printing 1 Courier Pl	Smyrna	TN	37167	**800-467-0444**	615-355-4000	626
Courier-Journal 525 W Broadway PO Box 740031	Louisville	KY	40201	**800-765-4011**	502-582-4011	531-2
Courier-Post 301 Cuthbert Blvd	Cherry Hill	NJ	08002	**800-677-6289**	856-663-6000	531-2
Courier-Tribune 500 Sunset Ave	Asheboro	NC	27203	**800-488-0444**	336-625-2101	531-2
Court Reporting Institute of Dallas 1341 W Mockingbird Ln Ste 200-E	Dallas	TX	75247	**866-382-1284**	214-350-9722	798
Court Reporting Institute of Houston 13101 NW Fwy Ste 100	Houston	TX	77040	**866-996-8300**	713-996-8300	798
Courtesy Assoc 2025 M St NW Ste 800	Washington	DC	20036	**800-647-4689**		186
Courtesy Building Services Inc 2154 W Northwest Hwy Ste 214	Dallas	TX	75220	**800-479-3853**	972-831-1444	103
Courtesy Chevrolet 1233 E Camelback Rd	Phoenix	AZ	85014	**877-295-4648**	602-235-0255	56
Courtesy Chrysler Jeep Dodge 9207 Adamo Dr E	Tampa	FL	33619	**866-343-9730**	813-620-4300	56
Courtroom Sciences Inc 4950 N O'Connor Rd	Irving	TX	75062	**800-514-5879**	972-717-1773	444
Courtyard Cafe 18 St Thomas St *Cust Svc	Toronto	ON	M5S3E7	**877-999-2767***	416-921-2921	669
Courtyard Fort Lauderdale Beach 440 Seabreeze Blvd	Fort Lauderdale	FL	33316	**888-236-2427**	954-524-8733	379
Coushatta Casino Resort 777 Coushatta Dr PO Box 1510	Kinder	LA	70648	**800-584-7263**		132
Cousineau Inc 3 Valley Rd PO Box 58	North Anson	ME	04958	**877-268-7463**	207-635-4445	447
Cousins Submarines Inc N83 W13400 Leon Rd	Menomonee Falls	WI	53051	**800-238-9736**	262-253-7700	668
Covalon Technologies Ltd 405 Britannia Rd E Ste 106	Mississauga	ON	L4Z3E6	**877-711-6055**	905-568-8400	582
Covance Inc 210 Carnegie Ctr *NYSE: CVD*	Princeton	NJ	08540	**888-268-2623**	609-419-2240	84
Covansys Corp 32605 W 12 Mile Rd Ste 250	Farmington Hills	MI	48334	**866-310-0950**	248-488-2088	182
Covanta Energy Corp 445 South St *NYSE: CVA*	Morristown	NJ	07960	**800-950-8749**	862-345-5000	785
Cove Haven Pocono Palace 5222 Milford Rd	East Stroudsburg	PA	18302	**877-822-3333**	800-432-9932	667
Cove Inn 900 Broad Ave S	Naples	FL	34102	**800-255-4365**	239-262-7161	379
Cove Lake State Park 110 Cove Lake Ln	Caryville	TN	37714	**800-250-8615**	423-566-9701	564
Covenant Care Home 600 Mount Moriah Church Rd	Lumberton	NC	28360	**877-708-7689**	910-738-7777	371
Covenant College 14049 Scenic Hwy	Lookout Mountain	GA	30750	**888-451-2683**	706-820-1560	167
Covenant Hospice 5041 N 12th Ave	Pensacola	FL	32504	**800-541-3072**	850-433-2155	371
Covenant House 5 Penn Plz Ste 2	New York	NY	10001	**800-999-9999**	212-727-4000	47-6
Covenant Transport Inc 400 Birmingham Hwy *NASDAQ: CVTI*	Chattanooga	TN	37419	**800-334-9686**	423-821-1212	778
Covenant Village of Golden Valley 5800 St Croix Ave	Minneapolis	MN	55422	**877-224-5051**	763-546-6125	670
Covenant Village of Turlock 2125 N Olive Ave	Turlock	CA	95382	**800-485-7844**	209-216-5610	670
Coventry First LLC 7111 Vly Green Rd	Fort Washington	PA	19034	**877-836-8300**		794
Coventry Health Care Inc 6705 Rockledge Dr Ste 900 *NYSE: CVH*	Bethesda	MD	20817	**866-667-3062**	301-581-0600	391-3
Coventry Health Care of Delaware Inc 750 Prides Crossing Ste 200	Newark	DE	19713	**800-833-7423**		391-3
Coventry Health Care of Georgia Inc 1100 Cir 75 Pkwy Ste 1400	Atlanta	GA	30339	**800-470-2004**	678-202-2100	391-3
Coventry Health Care of Iowa Inc 4320 114th St	Urbandale	IA	50322	**800-470-6352**	515-225-1234	391-3
Coventry Health Care of Kansas Inc 8320 Ward Pkwy	Kansas City	MO	64114	**800-969-3343**		391-3
Coventry Health Care of Louisiana Inc 1720 S Sykes Dr *Sales	Bismarck	ND	58504	**800-341-6613***		391-3
Coventry Health Care of Nebraska Inc 15950 W Dodge Rd Ste 100	Omaha	NE	68164	**855-449-2889**	402-498-9030	391-3
Coventry Lumber Inc 2030 Nooseneck Hill Rd	Coventry	RI	02816	**800-390-0919**	401-821-2800	193-3
Covera Solutions Inc 1021 Watervliet-Shaker Rd PO Box 13539	Albany	NY	12205	**866-526-8372**		257
Coverall Cleaning Concepts 5201 Congress Ave Ste 275	Boca Raton	FL	33487	**800-537-3371**	866-296-8944	151
Coverbind Corp 3200 Corporate Dr	Wilmington	NC	28405	**800-366-6060**	910-799-4116	607
Coverstar LLC 1795 West 200 North	Lindon	UT	84042	**800-617-7283**	801-373-4777	708
Covington Electric Co-op Inc 18836 US Hwy 84	Andalusia	AL	36421	**800-239-4121**	334-222-4121	247
Covington International Travel 4401 Dominion Blvd	Glen Allen	VA	23060	**800-922-9238**	804-747-7077	769
Covisint 1 Campus Martius Ste 700	Detroit	MI	48226	**800-229-4125**		180-4
Cowboy Village Resort 120 S Flat Creek Dr PO Box 38	Jackson	WY	83001	**800-962-4988**	307-733-3121	379
Coweta-Fayette Electric Membership Corp 807 Collinsworth Rd	Palmetto	GA	30268	**877-746-4362**	770-502-0226	247
Cowley County Community College & Area Vocational-Technical School PO Box 1147	Arkansas City	KS	67005	**800-593-2222**	620-442-0430	161
Cowtown Boots 11401 Gateway Blvd W	El Paso	TX	79936	**800-580-2698**	915-593-2929	302
Cowtown Bus Charters Inc 5504 Forest Hill Dr	Fort Worth	TX	76119	**877-287-4897**	817-531-3287	106
Cowtown Coliseum 121 E Exchange Ave	Fort Worth	TX	76164	**888-269-8696**	817-625-1025	718
Cox Arboretum MetroPark 6733 Springboro Pike	Dayton	OH	45449	**800-865-6543**	937-434-9005	96
Cox Communications Inc 1400 Lake Hearn Dr	Atlanta	GA	30319	**866-961-0027**	404-843-5000	115
Cox Industries Inc 860 Cannon Bridge Rd PO Box 1124	Orangeburg	SC	29116	**800-476-4401**	803-534-7467	816
Cox Interior Inc 1751 Old Columbia Rd	Campbellsville	KY	42718	**800-733-1751**		498
Cox Manufacturing Co 5500 N Loop 1604 E	San Antonio	TX	78247	**800-900-7981**	210-657-7731	620
Cox Media Group Tampa 11300 Fourth St N Ste 300	Saint Petersburg	FL	33716	**888-723-9388**	727-579-2000	642-122
Cox North America Inc 8181 Coleman Rd	Haslett	MI	48840	**800-822-8114**	517-339-3330	318
Cox Transportation Services Inc 10448 Dow Gil Rd	Ashland	VA	23005	**800-288-8118**	804-798-1477	778

Name	Address	City	State	Zip	Toll-Free	Phone	Class
Coyle Reproductions Inc	14949 Firestone Blvd	La Mirada	CA	90638	**866-269-5373**	714-690-8200	626
Coyne College Inc	330 N Green St	Chicago	IL	60607	**800-707-1922**	773-577-8100	762
Coyote Lake Feedyard Inc	1287 FM 1731	Muleshoe	TX	79347	**800-299-3321**	806-946-3321	10-1
Coyote Logistics LLC	191 E Deerpath Rd	Lake Forest	IL	60045	**877-626-9683**	847-295-2424	448
Cozad Asset Management Inc	2501 Galen Dr	Champaign	IL	61821	**800-437-1686**	217-356-8363	527
Cozen O'Connor	1900 Market St	Philadelphia	PA	19103	**800-523-2900**	215-665-2000	428
C-P Flexible Packaging	15 Grumbacher Rd	York	PA	17406	**800-815-0667**	717-764-1193	553
CP Franchising LLC	3300 University Dr	Coral Springs	FL	33065	**800-683-0206**	954-344-8060	770
CP Medical Inc	803 NE 25th Ave	Portland	OR	97232	**800-950-2763**	503-232-1555	475
CPA (College Parents of America)	2200 Wilson Blvd Ste 102-396	Arlington	VA	22201	**888-761-6702**		47-11
CPA (Catholic Press Assn)	205 W Monroe St Ste 470	Chicago	IL	60606	**800-777-7432**	312-380-6789	48-14
CPA Auto Dealer Consultants Assn (CADCA)	1801 W End Ave Ste 800	Nashville	TN	37203	**800-231-2524**	615-373-9880	48-1
CPAC (Cable Public Affairs Ch)	PO Box 81099	Ottawa	ON	K1P1B1	**877-287-2722**		736
CPAmerica International	11801 Research Dr	Alachua	FL	32615	**800-992-2324**	386-418-4001	48-1
CPAWS (Canadian Parks & Wilderness Society)	250 City Ctr Ave Ste 506	Ottawa	ON	K1R6K7	**800-333-9453**	613-569-7226	47-13
CPB (Corporation for Public Broadcasting)	401 Ninth St NW	Washington	DC	20004	**800-272-2190**	202-879-9600	306
CPB (First NBC)	29092 Kretel Rd	Lacombe	LA	70445	**800-423-7503**	985-819-1200	69
CPBI (Connecticut Public Broadcasting Inc)	1049 Asylum Ave	Hartford	CT	06105	**800-683-2112**	860-278-5310	629
CPC (Country Pride Co-op)	201 S Monroe PO Box 529	Winner	SD	57580	**888-325-7743**	605-842-2711	10-4
CPC Aeroscience Inc	2700 SW 14th St *Cust Svc	Pompano Beach	FL	33069	**800-327-1835***		144
CPC Logistics Inc	14528 S Outer 40 Rd Ste 210	Chesterfield	MO	63017	**800-274-3746**	314-542-2266	719
CPCU Society	720 Providence Rd	Malvern	PA	19355	**800-932-2728**		48-9
CPF (Cleft Palate Foundation)	1504 E Franklin St Ste 102	Chapel Hill	NC	27514	**800-242-5338**	919-933-9044	47-17
CPFD (Coastal Pacific Food Distributors Inc)	1015 Performance Dr	Stockton	CA	95206	**800-500-2611**	209-983-2454	298-8
CPH Engineers	500 W Fulton St	Sanford	FL	32771	**866-609-0688**		263
CPhA (California Pharmacists Assn)	4030 Lennane Dr	Sacramento	CA	95834	**866-365-7472**	916-779-1400	584
CPI (Companion Pets Inc)	2001 N Black Canyon Hwy	Phoenix	AZ	85009	**800-646-3611**	602-255-0166	577
CPI (Consumers Power Inc)	6990 W Hills Rd PO Box 1180	Philomath	OR	97370	**800-872-9036**	541-929-3124	247
CPI (Conifer Plastics Inc)	97 Witmer Rd	North Tonawanda	NY	14120	**800-635-3213**	716-693-2056	603
CPM Wolverine Proctor LLC	251 Gibraltar Rd	Horsham	PA	19044	**800-428-0846**	215-443-5200	299
CPP Inc	1055 Joaquin Rd Ste 200	Mountain View	CA	94043	**800-624-1765**	650-969-8901	634-2
CPR Institute for Dispute Resolution	575 Lexington Ave 21st Fl	New York	NY	10022	**866-723-1781**	212-949-6490	40
CPS (Comprehensive Pharmacy Services Inc)	6409 N Quail Hollow Rd	Memphis	TN	38120	**800-968-6962**	901-748-0470	196
Cps Building Company Ltd	4327 Red Bank Rd	Cincinnati	OH	45227	**877-295-9876**	513-271-9026	538
CPSC (Consumer Product Safety Commission)	4340 E W Hwy Ste 502	Bethesda	MD	20814	**800-638-2772**	301-504-7923	340-18
CPT (Central Petroleum Transport Inc)	6115 Mitchell St	Sioux City	IA	51111	**800-798-6357**	712-258-6357	778
CR Bard Inc Urological Div	8195 Industrial Blvd	Covington	GA	30014	**800-526-4455**	770-784-6100	475
CR Daniels Inc	3451 Ellicott Ctr Dr	Ellicott City	MD	21043	**800-933-2638**	410-461-2100	730
CR England & Sons Inc	4701 West 2100 South	Salt Lake City	UT	84120	**800-453-8826**	801-972-2712	778
CR Laurence Company Inc	2503 E Vernon Ave PO Box 58923	Los Angeles	CA	90058	**800-421-6144**	323-588-1281	193-2
Crabtree & Evelyn Ltd	102 Peake Brook Rd	Woodstock	CT	06281	**800-272-2873**	860-928-2761	217
Cracker Barrel Convenience Stores Inc	12221 Industriplex Blvd	Baton Rouge	LA	70809	**800-547-4151**	225-753-3200	206
Cracker Barrel Old Country Store Inc	PO Box 787 *NASDAQ: CBRL*	Lebanon	TN	37088	**800-333-9566**	615-444-5533	668
Crafco Inc	420 N Roosevelt Ave	Chandler	AZ	85226	**800-528-8242**	602-276-0406	45
Craft & Hobby Assn (CHA)	319 E 54th St	Elmwood Park	NJ	07407	**800-822-0494**	201-835-1200	47-18
Craft Inc	1929 County St PO Box 3049	South Attleboro	MA	02703	**800-827-2388**	508-761-7917	350
Craftmade International Inc	650 S Royal Ln *OTC: CRFT*	Coppell	TX	75019	**800-486-4892**	972-393-3800	36
Crafts 'n Things Magazine	PO Box 926	Sidney	OH	45365	**866-222-3621**		456-14
Crafts Technology	91 Joey Dr	Elk Grove Village	IL	60007	**800-323-6802**	847-758-3100	454
Craftsman Printing Inc	120 Citation Ct	Birmingham	AL	35209	**800-543-1051**	205-942-3939	626
Cragun's Conference & Golf Resort	11000 Cragun's Dr	Brainerd	MN	56401	**800-272-4867**		667
Craig Hospital	3425 S Clarkson St	Englewood	CO	80113	**800-247-0257**	303-789-8000	374-6
Craig Manufacturing Ltd	96 Mclean Ave	Hartland	NB	E7P2K5	**800-565-5007**	506-375-4493	479
Craig Test Boring Company Inc	5435 Harding Hwy PO Box 427	Mays Landing	NJ	08330	**800-584-2277**		263
Craig Transportation Co	26699 Eckel Rd	Perrysburg	OH	43551	**800-521-9119**	419-872-3333	778
Craighead Electric Co-op Corp	4314 Stadium Blvd PO Box 7503	Jonesboro	AR	72403	**800-794-5012**	870-932-8301	247
Crain Communications Inc	1155 Gratiot Ave	Detroit	MI	48207	**888-288-6954**	313-446-6000	634-9
Crain's Chicago Business Magazine	150 N Michigan Ave 16th Fl	Chicago	IL	60601	**877-812-1590**	312-649-5200	456-5
Crain's Cleveland Business Magazine	700 W St Clair Ave Ste 310	Cleveland	OH	44113	**888-909-9111**	216-522-1383	456-5
Crain's Detroit Business Magazine	1155 Gratiot Ave	Detroit	MI	48207	**888-909-9111**	313-446-6000	456-5
Crain's New York Business Magazine	685 Third Ave 3rd Fl	New York	NY	10017	**877-824-9379**	212-210-0100	456-5
Cramer Inc	1222 Quebec St	North Kansas City	MO	64116	**800-366-6700**		320-1
Cramer Products Inc	153 W Warren St	Gardner	KS	66030	**800-345-2231**	913-856-7511	476
Crandall Engineering Ltd	1077 St. George Blvd	Moncton	NB	E1E4C9	**866-857-2777**	506-857-2777	196
Crandall University	333 Gorge Rd	Moncton	NB	E1G3H9	**888-968-6228**	506-858-8970	783
Crane & Co Inc	30 S St *Cust Svc	Dalton	MA	01226	**800-268-2281***		551-2
Crane Company Dynalco Controls Div	3690 NW 53rd St	Fort Lauderdale	FL	33309	**800-368-6666**	954-739-4300	203
Crane Company Stockham Div	2129 Third Ave SE	Cullman	AL	35055	**800-786-2542**	256-775-3800	787
Crane Composites Inc	23525 W Eames St	Channahon	IL	60410	**800-435-0080**	815-467-8600	605
Crane Manufacturers Assn of America (CMAA)	8720 Red Oak Blvd Ste 201	Charlotte	NC	28217	**800-345-1815**	704-676-1190	48-13
Crane Nuclear Inc	2825 Cobb International Blvd	Kennesaw	GA	30152	**800-795-8013**	770-424-6343	471
Crane Worldwide Logistics LLC	1500 Rankin Rd	Houston	TX	77073	**888-870-2726**	281-443-2777	448
Cranel Inc	8999 Gemini Pkwy *General	Columbus	OH	43240	**800-288-3475***	614-431-8000	176
Cranesmart Systems Inc	4908 97 St NW	Edmonton	AB	T6E5S1	**888-562-3222**	780-437-2986	407
Craneveyor Corp	1524 Potrero Ave	South El Monte	CA	91733	**888-501-0050**		469
Cranmore Mountain Resort	1 Skimobile Rd PO Box 1640	North Conway	NH	03860	**800-786-6754**	603-356-5543	667
Cranston Machinery Company Inc	2251 SE Oak Grove Blvd	Oak Grove	OR	97267	**800-547-1012**	503-654-7751	555
Cranston Print Works Co	1381 Cranston St	Cranston	RI	02920	**800-876-2756**	401-943-4800	742-7
Cranwell Resort Spa & Golf Club	55 Lee Rd	Lenox	MA	01240	**800-272-6935**	413-637-1364	667
CRAssoc Inc	8580 Cinderbed Rd Ste 2400	Newington	VA	22122	**877-272-8960**	703-550-8145	462
Craters & Freighters	331 Corporate Cir Ste J	Golden	CO	80401	**800-736-3335**		311
Craven County Convention & Visitors Bureau	203 S Front St	New Bern	NC	28560	**800-437-5767**	252-637-9400	208
Crawdaddy's	1025 S Moorland Rd Ste 400	Brookfield	WI	53005	**800-727-9477**	414-778-2228	669
Crawford County	225 N Beaumont Rd	Prairie du Chien	WI	53821	**877-794-2372**	608-326-0200	338
Crawford Electric Co-op Inc	10301 N Service Rd PO Box 10	Bourbon	MO	65441	**800-677-2667**	573-732-4415	247
Crawford Industries LLC	1414 Crawford Dr	Crawfordsville	IN	47933	**800-428-0840**		547
Crawford Technologies Inc	45 St Clair Ave W Ste 102	Toronto	ON	M4V1K9	**866-679-0864**	416-923-0080	181
Crazy Shirts Inc	99-969 Iwaena St	Aiea	HI	96701	**800-771-2720**	808-487-9919	154-3
Crazy Woman Creek Bancorp Inc	PO Box 1020	Buffalo	WY	82834	**877-684-2766**	307-684-5591	360-2
CRB (Council of Real Estate Brokerage Managers)	430 N Michigan Ave	Chicago	IL	60611	**800-621-8738**		48-17
CRBC (Cambria-Rowe Business College)	221 Central Ave	Johnstown	PA	15902	**800-639-2273**	814-536-5168	798
CRC (Christian Reformed Church in North America)	2850 Kalamazoo Ave SE	Grand Rapids	MI	49560	**800-272-5125**	616-241-1691	47-20
CRC (Container Research Corp)	1 Hollow Hill Rd	Glen Riddle	PA	19037	**844-220-9574**	610-459-2160	200
CRC (Coordinating Research Council Inc)	3650 Mansell Rd Ste 140	Alpharetta	GA	30022	**800-445-8667**	678-795-0506	48-19
CRC Evans Pipeline International Inc	10700 E Independence St	Tulsa	OK	74116	**800-664-9224**	918-438-2100	192
CRC Industries Inc	885 Louis Dr *Cust Svc	Warminster	PA	18974	**800-556-5074***	215-674-4300	540
CRC Press LLC	6000 Broken Sound Pkwy NW Ste 300 *Cust Svc	Boca Raton	FL	33487	**800-272-7737***	561-994-0555	634-9
CRCA (Consumers' Research Council of America)	2020 Pennsylvania Ave NW Ste 300-A	Washington	DC	20006	**877-774-6337**	202-835-9698	47-10
Cream City Music	12505 W Bluemound Rd	Brookfield	WI	53005	**800-800-0087**	262-860-1800	525
Creamland Dairies Inc	PO Box 961447	Albuquerque	NM	87105	**800-395-7004**	505-247-0721	297-25
Cream-O-Land Dairy Inc	529 Cedar Ln	Florence	NJ	08518	**800-220-6455**	609-499-3601	298-4
Create-a-card Inc	16 Brasswood Rd	Saint James	NY	11780	**800-753-6867**	631-584-2273	534

Name / Address	City	State	ZIP	Toll-Free	Phone	Class
Creating Keepsakes Magazine 14850 Pony Express Rd	Bluffdale	UT	84065	**888-247-5282**	801-816-8300	456-14
Creation Engine 348 E Middlefield Rd	Mountain View	CA	94043	**800-431-8713**	650-934-0176	182
Creative Alliance Inc 437 W Jefferson St	Louisville	KY	40202	**800-525-0294**	502-584-8787	4
Creative Colors International Inc 19015 S Jodi Rd Ste E	Mokena	IL	60448	**800-933-2656**	708-478-1437	311
Creative Communications For The Parish Inc 1564 Fencorp Dr	Fenton	MO	63026	**800-325-9414**	636-305-9777	634-2
Creative Environments 8920 S Hardy Dr	Tempe	AZ	85284	**855-777-9305**	480-458-4100	422
Creative Financial Group (CFG) 16 Campus Blvd	Newtown Square	PA	19073	**800-893-4824**	610-325-6100	401
Creative Foam Corp 300 N Alloy Dr	Fenton	MI	48430	**800-529-4149**	810-629-4149	600
Creative Hobbies Inc 900 Creek Rd	Bellmawr	NJ	08031	**800-843-5456**	856-933-2540	43
Creative Impact Group Inc 801 Skokie Blvd Ste 108	Northbrook	IL	60062	**800-445-2171**	847-945-7401	186
Creative Kid Stuff 3939 E 46th St	Minneapolis	MN	55406	**800-353-0710**	612-929-2431	759
Creative Kids Magazine PO Box 8813	Waco	TX	76714	**800-998-2208**	254-756-3337	456-6
Creative Labs Inc 1901 McCarthy Blvd *Cust Svc	Milpitas	CA	95035	**800-998-1000***	408-428-6600	624
Creative Loafing Atlanta 384 Northyards Blvd Ste 600	Atlanta	GA	30313	**888-242-0208**	404-688-5623	531-5
Creative Logistics Solutions Inc 980 Mercantile Dr Ste J	Hanover	MD	21076	**800-407-0280**	410-793-0708	182
Creative Mktg International Corp 11460 Tomahawk Creek Pkwy	Leawood	KS	66211	**800-992-2642**	913-814-0510	391-2
Creative Outdoor Advertising 2402 Stouffville Rd	Gormley	ON	L0H1G0	**800-661-6088**		7
Creative Pultrusions Inc 214 Industrial Ln	Alum Bank	PA	15521	**888-274-7855**	814-839-4186	193-3
Creative Sign Designs 12801 Commodity Pl Ste 200	Tampa	FL	33626	**800-804-4809**	813-818-7100	318
Creative Teaching Press Inc 6262 Katella Ave	Cypress	CA	92649	**800-444-4287**	714-895-5047	245
Creative Training Techniques International Inc 14530 Martin Dr	Eden Prairie	MN	55344	**800-383-9210**	952-829-1954	763
Creativity for Kids 9450 Allen Dr	Cleveland	OH	44125	**800-311-8684**	216-643-4660	760
Credant Technologies Inc 15303 Dallas Pkwy Ste 1420	Addison	TX	75001	**800-929-8331**	972-458-5400	179
Credit Acceptance Corp 25505 W 12 Mile Rd	Southfield	MI	48034	**800-634-1506**	248-353-2700	216
Credit Card Systems Inc 180 Shepard Ave	Wheeling	IL	60090	**800-747-1269**	847-459-8320	702
Credit Control Services Inc (CCS) 2 Wells Ave Ste 1	Newton	MA	02459	**800-526-0532**	617-965-2000	159
Credit Management LP 4200 International Pkwy	Carrollton	TX	75007	**800-377-7713**		159
Credit Research Foundation (CRF) 8840 Columbia 100 Pkwy	Columbia	MD	21045	**866-265-3298**	410-740-5499	48-2
Credit Suisse 11 Madison Ave	New York	NY	10010	**800-222-8977**	212-325-2000	688
Credit Union Acceptance Company LLC 9601 Jones Rd Ste 108	Houston	TX	77065	**866-970-2822**	281-970-2822	221
Credit Union Directors Newsletter 5710 Mineral Pt Rd	Madison	WI	53705	**800-356-9655**	608-231-4000	530-1
Credit Union Executives Society (CUES) 5510 Research Pk Dr	Madison	WI	53711	**800-252-2664**	608-271-2664	48-2
Credit Union of Denver 9305 W Alameda Ave	Lakewood	CO	80226	**800-951-9014**	303-234-1700	69
Credit Union of Southern California PO Box 200	Whittier	CA	90608	**866-287-6225**	562-698-8326	221
Credit Union of Texas PO Box 517028	Dallas	TX	75251	**800-314-3828**	972-263-9497	221
Credit Valley Hospital 2200 Eglinton Ave W	Mississauga	ON	L5M2N1	**877-292-4284**	905-813-2200	374-2
Creditors Adjustment Bureau-LC Financial (CABLCF) 14226 Ventura Blvd	Sherman Oaks	CA	91423	**800-800-4523**	818-990-4800	159
Creditors Bureau Associates 420 College St	Macon	GA	31201	**866-949-4213**	478-750-1111	220
Cree Inc 4600 Silicon Dr *NASDAQ: CREE*	Durham	NC	27703	**800-533-2583**	919-313-5300	694
Creedmoor Psychiatric Ctr 79-25 Winchester Blvd	Queens Village	NY	11427	**800-597-8481**	718-464-7500	374-5
Creekside Inn 3400 El Camino Real	Palo Alto	CA	94306	**800-492-7335**	650-493-2411	379
Creform Corp PO Box 830	Greer	SC	29652	**800-839-8823**	864-989-1700	721
Creighton University 2500 California Plz	Omaha	NE	68178	**800-282-5835**	402-280-2700	167
Creighton University Medical Ctr 601 N 30th St	Omaha	NE	68131	**800-368-5097**	402-449-4000	374-3
Creor Group LLC Po Box 110398	Campbell	CA	95011	**877-774-4312**	408-248-4822	197
Crescendo Systems Corp 1600 Montgolfier	Laval	QC	H7T0A2	**800-724-2930**	450-973-8029	179
Crescent Cardboard Company LLC 100 W Willow Rd	Wheeling	IL	60090	**888-293-3956**	847-537-3400	559
Crescent City-Del Norte County Chamber of Commerce (CCDNCVB) 1001 Front St	Crescent City	CA	95531	**800-343-8300**	707-464-3174	208
Crescent Manufacturing Co 1310 Majestic Dr	Fremont	OH	43420	**800-537-1330**	419-332-6484	224
Cresco Lines Inc 15220 S Halsted St	Harvey	IL	60426	**800-323-4476**	708-339-1186	778
Cres-Cor 5925 Heisley Rd	Mentor	OH	44060	**877-273-7267**	440-350-1100	288
Crest Electronics Inc 3706 Alliance Dr	Greensboro	NC	27407	**888-502-7378**	336-855-6422	51
Crest Foods Company Inc 905 Main St	Ashton	IL	61006	**877-273-7893**	815-453-7411	297-17
Crest Healthcare Supply 195 Third St	Dassel	MN	55325	**800-328-8908**	320-275-3382	392
Crest Hotel & Suites 1670 James Ave	Miami Beach	FL	33139	**800-531-3880**	305-531-0321	379
Crest Ultrasonics Corp 10 Grumman Ave	Trenton	NJ	08628	**800-992-7378**	609-883-4000	780
Crested Butte Mountain Resort (CBMR) 12 Snowmass Rd PO Box 5700	Crested Butte	CO	81225	**877-547-5143**		667
Crestliner Inc 9040 Quaday Ave NE	Ostego	MN	55330	**866-301-8544**		89
Crestmark Bank 5480 Corporate Dr Ste 350	Troy	MI	48098	**888-999-8050**		274
Crestwood Advisors LLC 50 Federal St Ste 810	Boston	MA	02110	**877-273-7896**	617-523-8880	401
Crestwood Manor 50 Lacey Rd *General	Whiting	NJ	08759	**877-467-1652***	732-849-4900	670
Crete Carrier Corp 400 NW 56th St PO Box 81228 *Cust Svc	Lincoln	NE	68528	**800-998-4095***	402-475-9521	778
Creter Vault Corp 417 US Hwy 202	Flemington	NJ	08822	**800-352-4890**	908-782-7771	185
Creutzfeldt-Jakob Disease Foundation Inc 341 W 38th St Ste 501	New York	NY	10018	**800-659-1991**	212-719-5900	47-17
Crew Outfitters Inc 1001 Virginia Ave	Atlanta	GA	30354	**888-345-5353**		155
Crexendo Inc 1615 S 52nd St *OTC: CXDO*	Tempe	AZ	85281	**866-621-6111**	801-431-4695	38
CRF (Credit Research Foundation) 8840 Columbia 100 Pkwy	Columbia	MD	21045	**866-265-3298**	410-740-5499	48-2
CRG (Council for Responsible Genetics) 5 Upland Rd Ste 3	Cambridge	MA	02140	**888-591-3911**	617-868-0870	48-19
CRG Consulting 301 Moodie Dr Ste 325	Ottawa	ON	K2H9C4	**888-215-5147**	613-596-2910	196
CRG Global Inc 3 Signal Ave Ste A	Ormond Beach	FL	32174	**800-831-1718**	386-677-5644	666
Cricket Media Inc 30 Grove St Ste C	Peterborough	NH	03458	**800-821-0115**		456-6
Criminal Law Reporter 1801 S Bell St	Arlington	VA	22202	**800-372-1033**		530-7
Crissey Field State Recreation Site 1655 Hwy 101 N	Brookings	OR	97415	**800-551-6949**	541-469-2021	564
CRISTA Ministries 19303 Fremont Ave N *Cust Svc	Seattle	WA	98133	**800-346-9140***	206-546-7200	47-5
Cristek Interconnects Inc 5395 E Hunter Ave	Anaheim	CA	92807	**888-265-9162**	714-696-5200	813
Criswell College 4010 Gaston Ave	Dallas	TX	75246	**800-899-0012**	214-821-5433	167
Criterion Thread Company Inc 21744 98th Ave *General	Queens Village	NY	11429	**800-695-0080***	718-464-4200	593
Criticom Inc 4211 Forbes Blvd	Lanham	MD	20706	**800-449-3384**	301-306-0600	733
Criticom International Corp 715 W State Rd Ste 434	Longwood	FL	32750	**866-705-7705**		691
Critter Control Inc 9435 E Cherry Bend Rd	Traverse City	MI	49684	**800-451-6544**	231-947-2400	311
CRM Dynamics Inc 5800 Ambler Dr, Unit 106	Mississauga	ON	M4N2A5	**866-740-2424**		198
CRM Learning 2218 Faraday Ave Ste 110	Carlsbad	CA	92008	**800-421-0833**	760-431-9800	512
CRMC (Capital Research & Management Co) 333 S Hope St	Los Angeles	CA	90071	**800-421-4225**	213-486-9200	401
CRMC (Capital Regional Medical Ctr) 2626 Capital Medical Blvd	Tallahassee	FL	32308	**800-994-6610**	850-325-5000	374-3
CRMC (Colquitt Regional Medical Ctr) 3131 S Main St PO Box 40	Moultrie	GA	31768	**888-262-2762**	229-985-3420	374-3
CRN Digital Talk Radio 10487 Sunland Blvd	Sunland	CA	91040	**866-554-7387**	818-352-7152	736
Croatian National Tourist Office 350 Fifth Ave Ste 4003	New York	NY	10118	**800-829-4416**	212-279-8672	773
Crocker & Winsor Seafoods Inc PO Box 51905	Boston	MA	02205	**800-225-1597**	617-269-3100	297-14
Crocs Inc 6328 Monarch Pk Pl *NASDAQ: CROX*	Niwot	CO	80503	**866-306-3179**	303-848-7000	302
Croft LLC 107 Oliver Emmerich Dr	McComb	MS	39648	**800-437-8421**	601-684-6121	484
Crohn's & Colitis Foundation of America (CCFA) 386 Pk Ave S 17th Fl	New York	NY	10016	**800-932-2423**	212-685-3440	47-17
Cromers Inc 1700 Huger St	Columbia	SC	29201	**800-322-7688**		297-36
CropKing Inc 134 W Dr	Lodi	OH	44254	**800-321-5656**	330-302-4203	278
CropLife America 1156 15th St NW Ste 400	Washington	DC	20005	**800-266-9432**	202-296-1585	47-2
CROPP Co-op 1 Organic Way	LaFarge	WI	54639	**888-444-6455**		10-9
Crosbie & Company Inc 150 King St W Sun Life Financial Tower 15th Fl	Toronto	ON	M5H1J9	**866-873-7002**	416-362-7726	318
Crosby & Overton Inc 1610 W 17th St	Long Beach	CA	90813	**800-827-6729**	562-432-5445	665
Crosby Group, The 2801 Dawson Rd	Tulsa	OK	74110	**800-772-1500**	918-834-4611	469
Crosman Corp 7629 Rt 5 & 20	Bloomfield	NY	14469	**800-724-7486**	585-657-6161	286
Cross Automation Inc 2001 Oak Pkwy *General	Belmont	NC	28012	**800-272-7537***	704-523-2222	248
Cross Bros Inc 5255 Sheila St	Los Angeles	CA	90040	**866-939-1057**	323-266-2000	481
Cross Co 4400 Piedmont Pkwy	Greensboro	NC	27410	**800-858-1737**	336-856-6000	385
Cross Commerce Media Inc 130 Madison Ave	New York	NY	10016	**888-890-0020**		465

Name	Address	City	State	ZIP	Toll-Free	Phone	Class
Cross Country Healthcare Inc	6551 Pk of Commerce Blvd *NASDAQ: CCRN*	Boca Raton	FL	33487	**800-347-2264**	561-998-2232	719
Cross Country Home Services	1625 NW 136th Ave Ste 200 *Cust Svc	Sunrise	FL	33323	**800-778-8000***	954-845-2468	367
Cross Country Ski Areas Assn (CCSAA)	259 Bolton Rd	Winchester	NH	03470	**877-779-2754**	603-239-4341	47-22
Cross Creek Resort	3815 Pennsylvania 8	Titusville	PA	16354	**800-461-3173**	814-827-9611	379
Cross Financial Corp	74 Gilman Rd PO Box 1388	Bangor	ME	04401	**800-999-7345**	207-947-7345	390
Cross Insurance Center	515 Main St	Bangor	ME	04401	**800-745-3000**	207-561-8300	207
Cross Keys Village	2990 Carlisle Pk PO Box 128 *Mktg	New Oxford	PA	17350	**888-624-8242***	717-624-5350	670
Cross Oil Refining & Marketing Inc	484 E Sixth St	Smackover	AR	71762	**800-725-3066**	870-881-8700	579
Cross TV	370 W Camino Gardens Blvd Ste 300	Boca Raton	FL	33432	**877-276-7788**	561-367-7454	736
Crosscom National LLC	900 Deerfield Pkwy	Buffalo Grove	IL	60089	**888-471-6050**	847-520-9200	227
Crosscountry Courier Inc	PO Box 4030	Bismarck	ND	58502	**800-521-0287**	701-222-8498	545
Crosset Company Inc	10295 Toebben Dr	Independence	KY	41051	**800-347-4902**	859-283-5830	298-7
Crossett Inc	201 S Carver St *General	Warren	PA	16365	**800-876-2778***		778
Crosslake Communications	35910 County Rd 66 PO Box 70	Crosslake	MN	56442	**800-992-8220**	218-692-2777	387
Crossman Post Production LLC	35 Lone Hollow	Sandy	UT	84092	**888-553-1958**	801-553-1958	511
Crossmark Graphics Inc	16100 W Overland Dr	New Berlin	WI	53151	**800-236-1994**	262-821-1343	626
Crossmark Inc	5100 Legacy Dr	Plano	TX	75024	**877-699-6275**	469-814-1000	197
Crossmatch	720 Bay Rd Ste 100	Redwood City	CA	94063	**866-463-7792**	650-474-4000	82
Crossroads Bible College	601 N Shortridge Rd	Indianapolis	IN	46219	**800-822-3119**	317-352-8736	160
Crossroads College	920 Mayowood Rd SW	Rochester	MN	55902	**800-456-7651**	507-288-4563	160
Crossroads Systems Inc	8300 N MoPac Expy *NASDAQ: CRDS*	Austin	TX	78759	**800-643-7148**	512-349-0300	178
Crossville Cumberland County Chamber of Commerce	34 S Main St	Crossville	TN	38555	**877-465-3861**	931-484-8444	138
Crossville Porcelain Stone/USA	PO Box 1168	Crossville	TN	38557	**800-221-9093**	931-484-2110	749
Crossworld	306 Bala Ave	Bala Cynwyd	PA	19004	**888-785-0087**		47-20
Croswell Bus Lines Inc	975 W Main St	Williamsburg	OH	45176	**800-782-8747**	513-724-2206	106
Crouch Group Inc, The	300 N Carroll Blvd Ste 103	Denton	TX	76201	**888-211-0273**	940-383-1990	7
Crow Executive Air Inc	28331 Lemoyne Rd Toledo Metcalf Airport	Millbury	OH	43447	**800-972-2769**	419-838-6921	62
Crow Wing Co-op Power & Light Co	Hwy 371 N PO Box 507	Brainerd	MN	56401	**800-648-9401**	218-829-2827	247
Crow Wing County	326 Laurel St	Brainerd	MN	56401	**888-829-6680**	218-824-1067	338
Crow Wing State Park	3124 State Pk Rd	Brainerd	MN	56401	**888-646-6367**	218-825-3075	564
Crowder College	601 Laclede Ave	Neosho	MO	64850	**866-238-7788**	417-451-3223	161
Crowder Construction Company Inc	PO Box 30007	Charlotte	NC	28230	**800-849-2966**	704-372-3541	190-4
CrowdSource Solutions Inc	33 Bronze Pointe	Swansea	IL	62226	**855-276-9376**		630
Crowell Weedon & Co	1 Wilshire Blvd 26th Fl	Los Angeles	CA	90017	**800-227-0319**	213-620-1850	688
Crowley Maritime Corp	9487 Regency Square Blvd	Jacksonville	FL	32225	**800-276-9539**	904-727-2200	313
Crowley's Ridge College	100 College Dr	Paragould	AR	72450	**800-264-1096**	870-236-6901	161
Crown American Hotels Co	Pasquerilla Plz	Johnstown	PA	15907	**800-245-9295**	814-533-4600	379
Crown Battery Manufacturing Co	1445 Majestic Dr	Fremont	OH	43420	**800-487-2879**	419-334-7181	73
Crown Castle International Corp	1220 Augusta Dr Ste 500 *NYSE: CCI*	Houston	TX	77057	**877-486-9377**	713-570-3000	172
Crown Castle USA Inc	2000 Corporate Dr	Canonsburg	PA	15317	**877-486-9377**	724-416-2000	172
Crown College	8700 College View Dr	Saint Bonifacius	MN	55375	**800-346-9252**	952-446-4100	160
Crown Crafts Inc	916 S Burnside *NASDAQ: CRWS*	Gonzales	LA	70737	**800-433-9560**	225-647-9100	743
Crown Financial Ministries	601 Broad St SE	Gainesville	GA	30501	**800-722-1976**	770-534-1000	401
Crown Holdings Inc	1 Crown Way *NYSE: CCK*	Philadelphia	PA	19154	**800-523-3644**	215-698-5100	123
Crown Management Services Inc	1501 N Guillemard St	Pensacola	FL	32501	**800-844-5280**	850-438-7578	426
Crown Media Holdings Inc	12700 Ventura Blvd Ste 200 *NASDAQ: CRWN*	Studio City	CA	91604	**800-479-7328**	818-755-2400	736
Crown Micro Inc	48351 Fremont Blvd	Fremont	CA	94538	**800-963-7070**	510-490-8187	176
Crown Motors Ltd	196 Regent Blvd	Holland	MI	49423	**800-466-7000**	616-396-5268	56
Crown Packaging Corp	17854 Chesterfield Airport Rd	Chesterfield	MO	63005	**800-883-9400**	636-681-8000	547
Crown Plastics Co	116 May Dr	Harrison	OH	45030	**800-368-0238**	513-367-0238	599
Crown Point State Historic Site	21 Grandview Dr	Crown Point	NY	12928	**800-456-2267**	518-597-4666	564
Crown Products Company Inc	6390 Phillips Hwy	Jacksonville	FL	32216	**800-683-7144**	904-737-7144	695
Crown Reef Resort	2913 S Ocean Blvd	Myrtle Beach	SC	29577	**877-435-9125**	843-626-8077	379
Crown Roll Leaf Inc	91 Illinois Ave	Paterson	NJ	07503	**800-631-3831**	973-742-4000	296
Crown Travel & Cruises	240 Newton Rd Ste 106	Raleigh	NC	27615	**800-869-7447**	919-870-1986	769
Crowne Plaza Chateau Lacombe	10111 Bellamy Hill	Edmonton	AB	T5J1N7	**800-661-8801**	780-428-6611	379
Crowne Plaza Niagara Falls - Fallsview	5685 Falls Ave	Niagara Falls	ON	L2E6W7	**800-263-7135**	905-374-4447	378
Crowne Plaza Syracuse	701 E Genesee St	Syracuse	NY	13210	**888-227-6963**	315-479-7000	379
CrownTonka Inc	15600 37th Ave N Ste 100	Plymouth	MN	55446	**800-523-7337**	763-541-1410	662
Crozer-Keystone Health System (CKHS)	190 W Sproul Rd	Springfield	PA	19064	**800-254-3258**	610-328-8700	353
CRS (Catholic Relief Services)	228 W Lexington St	Baltimore	MD	21201	**800-235-2772**	410-625-2220	47-5
CRS Inc	4851 White Bear Pkwy	Saint Paul	MN	55110	**800-333-4949**	651-294-2700	111
CRS Jet Spares Inc	6701 NW 12th Ave	Fort Lauderdale	FL	33309	**800-338-5387**	954-972-2807	22
CRS Onesource	2803 Tamarack Rd PO Box 1984	Owensboro	KY	42302	**800-264-0710**	270-684-1469	298-11
CRST International Inc	3930 16th Ave SW PO Box 68	Cedar Rapids	IA	52406	**800-736-2778**		778
CRT Custom Products Inc	7532 Hickory Hills Ct	Whites Creek	TN	37189	**800-453-2533**	615-876-5490	759
CRU Acquisitions Group LLC	1000 SE Tech Ctr Dr Ste 160	Vancouver	WA	98683	**800-260-9800**	360-816-1800	175-8
Crucial Interactive Inc	21 Camden St 5th Fl	Toronto	ON	M5V1V2	**877-244-6562**	416-645-0135	197
Crucial Technology	3475 E Commercial Ct	Meridian	ID	83642	**800-336-8915**	208-363-5790	624
Crucible Materials Corp	575 State Fair Blvd	Syracuse	NY	13209	**800-365-1180**	315-487-4111	721
Cruise America	11 W Hampton Ave	Mesa	AZ	85210	**800-671-8042**	480-464-7300	119
Cruise Brokers	2803 W Busch Blvd Ste 100	Tampa	FL	33618	**800-409-1919**	813-288-9597	769
Cruise Brothers, The	950 Wellington Ave	Cranston	RI	02910	**800-827-7779**		770
Cruise Concepts	1329 Eniswood Pkwy	Palm Harbor	FL	34683	**800-752-7963**	727-784-7245	769
Cruise Connection LLC	7932 N Oak Ste 210	Kansas City	MO	64118	**800-572-0004**	816-420-8688	769
Cruise Connections Inc	3411 Healy Dr Ste D	Winston-Salem	NC	27103	**800-248-7447**		769
Cruise Deals.com	11111 Carmel Commons Blvd Ste 210	Charlotte	NC	28226	**800-668-6414**	704-542-6414	770
Cruise Lines International Assn (CLIA)	1201 F St NW Ste 250	Washington	DC	20004	**855-444-2542**	754-224-2200	47-23
Cruise People Inc	10191 W Sample Rd Ste 215	Coral Springs	FL	33065	**800-642-2469**	954-753-0069	769
Cruise People Ltd	1252 Lawrence Ave E Ste 210	Don Mills	ON	M3A1C3	**800-268-6523**	416-444-2410	769
Cruise Shop, The	700 Pasquinelli Dr Ste C	Westmont	IL	60559	**800-622-6456**	630-325-7447	769
Cruise Vacation Ctr	2042 Central Pk Ave	Yonkers	NY	10710	**800-803-7245**		769
Cruise Web Inc	3901 Calverton Blvd Ste 350	Calverton	MD	20705	**800-377-9383**	240-487-0155	769
Cruise West	3826 18th Ave W	Seattle	WA	98119	**888-862-8881**	206-283-9322	222
Cruisecheapcom	220 Congress Park Dr Ste 140	Delray Beach	FL	33445	**800-543-1915**	561-243-2100	770
CruiseOne Inc	1201 W Cypress Creek Rd Ste 100	Fort Lauderdale	FL	33309	**800-278-4731**		770
Cruises Cruises	6604 Antoine Dr	Houston	TX	77091	**800-245-9806**	713-681-9866	769
Cruises Inc	1201 W Cypress Creek Rd Ste 100 *Cust Svc	Fort Lauderdale	FL	33309	**888-282-1249***		769
Cruises.com	100 Fordham Rd Bldg C	Wilmington	MA	01887	**800-288-6006**		771
Cruising Gide Publications Inc	1130 Pinehurst Rd Ste B	Dunedin	FL	34698	**800-330-9542**	727-733-5322	5
Crum & Forster Insurance Inc	305 Madison Ave PO Box 1973	Morristown	NJ	07962	**800-690-5520**	973-490-6600	391-4
Crum Electric Supply Co	1165 W English Ave	Casper	WY	82601	**800-726-2239**	307-266-1278	248
Crump Insurance Services Inc	105 Eisenhower Pkwy	Roseland	NJ	07068	**800-222-0087**	973-461-2100	391-2
Crunch Fitness International	220 W 19th St	New York	NY	10011	**888-227-8624**	212-370-0998	354
Crusader Paper Company Inc	350 Holt Rd	North Andover	MA	01845	**800-421-0007**		553
Crutchfield Corp	1 Crutchfield Pk *Sales	Charlottesville	VA	22911	**888-955-6000***	434-817-1000	458
CRWRC (Christian Reformed World Relief Committee)	2850 Kalamazoo Ave SE	Grand Rapids	MI	49560	**800-552-7972**	616-241-1691	47-5
Crye-Leike Inc	6525 N Quail Hollow Rd	Memphis	TN	38120	**866-310-3102**		650
Cryobiology Inc	4830D Knightsbridge Blvd	Columbus	OH	43214	**800-359-4375**	614-451-4375	544

Alphabetical Section

Name / Address	Toll-Free	Phone	Class
Cryogenic Laboratories Inc 1944 Lexington Ave N . . . Roseville MN 55113	**800-466-2796**	651-489-8000	544
Cryolife Inc 1655 Roberts Blvd NW . . . Kennesaw GA 30144 *NYSE: CRY*	**800-438-8285**	770-419-3355	84
Cryovac Food Packaging & Food Solutions 100 Rogers Bridge Rd . . . Duncan SC 29334	**800-391-5645**		547
Crystal Beach Suites & Health Club 6985 Collins Ave . . . Miami Beach FL 33141	**888-643-4630**	305-865-9555	379
Crystal Cabinet Works Inc 1100 Crystal Dr . . . Princeton MN 55371	**800-347-5045**	763-389-4187	114
Crystal Communications Ltd 1525 Lakeville Dr Ste 230 . . . Kingwood TX 77339	**888-949-6603**	281-361-5199	198
Crystal Group Inc 850 Kacena Rd . . . Hiawatha IA 52233	**877-279-7863**	319-378-1636	178
Crystal Inn 185 S State St Ste 1300 . . . Salt Lake City UT 84111 *General	**800-662-2525***	801-320-7200	379
Crystal Inn Salt Lake City Downtown 230 W 500 S . . . Salt Lake City UT 84101	**800-662-2525**	801-328-4466	379
Crystal Lake Chamber of Commerce 427 W Virginia St . . . Crystal Lake IL 60014	**800-946-2248**	815-459-1300	138
Crystal Lake Manufacturing Inc 2225 Alabama 14 PO Box 159 . . . Autaugaville AL 36003	**800-633-8720**	334-365-3342	102
Crystal Lake State Park 96 Bellwater Ave . . . Barton VT 05822	**888-409-7579**	802-525-6205	564
Crystal Meth Anonymous General Service Organization (CMA) 4470 W Sunset Blvd Ste 107 PO Box 555 . . . Los Angeles CA 90027	**877-262-6691**		47-21
Crystal Mountain Resort 12500 Crystal Mtn Dr . . . Thompsonville MI 49683	**800-968-7686**	231-378-2000	667
Crystal River Preserve State Park 3266 N Sailboat Ave . . . Crystal River FL 34428	**800-326-3521**	352-563-0450	564
Crystal Rock Holdings Inc 1050 Buckingham St . . . Watertown CT 06795 *NYSE: AMEX*	**800-525-0070**	860-945-0661	79-2
Crystal Valley Coop 721 W Humphrey PO Box 210 . . . Lake Crystal MN 56055	**800-622-2910**	507-726-6455	278
Crystal Wealth Management System Ltd 3385 Harvester Rd Ste 200 . . . Burlington ON L7N3N2	**877-299-2854**	905-332-4414	794
Crystallex International Corp 8 King St E Ste 1201 . . . Toronto ON M5C1B5	**800-738-1577**	416-203-2448	501
Crystal-Like Plastics 21701 Plummer St . . . Chatsworth CA 91311	**800-554-6091**	323-849-1735	607
Crysteel Mfg Inc 52182 Ember Rd . . . Lake Crystal MN 56055 *Orders	**800-533-0494***	507-726-2728	469
Crysteel Truck Equipment Inc 55248 Ember Rd . . . Lake Crystal MN 56055 *General	**800-722-0588***	507-726-6041	778
Crystek Crystals Corp 12730 Commonwealth Dr . . . Fort Myers FL 33913	**800-237-3061**	239-561-3311	255
CS & P Technologies LP 18119 Telge Rd . . . Cypress TX 77429	**800-262-6103**	713-467-0869	638
CS Mott Children's Hospital 1500 E Medical Ctr Dr . . . Ann Arbor MI 48109	**800-211-8181**	734-936-4000	374-1
CSA Group 178 Rexdale Blvd . . . Toronto ON M9W1R3	**800-463-6727**	416-747-4000	318
CSBS (Conference of State Bank Supervisors) 1129 20th St NW 5th Fl . . . Washington DC 20036	**800-886-2727**	202-296-2840	48-7
CSC (Communications Supply Corp) 200 E Lies Rd . . . Carol Stream IL 60188	**800-468-2121**	630-221-6400	248
CSC (Curtis Steel Company LLC) 6504 Hurst St PO Box 7469 . . . Houston TX 77008	**800-749-4621**	713-861-4621	484
CSCOS (C & S Companies) 499 Col Eileen Collins Blvd . . . Syracuse NY 13212	**877-277-6583**	315-455-2000	263
CSE Corp 600 Seco Rd . . . Monroeville PA 15146	**800-245-2224**	412-856-9200	676
CSG (Council of State Governments) 2760 Research Pk Dr . . . Lexington KY 40511 *Sales	**800-800-1910***	859-244-8000	48-7
CSG (Community Services Group) 320 Highland Dr PO Box 597 . . . Mountville PA 17554	**877-907-7970**	717-285-7121	353
CSI (Christian Schools International) 3350 E Paris Ave SE . . . Grand Rapids MI 49512	**800-635-8288**	616-957-1070	48-5
CSI Aviation Services Inc 3700 Rio Grand Blvd NW . . . Albuquerque NM 87107	**800-765-9464**	505-761-9000	13
Csi Industries Inc 6910 W Ridge Rd . . . Fairview PA 16415	**800-937-9033**	814-474-9353	200
CSI International Inc 8120 State Rt 138 . . . Williamsport OH 43164	**800-795-4914**	740-420-5400	180-12
CSI Worldwide Inc 40 Regency Plz . . . Glen Mills PA 19342	**800-523-7118**	610-558-4500	186
CSM (Cambridge Street Metal Corp) 82 Stevens St . . . East Taunton MA 02718	**800-254-7580**	508-822-2278	491
CSM Metal Fabricating & Engineering Inc 1800 S San Pedro St . . . Los Angeles CA 90015	**800-272-4806**	213-748-7321	481
CSMC (Cedars-Sinai Medical Ctr) 8700 Beverly Blvd . . . Los Angeles CA 90048	**800-233-2771**	310-423-3277	374-3
CSP Inc 43 Manning Rd . . . Billerica MA 01821 *NASDAQ: CSPI*	**800-325-3110**	978-663-7598	175-1
CSRM (Cascade Steel Rolling Mills Inc) 3200 N Hwy 99 W PO Box 687 . . . McMinnville OR 97128	**800-283-2776**	503-472-4181	721
CSRS (D+H CollateralGuard RC) 4126 Norland Ave Ste 200 . . . Burnaby BC V5G3S8	**866-873-9780**	604-637-4000	632
CSS Laboratories Inc 1641 McGaw Ave . . . Irvine CA 92614	**800-852-2680**	949-852-8161	175-1
CSSA (Communications Supply Service Assn) 5700 Murray St . . . Little Rock AR 72209	**800-252-2772**	501-562-7666	48-20
CSS-Dynamac Corp 10301 Democracy Ln Ste 300 . . . Fairfax VA 22030	**800-888-4612**	703-691-4612	263
Cst Data 10725 John Price Rd . . . Charlotte NC 28273	**866-383-3282**	704-927-3282	227
CST/Berger Corp 255 W Fleming St . . . Watseka IL 60970	**800-435-1859**	815-432-5237	543
CSTE (Council of State & Territorial Epidemiologists) 2872 Woodcock Blvd Ste 303 . . . Atlanta GA 30341	**866-577-9956**	770-458-3811	48-7

Name / Address	Toll-Free	Phone	Class
CSTM (Mexico Tourism Board) 225 N Michigan Ave Ste 1800 . . . Chicago IL 60601 *General	**800-446-3942***		773
CSWE (Council on Social Work Education) 1701 Duke St . . . Alexandria VA 22314	**866-573-4235**	703-683-8080	48-5
CT Consultants Inc 8150 Sterling Ct . . . Mentor OH 44060	**800-925-0988**	440-951-9000	263
C&T Design & Equipment Company Inc 2750 Tobey Dr . . . Indianapolis IN 46219	**800-966-3374**	317-898-9602	406
Ct Gasket & Polymer Company Inc 12308 Cutten Rd . . . Houston TX 77066	**800-299-1685**		327
CT Lien Solutions 2727 Allen Pkwy Ste 1000 . . . Houston TX 77019	**800-833-5778**		632
CTAA (Community Transportation Assn of America) 1341 G St NW 10th Fl . . . Washington DC 20005	**800-891-0590**	202-628-1480	48-21
CTB Inc 611 N Higbee St PO Box 2000 . . . Milford IN 46542	**800-261-8651**	574-658-4191	275
CTE Solutions Inc 11 Holland Ave Ste 100 . . . Ottawa ON K1Y4S1	**800-699-4007**	613-798-5353	179
CTEC (Central Texas Electric Co-op Inc) 386 Friendship Ln PO Box 553 . . . Fredericksburg TX 78624 *General	**800-900-2832***	830-997-2126	247
CTG (Computer Task Group Inc) 800 Delaware Ave . . . Buffalo NY 14209 *OTC: CTG*	**800-992-5350**	716-882-8000	182
CTI (Cell Therapeutics Inc) 501 Elliott Ave W Ste 400 . . . Seattle WA 98119 *NASDAQ: CTIC*	**800-215-2355**	206-282-7100	84
CTI Inc 11105 Norrth Casa Grande Hwy . . . Rillito AZ 85654	**800-362-4952**	520-624-2348	778
CTJ (Citizens for Tax Justice) 1616 P St NW Ste 200-B . . . Washington DC 20036	**888-626-2622**	202-299-1066	47-7
CTL Distribution Inc 4201 Bonnie Mine Rd . . . Mulberry FL 33860	**800-237-9088**	863-428-2373	778
CTLGroup 5400 Old OrchaRd Rd . . . Skokie IL 60077	**800-522-2285**	847-965-7500	740
CTMC (Central Texas Medical Ctr) 1301 Wonder World Dr . . . San Marcos TX 78666	**800-927-9004**	512-353-8979	374-3
CTN (Christian Television Network Inc) 6922 142nd Ave N . . . Largo FL 33771	**800-716-7729**	727-535-5622	735
CTS Corp 905 W Blvd N . . . Elkhart IN 46514 *NYSE: CTS*	**800-757-6686**	574-293-7511	255
CTSI (Continental Traffic Service Inc) 5100 Poplar Ave 15th Fl . . . Memphis TN 38137	**888-836-5135**	901-766-1500	312
CTV-TV Ch 5 (CTV) 345 Graham Ave Ste 400 . . . Winnipeg MB R3C5S6	**800-461-1542**	204-788-3300	738-95
CU Conferences 8711 Watson Rd Ste 200 . . . St. Louis MO 63119	**888-465-6010**		387
CU*Answers 6000 28th St SE Ste 100 . . . Grand Rapids MI 49546	**800-327-3478**	616-285-5711	227
CUB (Concerned United Birthparents Inc) PO Box 503475 . . . San Diego CA 92150	**800-822-2777**		47-21
Cuba 315 Lexington Ave . . . New York NY 10016 *General	**800-553-3210***	212-689-7215	782
Cubeit Portable Storage Canada Inc 100 Canadian Rd . . . Scarborough ON M1R4Z5	**888-428-2348**		110
Cubic Corp 9333 Balboa Ave PO Box 85587 . . . San Diego CA 92186 *NYSE: CUB*	**800-937-5449**	858-277-6780	701
Cubic Defense Systems 9333 Balboa Ave . . . San Diego CA 92123	**800-937-5449**	858-277-6780	701
Cubic Transportation Systems Inc 5650 Kearny Mesa Rd . . . San Diego CA 92111	**800-937-5449**	858-268-3100	471
Cubix Corp 2800 Lockheed Way . . . Carson City NV 89706 *Sales	**800-829-0550***	775-888-1000	178
Cudahy Patrick Inc 1 Sweet Apple-Wood Ln . . . Cudahy WI 53110	**800-486-6900**	414-744-2000	472
CUE Inc 11 Leonberg Rd . . . Cranberry Township PA 16066	**800-283-4621**	724-772-5225	599
CUES (Credit Union Executives Society) 5510 Research Pk Dr . . . Madison WI 53711	**800-252-2664**	608-271-2664	48-2
CUES Inc 3600 Rio Vista Ave . . . Orlando FL 32805	**800-327-7791**	407-849-0190	203
Cuesta College PO Box 8106 . . . San Luis Obispo CA 93403	**800-675-2526**	805-546-3100	161
CUI Global Inc 20050 SW 112th Ave . . . Tualatin OR 97062 *NASDAQ: CUI*	**800-275-4899**	503-612-2300	360-3
Cuisinart 1 Cummings Pt Rd . . . Stamford CT 06902	**800-726-0190**	203-975-4609	36
Cuisine Magazine 2200 Grand Ave . . . Des Moines IA 50312	**800-311-3995**		456-11
Cuisine Solutions Inc 1501 Moran Rd Unit 100 . . . Sterling VA 20166 *OTC: CUSI*	**888-285-4679**	703-270-2900	297-36
Cuivre River Electric Co-op 1112 E Cherry St . . . Troy MO 63379	**800-392-3709**	636-528-8261	247
Culbertson Enterprises Inc (CEI) 600A Snyder Ave . . . West Chester PA 19382	**800-382-2685**	610-436-6400	191-7
Culinary Depot Inc 2 Melnick Dr . . . Monsey NY 10952	**888-845-8200**		406
Culinary Institute Alain & Marie LeNotre 7070 Allensby . . . Houston TX 77022	**888-536-6873**	713-692-0077	162
Culinary Institute of America 1946 Campus Dr . . . Hyde Park NY 12538 *Admissions	**800-285-4627***	845-452-9430	162
Culinary Institute of Charleston 7000 Rivers Ave . . . Charleston SC 29406	**877-349-7184**	843-574-6111	162
Culinary Software Services Inc 1900 Folsom St Ste 210 . . . Boulder CO 80302	**800-447-1466**	303-447-3334	179
Cullen, Weston, Pines & Bach LLP 122 W Washington Ave Ste 900 . . . Madison WI 53703	**866-443-8661**	608-807-0752	428
Cullen/Frost Bankers Inc 100 W Houston St . . . San Antonio TX 78205 *NYSE: CFR*	**800-562-6732**	210-220-4011	360-2

	City	State	ZIP	Toll-Free	Phone	Class
Culligan International Co 9399 W Higgins Rd Ste 1100	Rosemont	IL	60018	800-285-5442	847-430-2800	804
Cullinan Associates Inc 295 N Hubbards Ln 2nd Fl	Louisville	KY	40207	800-611-4841	502-893-0300	401
Cullman Area Chamber of Commerce 301 Second Ave SW	Cullman	AL	35055	800-313-5114	256-734-0454	138
Cullman Electric Co-op 1749 Eva Rd NE PO Box 1168	Cullman	AL	35055	800-242-1806	256-737-3201	247
Culpeper Baptist Retirement Community 12425 Village Loop	Culpeper	VA	22701	800-894-2411	540-825-2411	670
Culpeper National Cemetery 305 US Ave	Culpeper	VA	22701	800-827-1000	540-825-0027	135
Cultural Ctr for Language Studies 3191 Coral Way Ste 114	Miami	FL	33145	800-704-8181	305-529-2257	423
Cultural Experiences Abroad (CEA) 2999 N 44th St Ste 200	Phoenix	AZ	85018	800-266-4441	480-557-7900	758
Culver Academies 1300 Academy Rd	Culver	IN	46511	800-528-5837	574-842-7000	621
Culver City Unified School District (CCUSD) 4034 Irving Pl	Culver City	CA	90232	855-446-2673	310-842-4220	683
Culver Duck Farms Inc PO Box 910	Middlebury	IN	46540	800-825-9225	574-825-9537	10-7
Cumberland Chrysler Ctr 1550 Interstate Dr	Cookeville	TN	38501	888-277-4902		56
Cumberland County College 3322 College Dr	Vineland	NJ	08360	866-367-6232	856-691-8600	161
Cumberland County Public Library 300 Maiden Ln	Fayetteville	NC	28301	866-488-7386	910-483-1580	434-3
Cumberland Falls State Resort Park 7351 Hwy 90	Corbin	KY	40701	800-325-0063		564
Cumberland Furniture 321 Terminal St Sw	Grand Rapids	MI	49548	800-401-7877		322
Cumberland Gap National Historical Park 91 Bartlett Pk Rd PO Box 1848	Middlesboro	KY	40965	888-831-7526	606-248-2817	563
Cumberland Insurance Group 633 Shiloh Pike	Bridgeton	NJ	08302	800-232-6992		391-4
Cumberland Island National Seashore 101 Wheeler St	Saint Marys	GA	31558	877-860-6787	912-882-4336	563
Cumberland Mutual Fire Insurance Co 633 Shiloh Pk	Bridgeton	NJ	08302	800-232-6992		391-4
Cumberland Private Wealth Management Inc 99 Yorkville Ave Ste 300	Toronto	ON	M5R3K5	800-929-8296	416-929-1090	401
Cumberland Times-News 19 Baltimore St	Cumberland	MD	21502	800-742-8149	301-722-4600	531-2
Cumberland Truck Parts 15 Sylmar Rd	Nottingham	PA	19362	800-364-6995	610-932-1152	53
Cumberland University 1 Cumberland Sq	Lebanon	TN	37087	800-467-0562	615-444-2562	167
Cumberland Valley Co-op Assn 908 Mt Rock Rd	Shippensburg	PA	17257	800-488-2197	717-532-2197	446
Cumberland Valley Electric Inc 6219 N US Hwy 25 E	Gray	KY	40734	800-513-2677		247
Cumbre Inc 3333 Concours Ste 5100	Ontario	CA	91764	800-998-7986	909-484-2456	390
Cuming Corp 225 Bodwell St	Avon	MA	02322	800-432-6464	508-580-2660	536
Cuming County Public Power District 500 S Main St	West Point	NE	68788	877-572-2463	402-372-2463	247
Cummings Signs Inc 15 Century Blvd Ste 200	Nashville	TN	37214	800-489-7446		699
Cummins Construction Company Inc 1420 W Chestnut Ave	Enid	OK	73702	800-375-6001	580-233-6000	190-4
Cummins Facility Services 5202 Marion Waldo Rd	Prospect	OH	43342	800-451-5629	740-726-9800	103
Cummins Filtration 2931 Elm Hill Pike	Nashville	TN	37214	800-777-7064	615-367-0040	59
Cummins Inc 500 Jackson St PO Box 3005 *NYSE: CMI*	Columbus	IN	47201	800-343-7357	812-377-5000	264
Cummins Northwest LLC 811 SW Grady Way	Renton	WA	98055	800-274-0336	425-235-3400	14
Cummins Southern Plains Inc PO Box 90027	Arlington	TX	76004	800-516-4354	817-640-6801	385
Cummins-Allison Corp 852 Feehanville Dr	Mount Prospect	IL	60056	800-786-5528	847-299-9550	110
CUNA Mutual Group 5910 Mineral Pt Dr	Madison	WI	53705	800-937-2644	608-238-5851	360-4
Cunard Line Ltd 24303 Town Ctr Dr Ste 200	Valencia	CA	91355	800-728-6273	661-753-1000	222
Cunningham Brick Co Inc 701 N Main St	Lexington	NC	27292	800-672-6181	336-248-8541	149
Cunningham Manufacturing Co 318 S Webster St	Seattle	WA	98108	800-767-0038	206-767-3713	225
Cunningham Memorial Library 510 N 6 1/2 St	Terre Haute	IN	47809	800-851-4279	812-237-2580	434-6
CUNO Inc 400 Research Pkwy	Meriden	CT	06450	800-243-6894	203-237-5541	386
CUNY (City University of New York) 535 E 80th St	New York	NY	10075	877-769-7441	212-794-5555	784
CUPA-HR (College & University Professional Assn for Hum Res) 1811 Commons Pt Dr	Knoxville	TN	37932	877-287-2474	865-637-7673	48-5
Cupid Foundations Inc 475 Pk Ave S 17th Fl	New York	NY	10016	877-649-5283	212-686-6224	154-17
Curatel LLC 1605 W Olympic Blvd Ste 800	Los Angeles	CA	90015	866-287-2366		387
Curbstone Financial Management Corp 741 Chestnut St	Manchester	NH	03104	800-370-2872	603-624-8462	196
Curecanti National Recreation Area 102 Elk Creek	Gunnison	CO	81230	866-713-9688	970-641-2337	563
CureSearch for Children's Cancer 4600 East-West Hwy Ste 600	Bethesda	MD	20814	800-458-6223	301-718-0047	666
Curran Investment Management 30 S Pearl St Omni Plz 9th Fl	Albany	NY	12207	866-432-1246	518-391-4246	401
Current Analysis Inc 21335 Signal Hill Plz Ste 200	Sterling	VA	20164	877-787-8947	703-404-9200	180-1
Current Inc 30 Tyler St PO Box 120183	East Haven	CT	06512	877-436-6542	203-469-1337	598
Current USA Inc 1005 E Woodmen Rd *Cust Svc	Colorado Springs	CO	80920	800-848-2848*		458
Curriculum Assoc Inc 153 Rangeway Rd	North Billerica	MA	01862	800-225-0248		634-2
Curry College 1071 Blue Hill Ave	Milton	MA	02186	800-669-0686	617-333-2210	167
Curtain Call Costumes 333 E Seventh Ave	York	PA	17404	888-808-0801	717-852-6910	154-6
Curtis 1000 Inc 1725 Breckinridge Pkwy Ste 500	Duluth	GA	30096	877-287-8715	678-380-9095	265
Curtis Industries Inc 2400 S 43rd St PO Box 343925	Milwaukee	WI	53219	800-657-0853	414-649-4200	813
Curtis Industries LLC 111 Higgins St	Worcester	MA	01606	800-343-7676		515
Curtis Institute of Music 1726 Locust St	Philadelphia	PA	19103	800-640-4155	215-893-5252	167
Curtis Instruments Inc 200 Kisco Ave	Mount Kisco	NY	10549	800-777-3433	914-666-2971	250
Curtis M Phillips Ctr for the Performing Arts 315 Hull Rd PO Box 112750	Gainesville	FL	32611	800-905-2787	352-392-1900	571
Curtis Machine Company Inc 2500 E Trl St	Dodge City	KS	67801	800-835-9166	620-227-7164	707
Curtis Packing Co 2416 Randolph Ave	Greensboro	NC	27406	800-852-7890	336-275-7684	472
Curtis Restaurant Supply & Equipment Co 6577 E 40th St	Tulsa	OK	74145	800-766-2878	918-622-7390	301
Curtis Steel Company LLC (CSC) 6504 Hurst St PO Box 7469	Houston	TX	77008	800-749-4621	713-861-4621	484
Curtis, The 1405 Curtis St	Denver	CO	80202	800-525-6651	303-571-0300	379
Curtiss-Wright Corp 10 Waterview Blvd 2nd Fl *NYSE: CW*	Parsippany	NJ	07054	855-449-0995	973-541-3700	22
Curtis-Toledo Inc 1905 Kienlen Ave	Saint Louis	MO	63133	800-925-5431	314-383-1300	174
Cusack Wholesale Meat Inc 301 SW 12th St	Oklahoma City	OK	73109	800-241-6328	405-232-2114	298-9
Cushing-Malloy Inc 1350 N Main St	Ann Arbor	MI	48104	888-295-7244	734-663-8554	625
Custer Public Power District 625 E SE St PO Box 10	Broken Bow	NE	68822	888-749-2453	308-872-2451	247
Custom Accents 1940 Lunt Ave	Elk Grove Village	IL	60007	888-553-6789	847-640-4725	607
Custom Aluminum Products Inc 414 Div St	South Elgin	IL	60177	800-745-6333	847-717-5000	484
Custom Bldg Products 13001 Seal Beach Blvd	Seal Beach	CA	90740	800-272-8786	562-598-8808	3
Custom Brackets 32 Alpha Park	Cleveland	OH	44143	800-530-2289	440-446-0819	453
Custom Business Forms Inc 210 Edge Pl *General	Minneapolis	MN	55418	800-234-1221*	612-789-0002	109
Custom Cable Corp 242 Butler St	Westbury	NY	11590	800-832-3600	516-334-3600	115
Custom Cable Industries Inc 3221 Cherry Palm Dr	Tampa	FL	33619	800-552-2232	813-623-2232	191-4
Custom Chrome Inc 155 E Main Ave Ste 150	Morgan Hill	CA	95037	800-729-3332	408-778-0500	60
Custom Computer Specialists Inc (CCS) 70 Suffolk Ct	Hauppauge	NY	11788	800-598-8989	631-864-6699	182
Custom Coolers LLC 5609 Azle Ave	Fort Worth	TX	76114	800-627-0488	817-626-3737	662
Custom Drapery Blinds & Shutters 3402 E T C Jester	Houston	TX	77018	800-929-9211	713-225-9211	743
Custom Electronic Design & Installation Assn (CEDIA) 7150 Winton Dr Ste 300	Indianapolis	IN	46268	800-669-5329	317-328-4336	48-19
Custom Environmental Services Inc 8041 N I 70 Frontage Rd Unit 11	Arvada	CO	80002	800-310-7445	303-423-9949	665
Custom Fiberglass Mfg Corp *Snugtop* 1711 Harbor Ave PO Box 121	Long Beach	CA	90813	800-768-4867	562-432-5454	119
Custom Global Logistics LLC 317 W Lk St	Northlake	IL	60164	800-446-8336		315
Custom Hotel 8639 Lincoln Blvd	Los Angeles	CA	90045	877-287-8601	310-645-0400	379
Custom Medical Stock Photo Inc 3660 W Irving Pk Rd	Chicago	IL	60618	800-373-2677	773-267-3100	592
Custom Mold Engineering Inc 9780 S Franklin Dr	Franklin	WI	53132	800-448-2005	414-421-5444	755
Custom Pack Inc 662 Exton Cmns	Exton	PA	19341	800-722-7005	610-321-2525	600
Custom Paper Tubes Inc 15900 Industrial Pkwy	Cleveland	OH	44135	800-343-8823	216-362-2964	124
Custom Products of Litchfield Inc 1715 S Sibley Ave	Litchfield	MN	55355	800-222-5463	320-693-3221	275
Custom Toll Free 10940 Wilshire Blvd 17th Fl	Los Angeles	CA	90024	800-287-8664	800-933-3030	387
Custom Truck Accessories Inc 13408 Hwy 65 Ne	Ham Lake	MN	55304	800-333-1282	763-757-5326	53
Customer Communicator, The (TCC) 712 Main St Ste 187B	Boonton	NJ	07005	800-232-4317	973-265-2300	530-2
Customer Paradigm Inc 5353 Manhattan Cir Ste 103	Boulder	CO	80303	888-772-0777	303-499-9318	227
Customer Service Delivery Platform Corp 15615 Alton Pkwy Ste 310	Irvine	CA	92618	888-741-2737		179
Cutco Corp 1116 E State St	Olean	NY	14760	800-828-0448	716-372-3111	224
Cutera Inc 3240 Bayshore Blvd *NASDAQ: CUTR*	Brisbane	CA	94005	888-428-8372	415-657-5500	475
Cuthbert Greenhouses Inc 4900 Hendron Rd	Groveport	OH	43125	800-321-1939	614-836-3866	369
Cut-Heal Animal Care Products Inc 923 S Cedar Hill Rd	Cedar Hill	TX	75104	800-288-4325	972-293-9700	581
Cutler Majestic Theatre at Emerson College 219 Tremont St	Boston	MA	02116	888-627-7115	617-824-8000	571

Name / Address	City	State	ZIP	Toll-Free	Phone	Class
Cutlery & More LLC						
135 Prairie Lk Rd	East Dundee	IL	60118	**800-650-9866**		362
Cutten Realty Inc						
2120 Campton Rd Ste C	Eureka	CA	95503	**800-776-4458**	707-445-8811	650
Cutter & Buck Inc						
701 N 34th St Ste 400	Seattle	WA	98103	**800-713-7810**	888-338-9944	154-1
Cutter Aviation						
2802 E Old Tower Rd	Phoenix	AZ	85034	**800-234-5382**	602-273-1237	24
Cutter Consortium						
37 Broadway Ste 1	Arlington	MA	02474	**800-964-5118**	781-648-8700	530-3
Cutter Information Corp						
37 Broadway Ste 1	Arlington	MA	02474	**800-964-5118**	781-648-8700	634-9
Cutting Edge						
1825 Gillespie Way Ste 100	El Cajon	CA	92020	**800-257-1666**	619-258-7800	179
Cutting Edge Products LLC						
1000 Turk Hill Rd	Fairport	NY	14450	**800-497-0539**	252-830-5577	475
Cuyahoga Community College						
Eastern						
4250 Richmond Rd	Highland Hills	OH	44122	**800-954-8742**	216-987-2024	161
Metropolitan						
2900 Community College Ave	Cleveland	OH	44115	**800-954-8742**	216-987-4200	161
Western						
11000 Pleasant Valley Rd	Parma	OH	44130	**800-954-8742**	216-987-2800	161
Cuyahoga County Public Library						
2111 Snow Rd	Parma	OH	44134	**800-749-5560**	216-398-1800	434-3
Cuyahoga Falls News-Press						
1050 W Main St PO Box 5199	Kent	OH	44240	**800-560-9657**	330-541-9421	531-4
Cuyahoga Hills Juvenile Correctional Facility						
4321 Green Rd	Highland Hills	OH	44128	**800-872-3132**	216-464-8200	412
Cuyahoga Molded Plastics Corp						
1265 Babbitt Rd	Cleveland	OH	44132	**800-805-9549**	216-261-2744	603
Cuyahoga Valley National Park						
15610 Vaughn Rd	Brecksville	OH	44141	**800-445-9667**	216-524-1497	563
Cuyamaca College						
900 Rancho San Diego Pkwy	El Cajon	CA	92019	**800-234-1597**	619-660-4000	161
Cuyamaca Rancho State Park						
13652 Hwy 79	Julian	CA	92036	**800-444-7275**	760-765-0755	564
CVA (Connecticut Valley Arms)						
1685 Boggs Rd Ste 300	Duluth	GA	30096	**800-320-8767**	770-449-4687	286
CVB Financial Corp						
701 N Haven Ave PO Box 51000	Ontario	CA	91764	**888-222-5432**	909-980-4030	360-2
NASDAQ: CVBF						
CVD Diamond Corp						
2061 Piper Ln	London	ON	N5V3S5	**877-457-9903**	519-457-9903	480
CVEA (Copper Valley Electric Assn Inc)						
Mile 187 Glenn Hwy PO Box 45	Glennallen	AK	99588	**866-835-2832**	907-822-3211	247
CVMA (Canadian Veterinary Medical Assn)						
339 Booth St	Ottawa	ON	K1R7K1	**800-567-2862**	613-236-1162	48-8
CVS Corp 1 CVS Dr	Woonsocket	RI	02895	**888-607-4287***	401-765-1500	239
*Cust Svc						
CW (College of Westchester)						
325 Central Ave	White Plains	NY	10606	**800-660-7093**		798
C&W Enterprises Inc						
2522 SE Federal Hwy	Stuart	FL	34994	**844-241-6442**	772-287-5215	177
CWC Textron						
1085 W Sherman Blvd	Muskegon	MI	49441	**800-999-0853**	231-733-1331	59
CWCVB (Wausau Central Wisconsin Convention & Visitors Bureau)						
219 Jefferson St Ste B	Wausau	WI	54403	**888-948-4748**	715-355-8788	208
CWF (Canadian Wildlife Federation)						
350 Michael Cowpland Dr	Kanata	ON	K2M2W1	**800-563-9453**	613-599-9594	47-13
CWI Gifts & Crafts						
77 Cypress St SW	Reynoldsburg	OH	43068	**800-666-5858**	740-964-6210	43
CWPS Inc						
14120 A Sullyfield Cir	Chantilly	VA	20151	**877-297-7472**		182
CWPT (Civil War Preservation Trust)						
1331 H St NW Ste 1001	Washington	DC	20005	**888-606-1400**	202-367-1861	47-13
CWU (Church Women United)						
475 Riverside Dr Ste 243	New York	NY	10115	**800-298-5551**	212-870-2347	47-20
CXM (Chicago Extruded Metals Co)						
1601 S 54th Ave	Cicero	IL	60804	**800-323-8102***		484
*Cust Svc						
CXtec						
5404 S Bay Rd PO Box 4799	Syracuse	NY	13212	**800-767-3282***	315-476-3000	812
*Orders						
Cyanotech Corp						
73-4460 Queen Kaahumanu Hwy Ste 102	Kailua-Kona	HI	96740	**800-453-1187***	808-326-1353	478
NASDAQ: CYAN ■ *Sales						
Cyber Power Systems Inc						
4241 12th Ave E Ste 400	Shakopee	MN	55379	**877-297-6937**	952-403-9500	255
Cyber-Ark Software Inc						
60 Wells Ave	Newton	MA	02459	**888-808-9005**	617-965-1544	179
Cyberdata Corp						
3 Justin Ct	Monterey	CA	93940	**800-363-8010**	831-373-2601	178
Cyberex						
5900 Eastport Blvd	Richmond	VA	23231	**800-238-5000**	804-236-3300	255
Cyberonics Inc						
100 Cyberonics Blvd The Cyberonics Bldg.	Houston	TX	77058	**800-332-1375**	281-228-7262	476
NASDAQ: CYBX						
CyberOptics Corp						
5900 Golden Hills Dr	Minneapolis	MN	55416	**800-746-6315***	763-542-5000	250
NASDAQ: CYBE ■ *Cust Svc						
Cyber-Rain Inc						
6345 Balboa Blvd Ste 230	Encino	CA	91316	**877-888-1452**		407
Cybex International Inc						
10 Trotter Dr	Medway	MA	02053	**888-462-9239**	508-533-4300	269
NASDAQ: CYBI						
Cycle Country Access Corp						
205 N Depot St PO Box 107	Fox Lake	WI	53933	**800-841-2222***		29
*Sales						
Cycle World Magazine						
1499 Monrovia Ave	Newport Beach	CA	92663	**800-456-3084**	949-720-5300	456-3
Cycle-safe Inc						
5211 Cascade Rd Se Ste 210	Grand Rapids	MI	49546	**888-950-6531**	616-954-9977	709
Cyclonaire Corp						
2922 N Division Ave	York	NE	68467	**800-445-0730**	402-362-2000	209
Cyclone Drilling Inc						
PO Box 908	Gillette	WY	82717	**800-318-3724**	307-682-4161	539
Cyl-tec Inc						
971 W Industrial Dr	Aurora	IL	60506	**888-429-5832**	630-844-8800	740
Cyma Systems Inc						
2330 W University Dr Ste 4	Tempe	AZ	85281	**800-292-2962**		180-1
Cynergy Solutions LLC						
543 Country Club Dr Ste 538	Simi Valley	CA	93065	**877-296-3749**	805-416-1610	198
Cynosure Inc						
5 Carlisle Rd	Westford	MA	01886	**800-886-2966**	978-256-4200	424
NASDAQ: CYNO						
Cynthia C. & William E. Perry Pavilion						
9400 Turkey Lake Rd	Orlando	FL	32819	**800-447-1435**	321-842-8844	372
Cyphers Agency Inc, The						
53 Old Solomons Is Rd Ste G	Annapolis	MD	21401	**888-412-7469**		7
CypherWorX Inc						
3349 Monroe Ave	Rochester	NY	14618	**888-685-4440**		387
Cypremort Point State Park						
306 Beach Ln	Cypremort Point	LA	70538	**888-867-4510**	337-867-4510	564
Cypress Bayou Casino						
832 Martin Luther King Rd	Charenton	LA	70523	**800-284-4386**		451
Cypress Care Inc						
2736 Meadow Church Rd Ste 300	Duluth	GA	30097	**800-419-7191**		367
Cypress Hills National Cemetery						
625 Jamaica Ave	Brooklyn	NY	11208	**800-535-1117**	631-454-4949	135
Cypress Networks						
4125 Walker Ave Ste C	Greensboro	NC	27407	**866-625-3502**	336-841-3030	182
Cypress Security LLC						
478 Tehama St	San Francisco	CA	94103	**866-345-1277**		691
Cypress Semiconductor Corp						
198 Champion Ct	San Jose	CA	95134	**800-541-4736**	408-943-2600	694
NASDAQ: CY						
CYR Bus Lines						
153 Gilman Falls Ave	Old Town	ME	04468	**800-244-2335**	207-827-2335	106
Cyril Bath Co						
1610 Airport Rd	Monroe	NC	28110	**800-801-1418**	704-289-8531	455
Cystic Fibrosis Foundation						
6931 Arlington Rd Ste 200	Bethesda	MD	20814	**800-344-4823**	301-951-4422	47-17
Cytec Industries Inc						
5 Garret Mtn Plz	West Paterson	NJ	07424	**800-652-6013**	973-357-3100	144
NYSE: CYT						
Cytolab Pathology Services						
6825 216th St Sw	Lynnwood	WA	98036	**800-845-6167**	425-712-8020	415
CytoSport Inc						
4795 Industrial Way	Benicia	CA	94510	**888-313-1922**	707-751-3942	797
Czech Airlines						
1 Penn Plaza Ste 1416	New York	NY	10001	**855-359-2932**		25
Czech Airlines OK Plus						
147 W 35th St Ste 1505	New York	NY	10001	**855-359-2932**		26

D

Name / Address	City	State	ZIP	Toll-Free	Phone	Class
D & B						
103 JFK Pkwy	Short Hills	NJ	07078	**800-234-3867**	973-921-5500	634-2
NYSE: DNB						
D & D Commodities Ltd						
PO Box 359	Stephen	MN	56757	**800-543-3308**		446
D & D Distribution Services Inc						
789 Kings Mill Rd	York	PA	17403	**877-683-3358**	717-845-1646	801-1
D & D Foods Inc						
9425 N 48th St	Omaha	NE	68152	**800-208-0364**	402-571-4113	297-36
D & D Manufacturing Inc						
500 Territorial Dr	Bolingbrook	IL	60440	**888-300-6869**		755
D & H Distributing Company Inc						
2525 N Seventh St	Harrisburg	PA	17110	**800-340-1001**		176
D & R Sports Ctr Inc						
8178 W Main St	Kalamazoo	MI	49009	**800-992-1520**	269-372-2277	709
D & T Trucking Inc						
3686 140th St E PO Box 510	Rosemount	MN	55068	**800-624-8130**	651-480-7961	683
D & W Inc 941 Oak St	Elkhart	IN	46514	**800-255-0829**	574-264-9674	330
D F Richard Inc						
124 Broadway	Dover	NH	03821	**800-649-6457**	603-742-2020	317
D Hilton Assoc Inc						
9450 Grogans Mill Rd	Spring	TX	77380	**800-367-0433**	281-292-5088	196
D K Global						
420 Missouri Ct	Redlands	CA	92373	**866-375-2214**	909-747-0201	227
D L Evans Bank						
397 N Overland PO Box 1188	Burley	ID	83318	**888-873-9777**	208-678-9076	69
D M Bowman Inc						
10226 Governor Ln Blvd Ste 4009	Williamsport	MD	21795	**800-326-3274**	301-582-2784	778
D Net Internet Service						
208 E Palmer St	Franklin	NC	28734	**877-601-3638**	828-349-3638	227
D P Brown of Saginaw Inc						
2845 Universal Dr	Saginaw	MI	48603	**877-799-9400**	989-799-9400	393
D River State Recreation Site						
725 Summer St NE Ste C	Salem	OR	97301	**800-551-6949**	541-994-7341	564
D'Angelo Sandwich Shops						
600 Providence Hwy	Dedham	MA	02026	**800-727-2446**	781-461-1200	668
D'Arcy McGee's Irish Pub						
199 Four Valley Dr	Vaughan	ON	L4K0B8	**888-854-4402**	613-230-4433	669
D'Arrigo Bros Company of California Inc						
PO Box 850	Salinas	CA	93902	**800-995-5939***	831-455-4500	10-9
*Cust Svc						
D'vontz 7208 E 38th St	Tulsa	OK	74145	**877-322-3600**	918-622-3600	609
D'Youville College						
320 Porter Ave	Buffalo	NY	14201	**800-777-3921**	716-829-7600	167
D+H CollateralGuard RC (CSRS)						
4126 Norland Ave Ste 200	Burnaby	BC	V5G3S8	**866-873-9780**	604-637-4000	632
D. P. Curtis Trucking Inc						
1450 South Hwy 118	Richfield	UT	84701	**800-257-9151**		778
DA (Debtors Anonymous)						
PO Box 920888	Needham	MA	02492	**800-421-2383**	781-453-2743	47-21

Name / Address	City	State	ZIP	Toll-Free	Phone	Class
DA Davidson & Company Inc 8 Third St N	Great Falls	MT	59401	**800-332-5915**	406-727-4200	688
D-A Lubricant Co 1340 W 29th St	Indianapolis	IN	46208	**800-645-5823**	317-923-5321	540
Dabney S Lancaster Community College 1000 Dabney Dr PO Box 1000	Clifton Forge	VA	24422	**887-773-7522**	540-863-2800	161
Dabney State Recreation Area 725 Summer St NE Ste C	Salem	OR	97301	**800-551-6949**	503-695-2261	564
DAC (Dougherty Arts Ctr, The) 1110 Barton Springs Rd	Austin	TX	78704	**855-787-2227**	512-974-4000	49-1
DAC International Inc 6702 McNeil Dr	Austin	TX	78729	**800-527-2531**	512-331-5323	768
DAC Vision 3630 W Miller Ste 350	Garland	TX	75041	**800-800-1550**	972-677-2700	541
DACC (Dona Ana Branch Community College) 2800 N Sonoma Ranch Blvd PO Box 30001	Las Cruces	NM	88011	**800-903-7503**	575-528-7000	161
DACCO Transmission Parts 741 Dacco Dr PO Box 2789 *Cust Svc	Cookeville	TN	38502	**866-645-1452***	931-528-7581	59
Dacotah Paper Co 3940 15th Ave NW	Fargo	ND	58102	**800-270-6352**	701-281-1734	558
Dadant & Sons Inc 51 S Second St	Hamilton	IL	62341	**888-922-1293**	217-847-3324	121
Daedalus Books Inc 9645 Gerwig Ln	Columbia	MD	21046	**800-395-2665**	410-309-2706	95
Daemar Inc 861 Cranberry Ct	Oakville	ON	L6L6J7	**800-387-7115**	905-847-6500	350
Daemen College 4380 Main St	Amherst	NY	14226	**800-462-7652**	716-839-8225	167
DAG Media Inc 125-10 Queens Blvd Ste 14	Kew Gardens	NY	11415	**800-261-2799**	718-263-8454	634-6
Daggett Truck Line Inc 32717 County Rd 10	Frazee	MN	56544	**800-262-9393**	218-334-3711	778
Dahl Bros Canada Ltd 2600 S Sheridan Way	Mississauga	ON	L5J2M4	**800-268-5355**	905-822-2330	350
Dahle North America Inc 49 Vose Farm Rd Ste 110	Peterborough	NH	03458	**800-243-8145**	603-924-0003	533
Dahlsten Truck Line Inc 101 W Edgar PO Box 95	Clay Center	NE	68933	**800-228-4313**	402-762-3511	778
DAI (Denali Advance Integration) 17735 NE 65th St Ste 130	Redmond	WA	98052	**877-467-8008**	425-885-4000	182
Daikin America Inc 20 Olympic Dr *Cust Svc	Orangeburg	NY	10962	**800-365-9570***	845-365-9500	604-2
Dailey Marketing Group Inc 29829 Santa Margarita Pkwy Ste 100	Rancho Santa Margarita	CA	92688	**888-364-6584**	949-454-0751	7
Daily Advertiser, The 1100 Bertrand Dr	Lafayette	LA	70506	**800-526-8720**	337-289-6300	531-2
Daily American Republic 208 Poplar St PO Box 7	Poplar Bluff	MO	63901	**888-276-2242**	573-785-1414	531-2
Daily Breeze 5215 Torrance Blvd	Torrance	CA	90503	**800-253-2687**	310-540-5511	531-2
Daily Commercial 212 E Main St	Leesburg	FL	34748	**877-688-3028**	352-365-8200	531-2
Daily Courier 409 SE Seventh St	Grants Pass	OR	97526	**800-228-0457**	541-474-3700	531-2
Daily Environment Report 1801 S Bell St	Arlington	VA	22202	**800-372-1033**		530-5
Daily Express Inc 1072 Harrisburg Pk	Carlisle	PA	17013	**800-735-3136**	717-243-5757	778
Daily Gazette 2345 Maxon Rd Ext PO Box 1090	Schenectady	NY	12301	**800-262-2211**	518-374-4141	531-2
Daily Globe, The 118 E McLeod Ave PO Box 548	Ironwood	MI	49938	**800-236-2887**	906-932-2211	634-8
Daily Herald 155 E Algonquin Rd	Arlington Heights	IL	60005	**888-903-4070**	847-427-4300	531-2
Daily Journal 891 E Oak Rd	Vineland	NJ	08360	**800-222-0104**	856-691-5000	531-2
Daily Labor Report 1801 S Bell St	Arlington	VA	22202	**800-372-1033**		530-7
Daily Local News 250 N Bradford Ave	West Chester	PA	19382	**800-568-7355**	610-696-1775	531-2
Daily News 724 Bell Fork Rd PO Box 196	Jacksonville	NC	28541	**877-878-2120**	910-353-1171	531-2
Daily Nonpareil 535 W Broadway Ste 300	Council Bluffs	IA	51503	**800-283-1882**	712-328-1811	531-2
Daily Press 13891 Pk Ave PO Box 1389	Victorville	CA	92393	**844-287-3897**	760-241-7744	531-2
Daily Progress 685 W Rio Rd	Charlottesville	VA	22902	**866-469-4866**	434-978-7200	634-8
Daily Racing Form 100 Broadway 7th Fl *Cust Svc	New York	NY	10005	**800-306-3676***	212-366-7600	456-14
Daily Record 212 E Liberty St PO Box 918	Wooster	OH	44691	**800-686-2958**	330-264-1125	531-2
Daily Report for Executives 1801 S Bell St	Arlington	VA	22202	**800-372-1033**		530-2
Daily Sentinel PO Box 668	Grand Junction	CO	81502	**800-332-5832**	970-242-5050	531-2
Daily Star 102 Chestnut St PO Box 250	Oneonta	NY	13820	**800-721-1000**	607-432-1000	531-2
Daily Tax Report 1801 S Bell St	Arlington	VA	22202	**800-372-1033**		530-2
Daily Telegram 133 N Winter St	Adrian	MI	49221	**800-968-5111**	517-265-5111	531-2
Daily Times 618 Beam St	Salisbury	MD	21801	**877-335-6278**	410-749-7171	531-2
Daily World 315 S Michigan St	Aberdeen	WA	98520	**800-829-7880**	360-532-4000	531-2
DailyAccess Corp 307 University Blvd N Bldg 3 Ste 1500	Mobile	AL	36688	**877-859-5735**	251-665-1800	390
DailyFX 55 Water St 50th Fl	New York	NY	10041	**888-503-6739**	212-897-7660	401
DaimlerChrysler Corp Jeep Div PO Box 21-8004 *Cust Svc	Auburn Hills	MI	48321	**800-992-1997***		58
Dairiconcepts LP 3253 E Chestnut Expy	Springfield	MO	65802	**877-596-4374**	417-829-3400	297-5
Dairy Farmers of America Inc 10220 N Ambassador Dr	Kansas City	MO	64153	**888-332-6455**	816-801-6455	297-5
Dairy Herd Management 10901 W 84th Terr	Lenexa	KS	66214	**800-255-5113**	913-438-8700	456-1
Dairy Management Inc (DMI) 10255 W Higgins Rd Ste 900	Rosemont	IL	60018	**800-853-2479**		47-2
Dairy One 730 Warren Rd	Ithaca	NY	14850	**800-344-2697**	607-257-1272	11-2
Dairy Queen 7505 Metro Blvd	Minneapolis	MN	55439	**800-883-4279**	952-830-0200	381
Dairyamerica Inc 7815 N Palm Ave Ste 250	Fresno	CA	93711	**800-722-3110**	559-251-0992	48-18
Dairyland Insurance Co 1800 N Pt Dr *Sales	Stevens Point	WI	54481	**866-445-5364***	715-346-6000	391-4
Daisy IT Supplies Sales & Service 8575 Red Oak Ave	Rancho Cucamonga	CA	91730	**800-266-5585**	909-989-5585	111
Daisy Outdoor Products 400 W Stribling Dr	Rogers	AR	72756	**800-643-3458**	479-636-1200	708
Daisy Rock Guitars 16320 Roscoe Blvd Ste 100	Van Nuys	CA	91410	**877-693-2479**		526
Daiwa Corp 11137 Warland Dr	Cypress	CA	90630	**800-736-4653**	562-802-9589	708
DakoCytomation 6392 Via Real *Cust Svc	Carpinteria	CA	93013	**800-400-3256***	805-566-6655	233
Dakota Central Telecommunications Co-op 630 Fifth St N	Carrington	ND	58421	**800-771-0974**	701-652-3184	733
Dakota County Technical College 1300 E 145th St	Rosemount	MN	55068	**877-937-3282**	651-423-8301	798
Dakota Drug Inc 28 Main St N	Minot	ND	58703	**800-437-2018**	701-852-2141	240
Dakota Electric Assn 4300 220th St W	Farmington	MN	55024	**800-874-3409**	651-463-6144	247
Dakota Energy Co-op Inc PO Box 830	Huron	SD	57350	**800-353-8591**	605-352-8591	247
Dakota Gasification Co PO Box 5540	Bismarck	ND	58506	**866-747-3546**	701-221-4400	785
Dakota Granite Co 48391 150th St PO Box 1351	Milbank	SD	57252	**800-843-3333**	605-432-5580	722
Dakota Growers Pasta Company Inc 1 Pasta Ave	Carrington	ND	58421	**866-569-4411**	701-652-2855	297-31
Dakota Line Inc PO Box 476	Vermillion	SD	57069	**800-532-5682**	605-624-5228	778
Dakota Lions Sight & Health 4501 W 61st St Ste 201	Sioux Falls	SD	57107	**800-372-3751**	701-250-9390	271
Dakota Marble Inc 902 W 19th St	Yankton	SD	57078	**800-697-7241**	605-665-7241	722
Dakota Mfg Company Inc 1909 S Rowley St	Mitchell	SD	57301	**800-232-5682**	605-996-5571	777
Dakota Plains Co-op 151 Ninth Ave NW	Valley City	ND	58072	**800-288-7922**	701-845-0812	325
Dakota State University 820 N Washington Ave	Madison	SD	57042	**888-378-9988**	605-256-5139	167
Dakota Supply Group (DSG) 2601 Third Ave N	Fargo	ND	58102	**800-437-4702**	701-237-9440	248
Dakota Valley Electric Co-op 7296 Hwy 281	Edgeley	ND	58433	**800-342-4671**	701-493-2281	247
Dakota Wesleyan University 1200 W University Ave	Mitchell	SD	57301	**800-333-8506**	605-995-2600	167
Dakotacare 2600 W 49th St PO Box 7406	Sioux Falls	SD	57117	**800-325-5598**	605-334-4000	391-3
Daktronics Inc 201 Daktronics Dr *NASDAQ: DAKT*	Brookings	SD	57006	**800-325-8766**	605-692-0200	175-4
Dale Barton Agency Inc 1100 East 6600 South	Salt Lake City	UT	84121	**866-288-1666**	801-288-1600	390
Dale Carnegie & Assoc Inc 290 Motor Pkwy	Hauppauge	NY	11788	**800-231-5800**		763
Dale L Buchanan & Associates PC 6576 E Brainerd Rd	Chattanooga	TN	37421	**800-813-8783**	423-894-2552	428
Dale Laboratories 2960 Simms St	Hollywood	FL	33020	**800-327-1776**	954-925-0103	587
Dale Medical Products Inc PO Box 1556	Plainville	MA	02762	**800-343-3980**		475
Da-Lite Screen Company Inc 3100 N Detroit St	Warsaw	IN	46581	**800-622-3737**	574-267-8101	590
Dallas Baptist University 3000 Mtn Creek Pkwy	Dallas	TX	75211	**800-460-1328**	214-333-7100	167
Dallas Christian College 2700 Christian Pkwy	Dallas	TX	75234	**800-688-1029**	972-241-3371	160
Dallas Convention & Visitors Bureau 325 N St Paul St Ste 700	Dallas	TX	75201	**800-232-5527**	214-571-1000	208
Dallas Convention Ctr 650 S Griffin St	Dallas	TX	75202	**877-850-2100**	214-939-2750	207
Dallas County Hospital 610 10th St	Perry	IA	50220	**800-877-7541**	515-465-3547	374-3
Dallas Independent School District 3700 Ross Ave	Dallas	TX	75204	**866-796-3682**	972-925-3700	683
Dallas Institute of Funeral Service 3909 S Buckner Blvd	Dallas	TX	75227	**800-235-5444**	214-388-5466	798
Dallas Johnson Greenhouse Inc 2802 Twin City Dr	Council Bluffs	IA	51501	**800-445-4794**	712-366-0407	369
Dallas Love Field 8008 Cedar Springs Rd LB 16	Dallas	TX	75235	**877-359-8474**	214-670-5683	27
Dallas Market Ctr 2100 Stemmons Fwy Ste 113	Dallas	TX	75207	**800-325-6587**	214-655-6100	207
Dallas Morning News 508 Young St	Dallas	TX	75202	**800-431-0010**	214-977-8222	531-2
Dallas Opera 8350 N Central Expy Ste 210	Dallas	TX	75206	**888-353-4537**	214-443-1000	572-2
Dallas Theological Seminary 3909 Swiss Ave	Dallas	TX	75204	**800-992-0998**	800-387-9673	168-3

Name / Address	City	State	Zip	Toll-Free	Phone	Class
Dallas-Fort Worth International Airport (DFW) 3200 E Airfield Dr PO Box 619428	Dallas	TX	75261	**800-252-7522**	972-973-8888	27
Dallastown Area School District 700 New School Ln	Dallastown	PA	17313	**866-233-9796**	717-244-4021	683
Dalmac Oilfield Services Inc 4934 - 89 St	Edmonton	AB	T6E5K1	**888-632-5622**	780-988-8510	538
Dalmation Press 113 Seaboard Ln Ste C-250	Franklin	TN	37067	**800-815-8696**		634-2
Dal-Tile International Inc 7834 Hawn Fwy	Dallas	TX	75217	**800-933-8453**	214-398-1411	749
Dalton Enterprises Inc 131 Willow St	Cheshire	CT	06410	**800-851-5606**	203-272-3221	45
Dalton Gear Co 212 Colfax Ave N	Minneapolis	MN	55405	**800-328-7485**	612-374-2150	707
Dalton State College 650 N College Dr	Dalton	GA	30720	**800-829-4436**	706-272-4436	167
Daly City Public Library 40 Wembley Dr	Daly City	CA	94015	**888-227-7669**	650-991-8025	434-3
Daly Computers Inc 22521 Gateway Ctr Dr	Clarksburg	MD	20871	**800-955-3259**	301-670-0381	178
Daman Products Co Inc 1811 N Home St	Mishawaka	IN	46545	**800-959-7841**	574-259-7841	788
Damascus Bakery Inc 56 Gold St	Brooklyn	NY	11201	**800-367-7482**		67
Damascus Steel Casting Co Blockhouse Rd Run Extn	New Brighton	PA	15066	**800-920-2210**	724-846-2770	491
Damon Industries Inc 12435 Rockhill Ave NE	Alliance	OH	44601	**800-362-9850**	330-821-5310	150
Dan Schantz Farm & Greenhouses LLC 8025 Spinnerstown Rd	Zionsville	PA	18092	**800-451-3064**	610-967-2181	369
Dan Wolf Chevrolet of Naperville 1515 W Ogden Ave	Naperville	IL	60540	**800-243-8872**	630-596-1189	56
Dan'l Webster Inn 149 Main St	Sandwich	MA	02563	**800-444-3566**	508-888-3622	379
Dana Innovations 212 Avenida Fabricante	San Clemente	CA	92672	**800-582-7777**	949-492-7777	51
Dana Transport Inc 210 Essex Ave E	Avenel	NJ	07001	**800-733-3262**	732-750-9100	778
Dana-Farber Cancer Institute 44 Binney St	Boston	MA	02115	**866-408-3324**	617-632-3000	374-7
Dana-Farber Cancer Institute Stem Cell/Bone Marrow Transplant Program 450 Brookline Ave Dana 2	Boston	MA	02115	**866-408-3324**	617-632-3591	767
Danaher Corp 2200 Pennsylvania Ave NW Ste 800 *NYSE: DHR*	Washington	DC	20037	**800-833-9200**	202-828-0850	471
Danamark Watercare Ltd 2-90 Walker Dr	Brampton	ON	L6T4H6	**888-326-2627**		609
Danbury Hospital (DH) 24 Hospital Ave	Danbury	CT	06810	**800-516-3658**	203-739-7000	374-3
Danby Group LLP, The 3060-A Business Park Dr	Norcross	GA	30071	**800-262-2629**	770-416-9844	534
Dance Magazine 333 Seventh Ave 11th Fl	New York	NY	10001	**800-331-1750**	212-979-4800	456-9
Dance Theatre of Harlem Inc 466 W 152nd St	New York	NY	10031	**800-538-2538**	212-690-2800	572-1
Dane Media LLC 385 Sylvan Ave Ste 24	Englewood Cliffs	NJ	07632	**888-233-2863**		197
Danfords Hotel & Marina 25 E Broadway	Port Jefferson	NY	11777	**800-332-6367**		378
Daniel & Henry Co 1001 Highlands Plaza Dr W Ste 500	Saint Louis	MO	63110	**800-256-3462**	314-421-1525	390
Daniel & Stark Law Offices 100 W William Joel Bryan Pkwy	Bryan	TX	77803	**800-474-1233**	254-776-6200	428
Daniel & Yeager (D&Y) 6767 Old Madison Pk Ste 690	Huntsville	AL	35806	**800-955-1919**		268
Daniel Boone Regional Library 100 W Broadway	Columbia	MO	65203	**800-324-4806**	573-443-3161	434-3
Daniel F Young Inc 1235 Westlakes Dr Ste 255	Berwyn	PA	19312	**866-407-0083**	610-725-4000	448
Daniel Group Ltd, The 400 Clarice Ave Ste 200	Charlotte	NC	28204	**877-967-4242**		448
Daniel Measurement & Control Inc 5650 Brittmoore Rd	Houston	TX	77041	**800-518-1623**	713-467-6000	203
Daniel Smith Artist Materials PO Box 84268	Seattle	WA	98124	**800-426-6740**	206-223-9599	458
Daniel Webster College 20 University Dr	Nashua	NH	03063	**800-325-6876**	603-577-6000	167
Daniele Inc PO Box 106	Pascoag	RI	02859	**800-451-2535**	401-568-6228	297-26
Daniels & Roberts Inc 209 N Seacrest Blvd Ste 2	Boynton Beach	FL	33435	**800-488-0066**	561-241-0066	7
DANK (German-American National Congress) 4740 N Western Ave Ste 206	Chicago	IL	60625	**888-872-3265**	773-275-1100	47-14
Danly IEM 6779 Engle Rd Ste A-F	Cleveland	OH	44130	**800-652-6462**		755
Danner Shoe Manufacturing Co 17634 NE Airport *Cust Svc	Portland	OR	97230	**800-345-0430***	503-251-1100	302
Danny Herman Trucking Inc PO Box 55	Mountain City	TN	37683	**800-251-7500**	423-727-9061	448
Danos & Curole Marine Contractors Inc 13083 Louisiana 308	Larose	LA	70373	**800-487-5971**	985-693-3313	538
Danson Decor Inc 3425 Douglas B Floreani	St Laurent	QC	H4S1Y6	**800-363-1865**	514-335-2435	294
Dantom Systems Inc 29241 Beck Rd	Wixom	MI	48393	**866-536-2376**	248-567-7300	227
Danver 1 Grand St	Wallingford	CT	06492	**888-441-0537**	203-269-2300	320-1
Danville Ambulance Service Office 12 A St	Danville	PA	17821	**877-721-3671**	570-275-3031	30
Danville Area Community College 2000 E Main St	Danville	IL	61832	**877-342-3042**	217-443-3222	161
Danville Community College 1008 S Main St	Danville	VA	24541	**800-560-4291**	434-797-2222	161
Danville National Cemetery 1900 E Main St	Danville	IL	61832	**800-827-1000**	217-554-4550	135
Danville Public Library 319 N Vermilion St	Danville	IL	61832	**866-235-6096**	217-477-5220	434-3
Danville Regional Medical Ctr 142 S Main St	Danville	VA	24541	**800-688-3762**	434-799-2100	374-3
Danville Signal Processing Inc 38570 100th Ave	Cannon Falls	MN	55009	**877-230-5629**	507-263-5854	196
DAP Products Inc 2400 Boston St Ste 200 *Cust Svc	Baltimore	MD	21224	**800-543-3840***	410-675-2100	3
Dapper Tire Company Inc 4025 Lockridge St	San Diego	CA	92102	**800-266-7172**	619-266-1397	753
Daptiv 1008 Western Ave Ste 700	Seattle	WA	98101	**888-621-8361**	206-341-9117	38
Darby Dan Farm 3225 Old Frankfort Pk	Lexington	KY	40510	**888-321-0424**	859-254-0424	368
Dardanelle & Russellville Railroad Co 4416 S Arkansas Ave	Russellville	AR	72802	**888-877-7267**	479-968-6455	646
Dare 2 Share Ministries International PO Box 745323	Arvada	CO	80006	**800-462-8355**	303-425-1606	47-20
Dare Products Inc 860 Betterly Rd PO Box 157	Battle Creek	MI	49015	**800-922-3273**	269-965-2307	281
Darex 210 E Hersey St PO Box 730	Ashland	OR	97520	**800-597-6170**	541-488-2224	454
Darice Inc 13000 Darice Pkwy	Strongsville	OH	44149	**866-432-7423**		43
Darien Lake Theme Park Resort 9993 Allegheny Rd PO Box 91	Darien Center	NY	14040	**866-640-0652**	585-599-4641	32
Dark Horse Comics Inc 10956 SE Main St	Milwaukie	OR	97222	**800-862-0052**	503-652-8815	634-5
Darke Rural Electric Co-op Inc 1120 Fort Jefferson Rd	Greenville	OH	45331	**866-692-6330**	937-548-4114	247
Darling International Inc 251 O'Connor Ridge Blvd Ste 300 *NYSE: DAR*	Irving	TX	75038	**855-327-7761**	972-717-0300	297-12
Darlington Raceway 1301 Harry Bird Hwy	Darlington	SC	29532	**866-459-7223**		514
Darlington School 1014 Cave Spring Rd	Rome	GA	30161	**800-368-4437**	706-235-6051	621
Darlington Veneer Company Inc 225 Fourth St	Darlington	SC	29532	**800-845-2388**	843-393-3861	612
Darlingtonia State Natural Site 84505 Hwy 101 S	Florence	OR	97439	**800-551-6949**	541-997-3851	564
Darnall Army Medical Ctr 36000 Darnall Loop	Fort Hood	TX	76544	**800-305-6421**	254-288-8000	331-4
Daron Worldwide Trading Inc 24 Stewart Pl Unit 4	Fairfield	NJ	07004	**800-776-2324**	973-882-0035	759
Dar-Ran Furniture Industries 2402 Shore St	High Point	NC	27263	**800-334-7891**	336-861-2400	320-1
Darrow School 110 Darrow Rd	New Lebanon	NY	12125	**877-432-7769**	518-794-6000	621
Dart Aerospace Ltd 1270 Aberdeen St	Hawkesbury	ON	K6A1K7	**800-556-4166**	613-632-3336	21
Dart Appraisalcom 2600 W Big Beaver Rd Ste 540	Troy	MI	48084	**888-327-8123**		650
Dart Container Corp 500 Hogsback Rd	Mason	MI	48854	**800-248-5960**		600
Dart World Inc 140 Linwood St	Lynn	MA	01905	**800-225-2558**	781-581-6035	709
Dar-tech Inc 16485 Rockside Rd	Cleveland	OH	44137	**800-228-7347**	216-663-7600	145
Darton College 2400 Gillionville Rd	Albany	GA	31707	**866-775-1214**	229-430-6742	161
Darue of California Inc 14102 S Broadway	Los Angeles	CA	90061	**877-693-2783**	310-323-1350	154-20
Daryl Flood Inc 450 Airline Dr Ste 100	Coppell	TX	75019	**800-325-9340**	972-471-1496	188
DAS Inc 724 Lawn Rd	Palmyra	PA	17078	**866-622-7979**	717-964-3642	37
Dasco Pro Inc 340 Blackhawk Pk Ave	Rockford	IL	61104	**800-327-2690**	815-962-3727	756
Dash Point State Park 5700 SW Dash Pt Rd	Federal Way	WA	98023	**888-226-7688**	253-661-4955	564
Dash Tours 1024 Winnipeg St	Regina	SK	S4R8P8	**800-265-0000**	306-352-2222	758
Dashwood Industries Ltd 69323 Richmond St	Centralia	ON	N0M1K0	**800-265-4284**	519-228-6624	498
Dassault Falcon Jet Corp PO Box 2000	South Hackensack	NJ	07606	**800-527-2463**	201-440-6700	20
Dastmalchi Enterprises Inc 31 East Macarthur Crescent Ste 111	Santa Ana	CA	92707	**888-358-0331**		4
Data Access Corp 14000 SW 119th Ave	Miami	FL	33186	**800-451-3539**	305-238-0012	180-2
Data Dash Inc 3928 Delor St	Saint Louis	MO	63116	**800-211-5988**	314-832-5788	227
Data Device Corp 105 Wilbur Pl *Cust Svc	Bohemia	NY	11716	**800-332-5757***	631-567-5600	255
Data Exchange Corp 3600 Via Pescador	Camarillo	CA	93012	**800-237-7911**	805-388-1711	177
Data I/O Corp 6464 185th Ave NE Ste 101 *NASDAQ: DAIO*	Redmond	WA	98052	**800-426-1045**	425-881-6444	693
Data Impressions 17418 Studebaker Rd	Cerritos	CA	90703	**800-777-6488**	562-207-9050	176
Data Label Inc 1000 Spruce St	Terre Haute	IN	47807	**800-457-0676**	812-232-0408	413
Data Management Inc 537 New Britain Ave *Orders	Farmington	CT	06034	**800-243-1969***	860-677-8586	85
Data Management Marketing 3225 Jordan Blvd	Malabar	FL	32950	**888-266-4127**	321-725-8081	179
Data Papers Inc 468 Industrial Pk Rd	Muncy	PA	17756	**800-233-3032**		109
Data Partners Inc 12857 Banyan Creek Dr	Fort Myers	FL	33908	**866-423-1818**	239-267-8762	196
Data Path 318 McHenry Ave	Modesto	CA	95354	**888-693-2827**	209-521-0055	198

Name	Address	City	State	ZIP	Toll-Free	Phone	Class
Data Pro Acctg Software Inc	111 Second Ave NE Ste 1200	Saint Petersburg	FL	33701	800-237-6377	727-803-1500	180-1
Data Sales Company Inc	3450 W Burnsville Pkwy	Burnsville	MN	55337	800-328-2730	952-890-8838	176
Data Sciences International	119 14th St NW Ste 100	St. Paul	MN	55112	800-262-9687		666
Data Services Inc	31516 Winterplace Pkwy	Salisbury	MD	21804	800-432-4066	410-546-2206	227
Data Source Inc	1400 Universal Ave	Kansas City	MO	64120	877-846-9120	816-483-3282	109
Data Storage Systems Ctr (DSSC)	*Carnegie Mellon University ECE Dept* 5000 Forbes Ave	Pittsburgh	PA	15213	800-864-8287	412-268-6600	666
Data Systems Analysts Inc (DSA)	Eigth Neshaminy Interplex Ste 209	Trevose	PA	19053	877-422-4372	215-245-4800	182
Data Technology Inc	14225 Dayton Cir Ste 4 *General	Omaha	NE	68137	888-334-9300*	402-891-0711	546
Data Translation Inc	100 Locke Dr *OTC: DATX*	Marlborough	MA	01752	800-525-8528	508-481-3700	624
Data Transmission Network Corp	9110 W Dodge Rd Ste 200	Omaha	NE	68114	800-485-4000	402-390-2328	387
DataCard Corp	11111 Bren Rd W	Minnetonka	MN	55343	800-328-8623	952-933-1223	702
Datacolor	5 Princess Rd *General	Lawrenceville	NJ	08648	800-340-1007*	609-924-2189	419
DataDirect Networks	9351 Deering Ave	Chatsworth	CA	91311	800-837-2298	818-700-7600	175-8
Datafirst Corp	5124 Departure Dr	Raleigh	NC	27616	800-634-8504	919-876-6650	179
Dataflux Corp	940 NW Cary Pkwy Ste 201	Cary	NC	27513	800-727-0025	919-447-3000	179
Dataforth Corp	3331 E Hemisphere Loop	Tucson	AZ	85706	800-444-7644	520-741-1404	175-3
Dataium LLC	2525 Perimeter Pl Dr Ste 105	Nashville	TN	37214	877-896-3282		387
Dataline LLC	6703 Albunda Dr PO Box 50816	Knoxville	TN	37950	800-666-9858	865-588-7740	263
Datalink Corp	8170 Upland Cir *NASDAQ: DTLK*	Chanhassen	MN	55317	800-448-6314	952-944-3462	175-8
DataLink Interactive Inc	1120 Benfield Blvd Ste G	Millersville	MD	21108	888-565-3279	410-729-0440	182
Datalogic Scanning	959 Terry St	Eugene	OR	97402	800-695-5700	541-683-5700	175-7
Datalux Corp	155 Aviation Dr	Winchester	VA	22602	800-328-2589	540-662-1500	175-1
Datamann Inc	1994 Hartford Ave	Wilder	VT	05088	800-451-4263	802-295-6600	180-11
Datamark Graphics Inc	603 W Bailey St	Asheboro	NC	27203	888-629-6300		626
Datamark Inc	123 W Mills Ave Ste 400	El Paso	TX	79901	800-477-1944		227
Datamatics Management Services Inc	330 New Brunswick Ave	Fords	NJ	08863	800-673-0366	732-738-9600	180-1
Data-Matique	2110 Sherwin St	Garland	TX	75041	866-706-0981	972-272-3446	695
Datamax Corp	4501 Pkwy Commerce Blvd	Orlando	FL	32808	800-321-2233	407-578-8007	175-6
Datamax Office Systems Inc	6717 Waldemar Ave	Saint Louis	MO	63139	800-325-9299	314-633-1400	111
Datamine Internet Marketing Solutions Inc	330 S Lake St	Gary	IN	46403	877-328-2646	219-939-9987	7
DataMotion Inc	35 Airport Rd Ste 120	Morristown	NJ	07960	800-672-7233	973-455-1245	180-7
DataPipe	10 Exchange Pl	Jersey City	NJ	07302	877-773-3306	201-792-4847	806
Datapro Solutions Inc	6336 E Utah Ave	Spokane	WA	99212	888-658-6881	509-532-3530	182
Dataram Corp	777 Alexander Rd Ste 100 *NASDAQ: DRAM*	Princeton	NJ	08540	800-328-2726	609-799-0071	624
Datarealm Internet Services Inc	PO Box 1616	Hudson	WI	54016	877-227-3783		806
Dataserv Corp	8625 F St	Omaha	NE	68127	888-901-8700	402-339-8700	177
Datashield LLC	1440 Show Berry St	Park City	UT	84098	855-328-2744		198
Datassential	1762 Westwood Blvd Ste 250	Los Angeles	CA	90024	877-886-3687		465
Datasyst Engineering & Testing Services Inc	S14W33511 Hwy 18	Delafield	WI	53018	800-969-4050	262-968-4003	263
Datatech Labs	8000 e quincy ave	Denver	CO	80237	888-288-3282	303-770-3282	623
Datatel Inc	4375 Fair Lakes Ct	Fairfax	VA	22033	800-223-7036		180-10
Datatel Resources Corp	1729 Pennsylvania Ave	Monaca	PA	15061	800-245-2688	724-775-5300	109
DataViz Inc	612 Wheelers Farms Rd	Milford	CT	06460	800-733-0030	203-874-0085	180-12
Datawatch Corp	271 Mill Rd *NASDAQ: DWCH*	Chelmsford	MA	01824	800-445-3311	978-441-2200	180-12
Dates Weiser Furniture Corp	1700 Broadway St	Buffalo	NY	14212	800-466-7037	716-891-1700	322
DATTCO Inc	583 S St	New Britain	CT	06051	800-229-4879	860-229-4878	106
Datum Filing Systems Inc	89 Church Rd	Emigsville	PA	17318	800-828-8018	717-764-6350	288
Dauphin County	2 S Second St 3rd Fl.	Harrisburg	PA	17101	800-328-0058	717-780-6636	338
Dauphin North America	300 Myrtle Ave *Cust Svc	Boonton	NJ	07005	800-631-1186*	973-263-1100	320-1
Dauphine Orleans Hotel	415 Dauphine St	New Orleans	LA	70112	800-521-7111	504-586-1800	379
DAV (Disabled American Veterans)	3725 Alexandria Pike	Cold Spring	KY	41076	877-426-2838	859-441-7300	47-19
Davco Advertising Inc	89 N Kinzer Rd PO Box 288	Kinzers	PA	17535	800-283-2826	717-442-4155	7
Davco Technology LLC	1600 Woodland Dr PO Box 487	Saline	MI	48176	800-328-2611	734-429-5665	59
Dave & Buster's	3000 Oakwood Blvd	Hollywood	FL	33020	844-515-5157	954-923-5505	669
Dave & Buster's Inc	2481 Manana Dr	Dallas	TX	75220	800-842-5369	214-357-9588	657
Dave Thomas Foundation for Adoption	716 Mt Airyshire Blvd Ste 100	Columbus	OH	43235	800-275-3832		306
Dave White Chevrolet Inc	5880 Monroe St	Sylvania	OH	43560	800-893-5217	419-517-6111	56
Davenport & Co LLC	901 E Cary St 1 James Center Ste 1100	Richmond	VA	23219	800-846-6666	804-780-2000	688
Davenport Hotel, The	10 S Post St	Spokane	WA	99201	800-899-1482	509-455-8888	379
Davenport Insulation Inc	7400 Gateway Ct	Manassas	VA	20109	855-626-6459	703-631-7744	191-9
Davenport Machine Inc	167 Ames St	Rochester	NY	14611	800-344-5748	585-235-4545	454
Davenport University							
	Dearborn 4801 Oakman Blvd	Dearborn	MI	48126	800-585-1479	313-581-4400	167
	Flint 4318 Miller Rd Ste A	Flint	MI	48507	800-727-1443	810-732-9977	167
	Lansing 220 E Kalamazoo St	Lansing	MI	48933	800-686-1600	517-484-2600	167
	Lettinga Campus 6191 Kraft Ave SE	Grand Rapids	MI	49512	866-925-3884	616-698-7111	167
	Saginaw 5300 Bay Rd	Saginaw	MI	48604	800-968-8133	989-799-7800	167
	Warren 27650 Dequindre Rd	Warren	MI	48092	800-724-7708	586-558-8700	167
Davey Tree Expert Co	1500 N Mantua St	Kent	OH	44240	800-445-8733	330-673-9511	774
David A Smith Printing Inc	742 S 22nd St	Harrisburg	PA	17104	800-564-3117	717-564-3719	626
David A. Straz Jr Ctr for, The Performing Arts, The	1010 N WC MacInnes Pl	Tampa	FL	33602	800-955-1045	813-222-1000	571
David Berman Developments	340 Selby Ave	Ottawa	ON	K2A3X6	800-665-1809	613-728-6777	344
David Clark Company Inc	360 Franklin St *Cust Svc	Worcester	MA	01615	800-298-6235*	508-751-5800	575
David Evans & Assoc Inc (DEA)	2100 SW River Pkwy	Portland	OR	97201	800-721-1916	503-223-6663	263
David Grant US Air Force Medical Ctr	101 Bodin Cir	Travis AFB	CA	94535	800-264-3462	707-423-3735	331-4
David H Fell & Company Inc	6009 Bandini Blvd	Commerce	CA	90040	800-822-1996	323-722-9992	407
David Michael & Co Inc	10801 Decatur Rd	Philadelphia	PA	19154	800-363-5286	215-632-3100	297-15
David Suzuki Foundation	2211 Fourth Ave W	Vancouver	BC	V6K4S2	800-453-1533	604-732-4228	306
David Weekley Homes Inc	1111 N Post Oak Rd	Houston	TX	77055	800-390-6774	713-963-0500	651
David's Bridal Inc	1001 Washington St	Conshohocken	PA	19428	844-400-3222	610-943-5000	156-6
Davidsmeyer Bus Service Inc	2513 E Higgins Rd	Elk Grove Village	IL	60007	800-323-0312	847-437-3767	108
Davidson College	PO Box 7156	Davidson	NC	28035	800-768-0380	704-894-2000	167
Davidson Cos	8 Third St N PO Box 5015	Great Falls	MT	59401	800-332-5915	406-727-4200	688
Davidson County Community College	PO Box 1287	Lexington	NC	27293	800-233-4050	336-249-8186	161
Davidson Plyforms Inc	5505 33rd St SE	Grand Rapids	MI	49512	800-505-4732	616-956-0033	818
Davidson-Kennedy Co	800 Industrial Park Dr	Marietta	GA	30062	800-733-3434	770-427-9467	119
Davies Consulting Inc	6935 Wisconsin Ave Ste 600	Chevy Chase	MD	20815	800-811-8336	301-652-4535	196
Davies Molding LLC	350 Kehoe Blvd	Carol Stream	IL	60188	800-554-9208	630-510-8188	620
Davies Pearson PC	920 Fawcett Ave	Tacoma	WA	98401	800-439-1112	253-620-1500	428
Daviess County Metal Sales Inc	9929 E US Hwy 50	Cannelburg	IN	47519	800-279-4299	812-486-4299	695
Daviess-Martin County REMC	12628 E 75 N PO Box 430	Loogootee	IN	47553	800-762-7362	812-295-4200	247
Davis & Elkins College	100 Campus Dr	Elkins	WV	26241	800-624-3157	304-637-1900	167
Davis College	4747 Monroe St	Toledo	OH	43623	800-477-7021	419-473-2700	798
Davis Cos	325 Donald J Lynch Blvd	Marlborough	MA	01752	800-482-9494	763-231-0700	719
Davis Direct Inc	1241 Newell Pkwy	Montgomery	AL	36110	877-277-0878	334-277-0878	626
Davis Express Inc	PO Box 1276	Starke	FL	32091	800-874-4270		778
Davis Funds	2949 E Elvira Rd Ste 101	Tucson	AR	85756	800-279-0279		527
Davis Hospital & Medical Ctr (DHMC)	1600 W Antelope Dr	Layton	UT	84041	877-898-6080	801-807-1000	374-3
Davis Instrument Corp	3465 Diablo Ave	Hayward	CA	94545	800-678-3669	510-732-9229	471
Davis Law Firm	10500 Heitage Blvd Ste 102	San Antonio	TX	78201	800-770-0127	210-444-4444	428
Davis Memorial Hospital	812 Gorman Ave	Elkins	WV	26241	888-477-6895	304-636-3300	374-3
Davis Paint Company Inc	1311 Iron St PO Box 7589	North Kansas City	MO	64116	800-821-2029	816-471-4447	549
Davis Vision Inc	711 Troy-Schenectady Rd	Latham	NY	12110	800-999-5431		391-3

Name / Address	City	State	ZIP	Toll-Free	Phone	Class
Davisco International Inc 719 N Main St	Le Sueur	MN	56058	800-757-7611	507-665-8811	297-10
Davis-Ulmer Sprinkler Company Inc 1 Commerce Dr	Amherst	NY	14228	877-691-3200	716-691-3200	386
DaVita Inc 1551 Wewatta St *NYSE: DVA*	Denver	CO	80202	800-310-4872	303-405-2100	352
Davitt & Hanser Music Co 3015 Kustom Dr	Hebron	KY	41048	800-999-5558	859-817-7100	526
Davol Inc 100 Crossings Blvd *Cust Svc	Warwick	RI	02886	800-556-6756*		475
Davy Crockett Birthplace State Park 1245 Davy Crockett Pk Rd	Limestone	TN	37681	800-250-8615	423-257-2167	564
Daw Construction Group LLC 12552 South 125 West	Draper	UT	84020	800-748-4778	801-553-9111	188
Dawahares Inc 1845 Alexandria Dr	Lexington	KY	40504	800-677-9108	859-278-0422	156-2
Dawes Arboretum 7770 Jacksontown Rd SE	Newark	OH	43056	800-443-2937	740-323-2355	96
Dawn Food Products Inc 3333 Sargent Rd *Cust Svc	Jackson	MI	49201	800-292-1362*	517-789-4400	297-16
Dawson Community College 300 College Dr	Glendive	MT	59330	800-821-8320	406-377-3396	161
Dawson County Board of Education, The 517 Allen St	Dawsonville	GA	30534	866-632-9992	706-265-3246	683
Dawson Geophysical Co 508 W Wall St Ste 800 *NASDAQ: DWSN*	Midland	TX	79701	800-332-9766	432-684-3000	537
Dawson Public Power District 75191 Rd 433	Lexington	NE	68850	800-752-8305	308-324-2386	247
Day & Zimmermann Group Inc 1818 Market St	Philadelphia	PA	19130	877-319-0270	215-299-8000	725
Day Pitney LLP 242 Trumbull St	Hartford	CT	06103	866-667-6572	860-275-0100	428
Day Publishing Co 47 Eugene O'Neill Dr	New London	CT	06320	800-542-3354	860-442-2200	634-8
Daybreak Star Ctr 3801 W Government Way PO Box 99100	Seattle	WA	98199	800-321-4321	206-285-4425	49-1
Day-Glo Color Corp 4515 St Clair Ave	Cleveland	OH	44103	800-424-9300	216-391-7070	549
Daylight Donut Flour Company LLC 11707 E 11th St	Tulsa	OK	74128	800-331-2245	918-438-0800	67
Daylight Transport 1501 Hughes Way Ste 200	Long Beach	CA	90810	800-468-9999		778
Daymark Recovery Services Inc Stanly Center 1000 N First St Ste 1	Albemarle	NC	28001	866-275-9552	704-983-2117	724
Days Inn Hinton-Jasper Hotel 358 Smith St	Hinton	AB	T7V2A1	800-259-4827	780-817-1960	378
Days Inns Worldwide Inc 215 W 94th St Broadway	New York	NY	10025	800-225-3297	212-866-6400	379
DaySpa Magazine 7628 Densmore Ave	Van Nuys	CA	91406	800-442-5667	818-782-7328	456-21
DaySpring Cards Inc 21154 Hwy 16 E	Siloam Springs	AR	72761	800-944-8000	479-524-9301	129
Daystar Television Network 3901 Hwy 121 PO Box 610546	Bedford	TX	76021	800-329-0029	817-571-1229	736
Dayton Area Chamber of Commerce 1 Chamber Plaza Ste 200	Dayton	OH	45402	800-621-9131	937-226-1444	138
Dayton Art Institute 456 Belmonte Pk N	Dayton	OH	45405	800-272-8258	937-223-5277	519
Dayton Ballet 140 N Main St	Dayton	OH	45402	800-745-3000	937-449-5060	572-1
Dayton City Paper 126 N Main St Ste 240	Dayton	OH	45402	888-228-3630	937-222-8855	531-5
Dayton Contemporary Dance Co 840 Germantown St	Dayton	OH	45402	888-228-3630	937-228-3232	572-1
Dayton Daily News 1611 S Main St	Dayton	OH	45409	888-397-6397	937-225-2000	531-2
Dayton Foundation 40 N Main St Ste 500	Dayton	OH	45423	877-222-0410	937-222-0410	304
Dayton International Airport 3600 Terminal Dr Ste 300	Vandalia	OH	45377	877-359-3291	937-454-8200	27
Dayton National Cemetery 4100 W Third St	Dayton	OH	45428	800-273-8255	937-262-2115	135
Dayton Parts LLC 3500 Industrial Rd PO Box 5795 *Cust Svc	Harrisburg	PA	17110	800-225-2159*	717-255-8500	59
Dayton Philharmonic Orchestra 126 N Main St Ste 210	Dayton	OH	45402	888-228-3630	937-224-3521	572-3
Dayton Power & Light Co PO Box 1247	Dayton	OH	45401	800-433-8500	937-331-3900	785
Dayton Rehabilitation Institute 1 Elizabeth Pl	Dayton	OH	45417	800-765-4772	937-424-8200	724
Dayton Reliable Air Filter Inc 2294 N Moraine Dr *Orders	Dayton	OH	45439	800-699-0747*		17
Dayton Rogers Manufacturing Co 8401 W 35 W Service Dr	Minneapolis	MN	55449	800-677-8881	763-784-7714	487
Dayton Superior Corp 1125 Byers Rd	Miamisburg	OH	45342	800-745-3700	937-866-0711	350
Dayton T Brown Inc 1175 Church St	Bohemia	NY	11716	800-232-6300	631-589-6300	740
Dayton Va Medical Ctr 4100 W Third St	Dayton	OH	45428	800-368-8262	937-268-6511	374-8
Dayton/Montgomery County Convention & Visitors Bureau 1 Chamber Plz Ste A	Dayton	OH	45402	800-221-8235	937-226-8211	208
Daytona Beach Community College 1200 W International Speedway Blvd	Daytona Beach	FL	32114	877-822-6669	386-506-3000	161
Daytona Beach Resort & Conference Ctr 2700 N Atlantic Ave	Daytona Beach	FL	32118	800-654-6216	386-672-3770	379
Daytona Inn Beach Resort 219 S Atlantic Ave *General	Daytona Beach	FL	32118	800-874-1822*	386-252-3626	379

Name / Address	City	State	ZIP	Toll-Free	Phone	Class
Dayton-Phoenix Group Inc 1619 Kuntz Rd	Dayton	OH	45404	800-657-0707	937-496-3974	648
Dazian Inc 18 Central Blvd	South Hackensack	NJ	07606	877-232-9426		742-2
Dazor Lighting Solutions 2079 Congressional	Saint Louis	MO	63146	800-345-9103	314-652-2400	439
DB Aviation Inc 3550 N McAree Rd	Waukegan	IL	60087	888-362-6738	847-244-8504	62
DB Becker Company Inc 46 Leigh St	Clinton	NJ	08809	800-394-3991	908-730-6010	145
DB Root & Company Inc 436 Seventh Ave Ste 2800	Pittsburgh	PA	15219	888-227-0913	412-227-2800	196
D&B Sales & Marketing Solutions 460 Totten Pond Rd	Waltham	MA	02451	866-473-3932	781-672-9200	180-1
DBA Engineering Ltd 401 Hanlan Rd	Vaughan	ON	L4L3T1	800-819-8833	905-851-0090	258
DBI Inc 912 E Michigan Ave	Lansing	MI	48912	800-968-1324	517-485-3200	534
DBK Concepts Inc 12905 SW 129 Ave	Miami	FL	33186	800-725-7226	305-596-7226	177
DBS Bank Ltd 725 S Figueroa St	Los Angeles	CA	90017	800-209-4555	213-627-0222	69
DBSA (Depression & Bipolar Support Alliance) 730 N Franklin St Ste 501	Chicago	IL	60610	800-826-3632	312-642-0049	47-17
DBU (Duluth Business University) 4724 Mike Colalilo Dr	Duluth	MN	55807	800-777-8406	218-722-4000	798
DC Group Inc 1977 W River Rd N	Minneapolis	MN	55411	800-838-7927		765
DC Humphrys Inc 5744 Woodland Ave *Sales	Philadelphia	PA	19143	800-645-2059*	215-724-8181	730
DC Taylor Co 312 29th St NE	Cedar Rapids	IA	52402	800-876-6346	319-363-2073	191-12
DC Tuition Assistance Grant Program 810 First St NE	Washington	DC	20001	877-485-6751	202-727-2824	723
DCA (Diamond Council of America) 3212 W End Ave Ste 202	Nashville	TN	37203	877-283-5669	615-385-5301	48-4
DCAT (Drug Chemical & Associated Technologies Assn) 1 Washington Blvd Ste 7	Robbinsville	NJ	08691	800-640-3228	609-448-1000	48-19
DCCI (Dow Chemical Canada Inc) 450 First St SW Ste 2100	Calgary	AB	T2P5H1	800-447-4369	403-267-3500	143
DCEC (Delaware County Electric Co-op) 39 Elm St PO Box 471	Delhi	NY	13753	866-436-1223	607-746-2341	247
DCH (Delnor-Community Hospital) 300 Randall Rd	Geneva	IL	60134	800-223-9776	630-208-3000	374-3
DCH Honda of Nanuet 10 Rt 304	Nanuet	NY	10954	888-495-8660	845-623-1200	56
DCI (Drum Corps International) PO Box 3129 *Orders	Indianapolis	IN	46206	800-495-7469*	317-275-1212	47-4
DCL (Downey City Library) 11121 Brookshire Ave	Downey	CA	90241	877-846-3452	562-904-7360	434-3
DCM (Distribution Ctr Management) 712 Main St Ste 187B	Boonton	NJ	07005	800-232-4317	973-265-2300	530-2
DCOTA (Design Ctr of the Americas) 1855 Griffin Rd	Dania Beach	FL	33004	877-992-9204	954-920-7997	459
DCR Workforce Inc 7815 NW Beacon Sq Blvd Ste 224	Boca Raton	FL	33487	888-327-4867		198
Dcs Netlink 1800 Macauley Ave	Rice Lake	WI	54868	877-327-6385	715-236-7424	182
DCT (Diversified Chemical Technologies Inc) 15477 Woodrow Wilson St	Detroit	MI	48238	800-243-1424	313-867-5444	144
DD Bean & Sons Co 207 Peterborough St	Jaffrey	NH	03452	800-366-2824	603-532-8311	468
DD Jones Transfer & Warehouse Co Inc 2121 Old Greenbrier Rd	Chesapeake	VA	23320	800-335-4787	757-494-0225	801-1
D&D Sexton Inc PO Box 156	Carthage	MO	64836	800-743-0265	417-358-8727	778
DD Williamson & Company Inc 100 S Spring St	Louisville	KY	40206	800-227-2635	502-895-2438	297-15
DDA (Directory Distributing Assoc) 1602 Pk 370 Ct *General	Hazelwood	MO	63042	800-325-1964*	314-592-8600	94
Ddi System LLC 75 Glen Rd Ste 204	Sandy Hook	CT	06482	877-599-4334		181
De Marque inc 400 Boul Jean-Lesage Bureau 540	Quebec	QC	G1K8W1	888-458-9143	418-658-9143	176
De Ronde Tire Supply Inc 95 Rapin Pl	Buffalo	NY	14211	800-227-4647	716-897-6690	753
de Saisset Museum at Santa Clara University 500 El Camino Real	Santa Clara	CA	95053	866-554-6800	408-554-4528	519
De Soto National Memorial 8300 Desoto Memorial Hwy	Bradenton	FL	34209	888-831-7526	941-792-0458	563
De Wafelbakkers LLC 10000 Crystal Hill Rd.	North Little Rock	AR	72113	800-924-3391	501-791-3320	297-1
DEA (David Evans & Assoc Inc) 2100 SW River Pkwy	Portland	OR	97201	800-721-1916	503-223-6663	263
Deacon Industrial Supply Co Inc 165 Boro Line Rd	King of Prussia	PA	19406	800-726-9800	610-265-5322	385
Deaconess Hospital 600 Mary St	Evansville	IN	47747	800-677-3422	812-450-5000	374-3
Deaf Smith Electric Co-op Inc 1501 E First St	Hereford	TX	79045	800-687-8189	806-364-1166	247
Deal Interactive LLC 3 Park Ave 39th Fl	New York	NY	10016	888-415-4888		387
Deal LLC, The 20 Broad St *Cust Svc	New York	NY	10005	888-667-3325*	212-313-9325	634-9
Dealers Truck Equipment Co 2460 Midway St	Shreveport	LA	71108	800-259-7569	318-635-7567	515
DealersEdge PO Box 606	Barnegat Light	NJ	08006	800-321-5312	609-879-4456	530-13
DealerTrack Holdings Inc 1111 Marcus Ave Ste M04 *NASDAQ: TRAK*	Lake Success	NY	11042	877-357-8725	516-734-3600	180-10
DealNet Capital Corp 325 Milner Ave Ste 300	Toronto	ON	M1B5N1	855-912-3444		462

Name / Address	City	State	Zip	Toll-Free	Phone	Class
Dean Cluck Feedyard Inc 105 Dean Cluck Ave	Gruver	TX	79040	**888-458-4787**	806-733-5021	10-1
Dean College 99 Main St	Franklin	MA	02038	**877-879-3326**	508-541-1508	161
Dean Foods Co 2711 N Haskell Ave Ste 3400 *NYSE: DF*	Dallas	TX	75204	**800-395-7004**	214-303-3400	297-27
Dean Health Insurance Inc 1277 Deming Way	Madison	WI	53717	**800-279-1301**	608-836-1400	391-3
Dean Team Automotive Group Inc 15121 Manchester Rd	Ballwin	MO	63011	**888-699-0663**	636-227-0100	56
Dean Transportation Inc 4812 Aurelius Rd	Lansing	MI	48910	**800-282-3326**	517-319-8300	108
Dean Word Company Ltd 1245 River Rd PO Box 310330	New Braunfels	TX	78131	**800-683-3926**	830-625-2365	190-4
Deansteel Manufacturing Co 111 Merchant	San Antonio	TX	78204	**800-825-8271**	210-226-8271	236
Dearborn Chamber of Commerce 22100 Michigan Ave	Dearborn	MI	48124	**800-844-5440**	313-584-6100	138
Dearborn County Chamber of Commerce 320 Walnut St	Lawrenceburg	IN	47025	**800-322-8198**	812-537-0814	138
Dearborn Federal Credit Union 400 Town Ctr Dr	Dearborn	MI	48126	**888-336-2700**	313-336-2700	221
Dearborn Inn the - A Marriott Hotel 20301 Oakwood Blvd	Dearborn	MI	48124	**800-228-9290**	313-271-2700	379
Dearborn Times-Herald 13730 Michigan Ave	Dearborn	MI	48126	**866-468-7630**	313-584-4000	531-4
Dearth Motors Inc 520 Eigth St	Monroe	WI	53566	**877-495-5321**	608-325-3181	56
Death Valley National Park PO Box 579	Death Valley	CA	92328	**866-713-9688**	760-786-3200	563
Deauville Beach Resort 6701 Collins Ave	Miami Beach	FL	33141	**800-327-6656**	305-865-8511	667
DEB Inc 2815 Coliseum Centre Dr Ste 600	Charlotte	NC	28217	**800-248-7190**	704-263-4240	217
Deb-El Food Products LLC 2 Papetti Plaza	Elizabeth	NJ	07206	**800-421-0330**	908-351-0330	298-8
DeBourgh Manufacturing Co 27505 Otero Ave PO Box 981	La Junta	CO	81050	**800-328-8829**		288
DeBra-Kuempel 3976 Southern Ave	Cincinnati	OH	45227	**800-395-5741**	513-271-6500	191-10
DebtFolio Inc 35 Braintree Hill Office Park Ste 107	Braintree	MA	06084	**866-876-3654**		387
Debtors Anonymous (DA) PO Box 920888	Needham	MA	02492	**800-421-2383**	781-453-2743	47-21
DeCarolis Truck Rental Inc 333 Colfax St	Rochester	NY	14606	**800-666-1169**	585-254-1169	776
Decatur Area Convention & Visitors Bureau 202 E N St	Decatur	IL	62523	**800-331-4479**	217-423-7000	208
Decatur Computers Inc 1234 N Water St Ste B	Decatur	IL	62521	**800-429-7140**	217-475-0226	177
Decatur Co-op Assn 305 S York Ave	Oberlin	KS	67749	**800-886-2293**	785-475-2234	47-2
Decatur County Rural Electric Membership Corp 1430 W Main St PO Box 46	Greensburg	IN	47240	**800-844-7362**	812-663-3391	247
Decatur Daily 201 First Ave SE	Decatur	AL	35601	**888-353-4612**	256-353-4612	531-2
Decatur Memorial Hospital 2300 N Edward St	Decatur	IL	62526	**866-364-3600**	217-876-8121	374-3
Decatur/Morgan County Convention & Visitors Bureau (DMCCVB) 719 Sixth Ave SE PO Box 2349	Decatur	AL	35602	**800-232-5449**	256-350-2028	208
Deccofelt Corp 555 S Vermont Ave *Cust Svc	Glendora	CA	91741	**800-543-3226***	626-963-8511	742-2
Dechert LLP 2929 Arch St Cira Ctr	Philadelphia	PA	19104	**800-328-4880**	215-994-4000	428
Decision Systems Plus Inc 248 Spring Lake Dr Ste 170	Itasca	IL	60143	**800-676-7374**		182
DecisionOne Corp 426 W Lancaster Ave	Devon	PA	19333	**800-767-2876**	610-296-6000	177
DecisionPoint Systems Inc 19655 Descartes *OTC: DPSI*	Foothill Ranch	CA	92610	**800-336-3670**	949-465-0065	179
DecisionQuest 21535 Hawthorne Blvd Ste 310	Torrance	CA	90503	**877-833-2474**	310-618-9600	444
Decisive Business Systems Inc 7150 N Park Dr Ste 400	Pennsauken	NJ	08109	**866-203-8948**	856-910-0900	182
Decker Steel & Supply Inc 4500 Train Ave	Cleveland	OH	44102	**800-321-6100**	216-281-7900	491
Decker Tape Products Inc 6 Stewart Pl	Fairfield	NJ	07004	**800-227-5252**	973-227-5350	729
Decker Truck Line Inc 4000 Fifth Ave S	Fort Dodge	IA	50501	**800-247-2537**	515-576-4141	778
Deckers Outdoor Corp 495-A S Fairview Ave *NYSE: DECK*	Goleta	CA	93117	**877-337-8333**	805-967-7611	302
Declara Inc 977 Commercial St	Palo Alto	CA	94303	**877-216-0604**		387
Deco Chem Inc 3502 N Home St	Mishawaka	IN	46545	**888-332-6465**	574-259-3787	388
Deco Products Co 506 Sanford St	Decorah	IA	52101	**800-327-9751**	563-382-4264	309
DecoArt Inc 49 Cotton Ave	Stanford	KY	40484	**800-367-3047**	606-365-3193	42
Decoma International Inc *Magna Exteriors & Interiors* 50 Casmir Ct	Concord	ON	L4K4J5	**888-348-2398**	905-669-2888	488
Decor & You Inc 900 Main St S	Southbury	CT	06488	**800-477-3326**	203-264-3500	311
Decorating Den Systems Inc 8659 Commerce Dr	Easton	MD	21601	**800-332-3367**	410-822-9001	393
Decorative Crafts Inc 50 Chestnut St	Greenwich	CT	06830	**800-431-4455**	203-531-1500	361
Decore-ative Specialties Inc 2772 S Peck Rd	Monrovia	CA	91016	**800-729-7277**	626-254-9191	114
DeCoty Coffee Company Inc 1920 Austin St	San Angelo	TX	76903	**800-588-8001**		297-7
Dectro International Inc 1000 Blvd du Parc-Technologique	Quebec	QC	G1P4S3	**800-463-5566**	418-650-0303	474
Dectron International Inc 4300 Poirier Blvd	Montreal	QC	H4R2C5	**888-332-8766**	514-334-9609	360-3
Dedham Institution For Savings 55 Elm St PO Box 9107	Dedham	MA	02026	**888-289-0342**	781-329-6700	69
Dedicated Computing N26 W23880 Commerce Cir	Waukesha	WI	53188	**877-523-3301**	262-951-7200	175-1
Dedicated Distribution Inc 640 Miami Ave	Kansas City	KS	66105	**800-325-8367**	913-371-2200	474
Dee Cramer Inc 4221 E Baldwin Rd	Holly	MI	48442	**888-342-6995**	810-579-5000	191-12
Dee Electronics Inc 2500 16th Ave SW	Cedar Rapids	IA	52404	**800-747-3331**	319-365-7551	248
Dee Paper Box Company Inc 100 Broomall St	Chester	PA	19013	**800-359-0041**	610-876-9285	100
Deen Meats PO Box 4155 PO Box 4155	Fort Worth	TX	76164	**800-333-3953**	817-335-2257	298-9
Deep East Texas Council of Governments 274 e lamar st	Jasper	TX	75951	**800-256-6848**	409-384-5704	462
Deep East Texas Electric Co-op Inc 880 Texas Hwy 21 E PO Box 736	San Augustine	TX	75972	**800-392-5986**	936-275-2314	247
Deepwater Chemicals Inc 1210 Airpark Rd	Woodward	OK	73801	**800-854-4064**	580-256-0500	804
Deer Lodge Hotels Ltd 106 Circle Dr	Saskatoon	SK	S7L4L6	**800-578-7878**	306-242-8881	705
Deer Valley Federal Credit Union 16215 N 28th Ave	Phoenix	AZ	85053	**800-579-5051**	602-375-7300	221
Deer Valley Ranch 16825 County Rd 162	Nathrop	CO	81236	**877-897-1297**	719-395-2353	241
Deer Valley Resort Lodging PO Box 889	Park City	UT	84060	**800-558-3337**	435-645-6626	667
Deerfield Correctional Ctr 21360 Deerfield Dr	Capron	VA	23829	**800-560-4292**	434-658-4368	215
Deerfield Episcopal Retirement Community 1617 Hendersonville Rd	Asheville	NC	28803	**800-284-1531**	828-274-1531	670
Deerfield Spa 650 Resica Falls Rd	East Stroudsburg	PA	18302	**800-852-4494**	570-223-0160	704
Deerfoot Inn & Casino 1000 11500 35th St SE	Calgary	AB	T2Z3W4	**877-236-5225**	403-236-7529	379
Deerhurst Resort 1235 Deerhurst Dr *Sales	Huntsville	ON	P1H2E8	**800-461-6522***	705-789-6411	667
Deering Banjo Co 3733 Kenora Dr	Spring Valley	CA	91977	**800-845-7791**	619-464-8252	526
DeFehr Furniture Ltd 125 Furniture Pk	Winnipeg	MB	R2G1B9	**877-333-3471**	204-988-5630	320-2
Defender Industries Inc 42 Great Neck Rd	Waterford	CT	06385	**800-628-8225**	860-701-3400	768
Defenders of Wildlife 1130 17th St NW	Washington	DC	20036	**800-385-9712**	202-682-9400	47-3
Defense Commissary Agency 1300 E Ave	Fort Lee	VA	23801	**877-332-2471**	804-734-8000	340-3
Defense Contract Audit Agency 8725 John J Kingman Rd Ste 2135	Fort Belvoir	VA	22060	**855-414-5892**	703-767-3265	340-3
Defense Contract Management Agency 6350 Walker Ln Ste 300	Alexandria	VA	22310	**888-576-3262**		340-3
Defense Finance & Accounting Service 8899 E 56th St	Indianapolis	IN	46249	**888-332-7411**		731
Defense Information Systems Agency PO Box 4502	Arlington	VA	22204	**844-247-3457**		340-3
Defense Nuclear Facilities Safety Board 625 Indiana Ave NW Ste 700	Washington	DC	20004	**800-788-4016**	202-694-7000	340-18
Defense Research Institute (DRI) 55 W Monroe St Ste 20	Chicago	IL	60603	**866-525-6466**	312-795-1101	48-10
Defense Technical Information Ctr (DTIC) 8725 John J Kingman Rd Ste 0944	Fort Belvoir	VA	22060	**800-225-3842**	703-767-9100	340-3
Defense Technology/Federal Laboratories 1855 S Loop PO Box 248	Casper	WY	82601	**877-248-3835**	307-235-2136	286
Defense Threat Reduction Agency 8725 John T Kingman Rd MS 6201	Fort Belvoir	VA	22060	**800-701-5096**	703-767-5870	340-3
Deffenbaugh Industries Inc 2601 Midwest Dr	Kansas City	KS	66111	**800-631-3301**	913-631-3300	802
Defiance College 701 N Clinton St	Defiance	OH	43512	**800-520-4632**	419-784-4010	167
Defibtech LLC 741 Boston Post Rd Ste 201	Guilford	CT	06437	**866-333-4248**	203-453-4507	475
Deflect-O Corp 7035 E 86th St	Indianapolis	IN	46250	**800-428-4328**		533
Degesch America Inc PO Box 116	Weyers Cave	VA	24486	**800-330-2525**	540-234-9281	282
DeGraaf Nature Ctr 600 Graafschap Rd	Holland	MI	49423	**888-535-5792**	616-355-1057	49-4
DeGray Lake Resort State Park 2027 State Pk Entrance Rd	Bismarck	AR	71929	**800-737-8355**	501-865-2801	564
DeGrazia Gallery in the Sun 6300 N Swan Rd	Tucson	AZ	85718	**800-545-2185**	520-299-9191	519
Degree Controls Inc 18 Meadowbrook Dr	Milford	NH	03055	**877-334-7332**	603-672-8900	258
Dehart Marine Electronics Inc 134 W Carolina Ave	Memphis	TN	38103	**800-523-4278**	901-523-0945	181
Dehumidification Manufacturing Gp LLC 6609 Ave U	Houston	TX	77011	**866-736-8348**	713-939-1166	14
DEI Holdings Inc 1 Viper Way *OTC: DEIX*	Vista	CA	92081	**800-876-0800**	760-598-6200	51
Deighton Associates Ltd 223 Brock St N Unit 7	Whitby	ON	L1N4H6	**888-219-6605**	905-665-6605	263
Dejana Truck & Utility Equipment Company Inc 490 Pulaski Rd	Kings Park	NY	11754	**877-335-2621**	631-544-9000	778
DeKalb Chamber of Commerce 125 Clairemont Ave Ste 235	Tucker	GA	30084	**800-428-7337**	404-378-8000	138

Name / Address	City	State	ZIP	Toll-Free	Phone	Class
DeKalb County Public Library 215 Sycamore St	Decatur	GA	30030	**800-677-1116**	404-370-3070	434-3
DeKalb Public Library 309 Oak St	DeKalb	IL	60115	**888-268-2824**	815-756-9568	434-3
Del Amo Fashion Ctr 3525 Carson St	Torrance	CA	90503	**877-746-6642**	310-542-8525	459
Del Amo Hospital 23700 Camino Del Sol	Torrance	CA	90505	**800-533-5266**	310-530-1151	374-5
Del Mar Avionics 1601 Alton Pkwy Ste C	Irvine	CA	92606	**800-854-0481**	949-250-3200	528
Del Mar College *East* 101 Baldwin Blvd	Corpus Christi	TX	78404	**800-652-3357**	361-698-1200	161
Del Mar Die Casting Co 12901 S Western Ave	Gardena	CA	90249	**800-624-7468**	323-321-0600	309
Del Mar Scientific Acquisition Ltd 4951 Airport Pkwy Ste 803	Addison	TX	75001	**800-722-4270**	972-661-5160	203
Del Monte Foods Co 1 Maritime Plaza *Cust Svc	San Francisco	CA	94111	**800-543-3090***	415-247-3000	297-20
Del Monte Fresh Produce Co 241 Sevilla Ave *Cust Svc	Coral Gables	FL	33134	**800-950-3683***	305-520-8400	298-7
Del Monte Lodge Renaissance Rochester Hotel & Spa, The 41 N Main St	Pittsford	NY	14534	**866-237-5979**	585-381-9900	379
Del Rey Beach State Recreation Site 100 Peter Iredale Rd	Hammond	OR	97121	**800-551-6949**		564
Del Rio Chamber of Commerce (DRCoC) 1915 Veterans Blvd *General	Del Rio	TX	78840	**877-218-5117***	830-775-3551	138
Del Taco Inc 25521 Commercentre Dr Ste 200 *Cust Svc	Lake Forest	CA	92630	**800-852-7204***	949-462-9300	668
DelaGet LLC 6608 Flying Cloud Dr	Eden Prairie	MN	55344	**866-264-5050**		198
Delaine James Inc 10508C Boyer Blvd *Claims	Austin	TX	78758	**800-999-5333***	512-835-5333	86
Delair Group LLC 8600 River Rd	Delair	NJ	08110	**800-235-0185**	215-676-4068	726
DELAMAR Greenwich Harbor 500 Steamboat Rd	Greenwich	CT	06830	**866-335-2627**	203-661-9800	379
DeLand Area Chamber of Commerce 336 N Woodland Blvd	DeLand	FL	32720	**800-611-5207**	386-734-4331	138
Delaware *Agriculture Dept* 2320 S DuPont Hwy	Dover	DE	19901	**800-282-8685**	302-739-4811	339-8
Child Support Enforcement Div (DCSE) 84A Christiana Rd	New Castle	DE	19720	**800-464-4357**	302-577-7171	339-8
Emergency Management Agency 165 Brick Store Landing Rd	Smyrna	DE	19977	**877-729-3362**	302-659-3362	339-8
Parks & Recreation Div 89 Kings Hwy *Campground Resv	Dover	DE	19901	**877-987-2757***	302-739-9200	339-8
Tourism Office 99 Kings Hwy	Dover	DE	19901	**866-284-7483**	302-739-4271	339-8
Weights & Measures Office 2320 S DuPont Hwy	Dover	DE	19901	**800-282-8685**	302-739-4811	339-8
Delaware Art Museum 2301 Kentmere Pkwy	Wilmington	DE	19806	**866-232-3714**	302-571-9590	519
Delaware Assn of Realtors 134 E Water St	Dover	DE	19901	**800-305-4445**	302-734-4444	654
Delaware County Community College 901 Media Line Rd	Media	PA	19063	**800-908-9946**	610-359-5000	161
Delaware County Daily Times 500 Mildred Ave	Primos	PA	19018	**888-799-6299**	610-622-8800	531-2
Delaware County District Library 84 E Winter St	Delaware	OH	43015	**866-862-7286**	740-362-3861	434-3
Delaware County Electric Co-op (DCEC) 39 Elm St PO Box 471	Delhi	NY	13753	**866-436-1223**	607-746-2341	247
Delaware County Intermediate Unit 200 Yale Ave	Morton	PA	19070	**800-441-3215**	610-938-9000	683
Delaware County Memorial Hospital 501 N Lansdowne Ave	Drexel Hill	PA	19026	**877-884-1564**	610-284-8100	374-3
Delaware Div of Libraries 497 S Red Haven Ln	Dover	DE	19901	**800-829-4059**	302-739-4748	434-5
Delaware Electric Co-op Inc PO Box 600	Greenwood	DE	19950	**800-282-8595**	302-349-3147	247
Delaware Hospice Inc 3515 Silverside Rd	Wilmington	DE	19810	**800-838-9800**	302-478-5707	363
Delaware Mfg Industries Corp 3776 Commerce Ct	Wheatfield	NY	14120	**800-248-3642**	716-743-4360	264
Delaware North Cos Inc 40 Fountain Plz	Buffalo	NY	14202	**800-828-7240**	716-858-5000	187
Delaware Nurses Assn (DNA) 4765 Ogletown-Stanton Rd Ste L10	Newark	DE	19713	**800-626-4081**	302-733-5880	532
Delaware Psychiatric Ctr 1901 N Dupont Hwy Main Bldg	New Castle	DE	19720	**800-652-2929**	302-255-9399	374-5
Delaware State Bar Assn 405 N King St	Wilmington	DE	19801	**855-872-5911**	302-658-5279	71
Delaware State Chamber of Commerce 1201 N Orange St Ste 200 PO Box 671	Wilmington	DE	19899	**800-292-9507**	302-655-7221	139
Delaware State News 110 Galaxy Dr PO Box 737	Dover	DE	19903	**800-282-8586**	302-674-3600	531-2
Delaware State Park 5202 US Rt 23 N	Delaware	OH	43015	**866-644-6727**	740-548-4631	564
Delaware State University 1200 N DuPont Hwy *Admissions	Dover	DE	19901	**800-845-2544***	302-857-6351	167
Delaware Transit Corp 119 Lower Beach St Ste 100	Wilmington	DE	19805	**800-652-3278**	302-576-6000	467
Delaware Valley College 700 E Butler Ave	Doylestown	PA	18901	**800-233-5825**	215-489-2211	167
Delaware Valley Wholesale Florist Inc (DVWF) 520 Mantua Blvd N	Sewell	NJ	08080	**800-676-1212**	856-468-7000	295
Delco Diesel Services Inc 1100 S Agnew Ave	Oklahoma City	OK	73108	**800-256-0395**	405-232-3595	53

Name / Address	City	State	ZIP	Toll-Free	Phone	Class
Delden Manufacturing Company Inc 3530 N Kimball Dr	Kansas City	MO	64161	**800-821-3708**	816-413-1600	498
DeLeon's Bromeliads Co 13745 SW 216th St	Miami	FL	33170	**800-448-8649**	305-238-6028	369
Delfield Co 980 S Isabella Rd	Mount Pleasant	MI	48858	**800-733-8821**	989-773-7981	299
Deli Express 16101 W 78th St	Eden Prairie	MN	55344	**800-328-8184**		297-36
Delight Grecian Foods Inc 1201 Tonne Rd	Elk Grove Village	IL	60007	**800-621-4387**	847-364-1010	297-1
Delkor Systems Inc 8700 Rendova St NE	Circle Pines	MN	55014	**800-328-5558**	763-783-0855	546
Dell Inc 1 Dell Way *NASDAQ: DELL*	Round Rock	TX	78682	**800-879-3355**	512-338-4400	175-1
Dellenbach Motors 3111 S College Ave	Fort Collins	CO	80525	**866-963-5689**		56
Delmar International Inc 10636 Cote de Liesse	Montreal	QC	H8T1A5	**888-433-5627**	514-636-8800	315
Delmarva Foundation For Medical Care Inc (DFMC) 28464 Marlboro Ave	Easton	MD	21601	**800-999-3362**	410-822-0697	473
Delmarva Power PO Box 231 *Cust Svc	Wilmington	DE	19899	**800-898-8042***		785
Delmont Laboratories Inc 715 Harvard Ave PO Box 269	Swarthmore	PA	19081	**800-562-5541**	610-543-2747	581
Delnor-Community Hospital (DCH) 300 Randall Rd	Geneva	IL	60134	**800-223-9776**	630-208-3000	374-3
DeLorme 2 DeLorme Dr PO Box 298 *Sales	Yarmouth	ME	04096	**800-452-5931***	207-846-7000	634-1
Delphos Herald Inc 405 N Main St	Delphos	OH	45833	**800-589-6950**	419-695-0015	634-8
Delsey Luggage 6735 Business Pkwy Ste A	Elkridge	MD	21075	**800-558-3344**	410-796-5655	452
DelStar Technologies Inc 220 E St Elmo Rd	Austin	TX	78745	**800-521-6713**	512-447-7000	607
Delta Air Cargo PO Box 20559 Dept 670	Atlanta	GA	30320	**800-352-2737**		12
Delta Air Lines Inc 1030 Delta Blvd *NYSE: DAL*	Atlanta	GA	30354	**800-221-1212**	404-715-2600	25
Delta Apparel Inc 2750 Premier Pkwy Ste 100 *NYSE: DLA*	Duluth	GA	30097	**800-285-4456**	678-775-6900	154-3
Delta Blood Bank 65 N Commerce St	Stockton	CA	95202	**888-942-5663**	209-943-3830	88
Delta Carbona LP 376 Hollywood Ave Ste 208	Fairfield	NJ	07004	**888-746-5599**	973-808-6260	150
Delta Centrifugal Corp PO Box 1043 *Sales	Temple	TX	76503	**888-433-3100***	254-773-9055	308
Delta Chemical Corp 2601 Cannery Ave	Baltimore	MD	21226	**800-282-5322**	410-354-0100	144
Delta College 1961 Delta Rd	University Center	MI	48710	**888-636-4211**	989-686-9000	161
Delta Consolidated Industries Inc 4800 Krueger Dr	Jonesboro	AR	72401	**800-643-0084**	870-935-3711	487
Delta Cooling Towers Inc PO Box 315	Rockaway	NJ	07866	**800-289-3358**	973-586-2201	471
Delta Corporate Services Inc 129 Littleton Rd	Parsippany	NJ	07054	**800-335-8220**	973-334-6260	182
Delta County Area Chamber of Commerce 230 Ludington St	Escanaba	MI	49829	**800-221-2001**	906-786-2192	138
Delta Delta Delta Fraternity 2331 Brookhollow Plz Dr	Arlington	TX	76006	**877-746-7333**	817-633-8001	47-16
Delta Dental Insurance Company of Alaska PO Box 1809	Alpharetta	GA	30023	**800-521-2651**		391-3
Delta Dental of Arizona PO Box 43026	Phoenix	AZ	85080	**800-352-6132**		391-3
Delta Dental of Arkansas 1513 Country Club Rd PO Box 15965	Sherwood	AR	72120	**800-462-5410**	501-835-3400	391-3
Delta Dental of Colorado 4582 S Ulster St Ste 800	Denver	CO	80237	**800-233-0860**	303-741-9300	391-3
Delta Dental of Idaho 555 E Parkcenter Blvd PO Box 2870	Boise	ID	83706	**800-356-7586**	208-489-3580	391-3
Delta Dental of Indiana PO Box 30416	Lansing	MI	48909	**800-524-0149**		391-3
Delta Dental of Iowa 9000 Northpark Dr Ste 13 *Cust Svc	Johnston	IA	50131	**800-544-0718***	515-261-5500	391-3
Delta Dental of Kansas 1619 N Waterfront Pkwy PO Box 789769	Wichita	KS	67201	**800-234-3375**	316-264-4511	391-3
Delta Dental of Kentucky 10100 Linn Stn Rd PO Box 242810 *Cust Svc	Louisville	KY	40223	**800-955-2030***		391-3
Delta Dental of Louisiana PO Box 1803	Alpharetta	GA	30023	**800-422-4234**		391-3
Delta Dental of Maryland 1 Delta Dr	Mechanicsburg	PA	17055	**800-932-0783**	717-766-8500	391-3
Delta Dental of Massachusetts 465 Medford St *Cust Svc	Boston	MA	02129	**800-872-0500***	617-886-1000	391-3
Delta Dental of Michigan PO Box 30416	Lansing	MI	48909	**800-524-0149**		391-3
Delta Dental of Minnesota PO Box 330	Minneapolis	MN	55440	**800-553-9536**	651-406-5900	391-3
Delta Dental of Missouri 12399 Gravois Rd Ste 2	Saint Louis	MO	63127	**800-392-1167**	314-656-3000	391-3
Delta Dental of Montana PO Box 1803	Alpharetta	GA	30023	**800-422-4234**		391-3
Delta Dental of New Jersey 1639 State Rt 10	Parsippany	NJ	07054	**800-624-2633**	973-285-4000	391-3
Delta Dental of New Jersey Inc PO Box 222	Parsippany	NJ	07054	**800-452-9310**		391-3

Company / Address	City	State	ZIP	Toll-Free	Phone	Class
Delta Dental of New Mexico 2500 Louisiana Blvd NE Ste 600	Albuquerque	NM	87110	**800-999-0963**	505-883-4777	391-3
Delta Dental of New York 1 Delta Dr	Mechanicsburg	PA	17055	**800-932-0783**	717-766-8500	391-3
Delta Dental of Ohio PO Box 30416	Lansing	MI	48909	**800-524-0149**		391-3
Delta Dental of Oklahoma 16 NW 63rd St Ste 201	Oklahoma City	OK	73116	**800-522-0188**	405-607-2100	391-3
Delta Dental of Pennsylvania 1 Delta Dr	Mechanicsburg	PA	17055	**800-932-0783**		391-3
Delta Dental of Rhode Island 10 Charles St	Providence	RI	02904	**800-598-6684**	401-752-6000	391-3
Delta Dental of South Dakota 720 N Euclid Ave PO Box 1157	Pierre	SD	57501	**800-627-3961**	605-224-7345	391-3
Delta Dental of Tennessee 240 Venture Cir *Cust Svc	Nashville	TN	37228	**800-223-3104***	615-255-3175	391-3
Delta Dental of Virginia 4818 Starkey Rd	Roanoke	VA	24014	**800-367-3531**	540-989-8000	391-3
Delta Dental of West Virginia 1 Delta Dr	Mechanicsburg	PA	17055	**800-932-0783**	717-766-8500	391-3
Delta Dental of Wisconsin 2801 Hoover Rd PO Box 828	Stevens Point	WI	54481	**800-236-3713**	715-344-6087	391-3
Delta Dental of Wyoming 6234 Yellowstone Rd PO Box 29	Cheyenne	WY	82009	**800-735-3379**	307-632-3313	391-3
Delta Dental Plan of North Carolina 343 E Six Forks Rd Ste 180	Raleigh	NC	27609	**800-662-8856**	919-832-6015	391-3
Delta Downs Racetrack 2717 Delta Downs Dr	Vinton	LA	70668	**800-589-7441**		639
Delta Education LLC 80 NW Blvd	Nashua	NH	03063	**800-258-1302**	603-889-8899	245
Delta Employees Credit Union 1025 Virginia Ave	Atlanta	GA	30354	**800-544-3328**	404-715-4725	221
Delta Enterprises 114 W 26th St 8th Fl	New York	NY	10001	**800-377-3777**	212-736-7000	63
Delta King Riverboat Hotel 1000 Front St	Sacramento	CA	95814	**800-825-5464**	916-444-5464	379
Delta M Corp 1003 Larsen Dr	Oak Ridge	TN	37830	**800-922-0083**		407
Delta Natural Gas Co Inc 3617 Lexington Rd *NASDAQ: DGAS*	Winchester	KY	40391	**800-262-2012**	859-744-6171	785
Delta Oil & Gas Inc 700 W Pender St Ste 604	Vancouver	BC	V6C1G8	**866-355-3644**	604-602-1500	535
Delta Polymers Midwest Inc 6685 Sterling Dr N	Sterling Heights	MI	48312	**800-860-6848**	586-795-2900	602
Delta Sherbrooke Hotel & Conference Centre 2685 Rue King O	Sherbrooke	QC	J1L1C1	**800-268-1133**	819-822-1989	377
Delta Sigma Theta Sorority Inc 1707 New Hampshire Ave NW	Washington	DC	20009	**866-615-6464**	202-986-2400	47-16
Delta Star Inc 270 Industrial Rd	San Carlos	CA	94070	**800-892-8673**		765
Delta State University 1003 W Sunflower Rd	Cleveland	MS	38733	**800-468-6378**	662-846-4020	167
Delta T Inc 8323 Loch Lomond Dr	Pico Rivera	CA	90660	**800-928-5828**		611
Delta t Systems Inc 2171 State Rd 175	Richfield	WI	53076	**800-733-4204**	262-628-0331	358
Delta Tau Delta Fraternity 10000 Allisonville Rd	Fishers	IN	46038	**800-335-8795**	317-284-0203	47-16
Delta Theta Phi 225 Hillsborough St Ste 432	Raleigh	NC	27603	**800-783-2600**		47-16
Delta Waterfowl Foundation PO Box 3128	Bismarck	ND	58502	**888-987-3695**	701-222-8857	47-3
Delta Whistler Village Suites 4308 Main St	Whistler	BC	V0N1B4	**888-299-3987**	604-905-3987	667
Deltacom Inc 7037 Old Madison Pike	Huntsville	AL	35806	**800-239-3000**		733
deltathree Inc 75 Broad St *PINK: DDDC*	New York	NY	10004	**888-335-8230**	212-500-4850	733
DeltaTRAK Inc PO Box 398	Pleasanton	CA	94566	**800-962-6776**	925-249-2250	204
Deltec Homes Inc 69 Bingham Rd	Asheville	NC	28806	**800-642-2508**		188
Deltech Corp 11911 Scenic Hwy	Baton Rouge	LA	70807	**800-424-9300**	225-775-0150	604-1
Del-Tech Manufacturing Inc 9703 Penn Rd	Prince George	BC	V2N5T6	**800-736-7733**	250-564-3585	755
Deltek Inc 13880 Dulles Corner Ln *NASDAQ: PROJ*	Herndon	VA	20171	**800-456-2009**	703-734-8606	180-1
Deltona Corp 8014 SW 135th St Rd	Ocala	FL	34473	**800-333-5866**	352-347-2322	651
Deltrol Fluid Products 3001 Grant Ave	Bellwood	IL	60104	**800-477-9772**	708-547-0500	788
Deltronic Corp 3900 W Segerstrom Ave	Santa Ana	CA	92704	**800-451-6922**	714-545-5800	492
Deluxe Bldg Systems Inc 499 W Third St	Berwick	PA	18603	**800-843-7372**	570-752-5914	105
Deluxe Corp 3680 N Victoria St *NYSE: DLX*	Shoreview	MN	55126	**800-328-7205**	651-483-7111	360-3
Deluxe Stitcher Company Inc 3747 acorn ln	Franklin Park	IL	60131	**800-634-0810**		755
Delyse Inc 505 Reactor Way	Reno	NV	89502	**800-441-6887**	775-857-1811	297-9
DEMA (Diving Equipment & Marketing Assn) 3750 Convoy St Ste 310	San Diego	CA	92111	**800-862-3483**	858-616-6408	48-4
Demag Cranes & Components 29201 Aurora Rd	Solon	OH	44139	**866-920-3000**	440-248-2400	192
Demand Metric 562 Wellington St	London	ON	N6A3R5	**866-947-7744**	519-495-9619	465
Dematic 507 Plymouth Ave NE *Cust Svc	Grand Rapids	MI	49505	**877-725-7500***		469
DEMCO (Dixie Electric Membership Corp) PO Box 15659	Baton Rouge	LA	70895	**800-262-0221**	225-261-1221	247
DEMCO (Dethmers Manufacturing Co) 4010 320th St	Boyden	IA	51234	**800-543-3626**	712-725-2311	761
Demco Inc 4810 Forest Run Rd *Orders	Madison	WI	53704	**800-356-1200***	608-241-1201	559
Democrat & Chronicle 55 Exchange Blvd	Rochester	NY	14614	**800-790-9565**	585-232-7100	531-2
DeMolay International 10200 NW Ambassabor Dr *Orders	Kansas City	MO	64153	**800-336-6529***	816-891-8333	47-15
DeMontrond 888 I- 45 S *Sales	Conroe	TX	77304	**888-843-6583***	281-443-2500	56
DeMoulin Bros & Company Inc 1025 S Fourth St	Greenville	IL	62246	**800-228-8134**	618-664-2000	154-18
Demsey Manufacturing Co 78 New Wood Rd	Watertown	CT	06795	**800-533-6739**	860-274-6209	481
Den Hartog Industries Inc 4010 Hospers Dr S PO Box 425	Hospers	IA	51238	**800-342-3408**	712-752-8432	607
Denali Advance Integration (DAI) 17735 NE 65th St Ste 130	Redmond	WA	98052	**877-467-8008**	425-885-4000	182
Denali Commission 510 L St Ste 410	Anchorage	AK	99501	**888-480-4321**	907-271-1414	340-18
Denali State Park 7278 E Bogard Rd	Wasilla	AK	99654	**800-478-6196**	907-745-3975	564
Denbury Resources Inc 5320 Legacy Dr *NYSE: DNR* ■ *General	Plano	TX	75024	**800-348-9030***	972-673-2000	535
Dendreon Corp 301 2nd Ave *OTC: DNDNQ*	Seattle	WA	98101	**877-256-4545**	206-256-4545	84
Denier Electric Co Inc 10891 SR- 128	Harrison	OH	45030	**800-676-3282**	513-738-2641	247
Denim Group Ltd 1354 N Loop 1604 E Ste 110	San Antonio	TX	78232	**844-572-4400**		179
Deniro Marketing LLC 6777 Embarcadero Dr Ste 3	Stockton	CA	95219	**877-752-1458**	209-477-7676	197
Denison University 100 W College St	Granville	OH	43023	**800-336-4766**	740-587-6394	167
Denison University Doane Library 400 W Loop	Granville	OH	43023	**800-336-4766**	740-587-6235	434-6
Denmark *Consulate General* 875 N Michigan Ave Ste 3950	Chicago	IL	60611	**800-345-6541**		259
Den-Mat Corp 2727 Skyway Dr	Santa Maria	CA	93455	**800-433-6628**	805-922-8491	230
Dennis K Burke Inc 284 Eastern Ave PO Box 6069	Chelsea	MA	02150	**800-289-2875**	617-884-7800	448
Dennis Paper Co 910 Acorn Dr	Nashville	TN	37210	**800-441-5684**	615-883-9010	552
Dennis Supply Co PO Box 3376	Sioux City	IA	51102	**800-352-4618**	712-255-7637	663
Dennis Uniform Mfg Company Inc 135 SE Hawthorne Blvd	Portland	OR	97214	**800-854-6951**		154-18
Dennis, Corry, Porter & Smith LLP 14 Piedmont Ctr 3535 Piedmont Rd NE Ste 900	Atlanta	GA	30305	**800-735-0838**	404-365-0102	428
Denny's Corp 203 E Main St *NASDAQ: DENN* ■ *Cust Svc	Spartanburg	SC	29319	**800-733-6697***	864-597-8000	668
Denso North America Inc 9747 Whithorn Dr	Houston	TX	77095	**888-821-2300**	281-821-3355	145
Dent Clinic 711 48th Ave SE	Calgary	AB	T2G2A7	**888-722-3368**	403-255-3111	61-4
Dent Wizard International 4710 Earth City Expway	Bridgeton	MO	63044	**800-267-9369**	314-592-1800	61-4
Dental Economics Magazine 1421 S Sheridan Rd	Tulsa	OK	74112	**800-331-4463**		456-16
Dental Lifeline Network 1800 15th St Ste 100	Denver	CO	80202	**888-471-6334**	303-534-5360	47-17
Dental Technologies Inc (DTI) 5601 Arnold Rd	Dublin	CA	94568	**800-229-0936**	925-829-3611	415
DEN-TAL-EZ Group Inc 2 W Liberty Blvd Ste 160	Malvern	PA	19355	**866-383-4636**	610-725-8004	230
DEN-TAL-EZ Inc Equipment Div 2500 Hwy 31 S	Bay Minette	AL	36507	**800-383-4636**	251-937-6781	230
Dentists Insurance Co 1201 K St 17th Fl	Sacramento	CA	95814	**800-733-0634**	800-733-0633	391-5
Denton Chamber of Commerce 414 W Pkwy St	Denton	TX	76201	**800-747-2316**	940-382-9693	138
Denton Record-Chronicle 314 E Hickory St	Denton	TX	76201	**800-275-1722**	940-387-3811	531-2
Dentsply Caulk 38 W Clarke Ave	Milford	DE	19963	**800-532-2855**	302-422-4511	230
DENTSPLY International 221 W Philadelphia St PO Box 872	York	PA	17405	**800-800-2888**	717-845-7511	230
Dentsply International Inc 221 W Philadelphia St PO Box 872 *NASDAQ: XRAY*	York	PA	17405	**800-877-0020**	717-845-7511	230
Dentsply International Inc Tulsa Dental Div 5100 E Skelly Dr Ste 300	Tulsa	OK	74135	**800-662-1202**	918-493-6598	230
Denver Academy of Court Reporting 9051 Harlan St Ste 20	Westminster	CO	80031	**866-712-2425**	303-427-5292	798
Denver Ctr for the Performing Arts 1101 13th St	Denver	CO	80204	**800-641-1222**	303-893-4000	571
Denver Fire Dept Federal Credit Union (DFDFCU) 2201 Federal Blvd	Denver	CO	80211	**866-880-7770**	303-228-5300	221
Denver International Airport 8500 Pena Blvd	Denver	CO	80249	**800-247-2336**	303-342-2000	27
Denver International Film Festival 1510 York 3rd Fl	Denver	CO	80206	**866-293-1566**	303-595-3456	284
Denver Metro Convention & Visitors Bureau 1555 California St Ste 300	Denver	CO	80202	**800-480-2010**	303-892-1112	208
Denver Newspaper Agency 101 W Colfax Ave	Denver	CO	80202	**800-336-7678**	303-954-1010	634-8
Denver Performing Arts Complex 1400 Curtis St 1St Fl	Denver	CO	80204	**800-745-3000**	720-865-4220	571
Denver Public Schools 900 Grant St	Denver	CO	80203	**866-726-0033**	720-423-3200	683

Name / Address	City	State	ZIP	Toll-Free	Phone	Class
Denver Seminary 6399 S Santa Fe Dr	Littleton	CO	80120	800-922-3040	303-761-2482	168-3
Denver Veterans Affairs Medical Ctr 1055 Clermont St	Denver	CO	80220	888-336-8262	303-399-8020	374-8
Denver Wholesale Florists Co 4800 Dahlia St	Denver	CO	80216	800-829-8280	303-399-0970	295
Denver Wire Rope & Supply Inc 4100 Dahlia St	Denver	CO	80216	800-873-3697	303-377-5166	351
Department of Agriculture (USDA) 1400 Independence Ave SW	Washington	DC	20250	844-433-2774	202-720-3631	340-1
Department of Education						
Inspector General's Fraud & Abuse Hotline 400 Maryland Ave SW	Washington	DC	20202	800-647-8733		340-6
Office of Vocational & Adult Education 400 Maryland Ave SW Room 4W116	Washington	DC	20202	800-872-5327		340-6
Department of Energy (DOE) 1000 Independence Ave SW	Washington	DC	20585	800-342-5363	202-586-5450	340-7
Department of Health & Human Services (HHS) 330 Independence Ave SW	Washington	DC	20201	877-696-6775	202-619-0150	340-8
Ready Campaign 500 C St SW Ste 714	Washington	DC	20472	800-621-3362		340-9
Department of Housing & Urban Development (HUD) 451 Seventh St SW	Washington	DC	20410	800-569-4287	202-708-0685	340-10
Public Affairs Office 451 Seventh St SW	Washington	DC	20410	800-333-4636	202-708-0980	340-10
Department of Housing & Urban Development Regional Offices						
Boston 10 Cswy St 3rd Fl	Boston	MA	02222	800-225-5342	617-994-8200	340-10
Mid-Atlantic Region 100 Penn Sq E	Philadelphia	PA	19107	800-225-5342	215-656-0500	340-10
New York City Regional Office 26 Federal Plaza Ste 3541	New York	NY	10278	800-496-4294	212-264-8000	340-10
Pacific/Hawaii Region 600 Harrison St 3rd Fl	San Francisco	CA	94107	800-347-3739	415-489-6572	340-10
Rocky Mountain Region 1670 Bdwy 25th Fl	Denver	CO	80202	800-955-2232	303-672-5440	340-10
Department of Labor (DOL) 200 Constitution Ave NW	Washington	DC	20210	866-487-2365	202-693-4650	340-13
Department of Labor						
Job Corps 200 Constitution Ave NW Ste N4463	Washington	DC	20210	800-733-5627	202-693-3000	340-13
Office of Administrative Law Judges 200 Constitution Ave NW Ste 400 N	Washington	DC	20210	877-889-5627	202-693-7300	340-13
Public Affairs Office 200 Constitution Ave NW	Washington	DC	20210	866-487-2365	202-693-4650	340-13
Department of the Treasury 1500 Pennsylvania Ave NW	Washington	DC	20220	800-359-3898	202-622-2000	340-16
Department of Veterans Affairs (VA) 810 Vermont Ave NW *Cust Svc	Washington	DC	20420	800-827-1000*	202-461-7600	340-17
Public & Intergovernmental Affairs Office 810 Vermont Ave NW	Washington	DC	20420	800-273-8255		340-17
Departures Magazine 1120 Ave of the Americas	New York	NY	10036	888-424-0106	212-642-1999	456-22
DePaul University College of Law 25 E Jackson Blvd	Chicago	IL	60604	800-445-8667	312-362-8701	168-1
DePauw University 101 E Seminary St	Greencastle	IN	46135	800-447-2495	765-658-4006	167
DePauw University West Library 11 E Larabee St	Greencastle	IN	46135	800-447-2495	765-658-4420	434-6
DePelchin Children's Ctr 4950 Memorial Dr	Houston	TX	77007	888-730-2335	713-730-2335	47-6
Dependable Component Supply Corp 1003 E Newport Ctr Dr	Deerfield Beach	FL	33442	800-336-7100	954-283-5800	248
Dependable Highway Express Inc 2440 S 48th Ave	Phoenix	AZ	85043	800-472-2037	602-278-4401	448
Depobook Reporting Services 1600 G St Ste 101	Modesto	CA	95354	800-830-8885	209-544-6466	444
Depoe Bay Whale Center *Oregon Parks and Recreation Department* 58 US-101 198 NE 123rd St	Depoe Bay	OR	97341	800-551-6949	541-765-3304	564
Deposition Sciences Inc 3300 Coffey Ln	Santa Rosa	CA	95403	866-433-7724	707-573-6700	480
Depression & Bipolar Support Alliance (DBSA) 730 N Franklin St Ste 501	Chicago	IL	60610	800-826-3632	312-642-0049	47-17
Derby Industries LLC 4451 Robards Ln	Louisville	KY	40218	800-569-4812	502-451-7373	801-1
Derma Sciences Inc 214 Carnegie Ctr Ste 100	Princeton	NJ	08540	800-825-4325	609-514-4744	474
Dermatology Assoc of Atlanta 5555 Pchtrdnwyd Ste 190	Atlanta	GA	30324	800-233-0706	404-256-4457	374-7
Dermatran Health Solutions 1504 market st	Redding	CA	96001	855-675-5210		363
Dero Bike Racks Inc 504 Malcolm Ave SE Ste 100	Minneapolis	MN	55414	888-337-6729	612-359-0689	60
DeRoyal Industries Inc 200 DeBusk Ln	Powell	TN	37849	800-251-9864	865-938-7828	476
DeRoyal Textiles 141 E York St	Camden	SC	29020	800-845-1062	803-432-2403	742-1
Derr Flooring Company Inc 525 Davisville Rd PO Box 912	Willow Grove	PA	19090	800-523-3457	215-657-6300	361
Derrick Publishing Co 1510 W First St	Oil City	PA	16301	800-352-1002	814-676-7444	634-8
Der-Tex Corp 1 Lehner Rd	Saco	ME	04072	800-669-0364		742-2
Des Moines Area Community College						
Ankeny 2006 S Ankeny Blvd	Ankeny	IA	50021	800-362-2127	515-964-6200	161
Boone 1125 Hancock Dr	Boone	IA	50036	800-362-2127	515-432-7203	161
Carroll 906 N Grant Rd	Carroll	IA	51401	800-622-3334	712-792-1755	161
Urban/Des Moines 1100 Seventh St	Des Moines	IA	50314	800-622-3334	515-244-4226	161
Des Moines Independent School District 901 Walnut St	Des Moines	IA	50309	800-452-1111	515-242-7911	683
Des Moines International Airport 5800 Fleur Dr	Des Moines	IA	50321	877-686-0029	515-256-5050	27
Des Moines Register 715 Locust St	Des Moines	IA	50309	800-247-5346	515-284-8000	531-2
Des Plaines Public Library 1501 Ellinwood Ave	Des Plaines	IL	60016	800-829-1040	847-827-5551	434-3
DeSales University 2755 Stn Ave	Center Valley	PA	18034	877-433-7253	610-282-1100	167
Descartes Systems Group Inc 120 Randall Dr *TSE: DSG*	Waterloo	ON	N2V1C6	800-419-8495	519-746-8110	180-12
Deschutes Public Library 507 NW Wall St	Bend	OR	97701	855-268-3767	541-312-1020	434-3
Desco Dental Systems LLC 5005 W Loomis Rd Ste 100	Greenfield	WI	53220	800-392-7610	414-281-9192	179
Desco Plumbing & Heating Supply Inc 65 Worcester Rd	Etobicoke	ON	M9W5N7	800-564-5146	416-213-1555	611
Deseret Book Co 57 W S Temple	Salt Lake City	UT	84111	800-453-4532	801-534-1515	634-3
Deseret News 30 E 100 S Suite 400 PO Box 1257	Salt Lake City	UT	84110	800-999-7511	801-236-6000	531-2
Desert Botanical Garden 1201 N Galvin Pkwy	Phoenix	AZ	85008	888-314-9480	480-941-1225	96
Desert Canyon Golf Resort 1030 Desert Canyon Blvd	Orondo	WA	98843	800-258-4173	509-784-1111	667
Desert Dog Marketing LLC 4641 N 12th St Ste 200	Phoenix	AZ	85014	800-506-0398		227
Desert Hot Springs Spa Hotel 10805 Palm Dr	Desert Hot Springs	CA	92240	800-808-7727	760-329-6000	667
Desert Regional Medical Ctr 1150 N Indian Canyon Dr	Palm Springs	CA	92262	800-491-4990	760-323-6511	374-3
Desert Riviera Hotel 610 E Palm Canyon Dr	Palm Springs	CA	92264	866-270-8322	760-327-5314	379
Desert Sands Charter High School 44130 20th St W	Lancaster	CA	93534	877-360-5327		683
Desert Schools Federal Credit Union 148 N 48th St	Phoenix	AZ	85034	800-456-9171	602-433-7000	221
Desert Springs Marriott Resort & Spa 74855 Country Club Dr	Palm Desert	CA	92260	888-538-9459	760-341-2211	667
Desert Sun 750 N Gene Autry Trl	Palm Springs	CA	92263	800-233-3741	760-322-8889	531-2
Desert Sun Publishing Co PO Box 2734 *Advertising	Palm Springs	CA	92263	800-233-3741*	760-322-8889	634-8
Design Ctr of the Americas (DCOTA) 1855 Griffin Rd	Dania Beach	FL	33004	877-992-9204	954-920-7997	459
Design Design Inc 19 La Grave SE	Grand Rapids	MI	49503	800-334-3348	616-774-2448	129
Design Homes Inc 600 N Marquette Rd	Prairie du Chien	WI	53821	800-627-9443	608-326-6041	105
Design Institute of San Diego 8555 Commerce Ave	San Diego	CA	92121	800-619-4337	858-566-1200	167
Design It Yourself Gift Baskets LLC 7999 Hansen Rd Ste 204	Houston	TX	77061	800-589-7553	713-944-3440	128
Design News 225 Wyman St	Waltham	MA	02451	800-869-6882	763-746-2792	456-21
Design ProfessionalXL Group 2959 Salinas Hwy	Monterey	CA	93940	800-227-4284	831-649-5522	401
Design Strategy Corp 805 Third Ave 11th Fl	New York	NY	10022	800-331-8726	212-370-0000	182
Design Toscano Inc 1400 Morse Ave	Elk Grove Village	IL	60007	800-525-5141	847-952-0100	458
Design Within Reach Inc 711 Canal St 3rd fl 3rd Fl *OTC: DWRI*	Stamford	CT	06902	800-944-2233	203-614-0600	362
Design/Build Business Magazine 3030 Salt Creek Ln Ste 200	Arlington Heights	IL	60005	800-547-7377	847-454-2714	456-2
Designatronics Inc 2101 Jericho Tpke *Orders	New Hyde Park	NY	11040	800-345-1144*	516-328-3300	707
Designer Decal Inc 1120 E First Ave	Spokane	WA	99202	800-622-6333	509-535-0267	685
Designfax Magazine 2506 Tamiami Trail North	Nokomis	FL	34275	877-245-6247	941-966-9521	456-21
Designing Health Inc 28410 Witherspoon Pkwy	Valencia	CA	91355	800-774-7387	661-257-1705	478
Desire2Learn Inc 151 Charles SW Ste 400	Kitchener	ON	N2G1H6	888-772-0325	519-772-0325	176
Desktop Consulting Services 43311 Joy Rd	Canton	MI	48187	888-600-2731		177
DeskTop Labels 7277 Boone Ave N	Minneapolis	MN	55428	800-241-9730		413
Desmond Albany Hotel, The 660 Albany-Shaker Rd	Albany	NY	12211	800-448-3500	518-869-8100	669
Desoto Parish School District 201 Crosby St	Mansfield	LA	71052	888-741-0205	318-872-2836	683
DeSoto Public Library 211 E Pleasant Run Rd Ste C	DeSoto	TX	75115	800-886-9008	972-230-9656	434-3
Desoto Sales Inc 20945 Osborne St	Canoga Park	CA	91304	800-826-9779	818-998-0853	351
Despatch Industries Inc 8860 207th St W	Lakeville	MN	55044	800-726-0110	952-469-5424	319
DesPeres Hospital 2345 Dougherty Ferry Rd	Saint Louis	MO	63122	888-457-5203	314-966-9100	374-3
Dessert Innovations Inc 25-B Enterprise Blvd	Atlanta	GA	30336	800-359-7351	404-691-5000	297-2
DE-STA-CO 1025 Doris Rd	Auburn Hills	MI	48326	888-337-8226	248-836-6700	350
Destination Hotels & Resorts Inc 10333 E Dry Creek Rd Ste 450	Englewood	CO	80112	855-893-1011	303-799-3830	379
Destination Maternity Corp 456 N Fifth St *NASDAQ: DEST*	Philadelphia	PA	19123	800-466-6223	215-873-2200	156-6
Destination Resources 5435 Balboa Blvd Ste 106	Encino	CA	91316	800-422-6524	818-995-7915	186
Destiny Industries LLC 250 R W Bryant Rd	Moultrie	GA	31788	866-782-6600		504

Name / Address	City	State	ZIP	Toll-Free	Phone	Class
Destiny Solutions Inc						
40 Holly St	Toronto	ON	M4S3C3	**866-403-0500**	416-480-0500	227
Destron Fearing						
490 Villaume Ave	South Saint Paul	MN	55075	**800-328-0118**	651-455-1621	645
Detecto Scale Co						
203 E Daugherty St PO Box 151	Webb City	MO	64870	**800-641-2008**	417-673-4631	682
Detex Corp						
302 Detex Dr	New Braunfels	TX	78130	**800-729-3839**	830-629-2900	690
Dethmers Manufacturing Co (DEMCO)						
4010 320th St	Boyden	IA	51234	**800-543-3626**	712-725-2311	761
Detroit Edge Tool Co						
6570 E Nevada St	Detroit	MI	48234	**800-404-2038**	313-366-4120	492
Detroit Free Press						
615 W Lafayette Blvd	Detroit	MI	48226	**800-395-3300**	313-222-6400	531-2
Detroit Hoist Co						
6650 Sterling Dr N	Sterling Heights	MI	48312	**800-521-9126**	586-268-2600	469
Detroit Lakes Regional Chamber of Commerce						
700 Summit Ave	Detroit Lakes	MN	56501	**800-542-3992**	218-847-9202	138
Detroit Legal News Co						
1409 Allen Rd Ste B	Troy	MI	48083	**800-875-5275**	248-577-6100	634-8
Detroit Lions						
222 Republic Dr	Allen Park	MI	48101	**800-745-3000**	313-216-4000	713-3
Detroit Metropolitan Convention & Visitors Bureau						
211 W Fort St Ste 1000	Detroit	MI	48226	**877-424-5554**	313-202-1800	208
Detroit News						
615 W Lafayette Blvd	Detroit	MI	48226	**800-395-3300***	313-222-2300	531-2
*General						
Detroit Public Schools						
3031 W Grand Blvd	Detroit	MI	48202	**800-656-4673**	313-873-7927	683
Detroit Pump & Mfg Co						
450 Fair St Bldg D	Ferndale	MI	48220	**800-686-1662**	248-544-4242	385
Detroit Quality Brush Mfg						
32165 Schoolcraft Rd	Livonia	MI	48150	**800-722-3037**	734-525-5660	102
Detroit Radiant Product Co						
21400 Hoover Rd	Warren	MI	48089	**800-222-1100**	586-756-0950	319
Detroit Stoker Co						
1510 E First St	Monroe	MI	48161	**800-786-5374**	734-241-9500	319
Detroit Symphony Orchestra						
3711 Woodward Ave	Detroit	MI	48201	**800-434-6340**	313-576-5111	572-3
Detroit Tigers						
Comerica Pk 2100 Woodward Ave	Detroit	MI	48201	**866-800-1275**	313-962-4000	711
Devault Foods						
1 Devault Ln	Devault	PA	19432	**800-426-2874**	610-644-2536	298-8
Devcon Inc						
30 Endicott St	Danvers	MA	01923	**800-626-7226**	855-489-7262	3
Developers Diversified Realty Corp						
3300 Enterprise Pkwy	Beachwood	OH	44122	**877-225-5337**	216-755-5500	653
NYSE: DDR						
Development Dimensions International						
1225 Washington Pike	Bridgeville	PA	15017	**800-933-4463***	412-257-0600	195
*Mktg						
Development Director's Letter						
8204 Fenton St	Silver Spring	MD	20910	**800-666-6380**	301-588-6380	530-7
Devereux						
1291 Stanley Rd NW PO Box 1688	Kennesaw	GA	30156	**800-342-3357**	678-303-5233	374-1
Devereux Cleo Wallace						
8405 Church Ranch Blvd	Westminster	CO	80021	**800-456-2536**	303-466-7391	374-1
Devereux Hospital & Children's Ctr of Florida						
8000 Devereux Dr	Melbourne	FL	32940	**800-338-3738**	321-242-9100	374-1
DevFacto Technologies Inc						
2250 Scotia Place Tower 1 10060 Jasper Ave	Edmonton	AB	T5J3R8	**877-323-3832**	587-520-9118	462
deView Electronics USA Inc						
708 Vly Ridge Cir Ste 1	Lewisville	TX	75057	**877-433-8439**	214-222-3332	690
Devil's Den State Park						
11333 W Arkansas Hwy 74	West Fork	AR	72774	**888-742-8701**	479-761-3325	564
Devil's Head Resort & Convention Ctr						
S 6330 Bluff Rd	Merrimac	WI	53561	**800-472-6670**	608-493-2251	667
Devil's Lake State Recreation Area						
198 NE 123rd St	Lincoln City	OR	97367	**800-551-6949**		564
Devils Fork State Park						
161 Holcombe Cir	Salem	SC	29676	**866-345-7275**	864-944-2639	564
Devon Bank						
6445 N Western Ave	Chicago	IL	60645	**866-683-3866**		69
Devon Energy Corp						
20 N Broadway	Oklahoma City	OK	73102	**877-860-5820**	405-235-3611	535
NYSE: DVN						
DeVry University						
Calgary						
2700 Third Ave SE	Calgary	AB	T2A7W4	**800-363-5558***	403-235-3450	798
*General						
Colorado Springs						
1175 Kelly Johnson Blvd	Colorado Springs	CO	80920	**877-784-1997***	719-632-3000	798
*Help Line						
DeVry University Addison						
1221 N Swift Rd	Addison	IL	60101	**800-346-5420**	630-953-1300	798
DeVry University Federal Way						
3600 S 344th Way	Federal Way	WA	98001	**877-923-3879**	253-943-2800	798
DeVry University Fremont						
6600 Dumbarton Cir	Fremont	CA	94555	**800-363-5558**	510-574-1200	798
DeVry University Houston						
11125 Equity Dr	Houston	TX	77041	**866-338-7934**	713-973-3100	798
DeVry University Irving						
4800 Regent Blvd Ste 200	Irving	TX	75063	**800-633-3879**	972-929-6777	798
DeVry University Kansas City						
1310 E 104th St 2nd Fl	Kansas City	MO	64131	**800-821-3766**	816-941-0430	798
DeVry University Long Beach						
3880 Kilroy Airport Way	Long Beach	CA	90806	**800-597-1333**	562-997-5300	798
DeVry University Long Island City						
3020 Thomson Ave	Long Island	NY	11101	**888-713-3879**	718-472-2728	798
DeVry University North Brunswick						
630 US Hwy 1	North Brunswick	NJ	08902	**800-333-3879**		798
DeVry University Orlando						
4000 Millenia Blvd	Orlando	FL	32839	**888-857-5757**	407-345-2800	798
DeVry University Phoenix						
2149 W Dunlap Ave	Phoenix	AZ	85021	**800-528-0250***	602-870-9222	798
*Cust Svc						
DeVry University Pomona						
901 Corporate Ctr Dr	Pomona	CA	91768	**800-243-3660**	909-622-8866	798
DeVry University Sherman Oaks						
15301 Ventura Blvd Bldg D-100	Sherman Oaks	CA	91403	**888-610-0800**	818-713-8111	798
Dew Distribution Services Inc						
2201 Touhy Ave	Elk Grove Village	IL	60007	**800-837-3391**		647
DeWAL Industries Inc						
15 Ray Trainor Dr	Narragansett	RI	02882	**800-366-8356**	401-789-9736	729
Dew-El Corp						
10641 Paw Paw Dr	Holland	MI	49424	**800-443-3935**	616-396-6554	366
Dewey Ford Inc						
3055 SE Delaware Ave	Ankeny	IA	50021	**877-704-6793**		125
Dewey Services Inc						
939 E Union St	Pasadena	CA	91106	**877-339-3973**	626-568-9248	576
Dewied International Inc						
5010 IH- 10 E	San Antonio	TX	78219	**800-992-5600**	210-661-6161	297-26
Dewitt Products Co						
5860 Plumer Ave	Detroit	MI	48209	**800-962-8599***	313-554-0575	45
*Cust Svc						
DeWitt Wallace Decorative Arts Museum						
326 Francis St W	Williamsburg	VA	23185	**800-447-8679**		519
DexCom Inc						
6340 Sequence Dr	San Diego	CA	92121	**888-738-3646**	858-200-0200	84
NASDAQ: DXCM						
Dexter Axle						
2900 Industrial Pkwy	Elkhart	IN	46516	**800-522-7291**	574-295-7888	59
Dexter-Russell Inc						
44 River St	Southbridge	MA	01550	**800-343-6042**	508-765-0201	224
D&F Travel Inc						
338 Central Ave Ste 320	Dunkirk	NY	14048	**800-832-3516**		770
DFC (Duke Diet & Fitness Ctr)						
501 Douglas St	Durham	NC	27705	**800-235-3853**		704
DFDFCU (Denver Fire Dept Federal Credit Union)						
2201 Federal Blvd	Denver	CO	80211	**866-880-7770**	303-228-5300	221
DFMC (Delmarva Foundation For Medical Care Inc)						
28464 Marlboro Ave	Easton	MD	21601	**800-999-3362**	410-822-0697	473
DFS Group 500 Main St	Groton	MA	01471	**800-225-9528***		109
*General						
DFT Communications						
40 Temple St	Fredonia	NY	14063	**877-653-3100**	716-673-3000	387
DFW (Dallas-Fort Worth International Airport)						
3200 E Airfield Dr PO Box 619428	Dallas	TX	75261	**800-252-7522**	972-973-8888	27
DGA-PAC						
7920 W Sunset Blvd	Los Angeles	CA	90046	**800-421-4173**	310-289-2000	614
DGKR (DoubleTree Resort by Hilton Hotel Grand Key)						
3990 S Roosevelt Blvd	Key West	FL	33040	**888-844-0454**	305-293-1818	667
DGSE Cos Inc						
11311 Reeder Rd	Dallas	TX	75229	**800-527-5307**	972-484-3662	410
NYSE: DGSE						
DH (Dominican Hospital)						
1555 Soquel Dr	Santa Cruz	CA	95065	**866-466-1401**	831-462-7700	374-3
DH (Danbury Hospital)						
24 Hospital Ave	Danbury	CT	06810	**800-516-3658**	203-739-7000	374-3
DH Bader Management Services Inc						
14435 Cherry Ln Ct Ste 210	Laurel	MD	20707	**888-953-1955**	301-953-1955	650
Dh Web Inc						
11377 Robinwood Dr Ste D	Hagerstown	MD	21742	**877-567-6599**	301-733-7672	179
Dharma Trading Co						
1604 Fourth St	San Rafael	CA	94901	**800-542-5227**	415-456-1211	709
DHI Computing Service Inc						
1525 West 820 North PO Box 51427	Provo	UT	84601	**800-992-1344**	801-373-8518	180-11
DHI Mortgage Co Ltd						
10700 Pecan Park Blvd Ste 450	Austin	TX	78750	**800-315-8434**	512-502-0545	216
DHL Global Mail						
2700 S Commerce Pkwy Ste 400	Weston	FL	33331	**800-805-9306**	954-903-6300	545
DHMC (Davis Hospital & Medical Ctr)						
1600 W Antelope Dr	Layton	UT	84041	**877-898-6080**	801-807-1000	374-3
Di Graphics Inc						
4850 Ward Rd	Wheat Ridge	CO	80033	**800-433-2257**	303-425-0510	626
Diabetes Advisor Magazine						
1701 N Beauregard St	Alexandria	VA	22311	**800-342-2383**	800-806-7801	456-16
Diabetes Forecast Magazine						
1701 N Beauregard St	Alexandria	VA	22311	**800-676-4065**	703-549-1500	456-13
Diabetes Research Institute						
1450 NW Tenth Ave	Miami	FL	33136	**800-321-3437**	954-964-4040	666
Diablo Mfg Company Inc						
900 Golden Gate Terr PO Box 1108	Grass Valley	CA	95945	**800-551-2233***	530-272-2241	409
*Cust Svc						
Diablo Valley College						
321 Golf Club Rd	Pleasant Hill	CA	94523	**800-227-1060**	925-685-1230	161
Dial800 LLC						
9911 Pico Blvd Ste 1200	Los Angeles	CA	90035	**800-700-1987**	800-342-5800	226
Dialog						
2250 Perimeter Pk Dr Ste 300	Morrisville	NC	27560	**800-334-2564**	919-804-6400	387
Dialog, The						
1925 Delaware Ave	Wilmington	DE	19806	**877-225-7870**	302-573-3109	531-4
Dialogic Inc						
1504 Mccarthy Blvd	Milpitas	CA	95035	**800-755-4444**	408-750-9400	182
Diamond Aircraft Industries Inc						
1560 Crumlin Sideroad	London	ON	N5V1S2	**888-359-3220**	519-457-4000	20
Diamond Attachments LLC						
2801A S Mississippi	Atoka	OK	74525	**800-445-1917**	580-889-6202	789
Diamond Brand Canvas Products						
145 Cane Creek Industrial Pk Rd Ste 1	Fletcher	NC	28732	**800-459-6262***	828-684-9848	730
*Sales						
Diamond Chain Co						
402 Kentucky Ave	Indianapolis	IN	46225	**800-872-4246***	317-638-6431	619
*Cust Svc						
Diamond Coach Corp						
2300 W Fourth St PO Box 489	Oswego	KS	67356	**800-442-4645**	620-795-2191	515
Diamond Comic Distributors Inc						
1966 Greenspring Dr Ste 300	Timonium	MD	21093	**800-452-6642**	410-560-7100	634-5
Diamond Council of America (DCA)						
3212 W End Ave Ste 202	Nashville	TN	37203	**877-283-5669**	615-385-5301	48-4

Company	Address	City	State	ZIP	Toll-Free	Phone	Class
Diamond Drugs Inc	645 Kolter Dr	Indiana	PA	15701	**800-882-6337**	724-349-1111	233
Diamond Equipment Inc	1060 E Diamond Ave	Evansville	IN	47711	**800-258-4428**	812-425-4428	358
Diamond Head Inn	605 Diamond St	San Diego	CA	92109	**888-478-7829**	858-273-1900	379
Diamond Manufacturing Co	243 W Eigth St	Wyoming	PA	18644	**800-233-9601**	570-693-0300	487
Diamond Offshore Drilling Inc	15415 Katy Fwy *NYSE: DO*	Houston	TX	77094	**800-848-1980**	281-492-5300	539
Diamond Packaging Company Inc	111 Commerce Dr PO Box 23620	Rochester	NY	14692	**800-333-4079**	585-334-8030	100
Diamond Perforated Metals Inc	7300 W Sunnyview Ave	Visalia	CA	93291	**800-642-4334**	559-651-1889	487
Diamond Plastics Corp	1212 Johnstown Rd PO Box 1608	Grand Island	NE	68802	**800-782-7473**	308-384-4400	595
Diamond Power International Inc	2600 E Main St	Lancaster	OH	43130	**800-848-5086**	740-687-6500	386
Diamond Saw Works Inc	12290 Olean Rd	Chaffee	NY	14030	**800-828-1180**	716-496-7417	680
Diamond Services Corp	503 S DeGravelle Rd	Amelia	LA	70340	**800-879-1162**	985-631-2187	538
Diamond Tool & Die Inc	508 29th Ave	Oakland	CA	94601	**800-227-1084**	510-534-7050	755
Diamond V Mills Inc	PO Box 74570	Cedar Rapids	IA	52407	**800-373-7234**	319-366-0745	446
Diamond Vogel Paints	1110 Albany Pl SE PO Box 380	Orange City	IA	51041	**800-728-6435**	712-737-8880	549
Diamond Z Manufacturing	11299 Bass Ln	Caldwell	ID	83605	**800-949-2383**	208-585-2929	296
DiamondJacks Casino Resort	711 Diamond Jacks Blvd	Bossier City	LA	71111	**866-552-9629**	318-678-7777	132
DiamondRock Hospitality Co (DRHC)	3 Bethesda Metro Ctr Ste 1500 *NYSE: DRH*	Bethesda	MD	20814	**888-246-5941**	240-744-1150	652
Dian Fossey Gorilla Fund International	800 Cherokee Ave SE	Atlanta	GA	30315	**800-851-0203**	404-624-5881	47-3
Diana Wortham Theatre at Pack Place	2 S Pack Sq	Asheville	NC	28801	**800-999-2160**	828-257-4530	571
Diane Von Furstenberg	440 W 14th St	New York	NY	10014	**888-472-2383**	212-741-6607	279
DIANON Systems Inc	1 Forest Pkwy	Shelton	CT	06484	**800-328-2666**	203-926-7100	418
DiaSorin Inc	1951 NW Ave	Stillwater	MN	55082	**855-677-0600**	651-439-9710	233
DiAZiT Company Inc	941 US 1 Hwy *Cust Svc	Youngsville	NC	27596	**800-334-6641***	919-556-5188	699
DiCarlo Distributors Inc	1630 N Ocean Ave	Holtsville	NY	11742	**800-342-2756**	631-758-6000	298-8
Dice Inc	4101 NW Urbandale Dr	Urbandale	IA	50322	**877-386-3323**	515-280-1144	262
Dick Blick Co	PO Box 1267 *Orders	Galesburg	IL	61402	**800-447-8192***	309-343-6181	44
Dick Brantmeier Ford Inc	3624 Kohler Memorial Dr	Sheboygan	WI	53082	**800-498-6111**	920-458-6111	56
Dick Gores Rv World	14590 Duval Pl W	Jacksonville	FL	32218	**800-635-7008**	904-741-5100	515
Dick Lavy Trucking Inc	8848 State Rt 121	Bradford	OH	45308	**800-345-5289**	937-448-2104	778
Dicke Safety Products	1201 Warren Ave	Downers Grove	IL	60515	**877-891-0050**	630-969-0050	360-3
Dickens Books Ltd	219 N Milwaukee St	Milwaukee	WI	53202	**800-236-7323**		95
Dickenson County School District	PO Box 1127	Clintwood	VA	24228	**866-632-9992**	276-926-4643	683
Dickey Transport	401 E Fourth St	Packwood	IA	52580	**800-247-1081**	319-695-3601	578
DICKEY-John Corp	5200 Dickey-John Rd	Auburn	IL	62615	**800-637-2952**	217-438-3371	636
Dickinson Area Partnership	600 S Stephenson Ave	Iron Mountain	MI	49801	**888-543-2139**	906-774-2002	138
Dickinson College	PO Box 1773	Carlisle	PA	17013	**800-644-1773**	717-243-5121	167
Dickinson Convention & Visitors Bureau	72 E Museum Dr	Dickinson	ND	58601	**800-279-7391**	701-483-4988	208
Dickinson Homes Inc	404 N Stephenson Ave Hwy US-2 PO Box 2245	Iron Mountain	MI	49801	**800-438-4687**	906-774-2186	105
Dickinson State University	291 Campus Dr	Dickinson	ND	58601	**800-279-4295**	701-483-2507	167
Dickman Directories Inc	6145 Columbus Pk	Lewis Center	OH	43035	**877-836-4154**	740-548-6130	634-6
Dickson Co	930 S Westwood Ave	Addison	IL	60101	**800-757-3747**	630-543-3747	203
Dickson County Chamber of Commerce	119 Hwy 70 E	Dickson	TN	37055	**877-718-4967**	615-446-2349	138
Dickstein Shapiro LLP	1825 Eye St NW	Washington	DC	20006	**800-203-3447**	202-420-2200	428
Didax Inc	395 Main St	Rowley	MA	01969	**800-458-0024**	978-948-2340	245
Diebold Inc	5995 Mayfair Rd *NYSE: DBD*	North Canton	OH	44720	**800-999-3600**	330-490-4000	799
Dielectrics Industries Inc	300 Burnett Rd	Chicopee	MA	01020	**800-472-7286**	413-594-8111	599
Dieterich-Post Co	616 Monterey Pass Rd	Monterey Park	CA	91754	**800-955-3729**	626-289-5021	111
Dietz & Watson Inc	5701 Tacony St	Philadelphia	PA	19135	**800-333-1974**	215-831-9000	297-26
Diffenbaugh Inc	6865 Airport Dr	Riverside	CA	92504	**800-394-5334**	951-351-6865	188
Dig Corp	1210 Activity Dr	Vista	CA	92081	**800-322-9146**	760-727-0914	275
Digestive Care Inc	1120 Win Dr	Bethlehem	PA	18017	**877-882-5950**	610-882-0349	233
Digi International Inc	11001 Bren Rd E *NASDAQ: DGII*	Minnetonka	MN	55343	**877-912-3444**	952-912-3444	178
Digi-Key Corp	701 Brooks Ave S	Thief River Falls	MN	56701	**800-344-4539**	218-681-6674	248
DigiLink Inc	840 S Pickett St	Alexandria	VA	22304	**877-806-3444**	703-340-1800	176
Digimarc Corp	9405 SW Gemini Dr *NASDAQ: DMRC*	Beaverton	OR	97008	**800-344-4627**	503-469-4800	180-12
Digipen Institute of Technology	5001 150th Ave Ne	Redmond	WA	98052	**866-478-5236**	425-558-0299	167
Digirad Corp	13950 Stowe Dr *NASDAQ: DRAD*	Poway	CA	92064	**800-947-6134**	858-726-1600	382
Digiscribe International LLC	150 Clearbrook Rd Ste 125	Elmsford	NY	10523	**800-686-7577**		228
Digistream Investigation	417 mace blvd	Davis	CA	95618	**800-747-4329**		691
Digital Celerity LLC	548 Market St Ste 22067	San Francisco	CA	94104	**888-963-8876**		182
Digital ChoreoGraphics	PO Box 8268	Newport Beach	CA	92658	**800-548-1969**	949-548-1969	179
Digital Design Inc	67 Sand Pk Rd	Cedar Grove	NJ	07009	**800-967-7746**	973-857-0900	175-6
Digital Dialogue LLC	3252 University Dr Ste 165	Auburn Hills	MI	48326	**800-205-4268**		393
Digital Employees' Federal Credit Union	220 Donald Lynch Blvd	Marlborough	MA	01752	**800-328-8797**	508-263-6700	221
Digital Engineering Systems Corp	2450 Scott Blvd Ste 300	Santa Clara	CA	95050	**888-788-1898**	408-970-8551	759
Digital Excellence	300 York Ave	Saint Paul	MN	55101	**800-608-8008**	651-772-5100	656
Digital I-Olle	1424 30th St	San Diego	CA	92154	**866-423-4433**	619-423-4433	179
Digital Machining Systems LLC	929 Ridge Rd	Duson	LA	70529	**800-530-8945**	337-984-6013	453
Digital Measures	301 N Broadway 4th Fl	Milwaukee	WI	53202	**866-348-5677**		182
Digital Monitoring Products Inc	2500 N Partnership Blvd	Springfield	MO	65803	**800-641-4282**	417-831-9362	666
Digital Peripheral Solutions Inc	8015 E Crystal Dr	Anaheim	CA	92807	**877-998-3440**		175-8
Digital Photographer Magazine	12121 Wilshire Blvd 12th Fl	Los Angeles	CA	90025	**800-537-4619**	310-820-1500	456-14
Digital Power Corp	41324 Christy St	Fremont	CA	94538	**866-344-7697**	510-353-4023	255
Digital River Inc	10380 Bren Rd W *NASDAQ: DRIV*	Minnetonka	MN	55343	**800-598-7450**		38
Digital Room Inc	8000 Haskell Ave	Van Nuys	CA	91406	**866-266-5047**		626
Digital Security Controls (DSC)	3301 Langstaff Rd	Concord	ON	L4K4L2	**888-888-7838**	905-760-3000	690
Digital Solutions Inc	955 SE Olson Dr *Cust Svc	Waukee	IA	50263	**888-464-8770***	515-987-6227	180-11
Digital Storage Inc	7611 Green Meadows Dr	Lewis Center	OH	43035	**800-232-3475**	740-548-7179	176
Digital Street Inc	69550 Highway 111 Ste 201	Rancho Mirage	CA	92270	**866-464-5100**		462
Digital Voice Corp	1201 S Beltline Rd Ste 150 *Cust Svc	Coppell	TX	75019	**800-777-8329***	469-635-6500	732
DigitalWork Inc	14300 N Northsight Blvd Ste 206	Scottsdale	AZ	85260	**877-496-7571**		38
Digitec Inc	2731 Van Dorn Rd	Milford	NE	68405	**888-761-3382**	402-761-3382	666
Dignity Memorial	1929 Allen Pkwy	Houston	TX	77019	**800-894-2024**	713-522-5141	509
DignityUSA Inc	PO Box 376	Medford	MA	02155	**800-877-8797**	202-861-0017	47-21
DII (Doucette Industries Inc)	20 Leigh Dr	York	PA	17406	**800-445-7511**	717-845-8746	14
Dilley Manufacturing Co	215 E Third St	Des Moines	IA	50309	**800-247-5087**	515-288-7289	85
Dilmar Oil Company Inc	1951 W Darlington St PO Box 5629	Florence	SC	29501	**800-922-5823**		778
Dimco Steel Inc	3901 S Lamar St	Dallas	TX	75215	**877-428-8336**	214-428-8336	684
Dime Bank, The	820 Church St PO Box 509	Honesdale	PA	18431	**888-469-3463**	570-253-1902	69
Dime Community Bancshares Inc	209 Havemeyer St *NASDAQ: DCOM*	Brooklyn	NY	11211	**800-321-3463**	718-782-6200	360-2
Dimension Consulting Inc	2620 Second Ave Ste 9D	San Diego	CA	92103	**855-222-6444**	703-636-0933	198
Dinah's Garden Hotel	4261 El Camino Real	Palo Alto	CA	94306	**800-227-8220**	650-493-2844	379
Diners Club International	111 W Monroe	Chicago	IL	60603	**800-234-6377**		219
Dings Co	4740 W Electric Ave	Milwaukee	WI	53219	**800-494-1918**	414-672-7830	386
Dinkel's Bakery	3329 N Lincoln Ave *Orders	Chicago	IL	60657	**800-822-8817***	773-281-7300	297-1
Dinklage Feedyards	PO Box 274	Sidney	NE	69162	**888-343-5940**	308-254-5940	10-1
Dino's Trucking Inc	9615 Continental Indus Dr	Saint Louis	MO	63123	**800-771-7805**	314-631-3001	778
Diocese of Greensburg	723 E Pittsburgh St	Greensburg	PA	15601	**866-409-6455**	724-837-0901	47-20
Diocese of Rochester	1150 Buffalo Rd	Roch	NY	14624	**800-388-7177**	585-328-3210	47-20
Diocese of St. Augustine Inc	11625 Old St Augustine	Jacksonville	FL	32258	**800-775-4659**	904-262-3200	47-20

Name	Address	City	State	ZIP	Toll-Free	Phone	Class
Diocese of Steubenville Catholic Charities	PO Box 969	Steubenville	OH	43952	**800-339-7890**	740-282-3631	634-8
Dipert Travel & Transportation Ltd	PO Box 580	Arlington	TX	76004	**800-433-5335**		758
Dircks Moving Services Inc	4340 W Mohave St	Phoenix	AZ	85043	**800-523-5038**	602-267-9401	778
Direct Connection Printing & Mailing	1968 Yeager Ave	La Verne	CA	91750	**800-420-9937**	909-392-2334	626
Direct Holdings Americas Inc	8280 Willow Oaks Corporate Dr	Fairfax	VA	22031	**800-950-7887**		94
Direct Internet Access	141 Desiard St PO Box 7263	Monroe	LA	71201	**800-296-2249**		398
Direct Marketing Assn Inc (DMA)	1120 Ave of the Americas	New York	NY	10036	**855-422-0749**	212-768-7277	48-18
Direct Online Marketing	4727 Jacob St	Wheeling	WV	26003	**800-979-3177**	304-214-4850	227
Direct Relief International	27 S La Patera Ln	Goleta	CA	93117	**800-676-1638**	805-964-4767	47-5
Direct Source Inc	8176 Mallory Ct	Chanhassen	MN	55317	**800-934-8055**	952-934-8000	180-5
Direct Sports Inc	1720 Curve Rd	Pearisburg	VA	24134	**800-456-0072**		709
Direct Travel	95 New Jersey 17	Paramus	NJ	07652	**800-831-1366**	201-847-9000	769
DirectBuy Inc	8450 Broadway	Merrillville	IN	46410	**800-320-3462**	219-736-1100	311
Directec Corp	1650 Lyndon Farm Ct Ste 202	Louisville	KY	40223	**800-588-7800**	502-357-5000	198
DirectEmployers.com	9002 N Purdue Rd Quad III Ste 100	Indianapolis	IN	46268	**866-268-6206**	317-874-9000	393
DirectMailcom	201 Skipjack Rd	Prince Frederick	MD	20678	**866-284-5816**	301-855-1700	5
Directors Guild of America	7920 W Sunset Blvd	Los Angeles	CA	90046	**800-421-4173**	310-289-2000	414
Directory Distributing Assoc (DDA)	1602 Pk 370 Ct *General	Hazelwood	MO	63042	**800-325-1964***	314-592-8600	94
Directory One Inc	9135 Katy Fwy Ste 204	Houston	TX	77024	**800-477-1324**	713-465-0051	227
DIRECTV Inc	2230 E Imperial Hwy *Cust Svc	El Segundo	CA	90245	**800-531-5000***	310-535-5000	115
DirectWest Corp	2550 Sandra Schmirler Way Ste 200	Regina	SK	S4W1A1	**800-667-8201**	306-777-0333	227
Dirks Group, The	3802 Hummingbird Rd	Wausau	WI	54401	**800-866-1486**	715-848-9865	182
Dirxion LLC	1859 Bowles Ave Ste 100	Fenton	MO	63026	**888-391-0202**	636-717-2300	176
DIS Corp	1315 Cornwall Ave *Cust Svc	Bellingham	WA	98225	**800-426-8870***	360-733-7610	180-10
Disa Systems Inc	150 Transit Ave	Thomasville	NC	27360	**800-845-8508**	336-889-9187	18
Disability Funding Week	8204 Fenton St	Silver Spring	MD	20910	**800-666-6380**		530-8
Disability Law Compliance Report	610 Opperman Dr *Cust Svc	Eagan	MN	55123	**800-328-4880***	651-687-7000	530-7
Disability Rights Ctr Inc	18 Low Ave	Concord	NH	03301	**800-834-1721**	603-228-0432	47-17
Disabled & Alone/Life Services for the Handicapped	1440 Broadway 23rd Floor	New York	NY	10018	**800-995-0066**	212-532-6740	47-17
Disabled American Veterans (DAV)	3725 Alexandria Pike	Cold Spring	KY	41076	**877-426-2838**	859-441-7300	47-19
Disabled Sports USA (DS/USA)	451 Hungerford Dr Ste 100	Rockville	MD	20850	**800-543-2754**	301-217-0960	47-22
Disaster News Network (DNN)	PO Box 1746	Ellicott City	MD	21041	**888-384-3028**	443-393-3330	529
Disc Makers	7905 N Rt 130	Pennsauken	NJ	08110	**800-468-9353**	856-663-9030	175-8
Disco Inc	1895 Brannan Rd	McDonough	GA	30253	**800-325-1051**	770-474-7575	507
Discount Car & Truck Rentals Ltd	720 Arrow Rd	North York	ON	M9M2M1	**866-742-5968**		125
Discount Drug Mart Inc	211 Commerce Dr	Medina	OH	44256	**800-833-6278**	330-725-2340	239
Discount Labels Inc	4115 Profit Ct	New Albany	IN	47150	**800-995-9500**		413
Discount RampsCom LLC	760 S Indiana Ave	West Bend	WI	53095	**888-651-3431**	262-338-3431	479
Discount School Supplies	2 Lower Ragsdale Rd Ste 125	Monterey	CA	93940	**800-919-5238**		759
DiscountMugs.com	12610 NW 115th Ave	Medley	FL	33178	**800-569-1980**		688
Discover Bank	PO Box 30416	Salt Lake City	UT	84130	**800-347-7000**	302-323-7810	69
Discover Communications Inc	30 Victoria Crescent	Brampton	ON	L6T1E4	**888-456-8989**	905-455-5600	226
Discover Group Inc	2741 W 23rd St	Brooklyn	NY	11224	**866-456-6555**	718-456-4500	534
Discover Klamath	205 Riverside Dr Ste B	Klamath Falls	OR	97601	**800-445-6728**	541-882-1501	208
Discovery Communications Inc	1 Discovery Pl *NASDAQ: DISCA*	Silver Spring	MD	20910	**877-324-5850**	240-662-2000	736
Discovery Cove	6000 Discovery Cove Way	Orlando	FL	32821	**877-434-7268**	407-370-1280	821
Discovery Cruises Inc	1775 NW 70th Ave	Miami	FL	33126	**800-866-8687**	305-477-2867	222
Discovery Ctr of Springfield	438 E St Louis St	Springfield	MO	65806	**888-636-4395**	417-862-9910	520
Discovery Place	301 N Tryon St	Charlotte	NC	28202	**800-935-0553**	704-372-6261	520
Discovery Research Group	6975 Union Pk Ctr Ste 150	Midvale	UT	84047	**800-678-3748**		227
Disguise	12120 Kear Pl	Poway	CA	92064	**877-875-2557**	858-391-3600	154-6

Name	Address	City	State	ZIP	Toll-Free	Phone	Class
DISH Network LLC	9601 S Meridian Blvd *NASDAQ: DISH*	Englewood	CO	80112	**800-823-4929**		115
Disney Consumer Products	500 S Buena Vista St *PR	Burbank	CA	91521	**855-553-4763***	818-560-1000	634-9
Disney Vacation Club	1390 Celebration Blvd	Celebration	FL	34747	**800-500-3990**	407-566-3100	751
Disney's California Adventure	1313 S Disneyland Dr	Anaheim	CA	92802	**800-225-2024**	714-781-7290	32
Disney's Grand Floridian Spa	4401 Floridian Wy	Lake Buena Vista	FL	32830	**800-169-0730**	407-824-2332	705
Disney/Little Blue State Park	Hwy 28 E	Disney	OK	74340	**800-622-6317**	918-435-8066	564
Dispatch Printing Co	34 S Third St	Columbus	OH	43215	**800-282-0263**	614-461-5000	634-8
Dispatch, The	116 E Market St	Blairsville	PA	15717	**800-221-9282**	724-459-6100	531-2
Dispensing Dynamics International	1020 Bixby Dr	City of Industry	CA	91745	**800-888-3698**	626-961-3691	609
Display Smart LLC	801 W 27th Terr	Lawrence	KS	66046	**888-843-1870**	785-843-1869	235
Display Technologies LLC	1111 Marcus Ave Ste M68	Lake Success	NY	11042	**800-424-4220**		235
Disston Precision Inc	6795 State Rd *Cust Svc	Philadelphia	PA	19135	**800-238-1007***	215-338-1200	680
Distillata Co	1608 E 24th St *Cust Svc	Cleveland	OH	44114	**800-999-2906***	216-771-2900	803
Distinctive Dental Studio Ltd. Inc	1504 Wall St	Naperville	IL	60563	**800-552-7890**	630-369-4600	415
Distinctive Designs International Inc	120 Sibley Dr	Russellville	AL	35654	**800-243-4787**	256-332-7390	295
Distinguished Programs Group LLC, The	1180 Ave Of The Americas 16th Fl	New York	NY	10036	**888-355-4626**	212-297-3100	390
Distribution & Marking Services Inc (DMSI)	10709 Granite St Ste Q	Charlotte	NC	28273	**844-325-3741**	704-749-7300	448
Distribution Ctr Management (DCM)	712 Main St Ste 187B	Boonton	NJ	07005	**800-232-4317**	973-265-2300	530-2
District of Columbia *Convention & Tourism Corp*	901 7th St NW 4th Fl	Washington	DC	20001	**800-422-8644**	202-789-7000	339-9
District of Columbia Bar, The	1101 K St NW Ste 200	Washington	DC	20005	**877-333-2227**	202-737-4700	71
DIT-MCO International Corp	5612 Brighton Terr	Kansas City	MO	64130	**800-821-3487**	816-444-9700	250
Dittrick Museum of Medical History	11000 Euclid Ave	Cleveland	OH	44106	**800-368-4723**	216-368-3648	519
Divers Academy International	1500 Liberty Pl	Erial	NJ	08081	**800-238-3483**		798
Diverse Power Inc	1400 S Davis Rd	LaGrange	GA	30241	**800-845-8362**	706-845-2000	247
Diversified Chemical Technologies Inc (DCT)	15477 Woodrow Wilson St	Detroit	MI	48238	**800-243-1424**	313-867-5444	144
Diversified Electronics Co Inc	PO Box 566	Forest Park	GA	30298	**800-646-7278**	404-361-4840	248
Diversified Funding Services Inc	125 Habersham Dr Ste C	Fayetteville	GA	30214	**888-603-0055**	770-603-0055	274
Diversified Hum Res Inc	3020 E Camelback Rd Ste 213	Phoenix	AZ	85016	**888-870-5588**	480-941-5588	630
Diversified Labeling Solutions	1285 Hamilton Pkwy	Itasca	IL	60143	**800-397-3013**	630-625-1225	551-1
Diversified Lenders Inc	5607 S Ave Q	Lubbock	TX	79412	**800-288-3024**		196
Diversified Maintenance Systems Inc	5110 Eisenhower Blvd Ste250	Tampa	FL	33634	**800-351-1557**	813-383-0238	151
Diversified Search Cos	2005 Market St 33rd Fl	Philadelphia	PA	19103	**800-423-3932**	215-732-6666	268
DiversiTech Inc	6650 Sugarloaf Pkwy Ste 100	Duluth	GA	30097	**800-995-2222**	678-542-3600	14
Dividend Capital Trust	518 17th St Ste 1700	Denver	CO	80202	**866-324-7348**	303-228-2200	652
Divine Word College	102 Jacoby Dr SW	Epworth	IA	52045	**800-553-3321**	563-876-3353	167
Diving Equipment & Marketing Assn (DEMA)	3750 Convoy St Ste 310	San Diego	CA	92111	**800-862-3483**	858-616-6408	48-4
Divisions Maintenance Group Inc	1 RiverFrnt Pl Ste 510	Newport	KY	41071	**877-448-9730**		194
DIX (Downtown Idea Exchange)	712 Main St Ste 187B	Boonton	NJ	07005	**800-232-4317**	973-265-2300	530-2
Dixie Construction Products Inc	970 Huff Rd NW	Atlanta	GA	30318	**800-992-1180**	404-351-1100	351
Dixie Electric Co-op	9100 Atlanta Hwy	Montgomery	AL	36117	**888-349-4332**	334-288-1163	247
Dixie Electric Membership Corp (DEMCO)	PO Box 15659	Baton Rouge	LA	70895	**800-262-0221**	225-261-1221	247
Dixie Electric Power Assn	PO Box 88	Laurel	MS	39441	**888-465-9209**	601-425-2535	247
Dixie Group Inc	104 Nowlin Ln Ste 101 *NASDAQ: DXYN*	Chattanooga	TN	37421	**800-289-4811**	423-510-7000	130
Dixie Gun Works Inc	1412 W Reelfoot Ave PO Box 130 *Orders	Union City	TN	38281	**800-238-6785***	731-885-0700	709
Dixie Industries	3510 N Orchard Knob Ave	Chattanooga	TN	37406	**800-933-4943**	423-698-3323	350
Dixie Pipe Sales Inc	2407 Broiller	Houston	TX	77054	**800-733-3494**	713-796-2021	489
Dixie State University	225 S 700 E	Saint George	UT	84770	**855-628-8140**	435-652-7500	167
Dixie Store Fixtures & Sales Company Inc	2425 First Ave N	Birmingham	AL	35203	**800-323-4943**	205-322-2442	288
Dixie-Escalante Rural Electric Assn	71 E Hwy 56	Beryl	UT	84714	**800-874-0904**	435-439-5311	247
Dixie-Narco Inc	3330 Dixie-Narco Blvd	Williston	SC	29853	**800-688-9090**	803-266-5000	54

Name / Address	City	State	Zip	Toll-Free	Phone	Class
Dixon Ticonderoga Co 195 International Pkwy	Heathrow	FL	32746	**800-824-9430**	407-829-9000	570
DJ & A PC 3203 S Russell St	Missoula	MT	59801	**800-398-3522**	406-721-4320	258
DJ Jacobetti Home for Veterans 425 Fisher St	Marquette	MI	49855	**800-433-6760**	906-226-3576	791
DJ Orthopedics Inc 1430 Decision St	Vista	CA	92081	**800-321-9549**	760-727-1280	476
DKRW Advanced Fuels LLC 5444 Westheimer Ste 1560	Houston	TX	77056	**855-876-4595**		535
D&L Art Glass Supply 1440 W 52nd Ave	Denver	CO	80221	**800-525-0940**	303-449-8737	43
D-Link Systems Inc 17595 Mt Herrmann St	Fountain Valley	CA	92708	**800-326-1688**	714-885-6000	178
Dlt Solutions 13861 Sunrise Valley Dr Ste 400	Herndon	VA	20171	**800-262-4358**	703-709-7172	176
DLZ Corp 6121 Huntley Rd	Columbus	OH	43229	**800-336-5352**	614-888-0040	263
DM Figley Company Inc 10 Kelly Ct	Menlo Park	CA	94025	**800-292-9919**	650-329-8700	145
DM Transportation Management Services Inc 740 Reading Ave	Boyertown	PA	19512	**888-399-0162**	610-367-0162	196
DMA (Direct Marketing Assn Inc) 1120 Ave of the Americas	New York	NY	10036	**855-422-0749**	212-768-7277	48-18
DMCCVB (Decatur/Morgan County Convention & Visitors Bureau) 719 Sixth Ave SE PO Box 2349	Decatur	AL	35602	**800-232-5449**	256-350-2028	208
D-M-E Co 29111 Stephenson Hwy	Madison Heights	MI	48071	**800-626-6653**	248-398-6000	603
DME-Direct Inc 28486 Westinghouse Pl Ste 120	Valencia	CA	91355	**877-721-7701**		196
DMI (Dairy Management Inc) 10255 W Higgins Rd Ste 900	Rosemont	IL	60018	**800-853-2479**		47-2
DMS Facility Services Inc 417 East Huntington Dr	Monrovia	CA	91016	**800-443-8677**	626-305-8500	103
DMS Laboratories Inc 2 Darts Mill Rd	Flemington	NJ	08822	**800-567-4367**	908-782-3353	581
DMS Pharmaceutical Group Inc 810 Busse Hwy	Park Ridge	IL	60068	**877-788-1100**	847-518-1100	233
DMSI (Distribution & Marking Services Inc) 10709 Granite St Ste Q	Charlotte	NC	28273	**844-325-3741**	704-749-7300	448
DN Tanks 351 Cypress Ln	El Cajon	CA	92020	**800-227-8181**	619-440-8181	185
DNA (Delaware Nurses Assn) 4765 Ogletown-Stanton Rd Ste L10	Newark	DE	19713	**800-626-4081**	302-733-5880	532
DNA Diagnostics Ctr 1 DDC Way	Fairfield	OH	45014	**800-362-2368**	513-881-7800	417
DNA Paternity Lab of Utah 2749 E Parleys Way Ste 100	Salt Lake City	UT	84109	**800-362-5559**	801-466-3872	417
DNN (Disaster News Network) PO Box 1746	Ellicott City	MD	21041	**888-384-3028**	443-393-3330	529
Doane College 1014 Boswell Ave	Crete	NE	68333	**800-333-6263**	402-826-2161	167
Grand Island 3180 W US Hwy 34	Grand Island	NE	68801	**800-333-6263**	308-398-0800	167
Lincoln 303 N 52nd St	Lincoln	NE	68504	**888-803-6263**	402-466-4774	167
DOAR Litigation Consulting 170 Earle Ave	Lynbrook	NY	11563	**800-875-8705**	516-823-4000	444
Dober Chemical Group 11230 Katherine Crossing Ste 100	Woodridge	IL	60517	**800-323-4983**	630-410-7300	144
Doble Engineering Co Inc 85 Walnut St	Watertown	MA	02472	**888-443-6253**	617-926-4900	250
Doc 2 E-file Inc 4500 S Wayside Dr Ste 102	Houston	TX	77087	**888-649-2006**	713-649-2006	227
DocAuto Inc 3500 Pkwy Ln Ste 270	Norcross	GA	30092	**800-362-2886**	770-242-6747	387
Docken & Co 900-800 6 Ave Sw	Calgary	AB	T2P3G3	**877-269-3612**	403-269-3612	428
Doctors Foster & Smith Inc 2253 Air Pk Rd PO Box 100	Rhinelander	WI	54501	**800-826-7206**	715-369-3305	577
Doctors Hospital 5100 W Broad St	Columbus	OH	43228	**800-432-3309**	614-544-1000	374-3
Doctors Hospital at White Rock Lake 9440 Poppy Dr	Dallas	TX	75218	**866-893-8446**	214-820-0111	374-3
Doctors Hospital of Laredo 10700 McPherson Rd	Laredo	TX	78045	**844-244-4874**	956-523-2000	374-3
Doctors Without Borders USA Inc 333 Seventh Ave 2nd Fl	New York	NY	10001	**888-392-0392**	212-679-6800	47-5
Doctors' Co, The 185 Greenwood Rd	Napa	CA	94558	**800-421-2368**		391-5
Docufree Corp 1175 Northmeadow Pkwy Ste 140	Roswell	GA	30076	**877-220-4350**	770-643-2900	227
Document Security Systems Inc 200 Canal View Blvd Ste 300 *NYSE: DSS*	Rochester	NY	14623	**877-407-8031**	585-325-3610	180-10
Doc-U-Search Inc 63 Pleasant St PO Box 777	Concord	NH	03301	**800-332-3034**		632
Dodd Camera 2077 E 30th St	Cleveland	OH	44115	**800-507-1676**	216-361-6800	118
Dodge & Cox Funds 30 Dan Rd PO Box 8422	Canton	MA	02021	**800-621-3979**		527
Dodge City Community College 2501 N 14th Ave	Dodge City	KS	67801	**800-367-3222**	620-225-1321	161
Dodger Industries 2075 Stultz Rd PO Box 711 *Cust Svc	Martinsville	VA	24112	**800-247-7879***		154-1
DOE (Department of Energy) 1000 Independence Ave SW	Washington	DC	20585	**800-342-5363**	202-586-5450	340-7
Doe Run Co, The 1801 Pk 270 Dr Ste 300	Saint Louis	MO	63146	**800-356-3786**	314-453-7100	484
Doerfer Engineering Corp PO Box 816	Waverly	IA	50677	**877-483-4700**		263
Dog Fancy Magazine 3 Burroughs *Cust Svc	Irvine	CA	92618	**800-546-7730***	949-855-8822	456-14
Dogwood Hills Golf Resort 1252 State Hwy KK	Osage Beach	MO	65065	**800-220-6571**	573-348-3153	667

Name / Address	City	State	Zip	Toll-Free	Phone	Class
Dogwood Productions Inc 757 Government St	Mobile	AL	36602	**800-254-9903**	251-476-0858	7
Doherty Employment Group 7625 Parklawn Ave *Sales	Edina	MN	55435	**888-297-0495***	952-832-8383	630
Dohrn Transfer Co 625 Third Ave	Rock Island	IL	61201	**888-364-7621**	309-794-0723	448
Doka USA Ltd 214 Gates Rd	Little Ferry	NJ	07643	**877-365-2872**	201-329-7839	193-3
DOL (Department of Labor) 200 Constitution Ave NW	Washington	DC	20210	**866-487-2365**	202-693-4650	340-13
Dolce Atlanta-Peachtree 201 Aberdeen Pkwy	Peachtree City	GA	30269	**800-983-6523**	770-487-2666	377
Dolce Hayes Mansion 200 Edenvale Ave	San Jose	CA	95136	**866-981-3300**	408-226-3200	377
Dole Food Company Hawaii 802 Mapunapuna St	Honolulu	HI	96819	**800-697-9100**	808-861-8015	298-7
Dole Food Company Inc 1 Dole Dr *NYSE: DOLE*	Westlake Village	CA	91362	**800-232-8888**	818-879-6600	316-4
Dole Refrigerating Co 1420 Higgs Rd	Lewisburg	TN	37091	**800-251-8990**	931-359-6211	662
Dolese Bros Co 20 NW 13th St	Oklahoma City	OK	73103	**800-375-2311**	405-235-2311	185
Dollar Bank FSB 225 Forbes Ave	Pittsburgh	PA	15222	**800-828-5527**		69
Dollar General Corp 100 Mission Ridge *NYSE: DG*	Goodlettsville	TN	37072	**800-777-1410**	615-855-4000	789
Dollar Loan Ctr LLC 6122 W Sahara Ave	Las Vegas	NV	89146	**866-550-4352**	702-693-5626	216
Dollar Rent A Car Inc 5330 E 31st St	Tulsa	OK	74135	**800-800-4000**	918-669-3000	125
Dollar Thrifty Automotive Group Inc 5330 E 31st St PO Box 35985	Tulsa	OK	74135	**800-334-1705**	918-660-7700	125
Dollar Tree Stores Inc 500 Volvo Pkwy *NASDAQ: DLTR*	Chesapeake	VA	23320	**877-530-8733**		789
Dollars for Scholars Scholarship America 1 Scholarship Way	Saint Peter	MN	56082	**800-248-8080**	507-931-1682	723
Dollywood 2700 Dollywood Parks Blvd.	Pigeon Forge	TN	37863	**800-365-5996**		32
Dolphin Beach Resort 4900 Gulf Blvd	Saint Pete Beach	FL	33706	**800-237-8916**	727-360-7011	379
Dolphin Carpet & Tile 3550 NW 77th Ct	Miami	FL	33122	**800-639-3566**	305-591-4141	292
Dolphin Inn 1705 Atlantic Ave	Virginia Beach	VA	23451	**800-365-3467**	757-491-1420	379
Dolphin Shirt Co 757 Buckley Rd	San Luis Obispo	CA	93401	**800-377-3256**	805-541-2566	626
Dolphin Swim School Inc 1530 El Camino Ave	Sacramento	CA	95815	**800-436-5744**	916-929-8188	709
Dolphins Plus Inc 31 Corrine Pl	Key Largo	FL	33037	**866-860-7946**	305-451-1993	802
Domain Assoc 1 Palmer Sq Ste 515	Princeton	NJ	08542	**866-803-9204**	609-683-5656	790
Domaine Chandon Inc 1 California Dr	Yountville	CA	94599	**888-242-6366**		79-3
Domain-It! 9891 Montgomery Rd *General	Cincinnati	OH	45242	**866-269-2355***	513-351-4222	396
DomainPeople Inc 550 Burrard St Ste 200 Bentall Twr 5	Vancouver	BC	V6C2B5	**877-734-3667**	604-639-1680	396
Dome Printing 340 Commerce Cir	Sacramento	CA	95815	**800-343-3139**		626
Domengeaux Wright Roy & Edwards LLC 556 Jefferson St Ste 500	Lafayette	LA	70501	**800-375-6186**	337-233-3033	428
Domestic Linen Supply & Laundry Co Inc 30555 NW Hwy	Farmington Hills	MI	48334	**800-344-3555**	248-737-2000	442
Domestic Securities Inc 160 Summit Ave	Montvale	NJ	07645	**877-690-2274**	201-505-9855	688
Dometic Corp 2320 Industrial Pkwy	Elkhart	IN	46516	**800-544-4881**	574-294-2511	14
Domini Social Investments PO Box 9785	Providence	RI	02940	**800-582-6757**		527
Dominican College 470 Western Hwy	Orangeburg	NY	10962	**866-432-4636**	845-359-7800	167
Dominican Hospital (DH) 1555 Soquel Dr	Santa Cruz	CA	95065	**866-466-1401**	831-462-7700	374-3
Dominican School of Philosophy & Theology 2301 Vine St	Berkeley	CA	94708	**888-450-3778**	510-849-2030	168-3
Dominican University 7900 W Div St	River Forest	IL	60305	**800-828-8475**	708-366-2490	167
Dominican University of California 50 Acacia Ave *Admissions	San Rafael	CA	94901	**888-323-6763***	415-457-4440	167
Dominion Aviation Services Inc 7511 Airfield Dr	Richmond	VA	23237	**800-366-7793**	804-271-7793	578
Dominion Bldg Products 6949 Fairbanks N Houston Rd	Houston	TX	77040	**800-826-2617**		236
Dominion East Ohio PO Box 26532 *Cust Svc	Richmond	VA	23261	**800-362-7557***		785
Dominion Electric Supply Company Inc 5053 Lee Hwy	Arlington	VA	22207	**800-525-5006**	703-536-4400	248
Dominion Hope 701 E Cary St	Richmond	VA	23219	**866-366-4357**	888-366-8280	785
Dominion Lending Centres Inc 2215 Coquitlam Ave	Port Coquitlam	BC	V3B1J6	**866-928-6810**		508
Dominion North Carolina Power 701 E Cary St	Richmond	VA	23219	**888-667-3000**	757-857-2112	785
Dominion Resources Inc 120 Tredegar St *NYSE: D*	Richmond	VA	23219	**800-552-4034**	804-819-2000	360-5
Dominion Veterinary Laboratories Inc 1199 Sanford St	Winnipeg	MB	R3E3A1	**800-465-7122**	204-589-7361	581

Name / Address	City	State	ZIP	Toll-Free	Phone	Class
Dominion Virginia Power 120 Tredegar St	Richmond	VA	23219	**800-688-4673**		785
Domino's Pizza Inc 30 Frank Lloyd Wright Dr *NYSE: DPZ*	Ann Arbor	MI	48106	**800-253-8182**	734-930-3030	668
Domtar Corp 395 de Maisonneuve W *NYSE: UFS*	Montreal	QC	H3A1L6	**877-848-4466**	514-848-5555	681
Domtech Inc 40 East Davis St	Trenton	ON	K8V6S4	**888-278-8258**	613-394-4884	491
Don CeSar Beach Resort - A Loews Hotel 3400 Gulf Blvd	Saint Pete Beach	FL	33706	**888-430-4999**	727-360-1881	667
Don Garlits Museums 13700 SW 16th Ave	Ocala	FL	34473	**877-271-3278**	352-245-8661	521
Don Hummer Trucking Corp 1486 Hwy 6 NW PO Box 310	Oxford	IA	52322	**866-248-6637**	319-828-2000	778
Don Hutson Organization 516 Tennessee St Ste 219	Memphis	TN	38103	**800-647-9166**	901-767-0000	763
Don Laughlin's Riverside Resort & Casino 1650 Casino Dr	Laughlin	NV	89029	**800-227-3849**	702-298-2535	132
Don McGill Toyota Inc 11800 Katy Fwy	Houston	TX	77079	**877-259-6888**	281-496-2000	56
Don Pepino Sales Co 123 Railroad Ave	Williamstown	NJ	08094	**888-281-6400**	856-629-7429	297-20
Don Stevens Inc 980 Discovery Rd	Eagan	MN	55121	**800-444-2299**	651-452-0872	663
Don Young Co 8181 Ambassador Row	Dallas	TX	75247	**800-367-0390**	214-630-0934	479
Dona Ana Branch Community College (DACC) 2800 N Sonoma Ranch Blvd PO Box 30001	Las Cruces	NM	88011	**800-903-7503**	575-528-7000	161
Donan Engineering Co Inc 11321 Plantside Dr	Louisville	KY	40299	**800-482-5611**		400
Donatello, The 501 Post St	San Francisco	CA	94102	**800-258-2366**	415-441-7100	379
Donati Law Firm LLP 1545 Union Ave	Memphis	TN	38104	**800-521-0578**	901-278-1004	428
Donatos Pizza 935 Taylor Stn Rd	Columbus	OH	43230	**800-366-2867**		668
Donegal Group Inc 1195 River Rd *NASDAQ: DGICA*	Marietta	PA	17547	**800-877-0600**	717-426-1931	360-4
Donegal Mutual Insurance Co 1195 River Rd PO Box 302	Marietta	PA	17547	**800-877-0600**	717-426-1931	391-4
Donelson-Hermitage Chamber of Commerce 125 Donelson Pike PO Box 140200	Nashville	TN	37214	**800-688-9889**	615-883-7896	138
Donlen Corp 2315 Sanders Rd	Northbrook	IL	60062	**800-323-1483**	847-714-1400	291
Donna Karan International Inc 550 Seventh Ave *General	New York	NY	10018	**877-316-0975***	212-789-1500	154-20
Donnelly College 608 N 18th St	Kansas City	KS	66102	**800-908-9946**	913-621-6070	161
Donning Company Publishers 184 Business Pk Dr Ste 206	Virginia Beach	VA	23462	**800-296-8572**		634-2
Donor Alliance Inc 720 S Colorado Blvd Ste 800-N	Denver	CO	80246	**888-868-4747**	303-329-4747	544
Donor Network of Arizona 201 W Coolidge St	Phoenix	AZ	85013	**800-447-9477**	602-222-2200	271
Donor Network West 12667 Alcosta Blvd Ste 600	Oakland	CA	94607	**888-570-9400**	925-480-3101	544
Donovan Marine Inc 6316 Humphreys St	Harahan	LA	70123	**800-347-4464**	504-488-5731	768
Donriver Inc 2633 McKinney Ave Ste 130-101	Dallas	TX	75204	**866-733-1684**		198
Donzi Marine 1653 WhichaRds Beach Rd	Washington	NC	27889	**800-624-3304**		89
Dooney & Bourke Inc 1 Regent St *Cust Svc	East Norwalk	CT	06855	**800-347-5000***	203-853-7515	430
Door Components Inc 7980 Redwood Ave	Fontana	CA	92336	**866-989-3667**	909-770-5700	236
Door Engineering & Mfg LLC 400 Cherry St	Kasota	MN	56050	**800-959-1352**	507-931-6910	350
Door Systems Inc PO Box 511	Framingham	MA	01704	**800-545-3667**	508-875-3508	193-3
Doormark Inc 430 Goolsby Blvd	Deerfield Beach	FL	33442	**888-969-0124**	954-418-4700	114
Doral Arrowwood Conference Resort 975 Anderson Hill Rd	Rye Brook	NY	10573	**844-211-0512**	844-214-5500	377
Doral Financial Corp 1441 F D Roosevelt Ave *NYSE: DRL*	San Juan	PR	00920	**866-296-3743**	787-749-4949	360-2
Doral Golf Resort & Spa 4400 NW 87th Ave	Miami	FL	33178	**800-713-6725**	305-592-2000	667
Dorchester County 501 Ct Ln	Cambridge	MD	21613	**800-272-9829**	410-228-1700	338
Dordt College 498 Fourth Ave NE	Sioux Center	IA	51250	**800-343-6738**	712-722-6080	167
Dorel Juvenile Group USA 2525 State St	Columbus	IN	47201	**800-544-1108**	812-372-0141	63
Dorling Kindersley Publishing 375 Hudson St *Cust Svc	New York	NY	10014	**800-631-8571***	646-674-4047	634-2
DORMA Architectural Hardware DORMA Dr Drawer AC	Reamstown	PA	17567	**800-523-8483**	717-336-3881	487
DORMA Group North America Dorma Dr	Reamstown	PA	17567	**800-523-8483**	717-336-3881	350
Dorman Products Inc 3400 E Walnut St *NASDAQ: DORM*	Colmar	PA	18915	**800-523-2492**	215-997-1800	59
Dormont Manufacturing Co 6015 Enterprise Dr	Export	PA	15632	**800-367-6668**		370
Dornbracht Americas Inc 1700 Executive Dr S Ste 600	Duluth	GA	30096	**800-774-1181**		609
Dorney Park & Wildwater Kingdom 3830 Dorney Pk Rd	Allentown	PA	18104	**800-747-0561**	610-395-3724	32
Dornier MedTech America Inc 1155 Roberts Blvd	Kennesaw	GA	30144	**800-367-6437**	770-426-1315	382
Dorris Lumber & Moulding Co, The 2601 Redding Ave	Sacramento	CA	95820	**800-827-5823**	916-452-7531	498
Dorsett & Jackson Inc 3800 Noakes St	Los Angeles	CA	90023	**800-871-8365**	323-268-1815	145
Dorsett Industries Inc 1304 May St PO Box 805	Dalton	GA	30721	**800-241-4035**	706-278-1961	130
Dorsey & Whitney LLP 50 S Sixth St Ste 1500	Minneapolis	MN	55402	**800-759-4929**	612-340-2600	428
Doskocil Mfg Company Inc PO Box 1246	Arlington	TX	76004	**877-738-6283**		577
Doss Aviation Inc 3670 Rebecca Ln	Colorado Springs	CO	80917	**888-803-4415**	719-570-9804	578
Dostal Alley Casino 1 Dostal Alley	Central City	CO	80427	**888-949-2757**	303-582-1610	132
Dot Com Holdings of Buffalo Inc 1460 Military Rd	Buffalo	NY	14217	**877-636-3673**		688
Dot Foods Inc 1 Dot Way PO Box 192	Mount Sterling	IL	62353	**800-366-3687**	217-773-4411	298-6
Dot Hill Systems Corp 1351 S Sunset St *NASDAQ: HILL*	Longmont	CO	80501	**800-872-2783**	303-845-3200	178
Dothan Area Chamber of Commerce 102 Jamestown Blvd	Dothan	AL	36301	**800-221-1027**	334-792-5138	138
Dothan Area Convention & Visitors Bureau 3311 Ross Clark Cir	Dothan	AL	36301	**888-449-0212**	334-794-6622	208
Dothan Chrysler-Dodge Inc 4074 Ross Clark Cir NW	Dothan	AL	36303	**877-674-9574**		56
Dothan Eagle PO Box 1968	Dothan	AL	36302	**800-811-1771**	334-792-3141	531-2
Dot-Line Transportation PO Box 8739	Fountain Valley	CA	92728	**800-423-3780**	323-780-9010	190-5
Dotronix Inc 160 First St SE	New Brighton	MN	55112	**800-720-7218**	651-633-1742	175-4
Dotster 8100 NE Pkwy Dr Ste 300 PO Box 821066	Vancouver	WA	98682	**800-401-5250**	360-449-5800	396
Dotster Inc PO Box 821066	Vancouver	WA	98682	**800-401-5250**	360-253-2210	396
Double Diamond Co 5495 Belt Line Rd Ste 200	Dallas	TX	75254	**800-324-7438**	214-706-9801	651
Double Eagle Hotel & Casino 442 E Bennett Ave	Cripple Creek	CO	80813	**800-711-7234**	719-689-5000	132
Double H Plastics Inc 50 W St Rd	Warminster	PA	18974	**800-523-3932**	215-674-4100	603
Doublehorn Communications 1802 W Sixth St	Austin	TX	78703	**855-618-6423**	214-283-1400	226
Doubletree Claremont 555 W Foothill Blvd	Claremont	CA	91711	**800-222-8733**	909-626-2411	379
Doubletree Hotel Downtown Wilmington Legal District 700 N King St	Wilmington	DE	19801	**800-222-8733**	302-655-0400	379
Doubletree North Shore Hotel 9599 Skokie Blvd	Skokie	IL	60077	**800-445-8667**	847-679-7000	379
Doubletree Paradise Valley Resort 5401 N Scottsdale Rd	Scottsdale	AZ	85250	**800-222-8733**	480-947-5400	667
DoubleTree Resort by Hilton Hotel Grand Key (DGKR) 3990 S Roosevelt Blvd	Key West	FL	33040	**888-844-0454**	305-293-1818	667
Doucette Industries Inc (DII) 20 Leigh Dr	York	PA	17406	**800-445-7511**	717-845-8746	14
Doug Mockett & Company Inc 1915 Abalone Ave	Torrance	CA	90501	**800-523-1269**	310-318-2491	350
Doug Varone & Dancers 37 W 32nd St	New York	NY	10001	**800-366-2100**	212-279-3344	572-1
Dougherty & Company LLC 90 S Seventh St Ste 4300	Minneapolis	MN	55402	**800-328-4000**	612-376-4000	688
Dougherty Arts Ctr, The (DAC) 1110 Barton Springs Rd	Austin	TX	78704	**855-787-2227**	512-974-4000	49-1
Douglas & London P C 59 Maiden Ln Fl 6	New York	NY	10038	**888-596-9790**		444
Douglas Baldwin & Assoc PO Box 1249	La Canada	CA	91012	**800-392-3950**	818-952-4433	400
Douglas Battery Manufacturing Co 500 Battery Dr	Winston-Salem	NC	27107	**800-368-4527**		73
Douglas Bros 423 Riverside Industrial Pkwy	Portland	ME	04103	**800-341-0926**	207-797-6771	594
Douglas Cuddle Toys Company Inc 69 Krif Rd PO Box D	Keene	NH	03431	**800-992-9002**	603-352-3414	760
Douglas Industries Co 3441 S 11th Ave	Eldridge	IA	52748	**800-553-8907**	563-285-4162	708
Douglas Laboratories Inc 600 Boyce Rd	Pittsburgh	PA	15205	**800-245-4440**		797
Douglas Press Inc 2810 Madison St	Bellwood	IL	60104	**800-323-0705**	708-547-8400	323
Douglas Stewart Co, The 2402 Advance Rd	Madison	WI	53718	**800-279-2795**	608-221-1155	533
Douglas/Quikut Co 118 E Douglas Rd	Walnut Ridge	AR	72476	**800-982-5233**		224
Douglas-Coffee County Chamber of Commerce 211 S Gaskin Ave	Douglas	GA	31533	**888-426-3334**	912-384-1873	138
Douglas-Guardian Services Corp 14800 St Mary's Ln	Houston	TX	77079	**800-255-0552**	281-531-0500	399
Douglass Colony Group Inc 5901 E 58th Ave	Commerce	CO	80022	**877-288-0650**	303-288-2635	191-12
Douglass Truck Bodies Inc 231 21st St	Bakersfield	CA	93301	**800-635-7641**	661-327-0258	515
Douthat State Park 14239 Douthat State Pk Rd *General	Millboro	VA	24460	**800-933-7275***	540-862-8100	564
Douthitt Corp 245 Adair St	Detroit	MI	48207	**800-368-8448**	313-259-1565	590
Dove Cleaners Inc 1560 Yonge St	Toronto	ON	M4T2S9	**866-999-3683**	416-413-7900	426
Dove Manufacturing Plant 1 2525 N Sixth St	Vincennes	IN	47591	**866-444-3272**	812-886-4312	202
Dover Chemical Corp 3676 Davis Rd NW *General	Dover	OH	44622	**800-321-8805***	330-343-7711	144

Alphabetical Section

Name	Address	City	State	ZIP	Toll-Free	Phone	Class
Dover Downs Hotel & Casino	1131 N DuPont Hwy *NYSE: DDE*	Dover	DE	19901	**800-711-5882**	302-674-4600	639
Dover International Speedway	1131 N DuPont Hwy PO Box 843	Dover	DE	19901	**800-441-7223**	302-883-6500	639
Dover Post	1196 S Little Creek Rd	Dover	DE	19901	**800-942-1616**	302-678-3616	531-4
Dover Saddlery Inc	525 Great Rd PO Box 1100 *NASDAQ: DOVR*	Littleton	MA	01460	**800-406-8204**	978-952-8062	708
DOVICO Software Inc	236 St George St Ste 119	Moncton	NB	E1C1W1	**800-618-8463**	506-855-4477	181
Dow AgroSciences LLC	9330 Zionsville Rd	Indianapolis	IN	46268	**800-331-6451**	317-337-3000	282
Dow Chemical Canada Inc (DCCI)	450 First St SW Ste 2100	Calgary	AB	T2P5H1	**800-447-4369**	403-267-3500	143
Dow Chemical Co	2030 Dow Ctr *NYSE: DOW* ■ *Cust Svc	Midland	MI	48674	**800-422-8193***	989-636-1463	143
Dow Chemical Company Foundation	2030 Dow Ctr	Midland	MI	48674	**800-331-6451**	989-636-1000	305
Dow Chemical Company, The	1881 W Oak Pkwy	Marietta	GA	30062	**800-331-6451**	770-428-2684	600
Dow Corning Corp	PO Box 994 *Cust Svc	Midland	MI	48686	**800-248-2481***	989-496-4000	143
Dow Cover Co Inc	373 Lexington Ave	New Haven	CT	06513	**800-735-8877**	203-469-5394	349
Dow Electronics Inc	8603 E Adamo Dr	Tampa	FL	33619	**800-627-2900**	813-626-5195	248
Dow Liquid Separations	PO Box 1206	Midland	MI	48642	**800-447-4369**	989-636-1000	804
Dow Theory Forecasts	7412 Calumet Ave	Hammond	IN	46324	**800-233-5922**		530-9
Dow-Key Microwave Corp	4822 McGrath St	Ventura	CA	93003	**800-266-3695**	805-650-0260	255
Dowling College	150 Idle Hour Blvd	Oakdale	NY	11769	**800-369-5464**	631-244-3000	167
Dowling Graphics Inc	12920 Automobile Blvd	Clearwater	FL	33762	**800-749-6933**	727-573-5997	626
Down Beat Magazine	102 N Haven Rd	Elmhurst	IL	60126	**800-554-7470**	651-251-9682	456-9
Down East	680 Commercial St	Rockport	ME	04856	**800-766-1670**	207-594-9544	456-22
Down Under Linen & Bedding Ctr	5170 Dixie Rd	Mississauga	ON	L4W1E3	**888-624-6484**	905-624-5854	361
Downeast Graphics & Printing Inc	477 Washington Jct Rd	Ellsworth	ME	04605	**800-427-5582**	207-667-5582	626
Downey Chamber of Commerce	11131 Brookshire Ave	Downey	CA	90241	**888-201-0995**	562-923-2191	138
Downey City Library (DCL)	11121 Brookshire Ave	Downey	CA	90241	**877-846-3452**	562-904-7360	434-3
Downing Displays Inc	550 Techne Ctr Dr	Milford	OH	45150	**800-883-1800**	513-248-9800	234
Downs Crane & Hoist Company Inc	8827 Juniper St	Los Angeles	CA	90002	**800-748-5994**	323-589-6061	469
Downtown Athletic Store Inc	1180 Seminole Trail Ste 210	Charlottesville	VA	22901	**800-348-2649**	434-975-3696	709
Downtown Erie Hotel	18 W 18th St	Erie	PA	16501	**800-832-9101**	814-456-2961	379
Downtown Idea Exchange (DIX)	712 Main St Ste 187B	Boonton	NJ	07005	**800-232-4317**	973-265-2300	530-2
DoxTek Inc	264 W Center St	Orem	UT	84057	**877-705-7226**		227
Doyle Security Systems Inc	792 Calkins Rd	Rochester	NY	14623	**866-463-6953**	585-244-3400	690
Doyon Drilling Inc	11500 C St Ste 200	Anchorage	AK	99515	**800-478-9675**	907-563-5530	539
Doyon Ltd	1 Doyon Pl Ste 300	Fairbanks	AK	99701	**888-478-4755**	907-459-2000	535
Dp Murphy Company Inc	945 Grand Blvd	Deer Park	NY	11729	**800-424-8724**	631-673-9400	5
DP Technology Corp	1150 Avenida Acaso	Camarillo	CA	93012	**800-627-8479**	805-388-6000	180-5
D-Patrick Motoplex Inc	200 N Green River Rd	Evansville	IN	47715	**800-831-6870**	812-473-6500	56
DPC DATA Inc	103 Eisenhower Pkwy Ste 300	Roseland	NJ	07068	**800-996-4747**	201-346-0701	176
DPE Systems Inc	425 Pontius Ave N Ste 430	Seattle	WA	98109	**800-541-6566**	206-223-3737	182
DPEC Capital Inc	135 Fifth Ave	New York	NY	10010	**844-574-3577**	301-590-6500	405
DPF Data Services Group Inc	1990 Swarthmore Ave	Lakewood	NJ	08701	**800-431-4416**	732-370-8840	227
DPL Group, The	53 Clark Rd	Rothesay	NB	E2E2K9	**800-561-8880**	506-847-2347	387
DPL Inc	1065 Woodman Dr *NYSE: DPL*	Dayton	OH	45432	**800-433-8500**	800-736-3001	360-5
DPNM (New Mexico Democratic Party)	8214 Second St NW ste A	Albuquerque	NM	87114	**800-624-2457**	505-830-3650	615-1
DPSI Inc	1801 Stanley Rd Ste 301	Greensboro	NC	27407	**800-897-7233**	336-854-7700	180-11
DPT Laboratories Ltd	318 McCullough	San Antonio	TX	78215	**866-225-5378**	210-476-8150	582
Dr Delphinium Designs & Events	5806 W Lovers Ln & Tollway	Dallas	TX	75225	**800-783-8790**	214-522-9911	294
Dr Fresh Inc	6645 Caballero Blvd	Buena Park	CA	90620	**866-373-7371**	714-690-1573	474
DR Horton Inc	301 Commerce St Ste 500 *NYSE: DHI*	Fort Worth	TX	76102	**800-846-7866**	817-390-8200	651
Dr Kern USA Inc	221 S Franklin Rd	Indianapolis	IN	46219	**800-908-9885**	317-472-0873	75
Dr Pepper/Seven-Up Inc	5301 Legacy Dr	Plano	TX	75024	**800-696-5891**	972-673-7000	79-2
DR Sperry & Co	623 Rathbone Ave	Aurora	IL	60506	**888-997-9297**	630-892-4361	455
Dr Tax Software Inc	3333 Graham Blvd Ste 222	Montreal	QC	H3R3L5	**800-663-7829**	514-733-8355	182
Dr Vinyl & Assoc Ltd	1350 SE Hamblen Rd *General	Lees Summit	MO	64081	**800-531-6600***	816-525-6060	61-1
Dr. Sinatra	95 Old Shoals Rd	Arden	NC	28704	**800-304-1708**		530-8
Draeger Medical Inc	3135 Quarry Rd	Telford	PA	18969	**800-437-2437**		252
Drago Supply Co	740 Houston Ave	Port Arthur	TX	77640	**877-609-7975**	409-983-4911	385
Dragon Claw USA Inc	16033 Arrow Hwy	Irwindale	CA	91706	**800-238-5296**	626-480-0068	278
Drake Ctr	151 W Galbraith Rd	Cincinnati	OH	45216	**800-948-0003**	513-418-2500	374-6
Drake Hotel, The	140 E Walton Pl	Chicago	IL	60611	**800-553-7253**	312-787-2200	379
Drake Petroleum Co Inc	221 Quinebaug Rd	North Grosvenordale	CT	06255	**800-243-6366**		578
Drake Software	235 E Palmer St	Franklin	NC	28734	**800-890-9500**		180-1
Drake University	2507 University Ave	Des Moines	IA	50311	**800-443-7253**	515-271-3181	167
Drake University School of Law	2507 University Ave	Des Moines	IA	50311	**800-443-7253**	515-271-2824	168-1
Drake-Scruggs Equipment Inc	2000 S Dirksen Pkwy	Springfield	IL	62703	**877-799-0398**	217-753-3871	469
Drama Book Shop Inc	250 E 40th St Frnt 2	New York	NY	10018	**800-322-0595**	212-944-0595	95
Dramatists Guild of America Inc	1501 Broadway Ste 701	New York	NY	10036	**800-289-9366**	212-398-9366	47-4
Dramm & Echter Inc	1150 Quail Gardens Dr	Encinitas	CA	92024	**800-854-7021**	760-436-0188	369
Dranetz-BMI	1000 New Durham Rd	Edison	NJ	08818	**800-372-6832**	732-287-3680	250
Draper Knitting Co	28 Draper Ln	Canton	MA	02021	**800-808-7707**	781-828-0029	742-4
Draper Shade & Screen Co	411 S Pearl St	Spiceland	IN	47385	**800-238-7999**	765-987-7999	590
Drapers & Damons	9 Pasteur Ste 200	Irvine	CA	92618	**800-843-1174**		156-6
DRAXIMAGE Inc	16751 Transcanada Hwy	Kirkland	QC	H9H4J4	**888-633-5343**	514-630-7080	240
Drayton Group	2295 N Opdyke Rd Ste D	Auburn Hills	MI	48326	**888-655-4442**		103
DRCoC (Del Rio Chamber of Commerce)	1915 Veterans Blvd *General	Del Rio	TX	78840	**877-218-5117***	830-775-3551	138
Dreamland BBQ	1427 14th Ave S	Birmingham	AL	35205	**800-752-0544**	205-933-2133	669
DreamMaker Bath & Kitchen by Worldwide	510 N Valley Mills Dr Ste 304	Waco	TX	76710	**800-583-2133**		191-11
Dreamworld Backdrops	6450 Lusk Blvd Ste E-106	San Diego	CA	92121	**800-737-9869**		720
Drees Co	211 Grandview Dr	Fort Mitchell	KY	41017	**866-265-2980**	859-578-4200	189
Dreher Island State Recreation Area	3677 State Pk Rd	Prosperity	SC	29127	**866-345-7275**	803-364-4152	564
Dremel Inc	4915 21st St	Racine	WI	53406	**800-437-3635**	262-554-1390	757
Dresser & Associates Inc	243 US Route 1	Scarborough	ME	04074	**866-885-7212**	207-885-0809	462
Dreumex USA	3445 BoaRd Rd	York	PA	17406	**800-233-9382**	717-767-6881	150
Drew Shoe Corp	252 Quarry Rd	Lancaster	OH	43130	**800-837-3739**	740-653-4271	302
Drexel University	3141 Chestnut St *Admissions	Philadelphia	PA	19104	**866-358-1010***	215-895-2000	167
Drexel University Hagerty Library	33rd St & Market St	Philadelphia	PA	19104	**888-278-8825**	215-895-2767	434-6
Dreyfus Family of Funds	PO Box 55299	Boston	MA	02205	**800-843-5466**		527
Dreyfus-Cortney & Lowery Bros Rigging	4400 N Galvez St	New Orleans	LA	70117	**800-228-7660**	504-944-3366	768
Dreyfuss Planetarium	49 Washington St	Newark	NJ	07102	**888-370-6765**	973-596-6529	597
DRHC (DiamondRock Hospitality Co)	3 Bethesda Metro Ctr Ste 1500 *NYSE: DRH*	Bethesda	MD	20814	**888-246-5941**	240-744-1150	652
DRI (Defense Research Institute)	55 W Monroe St Ste 20	Chicago	IL	60603	**866-525-6466**	312-795-1101	48-10
Dri Mark Products Inc	999 S Oyster Bay Rd Ste 312	Bethpage	NY	11714	**800-645-9118**	516-484-6200	570
Driehaus Capital Management Inc	25 E Erie St	Chicago	IL	60611	**800-688-8819**	312-587-3800	401
Driftwood Beach State Recreation Site	5580 S Coast Hwy	Newport	OR	97366	**800-551-6949**		564
Driftwood Hotel	435 Willoughby Ave	Juneau	AK	99801	**800-544-2239**	907-586-2280	379
Driftwood Shores Resort	88416 First Ave	Florence	OR	97439	**800-422-5091**	541-997-8263	379
Drillers Service Inc	1792 Highland Ave NE	Hickory	NC	28601	**800-334-2308**	828-322-1100	536
Dril-Quip Inc	13550 Hempstead Hwy *NYSE: DRQ*	Houston	TX	77040	**877-316-2631**	713-939-7711	536
Drink More Water Store	7595-A Rickenbacker Dr	Gaithersburg	MD	20879	**800-697-2070**		14
DRIP Investor	7412 Calumet Ave	Hammond	IN	46324	**800-233-5922**	219-852-3200	530-9
Dripping Springs State Park	16830 Dripping Springs Rd	Okmulgee	OK	74447	**800-622-6317**	918-756-5971	564
Driscoll Children's Hospital	3533 S Alameda St	Corpus Christi	TX	78411	**800-324-5683**	361-694-5000	374-1
Driscoll Strawberry Assoc Inc	345 Westridge Dr	Watsonville	CA	95077	**800-871-3333**		316-1

Name / Address	City	State	Zip	Toll-Free	Phone	Class
Driskill Hotel 604 Brazos St	Austin	TX	78701	**800-252-9367**	512-474-5911	379
DRISTEEM Corp 14949 Technology Dr	Eden Prairie	MN	55344	**800-328-4447**	952-949-2415	14
Drive Thru Technology Inc 1755 N Main St	Los Angeles	CA	90031	**800-933-8388**	323-576-1400	175-1
Drive Train Industries Inc 5555 Joliet St	Denver	CO	80239	**800-525-6177**	303-292-5176	60
Drivekore Inc 101 Wesley Dr	Mechanicsburg	PA	17055	**800-382-1311**	717-697-7440	350
Driveline Holdings Inc 700 Freeport Pkwy Ste 100	Coppell	TX	75019	**888-123-4567**		197
DriverDO LLC 734 Massachusetts St	Lawrence	KS	66044	**844-366-6837**		226
Drivers License Guide Co 1492 Oddstad Dr	Redwood City	CA	94063	**800-227-8827**	650-369-4849	634-10
DriveTime Corp 4020 E Indian School Rd	Phoenix	AZ	85018	**888-418-1212**		56
Driving Records Facilities PO Box 1086	Glen Burnie	MD	21061	**800-772-5510**		632
DrivingSales LLC 8871 S Sandy Pkwy Ste 250	Sandy	UT	84070	**866-943-8371**		387
DRMP (Dyer Riddle Mills & Precourt Inc) 941 Lk Baldwin Ln	Orlando	FL	32814	**800-375-3767**	407-896-0594	263
Dropbox Inc 401 S 9th St	Ironton	OH	45638	**888-388-7768**		479
Drowsy Water Ranch PO Box 147	Granby	CO	80446	**800-845-2292**	970-725-3456	241
DRS C3 Systems LLC 400 Professional Dr	Gaithersburg	MD	20879	**800-694-5005**	301-921-8100	528
DRS Sustainment Systems Inc 7375 Industrial Rd	Florence	KY	41042	**800-694-5005**	859-372-8204	14
DRS Technologies Inc 5 Sylvan Way	Parsippany	NJ	07054	**800-694-5005**	973-898-1500	528
DRS Training & Control Systems 645 Anchors St NW	Fort Walton Beach	FL	32548	**800-694-5005**	850-302-3000	528
Drug Chemical & Associated Technologies Assn (DCAT) 1 Washington Blvd Ste 7	Robbinsville	NJ	08691	**800-640-3228**	609-448-1000	48-19
Drug Package Inc 901 Drug Package Ln	O'Fallon	MO	63366	**800-325-6137**		626
Drug Topics Magazine 24950 Country Club Blvd Ste 200 *Cust Svc	North Olmsted	OH	44070	**877-922-2022***	440-891-2792	456-5
DrugScan Inc 200 Precision Rd Ste 200 PO Box 347	Horsham	PA	19044	**800-235-4890**		416
Drugstore.com Inc 411 108th Ave NE Ste 1400	Bellevue	WA	98004	**800-378-4786**		239
Drum Corps International (DCI) PO Box 3129 *Orders	Indianapolis	IN	46206	**800-495-7469***	317-275-1212	47-4
Drummer & Wright Cnty Journal 108 Central Ave	Buffalo	MN	55313	**800-880-5047**	763-682-1221	531-3
Drury Hotels Company LLC 721 Emerson Rd Ste 400	Saint Louis	MO	63141	**800-378-7946**	314-429-2255	379
Drury University 900 N Benton Ave	Springfield	MO	65802	**800-922-2274**	417-873-7879	167
Druva Software Inc 150 Mathilda Place, STE 450	Sunnyvale	CA	94086	**888-248-4976**		387
Drycleaning & Laundry Institute 14700 Sweitzer Ln	Laurel	MD	20707	**800-638-2627**	301-622-1900	48-4
Drysdales Inc 3220 S Memorial Dr	Tulsa	OK	74145	**800-444-6481**	918-664-6481	329
Dryvit Systems Inc 1 Energy Way	West Warwick	RI	02893	**800-556-7752**	401-822-4100	389
DS Brown Co 300 E Cherry St	North Baltimore	OH	45872	**800-848-1730**	419-257-3561	193-2
D-S Pipe & Supply Company Inc 1301 Wicomico St Ste 3	Baltimore	MD	21230	**800-368-8880**	410-539-8000	611
DS Waters of America Inc 5660 New Northside Dr Ste 500 *Cust Svc	Atlanta	GA	30328	**800-201-6218***		803
DS/USA (Disabled Sports USA) 451 Hungerford Dr Ste 100	Rockville	MD	20850	**800-543-2754**	301-217-0960	47-22
DSA (Data Systems Analysts Inc) Eigth Neshaminy Interplex Ste 209	Trevose	PA	19053	**877-422-4372**	215-245-4800	182
DSC (Digital Security Controls) 3301 Langstaff Rd	Concord	ON	L4K4L2	**888-888-7838**	905-760-3000	690
DSC Logistics 1750 S Wolf Rd	Des Plaines	IL	60018	**800-372-1960**		448
DSG (Dakota Supply Group) 2601 Third Ave N	Fargo	ND	58102	**800-437-4702**	701-237-9440	248
DSG Tag Systems Inc 5455 152nd St Ste 214	Surrey	BC	V3S5A5	**877-589-8806**		387
DSLextreme.com 21540 Plummer St Ste A	Chatsworth	CA	91311	**866-243-8638**		398
DSM Chemicals North America Inc 1 Columbia Nitrogen Rd	Augusta	GA	30901	**800-526-0189**	706-849-6600	143
DSM Desotech Inc 1122 St Charles St	Elgin	IL	60120	**800-222-7189**	847-697-0400	144
DSM Engineering Plastics Inc 2267 W Mill Rd	Evansville	IN	47720	**800-333-4237**	812-435-7500	604-2
DSM Food Specialties Inc 45 Waterview Blvd	Parsippany	NJ	07054	**800-526-0189**	973-257-1063	297-42
DSN Group Inc 152 Lorraine Dr	Lake Zurich	IL	60047	**888-445-2919**		524
DS&O Electric Cooperative Inc 129 W Main St PO Box 286	Solomon	KS	67480	**800-376-3533**	785-655-2011	247
DSSC (Data Storage Systems Ctr) *Carnegie Mellon University ECE Dept* 5000 Forbes Ave	Pittsburgh	PA	15213	**800-864-8287**	412-268-6600	666
DST Controls 651 Stone Rd	Benicia	CA	94510	**800-251-0773**	707-745-5117	205
DST Output 5220 Robert J Mathews Pkwy	El Dorado Hills	CA	95762	**800-441-7587**	916-939-4960	495
DSX Access Systems Inc 10731 Rockwall Rd	Dallas	TX	75238	**888-419-8353**	214-553-6140	691
D-Ta Systems Inc 2500 Lancaster Rd	Ottawa	ON	K1B4S5	**877-382-3222**	613-745-8713	179
DTE Energy Co 1 Energy Plz *NYSE: DTE*	Detroit	MI	48226	**800-477-4747**	313-235-4000	360-5
DTI (Dental Technologies Inc) 5601 Arnold Rd	Dublin	CA	94568	**800-229-0936**	925-829-3611	415
DTIC (Defense Technical Information Ctr) 8725 John J Kingman Rd Ste 0944	Fort Belvoir	VA	22060	**800-225-3842**	703-767-9100	340-3
DTM Systems Inc 2323 Boundary Rd Unit 130	Vancouver	BC	V5M4V8	**888-655-3282**	604-257-6700	181
Dtreds LLC 1329 Shepard Dr Ste 2	Sterling	VA	20164	**877-694-7766**		226
Dts Cos Inc 1640 Monad Rd	Billings	MT	59101	**800-755-5855**	406-245-4695	778
Du Page Airport Authority 2700 International Dr Ste 200	West Chicago	IL	60185	**800-208-5690**	630-584-2211	27
Dualite Sales & Service Inc 1 Dualite Ln	Williamsburg	OH	45176	**800-543-7271**	513-724-7100	699
Dual-Lite Inc 701 Millennium Blvd	Greenville	SC	29607	**866-898-0131**	864-678-1000	439
Duane's 3649 Mission Inn Ave	Riverside	CA	92501	**800-843-7755**	951-784-0300	669
Duarte Unified School District 1620 Huntington Dr	Duarte	CA	91010	**888-225-7377**	626-599-5000	683
Dublin Convention & Visitors Bureau 9 S High St	Dublin	OH	43017	**800-245-8387**	614-792-7666	208
Dublin Villager 7801 N Central Dr	Lewis Center	OH	43035	**866-790-4502**	740-888-6100	531-4
Dublin-Laurens County Chamber of Commerce 1200 Bellvue	Dublin	GA	31021	**800-829-4933**	478-272-5546	138
DuBois Business College 1 Beaver Dr	Du Bois	PA	15801	**800-692-6213**	814-371-6920	798
Dubois Chemicals 3630 E Kemper Rd	Cincinnati	OH	45241	**800-438-2647**		150
Dubose National Energy Services Inc PO Box 499	Clinton	NC	28329	**800-590-2150**	910-590-2151	491
Dubuque Area Chamber of Commerce 300 Main St Ste 200	Dubuque	IA	52001	**800-798-4748**	563-557-9200	138
Dubuque Symphony Orchestra 2728 Asbury Rd Ste 900	Dubuque	IA	52001	**866-803-9280**	563-557-1677	572-3
Duca Financial Services Credit Union Ltd 5290 Yonge St	Toronto	ON	M2N5P9	**866-900-3822**	416-223-8502	221
Duckback Products 2644 Hegan Ln PO Box 980	Chico	CA	95927	**800-825-5382**		549
Ducks Unlimited Magazine 1 Waterfowl Way	Memphis	TN	38120	**800-453-8257**	901-758-3825	456-20
Ducommun Inc 23301 Wilmington Ave *NYSE: DCO*	Carson	CA	90745	**800-522-6645**	310-513-7280	205
Duct-O-Wire Co 345 Adams Cir	Corona	CA	92882	**800-752-6001**	951-735-8220	205
Dude Ranchers' Assn 1122 12th St PO Box 2307	Cody	WY	82414	**866-399-2339**	307-587-2339	47-23
Dudnyk 5 Walnut Grove Dr Ste 280	Horsham	PA	19044	**800-767-3263**	215-443-9406	4
Due North Consulting Inc 105 Owens Pkwy Ste C	Birmingham	AL	35244	**800-899-2676**	205-989-9394	198
Dueck Auto Group 12100 Featherstone Way	Richmond	BC	V6W1K9	**877-993-8325**	604-273-1311	56
Dueco N4 W22610 Bluemound Rd	Waukesha	WI	53186	**800-558-4004**	262-547-8500	385
Duff & Phelps Investment Management Co 200 S Wacker Dr Ste 500	Chicago	IL	60606	**800-338-8214**	312-263-2610	401
Duffield Assoc Inc 5400 Limestone Rd	Wilmington	DE	19808	**877-732-9633**	302-239-6634	188
Duininck Inc 408 Sixth St PO Box 208 *General	Prinsburg	MN	56281	**800-328-8949***		190-4
Duke Diet & Fitness Ctr (DFC) 501 Douglas St	Durham	NC	27705	**800-235-3853**		704
Duke Energy Corp 550 S Tryon St Mail Drop WP 890	Charlotte	NC	28202	**800-521-2232**	713-627-5400	785
Duke Manufacturing Co 2305 N Broadway	Saint Louis	MO	63102	**800-735-3853**	314-231-1130	299
Duke Towers- All Condominium Hotel 807 W Trinity Ave	Durham	NC	27701	**866-385-3869**	919-687-4444	379
Duke University Divinity School 407 Chapel Drive PO Box 90968	Durham	NC	27708	**800-367-3853**	919-660-3400	168-3
Duke University Press 905 W Main St Ste 18-B *Cust Svc	Durham	NC	27701	**888-651-0122***	919-687-3600	634-4
Duke University School of Law 201 Science Dr PO Box 90362	Durham	NC	27708	**888-529-2586**	919-613-7006	168-1
Duke University School of Medicine Office of Admissions DUMC 3710	Durham	NC	27710	**888-275-3853**	919-684-2985	168-2
Duke's 8th Avenue Hotel 630 W Eigth Ave	Anchorage	AK	99501	**800-478-4837**	907-274-6213	379
Dulles Aviation Inc 10501 Observation Rd Manassas Regl Airport	Manassas	VA	20110	**888-835-9324**	703-361-2171	62
Dultmeier Sales LLC 13808 Industrial Rd	Omaha	NE	68137	**888-677-5054**	402-333-1444	429
Duluth Area Chamber of Commerce 5 W First St Ste 101	Duluth	MN	55802	**800-385-8842**	218-722-5501	138
Duluth Business University (DBU) 4724 Mike Colalilo Dr	Duluth	MN	55807	**800-777-8406**	218-722-4000	798
Duluth Convention & Visitors Bureau 21 W Superior St Ste 100	Duluth	MN	55802	**800-438-5884**	218-722-4011	208
Duluth Entertainment Convention Ctr 350 Harbor Dr	Duluth	MN	55802	**800-628-8385**	218-722-5573	207
Duluth International Airport 4701 Grinden Dr	Duluth	MN	55811	**855-787-2227**	218-727-2968	27

Name / Address	City	State	Zip	Toll-Free	Phone	Class
Duluth News-Tribune 424 W First St *Circ	Duluth	MN	55802	**800-456-8080***	218-723-5281	531-2
Duluth Pack 365 Canal Park Dr	Duluth	MN	55802	**800-777-4439**	218-722-1707	709
Dumbell Man Fitness Equipment, The 655 Hawaii Ave	Torrance	CA	90503	**800-432-6266**	310-381-2900	354
DuMor Inc PO Box 142	Mifflintown	PA	17059	**800-598-4018**	717-436-2106	320-4
Dumore Corp 1030 Veterans St	Mauston	WI	53948	**888-467-8288**	608-847-6420	517
Dunbar Mechanical Inc 2806 N Reynolds Rd	Toledo	OH	43615	**800-719-2201**	419-537-1900	191-10
Dunbarton Corp PO Box 8577	Dothan	AL	36304	**800-633-7553**		236
Duncan & Son Lines Inc 23860 W US Hwy 85	Buckeye	AZ	85326	**800-528-4283**	623-386-4511	778
Duncan Aviation Inc 3701 Aviation Rd	Lincoln	NE	68524	**800-228-4277**	402-475-2611	24
Duncan Disposal Co *Arlington* 1212 Harrison Ave	Arlington	TX	76011	**800-766-1758**	817-317-2000	802
Duncan Enterprises 5673 E Shields Ave	Fresno	CA	93727	**800-438-6226**	559-291-4444	42
Duncan Hill Travel Ltd 2700 Beverly St	Duncan	BC	V9L5C7	**888-748-0391**	250-748-0391	773
Duncan Industrial Solutions 3450 S MacArthur Blvd	Oklahoma City	OK	73179	**800-375-9470**	405-688-2300	385
Duncan Solutions Inc 633 W Wisconsin Ave Ste 1600	Milwaukee	WI	53203	**888-993-8622**		494
Duncan Supply Company Inc 910 N Illinois St	Indianapolis	IN	46204	**800-382-5528**	317-634-1335	611
Duncan Valley Electric Co-op Inc PO Box 440	Duncan	AZ	85534	**800-669-2503**	928-359-2503	247
Duncan-Parnell Inc 900 S McDowell St	Charlotte	NC	28204	**800-849-7708**	704-372-7766	112
Dundee Internet Service Inc 168 Riley St	Dundee	MI	48131	**888-222-8485**	734-529-5331	227
Dunes Manor Hotel 2800 Baltimore Ave	Ocean City	MD	21842	**800-523-2888**	410-289-1100	379
Dungan Engineering pa 1574 Hwy 98 E	Columbia	MS	39429	**800-368-2573**	601-731-2600	258
Dunhill Hotel 237 N Tryon St	Charlotte	NC	28202	**800-354-4141**	704-332-4141	379
Dunkin' Donuts 130 Royall St *Cust Svc	Canton	MA	02021	**800-859-5339***	781-737-3000	67
Dunkin's Diamonds Inc 897 Hebron Rd	Heath	OH	43056	**877-343-4883**		410
Dunkley International Inc 1910 Lake St	Kalamazoo	MI	49001	**800-666-1264**	269-343-5583	299
Dunlap Industries Inc 297 Industrial Park Rd	Dunlap	TN	37327	**800-251-7214**		593
Dunlap Oil Company Inc 759 S Haskell Ave	Willcox	AZ	85643	**800-854-1646**	520-384-2248	325
Dunlop Tires 3045 Sheridan Dr	Amherst	NY	14226	**800-845-8378**	800-522-7458	752
Dunmore Corp 145 Wharton Rd	Bristol	PA	19007	**800-444-0242**	215-781-8895	599
Dunn Energy Co-op PO Box 220	Menomonie	WI	54751	**800-924-0630**	715-232-6240	247
Dunn Manufacturing Inc 1400 Goldmine Rd	Monroe	NC	28110	**800-868-7111**	704-283-2147	9
Dunn School 2555 Hwy 154 PO Box 98	Los Olivos	CA	93441	**800-287-9197**	805-688-6471	621
Dunn-Edwards Corp 4885 E 52nd Pl	Los Angeles	CA	90058	**800-537-4098**	323-771-3330	549
Dunwoody College of Technology 818 Dunwoody Blvd	Minneapolis	MN	55403	**800-292-4625**	612-374-5800	798
Duo Fast Northeast 22 Tolland St	East Hartford	CT	06108	**888-399-5712**	860-289-6861	350
Duo-Fast Corp 2400 Galvin Dr *Cust Svc	Elgin	IL	60123	**888-386-3278***	847-783-5500	756
Duo-Safety Ladder Corp 513 W Ninth Ave	Oshkosh	WI	54902	**877-386-5377**	920-231-2740	421
Dupaco Community Credit Union 3999 Pennsylvania Ave	Dubuque	IA	52002	**800-373-7600**	563-557-7600	221
DuPage Convention & Visitors Bureau 915 Harger Rd Ste 240	Oak Brook	IL	60523	**800-232-0502**	630-575-8070	208
Dupli Graphics Corp 6761 Thompson Rd N	Syracuse	NY	13211	**800-724-2477**		626
Dupli-Systems Inc 8260 Dow Cir	Strongsville	OH	44136	**800-321-1610**	440-234-9415	109
DuPont Advanced Fibers Systems 5401 Jefferson Davis Hwy	Richmond	VA	23234	**800-441-7515**	804-383-3845	604-1
DuPont Automotive 950 Stephenson Hwy PO Box 7013	Troy	MI	48007	**800-533-1313**	248-583-8000	549
DuPont Chemical Solutions 1007 Market St	Wilmington	DE	19898	**800-441-7515**	302-774-1000	144
DuPont Crop Protection PO Box 80705	Wilmington	DE	19880	**888-638-7668**	302-774-1000	282
DuPont Engineering Polymers Lancaster Pike Rt 141 Barley Mill Plz Bldg 22	Wilmington	DE	19805	**800-441-7515**	302-999-4592	604-2
DuPont Packaging & Industrial Polymers Barley Mill Plaza 26-2122 PO Box 80026	Wilmington	DE	19880	**800-438-7225**	703-305-7666	547
DuPont Performance Coatings 1007 Market St	Wilmington	DE	19898	**800-441-7515**	302-774-1000	549
DuPont Qualicon Henry Clay Rd Bldg 400 Rt 141 PO Box 80400	Wilmington	DE	19880	**800-863-6842**	302-695-5300	233
DuPont Surfaces 4417 Lancaster Pk CRP 728/3105	Wilmington	DE	19805	**800-448-9835**	302-774-1000	598
DuPont Theatre 1007 N Market St	Wilmington	DE	19801	**800-338-0881**	302-656-4401	571
DuPont Titanium Technologies 1007 Market St	Wilmington	DE	19898	**800-441-7515**	302-774-1000	142
Duquesne Light Holdings Inc 411 Seventh Ave	Pittsburgh	PA	15219	**888-393-7000**	412-393-7000	360-5
Duquesne University 600 Forbes Ave	Pittsburgh	PA	15282	**800-456-0590**	412-396-6000	167
DuQuoin Tourism Commission 20 N Chestnut St PO Box 1037	Du Quoin	IL	62832	**800-455-9570**	618-542-8338	208
Dura Wax Co 4101 W Albany St	McHenry	IL	60050	**800-435-5705**	815-385-5000	150
Durable Products Inc PO Box 826	Crossville	TN	38557	**800-373-3502**	931-484-3502	674
Duracell 14 Research Dr	Bethel	CT	06801	**800-551-2355**	800-544-5454	73
Duraclean International Inc 220 W Campus Dr	Arlington Heights	IL	60004	**800-862-5326**	847-704-7100	151
DuraColor 1840 Oakdale Ave	Racine	WI	53406	**877-899-7900**		626
Duracote Corp 350 N Diamond St	Ravenna	OH	44266	**800-321-2252**	330-296-3487	742-2
Duralee Fabrics Ltd Inc 1775 Fifth Ave *Cust Svc	Bay Shore	NY	11706	**800-275-3872***	631-273-8800	593
DuraLine Imaging Inc 110 Commercial Blvd	Flat Rock	NC	28731	**800-982-3872**	828-692-1301	627
Duran Human Capital Partners Inc 300 Orchard City Dr Ste 142	Campbell	CA	95008	**800-287-9682**	408-540-0070	719
Durand Forms Inc 6200 Equitable Rd	Kansas City	MO	64120	**800-545-6342**		695
Durango Area Tourism Office 111 S Camino del Rio	Durango	CO	81301	**800-525-8855**	970-247-3500	208
Durango Arts Ctr 802 E Second Ave	Durango	CO	81301	**800-838-3006**	970-259-2606	49-1
Durango Herald 1275 Main Ave	Durango	CO	81301	**800-530-8318**	970-247-3504	531-2
Durant Bancorp / First United Bank 1400 W Main	Durant	OK	74701	**800-924-4427**	580-924-2211	69
Dura-Stress Inc 11325 County Rd 44 *General	Leesburg	FL	34788	**800-342-9239***	352-787-1422	185
DuraTech Industries International Inc PO Box 1940	Jamestown	ND	58401	**800-243-4601**	701-252-4601	275
Duravit USA Inc 2205 Northmont Pkwy Ste 200	Duluth	GA	30096	**888-387-2848**	770-931-3575	611
Durham Academy Inc 3130 Pickett Rd	Durham	NC	27705	**888-904-9149**	919-489-9118	683
Durham Convention & Visitors Bureau 101 E Morgan St	Durham	NC	27701	**800-446-8604**	919-687-0288	208
Durham Cos Inc 6300 Transit Rd	Depew	NY	14043	**800-633-7724**	716-684-3333	719
Durham Manufacturing Co 201 Main St	Durham	CT	06422	**800-243-3774**	860-349-3427	288
Durkan Patterned Carpet Inc 405 Virgil Dr	Dalton	GA	30721	**800-981-2009**		130
Duro Dyne Corp 81 Spence St	Bay Shore	NY	11706	**800-899-3876**	631-249-9000	14
Durocher Auto Sales Inc 4651 Rt 9	Plattsburgh	NY	12901	**877-215-8954**	888-635-4599	56
Durr Marketing Assoc Inc PO Box 17600	Pittsburgh	PA	15235	**800-937-3877**		145
Durrset Amigos Ltd 4669 Hwy 90 W	San Antonio	TX	78237	**800-580-3477**	210-798-5360	297-36
Dury's 701 Ewing Ave	Nashville	TN	37203	**800-824-2379**	615-255-3456	118
DUSA Pharmaceuticals Inc 25 Upton Dr *NASDAQ: DUSA*	Wilmington	MA	01887	**877-533-3872**	978-657-7500	84
Dutailier Group Inc 299 Rue Chaput	Sainte-Pie	QC	J0H1W0	**800-363-9817**	450-772-2403	320-2
Dutch Gold Honey Inc 2220 Dutch Gold Dr	Lancaster	PA	17601	**800-846-2753**	717-393-1716	297-24
Dutch Valley Bulk Food Distributors Inc 7615 Lancaster Ave	Myerstown	PA	17067	**800-733-4191**	717-933-4191	298-8
Dutch Wonderland Family Amusement Park 2249 Lincoln Hwy E	Lancaster	PA	17602	**866-386-2839**	717-291-1888	32
Dutchess County Regional Chamber of Commerce 1 Civic Ctr Plaza Ste 400	Poughkeepsie	NY	12601	**800-817-2918**	845-454-1700	138
Dutchmen Mfg Inc 2164 Caragana Ct PO Box 2164	Goshen	IN	46527	**866-425-4369**	574-537-0600	119
Dutt & Wagner of Virginia Inc 1142 W Main St	Abingdon	VA	24210	**800-688-2116**	276-628-2116	298-10
Duvinage Corp 60 W Oak Ridge Dr	Hagerstown	MD	21740	**800-541-2645**	301-733-8255	490
DuVoice Corp 608 State St S Ste 100	Kirkland	WA	98033	**800-888-1057**	425-889-9790	227
DVD Empire 2140 Woodland Rd	Warrendale	PA	15086	**888-383-1880**		795
DVWF (Delaware Valley Wholesale Florist Inc) 520 Mantua Blvd N	Sewell	NJ	08080	**800-676-1212**	856-468-7000	295
DW Green Co 8100 S Priest Dr	Tempe	AZ	85284	**800-253-7146**	480-491-8483	4
Dwfritz Automation Inc 12100 SW Tualatin Rd	Wilsonville	OR	97070	**800-763-4161**	503-598-9393	538
Dwight D Eisenhower Presidential Library & Museum 200 SE Fourth St	Abilene	KS	67410	**877-746-4453**	785-263-6700	434-2
Dwight D Eisenhower V A Medical Ctr 4101 South 4th St	Leavenworth	KS	66048	**800-952-8387**	913-682-2000	374-8
Dwyer Products Corp 1226 Michael Dr Ste F	Wood Dale	IL	60191	**800-822-0092**	630-741-7900	35
DXP Enterprises Inc 7272 Pinemont Dr *NASDAQ: DXPE*	Houston	TX	77040	**800-830-3973**	713-996-4700	385
DXStorm.com Inc 824 Winston Churchill Blvd	Oakville	ON	L6J7X2	**877-397-8676**	905-842-8262	226
D&Y (Daniel & Yeager) 6767 Old Madison Pk Ste 690	Huntsville	AL	35806	**800-955-1919**		268
Dyad Constructors Inc 8505 Holt St	Houston	TX	77054	**800-803-9202**	713-799-9380	188

Company	Address	City	State	Zip	Toll-Free	Phone	Class
Dyatech LLC	805 S Wheatley St Ste 600	Ridgeland	MS	39157	**866-651-4222**	601-914-1004	390
Dycor Technologies Ltd	1851 94 St	Edmonton	AB	T6N1E6	**800-663-9267**	780-486-0091	666
Dyer Riddle Mills & Precourt Inc (DRMP)	941 Lk Baldwin Ln	Orlando	FL	32814	**800-375-3767**	407-896-0594	263
Dymax Corp	318 Industrial Ln	Torrington	CT	06790	**877-396-2963**	860-482-1010	3
Dynabrade Inc	8989 Sheridan Dr *Cust Svc	Clarence	NY	14031	**800-828-7333***	716-631-0100	757
Dynadot LLC	PO Box 345 *Cust Svc	San Mateo	CA	94401	**866-652-2039***	650-585-1961	396
Dynalectric Corp	4462 Corporate Ctr Dr	Los Alamitos	CA	90720	**866-890-7794**	714-828-7000	191-4
DynaLifeDX Diagnostic Laboratory Services	10150 - 102 St Ste 200	Edmonton	AB	T5J5E2	**800-661-9876**	780-451-3702	415
Dynaloy LLC	6445 Olivia Ln	Indianapolis	IN	46226	**800-669-5709**	317-788-5694	144
Dynamation Research Inc	2301 Pontius Ave	Los Angeles	CA	90064	**800-726-7997**	310-477-1224	350
Dynamet Inc	195 Museum Rd	Washington	PA	15301	**800-237-9655**	724-228-1000	484
DynaMetric Inc	717 S Myrtle Ave	Monrovia	CA	91016	**800-525-6925**	626-358-2559	732
Dynamex Inc	5429 LBJ Fwy Ste 1000 *Cust Svc	Dallas	TX	75240	**888-478-1660***	214-560-9000	545
Dynamic Computer Corp	23400 Industrial Pk Ct	Farmington Hills	MI	48335	**866-257-2111**	248-473-2200	176
Dynamic Design Solutions Inc	3565 Centre Cir	Fort Mill	SC	29715	**866-337-2010**	803-548-3609	258
Dynamic Homes LLC	525 Roosevelt Ave	Detroit Lakes	MN	56501	**800-492-4833**	218-847-2611	105
Dynamic Instruments Inc	3860 Calle Fortunada	San Diego	CA	92123	**800-793-3358**	858-278-4900	51
Dynamic Network Factory Inc	21353 Cabot Blvd	Hayward	CA	94545	**800-947-4742**	510-265-1122	175-8
Dynamicard	332 S Juniper St Ste 101	Escondido	CA	92025	**800-928-7670**		5
Dynamics Edge Inc	2635 N First St Ste #148	San Jose	CA	95134	**800-453-5961**		198
Dynapar	1675 Delany Rd *General	Gurnee	IL	60031	**800-873-8731***		799
Dynaquip Controls	10 Harris Industrial Pk	Saint Clair	MO	63077	**800-545-3636**	636-629-3700	788
Dynarex Corporation	10 Glenshaw St	Orangeburg	NY	10962	**888-335-7500**	845-365-8200	476
Dynaric Inc	5740 Bayside Rd	Virginia Beach	VA	23455	**800-526-0827**		546
Dynasplint Systems Inc	770 Ritchie Hwy Ste W21	Severna Park	MD	21146	**800-638-6771**	410-544-9530	266-4
Dynasty Suites	1235 W Colton Ave *General	Redlands	CA	92374	**800-874-8958***	909-793-6648	379
Dynatem Inc	23263 Madero Ste C	Mission Viejo	CA	92691	**800-543-3830**	949-855-3235	624
Dynatronics Corp	7030 Pk Centre Dr *NASDAQ: DYNT*	Salt Lake City	UT	84121	**800-874-6251**	801-568-7000	252
Dynavax Technologies Corp	2929 Seventh St Ste 100 *NASDAQ: DVAX*	Berkeley	CA	94710	**877-848-5100**	510-848-5100	582
Dynegy Inc	601 Travis St Ste 1400 *NYSE: DYN*	Houston	TX	77002	**800-633-4704**	713-507-6400	360-5
Dynetics Engineering Corp	515 Bond St	Lincolnshire	IL	60069	**800-888-8110**	847-541-7300	110
Dynisco LLC	38 Forge Pkwy *General	Franklin	MA	02038	**800-396-4726***	508-541-9400	471
Dyno Nobel Inc	2795 E Cottonwood Pkwy Ste 500	Salt Lake City	UT	84121	**800-473-2675**	801-364-4800	270
Dyonyx LP	1235 N Loop W *General	Houston	TX	77008	**855-749-6758***	713-485-7000	182
Dystonia Medical Research Foundation	1 E Wacker Dr Ste 2810 *General	Chicago	IL	60601	**800-377-3978***	312-755-0198	47-17
Dywidag Systems International	320 Marmon Dr	Bolingbrook	IL	60440	**800-457-7633**	630-739-1100	191-3

E

Company	Address	City	State	Zip	Toll-Free	Phone	Class
E & M Bindery Inc	11 Peekay Dr	Clifton	NJ	07014	**800-736-2463**	973-777-9300	625
E C S	2741 S 21st Ave	Broadview	IL	60155	**800-621-0759**	708-338-9700	258
E Dillon & Co	2522 Swords Creek Rd PO Box 160	Swords Creek	VA	24649	**800-234-8970**	276-873-6816	185
E Fougera & Co	60 Baylis Rd	Melville	NY	11747	**800-645-9833**	631-454-6996	583
E Gluck Corp	60-15 Little Neck Pkwy	Little Neck	NY	11362	**800-840-2933**	718-784-0700	152
E H Lynn Industries Inc	524 Anderson Dr	Romeoville	IL	60446	**800-633-2948**	815-328-8800	788
E Hofmann Plastics	51 Centennial Rd	Orangeville	ON	L9W3R1	**855-452-4014**		602
E J Harrison & Sons	PO Box 4009	Ventura	CA	93007	**800-418-7274**	805-647-1414	802
E Pi Bio Analytical	9095 W Harristown Blvd	Niantic	IL	62551	**866-963-2143**	217-963-2143	740
E S Robbins Corp	2802 Avalon Ave	Muscle Shoals	AL	35661	**866-934-6018**	256-248-2400	599
E Sam Jones Distributor Inc	4898 S Atlanta Rd	Smyrna	GA	30080	**800-624-9849**	404-351-3250	248
E Tour & Travel	3626 Quadrangle Blvd Ste 400 *Sales	Orlando	FL	32817	**800-339-5120***	407-515-2400	769
E Z Grout Corp	405 Watertown Rd	Waterford	OH	45786	**888-344-7688**	740-749-3512	134
E*Trade Bank	671 N Glebe Rd	Arlington	VA	22203	**800-387-2331**	877-800-1208	69
E*Trade Financial Corp	1271 Ave of the Americas 14th Fl *NASDAQ: ETFC*	New York	NY	10020	**800-387-2331**		688
E*Trade Financial Corp Corporate Services	4500 Bohannon Dr	Menlo Park	CA	94025	**800-786-2575**	650-331-6000	180-1
E.S. Fox Ltd	9127 Montrose Rd	Niagara Falls	ON	L2E7J9	**866-233-8933**	905-354-3700	263
E/The Environmental Magazine	28 Knight St PO Box 5098	Norwalk	CT	06851	**800-321-6742**	203-854-5559	456-19
E2 Consulting Engineers Inc	450 E 17th Ave Ste 200	Denver	CO	80203	**888-835-9400**	303-232-9800	263
EAA (Experimental Aircraft Assn)	3000 Poberezny Rd	Oshkosh	WI	54902	**800-236-4800**	920-426-4800	47-18
EAA AirVenture Museum	3000 Poberezny Rd	Oshkosh	WI	54902	**888-322-3229**	920-426-4800	519
eAcceleration Corp	1050 NE Hostmark St Ste 100-B *Sales	Poulsbo	WA	98370	**800-803-4588***	360-779-6301	180-7
EADS Group	1126 Eigth Ave	Altoona	PA	16602	**800-626-0904**	814-944-5035	263
EADS North American Defense Test & Services Inc	4 Goodyear *Cust Svc	Irvine	CA	92618	**800-722-2528***	949-859-8999	250
Eagan Convention & Visitors Bureau	1501 Central Pkwy	Eagan	MN	55121	**866-324-2620**	651-675-5546	208
Eagan Insurance Agency Inc	2629 N Cswy Blvd	Metairie	LA	70002	**888-882-9600**	504-836-9600	390
Eagle Affiliates Inc	1000 S Second St	Plainfield	NJ	07063	**800-237-9255**	908-757-4464	606
Eagle Asset Management	880 Carillon Pkwy	Saint Petersburg	FL	33716	**800-237-3101**		401
Eagle Aviation	2861 Aviation Way Columbia Metropolitan Airport	West Columbia	SC	29170	**800-849-3245**	803-822-5555	62
Eagle Bancorp Inc	7815 Woodmont Ave *NASDAQ: EGBN*	Bethesda	MD	20814	**800-364-8313**	240-497-2044	360-2
Eagle Burgmann Industries LP	10035 Brookriver Dr *General	Houston	TX	77040	**800-303-7735***		327
Eagle Cleaning Service Inc	525 Belview St	Bessemer	AL	35020	**877-864-5696**	205-424-5252	103
Eagle Communications Inc	2703 Hall St Ste 15 Ste 15	Hays	KS	67601	**877-613-2453**	785-625-5910	640
Eagle Comtronics Inc	7665 Henry Clay Blvd	Liverpool	NY	13088	**800-448-7474**	315-622-3402	645
Eagle Copters Ltd	823 Mctavish Rd NE	Calgary	AB	T2E7G9	**800-564-6469**	403-250-7370	359
Eagle Energy Trust	500 4 Ave SW Ste 2710	Calgary	AB	T2P2V6	**855-531-1575**	403-531-1575	535
Eagle Family Foods Inc	1 Strawberry Ln	Orrville	OH	44667	**888-656-3245**		297-27
Eagle Grips Inc	460 Randy Rd	Carol Stream	IL	60188	**800-323-6144**	630-260-0400	709
Eagle Group Inc	100 Industrial Blvd	Clayton	DE	19938	**800-441-8440**	302-653-3000	301
Eagle Magazine	1623 Gateway Cir S	Grove City	OH	43123	**800-648-5080**	614-883-2200	456-10
Eagle Marketing Inc Perfume Originals Products Div	2412 Sequoia Pk	Yukon	OK	73099	**800-233-7424**		573
Eagle Mountain Casino	681 S Tule Resv Rd	Porterville	CA	93257	**800-903-3353**	559-788-6220	132
Eagle Mountain House	179 Carter Notch Rd PO Box 804	Jackson	NH	03846	**800-966-5779**	603-383-9111	379
Eagle One Golf Products Inc	1340 N Jefferson St	Anaheim	CA	92807	**800-448-4409**	714-983-0050	708
Eagle Pack Pet Foods Inc	200 Ames Pond Dr	Tewksbury	MA	01876	**800-255-5959**	574-259-7834	577
Eagle Parts & Products Inc	1411 Marvin Griffin Rd	Augusta	GA	30906	**888-972-9911**	706-790-6687	60
Eagle Pass Chamber of Commerce	400 E Garrison St	Eagle Pass	TX	78852	**888-355-3224**	830-773-3224	138
Eagle Point National Cemetery	2763 Riley Rd	Eagle Point	OR	97524	**800-535-1117**	541-826-2511	135
Eagle Point Software Corp	4131 Westmark Dr	Dubuque	IA	52002	**800-678-6565**	563-556-8392	180-10
Eagle Professional Resources Inc	67 Yonge St Ste 200	Toronto	ON	M5E1J8	**800-281-2339**	613-234-1810	719
Eagle Publishing Co	75 S Church St	Pittsfield	MA	01201	**800-245-0254**	413-447-7311	634-8
Eagle Radio Inc	2703 Hall St Ste 15	Hays	KS	67601	**877-613-2453**		640
Eagle Ridge Inn & Resort	444 Eagle Ridge Dr	Galena	IL	61036	**800-892-2269**	815-777-2444	667
Eagle Roller Mill Co	1101 Airport Rd	Shelby	NC	28150	**800-223-9108**	704-487-5061	446
Eagle Transport Corp	300 S Wesleyan Blvd Ste 202	Rocky Mount	NC	27804	**800-776-9937**	252-937-2464	778
Eagle's Flight, Creative Training Excellence Inc	489 Clair Rd W	Guelph	ON	N1L0H7	**800-567-8079**	519-767-1747	462
Eagle-Picher Minerals Inc	9785 Gateway Dr Ste 1000 *Cust Svc	Reno	NV	89521	**800-228-3865***	775-824-7600	499

Name	Address	City	State	ZIP	Toll-Free	Phone	Class
Eagleville Hospital	100 Eagleville Rd *General	Eagleville	PA	19408	**800-255-2019***	610-539-6000	724
Eaglewood Resort & Spa	1401 Nordic Rd	Itasca	IL	60143	**877-285-6150**	630-773-1400	667
EAI Inc Environmental Management Service	50 Prescott St	Jersey City	NJ	07304	**800-886-3241**	201-395-0010	196
Eakes Office Plus	617 W Third St	Grand Island	NE	68801	**800-652-9396**	308-382-8026	534
EANGUS (Enlisted Assn of the National Guard of the US)	3133 Mt Vernon Ave	Alexandria	VA	22305	**800-234-3264**	703-519-3846	47-19
EAP Consultants Inc	3901 Roswell Rd Ste 340	Marietta	GA	30062	**800-869-0276**	770-951-9970	461
EAP Systems	500 W Cummings Pk	Woburn	MA	01801	**800-535-4841**	781-935-8850	461
Earhart Petroleum Inc	1494 Lytle Rd	Troy	OH	45373	**800-686-2928**	937-335-2928	578
Earl Burns Miller Japanese Garden	1250 Bellflower Blvd	Long Beach	CA	90840	**800-985-8880**	562-985-8885	96
Earl G Graves Ltd	130 Fifth Ave 10th Fl *Cust Svc	New York	NY	10011	**800-727-7777***	212-242-8000	634-9
Earl Industries LLC	2 Harper Ave	Portsmouth	VA	23707	**800-433-8442**	757-215-2500	696
Earl L Henderson Trucking Inc	206 W Main St	Salem	IL	62881	**800-447-8084**	618-548-4667	778
Earl May Seed & Nursery	208 N Elm St	Shenandoah	IA	51603	**877-800-5556**	712-246-1020	324
Earl's Apparel Inc	908 S Fourth St	Crockett	TX	75835	**800-527-3148**	936-544-5521	154-18
Earle M Jorgensen Co	10650 S Alameda St *Sales	Lynwood	CA	90262	**800-336-5365***	323-567-1122	489
Earlham College	801 National Rd W	Richmond	IN	47374	**800-327-5426**	765-983-1600	167
Earlham School of Religion	228 College Ave	Richmond	IN	47374	**800-432-1377**	765-983-1423	168-3
Early Bird, The	5312 Sebring Warner Rd	Greenville	OH	45331	**866-627-4557**	937-548-3330	531-4
Early Childhood Report	360 Hiatt Dr	Palm Beach Gardens	FL	33418	**800-621-5463**	561-622-6520	530-4
Earnest Machine Products Co	12502 Plz Dr	Cleveland	OH	44130	**800-327-6378**	216-362-1100	351
Earnest Partners LLC	1180 Peachtree St Ste 2300	Atlanta	GA	30309	**800-322-0068**	404-815-8772	401
Earnhardt Auto Centers	7300 W Orchid Ln	Chandler	AZ	85226	**888-378-7711**	480-926-4000	56
Earth Island	9201 Owensmouth Ave	Chatsworth	CA	91311	**888-394-3949**	818-725-2820	297-33
Earth Share	7735 Old Georgetown Rd Ste 900	Bethesda	MD	20814	**800-875-3863**	240-333-0300	47-13
Earth Systems Services Inc	895 Aerovista Pl Ste 102	San Luis Obispo	CA	93401	**866-781-0112**	805-781-0112	194
Earthbound Farm	1721 San Juan Hwy	San Juan Bautista	CA	95045	**800-690-3200**	831-623-7880	10-9
EarthLink Inc	1375 Peachtree St NE *NASDAQ: ELNK*	Atlanta	GA	30309	**866-383-3080**	404-815-0770	398
EarthRes Group Inc	6912 Old Easton Rd PO Box 468	Pipersville	PA	18947	**800-264-4553**	215-766-1211	263
EarthRights International	1612 K St NW Ste 401	Washington	DC	20006	**888-224-9043**	202-466-5188	47-13
Earthwatch Institute	114 Western Ave	Boston	MA	02134	**800-776-0188**	978-461-0081	47-13
EarthWay Products Inc	1009 Maple St	Bristol	IN	46507	**800-294-0671**	574-848-7491	429
East Arkansas Community College	1700 Newcastle Rd	Forrest City	AR	72335	**877-797-3222**	870-633-4480	161
East Balt Inc	1801 W 31st Pl	Chicago	IL	60608	**800-621-8555**	773-376-4444	67
East Bay Chamber of Commerce	16 Cutler St Ste 102	Warren	RI	02885	**877-797-9790**	401-245-0750	138
East Bay Ford Truck Sales Inc	70 Hegenberger Loop	Oakland	CA	94621	**888-219-8551**	510-272-4400	56
East Bay Tire Co	2200 Huntington Dr Unit C	Fairfield	CA	94533	**800-831-8473**	707-437-4700	753
East Boston Savings Bank	10 Meridian St	Boston	MA	02128	**800-657-3272**	617-567-1500	69
East Brunswick Public Library	2 Jean Walling Civic Ctr	East Brunswick	NJ	08816	**800-829-1040**	732-390-6950	434-3
East Canyon Hotel & Spa	288 E Camino Monte Vista	Palm Springs	CA	92262	**877-324-6835**	760-320-1928	379
East Central College	1964 Prairie Dell Rd	Union	MO	63084	**800-392-6848**	636-583-5193	161
East Central Community College	PO Box 129	Decatur	MS	39327	**877-462-3222**	601-635-2111	161
East Central Energy	PO Box 39	Braham	MN	55006	**800-254-7944**		247
East Coast Metal Distributors, Inc	1313 South Briggs Ave	Durham	NC	27703	**844-227-9531**		611
East Coast Metals	171 Ruth Rd	Harleysville	PA	19438	**800-355-2060**	215-256-9550	491
East Coast Security Services Inc	68 Stiles Rd	Salem	NH	03079	**800-639-2086**	603-898-6823	691
East End Hospice	481 Westhampton-Riverhead Rd PO Box 1048	WestHampton Beach	NY	11978	**877-513-0099**	631-288-8400	371
East Georgia College	131 College Cir	Swainsboro	GA	30401	**800-715-4255**	478-289-2000	161
East Georgia Regional Medical Ctr (EGRMC)	1499 Fair Rd	Statesboro	GA	30458	**844-455-8708**	912-486-1000	374-3
East Hampton Star Inc, The	153 Main St PO Box 5002	East Hampton	NY	11937	**844-324-0777**	631-324-0002	634-8
East Jefferson General Hospital (EJGH)	4200 Houma Blvd	Metairie	LA	70006	**866-280-7737**	504-454-4000	374-3
East Jordan Plastics Inc	PO Box 575	East Jordan	MI	49727	**800-353-1190**		601
East Lion Corp	318 Brea Canyon Rd	City of Industry	CA	91789	**877-939-1818**	626-912-1818	302
East Maine School District 63 (EMSD)	10150 Dee Rd	Des Plaines	IL	60016	**866-752-6850**	847-299-1900	683
East Mfg Corp	1871 State Rt 44 PO Box 277	Randolph	OH	44265	**888-405-3278**	330-325-9921	777
East Orange Campus of the VA New Jersey Health Care System (NJHCS)	385 Tremont Ave *General	East Orange	NJ	07018	**844-872-4681***		374-8
East Side Moving & Storage	4836 SE Powell Blvd	Portland	OR	97206	**800-547-4600**	503-777-4181	518
East Side Plating Inc	8400 SE 26th Pl	Portland	OR	97202	**800-394-8554**	503-654-3774	480
East St Tammany Chamber of Commerce	118 W Hall Ave	Slidell	LA	70460	**800-870-3673**	985-643-5678	138
East Stroudsburg University	200 Prospect St *Admissions	East Stroudsburg	PA	18301	**877-230-5547***	570-422-3542	167
East Stroudsburg University Kemp Library	200 Prospect St	East Stroudsburg	PA	18301	**877-422-1378**	570-422-3465	434-6
East Teak Trading Group Inc	1106 Drake Rd	Donalds	SC	29638	**800-338-5636**	864-379-2111	350
East Tennessee Public Communications Corp	1611 E Magnolia Ave	Knoxville	TN	37917	**844-686-2378**	865-595-0220	629
East Tennessee State University	PO Box 70731	Johnson City	TN	37614	**800-462-3878**	423-439-4213	167
East Texas Baptist University	1209 N Grove St	Marshall	TX	75670	**800-804-3828**	903-935-7963	167
East Valley Tribune	120 W First Ave	Mesa	AZ	85210	**877-728-5414**	480-898-6500	531-2
East Valley Water District	3654 E Highland Ave Ste 18	Highland	CA	92346	**866-275-3772**	909-889-9501	804
East West Bancorp Inc	1881 W Main St *NASDAQ: EWBC*	Alhambra	CA	91801	**888-895-5650**	626-308-2012	360-2
East West Label Co	1000 E Hector St	Conshohocken	PA	19428	**800-441-7333**	610-825-0410	413
East-Central Iowa Rural Electric Co-op	2400 Bing Miller Ln	Urbana	IA	52345	**877-850-4343**	319-443-4343	247
Eastco Multi Media Solutions Inc	3646 California Rd	Orchard Park	NY	14127	**800-365-8273**	716-662-0536	513
Easter Owens Electric Co	6692 Fig St	Arvada	CO	80004	**866-204-3707**	303-431-0111	205
Easter Seals	230 W Monroe St Ste 1800	Chicago	IL	60606	**800-221-6827**	312-726-6200	47-17
Eastern Arizona College	615 N Stadium Ave	Thatcher	AZ	85552	**800-678-3808**	928-428-8472	161
Eastern Bank	1 Eastern Pl	Lynn	MA	01901	**800-327-8376**	781-599-2100	69
Eastern Bank Corp	265 Franklin St *Cust Svc	Boston	MA	02110	**800-327-8376***	617-897-1008	360-2
Eastern Business Forms Inc	PO Box 10	Mauldin	SC	29662	**800-387-2648**		109
Eastern Carolina Nissan	3315 Hwy 70 E	New Bern	NC	28564	**888-944-7822**	252-636-1000	56
Eastern Concrete Materials Inc	475 Market St	Elmwood Park	NJ	07407	**800-822-7242**	201-797-7979	184
Eastern Connecticut State University	83 Windham St *Admissions	Willimantic	CT	06226	**877-353-3278***	860-465-5000	167
Eastern Connecticut State University Smith Library	83 Windham St	Willimantic	CT	06226	**800-578-1449**	860-465-4506	434-6
Eastern Floral & Gift Shop	818 Butterworth St SW	Grand Rapids	MI	49504	**800-494-2202**	616-949-2200	294
Eastern Foods Inc	1000 Naturally Fresh Blvd	Atlanta	GA	30349	**800-765-1950**		297-19
Eastern Gateway Community College	4000 Sunset Blvd	Steubenville	OH	43952	**800-682-6553**	740-264-5591	798
Eastern Idaho Technical College	1600 S 25th E	Idaho Falls	ID	83404	**800-662-0261**	208-524-3000	798
Eastern Illini Electric Co-op	330 W Ottawa PO Box 96	Paxton	IL	60957	**800-824-5102**	217-379-2131	247
Eastern Illinois University	600 Lincoln Ave *Admissions	Charleston	IL	61920	**800-252-5711***	217-581-2223	167
Eastern Iowa Light & Power Co-op	600 E Fifth St PO Box 3003	Wilton	IA	52778	**800-728-1242**	563-732-2211	247
Eastern Kentucky University	521 Lancaster Ave	Richmond	KY	40475	**800-465-9191**	859-622-2106	167
Eastern Lift Truck Company Inc	549 E Linwood Ave	Maple Shade	NJ	08052	**866-980-7175**	856-779-8880	385
Eastern Maine Community College	354 Hogan Rd	Bangor	ME	04401	**800-286-9357**	207-974-4600	798
Eastern Maine Electric Co-op Inc	21 Union St	Calais	ME	04619	**800-696-7444**	207-454-7555	247
Eastern Maine Healthcare Systems (EMHS)	43 Whiting Hill Rd	Brewer	ME	04412	**844-364-4473**	207-973-7050	353
Eastern Mennonite University	1200 Pk Rd *Admissions	Harrisonburg	VA	22802	**800-368-2665***	540-432-4118	167
Eastern Metal/USA-SIGN	1430 Sullivan St *Sales	Elmira	NY	14901	**800-872-7446***	607-734-2295	699
Eastern Michigan University	1000 College Pl	Ypsilanti	MI	48197	**800-468-6368**	734-487-1849	167
Eastern Michigan University Halle Library	955 W Cir Dr	Ypsilanti	MI	48197	**888-888-3465**	734-487-0020	434-6
Eastern Mountain Sports	1 Vose Farm Rd	Peterborough	NH	03458	**888-463-6367**	603-924-7231	709
Eastern Nazarene College	23 E Elm Ave	Quincy	MA	02170	**800-883-6288**	617-745-3000	167
Eastern New Mexico Medical Ctr	405 W Country Club Rd	Roswell	NM	88201	**800-222-1222**	575-622-8170	374-3
Eastern New Mexico University	1500 S Ave K Stn 6	Portales	NM	88130	**800-367-3668**	575-562-1011	167

Company / Address	City	State	ZIP	Toll-Free	Phone	Class
Eastern New Mexico University Roswell 52 University Blvd PO Box 6000	Roswell	NM	88202	**800-243-6687**		161
Eastern Oregon University 1 University Blvd	La Grande	OR	97850	**800-452-8639**	541-962-3393	167
Eastern Pennsylvania Supply Co 700 Scott St	Wilkes-Barre	PA	18705	**800-432-8075**	570-823-1181	611
Eastern Security Inc 303 Wyman St Ste 300	Waltham	MA	02451	**888-491-8181**		400
Eastern Shore Natural Gas Co 1110 Forest Ave Ste 201	Dover	DE	19904	**877-650-1257**	302-734-6720	785
Eastern State Hospital (ESH) 4601 Ironbound Rd	Williamsburg	VA	23188	**800-994-6610**	757-253-5161	374-5
Eastern University 1300 Eagle Rd *Admissions	Wayne	PA	19087	**800-452-0996***	610-341-5800	167
Eastern Virginia Bankshares Inc 330 Hospital Rd *NASDAQ: EVBS* ■ *General	Tappahannock	VA	22560	**866-296-3743***	804-443-8400	360-2
Eastern West Virginia Community & Technical College 316 Eastern Dr	Moorefield	WV	26836	**877-982-2322**	304-434-8000	161
Eastern Wholesale Fence Co Inc 274 Middle Island Rd	Medford	NY	11763	**800-339-3362**	631-698-0900	193-2
Eastern Wyoming College 3200 W 'C' St	Torrington	WY	82240	**800-658-3195**	307-532-8200	161
Eastex Environmental Lab Inc 1119 S University Dr PO Box 631375	Nacogdoches	TX	75961	**800-525-0508**	936-569-8879	198
Eastex Telephone Co-op Inc PO Box 150	Henderson	TX	75653	**800-232-7839**	903-854-1000	733
Eastfield College 3737 Motley Dr	Mesquite	TX	75150	**800-260-8000**	972-860-7100	161
Eastland Shoe Mfg Corp 4 Meeting House Rd	Freeport	ME	04032	**888-988-1998**	207-865-6314	302
Eastman Chemical Co 200 S Wilcox Dr *NYSE: EMN* ■ *Cust Svc	Kingsport	TN	37660	**800-327-8626***	423-229-2000	143
Eastman Machine Co 779 Washington St	Buffalo	NY	14203	**800-872-5571**	716-856-2200	741
Eastridge Workforce Solutions 2375 Northside Dr Ste 360	San Diego	CA	92108	**877-862-2632**	619-296-8735	731
Eastside Union School District 45006 30th St E	Lancaster	CA	93535	**877-263-7995**	661-952-1200	683
East-West University 816 S Michigan Ave	Chicago	IL	60605	**877-398-9376**	312-939-0111	167
Easy Ice LLC 925 W Washington St Ste 100	Marquette	MI	49855	**866-327-9423**		789
easyDNS 219 Dufferin St Ste 304A	Toronto	ON	M6K3J1	**888-677-4741**	416-535-8672	396
Easyriders Magazine 28210 Dorothy Dr	Agoura Hills	CA	91301	**800-323-3484**	818-889-8740	456-3
Easyturf 2750 La Mirada Dr	Vista	CA	92081	**866-353-3518**	760-789-7772	607
Eat With Us PO Box 1368	Columbus	MS	39703	**888-222-9550**	662-327-6982	669
Eat'n Park Hospitality Group Inc 285 E Waterfront Dr PO Box 3000	Homestead	PA	15120	**800-947-4033**	412-461-2000	668
EATELCORP Inc 913 S Burnside Ave	Gonzales	LA	70737	**800-621-4211**	225-621-4300	733
Eaton Farm Confectioners Inc 30 Burbank Rd	Sutton	MA	01590	**800-343-9300**	508-865-5235	297-8
Eaton Metal Products Co 4803 York St	Denver	CO	80216	**800-208-2657**	303-296-4800	90
Eaton Office Supply Company Inc 180 John Glenn Dr	Buffalo	NY	14228	**800-365-3237**	716-691-6100	533
Eaton Steel Corp 10221 Capital Ave	Oak Park	MI	48237	**800-527-3851**	248-398-3434	491
Eaton Vance Mutual Funds 2 International Pl	Boston	MA	02110	**800-225-6265**	617-482-8260	527
Eatons' Ranch 270 Eatons' Ranch Rd	Wolf	WY	82844	**800-210-1049**	307-655-9285	241
EatStreet Inc 131 W Wilson St Ste 400	Madison	WI	53715	**866-654-8777**		387
Eau Claire Press Co 701 S Farwell St	Eau Claire	WI	54701	**800-236-8808**	715-833-9200	634-8
EB Bradley Co 5080 S Alameda St	Los Angeles	CA	90058	**800-533-3030**	323-585-9201	351
EBAA (Eye Bank Assn of America) 1015 18th St NW Ste 1010	Washington	DC	20036	**888-491-8833**	202-775-4999	48-8
Ebara Technologies Inc 51 Main Ave	Sacramento	CA	95838	**800-535-5376**	916-920-5451	693
eBay Inc 2065 Hamilton Ave *NASDAQ: EBAY*	San Jose	CA	95125	**800-322-9266**	408-376-7400	50
Ebbtide Corp 2545 Jones Creek Rd	White Bluff	TN	37187	**866-467-4010**	615-797-3193	89
Eberbach Corp 505 S Maple Rd	Ann Arbor	MI	48103	**800-422-2558**	734-665-8877	419
Eberhard Hardware Manufacturing Ltd 1523 Bellmill Rd	Tillsonburg	ON	N4G0C9	**800-567-3344**	519-688-3443	350
Eberhard Mfg Co PO Box 368012	Cleveland	OH	44149	**800-334-6706**	440-238-9720	350
Ebix Inc 5 Concourse Pkwy Ste 3200 *NASDAQ: EBIX*	Atlanta	GA	30328	**800-755-2326**	678-281-2020	180-11
Ebonite International Inc PO Box 746	Hopkinsville	KY	42241	**800-326-6483**	270-881-1200	708
EBSCO Creative Concepts 3500 Blue Lake Dr Ste 150	Birmingham	AL	35243	**800-756-7023**	205-262-2696	9
EBSCO Industries Inc 5724 Hwy 280	Birmingham	AL	35242	**800-653-2726**	205-991-6600	187
EBSCO Industries Inc Vulcan Information Packaging Div PO Box 29	Vincent	AL	35178	**800-633-4526**		85
EBSCO Information Services PO Box 1943	Birmingham	AL	35201	**800-758-5995**	205-991-6600	387
EBSCO Publishing Inc 10 Estes St	Ipswich	MA	01938	**800-653-2726**	978-356-6500	634-10
EBSCO Subscription Services 110 Olmsted St Ste 100	Birmingham	AL	35242	**800-653-2726**	205-995-1596	94
E-Builder Inc 1800 NW 69 Ave Ste 201	Plantation	FL	33313	**800-580-9322**	954-556-6701	38
Ebus Inc 9250 Washburn Rd	Downey	CA	90242	**888-925-4263**	562-904-3474	515
EBUSINESS STRATEGIS LLC 18318 Fern Trl Ctr	Houston	TX	77084	**888-647-3249**	281-647-6183	462
eBX LLC 65 Franklin St Ste 201	Boston	MA	02110	**800-958-4813**	617-350-1600	688
Eby Co 4300 H St	Philadelphia	PA	19124	**800-329-3430**	215-537-4700	255
Eby-Brown Co 280 W Shuman Blvd Ste 280	Naperville	IL	60563	**800-553-8249**	630-778-2800	754
EC Co PO Box 10286	Portland	OR	97296	**800-462-3370**	800-659-3511	191-4
EC Ernst Inc 132 Log Canoe Cir	Stevensville	MD	21666	**800-683-7770**	301-350-7770	191-4
ECA (Evangelical Church Alliance) 205 W Broadway St PO Box 9	Bradley	IL	60915	**888-855-6060**	815-937-0720	47-20
Ecampusalberta 1301 16 Ave Nw	Calgary	AB	T2M0L4	**877-284-7248**	403-284-8777	683
ECCB (Erie 2-Chautauqua Cattaraugus Boces) 8685 Erie Rd	Angola	NY	14006	**800-228-1184**	716-549-4454	683
Ecclesia College 9653 Nations Dr	Springdale	AR	72762	**800-735-9926**	479-248-7236	160
ECCO 833 W Diamond St	Boise	ID	83705	**800-635-5900**	208-395-8000	698
Ecco Business Systems Inc 60 W 38th St 4th Fl	New York	NY	10018	**800-558-6777**	212-921-4545	110
Ecessa Corp 13755 1st Ave N Ste 100	Plymouth	MN	55441	**800-669-6242**	763-694-9949	732
ECFA (Evangelical Council for Financial Accountability) 440 W Jubal Early Dr Ste 130	Winchester	VA	22601	**800-323-9473**	540-535-0103	47-5
ECG Management Consultants Inc 1111 Third Ave Ste 2700	Seattle	WA	98101	**800-729-7635**	206-689-2200	196
Echelon Corp 550 Meridian Ave *NASDAQ: ELON*	San Jose	CA	95126	**888-324-3566**	408-938-5200	178
Echo 230A Sunrise Ave	Palm Beach	FL	33480	**855-435-0061**		669
Echo Design Group 10 E 40th St 16th Fl *General	New York	NY	10016	**800-327-3896***	212-686-8771	154-12
Echo Global Logistics Inc 600 W Chicago Ave Ste 725	Chicago	IL	60654	**800-354-7993**		196
Echo Inc 400 Oakwood Rd	Lake Zurich	IL	60047	**800-673-1558**	847-540-8400	429
Echo Lake Farm Produce Co PO Box 279	Burlington	WI	53105	**800-888-3447**		10-7
Echomountain Llc 1483 Patriot Blvd	Glenview	IL	60026	**877-311-1980**		182
Echota Fabrics Inc 1394 US 41 N	Calhoun	GA	30701	**800-763-9750**	706-629-9750	743
ECI (Engine Components Inc) 9503 Middlex	San Antonio	TX	78217	**800-324-2359**	210-820-8101	21
ECII (Engineered Controls International Inc) 100 Rego Dr PO Box 247	Elon	NC	27244	**800-650-0061**	336-449-7707	787
eCivis Inc 418 N Fair Oaks Ave Ste 301	Pasadena	CA	91103	**877-232-4847**		68
Eckards Home Improvement 2402 N Belt Hwy	Saint Joseph	MO	64506	**800-264-2794**	816-279-4522	292
Eckel Mfg Company Inc 8035 N County Rd W	Odessa	TX	79764	**800-654-4779**	432-362-4336	225
Eckenrod Ford Lincoln Mercury of Cullman Inc 5255 Alabama Hwy 157	Cullman	AL	35058	**888-470-7346**	256-734-3361	56
Eckerd College 4200 54th Ave S *Admissions	Saint Petersburg	FL	33711	**800-456-9009***	727-867-1166	167
Eckhart & Company Inc 4011 W 54th St	Indianapolis	IN	46254	**800-443-3791**	317-347-2665	85
Eclectic Products Inc 1075 Arrowsmith St PO Box 2280	Eugene	OR	97402	**800-693-4667**		3
Eclectik 1332 W Lake St	Chicago	IL	60607	**866-308-1231**	312-676-2442	129
Eclipse Inc 1665 Elmwood Rd	Rockford	IL	61103	**888-826-3473**	815-877-3031	319
Eclipse Marketing Services Inc 240 Cedar Knolls Rd Ste 100	Cedar Knolls	NJ	07927	**800-837-4648**		197
ECMD Inc 2 Grandview St	North Wilkesboro	NC	28659	**888-222-3961**	336-667-5976	688
Ecoa Industrial Products 5051 NW 37th Ave	Miami	FL	33142	**800-433-3833**		358
Ecodyne Ltd 4475 Corporate Dr	Burlington	ON	L7L5T9	**888-326-3963**	905-332-1404	386
ECOF (Eye Centers of Florida) 4101 Evans Ave	Fort Myers	FL	33901	**888-393-2455**	239-939-3456	796
Ecojustice Canada 131 Water St Ste 214	Vancouver	BC	V6B4M3	**800-926-7744**	604-685-5618	47-13
eCollect LLC 5000 Euclid Ave Ste 4403	Cleveland	OH	44103	**888-569-6001**		393
Ecolo Odor Control Technologies Inc 59 Penn Dr	Toronto	ON	M9L2A6	**800-667-6355**	416-740-3900	103
Ecom Enterprises Inc 1230 Oakmead Pkwy Ste 318	Sunnyvale	CA	94085	**877-955-3266**	408-720-9194	182
e-Commerce Law & Strategy 1617 JFK Blvd Ste 1750	Philadelphia	PA	19103	**877-256-2472**	215-557-2300	530-7
E-Commerce Times (ECT) 16133 Ventura Blvd Ste 700	Encino	CA	91436	**877-328-5500**	818-461-9700	456-5
Econo Foods 1600 Stephenson	Iron Mountain	MI	49801	**877-295-4558**	906-774-1911	345
Econoco Corp 300 Karin Ln	Hicksville	NY	11801	**800-645-7032**	516-935-7700	288
Econ-o-copy Inc 4437 Trenton St Ste A	Metairie	LA	70006	**877-256-0310**	504-457-0032	534
Econolite Control Products Inc 3360 E La Palma Av	Anaheim	CA	92806	**800-225-6480**	714-630-3700	698
Economic Development Administration 1401 Constitution Ave NW	Washington	DC	20230	**888-469-3146**	202-482-2900	340-2
Economical Insurance Group, The 111 Westmount Rd S PO Box 2000	Waterloo	ON	N2J4S4	**800-265-2180**	519-570-8200	391-4

Name / Address	City	State	ZIP	Toll-Free	Phone	Class
Economy Spring & Stamping Co 29 DePaolo Dr	Southington	CT	06489	**800-237-5225**	860-621-7358	717
eContent Magazine 143 Old Marlton Pike Ste 3	Medford	NJ	08055	**800-300-9868**	609-654-6266	456-7
eCornell 950 Danby Rd Ste 150	Ithaca	NY	14850	**866-326-7635**	607-330-3200	244
eCredit 777 Yamato Rd Ste 500	Boca Raton	FL	33431	**800-276-2321**	561-226-9000	180-1
ECRI Institute 5200 Butler Pike	Plymouth Meeting	PA	19462	**866-247-3004**	610-825-6000	47-17
ECRM Inc 554 Clark Rd	Tewksbury	MA	01876	**800-537-3276**	978-851-0207	110
ECS (Electronic Cash Systems Inc) 30352 Esperanza	Rancho Santa Margarita	CA	92688	**888-327-2860**	949-888-8580	55
ECS & R 3237 Us Hwy 19	Cochranton	PA	16314	**866-815-0016**	814-425-7773	198
ECS Financial Services Inc 3400 Dundee Rd	Northbrook	IL	60062	**800-826-7070**	847-291-1333	2
ECT (E-Commerce Times) 16133 Ventura Blvd Ste 700	Encino	CA	91436	**877-328-5500**	818-461-9700	456-5
Ectaco Inc 31-21 31st St	Long Island	NY	11106	**800-710-7920**	718-728-6110	175-1
ECU (Educators Credit Union) 1400 N Newman Rd PO Box 081040	Racine	WI	53406	**800-236-5898**	262-886-5900	221
ECWA (Erie County Water Authority) 295 Main St Rm 350	Buffalo	NY	14203	**855-748-1076**	716-849-8484	785
Ed Bozarth Chevrolet Inc 2001 S Havana St	Aurora	CO	80014	**877-626-9358**		56
ED Etnyre & Co 1333 S Daysville Rd	Oregon	IL	61061	**800-995-2116**	815-732-2116	192
Ed Fagan Inc 769 Susquehanna Ave	Franklin Lakes	NJ	07417	**800-335-6827**	201-891-4003	491
Ed Martin Inc 3800 E 96th St	Indianapolis	IN	46240	**800-211-5410**	317-846-3800	56
Ed Necco & Assoc 178 Private Dr	South Point	OH	45680	**866-996-3226**	513-771-9600	764
Ed Staub & Sons Petroleum Inc 1301 Esplanade Ave	Klamath Falls	OR	97601	**800-435-3835**		317
EDC (Education Development Ctr Inc) 55 Chapel St	Newton	MA	02458	**800-225-4276**	617-969-7100	47-11
Edco & Arrowhead Products Inc 8700 Excelsior Blvd	Hopkins	MN	55343	**800-333-2580**	952-945-2680	695
Eddie Bauer LLC PO Box 7001 *Orders	Groveport	OH	43125	**800-426-8020***		156-4
Eddington Thread Manufacturing Co PO Box 446	Bensalem	PA	19020	**800-220-8901**	215-639-8900	742-9
Eddy Packing Company Inc 404 Airport Dr	Yoakum	TX	77995	**800-292-2361**	361-293-2361	472
Edelbrock Corp 2700 California St	Torrance	CA	90503	**800-739-3737**	310-781-2222	59
Eden Foods Inc 701 Tecumseh Rd *Cust Svc	Clinton	MI	49236	**800-248-0320***	517-456-7424	297-36
Eden House 1015 Fleming St	Key West	FL	33040	**800-533-5397**		379
Eden Roc - A Renaissance Beach Resort & Spa 4525 Collins Ave	Miami Beach	FL	33140	**855-433-3676**	305-531-0000	667
Eden Stone Company Inc W4520 Lime Rd	Eden	WI	53019	**800-472-2521**	920-477-2521	502-6
Eden Theological Seminary 475 E Lockwood Ave	Saint Louis	MO	63119	**800-969-3627**	314-961-3627	168-3
Eder Flag Mfg Company Inc 1000 W Rawson Ave	Oak Creek	WI	53154	**800-558-6044**	414-764-3522	289
Edgar Allan Poe Museum 1914 E Main St	Richmond	VA	23223	**888-213-2763**	804-648-5523	519
Edgar Evins State Park 1630 Edgar Evins State Pk Rd	Silver Point	TN	38582	**800-250-8619**	931-858-2446	564
Edgar Lomax Co 6564 Loisdale Ct Ste 310	Springfield	VA	22150	**866-205-0524**	703-719-0026	401
EDGAR Online Inc 11200 Rockville Pk Ste 310 *NASDAQ: EDGR*	Rockville	MD	20852	**800-732-0330**	301-287-0300	404
Edge Electronics Inc 75 Orville Dr	Bohemia	NY	11716	**800-647-3343**	631-471-3343	175-8
Edge Information Management Inc 1682 W Hibiscus Blvd	Melbourne	FL	32901	**800-725-3343**	321-722-3343	632
EDge Interactive Inc 67 Mowat Ave Ste 533	Toronto	ON	M6K3E3	**800-211-5577**	416-494-3343	226
Edge Products 1080 S Depot Dr	Ogden	UT	84404	**888-360-3343**	801-476-3343	249
Edge Systems LLC 3S721 W Ave Ste 200 *Tech Supp	Warrenville	IL	60555	**800-352-3343***	630-810-9669	179
Edge Technologies Inc 3702 Pender Dr Ste 250	Fairfax	VA	22030	**888-771-3343**	703-691-7900	180-1
Edgecombe-Martin County Electric Membership Corp NC Hwy 33 E	Tarboro	NC	27886	**800-445-6486**	252-823-2171	247
Edgemark Partners 4510 cox rd	Glen Allen	VA	23060	**800-488-0289**	804-967-2000	462
Edgemont Pharmaceuticals LLC 1250 Capital of Texas Hwy S Bldg 3 Ste 400	Austin	TX	78746	**888-594-4332**	512-550-8555	233
Edgen Corp 18444 Highland Rd	Baton Rouge	LA	70809	**866-334-3648**	225-756-9868	385
Edgenet Inc 2948 Sidco Dr	Atlanta	GA	30326	**877-334-3638**	615-371-3848	179
Edgewater Beach Hotel 1901 Gulf Shore Blvd N	Naples	FL	34102	**866-624-1695**	888-564-1308	379
Edgewater Hotel 2411 Alaskan Way Pier 67	Seattle	WA	98121	**800-624-0670**	206-728-7000	379
Edgewater Hotel & Casino 2020 S Casino Dr *Resv	Laughlin	NV	89029	**866-352-3553***	702-298-2453	132
Edgewater Pointe Estates 23315 Blue Water Cir *General	Boca Raton	FL	33433	**888-339-2287***	561-391-6305	670

Name / Address	City	State	ZIP	Toll-Free	Phone	Class
Edgewater Resort 200 Edgewater Cir	Hot Springs	AR	71913	**800-234-3687**	501-767-3311	379
Edgewater Resort & Waterpark 2400 London Rd	Duluth	MN	55812	**800-777-7925**	218-728-3601	379
Edgewood College 1000 Edgewood College Dr	Madison	WI	53711	**800-444-4861**	608-663-2294	167
Edible Arrangements LLC 95 Barnes Rd *Cust Svc	Wallingford	CT	06492	**877-363-7848***	304-894-8901	311
Edimer Pharmaceuticals Inc 55 Cambridge Pkwy Ste 102W	Cambridge	MA	02142	**866-334-4240**	617-758-4300	233
Edinboro University of Pennsylvania 200 E Normal St	Edinboro	PA	16444	**888-846-2676**	814-732-2761	167
Edinboro University of Pennsylvania Baron-Forness Library (EUB) 200 Tartan Rd	Edinboro	PA	16444	**888-845-2890**	814-732-2273	434-6
Edinburg Chamber of Commerce 602 W University Dr	Edinburg	TX	78540	**800-800-7214**	956-383-4974	138
Edinburg Regional Medical Ctr (ERMC) 1102 W Trenton Rd	Edinburg	TX	78539	**800-465-5585**	956-388-6000	374-3
e-Discovery Law & Strategy 1617 JFK Blvd Ste 1750	Philadelphia	PA	19103	**877-256-2472**	215-557-2300	530-7
Edison Biotechnology Institute Ohio University Konneker Research Laboratories The Ridges	Athens	OH	45701	**800-444-2420**	740-593-4713	666
Edison Chouest Offshore 16201 E Main St	Galliano	LA	70354	**866-925-5161**	985-601-4444	464
Edison College *Charlotte* 26300 Airport Rd	Punta Gorda	FL	33950	**800-749-2322**	941-637-5629	161
Edison Community College 1973 Edison Dr	Piqua	OH	45356	**888-442-4551**	937-778-8600	161
Edison Electric Institute (EEI) 701 Pennsylvania Ave NW	Washington	DC	20004	**800-649-1202**	202-508-5000	47-12
Edison International 2244 Walnut Grove Ave *NYSE: EIX* ■ *Cust Svc	Rosemead	CA	91770	**800-655-4555***	626-302-1212	360-5
Edison Properties LLC 100 Washington St	Newark	NJ	07102	**888-727-5327**	973-643-0895	561
eDist 97 McKee Dr	Mahwah	NJ	07430	**800-800-6624**	201-512-1400	690
Edisto Beach State Park 8377 State Cabin Rd	Edisto Island	SC	29438	**800-315-3087**	843-869-2756	564
Edisto Electric Co-op Inc 896 Calhoun St	Bamberg	SC	29003	**800-433-3292**	803-245-5141	247
Edith J Carrier Arboretum & Botanical Gardens at James Madison University 780 University Blvd MSC 3705	Harrisonburg	VA	22807	**888-568-2586**	540-568-3194	96
Editor & Publisher Magazine 17782 Cowan Ste C	Irvine	CA	92614	**855-896-7433**	949-660-6150	456-5
Editorial Freelancers Assn (EFA) 71 W 23rd St 4th Fl	New York	NY	10010	**866-929-5400**	212-929-5400	48-16
Edlund Company Inc 159 Industrial Pkwy	Burlington	VT	05401	**800-772-2126**	802-862-9661	299
EDM Zap Parts Inc 1108 Front St Ste 2	Lisle	IL	60532	**800-759-2839**	630-852-1699	695
EDMC (Education Management Corp) 210 Sixth Ave 33rd Fl *NASDAQ: EDMC*	Pittsburgh	PA	15222	**800-275-2440**	412-562-0900	244
Edmo Distributors Inc 12830 E Mirabeau Pkwy	Spokane Valley	WA	99216	**800-235-3300**	509-535-8280	768
Edmonds Community College 20000 68th Ave W	Lynnwood	WA	98036	**866-886-4854**	425-640-1500	161
Edmonds Harbor Inn & Suites 130 W Dayton	Edmonds	WA	98020	**800-441-8033**	425-771-5021	379
Edmonton International Airport 8340 Sparrow Crescent	Edmonton	AB	T9E8B7	**800-854-9517**	780-800-0622	27
Edmonton Journal 10006 - 101 St	Edmonton	AB	T5J2S6	**800-232-9486**	780-429-5100	531-1
Edmonton Oilers 11230 110th St	Edmonton	AB	T5G3H7	**866-414-4625**	780-414-4000	714
Edmonton Sun 4990 92nd Ave Ste 250	Edmonton	AB	T6B3A1	**877-468-2401**	780-468-0100	531-1
Edmonton Symphony Orchestra 9720 102nd Ave	Edmonton	AB	T5J4B2	**800-563-5081**	780-428-1108	572-3
Edmund Optics Inc 101 E Gloucester Pk	Barrington	NJ	08007	**800-363-1992**	856-547-3488	543
Edmunds Gages 45 Spring Ln	Farmington	CT	06032	**800-878-1622**	860-677-2813	492
EDN Magazine 303 Second St *Orders	San Francisco	CA	94107	**800-446-6551***	415-947-6000	456-21
Edo Japan International Inc 32 St SE Ste 4838	Calgary	AB	T2B2S6	**888-336-9888**	403-215-8800	668
Edom Laboratories Inc 100 E Jefryn Blvd Ste M	Deer Park	NY	11729	**800-723-3366**	631-586-2266	797
Edon Farmers Co-op Assn Inc 205 S Michigan PO Box 308	Edon	OH	43518	**800-878-4093**	419-272-2121	278
Edro Corp 37 Commerce St *Sales	East Berlin	CT	06023	**800-628-6434***	860-828-0311	427
EDS (IEEE Electron Devices Society) IEEE Operations Ctr 445 Hoes Ln	Piscataway	NJ	08854	**800-678-4333**	732-981-0060	48-19
Edstrom Industries Inc 819 Bakke Ave	Waterford	WI	53185	**800-558-5913**	262-534-5181	420
Education Ctr Inc 3515 W Market St Ste 200	Greensboro	NC	27403	**800-714-7991**	336-854-0309	245
Education Development Ctr Inc (EDC) 55 Chapel St	Newton	MA	02458	**800-225-4276**	617-969-7100	47-11
Education Grants Alert 360 Hiatt Dr	Palm Beach Gardens	FL	33418	**800-621-5463**	561-622-6520	530-4
Education Management Corp (EDMC) 210 Sixth Ave 33rd Fl *NASDAQ: EDMC*	Pittsburgh	PA	15222	**800-275-2440**	412-562-0900	244
Education Management Solutions Inc 436 Creamery Way Ste 300	Exton	PA	19341	**877-367-5050**	610-701-7002	180-7
Education Management Systems Inc 4110 Shipyard Blvd	Wilmington	NC	28403	**800-541-8999**	910-799-0121	179

Name / Address	City	State	Zip	Toll-Free	Phone	Class
Education Resource Information Ctr (ERIC) c/o CSC 655 15th St NW Ste 500	Washington	DC	20005	**800-538-3742**		199
Education Week Magazine 6935 Arlington Rd	Bethesda	MD	20814	**800-346-1834**	301-280-3100	456-8
Educational Development Corp 10302 E 55th Pl *NASDAQ: EDUC*	Tulsa	OK	74146	**800-475-4522**	918-622-4522	94
Educational Employees Credit Union PO Box 5242	Fresno	CA	93755	**800-538-3328**	559-437-7700	221
Educational Housing Services Inc 55 Clark St	Brooklyn	NY	11201	**800-385-1689**	212-977-7622	48-5
Educational Insights Inc 380 N Fairway Dr	Vernon Hills	IL	60061	**800-995-4436**		245
Educational Leadership Magazine 1703 N Beauregard St	Alexandria	VA	22311	**800-933-2723**	703-578-9600	456-8
Educational Media Foundation 5700 W Oaks Blvd *General	Rocklin	CA	95765	**800-525-5683***	916-251-1600	640
Educational Research Newsletter PO Box 2347	South Portland	ME	04116	**800-321-7471**	207-632-1954	530-4
Educational Tours 1123 Sterling Rd	Inverness	FL	34450	**800-343-9003**		758
Educational Travel Consultants (ETC) PO Box 1580	Hendersonville	NC	28793	**800-247-7969**	828-693-0412	758
Educators Credit Union (ECU) 1400 N Newman Rd PO Box 081040	Racine	WI	53406	**800-236-5898**	262-886-5900	221
Educators Publishing Service Inc (EPS) 625 Mt Auburn St Third Fl PO Box 9031	Cambridge	MA	02139	**800-225-5750**		634-2
Educators Resource Inc 2575 Schillingers Rd *Cust Svc	Semmes	AL	36575	**800-868-2368***		245
Edufii Inc 2078 Parker St Ste 200	San Luis Obispo	CA	93401	**800-439-8505**		387
EdVenture Children's Museum 211 Gervais St	Columbia	SC	29201	**888-236-2427**	803-779-3100	520
EdVest PO Box 55244	Boston	MA	02205	**888-338-3789**		723
Edward A Sherman Publishing Co 101 Malbone Rd	Newport	RI	02840	**800-320-2378**	401-849-3300	634-8
Edward C Levy Co 9300 Dix Ave	Dearborn	MI	48120	**877-938-0007**	313-843-7200	502-5
Edward Don & Co 2500 S Harlem Ave *Cust Svc	North Riverside	IL	60546	**800-777-4366***		301
Edward J Darby & Son Inc 2200 N Eigth St PO Box 50049	Philadelphia	PA	19133	**800-875-6374**	215-236-2203	686
Edwards Industries LLC 6085 Marshalee Dr Ste 140	Elkridge	MD	21075	**800-556-2506**	443-561-0180	198
Edwards Instrument Co 530 S Hwy H	Elkhorn	WI	53121	**800-562-6838**	262-723-4221	526
Edwards Jet Ctr 1691 Aviation Pl	Billings	MT	59105	**866-353-8245**	406-252-0508	62
Edwards Lifesciences Corp 1 Edwards Way *NYSE: EW*	Irvine	CA	92614	**800-424-3278**	949-250-2500	582
Edwards Manufacturing Co 1107 Sykes St	Albert Lea	MN	56007	**800-373-8206**	507-373-8206	455
Edwin Gaynor Corp 200 Charles St	Stratford	CT	06615	**800-342-9667**	203-378-5545	813
Edwin L Heim Co 1918 Greenwood St	Harrisburg	PA	17104	**800-692-7316**	717-233-8711	191-4
Edwin Shaw Rehab 1621 Flickinger Rd	Akron	OH	44312	**800-221-4601**	330-784-1271	374-6
EE Schenck Co 6000 N Cutter Cir	Portland	OR	97217	**800-433-0722**	503-284-4124	593
EECO Switch 1240 Pioneer St Ste A	Brea	CA	92821	**800-854-3808**	714-835-6000	813
EEI (Edison Electric Institute) 701 Pennsylvania Ave NW	Washington	DC	20004	**800-649-1202**	202-508-5000	47-12
EEI (Environmental Enterprises Inc) 10163 Cincinnati Dayton Rd	Cincinnati	OH	45241	**800-722-2818**	513-772-2818	665
EEOC (Equal Employment Opportunity Commission) 1801 L St NW	Washington	DC	20507	**800-669-4000**	202-663-4191	340-18
EF Precision Design Inc 2301 Computer Rd	Willow Grove	PA	19090	**800-536-3900**	215-784-0861	755
EF Tours 2 Education Cir	Cambridge	MA	02141	**800-872-8439**	877-205-9909	758
EFA (Editorial Freelancers Assn) 71 W 23rd St 4th Fl	New York	NY	10010	**866-929-5400**	212-929-5400	48-16
EFC (Evangelical Fellowship of Canada) 600 Alden Rd Ste 300 Markham Industrial Pk	Markham	ON	L3R0E7	**866-302-3362**	905-479-5885	47-20
EFCO Corp 1000 County Rd	Monett	MO	65708	**800-221-4169**	417-235-3193	236
Effective Data Inc 1515 E Wdfield Rd	Schaumburg	IL	60173	**877-825-5233**	847-969-9300	227
Effective Solar Products LLC 601 Crescent Ave	Lockport	LA	70374	**888-824-0090**	985-532-0800	609
Efficas Inc 7007 Winchester Cir Ste 120	Boulder	CO	80301	**866-446-0388**	303-381-2070	577
Effingham Convention & Visitors Bureau 201 E Jefferson Ave	Effingham	IL	62401	**800-772-0750**	217-342-5305	208
Effingham County Chamber of Commerce 520 W Third St PO Box 1078	Springfield	GA	31329	**800-241-3333**	912-754-3301	138
Effingham Equity Inc 201 W Roadway Ave	Effingham	IL	62401	**800-223-1337**	217-342-4101	277
EFJohnson Technologies 1440 Corporate Dr	Irving	TX	75038	**800-328-3911**	972-819-0700	645
EFP Corp 223 Middleton Run Rd	Elkhart	IN	46516	**800-205-8537**	574-295-4690	603
EG Fisher Public Library 1289 Ingleside Ave	Athens	TN	37303	**800-552-6843**	423-745-7782	434-3
EG Penner Building Centres 200 Park Rd W	Steinbach	MB	R5G1A1	**800-353-8733**	204-326-1325	292
eGain Communications Corp 1252 Borregas Ave *NASDAQ: EGAN*	Mountain View	CA	94043	**888-603-4246**	408-636-4500	38
Egan Bernard & Co 1900 Old Dixie Hwy	Fort Pierce	FL	34946	**800-327-6676**		316-2
Egan Visual Inc 300 Hanlan Rd	Woodbridge	ON	L4L3P6	**888-609-8886**	905-851-2826	321
Egenera Inc 80 Central St	Boxborough	MA	01719	**866-301-3117**	978-206-6300	178
Egge Machine Company Inc 11707 Slauson Ave	Santa Fe Springs	CA	90670	**800-866-3443**	562-945-3419	453
Eglin Federal Credit Union 838 Eglin Pkwy NE	Fort Walton Beach	FL	32547	**800-367-6159**	850-862-0111	221
EGRMC (East Georgia Regional Medical Ctr) 1499 Fair Rd	Statesboro	GA	30458	**844-455-8708**	912-486-1000	374-3
EGS Electrical Group LLC 9377 W Higgins Rd	Rosemont	IL	60018	**800-621-1506**	847-268-6000	814
eGumBall Inc 8687 Research Dr Ste 200	Irvine	CA	92618	**800-890-8940**		197
EGW.com Inc 4075 Papazian Way *Cust Svc	Fremont	CA	94538	**800-546-4754***	510-668-0268	634-9
Egyptian Electric Co-op Assn PO Box 38	Steeleville	IL	62288	**800-606-1505**		247
Egyptian Stationers Inc 129 W Main St *Cust Svc	Belleville	IL	62220	**800-642-3949***	618-234-2323	534
EH Ashley & Company Inc 1 White Squadron Rd	Riverside	RI	02915	**800-735-7424**	401-431-0950	411
EH Wachs Co 600 Knightsbridge Pkwy	Lincolnshire	IL	60069	**800-323-8185**	847-537-8800	454
Ehlers & Assoc Inc 3060 Centre Pointe Dr	Roseville	MN	55113	**800-552-1171**	651-697-8500	196
Ehob Inc 250 N Belmont Ave	Indianapolis	IN	46222	**800-899-5553**	317-972-4600	476
Ehrhardt Tool & Machine Co 25 Central Industrial Dr	Granite City	IL	62040	**877-386-7856**	314-436-6900	755
EI Electronics LLC 1800 Shames Dr	Westbury	NY	11590	**877-346-3837**	516-334-0870	36
EIA (Environmental Information Assn) 6935 Wisconsin Ave Ste 306	Chevy Chase	MD	20815	**888-343-4342**	301-961-4999	47-13
Eide Industries Inc 16215 Piuma Ave	Cerritos	CA	90703	**800-422-6827**	562-402-8335	730
Eielson Air Force Base 354 Broadway St Unit 2B	Eielson AFB	AK	99702	**800-538-6647**	907-377-1110	496-1
Eigen Video 13366 Grass Vly Ave Ste A	Grass Valley	CA	95945	**888-924-2020**	530-274-1240	252
Eikos Inc 2 Master Dr	Franklin	MA	02038	**888-345-6712**	508-528-0300	666
EIS Electro Imaging Systems 6553 Las Positas Rd	Livermore	CA	94551	**800-207-4757**		534
Eisai Inc 100 Tice Blvd	Woodcliff Lake	NJ	07677	**866-613-4724**	201-692-1100	582
Eisenbach Consulting LLC 921 Shiloh Rd B-300	Tyler	TX	75703	**800-977-4020**		462
Eizo Nanao Technologies Inc 5710 Warland Dr	Cypress	CA	90630	**800-800-5202**	562-431-5011	175-4
EJ Group Inc 301 Spring St	East Jordan	MI	49727	**800-874-4100**	231-536-2261	308
EJ Thomas Performing Arts Hall 198 Hill St University of Akron	Akron	OH	44325	**800-745-3000**	330-972-7570	571
EJGH (East Jefferson General Hospital) 4200 Houma Blvd	Metairie	LA	70006	**866-280-7737**	504-454-4000	374-3
E&K Companies 343 Carol Ln	Elmhurst	IL	60126	**800-365-5760**	630-530-9001	191-9
Ekahau Inc 1851 Alexander Bell Dr Ste 300	Reston	VA	20191	**866-435-2428**		387
Ektron Inc 542 Amherst St (Rt 101A)	Nashua	NH	03063	**877-383-0885**	603-594-0249	6
El Al Israel Airlines Inc 15 E 26th St	New York	NY	10010	**800-223-6700**	212-852-0600	25
El Cajon Motors D/B/A El Cajon Ford 1595 E Main St	El Cajon	CA	92021	**877-375-1408**	619-579-8888	56
El Camino College 16007 Crenshaw Blvd	Torrance	CA	90506	**866-352-2646**	310-532-3670	161
El Camino Store, The 420 Athena Dr	Athens	GA	30601	**888-685-5987**	706-546-9217	56
El Caribe Resort 2125 S Atlantic Ave	Daytona Beach	FL	32118	**800-445-9889**	386-252-1558	705
El Centro Public Library 539 State St	El Centro	CA	92243	**877-482-5656**	760-337-4565	434-3
El Conquistador Resort & Golden Door Spa 1000 El Conquistador Ave *Resv	Fajardo	PR	00738	**888-543-1282***	787-863-1000	667
El Cortez Hotel & Casino 600 E Fremont St	Las Vegas	NV	89101	**800-634-6703**	702-385-5200	132
El Dorado County Chamber of Commerce 542 Main St	Placerville	CA	95667	**800-457-6279**	530-621-5885	138
El Dorado Furniture Corp 4200 NW 167th St	Miami	FL	33054	**888-451-7800**	305-624-2400	322
El Dorado Nature Ctr 7550 E Spring St	Long Beach	CA	90815	**800-662-8887**	562-570-1745	49-4
El Dorado Savings Bank 4040 El Dorado Rd	Placerville	CA	95667	**800-874-9779**	530-622-1492	69
El Dorado Trading Group Inc 760 San Antonio Rd	Palo Alto	CA	94303	**800-227-8292**		111
El Encanto Inc 2001 Fourth St SW PO Box 293	Albuquerque	NM	87103	**800-888-7336**	505-243-2722	297-36
El Fenix Corp 11075 Harry Hines Blvd	Dallas	TX	75229	**877-591-1918**	972-241-2171	668
EL Harvey & Sons Inc 68 Hopkinton Rd	Westborough	MA	01581	**800-321-3002**	508-836-3000	802
El Mar Plastics Inc 109 W 134th St	Los Angeles	CA	90061	**800-255-5210**	310-436-6444	602
El Matador Foods Inc 7201 Bayway Dr	Baytown	TX	77520	**800-470-2447**	281-424-4555	345
El Nuevo Herald 3511 NW 91st Ave	Doral	FL	33172	**866-949-6722**	305-376-3535	531-2

Name	Address	City	State	ZIP	Toll-Free	Phone	Class
El Paso Community College *Valle Verde*	919 Hunter Dr	El Paso	TX	79915	**800-531-8292**	915-831-2000	161
El Paso Convention & Performing Arts Ctr	1 Civic Ctr Plz	El Paso	TX	79901	**800-351-6024**	915-534-0600	207
El Paso Electric Co	100 N Stanton Stanton Tower *NYSE: EE*	El Paso	TX	79901	**800-351-1621**	915-543-5711	785
El Paso First Health Plans Inc	1145 Westmoreland Dr	El Paso	TX	79925	**877-532-3778**	915-532-3778	47-17
El Pollo Loco	3535 Harbor Blvd Ste 100	Costa Mesa	CA	92626	**877-375-4968**	714-599-5000	668
El Ran Furniture Ltd	2751 Transcanada Hwy	Pointe-Claire	QC	H9R1B4	**800-361-6546**	514-630-5656	320-2
El Rey Inn	1862 Cerillos Rd	Santa Fe	NM	87505	**800-521-1349**	505-982-1931	379
El Tovar Hotel	1 Main St	Grand Canyon	AZ	86023	**888-297-2757**	928-638-2631	379
Elaine P Nunez Community College	3710 Paris Rd	Chalmette	LA	70043	**866-825-1954**	504-278-7497	161
Elam Construction Inc	556 Struthers Ave	Grand Junction	CO	81501	**800-675-4598**	970-242-5370	190-4
Elan Financial Services	225 W Sta Sq Dr Ste 620	Pittsburgh	PA	15219	**877-935-2637**		401
Elan Hotel	8435 Beverly Blvd	Los Angeles	CA	90048	**866-203-2212**	323-658-6663	379
Elanco Animal Health	2500 Innovation Way	Greenfield	IN	46140	**877-352-6261**	317-276-2000	581
Elant Inc	46 Harriman Dr	Goshen	NY	10924	**800-501-3936**		390
Elantas PDG Inc	5200 N Second St	Saint Louis	MO	63147	**800-325-7492**	314-621-5700	144
Elat Chayyim	116 Johnson Rd	Falls Village	CT	06031	**800-398-2630**		671
Elavon	2 Concourse Pkwy Ste 300	Atlanta	GA	30328	**800-725-1243**	678-731-5000	180-4
eLawMarketing	25 Robert Pitt Dr Ste 209G	Monsey	NY	10952	**866-833-6245**		318
Elbeco Inc	4418 Pottsville Pk	Reading	PA	19605	**800-468-4654**	610-921-0651	154-18
ELCA (Evangelical Lutheran Church in America)	8765 W Higgins Rd	Chicago	IL	60631	**800-638-3522**	773-380-2700	47-20
Elco Corp	1000 Belt Line St	Cleveland	OH	44109	**800-321-0467**	216-749-2605	540
ELCO Mutual Life & Annuity	916 Sherwood Dr	Lake Bluff	IL	60044	**888-872-7954**	847-295-6000	391-2
Elder Wood Preserving Co Inc	334 Elder Wood Rd	Mansura	LA	71350	**866-606-2470**	318-964-2196	816
Eldercare Locator	1730 Rhode Island Ave NW Ste 1200	Washington	DC	20036	**800-677-1116**		199
Elderhostel Inc	11 Ave de Lafayette	Boston	MA	02111	**800-454-5768**		47-23
Elderly Instruments	1100 N Washington Ave	Lansing	MI	48906	**888-473-5810**	517-372-7890	525
ElderWood Senior Care	7 Limestone Dr	Williamsville	NY	14221	**888-826-9663**	716-633-3900	450
Eldorado Canyon State Park	9 Kneale Rd PO Box B	Eldorado Springs	CO	80025	**866-265-6447**	303-494-3943	564
Eldorado Gold Corp	550 Burrard St *NYSE: ELD*	Vanouver	BC	V6C2B5	**888-353-8166**	604-687-4018	501
Eldorado Hotel	309 W San Francisco St	Santa Fe	NM	87501	**800-955-4455**	505-988-4455	379
Eldorado Hotel Casino	345 N Virginia St *Resv	Reno	NV	89501	**800-879-8879***	775-786-5700	379
Eldorado National Inc	1655 Wall St	Salina	KS	67401	**800-850-1287**	909-591-9557	58
Eldorado Resort Casino Shreveport	451 Clyde Fant Pkwy	Shreveport	LA	71101	**877-602-0711**	318-220-0711	132
Eldridge Hotel	701 Massachusetts St	Lawrence	KS	66044	**800-527-0909**	785-749-5011	379
Eldridge Products Inc	2700 Garden Rd Bldg A	Monterey	CA	93940	**800-321-3569**	831-648-7777	203
Eleanor Roosevelt National Historic Site	4097 Albany Post Rd	Hyde Park	NY	12538	**800-337-8474**	845-229-9115	563
Eleanor Slater Hospital	14 Harrington Rd	Cranston	RI	02920	**800-438-8477**	401-462-2339	374-7
Election Systems & Software Inc	11208 John Galt Blvd *General	Omaha	NE	68137	**877-377-8683***	402-593-0101	799
Elections USA Inc	1927 E Saw Mill Rd	Quakertown	PA	18951	**800-789-8683**	215-538-0779	799
Electralloy Corp	175 Main St	Oil City	PA	16301	**800-458-7273**	814-678-4100	721
Electrex Inc	PO Box 948	Hutchinson	KS	67504	**800-319-3676**		255
Electric City Trolley Station & Museum	300 Cliff St	Scranton	PA	18503	**800-732-0999**	570-963-6590	519
Electric Heater Co	45 Seymour St	Stratford	CT	06615	**800-647-3165**	203-378-2659	35
Electric Mail Company Inc	3999 Henning Dr Ste 300	Burnaby	BC	V5C6P9	**866-950-5333**	604-482-1111	38
Electric Materials Co	50 S Washington St	North East	PA	16428	**800-356-2211**	814-725-9621	309
Electric Power Door	522 W 27th St	Hibbing	MN	55746	**800-346-5760**	218-263-8366	236
Electric Regulator Corp	6189 El Camino Real	Carlsbad	CA	92009	**800-458-6566**	760-438-7873	205
Electric Research & Mfg Co-op Inc	PO Box 1228	Dyersburg	TN	38025	**800-238-5587**	731-285-9121	765
Electric Supply & Equipment Co	1812 E Wendover Ave	Greensboro	NC	27405	**800-632-0268**	336-272-4123	248
Electric Supply Inc	4407 N Manhattan Ave	Tampa	FL	33614	**800-678-1894**	813-872-1894	248
Electric Utility Week	2 Penn Plz 25th Fl	New York	NY	10121	**800-752-8878**	212-904-3070	530-5
Electrical Distributing Inc	4600 NW St Helens Rd	Portland	OR	97210	**800-877-4229**	503-226-4044	37
Electri-Cord Mfg Co Inc	312 E Main St	Westfield	PA	16950	**888-278-8253**	814-367-2265	813
Electri-Flex Co	222 Central Ave	Roselle	IL	60172	**800-323-6174**	630-529-2920	814
Electro Brand Inc	1127 S Mannheim Rd Ste 305	Westchester	IL	60154	**800-982-3954**	708-338-4400	248
Electro Enterprises Inc	3601 N I-35 Service Rd	Oklahoma City	OK	73111	**800-324-6591**	405-427-6591	56
Electro Rent Corp	6060 Sepulveda Blvd *NASDAQ: ELRC* ■ *Sales	Van Nuys	CA	91411	**800-688-1111***	818-787-2100	266-1
Electro Scientific Industries Inc	13900 NW Science Pk Dr *NASDAQ: ESIO* ■ *Cust Svc	Portland	OR	97229	**800-331-4708***	503-641-4141	425
Electro Standards Laboratories Inc	36 Western Industrial Dr	Cranston	RI	02921	**877-943-1164**	401-943-1164	732
Electro Static Technology	31 Winterbrook Rd	Mechanic Falls	ME	04256	**866-738-1857**	207-998-5140	636
Electro Steam Generator Corp	50 Indel Ave PO Box 438	Rancocas	NJ	08073	**866-617-0764**	609-288-9071	264
Electrocon International Inc	405 Little Lk Dr	Ann Arbor	MI	48103	**888-240-4044**	734-761-8612	179
Electrocube Inc	3366 Pomona Blvd	Pomona	CA	91768	**800-515-1112**	909-595-4037	255
Electro-Flex Heat Inc	5 Northwood Rd	Bloomfield	CT	06002	**800-585-4213**	860-242-6287	357
Electrolux Appliances	PO Box 212237	Augusta	GA	30907	**877-435-3287**		35
Electrolux Home Care Products Inc	PO Box 3900 *Cust Svc	Peoria	IL	61612	**800-282-2886***		786
Electro-Matic Products Inc	23409 Industrial Pk Ct	Farmington Hills	MI	48335	**888-879-1088**	248-478-1182	248
Electro-Motive Diesel Inc	9301 W 55th St	La Grange	IL	60525	**800-255-5355**	708-387-6000	648
Electron Energy Corp	924 Links Ave	Landisville	PA	17538	**800-824-2735**	717-898-2294	457
Electronic Cash Systems Inc (ECS)	30352 Esperanza	Rancho Santa Margarita	CA	92688	**888-327-2860**	949-888-8580	55
Electronic Commerce & Law Report	1801 S Bell St	Arlington	VA	22202	**800-372-1033**		530-1
Electronic Component News	100 Enterprise Dr Ste 600	Rockaway	NJ	07866	**877-650-5160**	973-920-7000	456-21
Electronic Contracting Co	6501 N 70th St	Lincoln	NE	68507	**800-366-5320**	402-466-8274	191-4
Electronic Environments Corp	410 Forest St	Marlborough	MA	01752	**800-342-5332**	508-229-1400	176
Electronic Security Assn Inc (ESA)	2300 Vly View Ln Ste 230	Irving	TX	75062	**888-447-1689**	214-260-5970	48-3
Electronic Tele-Communications Inc	1915 MacArthur Rd *OTC: ETCIA*	Waukesha	WI	53188	**888-746-4382**	262-542-5600	732
Electronic Theatre Controls Inc	3031 Pleasantview Rd	Middleton	WI	53562	**800-688-4116**	608-831-4116	205
Electronic Transactions Association, The	1101 16th St NW Ste 402	Washington	DC	20036	**800-695-5509**	202-828-2635	136
Electronic Warfare Assoc Inc (EWA Inc)	13873 Pk Ctr Rd Ste 500 *General	Herndon	VA	20171	**888-392-0002***	703-904-5700	182
Electronics for Imaging Inc	303 Velocity Way *NASDAQ: EFII*	Foster City	CA	94404	**888-334-8650**	650-357-3500	178
Electronics Technicians Assn International (ETA)	5 Depot St	Greencastle	IN	46135	**800-288-3824**	765-653-8262	48-19
Electro-Sensors Inc	6111 Blue Cir Dr *NASDAQ: ELSE*	Minnetonka	MN	55343	**800-328-6170**	952-930-0100	494
Electrosonics	17150 15 Mile Rd	Fraser	MI	48026	**800-858-8448**	586-415-5555	177
Electroswitch	2010 Yonkers Rd	Raleigh	NC	27604	**888-768-2797**	919-833-0707	813
ElectroTech Inc	7101 Madison Ave W	Minneapolis	MN	55427	**800-544-4288**	763-544-4288	248
Electrovaya Inc	2645 Royal Windsor Dr *TSE: EFL*	Mississauga	ON	L5J1K9	**800-388-2865**	905-855-4610	175-1
Elegant Voyages	1802 Keesling Ct	San Jose	CA	95125	**800-555-3534**	408-239-0300	769
Elektrisola Inc	126 High St	Boscawen	NH	03303	**800-325-2022**	603-796-2114	811
Elementis Specialties Inc	469 Old Trenton Rd	East Windsor	NJ	08512	**800-866-6800**		142
Elenbaas Co	411 W Front St	Sumas	WA	98295	**800-808-6954**	360-988-5811	446
Elenco Electronics Inc	150 W Carpenter Ave	Wheeling	IL	60090	**800-533-2441**	847-541-3800	244
Eleni's	75 Ninth Ave	New York	NY	10011	**888-435-3647**		67
Elevating Boats LLC	201 Dean Ct	Houma	LA	70363	**800-843-2895**	985-868-9655	696
Elevator Equipment Corp	4035 Goodwin Ave	Los Angeles	CA	90039	**888-577-3326**	323-245-0147	258
ELF Fastening Systems Inc	29019 Solon Rd	Solon	OH	44139	**800-248-2376**	440-248-8655	280
Elgin Area Chamber of Commerce	31 S Grove Ave	Elgin	IL	60120	**800-621-3362**	847-741-5660	138
Elgin Area Convention & Visitors Bureau	60 S Grove Ave	Elgin	IL	60120	**800-217-5362**	847-695-7540	208
Elgin Community College	1700 Spartan Dr	Elgin	IL	60123	**855-850-2525**	847-697-1000	161
Elgin Molded Plastics	909 Grace St	Elgin	IL	60120	**800-548-5483**	847-931-2455	603
ELI (Environmental Law Institute)	2000 L St NW Ste 620	Washington	DC	20036	**800-433-5120**	202-939-3800	48-10
ELI Inc	2675 Paces Ferry Rd Se Ste 470	Atlanta	GA	30339	**800-497-7654**	770-319-7999	198

Name / Address	City	ST	ZIP	Toll-Free	Phone	Class
Eli Lilly & Co Lilly Corporate Ctr *NYSE: LLY* ■ *Prod Info	Indianapolis	IN	46285	**800-545-5979***	317-276-2000	582
Eli Lilly Canada Inc 3650 Danforth Ave	Toronto	ON	M1N2E8	**888-545-5972**	416-694-3221	582
Eli's Cheesecake Co 6701 W Forest Preserve Dr	Chicago	IL	60634	**800-999-8300**	773-736-3417	297-2
Eliason Corp 9229 Shaver Rd *Cust Svc	Portage	MI	49024	**800-828-3655***	269-327-7003	662
Elim Christian School 13020 S Central Ave	Palos Heights	IL	60463	**877-935-4627**	708-389-0555	683
Elim Park Place 140 Cook Hill Rd	Cheshire	CT	06410	**800-994-1776**	203-272-3547	670
Eliot Hotel, The 370 Commonwealth Ave	Boston	MA	02215	**800-443-5468**	617-267-1607	379
Eliot Rose Asset Management LLC 1000 Chapel View Blvd Ste 240	Cranston	RI	02920	**866-585-5100**	401-588-5100	401
Elisa Act Biotechnologies 109 Carpenter Dr	Sterling	VA	20165	**800-553-5472**		415
Elisabet Ney Museum 304 E 44th St	Austin	TX	78751	**800-680-7289**	512-458-2255	519
Elite Business Services PO Box 9630	Rancho Santa Fe	CA	92067	**800-204-3548**		763
Elite Coach 1685 W Main St	Ephrata	PA	17522	**800-722-6206**	717-733-7710	106
Elite Limousine Service Inc 1059 12th Ave Ste E	Honolulu	HI	96816	**800-776-2098**	808-735-2431	441
Elite Sportswear LP 2136 N 13th St *Cust Svc	Reading	PA	19604	**800-345-4087***	610-921-1469	154-1
Elitexpo Cargo Systems 845 Commerce Dr	South Elgin	IL	60177	**800-543-5484**		462
Elixir Industries Inc 24800 Chrisanta Dr Ste 210	Mission Viejo	CA	92691	**800-421-1942**	949-860-5000	236
Elizabeth Arden Inc 2400 NE 145th Ave 2nd Fl *NASDAQ: RDEN*	Miramar	FL	33027	**800-326-7337**	954-364-6900	573
Elizabeth Arden Red Door Spa at Mystic Marriott Hotel & Spa 625 N Rd	Groton	CT	06340	**866-449-7390**	860-446-2500	705
Elizabeth City State University 1704 Weeksville Rd *Admissions	Elizabeth City	NC	27909	**800-347-3278***	252-335-3400	167
Elizabeth Glaser Pediatric AIDS Foundation 1140 Connecticut Ave NW Ste 200	Washington	DC	20036	**888-499-4673**	202-296-9165	47-17
Elizabeth Hospice 150 W Crest St	Escondido	CA	92025	**800-797-2050**	760-737-2050	371
Elizabethtown Community & Technical College 600 College St Rd	Elizabethtown	KY	42701	**877-246-2322**	270-769-2371	161
Elizabethtown Gas Co 1 Elizabethtown Plz	Union	NJ	07083	**800-242-5830**	908-289-5000	785
Eljer Inc 1 Centennial Ave	Piscataway	NJ	08855	**800-442-1902**		610
Elk Country Inn 480 W Pearl St PO Box 1255	Jackson	WY	83001	**800-483-8667**	307-733-2364	379
Elk County PO Box 606	Howard	KS	67349	**877-504-2490**	620-374-2490	338
Elk Environmental Services 1420 Clarion St	Reading	PA	19601	**800-851-7156**	610-372-4760	198
Elk Grove Village Public Library 1001 Wellington Ave	Elk Grove Village	IL	60007	**800-252-8980**	847-439-0447	434-3
ELK Lighting Creativity 12 Willow Ln	Nesquehoning	PA	18240	**800-613-3261**		439
Elk Lighting Inc 12 Willow Lane	Nesquehoning	PA	18240	**866-283-1953**		439
Elk Mountain Ranch PO Box 910	Buena Vista	CO	81211	**800-432-8812**		241
ELK Products Inc 3266 Us 70 W	Connelly Springs	NC	28612	**800-797-9355**	828-397-4200	690
Elk River Systems Inc 777 E Main Ste 108	Bozeman	MT	59715	**888-771-0809**	406-632-4763	176
Elk Valley Rancheria 2332 Howland Hill Rd	Crescent City	CA	95531	**866-464-4680**	707-464-4680	706
Elkhart County Convention & Visitors Bureau 219 Caravan Dr	Elkhart	IN	46514	**800-262-8161**	574-262-8161	208
Elkhart Products Corp 1255 Oak St	Elkhart	IN	46514	**800-284-4851**	574-264-3181	594
Elkhorn Rural Public Power District 206 N Fourth St	Battle Creek	NE	68715	**800-675-2185**	402-675-2185	247
Elkins Constructors Inc 6104 S Gazebo Pk	Jacksonville	FL	32257	**800-772-1213**	904-353-6500	190-10
Elko Convention & Visitors Authority 700 Moren Way	Elko	NV	89801	**800-248-3556**	775-738-4091	207
Elks Magazine 2750 N Lakeview Ave	Chicago	IL	60614	**800-892-8384**	773-755-4700	456-10
Elle Magazine 1633 Broadway 44th Fl	New York	NY	10019	**800-876-8775**	212-903-5000	456-11
Ellenton Premium Outlets 5461 Factory Shops Blvd	Ellenton	FL	34222	**888-267-2121**	941-723-1150	459
Ellery Queen Mystery Magazine (EQMM) 267 Broadway 4th Fl	New York	NY	10007	**800-220-7443**		456-11
Ellie Fashion Group Inc 1447 Second St 3rd Fl	Santa Monica	CA	90401	**888-926-9615**		688
Ellie Mae Inc 4155 Hopyard Rd Ste 200	Pleasanton	CA	94588	**800-848-4904**	925-227-7000	179
Elliot Hospital 1 Elliot Way Ste 100	Manchester	NH	03103	**800-922-4999**	603-627-1669	374-3
Elliott & Frantz Inc 450 E Church Rd	King Of Prussia	PA	19406	**800-220-3025**	610-279-5200	358
Elliott Aviation Inc 6601 74th Ave PO Box 100	Milan	IL	61264	**800-447-6711**	309-799-3183	24
Elliott Bay Book Co 101 S Main St	Seattle	WA	98104	**800-962-5311**	206-624-6600	95
Elliott Company of Indianapolis Inc 9200 Zionsville Rd *Orders	Indianapolis	IN	46268	**800-545-1213***	317-291-1213	600
Elliott Davis Decosimo LLC 629 Market St Ste 100	Chattanooga	TN	37402	**800-782-8382**	423-756-7100	2
Elliott Davis LLC 200 E Broad St PO Box 6286	Greenville	SC	29606	**800-503-4721**	864-242-3370	2
Elliott Electric Supply Co 2526 N Stallings Dr PO Box 630610	Nacogdoches	TX	75963	**877-777-0242**	936-569-1184	248
Elliott Group 901 N Fourth St	Jeannette	PA	15644	**800-635-2208**	724-527-2811	174
Elliott Machine Works Inc 1351 Freese Works Pl	Galion	OH	44833	**800-299-0412**	419-468-4709	515
Elliott Wave International (EWI) PO Box 1618 *Cust Svc	Gainesville	GA	30503	**800-336-1618***	770-536-0309	634-9
Elliott Wave Theorist PO Box 1618	Gainesville	GA	30503	**800-336-1618**	770-536-0309	530-9
Elliott, Ostrander & Preston PC Union Bank Tower 707 SW Washington St Ste 1500	Portland	OR	97205	**866-716-3410**	503-224-7112	428
Ellis & Associates Inc 7064 Davis Creek Rd	Jacksonville	FL	32256	**800-273-0960**	904-880-0960	740
Ellis Coffee Co 2835 Bridge St	Philadelphia	PA	19137	**800-822-3984**	215-537-9500	298-11
Ellis Corp 1400 W Bryn Mawr Ave	Itasca	IL	60143	**800-611-6806**	630-250-9222	427
Ellis Ged & Bodden pa 7171 N Federal Hwy	Boca Raton	FL	33487	**888-342-3476**	561-995-1966	428
Ellis Management Services Inc 4324 N Beltine Rd	Irving	TX	75038	**888-988-3767**	972-256-3767	198
Ellmaker State Wayside 198 NE 123rd St	Newport	OR	97365	**800-551-6949**		564
Ellsworth Community College 1100 College Ave	Iowa Falls	IA	50126	**800-322-9235**	641-648-4611	161
Ellsworth Corp PO Box 1002	Germantown	WI	53022	**877-454-9224**	262-253-8600	145
Ellucian 4375 Fair Lakes Ct	Fairfax	VA	22033	**800-223-7036**	610-647-5930	180-10
Ellwood City Forge 800 Commercial Ave	Ellwood City	PA	16117	**800-843-0166**	724-752-0055	482
Elm Chevrolet Co Inc 301 E Church St	Elmira	NY	14901	**877-265-6708**	607-734-4141	56
ELM Resources 12950 Race Track Rd Ste 201	Tampa	FL	33626	**866-524-8198**		387
Elmer's Products Inc 1 Easton Oval	Columbus	OH	43219	**888-435-6377**		3
Elmet Technologies Inc 1560 Lisbon St	Lewiston	ME	04240	**800-343-8008**	207-333-6100	484
Elmhurst College 190 Prospect Ave	Elmhurst	IL	60126	**800-697-1871**	630-617-3400	167
Elmhurst Mutual Power & Light Co 120 132nd St S	Tacoma	WA	98444	**855-841-2178**	253-531-4646	247
Elmira College 1 Pk Pl *Admissions	Elmira	NY	14901	**800-935-6472***	607-735-1724	167
Elmira Psychiatric Ctr 100 Washington St	Elmira	NY	14901	**800-597-8481**	607-737-4711	374-5
Elmira Savings Bank 333 E Water St *NASDAQ: ESBK*	Elmira	NY	14901	**888-372-9299**	607-734-3374	69
ELMS College 291 Springfield St *Admissions	Chicopee	MA	01013	**800-255-3567***	413-592-3189	167
Elmwood Park Zoo 1661 Harding Blvd	Norristown	PA	19401	**800-652-4143**	610-277-3825	821
Elo TouchSystems Inc 301 Constitution Dr	Menlo Park	CA	94025	**800-557-1458**	650-361-4700	175-2
eLocal Listing LLC 28765 Single Oak Dr Ste 250	Temecula	CA	92590	**800-285-0484**		5
Elon University 100 Campus Dr	Elon	NC	27244	**800-334-8448**	336-278-2000	167
ELS Marketing Inc 3133 Orlando Dr	Mississauga	ON	L4V1C5	**877-612-2673**	905-612-1060	5
Elsevier Science Ltd 360 Pk Ave S	New York	NY	10010	**888-437-4636**	212-989-5800	634-9
Elster American Meter Co 2221 Industrial Rd	Nebraska City	NE	68410	**877-595-6254**	402-873-8200	494
Elte 80 Ronald Ave	Toronto	ON	M6E5A2	**888-276-3583**	416-785-7885	292
Elvis Presley Enterprises Inc 3734 Elvis Presley Blvd	Memphis	TN	38116	**800-238-2000**	901-332-3322	360-3
Elvis Presley's Heartbreak Hotel 3677 Elvis Presley Blvd	Memphis	TN	38116	**877-777-0606**	901-332-1000	379
Elward Construction Co 680 Harlan St	Lakewood	CO	80214	**800-933-5339**	303-239-6303	191-1
Elwood Corp High Performance Motors Group 2701 N Green Bay Rd	Racine	WI	53404	**800-558-9489**	262-637-6591	517
Elyria Mfg Corp 145 Northrup St PO Box 479	Elyria	OH	44035	**866-365-4171**	440-365-4171	620
Elzinga & Volkers 86 E Sixth St *General	Holland	MI	49423	**800-632-7734***	616-392-2383	683
Ema Brokerage LLC 1300 Rt 73 Ste 306	Mount Laurel	NJ	08054	**855-267-5867**	856-216-0211	688
eMag Solutions LLC 1120 Sanctuary Pkwy Ste 275	Alpharetta	GA	30305	**844-252-0113**	404-995-6060	180-12
Email Co, The 15 Kainona Ave	Toronto	ON	M3H3H4	**877-933-6245**		366
E-Markets Inc 807 Mountain Ave Ste 200	Berthoud	CO	80513	**877-674-7419**		38
Embassy Hotel & Suites 25 Cartier St	Ottawa	ON	K2P1J2	**800-661-5495**	613-237-2111	379
EmblemHealth Co 55 Water St	New York	NY	10041	**800-447-8255**	646-447-5000	391-3
EmbroidMe Inc 2121 Vista Pkwy	West Palm Beach	FL	33411	**877-877-0234**	561-640-7367	311
Embryotech Laboratories Inc 140 Hale St	Haverhill	MA	01830	**800-673-7500**	978-373-7300	740
Embry-Riddle Aeronautical University *Daytona Beach* 600 S Clyde Morris Blvd	Daytona Beach	FL	32114	**800-862-2416**	386-226-6000	167
Embry-Riddle Aeronautical University Prescott 3700 Willow Creek Rd	Prescott	AZ	86301	**800-888-3728**	928-777-3728	167

Alphabetical Section

Listing	City	State	ZIP	Toll-Free	Phone	Class
EMC (Grady Electric Membership Corp)						
1499 US Hwy 84 W	Cairo	GA	39828	**877-757-6060**	229-377-4182	247
EMC (IEEE Electromagnetic Compatibility Society)						
IEEE Operations Ctr 445 Hoes Ln	Piscataway	NJ	08854	**800-678-4333**	732-981-0060	48-19
EMC (Equipment Manufacturing Corp)						
14930 Marquardt Ave	Santa Fe Springs	CA	90670	**888-833-9000**	562-623-9394	386
EMC Corp						
2831 Mission College Blvd	Santa Clara	CA	95054	**877-534-2867***	408-566-2000	180-12
*Tech Supp						
EMC Corporation of Canada						
120 Adelaide St W 14th Fl Ste 1400	Toronto	ON	M5H1T1	**800-858-1410**	416-628-5973	387
EMC Insurance Group Inc						
717 Mulberry St	Des Moines	IA	50309	**800-447-2295**	515-280-2511	360-4
NASDAQ: EMCI						
EMCOR Group Inc						
301 Merritt 7 6th Fl	Norwalk	CT	06851	**866-890-7794**	203-849-7800	191-4
NYSE: EME						
EMCOR Services Betlem						
704 Clinton Ave South	Rochester	NY	14620	**800-423-8536**	585-271-5500	263
EMC-Paradigm Publishing Co						
875 Montreal Way	Saint Paul	MN	55102	**800-328-1452**	651-290-2800	634-2
EMD Serono Inc						
1 Technology Pl	Rockland	MA	02370	**800-283-8088**	781-982-9000	84
Emeco 805 W Elm Ave	Hanover	PA	17331	**800-366-5951**	717-637-5951	320-1
eMedia Music Corp						
664 NE Northlake Way	Seattle	WA	98105	**888-363-3424**	206-329-5657	182
eMedicine.com Inc						
8420 W Dodge Rd Ste 402	Omaha	NE	68114	**866-241-9601**	402-341-3222	356
Emerald City Graphics						
23328 66th Ave S	Kent	WA	98032	**877-631-5178***	253-520-2600	626
*General						
Emerald Downs						
2300 Emerald Downs Dr PO Box 617	Auburn	WA	98001	**888-931-8400**	253-288-7000	132
Emerald Kalama Chemical LLC						
1296 Third St NW	Kalama	WA	98625	**877-300-9545**	360-673-2550	297-15
Emerald Queen Casino (EQC)						
2024 E 29th St	Tacoma	WA	98404	**888-831-7655**	253-594-7777	132
Emerald Queen Hotel & Casino						
5700 Pacific Hwy E	Fife	WA	98424	**888-820-3555**	253-922-2000	379
Emerge Financial Wellness Inc						
530 Church St Ste 301	Nashville	TN	37219	**800-791-1725**		262
Emergency Ambulance Service International Inc						
3200 E Birch St Ste A	Brea	CA	92821	**800-400-0689**	714-990-1331	30
Emergency Nurses Assn (ENA)						
915 Lee St	Des Plaines	IL	60016	**800-900-9659**	847-460-4000	48-8
Emerson Climate Technologies - Retail Solutions						
1065 Big Shanty Rd NW Ste 100	Kennesaw	GA	30144	**800-829-2724**	770-425-2724	204
Emerson College						
10 Boylston Pl	Boston	MA	02116	**888-627-7115**	617-824-8500	167
Emerson Industrial Automation						
8000 W Florissant Ave PO Box 4100	St Louis	MO	63136	**888-213-0970**	952-995-8000	707
Emerson Network Power Connectivity Solutions						
1050 Dearborn Dr	Columbus	OH	43085	**800-275-3500**	614-888-0246	255
Emerson Process Management CSI						
835 Innovation Dr	Knoxville	TN	37932	**800-675-4726**	865-675-2110	471
Emerson Resort & Spa						
5340 Rt 28	Mount Tremper	NY	12457	**877-688-2828**	845-688-2828	379
Emerson Thomson & Bennett LLC						
1914 Akron Peninsula Rd	Akron	OH	44313	**800-822-8113**	330-434-9999	428
Emerson-Swan Inc						
300 Pond St	Randolph	MA	02368	**800-346-9219**	781-986-2000	611
Emery & Webb Inc						
989 Main St	Fishkill	NY	12524	**800-942-5818**	845-896-6727	390
Emery Air Charter Inc						
1 Airport Cir	Rockford	IL	61109	**800-435-8090**	815-968-8287	188
Emery Corp						
PO Box 1104	Morganton	NC	28680	**800-255-0537**	828-433-1536	455
Emery Winslow Scale Co						
73 Cogwheel Ln	Seymour	CT	06483	**800-891-3952**	203-881-9333	682
EMF Corp						
505 Pokagon Trl	Angola	IN	46703	**800-847-2818**	260-665-9541	255
Emf Inc 60 Foundry St	Keene	NH	03431	**800-992-3003**	603-352-8400	177
EMHS (Eastern Maine Healthcare Systems)						
43 Whiting Hill Rd	Brewer	ME	04412	**844-364-4473**	207-973-7050	353
Emily Morgan Hotel						
705 E Houston St	San Antonio	TX	78205	**800-824-6674**	210-225-5100	379
EMILY's List						
1800 M St NW Ste 375N	Washington	DC	20036	**800-683-6459**	202-326-1400	47-7
Eminence Speaker LLC						
838 Mulberry Pike PO Box 360	Eminence	KY	40019	**800-897-8373**	502-845-5622	51
EMK Consultants of Florida Inc						
7815 N Dale Mabry Hwy	Tampa	FL	33614	**800-347-2607**	813-931-8900	263
Emkay Inc						
805 W Thorndale Ave	Itasca	IL	60143	**800-621-2001**	630-250-7400	291
EMKF (Ewing Marion Kauffman Foundation)						
4801 Rockhill Rd	Kansas City	MO	64110	**800-385-1607**	816-932-1000	306
EMM (Episcopal Migration Ministries)						
815 Second Ave	New York	NY	10017	**800-334-7626**	212-716-6258	47-5
Emmanuel College						
181 Spring St	Franklin Springs	GA	30639	**800-860-8800**	706-245-7226	167
Emmaus Bible College						
2570 Asbury Rd	Dubuque	IA	52001	**800-397-2425**	563-588-8000	160
Emme E2MS LLC						
PO Box 2251	Bristol	CT	06011	**800-396-0523**		407
Emmet County						
200 Div St Ste 130	Petoskey	MI	49770	**866-731-1204**	231-348-1702	338
Emory & Henry College						
PO Box 10	Emory	VA	24327	**800-848-5493***	276-944-4121	167
*Admissions						
Emory Conference Ctr Hotel						
1615 Clifton Rd	Atlanta	GA	30329	**800-933-6679**	404-712-6000	377
Emory University						
201 Dowman Dr	Atlanta	GA	30322	**800-727-6036***	404-727-6036	167
*Admissions						
Emory University Oxford College						
201 Dowman Dr PO Box 1418	Atlanta	GA	30322	**800-723-8328**	404-727-6069	161

Listing	City	State	ZIP	Toll-Free	Phone	Class
Empire Bakery Equipment						
171 Greenwich St	Hempstead	NY	11550	**800-878-4070**	516-538-1210	453
Empire Bldg Materials Inc						
PO Box 220	Bozeman	MT	59771	**800-332-4577**	800-548-8201	193-2
Empire Building Services						
1570 E Edinger Ave	Santa Ana	CA	92705	**888-296-2078**	714-836-7700	136
Empire Comfort Systems Inc						
918 Freeburg Ave	Belleville	IL	62222	**800-851-3153**	618-233-7420	357
Empire Diamond Corp						
350 Fifth Ave Ste 4000	New York	NY	10118	**800-728-3425**	212-564-4777	411
Empire District Electric Co, The						
602 Joplin St PO Box 127	Joplin	MO	64802	**800-206-2300**	417-625-5100	785
NYSE: EDE						
Empire Electric Assn Inc						
801 N Broadway	Cortez	CO	81321	**800-709-3726**	970-565-4444	247
Empire Industries Inc						
180 Olcott St	Manchester	CT	06040	**800-243-4844**	860-647-1431	594
Empire Landmark Hotel & Conference Centre						
1400 Robson St	Vancouver	BC	V6G1B9	**800-830-6144**	604-687-0511	379
Empire Level Manufacturing Corp						
929 Empire Dr PO Box 800	Mukwonago	WI	53149	**800-558-0722**		756
Empire Livestock Marketing LLC						
5001 Brittonfield Pkwy	East Syracuse	NY	13057	**800-462-8802**	315-433-9129	445
Empire Safety & Supply Inc						
10624 Industrial Ave	Roseville	CA	95678	**800-995-1341**	916-781-3003	677
Empire Southwest Co						
1725 S Country Club Dr	Mesa	AZ	85210	**800-367-4731**	480-633-4000	358
Empire State Bldg						
350 Fifth Ave Ste 100	New York	NY	10118	**877-692-8439**	212-736-3100	49-3
Empire Telephone Corp						
34 Main St PO Box 349	Prattsburgh	NY	14873	**800-338-3300**	607-522-3712	733
Empire Vision Centers						
2921 Erie Blvd E	Syracuse	NY	13224	**877-959-4160**	315-446-5120	542
Empire West Inc						
9270 Graton Rd PO Box 511	Graton	CA	95444	**800-521-4261**	707-823-1190	601
EmpireWorks Inc						
1940 Olivera Rd.	Concord	CA	94520	**888-278-8200**		262
EmplawyerNet						
2331 Westwood Blvd	Los Angeles	CA	90064	**800-270-2688**		262
Employee Development Systems Inc						
7308 S Alton Way Ste 2J	Centennial	CO	80112	**800-282-3374**	303-221-0710	181
Employee Management Services						
435 Elm St	Cincinnati	OH	45202	**888-651-1536**	513-651-3244	630
Employer Flexible						
7850 N Sam Houston Parkway W Ste 100	Houston	TX	77064	**866-501-4942**		731
Employers Insurance Company of Nevada						
9790 Gateway Dr Ste 100	Reno	NV	89521	**888-682-6671**		390
Employers Resource Management Co						
1301 S Vista Ave Ste 200	Boise	ID	83705	**800-574-4668**	208-376-3000	569
Employment & Training Administration						
200 Constitution Ave NW	Washington	DC	20210	**866-487-2365**		340-13
Employment & Training Administration Regional Offices						
Region 3- Atlanta						
Federal Ctr 61 Forsyth St SW Rm 6M12	Atlanta	GA	20210	**877-872-5627**		340-13
Employment Discrimination Report						
1801 S Bell St	Arlington	VA	22202	**800-372-1033**		530-7
Employment Screening Services Inc						
627 E Sprague St Ste 100	Spokane	WA	99202	**800-473-7778**	509-624-3851	632
Employment Standards Administration						
200 Constitution Ave NW Rm S2321	Washington	DC	20210	**866-487-2365**	202-693-0200	340-13
Office of Labor-Management Standards (OLMS)						
200 Constitution Ave NW Rm N-1519	Washington	DC	20210	**866-487-2365**		340-13
EmploymentGuide.com						
150 Granby St	Norfolk	VA	23510	**877-876-4039**		262
Emporia Area Chamber of Commerce						
719 Commercial St	Emporia	KS	66801	**800-279-3730**	620-342-1600	138
Emporia State University						
1200 Commercial St	Emporia	KS	66801	**877-468-6378**	620-341-1200	167
Empress Software Inc						
11785 Beltsville Dr	Beltsville	MD	20705	**866-626-8888**	301-220-1919	180-2
Emprise Financial Corp						
257 N Broadway St PO Box 2970	Wichita	KS	67202	**800-201-7118***	316-383-4301	68
*Cust Svc						
EmpXtrack						
150 Motor Parkway Ste 401	Hauppauge	NY	11788	**888-840-2682**		40
Empyre Media						
1150 N Carroll Ave	Southlake	TX	76092	**866-996-9893**		5
EMS (IEEE Engineering Management Society)						
IEEE Operations Ctr 445 Hoes Ln	Piscataway	NJ	08854	**800-678-4333**	732-981-0060	48-19
EMSD (East Maine School District 63)						
10150 Dee Rd	Des Plaines	IL	60016	**866-752-6850**	847-299-1900	683
Ems-tech Inc						
699 Dundas St W	Belleville	ON	K8N4Z2	**844-450-8324**	613-966-6611	258
Emtek Products Inc						
15250 Stafford St	City of Industry	CA	91744	**800-356-2741**	626-961-0413	350
Emteq Inc						
5349 S Emmer Dr	New Berlin	WI	53151	**888-679-6170**	262-679-6170	24
Emulation Technology Inc						
759 Flynn Rd	Camarillo	CA	93012	**800-232-7837**	805-383-8480	203
ENA (Emergency Nurses Assn)						
915 Lee St	Des Plaines	IL	60016	**800-900-9659**	847-460-4000	48-8
Enbase LLC						
3303 Louisiana St Ste 210	Houston	TX	77006	**888-400-2719**		537
Enbridge Energy Partners LP						
1100 Louisiana Ste 3300	Houston	TX	77002	**800-481-2804**	713-821-2000	596
NYSE: EEP						
EnCana Corp						
500 Ctr St SE Po Box 2850	Calgary	AB	T2G1A6	**888-568-6322**	403-645-2000	535
NYSE: ECA						
Enchantment Resort						
525 Boynton Canyon Rd	Sedona	AZ	86336	**800-826-4180**		667
Encinitas Chamber of Commerce						
527 Encinitas Blvd	Encinitas	CA	92024	**800-953-6041**	760-753-6041	138

Company / Address	City	State	ZIP	Toll-Free	Phone	Class
Encision Inc 6797 Winchester Cir *OTC: ECIA*	Boulder	CO	80301	**800-998-0986**	303-444-2600	475
Enclave Suites of Orlando 6165 Carrier Dr	Orlando	FL	32819	**800-457-0077**	407-351-1155	379
Enclos Corp 2770 Blue Water Rd	Eagan	MN	55121	**888-234-2966**	651-796-6100	191-6
Encoder Products Co 464276 Hwy 95 S PO Box 249	Sagle	ID	83860	**800-366-5412**	208-263-8541	203
Encompass Group LLC 615 Macon Rd	McDonough	GA	30253	**800-284-4540**	770-957-1211	154-18
Encon Group Inc 500-1400 Blair Pl	Ottawa	ON	K1J9B8	**800-267-6684**	613-786-2000	390
Encon Safety Products Co 6825 W Sam Houston Pkwy N PO Box 3826	Houston	TX	77041	**800-283-6266**	713-466-1449	676
Encore Bank 3003 Tamiami Trail N Ste 100	Naples	FL	34103	**800-472-3272**	239-919-5888	69
Encore Capital Group Inc 3111 Camino Del Rio N Ste 300 *NASDAQ: ECPG*	San Diego	CA	92108	**877-445-4581**	858-560-2600	159
Encore Manufacturing Company Inc 2415 Ashland Ave	Beatrice	NE	68310	**800-267-4255**		429
Encore Medical Corp 9800 Metric Blvd	Austin	TX	78758	**800-456-8696**	512-832-9500	84
Encore Wire Corp 1329 Millwood Rd *NASDAQ: WIRE*	McKinney	TX	75069	**800-962-9473**	972-562-9473	811
Encyclopaedia Britannica Inc 331 N La Salle St	Chicago	IL	60654	**800-323-1229**	312-347-7159	634-2
Encyclopedia Britannica Inc 331 N Las Salle St *Cust Svc	Chicago	IL	60654	**800-323-1229***	312-347-7159	634-10
Enderes Tool Co 1103 Hershey St	Albert Lea	MN	56007	**800-874-7776**		756
Endevco Corp 30700 Rancho Viejo Rd	San Juan Capistrano	CA	92675	**800-982-6732**	949-493-8181	471
Endicott College 376 Hale St *Admissions	Beverly	MA	01915	**800-325-1114***	978-232-2021	167
Endo Pharmaceuticals Holdings Inc 100 Endo Blvd *Cust Svc	Chadds Ford	PA	19317	**800-462-3636***	610-558-9800	582
Endocrine Society 8401 Connecticut Ave Ste 900	Chevy Chase	MD	20815	**888-363-6274**	301-941-0200	48-8
Endologix Inc 11 Studebaker *NASDAQ: ELGX*	Irvine	CA	92618	**800-983-2284**	949-457-9546	475
Endometriosis Assn 8585 N 76th Pl	Milwaukee	WI	53223	**800-992-3636**	414-355-2200	47-17
Endot Industries Inc 60 Green Pond Rd	Rockaway	NJ	07866	**800-443-6368**	973-625-8500	595
Endotronix Inc 1005 Internationale Pkwy Ste 104	Woodridge	IL	60517	**877-363-6879**		740
Endress+Hauser Inc 2350 Endress Pl	Greenwood	IN	46143	**888-363-7377**	317-535-7138	203
Endries International Inc 714 W Ryan St PO Box 69	Brillion	WI	54110	**800-852-5821**	920-756-5381	385
Endura Products Inc 8817 W Market St	Colfax	NC	27235	**800-334-2006**	336-668-2472	238
Endurance Reinsurance Corp of America 750 Third Ave Fl 18 & 19	New York	NY	10017	**888-221-3894**	212-471-2800	391-4
Endurance Specialty Holdings Ltd 767 Third Ave 5th Fl *NYSE: ENH*	New York	NY	10017	**855-838-7792**	212-209-6500	390
Enduro Composites Inc 16602 Central Green Blvd	Houston	TX	77032	**800-231-7271**	713-358-4000	600
Eneflux Armtek Magnetics Inc 700 Hicksville Rd Ste 110	Bethpage	NY	11714	**877-363-3589**	516-576-3434	457
Enerac Inc 67 Bond St	Westbury	NY	11590	**800-695-3637**	516-997-2100	203
Enerbank USA Inc 1245 E Brickyard Rd Ste 600	Salt Lake City	UT	84106	**888-390-1220**		216
Enercon Engineering Inc 201 Altorfer Ln	East Peoria	IL	61611	**800-218-8831**	309-694-1418	205
Enerfab Inc 4955 Spring Grove Ave	Cincinnati	OH	45232	**800-772-5066**	513-641-0500	90
Enerflex Systems Ltd 1331 Macleod Trail SE Ste 904 *TSE: EFX*	Calgary	AB	T2G0K3	**800-242-3178**	403-387-6377	386
Ener-G Foods Inc 5960 First Ave S PO Box 84487	Seattle	WA	98124	**800-331-5222**	206-767-3928	297-36
Energen Corp 605 Richard Arrington Blvd N *NYSE: EGN*	Birmingham	AL	35203	**800-654-3206**	205-326-2700	360-5
Energy Alloys LLC 350 Glenborough Ste 300	Houston	TX	77067	**866-448-9831**	832-601-5800	489
Energy Concepts Inc 404 Washington Blvd	Mundelein	IL	60060	**800-621-1247**	847-837-8191	701
Energy Efficiency & Renewable Energy Information Ctr 1000 Independence Ave SW	Washington	DC	20585	**877-337-3463**	202-586-4849	199
Energy Focus Inc 32000 Aurora Rd *OTC: EFOI*	Solon	OH	44139	**800-327-7877**	440-715-1300	439
Energy Northwest 76 N Power Plant Loop	Richland	WA	99354	**800-468-6883**	509-372-5000	247
Energy Recovery Inc 1717 Doolittle Dr *NASDAQ: ERII*	San Leandro	CA	94577	**888-455-2263**	510-483-7370	804
Energy Transformation Systems Inc 43353 Osgood Rd	Fremont	CA	94539	**800-752-8208**	510-656-2012	765
Energy West Inc 1 First Ave S	Great Falls	MT	59401	**800-570-5688**	406-791-7500	785
EnergyExplorium 13339 Hagers Ferry Rd	Huntersville	NC	28078	**800-777-0003**	980-875-5600	519
EnergyUnited Electric Membership Corp PO Box 1831	Statesville	NC	28687	**800-522-3793**	704-873-5241	247
Enerpac PO Box 3241 *Cust Svc	Milwaukee	WI	53201	**800-433-2766***	262-293-1600	757
Enerplus Resources Fund 3000 Dome Tower 333 7th Ave SW Ste 3000	Calgary	AB	T2P2Z1	**800-319-6462**	403-298-2200	405
EnerSys 2366 Bernville Rd *NYSE: ENS*	Reading	PA	19605	**800-538-3627**	610-208-1991	73
EnerVision Inc 4170 Ashford Dunwoody Rd Ste 550	Atlanta	GA	30319	**888-999-8840**	678-510-2900	196
Enesco LLC 225 Windsor Dr	Itasca	IL	60143	**800-436-3726**	630-875-5300	334
Enflo Corp 315 Lake Ave	Bristol	CT	06010	**888-887-4093**	860-589-0014	599
Enforcer Products Inc PO Box 1060	Cartersville	GA	30120	**888-805-4357**		282
EngenderHealth 440 Ninth Ave 13th Fl	New York	NY	10001	**800-564-2872**	212-561-8000	47-17
Enghouse Systems Ltd 80 Tiverton Ct Ste 800 *TSE: ESL*	Markham	ON	L3R0G4	**866-206-0240**	905-946-3200	180-10
Engine Components Inc (ECI) 9503 Middlex	San Antonio	TX	78217	**800-324-2359**	210-820-8101	21
Engine Power Source Inc 348 Bryant Blvd	Rock Hill	SC	29732	**800-374-7522**	704-944-1999	517
Engineered Controls International Inc (ECII) 100 Rego Dr PO Box 247	Elon	NC	27244	**800-650-0061**	336-449-7707	787
Engineered Plastics Inc 211 Chase St	Gibsonville	NC	27249	**800-711-1740**	336-449-4121	601
Engineered Polymer Solutions Inc 1400 N State St	Marengo	IL	60152	**800-654-4242**		604-2
Engineered Polymers Corp (EPC) 1020 Maple Ave E	Mora	MN	55051	**800-388-2155**	320-679-3232	607
Engineered Products Co (EPCO) 601 Kelso St PO Box 108	Flint	MI	48506	**888-414-3726**	810-767-2050	350
Engineered Products Inc 500 Furman Hall Rd	Greenville	SC	29609	**888-301-1421**	864-234-4888	209
Engineered Protection Systems Inc 750 Front Ave NW	Grand Rapids	MI	49504	**800-966-9199**	616-459-0281	191-4
Engineered Storage Products Co 345 Harvestore Dr	DeKalb	IL	60115	**800-880-3663**	815-756-1551	90
Engineering & Environmental Consultants Inc 4625 E Ft Lowell Rd	Tucson	AZ	85712	**800-887-2103**	520-321-4625	263
Engineering Data Design Corp 105 Daventry Ln Ste 100	Louisville	KY	40223	**888-678-0683**	502-412-4000	258
Engineering News-Record (ENR) 350 fifth Ave Ste 6000	New York	NY	10118	**877-876-8208**	646-849-7100	456-21
Engineers Canada 180 Elgin St Ste 1100	Ottawa	ON	K2P2K3	**877-408-9273**	613-232-2474	47-1
Enginetech Inc 1205 W Crosby Rd	Carrollton	TX	75006	**800-869-8711**	972-245-0110	60
Engis Corp 105 W Hintz Rd	Wheeling	IL	60090	**800-993-6447**	847-808-9400	386
England Logistics Inc 1325 South 4700 West	Salt Lake City	UT	84104	**800-848-7810**	801-656-4500	196
Englander Northeast 12 Esquire Rd	North Billerica	MA	01862	**800-370-8700**		470
Englefield Oil Co 447 James Pkwy *Cust Svc	Heath	OH	43056	**800-837-4458***	740-928-8215	325
Englewood Electrical Supply 716 Belvedere Dr	Kokomo	IN	46901	**800-417-7543**	765-452-4087	248
Englewood Public Library 1000 Englewood Pkwy Englewood Civic Ctr 1st Fl	Englewood	CO	80110	**866-922-9006**	303-762-2560	434-3
Englewood-Cape Haze Area Chamber of Commerce 601 S Indiana Ave	Englewood	FL	34223	**800-603-7198**	941-474-5511	138
English Inn, The 677 S Michigan Rd	Eaton Rapids	MI	48827	**800-858-0598**	517-663-2500	669
Englund Marine & Industrial Supply Company Inc 95 Hamburg Ave PO Box 296	Astoria	OR	97103	**800-228-7051**	503-325-4341	223
Engman-Taylor Company Inc (ETCO) W142 N9351 Fountain Blvd	Menomonee Falls	WI	53051	**800-236-1975**	262-255-9300	385
Enhanced Software Products Inc 1811 N Hutchinson Rd	Spokane	WA	99212	**800-456-5750**	509-534-1514	227
Enid News & Eagle 227 W Broadway PO Box 3451	Enid	OK	73701	**800-299-6397**	580-548-8186	531-2
Enidine Inc 7 Centre Dr	Orchard Park	NY	14127	**800-852-8508**	716-662-1900	471
Enlisted Assn of the National Guard of the US (EANGUS) 3133 Mt Vernon Ave	Alexandria	VA	22305	**800-234-3264**	703-519-3846	47-19
Enloe Medical Ctr 1531 Esplanade	Chico	CA	95926	**800-822-8102**	530-332-7300	374-3
ENMAX Corp 141 50 Ave SE	Calgary	AB	T2G4S7	**877-571-7111**	403-514-3000	785
Ennis Inc PO Box D	Wolfe City	TX	75496	**800-527-1008**	972-775-9801	413
Enoch Manufacturing Co 14242 SE 82nd Dr	Clackamas	OR	97015	**888-659-2660**	503-659-2660	620
ENOCHS Examining Room Furniture PO Box 50559 *Cust Svc	Indianapolis	IN	46250	**800-428-2305***		320-3
Enor Corp 245 Livingston St	Northvale	NJ	07647	**800-977-6427**	201-750-1680	607
Enphase Energy Inc 1420 N Mcdowell Blvd	Petaluma	CA	94954	**877-797-4743**	707-763-4784	694
Enpro Inc 121 S LombaRd Rd	Addison	IL	60101	**800-323-2416**	630-629-3504	385
EnPro Industries Inc Fairbanks Morse Engine 701 White Ave	Beloit	WI	53511	**800-356-6955**		264
ENR (Engineering News-Record) 350 fifth Ave Ste 6000	New York	NY	10118	**877-876-8208**	646-849-7100	456-21
Ensave Energy Performance Inc 65 Millet St Ste 105	Richmond	VT	05477	**800-732-1399**		462

Name / Address	City	State	ZIP	Toll-Free	Phone	Class
ENSCO Inc						
3110 Fairview Pk Dr						
Ste 300	Falls Church	VA	22042	**800-367-2682**	703-321-9000	263
Ensearch Management Consultants						
905 E Cotati Ave	Cotati	CA	94931	**888-667-5627**		719
Ensemble Travel						
256 W 38th St 11th Fl	New York	NY	10018	**800-576-2378**	212-545-7460	770
Ensign Corp						
201 Ensign Rd	Bellevue	IA	52031	**888-797-8658**	563-872-3900	765
Ensinger Putnam Precision Molding						
11 Danco Rd	Putnam	CT	06260	**800-752-7865**	860-928-7911	603
Ent Federal Credit Union						
7250 Campus Dr	Colorado Springs	CO	80920	**800-525-9623**	719-574-1100	221
Entegee Inc						
70 BlanchaRd Rd Ste 102	Burlington	MA	01803	**800-368-3433**	781-221-5800	719
Entegris Inc						
129 Concord Rd Bldg 2	Billerica	MA	01821	**877-695-7654**	978-436-6500	693
NASDAQ: ENTG						
Entercom Communications Corp						
401 City Ave Ste 809	Bala Cynwyd	PA	19004	**800-776-9437**	610-660-5610	640
NYSE: ETM						
Enterey Inc						
9900 Irvine Ctr Dr Ste 100	Irvine	CA	92618	**800-691-2349**		462
Entergy Arkansas Inc						
425 W Capitol Ave	Little Rock	AR	72201	**800-368-3749**		785
Entergy Corp						
639 Loyola Ave	New Orleans	LA	70113	**800-368-3749**	504-576-4000	360-5
NYSE: ETR						
Entergy Louisiana Inc						
639 Loyola Ave	New Orleans	LA	70113	**800-368-3749***	504-576-6116	785
*Cust Svc						
Entergy New Orleans Inc						
639 Loyola Ave	New Orleans	LA	70113	**800-368-3749***		785
*Cust Svc						
Entergy Texas Inc						
350 Pine St	Beaumont	TX	77701	**800-368-3749**	409-981-3245	785
Entero Corp						
1040 Seventh Ave SW Ste 500	Calgary	AB	T2P3G9	**877-261-1820**	403-261-1820	179
Enterprise Bank of SC						
13497 Broxton Bridge Rd						
PO Box 8	Ehrhardt	SC	29081	**800-554-8969**	803-267-3191	69
Enterprise Community Partners Inc						
10227 Wincopin Cir	Columbia	MD	21044	**800-624-4298**	410-964-1230	47-5
Enterprise Financial Services Corp						
150 N Meramec Ave	Clayton	MO	63105	**800-396-8141**	314-725-5500	360-2
NASDAQ: EFSG						
Enterprise Rent-A-Car						
600 Corporate Pk Dr	Saint Louis	MO	63105	**844-377-0171**	314-512-5000	125
Enterprise Wireless Alliance (EWA)						
8484 Westpark Dr Ste 630	McLean	VA	22102	**800-482-8282**	703-528-5115	48-20
Enterprise-Ozark Community College						
1975 Ave C	Mobile	AL	36615	**877-701-0033**	251-438-2816	798
Entertainment Weekly Magazine						
1675 Broadway	New York	NY	10019	**800-828-6882**	212-522-5600	456-9
Enthermics Inc						
W164 N9221 Water St	Menomonee Falls	WI	53051	**800-862-9276**	262-251-8356	474
Enthone Inc						
350 Frontage Rd	West Haven	CT	06516	**800-431-2200**	203-934-8611	144
Entitle Direct Group Inc						
281 Tresser Blvd 6th Fl	Stamford	CT	06901	**877-936-8485**	203-724-1150	391-6
Entomological Society of America						
10001 Derekwood Ln Ste 100	Lanham	MD	20706	**800-523-8635**	301-731-4535	48-19
Entrepreneur Media Inc						
18061 Fitch	Irvine	CA	92614	**877-652-5295**	949-261-2325	634-9
Entrust Inc						
5400 LBJ Fwy Ste 1340	Dallas	TX	75240	**888-690-2424***	972-728-0447	180-12
*Sales						
Entwistle Co Dietzco Div						
6 Bigelow St	Hudson	MA	01749	**800-445-8909**	508-481-4000	555
EnviroLogix Inc						
500 Riverside Industrial Pkwy	Portland	ME	04103	**866-408-4597**	207-797-0300	740
Environics Analytics Group Ltd						
33 Bloor St E Ste 400	Toronto	ON	M4W3H1	**888-339-3304**	416-969-2733	197
Environment of Care Leader						
9737 Washintonian Blvd						
Ste 100	Gaithersburg	MD	20878	**800-929-4824***	301-287-2700	530-8
*Cust Svc						
Environment Reporter						
1801 S Bell St	Arlington	VA	22202	**800-372-1033**		530-5
Environmental & Safety Designs Inc						
5724 Summer Trees Dr	Memphis	TN	38134	**800-588-7962**	901-372-7962	194
Environmental Data Resources Inc						
440 Wheelers Farms Rd	Milford	CT	06460	**800-352-0050**	203-783-0300	387
Environmental Defense						
257 Pk Ave S	New York	NY	10010	**800-505-0703**	212-505-2100	47-13
Environmental Earthscapes Inc						
5075 S Swan Rd	Tucson	AZ	85706	**800-571-1575**	520-571-1575	422
Environmental Enterprises Inc (EEI)						
10163 Cincinnati Dayton Rd	Cincinnati	OH	45241	**800-722-2818**	513-772-2818	665
Environmental Health & Engineering Inc						
117 Fourth Ave	Needham	MA	02494	**800-825-5343**	781-247-4300	258
Environmental Industry Assn						
4301 Connecticut Ave NW						
Ste 300	Washington	DC	20008	**800-424-2869**	202-244-4700	47-12
Environmental Information Assn (EIA)						
6935 Wisconsin Ave Ste 306	Chevy Chase	MD	20815	**888-343-4342**	301-961-4999	47-13
Environmental Law Institute (ELI)						
2000 L St NW Ste 620	Washington	DC	20036	**800-433-5120**	202-939-3800	48-10
Environmental Management Inc						
5200 NE Hwy 33	Guthrie	OK	73044	**800-510-8510**	405-282-8510	666
US National Response Team						
1200 Pennsylvania Ave NW	Washington	DC	20593	**800-424-9346**	202-267-2675	340-18
Environmental Protection Agency Regional Offices						
Region 1						
1 Congress St Ste 1100	Boston	MA	02114	**888-372-7341**	617-918-1111	340-18
Region 3						
1650 Arch St	Philadelphia	PA	19103	**800-438-2474**	215-814-5000	340-18
Region 4						
Federal Ctr 61 Forsyth St SW	Atlanta	GA	30303	**800-241-1754**	404-562-9900	340-18
Region 6						
1445 Ross Ave Ste 1200	Dallas	TX	75202	**800-887-6063**	214-665-2200	340-18
Region 8						
1595 Wynkoop St	Denver	CO	80202	**800-227-8917**	303-312-6312	340-18
Region 9						
75 Hawthorne St	San Francisco	CA	94105	**866-372-9378**	415-947-8000	340-18
Region 10						
1200 Sixth Ave Ste 900	Seattle	WA	98101	**800-424-4372**	206-553-1200	340-18
Environmental Systems Research Institute Inc						
380 New York St	Redlands	CA	92373	**800-447-9778***	909-793-2853	180-10
*Sales						
Enviro-Tote Inc						
4 Cote Ln	Bedford	NH	03110	**800-868-3224**	603-647-7171	65
Envirovantage Inc						
629 Calef Hwy Ste 200	Epping	NH	03042	**800-640-5323**	603-679-9682	665
Envision Inc						
610 N Main St	Wichita	KS	67203	**888-425-7072**	316-440-1500	47-6
Envision Peripherals Inc (EPI)						
47490 Seabridge Dr	Fremont	CA	94538	**888-838-6388***	510-770-9988	175-4
*Tech Supp						
Envoy Plan Services Inc						
901 Calle Amanecer Ste 200	San Clemente	CA	92673	**800-248-8858**	949-366-5070	534
Enwood Structures Inc						
5724 McCrimmon Pkwy						
PO Box 2002	Morrisville	NC	27560	**800-777-8648**	919-518-0464	815
Enzo Biochem Inc						
527 Madison Ave	New York	NY	10022	**800-522-5052**	212-583-0100	233
NYSE: ENZ						
Enzo Life Sciences Inc						
10 Executive Blvd	Farmingdale	NY	11735	**800-942-0430**	631-694-7070	233
Enzymatic Therapy						
825 Challenger Dr	Green Bay	WI	54311	**800-783-2286**	920-469-1313	797
Eoa Inc						
1410 Jackson St	Oakland	CA	94612	**800-794-2482**	510-832-2852	263
Eoff Electric Company Inc						
3241 NW Industrial St	Portland	OR	97210	**800-285-3633**	503-222-9411	255
EOG Resources Inc						
1111 Bagby Sky Lobby 2	Houston	TX	77002	**877-363-3647**	713-651-7000	537
NYSE: EOG						
Eola Hills Wine Cellars						
501 S Pacific Hwy 99 W	Rickreall	OR	97371	**800-291-6730**	503-623-2405	49-6
Eos Systems Inc						
72 River Park St Ste 4	Needham	MA	02494	**855-453-2600**		182
EP Henry Corp						
201 Pk Ave	Woodbury	NJ	08096	**800-444-3679**	856-845-6200	185
EP Wealth Advisors Inc						
21515 Hawthorne Blvd Ste 1200	Torrance	CA	90503	**800-272-2328**	310-543-4559	196
Epac Software Technologies Inc						
42 Ladd St	East Greenwich	RI	02818	**888-336-3722**		179
E-pak Machinery Inc						
1535 S State Rd 39	La Porte	IN	46350	**800-328-0466**	219-393-5541	546
EPC (Engineered Polymers Corp)						
1020 Maple Ave E	Mora	MN	55051	**800-388-2155**	320-679-3232	607
EPCO (Engineered Products Co)						
601 Kelso St PO Box 108	Flint	MI	48506	**888-414-3726**	810-767-2050	350
EPCOS Inc						
485-B Rt 1 S Ste 200	Iselin	NJ	08830	**800-689-3717**		255
Epes Carriers Inc						
3400 Edgefield Ct	Greensboro	NC	27409	**800-869-3737**	336-668-3358	778
Ephor Group LLC						
24 E Greenway Plz Ste 440	Houston	TX	77046	**800-379-9330**		462
EPI (Envision Peripherals Inc)						
47490 Seabridge Dr	Fremont	CA	94538	**888-838-6388***	510-770-9988	175-4
*Tech Supp						
Epic AIR LLC						
22590 Nelson Rd	Bend	OR	97701	**888-359-3742**	541-318-8849	20
Epic Life Insurance Co						
1765 W Broadway	Madison	WI	53713	**800-236-8809***	608-223-2100	391-2
*Sales						
Epic Metals Corp						
11 Talbot Ave	Rankin	PA	15104	**877-696-3742**	412-351-3913	695
EPIEN Medical Inc						
4225 White Bear Pkwy Ste 600	St Paul	MN	55110	**888-884-4675**	651-653-3380	666
Epilepsy Foundation						
8301 Professional Pl E	Landover	MD	20785	**800-332-1000**	301-459-3700	47-17
Epilog Corp						
16371 Table Mtn Pkwy	Golden	CO	80403	**888-437-4564**	303-277-1188	543
Episcopal Church USA						
815 Second Ave	New York	NY	10017	**800-334-7626**	212-716-6000	47-20
Episcopal Diocese of West Texas						
111 Torcido Dr	San Antonio	TX	78209	**888-824-5387**	210-824-5387	47-20
Episcopal Divinity School						
99 Brattle St	Cambridge	MA	02138	**866-333-8742**	617-868-3450	168-3
Episcopal High School						
1200 N Quaker Ln	Alexandria	VA	22302	**877-933-4347**	703-933-4062	621
Episcopal Life Magazine						
815 Second Ave						
Episcopal Church Ctr	New York	NY	10017	**800-334-7626**	212-716-6000	456-18
Episcopal Migration Ministries (EMM)						
815 Second Ave	New York	NY	10017	**800-334-7626**	212-716-6258	47-5
Episcopal Relief & Development						
815 Second Ave	New York	NY	10017	**800-334-7626**	855-312-4325	47-5
Episcopal Theological Seminary of the Southwest (SSW)						
501 E 32nd PO Box 2247	Austin	TX	78705	**800-252-5400**	512-472-4133	168-3
Epitomics Inc						
863 Mitten Rd Ste 103	Burlingame	CA	94010	**888-772-2226**	650-583-6688	666
ePlus Inc						
13595 Dulles Technology Dr	Herndon	VA	20171	**888-482-1122**	703-984-8400	38
NASDAQ: PLUS						
Epoch Design						
17617 Ne 65th St Ste 2	Redmond	WA	98052	**800-589-7990**	425-284-0880	322
Epoch Senior Living						
51 Sawyer Rd Ste 500	Waltham	MA	02453	**877-376-2475**	781-891-0777	670
Epoque Hotels						
2500 NE 135th St Ste 502	North Miami	FL	33181	**866-376-7831**	305-538-9697	379
Eppinger Manufacturing Co						
6340 Schaefer Rd	Dearborn	MI	48126	**888-771-8277**	313-582-3205	708

Name / Address	City	State	ZIP	Toll-Free	Phone	Class
Epps Aviation Inc						
1 Aviation Way						
DeKalb Peachtree Airport	Atlanta	GA	30341	**800-241-6807**	770-458-9851	62
EPRI Journal						
3420 Hillview Ave	Palo Alto	CA	94304	**800-313-3774**	650-855-2121	456-21
Epro Tile Inc						
10890 E CR 6	Bloomville	OH	44818	**866-818-3776**		749
ePromos Promotional Products Inc						
120 Broadway Ste 1360	New York	NY	10271	**877-377-6667**	212-286-8008	94
EPS (Educators Publishing Service Inc)						
625 Mt Auburn St Third Fl						
PO Box 9031	Cambridge	MA	02139	**800-225-5750**		634-2
Epson America Inc						
3840 Kilroy Airport Way	Long Beach	CA	90806	**800-463-7766**	562-981-3840	175-6
Epson Electronics America Inc						
150 River Oaks Pkwy	San Jose	CA	95134	**800-228-3964**	408-922-0200	694
EQC (Emerald Queen Casino)						
2024 E 29th St	Tacoma	WA	98404	**888-831-7655**	253-594-7777	132
EQMM (Ellery Queen Mystery Magazine)						
267 Broadway 4th Fl	New York	NY	10007	**800-220-7443**		456-11
EQT Corp						
625 Liberty Ave Ste 1700	Pittsburgh	PA	15222	**800-242-1776**	412-553-5700	785
NYSE: EQT						
Equal Employment Opportunity Commission (EEOC)						
1801 L St NW	Washington	DC	20507	**800-669-4000**	202-663-4191	340-18
Equal Employment Opportunity Commission Regional Offices						
Atlanta District						
100 Alabama St SW Ste 4R30	Atlanta	GA	30303	**800-669-6820**		340-18
Birmingham District						
1130 22nd St S Ste 2000	Birmingham	AL	35205	**800-669-4000**	205-212-2100	340-18
Charlotte District						
129 W Trade St Ste 400	Charlotte	NC	28202	**800-669-4000**	704-344-6682	340-18
Chicago District						
500 W Madison St Ste 2800	Chicago	IL	60661	**800-669-4000**	312-353-2713	340-18
Dallas District						
207 S Houston St 3rd Fl	Dallas	TX	75202	**800-669-4000**	214-253-2700	340-18
Houston District						
1201 Louisiana St 6th Fl	Houston	TX	77002	**800-669-4000**		340-18
Los Angeles District						
255 E Temple St 4th Fl	Los Angeles	CA	90012	**800-669-4000**		340-18
New York District						
33 Whitehall St 5th Fl	New York	NY	10004	**866-408-8075**	212-336-3620	340-18
Philadelphia District						
801 Market St Ste 1300	Philadelphia	PA	19107	**800-669-4000**		340-18
Saint Louis District						
1222 Spruce St Rm 8.100	Saint Louis	MO	63103	**800-669-4000**	314-539-7800	340-18
San Francisco District						
450 Golden Gate Ave 5 W						
PO Box 36025	San Francisco	CA	94102	**800-669-4000**		340-18
Equal Rights Advocates (ERA)						
1170 Market St Ste 700	San Francisco	CA	94102	**800-839-4372**	415-621-0672	47-24
Equifax Credit Marketing Services						
1550 Peachtree St NW	Atlanta	GA	30309	**800-660-5125***	404-885-8000	220
NYSE: EFX ■ *Sales						
Equifax Inc						
1550 Peachtree St NW	Atlanta	GA	30309	**888-202-4025***	404-885-8000	220
NYSE: EFX ■ *Sales						
Equilibrium Inc						
100 Tamal Plz Ste 225	Corte Madera	CA	94925	**855-378-4542**	415-332-4343	180-8
Equine Canada						
2685 Queensview Dr	Ottawa	ON	K2B8K2	**866-282-8395**	613-248-3484	650
Equinox Fitness Holdings Inc						
895 Broadway	New York	NY	10003	**866-332-6549**	212-677-0180	354
Equinox, The						
3567 Main St	Manchester Village	VT	05254	**800-362-4747**	802-362-4700	667
Equipment Manufacturing Corp (EMC)						
14930 Marquardt Ave	Santa Fe Springs	CA	90670	**888-833-9000**	562-623-9394	386
Equipment Technology LLC						
341 NW 122nd St	Oklahoma City	OK	73114	**888-748-3841**		266-3
Equipoise Dental Laboratory Inc						
85 Portland Ave	Bergenfield	NJ	07621	**800-999-4950**	201-385-4750	418
EQUIPTO 225 Main St	Tatamy	PA	18085	**800-323-0801**	610-253-2775	288
Equipto Electronics Corp						
351 Woodlawn Ave	Aurora	IL	60506	**800-204-7225**	630-897-4691	256
Equis International						
90 South 400 West						
Ste 620	Salt Lake City	UT	84101	**800-882-3040***	801-265-9996	180-10
*Sales						
Equisport Agency Inc						
2306 Eastways Rd						
PO Box 269	Bloomfield Hills	MI	48304	**800-432-1215**	248-644-1215	391-1
Equitable Bank						
113 N Locust St	Grand Island	NE	68802	**800-641-5046**	308-382-3136	69
Equitable Gas Co						
PO Box 6766	Pittsburgh	PA	15212	**800-654-6335**		785
Equitable Life & Casualty Insurance Co						
3 Triad Ctr	Salt Lake City	UT	84180	**877-358-4060***		391-2
*Cust Svc						
Equity Co-op Livestock Sales Assn						
401 Commerce Ave	Baraboo	WI	53913	**800-362-3989**	608-356-8311	445
Equity Funding						
12505 Bel-Red Rd Ste 200	Bellevue	WA	98005	**866-332-3863**	425-283-1040	218
Equity Investment Corp						
3007 Piedmont Rd Ste 200	Atlanta	GA	30305	**877-342-0111**	404-239-0111	527
Equity Lifestyle Properties Inc						
2 N Riverside Plz Ste 800	Chicago	IL	60606	**800-274-7314**	312-279-1400	653
NYSE: ELS						
Equus Computer Systems Inc						
5801 Clearwater Dr	Minnetonka	MN	55343	**866-378-8727**	612-617-6200	175-1
Equus Magazine						
656 Quince OrchaRd Rd						
Ste 600	Gaithersburg	MD	20878	**800-829-5910***	301-977-3900	456-14
*Cust Svc						
EQUUS Total Return Inc						
700 Louisiana St 48th Fl	Houston	TX	77002	**888-323-4533**		790
ER Wagner Mfg Company Inc						
4611 N 32nd St	Milwaukee	WI	53209	**800-558-5596**	414-871-5080	350
ERA (Equal Rights Advocates)						
1170 Market St Ste 700	San Francisco	CA	94102	**800-839-4372**	415-621-0672	47-24
Era Helicopters LLC						
600 Airport Service Rd						
PO Box 6550	Lake Charles	LA	70606	**800-256-2372**	337-478-6131	13
ERA Wilder Realty						
120A Columbia Ave PO Box 610	Chapin	SC	29036	**866-593-7653**	803-345-6713	650
Erb Equipment Co Inc						
200 Erb Industrial Dr	Fenton	MO	63026	**800-634-9661**	636-349-0200	358
ERDC (US Army Engineer Research & Development Ctr)						
3909 Halls Ferry Rd	Vicksburg	MS	39180	**800-522-6937**	601-634-3188	666
Erect-A-Tube Inc						
701 W Pk St PO Box 100	Harvard	IL	60033	**800-624-9219**	815-943-4091	104
eResearch Technology Inc						
1818 Market St Ste 1000	Philadelphia	PA	19103	**800-704-9698**	215-972-0420	180-10
NASDAQ: ERT						
Ergodyne Corp						
1021 Bandana Blvd E Ste 220	Saint Paul	MN	55108	**800-225-8238**	651-642-9889	476
ErgoGenesis LLC						
1 BodyBilt Pl	Navasota	TX	77868	**800-364-5299**	936-825-1700	320-3
Ergotron Inc						
1181 Trapp Rd	Saint Paul	MN	55121	**800-888-8458***	651-681-7600	320-1
*Sales						
Erhard Bmw Of Bloomfield Hills						
4065 W Maple Rd	Bloomfield Hills	MI	48301	**888-481-4058**	248-642-6565	56
ERIC (Education Resource Information Ctr)						
c/o CSC						
655 15th St NW Ste 500	Washington	DC	20005	**800-538-3742**		199
Eric A. King						
301 Grant St Ste 4300	Pittsburgh	PA	15219	**888-742-2454**	281-667-4200	179
Eric Buchanan & Associates Pllc						
414 Mccallie Ave	Chattanooga	TN	37402	**877-634-2506**		444
Eric Electronics						
2220 Lundy Ave	San Jose	CA	95131	**800-495-3742***	408-432-1111	248
*General						
Erickson Air-Crane Co						
5550 SW Macadam Ave Ste 200	Portland	OR	97239	**877-870-5176**	503-505-5800	20
ERICO Products Inc						
34600 Solon Rd	Solon	OH	44139	**800-248-2677**	440-248-0100	813
Ericsson						
1 Telcordia Dr	Piscataway	NJ	08854	**800-521-2673**	732-699-2000	180-10
Erie 2-Chautauqua Cattaraugus Boces (ECCB)						
8685 Erie Rd	Angola	NY	14006	**800-228-1184**	716-549-4454	683
Erie County Water Authority (ECWA)						
295 Main St Rm 350	Buffalo	NY	14203	**855-748-1076**	716-849-8484	785
Erie Family Life Insurance Co						
100 Erie Insurance Pl	Erie	PA	16530	**800-458-0811**	814-870-2000	391-2
Erie Foods International Inc						
401 Seventh Ave PO Box 648	Erie	IL	61250	**800-447-1887**	309-659-2233	297-10
Erie Indemnity Co						
Erie Insurance Group						
100 Erie Insurance Pl	Erie	PA	16530	**800-458-0811**	814-870-2000	391-4
NASDAQ: ERIE						
Erie Insurance Exchange						
100 Erie Insurance Pl	Erie	PA	16530	**800-458-0811**	814-870-2000	391-4
Erie Insurance Property & Casualty Co						
100 Erie Insurance Pl	Erie	PA	16530	**800-458-0811**	814-870-2000	391-4
Erie Press Systems						
1253 W 12th St PO Box 4061	Erie	PA	16512	**800-222-3608**	814-455-3941	455
Erie Regional Chamber & Growth Partnership						
208 E Bayfront Pkwy	Erie	PA	16507	**888-300-3743**	814-454-7191	138
Erie Times-News						
205 W 12th St	Erie	PA	16534	**800-352-0043**	814-870-1600	531-2
Erie VA Medical Ctr						
135 E 38th St	Erie	PA	16504	**800-274-8387**	814-868-8661	374-8
Erie Vehicle Co						
60 E 51st St	Chicago	IL	60615	**888-550-3743**	773-536-6300	515
Erie Zoo 423 W 38th St	Erie	PA	16508	**877-371-5422**	814-864-4091	821
Erlanger Medical Ctr						
975 E Third St	Chattanooga	TN	37403	**877-849-8338**	423-778-7000	374-3
ERMC (Edinburg Regional Medical Ctr)						
1102 W Trenton Rd	Edinburg	TX	78539	**800-465-5585**	956-388-6000	374-3
Ernest F Mariani Company Inc						
573 West 2890 South	Salt Lake City	UT	84115	**800-453-2927**		663
Ernest Green & Son Ltd						
2395 Skymark Ave	Mississauga	ON	L4W4Y6	**800-387-7577**	905-629-8999	110
Ernest Maier Inc						
4700 Annapolis Rd	Bladensburg	MD	20710	**888-927-8303**	301-927-8300	185
Ernest Paper Products						
5777 Smithway St	Commerce	CA	90040	**800-233-7788**		558
Ernie Ball						
151 Suburban Rd	San Luis Obispo	CA	93401	**866-823-2255**	805-544-7726	526
Ernie Williams Ltd						
2613 Hwy 18 E	Algona	IA	50511	**888-535-4096**	515-295-3561	276
Ernst & Young						
Ernst & Young Tower 222 Bay St						
PO Box 251	Toronto	ON	M5K1J7	**800-291-3380**	416-864-1234	2
Ernst Enterprises Inc						
3361 Successful Way	Dayton	OH	45414	**800-353-1555**	937-233-5555	184
Ernst Publishing Co LLC						
1 Commerce Plaza 99 Washington Ave						
Ste 309	Albany	NY	12210	**800-345-3822**		634-9
ERS Industries Inc						
1005 Indian Church Rd	West Seneca	NY	14224	**800-993-6446**	716-675-2040	768
Erskine College						
2 Washington St	Due West	SC	29639	**888-359-4358***		167
*Admissions						
Erskine Theological Seminary						
2 Washington St PO Box 338	Due West	SC	29639	**888-359-4358**	864-379-8885	168-3
Ervin Industries Inc						
3893 Research Pk Dr	Ann Arbor	MI	48108	**800-748-0055**	734-769-4600	1
Ervin Leasing Co						
3893 Research Pk Dr	Ann Arbor	MI	48108	**800-748-0015**		266-3
Erwin-Keith Inc						
1529 Hwy 193	Wynne	AR	72396	**888-535-7333**	870-238-2079	10-4
ES (IEEE Education Society)						
IEEE Operations Ctr						
445 Hoes Ln	Piscataway	NJ	08854	**800-678-4333**	732-981-0060	48-19
ES Originals Inc						
440 9th Ave 7th Fl	New York	NY	10001	**800-677-6577***	212-736-8124	302
*General						

Alphabetical Section

	City	State	ZIP	Toll-Free	Phone	Class
ESA (Evangelicals for Social Action)						
PO Box 367	Wayne	PA	19087	800-650-6600	484-384-2990	47-7
ESA (Electronic Security Assn Inc)						
2300 Vly View Ln Ste 230	Irving	TX	75062	888-447-1689	214-260-5970	48-3
Esab Welding & Cutting Products Inc						
411 S Ebenezer Rd PO Box 100545	Florence	SC	29501	800-372-2123	843-669-4411	809
Escalade Inc						
817 Maxwell Ave	Evansville	IN	47711	800-426-1421*	812-467-1200	708
NASDAQ: ESCA ■ *Cust Svc						
Escalera Inc						
708 S Industrial Dr PO Box 1359	Yuba City	CA	95993	800-622-1359	530-673-6318	469
Escalon Premier Brands						
1905 McHenry Ave	Escalon	CA	95320	800-255-5750	209-838-7341	297-20
Escambia River Electric Co-op Inc						
3425 Florida 4	Jay	FL	32565	800-235-3848	850-675-4521	247
Escanaba Public Library						
400 Ludington St	Escanaba	MI	49829	800-992-9012	906-786-4463	434-3
Escapees RV Club						
100 Rainbow Dr	Livingston	TX	77399	800-231-9896	936-327-8873	47-23
Esco Corp						
2141 NW 25th Ave	Portland	OR	97210	800-523-3795	503-228-2141	192
ESCO Technologies Inc						
9900A Clayton Rd	Saint Louis	MO	63124	800-368-5948	314-213-7200	360-3
NYSE: ESE						
eScreen Inc						
7500 W 110th St Ste 500	Overland Park	KS	66210	800-881-0722	913-327-5915	387
ESD (Etiwanda School District)						
6061 E Ave	Etiwanda	CA	91739	800-300-1506	909-899-2451	683
ESE Inc						
3600 DownWind Dr	Marshfield	WI	54449	800-236-4778	715-387-4778	258
Eseeola Lodge, The						
175 Linville Ave PO Box 99	Linville	NC	28646	800-742-6717	828-733-4311	667
ESGR (National Committee for Employer Support of the Guard & Reserve)						
1555 Wilson Blvd Ste 319	Arlington	VA	22209	800-336-4590	703-696-1386	47-19
ESH (Eastern State Hospital)						
4601 Ironbound Rd	Williamsburg	VA	23188	800-994-6610	757-253-5161	374-5
eSignal						
3955 Pt Eden Way	Hayward	CA	94545	800-815-8256	510-266-6000	180-1
eSilicon Corp						
501 Macara Ave	Sunnyvale	CA	94085	877-769-2447	408-616-4600	255
Eskaton Village						
3939 Walnut Ave	Carmichael	CA	95608	800-300-3929	916-974-2000	670
Esker Inc						
1212 Deming Way Ste 350	Madison	WI	53717	800-368-5283	608-828-6000	180-12
ESL Instruction & Consulting Inc						
42 Broad St NW	Atlanta	GA	30303	877-579-2366	404-577-2366	423
Esmark Steel Group						
2500 Euclid Ave	Chicago Heights	IL	60411	800-323-0340	708-756-0400	360-3
Esmeralda County						
PO Box 547	Goldfield	NV	89013	800-884-4072	775-485-6309	338
eSoft Inc						
295 Interlocken Blvd Ste 500	Broomfield	CO	80021	866-233-2296	303-444-1600	178
ESOP Assn						
1726 M St NW Ste 501	Washington	DC	20036	866-366-3832	202-293-2971	48-12
ESOP Assn PAC						
1726 M St NW Ste 501	Washington	DC	20036	866-366-3832	202-293-2971	614
ESPE Mfg Company Inc						
9220 Ivanhoe St	Schiller Park	IL	60176	800-367-3773*	847-678-8950	350
*Cust Svc						
Esplanade Tours						
160 Commonwealth Ave Ste U-1A	Boston	MA	02116	800-628-4893	617-266-7465	758
Esplendor Resort at Rio Rico						
1069 Camino Caralampi	Rio Rico	AZ	85648	800-288-4746	520-281-1901	667
ESPN 545 Middle St	Bristol	CT	06010	877-710-3776		736
ESPN Classic Inc						
ESPN Plaza	Bristol	CT	06010	877-710-3776		736
ESPN Deportes						
2 Alhambra Plz 9th Fl	Coral Gables	FL	33134	800-337-6783	305-567-3797	736
Esprit Miami						
3043 NW 107th Ave	Miami	FL	33172	800-327-2320	305-591-2244	295
ESRI Canada Ltd						
12 Concorde Pl Ste 900	Toronto	ON	M3C3R8	866-625-4577	416-441-6035	176
Essco Inc						
1933 Highland Rd	Twinsburg	OH	44087	800-321-2664	216-524-4141	604-2
Essence Communications Inc						
135 W 50th St 4th Fl	New York	NY	10020	800-274-9398*		634-9
*Sales						
Essence Magazine						
135 W 50th St 4th Fl	New York	NY	10020	800-274-9398		456-11
Essentia Health						
502 E Second St	Duluth	MN	55805	855-469-6532	218-786-8376	374-3
Essential Technologies Inc						
1107 Hazeltine Blvd Ste 477	Chaska	MN	55318	800-818-1125	952-368-9001	177
Essentra PLC 3123 Stn Rd	Erie	PA	16510	800-847-0486	814-899-9263	153
Essex Crane Rental Corp						
1110 Lake Cook Rd Ste 220	Buffalo Grove	IL	60089	888-991-4100	847-215-6500	266-3
Essex Financial Services Inc						
176 Westbrook Rd	Essex	CT	06426	800-900-5972	860-767-4300	527
Essex Grain Products						
9 Lee Blvd	Frazer	PA	19355	800-441-1017	610-647-3800	298-11
Essex Meadows						
30 Bokum Rd	Essex	CT	06426	866-721-4838	860-767-7201	670
Essex Savings Bank						
PO Box 950	Essex	CT	06426	877-377-3922	860-767-4414	69
Essick Air Products Inc						
5800 Murray St	Little Rock	AR	72209	800-643-8341	501-562-1094	90
ESSROC Materials Inc						
3251 Bath Pike	Nazareth	PA	18064	800-437-7762	610-837-6725	134
Esterline Interface Technologies						
600 W Wilbur Ave	Coeur d'Alene	ID	83815	800-444-5923	208-765-8000	175-2
Esterline Mason						
13955 Balboa Blvd	Sylmar	CA	91342	800-232-7700	818-361-3366	503
Estes-Cox Corp						
1295 H St	Penrose	CO	81240	800-525-7561	719-372-6565	760
Estes-Winn Memorial Automobile Museum						
111 Grovewood Rd	Asheville	NC	28804	877-622-7238	828-253-7651	519
Estex Mfg Co Inc						
402 E Broad St PO Box 368	Fairburn	GA	30213	800-749-1224		730
Esther Price Candies Inc						
1709 Wayne Ave	Dayton	OH	45410	800-782-0326	937-253-2121	297-8
Estrada Hinojosa & Company Inc						
1717 Main St LB47	Dallas	TX	75201	800-676-5352	214-658-1670	401
ET Horn Co						
16050 Canary Ave	La Mirada	CA	90638	800-442-4676	714-523-8050	145
ETA (Evangelical Training Assn)						
PO Box 327	Wheaton	IL	60187	800-369-8291*		47-20
*General						
ETA (Electronics Technicians Assn International)						
5 Depot St	Greencastle	IN	46135	800-288-3824	765-653-8262	48-19
Eta Sigma Gamma						
2000 University Ave	Muncie	IN	47306	800-715-2559	765-285-2258	47-16
eTagz Inc						
108 1st Ave S Ste 450	Seattle	WA	98104	800-831-0399		5
ETC (Educational Travel Consultants)						
PO Box 1580	Hendersonville	NC	28793	800-247-7969	828-693-0412	758
ETCO (Engman-Taylor Company Inc)						
W142 N9351 Fountain Blvd	Menomonee Falls	WI	53051	800-236-1975	262-255-9300	385
ETCO Inc						
25 Bellows St	Warwick	RI	02888	800-689-3826	401-467-2400	813
ETCO Inc Automotive Products Div						
3004 62nd Ave E	Bradenton	FL	34203	800-689-3826	941-756-8426	249
Etegent Technologies Ltd						
1775 Mentor Ave	Cincinnati	OH	45212	800-860-4867	513-631-0579	263
Etera Solutions Llc						
354 TurnPk St Ste 203	Canton	MA	02021	888-536-6515		396
Eternabond						
75 E Div St	Mundelein	IL	60060	888-336-2663	847-837-9400	729
Eternity Healthcare Inc						
Ste 1 8755 Ash St	Vancouver	BC	V6P6T3	855-324-1110		475
Ethan Allen Hotel						
21 Lake Ave Ext	Danbury	CT	06811	800-742-1776	203-744-1776	379
Ethan Allen Interiors Inc						
Ethan Allen Dr	Danbury	CT	06811	888-324-3571		322
NYSE: ETH						
Etheridge Printing Co						
4434 Mcewen Rd	Dallas	TX	75244	800-834-2709	214-827-8151	393
Etiwanda School District (ESD)						
6061 E Ave	Etiwanda	CA	91739	800-300-1506	909-899-2451	683
Etobicoke Ironworks Ltd						
141 Rivalda Rd	Weston	ON	M9M2M6	866-274-6971	416-742-7111	479
ETS (Praxis Series Online Educational Testing Service Teaching & Learning Div)						
PO Box 6051	Princeton	NJ	08541	800-772-9476	609-771-7395	246
Ettore Products Co						
2100 N Loop Rd	Alameda	CA	94502	800-438-8673	510-748-4130	507
EUB (Edinboro University of Pennsylvania Baron-Forness Library)						
200 Tartan Rd	Edinboro	PA	16444	888-845-2890	814-732-2273	434-6
Eubanks Engineering Co						
3022 Inland Empire Blvd	Ontario	CA	91764	800-729-4208	909-483-2456	811
Eubel Brady & Suttman Asset Management Inc						
10100 Innovation Dr Ste 410	Dayton	OH	45342	800-391-1223	937-291-1223	196
Euclid Chemical Co						
19218 Redwood Rd	Cleveland	OH	44110	800-321-7628	216-531-9222	3
Euclid Heat Treating Co						
1340 E 222nd St	Euclid	OH	44117	800-962-2909	216-481-8444	483
Eufaula/Barbour County Chamber of Commerce						
333 E Broad St	Eufaula	AL	36027	800-524-7529	334-687-6664	138
Eugene Burger Management Corp						
6600 Hunter Dr	Rohnert Park	CA	94928	800-788-0233	707-584-5123	653
Eugene Cascades Coast						
754 Olive St	Eugene	OR	97440	800-547-5445	541-484-5307	208
Eugene Ernst Products Company Inc						
PO Box 925	Farmingdale	NJ	07727	800-992-2843	732-938-5641	494
Eugene O'Neill National Historic Site						
1000 Kuss Rd	Danville	CA	94526	866-945-7920	925-838-0249	563
Euler Hermes ACI						
800 Red Brook Blvd 4th Fl	Owings Mills	MD	21117	877-883-3224	410-753-0753	391-5
Eureka College						
300 E College Ave	Eureka	IL	61530	888-438-7352*	309-467-6350	167
*Admissions						
Eureka Homestead						
1922 Veterans Memorial Blvd	Metairie	LA	70005	855-858-5179	504-834-0242	68
Eureka Welding Alloys Inc						
2000 E Avis Dr	Madison Heights	MI	48071	800-962-8560	248-588-0001	809
Euro Lloyd Travel Inc						
1640 Hempstead Tpke	East Meadow	NY	11554	800-334-2724	516-228-4970	769
Euro Pacific Capital Inc						
88 Post Rd W 2nd Fl	Westport	CT	06880	800-727-7922	203-662-9700	69
Europa Restaurant						
1620 S Indian Trl	Palm Springs	CA	92264	800-245-2314	760-327-2314	669
Europe by Car						
40 Exchange Pl Ste 1720	New York	NY	10005	800-223-1516	212-581-3040	125
Euro-Pharm International Canada Inc						
9400 Boul Langelier	Montreal	QC	H1P3H8	888-929-0835	514-323-8757	233
EuroPharma Inc						
955 Challenger Dr	Green Bay	WI	54311	866-598-5487	920-406-6500	345
Euro-Suites Hotel						
University Centre 501 Chestnut Ridge Rd	Morgantown	WV	26505	800-678-4837		379
Eutectic Corp						
N 94 W 14355 Garwin Mace Dr	Menomonee Falls	WI	53051	800-558-8524	262-532-4677	809
ev3 Inc						
3033 Campus Dr	Plymouth	MN	55441	800-716-6700	763-398-7000	475
EVA Airways						
200 N Sepulveda Blvd Ste 1600	El Segundo	CA	90245	800-695-1188	310-362-6600	25
Evan B Donaldson Adoption Institute						
120 E 38th St	New York	NY	10016	800-837-2655	212-925-4089	47-6
Evan K Thalenberg Law Offices						
216 E Lexington St	Baltimore	MD	21202	800-778-1181	410-625-9100	428
Evana Automation						
5825 Old Boonville Hwy	Evansville	IN	47715	800-468-6774	812-479-8246	209
Evangel University						
1111 N Glenstone Ave	Springfield	MO	65802	800-382-6435	417-865-2815	167

	City	State	ZIP	Toll-Free	Phone	Class
Evangelical Church Alliance (ECA)						
205 W Broadway St PO Box 9	Bradley	IL	60915	**888-855-6060**	815-937-0720	47-20
Evangelical Council for Financial Accountability (ECFA)						
440 W Jubal Early Dr Ste 130	Winchester	VA	22601	**800-323-9473**	540-535-0103	47-5
Evangelical Fellowship of Canada (EFC)						
600 Alden Rd Ste 300 Markham Industrial Pk	Markham	ON	L3R0E7	**866-302-3362**	905-479-5885	47-20
Evangelical Free Church of America, The						
901 E 78th St	Minneapolis	MN	55420	**800-745-2202**	952-854-1300	47-20
Evangelical Lutheran Church in America (ELCA)						
8765 W Higgins Rd	Chicago	IL	60631	**800-638-3522**	773-380-2700	47-20
Evangelical School of Theology						
121 S College St	Myerstown	PA	17067	**800-532-5775**	717-866-5775	168-3
Evangelical Training Assn (ETA)						
PO Box 327	Wheaton	IL	60187	**800-369-8291***		47-20
*General						
Evangelicals for Social Action (ESA)						
PO Box 367	Wayne	PA	19087	**800-650-6600**	484-384-2990	47-7
Evan-Moor Educational Publishers Inc						
18 Lower Ragsdale Dr	Monterey	CA	93940	**800-777-4362**	831-649-5901	245
Evans & Sutherland Computer Corp						
770 Komas Dr	Salt Lake City	UT	84108	**800-327-5707***	801-588-1000	701
OTC: ESCC ■ *Sales						
Evans Bancorp Inc						
1 Grimsby Dr	Hamburg	NY	14075	**866-310-0763**	716-926-2000	360-2
NYSE: EVBN						
Evans Data Corp						
340 Soquel Ave	Santa Cruz	CA	95062	**800-831-3080**	831-425-8451	666
Evans Dedicated Systems Inc						
PO Box 9	Maywood	CA	90270	**800-427-6387**	323-725-2928	778
Evans Delivery Company Inc						
PO Box 268	Pottsville	PA	17901	**800-666-7885**	570-385-9048	312
Evans Distribution Systems						
18765 Seaway Dr	Melvindale	MI	48122	**800-653-8267**	313-388-3200	801-1
Evans Enterprises Inc						
1536 S Western Ave	Oklahoma City	OK	73109	**800-423-8267**	405-631-1344	248
Evans Food Group Ltd						
4118 S Halsted St	Chicago	IL	60609	**888-643-8267**	773-254-7400	297-35
Evans Tire & Service Centers Inc						
510 N Broadway	Escondido	CA	92025	**877-338-2678**		61-5
Evans-Sherratt Co						
13050 Northend Ave	Oak Park	MI	48237	**800-248-3826**	248-584-5500	474
Evanston Hospital						
2650 Ridge Ave	Evanston	IL	60201	**888-364-6400**	847-570-2000	374-3
Evanston Public Library						
1703 Orrington Ave	Evanston	IL	60201	**888-253-7003**	847-448-8600	434-3
Evansville Convention & Visitors Bureau						
401 SE Riverside Dr	Evansville	IN	47713	**800-433-3025**	812-421-2200	208
Evansville Courier & Press						
300 E Walnut St	Evansville	IN	47713	**800-288-3200**	812-424-7711	531-2
Evansville Teachers Federal Credit Union						
PO Box 5129	Evansville	IN	47716	**800-800-9271**	812-477-9271	221
Evco Plastics						
100 W N St PO Box 497	DeForest	WI	53532	**800-507-6000**		603
Evenflo Company Inc						
1801 Commerce Dr	Piqua	OH	45356	**800-233-5921**		63
Evening Observer						
8-10 E Second St PO Box 391	Dunkirk	NY	14048	**800-836-0931**	716-366-3000	531-2
Evening Sun						
135 Baltimore St PO Box 514	Hanover	PA	17331	**800-877-3786**	717-637-3736	531-2
Evensky & Katz LLC						
4000 Ponce de Leon Boulevard Ste 850	Coral Gables	FL	33146	**800-448-5435**	305-448-8882	196
Event Planning International Corp						
10900 Granite St	Charlotte	NC	28273	**800-940-2164**	980-233-3777	186
Event Producers Inc						
5724 Salmen St	New Orleans	LA	70123	**866-903-6949**	504-466-4066	513
EventRebels com Inc						
10013 Fox Den Rd	Ellicott City	MD	21042	**877-883-1786**		5
Eventure Interactive Inc						
3420 Bristol St Fl 6	Costa Mesa	CA	92626	**855-986-5669**		395
Ever-Bloom Inc						
4701 Foothill Rd	Carpinteria	CA	93013	**800-388-8112**	805-684-5566	369
Everbrite Inc						
4949 S 110th St PO Box 20020	Greenfield	WI	53220	**800-558-3888**	414-529-3500	699
Evercoat						
6600 Cornell Rd	Cincinnati	OH	45242	**800-729-7600**	513-489-7600	59
Everest College						
1010 W Sunshine St	Springfield	MO	65807	**888-223-8556**	417-864-7220	798
Everest College Alhambra						
2215 W Mission Rd	Alhambra	CA	91803	**888-223-8556**	626-979-4940	798
Everest College Anaheim						
511 N Brookhurst Ste 300	Anaheim	CA	92801	**888-224-6684**	714-953-6500	798
Everest College Aurora						
14280 E Jewell Ave Ste 100	Aurora	CO	80012	**888-223-8556**	303-745-6244	798
Everest College City of Industry						
12801 Crossroads Pkwy S	City of Industry	CA	91746	**888-224-6684**	562-908-2500	798
Everest College San Jose						
1245 S Winchester Blvd Ste 102	San Jose	CA	95128	**888-223-8556**	408-246-4171	798
Everest College Thornton						
9065 Grant St	Thornton	CO	80229	**888-223-8556**	303-457-2757	798
Everest Institute						
21107 Lahser Rd	Southfield	MI	48033	**800-611-2101***	248-799-9933	798
*General						
Everest Institute Long Beach						
2161 Technology Pl	Long Beach	CA	90810	**888-223-8556**	562-624-9530	798
Everest Re Group Ltd						
477 Martinsville Rd PO Box 830	Liberty Corner	NJ	07938	**800-269-6660**	908-604-3000	360-4
Everest Reinsurance Co						
477 Martinsville Rd	Liberty Corner	NJ	07938	**800-269-6660**	908-604-3000	391-5
Everest University						
Brandon						
3924 Coconut Palm Dr	Tampa	FL	33619	**888-223-8556***	813-621-0041	798
*Cust Svc						
Jacksonville						
8226 Phillips Hwy	Jacksonville	FL	32256	**800-611-2101**	904-731-4949	798
Lakeland						
995 E Memorial Blvd Ste 110	Lakeland	FL	33801	**888-223-8556**	863-686-1444	798
Largo 1199 E Bay Dr	Largo	FL	33770	**888-223-8556**	727-725-2688	798
North Orlando						
5421 Diplomat Cir	Orlando	FL	32810	**888-223-8556**	407-628-5870	798
Orange Park						
805 Wells Rd	Orange Park	FL	32073	**888-223-8556**	904-264-9122	798
Pompano Beach						
225 N Federal Hwy	Pompano Beach	FL	33062	**888-223-8556**	954-783-7339	798
South Orlando						
9200 Southpark Ctr Loop	Orlando	FL	32819	**800-611-2101**	407-851-2525	798
Tampa						
3319 W Hillsborough Ave	Tampa	FL	33614	**888-223-8556**	813-879-6000	798
Everett Community College						
2000 Tower St	Everett	WA	98201	**866-575-9027**	425-388-9100	161
Everett J Prescott Inc						
32 Prescott St	Gardiner	ME	04345	**800-357-2447**	207-582-1851	611
Everfast Inc						
203 Gale Ln	Kennett Square	PA	19348	**800-213-6366***	610-444-9700	272
*Cust Svc						
eVerge Group Inc						
4965 Preston Pk Blvd Ste 700	Plano	TX	75093	**888-548-1973**	972-608-1803	182
Everglades Boats						
544 Air Pk Rd	Edgewater	FL	32132	**800-368-5647**	386-409-2202	89
Evergreen Enterprises Inc						
5915 Midlothian Trnpk	Richmond	VA	23225	**800-774-3837**	804-231-1800	321
Evergreen FS Inc						
402 N Hershey Rd	Bloomington	IL	61704	**877-963-2392**	309-663-2392	278
Evergreen Hospice Services						
12822 124th Ln NE	Kirkland	WA	98034	**877-980-7500**	425-899-1070	371
Evergreen Lodge						
250 S Frontage Rd W	Vail	CO	81657	**800-284-8245**	970-476-7810	379
Evergreen Marriott Conference Resort						
4021 Lakeview Dr	Stone Mountain	GA	30083	**800-228-9290**	770-879-9900	377
Evergreen Resort						
7880 Mackinaw Trail	Cadillac	MI	49601	**800-634-7302**		667
Evergreen State College						
2700 Evergreen Pkwy	Olympia	WA	98505	**888-492-9480**	360-867-6000	167
Evergreen Woods						
88 Notch Hill Rd	North Branford	CT	06471	**866-413-6378***	203-488-8000	670
*General						
Evergreens, The						
309 Bridgeboro Rd	Moorestown	NJ	08057	**877-673-8234**	856-439-2000	670
Everhard Products Inc						
1016 Ninth St SW	Canton	OH	44707	**800-225-0984**	330-453-7786	756
EverHome Mortgage Co						
301 W Bay St	Jacksonville	FL	32202	**800-669-9721***	888-882-3837	508
*Cust Svc						
Everi Holdings Inc (GCA)						
7250 S Tenaya Way Ste 100	Las Vegas	NV	89113	**800-833-7110**	702-855-3000	55
NYSE: EVRI						
Everist Genomics Inc						
709 W Ellsworth Rd	Ann Arbor	MI	48108	**855-383-7478**		740
Everlaw						
2020 Milvia St Ste 220	Berkeley	CA	94704	**844-383-7529**		387
Everlube Products						
100 Cooper Cir	Peachtree City	GA	30269	**800-428-7802**	770-261-4800	480
Everprint International Inc						
18021 Cortney Ct	City of Industry	CA	91748	**800-984-5777**	626-839-2569	177
Everpure LLC						
1040 Muirfield Dr	Hanover Park	IL	60133	**800-323-7873**	630-307-3000	804
Eversource						
1 Nstar Way NW200	Westwood	MA	02090	**800-592-2000***	781-441-8011	785
*Cust Svc						
Eversource						
1 Federal St Bldg 111-4	Springfield	MA	01105	**800-286-2000**	413-785-5871	785
EverTrue LLC						
330 Congress St 2nd Fl	Boston	MA	02210	**855-387-8783**		387
Everwise Corp						
1178 Broadway 4th Fl	New York	NY	10001	**888-734-0011**		387
Everything Parking Inc						
1415 S Church St Ste T	Charlotte	NC	28203	**877-751-6683**	704-377-1755	107
EVH Mfg Company LLC						
4895 Red Bluff Rd	Loris	SC	29569	**888-990-2555**	843-756-2555	275
EVINE Live Inc						
6740 Shady Oak Rd	Eden Prairie	MN	55344	**800-676-5523**		736
Evo Exhibits						
399 Wegner Dr	West Chicago	IL	60185	**888-404-4224**	630-520-0710	7
Evogi Group Inc, The						
20645 N Pima Rd Bldg N Ste 130	Scottsdale	AZ	85255	**888-277-5573**		198
Evolution Computing						
7000 N 16th St Ste 120 514	Phoenix	AZ	85020	**800-874-4028**		180-5
Evolve Discovery Inc						
611 Mission St 4th Fl	San Francisco	CA	94105	**866-488-1032**	415-398-8600	112
EVS Ltd						
3702 W Sample St	South Bend	IN	46619	**800-364-3218**	574-233-5707	321
EW Kaufmann Co						
140 Wharton Rd	Bristol	PA	19007	**800-635-5358**	215-364-0240	145
EW Scripps Co						
312 Walnut St Ste 2800	Cincinnati	OH	45202	**800-888-3000**	513-977-3000	634-8
NYSE: SSP						
EW Wylie Corp						
1520 Second Ave NW	West Fargo	ND	58078	**800-437-4132***	701-282-5550	778
*Cust Svc						
EWA (Enterprise Wireless Alliance)						
8484 Westpark Dr Ste 630	McLean	VA	22102	**800-482-8282**	703-528-5115	48-20
EWA Inc (Electronic Warfare Assoc Inc)						
13873 Pk Ctr Rd Ste 500	Herndon	VA	20171	**888-392-0002***	703-904-5700	182
*General						
EWI (Executive Women International)						
3860 S 2300 E	Salt Lake City	UT	84109	**877-439-4669**	801-355-2800	48-12
EWI (Elliott Wave International)						
PO Box 1618	Gainesville	GA	30503	**800-336-1618***	770-536-0309	634-9
*Cust Svc						
Ewing Marion Kauffman Foundation (EMKF)						
4801 Rockhill Rd	Kansas City	MO	64110	**800-385-1607**	816-932-1000	306
eWorkplace Solutions Inc						
24461 Ridge Rt Dr Ste 210	Laguna Hills	CA	92653	**888-477-7989**	949-583-1646	180-8

Name / Address	City	State	ZIP	Toll-Free	Phone	Class
Exact Metrology Inc 11575 Goldcoast Dr	Cincinnati	OH	45246	**866-722-2600**	513-831-6620	358
Exactax Inc 2301 W Lincoln Ave Ste 100	Anaheim	CA	92801	**844-327-6740**	714-284-4802	731
Exactech Inc 2320 NW 66th Ct *NASDAQ: EXAC*	Gainesville	FL	32653	**800-392-2832**	352-377-1140	476
ExaDigm Inc 2871 Pullman St	Santa Ana	CA	92705	**800-933-0064**	949-486-0320	196
Exalpha Biologicals Inc 2 Shaker Rd Unit B101	Shirley	MA	01464	**800-395-1137**		233
Exar Corp 48720 Kato Rd *NYSE: EXAR*	Fremont	CA	94538	**855-755-1330**	510-668-7000	694
Excalibre Engineering 9201 Irvine Blvd	Irvine	CA	92618	**877-922-5427**	949-454-6603	740
Excalibur Extrusions Inc 110 E Crowther Ave	Placentia	CA	92870	**800-648-6804**	714-528-8834	595
Excalibur Hotel & Casino 3850 Las Vegas Blvd S	Las Vegas	NV	89109	**877-750-5464**	702-597-7777	132
Exceed Staffing LLC 363 N Sam Houston Pkwy E Ste 1100	Houston	TX	77550	**866-609-2884**	409-770-9000	195
Excel Bridge Manufacturing Co 12001 Shoemaker Ave	Santa Fe Springs	CA	90670	**800-548-0054**	562-944-0701	479
Excel Telecommunications 433 Las Colinas Blvd Ste 400	Irving	TX	75039	**877-668-0808**	972-910-1900	733
Excelda Manufacturing Co 12785 Emerson Dr	Brighton	MI	48116	**877-486-3801**	248-486-3800	144
Ex-Cell Metal Products Inc 11240 Melrose St	Franklin Park	IL	60131	**800-392-3557**	847-451-0451	288
Excelleris Technologies Inc 4445 Lougheed Hwy Ste 201	Burnaby	BC	V5C0E4	**866-728-4777**		44
Excelligence Learning Corp 2 Lower Ragsdale Dr Ste 125	Monterey	CA	93940	**800-627-2829**	831-333-5572	245
Excellon Automation Inc 20001 S Rancho Way	Rancho Dominguez	CA	90220	**800-392-3556**	310-668-7700	469
Excellus BlueCross BlueShield PO Box 22999	Rochester	NY	14692	**800-278-1247**	585-454-1700	391-3
Excellus BlueCross BlueShield of Central New York 333 Butternut Dr	Syracuse	NY	13214	**800-633-6066**	315-671-6400	391-3
Excelsior College 7 Columbia Cir	Albany	NY	12203	**888-647-2388**	518-464-8500	167
Excelsior Defense Inc 2232 Central Ave	Saint Petersburg	FL	33712	**877-955-4636**	727-527-9600	691
Excelsior Marking Products 888 W Waterloo Rd	Akron	OH	44314	**800-433-3615**	330-745-2300	466
Exchange State Bank 3992 Chandler St PO Box 68	Carsonville	MI	48419	**888-488-9300**	810-657-9333	69
Exchange, The 3911 S Walton Walker Blvd	Dallas	TX	75236	**800-527-2345**		789
EXCO Resources Inc 12377 Merit Dr Ste 1700 *NYSE: XCO*	Dallas	TX	75251	**888-788-9449**	214-368-2084	537
Exec Air Montana Inc 2430 Airport Rd	Helena	MT	59601	**800-513-2190**	406-442-2190	13
ExecSuite Third Ave SW Ste 702	Calgary	AB	T2P3B4	**800-667-4980**	403-294-5800	212
Execulink Telecom Inc 619 Main St N	Burgessville	ON	N0J1C0	**866-706-1994**		226
ExecUNet Inc 295 Westport Ave	Norwalk	CT	06851	**800-637-3126**	203-750-1030	262
Execusys Inc 6767 N Wickham Rd	Melbourne	FL	32940	**800-454-3081**	321-253-0077	179
Executive Car Leasing Inc 7807 Santa Monica Blvd	Los Angeles	CA	90046	**800-994-2277**	323-654-5000	291
Executive Enterprises Institute 12 Skyline Dr	Hawthorne	NY	10532	**877-334-4273**	914-517-1122	763
Executive Hotel Vintage Court 650 Bush St	San Francisco	CA	94108	**888-388-3932**	415-392-4666	379
Executive Inn 978 Phillips Ln	Louisville	KY	40209	**888-205-8144**	502-367-6161	379
Executive Inn Group Corp *Executive Hotels & Resorts* 1080 Howe St 8th Fl	Vancouver	BC	V6Z2T1	**866-642-6888**	604-642-5250	379
Executive Jet 4556 Airport Rd	Cincinnati	OH	45226	**877-356-5387**	513-979-6600	13
Executive Pacific Plaza Hotel 400 Spring St	Seattle	WA	98104	**888-388-3932**	206-623-3900	379
Executive Protection Institute 16 Penn Plz Ste 1570	New York	NY	10001	**800-947-5827**	212-268-4555	764
Executive Speakers Bureau 8567 Cordes Cir	Germantown	TN	38139	**800-754-9404**	901-754-9404	706
Executive Suite Hotel 4360 SpenaRd Rd	Anchorage	AK	99517	**888-315-2378**	907-243-6366	379
Executive Women International (EWI) 3860 S 2300 E	Salt Lake City	UT	84109	**877-439-4669**	801-355-2800	48-12
eXelate 7 W 22nd St 9th Fl	New York	NY	10010	**877-896-3282**	646-380-4400	465
Exerve Inc 2909 Langford Rd Ste 400B	Norcross	GA	30071	**800-364-0637**	770-447-1566	731
EXFO Inc 400 Godin Ave *NASDAQ: EXFO*	Quebec	QC	G1M2K2	**800-663-3936**	418-683-0211	250
Exhibit Concepts Inc 700 Crossroads Ct	Vandalia	OH	45377	**800-324-5063**		186
Exide Technologies 13000 Deerfield Pkwy Bldg 200 *NASDAQ: XIDE*	Milton	GA	30004	**888-563-6300**	678-566-9000	73
Exiss Aluminum Trailers Inc 900 East Trailer Blvd	El Reno	OK	73036	**877-553-9477**		119
Exocor Inc 271 Ridley Rd	St. Catharines	ON	L2R6P7	**888-317-2209**	905-704-0603	110
Exopack LLC 23810 China Lake Ct PO Box 5687	Katy	TX	77494	**877-447-3539**	864-596-7140	547
Exp Pharmaceutical Services Corp 48021 Warm Springs Blvd	Fremont	CA	94539	**800-350-0397**	510-476-0909	802
Expanding Light 14618 Tyler Foote Rd	Nevada City	CA	95959	**800-346-5350**	530-478-7518	671
Expanko Inc 180 Gordon Dr Ste 113	Exton	PA	19341	**800-345-6202**		293
Expansion Management Magazine 1300 E Ninth St	Cleveland	OH	44114	**866-505-7173**	216-696-7000	456-5
Expedient Communications 810 Parish St	Pittsburgh	PA	15220	**877-570-7827**	412-316-7800	398
Expedition Trips.com 6553 California Ave Sw	Seattle	WA	98136	**877-412-8527**	206-547-0700	770
Expeditor Systems Inc 4090 Nine McFarland Dr	Alpharetta	GA	30004	**800-226-8158**		474
Expeditors International of Washington Inc 1015 Third Ave 12th Fl *NASDAQ: EXPD*	Seattle	WA	98104	**800-284-7474**	206-674-3400	448
Experian Information Solutions Inc 475 Anton Blvd *Cust Svc	Costa Mesa	CA	92626	**888-397-3742***	714-830-7000	220
Experience Works Inc 4401 Wilson Blvd Ste 1100	Arlington	VA	22203	**866-397-9757**	703-522-7272	47-6
Experimental Aircraft Assn (EAA) 3000 Poberezny Rd	Oshkosh	WI	54902	**800-236-4800**	920-426-4800	47-18
Expert Choice Inc 1501 Lee Hwy Ste 302	Arlington	VA	22209	**888-259-6400**	703-243-5595	180-12
Expert Evidence Report 1801 S Bell St	Arlington	VA	22202	**800-372-1033**		530-7
Expert Global Solutions, Inc 507 Prudential Rd	Horsham	PA	19044	**877-217-4423**	215-441-3000	159
Expert Recruiters 883 Helmcken St	Vancouver	BC	V6Z1B1	**888-407-7799**	604-689-3600	262
Exploration Place 300 N McLean Blvd	Wichita	KS	67203	**877-904-1444**	316-660-0600	520
Exploratorium, The 3601 Lyon St	San Francisco	CA	94123	**800-232-9698**	415-561-0360	519
Explore Information Services LLC 2900 Lone Oak Pkwy Ste 140 PO Box 21636	St. Paul	MN	55121	**800-531-9125**		632
Explorica Inc 145 Tremont St	Boston	MA	02111	**888-310-7120**		758
Expo Group, The 5931 W Campus Cir Dr	Irving	TX	75063	**800-736-7775**	972-580-9000	186
Expo Square 4145 E 21st St	Tulsa	OK	74114	**877-781-2660**	918-744-1113	207
Expon Exhibits 909 Fee Dr	Sacramento	CA	95815	**800-783-9766**	916-924-1600	234
Exponent Inc 149 Commonwealth Dr *NASDAQ: EXPO*	Menlo Park	CA	94025	**888-656-3976**	650-326-9400	666
Exponent Telegram 324 Hewes Ave	Clarksburg	WV	26301	**800-982-6034**		531-2
Export-Import Bank of the US 811 Vermont Ave NW	Washington	DC	20571	**800-565-3946**	202-565-3946	340-18
Express 1 Limited Pkwy *NYSE: EXPR*	Columbus	OH	43230	**888-397-1980**		156-6
Express Employment Professionals 8516 NW Expy	Oklahoma City	OK	73162	**800-222-4057**	405-840-5000	719
Express Oil Change 1880 S Pk Dr	Hoover	AL	35244	**888-945-1771**	205-945-1771	61-5
Express-News Corp PO Box 2171	San Antonio	TX	78297	**800-555-1551**	210-250-3000	634-8
Express-Times 30 N Fourth St	Easton	PA	18042	**800-360-3601**	610-258-7171	531-2
Expressway Hotels 4303 17th Ave S	Fargo	ND	58103	**877-239-4303**	701-239-4303	379
Extended Care Hospital Westminster 206 Hospital Cir	Westminster	CA	92683	**800-236-9747**	714-891-2769	449
Extended Presence 3570 E 12th Ave Ste 200	Denver	CO	80206	**800-398-8957**	303-325-8600	318
Extended Stay America 11525 N Community House Rd Ste 100	Charlotte	NC	28277	**800-804-3724**	980-345-1600	379
Extended Stay Hotels *Crossland Economy Studios* 11525 N Community House Rd Ste 100	Charlotte	NC	28277	**800-804-3724**	980-345-1600	379
Extended StayAmerica 11525 N Community House Rd Ste 100	Charlotte	NC	28277	**800-804-3724**	980-345-1600	379
StudioPLUS Deluxe Studios 530 Woods Lake Rd	Greenville	SC	29607	**800-804-3724**	864-288-4300	379
Extensis 1800 SW First Ave Ste 500	Portland	OR	97201	**800-796-9798**	503-274-2020	179
Exterior Wood Inc 2685 Index St	Washougal	WA	98671	**800-222-1222**	360-835-8561	816
EXTOL International Inc 529 Terry Reiley Way	Pottsville	PA	17901	**800-542-7284**	570-628-5500	180-7
Extra Mile Mktg Inc 12600 SE 38th St Ste 205	Bellevue	WA	98006	**866-907-1753**	425-746-1572	196
Extreme Networks Inc 3585 Monroe St *NASDAQ: EXTR*	Santa Clara	CA	95051	**888-257-3000**	408-579-2800	178
Extreme Pita 2187 Dunwin Dr	Mississauga	ON	L5L1X2	**800-563-6688**	905-820-7887	311
Extreme Plastics Plus Inc 148 Roush Cir	Fairmont	WV	26554	**866-408-2837**		535
Extreme Reach Inc 75 2nd Ave Ste 720 *NASDAQ: DGIT*	Needham	MA	02494	**877-769-9382**	781-577-2016	510
Extron Electronics 1230 S Lewis St *Tech Supp	Anaheim	CA	92805	**800-633-9876***	714-491-1500	51
Extrude Hone Corp 235 Industry Blvd	Irwin	PA	15642	**800-835-3668**	724-863-5900	454
Extrudex Aluminum Ltd 411 Chrislea Rd	Woodbridge	ON	L4L8N4	**800-668-7210**	416-745-4444	491
Exxon Mobil Corp 5959 Las Colinas Blvd *NYSE: XOM*	Irving	TX	75039	**800-252-1800**	972-444-1000	535
Eyak Corp, The 360 W Benson Blvd Ste 210	Anchorage	AK	99503	**800-478-7161**	907-334-6971	360-3

Name / Address	City	State	Zip	Toll-Free	Phone	Class
Eyde Co 4660 S Hagadorn Ste 660	East Lansing	MI	48823	**800-422-3933**	517-351-2480	189
Eye Bank Assn of America (EBAA) 1015 18th St NW Ste 1010	Washington	DC	20036	**888-491-8833**	202-775-4999	48-8
Eye Bank for Sight Restoration Inc 120 Wall St 3rd Fl	New York	NY	10005	**866-287-3937**	212-742-9000	271
Eye Bank of British Columbia 2550 Willow St Eye Care Ctr 3rd Fl	Vancouver	BC	V5Z3N9	**800-667-2060**	604-875-4567	271
Eye Care for Animals 372 S Milwaukee Ave	Wheeling	IL	60090	**877-617-3937**	847-215-3933	239
Eye Center Surgeons & Associates Ll 401 Meridian St N Ste 200	Huntsville	AL	35801	**800-233-9083**	256-705-3937	239
Eye Centers of Florida (ECOF) 4101 Evans Ave	Fort Myers	FL	33901	**888-393-2455**	239-939-3456	796
Eye Communication Systems Inc 455 E Industrial Dr	Hartland	WI	53029	**800-558-2153**	262-367-1360	495
Eye Glass World Inc 2435 Commerce Ave Bldg 2200	Duluth	GA	30096	**800-637-3597**		542
Eye Lighting International NA 9150 Hendricks Rd *Cust Svc	Mentor	OH	44060	**888-665-2677***	440-350-7000	437
Eyefinity Inc 10875 International Dr Ste 200	Rancho Cordova	CA	95670	**877-448-0707**		179
Eye-Kraft Optical Inc 8 McLeland Rd	Saint Cloud	MN	56303	**888-455-2022**		541
Eye-Mart Express Inc 13800 Senlac Dr Ste 200	Farmers Branch	TX	75234	**888-372-2763**	972-488-2002	542
EyeMed Vision Care 4000 Luxottica Pl	Mason	OH	45040	**800-521-3605**	513-765-4321	391-3
eyeReturn Marketing 110 Eglinton Ave E Ste 705	Toronto	ON	M4P2Y1	**866-878-3335**	416-929-4834	5
Eyre Bus Service Inc 13600 Triadelphia Rd PO Box 239	Glenelg	MD	21737	**800-321-3973**	410-442-1330	106
EZ Loader Boat Trailers Inc 717 N Hamilton St	Spokane	WA	99202	**800-398-5623**	509-489-0181	761
EZ Trail Inc 1050 E Columbia St PO Box 168	Arthur	IL	61911	**800-677-2802**	217-543-3471	275
EZ8 Motels Inc 2484 Hotel Cir Pl	San Diego	CA	92108	**855-413-1222**	619-291-4824	705
ezCater Inc 101 Arch St Ste 1510	Boston	MA	02110	**800-488-1803**		387
EZCORP Inc 1901 Capital Pkwy *NASDAQ: EZPW*	Austin	TX	78746	**800-873-7296**	512-314-3400	568
Eze Castle Integration Inc 260 Franklin St 12th Fl	Boston	MA	02110	**800-752-1382**	617-217-3000	197
Eze Lap Diamond Products 3572 Arrowhead Dr	Carson City	NV	89706	**800-843-4815**	775-888-9500	695
Ezenia! Inc 14 Celina Ave Ste 17	Nashua	NH	03063	**800-966-2301**	781-505-2100	178
E-Z-GO 1451 Marvin Griffin Rd	Augusta	GA	30906	**800-241-5855**		515
E-Z-GO Division of Textron Inc 1451 Marvin Griffin Rd	Augusta	GA	30906	**800-241-5855**	706-798-4311	768

F

Name / Address	City	State	Zip	Toll-Free	Phone	Class
F & H Ribbon Co Inc 3010 S Pipeline Rd	Euless	TX	76040	**800-877-5775**		775
F & M Hat Co Inc 103 Walnut St PO Box 40	Denver	PA	17517	**800-953-4287**	717-336-5505	154-8
F C Kerbeck & Sons 100 Rt 73 N *General	Palmyra	NJ	08065	**855-846-1500***	856-829-8200	56
F E Myers 1101 Myers Pkwy	Ashland	OH	44805	**855-274-8947**	419-289-1144	638
F Mcconnell & Sons Inc 11102 Lincoln Hwy E	New Haven	IN	46774	**800-552-0835**	260-493-6607	298-8
F p i s Inc 220 Story Rd	Ocoee	FL	34761	**800-346-5977**	407-656-8818	7
F Visions Services 500 Greenwich St Fl 3	New York	NY	10013	**888-245-8333**	212-625-1616	120
F+W, A Content + eCommerce Co 10151 Carver Rd Ste 200 *Sales	Cincinnati	OH	45236	**800-289-0963***	513-531-2690	634-9
F-11 Photographic Supplies 16 E Main St	Bozeman	MT	59715	**888-548-0203**	406-586-3281	118
F5 Networks Inc 401 Elliott Ave W *NASDAQ: FFIV*	Seattle	WA	98119	**888-882-4447**	206-272-5555	178
FA Bartlett Tree Expert Co 1290 E Main St	Stamford	CT	06902	**877-227-8538**	203-323-1131	774
FA Davis Co 1915 Arch St	Philadelphia	PA	19103	**800-323-3555**	215-568-2270	634-2
FAA Credit Union PO Box 26406	Oklahoma City	OK	73126	**800-448-1990**	405-682-1990	221
Faa Federal Credit Union 3920 Whitebrook Dr	Memphis	TN	38118	**800-346-0069**	901-366-0066	221
Faac Inc 1229 Oak Valley Dr	Ann Arbor	MI	48108	**877-322-2387**	734-761-5836	701
FAAN (Food Allergy & Anaphylaxis Network) 11781 Lee Jackson Hwy Ste 160	Fairfax	VA	22033	**800-929-4040**	703-691-3179	47-17
Fabcon Inc 6111 Hwy 13 W	Savage	MN	55378	**800-727-4444**	952-890-4444	185
Fabian's Investment Resources 300 New Jersey Ave NW Ste 500	Washington	DC	20001	**800-950-8765**	267-295-8713	530-9
Fabral Inc 3449 Hempland Rd	Lancaster	PA	17601	**800-477-2741**	717-397-2741	479
Fabreeka International Inc 1023 Tpke St *Cust Svc	Stoughton	MA	02072	**800-322-7352***	781-341-3655	675
Fabricated Components Inc PO Box 431	Stroudsburg	PA	18360	**800-233-8163**	570-421-4110	481
Fabrication JR Tardif Inc 62 Blvd Cartier	Rivi Re-Du-Loup	QC	G5R6B2	**877-962-7273**	418-862-7273	275
Fabricators & Manufacturers Assn International (FMA) 833 Featherstone Rd	Rockford	IL	61107	**888-394-4362**	815-399-8700	48-13
Fabricut Inc 9303 E 46th St	Tulsa	OK	74145	**800-999-8200**	918-622-7700	361
Fabri-Form Co 200 S Friendship Dr	New Concord	OH	43762	**800-837-2574**	740-826-5000	601
Fabri-Kal Corp 600 Plastics Pl	Kalamazoo	MI	49001	**800-888-5054**	269-385-5050	601
Fabri-Quilt Inc 901 E 14th Ave	North Kansas City	MO	64116	**800-279-0622**	816-421-2000	260
Fabritech Inc 5740 Salmen St	New Orleans	LA	70123	**888-733-5009**	504-733-5009	742-8
FACC (Franklin Area Chamber of Commerce) 1259 Liberty St	Franklin	PA	16323	**888-547-2377**	814-432-5823	138
Face Stockholm Ltd 324 Joslen Blvd	Hudson	NY	12534	**888-334-3223**	518-828-6600	233
Facets Multimedia Inc 1517 W Fullerton Ave *Cust Svc	Chicago	IL	60614	**800-331-6197***	773-281-9075	510
Facility Solutions Group (FSG) 4401 Westgate Blvd Ste 310	Austin	TX	78745	**800-854-6465**	512-440-7985	248
Facing History & Ourselves 16 HuRd Rd	Brookline	MA	02445	**800-856-9039**	617-232-1595	47-11
Faction Media LLP 1730 Blake St Ste 200	Denver	CO	80202	**866-788-5306**		7
FactSet Research Systems Inc 601 Merritt 7 3rd Fl *NYSE: FDS*	Norwalk	CT	06851	**877-322-8738**	203-810-1000	404
FACVB (Fayetteville Area Convention & Visitors Bureau) 245 Person St	Fayetteville	NC	28301	**800-255-8217**	910-483-5311	208
FAE (New York State Society of Certified Public Accountant) 14 Wall St 19th Fl *General	New York	NY	10005	**800-537-3635***	212-719-8300	48-1
Faegre & Benson LLP 90 S Seventh St 2200 Wells Fargo Bldg	Minneapolis	MN	55402	**800-328-4393**	612-766-7000	428
FAF (Form-A-Feed Inc) 740 Bowman St	Stewart	MN	55385	**800-422-3649**	320-562-2413	446
Fafco Inc 435 Otterson Dr	Chico	CA	95928	**800-994-7652**	530-332-2100	90
Fager's Island Restaurant 201 60th St	Ocean City	MD	21842	**855-432-4377**	410-524-5500	669
FAHC (University of Vermont Medical Center, The) 111 Colchester Ave	Burlington	VT	05401	**800-358-1144**	802-847-0000	374-3
Fahlgren Inc 4030 Easton Station Ste 300	Columbus	OH	43219	**800-731-8927**	614-383-1500	4
FAIA (Pekin Insurance) 2505 Ct St	Pekin	IL	61558	**800-322-0160**	309-346-1161	391-4
FAIR (Federation for American Immigration Reform) 25 Massachusetts Ave NW Ste 330	Washington	DC	20009	**877-627-3247**	202-328-7004	47-7
Fair Grounds Race Course 1751 Gentilly Blvd	New Orleans	LA	70119	**800-262-7983**	504-944-5515	639
Fair Haven Beach State Park 14985 State Park Rd *General	Sterling	NY	13156	**800-456-2267***	315-947-5205	564
Fair Hills Resort 24270 County Hwy 20 *Resv	Detroit Lakes	MN	56501	**800-323-2849***	218-847-7638	667
Fair Isaac Corp 2665 Long Lake Rd Bldg C *NYSE: FICO* ■ *Cust Svc	Roseville	MN	55113	**888-342-6336***	612-758-5200	227
Fair Meadows at Tulsa 4609 E 21st St	Tulsa	OK	74114	**877-781-2660**	918-743-7223	639
Fair Oaks Hospital 5352 Linton Blvd	Delray Beach	FL	33484	**866-904-6871**	561-498-4440	374-5
Fair View Nursing Home 1714 W 16th St	Sedalia	MO	65301	**877-222-4114**	660-827-1594	371
Fair Winds Air Charter Inc 2525 SE Witham Field Hngr 7	Stuart	FL	34996	**800-989-9665**	772-288-4130	13
Fairbanks Convention & Visitors Bureau 101 Dunkel St Ste 111	Fairbanks	AK	99701	**800-327-5774**	907-456-5774	208
Fairbanks Correctional Ctr 1931 Eagan Ave	Fairbanks	AK	99701	**877-741-0741**	907-458-6700	215
Fairbanks Hospital 8102 Clearvista Pkwy	Indianapolis	IN	46256	**800-225-4673**	317-849-8222	724
Fairbanks Princess Riverside Lodge 4477 Pikes Landing Rd	Fairbanks	AK	99709	**800-426-0500**	907-455-4477	379
Fairbanks Scales Inc 821 Locust St	Kansas City	MO	64106	**800-451-4107**	816-471-0231	682
Fairbanks Youth Facility 1502 Wilbur St	Fairbanks	AK	99701	**800-478-2686**	907-451-2150	412
FairBridge Inns LLC 421 W Riverside Ave Ste 407	Spokane	WA	99201	**877-866-8090**		378
Fairchild Auto-mated Parts Inc 10 White St	Winsted	CT	06098	**800-927-2545**	860-379-2725	620
Fairchild Controls Corp 540 Highland St	Frederick	MD	21701	**800-695-5378**	301-228-3400	22
Fairchild Imaging Inc 1801 McCarthy Blvd	Milpitas	CA	95035	**800-325-6975**	408-433-2500	694
Fairchild Industrial Products Co 3920 Westpoint Blvd	Winston-Salem	NC	27103	**800-334-8422**	336-659-3400	203
Fairchild Semiconductor Corp 82 Running Hill Rd *NASDAQ: FCS*	South Portland	ME	04106	**800-341-0392**	207-775-8100	694
Fairfax County Convention & Visitors Bureau (FXVA) 3702 Pender Dr Ste 420	Fairfax	VA	22030	**800-732-4732**	703-790-0643	208
Fairfax Hospital 10200 NE 132nd St	Kirkland	WA	98034	**800-435-7221**	425-821-2000	374-5
Fairfax PET Imaging Ctr 8503 Arlington Blvd Ste 120 Lowr Level	Fairfax	VA	22031	**800-358-8831**	703-698-4441	767

Name / Address	City	State	ZIP	Toll-Free	Phone	Class
Fairfield Industries Inc 1111 Gillingham Ln	Sugar Land	TX	77478	**800-231-9809**	281-275-7500	471
Fairfield Medical Ctr (FMC) 401 N Ewing St	Lancaster	OH	43130	**800-548-2627**	740-687-8000	374-3
Fairfield Processing Corp 88 Rose Hill Ave	Danbury	CT	06810	**800-980-8000**	203-744-2090	604-1
Fairfield University Fairfield University 1073 N Benson Rd	Fairfield	CT	06824	**877-278-7396**	203-254-4010	571
Fairhaven 435 W Starin Rd	Whitewater	WI	53190	**877-624-2298**	262-473-2140	670
FairHope Hospice & Palliative Care Inc 282 Sells Rd	Lancaster	OH	43130	**800-994-7077**	740-654-7077	371
Fairlane Town Ctr 18900 Michigan Ave	Dearborn	MI	48126	**800-992-9500**		459
Fairleigh Dickinson University 285 Madison Ave	Madison	NJ	07940	**800-338-8803**	973-443-8500	167
Metropolitan 1000 River Rd	Teaneck	NJ	07666	**800-338-8803**	201-692-2000	167
FairMarket Life Settlements Corp 435 Ford Rd Ste 120	St Louis Park	MN	55426	**866-326-3757**		390
Fairmont Banff Springs PO Box 960	Banff	AB	T1L1J4	**800-441-1414**	403-762-2211	667
Fairmont Chateau Lake Louise 111 Lk Louise Dr	Lake Louise	AB	T0L1E0	**800-441-1414**	403-522-3511	667
Fairmont Chateau Whistler 4599 Chateau Blvd	Whistler	BC	V0N1B4	**800-441-1414**	604-938-8000	667
Fairmont Convention & Visitors Bureau 323 E Blue Earth Ave	Fairmont	MN	56031	**800-657-3280**	507-235-8585	208
Fairmont Hot Springs Resort 1500 Fairmont Rd	Fairmont	MT	59711	**800-332-3272**	406-797-3241	667
Fairmont Hotels & Resorts Inc 100 Wellington St W TD Ctr Ste 1600 *General	Toronto	ON	M5K1B7	**800-441-3313***	416-874-2600	379
Fairmont Kea Lani 4100 Wailea Alanui Dr	Maui	HI	96753	**800-659-4100**	808-875-4100	667
Fairmont Le Chateau Montebello 392 Notre Dame St	Montebello	QC	J0V1L0	**800-441-1414**	819-423-6341	667
Fairmont Orchid Hawaii 1 N Kaniku Dr	Kohala Coast	HI	96743	**800-845-9905**	808-885-2000	667
Fairmont San Francisco Hotel, The 950 Mason St	San Francisco	CA	94108	**800-257-7544**	415-772-5000	378
Fairmont Scottsdale Princess 7575 E Princess Dr	Scottsdale	AZ	85255	**800-257-7544**	480-585-4848	667
Fairmont Sonoma Mission Inn & Spa, The PO Box 1447	Sonoma	CA	95476	**866-540-4499**	707-938-9000	667
Fairmont State University 1201 Locust Ave *Admissions	Fairmont	WV	26554	**800-641-5678***	304-367-4892	167
Fairmount Behavioral Health System 561 Fairthorne Ave	Philadelphia	PA	19128	**800-235-0200**	215-487-4000	374-5
Fairmount Hotel, The 401 S Alamo St	San Antonio	TX	78205	**877-229-8808**	210-224-8800	379
FairPoint Communications Inc 521 E Morehead St Ste 250 *NASDAQ: FRP*	Charlotte	NC	28202	**866-740-2764**	704-344-8150	733
Fair-Rite Products Corp 1 Commerical Row PO Box J	Wallkill	NY	12589	**888-324-7748**	845-895-2055	251
Fairview Health Services 2450 Riverside Ave	Minneapolis	MN	55454	**800-824-1953**	612-672-6000	353
Fairview Hospice 2450 26th Ave S	Minneapolis	MN	55406	**800-285-5647**	612-728-2455	371
Fairview Hospital 18101 Lorain Ave	Cleveland	OH	44111	**800-801-2273**	216-444-0261	374-3
Fairview University Medical Ctr Mesabi 750 E 34th St	Hibbing	MN	55746	**888-870-8626**	218-262-4881	374-3
Fairview-Riverside State Park 119 Fairview Dr	Madisonville	LA	70447	**888-677-3247**	985-845-3318	564
Fairweather LLC 9525 King St	Anchorage	AK	99515	**800-319-8802**	907-346-3247	538
Fairwinds Federal Credit Union 3087 N Alafaya Trl	Orlando	FL	32826	**800-443-6887**	407-277-5045	221
Faith Baptist Bible College 1900 NW Fourth St	Ankeny	IA	50023	**800-409-3305**	515-964-0601	160
FaithTrust Institute 2400 N 45th St Ste 101	Seattle	WA	98103	**877-860-2255**	206-634-1903	47-17
Fakouri Electrical Engineering Inc 30001 Comercio	Rancho Santa Margarita	CA	92688	**800-669-8862**		263
Falcon Crest Aviation Supply Inc 8318 Braniff	Houston	TX	77061	**800-833-8229**	713-644-2290	258
Falcon Executive Aviation Inc 4766 E Falcon Dr	Mesa	AZ	85215	**800-237-2359**	480-832-0704	358
Falcon Express Inc 2250 E Church St	Philadelphia	PA	19124	**800-544-6566**	215-992-3140	778
Falcon Express Transportation Inc 6804 Virginia Manor Rd	Beltsville	MD	20705	**800-296-9696**	240-264-1215	315
Falcon Safety Products Inc 25 Imclone Dr	Branchburg	NJ	08876	**800-332-5266**	908-707-4900	150
Fall River Area Chamber of Commerce & Industry 200 Pocasset St	Fall River	MA	02721	**800-647-2824**	508-676-8226	138
Fall River Public Library 104 N Main St	Fall River	MA	02720	**800-331-3764**	508-324-2700	434-3
Fall River Rural Electric Co-op Inc 1150 N 3400 E	Ashton	ID	83420	**800-632-5726**	208-652-7431	247
Fallbrook Ctr 6633 Fallbrook Ave	West Hills	CA	91307	**866-718-1649**	818-885-9700	459
Fallon Community Health Plan Inc 10 Chestnut St Ste 7	Worcester	MA	01608	**800-333-2535**	508-799-2100	391-3
Fallsview Casino Resort 6380 Fallsview Blvd	Niagara Falls	ON	L2G7X5	**888-325-5788**		667
Falmouth Chamber of Commerce 20 Academy Ln	Falmouth	MA	02540	**800-526-8532**	508-548-8500	138
False Cape State Park 4001 Sandpiper Rd *General	Virginia Beach	VA	23456	**800-933-7275***	757-426-7128	564
Fam Funds 384 N Grand St PO Box 310	Cobleskill	NY	12043	**800-721-5391**	518-234-4393	318
FAME (Maine Finance Authority of Maine) 5 Community Dr PO Box 949	Augusta	ME	04332	**800-228-3734**	207-623-3263	723
Families Against Mandatory Minimums (FAMM) 1612 K St NW Ste 700	Washington	DC	20006	**800-435-7352**	202-822-6700	47-8
Families USA 1201 New York Ave NW Ste 1100	Washington	DC	20005	**888-392-5132**	202-628-3030	47-7
Familiprix Inc 6000 Rue Armand-Viau	Quebec	QC	G2C2C5	**800-463-5160**	418-847-3311	240
Family Brands International LLC 1001 Elm Hill Rd PO Box 429	Lenoir City	TN	37771	**800-356-4455**		297-26
Family Campers & RVers (FCRV) 4804 Transit Rd Bldg 2	Depew	NY	14043	**800-245-9755**	716-668-6242	47-23
Family Career & Community Leaders of America (FCCLA) 1910 Assn Dr	Reston	VA	20191	**800-234-4425**	703-476-4900	47-11
Family Caregiver Alliance (FCA) 180 Montgomery St Ste 900	San Francisco	CA	94104	**800-445-8106**	415-434-3388	47-17
Family Cir Magazine 375 Lexington Ave 9th Fl	New York	NY	10017	**800-627-4444**		456-11
Family Credit Counseling Service 111 N Wabash Ste 1408	Chicago	IL	60602	**800-994-3328**		40
Family Dollar Stores Inc PO Box 1017 *NYSE: FDO*	Charlotte	NC	28201	**866-377-6420**	704-847-6961	789
Family Handyman Magazine 2915 Commers Dr Ste 700	Eagan	MN	55121	**800-285-4961**		456-14
Family Home Hospice 1701 W Charleston Blvd	Las Vegas	NV	89102	**800-748-6773**	702-242-7000	371
Family Hospice & Palliative Care 50 Moffett St	Pittsburgh	PA	15243	**800-513-2148**	412-572-8800	371
Family Law Reporter 1801 S Bell St	Arlington	VA	22202	**800-372-1033**		530-7
Family Life Communications Inc PO Box 35300	Tucson	AZ	85740	**800-776-1070**		641
Family Motor Coach Assn (FMCA) 8291 Clough Pk	Cincinnati	OH	45244	**800-543-3622**	513-474-3622	47-23
Family Motor Coaching Magazine 8291 Clough Pk	Cincinnati	OH	45244	**800-543-3622**	513-474-3622	456-22
Family of the Americas Foundation PO Box 1170	Dunkirk	MD	20754	**800-443-3395**	301-627-3346	47-17
Family Practice Management 11400 Tomahawk Creek Pkwy	Leawood	KS	66211	**800-274-2237**	913-906-6000	456-16
Family Radio 290 Hegenberger Rd	Oakland	CA	94621	**800-543-1495**		640
Family Research Council (FRC) 801 G St NW	Washington	DC	20001	**800-225-4008**	202-393-2100	47-6
Family Stations Inc 290 Hegenberger Rd	Oakland	CA	94621	**800-543-1495**		643
Family Video 2500 Lehigh Ave	Glenview	IL	60026	**888-332-6843**	847-904-9000	795
Familymeds Inc 312 Farmington Ave	Farmington	CT	06032	**888-787-2800**		240
FamilySearch 35 N W Temple St	Salt Lake City	UT	84150	**866-406-1830**		387
FAMM (Families Against Mandatory Minimums) 1612 K St NW Ste 700	Washington	DC	20006	**800-435-7352**	202-822-6700	47-8
Famous Dave's Barbeque 181 Jennifer Rd	Annapolis	MD	21401	**877-833-9335**	410-224-2207	669
Famous Dave's of America Inc 12701 Whitewater Dr Ste 200 *NASDAQ: DAVE*	Minnetonka	MN	55343	**800-929-4040**	952-294-1300	668
Famous Footwear 247 Junction Rd *Cust Svc	Madison	WI	53717	**800-888-7198***	608-833-3340	302
Fannie Mae 3900 Wisconsin Ave NW *OTC: FNMA*	Washington	DC	20016	**800-732-6643**	202-752-7000	508
Fannin County Board of Education 2290 E First St	Blue Ridge	GA	30513	**800-308-2145**	706-632-3771	683
Fanning/Howey Assoc Inc 1200 Irmscher Blvd	Celina	OH	45822	**800-452-3573**	419-586-2292	263
Fantagraphics Books 7563 Lk City Way NE	Seattle	WA	98115	**800-657-1100**	206-524-1967	634-5
Fantastic Tours & Travel 6143 Jericho Tpke	Commack	NY	11725	**800-552-6262**	631-462-6262	758
Fan-Tastic Vent Corp 2083 S Almont Ave	Imlay City	MI	48444	**800-521-0298**	810-724-3818	36
Fantasy Diamond Corp 1550 W Carrol Ave	Chicago	IL	60607	**800-621-4445**	312-583-3200	410
Fantasy Springs Resort Casino 84-245 Indio Springs Pkwy *Cust Svc	Indio	CA	92203	**800-827-2946***	760-342-5000	132
Fantini Baking Company Inc 375 Washington St	Haverhill	MA	01832	**800-223-9037**	978-373-1273	297-1
Fantus Paper Products P.S. Greetings Inc 5730 N Tripp Ave *Sales	Chicago	IL	60646	**800-621-8823***	773-267-6069	129
FANUC America Corp 3900 W Hamlin Rd	Rochester Hills	MI	48309	**800-477-6268**	248-377-7000	386
Fanzz 2657 South 1030 West	Salt Lake City	UT	84119	**888-326-9946**	801-325-2700	709
Fapco Inc 216 Post Rd	Buchanan	MI	49107	**800-782-0167**	269-695-6889	548
FAPD (Federal APD Inc) 28100 Cabot Dr Ste 200	Novi	MI	48377	**877-992-7749**	248-374-9600	690
Far East Broadcasting Co Inc 15700 Imperial Hwy PO Box 1	La Mirada	CA	90638	**800-523-3480**		640
Fargo C'mon Inn Hotel 4338 20th Ave SW	Fargo	ND	58103	**800-334-1570**	701-277-9944	379
FARGODOME 1800 N University Dr	Fargo	ND	58102	**855-694-6367**	701-241-9100	718
Fargo-Moorhead Convention & Visitors Bureau 2001 44th St S	Fargo	ND	58103	**800-235-7654**	701-282-3653	208
Faribo Insurance Agency Inc 1404 Seventh St NW	Faribault	MN	55021	**888-923-0430**	507-334-3929	390
Farm & Home Oil Co 3115 State Rd	Telford	PA	18969	**800-776-7263**		317
Farm Boy Meats 2761 N Kentucky Ave	Evansville	IN	47711	**800-852-3976**	812-425-5231	472

	Toll-Free	Phone	Class
Farm Bureau Bank 2165 Green Vista Dr Ste 204 Sparks NV 89431	**800-492-3276**	775-673-4566	69
Farm Bureau Life Insurance Co 5400 University Ave West Des Moines IA 50266	**800-247-4170**	515-225-5400	391-2
Farm Business Consultants Inc 150 3015 Fifth Ave Ne Calgary AB T2A6T8	**800-265-1002**	403-735-6105	731
Farm Credit Council 50 F St NW Ste 900 Washington DC 20001	**866-632-9992**	202-626-8710	48-2
Farm Credit Leasing (FCL) 600 Hwy 169 S Ste 300 Minneapolis MN 55426	**800-444-2929**	952-417-7800	218
Farm Credit Of Central Florida Aca 115 S Missouri Ave Ste 400 Lakeland FL 33815	**800-533-2773**	863-682-4117	218
Farm Credit Of Northwest Florida Aca 5052 Hwy 90 Marianna FL 32446	**800-527-0647**	850-526-4910	218
Farm Credit of The Virginias Aca 106 Sangers Ln Staunton VA 24401	**800-559-1016**	540-886-3435	216
Farm Family Casualty Insurance Co PO Box 656 Albany NY 12201	**800-843-3276**	518-431-5000	391-4
Farm Family Life Insurance Co PO Box 656 Albany NY 12201	**800-948-3276**	518-431-5000	391-2
Farm Implement & Supply Company Inc 1200 S Washington Hwy 183 Plainville KS 67663	**888-589-6029**	785-434-4824	276
Farm Industry News 7900 International Dr Ste 300 Minneapolis MN 55425 *Cust Svc	**800-722-5334***	952-851-9329	456-1
Farm Journal 30 S 15th Ste 900 Philadelphia PA 19102	**800-331-9310**	215-557-8900	456-1
Farm Service Co-op 2308 Pine St Harlan IA 51537	**800-452-4372**	712-755-3185	278
Farm Show Magazine 20088 Kenwood Trial Lakeville MN 55044	**800-834-9665**		456-1
Farmdale Creamery Inc 1049 W Baseline St San Bernardino CA 92411	**800-346-7306**	909-889-3002	297-5
Farmer Boy Ag Systems Inc PO Box 435 Myerstown PA 17067	**800-845-3374**		276
Farmer Bros Co 20333 S Normandie Ave Torrance CA 90502 *NASDAQ: FARM*	**800-735-2878**	310-787-5200	297-7
Farmer State Bank of Sublette 303 S Pennsylvania Ave PO Box 20 Sublette IL 61367	**866-269-1722**	815-849-5242	360-2
Farmer's Co-op Assn 110 S Keokuk Wash Rd Keota IA 52248	**877-843-4893**	641-636-3748	47-2
Farmers Alliance Mutual Insurance Co 1122 N Main PO Box 1401 McPherson KS 67460	**800-362-1075**	620-241-2200	391-4
Farmers Bank, The 9 E Clinton St PO Box 129 Frankfort IN 46041	**800-932-7368**	765-654-8731	69
Farmers Capital Bank Corp PO Box 309 Frankfort KY 40602 *NASDAQ: FFKT*	**800-776-9437**	502-227-1668	360-2
Farmers Co-op 208 W Depot Dorchester NE 68343	**800-642-6439**	402-946-2211	277
Farmers Co-op Assn 105 Jackson St Jackson MN 56143	**800-864-3847**	507-847-4160	278
Farmers Co-op Union, The 225 S Broadway PO Box 159 Sterling KS 67579	**800-238-1843**	620-278-2141	11-1
Farmers Electric Co-op Inc 2000 E I-30 Greenville TX 75402	**800-541-2662**	903-455-1715	247
Farmers Fire Insurance Co 2875 Eastern Blvd York PA 17402	**800-537-0928**	717-751-4435	390
Farmers Insurance Exchange 4680 Wilshire Blvd Los Angeles CA 90010	**855-808-6599**	323-932-3200	391-4
Farmers Insurance Group 6060 W Manchester Ave Ste 302 Los Angeles CA 90045	**888-327-6335**		2
Farmers Mutual Hail Insurance Company of Iowa 6785 Westown Pkwy West Des Moines IA 50266	**800-247-5248**	515-282-9104	391-4
Farmers Mutual Insurance Company of Nebraska 1220 Lincoln Mall Lincoln NE 68508	**800-742-7433**	402-434-8300	391-4
Farmers Rice Co-op PO Box 15223 Sacramento CA 95851	**800-326-2799**	916-923-5100	297-23
Farmers Rural Electric Co-op Corp 504 S Broadway St Glasgow KY 42141	**800-253-2191**	270-651-2191	247
Farmers Supply Sales Inc 1409 E Ave Kalona IA 52247	**800-493-4917**	319-656-2291	276
Farmers Telecommunications Co-op (FTC) 144 McCurdy Ave N PO Box 217 Rainsville AL 35986	**866-638-2144**	256-638-2144	733
Farmers Telephone Co-op Inc 1101 E Main St Kingstree SC 29556	**888-218-5050**	843-382-2333	733
Farmers West 5300 Foothill Rd Carpinteria CA 93013	**800-549-0085**	805-684-5531	369
Farmers Win Coop (FFC) 110 N Jefferson Fredericksburg IA 50630	**800-562-8389**	563-237-5324	10-3
Farmers' Electric Co-op 201 W Business 36 PO Box 680 Chillicothe MO 64601	**800-279-0496**	660-646-4281	247
Farmington Convention & Visitors Bureau 3041 E Main St Farmington NM 87402	**800-448-1240**	505-326-7602	208
Farmington Press 218 N Washington St Farmington MO 63640	**800-455-0206**	573-756-8927	531-4
FarmLink Marketing Solutions Inc Suite 110-93 Lombard Ave Winnipeg MB R3B3B1	**877-376-5465**		197
FarmTek 1440 Field of Dreams Way Dyersville IA 52040	**800-327-6835**	563-875-2288	10-3
Farner-Bocken Co 1751 US Hwy 30 E PO Box 368 Carroll IA 51401	**800-274-8692**	712-792-3503	298-8
Farouk Systems Inc 250 Pennbright Dr Houston TX 77090	**800-237-9175**	281-876-2000	217
Farr Regional Library 1939 61st Ave Greeley CO 80634	**888-861-7323**	970-506-8550	434-3
Farr, Farr, Emerich, Hackett & Carr PA Earl D Farr Bldg 99 Nesbit St Punta Gorda FL 33950	**855-327-7529**	941-639-1158	428
Farrar Corp 142 W Burns St Norwich KS 67118	**800-536-2215**	620-478-2212	308
Farrel Corp 25 Main St Ansonia CT 06401	**800-800-7290**	203-736-5500	386
Farrell-Calhoun Inc 221 E Carolina Ave Memphis TN 38126	**888-832-7735**	901-526-2211	549
Farrey's Wholesale Hardware Company Inc 1850 NE 146th St North Miami FL 33181	**888-854-5483**	305-947-5451	361
Farris Evans Insurance Agency Inc 1568 Union Ave Memphis TN 38104	**800-395-8207**	901-274-5424	390
Farris Vaughan Wills & Murphy 700 W Georgia St Pacific Centre S 25th Fl PO Box 10026 Vancouver BC V7Y1B3	**877-684-9151**	604-684-9151	40
Farris, Riley & Pitt LLP 2025 Third Ave N Ste 400 Birmingham AL 35203	**888-580-5176**	205-324-1212	428
Farrs Better Foods 2575 South 300 West South Salt lake City UT 84115	**877-553-2777**	801-484-8724	297-25
Farwest Corrosion Control Co 1480 W Artesia Blvd Gardena CA 90248	**888-532-7937**	310-532-9524	263
FASB (Financial Acctg Standards Board) 401 Merritt 7 PO Box 5116 Norwalk CT 06856	**800-748-0659**	203-847-0700	48-1
FASCore LLC 8515 E Orchard Rd Greenwood Village CO 80111	**800-232-0859**	800-537-2033	534
FASEB (Federation of American Societies for Experimental Biology) 9650 Rockville Pk Bethesda MD 20814	**800-433-2732**	301-634-7000	48-19
Fashion Institute of Design & Merchandising			
Los Angeles 919 S Grand Ave Los Angeles CA 90015 *Admissions	**800-624-1200***	213-624-1200	163
Orange County 17590 Gillette Ave Irvine CA 92614	**888-974-3436**	949-851-6200	163
San Diego 350 Tenth Ave San Diego CA 92101	**800-243-3436**	619-235-2049	163
San Francisco 55 Stockton St San Francisco CA 94108	**800-422-3436**	415-675-5200	163
Fashion Island Shopping Ctr 401 Newport Ctr Dr Newport Beach CA 92660	**855-658-8527**	949-721-2000	459
Fashion Wallcoverings 4005 Carnegie Ave Cleveland OH 44103 *Orders	**800-362-9930***	216-432-1600	800
Fasig-Tipton Co Inc 2400 Newtown Pike Lexington KY 40511	**877-945-2020**	859-255-1555	50
Fasken Martineau DuMoulin LLP 333 Bay St Bay Adelaide Centre Ste 2400 PO Box 20 Toronto ON M5H2T6	**800-268-8424**	416-366-8381	40
Fast Company Magazine 7 World Trade Ctr New York NY 10007	**800-542-6029**	212-389-5300	456-5
Fast Heat Inc 776 Oaklawn Ave Elmhurst IL 60126	**877-747-8575**	630-833-5400	319
Fastbolt Corp 200 Louis St South Hackensack NJ 07606	**800-631-1980**	201-440-9100	350
Fastec Industrial 2219 Eddie Williams Rd Johnson City TN 37601	**800-837-2505**		351
Fastenal Co 2001 Theurer Blvd Winona MN 55987 *NASDAQ: FAST*	**877-507-7555**	507-454-5374	351
Fastener Supply Co 13410 S Ridge Dr PO Box 7369 Charlotte NC 28241	**800-888-9519**	704-596-7634	688
Fast-Fix Jewelry & Watch Repairs 451 Altamonte Ave Altamonte Springs FL 32701	**800-359-0407**	407-261-1595	311
FasTracKids International Ltd 6900 E Belleview Ave Ste 100 Greenwood Village CO 80111	**888-576-6888**	303-224-0200	311
FASTSIGNS International Inc 2542 Highlander Way Carrollton TX 75006	**800-327-8744**	972-447-0777	699
FastWeb Inc 444 N Michigan Ave Ste 600 Chicago IL 60611	**800-829-1040**	444-536-1212	723
Father Hennepin State Park 41294 Father Hennepin Pk Rd PO Box 397 Isle MN 56342	**888-646-6367**	320-676-8763	564
FAU (Florida Atlantic University) 777 Glades Rd Boca Raton FL 33431 *Admissions	**800-299-4328***	561-297-3000	167
Faulk & Winkler LLC 6811 Jefferson Hwy Baton Rouge LA 70806	**800-927-6811**	225-927-6811	196
Faulkner Information Services 7905 Browning Rd Pennsauken NJ 08109	**800-843-0460**	856-662-2070	634-11
Faulkner State Community College			
Bay Minette 1900 Hwy 31 S Bay Minette AL 36507	**800-381-3722**	251-580-2111	161
Fairhope 440 Fairhope Ave Fairhope AL 36532	**800-231-3752**	251-990-0420	161
Gulf Shores 3301 Gulf Shores Pkwy Gulf Shores AL 36542	**800-231-3752**	251-968-3101	161
Faulkner University 5345 Atlanta Hwy Montgomery AL 36109	**800-879-9816**	334-272-5820	167
Faultless Caster 3438 Briley Pk Blvd N Nashville TN 37207 *Cust Svc	**800-322-7359***		350
Fauquier Bank, The (TFB) 10 Courthouse Sq PO Box 561 Warrenton VA 20186	**800-638-3798**	540-347-2700	69
Fauquier Bankshares Inc 10 Courthouse Sq Warrenton VA 20186 *NASDAQ: FBSS*	**800-638-3798**	540-347-2700	360-2
Fauquier Times-Democrat 39 Culpeper St Warrenton VA 20186	**888-351-1660**	540-347-4222	531-4
Fauske & Assoc LLC 16w070 83rd St Burr Ridge IL 60527	**877-328-7531**	630-323-8750	194
Faxaway 417 Second Ave W Seattle WA 98119	**800-906-4329**	206-301-7000	733
FaxBack Inc 7007 SW Cardinal Ln Ste 105 Portland OR 97224	**800-329-2225**	503-597-5350	733
Fay School 48 Main St Southborough MA 01772	**800-933-2925**	508-485-0100	621
Fay Spofford & Thorndike LLC 5 Burlington Woods Burlington MA 01803	**800-835-8666**	781-221-1000	263
FAYBLOCK Materials Inc 130 Builders Blvd Fayetteville NC 28302	**800-326-9198**	910-323-9198	193-1
Fayette Chamber of Commerce 65 W Main St Uniontown PA 15401	**800-916-9365**	724-437-4571	138
Fayette County Board of Education 210 Stonewall Ave Fayetteville GA 30214	**800-550-5131**	770-460-3535	683

Name / Address	Toll-Free	Phone	Class
Fayette County Library			
216 W Market St .... Somerville TN 38068	**866-465-3591**	901-465-5248	434-3
Fayette County Public Library			
531 Summit St .... Oak Hill WV 25901	**855-275-5737**	304-465-0121	434-3
Fayette County Public Schools			
701 E Main St .... Lexington KY 40502	**877-597-2331**	859-381-4100	683
Fayette Electric Co-op Inc			
357 N Washington St .... La Grange TX 78945	**800-874-8290**	979-968-3181	247
Fayetteville Area Convention & Visitors Bureau (FACVB)			
245 Person St .... Fayetteville NC 28301	**800-255-8217**	910-483-5311	208
Fayetteville Observer			
458 Whitfield St .... Fayetteville NC 28306	**800-345-9895**	910-323-4848	531-2
Fayetteville Public Utilities			
408 W College St .... Fayetteville TN 37334	**800-379-2534**	931-433-1522	247
Fayetteville State University			
1200 Murchison Rd .... Fayetteville NC 28301	**800-222-2594***	910-672-1371	167
*Admissions			
Fayetteville Technical Community College			
2201 Hull Rd .... Fayetteville NC 28303	**877-245-5520**	910-678-8400	161
Fayetteville-Lincoln County Chamber of Commerce			
208 S Elk Ave .... Fayetteville TN 37334	**888-433-1238**	931-433-1234	138
FBFC (First Bank Financial Centre)			
155 W Wisconsin Ave			
PO Box 1004 .... Oconomowoc WI 53066	**888-569-9909**	262-569-9900	69
FBG Service Corp			
407 S 27th Ave .... Omaha NE 68131	**800-777-8326**	402-346-4422	103
FBLA-PBL (Future Business Leaders of America-Phi Beta Lambda Inc)			
1912 Assn Dr .... Reston VA 20191	**800-325-2946**		47-11
FBS (Fullerton Bldg Systems Inc)			
34620 250th St PO Box 308 .... Worthington MN 56187	**800-450-9782**	507-376-3128	815
FC Haab Company Inc			
2314 Market St .... Philadelphia PA 19103	**800-486-5663**	215-563-0800	317
FCA (Family Caregiver Alliance)			
180 Montgomery St Ste 900 .... San Francisco CA 94104	**800-445-8106**	415-434-3388	47-17
FCA (Fellowship of Christian Athletes)			
8701 Leeds Rd .... Kansas City MO 64129	**800-289-0909**	816-921-0909	47-22
FCA (First Co-op Assn)			
960 Riverview Dr PO Box 60 .... Cherokee IA 51012	**877-753-5400**	712-225-5400	446
FCC (First Community Corp)			
5455 Sunset Blvd .... Lexington SC 29072	**800-829-6372**	803-951-0555	360-2
NASDAQ: FCCO			
FCC (Federal Communications Commission)			
445 12th St SW .... Washington DC 20554	**888-225-5322**		340-18
FCC (Fremont Contract Carriers Inc)			
865 S Bud Blvd .... Fremont NE 68025	**800-228-9842**		448
FCC Services			
7951 E Maplewood Ave			
Ste 225 .... Greenwood Village CO 80111	**888-275-3227**		462
FCCI Insurance Group			
6300 University Pkwy .... Sarasota FL 34232	**800-226-3224**	941-907-3224	391-4
FCCLA (Family Career & Community Leaders of America)			
1910 Assn Dr .... Reston VA 20191	**800-234-4425**	703-476-4900	47-11
FCCU (First Community Credit Union)			
PO Box 1030 .... Chesterfield MO 63006	**800-767-8880**	636-728-3333	221
FCFC (First Community Financial Corp)			
4000 N Central Ave Ste 100 .... Phoenix AZ 85012	**877-777-4778**	602-265-7715	218
OTC: FMFP			
FCG (Florida City Gas)			
955 E 25th St .... Hialeah FL 33013	**800-993-7546**	305-691-8710	785
FCI Inc			
4661 Giles Rd .... Cleveland OH 44135	**800-321-1032**	216-251-5200	620
FCL (Farm Credit Leasing)			
600 Hwy 169 S Ste 300 .... Minneapolis MN 55426	**800-444-2929**	952-417-7800	218
FCL Graphics Inc			
4600 N Olcott Ave .... Harwood Heights IL 60706	**800-274-3380**	708-867-5500	626
FCNL (Friends Committee on National Legislation)			
245 Second St NE .... Washington DC 20002	**800-630-1330**	202-547-6000	614
FCPL (Flagler County Public Library)			
2500 Palm Coast Pkwy NW .... Palm Coast FL 32137	**877-863-5244**	386-446-6763	434-3
FCRV (Family Campers & RVers)			
4804 Transit Rd Bldg 2 .... Depew NY 14043	**800-245-9755**	716-668-6242	47-23
FCx Performance			
3000 E 14th Ave .... Columbus OH 43219	**800-253-6223**	614-324-6050	385
FD Lawrence Electric Company Inc			
3450 Beekman St .... Cincinnati OH 45223	**800-582-4490***	513-542-1100	248
*Cust Svc			
FD Roosevelt State Park			
2970 GA Hwy 190 .... Pine Mountain GA 31822	**800-864-7275**	706-663-4858	564
FDB (First DataBank Inc)			
701 Gateway Blvd			
Ste 600 .... South San Francisco CA 94080	**800-633-3453***		180-10
*General			
FDI Group Inc			
39500 High Pointe Blvd Ste 400 .... Novi MI 48375	**800-828-0759**		390
FDLI (Food & Drug Law Institute)			
1155 15th St NW Ste 800 .... Washington DC 20005	**800-956-6293**	202-371-1420	48-10
F&E Sportswear Corp			
1230 Newell Pkwy .... Montgomery AL 36110	**800-523-7762**	334-244-6477	685
Fearrington House			
2000 Fearrington Village Ctr .... Pittsboro NC 27312	**800-277-0130**	919-542-2121	379
Feather River College			
570 Golden Eagle Ave .... Quincy CA 95971	**800-442-9799**	530-283-0202	161
Featherlite Trailers			
Hwy 63 & 9 PO Box 320 .... Cresco IA 52136	**800-800-1230**	563-547-6000	777
Fechheimer Bros Company Inc			
4545 Malsbary Rd .... Cincinnati OH 45242	**800-543-1939**	513-793-5400	154-18
Federal APD Inc (FAPD)			
28100 Cabot Dr Ste 200 .... Novi MI 48377	**877-992-7749**	248-374-9600	690
Federal Assistance Monitor			
8204 Fenton St .... Silver Spring MD 20910	**800-666-6380**	301-588-6380	530-7
Federal Aviation Administration			
Aviation Research Div			
800 Independence Ave SW			
Rm 528A .... Washington DC 20591	**866-835-5322**	202-267-9251	666
Safety Hotline			
800 Independence Ave SW .... Washington DC 20591	**800-255-1111**		340-15
Federal Aviation Administration Northwest Mountain Region			
1601 Lind Ave SW .... Renton WA 98057	**800-220-5715**	425-227-2001	340-15
Federal Bldg Services Inc			
1641 Barclay Blvd .... Buffalo Grove IL 60089	**800-982-9234**	847-279-7360	151
Federal Block Corp			
247 Walsh Ave .... New Windsor NY 12553	**800-724-1999**	845-561-4108	185
Federal Bureau of Prisons			
National Institute of Corrections			
320 First St NW .... Washington DC 20534	**800-995-6423**	202-307-3106	340-12
National Institute of Corrections Information Cent			
11900 E Cornell Ave Unit C .... Aurora CO 80014	**800-877-1461**		340-12
Federal Business Products Inc			
95 Main Ave .... Clifton NJ 07014	**800-927-5123**	973-667-9800	109
Federal Cartridge Co			
900 Ehlen Dr .... Anoka MN 55303	**800-379-1732**		286
Federal Communications Commission (FCC)			
445 12th St SW .... Washington DC 20554	**888-225-5322**		340-18
Federal Computer Week Magazine			
3141 Fairview Pk Dr			
Ste 777 .... Falls Church VA 22042	**877-534-2208**	703-876-5100	456-7
Federal Contracts Report			
1801 S Bell St .... Arlington VA 22202	**800-372-1033**		530-7
Federal Correctional Complex			
Coleman			
846 NE 54th Terr .... Coleman FL 33521	**877-623-8426**	352-689-5000	214
Federal Correctional Institution			
Butner			
Old NC Hwy 75 PO Box 1000 .... Butner NC 27509	**877-623-8426**	919-575-4541	214
Englewood			
9595 W Quincy Ave .... Littleton CO 80123	**877-623-8426**	303-985-1566	214
Fairton			
655 Fairton-Millville Rd			
PO Box 280 .... Fairton NJ 08320	**877-623-8426**	856-453-1177	214
Forrest City			
1400 Dale Bumpers Rd .... Forrest City AR 72335	**877-623-8426**	870-630-6000	214
Loretto			
772 St Joseph St .... Loretto PA 15940	**877-623-8426**	814-472-4140	214
Manchester			
805 Fox Hollow Rd			
PO Box 4000 .... Manchester KY 40962	**877-623-8426**	606-598-1900	214
McKean			
6975 Rt 59 PO Box 8000 .... Lewis Run PA 16738	**877-623-8426**	814-362-8900	214
Yazoo City			
2225 Haley Barbour Pkwy			
PO Box 5050 .... Yazoo City MS 39194	**877-623-8426**	662-751-4800	214
Federal Deposit Insurance Corp			
550 17th St NW .... Washington DC 20429	**877-275-3342**	202-898-7192	340-18
Federal Deposit Insurance Corp Regional Offices			
Atlanta Area Office			
10 Tenth St NW Ste 800 .... Atlanta GA 30309	**800-765-3342**	678-916-2200	340-18
Boston Area Office			
15 Braintree Hill Office Pk			
Ste 300 .... Braintree MA 02184	**866-728-9953**	781-794-5500	340-18
Chicago Area Office			
300 S Riverside Plaza Ste 1700 .... Chicago IL 60606	**800-944-5343**	312-382-6000	340-18
Dallas Area Office			
1601 Bryan St .... Dallas TX 75201	**800-568-9161**	214-754-0098	340-18
Kansas City Area Office			
2345 Grand Blvd Ste 1200 .... Kansas City MO 64108	**800-209-7459**	816-234-8000	340-18
Memphis Area Office			
5100 Poplar Ave Ste 1900 .... Memphis TN 38137	**800-210-6354**	901-685-1603	340-18
New York Area Office			
350 5th Ave Ste 1200 .... New York NY 11215	**800-334-9593**	917-320-2500	340-18
San Francisco Area Office			
25 Jessie St at Ecker Sq			
Ste 2300 .... San Francisco CA 94105	**800-756-3558**	415-546-0160	340-18
SeaTac PO Box 13901 .... Seattle WA 98198	**877-623-8426**	206-870-5700	214
Federal EEO Advisor			
360 Hiatt Dr .... Palm Beach Gardens FL 33418	**800-341-7874**	561-622-6520	530-2
Federal Election Commission			
999 E St NW .... Washington DC 20463	**800-424-9530**	202-694-1100	267
Federal Emergency Management Agency (FEMA)			
500 C St SW .... Washington DC 20472	**800-621-3362**		340-9
FEMA for Kids			
500 C St SW Ste 714 .... Washington DC 20472	**800-621-3362**		340-9
National Flood Insurance Program			
500 C St SW .... Washington DC 20472	**888-379-9531**		340-9
Federal Emergency Management Agency Regional Offices (FEMA)			
Region 1 99 High St .... Boston MA 02110	**877-336-2734**	617-956-7551	340-9
Region 3			
1 Independence Mall			
615 Chestnut St 6th Fl .... Philadelphia PA 19106	**800-621-3362**	215-931-5500	340-9
Region 5			
536 S Clark St 6th Fl .... Chicago IL 60605	**877-336-2627**	312-408-5500	340-9
Region 6			
800 N Loop 288 .... Denton TX 76209	**800-426-5460**	940-898-5399	340-9
Region 9			
1111 Broadway Ste 1200 .... Oakland CA 94607	**877-336-2627**	510-627-7100	340-9
Federal Energy Regulatory Commission			
888 First St NE .... Washington DC 20426	**866-208-3372**	202-502-8004	340-7
Federal Energy Regulatory Commission Regional Offices			
Portland			
888 First St NE			
Fox Tower Ste 550 .... Washington DC 20426	**866-208-3372**	202-502-6088	340-7
Federal Equipment Co			
5298 River Rd .... Cincinnati OH 45233	**877-435-4723**	513-621-5260	174
Federal Express Europe Inc			
3610 Hacks Cross Rd .... Memphis TN 38125	**800-463-3339**	901-369-3600	545
Federal Flange			
4014 Pinemont St .... Houston TX 77018	**800-231-0150**	713-681-0606	482
Federal Foam Technologies Inc			
600 Wisconsin Dr .... New Richmond WI 54017	**800-898-9559**	715-246-9500	600
Federal Hearings & Appeals Services Inc			
117 W Main St .... Plymouth PA 18651	**800-664-7177**	570-779-5122	532
Federal Highway Administration			
National Highway Institute			
4600 Fairfax Dr Ste 800 .... Arlington VA 22203	**877-558-6873**	703-235-0500	340-15
Federal Industries Div Standex Corp			
215 Federal Ave .... Belleville WI 53508	**800-356-4206**		662
Federal Life Insurance Co Mutual			
3750 W Deerfield Rd .... Riverwoods IL 60015	**800-233-3750**	847-520-1900	391-2

	Toll-Free	Phone	Class
Federal Management Systems Inc			
462 K St NW .... Washington DC 20001	**877-637-8277**	202-842-3003	2
Federal Motor Carrier Safety Administration (FMCSA)			
1200 New Jersey Ave SE .... Washington DC 20590	**800-832-5660**		340-15
Federal Prison Camp			
Duluth			
6902 Airport Rd PO Box 1400 .... Duluth MN 55814	**877-623-8426**	218-722-8634	214
Montgomery			
Maxwell AFB .... Montgomery AL 36112	**877-623-8426**	334-293-2100	214
Federal Prison Industries Inc			
320 First St NW .... Washington DC 20534	**800-827-3168**		629
Federal Protection Inc			
2500 N Airport Commerce Ave			
.... Springfield MO 65803	**800-299-5400**		691
Federal Railroad Administration Regional Offices (FRA)			
Region 1			
55 Broadway Room 1077 .... Cambridge MA 02142	**800-724-5991**	617-494-2302	340-15
Region 2			
Baldwin Tower Ste 660			
1510 Chester Pike .... Crum Lynne PA 19022	**800-724-5992**	610-521-8200	340-15
Region 3			
61 Forsyth St SW Ste 16T20 .... Atlanta GA 30303	**800-724-5993**	404-562-3800	340-15
Region 4			
200 W Adams St .... Chicago IL 60606	**800-724-5040**	312-353-6203	340-15
Region 6			
901 Locust St Ste 464 .... Kansas City MO 64106	**800-724-5996**	816-329-3840	340-15
Region 8			
703 Broadway St Ste 650 .... Vancouver WA 98660	**800-724-5998**	360-696-7536	340-15
Federal Realty Investment Trust			
1626 E Jefferson St .... Rockville MD 20852	**800-658-8980**	301-998-8100	653
NYSE: FRT			
Federal Reserve Bank of Atlanta			
1000 Peachtree St NE .... Atlanta GA 30309	**888-500-7390**	404-498-8353	70
Birmingham Branch			
524 Liberty Pkwy .... Birmingham AL 35242	**800-257-7013**	205-968-6700	70
New Orleans Branch			
525 St Charles Ave .... New Orleans LA 70130	**877-638-7003**	504-593-3200	70
Federal Reserve Bank of Cleveland			
Cincinnati Branch			
150 E Fourth St .... Cincinnati OH 45202	**877-372-2457**	513-721-4787	70
Federal Reserve Bank of Dallas			
2200 N Pearl St PO Box 655906 .... Dallas TX 75201	**800-333-4460**	214-922-6000	70
El Paso Branch			
301 E Main St .... El Paso TX 79901	**800-333-4460**	915-521-5200	70
San Antonio Branch			
402 Dwyer Ave .... San Antonio TX 78204	**800-333-4460**	210-978-1200	70
Federal Reserve Bank of Kansas City			
1 Memorial Dr PO Box 1200 .... Kansas City MO 64198	**800-333-1010**	816-881-2000	70
Denver Branch			
1 Memorial Dr .... Kansas City MO 64198	**888-851-1920**		70
Oklahoma City Branch			
226 Dean A McGee Ave .... Oklahoma City OK 73102	**800-333-1030**	405-270-8400	70
Omaha Branch			
2201 Farnam St .... Omaha NE 68102	**800-333-1040**	402-221-5500	70
Federal Reserve Bank of Minneapolis			
90 Hennepin Ave .... Minneapolis MN 55401	**800-553-9656**	612-204-5000	70
Federal Reserve Bank of Philadelphia			
10 Independence Mall .... Philadelphia PA 19106	**877-574-1776**	215-574-6000	70
Federal Reserve Bank of Saint Louis			
701 Convention Plaza .... Saint Louis MO 63101	**800-333-0810**	314-444-8444	70
Little Rock Branch			
111 Ctr St			
Ste 1000 Stephens Bldg .... Little Rock AR 72201	**877-372-2457**	501-324-8300	70
Federal Reserve Bank of San Francisco (FRBSF)			
101 Market St .... San Francisco CA 94105	**800-227-4133**	415-974-2000	70
Portland Branch			
1500 SW First Ave Ste 100 .... Portland OR 97201	**800-227-4133**	503-276-3000	70
Salt Lake City Branch			
101 Market St .... San Francisco CA 94105	**800-227-4133**	415-974-2000	70
Federal Signal Corp Emergency Products Div			
2645 Federal Signal Dr .... University Park IL 60466	**800-264-3578**	708-534-3400	698
Federal Staffing Resources LLC			
2200 Somerville Rd Ste 300 .... Annapolis MD 21401	**866-886-2300**	410-990-0795	262
National Do Not Call Registry			
600 Pennsylvania Ave NW .... Washington DC 20580	**888-382-1222**		340-18
Federal Trade Commission Regional Offices			
East Central Region			
1111 Superior Ave Ste 200 .... Cleveland OH 44114	**877-382-4357**	216-263-3455	340-18
Midwest Region			
55 W Monroe St Ste 1825 .... Chicago IL 20580	**877-382-4357**		340-18
NortheastRegion			
1 Bowling Green Ste 318 .... New York NY 10004	**877-382-4357**	212-607-2829	340-18
Northwest Region			
915 Second Ave Rm 2896 .... Seattle WA 98174	**877-382-4357**		340-18
Southeast Region			
60 Forsyth St SW .... Atlanta GA 30303	**877-282-4357**	404-656-1390	340-18
Southwest Region			
1999 Bryan St Ste 2150 .... Dallas TX 75201	**877-382-4357**		340-18
Western Region			
901 Market St Ste 570 .... San Francisco CA 94103	**877-382-4357**		340-18
Federal Wage & Labor Institute			
7001 W 43rd St .... Houston TX 77092	**800-767-9243**	713-690-5676	750
Federal White Cement Ltd			
PO Box 1609 .... Woodstock ON N4S0A8	**800-265-1806***	519-485-5410	134
*Sales			
Federal-Mogul Corp			
27300 W 11 Mile Rd .... Southfield MI 48034	**800-325-8886***	248-354-7700	59
NASDAQ: FDML ■ *Cust Svc			
Federated Co-ops Inc			
502 S Second St .... Princeton MN 55371	**800-638-8228**	763-389-2582	578
Federated Group Inc			
3025 W Salt Creek Ln .... Arlington Heights IL 60005	**800-234-0011**	847-577-1200	345
Federated Insurance Cos			
121 E Pk Sq PO Box 328 .... Owatonna MN 55060	**800-533-0472**	507-455-5200	360-4
Federated Investors			
1001 Liberty Ave			
Federated Investors Twr .... Pittsburgh PA 15222	**800-245-0242**	412-288-1900	401
NYSE: FII			

	Toll-Free	Phone	Class
Federated Life Insurance Co			
121 E Pk Sq PO Box 328 .... Owatonna MN 55060	**800-533-0472**	507-455-5200	391-2
Federated Mutual Insurance Co			
121 E Pk Sq PO Box 328 .... Owatonna MN 55060	**800-533-0472**	507-455-5200	391-2
Federated Rural Electric Assn			
77100 US Hwy 71 PO Box 69 .... Jackson MN 56143	**800-321-3520**	507-847-3520	247
Federation Co-op			
108 N Water St .... Black River Falls WI 54615	**800-944-1784**	715-284-5354	278
Federation for American Immigration Reform (FAIR)			
25 Massachusetts Ave NW			
Ste 330 .... Washington DC 20009	**877-627-3247**	202-328-7004	47-7
Federation of American Societies for Experimental Biology (FASEB)			
9650 Rockville Pk .... Bethesda MD 20814	**800-433-2732**	301-634-7000	48-19
Federation of State Medical Boards of the US Inc (FSMB)			
400 Fuller Wiser Rd Ste 300 .... Euless TX 76039	**800-793-7939**	817-868-4000	48-8
FedEx 450 W First Ave .... Roselle NJ 07203	**800-463-3339**	406-252-6265	109
FedEx Corp			
3610 Hacks Cross Rd .... Memphis TN 38125	**800-463-3339**	901-369-3600	360-3
NYSE: FDX			
FedEx Custom Critical Inc			
1475 Boettler Rd .... Uniontown OH 44685	**800-463-3339***	234-310-4090	545
*Cust Svc			
FedEx Forum			
191 Beale St .... Memphis TN 38103	**866-648-4668**	901-205-1234	718
FedEx Supply Chain Services Inc			
5455 Darrow Rd .... Hudson OH 44236	**800-463-3339**	901-369-3600	448
Fedmet Resources Corp			
PO Box 278 .... Montreal QC H3Z2T2	**800-609-5711**	514-931-5711	661
Fednav Ltd			
1000 Rue de la GauchetiFre O			
Bureau 3500 .... Montreal QC H3B4W5	**800-678-4842***	514-878-6500	314
*General			
FedWorld.gov			
National Technical Information Service			
5285 Port Royal Rd .... Alexandria VA 22312	**800-553-6847**	703-605-6000	199
FEE (Foundation for Economic Education)			
30 S Broadway .... Irvington-on-Hudson NY 10533	**800-960-4333**	404-554-9980	631
Feeco International Inc			
3913 Algoma Rd .... Green Bay WI 54311	**800-373-9347**	920-468-1000	209
Feed the Children (FTC)			
PO Box 36 .... Oklahoma City OK 73101	**800-627-4556**	405-942-0228	47-5
Feesers Inc			
5561 Grayson Rd .... Harrisburg PA 17111	**800-326-2828**	717-564-4636	298-8
Feheley Fine Arts			
65 George St .... Toronto ON M5A4L8	**877-904-9114**	416-323-1373	41
FEI Behavioral Health			
11700 W Lk Pk Dr .... Milwaukee WI 53224	**800-782-1948**	414-359-1055	461
FEI Co			
5350 NE Dawson Creek Dr .... Hillsboro OR 97124	**866-693-3426***	503-726-7500	419
NASDAQ: FEIC ■ *Cust Svc			
Feingold Assn of the US			
37 Shell Rd 2nd Fl .... Rocky Point NY 11778	**800-321-3287**	631-369-9340	47-17
Feizy Import & Export Co Ltd			
1949 Stemmons Fwy .... Dallas TX 75207	**800-779-0877**	214-747-6000	292
Felbro Inc			
3666 E Olympic Blvd .... Los Angeles CA 90023	**800-733-5276**	323-263-8686	235
Feldmeier Equipment Inc			
6800 Townline Rd .... Syracuse NY 13211	**800-258-0118**	315-454-8608	299
Felician College			
262 S Main St .... Lodi NJ 07644	**888-442-4551**	201-559-6000	167
Rutherford			
223 Montross Ave .... Rutherford NJ 07070	**888-442-4551**	201-559-6000	167
Felix Neck Wildlife Sanctuary			
100 Felix Neck Dr .... Edgartown MA 02539	**866-627-2267**	508-627-4850	821
Felker Bros Corp			
22 N Chestnut Ave .... Marshfield WI 54449	**800-826-2304**	715-384-3121	489
Fellowes Inc			
1789 Norwood Ave .... Itasca IL 60143	**800-945-4545**	630-893-1600	110
Fellowship Hall Inc			
5140 Dunstan Rd .... Greensboro NC 27405	**800-659-3381**	336-621-3381	724
Fellowship of Christian Athletes (FCA)			
8701 Leeds Rd .... Kansas City MO 64129	**800-289-0909**	816-921-0909	47-22
Felly's Flowers Inc			
PO Box 6620 .... Madison WI 53716	**800-993-7673**		294
Felton Brush Inc			
7 Burton Dr .... Londonderry NH 03053	**800-258-9702**	603-425-0200	102
Felts Field Aviation Inc			
6205 E Rutter Ave .... Spokane WA 99212	**800-676-5538**	509-535-9011	62
FEM Electric Assn Inc			
PO Box 468 .... Ipswich SD 57451	**800-587-5880**	605-426-6891	247
FEMA (Federal Emergency Management Agency)			
500 C St SW .... Washington DC 20472	**800-621-3362**		340-9
FEMA (Federal Emergency Management Agency Regional Offices)			
Region 1 99 High St .... Boston MA 02110	**877-336-2734**	617-956-7551	340-9
Female Health Co			
515 N State St Ste 2225 .... Chicago IL 60654	**800-882-6655**	312-595-9123	476
Femco Machine Co			
754 S Main St Ext .... Punxsutawney PA 15767	**800-458-3445**	814-938-9763	453
Fender Musical Instruments Corp			
17600 N Perimeter Dr Ste 100 .... Scottsdale AZ 85255	**800-488-1818***	480-596-9690	526
*Cust Svc			
Fenner Drives			
311 W Stiegel St .... Manheim PA 17545	**800-243-3374***	717-665-2421	370
*Sales			
Fenton Art Glass Co			
700 Elizabeth St .... Williamstown WV 26187	**800-933-6766***	304-375-6122	334
*Cust Svc			
Fenway Park			
4 Yawkey Way .... Boston MA 02215	**877-733-7699**	617-226-6000	718
Fenwick Inn			
13801 Coastal Hwy .... Ocean City MD 21842	**800-492-1873**	410-250-1100	379
Ferguson Enterprises Inc			
12500 Jefferson Ave .... Newport News VA 23602	**800-721-2590**	757-874-7795	611
Ferguson Perforating & Wire Co			
130 Ernest St .... Providence RI 02905	**800-341-9800**	401-941-8876	482
Ferguson Supply & Box Manufacturing Co			
10820 Quality Dr .... Charlotte NC 28278	**800-821-1023**	704-597-0310	99
Ferguson Wellman Capital Management Inc			
888 S W Fifth Ave .... Portland OR 97204	**800-327-5765**	503-226-1444	527

Alphabetical Section

Name / Address	City	State	ZIP	Toll-Free	Phone	Class
Ferma Corp						
1265 Montecito Ave	Mountain View	CA	94043	**877-337-6211**	650-961-2742	191-16
Fernco Inc						
300 S Dayton St	Davison	MI	48423	**800-521-1283**	810-653-9626	595
Ferno-Washington Inc						
70 Weil Way	Wilmington	OH	45177	**800-733-3766**	937-382-1451	476
Fernwood Resort						
5785 Milford Rd	East Stroudsburg	PA	18302	**888-337-6966**		667
Feroleto Steel Company Inc						
300 Scofield Ave	Bridgeport	CT	06605	**800-243-2839**	203-366-3263	721
Ferrandino & Son Inc						
71 Carolyn Blvd	Farmingdale	NY	11735	**866-571-4609**	516-735-0097	609
Ferrara Fire Apparatus Inc						
PO Box 249	Holden	LA	70744	**800-443-9006**	225-567-7100	58
Ferrellgas Partners LP						
1 Liberty Plaza	Liberty	MO	64068	**888-337-7355**	816-792-1600	317
NYSE: FGP						
Ferring Pharmaceuticals Inc						
100 Interpace Pkwy	Parsippany	NJ	07054	**888-337-7464**	973-796-1600	240
Ferris School						
959 Centre Rd	Wilmington	DE	19805	**800-292-9582**	302-993-3800	412
Ferris State University						
1201 S State St	Big Rapids	MI	49307	**800-433-7747**	231-591-2000	167
FLITE Library						
1010 Campus Dr	Big Rapids	MI	49307	**800-433-7747**	231-591-3602	434-6
Traverse City						
2200 Dendrinos Dr Ste 200H	Traverse City	MI	49684	**866-857-1954**	231-995-1734	167
Ferro Corp						
6060 Parkland Blvd	Mayfield Heights	IN	44124	**800-321-3314**	216-875-5600	549
Ferro Corp Plastics Colorants Div						
6060 Parkland Blvd Ste 250	Mayfield Heights	OH	44124	**800-521-9094**	419-682-3311	549
Ferrum College						
215 Ferrum Mtn Rd	Ferrum	VA	24088	**800-868-9797**	540-365-2121	167
Ferry Plaza Wine Merchant Administration Offices						
101 The Embarcadero	San Francisco	CA	94105	**866-991-9400**	415-288-0470	443
FESCO Agencies NA Inc						
1000 Second Ave Ste 1310	Seattle	WA	98104	**800-275-3372**	206-583-0860	312
FESCO Ltd						
1000 Fesco Ave	Alice	TX	78332	**800-375-3479**	361-661-7000	538
Fesnak & Associates LLP						
1777 Sentry Pkwy W Ste 300	Blue Bell	PA	19422	**800-274-3978**	267-419-2200	731
Fess Parker's Doubletree Resort (FPDTR)						
633 E Cabrillo Blvd	Santa Barbara	CA	93103	**800-879-2929**	805-564-4333	667
Festiva Resorts						
1 Vance Gap Rd	Asheville	NC	28805	**866-933-7848***	828-254-3378	751
*Resv						
Festival Concert Hall						
North Dakota State University						
PO Box 5691	Fargo	ND	58105	**800-726-1724**	701-231-7932	571
Festival Flea Market Mall						
2900 W Sample Rd	Pompano Beach	FL	33073	**800-353-2627**	954-979-4555	459
Festival Inn, The						
1144 Ontario St	Stratford	ON	N5A6Z3	**800-463-3581**	519-273-1150	705
Festival Plaza						
101 Crockett St	Shreveport	LA	71101	**888-458-4748**	318-673-5100	207
Festive Holidays Inc						
5501 New Jersey Ave	Wildwood Crest	NJ	08260	**800-257-8920**	609-522-6316	758
Fetch Logistics Inc						
25 Northpointe Pkwy Ste 200	Amherst	NY	14228	**800-964-4940**	716-689-4556	312
Fey Industries Inc						
200 Fourth Ave N	Edgerton	MN	56128	**800-533-5340**	507-442-4311	85
FFB (First Financial Bancorp)						
255 E Fifth St Ste 700	Cincinnati	OH	45202	**877-322-9530**		360-2
NASDAQ: FFBC						
FFC (Farmers Win Coop)						
110 N Jefferson	Fredericksburg	IA	50630	**800-562-8389**	563-237-5324	10-3
FFD Financial Corp						
321 N Wooster Ave	Dover	OH	44622	**800-558-3424**	330-364-7777	360-2
OTC: FFDF						
FFE Transportation Inc						
1145 Empire Central Pl	Dallas	TX	75247	**800-569-9200**	214-630-8090	778
FFF Enterprises Inc						
41093 County Ctr Dr	Temecula	CA	92591	**800-843-7477**	951-296-2500	5
FFP (Food for the Poor Inc)						
6401 Lyons Rd	Coconut Creek	FL	33073	**800-427-9104**	954-427-2222	47-5
FFSI (First Financial Services Inc)						
6230 Fairview Rd Ste 450	Charlotte	NC	28210	**866-506-9090**		508
FFW Corp						
1205 N Cass St	Wabash	IN	46992	**800-377-4984**	260-563-3185	360-2
OTC: FFWC						
FGI (FOIA Group Inc)						
1250 Connecticut Ave NW Ste 200	Washington	DC	20036	**888-461-7951**		387
FGS (Freedom Graphic Systems Inc)						
1101 S Janesville St	Milton	WI	53563	**800-334-3540**		109
FH Bonn Co						
4300 Gateway Blvd	Springfield	OH	45502	**800-323-0143**	937-323-7024	742-3
Fhm Insurance Co						
4601 Touchton Rd E Bldg 300 Ste 3150	Jacksonville	FL	32246	**800-393-0001**	904-724-9890	391-4
FHN Memorial Hospital						
1045 W Stephenson St	Freeport	IL	61032	**800-747-4131**	815-599-6000	374-3
Fibar Group LLC, The						
80 Business Park Dr Suit 300	Armonk	NY	10504	**800-342-2721**	914-273-8770	709
Fiber Instruments Sales Inc						
161 Clear Rd	Oriskany	NY	13424	**800-500-0347***	315-736-2206	471
*Sales						
Fiber Optic Center New Trust						
23 Centre St	New Bedford	MA	02740	**800-473-4237**	508-992-6464	248
Fiber SenSys LLC						
2925 NW Aloclek Dr Ste 120	Hillsboro	OR	97124	**800-641-8150**	503-692-4430	690
Fibercomm Lc						
1605 Ninth St	Sioux City	IA	51101	**800-836-2472**	712-224-2020	115
Fiberglass Specialties Inc						
PO Box 1340	Henderson	TX	75653	**800-527-1459**	903-657-6522	607
Fibergrate Composite Structures Inc						
5151 Beltline Rd Ste 700	Dallas	TX	75254	**800-527-4043**	972-250-1633	605
FiberMark North America, Inc.						
161 Wellington Rd	Brattleboro	VT	05302	**800-784-8558***	802-257-0365	560
*Cust Svc						
Fibernetics Corp						
605 Boxwood Dr	Cambridge	ON	N3E1A5	**866-973-4237**	519-489-6700	226
Fiberoptics Technology Inc						
1 Quassett Rd	Pomfret	CT	06258	**800-433-5248***	860-928-0443	331
*Cust Svc						
Fiber-Tech Industries Inc						
2000 Kenskill Ave	Washington Court House	OH	43160	**800-879-4377**	740-335-9400	612
Fiberwave Corp						
140 58th St Bldg B Unit 6E	Brooklyn	NY	11220	**800-280-9011**	718-802-9011	811
Fibre Noire Internet Inc						
550 Ave Beaumont Ste 320	Montreal	QC	H3N1V1	**877-907-3002**		226
Fibre-Metal						
2000 Plainfield Pk	Cranston	RI	02921	**800-430-4110**		575
Fidelifacts						
42 Broadway Ste 1548	New York	NY	10004	**800-678-0007**	212-425-1520	632
Fidelity Advisor Funds						
PO Box 770002	Cincinnati	OH	45277	**800-522-7297**		527
Fidelity Bancshares Nc Inc						
PO Box 8	Fuquay Varina	NC	27526	**800-816-9608**	919-552-2242	69
Fidelity Bank						
100 E English St	Wichita	KS	67201	**800-658-1637**		69
Fidelity Engineering Corp						
25 Loveton Cir PO Box 2500	Sparks	MD	21152	**800-787-6000**	410-771-9400	14
Fidelity Exploration & Production Co						
1801 California St Ste 2500	Denver	CO	80202	**800-986-3133**	303-893-3133	537
Fidelity Federal Bancorp						
18 NW Fourth St	Evansville	IN	47708	**800-280-8280**	812-424-0921	360-2
OTC: FDLB						
Fidelity Investment Funds						
PO Box 770001	Cincinnati	OH	45277	**800-343-3548**		527
Fidelity Investments Charitable Gift Fund						
PO Box 770001	Cincinnati	OH	45277	**800-262-6039**		405
Fidelity Investments Institutional Operations Company Inc						
PO Box 770002	Cincinnati	OH	45277	**877-208-0098**		527
Fidelity Investments Institutional Services Company Inc						
82 Devonshire St	Boston	MA	02109	**800-343-3548**	617-563-9840	401
Fidelity National Title Group Inc						
601 Riverside Ave	Jacksonville	FL	32204	**888-866-3684**	904-854-8100	391-6
Fidelity National Title Insurance Co						
7025 N Scottsdale Rd	Scottsdale	AZ	85258	**888-934-3354**	480-344-6400	391-6
Fidelity National Title Insurance Company of Oregon						
900 SW Fifth Ave Mezzanine Level	Portland	OR	97204	**888-934-3354**	503-223-8338	391-6
Fidelity Partnership 1995						
483 Bay St Ste 200	Toronto	ON	M5G2N7	**800-263-4077**	416-307-5200	527
Fiducial						
1370 Ave of the Americas 31st Fl	New York	NY	10019	**866-343-8242**	212-207-4700	731
Fiducial						
10100 Old Columbia Rd	Columbia	MD	21046	**800-323-9000**	410-290-8296	731
Fiduciary Management Inc of Milwaukee						
100 E Wisconsin Ave Ste 2200	Milwaukee	WI	53202	**800-264-7684**	414-226-4545	401
Field Law						
10235 101 St Nw Ste 2000	Edmonton	AB	T5J3G1	**800-222-6479**	780-423-3003	428
Field Nation LLC						
310 Fourth Ave S Ste 8100	Minneapolis	MN	55415	**877-573-4353**		318
Field Paper Co						
3950 D St	Omaha	NE	68107	**800-969-3435**	402-733-3600	552
Field System Machining Inc						
720 Schneider Dr	South Elgin	IL	60177	**800-789-2814**	847-468-1313	491
Field Trip Factory						
2211 N Elston Ave Ste 304	Chicago	IL	60614	**800-987-6409**		298-8
Fieldale Farms Corp						
555 Broiler Blvd	Baldwin	GA	30511	**800-241-5400**	706-778-5100	618
Fieldpoint Private Bank & Trust						
100 Field Pt Rd	Greenwich	CT	06830	**877-438-4338**	203-413-9300	688
Fields Company LLC						
2240 Taylor Way	Tacoma	WA	98421	**800-627-4098**		45
Fiesta Henderson						
777 W Lk Mead Pkwy	Henderson	NV	89015	**888-899-7770**	702-558-7000	379
Fiesta Rancho Casino Hotel						
2400 N Rancho Dr	Las Vegas	NV	89130	**800-731-7333***	702-631-7000	132
*Resv						
Fiesta San Antonio Commission Inc, The						
2611 Broadway St	San Antonio	TX	78215	**877-723-4378**	210-227-5191	718
Fifield Land Co						
4307 Fifield Rd	Brawley	CA	92227	**800-536-6395**	760-344-6391	278
Fifth Third Bank Central Ohio						
21 E State St	Columbus	OH	43215	**866-671-5353**	800-972-3030	69
Figaro's Italian Pizza Inc						
1500 Liberty St SE Ste 160	Salem	OR	97302	**888-344-2767**	503-371-9318	668
Fiji Embassy						
1707 L St NW Ste 200	Washington	DC	20036	**800-932-3454**	202-337-8320	259
Fiji Visitors Bureau						
5777 W Century Blvd Ste 220	Los Angeles	CA	90045	**800-932-3454**	310-568-1616	773
Fiji Water Company LLC						
11444 W Olympic Blvd 2nd Fl	Los Angeles	CA	90064	**888-426-3454**	310-312-2850	79-2
Fike Corp						
704 SW Tenth St	Blue Springs	MO	64015	**877-342-3453**	816-229-3405	285
704 SW Tenth St	Blue Springs	MO	64015	**877-342-3453**	816-229-3405	747
File Keepers LLC						
6277 E Slauson Ave	Los Angeles	CA	90040	**800-332-3453**	323-728-3133	462
FileMaker Inc						
5201 Patrick Henry Dr	Santa Clara	CA	95054	**800-325-2747***	408-987-7000	180-1
*Cust Svc						
Fillauer Inc						
PO Box 5189	Chattanooga	TN	37406	**800-251-6398**	423-624-0946	476
Fillip Metal Cabinet Co						
4500 W 47th St	Chicago	IL	60632	**800-535-0733**	773-733-7527	320-1
Fillmore Glen State Park						
1686 St Rt 38	Moravia	NY	13118	**800-456-2267**	315-497-0130	564
Film Comment Magazine						
165 W 65th St	New York	NY	10023	**888-313-6085**	212-875-5610	456-9
Filoli 86 Canada Rd	Woodside	CA	94062	**866-691-9080**	650-364-8300	96

Alphabetical Section

Name / Address	City	State	ZIP	Toll-Free	Phone	Class
Filter Talent						
1425 4th Ave Ste 1000	Seattle	WA	98101	**800-336-0809**		262
FilterBoxx Water & Environmental Corp						
5716 Burbank Rd SE	Calgary	AB	T2H1Z4	**877-868-4747**	403-203-4747	318
Filterspun						
624 N Fairfield St	Amarillo	TX	79107	**800-323-5431**	806-383-3840	804
Filtertek Inc						
11411 Price Rd	Hebron	IL	60034	**800-248-2461**	815-648-1001	603
Filtration Group Inc						
912 E Washington St	Joliet	IL	60433	**877-603-1003**	815-726-4600	18
Filtration Lab Inc						
193 Rang De L Eglise	Saint Ligouri	QC	J0K2X0	**800-738-0168**	450-754-4222	789
FIMAC Solutions LLC						
Denver Technological Ctr 5299 DTC Blvd Ste 950	Greenwood Village	CO	80111	**877-789-5905**	303-320-1900	688
Fimc Commercial Realty						
1619 S Tyler St	Amarillo	TX	79102	**800-658-2616**	806-358-7151	650
Fin Pan Inc						
3255 Symmes Rd	Hamilton	OH	45015	**800-833-6444**	513-870-9200	185
FinAid Page LLC						
PO Box 2056	Cranberry Township	PA	16066	**800-433-3243**	724-538-4500	723
Final Draft Inc						
26707 W Agoura Rd Ste 205	Calabasas	CA	91302	**800-231-4055**	818-995-8995	180-10
Finance & Commerce						
730 Second Ave S US Trust Bldg Ste 100	Minneapolis	MN	55402	**800-451-9998**	612-333-4244	456-5
Finance Ctr Federal Credit Union						
PO Box 26501	Indianapolis	IN	46226	**800-473-2328**	317-916-7700	221
Finance Factors Ltd						
1164 Bishop St	Honolulu	HI	96813	**800-648-7136**	808-548-4940	216
Financial & Realty Services LLC						
1110 Bonifant St Ste 301	Silver Spring	MD	20910	**800-650-9714**	301-650-9112	273
Financial Acctg Standards Board (FASB)						
401 Merritt 7 PO Box 5116	Norwalk	CT	06856	**800-748-0659**	203-847-0700	48-1
Financial Advisory Service Inc						
4747 W 135th St	Leawood	KS	66224	**888-700-9230**	913-239-2300	196
Financial Engines Inc						
1804 Embarcadero Rd	Palo Alto	CA	94303	**888-443-8577**	408-498-6000	180-10
NASDAQ: FNGN						
Financial Guaranty Insurance Co						
125 Pk Ave 6th Fl	New York	NY	10017	**800-352-0001**	212-312-3000	391-5
Financial Institutions Inc						
220 Liberty St	Warsaw	NY	14569	**866-296-3743**	585-786-1100	360-2
NASDAQ: FISI						
Financial Managers Society (FMS)						
100 W Monroe St Ste 810	Chicago	IL	60603	**800-275-4367***	312-578-1300	48-2
*Cust Svc						
Financial Pacific Co						
3455 S 344th Way Ste 300	Federal Way	WA	98001	**800-447-7107**		218
Financial Partners Credit Union						
PO Box 7005	Downey	CA	90241	**800-950-7328**	562-923-0311	221
Financial Planning Assn (FPA)						
7535 E Hampden Ave Ste 600	Denver	CO	80231	**800-322-4237**	303-759-4900	48-2
Financial Publishing Co						
PO Box 570	South Bend	IN	46624	**800-433-0090***	574-243-6040	634-2
*Cust Svc						
Financial Service Corp						
2300 Windy Ridge Pkwy Ste 1100	Atlanta	GA	30339	**800-547-2382**		688
Financial Times						
1330 Ave of the Americas	New York	NY	10019	**800-628-8088**	212-641-6500	531-2
FinancialCAD Corp						
13450 102nd Ave Ste 1750	Surrey	BC	V3T5X3	**800-304-0702**	604-957-1200	38
FINCA (Foundation for International Community Assistance)						
1201 15th St NW 8th fl	Washington	DC	20005	**855-903-4622**	202-682-1510	47-5
Fincantieri Marine Systems North America Inc						
800-C Principal Ct	Chesapeake	VA	23320	**877-436-7643**	757-548-6000	688
Finch Paper LLC						
1 Glen St	Glens Falls	NY	12801	**800-833-9983**	518-793-2541	556
Finck Cigar Co						
414 Vera Cruz St	San Antonio	TX	78207	**800-221-0638***	210-226-4191	754
*Orders						
Find the Children						
2656 29th St Ste 203	Santa Monica	CA	90405	**888-477-6721**	310-314-3213	47-6
Findings Inc						
160 Water St	Keene	NH	03431	**800-225-2706**	603-352-3717	407
Findlay Automobile Club						
1550 Tiffin Ave	Findlay	OH	45840	**800-222-4357**	419-422-4961	52
Findlay Inn & Conference Ctr						
200 E Main Cross St	Findlay	OH	45840	**800-825-1455***	419-422-5682	379
*Cust Svc						
Fine Homebuilding Magazine						
63 S Main St PO Box 5506	Newtown	CT	06470	**800-283-7252**	203-426-8171	456-21
Fine Line Production						
2221 Regal Pkwy	Euless	TX	76040	**800-887-5625**	817-267-6750	482
Fine Organics Corp						
420 Kuller Rd PO Box 2277	Clifton	NJ	07015	**800-526-7480**	973-478-1000	150
Fine Woodworking Magazine						
63 S Main St PO Box 5506	Newtown	CT	06470	**800-283-7252**	203-426-8171	456-14
Fineline Printing Group						
8081 Zionsville Rd	Indianapolis	IN	46268	**877-334-7687**	317-872-4490	626
Finger Lakes Gaming & Race Track						
5857 Rt 96	Farmington	NY	14425	**877-846-7369**	585-924-3232	639
Finger Lakes Library System						
119 E Green St	Ithaca	NY	14850	**800-909-3557**	607-273-4074	434-3
Finger Lakes Times						
218 Genesse St PO Box 393	Geneva	NY	14456	**800-388-6652**	315-789-3333	634-8
Finger Lakes Visitors Connection						
25 Gorham St	Canandaigua	NY	14424	**877-386-4669**	585-394-3915	208
Fingerhut						
6509 Flying Cloud Dr	Eden Prairie	MN	55344	**800-208-2500**		458
Finish Line Ford Inc						
2211 W Pioneer Pkwy	Peoria	IL	61615	**888-841-4002**	309-693-2525	56
Finish Line Inc, The						
3308 N Mitthoeffer Rd	Indianapolis	IN	46235	**888-777-3949**	317-899-1022	302
NASDAQ: FINL						
FinishMaster Inc						
115 W Washington St 700 S	Indianapolis	IN	46204	**888-311-3678**	317-237-3678	549
Finken Plumbing Heating & Cooling						
628 19th Ave NE	Saint Joseph	MN	56374	**877-346-5367**	320-258-2005	609
Finks Jewelry Inc						
3545 Electric Rd	Roanoke	VA	24018	**800-699-7464**	540-342-2991	410
Finlandia Sauna Products Inc						
14010 Sw 72nd Ave Ste B	Portland	OR	97224	**800-354-3342**	503-684-8289	709
Finlandia University						
601 Quincy St	Hancock	MI	49930	**800-682-7604**	906-482-5300	167
Finley Hospital						
350 N Grandview Ave	Dubuque	IA	52001	**800-582-1891**	563-582-1881	374-3
Finn Corp						
9281 Le St Dr	Fairfield	OH	45014	**800-543-7166**	513-874-2818	275
Finn's Point National Cemetery						
454 Ft. Mott Rd	Pennsville	NJ	08070	**800-827-1000**	215-504-5610	135
Finney County Convention & Visitors Bureau						
1511 E Fulton Terr	Garden City	KS	67846	**866-267-4638**	620-275-1900	208
Finnleo Sauna						
575 Cokato St E	Cokato	MN	55321	**800-346-6536**		320-2
FINRA 1735 K St NW	Washington	DC	20006	**800-289-9999**	202-728-8000	48-2
Finzer Roller Co						
129 Rawls Rd	Des Plaines	IL	60018	**888-486-1900**	847-390-6200	675
Fire & Life Safety America						
3017 Vernon Rd	Richmond	VA	23228	**800-252-5069**	804-222-1381	285
3017 Vernon Rd	Richmond	VA	23228	**800-252-5069**	804-222-1381	747
Fire Fighter Sales & Service Co						
791 Commonwealth Dr	Warrendale	PA	15086	**888-412-3473**	724-720-6000	609
Firecom Inc						
39-27 59th St	Woodside	NY	11377	**888-347-3269**	718-899-6100	285
39-27 59th St	Woodside	NY	11377	**888-347-3269**	718-899-6100	747
Fire-End & Croker Corp						
7 Westchester Plz	Elmsford	NY	10523	**800-759-3473**	914-592-3640	575
Firefighters Community Credit Union Inc						
2300 St Clair Ave NE	Cleveland	OH	44114	**800-621-4644**	216-621-4644	221
FireKing Security Group						
101 Security Pkwy	New Albany	IN	47150	**800-457-2424**	812-948-8400	690
Firelands Electric Co-op Inc						
1 Energy Pl PO Box 32	New London	OH	44851	**800-533-8658**	419-929-1571	247
Firelands Regional Medical Ctr						
1111 Hayes Ave	Sandusky	OH	44870	**800-342-1177**	419-557-7400	374-3
Fireman's Fund Insurance Co						
1465 N McDowell Blvd	Petaluma	CA	94954	**866-386-3932**		391-5
Fireside Hearth & Home						
7571 215th St W	Lakeville	MN	55044	**800-669-4328**	651-452-3399	110
Fireside Inn & Suites						
25 Airport Rd	West Lebanon	NH	03784	**877-258-5900**	603-298-5900	379
FireSky Resort & Spa						
4925 N Scottsdale Rd	Scottsdale	AZ	85251	**800-528-7867**	480-945-7666	667
Firestone Fibers & Textiles Co						
100 Firestone Ln PO Box 1369	Kings Mountain	NC	28086	**800-441-1336**	704-734-2132	742-3
Firestone Industrial Products Co						
250 W 96th St	Indianapolis	IN	46260	**800-888-0650**	317-818-8600	59
Fireworks Fine Crafts Gallery						
3307 Utah Ave S	Seattle	WA	98134	**800-505-8882**	206-682-8707	519
Firm Consulting Group						
2107 W Cass St Ste B	Tampa	FL	33606	**877-636-9525**		462
FIRST						
200 Bedford St	Manchester	NH	03101	**800-871-8326**	603-666-3906	47-11
First Act Inc						
745 Boylston St	Boston	MA	02116	**888-551-1115**	617-226-7888	525
First Action Security Security Team Inc						
18702 Crestwood Dr	Hagerstown	MD	21742	**800-372-7447***	301-797-2124	690
*Cust Svc						
First Alarm Security & Patrol Inc						
1111 Estates Dr	Aptos	CA	95003	**800-684-1111**	831-476-1111	691
First Alert Inc						
3901 Liberty St Rd	Aurora	IL	60504	**800-323-9005**	630-851-7330	285
3901 Liberty St Rd	Aurora	IL	60504	**800-323-9005**	630-851-7330	747
First American Bank & Trust						
2785 Hwy 20 W PO Box 550	Vacherie	LA	70090	**800-738-2265**	225-265-2265	69
First American Bank Corp						
1650 Louis Ave	Elk Grove Village	IL	60009	**866-449-1150**	847-952-3700	360-2
First American Corp						
1 First American Way	Santa Ana	CA	92707	**800-854-3643**	714-250-3000	391-6
NYSE: FAF						
First American Funds						
PO Box 701	Milwaukee	WI	53201	**800-677-3863**		527
First American Home Buyers Protection Corp						
7833 Haskell Ave PO Box 10180	Van Nuys	CA	91410	**800-444-9030**	818-781-5050	367
First Bancorp						
341 N Main St	Troy	NC	27371	**800-548-9377**	910-576-6171	360-2
NASDAQ: FBNC						
First Banctrust Corp						
101 S Central Ave	Paris	IL	61944	**800-228-6381**	217-465-6381	360-2
OTC: FIRT						
First Bank Financial Centre (FBFC)						
155 W Wisconsin Ave PO Box 1004	Oconomowoc	WI	53066	**888-569-9909**	262-569-9900	69
First Bank Muleshoe						
202 S 1st PO Box 565	Muleshoe	TX	79347	**888-653-9558**	806-272-4515	69
First Bank Of Highland Park						
1835 First St PO Box 546	Highland Park	IL	60035	**877-651-7800**	847-432-7800	683
First Banks Inc						
135 N Meramec Ave	Clayton	MO	63105	**800-760-2265**	314-854-4600	360-2
First Busey Corp						
100 W University Ave	Champaign	IL	61820	**800-672-8739**	217-365-4516	360-2
NASDAQ: BUSE						
First Business Financial Services Inc						
401 Charmany Dr	Madison	WI	53719	**888-455-2263**	608-238-8008	69
NASDAQ: FBIZ						
First Calgary Savings						
510 16th Ave NE	Calgary	AB	T2E1K4	**866-923-4778**		69
First Candle						
1314 Bedford Ave Ste 210	Baltimore	MD	21208	**800-221-7437**	410-653-8226	47-17
First Carolina Corporate Credit Union						
7900 Triad Ctr Dr Ste 410	Greensboro	NC	27409	**800-585-4317**		218
First Cash Financial Services Inc						
690 E Lamar Blvd Ste 400	Arlington	TX	76011	**800-290-4598**	817-460-3947	568
NASDAQ: FCFS						
First Century Bank NA						
500 Federal St	Bluefield	WV	24701	**877-214-9426**	304-325-8181	69

Name / Address	City	State	ZIP	Toll-Free	Phone	Class
First Chemical Corp 1001 Industrial Rd	Pascagoula	MS	39581	**877-243-6178**	228-762-0870	143
First Choice Health Plan 600 University St Ste 1400	Seattle	WA	98101	**800-467-5281**		391-3
First Church of Christ Scientist 210 Massachusetts Ave P05-10	Boston	MA	02115	**800-288-7155**	617-450-2000	47-20
First Citizens Bancorp Inc PO Box 29 *OTC: FCBN*	Columbia	SC	29202	**888-612-4444**	919-716-4588	360-2
First Citizens Bank 350 S Beverly D Ste 150	Beverly Hills	CA	90212	**888-323-4732**		360-2
First Citizens Bank & Trust Co Inc 1230 Main St	Columbia	SC	29201	**888-612-4444**	919-716-4588	69
First Citizens National Bank Charitable Foundation PO Box 1708	Mason City	IA	50402	**800-423-1602**	641-423-1600	360-2
First Class Services Inc 9355 US Hwy 60 E *General	Lewisport	KY	42351	**800-467-8684***	270-295-3746	778
First Command Financial Services Inc 1 FirstComm Plz	Fort Worth	TX	76109	**800-443-2104**	817-731-8621	196
First Commonwealth Financial Corp 601 Philadelphia St *NYSE: FCF*	Indiana	PA	15701	**800-711-2265**	724-349-7220	360-2
First Community Corp (FCC) 5455 Sunset Blvd *NASDAQ: FCCO*	Lexington	SC	29072	**800-829-6372**	803-951-0555	360-2
First Community Credit Union (FCCU) PO Box 1030	Chesterfield	MO	63006	**800-767-8880**	636-728-3333	221
First Community Financial Corp (FCFC) 4000 N Central Ave Ste 100 *OTC: FMFP*	Phoenix	AZ	85012	**877-777-4778**	602-265-7715	218
First Community Village 1800 Riverside Dr	Columbus	OH	43212	**877-364-2570**	614-324-4455	670
First Co-op Assn (FCA) 960 Riverview Dr PO Box 60	Cherokee	IA	51012	**877-753-5400**	712-225-5400	446
First Corporate Sedans Inc 60 E 42nd St Ste 2424	New York	NY	10165	**800-473-8876**	212-972-2282	317
First DataBank Inc (FDB) 701 Gateway Blvd Ste 600 *General	South San Francisco	CA	94080	**800-633-3453***		180-10
First Defiance Financial Corp 601 Clinton St *NASDAQ: FDEF*	Defiance	OH	43512	**800-472-6292**	419-782-5015	360-2
First Dental Health 5771 Copley Dr Ste 101	San Diego	CA	92111	**800-334-7244**		415
First Draft 316 N Michigan Ave Ste 400	Chicago	IL	60601	**800-878-5331**	800-493-4867	530-11
First Eastern Mortgage Corp 100 Brickstone Sq	Andover	MA	01810	**800-777-2240**	978-749-3100	508
First Electric Co-op Corp 1000 S JP Wright Loop Rd	Jacksonville	AR	72076	**800-489-7405**	501-982-4545	247
First Environment Inc 91 Fulton St	Boonton	NJ	07005	**800-486-5869**	973-334-0003	194
First Equipment Co PO Box 2129	Addison	TX	75001	**888-780-8631**	972-380-2300	266-1
First Equity Mortgage Bankers 9300 S Dadeland Blvd Ste 500	Miami	FL	33156	**800-973-3654**	305-666-3333	508
First Farmers & Merchants National Bank 816 S Garden St PO Box 1148 *OTC: FIME*	Columbia	TN	38401	**800-882-8378**	931-388-3145	683
First Federal Bank Fsb 6900 N Executive Dr	Kansas City	MO	64120	**888-651-4759**	816-241-7800	69
First Federal Lakewood 14806 Detroit Ave	Lakewood	OH	44107	**800-966-7300**	216-529-2700	69
First Federal of Northern Michigan 100 S Second Ave *NASDAQ: FFNM*	Alpena	MI	49707	**800-916-8800**	989-356-9041	70
First Financial Bancorp (FFB) 255 E Fifth St Ste 700 *NASDAQ: FFBC*	Cincinnati	OH	45202	**877-322-9530**		360-2
First Financial Bank 1 First Financial Plz	Terre Haute	IN	47807	**800-511-0045**	812-238-6000	69
First Financial Bankshares Inc PO Box 701 *NASDAQ: FFIN*	Abilene	TX	79604	**888-588-2623**	325-627-7155	360-2
First Financial Corp 1 First Financial Plz *NASDAQ: THFF*	Terre Haute	IN	47807	**800-511-0045**	812-238-6000	360-2
First Financial Services Inc (FFSI) 6230 Fairview Rd Ste 450	Charlotte	NC	28210	**866-506-9090**		508
First Foundation Bank 18101 Von Karman Ave Ste 750	Irvine	CA	92612	**800-224-7931**	949-202-4100	69
First FSB 633 La Salle St	Ottawa	IL	61350	**800-443-8780**	815-434-3500	70
First FSB of Frankfort 216 W Main St PO Box 535	Frankfort	KY	40602	**888-818-3372**	502-223-1638	360-2
First Gold Hotel 270 Main St	Deadwood	SD	57732	**800-274-1876**	605-578-9777	379
First Hawaiian Bank 999 Bishop St	Honolulu	HI	96813	**888-844-4444**	808-525-6340	69
First Health Group Corp *Coventry* 3200 Highland Ave	Downers Grove	IL	60515	**800-247-2898**	630-737-7900	462
First Horizon National Corp 165 Madison *NYSE: FHN*	Memphis	TN	38103	**800-489-4040**	901-523-4444	360-2
First Insurance Company of Hawaii Ltd 1100 Ward Ave PO Box 2866	Honolulu	HI	96803	**800-272-5202**	808-527-7777	391-4
First Insurance Funding Corp 450 Skokie Blvd Ste 1000	Northbrook	IL	60062	**800-837-3707**		216
First Interstate Bancsystem Inc 401 N 31st St *NASDAQ: FIBK*	Billings	MT	59101	**888-752-3341**	406-255-5000	360-2
First Interstate Bank 401 N 31st St	Billings	MT	59101	**888-752-3341**	406-255-5000	69
First Jackson Bank 43243 Us Hwy 72	Stevenson	AL	35772	**888-950-2265**	256-437-2107	69
First Lease Inc 1 Walnut Grove Dr Ste 300	Horsham	PA	19044	**866-493-4778**		266-4
First Mercantile Trust Co 57 Germantown Ct 4th Fl	Cordova	TN	38018	**800-753-3682**	901-753-9080	69
First Merchants Corp 200 E Jackson St *NASDAQ: FRME*	Muncie	IN	47305	**800-205-3464**	765-747-1500	360-2
First Midwest Bancorp Inc 1 Pierce Pl Ste 1500 *NASDAQ: FMBI*	Itasca	IL	60143	**800-322-3623**	630-875-7200	360-2
First National Bank PO Box 578	Fort Collins	CO	80521	**800-883-8773**	970-495-9450	69
First National Bank Alaska 101 W 36 Ave PO Box 100720 *OTC: FBAK*	Anchorage	AK	99510	**800-856-4362**	907-777-4362	69
First National Bank Creston PO Box 445	Creston	IA	50801	**877-782-2195**	641-782-2195	69
First National Bank of Omaha 1620 Dodge St	Omaha	NE	68197	**800-462-5266**	402-341-0500	69
First National Bank of Oneida, The 18418 Alberta St PO Box 4699	Oneida	TN	37841	**866-546-8273**	423-569-8586	69
First National Bank of Santa Fe PO Box 609	Santa Fe	NM	87504	**888-912-2265**	505-992-2000	69
First National Bankers Bankshares Inc (FNBB) 7813 Office Pk Blvd	Baton Rouge	LA	70809	**800-421-6182**	225-924-8015	69
First National Lincoln Corp 223 Main St PO Box 940	Damariscotta	ME	04543	**800-564-3195**	207-563-3195	360-2
First National of Nebraska Inc PO BOX 2490	Omaha	NE	68197	**800-688-7070**	402-341-0500	360-2
First Nations Development Institute 2217 Princess Anne St Ste 111-1	Fredericksburg	VA	22401	**888-371-3686**	540-371-5615	47-14
First Nations University of Canada *Northern* 1301 Central Ave	Prince Albert	SK	S6V4W1	**800-267-6303**	306-765-3333	783
Saskatoon 226 20th St E	Saskatoon	SK	S7K0A6	**800-267-6303**	306-931-1800	783
First NBC (CPB) 29092 Kretel Rd	Lacombe	LA	70445	**800-423-7503**	985-819-1200	69
First Niagara Ctr 1 Seymour Knox III Plz	Buffalo	NY	14203	**888-223-6000**	716-855-4100	718
First Niagara Financial Group 726 Exchange St Ste 618	Buffalo	NY	14210	**800-421-0004**	716-625-7500	69
First Niagara RISK Management 1215 Manor Dr	Mechanicsburg	PA	17055	**800-421-0004**	717-795-8666	196
First of Long Island Corp 10 Glen Head Ave *NASDAQ: FLIC*	Glen Head	NY	11545	**800-554-8969**	516-671-4900	360-2
First Office 1204 E Sixth St	Huntingburg	IN	47542	**800-983-4415**		320-1
First Pacific Advisors Inc 11400 W Olympic Blvd Ste 1200	Los Angeles	CA	90064	**800-982-4372**	310-473-0225	401
First Palmetto Savings Bank Fsb PO Box 430	Camden	SC	29021	**800-922-7411**	803-432-2265	69
First Priority Health 19 N Main St	Wilkes-Barre	PA	18711	**800-822-8753**		391-3
First Priority Inc 1590 Todd Farm Dr	Elgin	IL	60123	**800-650-4899**	847-289-1600	582
First Quality Products Inc 121 N Rd	Mcelhattan	PA	17748	**800-227-3551**	570-769-6900	475
First Quantum Minerals Ltd 543 Granville St 8th Fl *TSE: FM*	Vancouver	BC	V6C1X8	**888-688-6577**	604-688-6577	501
First Regional Library 370 W Commerce St	Hernando	MS	38632	**800-446-0892**	662-429-4439	434-3
First Reliance Holdings LLC 275 N Pointe Pkwy Ste 60	Amherst	NY	14228	**877-495-8938**		393
First Republic Bank 111 Pine St *NYSE: FRC*	San Francisco	CA	94111	**800-392-1400**	415-392-1400	69
First Run Features 630 Ninth Ave Ste 1213	New York	NY	10036	**800-229-8575**	212-243-0600	510
First Savings Bank 2804 N Telshor Blvd	Las Cruces	NM	88011	**800-555-6895**	575-521-7931	69
First Security Bank of Missoula 1704 Dearborn PO Box 4506	Missoula	MT	59801	**888-782-3115**	406-728-3115	69
First Shore Federal 106-108 S Div St PO Box 4248	Salisbury	MD	21803	**800-634-6309**	410-546-1101	70
First South Bancorp Inc 1311 Carolina Ave *NASDAQ: FSBK*	Washington	NC	27889	**800-946-4178**	252-946-4178	360-2
First Southern Bank 301 S Ct St *General	Florence	AL	35630	**800-625-7131***	256-718-4200	360-2
First State Bank 708 Azalea Dr PO Box 506	Waynesboro	MS	39367	**866-408-3582**		69
First State Bank & Trust Co 1005 E 23rd St	Fremont	NE	68025	**888-674-4344**	402-721-2500	69
First State Bank of Kansas City 650 Kansas Ave	Kansas City	KS	66105	**800-883-1242**	913-371-1242	69
First Supply LLC 6800 Gisholt Dr	Madison	WI	53713	**800-236-9795**	608-222-7799	611
First Tennessee Bank 165 Madison Ave	Memphis	TN	38103	**800-382-5465**	901-523-4883	69
First Texas Bank 501 E Third St	Lampasas	TX	76550	**866-220-1598**	512-556-3691	69
First to The Finish Inc 1325 N Broad St	Carlinville	IL	62626	**800-747-9013**		709
First Truck Centre Inc 11313 170 St	Edmonton	AB	T5M3P5	**888-882-8530**	780-413-8800	56
First United Corp 19 S Second St *NASDAQ: FUNC*	Oakland	MD	21550	**888-692-2654**		360-2
First UNUM Life Insurance Co 2211 Congress St	Portland	ME	04122	**800-633-7491**	207-575-2211	391-2
First Western Bank & Trust PO Box 1090	Minot	ND	58702	**800-688-2584**	701-852-3711	69

Name / Address	City	State	ZIP	Toll-Free	Phone	Class
Firstbase Services Ltd 34609 Delair Rd	Abbotsford	BC	V2S2E1	**800-758-2922**	604-850-5334	344
FirstCare 1901 W Loop 289 Ste #9	Lubbock	TX	79407	**800-884-4901**	806-784-4300	391-2
FirstCom Music 1325 Capital Pkwy Ste 109 *Cust Svc	Carrollton	TX	75006	**800-858-8880***	972-446-8742	524
FirstEnergy Corp 76 S Main St *NYSE: FE*	Akron	OH	44308	**800-633-4766**		360-5
Firstexpress Inc 1135 Freightliner Dr	Nashville	TN	37210	**800-848-9203**		778
FirstFed Bancorp Inc 1630 Fourth Ave N PO Box 340	Bessemer	AL	35020	**800-436-5112**	205-428-8472	360-2
First-Knox National Bank 1 S Main St	Mount Vernon	OH	43050	**800-837-5266**	740-399-5500	69
Firstrust Savings Bank 15 E Ridge Pike 4th Fl	Conshohocken	PA	19428	**800-220-2265**	610-941-9898	69
Firstwave Technologies Inc 6263 N Scottsdale Rd Ste 180	Scottsdale	AZ	85250	**800-540-6061**	678-672-3112	180-11
Fisc Investment Services Corp 1849 Clairmont Rd	Decatur	GA	30033	**800-241-3203**	404-321-1212	688
Fischer Environmental Service Inc 1980 Surgi Dr	Mandeville	LA	70448	**800-391-2565**		576
Fischer Francis Trees & Watts Inc 200 Pk Ave 11th Fl	New York	NY	10166	**866-392-4090**	212-681-3000	401
Fischer International Systems Corp 9045 Strada Stell Ct Ste 201 *Tech Supp	Naples	FL	34109	**800-776-7258***	239-643-1500	180-1
Fiserv Inc 255 Fiserv Dr PO Box 979 *NASDAQ: FISV* ■ *Sales	Brookfield	WI	53008	**800-872-7882***	262-879-5000	68
Fisgard Capital Corp 3378 Douglas St	Victoria	BC	V8Z3L3	**866-382-9255**	250-382-9255	688
Fish & Richardson PC 1 Marina Park Dr	Boston	MA	02110	**800-818-5070**	617-542-5070	428
Fish Oven & Equipment Corp 120 W Kent Ave	Wauconda	IL	60084	**877-526-8720**	847-526-8686	299
Fish Window Cleaning Services Inc 200 Enchanted Pkwy	Manchester	MO	63021	**877-707-3474**	636-779-1500	311
Fisher & Arnold Inc 9180 Crestwyn Hills Dr	Memphis	TN	38125	**888-583-9724**	901-748-1811	196
Fisher & Ludlow Tru-Weld Grating 2000 Corporate Dr Ste 400	Wexford	PA	15090	**800-334-2047**	724-934-5320	490
Fisher & Paykel Appliances Inc 5900 Skylab Rd	Huntington Beach	CA	92647	**888-936-7872**		35
Fisher & Paykel Healthcare Inc 173 Technology Dr Ste 100	Irvine	CA	92618	**800-446-3908**	949-453-4000	252
Fisher Canvas Products Inc 415 St Mary St	Burlington	NJ	08016	**800-892-6688**		730
Fisher College 118 Beacon St	Boston	MA	02116	**866-266-6007**	617-236-8800	161
Fisher Container Corp 1111 Busch Pkwy	Buffalo Grove	IL	60089	**800-837-2247**	847-541-0000	547
Fisher Group Inc 3571 South 300 West	Salt Lake City	UT	84115	**800-365-8920**		393
Fisher Investments 13100 Skyline Blvd	Woodside	CA	94062	**800-550-1071**		401
Fisher Island Club & Resort 1 Fisher Island Dr *Resv	Miami	FL	33109	**800-537-3708***	305-535-6000	667
Fisher Manufacturing Co PO Box 60	Tulare	CA	93275	**800-421-6162**		608
Fisher Research Laboratory Inc 1465H Henry Brennan Ste H	El Paso	TX	79936	**800-685-5050**	915-225-0333	471
Fisher Sand & Gravel Co 3948 First ST SW	Underwood	ND	58576	**800-932-8740**	701-442-5600	502-4
Fisher Science Education 4500 Turnberry Dr	Hanover Park	IL	60133	**800-955-1177**	800-766-7000	245
Fisher Scientific Company Inc 112 Colonnade Rd	Ottawa	ON	K2E7L6	**800-234-7437**	613-226-8874	419
Fisher Textiles Inc 139 Business Pk Dr	Indian Trail	NC	28079	**800-554-8886**	704-821-8870	742-6
Fisheries Museum of the Atlantic 68 Bluenose Dr PO Box 1363	Lunenburg	NS	B0J2C0	**866-579-4909**	902-634-4794	519
Fisheries Supply Co 1900 N Northlake Way	Seattle	WA	98103	**800-426-6930**	206-632-4462	768
Fisherman's Wharf Inn 22 Commercial St	Boothbay Harbor	ME	04538	**800-628-6872**	207-633-5090	379
Fisher-Price Inc 636 Girard Ave	East Aurora	NY	14052	**800-432-5437**	716-687-3000	760
Fisher-Titus Medical Ctr (FTMC) 272 Benedict Ave	Norwalk	OH	44857	**800-589-3862**	419-668-8101	374-3
FishHound LLC 15720 Ventura Blvd Ste 220	Encino	CA	91436	**800-469-0224**		387
Fisk University 1000 17th Ave N	Nashville	TN	37208	**888-702-0022**	615-329-8500	167
Fiskars Brands Inc 2537 Daniels St	Madison	WI	53718	**866-348-5661**		224
Fiske Bros Refining Co 129 Lockwood St	Newark	NJ	07105	**800-733-4755**	973-589-9150	540
Fit America MD 4864 Arthur Kill Rd	Staten Island	NY	10309	**800-940-7546**	718-227-4980	808
Fitch Co 2201 Russell St	Baltimore	MD	21230	**800-933-4824**	410-539-1953	406
Fitch Ratings Inc 1 State St Plz	New York	NY	10004	**800-753-4824**	212-908-0500	220
Fitger's Brewery Complex 600 E Superior St	Duluth	MN	55802	**888-348-4377**	218-722-8826	669
Fitger's Brewery Museum 600 E Superior St	Duluth	MN	55802	**888-348-4377**	218-722-8826	519
Fitger's Inn 600 E Superior St	Duluth	MN	55802	**888-348-4377**	218-722-8826	379
Fitness Club Warehouse Inc 2210 S Sepulveda Blvd	Los Angeles	CA	90064	**800-348-4537**	310-235-2040	709
Fitness Depot 1808 Lower Roswell Rd	Marietta	GA	30068	**800-974-6828**	770-971-6828	354
Fitness Rx for Men Magazine 21 Bennetts Rd	Setauket	NY	11733	**800-653-1151**	631-751-9696	456-13
Fitness Zone 3439 Colonnade Pkwy Se 800	Birmingham	AL	35243	**800-875-9145**		709
Fitzgerald Auto Mall 10915 Georgia Ave	Wheaton	MD	20902	**855-776-0552**		56
Fitzgerald Contractors Inc 7103 St Vincent Ave	Shreveport	LA	71106	**800-259-3264**	318-869-3262	191-10
Fitzgeralds Casino & Hotel Tunica 711 Lucky Ln	Robinsonville	MS	38664	**888-766-5825**	662-363-5825	132
Fitzpatrick Manhattan Hotel 687 Lexington Ave	New York	NY	10022	**800-367-7701**	212-355-0100	379
Five Below Inc 1818 Market St Ste 2000	Philadelphia	PA	19103	**866-935-8852**	215-546-7909	760
Five Star Dodge 3068 Riverside Dr	Macon	GA	31210	**877-748-9845**	478-474-3700	56
Five Star Electric of Houston Inc 19424 Pk Row Ste 100	Houston	TX	77084	**888-492-7090**	281-492-7090	517
Five Star Food Service Inc 6005 Century Oaks Dr Ste 100	Chattanooga	TN	37416	**800-327-0043**	423-643-2600	300
Five Star Quality Care Inc 400 Centre St *NYSE: FVE*	Newton	MA	02458	**866-230-1286**	617-796-8387	450
Five Star Trucking Inc 4380 Glenbrook Rd	Willoughby	OH	44094	**800-321-3658**	440-953-9300	778
FIX Flyer LLC 225 Broadway Ste 1600	New York	NY	10007	**888-349-3593**		253
Fixtureworks LLC 33792 Doreka	Fraser	MI	48026	**888-794-8687**	586-294-1188	453
FJC 520 Eighth Ave 20th Fl	New York	NY	10018	**888-448-3352**	212-714-0001	306
FJC Security Services Inc 275 Jericho Tpke	Floral Park	NY	11001	**888-832-6352**	516-328-6000	691
Fkg Oil Co 721 W Main	Belleville	IL	62220	**800-873-3546**	618-233-6754	206
FL Crane & Sons Inc 508 S Spring St PO Box 428	Fulton	MS	38843	**800-748-9523**	662-862-2172	191-9
FL Emmert Co Inc 2007 Dunlap St	Cincinnati	OH	45214	**800-441-3343**	513-721-5808	446
FL Smidth Inc 2040 Ave C	Bethlehem	PA	18017	**800-523-9482**	610-264-6011	469
FLA (Forest Landowners Assn) 900 Cir 75 Pkwy Ste 205	Atlanta	GA	30339	**800-325-2954**	404-325-2954	47-13
Flagler College 74 King St *Admissions	Saint Augustine	FL	32084	**800-304-4208***	904-829-6481	167
Flagler County Public Library (FCPL) 2500 Palm Coast Pkwy NW	Palm Coast	FL	32137	**877-863-5244**	386-446-6763	434-3
Flagship All Suites Resort 60 N Maine Ave	Atlantic City	NJ	08401	**800-647-7890**	609-343-7447	379
Flagship Fire Inc 1500 15th Ave dr e	Palmetto	FL	34221	**866-242-3307**	941-723-7230	136
Flagship Press Inc 150 Flagship Dr	North Andover	MA	01845	**800-733-1520**	978-975-3100	626
Flagstaff Convention & Visitors Bureau 323 W Aspen Ave	Flagstaff	AZ	86001	**800-217-2367**	928-779-7611	208
Flagstaff Pulliam Airport 6200 S Pulliam Dr	Flagstaff	AZ	86001	**800-463-1389**	928-556-1234	27
Flagstaff Symphony Orchestra 113 E Aspen Ave # A	Flagstaff	AZ	86001	**888-520-7214**	928-774-5107	572-3
Flagstar Bank FSB 5151 Corporate Dr	Troy	MI	48098	**800-945-7700**	248-312-2000	69
FlagZone LLC 105A Industrial Dr	Gilbertsville	PA	19525	**800-976-4201**		260
Flambeau Inc 15981 Valplast Rd	Middlefield	OH	44062	**800-457-5252**	440-632-1631	603
Flame Enterprises Inc 21500 Gledhill St	Chatsworth	CA	91311	**800-854-2255**	818-700-2905	248
Flame Retardancy News 49 Walnut Pk Bldg 2	Wellesley	MA	02481	**866-285-7215**	781-489-7301	530-12
Flamers Charbroiled Hamburgers 1515 International Pkwy Ste 2013	Heathrow	FL	32746	**866-749-4889**	407-574-8363	668
Flamingo Gardens 3750 S Flamingo Rd	Davie	FL	33330	**800-435-7352**	954-473-2955	96
Flamingo Resort Hotel & Conference Ctr 2777 Fourth St	Santa Rosa	CA	95405	**800-848-8300**	707-545-8530	667
Flanders Corp 531 Flanders Filters Rd *OTC: FLDR*	Washington	NC	27889	**800-637-2803**	252-946-8081	18
FLANDERS Inc 8101 Baumgart Rd PO Box 23130	Evansville	IN	47724	**855-875-5888**	812-867-7421	517
Flash Technology Corp 332 Nichol Mill Ln	Franklin	TN	37067	**888-313-5274**	615-503-2000	528
Flat Rock Playhouse 2661 Greenville Hwy	Flat Rock	NC	28731	**866-732-8008**	828-693-0731	571
Flathead Convention & Visitors Bureau 15 Depot Pk	Kalispell	MT	59901	**800-543-3105**	406-756-9091	208
Flathead Electric Co-op Inc 2510 Hwy 2 E	Kalispell	MT	59901	**800-735-8489**	406-751-4483	247
Flathead Valley Community College 777 Grandview Dr	Kalispell	MT	59901	**800-313-3822**	406-756-3822	161
Flatout Inc 1422 Woodland Dr	Saline	MI	48176	**866-944-5445**	734-944-4262	297
Flavor Dynamics Inc 640 Montrose Ave	South Plainfield	NJ	07080	**888-271-8424**	908-822-8855	298-8
Flax Art & Design 1699 Market St	San Francisco	CA	94103	**844-352-9278**	415-552-2355	44
Fleet Engineers Inc 1800 E Keating Ave *Cust Svc	Muskegon	MI	49442	**800-333-7890***	231-777-2537	515
Fleet Equipment Corp 567 Commerce St	Franklin Lakes	NJ	07417	**800-631-0873**	201-337-3294	515
Fleet Landing Retirement Community 1 Fleet Landing Blvd *General	Atlantic Beach	FL	32233	**877-591-6547***	904-246-9900	670

Name / Address	City	State	Zip	Toll-Free	Phone	Class
Fleet Reserve Assn (FRA) 125 NW St	Alexandria	VA	22314	**800-372-1924**	703-683-1400	47-19
FleetBoss Global Positioning Solutions Inc 241 O'Brien Rd	Fern Park	FL	32730	**877-265-9559**	407-265-9559	732
Fleetwash Inc PO Box 1577	West Caldwell	NJ	07007	**800-847-3735**		61-1
Fleetwood Group Inc 11832 James St	Holland	MI	49424	**800-257-6390**	616-396-1142	320-3
Fleetwood Homes of Idaho Inc 2611 E Comstock Ave	Nampa	ID	83687	**800-334-8958**	208-466-2438	504
Fleetwood Homes of Virginia Inc 90 Weaver St	Rocky Mount	VA	24151	**866-890-6206**	540-483-5171	504
Fleetwood-Signode 3624 W Lake Ave	Glenview	IL	60026	**800-862-7997**	630-268-9999	558
Fleming College 200 Albert St S	Lindsay	ON	K9V5E6	**866-353-6464**	705-324-9144	161
Fleming Door Products Ltd 101 Ashbridge Cir	Woodbridge	ON	L4L3R5	**800-263-7515**		236
Flesh Co 2118 59th St	Saint Louis	MO	63110	**800-869-3330**	314-781-4400	109
Fletch's Inc 825 Charlevoix Ave PO Box 265	Petoskey	MI	49770	**877-238-0816**	231-347-9651	56
FletchAir Inc 103 Turkey Run Ln	Comfort	TX	78013	**800-329-4647**	830-995-5900	22
Fletcher Jones Imports 7300 W Sahara Ave	Las Vegas	NV	89117	**888-927-3675**	702-364-2700	56
Fletcher Music Centers Inc 3966 Airway Cir	Clearwater	FL	33762	**800-258-1088**	727-571-1088	525
Fletcher'S Medical Supplies Inc 6851 S Distribution Ave	Jacksonville	FL	32256	**855-541-7809**	904-387-4481	363
Fletcher-Terry Company Inc 65 Spring Ln *Cust Svc	Farmington	CT	06032	**800-843-3826***	860-677-7331	756
Flex Checks Inc PO Box 141215	Grand Rapids	MI	49514	**866-791-7900**	616-791-7900	2
Flex Foam 617 N 21st Ave	Phoenix	AZ	85009	**800-266-3626**	602-252-5819	130
Flex Hr 10700 Medlock Bridge Rd Ste 206	Johns Creek	GA	30097	**877-735-3947**	770-814-4225	354
Flex Magazine 21100 Erwin St	Woodland Hills	CA	91367	**877-527-8342**	412-235-0203	456-13
Flexaust Co 1510 Armstrong Rd	Warsaw	IN	46580	**800-343-0428**	574-267-7909	370
Flexbar Machine Corp 250 Gibbs Rd	Islandia	NY	11749	**800-879-7575**	631-582-8440	695
Flex-Cable Inc 5822 N Henkel Rd	Howard City	MI	49329	**800-245-3539**	231-937-8000	814
FlexHead Industries Inc 56 Lowland St	Holliston	MA	01746	**800-829-6975**	508-893-9596	51
Flexible Materials Inc 1202 Port Rd	Jeffersonville	IN	47130	**800-244-6492**	812-280-7000	612
Flexible Plan Investments Ltd 3883 Telegraph Rd Ste 100	Bloomfield Hills	MI	48302	**800-347-3539**	248-642-6640	401
Flexible Steel Lacing Co 2525 Wisconsin Ave	Downers Grove	IL	60515	**800-323-3444**	630-971-0150	209
Flexible-Montisa 323 Acorn St *Cust Svc	Plainwell	MI	49080	**800-875-6836***	269-924-0730	320-1
Flexicon Corp 2400 Emrick Blvd	Bethlehem	PA	18020	**888-353-9426**	610-814-2400	546
Flexicore of Texas PO Box 450049	Houston	TX	77245	**888-359-4267**	281-437-5700	185
FlexiInternational Software Inc 2 Enterprise Dr *OTC: FLXI*	Shelton	CT	06484	**800-353-9492**	203-925-3040	180-1
Flexi-Van Leasing Inc 251 Monroe Ave	Kenilworth	NJ	07033	**866-965-9288**	908-276-8000	266-5
Flexmag Industries Inc 107 Industry Rd	Marietta	OH	45750	**800-543-4426**	740-374-8024	457
Flex-N-Gate Corp 1306 E University Ave	Urbana	IL	61802	**800-398-1496**	217-278-2600	59
Flexo Impressions 8647 Eagle Creek Pkwy	Savage	MN	55378	**800-752-2357**	952-884-9442	626
Flex-O-Lite Inc 50 Crestwood Executive Ctr Ste 522	Saint Louis	MO	63126	**800-325-9525**		332
Flexospan Steel Buildings Inc 253 Railroad St	Sandy Lake	PA	16145	**800-245-0396**	724-376-7221	105
Flex-Pay Business Services Inc 723 Coliseum Dr Ste 200	Winston-Salem	NC	27106	**800-457-2143**	336-773-0128	196
FlexShopper Inc 2700 N Military Trl Ste 200	Boca Raton	FL	33431	**855-353-9289**		23
FLEXSTAR Packaging Inc 13320 River Rd	Richmond	BC	V6V1W7	**800-663-1177**	604-273-9277	600
Flexsys America LP 260 Springside Dr	Akron	OH	44333	**800-455-5622**	330-666-4111	674
Flextron Industries Inc 720 Mt Rd	Aston	PA	19014	**800-633-2181**	610-459-4600	547
Flex-Y-Plan Industries Inc 6960 W Ridge Rd *Cust Svc	Fairview	PA	16415	**800-458-0552***	814-474-1565	320-1
Flight Dimensions International Inc 4835 Cordell Ave Ste 150	Bethesda	MD	20814	**866-235-6870**	301-634-8201	21
Flight Light Inc 2708 47th Ave	Sacramento	CA	95822	**800-806-3548**	916-394-2800	62
Flight Systems Inc 505 Fishing Creek Rd	Lewisberry	PA	17339	**800-403-3728**	717-932-9900	249
Flightstar Corp 7 Airport Rd Willard Airport	Savoy	IL	61874	**800-747-4777**	217-351-7700	13
Flinchbaugh Engineering Inc 4387 Run Way	York	PA	17406	**866-967-5334**	717-755-1900	486
Flint & Walling Inc 95 N Oak St *Sales	Kendallville	IN	46755	**800-345-9422***	260-347-1600	638
Flint Cultural Ctr Corp 1310 E Kearsley St	Flint	MI	48503	**800-214-7275**	810-237-7333	49-1
Flint Energies 3 S Macon St	Reynolds	GA	31076	**800-342-3616**	478-847-3415	247
Flint Journal 200 E First St *Circ	Flint	MI	48502	**800-875-6200***	810-766-6100	531-2
Flint River Mills Inc 1100 Dothan Rd *Cust Svc	Bainbridge	GA	39817	**800-841-8502***	229-246-2232	446
Flint Surveying & Engineering Company Inc 5370 Miller Rd	Swartz Creek	MI	48473	**800-624-6089**	810-230-1333	263
Flintco LLC 1624 W 21st St	Tulsa	OK	74107	**800-947-2828**	918-587-8451	188
Flippen Group, The 1199 Haywood Dr	College Station	TX	77845	**800-316-4311**	979-693-7660	462
FLIR Systems Inc 27700-A SW Pkwy Ave *NASDAQ: FLIR*	Wilsonville	OR	97070	**877-773-3547**	503-498-3547	528
Floor Coverings International 5250 Triangle Pwy Ste 100 *Sales	Norcross	GA	30092	**800-955-4324***	770-874-7600	292
Flooring Sales Group 1251 First Ave S	Seattle	WA	98134	**877-478-3577**	206-624-7800	292
Flora Mfg & Distributing Ltd 7400 Fraser Park Dr	Burnaby	BC	V5J5B9	**888-436-6697**	604-436-6000	478
Florence Convention & Visitors Bureau 3290 W Radio Dr *General	Florence	SC	29501	**800-325-9005***	843-664-0330	208
Florence Eiseman company LLC 1966 S Fourth St	Milwaukee	WI	53204	**800-558-9013**		154-4
Florence Events Ctr 715 Quince St	Florence	OR	97439	**888-968-4086**	541-997-1994	207
Florence National Cemetery 803 E National Cemetery Rd	Florence	SC	29506	**877-907-8585**	843-669-8783	135
Florence-Darlington Technical College 2715 W Lucas St	Florence	SC	29502	**800-228-5745**	843-661-8324	798
Florentine Opera Co 700 N Water St Ste 950	Milwaukee	WI	53202	**800-326-7372**	414-291-5700	572-2
Florestone Products Company Inc 2851 Falcon Dr	Madera	CA	93637	**800-446-8827**	559-661-4171	609
Florexpo LLC 1960 Kellogg Ave	Carlsbad	CA	92008	**800-830-3567**		706
Florida						
Attorney General State Capitol PL-01	Tallahassee	FL	32399	**866-966-7226**	850-487-1963	339-10
Business & Professional Regulation Dept 1940 N Monroe St	Tallahassee	FL	32399	**866-532-1440**	850-487-1395	339-10
Consumer Services Div 2005 Apalachee Pkwy	Tallahassee	FL	32399	**800-435-7352**		339-10
Education Dept 325 W Gaines St Ste 1514	Tallahassee	FL	32399	**800-445-6739**	850-245-0505	339-10
Financial Services Dept 200 E Gaines St	Tallahassee	FL	32399	**800-342-2762**	850-413-3100	339-10
Insurance Regulation Office 200 E Gaines St	Tallahassee	FL	32301	**800-342-2762**	850-413-3140	339-10
Recreation & Parks Div 3900 Commonwealth Blvd MS 500 *Campground Resv	Tallahassee	FL	32399	**800-326-3521***	850-245-2157	339-10
Secretary of State RA Gray Bldg 500 S Bronough St	Tallahassee	FL	32399	**800-955-8771**	850-245-6500	339-10
Vocational Rehabilitation Services Div 2002 Old St Augustine Rd Bldg A	Tallahassee	FL	32301	**800-451-4327**	850-245-3399	339-10
Florida A & M University 1700 Lee Hall Dr Rm G-7 Foote-Hilyer Administration Ctr	Tallahassee	FL	32307	**866-642-1198**	850-599-3000	167
Coleman Memorial Library 1500 S Martin Luther King Blvd	Tallahassee	FL	32307	**800-540-6754**	850-599-3370	434-6
Florida Academy of Family Physicians 6720 Atlantic Blvd.	Jacksonville	FL	32211	**800-223-3237**		77
Florida Aquarium 701 Channelside Dr	Tampa	FL	33602	**800-353-4741**	813-273-4000	39
Florida Assn of Realtors 7025 Augusta National Dr	Orlando	FL	32822	**800-669-4327**	407-438-1400	654
Florida Atlantic University (FAU) 777 Glades Rd *Admissions	Boca Raton	FL	33431	**800-299-4328***	561-297-3000	167
Davie 3200 College Ave	Davie	FL	33314	**800-764-2222**	954-236-1000	167
Fort Lauderdale 111 E Las Olas Blvd	Fort Lauderdale	FL	33301	**800-764-2222**	954-201-7350	167
MacArthur 5353 Parkside Dr	Jupiter	FL	33458	**888-328-2586**	561-799-8500	167
Florida Bar 651 E Jefferson St	Tallahassee	FL	32399	**800-342-8060**	850-561-5600	71
Florida Bar Journal 651 E Jefferson St	Tallahassee	FL	32399	**800-342-8060**	850-561-5600	456-15
Florida Bill Status 111 W Madison St Rm 704	Tallahassee	FL	32399	**800-342-1827**	850-488-4371	433
Florida Chamber of Commerce 136 S Bronough St PO Box 11309	Tallahassee	FL	32302	**877-521-1230**	850-521-1200	139
Florida Christian College 1011 Bill Beck Blvd	Kissimmee	FL	34744	**888-468-6322**	407-847-8966	160
Florida City Gas (FCG) 955 E 25th St	Hialeah	FL	33013	**800-993-7546**	305-691-8710	785
Florida Coastal School of Law 8787 Bay Pine Rd	Jacksonville	FL	32256	**877-210-2591**	904-680-7700	168-1
Florida College 119 N Glen Arven Ave	Temple Terrace	FL	33617	**800-326-7655**	813-988-5131	167
Florida Community College at Jacksonville						
Downtown 101 State St W	Jacksonville	FL	32202	**877-633-5950**	904-633-8100	161
Florida Council Against Sexual Violence Inc 1820 E Park Ave Ste 100	Tallahassee	FL	32301	**888-956-7273**	850-297-2000	40
Florida Democratic Party 214 S Bronough St	Tallahassee	FL	32301	**855-352-7233**	850-222-3411	615-1

Name / Address	City	State	Zip	Toll-Free	Phone	Class
Florida Dental Assn 1111 E Tennessee St	Tallahassee	FL	32308	**800-877-9922**	850-681-3629	229
Florida Detroit Diesel-Allison Inc 5040 University Blvd W	Jacksonville	FL	32216	**888-812-4440**	904-737-7330	385
Florida Family Insurance Services LLC 27599 Riverview Ctr Blvd Ste 100 PO Box 136001	Bonita Springs	FL	34136	**888-850-4663**	239-495-4700	391-4
Florida Farm Bureau Insurance Cos 5700 SW 34th St	Gainesville	FL	32608	**866-275-7322**	352-378-1321	391-4
Florida Grand Opera 8390 NW 25th St	Miami	FL	33122	**800-741-1010**	305-854-1643	572-2
Florida Handling Systems Inc 2651 State Rd 60 W	Bartow	FL	33830	**800-664-3380**	863-534-1212	358
Florida Heritage Museum 167 San Marco Ave	Saint Augustine	FL	32084	**800-268-7252**	904-829-9729	519
Florida Holocaust Museum 55 Fifth St S	Saint Petersburg	FL	33701	**800-388-4069**	727-820-0100	519
Florida Hospital Heartland Medical Ctr 4200 Sun 'n Lake Blvd PO Box 9400	Sebring	FL	33871	**800-756-4447**	863-314-4466	374-3
Florida Institute of Technology 150 W University Blvd	Melbourne	FL	32901	**800-888-4348**	321-674-8000	167
Florida International University 11200 SW Eigth St	Miami	FL	33199	**800-677-6337**	305-348-2000	167
Florida Keys Community College 5901 College Rd	Key West	FL	33040	**866-567-2665**	305-296-9081	161
Florida Keys Electric Co-op Assn 91630 Overseas Hwy	Tavernier	FL	33070	**800-858-8845**	305-852-2431	247
Florida Memorial University 15800 NW 42nd Ave	Miami Gardens	FL	33054	**800-822-1362**	305-626-3600	167
Florida National Cemetery 6502 SW 102nd Ave	Bushnell	FL	33513	**877-907-8585**	352-793-7740	135
Florida Newsclips LLC PO Box 2190	Palm Harbor	FL	34682	**800-442-0332**		623
Florida Pneumatic Manufacturing Corp 851 Jupiter Pk Ln	Jupiter	FL	33458	**800-327-9403**	561-744-9500	757
Florida Prepaid College Board PO Box 6567	Tallahassee	FL	32314	**800-552-4723**		723
Florida Presbyterian Homes 16 Lk Hunter Dr	Lakeland	FL	33803	**866-294-3352**	863-688-5521	670
Florida Public Utilities Co (FPUC) 401 S Dixie Hwy	West Palm Beach	FL	33401	**800-427-7712**		785
Florida Repertory Theatre Inc 2267 Bay St	Fort Myers	FL	33901	**877-787-8053**	239-332-4665	718
Florida School Choice Fund Inc PO Box 1670	Jacksonville	FL	33601	**877-735-7837**		306
Florida Solar Energy Ctr 1679 Clearlake Rd	Cocoa	FL	32922	**877-777-4778**	321-638-1000	666
Florida Southern College 111 Lk Hollingsworth Dr *Admissions	Lakeland	FL	33801	**800-274-4131***	863-680-4131	167
Florida Student Financial Assistance Office 1940 N Monroe St Ste 70	Tallahassee	FL	32303	**888-827-2004**	850-410-5200	723
Florida Surplus Lines Service Office 1441 Maclay Commerce Dr	Tallahassee	FL	32312	**800-562-4496**	850-224-7676	40
Florida Technical College 12900 Challenger Pkwy *General	Orlando	FL	32826	**888-678-2929***	407-447-7300	798
Florida Tile Industries Inc 998 Governors Ln Ste 300 *Cust Svc	Lexington	KY	40513	**800-352-8453***	859-219-5200	749
Florida Times-Union 1 Riverside Ave	Jacksonville	FL	32202	**800-472-6397**	904-359-4111	531-2
Florida Venture Forum Inc, The 707 W Azeele St	Tampa	FL	33606	**888-375-7136**	813-335-8116	136
Florist Distributing Inc 2403 Bell Ave	Des Moines	IA	50321	**800-373-3741**	515-243-5228	295
Florsheim Inc 333 W Estabrook Blvd	Glendale	WI	53212	**866-454-0449**		302
Flow Dry Technology Inc 379 Albert Rd PO Box 190	Brookville	OH	45309	**800-533-0077**	937-833-2161	327
Flow International Corp 23500 64th Ave S *NASDAQ: FLOW*	Kent	WA	98032	**800-446-3569**	253-850-3500	454
Flower City Tissue Mills Inc 700 Driving Pk Ave	Rochester	NY	14613	**800-595-2030**	585-458-9200	547
Flower Patch Inc 4370 S 300 W *General	Murray	UT	84107	**888-865-6858***	801-747-2824	294
Flower Pot Florists 2314 N Broadway St	Knoxville	TN	37917	**800-824-7792**	865-523-5121	294
Flowers Auto Parts Co 935 Hwy 70 SE *Cust Svc	Hickory	NC	28602	**800-538-6272***	828-322-5414	60
Flowers by Sleeman for All Seasons & Reasons Ltd 1201 Memorial Rd	Houghton	MI	49931	**800-400-4023**	906-482-4023	294
Flowers Hospital 4370 W Main St	Dothan	AL	36305	**877-456-9617**	334-793-5000	374-3
Flow-Eze Co 3209 Auburn St	Rockford	IL	61101	**800-435-4873**	815-965-1062	685
Flowserve Corp 5215 N O'Connor Blvd Ste 2300 *NYSE: FLS*	Irving	TX	75039	**800-350-1082**	972-443-6500	638
Floyd Bell Inc 720 Dearborn Park Ln	Columbus	OH	43085	**888-356-9323**	614-294-4000	248
Floyd Blinsky Trucking Inc 210 Keys Rd	Yakima	WA	98901	**800-537-9599**	509-457-3484	683
Floyd Browne Group 3875 Embassy Parkway *General	Akron	OH	44333	**800-362-2764***	330-375-0800	195
Floyd E Tut Fann State Veterans Home 2701 Meridian St	Huntsville	AL	35811	**855-212-8028**	256-851-2807	791
Floyd Medical Ctr 304 Turner McCall Blvd	Rome	GA	30165	**866-874-2772**	706-509-5000	374-3
Floyd Memorial Hospital 1850 State St	New Albany	IN	47150	**800-423-1513**	812-944-7701	374-3
Fluent Home Ltd 7319 104 St NW	Edmonton	AB	T6E4B9	**855-238-4826**		691
Fluid Components International 1755 La Costa Meadows Dr	San Marcos	CA	92078	**800-863-8703**	760-744-6950	203
Fluid Innovation Inc 911 N RR 620 Ste 205	Austin	TX	78734	**866-934-7779**		807
Fluid Management Inc 1023 S Wheeling Rd	Wheeling	IL	60090	**800-462-2466**	847-537-0880	386
Fluid Metering Inc 5 Aerial Way Ste 500	Syosset	NY	11791	**800-223-3388**	516-922-6050	637
Fluidmaster Inc 30800 Rancho Viejo Rd	San Juan Capistrano	CA	92675	**800-631-2011**	949-728-2000	608
Fluidware 12 York St 2nd Fl	Ottawa	ON	K1N5S6	**866-218-5127**		387
Fluke Biomedical 6920 Seaway Blvd	Everett	WA	98203	**800-443-5853**	425-446-6945	250
Fluke Corp 6920 Seaway Blvd	Everett	WA	98203	**877-355-3225**	425-446-6100	250
Fluke Networks Inc 6920 Seaway Blvd	Everett	WA	98203	**800-283-5853**	425-446-4519	250
Fluor Corp 6700 Las Colinas Blvd	Irving	TX	75039	**800-405-6637**	469-398-7000	196
Flushing Financial Corp 1979 Marcus Ave *NASDAQ: FFIC*	New Hyde Park	NY	11042	**800-581-2889**	718-961-5400	360-2
FlyData Inc 1043 N Shoreline Blvd Ste 200	Mountain View	CA	94043	**855-427-9787**		623
Flyer.Com 201 Kelsey Ln	Tampa	FL	33619	**800-995-4433**	813-626-9430	634-10
Flying E Ranch 2801 W Wickenburg Way	Wickenburg	AZ	85390	**888-684-2650**	928-684-2690	241
Flying Leatherneck Aviation Museum Anderson Ave MCAS Miramar	San Diego	CA	92145	**877-359-8762**	858-693-1723	519
Flying Magazine 460 N. Orlando Ave. Ste 200 *Cust Svc	Winter Park	FL	32789	**800-678-0797***	407-628-4802	456-14
Flying W Ranch Inc 3330 Chuckwagon Rd	Colorado Springs	CO	80919	**800-232-3599**	719-598-4000	669
F&M Bank PO Box 1130	Clarksville	TN	37041	**800-645-4199**	931-645-2400	69
FM Brown's Sons Inc 205 Woodrow Ave PO Box 2116	Sinking Spring	PA	19608	**800-334-8816**	610-678-4567	446
FM Global 270 Central Ave PO Box 7500	Johnston	RI	02919	**800-343-7722**	401-275-3000	391-4
F&M Mafco Inc PO Box 11013	Cincinnati	OH	45211	**800-333-2151**	513-367-2151	192
FM NEWS 101 KXL 1211 SW Fifth Ave Ste 6	Portland	OR	97204	**877-733-1011**	503-517-6000	642-93
FMA (Fabricators & Manufacturers Assn International) 833 Featherstone Rd	Rockford	IL	61107	**888-394-4362**	815-399-8700	48-13
FMA Alliance Ltd 80 Garden Ctr Ste 3	Broomfield	CO	80020	**800-955-5598**	281-931-5050	159
FMC (Fairfield Medical Ctr) 401 N Ewing St	Lancaster	OH	43130	**800-548-2627**	740-687-8000	374-3
FMC Corp 2929 Walnut St *NYSE: FMC*	Philadelphia	PA	19104	**888-548-4486**	215-299-6000	142
FMC Technologies Inc 1803 Gears Rd *NYSE: FTI*	Houston	TX	77067	**800-356-4898**	281-591-4000	536
FMCA (Family Motor Coach Assn) 8291 Clough Pk	Cincinnati	OH	45244	**800-543-3622**	513-474-3622	47-23
FMCI (Grassley Group, The) 409 Washington St Ste A	Cedar Falls	IA	50613	**866-619-5580**		46
FMCSA (Federal Motor Carrier Safety Administration) 1200 New Jersey Ave SE	Washington	DC	20590	**800-832-5660**		340-15
FMG Enterprises Inc 1125 Memorex Dr	Santa Clara	CA	95050	**800-327-6177**	408-982-0110	638
FMI (Food Marketing Institute) 2345 Crystal Dr Ste 800	Arlington	VA	22202	**800-732-2639**	202-220-0600	48-18
FMI Corp 5171 Glenwood Ave Ste 200 *General	Raleigh	NC	27612	**800-669-1364***	919-787-8400	196
FMR Corp 82 Devonshire St	Boston	MA	02109	**800-343-3548**		401
FMS (Financial Managers Society) 100 W Monroe St Ste 810 *Cust Svc	Chicago	IL	60603	**800-275-4367***	312-578-1300	48-2
FMS Inc 8150 Leesburg Pk Ste 600	Vienna	VA	22182	**866-367-7801**	703-356-4700	180-2
FNBB (First National Bankers Bankshares Inc) 7813 Office Pk Blvd	Baton Rouge	LA	70809	**800-421-6182**	225-924-8015	69
FNW Industrial Plastics Inc 12500 Jefferson Ave PO Box 2778	Newport News	VA	23602	**800-721-2590**	757-874-7795	601
FOA (Friends of Animals Inc) 777 Post Rd Ste 205	Darien	CT	06820	**800-321-7387**	203-656-1522	47-3
Foam Molders & Specialty Corp 20004 State Rd	Cerritos	CA	90703	**800-378-8987**		600
Focus Camera Inc 905 McDonald Ave	Brooklyn	NY	11218	**800-221-0828**	718-437-8810	118
Focus Direct LLC 9707 Broadway	San Antonio	TX	78217	**800-555-1551**	210-805-9185	5
Focus Logistics Inc 1311 Howard Dr	West Chicago	IL	60185	**877-924-3600**	630-231-8200	315
Focus on the Family 8605 Explorer Dr *Sales	Colorado Springs	CO	80920	**800-232-6459***	719-531-3400	47-6
Focus Receivables Management LLC 1130 Northchase Pkwy Ste 150	Marietta	GA	30067	**877-362-8766**	678-305-9606	159
Focus Strategic Communications Inc 2474 Waterford St	Oakville	ON	L6L5E6	**866-263-6287**	905-825-8757	93
Foellinger-Freimann Botanical Conservatory 1100 S Calhoun St	Fort Wayne	IN	46802	**866-220-8842**	260-427-6440	96
Fogarty Creek State Recreation Area 725 Summer St NE Ste C	Salem	OR	97341	**800-551-6949**		564
FOI Services Inc 704 Quince OrchaRd Rd Ste 275	Gaithersburg	MD	20878	**800-654-1147**	301-975-9400	387

	City	State	ZIP	Toll-Free	Phone	Class
FOIA Group Inc (FGI) 1250 Connecticut Ave NW Ste 200	Washington	DC	20036	**888-461-7951**		387
Folbot Inc 4209 Pace St	Charleston	SC	29405	**800-533-5099**	843-744-3483	708
Foley & Lardner LLP 777 E Wisconsin Ave	Milwaukee	WI	53202	**855-225-5341**	414-271-2400	428
Foley House Inn 14 W Hull St Chippewa Sq	Savannah	GA	31401	**800-647-3708**	912-232-6622	379
Foley Inc 855 Centennial Ave	Piscataway	NJ	08854	**888-417-6464**	732-885-5555	61-7
Folger Adam Security Inc 4634 S Presa St	San Antonio	TX	78223	**888-745-0530**	210-533-1231	350
Folk Art Ctr PO Box 9545	Asheville	NC	28815	**888-672-7717**	828-298-7928	519
Follett Corp 3 Westbrook Corporate Center Ste 200	Westchester	IL	60154	**800-365-5388**	708-884-0000	94
Follett Educational Services 1433 International Pkwy	Woodridge	IL	60517	**800-621-4272**	630-972-5600	94
Follett Higher Education Group 3 Westbrook Corporate Ctr Ste 200	Westchester	IL	60154	**800-323-4506**		95
Follett Software Co 1391 Corporate Dr	McHenry	IL	60050	**800-323-3397**	815-759-1700	180-10
Folsom Lake Ford 12755 Folsom Blvd	Folsom	CA	95630	**800-730-0457**	916-353-2000	56
Fomo Products Inc 2775 Barber Rd	Norton	OH	44203	**800-321-5585**	330-753-4585	600
Fond du Lac Area Assn of Commerce 207 N Main St	Fond du Lac	WI	54935	**800-279-8811**	920-921-9500	138
Fond du Lac Band of Lake Superior Chippewa 1720 Big Lake Rd	Cloquet	MN	55720	**888-888-6007**	218-879-4593	131
Fond du Lac Convention & Visitors Bureau 171 S Pioneer Rd	Fond du Lac	WI	54935	**800-937-9123**	920-923-3010	208
Fond du Lac Tribal & Community College 2101 14th St	Cloquet	MN	55720	**800-657-3712**	218-879-0800	164
Fondaction Bureau 103 2175 Blvd de Maisonneuve Est	Montreal	QC	H2K4S3	**800-253-6665**	514-525-5505	527
Fontaine Fifth Wheel 7574 Commerce Cir	Trussville	AL	35173	**800-874-9780**	205-661-4900	59
Fontaine Modification Co 9827 Mt Holly Rd	Charlotte	NC	28214	**800-366-8246**	704-391-1355	515
Fontaine Trailer Co 430 Letson Rd PO Box 619	Haleyville	AL	35565	**800-821-6535**	205-486-5251	777
Fontaine Truck Equipment Co 7574 Commerce Cir	Trussville	AL	35173	**800-874-9780**	205-661-4900	515
Fontainebleau Miami Beach 4441 Collins Ave	Miami Beach	FL	33140	**800-548-8886**	305-538-2000	667
Fontainebleau State Park 67825 US Hwy 190	Mandeville	LA	70448	**888-677-3668**	985-624-4443	564
Fontana Village Resort 300 Woods Rd PO Box 68	Fontana Dam	NC	28733	**800-849-2258**	828-498-2211	667
Food & Drug Administration *Center for Devices & Radiological Health (CDRH)* 10903 New Hampshire Ave WO66-5429	Silver Spring	MD	20993	**800-638-2041**	301-796-7100	340-8
Center for Food Safety & Applied Nutrition 5100 Paint Branch Pkwy	College Park	MD	20740	**888-723-3366**		340-8
National Center for Toxicological Research 3900 N Ctr Rd	Jefferson	AR	72079	**800-638-3321**	870-543-7000	340-8
Pacific Region 1301 Clay St Ste 1180N	Oakland	CA	94612	**877-696-6775**		340-8
Food & Drug Law Institute (FDLI) 1155 15th St NW Ste 800	Washington	DC	20005	**800-956-6293**	202-371-1420	48-10
Food & Nutrition Service *Food Stamp Program* 3101 Pk Ctr Dr	Alexandria	VA	22302	**800-221-5689**	703-305-2022	340-1
Food & Wine Magazine 1120 Ave of the Americas Ste 9	New York	NY	10036	**800-333-6569**	813-979-6625	456-11
Food Allergy & Anaphylaxis Network (FAAN) 11781 Lee Jackson Hwy Ste 160	Fairfax	VA	22033	**800-929-4040**	703-691-3179	47-17
Food Bank For New York City 39 Broadway 10th Fl	New York	NY	10006	**866-692-3663**	212-566-7855	300
Food City 1005 N Arizona Ave	Chandler	AZ	85224	**800-755-7292**	480-857-2198	345
Food Consulting Co, The 13724 Recuerdo Dr	Del Mar	CA	92014	**800-793-2844**	858-793-4658	472
Food for the Poor Inc (FFP) 6401 Lyons Rd	Coconut Creek	FL	33073	**800-427-9104**	954-427-2222	47-5
Food Ingredient News 49 Walnut Pk Bldg 2	Wellesley	MA	02481	**866-285-7215**	781-489-7301	530-12
Food Marketing Institute (FMI) 2345 Crystal Dr Ste 800	Arlington	VA	22202	**800-732-2639**	202-220-0600	48-18
Food Processing Magazine 555 W Pierce Rd Ste 301	Itasca	IL	60143	**800-755-5505**	630-467-1300	456-21
Food Processing Suppliers Assn (FPSA) 1451 Dolley Madison Blvd Ste 101	McLean	VA	22101	**855-670-4787**	703-761-2600	48-13
Food Services of America Inc 16100 N 71st St Ste 400	Scottsdale	AZ	85254	**800-528-9346**	480-927-4000	298-8
Food Warming Equipment Company Inc 7900 S Rt 31 *Sales	Crystal Lake	IL	60014	**800-222-4393***	815-459-7500	299
FoodChek Systems Inc 1414 8 St. S.W. Ste 450	Calgary	AB	T2R1J6	**877-298-0208**	403-269-9424	407
Foodscience Corp 20 New England Dr Ste 10	Essex Junction	VT	05452	**800-451-5190**	802-878-5508	797
Foot Locker Inc 112 W 34th St *NYSE: FL*	New York	NY	10120	**800-952-5210**	212-720-3700	302
Foot of the Mountain Motel 200 W Arapahoe Ave	Boulder	CO	80302	**866-773-5489**	303-442-5688	379
Foothill College 12345 El Monte Rd	Los Altos Hills	CA	94022	**800-234-1597**	650-949-7777	161
Foothills Asset Management Ltd 8767 E Via de Ventura Ste 175	Scottsdale	AZ	85258	**800-663-9870**	480-777-9870	401
Foothills Inn 1625 N La Crosse St	Rapid City	SD	57701	**877-428-5666**	605-348-5640	379
Footstar Inc 933 MacArthur Blvd	Mahwah	NJ	07430	**800-322-2885**	201-934-2000	302
FOP (Fraternal Order of Police) 701 Marriott Dr	Nashville	TN	37214	**800-451-2711**	615-399-0900	47-15
For Eyes/Insight Optical 285 W 74th Pl	Hialeah	FL	33014	**877-688-9891**	305-557-9004	542
Forbes Hospice 4800 Friendship Ave	Pittsburgh	PA	15224	**800-381-8080**	412-578-5000	371
Forbes Inc 60 Fifth Ave	New York	NY	10011	**800-295-0893**	212-620-2200	634-9
Forbes Magazine 60 Fifth Ave	New York	NY	10011	**800-295-0893**	212-366-8900	456-5
Forbes Snyder Tristate Cash 54 Northampton St	Easthampton	MA	01027	**800-222-4064**	413-529-2950	255
Forbo Flooring Systems 8 Maplewood Dr Humboldt Industrial Pk *Cust Svc	Hazleton	PA	18202	**800-842-7839***		293
Force 3 Inc 2151 Priest Bridge Dr	Crofton	MD	21114	**800-391-0204**	301-261-0204	182
Force Control Industries Inc 3660 Dixie Hwy	Fairfield	OH	45014	**800-829-3244**	513-868-0900	619
Force Flow Inc 2430 Stanwell Dr	Concord	CA	94520	**800-893-6723**		362
Force10 Networks Inc 1415 N McDowell Blvd	Petaluma	CA	94954	**866-600-5100**	707-665-4400	679
Ford Audio-Video Systems Inc 4800 W I-40	Oklahoma City	OK	73128	**800-654-6744**	405-946-9966	51
Ford Equity Research Inc 11722 Sorrento Vly Rd Ste I	San Diego	CA	92121	**800-842-0207**	858-755-1327	401
Ford Fasteners Inc 110 S Newman St	Hackensack	NJ	07601	**800-272-3673**	201-487-3151	280
Ford Hotel Supply Company Inc 2204 N Broadway	Saint Louis	MO	63102	**800-472-3673**	314-231-8400	705
Ford Motor Co PO Box 6248 *NYSE: F*	Dearborn	MI	48126	**800-392-3673**	313-845-8540	58
Ford Motor Credit Co 1 American Rd	Dearborn	MI	48121	**800-727-7000**	313-322-3000	216
Ford of Montebello Inc 2747 Via Campo	Montebello	CA	90640	**888-313-2305**	323-838-6920	56
Ford of Ocala Inc 2816 NW Pine Ave	Ocala	FL	34475	**888-255-1788**	352-732-4800	515
FordDirect 1740 Us Hwy 60 PO Box 700	Republic	MO	65738	**888-865-2576**	417-732-2626	56
Fordham Auto Sales Inc 236 W Fordham Rd	Bronx	NY	10468	**800-407-1153**		56
Fordham Equipment Co 1204 Village Market Place Ste 262	Morrisville	NC	27560	**866-467-0708**	919-467-0708	320-3
Fordham University 441 E Fordham Rd	Bronx	NY	10458	**800-367-3426**	718-817-3240	167
College at Lincoln Ctr 113 W 60th St	New York	NY	10023	**800-367-3426**	212-636-6710	167
Westchester 400 Westchester Ave	West Harrison	NY	10604	**800-606-6090**	914-332-8295	167
Fordia Inc 2745 de Miniac Ville Saint Laurent	Saint Laurent	QC	H4S1E5	**800-768-7274**	514-336-9211	358
Forecast International 22 Commerce Rd	Newtown	CT	06470	**800-451-4975**	203-426-0800	634-10
Foreign Affairs 58 E 68th St *Cust Svc	New York	NY	10065	**800-829-5539***	212-434-9527	456-17
Foreign Candy Company Inc 1 Foreign Candy Dr	Hull	IA	51239	**800-831-8541**	712-439-1496	298-3
Foreign Policy Assn (FPA) 470 Pk Ave S	New York	NY	10016	**800-628-5754**	212-481-8100	47-7
Foremost Farms USA E10889A Penny Ln	Baraboo	WI	53913	**800-362-9196**	608-355-8700	297-10
Foremost Industries Inc 2375 Buchanan Trl W	Greencastle	PA	17225	**877-284-5334**	717-597-7166	105
Foremost Insurance Co 5600 Beech Tree Ln	Caledonia	MI	49316	**800-532-4221**		391-4
Foremostco Inc 8457 NW 66th St	Miami	FL	33166	**800-421-8986**	305-592-8986	692
Forensic Fluids Laboratories Inc 225 Parsons St	Kalamazoo	MI	49007	**866-492-2517**	269-492-7700	740
Forensic It 57 E Southcrest Cir	Edwardsville	IL	62025	**877-483-3284**	314-677-3950	740
Forest at Duke 2701 Pickett Rd	Durham	NC	27705	**800-474-0258**	919-490-8000	670
Forest City Trading Group LLC 10250 SW Greenburg Rd Ste 300	Portland	OR	97223	**800-767-3284**	503-246-8500	193-3
Forest Hills Journal 394 WaRds Corner Rd Ste 170	Loveland	OH	45140	**888-894-2113**	513-248-8600	531-4
Forest Lake Area School District 6100 210th St N	Forest Lake	MN	55025	**866-632-9992**	651-982-8100	683
Forest Landowners Assn (FLA) 900 Cir 75 Pkwy Ste 205	Atlanta	GA	30339	**800-325-2954**	404-325-2954	47-13
Forest Lawn Memorial-Parks & Mortuaries 1712 S Glendale Ave	Glendale	CA	91205	**800-204-3131**	323-254-3131	509
Forest Pharmaceutical Inc 13600 Shoreline Dr	Earth City	MO	63045	**800-678-1605**	314-493-7000	582
Forest Preserve Dist of Dupage County 1717 31st St	Oak Brook	IL	60523	**800-526-0857**	630-616-8424	228
Forest Service (USFS) 1400 Independence Ave SW	Washington	DC	20050	**800-832-1355**	202-205-8333	340-1
Forest Service Employees for Environmental Ethics (FSEEE) PO Box 11615	Eugene	OR	97440	**800-270-7504**	541-484-2692	48-7
Forest Service Regional Offices *Region 8 (Southern Region)* 1720 Peachtree St Ste 760S	Atlanta	GA	30309	**877-372-7248**	404-347-4177	340-1
Forestry Suppliers Inc 205 W Rankin St *Cust Svc	Jackson	MS	39201	**800-752-8460***	601-354-3565	458

Name / Address	City	State	ZIP	Toll-Free	Phone	Class
Forestville/Mystery Cave State Park 21071 County 118	Preston	MN	55965	**888-646-6367**	507-352-5111	564
Foretravel Motorcoach Inc 1221 NW Stallings Dr	Nacogdoches	TX	75964	**800-955-6226**	936-564-8367	119
Forever 21 Inc 2001 S Alameda St *Cust Svc	Los Angeles	CA	90058	**800-966-1355***	213-741-5100	156-6
Forever Living Products International Inc 7501 E McCormick Pkwy	Scottsdale	AZ	85258	**888-440-2563**	480-998-8888	217
Forever Spring 2629 E Craig Rd Ste E	Las Vegas	NV	89030	**800-523-4334**	702-633-4283	240
Forex Newscom 55 Water St 50th Fl	New York	NY	10041	**888-503-6739**		387
Forged Products Inc (FPI) 6505 N Houston Rosslyn Rd	Houston	TX	77091	**800-876-3416**	713-462-3416	482
Forkardt 2155 Traverse Field Dr	Traverse City	MI	49686	**800-544-3823**	231-995-8300	492
Forked Deer Electric Co-op PO Box 67	Halls	TN	38040	**844-333-2729**	731-836-7508	247
Forklifts of Minnesota Inc 2201 W 94th St	Bloomington	MN	55431	**800-752-4300**	952-887-5400	385
Forks of Cheat Winery 2811 Stewart Town Rd	Morgantown	WV	26508	**877-989-4637**	304-598-2019	49-6
Form-A-Feed Inc (FAF) 740 Bowman St	Stewart	MN	55385	**800-422-3649**	320-562-2413	446
Formaggio Kitchen on Line LLC 244 Huron Ave	Cambridge	MA	02138	**888-212-3224**	617-354-4750	294
Formall Inc 3908 Fountain Vly Dr	Knoxville	TN	37918	**800-643-3676**	865-922-7514	601
Formax Manufacturing Corp 168 Wealthy St SW	Grand Rapids	MI	49503	**800-242-2833**	616-456-5458	1
Former Governors' Mansion State Historic Site 612 E Blvd Ave	Bismarck	ND	58505	**866-243-5352**	701-328-2666	564
Formers by Ernie Inc 7905 Almeda Genoa Rd Ste B	Houston	TX	77075	**866-991-3455**	713-991-3455	358
Formetco Inc 2963 Pleasant Hill Rd	Duluth	GA	30096	**800-367-6382**	770-476-7000	699
Formflex Inc PO Box 218	Bloomingdale	IN	47832	**800-255-7659**		85
Formica Corp 10155 Reading Rd	Cincinnati	OH	45241	**800-367-6422**	513-786-3400	598
Forms Manufacturers Inc 312 E Forest Ave	Girard	KS	66743	**800-835-0614**	620-724-8225	109
Formtek Metal Forming Inc 4899 Commerce Pkwy	Cleveland	OH	44128	**800-631-0520**	216-292-4460	672
Formula Ford Inc 265 River St	Montpelier	VT	05602	**888-872-9439**	802-223-5201	56
Formula Growth Ltd 1010 Sherbrooke St W Ste 2300	Montreal	QC	H3A2R7	**877-343-6654**	514-288-5136	401
Forney Corp 16479 N Dallas Pkwy Ste 600 *Cust Svc	Addison	TX	75001	**800-356-7740***	972-458-6100	203
Forney Industries Inc 1830 LaPorte Ave	Fort Collins	CO	80521	**800-521-6038**		809
Forrest General Hospital 6051 US Hwy 49	Hattiesburg	MS	39402	**800-503-5980**	601-288-7000	374-3
Forrest Hills Mountain Resort & Conference Ctr 135 Forrest Hills Rd	Dahlonega	GA	30533	**800-654-6313**	706-864-6456	667
Forsbergs Inc 1210 Pennington Ave PO Box 510 *Cust Svc	Thief River Falls	MN	56701	**800-654-1927***	218-681-1927	275
Forsyth County Public Library 201 N Chestnut St FL 5	Winston-Salem	NC	27101	**866-345-1884**	336-703-2665	434-3
Forsyth Technical Community College 2100 Silas Creek Pkwy	Winston-Salem	NC	27103	**800-870-3676**	336-723-0371	798
Fort Bliss National Cemetery PO Box 6342	El Paso	TX	79906	**800-273-8255**	915-564-0201	135
Fort Bragg Unified School District 312 S Lincoln St	Fort Bragg	CA	95437	**800-734-7793**	707-961-2850	683
Fort Caspar Museum 4001 Fort Caspar Rd	Casper	WY	82604	**800-877-7353**	307-235-8462	519
Fort Cobb Lake State Park 27022 Copperhead Rd	Fort Cobb	OK	73038	**800-622-6317**	405-643-2249	564
Fort Collins Area Chamber of Commerce 225 S Meldrum St	Fort Collins	CO	80521	**877-652-8607**	970-482-3746	138
Fort Collins Convention & Visitors Bureau 19 Old Town Sq Ste 137	Fort Collins	CO	80524	**800-274-3678**	970-232-3840	208
Fort Custer National Cemetery 15501 Dickman Rd	Augusta	MI	49012	**800-273-8255**	269-731-4164	135
Fort Edward Express Company Inc 1402 Rt 9	Fort Edward	NY	12828	**800-342-1233**	518-792-6571	778
Fort Erie Race Track 230 Catherine St PO Box 1130	Fort Erie	ON	L2A5N9	**800-295-3770**	905-871-3200	639
Fort Garry, The 222 Broadway	Winnipeg	MB	R3C0R3	**800-665-8088**	204-942-8251	379
Fort Hays State University 600 Pk St *Admissions	Hays	KS	67601	**800-628-3478***	785-628-4000	167
Fort Henry National Historic Site PO Box 213 *Cust Svc	Kingston	ON	K7L4V8	**800-437-2233***	613-542-7388	519
Fort Jesup State Historic Site 32 Geoghagan Rd	Many	LA	71449	**888-677-5378**	318-256-4117	564
Fort Knox Federal Credit Union PO Box 900	Radcliff	KY	40159	**800-756-3678**	502-942-0254	221
Fort Lauderdale Hospital 1601 E Las Olas Blvd	Fort Lauderdale	FL	33301	**800-585-7527**	954-463-4321	374-5
Fort Lauderdale/Hollywood International Airport 100 Aviation Blvd	Fort Lauderdale	FL	33315	**866-682-2258**	954-359-1200	27
Fort Leonard Wood Bldg 744	Fort Leonard Wood	MO	65473	**800-350-7746**	573-596-0131	496-2
Fort Lewis College 1000 Rim Dr	Durango	CO	81301	**877-352-2656**	970-247-7010	167
Fort Madison 614 Ninth St	Fort Madison	IA	52627	**800-210-8687**	319-372-5471	208
Fort Marcy Hotel Suites 321 Kearney Ave	Santa Fe	NM	87501	**888-667-2775**	505-988-2800	379
Fort McAllister State Historic Park 3894 Ft McAllister Rd	Richmond Hill	GA	31324	**800-864-7275**	912-727-2339	564
Fort McDowell Casino 10424 N Ft McDowell Rd	Fort Mcdowell	AZ	85264	**800-843-3678**		132
Fort McHenry National Monument & Historic Shrine 2400 E Fort Ave	Baltimore	MD	21230	**866-945-7920**	410-962-4290	519
Fort Meigs State Memorial 29100 W River Rd	Perrysburg	OH	43551	**800-283-8916**	419-874-4121	49-2
Fort Morgan Area Chamber of Commerce 300 Main St	Fort Morgan	CO	80701	**800-354-8660**	970-867-6702	138
Fort Myers Beach Chamber of Commerce 17200 San Carlos Blvd	Fort Myers Beach	FL	33931	**866-998-9250**	239-454-7500	138
Fort Orange Press Inc 11 Sand Creek Rd	Albany	NY	12205	**800-777-3233**	518-489-3233	626
Fort Pillow State Historic Park 3122 Pk Rd	Henning	TN	38041	**800-250-8615**	731-738-5581	564
Fort Pitt Capital Group Inc 680 Andersen Dr Foster Plz Ten	Pittsburgh	PA	15220	**800-471-5827**	412-921-1822	527
Fort Polk 2030 14th St	Fort Polk	LA	71459	**800-752-4658**	337-531-2911	496-2
Fort Pulaski National Monument US Hwy 80 E	Savannah	GA	31410	**800-228-5150**	912-786-5787	563
Fort Ridgely State Park 72158 County Rd 30	Fairfax	MN	55332	**888-646-6367**	507-426-7840	564
Fort Riley 405 Pershing Ct	Fort Riley	KS	66442	**800-273-8255**	785-239-2022	496-2
Fort Rock State Natural Area 725 Summer St NE Ste C	Salem	OR	97739	**800-551-6949**		564
Fort Saint Jean Baptiste State Historic Site 155 Jefferson St	Natchitoches	LA	71457	**888-677-7853**	318-357-3101	564
Fort Scott Community College 2108 S Horton St	Fort Scott	KS	66701	**800-874-3722**	620-223-2700	161
Fort Smith Convention & Visitors Bureau 2 N 'B'	Fort Smith	AR	72901	**800-637-1477**	479-783-8888	208
Fort Smith National Cemetery 522 Garland Ave	Fort Smith	AR	72901	**800-535-1117**	479-783-5345	135
Fort Smith Public Library 3201 Rogers Ave	Fort Smith	AR	72903	**866-660-0885**	479-783-0229	434-3
Fort Smith Regional Airport 6700 McKennon Blvd Ste 200	Fort Smith	AR	72903	**800-992-7433**	479-452-7000	27
Fort Snelling State Park 101 Snelling Lake Rd	Saint Paul	MN	55111	**888-646-6367**	612-725-2389	564
Fort Valley State University 1005 State University Dr	Fort Valley	GA	31030	**877-462-3878**	478-825-6211	167
Fort Vancouver National Historic Site 612 E Reserve St	Vancouver	WA	98661	**800-832-3599**	360-816-6230	563
Fort Washington Investment Advisors Inc 303 Broadway Ste 1200	Cincinnati	OH	45202	**888-244-8167**	513-361-7600	401
Fort Wayne Newspapers Inc 600 W Main St	Fort Wayne	IN	46802	**800-444-3303**	260-461-8444	634-8
Fort Wayne/Allen County Convention & Visitors Bureau 927 S Harrison St	Fort Wayne	IN	46802	**800-767-7752**	260-424-3700	208
Fort Worth Chamber of Commerce 777 Taylor St Ste 900	Fort Worth	TX	76102	**800-433-5747**	817-336-2491	138
Fort Worth City Credit Union PO Box 100099	Fort Worth	TX	76185	**888-732-3085**	817-732-2803	221
Fort Worth Community Credit Union 1905 Forest Ridge Dr PO Box 210848	Bedford	TX	76021	**800-817-8234**	817-835-5000	221
Fort Worth Convention & Visitors Bureau 111 W Fourth St Ste 200	Fort Worth	TX	76102	**800-433-5747**	817-336-8791	208
Fort Worth Convention Ctr 1201 Houston St	Fort Worth	TX	76102	**866-630-2588**	817-392-6338	207
Fort Worth Museum of Science & History 1600 Gendy St	Fort Worth	TX	76107	**888-255-9300**	817-255-9300	519
Fort Worth Opera 1300 Gendy St	Fort Worth	TX	76107	**877-396-7372**	817-731-0833	572-2
Forte Data Systems Inc 3330 Paddock Pkwy	Suwanee	GA	30024	**800-571-8702**	678-208-0206	227
Forth Inc 5959 W Century Blvd Ste 700	Los Angeles	CA	90045	**800-553-6784**	310-999-6784	180-2
Forthea 3355 W Alabama St Ste 1230	Houston	TX	77098	**800-882-5905**	713-568-2763	5
Fortifiber Building Systems Group 300 Industrial Dr	Fernley	NV	89408	**800-773-4777**	775-333-6400	551-1
Fortin Consulting Inc 215 Hamel Rd	Hamel	MN	55340	**844-273-3117**	763-478-3606	198
Fortitude Business Solutions LLC PO Box 2095	Daphne	AL	36526	**877-577-2644**		393
Fortrend Corp 687 N Pastoria Ave	Sunnyvale	CA	94085	**888-937-3637**	408-734-9311	693
Fortress Integrated Technologies 100 Delawanna Ave	Clifton	NJ	07014	**888-734-9320**	973-572-1070	806
Fortress Technology Inc 51 Grand Marshall Dr	Toronto	ON	M1B5N6	**888-220-8737**	416-754-2898	690
Fortun Insurance Agency Inc 365 Palermo Ave	Coral Gables	FL	33134	**877-643-2055**	305-445-3535	390
Fortune Bay Resort & Casino 1430 Bois Forte Rd	Tower	MN	55790	**800-992-7529**	218-753-6400	451
Fortune Brands Inc 520 Lk Cook Rd *NYSE: FBHS*	Deerfield	IL	60015	**800-225-2719**	847-484-4400	187
Forum Credit Union PO Box 50738	Indianapolis	IN	46250	**800-382-5414**	317-558-6000	221
Forum Publishing Co 383 E Main St	Centerport	NY	11721	**800-635-7654**	631-754-5000	634-9
Forum, The 101 N Fifth St	Fargo	ND	58102	**800-274-5445**	701-235-7311	531-2
Forward Air Corp 430 Airport Rd PO Box 1058 *NASDAQ: FWRD*	Greeneville	TN	37744	**800-726-6654**	423-636-7100	778
Forward Corp 219 N Front St	Standish	MI	48658	**800-664-4501**	989-846-4501	325
Forward Technology Inc 260 Jenks Ave *Cust Svc	Cokato	MN	55321	**800-307-6040***	320-286-2578	386

Name / Address	Toll-Free	Phone	Class
Foss Maritime Co 1151 Fairview Ave N ... Seattle WA 98119	**800-562-2711**		464
Foss Mfg Co LLC 11 Merrill Industrial Dr ... Hampton NH 03842	**800-343-3277**	603-929-6000	742-6
Foss National Leasing 7200 Yonge St ... Thornhill ON L4J1V8	**800-461-3677**	905-886-4244	125
Foss State Park 10252 Hwy 44 ... Foss OK 73647	**800-622-6317**	580-592-4433	564
Fosta-Tek Optics Inc 320 Hamilton St ... Leominster MA 01453	**866-221-9157**	978-534-6511	543
Foster City Flowers & Gifts 1160 Chess Dr Ste 1 ... Foster City CA 94404	**800-970-7673**	650-573-6607	294
Foster Construction Products Inc 1105 S Frontenac St ... Aurora IL 60504	**800-231-9541**		3
Foster Farms Inc PO Box 306 PO Box 457 ... Livingston CA 95334	**800-255-7227**		10-7
Foster Grandparent Program c/o Senior Corps 1201 New York Ave NW ... Washington DC 20525	**800-424-8867**	202-606-5000	199
Foster Lake & Pond Management Inc 9020 White Oak Rd PO Box 1294 ... Garner NC 27529	**888-525-6348**	919-772-8548	462
Foster Pepper Pllc 1111 Third Ave Ste 3400 ... Seattle WA 98101	**800-995-5902**	206-447-4400	428
Foster Thomas Inc 1788 Forest Dr ... Annapolis MD 21401	**800-372-3626**		391-3
Foster's Daily Democrat 150 Venture Dr ... Dover NH 03820	**800-660-8310**	603-742-4455	531-2
Fotoprint 975 Pandora Ave ... Victoria BC V8V3P4	**888-382-8211**	250-382-8218	626
Foundation Constructors Inc 81 Big Break Rd PO Box 97 ... Oakley CA 94561	**800-841-8740**	925-754-6633	191-5
Foundation Ctr 79 Fifth Ave 2nd Fl ... New York NY 10003	**800-424-9836**	212-620-4230	47-11
Foundation Fighting Blindness 11435 Cron Hill Dr ... Owings Mills MD 21117	**800-683-5555**	410-568-0150	47-17
Foundation for Economic Education (FEE) 30 S Broadway ... Irvington-on-Hudson NY 10533	**800-960-4333**	404-554-9980	631
Foundation for International Community Assistance (FINCA) 1201 15th St NW 8th fl ... Washington DC 20005	**855-903-4622**	202-682-1510	47-5
Foundation for the Carolinas 217 S Tryon St ... Charlotte NC 28202	**800-973-7244**	704-973-4500	304
Foundation Laboratory 1716 W Holt Ave ... Pomona CA 91768	**800-843-7190**	909-623-9301	415
Foundation Technologies Inc 1400 Progress Industrial Blvd ... Lawrenceville GA 30043	**800-773-2368**	678-407-4640	193-1
Founders Federal Credit Union 607 N Main St ... Lancaster SC 29720 *Tech Supp	**888-918-7403***	803-289-5927	221
Founders Inn 5641 Indian River Rd ... Virginia Beach VA 23464	**800-926-4466**	757-424-5511	377
Fountain Industries Co 922 E 14th St ... Albert Lea MN 56007	**800-328-3594**	507-373-2351	110
Fountain Valley Regional Hospital & Medical Ctr 17100 Euclid St ... Fountain Valley CA 92708	**866-904-6871**	714-966-7200	374-3
Fountainhead College of Technology 3203 Tazewell Pk ... Knoxville TN 37918	**888-218-7335**	865-688-9422	798
Fountainhead Group Inc 23 Garden St ... New York Mills NY 13417	**800-311-9903**	315-736-0037	174
Four County Electric Membership Corp 1822 NC Hwy 53 W PO Box 667 ... Burgaw NC 28425	**888-368-7289**	910-259-2171	247
Four Oaks Bank & Trust Co PO Box 309 ... Four Oaks NC 27524	**877-963-6257**	919-963-2177	69
Four Points by Sheraton Charlotte 315 E Woodlawn Rd ... Charlotte NC 28217	**800-368-7764**	704-522-0852	379
Four Points by Sheraton French Quarter 541 Bourbon St ... New Orleans LA 70130	**866-716-8133**	504-524-7611	379
Four Queens Hotel & Casino 202 Fremont St ... Las Vegas NV 89101	**800-634-6045**	702-385-4011	379
Four Sails Resort Hotel 3301 Atlantic Ave ... Virginia Beach VA 23451	**800-227-4213**	757-491-8100	379
Four Seasons Hospice & Palliative Care 571 S Allen Rd ... Flat Rock NC 28731	**866-466-9734**	828-692-6178	371
Four Seasons Hotels & Resorts 1165 Leslie St ... Toronto ON M3C2K8	**800-332-3442**	416-449-1750	751
Four Seasons Hotels Inc 1165 Leslie St ... Toronto ON M3C2K8	**800-332-3442**	416-449-1750	379
Four Seasons Inc 1801 Waters Ridge Dr ... Lewisville TX 75057	**888-505-4567**	972-316-8100	611
Four Seasons Resort & Club Dallas at Las Colinas 4150 N MacArthur Blvd ... Irving TX 75038	**800-332-3442**	972-717-0700	667
Four Seasons Resort Hualalai 100 Ka'upulehu Dr ... Kailua-Kona HI 96740	**888-340-5662**	808-325-8000	667
Four Seasons Resort Jackson Hole 7680 Granite Loop Rd PO Box 544 ... Teton Village WY 83025	**800-914-5110**	307-732-5000	667
Four Seasons Resort Maui at Wailea 3900 Wailea Alanui Dr ... Wailea HI 96753	**800-334-6284**	808-874-8000	667
Four Seasons Resort Palm Beach 2800 S Ocean Blvd ... Palm Beach FL 33480	**800-432-2335**	561-582-2800	667
Four Seasons Resort Santa Barbara 1260 Ch Dr ... Santa Barbara CA 93108	**800-819-5053**	805-969-2261	667
Four Seasons Resort Scottsdale at Troon North 10600 E Crescent Moon Dr ... Scottsdale AZ 85262	**800-332-3442**	480-515-5700	667
Four Seasons Solar Products LLC 5005 Veterans Memorial Hwy ... Holbrook NY 11741	**800-368-7732**	631-563-4000	104
Four Seasons Spa at the Four Seasons Hotel Las Vegas 3960 Las Vegas Blvd S ... Las Vegas NV 89119	**800-332-3442**	702-632-5302	705
Four Seasons Spa at the Four Seasons Hotel Los Angeles at Beverly Hills 300 S Doheny Dr ... Los Angeles CA 90048	**800-819-5053**	310-786-2229	705
Four Seasons Spa at the Four Seasons Resort Jackson Hole 7680 Granite Loop Rd PO Box 544 ... Teton Village WY 83025	**800-819-5053**	307-732-5120	705
Four Seasons Spa at the Four Seasons Resort Maui 3900 Wailea Alanui Dr ... Wailea HI 96753	**800-334-6284**	808-874-2925	705
Four Seasons Spa at the Four Seasons Resort Santa Barbara 1260 Ch Dr ... Santa Barbara CA 93108 *General	**800-819-5053***	805-565-8250	705
Four Wheel Campers 1460 Churchill Downs Ave ... Woodland CA 95776	**800-242-1442**	530-666-1442	119
Four Winds Casino Resort 11111 Wilson Rd ... New Buffalo MI 49117	**866-494-6371**		131
Four Winds Hospital 800 Cross River Rd ... Katonah NY 10536	**800-528-6624**	914-763-8151	374-5
Foursome Inc 3570 Vicksveurg Ln N Ste 100 ... Plymouth MN 55447	**888-368-7766**	763-473-4667	156-2
Fourwinds Resort & Marina 9301 Fairfax Rd ... Bloomington IN 47401	**800-824-2628**	812-824-2628	667
Fowler State Bank 300 E Fifth St PO Box 511 ... Fowler IN 47944	**800-439-3951**	765-884-1200	69
Fowler's Chocolate Co 100 River Rock Dr Ste 102 ... Buffalo NY 14207	**800-824-2263**	716-877-9983	297-8
Fownes Bros & Company Inc 16 E 34th St ... New York NY 10016 *All	**800-345-6837***	212-683-0150	154-7
Fox Chase Cancer Ctr 333 Cottman Ave ... Philadelphia PA 19111	**888-369-2427**	215-728-6900	374-7
Fox Cities Chamber of Commerce & Industry 125 N Superior St ... Appleton WI 54911	**888-249-2587**	920-734-7101	138
Fox Cities Convention & Visitors Bureau 3433 W College Ave ... Appleton WI 54914	**800-236-6673**	920-734-3358	208
Fox Creek Leather Inc 2029 Elk Creek Pkwy ... Independence VA 24348	**800-766-4165**	276-773-3131	709
Fox Harb'r Resort & Spa 1337 Fox Harbour Rd ... Wallace NS B0K1Y0	**866-257-1801**	902-257-1801	705
Fox Hills Resort & Convention Ctr 250 W Church St ... Mishicot WI 54228	**800-950-7615**	920-755-2376	667
Fox Industries Inc 3100 Falls Cliff Rd ... Baltimore MD 21211	**888-760-0369**	410-243-8856	3
Fox Pool Corp 3490 BoaRd Rd ... York PA 17406	**800-723-1011**	717-764-8581	726
Fox River Mills Inc 227 Poplar Stq PO Box 298 ... Osage IA 50461	**800-247-1815**	641-732-3798	154-9
Fox Run Vineyards 670 State Rt 14 ... Penn Yan NY 14527	**800-636-9786**	315-536-4616	443
Fox Service Co PO Box 19047 ... Austin TX 78760	**866-668-4749**	512-442-6782	191-10
Fox Theatre 660 Peachtree St NE ... Atlanta GA 30308	**855-285-8499**	404-881-2100	571
Fox Valley Spring Company Inc N915 Craftsmen Dr ... Greenville WI 54942	**800-776-2645**	920-757-7777	491
Fox Valley Technical College 1825 N Bluemound Dr PO Box 2277 ... Appleton WI 54912	**800-735-3882**	920-735-5600	798
Fox's Pizza Den Inc 4425 Willaim Penn Hwy ... Murrysville PA 15668	**800-899-3697**	724-733-7888	668
Foxcom Inc 136 Main St Ste 300b ... Princeton NJ 08540	**866-663-7284**	609-514-1800	248
Foxcroft School 22407 Foxhound Ln ... Middleburg VA 20117	**800-858-2364**	540-687-5555	621
Foxdale Village 500 E Marylyn Ave ... State College PA 16801	**800-253-4951**	814-272-2117	670
Foxes Music Co 416 S Washington St ... Falls Church VA 22046	**800-446-4414**	703-533-7393	525
Foxworth-Galbraith Lumber Co 4965 Preston Pk Blvd Ste 400 ... Plano TX 75093	**800-688-8082**	972-665-2400	193-3
Foxx Equipment Co 421 Southwest Blvd ... Kansas City MO 64108	**800-821-2254**	816-421-3600	358
Foxy 104.3 Fm 8001-101 Creedmoor Rd ... Raleigh NC 27613	**800-321-5975**	919-848-9736	642-95
Foxy 107.1 8001-101 Creedmoor Rd ... Raleigh NC 27613	**800-467-3699**	919-848-9736	642-95
FP Mailing Solutions 140 N Mitchell Ct ... Addison IL 60101	**800-341-6052**	630-827-5500	111
FPA (Foreign Policy Assn) 470 Pk Ave S ... New York NY 10016	**800-628-5754**	212-481-8100	47-7
FPA (Financial Planning Assn) 7535 E Hampden Ave Ste 600 ... Denver CO 80231	**800-322-4237**	303-759-4900	48-2
FPC Flexible Packaging Corp 1891 Eglinton Ave E ... Toronto ON M1L2L7	**888-288-7386**	416-288-3060	547
FPDTR (Fess Parker's Doubletree Resort) 633 E Cabrillo Blvd ... Santa Barbara CA 93103	**800-879-2929**	805-564-4333	667
FPI (Forged Products Inc) 6505 N Houston Rosslyn Rd ... Houston TX 77091	**800-876-3416**	713-462-3416	482
FPL Group Inc *NextEra Energy Inc* 700 Universe Blvd ... Juno Beach FL 33408 *NYSE: NEE*	**888-218-4392**	561-694-4000	360-5
FPM LLC 1501 S Lively Blvd ... Elk Grove Village IL 60007	**877-437-6432**	847-228-2525	483
FPMI Solutions Inc 1033 N Fairfax St Ste 200 ... Alexandria VA 22314	**888-644-3764**		195
FPSA (Food Processing Suppliers Assn) 1451 Dolley Madison Blvd Ste 101 ... McLean VA 22101	**855-670-4787**	703-761-2600	48-13
FPUC (Florida Public Utilities Co) 401 S Dixie Hwy ... West Palm Beach FL 33401	**800-427-7712**		785
FRA (Fleet Reserve Assn) 125 NW St ... Alexandria VA 22314	**800-372-1924**	703-683-1400	47-19
FRA (Federal Railroad Administration Regional Offices) *Region 1* 55 Broadway Room 1077 ... Cambridge MA 02142	**800-724-5991**	617-494-2302	340-15
FRA Today 125 NW St ... Alexandria VA 22314	**800-372-1924**	703-683-1400	456-12
Frac Tech Services LLC 301 E 18th St ... Cisco TX 76437	**866-877-1008**	817-850-1008	144
Framingham Heart Study 73 Mt Wayte Ave Ste 2 ... Framingham MA 01702	**800-854-7582**	508-935-3418	666
Framingham State College 100 State St PO Box 9101 ... Framingham MA 01701	**866-361-8970**	508-620-1220	167
France *Consulate General* 205 N Michigan Ave Ste 3700 ... Chicago IL 60601	**866-858-4430**	312-327-5200	259
Consulate General 1395 Brickell Ave Ste 1050 ... Miami FL 33131	**877-624-8737**	305-403-4185	259
Consulate General 777 Post Oak Blvd Ste 600 ... Houston TX 77056	**888-902-5322**	713-572-2799	259

	City	State	ZIP	Toll-Free	Phone	Class
Consulate General						
934 Fifth Ave	New York	NY	10021	**800-772-1213**	212-606-3600	259
Consulate General						
540 Bush St	San Francisco	CA	94108	**800-553-4133**	415-397-4330	259
Consulate General						
3475 Piedmont Rd NE Ste 1840	Atlanta	GA	30305	**888-937-2623**	404-495-1660	259
Embassy						
4101 Reservoir Rd NW	Washington	DC	20007	**800-622-6232**	202-944-6000	259
Franchise Brands LLC						
325 Bic Dr	Milford	CT	06461	**800-797-2308**		462
Franchise Co, The (TFC)						
5399 Eglinton Ave W Ste 110	Etobicoke	ON	M9C5K9	**800-294-5591**	416-620-3960	462
Franchise Handbook						
5555 N Port Washington Rd Ste 305	Milwaukee	WI	53217	**800-272-0246**	414-882-2878	456-11
Franchise Information Services Inc						
4075 Wilson Boulevard Ste 410	Arlington	VA	22203	**800-485-9570**	703-740-4700	387
Franchising Business & Law Alert						
1617 JFK Blvd Ste 1750	Philadelphia	PA	19103	**877-256-2472**	215-557-2300	530-7
Franchising World Magazine						
1501 K St NW Ste 350	Washington	DC	20005	**800-543-1038**	202-628-8000	456-5
Franchoice Inc						
7500 Flying Cloud Dr	Eden Prairie	MN	55344	**877-396-4238**	952-345-8400	196
Francis Investment Counsel LLC						
21180 W Capitol Dr	Pewaukee	WI	53072	**866-232-6457**		794
Francis Marion Hotel, The						
387 King St	Charleston	SC	29403	**877-756-2121**	843-722-0600	379
Francis Marion University						
PO Box 100547	Florence	SC	29501	**800-368-7551**	843-661-1231	167
Francis Marion University Rogers Library						
PO Box 100547	Florence	SC	29502	**800-368-7551**		434-6
Francis Scott Key Family Resort						
12806 Ocean Gateway	Ocean City	MD	21842	**800-213-0088**	410-213-0088	667
Franciscan Oaks						
19 Pocono Rd	Denville	NJ	07834	**800-237-3330**	973-586-6000	670
Franciscan School of Theology						
1712 Euclid Ave	Berkeley	CA	94709	**855-355-1550**	760-547-1800	168-3
Franciscan Sisters of Chicago Inc						
11500 Theresa Dr	Lemont	IL	60439	**800-524-6126**		47-20
Franciscan St. Elizabeth Health						
1501 Hartford St	Lafayette	IN	47904	**800-371-6011**	765-423-6011	374-3
Francisco Grande Hotel & Golf Resort						
26000 Gila Bend Hwy	Casa Grande	AZ	85222	**800-237-4238***	520-836-6444	667
*General						
Frank & Teressa's Anchor Bar & Restaurant						
651 Delaware Ave	Buffalo	NY	14202	**866-248-9623**	716-883-1134	669
Frank B Fuhrer Wholesale Co						
3100 E Carson St	Pittsburgh	PA	15203	**800-837-2212**	412-488-8844	80-1
Frank C. Alegre Trucking Inc						
PO Box 1508	Lodi	CA	95241	**800-769-2440**	209-334-2112	778
Frank Edmunds & Co						
6111 S Sayre	Chicago	IL	60638	**800-447-3516**	773-586-2772	818
Frank Jackson State Park						
100 Jerry Adams Dr	Opp	AL	36467	**800-760-4089**	334-493-6988	564
Frank Lloyd Wright's Martin House Complex						
125 Jewett Pkwy	Buffalo	NY	14214	**877-377-3858**	716-856-3858	49-2
Frank Lynn & Associates Inc						
500 Park Blvd Ste 1300	Itasca	IL	60143	**800-245-5966**	312-263-7888	198
Frank Mayer & Assoc Inc						
1975 Wisconsin Ave	Grafton	WI	53024	**855-294-2875**		235
Frank Miller Lumber Company Inc						
1690 Frank Miller Rd	Union City	IN	47390	**800-345-2643**	765-964-3196	193-3
Frank Paxton Lumber Co						
7455 Dawson Rd	Cincinnati	OH	45243	**800-325-9800**	513-984-8200	193-3
Frank Roberts & Sons Inc						
1130 Robertsville Rd	Punxsutawney	PA	15767	**800-262-8955**	814-938-5000	193-4
Frankel Lois (Rep D - FL)						
1037 Longworth Bldg	Washington	DC	20515	**866-264-0957**	202-225-9890	342-2
Frankenmuth Convention & Visitors Bureau						
635 S Main St	Frankenmuth	MI	48734	**800-386-8696**	989-652-6106	208
Frankenmuth Insurance						
1 Mutual Ave	Frankenmuth	MI	48787	**800-234-4433**	989-652-6121	391-4
Frankfort Regional Medical Ctr						
299 King's Daughters Dr	Frankfort	KY	40601	**888-696-4505**	502-875-5240	374-3
Frankfort/Franklin County Tourist & Convention Commission						
100 Capitol Ave	Frankfort	KY	40601	**800-960-7200**	502-875-8687	208
Franklin & Marshall College						
PO Box 3003	Lancaster	PA	17604	**877-678-9111**	717-291-3951	167
Franklin & Marshall College Shadek-Fackenthal Library						
450 College Ave	Lancaster	PA	17604	**866-366-7655**	717-291-4223	434-6
Franklin Area Chamber of Commerce (FACC)						
1259 Liberty St	Franklin	PA	16323	**888-547-2377**	814-432-5823	138
Franklin College						
101 Branigin Blvd	Franklin	IN	46131	**800-852-0232**	317-738-8000	167
Franklin Community Health Network						
111 Franklin Health Commons	Farmington	ME	04938	**800-398-6031**	207-778-6031	374-3
Franklin County						
355 W Main St	Malone	NY	12953	**800-397-8686**	518-483-6770	338
Franklin Covey Co						
2200 West PkwyBlvd	Salt Lake City	UT	84119	**800-827-1776**	801-817-1776	763
NYSE: FC						
Franklin Credit Management Corp						
101 Hudson St	Jersey City	NJ	07302	**800-255-5897**	201-604-1800	216
Franklin D Roosevelt Presidential Library & Museum						
4079 Albany Post Rd	Hyde Park	NY	12538	**800-337-8474**	845-486-7770	434-2
Franklin Electric Co Inc						
9255 Coverdale Rd	Fort Wayne	IN	46809	**800-962-3787**	260-824-2900	517
NASDAQ: FELE						
Franklin Electric Co-op Inc						
225 Franklin St NW	Russellville	AL	35653	**800-410-2732**	256-332-2730	247
Franklin Empire Inc						
8421 Darnley Rd	Montreal	QC	H4T2B2	**800-361-5044**	514-341-9720	255
Franklin Fibre-Lamitex Corp						
903 E 13th St	Wilmington	DE	19802	**800-233-9739**	302-652-3621	598
Franklin Homes Inc						
10655 Hwy 43	Russellville	AL	35653	**800-332-4511**		504
Franklin Imaging LLC						
500 Schrock Rd	Columbus	OH	43229	**877-885-6894**	614-885-6894	626
Franklin Institute Science Museum						
222 N 20th St	Philadelphia	PA	19103	**800-732-0999**	215-448-1200	519
Franklin International						
2020 Bruck St	Columbus	OH	43207	**800-877-4583**	614-443-0241	3
Franklin Local School District						
PO Box 428	Duncan Falls	OH	43734	**800-846-4976**	740-674-5203	683
Franklin Mills						
1455 Franklin Mills Cir	Philadelphia	PA	19154	**877-746-6642***	215-632-1500	459
*General						
Franklin Mutual Insurance Co						
5 Broad St	Branchville	NJ	07826	**800-842-0551**	973-948-3120	391-4
Franklin Pierce University						
Concord 5 Chenell Dr	Concord	NH	03301	**800-437-0048**	603-228-1155	167
Keene 17 Bradco St	Keene	NH	03431	**800-325-1090**	603-899-4000	167
Lebanon						
24 Airport Rd Ste 19	West Lebanon	NH	03784	**800-325-1090**	603-298-5549	167
Manchester						
670 N Commercial St	Manchester	NH	03101	**800-437-0048***	603-626-4972	167
*Admissions						
Portsmouth						
73 Corporate Dr	Portsmouth	NH	03801	**800-325-1090**	603-433-2000	167
Rindge						
40 University Dr	Rindge	NH	03461	**800-437-0048***	603-899-4000	167
*Admissions						
Franklin Resources Inc						
1 Franklin Pkwy Bdge 970 1st Fl	San Mateo	CA	94403	**800-632-2301**	650-312-2000	401
NYSE: BEN						
Franklin Rural Electric Co-op						
1560 Hwy 65 PO Box 437	Hampton	IA	50441	**800-750-3557**	641-456-2557	247
Franklin Sports Inc						
17 Campanelli Pkwy PO Box 508	Stoughton	MA	02072	**800-225-8649**	781-344-1111	708
Franklin Square Hospital Ctr						
9000 Franklin Sq Dr	Baltimore	MD	21237	**888-404-3549**	443-777-7000	374-3
Franklin Street Properties Corp						
401 Edgewater Pl Ste 200	Wakefield	MA	01880	**877-686-9496**	781-557-1300	652
NYSE: FSP						
Franklin Templeton Investments						
3344 Quality Dr	Rancho Cordova	CA	95670	**800-632-2350**	650-312-2000	688
Franklin University						
201 S Grant Ave	Columbus	OH	43215	**877-341-6300**	614-797-4700	167
Franklin, The						
164 E 87th St	New York	NY	10128	**800-607-4009**	212-369-1000	379
Franks Supply Company Inc						
3311 Stanford Dr NE	Albuquerque	NM	87107	**800-432-5254**	505-884-0000	358
Frankston Packaging						
699 N Frankston Hwy	Frankston	TX	75763	**800-881-1495**	903-876-2550	556
FRAN-PAC						
1501 K St Ste 350	Washington	DC	20005	**800-543-1038**	202-628-8000	614
Frantz Group Inc, The						
1245 Cheyenne Ave	Grafton	WI	53024	**800-707-0064**	262-204-6000	197
Fraser Stryker PC LLO						
500 Energy Plz 409 S 17th St	Omaha	NE	68102	**800-544-6041**	402-341-6000	428
Fraternal Order of Alaska State Troopers Museum						
245 W Fifth Ave	Anchorage	AK	99501	**800-770-5050**	907-279-5050	519
Fraternal Order of Police (FOP)						
701 Marriott Dr	Nashville	TN	37214	**800-451-2711**	615-399-0900	47-15
Frazier Industrial Co						
91 Fairview Ave	Long Valley	NJ	07853	**800-859-1342**	908-876-3001	288
Frazier Rehabilitation Institute						
220 Abraham Flexner Way	Louisville	KY	40202	**800-333-2230**	502-582-7400	374-6
FRBSF (Federal Reserve Bank of San Francisco)						
101 Market St	San Francisco	CA	94105	**800-227-4133**	415-974-2000	70
FRC (Family Research Council)						
801 G St NW	Washington	DC	20001	**800-225-4008**	202-393-2100	47-6
FRCC (Front Range Community College)						
Boulder County						
2190 Miller Dr	Longmont	CO	80501	**888-800-9198**	303-678-3722	161
Fred C ChurchInc						
41 Wellman St	Lowell	MA	01851	**800-225-1865**	978-458-1865	390
Fred Loya Insurance						
1800 Lee Trevino Ste 201	El Paso	TX	79936	**800-554-0595**	915-590-5692	390
Fred M Schildwachter & Sons Inc						
1400 Ferris Pl	Bronx	NY	10461	**800-642-3646**	718-828-2500	317
Fred Pryor Seminars						
9757 Metcalf Ave	Overland Park	KS	66212	**800-780-8476**		763
Fred Usinger Inc						
1030 N Old World Third St	Milwaukee	WI	53203	**800-558-9998**	414-276-9100	297-26
Fred Weber Inc						
2320 Creve Coeur Mill Rd	Maryland Heights	MO	63043	**866-739-8855**	314-344-0070	190-4
Fred's Inc						
4300 New Getwell Rd	Memphis	TN	38118	**800-374-7417**	901-365-8880	231
NASDAQ: FRED						
Freddie Mac						
8200 Jones Branch Dr	McLean	VA	22102	**800-424-5401**	703-903-2000	508
North Central Region						
333 W Wacker Dr Ste 2500	Chicago	IL	60606	**800-373-3343**	312-407-7400	508
Northeast Region						
8200 Jones Branch Dr	McLean	VA	22102	**800-373-3343**	703-903-2000	508
Southeast/Southwest Region						
2300 Windy Ridge Pkwy Ste 200N	Atlanta	GA	30339	**800-373-3343**	770-857-8800	508
Frederick Goldman Inc						
154 W 14th St	New York	NY	10011	**800-221-3232**		411
Frederick Motor Co, The						
1 Waverley Dr	Frederick	MD	21702	**800-734-9118**		56
Frederick News Post						
200 E Patrick St	Frederick	MD	21701	**800-486-1177**	301-662-1177	531-2
Frederick Taylor University						
346 Rheem Blvd Ste 203	Moraga	CA	94556	**800-988-4622**		506
Frederick Wildman & Sons Ltd						
307 E 53rd St	New York	NY	10022	**800-733-9463***	212-355-0700	80-3
*General						
Frederick's of Hollywood Inc						
PO Box 2949	Phoenix	AZ	85062	**855-655-2514**	800-323-9525	156-6
Fredericksburg Chamber of Commerce						
302 E Austin St	Fredericksburg	TX	78624	**888-997-3600**	830-997-6523	208
Fredericksburg City Public Schools						
817 Princess Anne St	Fredericksburg	VA	22401	**800-846-4464**	540-372-1130	683

Name	Address	City	State	ZIP	Toll-Free	Phone	Class
Fredericksburg Regional Chamber of Commerce	2300 Fall Hill Ave Ste 240	Fredericksburg	VA	22401	**888-338-0252**	540-373-9400	138
Frederik Meijer Gardens & Sculpture Park	1000 E Beltline Ave NE	Grand Rapids	MI	49525	**877-975-3171**	616-957-1580	96
Free Flow Packaging International Inc	1090 Mills Way	Redwood City	CA	94063	**800-866-9946**	650-261-5300	600
Free Lance Star	616 Amelia St	Fredericksburg	VA	22401	**800-877-0500**	540-374-5000	531-2
Free Library of Philadelphia	1901 Vine St	Philadelphia	PA	19103	**800-732-0999**	215-686-5322	434-3
Free Methodist Foundation, The	8050 Spring Arbor Rd	Spring Arbor	MI	49283	**800-325-8975**	517-750-2727	306
Free Press	418 S Second St	Mankato	MN	56001	**800-657-4662**	507-625-4451	531-2
Free Service Tire Co Inc	PO Box 6187	Johnson City	TN	37602	**855-646-1423**	423-979-2250	753
Free Spirit Publishing Inc	217 Fifth Ave N Ste 200	Minneapolis	MN	55401	**800-735-7323**	612-338-2068	634-2
Free Will Baptist Bible College	3606 W End Ave	Nashville	TN	37205	**888-979-3524**	615-844-5000	160
Freeborn-Mower Co-op Services	2501 E Main St	Albert Lea	MN	56007	**800-734-6421**	507-373-6421	247
Freed-Hardeman University	158 E Main St	Henderson	TN	38340	**800-348-3481**	731-989-6651	167
Freedman Financial Associates Inc	8 Essex Ctr Dr 3rd Fl	Peabody	MA	01960	**800-588-8108**	978-531-8108	253
Freedman Seating Co	4545 W Augusta Blvd	Chicago	IL	60651	**800-443-4540**	773-524-2440	687
Freedom 95 Radio	645 Industrial Dr	Franklin	IN	46131	**800-278-9200**	317-736-4040	643
Freedom Communications Inc	17666 Fitch	Irvine	CA	92614	**855-862-7238**	949-253-2300	634-8
Freedom from Hunger	1460 Drew Ave Ste 300	Davis	CA	95618	**800-708-2555**	530-758-6200	47-5
Freedom Graphic Systems Inc (FGS)	1101 S Janesville St	Milton	WI	53563	**800-334-3540**		109
Freedom Greeting Card Company Inc	774 American Dr *Sales	Bensalem	PA	19020	**800-359-3301***	215-604-0300	129
Freedom Investments Inc	375 Raritan Ctr Pkwy	Edison	NJ	08837	**800-944-4033**		688
Freedom Medical Inc	219 Welsh Pool Rd	Exton	PA	19341	**800-784-8849**	610-903-0200	266-4
Freedom Scientific Inc	11800 31st Court N	St. Petersburg	FL	33716	**800-444-4443**	727-803-8000	179
Freedom Village	23442 El Toro Rd	Lake Forest	CA	92630	**800-584-8084**	949-472-4700	670
FreedomWorks	400 N Capitol St NW Ste 765	Washington	DC	20001	**888-564-6273**	202-783-3870	47-7
Freelin-Wade Co	1730 NE Miller St	McMinnville	OR	97128	**888-373-9233**	503-434-5561	370
Freeman Gas Inc	1186 Asheville Hwy	Spartanburg	SC	29303	**800-277-5730**	864-582-5475	357
Freeman Jewelers Inc	76 Merchants Row	Rutland	VT	05701	**800-451-4167**	802-773-2792	410
Freeman Manufacturing Co	900 W Chicago Rd	Sturgis	MI	49091	**800-253-2091**	269-651-2371	476
Freeman Mfg & Supply Co	1101 Moore Rd	Avon	OH	44011	**800-321-8511**	440-934-1902	566
Freeman's Flowers & Event Consultants	2934 Duniven Cir	Amarillo	TX	79109	**800-846-3104**	806-355-4451	294
Freeman, The	30 S Broadway *Sales	Irvington-on-Hudson	NY	10533	**800-960-4333***	914-591-7230	456-17
Freeservers.com	1253 N Research Way Ste Q-2500	Orem	UT	84097	**800-396-1999**		806
Freestone Inn at Wilson Ranch	31 Early Winters Dr	Mazama	WA	98833	**800-639-3809**	509-996-3906	667
Freestyle Photo Biz	5124 Sunset Blvd	Hollywood	CA	90027	**800-292-6137**		589
FreeWave Technologies Inc	1880 S Flatiron Ct Ste F *Cust Svc	Boulder	CO	80301	**866-923-6168***	303-444-3862	175-3
Freight Logistics Inc	PO Box 1712	Medford	OR	97501	**800-866-7882**	541-734-5617	312
FreightCar America Inc	17 Johns St *NASDAQ: RAIL*	Johnstown	PA	15901	**800-458-2235**		648
Freightliner of Hartford Inc	222 Roberts St	East Hartford	CT	06108	**800-453-6967**	860-289-0201	56
Freightliner Specialty Vehicles Inc	2300 S 13th St	Clinton	OK	73601	**800-358-7624**	580-323-4100	58
FreightPros	3307 Northland Dr Ste 360	Austin	TX	78731	**888-297-6968**		477
Freightquote.com Inc	16025 W 113th St	Lenexa	KS	66219	**800-323-5441**		313
Fremont Bank	PO Box 5101	Fremont	CA	94538	**800-359-2265**	510-792-2300	69
Fremont Contract Carriers Inc (FCC)	865 S Bud Blvd	Fremont	NE	68025	**800-228-9842**		448
Fremont County	450 N Second St	Lander	WY	82520	**800-967-2297**	307-332-2405	338
Fremont Hotel & Casino	200 Fremont St	Las Vegas	NV	89101	**800-634-6460**	702-385-3232	132
Fremont Industries Inc	4400 Vly Industrial Blvd N PO Box 67	Shakopee	MN	55379	**800-436-1238**	952-445-4121	144
Fremont Main Library	2400 Stevenson Blvd	Fremont	CA	94538	**800-434-0222**	510-745-1400	434-3
Fremont Public Schools	220 W Pine St	Fremont	MI	49412	**800-822-9433**	231-924-2350	683
Fremont Unified School District	PO Box 5008	Fremont	CA	94537	**800-544-5248**	510-657-2350	683
Fremont/Sandusky County Convention & Visitors Bureau	712 N St Ste 102	Fremont	OH	43420	**800-255-8070**	419-332-4470	208
French Country Waterways Ltd	24 Bay Rd	Duxbury	MA	02332	**800-222-1236**	781-934-2454	223
French Culinary Institute	462 Broadway	New York	NY	10013	**888-324-2433**		162
French Lick Resort	8670 W State Rd 56	French Lick	IN	47432	**888-936-9360**	812-936-9300	667
French Quarter Suites Hotel	1119 N Rampart St	New Orleans	LA	70116	**800-457-2253**	504-524-7725	379
French-American Chamber of Commerce in New York	1350 Broadway Ste 2101	New York	NY	10018	**800-821-2241**	212-867-0123	136
Frenchman Valley Farmers Co-op Exchange	202 Broadway	Imperial	NE	69033	**800-538-2667**	308-882-3200	278
Fresenius Medical Care North America	920 Winter St	Waltham	MA	02451	**800-662-1237**	781-699-9000	352
Fresh Air Educators Inc	203-1568 Carling Ave	Ottawa	ON	K1Z7M4	**866-495-4868**		246
Fresh Air Fund	633 Third Ave 14th Fl	New York	NY	10017	**800-367-0003**		241
Fresh Del Monte Produce Co	241 Sevilla Ave PO Box 149222 *NYSE: FDP* ■ *Cust Svc	Coral Gables	FL	33134	**800-950-3683***	305-520-8400	360-3
Fresh Express Inc	4757 The Grove Rd Ste 1212 *Cust Svc	Windermere	NC	34786	**800-242-5472***		11-1
FreshDirect Inc	23-30 Borden Ave	Long Island	NY	11101	**866-511-1240**	718-928-1000	345
FreshGrade Inc	301-1447 Ellis St	Kelowna	BC	V1Y2A3	**877-957-7757**		226
Freshwater Farm Products LLC	4554 State Hwy 12 E PO Box 850	Belzoni	MS	39038	**800-748-9338**	662-247-4205	297-14
Freshwater Society	2500 Shadywood Rd	Excelsior	MN	55331	**888-471-9773**	952-471-9773	47-13
Freskeeto Frozen Foods Inc	8019 Rt 209	Ellenville	NY	12428	**800-356-3663**	845-647-5111	297-18
Fresno & Clovis Convention & Visitors Bureau	1550 E Shaw Ave Ste 101	Fresno	CA	93710	**800-788-0836**	559-981-5500	208
Fresno Bee	1626 E St	Fresno	CA	93786	**800-877-3400**	559-441-6111	531-2
Fresno City College	1101 E University Ave	Fresno	CA	93741	**866-245-3276**	559-442-4600	161
Fresno Distributing Company Inc	2055 E McKinley Ave	Fresno	CA	93703	**800-655-2542**	559-442-8800	611
Fresno District Fair	1121 S Chance Ave	Fresno	CA	93702	**866-275-3772**	559-650-3247	639
Fresno Valves & Castings Inc	7736 E Springfield Ave PO Box 40	Selma	CA	93662	**800-333-1658**	559-834-2511	788
Fresno Yosemite International Airport	5175 E Clinton Way	Fresno	CA	93727	**800-244-2359**	559-621-4500	27
Freud America Inc	218 Feld Ave	High Point	NC	27263	**800-334-4107**	336-434-3171	350
Freundlich Supply Co Inc	2200 Arthur Kill Rd	Staten Island	NY	10309	**800-221-0260**	718-356-1500	768
Freyberg Hinkle Ashland Powers & Stowell Sc CPA	15420 W Capitol Dr	Brookfield	WI	53005	**800-413-8799**	262-784-6210	2
Friary of Lakeview Ctr, The	4400 Hickory Shores Blvd	Gulf Breeze	FL	32563	**800-332-2271**	850-932-9375	724
Frick Hospital	508 S Church St	Mount Pleasant	PA	15666	**877-771-1234**	724-547-1500	374-3
Fridgedoor.com	65 School St	Quincy	MA	02169	**800-955-3741**	617-770-7913	329
Frieda's Inc	4465 Corporate Ctr Dr	Los Alamitos	CA	90720	**800-241-1771**	714-826-6100	298-7
Friedberg Smith & Co PC	855 Main St	Bridgeport	CT	06604	**800-772-1213**	203-366-5876	2
Friedman Billings Ramsey Group Inc	1300 N 17th St Ste 1400	Arlington	VA	22209	**800-846-5050**	703-312-9500	688
Friedman Bros Decorative Arts	9015 NW 105th Way	Medley	FL	33178	**800-327-1065**	305-887-3170	334
Friedman Electric	1321 Wyoming Ave	Exeter	PA	18643	**800-545-5517**	570-654-3371	248
Friedman LLP	1700 Broadway	New York	NY	10019	**800-372-1033**	212-842-7000	2
Friedrich	10001 Reunion Pl Ste 500	San Antonio	TX	78216	**800-541-6645**	210-546-0500	14
Friend Tire Co	11 Industrial Dr	Monett	MO	65708	**800-950-8473**		753
Friend's Professional Stationery Inc	1535 Lewis Ave	Zion	IL	60099	**800-323-4394**		534
Friendfinder Network Inc	6800 Broken Sound Pkwy Ste 200 *TSE: FFN*	Boca Raton	FL	33487	**888-575-8383**	561-912-7000	228
Friendly Cruises	3081 S Sycamore Village Dr	Superstition Mountain	AZ	85118	**888-842-1786**	480-358-1496	769
Friendly Excursions Inc	PO Box 69	Sunland	CA	91041	**800-775-5018**	818-353-7726	758
Friendly Ice Cream Corp	1855 Boston Rd	Wilbraham	MA	01095	**800-966-9970**	413-731-4000	668
Friends Committee on National Legislation (FCNL)	245 Second St NE	Washington	DC	20002	**800-630-1330**	202-547-6000	614
Friends General Conference	1216 Arch St Ste 2B	Philadelphia	PA	19107	**800-966-4556**	215-561-1700	47-20
Friends Hospital	4641 Roosevelt Blvd	Philadelphia	PA	19124	**800-889-0548**	215-831-4600	374-5
Friends of Animals Inc (FOA)	777 Post Rd Ste 205	Darien	CT	06820	**800-321-7387**	203-656-1522	47-3
Friends of the Earth	1717 Massachusetts Ave NW Ste 600	Washington	DC	20036	**877-843-8687**	202-783-7400	47-13
Friends of the Earth Magazine	1100 15th St NW	Washington	DC	20005	**877-843-8687**	202-783-7400	456-19
Friends of the River	1418 20th St Ste 100	Sacramento	CA	95811	**888-464-2477**	916-442-3155	47-13
Friends Research Institute Inc	1040 Pk Ave Ste 103	Baltimore	MD	21201	**800-822-3677**	410-823-5116	666
Social Research Ctr	1040 Pk Ave Ste 103	Baltimore	MD	21201	**800-705-7757**	410-837-3977	666
Friends University	2100 University St	Wichita	KS	67213	**800-794-6945**	316-295-5000	167

	City	State	Zip	Toll-Free	Phone	Class
Friendship Manor 1209 21st Ave	Rock Island	IL	61201	**888-382-1222**	309-786-9667	670
Friendship Village Kalamazoo 1400 N Drake Rd	Kalamazoo	MI	49006	**800-613-3984**	269-381-0560	670
Friendship Village of Tempe 2645 E Southern Ave	Tempe	AZ	85282	**800-824-1112**	480-831-5000	670
Friendsview Retirement Community 1301 E Fulton St	Newberg	OR	97132	**866-307-4371**	503-538-3144	670
Friendswood Public Library 416 S Friendswood Dr	Friendswood	TX	77546	**800-696-3493**	281-482-7135	434-3
Fringe Benefits Management Co 3101 Sessions Rd	Tallahassee	FL	32303	**800-872-0345**	850-425-6200	390
Friona Feedyard 2370 FM 3140	Friona	TX	79035	**800-658-6014**	806-265-3574	10-1
Friona Industries LP 500 S Taylor St Ste 601	Amarillo	TX	79101	**800-658-6014**	806-374-1811	10-1
Frisch's Restaurants Inc 2800 Gilbert Ave *NYSE: FRS*	Cincinnati	OH	45206	**800-873-3633**	513-961-2660	668
Frit Industries Inc 1792 Jodie Parker Rd	Ozark	AL	36360	**800-633-7685**	334-774-2515	282
Frito-Lay North America 7701 Legacy Dr	Plano	TX	75024	**800-352-4477**	972-334-7000	297-35
Fritz Industries Inc 180 Gordon Dr Ste 113	Exton	PA	19341	**800-345-6202**		185
FRL Furniture 460 Grand Blvd	Westbury	NY	11590	**800-529-4375**	516-333-4400	662
Froedtert Hospital Bone Marrow Transplant Program 9200 W Wisconsin Ave	Milwaukee	WI	53226	**800-272-3666**	414-805-3666	767
Frog Street Press Inc 800 Industrial Blvd Ste 100	Grapevine	TX	76051	**800-884-3764**		245
Frog Switch & Mfg Co 600 E High St	Carlisle	PA	17013	**800-233-7194**	717-243-2454	308
Fromm Electric Supply Corp 2101 Centre Ave PO Box 15147	Reading	PA	19605	**800-360-4441**	610-374-4441	248
Front End Audio 130 Hunter Village Dr Ste D	Irmo	SC	29063	**888-228-4530**	803-748-0914	525
Front Porch Communities & Services 303 N Glenoaks Blvd	Burbank	CA	91502	**800-233-3709**		449
Front Range Community College (FRCC) *Boulder County* 2190 Miller Dr	Longmont	CO	80501	**888-800-9198**	303-678-3722	161
Larimer 4616 S Shields St	Fort Collins	CO	80526	**888-800-9198**	970-226-2500	161
Front Row USA Entertainment 900 N Federal Hwy Ste 200	Hallandale	FL	33009	**800-277-8499**	305-940-8499	748
Front Runner Consulting LLC 6850 O'Bannon Bluff	Loveland	OH	45140	**877-328-3360**	513-697-6850	196
Front Street Capital 33 Yonge St Ste 600	Toronto	ON	M5E1G4	**800-513-2832**	416-364-1990	401
Frontenac Bank 3330 Rider Trl S	Earth City	MO	63045	**877-205-5777**	314-298-8200	69
Frontenac State Park 29223 County 28 Blvd	Frontenac	MN	55026	**888-646-6367**	651-345-3401	564
Frontera Foods Inc 449 N Clark St Ste 205	Chicago	IL	60654	**800-509-4441**	312-595-1624	345
Frontier Adjusters of America Inc 4745 N Seventh St Ste 320	Phoenix	AZ	85014	**800-426-7228**		390
Frontier Airlines Ctr 400 W Wisconsin Ave	Milwaukee	WI	53203	**800-745-3000**	414-908-6000	207
Frontier Airlines Inc 7001 Tower Rd	Denver	CO	80249	**800-265-5505**	720-374-4200	360-1
Frontier Communications Corp 3 High Ridge Pk *NASDAQ: FTR*	Stamford	CT	06905	**800-877-4390**	203-614-5600	733
Frontier Computer Corp 1275 Business Pk Dr	Traverse City	MI	49686	**866-226-6344**	231-929-1386	182
Frontier Consulting Inc 10101 SW Fwy Ste 202	Houston	TX	77074	**877-324-8729**	713-778-0799	182
Frontier Co-op 211 S Lincoln PO Box 37	Brainard	NE	68626	**800-869-0379**	402-545-2811	277
Frontier Electronic Systems Corp 4500 W Sixth Ave	Stillwater	OK	74074	**800-677-1769**	405-624-1769	528
Frontier Investment Management Co 8401 N Central Expy Ste 300	Dallas	TX	75225	**800-553-8034**	972-934-2590	401
Frontier Logistics LP 1806 S 16th St	La Porte	TX	77571	**800-610-6808**		312
Frontier Metal Stamping Inc 3764 Puritan Way	Erie	CO	80516	**888-316-1266**	303-458-5129	482
Frontier Natural Products Co-op 3021 78th St PO Box 299	Norway	IA	52318	**800-669-3275**	319-227-7996	297-37
Frontier Networks Inc 530 Kipling Ave	Toronto	ON	M8Z5E3	**866-833-2323**	416-847-5240	387
Frontier Power Co 770 S 2nd St PO Box 280	Coshocton	OH	43812	**800-624-8050**	740-622-6755	247
Frontier-Kemper Constructors Inc 1695 Allen Rd	Evansville	IN	47710	**877-554-8600**	812-426-2741	190-10
Frontiers International Travel PO Box 959	Wexford	PA	15090	**800-245-1950**	724-935-1577	758
Frontline Communications PO Box 98	Orangeburg	NY	10962	**888-376-6854**		398
Frontline Group of Texas LLC 15021 Katy Fwy Ste 575	Houston	TX	77094	**800-285-5512**	281-453-6000	763
FrontPage Local 1660 Hotel Cir N Ste 600	San Diego	CA	92108	**800-521-7338**		630
Frosch International Travel Inc 1 Greenway Plz Ste 800	Houston	TX	77046	**800-866-1623**		770
Frost & Sullivan 7550 IH 10 W Ste 400	San Antonio	TX	78229	**877-463-7678**	210-348-1000	530-12
Frost Brown Todd LLC 201 E Fifth St 2200 PNC Ctr	Cincinnati	OH	45202	**866-559-6446**	513-651-6800	428
Frozen Head State Natural Area 964 Flat Fork Rd	Wartburg	TN	37887	**800-250-8615**	423-346-3318	564
Fruit Co, The 2900 Van Horn Dr	Hood River	OR	97031	**800-387-3100**	541-387-3100	294
Fruit of the Loom Inc 1 Fruit of the Loom Dr PO Box 90015	Bowling Green	KY	42102	**888-378-4829**	270-781-6400	154-3
Fruitridge Printing & Lithograph Inc 3258 Stockton Blvd	Sacramento	CA	95820	**800-835-4846**	916-452-9213	626
Frullati Cafe & Bakery 9311 E Via de Ventura	Scottsdale	AZ	85258	**866-452-4252**	480-362-4800	668
Frutarom Corp 9500 Railroad Ave	North Bergen	NJ	07047	**866-229-7198**	201-861-9500	297-15
Fruth Pharmacy Inc 4016 Ohio River Rd	Point Pleasant	WV	25550	**800-438-5390**	304-675-1612	239
Fry's Food Stores of Arizona Inc 500 S 99th Ave	Tolleson	AZ	85353	**866-221-4141**		345
Fryer-Knowles Inc 205 S Dawson St	Seattle	WA	98108	**800-544-6052**	206-767-7710	293
Frymaster LLC 8700 Line Ave *Cust Svc	Shreveport	LA	71106	**800-221-4583***	318-865-1711	299
Fry-Wagner Moving & Storage Co 3700 Rider Trl S	Earth City	MO	63045	**800-899-4035**	314-291-4100	778
FS Tool Corp 71 Hobbs Gate	Markham	ON	L3R9T9	**800-387-9723**	905-475-1999	695
FSB Warner Financial 1001 Peoples Sq	Waterloo	IA	50702	**800-747-9999**	319-235-6561	688
FSEEE (Forest Service Employees for Environmental Ethics) PO Box 11615	Eugene	OR	97440	**800-270-7504**	541-484-2692	48-7
FSG (Facility Solutions Group) 4401 Westgate Blvd Ste 310	Austin	TX	78745	**800-854-6465**	512-440-7985	248
FSG Lighting 4401 Westgate Blvd Ste 310	Austin	TX	78745	**800-854-6465**	512-440-7985	248
FSI Technologies Inc 668 E Western Ave	Lombard	IL	60148	**800-468-6009**	630-932-9380	205
FSMB (Federation of State Medical Boards of the US Inc) 400 Fuller Wiser Rd Ste 300	Euless	TX	76039	**800-793-7939**	817-868-4000	48-8
FSNA 1052 St Laurent Blvd	Ottawa	ON	K1K3B4	**855-304-4700**	613-745-2559	136
FTC (Farmers Telecommunications Co-op) 144 McCurdy Ave N PO Box 217	Rainsville	AL	35986	**866-638-2144**	256-638-2144	733
FTC (Feed the Children) PO Box 36	Oklahoma City	OK	73101	**800-627-4556**	405-942-0228	47-5
FTD Inc 3113 Woodcreek Dr *Cust Svc	Downers Grove	IL	60515	**800-736-3383***		294
FTG Inc 725 Marshall Phelps Rd	Windsor	CT	06095	**888-610-6020**	860-610-6000	248
FTI Consulting 909 Commerce Rd Ste 1400 *NYSE: FCN*	Annapolis	MD	21401	**800-334-5701**	410-224-8770	444
FTJ FundChoice LLC 2300 Litton Ln Ste 102	Hebron	KY	41048	**800-379-2513**		387
FTMC (Fisher-Titus Medical Ctr) 272 Benedict Ave	Norwalk	OH	44857	**800-589-3862**	419-668-8101	374-3
Fuchs North America 9740 Reisterstown Rd	Owings Mills	MD	21117	**800-365-3229**	410-363-1700	297-37
Fuego 330 E Palace Ave *Sales	Santa Fe	NM	87501	**855-811-0050***	505-986-0000	669
Fuel Education LLC 2300 Corporate Park Dr	Herndon	VA	20171	**800-222-2811**	844-251-4687	180-3
Fuel Tech Inc 27601 Bella Vista Pkwy *NASDAQ: FTEK* ■ *General	Warrenville	IL	60555	**800-666-9688***	630-845-4500	18
FuelFX LLC 5205 Spruce St	Bellaire	TX	77401	**877-255-2543**		197
Fugro-Roadware Inc 2505 Meadowvale Blvd	Mississauga	ON	L5N5S2	**800-828-2726**	905-567-2870	407
Fuji Health Science Inc 3 Terri Ln Ste 12	Burlington	NJ	08016	**877-385-4777**	609-386-3030	298-8
FUJIFILM Graphic System USA Inc 45 Crosby Dr	Bedford	MA	01730	**800-755-3854**	781-271-4400	385
Fujitsu America Inc 1250 E Arques Ave	Sunnyvale	CA	94085	**800-538-8460**	408-746-6200	732
Fujitsu Computer Products of America Inc 1255 E Arques Ave	Sunnyvale	CA	94085	**800-626-4686**	408-746-7000	175-8
Fujitsu Computer Systems Corp 1250 E Arques Ave	Sunnyvale	CA	94085	**800-538-8460**	408-746-6000	178
Fujitsu Consulting 1250 E Arques Ave	Sunnyvale	CA	94085	**800-831-3183**		182
Fujitsu General America Inc 353 Rt 46 W	Fairfield	NJ	07004	**888-888-3424**	973-575-0380	609
Fujitsu Ten Corp of America 19600 S Vermont Ave	Torrance	CA	90502	**800-233-2216**	310-327-2151	51
Fulbright & Jaworski LLP 1301 McKinney St Ste 5100	Houston	TX	77010	**866-385-2744**	713-651-5151	428
Fulflex Inc 32 Justin Holden Dr	Brattleboro	VT	05301	**800-283-2500**	802-257-5256	742-5
Fulghum Industries 317 S Main St	Wadley	GA	30477	**800-841-5980**	478-252-5223	681
Full Access Brokerage 1240 Charnelton St	Eugene	OR	97401	**866-890-5743**	541-284-5070	688
Full Sail University 3300 University Blvd Ste 160	Winter Park	FL	32792	**800-226-7625**	407-679-6333	798
Fullen Dock & Warehouse Inc 382 Klinke Rd	Memphis	TN	38127	**800-467-7104**	901-358-9544	193-1
Fuller Brush Co, The PO Box 729 1 Fuller Way *Cust Svc	Great Bend	KS	67530	**800-522-0499***	620-792-1711	102
Fuller Industrial 65 Nelson Rd	Lively	ON	P3Y1P4	**888-524-3777**	705-682-2777	594
Fuller Theological Seminary 135 N Oakland Ave	Pasadena	CA	91182	**800-235-2222**	626-584-5200	168-3
Fullerton Bldg Systems Inc (FBS) 34620 250th St PO Box 308	Worthington	MN	56187	**800-450-9782**	507-376-3128	815
Fullerton Tool Company Inc 121 Perry St	Saginaw	MI	48602	**855-722-7243**	989-799-4550	492
Fulmer Co 122 Gayoso Ave	Memphis	TN	38103	**844-438-5637**	901-525-5711	516
Fulton Corp 303 Eigth Ave	Fulton	IL	61252	**800-252-0002**		350
Fulton Industries Inc 135 E Linfoot St PO Box 377	Wauseon	OH	43567	**800-537-5012**	419-335-3015	439

Company	Address	City	State	ZIP	Toll-Free	Phone	Class
Fulton Opera House Foundation	12 N Prince St PO Box 1865	Lancaster	PA	17603	**888-480-1265**	717-397-7425	571
Fulton School District 58	2 Hornet Dr	Fulton	MO	65251	**800-456-2634**	573-590-8000	683
Fun 101.3 FM	1996 Auction Rd	Manheim	PA	17545	**877-870-5678**	717-653-0800	643
Fun Town Splash Town USA Inc	US Rt 1 774 Portland Rd	Saco	ME	04072	**800-843-5678**	207-284-5139	32
Fundcraft Publishing Inc	410 Hwy 72 W	Collierville	TN	38027	**800-964-5715**	901-853-7070	626
FundThrough Inc	260 Spadina Ave Ste 400	Toronto	ON	M5T2E4	**800-766-0460**		226
Funeral Consumers Alliance	33 Patchen Rd	South Burlington	VT	05403	**800-765-0107**	802-865-8300	47-10
Funeral Service Insider	3349 Hwy 138 Bldg D Ste D	Wall	NJ	07719	**800-500-4585**		530-13
Funnel Science Internet Marketing LLC	1802 N Carson St	Carson City	NV	89701	**877-301-0001**		5
Furman Sound LLC	1690 Corporate Cir	Petaluma	CA	94954	**877-486-4738**	707-763-1010	51
Furmanite America	101 Old Underwood Rd	La Porte	TX	77571	**800-444-5572**	281-842-5100	453
Furmano Foods Inc	770 Cannery Rd PO Box 500	Northumberland	PA	17857	**877-877-6032**	570-473-3516	297-20
Furnace Creek Inn & Ranch Resort	Hwy 190	Death Valley	CA	92328	**800-236-7916**	760-786-2345	667
Furniture Medic	3839 S Forest Hill Irene Rd	Memphis	TN	38125	**800-877-9933**		311
Furniture Outlets USA Inc	140 E Hinks Ln	Sioux Falls	SD	57104	**877-395-8998**	605-336-5000	292
FurnitureDealer.net Inc	PO Box 22251	Eagan	MN	55122	**866-387-6357**		529
Furst-McNess Co	120 E Clark St	Freeport	IL	61032	**800-435-5100**	815-235-6151	446
Fusion Inc	4658 E 355th St	Willoughby	OH	44094	**800-626-9501**	440-946-3300	386
Fusion Optix Inc	19 Wheeling Ave	Woburn	MA	01801	**866-506-8300**	781-995-0805	607
Fusion Solutions Inc	16901 N Dallas Pkwy Ste 114	Dallas	TX	75001	**888-817-1951**	972-764-1708	196
Fusion Telecommunications International Inc	420 Lexington Ave Ste 1718 *OTC: FSNN*	New York	NY	10170	**888-301-1721**	212-201-2400	733
FusionStorm	2 Bryant St Ste 150	San Francisco	CA	94105	**800-228-8324**	415-623-2626	179
Fuss & O'Neill Consulting Engineers Inc	146 Hartford Rd	Manchester	CT	06040	**800-286-2469**	860-646-2469	263
FUTEK Advanced Sensor Technology Inc	10 Thomas	Irvine	CA	92618	**800-233-8835**	949-465-0900	258
Futrend Technology Inc	8605 Westwood Ctr Dr Ste 502	Vienna	VA	22182	**866-388-7363**	703-556-0016	179
Future Business Leaders of America-Phi Beta Lambda Inc (FBLA-PBL)	1912 Assn Dr	Reston	VA	20191	**800-325-2946**		47-11
Future Electronics	237 Hymus Blvd *Cust Svc	Pointe-Claire	QC	H9R5C7	**800-675-1619***	514-694-7710	248
Future Foam Inc	1610 Ave N Council Bluffs	Council Bluffs	IA	51501	**800-733-8061**	712-323-9122	600
Future of Flight Foundation	8415 Paine Field Blvd	Mukilteo	WA	98275	**888-467-4777**	425-438-8100	128
Futurebiotics LLC	70 Commerce Dr	Hauppauge	NY	11788	**800-367-5433**	631-273-6300	797
Futurecom Systems Group Inc	3277 Langstaff Rd	Concord	ON	L4K5P8	**800-701-9180**	905-660-5548	248
FutureSoft Inc	1660 Townhurst Dr Ste E	Houston	TX	77043	**800-989-8908**	281-496-9400	180-7
Futurex Inc	864 Old Boerne Rd	Bulverde	TX	78163	**800-251-5112**	830-980-9782	178
Futurist Magazine	7910 Woodmont Ave Ste 450	Bethesda	MD	20814	**800-989-8274**	301-656-8274	456-11
FW Gartner Thermal Spraying Ltd	25 Southbelt Industrial Dr	Houston	TX	77047	**888-439-4872**	713-225-0010	480
FW Webb Co	160 Middlesex Tpke	Bedford	MA	01730	**800-343-7555**	781-272-6600	385
FXCM Inc	32 Old Slip *NYSE: FXCM*	New York	NY	10005	**888-503-6739**	212-897-7660	180-10
FXI	1400 N Providence Rd	Media	PA	19063	**800-355-3626**	610-744-2300	600
FXVA (Fairfax County Convention & Visitors Bureau)	3702 Pender Dr Ste 420	Fairfax	VA	22030	**800-732-4732**	703-790-0643	208
Fyda Freightliner Youngstown Inc	5260 76th Dr	Youngstown	OH	44515	**800-837-3932**	330-797-0224	61-5

G

Company	Address	City	State	ZIP	Toll-Free	Phone	Class
G & D Transportation Inc	50 Commerce Dr	Morton	IL	61550	**800-451-6680**		188
G & G Fitness Equipment Inc	7350 Transit Rd	Williamsville	NY	14221	**800-537-0516**	716-633-2527	354
G & H Decoys Inc	PO Box 1208 *Orders	Henryetta	OK	74437	**800-443-3269***	918-652-3314	708
G & H Wire Company Inc	2165 Earlywood Dr	Franklin	IN	46131	**800-526-1026**	317-346-6655	230
G & J Land & Marine Food Distributors	506 Front St	Morgan City	LA	70380	**800-256-9187**	985-385-2620	345
G & K Services Inc	5995 Opus Pkwy Ste 500	Minnetonka	MN	55343	**800-452-2737**	952-912-5500	442
G & O Thermal Supply Co	5435 N Northwest Hwy	Chicago	IL	60630	**800-621-4997**	773-763-1300	110
G & T Industries Inc	1001 76th St SW	Byron Center	MI	49315	**800-968-6035**		600
G & W Laboratories Inc	111 Coolidge St	South Plainfield	NJ	07080	**800-922-1038**	908-753-2000	582
G G Schmitt & Sons Inc	2821 Old Tree Dr	Lancaster	PA	17603	**866-724-6488**	717-394-3701	350
G r Manufacturing Inc	4800 Commerce Dr	Trussville	AL	35173	**800-841-8001**	205-655-8001	298-8
G Robert Cotton Correctional Facility	3500 N Elm Rd	Jackson	MI	49201	**855-444-3911**	517-780-5000	215
G2 Web Services LLC	1750 112th Ave NE Ste C101	Bellevue	WA	98004	**888-788-5353**	425-749-4040	182
G3 Communications	411 State Rt 17 S Ste 410	Hasbrouck Heights	NJ	07604	**888-603-3626**		197
G6 Hospitality LLC *Motel 6*	4001 International Pkwy	Carrollton	TX	75007	**800-466-8356**	972-360-9000	379
GA Braun Inc	461 E Brighton Ave	Syracuse	NY	13212	**800-432-7286**	315-475-3123	427
G&A Partners	4801 Woodway Dr Ste 210W	Houston	TX	77056	**800-253-8562**	713-784-1181	719
GA Wintzer & Son Co	204 W Auglaize St	Wapakoneta	OH	45895	**800-331-1801**	419-739-4900	297-12
GableSigns Inc	7440 Ft Smallwood Rd	Baltimore	MD	21226	**800-854-0568**	410-255-6400	699
Gabriel Roeder Smith & Co	1 Towne Sq Ste 800	Southfield	MI	48076	**800-521-0498**	248-799-9000	195
Gachman Metals & Recycling Company Inc	2600 Shamrock Ave	Fort Worth	TX	76107	**800-749-0423**	817-334-0211	684
Gaco Western Inc	200 W Mercer St Ste 202	Seattle	WA	98119	**800-456-4226**	206-575-0450	600
Gadabout Vacations	1801 E Tahquitz Canyon Way Ste 100	Palm Springs	CA	92262	**800-952-5068**	760-325-5556	758
Gadsden & Etowah County Chamber	1 Commerce Sq	Gadsden	AL	35901	**800-659-2955**	256-543-3472	138
Gadsden County Chamber of Commerce	208 N Adams St	Quincy	FL	32351	**800-627-9231**	850-627-9231	138
Gadsden State Community College	1001 George Wallace Dr PO Box 227	Gadsden	AL	35902	**800-226-5563**	256-549-8200	161
Gadsden Times	401 Locust St	Gadsden	AL	35901	**800-762-2464**	256-549-2000	531-2
GAF Materials Corp	1361 Alps Rd	Wayne	NJ	07470	**800-365-7353**	973-628-3000	45
Gaiam Inc	833 W S Boulder Rd Ste C *NASDAQ: GAIA*	Louisville	CO	80027	**877-989-6321**	303-222-3600	458
Gaines Motor Lines Inc	2349 13th Ave SW PO Box 1549	Hickory	NC	28603	**800-438-7311**	828-322-2000	188
Gainesville Area Chamber of Commerce	300 E University Ave Ste 100	Gainesville	FL	32601	**888-795-2707**	352-334-7100	138
Gainesville City Schools	508 Oak St	Gainesville	GA	30501	**800-533-0682**	770-536-5275	683
Gainesville Times	345 Green St NW	Gainesville	GA	30501	**800-395-5005**	770-532-1234	531-2
Gainey Suites Hotel	7300 E Gainey	Scottsdale	AZ	85258	**800-970-4666**	480-922-6969	378
GAI-Tronics Corp	400 E Wyomissing Ave	Mohnton	PA	19540	**800-492-1212**	610-777-1374	732
Galasso's Inc	10820 San Sevaine Way	Mira Loma	CA	91752	**800-339-7494**	951-360-1211	67
Galaxie Coffee Services	110 Sea Ln	Farmingdale	NY	11735	**800-564-9104**	631-694-2688	112
Galaxie Defense Marketing Services	5330 Napa St	San Diego	CA	92110	**888-711-3427**	619-299-9950	188
Galaxy Hotel Systems LLC	15621 Red Hill Ave Ste 100	Tustin	CA	92780	**800-624-2953**	714-258-5800	180-11
Galaxy Nutritional Foods Inc	66 Whitecap Dr	North Kingstown	RI	02852	**800-441-9419**	401-667-5000	297-5
Galaxy Software Solutions Inc	5820 N Lilley Rd Ste 8	Canton	MI	48187	**877-269-4774**	734-983-9030	262
Galco Industrial Electronics Inc	26010 Pinehurst Dr	Madison Heights	MI	48071	**888-783-4611**	248-542-9090	248
Galderma Laboratories Inc	14501 N Fwy	Fort Worth	TX	76177	**866-735-4137**	817-961-5000	582
Gale Cengage Learning	27500 Drake Rd *Cust Svc	Farmington Hills	MI	48331	**800-877-4253***	248-699-4253	634-2
Gale Force Petroleum Inc	100 King St W Ste 5700	Toronto	ON	M5X1C7	**888-440-3411**		318
Galecki Financial Management Inc	7743 W Jefferson Blvd	Fort Wayne	IN	46804	**800-838-6441**	260-436-8525	527
Galectin Therapeutics	4960 Peachtree Industrial Blvd Ste 240	Norcross	GA	02459	**888-286-8010**	617-559-0033	84
Galena Gazette	716 S Bench St	Galena	IL	61036	**800-373-6397**	815-777-0019	531-4
Galena/Jo Daviess County Convention & Visitors Bureau (GJDCCVB)	101 Bouthillier St *General	Galena	IL	61036	**800-747-9377***	815-777-3557	208
Galesburg Area Convention & Visitors Bureau	2163 E Main St	Galesburg	IL	61401	**800-916-3330**	309-343-2485	208
Galesburg Printing & Publishing Co	140 S Prairie St	Galesburg	IL	61401	**800-733-2767**	309-343-7181	634-8
Galison Publishing LLC	28 W 44th St Ste 1411	New York	NY	10036	**800-670-7441**	212-354-8840	129
Gallade Chemical Inc	1230 E St Gertrude Pl	Santa Ana	CA	92707	**888-830-9092**	714-546-9901	145
Gallagher Asphalt Corp	18100 S Indiana Ave	Thornton	IL	60476	**800-536-7160**	708-877-7160	190-4
Gallagher Corp	3908 Morrison Dr	Gurnee	IL	60031	**800-524-8597**	847-249-3440	604-2
Gallagher, Gams, Pryor, Tallan & Littrell LLP	471 E Broad St 19th Fl	Columbus	OH	43215	**866-378-1624**	614-228-5151	428
Gallant Greetings Corp	4300 United Pkwy	Schiller Park	IL	60176	**800-621-4279**	847-671-6500	129

Name / Address	City	State	ZIP	Toll-Free	Phone	Class
Gallaudet University 800 Florida Ave NE	Washington	DC	20002	**800-995-0550**	202-651-5000	167
Gallaudet University Library 800 Florida Ave NE	Washington	DC	20002	**800-995-0550**	202-651-5217	434-6
Gallaudet University Press 800 Florida Ave NE	Washington	DC	20002	**800-621-2736**	202-651-5488	634-4
Gallegos Corp PO Box 821	Vail	CO	81658	**800-425-5346**	970-926-3737	191-7
Galleon Resort & Marina 617 Front St	Key West	FL	33040	**800-544-3030**	305-296-7711	667
Gallery 78 Inc 796 Queen St	Fredericton	NB	E3B1C6	**888-883-8322**	506-454-5192	41
Gallery of History Inc 3601 W Sahara Ave	Las Vegas	NV	89102	**800-425-5379**	702-364-1000	50
Galliard Capital Management Inc 800 La Salle Ave Ste 1100	Minneapolis	MN	55402	**800-717-1617**	612-667-3220	402
Galliker Dairy Company Inc 143 Donald Ln	Johnstown	PA	15907	**800-477-6455**	814-266-8702	297-27
Gallina LLP 925 Highland Pointe Dr Ste 450	Roseville	CA	95678	**877-638-1188**	916-638-1188	2
Gallo Salame 2411 Baumann Ave	San Lorenzo	CA	94580	**800-988-6464**		297-26
Galls Inc 2680 Palumbo Dr	Lexington	KY	40509	**800-477-7766**	859-266-7227	575
Gallup Inc 1001 Gallup Dr	Omaha	NE	68102	**888-500-8282**	402-951-2003	465
Gallup Organization 901 F St NW	Washington	DC	20004	**877-242-5587**	202-715-3030	465
Galpin Motors Inc 15505 Roscoe Blvd	North Hills	CA	91343	**800-256-7137**	818-787-3800	56
Galt House Hotel 140 N Fourth St	Louisville	KY	40202	**800-843-4258**	502-589-5200	379
Galvan Industries Inc 7320 Millbrook Rd *General	Harrisburg	NC	28075	**800-277-5678***	704-455-5102	480
Galvanic Applied Sciences USA Inc 41 Wellman St	Lowell	MA	01851	**866-252-8470**	978-848-2701	203
Galveston Central Appraisal District 9850 Emmett F Lowry Expy Ste A	Texas City	TX	77591	**866-277-4725**	409-935-1980	318
Galveston College 4015 Ave Q	Galveston	TX	77550	**866-483-4242**	409-763-6551	161
Galveston County Daily News 8522 Teichman Rd PO Box 628	Galveston	TX	77553	**800-561-3611**	409-683-5200	531-2
Galveston Independent School District (GISD) 3904 Ave PO Box 660	Galveston	TX	77550	**877-262-1492**	409-766-5100	683
Galvestonian Condominium Association 1401 E Beach Dr	Galveston	TX	77550	**888-526-6161**	409-765-6161	705
GAMA (General Aviation Manufacturers Assn) 1400 K St NW Ste 801	Washington	DC	20005	**866-427-3287**	202-393-1500	48-21
GAMA International 2901 Telestar Ct *Cust Svc	Falls Church	VA	22042	**800-345-2687***		48-9
Gamajet Cleaning Systems Inc 604 Jeffers Cir *Sales	Exton	PA	19341	**877-426-2538***	610-408-9940	386
Gambrill State Park 8602 Gambrill Pk Rd	Frederick	MD	21702	**800-830-3974**	301-271-7574	564
Gambrinus Co, The 14800 San Pedro Ave 3rd Fl	San Antonio	TX	78232	**800-596-6486**	210-490-9128	80-1
Gambro BCT 10811 W Collins Ave	Lakewood	CO	80215	**877-339-4228**	303-231-4357	419
Gambro Renal Products 14143 Denver W Pkwy	Lakewood	CO	80401	**800-525-2623**	303-232-6800	252
GAMCO Investors Inc 1 Corporate Ctr *NYSE: GBL*	Rye	NY	10580	**800-422-3554**	914-921-5100	527
GamePlan Financial Marketing LLC 300 ParkBrooke Pl Ste 200 *Cust Svc	Woodstock	GA	30189	**800-886-4757***	678-238-0601	402
GameStop Corp 625 Westport Pkwy *NYSE: GME*	Grapevine	TX	76051	**800-883-8895**	817-424-2000	181
Gamewell FCI 12 Clintonville Rd	Northford	CT	06472	**800-606-1983**	203-484-7161	285
12 Clintonville Rd	Northford	CT	06472	**800-606-1983**	203-484-7161	747
Gaming Partners International Corp 1700 Industrial Rd *NASDAQ: GPIC*	Las Vegas	NV	89102	**800-728-5766**	702-384-2425	323
Gamla Enterprises North America Inc 875 Ave of The Americas Ste 205	New York	NY	10001	**800-442-6526**	212-947-3790	37
Gamma Beta Phi Society 78 Mitchell Rd Ste A	Oak Ridge	TN	37830	**800-628-9920**	865-483-6212	47-16
Gamma Dynacare Medical Laboratories Inc 115 Midair Ct	Brampton	ON	L6T5M3	**800-668-2714**		415
Gamma Sports 200 Waterfront Dr	Pittsburgh	PA	15222	**800-333-0337**	412-323-0335	708
GANA (Glass Assn of North America) 800 SW Jackson St Ste 1500	Topeka	KS	66612	**877-275-2421**	785-271-0208	48-13
Gandy Co 528 Gandrud Rd	Owatonna	MN	55060	**800-443-2476**	507-451-5430	275
Gandy's Dairies Inc 201 University Blvd	Lubbock	TX	79415	**877-382-4357**	806-762-8844	297-25
Ganesh Machinery 20869 Plummer St	Chatsworth	CA	91311	**888-542-6374**	818-349-9166	385
Gannett Fleming Inc 207 Senate Ave	Camp Hill	PA	17011	**800-233-1055**	717-763-7211	263
Gannett Welsh & Kotler LLC 222 Berkeley St 15th Fl	Boston	MA	02116	**800-225-4236**	617-236-8900	401
Gannon University 109 University Sq *Admissions	Erie	PA	16541	**800-426-6668***	814-871-7000	167
Gans Ink & Supply Company Inc 1441 Boyd St	Los Angeles	CA	90033	**800-421-6167**	323-264-2200	388
Gant Travel Management 400 W Seventh St Ste 233 *Cust Svc	Bloomington	IN	47404	**800-742-4198***		769
Gap Inc 2 Folsom St *NYSE: GPS*	San Francisco	CA	94105	**800-333-7899**	650-952-4400	156-4
Garaga Inc 8500 25th Ave	St Georges	QC	G6A1K5	**800-464-2724**	418-227-2828	479
Garan Lucow Miller PC 1000 Woodbridge St	Detroit	MI	48207	**800-875-1530**	313-446-1530	428
GARBC (General Assn of Regular Baptist Churches) 1300 N Meacham Rd	Schaumburg	IL	60173	**888-588-1600**	847-585-0816	47-20
Garco Bldg Systems 2714 S Garfield Rd	Airway Heights	WA	99001	**800-941-2291**	509-244-5611	104
Garda World Security Corp 1390 Barre St *TSE: GW*	Montreal	QC	H3C1N4	**800-859-1599**	514-281-2811	691
Gardco Lighting 1611 Clovis Barker Rd	San Marcos	TX	78666	**800-227-0758**	512-753-1000	439
Garden City Community College 801 N Campus Dr	Garden City	KS	67846	**800-658-1696**	620-276-7611	161
Garden City Feed Yard 1805 W Annie Scheer Rd	Garden City	KS	67846	**800-272-4191**	620-275-4191	10-1
Garden City Group LLC 105 Maxess Rd	Melville	NY	11747	**888-404-8013**	631-470-5000	428
Garden City Hotel 45 Seventh St	Garden City	NY	11530	**877-549-0400**	516-747-3000	379
Garden Court Hotel 520 Cowper St	Palo Alto	CA	94301	**800-824-9028**	650-322-9000	379
Garden Fresh Restaurant Corp 15822 Bernardo Ctr Dr Ste A	San Diego	CA	92127	**800-874-1600**	858-675-1600	668
Garden Grove Chamber of Commerce 12866 Main St Ste 102	Garden Grove	CA	92840	**800-959-5560**	714-638-7950	138
Garden of Life Inc 5500 Village Blvd Ste 102	West Palm Beach	FL	33407	**866-465-0051**		797
Garden Place Hotel 6461 Transit Rd	Depew	NY	14043	**877-456-4097**	716-683-7990	379
Garden Spa at MacArthur Place 29 E MacArthur St	Sonoma	CA	95476	**800-722-1866**	707-933-3193	705
Garden State Community Bank (GSCB) 36 Ferry St *NYSE: NYB*	Newark	NJ	07105	**877-786-6560**	973-589-8616	69
Garden State Engine & Equipment Co 3509 US Hwy 22	Somerville	NJ	08876	**800-479-3857**	908-534-5444	358
Garden State Growers 99 Locust Grove Rd	Pittstown	NJ	08867	**800-288-8484**	908-730-8888	369
Gardena Valley News 15005 S Vermont Ave	Gardena	CA	90247	**800-329-6351**	310-329-6351	531-4
Gardener's Supply Co 128 Intervale Rd	Burlington	VT	05401	**800-863-1700**	802-660-3500	324
Gardens Alive Inc 5100 Schenley Pl	Lawrenceburg	IN	47025	**800-222-1222**	513-354-1482	458
Gardens Hotel 526 Angela St	Key West	FL	33040	**800-526-2664**	305-294-2661	379
Gardens of the American Rose Ctr 8877 Jefferson-Paige Rd	Shreveport	LA	71119	**800-637-6534**	318-938-5402	96
Gardenside Ltd 808 Anthony St Ste 140	Berkeley	CA	94710	**888-999-8325**	415-455-4500	320-4
Gardner Denver Nash 1800 Gardner Expy	Quincy	IL	62305	**800-637-5729**	217-222-5400	174
Gardner Glass Products Inc 301 Elkin Hwy PO Box 1570	North Wilkesboro	NC	28659	**800-334-7267**		334
Gardner Inc 3641 Interchange Rd	Columbus	OH	43204	**800-848-8946**	614-456-4000	276
Gardner Publications Inc 6915 Valley Ave	Cincinnati	OH	45244	**800-950-8020**	513-527-8800	634-9
Gardner Village 1100 West 7800 South	West Jordan	UT	84088	**800-662-4335**	801-566-8903	459
Gardner-Gibson PO Box 5449	Tampa	FL	33675	**800-237-1155**	813-248-2101	45
Gardners Candies Inc 2600 Adams Ave PO Box E	Tyrone	PA	16686	**800-242-2639**	814-684-3925	122
Gardner-Webb University PO Box 817	Boiling Springs	NC	28017	**800-253-6472**	704-406-4498	167
Gare Inc 165 Rosemont St	Haverhill	MA	01832	**888-289-4273**	978-373-9131	42
Gared Sports Inc 707 N Second St Ste 202	Saint Louis	MO	63102	**800-325-2682**	314-421-0044	708
Garfield Refining Co 810 East Cayuga St	Philadelphia	PA	19124	**800-523-0968**		410
Gargoyles Inc 500 George Washington Hwy	Smithfield	RI	02917	**866-807-0195**	401-231-3800	541
Garkane Energy Co-op Inc 120 West 300 South PO Box 465	Loa	UT	84747	**800-747-5403**	435-836-2795	247
Garland C Norris Co 1101 Terry Rd	Apex	NC	27502	**800-331-8920**	919-387-1059	558
Garland Commercial Industries 185 S St	Freeland	PA	18224	**800-424-2411**	570-636-1000	299
Garland Company Inc 3800 E 91st St	Cleveland	OH	44105	**800-321-9336**	216-641-7500	45
Garland Independent School District (GISD) 501 S Jupiter PO Box 469026	Garland	TX	75046	**800-252-5555**	972-494-8201	683
Garland Resort 4700 N Red Oak Rd	Lewiston	MI	49756	**877-442-7526**	989-786-2211	667
Garland Sales Inc PO Box 1870	Dalton	GA	30720	**800-524-0361**	706-278-7880	130
Garland, The 4222 Vineland Ave	North Hollywood	CA	91602	**800-238-3759**	818-980-8000	379
Garlich Printing Co 525 Rudder Rd	Fenton	MO	63026	**800-276-2622**	636-349-8000	625
Garmin Ltd 1200 E 151st St *NASDAQ: GRMN*	Olathe	KS	66062	**888-442-7646**	913-397-8200	528
Garner Industries Inc 7201 N 98th St PO Box 29709	Lincoln	NE	68507	**800-228-0275**	402-434-9100	607
Garnet Hill Inc 231 Main St	Franconia	NH	03580	**800-870-3513**	603-823-5545	742-1
Garr Tool Co 7800 N Alger Rd	Alma	MI	48801	**800-248-9003**	989-463-6171	492

Name / Address	City	State	ZIP	Toll-Free	Phone	Class
Garrett College 687 Mosser Rd	McHenry	MD	21541	**866-554-2773**	301-387-3000	161
Garrett County Chamber of Commerce 15 Visitors Ctr Dr	McHenry	MD	21541	**888-387-5237**	301-387-4386	138
Garrett Metal Detectors 1881 W State St	Garland	TX	75042	**800-234-6151**	972-494-6151	471
Garrett's Desert Inn 311 Old Santa Fe Trl	Santa Fe	NM	87501	**800-888-2145**	505-982-1851	379
Garrity Print Solutions 109 Research Dr	Harahan	LA	70123	**877-568-1555**	504-733-9654	626
Garry Packing Inc 11272 E Central Ave	Del Rey	CA	93616	**800-248-2126**	559-888-2126	297-18
Garsite LLC 539 S Tenth St	Kansas City	KS	66105	**888-427-7483**	913-342-5600	21
Gartner Inc 56 Top Gallant Rd *NYSE: IT*	Stamford	CT	06902	**866-471-2526**	203-964-0096	465
Garton Tractor Inc 2400 N Golden State Blvd	Turlock	CA	95382	**877-872-2767**	209-632-3931	276
Garvan Woodland Gardens 550 Arkridge Rd PO Box 22240	Hot Springs	AR	71903	**800-366-4664**	501-262-9300	96
Garvey Corp 208 S Rt 73	Blue Anchor	NJ	08037	**800-257-8581**	609-561-2450	209
Garvey Wholesale Beverage Inc 2542 San Gabriel Blvd	Rosemead	CA	91770	**800-287-2075**	626-280-5244	79-3
Garvin-Allen Solutions Ltd Unit 12 155 Chain Lk Dr	Halifax	NS	B3S1B3	**877-325-9062**	902-453-3554	182
Gary Plastic Packaging Corp 1340 Viele Ave	Bronx	NY	10474	**800-221-8150**	718-893-2200	599
Gary Soren Smith Ctr for the Fine & Performing Arts *Ohlone College* 43600 Mission Blvd	Fremont	CA	94539	**800-309-2131**	510-659-6031	571
GAS (Glass Art Society) 6512 23rd Ave NW Ste 329	Seattle	WA	98121	**800-636-2377**	206-382-1305	47-4
Gas Co, The 515 Kamake'e St	Honolulu	HI	96814	**866-499-3941**	808-535-5933	785
Gas Daily 1200 G St NW Ste 1000	Washington	DC	20005	**800-752-8878**	202-383-2000	530-5
Gas Equipment Company Inc 11616 Harry Hines Blvd	Dallas	TX	75229	**800-821-1829**	972-241-2333	385
Gas Technology Energy Concepts LLC 401 William L Gaiter Pkwy Ste 4	Buffalo	NY	14215	**800-451-8294**		174
Gas Transmission-Northwest 1400 SW Fifth Ave Ste 900	Portland	OR	97201	**888-750-6275**		326
GasAmerica Services Inc 2700 W Main St	Greenfield	IN	46140	**800-643-1948**	317-468-2515	325
Gasboy International Inc 7300 W Friendly Ave *Sales	Greensboro	NC	27420	**800-444-5579***	336-547-5000	636
Gascosage Electric Co-op 803 S Hwy 28 PO Box G	Dixon	MO	65459	**866-568-8243**	573-759-7146	247
Gas-Fired Products Inc 305 Doggett St	Charlotte	NC	28203	**800-830-3983**	704-372-3485	319
Gaska-Tape Inc 1810 W Lusher Ave	Elkhart	IN	46517	**800-423-1571**	574-294-5431	729
Gasket Manufacturing Co 18001 Main St	Gardena	CA	90248	**800-442-7538**	310-217-5600	327
Gaskets Inc 301 W Hwy 16	Rio	WI	53960	**800-558-1833**	920-992-3137	327
Gaslamp Plaza Suites 520 E St	San Diego	CA	92101	**800-874-8770**	619-232-9500	379
Gaspard Inc 200 N Janacek Rd	Brookfield	WI	53045	**800-784-6868**	262-784-6800	154-13
Gassaway Mansion 106 Dupont Dr	Greenville	SC	29607	**888-912-7469**	864-271-0188	49-2
Gassco 7515 Lindsay Rd	Bakersfield	CA	93313	**800-390-7837**	661-832-7406	578
Gaston Chamber of Commerce 601 W Franklin Blvd	Gastonia	NC	28052	**800-933-3909**	704-864-2621	138
Gaston College 201 Hwy 321-S	Dallas	NC	28034	**800-634-7854**	704-922-6200	161
Gaston County Public Library 1555 E Garrison Blvd	Gastonia	NC	28054	**888-241-3115**	704-868-2164	434-3
Gaston County Travel & Tourism 620 N Main St	Belmont	NC	28012	**800-849-9994**	704-825-4044	208
Gaston Gazette 1893 Remount Rd	Gastonia	NC	28054	**800-527-5226**	704-869-1700	531-2
Gastonian, The 220 E Gaston St	Savannah	GA	31401	**800-322-6603**	912-232-2869	379
Gatan Inc 5794 W Las Positas Blvd	Pleasanton	CA	94588	**888-887-3377**	925-463-0200	419
Gatco Inc 1550 Factor Ave	San Leandro	CA	94577	**800-227-5640**	510-352-8770	785
Gate Petroleum Co 9540 San Jose Blvd PO Box 23627	Jacksonville	FL	32241	**866-571-1982**	904-737-7220	325
Gatekeeper Systems Inc 8 Studebaker	Irvine	CA	92618	**888-808-9433**	949-453-1940	201
Gates Albert Inc 3434 Union St	North Chili	NY	14514	**800-937-9311**	585-594-9401	620
Gates Bar-B-Q 4621 Paseo Blvd	Kansas City	MO	64110	**800-662-7427**	816-923-0900	668
Gates Corp 1551 Wewatta St	Denver	CO	80202	**800-709-6001**	303-744-1911	370
Gates County 200 Ct St	Gatesville	NC	27938	**800-272-9829**	252-357-2411	338
Gates Family Foundation 1390 Lawrence St	Denver	CO	80204	**866-590-4377**	303-722-1881	306
Gates of the Arctic National Park & Preserve 4175 Geist Rd	Fairbanks	AK	99709	**866-869-6887**	907-457-5752	563
Gateway Arch 50 S Leonor K Sullivan Blvd	Saint Louis	MO	63102	**877-982-1410**		49-3
Gateway Community & Technical College (GCTC) 1025 Amsterdam Rd	Covington	KY	41011	**855-346-4282**	859-441-4500	798
GateWay Community College 108 N 40th St	Phoenix	AZ	85034	**888-994-4433**	602-286-8000	161
Gateway Ctr 1 Gateway Dr	Collinsville	IL	62234	**800-289-2388**	618-345-8998	207
Gateway Foundation Inc 1080 E Pk St	Carbondale	IL	62901	**877-505-4673**		724
Gateway Inc 7565 Irvine Ctr Dr	Irvine	CA	92618	**800-846-2000**	949-471-7040	175-1
Gateway Industrial Power Inc 921 Fournie Ln	Collinsville	IL	62234	**888-865-8675**	618-345-0123	56
Gateway Limousines 1550 Gilbreth Rd	Burlingame	CA	94010	**800-486-7077**	650-697-5548	441
Gateway Mortgage Group LLC 6910 E 14th St	Tulsa	OK	74112	**877-406-8109**	918-712-9000	216
Gateway News 1050 West Main St	Kent	OH	44240	**800-560-9657**	330-541-9400	531-4
Gateway Newstands 240 Chrislea Rd	Woodbridge	ON	L4L8V1	**800-942-5351**	905-851-9652	529
Gateway Regional Medical Ctr (GRMC) 2100 Madison Ave *General	Granite City	IL	62040	**800-422-6237***	618-798-3000	374-3
Gateway Shoe Co 910 Kehro Mill Rd Ste 112	Ballwin	MO	63011	**800-539-6063**	636-256-7050	302
Gateway Supply Company Inc 1312 Hamrick St	Columbia	SC	29202	**800-922-5312**	803-771-7160	611
Gateway Technical College 3520 30th Ave	Kenosha	WI	53144	**800-247-7122**	262-564-2200	798
Gateway Travel Service Inc 28470 W 13 Mile Rd Ste 200	Farmington Hills	MI	48334	**800-423-4898**	248-432-8600	770
Gateways Inn 51 Walker St	Lenox	MA	01240	**888-492-9466**	413-637-2532	379
Gator Park 24050 SW Eigth St	Miami	FL	33194	**800-559-2205**	305-559-2255	821
Gatorade Sports Science Institute 617 W Main St	Barrington	IL	60010	**800-616-4774**		666
Gatorland 14501 S Orange Blossom Trl	Orlando	FL	32837	**800-393-5297**	407-855-5496	821
GATRA 2 Oak St	Taunton	MA	02780	**800-483-2500**	508-823-8828	107
Gaucho's Churrascaria 62 Lowell St	Manchester	NH	03101	**866-669-9460**	603-669-9460	669
Gavel International Corp 300 Tri State International Ste 320	Lincolnshire	IL	60069	**800-544-2835**	847-945-8150	186
Gay Men's Health Crisis (GMHC) 119 W 24th St	New York	NY	10011	**800-243-7692**	212-367-1000	47-17
Gayla Industries Inc PO Box 920800	Houston	TX	77292	**800-231-7508**		760
Gaylor Electric 5750 Castle Creek Pkwy N Dr Ste 400	Indianapolis	IN	46250	**800-878-0577**	317-843-0577	191-4
Gaylord Bros 7282 William Barry Blvd	Syracuse	NY	13212	**800-345-5330**	315-457-5070	320-3
Gaylord Hospital Gaylord Farms Rd PO Box 400	Wallingford	CT	06492	**866-429-5673**	203-284-2800	374-6
Gaylord Industries Inc 10900 SW Avery St	Tualatin	OR	97062	**800-547-9696**	503-691-2010	18
Gaylord Manufacturing Co 1088 Montclaire Dr	Ceres	CA	95307	**800-375-0091**	209-538-3313	814
Gaylord Opryland Hotel & Convention Ctr 2800 Opryland Dr	Nashville	TN	37214	**888-236-2427**	615-889-1000	379
Gaymar Industries Inc 10 Centre Dr	Orchard Park	NY	14127	**800-828-7341**	716-662-2551	475
Gaytan Foods 15430 Proctor Ave	City Of Industry	CA	91745	**800-242-9826**	626-330-4553	297-26
Gazette Newspapers Inc 9030 Comprint Ct	Gaithersburg	MD	20877	**888-670-7100**	301-948-3120	634-8
Gazette Publishing Inc 1114 Broadway	Wheaton	MN	56296	**800-567-8303**	320-563-8146	626
Gazette, The 501 Second Ave SE	Cedar Rapids	IA	52401	**800-397-8333**	319-398-8333	531-2
GB Tubulars Inc 950 Threadneedle St Ste 130	Houston	TX	77079	**888-245-3848**	713-465-3585	491
GBCVB (Greater Boston Convention & Visitors Bureau) 2 Copley Pl Ste 105	Boston	MA	02116	**888-733-2678**	617-536-4100	208
GBH Communications Inc 1309 S Myrtle Ave	Monrovia	CA	91016	**800-222-5424**		248
GBPD (Guardian Building Products) 979 Batesville Rd	Greer	SC	29651	**800-569-4262**	864-297-6101	193-3
GBS Corp 7233 Freedom Ave NW	North Canton	OH	44720	**800-552-2427**	330-494-5330	533
GBS Filing Solutions 224 Morges Rd	Malvern	OH	44644	**800-873-4427**	330-494-5330	559
Gbsa Inc 2710 N ave	Bridgeport	CT	06604	**800-544-0005**	203-549-0060	7
GBTA (Global Business Travel Assn, The) 123 N Pitt St	Alexandria	VA	22314	**888-574-6447**	703-684-0836	47-23
GC America Inc 3737 W 127th St *Cust Svc	Alsip	IL	60803	**800-323-7063***	708-597-0900	230
GC Services LP 6330 Gulfton St	Houston	TX	77081	**800-756-6524**	713-777-4441	159
GCA (Everi Holdings Inc) 7250 S Tenaya Way Ste 100 *NYSE: EVRI*	Las Vegas	NV	89113	**800-833-7110**	702-855-3000	55
GCA Services Group 1350 Euclid Ave Ste 1500	Cleveland	OH	44115	**800-422-8760**		151
GCEC (Grayson-Collin Electric Co-op) PO Box 548	Van Alstyne	TX	75495	**800-967-5235**	903-482-7100	247
GCF (General Credit Forms Inc) 3595 Rider Trl S	Earth City	MO	63045	**888-423-6397**	314-216-8600	109
GCS (Georgia Cancer Specialists Pc) 1872 Montreal Rd	Tucker	GA	30084	**800-491-5991**	770-496-9443	374-7
GCS Service Inc 370 Wabasha St N	St. Paul	MN	55102	**800-822-2303**		393
GCSAA (Golf Course Superintendents Assn of America) 1421 Research Pk Dr	Lawrence	KS	66049	**800-472-7878**	785-841-2240	47-2
GCTC (Gateway Community & Technical College) 1025 Amsterdam Rd	Covington	KY	41011	**855-346-4282**	859-441-4500	798

Company	City	State	ZIP	Toll-Free	Phone	Class
GCube Insurance Services Inc 3101 Wcoast Hwy Ste 100	Newport Beach	CA	92663	**877-903-4777**	949-515-9981	390
GE Analytical Instruments Inc 6060 Spine Rd	Boulder	CO	80301	**800-255-6964**	303-444-2009	690
GE Betz 4636 Somerton Rd *Cust Svc	Trevose	PA	19053	**866-439-2837***	215-355-3300	144
GE Capital Solutions Franchise Finance 8377 E Hartford Dr Ste 200	Scottsdale	AZ	85255	**866-438-4333**		652
GE Fanuc Embedded Systems Inc 7401 Snaproll NE	Albuquerque	NM	87109	**888-790-1820**	505-875-0600	624
GE Healthcare Information Technologies 8200 W Tower Ave	Milwaukee	WI	53223	**800-558-5102**	414-355-5000	252
GE Infrastructure Sensing 1100 Technology Pk Dr	Billerica	MA	01821	**800-833-9438**	978-437-1000	203
GE Lighting Systems Inc 3010 Spartanburg Hwy	East Flat Rock	NC	28726	**888-694-3533**	828-693-2000	439
GE Rail Car Services 161 N Clark St 7th Fl	Chicago	IL	60601	**800-626-2000**	312-853-5000	266-5
GE Richards Graphic Supplies Company Inc 928 Links Ave	Landisville	PA	17538	**800-233-0410**	717-898-3151	688
GE Transportation Rail 2901 E Lake Rd *Prod Info	Erie	PA	16531	**800-285-6545***	814-875-2234	648
GE Vendor Financial Services 1719 Rt 10 E Ste 306	Parsippany	NJ	07054	**800-626-2000**	203-373-2039	218
GE Water & Process Technologies 4636 Somerton Rd	Trevose	PA	19053	**866-439-2837**	215-355-3300	804
Gear Energy Ltd 2600 500 - Fourth Ave SW	Calgary	AB	T2P2V6	**877-494-3430**	403-538-8435	535
Gear for Sports Inc 9700 Commerce Pkwy	Lenexa	KS	66219	**800-255-1065**	913-693-3200	154-1
Gearhart By the Sea 1157 N Marion Ave	Gearhart	OR	97138	**800-547-0115**	503-738-8331	667
Geary Pacific Corp 1908 N Enterprise St	Orange	CA	92865	**800-444-3279**	714-279-2950	688
GEARYS Beverly Hills 351 N Beverly Dr	Beverly Hills	CA	90210	**800-793-6670**	310-273-4741	362
Geauga County Transit 12555 Merritt Rd *Cust Svc	Chardon	OH	44024	**888-287-7190***	440-279-2150	107
GeBBS Healthcare Solutions Inc 560 Sylvan Ave Second Fl	Englewood Cliffs	NJ	07632	**888-539-4282**		179
Gebco Insurance Assoc 8600 LaSalle Rd Ste 338	Towson	MD	21286	**800-464-3226**	410-668-3100	390
GEFCO (GEFCO Inc) 2215 S Van Buren	Enid	OK	73703	**800-759-7441**	580-234-4141	536
GEFCO Inc (GEFCO) 2215 S Van Buren	Enid	OK	73703	**800-759-7441**	580-234-4141	536
Gefran ISI Inc 8 Lowell Ave	Winchester	MA	01890	**888-888-4474**	781-729-5249	203
Gehl's Guernsey Farms Inc N116 W15970 Main St	Germantown	WI	53022	**800-521-2873**	262-251-8572	297-10
Gehr Industries 7400 E Slauson Ave	Los Angeles	CA	90040	**800-688-6606**	323-728-5558	811
GEI Consultants Inc 400 Unicorn Pk Dr	Woburn	MA	01801	**888-434-9679**	781-721-4000	263
Geiger International Inc 6095 Fulton Industrial Blvd SW	Atlanta	GA	30336	**800-456-6452**	404-344-1100	320-1
Geisinger Health Plan 100 N Academy Ave	Danville	PA	17822	**800-447-4000**	570-271-8760	391-3
Gelita USA Inc PO Box 927	Sioux City	IA	51102	**800-223-9244**	712-943-5516	297-22
Gelmart Industries Inc 136 Madison Ave 4th Fl *General	New York	NY	10016	**800-746-0014***	212-743-6900	154-17
Gel-Pak LLC 31398 Huntwood Ave	Hayward	CA	94544	**888-621-4147**	510-576-2220	694
Gem Dandy Inc 200 W Academy St	Madison	NC	27025	**800-334-5101**	336-548-9624	154-2
GEM Edwards Inc 5640 Hudson Industrial Pkwy PO Box 429	Hudson	OH	44236	**800-733-7976**		475
GEM Group 9 International Way	Lawrence	MA	01843	**800-800-3200**	978-691-2000	66
Gem State Paper & Supply Co 1801 Highland Ave E	Twin Falls	ID	83303	**800-727-2737**	208-733-6081	558
Gemex Systems Inc 6040 W Executive Dr Ste A	Mequon	WI	53092	**866-694-3639**	262-242-1111	411
Gemini Coatings Inc 421 SE 27th St	El Reno	OK	73036	**800-262-5710**	405-262-5710	549
Gemini Inc 103 Mensing Way	Cannon Falls	MN	55009	**800-538-8377**	507-263-3957	699
Gemini Valve 2 Otter Ct	Raymond	NH	03077	**800-370-0936**	603-895-4761	787
Gemmel Pharmacy Group Inc 143 N Euclid Ave	Ontario	CA	91762	**888-302-0229**	909-988-0591	239
Gemological Institute of America (GIA) 5345 Armada Dr	Carlsbad	CA	92008	**800-421-7250**	760-603-4000	48-4
Gems Sensors Inc 1 Cowles Rd	Plainville	CT	06062	**800-378-1600**	860-747-3000	203
Gemstone Systems Inc 1260 NW Waterhouse Ave Ste 200	Beaverton	OR	97006	**800-243-4772**	503-533-3000	180-1
Gemtex Abrasives 234 Belfield Rd	Toronto	ON	M9W1H3	**800-387-5100**	416-245-5605	1
Gemtor Inc 1 Johnson Ave	Matawan	NJ	07747	**800-405-9048**	732-583-6200	676
Genaera Corp 5110 Campus Dr	Plymouth Meeting	PA	19462	**800-299-9156**	610-941-4020	84
GenBio 15222 Ave of Science Ste A *Tech Supp	San Diego	CA	92128	**800-288-4368***	858-592-9300	233
Gencor Industries Inc 5201 N Orange Blossom Trail *NASDAQ: GENC* ■ *General	Orlando	FL	32810	**888-887-1266***	407-290-6000	192
Gene Codes Corp 775 Technology Dr	Ann Arbor	MI	48108	**800-497-4939**	734-769-7249	179
Genealogy.com 360 West 4800 North	Provo	UT	84604	**800-262-3787**	801-705-7000	397
Genemed Biotechnologies Inc 458 Carlton Ct S San Francisco	San Francisco	CA	94080	**877-436-3633**	650-952-0110	666
Geneos Wealth Management Inc 9055 E Mineral Cir Ste 200	Centennial	CO	80112	**888-812-5043**	303-785-8470	688
Generac Power Systems Inc PO Box 8	Waukesha	WI	53187	**888-436-3722**	262-544-4811	517
General Air Service & Supply Company Inc 1105 Zuni St	Denver	CO	80204	**877-782-8434**	303-892-7003	145
General Assn of Regular Baptist Churches (GARBC) 1300 N Meacham Rd	Schaumburg	IL	60173	**888-588-1600**	847-585-0816	47-20
General Atomics 3550 General Atomics Ct PO Box 85608	San Diego	CA	92121	**800-669-6820**	858-455-3000	666
General Aviation Manufacturers Assn (GAMA) 1400 K St NW Ste 801	Washington	DC	20005	**866-427-3287**	202-393-1500	48-21
General Bearing Corp 44 High St *Sales	West Nyack	NY	10994	**800-431-1766***	845-358-6000	74
General Body Manufacturing Co 7110 Jensen Dr	Houston	TX	77093	**800-395-8585**	713-692-5177	515
General Butler State Resort Park 1608 US Hwy 227	Carrollton	KY	41008	**866-462-8853**	502-732-4384	667
General Cable Corp 4 Tesseneer Dr *NYSE: BGC*	Highland Heights	KY	41076	**800-572-8000**	859-572-8000	812
General Carbide Corp 1151 Garden St	Greensburg	PA	15601	**800-245-2465**	724-836-3000	755
General Communication Inc 2550 Denali St Ste 1000 *NASDAQ: GNCMA*	Anchorage	AK	99503	**800-770-7886**	907-265-5600	733
General Credit Forms Inc (GCF) 3595 Rider Trl S	Earth City	MO	63045	**888-423-6397**	314-216-8600	109
General Data Co Inc 4354 Ferguson Dr	Cincinnati	OH	45245	**800-733-5252**	513-752-7978	176
General Devices Company Inc 1410 S Post Rd	Indianapolis	IN	46239	**800-821-3520**	317-897-7000	203
General Die Casters Inc 2150 Highland Rd	Twinsburg	OH	44087	**800-332-2278**	330-657-2300	309
General Digital Corp 8 Nutmeg Rd S	South Windsor	CT	06074	**800-952-2535**	860-282-2900	175-4
General Dynamics C4 Systems 400 John Quincy Adams Rd Bldg 80	Taunton	MA	02780	**877-449-0600**		180-10
General Dynamics Information Technology 3211 Jermantown Rd	Fairfax	VA	22030	**800-242-0230**	703-246-0200	182
General Dynamics SATCOM Technologies 3111 Fujita St	Torrance	CA	90505	**888-874-7646**	828-464-4141	645
General Dynamics SATCOM Technologies 1500 Prodelin Dr	Newton	NC	28658	**888-874-7646**	828-464-4141	645
General Econopak Inc 1725 N Sixth St	Philadelphia	PA	19122	**888-871-8568**	215-763-8200	575
General Educational Development Testing Service *American Council on Education* 1 Dupont Cir NW	Washington	DC	20036	**866-205-6267**	202-939-9300	246
General Electrodynamics Corporation Inc 8000 Calendar Rd	Arlington	TX	76001	**800-551-6038**	817-572-0366	22
General Equipment & Supplies Inc 4300 Main Ave	Fargo	ND	58103	**800-437-2924**	701-282-2662	358
General Equipment Co 620 Alexander Dr SW PO Box 334 *Cust Svc	Owatonna	MN	55060	**800-533-0524***	507-451-5510	386
General Fasteners Co 37584 Amrhein Rd Ste 150	Livonia	MI	48150	**800-945-2658**	734-452-2400	351
General Federation of Women's Clubs (GFWC) 1734 N St NW	Washington	DC	20036	**800-443-4392**	202-347-3168	47-24
General Filters Inc 43800 Grand River Ave	Novi	MI	48375	**866-476-5101**		18
General Formulations Inc 309 S Union St	Sparta	MI	49345	**800-253-3664**	616-887-7387	599
General Growth Properties Inc 110 N Wacker Dr *NYSE: GGP*	Chicago	IL	60606	**888-395-8037**	312-960-5000	653
General Healthcare Resources Inc 2250 Hickory Rd Ste 240	Plymouth Meeting	PA	19462	**800-879-4471**	610-834-1122	363
General Hearing Corp 175 Brookhollow Esplanade	Harahan	LA	70123	**800-824-3021**	504-733-3767	239
General Insulation Company Inc 278 Mystic Ave Ste 209	Medford	MA	02155	**800-229-9148**	781-391-2070	193-4
General Loose Leaf Bindery Co 3811 Hawthorn Ct	Waukegan	IL	60087	**800-621-0493**	847-244-9700	85
General Machine Products Company Inc 3111 Old Lincoln Hwy *Tech Supp	Trevose	PA	19053	**800-345-6009***	215-357-5500	756
General Magnaplate Corp 1331 Us Rt 1	Linden	NJ	07036	**800-441-6173**	908-862-6200	486
General Mills Foundation PO Box 9452	Minneapolis	MN	55440	**800-248-7310**		305
General Mills Inc 1 General Mills Blvd *NYSE: GIS*	Minneapolis	MN	55426	**800-248-7310**		300
General Motors Acceptance Corp (GMAC) 200 Renaissance Ctr	Detroit	MI	48265	**800-200-4622**	877-320-2559	216
General Motors Corp Buick Motor Div 300 Renaissance Ctr PO Box 33136 *Cust Svc	Detroit	MI	48265	**800-521-7300***		58
General Motors Foundation Inc PO Box 33170	Detroit	MI	48232	**800-222-1020**		305
General Pet Supply Inc 7711 N 81st St	Milwaukee	WI	53223	**800-433-9786**	414-365-3400	94
General Plastic Extrusions Inc 1238 Kasson Dr	Prescott	WI	54021	**800-532-3888**	715-262-3806	547
General Plastics Mfg Co 4910 S Burlington Way	Tacoma	WA	98409	**800-806-6051**	253-473-5000	600

Name / Address	City	State	ZIP	Toll-Free	Phone	Class
General Plug & Mfg Co Inc 455 Main St	Grafton	OH	44044	**800-289-7584**	440-926-2411	594
General Produce Co 1330 N 'B' St	Sacramento	CA	95814	**800-366-4991**	916-441-6431	298-7
General Revenue Corp 4660 Duke Dr Ste 300	Mason	OH	45040	**800-234-6258**		159
Federal Citizen Information Center PO Box 100	Pueblo	CO	81009	**888-878-3256**		340-18
General Services Administration Regional Offices						
Region 1 - New England 10 Cswy St Rm 1010 Thomas P O'Neill Federal Bldg.	Boston	MA	02222	**866-734-1727**	617-565-5860	340-18
Region 3 - Mid-Atlantic Strawbridge Bldg 20 N 8th St	Philadelphia	PA	19107	**800-333-4636**	215-446-5100	340-18
Region 4 - Southeast Sunbelt 1800 F St NW Ste 600	Washington	DC	20405	**800-333-4636**		340-18
Region 8 - Rocky Mountain Denver Federal Ctr Bldg 41	Denver	CO	80225	**888-999-4777**	303-236-7329	340-18
General Shale Products LLC 3015 Bristol Hwy	Johnson City	TN	37601	**800-414-4661**	423-282-4661	149
General Star National Insurance Co 695 E Main St Financial Ctr	Stamford	CT	06901	**800-624-5237**	203-328-5000	391-4
General Steamship Agencies Inc 575 Redwood Hwy Ste 200	Mill Valley	CA	94941	**855-859-3123**	415-389-5200	464
General Steel Inc PO Box 1503	Macon	GA	31202	**800-476-2794**	478-746-2794	491
General Theological Seminary 440 W 21st St	New York	NY	10011	**888-487-5649**	212-243-5150	168-3
General Tool & Supply Co Inc 2705 NW Nicolai St	Portland	OR	97210	**800-526-9328**	503-226-3411	385
General Tool Co 101 Landy Ln	Cincinnati	OH	45215	**800-314-9817**	513-733-5500	755
General Tools Mfg Company LLC 80 White St	New York	NY	10013	**800-697-8665**	212-431-6100	756
General Tours 53 Summer St	Keene	NH	03431	**800-221-2216**		758
General Truck Parts & Equipment Co 3835 W 42nd St	Chicago	IL	60632	**800-621-3914**	773-247-6900	60
General Vision Services LLC 520 Eigth Ave 9th Fl	New York	NY	10018	**855-653-0586**	212-729-5300	542
General Wax & Candle Co 6863 Beck Ave PO Box 9398	North Hollywood	CA	91605	**800-929-7867**	818-765-5800	121
General Wire Spring Co 1101 Thompson Ave	McKees Rocks	PA	15136	**800-245-6200**	412-771-6300	716
Generations United (GU) 1333 H St NW Ste 500-W	Washington	DC	20005	**800-677-1116**	202-289-3979	47-6
Generex Biotechnology Corp 555 Richmond St W Ste 202 *OTC: GNBT*	Toronto	ON	M5J2G2	**800-391-6755**	416-364-2551	84
Generic Pharmaceutical Assn (GPhA) 2300 Clarendon Blvd Ste 400	Arlington	VA	22201	**800-859-8003**	703-647-2480	48-19
Genesee Community College 1 College Rd	Batavia	NY	14020	**866-225-5422**	585-343-0068	161
Genesee County Chamber of Commerce 210 E Main St	Batavia	NY	14020	**877-788-6846**	585-343-7440	138
Genesee County Parks & Recreation 5045 Stanley Rd	Flint	MI	48506	**800-648-7275**	810-736-7100	49-4
Genesee District Library G-4195 W Pasadena Ave	Flint	MI	48504	**866-732-1120**	810-732-0110	434-3
Genesee Regional Chamber of Commerce 519 S Saginaw St Ste 200	Flint	MI	48502	**800-829-3676**	810-600-1404	138
Genesee Valley Ctr 3341 S Linden Rd	Flint	MI	48507	**866-236-1128**	810-732-4000	459
Genesis Biosystems Inc 1500 Eagle Ct # 75057	Lewisville	TX	75057	**888-577-7335**	972-315-7888	76
Genesis Capital LLC 3414 Peachtree Rd Ne Ste 700	Atlanta	GA	30326	**800-998-8479**	404-816-7540	69
Genesis Corp 950 Third Ave Fl 26	New York	NY	10022	**800-261-1776**	212-688-5522	182
Genesis Energy LP 919 Milam Ste 2100 *NYSE: GEL*	Houston	TX	77002	**800-284-3365**	713-860-2500	596
Genesis HealthCare Corp 101 E State St	Kennett Square	PA	19348	**800-944-7776**	610-444-6350	450
Genesis Home Care Inc 116 E Heritage Dr	Tyler	TX	75703	**800-947-0273**	903-509-3374	363
Genesis Medical Ctr Illini Campus 801 Illini Dr	Silvis	IL	61282	**800-250-6020**	309-792-9363	374-3
Genesis Publisher Services 3310 Eagle Pk Dr NE Ste 200	Grand Rapids	MI	49525	**800-828-1022**	616-831-2800	634-6
Genesisfour Corp 7747 Ten Acre Rd	Andrews	SC	29510	**800-937-4364**	843-461-4117	179
Genesys Telecommunications Laboratories Inc 2001 Junipero Serra Blvd	Daly City	CA	94014	**888-436-3797**	650-466-1100	732
Genetec Inc 2280 Alfred-Nobel Blvd Ste 400	Montreal	QC	H4S2A4	**866-684-8006**	514-332-4000	227
Genetic Engineering News 140 Huguenot St 3rd Fl	New Rochelle	NY	10801	**888-211-4235**	914-740-2100	530-12
Genetic Profiles Corp 10675 Treena St Ste 103	San Diego	CA	92131	**800-551-7763**		417
Genetica DNA Laboratories Inc 8740 Montgomery Rd	Cincinnati	OH	45236	**800-433-6848**	513-985-9777	417
Genetics Associates Inc 1916 Patterson St Ste 400	Nashville	TN	37203	**800-331-4363**	615-327-4532	415
Genetics Society of America (GSA) 9650 Rockville Pk	Bethesda	MD	20814	**866-486-4363**	301-634-7300	48-19
Genetrack Biolabs Inc 401-1508 Broadway W	Vancouver	BC	V6J1W8	**888-828-1899**	604-325-7282	418
Geneva Capital LLC 522 Broadway St Ste 4	Alexandria	MN	56308	**800-408-9352**		196
Geneva College 3200 College Ave	Beaver Falls	PA	15010	**800-847-8255**	724-847-6500	167
Geneva on the Lake 1001 Lochland Rd	Geneva	NY	14456	**800-343-6382**	315-789-7190	379
Geneva Rock Products Inc 302 W 5400 S Ste 200	Murray	UT	84107	**855-614-6497**	801-281-7900	184
Geneva Scientific Inc 11 N Batavia Ave	Batavia	IL	60510	**800-338-2697**		385
Genex Co-op Inc/CRI 117 E Green Bay St	Shawano	WI	54166	**888-333-1783**	715-526-2141	11-2
Genex Services Inc 440 E Swedesford Rd Ste 1000	Wayne	PA	19087	**888-464-3639**	610-964-5100	196
Genghis Grill 18900 Dallas Pkwy Ste 150	Dallas	TX	75244	**888-436-4447**		669
Genie Co 1 Door Dr PO Box 67	Mount Hope	OH	44660	**800-354-3643**		350
Genie Industries Inc 18340 NE 76th St	Redmond	WA	98052	**800-536-1800**	425-881-1800	469
Genie Repros Inc 2211 Hamilton Ave	Cleveland	OH	44114	**877-496-6611**	216-696-6677	626
Genieco Inc 200 N Laflin St	Chicago	IL	60607	**800-223-8217**	312-421-2383	144
Genius Jones Inc 49 NE 39th St	Miami	FL	33137	**866-436-4875**		176
Genoa Business Forms Inc 445 Pk Ave	Sycamore	IL	60178	**800-383-2801**		109
Genomic Health Inc 101 Galveston Dr *NASDAQ: GHDX*	Redwood City	CA	94063	**866-662-6897**	650-556-9300	84
Genova Diagnostics 63 Zillicoa St	Asheville	NC	28801	**800-522-4762**	828-253-0621	418
Genova Products Inc 7034 E Court St	Davison	MI	48423	**800-521-7488**	810-744-4500	607
Genpak Carthage 505 E Cotton St	Carthage	TX	75633	**800-626-6695**	903-693-7151	301
Genpak Corp 68 Warren St	Glens Falls	NY	12801	**800-626-6695**	518-798-9511	547
GenPore 1136 Morgantown Rd PO Box 380	Reading	PA	19607	**800-654-4391**	610-374-5171	607
Gen-Probe Inc 10210 Genetic Ctr Dr	San Diego	CA	92121	**800-523-5001**	858-410-8000	233
GenQuest DNA Analysis Laboratory 133 Coney Island Dr	Sparks	NV	89431	**877-362-5227**	775-358-0652	417
Gensco Equipment (1990) Inc 53 Carlaw Ave	Toronto	ON	M4M2R6	**800-268-6797**	416-465-7521	260
Gensco Inc 4402 20th St E	Tacoma	WA	98424	**877-620-8203**	253-620-8203	611
GenServe Inc 80 Sweeneydale Ave	Bay Shore	NY	11706	**800-247-7215**	631-435-0437	110
Gentec Inc 2625 Dalton	Quebec	QC	G1P3S9	**800-463-4480**	418-651-8000	205
Gentek Bldg Products Inc 11 Craigwood Rd	Avenel	NJ	07001	**800-548-4542**	732-381-0900	695
Gentex Optics Inc 324 Main St	Simpson	PA	18407	**800-736-0554**	570-282-3550	541
Genzyme Corp 500 Kendall St	Cambridge	MA	02142	**800-745-4447**	617-252-7500	84
Genzyme Genetics 3400 Computer Dr	Westborough	MA	01581	**800-255-7357**	508-898-9001	417
GEO Drilling Fluids Inc 1431 Union Ave	Bakersfield	CA	93305	**800-438-7436**	661-325-5919	539
Geo Products LLC 8615 Golden Spike Ln	Houston	TX	77086	**800-434-4743**	281-820-5493	817
Geocel Corp PO Box 398	Elkhart	IN	46515	**800-348-7615**	574-264-0645	3
Geocomp Corp 1145 Massachusetts Ave *Cust Svc	Boxborough	MA	01719	**800-822-2669***	978-635-0012	180-5
GeoEngineers Inc 8410 154th Ave NE	Redmond	WA	98052	**888-624-8373**	425-861-6000	263
Geoforce Inc 750 Canyon Dr Ste 140	Coppell	TX	75019	**888-574-3878**	972-546-3878	535
Geographics 108 Main St 3rd Fl	Norwalk	CT	06851	**800-436-4919**		551-2
Geo-instruments Inc 24 Celestial Dr	Narragansett	RI	02882	**800-477-2506**		462
Geological Museum 1000 E University Ave	Laramie	WY	82071	**800-842-2776**	307-766-2646	519
Geological Society of America, The (GSA) 3300 Penrose Pl PO Box 9140	Boulder	CO	80301	**800-472-1988**	303-357-1000	48-19
GeoLogics Corp 5285 Shawnee Rd Ste 300	Alexandria	VA	22312	**800-684-3455**	703-750-4000	182
Geomet Technologies LLC 20251 Century Blvd	Germantown	MD	20874	**877-407-8033**	301-428-9898	195
Geophysical Research Letter 2000 Florida Ave NW	Washington	DC	20009	**800-966-2481**	202-462-6900	530-12
Geophysics GPR International Inc 100 - 2545 Delorimier Stree	Longueuil	QC	J4K3P7	**800-672-4774**	450-679-2400	725
GeoResources Inc 110 Cypress Stn Dr Ste 220 *NASDAQ: GEOI*	Williston	ND	58802	**855-538-0599**	281-537-9920	535
George E DeLallo Co Inc 6390 Rt 30	Jeannette	PA	15644	**877-335-2556**	724-523-6577	298-8
George Fox Evangelical Seminary 12753 SW 68th Ave	Portland	OR	97223	**800-493-4937**	503-554-6150	168-3
George Fox University 414 N Meridian St	Newberg	OR	97132	**800-765-4369**	503-538-8383	167
George H. Crosby Manitou State Park c/o Tettegouche State Pk 5702 Hwy 61	Silver Bay	MN	55614	**888-646-6367**	218-226-6365	564
George Heinl & Co 201 Church St	Toronto	ON	M5B1Y7	**800-387-7858**	416-363-0093	526
George J Foster Co Inc 150 Venture Dr	Dover	NH	03820	**800-462-2265**	603-742-4455	634-8
George K Baum & Co 4801 Main St Ste 500 Ste 500	Kansas City	MO	64112	**800-821-7195**	816-474-1100	688
George Kelk Corp 48 Lesmill Rd	Toronto	ON	M3B2T5	**888-275-5355**	416-445-5850	407
George Koch Sons LLC 10 S 11th Ave	Evansville	IN	47712	**888-873-5624**	812-465-9600	386
George L Throop Co 444 N Fair Oaks Ave	Pasadena	CA	91103	**800-796-0285**	626-796-0285	185
George Mason Mortgage Corp 4100 Monu Crnr Dr Ste 100	Fairfax	VA	22030	**800-867-6859**	703-273-2600	508

Name / Address	City	State	ZIP	Toll-Free	Phone	Class
George Mason University						
4400 University Dr	Fairfax	VA	22030	**888-627-6612**	703-993-1000	167
George Patton Assoc Inc						
55 Broadcommon Rd	Bristol	RI	02809	**800-572-2194**	401-247-0333	699
George R Brown Convention Ctr						
1001 Avenida de Las Americas	Houston	TX	77010	**800-427-4697**	713-853-8000	207
George R Peters Assoc Inc						
PO Box 850	Troy	MI	48099	**800-929-5972**	248-524-2211	248
George Risk Industries Inc						
802 S Elm St	Kimball	NE	69145	**800-523-1227***	308-235-4645	690
OTC: RSKIA ■ *Sales						
George S Coyne Chemical Co						
3015 State Rd	Croydon	PA	19021	**800-523-1230**	215-785-3000	145
George School						
1690 Newtown-Langhorne Rd	Newtown	PA	18940	**888-804-1300**	215-579-6547	621
George STREET Photo & Video LLC						
230 W Huron St Ste 3W	Chicago	IL	60654	**866-831-4103**		589
George T. Bagby State Park & Lodge						
330 Bagby Pkwy	Fort Gaines	GA	39851	**877-591-5575**	229-768-2571	564
George Uhe Company Inc						
219 River Dr	Garfield	NJ	07026	**800-850-4075**	201-843-4000	478
George Washington Masonic National Memorial						
101 Callahan Dr	Alexandria	VA	22301	**800-435-7352**	703-683-2007	49-3
George Washington University						
2121 'I' St NW	Washington	DC	20052	**866-498-3382**	202-994-1000	167
Mount Vernon College						
2100 Foxhall Rd NW	Washington	DC	20007	**800-447-3765**	202-994-1000	167
George Washington University Hospital						
900 23rd St NW	Washington	DC	20037	**888-449-3627**	202-715-4000	374-3
George Washington University Inn						
824 New Hampshire Ave NW	Washington	DC	20037	**800-424-9671**	202-337-6620	379
George Washington University School of Medicine & Health Sciences						
2300 'I' St NW Ross Hall 716	Washington	DC	20037	**866-846-1107**	202-994-3506	168-2
George Weston Ltd						
22 St Clair Ave E	Toronto	ON	M4T2S7	**800-564-6253**	416-922-2500	360-3
TSE: WN						
Georgeson Securities Corp						
480 Washington Blvd 27th Fl	Jersey City	NJ	07310	**800-428-0717**		688
Georgetown College						
400 E College St	Georgetown	KY	40324	**800-788-9985***	502-863-8000	167
*Admissions						
Georgetown Convention & Visitors Bureau						
1101 N College St	Georgetown	TX	78626	**800-436-8696**	512-930-3545	208
Georgetown County Chamber of Commerce						
531 Front St	Georgetown	SC	29440	**800-777-7705**	843-546-8436	138
Georgetown Inn						
1310 Wisconsin Ave	Washington	DC	20007	**866-971-6618**	202-333-8900	379
Georgetown Railroad Co						
5300 S IH-35 PO Box 529	Georgetown	TX	78626	**888-456-6777**	512-863-2538	646
Georgetown Times						
615 Front St	Georgetown	SC	29440	**800-772-1213**	843-546-4148	531-4
Georgetown University Hotel & Conference Ctr						
3800 Reservoir Rd NW	Washington	DC	20057	**888-902-1606**	202-687-3200	377
Georgia						
Arts Council						
260 14th St NW Ste 401	Atlanta	GA	30318	**800-222-6006**	404-685-2400	339-11
Corrections Dept						
300 Patrol Rd Forsyth	Atlanta	GA	31029	**888-343-5627**	404-656-4661	339-11
Emergency Management Agency (GEMA)						
935 E Confederate Ave SE						
PO Box 18055	Atlanta	GA	30316	**800-879-4362**	404-635-7000	339-11
Environmental Protection Div						
2 Martin Luther King Jr Dr						
Ste 1152 E Tower	Atlanta	GA	30334	**888-373-5947**	404-657-5947	339-11
Governor's Office of Consumer Protection						
2 ML King Jr Dr Ste 356	Atlanta	GA	30334	**800-869-1123**		339-11
Securities & Business Regulation Div						
2 Martin Luther King Jr Dr						
W Tower Ste 802	Atlanta	GA	30334	**844-753-7825**	478-207-2440	339-11
State Government Information						
7 Martin Luther King JrDr						
Ste 643	Atlanta	GA	30303	**800-436-7442**	678-436-7442	339-11
Tourism Div						
75 Fifth St NW Ste 1200	Atlanta	GA	30308	**800-255-0056***	404-962-4000	339-11
*Resv						
Georgia Assn of Realtors						
3200 Presidential Dr	Atlanta	GA	30340	**866-280-0576**	770-451-1831	654
Georgia Bar Journal						
104 Marietta St NW Ste 100	Atlanta	GA	30303	**866-773-2782**	404-527-8700	456-15
Georgia Boot Inc						
39 E Canal St	Nelsonville	OH	45764	**877-795-2410**	740-753-1951	302
Georgia Cancer Specialists Pc (GCS)						
1872 Montreal Rd	Tucker	GA	30084	**800-491-5991**	770-496-9443	374-7
Georgia Chamber of Commerce						
233 Peachtree St NE Ste 2000	Atlanta	GA	30303	**800-241-2286**	404-223-2264	139
Georgia College & State University						
231 W Hancock St CB 23	Milledgeville	GA	31061	**800-342-0471**	478-445-5004	167
Macon 433 Cherry St	Macon	GA	31206	**800-342-0471**	478-752-4278	167
Georgia Correctional Industries						
2984 Clifton Springs Rd	Decatur	GA	30034	**800-282-7130**	404-244-5100	629
Georgia Crown Distributing Co						
100 Georgia Crown Dr	McDonough	GA	30253	**800-342-2350**	770-302-3000	80-3
Georgia Cu Affiliates						
6705 Sugarloaf Pkwy Ste 200	Duluth	GA	30097	**800-768-4282**	770-476-9625	221
Georgia Dental Assn						
7000 Peachtree Dnwdy Rd NE						
Ste 200 Bldg 17	Atlanta	GA	30328	**800-432-4357**	404-636-7553	229
Georgia Dome						
1 Georgia Dome Dr NW	Atlanta	GA	30313	**888-333-4406**	404-223-9200	718
Georgia Farm Bureau News						
1620 Bass Rd	Macon	GA	31210	**800-342-1192**	478-474-8411	456-1
Georgia Hardy Tours						
20 Eglinton Ave East	Toronto	ON	M4R1K8	**800-813-4509**	416-483-7533	770
Georgia Highlands College						
Cartersville						
5441 Hwy 20 NE	Cartersville	GA	30121	**800-332-2406**	678-872-8000	161
Floyd 3175 Cedartown Hwy	Rome	GA	30161	**800-332-2406**	706-802-5000	161
Georgia Institute of Technology Library						
225 N Ave NW	Atlanta	GA	30332	**888-225-7804**	404-894-4500	434-6
Georgia International Convention Ctr						
2000 Convention Ctr Concourse	College Park	GA	30337	**888-331-4422**	770-997-3566	207
Georgia Lottery Corp						
250 Williams St NW Ste 3000	Atlanta	GA	30303	**800-425-8259**	404-215-5000	451
Georgia Military College						
201 E Green St	Milledgeville	GA	31061	**800-342-0413**	478-387-4900	161
Georgia Municipal Association						
201 Pryor St SW	Atlanta	GA	30303	**888-488-4462**	404-688-0472	532
Georgia Northwestern Technical College Foundation Inc						
1 Maurice Culberson Dr Sw	Rome	GA	30161	**866-983-4682**	706-295-6842	306
Georgia Nurses Assn (GNA)						
3032 Briarcliff Rd NE	Atlanta	GA	30329	**800-324-0462**	404-325-5536	532
Georgia Pharmacy Assn (GPhA)						
50 Lenox Pointe NE	Atlanta	GA	30324	**888-871-5590**	404-231-5074	584
Georgia Ports Authority						
PO Box 2406	Savannah	GA	31402	**800-342-8012**	912-964-3811	617
Georgia Power Co						
241 Ralph McGill Blvd NE	Atlanta	GA	30308	**866-506-5333***	404-506-5000	785
*Cust Svc						
Georgia Printco						
90 S Oak St	Lakeland	GA	31635	**866-572-0146**		626
Georgia Public Broadcasting (GPB)						
260 14th St NW	Atlanta	GA	30318	**800-222-6006**		629
Georgia Public Library						
1800 Century Pl NE Ste 150	Atlanta	GA	30345	**800-248-6701**	404-235-7200	31
Georgia Regional Hospital at Savannah						
1915 Eisenhower Dr	Savannah	GA	31406	**800-436-7442**	912-356-2011	374-5
Georgia Society of Cpa's						
3353 Peachtree Rd NE Ste 400	Alpharetta	GA	30326	**800-330-8889**	404-231-8676	136
Georgia Southwestern State University						
800 Gsw State University Dr	Americus	GA	31709	**800-338-0082***	229-928-1273	167
*Admissions						
Georgia Student Finance Commission						
2082 E Exchange Pl Ste 200	Tucker	GA	30084	**800-505-4732**	770-724-9000	723
Georgia Transparency & Campaign Finance Commission						
200 Piedmont Ave SE Ste 1402	Atlanta	GA	30334	**866-589-7327**	404-463-1980	267
Georgia Veterinary Medical Assn						
233 Peachtree St NE Ste 2205	Atlanta	GA	30303	**800-853-1625**	678-309-9800	793
Georgia's Own Credit Union						
1155 Peachtree St NE Ste 400	Atlanta	GA	30309	**800-533-2062**	404-874-1166	221
Georgian Court Hotel						
773 Beatty St	Vancouver	BC	V6B2M4	**800-663-1155**	604-682-5555	379
Georgian Court University						
900 Lakewood Ave	Lakewood	NJ	08701	**800-458-8422**		167
Georgian Hotel						
1415 Ocean Ave	Santa Monica	CA	90401	**800-538-8147**	310-395-9945	379
Georgian Plantation Shutter Co						
455 Wilbanks Dr	Ball Ground	GA	30107	**888-684-0382**	678-454-1100	361
Georgian Resort						
384 Canada St	Lake George	NY	12845	**800-525-3436**	518-668-5401	379
Georgian Terrace Hotel						
659 Peachtree St NE	Atlanta	GA	30308	**800-651-2316**	404-897-1991	379
Georgian, The						
411 University St	Seattle	WA	98101	**888-363-5022**	206-621-7889	669
Georgie's Ceramic & Clay Company Inc						
756 NE Lombard St	Portland	OR	97211	**800-999-2529**	503-283-1353	42
Geoscape International Inc						
2100 W Flagler St	Miami	FL	33135	**888-211-9353**		182
GEOSPAN Corp						
10900 73rd Ave N Ste 136	Minneapolis	MN	55369	**800-436-7726**	763-493-9320	227
GeoSyntec Consultants Inc						
5901 Broken Sound Pkwy NW						
Ste 300	Boca Raton	FL	33487	**866-676-1101**	561-995-0900	263
Geotab Inc						
1081 S Service Rd W	Oakville	ON	L6L6K3	**877-436-8221**	416-434-4309	387
Geotech Environmental Equipment Inc						
2650 E 40th Ave	Denver	CO	80205	**800-833-7958**	303-320-4764	203
Geotek Engineering & Testing Services Inc						
909 E 50th St N	Sioux Falls	SD	57104	**800-354-5512**	605-335-5512	258
GeoTrust Inc						
350 Ellis St Bldg J	Mountain View	CA	94043	**866-511-4141**	650-426-5010	180-7
Gerald H Phipps						
5995 Greenwood Florida Plaza Blvd						
Ste 100	Greenwood Village	CO	80111	**866-487-2365**	303-571-5377	188
Gerald R Ford Conservation Ctr						
1326 S 32nd St	Omaha	NE	68105	**800-634-6932**	402-595-1180	49-1
Gerald R Ford International Airport						
5500 44th St SE	Grand Rapids	MI	49512	**866-289-9673**	616-233-6000	27
Gerald R Ford Museum						
303 Pearl St NW	Grand Rapids	MI	49504	**800-888-9487**	616-254-0400	519
Gerard Daniel Worldwide						
34 Barnhart Dr	Hanover	PA	17331	**800-232-3332**	717-637-5901	686
Gerber Auto Collision & Glass Centers Inc						
8250 Skokie Blvd	Skokie	IL	60077	**877-743-7237**	847-679-0510	61-4
Gerber Childrenswear Inc						
7005 Pelham Rd Ste D	Greenville	SC	29602	**800-642-4452**	864-987-5200	154-4
Gerber Collision & Glass						
44700 Enterprise Dr	Clinton Township	MI	48038	**877-743-7237***	586-954-3850	61-4
*General						
Gerber Life Insurance Co						
1311 Mamaroneck Ave	White Plains	NY	10605	**800-704-2180**	914-272-4000	391-2
Gerber Plumbing Fixtures LLC						
2500 International Pkwy	Woodridge	IL	60517	**888-648-6466**		610
Gerber Products Co						
445 State St	Fremont	MI	49412	**800-284-9488**		297-36
Gerber Technology Inc						
24 Industrial Pk Rd W	Tolland	CT	06084	**800-826-3243**	860-871-8082	741
Gerber Tours Inc						
100 Crossways Park Dr W						
Ste 400	Woodbury	NY	11797	**800-645-9145**	516-826-5000	758
Gerdau AmeriSteel Corp						
4221 W Boy Scout Blvd Ste 600	Tampa	FL	33607	**800-876-7833***	813-286-8383	721
*Sales						
Gerhart Systems & Controls Corp						
754 Roble Rd Ste 140	Allentown	PA	18109	**888-437-4278**	610-264-2800	636
Gerloff Company Inc						
14955 Bulverde Rd	San Antonio	TX	78247	**800-486-3621**	210-490-2777	188

Name	Address	City	State	Zip	Toll-Free	Phone	Class
German American Bancorp	711 Main St *NASDAQ: GABC*	Jasper	IN	47546	**800-482-1314**	812-482-1314	360-2
German Marshall Fund of the United States	1744 R St NW	Washington	DC	20009	**800-276-5680**	202-745-3950	782
German-American National Congress (DANK)	4740 N Western Ave Ste 206	Chicago	IL	60625	**888-872-3265**	773-275-1100	47-14
GermanDeli.com	601 Westport Pkwy, Ste 100	Grapevine	TX	76051	**877-437-6269**	817-410-9955	345
Germania Farm Mutual Insurance Assn	507 Hwy 290 E	Brenham	TX	77833	**800-392-2202**	979-836-5224	391-4
Germany *Consulate General*	285 Peachtree Ctr Ave NE Ste 901	Atlanta	GA	30303	**866-687-8561**	404-659-4760	259
Germiphene Corp	1379 Colborne St E PO Box 1748	Brantford	ON	N3T5M1	**800-265-9931**	519-759-7100	582
Gerontological Society of America, The	1220 L St NW Ste 901	Washington	DC	20005	**800-677-1116**	202-842-1275	48-8
Gerrity Baker Williams Inc	3 Goldmine Rd	Flanders	NJ	07836	**800-548-2329**	973-426-1500	390
Gerry Cosby & Company Inc	11 Pennsylvania Plz	New York	NY	10001	**877-563-6464**	212-563-6464	709
Gershman, Brickner & Bratton Inc	8550 Arlington Blvd Ste 304	Fairfax	VA	22031	**800-573-5801**	703-573-5800	194
Gerson Co	1450 S Lone Elm Rd	Olathe	KS	66061	**800-444-8172**	913-262-7400	411
Gertrude Hawk Chocolates Inc	9 Keystone Pk	Dunmore	PA	18512	**866-932-4295**	800-822-2032	297-8
GES (Grangeville Environmental Services) *GES Property Pros LLC*	585 McAllister St	Hanover	PA	17331	**866-437-5151**	717-637-6152	83
GES Exposition Services	7000 Lindell Rd	Las Vegas	NV	89118	**800-443-9767**	702-515-5500	186
GES Global Energy Services Inc	3220 Cypress Creek Pkwy	Houston	TX	77068	**888-523-6797**		192
Gesa Credit Union	51 Gage Blvd PO Box 500	Richland	WA	99352	**888-946-4372**	509-946-1611	221
Gessner Products Company Inc	241 N Main St	Ambler	PA	19002	**800-874-7808**	215-646-7667	607
GET Engineering Corp	9350 Bond Ave	El Cajon	CA	92021	**877-494-1820**	619-443-8295	205
Get Noticed Promotions Inc	152 Sonwil Dr	Buffalo	NY	14225	**877-296-7179**	716-688-8152	128
Getconnect	14114 Dallas Pkwy Ste 430	Dallas	TX	75254	**888-200-1831**		366
Gettysburg College	300 N Washington St	Gettysburg	PA	17325	**800-431-0803**	717-337-6000	167
Gettysburg Convention & Visitors Bureau	571 W Middle St	Gettysburg	PA	17325	**800-337-5015**	717-334-6274	208
Gettysburg Hotel	1 Lincoln Sq Best Western Gettysburg Hotel	Gettysburg	PA	17325	**866-378-1797**	717-337-2000	669
Gettysburg-Adams County Area Chamber of Commerce	18 Carlisle St Ste 203	Gettysburg	PA	17325	**800-699-1176**	717-334-8151	138
Getzen Company Inc	530 S Cty Hwy H PO Box 440	Elkhorn	WI	53121	**800-366-5584**	262-723-4221	526
GF Health Products Inc	2935 NE Pkwy	Atlanta	GA	30360	**800-347-5678**	770-447-1609	476
GF Machining Solutions	560 Bond St	Lincolnshire	IL	60069	**800-282-1336**	847-913-5300	454
GFC Leasing Co	2675 Research Pk Dr	Madison	WI	53711	**800-333-5905**	800-677-7877	266-2
GfG Instrumentation Inc	1194 Oak Vly Dr Ste 20	Ann Arbor	MI	48108	**800-959-0329**	734-769-0573	203
GFI Genfare	751 Pratt Blvd	Elk Grove Village	IL	60007	**877-247-3797**	847-593-8855	471
GFI Group Inc	55 Water St *NYSE: GFIG*	New York	NY	10041	**888-750-5884**	212-968-4100	171
GFWC (General Federation of Women's Clubs)	1734 N St NW	Washington	DC	20036	**800-443-4392**	202-347-3168	47-24
GGB North America	700 Mid Atlantic Pkwy PO Box 189	Thorofare	NJ	08086	**888-840-2349**	856-848-3200	619
GGS Technical Publications Services	3265 Farmtrail Rd	York	PA	17406	**800-927-4474**	717-764-2222	779
Ghafari Assoc Inc	17101 Michigan Ave	Dearborn	MI	48126	**800-289-7822**	313-441-3000	263
Gheens Science Hall & Rauch Planetarium	Rauch Planetarium University of Louisville	Louisville	KY	40292	**800-996-7566**	502-852-6664	597
Ghent Manufacturing Inc	2999 Henkle Dr	Lebanon	OH	45036	**800-543-0550**	513-932-3445	245
GHG Corp	960 Clear Lk City Blvd	Webster	TX	77598	**866-380-4146**	281-488-8806	180-10
Ghirardelli Chocolate Co	1111 139th Ave	San Leandro	CA	94578	**800-877-9338**		297-8
Ghost Armor LLC	1470 N Horne St	Gilbert	AZ	85233	**888-960-2766**	480-921-3161	789
GHS (Greenville Hospital System)	701 Grove Rd	Greenville	SC	29605	**877-447-4636**	864-455-8976	353
GHS Corp	2813 Wilber Ave	Battle Creek	MI	49037	**800-388-4447**		526
GHS Interactive Security Inc	2081 Arena Blvd Ste 260	Sacramento	CA	95834	**855-208-2447**		691
GHX (Global Health Care Exchange LLC)	1315 W Century Dr	Louisville	CO	80027	**800-968-7449**	720-887-7000	227
GIA (Gemological Institute of America)	5345 Armada Dr	Carlsbad	CA	92008	**800-421-7250**	760-603-4000	48-4
Giant Eagle Inc	101 Kappa Dr *Cust Svc	Pittsburgh	PA	15238	**800-553-2324***	412-963-6200	345
Giant Food Inc	8301 Professional Pl Ste 115	Landover	MD	20785	**888-469-4426**		345
Giant Food Stores Inc	1149 Harrisburg Pike	Carlisle	PA	17013	**888-814-4268**	717-249-4000	345
Giant Resource Recovery Company Inc	654 Judge St PO Box 352	Harleyville	SC	29488	**800-637-4023**	803-496-2200	194
Giant Springs State Park	4600 Giant Springs Rd	Great Falls	MT	59405	**855-922-6768**	406-454-5840	564
Giantbank.com	6300 NE First Ave	Fort Lauderdale	FL	33334	**877-446-4200**	954-958-0001	69
Gibbs & Assoc	323 Science Dr *Cust Svc	Moorpark	CA	93021	**800-654-9399***	805-523-0004	180-5
Gibbs Wire & Steel Company Inc	Metals Dr PO Box 520	Southington	CT	06489	**800-800-4422**	860-621-0121	491
Gibraltar Industries Inc	3556 Lakeshore Rd *NASDAQ: ROCK*	Buffalo	NY	14219	**800-247-8368**	716-826-6500	721
Gibraltar Steel Furniture Inc	9976 Westwanda Dr	Beverly Hills	CA	90210	**800-416-3635**	310-276-8889	322
Gibson & Barnes	1900 Weld Blvd Ste 140 *Sales	El Cajon	CA	92020	**800-748-6693***	619-440-6977	154-18
Gibson Arnold & Assoc	5433 Westheimer Rd Ste 1016	Houston	TX	77056	**800-879-2007**	713-572-3000	719
Gibson Dunn & Crutcher LLP	333 S Grand Ave Ste 4600	Los Angeles	CA	90071	**888-203-1112**	213-229-7000	428
Gibson Guitar Corp	309 Plus Pk Blvd	Nashville	TN	37217	**800-444-2766**	615-871-4500	526
Gibson Laboratories Inc	1040 Manchester St	Lexington	KY	40508	**800-477-4763**	859-254-9500	233
Gibson Piano Ventures Inc	309 Plus Pk Blvd	Nashville	TN	37217	**800-444-2766**	615-871-4500	526
Gideon Putnam Resort & Spa	24 Gideon Putnam Rd	Saratoga Springs	NY	12866	**800-452-7275**	518-584-3000	379
Giffin Koerth Inc	40 University Ave Ste 800	Toronto	ON	M5J1T1	**800-564-5313**	416-368-1700	258
Gift of Hope Organ & Tissue Donor Network	425 Spring Lake Dr	Itasca	IL	60143	**877-577-3747**	630-758-2600	544
Gift of Life Bone Marrow Foundation	800 Yamato Rd Ste 101	Boca Raton	FL	33431	**800-962-7769**	561-982-2900	47-17
Gift of Life Donor Program	401 N Third St	Philadelphia	PA	19123	**800-543-6391**	215-557-8090	544
Gift of Life Foundation	3861 Research Park Dr	Ann Arbor	MI	48108	**866-500-5801**	734-973-1577	294
Gift of Life Transplant House	705 Second St SW	Rochester	MN	55902	**800-479-7824**	507-288-7470	372
Gift Wrap Co	338 Industrial Blvd *General	Midway	GA	31320	**800-443-4429***		547
GiftCertificates.com	11510 Blondo St	Omaha	NE	68164	**800-773-7368**		328
Gifts for You LLC	2425 Curtiss St	Downers Grove	IL	60515	**866-443-8748**	630-771-0095	294
Giftware News	704 N Wells St	Chicago	IL	60654	**800-229-1967**	312-849-2220	456-21
Gigasonic	260 E Gish Rd	San Jose	CA	95112	**888-246-4442**	408-573-1400	525
Giga-Tronics Inc	4650 Norris Canyon Rd *NASDAQ: GIGA*	San Ramon	CA	94583	**800-726-4442**	925-328-4650	250
GigMasters.com Inc	33 S Main St	Norwalk	CT	06854	**866-342-9794**		387
Gil Tours Travel Inc	1511 Walnut St 2nd Fl	Philadelphia	PA	19102	**800-223-3855**	215-568-6655	769
Gila County	1400 E Ash St	Globe	AZ	85501	**800-304-4452**	928-425-3231	338
Gilbane Bldg Co	7 Jackson Walkway	Providence	RI	02903	**800-445-2263**	401-456-5800	190-7
Gilbane Bldg Co New England Regional Office	7 Jackson Walkway	Providence	RI	02903	**800-445-2263**	401-456-5800	188
Gilbane Bldg Company Mid-Atlantic Regional Office	7901 Sandy Spring Rd Ste 500	Laurel	MD	20707	**800-445-2263**	410-649-1750	188
Gilbane Bldg Company Southwest Regional Office	1331 Lamar St Ste 1170	Houston	TX	77010	**800-445-2263**	713-209-1873	188
Gilbane Inc	7 Jackson Walkway	Providence	RI	02903	**800-445-2263**	401-456-5890	651
Gilbert Displays Inc	110 Spagnoli Rd	Melville	NY	11747	**855-577-1100**	631-577-1100	234
Gilbert Industries Inc	5611 Krueger Dr	Jonesboro	AR	72401	**800-643-0400**	870-932-6070	576
Gilbreth Packaging Systems	3001 State Rd	Croydon	PA	19021	**800-630-2413**		413
Gilchrist Hospice Care	11311 McCormick Rd	Hunt Valley	MD	21031	**800-735-2258**	443-849-8200	371
Gilcrease Museum	1400 N Gilcrease Museum Rd	Tulsa	OK	74127	**888-655-2278**	918-596-2700	519
Gilead Sciences Inc	333 Lakeside Dr *NASDAQ: GILD*	Foster City	CA	94404	**800-445-3235**	650-574-3000	84
Giles & Ransome Inc Ransome Engine Power Div	2975 Galloway Rd	Bensalem	PA	19020	**877-726-7663**	215-639-4300	276
Giles Engineering Assoc Inc	N8 W22350 Johnson Dr	Waukesha	WI	53186	**800-782-0610**	262-544-0118	258
Gill Athletics Inc	2808 Gemini Ct *Cust Svc	Champaign	IL	61822	**800-637-3090***	217-367-8438	708
Gillespie County Fairgrounds	530 Fair Dr PO Box 526	Fredericksburg	TX	78624	**800-280-9531**	830-997-2359	639
Gillespie Graphics	27676 SW Pkwy Ave	Wilsonville	OR	97070	**800-547-6841**	503-682-1122	685
Gillespie Museum of Minerals	421 N Woodland Blvd Unit 8403	DeLand	FL	32723	**800-688-0101**	386-822-7330	519
Gillespie, Prudhon & Associates Inc	16111 Se 106th Ave Ste 100	Clackamas	OR	97015	**800-595-2145**	503-657-0424	263
Gillette Children's Specialty Healthcare	200 E University Ave	Saint Paul	MN	55101	**800-719-4040**	651-291-2848	374-1
Gillig Corp	25800 Clawiter Rd	Hayward	CA	94545	**800-735-1500**	510-785-1500	515
Gilligan & Ferneman LLC	1754 Business Ctr Ln	Kissimmee	FL	34758	**800-720-4152**		318
Gillman Cos	10595 W Sam Houston Pkwy S	Houston	TX	77099	**888-532-8956**	713-776-7000	56

Company / Address	City	State	ZIP	Toll-Free	Phone	Class
Gillmore Security Systems Inc 26165 Broadway Ave	Cleveland	OH	44146	**800-899-8995**	440-232-1000	691
Gilman & Pastor LLP 63 Atlantic Ave 3rd Fl	Boston	MA	02110	**877-428-7374**	617-742-9700	194
Gilman USA 1230 Cheyenne Ave PO Box 5	Grafton	WI	53024	**800-445-6267**	262-377-2434	492
Gilmore Entertainment Group 8901-A Business 17 N	Myrtle Beach	SC	29572	**800-843-6779**	843-913-4000	183
Gilmour Academy 34001 Cedar Rd	Gates Mills	OH	44040	**800-533-5140**	440-442-1104	621
Gilmour Mfg Group 2537 Daniels St Somerset *Cust Svc	Madison	WI	53718	**866-348-5661***		429
Gilroy Chevrolet Cadillac Inc 6720 Bear Cat Ct	Gilroy	CA	95020	**800-201-7241**	408-842-9301	56
Gilsbar Inc PO Box 998	Covington	LA	70434	**800-445-7227**	985-892-3520	461
Gina B Designs Inc 12700 Industrial Pk Blvd Ste 40	Plymouth	MN	55441	**800-228-4856**	763-559-7595	129
Ginger Cove 4000 River Crescent Dr	Annapolis	MD	21401	**800-299-2683**	410-266-7300	670
Gino Morena Enterprises LLC 111 Starlite St	South San Francisco	CA	94080	**800-227-6905**		76
Ginsberg's Foods Inc 29 Ginsberg Ln PO Box 17	Hudson	NY	12534	**800-999-6006**	518-828-4004	355
Giordano s Solid Waste Removal 110 N Mill Rd	Vineland	NJ	08360	**800-636-8625**	856-696-2068	658
Giorgio Foods Inc PO Box 96	Temple	PA	19560	**800-220-2139**	610-926-2139	297-20
Giovanni's Restaurant & Convention Ctr 610 N Bell School Rd	Rockford	IL	61107	**877-926-8300**	815-398-6411	669
Girl Scouts of the USA 420 Fifth Ave	New York	NY	10018	**800-478-7248**	212-852-8000	47-15
Girls Inc 120 Wall St 3rd Fl	New York	NY	10005	**800-374-4475**	212-509-2000	47-24
Girls' Life Acqusition Co 4529 Hartford Rd	Baltimore	MD	21214	**800-931-2237**	410-426-9600	456-6
Giroux Glass Inc 850 W Washington Blvd	Los Angeles	CA	90015	**800-684-5277**	213-747-7406	191-6
GISD (Garland Independent School District) 501 S Jupiter PO Box 469026	Garland	TX	75046	**800-252-5555**	972-494-8201	683
GISD (Galveston Independent School District) 3904 Ave PO Box 660	Galveston	TX	77550	**877-262-1492**	409-766-5100	683
Giselle's Travel Inc 1300 Ethan Way Ste 100	Sacramento	CA	95825	**800-782-5545**	916-922-5500	769
Gislason & Hunter LLP 2700 S Broadway	New Ulm	MN	56073	**800-469-0234**	507-354-3111	428
Gitman & Co 2309 Chestnut St	Ashland	PA	17921	**800-526-3929**	570-875-3100	154-11
Gitman Bros Shirt Company Inc 2309 Chestnut St 19th Fl *General	Ashland	PA	10019	**800-526-3929***	212-581-6968	154-11
GIW Industries Inc 5000 Wrightsboro Rd	Grovetown	GA	30813	**888-832-4449**	706-863-1011	638
GJDCCVB (Galena/Jo Daviess County Convention & Visitors Bureau) 101 Bouthillier St *General	Galena	IL	61036	**800-747-9377***	815-777-3557	208
GK Industries Ltd 50 Precidio Ct	Brampton	ON	L6S6E3	**800-463-8889**	905-799-1972	60
GKG (Global Knowledge Group Inc) 302 N Bryan Ave	Bryan	TX	77803	**866-776-7584**		806
G-L Veneer Co Inc 2224 E Slauson Ave	Huntington Park	CA	90255	**800-588-5003**	323-582-5203	612
Glacial Energy 2701 N Dallas Pkwy Ste 120	Plano	TX	75093	**877-569-2841**		194
Glacial Lakes Energy LLC 301 20th Ave SE PO Box 933	Watertown	SD	57201	**866-934-2676**	605-882-8480	578
Glacial Lakes State Park 25022 County Rd 41	Starbuck	MN	56381	**888-646-6367**	320-239-2860	564
Glacial Ridge Hospital Foundation Inc 10 Fourth Ave SE	Glenwood	MN	56334	**866-667-4747**	320-634-4521	374-3
Glacial Waters Spa at Grand View Lodge 23521 Nokomis Ave	Nisswa	MN	56468	**866-801-2951**	218-963-2234	705
Glacier Bancorp Inc PO Box 27 *NASDAQ: GBCI*	Kalispell	MT	59903	**800-735-4371**	406-756-4200	360-2
Glacier Clear Enterprises Inc 3291 Thomas St *Cust Svc	Innisfil	ON	L9S3W3	**800-668-5118***	705-436-6363	803
Glacier Electric Co-op Inc 410 E Main St	Cut Bank	MT	59427	**800-347-6795**	406-873-5566	247
Glacier National Park PO Box 350	Revelstoke	BC	V0E2S0	**866-787-6221**	250-837-7500	562
Glacier Water Services Inc 1385 Pk Ctr Dr *OTC: GWSV*	Vista	CA	92081	**800-452-2437**	760-560-1111	54
Glade & Grove Supply Inc 305 CR 17 W PO Box 760	Avon Park	FL	33826	**800-433-4451**	561-996-3095	276
Glade Springs Resort 255 Resort Dr	Daniels	WV	25832	**866-562-8054**		667
Gladstone Dodge 5610 N Oak Trafficway	Gladstone	MO	64118	**866-695-2043**		56
Gladstone School District 115 17789 Webster Rd	Gladstone	OR	97027	**800-328-0272**	503-655-2777	683
Glamos Wire Products Company Inc 5561 N 152nd St	Hugo	MN	55038	**800-328-5062**	651-429-5386	72
Glance Networks Inc 1167 Massachusetts Ave	Arlington	MA	02476	**877-452-6236**	781-646-8505	227
Glancy Prongay & Murray LLP 1801 Ave Of The Stars	Los Angeles	CA	90067	**888-773-9224**	310-201-9150	428
Glasgow Inc 104 Willow Grove Ave	Glenside	PA	19038	**877-222-5514**	215-884-8800	190-4
Glasgow-Barren County Chamber of Commerce 118 E Public Sq	Glasgow	KY	42141	**800-264-3161**	270-651-3161	138
Glass Art Society (GAS) 6512 23rd Ave NW Ste 329	Seattle	WA	98121	**800-636-2377**	206-382-1305	47-4
Glass Assn of North America (GANA) 800 SW Jackson St Ste 1500	Topeka	KS	66612	**877-275-2421**	785-271-0208	48-13
Glass House Inn 3202 W 26th St	Erie	PA	16506	**800-956-7222**	814-833-7751	379
Glass Molders Pottery Plastics & Allied Workers International Union 608 E Baltimore Pike	Media	PA	19063	**855-670-4787**	610-565-5051	414
GlassCraft Door Co 2002 Brittmoore Rd	Houston	TX	77043	**800-766-2196**	713-690-8282	236
Glassmere Fuel Service Inc 1967 Saxonburg Blvd	Tarentum	PA	15084	**800-235-9054**	724-265-4646	317
Glasteel-stabilit America Inc 285 Industrial Dr	Moscow	TN	38057	**800-238-5546**	901-877-3010	607
Glastender Inc 5400 N Michigan Rd	Saginaw	MI	48604	**800-748-0423**	989-752-4275	386
Glastic Corp 4321 Glenridge Rd	Cleveland	OH	44121	**800-360-1319**	216-486-0100	605
Glastonbury Citizen Inc PO Box 373	Glastonbury	CT	06033	**860-537-1772**	860-633-4691	634-8
Glastonbury Southern Gage 46 Industrial Pk Rd	Erin	TN	37061	**800-251-4243**	931-289-4243	492
Glauber Equipment Corp 1600 Commerce Pkwy	Lancaster	NY	14086	**888-452-8237**	716-681-1234	358
Glaucoma Research Foundation 251 Post St Ste 600	San Francisco	CA	94108	**800-826-6693**	415-986-3162	47-17
Glaval Bus 914 County Rd 1	Elkhart	IN	46514	**800-445-2825**	574-262-2212	58
GlaxoSmithKline Inc 7333 Mississauga Rd N	Mississauga	ON	L5N6L4	**800-387-7374**	905-819-3000	582
Glazer's Wholesale Drug Company Inc 14911 Quorum Dr Ste 400	Dallas	TX	75254	**800-275-2854**	972-392-8200	80-3
Glaz-Tech Industries Inc 2207 E Elvira Rd	Tucson	AZ	85756	**800-755-8062**	520-629-0268	330
GLC (God's Learning Ch) PO Box 61000	Midland	TX	79711	**800-707-0420**	432-563-0420	736
GLE Associates Inc 5405 Cypress Center Dr Ste 110	Tampa	FL	33609	**888-453-4531**	813-241-8350	194
Gleason Corp 1000 University Ave	Rochester	NY	14607	**800-727-6333**	585-473-1000	454
Gleason M & M Precision Systems Corp 300 Progress Rd	Dayton	OH	45449	**800-727-6333**	937-859-8273	250
Gleason Reel Corp 600 S Clark St	Mayville	WI	53050	**888-504-5151**	920-387-4120	116
Glen Cove Mansion Hotel & Conference Ctr 200 Dosoris Ln	Glen Cove	NY	11542	**877-782-9426**	516-671-6400	377
Glen Eden Corp 25999 Glen Eden Rd	Corona	CA	92883	**800-843-6833**	951-277-4650	120
Glen Ellyn Chamber of Commerce 800 Roosevelt Rd Bldg D Ste 108	Glen Ellyn	IL	60137	**800-622-9000**	630-469-0907	138
Glen Grove Suites 2837 Yonge St	Toronto	ON	M4N2J6	**800-565-3024**	416-489-8441	379
Glen Meadows 11630 Glen Arm Rd	Glen Arm	MD	21057	**800-630-4689**		670
Glen Mills Schools PO Box 5001	Concordville	PA	19331	**800-441-2064**	610-459-8100	622
Glen Oaks Community College 62249 Shimmel Rd	Centreville	MI	49032	**888-994-7818**	269-467-9945	161
Glen Research Corp 22825 Davis Dr	Sterling	VA	20164	**800-327-4536**	703-437-6191	666
Glenair Inc 1211 Air Way	Glendale	CA	91201	**888-465-4094**	818-247-6000	813
Glenbeigh Health Source 2863 SR 45	Rock Creek	OH	44084	**800-234-1001**	440-563-3400	724
Glencoe/McGraw-Hill 8787 Orion Pl	Columbus	OH	43240	**800-848-1567**		634-2
Glencrest Farm 1576 Moores Mill Rd PO Box 4468	Midway	KY	40347	**800-903-0136**	859-233-7032	368
Glendale Community College 1500 N Verdugo Rd	Glendale	CA	91208	**866-251-1977**	818-240-1000	161
Glendinning Marine Products 740 Century Cir	Conway	SC	29526	**800-500-2380**	843-399-6146	205
Glendora Chamber of Commerce 131 E Foothill Blvd	Glendora	CA	91741	**800-926-4478**	626-963-4128	138
Glendora Highlander Press 1210 N Azusa Canyon Rd	West Covina	CA	91790	**800-788-1200**	626-962-8811	531-4
Glendora Public Library & Cultural Ctr 140 S Glendora Ave	Glendora	CA	91741	**866-275-3772**	626-852-4891	434-3
Glendorn 1000 Glendorn Dr	Bradford	PA	16701	**800-843-8568**	814-362-6511	379
Gleneden Beach State Recreation Site 198 NE 123rd St	Newport	OR	97365	**800-551-6949**		564
Glenerin Inn, The 1695 The Collegeway	Mississauga	ON	L5L3S7	**877-991-9971**	905-828-6103	379
Glenmede Funds 1650 Market St Ste 1200	Philadelphia	PA	19103	**800-966-3200**	215-419-6000	527
Glenmore Inn 2720 Glenmore Trl SE	Calgary	AB	T2C2E6	**800-661-3163**	403-279-8611	379
Glenn O Hawbaker Inc 1952 Waddle Rd Ste 203	State College	PA	16803	**800-221-1355**	814-237-1444	45
GlenOaks Hospital 701 Winthrop Ave	Glendale Heights	IL	60139	**866-751-7127**	630-545-8000	374-3
Glenro Inc 39 McBride Ave	Paterson	NJ	07501	**888-453-6761**	973-279-5900	319
Glenrock International Inc 985 E Linden Ave	Linden	NJ	07036	**800-453-6762**	908-862-3433	722
Glens Falls Hospital 100 Pk St	Glens Falls	NY	12801	**800-994-6610**	518-926-1000	374-3
Glensheen Mansion 3300 London Rd	Duluth	MN	55804	**888-454-4536**	218-726-8910	49-2
Glentek Inc 208 Standard St	El Segundo	CA	90245	**877-470-6742**	310-322-3026	517
Glenville State College 200 High St *Admissions	Glenville	WV	26351	**800-924-2010***	304-462-7361	167
Glenwood LLC 111 Cedar Ln	Englewood	NJ	07631	**800-542-0772**	201-569-0050	583
Glenwood State Bank 5 E Minnesota Ave PO Box 197	Glenwood	MN	56334	**800-207-7333**	320-634-5111	69
Glessner House Museum 1800 S Prairie Ave	Chicago	IL	60616	**800-657-0687**	312-326-1480	519

Name / Address	City	State	ZIP	Toll-Free	Phone	Class
Glidden House 1901 Ford Dr	Cleveland	OH	44106	866-812-4537	216-231-8900	379
Glidewell Laboratories Inc 4141 MacArthur Blvd	Newport Beach	CA	92660	800-854-7256		740
Glimmerglass Festival 7300 State Hwy 80 PO Box 191	Cooperstown	NY	13326	866-568-2388	607-547-0700	572-2
Glimmerglass Networks Inc 26142 Eden Landing Rd	Hayward	CA	94545	877-723-1900	510-723-1900	180-10
Glines & Rhodes Inc 189 E St	Attleboro	MA	02703	800-343-1196	508-226-2000	484
GLK Foods LLC 11 Clark St	Shortsville	NY	14548	855-572-8800		297-19
GLM Industries LP 1508 - Eighth St	Nisku	AB	T9E7S6	800-661-9828	780-955-2233	479
Global Air Response 5919 Approach Rd	Sarasota	FL	34238	800-631-6565		30
Global Business Travel Assn, The (GBTA) 123 N Pitt St	Alexandria	VA	22314	888-574-6447	703-684-0836	47-23
Global Cash Card 7 Corporate Park Ste 130	Irvine	CA	92606	888-220-4477	949-751-0360	401
Global Computer Supplies Inc 11 Harbor Pk Dr	Port Washington	NY	11050	800-446-9662	888-278-4437	176
Global Consultants Inc 25 Airport Rd	Morristown	NJ	07960	877-264-6424	973-889-5200	182
Global Electronic Music Marketplace PO Box 4062	Palm Springs	CA	92263	800-207-4366		524
Global Elite Group 825 E Gate Blvd Ste 301	Garden City	NY	11530	877-425-0999	516-414-0487	691
Global Equipment Marketing Inc PO Box 810483	Boca Raton	FL	33481	866-750-8662	561-750-8662	358
Global Exchange 2017 Mission St Ste 303	San Francisco	CA	94110	800-497-1994	415-255-7296	47-7
Global Filtration Inc 9207 Emmott St	Houston	TX	77040	888-717-0888	713-856-9800	56
Global Ground Support LLC 540 Old Hwy 56	Olathe	KS	66061	888-780-0303	913-780-0300	22
Global Health Care Exchange LLC (GHX) 1315 W Century Dr	Louisville	CO	80027	800-968-7449	720-887-7000	227
Global Help Desk Services Inc 2080 Silas Deane Hwy	Rocky Hill	CT	06067	800-770-1075		182
Global HR Research LLC 24201 Walden Ctr Dr Ste 206	Bonita Springs	FL	34134	800-790-1205	239-274-0048	262
Global Imaging Systems Inc 3820 Northdale Blvd Ste 200A	Tampa	FL	33624	888-628-7834	813-960-5508	111
Global Industries Inc 17 W Stow Rd	Marlton	NJ	08053	800-220-1900	856-596-3390	320-1
Global Knowledge Group Inc (GKG) 302 N Bryan Ave	Bryan	TX	77803	866-776-7584		806
Global Knowledge Training LLC 9000 Regency Pkwy Ste 500	Cary	NC	27518	800-268-7737	919-461-8600	762
Global Market Perspective PO Box 1618	Gainesville	GA	30503	800-336-1618	770-536-0309	530-9
Global Maxfin Investments Inc 100 Mural St Ste 201	Richmond Hill	ON	L4B1J3	866-666-5266	416-741-1544	688
Global Medical Imaging LLC 222 Rampart St	Charlotte	NC	28203	800-958-9986		474
Global Medical LLC 8332 Bristol Ct Ste 108	Jessup	MD	20794	800-528-1001		474
Global Nest LLC 281 State Rt 79 N Ste 208	Morganville	NJ	07751	866-850-5872	732-333-5848	179
Global Neuro-Diagnostics LP 2670 Firewheel Dr Ste B	Flower Mound	TX	75028	866-848-2522		418
Global Pacific Financial Services Ltd 10430 144 St	Surrey	BC	V3T4V5	800-561-1177		318
Global Partners LP 800 S St Ste 200 *NYSE: GLP*	Waltham	MA	02454	800-685-7222	781-894-8800	578
Global Payments Inc 10 Glenlake Pkwy N Twr *NYSE: GPN*	Atlanta	GA	30328	800-560-2960	770-829-8000	257
Global Power Report 2 Penn Plz 25th Fl	New York	NY	10121	800-752-8878		530-5
Global R&D Consulting Group 3200 Autoroute Laval Ouest	Laval	GA	30022	866-770-5577		393
Global Reach Internet Productions LLC 2321 N Loop Dr Ste 101	Ames	IA	50010	877-254-9828	515-996-0996	179
Global Relay Communications Inc 220 cambie St	Vancouver	BC	V6B2M9	866-484-6630	604-484-6630	226
Global Search Network Inc 118 S Fremont Ave	Tampa	FL	33606	800-254-3398	813-832-8300	195
Global Shop Solutions Inc 975 Evergreen Cir *Sales	The Woodlands	TX	77380	800-364-5958*	281-681-1959	180-1
Global Software Inc 3201 Beechleaf Ct Ste 170	Raleigh	NC	27604	800-326-3444	919-872-7800	180-1
Global Solar Energy Inc 8500 S Rita Rd	Tucson	AZ	85747	866-999-8422	520-546-6313	694
Global Technology Resources Inc 990 S Bdwy Ste 300	Denver	CO	80209	877-603-1984	303-455-8800	182
Global Travel 900 W Jefferson St	Boise	ID	83702	800-584-8888	208-387-1000	769
Global Travel International 2600 Lk Lucien Dr Ste 201	Maitland	FL	32751	800-715-4440	407-660-7800	770
Global University 1211 S Glenstone Ave	Springfield	MO	65804	800-443-1083	417-862-9533	764
GlobalDie 1130 Minot Ave PO Box 1120	Auburn	ME	04211	800-910-3747	207-514-7252	755
Globalspec Inc 350 Jordan Rd	Troy	NY	12180	800-261-2052	518-880-0200	182
Globalstar LP 3200 Zanker Rd Bldg 260	San Jose	CA	95134	877-728-7466	408-933-4000	679
Globe Consultants Inc 3112 Porter St Ste D	Soquel	CA	95073	800-208-0663		195
Globe Electronic Hardware Inc 34-24 56th St	Woodside	NY	11377	800-221-1505	718-457-0303	205
Globe Food Equipment Co 2153 Dryden Rd	Dayton	OH	45439	800-347-5423	937-299-5493	299
Globe Mfg Co 37 Loudon Rd	Pittsfield	NH	03263	800-232-8323	603-435-8323	575
Globe Motors Inc 2275 Stanley Ave	Dayton	OH	45404	800-433-5700	937-228-3171	56
Globe Ticket & Label Co 11 Eisenhower Ln S	Lombard	IL	60148	800-523-5968		626
Globecomm Systems Inc 45 Oser Ave *NASDAQ: GCOM*	Hauppauge	NY	11788	866-499-0223	631-231-9800	645
Globe-Gazette 300 N Washington St PO Box 271	Mason City	IA	50402	800-421-0546	641-421-0500	531-2
Globex Corp 3620 Stutz Dr	Canfield	OH	44406	800-533-8610	330-533-0030	258
Globus 5301 S Federal Cir	Littleton	CO	80123	866-755-8581		758
Glo-Quartz Electric Heater Company Inc 7084 Maple St *Sales	Mentor	OH	44060	800-321-3574*	440-255-9701	319
Glorietta Bay Inn 1630 Glorietta Blvd	Coronado	CA	92118	800-283-9383	619-435-3101	379
Glorybee Foods Inc 120 N Seneca Rd	Eugene	OR	97402	800-456-7923	541-689-0913	297-24
Glover Sales Group LLC 221 Cockeysville Rd	Cockeysville	MD	21030	800-966-9016	410-771-8000	321
Gloves Inc 1950 Collins Boulevard	Austell	MA	30106	800-476-4568	770-944-9186	154-7
Glovia International Inc 2250 E Imperial Hwy Ste 200	El Segundo	CA	90245	888-245-6842	310-563-7000	180-1
GLS (Government Liaison Services Inc) 200 N Glebe Rd Ste 321	Arlington	VA	22203	800-642-6564	703-524-8200	632
Gls Group Inc 27850 Detroit Rd	Westlake	OH	44145	800-955-9435	440-899-7770	186
GM Nameplate Inc 2040 15th Ave W	Seattle	WA	98119	800-366-7668	206-284-2200	480
GMAC (General Motors Acceptance Corp) 200 Renaissance Ctr	Detroit	MI	48265	800-200-4622	877-320-2559	216
GMAC (Graduate Management Admission Council) 11921 Freedom Dr Ste 300	Reston	VA	20190	866-505-6559	703-668-9600	47-11
GMAC Insurance Holdings Inc PO Box 3199	Winston-Salem	NC	27102	888-293-5108		360-4
GMHC (Gay Men's Health Crisis) 119 W 24th St	New York	NY	10011	800-243-7692	212-367-1000	47-17
GMI Building Services Inc 8001 Vickers St	San Diego	CA	92111	866-803-4464		258
GMI Composites Inc 1355 W Sherman Blvd	Muskegon	MI	49441	800-330-4045	231-755-1611	605
GMP Metal Products Inc 3883 Delor St	Saint Louis	MO	63116	800-325-9808	314-481-0300	275
GN Diamond LLC 800 Chestnut St	Philadelphia	PA	19107	800-724-8810	215-925-0217	410
GN ReSound North America 8001 E Bloomington Fwy	Bloomington	MN	55420	888-735-4327		252
GN US Inc 77 NE Blvd	Nashua	NH	03062	800-327-2230	603-598-1100	732
GNA (Georgia Nurses Assn) 3032 Briarcliff Rd NE	Atlanta	GA	30329	800-324-0462	404-325-5536	532
GNC Inc 300 Sixth Ave 14th Fl *NYSE: GNC*	Pittsburgh	PA	15222	877-462-4700		355
GNFCC (Greater North Fulton Chamber of Commerce) 11605 Haynes Bridge Rd Ste 100	Alpharetta	GA	30009	866-840-5770	770-993-8806	138
Go 2 Group 138 N Hickory Ave	Bel Air	MD	21014	877-442-4669	410-879-8102	179
GO Carlson Inc 350 Marshallton Thorndale Rd	Downingtown	PA	19335	800-338-5622	610-384-2800	721
Go Edit Inc 5614 Cahuenga Blvd	North Hollywood	CA	91601	800-833-9200	818-284-6260	511
Go Medico 1515 S 75th St	Omaha	NE	68124	800-228-6080	402-391-6900	391-2
Go Next 8000 W 78th St Ste 345	Minneapolis	MN	55439	800-842-9023	952-918-8950	758
GO Transit 20 Bay St Ste 600	Toronto	ON	M5J2W3	888-438-6646	416-869-3200	467
Go...With Jo! Tours & Travel Inc 910 Dixieland Rd	Harlingen	TX	78552	800-999-1446	956-423-1446	758
Goal Sporting Goods Inc 37 Industrial Pk Rd PO Box 236	Essex	CT	06426	800-334-4625		708
GoalLine Solutions 3115 Harvester Rd Ste 200	Burlington	ON	L7N3H8	866-788-4625		197
Goals & Poles 7575 Jefferson Hwy	Baton Rouge	LA	70806	800-275-0317	225-923-0622	708
Goalsetter Systems Inc 1041 Cordova Ave	Lynnville	IA	50153	800-362-4625		708
Gobin's Inc 615 N Santa Fe Ave	Pueblo	CO	81003	800-425-2324	719-544-2324	534
God's Bible School & College 1810 Young St	Cincinnati	OH	45202	800-486-4637	513-721-7944	160
God's Learning Ch (GLC) PO Box 61000	Midland	TX	79711	800-707-0420	432-563-0420	736
Goddard College 123 Pitkin Rd	Plainfield	VT	05667	800-468-4888	802-454-8311	167
Goddard Institute for Space Studies 2880 Broadway	New York	NY	10025	888-661-1620	212-678-5510	666
Goddard Systems Inc 1016 W Ninth Ave	King of Prussia	PA	19406	800-463-3273	610-265-8510	311
Godfrey Trucking Inc 6173 West 2100 South	West Valley City	UT	84128	800-444-7669	801-972-0660	778
Goethe Institut Atlanta/German Cultural Ctr 1197 Peachtree St NE	Atlanta	GA	30361	888-446-3843	404-892-2388	519
Goetz Printing Co, The 7939 Angus Ct	Springfield	VA	22153	866-245-0977	703-569-8232	626
Goetze Dental 3939 NE 33 Terrace	Kansas City	MO	64117	800-692-0804	816-413-1200	474

Name / Address	City	State	Zip	Toll-Free	Phone	Class
Goetze's Candy Company Inc 3900 E Monument St	Baltimore	MD	21205	800-295-8058*	410-342-2010	297-8
*Orders						
GOG (Gynecologic Oncology Group) 1600 JFK Blvd Ste 1020	Philadelphia	PA	19103	800-225-3053	215-854-0770	48-8
Gogebic Community College E 4946 Jackson Rd	Ironwood	MI	49938	800-682-5910	906-932-4231	161
GOGO WorldWide Vacations 69 Spring St	Ramsey	NJ	07446	800-254-3477		769
GOJO Industries Inc 1 GOJO Plz Ste 500	Akron	OH	44311	800-321-9647	330-255-6000	217
Gokeyless 3646 Cargo Rd	Vandalia	OH	45377	877-439-5377	937-890-2333	40
Gold Canyon Golf Resort 6100 S Kings Ranch Rd	Gold Canyon	AZ	85118	800-827-5281	480-982-9090	667
Gold Coast Freightways Inc 12250 NW 28th Ave	Miami	FL	33167	877-465-3585	305-687-3560	312
Gold Coast Hotel & Casino 4000 W Flamingo Rd	Las Vegas	NV	89103	800-331-5334	702-367-7111	132
Gold Coast Ingredients Inc 2429 Yates Ave	Commerce	CA	90040	800-352-8673	323-724-8935	298-8
Gold Coast Tours 105 Gemini Ave	Brea	CA	92821	800-638-6427	714-449-6888	106
Gold Dust West Carson City 2171 E William St	Carson City	NV	89701	877-519-5567	775-885-9000	132
Gold Eagle Co 4400 S Kildare Ave	Chicago	IL	60632	800-367-3245		144
Gold Mechanical Inc 4735 W Division St	Springfield	MO	65802	877-873-9770	417-873-9770	191-10
Gold Medal PO Box 9452	Minneapolis	MN	55440	800-248-7310		297-23
Gold Medal Bakery Inc 1397 Bay St	Fall River	MA	02724	800-642-7568	508-674-5766	67
Gold Newsletter PO Box 84900	Phoenix	AZ	85071	800-877-8847		530-9
Gold Ranch Casino & RV Resort 350 Gold Ranch Rd	Verdi	NV	89439	877-914-6789	775-345-6789	132
Gold Reserve Inc 926 W Sprague Ave Ste 200	Spokane	WA	99201	800-625-9550	509-623-1500	501
TSE: GRZ						
Gold Room 127 N Franklin St	Juneau	AK	99801	800-544-0970	907-586-2660	669
Gold Standard Enterprises Inc 5100 W Dempster St	Skokie	IL	60077	888-942-9463	847-674-4200	443
Gold Star Chili 650 Lunken Pk Dr	Cincinnati	OH	45226	800-643-0465	513-231-4541	668
Gold Star FS Inc 101 NE St	Cambridge	IL	61238	800-443-8497	309-937-3369	278
Gold Stars Speakers Bureau 7478 N La Cholla Blvd	Tucson	AZ	85741	800-844-4384	520-742-4384	197
Gold Strike Casino Resort 1010 Casino Ctr Dr	Tunica Resorts	MS	38664	888-245-7829*	662-357-1111	132
*Resv						
Gold Strike Hotel & Gambling Hall 1 Main St	Jean	NV	89019	800-634-1359	702-477-5000	132
Goldbelt Hotel Juneau 51 Egan Dr	Juneau	AK	99801	888-478-6909	907-586-6900	379
Goldberg Weisman Cairo 1 E Wacker Dr Ste 3800	Chicago	IL	60601	800-464-4772	312-464-1234	428
Goldbug Inc 18245 E 40th Ave	Aurora	CO	80011	800-942-9442	303-371-2535	156-1
Goldcorp Inc 666 Burrard St Ste 3400	Vancouver	BC	V6C2X8	800-567-6223	604-696-3000	501
NYSE: G						
Goldcrest Wallcoverings PO Box 245	Slingerlands	NY	12159	800-535-9513	518-478-7214	800
Gold-Eagle Co-op PO Box 280 PO Box 280	Goldfield	IA	50542	800-825-3331		10-3
Goldec Hamm's Manufacturing Ltd 6760 65 Ave	Red Deer	AB	T4P1A5	800-661-1665	403-343-6607	393
Golden Anchor Travel 1909 Southwood St	Sarasota	FL	34231	800-299-1125	941-922-4070	773
Golden Artists Colors Inc 188 Bell Rd	New Berlin	NY	13411	800-959-6543	607-847-6154	42
Golden Door 777 Deer Springs Rd	San Marcos	CA	92069	866-420-6414	760-744-5777	704
Golden Eagle Insurance Corp 525 B St	San Diego	CA	92101	888-398-8924	610-832-8240	391-4
Golden Eagle Resort 511 Mountain Rd PO Box 1090	Stowe	VT	05672	800-626-1010	802-253-4811	379
Golden Flake Snack Foods Inc 1 Golden Flake Dr	Birmingham	AL	35205	800-239-2447	205-323-6161	297-35
Golden Foods/Golden Brands LLC 2520 Seventh St Rd	Louisville	KY	40208	800-622-3055	502-636-3712	297-30
Golden Gate Baptist Theological Seminary 201 Seminary Dr	Mill Valley	CA	94941	888-442-8701	415-380-1300	168-3
Golden Gate Bridge Golden Gate Bridge Toll Plz Presidio Stn PO Box 9000	San Francisco	CA	94129	877-229-8655	415-921-5858	49-3
Golden Gate Canyon State Park 92 Crawford Gulch Rd	Golden	CO	80403	866-265-6447	303-582-3707	564
Golden Gate University						
Roseville 7 Sierra Gate Plz Ste 101	Roseville	CA	95678	800-448-4968	916-648-1446	798
San Francisco 536 Mission St	San Francisco	CA	94105	800-448-4968	415-442-7000	798
Golden Gate University School of Law 536 Mission St	San Francisco	CA	94105	800-448-4968	415-442-6600	168-1
Golden Grain Energy LLC 1822 43rd St SW	Mason City	IA	50401	888-443-2676	641-423-8525	10-4
Golden Hotel, The 800 11th St	Golden	CO	80401	800-233-7214	303-279-0100	379
Golden Neo-Life Diamite International 3500 Gateway Blvd	Fremont	CA	94538	800-432-5842		366
Golden Nugget Hotel 129 E Fremont St	Las Vegas	NV	89101	800-634-3454	702-385-7111	667
Golden Nugget Hotels & Casinos 151 Beach Blvd	Biloxi	MS	39530	800-777-7568	228-435-5400	132
Golden Nugget Laughlin 2300 S Casino Dr	Laughlin	NV	89029	800-950-7700	702-298-7111	132
Golden Oaks Village 5801 N Oakwood Rd	Enid	OK	73703	800-259-0914	580-249-2600	670
Golden Sands General Contractors Inc 2500 NW 39 St	Miami	FL	33142	888-994-4742	305-633-3336	188
Golden Spike Equipment Co 1352 W Main St PO Box 70	Tremonton	UT	84337	800-821-4474	435-257-5346	276
Golden Sports Tours 301 W Parker Rd Ste 206	Plano	TX	75023	800-966-8258		769
Golden Star Inc 4770 N Belleview Ave Ste 209	Kansas City	MO	64116	800-821-2792	816-842-0233	507
Golden Star Resources Ltd 150 King St W Ste 1200	Toronto	ON	M5H1J9	800-553-8436	303-830-9000	501
NYSE: GSS						
Golden State Medical Supply Inc 5187 Camino Ruiz	Camarillo	CA	93012	800-284-8633	805-477-9866	233
Golden State Warriors 1011 Broadway	Oakland	CA	94607	866-648-4668	510-986-2200	712-1
Golden Valley Bank Community Foundation 190 Cohasset Rd Ste 170	Chico	CA	95926	800-808-2070	530-894-1000	69
Golden Valley Electrical Assn Inc 758 Illinois St	Fairbanks	AK	99701	800-770-4832	907-452-1151	247
Golden Valley Memorial Hospital 1600 N Second St	Clinton	MO	64735	888-225-6903	660-885-5511	374-3
Golden West Casino 1001 S Union Ave	Bakersfield	CA	93307	800-267-3983	661-324-6936	132
Golden West Telecommunications 415 Crown St PO Box 411	Wall	SD	57790	866-279-2161	605-279-2161	733
Goldener Hirsch Inn 7570 Royal St E	Park City	UT	84060	800-252-3373*	435-649-7770	379
*Cust Svc						
GoldenRAM Computer Products 13 Whatney	Irvine	CA	92618	800-222-8861	949-460-9000	624
Golden-Tech International Inc 2461 152nd Ave NE	Redmond	WA	98052	800-311-8090	425-869-1461	298-5
Goldey Beacom College 4701 Limestone Rd	Wilmington	DE	19808	800-833-4877	302-998-8814	167
Goldline International Inc 1601 Cloverfield Blvd 100 S Tower	Santa Monica	CA	90404	877-376-2646	310-587-1423	490
Goldman Sachs 200 W St	New York	NY	10282	800-526-7384	212-902-1000	527
NYSE: GS						
Goldman Sachs Asset Management (GSAM) 200 W St	New York	NY	10282	800-526-7384	212-902-1000	401
Goldmark Group Inc, The 1155 Bloomfield Ave	Clifton	NJ	07012	800-632-9632	973-777-5720	344
Goldsmith & Eggleton Inc 300 First St	Wadsworth	OH	44281	800-321-0954	330-336-6616	604-2
Goleta Valley Chamber of Commerce 271 N Fairview Ave Ste 104	Goleta	CA	93117	800-646-5382	805-967-2500	138
Golf Course Superintendents Assn of America (GCSAA) 1421 Research Pk Dr	Lawrence	KS	66049	800-472-7878	785-841-2240	47-2
Golf Etc of America Inc 2201 Commercial Ln	Granbury	TX	76048	800-806-8633	817-579-5263	709
Golf Shack Inc 1631 N Bell School Rd	Rockford	IL	61107	888-446-5390	815-397-3709	709
GolfBC Holdings Inc 1800-1030 W Georgia St	Vancouver	BC	V6E2Y3	800-446-5322		785
Golflogix Inc 15685 N Greenway-Hayden Loop Ste 100A	Scottsdale	AZ	85260	877-977-0162		147
Golfsmith International Inc 11000 N IH-35	Austin	TX	78753	800-396-0099*	512-821-4050	709
*Sales						
GolfWorks, The 4820 Jacksontown Rd PO Box 3008	Newark	OH	43055	800-848-8358	740-328-4193	708
Golub Corp 461 Nott St	Schenectady	NY	12308	800-666-7667		345
gomembers Inc 1155 Perimeter Center West	Atlanta	GA	30338	855-411-2783		180-10
Gompers & Assoc PLLC 117 Edgington Ln	Wheeling	WV	26003	844-805-9844	304-242-9300	2
Gonnella Baking Co 1001 W Chicago Ave	Chicago	IL	60642	800-262-3442	312-733-2020	67
Gonzaga University 502 E Boone Ave	Spokane	WA	99258	800-986-9585	509-323-6572	167
Gonzaga University Foley Library 502 E Boone Ave	Spokane	WA	99258	800-498-5941	509-323-5931	434-6
Gonzaga University School of Law 721 N Cincinnati St PO Box 3528	Spokane	WA	99220	800-793-1710*	509-313-3700	168-1
*Admissions						
Gonzales Inquirer, The 1000 Civic Ctr Loop	San Marcos	TX	78666	800-210-5909	830-672-2861	787
Good Eats Inc 12200 Stemmons Fwy Ste 100	Dallas	TX	75234	800-275-1337	972-241-5500	668
Good Hotel						
Good Hotel 112 Seventh St	San Francisco	CA	94103	800-444-5819	415-621-7001	379
Good Leads 224 Main St Unit 2B	Salem	NH	03079	866-894-5323	603-870-8150	393
Good Printers Inc 213 Dry River Rd	Bridgewater	VA	22812	800-296-3731	540-828-4663	176
Good Sam Club PO Box 6888	Englewood	CO	80155	800-234-3450		47-23
Good Samaritan Hospice 2408 Electric Rd	Roanoke	VA	24018	888-466-7809	540-776-0198	371
Good Samaritan Hospital 10 E 31st St	Kearney	NE	68847	800-277-4306	308-865-7100	374-3
Good Samaritan Hospital of Maryland 5601 Loch Raven Blvd	Baltimore	MD	21239	855-633-5655	410-532-8000	374-3
Good Samaritan Regional Medical Ctr 3600 NW Samaritan Dr	Corvallis	OR	97330	888-872-0760	541-768-5111	374-3
Good Time Tours 455 Corday St	Pensacola	FL	32503	800-446-0886	850-476-0046	758
Good Times Travel Inc 17132 Magnolia St	Fountain Valley	CA	92708	888-488-2287	714-848-1255	758

Name / Address	City	State	Zip	Toll-Free	Phone	Class
Good Will Publishers Inc PO Box 269	Gastonia	NC	28052	**800-219-4663**	704-865-1256	634-2
Good Zoo & Benedum Planetarium 465 Lodge Dr	Wheeling	WV	26003	**800-624-6988**	304-243-4030	821
Goodall Manufacturing Co 7558 Washington Ave S	Eden Prairie	MN	55344	**800-328-7730**	952-941-6666	249
Goodell Devries Leech & Dann LLP 1 S St 20th Fl	Baltimore	MD	21202	**888-229-4354**	410-783-4000	428
Goodfellow Inc 225 Goodfellow St	Delson	QC	J5B1V5	**800-361-6503**	450-635-6511	815
Goodheart-Willcox Publisher 18604 W Creek Dr	Tinley Park	IL	60477	**800-323-0440**	708-687-5000	634-2
Goodhue County Co-op Electric Assn 1410 Northstar Dr	Zumbrota	MN	55992	**800-927-6864**	507-732-5117	247
Goodin Co 2700 N Second St	Minneapolis	MN	55411	**800-328-8433**	612-588-7811	611
Gooding Company Inc 5568 Davison Rd	Lockport	NY	14094	**800-769-7768**	716-434-5501	626
Goodman Correctional Institution 4556 Broad River Rd	Columbia	SC	29210	**866-230-7761**	803-896-8565	215
Goodman Factors 3010 LBJ Fwy Ste 140	Dallas	TX	75234	**877-446-6362**	972-241-3297	274
Good-Nite Inn Fremont 4135 Cushing Pkwy	Fremont	CA	94538	**800-648-3466**	510-656-9307	379
Goodrich Corp 2730 W Tyvola Rd 4 Coliseum Ctr *NYSE: GR*	Charlotte	NC	28217	**800-735-7899**	704-423-7000	528
Goodrich Corp Aircraft Interior Products Div 3420 S Seventh St	Phoenix	AZ	85040	**877-808-7575**	602-243-2200	22
Goodwill Industries International Inc 15810 Indianola Dr	Rockville	MD	20855	**800-741-0197**	301-530-6500	47-5
Goodwill Industries of Akron Ohio Inc, The 570 E Waterloo Rd	Akron	OH	44319	**800-989-8428**	330-724-6995	195
Goodwill Industries of Central Texas 1015 Norwood Pk Blvd	Austin	TX	78753	**800-735-2989**	512-637-7106	47-15
Goodyear Tire & Rubber Co 200 Innovation Way *NASDAQ: GT* ■ *Cust Svc	Akron	OH	44316	**800-321-2136***	330-796-2121	752
Goold Health Systems Inc PO Box 1090	Augusta	ME	04332	**800-832-9672**	207-622-7153	227
Goose Creek State Park 2190 Camp Leach Rd	Washington	NC	27889	**877-722-6762**	252-923-2191	564
Gooseberry Falls State Park 3206 Hwy 61	Two Harbors	MN	55616	**888-646-6367**	218-834-3855	564
Gooseneck Trailer Mfg Co 4400 E Hwy 21 PO Box 832 *Cust Svc	Bryan	TX	77808	**800-688-5490***	979-778-0034	761
Gopher Sign Co 1310 Randolph Ave	Saint Paul	MN	55105	**800-383-3156**	651-698-5095	699
Gordman 12100 W Ctr Rd	Omaha	NE	68144	**855-290-6454**	402-691-4000	231
Gordon Brush Mfg Company Inc 6247 Randolph St	Commerce	CA	90040	**800-950-7950**	323-724-7777	102
Gordon College 255 Grapevine Rd	Wenham	MA	01984	**800-343-1379**	978-927-2300	167
Gordon County Chamber of Commerce 300 S Wall St	Calhoun	GA	30701	**800-887-3811**	706-625-3200	138
Gordon Paper Company Inc PO Box 1806	Norfolk	VA	23501	**800-457-7366**	757-464-3581	551-2
Gordon Trucking Inc 151 Stewart Rd SW	Pacific	WA	98047	**800-426-8486**	253-863-7777	778
Gordon-Conwell Theological Seminary 130 Essex St	South Hamilton	MA	01982	**800-428-7329**	978-468-7111	168-3
Gorton's Inc 128 Rogers St	Gloucester	MA	01930	**800-222-6846**	978-283-3000	297-14
Goshen Chamber of Commerce 232 S Main St	Goshen	IN	46526	**800-307-4204**	574-533-2102	138
Goshen College 1700 S Main St	Goshen	IN	46526	**800-348-7422**	574-535-7000	167
Goshen News 114 S Main St PO Box 569	Goshen	IN	46527	**800-487-2151**	574-533-2151	531-2
Gosiger Inc 108 McDonough St	Dayton	OH	45402	**877-288-1538**	937-228-5174	385
GoSolo Technologies Inc 5410 Mariner St Ste 175	Tampa	FL	33609	**866-246-7656**		616
Gospel Light Publications 1957 Eastman Ave	Ventura	CA	93003	**800-446-7735**	805-644-9721	634-3
Gospel Publishing House 1445 N Boonville Ave *Orders	Springfield	MO	65802	**800-641-4310***	417-862-2781	625
Goss Inc 1511 William Flynn Hwy	Glenshaw	PA	15116	**800-367-4677**	412-486-6100	809
Gossen /Corp 2030 W Bender Rd	Milwaukee	WI	53209	**800-558-8984**	414-228-9800	193-2
Gossner Foods Inc 1051 N 1000 W	Logan	UT	84321	**800-944-0454**	435-713-6100	297-5
GOTCO International Inc 11410 Spring Cypress Rd	Tomball	TX	77375	**800-683-7746**	281-376-3784	538
Gotham Distributing Corp 60 Portland Rd	Conshohocken	PA	19428	**800-446-8426**	610-649-7650	522
GotPrint 7651 N San Fernando Rd	Burbank	CA	91505	**877-922-7374**	818-252-3000	779
Gottlieb Martin & Associates Inc 4932 Sunbeam Rd	Jacksonville	FL	32257	**800-833-9986**	904-346-3088	462
Goucher College 1021 Dulaney Vly Rd	Towson	MD	21204	**800-468-2437**	410-337-6000	167
Gougler Industries Inc 711 Lake St	Kent	OH	44240	**800-527-2282**	330-673-5826	386
Gould & Goodrich Leather Inc 709 E McNeil St	Lillington	NC	27546	**800-277-0732**	910-893-2071	431
Gould Technology LLC 1121 Benfield Blvd Stes J-P	Millersville	MD	21108	**800-544-6853**	410-987-5600	543
Goulds Pumps Inc Goulds Water Technologies Group 240 Fall St	Seneca Falls	NY	13148	**800-327-7700**	315-568-2811	787
Gouverneur Hotel Montreal (Place-Dupuis) 1000 Sherbrooke St W Ste 2300	Montreal	QC	H3A3R3	**888-910-1111**		379

Name / Address	City	State	Zip	Toll-Free	Phone	Class
Govconnection Inc 7503 Standish Pl	Rockville	MD	20855	**800-998-0009**		181
Gove Group Real Estate LLC 70 Portsmouth Ave	Stratham	NH	03885	**866-778-6400**	603-778-6400	650
Governing Magazine 1100 Connecticut Ave NW Ste 1300	Washington	DC	20036	**800-940-6039**	202-862-8802	456-12
Government Employee Relations Report 1801 S Bell St	Arlington	VA	22202	**800-372-1033**		530-2
Government Island State Recreation Area 725 Summer St NE Ste C	Salem	OR	97301	**800-551-6949**		564
Government Liaison Services Inc (GLS) 200 N Glebe Rd Ste 321	Arlington	VA	22203	**800-642-6564**	703-524-8200	632
Government Research Service 1516 SW Boswell Ave	Topeka	KS	66604	**800-346-6898**	785-232-7720	634-2
Governor Calvert House 58 State Cir	Annapolis	MD	21401	**800-847-8882**	410-263-2641	379
Governor Daniel Dunklin's Grave State Historic Site 104 Dunklin Dr 2901 Hwy 61	Herculaneum	MO	65102	**800-334-6946**		564
Governor Patterson Memorial State Recreation Site 5580 S Coast Hwy 5580 S Coast Hwy	Waldport	OR	97394	**800-551-6949**		564
Governor's Inn 210 Richards Blvd	Sacramento	CA	95811	**800-999-6689**	916-448-7224	379
Governors State University 1 University Pkwy	University Park	IL	06048	**800-478-8478**	708-534-5000	167
Gowan Company LLC PO Box 5569	Yuma	AZ	85366	**800-883-1844**	928-783-8844	278
Gowans-Knight Co Inc 49 Knight St	Watertown	CT	06795	**800-352-4871**	860-274-8801	515
Goway Travel Ltd 3284 Yonge St Ste 300	Toronto	ON	M4N3M7	**800-665-4432**	416-322-1034	770
Goyette Mechanical Co 3842 Gorey Ave	Flint	MI	48501	**877-469-3883**	810-743-6883	191-10
GP Strategies Corp 11000 Broken Land Parkway Ste 200	Columbia	MD	21044	**888-843-4784**	443-367-9600	182
Gpa Specialty Printable Sbstrt 8740 W 50th St	McCook	IL	60525	**800-395-9000**	773-650-2020	552
GPB (Georgia Public Broadcasting) 260 14th St NW	Atlanta	GA	30318	**800-222-6006**		629
GPB Education 260 14th St NW	Atlanta	GA	30318	**888-501-8960**	404-685-2550	629
GPCCVB (Greenville-Pitt County Convention & Visitors Bureau) 417 Cotanche St Ste 100	Greenville	NC	27858	**800-537-5564**	252-329-4200	208
GPhA (Generic Pharmaceutical Assn) 2300 Clarendon Blvd Ste 400	Arlington	VA	22201	**800-859-8003**	703-647-2480	48-19
GPhA (Georgia Pharmacy Assn) 50 Lenox Pointe NE	Atlanta	GA	30324	**888-871-5590**	404-231-5074	584
GPK Products Inc 1601 43rd St NW	Fargo	ND	58102	**800-437-4670**	701-277-3225	607
GPO (US Government Printing Office Bookstore) 732 N Capitol St NW	Washington	DC	20401	**866-512-1800**	202-512-1800	342
GRAA (Greater Rockford Auto Auction Inc) 5937 Sandy Hollow Rd	Rockford	IL	61109	**800-830-4722**	815-874-7800	50
Graber Olive House Inc 315 E Fourth St	Ontario	CA	91764	**800-996-5483**		336
Grabill Cabinet Company Inc 13844 Sawmill Dr	Grabill	IN	46741	**877-472-2782**		114
Grace Bible College 1011 Aldon St SW PO Box 910	Grand Rapids	MI	49509	**800-968-1887**	616-538-2330	160
Grace College 200 Seminary Dr	Winona Lake	IN	46590	**800-544-7223**	574-372-5100	167
Grace Communion International PO Box 5005	Glendora	CA	91740	**800-423-4444**	626-650-2300	634-9
Grace Davison 7500 Grace Dr	Columbia	MD	21044	**800-638-6014**	410-531-4000	144
Grace Hospice 6400 S Lewis Ave Ste 1000	Tulsa	OK	74136	**800-659-0307**	918-744-7223	371
Grace Theological Seminary 200 Seminary Dr	Winona Lake	IN	46590	**800-544-7223**	574-372-5100	168-3
Grace University 1311 S Ninth St	Omaha	NE	68108	**800-383-1422**	402-449-2800	160
Graceland (Elvis Presley Mansion) 3734 Elvis Presley Blvd	Memphis	TN	38116	**800-238-2000**	901-332-3322	519
Graceland Fruit Inc 1123 Main St	Frankfort	MI	49635	**800-352-7181**	231-352-7181	297-18
Graceland University 1 University Pl	Lamoni	IA	50140	**800-859-1215**	641-784-5000	167
Graceland University Independence 1401 W Truman Rd	Independence	MO	64050	**800-833-0524**	816-833-0524	167
Gracious Home 1220 Third Ave	New York	NY	10021	**800-338-7809**	212-517-6300	362
Gracious Living Corp 7200 Martin Grove Rd	Woodbridge	ON	L4L9J3	**800-465-5660**	905-264-5660	322
Graco Inc 88 11th Ave NE PO Box 1441 *NYSE: GGG* ■ *Cust Svc	Minneapolis	MN	55413	**800-328-0211***	612-623-6000	638
Gradall Industries Inc 406 Mill Ave SW	New Philadelphia	OH	44663	**800-382-8302**	330-339-2211	192
Grade Finders Inc PO Box 944	Exton	PA	19341	**800-777-8074**	610-524-7070	634-2
Graduate Management Admission Council (GMAC) 11921 Freedom Dr Ste 300	Reston	VA	20190	**866-505-6559**	703-668-9600	47-11
Graduate Theological Union 2400 Ridge Rd	Berkeley	CA	94709	**800-826-4488**	510-649-2400	168-3
Grady Electric Membership Corp (EMC) 1499 US Hwy 84 W	Cairo	GA	39828	**877-757-6060**	229-377-4182	247
Grady Management Inc 8630 Fenton St Ste 625	Silver Spring	MD	20910	**800-544-7239**	301-587-3330	653
Grady Memorial Hospital 2220 Iowa Ave	Chickasha	OK	73018	**800-299-9665**	405-224-2300	374-3
Graebel Van Lines Inc 16346 Airport Cir	Aurora	CO	80011	**800-568-0031**	303-214-6683	518
Graeter's Inc 2145 Reading Rd	Cincinnati	OH	45202	**800-721-3323**	513-721-3323	297-25

Name / Address	City	State	ZIP	Toll-Free	Phone	Class
Graf & Sons Whlse. Dept Inc 4050 S Clark St	Mexico	MO	65265	**800-531-2666**	573-581-2266	709
Graff Truck Centers Inc 1401 S Saginaw St	Flint	MI	48503	**888-870-4203**	810-239-8300	56
Grafton National Cemetery 431 Walnut St	Grafton	WV	26354	**800-535-1117**	304-265-2044	135
Grafton on Sunset 8462 W Sunset Blvd	West Hollywood	CA	90069	**800-821-3660**	323-654-4600	379
Graham Architectural Products Corp 1551 Mt Rose Ave	York	PA	17403	**800-755-6274**	717-849-8100	236
Graham Co, The 1 Penn Sq W 25th Fl.	Philadelphia	PA	19102	**888-472-4262**	215-567-6300	390
Graham Corp 20 Florence Ave *NYSE: GHM* ■ *Orders	Batavia	NY	14020	**800-828-8150***	585-343-2216	386
Graham County 34 Wall St Ste 407	Asheville	NC	28801	**866-962-6246**	828-255-0182	338
Graham County Chamber of Commerce 1111 Thatcher Blvd	Safford	AZ	85546	**888-837-1841**	928-428-2511	138
Graham County Electric Inc 9 W Center St	Pima	AZ	85543	**800-577-9266**	928-485-2451	247
Graham Medical Products 2273 Larsen Rd *Cust Svc	Green Bay	WI	54303	**800-558-6765***	920-494-8701	575
Graham, The 1075 Thomas Jefferson St NW	Washington	DC	20007	**855-341-1292**	202-337-0900	379
Grain Belt Supply Company Inc PO Box 615	Salina	KS	67402	**800-447-0522**	785-827-4491	479
Grain Dealers Mutual Insurance Co 6201 Corporate Dr	Indianapolis	IN	46278	**800-428-7081**	317-388-4500	391-4
Grambling State University 403 Main St	Grambling	LA	71245	**800-569-4714**	318-247-3811	167
Gramercy Park Hotel 2 Lexington Ave	New York	NY	10010	**866-784-1300**	212-920-3300	379
Grammer Industries Inc 6320 E State St	Columbus	IN	47201	**800-333-7410**	812-579-5655	778
Grammy Magazine 3030 Olympic Blvd	Santa Monica	CA	90404	**800-423-2017**	310-392-3777	456-9
Grand 1894 Opera House 2020 Postoffice St	Galveston	TX	77550	**800-821-1894**	409-765-1894	571
Grand Aerie Fraternal Order of Eagles 1623 Gateway Cir S	Grove City	OH	43123	**877-829-5500**	614-883-2200	47-15
Grand Aire Express Inc 11777 W Airport Service Rd	Swanton	OH	43558	**800-704-7263**		62
Grand America Hotel 555 S Main St	Salt Lake City	UT	84111	**800-621-4505**	801-258-6000	379
Grand Blanc Cement Products 10709 Ctr Rd	Grand Blanc	MI	48439	**800-875-7500**	810-694-7500	185
Grand Canyon University 3300 W Camelback Rd	Phoenix	AZ	85017	**800-800-9776**	602-639-7500	167
Grand Casino Hinckley 777 Lady Luck Dr	Hinckley	MN	55037	**800-472-6321**		132
Grand Casino Mille Lacs 777 Grand Ave PO Box 343	Onamia	MN	56359	**800-626-5825**		132
Grand Country Inn Grand Country Sq 1945 W Hwy 76	Branson	MO	65616	**888-505-4096**	417-335-3535	379
Grand Del Mar 5300 Grand Del Mar Ct	San Diego	CA	92130	**855-314-2030**	858-314-2000	379
Grand Electric Co-op Inc 801 Coleman Ave PO Box 39	Bison	SD	57620	**800-592-1803**	605-244-5211	247
Grand European Tours 6000 Meadows Rd Ste 520	Lake Oswego	OR	97035	**877-622-9109**	503-718-2262	758
Grand Forks Chamber of Commerce 202 N Third St	Grand Forks	ND	58203	**855-233-6362**	701-772-7271	138
Grand Gateway Hotel 1721 N LaCrosse St	Rapid City	SD	57701	**866-742-1300**	605-342-8853	379
Grand Geneva Resort & Spa 7036 Grand Geneva Way	Lake Geneva	WI	53147	**800-558-3417**	262-248-8811	667
Grand Harbor Resort & Waterpark 350 Bell St	Dubuque	IA	52001	**866-690-4006**	563-690-4000	667
Grand Hotel Marriott Resort Golf Club & Spa 1 Grand Blvd PO Box 639	Point Clear	AL	36564	**800-544-9933**	251-928-9201	705
Grand Hotel Minneapolis, The 615 Second Ave S	Minneapolis	MN	55402	**866-843-4726**	612-288-8888	379
Grand Hotel of Cape May Beach Ave	Cape May	NJ	08204	**800-257-8550**	609-884-5611	379
Grand Hyatt Kauai Resort & Spa 1571 Poipu Rd	Koloa	HI	96756	**800-233-1234**	808-742-1234	667
Grand Island Independent 422 W First St	Grand Island	NE	68801	**800-658-3160**	308-382-1000	531-2
Grand Island Veterans' Home 2300 W Capital Ave	Grand Island	NE	68803	**800-358-8802**	308-385-6252	791
Grand Isle State Park Admiral Craik Dr	Grand Isle	LA	70358	**888-787-2559**	985-787-2559	564
Grand Junction Area Chamber of Commerce 360 Grand Ave	Grand Junction	CO	81501	**800-352-5286**	970-242-3214	138
Grand Junction Visitors & Convention Bureau 740 Horizon Dr	Grand Junction	CO	81506	**800-962-2547**	970-244-1480	208
Grand Lake Gardens 401 Santa Clara Ave	Oakland	CA	94610	**800-416-6091**		670
Grand Lodge Crested Butte 6 Emmons Rd	Crested Butte	CO	81225	**877-547-5143**	970-349-8000	667
Grand Oaks Hotel 2315 Green Mountain Dr	Branson	MO	65616	**800-553-6423**		379
Grand Ole Opry 2804 Opryland Dr	Nashville	TN	37214	**800-733-6779**	615-871-6779	571
Grand Pacific Palisades Resort & Hotel 5805 Armada Dr	Carlsbad	CA	92008	**800-725-4723**	760-827-3200	667
Grand Palms Hotel & Golf Resort 110 Grand Palms Dr	Pembroke Pines	FL	33027	**800-327-9246**	954-431-8800	667
Grand Portage Lodge & Casino PO Box 233	Grand Portage	MN	55605	**800-543-1384**	218-475-2401	667
Grand Portage State Park 9393 E Hwy 61	Grand Portage	MN	55605	**888-646-6367**	218-475-2360	564
Grand Rapids Area Chamber of Commerce 1 NW Third St	Grand Rapids	MN	55744	**800-472-6366**	218-326-6619	138
Grand Rapids Art Museum 101 Monroe Ctr	Grand Rapids	MI	49503	**800-272-8258**	616-831-1000	519
Grand Rapids Civic Theatre 30 N Div Ave	Grand Rapids	MI	49503	**888-823-6837**	616-222-6650	571
Grand Rapids Label Co 2351 Oak Industrial Dr NE	Grand Rapids	MI	49505	**800-552-5215**	616-459-8134	413
Grand Rapids Scale Company Inc 4215 Stafford Ave Sw	Grand Rapids	MI	49548	**800-348-5701**	616-538-7080	362
Grand Rapids/Kent County Convention & Visitors Bureau 171 Monroe Ave NW Ste 700	Grand Rapids	MI	49503	**800-678-9859**	616-459-8287	208
Grand Sierra Resort & Casino 2500 E Second St	Reno	NV	89595	**800-501-2651**	775-789-2000	667
Grand Strand Regional Medical Ctr 809 82nd Pkwy	Myrtle Beach	SC	29572	**800-342-2383**	843-692-1000	374-3
Grand Summit Hotel 570 Springfield Ave	Summit	NJ	07901	**800-346-0773**	908-273-3000	379
Grand Targhee Resort 3300 E Ski Hill Rd	Alta	WY	83414	**800-827-4433**	307-353-2300	667
Grand Teton Lodge Co 5 Miles N Hwy 89 PO Box 250 *Resv	Moran	WY	83013	**800-628-9988***	307-543-2811	667
Grand Traverse Resort & Spa 100 Grand Traverse Blvd PO Box 404	Acme	MI	49610	**800-236-1577**	231-534-6000	667
Grand Valley Rural Power Lines Inc 845 22 Rd PO Box 190	Grand Junction	CO	81505	**877-760-7435**	970-242-0040	247
Grand Valley State University 1 Campus Dr	Allendale	MI	49401	**800-748-0246**	616-331-5000	167
Grand Valley State University Zumberge Library 1 Campus Dr	Allendale	MI	49401	**800-879-0581**	616-331-3252	434-6
Grand View College 1200 Grandview Ave	Des Moines	IA	50316	**800-444-6083**	515-263-2800	167
Grand View Lodge 23521 Nokomis Ave	Nisswa	MN	56468	**866-801-2951**	218-963-2234	667
Grand View Media Group Inc (GVMG) 200 Croft St Ste 1	Birmingham	AL	35242	**888-431-2877**	205-408-3700	634-9
Grand Wailea Resort & Spa 3850 Wailea Alanui Dr	Wailea	HI	96753	**800-888-6100**	808-875-1234	667
Grand, The 818 N Market St	Wilmington	DE	19801	**800-374-7263**	302-658-7897	571
Grande Cheese Co 301 E Main St	Lomira	WI	53048	**800-772-3210**		297-5
Grande Colonial 910 Prospect St	La Jolla	CA	92037	**888-828-5498**		379
Grande Prairie Public Library 3479 W 183rd St	Hazel Crest	IL	60429	**800-321-9511**	708-798-5563	434-3
Grandite Inc PO Box 47133	Quebec	QC	G1S4X1	**866-808-3932**	581-318-2018	180-1
GrandLife Hotels Inc 310 W Broadway	New York	NY	10013	**800-965-3000**	212-965-3000	378
Grandma's Saloon & Grill 522 Lake Ave S	Duluth	MN	55802	**800-706-7672**	218-727-4192	669
Grandmother's Buttons Museum 9814 Royal St	Saint Francisville	LA	70775	**800-580-6941**	225-635-4107	519
Grandover Resort & Conference Ctr 1000 Club Rd	Greensboro	NC	27407	**800-472-6301**	336-294-1800	377
Grandview Products Co 1601 Superior Dr	Parsons	KS	67357	**800-247-9105**	620-421-6950	114
Grandwell Industries Inc 6109 S NC HWY 55 *Cust Svc	Fuquay Varina	NC	27526	**800-338-6554***	919-557-1221	699
Grange Insurance 671 S High St	Columbus	OH	43206	**800-422-0550**		391-2
Grange Mutual Casualty Co 671 S High St	Columbus	OH	43206	**800-422-0550**		391-4
Grangetto's Farm & Garden Supply Co 1105 W Mission Ave	Escondido	CA	92025	**800-536-4671**	760-745-4671	278
Grangeville Environmental Services (GES) *GES Property Pros LLC* 585 McAllister St	Hanover	PA	17331	**866-437-5151**	717-637-6152	83
Granite City Electric Supply Co 19 Quincy Ave	Quincy	MA	02169	**800-850-9400**	617-472-6500	362
Granite Falls Energy LLC 15045 Hwy 23 SE	Granite Falls	MN	56241	**877-485-8595**	320-564-3100	298-8
Granite Falls School District 307 N Alder Ave	Granite Falls	WA	98252	**888-651-8931**	360-691-7717	683
Granite Farms Estates 1343 W Baltimore Pike	Media	PA	19063	**888-499-2287**	610-358-3440	670
Granite Group Wholesalers LLC 6 Storrs St	Concord	NH	03301	**800-258-3690**	603-224-1901	611
Granite Knitwear Inc 805 S Salberry Ave Hwy 52S *Cust Svc	Granite Quarry	NC	28072	**800-476-9944***	704-279-5526	154-11
Granite Security Products Inc 4801 Esco Dr	Fort Worth	TX	76140	**877-948-6723**	469-735-4901	350
Granite State College 8 Old Suncook Rd	Concord	NH	03301	**888-228-3000**	603-228-3000	167
Berlin 25 Hall St Rm 144	Concord	NH	03301	**855-472-4255**	603-447-3970	167
Granite State Independent Living Foundation 21 Chenell Dr	Concord	NH	03301	**800-826-3700**	603-228-9680	306
Granite State Manufacturing Co 124 Joliette St	Manchester	NH	03102	**800-464-7646**		453
Granite Telecommunications LLC 100 Newport Ave Ext	Quincy	MA	02171	**866-847-1500**	617-933-5500	733
Graniterock Co 350 Technology Dr PO Box 50001	Watsonville	CA	95077	**888-762-5100**	831-768-2000	193-1
Grant & Weber Inc 26610 Agoura Rd Ste 209	Calabasas	CA	91302	**800-333-1656**	818-871-7700	393
Grant Assembly Technologies 90 Silliman Ave	Bridgeport	CT	06605	**800-227-2150**	203-366-4557	455
Grant Bennett Accountants 1375 Exposition Blvd Ste 230	Sacramento	CA	95815	**888-763-7323**	916-922-5109	2
Grant County 35 C St NW PO Box 37	Ephrata	WA	98823	**800-572-0119**	509-754-2011	338
Grant Plaza Hotel 465 Grant Ave	San Francisco	CA	94108	**800-472-6899**	415-434-3883	379
Grants Manager Network 1666 K St NW Ste 440	Washington	DC	02006	**888-466-1996**	504-834-9656	136

Name / Address	City	State	Zip	Toll-Free	Phone	Class
Grants Pass Chamber of Commerce 1995 NW Vine St PO Box 970	Grants Pass	OR	97526	**800-547-5927**	541-476-7717	138
Grants Pass Visitors & Convention Bureau 1995 NW Vine St	Grants Pass	OR	97526	**800-547-5927**	541-476-7574	208
Grants State Bank 824 W Santa Fe Ave PO Box 1088	Grants	NM	87020	**877-285-6611**	505-285-6611	69
Grants.gov *Dept of Health & Human Services* 200 Independence Ave SW HHH Bldg	Washington	DC	20201	**800-518-4726**		199
Grants/Cibola County Chamber of Commerce 100 N Iron Ave	Grants	NM	87020	**866-270-5110**	505-287-4802	138
Granville Island Hotel 1253 Johnston St *Resv	Vancouver	BC	V6H3R9	**800-663-1840***	604-683-7373	379
Grapevine Chamber of Commerce 200 Vine St	Grapevine	TX	76051	**866-322-8667**	817-481-1522	138
Grapevine Convention Ctr, The 1209 S Main St	Grapevine	TX	76051	**866-782-7897**	817-410-3459	207
Graphel Corp 6115 Centre Pk Dr PO Box 369	West Chester	OH	45071	**800-255-1104**	513-779-6166	499
Graphic Controls LLC 400 Exchange St	Buffalo	NY	14204	**800-669-1535**		627
Graphic Packaging International 1500 Riveredge Parkway NW Ste 100 *NYSE: GPK*	Atlanta	GA	30328	**888-548-8395**	770-240-7200	100
Graphic Products Inc PO Box 4030	Beaverton	OR	97076	**888-326-9244**	503-644-5572	176
Graphic Reproduction 1381 Franquette Ave Bldg B1	Concord	CA	94520	**800-498-9939**	925-674-0900	344
Graphic Specialties Inc 3110 Washington Ave N	Minneapolis	MN	55411	**800-486-4605**	612-522-5287	699
Graphics Type & Color Enterprises Inc 2300 NW Seventh Ave	Miami	FL	33127	**800-433-9298**	305-591-7600	626
Graphique De France 9 State St *Sales	Woburn	MA	01801	**800-444-1464***	781-935-3405	129
Graphite Sales Inc 16710 W Pk Cir Dr	Chagrin Falls	OH	44023	**800-321-4147**	440-543-8221	499
Graphnet Inc 40 Fultron St 28th Fl	New York	NY	10038	**800-327-1800**	212-994-1100	733
Grass America Inc 1202 Hwy 66 S	Kernersville	NC	27284	**800-334-3512**		350
Grassland Dairy Products Company Inc N 8790 Fairgrounds Ave PO Box 160	Greenwood	WI	54437	**800-428-8837**	715-267-6182	297-3
Grassland Equipment & Irrigation Corp 892-898 Troy Schenectady Rd	Latham	NY	12110	**800-564-5587**	518-785-5841	429
Grassley Group, The (FMCI) 409 Washington St Ste A	Cedar Falls	IA	50613	**866-619-5580**		46
Grassroots Motorsports Magazine 915 Ridgewood Ave	Holly Hill	FL	32117	**800-520-8292**	386-239-0523	456-3
Gratz College 7605 Old York Rd	Melrose Park	PA	19027	**800-475-4635**	215-635-7300	167
Gratz Park Inn 120 W Second St	Lexington	KY	40507	**800-752-4166**	859-231-1777	669
Graver Technologies LLC 200 Lake Dr	Newark	DE	19702	**800-249-1990**	302-731-1700	804
Graver Water Systems 675 Central Ave Ste 3	New Providence	NJ	07974	**877-472-8379**	908-516-1400	804
Graves Lumber Co 1315 S Cleveland-Massillon Rd	Copley	OH	44321	**877-500-5515**	330-666-1115	498
Graves Piano & Organ Company Inc 5798 Karl Rd	Columbus	OH	43229	**800-686-4322**	614-847-4322	525
Gravograph-New Hermes Inc 2200 Northmont Pkwy	Duluth	GA	30096	**800-843-7637**	770-623-0331	628
Gray & Sons Inc 430 W Padonia Rd	Timonium	MD	21093	**800-254-0752**	410-771-4311	190-4
Gray Construction 10 Quality St	Lexington	KY	40507	**800-814-8468**	859-281-5000	188
Gray Glass Co 217-44 98th Ave	Queens Village	NY	11429	**800-523-3320**	718-217-2943	330
Gray Line Worldwide 1835 Gaylord St	Denver	CO	80206	**800-472-9546**	303-394-6920	758
Gray Television Inc 4370 Peachtree Rd NE *NYSE: GTN*	Atlanta	GA	30319	**888-835-2869**	404-504-9828	735
Gray Transportation Inc 2459 GT Dr	Waterloo	IA	50703	**800-234-3930**	319-234-3930	683
Graybar Electric Co Inc 34 N Meramec Ave	Saint Louis	MO	63105	**800-472-9227**	314-573-9200	248
Grayling Industries 1008 Branch Dr	Alpharetta	GA	30004	**800-635-1551**	770-751-9095	547
Graylyn International Conference Center Inc 1900 Reynolda Rd	Winston-Salem	NC	27106	**800-472-9596**	336-758-2600	186
Graymills Corp 3705 N Lincoln Ave	Chicago	IL	60613	**877-465-7867**	773-477-4100	638
Graymont Inc 10991 Shellbridge Way Ste 200	Richmond	BC	V6X3C6	**866-207-4292**	604-276-9331	440
Grays Harbor Chamber of Commerce 506 Duffy St	Aberdeen	WA	98520	**800-321-1924**	360-532-1924	138
Grays Harbor College 1620 Edward P Smith Dr	Aberdeen	WA	98520	**800-562-4830**	360-532-9020	161
Grays Harbor Raceway 32 Elma McCleary Rd PO Box 911	Elma	WA	98541	**800-667-7711**	360-482-4374	639
Grays Harbor Tourism PO Box 1229	Elma	WA	98541	**800-621-9625**	360-482-2651	208
Grayson Rural Electric Co-op Corp 109 Bagby Pk	Grayson	KY	41143	**800-562-3532**	606-474-5136	247
Grayson-Collin Electric Co-op (GCEC) PO Box 548	Van Alstyne	TX	75495	**800-967-5235**	903-482-7100	247
GrayWolf Sensing Solutions LLC 6 Research Dr	Shelton	CT	06484	**800-218-7997**	203-402-0477	419
GRE America Inc 425 Harbor Blvd	Belmont	CA	94002	**800-233-5973**	650-591-1400	175-3
Grease Monkey International 7450 E Progress Pl	Greenwood Village	CO	80111	**800-822-7706**	303-308-1660	61-5
Great American Bancorp Inc 1311 S Neil St *OTC: GTPS*	Champaign	IL	61820	**800-962-4284**	217-356-2265	360-2
Great American Cookie Company Inc 3300 Chambers Rd Ste 170	Horseheads	NY	14845	**877-639-2361**		67
Great American Group Inc 21860 Burbank Blvd Ste 300 *OTC: GAMR*	Woodland Hills	CA	91367	**800-454-7328**	818-884-3737	653
Great American Supplemental Benefits PO Box 26580	Austin	TX	78755	**866-459-4272**		391-3
Great Arrow Graphics 2495 Main St Ste 457	Buffalo	NY	14214	**800-835-0490**	716-836-0408	129
Great Basin College 1500 College Pkwy	Elko	NV	89801	**888-590-6726**	775-738-8493	167
Great Basin Scientific Inc 420 E S Temple Ste A	Salt Lake City	UT	84111	**888-360-4022**	801-990-1055	475
Great Books Foundation 35 E Wacker Dr Ste 400	Chicago	IL	60601	**800-222-5870**	312-332-5870	47-11
Great Canadian Dollar Store (1993) Ltd 2957 Jutland Rd Ste 101	Victoria	BC	V8T5J9	**877-388-0123**	250-388-0123	789
Great Clips Inc 7700 France Ave S Ste 425	Minneapolis	MN	55435	**800-999-5959**	952-893-9088	76
Great Day Improvements LLC 700 E Highland Rd	Macedonia	OH	44056	**800-230-8301**	330-468-0700	238
Great Divide Lodge 550 Village Rd PO Box 8059	Breckenridge	CO	80424	**888-400-9590**	970-547-5550	379
Great Events & TEAMS Inc 2170 S Parker Rd Ste 290	Denver	CO	80231	**866-706-7814**	303-394-2022	186
Great Falls Area Chamber of Commerce 100 First Ave N	Great Falls	MT	59401	**800-735-8535**	406-761-4434	138
Great Falls Marketing LLC 121 Mill St	Auburn	ME	04210	**800-221-8895**		197
Great Falls Tribune 205 River Dr S	Great Falls	MT	59405	**800-438-6600**	406-791-1444	531-2
Great Harvest Bread Co 28 S Montana St	Dillon	MT	59725	**800-442-0424**	406-683-6842	67
Great Lakes Aviation Ltd 1022 Airport Pkwy *OTC: GLUX*	Cheyenne	WY	82001	**800-554-5111**	307-432-7000	25
Great Lakes Christian College 6211 W Willow Hwy *Admissions	Lansing	MI	48917	**800-937-4522***	517-321-0242	160
Great Lakes Crossing Outlets 4000 Baldwin Rd	Auburn Hills	MI	48326	**877-746-7452**	248-454-5000	49-5
Great Lakes Cruise Co 3270 Washtenaw Ave	Ann Arbor	MI	48104	**888-891-0203**		222
Great Lakes Dart Manufacturing Inc S84 W19093 Enterprise Dr	Muskego	WI	53150	**800-225-7593**	262-679-8730	759
Great Lakes Energy Co-op 1323 Boyne Ave	Boyne City	MI	49712	**888-485-2537**		247
Great Lakes Filters 301 Arch Ave	Hillsdale	MI	49242	**800-521-8565**		18
Great Lakes Institute of Technology Toni & Guy Hairdressing Academy 5100 Peach St	Erie	PA	16509	**800-394-4548**	814-864-6666	167
Great Lakes Mall 7850 Mentor Ave	Mentor	OH	44060	**877-746-6642**	440-255-6900	459
Great Lakes Orthodontic Laboratories Div 200 Cooper Ave	Tonawanda	NY	14150	**800-828-7626**		230
Great Lakes Packaging Corp W 190 N 11393 Carnegie Dr	Germantown	WI	53022	**800-261-4572**	262-255-2100	99
Great Lakes Towing Co 4500 Div Ave	Cleveland	OH	44102	**800-321-3663**	216-621-4854	464
Great Neck Saw Manufacturing Inc 165 E Second St *Cust Svc	Mineola	NY	11501	**800-457-0600***	516-746-5352	680
Great Northern Corp 395 Stroebe Rd	Appleton	WI	54914	**800-236-3671**	920-739-3671	99
Great Northern Insurance Co 15 Mtn View Rd *Cust Svc	Warren	NJ	07059	**800-252-4670***	908-903-2000	391-4
Great Northern Iron Ore Properties 332 Minnesota St Rm W1290 *NYSE: GNI*	Saint Paul	MN	55101	**800-468-9716**	651-224-2385	673
Great Pacific Fixed Income Securities Inc 151 Kalmus Dr Ste H-8	Costa Mesa	CA	92626	**800-284-4804**	714-619-3000	688
Great Plains Coca-Cola Bottling Company Inc 600 N May Ave	Oklahoma City	OK	73107	**800-753-2653**	405-280-2000	79-2
Great Plains Health Alliance Inc 625 Third St	Phillipsburg	KS	67661	**800-432-2779**	785-543-2111	353
Great Plains Industries Inc 5252 E 36th St N *Sales	Wichita	KS	67220	**800-835-0113***	316-686-7361	638
Great Plains Laboratory Inc 11813 W 77th St	Overland Park	KS	66214	**800-288-0383**	913-341-8949	418
Great Plains Nature Ctr 6232 E 29th St N	Wichita	KS	67220	**800-222-1222**	316-683-5499	49-4
Great Plains State Park 22487 E 1566 Rd	Mountain Park	OK	73559	**800-622-6317**	580-569-2032	564
Great Plains Tribal Chairmen's Health Board 1770 Rand Rd	Rapid City	SD	57702	**800-745-3466**	605-721-1922	196
Great Planes Model Distributors PO Box 9021	Champaign	IL	61826	**800-637-7660**	217-398-3630	760
Great River Bluffs State Park 43605 Kipp Dr	Winona	MN	55987	**888-646-6367**	507-643-6849	564
Great River Energy 12300 Elm Creek Blvd	Maple Grove	MN	55369	**888-521-0130**	763-445-5000	247
Great Salt Lake Book Festival Utah Humanities Council 202 W 300 N	Salt Lake City	UT	84103	**877-786-7598**	801-359-9670	283
Great Seats Inc 7338 Baltimore Ave Ste 108A	College Park	MD	20740	**800-664-5056**	301-985-6250	748
Great Skate Hockey Supl Co 3395 Sheridan Dr	Buffalo	NY	14226	**800-828-7496**	716-838-5100	709
Great Source Education Group 181 Ballardvale St	Wilmington	MA	01887	**800-289-4490**		245
Great South Texas Corp 814 Arion Pkwy	San Antonio	TX	78216	**800-531-3858**	210-369-0300	179

Name / Address	City	State	ZIP	Toll-Free	Phone	Class
Great Steak & Potato Co 9311 E Via de Ventura	Scottsdale	AZ	85258	**866-452-4252**	480-362-4800	668
Great West Casualty Co 1100 W 29th St PO Box 277	South Sioux City	NE	68776	**800-228-8602**	402-494-2411	391-4
Great Western Bank 6015 NW Radial Hwy	Omaha	NE	68104	**800-952-2043**	402-952-6000	69
Great Western Mfg Co Inc 2017 S Fourth St PO Box 149	Leavenworth	KS	66048	**800-682-3121**	913-682-2291	299
Great Wolf Lodge Williamsburg 549 E Rochambeau Dr	Williamsburg	VA	23188	**800-551-9653**	757-229-9700	667
Greater Atlanta Christian 1575 Indian Trl Lilburn Rd	Norcross	GA	30093	**800-450-1327**	770-243-2000	47-20
Greater Atlantic City Chamber 12 S Virginia Ave	Atlantic City	NJ	08401	**800-123-4567**	609-345-4524	138
Greater Augusta Regional Chamber of Commerce 30 Ladd Rd PO Box 1107	Fishersville	VA	22939	**866-922-2514**	540-324-1133	138
Greater Austin Chamber of Commerce 535 E 5th St	Austin	TX	78701	**888-409-5380**	512-478-9383	138
Greater Bakersfield Convention & Visitors Bureau 515 Truxtun Ave	Bakersfield	CA	93301	**866-425-7353**	661-852-7282	208
Greater Bangor Convention & Visitors Bureau 40 Harlow St	Bangor	ME	04401	**800-916-6673**	207-947-5205	208
Greater Beloit Chamber of Commerce 500 Public Ave	Beloit	WI	53511	**866-981-5969**	608-365-8835	138
Greater Bethesda-Chevy Chase Chamber of Commerce 7910 Woodmont Ave Ste 1204	Bethesda	MD	20814	**800-333-6778**	301-652-4900	138
Greater Birmingham Convention & Visitors Bureau 2200 Ninth Ave N	Birmingham	AL	35203	**800-458-8085**	205-458-8000	208
Greater Boca Raton Chamber of Commerce 1800 N Dixie Hwy	Boca Raton	FL	33432	**800-435-7352**	561-395-4433	138
Greater Boston Chamber of Commerce 265 Franklin St	Boston	MA	02110	**800-476-3094**	617-227-4500	138
Greater Boston Convention & Visitors Bureau (GBCVB) 2 Copley Pl Ste 105	Boston	MA	02116	**888-733-2678**	617-536-4100	208
Greater Bridgeport Conference & Vistors Ctr 164 W Main St	Bridgeport	WV	26330	**800-368-4324**	304-842-7272	208
Greater Bristol Chamber of Commerce 200 Main St	Bristol	CT	06010	**855-344-1874**	860-584-4718	138
Greater Cedar Creek Lake Area Chamber of Commerce 604 S Third St Ste E	Mabank	TX	75147	**800-331-6844**	903-887-3152	138
Greater Cedar Valley Chamber of Commerce 10 W 4th St Ste 310	Waterloo	IA	50703	**800-288-1047**	319-232-1156	138
Greater Cincinnati Convention & Visitors Bureau 525 Vine St Ste 1500	Cincinnati	OH	45202	**800-543-2613**	513-621-2142	208
Greater Cleveland Partnership 1240 Huron Rd E Ste 300	Cleveland	OH	44115	**888-304-4769**	216-621-3300	138
Greater Columbus Chamber of Commerce 1200 Sixth Ave PO Box 1200	Columbus	GA	31902	**800-360-8552**	706-327-1566	138
Greater Columbus Convention & Visitors Bureau 277 W Nationwide Blvd Ste 125	Columbus	OH	43215	**866-397-2657**	614-221-6623	208
Greater Columbus Convention Ctr 400 N High St	Columbus	OH	43215	**800-626-0241**	614-827-2500	207
Greater Concord Chamber of Commerce 2280 Diamond Blvd Ste 200	Concord	CA	94520	**800-427-8686**	925-685-1181	138
Greater Deerfield Beach Chamber of Commerce 1601 E Hillsboro Blvd	Deerfield Beach	FL	33441	**866-551-9805**	954-427-1050	138
Greater Des Moines Convention & Visitors Bureau 400 Locust St Ste 265	Des Moines	IA	50309	**800-451-2625**	515-286-4960	208
Greater Des Moines Partnership 700 Locust St Ste 100	Des Moines	IA	50309	**866-487-9243**	515-286-4950	138
Greater East Aurora Chamber of Commerce 652 Main St	East Aurora	NY	14052	**800-441-2881**	716-652-8444	138
Greater Enid Chamber of Commerce PO Box 907	Enid	OK	73702	**877-334-2665**	580-237-2494	138
Greater Eureka Chamber of Commerce, The 2112 Broadway	Eureka	CA	95501	**866-267-4255**	707-442-3738	138
Greater Fort Lauderdale Chamber of Commerce 512 NE Third Ave	Fort Lauderdale	FL	33301	**800-683-8338**	954-462-6000	138
Greater Fort Lauderdale Convention & Visitors Bureau 100 E Broward Blvd Ste 200	Fort Lauderdale	FL	33301	**877-272-5465**	954-765-4466	208
Greater Fort Myers Chamber of Commerce 2310 Edwards Dr	Fort Myers	FL	33901	**800-366-3622**	239-332-3624	138
Greater Giving Inc 1920 N W Amberglen Pkwy Ste 140	Beaverton	OR	97006	**800-276-5992**		318
Greater Grand Forks Convention & Visitors Bureau 4251 Gateway Dr	Grand Forks	ND	58203	**800-866-4566**	701-746-0444	208
Greater Greenville Chamber of Commerce 24 Cleveland St	Greenville	SC	29601	**866-485-5262**	864-242-1050	138
Greater Greenville Convention & Visitors Bureau 148 River St Ste 222	Greenville	SC	29601	**800-351-7180**	864-421-0000	208
Greater Greenwood Chamber of Commerce 65 Airport Pkwy	Greenwood	IN	46143	**800-462-7585**	317-888-4856	138
Greater Hartsville Chamber of Commerce PO Box 578	Hartsville	SC	29551	**866-747-0060**	843-332-6401	138
Greater Houston Convention & Visitors Bureau 901 Bagby St Ste 100	Houston	TX	77002	**800-446-8786**	713-437-5200	208
Greater Hutchinson Convention & Visitors Bureau 117 N Walnut St PO Box 519	Hutchinson	KS	67504	**800-691-4262**	620-662-3391	208
Greater Jackson Chamber of Commerce 141 S Jackson St	Jackson	MI	49201	**800-366-3699**	517-782-8221	138
Greater Jackson County Chamber of Commerce PO Box 973	Scottsboro	AL	35768	**800-259-5508**	256-259-5500	138
Greater Johnstown/Cambria County Chamber of Commerce 245 Market St Ste 100	Johnstown	PA	15901	**800-790-4522**	814-536-5107	138
Greater Johnstown/Cambria County Convention & Visitors Bureau 111 Roosevelt Blvd Ste A	Johnstown	PA	15906	**800-237-8590**	814-536-7993	208
Greater Killeen Chamber of Commerce 1 Santa Fe Plz	Killeen	TX	76540	**866-790-4769**	254-526-9551	138
Greater Lansing Convention & Visitors Bureau 500 E Michigan Ave Ste 180	Lansing	MI	48912	**888-252-6746**	517-487-0077	208
Greater Lawrence County Area Chamber of Commerce 216 Collins Ave	South Point	OH	45680	**800-408-1334**	740-377-4550	138
Greater Lawrence Township Chamber of Commerce 9120 Otis Ave Ste 100	Indianapolis	IN	46216	**800-473-2328**	317-541-9876	138
Greater Lehigh Valley Chamber of Commerce 840 Hamilton St Ste 205	Allentown	PA	18101	**800-845-7941**	610-841-5800	138
Greater Limestone County Chamber of Commerce 101 S Beaty St	Athens	AL	35611	**866-953-6565**	256-232-2600	138
Greater Lowell Chamber of Commerce 131 Merrimack St	Lowell	MA	01852	**800-338-0221**	978-459-8154	138
Greater Madison Convention & Visitors Bureau 615 E Washington Ave	Madison	WI	53703	**800-373-6376**	608-255-2537	208
Greater Mankato Growth 1961 Premier Dr	Mankato	MN	56001	**800-697-0652**	507-385-6640	208
Greater Marathon Chamber of Commerce 12222 Overseas Hwy	Marathon	FL	33050	**800-262-7284**	305-743-5417	138
Greater Menomonie Area Chamber of Commerce 342 E Main St	Menomonie	WI	54751	**800-283-1862**	715-235-9087	138
Greater Merced Chamber of Commerce 1640 N St Ste 120	Merced	CA	95340	**800-877-2345**	209-384-7092	138
Greater Meriden Chamber of Commerce 3 Colony St Ste 301	Meriden	CT	06451	**877-283-8158**	203-235-7901	138
Greater Merrimack Valley Convention & Visitors Bureau 40 French St 2nd Fl	Lowell	MA	01852	**800-443-3332**	978-459-6150	208
Greater Miami Chamber of Commerce 1601 Biscayne Blvd	Miami	FL	33132	**888-660-5955**	305-350-7700	138
Greater Miami Convention & Visitors Bureau 701 Brickell Ave Ste 2700	Miami	FL	33131	**800-933-8448**	305-539-3000	208
Greater Milwaukee Convention & Visitors Bureau 648 N Plankinton Ave Ste 425	Milwaukee	WI	53203	**800-554-1448**	414-273-7222	208
Greater Monmouth Chamber of Commerce 57 Schanck Rd Ste C-3	Freehold	NJ	07728	**800-700-6400**	732-462-3030	138
Greater Monticello Chamber of Commerce 116 N Main St	Monticello	IN	47960	**800-541-7906**	574-583-7220	138
Greater Morgantown Convention & Visitors Bureau 68 Donley St	Morgantown	WV	26501	**800-458-7373**	304-292-5081	208
Greater Mount Airy Chamber of Commerce 200 N Main St	Mount Airy	NC	27030	**800-948-0949**	336-786-6116	138
Greater Muskogee Area Chamber of Commerce PO Box 797	Muskogee	OK	74402	**866-381-6543**	918-682-2401	138
Greater Naples Marco Island Everglades Convention & Visitors Bureau 2800 Horseshoe Dr	Naples	FL	34104	**800-688-3600**	239-252-2384	208
Greater New Braunfels Chamber of Commerce Inc, The 390 S Seguin Ave PO Box 311417	New Braunfels	TX	78130	**800-572-2626**	830-625-2385	208
Greater New Orleans Hotel & Lodging Assn 2020 St Charles Ave 5th Fl	New Orleans	LA	70130	**866-366-1121**	504-525-2264	376
Greater Newport Chamber of Commerce 555 SW Coast Hwy	Newport	OR	97365	**800-262-7844**	541-265-8801	138
Greater North Fulton Chamber of Commerce (GNFCC) 11605 Haynes Bridge Rd Ste 100	Alpharetta	GA	30009	**866-840-5770**	770-993-8806	138
Greater Northampton Chamber of Commerce 99 Pleasant St	NorthHampton	MA	01060	**800-392-6090**	413-584-1900	138
Greater Ny Dental Meeting 518 Fifth Ave Fl 3	New York	NY	10036	**844-797-7469**	212-398-6922	196
Greater O'Hare Assn of Industry & Commerce PO Box 1516	Elk Grove Village	IL	60009	**877-355-4768**	630-773-2944	138
Greater Ocean City Chamber of Commerce 12320 Ocean Gateway	Ocean City	MD	21842	**888-626-3386**	410-213-0144	138
Greater Omaha Convention & Visitors Bureau 1001 Farnam St Ste 200	Omaha	NE	68102	**866-937-6624**	402-444-4660	208
Greater Omaha Packing Company Inc 3001 L St	Omaha	NE	68107	**800-747-5400**	402-731-1700	472
Greater Parkersburg Convention & Visitors Bureau 350 Seventh St	Parkersburg	WV	26101	**800-752-4982**	304-428-1130	208
Greater Paterson Chamber of Commerce 100 Hamilton Plaza Ste 1201	Paterson	NJ	07505	**800-220-2892**	973-881-7300	138
Greater Peterborough Chamber of Commerce 175 George St N	Peterborough	ON	K9J3G6	**877-640-4037**	705-748-9771	137
Greater Phoenix Convention & Visitors Bureau 400 E Van Buren St Ste 600	Phoenix	AZ	85004	**877-225-5749**	602-254-6500	208
Greater Pittsburgh Chamber of Commerce 425 Sixth Ave Ste 1100	Pittsburgh	PA	15219	**877-392-1300**	412-392-4500	138
Greater Pittsburgh Convention & Visitors Bureau 120 Fifth Ave 5th Ave Pl, 1st Level	Pittsburgh	PA	15222	**800-359-0758**	412-281-7711	208
Greater Plant City Chamber of Commerce 106 N Evers St	Plant City	FL	33563	**800-760-2315**	813-754-3707	138
Greater Pueblo Chamber of Commerce 302 N Santa Fe Ave	Pueblo	CO	81003	**800-233-3446**	719-542-1704	138
Greater Raleigh Chamber of Commerce PO Box 2978	Raleigh	NC	27602	**888-456-8535**	919-664-7000	138
Greater Raleigh Convention & Visitors Bureau 421 Fayetteville St Mall Ste 1505	Raleigh	NC	27602	**800-849-8499**	919-834-5900	208
Greater Renton Chamber of Commerce 625 S Fourth St	Renton	WA	98057	**877-467-3686**	425-226-4560	138
Greater Reston Chamber of Commerce 1763 Fountain Dr	Reston	VA	20190	**888-274-2912**	703-707-9045	138
Greater Rockford Airport 60 Airport Dr	Rockford	IL	61109	**800-517-2000**	815-969-4000	27
Greater Rockford Auto Auction Inc (GRAA) 5937 Sandy Hollow Rd	Rockford	IL	61109	**800-830-4722**	815-874-7800	50
Greater Rome Convention & Visitors Bureau 402 Civics Ctr Dr	Rome	GA	30161	**800-444-1834**	706-295-5576	208
Greater Saint Charles Convention & Visitors Bureau 230 S Main St	Saint Charles	MO	63301	**800-366-2427**	636-946-7776	208
Greater San Antonio Chamber of Commerce 602 E Commerce St	San Antonio	TX	78205	**888-828-8680**	210-229-2100	138
Greater Seattle Chamber of Commerce 1301 Fifth Ave Ste 1500	Seattle	WA	98101	**866-978-2997**	206-389-7200	138
Greater Shawnee Area Chamber of Commerce 131 N Bell Ave	Shawnee	OK	74801	**800-762-7695**	405-273-6092	138
Greater Shreveport Chamber of Commerce 400 Edwards St	Shreveport	LA	71101	**800-448-5432**	318-677-2500	138
Greater Sierra Vista Area Chamber of Commerce 21 E Wilcox Dr	Sierra Vista	AZ	85635	**800-288-3861**	520-458-6940	138
Greater Spokane Inc 801 W Riverside Ave Ste 100	Spokane	WA	99201	**800-776-5263**	509-624-1393	138
Greater Springfield Convention & Visitors Bureau 1441 Main St	Springfield	MA	01103	**800-723-1548**	413-787-1548	208

Name	Address	City	State	ZIP	Toll-Free	Phone	Class
Greater Starkville Development Partnership	200 E Main St	Starkville	MS	39759	**800-649-8687**	662-323-3322	138
Greater Susquehanna Valley Chamber of Commerce	2859 N Susquehanna Trl PO Box 10	Shamokin Dam	PA	17876	**800-410-2880**	570-743-4100	138
Greater Tacoma Convention & Trade Ctr	1500 Broadway	Tacoma	WA	98402	**800-745-3000**	253-830-6601	207
Greater Talent Network Inc	437 Fifth Ave	New York	NY	10016	**800-326-4211**	212-645-4200	706
Greater Tampa Chamber of Commerce	201 N Franklin St Ste 201	Tampa	FL	33602	**800-707-8846**	813-228-7777	138
Greater Toledo Convention & Visitors Bureau	401 Jefferson Ave	Toledo	OH	43604	**800-243-4667**	419-321-6404	208
Greater Vineland Chamber of Commerce	2115 S Delsea Dr	Vineland	NJ	08360	**800-922-1766**	856-691-7400	138
Greater Watertown-North Country Chamber of Commerce	1241 Coffeen St	Watertown	NY	13601	**800-924-5145**	315-788-4400	138
Greater Wilkes-Barre Chamber of Business & Industry	2 Public Sq PO Box 5340	Wilkes-Barre	PA	18710	**800-701-8449**	570-823-2101	138
Greater Wilmington Chamber of Commerce	1 Estell Lee Pl	Wilmington	NC	28401	**800-829-4477**	910-762-2611	138
Greater Wilmington Convention & Visitors Bureau	100 W Tenth St Ste 20	Wilmington	DE	19801	**800-489-6664**		208
Greater Woodfield Convention & Visitors Bureau	1375 E Woodfield Rd Ste 120	Schaumburg	IL	60173	**800-847-4849**	847-490-1010	208
Greater Yellowstone Coalition (GYC)	215 S Wallace Ave Ste 2	Bozeman	MT	59715	**800-775-1834**	406-586-1593	47-13
Great-West Life & Annuity Insurance Co	8515 E OrchaRd Rd	Greenwood Village	CO	80111	**800-537-2033**	303-737-3000	391-2
Great-West Life Assurance Co	100 Osborne St	Winnipeg	MB	R3C3A5	**800-990-6654**	204-946-1190	391-2
Greek Catholic Union of the USA	5400 Tuscarawas Rd	Beaver	PA	15009	**800-722-4428**	724-495-3400	391-2
Greeley & Hansen	100 S Wacker Dr Ste 1400	Chicago	IL	60606	**800-837-9779**	312-558-9000	263
Greeley Convention & Visitors Bureau	902 Seventh Ave	Greeley	CO	80631	**800-449-3866**	970-352-3567	208
Greeley County	510 Broadway PO Box 656	Tribune	KS	67879	**888-204-1781**	620-376-2548	338
Greeley-Weld Chamber of Commerce	902 Seventh Ave	Greeley	CO	80631	**800-449-3866**	970-352-3566	138
Green Bay Botanical Garden	2600 Larsen Rd	Green Bay	WI	54303	**877-355-4224**	920-490-9457	96
Green Bay Drop Forge	1341 State St	Green Bay	WI	54304	**800-824-4896**	920-432-6401	482
Green Bay Packaging Inc	1700 Webster Ct	Green Bay	WI	54302	**800-236-8400**	920-433-5111	547
Green Bay Press-Gazette	PO Box 23430	Green Bay	WI	54305	**800-422-7128**	920-431-8400	531-2
Green County	1016 16th Ave	Monroe	WI	53566	**800-947-3529**	608-328-9430	338
Green Depot Inc	1 Ivy Hill Rd	Brooklyn	NY	11211	**800-238-5008**	718-782-2991	429
Green Earth Cleaning	51 W 135th St	Kansas City	MO	64145	**877-926-0895**	816-926-0895	115
Green Field Paper Co	7196 Clairemont Mesa Blvd	San Diego	CA	92111	**888-402-9979**	858-565-2585	556
Green Foods Corp	2220 Camino Del Sol	Oxnard	CA	93030	**800-777-4430**	805-983-7470	297-25
Green Hills Antique Mall	4108 Hillsboro Pk	Nashville	TN	37215	**888-316-6255**	615-383-9851	459
Green Hills Software Inc	30 W Sola St	Santa Barbara	CA	93101	**800-765-4733**	805-965-6044	180-2
Green Lawn Fertilizing Inc	1004 Saunders Ln	West Chester	PA	19380	**888-581-5296**		576
Green Line Hose & Fittings (B.C.) Ltd	1477 Derwent Way	Delta	BC	V3M6N3	**800-665-5444**	604-525-6700	358
Green Mountain at Fox Run	262 Fox Ln PO Box 358	Ludlow	VT	05149	**800-448-8106**	802-228-8885	704
Green Mountain College	1 Brennan Cir *Admissions	Poultney	VT	05764	**800-776-6675***	802-287-8000	167
Green Mountain Inn	18 Main St PO Box 60	Stowe	VT	05672	**800-253-7302**	802-253-7301	379
Green Mountain Power Corp	163 Acorn Ln	Colchester	VT	05446	**888-835-4672**	802-864-5731	785
Green Oaks Hospital	7808 Clodus Fields Dr	Dallas	TX	75251	**800-866-6554**	972-991-9504	374-5
Green Plains Renewable Energy Inc	450 Regency Pkwy Ste 400 *NASDAQ: GPRE*	Omaha	NE	68114	**877-886-2288**	402-884-8700	142
Green Room at the Hotel duPont	11th & Market St	Wilmington	DE	19801	**800-441-9019**	302-594-3100	669
Green Tortoise Adventure Travel & Hostels	494 Broadway	San Francisco	CA	94133	**800-867-8647**	415-834-1000	758
Green Valley Floral Co	24999 Potter Rd	Salinas	CA	93908	**800-228-1255**	831-424-7691	369
Green Valley Ranch Resort Casino & Spa	2300 Paseo Verde Pkwy *Resv	Henderson	NV	89052	**866-782-9487***	702-617-7777	379
Green Valley Spa & Resort	1871 W Canyon View Dr	Saint George	UT	84770	**800-237-1068**		704
Greenbelt Electric Co-op Inc	PO Box 948	Wellington	TX	79095	**800-527-3082**	806-447-2536	247
Greenbriar Inn, The	8735 N Foothills Hwy	Boulder	CO	80302	**800-253-1474**	303-440-7979	669
Greenbrier Co	1 Centerpointe Dr Ste 200 *NYSE: GBX*	Lake Oswego	OR	97035	**800-343-7188**	503-684-7000	648
Greenbrier County	200 W Washington St	Lewisburg	WV	24901	**800-833-2068**	304-647-6602	338
Greenbrier County Convention & Visitors Bureau	200 W Washington St	Lewisburg	WV	24901	**800-833-2068**	304-645-1000	208
Greenbrier Farms Inc	225 Sign Pine Rd	Chesapeake	VA	23322	**800-829-2141**	757-421-2141	324
Greenbrier, The	300 W Main St	White Sulphur Springs	WV	24986	**800-453-4858**	304-536-1110	667
Greenbusch Group Inc	1900 W Nickerson St Ste 201	Seattle	WA	98119	**855-476-2874**	206-378-0569	198
Greene County Bancorp Inc	302 Main St *NASDAQ: GCBC*	Catskill	NY	12414	**888-439-4272**	518-943-2600	360-2
Greene County Convention & Visitors Bureau	1221 Meadowbridge Dr	Beavercreek	OH	45434	**800-733-9109**	937-429-9100	208
Greenerd Press & Machine Company Inc	41 Crown St PO Box 886	Nashua	NH	03061	**800-877-9110**	603-889-4101	455
Greeneville Light & Power System	PO Box 1690	Greeneville	TN	37744	**866-466-1438**	423-636-6200	247
Greenfield Savings Bank	400 Main St PO Box 1537	Greenfield	MA	01302	**888-324-3191**	413-774-3191	69
Greenfield Village	20900 Oakwood Blvd	Dearborn	MI	48124	**800-835-5237**	313-271-1620	519
GreenGeeks LLC	5739 Kanan Rd Ste 300	Agoura Hills	CA	91301	**877-326-7483**	310-496-8946	227
Greenheart Farms Inc	902 Zenon Way	Arroyo Grande	CA	93420	**800-549-5531**	805-481-2234	10-9
Greenheck Fan Corp	1100 Greenheck Dr PO Box 410	Schofield	WI	54476	**800-355-5354**	715-359-6171	18
Greenhorn Creek Guest Ranch	2116 Greenhorn Ranch Rd	Quincy	CA	95971	**800-334-6939**	530-283-0930	241
Greenhorn Creek Resort	711 McCauley Ranch Rd	Angels Camp	CA	95222	**888-736-5900**	209-729-8111	667
Greenleaf Ctr	2209 Pineview Dr	Valdosta	GA	31602	**800-247-2747**	229-671-6700	724
Greenleaf Nursery Co	28406 Hwy 82	Park Hill	OK	74451	**800-331-2982**	918-457-5172	369
Greenlee Textron	1390 Aspen Way	Vista	CA	92081	**800-642-2155**	760-598-8900	255
Greenlee Textron Inc	4455 Boeing Dr	Rockford	IL	61109	**800-435-0786**		757
Greenline Equipment	14750 S Pony Express Rd	Bluffdale	UT	84065	**888-201-5500**	801-966-4231	276
GreenLine Paper Company Inc	631 S Pine St	York	PA	17403	**800-641-1117**	717-845-8697	552
GreenMan Technologies Inc	7 Kimball Ln Bldg A	Lynnfield	MA	01940	**866-994-7697**	781-224-2411	658
Greenpages Inc	33 Badgers Island W	Kittery	ME	03904	**888-687-4876**	207-439-7310	182
Greenpath Inc	36500 Corporate Dr	Farmington Hills	MI	48331	**800-550-1961**	248-553-5400	808
Greenpeace Canada	33 Cecil St	Toronto	ON	M5T1N1	**800-320-7183**	416-597-8408	47-13
Greenpeace USA	702 H St NW Ste 300	Washington	DC	20001	**800-326-0959**	202-462-1177	47-13
Greensboro Area Convention & Visitors Bureau	2200 Pinecroft Rd Ste 200	Greensboro	NC	27407	**800-344-2282**	336-274-2282	208
Greensboro College	815 W Market St	Greensboro	NC	27401	**800-346-8226**	336-272-7102	167
Greenscape Pump Services Inc	1425 Whitlock Ln Ste 108	Carrollton	TX	75006	**877-401-4774**	972-446-0037	611
GreenSky Trade Credit LLC	1797 Northeast Expy Ste 100	Atlanta	GA	30329	**866-936-0602**		226
Greenstone Farm Credit Services Aca	3515 West Rd	East Lansing	MI	48823	**800-444-3276**	800-968-0061	218
Greentec International Inc	95 Struck Ct	Cambridge	ON	N1R8L2	**888-858-1515**	519-624-3300	658
Greenview Data Inc	8178 Jackson Rd	Ann Arbor	MI	48103	**800-458-3348**	734-426-7500	198
Greenview Regional Hospital	1801 Ashley Cir	Bowling Green	KY	42104	**800-605-1466**	270-793-1000	374-3
Greenville Area Chamber of Commerce	1 Depot Sq	Greenville	AL	36037	**800-959-0717**	334-382-3251	138
Greenville City Hall	206 S Main St	Greenville	SC	29601	**800-829-4477**	864-232-2273	337
Greenville College	315 E College Ave	Greenville	IL	62246	**800-345-4440**	618-664-7100	167
Greenville County Library	25 Heritage Green Pl	Greenville	SC	29601	**866-275-7273**	864-242-5000	434-3
Greenville First Bank	100 Verdae Blvd Ste 100	Greenville	SC	29072	**877-679-9646**	864-679-9000	69
Greenville Hospital System (GHS)	701 Grove Rd	Greenville	SC	29605	**877-447-4636**	864-455-8976	353
Greenville News	305 S Main St	Greenville	SC	29601	**800-800-5116**	864-298-4100	531-2
Greenville Technical College							
Barton	506 S Pleasantburg Dr *All	Greenville	SC	29607	**800-723-0673***	864-250-8000	161
Greer	2522 Locust Hill Rd	Taylors	SC	29687	**800-723-0673**		161
Greenville Zoo	150 Cleveland Pk Dr	Greenville	SC	29601	**800-877-8339**	864-467-4300	821
Greenville-Pitt County Convention & Visitors Bureau (GPCCVB)	417 Cotanche St Ste 100	Greenville	NC	27858	**800-537-5564**	252-329-4200	208
Greenville-Spartanburg Airport (GSP)	2000 GSP Dr Ste 1	Greer	SC	29651	**800-331-1212**	864-877-7426	27
Greenwald Industries	212 Middlesex Ave	Chester	CT	06412	**800-221-0982**	860-526-0800	494
Greenwich Assoc LLC	6 High Ridge Pk	Stamford	CT	06905	**800-704-1027**	203-629-1200	196
Greenwich Hospital	5 Perryridge Rd	Greenwich	CT	06830	**800-657-8355**	203-863-3000	374-3
Greenwood Convention & Visitors Bureau	111 E Market St	Greenwood	MS	38930	**800-748-9064**	662-453-9197	208
Greenwood King Properties 2 Inc	1616 S Voss Rd Ste 900	Houston	TX	77057	**800-403-0888**	713-784-0888	198
Greenwood Mop & Broom Inc	312 Palmer St	Greenwood	SC	29646	**800-635-6849**	864-227-8411	102
Greenwood Park Mall	1251 US Hwy 31 N	Greenwood	IN	46142	**877-746-6642**	317-881-6758	459
Greenwood Plantation	6838 Highland Rd	Saint Francisville	LA	70775	**800-259-4475**	225-655-4475	49-2
Greenwood Racing Inc	3001 St Rd	Bensalem	PA	19020	**888-238-2946**	215-639-9000	360-2

Name / Address	City	State	ZIP	Toll-Free	Phone	Class
Greenwood School 14 Greenwood Ln	Putney	VT	05346	**800-380-9218**	802-387-4545	621
Greenwood School District 50 1855 Calhoun Rd PO Box 248	Greenwood	SC	29648	**888-260-9430**	864-941-5400	683
Greenwood-Heinemann 361 Hanover St	Portsmouth	NH	03801	**800-541-2086**	603-431-7894	634-2
Greenwood-Leflore County Chamber of Commerce 402 Hwy 82	Greenwood	MS	38930	**800-844-7483**	662-453-4152	138
Greer Garson Theatre Ctr 1600 St Michael's Dr College of Santa Fe	Santa Fe	NM	87505	**800-456-2673**	505-473-6011	571
Greer Laboratories Inc 639 Nuway Cir NE PO Box 800 *Cust Svc	Lenoir	NC	28645	**800-378-3906***	828-754-5327	478
Greer Steel Co 624 Blvd *Sales	Dover	OH	44622	**800-388-2868***	330-343-8811	721
Greeters of Hawaii Ltd 300 Rodgers Blvd Ste 266	Honolulu	HI	96819	**800-366-8559**	808-836-0161	294
Greg Norman Collection 134 W 37th St Ste 4	New York	NY	10018	**888-667-6264**		154-11
Gregg Appliances Inc 4151 E 96th St *NYSE: HGG*	Indianapolis	IN	46240	**800-284-7344**	317-848-8710	34
Gregg Investigations Inc 500 E Milwaukee St	Janesville	WI	53545	**800-866-1976**		400
Gregory Poole Equipment Co 4807 Beryl Rd PO Box 469	Raleigh	NC	27606	**800-451-7278**	919-828-0641	386
Greif Inc 425 Winter Rd *NYSE: GEF*	Delaware	OH	43015	**877-781-9797**	740-549-6000	200
Gresham Petroleum Co 415 Pershing Ave P O Box 690	Indianola	MS	38751	**800-748-8934**	662-884-5000	580
Gressco Ltd 328 Moravian Vly Rd	Waunakee	WI	53597	**800-345-3480**	608-849-6300	322
Gretz Beer Co 710 E Main St *General	Norristown	PA	19401	**800-310-5099***	610-275-0285	80-1
Grey Bonnet Inn 831 Rt 100 N	Killington	VT	05751	**800-342-2086**		379
Grey House Publishing 4919 Rt 22 PO Box 56	Amenia	NY	12501	**800-562-2139**	518-789-8700	634-2
Greyfield Inn 4 N Second St Ste 300	Fernandina Beach	FL	32034	**866-401-8581**	904-261-6408	379
Greyhound Canada Transportation Corp 1111 International Blvd Ste 700	Burlington	ON	L7L6W1	**800-661-8747**		106
Greyhound Hall of Fame 407 S Buckeye Ave	Abilene	KS	67410	**800-932-7881**	785-263-3000	521
Greylock Federal Credit Union 150 W St	Pittsfield	MA	01201	**800-207-5555**	413-236-4000	221
Greyston Bakery Inc 104 Alexander St	Yonkers	NY	10701	**800-289-2253**	914-375-1510	297-1
Greystone Construction Co 500 S Marschall Rd Ste 300	Shakopee	MN	55379	**888-742-6837**	952-496-2227	188
Greystone Investment Management LLC 3805 Edwards Rd Ste 180	Cincinnati	OH	45209	**877-293-0908**	513-731-8444	527
Greystone Managed Investments Inc 300 Park Centre 1230 Blackfoot Dr	Regina	SK	S4S7G4	**800-213-4286**	306-779-6400	401
Greystone of Lincoln Inc 7 Wellington Rd	Lincoln	RI	02865	**800-446-1761**	401-333-0444	620
GRFI Ltd 400 E Randolph St Ste 700	Chicago	IL	60601	**888-856-5161**		465
Gridstore Inc 1975 W El Camino Real Ste 306	Mountain View	CA	94040	**855-786-7065**	650-316-5515	175-8
Gries Seed Farms Inc 2348 N Fifth St	Fremont	OH	43420	**800-472-4797**	419-332-5571	692
Griesbach Diamond Water N1022 Quality Dr	Greenville	WI	54942	**800-236-8931**	920-757-5440	103
Griffin Gate Marriott Resort 1800 Newtown Pk	Lexington	KY	40511	**800-228-9290**	859-231-5100	667
Griffin Memorial Hospital 900 E Main St *General	Norman	OK	73071	**800-955-3468***	405-321-4880	374-5
Griffin Tabor Communications 8445 camino santa fe	San Diego	CA	92121	**800-795-4472**	858-625-0070	5
Griffin Thermal Products 100 Hurricane Creek Rd	Piedmont	SC	29673	**800-722-3723**	864-845-5000	59
Griffin Transport Services 5360 Capital Ct	Reno	NV	89502	**800-361-5028**	775-331-8010	448
Griffith Rubber Mills 2625 NW Industrial St	Portland	OR	97210	**800-321-9677**	503-226-6971	675
Grifols USA LLC 2410 Lillyvale Ave	Los Angeles	CA	90032	**888-474-3657**		84
Grill 225 225 E Bay St	Charleston	SC	29401	**877-440-2250**	843-266-4222	669
Grill at Hacienda del Sol 5501 N Hacienda del Sol Rd	Tucson	AZ	85718	**800-728-6514**	520-529-3500	669
Grimmway Farms Inc PO Box 81498	Bakersfield	CA	93380	**800-301-3101**		10-9
Grimstad S84w18887 Enterprise Dr	Muskego	WI	53150	**877-474-6782**	414-422-2300	358
Grindmaster Crathco Systems Inc 4003 Collins Ln	Louisville	KY	40245	**800-695-4500**	502-425-4776	299
Grinnell College 1115 8th Ave	Grinnell	IA	50112	**800-247-0113**	641-269-3600	167
Grinnell College Burling Library 6th Ave High St	Grinnell	IA	50112	**800-247-0113**	641-269-3371	434-6
Grinnell Mutual Reinsurance Co 4215 Hwy 146 PO Box 790	Grinnell	IA	50112	**800-362-2041**	641-269-8000	391-4
Griswold Corp 1 River St PO Box 638	Moosup	CT	06354	**800-472-8788**	860-564-3321	674
Griswold Machine & Engineering Inc 8530 M 60	Union City	MI	49094	**800-248-2054**	517-741-4300	474
Griswold Special Care Inc 717 Bethlehem Pike Ste 300	Erdenheim	PA	19038	**855-303-9470**	215-402-0200	311
Grit Commercial Printing Inc 80 Choate Cir	Montoursville	PA	17754	**800-872-0409**	570-368-8021	626
Grizzly & Wolf Discovery Ctr 201 S Canyon St	West Yellowstone	MT	59758	**800-257-2570**	406-646-7001	821
GRMC (Gateway Regional Medical Ctr) 2100 Madison Ave *General	Granite City	IL	62040	**800-422-6237***	618-798-3000	374-3
Grob Inc 1731 Tenth Ave	Grafton	WI	53024	**800-225-6481**	262-377-1400	454
Grobet File Company of America Inc 750 Washington Ave	Carlstadt	NJ	07072	**800-847-4188**	201-939-6700	756
Grocery People Ltd, The 14505 Yellowhead Trl	Edmonton	AB	T5L3C4	**800-461-9401**	780-447-5700	298-8
Grocery Supply Co 130 Hillcrest Dr	Sulphur Springs	TX	75482	**800-231-1938**	903-885-7621	298-8
Groendyke Transport Inc 2510 Rock Island Blvd	Enid	OK	73701	**800-843-2103**	580-234-4663	778
Grogans Health Care Supply Inc 1016 S Broadway St	Lexington	KY	40504	**800-365-1020**	859-254-6661	474
Grohe America Inc 241 Covington Dr	Bloomingdale	IL	60108	**800-444-7643**	630-582-7711	608
Groovfold Inc 1050 W State St	Newcomerstown	OH	43832	**800-367-1133**	740-498-8363	310
Grosh Scenic Rentals 4114 Sunset Blvd	Los Angeles	CA	90029	**877-363-7998**		720
Gros-Ite Industries 1790 New Britain Ave	Farmington	CT	06032	**877-777-4778**	860-677-2603	21
Gross Mendelsohn & Assoc pa 36 S Charles St 18th fl	Baltimore	MD	21201	**800-899-4623**	410-685-5512	2
Grossenburg Implement Inc 31341 US Hwy 18	Winner	SD	57580	**800-658-3440**	605-842-2040	276
Grossinger Motors 1430 Fort Jesse Rd	Normal	IL	61761	**888-719-0095**		56
Grossman Iron & Steel 5 N Market St	Saint Louis	MO	63102	**800-969-9423**	314-231-9423	684
Grote Industries Inc 2600 Lanier Dr	Madison	IN	47250	**800-628-0809**	812-273-2121	59
Groth Corp 13650 N Promenade Blvd	Stafford	TX	77477	**800-354-7684**	281-295-6800	787
Grotto Ristorante 129 E Fremont St	Las Vegas	NV	89101	**800-634-3454**	702-385-7111	669
Grounds For Play Inc 1401 E Dallas St	Mansfield	TX	76063	**800-552-7529**		346
Group 1 Automotive Inc 800 Gessner Ste 500 *NYSE: GPI*	Houston	TX	77024	**888-707-4094**	713-647-5700	56
Group Dekko Services LLC 2505 Dekko Dr	Garrett	IN	46738	**800-829-3101**	260-357-3621	813
Group Health Co-op 320 Westlake Ave N Ste 100	Seattle	WA	98109	**888-901-4636**	206-448-5600	391-3
Group Management Services Inc 3296 Columbia Rd Ste 101	Richfield	OH	44286	**888-823-2084**	330-659-0100	462
Group O Inc 4905 77th Ave *Cust Svc	Milan	IL	61264	**800-752-0730***	309-736-8300	112
Groupe Lacasse LLC 99 St-Pierre St	Sainte-Pie	QC	J0H1W0	**888-522-2773**	450-772-2495	320-1
Groupe Riotel Hospitality Inc 250 Ave du Phare Est	Matane	QC	G4W3N4	**877-566-2651**	418-566-2651	705
Grove Consultants International, The 1000 Oreilly Ave	San Francisco	CA	94129	**800-494-7683**	415-561-2500	462
Grove Park Inn Resort & Spa 290 Macon Ave	Asheville	NC	28804	**800-438-5800**	828-252-2711	667
Grove Printing Corp 4225 Howard Ave	Kensington	MD	20895	**877-290-5793**	301-571-1024	626
Grove, The 189 The Grove Dr	Los Angeles	CA	90036	**888-315-8883**	323-900-8080	459
Grover Corp 2759 S 28th St	Milwaukee	WI	53234	**800-776-3602**	414-384-9472	127
GroveWare Technologies Ltd 90 Eglinton Ave E Ste 411	Toronto	ON	M4P2Y3	**877-701-9378**		318
Grower Direct Fresh Cut Flowers 6303 Wagner Rd	Edmonton	AB	T6E4N4	**877-277-4787**	780-436-7774	294
Growth Assn of Southwestern Illinois 5800 Godfrey Rd Alden Hall	Godfrey	IL	62035	**855-852-9460**	618-467-2280	138
Growth Coach, The 10700 Montgomery Rd Ste 300	Cincinnati	OH	45242	**888-292-7992**		311
Growth Products Ltd 80 Lafayette Ave	White Plains	NY	10603	**800-648-7626**	914-428-1316	278
GRSS (IEEE Geoscience & Remote Sensing Society) IEEE Operations Ctr 445 Hoes Ln	Piscataway	NJ	08854	**800-678-4333**	732-562-5550	48-19
Grubbs Infiniti Ltd 1661 Airport Fwy	Euless	TX	76040	**800-685-1111**	817-318-1200	56
Gruber Systems Inc 25636 Ave Stanford	Valencia	CA	91355	**800-257-4070**	661-257-4060	603
Gruma Corp 1159 Cottonwood L Ste 200	Irving	TX	75038	**800-147-8629**	972-232-5000	11-1
Grunau Company Inc 1100 W Anderson Ct	Oak Creek	WI	53154	**800-365-1920**	414-216-6900	191-10
Grundy County Chamber of Commerce & Industry 909 Liberty St	Morris	IL	60450	**800-892-1412**	815-942-0113	138
Grundy County Rural Electric Co-op 102 E 'G' Ave	Grundy Center	IA	50638	**800-390-7605**	319-824-5251	247
Grundy Electric Co-op Inc 4100 Oklahoma Ave	Trenton	MO	64683	**800-279-2249**	660-359-3941	247
Grupe Co 3255 W March Ln Ste 400	Stockton	CA	95219	**877-984-7873**	209-473-6000	189
GS Blodgett Corp 44 Lakeside Ave	Burlington	VT	05401	**800-331-5842**	802-658-6600	299
Gs Foods Inc 5925 S Alcoa Ave	Vernon	CA	90058	**800-273-6637**	323-581-6161	345
G-S Supplies 408 St Paul St	Rochester	NY	14605	**800-295-3050**	585-295-0250	543
GSA (Geological Society of America, The) 3300 Penrose Pl PO Box 9140	Boulder	CO	80301	**800-472-1988**	303-357-1000	48-19
GSA (Genetics Society of America) 9650 Rockville Pk	Bethesda	MD	20814	**866-486-4363**	301-634-7300	48-19
GSAM (Goldman Sachs Asset Management) 200 W St	New York	NY	10282	**800-526-7384**	212-902-1000	401

Alphabetical Section

Name / Address	City	State	Zip	Toll-Free	Phone	Class
Gsat Inc						
100 W Oak St Ste 200	Denton	TX	76201	**866-977-4728**	469-287-6771	182
GSB (Guilford Savings Bank)						
PO Box 369	Guilford	CT	06437	**866-878-1480**	203-453-2015	69
GSCB (Garden State Community Bank)						
36 Ferry St	Newark	NJ	07105	**877-786-6560**	973-589-8616	69
NYSE: NYB						
GSE Lining Technology Inc						
19103 Gundle Rd	Houston	TX	77073	**800-435-2008**	281-443-8564	599
GSE Systems Inc						
1332 Londontown Blvd Ste 200	Sykesville	MD	21784	**800-638-7912***	410-970-7800	180-1
NYSE: GVP ■ *Cust Svc						
GSI Group Inc						
125 Middlesex Tpke	Bedford	MA	01730	**800-342-3757**	781-266-5700	425
NASDAQ: GSIG						
GSP (Greenville-Spartanburg Airport)						
2000 GSP Dr Ste 1	Greer	SC	29651	**800-331-1212**	864-877-7426	27
Gst Information Technology Solutions						
13043 166th St	Cerritos	CA	90703	**800-833-0128**	562-345-8700	179
GT Water Products Inc						
5239 N Commerce Ave	Moorpark	CA	93021	**800-862-5647**	805-529-2900	606
GTE Federal Credit Union						
PO Box 172599	Tampa	FL	33672	**888-871-2690**	813-871-2690	221
GTI Corporate Travel						
111 Township Line Rd	Jenkintown	PA	19046	**800-223-3863**	215-379-6800	770
Gts Communications & Cabling Co						
11953 Prospect Rd	Strongsville	OH	44149	**877-487-8866**	440-878-8866	181
GTSI Corp						
2553 Dulles View Dr Ste 100	Herndon	VA	20171	**800-999-4874**	703-502-2000	176
NASDAQ: GTSI						
GTT Global						
600 Data Dr Ste 101	Plano	TX	75075	**800-485-6828**	972-239-5069	16
GTX Corp						
117 W Ninth St Ste 1214	Los Angeles	CA	90015	**877-489-3019**	213-489-3019	733
GU (Generations United)						
1333 H St NW Ste 500-W	Washington	DC	20005	**800-677-1116**	202-289-3979	47-6
Guadalupe Credit Union						
3601 Mimbres Ln	Santa Fe	NM	87507	**800-540-5382**	505-982-8942	221
Guadalupe Valley Electric Co-op Inc						
825 E Sarah Dewitt Dr	Gonzales	TX	78629	**800-223-4832**	830-857-1200	247
Guadalupe Valley Telephone Co-op (GVTC)						
36101 FM 3159	New Braunfels	TX	78132	**800-367-4882**	830-885-4411	733
Guarantee Trust Life Insurance Co						
1275 Milwaukee Ave	Glenview	IL	60025	**800-338-7452**	847-699-0600	391-2
Guaranteed Rate Inc						
3940 N Ravenswood	Chicago	IL	60613	**866-934-7283**	773-290-0505	216
Guaranty Bancshares Inc						
100 W Arkansas St						
PO Box 1158	Mount Pleasant	TX	75455	**888-572-9881**	903-572-9881	360-2
Guaranty Bank						
4000 W Brown Deer Rd	Brown Deer	WI	53209	**800-235-4636**	414-362-4000	69
Guaranty Bank & Trust Co						
PO Box 1807	Cedar Rapids	IA	52406	**800-362-2119**	319-286-6200	69
Guaranty State Bank & Trust Company Beloit Kansas, The						
201 S Mill St	Beloit	KS	67420	**888-738-8000**	785-738-3501	69
Guard Publishing Co						
PO Box 10188	Eugene	OR	97440	**800-377-7428**	541-485-1234	634-8
Guard Systems Inc						
1190 Monterey Pass Rd	Monterey Park	CA	91754	**800-606-6711**	323-881-6711	691
Guardair Corp						
47 Veterans Dr	Chicopee	MA	01022	**800-482-7324**	413-594-4400	174
Guardian Alarm						
20800 Southfield Rd	Southfield	MI	48075	**800-782-9688**	248-423-1000	690
Guardian Building Products (GBPD)						
979 Batesville Rd	Greer	SC	29651	**800-569-4262**	864-297-6101	193-3
Guardian Electric Mfg Company Inc						
1425 Lake Ave	Woodstock	IL	60098	**800-762-0369**	815-334-3600	205
Guardian Industries Corp						
2300 Harmon Rd	Auburn Hills	MI	48326	**800-822-5599**	248-340-1800	330
Guardian Life Insurance Company of America						
7 Hanover Sq	New York	NY	10004	**888-600-4667**	212-598-8000	391-2
Guardian Mobility Corp						
43 Auriga Dr	Ottawa	ON	K2E7Y8	**888-817-8159**	613-225-8885	645
Guardian Packaging Inc						
3615 Security St	Garland	TX	75042	**800-259-1502**	214-349-1500	600
Guardian Protection Services Inc						
174 Thorn Hill Rd	Warrendale	PA	15086	**877-314-7092***	855-779-2001	691
*Cust Svc						
Guard-Line Inc						
215 S Louise St PO Box 1030	Atlanta	TX	75551	**800-527-8822**	903-796-4111	154-7
guardNOW Inc						
16209 Victory Blvd Ste 302	Van Nuys	CA	91406	**877-482-7366**		691
Guenther House						
205 E Guenther St	San Antonio	TX	78204	**800-235-8186**	210-227-1061	49-2
Guerbet LLC						
120 W Seventh St Ste 108	Bloomington	IN	47404	**877-729-6679**	812-333-0059	233
Guernsey-Muskingum Electric Co-op						
17 S Liberty St	New Concord	OH	43762	**800-521-9879**	740-826-7661	247
Guest Communications Corp						
15009 W 101st Ter	Shawnee Mission	KS	66215	**800-637-8525**	913-888-1217	5
Guest Informant Magazine						
725 Broad St	Augusta	GA	30901	**800-622-6358**	706-724-0851	456-22
Guest Services Inc						
3055 Prosperity Ave	Fairfax	VA	22031	**800-345-7534**	703-849-9300	300
Guest Supply Inc						
4301 US Hwy 1						
PO Box 902	Monmouth Junction	NJ	08852	**800-446-7819***	609-514-9696	217
*Cust Svc						
Guggenheim Hermitage Museum						
3355 Las Vegas Blvd S						
Venetian Resort Hotel & Casino	Las Vegas	NV	89109	**800-329-6109**	212-423-3575	519
Guhring Inc						
1445 Commerce Ave	Brookfield	WI	53045	**800-776-6170**	262-784-6730	492
Guidance Software Inc						
215 N Marengo Ave 2nd Fl	Pasadena	CA	91101	**866-229-9199**	626-229-9191	180-10
Guida-Seibert Dairy Co						
433 Pk St	New Britain	CT	06051	**800-832-8929**	860-224-2404	297-27
Guide Dog Foundation for the Blind Inc						
371 E Jericho Tkpe	Smithtown	NY	11787	**800-548-4337**		47-17
Guide Dogs for the Blind						
350 Los Ranchitos Rd	San Rafael	CA	94903	**800-295-4050**	415-499-4000	47-17
Guide Dogs of America						
13445 Glenoaks Blvd	Sylmar	CA	91342	**800-459-4843**	818-362-5834	47-17
Guidecraft USA						
55508 Hwy 19 W	Winthrop	MN	55396	**800-524-3555**	507-647-5030	760
Guided Tours of Trois-Rivieres						
1457 Rue Notre Dame	Trois-Rivieres	QC	G9A4X4	**800-313-1123**	819-375-1122	773
GuideOne Mutual Insurance Co						
1111 Ashworth Rd	West Des Moines	IA	50265	**877-448-4331**	515-267-5000	391-4
Guidesoft Inc						
5875 Castle Creek Pkwy						
Ste 400	Indianapolis	IN	46250	**877-256-6948**	317-578-1700	40
Guild Mortgage Co						
5898 Copley Dr 4th & 5th Fl	San Diego	CA	92111	**800-365-4441**		508
Guildcraft Inc						
100 Fire Tower Dr	Tonawanda	NY	14150	**800-345-5563**		709
Guilford College						
5800 W Friendly Ave	Greensboro	NC	27410	**800-992-7759***	336-316-2000	167
*Admissions						
Guilford County Schools						
617 W Market St	Greensboro	NC	27401	**866-286-7337**	336-370-8100	683
Guilford Savings Bank (GSB)						
PO Box 369	Guilford	CT	06437	**866-878-1480**	203-453-2015	69
Guinness World Records Museum						
4943 Clifton Hill	Niagara Falls	ON	L2G3N5	**866-656-0310**	905-357-4330	519
Guitar Player Magazine						
28 E 28th St 12th Fl	New York	NY	10016	**800-289-9839***	212-378-0400	456-9
*Cust Svc						
Guittard Chocolate Co						
10 GuittaRd Rd	Burlingame	CA	94010	**800-468-2462**	650-697-4427	297-8
Gulf Business Forms Inc						
2460 S IH-35 PO Box 1073	San Marcos	TX	78667	**800-433-4853**	512-353-8313	109
Gulf Coast Bank						
4310 Johnston St	Lafayette	LA	70503	**800-722-5363**	337-989-1133	69
Gulf Coast Bank & Trust Co						
200 St Charles Ave	New Orleans	LA	70130	**800-223-2060**	504-561-6100	683
Gulf Coast Collection Bureau Inc						
5630 Marquesas Cir	Sarasota	FL	34233	**866-991-7358**	941-927-6999	159
Gulf Coast Community College						
5230 W Hwy 98	Panama City	FL	32401	**800-311-3685**	850-769-1551	161
Gulf Coast Electric Co-op Inc						
722 W Hwy 22 PO Box 220	Wewahitchka	FL	32465	**800-333-9392**	850-639-2216	247
Gulf Coast Machine & Supply Company Inc						
6817 Industrial Rd	Beaumont	TX	77705	**800-231-3032**	409-842-1311	721
Gulf Coast Medical Ctr						
13681 Doctors Way	Fort Myers	FL	33912	**800-809-9906**	239-343-1000	374-3
Gulf Coast Regional Blood Ctr						
1400 La Concha Ln	Houston	TX	77054	**888-482-5663**	713-790-1200	88
Gulf Coast Tmc						
7670 Hwy 10	Ethel	LA	70730	**866-683-6636**	225-683-6636	633
Gulf Coast Treatment Ctr						
1015 Mar-Walt Dr	Fort Walton Beach	FL	32547	**800-537-5433**	850-863-4160	374-1
Gulf Engineering LLC						
611 Hill St	Jefferson	LA	70121	**800-347-4749**	504-733-4868	190
Gulf Hills Hotel						
13701 Paso Rd	Ocean Springs	MS	39564	**866-875-4211**	228-875-4211	667
Gulf of Maine Research Institute, The						
350 Commercial St	Portland	ME	04101	**866-447-2111**	207-772-2321	465
Gulf Offshore Logistics LLC						
120 White Rose Dr	Raceland	LA	70394	**866-532-1060**		538
Gulf Stream Coach Inc						
503 S Oakland Ave PO Box 1005	Nappanee	IN	46550	**800-289-8787**	574-773-7761	119
Gulf Winds International Inc						
411 Brisbane St	Houston	TX	77061	**866-238-4909**	713-747-4909	801-1
Gulfside Hospice Inc						
6224 Lafayette St	New Port Richey	FL	34652	**800-561-4883**	727-845-5707	371
Gumbiner Savett Inc						
1723 Cloverfield Blvd	Santa Monica	CA	90404	**800-989-9798**	310-828-9798	2
Gump's						
135 Post St	San Francisco	CA	94108	**800-766-7628**	415-982-1616	362
Gun Parts Corp						
226 Williams Ln	Kingston	NY	12401	**866-686-7424**	845-679-4867	286
Gund Inc 1 Runyons Ln	Edison	NJ	08817	**800-448-4863***	732-248-1500	760
*Cust Svc						
Gundaker Property Management						
2458 Old Dorsett Rd						
Ste 100	Maryland Heights	MO	63043	**800-325-1978**	314-298-5200	653
Gundersen Lutheran at Home HomeCare & Hospice						
914 Green Bay St	La Crosse	WI	54601	**800-362-9567***	608-775-8400	371
*General						
Gundersen Lutheran Medical Ctr						
1836 S Ave	La Crosse	WI	54601	**800-362-9567**	608-782-7300	374-3
Gunite Corp						
302 Peoples Ave	Rockford	IL	61104	**800-677-3786**	815-964-3301	59
Gunlocke Company LLC						
1 Gunlocke Dr	Wayland	NY	14572	**800-828-6300***	585-728-5111	320-1
*Cust Svc						
Gunnebo-Johnson Corp						
1240 N Harvard Ave	Tulsa	OK	74115	**800-331-5460***	918-832-8933	469
*Sales						
Gunnison County Electric Assn Inc						
37250 W Hwy 50 PO Box 180	Gunnison	CO	81230	**800-726-3523**	970-641-3520	247
Gunster Yoakley & Stewart Pa						
777 S Flagler Dr						
Ste 500 E	West Palm Beach	FL	33401	**800-749-1980**	561-655-1980	428
Guntert & Zimmerman Construction Div Inc						
222 E Fourth St	Ripon	CA	95366	**800-733-2912**	209-599-0066	192
Gunther Mele Ltd						
30 Craig St	Brantford	ON	N3R7J1	**888-486-8437**	519-756-4330	600
Gupton-Jones College of Funeral Service						
5141 Snapfinger Woods Dr	Decatur	GA	30035	**800-848-5352**	770-593-2257	798
Gurstel Chargo LLP						
6681 Country Club Dr	Golden Valley	MN	55427	**877-750-6335**	763-267-6700	428
Guru.com						
5001 Baum Blvd Ste 760	Pittsburgh	PA	15213	**888-678-0136**	412-687-1316	262
Gurwitch Products LLC						
8 Greenway Plz Ste 7	Houston	TX	77046	**888-637-2437**	281-275-7000	217

Company / Address	City	State	Zip	Toll-Free	Phone	Class
Gustave A Larson Co PO Box 910	Pewaukee	WI	53072	**800-829-9609**	262-542-0200	663
Gustavus Adolphus College 800 W College Ave	Saint Peter	MN	56082	**800-487-8288**	507-933-8000	167
Guthrie Healthcare System 1 Guthrie Sq	Sayre	PA	18840	**888-448-8474**	570-887-4401	353
Guthrie Theater 818 S Second St *Resv	Minneapolis	MN	55415	**877-447-8243***	612-377-2224	571
Guthy-Renker Television Network 3340 Ocean Pk Blvd	Santa Monica	CA	90405	**888-651-6607**	310-581-6250	739
Gutsy Women Travel LLC 801 E Katella Ave	Anaheim	CA	92806	**866-464-8879**		758
Guttenplans Frozen Dough 100 Hwy 36 *General	Middletown	NJ	07748	**888-422-4357***	732-495-9480	297-2
Guy M Turner Inc 4514 S Holden Rd PO Box 7776	Greensboro	NC	27406	**800-432-4859**	336-294-4660	778
Guy Shavender Trucking Inc PO Box 206	Pantego	NC	27860	**800-682-2447**	252-943-3379	683
GVMG (Grand View Media Group Inc) 200 Croft St Ste 1	Birmingham	AL	35242	**888-431-2877**	205-408-3700	634-9
GVTC (Guadalupe Valley Telephone Co-op) 36101 FM 3159	New Braunfels	TX	78132	**800-367-4882**	830-885-4411	733
GWI Inc 8 Pomerleau St	Biddeford	ME	04005	**866-494-2020**	207-286-8686	607
Gwin's Travel Planners Inc 212 N Kirkwood Rd	Saint Louis	MO	63122	**800-433-9211**	314-822-1957	769
Gwynedd-Mercy College 1325 Sunneytown Pk PO Box 901 *Admissions	Gwynedd Valley	PA	19437	**800-342-5462***	215-646-7300	167
GXS Inc 9711 Washingtonian Blvd	Gaithersburg	MD	20878	**800-560-4347**	301-340-4000	180-4
GYC (Greater Yellowstone Coalition) 215 S Wallace Ave Ste 2	Bozeman	MT	59715	**800-775-1834**	406-586-1593	47-13
Gym Source 40 E 52nd St	New York	NY	10022	**800-496-3499**	212-688-4222	709
Gymboree Corp 500 Howard St *NASDAQ: GYMB*	San Francisco	CA	94105	**877-449-6932**	415-278-7000	156-1
Gynecologic Oncology Group (GOG) 1600 JFK Blvd Ste 1020	Philadelphia	PA	19103	**800-225-3053**	215-854-0770	48-8
Gypsum Express Ltd 8280 Sixty Rd PO Box 268	Baldwinsville	NY	13027	**800-621-7901**	315-638-2201	448
Gyration Inc 3601-B Calle Tecate	Camarillo	CA	93012	**888-340-0033**		175-2
Gyrodata Inc 23000 Northwest Lk Dr	Houston	TX	77095	**800-348-6063**	281-213-6300	192

H

Company / Address	City	State	Zip	Toll-Free	Phone	Class
H & C Tool Supply Corp 235 Mount Read Blvd	Rochester	NY	14611	**800-323-4624**	585-235-5700	350
H & E Equipment Services Inc 11100 Mead Rd *NASDAQ: HEES*	Baton Rouge	LA	70809	**866-467-3682**	225-298-5200	266-3
H & H Color Lab Inc 8906 E 67th St	Raytown	MO	64133	**800-821-1305**	816-358-6677	587
H & H Graphics Inc 854 N Prince St	Lancaster	PA	17603	**866-338-7569**	717-393-3941	344
H & H Industrial Corp 7612 Rt 130	Pennsauken	NJ	08110	**800-982-0341**	856-663-4444	695
H & H Publishing Company Inc 1231 Kapp Dr	Clearwater	FL	33765	**800-366-4079**	727-442-7760	246
H & H Swiss Screw Machine Products Company Inc 1478 Chestnut Ave	Hillside	NJ	07205	**800-826-9985**		620
H & L Tooth Company Inc 10055 E 56 St N	Tulsa	OK	74117	**800-458-6684**	918-272-0951	482
H & M International Transportation Inc 485B Rt 1 S	Iselin	NJ	08830	**800-446-4685**	732-510-4640	778
H & R 1871 60 Industrial Rowe	Gardner	MA	01440	**866-776-9292**		286
H & R Block Tax Services Inc 4400 Main St	Kansas City	MO	64111	**800-472-5625**		731
H & S Bakery Inc 601 S Caroline St	Baltimore	MD	21231	**800-959-7655**	410-276-7254	297-1
H & W Computer Systems Inc 6154 N Meeker Pl Ste 100	Boise	ID	83713	**800-338-6692**	208-377-0336	179
H & W Trucking Company Inc 1772 N Andy Griffith Pkwy PO Box 1545	Mount Airy	NC	27030	**800-334-9181**	336-789-2188	778
H B Fuller Construction Products Inc 1105 S Frontenac Rd	Aurora	IL	60504	**800-832-9002**		3
H Barber & Sons Inc 15 Raytkwich Rd	Naugatuck	CT	06770	**800-355-8318**	203-729-9000	665
H Company Computer Products Inc 16812 Hale Ave	Irvine	CA	92606	**800-726-2477**	949-833-3222	175-8
H E Whitlock Inc 4808 Dillon Dr PO Box 8030	Pueblo	CO	81008	**866-933-0709**		448
H Freeman & Son Inc 411 N Cranberry Rd	Westminster	MD	21157	**800-876-7700**	410-857-5774	154-11
H G Makelim Co 219 Shaw Rd	South San Francisco	CA	94080	**800-471-0590**	650-873-4757	385
H Gr Industrial Surplus 20001 Euclid Ave	Euclid	OH	44117	**866-447-7117**	216-486-4567	358
H Kramer & Co 1345 W 21st St	Chicago	IL	60608	**800-621-2305**	312-226-6600	484
H Lee Moffitt Cancer Ctr & Research Institute University of S Florida 12902 Magnolia Dr	Tampa	FL	33612	**800-456-3434**	888-663-3488	374-7

Company / Address	City	State	Zip	Toll-Free	Phone	Class
H Lee Moffitt Cancer Ctr & Research Institute Blood & Marrow Transplantation Program 12902 Magnolia Dr	Tampa	FL	33612	**888-663-3488**		767
H Muehlstein & Company Inc 10 Westport Rd	Wilton	CT	06897	**800-257-3746**	203-855-6000	602
H O Wolding Inc PO Box 217	Amherst	WI	54406	**800-950-0054**	715-824-5513	778
H Pearce Real Estate Co 393 State St	North Haven	CT	06473	**800-373-3411**	203-281-3400	650
H Smith Packing Corp 99 Ft Fairfield Rd	Presque Isle	ME	04769	**800-393-9898**	207-764-4540	298-7
H Stern Jewelers Inc 645 Fifth Ave	New York	NY	10022	**800-747-8376**	212-688-0300	410
H Wilson Co 2245 Delany Rd	Waukegan	IL	60087	**800-245-7224**		320-1
H. B. Van Duzer Forest State Scenic Corridor 198 NE 123rd St	Otis	OR	97368	**800-551-6949**		564
H. E. Murdock Co Inc 88 Main St	Waterville	ME	04901	**888-974-1805**	207-873-7036	410
H. T. Berry Co Inc PO Box B	Canton	MA	02021	**800-736-2206**	781-828-6000	558
H2 Engineering Surveying LLC 8880 N Hess St	Hayden	ID	83835	**877-700-9909**	208-772-6600	725
H2O Plus Inc 845 W Madison St *Cust Svc	Chicago	IL	60607	**800-242-2284***	312-850-9283	217
HA Guden Company Inc 99 Raynor Ave	Ronkonkoma	NY	11779	**800-344-6437**	631-737-2900	350
HA Logistics Inc 5175 Johnson Dr	Pleasanton	CA	94588	**800-449-5778**	925-251-9300	312
Haag Engineering Co 4949 W Royal Ln	Irving	TX	75063	**800-527-0168**	214-614-6500	263
Haas & Wilkerson Inc 4300 Shawnee Mission Pkwy	Fairway	KS	66205	**800-821-7703**	913-432-4400	390
Haas Automation Inc 2800 Sturgis Rd	Oxnard	CA	93030	**800-331-6746**	805-278-1800	453
Haas Cabinet Company Inc 625 W Utica St	Sellersburg	IN	47172	**800-457-6458**	812-246-4431	114
Habana Inn 2200 NW 40th St	Oklahoma City	OK	73112	**800-988-2221**	405-525-0730	379
Habanero Consulting Group Inc 510-1111 Melville St	Vancouver	BC	V6E3V6	**866-841-6201**	604-709-6201	227
Habasit ABT Inc 150 Industrial Pk Rd	Middletown	CT	06457	**800-522-2358**	860-632-2211	370
Habasit America 805 Satellite Blvd	Suwanee	GA	30024	**800-458-6431**		607
Habasit Belting Inc 1400 Clinton St	Buffalo	NY	14206	**800-325-1585**	716-824-8484	370
Habbersett Scrapple Inc 103 S Railroad Ave	Bridgeville	DE	19933	**800-338-4727**		297-26
Habco Beverage Systems Inc 501 Gordon Baker Rd	Toronto	ON	M2H2S6	**800-448-0244**	416-491-6008	801-1
Habersham County Chamber of Commerce 668 Clarkesville St	Cornelia	GA	30531	**800-835-2559**	706-778-4654	138
Habersham Electric Membership Corp 6135 Georgia 115	Clarkesville	GA	30523	**800-640-6812**	706-754-2114	247
Habersham Funding LLC 3495 Piedmont Rd NE Ste 910	Atlanta	GA	30305	**888-874-2402**	404-233-8275	794
Habitat for Humanity International Inc 121 Habitat St	Americus	GA	31709	**800-422-4828**	229-924-6935	47-5
Habitat Housewares 3801 Old Seward Hwy Ste 7	Anchorage	AK	99503	**800-770-1856**	907-561-1856	362
Habitat Suites 500 E Highland Mall Blvd	Austin	TX	78752	**800-535-4663**	512-467-6000	379
Habitec Security Inc 2926 S Republic Blvd	Toledo	OH	43615	**888-422-4832**	419-537-6768	691
HAC (Housing Assistance Council) 1025 Vermont Ave NW Ste 606	Washington	DC	20005	**866-234-2689**	202-842-8600	47-5
Hach Co PO Box 389	Loveland	CO	80539	**800-227-4224**	970-669-3050	419
Hachette Book Group 237 Pk Ave	New York	NY	10017	**800-759-0190**		634-2
Hacienda del Sol Guest Ranch Resort 5501 N Hacienda Del Sol Rd	Tucson	AZ	85718	**800-728-6514**	520-299-1501	667
Hacienda Home Centers Inc 1255 Bosque Farms Blvd	Bosque Farms	NM	87068	**800-944-0704**	505-869-2637	364
Hacienda Mexican Restaurants 1501 N Ironwood Dr	South Bend	IN	46635	**800-541-3227**		668
Hacienda The at Hotel Santa Fe 1501 Paseo del Peralta	Santa Fe	NM	87501	**855-825-9876**	505-955-7805	379
Hackbarth Delivery Service Inc 3504 Brookdale Dr N	Mobile	AL	36618	**800-277-3322**	251-478-1401	315
Hacker Johnson & Smith PA 500 N Wshore Blvd Ste 1000	Tampa	FL	33609	**800-366-7126**	813-286-2424	2
Hacklebarney State Park 119 Hacklebarney Rd 119 Hacklebarney Rd	Long Valley	NJ	07853	**800-659-4044**	908-638-6969	564
Hackney & Sons Inc 911 W 5th St PO Box 880	Washington	NC	27889	**800-763-0700**	252-946-6521	515
Hackworth Reprographics 1700 Liberty St	Chesapeake	VA	23324	**800-676-2424**	757-545-7675	112
HACU (Hispanic Assn of Colleges & Universities) 8415 Datapoint Dr Ste 400	San Antonio	TX	78229	**800-780-4228**	210-692-3805	48-5
Hader/Seitz Inc 15600 W Lincoln Ave	New Berlin	WI	53151	**877-388-2101**		225
Hadley House Co PO Box 219	Cokato	MN	55321	**800-423-5390**		634-10
Hadronics Inc 4570 Steel Pl	Cincinnati	OH	45209	**800-829-0826**	513-321-9350	480
Haeger Industries Inc 7 Maiden Ln *Cust Svc	Dundee	IL	60118	**800-288-2529***	847-426-3441	334
Haemonetics Corp 400 Wood Rd *NYSE: HAE*	Braintree	MA	02184	**800-225-5242**	781-848-7100	475
Hafele America Company Inc 3901 Cheyenne Dr *Cust Svc	Archdale	NC	27263	**800-423-3531***	336-889-2322	490
Hagemeyer North America Inc 1460 Tobias Gadson Blvd	Charleston	SC	29407	**877-462-7070**	843-745-2400	385

Alphabetical Section

Name / Address	City	State	ZIP	Toll-Free	Phone	Class
Hager Co 139 Victor St	Saint Louis	MO	63104	**800-325-9995**	314-772-4400	350
Hagerstown/Washington County Convention & Visitors Bureau 16 Public Sq	Hagerstown	MD	21740	**888-257-2600**	301-791-3246	208
Hagerty Insurance Agency LLC 141 River's Edge Dr Ste 200 PO Box 1303	Traverse City	MI	49684	**877-922-9701**	231-947-6868	391-4
Hagey Coach & Tours Nrt 210 Schoolhouse Rd	Souderton	PA	18964	**800-544-2439**	215-723-4381	758
Haggar Clothing Co 11511 Luna Rd 2 Colinas Crossing	Dallas	TX	75234	**877-841-2219**	214-352-8481	154-11
Haggard & Stocking Assoc 5318 Victory Dr	Indianapolis	IN	46203	**800-622-4824**	317-788-4661	385
Haggerty Enterprises Inc 370 Kimberly Dr	Carol Stream	IL	60188	**800-336-5282**	630-315-3300	334
Hagie Manufacturing Co PO Box 273	Clarion	IA	50525	**800-247-4885**	515-532-2861	275
Hagyard-Davidson-McGee Assoc PSC 4250 Iron Works Pike	Lexington	KY	40511	**888-323-7798**	859-255-8741	11-2
Hahn & Bowersock Corp 151 Kalmus Dr Ste L1	Costa Mesa	CA	92626	**800-660-3187**		444
Hahn Janice (Rep D - CA) 404 Cannon Bldg	Washington	DC	20515	**855-328-7332**	202-225-8220	342-2
Hahn Systems Co Inc 6312 SE Ave	Indianapolis	IN	46203	**800-201-4246**	317-243-3796	385
HAI (Helicopter Assn International) 1635 Prince St	Alexandria	VA	22314	**800-435-4976**	703-683-4646	48-21
HAI (Hohman Assoc Inc) 6951 W Little York	Houston	TX	77040	**800-324-0978**	713-896-0978	47-2
Haida Corp PO Box 89	Hydaburg	AK	99922	**800-478-3721**	907-285-3721	750
Hain Celestial Group Inc 4600 Sleepytime Dr *NASDAQ: HAIN*	Boulder	CO	80301	**800-434-4246**		298-11
Hainen Ford Inc 800 Hwy 5 S	Tipton	MO	65081	**888-526-6979**		56
Haines & Company Inc 8050 Freedom Ave	North Canton	OH	44720	**800-843-8452**		634-6
Haines City Citrus Growers Assn (HCCGA) 8 Railroad Ave PO Box 337 *Sales	Haines City	FL	33844	**800-327-6676***	863-422-1174	11-1
Hajoca Corp 127 Coulter Ave	Ardmore	PA	19003	**888-328-2383**	610-649-1430	611
Hal Leonard Corp 960 E Mark St	Winona	MN	55987	**800-321-3408**	507-454-2920	634-7
Hale Centre Theater 3333 S Decker Lake Dr	West Valley City	UT	84119	**877-829-5500**	801-984-9000	571
Hale Farm & Village 2686 Oakhill Rd PO Box 296	Bath	OH	44210	**800-589-9703**	330-666-3711	519
Hale Products Inc 700 Spring Mill Ave	Conshohocken	PA	19428	**800-220-4253**	610-825-6300	638
Hale Trailer Brake & Wheel Inc Rt 73 & Cooper Rd	Voorhees	NJ	08043	**800-232-6535**	856-768-1330	125
Halekulani Hotel 2199 Kalia Rd	Honolulu	HI	96815	**800-367-2343**	808-923-2311	379
Halex Co 23901 Aurora Rd	Bedford Heights	OH	44146	**800-749-3261**		309
Halex Corp 750 S Reservoir St	Pomona	CA	91766	**800-576-1636**	909-622-3537	350
Haley Bros Inc 6291 Orangethorpe Ave	Buena Park	CA	90620	**800-854-5951**	714-670-2112	238
Half Hitch Tackle Company Inc 2206 Thomas Dr	Panama City	FL	32408	**888-668-9810**	850-234-2621	709
Half Moon Bay Lodge & Conference Ctr 2400 S Cabrillo Hwy	Half Moon Bay	CA	94019	**800-710-0778**	650-726-9000	379
Half Moon Bay State Beach c/o San Mateo Coast Sector Office 95 Kelly Ave	Half Moon Bay	CA	94019	**800-444-7275**	650-726-8819	564
Halifax County Chamber of Commerce PO Box 399	South Boston	VA	24592	**800-283-0098**	434-572-3085	138
Halifax County Public Schools 1030 Mary Bethune St PO Box 1849	Halifax	VA	24558	**800-253-2687**	434-476-2171	683
Halifax Electric Membership Corp 208 Whitfield St	Enfield	NC	27823	**800-690-0522**	252-445-5111	247
Halifax Marriott Harborfront Hotel 1919 Upper Water St	Halifax	NS	B3J3J5	**800-450-4442**	902-421-1700	379
Hall County Schools 711 Green St NW Ste 100	Gainesville	GA	30501	**866-632-9992**	770-534-1080	683
Hall Signs Inc 4495 W Vernal Pk	Bloomington	IN	47404	**800-284-7446**		699
Halliburton House Inn 5184 Morris St	Halifax	NS	B3J1B3	**888-512-3344**	902-420-0658	379
Hallie Ford Museum of Art 700 State St	Salem	OR	97301	**844-232-7228**	503-370-6855	519
Hallmark Cards Inc 2501 McGee St	Kansas City	MO	64108	**800-425-5627**	816-274-5111	129
Hallmark Ch 12700 Ventura Blvd Ste 200	Studio City	CA	91604	**888-390-7474**	818-755-2400	736
Hallmark Corp Foundation 2501 McGee St	Kansas City	MO	64108	**800-425-5627**		305
Hallmark Inns & Resorts 15455 Hallmark Dr Ste 200	Lake Oswego	OR	97035	**888-448-4449**	503-635-4555	379
Hallmark International PO Box 419034	Kansas City	MO	64141	**800-425-5627**	816-274-5111	129
Hallmark Nameplate Inc 1717 E Lincoln Ave	Mount Dora	FL	32757	**800-874-9063**	352-383-8142	699
Halocarbon Products Corp PO Box 661	River Edge	NJ	07661	**800-338-5803**	201-262-8899	582
Halogen Software 495 March Rd	Kanata	ON	K2K3G1	**866-566-7778**	613-270-1011	180-1
Halsted Corp 51 Commerce Dr Ste 3	Cranbury	NJ	08512	**800-843-5184**	201-433-3323	66
Halston LLC 1201 W Fifth St 11th fl	Los Angeles	CA	90017	**844-425-7866**		156-2
Halyard Health 20202 Windrow Dr	Lake Forest	CA	92630	**800-448-3569**	949-206-2700	476
Hamacher Resource Group LLC 8801 W Heather Ave	Milwaukee	WI	53224	**800-888-0889**		363
Hamburg Sud North America Inc 465 S St	Morristown	NJ	07960	**888-228-8241**	973-775-5300	314
Hamilton Beach/Proctor-Silex Inc 4421 Waterfront Dr *Cust Svc	Glen Allen	VA	23060	**800-851-8900***	804-273-9777	36
Hamilton Capital Management 5025 Arlington Centre Blvd	Columbus	OH	43220	**888-833-5951**	614-273-1000	401
Hamilton Chevrolet 5800 E 14 Mile Rd	Warren	MI	48092	**888-466-7827**	586-264-1400	56
Hamilton City Employees Federal Credit Union 309 Ct St	Hamilton	OH	45011	**800-264-5578**	513-868-5881	221
Hamilton Co 4970 Energy Way	Reno	NV	89502	**800-648-5950**	775-858-3000	419
Hamilton College 198 College Hill Rd *Admissions	Clinton	NY	13323	**800-843-2655***	315-859-4421	167
Hamilton County Convention & Visitors Bureau Inc 37 E Main St	Carmel	IN	46032	**800-776-8687**	317-848-3181	208
Hamilton County Educational Service Ctr (HCESC) 11083 Hamilton Ave	Cincinnati	OH	45231	**800-964-8211**	513-674-4200	683
Hamilton County Electric Co-op Assn 420 N Rice St PO Box 753	Hamilton	TX	76531	**800-595-3401**	254-386-3123	247
Hamilton Ctr Inc PO Box 4323	Terre Haute	IN	47804	**800-742-0787**	812-231-8323	374-5
Hamilton Group 100 Elwood Davis Rd	North Syracuse	NY	13212	**800-351-3066**	315-413-0086	274
Hamilton Park Hotel & Conference Ctr 175 Pk Ave	Florham Park	NJ	07932	**877-999-3223**	973-377-2424	377
Hamilton Port Authority 605 James St N 6th Fl	Hamilton	ON	L8L1K1	**800-263-2131**	905-525-4330	617
Hamilton Sorter Co Inc 3158 Production Dr	Fairfield	OH	45014	**800-503-9966**	513-870-4400	288
Hamilton Telephone Co 1001 12th St	Aurora	NE	68818	**800-821-1831**	402-694-5101	115
Hamler State Bank 210 Randolph St PO Box 358	Hamler	OH	43524	**888-508-3955**	419-274-3955	69
Hamlin Beach State Park 1 Hamlin Beach Blvd W	Hamlin	NY	14464	**800-456-2267**	585-964-2462	564
Hamline University 1536 Hewitt Ave	Saint Paul	MN	55104	**800-753-9753**	651-523-2207	167
Hammacher Schlemmer & Co 9307 N Milwaukee Ave	Niles	IL	60714	**800-321-1484**		362
Hammel Green & Abrahamson Inc 701 Washington Ave N	Minneapolis	MN	55401	**888-442-8255**	612-758-4000	263
Hammelmann Corp 600 Progress Rd	Dayton	OH	45449	**800-783-4935**	937-859-8777	638
Hammer Nutrition Ltd 4952 Whitefish Stage Rd *Cust Svc	Whitefish	MT	59937	**800-336-1977***	406-862-1877	797
Hammerman Bros Inc 50 W 57th St 12th Fl	New York	NY	10019	**800-223-6436**	212-956-2800	409
Hammersmith Mfg & Sales Inc 401 Central Ave	Horton	KS	66439	**800-375-8245**	785-486-2121	90
Hammock Beach Resort 200 Ocean Crest Dr	Palm Coast	FL	32137	**866-841-0287**	386-246-5500	667
Hammond Communications Group Inc 173 Trade St	Lexington	KY	40511	**888-424-1878**	859-254-1878	512
Hammond Drives & Equipment Inc 8527 Midland Rd	Freeland	MI	48623	**888-695-2239**	989-695-2239	358
Hammond Electronics Inc 1230 W Central Blvd *Sales	Orlando	FL	32805	**800-929-3672***	407-849-6060	248
Hammond Suzuki USA Inc 743 Annoreno Dr	Addison	IL	60101	**888-765-2900**	630-543-0277	526
Hamon Research-Cottrell Inc 58 E Main St	Somerville	NJ	08876	**800-445-6578**	908-685-4000	386
Hampden-Sydney College PO Box 667 *Admissions	Hampden Sydney	VA	23943	**800-755-0733***	434-223-6120	167
Hampson Archeological Museum State Park PO Box 156	Wilson	AR	72395	**888-742-8701**	870-655-8622	564
Hampton Affiliates 9600 SW Barnes Rd Ste 200	Portland	OR	97225	**888-310-1464**	503-297-7691	681
Hampton Behavioral Health Center 650 Rancocas Rd	Westampton	NJ	08060	**800-603-6767**		724
Hampton Conventions & Visitors Bureau 1919 Commerce Dr Ste 290	Hampton	VA	23666	**800-487-8778**	757-722-1222	208
Hampton Inn Philadelphia Ctr City-Convention Ctr 1301 Race St	Philadelphia	PA	19107	**800-426-7866**	215-665-9100	207
Hampton Plantation State Historic Site 1950 Rutledge Rd	McClellanville	SC	29458	**800-315-3087**	843-546-9361	564
Hampton Products International Corp 50 Icon	Foothill Ranch	CA	92610	**800-562-5625**	949-472-4256	350
Hampton Securities Ltd 141 Adelaide St W Ste 1800	Toronto	ON	M5H3L5	**877-225-0229**	416-862-7800	688
Hampton University 100 E Queen St	Hampton	VA	23668	**800-624-3341**	757-727-5000	167
Hamptons Magazine 67 Hampton Rd Ste 201	SouthHampton	NY	11968	**866-891-3144**	631-283-7125	456-22
Hamrick Mills Inc 515 W Buford St PO Box 48	Gaffney	SC	29341	**800-600-4305**	864-489-4731	742-1
Hana Hou Magazine (Hawaiian Airlines) 1144 Tenth Ave Ste 401	Honolulu	HI	96816	**888-733-3336**	808-733-3333	456-22
Hanalei Bay Resort & Suites 5380 Honoiki Rd	Princeville	HI	96722	**877-344-0688**	808-826-6522	667
Hanauma Bay Nature Preserve 100 Hanauma Bay Rd	Honolulu	HI	96825	**800-690-6200**	808-396-4229	49-4
Hanchett Entry Systems Inc (HES) 22630 N 17th Ave	Phoenix	AZ	85027	**800-626-7590**	623-582-4626	690
Hanchett Manufacturing Inc 906 N State St	Big Rapids	MI	49307	**800-454-7463**	231-796-7678	454
Hancock County 12630 Broad St	Sparta	GA	31087	**800-255-0135**	706-444-5746	338
Hancock County Co-op Oil Assn 245 State St	Garner	IA	50438	**800-924-2667**	641-923-2635	345
Hancock Holding Co 2510 14th St	Gulfport	MS	39501	**800-522-6542**	228-868-4727	360-2

Name / Address	City	State	ZIP	Toll-Free	Phone	Class
Hancock-Wood Electric Co-op Inc (HWEC) 1399 Business Pk Dr S PO Box 190	North Baltimore	OH	45872	800-445-4840	419-257-3241	247
Hancor Inc PO Box 1047	Findlay	OH	45839	888-892-2694	419-422-6521	595
Handgards Inc 901 Hawkins Blvd	El Paso	TX	79915	800-351-8161		575
Handi-Ramp 510 N Ave	Libertyville	IL	60048	800-876-7267	847-680-7700	358
Handlery Hotel & Resort 950 Hotel Cir N	San Diego	CA	92108	800-676-6567	619-298-0511	667
Handlery Union Square Hotel 351 Geary St	San Francisco	CA	94102	800-995-4874	415-781-7800	379
Handley Industries Inc 2101 Brooklyn Rd	Jackson	MI	49203	800-870-5088	517-787-8821	201
Handy Hardware Wholesale Inc 8300 Tewantin Dr	Houston	TX	77061	800-364-3835	713-644-1495	351
Handy Store Fixtures Inc 337 Sherman Ave	Newark	NJ	07114	800-631-4280	973-242-1600	288
Handyman Connection Inc 11115 Kenwood Rd	Cincinnati	OH	45242	800-884-2639	513-771-3003	191-11
Handyman Matters Inc 12567 W Cedar Dr	Lakewood	CO	80228	866-349-6946	303-984-0177	311
HandyTrac Systems LLC 510 Staghorn Ct	Alpharetta	GA	30004	800-665-9994	678-990-2305	690
Hanes Cos Inc 500 N McLin Creek Rd	Conover	NC	28613	877-252-3052	828-464-4673	593
Hanger Orthopedic Group Inc 10910 Domain Dr Ste 300	Austin	TX	78758	877-442-6437	512-777-3800	352
Hanger Prosthetics & Orthopedics Inc 10910 Domain Dr Ste 300	Austin	TX	78758	877-442-6437		476
Hangsterfer's Laboratories Inc 175 Ogden Rd	Mantua	NJ	08051	800-433-5823	856-468-0216	540
Hankook Tire America Corp 1450 Valley Rd	Wayne	NJ	07470	800-426-8252	973-633-9000	752
Hanley Wood Market Intelligence 555 Anton Blvd Ste 950	Costa Mesa	CA	92626	800-938-8839	714-540-8500	195
Hanley-Wood LLC 1 Thomas Cir NW Ste 600	Washington	DC	20005	800-227-8839	202-452-0800	634-9
Hanmi Bank 3660 Wilshire Blvd Ste PH-A	Los Angeles	CA	90010	877-808-4266	213-382-2200	360-2
Hanna Andersson Corp 1010 NW Flanders St *Cust Svc	Portland	OR	97209	800-222-0544*		458
Hanna Steel Corp 3812 Commerce Ave PO Box 558	Fairfield	AL	35064	800-633-8252	205-780-1111	489
Hannaford Bros Co 145 Pleasant Hill Rd	Scarborough	ME	04074	800-213-9040		298-8
Hannay Reels Inc 553 SR 143	Westerlo	NY	12193	877-467-3357	518-797-3791	116
Hannibal Carbide Tool Inc 5000 Paris Gravel Rd	Hannibal	MO	63401	800-451-9436	573-221-2775	492
Hannibal Convention & Visitors Bureau 505 N Third St	Hannibal	MO	63401	866-263-4825	573-221-2477	208
Hannibal Industries Inc 3851 S Santa Fe Ave	Los Angeles	CA	90058	888-246-7074	323-588-4261	489
Hannibal Regional Hospital 6500 Hospital Dr	Hannibal	MO	63401	888-426-6425	573-248-1300	374-3
Hannibal-LaGrange College 2800 Palmyra Rd *Admissions	Hannibal	MO	63401	800-454-1119*	573-221-3675	167
Hannon Hydraulics LLC 625 N Loop 12	Irving	TX	75061	800-333-4266	972-438-2870	225
Hannon Security Services Inc 9036 Grand Ave S	Minneapolis	MN	55420	800-328-3877	952-881-5865	691
Hanover College 484 Ball Dr	Hanover	IN	47243	800-213-2178	812-866-7000	167
Hanover Foods Corp 1550 York St PO Box 334 *OTC: HNFSA*	Hanover	PA	17331	800-888-4646	717-632-6000	297-36
Hanover Hospital 300 Highland Ave	Hanover	PA	17331	800-673-2426	717-637-3711	374-3
Hanover Inn 2 E Wheelock St	Hanover	NH	03755	800-443-7024	603-643-4300	379
Hanover Insurance Co 440 Lincoln St	Worcester	MA	01653	800-853-0456	508-855-1000	391-4
Hans Johnsen Co 8901 Chancellor Row *Sales	Dallas	TX	75247	800-879-1515*	214-879-1550	351
Hansa GCR LLC 308 SW First Ave	Portland	OR	97204	800-755-7683	503-241-8036	197
Hanscom Inc 331 Market St	Warren	RI	02885	877-725-6788	401-247-1999	607
Hansen Architectural Systems 5500 Se Alexander St	Hillsboro	OR	97123	800-599-2965	503-356-0959	491
Hansen Beverage Co 2661 Green River Rd	Corona	CA	92879	877-265-3632	800-426-7367	298-8
Hansen Manufacturing Corp 5100 W 12th St	Sioux Falls	SD	57107	800-328-1785	605-332-3200	209
Hansen Surfboards 1105 S Coast Hwy 101	Encinitas	CA	92024	800-480-4754	760-753-6595	709
Hansen Technologies Corp 6827 High Grove Blvd	Burr Ridge	IL	60527	800-426-7368	630-325-1565	204
Hansgrohe Inc 1490 Bluegrass Lakes Pkwy	Alpharetta	GA	30004	800-334-0455	770-360-9880	608
Hanson Information System 2433 W White Oaks Dr	Springfield	IL	62704	888-245-8468	217-726-2400	179
Hanson Logistics 2900 S State St	Saint Joseph	MI	49085	888-772-1197	269-982-1390	448
Hanson Medical Systems Inc 1954 Howell Branch Rd Ste 203	Winter Park	FL	32792	877-671-3883	407-671-3883	474
Hapag-Lloyd America Inc 401 E Jackson St	Tampa	FL	33602	800-282-8977	813-276-4600	314
Hapco Inc 26252 Hillman Hwy	Abingdon	VA	24210	800-368-7171	276-628-7171	490
Hapman 6002 E N Ave	Kalamazoo	MI	49048	800-427-6260	269-343-1675	209

Name / Address	City	State	ZIP	Toll-Free	Phone	Class
Happy Time Tours & Travel 1475 Walsh St W	Thunder Bay	ON	P7E4X6	800-473-5955	807-473-5955	770
Hapuna Beach Prince Hotel 62-100 Kauna'oa Dr	Kamuela	HI	96743	800-882-6060	808-880-1111	667
Harbec Plastics Inc 369 SR- 104	Ontario	NY	14519	888-521-4416	585-265-0010	607
Harben Inc 2010 Ronald Regan Blvd	Cumming	GA	30041	800-327-5387	770-889-9535	638
Harbin Hot Springs 18424 Harbin Springs Rd PO Box 782	Middletown	CA	95461	800-622-2477	707-987-2477	671
Harbison-Fischer 901 N Crowley Rd	Crowley	TX	76036	800-364-7867	817-297-2211	536
Harbor Court Hotel 165 Steuart St	San Francisco	CA	94105	866-792-6283	415-882-1300	379
Harbor Credit Union 800 Weise St	Green Bay	WI	54302	800-827-4645	920-431-6688	221
Harbor Freight Tools 3491 Mission Oaks Blvd	Camarillo	CA	93011	800-444-3353	805-445-4791	351
Harbor Hospital Ctr 3001 S Hanover St	Baltimore	MD	21225	800-280-9006	410-350-3200	374-3
Harbor Hotel Provincetown 698 Commercial St Cape Cod	Provincetown	MA	02657	855-447-8696		378
Harbor Light Hospice 800 Roosevelt Rd Bldg C Ste 206	Glen Ellyn	IL	60137	800-419-0542	630-300-3716	371
Harbor Sales 1000 Harbor Ct	Sudlersville	MD	21668	800-345-1712		612
Harbor View Hotel 131 N Water St Martha's Vineyard PO Box 7	Edgartown	MA	02539	800-225-6005	508-627-7000	379
Harborlite 130 Castilian Dr	Santa Barbara	CA	93117	800-893-4445	805-562-0200	502-3
HarborOne Credit Union 770 Oak St PO Box 720	Brockton	MA	02301	800-244-7592	508-895-1000	221
Harborplace & the Gallery 201 E Pratt St	Baltimore	MD	21202	800-722-8614	410-332-4191	49-5
Harbors Home Health & Hospice 201 Seventh St	Hoquiam	WA	98550	800-772-1319	360-532-5454	371
Harborside Hotel & Marina 55 W St	Bar Harbor	ME	04609	800-328-5033	207-288-5033	379
Harborside Inn 1 Christie's Landing	Newport	RI	02840	800-427-9444	401-846-6600	379
Harborside Suites At Little Harbor 611 Destiny Dr	Ruskin	FL	33570	800-327-2773		667
Harbour Industries Inc 4744 Shelburne Rd PO Box 188	Shelburne	VT	05482	800-659-4733	802-985-3311	812
Harbour Towers Hotel & Suites 345 Quebec St	Victoria	BC	V8V1W4	800-663-5896	250-385-2405	378
Harbour's Edge 401 E Linton Blvd	Delray Beach	FL	33483	888-417-9281	561-272-7979	670
Harbourtowne Golf Resort & Conference Ctr 9784 Martingham Dr	Saint Michaels	MD	21663	800-446-9066	410-745-9066	667
Harco Company Ltd 5915 Coopers Ave	Mississauga	ON	L4Z1R9	800-387-9503	905-890-1220	34
Harco National Insurance Co PO Box 68309	Schaumburg	IL	60168	800-448-4642		391-4
Harcourt Equipment 313 Hwy 169 & 175 E	Harcourt	IA	50544	800-445-5646	515-354-5332	276
Harcourt Outlines Inc 7765 S 175 W PO Box 128	Milroy	IN	46156	800-428-6584		54
Harcourt Pencil Co 7765 S 175 W	Milroy	IN	46156	800-428-6584		570
Harcum College 750 Montgomery Ave	Bryn Mawr	PA	19010	800-650-0035	610-525-4100	161
Hard Mfg Company Inc 230 Grider St	Buffalo	NY	14215	800-873-4273		320-3
Hard Rock Cafe 45 Monroe St	Detroit	MI	48226	888-519-6683	313-964-7625	669
Hard Rock Cafe International Inc 6100 Old Pk Ln	Orlando	FL	32835	888-519-6683	407-445-7625	668
Hard Rock Hotel & Casino 4455 Paradise Rd	Las Vegas	NV	89169	800-693-7625	702-693-5000	667
Hard Rock Hotel & Casino Biloxi 777 Beach Blvd	Biloxi	MS	39530	877-877-6256	228-374-7625	132
Hard Rock Hotel at Universal Orlando Resort 5800 Universal Blvd	Orlando	FL	32819	888-430-4999	407-503-2000	667
Hard Rock Hotel San Diego 207 Fifth Ave	San Diego	CA	92101	866-751-7625	619-702-3000	379
HARDI Hydronic Heating & Cooling Council 3455 Mill Run Dr Ste 820	Hilliard	OH	43026	888-253-2128	614-345-4328	48-18
Hardi Inc 1500 W 76th St	Davenport	IA	52806	866-770-7063	563-386-1730	275
Hardin County 495 Main St	Savannah	TN	38372	800-552-3866	731-925-3921	338
Hardin County Chamber of Commerce (HCCBA) 225 S Detroit St	Kenton	OH	43326	888-642-7346	419-673-4131	138
Hardin's Florist Supply 329 W Bowman Ave	Liberty	NC	27298	800-672-8226	336-622-3035	294
Harding Instruments 7741 Wagner Rd NW	Edmonton	AB	T6E5X7	888-792-1171	780-462-7100	203
Harding University 915 E Market Ave	Searcy	AR	72149	800-477-4407	501-279-4000	167
Harding University Graduate School of Religion 915 E Market Ave	Searcy	AR	72143	800-477-4407	501-279-4407	168-3
Hardinge Inc 1 Hardinge Dr *NASDAQ: HDNG*	Elmira	NY	14902	800-843-8801	607-734-2281	454
Hardin-Simmons University 2200 Hickory St	Abilene	TX	79698	877-464-7889	325-670-1206	167
Hardware Distribution Warehouses Inc (HDW) 6900 Woolworth Rd *Cust Svc	Shreveport	LA	71129	800-256-8527*	318-686-8527	351
Hardware Suppliers of America Inc (HSI) 1400 E Fire Tower Rd	Greenville	NC	27858	800-334-5625		351
Hardwick Clothes Inc 3800 Old Tasso Rd	Cleveland	TN	37312	800-251-6392		154-11

Name / Address	City	State	ZIP	Toll-Free	Phone	Class
Hardwoods of Michigan Inc 430 Div St	Clinton	MI	49236	**800-327-2812**	517-456-7431	681
Hardy Corp 350 Industrial Dr	Birmingham	AL	35211	**800-289-4822**	205-252-7191	191-10
Hardy County 204 Washington St Rm 111	Moorefield	WV	26836	**800-222-1222**	304-530-0250	338
Harford County Chamber of Commerce 108 S Bond St	Bel Air	MD	21014	**800-682-8536**	410-838-2020	138
Harford County Public Library 1221-A Brass Mill Rd	Belcamp	MD	21017	**800-944-7403**	410-575-6761	434-3
Hargrave Military Academy (HMA) 200 Military Dr	Chatham	VA	24531	**800-432-2480**	434-432-2481	621
Hargray Communications 856 William Hilton Pkwy PO Box 5986	Hilton Head Island	SC	29938	**800-726-1266**	843-341-1501	733
Harkcon 1390 Chain Bridge Rd 570	Mclean	VA	22101	**800-499-6456**		462
Harkins Builders Inc 2201 Warwick Way	Marriottsville	MD	21104	**800-227-2345**	410-750-2600	188
Harlan ARH Hospital 81 Ballpark Rd	Harlan	KY	40831	**800-274-9375**	606-573-8100	374-3
Harlan County 311 Main St	Alma	NE	68920	**800-762-5498**		338
Harlan Materials Handling Corp 27 Stanley Rd	Kansas City	KS	66115	**800-255-4262**	913-342-5650	469
Harlem Globetrotters International Inc 400 E Van Buren St Ste 300	Phoenix	AZ	85004	**800-641-4667**	602-258-0000	183
Harlequin Enterprises Ltd 225 Duncan Mill Rd	Don Mills	ON	M3B3K9	**888-343-9777**	416-445-5860	634-2
Harlequin-Silhouette Books 233 Broadway Ste 1001	New York	NY	10279	**800-873-8635**	212-553-4200	634-2
Harley-Davidson Financial Services Inc PO Box 21489	Carson City	NV	89721	**888-691-4337**		216
Harleysville Group Inc 355 Maple Ave *NASDAQ: HGIC*	Harleysville	PA	19438	**800-523-6344**	215-256-5000	360-4
Harleysville Insurance Co of New Jersey 112 W Park Dr	Mount Laurel	NJ	08054	**800-322-5521**	856-642-9779	391-4
Harleysville Mutual Insurance Co 355 Maple Ave	Harleysville	PA	19438	**800-523-6344**	215-256-5000	391-2
Harleysville Savings Financial Corp 271 Main St *NASDAQ: HARL*	Harleysville	PA	19438	**888-256-8828**	215-256-8828	360-2
Harleysville Worcester Insurance Co 120 Front St Ste 400	Worcester	MA	01608	**800-225-7387**	508-754-6666	391-4
Harlo Corp PO Box 129	Grandville	MI	49468	**800-391-4151**	616-538-0550	469
Harman International Industries Inc 400 Atlantic St 15th Fl *NYSE: HAR*	Stamford	CT	06901	**800-473-0602**	203-328-3500	51
Harman, Claytor, Corrigan & Wellman A Professional Corp PO Box 70280	Richmond	VA	23255	**877-747-4229**	804-747-5200	428
Harmon Electric Assn Inc (HEA) 114 N First St PO Box 393	Hollis	OK	73550	**800-643-7769**	580-688-3342	247
Harmon Stores Inc 650 Liberty Ave	Union	NJ	07083	**866-427-6661**		239
Harmonic Drive LLC 247 Lynnfield St	Peabody	MA	01960	**800-921-3332**	978-532-1800	60
Harmonic Inc 4300 N First St *NASDAQ: HLIT*	San Jose	CA	95134	**800-322-2885**	408-542-2500	645
Harmonie State Park 3451 Harmonie State Pk Rd	New Harmony	IN	47631	**866-622-6746**	812-682-4821	564
Harmony Dental Lab 758 W Duval St	Jacksonville	FL	32202	**888-354-3594**	904-354-4467	418
Harmony Foundation Inc 1600 Fish Hatchery Rd	Estes Park	CO	80517	**866-686-7867**	970-586-4491	724
Harms Charters 532 S Vly View Rd	Sioux Falls	SD	57106	**800-678-6543**	605-336-3339	106
Harnack Co 6016 Nordic Dr *Cust Svc	Cedar Falls	IA	50613	**800-772-2022***	319-277-0660	429
Harnett County Board of Education 1008 11th St PO Box 1029	Lillington	NC	27546	**800-942-3767**	910-893-8151	683
Harney Rock & Paving Co 457 S Date Ave	Burns	OR	97720	**888-298-2681**	541-573-7855	502-5
Harold G Butzer Inc 730 Wicker Ln	Jefferson City	MO	65109	**800-769-1065**	573-636-4115	191-10
Harold Levinson Assoc (HLA) 21 Banfi Plz	Farmingdale	NY	11735	**800-325-2512**	631-962-2400	298-3
Harper Brush Works Inc 400 N Second St	Fairfield	IA	52556	**800-223-7894**	641-472-5186	102
Harper County 201 N Jennings Ave	Anthony	KS	67003	**877-537-2110**	620-842-5555	338
Harper Engraving & Printing Co 2626 Fisher Rd	Columbus	OH	43204	**800-848-5196**	614-276-0700	626
Harper Motors Inc 200 Hwy 531	Minden	LA	71055	**800-259-0395**	318-377-0395	200
Harper Trucks Inc PO Box 12330	Wichita	KS	67277	**800-835-4099**	316-942-1381	469
Harper's Magazine 666 Broadway 11th Fl	New York	NY	10012	**800-444-4653**	212-420-5720	456-11
HarperCollins Publishers Inc 10 E 53rd St	New York	NY	10022	**800-242-7737**	212-207-7000	634-2
Harrah's Ak-Chin Casino Resort 15406 Maricopa Rd *General	Maricopa	AZ	85139	**800-427-7247***	480-802-5000	667
Harrah's Cherokee Casino & Hotel 777 Casino Dr *General	Cherokee	NC	28719	**877-811-0777***	828-497-7777	132
Harrah's Council Bluffs 1 Harrahs Blvd	Council Bluffs	IA	51501	**800-342-7724**	712-329-6000	132
Harrah's Joliet 151 N Joliet St	Joliet	IL	60432	**800-522-4700**	815-740-7800	132
Harrah's Laughlin 2900 S Casino Dr	Laughlin	NV	89029	**800-427-7247**	702-298-4600	132
Harrah's New Orleans 8 Canal St	New Orleans	LA	70130	**800-427-7247**	504-533-6000	132
Harrah's Resort Atlantic City 777 Harrah's Blvd	Atlantic City	NJ	08401	**800-342-7724**	609-441-5000	132
Harrah's Rincon Casino & Resort 777 Harrah's Rincon Way	Valley Center	CA	92082	**800-522-4700**	760-751-3100	667
Harrah's Tunica 1021 Casino Ctr Dr	Robinsonville	MS	38664	**800-946-4946**	800-303-7463	132
Harrang Long Gary Rudnick PC 360 E 10th Ave Ste 300	Eugene	OR	97401	**800-315-4172**	541-485-0220	428
Harraseeket Inn 162 Main St	Freeport	ME	04032	**800-342-6423**	207-865-9377	379
Harri Plumbing & Heating Inc 809 W 12th St	Juneau	AK	99801	**800-478-3190**	907-586-3190	611
Harriman State Park 3489 Green Canyon Rd	Island Park	ID	83429	**866-634-3246**	208-558-7368	564
Harrington College of Design 200 W Madison St	Chicago	IL	60606	**866-590-4423**		167
Harrington Hoists Inc 401 W End Ave	Manheim	PA	17545	**800-233-3010**	717-665-2000	386
Harrington Industrial Plastics LLC 14480 Yorba Ave	Chino	CA	91710	**800-213-4528**	909-597-8641	385
Harrington Memorial Hospital (HMH) 100 S St	Southbridge	MA	01550	**800-416-6072**	508-765-9771	374-3
Harrington Raceway 15 W Rider Rd	Harrington	DE	19952	**888-887-5687**	302-398-7223	639
Harris Assoc LP 111 South Wacker Dr Ste 4600	Chicago	IL	60606	**800-731-0700**	312-646-3600	401
Harris Connect LLC 1511 Rt 22 Ste C-25	Brewster	NY	10509	**800-516-4915**		634-2
Harris Corp 1025 W NASA Blvd *NYSE: HRS*	Melbourne	FL	32919	**800-442-7747**	321-727-9100	645
Harris Corp RF Communications Div 1680 University Ave	Rochester	NY	14610	**866-264-8040**	585-244-5830	645
Harris County 112 S College St PO Box 426	Hamilton	GA	31811	**888-478-0010**	706-628-0010	338
Harris Farms Inc 27366 W Oakland Ave	Coalinga	CA	93210	**800-311-6211**	559-884-2859	10-9
Harris Financial Services Inc 940 Spokane Ave	Whitefish	MT	59937	**800-735-7895**	406-862-4400	688
Harris Industries Inc 5181 Argosy Ave	Huntington Beach	CA	92649	**800-222-6866**	714-898-8048	729
Harris Miniature Golf 141 W Burk Ave	Wildwood	NJ	08260	**888-294-6530**	609-522-4200	190-3
Harris Moran Seed Co PO Box 4938	Modesto	CA	95352	**800-808-7333**	800-320-4672	692
Harris myCFO Inc 2200 Geng Rd Ste 100	Palo Alto	CA	94303	**866-966-1130**	650-210-5000	404
Harris Products Group 4501 Quality Pl	Mason	OH	45040	**800-733-4043**	513-754-2000	809
Harris Ranch Beef Co 16277 S McCall Ave PO Box 220	Selma	CA	93662	**800-742-1955**		472
Harris Soup Co, The 17711 NE Riverside Pkwy	Portland	OR	97230	**800-307-7687**	503-257-7687	298-8
Harris Teeter Inc PO Box 10100 *NYSE: HTSI*	Mathews	NC	28106	**800-432-6111**	704-844-3100	187
Harris Wyatt & Amala Attorneys at Law 5778 Commercial St Se	Salem	OR	97306	**800-853-2144**	503-378-7744	428
Harrisburg Area Community College 1 HACC Dr	Harrisburg	PA	17110	**800-222-4222**	717-780-2300	161
Gettysburg 731 Old Harrisburg Rd	Gettysburg	PA	17325	**800-222-4222**	717-337-3855	161
Lebanon 735 Cumberland St	Lebanon	PA	17042	**800-222-4222**	717-270-4222	161
Harrisburg Dairies Inc 2001 Herr St	Harrisburg	PA	17105	**800-692-7429**	717-233-8701	297-27
Harrisburg Hospital 111 S Front St	Harrisburg	PA	17101	**888-782-5678**	717-782-3131	374-3
Harrisburg International Airport 1 Terminal Dr Ste 300	Middletown	PA	17057	**888-235-9442**	717-948-3900	27
Harrisburg Regional Chamber 3211 N Front St Ste 201	Harrisburg	PA	17110	**877-883-8339**	717-232-4099	138
HarrisData 13555 Bishops Ct Ste 300	Brookfield	WI	53005	**800-225-0585**	262-784-9099	180-1
Harrison Hot Springs Resort & Spa 100 Esplanade Ave	Harrison Hot Springs	BC	V0M1K0	**800-663-2266**	604-796-2244	667
Harrison Memorial Hospital 2520 Cherry Ave	Bremerton	WA	98310	**866-844-9355**	360-377-3911	374-3
Harrison Paint Co 1329 Harrison Ave SW	Canton	OH	44706	**800-321-0680**	330-455-5125	549
Harrison Steel Castings Co Inc 900 S Mound St	Attica	IN	47918	**800-659-4722**	765-762-2481	308
Harrisonville Telephone Co 213 S Main St PO Box 149	Waterloo	IL	62298	**888-482-8353**	618-939-6112	733
Harrogate 400 Locust St	Lakewood	NJ	08701	**888-551-5531**	732-905-7070	670
Harry & David Holdings Inc 2500 S Pacific Hwy *Cust Svc	Medford	OR	97501	**877-322-1200***		336
Harry Cooper Supply Company Inc 605 N Sherman Pkwy	Springfield	MO	65802	**800-426-6737**	417-865-8392	611
Harry Davis & Co 1725 Blvd of Allies	Pittsburgh	PA	15219	**800-775-2289**	412-765-1170	50
Harry G Barr Co 6500 S Zero St	Fort Smith	AR	72903	**800-829-2277**	479-646-7891	237
Harry Hynes Memorial Hospice 313 S Market St	Wichita	KS	67202	**800-767-4965**	316-265-9441	371
Harry Klitzner Co, The 530 Wellington Ave Ste 11	Cranston	RI	02910	**800-621-0161**		409
Harry London Candies Inc 5353 Lauby Rd *Cust Svc	North Canton	OH	44720	**800-333-3629***	330-494-0833	297-8
Harry Ritchie's Jewelers Inc 956 Willamette St *Cust Svc	Eugene	OR	97401	**800-935-2850***	541-686-1787	410
Harry S Truman College 1145 W Wilson Ave	Chicago	IL	60640	**877-863-6339**	773-878-1700	161

Name / Address	City	State	ZIP	Toll-Free	Phone	Class
Harry S Truman Memorial Veterans Hospital 800 Hospital Dr	Columbia	MO	65201	**877-222-8387**	573-814-6000	374-8
Harry S Truman National Historic Site 223 N Main St	Independence	MO	64050	**877-642-4743**	816-254-2720	563
Harry S Truman Presidential Library & Museum 500 W Hwy 24	Independence	MO	64050	**800-833-1225**	816-268-8200	434-2
Harry S Truman's Little White House Museum 111 Front St	Key West	FL	33040	**800-435-7352**	305-294-9911	519
Harry Winston Inc 718 Fifth Ave	New York	NY	10019	**800-988-4110**	212-399-1000	409
Harsco Corp 350 Poplar Church Rd *NYSE: HSC*	Camp Hill	PA	17011	**866-470-3900**	717-763-7064	187
Harsco Industrial Air-X-Changers 5215 Arkansas Rd	Catoosa	OK	74015	**800-404-3904**	918-619-8000	90
Hart & Price Corp PO Box 36368	Dallas	TX	75235	**800-777-9129**	214-521-9129	663
Hart Corp 900 Jaymor Rd	SouthHampton	PA	18966	**800-368-4278**	215-322-5100	650
Hart Electric Membership Corp 1071 Elberton Hwy	Hartwell	GA	30643	**800-241-4109**	706-376-4714	247
Hart Industries Inc 11412 Cronridge Dr	Owings Mills	MD	21117	**800-638-2700**	410-581-1900	626
Hart InterCivic 15500 Wells Port Dr PO Box 80649	Austin	TX	78708	**800-223-4278**	512-252-6400	799
Hart Petroleum 323 Skidmores Rd	Deer Park	NY	11729	**800-796-3342**	631-667-3200	579
Hart Publications Inc 1616 S Voss Rd Ste 1000	Houston	TX	77057	**800-874-2544**	713-260-6400	634-9
Hart Schaffner Marx (HSM) 1680 E Touhy Ave	Des Plaines	IL	60018	**800-327-4466**		154-11
Hart Scientific Inc 799 E Utah Vly Dr	American Fork	UT	84003	**800-438-4278**	801-763-1600	203
Harte Nissan Inc 165 W Service Rd	Hartford	CT	06120	**866-687-8971**	860-549-2800	56
Harte-Hanks Inc 9601 McAllister Fwy Ste 610 *NYSE: HHS*	San Antonio	TX	78216	**800-456-9748**	210-829-9000	5
Harte-Hanks Response Management 2800 Wells Branch Pkwy	Austin	TX	78728	**800-456-9748**	512-434-1100	734
Hartford Computer Group Inc 10440 Little Patuxent Pkwy 3rd Fl	Columbia	MD	21044	**800-370-5849**	410-740-3020	182
Hartford Courant 285 Broad St	Hartford	CT	06115	**800-524-4242**	860-241-6200	531-2
Hartford Electric Supply Co (HESCO) 30 Inwood Rd Ste 1	Rocky Hill	CT	06067	**800-969-5444**	860-236-6363	248
Hartford Financial Services Group Inc 690 Asylum Ave *NYSE: HIG*	Hartford	CT	06115	**866-553-5663**	860-547-5000	360-4
Hartford Hospital 80 Seymour St	Hartford	CT	06102	**800-545-7664**	860-545-5000	374-3
Hartford Life & Accident Insurance Co 1 Hartford Plz	Hartford	CT	06155	**877-896-9320**	860-547-5000	391-2
Hartford Mutual Funds 30 Dan Rd Ste 55022	Canton	MA	02021	**888-843-7824**		527
Hartford Seminary 77 Sherman St	Hartford	CT	06105	**877-860-2255**	860-509-9500	167
Hartford's Omni Auto Plan PO Box 105440	Atlanta	GA	30348	**800-243-5860**	770-952-4500	391-4
Hartnell College 156 Homestead Ave	Salinas	CA	93901	**888-678-2871**	831-755-6700	161
Hartness House Inn 30 Orchard St	Springfield	VT	05156	**800-732-4789**	802-885-2115	379
Hartness International Inc 1200 Garlington Rd PO Box 26509	Greenville	SC	29616	**800-845-8791**	864-297-1200	546
Hartnett Law Firm, The 2920 N Pearl St	Dallas	TX	75201	**800-900-9702**	214-742-4655	428
Harts Nursery of Jefferson Inc 4049 Jefferson-Scio Rd	Jefferson	OR	97352	**800-356-9335**	541-327-3366	369
Hartsfield-Jackson Atlanta International Airport 6000 N Terminal Pkwy Ste 4000	Atlanta	GA	30320	**800-897-1910**	404-530-6600	27
Hartson-kennedy Cabinet Top Company Inc 522 W 22nd St PO Box 3095	Marion	IN	46953	**800-388-8144**	765-668-8144	598
Hartung Agalite Glass Co 17830 W Valley Hwy	Seattle	WA	98188	**800-552-2227**	425-656-2626	330
Hartung Bros Inc 708 Heartland Trl Ste 2000	Madison	WI	53717	**800-362-2522**	608-829-6000	10-9
Hartung Glass Industries 10450 SW Ridder Rd	Wilsonville	OR	97070	**800-552-2227**	503-682-3846	330
Hartwell Medical Corp 6354 Corte Del Abeto Ste F	Carlsbad	CA	92011	**800-633-5900**	760-438-5500	475
Hartwick College 1 Hartwick Dr	Oneonta	NY	13820	**888-427-8942**	607-431-4150	167
Harty Press Inc, The PO Box 324	New Haven	CT	06513	**800-654-0562**	203-562-5112	626
Hartz Mountain Corp, The 400 Plz Dr	Secaucus	NJ	07094	**800-275-1414**		577
Hartzell Engine Technologies LLC 2900 Selma Hwy	Montgomery	AL	36108	**877-359-5355**	334-386-5400	21
Hartzell Fan Inc 910 S Downing St	Piqua	OH	45356	**800-336-3267**	937-773-7411	18
Hartzell Propeller Inc 1 Propeller Pl	Piqua	OH	45356	**800-942-7767**	937-778-4200	22
Harvard Bioscience Inc 84 October Hill Rd *NASDAQ: HBIO*	Holliston	MA	01746	**800-272-2775**	508-893-8999	419
Harvard Book Store Inc 1256 Massachusetts Ave	Cambridge	MA	02138	**800-542-7323**	617-661-1515	95
Harvard Business Review 60 Harvard Way	Boston	MA	02163	**800-274-3214**	617-783-7500	456-5
Harvard Business School Publishing 60 Harvard Way	Boston	MA	02163	**800-795-5200**		634-4
Harvard Educational Review 8 Story St 1st Fl	Cambridge	MA	02138	**877-930-4473**	617-495-3432	456-8
Harvard Medical School 25 Shattuck St	Boston	MA	02115	**866-606-0573**	617-432-1550	168-2
Harvard Pilgrim Health Care Inc 93 Worcester St	Wellesley	MA	02481	**888-888-4742**	617-509-1000	391-3
Harvard Square Hotel 110 Mt Auburn St Harvard Sq	Cambridge	MA	02138	**800-458-5886**	617-864-5200	379
Harvard University Press 79 Garden St	Cambridge	MA	02138	**800-405-1619**	617-495-2600	634-4
Harvard Women's Health Watch PO Box 9308	Big Sandy	TX	75755	**877-649-9457**		530-8
Harvest Energy Trust 700 2nd St SW Ste 2100	Calgary	AB	T2P2W1	**866-666-1178**	403-265-1178	673
Harvest Inn 1 Main St	Saint Helena	CA	94574	**800-950-8466**	707-963-9463	379
Harvest Land Co-op 711 Front St PO Box 278	Morgan	MN	56266	**800-245-5819**	507-249-3196	446
Harvest Partners 280 Pk Ave 25th Fl	New York	NY	10017	**866-771-1000**	212-599-6300	790
Harvey Cadillac Co 2600 28th St SE *Sales	Grand Rapids	MI	49512	**877-845-1557***	616-949-1140	56
Harvey Industries Inc 1400 Main St	Waltham	MA	02451	**800-598-5400**		193-4
Harvey Mudd College 301 Platt Blvd Kingston Hall	Claremont	CA	91711	**877-827-5462**	909-621-8011	167
Harvey Software Inc 7050 Winkler Rd Ste 104	Fort Myers	FL	33919	**800-231-0296**		179
Harvey Watt & Co 475 N Central Ave	Atlanta	GA	30354	**800-241-6103**	404-767-7501	391-2
Harveys Lake Tahoe Hwy 50 at Stateline Ave PO Box 128	Lake Tahoe	NV	89449	**800-522-4700**	775-588-6611	132
Hasbro Inc 1027 Newport Ave *NASDAQ: HAS*	Pawtucket	RI	02861	**800-242-7276**	401-431-8697	760
Hasco Oil Company Inc 2800 Temple Ave	Long Beach	CA	90806	**800-456-8491**	562-595-8491	578
Haskel International Inc 100 E Graham Pl	Burbank	CA	91502	**800-743-2720**	818-843-4000	638
Haskell Co 111 Riverside Ave	Jacksonville	FL	32202	**800-622-4326**	904-791-4500	190-7
Hassayampa Inn 122 E Gurley St *Cust Svc	Prescott	AZ	86301	**800-322-1927***		379
Hastings & Sons Publishing 38 Exchange St	Lynn	MA	01901	**800-243-4636**	781-593-7700	634-8
Hastings Area Chamber of Commerce & Tourism Bureau 111 E Third St	Hastings	MN	55033	**888-612-6122**	651-437-6775	138
Hastings Bus Co 425 31st St E	Hastings	MN	55033	**800-210-6362**	651-437-1888	108
Hastings College 710 N Turner Ave	Hastings	NE	68901	**800-532-7642**	402-463-2402	167
Hastings Entertainment Inc 3601 Plains Blvd *NASDAQ: HAST* ■ *Cust Svc	Amarillo	TX	79102	**877-427-8464***		95
Hastings Equity Grain Bin Mfg Co 1900 Summit Ave	Hastings	NE	68901	**888-883-2189**	402-462-2189	275
Hastings House Country House Hotel 160 Upper Ganges Rd	Salt Spring Island	BC	V8K2S2	**800-661-9255**	250-537-2362	379
Hastings HVAC Inc 3606 Yost Ave PO Box 669 *Cust Svc	Hastings	NE	68902	**800-228-4243***	402-463-9821	14
Hastings Manufacturing Co 325 N Hanover St	Hastings	MI	49058	**800-776-1088**	269-945-2491	127
Hastings Veterans Home 1200 E 18th St	Hastings	MN	55033	**877-838-3803**	651-438-8500	791
Hat World Corp 7555 Woodland Dr	Indianapolis	IN	46278	**888-564-4287**		156-5
Hatboro-Horsham School District 229 Meetinghouse Rd	Horsham	PA	19044	**866-771-3170**	215-672-5660	683
Hatch & Kirk Inc 5111 Leary Ave NW	Seattle	WA	98107	**800-426-2818**	206-783-2766	264
HatchBeauty Agency LLC 1715 18th St	Santa Monica	CA	90404	**877-428-2424**		197
Hatfield Quality Meats Inc 2700 Clemens Rd	Hatfield	PA	19440	**800-743-1191**	215-368-2500	472
Hatteras Hammocks Inc 305 Industrial Blvd	Greenville	NC	27834	**800-643-3522**	252-758-0641	320-4
Hattiesburg American 825 N Main St	Hattiesburg	MS	39401	**800-844-2637**	601-582-4321	531-2
Hattiesburg-Laurel Regional Airport 1002 Terminal Dr	Moselle	MS	39459	**800-433-7300**	601-649-2444	27
Hatton Brown Publishers Inc PO Box 2268	Montgomery	AL	36102	**800-669-5613**	334-834-1170	634-9
Hauck & Assoc Inc 1025 Thomas Jefferson St Ste 500 E	Washington	DC	20007	**800-767-7777**	202-452-8100	46
Hauppauge Computer Works Inc 91 Cabot Ct	Hauppauge	NY	11788	**800-443-6284**	631-434-1600	624
Hauppauge Digital Inc 91 Cabot Ct *OTC: HAUP*	Hauppauge	NY	11788	**800-443-6284**	631-434-1600	624
Hause Machines 809 S Pleasant St	Montpelier	OH	43543	**800-932-8665**	419-485-3158	454
Hausmann Industries Inc 130 Union St	Northvale	NJ	07647	**888-428-7626**	201-767-0255	320-1
Havenwood-Heritage Heights Havenwood Campus 33 Christian Ave	Concord	NH	03301	**800-457-6833**	603-224-5363	670
Havenwoods State Forest 6141 N Hopkins St	Milwaukee	WI	53209	**888-936-7463**	414-527-0232	564
Havenwyck Hospital 1525 University Dr	Auburn Hills	MI	48326	**800-401-2727**	248-373-9200	374-5
Haverford Trust Co 3 Radnor Corp Ctr Ste 450	Radnor	PA	19087	**888-995-1979**	610-995-8700	405
Haverhill Gazette 100 Turnpike St	N Andover	MA	01831	**888-411-3245**	978-946-2000	531-2
Haverty Furniture Cos Inc 780 Johnson Ferry Rd NE Ste 800 *NYSE: HVT*	Atlanta	GA	30342	**888-428-3789**	404-443-2900	322
Haviland Enterprises Inc 421 Ann St NW	Grand Rapids	MI	49504	**800-456-1134**	616-361-6691	145

Alphabetical Section

Listing	City	State	ZIP	Toll-Free	Phone	Class
Hawaii						
Child Support Enforcement Agency 601 Kamokila Blvd Ste 251	Kapolei	HI	96707	888-317-9081		339-12
Taxation Dept 830 Punchbowl St Rm 221	Honolulu	HI	96813	800-222-3229	808-587-4242	339-12
Vocational Rehabilitation Div 1901 Bachelot St	Honolulu	HI	96817	800-316-8005	808-586-9744	339-12
Hawaii Assn of Realtors 1136 12th Ave Ste 220	Honolulu	HI	96816	866-693-6767	808-733-7060	654
Hawaii Bar Journal 1100 Alakea St Ste 1000	Honolulu	HI	96813	888-586-1056	808-537-1868	456-15
Hawaii Coffee Company Inc 1555 Kalani St	Honolulu	HI	96817	800-338-8353	808-847-3600	158
Hawaii Community Foundation 65-1279 Kawaihae Rd	Kamuela	HI	96743	888-731-3863	808-537-6333	304
Hawaii Convention Ctr 1801 Kalakaua Ave	Honolulu	HI	96815	800-295-6603	808-943-3500	207
Hawaii Democratic Party 1050 Ala Moana Blvd Ste D-26	Honolulu	HI	96814	844-596-2980	808-596-2980	615-1
Hawaii Dental Assn 1345 S Beretania St Ste 301	Honolulu	HI	96814	800-359-6725	808-593-7956	229
Hawaii Dental Service 700 Bishop St Ste 700	Honolulu	HI	96813	800-232-2533	808-521-1431	391-3
Hawaii Dept of Education Honolulu District Office 4967 Kilauea Ave	Honolulu	HI	96816	800-437-8641	808-733-4950	683
Hawaii Information Consortium (HIC) 201 Merchant St Ste 1805	Honolulu	HI	96813	800-295-0089	808-695-4620	564
Hawaii Island Chamber of Commerce 117 Keawe St	Hilo	HI	96720	877-482-4411	808-935-7178	138
Hawaii Medical Assn 1360 S Beretania St	Honolulu	HI	96816	888-536-2792	808-536-7702	473
Hawaii Medical Service Assn 818 Keeaumoku St	Honolulu	HI	96822	800-776-4672	808-948-6111	391-3
Hawaii National Bank 45 N King St	Honolulu	HI	96817	800-528-2273	808-528-7711	68
Hawaii Nurses Assn (HNA) 949 Kapiolani Blvd Ste 107	Honolulu	HI	96814	800-617-2677	808-531-1628	532
Hawaii Nut & Bolt Inc 905 Ahua St	Honolulu	HI	96819	800-764-6887	808-834-1919	351
Hawaii Pacific University 1164 Bishop St Ste 200	Honolulu	HI	96813	866-225-5478	808-544-0200	167
Meader Library 1060 Bishop St	Honolulu	HI	96813	866-225-5478	808-544-0210	434-6
Windward Hawaii Loa 1164 Bishop St *Admissions	Honolulu	HI	96813	866-225-5478*	808-544-0200	167
Hawaii Planing Mill Ltd (HPM) 16-166 Melekahiwa St	Keaau	HI	96749	877-841-7633	808-966-5693	193-3
Hawaii Postsecondary Education Commission 2444 Dole St Bachman Hall Rm 209	Honolulu	HI	96822	877-531-2333	808-956-8213	723
Hawaii Preparatory Academy 65-1692 Kohala Mountain Rd	Kamuela	HI	96743	800-644-4481	808-885-7321	621
Hawaii Prince Hotel Waikiki, The 100 Holomoana St	Honolulu	HI	96815	888-977-4623		667
Hawaii Public Television 2350 Dole St	Honolulu	HI	96822	800-238-4847	808-973-1000	629
Hawaii Visitors & Convention Bureau 2270 Kalakaua Ave Ste 801	Honolulu	HI	96815	800-464-2924		208
Hawaii's Best Bed & Breakfasts 571 Pauku St	Kailua	HI	96734	800-262-9912	808-263-3100	376
Hawaiian Airlines HawaiianMiles PO Box 30008	Honolulu	HI	96820	877-426-4537		26
Hawaiian Airlines Inc 3375 Koapaka St Ste G350	Honolulu	HI	96819	800-367-5320	808-835-3700	25
Hawaiian Electric Industries Inc 1001 Bishop St Ste 2900	Honolulu	HI	96813	877-871-8461	808-543-5662	785
Hawaiian Inn 2301 S Atlantic Ave	Daytona Beach Shores	FL	32118	800-922-3023	386-255-5411	379
Hawaiian Isles Kona Coffee Co 2839 Mokumoa St *Orders	Honolulu	HI	96819	800-657-7716*	808-839-3255	297-7
Hawaiian Tug & Barge 1331 N Nimitz Hwy PO Box 3288	Honolulu	HI	96817	800-572-2743	808-543-9311	464
Hawk Eye, The 800 S Main St PO Box 10	Burlington	IA	52601	800-397-1708	319-754-8461	531-2
Hawk Inn & Mountain Resort 75 Billings Rd	Plymouth	VT	05056	800-685-4295	802-672-3811	667
Hawk's Cay Resort & Marina 61 Hawk's Cay Blvd	Duck Key	FL	33050	888-395-5539	305-743-7000	667
Hawker Powersource Inc 9404 Ooltewah Industrial Dr PO Box 808	Ooltewah	TN	37363	800-238-8658	423-238-5700	73
Hawkeye Community College 1501 E Orange Rd	Waterloo	IA	50704	800-670-4769	319-296-2320	161
Hawkeye REC 24049 Iowa 9	Cresco	IA	52136	800-658-2243	563-547-3801	247
Hawkeye Stages Inc 703 Dudley St	Decorah	IA	52101	877-464-2954	563-382-3639	106
Hawkins Inc 3100 E Hennepin Ave *NASDAQ: HWKN*	Minneapolis	MN	55413	800-328-5460	612-331-6910	142
Hawkins Traffic Safety Supply 1255 E Shore Hwy	Berkeley	CA	94710	800-772-3995	800-236-0112	676
Hawley Mountain Guest Ranch 4188 Main Boulder Rd	McLeod	MT	59052	877-496-7848	406-932-5791	241
Haworth Inc 1 Haworth Ctr	Holland	MI	49423	800-344-2600	616-393-3000	320-1
Haws Corp 1455 Kleppe Ln	Sparks	NV	89431	888-640-4297	775-359-4712	662
Hawthorn Ctr 18471 Haggerty Rd	Northville	MI	48167	855-444-3911	248-349-3000	374-1
Hawthorne Chamber of Commerce 12519 Crenshaw Blvd	Hawthorne	CA	90250	800-977-4770	310-676-1163	138
Hawthorne Hotel 18 Washington Sq W	Salem	MA	01970	800-729-7829	978-744-4080	379
Hawthorne Inn & Conference Ctr 420 High St	Winston-Salem	NC	27101	877-777-3099	336-777-3000	379

Listing	City	State	ZIP	Toll-Free	Phone	Class
Hawthorne Machinery Co 16945 Camino San Bernardo	San Diego	CA	92127	800-437-4228	858-674-7000	266-3
Hay Group Inc 1650 Arch St Ste 2300	Philadelphia	PA	19107	800-716-4429	215-861-2000	196
Hay House Inc PO Box 5100	Carlsbad	CA	92018	800-654-5126	760-431-7695	634-3
Hayden Automotive 1801 Waters Ridge Dr	Lewisville	TX	75057	888-505-4567		59
Hayden Twist Drill & Tool Company Inc 22822 Globe St	Warren	MI	48089	800-521-1780	586-754-7700	492
Hayes & Stolz Industrial Manufacturing Co 3521 Hemphill St PO Box 11217	Fort Worth	TX	76110	800-725-7272	817-926-3391	299
Hayes Handpiece Franchises Inc 5375 Avenida Encinas Ste C	Carlsbad	CA	92008	800-228-0521	760-602-0521	311
Hayes School Publishing Co Inc 321 Pennwood Ave	Pittsburgh	PA	15221	800-926-0704	412-371-2373	245
Hayes Specialties Corp 1761 E Genesee	Saginaw	MI	48601	800-248-3603	989-755-6541	329
Haynes International Inc 1020 W Pk Ave PO Box 9013 *NASDAQ: HAYN*	Kokomo	IN	46904	800-354-0806	765-456-6000	484
Hays Convention & Visitors Bureau 2700 Vine St PO Box 490	Hays	KS	67601	800-569-4505	785-628-8202	208
Hays Fluid Controls 114 Eason Rd	Dallas	NC	28034	800-354-4297	704-922-9565	788
Hays Medical Ctr (HMC) 2220 Canterbury Dr	Hays	KS	67601	800-248-0073	785-650-2759	374-3
Haystak Digital Marketing LLC 1514 Broadway Ste 201	Fort Myers	FL	33901	866-292-0194		5
Hayward Baker Inc 1130 Annapolis Rd Ste 202	Odenton	MD	21113	800-456-6548	410-551-8200	191-5
Haywood Community College 185 Freedlander Dr	Clyde	NC	28721	866-468-6422	828-627-2821	161
Haywood County Chamber of Commerce 28 Walnut St	Waynesville	NC	28786	877-456-3073	828-456-3021	138
Haywood Electric Membership Corp 376 Grindstone Rd	Waynesville	NC	28785	800-951-6088	828-452-2281	247
Haywood Securities Inc Waterfront Centre 200 Burrard St Ste 700	Vancouver	BC	V6C3L6	800-663-9499	604-697-7100	401
Hazard Community & Technical College 1 Community College Dr	Hazard	KY	41701	800-246-7521	606-436-5721	161
Hazard Campus 101 Vo Tech Dr	Hazard	KY	41701	800-246-7521	606-436-5721	161
Lees Campus 601 Jefferson Ave	Jackson	KY	41339	800-246-7521	606-666-7521	161
Hazel Park Raceway 1650 E 10 Mile Rd	Hazel Park	MI	48030	800-794-8001	248-398-1000	639
Hazelden Chicago 867 N Dearborn St	Chicago	IL	60610	800-257-7810	312-943-3534	724
Hazelden Ctr for Youth & Families (HCYF) 11505 36th Ave N	Plymouth	MN	55441	800-257-7810	763-509-3800	724
Hazelden Foundation 15251 Pleasant Vly Rd	Center City	MN	55012	800-257-7810	651-213-4200	724
Hazelden New York 322 Eigth Ave 12th Fl	New York	NY	10001	800-257-7800	212-420-9520	724
Hazelden Springbrook 1901 Esther St	Newberg	OR	97132	866-866-4662	503-554-4300	724
Hazelnut Growers of Oregon 401 N 26th Ave	Cornelius	OR	97113	800-273-4676	503-648-4176	11-1
Hazen & Sawyer PC 498 Seventh Ave 11th Fl	New York	NY	10018	800-858-9876	212-777-8400	263
Hazen Transport Inc 27050 Wick Rd	Taylor	MI	48180	800-251-2120	313-292-2120	778
Hazle Park Packing Co 260 Washington Ave Hazle Pk	Hazletownship	PA	18202	800-238-4331	570-455-7571	297-26
Hazleton Standard Speaker 21 N Wyoming St *Cust Svc	Hazleton	PA	18201	800-843-6680*	570-455-3636	531-2
HB Communications Inc 60 Dodge Ave	North Haven	CT	06473	800-243-4414	203-234-9246	37
HB Fuller Co 1200 Willow Lk Blvd PO Box 64683 *NYSE: FUL*	Saint Paul	MN	55164	888-423-8553	651-236-5900	3
HB Mellott Estate Inc 100 Mellott Dr	Warfordsburg	PA	17267	800-634-5634	301-678-2050	502-5
HB Rentals LC 5813 Hwy 90 E	Broussard	LA	70518	800-262-6790	337-839-1641	266-3
HBD Inc 3901 Riverdale Rd	Greensboro	NC	27406	800-403-2247	336-275-4800	66
HBD/Thermoid Inc 1301 W Sandusky Ave	Bellefontaine	OH	43311	800-543-8070	937-593-5010	370
HB&G Inc PO Box 589	Troy	AL	36081	800-264-4424	334-566-5000	498
HBI (Hickory Brands Inc) 429 27th St NW	Hickory	NC	28601	800-438-5777		742-5
HBP (Huttig Bldg Products Inc) 555 Maryville University Dr Ste 400 *OTC: HBPI*	Saint Louis	MO	63141	800-325-4466	314-216-2600	498
HBPL (Huntington Beach Public Library) 7111 Talbert Ave	Huntington Beach	CA	92648	800-565-0148	714-842-4481	434-3
HCA Midwest Health System 903 E 104th St Ste 500	Kansas City	MO	64131	800-386-9355	816-508-4000	353
HCAA (National CPA Health Care Advisors Assn) 1801 W End Ave Ste 800	Nashville	TN	37203	800-231-2524	615-373-9880	48-1
HCC Inc 1501 First Ave	Mendota	IL	61342	800-548-6633	815-539-9371	275
HCC Life Insurance Co 225 Townpark Dr Ste 145	Kennesaw	GA	30144	800-447-0460	770-973-9851	391-2
HCCBA (Hardin County Chamber of Commerce) 225 S Detroit St	Kenton	OH	43326	888-642-7346	419-673-4131	138
HCCGA (Haines City Citrus Growers Assn) 8 Railroad Ave PO Box 337 *Sales	Haines City	FL	33844	800-327-6676*	863-422-1174	11-1
HCESC (Hamilton County Educational Service Ctr) 11083 Hamilton Ave	Cincinnati	OH	45231	800-964-8211	513-674-4200	683

				Toll-Free	Phone	Class
HCI (Health Communications Inc)						
3201 SW 15th St	Deerfield Beach	FL	33442	**800-441-5569***	954-360-0909	634-2
*Cust Svc						
HCI Group, The						
6440 Southpoint Pkwy Ste 300	Jacksonville	FL	32216	**866-793-2484**	904-337-6300	198
Hcpro Inc						
75 Sylvan St Ste A-10	Danvers	MA	01923	**800-650-6787**		197
HCREC (Humboldt County Rural Electric Co-op)						
1210 13th St N	Humboldt	IA	50548	**800-452-1111**	515-332-1616	247
HCSG (Healthcare Services Group Inc)						
3220 Tillman Dr Ste 300	Bensalem	PA	19020	**800-486-3289**	215-639-4274	442
HCYF (Hazelden Ctr for Youth & Families)						
11505 36th Ave N	Plymouth	MN	55441	**800-257-7810**	763-509-3800	724
H-D Electric Co-op Inc						
423 Third Ave S	Clear Lake	SD	57226	**800-781-7474**	605-874-2171	247
HD Hudson Manufacturing Co						
500 N Michigan Ave	Chicago	IL	60611	**800-977-7293**	312-644-2830	275
HD Supply Waterworks Ltd						
PO Box 1419	Thomasville	GA	31799	**800-492-6909**	800-950-7659	385
HD Vest Financial Services						
6333 N State Hwy 161 4th Fl	Irving	TX	75038	**866-218-8206**	972-870-6000	401
HDR Engineering Inc						
8404 Indian Hills Dr	Omaha	NE	68114	**800-366-4411**	402-399-1000	263
HDSA (Huntington's Disease Society of America)						
505 Eigth Ave Ste 902	New York	NY	10018	**800-345-4372**	212-242-1968	47-17
HDT Global						
30500 Aurora Rd Ste 100	Solon	OH	44139	**800-969-8527**	216-438-6111	15
HDW (Hardware Distribution Warehouses Inc)						
6900 Woolworth Rd	Shreveport	LA	71129	**800-256-8527***	318-686-8527	351
*Cust Svc						
HE Neumann Inc						
100 Middle Creek Rd	Triadelphia	WV	26059	**800-627-5312**	304-232-3040	191-10
HE Williams Inc						
831 W Fairview Ave	Carthage	MO	64836	**866-358-4065**	417-358-4065	439
HEA (Harmon Electric Assn Inc)						
114 N First St PO Box 393	Hollis	OK	73550	**800-643-7769**	580-688-3342	247
HEAD USA Inc						
1 Selleck St	Norwalk	CT	06855	**800-874-3235**		708
Headquarter Toyota						
5895 NW 167th St	Miami	FL	33015	**800-549-0947**	305-364-9800	56
Headsets Direct Inc						
1454 W Gurley St Ste A	Prescott	AZ	86305	**800-914-7996**	928-777-9100	248
Headstart Hair For Men Inc						
3395 Cypress Gardens Rd	Winter Haven	FL	33884	**800-645-6525**	863-324-5559	348
Healing the Children (HTC)						
2624 W Beacon Ave	Spokane	WA	99208	**888-233-9527**	509-327-4281	47-5
Health & Environment Dept						
130 S Market St Ste 6050	Wichita	KS	67202	**800-842-0078**	316-337-6020	802
Health & Safety Institute Inc						
1450 Westec Dr	Eugene	OR	97402	**800-447-3177**		762
Health After 50						
750 Third Ave Fl 6	New York	NY	10017	**800-829-0422**		530-8
Health Alliance Plan						
2850 W Grand Blvd	Detroit	MI	48202	**800-422-4641**	313-872-8100	391-3
Health Care Daily Report						
1801 S Bell St	Arlington	VA	22202	**800-372-1033**		530-8
Health Care Property Investors Inc						
1920 Main St Ste 1200	Irvine	CA	92614	**800-690-6903**	949-407-0700	653
Health Care Software Inc						
PO Box 2430	Farmingdale	NJ	07727	**800-524-1038**		179
Health Coalition Inc						
8320 NW 30th Terr	Doral	FL	33122	**800-456-7283**	305-662-2988	240
Health Communications Inc (HCI)						
3201 SW 15th St	Deerfield Beach	FL	33442	**800-441-5569***	954-360-0909	634-2
*Cust Svc						
Health Facilities Management Magazine						
155 N Wacker Dr Ste 400	Chicago	IL	60606	**800-621-6902**	312-893-6800	456-5
Health Forum						
155 North Wacker Drive Ste 400	Chicago	IL	60606	**800-621-6902**	312-893-6800	634-11
Health Industry Business Communications Council (HIBCC)						
2525 E Arizona Biltmore Cir Ste 127	Phoenix	AZ	85016	**800-755-5505**	602-381-1091	48-8
Health Industry Distributors Assn (HIDA)						
310 Montgomery St	Alexandria	VA	22314	**800-549-4432**	703-549-4432	48-18
Health Law Reporter						
1801 S Bell St	Arlington	VA	22202	**800-372-1033**		530-7
Health Law Week						
590 Dutch Vly Rd NE	Atlanta	GA	30324	**800-926-7926**	404-881-1141	530-8
Health Management Systems Inc						
401 Pk Ave S	New York	NY	10016	**877-357-3268**	212-857-5000	227
Health Net Inc						
21650 Oxnard St	Woodland Hills	CA	91367	**800-848-4747**	818-676-6000	391-3
NYSE: HNT						
Health Net Of Arizona Inc						
1230 W Washington St	Tempe	AZ	85281	**800-291-6911**	602-794-1400	353
Health Network Laboratory						
2024 Lehigh St	Allentown	PA	18103	**877-402-4221**	610-402-8170	418
Health Partners						
8170 33rd Ave S	Minneapolis	MN	55425	**800-247-7015**	952-883-6877	371
Health Physics Society						
1313 Dolley Madison Blvd Ste 402	McLean	VA	22101	**888-624-8373**	703-790-1745	47-17
Health Resources & Services Administration (HRSA)						
5600 Fishers Ln	Rockville	MD	20857	**888-275-4772**	301-443-2216	340-8
Health Smart Rx						
1301 E Ninth St	Cleveland	OH	44114	**800-681-6912**		585
Health Tradition Health Plan						
1808 E Main St	Onalaska	WI	54650	**800-545-8499**	608-781-9692	391-3
HealthAmerica Pennsylvania Inc						
3721 Tecport Dr PO Box 67103	Harrisburg	PA	17111	**800-788-6445**		391-3
HealthAxis Inc						
7301 N State Hwy 161	Irving	TX	75039	**888-974-2947**	972-443-5000	462
Healthcare Automation Inc						
41 Sharpe Dr	Cranston	RI	02920	**800-738-8850**	401-572-3040	179
Healthcare Disparities Report						
8204 Fenton St	Silver Spring	MD	20910	**800-666-6380**	301-588-6385	530-8
Healthcare Financial Management Assn (HFMA)						
2 Westbrook Corporate Ctr Ste 700	Westchester	IL	60154	**800-252-4362**	708-531-9600	48-8
Healthcare Management Systems Inc (HMS)						
3102 W End Ave Ste 400	Nashville	TN	37203	**800-383-3317**	615-383-7300	387
Healthcare Services Group Inc (HCSG)						
3220 Tillman Dr Ste 300	Bensalem	PA	19020	**800-486-3289**	215-639-4274	442
HealthCare USA						
10 S Broadway Ste 1200	Saint Louis	MO	63102	**800-213-7792**	314-241-5300	391-3
HealthCareSource Inc						
100 Sylvan Rd Ste 100	Woburn	MA	01801	**800-869-5200**		262
Healthcom						
1600 W Jackson St	Sullivan	IL	61951	**800-525-6237**		474
HealthDrive Corp						
888 Worcester St	Wellesley	MA	02482	**888-964-6681**		352
HealthForce Ontario Marketing & Recruitment Agency						
163 Queen St E	Toronto	ON	M5A1S1	**800-596-4046**	416-862-2200	262
Healthforce Partners Inc						
18323 Bothell Everett Hwy	Bothell	WA	98012	**877-437-2497**	425-806-5700	196
HealthMEDX						
5100 N Towne Ctr Dr	Ozark	MO	65721	**877-875-1200**	417-582-1816	38
HealthPartners Inc						
PO Box 1309	Minneapolis	MN	55440	**800-883-2177**	952-883-5000	391-3
Healthplex Inc						
333 Earl Ovington Blvd	Uniondale	NY	11553	**800-468-0608***	516-542-2200	391-3
*Cust Svc						
HealthPlus of Michigan						
2050 S Linden Rd	Flint	MI	48532	**800-332-9161**	810-230-2000	391-3
Healthpoint						
3909 Hulen St	Fort Worth	TX	76107	**800-441-8227***	817-900-4000	583
*Cust Svc						
HealthSCOPE Benefits Inc						
27 Corporate Hill Dr	Little Rock	AR	72205	**877-240-0135**	501-225-1551	390
HealthSource Saginaw						
3340 Hospital Rd	Saginaw	MI	48603	**800-662-6848**	989-790-7700	724
HealthSouth Chattanooga Rehabilitation Hospital						
3660 Grandview Pkwy Ste 200	Birmingham	AL	35243	**800-765-4772**	205-967-7116	374-6
HealthSouth Corp						
3660 Grandview Pkwy Ste 200	Birmingham	AL	35243	**800-765-4772**	205-967-7116	352
NYSE: HLS						
HealthSouth Harmarville Rehabilitation Hospital						
320 Guys Run Rd	Pittsburgh	PA	15238	**800-765-4772**	412-828-1300	374-6
HealthSouth Hospital of Pittsburgh						
320 Guys Run Rd	Pittsburgh	PA	15238	**800-765-4772**	412-828-1300	374-6
HealthSouth MountainView Regional Rehabilitation Hospital						
1160 Van Voorhis Rd	Morgantown	WV	26505	**800-388-2451**	304-598-1100	374-6
HealthSouth Nittany Valley Rehabilitation Hospital						
550 W College Ave	Pleasant Gap	PA	16823	**800-842-6026**	814-359-3421	374-6
HealthSouth Rehabilitation Hospital of Altoona						
2005 Vly View Blvd	Altoona	PA	16602	**800-873-4220**	814-944-3535	374-6
HealthSouth Rehabilitation Hospital of Austin						
1215 Red River	Austin	TX	78701	**800-765-4772**	512-474-5700	374-6
HealthSouth Rehabilitation Hospital of Erie						
143 E Second St	Erie	PA	16507	**800-765-4772**	814-878-1230	374-6
HealthSouth Rehabilitation Hospital of Kingsport						
113 Cassel Dr	Kingsport	TN	37660	**800-454-7422**	423-246-7240	374-6
Healthspace USA Inc						
4860 Cox Rd Ste 200	Glen Allen	VA	23060	**866-860-4224**	804-935-8532	203
HealthStream Inc						
209 Tenth Ave S Ste 450	Nashville	TN	37203	**800-933-9293**	615-301-3100	763
NASDAQ: HSTM						
Healthtrax Fitness & Wellness						
2345 Main St	Glastonbury	CT	06033	**800-998-0880**	860-652-7066	354
HealthTronics Inc						
9825 Spectrum Dr Bldg 3	Austin	TX	78717	**888-252-6575**	512-328-2892	252
Healthways Inc						
701 Cool Springs Blvd	Franklin	TN	37067	**800-327-3822**		352
NASDAQ: HWAY						
Healthy Directions LLC						
7811 Montrose Rd	Potomac	MD	20854	**866-599-9491**		634-9
Healthy Pet						
6960 Salashan Pkwy	Ferndale	WA	98248	**800-242-2287**	360-734-7415	577
Healy Group Inc, The						
53800 Generations Dr	South Bend	IN	46635	**800-667-4613**	574-271-6000	390
Hearing Loss Assn of America						
7910 Woodmont Ave Ste 1200	Bethesda	MD	20814	**800-221-6827**	301-657-2248	47-17
Hearn Kirkwood						
7251 Standard Dr	Hanover	MD	21076	**800-777-9489***	410-712-6000	298-7
*General						
Hearn Paper Co						
556 N Meridian Rd	Youngstown	OH	44509	**800-225-2989**	330-792-6533	552
Hearst Foundation, The						
300 W 57th St 26th Fl	New York	NY	10019	**800-841-7048**	212-649-3750	306
Hearst San Simeon State Historical Monument						
750 Hearst Castle Rd	San Simeon	CA	93452	**800-444-4445**	805-927-2020	564
Heart & Soul Magazine						
15480 Annapolis Rd Ste 202-225	Bowie	MD	20715	**800-834-8813**		456-13
Heart of Lancaster Regional Medical Ctr						
1500 Highland Dr	Lititz	PA	17543	**800-999-6673**	717-625-5000	374-3
Heart Six Ranch						
16985 Buffalo Vly Rd PO Box 70	Moran	WY	83013	**888-543-2477**		241
Hearth & Home Technologies Inc						
7571 215th St W	Lakeville	MN	55044	**888-427-3973**	952-985-6000	357
Heartland Blood Centers						
1200 N Highland Ave	Aurora	IL	60506	**800-786-4483**	630-892-7055	88
Heartland Co-op						
2829 Westown Pkwy Ste 350	West Des Moines	IA	50266	**800-513-3938**	515-225-1334	277
Heartland Equipment Inc						
2100 N Falls Blvd	Wynne	AR	72396	**800-530-7617**		275
Heartland Express Inc						
901 N Kansas Ave	North Liberty	IA	52317	**800-654-1175**		778
NASDAQ: HTLD						
Heartland Financial USA Inc						
1398 Central Ave	Dubuque	IA	52001	**888-739-2100**	563-589-2100	360-2
NASDAQ: HTLF						
Heartland Funds						
789 N Water St Ste 500	Milwaukee	WI	53202	**800-432-7856**	414-347-7777	527
Heartland Hands-Hope Hospice						
137 N Belt Hwy	Saint Joseph	MO	64506	**800-443-1143**	816-271-7190	371
Heartland Hospice Services						
333 N Summit St	Toledo	OH	43604	**800-366-1232**	419-252-5500	371

Name	Address	City	State	ZIP	Toll-Free	Phone	Class
Heartland Inns	87-2nd St *Resv	Coralville	IA	52241	800-334-3277*	319-351-8132	379
Heartland Label Printers Inc	1700 Stephen St *General	Little Chute	WI	54140	800-236-7914*		248
Heartland Lions Eye Bank	10100 N Ambassador Dr Ste 200	Kansas City	MO	64153	800-756-4824	816-454-5454	271
Heartland Meat Company Inc	3461 Main St	Chula Vista	CA	91911	888-407-3668	619-407-3668	298-9
Heartland Paper Co	808 W Cherokee St *Cust Svc	Sioux Falls	SD	57104	800-843-7922*	605-336-1190	558
Heartland Park Topeka	7530 SW Topeka Blvd	Topeka	KS	66619	800-437-2237	785-862-4781	514
Heartland Payment Systems Inc	90 Nassau St 2nd Fl *NYSE: HPY*	Princeton	NJ	08542	888-798-3131	609-683-3831	253
Heartland Petroleum LLC	4001 E Fifth Ave	Columbus	OH	43219	800-889-7831	614-441-4001	578
Heartland Power Co-op	216 Jackson St PO Box 65	Thompson	IA	50478	888-584-9732	641-584-2251	247
Heartland Rural Electric Co-op	110 Enterprise St	Girard	KS	66743	888-835-9585	620-724-8251	247
Heartland Spa	1237 E 1600 N Rd	Gilman	IL	60938	800-545-4853		704
Heartline Fitness Products Inc	8041 Cessna Ave Ste 200	Gaithersburg	MD	20879	800-262-3348	301-921-0661	269
Heat & Control Inc	21121 Cabot Blvd	Hayward	CA	94545	800-227-5980	510-259-0500	299
Heat Seal LLC	4580 E 71st St	Cleveland	OH	44125	800-342-6329	216-341-2022	546
Heatcraft Refrigeration Products	2175 W Pk Pl Blvd	Stone Mountain	GA	30087	800-321-1881	770-465-5600	662
Heath Consultants Inc	9030 Monroe Rd	Houston	TX	77061	800-432-8487	713-844-1300	194
HeatMax Inc	505 Hill Rd PO Box 1191	Dalton	GA	30721	800-432-8629	706-226-1800	575
Heatrex Inc	PO Box 515	Meadville	PA	16335	800-394-6589	814-724-1800	319
Heaven's Best Carpet & Upholstery Cleaning	PO Box 607	Rexburg	ID	83440	800-359-2095	208-359-1106	151
Heavy Machines Inc	3926 E Rains Rd	Memphis	TN	38118	888-366-9028	901-260-2200	358
Hebeler Corp	2000 Military Rd	Tonawanda	NY	14150	800-486-4709	716-873-9300	619
Hebrew Immigrant Aid Society (HIAS)	333 Seventh Ave 16th Fl	New York	NY	10001	800-442-7714	212-967-4100	47-5
Hebrew Union College Los Angeles	3077 University Ave	Los Angeles	CA	90007	800-899-0925	213-749-3424	167
Hebron Academy	339 Rd PO Box 309	Hebron	ME	04238	888-432-7664	207-966-2100	621
Heceta Head Lighthouse State Scenic Viewpoint	93111 Hwy 101 N	Florence	OR	97439	800-551-6949		564
Hecla Mining Co	800 W Pender St Ste 970 *NYSE: HL*	Vancouver	BC	V6C2V6	800-432-5291	604-682-6201	501
Hed Cycling Products	1735 Terrace Dr	Roseville	MN	55113	888-246-3639	651-653-0202	516
Hedahls Inc	100 East Broadway	Bismarck	ND	58502	800-433-2457	701-223-8393	60
Hedwin Corp	1600 Roland Heights Ave	Baltimore	MD	21211	800-638-1012	410-467-8209	201
Heely-Brown Company Inc	1280 Chattahoochee Ave	Atlanta	GA	30318	800-241-4628	404-352-0022	45
Heerema Co	200 Sixth Ave	Hawthorne	NJ	07506	800-346-4729	973-423-0505	709
Heery International Inc	999 Peachtree St NE	Atlanta	GA	30309	866-840-3940	404-881-9880	263
Heffel Gallery Ltd	2247 Granville St	Vancouver	BC	V6H3G1	800-528-9608	604-732-6505	41
HEI Inc	1495 Steiger Lk Ln	Victoria	MN	55386	866-720-2397	952-443-2500	694
Heidel House Resort	643 Illinois Ave	Green Lake	WI	54941	800-444-2812	920-294-3344	667
Heidelberg University	310 E Market St	Tiffin	OH	44883	800-434-3352	419-448-2000	167
Heidelberg USA Inc	1000 Gutenberg Dr *Cust Svc	Kennesaw	GA	30144	888-472-9655*	770-419-6500	628
Heidler Roofing Services Inc	2120 Alpha Dr	York	PA	17408	866-792-3549	717-792-3549	191-12
Heifer International	1 World Ave	Little Rock	AR	72202	800-422-0474	501-907-2600	47-5
Heil Environmental Ltd	2030 Hamilton Pl Blvd Ste 200	Chattanooga	TN	37421	866-367-4345	423-899-9100	515
Heilind Electronics Inc	58 Jonspin Rd	Wilmington	MA	01887	800-400-7041	978-657-4870	248
Heim LP	6360 W 73rd St	Chicago	IL	60638	800-927-9393	708-496-7450	455
Heinen's Inc	4540 Richmond Rd	Cleveland	OH	44128	855-475-2300		345
Heiners Bakery Inc	1300 Adams Ave	Huntington	WV	25704	800-776-8411	304-523-8411	297-1
Heinrich Envelope Corp	925 Zane Ave N	Minneapolis	MN	55422	800-346-7957	763-544-3571	265
Heintz & Weber Co Inc	150 Reading Ave	Buffalo	NY	14220	800-438-6878	716-852-7171	297-41
Heinz Hall for the Performing Arts	600 Penn Ave	Pittsburgh	PA	15222	800-743-8560	412-392-4900	571
Helac Corp	225 Battersby Ave	Enumclaw	WA	98022	800-327-2589	360-825-1601	225
Helen B Hoffman Plantation Library	501 N Fig Tree Ln	Plantation	FL	33317	800-774-5866	954-797-2140	434-3
Helen DeVos Children's Hospital	100 Michigan St NE	Grand Rapids	MI	49503	800-222-1222	616-391-9000	374-1
Helen DeVos Children's Hospital Pediatric Hematology/Oncology Program	100 Michigan NE	Grand Rapids	MI	49503	866-989-7999	616-391-9000	767
Helen Hayes Theatre	240 W 44th St	New York	NY	10036	800-447-7400	212-239-6200	744
Helen Keller International	352 Pk Ave S Ste 1200	New York	NY	10010	877-535-5374	212-532-0544	47-5
Helena Area Chamber of Commerce	225 Cruse Ave	Helena	MT	59601	800-743-5362	406-442-4120	138
Helena Laboratories Inc	1530 Lindbergh Dr	Beaumont	TX	77704	800-231-5663	409-842-3714	233
Helical Products Co Inc	901 W McCoy Ln	Santa Maria	CA	93455	877-353-9873	805-928-3851	619
Helicopter Assn International (HAI)	1635 Prince St	Alexandria	VA	22314	800-435-4976	703-683-4646	48-21
Helicopter Support Inc (HSI)	124 Quarry Rd	Trumbull	CT	06611	800-795-6051	203-416-4000	768
Heliene Inc	520 Allen'S Side Rd	Sault Sainte Marie	ON	P6A6K4	855-363-2797	705-575-6556	255
Heli-Mart Inc	3184 Airway Ave Unit E	Costa Mesa	CA	92626	800-826-6899	714-755-2999	768
Heliodyne Corp	4910 Seaport Ave	Richmond	CA	94804	888-878-8750	510-237-9614	322
Helix Energy Solutions Inc	400 N Sam Houston Pkwy E Ste 400 *NYSE: HLX*	Houston	TX	77060	888-345-2347	281-618-0400	538
Helixstorm Inc	41619 Margarita Rd Ste 202	Temecula	CA	92591	888-434-3549		387
Hello Direct Inc	77 NE Blvd	Nashua	NH	03062	800-435-5634		458
HelloWorld	3000 Town center ste 2100	South Field	MI	48075	877-837-7493		7
Helly Hansen US Inc	4104 C St NE Ste 200	Auburn	WA	98002	800-435-5901		154-5
Helmel Engineering Products Inc	6520 Lockport Rd	Niagara Falls	NY	14305	800-237-8266	716-297-8644	176
Helmerich & Payne Inc	1437 S Boulder Ave *NYSE: HP*	Tulsa	OK	74119	800-205-4913	918-742-5531	539
Help At Home Inc	1 N State St Ste 800	Chicago	IL	60602	800-404-3191	312-762-0900	363
HELP USA	5 Hanover Sq	New York	NY	10004	800-311-7999	212-400-7000	47-5
Helpjuice Inc	211 E Seventh St Ste 620	Austin	TX	78701	888-256-0808	888-230-3420	387
Helton Industries Ltd	30840 Peardonville Rd	Abbotsford	BC	V2T6K2	877-300-7412	604-854-3660	350
Helvoet Pharma Inc	9012 Pennsauken Hwy	Pennsauken	NJ	08110	800-874-3586	856-663-2202	476
Helwig Carbon Products Inc	8900 W Tower Ave	Milwaukee	WI	53224	800-365-3113	414-354-2411	126
Helzberg Diamonds	1825 Swift Ave	North Kansas City	MO	64116	800-435-9237	816-842-7780	410
Hemacare Corp	15350 Sherman Way Ste 350	Van Nuys	CA	91406	877-310-0717	818-226-1968	88
Hemagen Diagnostics Inc	9033 Red Branch Rd *OTC: HMGN*	Columbia	MD	21045	800-436-2436	443-367-5500	233
Hemenway's Seafood Grille	121 S Main St	Providence	RI	02903	888-759-5557	401-351-8570	669
Hemispheres Restaurant & Bistro	108 Chestnut St	Toronto	ON	M5G1R3	800-668-6600	416-599-8000	669
Hemmings Motor News	222 Main St	Bennington	VT	05201	800-227-4373	802-442-3101	456-3
Henderson Auctions	13340 Florida Blvd PO Box 336	Livingston	LA	70754	800-334-7443	225-686-2252	50
Henderson Community College	2660 S Green St	Henderson	KY	42420	800-696-9958	270-827-1867	161
Henderson Convention Ctr	200 S Water St	Henderson	NV	89015	877-775-5252	702-267-2171	207
Henderson County Public Library	301 N Washington St	Hendersonville	NC	28739	866-866-2362	828-697-4725	434-3
Henderson County Tourist Commission	101 N Water St Ste B	Henderson	KY	42420	800-648-3128	270-826-3128	208
Henderson County Travel & Tourism	201 S Main St	Hendersonville	NC	28792	800-828-4244	828-693-9708	208
Henderson Glass Inc	715 S Blvd E	Rochester Hills	MI	48307	800-694-0672		332
Henderson Hills Baptist Church	1200 E I 35 Frontage Rd	Edmond	OK	73034	877-901-4639	405-341-4639	47-20
Henderson Manufacturing Inc	1085 S Third St	Manchester	IA	52057	800-359-4970	563-927-2828	275
Henderson Sewing Machine Company Inc	Waits Dr Industrial Park	Andalusia	AL	36420	800-824-5113	334-222-2451	358
Henderson State University	1100 Henderson St	Arkadelphia	AR	71999	800-228-7333	870-230-5000	167
Henderson Wheel & Warehouse Supply	1825 South 300 West	Salt Lake City	UT	84115	800-748-5111	801-486-2073	60
Hendrick Buick GMC Cadillac	1151 W 104th St	Kansas City	MO	64114	888-255-9362	877-584-7140	56
Hendrick Hospice Care	1682 Hickory St	Abilene	TX	79601	800-622-8516	325-677-8516	371
Hendrick Manufacturing Co	1 Seventh Ave *Cust Svc	Carbondale	PA	18407	800-225-7373*		487
Hendrick Motorsports Museum	4400 Papa Joe Hendrick Blvd	Charlotte	NC	28262	877-467-4890		521
Hendricks County Flyer	8109 Kingston St Ste 500	Avon	IN	46123	800-359-3747	317-272-5800	531-4
Hendricks Power Co-op	86 N County Rd 500 E	Avon	IN	46123	800-876-5473	317-745-5473	247
Hendrickson International	800 S Frontage Rd	Woodridge	IL	60517	855-743-3733	630-910-2800	59
Hendrix College	1600 Washington Ave	Conway	AR	72032	800-277-9017	501-329-6811	167
Hengehold Capital Management LLC	6116 Harrison Ave	Cincinnati	OH	45247	877-598-5120	513-598-5120	401

Name	Address	City	State	ZIP	Toll-Free	Phone	Class
Henkel Corp	1 Henkel Way *Cust Svc	Rocky Hill	CT	06067	**800-243-4874***	860-571-5100	3
Henkels & McCoy Inc	985 Jolly Rd	Blue Bell	PA	19422	**888-436-5357**	215-283-7600	190-10
Henley Park Hotel	926 Massachusetts Ave NW	Washington	DC	20001	**800-222-8474**	202-638-5200	379
Henlopen Hotel	511 N Boardwalk	Rehoboth Beach	DE	19971	**800-441-8450**	302-227-2551	379
Henneman Engineering	1605 S State St	Champaign	IL	61820	**888-616-0216**	217-359-1514	263
Hennepin Technical College	9000 Brooklyn Blvd	Brooklyn Park	MN	55445	**800-345-4655**	952-995-1300	798
Hennessy Industries Inc	1601 JP Hennesey Dr	La Vergne	TN	37086	**800-688-6359**	855-876-3864	59
Hennis Care Centre	1720 Cross St	Dover	OH	44622	**800-241-1044**	330-364-8849	449
Henny Penny Corp	1219 US 35 W PO Box 60	Eaton	OH	45320	**800-417-8417**	937-456-8400	299
Henri Bendel Inc	712 Fifth Ave	New York	NY	10019	**866-875-7975**	212-247-1100	156-6
Henricus Historical Park	Henricus Pk Rd	Chester	VA	23836	**800-514-3849**	804-748-1613	519
Henry A Bromelkamp & Co	106 E 24th St	Minneapolis	MN	55404	**877-767-6703**	612-870-9087	182
Henry B Gonzalez Convention Ctr	200 E Market St	San Antonio	TX	78205	**877-504-8895**	210-207-8500	207
Henry Brick Co Inc	3409 Water Ave	Selma	AL	36703	**800-218-3906**	334-875-2600	149
Henry Co	909 N Sepulveda Blvd Ste 650	El Segundo	CA	90245	**800-598-7663**	310-955-9200	45
Henry County Public Library System	1001 Florence McGarity Blvd	McDonough	GA	30252	**877-527-3712**	770-954-2806	434-3
Henry Equestrian Insurance Brokers	28 Victoria St	Aurora	ON	L4G1P9	**800-565-4321**	905-727-1144	391-1
Henry Ford Community College	5101 Evergreen Rd	Dearborn	MI	48128	**800-585-4322**	313-845-9600	161
Henry Ford Health System	1 Ford Pl	Detroit	MI	48202	**800-436-7936**		353
Henry Ford Hospital	2799 W Grand Blvd	Detroit	MI	48202	**800-999-4340**	313-916-2600	374-3
Henry Ford Museum	20900 Oakwood Blvd	Dearborn	MI	48124	**800-835-5237**	313-271-1620	519
Henry Ford OptimEyes	655 W 13-Mile Rd	Madison Heights	MI	48071	**800-393-2273**	248-588-9300	542
Henry Glass & Co	49 W 37th St	New York	NY	10018	**800-294-9495**	917-229-1080	742-1
Henry Pratt Co	401 S Highland Ave	Aurora	IL	60506	**877-436-7977**	630-844-4000	788
Henry Products Inc	302 S 23rd Ave	Phoenix	AZ	85009	**800-525-5533**	602-253-3191	193-1
Henry Quentzel Plumbing Supply Co	379 Throop Ave	Brooklyn	NY	11221	**800-889-2294**	718-455-6600	611
Henry Schein Inc	135 Duryea Rd *NASDAQ: HSIC*	Melville	NY	11747	**800-582-2702**	631-843-5500	474
Henry Technologies	701 S Main St	Chatham	IL	62629	**800-964-3679**	217-483-2406	14
Henry Troemner LLC	201 Wolf Dr	Thorofare	NJ	08086	**800-352-7705**	856-686-1600	475
Hensley Industries Inc	2108 Joe Field Rd PO Box 29779	Dallas	TX	75229	**888-406-6262**	972-241-2321	192
Hentzen Coatings Inc	6937 W Mill Rd	Milwaukee	WI	53218	**800-236-6589**	414-353-4200	549
Hepaco Inc	2711 Burch Dr PO Box 26308	Charlotte	NC	28269	**800-888-7689**	704-598-9782	691
Hepatitis Foundation International (HFI)	504 Blick Dr	Silver Spring	MD	20904	**800-891-0707**	301-622-4200	47-17
Her Interactive Inc	1150 114th Ave SE Ste 200 *Orders	Bellevue	WA	98004	**800-461-8787***	425-460-8787	180-6
Heraeus	300 Heraeus Way *General	South Bend	IN	46614	**800-431-1785***		230
Herald & Review	601 E Williams St	Decatur	IL	62523	**800-437-2533**	217-429-5151	531-2
Herald Bulletin	1133 Jackson St	Anderson	IN	46016	**800-750-5049**	765-622-1212	531-2
Herald Democrat	603 S Sam Rayburn Fwy	Sherman	TX	75090	**800-827-7183**	903-893-8181	531-2
Herald Journal	75 W 300 N	Logan	UT	84321	**800-275-0423**	435-752-2121	531-2
Herald Publishing Co	PO Box 153	Houston	TX	77001	**888-421-1866**	713-630-0391	634-8
Herald Times Reporter	902 Franklin St	Manitowoc	WI	54221	**800-783-7323**	920-684-4433	531-2
Herald, The	52 S Dock St	Sharon	PA	16146	**800-981-1692**	724-981-6100	531-2
Herald-Dispatch	946 Fifth Ave	Huntington	WV	25701	**800-444-2446**	304-526-4000	531-2
Herald-Mail Co, The	100 Summit Ave PO Box 439	Hagerstown	MD	21741	**800-626-6397**	301-733-5131	634-8
Herald-Palladium	3450 Hollywood Rd	Saint Joseph	MI	49085	**800-356-4262**	269-429-2400	531-2
Herald-Standard	8 E Church St	Uniontown	PA	15401	**800-342-8254**	724-439-7500	531-2
Herald-Star	401 Herald Sq	Steubenville	OH	43952	**800-526-7987**	740-283-4711	634-8
Herald-Sun, The	2828 Pickett Rd	Durham	NC	27705	**866-348-6479**	919-419-6500	531-2
Herb Chambers I 95 Inc	107 Andover St	Danvers	MA	01923	**877-907-1965**		56
Herb Gordon Nissan	3131 Automobile Blvd	Silver Spring	MD	20904	**844-249-4077**	866-399-7502	56
Herb Research Foundation (HRF)	4140 15th St	Boulder	CO	80304	**800-748-2617**	303-449-2265	47-17
Herbalist, The	2106 NE 65th St	Seattle	WA	98115	**800-694-3727**	206-523-2600	797
Herber Aircraft Service Inc	1401 E Franklin Ave	El Segundo	CA	90245	**800-544-0050**	310-322-9575	479
Herbert H. Landy Insurance Agency Inc	75 Second Ave Ste 410	Needham	MA	02494	**800-336-5422**		390
Hercules Chemical Company Inc	111 S St	Passaic	NJ	07055	**800-221-9330**	973-778-5000	3
Hercules Engine Components Co	2770 S Erie St	Massillon	OH	44646	**800-345-0662**	330-830-2498	264
Hercules Industries Inc	1310 W Evans Ave	Denver	CO	80223	**800-356-5350**	303-937-1000	611
Hercules Manufacturing Co	800 Bob Posey St	Henderson	KY	42420	**800-633-3031**	270-826-9501	515
Hercules Offshore Inc	9 Greenway Plaza Ste 2200 *NASDAQ: HERO*	Houston	TX	77046	**888-647-1715**	713-350-5100	539
Hercules Tire & Rubber Co	16380 E US Rt 224 - 200	Findlay	OH	45840	**800-677-9535**	419-425-6400	752
Herc-U-Lift Inc	5655 Hwy 12 W PO Box 69	Maple Plain	MN	55359	**800-362-3500**	763-479-2501	385
Herculite Products Inc	105 E Sinking Springs Ln *Cust Svc	Emigsville	PA	17318	**800-772-0036***	717-764-1192	742-2
Heritage Bags	1648 Diplomat Dr	Carrollton	TX	75006	**800-527-2247**		65
Heritage Bank	101 N Main St	Jonesboro	GA	30236	**866-971-0106**	770-478-8881	360-2
Heritage Bible College	1747 Bud Hawkins Rd PO Box 1628	Dunn	NC	28334	**800-297-6351**	910-892-3178	167
Heritage Canada Foundation	5 Blackburn Ave	Ottawa	ON	K1N8A2	**866-964-1066**	613-237-1066	47-13
Heritage Christian University	3625 Helton Dr PO Box HCU	Florence	AL	35630	**800-367-3565**	256-766-6610	160
Heritage Club	2020 S Monroe St	Denver	CO	80210	**888-221-7317**	303-758-3017	670
Heritage Co, The	2402 Wildwood Ave Ste 500	North Little Rock	AR	72120	**800-643-8822**	501-835-5000	5
Heritage College & Seminary	175 Holiday Inn Dr	Cambridge	ON	N3C3T2	**800-465-1961**	519-651-2869	783
Heritage Commerce Corp	150 Almaden Blvd *NASDAQ: HTBK*	San Jose	CA	95113	**800-468-9716**	408-947-6900	360-2
Heritage Corridor Convention & Visitors Bureau	339 W Jefferson St	Joliet	IL	60435	**800-926-2262**	815-727-2323	208
Heritage Ctr	1201 W Buena Vista Rd	Evansville	IN	47710	**800-704-0700**	812-429-0700	449
Heritage Financial Corp	201 Fifth Ave SW *NASDAQ: HFWA*	Olympia	WA	98501	**800-962-4284**	360-943-1500	360-2
Heritage Foods LLC	4002 Westminster Ave *Orders	Santa Ana	CA	92703	**800-321-5960***	714-775-5000	297-27
Heritage Ford Inc	2100 Sisk Rd	Modesto	CA	95350	**888-323-9990**	209-529-5110	56
Heritage Foundation	214 Massachusetts Ave NE	Washington	DC	20002	**800-546-2843**	202-546-4400	631
Heritage Global Solutions Inc	230 N Maryland Ave	Glendale	CA	91206	**800-915-4474**	818-547-4474	198
Heritage Group Inc	1101 12th St	Aurora	NE	68818	**888-463-6611**	402-694-3136	69
Heritage Hill State Historical Park	2640 S Webster Ave	Green Bay	WI	54301	**800-721-5150**	920-448-5150	564
Heritage Hills Golf Resort & Conference Ctr	2700 Mt Rose Ave	York	PA	17402	**877-782-9752**	717-755-0123	667
Heritage Hospice	120 Enterprise Dr PO Box 1213	Danville	KY	40423	**800-203-6633**	859-236-2425	371
Heritage Inn, The	34521 Postal Ln	Lewes	DE	19958	**800-669-9399**		379
Heritage Mint Ltd	PO Box 13750	Scottsdale	AZ	85267	**888-860-6245**	480-860-1300	728
Heritage of the Americas Museum	12110 Cuyamaca College Dr W	El Cajon	CA	92019	**800-234-1597**	619-670-5194	519
Heritage Office Furnishings	1588 Rand Ave	Vancouver	BC	V6P3G2	**888-775-4555**	604-688-2381	321
Heritage Place Inc	2829 S MacArthur	Oklahoma City	OK	73128	**888-343-9831**	405-682-4551	50
Heritage Plastics Inc	1002 Hunt St	Picayune	MS	39466	**800-245-4623**	601-798-8663	604-2
Heritage Square Museum	3800 Homer St	Los Angeles	CA	90031	**800-375-1771**	323-225-2700	519
Heritage Summit HealthCare of Florida Inc	PO Box 2928	Lakeland	FL	33806	**800-282-7644**	863-665-6629	391-3
Heritage University	3240 Ft Rd	Toppenish	WA	98948	**888-272-6190**	509-865-8500	167
Heritage Valley Health System	1000 Dutch Ridge Rd	Beaver	PA	15009	**877-771-4847**	724-728-7000	374-3
Heritage-Crystal Clean Inc	2175 Pt Blvd Ste 375	Elgin	IL	60123	**877-938-7948**	847-836-5670	150
Herkimer County Chamber of Commerce	28 W Main St	Mohawk	NY	13407	**877-984-4636**	315-866-7820	138
Herkimer County Community College	100 Reservoir Rd	Herkimer	NY	13350	**844-464-4375**	315-866-0300	161
Herlache Enterprises	6417 W 87th St Ste 3	Oak Lawn	IL	60453	**888-446-8854**		228
Herman Davis State Park	Corner of Ark 18 Baltimore St	Manila	AR	72201	**888-287-2757**		564
Herman Goldner Co Inc	7777 Brewster Ave	Philadelphia	PA	19153	**800-355-5997**	215-365-5400	191-10
Herman H Sticht Company Inc	45 Main St Ste 701	Brooklyn	NY	11201	**800-221-3203**	718-852-7602	471
Herman Herman Katz & Cotlar LLP	820 Okeefe Ave	New Orleans	LA	70113	**844-943-7626**	504-581-4892	428
Herman Miller for Health Care	855 E Main Ave PO Box 302	Zeeland	MI	49464	**888-443-4357**	616-654-3000	320-3
Herman Miller Inc	855 E Main Ave *NASDAQ: MLHR*	Zeeland	MI	49464	**888-443-4357**	616-654-3000	320-1
Herman's Inc	2820 Blackhawk Rd	Rock Island	IL	61201	**800-447-1295**	309-788-9568	155

Name / Address	City	State	ZIP	Toll-Free	Phone	Class
Hermann Oak Leather Co 4050 N First St	Saint Louis	MO	63147	**800-325-7950**	314-421-1173	432
Hermell Products Inc 9 Britton Dr	Bloomfield	CT	06002	**800-233-2342**	860-242-6550	476
Hermes Abrasives Ltd PO Box 2389	Virginia Beach	VA	23450	**800-464-8314**	757-486-6623	1
Hermitage Hotel 231 Sixth Ave N	Nashville	TN	37219	**888-888-9414**	615-244-3121	379
hermo Fisher Scientific Inc 8365 Valley Pike PO Box 307	Middletown	VA	22645	**800-528-0494**	800-556-2323	233
Hermosa Inn 5532 N Palo Cristi Rd	Paradise Valley	AZ	85253	**800-241-1210**	602-955-8614	379
Herndon Plant Oakley Ltd 800 N Shoreline Blvd Ste 2200 South	Corpus Christi	TX	78401	**800-888-4894**	361-888-7611	401
Heroix Corp 165 Bay State Dr	Braintree	MA	02184	**800-229-6500**	781-848-1701	180-12
Herold's Salads Inc 17512 Miles Ave	Cleveland	OH	44128	**800-427-2523**	216-991-7500	297-33
Heron Point of Chestertown 501 E Campus Ave	Chestertown	MD	21620	**800-327-9138**	410-778-7300	670
Herpes Resource Center, The (HRC) PO Box 13827	Research Triangle Park	NC	27709	**877-478-5868**	919-361-8400	47-17
Herr Foods Inc 20 Herr Dr PO Box 300	Nottingham	PA	19362	**800-344-3777**	610-932-9330	297-35
Herr Tavern & Public House 900 Chambersburg Rd	Gettysburg	PA	17325	**800-362-9849**	717-334-4332	669
Herrschners Inc 2800 Hoover Rd	Stevens Point	WI	54481	**800-713-1239**	715-341-8686	260
HERS (Hysterectomy Educational Resources & Services Foundation) 422 Bryn Mawr Ave	Bala Cynwyd	PA	19004	**888-750-4377**	610-667-7757	47-17
Hersam Acorn Newspapers 16 Bailey Ave	Ridgefield	CT	06877	**800-372-2790**	203-438-6544	634-8
Herschel-Adams Inc 1301 N 14th St	Indianola	IA	50125	**800-247-2167**		275
Hershey Co 100 Crystal A Dr *NYSE: HSY* ■ *Cust Svc	Hershey	PA	17033	**800-468-1714***		297-8
Hershey Creamery Co 301 S Cameron St	Harrisburg	PA	17101	**888-240-1905**	717-238-8134	297-25
Hershey Entertainment & Resorts Co 100 W Hersheypark Dr	Hershey	PA	17033	**800-437-7439**		31
Hershey Harrisburg Region Visitors Bureau 3211 N Front St Ste 301-A	Harrisburg	PA	17110	**877-727-8573**	717-231-7788	208
Hershey Lodge 325 University Dr	Hershey	PA	17033	**844-330-1802**	717-533-3311	379
Hersheypark 100 Hershey Pk Dr	Hershey	PA	17033	**844-330-1813**	717-534-3900	32
Herson's Inc 15525 Frederick Rd	Rockville	MD	20855	**888-203-8318**		56
Hertz Equipment Rental Corp 225 Brae Blvd	Park Ridge	NJ	07656	**800-654-3131**	201-307-2000	266-3
Hertz Global Holdings Inc 225 Brae Blvd *NYSE: HTZ*	Park Ridge	NJ	07656	**800-654-3131**	201-307-2000	125
Hertz Schram & Saretsky Pc 1760 S Telegraph Rd Ste 300	Bloomfield Hills	MI	48302	**866-775-5987**	248-335-5000	428
Herweck's Art & Drafting Supplies 300 Broadway St	San Antonio	TX	78205	**800-725-1349**	210-227-1349	44
Herzing College *Atlanta* 3393 Peachtree Rd Ste 1003	Atlanta	GA	30326	**800-573-4533**	404-816-4533	798
Herzing College Birmingham 280 W Valley Ave	Birmingham	AL	35209	**800-425-9432**	205-916-2800	798
Herzing College Madison 5218 E Terr Dr	Madison	WI	53718	**800-582-1227**	608-249-6611	798
Herzog Contracting Corp 600 S Riverside Rd	Saint Joseph	MO	64507	**800-541-7846**	816-233-9001	190-4
HES (Hanchett Entry Systems Inc) 22630 N 17th Ave	Phoenix	AZ	85027	**800-626-7590**	623-582-4626	690
HESCO (Hartford Electric Supply Co) 30 Inwood Rd Ste 1	Rocky Hill	CT	06067	**800-969-5444**	860-236-6363	248
Heska Corp 3760 Rocky Mtn Ave *NASDAQ: HSKA*	Loveland	CO	80538	**800-464-3752**	970-493-7272	581
Hesperia Chamber of Commerce 16816 Main St Ste D	Hesperia	CA	92345	**855-574-7337**	760-244-2135	138
HESS Construction + Engineering Services Inc 804 W Diamond Ave Ste 300	Gaithersburg	MD	20878	**800-544-6056**	301-670-9000	258
Hesse Inc 6700 St John Ave	Kansas City	MO	64123	**800-821-5562**	816-483-7808	777
Hesselgrave International PO Box 30768	Bellingham	WA	98228	**800-457-5522**	360-734-3570	758
Hesser College 3 Sundial Ave	Manchester	NH	03103	**888-971-2190**	603-668-6660	167
Hesston College 325 S College Dr PO Box 3000	Hesston	KS	67062	**800-995-2757**	620-327-4221	161
Heubel Material Handling Inc 6311 NE Equitable Rd	Kansas City	MO	64120	**800-283-4177**		768
Hewlett-Packard (Canada) Ltd (HP) 5150 Spectrum Way	Mississauga	ON	L4W5G1	**888-447-4636**	905-206-4725	175-1
Hewlett-Packard Co 3000 Hanover St *NYSE: HPQ* ■ *Sales	Palo Alto	CA	94304	**800-752-0900***	650-857-1501	175-1
Hexagon Metrology Inc 250 Circuit Dr	North Kingstown	RI	02852	**800-343-7933**	401-886-2000	471
Hexaware Technologies Inc 1095 Cranbury Rd	Jamesburg	NJ	08831	**866-746-2133**	609-409-6950	182
Hexcel Corp 281 Tresser Blvd 16th Fl *NYSE: HXL*	Stamford	CT	06901	**800-444-3923**	800-688-7734	604-1
Heyburn State Park 57 Chatcolet Rd	Plummer	ID	83851	**866-634-3246**	208-686-1308	564
Heyco Products 1800 Industrial Way N	Toms River	NJ	08755	**800-526-4182**	732-286-1800	487
Heyman HospiceCare 420 E Second Ave	Rome	GA	30161	**800-324-1078**	706-509-3200	371
Heymann Performing Arts Ctr 1373 S College Rd	Lafayette	LA	70503	**800-745-3000**	337-291-5540	571
Heyrman Printing LLC 2083 Holmgren Way	Green Bay	WI	54304	**800-236-4815**	920-499-4815	626
HF Financial Corp 225 S Main Ave *NASDAQ: HFFC*	Sioux Falls	SD	57104	**800-244-2149**	605-333-7556	360-2
HF Group Inc 203 W Artesia Blvd	Compton	CA	90220	**800-421-5000**	310-605-0755	495
HFA (Hospice Foundation of America) 1710 Rhode Island Ave NW Ste 400	Washington	DC	20036	**800-854-3402**	202-457-5811	48-8
HFES (Human Factors & Ergonomics Society) 1124 Montana Ave Ste B PO Box 1369	Santa Monica	CA	90406	**800-233-1234**	310-394-1811	47-17
HFI (Hepatitis Foundation International) 504 Blick Dr	Silver Spring	MD	20904	**800-891-0707**	301-622-4200	47-17
HFIA (Home Furnishings Independents Assn) 2050 Stemmons World Fwy Ste 292	Dallas	TX	75207	**800-422-3778**		48-4
HFMA (Healthcare Financial Management Assn) 2 Westbrook Corporate Ctr Ste 700	Westchester	IL	60154	**800-252-4362**	708-531-9600	48-8
HFTP (Hospitality Financial & Technology Professionals) 11709 Boulder Ln Ste 110	Austin	TX	78726	**800-646-4387**	512-249-5333	48-1
Hfw Industries Inc 196 Philadelphia St PO Box 8	Buffalo	NY	14207	**800-937-9311**	716-875-3380	386
Hg Solutions 3701 S Lawrence St	Tacoma	WA	98409	**866-988-2626**	253-588-2626	462
HGI Skydyne 100 River Rd	Port Jervis	NY	12771	**800-428-2273**		201
HH Angus & Assoc Ltd 1127 Leslie St	Toronto	ON	M3C2J6	**866-955-8201**	416-443-8200	258
HH Arnold Co Inc 529 Liberty St	Rockland	MA	02370	**866-868-9603**	781-878-0346	741
HH Brown Shoe Company Inc 124 W Putnam Ave	Greenwich	CT	06830	**888-444-2769**	203-661-2424	302
HHI (Hoag Hospital Irvine) 16200 Sand Canyon Ave	Irvine	CA	92618	**800-309-9729**	949-764-4624	374-3
HHS (Department of Health & Human Services) 330 Independence Ave SW	Washington	DC	20201	**877-696-6775**	202-619-0150	340-8
Hi Tech Data Floors Inc 1885 Swarthmore Ave	Lakewood	NJ	08701	**800-544-8321**	732-905-1799	292
Hi Tech Seals Inc 9211-41 Ave	Edmonton	AB	T6E6R5	**800-661-6055**	780-438-6055	350
HI TecMetal Group Inc 1101 E 55th St	Cleveland	OH	44103	**877-484-2867**	216-881-8100	483
HIAS (Hebrew Immigrant Aid Society) 333 Seventh Ave 16th Fl	New York	NY	10001	**800-442-7714**	212-967-4100	47-5
HI-AYH (Hostelling International USA - American Youth Hostels) 8401 Colesville Rd Ste 600	Silver Spring	MD	20910	**800-725-2331**	301-495-1240	47-23
Hibbing Community College 1515 E 25th St	Hibbing	MN	55746	**800-224-4422**	218-262-7200	161
Hibbs Hallmark & Co 501 Shelley Dr	Tyler	TX	75701	**800-765-6767**		390
HIBCC (Health Industry Business Communications Council) 2525 E Arizona Biltmore Cir Ste 127	Phoenix	AZ	85016	**800-755-5505**	602-381-1091	48-8
Hibco Plastics Inc 1820 Us 601 Hwy	Yadkinville	NC	27055	**800-849-8683**	336-463-2391	600
HIC (Hawaii Information Consortium) 201 Merchant St Ste 1805	Honolulu	HI	96813	**800-295-0089**	808-695-4620	564
Hickey Freeman 1155 N Clinton Ave *Cust Svc	Rochester	NY	14621	**844-755-7344***	585-467-7021	154-11
Hickman-Fulton Counties Rural Electric Co-op Corp 1702 Moscow Ave	Hickman	KY	42050	**800-633-1391**	270-236-2521	247
Hickok Inc 10514 Dupont Ave *OTC: HICKA*	Cleveland	OH	44108	**800-342-5080**	216-541-8060	250
Hickory Brands Inc (HBI) 429 27th St NW	Hickory	NC	28601	**800-438-5777**		742-5
Hickory Daily Record 1100 Pk Pl	Hickory	NC	28602	**800-849-8586**	828-322-4510	531-2
Hickory Farms Inc 811 Madison Ave	Toledo	OH	43604	**800-753-8558**		336
Hickory Knob State Resort Park 1591 Resort Dr	McCormick	SC	29835	**800-491-1764**	864-391-2450	564
Hickory Metro Convention & Visitors Bureau 1960 13th Ave Dr SE	Hickory	NC	28602	**800-509-2444**	828-322-1335	208
Hickory Motor Speedway 3130 Hwy 70 SE	Newton	NC	28658	**800-843-8725**	828-464-3655	514
Hickory Point Bank & Trust FSB PO Box 2548 *Cust Svc	Decatur	IL	62525	**800-872-0081***	217-875-3131	69
Hickory Printing Group Inc 725 Reese Dr SW	Conover	NC	28613	**800-442-5679**	828-465-3431	626
Hickory Ridge Marriott Conference Hotel 10400 Fernwood Rd	Bethesda	IL	20817	**800-334-0344**	301-380-3000	377
Hickory Springs Mfg Co 235 Second Ave NW	Hickory	NC	28601	**800-438-5341**		717
HID Global Corp 611 Center Ridge Dr	Austin	TX	78753	**800-237-7769**	512-776-9000	180-12
HIDA (Health Industry Distributors Assn) 310 Montgomery St	Alexandria	VA	22314	**800-549-4432**	703-549-4432	48-18
Hidalgo County 100 N Closner	Edinburg	TX	78539	**888-318-2811**	956-318-2100	338
Hidden Valley Resort & Conference Ctr 1 Craighead Dr PO Box 4420	Hidden Valley	PA	15502	**800-452-2223**	814-443-8000	377
Hideout at Flitner Ranch Resort PO Box 206	Shell	WY	82441	**800-354-8637**	307-765-2080	241
Hie Electronics Inc 321 N Central Expy Ste 260	Mckinney	TX	75070	**888-782-7937**	972-542-2327	175-8
Higdon Florist 201 E 32nd St	Joplin	MO	64804	**800-641-4726**	417-624-7171	294
High Concrete Structures Inc 125 Denver Rd	Denver	PA	17517	**800-773-2278**	717-336-9300	185

Name / Address	City	State	ZIP	Toll-Free	Phone	Class
High Country Bancorp Inc 7360 W Hwy 50 PO Box 309 *OTC: HCBC*	Salida	CO	81201	**800-201-0557**	719-539-2516	360-2
High Country News 119 Grand Ave	Paonia	CO	81428	**800-311-5852**	970-527-4898	531-3
High Country Transportation Inc PO Box 700	Cortez	CO	81321	**800-635-7687**		778
High Desert Museum 59800 S Hwy 97	Bend	OR	97702	**866-632-9992**	541-382-4754	519
High End Systems Inc 2105 Gracy Farms Ln	Austin	TX	78758	**800-890-8989**	512-836-2242	439
High Hampton Inn & Country Club 1525 Hwy 107 S	Cashiers	NC	28717	**800-334-2551**	828-743-2450	667
High Peaks Resort 2384 Saranac Ave	Lake Placid	NY	12946	**800-755-5598**	518-523-4411	667
High Performance Computing Collaboratory PO Box 9627	Mississippi State	MS	39762	**800-521-4041**	662-325-8278	666
High Plains Livestock Exchange LLC 28601 US Hwy 34	Brush	CO	80723	**866-842-5115**	970-842-5115	445
High Plains Power Inc 1775 E Monroe PO Box 713	Riverton	WY	82501	**800-445-0613**	307-856-9426	247
High Plains Publishers Inc 1500 W Wyatt Earp Blvd	Dodge City	KS	67801	**800-452-7171**	620-227-7171	634-8
High Point Chamber of Commerce 1634 N Main St	High Point	NC	27262	**844-704-3663**	336-882-5000	138
High Point Convention & Visitors Bureau 300 S Main St	High Point	NC	27260	**800-720-5255**	336-884-5255	208
High Point Furniture Industries Inc 1104 Bedford St PO Box 2063	High Point	NC	27261	**800-447-3462**	336-431-7101	320-1
High Point Public Library (HPPL) 901 N Main St	High Point	NC	27262	**877-772-8346**	336-883-3660	434-3
High Point Regional Health System (HPRHS) 601 N Elm St PO Box HP-5	High Point	NC	27262	**877-878-7644**	336-878-6000	374-3
High Point University 833 Montlieu Ave	High Point	NC	27262	**800-345-6993**	336-841-9216	167
High Power Technical Services Inc (HPTS) 2230 Ampere Dr	Louisville	KY	40299	**866-310-5377**		115
High Speed Productions Inc 1303 Underwood Ave	San Francisco	CA	94124	**888-520-9099**	415-822-3083	513
High Vacuum Apparatus LLC (HVA) 12880 Moya Blvd	Reno	NV	89506	**800-551-4422**	775-359-4442	787
High West Energy Inc (HWE) 6270 County Rd 212	Pine Bluffs	WY	82082	**888-834-1657**	307-245-3261	247
Higher Ed Growth LLC 5400 S Lakeshore Dr Ste 101	Tempe	AZ	85283	**866-433-8532**		448
HighJump Software 5600 W 83rd St Ste 600	Minneapolis	MN	55437	**800-328-3271**	952-947-4088	180-1
Highland Computer Forms Inc 1025 W Main St	Hillsboro	OH	45133	**800-669-5213**	937-393-4215	109
Highland Ridge Hospital 7309 South 180 West	Midvale	UT	84047	**800-821-4357**	801-569-2153	724
Highlands Pathology Consultants Pc 2175 Hwy 75 Ste 4	Blountville	TN	37617	**877-696-6775**	423-323-5290	415
Highlands Today 315 US Hwy 27 N *General	Sebring	FL	33870	**866-607-2187***	863-386-5800	531-2
Highlights for Children Inc 1800 Watermark Dr *Cust Svc	Columbus	OH	43216	**800-255-9517***	614-486-0631	634-9
Highline Electric Assn 1300 S Interocean Ave	Holyoke	CO	80734	**800-816-2236**	970-854-2236	247
Highmark Inc 120 Fifth Ave Pl	Pittsburgh	PA	15222	**800-992-0246**	412-544-7000	391-3
Highway Machine Company Inc (HMC) 3010 S Old US Hwy 41	Princeton	IN	47670	**866-990-9462**	812-385-3639	453
Highway To Health Inc 1 Radnor Corporate Ctr Ste 100	Radnor	PA	19087	**888-243-2358**		391-7
Highwoods Properties Inc 3100 Smoketree Ct Ste 600 *NYSE: HIW*	Raleigh	NC	27604	**866-449-6637**	919-872-4924	653
Hiland Dairy Co PO Box 2270	Springfield	MO	65801	**800-641-4022**	417-862-9311	297-27
Hilbert College 5200 S Pk Ave	Hamburg	NY	14075	**800-649-8003**	716-649-7900	167
Hilco Electric Co-op Inc 115 E Main PO Box 127	Itasca	TX	76055	**800-338-6425**	254-687-2331	247
Hilford Moving & Storage 1595 Arundell Ave	Ventura	CA	93003	**800-739-6683**	805-642-0221	518
Hilgard House Hotel & Suites 927 Hilgard Ave	Los Angeles	CA	90024	**800-826-3934**	310-208-3945	379
Hilgraeve Inc 115 E Elm Ave *Sales	Monroe	MI	48162	**800-826-2760***	734-243-0576	180-7
Hill & Griffith Co 1085 Summer St	Cincinnati	OH	45204	**800-543-0425**	513-921-1075	499
Hill & Valley Inc 3915 9th St	Rock Island	IL	61201	**800-480-0055**	309-793-0161	67
Hill Barth & King LLC 7680 Market St	Youngstown	OH	44512	**800-733-8613**	330-758-8613	2
Hill Bros Chemical Co 1675 N Main St	Orange	CA	92867	**800-994-8801**	714-998-8800	145
Hill County Electric Co-op Inc PO Box 2330	Havre	MT	59501	**877-394-7804**		247
Hill Crest Behavioral Health Services 6869 Fifth Ave S	Birmingham	AL	35212	**800-292-8553**	205-833-9000	374-5
Hill Mfg Company Inc 1500 Jonesboro Rd SE	Atlanta	GA	30315	**800-445-5123**	404-522-8364	150
Hill PHOENIX Inc 1003 Sigman Rd	Conyers	GA	30013	**800-518-6630**	770-285-3264	662
Hill Physicians Medical Group Inc 2409 Camino Ramon PO Box 5080	San Ramon	CA	94583	**800-445-5747**	925-820-8300	462
Hill School 717 E High St	Pottstown	PA	19464	**877-651-2800**	610-326-1000	621
Hill Wood Products Inc 9483 Ashawa Rd	Cook	MN	55723	**800-788-9689**	218-666-5933	550
Hillcrest Baptist Medical Ctr 3000 Herring Ave	Waco	TX	76708	**800-793-6030**	254-202-2000	374-3

Name / Address	City	State	ZIP	Toll-Free	Phone	Class
Hillcrest Foods 2695 E 40th St	Cleveland	OH	44115	**800-952-4344**	216-361-4625	298-4
Hillcrest Garden 95 W Century Rd	Paramus	NJ	07652	**800-437-7000**	201-599-3030	294
Hillcrest Historic District Markham & Kavanaugh	Little Rock	AR	72216	**877-637-0037**	501-371-0075	49-5
Hiller Aviation Museum 601 Skyway Rd	San Carlos	CA	94070	**888-500-1555**	650-654-0200	519
Hillerich & Bradsby Company Inc 800 W Main St	Louisville	KY	40202	**800-282-2287**	502-585-5226	708
Hilliard This Week 7801 N Central Dr	Lewis Center	OH	43035	**888-837-4342**	740-888-6100	531-4
Hillman Group Inc 10590 Hamilton Ave	Cincinnati	OH	45231	**800-800-4900**	513-851-4900	351
Hill-Rom Services Inc 1069 SR 46 E	Batesville	IN	47006	**800-267-2337**	812-934-7777	320-3
Hills Bank & Trust Co 131 Main St PO Box 70	Hills	IA	52235	**800-445-5725**	319-679-2291	69
Hills Materials Co 3975 Sturgis Rd	Rapid City	SD	57702	**800-325-7056**	605-394-3300	502-4
Hillsboro Equipment Inc E18898 Hwy 33	Hillsboro	WI	54634	**800-521-5133**	608-489-2275	276
Hillsboro Public Library 2850 NE Brookwood Pkwy	Hillsboro	OR	97124	**855-870-0049**	503-615-6500	434-3
Hillsborough Community College *Dale Mabry* 4001 Tampa Bay Blvd	Tampa	FL	33614	**866-253-7077**	813-253-7000	161
Hillsborough County Public Schools 901 E Kennedy Blvd	Tampa	FL	33602	**800-962-2873**	813-272-4000	683
Hillsborough Township Board of Education 379 S Branch Rd	Hillsborough	NJ	08844	**800-272-1325**	908-431-6600	683
Hillsdale College 33 E College St	Hillsdale	MI	49242	**888-886-1174**	517-437-7341	167
Hillsdale Free Will Baptist College PO Box 7208	Moore	OK	73153	**800-460-6328**	405-912-9000	167
Hillshire Brands 2200 W Don Tyson Pkwy	Springdale	AR	72762	**800-323-7117**	479-290-6397	217
Hillside Candy Co 35 Hillside Ave	Hillside	NJ	07205	**800-524-1304**	973-926-2300	297-8
Hillside School 404 Robin Hill Rd	Marlborough	MA	01752	**800-344-8328**	508-485-2824	621
Hillstone Restaurant Group 147 S Beverly Dr	Beverly Hills	CA	90212	**800-230-9787**	310-385-7343	668
Hilltop Inn of Vermont 3472 Airport Rd	Montpelier	VT	05602	**877-609-0003**	802-229-5766	379
Hillyard Chemical Company Inc 302 N Fourth St PO Box 909	Saint Joseph	MO	64501	**800-365-1555**	816-233-1321	150
Hilman Inc 12 Timber Ln *Cust Svc	Marlboro	NJ	07746	**888-276-5548***	732-462-6277	469
Hilmar Cheese Company Inc PO Box 910	Hilmar	CA	95324	**888-300-4465**	209-667-6076	297-5
Hilti Inc 5400 S 122nd E Ave *Cust Svc	Tulsa	OK	74146	**800-879-8000***	918-252-6000	757
Hilton Galveston Island Resort 5400 Seawall Blvd	Galveston	TX	77551	**800-475-3386**	409-744-5000	667
Hilton Grand Vacations Company LLC 6355 Metro W Blvd Ste 180	Orlando	FL	32835	**800-230-7068**	407-722-3100	751
Hilton Hawaiian Village 2005 Kalia Rd	Honolulu	HI	96815	**800-445-8667**	808-949-4321	667
Hilton Head Health Institute 14 Valencia Rd	Hilton Head Island	SC	29928	**800-292-2440**	843-785-3919	704
Hilton Head Island Beach & Tennis Resort 40 Folly Field Rd *Resv	Hilton Head Island	SC	29928	**800-475-2631***	843-842-4402	667
Hilton Head Island Visitors & Convention Bureau 1 Chamber Dr PO Box 5647	Hilton Head Island	SC	29938	**800-523-3373**	843-785-3673	208
Hilton Head Island-Bluffton Chamber of Commerce 1 Chamber Dr	Hilton Head Island	SC	29928	**800-523-3373**	843-785-3673	138
Hilton Head Library 11 Beach City Rd	Hilton Head Island	SC	29926	**800-860-1444**	843-255-6500	434-3
Hilton Myrtle Beach Resort 10000 Beach Club Dr	Myrtle Beach	SC	29572	**800-445-8667**	843-449-5000	667
Hilton San Diego Resort 1775 E Mission Bay Dr	San Diego	CA	92109	**800-445-8667**	619-276-4010	667
Hilton Sandestin Beach Golf Resort & Spa 4000 Sandestin Blvd S	Destin	FL	32550	**800-559-1805**	850-267-9500	667
Hilton Scranton & Conference Ctr 100 Adams Ave	Scranton	PA	18503	**800-445-8667**	570-343-3000	377
Hilton Sedona Resort & Spa 90 Ridge Trl Dr *General	Sedona	AZ	86351	**877-273-3762***	928-284-4040	667
Hilton Short Hills 41 JFK Pkwy	Short Hills	NJ	07078	**800-445-8667**	973-379-0100	705
Hilton Suites Toronto/Markham Conference Centre & Spa 8500 Warden Ave	Markham	ON	L6G1A5	**800-445-8667**	905-470-8500	705
Hilton Waikoloa Village 425 Waikoloa Beach Dr	Waikoloa	HI	96738	**866-931-1679**	808-886-1234	667
Hilton Whistler Resort & Spa 4050 Whistler Way	Whistler	BC	V0N1B4	**800-515-4050**	604-932-1982	667
Hilton Worldwide 7930 Jones Branch Dr	McLean	VA	22102	**800-445-8667**	703-883-1000	379
Himoinsa Power Systems Inc 16002 W 110th St	Lenexa	KS	66219	**866-710-2988**	913-495-5557	517
Hinckley Co, The 1 Little Harbor Landing	Portsmouth	RI	02871	**866-446-2553**	401-683-7005	89
Hinda Incentives Inc 2440 W 34th St	Chicago	IL	60608	**866-487-2365**	773-890-5900	763
Hindley Mfg Company Inc 9 Havens St	Cumberland	RI	02864	**800-323-9031**	401-722-2550	350
Hinds Community College 501 E Main St PO Box 1100	Raymond	MS	39154	**800-446-3722**	601-857-5261	161
Hinds Hospice 1616 W Shaw Ste C-1	Fresno	CA	93711	**800-400-4677**	559-248-8591	371
Hines Interest LP 2800 Post Oak Blvd	Houston	TX	77056	**888-782-7937**	713-621-8000	651

Name / Address	City	State	Zip	Toll-Free	Phone	Class
Hines Nut Co Inc 990 S St Paul St	Dallas	TX	75201	**800-561-6374**	214-939-0253	297-28
Hines Park Lincoln Inc 40601 Ann Arbor Rd	Plymouth	MI	48170	**866-979-3919**		56
Hingham Mutual Fire Insurance Co 230 Beal St	Hingham	MA	02043	**800-341-8200**	781-749-0841	391-4
Hiniker Co 58766 240th St	Mankato	MN	56002	**800-433-5620**	507-625-6621	275
Hinkle Insurance Agency Inc 600 Olde Hickory Rd Ste 200	Lancaster	PA	17601	**877-408-1418**	717-560-9733	390
Hinkley Lighting 12600 Berea Rd	Cleveland	OH	44111	**800-446-5539**	216-671-3300	439
Hinsdale County 311 N Henson St	Lake City	CO	81235	**877-944-7575**	970-944-2225	338
Hinshaws Acura/Honda 5955 20th St E	Fife	WA	98424	**800-752-2872**	253-922-8830	56
Hinton Lakeview Inns & Suites 500 Smith St	Hinton	AB	T7V2A1	**877-355-3500**	780-865-2575	378
Hippocrates Health Institute Life-Change Ctr 1443 Palmdale Ct	West Palm Beach	FL	33411	**800-842-2125**	561-471-8876	704
Hiram College PO Box 67 *Admissions	Hiram	OH	44234	**800-362-5280***	330-569-5169	167
Hire Image LLC 6 Alcazar Ave	Johnston	RI	02919	**888-433-0090**	401-490-2202	719
Hiregenics 47742 Van Dyke Ave	Shelby Township	MI	48317	**866-315-5489**		569
Hireko Trading Company Inc 16185 Stephens St	City of Industry	CA	91745	**800-367-8912**		708
HireRight Inc 5151 California Ave	Irvine	CA	92617	**800-400-2761**	949-428-5800	632
Hirschbach Motor Lines Inc 18355 US Hwy 20	East Dubuque	IL	61025	**800-554-2969**	402-494-5000	778
Hirsh Industries Inc 3636 Westown Pkwy Ste 100	West Des Moines	IA	50266	**800-383-7414**	515-299-3200	320-1
Hirzel Canning Company & Farms 411 Lemoyne Rd	Northwood	OH	43619	**800-837-1631**	419-693-0531	297-20
Hispanic Assn of Colleges & Universities (HACU) 8415 Datapoint Dr Ste 400	San Antonio	TX	78229	**800-780-4228**	210-692-3805	48-5
Historic Bullock Hotel 633 Main St	Deadwood	SD	57732	**800-336-1876**		379
Historic French Market Inn 509 Decatur St	New Orleans	LA	70130	**800-366-2743**	504-561-5621	379
Historic Inns of Annapolis 58 State Cir	Annapolis	MD	21401	**800-847-8882**	410-263-2641	379
Historic Jonesborough Visitors Ctr & Museum 117 Boone St	Jonesborough	TN	37659	**866-401-4223**	423-753-1010	519
Historic New England 141 Cambridge St	Boston	MA	02114	**800-722-2256**	617-227-3956	47-13
Historic Old Town Fort Collins 19 Old Town Sq Ste 230	Fort Collins	CO	80524	**866-203-5939**	970-484-6500	459
Historic Rock Ford Plantation 881 Rockford Rd	Lancaster	PA	17602	**800-732-0999**	717-392-7223	49-2
Historic Roswell District 617 Atlanta St	Roswell	GA	30075	**800-776-7935**		49-2
Historic Tours of America Inc 201 Front St Ste 224 *General	Key West	FL	33040	**800-844-7601***	305-296-3609	758
Historic Trinity Lutheran Church 1345 Gratiot Ave	Detroit	MI	48207	**800-268-3058**	313-567-3100	49
Historical Lawmen Museum 845 Motel Blvd	Las Cruces	NM	88007	**800-332-2121**	575-525-1911	519
Historical Research Ctr Inc 2107 Corporate Dr	Boynton Beach	FL	33426	**800-985-9956**		328
History Ch *A&E Television Networks LLC* 235 E 45th St 2nd Fl	New York	NY	10017	**888-371-5848**	212-210-1400	736
Hit Promotional Products Inc 7150 Bryan Dairy Rd	Largo	FL	33777	**800-237-6305**	727-541-5561	9
Hitachi America Ltd 50 Prospect Ave	Tarrytown	NY	10591	**800-448-2244**	914-332-5800	187
Hitachi America Ltd Computer Div 2000 Sierra Pt Pkwy	Brisbane	CA	94005	**800-448-2244**		175-8
Hitachi Canada Ltd 5450 Explore Dr Ste 501	Mississauga	ON	L4W5N1	**877-248-4237**	905-629-9300	255
Hitachi Chemical Diagnostics 630 Clyde Ct	Mountain View	CA	94043	**800-233-6278**	650-961-5501	233
Hitachi Data Systems Corp 750 Central Expy	Santa Clara	CA	95050	**877-437-3849**	408-970-1000	175-8
Hitachi Kokusai Electric America Ltd 150 Crossways Pk Dr	Woodbury	NY	11797	**855-490-5124**	516-921-7200	645
Hitachi Medical Systems America Inc 1959 Summit Commerce Pk	Twinsburg	OH	44087	**800-800-3106**	330-425-1313	382
Hitachi Metals America Ltd 2 Manhattanville Rd Ste 301	Purchase	NY	10577	**800-777-5757**	914-694-9200	308
Hitch Enterprises Inc 309 Northridge Cir PO Box 1308	Guymon	OK	73942	**800-951-2533**	580-338-8575	360-3
HITCO Carbon Composites Inc 1600 W 135th St	Gardena	CA	90249	**800-421-5444**	310-527-0700	503
Hite Co 3101 Beale Ave	Altoona	PA	16601	**800-252-3598**	814-944-6121	248
HITEC Group Ltd 1743 Quincy Ave Unit 155	Naperville	IL	60540	**800-288-8303**		248
Hi-Tech Fabrication Inc Leesville Industrial Park 8900 Midway W Rd	Raleigh	NC	27617	**800-359-7249**	919-781-2552	695
Hi-Tech Systems Engineering Co 2700 Old Centre Rd	Portage	MI	49024	**866-312-1893**	269-488-7788	263
Hitt Marking Devices Inc 3231 W MacArthur Blvd	Santa Ana	CA	92704	**800-969-6699**	714-979-1405	466
Hive Modern Design 820 nw glisan st	Portland	OR	97209	**866-663-4483**	503-242-1967	136
Hivelocity Ventures Corp 8010 Woodland Ctr Blvd Ste 700	Tampa	FL	33614	**888-869-4678**	813-471-0355	227
Hiwassee College 225 Hiwassee College Dr	Madisonville	TN	37354	**800-356-2187**	423-442-2001	161
Hix Corp 1201 E 27th Terr	Pittsburg	KS	66762	**800-835-0606**	620-231-8568	741
Hixardt Technologies Inc 119 W Intendencia St	Pensacola	FL	32502	**866-985-3282**	850-439-3282	182
HJ Heinz Co 1 PPG Pl Ste 3100	Pittsburgh	PA	15230	**800-255-5750**	412-456-5700	297-20
HK Systems Inc 2855 S James Dr	New Berlin	WI	53151	**800-424-7365**	262-860-7000	180-1
HKA Enterprises Inc 337 Spartangreen Blvd	Duncan	SC	29334	**800-825-5452**	864-661-5100	194
Hkm Direct Market Communications Inc 5501 Cass Ave *General	Cleveland	OH	44102	**800-860-4456***	216-651-9500	5
HL Dalis Inc 35-35 24th St	Long Island	NY	11106	**800-453-2547**	718-361-1100	248
HL Turner Group Inc, The 27 Locke Rd	Concord	NH	03301	**800-305-2289**	603-228-1122	263
HLA (Harold Levinson Assoc) 21 Banfi Plz	Farmingdale	NY	11735	**800-325-2512**	631-962-2400	298-3
HLC Hotels Inc 7080 Abercorn St PO Box 13069	Savannah	GA	31416	**800-344-4378**	912-352-4493	379
HLI (Human Life International) 4 Family Life Ln *Orders	Front Royal	VA	22630	**800-549-5433***	540-635-7884	47-6
Hli Properties Inc 1003 Central Ave	Fort Dodge	IA	50501	**800-247-2000**	515-955-1600	634-9
HM Royal Inc 689 Pennington Ave	Trenton	NJ	08618	**800-257-9452**	609-396-9176	145
HM Stauffer & Sons Inc 33 Glenola Dr PO Box 567	Leola	PA	17540	**800-662-2226**	717-656-2811	815
HMA (Hargrave Military Academy) 200 Military Dr	Chatham	VA	24531	**800-432-2480**	434-432-2481	621
HMC (Highway Machine Company Inc) 3010 S Old US Hwy 41	Princeton	IN	47670	**866-990-9462**	812-385-3639	453
HMC (Hays Medical Ctr) 2220 Canterbury Dr	Hays	KS	67601	**800-248-0073**	785-650-2759	374-3
HMC Archtiect 3546 Councours St	Ontario	CA	91764	**800-350-9979**	909-989-9979	263
HMH (Harrington Memorial Hospital) 100 S St	Southbridge	MA	01550	**800-416-6072**	508-765-9771	374-3
HMJ Inc 212 W Colfax Ave	South Bend	IN	46601	**800-347-7986**	574-232-3061	770
HMN Financial Inc 1016 Civic Ctr Dr NW *NASDAQ: HMNF*	Rochester	MN	55901	**888-257-2000**	507-535-1309	360-2
HMS (Healthcare Management Systems Inc) 3102 W End Ave Ste 400	Nashville	TN	37203	**800-383-3317**	615-383-7300	387
HNA (Hawaii Nurses Assn) 949 Kapiolani Blvd Ste 107	Honolulu	HI	96814	**800-617-2677**	808-531-1628	532
HNA (Hockey North America) 45570 Shepard Dr	Sterling	VA	20164	**800-446-2539**	703-430-8100	47-22
HO Bostrom Company Inc 818 Progress Ave	Waukesha	WI	53186	**800-332-5415**	262-542-0222	687
HO Trerice Co 12950 W Eight-Mile Rd	Oak Park	MI	48237	**888-873-7423**	248-399-8000	203
Hoag Hospital Irvine (HHI) 16200 Sand Canyon Ave	Irvine	CA	92618	**800-309-9729**	949-764-4624	374-3
Hoard's Dairyman Magazine 28 Milwaukee Ave W PO Box 801	Fort Atkinson	WI	53538	**800-245-8222**	920-563-5551	456-1
Hoban & Assoc Dba Coast Real Estate Services 2829 Rucker Ave	Everett	WA	98201	**800-339-3634**	425-339-3638	650
Hobart & William Smith Colleges 300 Pulteney St *Admissions	Geneva	NY	14456	**800-852-2256***	315-781-3000	167
Hobart Bros Co 101 Trade Sq E	Troy	OH	45373	**800-424-1543**	937-332-4000	809
Hobart Corp 701 S Ridge Ave *Cust Svc	Troy	OH	45374	**800-333-7447***	937-332-3000	299
Hobas Pipe USA LP 1413 E Richey Rd	Houston	TX	77073	**800-856-7473**	281-821-2200	595
Hobbs Bonded Fibers Inc 200 Commerce Dr	Waco	TX	76710	**800-433-3357**	254-741-0040	742-6
Hobbs Chamber of Commerce 400 N Marland Blvd	Hobbs	NM	88240	**800-658-6291**	575-397-3202	138
Hobby Lobby Creative Centers 7707 SW 44th St	Oklahoma City	OK	73179	**855-329-7060**	405-745-1100	44
Hobe Sound Bible College PO Box 1065	Hobe Sound	FL	33475	**800-881-5534**	772-546-5534	160
Hobie Cat Co 4925 Oceanside Blvd	Oceanside	CA	92056	**800-462-4349**	760-758-9100	89
Hobson & Motzer Inc 30 Air Line Dr	Durham	CT	06422	**800-476-5111**	860-349-1756	487
Hobsons CollegeView 50 E Business Way Ste 300	Cincinnati	OH	45241	**800-927-8439**		634-9
Ho-Chunk Casino S 3214 County Rd BD	Baraboo	WI	53913	**800-746-2486**		132
Hockessin Library 1023 Valley Rd	Hockessin	DE	19707	**888-352-7722**	302-239-5160	434-3
Hockey News Magazine 25 Sheppard Ave Ste 100	Toronto	ON	M2N6S7	**888-361-9768**	514-848-7000	456-20
Hockey North America (HNA) 45570 Shepard Dr	Sterling	VA	20164	**800-446-2539**	703-430-8100	47-22
Hocking College 3301 Hocking Pkwy	Nelsonville	OH	45764	**877-462-5464**	740-753-3591	798
Hocking Valley Bank 7 W Stimson Ave	Athens	OH	45701	**888-482-5854**	740-592-4441	69
Hodell-natco Industries Inc 7825 Hub Pkwy	Cleveland	OH	44125	**800-321-4862**	216-447-0165	351
Hodge Products Inc PO Box 1326	El Cajon	CA	92020	**800-778-2217**		296
Hodges University 2655 Northbrooke Dr	Naples	FL	34119	**800-466-8017**	239-513-1122	167
Fort Myers 4501 Colonial Blvd	Fort Myers	FL	33966	**800-466-0019**	239-938-7701	167
Hodgson Mill Inc 1100 Stevens Ave	Effingham	IL	62401	**800-347-0105**	217-347-0105	297-23
Hoegemeyer Hybrids Inc 1755 Hoegemeyer Rd	Hooper	NE	68031	**800-245-4631**	402-654-3399	10-4

Name / Address	City	State	ZIP	Toll-Free	Phone	Class
Hoffman California Fabrics Inc 25792 Obrero Dr	Mission Viejo	CA	92691	800-547-0100		593
Hoffman Memorial State Wayside PO Box 569	Mytrle Point	OR	97458	800-551-6949		564
Hoffman Products 9600 Vly View Rd	Macedonia	OH	44056	800-645-2014	216-525-4320	813
Hoffmann Hospice of the Valley 8501 Brimhall Rd Bldg 100	Bakersfield	CA	93312	888-833-3900	661-410-1010	371
Hoffmann-LaRoche Inc 340 Kingsland St	Nutley	NJ	07110	800-526-6367	973-235-5000	582
Hoffmaster 2920 N Main St	Oshkosh	WI	54901	800-327-9774	920-235-9330	557
Hofstra University 1000 Fulton Ave	Hempstead	NY	11549	800-463-7872	516-463-6600	167
Hog Slat 315 S Sycamore St	Flora	IN	46929	800-949-4647	574-967-3776	446
Hog Slat Inc PO Box 300	Newton Grove	NC	28366	800-949-4647	910-594-0219	10-5
Hogan-Knotts Financial Group, The 298 Broad St	Red Bank	NJ	07701	800-801-3190	732-842-7400	688
Hoggan Health Industries Inc 8020 South 1300 West	West Jordan	UT	84088	800-678-7888	801-572-6500	269
Hogue Cellars 2800 Lee Rd	Prosser	WA	99350	800-565-9779		79-3
Hohman Assoc Inc (HAI) 6951 W Little York	Houston	TX	77040	800-324-0978	713-896-0978	47-2
Hohmann & Barnard Inc 30 Rasons Ct	Hauppauge	NY	11788	800-645-0616	631-234-0600	280
Hohner Inc 1000 Technology Pk Dr	Glen Allen	VA	23059	800-446-6010	804-515-1900	526
Hohokam Pima National Monument c/o Casa Grande Ruins National Monument 1100 W Ruins Dr	Coolidge	AZ	85228	866-705-5711	520-723-3172	563
Hoigaards Inc 5425 Excelsior Blvd	Minneapolis	MN	55416	800-266-8157	952-929-1351	709
Hoist Fitness Systems Inc 9990 Empire St Ste 130	San Diego	CA	92126	800-548-5438	858-578-7676	269
Holabird Sports LLC 9220 Pulaski Hwy	Middle River	MD	21220	866-860-1416	410-687-6400	709
Holaday Circuits Inc 11126 Bren Rd W	Minnetonka	MN	55343	800-362-3303	952-933-3303	624
Holderness School Chapel Ln PO Box 1879	Plymouth	NH	03264	877-262-1492	603-536-1747	621
Hole in One International 6195 Ridgeview Ct Ste A	Reno	NV	89519	800-827-2249	775-828-4653	758
Holiday Acres Resort 4060 S Shore Dr PO Box 460	Rhinelander	WI	54501	800-261-1500	715-369-1500	667
Holiday Builders Inc 2293 W Eau Gallie Blvd	Melbourne	FL	32935	866-431-2533	321-610-5172	651
Holiday Cos 4567 American Blvd W PO Box 1224	Bloomington	MN	55437	800-745-7411	952-830-8700	187
Holiday Diver Inc 180 Gulf Stream Way	Dania Beach	FL	33004	800-348-3872	954-925-7630	709
Holiday Express Corp 721 S 28th St	Estherville	IA	51334	800-831-5078	712-362-5812	683
Holiday Hair 7201 Metro Blvd	Minneapolis	MN	55439	800-345-7811		76
Holiday Inn 301 Government St	Mobile	AL	36602	888-465-4329	251-694-0100	379
Holiday Inn Baltimore Inner Harbor Hotel 301 W Lombard St	Baltimore	MD	21201	877-834-3613	410-685-3500	378
Holiday Inn Express & Suites 5001 Brougham Dr	Drayton Valley	AB	T7A0A1	877-444-3110	780-515-9888	376
Holiday Inn Express & Suites Oceanfront 3301 S Atlantic Ave	Daytona Beach Shores	FL	32118	800-633-8464	386-767-1711	667
Holiday Inn Express DFW North 4550 W John Carpenter Fwy	Irving	TX	75063	800-465-4329		379
Holiday Inn Resort Daytona Beach Oceanfront 1615 S Atlantic Ave	Daytona Beach	FL	32118	800-874-0975	386-255-0921	379
Holiday Inn Resort Lake Buena Vista 13351 SR 535 *Sales	Orlando	FL	32821	866-808-8833*	407-239-4500	667
Holiday Inn SunSpree Resort Wrightsville Beach 1706 N Lumina Ave	Wrightsville Beach	NC	28480	888-211-9874	910-256-2231	667
Holiday Isle Beach Resort & Marina 84001 Overseas Hwy	Islamorada	FL	33036	877-712-2842	305-664-2321	667
Holiday Retirement Corp 5885 Meadows Rd Ste 500	Lake Oswego	OR	97035	800-322-0999	503-370-7070	653
Holiday River Expeditions 544 East 3900 South	Salt Lake City	UT	84107	800-624-6323	801-266-2087	758
Holiday Stationstores 4567 American Blvd W	Bloomington	MN	55437	800-745-7411	952-830-8700	206
Holiday Trails Resorts (Western) Inc 53730 Bridal Falls Rd	Rosedale	BC	V0X1X1	800-663-2265	604-794-7876	120
Holiday Tree Farms Inc 800 NW Cornell Ave	Corvallis	OR	97330	800-289-3684	541-753-3236	750
Holiday Valley Resort 6557 Holiday Valley Rd PO Box 370	Ellicottville	NY	14731	800-323-0020	716-699-2345	667
Holiday World & Splashin' Safari 452 E Christmas Blvd	Santa Claus	IN	47579	877-463-2645	812-937-4401	32
Holland America Line 300 Elliott Ave W	Seattle	WA	98119	800-426-0327	206-281-3535	222
Holland Area Convention & Visitors Bureau 76 E Eigth St	Holland	MI	49423	800-506-1299	616-394-0000	208
Holland Bowl Mill 120 James St	Holland	MI	49424	800-774-1230	616-396-6513	281
Holland Capital Management LP 303 W Madison St Ste 700	Chicago	IL	60606	800-295-9779	312-553-4830	401
Holland Mfg Co Inc 15 Main St PO Box 404	Succasunna	NJ	07876	800-345-0492	973-584-8141	729
Holland NASCAR Motorsports Complex 11586 Holland Glenwood Rd	Holland	NY	14080	866-655-0257	716-537-2272	514
Holland Sentinel 54 W Eigth St	Holland	MI	49423	800-633-4227	616-392-2311	531-2
Hollander Home Fashions Corp 6501 Congress Avenue Ste 300	Boca Raton	FL	33487	800-233-7666	561-997-6900	743
Hollar & Greene Produce Co Inc 230 Cabbage Rd PO Box 3500	Boone	NC	28607	800-222-1077	828-264-2177	298-7
Holley Performance Products Inc 1801 Russellville Rd *Sales	Bowling Green	KY	42101	800-638-0032*	270-782-2900	127
Holliday Lake State Park 2759 State Pk Rd	Appomattox	VA	24522	800-933-7275	434-248-6308	564
Hollins University PO BOX 9707 *Admissions	Roanoke	VA	24020	800-456-9595*	540-362-6401	167
Hollis Marketing 2130 Brenner St	Saginaw	MI	48602	866-797-3301	989-797-3300	197
Hollister Inc 2000 Hollister Dr	Libertyville	IL	60048	800-323-4060	847-680-1000	476
Hollister Moving & Storage 1650 Lana Way	Hollister	CA	95023	800-767-8580	831-637-6250	518
Holloman Corp 333 N Sam Houston Pkwy E Ste 600	Houston	TX	77060	800-521-2461	281-878-2600	188
Holloway Sportswear Inc 2633 Campbell Rd	Sidney	OH	45365	800-331-5156		154-5
Holly Energy Partners LP 100 Crescent Ct Ste 1600	Dallas	TX	75201	800-642-1687	214-871-3555	360-5
Holly Hill Hospital 3019 Falstaff Rd	Raleigh	NC	27610	800-447-1800	919-250-7000	374-5
Holly Poultry Inc 2221 Berlin St	Baltimore	MD	21230	800-342-9464	410-727-6210	345
Holly Shores Best Holiday 491 Route 9	Cape May	NJ	08204	877-494-6559	609-886-1234	705
Hollyhock PO Box 127	Mansons Landing	BC	V0P1K0	800-933-6339	250-935-6576	671
Hollywood Bowl 2301 N Highland Ave	Hollywood	CA	90068	800-745-3000	323-850-2000	571
Hollywood Casino at Charles Town Races 750 Hollywood Dr	Charles Town	WV	25414	800-795-7001	304-725-7001	639
Hollywood Casino Baton Rouge 1717 River Rd N	Baton Rouge	LA	70802	800-447-6843	225-709-7777	132
Hollywood Casino Bay Saint Louis 711 Hollywood Blvd	Bay Saint Louis	MS	39520	866-758-2591		132
Hollywood Casino Joliet 777 Hollywood Blvd	Joliet	IL	60436	800-426-2537		132
Hollywood Reporter 5055 Wilshire Blvd Ste 600	Los Angeles	CA	90036	866-525-2150	323-525-2000	456-9
Hollywood Wax Museum 6767 Hollywood Blvd	Hollywood	CA	90028	800-214-3661	323-462-5991	519
Hol-Mac Corp 2730-A Hwy 15 PO Box 349	Bay Springs	MS	39422	800-844-3019	601-764-4121	225
Holman Cadillac Co 1200 Rt 73 S	Mount Laurel	NJ	08054	866-865-6973	856-778-1000	56
Holman Group 9451 Corbin Ave	Northridge	CA	91324	800-321-2843	818-704-1444	461
Holman Transportation Services Inc 1010 Holman Ct	Caldwell	ID	83605	800-375-2416	208-454-0779	778
Holmberg Farms Inc 13430 Hobson Simmons Rd	Lithia	FL	33547	800-282-3562		295
Holmes Community College PO Box 399	Goodman	MS	39079	800-465-6374	662-472-2312	161
Holmes Murphy & Assoc Inc 3001 Westown Pkwy	West Des Moines	IA	50266	800-247-7756	515-223-6800	390
Holmes Regional Medical Ctr 1350 Hickory St	Melbourne	FL	32901	800-716-7737	321-434-7000	374-3
Holmes-Wayne Electric Co-op Inc 6060 Ohio 83	Millersburg	OH	44654	866-674-1055	330-674-1055	247
Holocaust Memorial Ctr 28123 OrchaRd Lake Rd	Farmington Hills	MI	48334	800-875-5275	248-553-2400	519
Hologic Inc 35 Crosby Dr *NASDAQ: HOLX*	Bedford	MA	01730	800-523-5001	781-999-7300	382
Holophane 214 Oakwood Ave PO Box 3004	Newark	OH	43058	866-465-6742	740-345-9631	439
Holstein Assn USA Inc 1 Holstein Pl PO Box 808 *Orders	Brattleboro	VT	05302	800-952-5200*	802-254-4551	47-2
Holsum Bakery Inc 2322 W Lincoln St	Phoenix	AZ	85009	800-755-8167	602-252-2351	67
Holt & Bugbee Co 1600 Shawsheen St	Tewksbury	MA	01876	800-325-6010	978-851-7201	193-3
HOLT Texas Ltd 3302 S WW White Rd	San Antonio	TX	78222	800-275-4658	210-648-1111	276
Holts Cigar Co 1522 Walnut St	Philadelphia	PA	19102	800-523-1641	215-732-8500	754
Holtzbrinck Publishers 175 Fifth Ave	New York	NY	10010	800-221-7945	646-307-5151	634-2
Holum & Sons Company Inc 740 Burr Oak Dr	Westmont	IL	60559	800-447-4479	630-654-8222	85
Holy Cross Energy PO Box 2150	Glenwood Springs	CO	81602	877-833-2555	970-945-5491	247
Holy Cross Family Ministries 518 Washington St	North Easton	MA	02356	800-299-7729	508-238-4095	47-20
Holy Cross Hospital 1500 Forest Glen Rd	Silver Spring	MD	20910	800-358-9001	301-754-7000	374-3
Holy Family Memorial Medical Ctr 2300 Western Ave PO Box 1450	Manitowoc	WI	54220	800-994-3662	920-320-2011	374-3
Holy Family University 9801 Frankford Ave	Philadelphia	PA	19114	800-422-0010	215-637-7700	167
Holy Names University 3500 Mountain Blvd	Oakland	CA	94619	800-430-1321	510-436-1000	167
Holy Redeemer Home Care & Hospice 12265 Townsend Rd Ste 400	Philadelphia	PA	19154	888-678-8678		371
Holy Redeemer Hospital & Medical Ctr 1648 Huntingdon Pk	Meadowbrook	PA	19046	800-818-4747	215-947-3000	374-3
Holy Rosary Healthcare 2600 Wilson St	Miles City	MT	59301	800-843-3820	406-233-2600	374-3
Holyoke Community College 303 Homestead Ave	Holyoke	MA	01040	877-442-6222	413-538-7000	161

Alphabetical Section

Name / Address	City	State	ZIP	Toll-Free	Phone	Class
Holz Rubber Company Inc 1129 S Sacramento St	Lodi	CA	95240	800-285-1600	209-368-7171	675
Homasote Co 932 Lower Ferry Rd PO Box 7240 *OTC: HMTC*	West Trenton	NJ	08628	800-257-9491	609-883-3300	817
Home & Garden Showplace 8600 W Bryn Mawr	Chicago	IL	60631	877-502-4641	773-695-5000	324
Home Automated Living Inc 14401 Sweitzer Ln 6th Fl	Laurel	MD	20707	800-935-5313	301-498-6000	176
Home Bound Healthcare Inc 1615 Vollmer Rd	Flossmoor	IL	60422	800-444-7028	708-798-0800	363
Home Capital Group Inc 145 King St W Ste 2300 *TSE: HCG*	Toronto	ON	M5H1J8	800-990-7881	416-360-4663	360-3
Home Care Industries Inc ALFCO Div 1 Lisbon St *Cust Svc	Clifton	NJ	07013	800-325-1908*	973-365-1600	18
Home City Financial Corp 2454 N Limestone St *OTC: HCFL*	Springfield	OH	45503	866-421-2331	937-390-0470	360-2
Home Depot Inc 2455 Paces Ferry Rd NW *NYSE: HD* ■ *Cust Svc	Atlanta	GA	30339	800-553-3199*	770-433-8211	364
Home Depot Supply 3100 Cumberland Blvd Ste 1480	Atlanta	GA	30339	855-615-8372	770-852-9000	351
Home Design Outlet Center 400 County Ave	Secaucus	NJ	07094	800-701-0388		361
Home Dynamix LLC 1 Carol Pl	Moonachie	NJ	07074	800-726-9290	201-807-0111	130
Home Entertainment Distribution Inc 120 Shawmut Rd	Canton	MA	02021	800-343-9619	888-567-7557	37
Home Essentials & Beyond Inc 200 Theodore Conrad Dr	Jersey City	NJ	07305	800-417-6218	732-590-3600	361
Home Federal Bank 225 S Main Ave	Sioux Falls	SD	57104	800-244-2149	605-336-2470	69
Home Furnishings Independents Assn (HFIA) 2050 Stemmons World Fwy Ste 292	Dallas	TX	75207	800-422-3778		48-4
Home Furniture Mart 5301 Sheila St	Commerce	CA	90040	888-936-6673	909-627-5705	789
Home Health & Hospice Care 7 Executive Park Dr	Merrimack	NH	03054	800-887-5973	603-882-2941	371
Home Health Line 11300 Rockville Pk Ste 1100	Rockville	MD	20852	800-929-4824	301-287-2700	530-8
Home Hospice Care of Rhode Island 1085 N Main St	Providence	RI	02904	800-338-6555	401-415-4200	371
Home Hospice of Grayson County 505 W Ctr St	Sherman	TX	75090	888-233-7455	903-868-9315	371
Home Instead Inc 13323 California St	Omaha	NE	68154	888-484-5759	402-498-4466	363
Home IV Care & Nutritional Service 30 Ebco Cir Ste 102	Waynesboro	VA	22980	800-552-6576		363
Home Market Foods Inc 140 Morgan Dr	Norwood	MA	02062	800-367-8325	781-948-1500	297-36
Home Media Retailing 4590 MacArthur Ste 500	Newport Beach	CA	92660	800-371-6897	714-759-4661	456-21
Home News Enterprises 333 Second St	Columbus	IN	47201	800-876-7811		634-8
Home News Tribune 92 E Main St Ste 202	Somerville	NJ	08876	800-627-4663	732-246-5500	531-2
Home Paramount Pest Control Cos Inc PO Box 850	Forest Hill	MD	21050	888-888-4663	410-510-0700	576
Home Products International Inc 4501 W 47th St	Chicago	IL	60632	800-327-3534	773-890-1010	606
Home Ranch PO Box 822	Clark	CO	80428	800-688-2982	970-879-1780	241
Home Savings & Loan Company of Youngstown 275 W Federal St	Youngstown	OH	44503	888-822-4751	330-742-0500	69
Home Security of America Inc 310 N Midvale Blvd	Madison	WI	53705	800-367-1448		367
Home Staff Inc 5517 N Cumberland Ave Ste 915	Chicago	IL	60656	800-806-6924	773-467-6002	363
HomeAdvisor 14023 Denver W Pkwy Ste 200	Golden	CO	80401	800-474-1596	303-963-7200	397
HomeCare & Hospice 1225 W State St	Olean	NY	14760	800-339-7011	716-372-5735	371
HomeCare of East Alabama Medical Ctr 665 Opelika Rd	Auburn	AL	36830	866-542-4768	334-826-3131	371
HomeGain.com Inc 6001 Shellmound St Ste 550	Emeryville	CA	94608	888-542-0800	510-655-0800	650
Homeland Security Funding Week 8204 Fenton St	Silver Spring	MD	20910	800-666-6380	301-588-6380	530-7
HomEquity Bank 1881 Yonge St Ste 300	Toronto	ON	M4S3C4	866-522-2447	416-925-4757	68
Homer Electric Assn Inc 3977 Lake St	Homer	AK	99603	800-478-8551	907-235-8551	247
Homer Laughlin China Co 672 Fiesta Dr	Newell	WV	26050	800-452-4462	304-387-1300	728
Homer Optical Company Inc 2401 Linden Ln	Silver Spring	MD	20910	800-627-2710	301-585-9060	541
Homereach Hospice 800 McConnell Dr	Columbus	OH	43214	800-837-2455	614-566-5377	371
Homes & Land Magazine Affiliates LLC 1830 E Pk Ave	Tallahassee	FL	32301	800-277-7800	850-575-0189	634-9
Homes by Keystone Inc 13338 Midvale Rd PO Box 69	Waynesboro	PA	17268	800-890-7926		105
Homes.com Inc 150 Granby St	Norfolk	VA	23510	866-675-1058		387
HomeServices of America Inc 333 S Seventh St 27th Fl	Minneapolis	MN	55402	888-485-0018		650
Homestead Mills 221 N River St PO Box 1115	Cook	MN	55723	800-652-5233	218-666-5233	297-4
Homestead Resort 700 N Homestead Dr	Midway	UT	84049	888-327-7220		667
Homestead Technologies Inc 180 Jefferson Dr	Menlo Park	CA	94025	800-797-2958	650-944-3100	806
HomeSteps 500 Plano Pkwy	Carrollton	TX	75010	800-972-7555		508
HomeStreet Bank 601 Union St 2 Union Sq Ste 2000	Seattle	WA	98101	800-654-1075	206-623-3050	69
HomeTeam Inspection Service Inc 575 Chamber Dr	Milford	OH	45150	800-598-5297		365
Hometown America LLC 150 N Wacker Dr Ste 2800	Chicago	IL	60606	888-735-4310	312-604-7500	504
Hometown Bank 245 N Peters Ave	Fond du Lac	WI	54935	877-261-2220	920-907-2220	69
Hometown Sportswear Inc 3692 Us Rt 60 E	Barboursville	WV	25504	888-770-7223	304-736-4021	709
Hometrust Bank, The PO Box 10	Asheville	NC	28802	800-627-1632	828-259-3939	69
HomeVestors of America Inc 6500 Greenville Ave Ste 400	Dallas	TX	75206	866-200-6475	972-761-0046	311
Homewatch International Inc 7100 E Belleview Ave Ste 303	Greenwood Village	CO	80111	800-777-9770	303-758-5111	363
Homewood at Williamsport 16505 Virginia Ave	Williamsport	MD	21795	877-849-9244	301-582-1750	670
Homewood FSB 3228-30 Eastern Ave	Baltimore	MD	21224	800-554-8969	410-327-5220	69
HON Co 200 Oak St	Muscatine	IA	52761	800-553-8230	563-272-7100	320-1
Honda Ctr 2695 E Katella Ave	Anaheim	CA	92806	877-945-3946	714-704-2400	718
Honda of Santa Monica 1726 Santa Monica Blvd	Santa Monica	CA	90404	800-269-2031	310-264-4900	56
Honda World 10645 Studebaker Rd	Downey	CA	90241	888-458-9404	562-929-7000	56
Hondros College 4140 Executive Pkwy	Westerville	OH	43081	888-466-3767		167
Honduras *Embassy* 3007 Tilden St NW	Washington	DC	20008	800-375-5283	202-966-7702	259
Honegger Ringger & Company Inc 1905 N Main St	Bluffton	IN	46714	888-853-5906	260-824-4107	2
Honey Acres 1557 Hwy 67 N	Ashippun	WI	53003	800-558-7745		297-24
Honey Creek State Park 901 State Pk Rd	Grove	OK	74344	800-622-6317	918-786-9447	564
Honey Dew Assoc Inc 2 Taunton St	Plainville	MA	02762	800-946-6393	508-699-3900	67
Honeys Place Inc 640 Glenoaks Blvd	San Fernando	CA	91340	800-910-3246	818-256-1101	233
Honeytree Inc 8570 M 50	Onsted	MI	49265	800-968-1889	517-467-2482	297-24
Honeyville Grain Inc 11600 Dayton Dr	Rancho Cucamonga	CA	91730	888-810-3212	909-980-9500	297-4
Honeyville Metal Inc 4200 S 900 W	Topeka	IN	46571	800-593-8377	260-593-2266	18
Honeywell 101 Columbia Rd	Morristown	NJ	07960	800-822-7673	973-455-2000	144
Honeywell Aerospace 3520 Westmoor St	South Bend	IN	46628	800-707-4555	574-231-2000	22
Honeywell Fire Solutions 1 Fire-Lite Pl	Northford	CT	06472	800-627-3473	203-484-7161	285
1 Fire-Lite Pl	Northford	CT	06472	800-627-3473	203-484-7161	747
Honeywell Fluorine Products 101 Columbia Rd	Morristown	NJ	07962	800-951-1527	973-455-2000	144
Honeywell International Inc 101 Columbia Rd PO Box M6/LM *NYSE: HON*	Morristown	NJ	07962	877-841-2840	480-353-3020	732
Honeywell Safety Products 2000 Plainfield Pike *Cust Svc	Cranston	RI	02921	800-430-4110*	401-943-4400	575
Honeywell Security Group 2 Corporate Ctr Dr Ste 100	Melville	NY	11747	800-467-5875	516-577-2000	690
Honeywell Sensing & Control 11 W Spring St *Cust Svc	Freeport	IL	61032	800-537-6945*	815-235-5500	205
Honeywell Specialty Materials 101 Columbia Rd	Morristown	NJ	07962	800-222-0094	973-455-2145	604-1
Honeywood Winery 1350 Hines St SE	Salem	OR	97302	800-726-4101	503-362-4111	49-6
Hong Kong Tourism Board 5670 Wilshire Blvd Ste 1230	Los Angeles	CA	90036	800-282-4582	323-938-4582	773
Honkamp Krueger & Company PC 2345 JFK Rd PO Box 699	Dubuque	IA	52004	888-556-0123	563-556-0123	2
Honolulu Academy of Arts 900 S Beretania St	Honolulu	HI	96814	866-385-3849	808-532-8700	519
Honolulu Advertiser 500 Ala Moana Blvd	Honolulu	HI	96813	800-801-5999	808-529-4747	531-2
Honolulu Magazine 1000 Bishop St Ste 405	Honolulu	HI	96813	800-788-4230	808-534-7546	456-22
Honolulu Publishing Co Ltd 707 Richards St Ste PH3	Honolulu	HI	96813	800-272-5245	808-524-7400	634-9
Honor Foods 1801 N Fifth St	Philadelphia	PA	19122	800-462-2890	215-236-1700	298-8
Hoober Inc 3452 Old Philadelphia Pk PO Box 518	Intercourse	PA	17534	800-732-0017	717-768-8231	276
Hood College 401 Rosemont Ave	Frederick	MD	21701	800-922-1599	301-696-3400	167
Hood County Public Library 222 N Travis St	Granbury	TX	76048	800-452-9292	817-573-3569	434-3
Hood Packaging Corp 25 Woodgreen Pl	Madison	MS	39110	800-321-8115	601-853-7260	64
Hooker Furniture Corp 440 E Commonwealth Blvd *NASDAQ: HOFT* ■ *Cust Svc	Martinsville	VA	24112	800-422-1511*	276-632-0459	320-2
Hooper Corp 2030 Pennsylvania Ave	Madison	WI	53704	877-630-7554	608-249-0451	191-10
Hooper Handling Inc 5590 Camp Rd	Hamburg	NY	14075	800-649-5590	716-649-5590	358
Hoosier Co 5421 W 86th St PO Box 681064	Indianapolis	IN	46268	800-521-4184	317-872-8125	288
Hoosier Park Racing & Casino 4500 Dan Patch Cir	Anderson	IN	46013	800-526-7223	765-642-7223	639

Name / Address	City	State	Zip	Toll-Free	Phone	Class
Hooters Casino Hotel 115 E Tropicana Ave	Las Vegas	NV	89109	**866-584-6687**	702-739-9000	132
Hoover & Strong Inc 10700 Trade Rd *Cust Svc	North Chesterfield	VA	23236	**800-759-9997***		484
Hoover Construction Co Inc PO Box 1007	Virginia	MN	55792	**800-741-0970**	218-741-3280	190-4
Hoover Toyota 2686 Hwy 150	Hoover	AL	35244	**866-980-8082**	205-978-2600	56
Hoover's Inc 5800 Airport Blvd	Austin	TX	78752	**800-486-8666**	512-374-4500	634-6
Hop-A-Jet Inc 5525 NW 15th Ave Ste 150	Fort Lauderdale	FL	33309	**800-556-6633**	954-771-5779	13
Hope College 69 E Tenth St PO Box 9000 *Admissions	Holland	MI	49422	**800-968-7850***	616-395-7850	167
Hope College Van Wylen Library 53 Graves Pl	Holland	MI	49423	**800-968-7850**	616-395-7790	434-6
Hope Global Engineered Textile Solutions 50 Martin St *General	Cumberland	RI	02864	**800-854-7139***	401-333-8990	742-5
Hope Hospice 9470 HealthPark Cir	Fort Myers	FL	33908	**800-835-1673**	239-482-4673	371
Hope International University 2500 E Nutwood Ave	Fullerton	CA	92831	**866-722-4673**	714-879-3901	167
Hope Network 3075 Orchard Vista Dr SE	Grand Rapids	MI	49546	**800-695-7273**	616-301-8000	449
Hope Pharmaceuticals Inc 16416 N 92nd St Ste 125	Scottsdale	AZ	85260	**800-755-9595**		582
Hopewell Furnace National Historic Site 2 Mark Bird Ln	Elverson	PA	19520	**866-705-5711**	610-582-8773	563
Hopkins & Carley A Law Corp PO Box 1469	San Jose	CA	95109	**800-829-3676**	408-286-9800	428
Hopkins Ctr for the Arts 6041 Wilson Hall	Hanover	NH	03755	**800-451-4067**	603-646-2422	571
Hopkins Manufacturing Corp 428 Peyton St	Emporia	KS	66801	**800-524-1458**	620-342-7320	59
Hopkins Sporting Goods Inc 5485 NW Beaver Dr	Johnston	IA	50131	**800-362-2937**	515-270-0132	709
Hopkins-Carter Company Inc 3300 NW 21st St	Miami	FL	33142	**800-595-9656**	305-635-7377	464
Hopkinsville Community College 720 N Dr	Hopkinsville	KY	42240	**866-534-2224**	270-886-3921	161
Hopkinsville-Christian County Chamber of Commerce 2800 Port Campbell Blvd	Hopkinsville	KY	42240	**800-842-9959**	270-885-9096	138
Horace Mann Educators Corp 1 Horace Mann Plz *NYSE: HMN*	Springfield	IL	62715	**800-999-1030**	217-789-2500	360-4
Horace Mann Life Insurance Co 1 Horace Mann Plaza	Springfield	IL	62715	**800-999-1030**	217-789-2500	391-2
Horiba Instruments Inc 17671 Armstrong Ave	Irvine	CA	92614	**800-446-7422**	949-250-4811	419
Horizon Air Freight Inc 152-15 Rockaway Blvd	Jamaica	NY	11434	**800-221-6028**	718-528-3800	448
Horizon Books 243 E Front St	Traverse City	MI	49684	**800-587-2147**	231-946-7290	95
Horizon Convention Ctr 401 S High St	Muncie	IN	47305	**888-288-8860**	765-288-8860	207
Horizon Credit Union 13224 E Mansfield Ste 300	Spokane Valley	WA	99216	**800-808-6402**		221
Horizon Freight System Inc 6600 Bessemer Ave	Cleveland	OH	44127	**800-480-6829**	216-341-7410	467
Horizon Paper Co Inc 1010 Washington Blvd	Stamford	CT	06901	**866-358-0855**	203-358-0855	551-1
Horizon Services Co 250 Governor St	East Hartford	CT	06108	**800-949-5323**		103
Horizon Termite & Pest Control Corp 45 Cross Ave	Midland Park	NJ	07432	**888-612-2847**	201-447-2530	576
Horizon USA Data Supplies Inc 1595 Meadow Wood Ln Ste 1	Reno	NV	89502	**800-325-1199**	775-858-2300	176
Horizons Window Fashions Inc 1705 Waukegan Rd	Waukegan	IL	60085	**800-858-2352**		361
Hormel Foods Corp 1 Hormel Pl *NYSE: HRL*	Austin	MN	55912	**800-523-4635**	507-437-5611	297-26
Hornady Manufacturing Co 3625 W Old Potash Hwy	Grand Island	NE	68803	**800-338-3220**	308-382-1390	286
Hornbeck Offshore Services Inc 103 Northpark Blvd Ste 300 *NYSE: HOS*	Covington	LA	70433	**800-642-9816**	985-727-2000	464
Horner Millwork Corp 1255 Grand Army Hwy	Somerset	MA	02726	**800-543-5403**	508-679-6479	498
Hornerxpress Inc 5755 Powerline Rd	Fort Lauderdale	FL	33309	**800-432-6966**	954-772-6966	726
Hornor Townsend & Kent Inc (HTK) 600 Dresher Rd Ste C1C	Horsham	PA	19044	**800-289-9999**		402
Hornung's Golf Products Inc 815 Morris St	Fond du Lac	WI	54935	**800-323-3569**	920-922-2640	329
Horowitt, Darryl J. - Coleman & Horowitt LLP 499 W Shaw Ave Ste 116	Fresno	CA	93704	**800-891-8362**	559-248-4820	428
Horry Telephone Co-op Inc (HTC) 3480 Hwy 701 N PO Box 1820	Conway	SC	29528	**800-824-6779**	843-365-2151	733
Horry-Georgetown Technical College 2050 E Hwy 501	Conway	SC	29526	**855-544-4482**	843-347-3186	798
Grand Strand Campus 743 Hemlock Ave	Myrtle Beach	SC	29577	**855-544-4482**	843-477-0808	798
Horse Illustrated Magazine 3 Burroughs	Irvine	CA	92618	**888-588-4677**	949-855-8822	456-14
Horse Prairie Ranch 3300 Bachelor Mountain Rd	Dillon	MT	59725	**888-726-2454**	406-681-3166	241
Horsehead Corp 4955 Steubenville Pk Ste 405	Pittsburgh	PA	15205	**800-648-8897**	724-774-1020	142
HorseLoverZ com 254 N Cedar St	Hazleton	PA	18201	**877-804-7810**	570-579-0054	156-5
Horseshoe Bend Regional Library 207 NW St	Dadeville	AL	36853	**855-336-0333**	256-825-9232	434-3
Horseshoe Casino 777 Casino Ctr Dr	Hammond	IN	46320	**800-522-4700**	219-473-7000	132
Horseshoe Valley Resort Ltd 1101 Horseshoe Vly Rd - Comp 10 RR 1	Barrie	ON	L4M4Y8	**800-461-5627**	705-835-2790	378
Horsham Clinic 722 E Butler Pk	Ambler	PA	19002	**800-237-4447**	215-643-7800	374-5
Horspool & Romine Manufacturing Inc 5850 Marshall St	Oakland	CA	94608	**800-446-2263**		620
Hortica Insurance 1 Horticultural Ln PO Box 428	Edwardsville	IL	62025	**800-851-7740**	618-656-4240	391-4
Horton Emergency Vehicles 3800 McDowell Rd	Grove City	OH	43123	**800-282-5113**	614-539-8181	58
Horton Grand Hotel 311 Island Ave	San Diego	CA	92101	**800-542-1886**	619-544-1886	379
Horton Group, The 10320 Orland Pkwy	Orland Park	IL	60467	**800-383-8283**	708-845-3000	390
Horton Homes Inc 101 Industrial Blvd	Eatonton	GA	31024	**800-657-4000**	706-485-8506	504
Horton Inc 2565 Walnut St	Saint Paul	MN	55113	**800-621-1320**	651-361-6400	619
Horwith Trucks Inc PO Box 7	NorthHampton	PA	18067	**800-220-8807**	610-261-2220	56
Hosanna 2421 Aztec Rd Ne	Albuquerque	NM	87107	**800-545-6552**	505-881-3321	95
Hosokawa Polymer Systems 63 Fuller Way	Berlin	CT	06037	**800-233-6112**	860-828-0541	386
Hosparus Inc 502 Hausfeldt Ln	New Albany	IN	47150	**800-895-5633**	812-945-4596	371
Hospi Tel Manufacturing Corp 545 N Arlington Ave Ste 7	East Orange	NJ	07017	**800-631-0462**	973-678-7100	474
Hospice & Palliative Care of Cape Cod Inc 765 Attucks Ln	Hyannis	MA	02601	**800-642-2423**	508-957-0200	371
Hospice & Palliative Care of Northern Colorado 2726 W 11th St Rd	Greeley	CO	80634	**800-564-5563**	970-352-8487	371
Hospice & Palliative Care of Western Colorado 2754 Compass Dr Ste 377	Grand Junction	CO	81506	**866-310-8900**	970-241-2212	371
Hospice & Palliative CareCenter 101 Hospice Ln	Winston-Salem	NC	27103	**888-876-3663**	336-768-3972	371
Hospice Alliance 10220 Prairie Ridge Blvd	Pleasant Prairie	WI	53158	**800-830-8344**	262-652-4400	371
Hospice at Home 4025 Health Pk Ln	Saint Joseph	MI	49085	**800-717-3811**	269-429-7100	371
Hospice at the Texas Medical Ctr 1905 Holcombe Blvd	Houston	TX	77030	**800-630-7894**	713-467-7423	371
Hospice Atlanta-Visiting Nurse Health System 1244 Pk Vista Dr	Atlanta	GA	30319	**866-374-4776**	404-869-3000	371
Hospice Austin 4107 Spicewood Springs Rd Ste 100	Austin	TX	78759	**800-445-3261**	512-342-4700	371
Hospice Brazos Valley 502 W 26th St	Bryan	TX	77803	**800-824-2326**	979-821-2266	371
Hospice by the Sea 1531 W Palmetto Pk Rd	Boca Raton	FL	33486	**800-633-2577**	561-395-5031	371
Hospice Care 100 Sylvan Rd	Woburn	MA	01801	**866-279-7103**	781-569-2888	371
Hospice Care Inc 4277 Middle Settlement Rd	New Hartford	NY	13413	**800-317-5661**	315-735-6484	371
Hospice Care Network 99 Sunnyside Blvd	Woodbury	NY	11797	**800-405-6731**	516-832-7100	371
Hospice Community Care PO Box 993	Rock Hill	SC	29731	**800-895-2273**	803-329-1500	371
Hospice Education Institute 3 Unity Sq PO Box 98	Machiasport	ME	04655	**800-331-1620**	207-255-8800	47-17
Hospice Family Care 550 E Main St	Batavia	NY	14020	**800-719-7129**	585-343-7596	371
Hospice Foundation of America (HFA) 1710 Rhode Island Ave NW Ste 400	Washington	DC	20036	**800-854-3402**	202-457-5811	48-8
Hospice Home Care 2200 S Bowman	Little Rock	AR	72211	**800-479-1219**	501-296-9043	371
Hospice House Foundation Inc 903 n sam houston ave	Odessa	TX	79761	**877-428-3581**	432-580-0067	371
Hospice Ministries 450 Towne Ctr Blvd	Ridgeland	MS	39157	**800-273-7724**	601-898-1053	371
Hospice of Acadiana 2600 Johnston St Ste 200	Lafayette	LA	70503	**800-738-2226**	337-232-1234	371
Hospice of Alamance Caswell 914 Chapel Hill Rd	Burlington	NC	27215	**800-588-8879**	336-532-0100	371
Hospice of Arizona 19820 N Seventh Ave Ste 130	Phoenix	AZ	85027	**888-330-8560**	602-678-1313	371
Hospice of Baton Rouge 9063 Siegen Ln	Baton Rouge	LA	70810	**888-447-0433**	225-767-4673	371
Hospice of Boulder County 2594 Trlridge Dr E	Lafayette	CO	80026	**877-986-4766**	303-449-7740	371
Hospice of Central Ohio 2269 Cherry Vly Rd	Newark	OH	43055	**800-804-2505**	740-344-0311	371
Hospice of Central Pennsylvania 1320 Linglestown Rd	Harrisburg	PA	17110	**866-779-7374**	717-732-1000	371
Hospice of Chattanooga 4411 Oakwood Dr	Chattanooga	TN	37416	**800-267-6828**	423-892-4289	371
Hospice of Cincinnati 4360 Cooper Rd	Cincinnati	OH	45242	**800-691-7255**	513-891-7700	371
Hospice of Dayton 324 Wilmington Ave	Dayton	OH	45420	**800-653-4490**	937-256-4490	371
Hospice of East Texas 4111 University Blvd	Tyler	TX	75701	**800-777-9860**	903-266-3400	371
Hospice of Henry Ford Health System 2799 W Grand Blvd	Detroit	MI	48202	**800-436-7936**	248-585-5270	371
Hospice of Holland Inc 270 Hoover Blvd	Holland	MI	49423	**800-255-3522**	616-396-2972	371
Hospice of Huntington 1101 Sixth Ave	Huntington	WV	25701	**800-788-5480**	304-529-4217	371
Hospice of Kankakee Valley Inc 482 Main St Nw	Bourbonnais	IL	60914	**855-871-4695**	815-939-4141	371

Name / Address	City	State	ZIP	Toll-Free	Phone	Class
Hospice of Lake & Sumter Inc 2445 Ln Pk Rd	Tavares	FL	32778	**888-728-6234**	352-343-1341	371
Hospice of Lake Cumberland 100 Pkwy Dr	Somerset	KY	42503	**800-937-9596**	606-679-4389	371
Hospice of Lancaster County 685 Good Dr PO Box 4125	Lancaster	PA	17604	**888-236-9563**	717-295-3900	371
Hospice of Lansing 4052 Legacy Pkwy Ste 200	Lansing	MI	48911	**877-882-4500**	517-882-4500	371
Hospice of Lincolnland 1000 Health Ctr Dr	Mattoon	IL	61938	**800-454-4055**		371
Hospice of Marion County 3231 SW 34th Ave	Ocala	FL	34474	**888-482-5018**	352-873-7400	371
Hospice of Marshall County 408 Martling Rd	Albertville	AL	35951	**888-334-9336**	256-891-7724	371
Hospice of Medina County 5075 Windfall Rd	Medina	OH	44256	**800-700-4771**	330-722-4771	371
Hospice of Miami County 550 Summit Ave Ste 101	Troy	OH	45373	**800-372-0009**	937-335-5191	371
Hospice of Michigan 400 Mack Ave	Detroit	MI	48201	**888-247-5701**	313-578-5000	371
Hospice of Midland 911 W Texas Ave	Midland	TX	79701	**800-339-1180**	432-682-2855	371
Hospice of NE Georgia Medical Ctr 2150 Limestone Pkwy Ste 222	Gainesville	GA	30501	**888-572-3900**	770-533-8888	371
Hospice of New Jersey 400 Broadacres Dr 1St Fl	Bloomfield	NJ	07003	**800-501-0451**	973-893-0818	371
Hospice of North Central Ohio 1050 Dauch Dr	Ashland	OH	44805	**800-952-2207**	419-281-7107	371
Hospice of Northeast Florida 4266 Sunbeam Rd	Jacksonville	FL	32257	**866-253-6681**	904-268-5200	371
Hospice of Northwest Ohio 30000 E River Rd	Perrysburg	OH	43551	**866-661-4001**	419-661-4001	371
Hospice of Orange & Sullivan Counties 800 Stony Brook Ct	Newburgh	NY	12550	**800-924-0157**	845-561-6111	371
Hospice of Palm Beach County 5300 E Ave	West Palm Beach	FL	33407	**800-287-4722**	561-848-5200	371
Hospice of Redlands Community Hospital 350 Terracina Blvd	Redlands	CA	92373	**888-397-4999**	909-335-5643	371
Hospice of Reno County 1600 N Lorraine	Hutchinson	KS	67502	**800-267-6891**	620-665-2473	371
Hospice of Rutherford County 374 Hudlow Rd PO Box 336	Forest City	NC	28043	**800-218-2273**	828-245-0095	371
Hospice of Saint Francis Inc 1250 Grumman Pl Ste B	Titusville	FL	32780	**866-269-4240**	321-269-4240	371
Hospice of Saint Lawrence Valley 6805 State Hwy 11	Potsdam	NY	13676	**888-827-1000**	315-265-3105	371
Hospice of San Angelo 36 E Twohig St PO Box 471	San Angelo	TX	76903	**800-499-6524**	325-658-6524	371
Hospice of Siouxland 4300 Hamilton Blvd	Sioux City	IA	51104	**800-383-4545**	712-233-4100	371
Hospice of South Texas 605 E Locust Ave	Victoria	TX	77901	**800-874-6908**	361-572-4300	371
Hospice of Southeastern Connecticut Inc 227 Dunham St	Norwich	CT	06360	**877-654-4035**	860-848-5699	371
Hospice of Southern Illinois 305 S Illinois St	Belleville	IL	62220	**800-233-1708**	618-235-1703	371
Hospice of Southern Kentucky 5872 Scottsville Rd	Bowling Green	KY	42104	**800-344-9479**	270-782-3402	371
Hospice of Southwest Georgia 114 A Mimosa Dr	Thomasville	GA	31792	**800-290-6567**	229-584-5500	371
Hospice of Spokane 121 S Arthur St	Spokane	WA	99202	**800-467-7423**	509-456-0438	371
Hospice of Stanly County 960 N First St	Albemarle	NC	28001	**800-230-4236**	704-983-4216	371
Hospice of the Bluegrass 2312 Alexandria Dr	Lexington	KY	40504	**800-876-6005**	859-276-5344	371
Hospice of the Calumet Area 600 Superior Ave	Munster	IN	46321	**888-303-0180**	219-922-2732	371
Hospice of the Chesapeake 445 Defense Hwy *General	Annapolis	MD	21401	**877-462-1101***	410-987-2003	371
Hospice of the Cleveland Clinic 6801 Brecksville Rd Ste 10	Independence	OH	44131	**800-263-0403**	216-444-9819	371
Hospice of the Comforter 480 W Central Pkwy	Altamonte Springs	FL	32714	**877-696-6775**	407-682-0808	371
Hospice of the North Shore 75 Sylvan St Ste B102	Danvers	MA	01923	**888-283-1722**	978-774-7566	371
Hospice of the Panhandle 330 Hospice Ln	Kearneysville	WV	25430	**800-345-6538**	304-264-0406	371
Hospice of the Piedmont 675 Peter Jefferson Pkwy Ste 300	Charlottesville	VA	22911	**800-975-5501**	434-817-6900	371
Hospice of the Red River Valley 1701 38th St S Ste 101	Fargo	ND	58103	**800-237-4629**	701-356-1500	371
Hospice of the Treasure Coast 5090 Dunn Rd	Fort Pierce	FL	34981	**800-299-4677**	772-462-8900	371
Hospice of the Upstate 1835 Rogers Rd	Anderson	SC	29621	**800-261-8636**	864-224-3358	371
Hospice of the Valley 240 Johnston St SE	Decatur	AL	35601	**877-260-3657**	256-350-5585	371
Hospice of the Western Reserve 300 E 185th St	Cleveland	OH	44119	**800-707-8922**	216-383-2222	371
Hospice of Visiting Nurse Service 3358 Ridgewood Rd	Akron	OH	44333	**800-335-1455**	330-665-1455	371
Hospice of Wake County Inc 250 Hospice Cir	Raleigh	NC	27607	**888-900-3959**	919-828-0890	371
Hospice of West Alabama 3851 Loop Rd	Tuscaloosa	AL	35404	**877-362-7522**	205-523-0101	371
Hospice of Wichita Falls 4909 Johnson Rd	Wichita Falls	TX	76310	**800-378-2822**	940-691-0982	371
Hospice Savannah Inc PO Box 13190	Savannah	GA	31416	**888-355-4911**	912-355-2289	371
HospiceCare 5395 E Cheryl Pkwy	Madison	WI	53711	**800-553-4289**	608-276-4660	371
Hospira Inc 275 N Field Dr *NYSE: HSP*	Lake Forest	IL	60045	**877-946-7747**	224-212-2000	476
Hospital Billing & Collection Service Ltd 118 Lukens Dr	New Castle	DE	19720	**877-254-9580**	302-552-8000	159
Hospital Forms & Systems Corp 8900 Ambassador Row	Dallas	TX	75247	**800-527-5081**	214-634-8900	109
Hospital Litigation Reporter 590 Dutch Vly Rd NE	Atlanta	GA	30324	**800-926-7926**	404-881-1141	530-7
Hospital Marketing Services Company Inc 162 Great Hill Rd	Naugatuck	CT	06770	**800-786-5094**	203-723-1466	475
Hospital of Saint Raphael 1450 Chapel St	New Haven	CT	06511	**888-700-6543**	203-789-3000	374-3
Hospital of the University of Pennsylvania 3400 Spruce St	Philadelphia	PA	19104	**800-789-7366**	215-662-4000	374-3
Hospitality Financial & Technology Professionals (HFTP) 11709 Boulder Ln Ste 110	Austin	TX	78726	**800-646-4387**	512-249-5333	48-1
Hospitality International Inc 1726 Montreal Cir	Tucker	GA	30084	**800-251-1962**		379
Master Hosts Inns & Resorts 1726 Montreal Cir	Tucker	GA	30084	**800-247-4677**		379
Passport Inn 1726 Montreal Cir	Tucker	GA	30084	**800-251-1962**		379
Red Carpet Inn 1726 Montreal Cir	Tucker	GA	30084	**800-247-4677**		379
Scottish Inns 1726 Montreal Cir	Tucker	GA	30084	**800-251-1962**		379
Hospitality Law 360 Hiatt Dr	Palm Beach Gardens	FL	33418	**800-621-5463**	561-622-6520	530-7
Hospitality Suites Resort 409 N Scottsdale Rd	Scottsdale	AZ	85257	**800-445-5115**	480-949-5115	379
Hospitals & Health Networks Magazine 155 N Wacker Ste 400	Chicago	IL	60606	**800-621-6902**	312-893-6800	456-5
Hoss's Steak & Sea House 170 Patchway Rd	Duncansville	PA	16635	**800-992-4677**	814-695-7600	668
Host Department LLC 45277 Fremont Blvd Ste 11	Fremont	CA	94538	**866-887-4678**		387
Host Depot Inc 4613 N University Dr Ste 227	Coral Springs	FL	33067	**888-340-3527**	954-340-3527	806
Hostcentric Inc 70 BlanchaRd Rd 3rd Fl *Tech Supp	Burlington	MA	01803	**866-897-5418***	602-716-5396	806
Hostedware Corp 16 Technology Dr Ste 116	Irvine	CA	92618	**800-211-6967**	949-585-1500	806
Hostelling International USA - American Youth Hostels (HI-AYH) 8401 Colesville Rd Ste 600	Silver Spring	MD	20910	**800-725-2331**	301-495-1240	47-23
Hostos Community College 500 Grand Concourse	Bronx	NY	10451	**888-993-7650**	718-518-4444	161
Hostway Corp 100 N Riverside Plaza 8th Fl	Chicago	IL	60606	**866-467-8929**	312-238-0125	806
Hot Dog on a Stick 5942 Priestly Dr	Carlsbad	CA	92008	**877-639-2361**	760-930-0456	668
Hot Rod Magazine 6420 Wilshire Blvd *Orders	Los Angeles	CA	90048	**800-800-4681***	323-782-2000	456-3
Hot Rod Network 774 S Placentia Ave	Placentia	CA	92870	**800-926-8207**		456-3
Hot Rooms 875 N. Michigan Ave Ste 3100	Chicago	IL	60611	**800-468-3500**	773-468-7666	376
Hot Shot Delivery Inc 747 N Shepherd Dr Ste 100 PO Box 701189	Houston	TX	77007	**866-261-3184**	713-869-5525	545
Hot Springs Convention & Visitors Bureau 134 Convention Blvd	Hot Springs	AR	71901	**800-543-2284**	501-321-2277	208
Hot Springs Convention Ctr (HSCVB) 134 Convention Blvd PO Box 6000	Hot Springs	AR	71902	**800-625-7576**	501-321-2277	207
Hot Springs Lodge & Pool 415 E Sixth St PO Box 308	Glenwood Springs	CO	81602	**800-537-7946**	970-945-6571	667
Hot Springs Memorial Field 525 Airport Rd	Hot Springs	AR	71913	**800-992-7433**	501-321-6750	27
Hot Stuff Pizza 2930 W Maple St	Sioux Falls	SD	57107	**800-336-1320**	605-336-6961	67
Hotel & Restaurant Supply Inc 5020 Arundel Rd PO Box 6	Meridian	MS	39302	**800-782-6651**	601-482-7127	301
Hotel & Suites Normandin 4700 Pierre-Bertrand Blvd	Quebec	QC	G2J1A4	**800-463-6721**	418-622-1611	379
Hotel 1000 1000 First Ave	Seattle	WA	98104	**877-315-1088**	206-957-1000	379
Hotel 140 140 Clarendon St	Boston	MA	02116	**800-714-0140**	617-585-5600	379
Hotel 43 981 Grove St	Boise	ID	83702	**800-243-4622**	208-342-4622	379
Hotel 71 71 St Pierre St	Quebec	QC	G1K4A4	**888-692-1171**	418-692-1171	379
Hotel Abri 127 Ellis St	San Francisco	CA	94102	**866-778-6169**	415-392-8800	379
Hotel Adagio 550 Geary St	San Francisco	CA	94102	**855-687-7262**	415-775-5000	379
Hotel Allegro Chicago 171 W Randolph St	Chicago	IL	60601	**800-643-1500**	312-236-0123	379
Hotel Ambassadeur 3401 Blvd Ste-Anne	Quebec	QC	G1E3L4	**800-363-4619**	418-666-2828	379
Hotel Ambassador 1324 S Main St *General	Tulsa	OK	74119	**888-408-8282***	918-587-8200	379
Hotel Andra 2000 Fourth Ave	Seattle	WA	98121	**877-448-8600**	206-448-8600	379
Hotel at Auburn University & Dixon Conference Ctr, The 241 S College St	Auburn	AL	36830	**800-228-2876**	334-821-8200	377
Hotel at Old Town Wichita 830 E First St	Wichita	KS	67202	**877-265-3869**	316-267-4800	379
Hotel Avante 860 E El Camino Real	Mountain View	CA	94040	**800-538-1600**	650-940-1000	379
Hotel Beacon 2130 Broadway	New York	NY	10023	**800-572-4969**	212-787-1100	379
Hotel Bedford 118 E 40th St	New York	NY	10016	**800-221-6881**	212-697-4800	379
Hotel Bel-Air 701 Stone Canyon Rd	Los Angeles	CA	90077	**800-648-4097**	310-472-1211	379

Name / Address	City	State	Zip	Toll-Free	Phone	Class
Hotel Bijou 111 Mason St	San Francisco	CA	94102	**877-568-2733**	415-771-1200	379
Hotel Blue 717 Central Ave Nw	Albuquerque	NM	87102	**877-878-4868**	505-924-2400	378
Hotel Boulderado 2115 13th St	Boulder	CO	80302	**800-433-4344**	303-442-4344	379
Hotel Burnham 1 W Washington St	Chicago	IL	60602	**866-690-1986**	312-782-1111	379
Hotel Captain Cook 939 W Fifth Ave	Anchorage	AK	99501	**800-843-1950**	907-276-6000	379
Hotel Chateau Bellevue 16 Rue de la Porte	Quebec	QC	G1R4M9	**877-849-1877**	418-692-2573	379
Hotel Chateau Laurier 1220 Pl George-V Ouest	Quebec	QC	G1R5B8	**877-522-8108**	418-522-8108	379
Hotel Cheribourg 2603 Ch du Parc	Orford	QC	J1X8C8	**877-845-5344**	819-843-3308	667
Hotel Classique 2815 Laurier Blvd	Quebec	QC	G1V4H3	**800-463-1885**	418-658-2793	379
Hotel Colorado 526 Pine St	Glenwood Springs	CO	81601	**800-544-3998**	970-945-6511	379
Hotel Commonwealth 500 Commonwealth Ave	Boston	MA	02215	**866-784-4000**	617-933-5000	379
Hotel Congress 311 E Congress St	Tucson	AZ	85701	**800-722-8848**	520-622-8848	379
Hotel Contessa 306 W Market St	San Antonio	TX	78205	**866-435-0900**	210-229-9222	379
Hotel de Anza 233 W Santa Clara St	San Jose	CA	95113	**800-843-3700**	408-286-1000	379
Hotel Deca 4507 Brooklyn Ave NE	Seattle	WA	98105	**800-899-0251**	206-634-2000	379
Hotel Del Coronado 1500 Orange Ave	Coronado	CA	92118	**800-468-3533**	619-435-6611	667
Hotel Del Sol 3100 Webster St	San Francisco	CA	94123	**877-433-5765**	415-921-5520	379
Hotel Deluxe 729 SW 15th Ave	Portland	OR	97205	**866-895-2094**	503-219-2094	379
Hotel Derek 2525 W Loop S	Houston	TX	77027	**866-292-4100**	713-961-3000	379
Hotel Dieu Hospital 166 Brock St	Kingston	ON	K7L5G2	**855-544-3400**	613-544-3310	374-2
Hotel Drisco 2901 Pacific Ave	San Francisco	CA	94115	**800-738-7477**	415-346-2880	379
Hotel du Lac 121 Rue Cuttle	Mont-Tremblant	QC	J8E1B9	**800-567-8341**	819-425-2731	667
Hotel du Pont 11th & Market Sts	Wilmington	DE	19801	**800-441-9019**	302-594-3100	379
Hotel Durant 2600 Durant Ave	Berkeley	CA	94704	**800-738-7477**	510-845-8981	379
Hotel Edison 228 W 47th St	New York	NY	10036	**800-637-7070**	212-840-5000	379
Hotel Encanto de Las Cruces 705 S Telshor Blvd	Las Cruces	NM	88011	**866-383-0443**	575-522-4300	379
Hotel Galvez - A Wyndham Historic Hotel 2024 Seawall Blvd	Galveston	TX	77550	**800-996-3426**	409-765-7721	379
Hotel George 15 E St NW *General	Washington	DC	20001	**800-546-7866***	202-347-4200	379
Hotel Grand Pacific 463 Belleville St	Victoria	BC	V8V1X3	**800-663-7550**	250-386-0450	379
Hotel Grand Victorian 2325 W Hwy 76	Branson	MO	65616	**800-324-8751**	417-336-2935	379
Hotel Granduca 1080 Uptown Pk Blvd	Houston	TX	77056	**888-472-6382**	713-418-1000	379
Hotel Griffon 155 Steuart St	San Francisco	CA	94105	**800-321-2201**	415-495-2100	379
Hotel Jerome 330 E Main St	Aspen	CO	81611	**855-331-7213**		379
Hotel La Rose 308 Wilson St	Santa Rosa	CA	95401	**800-527-6738**	707-579-3200	379
Hotel Le Bleu 370 Fourth Ave	Brooklyn	NY	11215	**866-427-6073**	718-625-1500	379
Hotel Le Cantlie Suites 1110 Sherbrooke St W	Montreal	QC	H3A1G9	**800-567-1110**	514-842-2000	379
Hotel Le Capitole 972 St Jean St	Quebec	QC	G1R1R5	**800-261-9903**	418-694-4444	379
Hotel Le Clos Saint-Louis 69 St Louis St	Quebec	QC	G1R3Z2	**800-461-1311**	418-694-1311	379
Hotel Le Germain Toronto 30 Mercer St	Toronto	ON	M5V1H3	**866-345-9501**	416-345-9500	379
Hotel Le Marais 717 Conti St	New Orleans	LA	70130	**800-935-8740**	504-525-2300	379
Hotel le Priori 15 du Sault-au-Matelot St	Quebec	QC	G1K3Y7	**800-351-3992**	418-692-3992	379
Hotel Le Soleil 567 Hornby St	Vancouver	BC	V6C2E8	**877-632-3030**	604-632-3000	379
Hotel Le St-James 355 St Jacques St	Montreal	QC	H2Y1N9	**866-841-3111**	514-841-3111	379
Hotel Lombardy 2019 Pennsylvania Ave NW	Washington	DC	20006	**800-424-5486**	202-828-2600	379
Hotel Lord-Berri 1199 Berri St	Montreal	QC	H2L4C6	**888-363-0363**	514-845-9236	379
Hotel Lucia 400 SW Broadway	Portland	OR	97205	**877-225-1717**	503-225-1717	379
Hotel Lumen 6101 Hillcrest Ave	Dallas	TX	75205	**800-908-1140**	214-219-2400	379
Hotel Lusso 808 West Sprague Avenue *General	Spokane	WA	99201	**800-899-1482***	509-747-9750	379
Hotel Madera 1310 New Hampshire Ave NW	Washington	DC	20036	**800-546-7866**	202-296-7600	379
Hotel Manoir Victoria 44 Cote du Palais	Quebec	QC	G1R4H8	**800-463-6283**	418-692-1030	379
Hotel Mark Twain 345 Taylor St	San Francisco	CA	94102	**877-854-4106**	415-673-2332	379
Hotel Marlowe Cambridge 25 Edwind H Land Blvd	Cambridge	MA	02141	**800-825-7140**	617-868-8000	379
Hotel Max 620 Stewart St	Seattle	WA	98101	**866-833-6299**	206-728-6299	379
Hotel Mead 451 E Grand Ave	Wisconsin Rapids	WI	54494	**800-843-6323**	715-423-1500	379
Hotel Mela 120 W 44th St	New York	NY	10036	**877-452-6352**	212-710-7000	379
Hotel Metro 411 E Mason St	Milwaukee	WI	53202	**877-638-7620**	414-272-1937	379
Hotel Monaco Chicago 225 N Wabash Ave	Chicago	IL	60601	**866-610-0081**	312-960-8500	379
Hotel Monaco Denver 1717 Champa St	Denver	CO	80202	**800-990-1303**	303-296-1717	379
Hotel Monaco Portland 506 SW Washington at Fifth Ave	Portland	OR	97204	**866-861-9514**	503-222-0001	379
Hotel Monaco Salt Lake City 15 West 200 South *Resv	Salt Lake City	UT	84101	**800-805-1801***	801-595-0000	379
Hotel Monaco Seattle 1101 Fourth Ave	Seattle	WA	98101	**800-715-6513**	206-621-1770	379
Hotel Monte Vista 100 N San Francisco St	Flagstaff	AZ	86001	**800-545-3068**	928-779-6971	379
Hotel Monteleone 214 Royal St	New Orleans	LA	70130	**866-338-4684**	504-523-3341	379
Hotel Mortagne 1228 Rue Nobel	Boucherville	QC	J4B5H1	**877-655-9966**	450-655-9966	705
Hotel Murano 1320 Broadway Plz	Tacoma	WA	98402	**888-862-3255**	253-238-8000	379
Hotel Nikko San Francisco 222 Mason St	San Francisco	CA	94102	**866-636-4556**	415-394-1111	379
Hotel Northampton 36 King St	NorthHampton	MA	01060	**800-547-3529**	413-584-3100	379
Hotel Oceana *Santa Barbara* 202 W Cabrillo Blvd	Santa Barbara	CA	93101	**800-965-9776**	805-965-4577	379
Hotel Omni Mont-Royal 1050 Sherbrooke St W	Montreal	QC	H3A2R6	**800-843-6664**	514-284-1110	379
Hotel Orrington 1710 Orrington Ave	Evanston	IL	60201	**888-677-4648**	847-866-8700	379
Hotel Pacific 300 Pacific St	Monterey	CA	93940	**800-554-5542**	831-373-5700	379
Hotel Phillips 106 W 12th St	Kansas City	MO	64105	**877-704-5341**	816-221-7000	379
Hotel Plaza Athenee 37 E 64th St	New York	NY	10065	**800-447-8800**	212-734-9100	379
Hotel Plaza Quebec 3031 Laurier Blvd	Sainte-Foy	QC	G1V2M2	**800-567-5276**	418-658-2727	379
Hotel Plaza Real 125 Washington Ave	Santa Fe	NM	87501	**855-752-9273**	505-988-4900	379
Hotel Preston 733 Briley Pkwy	Nashville	TN	37217	**800-407-4324**	615-361-5900	379
Hotel Provincial 1024 Rue Chartres	New Orleans	LA	70116	**800-535-7922**	504-581-4995	379
Hotel Rex 562 Sutter St *Resv	San Francisco	CA	94102	**800-433-4434***	415-433-4434	379
Hotel Rodney 142 Second St	Lewes	DE	19958	**800-824-8754**	302-645-6466	379
Hotel Roger Williams 131 Madison Ave *Resv	New York	NY	10016	**888-448-7788***	212-448-7000	379
Hotel Rouge 1315 16th St NW	Washington	DC	20036	**800-738-1202**	202-232-8000	379
Hotel Royal Plaza 1905 Hotel Plaza Blvd	Lake Buena Vista	FL	32830	**888-662-4683**	407-828-2828	379
Hotel Ruby Foo's 7655 Decarie Blvd	Montreal	QC	H4P2H2	**800-361-5419**	514-731-7701	379
Hotel Saint Francis 210 Don Gaspar Ave	Santa Fe	NM	87501	**800-529-5700**	505-983-5700	379
Hotel Saint Marie 827 Toulouse St	New Orleans	LA	70112	**800-366-2743**	504-561-8951	379
Hotel San Carlos 202 N Central Ave	Phoenix	AZ	85004	**866-253-4121**	602-253-4121	379
Hotel Santa Barbara 533 State St	Santa Barbara	CA	93101	**888-259-7700**	805-957-9300	379
Hotel Santa Fe 1501 Paseo de Peralta	Santa Fe	NM	87501	**855-825-9876**	505-982-1200	379
Hotel Sax Chicago 333 N Dearborn St	Chicago	IL	60610	**855-880-1240**	312-245-0333	379
Hotel Sepia 3135 Ch St-Louis	Sainte-Foy	QC	G1W1R9	**888-301-6837**	418-653-4941	379
Hotel Shangri La 1301 Ocean Ave	Santa Monica	CA	90401	**877-999-1301**	310-394-2791	378
Hotel Shelley 844 Collins Ave	Miami Beach	FL	33139	**877-762-3477**	305-531-3341	379
Hotel Solamar 435 Sixth Ave	San Diego	CA	92101	**877-230-0300**	619-819-9500	379
Hotel Strasburg, The 213 S Holliday St	Strasburg	VA	22657	**800-348-8327**	540-465-9191	379
Hotel Teatro 1100 14th St	Denver	CO	80202	**888-727-1200**	303-228-1100	379
Hotel The Queen Mary 1126 Queens Hwy	Long Beach	CA	90802	**877-342-0738**	562-435-3511	379
Hotel Triton 342 Grant Ave	San Francisco	CA	94108	**800-800-1299**	415-394-0500	379
Hotel Universel 2300 Ch St-Foy	Quebec	QC	G1V1S5	**800-463-4495**	418-653-5250	379
Hotel Utica 102 Lafayette St	Utica	NY	13502	**877-906-1912**	315-724-7829	379
Hotel Valencia Riverwalk 150 E Houston St	San Antonio	TX	78205	**855-596-3387**	210-227-9700	705
Hotel Valencia Santana Row 355 Santana Row	San Jose	CA	95128	**866-842-0100**	408-551-0010	379
Hotel Valley Ho 6850 E Main St	Scottsdale	AZ	85251	**866-882-4484**	480-376-4600	379
Hotel Viking 1 Bellevue Ave	Newport	RI	02840	**800-556-7126**	401-847-3300	379
Hotel Vintage Park 1100 Fifth Ave	Seattle	WA	98101	**800-853-3914**	206-624-8000	379

Name / Address	City	State	Zip	Toll-Free	Phone	Class
Hotel Wales 1295 Madison Ave	New York	NY	10128	866-925-3746	212-876-6000	379
Hotel XIXe Siecle *Lhotel* 262 St Jacques St W	Vieux-Quebec	QC	H2Y1N1	877-553-0019	514-985-0019	379
Hotel ZaZa Dallas 2332 Leonard St	Dallas	TX	75201	800-597-8399	214-468-8399	379
Hotel ZaZa Houston 5701 Main St *Resv	Houston	TX	77005	888-880-3244*	713-526-1991	379
Hotelrooms.com Inc 108-18 Queens Blvd	Forest Hills	NY	11375	800-486-7000	718-730-6000	397
Hotels Etc Inc 7712 Hampton Pl Bldg 11C	Loganville	GA	30052	877-967-7283		377
Hot-Line Freight System Inc PO Box 205	West Salem	WI	54669	800-468-4686	608-486-1600	778
Hotpadscom PO Box 53104	Washington	DC	20009	888-876-1992	202-232-1581	650
Hotwire Communications LLC 1 Belmont Ave Ste 1100	Bala Cynwyd	PA	19004	800-355-5668	800-409-4733	226
Hotwire.com 655 Montgomery St Ste 600 *Cust Svc	San Francisco	CA	94111	866-468-9473*	415-343-8400	771
Houchen Bindery Ltd 340 First St	Utica	NE	68456	800-869-0420	402-534-2261	625
Houff Transfer Inc 46 Houff Rd	Weyers Cave	VA	24486	800-476-4683	540-234-9233	778
Hougen Manufacturing Inc 3001 Hougen Dr *Orders	Swartz Creek	MI	48473	800-426-7818*	810-635-7111	492
Houghton Chemical Corp 52 Cambridge St	Allston	MA	02134	800-777-2466	617-254-1010	144
Houghton College 1 Willard Ave PO Box 128	Houghton	NY	14744	800-777-2556	585-567-9200	167
Houghton International Inc 945 Madison Ave PO Box 930	Valley Forge	PA	19482	888-459-9844	610-666-4000	3
Houma Area Convention & Visitors Bureau 114 Tourist Dr	Gray	LA	70359	800-688-2732	985-868-2732	208
Houmas House Plantation & Gardens 40136 Hwy 942	Darrow	LA	70725	800-979-3370	225-473-7841	49-2
Housatonic Community College 900 Lafayette Blvd	Bridgeport	CT	06604	866-733-2463	203-332-5000	161
House Foods America Corp 7351 Orangewood Ave	Garden Grove	CA	92841	877-333-7077	714-901-4350	297-20
House of Brick Technologies LLC 9300 Underwood Ave Ste 300	Omaha	NE	68114	877-780-7038	402-445-0764	182
House of Flavors Inc 110 N William St	Ludington	MI	49431	800-930-7740	231-845-7369	380
House of Raeford Farms Inc 520 E Central Ave	Raeford	NC	28376	800-888-7539	910-875-5161	618
House-Autry Mills Inc 7000 US Hwy 301 S	Four Oaks	NC	27524	800-849-0802		297-23
House-Hasson Hardware Inc 3125 Water Plant Rd	Knoxville	TN	37914	800-333-0520	865-525-0471	351
HouseMaster 92 E Main St Ste 301	Somerville	NJ	08876	800-526-3939	732-469-6565	365
Housh-the Home Energy Experts 18 South Main St	Monroe	OH	45050	866-611-5752	513-793-6374	609
Housing Assistance Council (HAC) 1025 Vermont Ave NW Ste 606	Washington	DC	20005	866-234-2689	202-842-8600	47-5
Housing Authority Risk Retention Group Inc PO Box 189	Cheshire	CT	06410	800-873-0242	203-272-8220	390
Houston Arboretum & Nature Ctr 4501 Woodway Dr	Houston	TX	77024	866-510-7219	713-681-8433	49-4
Houston Area Safety Council 1301 W 13th St	Deer Park	TX	77536	888-955-7233	281-476-9900	136
Houston Astros Minute Maid Pk 501 Crawford St	Houston	TX	77002	800-771-2303	713-259-8000	711
Houston Ballet 601 Preston St	Houston	TX	77002	800-828-2787	713-523-6300	572-1
Houston Baptist University 7502 Fondren Rd *Admissions	Houston	TX	77074	800-969-3210*	281-649-3000	167
Houston Chronicle 801 Texas Ave	Houston	TX	77002	800-735-3800	713-362-7171	531-2
Houston Food Bank, The 535 Portwall St	Houston	TX	77029	866-384-4277	713-223-3700	325
Houston Grand Opera 510 Preston St	Houston	TX	77002	800-626-7372	713-546-0200	572-2
Houston Harris Div Patrol Inc 6420 Richmond Ave	Houston	TX	77057	877-975-9922	713-975-9922	691
Houston Independent School District 228 McCarty St	Houston	TX	77029	800-446-2821	713-556-6000	683
Houston LifeStyle Magazine 10707 Corporate Dr Ste 170	Stafford	TX	77477	866-505-4456	281-240-2445	456-22
Houston Mfg Specialty Company Inc 9909 Wallisville Rd	Houston	TX	77013	800-231-6030	713-675-7400	327
Houston Press 1621 Milam St Ste 100	Houston	TX	77002	877-926-8300	713-280-2400	531-5
Houston Public Library 500 McKinney St	Houston	TX	77002	800-318-2596	832-393-1313	434-3
Houston Rockets 1510 Polk St	Houston	TX	77002	866-648-4668	713-758-7200	712-1
Houston Service Industries Inc 7901 Hansen Rd	Houston	TX	77061	800-725-2291	713-947-1623	18
Houston Wire & Cable Co (HWC) 10201 N Loop E	Houston	TX	77029	800-468-9473	713-609-2100	248
Houstonian Hotel Club & Spa 111 N Post Oak Ln *Resv	Houston	TX	77024	800-231-2759*	713-680-2626	667
Hoveround Corp 2151 Whitfield Industrial Way	Sarasota	FL	34243	800-542-7236	941-739-6200	476
HOW Design Magazine 4700 E Galbraith Rd *Cust Svc	Cincinnati	OH	45236	800-333-1115*	513-531-2690	456-2
Howard Bros Florists 8700 S Pennsylvania Ave	Oklahoma City	OK	73159	800-648-0524	405-632-4747	294
Howard College 1001 Birdwell Ln	Big Spring	TX	79720	877-898-3833	432-264-5000	161

Name / Address	City	State	Zip	Toll-Free	Phone	Class
Howard County General Hospital 5755 Cedar Ln	Columbia	MD	21044	866-323-4615	410-740-7890	374-3
Howard County Tourism Council 8267 Main St Side Entrance	Ellicott City	MD	21043	866-313-6300	410-313-1900	208
Howard Electric Co-op 205 Hwy 5 & 240 N PO Box 391	Fayette	MO	65248	877-352-0122	660-248-3311	247
Howard F Baer Inc 1301 Foster Ave	Nashville	TN	37210	800-447-7430	615-255-7351	778
Howard Greeley Rural Power 422 Howard Ave PO Box 105	Saint Paul	NE	68873	800-280-4962	308-754-4457	247
Howard Leight Industries 7828 Waterville Rd	San Diego	CA	92154	800-430-5490		476
Howard Payne University 1000 Fisk Ave	Brownwood	TX	76801	800-950-8465	325-646-2502	167
Howard Precision Metals Inc PO Box 240127	Milwaukee	WI	53224	800-444-0311	414-355-9611	491
Howard Sheppard Inc PO Box 797	Sandersville	GA	31082	800-846-1726	478-552-5127	778
Howard Simon & Associates Inc 304 Saunders Rd	Riverwoods	IL	60015	800-424-7526	847-945-0340	462
Howard Systems International 2777 Summer St	Stamford	CT	06905	800-326-4860		182
Howard Uniform Co 1915 Annapolis Rd	Baltimore	MD	21230	800-628-8299	410-727-3086	154-18
Howard University 2400 Sixth St NW	Washington	DC	20059	800-822-6363	202-806-6100	167
Howard University School of Divinity 1400 Shepherd St NE	Washington	DC	20017	800-822-6363	202-806-0500	168-3
Howard University School of Law 2900 Van Ness St NW	Washington	DC	20008	800-829-9019	202-806-8000	168-1
HowardSoft 7852 Ivanhoe Ave	La Jolla	CA	92037	800-248-2937	858-454-0121	180-9
Howco Metals Management 9611 Telge Rd	Houston	TX	77095	800-392-7720	281-649-8800	308
Howden Buffalo Inc 7909 Parklane Rd Ste 300	Columbia	SC	29223	866-757-0908	803-741-2700	18
Howe Military School PO Box 240	Howe	IN	46746	888-462-4693	260-562-2131	621
Howell Tractor & Equipment LLC 480 Blaine St	Gary	IN	46406	800-852-8816		789
Howell's Craftand Imports 6030 NE 112th Ave	Portland	OR	97220	800-547-0368		43
Howell's Motor Freight Inc PO Box 12308	Roanoke	VA	24024	800-444-0585	540-966-3200	778
Howell-Oregon Electric Co-op Inc 6327 N US Hwy 63 PO Box 649	West Plains	MO	65775	855-385-9903	417-256-2131	247
HowGood Inc 33 Flatbush Ave 5th Fl	Brooklyn	NY	11217	888-601-3015		462
Howred Corp 7887 San Felipe St Ste 122	Houston	TX	77063	800-535-5053	713-781-3980	193-4
Hoxworth Blood Ctr University of Cincinnati Medical Ctr 3130 Highland Ave ML0055	Cincinnati	OH	45267	800-265-1515	513-558-1200	88
HP (Hewlett-Packard (Canada) Ltd) 5150 Spectrum Way	Mississauga	ON	L4W5G1	888-447-4636	905-206-4725	175-1
HP Hotels Inc 1 Chase Corporate Dr Ste 210	Birmingham	AL	35244	800-576-3467	205-879-7004	379
H-P Products Inc 512 W Gorgas St	Louisville	OH	44641	800-822-8356	330-875-5556	594
HPC Foods Ltd 288 Libby St	Honolulu	HI	96819	877-370-0919	808-848-2431	297-21
HPD, LLC 23563 W Main St	Plainfield	IL	60544	866-362-0993	815-609-2000	263
HPH Corp 1529 SE 47th Terr	Cape Coral	FL	33904	800-654-9884	239-540-0085	348
HPL Stampings Inc 425 Enterprise Pkwy	Lake Zurich	IL	60047	800-927-0397	847-540-1400	487
HPM (Hawaii Planing Mill Ltd) 16-166 Melekahiwa St	Keaau	HI	96749	877-841-7633	808-966-5693	193-3
HPPL (High Point Public Library) 901 N Main St	High Point	NC	27262	877-772-8346	336-883-3660	434-3
HPRHS (High Point Regional Health System) 601 N Elm St PO Box HP-5	High Point	NC	27262	877-878-7644	336-878-6000	374-3
HPTS (High Power Technical Services Inc) 2230 Ampere Dr	Louisville	KY	40299	866-310-5377		115
H&R Construction Parts & Equipment Inc 20 Milburn St	Buffalo	NY	14212	800-333-0650	716-891-4311	56
HR Focal Point LLC 5151 Headquarters Dr Ste 135	Plano	TX	75024	855-464-4737		198
HR People & Strategy (HRPS) 401 N Michigan Ave Ste 2200	Chicago	IL	60611	800-337-9517	312-321-6805	48-12
HR Works Inc 200 WillowBrook Ofc Park	Fairport	NY	14450	877-219-9062	585-381-8340	262
HRC (Herpes Resource Center, The) PO Box 13827	Research Triangle Park	NC	27709	877-478-5868	919-361-8400	47-17
Hrd Discount Book Society 2002 Renaissance Blvd	King Of Prussia	PA	19406	800-633-4533	610-279-2002	198
HRF (Herb Research Foundation) 4140 15th St	Boulder	CO	80304	800-748-2617	303-449-2265	47-17
HRI Inc 1750 W College Ave	State College	PA	16801	877-474-9999	814-238-5071	190-4
HRMagazine 1800 Duke St	Alexandria	VA	22314	800-283-7476	703-548-3440	456-5
HRP Associates Inc 197 Scott Swamp Rd	Farmington	CT	06032	800-246-9021		263
HRPS (HR People & Strategy) 401 N Michigan Ave Ste 2200	Chicago	IL	60611	800-337-9517	312-321-6805	48-12
HRSA (Health Resources & Services Administration) 5600 Fishers Ln	Rockville	MD	20857	888-275-4772	301-443-2216	340-8
Hru Inc. Technical Resources 3451 Dunckel Rd	Lansing	MI	48911	888-205-3446	517-272-5888	462
H&S Constructors Inc 1616 Valero Way	Corpus Christi	TX	78469	800-727-8602	361-289-5272	258
HSB Group Inc 1 State St	Hartford	CT	06103	800-472-1866	860-722-1866	391-4
HSBC Bank USA 2929 Walden Ave	Depew	NY	14043	800-338-4626		508

Name / Address	City	State	ZIP	Toll-Free	Phone	Class
HSBC North America Holdings Inc 2700 Sanders Rd	Prospect Heights	IL	60070	800-975-4722	847-564-5000	360-2
HSC Pediatric Ctr 1731 Bunker Hill Rd NE	Washington	DC	20017	800-226-4444	202-832-4400	374-1
HSCVB (Hot Springs Convention Ctr) 134 Convention Blvd PO Box 6000	Hot Springs	AR	71902	800-625-7576	501-321-2277	207
HSI (Helicopter Support Inc) 124 Quarry Rd	Trumbull	CT	06611	800-795-6051	203-416-4000	768
HSI (Hardware Suppliers of America Inc) 1400 E Fire Tower Rd	Greenville	NC	27858	800-334-5625		351
HSM (Hart Schaffner Marx) 1680 E Touhy Ave	Des Plaines	IL	60018	800-327-4466		154-11
HSQ Technology 26227 Research Rd	Hayward	CA	94545	800-486-6684	510-259-1334	203
HT Hackney Co 502 S Gay St PO Box 238	Knoxville	TN	37901	800-406-1291	865-546-1291	187
HTC (Healing the Children) 2624 W Beacon Ave	Spokane	WA	99208	888-233-9527	509-327-4281	47-5
HTC (Horry Telephone Co-op Inc) 3480 Hwy 701 N PO Box 1820	Conway	SC	29528	800-824-6779	843-365-2151	733
HTK (Hornor Townsend & Kent Inc) 600 Dresher Rd Ste C1C	Horsham	PA	19044	800-289-9999		402
HTT Inc. 1828 Oakland Ave	Sheboygan	WI	53081	866-270-4710	920-453-5300	487
Hub City Inc 2914 Industrial Ave	Aberdeen	SD	57401	800-482-2489	605-225-0360	707
Hub Folding Box Co Inc 774 Norfolk St	Mansfield	MA	02048	800-334-1113	508-339-0005	100
Hub Group Inc 2000 Clearwater Dr *NASDAQ: HUBG*	Oak Brook	IL	60523	800-377-5833	630-271-3600	448
Hub International Ltd 1065 Ave of the Americas	New York	NY	10018	800-456-5293	212-338-2000	390
Hub Pattern Corp 2113 Salem Ave	Roanoke	VA	24016	800-482-3505	540-342-3505	566
HUB Technical Services 44 Norfolk Ave Ste 4	South Easton	MA	02375	877-482-8324	508-238-9887	182
Hubbard & Drake General Mechanical Contractors Inc PO Box 1867	Decatur	AL	35602	800-353-9245	256-353-9244	191-10
Hubbard Feeds Inc 111 W Cherry St Ste 500	Mankato	MN	56001	800-869-7219	507-388-9400	446
Hubbard House, The 29 W Miller St	Orlando	FL	32806	800-648-3818	407-649-6886	372
Hubbard Publishing Co 127 E Chillicothe Ave PO Box 40	Bellefontaine	OH	43311	866-632-9992	937-592-3060	634-8
Hubbard-Hall Inc 563 S Leonard St	Waterbury	CT	06708	800-331-6871	203-756-5521	145
Hubbell Power Systems Inc 210 N Allen St	Centralia	MO	65240	800-346-3062	573-682-5521	255
Hubbell Premise Wiring Inc 23 Clara Dr	Mystic	CT	06355	800-626-0005		813
Hubbell RACO 3902 W Sample St	South Bend	IN	46619	800-722-6437	574-234-7151	814
Hubbell Wiring Device-Kellems 40 Waterview Dr *Cust Svc	Shelton	CT	06484	800-288-6000*	203-882-4800	813
Huber's Orchard & Winery 19816 Huber Rd	Borden	IN	47106	800-345-9463	812-923-9463	49-6
Huckstep & Assoc LLC 3734 S Ave Ste E	Springfield	MO	65807	800-269-6466	417-889-8991	2
HUD (Department of Housing & Urban Development) 451 Seventh St SW	Washington	DC	20410	800-569-4287	202-708-0685	340-10
HUD Office of Fair Housing & Equal Opportunity 451 Seventh St SW	Washington	DC	20410	800-669-9777	202-708-1112	340-10
Housing Discrimination Hotline 451 Seventh St SW	Washington	DC	20410	800-333-4636	202-708-1112	340-10
HUD Office of Public & Indian Housing 451 Seventh St SW Rm 4100	Washington	DC	20410	800-955-2232	202-708-0950	340-10
Real Estate Assessment Ctr 550 12th St SW Ste 100	Washington	DC	20410	888-245-4860	202-708-1112	340-10
Hudson City Savings Bank W 80 Century Rd	Paramus	NJ	07652	800-222-0194	201-967-1900	69
Hudson Color Concentrates Inc 50 Francis St	Leominster	MA	01453	888-858-9065	978-537-3538	549
Hudson Institute 1015 15th St NW Ste 600	Washington	DC	20005	888-554-1325	202-974-2400	631
Hudson Lock Inc 81 Apsley St	Hudson	MA	01749	800-434-8960		350
Hudson Printing & Graphic Design 611 S Mobberly Ave	Longview	TX	75602	800-530-4888	903-758-1773	344
Hudson River Fruit Distributors 65 Old Indian Rd	Milton	NY	12547	800-640-2774		316-3
Hudson River Islands State Park Schodack Island State Pk	Schodack Landing	NY	12156	800-456-2267	518-732-0187	564
Hudson Valley Community College 80 Vandenburgh Ave	Troy	NY	12180	877-325-4822	518-629-4822	161
Hudson Valley Federal Credit Union 159 Barnegat Rd	Poughkeepsie	NY	12601	800-468-3011	845-463-3011	221
Hudson Valve Company Inc 5301 Office Pk Dr Ste 330	Bakersfield	CA	93309	800-748-6218	661-869-1126	787
Hudson's on the Bend 3509 Ranch Rd 620 N	Austin	TX	78734	800-996-7655	512-266-1369	669
Hudspeth County 109 Brown St	Sierra Blanca	TX	79851	888-368-4689	915-369-2331	338
Hueco Tanks State Historic Site 6900 Hueco Tanks Rd Ste 1	El Paso	TX	79938	800-792-1112	915-857-1135	564
Hueneme Elementary School Dist 205 N Ventura Rd	Port Hueneme	CA	93041	866-431-2478	805-488-3588	683
Hufcor Inc 2101 Kennedy Rd	Janesville	WI	53545	800-356-6968	608-756-1241	288
Huffman Corp 1050 Huffman Way	Clover	SC	29710	888-483-3626	803-222-4561	454
Huffman Laboratories Inc 4630 Indiana St	Golden	CO	80403	877-886-6225	303-278-4455	740
Huffy Bicycle Co 6551 Centerville Business Pkwy	Centerville	OH	45459	800-872-2453	937-865-2800	81
Hu-Friedy Mfg Company Inc 3232 N Rockwell St	Chicago	IL	60618	800-483-7433	773-975-6100	230
Hughes Bros Inc 210 N 13th St PO Box 159	Seward	NE	68434	800-869-0359	402-643-2991	814
Hughes Corp Weschler Instruments Div 16900 Foltz Pkwy	Cleveland	OH	44149	800-557-0064	440-238-2550	250
Hughes Federal Credit Union Inc PO Box 11900	Tucson	AZ	85734	866-760-3156	520-794-8341	221
Hughes Network Systems LLC 11717 Exploration Ln	Germantown	MD	20876	800-461-9330	301-428-5500	732
Hughes Supply Company of Thomasville Inc 175 Kanoy Rd PO Box 1003	Thomasville	NC	27360	800-747-8141	336-475-8146	453
HughesNet 11717 Exploration Ln	Germantown	MD	20876	866-347-3292	301-428-5500	398
Hughston Orthopedic Hospital 100 Frist Ct	Columbus	GA	31908	855-795-3609	706-494-2100	374-7
Hugoton Royalty Trust 2911 Turtle Creek Blvd, Ste 850 PO Box 962020 *NYSE: HGT*	Dallas	TX	75219	855-588-7839	214-209-2400	673
Huhtamaki Inc North America 9201 Packaging Dr	DeSoto	KS	66018	800-255-4243	913-583-3025	547
Huitt-Zollars Inc 1717 McKinney Ave Ste 1400	Dallas	TX	75202	866-667-6572	214-871-3311	263
Huka Productions LLC 924 Valmont St Ste 103	New Orleans	LA	70115	888-512-7469		197
Hull Lift Truck Inc 28747 Old US 33 W	Elkhart	IN	46516	888-284-0364	574-293-8651	385
Hultgren Implements Inc 5698 State Hwy 175	Ida Grove	IA	51445	800-827-1650	712-364-3105	276
Human Arc Corp 1457 East 40th St	Cleveland	OH	44103	800-828-6453	216-431-5200	390
Human Capital 2055 Crooks Rd Lowr Level	Rochester Hills	MI	48309	888-736-9071		630
Human Factors & Ergonomics Society (HFES) 1124 Montana Ave Ste B PO Box 1369	Santa Monica	CA	90406	800-233-1234	310-394-1811	47-17
Human Factors International Inc 410 W Lowe Ave	Fairfield	IA	52556	800-242-4480	641-472-4480	179
Human Growth Foundation 997 Glen Cove Ave Ste 5	Glen Head	NY	11545	800-451-6434	516-671-4041	47-17
Human Kinetics 1607 N Market St	Champaign	IL	61820	800-747-4457	217-351-5076	634-2
Human Life International (HLI) 4 Family Life Ln *Orders	Front Royal	VA	22630	800-549-5433*	540-635-7884	47-6
Human Movement LLC 1111 S St	Louisville	CO	80027	855-464-6601		234
Human Resource Development Press Inc 22 Amherst Rd	Amherst	MA	01002	800-822-2801	413-253-3488	196
Human Rights Campaign 1640 Rhode Island Ave NW	Washington	DC	20036	800-777-4723	202-628-4160	47-8
Human Touch 3030 Walnut Ave	Long Beach	CA	90807	800-742-5493	562-426-8700	320-2
Humana Foundation Inc 500 W Main St Ste 208	Louisville	KY	40202	888-431-4748	502-580-4140	305
Humana Inc 500 W Main St *NYSE: HUM*	Louisville	KY	40202	800-486-2620	502-580-1000	391-3
Humana Military Healthcare Services 500 W Main St *General	Louisville	KY	40201	800-444-5445*		391-3
Humboldt County Convention & Visitors Bureau 1034 Second St	Eureka	CA	95501	800-346-3482	707-443-5097	208
Humboldt County Rural Electric Co-op (HCREC) 1210 13th St N	Humboldt	IA	50548	800-452-1111	515-332-1616	247
Humboldt Manufacturing Co 875 Tollgate Rd	Elgin	IL	60123	800-544-7220	708-456-6300	407
Humboldt State University 1 Harpst St	Arcata	CA	95521	866-850-9556	707-826-3011	167
Humco Holding Group Inc 7400 Alumax Dr	Texarkana	TX	75501	800-662-3435	903-334-6200	582
Hume Travel Corp 401 WGeorgia St Ste 1680	Vancouver	BC	V6B5A1	800-663-9787	604-682-7581	770
Hummert International Inc 4500 Earth City Expy	Earth City	MO	63045	800-325-3055	314-506-4500	278
Humphrey Products Co 5070 E N Ave PO Box 2008	Kalamazoo	MI	49048	800-477-8707	269-381-5500	787
Humphrey's Half Moon Inn & Suites 2303 Shelter Island Dr	San Diego	CA	92106	800-542-7400	619-224-3411	379
Humphreys College 6650 Inglewood Ave	Stockton	CA	95207	800-433-3243	209-478-0800	167
Hunger Project, The 5 Union Sq W	New York	NY	10003	800-228-6691	212-251-9100	47-5
Hunt & Sons Inc 5750 S Watt Ave	Sacramento	CA	95829	800-734-2999	916-383-4868	325
Hunt Consolidated Inc 1900 N Akard St	Dallas	TX	75201	800-424-9300	214-978-8000	360-3
Hunt Forest Products 401 E Reynolds Dr PO Box 1263	Ruston	LA	71273	800-390-8589	318-255-2245	681
Hunt Guillot & Assoc LLC 603 Reynolds Dr	Ruston	LA	71270	866-255-6825	318-255-6825	258
Hunt Insurance Agency Inc 12000 S Harlem Ave	Palos Heights	IL	60463	800-772-6484	708-361-5300	390
Hunt Midwest Enterprises Inc 8300 NE Underground Dr	Kansas City	MO	64161	800-551-6877	816-455-2500	653
Hunt Midwest Mining Inc 8300 NE Underground Dr	Kansas City	MO	64161	800-551-6877	816-455-2500	502-5
Hunt Midwest Residential Development 8300 NE Underground Dr	Kansas City	MO	64161	800-551-6877	816-455-2500	651
Hunt Pan Am Aviation Inc 505 Amelia Earhart Dr	Brownsville	TX	78521	800-888-7524	956-542-9111	62
Hunt Regional Healthcare 4215 Joe Ramsey Blvd	Greenville	TX	75401	855-854-2283	903-408-5000	374-3

Name / Address	City	State	ZIP	Toll-Free	Phone	Class
Hunter Business Group LLC 4650 N Port Washington Rd	Milwaukee	WI	53212	**800-423-4010**		197
Hunter Company Inc 3300 W 71st Ave	Westminster	CO	80030	**800-676-4868**	303-427-4626	708
Hunter Contracting Co 701 N Cooper Rd	Gilbert	AZ	85233	**877-992-0521**	480-892-0521	190-4
Hunter Display 14 Hewlett Ave	East Patchogue	NY	11772	**800-767-2110**	631-475-5900	235
Hunter Douglas Inc 1 Hunter Douglas Dr	Cumberland	MD	21502	**800-365-3399**	301-722-7700	86
Hunter Engineering Co 11250 Hunter Dr	Bridgeton	MO	63044	**800-448-6848**	314-731-3020	61-5
Hunter Fan Co 7130 Goodlett Farms Pkwy Ste 400	Memphis	TN	38016	**888-830-1326**	901-743-1360	36
Hunter Heavy Equipment Inc 2829 Texas Ave	Texas City	TX	77590	**800-562-7368**	409-945-2382	192
Hunter Public Relations 41 Madison Ave 5th Fl	New York	NY	10010	**866-395-7710**	212-679-6600	633
Hunter Travel Managers 4683 Chabot Dr Ste 385	Pleasanton	CA	94588	**800-876-8785**	925-463-0560	770
Hunter Woodworks Inc 21038 S Wilmington Ave PO Box 4937	Carson	CA	90749	**800-966-4751**	323-775-2544	550
Hunterdon County Democrat 8 Minneakoning Rd	Flemington	NJ	08822	**888-782-7533**	908-782-4747	531-4
Hunting Island State Park 2555 Sea Island Pkwy	Hunting Island	SC	29920	**800-315-3087**	843-838-2011	564
Huntingdon College 1500 E Fairview Ave *Admissions	Montgomery	AL	36106	**800-763-0313***	334-833-4497	167
Huntingdon County Visitors Bureau 6993 Seven Pt Rd Ste 2	Hesston	PA	16647	**888-729-7869**	814-658-0060	208
Huntington Bancshares Inc 7 Easton Oval *NASDAQ: HBAN*	Columbus	OH	43219	**800-480-2265**		360-2
Huntington Beach Marketing & Visitors Bureau 301 Main St Ste 208	Huntington Beach	CA	92648	**800-729-6232**	714-969-3492	208
Huntington Beach Public Library (HBPL) 7111 Talbert Ave	Huntington Beach	CA	92648	**800-565-0148**	714-842-4481	434-3
Huntington Beach State Park 16148 Ocean Hwy	Murrells Inlet	SC	29576	**800-491-1764**	843-237-4440	564
Huntington County Visitors & Convention Bureau 407 N Jefferson St	Huntington	IN	46750	**800-848-4282**	260-359-8687	208
Huntington Junior College 900 Fifth Ave	Huntington	WV	25701	**800-344-4522**	304-697-7550	798
Huntington Learning Centers Inc 496 Kinderkamack Rd	Oradell	NJ	07649	**800-653-8400**	201-261-8400	147
Huntington Mortgage Co 7575 Huntington Pk Dr	Columbus	OH	43235	**800-323-4695**	614-480-6505	508
Huntington National Bank 41 S High St Huntington Ctr	Columbus	OH	43287	**800-480-2265**	614-480-8300	69
Huntington Park Rubber Stamp 2761 E Slauson Ave PO Box 519	Huntington Park	CA	90255	**800-882-0029**	323-582-6461	466
Huntington State Park PO Box 1343	Huntington	UT	84528	**800-322-3770**	435-687-2491	564
Huntington Township Chamber of Commerce 164 Main St	Huntington	NY	11743	**888-962-9932**	631-423-6100	138
Huntington University 2303 College Ave *Admissions	Huntington	IN	46750	**800-642-6493***	260-356-6000	167
Huntington Veterans Affairs Medical Ctr 1540 Spring Valley Dr	Huntington	WV	25704	**800-827-8244**	304-429-6741	374-8
Huntington's Disease Society of America (HDSA) 505 Eigth Ave Ste 902	New York	NY	10018	**800-345-4372**	212-242-1968	47-17
Huntleigh Securities Corp 7800 Forsyth Blvd 5th Fl	Saint Louis	MO	63105	**800-727-5405**	314-236-2400	688
Huntsman Corp 500 Huntsman Way *NYSE: HUN*	Salt Lake City	UT	84108	**888-490-8484**	801-584-5700	604-2
Huntsville Board of Education 200 White St	Huntsville	AL	35801	**877-517-0020**	256-428-6800	683
Huntsville Botanical Garden 4747 Bob Wallace Ave	Huntsville	AL	35805	**800-300-4916**	256-830-4447	96
Huntsville Museum of Art 300 Church St SW	Huntsville	AL	35801	**800-786-9095**	256-535-4350	519
Huntsville Times 2317 S Memorial Pkwy	Huntsville	AL	35801	**800-239-5271**	256-532-4000	531-2
Huntsville/Madison County Convention & Visitor's Bureau 500 Church St Ste 1	Huntsville	AL	35801	**800-843-0468**	256-551-2230	208
Huntsville-Walker County Chamber of Commerce 1327 11th St	Huntsville	TX	77340	**800-289-0389**	936-295-8113	138
Huntwood Industries 23800 E Apple Way	Liberty Lake	WA	99019	**800-873-7350**	509-924-5858	114
Huot Manufacturing Co 550 Wheeler St N	Saint Paul	MN	55104	**800-832-3838**	651-646-1869	320-1
Hurckman Mechanical Industries Inc PO Box 10977	Green Bay	WI	54307	**844-499-8771**	920-499-8771	191-10
Hurco Cos Inc 1 Technology Way *NASDAQ: HURC* ■ *Sales	Indianapolis	IN	46268	**800-634-2416***	317-293-5309	454
Hurley Medical Ctr 1 Hurley Plz	Flint	MI	48503	**800-336-8999**	810-262-9000	374-3
Huron Chamber & Visitors Bureau 1725 Dakota Ave S	Huron	SD	57350	**800-487-6673**	605-352-0000	208
Huron Machine Products Inc 228 SW 21st Terr	Fort Lauderdale	FL	33312	**800-327-8186**		492
Huron Valley Correctional Facility 3201 Bemis Rd	Ypsilanti	MI	48197	**855-444-3911**	734-572-9900	215
Hurst Boiler & Welding Company Inc 100 Boilermaker Ln	Coolidge	GA	31738	**877-994-8778**	229-346-3545	90
Hurst Chemical Co 2360 Eastman Ave Ste 108 *Cust Svc	Oxnard	CA	93030	**800-723-2004***		627
Hurst Farm Supply Inc 105 Ave D	Abernathy	TX	79311	**800-535-8903**	806-298-2541	276
Hurst Group 257 E Short St	Lexington	KY	40507	**800-926-4423**	859-255-4422	534
Hurst Place 209 Limeridge Rd E	Hamilton	ON	L9A2S6	**888-521-8300**	289-426-5302	461
Hurst Public Library 901 Precinct Line Rd	Hurst	TX	76053	**800-344-8377**	817-788-7300	434-3
Hurtigruten 405 Pk Ave	New York	NY	10022	**866-552-0371**	212-319-1300	222
Hurwitz-Mintz Furniture Co 1751 Airline Dr	Metairie	LA	70001	**888-957-9555**	504-378-1000	322
Huse Publishing Co 525 Norfolk Ave PO Box 977	Norfolk	NE	68701	**877-371-1020**	402-371-1020	634-8
Hush Puppies Co 9341 Courtland Dr NE	Rockford	MI	49351	**866-699-7365**	616-866-5500	302
Husky Energy Inc 707 Eigth Ave SW PO Box 6525 *TSE: HSE*	Calgary	AB	T2P3G7	**877-262-2111**	403-298-6111	535
Husky Injection Molding Systems Ltd 500 Queen St S	Bolton	ON	L7E5S5	**800-465-4875**	905-951-5000	386
Husqvarna Construction Products 17400 W 119th St	Olathe	KS	66061	**800-288-5040**		492
Hussey Copper Ltd 100 Washington St	Leetsdale	PA	15056	**800-733-8866**	724-251-4200	484
Hussey Seating Co 38 Dyer St Ext	North Berwick	ME	03906	**800-341-0401**	207-676-2271	320-3
Hussmann Corp 12999 St Charles Rock Rd	Bridgeton	MO	63044	**800-592-2060**	314-291-2000	662
Husson College 1 College Cir	Bangor	ME	04401	**800-448-7766**	207-941-7000	167
Hussong Manufacturing Company Inc 204 Industrial Park Rd	Lakefield	MN	56150	**800-253-4904**	507-662-6641	362
Hussung Mechanical Contractors 6913 Enterprise Dr	Louisville	KY	40214	**800-446-2738**	502-375-3500	609
Huston-Tillotson University 900 Chicon St	Austin	TX	78702	**877-487-8702**	512-505-3000	167
Hutchens Construction Co 1007 Main St	Cassville	MO	65625	**888-728-3482**	417-847-2489	190-4
Hutchens Industries Inc 215 N Patterson Ave	Springfield	MO	65802	**800-654-8824**	417-862-5012	59
Hutchinson Aerospace & Industry Inc 82 S St	Hopkinton	MA	01748	**800-227-7962**	508-417-7000	674
Hutchinson Community College & Area Vocational School 1300 N Plum St	Hutchinson	KS	67501	**800-289-3501**	620-665-3500	161
Hutchinson Co-Op PO Box 158	Hutchinson	MN	55350	**800-795-1299**	320-587-4647	278
Hutchinson Manufacturing Inc 720 Hwy 7 W PO Box 487	Hutchinson	MN	55350	**800-795-1276**	320-587-4653	695
Hutchinson News 300 W Second St	Hutchinson	KS	67504	**800-766-3311**	620-694-5700	531-2
Hutchinson Regional Healthcare System 1701 E 23rd Ave	Hutchinson	KS	67502	**800-267-6891**	620-665-2000	374-3
Hutchinson Technology Inc 40 W Highland Pk Dr *NASDAQ: HTCH*	Hutchinson	MN	55350	**800-419-1007**	320-587-3797	255
Hutchinson Zoo 6 Emerson Loop E	Hutchinson	KS	67501	**800-362-3247**	620-694-2693	821
Hutchinson/Mayrath/TerraTrack Industries 514 W Crawford PO Box 629	Clay Center	KS	67432	**800-523-6993**	785-632-2161	275
Hutchinson/Reno County Chamber of Commerce 117 N Walnut St	Hutchinson	KS	67501	**800-691-4262**	620-662-3391	138
Hutchison Inc 7460 Hwy 85 PO Box 1158	Adams City	CO	80022	**800-525-0121**	303-287-2826	193-3
Hutson 306 Andrus Dr	Murray	KY	42071	**866-488-7662**	270-886-3994	429
Huttig Bldg Products Inc (HBP) 555 Maryville University Dr Ste 400 *OTC: HBPI*	Saint Louis	MO	63141	**800-325-4466**	314-216-2600	498
Huxley Communications Cooperative 102 n main ave	Huxley	IA	50124	**800-231-4922**	515-597-2212	226
HVA (High Vacuum Apparatus LLC) 12880 Moya Blvd	Reno	NV	89506	**800-551-4422**	775-359-4442	787
HVB AE Power Systems Inc 7250 Mcginnis Ferry Rd	Suwanee	GA	30024	**866-362-0798**	770-495-1755	727
HVH Transportation Inc 181 E 56th Ave Ste 200	Denver	CO	80216	**800-525-4844**	303-292-3656	778
HW Wilson Co 10 Estes St	Ipswich	MA	01938	**800-653-2726**	978-356-6500	634-2
HWC (Houston Wire & Cable Co) 10201 N Loop E	Houston	TX	77029	**800-468-9473**	713-609-2100	248
HWE (High West Energy Inc) 6270 County Rd 212	Pine Bluffs	WY	82082	**888-834-1657**	307-245-3261	247
HWEC (Hancock-Wood Electric Co-op Inc) 1399 Business Pk Dr S PO Box 190	North Baltimore	OH	45872	**800-445-4840**	419-257-3241	247
HWH Corp 2096 Moscow Rd	Moscow	IA	52760	**800-321-3494**	563-724-3396	59
Hyannis Holiday Motel 131 Ocean St	Hyannis	MA	02601	**800-423-1551**	508-775-1639	379
Hyannis Travel Inn 18 N St	Hyannis	MA	02601	**800-352-7190**	508-775-8200	379
Hyatt Carmel Highlands 120 Highlands Dr	Carmel	CA	93923	**800-633-7313**	831-620-1234	379
Hyatt Gold Passport Program 9805 Q St PO Box 27089	Omaha	NE	68127	**800-233-1234**		378
Hyatt Hotels Corp 71 S Wacker Dr *NYSE: H*	Chicago	IL	60606	**888-591-1234**	312-750-1234	379
Grand Hyatt Hotels 71 S Wacker Dr *Resv	Chicago	IL	60606	**800-233-1234***	312-750-1234	379
Hyatt Place Hotels 71 S Wacker Dr	Chicago	IL	60606	**888-492-8847**	312-750-1234	379
Hyatt Regency Hotels 71 S Wacker Dr *Resv	Chicago	IL	60606	**800-233-1234***	312-750-1234	379
Park Hyatt Hotels 71 S Wacker Dr *Resv	Chicago	IL	60606	**800-233-1234***	312-750-1234	379
Hyatt Place New York Midtown South 52-54 W 36th	New York	NY	10015	**888-492-8847**		377

Name / Address	City	State	Zip	Toll-Free	Phone	Class
Hyatt Regency Huntington Beach Resort & Spa 21500 Pacific Coast Hwy	Huntington Beach	CA	92648	**800-633-7313**	714-698-1234	669
Hyatt Regency Lake Tahoe Resort & Casino 111 Country Club Dr	Incline Village	NV	89451	**800-233-1234**	775-832-1234	132
Hyatt Regency Maui Resort & Spa 200 Nohea Kai Dr	Lahaina	HI	96761	**800-633-7313**	808-661-1234	667
Hyatt Regency Scottsdale Resort at Gainey Ranch 7500 E Doubletree Ranch Rd	Scottsdale	AZ	85258	**800-233-1234**	480-483-5558	705
Hyatt Vacation Ownership Inc 140 Fountain Pkwy N Ste 570	Saint Petersburg	FL	33716	**800-926-4447**	727-803-9400	751
Hycor Biomedical Inc 7272 Chapman Ave *Cust Svc	Garden Grove	CA	92841	**800-382-2527***		233
Hyde Tools Co 54 Eastford Rd	Southbridge	MA	01550	**800-872-4933**	508-764-4344	756
Hydra-Fab Fluid Power Inc 3585 Laird Rd Unit 5	Mississauga	ON	L5L5Z8	**866-466-9866**	905-569-1819	358
Hydraforce Inc 500 Barclay Blvd	Lincolnshire	IL	60069	**877-237-9101**	847-793-2300	788
Hydrel 12881 Bradley Ave	Sylmar	CA	91342	**866-533-9901**		439
Hydrite Chemical Co 300 N Patrick Blvd	Brookfield	WI	53045	**800-543-4560**	262-792-1450	145
Hydro Aluminum North America 999 Corporate Blvd Ste 100	Linthicum	MD	21090	**888-935-5752**		489
Hydro Carbide 4439 State Rte 982	Latrobe	PA	15650	**800-245-2476**	724-539-9701	755
Hydro One Inc 483 Bay St 15th Fl	Toronto	ON	M5G2P5	**888-664-9376**	416-345-5000	785
Hydro Systems Inc 29132 Ave Paine	Valencia	CA	91355	**800-747-9990**	661-775-0686	375
HydroCAD Software Solutions LLC PO Box 477	Chocorua	NH	03817	**800-927-7246**	603-323-8666	180-8
HYDRO-FIT Inc 160 Madison St *Cust Svc	Eugene	OR	97402	**800-346-7295***	541-484-4361	269
Hydro-flo Products Inc 3655 N 124th St	Brookfield	WI	53005	**800-843-3569**	262-781-2810	611
Hydrolevel Co 83 Water St	New Haven	CT	06511	**800-654-0768**	203-776-0473	205
Hydromatic Pump Co 740 E Ninth St	Ashland	OH	44805	**888-957-8677**		638
HydroPressure Cleaning Inc 413 Dawson Dr	Camarillo	CA	93012	**800-934-2399**		638
Hydroseal Valve Co Inc 1500 SE 89th St	Oklahoma City	OK	73149	**800-398-2493**	405-631-1533	787
Hydrotex Inc 12920 Senlac D Ste 190	Farmers Branch	TX	75234	**800-527-9439**		540
Hydro-Thermal Corp 400 Pilot Ct	Waukesha	WI	53188	**800-952-0121**	262-548-8900	386
Hygenic Corp 1245 Home Ave	Akron	OH	44310	**800-321-2135**	330-633-8460	230
hygiena LLC 941 Avenida Acaso	Camarillo	CA	93012	**877-494-4364**	805-388-8007	419
Hygieneering Inc 7575 Plz Ct	Willowbrook	IL	60527	**800-444-7154**	630-654-2550	462
Hygolet Inc 349 SE Second Ave	Deerfield Beach	FL	33441	**800-494-6538**	954-481-8601	607
Hygrade Metal Moulding Manufacturing Corp 1990 Highland Ave	Bethlehem	PA	18020	**800-645-9475**	610-866-2441	236
Hy-Grade Precast Concrete 2411 First St	St Catharines	ON	L2R6P7	**800-229-8568**	905-684-8568	185
Hygrade Precision Technologies Inc 329 Cooke St	Plainville	CT	06062	**800-457-1666**	860-747-5773	755
HyGreen Inc 3630 SW 47th Ave Ste 100	Gainesville	FL	32608	**877-574-9473**		740
Hy-Ko Products Co 60 Meadow Ln	Northfield	OH	44067	**800-292-0550**	330-467-7446	699
Hyland Software Inc 28500 Clemens Rd	Westlake	OH	44145	**888-495-2638**	440-788-5000	180-7
Hylant Group 811 Madison Ave	Toledo	OH	43624	**800-249-5268**	419-255-1020	390
Hynes Industries 3760 Oakwood	Youngstown	OH	44515	**800-321-9257**		491
HyperDisk Marketing Inc 18251 McDurmott W Ste A	Irvine	CA	92614	**800-241-1210**	949-442-9850	179
Hyperion Capital Management Inc 200 Vessey St 3 World Financial Ctr	New York	NY	10281	**800-497-3746**	212-549-8400	401
Hypertension Diagnostics Inc 730 Bldg Ste 295	Minneapolis	MN	55402	**888-785-7392**	651-687-9999	475
Hypertherm Inc 21 Great Hollow Rd PO Box 5010	Hanover	NH	03755	**800-643-0030**	603-643-3441	454
Hypneumat Inc 5900 W Franklin Dr	Franklin	WI	53132	**800-228-9949**	414-423-7400	454
Hypro 375 Fifth Ave NW *Cust Svc	New Brighton	MN	55112	**800-424-9776***	651-766-6300	638
Hyson Products 10367 Brecksville Rd	Brecksville	OH	44141	**800-876-4976**	440-526-5900	788
Hysterectomy Educational Resources & Services Foundation (HERS) 422 Bryn Mawr Ave	Bala Cynwyd	PA	19004	**888-750-4377**	610-667-7757	47-17
Hy-Tape International Inc PO Box 540	Patterson	NY	12563	**800-248-0101**		476
Hyundai Motor America 10550 Talbert Ave *Cust Svc	Fountain Valley	CA	92708	**800-633-5151***	714-965-3000	58

I

Name / Address	City	State	Zip	Toll-Free	Phone	Class
I & I Sling Inc PO Box 2423	Aston	PA	19014	**800-874-3539**	610-485-8500	210
I Am Athlete LLC PO Box 667	Santa Monica	CA	90406	**877-462-7979**		387
I B M Southeast Employees Federal Credit Union PO Box 5090	Boca Raton	FL	33431	**888-567-8688**	561-982-4700	221
I D Booth Inc PO Box 579	Elmira	NY	14902	**888-432-6684**	607-733-9121	611
I Imagine Studio Inc 152 W Huron Ste 100	Chicago	IL	60654	**855-792-7263**	847-467-0308	5
I Rice & Company Inc 11500 Roosevelt Blvd Bldg D	Philadelphia	PA	19116	**800-232-6022**	215-673-7423	297-15
I Wireless 4135 NW Urbandale Dr *Cust Svc	Urbandale	IA	50322	**888-550-4497***	515-258-7000	732
i Wireless Ctr 1201 River Dr	Moline	IL	61265	**800-745-3000**	309-764-2001	718
I. s Outsource Inc 19119 N Creek Pkwy Ste 200	Bothell	WA	98011	**800-240-2821**	206-374-0251	179
I.B.I.S. Inc 30 Technology Pkwy S Ste 400	Norcross	GA	30092	**866-714-8422**	770-368-4000	693
I.T. Blueprint Solutions Consulting Inc 170-422 Richards St	Vancouver	BC	V6B2Z4	**866-261-8981**		198
IAABO (International Assn of Approved Basketball Officials) PO Box 355	Carlisle	PA	17013	**800-526-1379**	717-713-8129	47-22
IAAI (International Assn of Arson Investigators) 2111 Baldwin Ave # 203	Crofton	MD	21114	**800-468-4224**	410-451-3473	48-7
IAAO (International Assn of Assessing Officers) 314 W Tenth St	Kansas City	MO	64105	**800-616-4226**	816-701-8100	48-7
IABC (International Assn of Business Communicators) 155 Montgomery St Ste 1210	San Francisco	CA	94104	**800-766-4222**	415-544-4700	48-12
IAC Industries 895 Beacon St	Brea	CA	92821	**800-989-1422**	714-990-8997	320-1
IACP (International Assn of Culinary Professionals) 1221 Ave of the Americas 42nd fl	New York	NY	10020	**800-928-4227**	866-358-2524	48-6
IACP (International Academy of Compounding Pharmacists) 4638 Riverstone Blvd	Missouri City	TX	77459	**800-927-4227**	281-933-8400	48-8
IACP (International Assn of Chiefs of Police) 44 Canal Ctr Plz Ste 200	Alexandria	VA	22314	**800-843-4227**	703-836-6767	48-7
IAEE (International Assn of Exhibitions & Events) 12700 Park Central Dr Ste 308	Dallas	TX	75251	**866-266-3378**	972-458-8002	48-18
IAEI (International Assn of Electrical Inspectors) 901 Waterfall Way Ste 602	Richardson	TX	75080	**800-786-4234**	972-235-1455	48-3
IAFC (International Assn of Fire Chiefs) 4025 Fair Ridge Dr Ste 300	Fairfax	VA	22033	**866-385-9110**	703-273-0911	48-7
IAFE (International Assn of Fairs & Expositions, The) 3043 E Cairo	Springfield	MO	65802	**800-516-0313**	417-862-5771	47-23
IAFP (International Assn for Food Protection) 6200 Aurora Ave Ste 200W *General	Des Moines	IA	50322	**800-369-6337***	515-276-3344	48-6
IAHB (Institute for the Advancement of Human Behavior) PO BOX 5527	Santa Rosa	CA	95402	**800-258-8411**	650-851-8411	48-8
IAIA (Institute of American Indian Arts) 83 Avan Nu Po Rd	Santa Fe	NM	87508	**800-804-6422**	505-424-2300	164
IAMFC (International Assn of Marriage & Family Counselors) 5999 Stevenson Ave	Alexandria	VA	22304	**800-347-6647**		48-15
IAMGOLD Corp 401 Bay St Ste 3200 PO Box 153 *TSE: IMG*	Toronto	ON	M5H2Y4	**888-464-9999**	416-360-4710	501
IAMS Co 3700 Ohio 65 *Cust Svc	Leipsic	OH	45856	**800-675-3849***	419-943-4267	577
IANA (Intermodal Assn of North America) 11785 Beltsville Dr Ste 1100	Calverton	MD	20705	**877-438-8442**	301-982-3400	48-21
IAP Worldwide Services Inc 7315 N Atlantic Ave	Cape Canaveral	FL	32920	**877-296-8010**	321-784-7100	273
IAPA (International Airline Passengers Assn) PO Box 700188	Dallas	TX	75370	**800-821-4272**	972-404-9980	47-23
IAPES (International Assn of Workforce Professionals) 1801 Louisville Rd	Frankfort	KY	40601	**888-898-9960**	502-223-4459	48-12
IAPMO (International Assn of Plumbing & Mechanical Officials) 4755 E Philadelphia St	Ontario	CA	91761	**877-427-6601**	909-472-4100	48-7
IASIS Healthcare Corp 117 Seaboard Ln Bldg E	Franklin	TN	37067	**877-898-6080**	615-844-2747	353
IASP (International Assn for the Study of Pain) 111 Queen Anne Ave N Ste 501	Seattle	WA	98109	**866-574-2654**	206-283-0311	47-17
IATSE (International Alliance of Theatrical Stage Employees Moving Picture Technicians) 1430 Broadway 20th Fl	New York	NY	10018	**800-456-3863**	212-730-1770	414
IATSE PAC 1430 Broadway 20th Fl	New York	NY	10018	**844-422-9273**	212-730-1770	614
IAVM (International Assn of Venue Managers Inc) 635 Fritz Dr Ste 100	Coppell	TX	75019	**800-935-4226**	972-906-7441	48-12
IBA (Institute of Business Appraisers) 1111 BrickyaRd Rd Ste 200	Salt Lake City	UT	84106	**800-299-4130**		48-17
Ibaset 27442 Portola Pkwy	Foothill Ranch	CA	92610	**877-422-7381**	949-598-5200	182
Ibb Design Group 5798 Genesis Ct	Frisco	TX	75034	**800-355-9195**	214-618-6600	136
IBC Advanced Alloys Corp 570 Granville St Ste 1200	Vancouver	BC	V6C3P1	**800-373-3251**	604-685-6263	501
IBERIABANK Corp 200 W Congress St *NASDAQ: IBKC*	Lafayette	LA	70501	**800-968-0801**		360-2
Iberville Parish Chamber of Commerce 23675 Church St	Plaquemine	LA	70764	**800-266-2692**	225-687-3560	138
IBHS (Institute for Business & Home Safety) 4775 E Fowler Ave	Tampa	FL	33617	**866-657-4247**	813-286-3400	48-9

Alphabetical Section

Name / Address	Toll-Free	Phone	Class
IBISWorld Inc 11755 Wilshire blvd 11th fl .... Los Angeles CA 90025	800-330-3772		387
IBM (International Business Machines Corp) 1 New OrchaRd Rd .... Armonk NY 10504 *NYSE: IBM*	800-426-4968	914-499-1900	175-1
IBS (International Biometric Society) 1444 'I' St NW Ste 700 .... Washington DC 20005	800-262-1171	202-712-9049	48-19
IBS (International Bible Society) *Biblica* 1820 Jet Stream Dr .... Colorado Springs CO 80921 *Cust Svc	800-524-1588*	719-488-9200	47-20
IBS Direct 431 Yerkes Rd .... King of Prussia PA 19406	800-220-1255	610-265-8210	109
IBS Electronics Inc 3506 W Lk Ctr Dr Ste D .... Santa Ana CA 92704	800-527-2888	714-751-6633	248
IBT Enterprises LLC 1770 Indian Trail Rd Ste 300 .... Norcross GA 30093	877-242-8428	770-381-2023	196
IBT Inc 9400 W 55th St .... Merriam KS 66203	800-332-2114	913-677-3151	385
IBU (Inlandboatmen's Union of the Pacific) 1711 W Nickerson St Ste D .... Seattle WA 98119	800-562-6000	206-284-6001	414
IBWA (International Bottled Water Assn) 1700 Diagonal Rd Ste 650 .... Alexandria VA 22314	800-928-3711	703-683-5213	48-6
ICA (International Chiropractors Assn) 6400 Arlington Blvd Ste 800 .... Falls Church VA 22042	800-423-4690	703-528-5000	48-8
ICA (Independent Charities of America) 1100 Larkspur Landing Cir Ste 340 .... Larkspur CA 94939	800-477-0733	415-925-2600	47-5
ICAC (Institute of Clean Air Cos) 1730 M St NW Ste 206 .... Washington DC 20036	800-631-9505	202-457-0911	47-12
iCAD Inc 98 Spit Brook Rd Ste 100 .... Nashua NH 03062 *NASDAQ: ICAD*	866-280-2239	603-882-5200	382
Icahn Enterprises LP 767 Fifth Ave 47th Fl .... New York NY 10153 *NASDAQ: IEP*	800-255-2737	212-702-4300	360-3
ICAM Technologies Corp 21500 Nassr St .... Sainte-anne-de-bellevue QC H9X4C1	800-827-4226	514-697-8033	181
Icare Industries Inc 4399 35th St N .... Saint Petersburg FL 33714	877-422-7352	727-526-0501	541
IcareLabs 4399 35th St N .... Saint Petersburg FL 33714	877-422-7352		541
ICBA (Independent Community Bankers of America) 1615 L St NW Ste 900 .... Washington DC 20036	800-422-8439	202-659-8111	48-2
ICC (International Code Council) 500 New Jersey Ave NW 6th Fl .... Washington DC 20001	888-422-7233	202-370-1800	48-3
ICC Chemical Corp 460 Pk Ave .... New York NY 10022	800-422-1720	212-521-1700	145
ICC Industries Inc 460 Pk Ave .... New York NY 10022	800-422-1720	212-521-1700	143
ICCFA (International Cemetery Cremation & Funeral Assn) 107 Carpenter Dr Ste 100 .... Sterling VA 20164	800-645-7700	703-391-8400	48-4
ICCP (Institute for Certification of Computing Professionals) 2400 E Devon Ave Ste 281 .... Des Plaines IL 60018	800-843-8227	847-299-4227	47-9
ICD (International College of Dentists) 51 Monroe St Ste 1400 .... Rockville MD 20850	800-533-6825	301-251-8861	48-8
ICD (Industrial Controls Distributors Inc) 1776 Bloomsbury Ave .... Ocean NJ 07712 *Sales	800-281-4788*	732-918-9000	385
ICE (US Immigration & Customs Enforcement) 425 'I' St NW .... Washington DC 20536	866-347-2423	202-514-1900	340-9
Ice Technologies Inc 411 SE Ninth St .... Pella IA 50219	877-754-8420	641-628-8724	182
Icelandair North America 1900 Crown Colony Dr .... Quincy MA 02169	800-223-5500		26
Icemakers Inc 3711 Fifth Ct N .... Birmingham AL 35222 *General	800-467-2181*	205-591-2791	380
Ice-O-Matic 11100 E 45th Ave .... Denver CO 80239	800-423-3367	303-371-3737	662
Iceptstechnology Group Inc 1301 Fulling Mill Rd .... Middletown PA 17057	888-477-7989	717-704-1000	176
ICF (International Contract Furnishings Inc) 19 Ohio Ave .... Norwich CT 06360	800-237-1625	860-886-1700	322
ICFG (International Church of the Foursquare Gospel) 1910 W Sunset Blvd PO Box 26902 .... Los Angeles CA 90026	888-635-4234	213-989-4234	47-20
ICFL (Idaho Commission for Libraries) 325 W State St .... Boise ID 83702	800-458-3271	208-334-2150	434-5
ICG Link Inc 7003 Chadwick Dr Ste 111 .... Brentwood TN 37027	877-397-7605	615-370-1530	353
ICG/Holliston 905 Holliston Mills Rd .... Church Hill TN 37642	800-251-0451	423-357-6141	742-2
ICIA (International Communications Industries Assn) 11242 Waples Mill Rd Ste 200 .... Fairfax VA 22030	800-659-7469	703-273-7200	48-20
iCIMS Inc 90 Matawan Rd Pkwy 120 5th Fl .... Matawan NJ 07747	800-889-4422	732-847-1941	180-1
ICLA (International Collegiate Licensing Assn) 24651 Detroit Rd .... Westlake OH 44145	877-887-2261	440-892-4000	47-22
ICM Asset Management Inc 601 W Main Ave .... Spokane WA 99201	800-488-4075	509-455-3588	401
Icm Controls Corp 7313 William Barry Blvd .... North Syracuse NY 13212	800-365-5525	315-233-5266	205
ICM Inc 310 N First St .... Colwich KS 67030	877-456-8588	316-796-0900	462
ICMA (International City/County Management Assn) 777 N Capitol St NE Ste 500 .... Washington DC 20002	800-745-8780	202-289-4262	48-7
ICMARC 777 N Capitol St NE Ste 600 .... Washington DC 20002 *General	800-669-7471*	202-962-4600	527
ICOI (International Congress of Oral Implantologists) 248 Lorraine Ave 3rd Fl .... Upper Montclair NJ 07043	800-442-0525	973-783-6300	48-8
iCollector Technologies Inc 1750 Coast Meridian Rd Ste 114 .... Port Coquitlam BC V3C6R8	866-313-0123	604-941-2221	50
ICOM America Inc 2380 116th Ave NE .... Bellevue WA 98004	800-872-4266	425-454-8155	645

Name / Address	Toll-Free	Phone	Class
ICON Advisers Inc 5299 DTC Blvd Ste 1200 .... Greenwood Village CO 80111	800-828-4881	303-790-1600	401
ICON Health & Fitness Inc 1500 South 1000 West .... Logan UT 84321	800-999-3756	435-750-5000	269
Icon Identity Solutions 1418 Elmhurst Rd .... Elk Grove Village IL 60007	888-724-0380		699
Iconixx Software 3420 Executive Ctr Dr Ste 250 .... Austin TX 78731	877-426-6499		182
Iconma LLC 850 Stephenson Hwy Ste 612 .... Troy MI 48083	888-451-2519		630
Icor Technology Inc 935 Ages Dr .... Ottawa ON K1G6L3	877-483-7978	613-745-3600	688
ICPI (Interlocking Concrete Pavement Institute) 14801 Murdock St Ste 2300 .... Chantilly VA 20151	800-241-3652	202-712-9036	48-3
ICPM (Institute of Certified Professional Managers) James Madison University MSC 5504 .... Harrisonburg VA 22807	800-460-8013	540-568-3247	48-12
ICS (Information & Computing Services Inc) 1650 Prudential Dr Ste 300 .... Jacksonville FL 32207	800-676-4427	904-399-8500	180-1
ICS Blount Inc 4909 SE International Way .... Portland OR 97222	800-321-1240		680
ICS Marketing Services Inc 4225 Legacy Pkwy .... Lansing MI 48911	888-394-1890	517-394-1890	197
ICTC (Inter-Community Telephone Co) PO Box 8 .... Nome ND 58062	800-350-9137	701-924-8815	733
ICU Medical Inc 951 Calle Amanecer .... San Clemente CA 92673 *NASDAQ: ICUI*	800-824-7890	949-366-2183	476
ICW Group 11455 El Camino Real .... San Diego CA 92130	800-877-1111	858-350-2400	391-4
ICWM (Institute of Caster & Wheel Manufacturers) 8720 Red Oak Blvd Ste 201 .... Charlotte NC 28217	877-522-5431	704-676-1190	48-13
IcwUSACom Inc 1487 Kingsley Dr .... Medford OR 97504	800-558-4435	541-608-2824	322
ID Systems Inc 123 Tice Blvd Ste 101 .... Woodcliff Lake NJ 07677 *NASDAQ: IDSY*	866-410-0152	201-996-9000	645
IDA (In Defense of Animals) 3010 Kerner Blvd .... San Rafael CA 94901	800-705-0425	415-448-0048	47-3
IDA (International Dyslexia Assn, The) 40 York Rd 4th Fl .... Towson MD 21204	800-222-3123	410-296-0232	47-17
Idaho			
Aging Commission (ICOA) 341 W Washington Fl 3 PO Box 83720 .... Boise ID 83702	800-926-2588	208-334-3833	339-13
Arts Commission 2410 Old Penitentiary Rd .... Boise ID 83712	800-278-3863	208-334-2119	339-13
Board of Medicine 1755 N Westgate Dr Ste 140 PO Box 83720 .... Boise ID 83704	800-333-0073	208-327-7000	339-13
Crime Victims Compensation Program PO Box 83720 .... Boise ID 83720	800-950-2110	208-334-6000	339-13
Department of Commerce 700 W State St PO Box 83720 .... Boise ID 83720	800-842-5858	208-334-2470	339-13
Homeland Security Bureau 4040 W Guard St Bldg 600 .... Boise ID 83705	800-344-0984	208-422-3040	339-13
Housing & Finance Assn 565 W Myrtle Ave .... Boise ID 83702	800-526-7145	208-331-4882	339-13
Parks & Recreation Dept 5657 Warm Springs Ave .... Boise ID 83716	855-514-2429		339-13
Public Utilities Commission PO Box 83720 .... Boise ID 83720	800-432-0369	208-334-0300	339-13
Real Estate Commission 575 E Parkcenter Blvd Ste 180 .... Boise ID 83706	866-447-5411	208-334-3285	339-13
Tax Commission 800 E Pk Blvd .... Boise ID 83712	800-972-7660	208-334-7660	339-13
Tourism Development Div 700 W State St PO Box 83720 .... Boise ID 83720 *General	800-847-4843*	208-334-2470	339-13
Idaho Assn of Realtors 10116 W Overland Rd .... Boise ID 83702	800-621-7553	208-342-3585	654
Idaho Botanical Garden 2355 N Penitentiary Rd .... Boise ID 83712	877-527-8233	208-343-8649	96
Idaho Commission for Libraries (ICFL) 325 W State St .... Boise ID 83702	800-458-3271	208-334-2150	434-5
Idaho Community Foundation Inc 210 W State St .... Boise ID 83702	800-657-5357	208-342-3535	306
Idaho County Light & Power Co-op 1065 Hwy 13 .... Grangeville ID 83530	877-212-0424	208-983-1610	247
Idaho Democratic Party 943 W Overland Rd .... Meridian ID 83642	800-626-0471	208-336-1815	615-1
Idaho Falls School District 91 Education Foundation Inc 690 John Adams Pkwy .... Idaho Falls ID 83401	888-993-7120	208-525-7500	683
Idaho Lions Eye Bank 1090 N Cole Rd .... Boise ID 83704	800-546-6889	208-338-5466	271
Idaho Lottery 1199 Shoreline Ln Ste 100 .... Boise ID 83702	800-432-5688	208-334-2600	451
Idaho National Laboratory (INL) 2525 Fremont Ave .... Idaho Falls ID 83402	866-495-7440		666
Idaho Nurses Assn (INA) 1850 E Southern Ave Ste 1 .... Tempe AZ 85224	888-721-8904		532
Idaho Pacific Lumber Co (IdaPac) 7255 Franklin Rd .... Boise ID 83709	800-231-2310	208-375-8052	193-3
Idaho Power Co 1221 W Idaho St .... Boise ID 83702	800-488-6151	208-388-2200	785
Idaho Public Television (IPTV) 1455 N Orchard St .... Boise ID 83706	800-543-6868	208-373-7220	629
Idaho State Bar 525 W Jefferson St .... Boise ID 83702	800-221-3295	208-334-4500	71
Idaho State Journal 305 S Arthur Ave .... Pocatello ID 83204	800-669-9777	208-232-4161	531-2
Idaho State Veterans Home-Lewiston 821 21st Ave .... Lewiston ID 83501	877-222-8387	208-799-3422	791
Idaho State Veterans Home-Pocatello 1957 Alvin Ricken Dr .... Pocatello ID 83201	877-222-8387	208-236-6340	791
Idaho Statesman PO Box 40 .... Boise ID 83707	800-635-8934	208-377-6400	531-2

Name / Address	City	State	Zip	Toll-Free	Phone	Class
Idaho-Pacific Corp 4723 E 100 N PO Box 478 *Sales	Ririe	ID	83443	**800-238-5503***	208-538-6971	297-18
IdaPac (Idaho Pacific Lumber Co) 7255 Franklin Rd	Boise	ID	83709	**800-231-2310**	208-375-8052	193-3
IDC (International Data Corp) 5 Speen St	Framingham	MA	01701	**800-343-4952**	508-872-8200	465
IDD Process & Packaging 5450 Tech Cir	Moorpark	CA	93021	**800-621-4144**	805-529-9890	263
IDDBA (International Dairy-Deli-Bakery Assn) 636 Science Dr	Madison	WI	53705	**877-399-4925**	608-238-7908	48-6
IDEA Inc 10455 Pacific Ctr Ct	San Diego	CA	92121	**800-999-4332**	858-535-8979	47-22
Idea Works Inc, The 100 W Briarwood Ln	Columbia	MO	65203	**800-537-4866**	573-445-4554	179
Ideal Adv & Printing 116 N Winnebago St	Rockford	IL	61101	**800-208-0294**	815-965-1713	4
Ideal Chemical & Supply Co 4025 Air Pk St	Memphis	TN	38118	**800-232-6776**	901-363-7720	145
Ideal Industries Inc 1375 Pk Ave	Sycamore	IL	60178	**800-435-0705**	815-895-5181	814
Ideal Jacobs Corp 515 Valley St	Maplewood	NJ	07040	**877-873-4332**	973-275-5100	626
Ideal Pet Products Inc 24735 Ave Rockefeller	Valencia	CA	91355	**800-378-4385**	661-294-2266	607
Ideal Shield LLC 2525 Clark St	Detroit	MI	48209	**866-825-8659**	313-842-7290	296
Ideal Software Systems Inc 4909 29th Ave	Meridian	MS	39305	**800-964-3325**	601-693-1673	179
Ideal Tape Co 1400 Middlesex St	Lowell	MA	01851	**800-284-3325**		476
Idealease Inc 430 N Rand Rd	North Barrington	IL	60010	**800-435-3273**	847-304-6000	776
Idealliance 1600 Duke St Ste 420	Alexandria	VA	22314	**800-255-8141**	952-896-1908	48-16
Idealogical Systems Inc 2900 John St	Markham	ON	L3R5G3	**855-554-4332**	905-474-0772	182
Idealstor LLC 12400 St Hwy 71 W Ste 350-364	Austin	TX	78738	**888-864-3257**	512-279-4321	175-8
IdeaTek Communications LLC 10400 E 69th St PO Box 258	Buhler	KS	67522	**855-433-2835**		387
IDEC Corp 1175 Elko Dr	Sunnyvale	CA	94089	**800-262-4332**	408-747-0550	205
Idegy 3990 Business Park Dr	Columbus	OH	43204	**888-421-2288**	614-545-5000	186
Idenix Pharmaceuticals Inc 320 Bent St 4th fl *NYSE: MRK*	Cambridge	MA	02141	**800-770-4674**	908-423-1000	84
Ident-A-Kid Services of America 1780 102nd Ave N Ste 100	Saint Petersburg	FL	33716	**800-890-1000**	727-577-4646	311
Identatronics Inc 165 N Lively Blvd *Cust Svc	Elk Grove Village	IL	60007	**800-323-5403***	847-437-2654	590
IDenticard Systems Inc 25 Race Ave FL 1	Lancaster	PA	17603	**800-233-0298**	717-569-5797	690
Identification Plates Inc 1555 High Point Dr	Mesquite	TX	75149	**800-395-2570**	972-216-1616	411
Identigene LLC 2495 South West Temple	Salt Lake City	UT	84115	**888-404-4363**	801-462-1401	418
Identity Automation LP 8833 N Sam Houston Pkwy W	Houston	TX	77064	**877-221-8401**		358
Identity Genetics Inc 47927 213th St	Aurora	SD	57002	**800-861-1054**		417
Identity Theft Resource Center 3625 Ruffin Rd Ste 204	San Diego	CA	92123	**888-400-5530**	858-693-7935	630
IDEO 100 Forest Ave	Palo Alto	CA	94301	**866-369-9888**	650-289-3400	263
IDEXX Laboratories Inc 1 IDEXX Dr *NASDAQ: IDXX*	Westbrook	ME	04092	**800-548-6733**	207-556-0300	233
IDF (Immune Deficiency Foundation) 40 W Chesapeake Ave Ste 308	Towson	MD	21204	**800-296-4433**	410-321-6647	47-17
IDFW (Institute for a Drug-Free Workplace) 10701 Parkridge Blvd Ste 300	Reston	VA	20191	**877-696-6775**	703-391-7222	48-12
IDG (International Data Group Inc) 1 Exeter Plaza 15th Fl *Orders	Boston	MA	02116	**800-343-4952***	617-534-1200	634-9
IDI Distributors Inc 8303 Audubon Rd	Chanhassen	MN	55317	**888-843-1318**	952-279-6400	688
iDirect Technologies Inc 13865 Sunrise Valley Dr Ste 100	Herndon	VA	20171	**888-362-5475**	703-648-8118	732
IDP (Insurance Data Processing Inc) 8101 Washington Ln	Wyncote	PA	19095	**800-523-6745**	215-885-2150	180-11
IDSA (Infectious Diseases Society of America) 1300 Wilson Blvd Ste 300	Arlington	VA	22209	**888-844-4372**	703-299-0200	48-8
IDT|RPM Consulting Services 1009 W Hawthorn Dr	Itasca	IL	60143	**877-722-6438**	630-875-1100	198
IEAP (Interface EAP Inc) 10370 Richmond Ave Ste 1100 PO Box 421879	Houston	TX	77042	**800-324-4327**	713-781-3364	461
IEEE Broadcast Technology Society (BTS) 445 Hoes Ln	Piscataway	NJ	08854	**800-678-4333**	732-562-5407	48-19
IEEE Computer Graphics & Applications Magazine 10662 Los Vaqueros Cir PO Box 3014	Los Alamitos	CA	90720	**800-272-6657**	714-821-8380	456-7
IEEE Computer Society 2001 L St NW Ste 700	Washington	DC	20036	**800-272-6657**	202-371-0101	48-19
IEEE Computer Society Press 10662 Los Vaqueros Cir PO Box 3014	Los Alamitos	CA	90720	**800-272-6657**	714-821-8380	634-9
IEEE Consumer Electronics Society (CES) 445 Hoes Ln	Piscataway	NJ	08854	**800-678-4333**	732-981-0060	48-19
IEEE Education Society (ES) IEEE Operations Ctr 445 Hoes Ln	Piscataway	NJ	08854	**800-678-4333**	732-981-0060	48-19
IEEE Electromagnetic Compatibility Society (EMC) IEEE Operations Ctr 445 Hoes Ln	Piscataway	NJ	08854	**800-678-4333**	732-981-0060	48-19
IEEE Electron Devices Society (EDS) IEEE Operations Ctr 445 Hoes Ln	Piscataway	NJ	08854	**800-678-4333**	732-981-0060	48-19
IEEE Engineering Management Society (EMS) IEEE Operations Ctr 445 Hoes Ln	Piscataway	NJ	08854	**800-678-4333**	732-981-0060	48-19
IEEE Geoscience & Remote Sensing Society (GRSS) IEEE Operations Ctr 445 Hoes Ln	Piscataway	NJ	08854	**800-678-4333**	732-562-5550	48-19
IEEE Industrial Electronics Society (IES) IEEE Operations Ctr 445 Hoes Ln	Piscataway	NJ	08854	**800-678-4333**	732-981-0060	48-19
IEEE Instrumentation & Measurement Society (IM) 445 Hoes Ln	Piscataway	NJ	08854	**800-327-6677**	732-562-3844	48-19
IEEE Magnetics Society 445 Hoes Ln PO Box 459	Piscataway	NJ	08855	**800-678-4333**	908-981-0060	48-19
IEEE Micro Magazine 10662 Los Vaqueros Cir PO Box 3014	Los Alamitos	CA	90720	**800-272-6657**	714-821-8380	456-7
IEEE Microwave Theory & Techniques Society (MTT-S) 5829 Bellanca Dr	Elkridge	MD	21075	**800-678-4333**	410-796-5866	48-19
IEEE Nuclear & Plasma Sciences Society (NPSS) 445 Hoes Ln	Piscataway	NJ	08854	**800-678-4333**	732-562-5501	48-19
IEEE Power Engineering Society (PES) IEEE Operations Ctr 445 Hoes Ln	Piscataway	NJ	08854	**800-678-4333**	732-562-3883	48-19
IEEE Product Safety Engineering Society IEEE Operations Ctr 445 Hoes Ln	Piscataway	NJ	08854	**800-678-4333**	732-981-0060	48-19
IEEE Reliability Society (RS) IEEE Operations Ctr 445 Hoes Ln	Piscataway	NJ	08854	**800-678-4333**	732-981-0060	48-19
IEEE Signal Processing Society IEEE Operations Ctr 445 Hoes Ln	Piscataway	NJ	08854	**800-678-4333**	732-981-0060	48-19
IEEE Society on Social Implications of Technology (SSIT) IEEE Operations Ctr 445 Hoes Ln	Piscataway	NJ	08854	**800-678-4333**	732-981-0060	48-19
IEEE Solid State Circuits Society (SSCS) 445 Hoes Ln	Piscataway	NJ	08854	**800-678-4333**	732-981-3400	48-19
IEEE Ultrasonics Ferroelectrics & Frequency Control Society IEEE Operations Ctr 445 Hoes Ln	Piscataway	NJ	08854	**800-678-4333**	732-981-0060	48-19
IEHA (International Executive Housekeepers Assn) 1001 Eastwind Dr Ste 301	Westerville	OH	43081	**800-200-6342**	614-895-7166	48-4
IEP Technologies LLC 400 Main St	Ashland	MA	01721	**855-793-8407**		665
IES (IEEE Industrial Electronics Society) IEEE Operations Ctr 445 Hoes Ln	Piscataway	NJ	08854	**800-678-4333**	732-981-0060	48-19
IeSmart Systems LLC 15200 E Hardy Rd	Houston	TX	77032	**866-437-6278**	281-447-6278	198
IEWC (Industrial Electric Wire & Cable Inc) 5001 S Towne Dr	New Berlin	WI	53151	**800-344-2323**	262-782-2323	248
IFA (International Franchise Assn) 1501 K St NW Ste 350	Washington	DC	20005	**800-543-1038**	202-628-8000	48-18
IFAI (Industrial Fabrics Assn International) 1801 County Rd 'B' W	Roseville	MN	55113	**800-225-4324**	651-222-2508	48-13
IFAW (International Fund for Animal Welfare) 290 Summer St	Yarmouth Port	MA	02675	**800-932-4329**	508-744-2000	47-3
IFCA International 3520 Fairlane Ave SW	Grandville	MI	49418	**800-347-1840**	616-531-1840	47-20
IFEBP (International Foundation of Employee Benefit Plans) 18700 W Bluemound Rd	Brookfield	WI	53045	**888-334-3327**	262-786-6700	262
IFIC (International Fidelity Insurance Co) 1 Newark Ctr 20th Fl	Newark	NJ	07102	**800-333-4167**	973-624-7200	391-5
IFIC (International Food Information Council Foundation) 1100 Connecticut Ave NW Ste 430	Washington	DC	20036	**888-723-3366**	202-296-6540	48-6
Ifocus Consulting Inc 100 39th St Ste 201	Astoria	OR	97103	**888-308-6192**	503-338-7443	198
Ifrah Financial Services Inc 17300 Chenal Pkwy Ste 150	Little Rock	AR	72223	**800-954-3724**	501-821-7733	253
IFS Financial Services Inc 250 Brownlow Ave Ste 1	Dartmouth	NS	B3B1W9	**800-565-1153**	902-481-6106	318
IFS North America Inc 300 Pk Blvd Ste 555	Chicago	IL	60143	**888-437-4968**		180-1
IFT (Institute of Food Technologists) 525 W Van Buren St Ste 1000	Chicago	IL	60607	**800-438-3663**	312-782-8424	48-6
IG Inc 720 S Sara Rd	Mustang	OK	73064	**800-654-8433**	405-376-9393	327
IGA Inc 8725 W Higgins Rd Ste 350	Chicago	IL	60631	**800-321-5442**	773-693-4520	345
Igenex 795 San Antonio Rd	Palo Alto	CA	94303	**800-832-3200**	650-424-1191	418
IGI (Information Gatekeepers Inc) 1340 Soldiers Field Rd Ste 2	Brighton	MA	02135	**800-323-1088**	617-782-5033	634-11
IGI (Insight Global Inc) 4170 Ashford Dunwoody Rd Ste 250	Atlanta	GA	30319	**888-336-7463**	404-257-7900	195
Igloo Products Corp 777 Igloo Rd	Katy	TX	77494	**866-509-3503**	713-584-6800	606
IGLTA (International Gay & Lesbian Travel Assn) 1201 NE 26th St Ste 103	Fort Lauderdale	FL	33305	**888-789-3090**	954-630-1637	47-23
IGM Financial Inc 447 Portage Ave 1 Canada Ctr *NYSE: IGM*	Winnipeg	MB	R3B3H5	**888-746-6344**		401
Ignify Inc 200 Pine Ave 4th Fl	Long Beach	CA	90802	**888-599-4332**	562-219-2000	179
Ignition Systems & Controls LP 6300 W Hwy 80	Midland	TX	79706	**800-777-5559**	432-697-6472	249
iGo Inc 17800 N Perimeter Dr Ste 200 *NASDAQ: IGOI*	Scottsdale	AZ	85255	**888-205-0093**	480-596-0061	178
I-Go Van & Storage 9820 S 142nd St	Omaha	NE	68138	**800-228-9276**	402-891-1222	518
iGov Technologies Inc 9211 Palm River Rd Ste 110	Tampa	FL	33619	**800-777-9375**	813-612-9470	228
IGS (Institute of General Semantics) 72-11 Austin St	Forest Hills	NY	11375	**800-346-1359**	212-729-7973	47-11

	Toll-Free	Phone	Class
IGS (Industrial Gasket & Shim Company Inc)			
200 Country Club Rd . . . . Meadow Lands PA 15347	**800-229-1447**	724-222-5800	327
IGSHPA (International Ground Source Heat Pump Assn)			
Oklahoma State University			
374 Cordell S . . . . Stillwater OK 74078	**800-626-4747**	405-744-5175	48-13
IGT (International Game Technology)			
9295 Prototype Dr . . . . Reno NV 89521	**800-522-4700**	775-448-7777	323
NYSE: IGT			
IHA (International Housewares Assn)			
6400 Shafer Ct Ste 650 . . . . Rosemont IL 60018	**800-752-1052**	847-292-4200	48-4
IHC (International Homes of Cedar Inc)			
PO Box 886 . . . . Woodinville WA 98072	**800-767-7674**	360-668-8511	105
iHealth Lab Inc			
719 N Shoreline Blvd . . . . Mountain View CA 94043	**855-816-7705**		740
iHeartMedia, Inc			
200 E Basse Rd . . . . San Antonio TX 78209	**800-829-6551**	210-822-2828	187
IHG (InterContinental Hotels Group)			
3 Ravinia Dr Ste 100 . . . . Atlanta GA 30346	**800-621-0555**	770-604-2000	379
IHI (Institute for Healthcare Improvement)			
20 University Rd 7th Fl . . . . Cambridge MA 02138	**866-787-0831**	617-301-4800	48-8
IHL Consulting Group			
1064 Cedarview Ln . . . . Franklin TN 37067	**888-445-6777**	615-591-2955	462
IHLIC (Investors Heritage Life Insurance Co)			
200 Capital Ave PO Box 717 . . . . Frankfort KY 40602	**800-422-2011**	502-223-2361	391-2
IHMM (Institute of Hazardous Materials Management)			
11900 Parklawn Dr Ste 450 . . . . Rockville MD 20852	**800-437-0137**	301-984-8969	47-12
IHOP Corp			
450 N Brand Blvd . . . . Glendale CA 91203	**866-444-5144**	818-240-6055	668
IHRIM (International Assn for Human Resource Information Management Inc)			
PO Box 1086 . . . . Burlington MA 01803	**800-804-3983**		48-12
IHRSA (International Health Racquet & Sportsclub Assn)			
70 Fargo St . . . . Boston MA 02210	**800-228-4772**	617-951-0055	47-22
IHS (International Hearing Society)			
16880 Middlebelt Rd Ste 4 . . . . Livonia MI 48154	**800-521-5247**	734-522-7200	47-17
IHS Energy Group			
15 Inverness Way E . . . . Englewood CO 80112	**800-447-2273**	303-736-3000	180-10
IHS Inc			
321 Inverness Dr S . . . . Englewood CO 80112	**800-525-7052**	303-790-0600	180-11
NYSE: IHS			
IIABA (Independent Insurance Agents & Brokers of America Inc)			
127 S Peyton St . . . . Alexandria VA 22314	**800-221-7917**	703-683-4422	48-9
IID (Imperial Irrigation District)			
PO Box 937 . . . . Imperial CA 92251	**800-303-7756**	760-482-9600	205
IIDA (International Interior Design Assn)			
222 Merchandise Mart Plz			
Ste 567 . . . . Chicago IL 60654	**888-799-4432**	312-467-1950	47-4
IIE (Institute of Industrial Engineers)			
3577 PkwyLn Ste 200 . . . . Norcross GA 30092	**800-494-0460***	770-449-0460	48-13
*Cust Svc			
IIG (Industrial Insulation Group LLC)			
2100 Line St . . . . Brunswick GA 31520	**800-334-7997**	303-978-2000	389
III (Insurance Information Institute Inc)			
110 William St . . . . New York NY 10038	**877-263-7995**	212-346-5500	48-9
IIMC (International Institute of Municipal Clerks)			
8331 Utica Ave Ste 200 . . . . . . Rancho Cucamonga CA 91730	**800-251-1639**	909-944-4162	48-7
IIS Group LLC			
1015 Virginia Dr			
Ste 1 W . . . . Fort Washington PA 19034	**855-443-5777**		177
IJO (Independent Jewelers Organization)			
136 Old Post Rd . . . . Southport CT 06890	**800-624-9252**		48-4
Ika-Works Inc			
2635 Northchase Pkwy SE . . . . Wilmington NC 28405	**800-733-3037**	910-452-7059	420
IKEA			
420 Alan Wood Rd . . . . Conshohocken PA 19428	**800-434-4532**	610-834-0180	322
Ikegami Electronics USA Inc			
37 Brook Ave . . . . Maywood NJ 07607	**800-368-9171**	201-368-9171	645
Ikonisys Inc			
5 Science Park . . . . New Haven CT 06511	**866-456-6832**	203-776-0791	740
Il Fornaio America Corp			
770 Tamalpais Dr Ste 400 . . . . Corte Madera CA 94925	**888-454-6246**	415-945-0500	668
ILA (Illinois Library Assn)			
33 W Grand Ave Ste 301 . . . . Chicago IL 60610	**877-565-1896**	312-644-1896	435
ILAA (International Lawyers in Alcoholics Anonymous)			
415-1080 Mainland St . . . . Vancouver BC V6B2T4	**888-685-2171**	604-685-2171	47-21
Ilan Systems			
1107 Fair Oaks Ave . . . . South Pasadena CA 91030	**800-678-3526**		182
ILC Dover Inc			
1 Moonwalker Rd . . . . Frederica DE 19946	**800-631-9567**	302-335-3911	575
ILC Resources			
3301 106th Cir . . . . Urbandale IA 50322	**800-247-2133**	515-243-8106	502-3
iLeads.com LLC			
567 San Nicolas Dr			
Ste 180 . . . . Newport Beach CA 92660	**877-245-3237**		226
Ilene Industries Inc			
301 Stanley Blvd . . . . Shelbyville TN 37160	**800-251-1602**	931-684-8731	327
Ilex Construction & Woodworking			
3801 Northampton St NW Ste 3 . . . . . . Washington DC 20015	**866-551-4539**	410-820-4393	683
Iliff School of Theology			
2201 S University Blvd . . . . Denver CO 80210	**800-678-3360**	303-744-1287	168-3
Ilikai Hotel & Suites			
1777 Ala Moana Blvd . . . . Honolulu HI 96815	**866-536-7973**	808-949-3811	379
iLinc Communications Inc			
2999 N 44th St Ste 650 . . . . Phoenix AZ 85018	**800-767-9054**	602-952-1200	178
Illinois			
Child Support Enforcement Div			
509 S Sixth St . . . . Springfield IL 62701	**800-447-4278**		339-14
Crime Victims Services Div			
100 W Randolf Rd 13th Fl . . . . Chicago IL 60601	**800-228-3368**	312-814-2581	339-14
Human Services Dept			
100 S Grand Ave E 3rd Fl . . . . Springfield IL 62762	**800-843-6154**	217-557-1601	339-14
Mental Health Div			
100 W Randolf St Ste 3-400 . . . . Chicago IL 60601	**800-252-2923**	312-814-2811	339-14
Revenue Dept			
101 W Jefferson St . . . . Springfield IL 62702	**800-732-8866**	217-782-3336	339-14
Secretary of State			
213 State Capitol . . . . Springfield IL 62756	**800-252-8980**	217-782-2201	339-14
Tourism Bureau			
100 W Randolph St Ste 3-400 . . . . Chicago IL 60601	**800-226-6632**	312-814-4732	339-14
Veterans Affairs Dept			
James R. Thompson Ctr 100 W Randolph			
Ste 5-570 . . . . Chicago IL 60601	**800-437-9824**	312-814-5391	339-14
Workers' Compensation Commission			
100 W Randolph St 8th Fl . . . . Chicago IL 60601	**866-352-3033**	312-814-6611	339-14
Illinois Auto Electric Co			
700 Enterprise St . . . . Aurora IL 60504	**800-683-8484**	630-862-3300	385
Illinois Blueprint Corp			
800 SW Jefferson Ave . . . . Peoria IL 61605	**800-747-7070**	309-676-1300	242
Illinois College			
1101 W College Ave . . . . Jacksonville IL 62650	**866-464-5265***	217-245-3030	167
*Admissions			
Illinois Fair Plan Association			
130 East Randolph PO Box 81469 . . . . Chicago IL 60601	**800-972-4480**	312-861-0385	688
Illinois Glove Co			
3701 Commercial Ave . . . . Northbrook IL 60062	**800-342-5458**	847-291-1700	154-7
Illinois Health Care Association			
1029 S Fourth St . . . . Springfield IL 62703	**800-252-8988**	217-528-6455	532
Illinois Institute of Art			
Chicago			
350 N Orleans St Ste 136-L . . . . Chicago IL 60654	**800-351-3450**	312-280-3500	163
Schaumburg			
1000 N Plz Dr . . . . Schaumburg IL 60173	**800-314-3450**	847-619-3450	163
Illinois Institute of Technology			
10 W 33rd St . . . . Chicago IL 60616	**800-448-2329**	312-567-3025	167
Illinois International Port District			
3600 E 95th St . . . . Chicago IL 60617	**800-843-7678**	773-646-4400	617
Illinois Library Assn (ILA)			
33 W Grand Ave Ste 301 . . . . Chicago IL 60610	**877-565-1896**	312-644-1896	435
Illinois Lottery			
101 W Jefferson St . . . . Springfield IL 62702	**800-252-1775**	217-524-6435	451
Illinois Mutual Life Insurance Co			
300 SW Adams St . . . . Peoria IL 61634	**800-380-6688**	309-674-8255	391-2
Illinois National Bank			
322 E Capitol . . . . Springfield IL 62701	**877-771-2316**	217-747-5500	69
Illinois Nurses Assn (INA)			
105 W Adams St Ste 2101 . . . . Chicago IL 60603	**800-262-2500**	312-419-2900	532
Illinois Rural Electric Co-op			
2 S Main St . . . . Winchester IL 62694	**800-468-4732**	217-742-3128	247
Illinois State Bar Assn			
424 S Second St . . . . Springfield IL 62701	**800-252-8908**	217-525-1760	71
Illinois State Dental Society			
1010 S Second St . . . . Springfield IL 62704	**888-286-2447**	217-525-1406	229
Illinois State Library			
300 S Second St . . . . Springfield IL 62701	**800-665-5576**	217-782-2994	434-5
Illinois State Medical Inter-Insurance Exchange (ISMIE)			
20 N Michigan Ave Ste 700 . . . . Chicago IL 60602	**800-782-4767**	312-782-2749	391-5
Illinois State Medical Society			
20 N Michigan Ave Ste 700 . . . . Chicago IL 60602	**800-782-4767**	312-782-1654	473
Illinois State Military Museum			
1301 N MacArthur Blvd . . . . Springfield IL 62702	**800-732-8868**	217-761-3910	519
Illinois State University			
North and School Streets			
Hovey Hall 201 . . . . Normal IL 61790	**800-366-2478***	309-438-2111	167
*Admissions			
Illinois Student Assistance Commission			
1755 Lake Cook Rd . . . . Deerfield IL 60015	**800-899-4722**	847-948-8500	723
Illinois Symphony Orchestera			
524 E Capitol Ave . . . . Springfield IL 62701	**800-401-7222**	217-522-2838	572-3
Illinois Veterans Home-Anna			
792 N Main St . . . . Anna IL 62906	**888-261-3336**	618-833-6302	791
Illinois Wesleyan University			
1312 Pk St . . . . Bloomington IL 61701	**800-332-2498***	309-556-3031	167
*Admissions			
Illinois Wholesale Cash Register Inc			
2790 Pinnacle Dr . . . . Elgin IL 60124	**800-544-5493**	847-310-4200	111
Illumina Inc			
9885 Towne Centre Dr . . . . San Diego CA 92121	**800-809-4566**	858-202-4500	419
NASDAQ: ILMN			
ILMO Products Company Inc			
7 Eastgate Dr . . . . Jacksonville IL 62650	**888-243-9353**	217-245-2183	358
iLookabout Corp			
383 Richmond St Ste 408 . . . . London ON N6A3C4	**866-963-2015**	519-963-2015	179
ILS (International Launch Services)			
1875 Explorer St Ste 700 . . . . Reston VA 20190	**800-852-4980**	571-633-7400	503
ILSCO			
4730 Madison Rd . . . . Cincinnati OH 45227	**800-776-9775***	513-533-6200	813
*Sales			
ILX Lightwave Corp			
31950 E Frontage Rd . . . . Bozeman MT 59715	**800-459-9459**	406-586-1244	250
IM (IEEE Instrumentation & Measurement Society)			
445 Hoes Ln . . . . Piscataway NJ 08854	**800-327-6677**	732-562-3844	48-19
IMA (Institute of Management Accountants Inc)			
10 Paragon Dr Ste 1 . . . . Montvale NJ 07645	**800-638-4427**	201-573-9000	48-1
IMA (Interchurch Medical Assistance Inc)			
500 Main St PO Box 429 . . . . New Windsor MD 21776	**877-241-7952**	410-635-8720	47-5
Image API LLC			
2002 Old St Augustine Rd			
Bldg D . . . . Tallahassee FL 32301	**877-560-4274**	850-222-1400	179
Image Iv Systems Inc			
512 S Varney St . . . . Burbank CA 91502	**800-473-5424**	818-841-0756	366
Image Labs International			
PO Box 1545 . . . . Belgrade MT 59714	**800-785-5995**	406-585-7225	180-8
Image One Corp			
13201 Capital Ave . . . . Oak Park MI 48237	**800-799-5377**	248-414-9955	627
Image Sport Inc			
1115 SE Westbrooke Dr . . . . Waukee IA 50263	**800-919-0520**	515-987-7699	685
Image Works			
PO Box 443 . . . . Woodstock NY 12498	**800-475-8801**	845-679-8500	592
imageMEDIA Inc			
425 E Spruce . . . . St Tarpon Springs FL 34689	**866-885-4468**	727-772-8889	626
ImageWorks			
250 Clearbrook Rd . . . . Elmsford NY 10523	**800-592-6666**	914-592-6100	382
Imagine Advertising & Publishing Inc			
6141 Crooked Creek Rd . . . . Norcross GA 30092	**866-832-3214**	770-734-0966	393
Imagine GPS Inc			
6847 S Ea Ste 104 . . . . Las Vegas NV 89119	**866-477-2489**	702-990-5600	645
Imaginet Resources Corp			
233 Portage Ave . . . . Winnipeg MB R3B2A7	**800-989-6022**	204-989-6022	179

Name / Address	City	State	Zip	Toll-Free	Phone	Class
Imaging Business Machines LLC 2750 Crestwood Blvd	Birmingham	AL	35210	**877-627-8325**	205-439-7100	110
Imaging Healthcare Specialists Medical Group Inc 6256 Greenwich Dr Ste 150	San Diego	CA	92122	**866-558-4320**		415
Imaging Supplies Company Inc 804 Woodland Ave	Sanford	NC	27330	**800-518-1152**	919-776-1152	588
iMakeNews Inc 200 Fifth Ave	Waltham	MA	02451	**866-964-6397**	781-890-4700	182
I-many Inc 1735 Market St 37th Fl	Philadelphia	PA	19103	**877-774-2451**	215-344-1900	180-1
Imation Corp 1 Imation Pl *NYSE: IMN*	Oakdale	MN	55128	**888-466-3456**	651-704-4000	656
IMBA (International Mountain Bicycling Assn) 4888 Pearl E Cir Ste 200E	Boulder	CO	80301	**888-442-4622**	303-545-9011	47-23
IMC (InterAmerican Motor Corp) 8901 Canoga Ave	Canoga Park	CA	91304	**800-874-8925**	818-678-1200	60
IMC (International Medical Corps) 1919 Santa Monica Blvd Ste 400	Santa Monica	CA	90404	**800-481-4462**	310-826-7800	47-5
IMC Networks Corp 19772 Pauling	Foothill Ranch	CA	92610	**800-624-1070**	949-465-3000	178
IMC USA (Institute of Management Consultants USA Inc) 2025 M St NW Ste 800	Washington	DC	20036	**800-221-2557**	202-367-1134	48-12
IMCA (Investment Management Consultants Assn) 5619 DTC Pkwy Ste 500	Greenwood Village	CO	80111	**800-250-9083**	303-770-3377	48-2
IMCOR-Interstate Mechanical Corp 1841 E Washington St	Phoenix	AZ	85034	**800-628-0211**	602-257-1319	191-10
IMCU (Indiana Members Credit Union) 7110 W Tenth St	Indianapolis	IN	46214	**800-556-9268**	317-248-8556	221
IME (Institute of Makers of Explosives) 1120 19th St NW Ste 310	Washington	DC	20036	**800-461-8841**	202-429-9280	48-13
Imecom Group 8 Governor Wentworth Hwy	Wolfeboro	NH	03894	**800-329-9099**	603-569-0600	180-7
Imedex Inc 4325 Alexander Dr	Alpharetta	GA	30022	**800-243-6969**	770-751-7332	798
iMemories 9181 E Bell Rd	Scottsdale	AZ	85260	**800-845-7986**		587
Imerys USA Inc 100 Mansell Ct E Ste 300	Roswell	GA	30076	**800-843-3222**	770-645-3300	502-2
IMETCO (Innovative Metals Company Inc) 4648 S Old Peachtree Rd	Norcross	GA	30084	**800-646-3826**	770-908-1030	45
iMethods LLC 10748 Deerwood Park Blvd Ste 150	Jacksonville	FL	32256	**888-306-2261**		198
Imex Veterinary Inc 1001 Mckesson Dr	Longview	TX	75604	**800-828-4639**	903-295-2196	792
IMG (International Motor Coach Group Inc) 8695 College Blvd Ste 260	Overland Park	KS	66210	**888-447-3466**	913-906-0111	48-21
Imh Financial Corp 7001 N Scottsdale Rd Ste 2050	Scottsdale	AZ	85253	**800-510-6445**	480-840-8400	218
IMI (International Masonry Institute) 17101 Science Dr	Bowie	MD	20715	**800-803-0295**		48-3
IMI Cornelius Inc 101 Broadway St W	Osseo	MN	55369	**800-238-3600**	763-488-8200	662
IMI Data Search Inc 275 E Hillcrest Dr Ste 102	Thousand Oaks	CA	91360	**800-860-7779**	805-495-1149	632
I-Minerals Inc 880 - 580 Hornby St	Vancouver	BC	V6C3B6	**877-303-6573**	604-303-6573	502-2
IMLA (International Municipal Lawyers Assn) 7910 Woodmont Ave Ste 1440	Bethesda	MD	20814	**800-942-7732**	202-466-5424	48-10
Immaculata University 1145 King Rd	Immaculata	PA	19345	**877-428-6329**	610-647-4400	167
Immedia Inc 3311 Broadway St NE	Minneapolis	MN	55413	**866-832-2734**	612-524-3400	626
Immediate Mailing Services Inc 245 Commerce Blvd	Liverpool	NY	13088	**800-466-4189**		5
Immediatek Inc(NDA) 3301 Airport Fwy Ste 200	Bedford	TX	76021	**888-661-6565**		226
Immtech Pharmaceuticals 1 N End Ave	New York	NY	10282	**877-898-8038**	212-791-2911	582
ImmucorGamma Inc 3130 Gateway Dr PO Box 5625 *NASDAQ: BLUD* ■ *Cust Svc	Norcross	GA	30091	**800-829-2553***	770-441-2051	233
Immune Deficiency Foundation (IDF) 40 W Chesapeake Ave Ste 308	Towson	MD	21204	**800-296-4433**	410-321-6647	47-17
Immuno Concepts NA Ltd 9825 Goethe Rd Ste 350	Sacramento	CA	95827	**800-251-5115**	916-363-2649	740
ImmunoDiagnostics Inc 1 Presidential Way Ste 104	Woburn	MA	01801	**800-573-1700**	781-938-6300	233
Immunomedics Inc 300 American Rd *NASDAQ: IMMU*	Morris Plains	NJ	07950	**800-327-7211**	973-605-8200	84
Immuno-Mycologics Inc (IMMY) 2700 Technology Pl	Norman	OK	73071	**800-654-3639**	405-360-4669	233
Immunovision Inc 1820 Ford Ave	Springdale	AR	72764	**800-541-0960**	479-751-7005	233
IMMVAC Inc 6080 Bass Ln	Columbia	MO	65201	**800-944-7563**	573-443-5363	581
IMMY (Immuno-Mycologics Inc) 2700 Technology Pl	Norman	OK	73071	**800-654-3639**	405-360-4669	233
Imo Pump 1710 Airport Rd	Monroe	NC	28110	**888-478-6996**	704-289-6511	638
iMomentous 20 Gibraltar Rd Ste 109	Horsham	PA	19044	**888-985-7755**		198
iMortgage Services Inc 2570 Boyce Plz Rd Boyce Plz Iii	Pittsburgh	PA	15241	**888-575-8555**	412-220-7330	216
Impac Mortgage Holdings Inc 19500 Jamboree Rd *NYSE: IMH*	Irvine	CA	92612	**800-597-4101**	949-475-3600	652
Impact Drug & Alcohol Treatment Ctr 1680 N Fair Oaks Ave PO Box 93607	Pasadena	CA	91103	**866-734-4200**	626-798-0884	724
Impact Guns 2710 South 1900 West	Ogden	UT	84401	**888-505-3086**	801-393-2474	681
Impact Label Corp 3434 S Burdick St	Kalamazoo	MI	49001	**800-820-0362**	269-381-4280	413
Impact Products LLC 2840 Centennial Rd *Cust Svc	Toledo	OH	43617	**800-333-1541***	419-841-2891	150
Impact Seven Inc 147 Lk Almena Dr	Almena	WI	54805	**800-685-9353**	715-357-3334	402
Impatica Inc 2430 Don Reid Dr Ste 200	Ottawa	ON	K1H1E1	**800-548-3475**	613-736-9982	227
Impax Laboratories Inc 30831 Hun2od Ave *NASDAQ: IPXL*	Hayward	CA	94544	**877-994-6729**	510-240-6450	583
Imperial Bedding Co 720 11th St PO Box 5347	Huntington	WV	25703	**800-529-3321**	304-529-3321	470
Imperial Graphics Inc 3100 Walkent Dr NW	Grand Rapids	MI	49544	**800-777-2591**		109
Imperial Industries Inc 505 Industrial Pk Ave	Rothschild	WI	54474	**800-558-2945**	715-359-0200	104
Imperial Irrigation District (IID) PO Box 937	Imperial	CA	92251	**800-303-7756**	760-482-9600	205
Imperial Manufacturing Group Inc 40 Industrial Park St	Richibucto	NB	E4W4A4	**800-561-3100**	506-523-9117	609
Imperial of Waikiki 205 Lewers St	Honolulu	HI	96815	**800-347-2582**	808-923-1827	379
Imperial Oil Resources Ltd 237 Fourth Ave SW PO Box 2480 Stn M	Calgary	AB	T2P3M9	**800-567-3776**		579
Imperial PFS (UPAC) 8245 Nieman Rd	Lenexa	KS	66214	**800-877-7848**	913-894-6150	218
Imperial Pools Inc 33 Wade Rd	Latham	NY	12110	**800-444-9977**	518-786-1200	726
Imperial Theatre 249 W 45th St	New York	NY	10036	**800-447-7400**	212-239-6200	744
Imperial Trading Co Inc 701 Edwards Ave *Cust Svc	Elmwood	LA	70123	**800-775-4504***	504-733-1400	298-8
Imperial Woodworks Inc PO Box 7835 PO Box 7835	Waco	TX	76714	**800-234-6624**		320-3
Implant Sciences Corp 500 Research Dr *OTC: IMSC*	Wilmington	MA	01887	**877-732-7333**	978-752-1700	475
Implement Sales Company LLC 1574 Stone Ridge Dr	Stone Mountain	GA	30083	**800-955-9592**	770-908-9439	276
Impo International Inc PO Box 639	Santa Maria	CA	93456	**800-367-4676**		302
IMPRES Technology Solutions Inc 10330 Pioneer Blvd Ste 280	Santa Fe Springs	CA	90670	**800-652-9686**	562-298-4030	198
Imprimis Group Inc 4835 Lyndon B Johnson Fwy	Dallas	TX	75244	**888-772-9682**	972-419-1700	344
Improv Asylum 216 Hanover St	Boston	MA	02113	**888-396-6887**	617-263-6887	521
Improve Group Inc, The 1385 Mendota Heights Rd Ste 200b	Mendota Heights	MN	55120	**877-467-7847**		198
Improved Construction Methods 1040 N Redmond Rd	Jacksonville	AR	72076	**877-494-5793**		358
Impulse Technologies Ltd 920 Gana Crt	Mississauga	ON	L5S1Z4	**800-667-5475**	905-564-9266	688
IMS Inc 340 Progress Dr *General	Manchester	CT	06040	**800-264-9837***	860-649-4415	248
IMSA (International Municipal Signal Assn) 165 E Union St PO Box 539	Newark	NY	14513	**800-723-4672**	315-331-2182	48-7
IMT (Iowa Mold Tooling Co Inc) 500 W US Hwy 18	Garner	IA	50438	**800-247-5958**	641-923-3711	469
IMT Group, The PO Box 1336	Des Moines	IA	50266	**800-274-3531**		391-4
Imtech Graphics Inc 545 Dell Rd	Carlstadt	NJ	07072	**800-468-3240**		779
IMVU Inc PO Box 390012	Mountain View	CA	94039	**866-761-0975**	650-321-8334	387
In Defense of Animals (IDA) 3010 Kerner Blvd	San Rafael	CA	94901	**800-705-0425**	415-448-0048	47-3
In The Swim Inc 320 Industrial Dr	West Chicago	IL	60185	**800-288-7946**	630-876-0040	709
In Touch Business Consultants 11370 66th St 132	Largo	FL	33773	**877-676-5492**		462
INA (Idaho Nurses Assn) 1850 E Southern Ave Ste 1	Tempe	AZ	85224	**888-721-8904**		532
INA (Illinois Nurses Assn) 105 W Adams St Ste 2101	Chicago	IL	60603	**800-262-2500**	312-419-2900	532
InBios International Inc 562 First Ave S Ste 600	Seattle	WA	98104	**866-462-4671**	206-344-5821	465
Inc Magazine 7 World Trade Ctr	New York	NY	10007	**800-234-0999**	212-389-5377	456-5
Inca Engineers Inc 400 112th Ave NE Ste 400	Bellevue	WA	98004	**800-825-4622**	425-635-1000	196
Incentive Publications Inc 2400 Crestmoor Dr *Mktg	Nashville	TN	37215	**800-967-5325***	615-385-2934	245
Incepture Inc 8381 Dix Ellis Trail Ste 105	Jacksonville	FL	32225	**877-347-7151**		262
Incline Village/Crystal Bay Visitors Bureau 969 Tahoe Blvd	Incline Village	NV	89451	**800-468-2463**	775-832-1606	208
InComm Conferencing Inc 208 Harristown Rd Ste 101	Glen Rock	NJ	07452	**877-804-2062**		387
Incontact Inc 7730 S Union Pk Ave Ste 500 *NASDAQ: SAAS*	Salt Lake City	UT	84047	**800-363-6177**	801-320-3200	180-11
Incontrol Technology Inc 1651 e main st	El Cajon	CA	92021	**888-508-1288**	619-270-1260	227
InCycle Software Inc 545 Promenade du Centropolis Ste 220	Laval	QC	H7T0A3	**800-565-0510**	450-682-4777	182
Indaco Metal 3 American Way	Shawnee	OK	74804	**877-750-5614**	877-300-7334	105

Name / Address	City	State	Zip	Toll-Free	Phone	Class
Indeck Power Equipment Co						
1111 Willis Ave	Wheeling	IL	60090	800-446-3325	847-541-8300	385
Indelco Plastics Corp						
6530 Cambridge St	Minneapolis	MN	55426	800-486-6456	952-925-5075	604-2
Indel-Davis Inc						
4401 S Jackson Ave	Tulsa	OK	74107	800-331-6300	918-587-2151	538
Independant Insurance Services In						
3956 N Pine St	Davenport	IA	52806	800-373-1562	563-383-5555	390
Independence Blue Cross						
1901 Market St	Philadelphia	PA	19103	800-275-2583		391-3
Independence Community College						
1057 W College Ave						
PO Box 708	Independence	KS	67301	800-842-6063	620-331-4100	161
Independence Excavating Inc						
5720 Schaaf Rd	Independence	OH	44131	800-524-3478	216-524-1700	191-5
Independent Agent Magazine						
127 S Peyton St	Alexandria	VA	22314	800-221-7917		456-5
Independent Bank Corp						
230 W Main St	Ionia	MI	48846	888-300-3193	616-527-2400	360-2
NASDAQ: IBCP						
Independent Charities of America (ICA)						
1100 Larkspur Landing Cir						
Ste 340	Larkspur	CA	94939	800-477-0733	415-925-2600	47-5
Independent Chemical Corp						
79-51 Cooper Ave	Glendale	NY	11385	800-892-2578	718-894-0700	145
Independent Community Bankers of America (ICBA)						
1615 L St NW Ste 900	Washington	DC	20036	800-422-8439	202-659-8111	48-2
Independent Electric Supply Inc						
1370 Bayport Ave	San Carlos	CA	94070	855-437-4968	650-594-9440	248
Independent Health						
511 Farber Lakes Dr	Buffalo	NY	14221	800-247-1466	716-631-3001	391-3
Independent Ink Inc						
13700 Gramercy Pl	Gardena	CA	90249	800-446-5538	310-523-4657	388
Independent Institute						
100 Swan Way	Oakland	CA	94621	800-927-8733	510-632-1366	631
Independent Insurance Agents & Brokers of America Inc (IIABA)						
127 S Peyton St	Alexandria	VA	22314	800-221-7917	703-683-4422	48-9
Independent Jewelers Organization (IJO)						
136 Old Post Rd	Southport	CT	06890	800-624-9252		48-4
Independent Order of Foresters (IOF)						
789 Don Mills Rd	Toronto	ON	M3C1T9	800-828-1540	416-429-3000	47-5
Independent Order of Odd Fellows						
422 N Trade St	Winston-Salem	NC	27101	800-235-8358	336-725-5955	47-15
Independent Petroleum Assn of America (IPAA)						
1201 15th St NW Ste 300	Washington	DC	20005	800-433-2851	202-857-4722	47-12
Independent Protection Company Inc						
1607 S Main St	Goshen	IN	46526	800-860-8388	574-533-4116	813
Independent Publishers Group						
814 N Franklin St	Chicago	IL	60610	800-888-4741*	312-337-0747	94
*Orders						
Independent Publishing Co						
1000 Williamston Rd	Anderson	SC	29621	800-859-6397	864-224-4321	634-8
Independent Record						
317 Cruse Ave	Helena	MT	59601	800-523-2272	406-447-4000	531-2
Independent Rental Inc						
2020 S Cushman St	Fairbanks	AK	99701	888-456-6595		266-2
Independent Sector						
1602 L St NW Ste 900	Washington	DC	20036	888-737-9477	202-467-6100	47-5
Independent Television Service (ITVS)						
651 Brannan St Ste 410	San Francisco	CA	94107	800-621-6196	415-356-8383	739
Independent, The						
2250 First St	Livermore	CA	94550	877-952-3588	925-447-8700	531-4
Indera Mills Co						
350 W Maple St PO Box 309	Yadkinville	NC	27055	800-334-8605	336-679-4440	154-17
Index Fresh Inc						
18184 Slover Ave	Bloomington	CA	92316	800-352-6931	909-877-0999	11-1
Index Funds Advisors Inc						
19200 Von Karman Ave Ste 150	Irvine	CA	92612	888-643-3133	949-502-0050	688
Consulate General						
540 Arguello Blvd	San Francisco	CA	94118	866-978-0055	415-668-0662	259
India Tourist Office						
3550 Wilshire Blvd Ste 204	Los Angeles	CA	90010	800-425-1414*	213-380-8855	773
*General						
Indian Arts & Crafts Board						
Dept of the Interior 1849 C St NW						
MS 2528-MIB	Washington	DC	20240	888-278-3253	202-208-3773	340-18
Indian Bible College						
2918 N Aris Ave	Flagstaff	AZ	86004	866-503-7789	928-774-3890	167
Indian Capital Technology Ctr						
2403 N 41st St E	Muskogee	OK	74403	800-757-0877	918-687-6383	798
Indian Creek Fabricators						
1350 Commerce Pk Dr	Tipp City	OH	45371	877-769-5880	937-667-5818	755
Indian Electric Co-op Inc						
2506 E Hwy 64	Cleveland	OK	74020	800-482-2750	918-358-2514	247
Indian Harvest Specialtifoods Inc						
1012 Paul Bunyan Dr SE	Bemidji	MN	56601	800-346-7032*		297-23
*Orders						
Indian Head Industries Inc						
8530 Cliff Cameron Dr	Charlotte	NC	28269	800-527-1534	704-547-7411	59
Indian Hills Community College						
525 Grandview Ave	Ottumwa	IA	52501	800-726-2585	641-683-5111	161
Indian Pueblo Cultural Ctr						
2401 12th St NW	Albuquerque	NM	87104	866-855-7902	505-843-7270	519
Indian River County Chamber of Commerce						
1216 21st St	Vero Beach	FL	32960	877-646-6889	772-567-3491	138
Indian River Estates						
2250 Indian Creek Blvd W	Vero Beach	FL	32966	800-544-0277*	772-562-7400	670
*Mktg						
Indian River Lifesaving Station Museum						
25039 Costal Hwy	Rehoboth Beach	DE	19971	877-987-2757	302-227-6991	519
Indian River State College (IRSC)						
3209 Virginia Ave	Fort Pierce	FL	34981	866-792-4772	772-462-4772	161
Indian River Transport Co						
2580 Executive Rd	Winter Haven	FL	33884	800-877-2430	863-324-2430	778
Indian Springs Resort & Spa						
1712 Lincoln Ave	Calistoga	CA	94515	800-877-3623	707-942-4913	667
Indian Springs School						
190 Woodward Dr	Pelham	AL	35124	888-843-9477*	205-988-3350	621
*General						
Indian Summer Carpet Mills Inc						
601 Callahan Rd PO Box 3577	Dalton	GA	30719	800-824-4010	706-277-6277	130
Indian Temple Mound Museum						
107 Miracle Strip Pkwy SW						
	Fort Walton Beach	FL	32548	866-847-1301	850-833-9500	519
Indian Trails Inc						
109 E Comstock St	Owosso	MI	48867	800-292-3831	989-725-5105	106
Indian Valley Industries Inc						
PO Box 810	Johnson City	NY	13790	800-659-5111	607-729-5111	66
Indian Wells Resort Hotel						
76-661 Hwy 111	Indian Wells	CA	92210	800-248-3220	760-345-6466	667
Indiana						
Child Support Bureau						
402 W Washington St	Indianapolis	IN	46204	800-840-8757	317-232-2350	339-15
Consumer Protection Div						
402 W Washington St 5th Fl.	Indianapolis	IN	46204	800-382-5516	317-232-6330	339-15
Disability Aging & Rehabilitative Services Div						
402 W Washington St						
Rm W451	Indianapolis	IN	46204	800-545-7763	317-232-1147	339-15
Environmental Management Dept						
100 N Senate Ave Rm 1301	Indianapolis	IN	46204	800-451-6027	317-232-8611	339-15
Family & Social Services Admin						
402 W Washington St Rm W461						
PO Box 7083	Indianapolis	IN	46207	800-545-7763		339-15
General Assembly						
State House						
200 W Washington St.	Indianapolis	IN	46204	800-382-9842	317-232-9600	339-15
Insurance Dept						
311 W Washington St						
Ste 300	Indianapolis	IN	46204	800-622-4461*	317-232-2385	339-15
*Cust Svc						
State Government Information						
402 W Washington St						
Rm W160A	Indianapolis	IN	46204	800-457-8283	317-233-0800	339-15
State Parks & Reservoirs Div						
402 W Washington St						
Rm W298	Indianapolis	IN	46204	800-622-4931	317-232-4124	339-15
Tourism Development Office						
1 N Capitol Ave Ste 100	Indianapolis	IN	46204	800-457-8283	317-232-8860	339-15
Victims Services Div						
101 W Washington St						
Ste 1170 East Tower	Indianapolis	IN	46204	800-353-1484	317-232-1233	339-15
Indiana Assn of Realtors						
7301 N Shadeland Ave Ste A	Indianapolis	IN	46250	800-284-0084	317-842-0890	654
Indiana Association of School Principals Inc						
11025 E 25th St	Indianapolis	IN	46229	800-285-2188	317-891-9900	532
Indiana County						
350 N Fourth St	Indiana	PA	15701	888-559-6355	724-465-3805	338
Indiana County Tourist Bureau						
2334 Oakland Ave Ste 68	Indiana	PA	15701	877-746-3426	724-463-7505	208
Indiana Credit Union League						
5975 Castle Creek Parkway N						
Ste 300	Indianapolis	IN	46250	800-285-5300	317-594-5300	221
Indiana Democratic Party						
115 W Washington St						
Ste 1165	Indianapolis	IN	46204	800-223-3387	317-231-7100	615-1
Indiana Dental Assn						
401 W Michigan St	Indianapolis	IN	46202	800-562-5646	317-634-2610	229
Indiana Dimension Inc						
1621 W Market St	Logansport	IN	46947	888-875-4434		681
Indiana Donor Network						
3760 Guion Rd	Indianapolis	IN	46222	888-275-4676	317-685-0389	544
Indiana Dunes the Casual Coast						
1215 N State Rd 49	Porter	IN	46304	800-283-8687	219-926-2255	208
Indiana Farm Bureau Insurance Co						
225 SE St PO Box 1250	Indianapolis	IN	46206	800-723-3276	317-692-7200	391-2
Indiana Farmers Mutual Insurance Co						
10 W 106th St	Indianapolis	IN	46290	800-666-6460	317-846-4211	391-4
Indiana Fever						
Conseco Fieldhouse						
125 S Pennsylvania St	Indianapolis	IN	46204	877-275-9007	317-917-2500	712-2
Indiana Furniture						
1224 Mill St	Jasper	IN	47546	800-422-5727	812-482-5727	320-1
Indiana Lottery						
201 S Capitol Ave Ste 1100	Indianapolis	IN	46225	800-955-6886	317-264-4800	339-15
Indiana Members Credit Union (IMCU)						
7110 W Tenth St	Indianapolis	IN	46214	800-556-9268	317-248-8556	221
Indiana Pharmacists Alliance						
729 N Pennsylvania St	Indianapolis	IN	46204	800-516-0313	317-634-4968	584
Indiana Port Commission						
150 W Market St Ste 100	Indianapolis	IN	46204	800-232-7678	317-232-9200	617
Indiana Printing & Publishing Co						
899 Water St PO Box 10	Indiana	PA	15701	800-262-3077	724-465-5555	634-8
Indiana Rail Road Co, The						
101 W Ohio St Ste 1600	Indianapolis	IN	46204	888-596-2121	317-262-5140	647
Indiana Ribbon Inc						
106 N Second St	Wolcott	IN	47995	800-531-3100	219-279-2112	547
Indiana State Bar Assn						
1 Indiana Sq Ste 530	Indianapolis	IN	46204	800-266-2581	317-639-5465	71
Indiana State Medical Assn						
322 Canal Walk	Indianapolis	IN	46202	800-257-4762	317-261-2060	473
Indiana State University						
200 N Seventh St	Terre Haute	IN	47809	800-468-6478		167
Indiana Students Assistance Commission						
150 W Market St Ste 500	Indianapolis	IN	46204	888-528-4719	317-232-2350	723
Indiana Tech						
1600 E Washington Blvd	Fort Wayne	IN	46803	800-937-2448	260-422-5561	167
Indiana Trust & Investment Management Co						
4045 Edison Lakes Pkwy						
Ste 100	Mishawaka	IN	46545	800-362-7905	574-271-0374	794
Indiana University						
East						
2325 Chester Blvd	Richmond	IN	47374	800-959-3278	765-973-8208	167
Kokomo						
2300 S Washington St PO Box 9003	Kokomo	IN	46904	888-875-4485	765-455-9217	167
Northwest 3400 Broadway	Gary	IN	46408	888-968-7486	219-980-6500	167
South Bend						
1700 Mishawaka Ave						
PO Box 7111	South Bend	IN	46634	877-462-4872	574-520-4870	167

Company / Address	City	State	ZIP	Toll-Free	Phone	Class
Southeast						
4201 Grant Line Rd	New Albany	IN	47150	**800-852-8835**	812-941-2212	167
Indiana University Cancer Ctr Bone Marrow & Stem Cell Transplant Team						
550 N University Blvd	Indianapolis	IN	46202	**888-600-4822**	317-948-6997	767
Indiana University Hospital						
550 N University Blvd	Indianapolis	IN	46202	**800-248-1199**	317-274-5000	374-3
Indiana University of Pennsylvania						
1011 S Dr Sutton Hall Ste 117	Indiana	PA	15705	**800-442-6830**	724-357-2230	167
Indiana University of Pennsylvania Stapleton Library						
1011 S Dr	Indiana	PA	15705	**888-342-2383**	724-357-2340	434-6
Indiana University Press						
601 N Morton St	Bloomington	IN	47404	**800-842-6796**	812-855-8817	634-4
Indiana University-Purdue University						
Fort Wayne						
2101 E Coliseum Blvd	Fort Wayne	IN	46805	**800-324-4739**	260-481-6100	167
Indiana University-Purdue University Indianapolis						
Library						
755 W Michigan St	Indianapolis	IN	46202	**888-422-0499**	317-274-0462	434-6
Indiana Veterinary Medical Assn						
201 S Capitol Ave Ste 405	Indianapolis	IN	46225	**800-270-0747**	317-974-0888	793
Indiana Wesleyan University						
4201 S Washington St	Marion	IN	46953	**800-332-6901**	765-677-2138	167
Indiana Workforce Development Dept						
10 N Senate Ave	Indianapolis	IN	46204	**800-891-6499**	317-232-7670	261
Indianapolis Business Journal						
41 E Washington St Ste 200	Indianapolis	IN	46204	**800-428-7081**	317-634-6200	456-5
Indianapolis Colts						
7001 W 56th St	Indianapolis	IN	46254	**800-805-2658**	317-297-2658	713-3
Indianapolis Convention & Visitors Assn						
200 S Capitol Ave Ste 300	Indianapolis	IN	46225	**800-862-6912**	317-262-3000	208
Indianapolis Fruit Company Inc						
4501 Massachusetts Ave	Indianapolis	IN	46218	**800-377-2425**	317-546-2425	298-7
Indianapolis Monthly Magazine						
40 Monument Cir Ste 100	Indianapolis	IN	46204	**888-403-9005***	317-237-9288	456-22
*Circ						
Indianapolis Star						
307 N Pennsylvania St	Indianapolis	IN	46204	**800-669-7827**	317-444-4000	531-2
Indianapolis Symphony Orchestra						
45 Monument Cir	Indianapolis	IN	46204	**800-366-8457**	317-262-1100	572-3
Indianhead Federated Library System						
1538 Truax Blvd	Eau Claire	WI	54703	**800-321-5427**	715-839-5082	434-3
Indianhead Mountain Resort						
500 Indianhead Rd	Wakefield	MI	49968	**800-346-3426**		667
Indigo Books & Music Inc						
468 King St W Ste 500	Toronto	ON	M5V1L8	**800-832-7569***	416-364-4499	95
NYSE: IDG ■ *Cust Svc						
Indigo Dynamic Networks Llc						
2413 W Algonquin Rd	Algonquin	IL	60102	**888-464-6344**		182
Indigo Inn						
1 Maiden Ln	Charleston	SC	29401	**800-845-7639**	843-577-5900	379
Indigo Rose Corp						
123 Bannatyne Ave Ste 200	Winnipeg	MB	R3B0R3	**800-665-9668**	204-946-0263	181
Individual Software Inc						
4255 HopyaRd Rd Ste 2	Pleasanton	CA	94588	**800-822-3522**	925-734-6767	180-3
Indoff Inc						
11816 Lackland Rd	Saint Louis	MO	63146	**800-486-7867**	314-997-1122	385
Indoor Purification Systems Inc						
Surround Air Div						
334 N Marshall Way Ste C	Layton	UT	84041	**888-812-1516**	801-547-1162	17
Inductoheat Inc						
32251 N Avis Dr	Madison Heights	MI	48071	**800-624-6297**	248-585-9393	319
Inductotherm Group						
10 Indel Ave PO Box 157	Rancocas	NJ	08073	**800-257-9527**	609-267-9000	319
Indus International Inc						
340 S Oak St PO Box 890	West Salem	WI	54669	**800-843-9377**	608-786-0300	495
Indusco Group						
1200 W Hamburg St	Baltimore	MD	21230	**800-727-0665**	410-727-0665	469
Industrial Alliance Insurance & Financial Services						
1080 Grande Allee W						
PO Box 1907 Stn Therminus	Quebec	QC	G1K7M3	**800-463-6236**	418-684-5000	391-2
Industrial Battery & Charger Inc						
5831 Orr Rd	Charlotte	NC	28213	**800-833-8412**	704-597-7330	73
Industrial Brush Company Inc						
105 Clinton Rd	Fairfield	NJ	07004	**800-241-9860**	973-575-0455	102
Industrial Chemicals Inc						
2042 Montreat Dr	Vestavia	AL	35216	**800-476-2042***	205-823-7330	145
*Cust Svc						
Industrial Commodities Inc						
PO Box 4380	Glen Allen	VA	23060	**800-523-7902**		298-11
Industrial Container Services						
7152 First Ave S	Seattle	WA	98108	**800-273-3786**	206-763-2345	200
Industrial Contractors Inc						
701 Ch Dr	Bismarck	ND	58501	**800-467-3089**	701-258-9908	191-10
Industrial Controls Distributors Inc (ICD)						
1776 Bloomsbury Ave	Ocean	NJ	07712	**800-281-4788***	732-918-9000	385
*Sales						
Industrial Custom Products Inc						
2801 37th Ave NE	Minneapolis	MN	55421	**800-654-0886**	612-781-2255	327
Industrial Data Systems Inc						
3822 E La Palma Ave	Anaheim	CA	92807	**800-854-3311**	714-921-9212	682
Industrial Diesel Inc						
8705 Harmon Rd	Fort Worth	TX	76177	**800-323-3659**	817-232-1071	385
Industrial Door Company Inc						
360 Coon Rapids Blvd	Minneapolis	MN	55433	**888-798-0199**	763-786-4730	238
Industrial Electric Wire & Cable Inc (IEWC)						
5001 S Towne Dr	New Berlin	WI	53151	**800-344-2323**	262-782-2323	248
Industrial Fabrics Assn International (IFAI)						
1801 County Rd 'B' W	Roseville	MN	55113	**800-225-4324**	651-222-2508	48-13
Industrial Gasket & Shim Company Inc (IGS)						
200 Country Club Rd	Meadow Lands	PA	15347	**800-229-1447**	724-222-5800	327
Industrial Hardware & Specialties Inc						
178 Kentucky Ave	Paterson	NJ	07503	**800-684-4010**	973-684-4010	351
Industrial Insulation Group LLC (IIG)						
2100 Line St	Brunswick	GA	31520	**800-334-7997**	303-978-2000	389
Industrial Louvers Inc						
511 Seventh St S	Delano	MN	55328	**800-328-3421**	763-972-2981	695
Industrial Material Corp						
7701 Harborside Dr	Galveston	TX	77554	**800-701-4462**	409-744-4538	491

Company / Address	City	State	ZIP	Toll-Free	Phone	Class
Industrial Paper Tube Inc						
1335 E Bay Ave	Bronx	NY	10474	**800-345-0960**		124
Industrial Piping Inc						
800 Culp Rd	Pineville	NC	28134	**800-951-0988**	704-588-1100	191-10
Industrial Power & Lighting Corp						
60 Depost St Ste 500	Buffalo	NY	14206	**800-639-3702**	716-854-1811	191-4
Industrial Revolution Inc						
9225 151st Ave NE	Redmond	WA	98052	**888-297-6062**	425-883-6600	695
Industrial Rubber Works						
1700 Nicholas Blvd	Elk Grove Village	IL	60007	**800-852-1855**	847-952-1800	370
Industrial Scientific Corp						
7848 Steubenville Pk	Oakdale	PA	15071	**800-338-3287**	412-788-4353	203
Industrial Soap Co						
722 S Vandeventer Ave	Saint Louis	MO	63110	**800-405-7627**	314-241-6363	406
Industrial Steel Treating Inc						
613 Carroll St	Jackson	MI	49202	**800-253-9534**		483
Industrial Tectonics Inc						
7222 Huron River Dr	Dexter	MI	48130	**866-816-8904**	734-426-4681	484
Industrial Timber & Lumber Corp (ITL)						
23925 Commerce Pk Rd	Beachwood	OH	44122	**800-829-9663**	216-831-3140	681
Industrial Tool Inc						
9210 52nd Ave N	New Hope	MN	55428	**800-776-4455***	763-533-7244	453
*Sales						
Industrial Tools Inc (ITI)						
1111 S Rose Ave	Oxnard	CA	93033	**800-266-5561**	805-483-1111	492
Industrial Towel & Uniform Inc						
2700 S 160th St	New Berlin	WI	53151	**800-767-2487**	262-782-1950	442
Industrial Tube & Steel Corp						
4658 Crystal Pkwy	Kent	OH	44240	**800-662-9567**	330-474-5530	688
Industrial Welders & Machinists Inc						
610 Opperman Dr	Eagan	MN	55123	**800-455-4565**		809
Industries for the Blind						
445 S Curtis Rd	West Allis	WI	53214	**800-642-8778**	414-778-3040	102
Industronics Service Co						
489 Sullivan Ave	South Windsor	CT	06074	**800-878-1551**	860-289-1551	319
Industry Specific Solutions LLC						
24901 Northwestern Hwy						
Ste 400	Southfield	MI	48075	**877-356-3450**		262
Industry-Railway Suppliers Inc						
811 Golf Ln	Bensenville	IL	60106	**800-728-0029**	630-766-5708	768
Inertia Dynamics Inc						
31 Industrial Pk Rd	New Hartford	CT	06057	**800-800-6445**	860-482-4444	205
Inetsolution						
250 Monroe NW Ste 400	Grand Rapids	MI	49503	**855-728-5839**	586-726-9490	182
INetU Inc						
744 Roble Rd	Allentown	PA	18109	**888-664-6388**	610-266-7441	806
Infantino LLC						
4920 Carroll Canyon Rd						
Ste 200	San Diego	CA	92121	**800-840-4916**		63
Infectious Diseases Society of America (IDSA)						
1300 Wilson Blvd Ste 300	Arlington	VA	22209	**888-844-4372**	703-299-0200	48-8
Infinera Corp						
140 Caspian Ct	Sunnyvale	CA	94089	**877-742-3427**	408-572-5200	732
NASDAQ: INFN						
Infinite Graphics Inc						
4611 E Lake St	Minneapolis	MN	55406	**800-679-0676**	612-721-6283	180-5
OTC: INFG						
Influence Technologies Inc						
1342 La Colina Dr	Tustin	CA	92780	**877-420-2766**		393
Info Cubic LLC						
9250 E Costilla Ave						
Ste 525	Greenwood Village	CO	80112	**877-360-4636**	303-220-0170	318
Info Tech Inc						
5700 SW 34th St Ste 1235	Gainesville	FL	32608	**888-352-2439**	352-381-4400	180-10
Info. Quality Healthcare						
385b Highland Colony Pkwy						
Ste 504	Ridgeland	MS	39157	**800-844-0500**	601-957-1575	136
Infoaccess.net LLC						
8801 E Pleasant Vly Rd	Cleveland	OH	44131	**800-255-0253**	216-328-0100	179
InfoCision Management Corp						
325 Springside Dr	Akron	OH	44333	**800-210-6269**	330-668-1400	734
InFocus Corp						
13190 SW 68th Pkwy Ste 200	Portland	OR	97223	**877-388-8385**	503-207-4700	590
INFOCUS Marketing Inc						
4245 Sigler Rd	Warrenton	VA	20187	**800-708-5478**		462
infoGroup Inc						
1020 E First St	Papillion	NE	68046	**866-414-7848**	402-836-5290	5
Infogrow Corp						
2140 Front St	Cuyahoga Falls	OH	44221	**800-897-9807**		198
InfoMart Inc						
1582 Terrell Mill Rd	Marietta	GA	30067	**800-800-3774**	770-984-2727	195
InfoMine Inc						
580 Hornby St Ste 900	Vancouver	BC	V6C3B6	**888-683-2037**	604-683-2037	227
InfoNow Corp						
1875 Lawrence St Ste 1200	Denver	CO	80202	**855-524-3282**	303-293-0212	180-7
Infor Global Solutions						
13560 Morris Rd Ste 4100	Alpharetta	GA	30004	**866-244-5479**	678-319-8000	180-10
Informant Technologies Inc						
19 Jenkins Ave Ste 200	Lansdale	PA	19446	**877-503-4636**	215-412-9165	179
Informatica Corp						
100 Cardinal Way	Redwood City	CA	94063	**800-653-3871**	650-385-5000	180-1
NASDAQ: INFA						
Information & Computing Services Inc (ICS)						
1650 Prudential Dr Ste 300	Jacksonville	FL	32207	**800-676-4427**	904-399-8500	180-1
Information Builders Inc						
2 Penn Plz	New York	NY	10121	**800-969-4636**	212-736-4433	180-7
Information Gatekeepers Inc (IGI)						
1340 Soldiers Field Rd Ste 2	Brighton	MA	02135	**800-323-1088**	617-782-5033	634-11
Information Management Systems Inc						
114 W Main St Ste 211						
PO Box 2924	New Britain	CT	06050	**888-403-8347**	860-229-1119	632
Information Network Assoc Inc						
5235 N Front St	Harrisburg	PA	17110	**800-443-0824**	717-599-5505	691
Information Resources Inc						
150 N Clinton St	Chicago	IL	60661	**866-262-5973**	312-726-1221	465
Information Systems Audit & Control Assn (ISACA)						
3701 Algonquin Rd						
Ste 1010	Rolling Meadows	IL	60008	**888-491-8833**	847-253-1545	47-9

Name / Address	City	State	ZIP	Toll-Free	Phone	Class
Information Today Inc						
143 Old Marlton Pike	Medford	NJ	08055	**800-300-9868**	609-654-6266	634-9
Information Today Magazine						
143 Old Marlton Pk	Medford	NJ	08055	**800-300-9868**	609-654-6266	456-7
InformationWeek Magazine						
600 Community Dr	Manhasset	NY	11030	**855-569-5945**	516-562-5000	456-7
INFORMS (Institute for Operations Research & the Management Sciences)						
7240 Pkwy Dr Ste 300	Hanover	MD	21076	**800-446-3676**	443-757-3500	48-19
Infosight Corp						
PO Box 5000	Chillicothe	OH	45601	**800-401-0716**	740-642-3600	466
Infosource Inc						
1300 City View Ctr	Oviedo	FL	32765	**800-393-4636**	407-796-5200	179
InfoTech Enterprises America Inc						
330 Roberts St Ste 102	East Hartford	CT	06108	**866-746-2133**	860-528-5430	258
infoUSA Inc						
5711 S 86th Cir	Omaha	NE	68127	**800-321-0869**	800-835-5856	387
InfoVista Corp						
12950 Worldgate Dr Ste 250	Herndon	VA	20170	**866-921-9219**	703-435-2435	180-1
InfoWorld Inc						
501 Second St Fl 6	San Francisco	CA	94107	**800-227-8365**	415-243-4344	456-7
InfoWorld Media Group Inc						
501 Second St 6 Fl	San Francisco	CA	94107	**800-227-8365**	415-243-0500	634-9
InfraRed Imaging Systems Inc						
22718 Holycross Epps Rd	Marysville	OH	43040	**888-987-5768**		94
Infrastructure Networks Inc						
1718 Fry Rd Ste 116	Houston	TX	77084	**855-333-4638**	281-740-3226	387
Infusion Nurses Society (INS)						
315 Norwood Pk S	Norwood	MA	02062	**800-694-0298**	781-440-9408	48-8
InfySource Ltd						
8345 NW 66th St	Miami	FL	33166	**800-275-7503**		623
ING Funds						
7337 E Doubletree Ranch Rd	Scottsdale	AZ	85258	**800-992-0180**		527
Ingenuity Ieq						
3600 Centennial Dr	Midland	MI	48642	**800-669-9726**	989-496-2233	609
Ingersoll Rand Air Solutions Group						
800-D Beaty St	Davidson	NC	28036	**800-866-5457**		174
Ingle International						
460 Richmond St W Ste 100	Toronto	ON	M5V1Y1	**800-360-3234**	416-730-8488	391-7
Ingles Markets Inc						
2913 US Hwy 70 W	Black Mountain	NC	28711	**800-635-5066**	828-669-2941	345
NASDAQ: IMKTA						
Ingleside Inn						
200 W Ramon Rd	Palm Springs	CA	92264	**800-772-6655**	760-325-0046	379
Ingot Metal Company Ltd						
111 Fenmar Dr	Weston	ON	M9L1M3	**800-567-7774**	416-749-1372	480
Ingram Book Group						
1 Ingram Blvd	La Vergne	TN	37086	**800-937-8000**	615-793-5000	94
Ingram Entertainment Inc						
2 Ingram Blvd	La Vergne	TN	37089	**800-621-1333**	615-287-4000	510
Ingram Micro Inc						
1600 E St Andrew Pl	Santa Ana	CA	92705	**800-456-8000***	714-566-1000	176
NYSE: IM ■ *Sales						
Ingram Park Mall						
6301 NW Loop 410	San Antonio	TX	78238	**877-746-6642**	210-684-9570	459
Injured Workers Insurance Fund						
8722 Loch Raven Blvd	Towson	MD	21286	**800-264-4943**	410-494-2000	391-4
Ink Technology Corp						
18320 Lanken Ave	Cleveland	OH	44119	**800-633-2826**	216-486-6720	627
INL (Idaho National Laboratory)						
2525 Fremont Ave	Idaho Falls	ID	83402	**866-495-7440**		666
Inland Arts & Graphics Inc						
14440 Edison Dr	New Lenox	IL	60451	**800-437-6003**		626
Inland Empire Paper Co						
3320 N Argonne	Millwood	WA	99212	**866-437-7711**	509-924-1911	556
Inland Group Inc						
2901 Butterfield Rd	Oak Brook	IL	60523	**800-826-8228**	630-218-8000	653
Inland Mortgage Corp						
2901 Butterfield Rd	Oak Brook	IL	60523	**800-826-8228**	630-218-8000	508
Inland Northwest Blood Ctr						
210 W Cataldo Ave	Spokane	WA	99201	**800-423-0151**	509-624-0151	88
Inland Plywood Co						
375 N Cass Ave	Pontiac	MI	48342	**800-521-4355**	248-334-4706	612
Inland Power & Light Company Inc						
10110 W Hallett Rd	Spokane	WA	99224	**800-747-7151**	509-747-7151	247
Inland Real Estate Corp						
2901 Butterfield Rd	Oak Brook	IL	60523	**888-331-4732**	630-218-8000	652
NYSE: IRC						
Inland Real Estate Development Corp						
2901 Butterfield Rd	Oak Brook	IL	60523	**866-954-5692**	630-218-8000	651
Inland Seafood Corp						
1651 Montreal Cir	Tucker	GA	30084	**800-883-3474**	404-350-5850	298-5
Inland Technologies Inc						
14 Queen St PO Box 253	Truro	NS	B2N5C1	**877-633-5263**	902-895-6346	194
Inlandboatmen's Union of the Pacific (IBU)						
1711 W Nickerson St Ste D	Seattle	WA	98119	**800-562-6000**	206-284-6001	414
Inlet Tower Suites						
1200 L St	Anchorage	AK	99501	**800-544-0786**	907-276-0110	379
Inline Fibreglass Ltd						
30 Constellation Ct	Toronto	ON	M9W1K1	**866-566-5656**	416-679-1171	498
Inline Plastics Corp						
42 Canal St	Shelton	CT	06484	**800-826-5567**	203-924-2015	601
Inman News						
1100 Marina Village Pkwy Ste 102	Alameda	CA	94501	**800-775-4662**	510-658-9252	529
Inmedius Inc						
2247 Babcock Blvd	Pittsburgh	PA	15237	**800-697-7110**		179
Inn & Spa at Loretto						
211 Old Santa Fe Trl	Santa Fe	NM	87501	**800-727-5531**	505-988-5531	379
Inn Above Tide, The						
30 El Portal	Sausalito	CA	94965	**800-893-8433**	415-332-9535	379
Inn at Aspen						
38750 Hwy 82	Aspen	CO	81611	**800-222-7736**		377
Inn at Bay Harbor, The						
3600 Village Harbor Dr	Bay Harbor	MI	49770	**800-462-6963**	231-439-4000	667
Inn at Camachee Harbor						
201 Yacht Club Dr	Saint Augustine	FL	32084	**800-688-5379**	904-825-0003	379
Inn at Gig Harbor						
3211 56th St NW	Gig Harbor	WA	98335	**800-795-9980**	253-858-1111	379
Inn at Harbour Town						
7 Lighthouse Ln	Hilton Head Island	SC	29928	**800-732-7463***	843-363-8100	379
*Resv						
Inn at Langley						
400 First St PO Box 835	Langley	WA	98260	**800-843-3779**	360-221-3033	379
Inn at Mamas Fish House						
799 Poho Pl	Paia	HI	96779	**800-860-4852**	808-579-8488	378
Inn at Montchanin Village						
528 Montchanin Rd	Montchanin	DE	19710	**800-269-2473**	302-888-2133	379
Inn at Morro Bay						
60 State Pk Rd	Morro Bay	CA	93442	**800-321-9566**	805-772-5651	379
Inn at Otter Crest						
301 Otter Crest Loop	Otter Rock	OR	97369	**800-452-2101**	541-765-2111	379
Inn at Pelican Bay						
800 Vanderbilt Beach Rd	Naples	FL	34108	**800-597-8770**	239-597-8777	379
Inn at Perry Cabin						
308 Watkins Ln	Saint Michaels	MD	21663	**800-722-2949**	410-745-2200	379
Inn at Rancho Santa Fe						
5951 Linea Del Cielo PO Box 869	Rancho Santa Fe	CA	92067	**800-843-4661**	858-756-1131	667
Inn at Reading, The						
1040 N Pk Rd	Wyomissing	PA	19610	**800-383-9713**	610-372-7811	379
Inn at Saint John						
939 Congress St	Portland	ME	04102	**800-636-9127**	207-773-6481	379
Inn at Spanish Bay, The						
2700 17-Mile Dr	Pebble Beach	CA	93953	**800-654-9300**	831-647-7500	667
Inn at Spanish Head						
4009 SW Hwy 101	Lincoln City	OR	97367	**800-452-8127**	541-996-2161	379
Inn at Stratton Mountain						
5 Village Lodge Rd	Stratton Mountain	VT	05155	**800-787-2886**	802-297-2500	667
Inn at the Market						
86 Pine St	Seattle	WA	98101	**800-446-4484**	206-443-3600	379
Inn At The Quay						
900 Quayside Dr	New Westminster	BC	V3M6G1	**800-663-2001**	604-520-1776	379
Inn at Union Square						
440 Post St	San Francisco	CA	94102	**800-288-4346**	415-397-3510	379
Inn at Virginia Mason						
1006 Spring St	Seattle	WA	98104	**800-283-6453**	206-583-6453	372
Inn at Virginia Tech & Skelton Conference Ctr						
901 Prices Fork Rd	Blacksburg	VA	24061	**877-200-3360**	540-231-8000	377
Inn at, The Tides, The						
800 Coast Hwy 1	Bodega Bay	CA	94923	**800-541-7788**	707-875-2751	379
Inn by the Lake						
3300 Lk Tahoe Blvd	South Lake Tahoe	CA	96150	**800-877-1466**	530-542-0330	379
Inn by the Sea						
40 Bowery Beach Rd	Cape Elizabeth	ME	04107	**800-888-4287**	207-799-3134	667
Inn of Long Beach						
185 Atlantic Ave	Long Beach	CA	90802	**800-230-7500**	562-435-3791	379
Inn of the Anasazi						
113 Washington Ave	Santa Fe	NM	87501	**888-767-3966**	505-988-3030	379
Inn of the Governors						
101 W Alameda St	Santa Fe	NM	87501	**800-234-4534**	505-982-4333	379
Inn of the Hills River Resort						
1001 Junction Hwy	Kerrville	TX	78028	**800-292-5690**	830-895-5000	667
Inn of the Mountain Gods						
287 Carrizo Canyon Rd	Mescalero	NM	88340	**800-545-9011**		667
Inn on Biltmore Estate						
1 Antler Hill Rd	Asheville	NC	28803	**800-411-3812**	828-225-1600	379
Inn on Fifth						
699 Fifth Ave S	Naples	FL	34102	**888-403-8778**	239-403-8777	379
Inn on Gitche Gumee						
8517 Congdon Blvd	Duluth	MN	55804	**800-317-4979**	218-525-4979	379
Inn on Lake Superior						
350 Canal Pk Dr	Duluth	MN	55802	**888-668-4352**	218-726-1111	379
Inn on the Alameda						
303 E Alameda St	Santa Fe	NM	87501	**888-984-2121**	505-984-2121	379
Inn on the Paseo						
630 Paseo de Peralta	Santa Fe	NM	87501	**855-984-8200**	505-984-8200	379
Inner Traditions International						
1 Pk Row	Rochester	VT	05767	**800-246-8648**	802-767-3174	634-2
Innis Maggiore Group Inc						
4715 Whipple Ave NW	Canton	OH	44718	**800-460-4111**	330-492-5500	4
Innisbrook Resort & Golf Club						
36750 US Hwy 19 N	Palm Harbor	FL	34684	**800-492-6899**	727-942-2000	667
Innodata-Isogen Inc						
3 University Plz Dr	Hackensack	NJ	07601	**877-454-8400**	201-371-8000	180-12
NASDAQ: INOD						
Innotap						
200 North Warner Rd Ste 210	King of Prussia	PA	19406	**855-438-4666**		227
In-N-Out Burger Inc						
4199 Campus Dr 9th Fl	Irvine	CA	92612	**800-786-1000***	949-509-6200	668
*Cust Svc						
Innovadex LLC						
7930 Santa Fe 3rd Fl	Overland Park	KS	66204	**877-292-7279**	913-307-9010	393
Innovairre Communications LLC						
825 Hylton Rd	Pennsauken	NJ	08110	**856-663-2500**		465
Innovate E-Commerce Inc						
160 N Craig St	Pittsburgh	PA	15213	**888-771-9606**		630
Innovative Data Management Systems LLC						
4006 W Azeele St	Tampa	FL	33609	**866-706-4588**	813-207-2025	179
Innovative Enterprises Inc						
25 Town & Country Dr	Washington	MO	63090	**800-280-0300**	636-390-0300	547
Innovative Fluid Handling Systems						
3300 E Rock Falls Rd	Rock Falls	IL	61071	**800-435-7003**	815-626-1018	200
Innovative Hearth Products						
2701 S Harbor Blvd	Santa Ana	CA	92704	**866-328-4537**		361
Innovative Industrial Solutions Inc						
2830 Skyline Dr	Russellville	AR	72802	**888-684-8249**	479-968-4266	691
Innovative Information Solutions Inc						
61 I- Ln	Waterbury	CT	06705	**800-343-8121**	203-756-4243	181
Innovative Metals Company Inc (IMETCO)						
4648 S Old Peachtree Rd	Norcross	GA	30084	**800-646-3826**	770-908-1030	45
Innovative Solutions & Support Inc						
720 Pennsylvania Dr	Exton	PA	19341	**866-359-7876**	610-646-9800	528
NASDAQ: ISSC						
Innovative Stamping Corp						
2068 E Gladwick St	Compton	CA	90220	**800-400-0047**	310-537-6996	487

Company	Address	City	State	ZIP	Toll-Free	Phone	Class
Innovative Systems Group Inc	799 Roosevelt Rd	Glen Ellyn	IL	60137	**800-739-2400**	630-858-8500	179
Innovative Systems Inc	790 Holiday Dr Bldg 11	Pittsburgh	PA	15220	**800-622-6390**	412-937-9300	180-1
Innovative Technologies Corp (ITC)	1020 Woodman Dr Ste 100	Dayton	OH	45432	**800-745-8050**	937-252-2145	180-10
Innovative Telecom Solutions Inc	9 Vela Way	Edgewater	NJ	07020	**800-510-3000**		387
Innovent Air Handling Equipment	60 28th Ave N	Minneapolis	MN	55411	**877-218-4129**	612-877-4800	358
Innovize Inc	500 Oak Grove Pkwy	Saint Paul	MN	55127	**877-605-6580**		601
Inns at Mill Falls	312 Daniel Webster Hwy	Meredith	NH	03253	**800-622-6455**		379
InnSuites Hospitality Trust	1625 E Northern Ave Ste 105 *NYSE: IHT*	Phoenix	AZ	85020	**800-842-4242**	602-944-1500	652
InnSuites Hospitality Trust InnSuites Hotels & Suites	475 N Granada Ave	Tucson	AZ	85701	**800-842-4242**	520-622-0923	379
InnSuites Hotel Tempe/Phoenix Airport	1651 W Baseline Rd	Tempe	AZ	85283	**800-841-4242**	480-897-7900	379
Inolex Chemical Co	2101 S Swanson St *Cust Svc	Philadelphia	PA	19148	**800-521-9891***	215-271-0800	143
Inova Diagnostics Inc	9900 Old Grove Rd	San Diego	CA	92131	**800-545-9495**	858-586-9900	233
Inova Health System	8110 Gatehouse Rd	Falls Church	VA	22042	**855-694-6682**		353
Inova Payroll Inc	176 Thompson Ln Ste 204	Nashville	TN	37211	**888-244-6106**	615-921-0600	731
Inova Solutions Inc	110 Avon St	Charlottesville	VA	22902	**800-637-1077**	434-817-8000	180-1
In-O-Vate Technologies Inc	810 Saturn St Ste 21	Jupiter	FL	33477	**888-443-7937**	561-743-8696	193-1
Inovatia Laboratories LLC	120 E Davis St	Fayette	MO	65248	**800-280-1912**	660-248-1911	740
Inovex Industries Inc	45681 Oakbrook Ct Ste 102	Sterling	VA	20166	**888-374-3366**	703-421-9778	3
Inovio Pharmaceuticals Inc	660 W Germantown Pk Ste 110 *NASDAQ: INOVIO*	Plymouth	PA	19462	**877-446-6846**	267-440-4200	252
Inovise Medical Inc	8770 SW Nimbus Ave Ste D	Beaverton	OR	97008	**877-466-8473**	503-431-3800	475
InPath Devices	3610 Dodge St Ste 200	Omaha	NE	68131	**800-988-1914**	402-345-9200	175-7
In-place Machining Company Inc	3811 N Holton St	Milwaukee	WI	53212	**800-833-3575**	414-562-2000	695
Inpower LLC	3555 Africa Rd	Galena	OH	43021	**866-548-0965**	740-548-0965	350
Input 1 LLC	6200 Canoga Ave Ste 400	Woodland Hills	CA	91367	**888-882-2554**	818-713-2303	180-10
Inquipco	2730 N Nellis Blvd	Las Vegas	NV	89115	**800-598-3465**	702-644-1700	192
Inquiries Inc	129 N W St	Easton	MD	21601	**866-987-3767**	410-819-3711	400
Inquiry Systems Inc	1195 Goodale Blvd	Columbus	OH	43212	**800-508-1116**	614-464-3800	197
INS (Infusion Nurses Society)	315 Norwood Pk S	Norwood	MA	02062	**800-694-0298**	781-440-9408	48-8
Inscape Publishing Inc	6465 Wayzata Blvd Ste 800	Minneapolis	MN	55426	**877-735-8383**	763-765-2222	180-3
Insco Distributing Inc	12501 Network Blvd	San Antonio	TX	78249	**855-282-4295**	210-690-8400	663
Inside FERC	2 Penn Plz 25th Fl	New York	NY	10121	**800-752-8878**		530-5
Inside NRC	2 Penn Plz 25th Fl	New York	NY	10121	**800-752-8878**		530-5
Inside Washington Publishers	1919 S Eads St Ste 201	Arlington	VA	22202	**800-424-9068**	703-416-8500	634-9
InsideFlyer Magazine	1930 Frequent Flyer Pt	Colorado Springs	CO	80915	**888-407-4747**	719-597-8889	456-22
Insight	444 Scott Dr	Bloomingdale	IL	60108	**800-467-4448**		195
Insight Computing LLC	448 Ignacio Blvd Ste 490	Novato	CA	94949	**800-380-8985**	415-898-5411	177
Insight Enterprises Inc	6820 S Harl Ave *NASDAQ: NSIT*	Tempe	AZ	85283	**800-467-4448**	480-333-3000	181
Insight Global Inc (IGI)	4170 Ashford Dunwoody Rd Ste 250	Atlanta	GA	30319	**888-336-7463**	404-257-7900	195
Insight Information	214 King St W Ste 300	Toronto	ON	M5H3S6	**888-777-1707**	416-777-2020	763
Insight Investments Corp	611 Anton Blvd Ste 700	Costa Mesa	CA	92626	**888-442-1441**	714-939-2300	623
Insight Media	2162 Broadway	New York	NY	10024	**800-233-9910**	212-721-6316	510
Insight Technology Inc	9 Akira Way	Londonderry	NH	03053	**866-509-2040**	603-626-4800	21
Insignia Systems Inc	8799 Brooklyn Blvd *NASDAQ: ISIG*	Minneapolis	MN	55445	**800-874-4648**	763-392-6200	699
In-Sink-Erator	4700 21st St	Racine	WI	53406	**800-558-5712**	262-554-5432	35
Insituform Technologies Inc	17988 Edison Ave *Cust Svc	St. Louis	MO	63005	**800-234-2992***	636-530-8000	190-10
Insl-X Products Corp	101 Paragon Dr *Cust Svc	Montvale	NJ	07645	**800-225-5554***		549
Insparisk LLC	71-19 80th St Ste 8205	Glendale	NY	11385	**888-464-6772**		365
Insperity Inc	19001 Crescent Springs Dr	Kingwood	TX	77339	**800-237-3170**	866-715-3552	462
Inspirage Inc	600 108th Ave NE Ste 540	Bellevue	WA	98004	**855-517-4250**		630
Inspiration Software Inc	6443 SW Beaverton Hillsdale Hwy Ste 370	Portland	OR	97221	**800-877-4292**	503-297-3004	180-1
Inspired eLearning Inc	613 NW Loop 410 Ste 530	San Antonio	TX	78216	**800-631-2078**	210-579-0224	227
InstaGift LLC	117 West Glenwood Dr	Birmingham	AL	35209	**877-870-3463**		393
Instant Imprints	5897 Oberlin Dr Ste 200	San Diego	CA	92121	**800-542-3437**	858-642-4848	311
Instantel Inc	309 Legget Dr	Ottawa	ON	K2K3A3	**800-267-9111**	613-592-4642	255
Instantiations Inc	Officers Row Ste 1325B	Vancouver	WA	98661	**855-476-2558**	503-649-3836	180-2
Instantwhip Foods Inc	2200 Cardigan Ave *Cust Svc	Columbus	OH	43215	**800-544-9447***	614-488-2536	297-10
Insteel Industries Inc	1373 Boggs Dr *NASDAQ: IIIN*	Mount Airy	NC	27030	**800-334-9504**	336-786-2141	811
Institute for a Drug-Free Workplace (IDFW)	10701 Parkridge Blvd Ste 300	Reston	VA	20191	**877-696-6775**	703-391-7222	48-12
Institute for Astronomy	University of Hawaii 2680 Woodlawn Dr	Honolulu	HI	96822	**800-351-1330**	808-956-8312	666
Institute for Business & Home Safety (IBHS)	4775 E Fowler Ave	Tampa	FL	33617	**866-657-4247**	813-286-3400	48-9
Institute for Certification of Computing Professionals (ICCP)	2400 E Devon Ave Ste 281	Des Plaines	IL	60018	**800-843-8227**	847-299-4227	47-9
Institute for Corporate Productivity Inc	411 First Ave S Ste 403	Seattle	WA	98104	**866-375-4427**	206-624-6565	465
Institute for Healthcare Improvement (IHI)	20 University Rd 7th Fl	Cambridge	MA	02138	**866-787-0831**	617-301-4800	48-8
Institute for Humane Studies	3434 Washington Blvd Ste 440	Arlington	VA	22201	**800-697-8799**	703-993-4880	631
Institute for Justice	901 N Glebe Rd Ste 900	Arlington	VA	22203	**888-322-6397**	703-682-9320	631
Institute For Natural Resources	PO Box 5757	Concord	CA	94524	**877-246-6336**	925-609-2820	21
Institute for Operations Research & the Management Sciences (INFORMS)	7240 Pkwy Dr Ste 300	Hanover	MD	21076	**800-446-3676**	443-757-3500	48-19
Institute for Policy Studies (IPS)	1112 16th St NW Ste 600	Washington	DC	20036	**877-564-6833**	202-234-9382	631
Institute for Research on Poverty	University of Wisconsin Madison 1180 Observatory Dr 3412 William H Sewell Social Sciences Bldg	Madison	WI	53706	**866-301-1753**	608-262-6358	666
Institute for Supply Management (ISM)	2055 Centennial Cir *Cust Svc	Tempe	AZ	85284	**800-888-6276***	480-752-6276	48-12
Institute for Systems Research	University of Maryland 2173 AV Williams Bldg	College Park	MD	20742	**866-675-8967**	301-405-6615	666
Institute for the Advancement of Human Behavior (IAHB)	PO BOX 5527	Santa Rosa	CA	95402	**800-258-8411**	650-851-8411	48-8
Institute of American Indian Arts (IAIA)	83 Avan Nu Po Rd	Santa Fe	NM	87508	**800-804-6422**	505-424-2300	164
Institute of Business Appraisers (IBA)	1111 BrickyaRd Rd Ste 200	Salt Lake City	UT	84106	**800-299-4130**		48-17
Institute of Caster & Wheel Manufacturers (ICWM)	8720 Red Oak Blvd Ste 201	Charlotte	NC	28217	**877-522-5431**	704-676-1190	48-13
Institute of Certified Professional Managers (ICPM)	James Madison University MSC 5504	Harrisonburg	VA	22807	**800-460-8013**	540-568-3247	48-12
Institute of Clean Air Cos (ICAC)	1730 M St NW Ste 206	Washington	DC	20036	**800-631-9505**	202-457-0911	47-12
Institute of Corporate Directors	602 - 40 University Ave	Toronto	ON	M5J1T1	**877-593-7741**	416-593-7741	161
Institute of Culinary Education	50 W 23rd St	New York	NY	10010	**800-522-4610**	212-847-0700	162
Institute of Food Technologists (IFT)	525 W Van Buren St Ste 1000	Chicago	IL	60607	**800-438-3663**	312-782-8424	48-6
Institute of General Semantics (IGS)	72-11 Austin St	Forest Hills	NY	11375	**800-346-1359**	212-729-7973	47-11
Institute of Gerontology	University of Michigan 300 N Ingalls St	Ann Arbor	MI	48109	**877-865-2167**	734-936-2107	666
Institute of Government & Public Affairs	Univ of Illinois 1007 W Nevada St	Urbana	IL	61801	**866-794-3340**	217-333-3340	631
Institute of Hazardous Materials Management (IHMM)	11900 Parklawn Dr Ste 450	Rockville	MD	20852	**800-437-0137**	301-984-8969	47-12
Institute of Industrial Engineers (IIE)	3577 PkwyLn Ste 200 *Cust Svc	Norcross	GA	30092	**800-494-0460***	770-449-0460	48-13
Institute of Makers of Explosives (IME)	1120 19th St NW Ste 310	Washington	DC	20036	**800-461-8841**	202-429-9280	48-13
Institute of Management Accountants Inc (IMA)	10 Paragon Dr Ste 1	Montvale	NJ	07645	**800-638-4427**	201-573-9000	48-1
Institute of Management Consultants USA Inc (IMC USA)	2025 M St NW Ste 800	Washington	DC	20036	**800-221-2557**	202-367-1134	48-12
Institute of Materials Science	University of Connecticut 97 N Eagleville Rd	Storrs	CT	06269	**800-528-7411**	860-486-4623	666
Institute of Navigation Inc (ION)	8551 Rixlew Ln Ste 360	Manassas	VA	20109	**800-696-7353**	703-366-2723	48-21
Institute of Packaging Professionals (IoPP)	1833 Centre Point Cir Ste 123	Naperville	IL	60563	**800-432-4085**	630-544-5050	48-13
Institute of Real Estate Management (IREM)	430 N Michigan Ave	Chicago	IL	60611	**800-837-0706**	312-329-6000	48-17
Institute of Scrap Recycling Industries Magazine	1615 L St NW Ste 6000	Washington	DC	20036	**800-767-7236**	202-662-8500	456-21
Institute of Texan Cultures	801 E Durango Blvd	San Antonio	TX	78205	**800-447-3372**	210-458-2300	519
Institute of World Politics	1521 16th St NW	Washington	DC	20036	**888-566-9497**	202-462-2101	631
Institutional Investor Newsletters	225 Pk Ave S 8th Fl	New York	NY	10003	**800-437-9997**	212-224-3300	634-9

Alphabetical Section

	Toll-Free	Phone	Class
Institutional Wholesale Co 535 Dry Vly Rd . . . Cookeville TN 38506	800-239-9588	931-537-4000	300
Instrument Sales & Service Inc 16427 NE Airport Way . . . Portland OR 97230	800-333-7976	503-239-0754	60
Instrumentation Laboratory Inc 180 Hartwell Rd . . . Bedford MA 01730 *Sales	800-955-9525*	781-861-0710	419
Insulet Corp 9 Oak Park Dr . . . Bedford MA 01730	800-591-3455	781-457-5000	475
Insulfab Plastics Inc 834 Hayne St . . . Spartanburg SC 29301	800-845-7599	864-582-7506	598
Insultab Inc 45 Industrial Pkwy . . . Woburn MA 01801 *Cust Svc	800-468-4822*	781-935-0800	598
Insurance Auto Auctions Inc 2 Westbrook Corporate Ctr Ste 500 . . . Westchester IL 60154	800-872-1501	708-492-7000	50
Insurance Company of the West 11455 El Camino Real . . . San Diego CA 92130	800-877-1111	858-350-2400	391-4
Insurance Consultants International 19760 Knights Crossing Ste 1C . . . Monument CO 80132	800-576-2674	719-573-9080	391-7
Insurance Coverage Law Bulletin, The 1617 JFK Blvd Ste 1750 . . . Philadelphia PA 19103	877-256-2472	215-557-2300	530-7
Insurance Data Processing Inc (IDP) 8101 Washington Ln . . . Wyncote PA 19095	800-523-6745	215-885-2150	180-11
Insurance Information Institute Inc (III) 110 William St . . . New York NY 10038	877-263-7995	212-346-5500	48-9
Insurance Institute for Highway Safety 1005 N Glebe Rd Ste 800 . . . Arlington VA 22201	888-327-4236	703-247-1500	48-9
Insurance Marketing Agencies Inc 306 Main St . . . Worcester MA 01608	800-891-1226	508-753-7233	391-2
Insurance Research Council (IRC) 718 Providence Rd . . . Malvern PA 19355	800-644-2101	610-644-2212	48-9
Insurance Services Office Inc (ISO) 545 Washington Blvd . . . Jersey City NJ 07310	800-888-4476	201-469-2000	390
InsurBanc 10 Executive Dr . . . Farmington CT 06032	866-467-2262	860-677-9701	69
Insurity Inc 170 Huyshope Ave . . . Hartford CT 06106	866-476-2606	860-616-7721	179
InsWeb Inc 11290 Pyrites Way . . . Gold River CA 95670	866-697-9085	916-853-3300	113
INTA (International Trademark Assn) 655 Third Ave 10th Fl . . . New York NY 10017	800-995-3579	212-768-9887	48-12
Intacct Corp 300 Park Ave Ste 1400 . . . San Jose CA 95110	877-437-7765	408-878-0900	38
Intact Info Solutions LLC 1370 Vly Vista Dr Ste 265 . . . Diamond Bar CA 91765	888-986-7736	909-396-9200	198
Intact Insurance 700 University Ave Mn 3 Ste 1500 . . . Toronto ON M5G0A1	877-341-1464	844-489-3768	391-4
Intaglio LLC 5809 Cross Roads Commerce Pkwy Ste 200 . . . Grand Rapids MI 49519	800-632-9153	616-243-3300	512
Intec Video Systems Inc 23301 Vista Grande Dr . . . Laguna Hills CA 92653	800-468-3254	949-859-3800	691
Intedge Mfg 1875 Chumley Rd . . . Woodruff SC 29388	866-969-9605	864-969-9601	301
Integra Capital Ltd 2020 Winston Park Dr Ste 200 . . . Oakville ON L6H6X7	800-363-2480	905-829-1131	401
Integra Information Technologies Inc 101 South 27th St . . . Boise ID 83702	800-444-8688	208-336-2720	198
Integra LifeSciences Holdings Corp 311 Enterprise Dr . . . Plainsboro NJ 08536 *NASDAQ: IART*	800-654-2873	609-275-0500	84
Integra Telecom Inc 1201 NE Lloyd Blvd Ste 500 . . . Portland OR 97232 *General	866-468-3472*	503-453-8000	733
IntegraCare Holdings Inc 2559 SW Grapevine Pkwy Ste 300 . . . Grapevine TX 76051	800-735-2988	817-310-4999	363
IntegraColor 3210 Innovative Way . . . Mesquite TX 75149	800-933-9511	972-289-0705	626
integraSoft Inc 2547 Tech Dr . . . Bettendorf IA 52722	877-630-7960	563-332-5030	198
Integrated Biometrics Inc 121 Broadcast Dr . . . Spartanburg SC 29303	888-840-8034	864-990-3711	690
Integrated BioPharma Inc 225 Long Ave . . . Hillside NJ 07205 *OTC: INBP*	888-319-6962	973-926-0816	797
Integrated Business Systems & Services Inc 1601 Shop Rd Ste E . . . Columbia SC 29201	800-553-1038	803-736-5595	180-1
Integrated Device Technology Inc 6024 Silver Creek Vly Rd . . . San Jose CA 95138 *NASDAQ: IDTI*	800-345-7015	408-284-8200	694
Integrated Flow Solutions LLC 6461 Reynolds Rd . . . Tyler TX 75708	800-859-7867	903-595-6511	638
Integrated Magnetics Inc 11248 Playa Ct . . . Culver City CA 90230	800-421-6692	310-391-7213	255
Integrated Regional Laboratories Inc 5361 NW 33rd Ave . . . Ft. Lauderdale FL 33309	800-522-0232		415
Integrated Silicon Solution Inc (ISSI) 1940 Zanker Rd . . . San Jose CA 95112 *NASDAQ: ISSI*	800-379-4774	408-969-6600	694
Integrated Support Command Miami Beach 100 MacArthur Cswy . . . Miami Beach FL 33139	866-772-8724	305-535-4300	157
Integrated Systems Analysts Inc 2001 N Beauregard St Ste 600 . . . Alexandria VA 22311	800-929-1024	703-824-0700	182
Integration Technologies Group Inc 2745 Hartland Rd Ste 200 . . . Falls Church VA 22043	800-835-7823	703-698-8282	177
Integretel Inc 5883 Rue Ferrari . . . San Jose CA 95138	888-302-2750	408-362-4000	734
INTEGRIS Baptist Regional Health Ctr 200 Second Ave SW . . . Miami OK 74355	888-951-2277	918-542-6611	374-3
INTEGRIS Bass Baptist Health Ctr 600 S Monroe . . . Enid OK 73701	888-951-2277	580-233-2300	374-3
INTEGRIS Health Inc 3300 NW Expy . . . Oklahoma City OK 73112	888-951-2277	405-951-2277	353
INTEGRIS Southwest Medical Ctr 4401 S Western St . . . Oklahoma City OK 73109	888-949-3816	405-636-7000	374-3

	Toll-Free	Phone	Class
Integrity Music 4050 Lee Vance View . . . Colorado Springs CO 80918	888-888-4726	719-536-0100	655
Integrity Staffing Solutions Inc 700 Prides Crossing Ste 300 . . . Newark DE 19713	888-458-8367	302-661-8776	719
Integrity Systems & Solutions LLC 1247 Highland Ave Ste 202 . . . Cheshire CT 06410	866-446-8797	203-271-7971	179
Intek Plastic Inc 1000 Spiral Blvd . . . Hastings MN 55033	888-468-3531		327
Intel Corp 2200 Mission College Blvd . . . Santa Clara CA 95052 *NASDAQ: INTC* ■ *Cust Svc	800-628-8686*	408-765-8080	694
Intel Museum 2200 Mission College Blvd . . . Santa Clara CA 95052	800-628-8686	408-765-0503	519
Intellect Resources Inc 3824 N Elm St Ste 102 . . . Greensboro NC 27455	877-554-8911		262
Intelletrace Inc 448 Ignacio Blvd . . . Novato CA 94945	800-618-5877		387
Intellicom Computer Consulting 1702 Second Ave . . . Kearney NE 68847	877-501-3375	308-237-0684	182
Intelligencer Journal 8 W King St PO Box 1328 . . . Lancaster PA 17603	800-809-4666	717-291-8622	531-2
Intelligencer Printing Co 330 Eden Rd . . . Lancaster PA 17601	800-233-0107		626
Intelligent Computer Solutions Inc 9350 Eton Ave . . . Chatsworth CA 91311	888-994-4678	818-998-5805	176
Intelligent Decisions Inc 21445 Beaumeade Cir . . . Ashburn VA 20147	800-929-8331	703-554-1600	182
Intelligent Mechatronic Systems Inc 435 King St N . . . Waterloo ON N2J2Z5	866-818-6637	519-745-8887	666
Intelligent Transportation Society of America (ITS) 1100 17th St NW Ste 1200 . . . Washington DC 20036	800-374-8472	202-484-4847	48-21
Intelligrated Products 475 E High St PO Box 899 . . . London OH 43140	866-936-7300	513-701-7300	209
IntelliNet Technologies Inc 1990 W New Haven Ave Ste 303 . . . Melbourne FL 32904	888-726-0686	321-726-0686	180-7
IntelliSoft Group LLC 61 Spit Brook Rd . . . Nashua NH 03060	888-634-4464		182
Interaction Assoc 70 Fargo St Ste 908 . . . Boston MA 02210	800-347-8352	617-234-2700	196
Interactive Business Systems Inc 2625 Butterfield Rd . . . Oak Brook IL 60523	800-555-5427	630-571-9100	182
Interactive Data Corp 32 Crosby Dr . . . Bedford MA 01730	800-228-9715	781-687-8500	634-10
Interactive Digital Solutions Inc 14701 Cumberland Rd Ste 400 . . . Noblesville IN 46060	877-880-0022	317-770-3521	51
Interactive Intelligence Inc 7601 Interactive Way . . . Indianapolis IN 46278 *NASDAQ: ININ*	800-267-1364	317-872-3000	180-7
Interactive Medical Connections Inc 700 Gemini St Ste 110 . . . Houston TX 77058	800-480-8040	281-486-4434	415
Interactive Services Group Inc 600 Delran Pkwy Ste C . . . Delran NJ 08075	800-566-3310		177
Inter-American Development Bank 1300 New York Ave NW . . . Washington DC 20577	877-782-7432	202-623-1000	781
InterAmerican Motor Corp (IMC) 8901 Canoga Ave . . . Canoga Park CA 91304	800-874-8925	818-678-1200	60
Interbond Corp of America 3200 SW 42nd St . . . Fort Lauderdale FL 33312	800-432-8579		34
InterCall 8420 W Bryn Mawr Ste 1100 . . . Chicago IL 60631	800-374-2441	773-399-1600	733
Intercept Energy Services Inc 11464 - 149 St . . . Edmonton AB T5M1W7	877-975-0558		537
Interchem Corp 120 Rt 17 N . . . Paramus NJ 07652	800-261-7332	201-261-7333	478
Interchurch Medical Assistance Inc (IMA) 500 Main St PO Box 429 . . . New Windsor MD 21776	877-241-7952	410-635-8720	47-5
Intercollegiate Studies Institute (ISI) 3901 Centerville Rd . . . Wilmington DE 19807	800-526-7022	302-652-4600	47-11
Inter-Community Telephone Co (ICTC) PO Box 8 . . . Nome ND 58062	800-350-9137	701-924-8815	733
Intercomp Co 3839 County Rd 116 . . . Medina MN 55340	800-328-3336	763-476-2531	682
InterContinental Hotels Group (IHG) 3 Ravinia Dr Ste 100 . . . Atlanta GA 30346	800-621-0555	770-604-2000	379
Holiday Inn Hotels & Resorts 3 Ravinia Dr Ste 100 . . . Atlanta GA 30346	800-725-8232	770-604-2000	379
Hotel Indigo 3 Ravinia Dr Ste 100 . . . Atlanta GA 30346	800-334-5194	770-604-2000	379
Staybridge Suites 3 Ravinia Dr Ste 100 . . . Atlanta GA 30346	800-465-4329	770-604-2000	379
Intercontinental San Francisco 888 Howard St . . . San Francisco CA 94103	888-811-4273		378
Inter-County Bakers Inc 1095 Long Island Ave . . . Deer Park NY 11729	800-696-1350	631-957-1350	69
Inter-County Energy Co-op 1009 Hustonville Rd . . . Danville KY 40422	888-266-7322	859-236-4561	247
Interdenominational Theological Ctr 700 Martin Luther King Jr Dr . . . Atlanta GA 30314	800-908-9946	404-527-7700	169
InterDev LLC 2650 Holcomb Bridge Rd Ste 310 . . . Alpharetta GA 30022	877-841-8069	770-643-4400	182
Interdom LLC 11800 S 75th Ave Ste 2N . . . Palos Heights IL 60463	800-935-0851		312
Interface EAP Inc (IEAP) 10370 Richmond Ave Ste 1100 PO Box 421879 . . . Houston TX 77042	800-324-4327	713-781-3364	461
Interface Inc 7401 E Butherus Dr . . . Scottsdale AZ 85260	800-947-5598	480-948-5555	471
Interface Security Systems LLC 6340 International Pkwy Ste 100 . . . Plano TX 75093	866-593-3480	972-996-2800	690
Interface Solutions Inc 216 Wohlsen Way . . . Lancaster PA 17603	800-942-7538		327
Interfaith Alliance 1212 New York Ave NW Ste 1250 . . . Washington DC 20005	800-510-0969	202-238-3300	47-7
Interfaith Ministries for Greater Houston 3217 Montrose Blvd . . . Houston TX 77006	800-511-0999	713-533-4900	47-20
Intergraph Corp 19 Interpro Rd . . . Madison AL 35758	800-345-4856	256-730-2000	180-5

Listing	City	State	ZIP	Toll-Free	Phone	Class
Interim HealthCare Inc						
1601 Sawgrass Corporate Pkwy	Sunrise	FL	33323	**800-338-7786**	954-858-6000	719
Interior Design Services Inc						
209 Powell Pl	Brentwood	TN	37027	**800-433-7446**	615-376-1200	322
Interlaken Inn						
74 Interlaken Rd Rt 12	Lakeville	CT	06039	**800-222-2909**	860-435-9878	667
Interlectric Corp						
1401 Lexington Ave	Warren	PA	16365	**800-722-2184**	814-723-6061	437
Interleukin Genetics Inc						
135 Beaver St	Waltham	MA	02452	**866-990-4363***	781-398-0700	233
OTC: ILIU ■ *Cust Svc						
Interlink Network Systems Inc						
495 Cranbury Rd	East Brunswick	NJ	08816	**877-872-6947**	732-846-2226	258
Interlocking Concrete Pavement Institute (ICPI)						
14801 Murdock St Ste 2300	Chantilly	VA	20151	**800-241-3652**	202-712-9036	48-3
Interlog USA Inc						
2818A Anthony Ln S	Minneapolis	MN	55418	**800-603-6030**	612-789-3456	314
Intermark Group Inc						
101 25th St N	Birmingham	AL	35243	**800-624-9239**	205-803-0000	4
Intermec Technologies Corp						
6001 36th Ave W	Everett	WA	98203	**800-934-3163***	425-348-2600	226
*Sales						
InterMetro Industries Corp						
651 N Washington St	Wilkes-Barre	PA	18705	**800-992-1776***	570-825-2741	72
*Cust Svc						
Intermodal Assn of North America (IANA)						
11785 Beltsville Dr Ste 1100	Calverton	MD	20705	**877-438-8442**	301-982-3400	48-21
Intermolecular Inc						
3011 N First St	San Jose	CA	95134	**877-251-1860**	408-582-5700	694
Intermountain Air LLC						
301 N 2370 W	Salt Lake City	UT	84116	**800-433-9617**	801-322-1645	768
Intermountain Gas Co Inc						
555 S Cole Rd	Boise	ID	83709	**800-548-3679***	208-377-6840	785
*Cust Svc						
Intermountain HealthCare						
36 S State St	Salt Lake City	UT	84111	**800-843-7820***	801-442-2000	353
*Hum Res						
Intermountain Healthcare Logan Regional Hospital						
500 E 1400 N	Logan	UT	84341	**800-442-4845**	435-716-1000	374-3
Intermountain Rural Electric Assn						
5496 Hwy 85	Sedalia	CO	80135	**800-332-9540**	303-688-3100	247
Internal Medicine News						
5635 Fishers Ln Ste 6000	Rockville	MD	20852	**877-524-9336**	240-221-2400	456-16
Internal Revenue Service (IRS)						
1111 Constitution Ave NW	Washington	DC	20224	**800-829-1040**	202-622-9511	340-16
Taxpayer Advocate Service						
77 K St NE Ste 1500	Washington	DC	20002	**877-777-4778**	202-803-9000	340-16
Internap Network Services Corp						
250 Williams St Ste E-100	Atlanta	GA	30303	**877-843-7627**	404-302-9700	38
NASDAQ: INAP						
International Academy of Compounding Pharmacists (IACP)						
4638 Riverstone Blvd	Missouri City	TX	77459	**800-927-4227**	281-933-8400	48-8
International Academy of Design & Technology						
Chicago						
1 N State St Ste 500	Chicago	IL	60602	**888-318-6111**	312-386-7681	163
Las Vegas						
2495 Village View Dr	Henderson	NV	89074	**866-400-4238**	702-990-0150	163
International Aid Inc						
17011 W Hickory St	Spring Lake	MI	49456	**800-968-7490**	616-846-7490	47-5
International Air Transport Assn						
800 Pl Victoria PO Box 113	Montreal	QC	H4Z1M1	**800-716-6326**	514-874-0202	48-21
International Airline Passengers Assn (IAPA)						
PO Box 700188	Dallas	TX	75370	**800-821-4272**	972-404-9980	47-23
International Alliance for Women (TIAW)						
1101 Pennsylvania Ave						
NW Fl 6	Washington	DC	20004	**888-712-5200**		47-24
International Alliance of Theatrical Stage Employees Moving Picture Technicians (IATSE)						
1430 Broadway 20th Fl	New York	NY	10018	**800-456-3863**	212-730-1770	414
International Assn for Food Protection (IAFP)						
6200 Aurora Ave Ste 200W	Des Moines	IA	50322	**800-369-6337***	515-276-3344	48-6
*General						
International Assn for Human Resource Information Management Inc (IHRIM)						
PO Box 1086	Burlington	MA	01803	**800-804-3983**		48-12
International Assn for the Study of Pain (IASP)						
111 Queen Anne Ave N Ste 501	Seattle	WA	98109	**866-574-2654**	206-283-0311	47-17
International Assn of Approved Basketball Officials (IAABO)						
PO Box 355	Carlisle	PA	17013	**800-526-1379**	717-713-8129	47-22
International Assn of Arson Investigators (IAAI)						
2111 Baldwin Ave # 203	Crofton	MD	21114	**800-468-4224**	410-451-3473	48-7
International Assn of Assessing Officers (IAAO)						
314 W Tenth St	Kansas City	MO	64105	**800-616-4226**	816-701-8100	48-7
International Assn of Bridge Structural Ornamental & Reinforcing Iron Workers						
1750 New York Ave NW Ste 400	Washington	DC	20006	**800-368-0105**	202-383-4800	414
International Assn of Business Communicators (IABC)						
155 Montgomery St						
Ste 1210	San Francisco	CA	94104	**800-766-4222**	415-544-4700	48-12
International Assn of Chiefs of Police (IACP)						
44 Canal Ctr Plz Ste 200	Alexandria	VA	22314	**800-843-4227**	703-836-6767	48-7
International Assn of Culinary Professionals (IACP)						
1221 Ave of the Americas						
42nd fl	New York	NY	10020	**800-928-4227**	866-358-2524	48-6
International Assn of Electrical Inspectors (IAEI)						
901 Waterfall Way Ste 602	Richardson	TX	75080	**800-786-4234**	972-235-1455	48-3
International Assn of Exhibitions & Events (IAEE)						
12700 Park Central Dr Ste 308	Dallas	TX	75251	**866-266-3378**	972-458-8002	48-18
International Assn of Fairs & Expositions, The (IAFE)						
3043 E Cairo	Springfield	MO	65802	**800-516-0313**	417-862-5771	47-23
International Assn of Fire Chiefs (IAFC)						
4025 Fair Ridge Dr Ste 300	Fairfax	VA	22033	**866-385-9110**	703-273-0911	48-7
International Assn of Lions Clubs						
300 W 22nd St	Oak Brook	IL	60523	**800-710-7822**	630-571-5466	47-15
International Assn of Marriage & Family Counselors (IAMFC)						
5999 Stevenson Ave	Alexandria	VA	22304	**800-347-6647**		48-15
International Assn of Plumbing & Mechanical Officials (IAPMO)						
4755 E Philadelphia St	Ontario	CA	91761	**877-427-6601**	909-472-4100	48-7
International Assn of Venue Managers Inc (IAVM)						
635 Fritz Dr Ste 100	Coppell	TX	75019	**800-935-4226**	972-906-7441	48-12
International Assn of Workforce Professionals (IAPES)						
1801 Louisville Rd	Frankfort	KY	40601	**888-898-9960**	502-223-4459	48-12

Listing	City	State	ZIP	Toll-Free	Phone	Class
International Baptist College						
2211 W Germann Rd	Chandler	AZ	85286	**800-422-4858***	480-245-7900	167
*General						
International Bible Society (IBS)						
Biblica						
1820 Jet Stream Dr	Colorado Springs	CO	80921	**800-524-1588***	719-488-9200	47-20
*Cust Svc						
International Biometric Society (IBS)						
1444 'I' St NW Ste 700	Washington	DC	20005	**800-262-1171**	202-712-9049	48-19
International Bottled Water Assn (IBWA)						
1700 Diagonal Rd Ste 650	Alexandria	VA	22314	**800-928-3711**	703-683-5213	48-6
International Boundary & Water Commission - US & Mexico						
4171 N Mesa Ste C-100	El Paso	TX	79902	**800-262-8857**	915-832-4101	340-14
International Bowling Museum & Hall of Fame						
621 Six Flags Dr	Arlington	TX	76011	**800-514-2695**	817-385-8215	521
International Business & Finance Daily						
1801 S Bell St	Arlington	VA	22202	**800-372-1033**		530-1
International Business College						
5699 Coventry Ln	Fort Wayne	IN	46804	**800-589-6363**	260-459-4500	798
International Business Machines Corp (IBM)						
1 New OrchaRd Rd	Armonk	NY	10504	**800-426-4968**	914-499-1900	175-1
NYSE: IBM						
International Carwash Assn						
230 E Ohio St	Chicago	IL	60611	**888-422-8422**		48-21
International Cemetery Cremation & Funeral Assn (ICCFA)						
107 Carpenter Dr Ste 100	Sterling	VA	20164	**800-645-7700**	703-391-8400	48-4
International Ceramic Engineering						
235 Brooks St	Worcester	MA	01606	**800-779-3321**	508-853-4700	251
International Chauffeured Service Worldwide						
53 E 34th St	New York	NY	10016	**800-266-5254**	212-213-0302	441
International Chemical Co						
2628 N Mascher St	Philadelphia	PA	19133	**888-225-5422**	215-739-2313	144
International Chimney Corp						
55 S Long St	Williamsville	NY	14221	**800-828-1446**		191-7
International Chiropractors Assn (ICA)						
6400 Arlington Blvd						
Ste 800	Falls Church	VA	22042	**800-423-4690**	703-528-5000	48-8
International Church of the Foursquare Gospel (ICFG)						
1910 W Sunset Blvd						
PO Box 26902	Los Angeles	CA	90026	**888-635-4234**	213-989-4234	47-20
International City/County Management Assn (ICMA)						
777 N Capitol St NE Ste 500	Washington	DC	20002	**800-745-8780**	202-289-4262	48-7
International Civil Rights Ctr & Museum						
134 S Elm St	Greensboro	NC	27401	**800-748-7116**	336-274-9199	519
International Coatings Co						
13929 166th St	Cerritos	CA	90703	**800-423-4103**	562-926-1010	388
International Code Council (ICC)						
500 New Jersey Ave NW 6th Fl	Washington	DC	20001	**888-422-7233**	202-370-1800	48-3
International Cold Storage Company Inc						
215 E 13th St	Andover	KS	67002	**800-835-0001**	316-733-1385	662
International College of Dentists (ICD)						
51 Monroe St Ste 1400	Rockville	MD	20850	**800-533-6825**	301-251-8861	48-8
International Collegiate Licensing Assn (ICLA)						
24651 Detroit Rd	Westlake	OH	44145	**877-887-2261**	440-892-4000	47-22
International Communications Industries Assn (ICIA)						
11242 Waples Mill Rd Ste 200	Fairfax	VA	22030	**800-659-7469**	703-273-7200	48-20
International Conference of Funeral Service Examining Boards Inc						
1885 Shelby Ln	Fayetteville	AR	72704	**800-709-0180**	479-442-7076	48-7
International Congress of Oral Implantologists (ICOI)						
248 Lorraine Ave 3rd Fl	Upper Montclair	NJ	07043	**800-442-0525**	973-783-6300	48-8
International Contract Furnishings Inc (ICF)						
19 Ohio Ave	Norwich	CT	06360	**800-237-1625**	860-886-1700	322
International Converter Inc						
17153 Industrial Hwy	Caldwell	OH	43724	**800-848-6623**	740-732-5665	553
International Cornea Project						
9246 Lightwave Ave Ste 120	San Diego	CA	92123	**800-393-2265**	858-694-0400	271
International Dairy Queen Corp						
7505 Metro Blvd	Minneapolis	MN	55439	**866-793-7582**	952-830-0200	668
International Dairy-Deli-Bakery Assn (IDDBA)						
636 Science Dr	Madison	WI	53705	**877-399-4925**	608-238-7908	48-6
International Data Corp (IDC)						
5 Speen St	Framingham	MA	01701	**800-343-4952**	508-872-8200	465
International Data Group Inc (IDG)						
1 Exeter Plaza 15th Fl	Boston	MA	02116	**800-343-4952***	617-534-1200	634-9
*Orders						
International Delivery Solutions LLC						
7340 S Howell Ave	Milwaukee	WI	53154	**877-437-8722**		5
International Dyslexia Assn, The (IDA)						
40 York Rd 4th Fl	Towson	MD	21204	**800-222-3123**	410-296-0232	47-17
International Engraved Graphics Assn						
305 Plus Pk Blvd	Nashville	TN	37217	**800-821-3138**		48-4
International Executive Housekeepers Assn (IEHA)						
1001 Eastwind Dr Ste 301	Westerville	OH	43081	**800-200-6342**	614-895-7166	48-4
International Exposition Ctr						
1-X Ctr Dr	Cleveland	OH	44135	**855-436-8683**	216-676-6000	207
International Extrusions Inc						
5800 Venoy Rd	Garden City	MI	48135	**800-242-8876**	734-427-8700	481
International Federation of Accountants						
545 Fifth Ave 14th Fl	New York	NY	10017	**888-272-2001**	212-286-9344	48-1
International Fiber Corp						
50 Bridge St	North Tonawanda	NY	14120	**888-698-1936**	716-693-4040	604-1
International Fidelity Insurance Co (IFIC)						
1 Newark Ctr 20th Fl	Newark	NJ	07102	**800-333-4167**	973-624-7200	391-5
International Food Information Council Foundation (IFIC)						
1100 Connecticut Ave NW						
Ste 430	Washington	DC	20036	**888-723-3366**	202-296-6540	48-6
International Foundation of Employee Benefit Plans (IFEBP)						
18700 W Bluemound Rd	Brookfield	WI	53045	**888-334-3327**	262-786-6700	262
International Franchise Assn (IFA)						
1501 K St NW Ste 350	Washington	DC	20005	**800-543-1038**	202-628-8000	48-18
International Fraternity of Phi Gamma Delta						
1201 Red Mile Rd PO Box 4599	Lexington	KY	40544	**888-668-4293**	859-255-1848	47-16
International Fund for Animal Welfare (IFAW)						
290 Summer St	Yarmouth Port	MA	02675	**800-932-4329**	508-744-2000	47-3
International Game Technology (IGT)						
9295 Prototype Dr	Reno	NV	89521	**800-522-4700**	775-448-7777	323
NYSE: IGT						
International Gay & Lesbian Travel Assn (IGLTA)						
1201 NE 26th St Ste 103	Fort Lauderdale	FL	33305	**888-789-3090**	954-630-1637	47-23

Name / Address	City	State	ZIP	Toll-Free	Phone	Class
International Gourmet Foods Inc 7520 Fullerton Rd	Springfield	VA	22153	800-522-0377	703-569-4520	345
International Ground Source Heat Pump Assn (IGSHPA) Oklahoma State University 374 Cordell S	Stillwater	OK	74078	800-626-4747	405-744-5175	48-13
International Group Inc 85 Old Eagle School Rd	Wayne	PA	19087	800-852-6537	610-687-9030	579
International Health Racquet & Sportsclub Assn (IHRSA) 70 Fargo St	Boston	MA	02210	800-228-4772	617-951-0055	47-22
International Hearing Society (IHS) 16880 Middlebelt Rd Ste 4	Livonia	MI	48154	800-521-5247	734-522-7200	47-17
International Homes of Cedar Inc (IHC) PO Box 886	Woodinville	WA	98072	800-767-7674	360-668-8511	105
International Hotel 20 Second Ave SW	Rochester	MN	55902	800-940-6811		379
International House Hotel 221 Camp St	New Orleans	LA	70130	800-633-5770	504-553-9550	379
International Housewares Assn (IHA) 6400 Shafer Ct Ste 650	Rosemont	IL	60018	800-752-1052	847-292-4200	48-4
International Imaging Materials Inc 310 Commerce Dr	Amherst	NY	14228	888-464-4625	716-691-6333	533
International Immunology Corp 25549 Adams Ave	Murrieta	CA	92562	800-843-2853	951-677-5629	233
International Institute of Ammonia Refrigeration 1001 N Fairfax St Ste 503	Alexandria	VA	22314	800-937-8461	703-312-4200	48-3
International Institute of Municipal Clerks (IIMC) 8331 Utica Ave Ste 200	Rancho Cucamonga	CA	91730	800-251-1639	909-944-4162	48-7
International Interior Design Assn (IIDA) 222 Merchandise Mart Plz Ste 567	Chicago	IL	60654	888-799-4432	312-467-1950	47-4
International Investigators Inc 3216 N Pennsylvania St	Indianapolis	IN	46205	800-403-8111	317-925-1496	400
International Isotopes Inc 4137 Commerce Cir *OTC: INIS*	Idaho Falls	ID	83401	800-699-3108	208-524-5300	233
International Jet Aviation Services 8511 Aviator Ln	Centennial	CO	80112	800-858-5891	303-790-0414	13
International Label & Printing Company Inc 2550 United Ln	Elk Grove Village	IL	60007	800-244-1442		413
International Launch Services (ILS) 1875 Explorer St Ste 700	Reston	VA	20190	800-852-4980	571-633-7400	503
International Lawyers in Alcoholics Anonymous (ILAA) 415-1080 Mainland St	Vancouver	BC	V6B2T4	888-685-2171	604-685-2171	47-21
International Longshore & Warehouse Union 1188 Franklin St 4th Fl	San Francisco	CA	94109	866-266-0013	415-775-0533	414
International Manufacturing Group Inc 879 F St Ste 120	West Sacramento	CA	95605	800-775-6412		474
International Masonry Institute (IMI) 17101 Science Dr	Bowie	MD	20715	800-803-0295		48-3
International Medical Corps (IMC) 1919 Santa Monica Blvd Ste 400	Santa Monica	CA	90404	800-481-4462	310-826-7800	47-5
International Medical Device Regulatory Monitor 300 N Washington St Ste 200	Falls Church	VA	22046	888-838-5578	703-538-7600	530-8
International Meeting Managers Inc 4550 Post Oak Pl Ste 342	Houston	TX	77027	800-423-7175	713-965-0566	186
International Metal Hose Co 520 Goodrich Rd	Bellevue	OH	44811	800-458-6855	419-483-7690	489
International Mold Steel Inc 6796 Powerline Dr	Florence	KY	41042	800-625-6653	859-342-6000	491
International Montessori Council & The Montessori Foundation 19600 Florida 64 PO Box 130	Bradenton	FL	34212	800-655-5843	941-729-9565	47-11
International Motor Coach Group Inc (IMG) 8695 College Blvd Ste 260	Overland Park	KS	66210	888-447-3466	913-906-0111	48-21
International Mountain Bicycling Assn (IMBA) 4888 Pearl E Cir Ste 200E	Boulder	CO	80301	888-442-4622	303-545-9011	47-23
International Municipal Lawyers Assn (IMLA) 7910 Woodmont Ave Ste 1440	Bethesda	MD	20814	800-942-7732	202-466-5424	48-10
International Municipal Signal Assn (IMSA) 165 E Union St PO Box 539	Newark	NY	14513	800-723-4672	315-331-2182	48-7
International Museum of the Horse 4089 Iron Works Pkwy	Lexington	KY	40511	800-678-8813	859-259-4232	519
International Order of the Golden Rule (OGR) 3520 Executive Ctr Dr Ste 300	Austin	TX	78731	800-637-8030	512-334-5504	48-4
International Organization of Masters Mates & Pilots 700 Maritime Blvd	Linthicum Heights	MD	21090	877-667-5522	410-850-8700	414
International Orthodox Christian Charities (IOCC) 110 W Rd Ste 360	Towson	MD	21204	877-803-4622	410-243-9820	47-5
International Paper Co 6400 Poplar Ave *NYSE: IP* ■ *Prod Info	Memphis	TN	38197	800-223-1268*	901-419-9000	556
International Pentecostal Holiness Church (IPHC) PO Box 12609	Oklahoma City	OK	73157	888-474-2966	405-787-7110	47-20
International Planned Parenthood Federation - Western Hemisphere Region (IPPF/WHR) 125 Maiden Ln 9th Fl	New York	NY	10005	866-477-3947	212-248-6400	47-5
International Plant Nutrition Institute (IPNI) 3500 PkwyLn Ste 550	Norcross	GA	30092	800-521-3044	770-447-0335	47-2
International Plastics Inc 185 Commerce Ctr	Greenville	SC	29615	800-820-4722	864-297-8000	345
International Playthings Inc 75D Lackawanna Ave	Parsippany	NJ	07054	800-631-1272	973-316-2500	760
International Poly Bag Inc 990 Pk Ctr Dr Ste F & G	Vista	CA	92081	800-976-5922	760-598-2468	65
International Port of Dutch Harbor PO Box 610	Unalaska	AK	99685	800-526-6731	907-581-1251	617
International Public Management Assn for Hum Res (IPMA-HR) 1617 Duke St	Alexandria	VA	22314	800-381-8378	703-549-7100	48-12
International Reprographic Assn (IRgA) 401 N Michigan Ave Ste 2200	Chicago	IL	60611	800-833-4742	312-245-1026	48-16
International Rescue Committee (IRC) 122 E 42nd St 12th Fl	New York	NY	10168	800-435-7352	212-551-3000	47-5
International Revolving Door Co 2138 N Sixth Ave	Evansville	IN	47710	800-745-4726	812-425-3311	236
International Safe Transit Assn (ISTA) 1400 Abbott Rd Ste 160	East Lansing	MI	48823	888-299-2208	517-333-3437	48-21
International Sanitary Supply Assn (ISSA) 3300 Dundee Rd	Northbrook	IL	60062	800-225-4772	847-982-0800	48-18
International Shipholding Corp 11 N Water Ste 18290 *NYSE: ISH*	Mobile	AL	36602	800-826-3513	251-243-9100	314
International Sight Restoration Inc 3808 Gunn Hwy Ste B	Tampa	FL	33618	877-477-3210	813-264-6003	271
International Sign Assn (ISA) 1001 N Fairfax St Ste 301	Alexandria	VA	22314	866-949-7446	703-836-4012	48-4
International Snowmobile Hall of Fame 1521 N Railroad St	Eagle River	WI	54521	800-746-8963	715-479-2186	521
International Society for Animal Rights (ISAR) PO Box F	Clarks Summit	PA	18411	888-589-6397	570-586-2200	47-3
International Society for Heart & Lung Transplantation (ISHLT) 14673 Midway Rd Ste 200	Addison	TX	75001	888-722-2220	972-490-9495	48-8
International Society for Magnetic Resonance in Medicine (ISMRM) 2030 Addison St Ste 700	Berkeley	CA	94704	800-445-8667	510-841-1899	48-8
International Society for Performance Improvement (ISPI) PO Box 13035	Silver Spring	MD	20910	800-825-7550	301-587-8570	48-12
International Society for Peritoneal Dialysis (ISPD) 66 Martin St	Milton	ON	L9T2R2	888-834-1001	905-875-2456	48-8
International Society for Pharmacoeconomics & Outcomes Research (ISPOR) 3100 Princeton Pk Bldg 3 Ste E	Lawrenceville	NJ	08648	800-992-0643	609-219-0773	48-8
International Society for Pharmacoepidemiology (ISPE) 5272 River Rd Ste 630	Bethesda	MD	20816	888-887-7955	301-718-6500	48-8
International Society for Technology in Education (ISTE) 1530 Wilson Blvd Ste 730 *General	Arlington	VA	22209	800-336-5191*	202-861-7777	48-5
International Society for Traumatic Stress Studies (ISTSS) 111 Deer Lk Rd Ste 100	Deerfield	IL	60015	877-469-7873	847-480-9028	48-15
International Society of Arboriculture (ISA) PO Box 3129	Champaign	IL	61826	888-472-8733	217-355-9411	47-2
International Society of Certified Electronics Technicians (ISCET) 3608 Pershing Ave	Fort Worth	TX	76107	800-946-0201	817-921-9101	48-19
International Society of Certified Employee Benefit Specialists (ISCEBS) 18700 W Bluemond Rd PO Box 209	Brookfield	WI	53008	888-334-3327	262-786-8771	48-12
International Society of Fire Service Instructors (ISFSI) 14001C St Germain Dr	Centreville	VA	20121	800-435-0005		48-7
International Society of Refractive Surgery (ISRS) 655 Beach St PO Box 7424	San Francisco	CA	94109	866-561-8558	415-561-8581	48-8
International Society of Tropical Foresters (ISTF) 5400 Grosvenor Ln	Bethesda	MD	20814	866-897-8720	301-530-4514	47-13
International SOS Assistance Inc 3600 Horizon Blvd Ste 300	Trevose	PA	19053	800-441-2668	215-244-1500	391-7
International Specialty Products Inc (ISP) 1361 Alps Rd	Wayne	NJ	07470	800-622-4423	973-628-4000	143
International Tax Monitor 1801 S Bell St	Arlington	VA	22202	800-372-1033		530-1
International Tennis Hall of Fame & Museum 194 Bellevue Ave	Newport	RI	02840	800-745-3000	401-849-3990	521
International Trademark Assn (INTA) 655 Third Ave 10th Fl	New York	NY	10017	800-995-3579	212-768-9887	48-12
International Training Inc 1045 Ne Industrial Blvd	Jensen Beach	FL	34957	888-778-9073	207-729-4201	31
International Transplant Nurses Society (ITNS) 1739 E Carson St PO Box 351	Pittsburgh	PA	15203	800-776-8636	412-343-4867	48-8
International Travel Systems Inc 64 Madison Ave	Wood-Ridge	NJ	07075	800-258-0135	201-727-0470	16
International Union of Bricklayers & Allied Craftworkers (BAC) 1776 eye St NW	Washington	DC	20006	888-880-8222	202-783-3788	414
International Union of Painters & Allied Trades (IUPAT) 7234 Pkwy Dr	Hanover	MD	21076	800-554-2479	410-564-5900	414
International Union of Police Assn 1549 Ringling Blvd Ste 600	Sarasota	FL	34236	800-247-4872	941-487-2560	414
International Union Security Police & Fire Professionals of America (SPFPA) 25510 Kelly Rd	Roseville	MI	48066	800-228-7492	586-772-7250	414
International Violin Co Ltd 1421 Clarkview Rd	Baltimore	MD	21209	800-542-3538	410-832-2525	525
International Visual Corp (IVC) 11500 Blvd Armand Bombardier	Montreal	QC	H1E2W9	866-643-0570	514-643-0570	288
International Window Corp 5625 E Firestone Blvd	South Gate	CA	90280	800-477-4032	562-928-6411	236
International Women's Air & Space Museum 1501 N Marginal Rd Burke Lakefront Airport	Cleveland	OH	44114	877-287-4752	216-623-1111	519
International Wood Products Assn (IWPA) 4214 King St	Alexandria	VA	22302	855-435-0005	703-820-6696	48-3
Internet Business Network 303 Ross Dr	Mill Valley	CA	94941	866-497-6747	415-377-2255	634-9
Internet Law & Strategy 1617 JFK Blvd Ste 1750	Philadelphia	PA	19103	877-256-2472	215-557-2300	530-7
Internet Matrix Inc 10179 Huennekens St	San Diego	CA	92121	800-462-8749		7
Internet Nebraska Inc 1719 N Cotner Blvd Ste B	Lincoln	NE	68505	800-438-4638	402-434-8680	227
InternetSafety.com Inc 3979 S Main St Ste 230	Acworth	GA	30101	877-944-8080		180-7
Inter-Pacific Corp 2257 Colby Ave	Los Angeles	CA	90064	877-605-8414	310-473-7591	302
Interphase Corp 4240 International Pkwy Ste 105 *NASDAQ: INPH*	Carrollton	TX	75007	800-327-8638	214-654-5000	178
Interplastic Corp 1225 Wolters Blvd	Saint Paul	MN	55110	800-736-5497	651-481-6860	604-2
Interpoint Corp PO Box 97005	Redmond	WA	98073	800-822-8782	425-882-3100	255
Interpreters Unlimited Inc 11199 Sorrento Vly Rd Ste 203	San Diego	CA	92121	800-726-9891		766
Interprint Inc 12350 US Hwy 19 N	Clearwater	FL	33764	800-749-5152	727-531-8957	626
Interprint LLC 7111 Hayvenhurst Ave	Van Nuys	CA	91406	800-926-9873	818-989-3600	626
InterraTech Corp PO Box 4	Mount Ephraim	NJ	08059	888-589-4889	856-854-5100	180-1
Intersect Media Solutions 766 N Sun Dr Ste 2000	Lake Mary	FL	32746	866-404-5913		197

Name / Address	City	State	ZIP	Toll-Free	Phone	Class
Intersections Inc						
3901 Stonecroft Blvd	Chantilly	VA	20151	**800-695-7536**	703-488-6100	219
NASDAQ: INTX						
Interserve USA						
PO Box 418	Upper Darby	PA	19082	**800-809-4440**	610-352-0581	47-20
Intersil Corp						
1001 Murphy Ranch Rd	Milpitas	CA	95035	**888-468-3774**	408-432-8888	694
NASDAQ: ISIL						
Interstate Aviation						
62 Johnson Ave	Plainville	CT	06062	**800-573-5519**	860-747-5519	62
Interstate Batteries						
12770 Merit Dr Ste 400	Dallas	TX	75251	**800-541-8419**	972-991-1444	60
Interstate Chemical Co Inc						
2797 Freedland Rd	Hermitage	PA	16148	**800-422-2436**	724-981-3771	142
Interstate Connecting Components Inc						
120 Mt Holly By Pass	Lumberton	NJ	08048	**888-899-1990**	800-422-3911	248
Interstate Distributor Co						
11707 21st Ave S	Tacoma	WA	98444	**800-426-8560**		778
Interstate Electrical Supply Inc						
2300 Second Ave	Columbus	GA	31901	**800-903-4409**	706-324-1000	248
Interstate Electronics Corp						
602 E Vermont Ave PO Box 3117	Anaheim	CA	92803	**800-854-6979**	714-758-0500	528
Interstate Transport Inc						
324 First Ave N	St Petersburg	FL	33701	**866-281-1281**	727-822-9999	648
Interstates Construction Services Inc						
1520 N Main Ave	Sioux Center	IA	51250	**800-827-1662**	712-722-1662	191-4
Interstock Premium Cabinets LLC						
6300 Bristol Pike	Levittown	PA	19057	**800-896-9842**	267-288-1200	742-9
Interstyle Ceramics & Glass Ltd						
3625 Brighton Ave	Burnaby	BC	V5A3H5	**800-667-1566**	604-421-7229	749
Intertek Group PLC						
801 Travis St Ste 1500	Houston	TX	77002	**800-967-5352**	713-407-3500	263
Intertrade Industries Ltd						
14600 Commerce Ln	Huntington Beach	CA	92649	**800-944-9277**	714-894-5566	600
InterTrust Technologies Corp						
920 Stewart Dr Ste 100	Sunnyvale	CA	94085	**800-393-2272**	408-616-1600	180-12
Interval International Inc						
6262 Sunset Dr PO Box 431920	Miami	FL	33143	**800-828-8200**	305-666-1861	751
InterVarsity Christian Fellowship/USA						
6400 Schroeder Rd	Madison	WI	53711	**866-734-4823**	608-274-9001	47-20
Intervest Construction Inc						
2379 Beville Rd	Daytona Beach	FL	32119	**855-215-2974**	844-349-6401	651
Interview Magazine						
575 Broadway 5th Fl	New York	NY	10012	**800-925-9574**	212-941-2900	456-11
InterVision Systems Technologies Inc						
2270 Martin Ave	Santa Clara	CA	95050	**800-787-6707**	408-980-8550	182
InterWest Insurance Services Inc						
3636 American River Dr						
2nd Fl	Sacramento	CA	95864	**800-444-4134**	916-679-2960	390
InterWest Partners						
2710 Sand Hill Rd 2nd Fl	Menlo Park	CA	94025	**866-803-9204**	650-854-8585	790
InterWorks Inc						
1425 S Sangre Rd	Stillwater	OK	74074	**866-490-9643**	405-624-3214	182
Intex Recreation Corp						
1665 Hughes Way PO Box 1440	Long Beach	CA	90801	**800-234-6839***		708
*Cust Svc						
Intland GmbH						
968 Inverness Way	Sunnyvale	CA	94087	**866-468-5210**		393
In-Touch Insight Systems Inc						
400 March Rd	Ottawa	ON	K2K3H4	**800-263-2980**		179
Intradiem						
3650 Mansell Rd Ste 500	Alpharetta	GA	30022	**888-566-9457**	678-356-3500	180-10
Intrado Inc						
1601 Dry Creek Dr	Longmont	CO	80503	**877-262-3775**	720-494-5800	733
IntraLinks Inc						
150 E 42nd St Ste 8	New York	NY	10017	**888-546-5383**	212-543-7700	38
Intratek Computer Inc						
5431 Industrial Dr	Huntington Beach	CA	92649	**800-892-8282**		177
Intrepid Control Systems Inc						
5700 18 Mile Rd	Sterling Heights	MI	48314	**800-859-6265**	586-731-7950	182
Intrepid Potash Inc						
700 17th St Ste 1700	Denver	CO	80202	**800-451-2888**	303-296-3006	282
NYSE: IPI						
Intrepid Sea-Air-Space Museum						
W 46th St & 12th Ave Pier 86	New York	NY	10036	**877-957-7447**	212-245-0072	519
Intrinsix Corp						
100 Campus Dr	Marlborough	MA	01752	**800-783-0330**	508-658-7600	263
Intronix Technologies Inc						
26 McEwan Dr West Unit 15	Bolton	ON	L7E1E6	**800-819-9996**	905-951-3361	318
Intrusion Inc						
1101 E Arapaho Rd	Richardson	TX	75081	**888-637-7770**	972-234-6400	180-12
Intsel Steel Distributors LP						
11310 W Little York	Houston	TX	77041	**800-762-3316**	713-937-9500	721
Intuit Inc						
2632 Marine Way	Mountain View	CA	94043	**800-446-8848***	650-944-6000	180-9
NASDAQ: INTU ■ *Cust Svc						
Intuitive Surgical Inc						
1266 Kifer Rd Bldg 101	Sunnyvale	CA	94086	**888-868-4647**	408-523-2100	475
NASDAQ: ISRG						
Inuit Gallery of Vancouver Ltd						
206 Cambie St Gastown	Vancouver	BC	V6B2M9	**888-615-8399**	604-688-7323	41
Invacare Corp						
1 Invacare Way	Elyria	OH	44036	**800-333-6900**	440-329-6000	476
NYSE: IVC						
Invenio Marketing Solutions Inc						
2201 Donley Dr Ste 200	Austin	TX	78758	**800-926-1754**	512-990-2000	197
Invent Now, Inc						
3701 Highland Park NW	North Canton	OH	44720	**800-968-4332**		519
Inventory Sales Co						
9777 Reavis Rd	St Louis	MO	63123	**866-417-3801**	314-776-6200	350
Inver Hills Community College						
2500 80th St E	Inver Grove Heights	MN	55076	**866-576-0689**	651-450-8500	161
Inverness Hotel & Golf Club						
200 Inverness Dr W	Englewood	CO	80112	**800-346-4891**	303-799-5800	667
Invesco						
11 Greenway Plaza Ste 100	Houston	TX	77046	**800-959-4246**	713-626-1919	527
INVESCO Private Capital Inc						
1166 Ave of the Americas						
26th Fl	New York	NY	10036	**800-959-4246**	212-278-9000	790
Invesco Trimark Ltd						
5140 Yonge St Ste 800	Toronto	ON	M2N6X7	**800-874-6275**	416-590-9855	527
Investment Management Consultants Assn (IMCA)						
5619 DTC Pkwy Ste 500	Greenwood Village	CO	80111	**800-250-9083**	303-770-3377	48-2
Investment Scorecard Inc						
601 Grassmere Park Dr Ste 1	Nashville	TN	37211	**800-555-6035**	615-301-1975	401
Investor's Business Daily						
12655 Beatrice St	Los Angeles	CA	90066	**800-831-2525**	310-448-6000	531-2
Investorldeas com						
145 Tyee Dr Number 1573	Point Roberts	WA	98281	**800-665-0411**		465
InvestorPlace.com						
2420A Gehman Ln						
2420A Gehman Ln	Lancaster	PA	17602	**800-219-8592**		404
Investors Heritage Life Insurance Co (IHLIC)						
200 Capital Ave PO Box 717	Frankfort	KY	40602	**800-422-2011**	502-223-2361	391-2
Investors Savings Bank						
101 Wood Ave S	Iselin	NJ	08830	**855-422-6548**	973-924-5100	69
NASDAQ: ISBC						
Investors Title Co						
121 N Columbia St	Chapel Hill	NC	27514	**800-326-4842**	919-968-2200	360-4
NASDAQ: ITIC						
Investrade Discount Securities						
950 N Milwaukee Ave Ste 102	Glenview	IL	60025	**800-498-7120***	847-375-6080	688
*Cust Svc						
Invincible Office Furniture Co						
842 S 26th St PO Box 1117	Manitowoc	WI	54220	**877-682-4601**	920-682-4601	320-1
Invisible Hand Networks Inc						
670 Broadway Ste 302	New York	NY	10012	**866-637-5286**	212-400-7416	393
INVISTA						
4123 E 37th St N	Wichita	KS	67220	**877-446-8478**	316-828-1000	604-1
InVite Health Inc						
1 Garden State Plz	Paramus	NJ	07652	**800-349-0929**	201-587-2222	345
Invitechange LLC						
110 Third Ave N Ste 102	Edmonds	WA	98020	**877-228-2622**	425-778-3505	763
Inviting Home.com						
4700 SW 51st St Unit 219	Davie	FL	33314	**866-751-6606**	781-444-8001	322
InVitro International						
330 E Orangethorpe Ave Ste D	Placentia	CA	92870	**800-246-8487**	949-851-8356	233
Invivoscribe Technologies Inc						
6330 Nancy Ridge Dr Ste 106	San Diego	CA	92121	**866-623-8105**	858-224-6600	233
Invoke Solutions Inc						
375 Totten Pond Rd	Waltham	MA	02451	**866-687-4367**	781-810-2700	465
InVue Security Products Inc						
10715 Sikes Pl Ste 200	Charlotte	NC	28277	**888-257-4272**	704-206-7849	255
IOA Re Inc						
190 W Germantown Pk						
Ste 200	East Norriton	PA	19401	**800-462-2300**	610-940-9000	391-3
IOActive Inc						
701 Fifth Ave Ste 6850	Seattle	WA	98104	**866-760-0222**	206-784-4313	182
IOCC (International Orthodox Christian Charities)						
110 W Rd Ste 360	Towson	MD	21204	**877-803-4622**	410-243-9820	47-5
IOF (Independent Order of Foresters)						
789 Don Mills Rd	Toronto	ON	M3C1T9	**800-828-1540**	416-429-3000	47-5
Iolani School						
563 Kamoku St	Honolulu	HI	96826	**888-879-8970**	808-949-5355	622
Ioline Corp						
14140 NE 200th St	Woodinville	WA	98072	**800-598-0029**	425-398-8282	741
Iomosaic Corp						
93 Stiles Rd	Salem	NH	03079	**844-466-6724**	603-893-7009	198
ION (Institute of Navigation Inc)						
8551 Rixlew Ln Ste 360	Manassas	VA	20109	**800-696-7353**	703-366-2723	48-21
Ion Media Networks						
601 Clearwater Pk Rd	West Palm Beach	FL	33401	**800-987-9936**	561-659-4122	736
Ion Networks Inc						
120 Corporate Blvd						
Ste A	South Plainfield	NJ	07080	**800-722-8986**	908-546-3900	180-7
Iona College						
715 N Ave	New Rochelle	NY	10801	**800-264-6350**	914-633-2502	167
IoPP (Institute of Packaging Professionals)						
1833 Centre Point Cir						
Ste 123	Naperville	IL	60563	**800-432-4085**	630-544-5050	48-13
Iowa						
Adult Children & Family Services Div						
1305 E Walnut St	Des Moines	IA	50319	**800-735-2942**	515-281-8746	339-16
Child Support Recovery Unit						
PO Box 9125	Des Moines	IA	50306	**888-229-9223**		339-16
Consumer Protection Div						
1305 E Walnut St 2nd Fl	Des Moines	IA	50319	**888-777-4590**	515-281-5926	339-16
Elder Affairs Dept						
510 E 12th St Ste 2	Des Moines	IA	50309	**800-532-3213**	515-242-3333	339-16
Motor Vehicle Div						
100 Euclid Ave PO Box 9204	Des Moines	IA	50306	**800-532-1121**	515-244-9124	339-16
Revenue & Finance Dept						
1305 E Walnut	Des Moines	IA	50319	**800-367-3388**	515-281-3204	339-16
Utilities Board						
1375 E Ct Ave Rm 69	Des Moines	IA	50319	**877-565-4450**	515-725-7300	339-16
Iowa Assn of Business & Industry						
400 E Ct Ave Ste 100	Des Moines	IA	50309	**800-383-4224**	515-280-8000	139
Iowa Assn of Realtors						
1370 NW 114th St Ste 100	Clive	IA	50325	**800-532-1515**	515-453-1064	654
Iowa Central Community College						
2031 Quail Ave	Fort Dodge	IA	50501	**800-362-2793**	515-576-7201	161
Iowa City Public Library						
123 S Linn St	Iowa City	IA	52240	**866-862-6877**	319-356-5200	434-3
Iowa City/Coralville Area Convention & Visitors Bureau						
900 First Ave Hayden Fry Way						
	Coralville	IA	52241	**800-283-6592**	319-337-6592	208
Iowa College Student Aid Commission						
603 E 12th St Fl 5th	Des Moines	IA	50319	**800-383-4222**	515-725-3400	723
Iowa Dental Assn						
8797 NW 54th Ave Ste 100	Johnston	IA	50131	**800-828-2181**	515-331-2298	229
Iowa Farm Bureau Spokesman Magazine						
5400 University Ave	West Des Moines	IA	50266	**866-598-3693**	515-225-5413	456-1
Iowa Gold Star Military Museum						
7105 NW 70th Ave	Johnston	IA	50131	**800-294-6607**	515-252-4531	519
Iowa Interstate Railroad						
5900 Sixth St SW	Cedar Rapids	IA	52404	**800-321-3884**	319-298-5400	646
Iowa Lakes Community College						
300 S 18th St	Estherville	IA	51334	**800-242-5106**	712-362-2604	161

Name	Address	City	State	Zip	Toll-Free	Phone	Class
Iowa Lakes Electric Co-op	702 S First St	Estherville	IA	51334	**800-225-4532**	712-362-7870	247
Iowa Legal Aid	1111 Ninth St Ste 230	Des Moines	IA	50314	**800-992-8161**	515-243-2151	428
Iowa Medical Society	1001 Grand Ave	West Des Moines	IA	50265	**800-747-3070**	515-223-1401	473
Iowa Mold Tooling Co Inc (IMT)	500 W US Hwy 18	Garner	IA	50438	**800-247-5958**	641-923-3711	469
Iowa Mortgage Association	8800 Nw 62nd Ave	Johnston	IA	50131	**800-800-2353**	515-286-4352	532
Iowa Pharmacy Assn	8515 Douglas Ave Ste 16	Des Moines	IA	50322	**866-512-1800**	515-270-0713	584
Iowa Prison Industries (IPI)	1445 E Grand Ave	Des Moines	IA	50316	**800-670-4537**	515-242-5770	629
Iowa Public Television	6450 Corporate Dr	Johnston	IA	50131	**800-532-1290**	515-242-3100	
Iowa Realty Company Inc	3501 Westown Pkwy	West Des Moines	IA	50266	**800-247-2430**	515-453-6222	650
Iowa Soybean Association	4554 114th st	Urbandale	IA	50322	**800-383-1423**	515-251-8640	136
Iowa State Penitentiary	Ave E & 1st St PO Box 409	Fort Madison	IA	52627	**800-382-0019**	319-372-1908	215
Iowa State Savings Bank	401 W Adams St	Creston	IA	50801	**888-508-0142**	641-782-1000	69
Iowa State University	100 Alumni Hall *Admissions	Ames	IA	50011	**800-262-3810***	515-294-4111	167
Iowa Veterans Home	1301 Summit St Bldg 3465	Marshalltown	IA	50131	**800-838-4692**	515-252-4698	791
Iowa Veterinary Medical Assn	1605 N Ankeny Blvd Ste 110	Ankeny	IA	50023	**800-369-9564**	515-965-9237	793
Iowa Wesleyan College	601 N Main St	Mount Pleasant	IA	52641	**800-582-2383**		167
Iowa Western Community College *Clarinda*	923 E Washington St	Clarinda	IA	51632	**800-521-2073**	712-542-5117	161
Iowa Workforce Development	1000 E Grand Ave	Des Moines	IA	50319	**800-562-4692**	515-281-5387	261
IP Casino Resort & Spa	850 Bayview Ave *Resv	Biloxi	MS	39530	**888-946-2847***	228-436-3000	132
IPAA (Independent Petroleum Assn of America)	1201 15th St NW Ste 300	Washington	DC	20005	**800-433-2851**	202-857-4722	47-12
iPass Inc	3800 Bridge Pkwy *NASDAQ: IPAS*	Redwood Shores	CA	94065	**877-236-3807**	650-232-4100	394
IPC Securities Corp	2680 Skymark Ave Ste 700	Mississauga	ON	L4W5L6	**877-212-9799**	905-212-9788	689
IPC Technologies Inc	7200 Glen Forest Dr Ste 100	Richmond	VA	23226	**877-947-2835**	804-622-7288	719
ipDataTel LLC	13110 SW Fwy	Sugar Land	TX	77478	**866-896-1818**	713-452-2700	255
IPG Photonics Corp	50 Old Webster Rd *NASDAQ: IPGP*	Oxford	MA	01540	**877-980-1550**	508-373-1100	425
IPHC (International Pentecostal Holiness Church)	PO Box 12609	Oklahoma City	OK	73157	**888-474-2966**	405-787-7110	47-20
IPI (Iowa Prison Industries)	1445 E Grand Ave	Des Moines	IA	50316	**800-670-4537**	515-242-5770	629
IPMA-HR (International Public Management Assn for Hum Res)	1617 Duke St	Alexandria	VA	22314	**800-381-8378**	703-549-7100	48-12
IPNI (International Plant Nutrition Institute)	3500 PkwyLn Ste 550	Norcross	GA	30092	**800-521-3044**	770-447-0335	47-2
IPPF/WHR (International Planned Parenthood Federation - Western Hemisphere Region)	125 Maiden Ln 9th Fl	New York	NY	10005	**866-477-3947**	212-248-6400	47-5
IPS (Institute for Policy Studies)	1112 16th St NW Ste 600	Washington	DC	20036	**877-564-6833**	202-234-9382	631
IPS Corp	455 W Victoria St	Compton	CA	90220	**800-888-8312**	310-898-3300	3
Ipsen Inc	PO Box 6266	Rockford	IL	61125	**800-727-7625**	815-332-4941	319
Ipsenault Co, The	3791 River Rd N Ste F	Keizer	OR	97303	**866-240-7032**	503-390-8968	197
Ipss Inc	150 Isabella St	Ottawa	ON	K1S1V7	**866-532-2207**	613-232-2228	691
Ipswich Shellfish Co Inc	8 Hayward St	Ipswich	MA	01938	**800-477-9424**	978-356-4371	298-5
Ipswitch Inc	83 Hartwell Ave	Lexington	MA	02421	**800-793-4825**	781-676-5700	180-12
IPTV (Idaho Public Television)	1455 N Orchard St	Boise	ID	83706	**800-543-6868**	208-373-7220	629
IQ Systems Inc	5595 Equity Ave Ste 300	Reno	NV	89502	**866-842-4748**	775-352-2301	462
IQware Inc	5850 Coral Ridge Dr Ste 309	Coral Springs	FL	33076	**877-698-5151**	954-698-5151	182
Ira Green Inc	177 Georgia Ave *General	Providence	RI	02905	**800-663-7487***	401-467-4770	409
IRC (International Rescue Committee)	122 E 42nd St 12th Fl	New York	NY	10168	**800-435-7352**	212-551-3000	47-5
IRC (Insurance Research Council)	718 Providence Rd	Malvern	PA	19355	**800-644-2101**	610-644-2212	48-9
Iredale Mineral Cosmetics Ltd	28 Church St	Great Barrington	MA	01230	**877-869-9420**	413-528-1078	240
Ireland *Embassy*	2234 Massachusetts Ave NW	Washington	DC	20008	**866-560-1050**	202-462-3939	259
IREM (Institute of Real Estate Management)	430 N Michigan Ave	Chicago	IL	60611	**800-837-0706**	312-329-6000	48-17
Irex Contracting Group	120 N Lime St	Lancaster	PA	17608	**800-487-7255**		191-9
IRgA (International Reprographic Assn)	401 N Michigan Ave Ste 2200	Chicago	IL	60611	**800-833-4742**	312-245-1026	48-16
Iridex Corp	1212 Terra Bella Ave *NASDAQ: IRIX* ■ *Cust Svc	Mountain View	CA	94043	**800-388-4747***	650-940-4700	424
Iris Group Inc, The	1675 Faraday Ave	Carlsbad	CA	92008	**800-347-1103**	760-431-1103	4
Iris USA Inc	11111 80th Ave	Pleasant Prairie	WI	53158	**800-320-4747**	262-612-1000	606
Iron & Metals Inc	5555 Franklin St	Denver	CO	80216	**800-776-7910**	303-292-5555	684
Iron City Distributing Co	2670 Commercial Ave *Cust Svc	Mingo Junction	OH	43938	**800-759-2671***	740-598-4171	80-1
Iron City Pipe & Supply	330 E Broadway St	Jackson	OH	45640	**877-286-7447**	740-286-8080	609
Iron City Uniform Rental	6640 Frankstown Ave	Pittsburgh	PA	15206	**800-532-2010**	412-661-2001	442
Iron Horse Energy Services Inc	1901 Dirkson Dr NE	Redcliff	AB	T0J2P0	**877-526-4666**	403-526-4600	539
Iron Mountain	745 Atlantic Ave *NYSE: IRM*	Boston	MA	02111	**800-899-4766**		801-1
Iron Range Tourism Bureau	403 N First St	Virginia	MN	55792	**800-777-8497**	218-749-8161	208
Iron Tribe Franchise LLC	300 27th St S	Birmingham	AL	35233	**855-226-8699**	205-226-8669	354
Ironman Magazine	1701 Ives Ave	Oxnard	CA	93033	**800-447-0008**	805-385-3500	456-13
IronMaster LLC	14562 167th Ave SE	Monroe	WA	98272	**800-533-3339**	360-217-7780	269
Ironplanet Inc	3825 Hopyard Rd Ste 250 *Cust Svc	Pleasanton	CA	94588	**888-433-5426***	925-225-8600	50
Ironworkers Political Action League	1750 New York Ave NW Ste 400	Washington	DC	20006	**800-368-0105**	202-383-4800	614
Iroquois Gas Transmission System LP	1 Corporate Dr Ste 600	Shelton	CT	06484	**800-888-3982**	203-925-7200	326
Iroquois New York	49 W 44th St	New York City	NY	10036	**800-332-7220**	212-840-3080	379
Iroquois Products of Chicago	2220 W 56th St	Chicago	IL	60636	**800-453-3355**		201
Irresistibles	7 Hawkes St	Marblehead	MA	01945	**800-555-9865**	781-631-1248	156-6
IRS (Internal Revenue Service)	1111 Constitution Ave NW	Washington	DC	20224	**800-829-1040**	202-622-9511	340-16
IRS Practice Adviser	1801 S Bell St	Arlington	VA	22202	**800-372-1033**		530-7
IRSC (Indian River State College)	3209 Virginia Ave	Fort Pierce	FL	34981	**866-792-4772**	772-462-4772	161
Irvine Access Floors Inc	9425 Washington Blvd	Laurel	MD	20723	**800-969-8870**	301-617-9333	490
Irvine Chamber of Commerce	2485 McCabe Way Ste 150 *General	Irvine	CA	92614	**800-321-2211***	949-660-9112	138
Irvine Scientific	2511 Daimler St	Santa Ana	CA	92705	**800-577-6097**	949-261-7800	84
Irvine Technology Corp	201 E Sandpointe Ave Ste 300	Santa Ana	CA	92707	**866-322-4482**		196
Irving Convention & Visitors Bureau	500 W Las Colinas Blvd	Irving	TX	75039	**800-247-8464**	972-252-7476	208
Irving Mall	3880 Irving Mall	Irving	TX	75062	**877-746-6642**	972-255-0571	459
Irvington General Hospital	95 Old Short Hills Rd	West Orange	NJ	07052	**888-724-7123**		374-3
Irwin Electric Membership Corp	915 W Fourth St	Ocilla	GA	31774	**800-237-3745**	229-468-7415	247
Irwin Naturals	5310 Beethoven St	Los Angeles	CA	90066	**800-297-3273**	310-306-3636	797
Irwin Seating Company Inc	3251 Fruit Ridge NW	Grand Rapids	MI	49544	**866-464-7946**	616-574-7400	320-3
ISA (International Sign Assn)	1001 N Fairfax St Ste 301	Alexandria	VA	22314	**866-949-7446**	703-836-4012	48-4
ISA (International Society of Arboriculture)	PO Box 3129	Champaign	IL	61826	**888-472-8733**	217-355-9411	47-2
Isaak Bond Investments Inc	3900 S Wadsworth Blvd Ste 590	Lakewood	CO	80235	**800-279-4426**	303-623-7500	688
Isabel Bloom LLC	736 Federal St Ste 2100	Davenport	IA	52803	**800-273-5436**		185
ISACA (Information Systems Audit & Control Assn)	3701 Algonquin Rd Ste 1010	Rolling Meadows	IL	60008	**888-491-8833**	847-253-1545	47-9
Isagenix International LLC	2225 S Price Rd	Chandler	AZ	85286	**877-877-8111**	480-889-5747	297-11
ISAR (International Society for Animal Rights)	PO Box F	Clarks Summit	PA	18411	**888-589-6397**	570-586-2200	47-3
Isc Sales Inc	4421 Tradition Trl	Plano	TX	75093	**800-836-7472**	972-964-2700	179
ISCEBS (International Society of Certified Employee Benefit Specialists)	18700 W Bluemound Rd PO Box 209	Brookfield	WI	53008	**888-334-3327**	262-786-8771	48-12
ISCET (International Society of Certified Electronics Technicians)	3608 Pershing Ave	Fort Worth	TX	76107	**800-946-0201**	817-921-9101	48-19
ISCO Inc	4700 Superior St PO Box 82531	Lincoln	NE	68501	**800-228-4250**	402-464-0231	419
Isco Industries	926 Baxter Ave PO Box 4545	Louisville	KY	40204	**800-345-4726**	502-583-6591	595
ISCO International LLC	1450 Arthur Ave Ste A	Elk Grove Village	IL	60007	**888-948-4726**	224-222-1666	732
isekurity Inc	24663 Mound Rd	Warren	MI	48091	**877-838-5734**		691
iSelect Internet Inc	1420 W Kettleman Ln Ste E	Lodi	CA	95242	**877-837-1427**	209-334-0496	398
ISFSI (International Society of Fire Service Instructors)	14001C St Germain Dr	Centreville	VA	20121	**800-435-0005**		48-7
ISG Novasoft (ISGN)	600 A N John Rodes Blvd	Melbourne	FL	32934	**800-462-5545**	800-939-8258	180-1
ISGN (ISG Novasoft)	600 A N John Rodes Blvd	Melbourne	FL	32934	**800-462-5545**	800-939-8258	180-1
ISHLT (International Society for Heart & Lung Transplantation)	14673 Midway Rd Ste 200	Addison	TX	75001	**888-722-2220**	972-490-9495	48-8
ISI (Intercollegiate Studies Institute)	3901 Centerville Rd	Wilmington	DE	19807	**800-526-7022**	302-652-4600	47-11
ISI Commercial Refrigeration LP	640 W 6th St	Houston	TX	77007	**800-777-5070**	214-631-7980	663

Name / Address	City	State	Zip	Toll-Free	Phone	Class
Isis It Inc						
88 Vilcom Ctr Dr Ste 180	Chapel Hill	NC	27514	**877-970-4747**	919-932-6150	182
iSky						
1700 Pennsylvania Ave NW						
Ste 560	Washington	DC	20006	**855-475-4759**		734
Islamorada Chamber of Commerce						
PO Box 915	Islamorada	FL	33036	**800-322-5397**	305-664-4503	138
Islamorada Fish Co						
81532 Overseas Hwy						
PO Box 283	Islamorada	FL	33036	**800-258-2559**		669
Island Express Helicopter Service						
1175 Queens Hwy S	Long Beach	CA	90802	**800-228-2566***	310-510-2525	359
*Cust Svc						
Island Federal Credit Union						
120 Motor Pkwy	Hauppauge	NY	11788	**800-475-5263**	631-851-1100	221
Island Hotel, The						
690 Newport Ctr Dr	Newport Beach	CA	92660	**866-554-4620**	949-759-0808	379
Island Lincoln-Mercury Inc						
1850 E Merritt Island Cswy						
	Merritt Island	FL	32952	**800-392-3673**	321-452-9220	56
Island Oasis						
141 Norfolk St PO Box 769	Walpole	MA	02081	**800-777-4752**	508-660-1176	300
Island Pacific Inc						
17310 Red Hill Ave Ste 320	Irvine	CA	92614	**800-994-3847**		180-10
Island Packet						
10 Buck Island Rd	Bluffton	SC	29910	**877-706-8100**	843-706-8100	531-2
Island Press						
2000 M St NW Ste 650	Washington	DC	20036	**800-621-2736**	202-232-7933	634-2
Island Surf						
1450 Miracle Strip Pkwy SE						
	Fort Walton Beach	FL	32548	**800-272-2065**		709
Island View Casino Resort						
3300 W Beach Blvd PO Box 1600	Gulfport	MS	39502	**888-777-9696***	228-314-2100	132
*General						
Island Windjammers Inc						
165 Shaw Dr	Acworth	GA	30102	**877-772-4549**		31
Islands in the Sun Cruises & Tours Inc						
121 Bayview	Grasonville	MD	21638	**800-278-7786**	410-827-3812	769
Islands Magazine						
460 N Orlando Ave Ste 200	Winter Park	FL	32789	**800-250-1523**	515-237-3697	456-22
ISLC Inc						
14 Savannah Hwy	Beaufort	SC	29906	**888-828-4752**	843-770-1000	387
Isle of Capri Casino						
1800 E Front St	Kansas City	MO	64120	**800-843-4753**	816-855-7777	132
Isle of Capri Casino Hotel Lake Charles						
100 W Lake Ave	Westlake	LA	70669	**800-843-4753**		132
ISM (Institute for Supply Management)						
2055 Centennial Cir	Tempe	AZ	85284	**800-888-6276***	480-752-6276	48-12
*Cust Svc						
ISMIE (Illinois State Medical Inter-Insurance Exchange)						
20 N Michigan Ave Ste 700	Chicago	IL	60602	**800-782-4767**	312-782-2749	391-5
ISMRM (International Society for Magnetic Resonance in Medicine)						
2030 Addison St Ste 700	Berkeley	CA	94704	**800-445-8667**	510-841-1899	48-8
ISN Global Enterprises Inc						
Po Box 1391	Claremont	CA	91711	**877-376-4476**	909-670-0601	194
ISO (Insurance Services Office Inc)						
545 Washington Blvd	Jersey City	NJ	07310	**800-888-4476**	201-469-2000	390
Isolatek International Inc						
41 Furnace St	Stanhope	NJ	07874	**800-631-9600**	973-347-1200	389
Isolite Systems						
111 Castilian Dr	Santa Barbara	CA	93117	**800-560-6066**	805-560-9888	230
IsoRay Medical Inc						
350 Hills St Ste 106	Richland	WA	99354	**877-447-6729**	509-375-1202	360-3
Iso-Tex Diagnostics Inc						
PO Box 909	Friendswood	TX	77549	**800-477-4839**		233
ISP (International Specialty Products Inc)						
1361 Alps Rd	Wayne	NJ	07470	**800-622-4423**	973-628-4000	143
ISPD (International Society for Peritoneal Dialysis)						
66 Martin St	Milton	ON	L9T2R2	**888-834-1001**	905-875-2456	48-8
ISPE (International Society for Pharmacoepidemiology)						
5272 River Rd Ste 630	Bethesda	MD	20816	**888-887-7955**	301-718-6500	48-8
ISPI (International Society for Performance Improvement)						
PO Box 13035	Silver Spring	MD	20910	**800-825-7550**	301-587-8570	48-12
ISPOR (International Society for Pharmacoeconomics & Outcomes Research)						
3100 Princeton Pk						
Bldg 3 Ste E	Lawrenceville	NJ	08648	**800-992-0643**	609-219-0773	48-8
Israel Government Tourist Office						
800 Second Ave 16th Fl	New York	NY	10017	**877-248-8687**	212-499-5660	773
Isram World of Travel Inc						
90 John St Ste 602	New York	NY	10038	**800-223-7460**		758
ISRS (International Society of Refractive Surgery)						
655 Beach St PO Box 7424	San Francisco	CA	94109	**866-561-8558**	415-561-8581	48-8
ISSA (International Sanitary Supply Assn)						
3300 Dundee Rd	Northbrook	IL	60062	**800-225-4772**	847-982-0800	48-18
ISSI (Integrated Silicon Solution Inc)						
1940 Zanker Rd	San Jose	CA	95112	**800-379-4774**	408-969-6600	694
NASDAQ: ISSI						
Issuer Direct Corp						
500 Perimeter Park Dr Ste D	Morrisville	NC	27560	**877-481-4014**		318
ISTA (International Safe Transit Assn)						
1400 Abbott Rd Ste 160	East Lansing	MI	48823	**888-299-2208**	517-333-3437	48-21
ISTA Advocate Magazine						
150 W Market St Ste 900	Indianapolis	IN	46204	**800-382-4037**	317-263-3400	456-8
iStar Financial Inc						
1114 Ave of the Americas						
39th Fl	New York	NY	10036	**888-603-5847**	212-930-9400	218
NYSE: STAR						
ISTE (International Society for Technology in Education)						
1530 Wilson Blvd Ste 730	Arlington	VA	22209	**800-336-5191***	202-861-7777	48-5
*General						
ISTF (International Society of Tropical Foresters)						
5400 Grosvenor Ln	Bethesda	MD	20814	**866-897-8720**	301-530-4514	47-13
ISTSS (International Society for Traumatic Stress Studies)						
111 Deer Lk Rd Ste 100	Deerfield	IL	60015	**877-469-7873**	847-480-9028	48-15
It Doctors						
2175 Northdale Blvd Nw	Minneapolis	MN	55433	**888-472-2287**	763-267-6980	179
It4ce Inc						
1200 Aerowood Dr	Mississauga	ON	L4W2S7	**877-470-0008**	905-206-9947	762
ITAGroup						
4600 Westown Pkwy	West Des Moines	IA	50266	**800-257-1985**		384
Italgrani USA Inc						
7900 Van Buren St	Saint Louis	MO	63111	**800-274-1274**	314-638-1447	277
iTalkBB Canada Inc						
109 - 235 Yorkland Blvd	North York	ON	M2J4Y8	**877-482-5522**		226
Italy						
Consulate General						
150 S Independence Mall W						
Public Ledger Bldg Ste 1026	Philadelphia	PA	19106	**800-531-0840**	215-592-7329	259
Consulate General						
1300 Post Oak Blvd Ste 660	Houston	TX	77056	**800-637-9314**	713-850-7520	259
Consulate General						
600 Atlantic Ave 17th Fl	Boston	MA	02210	**888-225-5427**	617-722-9201	259
Embassy						
3000 Whitehaven St NW	Washington	DC	20008	**800-222-1222**	202-612-4400	259
Italy-America Chamber of Commerce Southeast Inc						
2 S Biscayne Blvd Ste 1880	Miami	FL	33131	**800-428-3003**	305-577-9868	136
Itasca Community College						
1851 E Us Hwy 169	Grand Rapids	MN	55744	**800-996-6422**	218-327-4460	161
Itasca-Mantrap Co-op Electrical Assn						
16930 County Rd 6	Park Rapids	MN	56470	**888-713-3377**	218-732-3377	247
Itawamba Community College						
Fulton 602 W Hill St	Fulton	MS	38843	**800-433-3243**	662-862-8000	161
ITC (Innovative Technologies Corp)						
1020 Woodman Dr Ste 100	Dayton	OH	45432	**800-745-8050**	937-252-2145	180-10
ITC Learning Corp						
1616 Anderson Rd Ste 109	McLean	VA	22102	**800-638-3757**		763
Itech Digital LLC						
4287 W 96th St	Indianapolis	IN	46268	**866-733-6673**	317-704-0440	691
Iten Industries						
4602 Benefit Ave	Ashtabula	OH	44004	**800-227-4836***	440-997-6134	598
*Orders						
Itergy International Inc						
2075 University Ste 700	Montreal	QC	H3A2L1	**866-522-5881**	514-845-5881	182
Iteris Inc						
1700 Carnegie Ave Ste 100	Santa Ana	CA	92705	**888-254-5487**	949-270-9400	645
NYSE: ITI						
ITG Inc						
1 Liberty Plz 165 Broadway	New York	NY	10006	**800-215-4484**	212-588-4000	688
Ithaca College						
953 Danby Rd	Ithaca	NY	14850	**800-429-4274***	607-274-3124	167
*Admissions						
Ithaca/Tompkins County Convention & Visitors Bureau						
904 E Shore Dr	Ithaca	NY	14850	**800-284-8422**	607-272-1313	208
ITI (Industrial Tools Inc)						
1111 S Rose Ave	Oxnard	CA	93033	**800-266-5561**	805-483-1111	492
ITL (Industrial Timber & Lumber Corp)						
23925 Commerce Pk Rd	Beachwood	OH	44122	**800-829-9663**	216-831-3140	681
ITNS (International Transplant Nurses Society)						
1739 E Carson St PO Box 351	Pittsburgh	PA	15203	**800-776-8636**	412-343-4867	48-8
Itology.com Ltd						
214 - 11 Ave SE Ste 210	Calgary	AB	T2G0X8	**877-226-7726**	403-226-3040	179
ITR Group Inc						
2520 Lexington Ave S Ste 500	Saint Paul	MN	55120	**866-290-3423**		195
Itron Inc						
2111 N Molter Rd	Liberty Lake	WA	99019	**800-635-5461**	509-924-9900	250
NASDAQ: ITRI						
ITS (Intelligent Transportation Society of America)						
1100 17th St NW Ste 1200	Washington	DC	20036	**800-374-8472**	202-484-4847	48-21
ITSource Technology Inc						
1401 Los Gamos Dr Ste 102	San Rafael	CA	94903	**866-548-4911**	415-472-5700	182
ITT Educational Services Inc						
13000 N Meridian St	Carmel	IN	46032	**800-388-3368**	317-706-9200	244
NYSE: ESI						
ITT Goulds Pumps Industries/Goulds Industrial Pumps Group						
240 Fall St	Seneca Falls	NY	13148	**800-327-7700**	315-568-2811	787
ITT Industries Inc						
1133 Westchester Ave	White Plains	NY	10604	**800-254-2823**	914-641-2000	255
NYSE: ITT						
ITT Industries Inc Engineered Valves Div						
33 Centerville Rd	Lancaster	PA	17603	**800-366-1111**	717-509-2200	787
ITT Night Vision & Imaging						
7635 Plantation Rd	Roanoke	VA	24019	**800-448-8678**	540-563-0371	543
ITT Standard						
175 Standard Pkwy	Cheektowaga	NY	14227	**800-447-7700**	800-281-4111	90
ITT Technical Institute						
Lathrop						
16916 S Harlan Rd	Lathrop	CA	95330	**800-346-1786**	209-858-0077	798
Oxnard						
2051 Solar Dr Ste 150	Oxnard	CA	93036	**800-530-1582**	805-988-0143	798
Rancho Cordova						
10863 Gold Ctr Dr	Rancho Cordova	CA	95670	**800-488-8466**	916-851-3900	798
San Bernardino						
670 Carnegie Dr	San Bernardino	CA	92408	**800-888-3801**	909-806-4600	798
San Dimas						
650 W Cienega Ave	San Dimas	CA	91773	**800-414-6522**	909-971-2300	798
Sylmar						
12669 Encinitas Ave	Sylmar	CA	91342	**800-363-2086**	818-364-5151	798
ITT Technical Institute Albany						
13 Airline Dr	Albany	NY	12205	**800-489-1191**	518-452-9300	798
ITT Technical Institute Albuquerque						
5100 Masthead St NE	Albuquerque	NM	87109	**800-636-1114**	505-828-1114	798
ITT Technical Institute Arlington						
551 Ryan Plz Dr	Arlington	TX	76011	**888-288-4950**	817-794-5100	798
ITT Technical Institute Arnold						
1930 Meyer Drury Dr	Arnold	MO	63010	**888-488-1082**	636-464-6600	798
ITT Technical Institute Austin						
6330 Hwy 290 E Ste 150	Austin	TX	78723	**800-431-0677**	512-467-6800	798
ITT Technical Institute Birmingham						
6270 Pk S Dr	Bessemer	AL	35022	**800-488-7033**	205-497-5700	798
ITT Technical Institute Boise						
12302 W Explorer Dr	Boise	ID	83713	**800-666-4888**	208-322-8844	798
ITT Technical Institute Canton						
1905 S Haggerty Rd	Canton	MI	48188	**800-247-4477**	734-397-7800	798
ITT Technical Institute Cordova						
7260 Goodlett Farms Pkwy	Cordova	TN	38016	**866-444-5141**	901-381-0200	798
ITT Technical Institute Dayton						
3325 S- Eight Rd	Dayton	OH	45414	**800-568-3241**	937-264-7700	798

Name / Address	City	State	ZIP	Toll-Free	Phone	Class
ITT Technical Institute Earth City						
3640 Corporate Trl Dr	Earth City	MO	63045	**800-235-5488**	314-298-7800	798
ITT Technical Institute Fort Lauderdale						
3401 S University Dr	Fort Lauderdale	FL	33328	**800-488-7797**	954-476-9300	798
ITT Technical Institute Fort Wayne						
2810 Dupont Commerce Ct	Fort Wayne	IN	46825	**800-866-4488**	260-497-6200	798
ITT Technical Institute Getzville						
2295 Millersport Hwy	Getzville	NY	14068	**800-469-7593**	716-689-2200	798
ITT Technical Institute Grand Rapids						
1980 Metro Ct SW	Wyoming	MI	49519	**800-632-4676**	616-406-1200	798
ITT Technical Institute Greenville						
6 Independence Pointe Independence Corporate Pk	Greenville	SC	29615	**800-932-4488**	864-288-0777	798
ITT Technical Institute Harrisburg						
449 Eisenhower Blvd Ste 100	Harrisburg	PA	17111	**800-847-4756**	717-565-1700	798
ITT Technical Institute Henderson						
2300 Corporate Cir Ste 150	Henderson	NV	89074	**800-488-8459**	702-558-5404	798
ITT Technical Institute High Point						
4050 Piedmont Pkwy	High Point	NC	27265	**877-536-5231**	336-819-5900	798
ITT Technical Institute Houston						
15651 N Fwy	Houston	TX	77090	**800-879-6486**	281-873-0512	798
ITT Technical Institute Indianapolis						
9511 Angola Ct	Indianapolis	IN	46268	**800-937-4488**	317-875-8640	798
ITT Technical Institute Jacksonville						
7011 AC Skinner Pkwy Ste 140	Jacksonville	FL	32256	**800-318-1264**	904-573-9100	798
ITT Technical Institute Kansas City						
9150 E 41st Terr	Kansas City	MO	64133	**877-488-1442**	816-276-1400	798
ITT Technical Institute Kennesaw						
2065 Baker Rd NW	Kennesaw	GA	30144	**800-564-9771**	770-426-2300	798
ITT Technical Institute Liverpool						
235 Greenfield Pkwy	Liverpool	NY	13088	**877-488-0011**	315-461-8000	798
ITT Technical Institute Louisville						
9500 Ormsby Stn Rd Ste 100	Louisville	KY	40223	**888-790-7427**	502-327-7424	798
ITT Technical Institute Murray						
920 Levoy Dr	Murray	UT	84123	**800-365-2136**	801-263-3313	798
ITT Technical Institute Nashville						
2845 Elm Hill Pk	Nashville	TN	37214	**800-331-8386**	615-889-8700	798
ITT Technical Institute Newburgh						
10999 Stahl Rd	Newburgh	IN	47630	**800-832-4488**	812-858-1600	798
ITT Technical Institute Norfolk						
5425 Robin Hood Rd Ste 100	Norfolk	VA	23513	**888-253-8324**	757-466-1260	798
ITT Technical Institute Norwood						
4750 Wesley Ave	Norwood	OH	45212	**800-314-8324**	513-531-8300	798
ITT Technical Institute Omaha						
1120 N 103rd Plz Ste 200	Omaha	NE	68114	**800-677-9260**	402-331-2900	798
ITT Technical Institute Owings Mills						
11301 Red Run Blvd	Owings Mills	MD	21117	**877-411-6782**	443-394-7115	798
ITT Technical Institute Portland						
9500 NE Cascades Pkwy	Portland	OR	97220	**800-234-5488**	503-255-6500	798
ITT Technical Institute Richardson						
2101 Waterview Pkwy	Richardson	TX	75080	**888-488-5761**	972-690-9100	798
ITT Technical Institute Richmond						
300 Gateway Centre Pkwy	Richmond	VA	23235	**888-330-4888**	804-330-4992	798
ITT Technical Institute San Antonio						
5700 NW Pkwy	San Antonio	TX	78249	**800-880-0570**	210-694-4612	798
ITT Technical Institute Seattle						
12720 Gateway Dr Ste 100	Seattle	WA	98168	**800-422-2029**	206-244-3300	798
ITT Technical Institute Springfield						
7300 Boston Blvd	Springfield	VA	22153	**866-817-8324**	703-440-9535	798
ITT Technical Institute Strongsville						
14955 Sprague Rd	Strongsville	OH	44136	**800-331-1488**	440-234-9091	798
ITT Technical Institute Tampa						
4809 Memorial Hwy	Tampa	FL	33634	**800-825-2831**	813-885-2244	798
ITT Technical Institute Tempe						
5005 S Wendler Dr	Tempe	AZ	85282	**800-879-4881**	602-437-7500	798
ITT Technical Institute Troy						
1522 E Big Beaver Rd	Troy	MI	48083	**800-832-6817**	248-524-1800	798
ITT Technical Institute Tucson						
1455 W River Rd	Tucson	AZ	85704	**800-870-9730**	520-408-7488	798
ITT Technical Institute Warrensville Heights						
4700 Richmond Rd	Warrensville Heights	OH	44128	**800-741-3494**	216-896-6500	798
ITT Technical Institute Wilmington						
200 Ballardvale St Ste 200	Wilmington	MA	01887	**800-430-5097**	978-658-2636	798
ITT Technical Institute Youngstown						
1030 N Meridian Rd	Youngstown	OH	44509	**800-832-5001**	330-270-1600	798
ITVS (Independent Television Service)						
651 Brannan St Ste 410	San Francisco	CA	94107	**800-621-6196**	415-356-8383	739
ITW Brands						
955 National Pkwy Ste 95500	Schaumburg	IL	60173	**877-489-2726**	847-944-2260	280
ITW Buildex						
1349 W Bryn Mawr	Itasca	IL	60143	**800-284-5339**	630-595-3500	280
ITW Dymon						
805 E Old 56 Hwy	Olathe	KS	66061	**800-443-9536**	913-829-6296	150
ITW Insulation Systems						
1370 E 40th St Ste 1 Bldg 7	Houston	TX	77022	**800-231-1024**		389
ITW Polymers Sealants North America						
111 S Nursery R	Irving	TX	75060	**888-751-0409***	972-438-9111	3
*Hotline						
ITW Rocol North America						
3650 W Lake Ave	Glenview	IL	60026	**800-452-5823**	847-657-5278	540
ITW Switches						
195 E Algonquin Rd	Des Plaines	IL	60016	**800-544-3354**	847-876-9400	727
ITW Vortec						
10125 Carver Rd	Cincinnati	OH	45242	**800-441-7475**	513-891-7485	14
Itx Corp						
1169 Pittsford Victor Rd Ste 100	Pittsford	NY	14534	**800-600-7785**	585-899-4888	226
iUniverse						
1663 Liberty Dr	Bloomington	IN	47403	**800-288-4677**	812-330-2909	634-2
IUPAT (International Union of Painters & Allied Trades)						
7234 Pkwy Dr	Hanover	MD	21076	**800-554-2479**	410-564-5900	414
IV Most Consulting Inc						
33 Park Dr	Mt Kisco	NY	10549	**800-448-6678**		179
iv3 Solutions Corp						
50 Minthorn Blvd Ste 301	Markham	ON	L3T7X8	**877-995-2651**		365
Ivan Franko Museum						
1040 - 555 Main St 595 Pritchard Ave	Winnipeg	MB	R3B1C3	**866-747-9323**	204-947-1782	519
IVC (International Visual Corp)						
11500 Blvd Armand Bombardier	Montreal	QC	H1E2W9	**866-643-0570**	514-643-0570	288
IVCi LLC						
601 Old Willets Path	Hauppauge	NY	11788	**800-224-7083**	631-273-5800	733
Ivenuecom						
9925 Painter Ave Ste A	Whittier	CA	90605	**800-683-8314**		179
Ivers-Lee Inc						
31 Hansen S	Brampton	ON	L6W3H7	**800-265-1009**	905-451-5535	84
Ivey Spencer Leadership Centre						
551 Windermere Rd	London	ON	N5X2T1	**888-678-6926**	519-679-4546	377
Ivinson Memorial Hospital						
255 N 30th St	Laramie	WY	82072	**877-858-0990**	307-742-2141	374-3
Ivory Homes						
970 E Woodoak Ln	Salt Lake City	UT	84117	**888-455-5561**		651
IVY Biomedical Systems Inc						
11 Business Pk Dr	Branford	CT	06405	**800-247-4614**	203-481-4183	252
Ivy Tech Columbus College						
Columbus						
4475 Central Ave	Columbus	IN	47203	**800-922-4838**	812-372-9925	798
Ivy Tech Community College						
Bloomington						
200 Daniels Way	Bloomington	IN	47404	**866-447-0700**	812-330-6137	798
Central Indiana						
50 W Fall Creek Pkwy N Dr	Indianapolis	IN	46208	**888-489-5463**	317-921-4800	798
Kokomo						
1815 E Morgan St	Kokomo	IN	46901	**800-459-0561**	765-459-0561	798
Muncie 4301 S Cowan Rd	Muncie	IN	47302	**800-589-8324**	765-289-2291	798
North Central						
220 Dean Johnson Blvd	South Bend	IN	46601	**888-489-3478**	574-289-7001	798
Northwest						
1440 E 35th Ave	Gary	IN	46409	**888-489-5463**	219-981-1111	798
Richmond						
2357 Chester Blvd	Richmond	IN	47374	**800-659-4562**	765-966-2656	798
Southeast						
590 Ivy Tech Dr	Madison	IN	47250	**800-403-2190**	812-265-2580	798
Southern Indiana						
8204 old Indiana 311	Sellersburg	IN	47172	**800-321-9021**	812-246-3301	798
Wabash Valley						
8000 S Education Dr	Terre Haute	IN	47802	**888-489-5463**	812-298-2293	798
iWay Software						
2 Penn Plz	New York	NY	10121	**800-736-6130**	212-736-4433	196
IWLA (Izaak Walton League of America)						
707 Conservation Ln	Gaithersburg	MD	20878	**800-453-5463**	301-548-0150	47-13
IWPA (International Wood Products Assn)						
4214 King St	Alexandria	VA	22302	**855-435-0005**	703-820-6696	48-3
Ixia						
26601 W Agoura Rd	Calabasas	CA	91302	**877-367-4942**	818-871-1800	250
NASDAQ: XXIA						
Izaak Walton League of America (IWLA)						
707 Conservation Ln	Gaithersburg	MD	20878	**800-453-5463**	301-548-0150	47-13
Izzydesign						
17237 Van Wagoner Rd	Spring Lake	MI	49456	**800-543-5449**	616-916-9369	320-1

J

Name / Address	City	State	ZIP	Toll-Free	Phone	Class
J & A Freight Systems Inc						
4704 Irving Park Rd Ste 8	Chicago	IL	60641	**877-668-3378**		312
J & A Printing Inc						
PO Box 457	Hiawatha	IA	52233	**800-793-1781**	319-393-1781	626
J & E Supply & Fastner Company Inc						
1903 SE 59th St	Oklahoma City	OK	73129	**800-677-7922**	405-670-1234	351
J & J Industries Inc						
818 J & J Dr PO Box 1287	Dalton	GA	30721	**800-241-4586**	706-529-2100	130
J & J Security Services Corp						
2922 Howland Blvd Ste 2	Deltona	FL	32725	**877-532-7233**	386-789-5555	691
J & J Snack Foods Corp						
6000 Central Hwy	Pennsauken	NJ	08109	**800-486-9533**	856-665-9533	297-25
NASDAQ: JJSF						
J & M Industries Inc						
300 Ponchatoula Pkwy	Ponchatoula	LA	70454	**800-989-1002**	985-386-6000	66
J & M Plating Inc						
4500 Kishwaukee St	Rockford	IL	61109	**877-344-3044**	815-964-4975	480
J Alexander's Corp						
3401 W End Ave Ste 260	Nashville	TN	37203	**888-528-1991**	615-269-1900	668
NASDAQ: JAX						
J C Steele & Sons Inc						
710 S Mulberry St	Statesville	NC	28677	**800-278-3353**	704-872-3681	453
J Crew Group Inc						
770 Broadway	New York	NY	10003	**800-562-0258**	212-209-2500	458
J D'Addario & Company Inc						
595 Smith St	Farmingdale	NY	11735	**800-323-2746**	631-439-3300	526
J Edgar Eubanks & Assoc						
1 Windsor Cove Ste 305	Columbia	SC	29223	**800-445-8629**	803-252-5646	46
J Fletcher Creamer & Son Inc						
101 E Broadway	Hackensack	NJ	07601	**800-835-9801**	201-488-9800	191-5
J Freirich Foods Inc						
815 W Kerr St PO Box 1529	Salisbury	NC	28144	**800-554-4788**	704-636-2621	472
J HI Mail Marketing						
3100 Borham Ave	Stevens Point	WI	54481	**800-236-0581**	715-341-0581	197
J K Consulting						
990 E Ninth St	Lockport	IL	60441	**866-634-9633**	815-588-4530	198
J L Business Interiors Inc						
515 Schoenhaar Dr PO Box 303	West Bend	WI	53090	**866-338-5524**	262-338-2221	321
J McLaughlin						
236250 Greenpoint Ave 2nd Fl	Brooklyn	NY	10021	**844-532-5625**	212-879-9565	156-4
J O Galloup Co						
3838 Clay Ave SW	Wyoming	MI	49548	**888-755-3110**	269-965-4005	193-2
J P Noonan Transportation Inc						
415 W St	West Bridgewater	MA	02379	**800-922-8026**	508-583-2880	778

Name / Address	City	State	ZIP	Toll-Free	Phone	Class
J Polep Distribution Services Inc 705 Meadow St	Chicopee	MA	01013	**800-447-6537**	413-592-4141	754
J Robert Scott Inc 500 N Oak St	Inglewood	CA	90302	**877-207-5130**	310-680-4300	320-4
J S Logistics 4550 Gustine Ave	Saint Louis	MO	63116	**800-814-2634**	314-832-6008	315
J Smith Lanier & Co 300 W Tenth St	West Point	GA	31833	**800-226-4522**	706-645-2211	390
J Sosnick & Sons Inc 258 Littlefield Ave	South San Francisco	CA	94080	**800-223-2194**	650-952-2226	298-11
J. C. Macelroy Company Inc PO Box 850	Piscataway	NJ	08855	**800-622-3576**	732-572-7100	479
J. Ennis Fabrics Ltd 12122 - 68 St	Edmonton	AB	T5B1R1	**800-663-6647**		406
J. H. Bennett & Company Inc PO Box 8028 *General	Novi	MI	48376	**800-837-5426***	248-596-5100	385
J. Knipper & Company Inc 1 Healthcare Way	Lakewood	NJ	08701	**888-564-7737**	732-905-7878	197
J.M. Bozeman Enterprises Inc 166 Seltzer Ln *General	Malvern	AR	72104	**800-472-1836***	501-844-4060	683
J2 Global Communications Inc 6922 Hollywood Blvd 8th Fl *Sales	Los Angeles	CA	90028	**888-718-2000***	323-860-9200	733
JA (Jewelers of America) 52 Vanderbilt Ave 19th Fl	New York	NY	10017	**800-223-0673**	646-658-0246	48-4
JA Billipp Co 6925 Portwest Dr Ste 130	Houston	TX	77024	**800-216-9013**	713-426-5000	651
Jaapharm Canada Inc 510 Rowntree Dairy Rd Bldg B	Woodbridge	ON	L4L8H2	**800-465-9587**	905-851-7885	582
Jabil Circuit Inc 10560 ML King St N *NYSE: JBL*	Saint Petersburg	FL	33716	**877-217-6328**	727-577-9749	624
Jabo Supply Corp 5164 County Rd 64/66	Huntington	WV	25705	**800-334-5226**	304-736-8333	385
JACAN (Junior Achievement of Canada) 1 Eva Rd Ste 218	Toronto	ON	M9C4Z5	**800-265-0699**	416-622-4602	47-11
Jace Holdings Ltd 6649 Butler Crescent	Saanichton	BC	V8M1Z7	**800-667-8280**	250-483-1715	298-8
Jack B Kelley Inc 801 S Fillmore St Ste 505	Amarillo	TX	79101	**800-225-5525**	806-353-3553	778
Jack B Parson Cos 2350 South 1900 West	Ogden	UT	84401	**888-672-7766**	801-731-1111	190-4
Jack Becker Distributors Inc 6800 Suemac Pl	Jacksonville	FL	32254	**800-488-8411**		580
Jack Conway 137 Washington St	Norwell	MA	02061	**800-283-1030**	781-871-0080	650
Jack Henry & Assoc Inc 663 W Hwy 60 PO Box 807 *NASDAQ: JKHY*	Monett	MO	65708	**800-299-4222**	417-235-6652	180-11
Jack in the Box Inc 9330 Balboa Ave *NASDAQ: JACK*	San Diego	CA	92123	**800-955-5225**	858-571-2121	668
Jack London Inn 444 Embarcadero W	Oakland	CA	94607	**800-549-8780**	510-444-2032	379
Jack O'Dwyer's PR Newsletter 271 Madison Ave Ste 600	New York	NY	10016	**866-395-7710**	212-679-2471	530-11
Jack Ogren & Company Inc 6929 Hohman Ave	Hammond	IN	46324	**888-489-4235**	219-933-0076	390
Jack Richeson & Company Inc 557 Marcella Dr	Kimberly	WI	54136	**800-233-2404**	920-738-0744	42
Jack Williams Tire Co Inc PO Box 3655	Scranton	PA	18505	**800-833-5051**		61-5
Jack's Family Restaurants Inc 2831 19th St S	Homewood	AL	35209	**888-795-2707**	205-879-9321	668
Jacknob Corp 290 Oser Ave PO Box 18032	Hauppauge	NY	11788	**800-424-7495**	631-546-6560	350
Jacko Law Group PC 5920 Friars Rd Ste 208	San Diego	CA	92108	**866-497-2298**	619-298-2880	428
Jackpot Junction Casino Hotel 39375 County Hwy 24 PO Box 420	Morton	MN	56270	**800-946-2274**	507-697-8000	132
Jackson & Perkins 2 Floral Ave *Cust Svc	Hodges	SC	29653	**800-292-4769***		458
Jackson Area Chamber of Commerce 197 Auditorium St	Jackson	TN	38301	**866-262-8867**	731-423-2200	138
Jackson Citizen Patriot 100 E Michigan Ave Ste 100	Jackson	MI	49201	**877-213-3754**		531-2
Jackson Community College 2111 Emmons Rd	Jackson	MI	49201	**888-522-7344**	517-787-0800	161
Hillsdale 3120 W Carleton Rd PO Box 712	Hillsdale	MI	49242	**888-522-7344**	517-437-3343	161
Jackson County 3405 S Main St PO Box 155	Newport	AR	72043	**800-234-1040**	870-523-6011	338
Jackson County Area Chamber of Commerce 270 Athens St PO Box 629	Jefferson	GA	30549	**800-243-6921**	706-387-0300	138
Jackson County Chamber of Commerce 773 W Main St	Sylva	NC	28779	**800-962-1911**	828-586-2155	138
Jackson County Convention & Visitors Bureau 141 S Jackson St	Jackson	MI	49201	**800-245-5282**	517-764-4440	208
Jackson County Memorial Hospital 1200 E Pecan St	Altus	OK	73521	**800-595-0455**	580-379-5000	374-3
Jackson County Public Library (JCPL) 303 W Second St	Seymour	IN	47274	**877-275-7673**	812-522-3412	434-3
Jackson County Rural Electric Membership Corp 274 E Base Rd	Brownstown	IN	47220	**800-288-4458**	812-358-4458	247
Jackson County School District 6 300 Ash St	Central Point	OR	97502	**800-978-3040**	541-494-6200	683
Jackson County School System 1660 Winder Hwy	Jefferson	GA	30549	**800-760-3727**	706-367-5151	683
Jackson Electric Co-op N6868 County Rd F PO Box 546	Black River Falls	WI	54615	**800-370-4607**	715-284-5385	247
Jackson Electric Membership Corp 850 Commerce Rd	Jefferson	GA	30549	**800-462-3691**	706-367-5281	247
Jackson Energy Co-op 115 Jackson Energy Ln	McKee	KY	40447	**800-262-7480**	606-364-1000	247
Jackson George N Ltd 1139 Mcdermot Ave	Winnipeg	MB	R3E0V2	**800-665-8978**	204-786-3821	361
Jackson Hewitt Inc 3 Sylvan Way Ste 301 *OTC: JHTXQ*	Parsippany	NJ	07054	**800-234-1040**		731
Jackson Hole Central Reservations (JHCR) 140 E Broadway Ste 24 PO Box 2618	Jackson	WY	83001	**888-838-6606**	307-733-4005	376
Jackson Hole Lodge 420 W Broadway PO Box 1805	Jackson	WY	83001	**800-604-9404**	307-733-2992	379
Jackson Hole Mountain Resort 3395 Cody Ln PO Box 290	Teton Village	WY	83025	**800-450-0477**	307-733-2292	667
Jackson HoleResort Lodging 3200 W McCollister Dr PO Box 510	Teton Village	WY	83025	**800-443-8613**	307-733-3990	667
Jackson ImmunoResearch Laboratories Inc 872 W Baltimore Pk PO Box 9	West Grove	PA	19390	**800-367-5296**	610-869-4024	233
Jackson International Airport 100 International Dr Ste 300	Jackson	MS	39208	**800-227-7368**	601-939-5631	27
Jackson Laboratory, The 600 Main St	Bar Harbor	ME	04609	**800-422-6423**	207-288-6000	666
Jackson Lake Lodge PO Box 250	Moran	WY	83013	**800-628-9988**	307-543-2811	667
Jackson Marking Products Co 9105 N Rainbow Ln	Mount Vernon	IL	62864	**800-782-6722**	618-242-1334	466
Jackson Mattress Company Inc 3154 Camden Rd	Fayetteville	NC	28306	**800-763-7378**	910-425-0131	470
Jackson National Life Insurance Co 1 Corporate Way	Lansing	MI	48951	**800-644-4565**	517-381-5500	391-2
Jackson Oil & Solvents Inc 1970 Kentucky Ave	Indianapolis	IN	46221	**800-221-4603**	317-636-4421	540
Jackson Purchase Ag Credit Assn PO Box 309	Mayfield	KY	42066	**877-422-4203**	270-247-5613	218
Jackson Purchase Energy Corp 2900 Irvin Cobb Dr	Paducah	KY	42002	**800-633-4044**	270-442-7321	247
Jackson Purchase Medical Ctr 1099 Medical Ctr Cir	Mayfield	KY	42066	**800-994-6610**	270-251-4100	374-3
Jackson State University 1400 John R Lynch St	Jackson	MS	39217	**800-848-6817**	601-979-2121	167
Jackson Sun 245 W LaFayette St	Jackson	TN	38301	**800-372-3922**	731-427-3333	531-2
Jackson Tube Service Inc 8210 Industry Pk Dr	Piqua	OH	45356	**800-543-8910**	937-773-8550	489
Jacksonport State Park 1 Capitol Mall	Newport	AR	72112	**888-287-2757**	870-523-2143	564
Jacksonville Area Chamber of Commerce 310 E State St	Jacksonville	IL	62650	**800-593-5678**	217-243-5678	138
Jacksonville Chamber of Commerce 200 Dupree Dr	Jacksonville	AR	72076	**888-857-3019**	501-982-1511	138
Jacksonville Convention & Visitors Bureau 310 E State St	Jacksonville	IL	62650	**800-593-5678**	217-243-5678	208
Jacksonville Independent School District PO Box 631	Jacksonville	TX	75766	**800-583-6908**	903-586-6511	683
Jacksonville Magazine 1261 King St	Jacksonville	FL	32204	**800-962-0214**	904-389-3622	456-22
Jacksonville State University 700 Pelham Rd N	Jacksonville	AL	36265	**800-231-5291**	256-782-5781	167
Jacksonville University 2800 University Blvd N	Jacksonville	FL	32211	**800-225-2027**	904-256-8000	167
Jacksonville/Onslow Chamber of Commerce 1099 Gum Branch Rd	Jacksonville	NC	28541	**800-877-8339**	910-347-3141	138
Jacmel Jewelry Inc 3030 47th Ave	Long Island	NY	11101	**800-945-4300**		409
Jaco Electronics Inc 415 Oser Ave *OTC: JACO*	Hauppauge	NY	11788	**877-373-5226**		248
Jacob Holtz Co 10 Industrial Hwy MS-6 Airport Business Complex B	Lester	PA	19029	**800-445-4337**	215-423-2800	350
Jacob Leinenkugel Brewing Co 124 E Elm St *General	Chippewa Falls	WI	54729	**888-534-6437***	715-723-5558	101
Jacob Stern & Sons Inc 1464 E Valley Rd *Cust Svc	Santa Barbara	CA	93108	**800-223-7054***	805-565-1411	297-12
Jacobs Theatre 242 W 45th St	New York	NY	10036	**800-447-7400**	212-239-6200	744
Jacobsen Homes 600 Packard Ct	Safety Harbor	FL	34695	**800-843-1559**	727-726-1138	504
Jacquelyn Wigs 15 W 37th St 4th Fl	New York	NY	10018	**800-272-2424**	212-302-2266	348
Jade Engineered Plastic Inc 121 Broadcommon Rd	Bristol	RI	02809	**800-557-9155**	401-253-4440	327
JAE Electronics Inc 142 Technology Dr Ste 100	Irvine	CA	92618	**800-523-7278**	949-753-2600	255
Jaeckle Wholesale Inc 4101 Owl Creek Dr	Madison	WI	53718	**800-236-7225**	608-838-5400	193-1
Jafra Cosmetics International 2451 Townsgate Rd	Westlake Village	CA	91361	**800-551-2345**	805-449-3000	217
Jagemann Stamping Co 5757 W Custer St	Manitowoc	WI	54220	**888-337-7853**	920-682-4633	487
Jaipur Rugs Inc 2775 Pacific Dr	Norcross	GA	30071	**888-676-7330**	404-351-2360	130
JAK Enterprises Inc 8309 N Knoxville Ave	Peoria	IL	61615	**800-752-3295**	309-692-8222	542
Jake A Parrott Insurance Agency Inc 2508 N Herritage St	Kinston	NC	28501	**800-727-7688**	252-523-1041	390
Jake's Famous Crawfish 401 SW 12th Ave SW Stark	Portland	OR	97205	**800-552-6379**	503-226-1419	669
Jaken Company Inc 14420 My ford rf	Irvine	CA	90623	**800-401-7225**	714-522-1700	288
Jakes Crane & Rigging Inc 6109 Dean Martin Dr	Las Vegas	NV	89118	**800-872-5253**	702-872-5253	192
JAKKS Pacific Inc 21749 Baker Pkwy *NASDAQ: JAKK*	Walnut	CA	91789	**877-875-2557**	909-594-7771	760
JAMA (Journal of the American Medical Assn) PO Box 10946	Chicago	IL	60654	**800-262-2350**	312-670-7827	456-16

Name / Address	City	State	ZIP	Toll-Free	Phone	Class
Jamaica Tourist Board 5201 Blue Lagoon Dr Ste 670	Miami	FL	33126	**800-526-2422**	305-665-0557	773
Jamak Fabrication Inc 1401 N Bowie Dr	Weatherford	TX	76086	**800-543-4747**	817-594-8771	675
James A Scott & Son Inc PO Box 10489	Lynchburg	VA	24506	**800-365-0101**	434-832-2100	391-4
James Austin Co 115 Downieville Rd PO Box 827	Mars	PA	16046	**800-245-1942**	724-625-1535	150
James Avery Craftsman Inc 145 Avery Rd N	Kerrville	TX	78029	**800-283-1770**	830-895-1122	409
James Candy Co 1519 Boardwalk *Orders	Atlantic City	NJ	08401	**800-441-1404***	609-344-1519	297-8
James Chicago, The 55 E Ontario	Chicago	IL	60611	**888-526-3778**	312-337-1000	379
James D Morrissey Inc 9119 Frankford Ave	Philadelphia	PA	19114	**877-536-6857**	215-357-5505	190-4
James Gettys Hotel 27 Chambersburg St	Gettysburg	PA	17325	**888-900-5275**	717-337-1334	379
James Graham Brown Cancer Ctr 529 S Jackson St	Louisville	KY	40202	**866-530-5516**	502-562-4369	767
James Greene & Assoc Inc 275 W Kiehl Ave	Sherwood	AR	72120	**800-422-3384**	501-834-4001	390
James H Quillen Veterans Affairs Medical Ctr Corner of Lamont & Veterans Way PO Box 4000	Mountain Home	TN	37684	**877-573-3529**	423-926-1171	374-8
James Hardie Bldg Products 26300 La Alameda Ave Ste 400	Mission Viejo	CA	92691	**888-542-7343**	949-348-1800	193-4
James J Hill House 240 Summit Ave	Saint Paul	MN	55102	**888-727-8386**	651-297-2555	49-2
James L Allen Ctr 2169 Campus Dr	Evanston	IL	60208	**877-755-2227**	847-467-7000	377
James L. Taylor Manufacturing Co 108 Parker Ave	Poughkeepsie	NY	12601	**800-952-1320**	845-452-3780	819
James Lane Air Conditioning Company Inc 5024 Old Jacksboro Hwy	Wichita Falls	TX	76302	**800-460-2204**	940-766-0244	609
James Machine Works LLC 1521 Adams St	Monroe	LA	71201	**800-259-6104**	318-322-6104	191-1
James Skinner Baking Co 4657 G St	Omaha	NE	68117	**800-358-7428**	402-734-1672	297-2
James Wood Motors Inc 2111 Us Hwy 287 S	Decatur	TX	76234	**888-833-7230**	940-627-2177	56
Jameson Inns *Jameson Inns* 115 Ann Denard Dr	Washington	GA	30673	**800-526-3766**	706-678-7925	379
Jamestown Business College 7 Fairmount Ave PO Box 429	Jamestown	NY	14702	**877-557-2575**	716-664-5100	798
Jamestown College 6000 College Ln	Jamestown	ND	58405	**800-336-2554**	701-252-3467	167
Jamestown Community College 525 Faulkner St PO Box 20	Jamestown	NY	14702	**800-388-8557**	716-338-1000	161
Cattaraugus County 260 N Union St PO Box 5901	Olean	NY	14760	**800-388-9776**	716-376-7500	161
Jamestown Promotions & Tourism Ctr 404 Louis L'Amour Ln	Jamestown	ND	58401	**800-222-4766**	701-251-9145	208
Jamesway Incubator Co Inc 30 High Ridge Ct	Cambridge	ON	N1R7L3	**800-438-8077**	519-624-4646	275
Jamison Bedding Inc PO Box 681948 *Cust Svc	Franklin	TN	37068	**800-255-1883***	615-794-1883	470
Jamison Door Co 55 JV Jamison Dr	Hagerstown	MD	21740	**800-532-3667**	301-733-3100	236
JAMS/Endispute 500 N State College Blvd 14th Fl	Orange	CA	92868	**800-352-5267**	714-939-1300	40
JAMZ-FM 93.9 (CHR) 650 Iwilei Rd Ste 400	Honolulu	HI	96817	**800-745-3000**	808-550-9200	642-54
Jan Cos 35 Sockanosset Cross Rd	Cranston	RI	02920	**888-693-6844**	401-946-4000	668
Jan Marini Skin Research Inc 6951 Via Del Oro	San Jose	CA	95119	**800-347-2223**	408-362-0130	217
Jan's Mountain Outfitters 1600 Pk Ave PO Box 280	Park City	UT	84060	**800-745-1020**	435-649-4949	709
Janalent Corp 7582 Las Vegas Blvd. S. Ste. 580 Ste	Las Vegas	NV	89123	**888-290-4870**		198
Janazzo Services Corp 140 Norton St Rt 10 PO Box 469	Milldale	CT	06467	**800-297-3931**	860-621-7381	191-10
Jane Addams Hull-House Museum 800 S Halsted St	Chicago	IL	60607	**800-625-2013**	312-413-5353	49-2
Jane Goodall Institute for Wildlife Research Education & Conservation (JGI) 1595 Spring Hill Rd Ste 550	Vienna	VA	22182	**800-592-5263**	703-682-9220	47-3
Jane Rose Reporting 80 Fifth Ave	New York	NY	10011	**800-825-3341**	212-727-7773	444
Jane's Information Group 110 N Royal St Ste 200	Alexandria	VA	22314	**800-824-0768**	703-683-3700	634-2
Janell Inc 6130 Cornell Rd	Cincinnati	OH	45242	**888-489-9111**	513-489-9111	358
Janes Island State Park 26280 Alfred Lawson Dr	Crisfield	MD	21817	**877-620-8367**	410-968-1565	564
Janesville Gazette 1 S Parker Dr PO Box 5001	Janesville	WI	53547	**800-362-6712**	608-754-3311	531-2
Janesville Sand & Gravel Co (JSG) 1110 Harding St	Janesville	WI	53547	**800-955-7702**	608-754-7701	502-4
Janesway Electronic Corp 404 N Terr Ave	Mount Vernon	NY	10552	**800-431-1348**	914-699-6710	248
Janet Mcafee Real Estate 9889 Clayton Rd	Saint Louis	MO	63124	**888-991-4800**	314-997-4800	650
Jani-King International Inc 16885 Dallas Pkwy	Addison	TX	75001	**800-526-4546**	972-991-0900	151
Jankovich Co, The Berth 74	San Pedro	CA	90731	**800-836-5355**		537
Janlynn Corp 2070 Westover Rd	Chicopee	MA	01022	**800-445-5565**	413-206-0002	593
Janney Montgomery Scott LLC 1801 Market St	Philadelphia	PA	19103	**800-526-6397**	215-665-6000	688
Jan-Pro International Inc (JPI) 2520 Northwinds Pkwy Ste 375	Alpharetta	GA	30009	**866-355-1064**	678-336-1780	151

Name / Address	City	State	ZIP	Toll-Free	Phone	Class
Janson Industries 1200 Garfield Ave SW	Canton	OH	44706	**800-548-8982**	330-455-7029	720
Janssen Pharmaceutica Inc 1125 Trenton-Harbourton Rd	Titusville	NJ	08560	**800-526-7736**	609-730-2000	582
Jantek Industries 230 Rt 70	Medford	NJ	08055	**888-782-7937**	609-654-1030	236
Japan Travel Bureau USA Inc 156 W 56th St	New York	NY	10019	**800-235-3523**	212-698-4900	769
Japanese American National Museum 369 E First St	Los Angeles	CA	90012	**800-461-5266**	213-625-0414	519
Jarden Consumer Solutions 2381 Executive Ctr Dr	Boca Raton	FL	33431	**800-777-5452**	561-912-4100	36
Jarden Home Brands 14611 W Commerce Rd *Cust Svc	Daleville	IN	47334	**800-240-3340***	765-557-3000	818
Jared Coffin House 29 Broad St *Cust Svc	Nantucket	MA	02554	**800-248-2405***	508-228-2400	379
Jaro Transportation Services Inc 975 Post Rd	Warren	OH	44483	**800-451-3447**	330-393-5659	778
Jarrard Phillips Cate & Hancock Inc 219 Ward Cir	Brentwood	TN	37027	**888-844-6274**	312-419-0575	7
Jarrow Formulas Inc 1824 S Robertson Blvd	Los Angeles	CA	90035	**800-726-0886**	310-204-6936	797
Jarvis Caster Co 881 Lower Brownsville Rd	Jackson	TN	38301	**800-995-9876**		350
JAS (Jo-Ann Stores Inc) 5555 Darrow Rd	Hudson	OH	44236	**888-739-4120**	330-656-2600	272
Jas. D. Collier & Co 606 S Mendenhall Rd Ste 200 *General	Memphis	TN	38117	**800-511-1548***		390
Jasco Products Inc 10 E Memorial Rd	Oklahoma City	OK	73114	**800-654-8483**	405-752-0710	248
Jason International Inc 8328 MacArthur Dr	North Little Rock	AR	72118	**800-255-5766**	501-771-4477	375
Jasper County Rural Electric Membership Corp 280 E 400 S	Rensselaer	IN	47978	**888-866-7362**	219-866-4601	247
Jasper Desk Co 415 E Sixth St *Cust Svc	Jasper	IN	47546	**800-365-7994***	812-482-4132	320-1
JASPER Engines & Transmissions 815 Wernsing Rd PO Box 650	Jasper	IN	47547	**800-827-7455**	812-482-1041	59
Jasper Rubber Products Inc 1010 First Ave	Jasper	IN	47546	**800-457-7457**	812-482-3242	675
Jasper Seating Company Inc *Jasper Group* 225 Clay St	Jasper	IN	47546	**800-622-5661**	812-482-3204	320-1
Jasper Wyman & Son PO Box 100 *Sales	Milbridge	ME	04658	**800-341-1758***		316-1
Jatheon Technologies Inc British Colonial Bldg 8 Wellington St E Mezzanine Level	Toronto	ON	M5E1C5	**888-528-4366**	416-840-0418	401
Java Dave's Executive Coffee Service 6239 E 15th St	Tulsa	OK	74112	**800-725-7315**	918-836-5570	112
Jay Cee Sales & Rivet Inc 32861 Chesley Dr	Farmington	MI	48336	**800-521-6777**	248-478-2150	351
Jay County Rural Electric Membership Corp 484 S 200 W PO Box 904	Portland	IN	47371	**800-835-7362**	260-726-7121	247
Jay Peak Resort 830 Jay Peak Rd	Jay	VT	05859	**800-451-4449**	802-988-2611	667
Jay Roberts Jewelers 515 Rt 73 S	Marlton	NJ	08053	**888-828-8463**	856-596-8600	410
Jayco Inc 903 S Main St *Cust Svc	Middlebury	IN	46540	**800-283-8267***	574-825-5861	119
Jayhawk Bowling Supply Inc 355 N Iowa St PO Box 685	Lawrence	KS	66044	**800-255-6436**	785-842-3237	708
Jaynes Corp 2906 Broadway NE	Albuquerque	NM	87107	**800-393-6343**	505-345-8591	188
Jaypro Sports Inc 976 Hartford Tpke *Cust Svc	Waterford	CT	06385	**800-243-0533***	860-447-3001	346
Jayson Home & Garden 1885 N Clybourn Ave	Chicago	IL	60614	**800-472-1885**	773-248-8180	322
Jazz Pharmaceuticals Inc 3180 Porter Dr	Palo Alto	CA	94304	**866-997-3688**	650-496-3777	582
Jazzercise Inc 2460 Impala Dr *Cust Svc	Carlsbad	CA	92010	**800-348-4748***	760-476-1750	808
Jazziz Magazine 2650 N Military Trail Ste 140	Boca Raton	FL	33431	**888-852-9987**	561-893-6868	456-9
JazzTimes Magazine 85 Quincy Ave Ste 2	Quincy	MA	02169	**800-437-5828**	617-706-9110	456-9
JB Hunt Transport Services Inc 615 JB Hunt Corporate Dr *NASDAQ: JBHT*	Lowell	AR	72745	**800-643-3622**	479-820-0000	448
JB Martin Co 645 Fifth Ave Ste 400	New York	NY	10022	**800-223-0525**	212-421-2020	742-1
J&B Medical Supply Co Inc 50496 W Pontiac Trail	Wixom	MI	48393	**800-980-0047**	248-896-6210	240
JB Sandlin Cos 5137 Davis Blvd	Fort Worth	TX	76180	**800-821-4663**	817-281-3509	189
JBFCS (Jewish Board of Family & Children Services) 120 W 57th St	New York	NY	10019	**888-523-2769**	212-582-9100	47-6
JBL Professional 8500 Balboa Blvd	Northridge	CA	91329	**800-852-5776**	818-894-8850	51
JBMH (Joseph Brant Memorial Hospital) 1230 N Shore Blvd	Burlington	ON	L7S1W7	**800-810-0000**	905-632-3730	374-2
JBS United Inc 4310 State Rd 38 W	Sheridan	IN	46069	**800-382-9909**	317-758-4495	446
JC Newman Cigar Co 2701 16th St *Orders	Tampa	FL	33605	**800-477-1884***	813-248-2124	754
JC Penney Optical Co 821 N Central Expressway	Plano	TX	75075	**866-435-7111**	972-516-1393	542

Listing	Toll-Free	Phone	Class
JC Raulston Arboretum North Carolina State University PO Box 7522 .... Raleigh NC 27695	888-842-2442	919-513-7457	96
JC Whitney 761 Progress Pkwy .... La Salle IL 61301	866-529-5530		458
JCI (Junior Chamber International) 15645 Olive Blvd .... Chesterfield MO 63017	800-905-5499	636-449-3100	47-7
JCPL (Jackson County Public Library) 303 W Second St .... Seymour IN 47274	877-275-7673	812-522-3412	434-3
JCSI Corporate Staffing 2 South St .... Grafton MA 01519	888-527-4462	774-760-1800	262
JD Calato Mfg Company Inc 4501 Hyde Pk Blvd .... Niagara Falls NY 14305 *Cust Svc	800-358-4590*	716-285-3546	526
JD Equipment Inc 1660 US 42 NE .... London OH 43140	800-659-5646	614-879-6620	276
JD Ford & Company LLC 650 S Cherry St Ste 1200 .... Denver CO 80246	888-999-9495	303-333-3673	688
JD Gould Co Inc 4707 Massachusetts Ave .... Indianapolis IN 46218	800-634-6853		788
JD Heiskell & Co 116 W Cedar St .... Tulare CA 93274	800-366-1886	559-685-6100	446
JD McCarty Ctr for Children with Developmental Disabilities 2002 E Robinson St .... Norman OK 73071	800-777-1272	405-307-2800	374-1
JD Power & Assoc 2625 Townsgate Rd Ste 100 .... Westlake Village CA 91361	800-274-5372	805-418-8000	465
Jdk Consulting 4924 Balboa Blvd Ste 487 .... Encino CA 91316	855-535-7877	818-705-8050	198
JDR Microdevices Inc 229 Polaris Ave Ste 17 .... Mountain View CA 94043	800-538-5000	650-625-1400	458
JDRF (Juvenile Diabetes Research Foundation International) 120 Wall St .... New York NY 10005	800-533-2873	212-785-9500	47-17
JE Adams Industries Ltd 1025 63rd Ave Sw .... Cedar Rapids IA 52404	800-553-8861	319-363-0237	53
JE Herndon Company Inc 1020 J E Herndon Access Rd .... Kings Mountain NC 28086	800-277-0500	704-739-4711	742-8
JE Sawyer & Company Inc 64 Glen St .... Glens Falls NY 12801	800-724-3983		611
Jean Coutu Group (PJC) Inc 530 Rue Beriault .... Longueuil QC J4G1S8 *TSE: PJC.A*	877-695-6175	450-646-9760	239
Jean Paree Weegs Inc 4041 South 700 East Ste 2 .... Salt Lake City UT 84107 *Orders	800-422-9447*		348
Jeansonne & Remondet LLC 365 Canal St Ste 1600 .... New Orleans LA 70130	800-446-2745	337-237-4370	428
Jedson Engineering 705 Central Ave .... Cincinnati OH 45202	866-729-3945	513-965-5999	258
Jeff Davis Bancshares Inc 507 N Main St PO Box 730 .... Jennings LA 70546 *OTC: JDVB*	800-789-5159	337-824-3424	69
Jefferds Corp 2070 Winfield Rd .... Saint Albans WV 25177	888-848-6216	304-755-8111	385
Jefferies Socks 2203 Tucker St .... Burlington NC 27215	800-334-6831	336-226-7315	154-9
Jeffers Inc 310 W Saunders Rd PO Box 100 .... Dothan AL 36301	800-533-3377	334-793-6257	577
Jefferson Barracks County Park 345 N Dr .... Saint Louis MO 63125	800-735-2966	314-615-8800	49-4
Jefferson Barracks National Cemetery 2900 Sheridan Rd .... Saint Louis MO 63125	800-827-1000	314-845-8320	135
Jefferson City Area Chamber of Commerce 213 Adams St .... Jefferson City MO 65101	866-223-6535	573-634-3616	138
Jefferson City Convention & Visitors Bureau 700 E Capitol Ave .... Jefferson City MO 65101	800-769-4183	573-632-2820	208
Jefferson City National Cemetery 1024 E McCarty St .... Jefferson City MO 65101	877-907-8585	314-845-8320	135
Jefferson City News Tribune 210 Monroe St .... Jefferson City MO 65101	888-892-6333	573-636-3131	531-2
Jefferson College of Health Sciences 101 Elm Ave SE .... Roanoke VA 24031	888-985-8483	540-985-8483	798
Jefferson Community & Technical College 109 E Broadway .... Louisville KY 40202	855-246-5282	502-213-5333	161
Jefferson Community College 1220 Coffeen St .... Watertown NY 13601	888-435-6522	315-786-2200	161
Jefferson County PO Box 890 .... Dandridge TN 37725	877-237-3847	865-397-9642	338
Jefferson County Chamber of Commerce 532 Patriot Dr .... Dandridge TN 37725	877-237-3847	865-397-9642	138
Jefferson County Convention & Visitors Bureau 37 Washington Ct .... Harpers Ferry WV 25425	866-435-5698	304-535-2627	208
Jefferson County Journal 1405 N Truman Blvd .... Festus MO 63028	800-365-0820	636-937-9811	531-4
Jefferson Ctr 541 Luck Ave Ste 221 .... Roanoke VA 24016	866-345-2550	540-343-2624	571
Jefferson Davis Electric Co-op 906 N Lk Arthur Ave PO Box 1229 .... Jennings LA 70546	800-256-5332	337-824-4330	247
Jefferson Energy Co-op 3077 Hwy 17 PO Box 457 .... North Wrens GA 30833	877-533-3377	706-547-2167	247
Jefferson Hotel 101 W Franklin St .... Richmond VA 23220	800-424-8014	804-788-8000	379
Jefferson Hotel Washington Dc, The 1200 16th St Nw .... Washington DC 20036	877-313-9749	202-448-2300	705
Jefferson Medical College of Thomas Jefferson University 1015 Walnut St .... Philadelphia PA 19107	800-533-3669	215-955-6983	168-2
Jefferson National Expansion Memorial 11 N Fourth St .... Saint Louis MO 63102	855-733-4522	314-655-1700	563
Jefferson Partners LP 2100 E 26th St .... Minneapolis MN 55404 *Cust Svc	800-767-5333*	612-359-3400	107
Jefferson State Community College 2601 Carson Rd .... Birmingham AL 35215	800-239-5900	205-853-1200	161
Jefferson-Madison Regional Library 201 E Market St .... Charlottesville VA 22902	866-979-1555	434-979-7151	434-3

Listing	Toll-Free	Phone	Class
Jeffrey Byrne & Associates 4042 Central St .... Kansas City MO 64111	800-222-9233		40
Jeffrey Hale - St Brigid's Hospital 1250 ch Sainte-Foy .... Quebec QC G1S2M6	888-984-5333	418-684-5333	374-2
Jeffrey Matthews Financial Group LLC, The 308 Vreeland Rd Ste 210 .... Florham Park NJ 07932	888-467-3636	973-805-6222	401
JEGS Performance Auto Parts 101 Jeg'S Pl .... Delaware OH 43015	800-345-4545	614-294-5050	60
Jekyll Island Club Hotel 371 Riverview Dr .... Jekyll Island GA 31527	800-535-9547	912-635-2600	667
Jel Sert Co Rt 59 & Conde St .... West Chicago IL 60185	800-323-2592	630-876-4838	297-15
Jeld-Wen Inc PO Box 1329 .... Klamath Falls OR 97601	800-535-3936		498
Jelliff Corp 354 Pequot Ave .... Southport CT 06890	800-243-0052	203-259-1615	686
Jelly Belly Candy Co 1 Jelly Belly Ln .... Fairfield CA 94533	800-323-9380	707-428-2800	297-8
Jem Engineering LLC 8683 Cherry Ln .... Laurel MD 20707	877-317-1070	301-317-1070	645
JEM Strapping Systems 116 Shaver St .... Brantford ON N3T5M1	877-536-6584	519-754-5432	654
Jemez Mountains Electric Co-op PO Box 128 .... Espanola NM 87532	888-755-2105	505-753-2105	247
Jena Communications 125 Stokes Ave .... Stroudsburg PA 18360	800-367-5362	570-476-6900	626
Jencast PO Box 1509 .... Coffeyville KS 67337	800-331-2662	620-251-5700	308
Jenkins Electric Inc 5933 Brookshire Blvd .... Charlotte NC 28216	800-438-3003		255
Jenkins Fenstermaker PLLC 325 Eighth St .... Huntington WV 25701	866-617-4736	304-523-2100	428
Jenkins Mfg Company Inc 1608 Frank Akers Rd .... Anniston AL 36207	800-633-2323	256-831-7000	238
Jennie Stuart Medical Ctr 320 W 18th St PO Box 2400 .... Hopkinsville KY 42241	800-887-5762	270-887-0100	374-3
Jennie-O Turkey Store 2505 Willmar Ave SW .... Willmar MN 56201	800-621-3505	320-235-2622	618
Jennings County Chamber of Commerce 203 N State St PO Box 340 .... North Vernon IN 47265	866-382-4968	812-346-2339	138
Jennings County Schools 34 W Main St .... North Vernon IN 47265	866-346-3724	812-346-4483	683
Jenny Craig International Inc 5770 Fleet St .... Carlsbad CA 92008	800-443-2331	760-696-4000	808
Jenny Wiley State Resort Park 75 Theatre Ct .... Prestonsburg KY 41653	800-325-0142		564
Jensen Distribution Services PO Box 3708 .... Spokane WA 99220 *General	800-234-1321*		351
Jensen Precast 625 Bergin Way .... Sparks NV 89431	800-648-1134	775-359-6200	185
Jenzabar Inc 101 Huntington Ave Ste 2200 .... Boston MA 02199	800-593-0028	617-492-9099	180-10
Jeppesen Sanderson Inc 55 Inverness Dr E .... Englewood CO 80112	800-621-5377	303-799-9090	634-2
Jergens Inc 15700 S Waterloo Rd .... Cleveland OH 44110	800-537-4367	877-486-1454	492
Jerith Mfg Company Inc 14400 McNulty Rd .... Philadelphia PA 19154	800-344-2242	215-676-4068	490
Jerome Cheese Co 547 W Nez Perce .... Jerome ID 83338	800-757-7611	208-324-8806	297-5
Jerome's Furniture Warehouse 16960 Mesamint St .... San Diego CA 92127	866-633-4094		322
Jerry L Pettis Memorial Veterans Affairs Medical Ctr 11201 Benton St .... Loma Linda CA 92357	800-827-1000	909-825-7084	374-8
Jerry Lipps Inc 3888 Nash Rd .... Cape Girardeau MO 63702	800-325-3331	573-335-8204	778
Jerry Pate Turf & Irrigation Inc 301 Schubert Dr .... Pensacola FL 32504	800-700-7004	850-479-4653	276
Jerry's Marine Service 100 SW 16th St .... Fort Lauderdale FL 33315	800-432-2231		768
Jerry's Sport Ctr Inc 100 Capital Rd .... Jenkins Township PA 18640	800-234-2612		708
Jerry's Systems Inc 702 Russell Ave Ste 306 .... Gaithersburg MD 20877	800-990-9176		668
Jersey Cape Realty Inc 739 Washington St .... Cape May NJ 08204	800-643-0043	609-884-5800	650
Jersey City Free Public Library 472 Jersey Ave .... Jersey City NJ 07302	800-443-0315	201-547-4501	434-3
Jersey Shore State Bank 300 Market St PO Box 967 .... Williamsport PA 17701	888-412-5772	570-322-1111	69
Jersey Shore Steel Co 70 Maryland Ave PO Box 5055 .... Jersey Shore PA 17740	800-833-0277	570-753-3000	721
Jersey Shore University Medical Ctr 1945 Rt 33 .... Neptune NJ 07753	800-560-9990	732-775-5500	374-3
Jesco-Wipco Industries Inc 950 Anderson Rd PO Box 388 .... Litchfield MI 49252	800-455-0019	517-542-2903	288
Jesse Engineering Co 1840 Marine View Dr .... Tacoma WA 98422	800-468-3595	253-922-7433	479
Jesuit School of Theology at Berkeley 1735 LeRoy Ave .... Berkeley CA 94709	800-824-0122	510-549-5000	168-3
Jet Aviation 112 Charles A Lindbergh Dr .... Teterboro NJ 07608	800-538-0832	201-288-8400	24
Jet Industries Inc 1935 Silverton Rd NE PO Box 7362 .... Salem OR 97303	800-659-0620	503-363-2334	609
Jet Resource Inc 455 Wilmer Ave Lunken Airport Hngr 27 .... Cincinnati OH 45226	800-404-5387	513-871-1554	13
Jet Star Inc 10825 Andrade Dr .... Zionsville IN 46077	800-969-4222	317-873-4222	778
JetBlue Airways Corp 118-29 Queens Blvd .... Forest Hills NY 11375 *NASDAQ: JBLU*	800-538-2583	718-286-7900	360-1
Jet-Lube Inc 4849 Homestead Rd Ste 232 .... Houston TX 77226	800-538-5823	713-670-5700	540
Jetstream of Houston LLP 4930 Cranswick .... Houston TX 77041	800-231-8192	713-462-7000	788

Name / Address	City	State	Zip	Toll-Free	Phone	Class
JetSuite 18952 MacArthur Blvd	Irvine	CA	92612	**866-779-7770**		13
Jeunesse Global LLC 650 Douglas Ave	Altamonte Springs	FL	32714	**800-400-2676**	407-215-7414	75
Jewel Case Corp 110 Dupont Dr	Providence	RI	02907	**800-441-4447**	401-943-1400	201
Jewel-Craft Inc 4122 Olympic Blvd	Erlanger	KY	41018	**800-525-5482**	859-282-2400	411
Jewelers of America (JA) 52 Vanderbilt Ave 19th Fl	New York	NY	10017	**800-223-0673**	646-658-0246	48-4
Jewelers Shipping Assn (JSA) 125 Carlsbad St	Cranston	RI	02920	**800-688-4572**	401-943-6020	48-21
Jewell Instruments LLC 850 Perimeter Rd	Manchester	NH	03103	**800-227-5955**	603-669-6400	528
Jewell Tool Technology 3129 State St	Bettendorf	IA	52722	**800-831-8665**	563-355-5010	453
JewelryWeb.com Inc 98 Cuttermill Rd Ste 464	Great Neck	NY	11021	**800-955-9245**	516-482-3982	410
Jewett-Cameron Trading Company Ltd 32275 NW Hillcrest PO Box 1010 *NASDAQ: JCTCF*	North Plains	OR	97133	**800-547-5877**	503-647-0110	193-3
Jewish Board of Family & Children Services (JBFCS) 120 W 57th St	New York	NY	10019	**888-523-2769**	212-582-9100	47-6
Jewish Home Lifecare 120 W 106th St	New York	NY	10025	**800-544-0304**	212-870-5000	449
Jewish Hospital & St Mary's HealthCare 200 Abraham Flexner Way	Louisville	KY	40202	**800-451-3637**	502-587-4011	374-5
Jewish Museum of Maryland 15 Lloyd St *All	Baltimore	MD	21202	**800-235-4045***	410-732-6400	519
Jewish National Fund (JNF) 42 E 69th St	New York	NY	10021	**800-542-8733**	212-879-9300	47-20
Jewish Publication Society 2100 Arch St 2nd Fl	Philadelphia	PA	19103	**800-234-3151**	215-832-0600	634-3
Jewish Reconstructionist Federation (JRF) 101 Greenwood Ave	Jenkintown	PA	19046	**877-226-7573**	215-885-5601	47-20
Jewish United Fund/Jewish Federation of Metropolitan Chicago (JUF) 30 S Wells St	Chicago	IL	60606	**855-275-5237**	312-346-6700	47-20
Jews for Jesus 60 Haight St	San Francisco	CA	94102	**800-366-5521**	415-864-2600	47-20
JF Ahern Co 855 Morris St	Fond du Lac	WI	54935	**800-532-0155**	920-921-9020	191-10
JF Drake State Technical College 3421 Meridian St N	Huntsville	AL	35811	**888-413-7253**	256-539-8161	798
JF Shea Construction Inc 655 Brea Canyon Rd	Walnut	CA	91789	**888-779-7333**	909-594-9500	190-4
JF White Contracting Co 10 Burr St	Framingham	MA	01701	**866-539-4400**	508-879-4700	190-4
JFKL (John F Kennedy Library) 190 W 49th St	Hialeah	FL	33012	**877-738-5622**	305-821-2700	434-3
JFP (Joyner Fine Properties) 2727 Enterprise Pkwy	Richmond	VA	23294	**800-446-3858**	804-270-9440	650
JG Tax Group 1430 S Federal Hwy	Deerfield Beach	FL	33441	**866-477-5291**		731
JGI (Jane Goodall Institute for Wildlife Research Education & Conservation) 1595 Spring Hill Rd Ste 550	Vienna	VA	22182	**800-592-5263**	703-682-9220	47-3
JH Baxter & Co PO Box 5902	San Mateo	CA	94402	**800-556-1098**	650-349-0201	816
JH Fletcher & Co Inc 402 High St	Huntington	WV	25705	**800-327-6203**	304-525-7811	192
JH Industries Inc 1981 E Aurora Rd	Twinsburg	OH	44087	**800-321-4968**	330-963-4105	479
JH Larson Co 10200 51st Ave N	Plymouth	MN	55442	**800-292-7970**	763-545-1717	248
JH Routh Packing Company Inc 4413 W Bogart Rd	Sandusky	OH	44870	**800-446-6759**	419-626-2251	472
JH Technology Inc 5107 Lena Rd Unit 111	Bradenton	FL	34211	**800-808-0300**	941-758-7710	196
JH Walker Trucking Company Inc 152 N Hollywood Rd	Houma	LA	70364	**800-535-5992**	985-868-8330	778
JHCR (Jackson Hole Central Reservations) 140 E Broadway Ste 24 PO Box 2618	Jackson	WY	83001	**888-838-6606**	307-733-4005	376
JHL Industries 10012 Nevada Ave	Chatsworth	CA	91311	**800-255-6636**	818-882-2233	729
Jiffy Lube PO Box 4427	Houston	TX	77210	**800-344-6933**		61-5
Jim Bishop Cabinets Inc 5640 Bell Rd	Montgomery	AL	36116	**800-410-2444**		114
Jim Palmer Trucking Inc 9730 Derby Dr	Missoula	MT	59801	**888-698-3422**	406-721-5151	778
Jimbo's Jumbos Inc 185 Peanut Dr PO Box 465 *General	Edenton	NC	27932	**800-334-4771***		297-32
Jimmie Davis State Park 1209 State Pk Rd	Chatham	LA	71226	**888-677-2263**	318-249-2595	564
Jimmy John's Franchise Inc 2212 Fox Dr	Champaign	IL	61820	**800-546-6904**	217-356-9900	668
Jimmy Swaggart Ministries (JSM) 8919 World Ministry Blvd PO Box 262550 *Orders	Baton Rouge	LA	70810	**800-288-8350***	225-768-8300	47-20
Jive Communications Inc 1275 West 1600 North Ste 100	Orem	UT	84057	**866-768-5429**		181
JJ Haines & Company Inc 6950 Aviation Blvd	Glen Burnie	MD	21061	**800-922-9248**		361
JJ Keller & Assoc Inc 3003 Breezewood Ln PO Box 368	Neenah	WI	54957	**800-558-5011**	920-722-2848	634-11
JJ MacKay Canada Ltd 1342 Abercrombie Rd	New Glasgow	NS	B2H5C6	**888-462-2529**	902-752-5124	768
JJB Hilliard WL Lyons Inc 500 W Jefferson St	Louisville	KY	40202	**800-444-1854**	502-588-8400	688
JL Clark Mfg Co 923 23rd Ave	Rockford	IL	61104	**877-482-5275**	815-962-8861	123
JL Clark Mfg Co Lancaster Div 303 N Plum St	Lancaster	PA	17602	**877-482-5275**	717-392-4125	123
JL Industries Inc 4450 W 78th St Cir	Bloomington	MN	55435	**800-554-6077**	952-835-6850	288
JLM Couture Inc 525 Seventh Ave Ste 1703	New York	NY	10018	**800-924-6475**	212-221-8203	154-20
JLS Mailing Services Inc 672 Crescent St	Brockton	MA	02302	**866-557-6245**	508-313-1000	5
JM Eventsonline ca Inc 155 Colonnade Rd Ste 17	Ottawa	ON	K2E7K1	**866-638-3687**		226
JM Huber Corp 499 Thornall St 8th Fl	Edison	NJ	08837	**877-418-0038**	732-549-8600	535
JM Manufacturing Company Inc 5200 West Century Blvd	Los Angeles	CA	90045	**800-621-4404**		595
JM Smucker Co 1 Strawberry Ln *NYSE: SJM*	Orrville	OH	44667	**888-550-9555**	330-682-3000	297-20
JM Swank Co 395 Herky St	North Liberty	IA	52317	**800-593-6333**	319-626-3683	298-8
JM Test Systems Inc 7323 Tom Dr	Baton Rouge	LA	70806	**800-353-3411**	225-925-2029	740
JM Turner Engineering Inc 1325 College Ave	Santa Rosa	CA	95404	**800-514-4220**	707-528-4503	258
J-Mar Enterprises Inc PO Box 4143	Bismarck	ND	58502	**800-446-8283**	701-222-4518	778
Jmd Group LLC 720 Walnut St	Chattanooga	TN	37402	**866-251-0361**	423-265-8111	390
JMFA (M Floyd John & Assoc Inc) 125 N Burnett Dr	Baytown	TX	77520	**800-809-2307**		196
JMG Security Systems Inc 17150 Newhope St Ste 109	Fountain Valley	CA	92708	**800-900-4564**	714-545-8882	691
JMMC (John Muir Medical Ctr) 1601 Ygnacio Valley Rd	Walnut Creek	CA	94598	**844-398-5376**	925-939-3000	374-3
JMP Engineering Inc 4026 Meadowbrook Dr Unit 143	London	ON	N6L1C9	**855-228-8668**	519-652-2741	263
JMT (Johnson Mirmiran & Thompson) 72 Loveton Cir	Sparks	MD	21152	**800-472-2310**	410-329-3100	263
JNF (Jewish National Fund) 42 E 69th St	New York	NY	10021	**800-542-8733**	212-879-9300	47-20
JNJ Express Inc 3935 Old Getwell Rd PO Box 30983	Memphis	TN	38130	**888-383-7157**	901-362-3444	778
Joan & Sanford Weill Medical College of Cornell University 445 E 69th St	New York	NY	10021	**800-422-0711**	212-746-5454	168-2
Joan C Edwards School of Medicine at Marshall University 1600 Medical Ctr Dr	Huntington	WV	25701	**877-691-1600**	304-691-1700	168-2
Jo-Ann Fabrics & Crafts 5555 Darrow Rd	Hudson	OH	44236	**888-739-4120**	330-656-2600	272
Jo-Ann Stores Inc (JAS) 5555 Darrow Rd	Hudson	OH	44236	**888-739-4120**	330-656-2600	272
JobDiva 116 John St. Ste 1406	New York	NY	10038	**866-562-3482**		393
Jobe Hastings & Assoc CPA's 745 S Church St Ste 105	Murfreesboro	TN	37133	**866-207-2384**	615-893-7777	2
Jobelephantcom Inc 5443 Fremontia Ln	San Diego	CA	92115	**800-311-0563**	619-795-0837	7
JobHive Inc 701 E Bridger Ave Ste 400	Las Vegas	NV	89101	**855-562-4483**		262
JobMonkey Inc PO Box 3956	Seattle	WA	98124	**800-230-1095**		262
Jobscope Corp 355 Woodruff Rd	Greenville	SC	29607	**800-443-5794**		180-11
JOC (Johnson Oil Co) 1113 E Sara DeWitt Dr	Gonzales	TX	78629	**800-284-2432**		578
Jo-Carroll Energy 793 US Hwy 20 W	Elizabeth	IL	61028	**800-858-5522**	815-858-2207	247
Jockey International Inc 2300 60th St PO Box 1417	Kenosha	WI	53140	**800-562-5391**		154-17
Jockeys' Guild Inc 103 Wind Haven Dr Ste 200	Nicholasville	KY	40356	**866-465-6257**	859-305-0606	47-22
Joe Holland Chevrolet Inc 210 Maccorkle Ave SW	South Charleston	WV	25303	**855-468-9491**	304-744-1561	56
Joe Van Horn Chevrolet Inc PO Box 238	Plymouth	WI	53073	**800-236-1415**	920-893-6361	56
Joe Wheeler Electric Membership Corp PO Box 460	Trinity	AL	35673	**800-239-6518**	256-552-2300	247
Joe Wheeler Resort Lodge & Convention Ctr 4401 McLean Dr	Rogersville	AL	35652	**800-544-5639**	256-247-5461	667
Joe's Jeans Inc 2340 S Eastern Ave *NASDAQ: JOEZ*	Commerce	CA	90040	**877-528-5637**	323-837-3700	156-4
Joe's Stone Crab 11 Washington Ave	Miami Beach	FL	33139	**800-780-2722**	305-673-0365	669
Joerns Healthcare 5001 Joerns Dr	Stevens Point	WI	54481	**800-826-0270**	715-341-3600	320-3
Joey's Only Seafood Franchising Corp 514-42nd Ave SE	Calgary	AB	T2G1Y6	**800-661-2123**	403-243-4584	668
Joffrey's Coffee & Tea Co 3803 Corporex Pk Dr	Tampa	FL	33619	**800-458-5282**	813-250-0404	298-11
Johanna Foods Inc 20 Johanna Farm Rd PO Box 272	Flemington	NJ	08822	**800-727-6700**	908-788-2200	297-20
Johannes Flowers Inc 4990 Foothill Rd	Carpinteria	CA	93013	**800-365-9476**	805-684-5686	369
Johanson Mfg Corp 301 Rockaway Valley Rd	Boonton	NJ	07005	**800-477-1272**	973-334-2676	255
John A Van Den Bosch Co 4511 Holland Ave	Holland	MI	49424	**800-968-6477**		446
John Amico Haircare Products 4731 W 136th St	Crestwood	IL	60445	**800-676-5264**	708-824-4000	217
John Anson Ford Theatres 2580 Cahuenga Blvd E	Hollywood	CA	90068	**800-352-0050**	323-461-3673	571
John B Hynes Veterans Memorial Convention Ctr 900 Boylston St	Boston	MA	02115	**800-392-6089**	617-954-2000	207
John B Malouf Inc 8201 Quaker Ave Ste 106	Lubbock	TX	79424	**800-658-9500**	806-794-9500	156-4
John B Sanfilippo & Son Inc 1703 N Randall Rd *NASDAQ: JBSS*	Elgin	IL	60123	**800-874-8734**	847-289-1800	297-28
John Bean Co 309 Exchange Ave	Conway	AR	72032	**800-225-5786**	501-450-1500	59

Name / Address	City	State	ZIP	Toll-Free	Phone	Class
John Boos & Co 3601 S Banker St PO Box 609	Effingham	IL	62401	**888-431-2667**	217-347-7701	288
John Boyd Thacher State Park 1 Hailes Cave Rd	Voorheesville	NY	12186	**800-456-2267**	518-872-1237	564
John Brown University 2000 W University St *Admissions	Siloam Springs	AR	72761	**877-528-4636***	479-524-9500	167
John C. Heath, Attorney at Law PLLC 360 N Cutler Dr	Salt Lake City	UT	84054	**800-756-9681**		428
John Carroll School, The 703 Churchville Rd	Bel Air	MD	21014	**800-422-0010**	410-879-2480	683
John Carroll University 20700 N Pk Blvd	Cleveland	OH	44118	**888-335-6800**	216-397-1886	167
John Cooper School 1 John Cooper Dr	The Woodlands	TX	77381	**800-295-1162**	281-367-0900	683
John D Archbold Memorial Hospital 915 Gordon Ave	Thomasville	GA	31792	**800-341-1009**	229-228-2000	374-3
John Daugherty Realtors 520 Post Oak Blvd 6th Fl	Houston	TX	77027	**800-231-2821**	713-626-3930	650
John Day Co 6263 Abbott Dr	Omaha	NE	68110	**800-767-2273**	402-455-8000	276
John Deere Coffeyville Works Inc 2624 N US Hwy	Coffeyville	KS	67337	**800-844-1337**		619
John Deere Credit Co 6400 NW 86th St	Johnston	IA	50131	**800-275-5322**	515-267-3000	218
John Deere Planetarium 820 38th St Augustana College	Rock Island	IL	61201	**800-798-8100**	309-794-7327	597
John Deere Power Systems 3801 W Ridgeway Ave PO Box 5100	Waterloo	IA	50704	**800-533-6446**		264
John E Conner Museum 905 W Santa Gertrudis Ave 700 University Blvd.	Kingsville	TX	78363	**800-726-8192**	361-593-2810	519
John E Jones Oil Co Inc 1016 S Cedar PO Box 546	Stockton	KS	67669	**800-323-9821**	785-425-6746	188
John E Koerner & Company Inc 4820 Jefferson Hwy	New Orleans	LA	70121	**800-333-1913**		298-11
John F Buchan Homes 2821 Northup Way Ste 100	Bellevue	WA	98004	**866-528-2426**	425-827-2266	651
John F Kennedy Ctr for the Performing Arts 2700 F St NW	Washington	DC	20566	**800-444-1324**	202-416-8000	571
John F Kennedy Library (JFKL) 190 W 49th St	Hialeah	FL	33012	**877-738-5622**	305-821-2700	434-3
John F Kennedy Presidential Library & Museum Columbia Pt	Boston	MA	02125	**866-535-1960**	617-514-1600	434-2
John F Kennedy University 100 Ellinwood Way	Pleasant Hill	CA	94523	**800-696-5358**	925-969-3300	167
John F. Kennedy Space Ctr	Kennedy Space Center	FL	32899	**866-737-5235**	321-867-5000	666
John Fabick Tractor Co 1 Fabick Dr *Cust Svc	Fenton	MO	63026	**800-845-9188***	636-343-5900	358
John Hancock Funds 601 Congress St	Boston	MA	02210	**800-338-8080**	617-375-1500	527
John Hancock New York 100 Summit Lake Dr	Valhalla	NY	10595	**800-732-5543**	877-391-3748	391-2
John Henry Co 5800 W Grand River Ave	Lansing	MI	48906	**800-748-0517**	517-323-9000	625
John J Pershing Veterans Affairs Medical Ctr 1500 N Westwood Blvd	Poplar Bluff	MO	63901	**888-557-8262**	573-686-4151	374-8
John Jay Homestead State Historic Site PO Box 832	Katonah	NY	10536	**800-456-2267**	914-232-5651	564
John Johnson Co 274 S Waterman St	Detroit	MI	48209	**800-991-1394**	313-496-0600	730
John Knox Village 651 SW Sixth St	Pompano Beach	FL	33060	**800-998-5669**		670
John M Frey Co Inc 2735 62nd St Ct	Bettendorf	IA	52722	**800-397-3739**	563-332-9200	611
John M. Campbell & Co 1215 Crossroads Blvd	Norman	OK	73072	**800-821-5933**	405-321-1383	263
John Marshall Law School 315 S Plymouth Ct	Chicago	IL	60604	**800-285-2221**	312-427-2737	168-1
John Morrell & Co 805 E Kemper Rd	Cincinnati	OH	45246	**800-722-1127**	513-346-3540	472
John Muir Medical Ctr (JMMC) 1601 Ygnacio Valley Rd	Walnut Creek	CA	94598	**844-398-5376**	925-939-3000	374-3
John Paul Jones State Historic Site c/o Bureau of Parks & Lands	Bangor	ME	04401	**800-452-1942**	207-941-4014	564
John Paul Mitchell Systems 1888 Century Park E ste 1600 *Cust Svc	Los Angeles	CA	90067	**800-793-8790***		217
John Paul Pet Salon 32861 Camino Capistrano Ste F	San Juan Capistrano	CA	92675	**855-577-7669**		792
John R Hess & Company Inc 400 Stn St PO Box 3615	Cranston	RI	02910	**800-828-4377**	401-785-9300	145
John R White Company Inc PO Box 10043	Birmingham	AL	35202	**800-245-1183**	205-595-8381	145
John Reyer Shoe Store 40 S Water Ave *Cust Svc	Sharon	PA	16146	**800-245-1550***		302
John Roberts Co 9687 E River Rd	Coon Rapids	MN	55433	**800-551-1534**	763-755-5500	626
John S Knight Ctr 77 E Mill St	Akron	OH	44308	**800-245-4254**	330-374-8900	207
John T Cyr & Sons Inc 153 Gilman Falls Ave	Old Town	ME	04468	**800-244-2335**	207-827-2335	108
John Volpi & Company Inc 5263 Northrup Ave	St Louis	MO	63110	**800-288-3439**	314-772-8550	297-10
John W Danforth Co 300 Colvin Woods Pkwy	Tonawanda	NY	14150	**800-888-6119**	716-832-1940	191-10
John Watson Chevrolet 3535 Wall Ave	Ogden	UT	84401	**866-647-9930**	801-394-2611	56
John Wieland Homes & Neighborhoods 4125 Atlanta Rd SE	Smyrna	GA	30080	**800-376-4663**	770-996-2400	651
John Wiley & Sons Inc 111 River St *NYSE: JW/A* ■ *Sales	Hoboken	NJ	07030	**800-225-5945***	201-748-6000	634-2
John Wolf Florist 6228 Waters Ave	Savannah	GA	31406	**800-944-6435**	912-352-9843	294
John Zink Company LLC 11920 E Apache St	Tulsa	OK	74116	**800-421-9242**	918-234-1800	357
John-Kenyon Eye Ctr 1305 Wall St	Jeffersonville	IN	47130	**800-342-5393**		796
Johnny's Fine Foods Inc 319 E 25th St *General	Tacoma	WA	98421	**800-962-1462***	253-383-4597	297-37
Johnny's Selected Seeds 955 Benton Ave	Winslow	ME	04901	**877-564-6697**	207-861-3900	692
Johns Dental Laboratory Inc 423 S 13th St	Terre Haute	IN	47807	**800-457-0504**	812-232-6026	383
Johns Eastern Co Inc PO Box 110259 Lakewood Branch *General	Sarasota	FL	34211	**877-326-5326***	941-907-3100	390
Johns Hopkins University Press 2715 N Charles St *Orders	Baltimore	MD	21218	**800-537-5487***	410-516-6900	634-4
Johns Manville Corp 717 17th St PO Box 5108 *Prod Info	Denver	CO	80217	**800-654-3103***	303-978-2000	389
Johnson & Johnson Consumer Products Co 199 Grandview Rd	Skillman	NJ	08558	**866-565-2229**	908-874-1000	217
Johnson & Johnson Inc 7101 Notre-Dame E	Montreal	QC	H1N2G4	**800-361-8990**	514-251-5100	217
Johnson & Johnson Vision Care Inc 7500 Centurion Pkwy	Jacksonville	FL	32256	**800-843-2020**	800-874-5278	541
Johnson & Wales University *Providence* 8 Abbott Pk Pl	Providence	RI	02903	**800-342-5598**	401-598-1000	167
Johnson & Wales University Charlotte 801 W Trade St	Charlotte	NC	28202	**866-598-2427**	980-598-1100	167
Johnson & Wales University Denver 7150 E Montview Blvd	Denver	CO	80220	**877-598-3368**	303-256-9300	167
Johnson & Wales University North Miami 1701 NE 127th St	North Miami	FL	33181	**866-598-3567**	800-342-5598	167
Johnson Bros Bakery Supply 10731 N Interstate 35	San Antonio	TX	78233	**877-446-2767**	800-590-2575	298-8
Johnson C Smith University 100 Beatties Ford Rd *Admissions	Charlotte	NC	28216	**800-782-7303***	704-378-1000	167
Johnson College 3427 N Main Ave	Scranton	PA	18508	**800-293-9675**	570-342-6404	798
Johnson Controls Systems 9410 Bunsen Pkwy Ste 100-B	Louisville	KY	40220	**800-765-7773**	502-671-7300	204
Johnson County 111 S Cherry St Ste 1200	Olathe	KS	66061	**800-766-3777**	913-715-0775	338
Johnson County Community College 12345 College Blvd	Overland Park	KS	66210	**866-896-5893**	913-469-8500	161
Johnson County Library PO Box 2933	Shawnee Mission	KS	66201	**800-386-8501**	913-826-4600	434-3
Johnson County Rural Electric Membership Corp 750 International Dr	Franklin	IN	46131	**800-382-5544**	317-736-6174	247
Johnson Electric Coil Co 821 Watson St	Antigo	WI	54409	**800-826-9741**	715-627-4367	765
Johnson Engineering Inc 2122 Johnson St	Fort Myers	FL	33901	**866-367-4400**	239-334-0046	258
Johnson Gas Appliance Co 520 E Ave NW	Cedar Rapids	IA	52405	**800-553-5422**	319-365-5267	319
Johnson Industries 5944 Peachtree Corners E *Orders	Norcross	GA	30071	**800-922-8111***	770-441-1128	60
Johnson Investment Counsel Inc 3777 W Fork Rd	Cincinnati	OH	45247	**800-541-0170**	513-661-3100	401
Johnson Matthey Medical Products 1401 King Rd	West Chester	PA	19380	**800-442-1405**	610-648-8000	475
Johnson Matthey Pharma Services 25 Patton Rd	Devens	MA	01434	**800-444-8544**	978-784-5000	478
Johnson Mirmiran & Thompson (JMT) 72 Loveton Cir	Sparks	MD	21152	**800-472-2310**	410-329-3100	263
Johnson Motors Inc 1891 Blinker Pkwy	Du Bois	PA	15801	**800-537-1768**	814-371-4444	56
Johnson Oil Co (JOC) 1113 E Sara DeWitt Dr	Gonzales	TX	78629	**800-284-2432**		578
Johnson Outdoors Inc 555 Main St *NASDAQ: JOUT*	Racine	WI	53403	**800-468-9716**	262-631-6600	708
Johnson Refrigerated Truck Bodies 215 E Allen St *Sales	Rice Lake	WI	54868	**800-922-8360***	715-234-7071	515
Johnson Scale Company Inc 36 Stiles Ln	Pine Brook	NJ	07058	**800-572-2531**		682
Johnson State College 337 College Hill	Johnson	VT	05656	**800-635-2356**	802-635-2356	167
Johnson Storage & Moving Co 221 Broadway	Denver	CO	80202	**800-289-6683**	303-778-6683	518
Johnson Supply Inc 10151 Stella Link Rd	Houston	TX	77025	**800-833-5455**	713-830-2499	611
Johnson University 7900 Johnson Dr	Knoxville	TN	37998	**800-827-2122**	865-573-4517	160
Johnson Wholesale Floors Inc 1874 Defoor Ave NW	Atlanta	GA	30318	**800-345-9318**	404-352-2700	130
Johnson Youth Ctr 3252 Hospital Dr	Juneau	AK	99801	**800-780-9972**	907-586-9433	412
Johnson's Garden Centers 2707 W 13th St	Wichita	KS	67203	**888-542-8463**	316-942-1443	324
Johnsonite Inc 16910 Munn Rd	Chagrin Falls	OH	44023	**800-899-8916**	440-543-8916	130
Johnsonville Sausage LLC PO Box 906	Sheboygan Falls	WI	53085	**888-556-2728**		297-26
Johnston & Murphy Inc 1415 Murfreesboro Rd	Nashville	TN	37217	**800-424-2854**	615-367-7168	302
Johnston County Convention & Visitors Bureau 235 E Market St	Smithfield	NC	27577	**800-441-7829**	919-989-8687	208

Name / Address	City	State	Zip	Toll-Free	Phone	Class
Johnston Paper Co 2 Eagle Dr	Auburn	NY	13021	**800-800-7123**	315-253-8435	558
Johnston the Florist Inc 14179 Lincoln Way	North Huntingdon	PA	15642	**800-356-9371**	412-751-2821	294
Joliet Area Community Hospice 250 Water Stone Cir	Joliet	IL	60431	**800-360-1817**	815-740-4104	371
Joliet Equipment Corp 1 Doris Ave	Joliet	IL	60433	**800-435-9350**	815-727-6606	517
Joliet Junior College *North* 1215 Houbolt Rd	Joliet	IL	60431	**800-899-4722**	815-729-9020	161
Joliet Region Chamber of Commerce & Industry 63 N Chicago St	Joliet	IL	60432	**877-499-9669**	815-727-5371	138
Jolly Hotel Madison Towers 22 E 38th St *Resv	New York	NY	10016	**888-726-0528***	212-802-0600	379
Jolly Roger Inn 640 W Katella Ave	Anaheim	CA	92802	**888-296-5986**	714-782-7500	379
Jolt Consulting Group 112 Spring St Ste 301	Saratoga Springs	NY	12866	**877-249-6262**		462
Jomax LLC 14100 N 83rd Ave Ste 235	Peoria	AZ	85381	**888-866-0721**		393
Jon Renau Collection 2510 Island View Way	Vista	CA	92081	**800-462-9447**	760-598-0067	348
Jon's Nursery Inc 24546 Nursery Way	Eustis	FL	32736	**800-322-4289**	352-357-4289	294
Jonah Group Ltd, The 461 King St W 3rd Fl	Toronto	ON	M5V1K4	**888-594-6260**	416-304-0860	181
Jonas Fitness Inc 16969 n texas ave	Webster	TX	77598	**800-324-9800**		354
Jonathan Lord Corp 87 Carlough Rd	Bohemia	NY	11716	**800-814-7517**	631-563-4445	298-8
Jones Apparel Group Inc Jones New York Collection Div 1411 Broadway	New York	NY	10018	**800-999-1877**	212-355-4449	154-20
Jones College 5353 Arlington Expy	Jacksonville	FL	32211	**800-331-0176**	904-743-1122	167
Jones Dairy Farm 800 Jones Ave	Fort Atkinson	WI	53538	**800-635-6637**	920-563-2431	297-26
Jones Environmental Inc 708 Milam St Ste 100	Shreveport	LA	71101	**877-345-4534**	318-226-8444	198
Jones Eye Clinic 4405 Hamilton Blvd	Sioux City	IA	51104	**800-334-2015**	712-239-3937	796
Jones Hamilton Co 30354 Tracy Rd	Walbridge	OH	43465	**888-858-4425**	419-666-9838	142
Jones International Ltd 9697 E Mineral Ave	Centennial	CO	80112	**800-525-7002**		641
Jones Metal Products Co 200 N Ctr St	West Lafayette	OH	43845	**888-868-6535**	740-545-6381	755
Jones Metal Products Inc 3201 Third Ave	Mankato	MN	56001	**800-967-1750**	507-625-4436	695
Jones Motor Company Inc 900 W Bridge St PO Box 137	Spring City	PA	19475	**800-825-6637**	610-948-7900	778
Jones Soda Co 66 S Hanford St Ste 150 *OTC: JSDA*	Seattle	WA	98134	**800-690-6903**	206-624-3357	79-2
Jonesboro Sun 518 Carson St	Jonesboro	AR	72401	**800-237-5341**	870-935-5525	531-2
Jones-Onslow Electric Membership Corp 259 Western Blvd	Jacksonville	NC	28546	**800-682-1515**	910-353-1940	247
JOPERD (Journal of Physical Education Recreation & Dance) 1900 Assn Dr	Reston	VA	20191	**800-213-7193**	703-476-3400	456-8
Joplin Globe 117 E Fourth St	Joplin	MO	64801	**800-444-8514**	417-623-3480	531-2
Jordan Hospital 275 Sandwich St	Plymouth	MA	02360	**800-256-7326**	508-746-2000	374-3
Jordan Lake State Recreation Area 280 State Pk Rd	Apex	NC	27523	**877-722-6762**	919-362-0586	564
Jordan Tourism Board (JTB) 1307 Dolley Madison Blvd Ste 2A	McLean	VA	22101	**877-733-5673**	703-243-7404	773
Jordano's Inc 550 S Patterson Ave	Santa Barbara	CA	93111	**800-325-2278**	805-964-0611	298-8
Jorgensen Conveyors Inc 10303 N Baehr Rd	Mequon	WI	53092	**800-325-7705**	262-242-3089	209
Jorgensen Forge Corp 8531 E Marginal Way S	Tukwila	WA	98108	**800-231-5382**	206-762-1100	482
Jorgensen Laboratories Inc 1450 Van Buren Ave	Loveland	CO	80538	**800-525-5614**	970-669-2500	474
Jos A Bank Clothiers 500 Hanover Pk *Cust Svc	Hampstead	MD	21074	**800-999-7472***	410-239-2700	154-11
Josam Co 525 W US Hwy 20	Michigan City	IN	46360	**800-365-6726**	219-872-5531	608
Joseph Blank Inc 62 W 47th St Ste 808	New York	NY	10036	**800-223-7666**	212-575-9050	411
Joseph Brant Memorial Hospital (JBMH) 1230 N Shore Blvd	Burlington	ON	L7S1W7	**800-810-0000**	905-632-3730	374-2
Joseph H. Stewart State Recreation Area 35251 Hwy 62	Prospect	OR	97536	**800-452-5687**	541-560-3334	564
Joseph Meyerhoff Symphony Hall 1212 Cathedral St	Baltimore	MD	21201	**877-276-1444**	410-783-8100	571
Joseph, Greenwald & Laake PA 6404 Ivy Ln Ste 400	Rockville	MD	20770	**877-412-7429**	301-220-2200	428
Josephine County Fairgrounds 1451 Fairgrounds Rd PO Box 672	Grants Pass	OR	97527	**800-773-1162**	541-476-3215	639
Joslyn Sunbank Co LLC 1740 Commerce Way	Paso Robles	CA	93446	**800-523-0727**	805-238-2840	814
Jostens Inc 3601 Minnesota Ave Ste 400	Minneapolis	MN	55435	**800-235-4774**	952-830-3300	409
Jottan Inc PO Box 166	Florence	NJ	08518	**800-364-4234**	609-447-6200	191-12
Joule Inc 1245 US Rt 1 S	Edison	NJ	08837	**800-341-0341**	732-548-5444	719
Journal & Courier 217 N Sixth St *News Rm	Lafayette	IN	47901	**800-407-5813***	765-423-5511	531-2
Journal Gazette 600 W Main St	Fort Wayne	IN	46802	**888-966-4532**	260-461-8773	531-2
Journal Graphics Inc 2840 NW 35th Ave	Portland	OR	97210	**888-609-6051**	503-790-9100	634-8
Journal Inquirer 306 Progress Dr PO Box 510	Manchester	CT	06045	**800-237-3606**	860-646-0500	531-2
Journal Le Droit 47 Clarence St	Ottawa	ON	K1N9K1	**800-267-6961**	613-562-0555	531-1
Journal of Accountancy 220 Leigh Farm Rd	Durham	NC	27707	**888-777-7077**		456-5
Journal of Employee Communication Management 316 N Michigan Ave Ste 400	Chicago	IL	60601	**800-878-5331**	312-960-4100	530-2
Journal of Financial Planning Assn 7535 E Hampden Ave Ste 600	Denver	CO	80231	**800-322-4237**	303-759-4900	456-5
Journal of Petroleum Technology 222 Palisades Creek Dr	Richardson	TX	75080	**800-456-6863**	972-952-9393	456-21
Journal of Physical Education Recreation & Dance (JOPERD) 1900 Assn Dr	Reston	VA	20191	**800-213-7193**	703-476-3400	456-8
Journal of Practical Nursing (JPN) 1940 Duke St Ste 200	Alexandria	VA	22314	**800-655-4845**	703-933-1003	456-16
Journal of Property Management 430 N Michigan Ave	Chicago	IL	60611	**800-837-0706**		456-5
Journal of Protective Coatings & Linings 2100 Wharton St Ste 310	Pittsburgh	PA	15203	**800-837-8303**	412-431-8300	456-21
Journal of the American Dietetic Assn 1600 John F Kennedy Blvd	Philadelphia	PA	19103	**800-654-2452**		456-16
Journal of the American Medical Assn (JAMA) PO Box 10946	Chicago	IL	60654	**800-262-2350**	312-670-7827	456-16
Journal of the American Pharmacists Assn 2215 Constitution Ave NW	Washington	DC	20037	**800-237-2742**	202-628-4410	456-16
Journal of the Kansas Bar Assn 1200 SW Harrison St	Topeka	KS	66612	**800-928-3111**	785-234-5696	456-15
Journal of the Louisiana State Medical Society 6767 Perkins Rd Ste 100	Baton Rouge	LA	70808	**800-375-9508**	225-763-8500	456-16
Journal of the Medical Assn of Georgia 1849 The Exchange Ste 200	Atlanta	GA	30339	**800-282-0224**	678-303-9290	456-16
Journal of the Mississippi State Medical Assn PO Box 2548	Ridgeland	MS	39158	**800-898-0251**	601-853-6733	456-16
Journal of the Philosophy of Sport 1607 N Market St	Champaign	IL	61820	**800-747-4457**	217-351-5076	456-20
Journal Publishing Co 1242 S Green St	Tupelo	MS	38804	**800-264-6397**	662-842-2611	634-8
Journal, The 207 W King St	Martinsburg	WV	25402	**800-448-1895**	304-263-8931	531-2
Journal-Standard 27 S State Ave	Freeport	IL	61032	**800-325-6397**	815-232-1171	531-2
Journey Education Marketing Inc 13755 Hutton Dr Ste 500	Dallas	TX	75234	**800-874-9001**	972-481-2000	176
Journey Museum 222 New York St	Rapid City	SD	57701	**877-343-8220**	605-394-6923	519
Journyx Inc 7600 Burnet Rd Ste. 300	Austin	TX	78757	**800-755-9878**	512-834-8888	38
Joy Cone Co 3435 Lamor Rd	Hermitage	PA	16148	**800-242-2663**	724-962-5747	297-9
Joy Dog Food PO Box 305	Pinckneyville	IL	62274	**800-245-4125**		577
Joyce Florist 2729 S Hampton Rd	Dallas	TX	75224	**800-527-1520**	214-942-1776	294
Joyce Koons Buick Gmc 10660 Automotive Dr	Manassas	VA	20109	**866-755-0072**		515
Joyce Motors Corp 3166 SR- 10	Denville	NJ	07834	**844-332-5955**	973-361-3000	56
Joyce Windows 1125 Berea Industrial Pkwy	Berea	OH	44017	**800-824-7988**	440-239-9100	236
Joyner Fine Properties (JFP) 2727 Enterprise Pkwy	Richmond	VA	23294	**800-446-3858**	804-270-9440	650
JP Everhart & Co PO Box 2683	Waco	TX	76702	**888-622-8575**		391-5
JP Maguire Assoc Inc 266 Brookside Rd	Waterbury	CT	06708	**877-576-2484**	203-755-2297	83
Jp Mchale Pest Management Inc 241 Bleakley Ave	Buchanan	NY	10511	**800-479-2284**		576
JPI (Jan-Pro International Inc) 2520 Northwinds Pkwy Ste 375	Alpharetta	GA	30009	**866-355-1064**	678-336-1780	151
JPMorgan Fleming Asset Management PO Box 8528	Boston	MA	02266	**800-480-4111**		401
JPN (Journal of Practical Nursing) 1940 Duke St Ste 200	Alexandria	VA	22314	**800-655-4845**	703-933-1003	456-16
JR Filanc Construction Company Inc 740 N Andreasen Dr	Escondido	CA	92029	**877-225-5428**	760-941-7130	190-10
JR O'Dwyer Co 271 Madison Ave 6th Fl	New York	NY	10016	**866-395-7710**	212-679-2471	634-9
JR Realty 101 E Horizon Dr	Henderson	NV	89015	**800-541-6780**	702-564-5142	650
JR Simplot Co 999 W Main St Ste 1300	Boise	ID	83702	**800-832-8893**	208-336-2110	297-21
JR Watkins Inc 150 Liberty St PO Box 5570	Winona	MN	55987	**800-243-9423**	507-457-3300	366
Jra Financial Advisors 7373 Kirkwood Ct Ste 300	Maple Grove	MN	55369	**800-278-5988**	763-315-8000	401
JRF (Jewish Reconstructionist Federation) 101 Greenwood Ave	Jenkintown	PA	19046	**877-226-7573**	215-885-5601	47-20
JRM Industries Inc 1 Mattimore St	Passaic	NJ	07055	**800-533-2697**	973-779-9340	742-5
JS Paluch Company Inc 3708 River Rd Ste 400	Franklin Park	IL	60131	**800-621-5197**	847-678-9300	40
JSA (Junior State of America) 400 S El Camino Real Ste 300	San Mateo	CA	94402	**800-334-5353**	650-347-1600	47-11
JSA (Jewelers Shipping Assn) 125 Carlsbad St	Cranston	RI	02920	**800-688-4572**	401-943-6020	48-21
Jsa Technologies 201 Main St Ste 1320	Fort Worth	TX	76102	**877-572-8324**		396
JSG (Janesville Sand & Gravel Co) 1110 Harding St	Janesville	WI	53547	**800-955-7702**	608-754-7701	502-4
JSJ Corp Dake Div 724 Robbins Rd	Grand Haven	MI	49417	**800-846-3253**	616-842-7110	351
JSM (Jimmy Swaggart Ministries) 8919 World Ministry Blvd PO Box 262550 *Orders	Baton Rouge	LA	70810	**800-288-8350***	225-768-8300	47-20

Company	Address	City	State	Zip	Toll-Free	Phone	Class
JT Mega	4020 Minnetonka Blvd	Minneapolis	MN	55416	**800-923-6342**	952-929-1370	7
JTB (Jordan Tourism Board)	1307 Dolley Madison Blvd Ste 2A	McLean	VA	22101	**877-733-5673**	703-243-7404	773
JTech Communications Inc	6413 Congress Ave Ste 150	Boca Raton	FL	33487	**800-321-6221**		732
JTEKT Corporation	29570 Clemens Rd *Cust Svc	Westlake	OH	44145	**800-263-5163***	440-835-1000	74
Juanita K Hammons Hall for the Performing Arts	901 S National Ave	Springfield	MO	65897	**888-476-7849**	417-836-6776	571
Juanita's Foods Inc	PO Box 847 PO Box 847	Wilmington	CA	90748	**800-303-2965**		297-36
Jubitz Corp	33 NE Middlefield Rd	Portland	OR	97211	**800-523-0600**	503-283-1111	325
Judaica Press Inc	123 Ditmas Ave	Brooklyn	NY	11218	**800-972-6201**	718-972-6200	634-2
Judd Wire Inc	124 Tpke Rd *Cust Svc	Turners Falls	MA	01376	**800-545-5833***	413-863-4357	812
Judge Group Inc	300 Conshohocken State Rd Ste 300	West Conshohocken	PA	19428	**888-228-7162**	610-667-7700	719
Judicate West	1851 E First St Ste 1600	Santa Ana	CA	92705	**800-488-8805**	714-834-1340	40
Judicial Watch Inc	425 Third St SW Ste 800	Washington	DC	20024	**888-593-8442**	202-646-5172	47-7
Judson College	302 Bibb St *Admissions	Marion	AL	36756	**800-447-9472***	334-683-5110	167
Judson Park	23600 Marine View Dr S	Des Moines	WA	98198	**800-401-4113**	206-824-4000	670
Judson University	1151 N State St *Admissions	Elgin	IL	60123	**800-879-5376***	847-628-2500	167
JUF (Jewish United Fund/Jewish Federation of Metropolitan Chicago)	30 S Wells St	Chicago	IL	60606	**855-275-5237**	312-346-6700	47-20
Jugs Sports	11885 SW Herman Rd	Tualatin	OR	97062	**800-547-6843**		708
Juice It Up! Franchise Corp	17915 Sky Pk Cir Ste J	Irvine	CA	92614	**888-705-8423**	949-475-0146	311
Julian Charter School Inc	1704 Cape Horn	Julian	CA	92036	**866-853-0003**	760-765-3847	683
Julian Tours	1721 Crestwood Dr	Alexandria	VA	22302	**800-541-7936**	703-379-2300	758
Julie Inc	3275 Executive Dr	Joliet	IL	60431	**800-892-0123**	815-741-5000	734
Julius Koch USA Inc	387 Church St *Sales	New Bedford	MA	02745	**800-522-3652***	508-995-9565	742-5
July Business Services	215 Mary Ave Ste 302	Waco	TX	76701	**888-333-5859**		40
Jump River Electric Co-op	PO Box 99	Ladysmith	WI	54848	**866-273-5111**	715-532-5524	247
Juneau Chamber of Commerce	9301 Glacier Hwy Ste 110	Juneau	AK	99801	**888-581-2201**	907-463-3488	138
Juneau Convention & Visitors Bureau	101 Egan Dr	Juneau	AK	99801	**888-581-2201**	907-586-1737	208
Juneau International Airport	1873 Shell Simmons Dr Ste 200	Juneau	AK	99801	**800-478-4176**	907-789-7821	27
Juneau Public Libraries	292 Marine Way	Juneau	AK	99801	**800-478-4176**	907-586-5324	434-3
Jungle Adventures	26205 E Colonial Dr	Christmas	FL	32709	**877-424-2867**	407-568-2885	821
Juniata College	1700 Moore St	Huntingdon	PA	16652	**877-586-4282**	814-641-3000	167
Juniata Valley Area Chamber of Commerce	1 W Market St	Lewistown	PA	17044	**866-377-1234**	717-248-6713	138
Junior Achievement of Canada (JACAN)	1 Eva Rd Ste 218	Toronto	ON	M9C4Z5	**800-265-0699**	416-622-4602	47-11
Junior Chamber International (JCI)	15645 Olive Blvd	Chesterfield	MO	63017	**800-905-5499**	636-449-3100	47-7
Junior State of America (JSA)	400 S El Camino Real Ste 300	San Mateo	CA	94402	**800-334-5353**	650-347-1600	47-11
Juniper Networks Inc	1194 N Mathilda Ave *NYSE: JNPR*	Sunnyvale	CA	94089	**888-586-4737**	408-745-2000	178
Juniper Pharmaceuticals Inc	33 Arch St *NASDAQ: CBRX*	Boston	MA	02110	**866-566-5636**	973-994-3999	582
Jupiter Aluminum Corp	4825 Scott St	Schiller Park	IL	60176	**800-392-7265**	847-928-5930	658
Jupiter Beach Resort	5 N A1A	Jupiter	FL	33477	**877-389-0571**	561-746-2511	667
Juran Institute Inc	160 Main St Ste 100	Southington	CT	06489	**800-338-7726**	203-267-3445	112
Jurlique Spa	4925 N Scottsdale Rd	Scottsdale	AZ	85251	**800-528-7867**	480-424-6072	705
Jury Research Institute	2617 Danville Blvd PO Box 100	Alamo	CA	94507	**800-233-5879**	925-932-5663	444
Just Born Inc	1300 Stefko Blvd	Bethlehem	PA	18017	**800-445-5787**	610-867-7568	297-8
Justifacts Credential Verification Inc	5250 Logan Ferry Rd	Murrysville	PA	15668	**800-356-6885**	412-798-4790	706
Justin Boot Co Inc	610 W Daggett St *Cust Svc	Fort Worth	TX	76104	**800-548-1021***	817-332-7797	302
Justin P. Wilson Cumberland Trail State Park	220 Pk Rd	Caryville	TN	38555	**800-342-3145**	423-566-2229	564
Justiss Oil Company Inc	1120 E Oak St	Jena	LA	71342	**800-256-2501**	318-992-4111	539
Justrite Manufacturing Co	2454 E Dempster St Ste 300	Des Plaines	IL	60016	**800-798-9250**	847-298-9250	200
Juvenile Diabetes Research Foundation International (JDRF)	120 Wall St	New York	NY	10005	**800-533-2873**	212-785-9500	47-17
JVC Professional Products Co	1700 Valley Rd	Wayne	NJ	07470	**800-252-5722**	973-317-5000	51
JW Aluminum	435 Old Mt Holly Rd *Sales	Mount Holly	SC	29445	**877-586-5314***		484
JW Jung Seed Co	335 S High St	Randolph	WI	53956	**800-297-3123**		692
JW Marriott Desert Ridge Resort & Spa	5350 E Marriott Dr	Phoenix	AZ	85054	**800-845-5279**	480-293-5000	667
JW Marriott Orlando Grande Lakes Resort	4040 Central Florida Pkwy	Orlando	FL	32837	**800-576-5750**	407-206-2300	667
JW Marriott Resort Las Vegas	221 N Rampart Blvd	Las Vegas	NV	89144	**877-869-8777**	702-869-7777	667
JW Pepper & Son Inc	2480 Industrial Blvd	Paoli	PA	19301	**800-345-6296**	610-648-0500	525
JW Peters Inc	500 W Market St	Burlington	WI	53105	**866-265-7888**	262-806-9009	185
JW Speaker Corp	N 120 W 19434 Freistadt Rd PO Box 1011	Germantown	WI	53022	**800-558-7288**	262-251-6660	438
JW Starr Pass Resort & Spa	3800 W Starr Pass Blvd	Tucson	AZ	85745	**800-845-5279**	520-792-3500	705
JWCI (Providence Health & Services)	2200 Santa Monica Blvd	Santa Monica	CA	90404	**800-262-6259**	310-582-7450	666
JWF Industries	84 Iron St PO Box 1286	Johnstown	PA	15907	**800-225-9359**	814-539-6922	809

K

Company	Address	City	State	Zip	Toll-Free	Phone	Class
K A Hamilton & Assoc	159 Perry Hwy Ste 100	Pittsburgh	PA	15229	**800-746-4726**	412-459-0122	262
K D M Enterprise LLC	820 Commerce Pkwy	Carpentersville	IL	60110	**877-591-9768**	847-783-0333	556
K Line America Inc	8730 Stony Pt Pkwy Ste 400	Richmond	VA	23235	**800-609-3221**	804-560-3600	314
K Rcr Tv News Channel 7 Tv	755 Auditorium Dr	Redding	CA	96001	**800-222-5727**	530-243-7777	739
K12 Inc	2300 Corporate Pk Dr *NYSE: LRN*	Herndon	VA	20171	**866-512-2273**	703-483-7000	683
K2 Industrial Services	5233 Hohman Ave	Hammond	IN	46320	**866-524-6387**	219-933-5300	191-8
K2 Sports	4201 Sixth Ave S	Seattle	WA	98108	**800-426-1617**	206-805-4800	708
KA (Kraus-Anderson Co)	523 S Eigth St	Minneapolis	MN	55404	**888-547-3983**	612-305-2934	187
KA Steel Chemicals Inc	15185 Main St PO Box 729	Lemont	IL	60439	**800-677-8335**	630-257-3900	145
Kaba Ilco Corp	400 Jeffreys Rd	Rocky Mount	NC	27804	**800-334-1381**	252-446-3321	350
KA-BAR Knives Inc	200 Homer St	Olean	NY	14760	**800-282-0130**	716-372-5952	224
KABB-TV Ch 29 (Fox)	4335 NW Loop 410	San Antonio	TX	78229	**888-538-8541**	210-366-1129	738-72
KABC-AM 790 (N/T)	3321 S La Cienega Blvd PO Box 790	Los Angeles	CA	90016	**800-222-5222**	310-840-4900	642-69
KABX-FM 97.5 (Oldies)	1020 W Main St	Merced	CA	95340	**800-350-3777**	209-723-2191	643
KABZ-FM 103.7 (N/T)	2400 Cottondale Ln	Little Rock	AR	72202	**800-477-1037**	501-661-1037	642-68
KACV-FM 90 (Alt)	PO Box 447	Amarillo	TX	79178	**800-766-0176**		642-5
Kadlec Regional Medical Ctr	888 Swift Blvd	Richland	WA	99352	**800-780-6067**	509-946-4611	374-3
Kaepa USA Inc	9050 Autobahn Dr Ste 500	Dallas	TX	75237	**800-880-9200**		302
Kaeser & Blair Inc	4236 Grissom Dr	Batavia	OH	45103	**800-642-0790**		366
KAFL Inc	85 Allen St Ste 300	Rochester	NY	14608	**800-272-6488**	585-271-6400	390
KAFT-TV Ch 13 (PBS)	350 S Donaghey Ave	Conway	AR	72034	**800-662-2386**	501-682-2386	
KAG (Kenan Advantage Group Inc)	4366 Mt Pleasant St NW	North Canton	OH	44720	**800-969-5419**	330-491-0474	778
KAG West	4076 Seaport Blvd	West Sacramento	CA	95691	**800-547-1587**	916-371-8241	778
Kagan	981 Calle Amanecer	San Clemente	CA	92673	**800-933-2667**	949-369-6310	529
Kahala Mandarin Oriental Hotel Hawaii Resort	5000 Kahala Ave	Honolulu	HI	96816	**800-367-2525**	808-739-8888	379
Kahala Travel	3838 Camino Del Rio N Ste 300	San Diego	CA	92108	**800-852-8338**	619-282-8300	770
Kahiki Foods Inc	1100 Morrison Rd	Columbus	OH	43230	**855-524-4540**	614-322-3180	297-36
Kahn Litwin Renza & Company Ltd	951 N Main St	Providence	RI	02904	**888-557-8557**	401-274-2001	2
Kahului Airport	1 Kahului Airport Rd	Kahului	HI	96732	**800-321-3712**	808-872-3830	27
Kahuna Inc	555 Bryant St Ste 322	Palo Alto	CA	94301	**844-465-2486**		387
KAI (Kingsway America Inc)	150 NW Pt Blvd	Elk Grove Village	IL	60007	**800-232-0631**	847-700-9100	360-4
Kai	20 Jay St Ste 530	Brooklyn	NY	11201	**888-832-7832**	718-250-4000	669
Kailua Chamber of Commerce	600 Kailua Rd Ste 107	Kailua	HI	96734	**888-261-7997**	808-261-2727	138
Kaiser Aluminum Corp	27422 Portola Pkwy Ste 200 *Sales	Foothill Ranch	CA	92610	**800-873-2011***	949-614-1740	484
Kaiser Foundation Health Plan Inc	1 Kaiser Plz	Oakland	CA	94612	**800-464-4000**	408-972-3000	391-3

Name	Address	City	State	Zip	Toll-Free	Phone	Class
Kaiser Permanente	3495 Piedmont Rd NE Piedmont Ctr Bldg 9	Atlanta	GA	30305	800-611-1811	404-364-7000	391-3
Kaiser Permanente Foundation Hospital	9400 E Rosecrans Ave	Bellflower	CA	90706	866-279-8954	562-461-3000	374-3
Kaiser Permanente Harbor City Medical Ctr	25825 S Vermont Ave	Harbor City	CA	90710	800-464-4000	310-325-5111	374-3
Kaiser Permanente Hawaii	711 Kapiolani Blvd	Honolulu	HI	96813	800-966-5955	808-432-0000	391-3
Kaiser Permanente Hospital	441 N Lakeview Ave	Anaheim	CA	92807	800-464-4000	714-279-4000	374-3
Kaiser Permanente Medical Center-South Sacramento	6600 Bruceville Rd	Sacramento	CA	95823	800-464-4000	916-688-2000	374-3
Kaiser Permanente Medical Ctr	1200 El Camino Real	South San Francisco	CA	94080	800-464-4000	650-742-2000	374-3
Kaiser Permanente Northwest	500 NE Multnomah St Ste 100	Portland	OR	97232	800-813-2000	503-813-2000	391-3
Kaiser Permanente Parma Medical Ctr	12301 Snow Rd	Cleveland	OH	44130	800-524-7372	216-362-2000	374-3
Kaiser Permanente Riverside Medical Ctr	10800 Magnolia Ave *Cust Svc	Riverside	CA	92505	800-464-4000*	951-353-2000	374-3
Kaiser Permanente Walnut Creek Medical Ctr	1425 S Main St	Walnut Creek	CA	94596	800-464-4000	925-295-4000	374-3
KaiserAir Inc	8735 Earhart Rd PO Box 2626	Oakland	CA	94621	800-538-2625	510-569-9622	13
Kalamazoo College	1200 Academy St *Admissions	Kalamazoo	MI	49006	800-253-3602*	269-337-7166	167
Kalamazoo County Convention & Visitors Bureau	141 E Michigan Ave Ste 100	Kalamazoo	MI	49007	800-888-0509	269-488-9000	208
Kalamazoo Gazette	401 S Burdick St	Kalamazoo	MI	49007	800-466-6397	269-345-3511	531-2
Kalamazoo Psychiatric Hospital	1312 Oakland Dr	Kalamazoo	MI	49008	888-509-7007	269-337-3000	374-5
Kalamazoo Technical Furniture	6450 Vly Industrial Dr	Kalamazoo	MI	49009	800-832-5227		420
Kalani Oceanside Retreat	12-6860 Kapoho Kalapana Rd	Pahoa	HI	96778	800-800-6886	808-965-7828	671
Kaleo Software Inc	2041 Rosecrans Ave Ste 245	El Segundo	CA	90245	888-937-8945		387
Kalibrate Technologies PLC	25B Hanover Rd *Cust Svc	Florham Park	NJ	07932	800-727-6774*	973-549-1850	180-11
Kalido	1 Wall St Ste 3	Burlington	MA	01803	866-466-3849	781-202-3200	180-1
Kalispell Regional Medical Ctr	310 Sunnyview Ln	Kalispell	MT	59901	800-228-1574	406-752-5111	374-3
Kalitta Charters LLC	843 Willow Run Airport	Ypsilanti	MI	48198	800-525-4882	734-544-3400	21
Kalitta Flying Service	818 Willow Run Airport	Ypsilanti	MI	48198	800-521-1590	734-484-0088	12
Kallista Inc	1227 N Eigth St Ste 2 *Cust Svc	Sheboygan	WI	53081	888-452-5547*	920-457-4441	375
Kallman Worldwide Inc	4 N St Ste 800	Waldwick	NJ	07463	877-492-7028	201-251-2600	208
Kalman Floor Company Inc	1202 Bergen Pkwy Ste 110	Evergreen	CO	80439	800-525-7840	303-674-2290	191-2
Kalsec Inc	3713 W Main St	Kalamazoo	MI	49006	800-323-9320	269-349-9711	297-15
Kalwall Corp	1111 Candia Rd PO Box 237	Manchester	NH	03105	800-258-9777	603-627-3861	607
Kam Wah Chung State Heritage Site (KWC)	725 Summer St NE Ste C	Salem	OR	97301	800-551-6949	503-986-0707	564
Kam's	4500 Montrose Blvd	Houston	TX	77006	800-510-3663	713-529-5057	669
Kaman Corp	PO Box 1 *NYSE: KAMN*	Bloomfield	CT	06002	866-450-3663	860-243-7100	187
Kamatics Corp	1330 Blue Hills Ave	Bloomfield	CT	06002	866-540-5760	860-243-9704	619
KaMMCO (Kansas Medical Mutual Insurance Co)	623 SW Tenth Ave Ste 200	Topeka	KS	66612	800-232-2259	785-232-2224	391-5
Kampgrounds of America Inc (KOA)	PO Box 30558	Billings	MT	59114	888-562-0000		120
Kanatek Technologies Inc	535 Legget Dr Ste 400	Kanata	ON	K2K3B8	800-526-2821	613-591-1482	182
Kanawha Hospice Care	1606 Kanawha Blvd W	Charleston	WV	25387	800-560-8523	304-768-8523	371
Kanawha Scales & Systems Inc	Rock Branch Industrial Pk 303 Jacobson Dr	Poca	WV	25159	800-955-8321	304-755-8321	361
Kane County	78 S 100 E	Kanab	UT	84741	800-733-5263	435-644-5033	338
Kane Graphical Corp	2255 W Logan Blvd	Chicago	IL	60647	800-992-2921		344
Kane Manufacturing Corp	515 N Fraley St	Kane	PA	16735	800-952-6399	814-837-6464	236
Kane Reid Securities Group Inc	13024 Ballantyne Corporate Pl Ste 500	Charlotte	NC	28277	877-495-5464		688
Kane Transport Inc	40925 403rd Ave	Sauk Centre	MN	56378	800-892-8557	320-352-2762	766
Kanebridge Corp	153 Bauer Dr	Oakland	NJ	07436	888-222-9221	201-337-2300	350
Kanequip Inc	1451 S Second Ave	Dodge City	KS	67801	800-359-1108	620-225-0016	429
Kanguru Solutions	1360 Main St *Sales	Millis	MA	02054	888-526-4878*	508-376-4245	175-8
Kankakee Community College	100 College Dr	Kankakee	IL	60901	800-526-0844	815-802-8100	161
Kann Manufacturing Corp	PO Box 400	Guttenberg	IA	52052	800-806-5266	563-252-2035	515
Kansas							
Consumer Protection Div	534 S Kansas Ave Ste 1210	Topeka	KS	66603	800-452-6727	785-296-5059	339-17
Healing Arts Board	800 SW Jackson Lower Level Ste A	Topeka	KS	66612	888-886-7205	785-296-7413	339-17
Insurance Dept	420 SW Ninth St	Topeka	KS	66612	800-432-2484	785-296-3071	339-17
Travel & Tourism Development Div	1020 S Kansas Ave Ste 200	Topeka	KS	66612	800-252-6727	785-296-2009	339-17
Treasurer	900 SW Jackson St Ste 201	Topeka	KS	66612	800-432-0386	785-296-3171	339-17
Workers' Compensation Div	401 SW Topeka Blvd Ste 2	Topeka	KS	66603	800-332-0353	785-296-4000	339-17
Kansas Assn of Realtors	3644 SW Burlingame Rd	Topeka	KS	66611	800-366-0069	785-267-3610	654
Kansas Bar Assn	1200 SW Harrison St	Topeka	KS	66612	800-928-3111	785-234-5696	71
Kansas Children's Service League (KCSL)	3545 SW 5th	Topeka	KS	66606	877-530-5275	785-274-3100	47-6
Kansas City Art Institute	4415 Warwick Blvd	Kansas City	MO	64111	800-522-5224	816-474-5224	163
Kansas City Aviation Ctr Inc	15325 S Pflumm Rd	Olathe	KS	66062	800-720-5222	913-782-0530	62
Kansas City Chiefs	Arrowhead Stadium 1 Arrowhead Dr	Kansas City	MO	64129	800-332-6048	816-920-9300	713-3
Kansas City Convention & Entertainment Centers	301 W 13th St	Kansas City	MO	64105	800-767-7700	816-513-5000	207
Kansas City Convention & Visitors Assn	1100 Main St Ste 2200	Kansas City	MO	64105	800-767-7700	816-221-5242	208
Kansas City Kansas Convention & Visitors Bureau Inc	901 N Eigth St PO Box 171517	Kansas City	KS	66117	800-264-1563	913-321-5800	208
Kansas City Life Insurance Co	3520 Broadway *NASDAQ: KCLI*	Kansas City	MO	64111	800-821-6164	816-753-7000	360-4
Kansas City Peterbilt Inc	8915 Woodend Rd	Kansas City	KS	66111	800-489-1122	913-441-2888	61-5
Kansas City Power & Light Co	1200 Main	Kansas City	MO	64141	888-471-5275	816-556-2200	785
Kansas City Royals	Kauffman Stadium 1 Royal Way *Sales	Kansas City	MO	64129	800-676-9257*	816-921-8000	711
Kansas City Southern Railway Co	427 W 12th St	Kansas City	MO	64105	800-468-6527	816-983-1303	646
Kansas City Star	1729 Grand Ave	Kansas City	MO	64108	877-962-7827		531-2
Kansas City Symphony	1703 Wyandotte Ste 200	Kansas City	MO	64108	877-829-5590	816-471-1100	572-3
Kansas Cosmosphere & Space Ctr	1100 N Plum St	Hutchinson	KS	67501	800-397-0330	620-662-2305	520
Kansas Expocentre	1 Expocentre Dr	Topeka	KS	66612	800-745-3000	785-235-1986	207
Kansas Gas Service	7421 W 129th St	Overland Park	KS	66213	888-482-4950		785
Kansas Health Foundation	309 E Douglas	Wichita	KS	67202	800-373-7681	316-262-7676	306
Kansas Living Magazine	2627 KFB Plz	Manhattan	KS	66503	800-406-3053	785-587-6000	456-1
Kansas Lottery	128 N Kansas Ave	Topeka	KS	66603	800-544-9467	785-296-5700	451
Kansas Medical Mutual Insurance Co (KaMMCO)	623 SW Tenth Ave Ste 200	Topeka	KS	66612	800-232-2259	785-232-2224	391-5
Kansas Medical Society	623 SW Tenth Ave	Topeka	KS	66612	800-332-0156	785-235-2383	473
Kansas Museum of History	6425 SW Sixth St	Topeka	KS	66615	800-279-3730	785-272-8681	519
Kansas Pharmacists Assn	1020 SW Fairlawn Rd	Topeka	KS	66604	888-792-6273	785-228-2327	584
Kansas Press Assn Inc	5423 SW Seventh St	Topeka	KS	66606	855-572-1863	785-271-5304	529
Kansas State University	119 Anderson Hall *Admissions	Manhattan	KS	66506	800-432-8270*	785-532-6250	167
Kansas Veterinary Medical Assn	816 SW Tyler St Ste 200	Topeka	KS	66612	888-545-5862	785-233-4141	793
Kansas Wesleyan University	100 E Claflin Ave	Salina	KS	67401	800-874-1154	785-827-5541	167
Kanto Corp	13424 N Woodrush Way	Portland	OR	97203	866-609-5571	503-283-0405	142
Kantola Productions LLC	55 Sunnyside Ave	Mill Valley	CA	94941	800-280-1180	415-381-9363	513
KANU-FM 91.5 (NPR)	1120 W 11th St Kansas Public Radio	Lawrence	KS	66044	888-577-5268	785-864-4530	643
Kanzaki Specialty Papers	1 Monarch Pl Ste 800	Springfield	MA	01144	888-526-9254		553
Kao Specialties Americas LLC	243 Woodbine St PO Box 2316	High Point	NC	27261	800-727-2214	336-884-2214	144
Kapalua Villas, The	2000 Village Rd	Lahaina	HI	96761	800-545-0018	808-665-9170	667
Kaplan & Zubrin Inc	146 Kaighns Ave	Camden	NJ	08103	800-248-1736	856-964-1083	297-19
Kaplan Early Learning Co	1310 Lewisville-Clemmons Rd	Lewisville	NC	27023	800-334-2014	336-766-7374	245
Kaplan Inc	6301 Kaplan University Ave *Cust Svc	Fort Lauderdale	FL	33309	800-258-2432*	954-515-3993	246
Kaplan Telephone Company Inc (KTC)	220 N Cushing Ave	Kaplan	LA	70548	866-643-7171	337-643-7171	733
Kaplan University	6301 Kaplan University Ave	Fort Lauderdale	FL	33309	866-527-5268		798
Kaplan University Lincoln	1821 K St	Lincoln	NE	68508	800-987-7734		798
Kaplan University Omaha	5425 N 103rd St	Omaha	NE	68134	800-987-7734	402-572-8500	798
Kappa Alpha Order	115 Liberty Hall Rd	Lexington	VA	24450	888-922-6335	540-463-1865	47-16

Name / Address	City	State	ZIP	Toll-Free	Phone	Class
Kappa Alpha Theta Fraternity 8740 Founders Rd	Indianapolis	IN	46268	**800-526-1870**	317-876-1870	47-16
Kappa Delta Pi 3707 Woodview Trace	Indianapolis	IN	46268	**800-284-3167**	317-871-4900	47-16
Kappa Delta Sorority 3205 Players Ln	Memphis	TN	38125	**800-536-1897**	901-748-1897	47-16
Kappa Kappa Gamma PO Box 38	Columbus	OH	43216	**866-554-1870**	614-228-6515	47-16
Kappler Inc 115 Grimes Dr PO Box 490	Guntersville	AL	35976	**800-600-4019**	256-505-4005	575
Kar's Nuts 1200 E 14 Mile Rd	Madison Heights	MI	48071	**800-527-6887**	248-588-1903	297-28
Karas & Karas Glass Company Inc 455 Dorchester Ave	Boston	MA	02127	**800-888-1235**	617-268-8800	191-6
Karbone Inc 130 W 42nd St 9th Fl	New York	NY	10036	**800-728-2056**	646-291-2900	194
Kardex Systems Inc 114 Westview Ave	Marietta	OH	45750	**800-639-5805**	740-374-9300	288
Karen Ann Quinlan Hospice 99 Sparta Ave	Newton	NJ	07860	**800-882-1117**	973-383-0115	371
KARE-TV Ch 11 (NBC) 8811 State Hwy 55	Golden Valley	MN	55427	**888-966-4532**	763-546-1111	
Karges Furniture Company Inc 1501 W Maryland St	Evansville	IN	47710	**800-252-7437**	812-425-2291	288
Karl Storz Endoscopy-america Inc 600 Corporate Pt	Culver City	CA	90230	**800-321-1304**	310-338-8100	474
Karl W Richter Inc 350 Middlefield Rd	Toronto	ON	M1S5B1	**877-597-8665**	416-757-8951	351
Karl's Transport Inc PO Box 333	Antigo	WI	54409	**800-922-8707**	715-623-2033	467
Karmanos Cancer Institute Bone Marrow/Stem Cell Transplant Program 4100 John R	Detroit	MI	48201	**800-527-6266**		767
Karnak Corp, The 330 Central Ave	Clark	NJ	07066	**800-526-4236**	732-388-0300	45
Karnes Electric Co-op Inc 1007 N Hwy 123	Karnes City	TX	78118	**888-807-3952**	830-780-3952	247
Karpel Computer Systems Inc 770 Spirit of St	Saint Louis	MO	63005	**888-294-7886**	314-892-6300	179
Karthauser & Sons Inc W 147 N 11100 Fond du Lac Ave	Germantown	WI	53022	**800-338-8620**	262-255-7815	295
Kasa Industrial Controls Inc 418 E Ave B	Salina	KS	67401	**800-755-5272**	785-825-7181	727
Kaseya Corp 400 Totten Pond Rd Ste 200	Waltham	MA	02451	**877-926-0001**		198
Kaslen Textiles 6099 Triangle Dr	Commerce	CA	90040	**800-777-5789**	323-588-7700	743
Kason Industries Inc 57 Amlajack Blvd	Newnan	GA	30265	**800-935-3550**	770-304-3000	350
Katalyst Surgical LLC 754 Goddard Ave	Chesterfield	MO	63005	**888-452-8259**		688
Kate B Reynolds Charitable Trust 128 Reynolda Village	Winston-Salem	NC	27106	**800-485-9080**	336-397-5500	306
Kate Spade 135 5th Ave	New York	NY	10010	**866-999-5283**	212-358-0420	349
Katharine Beecher Candies 1250 Slate Hill Rd	Camp Hill	PA	17011	**800-233-7082**	717-761-5440	297-8
Katharine Ordway Preserve 4245 N Fairfax Dr Ste 100	Arlington	VA	22203	**800-628-6860**	203-226-4991	49-4
Katherine Shaw Bethea Hospital 403 E First St	Dixon	IL	61021	**800-582-9731**	815-288-5531	374-3
Katmai Coastal Bear Tours PO Box 1503	Homer	AK	99603	**800-532-8338**	907-235-8337	758
Katz Group 10104 103rd Ave Ste 1702 Bell Tower	Edmonton	AB	T5J0H8	**866-323-9695**	780-990-0505	239
Katz Law Office Ltd 2408 W Cermak Rd	Chicago	IL	60608	**866-352-3033**	773-847-8982	428
Kauai Community College 3-1901 Kaumualii Hwy	Lihue	HI	96766	**800-776-4816**	808-245-8311	161
Kauffman Stadium 1 Royal Way	Kansas City	MO	64129	**800-676-9257**	512-434-1542	718
Kaufman Company Inc 19 Walkhill Rd	Norwood	MA	02062	**800-338-8023**	781-255-1000	40
Kaufman Mfg Co 547 S 29th St PO Box 1056	Manitowoc	WI	54221	**800-420-6641**	920-684-6641	454
Kaufman Rossin & Co PA 2699 S Bayshore Dr	Miami	FL	33133	**866-357-9634**	305-858-5600	2
Kaw Valley Electric Co-op Inc 1100 SW Auburn Rd	Topeka	KS	66615	**800-794-2011**	785-478-3444	247
Kawada Hotel 200 S Hill St	Los Angeles	CA	90012	**800-752-9232**	213-621-4455	379
Kawasaki Motors Corp USA PO Box 25252	Santa Ana	CA	92799	**866-802-9381**	949-770-0400	708
Kaweah Delta Hospital 400 W Mineral King Ave	Visalia	CA	93291	**800-717-5670**	559-624-2000	374-3
Kay Chemical Co 8300 Capital Dr	Greensboro	NC	27409	**877-315-1115**	336-668-7290	150
Kay Dee Designs Inc 177 Skunk Hill Rd	Hope Valley	RI	02832	**800-537-3433**		743
Kay Dee Feed Company Inc 1919 Grand Ave *Cust Svc	Sioux City	IA	51106	**800-831-4815***	712-277-2011	446
Kay El Bar Guest Ranch PO Box 2480	Wickenburg	AZ	85358	**800-684-7583**	928-684-7593	241
Kay Electric Co-op (KEC) 300 W Doolin Ave	Blackwell	OK	74631	**800-535-1079**	580-363-1260	247
Kay Green Design Inc 859 Outer Rd	Orlando	FL	32814	**800-226-5186**	407-246-7155	393
Kay Jewelers 375 Ghent Rd	Akron	OH	44333	**800-681-8796**	330-668-5000	410
Kay Park Recreation Corp 1301 Pine St *Cust Svc	Janesville	IA	50647	**800-553-2476***		320-4
Kay Toledo Tag Inc PO Box 5038	Toledo	OH	43612	**800-822-8247**	419-729-5479	626
Kayem Foods Inc 75 Arlington St	Chelsea	MA	02150	**800-426-6100**	617-889-1600	297-26
Kaye-Smith 4101 Oakesdale Ave SW	Renton	WA	98057	**800-822-9987**	425-228-8600	109
Kayline Processing Inc 31 Coates St *Sales	Trenton	NJ	08611	**800-367-5546***	609-695-1449	599
Kaylor Dental Laboratory Inc 619 N Florence St	Wichita	KS	67212	**800-657-2549**	316-943-3226	415
Kayne Anderson Capital Advisors LP 1800 Ave of the Stars 3rd Fl	Los Angeles	CA	90067	**800-638-1496**		401
Kaytee Products Inc 521 Clay St	Chilton	WI	53014	**800-669-9580**	920-849-2321	577
KAZ Inc 250 Tpke Rd	Southborough	MA	01772	**800-477-0457**		36
Kazan, McClain, Abrams, Fernandez, Lyons & Farrise PLC Jack London Market 55 Harrison St Ste 400	Oakland	CA	94607	**877-995-6372**		465
KB Electronics Inc 12095 NW 39th St	Coral Springs	FL	33065	**800-221-6570**	954-346-4900	205
KB Home 10990 Wilshire Blvd 7th Fl *NYSE: KBH*	Los Angeles	CA	90024	**800-304-0657**	310-231-4000	651
KBACE Technologies Inc 6 Trafalgar Sq	Nashua	NH	03063	**800-334-4470**	603-821-7000	179
KBAC-FM 98.1 (AAA) 2502 Camino Entrada Ste C	Santa Fe	NM	87507	**888-321-5123**	505-988-5222	642-108
KBAY-FM 94.5 (AC) 190 Pk Ctr Plz Ste 200	San Jose	CA	95113	**800-948-5229**	408-287-5775	642-107
KBBY-FM 95.1 (AC) 1376 Walter St	Ventura	CA	93003	**888-288-9242**	805-642-8595	643
KBFB-FM 97.9 (Urban) 13331 Preston Rd Ste 1180	Dallas	TX	75240	**888-362-8683**	972-331-5400	642-36
KBH Corp, The 395 Anderson Blvd	Clarksdale	MS	38614	**800-843-5241**	662-624-5471	275
KBHC (Kristin Brooks Hope Ctr) 1250 24th St NW	Washington	DC	20037	**800-784-2433**	202-536-3200	47-17
KBHE-FM 89.3 (NPR) 555 N Dakota St PO Box 5000	Vermillion	SD	57069	**800-456-0766**	605-677-5861	643
KBHE-TV Ch 9 (PBS) 555 N Dakota St PO Box 5000	Vermillion	SD	57069	**800-333-0789**		
KBIA-FM 91.3 (NPR) 409 Jesse Hall	Columbia	MO	65211	**800-292-9136**	573-882-3431	643
KBME-TV Ch 3 (PBS) 207 N Fifth St	Fargo	ND	58102	**800-359-6900**	701-241-6900	738-30
KBNP-AM 1410 (N/T) 278 SW Arthur St	Portland	OR	97201	**888-214-9237**	503-223-6769	642-93
KBR Inc 601 Jefferson St	Houston	TX	77002	**888-203-1112**	713-753-2000	263
KBR Rural Public Power District 374 N Pine St PO Box 187	Ainsworth	NE	69210	**800-672-0009**	402-387-1120	247
KBRG-FM 100.3 (Span AC) 750 Battery St Ste 200	San Francisco	CA	94111	**888-808-1003**		643
KBT Inc 3885 W Michigan St	Sidney	OH	45365	**800-860-9455**		683
KBTC-TV Ch 28 (PBS) 2320 S 19th St	Tacoma	WA	98405	**888-596-5282**	253-680-7700	738-75
KBXL-FM 94.1 (Rel) 1440 S Weideman Ave	Boise	ID	83709	**877-207-2276**	208-377-3790	642-17
KBXX-FM 97.9 (Urban) 24 Greenway Plaza Ste 900	Houston	TX	77046	**888-407-4747**	713-623-2108	642-56
KBYU-TV Ch 11 (PBS) 2000 Ironton Blvd Brigham Young University	Provo	UT	84606	**800-298-5298**	801-422-8450	
KBYZ-FM 96.5 (CR) 4303 Memorial Hwy	Mandan	ND	58554	**888-663-9650**	701-663-9600	643
KC Electric Assn 422 Third Ave	Hugo	CO	80821	**800-700-3123**	719-743-2431	247
KCAQ-FM 104.7 (CHR) 2284 S Victoria Ave Ste 2G	Ventura	CA	93003	**877-440-1047**	805-289-1400	643
KCDU-FM 101.7 (AC) 60 Garden Ct Ste 300	Monterey	CA	93940	**800-365-8630**	831-658-5200	642-79
KCFR-FM 90.1 (NPR) 7409 S Alton Ct	Centennial	CO	80112	**800-722-4449**	303-871-9191	643
KCI (Kinetic Concepts Inc) PO Box 659508 *Cust Svc	San Antonio	TX	78265	**800-275-4524***		476
KCI Medical Canada Inc 75 Courtneypark Dr W Unit No 2	Mississauga	ON	L5W0E3	**800-668-5403**	905-565-7187	474
KCI Technologies Inc 936 Ridgebrook Rd	Sparks	MD	21152	**800-572-7496**	410-316-7800	263
KCLR-FM 99.3 (Ctry) 3215 Lemone Industrial Blvd Ste 200	Columbia	MO	65201	**800-455-5257**	573-875-1099	643
KCM Investment Advisors LLC 750 Lindaro St Ste 250	San Rafael	CA	94901	**888-287-5555**	415-461-7788	401
KCMQ-FM 96.7 (CR) 3215 Lemone Industrial Blvd Ste 200	Columbia	MO	65201	**800-455-1967**	573-875-1099	643
KCRG-TV Ch 9 (ABC) 501 Second Ave SE	Cedar Rapids	IA	52401	**800-332-5443**	319-398-8393	738-14
KCRW-FM 89.9 (NPR) 1900 Pico Blvd	Santa Monica	CA	90405	**877-527-9227**	310-450-5183	643
KCSD-FM 90.9 (NPR) 555 N Dakota St PO Box 5000	Vermillion	SD	57069	**800-456-0766**	605-677-5861	643
KCSL (Kansas Children's Service League) 3545 SW 5th	Topeka	KS	66606	**877-530-5275**	785-274-3100	47-6
KCTS-TV Ch 9 (PBS) 401 Mercer St	Seattle	WA	98109	**800-443-9991**	206-728-6463	738-75
KCUR-FM 89.3 (NPR) 4825 Troost Ave Ste 202	Kansas City	MO	64110	**855-778-5437**	816-235-1551	642-62
KCVB (Kingsport Convention & Visitors Bureau) 400 Clinchfield St Ste 100	Kingsport	TN	37660	**800-743-5282**	423-392-8820	208
KCWC-TV Ch 4 (PBS) 2660 Peck Ave	Riverton	WY	82501	**800-495-9788**	307-856-6944	
KDAQ-FM 89.9 (NPR) 1 University Pl PO Box 5250	Shreveport	LA	71115	**800-552-8502**	318-798-0102	642-112
KDC Technologies 27201 Tourney Rd Ste 201	Valencia	CA	91355	**877-532-1112**		198

Company / Address	City	State	ZIP	Toll-Free	Phone	Class
K-Dee Supply Inc 621 E Lake St	Lake Mills	WI	53551	800-268-3681	920-648-8202	777
KDIndustries 1525 E Lake Rd	Erie	PA	16511	800-840-9577	814-453-6761	662
KDLT-TV Ch 46 (NBC) 3600 S Westport Ave	Sioux Falls	SD	57106	800-727-5358	605-361-5555	738-77
KDON-FM 102.5 (CHR) 903 N Main St	Salinas	CA	93906	888-558-5366	831-755-8181	643
KDOT-FM 104.5 (Rock) 2900 Sutro St	Reno	NV	89512	800-227-1885	775-329-9261	642-96
KDR (National Fraternity of Kappa Delta Rho) 331 S Main St	Greensburg	PA	15601	800-536-5371	724-838-7100	47-16
KDSU-FM 91.9 (NPR) 207 Fifth St N	Fargo	ND	58102	800-359-6900	701-241-6900	642-44
KDVR-TV Ch 31 (Fox) 100 E Speer Blvd	Denver	CO	80203	888-397-3742	303-595-3131	738-23
KDWN-AM 720 (N/T) 1455 E Tropicana Ave Ste 800	Las Vegas	NV	89119	888-695-2664	702-730-0300	642-65
Kea Lani Spa at the Fairmont Kea Lani Maui 4100 Wailea Alanui Dr	Maui	HI	96753	800-659-4100	808-875-2229	705
KEA News 401 Capital Ave	Frankfort	KY	40601	800-231-4532	502-875-2889	456-8
Kean University 1000 Morris Ave Kean Hall	Union	NJ	07083	800-882-1037	908-737-7100	167
Keane Care Inc 8383 158th Ave NE Ste 100	Redmond	WA	98052	800-426-2675		180-11
KEAN-FM 105.1 (Ctry) 3911 S First St	Abilene	TX	79605	800-588-5326	325-676-5326	642-1
Kear IT Inc 1510-H Caton Ctr Dr	Baltimore	MD	21227	877-532-7481		393
Kearney Area Chamber of Commerce 1007 Second Ave PO Box 607	Kearney	NE	68848	800-227-8340	308-237-3101	138
Kearny FSB 120 Passaic Ave	Fairfield	NJ	07004	800-273-3406	973-244-4500	69
Keating Technologies Inc 25 Royal Crest Court Ste 120	Markham	ON	L3R9X4	877-532-8464	905-479-0230	462
KEC (Kay Electric Co-op) 300 W Doolin Ave	Blackwell	OK	74631	800-535-1079	580-363-1260	247
KEC (Kiamichi Electric Co-op Inc) 966 SW Hwy 2 PO Box 340	Wilburton	OK	74578	800-888-2731	918-465-2338	247
Keds Corp 1400 Industries Rd	Richmond	IN	47374	800-680-0966		302
KEDT-FM 90.3 (NPR) 4455 S Padre Island Dr Ste 38	Corpus Christi	TX	78411	800-307-5338	361-855-2213	642-35
KEDT-TV Ch 16 (PBS) 4455 S Padre Island Dr Ste 38	Corpus Christi	TX	78411	800-307-5338	361-855-2213	738-20
Keefe Real Estate 1155 E Geneva St	Delavan	WI	53115	800-690-2292	262-728-8757	650
Keeler Motor Car Co 1111 Troy Schenectady Rd	Latham	NY	12110	800-474-4197	518-785-4197	56
Keeley Investment Corp 401 S La Salle St Ste 1201	Chicago	IL	60605	800-533-5344	312-786-5000	171
Keen Technical Solutions LLC 800 Cottageview Dr Ste 1042	Traverse City	MI	49684	888-675-7772		194
Keenan & Assoc 2355 Crenshaw Blvd Ste 200 PO Box 4328	Torrance	CA	90501	800-654-8102	310-212-3344	390
Keene Publishing Corp PO Box 546	Keene	NH	03431	800-765-9994	603-352-1234	634-8
Keene State College 229 Main St	Keene	NH	03435	800-572-1909	603-352-1909	167
Keeney Manufacturing Co 1170 Main St *Cust Svc	Newington	CT	06111	800-243-0526*	860-666-3342	608
Keesler Federal Credit Union PO Box 7001	Biloxi	MS	39534	888-533-7537	228-385-5500	221
KEGA-FM 101.5 (Ctry) 50 West Broadway Ste 200	Salt Lake City	UT	84101	866-551-1015	801-524-2600	642-103
Kegel's Produce Inc 2851 Old Tree Dr	Lancaster	PA	17603	800-535-3435	717-392-6612	298-7
Kehoe Component Sales Inc 34 Foley Dr	Sodus	NY	14551	800-228-7223		248
Keilson-Dayton Co 107 Commerce Pk Dr	Dayton	OH	45404	800-759-3174	937-236-1070	754
Keim T S Inc 1249 N Ninth St PO Box 226	Sabetha	KS	66534	800-255-2450		778
Keiro Services 325 S Boyle Ave	Los Angeles	CA	90033	800-366-2624	323-980-7555	462
Keiser Homes 56 Mechanic Falls Rd Rte 121	Oxford	ME	04270	888-333-1748		105
Keiser University *Fort Lauderdale* 1500 W Commercial Blvd	Fort Lauderdale	FL	33309	800-749-4456	954-776-4456	798
Melbourne 900 S Babcock St	Melbourne	FL	32901	888-534-7379	321-409-4800	798
Sarasota 6151 Lk Osprey Dr	Sarasota	FL	34240	866-534-7372	941-907-3900	798
Keith & Schnars PA 6500 N Andrews Ave	Fort Lauderdale	FL	33309	800-488-1255	954-776-1616	263
Keith Titus Corp PO Box 920	Weedsport	NY	13166	800-233-2126	315-834-6681	778
Keithly-Williams Seeds Inc 420 Palm Ave	Holtville	CA	92250	800-533-3465	760-356-5533	692
Keller Army Community Hospital 900 Washington Rd	West Point	NY	10996	800-552-2907	845-938-7992	331-4
Keller Laboratories Inc 160 Larkin Williams Industrial Ct	Fenton	MO	63026	800-325-3056	636-600-4200	418
Keller Supply Company Inc 3209 17th Ave W	Seattle	WA	98119	800-285-3302	206-285-3300	611
Kellermeyer Co 475 W Woodland Cir	Bowling Green	OH	43402	800-445-7415	419-255-3022	406
Kelley & Ferraro LLP 2200 Key Tower 127 Pub Sq	Cleveland	OH	44114	800-398-1795	216-202-3450	428
Kelley Blue Book Company Inc 195 Technology Dr	Irvine	CA	92623	800-258-3266	949-770-7704	57
Kelley Manufacturing Co 80 Vernon Dr PO Box 1467	Tifton	GA	31793	800-444-5449	229-382-9393	275
Kellogg Co 1 Kellogg Sq PO Box 3599 *NYSE: K* ■ *Cust Svc	Battle Creek	MI	49016	800-962-1413*	269-961-2000	297-4
Kellogg Garden Products 350 W Sepulveda Blvd	Carson	CA	90745	800-232-2322		282
Kellogg Hotel & Conference Ctr 219 S Harrison Rd Michigan State University Campus	East Lansing	MI	48824	800-875-5090	517-432-4000	379
Kellogg Marine Supply Inc 5 Enterprise Dr	Old Lyme	CT	06371	800-243-9303	860-434-6002	768
Kelly Aerospace 1404 E S Blvd	Montgomery	AL	36116	888-461-6077	334-286-8551	249
Kelly Home Care Services Inc 999 W Big Beaver Rd	Troy	MI	48084	800-755-8636	248-362-4444	363
Kelly Mike Law Group LLC 500 Taylor St Ste 400	Columbia	SC	29201	866-692-0123	803-726-0123	428
Kelly Paper Co 288 Brea Canyon Rd	Walnut	CA	91789	800-675-3559		552
Kelly Pipe Company LLC 11680 Bloomfield Ave	Santa Fe Springs	CA	90670	800-305-3559	562-868-0456	594
Kelly Press Inc 1701 Cabin Branch Dr	Cheverly	MD	20785	888-535-5940	301-386-2800	626
Kelly Ryan Equipment Co 900 Kelly Ryan Dr	Blair	NE	68008	800-640-6967	402-426-2151	275
Kelly Systems Inc 422 N Western Ave	Chicago	IL	60612	800-258-8237	312-733-3224	469
Kelly's Janitorial Service Inc 228 Hazel Ave	Trenton	NJ	08638	800-227-0366	609-771-0365	258
Kelly's Pipe & Supply Co Inc 2124 Industrial Rd	Las Vegas	NV	89102	888-382-4957		611
Kelly-Moore Paint Company Inc 987 Commercial St	San Carlos	CA	94070	800-874-4436	650-592-8337	549
KELO-TV Ch 11 (CBS) 501 S Phillips Ave	Sioux Falls	SD	57104	800-888-5356	605-336-1100	738-77
Kelowna General Hospital (KGH) 2268 Pandosy St	Kelowna	BC	V1Y1T2	888-877-4442	250-862-4000	374-2
KELP-AM 1590 (Rel) 6900 Commerce St	El Paso	TX	79915	800-658-6299	915-779-0016	642-39
Kelser Corp 111 Roberts St Ste D	East Hartford	CT	06108	800-647-5316	860-528-9819	227
Kelsey Museum of Archaeology 434 S State St University of Michigan	Ann Arbor	MI	48109	800-562-3559	734-763-3559	519
Kelsey National Corp 3030 S Bundy Dr	Los Angeles	CA	90066	800-366-5656	310-390-1000	390
Keltic Transportation Inc 90 MacNaughton Ave Caledonia Industrial Park	Moncton	NB	E1H3L9	888-854-1233	506-854-1233	315
Kelty 6235 Lookout Rd	Boulder	CO	80301	800-423-2320	800-535-3589	63
Kelyniam Global Inc 97 River Rd	Canton	CT	06019	800-280-8192		252
KEM Electric Co-op Inc 107 S Broadway	Linton	ND	58552	800-472-2673	701-254-4666	247
Kemco Systems Inc 11500 47th St N	Clearwater	FL	33762	800-633-7055	727-573-2323	427
Kemin Industries Inc 2100 Maury St	Des Moines	IA	50317	800-777-8307	515-559-5100	446
Kemper Arena & American Royal Centers 1701 American Royal Ct	Kansas City	MO	64102	800-767-7700	816-221-5242	718
Kemps LLC 1270 Energy Ln	Saint Paul	MN	55108	800-322-9566	651-379-6500	297-27
Kemron Environmental Services Inc 8521 Leesburg Pike Ste 175	Vienna	VA	22182	888-429-3516	703-893-4106	194
Kemtah Group Inc 7601 Jefferson St NE Ste 120	Albuquerque	NM	87109	877-753-6824	505-346-4900	182
Kemwel Inc 39 Commercial St	Portland	ME	04112	800-678-0678	207-842-2285	125
Ken Fowler Motors 1265 Airport Pk Blvd	Ukiah	CA	95482	800-287-0107	707-468-0101	56
Ken Garff Automotive Group 405 S Main St	Salt Lake City	UT	84111	888-630-6838	801-257-3400	56
Ken Garner Manufacturing - Rho Inc 1201 E 28th St # B	Chattanooga	TN	37404	888-454-7207	423-698-6200	263
Ken Jones Tire Inc 73 Chandler St	Worcester	MA	01609	800-225-9513	508-755-5255	753
Ken's Flower Shop 140 W S Boundary St	Perrysburg	OH	43551	800-253-0100	419-874-1333	294
Kenall Mfg 1020 Lakeside Dr	Gurnee	IL	60031	800-453-6255	847-360-8200	439
Kenan Advantage Group Inc (KAG) 4366 Mt Pleasant St NW	North Canton	OH	44720	800-969-5419	330-491-0474	778
Kenan Transport Co 100 Europa Ctr Ste 320	Chapel Hill	NC	27517	866-821-3444	919-967-8221	778
Kenco Group Inc 2001 Riverside Dr	Chattanooga	TN	37406	800-758-3289		448
Kenda USA 7095 Americana Pkwy	Reynoldsburg	OH	43068	866-536-3287	614-866-9803	753
Kendal at Ithaca 2230 N Triphammer Rd	Ithaca	NY	14850	800-253-6325	607-266-5300	670
Kendal at Longwood & Crosslands PO Box 100	Kennett Square	PA	19348	800-216-1920	610-388-1441	670
Kendal at Oberlin 600 Kendal Dr *Mktg	Oberlin	OH	44074	800-548-9469*		670
Kendall & Davis Company Inc 3668 S Geyer Rd Ste 100	St. Louis	MO	63127	866-675-3755		262
Kendall College 900 N North Branch St	Chicago	IL	60622	888-905-3632	312-752-2000	162
Kendall College of Art & Design of Ferris State University 17 Fountain St NW	Grand Rapids	MI	49503	800-676-2787	616-451-2787	167
Kendall Electric Inc 131 Grand Trunk Ave	Battle Creek	MI	49037	800-632-5422	269-963-5585	248
Kendall Packaging Corp 10200 N Port Washington Rd	Mequon	WI	53092	800-237-0951	262-404-1200	599

Alphabetical Section

				Toll-Free	Phone	Class
Kendall/Hunt Publishing Co						
4050 Westmark Dr PO Box 1840	Dubuque	IA	52002	**800-228-0810***	563-589-1000	634-2
*Cust Svc						
Kendall-Jackson Wine Estates Ltd						
425 Aviation Blvd	Santa Rosa	CA	95403	**800-769-3649**	707-544-4000	79-3
Kendle International Inc						
441 Vine St 1200 Carew Twr	Cincinnati	OH	45202	**800-733-1572**	513-381-5550	666
Kendra Scott Design Inc						
1400 S Congress Ave Ste A-170	Austin	TX	78704	**866-677-7023**	512-499-8400	411
Kenergy Corp						
6402 Old Corydon Rd	Henderson	KY	42419	**800-844-4832**	270-826-3991	247
Kenilworth Aquatic Gardens						
1550 Anacostia Ave NE	Washington	DC	20019	**877-642-4743**	202-426-6905	96
Kenlake State Resort Park						
542 Kenlake Rd	Hardin	KY	42048	**800-325-0143**	270-474-2211	564
Kenlee Precision Corp						
1701 Inverness Ave	Baltimore	MD	21230	**800-969-5278**	410-525-3800	620
Ken-Mac Metals Inc						
17901 Englewood Dr	Cleveland	OH	44130	**800-831-9503**	440-234-7500	491
Kenmore Air Harbor Inc						
6321 NE 175th St	Kenmore	WA	98028	**866-435-9524**	425-486-1257	25
Kenmore Camera Inc						
18031 67th Ave NE PO Box 82467	Kenmore	WA	98028	**888-485-7447**	425-485-7447	118
Kenmore-Town of Tonawanda Chamber of Commerce						
3411 Delaware Ave	Kenmore	NY	14217	**888-710-6626**	716-874-1202	138
Kennametal Inc						
2879 Aero Pk Dr	Traverse City	MI	49686	**800-662-2131**	231-946-2100	1
NYSE: KMT						
Kennebec Savings Bank						
150 State St PO Box 50	Augusta	ME	04332	**888-303-7788**	207-622-5801	69
Kennebec Telephone Company Inc						
220 S Main St	Kennebec	SD	57544	**888-868-3390**	605-869-2220	733
Kennebec Valley Community College						
92 Western Ave	Fairfield	ME	04937	**800-528-5882**	207-453-5000	161
Kennedy Anthony M						
US Supreme Ct Bldg						
1 1st St NE	Washington	DC	20543	**800-772-1213**	202-479-3000	341-3
Kennedy Ctr Opera House Orchestra						
John F Kennedy Ctr for the Performing Arts						
2700 F St NW	Washington	DC	20566	**800-444-1324**		572-3
Kennedy Health System-Cherry Hill						
2201 Chapel Ave W	Cherry Hill	NJ	08002	**866-224-0264**	856-488-6500	374-3
Kennedy Krieger Institute						
707 N Broadway	Baltimore	MD	21205	**800-873-3377**	443-923-9200	374-1
Kennedy Manufacturing Co						
1260 Industrial Dr	Van Wert	OH	45891	**800-413-8665**	419-238-2442	487
Kennedy Office Supply						
4211-A Atlantic Ave	Raleigh	NC	27604	**800-733-9401**	919-878-5400	534
Kennedy Valve						
1021 E Water St	Elmira	NY	14902	**800-782-5831**	607-734-2211	787
Kennedy Wholesale Inc						
16014 Adelante St	Irwindale	CA	91706	**877-292-2639**	818-241-9977	298-3
Kennedy-Wilson Inc						
9701 Wilshire Blvd						
Ste 700	Beverly Hills	CA	90212	**800-522-6664**	310-887-6400	50
Kennesaw State University						
1000 Chastain Rd	Kennesaw	GA	30144	**888-875-3697**	770-423-6000	167
Kenneth Cole Productions Inc						
603 W 50th St	New York	NY	10019	**800-536-2653**	212-265-1500	302
NYSE: KCP						
Kenney Mfg Co						
1000 Jefferson Blvd	Warwick	RI	02886	**800-753-6639***	401-739-2200	86
*Cust Svc						
Kennickell Printing Co						
1700 E President St	Savannah	GA	31404	**800-673-6455**		626
Kennicott Bros						
452 N Ashland Ave	Chicago	IL	60622	**866-346-2826**	312-492-8200	295
Kenosha Area Convention & Visitors Bureau						
812 56th St	Kenosha	WI	53140	**800-654-7309**	262-654-7307	208
Kenosha Medical Ctr						
6308 Eigth Ave	Kenosha	WI	53143	**800-994-6610**	262-656-2011	374-3
Kenosha News						
5800 Seventh Ave	Kenosha	WI	53140	**800-292-2700**	262-657-1000	531-2
Kenosha Public Museum						
5500 First Ave	Kenosha	WI	53140	**888-258-9966**	262-653-4140	519
Kensey Nash Corp						
735 Pennsylvania Dr	Exton	PA	19341	**800-322-2885***	484-713-2100	475
NASDAQ: KNSY ■ *General						
Kensington Computer Products Group						
333 Twin Dolphin Dr						
6th Fl	Redwood Shores	CA	94065	**800-535-4242**	650-572-2700	175-2
Kensington Court Ann Arbor						
610 Hilton Blvd	Ann Arbor	MI	48108	**800-344-7829***	734-761-7800	379
*Orders						
Kensington Park Hotel						
450 Post St	San Francisco	CA	94102	**800-553-1900**	415-788-6400	379
Kensington Publishing Corp						
119 W 40th St	New York	NY	10018	**800-221-2647**	212-407-1500	634-2
Kensington Riverside Inn						
1126 Memorial Dr NW	Calgary	AB	T2N3E3	**877-313-3733**	403-228-4442	379
Kent Chamber of Commerce						
524 W Meeker St Ste 1	Kent	WA	98032	**800-321-2808**	253-854-1770	138
Kent County & Greater Dover Delaware Convention & Visitors Bureau						
435 N DuPont Hwy	Dover	DE	19901	**800-233-5368**	302-734-1736	208
Kent District Library						
814 W River Ctr Dr NE	Comstock Park	MI	49321	**877-243-2466**	616-784-2007	434-3
Kent Elastomer Products Inc						
1500 St Claire Ave	Kent	OH	44240	**800-331-4762***	330-673-1011	674
*Cust Svc						
Kent General Hospital						
640 S State St	Dover	DE	19901	**888-761-8300**	302-674-4700	374-3
Kent Hospital						
455 Toll Gate Rd	Warwick	RI	02886	**800-892-9291**	401-737-7000	374-3
Kent Quality Foods Inc						
703 Leonard St NW	Grand Rapids	MI	49504	**800-748-0141**		297-26
Kent School PO Box 2006	Kent	CT	06757	**800-538-5368**	860-927-6111	621
Kent Security Services Inc						
14600 Biscayne Blvd	North Miami Beach	FL	33181	**800-273-5368**	305-919-9400	691
Kent State University						
800 E. Summit St PO Box 5190	Kent	OH	44242	**800-988-5368**	330-672-2121	167
Ashtabula						
3300 Lake Rd W	Ashtabula	OH	44004	**800-988-5368**	440-964-3322	161
Stark						
6000 Frank Ave NW	North Canton	OH	44720	**800-988-5368**	330-499-9600	167
Trumbull Campus						
4314 Mahoning Ave NW	Warren	OH	44483	**800-988-5368**	330-847-0571	167
Tuscarawas						
330 University Dr NE	New Philadelphia	OH	44663	**800-988-5368**	330-339-3391	167
Kent State University Museum						
PO Box 5190	Kent	OH	44242	**800-988-5368**	330-672-3450	519
Kentec Inc						
3250 Centerville Hwy	Snellville	GA	30039	**800-241-0148**	770-985-1907	351
Kentec Medical Inc						
17871 Fitch	Irvine	CA	92614	**800-825-5996**	949-863-0810	474
Ken-Tron Manufacturing Inc						
PO Box 21250	Owensboro	KY	42304	**800-872-9336**	270-684-0431	487
Kentucky						
Arts Council						
500 Mero St						
21st Fl Capital Plaza Tower	Frankfort	KY	40601	**888-833-2787**	502-564-3757	339-18
Child Support Div						
730 Schenkel Ln	Frankfort	KY	40601	**800-248-1163**	502-564-2285	339-18
Consumer Protection Div						
1024 Capital Ctr Dr Ste 200	Frankfort	KY	40601	**888-432-9257**	502-696-5389	339-18
Crime Victims Compensation Board						
130 Brighton Pk Blvd	Frankfort	KY	40601	**800-469-2120**	502-573-2290	339-18
Education Professional Standards Board						
100 Airport Dr 3rd Fl	Frankfort	KY	40601	**888-598-7667**	502-564-4606	339-18
Financial Institutions Dept						
1025 Capital Ctr Dr Ste 200	Frankfort	KY	40601	**800-223-2579**	502-573-3390	339-18
Fish & Wildlife Resources Dept						
1 Game Farm Rd	Frankfort	KY	40601	**800-858-1549**	502-564-3400	339-18
General Assembly						
700 Capitol Ave						
State Capitol Bldg.	Frankfort	KY	40601	**800-372-7181**	502-564-8100	339-18
Historical Society						
100 W Broadway	Frankfort	KY	40601	**877-444-7867**	502-564-1792	339-18
Housing Corp						
1231 Louisville Rd	Frankfort	KY	40601	**800-633-8896**	502-564-7630	339-18
Insurance Dept						
215 W Main St	Frankfort	KY	40602	**800-595-6053**	502-564-3630	339-18
Public Service Commission						
PO Box 615	Frankfort	KY	40602	**800-772-4636**	502-564-3940	339-18
Real Estate Commission (KREC)						
10200 Linn Stn Rd Ste 201	Louisville	KY	40223	**888-373-3300***	502-429-7250	339-18
*General						
State Government Information						
229 W Main St Ste 400	Frankfort	KY	40601	**877-855-3573**	502-875-3733	339-18
Travel and Tourism Dept						
500 Mero St Ste 2200	Frankfort	KY	40601	**800-225-8747**	502-564-4930	339-18
Veterans Affairs Dept (KDVA)						
1111B Louisville Rd	Frankfort	KY	40601	**800-572-6245**	502-564-9203	339-18
Vocational Rehabilitation Dept						
275 E Main St MS 2E-K	Frankfort	KY	40601	**800-372-7172**	502-564-4440	339-18
Workers Claims Dept (DWC)						
657 Chamberlin Ave	Frankfort	KY	40601	**800-554-8601**	502-564-5550	339-18
Kentucky Assn of Realtors						
2801 Palumbo Dr Ste 202	Lexington	KY	40509	**800-264-2185**	859-263-7377	654
Kentucky Bank						
PO Box 157	Paris	KY	40362	**877-322-8228**	859-987-1795	69
Kentucky Bankers Association						
600 W Main St Ste 400	Louisville	KY	40202	**800-392-4045**	502-582-2453	532
Kentucky Chamber of Commerce						
464 Chenault Rd	Frankfort	KY	40601	**800-533-0127**	502-695-4700	139
Kentucky Christian University						
100 Academic Pkwy	Grayson	KY	41143	**800-522-3181***	606-474-3000	167
*Admissions						
Kentucky Correctional Industries						
1041 Leestown Rd	Frankfort	KY	40601	**800-828-9524**	502-573-1040	629
Kentucky Correctional Institution for Women						
3000 Ash Ave	Pewee Valley	KY	40056	**877-687-6818**	502-241-8454	215
Kentucky Dept for Libraries & Archives						
300 Coffee Tree Rd	Frankfort	KY	40602	**800-372-2968**	502-564-8300	434-5
Kentucky Derby Museum						
704 Central Ave	Louisville	KY	40208	**800-273-3729**	502-637-1111	519
Kentucky Educational Television (KET)						
600 Cooper Dr	Lexington	KY	40502	**800-432-0951**	859-258-7000	629
Kentucky Electric Steel LLC						
2704 S Big Run Rd W	Ashland	KY	41102	**800-333-3012**	606-929-1200	721
Kentucky Higher Education Assistance Authority (KHEAA)						
100 Airport Rd	Frankfort	KY	40602	**800-928-8926**		723
Kentucky Horse Park						
4089 Iron Works Pkwy	Lexington	KY	40511	**800-678-8813**	859-233-4303	821
Kentucky Hospital Association						
2501 Nelson Miller Pkwy						
Ste 200	Louisville	KY	40223	**800-945-4542**	502-426-6220	532
Kentucky International Convention Ctr						
221 S Fourth St	Louisville	KY	40202	**800-701-5831**	502-595-4381	207
Kentucky Lottery Corp						
1011 W Main St	Louisville	KY	40202	**800-937-8946**	502-560-1500	451
Kentucky Mountain Bible College						
855 Hwy 541	Jackson	KY	41339	**800-879-5622**	606-693-5000	160
Kentucky Opera Assn						
323 W Broadway Ste 601	Louisville	KY	40202	**800-690-9236**	502-584-4500	572-2
Kentucky Organ Donor Affiliates (KODA)						
10160 Linn Station Rd	Louisville	KY	40223	**800-525-3456**	502-581-9511	544
Kentucky Pharmacists Assn						
1228 US 127 S	Frankfort	KY	40601	**800-922-1557**	502-227-2303	584
Kentucky Post						
1720 Gilbert Ave	Cincinnati	OH	45202	**877-667-4265**	513-721-9900	531-2
Kentucky Press Assn						
101 Consumer Ln	Frankfort	KY	40601	**800-264-5721***	502-223-8821	623
*Cust Svc						
Kentucky Speedway						
1 Speedway Blvd	Sparta	KY	41086	**888-652-7223***	859-567-3400	514
*Resv						

Name / Address	City	State	ZIP	Toll-Free	Phone	Class
Kentucky State University 400 E Main St *Admissions	Frankfort	KY	40601	**800-325-1716***	502-597-6000	167
Kentucky Trailer 7201 Logistics Dr	Louisville	KY	40258	**888-598-7245**	502-637-2551	777
Kentucky Trailer Technologies 1240 N Pontiac Trial	Walled Lake	MI	48390	**866-638-6080**	248-960-9700	777
Kentucky Veterinary Medical Assn 108 Consumer Ln	Frankfort	KY	40601	**800-552-5862**	502-226-5862	793
Kentucky Wesleyan College 3000 Frederica St *Admissions	Owensboro	KY	42301	**800-999-0592***	270-852-3120	167
Kentwood Office Furniture Inc 3063 Breton Rd SE	Grand Rapids	MI	49512	**877-698-6250**	616-957-2320	321
Kenwood USA Corp 2201 E Dominguez St	Long Beach	CA	90810	**800-536-9663**	310-639-9000	645
Kenworth Northwest Inc 20220 International Blvd S	SeaTac	WA	98198	**800-562-0060**	206-433-5911	56
Kenworth of Indianapolis Inc 2929 S Holt Rd	Indianapolis	IN	46241	**800-827-8421**	317-247-8421	56
Kenworth Sales Co 2125 Constitution Blvd *General	West Valley City	UT	84119	**800-222-7831***	801-487-4161	778
Kenya Tourism Board 6033 West Century Blvd Ste 900	Los Angeles	CA	90045	**800-223-6486**	310-649-7718	773
Kenyon College 103 College Dr	Gambier	OH	43022	**800-848-2468**	740-427-5000	167
Kenyon Plastering Inc 4001 W Indian School Rd	Phoenix	AZ	85019	**800-949-4319**	602-233-1191	549
KEO Cutters Inc 25040 Easy St	Warren	MI	48089	**888-390-2050**	586-771-2050	492
Keokuk National Cemetery 1701 J St	Keokuk	IA	52632	**800-273-8255**	309-782-2094	135
Kepco Inc 131-38 Sanford Ave	Flushing	NY	11355	**800-526-2324**	718-461-7000	255
Kepner-Tregoe Inc PO Box 704	Princeton	NJ	08542	**800-537-6378**	609-921-2806	196
Ker & Downey Inc 6703 Hwy Blvd	Katy	TX	77494	**800-423-4236**	281-371-2500	758
KERA-FM 90.1 (NPR) 3000 Harry Hines Blvd	Dallas	TX	75201	**800-456-5372**	214-871-1390	642-36
Kerite Co 49 Day St	Seymour	CT	06483	**800-777-7483**	203-888-2591	811
Kerkau Manufacturing Co 1321 S Valley Ctr Dr	Bay City	MI	48706	**800-248-5060**	989-686-0350	462
Kerley & Sears Inc 4331 Cement Vly Rd	Midlothian	TX	76065	**800-346-4381**	972-775-3902	789
Kern County Board of Trade 2101 Oak St *General	Bakersfield	CA	93301	**800-787-9920***	661-868-5376	138
Kern Health Systems 9700 Stockdale Hwy	Bakersfield	CA	93311	**888-466-2219**	661-664-5000	233
Kern River Gas Transmission Co 2755 E Cottonwood Pkwy Ste 300	Salt Lake City	UT	84121	**800-420-7500**	801-937-6000	326
Kern Schools Federal Credit Union PO Box 9506	Bakersfield	CA	93389	**800-221-3311**	661-833-7900	221
Kerr Lakeside Inc 26841 Tungsten Rd	Euclid	OH	44132	**800-487-5377**	216-261-2100	620
Kerr Pump & Supply 12880 Cloverdale St	Oak Park	MI	48237	**800-482-8259**	248-543-3880	638
Kerrville Bus Co 1 S Main St	Del Rio	TX	78840	**800-474-3352**	830-775-7515	106
Kerrville Convention & Visitors Bureau 2108 Sidney Baker St	Kerrville	TX	78028	**800-221-7958**	830-792-3535	208
Kerrville National Cemetery 3600 Memorial Blvd	Kerrville	TX	78028	**800-273-8255**	210-820-3891	135
Kerrville State Hospital 721 Thompson Dr	Kerrville	TX	78028	**888-963-7111**	830-896-2211	374-5
Kerry's Nursery Inc 21840 SW 258th St	Homestead	FL	33031	**800-331-9127**		369
Kershaw County Chamber of Commerce 607 S Broad St	Camden	SC	29020	**800-968-4037**	803-432-2525	138
Kerusso Activewear Inc 402 Hwy 62 Spur	Berryville	AR	72616	**800-424-0943**	870-423-6242	685
Keryx Biopharmaceuticals Inc 750 Lexington Ave 20th Fl *NASDAQ: KERX*	New York	NY	10022	**800-903-0247**	212-531-5965	582
Kesler-Schaefer Auto Auction Inc 5333 W 46th St PO Box 53203	Indianapolis	IN	46254	**800-959-5722**	317-297-2300	515
KESQ-TV Ch 3 (ABC) 42650 Melanie Pl	Palm Desert	CA	92211	**888-776-8538**	760-318-8528	
Kesselman Jones 3411 Candelaria Rd Ne Ste G	Albuquerque	NM	87107	**866-219-4582**	505-266-3461	197
Kessler International 45 Rockefeller Plz Ste 2000	New York	NY	10111	**800-932-2221**	212-286-9100	400
Kessler Sign Co 5804 Poe Ave	Dayton	OH	45414	**800-686-1870**	937-898-0633	699
Kessler's Inc 1201 Hummel Ave	Lemoyne	PA	17043	**800-382-1328**	717-763-7162	297-26
Kester Inc 800 W Thorndale Ave	Itasca	IL	60143	**800-253-7837**	630-616-4000	144
Keswick Hall 701 Club Dr	Keswick	VA	22947	**888-778-2565**	434-979-3440	379
KET (Kentucky Educational Television) 600 Cooper Dr	Lexington	KY	40502	**800-432-0951**	859-258-7000	629
KETA-TV Ch 13 (PBS) PO Box 14190	Oklahoma City	OK	73113	**800-879-6382**	405-848-8501	738-55
Ketchikan Visitors Bureau 131 Front St	Ketchikan	AK	99901	**800-770-3300**	907-225-6166	208
KETC-TV Ch 9 (PBS) 3655 Olive St	Saint Louis	MO	63108	**855-482-5382**	314-512-9000	738-70
KETG-TV Ch 9 (PBS) 350 S Donaghey Ave	Conway	AR	72034	**800-662-2386**	501-682-2386	
KETS-TV Ch 2 (PBS) 350 S Donaghey Ave	Conway	AR	72034	**800-662-2386**	501-682-2386	

Name / Address	City	State	ZIP	Toll-Free	Phone	Class
Kett Engineering Corp 15500 Erwin St Ste 1029	Van Nuys	CA	91411	**877-372-6799**	818-908-5388	740
Kettering University 1700 University Ave	Flint	MI	48504	**800-955-4464**	810-762-9500	167
KETV-TV Ch 7 (ABC) 2665 Douglas St	Omaha	NE	68131	**800-279-5388**	402-345-7777	738-56
Keuka College 141 Central Ave *Admissions	Keuka Park	NY	14478	**866-632-9992***	315-279-5254	167
Keurig Inc 53 S Ave	Burlington	MA	01867	**866-901-2739**		101
Kewaunee Scientific Corp 2700 W Front St PO Box 1842 *NASDAQ: KEQU*	Statesville	NC	28687	**800-824-6626**	704-873-7202	420
Keweenaw Financial Corp 235 Quincy St	Hancock	MI	49930	**866-482-0404**	906-482-0404	360-2
KEX-AM 1190 (N/T) 13333 SW 68th Parkway Ste 310	Tigard	OR	97223	**888-457-4838**	503-323-6400	642-93
Key Air LLC 3 Juliano Dr Ste 201	Oxford	CT	06478	**888-539-2471**	203-264-0605	13
Key Bank 65 Dutch Hill Rd *Cust Svc	Orangeburg	NY	10962	**800-539-2968***		69
Key Bellevilles Inc 100 Key Ln	Leechburg	PA	15656	**800-245-3600**	724-295-5111	491
Key Club International 3636 Woodview Trace	Indianapolis	IN	46268	**800-549-2647**	317-875-8755	47-15
Key Container Corp 21 Campbell St	Pawtucket	RI	02861	**800-343-8811**	401-723-2000	99
Key Curriculum Press 1150 65th St	Emeryville	CA	94608	**800-338-3987**	510-595-7000	634-2
Key Equipment Finance 1000 S McCaslin Blvd	Superior	CO	80027	**888-301-6238**		218
Key Fire Hose Corp (KFH) PO Box 7107	Dothan	AL	36302	**800-447-5666**	334-671-5532	370
Key Industries Inc 400 Marble Rd	Fort Scott	KS	66701	**800-835-0365**	620-223-2000	154-18
Key Information Systems Inc 30077 Agoura Ct 1st fl	Agoura Hills	CA	91301	**877-442-3249**	818-992-8950	180-11
Key Largo Chamber of Commerce 106000 Overseas Hwy	Key Largo	FL	33037	**800-680-9701**	305-451-1414	138
Key Largo Grande Resort & Beach Club 97000 S Overseas Hwy *Resv	Key Largo	FL	33037	**888-871-3437***	305-852-5553	667
Key Largo Marriott Bay Resort 103800 Overseas Hwy *Resv	Key Largo	FL	33037	**888-731-9056***	305-453-0000	667
Key Lime Inn 725 Truman Ave	Key West	FL	33040	**800-549-4430**	305-294-5229	379
Key Magazine PO Box 111266	Memphis	TN	38111	**866-636-7447**	901-458-3912	456-22
Key Speakers Bureau Inc 3500 E Coast Hwy Ste 6	Corona del Mar	CA	92625	**800-675-1175**	949-675-7856	706
Key Technology Inc 150 Avery St *NASDAQ: KTEC*	Walla Walla	WA	99362	**877-341-5668**	509-529-2161	299
Key West Aloe 13095 N Telecom Pkwy	Tampa	FL	33637	**800-445-2563**		217
Key West Aquarium 1 Whitehead St	Key West	FL	33040	**888-544-5927**	305-296-2051	39
Key West Key 726 Passover Ln	Key West	FL	33040	**800-881-7321**		376
Key West Visitors Ctr 510 Greene St 1st Fl *General	Key West	FL	33040	**800-533-5397***	305-294-2587	208
Key: This Week in Chicago Magazine 222 W Ontario St Ste 420	Chicago	IL	60654	**877-866-0966**	312-943-0838	456-22
Keyano College 8115 Franklin Ave	Fort Mcmurray	AB	T9H2H7	**800-251-1408**	780-791-4800	95
Keyboard Magazine 28 E 28th St 12th Fl *Cust Svc	New York	NY	10016	**800-483-2433***	212-378-0400	456-9
KeyCorp 127 Public Sq *NYSE: KEY*	Cleveland	OH	44114	**800-539-9055**	216-689-8481	360-2
KEYE-TV Ch 42 (CBS) 10700 Metric Blvd	Austin	TX	78758	**800-621-3362**	512-835-0042	738-6
Keynote Systems Inc 777 Mariners Island Blvd *NASDAQ: KEYN*	San Mateo	CA	94404	**888-539-7978**	650-403-2400	180-7
KeyPoint Credit Union 2805 Bowers Ave	Santa Clara	CA	95051	**888-255-3637**	408-731-4100	221
Keyston Bros 2801 Academy Way Ste A	Sacramento	CA	95815	**800-453-1112**	916-927-5851	593
Keystone Aniline Corp 2501 W Fulton St	Chicago	IL	60612	**800-522-4393**	312-666-2015	142
Keystone Automotive Operations Inc 44 Tunkhannock Ave	Exeter	PA	18643	**800-521-9999**	570-655-4514	60
Keystone Aviation Services Inc 288 Christian St	Oxford	CT	06478	**866-436-2177**	203-264-6525	62
Keystone College 1 College Green	La Plume	PA	18440	**800-824-2764**	570-945-5141	167
Keystone Consolidated Industries Inc 7000 SW Adams St *Sales	Peoria	IL	61641	**800-447-6444***		811
Keystone Ctr 2001 Providence Ave	Chester	PA	19013	**800-558-9600**	610-876-9000	724
Keystone Dental Inc 144 Middlesex Tpke	Burlington	MA	01803	**866-902-9272**	781-328-3490	230
Keystone Electronics Corp 31-07 20th Rd	Astoria	NY	11105	**800-221-5510**	718-956-8900	350
Keystone Equities Group, The 1003 B Egypt Rd	Oaks	PA	19456	**800-715-9905**	610-415-6300	196
Keystone Industries 480 S Democrat Rd	Gibbstown	NJ	08027	**800-333-3131**	856-663-4700	474
Keystone Learning Systems LLC 6030 Daybreak Cir Ste A150 116	Clarksville	MD	21029	**800-949-5590**	410-800-4000	512

Name / Address	City	State	Zip	Toll-Free	Phone	Class
Keystone Payroll 355 Colonnade Blvd Ste C	State College	PA	16803	**877-717-2272**	814-234-2272	2
Keystone Pretzels 124 W Airport Rd	Lititz	PA	17543	**888-572-4500**		297-9
Keystone Property Group Inc 1 Presidential Blvd Ste 300	Bala Cynwyd	PA	19004	**866-980-1818**	610-980-7000	650
Keystone Resort 21996 Hwy 6 PO Box 38	Keystone	CO	80435	**877-625-1556**	970-496-2316	667
Keystone Retaining Wall Systems Inc 4444 W 78th St	Minneapolis	MN	55435	**800-642-3887**	952-897-1040	722
Keystone RV Co 2642 Hackberry Dr PO Box 2000	Goshen	IN	46527	**866-425-4369**	574-535-2100	119
Keystone State Park 1926 S Hwy 151	Sand Springs	OK	74063	**800-654-8240**	918-865-4991	564
KEYW Corp 7740 Milestone Pkwy Ste 400	Hanover	MD	21076	**800-340-1001**	443-733-1600	179
KF Industries Inc 1500 SE 89th St	Oklahoma City	OK	73149	**800-398-2493**	405-631-1533	787
KFAN-AM 1130 (Sports) 1600 Utica Ave S Ste 400	Minneapolis	MN	55416	**800-320-5326**	952-417-3000	642-77
KFBB-TV 3200 Old Havre Hwy	Black Eagle	MT	59414	**877-509-9785**	406-453-4377	
KFC Corp 1441 Gardiner Ln	Louisville	KY	40213	**800-225-5532**	920-923-2321	668
KFH (Key Fire Hose Corp) PO Box 7107	Dothan	AL	36302	**800-447-5666**	334-671-5532	370
KFJM-FM 90.7 (AAA) 207 N Fifth St	Fargo	ND	58102	**800-366-6888**	701-241-6900	643
KFMB-AM 760 (N/T) 7677 Engineer Rd	San Diego	CA	92111	**800-760-5362**	858-292-7600	642-105
KFME-TV Ch 13 (PBS) 207 N Fifth St	Fargo	ND	58102	**800-359-6900**	701-241-6900	738-30
KForce Government Soultions 2750 Prosperity Ave Ste 300	Fairfax	VA	22031	**800-200-7465**	703-245-7350	182
Kforce Inc 1001 E Palm Ave *NASDAQ: KFRC*	Tampa	FL	33605	**877-453-6723**	813-552-5000	719
KFRG-FM 95.1 (Ctry) 900 E Washington St Ste 315	Colton	CA	92324	**888-431-3764**	909-825-9525	643
KFRX-FM 106.3 (CHR) 3800 Cornhusker Hwy	Lincoln	NE	68504	**800-523-9101**	402-466-1234	642-67
Kfs Inc 1840 West Airfield Dr	Dallas	TX	75261	**800-364-4115**	817-488-4115	24
KFTV-TV Ch 21 (Uni) 601 W Univision Plaza	Fresno	CA	93650	**866-783-2645**	559-222-2121	738-33
KFXA-TV Ch 28 (Fox) 600 Old Marion Rd NE	Cedar Rapids	IA	52402	**800-222-5426**	800-462-8782	738-14
KGAN-TV Ch 2 (CBS) 600 Old Marion Rd NE	Cedar Rapids	IA	52402	**800-642-6140**	319-395-9060	738-14
KGFE-TV Ch 2 (PBS) 207 N Fifth St	Fargo	ND	58102	**800-359-6900**	701-241-6900	738-30
KGGI-FM 99.1 (CHR) 2030 Iowa Ave Ste A	Riverside	CA	92507	**866-991-5444**	951-684-1991	642-98
KGH (Kelowna General Hospital) 2268 Pandosy St	Kelowna	BC	V1Y1T2	**888-877-4442**	250-862-4000	374-2
KGNU-FM 88.5 (Var) 4700 Walnut St	Boulder	CO	80301	**800-737-3030**	303-449-4885	643
KGNZ-FM 88.1 (Rel) 542 Butternut St	Abilene	TX	79602	**800-588-8801**	325-673-3045	642-1
KGON-FM 92.3 (CR) 0700 SW Bancroft St	Portland	OR	97239	**800-222-9236**	503-223-1441	642-93
KGOU-FM 106.3 (NPR) 860 Van Vleet Oval Rm 300	Norman	OK	73019	**866-533-2470**	405-325-3388	643
KGS Steel Inc 3725 Pine Ln	Bessemer	AL	35022	**800-533-3846**	205-425-0800	491
KGW-TV Ch 8 (NBC) 1501 SW Jefferson St	Portland	OR	97201	**800-669-9777**	503-226-5000	738-63
KHBS-TV Ch 40 (ABC) 2415 N Albert Pike *General	Fort Smith	AR	72904	**855-253-7122***	479-783-4040	738-31
KHEAA (Kentucky Higher Education Assistance Authority) 100 Airport Rd	Frankfort	KY	40602	**800-928-8926**		723
KHIP-FM 104.3 (CR) 60 Garden Ct Ste 300	Monterey	CA	93940	**877-762-5104**	831-658-5200	642-79
Khong Guan Corp 30068 Eigenbrodt Way	Union City	CA	94587	**877-889-8968**	510-487-7800	197
KHON-TV Ch 2 (Fox) 88 Piikoi St	Honolulu	HI	96814	**877-926-8300**	808-591-4278	738-36
Khoury Inc 1129 Webster Ave PO Box 1746	Waco	TX	76703	**800-725-6765**	254-754-5481	320-1
KHS & S Contractors Inc 5422 Bay Ctr Dr Ste 200	Tampa	FL	33609	**866-991-7277**	813-628-9330	191-9
KHTK-AM 1140 (Sports) 5244 Madison Ave	Sacramento	CA	95841	**800-920-1140**	916-338-9200	642-101
KHTO-FM 96.7 125 Corporate Terr	Hot Springs	AR	71913	**888-507-9538**	501-525-9700	642-55
KHVH-AM 830 (N/T) 650 Iwilei Rd Ste 400	Honolulu	HI	96817	**888-565-8383**	808-550-9200	642-54
KI 1330 Bellevue St	Green Bay	WI	54302	**800-424-2432**	920-468-8100	320-1
Kiamichi Electric Co-op Inc (KEC) 966 SW Hwy 2 PO Box 340	Wilburton	OK	74578	**800-888-2731**	918-465-2338	247
Kiawah Island Golf Resort 1 Sancturay Beach Dr *Resv	Kiawah Island	SC	29455	**800-654-2924***	843-768-2121	667
Kibble Equipment 1150 S Victory Dr	Mankato	MN	56001	**800-624-8983**	507-387-8201	358
Kibow Biotech Inc 4781 W Chester Pike Newtown Business Ctr	Newtown Square	PA	19073	**888-271-2560**	610-353-5130	233
Kice Industries Inc 5500 N Mill Heights Dr	Wichita	KS	67219	**877-289-5423**	316-744-7151	209
Kichler Lighting 7711 E Pleasant Vly Rd PO Box 318010	Cleveland	OH	44131	**866-558-5706**		439
Kickhaefer Mfg Co (KMC) 1221 S Pk St PO Box 348	Port Washington	WI	53074	**800-822-6080**	262-377-5030	487
Kicking Horse Energy Inc 1520-700 6 Ave SW	Calgary	AB	T2P0T8	**877-672-2121**	403-234-8663	539
Kidango Inc 44000 Old Warm Springs Blvd	Fremont	CA	94538	**800-262-4252**	408-258-3710	306
KidCo Inc 1013 Technology Way	Libertyville	IL	60048	**800-553-5529**	847-549-8600	63
Kidde-Fenwal Inc 400 Main St *Hum Res	Ashland	MA	01721	**800-872-6527***	508-881-2000	204
Kidron Inc 13442 Emerson Rd	Kidron	OH	44636	**800-321-5421**	330-857-3011	515
Kids Help Phone 300-439 University Ave	Toronto	ON	M5G1Y8	**800-268-3062**	416-586-5437	136
Kids II 555 N Pt Ctr E Ste 600	Alpharetta	GA	30022	**800-230-8190**	770-751-0442	63
KidsPeace Orchard Hills Campus 5300 Kids Peace Dr	Orefield	PA	18069	**800-257-3223**		374-1
Kiefer Specialty Flooring Inc 2910 Falling Waters Blvd	Lindenhurst	IL	60046	**800-322-5448**	847-245-8450	361
Kieffer & Company Inc 3322 Washington Ave	Sheboygan	WI	53081	**800-458-4394**		699
KIII-TV Ch 3 (ABC) 5002 S Padre Island Dr	Corpus Christi	TX	78411	**800-882-9539**	361-986-8300	738-20
KIK Custom Products 2730 Middlebury St	Elkhart	IN	46516	**800-479-6603**	574-295-0000	144
KIK Pool Additives Inc 5160 E Airport Dr	Ontario	CA	91761	**800-745-4536**	909-390-9912	144
Kikusui America Inc 1633 Bayshore Hwy Ste 331	Burlingame	CA	94010	**877-876-2807**	650-259-5900	248
Kilian Community College 300 E Sixth St	Sioux Falls	SD	57103	**800-888-1147**	605-221-3100	161
Killen Group Inc 1189 Lancaster Ave	Berwyn	PA	19312	**877-454-5536**	610-296-7222	401
Killington Grand Resort Hotel & Conference Ctr 4763 Killington Rd	Killington	VT	05751	**800-621-6867**	802-422-5001	379
Killington Resort & Pico Mountain 4763 Killington Rd	Killington	VT	05751	**800-621-6867**	802-422-6200	667
Killion Industries Inc 1380 Poinsettia Ave	Vista	CA	92081	**800-421-5352**	760-727-5102	288
KILO-FM 94.3 (Rock) 1805 E Cheyenne Rd *General	Colorado Springs	CO	80905	**800-727-5456***	719-634-4896	642-31
Kilwins Quality Confections Inc (KQC) 1050 Bay View Rd	Petoskey	MI	49770	**888-454-5946**		122
Kim Hotstart Manufacturing Co 5723 E Alki Ave	Spokane	WA	99212	**800-224-5550**	509-536-8660	15
Kimball Electronics 13700 Reptron Blvd	Tampa	FL	33626	**800-903-8328**	813-814-5000	624
Kimball Electronics Group 1038 E 15th St	Jasper	IN	47549	**800-482-1616**	812-634-4200	624
Kimball Genetics Inc 8490 Upland Dr Ste 100	Englewood	CO	80112	**800-444-9111**		415
Kimball Hospitality 1180 E 16th St	Jasper	IN	47549	**800-634-9510**	276-666-8933	320-3
Kimball International Inc 1600 Royal St *NASDAQ: KBAL*	Jasper	IN	47549	**800-482-1616**	812-482-1600	187
Kimball Midwest 4800 Robert Rd	Columbus	OH	43228	**800-233-1294**	614-219-6100	385
Kimball Office Furniture Co 1600 Royal St	Jasper	IN	47549	**800-482-1818**		320-1
Kimball Terrace Inn 10 Huntington Rd	Northeast Harbor	ME	04662	**800-454-6225**	207-276-3383	379
Kimber Manufacturing Inc 555 Taxter Rd Ste 235	Elmsford	NY	10523	**888-243-4522**	406-758-2222	327
Kimberly Hotel 145 E 50th St	New York	NY	10022	**800-683-0400**	212-755-0400	379
Kimberly-Clark Corp 351 Phelps Dr *NYSE: KMB*	Irving	TX	75038	**888-525-8388**	972-281-1200	557
Kimco Realty Corp 3333 New Hyde Pk Rd *NYSE: KIM*	New Hyde Park	NY	11042	**800-645-6292**	516-869-9000	653
Kimco Staffing Services Inc 17872 Cowan Ave	Irvine	CA	92614	**800-649-5627**	949-752-6996	719
Kimoto Tech Inc PO Box 1783	Cedartown	GA	30125	**888-546-6861**	770-748-2643	599
Kimpton Hotel & Restaurant Group 422 SW Broadway	Portland	OR	97205	**800-263-2305**	503-228-1212	379
Kimpton Hotel & Restaurant Group LLC 222 Kearny St Ste 200	San Francisco	CA	94108	**800-546-7866**	415-397-5572	379
Kimpton Hotel & Restaurant Group, LLC 10050 S DeAnza Blvd	Cupertino	CA	95014	**800-499-1408**	415-397-5572	379
KIMT-TV Ch 3 (CBS) 112 N Pennsylvania Ave	Mason City	IA	50401	**800-323-4883**	641-423-2540	
Kimwood Corp 77684 Oregon 99	Cottage Grove	OR	97424	**800-942-4401**	541-942-4401	819
Kin Communications Inc 736 Granville St Ste 100	Vancouver	BC	V6Z1G3	**866-684-6730**	604-684-6730	226
Kinamed Inc 820 Flynn Rd	Camarillo	CA	93012	**800-827-5775**	805-384-2748	475
Kinaxis 700 Silver Seven Rd *General	Ottawa	ON	K2V1C3	**877-546-2947***	613-592-5780	180-10
Kincaid Coach Lines Inc 9207 Woodend Rd	Kansas City	KS	66111	**800-998-1901**	913-441-6200	758
Kincardine Cable TV Ltd 223 Bruce Ave	Kincardine	ON	N2Z2P2	**800-265-3064**	519-396-8880	115
Kinco International 4286 NE 185th Dr *General	Portland	OR	97230	**800-547-8410***		154-7
Kinder Morgan 1001 Louisiana St Ste 1000 *NYSE: KMI*	Houston	TX	77002	**800-247-4122**	713-369-9000	326
Kinder Morgan Bulk Terminals Inc 7116 Hwy 22	Sorrento	LA	70778	**800-232-1627**	225-675-5387	464
Kinder Morgan Energy Partners LP 500 Dallas St Ste 1000 *NYSE: KMI*	Houston	TX	77002	**866-208-3372**	713-369-9000	326
Kinder Morgan Inc KN Energy Retail Div 370 Van Gordon St	Lakewood	CO	80228	**800-232-1627**	303-989-1740	785

Name / Address	City	State	ZIP	Toll-Free	Phone	Class
Kinder Morgan Management LLC 500 Dallas St 1 Allen Ctr Ste 1000 *NYSE: KMI*	Houston	TX	77002	**800-781-4152**	713-369-9000	326
KinderCare Learning Centers Inc 650 NE Holladay St Ste 1400 PO Box 6760	Portland	OR	97232	**800-633-1488**		147
Kinderdance International Inc 5238 Valleypointe Pkwy	Roanoke	VA	24019	**800-554-2334**	321-984-4448	311
Kindred Healthcare Inc 680 S Fourth Ave *NYSE: KND*	Louisville	KY	40202	**800-545-0749**	502-596-7300	353
Kindred Hospital Atlanta 705 Juniper St	Atlanta	GA	30308	**800-255-0135**	404-873-2871	374-7
Kindred Hospital Greensboro 2401 Southside Blvd	Greensboro	NC	27406	**877-836-2671**	336-271-2800	449
Kindred Hospital Kansas City 8701 Troost Ave	Kansas City	MO	64131	**800-545-0749**	816-995-2000	374-7
Kindred Hospital Philadelphia 6129 Palmetto St	Philadelphia	PA	19111	**800-654-5988**	215-722-8555	449
Kindred Hospital Pittsburgh 7777 Steubenville Pk	Oakdale	PA	15071	**800-654-5988**	412-494-5500	449
Kinecta Federal Credit Union 1440 Rosecrans Ave PO Box 10003	Manhattan Beach	CA	90266	**800-854-9846**	310-643-5400	221
Kinesis Corp 22030 20th Ave SE Ste 102	Bothell	WA	98021	**800-454-6374**	425-402-8100	175-2
Kinetic Concepts Inc (KCI) PO Box 659508 *Cust Svc	San Antonio	TX	78265	**800-275-4524***		476
Kinetic Instrument Inc 17 Berkshire Blvd	Bethel	CT	06801	**800-233-2346**	203-743-0080	230
Kinetico Inc 10845 Kinsman Rd	Newbury	OH	44065	**800-944-9283**		804
Kinetics Mechanical Service Inc 6691 Brisa St	Livermore	CA	94550	**866-567-7378**	925-245-6200	609
King & Prince Beach & Golf Resort 201 Arnold Rd	Saint Simons Island	GA	31522	**800-342-0212**	912-638-3631	667
King & Prince Seafood Corp 1 King & Prince Blvd	Brunswick	GA	31520	**800-841-0205**	912-265-5155	297-14
King & Schickli PLLC 247 N Broadway	Lexington	KY	40507	**888-364-5712**	859-252-0889	428
KING 5 Television 333 Dexter Ave N	Seattle	WA	98109	**877-564-2261**	206-448-5555	738-75
King Architectural Metals Inc PO Box 271169	Dallas	TX	75227	**800-542-2379**		490
King Bio Pharmaceuticals Inc 3 Westside Dr	Asheville	NC	28806	**800-543-3245**	828-255-0201	582
King College 1350 King College Rd *Admissions	Bristol	TN	37620	**800-362-0014***	423-652-4861	167
King County 401 5th Ave Ste 800	Seattle	WA	98104	**800-325-6165**	206-296-1586	338
King Electrical Manufacturing Co 9131 Tenth Ave S	Seattle	WA	98108	**800-603-5464**	206-762-0400	36
King Engineering Corp 3201 S State St *Cust Svc	Ann Arbor	MI	48106	**800-242-8871***	734-662-5691	18
King Estate Winery 80854 Territorial Rd	Eugene	OR	97405	**800-884-4441**	541-942-9874	49-6
King Features Syndicate Inc 300 W 57th St 15th Fl	New York	NY	10019	**800-708-7311**	212-969-7550	529
King Industries Inc 1 Science Rd	Norwalk	CT	06852	**800-431-7900**	203-866-5551	144
King Kamehameha's Kona Beach Hotel 75-5660 Palani Rd	Kailua-Kona	HI	96740	**800-367-2111**	808-329-2911	379
King Koil Licensing Company Inc 7501 S Quincy St Ste 130	Willowbrook	IL	60527	**800-525-8331**		470
King Nut Co 31900 Solon Rd	Solon	OH	44139	**800-860-5464**	440-248-8484	297-28
King of Prussia Mall 160 N Gulph Rd	King of Prussia	PA	19406	**877-746-6642**	610-265-5727	459
King Pacific Lodge 255 W First St	North Vancouver	BC	V7M3G8	**855-825-9378**	604-987-5452	379
King Plastic Corp 1100 N Toledo Blade Blvd	North Port	FL	34288	**800-780-5502**	941-493-5502	607
King Precision Glass Inc 177 S Indian Hill Blvd	Claremont	CA	91711	**866-554-2773**	909-626-3526	332
King Relocation Services 13535 Larwin Cir	Santa Fe Springs	CA	90670	**800-854-3679**		518
King's College 133 N River St	Wilkes-Barre	PA	18711	**800-955-5777**	570-208-5858	167
King's College Library 322 Lamar Ave	Charlotte	NC	28204	**800-768-2255**	704-372-0266	167
King's Daughters Medical Ctr 2201 Lexington Ave	Ashland	KY	41101	**888-377-5362**	606-408-4000	374-3
King's Jewelry & Loan 800 S Vermont Ave	Los Angeles	CA	90005	**800-378-1111**	213-383-5555	410
King's Material Inc 650 12th Ave SW	Cedar Rapids	IA	52404	**800-332-5298**	319-363-0233	185
King's University College 9125 50th St	Edmonton	AB	T6B2H3	**800-661-8582**	780-465-3500	783
Kingbridge Centre, The 12750 Jane St	King City	ON	L7B1A3	**800-827-7221**	905-833-3086	377
Kingman Regional Medical Ctr (KRMC) 3269 Stockton Hill Rd	Kingman	AZ	86409	**877-757-2101**	928-757-2101	374-3
Kings Super Markets Inc 700 Lanidex Plaza	Parsippany	NJ	07054	**800-325-4647**		298-8
Kingsboro Psychiatric Ctr 681 Clarkson Ave	Brooklyn	NY	11203	**800-597-8481**		374-5
Kingsbury Inc 10385 Drummond Rd *Sales	Philadelphia	PA	19154	**866-581-5464***	215-824-4000	619
Kingsdown Inc 126 W Holt St *Cust Svc	Mebane	NC	27302	**800-354-5464***	919-563-3531	470
Kingsgate Marriott Conference Ctr at the University of Cincinnati 151 Goodman St	Cincinnati	OH	45219	**800-228-9290**	513-487-3800	377
Kingsley Plantation 11676 Palmetto Ave	Jacksonville	FL	32226	**877-874-2478**	904-251-3537	519
Kingsmill Resort & Spa 1010 Kingsmill Rd	Williamsburg	VA	23185	**800-832-5665**	757-253-1703	667
Kingsport Convention & Visitors Bureau (KCVB) 400 Clinchfield St Ste 100	Kingsport	TN	37660	**800-743-5282**	423-392-8820	208
Kingsport Times-News 701 Lynn Garden Dr	Kingsport	TN	37660	**800-251-0328**	423-246-8121	531-2
Kingston National Bank 2 N Main St PO Box 613	Kingston	OH	45644	**866-642-2191**	740-642-2191	69
Kingston Oil Supply Corp 2926 Rt 32 N	Saugerties	NY	12477	**800-755-6726**	845-247-2200	317
Kingston Technology Co 17600 Newhope St	Fountain Valley	CA	92708	**800-835-6575**	714-435-2600	290
Kingsway America Inc (KAI) 150 NW Pt Blvd	Elk Grove Village	IL	60007	**800-232-0631**	847-700-9100	360-4
Kingsway Charities 1119 Commonwealth Ave	Bristol	VA	24201	**800-321-9234**	276-466-3014	47-20
Kingswood Senior Living Community 10000 Wornall Rd *Sales	Kansas City	MO	64114	**888-942-2715***	816-942-0994	670
Kingwood College 20000 Kingwood Dr	Kingwood	TX	77339	**800-883-7939**	281-312-1600	161
Kinney Brick Co 100 Prosperity Rd PO Box 1804	Albuquerque	NM	87103	**800-464-4605**	505-877-4550	149
Kino International Corp 333 W 39th St Rm 503	New York	NY	10018	**800-562-3330**	212-629-6880	510
Kinray Inc 152-35 Tenth Ave	Whitestone	NY	11357	**800-854-6729**	718-767-1234	240
Kinross Gold Corp 25 York St 17th Fl *NYSE: KGC*	Toronto	ON	M5J2V5	**866-561-3636**	416-365-5123	501
Kinsight LLC 600 University Park Pl Ste 501	Birmingham	AL	35209	**866-871-3334**	205-871-3334	196
Kinsley & Sons Inc 24 S Church St Ste A *General	Union	MO	63084	**800-468-4428***		409
Kintetsu World Express USA Inc 1 Jericho Plz Ste 100	Jericho	NY	11753	**800-275-4045**	516-933-7100	448
KINT-FM 93.9 (Span) 5426 N Mesa St	El Paso	TX	79912	**866-560-5673**	915-581-1126	642-39
Kinyo Company Inc 14235 Lomitas Ave	La Puente	CA	91746	**800-735-4696**	626-333-3711	175-5
Kinzie Hotel 20 W Kinzie St	Chicago	IL	60654	**877-262-5341**	312-395-9000	379
KIOA-FM 93.3 (Oldies) 1416 Locust St	Des Moines	IA	50309	**877-984-8786**	515-280-1350	642-38
Kiolbassa Provision Co 1325 S Brazos St	San Antonio	TX	78207	**800-456-5465**	713-747-7383	297-26
Kiosk Information Systems Inc (KIS) 346 S Arthur Ave *General	Louisville	CO	80027	**800-509-5471***	303-466-5471	613
Kipin Industries Inc 4194 Green Garden Rd	Aliquippa	PA	15001	**800-782-8050**	724-495-6200	191-16
Kiplinger Agriculture Letter 1729 H St NW	Washington	DC	20006	**800-544-0155**	202-887-6400	530-13
Kipp Foundation 135 Main St Ste 1700	San Francisco	CA	94105	**866-345-5477**	415-399-1556	196
Kirby Agri Inc 500 Running Pump Rd PO Box 6277	Lancaster	PA	17607	**800-745-7524**	717-299-2541	282
Kirby Bldg Systems Inc 124 Kirby Dr	Portland	TN	37148	**800-348-7799**	615-325-4165	104
Kirby Co 1920 W 114th St	Cleveland	OH	44102	**800-437-7170**	216-228-2400	786
Kirk Integrated Marketing Services Ltd 11388 No 5 Rd Ste 110	Richmond	BC	V7A4E7	**888-275-5475**	604-279-8484	5
Kirk Rudy Inc 125 Lorraine Pkwy	Woodstock	GA	30188	**800-897-1910**	770-427-4203	546
Kirkegaard & Perry Laboratories Inc 910 Clopper Rd	Gaithersburg	MD	20878	**800-638-3167**	301-948-7755	233
Kirkham's Outdoor Products 3125 S State St	Salt Lake City	UT	84115	**800-453-7756**	801-486-4161	709
Kirkland & Ellis LLP 200 E Randolph Dr	Chicago	IL	60601	**800-647-7600**	312-861-2000	428
Kirkland's Inc 5310 Maryland Way *NASDAQ: KIRK*	Brentwood	TN	37027	**877-541-4855**		362
Kirkpatrick & Lockhart Preston Gates Ellis LLP 210 Sixth Ave	Pittsburgh	PA	15222	**800-452-8260**	412-355-6500	428
Kirkridge Retreat & Study Ctr 2495 Fox Gap Rd	Bangor	PA	18013	**800-231-2222**	610-588-1793	671
Kirkwood Bank & Trust Co 2911 N 14th St	Bismarck	ND	58503	**800-492-4955**	701-258-6550	69
Kirkwood Community College 6301 Kirkwood Blvd SW	Cedar Rapids	IA	52404	**800-332-2055**	319-398-5411	161
Kirkwood Library 6000 Kirkwood Hwy	Wilmington	DE	19808	**888-352-7722**	302-995-7663	434-3
Kirr Marbach & Co Investment Management 621 Washington St	Columbus	IN	47201	**800-808-9444**	812-376-9444	401
Kirtland Air Force Base 2000 Wyoming Blvd SE Ste A-1	Kirtland AFB	NM	87117	**877-246-1453**	505-846-5991	496-1
Kirtland Community College 10775 N St Helen Rd	Roscommon	MI	48653	**866-632-9992**	989-275-5000	161
Kirtley Technology Corp 9s531 Wilmette Ave	Darien	IL	60561	**888-757-0778**	630-512-0213	227
Kirwan Surgical Products Inc 180 Enterprise Dr	Marshfield	MA	02050	**888-547-9267**	781-834-9500	475
KIS (Kiosk Information Systems Inc) 346 S Arthur Ave *General	Louisville	CO	80027	**800-509-5471***	303-466-5471	613
Kish Bancorp Inc 4255 E Main St PO Box 917 *OTC: KISB*	Belleville	PA	17004	**888-554-4748**	717-935-2191	69
Kishwaukee College 21193 Malta Rd	Malta	IL	60150	**888-656-7329**	815-825-2086	161

Name / Address	City	State	Zip	Toll-Free	Phone	Class
Kishwaukee Community Hospital 1 Kish Hospital Dr	DeKalb	IL	60115	**800-397-1521**	815-756-1521	374-3
Kiski School 1888 Brett Ln	Saltsburg	PA	15681	**877-547-5448**	724-639-3586	621
Kiss the Cook Restaurant 72 Church St	Glendale	AZ	85301	**888-658-5477**	802-863-4226	669
KISS-FM 99.5 (Rock) 8122 Datapoint Dr Ste 600	San Antonio	TX	78229	**855-787-2227**	210-615-5400	642-104
Kissimmee Utility Authority Inc (KUA) 1701 W Carroll St	Kissimmee	FL	34741	**877-582-7700**	407-933-7777	785
Kistler-Morse Corp 150 Venture Blvd	Spartanburg	SC	29306	**800-426-9010**	864-574-2763	203
Kistner Concrete Products Inc 8713 Read Rd	East Pembroke	NY	14056	**800-809-2801**	585-762-8216	185
KISU-TV Ch 10 (PBS) 921 S Eighth Ave S-8111	Pocatello	ID	83209	**800-543-6868**	208-282-2857	738-61
KIT HomeBuilders West LLC 1124 Garber St	Caldwell	ID	83605	**800-859-0347**	208-454-5000	105
Kitano New York 66 Pk Ave E 38th St	New York	NY	10016	**800-548-2666**	212-885-7000	379
Kitchen Academy 6370 W Sunset Blvd	Hollywood	CA	90028	**866-548-2223**		162
Kitchen Collection Inc 71 E Water St *General	Chillicothe	OH	45601	**888-548-2651***	740-773-9150	362
Kitchen Tune-Up Inc 813 Cir Dr	Aberdeen	SD	57401	**800-333-6385**	605-225-4049	191-11
KITCO Fiber Optics Inc 5269 Cleveland St	Virginia Beach	VA	23462	**866-643-5220**	757-518-8100	609
Kite Realty Group Trust 30 S Meridian St Ste 1100 *NYSE: KRG*	Indianapolis	IN	46204	**888-577-5600**	317-577-5600	652
Kitsap Regional Library 1301 Sylvan Way	Bremerton	WA	98310	**877-883-9900**	360-405-9100	434-3
Kitsap Sun PO Box 259	Bremerton	WA	98337	**888-377-3711**	360-377-3711	531-2
KITS-FM 105.3 (Alt) 865 Battery St	San Francisco	CA	94111	**800-696-1053**		642-106
Kitt Peak National Observatory 950 N Cherry Ave	Tucson	AZ	85719	**888-809-4012**	520-318-8600	597
Kittery Trading Post 301 US 1	Kittery	ME	03904	**888-587-6246**	603-334-1157	156-2
Kittredge Equipment Co Inc 100 Bowles Rd	Agawam	MA	01001	**800-423-7082**	413-304-4100	301
Kitty Askins Hospice Ctr 107 Handley Pk Ct	Goldsboro	NC	27534	**800-692-4442**	919-735-5887	371
Kivort Steel 380 Hudson River Rd	Waterford	NY	12188	**800-462-2616**	518-590-7233	491
Kiwanis International Foundation 3636 Woodview Trace	Indianapolis	IN	46268	**800-549-2647**	317-875-8755	306
Kiwash Electric Co-op Inc 120 W First St	Cordell	OK	73632	**888-832-3362**	580-832-3361	247
Kiwi Ii Construction Inc 28177 Keller Rd	Murrieta	CA	92563	**877-465-4942**	951-301-8975	188
KIXI-AM 880 (Nost) 3650 131st Ave SE Ste 550	Bellevue	WA	98006	**866-880-5494**	425-562-8964	643
KJAQ-FM 96.5 (Var) 1000 Dexter Ave N Ste 100	Seattle	WA	98109	**866-416-5225**	206-805-1100	642-111
KJLA-TV Ch 57 (Ind) 2323 Corinth Ave	Los Angeles	CA	90064	**800-588-5788**	310-943-5288	738-46
KJR-AM 950 (Sports) 351 Elliott Ave W Ste 300	Seattle	WA	98119	**800-829-0950**	206-494-2000	642-111
KJUD-TV Ch 8 (ABC) 2700 E Tudor Rd	Anchorage	AK	99507	**877-304-1313**	907-561-1313	738-40
KKBQ-FM 92.9 (Ctry) 1990 Post Oak Blvd Ste 2300	Houston	TX	77056	**877-745-6591**	713-963-1200	642-56
KKFI-FM 90.1 (Var) 3901 Main St Ste 203	Kansas City	MO	64111	**888-931-0901**	816-931-3122	642-62
KKPT-FM 94.1 (CR) 2400 Cottondale Ln	Little Rock	AR	72202	**800-844-0094**	501-664-9410	642-68
KL Industries Inc 1790 Sun Dolphin Dr	Muskegon	MI	49444	**800-733-2727**	231-733-2725	708
Klafter's Inc 216 N Beaver St	New Castle	PA	16101	**800-922-1233**		754
Klamath County 305 Main St	Klamath Falls	OR	97601	**800-377-6094**	541-883-5134	338
KLAQ-FM 95.5 (Rock) 4180 N Mesa St	El Paso	TX	79902	**844-305-6210**	915-880-4955	642-39
Klass Ingredients Inc 3885 N Buffalo St	Orchard Park	NY	14127	**800-662-6577**	716-662-6665	345
KLAT-AM 1010 (Span N/T) 5100 SW Fwy	Houston	TX	77056	**800-646-6779**	713-407-1415	642-56
KLA-Tencor Corp 1 Technology Dr *NASDAQ: KLAC*	Milpitas	CA	95035	**800-600-2829**	408-875-3000	250
KLAZ-FM 105.9 (CHR) 208 Buena Vista Rd	Hot Springs	AR	71913	**800-621-3362**	501-525-4600	642-55
KLCA-FM 96.5 (Alt) 961 Matley Ln Ste 120	Reno	NV	89502	**855-354-9111**	775-829-1964	642-96
KLCC-FM 89.7 (NPR) 4000 E 30th Ave	Eugene	OR	97401	**800-922-3682**	541-463-6000	642-41
Kleet Lumber Company Inc 777 Pk Ave	Huntington	NY	11743	**800-696-5533**	631-427-7060	193-3
Klein & Company Corporate Housing Services Inc 914 Washington Ave	Golden	CO	80401	**800-208-9826**	303-796-2100	212
Klein Independent School District 7200 Spring Cypress Rd	Spring	TX	77379	**888-703-0083**	832-249-4000	683
Klein Steel Service 105 Vanguarden Pkwy *Cust Svc	Rochester	NY	14606	**800-477-6789***	585-328-4000	491
Klein Systems Group Ltd 360-4400 Dominion St	Burnaby	BC	V5G4G3	**877-689-7117**	604-689-7117	179
Klein Tools Inc 450 Bond St *Cust Svc	Lincolnshire	IL	60069	**800-553-4676***		756
Kleinschmidt Inc 450 Lake Cook Rd	Deerfield	IL	60015	**800-824-2330**	847-945-1000	38
Klemmer & Associates Leaders 1340 commerce st	Petaluma	CA	94954	**800-577-5447**	707-559-7722	462
KLFC-FM 88.1 (Rel) 205 W Atlantic St	Branson	MO	65616	**877-410-8592**	417-334-5532	642-19
Kline & Company Inc 35 Waterview Blvd Ste 305	Parsippany	NJ	07424	**800-290-5214**	973-435-6262	196
Kline & Specter A Professional Corp 1525 Locust St 19th Fl	Philadelphia	PA	19102	**800-243-1100**	215-772-1000	428
Klingberg Family Centers Inc 370 Linwood St	New Britain	CT	06052	**877-696-6775**	860-224-9113	47-15
Klingelhofer Corp 165 Mill Ln	Mountainside	NJ	07092	**800-879-5546**	908-232-7200	454
Klipsch LLC 137 Hempstead 278	Hope	AR	71801	**888-250-8561**		51
KLJ Computer Solutions Inc 115 Joseph Zatzman Dr	Dartmouth	NS	B3B1N3	**888-455-5669**		181
KLLM Inc 135 Riverview Dr	Richland	MS	39218	**800-925-5556**	800-925-1000	778
KLM Mechanical Service Inc PO Box 35121	Louisville	KY	40232	**866-466-4438**	502-955-2062	191-10
KLN Steel Products Co 2 Winnco Dr	San Antonio	TX	78218	**800-624-9101**	210-227-4747	320-3
KLNV-FM 106.5 (Span) 600 W Broadway Ste 2150	San Diego	CA	92101	**800-879-4278**	619-235-0600	642-105
KLO-AM 1430 (N/T) 257 East 200 South Ste 400	Salt Lake City	UT	84111	**866-627-1430**	801-364-9836	642-103
Klochko Equipment Rental Company Inc 2782 Corbin Ave	Melvindale	MI	48122	**800-783-7368**	313-386-7220	266-3
Kloppenberg & Co 2627 W Oxford Ave	Englewood	CO	80110	**800-346-3246**	303-761-1615	662
KLOS-FM 95.5 (CR) 3321 S La Cienega Blvd	Los Angeles	CA	90016	**800-955-5567**	310-840-4828	642-69
Klosterman Baking Company Inc 4760 Paddock Rd	Cincinnati	OH	45229	**877-301-1004**	513-242-1004	297-1
KLPB-TV Ch 24 (PBS) 7733 Perkins Rd	Baton Rouge	LA	70810	**800-272-8161**	225-767-5660	738-9
KLRN-TV Ch 9 (PBS) 501 Broadway St	San Antonio	TX	78215	**800-627-8193**	210-270-9000	738-72
Kluane National Park & Reserve of Canada PO Box 5495	Haines Junction	YT	Y0B1L0	**877-852-3100**	867-634-7250	562
Kluber Lubrication North America LP 32 Industrial Dr	Londonderry	NH	03053	**800-447-2238**	603-647-4104	540
KLUV-FM 98.7 (Oldies) 4131 N Central Expy Ste 1000	Dallas	TX	75204	**855-987-5588**	214-525-7000	642-36
KM Fabrics Inc 2 Waco St	Greenville	SC	29611	**800-873-7326**	864-295-2550	742-1
K&M Tire Inc 965 Spencerville Rd PO Box 279	Delphos	OH	45833	**877-879-5407**	419-695-1061	752
KMA One 6815 Meadowridge Ct	Alpharetta	GA	30005	**888-500-2536**	770-886-4000	366
K-Mac Enterprises Inc PO Box 6538	Fort Smith	AR	72906	**800-947-9277**	479-646-2053	668
KMAJ-AM 1440 (N/T) 825 S Kansas Ave Ste 100	Topeka	KS	66612	**877-297-1077**	785-272-2122	642-124
KMAJ-FM 107.7 (AC) 825 S Kansas Ave Ste 100	Topeka	KS	66612	**877-297-1077**	785-272-2122	642-124
KMAX-TV Ch 31 (CBS) 2713 Kovr Dr	West Sacramento	CA	95605	**800-374-8813**	916-374-1313	
KMC (Kickhaefer Mfg Co) 1221 S Pk St PO Box 348	Port Washington	WI	53074	**800-822-6080**	262-377-5030	487
KMC Controls Inc 19476 Industrial Dr	New Paris	IN	46553	**877-444-5622**	574-831-5250	204
KMI Diagnostics Inc 8201 Central Ave NE Ste P	Minneapolis	MN	55432	**888-564-3424**	763-231-3313	233
KMIZ-TV Ch 17 (ABC) 501 Business Loop 70 E	Columbia	MO	65201	**800-345-4109**	573-449-0917	
KMJ-AM 580 (N/T) 1071 W Shaw Ave	Fresno	CA	93711	**800-776-5858**	559-490-5800	642-48
KMJ-FM 105.9 1071 W Shaw Ave	Fresno	CA	93711	**800-491-1899**	559-490-5800	642-48
KMLO-FM 100.7 (Ctry) 214 W Pleasant Dr	Pierre	SD	57501	**800-658-5439**	605-224-8686	642-91
KMOS-TV Ch 6 (PBS) University of Central Missouri	Warrensburg	MO	64093	**800-753-3436**		
KMPH-TV Ch 26 (Fox) 5111 E McKinley Ave	Fresno	CA	93727	**800-101-2045**	559-453-8850	738-33
KMS Ventures Inc 1301 W 25th St Ste 300	Austin	TX	78705	**844-282-7433**	512-474-6312	264
Kmtelecom 18 Second Ave NW	Kasson	MN	55944	**888-232-3796**	507-634-2511	115
KMTV Action 3 News 10714 Mockingbird Dr	Omaha	NE	68127	**800-800-6619**	402-592-3333	738-56
KMVQ-FM 99.7 (AC) 865 Battery St	San Francisco	CA	94111	**888-456-9970**		642-106
KMW Ltd PO Box 327	Sterling	KS	67579	**800-445-7388**	620-278-3641	275
KMXB-FM 94.1 (AC) 7255 S Tenaya Way Ste 100	Las Vegas	NV	89113	**866-438-0220**	702-257-9400	642-65
Knaack Manufacturing Co 420 E Terra Cotta Ave	Crystal Lake	IL	60014	**800-456-7865**	815-459-6020	487
Knape & Vogt Manufacturing Co 2700 Oak Industrial Dr NE	Grand Rapids	MI	49505	**800-253-1561**	616-459-3311	350
Knappen Milling Co 110 S Water St	Augusta	MI	49012	**800-562-7736**	269-731-4141	297-23
Knauf Insulation 1 Knauf Dr	Shelbyville	IN	46176	**800-825-4434**	317-398-4434	389
KNAU-FM 88.7 (NPR) PO Box 5764 PO Box 5764	Flagstaff	AZ	86011	**800-523-5628**	928-523-5628	642-45
KNBA-FM 90.3 (NPR) 3600 San Geronimo Dr Ste 480	Anchorage	AK	99508	**888-278-5622**	907-793-3500	642-6
KNDR-FM 104.7 (Rel) 1400 NE Third St	Mandan	ND	58554	**800-767-5095**	701-663-2345	643
Knf Neuberger Inc 2 Black Forest Rd	Trenton	NJ	08691	**800-323-4340**	609-890-8600	420
Knife River Indian Villages National Historic Site 564 County Rd 37 PO Box 9	Stanton	ND	58571	**866-705-5711**	701-745-3300	563

Company	Address	City	State	ZIP	Toll-Free	Phone	Class
Knight Capital Group Inc	545 Washington Blvd	Jersey City	NJ	07310	800-544-7508	201-222-9400	688
NYSE: KCG							
Knight Electronics Inc	10557 Metric Dr	Dallas	TX	75243	800-323-2439	214-340-0265	196
Knight Hawk Coal LLC	500 Cutler-Trico Rd	Percy	IL	62272	855-611-2625	618-426-3662	500
Knight James E & Associates Pc	14825 Saint Marys Ln	Houston	TX	77079	800-772-1213	281-493-5080	731
Knight Publishing Co	600 S Tryon St	Charlotte	NC	28202	800-332-0686	704-358-5000	634-8
Knight Rifles	213 Dennis st Athens	Athens	TN	37303	866-518-4181		286
Knight Transportation Inc	5601 W Buckeye Rd	Phoenix	AZ	85043	800-489-2000	602-269-2000	778
NYSE: KNX							
Knights of Columbus	1 Columbus Plz	New Haven	CT	06510	800-380-9995*	203-752-4000	47-15
*Cust Svc							
Knippelmier Chevrolet Inc	1811 E Hwy 62 E	Blanchard	OK	73010	877-644-7255		56
KNIS-FM 91.3 (Rel)	PO Box 21888	Carson City	NV	89721	800-541-5647	775-883-5647	642-96
Knit Rite Inc	120 Osage Ave	Kansas City	KS	66105	800-821-3094	913-281-4600	475
Knitney Lines Inc	PO Box 350	Scranton	PA	18505	866-564-8639*	570-457-5060	312
*General							
KNME-TV Ch 5 (PBS)	1130 University Blvd NE, University of New Mexico	Albuquerque	NM	87102	800-328-5663	505-277-2121	738-2
KNML-AM 610 (Sports)	500 Fourth St NW 5th Fl	Albuquerque	NM	87102	888-922-0610	505-767-6700	642-4
Knob Hill Inn	960 N Main St PO Box 1327	Ketchum	ID	83340	800-526-8010	208-726-8010	379
Knockout Pest Control Inc	1009 Front St	Uniondale	NY	11553	800-244-7378	516-489-7817	576
Knoebels Amusement Resort	391 Knoebels Blvd	Elysburg	PA	17824	800-487-4386	570-672-2572	32
Knoll Inc	1235 Water St	East Greenville	PA	18041	800-343-5665*	215-679-7991	320-1
NYSE: KNL ■ *Cust Svc							
Knollwood	6200 Oregon Ave NW	Washington	DC	20015	800-541-4255	202-541-0400	670
Knopp Inc	1307 66th St	Emeryville	CA	94608	800-227-1848	510-653-1661	250
Knorr Beeswax Products Inc	14906 Via De La Valle	Del Mar	CA	92014	800-807-2337	760-431-2007	121
Knott's Berry Farm	8039 Beach Blvd	Buena Park	CA	90620	800-742-6427	714-220-5220	32
Knott's Berry Farm Resort	7675 Crescent Ave	Buena Park	CA	90620	866-752-2444	714-995-1111	667
Know Before You Go Reservations	8000 International Dr	Orlando	FL	32819	800-749-1993	407-352-9813	376
KnowEm LLC	58 Phoenix Ave	Morristown	NJ	07960	800-691-5669		5
Knowledge Information Solutions Inc	2877 Guardian Ln Ste 201	Virginia Beach	VA	23452	877-547-7248	757-463-0033	181
Knowledge Works Inc	5750 Old Orchard Rd Ste 250	Skokie	IL	60077	866-825-3400	847-853-6117	465
Knowles - Mcniff	12862 Garden Grove Blvd Ste C	Garden Grove	CA	92843	800-820-5254		179
Knox College	2 E S St	Galesburg	IL	61401	800-678-5669*	309-341-7000	167
*Admissions							
Knox County Convention & Visitors Bureau	107 S Main St	Mount Vernon	OH	43050	800-837-5282	740-392-6102	208
Knox Nursery Inc	940 Avalon Rd	Winter Garden	FL	34787	800-441-5669		369
Knox Services	2250 Fourth Ave	San Diego	CA	92101	800-995-6694	619-233-9700	626
Knoxville Civic Auditorium/Coliseum	500 Howard Baker Jr Ave	Knoxville	TN	37915	877-995-9961	865-215-8900	571
Knoxville News-Sentinel	2332 News Sentinel Dr	Knoxville	TN	37921	800-237-5821	865-521-8181	531-2
Knoxville Tourism & Sports Corp	301 S Gay St	Knoxville	TN	37902	800-727-8045	865-523-7263	208
KNPR-FM 89.5 (NPR)	1289 S Torrey Pines Dr	Las Vegas	NV	89146	888-258-9895	702-258-9895	642-65
KNRK-FM 94.7 (Alt)	0700 SW Bancroft St	Portland	OR	97239	800-777-0947	503-733-5470	642-93
KNWC-AM 96.5 (Rel)	6300 S Tallgrass Ave	Sioux Falls	SD	57108	888-569-5692	605-339-1270	642-113
KNWI-FM 107.1 (Rel)	3737 Woodland Ave Ste 300	West Des Moines	IA	50266	800-701-3123	515-327-1071	643
KNXV-TV Ch 15 (ABC)	515 N 44th St	Phoenix	AZ	85008	800-222-4357	602-273-1500	738-59
KO Prime	90 Tremont St	Boston	MA	02108	866-906-9090	617-772-0202	669
KOA (Kampgrounds of America Inc)	PO Box 30558	Billings	MT	59114	888-562-0000		120
KOAT-TV Ch 7 (ABC)	3801 Carlisle Blvd NE	Albuquerque	NM	87107	877-871-0165	505-884-7777	738-2
Kobelco Stewart Bolling Inc (KSBI)	1600 Terex Rd	Hudson	OH	44236	800-464-0064	330-655-3111	386
Koberg Beach State Recreation Site	725 Summer St NE Ste C	Salem	OR	97301	800-551-6949	503-986-0707	564
Kobussen Buses Ltd	W914 County Rd CE	Kaukauna	WI	54130	800-447-0116	920-766-0606	108
Koch Filter Corp	625 W Hill St	Louisville	KY	40208	800-757-5624	502-634-4796	18
Koch Foods Inc	1300 Higgins Rd Ste 100	Park Ridge	IL	60068	800-837-2778	847-384-5940	618
Koch Membrane Systems Inc	850 Main St	Wilmington	MA	01887	888-677-5624	978-694-7000	386
Koch Mineral Services LLC	4111 E 37th St N	Wichita	KS	67220	800-750-5834	316-828-5500	171
Koch Specialty Plant Services	12221 E Sam Houston Pkwy N	Houston	TX	77044	800-765-9177	713-427-7700	538
KODA (Kentucky Organ Donor Affiliates)	10160 Linn Station Rd	Louisville	KY	40223	800-525-3456	502-581-9511	544
Kodiak Port & Harbor	403 Marine Way	Kodiak	AK	99615	800-563-4254	907-486-8080	617
KODS-FM 103.7 (Oldies)	961 Matley Ln Ste 120	Reno	NV	89502	855-354-9111	775-829-1964	642-96
Koehler-Bright Star Inc	380 Stewart Rd	Hanover Township	PA	18706	800-788-1696*	570-825-1900	439
*Cust Svc							
Koeze Co	PO Box 9470	Grand Rapids	MI	49509	800-555-9688		297-8
Koger/Air Corp	PO Box 2098	Martinsville	VA	24113	800-368-2096	276-638-8821	150
Kohl & Frisch Ltd	7622 Keele St	Concord	ON	L4K2R5	800-265-2520		233
Kohl's Corp	N 56 W 17000 Ridgewood Dr	Menomonee Falls	WI	53051	855-564-5705	262-703-7000	231
NYSE: KSS							
Kohl's House at Children's Memorial Hospital	225 E Chicago Ave	Chicago	IL	60611	800-543-7362	312-227-4000	372
Kohler Canada Company Hytec Plumbing Products Div	4150 Spallumcheen Dr	Armstrong	BC	V0E1B6	800-871-8311	250-546-3067	609
Kohler Co Inc	444 Highland Dr	Kohler	WI	53044	800-456-4537	920-457-4441	187
Kohler Engines	444 Highland Dr	Kohler	WI	53044	800-544-2444	920-457-4441	264
Kohler Plumbing North America	444 Highland Dr	Kohler	WI	53044	800-456-4537	920-457-4441	608
Kohler Waters Spa	444 Highlands Dr	Kohler	WI	53044	866-928-3777	920-457-7777	705
Kohltech International Ltd	583 MacElmon Rd	Debert	NS	B0M1G0	800-565-4396	902-662-3100	750
KOI Warehouse Inc	2701 Spring Grove Ave	Cincinnati	OH	45225	800-354-0408	513-357-2400	53
Koike Aronson Inc	635 W Main St PO Box 307	Arcade	NY	14009	800-252-5232	585-492-2400	454
Kois Bros Equipment Company Inc	5200 Colorado Blvd	Commerce	CO	80022	800-672-6010	303-298-7370	386
Kokomo Opalescent Glass Co	1310 S Market St	Kokomo	IN	46902	877-475-6329	765-457-8136	330
Kokomo Tribune (KT)	300 N Union St PO Box 9014	Kokomo	IN	46901	800-382-0696	765-459-3121	531-2
Kokosing Construction Company Inc	17531 Waterford Rd PO Box 226	Fredericktown	OH	43019	800-800-6315	740-694-6315	190-4
Kokusai Semiconductor Equipment Corp	2460 N First St Ste 290	San Jose	CA	95131	800-800-5321	408-456-2750	693
Kolcraft Enterprises Inc	10832 NC Hwy 211 E	Aberdeen	NC	28315	800-453-7673*	910-944-9345	470
*Cust Svc							
Kolene Corp	12890 Westwood Ave	Detroit	MI	48223	800-521-4182	313-273-9220	144
Kolkhorst Petroleum Co	1685 E Washington	Navasota	TX	77868	800-548-6671	936-825-6868	317
KOLL-FM 105.5	3071 Continental Dr	West Palm Beach	FL	33407	888-415-1055	561-616-6600	642-129
Kollmorgen Corp Electro-Optical Div	50 Prince St	NorthHampton	MA	01060	877-282-1168	413-586-2330	543
Kollsman Inc	220 Daniel Webster Hwy	Merrimack	NH	03054	800-772-9603	603-889-2500	528
KOLN-TV Ch 10 (CBS)	840 N 40th	Lincoln	NE	68503	800-475-1011	402-467-4321	738-43
Kolosso Toyota	3000 W Wisconsin Ave	Appleton	WI	54914	877-756-2297	920-738-3666	56
Kolpak	2915 Tennessee Ave N	Parsons	TN	38363	800-826-7036	731-847-5328	662
Kolpin Powersports	9955 59th Ave N	Plymouth	MN	55442	877-956-5746	920-928-3118	708
Komet Of America Inc	2050 Mitchell Blvd	Schaumburg	IL	60193	800-865-6638	847-923-8400	620
Komline-Sanderson Engineering Corp	12 Holland Ave	Peapack	NJ	07977	800-225-5457	908-234-1000	386
KOMU-TV Ch 8 (NBC)	5550 Hwy 63 S	Columbia	MO	65201	800-286-3932	573-884-6397	
Kona Grill Inc	7150 E Camelback Rd Ste 220	Scottsdale	AZ	85251	866-328-5662	480-922-8100	668
NASDAQ: KONA							
Kona International Airport	73-200 Kupipi St	Kailua-Kona	HI	96740	800-321-3712	808-327-9520	27
Kona Kai Resort	1551 Shelter Island Dr	San Diego	CA	92106	800-566-2524	619-221-8000	379
Konami Gaming Inc	585 Trade Ctr Dr	Las Vegas	NV	89119	866-544-7568	702-616-1400	323
Konecranes America	7300 Chippewa Blvd	Houston	TX	77086	800-231-0241	281-445-2225	469
Koneta Inc	1400 Lunar Dr	Wapakoneta	OH	45895	800-331-0775	419-739-4200	674
Konop Cos	1725 Industrial Dr	Green Bay	WI	54302	800-770-0477	920-468-8517	297-34
Konsyl Pharmaceuticals Inc	8050 Industrial Pk Rd	Easton	MD	21601	800-356-6795	410-822-5192	582
Kontiki Beach Resort	2290 N Fulton Beach Rd	Rockport	TX	78382	800-388-0649	361-729-2318	378
Kontron Mobile Computing Inc	7631 Anagram Dr	Eden Prairie	MN	55344	888-343-5396	952-974-7000	175-1
KOOL-FM 94.5 (Oldies)	840 N Central Ave	Phoenix	AZ	85004	800-222-4357	602-260-9494	642-90
Koons Ford of Annapolis Inc	2540 Riva Rd	Annapolis	MD	21401	888-313-5524	410-224-2100	56
Koontz-Wagner Electric Company Inc	3801 Voorde Dr	South Bend	IN	46628	800-345-2051	574-232-2051	191-4
Kootenai Electric Co-op Inc	2451 W Dakota Ave	Hayden	ID	83835	800-240-0459	208-765-1200	247
Kop-Coat Inc	436 Seventh Ave, 1850 Koppers Bldg	Pittsburgh	PA	15219	800-221-4466	412-227-2426	549

Name / Address	City	State	Zip	Toll-Free	Phone	Class
Kopf Builders Inc 420 Avon Belden Rd	Avon Lake	OH	44012	**888-933-5673**	440-933-6908	189
KOPN-FM 89.5 (Var) 915 E Broadway	Columbia	MO	65201	**800-895-5676**	573-874-1139	643
Koppers Inc 436 Seventh Ave *NYSE: KOP*	Pittsburgh	PA	15219	**800-385-4406**	412-227-2001	816
KOR Water Inc 95 Enterprise Ste 310	Aliso Viejo	CA	92656	**877-708-7567**	714-708-7567	123
Koral Industries Inc 1504 S Kaufman St	Ennis	TX	75119	**800-627-2441**	972-875-6555	375
Korber Hats Inc 394 Kilburn St *Cust Svc	Fall River	MA	02724	**800-428-9911***	508-672-7033	154-8
Korea National Tourism Organization 2 Executive Dr Ste 750	Fort Lee	NJ	07024	**800-868-7567**	201-585-0909	773
Korea Republic of *Consulate General* 2033 Sixth Ave Ste 1125	Seattle	WA	98121	**800-375-5283**	206-441-1011	259
Korean Air 6101 W Imperial Hwy	Los Angeles	CA	90045	**800-438-5000**	310-417-5200	25
Korean Air Skypass 1813 Wilshire Blvd Ste 300	Los Angeles	CA	90057	**800-438-5000**	213-484-1900	26
Kor-it Inc 1964 Auburn Blvd	Sacramento	CA	95815	**888-727-4560**		192
Korn/Ferry International 1900 Ave of the Stars Ste 2600 *NYSE: KFY*	Los Angeles	CA	90067	**877-345-3610**	310-552-1834	268
Korney Board Aids Sporting 312 Harrison Ave	Roxton	TX	75477	**800-842-7772**	903-346-3269	709
Kornylak Corp 400 Heaton St	Hamilton	OH	45011	**800-837-5676**	513-863-1277	469
Kosciusko County Convention & Visitors Bureau (KOSCVB) 111 Capital Dr	Warsaw	IN	46582	**800-800-6090**	574-269-6090	208
KOSCVB (Kosciusko County Convention & Visitors Bureau) 111 Capital Dr	Warsaw	IN	46582	**800-800-6090**	574-269-6090	208
Koshin America Corp 1218 Remington Rd	Schaumburg	IL	60173	**800-634-4092**	847-310-0740	638
Koss Corp 4129 N Port Washington Ave *NASDAQ: KOSS*	Milwaukee	WI	53212	**800-872-5677**	414-964-5000	51
Koss Industrial Inc 1943 Commercial Way	Green Bay	WI	54311	**800-844-6261**	920-469-5300	297
KOTA-TV Ch 3 (ABC) 518 St Joseph St	Rapid City	SD	57701	**866-558-4554**	605-342-2000	738-65
Kotter International 5 Bennett St	Cambridge	MA	02138	**855-400-4712**	617-600-6787	462
KOTV-TV Ch 6 (CBS) PO Box 6	Tulsa	OK	74101	**888-434-8248**	918-732-6000	738-91
Kovack Securities Inc 6451 N Federal Hwy # 1201 Ste 1201	Fort Lauderdale	FL	33308	**800-711-4078**	954-782-4771	688
Kovasys Inc 500 Pl d'Armes Ste 1800	Montreal	QC	H2X2T7	**888-568-2747**		262
Koza Inc 2910 S Main St	Pearland	TX	77581	**800-594-5555**	281-485-1462	626
KOZK-TV Ch 21 (PBS) 901 S National Ave	Springfield	MO	65897	**866-684-5695**	417-836-3500	738-81
KPBS-FM 89.5 (NPR) San Diego State University 5200 Campanile Dr	San Diego	CA	92182	**888-399-5727**	619-265-6438	642-105
KPBS-TV Ch 15 (PBS) 5200 Campanile Dr	San Diego	CA	92182	**888-399-5727**	619-594-1515	738-73
KPDQ-FM 93.9 (Rel) 6400 SE Lake Rd Ste 350	Portland	OR	97222	**800-845-2162**	503-786-0600	642-93
KPDX-TV Ch 49 (MNT) 14975 NW Greenbrier Pkwy	Beaverton	OR	97006	**866-906-1249**	503-906-1249	
KPLO-FM 94.5 (Ctry) 214 W Pleasant Dr *General	Pierre	SD	57501	**800-658-5439***	605-224-8686	642-91
KPLO-TV Ch 6 (CBS) 501 S Phillips Ave	Sioux Falls	SD	57104	**800-888-5356**	605-336-1100	
KPLU-FM 88.5 (NPR) 12180 Pk Ave S	Tacoma	WA	98447	**800-677-5758**	253-535-7758	643
KPLZ-FM 101.5 (AC) 140 Fourth Ave N Ste 340	Seattle	WA	98109	**888-821-1015**	206-404-4000	642-111
KPRF-FM 98.7 (CHR) 6214 W 34th St	Amarillo	TX	79109	**866-930-5225**	806-355-9777	642-5
KPRS-FM 103.3 (Urban) 11131 Colorado Ave	Kansas City	MO	64137	**800-273-8255**	816-763-2040	642-62
KPRX-FM 89.1 (NPR) 3437 W Shaw Ave Ste 101	Fresno	CA	93711	**800-275-0764**	559-275-0764	642-48
KPTS-TV Ch 8 (PBS) 320 W 21 St	Wichita	KS	67203	**800-794-8498**	316-838-3090	738-94
KPTV-TV Ch 12 (Fox) 14975 NW Greenbrier Pkwy	Beaverton	OR	97006	**866-906-1249**	503-906-1249	
KPVU-FM 91.3 (NPR) Prairie View A & M University MS 1415	Prairie View	TX	77446	**877-241-1752**	936-261-3750	643
KPXO-TV Ch 66 (I) 875 Waimanu St Ste 630	Honolulu	HI	96813	**800-987-9936**	808-591-1275	738-36
KQC (Kilwins Quality Confections Inc) 1050 Bay View Rd	Petoskey	MI	49770	**888-454-5946**		122
KQED-FM 88.5 (NPR) 2601 Mariposa St	San Francisco	CA	94110	**800-723-3566**	415-864-2000	642-106
KQED-TV Ch 9 (PBS) 2601 Mariposa St	San Francisco	CA	94110	**866-573-3123**	415-864-2000	738-74
KQV-AM 1410 (N/T) 650 Smithfield St Ste 620 Ctr City Towers	Pittsburgh	PA	15222	**888-272-7229**	412-562-5900	642-92
Kraft Chemical Co 1975 N Hawthorne Ave	Melrose Park	IL	60160	**800-345-5200**	708-345-5200	145
Kraft Fluid Systems Inc 14300 Foltz Pkwy	Strongsville	OH	44149	**800-257-1155**	440-238-5545	638
Kraft Power Corp 199 Wildwood Ave	Woburn	MA	01801	**800-969-6121**	781-938-9100	517
Kraftmaid Cabinetry Inc 15535 S State Ave PO Box 1055	Middlefield	OH	44062	**888-562-7744**		114
Kraftware Corp 270 Cox St *Cust Svc	Roselle	NJ	07203	**800-221-1728***		606
Kramer Laboratories Inc 8778 SW Eigth St	Miami	FL	33174	**800-824-4894**	305-223-1287	582
Kramig Insulation 323 S Wayne Ave	Cincinnati	OH	45215	**888-579-0079**	513-761-4010	191-9
Krannert Ctr for the Performing Arts 500 S Goodwin Ave	Urbana	IL	61801	**800-527-2849**	217-333-6700	571
Kraton Performance Polymers Inc 15710 John F Kennedy Blvd Ste 300 *NYSE: KRA*	Houston	TX	77032	**800-457-2866**	281-504-4950	604-2
Kratos Defense & Security Solutions Inc 4820 Eastgate Mall Ste 200	San Diego	CA	92121	**877-548-7911**	858-332-3700	263
Kraus-Anderson Co (KA) 523 S Eigth St	Minneapolis	MN	55404	**888-547-3983**	612-305-2934	187
Kraus-Anderson Insurance 420 Gateway Blvd	Burnsville	MN	55337	**800-207-9261**	952-707-8200	390
KRBE-FM 104.1 (CHR) 9801 Westheimer Rd Ste 700	Houston	TX	77042	**888-955-2993**	713-266-1000	642-56
KRCC-FM 91.5 (NPR) 912 N Weber St	Colorado Springs	CO	80903	**800-748-2727**	719-473-4801	642-31
Kreamer Feed Inc PO Box 38	Kreamer	PA	17833	**800-767-4537**	570-374-8148	278
Kreative Carriers Transportation & Logistic Services Inc 61 Bluewater Rd	Bedford	NS	B4B1G8	**888-274-2444**		315
Kreher Steel Company LLC 1550 N 25th Ave	Melrose Park	IL	60160	**800-323-0745**		491
Krehling Industries Inc 1399 Hagy Way	Harrisburg	PA	17110	**800-839-1654**	717-232-7936	184
Kreider Farms 1461 Lancaster Rd	Manheim	PA	17545	**888-665-4415**	717-665-4415	10-2
Kreinik Manufacturing Company Inc 1708 Gihon Rd	Parkersburg	WV	26101	**800-537-2166**	304-422-8900	709
Kreisler Mfg Corp 180 Van Riper Ave	Elmwood Park	NJ	07407	**888-750-5834**	201-791-0700	21
KREM-TV Ch 2 (CBS) 4103 S Regal St	Spokane	WA	99223	**888-404-3922**	509-448-2000	738-79
Kress Employment Screening 320 Westcott St Ste 108	Houston	TX	77007	**888-636-3693**	713-880-3693	632
Krieger Specialty Products Co 4880 Gregg Rd	Pico Rivera	CA	90660	**866-203-5060**	562-695-0645	236
Krillion Inc 607A W Dana St	Mountain View	CA	94041	**877-784-0805**	949-784-0800	179
Kripalu Ctr for Yoga & Health 57 Interlaken Rd	Stockbridge	MA	01262	**800-741-7353**	413-448-3400	704
Krispy Kreme Doughnuts Corp 370 Knollwood St Ste 500 *NYSE: KKD*	Winston-Salem	NC	27103	**800-457-4779**	336-725-2981	67
Kristin Brooks Hope Ctr (KBHC) 1250 24th St NW	Washington	DC	20037	**800-784-2433**	202-536-3200	47-17
KRLD-AM 1080 (N/T) 4131 N Central Expy Ste 100	Dallas	TX	75204	**800-289-1080**	214-525-7000	642-36
KRMA-TV Ch 6 (PBS) 1089 Bannock St	Denver	CO	80204	**800-274-6666**	303-892-6666	738-23
KRMC (Kingman Regional Medical Ctr) 3269 Stockton Hill Rd	Kingman	AZ	86409	**877-757-2101**	928-757-2101	374-3
KRMG-AM 740 (N/T) 7136 S Yale Ave Ste 500	Tulsa	OK	74136	**855-297-9696**	918-493-7400	642-126
Kroger Co 1014 Vine St *NYSE: KR*	Cincinnati	OH	45202	**800-576-4377**	513-762-4000	345
Krohn Industries Inc PO Box 98	Carlstadt	NJ	07072	**800-526-6299**	201-933-9696	407
Kroll Background America Inc 100 Centerview Dr Ste 300	Nashville	TN	37214	**800-697-7189**	615-320-9800	632
Kroll Factual Data Inc 5200 Hahns Peak Dr	Loveland	CO	80538	**800-929-3400**	970-663-5700	220
Kroll Inc 600 Third Ave	New York	NY	10016	**800-675-3772**	212-593-1000	196
Kroll Ontrack Inc 9023 Columbine Rd	Eden Prairie	MN	55347	**800-872-2599**	952-937-5161	180-12
Krones Inc 9600 S 58th St PO Box 321801	Franklin	WI	53132	**800-752-3787**	414-409-4000	546
Kronos Inc 297 Billerica Rd	Chelmsford	MA	01824	**888-293-5549**	978-250-9800	180-11
Kronos Micronutrients 213 W Moxee Ave PO Box 1167	Moxee	WA	98936	**800-541-4086**	509-248-4911	282
Kronos Products Inc 1 Kronos Dr	Glendale Heights	IL	60139	**800-621-0099**		297-26
Kronos Worldwide Inc 5430 LBJ Freeway Ste 1700 *NYSE: KRO*	Houston	TX	75240	**800-866-5600**	281-423-3300	144
KROQ-FM 106.7 (Alt) 5901 Venice Blvd	Los Angeles	CA	90034	**800-520-1067**	323-930-1067	642-69
KROX-AM 1260 (Var) 208 S Main St	Crookston	MN	56716	**800-222-2537**	218-281-1140	643
Kroy LLC 3830 Kelley Ave *Cust Svc	Cleveland	OH	44114	**888-888-5769***	216-426-5600	175-6
KRQE-TV Ch 13 (CBS) 13 Broadcast Plz SW	Albuquerque	NM	87104	**800-283-4227**	505-243-2285	738-2
KRRO-FM 103.7 (Rock) 500 S Phillips Ave	Sioux Falls	SD	57104	**800-283-4867**	605-331-5350	642-113
KRTH-FM 101.1 (Oldies) 5670 Wilshire Blvd Ste 200	Los Angeles	CA	90036	**800-232-5784**	323-936-5784	642-69
Kruepke Trucking Inc 2881 Hwy P *Cust Svc	Jackson	WI	53037	**800-798-5000***	262-677-3155	778
Kruger Street Toy & Train Museum 144 Kruger St	Wheeling	WV	26003	**877-242-8133**	304-242-8133	519
Kruse Adhesive Tape Inc 1610 E McFadden Ave	Santa Ana	CA	92705	**800-992-7702**	714-640-2130	729
KRVK-FM 107.9 (Rock) 150 N Nichols Ave	Casper	WY	82601	**800-442-2256**	307-266-5252	642-22

Name	Address	City	State	ZIP	Toll-Free	Phone	Class
Kryptonite Kollectibles	1441 Plainfield Ave	Janesville	WI	53545	**877-646-1728**		789
KSA Engineers Inc	140 E Tyler St Ste 600 Ste 600	Longview	TX	75601	**877-572-3647**	903-236-7700	263
KSAN-FM 107.7 (Alt)	750 Battery St 3rd Fl	San Francisco	CA	94105	**888-303-2663**	415-995-6800	642-106
KSAZ-TV Ch 10 (Fox)	511 W Adams St	Phoenix	AZ	85003	**888-369-4762**	602-257-1234	738-59
KSBI (Kobelco Stewart Bolling Inc)	1600 Terex Rd	Hudson	OH	44236	**800-464-0064**	330-655-3111	386
Ksbj	1722 Treble Dr	Humble	TX	77338	**877-644-5725**	281-446-5725	115
Ksby-Tv	1772 Calle Joaquin	San Luis Obispo	CA	93405	**800-583-4135**	805-541-6666	115
KSCF-FM 103.7 (N/T)	8033 Linda Vista Rd	San Diego	CA	92111	**888-388-1037**	858-571-7600	642-105
KSGN-FM 89.7 (Rel)	2048 Orange Tree Ln Ste 200	Redlands	CA	92374	**888-897-5746**	909-583-2150	642-98
KSHB-TV Ch 41 (NBC)	4720 Oak St	Kansas City	MO	64112	**800-222-1222**	816-753-4141	738-41
KSKN-TV Ch 22 (CW)	4103 S Regal St	Spokane	WA	99223	**888-404-3922**	509-448-2000	738-79
KSKS-FM 93.7 (Ctry)	1071 W Shaw Ave	Fresno	CA	93711	**800-767-5477**	559-490-5800	642-48
KSLA-TV Ch 12 (CBS)	1812 Fairfield Ave	Shreveport	LA	71101	**800-444-5752**	318-222-1212	738-76
KSLR-AM 630 (Rel)	9601 McAllister Fwy Ste 1200	San Antonio	TX	78216	**800-247-4784**	210-344-8481	642-104
KSL-TV Ch 5 (NBC)	PO Box 1160	Salt Lake City	UT	84110	**800-862-9098**	801-575-5555	738-71
KSME-FM 96.1 (CHR)	4270 Byrd Dr	Loveland	CO	80538	**877-498-9600**	970-461-2560	643
KSMQ-TV Ch 15 (PBS)	2000 Eigth Ave NW	Austin	MN	55912	**800-658-2539**	507-433-0678	
KSMS-FM 90.5 (NPR)	Missouri State University 901 S National Ave	Springfield	MO	65804	**800-767-5768**	417-836-5878	642-118
KSMU-FM 91.1 (NPR)	Missouri State University 901 S National Ave	Springfield	MO	65897	**800-767-5768**	417-836-5878	642-118
KSNT-TV Ch 27 (NBC)	6835 NW Hwy 24	Topeka	KS	66618	**800-222-8477**	785-582-4000	738-85
KSNW-TV	833 N Main St	Wichita	KS	67203	**800-432-3924**	316-265-3333	738-94
KSPR-TV Ch 33 (ABC)	1359 St Louis St	Springfield	MO	65802	**877-248-6922**	417-831-1333	738-81
KSPS Public TV	3911 S Regal St	Spokane	WA	99223	**800-735-2377**	509-443-7800	738-79
KSTP-AM 1500 (N/T)	3415 University Ave	Saint Paul	MN	55114	**877-615-1500**	651-646-8255	642-77
KSTW-TV Ch 11 (CW)	1000 Dexter Ave N Ste 205	Seattle	WA	98109	**866-313-5789**	206-441-1111	
KSTX-FM 89.1 (NPR)	8401 Datapoint Dr Ste 800	San Antonio	TX	78229	**800-622-8977**	210-614-8977	642-104
KSWD-FM 100.3 (Rock)	5900 Wilshire Blvd Ste 1900	Los Angeles	CA	90036	**888-696-1003**	323-634-1800	642-69
KSWF-FM 100.5 (Ctry)	1856 S Glenstone Ave	Springfield	MO	65804	**844-289-7234**	417-890-5555	642-118
K-Swiss Inc	31248 Oak Crest Dr *NASDAQ: KSWS*	Westlake Village	CA	91361	**800-938-8000**	818-706-5100	302
KSWV-AM 810 (Span)	102 Taos St	Santa Fe	NM	87505	**800-873-3372**	505-983-3303	642-108
K-Systems Inc	2104 Aspen Dr	Mechanicsburg	PA	17055	**800-221-0204**	717-795-7711	180-1
KT (Kokomo Tribune)	300 N Union St PO Box 9014	Kokomo	IN	46901	**800-382-0696**	765-459-3121	531-2
KTAL-TV Ch 6 (NBC)	3150 N Market St	Shreveport	LA	71107	**800-259-4929**	318-629-6000	738-76
Kta-Tator Inc	115 Technology Dr	Pittsburgh	PA	15275	**800-582-4243**	412-788-1300	263
KTBN-TV Ch 40 (TBN)	2442 Michelle Dr	Tustin	CA	92780	**888-731-1000**	714-832-2950	
KTBS-TV Ch 3 (ABC)	312 E Kings Hwy	Shreveport	LA	71104	**866-543-3296**	318-861-5800	738-76
KTBY-TV Ch 4 (Fox)	2700 E Tudor Rd	Anchorage	AK	99507	**877-304-1313**	907-561-1313	738-3
KTC (Kaplan Telephone Company Inc)	220 N Cushing Ave	Kaplan	LA	70548	**866-643-7171**	337-643-7171	733
KTHT-FM	1990 Post Oak Blvd Ste 2300	Houston	TX	77056	**877-745-6591**	713-963-1200	642-56
KTHV-TV Ch 11 (CBS)	720 S Izard St	Little Rock	AR	72201	**800-621-3362**	501-376-1111	738-44
KTIK-AM 1350 (Sports)	1419 W Bannock St	Boise	ID	83702	**866-296-1350**	208-336-3670	642-17
KTKZ-AM 1380 (N/T)	1425 River Pk Dr Ste 520	Sacramento	CA	95815	**888-923-1380**	916-924-0710	642-101
KTOM-FM 92.7 (Ctry)	903 N Main St *General	Salinas	CA	93906	**800-660-5866***	831-755-8181	643
KTOZ-FM 95.5 (AC)	1856 S Glenstone Ave	Springfield	MO	65804	**800-757-9550**	417-890-5555	642-118
KTRC-AM 1260 (N/T)	2502 Camino Entrada Ste C	Santa Fe	NM	87507	**888-321-5123**	505-471-1067	642-108
KTRS-AM 550 (N/T)	638 Westport Plaza	Saint Louis	MO	63146	**888-550-5877**	314-453-5500	642-102
KTRS-FM 104.7 (CHR)	150 N Nichols Ave	Casper	WY	82601	**800-442-2256**	307-266-5252	642-22
KTSD-FM 91.1 (NPR)	555 N Dakota St PO Box 5000	Vermillion	SD	57069	**800-456-0766**	605-677-5861	643
KTSD-TV Ch 10 (PBS)	555 N Dakota St PO Box 5000	Vermillion	SD	57069	**800-333-0789**		
KTSF-TV Ch 26 (Ind)	100 Valley Dr	Brisbane	CA	94005	**800-772-1213**	415-468-2626	
KTTC-TV Ch 10 (NBC)	6301 Bandel Rd NW	Rochester	MN	55901	**800-288-1656**	507-288-4444	738-68
KTTS-FM 94.7 (Ctry)	2330 W Grand St	Springfield	MO	65802	**800-621-3362**	417-865-6614	642-118
K-Tube Technologies	13400 Kirkham Way	Poway	CA	92064	**800-394-0058**	858-513-9229	476
KTVB-TV Ch 7 (NBC)	5407 Fairview	Boise	ID	83706	**800-537-8939**	208-375-7277	738-12
KTVF-TV Ch 11 (NBC)	3650 Braddock St	Fairbanks	AK	99701	**855-255-5975**	907-458-1800	738-29
KTVQ-TV Ch 2 (CBS)	3203 Third Ave N	Billings	MT	59101	**800-908-4490**	406-252-5611	738-10
KTWB-FM 101.9 (Ctry)	500 S Phillips Ave	Sioux Falls	SD	57104	**888-293-2832**	605-331-5350	642-113
KTWU-TV Ch 11 (PBS)	1700 College	Topeka	KS	66621	**800-866-5898**	785-670-1111	738-85
KTXR-FM 101.3 (AC)	3000 E Chestnut Expy *General	Springfield	MO	65806	**855-586-8852***	417-862-3751	642-118
KTXY-FM 106.9 (AC)	3215 Lemone Industrial Blvd Ste 200	Columbia	MO	65201	**800-500-9107**	573-875-1099	643
KUA (Kissimmee Utility Authority Inc)	1701 W Carroll St	Kissimmee	FL	34741	**877-582-7700**	407-933-7777	785
KUAC FM/TV	PO Box 755620	Fairbanks	AK	99775	**800-727-6543**	907-474-7491	629
KUAC-FM 89.9 (NPR)	312 Tanana Dr Ste 202 PO Box 755620	Fairbanks	AK	99775	**800-727-6543**	907-474-7491	642-43
KUAC-TV Ch 9 (PBS)	University of Alaska PO Box 755620	Fairbanks	AK	99775	**800-727-6543**	907-474-7491	738-29
KUAD-FM 99.1 (Ctry)	600 Main St	Windsor	CO	80550	**800-500-2599**		643
KUAF 91.3 Public Radio	9 S School Ave	Fayetteville	AR	72701	**800-522-5823**	479-575-2556	643
Kubin-Nicholson Corp	8440 N 87th St	Milwaukee	WI	53224	**800-858-9557**	414-586-4300	8
Kubota Tractor Corp	3401 Del Amo Blvd	Torrance	CA	90503	**888-458-2682**	310-370-3370	275
Kubotek USA	2 Mt Royal Ave Ste 500	Marlborough	MA	01752	**800-372-3872**	508-229-2020	180-5
KUED-TV Ch 7 (PBS)	101 Wasatch Dr Rm 215	Salt Lake City	UT	84112	**800-477-5833**	801-581-7777	738-71
Kuehne & Nagel Inc	10 Exchange Pl	Jersey City	NJ	07302	**866-914-0444**	201-413-5500	448
Kugler Co	209 W Third St PO Box 1748	McCook	NE	69001	**800-445-9116**	308-345-2280	278
KUHF-FM 88.7 (Clas)	4343 Elgin St 3rd Fl	Houston	TX	77204	**877-252-0436**	713-743-0887	642-56
Kuhlman Corp	1845 Indian Woods Cir	Maumee	OH	43537	**800-669-3309**	419-897-6000	184
Kuhn Flowers Inc	3802 Beach Blvd	Jacksonville	FL	32207	**800-458-5846**	904-398-8601	294
Kula Hospital	100 Keokea Pl	Kula	HI	96790	**800-845-6733**	808-878-1221	449
Kultur International Films Ltd	PO Box 755	Forked River	NJ	08731	**888-329-2580**		512
Kumho Tire USA Inc	10299 Sixth St	Rancho Cucamonga	CA	91730	**800-445-8646**	909-428-3999	753
Kumon North America Inc	300 Frank W Burr Blvd Glenpointe Ctr E Ste 6	Teaneck	NJ	07666	**800-222-6284**	201-928-0444	147
KUNM-FM 89.9 (NPR)	1University of New Mexico MSC 06 3520	Albuquerque	NM	87131	**877-277-4806**	505-277-4806	642-4
Kuno Creative Group LLC	36901 American Wy Ste 2A	Avon	OH	44011	**800-303-0806**		4
Kuntzman Trucking Inc	13515 Oyster Rd	Alliance	OH	44601	**800-362-9779**	330-821-9160	778
KUOW-FM 94.9 (NPR)	4518 University Way NE Ste 310	Seattle	WA	98105	**800-289-5869**	206-543-2710	642-111
KUPX-TV Ch 16 (I)	466C Lawndale Dr	Salt Lake City	UT	84115	**888-467-2988**	801-474-0016	738-71
Kuraray America Inc	2625 Bay Area Blvd Ste 600	Houston	TX	77058	**800-423-9762**	281-909-5800	742-1
Kuriyama of America Inc	360 E State Pkwy	Schaumburg	IL	60173	**800-800-0320**	847-755-0360	193-2
Kurt Manufacturing Co	5280 Main St NE	Minneapolis	MN	55421	**800-458-7855**	763-572-1500	453
Kurt Weiss Greenhouses Inc	95 Main St	Center Moriches	NY	11934	**800-344-7805**	631-878-2500	369
Kurtz Bros Company Inc	400 Reed St PO Box 392	Clearfield	PA	16830	**800-252-3811**	814-765-6561	85
Kurtzon Lighting Inc	1420 S Talman Ave	Chicago	IL	60608	**800-837-8937**	773-277-2121	439
Kurz Electric Solutions Inc	1325 McMahon Dr	Neenah	WI	54956	**800-776-3629**	920-886-8200	707
KUSC-FM 91.5 (Clas)	1149 S Hill St Ste H100 PO Box 7913	Los Angeles	CA	90015	**877-587-2227**	213-225-7400	642-69
KUSD-TV Ch 2 (PBS)	555 N Dakota St PO Box 5000	Vermillion	SD	57069	**800-333-0789**		
KUSM-TV Ch 9 (PBS)	Visual Communications Bldg Rm 183	Bozeman	MT	59717	**800-426-8243**	406-994-3437	
KUSP-FM 88.9 (NPR)	203 Eigth Ave	Santa Cruz	CA	95062	**800-655-5877**	831-476-2800	643
Kussmaul Electronics Company Inc	170 Cherry Ave	West Sayville	NY	11796	**800-346-0857**	631-567-0314	258
Kustom Fl LLC	265 Hunt Park Cv	Longwood	FL	32750	**866-679-0699**		188
Kutoka Interactive Inc	225 Roy E Ste 100	Montreal	QC	H2W1M5	**877-858-8652**	514-849-4800	7
KUTV-TV Ch 2 (CBS)	299 S Main St Ste 150	Salt Lake City	UT	84111	**866-438-0220**	801-839-1234	738-71
Kutztown University	15200 Kutztown Rd	Kutztown	PA	19530	**877-628-1915**	610-683-4000	167
Kuukpik Corp	PO Box 89187	Nuiqsut	AK	99789	**866-480-6220**	907-480-6220	345
KUVO-FM 89.3 (Jazz)	2900 Welton St Ste 200	Denver	CO	80205	**800-574-5886**	303-480-9272	642-37

Name	Address	City	State	Zip	Toll-Free	Phone	Class
Kuwait Airways Oasis Club	400 Kelby St	Fort Lee	NJ	07024	**800-458-9248**	201-582-9222	26
Kuwait Embassy	2940 Tilden St NW	Washington	DC	20008	**800-688-9889**	202-966-0702	259
KUWJ-FM 90.3 (NPR)	1000 E University Ave	Laramie	WY	82071	**800-729-5897**	307-766-4240	643
KUWS-FM 91.3 (NPR)	1805 Catlin Ave	Superior	WI	54880	**800-300-8530**	715-394-8530	643
Kuyper College	3333 E Beltline Ave NE	Grand Rapids	MI	49525	**800-511-3749**	616-222-3000	160
KVAL Inc	825 Petaluma Blvd S	Petaluma	CA	94952	**800-553-5825**	707-762-7367	819
K-VA-T Food Stores Inc	PO Box 1158	Abingdon	VA	24212	**800-826-8451**	276-623-5100	345
KVCR-FM 91.9 (NPR)	701 S Mt Vernon Ave	San Bernardino	CA	92410	**800-533-5827**	909-384-4444	642-98
KVI-AM 570 (N/T)	140 Fourth Ave N Ste 340	Seattle	WA	98109	**888-312-5757**	206-404-4000	642-111
KVIA-TV Ch 7 (ABC)	4140 Rio Bravo St	El Paso	TX	79902	**800-433-7300**	915-496-7777	738-26
KVIE-TV Ch 6 (PBS)	2030 W El Camino Ave	Sacramento	CA	95833	**800-347-5843**	916-929-5843	738-69
KVIL-FM 103.7 (AC)	4131 N Central Expy Ste 1000	Dallas	TX	75204	**877-787-1037**	214-525-7000	642-36
KVKI-FM 96.5 (AC)	6341 W Port Ave	Shreveport	LA	71129	**800-487-1840**	318-688-1130	642-112
KVLC-FM 101.1 (Oldies)	101 Perkins Dr	Las Cruces	NM	88005	**877-527-1011**	575-527-1111	643
KVLY-TV Ch 11 (NBC)	1350 21st Ave S	Fargo	ND	58103	**800-450-5844**	701-237-5211	738-30
KVOR-AM 740 (N/T)	6805 Corporate Dr Ste 130	Colorado Springs	CO	80919	**800-232-6459**	719-540-0740	642-31
KVPR-FM 89.3 (NPR)	3437 W Shaw Ave Ste 101	Fresno	CA	93711	**800-275-0764**	559-275-0764	642-48
KWC (Kam Wah Chung State Heritage Site)	725 Summer St NE Ste C	Salem	OR	97301	**800-551-6949**	503-986-0707	564
KWCG Inc	12255 Pkwy Centre Dr	San Diego	CA	92064	**877-464-5924**		262
KWCH-TV Ch 12 (CBS)	2815 E 37th St N	Wichita	KS	67219	**888-512-6397**	316-838-1212	738-94
KWHE-TV Ch 14 (Ind)	1188 Bishop St Ste 502	Honolulu	HI	96813	**800-218-1414**	808-538-1414	738-36
Kwik Goal Ltd	140 Pacific Dr	Quakertown	PA	18951	**800-531-4252**	215-536-2200	708
Kwik Kafe Company Inc	204 Furnace St	Bluefield	VA	24605	**800-533-4066**	276-322-4691	366
Kwik Lok Corp	2712 S 16th Ave PO Box 9548	Yakima	WA	98909	**800-688-5945**	509-248-4770	299
Kwik-Covers LLC	811 Ridge Rd	Webster	NY	14580	**866-586-9620**	585-787-9620	362
Kwik-Wall Co	1010 E Edwards St	Springfield	IL	62703	**800-280-5945**	217-522-5553	288
KWIN-FM 97.7 (CHR)	3127 Transworld Dr Ste 270	Stockton	CA	95206	**800-585-5946**	209-507-8500	642-120
KWJ Engineering Inc	8430 Central Ave Ste C	Newark	CA	94560	**800-472-6626**	510-794-4296	690
KWJJ-FM 99.5 (Ctry)	0700 SW Bancroft St	Portland	OR	97239	**866-239-9653**	503-733-9653	642-93
KWPX-TV Ch 33 (I)	8112-C 304th Ave SE PO Box 426	Preston	WA	98050	**888-467-2988**	425-222-6010	
KWS Mfg Company Ltd	3041 Conveyor Dr	Burleson	TX	76028	**800-543-6558**	817-295-2247	209
KWTV-TV Ch 9 (CBS)	7401 N Kelley Ave	Oklahoma City	OK	73111	**888-550-5988**	405-843-6641	738-55
KWWL-TV Ch 7 (NBC)	500 E Fourth St	Waterloo	IA	50703	**800-947-7746**	319-291-1200	
KWYE-FM 101.1 (CHR)	1071 W Shaw Ave	Fresno	CA	93711	**800-345-9101**	559-490-5800	642-48
KWYR-FM 93.7 (AC)	PO Box 491	Winner	SD	57580	**800-388-5997**	605-842-3333	643
KWYY-FM 95.5 (Ctry)	150 N Nichols Ave	Casper	WY	82601	**800-339-4673**	307-266-5252	642-22
KXFG-FM 92.9 (Ctry)	900 E Washington Ste 315	Colton	CA	92324	**888-431-3764**	909-825-9525	643
KXJB-TV Ch 4 (CBS)	1350 21st Ave S	Fargo	ND	58103	**877-571-0774**	701-237-5211	738-30
KXLT-TV Ch 47 (Fox)	6301 Bandel Rd NW	Rochester	MN	55901	**800-452-4368**	507-252-4747	738-68
KXPR-FM 88.9 (Clas)	7055 Folsom Blvd	Sacramento	CA	95826	**877-480-5900**	916-278-8900	642-101
KXSC-FM 104.9 (Alt)	PO Box 6375	Artesia	CA	90702	**888-966-5332**	415-546-8710	642-107
KXTX-TV Ch 39 (Tele)	4805 Amon Carter Blvd	Fort Worth	TX	76155	**877-266-8365**		738-21
KYCC-FM 90.1 (Rel)	9019 W Ln	Stockton	CA	95210	**800-654-5254**	209-477-3690	642-120
KYE Systems Corp	1301 NW 84th Ave Ste 127	Doral	FL	33126	**800-488-3111**	305-468-9250	175-2
Kyocera Industrial Ceramics Corp	5713 E Fourth Plain Rd	Vancouver	WA	98661	**800-826-0527**	360-696-8950	251
Kyocera International Inc	8611 Balboa Ave	San Diego	CA	92123	**877-248-4237**	858-576-2600	360-3
Kyocera Solar Inc	7812 E Acoma Dr Ste 2	Scottsdale	AZ	85260	**800-544-6466**	480-948-8003	694
Kyocera Tycom Corp	3565 Cadillac	Costa Mesa	CA	92626	**800-823-7284**	714-428-3600	454
Kysela Pere Et Fils Ltd	331 Victory Rd	Winchester	VA	22602	**877-492-7917**	540-722-9228	79-3
Kysor Panel Systems	4201 N Beach St	Fort Worth	TX	76137	**800-633-3426**	817-281-5121	662
KYTV-TV Ch 3 (NBC)	PO Box 3500	Springfield	MO	65808	**888-476-6988**	417-268-3000	738-81
KYUR-TV Ch 13 (ABC)	2700 E Tudor Rd	Anchorage	AK	99507	**877-304-1313**	907-561-1313	738-3
KYXY-FM 96.5 (AC)	8033 Linda Vista Rd	San Diego	CA	92111	**888-560-9650**	858-571-7600	642-105
KYYY-FM 92.9 (AC)	3500 E Rosser Ave	Bismarck	ND	58501	**866-929-9393**	701-224-9393	642-16
KZHT-FM 97.1 (CHR)	2801 S Decker Lake Dr	Salt Lake City	UT	84119	**800-888-8499**	801-908-1300	642-103
KZOK-FM 102.5 (CR)	1000 Dexter Ave N	Seattle	WA	98109	**800-252-1025**	206-421-1025	642-111
KZZP-FM 104.7 (CHR)	4686 E Van Buren St Ste 300	Phoenix	AZ	85008	**877-541-1966**	602-374-6000	642-90

L

Name	Address	City	State	Zip	Toll-Free	Phone	Class
L & L Nursery Supply Co Inc	2552 Shenandoah Way	San Bernardino	CA	92407	**800-624-2517**	909-591-0461	295
L & M Radiator Inc	1414 E 37th St	Hibbing	MN	55746	**800-346-3500**	218-263-8993	60
L & N Federal Credit Union	9265 Smyrna Pkwy	Louisville	KY	40229	**800-443-2479**	502-368-5858	221
L & S Truck Ctr of Appleton Inc	330 N Bluemound Dr	Appleton	WI	54914	**888-617-3140**	920-749-1700	56
L B L Group	3631 S. Harbor Blvd Ste 200	Santa Ana	CA	92704	**800-451-8037**	657-232-0500	688
L B Plastics Inc	PO Box 907	Mooresville	NC	28115	**800-752-7739**	704-663-1543	609
L b Property Management	4730 Woodman Ave Ste 200	Sherman Oaks	CA	91423	**888-400-7080**		650
L Bornstein & Co Inc	321 Washington St	Somerville	MA	02143	**800-842-1111**	617-776-3555	361
L E Coppersmith Inc	525 S Douglas St	El Segundo	CA	90245	**888-827-4388**	310-607-8000	312
L M Scofield Co	6533 Bandini Blvd	Los Angeles	CA	90040	**800-800-9900**	323-720-3000	185
L Suzio Concrete Company Inc	975 Westfield Rd	Meriden	CT	06450	**888-789-4626**	203-237-8421	184
L Thorn Co Inc	6000 Grant Line Rd	New Albany	IN	47150	**800-662-4594**	812-246-4461	193-1
L' Appartement Hotel	455 Sherbrooke W	Montreal	QC	H3A1B7	**800-363-3010**	514-284-3634	379
L'Academie de Cuisine Inc	16006 Industrial Dr	Gaithersburg	MD	20877	**800-664-2433**	301-670-8670	162
L'Acadie-Nouvelle	476 St-Pierre W	Caraquet	NB	E1W1B7	**800-561-2255**	506-727-4444	531-1
L'Auberge de Sedona	301 L'Auberge Ln	Sedona	AZ	86336	**855-905-5745**	928-282-1661	669
L'Auberge Del Mar	1540 Camino del Mar PO Box 2880	Del Mar	CA	92014	**800-245-9757**	858-259-1515	667
L'Ermitage Beverly Hills Hotel	9291 Burton Way	Beverly Hills	CA	90210	**877-235-7582**	310-278-3344	379
L'Hotel du Vieux-Quebec	1190 St Jean St	Quebec	QC	G1R1S6	**800-361-7787**	418-692-1850	379
L'Hotel Quebec	3115 des Hotels Ave	Sainte-Foy	QC	G1W3Z6	**800-567-5276**	418-658-5120	379
L'Oreal USA	575 Fifth Ave	New York	NY	10017	**800-322-2036**	212-818-1500	217
L-3 Avionics Systems	5353 52nd St SE	Grand Rapids	MI	49512	**800-253-9525**	616-949-6600	528
L-3 Communications Corp	600 Third Ave 34-35 Fl. *NYSE: LLL*	New York	NY	10016	**800-351-8483**	212-697-1111	732
L-3 Communications Corp Aviation Recorders Div	6000 Fruitville Rd	Sarasota	FL	34232	**877-726-2228**	941-371-0811	528
L-3 Communications Corp Communication Systems East Div	1 Federal St	Camden	NJ	08103	**800-339-6197**	856-338-3000	528
L-3 Communications Corp Randtron Antenna Systems Div	130 Constitution Dr *Sales	Menlo Park	CA	94025	**866-900-7270***	650-326-9500	528
L-3 Communications ESSCO	90 Nemco Way	Ayer	MA	01432	**877-282-1168**	978-568-5100	645
L-3 Communications Flight International Aviation LLC	1 Lear Dr	Newport News	VA	23602	**800-358-4685**	757-886-5500	24
L-3 Communications Integrated Systems	10001 Jack Finney Blvd	Greenville	TX	75402	**877-282-1168**	903-455-3450	22
L-3 Communications Telemetry East Div	1515 Grundy's Ln	Bristol	PA	19007	**800-351-8483**	267-545-7000	645
L-3 Communications Telemetry West Div	9020 Balboa Ave	San Diego	CA	92123	**800-351-8483**	858-694-7500	645
La Beau Bros Inc	295 N Harrison Ave	Kankakee	IL	60901	**800-747-9519**	815-933-5519	56
La Belle Dodge Chrysler Jeep Inc	501 S Main St	Labelle	FL	33935	**800-226-1193**	863-675-2701	56
La Capitol Federal Credit Union	PO Box 3398	Baton Rouge	LA	70821	**800-522-2748**	225-342-5055	221
LA Care Health Plan	555 W Fifth St 29th Fl.	Los Angeles	CA	90013	**888-839-9909**	213-694-1250	391-3
La Cie Canada Tire Inc	21500 Transcanadienne	Baie-D'Urfe	QC	H9X4B7	**888-267-5097**	514-457-0155	752
La Crosse Area Convention & Visitors Bureau	410 Veterans Memorial Dr	La Crosse	WI	54601	**800-658-9424**	608-782-2366	208
La Crosse Graphics Inc	3025 East Ave S	La Crosse	WI	54601	**800-832-2503**	608-788-2500	626
La Crosse Tribune	401 N Third St	La Crosse	WI	54601	**800-262-0420**	608-782-9710	531-2
LA Darling Co	1401 Hwy 49B	Paragould	AR	72450	**800-643-3499**	870-239-9564	288
La Follette Utilities Board	302 N Tennessee Ave PO Box 1411	La Follette	TN	37766	**800-352-1340**	423-562-3316	247
La Fonda	100 E San Francisco St	Santa Fe	NM	87501	**800-523-5002**	505-982-5511	379
La Fontaine Bleue Inc	7514 S Ritchie Hwy	Glen Burnie	MD	21061	**877-778-6863**	410-760-4115	669
La Grande-Union County Chamber of Commerce	102 Elm St	La Grande	OR	97850	**800-848-9969**	541-963-8588	138

Name / Address	City	State	ZIP	Toll-Free	Phone	Class
La Habra Products Inc 4125 E La Palma Ave Ste 250	Anaheim	CA	92807	**866-516-0061**	714-778-2266	499
La Hacienda Treatment Ctr 145 La Hacienda Way	Hunt	TX	78024	**800-749-6160**	830-238-4222	724
La Jolla Beach & Tennis Club 2000 Spindrift Dr	La Jolla	CA	92037	**888-828-0948**	858-454-7126	667
La Jolla Nursing & Rehabilitation Ctr 2552 Torrey Pines Rd	La Jolla	CA	92037	**800-861-0086**	858-453-5810	449
La Leche League International Inc (LLLI) 957 N Plum Grove Rd	Schaumburg	IL	60173	**800-525-3243**	847-519-7730	47-17
La Marche Mfg Co 106 Bradrock Dr	Des Plaines	IL	60018	**888-232-9562**	847-299-1188	255
La Mesa Rv Ctr Inc 7430 Copley Pk Pl *Sales	San Diego	CA	92111	**888-509-4199***	858-874-8000	56
La Pensione Hotel 606 W Date St	San Diego	CA	92101	**800-232-4683**	619-236-8000	379
La Petite Bretonne Inc 1210 Boul Mich Le-Bohec	Blainville	QC	J7C5S4	**800-361-3381**	450-435-3381	298-8
La Plata Electric Assn Inc 45 Stewart St	Durango	CO	81303	**888-839-5732**	970-247-5786	247
La Playa Beach & Golf Resort 9891 Gulf Shore Dr	Naples	FL	34108	**800-237-6883**	239-597-3123	667
La Porte County 813 Lincolnway	La Porte	IN	46350	**800-654-3441**	219-326-6808	338
La Porte Hospital (LPH) 1007 Lincolnway PO Box 250	La Porte	IN	46350	**800-235-6204**	219-326-1234	374-3
La Posada de Santa Fe Resort & Spa 330 E Palace Ave	Santa Fe	NM	87501	**866-280-3810**	505-986-0000	667
La Posada Hotel & Suites 1000 Zaragoza St *Resv	Laredo	TX	78040	**800-444-2099***	956-722-1701	379
La Quinta Inn & Suites Secaucus Meadowlands 350 Lighting Way *General	Secaucus	NJ	07094	**800-753-3757***	201-863-8700	379
La Quinta Resort & Club 49-499 Eisenhower Dr	La Quinta	CA	92253	**800-598-3828**	760-564-4111	667
La Reina Inc 316 N Ford Blvd	Los Angeles	CA	90022	**800-367-7522**	323-268-2791	297-36
La Roche College 9000 Babcock Blvd *Admissions	Pittsburgh	PA	15237	**800-838-4572***	412-367-9300	167
La Rosa Del Monte Express Inc 1133-35 Tiffany St	Bronx	NY	10459	**800-452-7672**	718-991-3300	778
La Salle University 1900 W Olney Ave	Philadelphia	PA	19141	**800-328-1910**	215-951-1500	167
La Salsa Fresh Mexican Grill 320 Commerce Ste 100	Irvine	CA	92602	**866-452-7257**	949-270-8900	668
La Sierra University 4500 Riverwalk Pkwy	Riverside	CA	92515	**800-874-5587**	951-785-2000	167
La Touraine Inc 625 Broadway Ste 700	San Diego	CA	92101	**800-893-8871**		227
La Veta/Cuchara Chamber of Commerce 132 W Ryus Ave	La Veta	CO	81055	**866-277-5550**	719-742-3676	138
La Vida Llena 10501 Lagrima de Oro NE	Albuquerque	NM	87111	**800-922-1344**	505-293-4001	670
LA Weekly 6715 Sunset Blvd	Los Angeles	CA	90028	**866-789-6188**		531-5
Lab Products Inc 742 Sussex Ave PO Box 639	Seaford	DE	19973	**800-526-0469**	302-628-4300	72
LaBarge Coating LLC 211 N Bdwy Ste 3050	Saint Louis	MO	63102	**866-992-4191**	314-646-3400	538
Labatt Breweries of Canada 207 Queen's Quay W Ste 299 *Cust Svc	Toronto	ON	M5J1A7	**800-268-2337***	416-361-5050	101
Labcon North America Inc 3700 Lkeville Hwy	Petaluma	CA	94954	**800-227-1466**	707-766-2100	419
Labconco Corp 8811 Prospect Ave *Cust Svc	Kansas City	MO	64132	**800-821-5525***	816-333-8811	420
Label Systems Inc 4111 Lindbergh Dr	Addison	TX	75001	**800-220-9552**	972-387-4512	626
Label Works 2025 Lookout Dr	North Mankato	MN	56003	**800-522-3558**		626
Labelmaster Co 5724 N Pulaski Rd	Chicago	IL	60646	**800-621-5808**	773-478-0900	413
Labeltape Inc 5100 Beltway Dr SE	Caledonia	MI	49316	**800-928-4537**	616-698-1830	413
Labette Bank 4th & Huston PO Box 497	Altamont	KS	67330	**800-711-5311**	620-784-5311	69
Labette Community College 200 S 14th St	Parsons	KS	67357	**888-522-3883**	620-421-6700	161
LabOne Inc 10101 Renner Blvd	Lenexa	KS	66219	**800-646-7788**	913-888-1770	418
Labor Finders International Inc 11426 N Jog Rd	Palm Beach Gardens	FL	33418	**800-864-7749**	561-627-6507	719
Labor Law Center Inc 12534 Vly view st	Garden Grove	CA	92845	**800-745-9970**		136
Laboratory Corp of America Holdings 358 S Main St *NYSE: LH*	Burlington	NC	27215	**800-334-5161**	336-584-5171	418
Laboratory Institute of Merchandising 12 E 53rd St	New York	NY	10022	**800-677-1323**	212-752-1530	167
Laborchex Co, The 2506 Lakeland Dr Ste 200	Jackson	MS	39232	**800-880-0366**	601-664-6760	632
Labrada Nutrition 403 Century Plz Dr Ste 440	Houston	TX	77073	**800-832-9948**		797
Labrie Environmental Group 175 du Pont	Saint-Nicolas	QC	G7A2T3	**800-463-6638**	418-831-8250	515
LABS Inc 6933 S Revere Pkwy	Centennial	CO	80112	**866-393-2244**	720-528-4750	417
Lac Courte Oreilles Ojibwa Community College 13466 W Trepania Rd	Hayward	WI	54843	**888-526-6221**	715-634-4790	164
Lace For Less Inc 1500 Main Ave Ste 3	Clifton	NJ	07011	**800-533-5223**	973-478-2955	742-4
Lack's Valley Stores Ltd 1300 San Patricia St	Pharr	TX	78577	**800-870-6999**	956-702-3361	322
Lackawanna College 501 Vine St	Scranton	PA	18509	**877-346-3552**	570-961-7810	161
Lackawanna County Convention & Visitors Bureau 99 Glenmaura National Blvd	Scranton	PA	18507	**800-229-3526**	570-496-1701	208
Laclede Electric Co-op 1400 E Rt 66	Lebanon	MO	65536	**800-299-3164**	417-532-3164	247
Laclede Gas Co 720 Olive St	Saint Louis	MO	63101	**800-887-4173**	314-342-0500	785
La-Co/Markal Co 1201 Pratt Blvd	Elk Grove Village	IL	60007	**800-621-4025**	847-956-7600	466
LaCrosse Footwear Inc 17634 NE Airport *Cust Svc	Portland	OR	97230	**800-323-2668***		302
Lacrosse Hall of Fame & Museum 113 W University Pkwy	Baltimore	MD	21210	**866-877-7550**	410-235-6882	519
Lad Lake Inc W350s1401 Waterville Rd	Dousman	WI	53118	**877-965-2131**	262-965-2131	147
Ladenburg Thalmann Financial Services Inc 4400 Biscayne Blvd 12th Fl *NYSE: LTS*	Miami	FL	33137	**800-523-8425**	212-409-2000	688
Lady Bird Johnson Wildflower Ctr 4801 LaCrosse Ave	Austin	TX	78739	**877-945-3357**	512-292-4200	96
Lady Foot Locker (LFL) 112 W 34th St	New York	NY	10120	**800-991-6686**	212-720-3700	302
Lady Grace Stores Inc 139 Endicott St Ste 1	Denvers	MA	01923	**800-922-0504**	781-569-0727	156-6
Laetitia Vineyards & Winery Inc 453 Laetitia Vineyard Dr	Arroyo Grande	CA	93420	**888-809-8463**	805-481-1772	79-3
Lafayette Convention & Visitors Commission 1400 NW Evangeline Thwy	Lafayette	LA	70501	**800-346-1958**	337-232-3737	208
Lafayette Federal Credit Union (Inc) 3535 University Blvd W	Kensington	MD	20895	**800-888-6560**	301-929-7990	221
Lafayette Hotel 600 St Charles Ave	New Orleans	LA	70130	**800-366-2743**	504-524-4441	379
Lafayette Hotel & Suites San Diego 2223 El Cajon Blvd	San Diego	CA	92104	**800-468-3531**	619-296-2101	379
Lafayette Life Insurance Co 400 Broadway	Cincinnati	OH	45202	**800-443-8793**		391-2
Lafayette Museum 1122 Lafayette St	Lafayette	LA	70501	**800-346-1958**	337-234-2208	519
Lafayette Park Hotel 3287 Mt Diablo Blvd	Lafayette	CA	94549	**855-382-8632**	925-283-3700	379
Lafayette Steel Erector Inc 313 Westgate Rd	Lafayette	LA	70506	**877-234-9435**	337-234-9435	191-14
Lafayette Venetian Blind Inc 3000 Klondike Rd. PO Box 2838	West Lafayette	IN	47996	**800-342-5523**		86
Lafayette Wood-Works Inc 3004 Cameron St	Lafayette	LA	70506	**800-960-3311**	337-233-5250	498
Lafayette-West Lafayette Convention & Visitors Bureau 301 Frontage Rd	Lafayette	IN	47905	**800-872-6648**	765-447-9999	208
Laflamme Doors & Windows Corp 39 Industrielle	St. Apollinaire	QC	G0S2E0	**800-463-1922**		498
Lafontaine Honda 2245 S Telegraph Rd	Dearborn	MI	48124	**866-567-5088**		56
LaForce Inc 1060 W Mason St	Green Bay	WI	54303	**800-236-8858**	920-497-7100	236
Lafourche Parish 402 Green St PO Box 5548	Thibodaux	LA	70302	**800-834-8832**	985-446-8427	338
LaFrance Equipment Corp 516 Erie St	Elmira	NY	14904	**800-873-8808**	607-733-5511	677
Lago Mar Resort & Club 1700 S Ocean Ln	Fort Lauderdale	FL	33316	**855-209-5677**	954-678-3915	667
Lagoon & Pioneer Village 375 N Lagoon Dr	Farmington	UT	84025	**800-748-5246**	801-451-8000	32
LaGrange College 601 Broad St *Admissions	LaGrange	GA	30240	**800-593-2885***	706-880-8000	167
LaGrange County Rural Electric Membership Corp 1995 E US Hwy 20	LaGrange	IN	46761	**877-463-7165**	260-463-7165	247
Laguna Beach Visitors & Conference Bureau 381 Forest Ave	Laguna Beach	CA	92651	**800-877-1115**	949-497-9229	208
Laguna Cliffs Marriott Resort 25135 Pk Lantern	Dana Point	CA	92629	**800-545-7483**	949-661-5000	667
Laguna College of Art & Design 2222 Laguna Canyon Rd	Laguna Beach	CA	92651	**800-255-0762**	949-376-6000	167
Lahaina Shores Beach Resort 475 Front St	Lahaina	HI	96761	**866-934-9176**		378
Lahey Clinic Foundation Inc 41 Mall Rd	Burlington	MA	01805	**800-524-3955**	781-744-8000	374-3
Laird & Co 1 LaiRd Rd	Scobeyville	NJ	07724	**877-438-5247**	732-542-0312	79-1
Laird Noller Ford Inc 2245 SW Topeka Blvd	Topeka	KS	66611	**800-632-3673**	785-235-9211	515
Laird Norton Tyee 801 Second Ave Ste 1600	Seattle	WA	98104	**800-426-5105**	206-464-5100	401
Laird Plastics Inc 6800 Broken Sound Pkwy Ste 150	Boca Raton	FL	33487	**800-243-9696**	561-443-9100	602
Laitner Brush Co 1561 Laitner Dr *Cust Svc	Traverse City	MI	49686	**800-423-6805***	231-929-3300	102
Laitram LLC 200 Laitram Ln	Harahan	LA	70123	**800-535-7631**	504-733-6000	528
Lake Agassiz Regional Library (LARL) 118 Fifth St S PO Box 900	Moorhead	MN	56560	**800-247-0449**	218-233-3757	434-3
Lake Air 7709 Winpark Dr	Minneapolis	MN	55427	**888-785-2422**	763-546-0994	488
Lake Area Technical Institute 230 11th St NE PO Box 730	Watertown	SD	57201	**800-657-4344**	605-882-5284	161
Lake Arrowhead Resort & Spa 27984 Hwy 189	Lake Arrowhead	CA	92352	**800-800-6792**	909-336-1511	667
Lake Austin Spa Resort 1705 S Quinlan Pk Rd	Austin	TX	78732	**800-847-5637**	512-372-7380	705
Lake Barkley State Resort Park 3500 State Pk Rd	Cadiz	KY	42211	**800-325-1708**		564
Lake Barkley Tourist Commission 82 Days Inn Dr	Kuttawa	KY	42055	**800-355-3885**	270-388-5300	208
Lake Bistineau State Park 103 State Pk Rd	Doyline	LA	71023	**888-677-2478**	318-745-3503	564

Name / Address	City	State	ZIP	Toll-Free	Phone	Class
Lake Breeze Motel Resort 9000 Congdon Blvd	Duluth	MN	55804	**800-738-5884**	218-525-6808	667
Lake Bruin State Park 201 State Pk Rd	Saint Joseph	LA	71366	**888-677-2784**	318-766-3530	564
Lake Carmi State Park 460 Marsh Farm Rd *Resv	Enosburg Falls	VT	05450	**888-409-7579***	802-933-8383	564
Lake Cascade State Park 970 Dam Rd	Cascade	ID	83611	**866-634-3246**	208-382-6544	564
Lake Catherine Footwear 3770 Malvern Rd PO Box 6048	Hot Springs	AR	71901	**800-819-1901**		302
Lake Champlain Regional Chamber of Commerce 60 Main St Ste 100	Burlington	VT	05401	**877-686-5253**	802-863-3489	138
Lake Charles American Press Inc PO Box 2893	Lake Charles	LA	70602	**800-737-2283**	337-433-3000	634-8
Lake Charles Civic Ctr 900 Lakeshore Dr	Lake Charles	LA	70601	**888-620-1749**	337-491-1256	571
Lake Chicot State Park 2542 Hwy 257	Lake Village	AR	71653	**800-264-2430**	870-265-5480	564
Lake Claiborne State Park 225 State Pk Rd	Homer	LA	71040	**888-677-2524**	318-927-2976	564
Lake Country Power 2810 Elida Dr	Grand Rapids	MN	55744	**800-421-9959**		247
Lake County 895 Michigan Ave PO Box 130	Baldwin	MI	49304	**800-245-3240**	231-745-4331	338
Lake County Convention & Visitors Bureau 5465 W Grand Ave Ste 100	Gurnee	IL	60031	**800-525-3669**	847-662-2700	208
Lake D'Arbonne State Park 3628 Evergreen Rd	Farmerville	LA	71241	**888-677-5200**	318-368-2086	564
Lake Erie College 391 W Washington St	Painesville	OH	44077	**800-533-4996**	440-375-7050	167
Lake Erie Frozen Foods Co 1830 Orange Rd	Ashland	OH	44805	**800-766-8501**	419-289-9204	345
Lake Erie Graphics Inc 5372 W 130th St	Brook Park	OH	44142	**888-293-7397**	216-265-7575	626
Lake Erie Shores & Islands Welcome Ctr 770 SE Catawba Rd	Port Clinton	OH	43452	**800-441-1271**	419-734-4386	208
Lake Forest College 555 N Sheridan Rd	Lake Forest	IL	60045	**800-828-4751**	847-234-3100	167
Lake Greenwood State Recreation Area 302 State Pk Rd	Ninety Six	SC	29666	**866-345-7275**	864-543-3535	564
Lake Havasu Area Chamber of Commerce 314 London Bridge Rd	Lake Havasu City	AZ	86403	**800-307-3610**	928-855-4115	138
Lake Immunogenics Inc 348 Berg Rd	Ontario	NY	14519	**800-648-9990**		581
Lake Junaluska Assembly Lake Junaluska Conference Retreat Ctr 689 N Lakeshore Dr	Lake Junaluska	NC	28745	**800-482-1442**	828-452-2881	47-20
Lake Kegonsa State Park 2405 Door Creek Rd *General	Stoughton	WI	53589	**888-947-2757***	608-873-9695	564
Lake Lanier Islands Resort 7000 Holiday Rd	Buford	GA	30518	**800-840-5253**	770-945-8787	667
Lake Lawn Resort 2400 E Geneva St	Delavan	WI	53115	**800-338-5253**	262-728-7950	667
Lake Louise Inn 210 Village Rd PO Box 209	Lake Louise	AB	T0L1E0	**800-661-9237**	403-522-3791	379
Lake Lure Inn & Spa, The 2771 Memorial Hwy	Lake Lure	NC	28746	**888-434-4970**	828-625-2526	379
Lake Lurleen State Park 13226 Lake Lurleen Rd	Coker	AL	35452	**800-760-4089**	205-339-1558	564
Lake Michigan College						
Bertrand Crossing 1905 Foundation Dr	Niles	MI	49120	**800-252-1562**	269-695-1391	161
South Haven 125 Veterans Blvd	South Haven	MI	49090	**800-252-1562**	269-639-8442	161
Lake Morey Resort 1 Clubhouse Rd	Fairlee	VT	05045	**800-423-1211**	802-333-4311	667
Lake Murray Resort Park 3323 Lodge Rd	Ardmore	OK	73401	**800-622-6317**	580-223-6600	667
Lake Murray State Park 120 N Robinson Ave 6th Fl	Oklahoma City	OK	73152	**800-652-6552**		564
Lake Norman Chamber of Commerce 19900 W Catawba Ave Ste 101	Cornelius	NC	28031	**800-305-2508**	704-892-1922	138
Lake of the Ozarks Convention & Visitors Bureau 5815 Hwy 54 PO Box 1498	Osage Beach	MO	65065	**800-386-5253**	573-348-1599	208
Lake of the Torches Resort Casino 510 Old Abe Rd	Lac du Flambeau	WI	54538	**800-258-6724**	715-588-7070	132
Lake Owyhee State Park 725 Summer St NE Ste C	Salem	OR	97301	**800-551-6949**	503-986-0707	564
Lake Park Retirement Residences 1850 Alice St	Oakland	CA	94612	**866-384-3130**	510-835-5511	670
Lake Placid Convention & Visitors Bureau 2608 Main St	Lake Placid	NY	12946	**800-447-5224**	518-523-2445	208
Lake Placid Lodge 144 Lodge Way	Lake Placid	NY	12946	**877-523-2700**	518-523-2700	379
Lake Powell Resorts & Marinas 100 Lakeshore Dr	Page	AZ	86040	**800-622-6317**	888-896-3829	667
Lake Quassapaug Park 2132 Middlebury Rd	Middlebury	CT	06762	**800-367-7275**	203-758-2913	31
Lake Quinault Lodge 345 S Shore Rd	Quinault	WA	98575	**800-562-6672**	360-288-2900	667
Lake Region Co-op Electrical Assn 1401 S Broadway PO Box 643	Pelican Rapids	MN	56572	**800-552-7658**	218-863-1171	247
Lake Region Electric Assn Inc 1212 Main St	Webster	SD	57274	**800-657-5869**	605-345-3379	247
Lake Region Electric Co-op Inc 516 S Lake Region Rd	Hulbert	OK	74441	**800-364-5732**	918-772-2526	247
Lake Region Hospital 712 S Cascade St	Fergus Falls	MN	56537	**800-439-6424**	218-736-8000	374-3
Lake Region Mfg Company Inc 340 Lk Hazeltine Dr	Chaska	MN	55318	**866-899-1392**		475
Lake Region State College 1801 College Dr N	Devils Lake	ND	58301	**800-443-1313**	701-662-1514	161
Lake Seminole Square 8333 Seminole Blvd	Seminole	FL	33772	**866-785-9025**	727-228-7312	670
Lake Shore Cryotronics 575 McCorkle Blvd	Westerville	OH	43082	**877-969-0010**	614-891-2243	203
Lake Shore Industries Inc (LSI) 1817 Poplar St PO BOX 3427	Erie	PA	16508	**800-458-0463**		699
Lake Shore Railway Museum 31 Wall St Lake Shore Historical Society	North East	PA	16428	**800-945-0340**	814-725-1911	519
Lake Sunapee Bank 9 Main St PO Box 29	Newport	NH	03773	**800-281-5772**	603-863-5772	360-2
Lake Superior College 2101 Trinity Rd	Duluth	MN	55811	**800-432-2884**	218-733-7600	161
Lake Superior Ind Sch Dist 381 1640 2 Hwy	Two Harbors	MN	55616	**888-878-0136**	218-834-8201	683
Lake Superior State University 650 W Easterday Ave *Admissions	Sault Sainte Marie	MI	49783	**888-800-5778***	906-632-6841	167
Lake Tahoe Visitors Authority 3066 Lk Tahoe Blvd	South Lake Tahoe	CA	96150	**800-288-2463**	530-544-5050	208
Lake Wapello State Park 15248 Campground Rd	Drakesville	IA	52552	**866-495-4868**	641-722-3371	564
Lake Wissota State Park 18127 County Hwy O	Chippewa Falls	WI	54729	**800-847-9367**	715-382-4574	564
Lake Wister State Park 25567 US Hwy 270	Wister	OK	74966	**800-622-6317**	918-655-7212	564
Lakeland Bancorp Inc 250 Oak Ridge Rd *NASDAQ: LBAI*	Oak Ridge	NJ	07438	**866-224-1379**	973-697-2000	360-2
Lakeland College PO Box 359	Sheboygan	WI	53082	**800-569-2166**	920-565-2111	167
Lakeland Community College 7700 Clocktower Dr	Kirtland	OH	44094	**800-589-8520**	440-525-7000	161
Lakeland Financial Corp 202 E Ctr St *NASDAQ: LKFN*	Warsaw	IN	46580	**800-827-4522**	574-267-6144	360-2
Lakeland Industries Inc 701-7 Koehler Ave *NASDAQ: LAKE*	Ronkonkoma	NY	11779	**800-645-9291**	631-981-9700	575
Lakeland Medical Center-Niles 31 N St Joseph Ave	Niles	MI	49120	**800-968-0115**	269-683-5510	374-3
Lakeland Plastics Inc (LP) 1550 McCormick Blvd	Mundelein	IL	60060	**800-454-4006**	847-680-1550	598
Lakeland Village Beach & Mountain Resort 3535 Lake Tahoe Blvd	South Lake Tahoe	CA	96150	**888-484-7094**	530-544-1685	667
Lakepoint Resort State Park 104 Lakepoint Dr	Eufaula	AL	36027	**800-544-5253**	334-687-8011	564
Lakeport Regional Chamber of Commerce 875 Lakeport Blvd PO Box 295	Lakeport	CA	95453	**866-525-3767**	707-263-5092	138
Lakeridge Health Oshawa 1 Hospital Ct	Oshawa	ON	L1G2B9	**866-338-1778**	905-576-8711	374-2
Lakes Region Community College (LRCC) 379 Belmont Rd	Laconia	NH	03246	**800-357-2992**	603-524-3207	161
Lakeshirts Inc 750 Randolph Rd	Detroit Lakes	MN	56501	**800-627-2780**	218-847-2171	60
Lakeshore Chamber of Commerce 5246 Hohman Ave Ste 100	Hammond	IN	46320	**855-464-6368**	219-931-1000	138
Lakeshore Learning Materials 2695 E Dominguez St	Carson	CA	90895	**800-778-4456**		533
Lakeshore Technical College 1290 N Ave	Cleveland	WI	53015	**888-468-6582**	920-693-1000	798
Lakeside Bank 55 W Wacker Dr	Chicago	IL	60601	**866-892-1572**	312-435-5100	69
Lakeside Behavioral Health System 2911 Brunswick Rd	Memphis	TN	38133	**800-232-5253**	901-377-4700	374-5
Lakeside Foods Inc 808 Hamilton St	Manitowoc	WI	54220	**800-466-3834**	920-684-3356	297-20
Lakeside Inn 100 N Alexander St	Mount Dora	FL	32757	**800-556-5016**	352-383-4101	379
Lakeside International LLC 11000 W Silver Spring Rd	Milwaukee	WI	53225	**800-236-0444**	414-353-4800	56
Lakeside Manufacturing Inc 4900 W Electric Ave	West Milwaukee	WI	53219	**800-558-8565**	414-902-6400	320-1
Lakeside Process Controls Ltd 2475 Hogan Dr	Mississauga	ON	L5N0E9	**800-265-1005**	905-629-9340	110
Lakeside Toyota 3701 N Cswy Blvd *Sales	Metairie	LA	70002	**877-512-8274***	504-833-3311	56
Lakeview Golf Resort & Spa 1 Lakeview Dr	Morgantown	WV	26508	**800-624-8300**	304-594-1111	667
Lakeview on the Lake 8696 E Lake Rd	Erie	PA	16511	**888-558-8439**	814-899-6948	379
Lakeview Publishing of Elbow Lake Inc 35 Central Ave N	Elbow Lake	MN	56531	**877-852-2796**	218-685-5326	531-3
Lakeville Area Chamber of Commerce & Convention & Visitors Bureau 19950 Dodd Blvd Ste 101	Lakeville	MN	55044	**888-525-3845**	952-469-2020	138
Lakeville Journal Co LLC 33 Bissell St PO Box 1688	Lakeville	CT	06039	**800-553-2234**	860-435-9873	634-8
Lakewold Gardens 12317 Gravelly Lk Dr SW	Lakewood	WA	98499	**888-858-4106**	253-584-4106	96
Lakewood Health System 49725 County 83	Staples	MN	56479	**800-525-1033**	218-894-1515	363
Lakewood Hospital 14519 Detroit Ave	Lakewood	OH	44107	**866-588-2264**	216-521-4200	374-3
Lakewood Manor 1900 Lauderdale Dr	Richmond	VA	23238	**866-521-9100**	804-740-2900	670
Lakewood Shores Resort 7751 Cedar Lake Rd	Oscoda	MI	48750	**800-882-2493**	989-739-2073	667
Lakin Tire West Inc 15305 Spring Ave	Santa Fe Springs	CA	90670	**800-488-2752**	562-802-2752	753
LallyPak Inc 1209 Central Ave	Hillside	NJ	07205	**800-523-8484**	908-351-4141	547
Lam Research Corp 4650 Cushing Pkwy *NASDAQ: LRCX*	Fremont	CA	94538	**800-526-7678**	510-572-0200	693
Lamar Adv Co 5321 Corporate Blvd *NASDAQ: LAMR*	Baton Rouge	LA	70808	**800-235-2627**	225-926-1000	8
Lamar Community College 2401 S Main St	Lamar	CO	81052	**800-968-6920**	719-336-2248	161

Name	Address	City	State	Zip	Toll-Free	Phone	Class
Lamar County Chamber of Commerce	1125 Bonham St	Paris	TX	75460	800-727-4789	903-784-2501	138
Lamar County Electric Co-op Assn	1485 N Main St	Paris	TX	75460	800-252-8080	903-784-4303	247
Lamar State College *Port Arthur*	PO Box 310	Port Arthur	TX	77641	800-477-5872	409-983-4921	161
Lamartek Inc	175 NW Washington St *Orders	Lake City	FL	32055	800-495-1046*	386-752-1087	708
Lamaze International	2025 M St NW Ste 800	Washington	DC	20036	800-368-4404	202-367-1128	48-8
Lamb County Electric Co-op Inc	2415 S Phelps Ave	Littlefield	TX	79339	800-365-9000	806-385-5191	247
Lambda Legal Defense & Education Fund	120 Wall St Ste 1500	New York	NY	10005	866-542-8336	212-809-8585	47-8
Lambeau Telecom	1807 N Ctr St *Cust Svc	Beaver Dam	WI	53916	800-444-4014*	920-887-3148	733
Lambert Saint Louis International Airport	10701 Lambert International Blvd PO Box 10212	Saint Louis	MO	63145	855-787-2227	314-426-8000	27
Lambuth University	705 Lambuth Blvd	Jackson	TN	38301	800-526-2305	731-427-4725	167
Lamers Bus Lines Inc	2407 S Pt Rd	Green Bay	WI	54313	800-236-1240	920-496-3600	106
Lamesa Independent School District	PO Box 261	Lamesa	TX	79331	888-286-6700	806-872-5461	683
Lamey-Wellehan Inc	940 Turner St	Auburn	ME	04210	800-370-6900	207-784-6595	302
Laminar Consulting Services	424 S Olive St	Orange	CA	92866	888-531-9995		198
Laminate Technologies Inc	161 Maule Rd	Tiffin	OH	44883	800-231-2523		815
Laminated Wood Systems Inc (LWS)	1327 285th Rd PO Box 386	Seward	NE	68434	800-949-3526		815
Lamination Depot Inc	1505 E McFadden Ave	Santa Ana	CA	92705	800-925-0054	714-954-0632	534
Laminations	3010 E Venture Dr	Appleton	WI	54911	800-925-2626	920-831-0596	547
Laminators Inc	3255 Penn St	Hatfield	PA	19440	877-663-4277	215-723-8107	815
Lammes Candies Since 1885 Inc	PO Box 1885	Austin	TX	78767	800-252-1885	512-310-2223	297-8
Lamons Gasket Co	7300 Airport Blvd	Houston	TX	77061	800-231-6906	713-222-0284	327
Lamont Engineers	548 Main St	Cobleskill	NY	12043	800-882-9721	518-234-4028	196
Lamont Ltd	1530 Bluff Rd	Burlington	IA	52601	800-553-5621	319-753-5131	320-2
Lamothe House Hotel	621 Esplanade Ave	New Orleans	LA	70116	800-535-7815		379
LaMotte Co	802 Washington Ave	Chestertown	MD	21620	800-344-3100	410-778-3100	419
Lamplight Farms Inc	W140 N4900 Lilly Rd *Cust Svc	Menomonee Falls	WI	53051	888-473-1088*	262-781-9590	439
Lamson & Goodnow Mfg Co	45 Conway St	Shelburne Falls	MA	01370	800-872-6564	413-625-0201	224
Lamvin Inc	4675 N Ave	Oceanside	CA	92056	800-446-6329	760-806-6400	607
Lancaster Bible College	901 Eden Rd PO Box 83403	Lancaster	PA	17608	800-544-7335	717-569-7071	160
Lancaster City School District	345 E Mulberry St	Lancaster	OH	43130	888-647-4729	740-687-7300	683
Lancaster Colony Commercial Products Inc	3902 Indianola Ave	Columbus	OH	43214	800-292-7260	614-263-2850	301
Lancaster Distributing Co	1310 Union St *General	Spartanburg	SC	29302	800-845-8287*	864-583-3011	549
Lancaster Eagle-Gazette	138 W Chestnut St	Lancaster	OH	43130	877-513-7355	740-654-1321	531-2
Lancaster Host Resort	2300 Lincoln Hwy E *Resv	Lancaster	PA	17602	800-233-0121*	717-299-5500	667
Lancaster Hotel	701 Texas St	Houston	TX	77002	800-231-0336	713-228-9500	379
Lancaster Knives Inc	165 Ct St	Lancaster	NY	14086	800-869-9666	716-683-5050	492
Lancaster New Era	8 W King St PO Box 1328	Lancaster	PA	17603	800-809-4666	717-291-8811	531-2
Lancaster Newspapers Inc	8 W King St PO Box 1328	Lancaster	PA	17603	800-809-4666	717-291-8811	634-8
Lancaster Pump Co	1340 Manheim Pk	Lancaster	PA	17601	800-442-0786	717-397-3521	804
Lancaster Regional Medical Ctr	250 College Ave	Lancaster	PA	17603	877-456-9617	717-291-8211	374-3
Lancaster Theological Seminary	555 W James St	Lancaster	PA	17603	800-393-0654	717-393-0654	168-3
Lancaster Toyota Inc	5270 Manheim Pk	East Petersburg	PA	17520	888-424-1295		56
Lancer Corp	6655 Lancer Blvd	San Antonio	TX	78219	800-729-1500	210-310-7000	662
Lancer Label	301 S 74th St *Cust Svc	Omaha	NE	68114	800-228-7074*		413
Lancer Orthodontics Inc	1493 Poinsettia Bldg 143 *NYSE: LANZ* ■ *Cust Svc	Vista	CA	92081	800-854-2896*	760-744-5585	230
Lancore Technologies	11211 Richmond Ave	Houston	TX	77082	866-492-5800	281-493-5850	179
Land & Legal Solutions Inc	300 S Hamilton Ave	Greensburg	PA	15601	800-245-7900	724-853-8992	180-10
Land Coast Insulation Inc	4017 Second St	New Iberia	LA	70560	800-333-9424	337-367-7741	191-9
Land Line Magazine	1 NW Oodia Dr PO Box 1000	Grain Valley	MO	64029	800-444-5791	816-229-5791	456-21
Land O'Lakes Inc Dairyman's Div	400 S 'M' St	Tulare	CA	93274	800-328-4155	559-687-8287	297-27
Land O'Lakes Inc Western Feed Div	4001 Lexington Ave N	Arden Hills	MN	55126	800-328-9680		446
Land Rover North America Inc	555 MacArthur Blvd	Mahwah	NJ	07430	800-637-6837		58
Landaas & Co	411 E Wisconsin Ave 20th Fl	Milwaukee	WI	53202	800-236-1096	414-223-1099	401
Landair Corp	1110 Myers St	Greeneville	TN	37743	888-526-3247		778
Landajob Advertising & Marketing Talent	222 W Gregory Blvd Ste 304	Kansas City	MO	64114	800-931-8806	816-523-1881	197
Landauer Inc	2 Science Rd *NYSE: LDR*	Glenwood	IL	60425	800-323-8830	708-755-7000	575
Landec Ag LLC	201 N Michigan St	Oxford	IN	47971	800-241-7252	765-385-1000	282
Lander University	320 Stanley Ave *Admissions	Greenwood	SC	29649	800-922-1117*	864-388-8307	167
Landers Ford Inc	2082 W Poplar Ave	Collierville	TN	38017	888-281-5266		56
Landice Inc	111 Canfield Ave	Randolph	NJ	07869	800-526-3423	973-927-9010	475
Landis Gyr Inc	2800 Duncan Rd	Lafayette	IN	47904	888-390-5733	765-742-1001	250
Landiscor	7310 N 16th St Ste 275	Phoenix	AZ	85020	866-221-8578	602-248-8989	725
Landmark Aviation	3501 Aviation Ave *General	Sioux Falls	SD	57104	800-888-1646*	408-286-3832	62
Landmark Community Newspapers Inc	601 Taylorsville Rd	Shelbyville	KY	40065	800-939-9322	502-633-4334	634-8
Landmark Credit Union	5445 S Westridge Dr PO Box 510910	New Berlin	WI	53151	800-801-1449	262-796-4500	221
Landmark Financial Group LLC	181 Old Post Rd	Southport	CT	06890	800-437-4214	203-254-8422	253
Landmark Inn	230 N Front St *General	Marquette	MI	49855	888-752-6362*	906-228-2580	379
Landmark International Trucks Inc	4550 Rutledge Pk	Knoxville	TN	37914	800-968-9999	865-637-4881	778
Landmark Lincoln-Mercury Inc	5000 S Broadway	Englewood	CO	80113	888-318-9692	303-761-1560	56
Landmark Plastic Corp	1331 Kelly Ave	Akron	OH	44306	800-242-1183	330-785-2200	607
Landmark Resort	7643 Hillside Rd	Egg Harbor	WI	54209	800-273-7877	920-868-3205	667
Landmark School	429 Hale St PO Box 227	Prides Crossing	MA	01965	866-333-0859	978-236-3010	621
Landmark Structures LP	1665 Harmon Rd	Fort Worth	TX	76177	800-888-6816	817-439-8888	190-10
Landmark Theaters	2222 S Barrington Ave *Cust Svc	Los Angeles	CA	90064	888-724-6362*	310-473-6701	745
Landmark Tours	1304 University Ave NE Ste 201	Minneapolis	MN	55413	888-231-8735	651-490-5408	758
Landoll Corp	1900 N St *Cust Svc	Marysville	KS	66508	800-446-5175*	785-562-5381	469
Landor Assoc Ltd	1001 Front St	San Francisco	CA	94111	888-252-6367	415-365-1700	197
Landry's Restaurants Inc	1510 W Loop S	Houston	TX	77027	800-552-6379	713-850-1010	668
Lands' End Inc	1 Lands' End Ln *Orders	Dodgeville	WI	53595	800-963-4816*		458
Landsberg Orora	1640 S Greenwood Ave *Cust Svc	Montebello	CA	90640	888-526-3723*	323-832-2000	558
Landscape Concepts Management	31745 Alleghany Rd	Grayslake	IL	60030	866-655-3800	847-223-3800	422
Landscape Structures Inc	601 Seventh St S	Delano	MN	55328	800-328-0035	763-972-3391	346
Landshire Inc	12 Tucker Dr	Caseyville	IL	62232	800-969-2747	618-293-6525	297-34
Landstar Express America Inc	13410 Sutton Pk Dr S	Jacksonville	FL	32224	800-872-9400	904-398-9400	778
Landstar Inway Inc	13410 Sutton Pk Dr S	Jacksonville	FL	61102	800-435-7352	800-872-9400	778
Landstar Logistics Inc	13410 Sutton Pk Dr S	Jacksonville	FL	32224	800-872-9400	904-398-9400	448
Lane Aviation Corp	4389 International Gateway	Columbus	OH	43219	800-848-6263	614-237-3747	62
Lane Bryant Inc	3344 Morse Crossing *Cust Svc	Columbus	OH	43215	866-886-4731*	954-970-2205	156-6
Lane College	545 Ln Ave *Admissions	Jackson	TN	38301	800-960-7533*	731-426-7500	167
Lane Community College	4000 E 30th Ave	Eugene	OR	97405	800-321-2211	541-463-3000	161
	Florence 3149 Oak St	Florence	OR	97439	800-222-3290	541-997-8444	161
Lane Press Inc	87 Meadowland Dr PO Box 130	Burlington	VT	05402	800-733-3740	802-863-5555	626
Lane-Scott Electric Co-op Inc	410 S High	Dighton	KS	67839	800-407-2217	620-397-5327	247
Lang Dental Manufacturing Co	175 Messner Dr	Wheeling	IL	60090	800-222-5264	847-215-6622	230
Langdon Hall Country House Hotel & Spa	1 Langdon Dr	Cambridge	ON	N3H4R8	800-268-1898	519-740-2100	379
Langer Inc	2905 Veterans' Memorial Hwy	Ronkonkoma	NY	11779	800-645-5520		476
Langham Boston, The	250 Franklin St	Boston	MA	02110	800-791-7781	617-451-1900	379
Langley Federal Credit Union	1055 W Mercury Blvd	Hampton	VA	23666	800-826-7490	757-827-7200	221
Langley Porter Psychiatric Institute	401 Parnassus Ave	San Francisco	CA	94143	800-723-7140	415-476-7000	374-5

Name	Address	City	State	Zip	Toll-Free	Phone	Class
Langlois Co	10810 San Sevaine Way	Mira Loma	CA	91752	**800-962-5993**	951-360-3900	297-16
Lang-Mekra North America LLC	101 Tillessen Blvd	Ridgeway	SC	29130	**888-635-7248**	803-337-5264	332
Langston University	2013 Langston University PO Box 1500	Langston	OK	73050	**877-466-2231**		167
Langstons Co	2034 NW Seventh St	Oklahoma City	OK	73106	**800-658-2831**	405-235-9536	231
Language Engineering Co	135 Beaver St Ste 204	Waltham	MA	02452	**888-366-4532**	781-642-8900	180-3
Language Line Services	1 Lower Ragsdale Dr Bldg 2	Monterey	CA	93940	**800-752-6096**		766
Language Services Associates Inc	455 Business Ctr Dr - Ste 100	Horsham	PA	19044	**800-305-9673**		766
Lankenau Medical Ctr	100 E Lancaster Ave	Wynnewood	PA	19096	**866-225-5654**	484-476-2000	374-3
Lankota Inc	270 Wpark Ave	Huron	SD	57350	**866-526-5682**	605-352-4550	56
LANL (Los Alamos National Laboratory)	PO Box 1663	Los Alamos	NM	87545	**877-723-4101**	505-667-7000	666
Lanman Oil Co Inc	PO Box 108	Charleston	IL	61920	**800-677-2819**		578
Lannett Company Inc (LCI)	13200 Townsend Rd *NYSE: LCI*	Philadelphia	PA	19154	**800-325-9994**	215-333-9000	478
Lansco Colors	1 Blue Hill Plaza 11th Fl PO Box 1685	Pearl River	NY	10965	**800-526-2783**	845-507-5942	549
Lansdale School of Business	290 Wissahickon Ave	North Wales	PA	19454	**800-219-0486**	215-699-5700	798
Lansdowne Resort	44050 Woodridge Pkwy	Leesburg	VA	20176	**877-513-8400**	703-729-8400	377
Lansing Bldg Products	8501 Sanford Dr	Richmond	VA	23228	**800-768-5762**	804-266-8771	193-4
Lansing Community College	419 N Washington Sq	Lansing	MI	48933	**800-644-4522**	517-483-1957	161
Lansing State Journal	120 E Lenawee St	Lansing	MI	48919	**800-234-1719**	517-377-1000	531-2
Lansmont Corp	Ryan Ranch Research Pk 17 Mandeville Ct	Monterey	CA	93940	**800-526-7666**	831-655-6600	344
Lantal Textiles Inc	1300 Langenthal Dr PO Box 965	Rural Hall	NC	27045	**800-334-3309**	336-969-9551	742-1
Lantana Communications Corp	1700 Tech Centre Pkwy Ste 100	Arlington	TX	76014	**800-345-4211**		44
Lantech Inc	11000 Bluegrass Pkwy	Louisville	KY	40299	**800-866-0322**	502-815-9109	546
Lantern Lodge Motor Inn	411 N College St	Myerstown	PA	17067	**800-262-5564**	717-866-6536	379
Lantronix Inc	167 Technology Dr *NASDAQ: LTRX* ■ *Orders	Irvine	CA	92618	**800-526-8766***	949-453-3990	732
Lanxess Corp	111 RIDC Pk W Dr	Pittsburgh	PA	15275	**800-526-9377**	412-809-1000	604-3
Lanz Cabinet Shop Inc	3025 W Seventh Pl	Eugene	OR	97402	**800-788-6332**	541-485-4050	361
Lapeer Regional Hospital	1375 N Main St	Lapeer	MI	48446	**888-327-0671**	810-667-5500	374-3
Lapham-Hickey Steel Corp	5500 W 73rd St	Chicago	IL	60638	**800-323-8443**	708-496-6111	491
LaPine State Park	15800 State Recreation Rd	La Pine	OR	97739	**800-551-6949**		564
LaPlaya Resort & Suites	2500 N Atlantic Ave	Daytona Beach	FL	32118	**800-224-5052**	386-672-0990	379
LapLink Software Inc	600 108th Ave NE Ste 610	Bellevue	WA	98004	**800-343-8080**	425-952-6000	180-12
Lapmaster International LLC	501 W Algonquin Rd	Mount Prospect	IL	60056	**877-352-8637**	224-659-7101	490
LaPorte County Convention & Visitors Bureau	4073 S Franklin St	Michigan City	IN	46360	**800-634-2650**	219-872-5055	208
LaPorte Savings Bank, The	710 Indiana Ave	LaPorte	IN	46350	**866-362-7511**	219-362-7511	69
Laramie Area Chamber of Commerce	800 S Third St	Laramie	WY	82070	**866-876-1012**	307-745-7339	138
Laramie County Community College	1400 E College Dr	Cheyenne	WY	82007	**800-522-2993**	307-778-5222	161
Albany County	1125 Boulder Dr	Laramie	WY	82070	**800-522-2993**	307-721-5138	161
Laramie River Dude Ranch	25777 County Rd 103	Jelm	WY	82063	**800-551-5731**	970-435-5716	241
Larchmont Engineering & Irrigation Co	11 Larchmont Ln PO Box 66	Lexington	MA	02420	**877-862-2550**	781-862-2550	276
Larco	210 NE Tenth Ave *Cust Svc	Brainerd	MN	56401	**800-523-6996***	218-829-9797	255
Lard Oil Company Inc	914 Florida Blvd SW	Denham Springs	LA	70726	**800-738-7738**	225-664-3311	578
Laredo Morning Times	111 Esperanza Dr	Laredo	TX	78041	**800-232-7907**	956-728-2500	531-2
Laredo-Webb County Chamber of Commerce	2310 San Bernardo Ave	Laredo	TX	78042	**800-292-2122**	956-722-9895	138
Larkin Enterprises Inc	317 W Broadway PO Box 405	Lincoln	ME	04457	**800-990-5418**	207-794-8700	190
Larksfield Place	7373 E 29th St N	Wichita	KS	67226	**866-232-8484**	316-858-3910	670
LARL (Lake Agassiz Regional Library)	118 Fifth St S PO Box 900	Moorhead	MN	56560	**800-247-0449**	218-233-3757	434-3
LARON Inc	4255 Santa Fe Dr	Kingman	AZ	86401	**800-248-3430**	928-757-8424	258
Larsen Farms	2650 N 2375 E *Sales	Hamer	ID	83425	**800-767-6104***	208-662-5501	297-18
Larson Contracting Inc	508 West Main St	Lake Mills	IA	50450	**800-765-1426**	641-592-5800	191-3
Larson Design Group Inc	1000 Commerce Pk Dr Ste 201 PO Box 487	Williamsport	PA	17701	**877-323-6603**	570-323-6603	263
Larson King LLP	30 E Seventh St Ste 2800	Saint Paul	MN	55101	**877-373-5501**	651-312-6500	428
Larson Manufacturing Co	2333 Eastbrook Dr *Cust Svc	Brookings	SD	57006	**888-483-3768***	605-692-6115	237
Larson-Juhl	3900 Steve Reynolds Blvd	Norcross	GA	30093	**800-221-4123**		310
Larue Coffee	2631 S 156th Cir	Omaha	NE	68130	**800-658-4498**	402-333-9099	298-8
Las Cruces Convention & Visitors Bureau	211 N Water St	Las Cruces	NM	88001	**800-429-9488**	575-541-2444	208
Las Cruces Public Schools	505 S Main St Ste 249	Las Cruces	NM	88001	**888-222-1498**	575-527-5800	683
Las Cruces Sun-News	256 W Las Cruces Ave	Las Cruces	NM	88005	**877-827-7200**	575-541-5400	531-2
LAS Enterprises Inc	2413 L & A Rd	Metairie	LA	70001	**800-264-1527**	504-887-1515	189
Las Vegas Chamber of Commerce	575 Symphony Park Ave Ste 100	Las Vegas	NV	89105	**888-635-7272**	702-641-5822	138
Las Vegas Convention & Visitors Authority	3150 Paradise Rd	Las Vegas	NV	89109	**877-847-4858**	702-892-0711	208
Las Vegas Motor Speedway	7000 Las Vegas Blvd N	Las Vegas	NV	89115	**800-644-4444**	702-644-4444	514
LaSalle County	707 E Etna Rd	Ottawa	IL	61350	**800-247-5243**	815-433-3366	338
LaSalle Grill	115 W Colfax Ave	South Bend	IN	46601	**800-382-9323**	574-288-1155	669
LASCCO (Los Angeles Smoking & Curing Co)	1100 W Ewing St	Seattle	WA	98119	**800-365-8950**	206-285-6800	297-13
Lasco Fittings Inc	414 Morgan St PO Box 116	Brownsville	TN	38012	**800-776-2756**	731-772-3180	595
Lasell College	1844 Commonwealth Ave *Admissions	Newton	MA	02466	**888-527-3554***	617-243-2225	167
Laser Excel	N6323 Berlin Rd PO Box 279	Green Lake	WI	54941	**800-285-6544**	920-294-6544	453
Laser Image Inc	2451 N Stemmons Fwy	Dallas	TX	75207	**866-812-3491**		626
Laser Institute of America (LIA)	13501 Ingenuity Dr Ste 128	Orlando	FL	32826	**800-345-2737**	407-380-1553	48-19
Laser Pros International	1 International Ln	Rhinelander	WI	54501	**888-558-5277**	715-369-5995	176
Laser Technology Inc	7070 S Tucson Way	Englewood	CO	80112	**800-280-6113**	303-649-1000	494
LaserMax Corp	3495 Winton Pl	Rochester	NY	14623	**800-527-3703**	585-272-5420	543
Laserscope	3070 Orchard Dr	San Jose	CA	95134	**800-878-3399**	408-943-0636	424
LaserVue Eye Ctr	3540 Mendocino Ave Ste 200	Santa Rosa	CA	95403	**888-527-3745**	707-522-6200	796
Lashbrook Designs	131 E 13065 S	Draper	UT	84020	**888-252-7388**		411
Lasko Metal Products Inc	820 Lincoln Ave	West Chester	PA	19380	**800-233-0268**	610-692-7400	36
LasscoWizer Inc	485 Hague St	Rochester	NY	14606	**800-854-6595**	585-436-1934	628
Lassen County Chamber of Commerce	75 N Weatherlow St	Susanville	CA	96130	**877-686-7878**	530-257-4323	138
Lassonde Pappas	1 Colons Dr Ste 200	Carneys Point	NJ	08069	**800-257-7019**	856-455-1000	297-20
LassoSoft LLC	PO Box 33	Manchester	WA	98353	**888-286-7753**	954-302-3526	180-7
Lasting Impressions Inc	7406 43rd Ave NE	Marysville	WA	98270	**866-859-7625**	360-659-1255	626
LastMinuteTravel.com Inc	220 E Central Pkwy Ste 4000	Altamonte Springs	FL	32701	**800-442-0568**	407-667-8700	771
Lasvegastickets.com	5030 Paradise Rd Ste B108	Las Vegas	NV	89119	**800-597-7469**	702-597-1588	376
Latah Creek Winery	13030 E Indiana Ave	Spokane	WA	99216	**800-528-2427**	509-926-0164	49-6
Latham Hotel, The	135 S 17th St	Philadelphia	PA	19103	**877-528-4261**	215-563-7474	379
Latham Seed Co	131 180th St	Alexander	IA	50420	**877-465-2842**	641-692-3258	692
Lathem Time Corp	200 Selig Dr SW	Atlanta	GA	30336	**800-241-4990**	404-691-0400	110
Laticrete International Inc	91 Amity Rd	Bethany	CT	06524	**800-243-4788**	203-393-0010	3
Latigo Ranch	PO Box 237	Kremmling	CO	80459	**800-227-9655**	970-724-9008	241
Latin Business Assn (LBA)	120 S San Pedro St Ste 530	Los Angeles	CA	90012	**866-924-9757**	213-628-8510	48-12
Latina Media Ventures LLC	625 Madison Ave 3rd Fl	New York	NY	10022	**888-489-7753**	212-642-0200	456-11
Latitude Consulting Group Inc	100 E Michigan Ave Ste 200	Saline	MI	48176	**888-577-2797**		462
Latrobe Specialty Steel Co	2626 Ligonier St	Latrobe	PA	15650	**888-245-7856**	724-537-7711	491
Latta's School Supply	1502 Fourth Ave	Huntington	WV	25701	**800-624-3501**	304-523-8400	534
Latter Day Saints Business College	95 North 300 West	Salt Lake City	UT	84101	**800-999-5767**	801-524-8100	798
Lattice Inc	1751 S Naperville Rd Ste 100 *Sales	Wheaton	IL	60189	**800-444-4309***	630-949-3250	180-12
Lattice Semiconductor Corp	5555 NE Moore Ct *NASDAQ: LSCC*	Hillsboro	OR	97124	**800-528-8423**	503-268-8000	694
Laughing Elephant	3645 Interlake Ave N	Seattle	WA	98103	**800-354-0400**		129
Laughlin Air Force Base	561 Liberty Dr Ste 3	Laughlin AFB	TX	78843	**866-966-1020**	830-298-5988	496-1
Laughlin Memorial Hospital	1420 Tuscolum Blvd	Greeneville	TN	37745	**800-852-7157**	423-787-5000	374-3
Laughlin/Constable Inc	207 E Michigan St	Milwaukee	WI	53202	**800-432-8747**	414-272-2400	4

Name / Address	City	State	Zip	Toll-Free	Phone	Class
LaughStub LLC 2038 Armacost Ave	Los Angeles	CA	90025	**800-927-0939**		387
Launch Agency LP 4100 Midway Rd Ste 2110	Carrollton	TX	75007	**866-427-5013**	972-818-4100	4
Launch Pad 18130 Jorene Rd	Odessa	FL	33556	**888-920-3450**		181
Laura Ingalls Wilder Museum & Home 3068 Hwy A	Mansfield	MO	65704	**877-924-7126**		519
Laureate Education Inc 650 S Exeter St	Baltimore	MD	21202	**866-452-8732**	410-843-6100	244
Laurel Grocery Co Inc 129 Barbourville Rd	London	KY	40744	**800-467-6601**		298-8
Laurel Highlands Visitors Bureau 120 E Main St	Ligonier	PA	15658	**800-333-5661**	724-238-5661	208
Laurel Ink 911 N 145th St *Cust Svc	Seattle	WA	98133	**800-850-0081***		129
Laurel Inn 444 Presidio Ave	San Francisco	CA	94115	**800-552-8735**	415-346-7431	379
Laurel Lake Retirement Community 200 Laurel Lk Dr	Hudson	OH	44236	**866-650-2100**		670
Laurel Park Rt 198 & Racetrack Rd PO Box 130	Laurel	MD	20724	**800-638-1859**	301-725-0400	639
Laurel University 1215 Eastchester Dr	High Point	NC	27265	**855-528-7358**	336-887-3000	160
Laurelville Mennonite Church Ctr 941 Laurelville Ln	Mount Pleasant	PA	15666	**800-839-1021**	724-423-2056	671
Lauren Engineers & Constructors Inc 901 S First St	Abilene	TX	79602	**800-433-7300**	325-670-9660	263
Lauren Mfg 2228 Reiser Ave SE	New Philadelphia	OH	44663	**800-683-0676**	330-339-3373	675
Laurens County Chamber of Commerce 291 Professional Pk Rd	Clinton	SC	29325	**866-548-9674**	864-833-2716	138
Laurens Electric Co-op Inc 2254 S Carolina 14	Laurens	SC	29360	**800-942-3141**		247
Laurent Clerc National Deaf Education Ctr 800 Florida Ave NE	Washington	DC	20002	**866-637-0102**	202-651-5050	47-17
Laurentian Bank of Canada 1981 McGill College Ave *TSE: LB*	Montreal	QC	H3A3K3	**800-252-1846**	514-284-4500	69
Laurentian Bank Securities Inc 1981 McGill College Ave Ste 100	Montreal	QC	H3A3K3	**888-350-8577**	514-350-2800	401
Laurentian University 935 Ramsey Lake Rd	Sudbury	ON	P3E2C6	**800-461-4030**	705-675-1151	783
Laurie Raphael 117 Dalhousie St	Quebec	QC	G1K9C8	**877-876-4555**	418-692-4555	669
Laurin Publishing Co Inc 100 West St	Pittsfield	MA	01202	**877-422-7300**	413-499-0514	634-9
LAUSD (Los Angeles Unified School District) 333 S Beaudry Ave	Los Angeles	CA	90017	**877-772-6273**	213-241-1000	683
Lauterbach Group Inc W222 N5710 Miller Way *Sales	Sussex	WI	53089	**800-841-7301***	262-820-8130	553
Lava Beds National Monument 1 Indian Well Headquarters	Tulelake	CA	96134	**866-705-5711**	530-260-0537	563
Lava Hot Springs State Foundation 430 E Main St PO Box 669	Lava Hot Springs	ID	83246	**800-423-8597**	208-776-5221	49-4
Laval University 2325 Rue University	Quebec	QC	G1V0A6	**877-785-2825**	418-656-2131	783
Lavanture Products Co 22825 Gallatin Way	Elkhart	IN	46514	**800-348-7625**	574-264-0658	599
Lavelle Industries Inc 665 McHenry St	Burlington	WI	53105	**800-528-3553**	262-763-2434	675
LaVezzi Precision Inc 999 Regency Dr	Glendale Heights	IL	60139	**800-323-1772**	630-582-1230	453
Law Enforcement Assoc Corp (LEA) 120 Penmarc Dr Ste 125 *OTC: LAWEQ*	Raleigh	NC	27616	**800-354-9669**	919-872-6210	51
Law Enforcement Technology Magazine 1233 Janesville Ave	Fort Atkinson	WI	53538	**800-547-7377**		456-5
Law Engine 7660-H Fay Avenue Ste 342	La Jolla	CA	92037	**800-894-2889**	858-456-1234	397
Law Officer's Bulletin 610 Opperman Dr	Eagan	MN	55123	**800-344-5008**	651-687-7000	530-2
Law Technology News 120 Broadway 5th Fl *Cust Svc	New York	NY	10271	**800-888-8300***	212-457-7905	456-7
Lawgical Inc 11693 San Vicente Blvd Ste 910	Los Angeles	CA	90049	**800-811-4458**		197
Lawler Foods Ltd Inc PO Box 2558	Humble	TX	77347	**800-541-8285**	281-446-0059	297-1
Lawley Service Insurance 361 Delaware Ave *Cust Svc	Buffalo	NY	14202	**800-860-5741***	716-849-8618	390
Lawn Dawg Inc 39 Simon St., Unit 14	Nashua	NH	03060	**888-993-3294**		774
Lawn Doctor Inc 142 SR 34	Holmdel	NJ	07733	**800-845-0580**	800-631-5660	576
Lawn Equipment Parts Co 1475 River Rd	Marietta	PA	17547	**800-365-3726**	717-426-5200	429
Lawrence Academy Powderhouse Rd PO Box 992	Groton	MA	01450	**800-977-4698**	978-448-6535	621
Lawrence Behr Assoc Inc 3400 Tupper Dr	Greenville	NC	27834	**800-522-4464**	252-757-0279	198
Lawrence Companies (LTS) 872 Lee Hwy PO Box 7667	Roanoke	VA	24019	**800-336-9626**	540-966-4000	778
Lawrence County County Courthouse 430 Court St	New Castle	PA	16101	**855-564-6116**	724-658-2541	338
Lawrence County Tennessee Chamber of Commerce 25B Public Sqr PO Box 86	Lawrenceburg	TN	38464	**877-388-4911**	931-762-4911	138
Lawrence County Tourist Promotion Agency 229 S Jefferson St	New Castle	PA	16101	**888-284-7599**	724-654-8408	208
Lawrence Daily Journal-World Co 609 New Hampshire St PO Box 888	Lawrence	KS	66044	**800-578-8748**	785-843-1000	634-8
Lawrence Equipment Inc 2034 Peck Rd	El Monte	CA	91733	**800-423-4500**	626-442-2894	299
Lawrence Hall Chevrolet Inc 1385 S Danville Dr	Abilene	TX	79605	**800-568-7158**	325-695-8800	56
Lawrence Memorial Hospital (LMH) 325 Maine St	Lawrence	KS	66044	**800-749-4144**	785-505-5000	374-3
Lawrence Paper Co 2801 Lakeview Rd	Lawrence	KS	66049	**800-535-4553**	785-843-8111	99
Lawrence Public Library 707 Vermont St	Lawrence	KS	66044	**888-657-7323**	785-843-3833	434-3
Lawrence Public Schools 110 McDonald Dr	Lawrence	KS	66044	**800-772-1213**	785-832-5000	683
Lawrence Ragan Communications Inc 111 E Wacker Dr Ste 500	Chicago	IL	60601	**800-878-5331**	800-493-4867	634-9
Lawrence Technological University 21000 W 10-Mile Rd	Southfield	MI	48075	**800-225-5588**	248-204-3160	167
Lawrence University 115 S Drew St	Appleton	WI	54911	**800-432-5427**	920-832-7000	167
Lawrence University Mudd Library 711 E Boldt Way	Appleton	WI	54911	**800-432-5427**	920-832-6750	434-6
Lawrenceville School 2500 Main St PO Box 6008	Lawrenceville	NJ	08648	**800-735-2030**	609-896-0400	621
Lawry's Restaurants Inc 234 E Colorado Blvd Ste 500	Pasadena	CA	91101	**888-552-9797**	626-440-5234	668
Lawry's the Prime Rib 100 N La Cienega Blvd	Beverly Hills	CA	90211	**877-529-7984**	310-652-2827	669
Lawson State Community College *Bessemer* 1100 Ninth Ave SW	Bessemer	AL	35022	**800-373-4879**	205-925-2515	798
Lawton & Cates SC 10 E Doty St Ste 400	Madison	WI	53703	**800-900-4539**	608-282-6200	428
Lawton Industries Inc 4353 Pacific St	Rocklin	CA	95677	**800-692-2600**	916-624-7895	386
Lawton Public Library 110 SW Fourth St	Lawton	OK	73501	**855-895-8064**	580-581-3450	434-3
Lawton's Drug Stores Ltd 236 Brownlow Ave Ste 270	Dartmouth	NS	B3B1V5	**866-990-1599**	902-468-1000	233
Lawyers Diary & Manual 890 Mtn Ave Ste 300	New Providence	NJ	07974	**800-444-4041**	973-642-1440	634-2
Lawyers Weekly Inc 10 Milk St Ste 1000	Boston	MA	02108	**800-444-5297**	617-451-7300	531-3
Lawyers' Committee for Civil Rights Under Law 1401 New York Ave NW Ste 400	Washington	DC	20005	**888-299-5227**	202-662-8600	48-10
Lawyers' Travel Service 71 Fifth Ave *General	New York	NY	10003	**800-431-1112***		769
Lawyers.com Martindale-Hubbell 121 Chanlon Rd	New Providence	NJ	07974	**800-526-4902**	908-464-6800	173
Layer 3 Communications LLC 1555 Oakbrook Dr Ste 100	Norcross	GA	30093	**866-535-3924**	770-225-5300	254
Layne 4520 N State Rd 37 *All	Orleans	IN	47452	**855-529-6301***	812-865-3232	190-10
Layton Manufacturing Corp 825 Remsen Ave	Brooklyn	NY	11236	**800-545-8002**	718-498-6000	14
Lazard 30 Rockefeller Plz *NYSE: LAZ*	New York	NY	10112	**866-867-4070**	212-632-6000	688
Lazard Funds 30 Rockefeller Plz 57th Fl	New York	NY	10112	**800-823-6300**		527
La-Z-Boy Inc 1284 N Telegraph Rd *NYSE: LZB*	Monroe	MI	48162	**800-375-6890**	734-242-1444	320-2
Lazer Grant Inc 309 Mcdermot Ave	Winnipeg	MB	R3A1T3	**800-220-0005**	204-942-0300	2
Lazy L & B Ranch 1072 E Fork Rd *Cust Svc	Dubois	WY	82513	**800-453-9488***	307-455-2839	241
Lazzari Fuel Company LLC 11 Industrial Way	Brisbane	CA	94005	**800-242-7265**	415-467-2970	317
LB Foster Co 415 Holiday Dr *NASDAQ: FSTR*	Pittsburgh	PA	15220	**800-255-4500**		648
LB Furniture Industries LLC 99 S Third St	Hudson	NY	12534	**800-221-8752**	518-828-1501	320-3
L&B Transport LLC 708 US190 PO Box 74870	Port Allen	LA	70767	**800-545-9401**	225-387-0894	448
LB White Company Inc W 6636 LB White Rd	Onalaska	WI	54650	**800-345-7200**	608-783-5691	357
LBA (Latin Business Assn) 120 S San Pedro St Ste 530	Los Angeles	CA	90012	**866-924-9757**	213-628-8510	48-12
LBA Group Inc 3400 Tupper Dr	Greenville	NC	27834	**800-522-4464**	252-757-0279	263
LBCH (Louisiana Baptist Children's Home Inc) 7200 DeSiard St	Monroe	LA	71203	**877-345-7411**	318-343-2244	47-15
LBI Eyewear 20801 Nordhoff St *Cust Svc	Chatsworth	CA	91311	**800-423-5175***	818-407-1890	541
LBJ Library & Museum 2313 Red River St	Austin	TX	78705	**800-874-6451**	512-721-0216	434-2
LBS (Library Binding Service) 1801 Thompson Ave	Des Moines	IA	50316	**800-247-5323**	515-262-3191	91
LBT Inc 11502 "I" St	Omaha	NE	68137	**888-528-7278**	402-333-4900	777
LC King Mfg Company Inc 24 Seventh St	Bristol	TN	37620	**800-826-2510**	423-764-5188	154-18
LCA-Vision Inc 7840 Montgomery Rd *NASDAQ: LCAV*	Cincinnati	OH	45236	**800-688-4550**	513-792-9292	796
LCCR (Leadership Conference on Civil Rights) 1629 K St NW Ste 1000	Washington	DC	20006	**888-460-0813**	202-466-3311	47-8
LCD Lighting Inc 37 Robinson Blvd	Orange	CT	06477	**800-826-9465**	203-795-1520	437
LCH Paper Tube & Core Co 11930 Larc Industrial Blvd	Burnsville	MN	55337	**800-472-3477**	952-358-3587	124
LCI (Lannett Company Inc) 13200 Townsend Rd *NYSE: LCI*	Philadelphia	PA	19154	**800-325-9994**	215-333-9000	478

	City	State	Zip	Toll-Free	Phone	Class
LCMS (Lutheran Church Missouri Synod)						
1333 S Kirkwood Rd	Saint Louis	MO	63122	**888-843-5267**	314-965-9000	47-20
LCNB National Bank						
3209 W Galbraith Rd	Cincinnati	OH	45239	**800-344-2265**	513-932-1414	69
LCPS (Lenoir County Public School)						
2017 W Vernon Ave PO Box 729	Kinston	NC	28504	**888-684-8404**	252-527-1109	683
LCS Technologies Inc						
11230 Gold Express Dr Ste 310-140	Gold River	CA	95670	**855-277-5527**		623
LDA (Learning Disabilities Assn of America)						
4156 Library Rd	Pittsburgh	PA	15234	**888-300-6710**	412-341-1515	47-17
LDP Inc						
75 Kiwanis Blvd PO Box O	West Hazleton	PA	18201	**800-522-8413**		180-3
LDR Industries Inc						
600 N Kilbourn Ave	Chicago	IL	60624	**800-545-5230**	773-265-3000	608
LDS Hospital						
8th Ave & C St	Salt Lake City	UT	84143	**888-301-3880**	801-408-1100	374-3
Le Chamois						
4557 Blackcomb Way	Whistler	BC	V0N1B4	**866-944-7853**	604-932-8700	379
Le Cirque						
3600 Las Vegas Blvd S	Las Vegas	NV	89109	**888-987-6667**	702-693-7111	669
Le Cordon Bleu College of Culinary Arts						
Atlanta 1927 Lakeside Pkwy	Tucker	GA	30084	**888-549-8222**	770-938-4711	162
Las Vegas 1451 Ctr Crossing Rd	Las Vegas	NV	89144	**888-551-8222**	702-365-7690	162
Le Creuset of America Inc						
114 Bob Gifford Blvd	Early Branch	SC	29916	**877-418-5547**	803-943-4308	485
Le Devoir						
2050 Bleury St 9th Fl	Montreal	QC	H3A3M9	**800-463-7559**	514-985-3333	531-1
LE Johnson Products Inc						
2100 Sterling Ave	Elkhart	IN	46516	**800-837-5664**	574-293-5664	350
Le Mars Insurance Co						
PO Box 1608	Le Mars	IA	51031	**800-545-6480**		390
Le Meridian						
20 Sidney St	Cambridge	MA	02139	**800-543-4300**	617-577-0200	379
Le Meridien Chambers Minneapolis						
901 Hennepin Ave *General	Minneapolis	MN	55403	**877-782-0116***	612-767-6900	379
Le M,ridien Dallas, The Stoneleigh						
2927 Maple Ave	Dallas	TX	75201	**888-625-4988**	214-871-7111	379
Le Merigot - A JW Marriott Beach Hotel & Spa						
1740 Ocean Ave	Santa Monica	CA	90401	**888-539-7899**	310-395-9700	379
Le Montrose Suite Hotel						
900 Hammond St	West Hollywood	CA	90069	**800-776-0666**	310-855-1115	379
Le Moyne College						
1419 Salt Springs Rd *Admissions	Syracuse	NY	13214	**800-333-4733***	315-445-4100	167
Le Nouvel Montreal Hotel & Spa						
1740 Rene-Levesque Blvd W	Montreal	QC	H3H1R3	**800-363-6063**	514-931-8841	379
Le Parc Suite Hotel						
733 NW Knoll Dr *Resv	West Hollywood	CA	90069	**800-578-4837***	877-591-9556	379
Le Port-Royal Hotel & Suites						
144 St Pierre St	Quebec	QC	G1K8N8	**866-417-2777**	418-692-2777	379
Le Richelieu Hotel						
1234 Chartres St	New Orleans	LA	70116	**800-535-9653**	504-529-2492	379
Le Saint Sulpice						
414 Rue St Sulpice *General	Montreal	QC	H2Y2V5	**877-785-7423***	514-288-1000	379
Le Smith Co						
1030 E Wilson St PO Box 766	Bryan	OH	43506	**888-537-6484**	419-636-4555	350
Le Sueur Cheese Company Inc						
719 N Main St	Le Sueur	MN	56058	**800-247-0871**	507-665-3353	297-5
LEA (Law Enforcement Assoc Corp)						
120 Penmarc Dr Ste 125 *OTC: LAWEQ*	Raleigh	NC	27616	**800-354-9669**	919-872-6210	51
Lea Regional Medical Ctr						
5419 N Lovington Hwy	Hobbs	NM	88240	**877-492-8001**	575-492-5000	374-3
Leach International Corp						
6900 Orangethorpe Ave	Buena Park	CA	90622	**800-232-7700**	714-736-7598	205
Leaders LLC						
2 Portland Fish Pier Ste 214	Portland	ME	04101	**888-583-7770**		688
Leadership Conference on Civil Rights (LCCR)						
1629 K St NW Ste 1000	Washington	DC	20006	**888-460-0813**	202-466-3311	47-8
Leadership Directories Inc						
104 Fifth Ave 3rd Fl	New York	NY	10011	**800-627-0311**	212-627-4140	634-2
Leadership Journal						
465 Gundersen Dr	Carol Stream	IL	60188	**800-777-3136**	630-260-6200	456-5
Leadership Management Inc						
4567 Lk Shore Dr	Waco	TX	76710	**800-568-1241**	254-776-2060	763
Leadership Performance Sustainability Laboratories						
4647 Hugh Howell Rd	Tucker	GA	30084	**800-241-8334**		540
Leader-Telegram						
701 S Farwell St	Eau Claire	WI	54701	**800-236-8808**	715-833-9200	531-2
Leading Age						
2519 Connecticut Ave NW	Washington	DC	20008	**866-702-3278**	202-783-2242	47-6
Leading Authorities Inc						
1990 M St Ste 800	Washington	DC	20036	**800-773-2537**	202-783-0300	706
Leading Hotels of the World						
485 Lexington Ave Ste 401	New York	NY	10017	**800-745-8883**	212-515-5600	376
Leading Lady						
24050 Commerce Pk *Cust Svc	Beachwood	OH	44122	**800-321-4804***	216-464-5490	154-17
Leadman Electronic USA Inc						
382 Laurelwood Dr	Santa Clara	CA	95054	**877-532-3626**	408-738-1751	176
LeadRival						
1207 S White Chapel Blvd Ste 250	Southlake	TX	76092	**800-332-8017**		5
League to Save Lake Tahoe						
2608 Lake Tahoe Blvd	South Lake Tahoe	CA	96150	**888-844-9904**	530-541-5388	47-13
Leahi Hospital						
3675 Kilauea Ave	Honolulu	HI	96816	**800-845-6733**	808-733-8000	374-7
Leaktite Corp						
40 Francis St	Leominster	MA	01453	**800-392-0039**	978-537-8000	607
Leam Drilling Systems Inc						
2027a Airport Rd	Conroe	TX	77301	**800-426-5349**		538
Leamington District Chamber of Commerce						
318 Erie St S	Leamington	ON	N8H3C5	**800-393-3769**	519-326-2721	137
Leanin' Tree Museum of Western Art						
6055 Longbow Dr	Boulder	CO	80301	**800-525-0656**	303-530-1442	519
LeanLogistics Inc						
1351 S Waverly Rd	Holland	MI	49423	**866-584-7280**	616-738-6400	312
Leap/Carpenter/Kemps Insurance Agency						
3187 Collins Dr	Merced	CA	95348	**800-221-0864**	209-384-0727	390
LeapFrog Enterprises Inc						
6401 Hollis St Ste 100 *NYSE: LF*	Emeryville	CA	94608	**800-701-5327**	510-420-5000	760
Lear Capital Inc						
1990 S Bundy Dr Ste 600	Los Angeles	CA	90025	**800-576-9355**		253
Learning Care Group Inc						
21333 Haggerty Rd Ste 300	Novi	MI	48375	**877-817-3883**	248-697-9000	147
Learning Communications LLC						
5520 Trabuco Rd	Irvine	CA	92620	**800-622-3610**		512
Learning Disabilities Assn of America (LDA)						
4156 Library Rd	Pittsburgh	PA	15234	**888-300-6710**	412-341-1515	47-17
Learning Enhancement Corp						
200 S Wacker Dr Ste 3100	Chicago	IL	60606	**877-272-4610**	312-455-1758	227
Learning Express Inc						
29 Buena Vista St	Devens	MA	01434	**888-725-8697**	978-889-1000	759
Learning Research & Development Ctr (LRDC)						
University of Pittsburgh 3939 O'Hara St	Pittsburgh	PA	15260	**800-397-0071**	412-624-7020	666
Learning Resources						
380 N Fairway Dr	Vernon Hills	IL	60061	**800-222-3909**	847-573-8400	245
Learning Tree International Inc						
1831 Michael Faraday Dr *OTC: LTRE* ■ *Cust Svc	Reston	VA	20190	**800-843-8733***	703-709-9119	762
Learning Unlimited						
5810 E Skelly Dr Ste 500	Tulsa	OK	74135	**888-622-4203**	918-622-3292	462
Learning Wrap-Ups Inc						
1660 W Gordon Ave Ste 4	Layton	UT	84041	**800-992-4966**	801-497-0050	245
Lease Equity Appreciation Fund I LP						
110 S Poplar St Ste 101	Wilmington	DE	19801	**800-819-5556**		23
Lease Plan USA						
1165 Sanctuary Pkwy	Alpharetta	GA	30004	**800-457-8721**	770-933-9090	291
Leasing Assoc Inc						
12600 N Featherwood Dr Ste 400	Houston	TX	77034	**800-449-4807**	832-300-1300	291
Leather Industries of America (LIA)						
3050 K St NW Ste 400	Washington	DC	20007	**800-635-0617**	202-342-8497	48-4
Leathercraft						
PO Box 639	Conover	NC	28613	**800-627-1561**		320-2
Leatherman Tool Group Inc						
12106 NE Ainsworth Cir	Portland	OR	97220	**800-847-8665**	503-253-7826	756
Leatherock International Inc						
5285 Lovelock St	San Diego	CA	92110	**800-466-6667**	619-299-7625	432
Leatherup Com						
955 Venice Blvd	Los Angeles	CA	90015	**800-846-6010**	213-763-6185	227
Leave No Trace Ctr for Outdoor Ethics Inc						
1830 17th St	Boulder	CO	80302	**800-332-4100**	303-442-8222	47-23
Leavenworth County						
300 Walnut St	Leavenworth	KS	66048	**855-893-9533**	913-684-0421	338
Leavenworth-Jefferson Electric Co-op Inc						
507 N Union St	McLouth	KS	66054	**888-796-6111**		247
leavitt group Enterprises						
216 S 200 W	Cedar City	UT	84720	**800-264-8085**	435-586-6553	390
Leavitt Machinery & Rentals Inc						
24389 Fraser Hwy	Langley	BC	V2Z2L3	**877-850-6499**	604-607-4450	358
Leavitt Tube						
1717 W 115th St	Chicago	IL	60643	**800-532-8488**	773-239-7700	489
Lebanon Area Chamber of Commerce						
186 N Adams St	Lebanon	MO	65536	**888-588-5710**	417-588-3256	138
Lebanon Daily News						
718 Poplar St	Lebanon	PA	17042	**800-457-5929**	717-272-5611	531-2
Lebanon Seaboard Corp						
1600 E Cumberland St	Lebanon	PA	17042	**800-233-0628**	717-273-1685	282
Lebanon Valley College						
101 N College Ave	Annville	PA	17003	**866-582-4236**	717-867-6181	167
Lebenthal Wealth Advisors						
230 Park Ave Fl 32	New York	NY	10169	**877-425-6006**	212-425-6006	688
LEC (Lincoln Electric Co-op Inc)						
500 Osloski Rd PO Box 628	Eureka	MT	59917	**800-442-2994**	406-889-3301	247
Lechler Inc						
445 Kautz Rd *Cust Svc	Saint Charles	IL	60174	**800-777-2926***	630-377-6611	486
Leco Corp						
3000 Lakeview Ave	Saint Joseph	MI	49085	**800-292-6141**	269-985-5496	419
Leconte Wealth Management LLC						
703 William Blount Dr	Maryville	TN	37801	**888-236-6630**	865-379-8200	401
LeCroy Corp						
700 Chestnut Ridge Rd *NASDAQ: LCRY*	Chestnut Ridge	NY	10977	**800-553-2769**	845-425-2000	250
Lectrosonics Inc						
PO Box 15900	Rio Rancho	NM	87174	**800-821-1121**	505-892-4501	51
LED Supply Co						
747 Sheridan Blvd Unit 8E	Lakewood	CO	80214	**877-595-4769**		198
Ledalite Architectural Products						
19750-92A Ave	Langley	BC	V1M3B2	**800-665-5332**	604-888-6811	439
Ledger, The						
300 W Lime St	Lakeland	FL	33815	**888-431-7323**	863-802-7000	531-2
Ledtronics Inc						
23105 Kashiwa Ct	Torrance	CA	90505	**800-579-4875**	310-534-1505	437
Ledwell & Son Enterprises						
3300 Waco St	Texarkana	TX	75501	**888-533-9355**	903-838-6531	777
Lee & Cates Glass Inc						
5355 Shawland Rd	Jacksonville	FL	32254	**888-844-1989**	904-358-8555	191-6
Lee Brass Co						
1800 Golden Springs Rd *General	Anniston	AL	36207	**800-876-1811***		309
Lee Brick & Tile Co						
3704 Hawkins Ave PO Box 1027	Sanford	NC	27330	**800-672-7559**	919-774-4800	149
Lee Correctional Institution						
990 Wisacky Hwy	Bishopville	SC	29010	**877-846-3472**	803-428-2800	215
Lee County Electric Co-op Inc						
4980 Bayline Dr PO Box 3455	North Fort Myers	FL	33917	**800-282-1643**	239-995-2121	247
Lee County Visitors & Convention Bureau						
2201 Second St Ste 600	Fort Myers	FL	33901	**800-237-6444**	239-338-3500	208

Alphabetical Section

Alphabetical Section

Name / Address	City	State	ZIP	Toll-Free	Phone	Class
Lee Dan Communications Inc 155 Adams Ave	Hauppauge	NY	11788	**800-231-1414**	631-231-1414	392
Lee Hecht Harrison LLC 50 Tice Blvd	Woodcliff Lake	NJ	07677	**800-611-4544**		195
Lee Jeans 9001 W 67th St *Cust Svc	Merriam	KS	66202	**800-453-3348***	913-384-4000	154-10
Lee Kum Kee Inc 14841 Don Julian Rd *Orders	City of Industry	CA	91746	**800-654-5082***	626-709-1888	297-19
Lee Myles Auto Group 914 Fern Ave	Reading	PA	19607	**800-533-6953**		61-6
Lee Products Co 800 E 80th St	Bloomington	MN	55420	**800-989-3544**	952-854-3544	533
Lee Silsby Compounding Pharmacy 3216 Silsby Rd	Cleveland Heights	OH	44118	**800-918-8831**	216-321-4300	239
Lee Spring Company Inc 140 58th St Unit 3C	Brooklyn	NY	11220	**800-110-2500**	718-236-2222	717
Lee Supply Corp 6610 Guion Rd	Indianapolis	IN	46268	**800-873-1103**	317-290-2500	611
Lee University 1120 N Ocoee St	Cleveland	TN	37311	**800-533-9930**	423-614-8000	167
Lee's Morvillo Group 160 Niantic Ave	Providence	RI	02907	**800-821-1700**	401-353-1740	407
Lee's Summit Chamber of Commerce 220 SE Main St	Lees Summit	MO	64063	**888-816-5757**	816-524-2424	138
Leebaw Mfg Company Inc PO Box 553	Canfield	OH	44406	**800-841-8083**		469
Leech Lake Area Chamber of Commerce 205 Minnesota Ave E	Walker	MN	56484	**800-833-1118**	218-547-1313	138
Leech Lake Tribal College 6945 Little Wolf Rd PO Box 180	Cass Lake	MN	56633	**866-676-2772**	218-335-4200	164
Leeches USA Ltd 300 Shames Dr	Westbury	NY	11590	**800-645-3569**	516-333-2570	474
Leed Selling Tools Corp 9700 Hwy 57	Evansville	IN	47725	**855-687-5333**	812-867-4340	85
Leelanau County 8527 E Government Ctr Dr	Suttons Bay	MI	49682	**866-256-9711**	231-256-9824	338
Leelanau Fruit Co 2900 SW Bay Shore Dr	Suttons Bay	MI	49682	**800-431-0718**	231-271-3514	297-21
Leer LP 206 Leer St *Cust Svc	New Lisbon	WI	53950	**800-766-5337***	608-562-7100	662
Leerink Swann & Co 1 Federal St 37th Fl	Boston	MA	02110	**800-808-7525**		401
Lees-McRae College 191 Main St W	Banner Elk	NC	28604	**800-280-4562**	828-898-5241	167
Leeson Canada Inc 320 Superior Blvd	Mississauga	ON	L5T2N7	**800-563-0949**	905-670-4770	110
Leevac Shipyards Inc 111 Bunge St	Jennings	LA	70546	**800-244-3262**	337-824-2210	696
Leeward Community College 96-045 Ala Ike	Pearl City	HI	96782	**888-442-4551**	808-455-0011	161
Leff Electric 4700 Spring Rd	Cleveland	OH	44131	**800-686-5333**	216-432-3000	248
Leffler Energy Inc 15 Mt Joy St	Mount Joy	PA	17552	**800-984-1411**		578
LeFiell Manufacturing Co 13700 Firestone Blvd	Santa Fe Springs	CA	90670	**800-451-5971**	562-921-3411	489
Lefkowitz Garfinkel Champi & DeRienzo PC 10 Weybosset St	Providence	RI	02903	**800-927-5423**	401-421-4800	2
LeFleur's Bluff State Park 2140 Riverside Dr	Jackson	MS	39202	**800-237-6278**	601-987-3923	564
Legacy Bank 1580 E Cheyenne Mtn Blvd	Colorado Springs	CO	80906	**866-627-0800**	719-579-9150	69
Legacy Benefits Corp 350 Fifth Ave Ste 4320	New York	NY	10118	**800-875-1000**		794
Legacy Electronics Inc 1220 N Dakota St PO Box 348	Canton	SD	57013	**888-466-3853**	949-498-9600	176
Legacy Emanuel Hospital & Health Ctr 2801 N Gantenbein Ave	Portland	OR	97227	**888-598-4232**	503-413-2200	374-3
Legacy Golf Resort 6808 S 32nd St	Phoenix	AZ	85042	**888-828-3673**	602-305-5500	667
Legacy Good Samaritan Hospital 1015 NW 22nd Ave	Portland	OR	97210	**800-733-9959**	503-335-3500	374-3
Legacy Salmon Creek Hospital 2211 NE 139th St	Vancouver	WA	98686	**877-270-5566**	360-487-1000	374-3
Legal & General America Inc 1701 Research Blvd	Rockville	MD	20850	**800-638-8428**	301-279-4800	360-4
Legal Aid 126 W Adams St Fl 7	Jacksonville	FL	32202	**866-356-8371**	904-356-8371	428
Legal Aid Society of Palm Beach County Inc 423 Fern St Ste 200	West Palm Beach	FL	33401	**800-403-9353**	561-655-8944	428
Legal Club of America Corp 7771 W Oakland Park Blvd Ste 217	Sunrise	FL	33351	**800-316-5387**	954-377-0222	462
Legal Data Resources Inc 2816 W Summerdale Ave	Chicago	IL	60625	**844-732-2437**	773-561-2468	632
Legal Management: Journal of the Assn of Legal Administrators (ALA) 75 Tri State International Ste 222	Lincolnshire	IL	60069	**877-675-5571**	847-267-1252	456-15
LegalEase Inc 211 E 43rd St Ste 2203	New York	NY	10017	**800-393-1277**	212-393-9070	632
Legend Power Systems Inc 1480 Frances St	Vancouver	BC	V5L1Y9	**866-772-8797**	604-420-1500	765
Legend Seeds Inc PO Box 241	De Smet	SD	57231	**800-678-3346**	605-854-3346	278
Legendary Marketing 3729 S Lecanto Hwy	Lecanto	FL	34461	**800-827-1663**	352-527-3553	197
Legendary Whitetails 820 Enterprise Dr	Slinger	WI	53086	**800-875-9453**		361
Legends of England 3520 Roberts Cut Off Rd	Fort Worth	TX	76114	**800-578-1065**	817-236-3141	361
Legends of the Game Baseball Museum 1000 Ballpark Way	Arlington	TX	76011	**866-274-9053**		521
Legends Theater 1600 W Hwy 76	Branson	MO	65616	**800-374-7469**	417-339-3003	571
Legg Company Inc 325 E Tenth St *Sales	Halstead	KS	67056	**800-835-1003***		370
Legg Mason Inc (LMI) 100 International Dr *NYSE: LM*	Baltimore	MD	21202	**800-822-5544**	410-539-0000	688
Leggett & Platt Inc Number 1 Leggett Rd PO Box 757 *NYSE: LEG*	Carthage	MO	64836	**800-888-4569**	417-358-8131	717
Legion Lighting Company Inc 221 Glenmore Ave	Brooklyn	NY	11207	**800-453-4466**	718-498-1770	439
LEGO Systems Inc 555 Taylor Rd	Enfield	CT	06082	**877-518-5346**	860-763-6731	760
LEGOLAND California 1 Legoland Dr	Carlsbad	CA	92008	**877-534-6526**	760-438-5346	32
Lehigh Asphalt Paving & Construction Co Inc PO Box 549	Tamaqua	PA	18252	**877-222-5514**	570-668-4303	190-4
Lehigh Carbon Community College 4525 Education Pk Dr *General	Schnecksville	PA	18078	**800-414-3975***	610-799-2121	161
Morgan Ctr 234 High St	Tamaqua	PA	18252	**800-424-2460**	570-668-6880	161
Lehigh Fluid Power Inc 1413 Rt 179	Lambertville	NJ	08530	**800-257-9515**		638
Lehigh Inland Cement Ltd 12640 Inland Way *Orders	Edmonton	AB	T5V1K2	**800-252-9304***	780-420-2500	134
Lehigh Valley Health Network 700 E Broad St	Hazleton	PA	18201	**800-528-1234**	570-501-4000	374-3
Lehigh Valley Hospice 2166 S 12th St Ste 401	Allentown	PA	18103	**888-584-2273**	610-969-0300	371
Lehigh Valley International Airport 3311 Airport Rd	Allentown	PA	18109	**800-359-5842**	610-266-6000	27
Lehigh Valley Plastics Inc 187 N Commerce Way	Bethlehem	PA	18017	**800-354-5344**	484-893-5500	603
Lehigh Valley Visitor Ctr 840 Hamilton St Ste 200	Allentown	PA	18101	**800-747-0561**	610-882-9200	208
Lehman College 250 Bedford Pk Blvd W	Bronx	NY	10468	**800-311-5656**	718-960-8000	167
Lehman Hardware & Appliances Inc 4779 Kidron Rd	Dalton	OH	44618	**888-438-5346**		393
Lehman Trikes Inc 125 Industrial Dr *CVE: LHT*	Spearfish	SD	57783	**888-394-3357**	605-642-2111	516
Leica Geosystems Inc 3498 Kraft Ave SE *Sales	Grand Rapids	MI	49512	**800-367-9453***	616-977-4189	425
Leidenheimer Baking Co 1501 Simon Bolivar Ave	New Orleans	LA	70113	**800-259-9099**	504-525-1575	297-1
Leigh Baldwin & Company LLC 1 Hopper St Ste 1	Utica	NY	13501	**800-659-8044**	315-734-1410	688
Leisure Pro 42 W 18th St	New York	NY	10011	**800-637-6880**	212-645-1234	709
Leisure Sports Inc 7077 Koll Ctr Pkwy Ste 110	Pleasanton	CA	94566	**888-239-0930**	925-600-1966	379
Leisure Systems Inc 502 TechneCenter Dr Ste D	Milford	OH	45150	**866-928-9644**	513-831-2100	120
LeisureLink Inc 90 S 400 W Ste 300	Salt Lake City	UT	84101	**855-840-2249**		378
LEK Consulting 28 State St 16th Fl	Boston	MA	02109	**800-929-4535**	617-951-9500	196
LEKTRO Inc 1190 SE Flightline Dr	Warrenton	OR	97146	**800-535-8767**	503-861-2288	56
Lemco Tool Corp 1850 Metzger Ave	Cogan Station	PA	17728	**800-233-8713**	570-494-0620	453
Lemon Peak Marketing Services 500 W Putnam Ave Ste 400	Greenwich	CT	06831	**888-253-7348**		5
LemonStand eCommerce Inc 912-525 Seymour St	Vancouver	BC	V6B3H7	**855-332-0555**	604-558-0555	226
Len-Co Lumber Corp 1445 Seneca St	Buffalo	NY	14210	**800-258-4585**	716-822-0243	364
LendingTree Inc 11115 Rushmore Dr	Charlotte	NC	28277	**800-555-8733**	704-541-5351	508
Lenexpo Inc 1293 Mtn View Alviso Rd Ste A	Sunnyvale	CA	94089	**877-536-3976**	408-962-0515	255
Lenning & Company Inc 13924 Seal Beach Blvd Ste C	Seal Beach	CA	90740	**800-200-4829**	562-594-9729	2
Lennox Industries Inc 2100 Lake Pk Blvd *Cust Svc	Richardson	TX	75080	**800-953-6669***		15
Lennox International Inc 2140 Lake Pk Blvd *NYSE: LII*	Richardson	TX	75080	**800-953-6669**	972-497-5000	15
Lenoir Community College PO Box 188	Kinston	NC	28502	**866-866-2362**	252-527-6223	161
Lenoir County Public School (LCPS) 2017 W Vernon Ave PO Box 729	Kinston	NC	28504	**888-684-8404**	252-527-1109	683
Lenoir Mirror Company Inc 401 Kincaid St	Lenoir	NC	28645	**800-438-8204**	828-728-3271	332
Lenoir-Rhyne University 625 Seventh Ave NE	Hickory	NC	28601	**800-277-5721**	828-328-7300	167
Lenox Corp PO Box 2006	Bristol	PA	19007	**800-223-4311**		728
Lenox Hotel 61 Exeter St	Boston	MA	02116	**800-225-7676**	617-536-5300	379
LENSAR Inc 2800 Discovery Dr	Orlando	FL	32826	**888-536-7271**		474
LensCrafters Inc 4000 Luxottica Pl	Mason	OH	45040	**877-753-6727**	513-765-4321	542
Lenze 630 Douglas St	Uxbridge	MA	01569	**800-217-9100**	508-278-9100	707
Leo Wolleman Inc 45 W 45th St 10th Fl	New York	NY	10036	**800-223-5667**	212-840-1881	411
Leola Village Inn & Suites 38 Deborah Dr	Leola	PA	17540	**877-669-5094**	717-656-7002	379
Leominster Credit Union 20 Adams St	Leominster	MA	01453	**800-649-4646**	978-537-8021	221
Leon Max Inc 3100 New York Dr	Pasadena	CA	91107	**888-334-4629**	626-797-9991	154-20

Name / Address	City	State	Zip	Toll-Free	Phone	Class
Leon S McGoogan Library of Medicine University of Nebraska Medical Ctr 986705 Nebraska Medical Ctr	Omaha	NE	68198	**866-800-5209**	402-559-6221	434-1
Leona Group LLC 2125 University Pk Dr	Okemos	MI	48864	**800-656-6763**	517-333-9030	244
Leonard Paper Co 725 N Haven St *Cust Svc	Baltimore	MD	21205	**800-327-5547***		558
Leonard Valve Co 1360 Elmwood Ave	Cranston	RI	02910	**800-222-1208**	401-461-1200	787
Leppo Inc PO Box 154	Tallmadge	OH	44278	**800-453-7762**	330-633-3999	266-3
Lerner Publishing Group 1251 Washington Ave N	Minneapolis	MN	55401	**800-328-4929**		634-2
Lerner Research Institute 9500 Euclid Ave	Cleveland	OH	44195	**800-223-2273**	216-444-3900	666
LES (Loyd's Electric Supply Inc) 838 Stonetree Dr	Branson	MO	65616	**800-492-4030**	417-334-2171	248
Les Stanford Chevrolet Inc 21730 Michigan Ave	Dearborn	MI	48124	**800-836-0972**	313-457-0364	56
Les Suites Hotel Ottawa 130 Besserer St	Ottawa	ON	K1N9M9	**866-682-0879**	613-232-2000	379
Les Wilkins & Assoc Inc 6850 35th Ave NE	Seattle	WA	98115	**800-426-6634**	206-522-0908	474
Lesaffre Yeast Corp 7475 W Main St *Cust Svc	Milwaukee	WI	53214	**877-677-7000***		297-42
LeSaint Logistics 868 W Crossroads Pkwy	Romeoville	IL	60446	**877-566-9375**	630-243-5950	448
LeSea Broadcasting Corp 61300 S Ironwood Rd	South Bend	IN	46614	**800-365-3732**	574-291-8200	735
Lesley University 29 Everett St	Cambridge	MA	02138	**800-999-1959**	617-868-9600	167
Leslie Controls Inc 12501 Telecom Dr	Tampa	FL	33637	**800-323-8366**	813-978-1000	787
Lesman Instrument Co 135 Bernice Dr	Bensenville	IL	60106	**800-953-7626**	630-595-8400	386
Leson Chevrolet Co Inc 1501 Westbank Express	Harvey	LA	70058	**877-496-2420**	504-366-4381	515
Lesperance & Martineau 1440 Rue Sainte-catherine O	Montreal	QC	H3G1R8	**888-273-8387**	514-861-4831	428
Lester Bldg Systems LLC 1111 Second Ave S	Lester Prairie	MN	55354	**800-826-4439**	320-395-2531	105
Lester Inc 19 Business Pk Dr	Branford	CT	06405	**800-999-5265**	203-488-5265	734
Lester Sales Co Inc 4312 W Minnesota St	Indianapolis	IN	46241	**800-544-6183**	317-244-7811	248
Lester's Florist Inc 2100 Bull St	Savannah	GA	31401	**800-841-1103**	912-233-6066	294
LeTourneau University 2100 S Mobberly Ave	Longview	TX	75602	**800-759-8811**	903-233-3000	167
Level 3 Communications Inc 1025 Eldorado Blvd *NYSE: LVLT*	Broomfield	CO	80021	**877-453-8353**	720-888-1000	394
Level Interactive 241 Fourth Ave	Pittsburgh	PA	15222	**877-733-8625**		5
Levenger 420 S Congress Ave *Cust Svc	Delray Beach	FL	33445	**800-544-0880***	561-276-2436	458
Leventhal Ltd PO Box 564 *General	Fayetteville	NC	28302	**800-847-4095***		154-18
Levi Strauss & Co 1155 Battery St	San Francisco	CA	94111	**866-290-6064**	415-501-6000	154-10
Levinson Institute Inc 28 Main St Ste 100	Jaffrey	NH	03452	**800-290-5735**	603-532-4700	763
Levolor Kirsch Window Fashions 4110 Premier Dr	High Point	NC	27265	**800-752-9677**	336-812-8181	86
Levy Home Entertainment LLC 1420 Kensington Rd Ste 300	Oak Brook	IL	60523	**800-549-5389**	708-547-4400	529
Lew A. Cummings Company Inc 4 Peters Brook Dr	Hooksett	NH	03106	**800-647-0035**		626
Lew Jan Textile Corp 366 Veterans Memorial Hwy	Commack	NY	11725	**800-899-0531**		593
Lewcott Corp 86 Providence Rd *Sales	Millbury	MA	01527	**800-225-7725***	508-865-1791	604-2
Lewellen & Best Displays Inc 101 Knell St	Montgomery	IL	60538	**800-250-7565**	630-896-2500	393
Lewer Agency Inc 4534 Wornall Rd	Kansas City	MO	64111	**800-821-7715**		390
Lewin Group 3130 Fairview Pk Dr Ste 800	Falls Church	VA	22042	**877-227-5042**	703-269-5500	196
Lewis & Clark College 0615 SW Palatine Hill Rd *Admissions	Portland	OR	97219	**800-444-4111***	503-768-7040	167
Lewis & Clark Library 120 S Last Chance Gulch	Helena	MT	59601	**800-733-2767**	406-447-1690	434-3
Lewis & Clark State Recreation Site 725 Summer St NE Ste C	Salem	OR	97301	**800-551-6949**	503-986-0707	564
Lewis & Clark Trail Heritage Foundation 4201 Giant Springs Rd	Great Falls	MT	59405	**888-701-3434**	406-454-1234	47-23
Lewis & Knopf CPAs PC 5206 Gateway Centre Ste 100	Flint	MI	48507	**877-244-1787**	810-238-4617	2
Lewis & Michael Inc 1827 Woodman Dr	Dayton	OH	45420	**800-543-3524**	937-252-6683	188
Lewis County 499 US Hwy 33 E Ste 102	Weston	WV	26452	**800-296-7329**	304-269-7328	338
Lewis County Chamber of Commerce 7576 S State St	Lowville	NY	13367	**800-724-0242**	315-376-2213	138
Lewis County Rural Electric Co-op 18256 Hwy 16 PO Box 68	Lewistown	MO	63452	**888-454-4485**	573-215-4000	247
Lewis Direct Marketing 325 E Oliver St	Baltimore	MD	21202	**800-533-5394**	410-539-5100	5
Lewis Electric Supply Company Inc 1306 Second St PO Box 2237	Muscle Shoals	AL	35662	**800-239-0681**	256-383-0681	248
Lewis Goetz & Company Inc 1571 Grandview Ave	Paulsboro	NJ	08066	**800-257-6239**	856-579-1421	385
Lewis M Carter Mfg Co PO Box 428	Donalsonville	GA	39845	**800-332-8232**	229-524-2197	299
Lewis S. Mills High School 24 Lyon Rd	Burlington	CT	06013	**800-673-2411**	860-673-0423	683
Lewis Tree Service Inc 300 Lucius Gordon Dr	West Henrietta	NY	14586	**800-333-1593**	585-436-3208	774
Lewis University 1 University Pkwy Unit 297	Romeoville	IL	60446	**800-897-9000**	815-836-5250	167
Lewis Wagner 501 Indiana Ave #200	Indianapolis	IN	46202	**800-237-0505**	317-237-0500	428
Lewis-Clark State College 500 Eigth Ave	Lewiston	ID	83501	**800-933-5272**	208-792-5272	167
Lewis-Goetz & Co Inc 650 Washington Rd Ste 210	Pittsburgh	PA	15228	**800-989-0447**	412-341-7100	385
Lewiston Sales Inc 21241 Dutchmans Crossing Rd	Lewiston	MN	55952	**800-732-6334**	507-523-2112	445
Lewistown News-argus 521 W Main St	Lewistown	MT	59457	**800-879-5627**	406-535-3401	531-3
Lexar Media Inc 47300 Bayside Pkwy	Fremont	CA	94538	**877-747-4031**	510-413-1200	290
Lexel Imaging Systems Inc 1501 Newtown Pike	Lexington	KY	40511	**800-397-8121**	859-243-5500	255
Lexicon Pharmaceuticals Inc 8800 Technology Forest Pl *NASDAQ: LXRX*	The Woodlands	TX	77381	**855-828-4651**	281-863-3000	84
Lexicon Technologies Inc 2195 Eastview Pkwy	Conyers	GA	30013	**888-250-4075**		179
Lexinet Corp, The 701 N Union St	Council Grove	KS	66846	**800-767-1577**	620-767-7000	5
Lexington Convention & Visitors Bureau 301 E Vine St	Lexington	KY	40507	**800-845-3959**	859-233-7299	208
Lexington Corporate Properties Trust 1 Penn Plz Ste 4015	New York	NY	10119	**800-850-3948**	212-692-7200	653
Lexington Herald-Leader 100 Midland Ave	Lexington	KY	40508	**800-999-8881**	859-231-3100	531-2
Lexington Investment Mortgage Company LLC 2365 Harrodsburg Rd Ste B375	Lexington	KY	40504	**800-264-7073**	859-224-7073	688
Lexington Philharmonic 161 N Mill St	Lexington	KY	40507	**888-494-4226**	859-233-4226	572-3
Lexington Theological Seminary 631 S Limestone St	Lexington	KY	40508	**866-296-6087**	859-252-0361	168-3
Lexington Veteran Affairs Medical Center 1101 Veterans Dr	Lexington	KY	40502	**877-222-8387**	859-233-4511	391-3
Lexington Wealth Management 12 Waltham St	Lexington	MA	02421	**800-626-1566**	781-860-7745	401
LexisNexis Martindale-Hubbell 121 Chanlon Rd	New Providence	NJ	07974	**800-526-4902**		387
LexisNexis Matthew Bender 744 Broad St	Newark	NJ	07102	**800-252-9257**	973-820-2000	634-2
LexJet Corp 1680 Fruitville Rd 3rd Fl	Sarasota	FL	34236	**800-453-9538**	941-330-1210	627
Lexmark Carpet Mills Inc 285 Kraft Dr	Dalton	GA	30721	**800-871-3211**		130
Lexmark International Inc 740 W New Cir Rd *NYSE: LXK* ■ *Cust Svc	Lexington	KY	40550	**800-539-6275***	859-232-2000	175-6
Lexus of Memphis Inc 2600 Ridgeway Rd *Sales	Memphis	TN	38119	**877-876-9996***	901-362-8833	56
LFA (Lupus Foundation of America Inc) 2000 L St NW Ste 410	Washington	DC	20036	**800-558-0121**	202-349-1155	47-17
LFCU (Lockheed Federal Credit Union) 2340 Hollywood Way	Burbank	CA	91505	**800-328-5328**	818-565-2020	221
LFL (Lady Foot Locker) 112 W 34th St	New York	NY	10120	**800-991-6686**	212-720-3700	302
LG Barcus & Sons Inc 1430 State Ave	Kansas City	KS	66102	**800-255-0180**	913-621-1100	190-2
LG Electronics USA Inc 1000 Sylvan Ave *Tech Supp	Englewood Cliffs	NJ	07632	**800-243-0000***	201-816-2000	175-4
L&g Engineering Laboratory LLC 2100 W Expressway 83	Mercedes	TX	78570	**888-565-9813**	956-565-9813	740
LG Everist Inc 300 S Phillips Ave Ste 200	Sioux Falls	SD	57117	**800-843-7992**	605-334-5000	502-4
LG2 Environmental Solutions Inc 14785 Old St Augustine Rd Ste 4	Jacksonville	FL	32258	**800-435-0072**	904-288-8631	650
LHC Group LLC 901 Hugh Wallis Rd S *NASDAQ: LHCG*	Lafayette	LA	70508	**866-542-4768**	337-289-8188	363
LHR Services & Equipment Inc lc-disc 4200 Fm 1128 Rd	Pearland	TX	77584	**800-943-2324**	713-943-2324	607
Li Cor Inc PO Box 4425	Lincoln	NE	68504	**800-447-3576**	402-467-3576	419
LIA (Laser Institute of America) 13501 Ingenuity Dr Ste 128	Orlando	FL	32826	**800-345-2737**	407-380-1553	48-19
LIA (Leather Industries of America) 3050 K St NW Ste 400	Washington	DC	20007	**800-635-0617**	202-342-8497	48-4
Lia Auto Group, The 1258 Central Ave PO Box 5789	Albany	NY	12205	**855-212-7985**	518-489-2111	56
Liacouras Ctr 1776 N Broad St	Philadelphia	PA	19121	**800-298-4200**	215-204-2400	571
Libbey Inc 300 Madison Ave PO Box 10060 *NYSE: LBY*	Toledo	OH	43699	**888-794-8469**	419-325-2100	334
Liberal Party of Canada 81 Metcalfe St	Ottawa	ON	K1P6M8	**888-542-3725**		614
Libertarian Party 2600 Virginia Ave NW Ste 200	Washington	DC	20037	**800-353-2887**	202-333-0008	615
Liberty Bank 315 Main St	Middletown	CT	06457	**800-622-6732**	800-354-8950	69
Liberty Bank & Trust Co PO Box 60131	New Orleans	LA	70160	**800-883-3943**	504-240-5100	69
Liberty Brass Turning Company Inc 38-01 Queens Blvd	Long Island	NY	11101	**800-345-5939**	718-784-2911	620

Name / Address	City	State	ZIP	Toll-Free	Phone	Class
Liberty Ch 1971 University Blvd	Lynchburg	VA	24506	**800-332-1883**	434-582-2000	736
Liberty County Chamber of Commerce 425 W Oglethorpe Hwy	Hinesville	GA	31313	**855-846-3940**	912-368-4445	138
Liberty Diversified International Inc 5600 Hwy 169 N	New Hope	MN	55428	**800-421-1270**	763-536-6600	360-3
Liberty Drug & Surgical Inc 195 Main St	Chatham	NJ	07928	**877-816-0111**	973-635-6200	239
Liberty Forge Inc PO Box 1210	Liberty	TX	77575	**800-231-2377**		482
Liberty Fund Inc 8335 Allison Pt Trial Ste 300	Indianapolis	IN	46250	**800-955-8335**	317-842-0880	306
Liberty Hardware Mfg Corp 140 Business Pk Dr	Winston-Salem	NC	27107	**800-542-3789**		350
Liberty Hospital 2525 Glenn Hendren Dr	Liberty	MO	64068	**800-344-3829**	816-781-7200	374-3
Liberty Pumps Inc 7000 Apple Tree Ave	Bergen	NY	14416	**800-543-2550**	585-494-1817	638
Liberty Safe & Security Products Inc 1199 W Utah Ave	Payson	UT	84651	**800-247-5625**	801-925-1000	486
Liberty Savings Bank FSB 2251 Rombach Ave	Wilmington	OH	45177	**800-436-6300**		69
Liberty Tax Service Inc 1716 Corporate Landing Pkwy *Cust Svc	Virginia Beach	VA	23454	**800-790-3863***	757-493-8855	731
Liberty Toyota Scion 4397 Rt 130 S	Burlington	NJ	08016	**888-809-7798**	609-386-6300	515
Liberty Travel Inc 69 Spring St	Ramsey	NJ	07446	**888-271-1584**	201-934-3500	769
Liberty Tree Mall 100 Independence Way	Danvers	MA	01923	**877-746-6642**	978-777-0794	459
Liberty University 1971 University Blvd	Lynchburg	VA	24502	**800-543-5317**	434-582-2000	167
LibertyTree 100 Swan Way	Oakland	CA	94621	**800-927-8733**	510-632-1366	95
Libertyville Chevrolet Inc 1001 S Milwaukee Ave *Sales	Libertyville	IL	60048	**877-520-1807***	847-281-5330	515
Libman Co 220 N Sheldon St	Arcola	IL	61910	**877-818-3380**		102
Libra Industries Inc 7770 Div Dr	Mentor	OH	44060	**800-825-1674**	440-974-7770	624
Library & Information Technology Assn (LITA) 50 E Huron St	Chicago	IL	60611	**800-545-2433**	312-280-4270	48-11
Library Binding Service (LBS) 1801 Thompson Ave	Des Moines	IA	50316	**800-247-5323**	515-262-3191	91
Library Hotel 299 Madison Ave	New York	NY	10017	**877-793-7323**	212-983-4500	379
Library Journal 160 Varick St 11th Fl	New York	NY	10013	**800-588-1030**	646-380-0700	456-8
Library Leadership & Management Assn (LLAMA) 50 E Huron St	Chicago	IL	60611	**800-545-2433**		48-11
Library of Congress *National Library Service for the Blind & Physically Handicapped* 1291 Taylor St NW	Washington	DC	20011	**888-657-7323**	202-707-5100	342
US Copyright Office 101 Independence Ave SE	Washington	DC	20559	**877-476-0778**	202-707-3000	342
Library of Michigan, The 702 W Kalamazoo St PO Box 30007	Lansing	MI	48909	**800-726-7323**	517-373-1580	434-5
Library Reproduction Service 14214 S Figueroa St	Los Angeles	CA	90061	**800-255-5002**		625
Libyan Arab Jamahiriya 309-315 E 48th St	New York	NY	10017	**800-253-9646**	212-752-5775	782
LICH (Long Island College Hospital) 339 Hicks St	Brooklyn	NY	11201	**800-227-8922**	718-780-1000	374-3
Licking Valley Oil Inc PO Box 246	Butler	KY	41006	**800-899-9449**	859-472-7111	578
Licking Valley Rural Electric Co-op Corp 271 Main St	West Liberty	KY	41472	**800-596-6530**	606-743-3179	247
LICT Corp 401 Theodore Fremd Ave	Rye	NY	10580	**800-690-6903**	914-921-8821	733
Lido Van & Storage Co Inc 2152 Alton Pkwy Ste N	Irvine	CA	92606	**800-339-5436**	949-863-9000	518
Lieberman Software Corp 1900 Ave of the Stars Ste 425	Los Angeles	CA	90067	**800-829-6263**	310-550-8575	179
Liechty Farm Equipment Inc 1701 S Defiance St	Archbold	OH	43502	**800-272-5898**	419-445-1565	276
Lied Ctr for Performing Arts 301 N 12th St	Lincoln	NE	68588	**800-432-3231**	402-472-4700	571
Life Alert 16027 Ventura Blvd	Encino	CA	91436	**800-920-3410**	818-700-7000	574
Life Flight Network LLC 22285 Yellow Gate Ln NE	Aurora	OR	97002	**800-232-0911**	503-678-4364	13
Life Force International Corp 495 Raleigh Ave	El Cajon	CA	92064	**800-531-4877**	858-218-3200	345
Life Insurance Co of Alabama 302 Broad St	Gadsden	AL	35901	**800-226-2371**	256-543-2022	391-2
Life of the South Insurance Co 10151 Deerwood Pk Blvd Bldg 100	Jacksonville	FL	32256	**800-888-2738**	904-350-9660	391-5
Life Pacific College 1100 W Covina Blvd	San Dimas	CA	91773	**877-886-5433**	909-599-5433	160
Life Partners Inc (LPI) 204 Woodhew Dr	Waco	TX	76712	**800-368-5569**	254-751-7797	794
Life Settlement Solutions Inc 9201 Spectrum Ctr Blvd Ste 105	San Diego	CA	92123	**800-762-3387**	858-576-8067	794
Life University 1269 Barclay Cir	Marietta	GA	30060	**800-543-3203**	770-426-2884	167
Life-Assist Inc 11277 Sunrise Park Dr	Rancho Cordova	CA	95742	**800-824-6016**		474
LifeBanc 4775 Richmond Rd	Cleveland	OH	44128	**888-558-5433**	216-752-5433	544
Lifeblood Mid-South Regional Blood Ctr 1040 Madison Ave	Memphis	TN	38104	**888-543-3256**	901-522-8585	88
LifeCell Corp 1 Millennium Way	Branchburg	NJ	08876	**800-226-2714**		544
LifeCore Biomedical LLC 3515 Lyman Blvd *Cust Svc	Chaska	MN	55318	**800-348-4368***	952-368-4300	84
LifeCourse Associates Inc 9080 Eaton Park Rd	Great Falls	VA	22066	**866-537-4999**		195
LifeFone 16 Yellowstone Ave	White Plains	NY	10607	**888-687-0451**		574
LifeLearn Inc 367 Woodlawn Rd W Unit 9	Guelph	ON	N1H7K9	**888-770-2218**	519-767-5043	244
Lifeline Medical Assoc LLC 99 Cherry Hill Rd Ste 220	Parsippany	NJ	07054	**800-845-2785**	973-316-0307	374-3
Lifeline of Ohio 770 Kinnear Rd Ste 200	Columbus	OH	43212	**800-525-5667**	614-291-5667	544
Lifelink Foundation Inc 409 Bayshore Blvd	Tampa	FL	33606	**800-262-5775**	813-253-2640	363
LifeLink Tissue Bank 8510 Sunstate St	Tampa	FL	33634	**800-683-2400**	813-886-8111	544
LifeNet 1864 Concert Dr	Virginia Beach	VA	23453	**800-847-7831**	757-464-4761	544
LifeNet Health Northwest 501 SW 39th St	Renton	WA	98057	**800-858-2282**	425-981-8900	544
Lifenet Inc 6225 St Michaels Dr	Texarkana	TX	75503	**800-832-6395**	903-832-8531	30
Lifepath Hospice 3010 W Azeele St	Tampa	FL	33609	**800-209-2200**	813-877-2200	371
LifePoint Health 330 Seven Springs Way *NASDAQ: LPNT*	Brentwood	TN	37027	**888-982-9144**	615-920-7000	353
LifePoint Inc 3950 Faber Pl Dr	Charleston	SC	29405	**800-462-0755**	843-763-7755	271
LifeRing Secular Recovery 1440 Broadway Ste 312	Oakland	CA	94612	**800-811-4142**	510-763-0779	47-21
LifeScan Inc 1000 Gibraltar Dr	Milpitas	CA	95035	**800-227-8862**	408-263-9789	233
LifeScan Laboratory Inc 5255 W Golf	Skokie	IL	60077	**800-270-0037**		415
LifeServe Blood Ctr 431 E Locust St	Des Moines	IA	50309	**800-287-4903**		88
LifeShare Blood Centers 8910 Linwood Ave	Shreveport	LA	71106	**800-256-4483**	318-222-7770	88
LifeShare Community Blood Services 105 Cleveland St	Elyria	OH	44035	**800-317-5412**	440-322-5700	88
LifeShare of the Carolinas 1200 Ridgefield Blvd Ste 150	Asheville	NC	28806	**800-932-4483**	828-665-0107	271
LifeShare Transplant Donor Services of Oklahoma 4705 NW Expy	Oklahoma City	OK	73132	**888-580-5680**	405-840-5551	544
Lifesharing Community Organ & Tissue Donation 3465 Camino del Rio S Ste 410	San Diego	CA	92108	**866-797-2366**	619-521-1983	544
LifeSize Communications Inc 1601 S Mopac Expwy Ste 100	Austin	TX	78746	**877-543-3749**	512-347-9300	51
LifeSource Blood Services 2764 Aurora Ave	Naperville	IL	60540	**877-543-3768**		88
LifeSouth Community Blood Centers 4039 Newberry Rd	Gainesville	FL	32607	**888-795-2707**		88
LifeSouth Community Blood Centers Atlanta 4891 Ashford Dunwoody Rd	Atlanta	GA	30338	**888-795-2707**	404-329-1994	88
Lifespire 350 Fifth Ave Ste 301	New York	NY	10118	**800-221-5594**	212-741-0100	47-17
Lifespring Inc 460 Spring St	Jeffersonville	IN	47130	**800-456-2117**	812-280-2080	353
Lifetime Brands Inc 1000 Steward Ave *NASDAQ: LCUT*	Garden City	NY	11530	**800-252-3390**	516-683-6000	485
Lifetime Products Inc Freeport Ctr Bldg D-11 PO Box 160010	Clearfield	UT	84016	**800-242-3865**	801-776-1532	708
Lifetouch Church Directories 1371 Portland Way N	Galion	OH	44833	**800-521-4611**	419-468-4739	634-10
Lifeway Foods Inc 6431 W Oakton St *NASDAQ: LWAY*	Morton Grove	IL	60053	**877-281-3874**	847-967-1010	297-27
Lifewings Partners LLC 9198 Crestwyn Hills Dr	Memphis	TN	38125	**800-290-9314**		462
Lift-All Company Inc 1909 McFarland Dr	Landisville	PA	17538	**800-909-1964**	717-898-6615	469
Liftone 440 E Westinghouse Blvd	Charlotte	NC	28273	**855-543-8663**		469
Lifts West Condominium Resort Hotel PO Box 330	Red River	NM	87558	**800-221-1859**	505-754-2778	667
Ligature, The 4909 Alcoa Ave	Los Angeles	CA	90058	**800-944-5440**	323-585-6000	779
Light for Life Foundation International PO Box 644	Westminster	CO	80036	**800-273-8255**	303-429-3530	47-17
Light Impressions 100 Carlson Rd	Rochester	NY	14610	**800-975-6429**		627
Light Metals Corp 2740 Prairie St SW	Wyoming	MI	49509	**888-363-8257**	616-538-3030	484
Light Sources Inc 37 Robinson Blvd	Orange	CT	06477	**800-826-9465**	203-799-7877	437
LightEdge Solutions Inc 215 10th St Ste 1000	Des Moines	IA	50309	**877-771-3343**	515-471-1000	806
Lighthouse Club Hotel 201 60th St	Ocean City	MD	21842	**888-371-5400**	410-524-5400	379
Lighthouse Computer Services Inc 6 Blackstone Valley Pl Ste 205	Lincoln	RI	02865	**888-542-8030**	401-334-0799	182
Lighthouse Hospice 1040 Kings Hwy N Ste 100 *General	Cherry Hill	NJ	08034	**888-467-7423***	856-414-1155	371
Lighthouse Lodge & Suites 1150 Lighthouse Ave	Pacific Grove	CA	93950	**800-858-1249**		379
Lighting Quotient, The 114 Boston Post Rd	West Haven	CT	06516	**800-222-0193**	203-931-4455	439
Lightner Electronics Inc 1771 Beaver Dam Rd	Claysburg	PA	16625	**866-239-3888**	814-239-8323	188
Lightnin 135 Mt Read Blvd	Rochester	NY	14611	**877-247-3797**	585-436-5550	386

Name / Address	City	State	Zip	Toll-Free	Phone	Class
Lightning Source 1246 Heil Quaker Blvd	La Vergne	TN	37086	**800-509-4156**	615-213-5815	634-2
Lightning Transportation Inc 16820 Blake Rd	Hagerstown	MD	21740	**800-233-0624**	301-582-5700	778
Lightower Fiber Networks 80 Central St	Boxborough	MA	01719	**888-583-4237**	978-264-6000	733
Lightriver Technologies Inc 2150 John Glenn Dre Ste 200	Concord	CA	94520	**888-544-4825**	941-552-9410	679
Lightspeed Aviation Inc 6135 Jean Rd	Lake Oswego	OR	97035	**800-332-2421**	503-968-3113	645
Lignite Energy Council 1016 E Owens Ave	Bismarck	ND	58502	**800-932-7117**	701-258-7117	136
Lil' Drug Store Products Inc 1201 Continental Pl Ne	Cedar Rapids	IA	52402	**800-553-5022**		240
Lila Cockrell Theatre 200 E Market St *General	San Antonio	TX	78205	**877-504-8895***	210-207-8500	571
Lilleys' Landing Resort 367 River Ln	Branson	MO	65616	**866-545-5397**	417-334-6380	667
Lillie's Asian Cuisine 129 E Fremont St	Las Vegas	NV	89101	**800-634-3454**	702-385-7111	669
Lima Estates 411 N Middletown Rd	Media	PA	19063	**888-398-2287**	610-565-7020	670
Lima Memorial Hospital 1001 Bellefontaine Ave	Lima	OH	45804	**877-362-5672**	419-228-3335	374-3
Lima News 3515 Elida Rd	Lima	OH	45807	**800-686-9924**	419-223-1010	531-2
Lima/Allen County Convention & Visitors Bureau 144 S Main St Ste 101	Lima	OH	45801	**888-222-6075**	419-222-6075	208
Lime Rock Park 60 White Hollow Rd	Lakeville	CT	06039	**800-722-3577**	860-435-5000	514
Limestone College 1115 College Dr	Gaffney	SC	29340	**800-795-7151**	864-489-7151	167
Limoneira Co 1141 Cummings Rd *NASDAQ: LMNR*	Santa Paula	CA	93060	**866-321-8953**	805-525-5541	316-2
Limpert Bros Inc 202 NW Blvd PO Box 1480	Vineland	NJ	08362	**800-691-1353**	856-691-1353	297-15
LIMRA International Inc 300 Day Hill Rd	Windsor	CT	06095	**800-235-4672**	860-688-3358	48-9
Lincluden Investment Management 1275 N Service Rd W Ste 607	Oakville	ON	L6M3G4	**800-532-7071**	905-825-9000	527
Lincoln Botanical Garden & Arboretum (BGA) University of Nebraska 1309 N 17th St	Lincoln	NE	68588	**800-742-8800**	402-472-2679	96
Lincoln Christian College Seminary 100 Campus View Dr	Lincoln	IL	62656	**888-522-5228**	217-732-3168	168-3
Lincoln City Visitor & Convention Bureau 801 SW Hwy 101 Ste 401	Lincoln City	OR	97367	**800-452-2151**	541-996-1274	208
Lincoln College 300 Keokuk St	Lincoln	IL	62656	**800-569-0556**	217-732-3155	161
Lincoln College of Technology 7225 Winton Dr Bldg 128	Indianapolis	IN	46268	**800-228-6232**	317-632-5553	798
Lincoln Convention & Visitors Bureau 1135 M St Ste 300	Lincoln	NE	68508	**800-423-8212**	402-434-5335	208
Lincoln County PO Box 978	Brookhaven	MS	39602	**800-613-4667**	601-833-1411	338
Lincoln Ctr Theater 150 W 65th St	New York	NY	10023	**800-432-7250**		746
Lincoln Educational Services 85 Sigourney St	Hartford	CT	06105	**800-762-4337**	800-254-0547	162
Suffield 8 PROGRESS DR	Shelton	CT	06484	**800-254-0547**	203-929-0592	162
Lincoln Electric Co 22801 St Clair Ave	Cleveland	OH	44117	**888-935-3878**	216-481-8100	809
Lincoln Electric Co-op Inc (LEC) 500 Osloski Rd PO Box 628	Eureka	MT	59917	**800-442-2994**	406-889-3301	247
Lincoln FSB 1101 N St 68508	Lincoln	NE	68501	**800-333-2158**	402-474-1400	70
Lincoln General Insurance Co 3501 Concord Rd	York	PA	17402	**800-876-3350**	717-757-0000	390
Lincoln Heritage Life Insurance Co 4343 E Camelback Rd Ste 400 Ste 400	Phoenix	AZ	85018	**800-438-7180**	602-957-1650	391-2
Lincoln Journal-Star 926 P St	Lincoln	NE	68508	**800-742-7315**	402-475-4200	531-2
Lincoln Laboratory Massachusetts Institute of Technology 244 Wood St	Lexington	MA	02420	**800-445-8667**	781-981-5500	666
Lincoln Land Community College 5250 Shepherd Rd PO Box 19256	Springfield	IL	62794	**800-727-4161**	217-786-2200	161
Lincoln Land Oil Co PO Box 4307	Springfield	IL	62708	**800-238-4912**	217-523-5050	317
Lincoln Memorial University 6965 Cumberland Gap Pkwy	Harrogate	TN	37752	**800-325-0900**	423-869-3611	167
Lincoln National Corp (LNC) 150 N Radnor-Chester Rd *NYSE: LNC*	Radnor	PA	19087	**877-275-5462**	484-583-1400	360-4
Lincoln National Life Insurance Co 1300 S Clinton St	Fort Wayne	IN	46802	**800-454-6265**		391-2
Lincoln State Park Hwy 162 PO Box 216	Lincoln City	IN	47552	**877-478-3657**	812-937-4710	564
Lincoln Trail College 11220 State Hwy 1	Robinson	IL	62454	**866-582-4322**	618-544-8657	161
Lincoln University 820 Chestnut St B-7 Young Hall *Admissions	Jefferson City	MO	65102	**800-521-5052***	573-681-5599	167
Lincoln Wood Products Inc 1400 W Taylor St PO Box 375	Merrill	WI	54452	**800-967-2461**		238
Lincoln-Mercury Co PO Box 6128	Dearborn	MI	48121	**800-521-4140**		58
Linda Hall Library 5109 Cherry St	Kansas City	MO	64110	**800-662-1545**	816-363-4600	434-3
Lindal Cedar Homes Inc 4300 S 104th Pl *Prod Info	Seattle	WA	98178	**800-426-0536***	206-725-0900	105
Lindamar Industries Inc 1603 Commerce Way	Paso Robles	CA	93446	**800-235-1811**	805-237-1910	362
Lindblad Expeditions 96 Morton St 9th Fl	New York	NY	10014	**800-397-3348**	212-765-7740	758
Lindeblad Piano Restoration 101 Us 46	Pine Brook	NJ	07058	**888-587-4266**		526
Linden Hall School for Girls 212 E Main St	Lititz	PA	17543	**800-258-5778**	717-626-8512	621
Linden Publishing 2006 S Mary St *Sales	Fresno	CA	93721	**800-345-4447***	559-233-6633	634-2
Linden Row Inn 100 E Franklin St	Richmond	VA	23219	**800-348-7424**	804-783-7000	379
Linden Warehouse & Distribution Co Inc 1300 Lower Rd	Linden	NJ	07036	**800-333-2855**	908-862-1400	778
Lindenmeyr Book Publishing Papers 521 Fifth Ave	New York	NY	10175	**800-842-8480**		552
Lindenmeyr Munroe 14 Research Pkwy	Wallingford	CT	06492	**800-842-8480**		552
Lindenmeyr Munroe Central Central National-Gottesman Inc 3 Manhattanville Rd	Purchase	NY	10577	**800-221-3042**		552
Lindenmeyr Munroe Paper Corp 115 Moonachie Ave	Moonachie	NJ	07074	**800-221-3042**	201-440-6491	552
Lindenwood University 209 S Kingshighway	Saint Charles	MO	63301	**877-615-8212**	636-949-2000	167
Lindey's Prime Steak House 3600 N Snelling Ave	Arden Hills	MN	55112	**866-491-0538**	651-633-9813	669
LINDO Systems Inc 1415 N Dayton St *Sales	Chicago	IL	60622	**800-441-2378***	312-988-7422	180-5
Lindquist Steels Inc 1050 Woodend Rd	Stratford	CT	06615	**800-243-9637**		491
Lindsay Corp 2222 N 111th St *NYSE: LNN*	Omaha	NE	68164	**866-404-5049**	402-829-6800	275
Lindsay Manufacturing Inc PO Box 1708	Ponca City	OK	74602	**800-546-3729**	580-762-2457	786
Lindsey & Company Inc 2302 Llama Dr	Searcy	AR	72143	**800-890-7058**	501-268-5324	176
Lindsey Wilson College 210 Lindsey Wilson St	Columbia	KY	42728	**800-264-0138**	270-384-2126	167
Lindt & Sprungli USA 1 Fine Chocolate Pl	Stratham	NH	03885	**877-695-4638**	603-778-8100	297-8
Lineage Power Corp 601 Shiloh Rd	Plano	TX	75074	**877-546-3243**	972-244-9288	785
Lineagen Inc 2677 E Parleys Way	Salt Lake City	UT	84109	**888-888-6736**	801-931-6200	666
Linear Laboratories 42025 Osgood Rd	Fremont	CA	94539	**800-536-0262**	510-226-0488	203
Linear Technology Corp 1630 McCarthy Blvd *NASDAQ: LLTC*	Milpitas	CA	95035	**888-500-6973**	408-432-1900	694
Linemaster Switch Corp 29 Plaine Hill Rd	Woodstock	CT	06281	**800-974-3668**	860-974-1000	484
Linen Chest Inc 4455 AutoRt Des Laurentides	Laval	QC	H7L5X8	**800-363-3832**	514-341-7077	364
Linetec 725 S 75th Ave	Wausau	WI	54401	**888-717-1472**	715-843-4100	479
Linfield College 900 SE Baker St *Admissions	McMinnville	OR	97128	**800-640-2287***	503-883-2213	167
Lingo Inc 7901 Jones Branch Dr 9th Fl	Mclean	VA	22102	**888-546-4699**		387
Lingo Manufacturing Co 7400 Industrial Rd *Cust Svc	Florence	KY	41042	**800-354-9771***	859-371-2662	235
Lingo Media Corp 151 Bloor St W Ste 703	Toronto	ON	M5S1S4	**866-927-7011**	416-927-7000	244
Lingua School Inc 225 E Las Olas Blvd 6th Fl	Fort Lauderdale	FL	33301	**888-654-6482**	954-577-9955	423
Linguistics Systems Inc 201 Broadway	Cambridge	MA	02139	**877-654-5006**		766
Link Electronics Inc 2137 Rust Ave	Cape Girardeau	MO	63703	**800-776-4411**	573-334-4433	115
Link Energy LLC 39 Rivalda Rd 2nd Fl	Toronto	ON	M9M2M4	**855-444-5465**		580
Link-Burns Mfg Company Inc 253 American Way	Voorhees	NJ	08043	**800-457-4358**	856-429-6844	695
Linkus Enterprises Inc 5595 W San Madele Ave	Fresno	CA	93722	**888-854-6587**	559-256-6600	679
Linn Gear Co 100 N Eigth St PO Box 397	Lebanon	OR	97355	**800-547-2471**	541-259-1211	619
LINQ Services 1200 Steuart St Unit C3	Baltimore	MD	21230	**800-421-5467**		387
Linscomb & Williams Inc 1400 Post Oak Blvd Ste 1000	Houston	TX	77056	**800-960-1200**	713-840-1000	401
Linsly School 60 Knox Ln	Wheeling	WV	26003	**866-648-1893**	304-233-3260	621
Lintern Corp 8685 Stn St	Mentor	OH	44060	**800-321-3638**	440-255-9333	14
Linville Caverns Inc 19929 US 221 N	Marion	NC	28752	**800-419-0540**		49-4
Lion Apparel Inc 7200 Poe Ave Ste 400	Dayton	OH	45414	**800-548-6614**	937-898-1949	154-18
Lion Brand Yarn Co 135 Kero Rd	Carlstadt	NJ	07072	**800-795-5466**	212-243-8995	742-9
Lion Bros Company Inc 300 Red Brook Blvd *Cust Svc	Owings Mills	MD	21117	**800-365-6543***		260
Lion Inc 200 Martin Ln Ste A	Elk Grove	IL	60007	**800-867-6320**	872-228-5466	508
Lion Magazine 300 W 22nd St *Circ	Oak Brook	IL	60523	**800-710-7822***	630-571-5466	456-10
Lionel .com LLC 26750 23 Mile Rd	Chesterfield	MI	48051	**800-454-6635**	586-949-4100	760
Lionetti Assoc 450 S Front St	Elizabeth	NJ	07202	**800-734-0910**	908-820-8800	684
Lionheart Publishing Inc 506 Roswell St	Marietta	GA	30060	**888-303-5639**		634-9

Name / Address	City	State	ZIP	Toll-Free	Phone	Class
Lions Eye Bank of Manitoba & Northwest Ontario Inc 691 Wolseley Ave	Winnipeg	MB	R3G1C3	**800-552-6820**	204-788-8507	271
Lions Eye Bank of Nebraska Inc *University of Nebraska Medical Ctr* 985541 Nebraska Medical Ctr	Omaha	NE	68198	**800-225-7244**	402-559-4039	271
Lions Eye Bank of Wisconsin 2401 American Ln	Madison	WI	53704	**877-233-2354**	608-233-2354	271
Lions Gate Hospital 231 E 15th St	North Vancouver	BC	V7L2L7	**800-984-1131**	604-988-3131	374-2
Lions Medical Eye Bank & Research Ctr of Eastern Virginia Inc 600 Gresham Dr	Norfolk	VA	23507	**800-453-6059**		271
LiphaTech Inc 3600 W Elm St	Milwaukee	WI	53209	**888-331-7900**		84
Lipinski Landscape & Irrigation Contractors Inc 100 Sharp Rd	Marlton	NJ	08053	**800-644-6035**		422
Lipper International Inc 235 Washington St	Wallingford	CT	06492	**800-243-3129**	203-269-8588	728
Lippincott Marine 3420 Main St	Grasonville	MD	33701	**877-437-4193**	410-827-9300	695
Lipscomb University 3901 Granny White Pk	Nashville	TN	37204	**800-333-4358**	615-966-1000	167
Lipten Company LLC 28054 Ctr Oaks Ct	Wixom	MI	48393	**800-860-0790**	248-374-8910	385
Liquid Transport Corp 8470 Allison Pt Blvd Ste 400	Indianapolis	IN	46250	**800-942-3175**	317-841-4200	778
Liquidity Services Inc 1920 L St NW 6th Fl *NASDAQ: LQDT*	Washington	DC	20036	**800-310-4604**	202-467-6868	50
Liquidmetal Technologies Inc (LQMT) 30452 Esperanza *OTC: LQMT*	Rancho Santa Margarita	CA	92688	**888-203-1112**	949-635-2100	481
Lisa Motor Lines 1145 Empire Central Pl PO Box 655888	Dallas	TX	75247	**800-569-9200**	214-630-8090	778
LISI Inc 1600 W Hillsdale Blvd	San Mateo	CA	94402	**866-570-5474**	650-348-4131	390
Lisle Convention & Visitors Bureau 925 Burlington Ave	Lisle	IL	60532	**800-733-9811**	630-769-1000	208
List Industries Inc 401 Jim Moran Blvd	Deerfield Beach	FL	33442	**800-776-1342**	954-429-9155	320-3
Lista International Corp 106 Lowland St *Cust Svc	Holliston	MA	01746	**800-722-3020***	508-429-1350	288
Listel Hotel, The 1300 Robson St	Vancouver	BC	V6E1C5	**800-663-5491**	604-684-8461	379
Listo Pencil Corp 1925 Union St	Alameda	CA	94501	**800-547-8648**	510-522-2910	570
LITA (Library & Information Technology Assn) 50 E Huron St	Chicago	IL	60611	**800-545-2433**	312-280-4270	48-11
Litchfield Beach & Golf Resort 14276 Ocean Hwy	Pawleys Island	SC	29585	**888-766-4633**	843-237-3000	667
Litehaus Systems Inc 7445 132nd St Ste 2010	Surrey	BC	V3W1J8	**866-771-0044**		807
Litehouse Inc 1109 N Ella Ave	Sandpoint	ID	83864	**800-669-3169**	208-265-3700	297-19
Litelab Corp 251 Elm St	Buffalo	NY	14203	**800-238-4120**	716-856-4491	362
Litetronics International Inc 4101 W 123rd St	Alsip	IL	60803	**800-860-3392**	708-389-8000	437
Lithia Motors Inc 360 E Jackson St *NYSE: LAD*	Medford	OR	97501	**866-318-9660**		56
Litho-Krome Co 5700 Old Brim Dr	Midland	GA	31820	**800-572-8028**	706-562-7900	626
Lithonia Lighting 1 Lithonia Way	Conyers	GA	30012	**800-858-7763**	770-922-9000	439
Lith-O-Roll Corp 9521 Telstar Ave	El Monte	CA	91731	**800-423-4176**	626-579-0340	453
Lititz Mutual Insurance Co 2 N Broad St PO Box 900	Lititz	PA	17543	**800-626-4751**	717-626-4751	391-4
Littau Harvester Inc 855 Rogue Ave	Stayton	OR	97383	**866-262-2495**	503-769-5953	276
Littelfuse Inc 8755 W Higgins Rd Ste 500 *NASDAQ: LFUS* ■ *Sales	Chicago	IL	60631	**800-227-0029***	773-628-1000	727
Little America Hotel & Resort Cheyenne 2800 W Lincolnway	Cheyenne	WY	82009	**800-445-6945**	307-775-8400	379
Little America Hotel & Towers Salt Lake City 555 S Main St	Salt Lake City	UT	84101	**800-453-9450**	801-258-6568	379
Little America Hotel Flagstaff 2515 E Butler Ave	Flagstaff	AZ	86004	**800-352-4386**	928-779-7900	379
Little America Hotels & Resorts 500 S Main St	Salt Lake City	UT	84101	**800-281-7899**	801-596-5700	379
Little Bank Inc, The 804 Carey Rd *OTC: LTLB*	Kinston	NC	28501	**855-449-0975**	252-939-9990	69
Little Brown & Co 237 Pk Ave *Cust Svc	New York	NY	10017	**800-759-0190***	212-364-1100	634-2
Little Caesars Inc 2211 Woodward Ave	Detroit	MI	48201	**800-722-3727**	313-983-6409	668
Little Creek Casino Resort 91 W State Rt 108	Shelton	WA	98584	**800-667-7711**	360-427-7711	667
Little Falls Granite Works 10802 Hwy 10	Little Falls	MN	56345	**800-862-2417**		722
Little Gym International Inc 7001 N Scottsdale Rd *General	Paradise Valley	AZ	85253	**888-228-2878***		354
Little Kids Inc 225 Chapman St Ste 202	Providence	RI	02905	**800-545-5437**	401-454-7600	607
Little Nell, The 675 E Durant Ave	Aspen	CO	81611	**888-843-6355**	970-920-4600	379
Little Ocmulgee Electric Membership Corp 26 W Railroad Ave	Alamo	GA	30411	**800-342-1290**	912-568-7171	247
Little Palm Island Resort & Spa 28500 Overseas Hwy	Little Torch Key	FL	33042	**800-343-8567**	305-872-2524	667
Little Pee Dee State Park 1298 State Pk Rd	Dillon	SC	29536	**800-491-1764**	843-774-8872	564
Little River Electric Co-op Inc (LRECI) PO Box 220	Abbeville	SC	29620	**800-459-2141**	864-366-2141	247
Little Rock Air Force Base 1250 Thomas Ave	Little Rock AFB	AR	72099	**800-557-6815**	501-987-1110	496-1
Little Rock Convention & Visitors Bureau 426 W Markham St PO Box 3232	Little Rock	AR	72203	**800-844-4781**	501-376-4781	208
Little Talbot Island State Park 12157 Heckscher Dr	Jacksonville	FL	32226	**800-326-3521**	904-251-2320	564
Little Tikes Co, The 2180 Barlow Rd *Cust Svc	Hudson	OH	44236	**800-321-0183***		760
Little White House State Historic Site 401 Little White House Rd	Warm Springs	GA	31830	**800-864-7275**	706-655-5870	564
Littlefield Feedyard Farm to Market 37	Littlefield	TX	79339	**800-658-6014**	806-385-5141	10-1
Littleford Day Inc 7451 Empire Dr	Florence	KY	41042	**800-365-8555**	859-525-7600	386
Littler Mendelson PC 650 California St 20th Fl	San Francisco	CA	94108	**888-548-8537**	415-433-1940	428
Littlestown Foundry Inc 150 Charles St PO Box 69	Littlestown	PA	17340	**800-471-0844**	717-359-4141	309
Littleton Coin Company LLC 1309 Mt Eustis Rd	Littleton	NH	03561	**800-645-3122**	603-444-5386	49-3
Litton Engineering Laboratories 200 Litton Dr Ste 200	Grass Valley	CA	95945	**800-821-8866**	530-273-6176	453
Liturgical Publications Inc 2875 S James Dr	New Berlin	WI	53151	**800-876-4574**	262-785-1188	634-9
Live Design 249 W 17th St *Sales	New York	NY	10011	**866-505-7173***	212-204-4272	456-9
Livecareer Inc 1432 Washington St	San Francisco	CA	94109	**800-652-8430**		396
Livengrin Foundation 4833 Hulmeville Rd	Bensalem	PA	19020	**800-245-4746**	215-638-5200	724
Livestock Marketing Assn (LMA) 10510 N Ambassador Dr	Kansas City	MO	64153	**800-821-2048**	816-891-0502	47-2
Living Assistance Services Inc 937 Haverford Rd Ste 200	Bryn Mawr	PA	19010	**800-365-4189**		311
Living Bank PO Box 6725	Houston	TX	77027	**800-528-2971**	713-961-9431	47-17
Living Color Enterprises Inc 6850 NW 12th Ave	Fort Lauderdale	FL	33309	**800-878-9511**	954-970-9511	40
Living Earth Crafts 3210 Executive Ridge Dr	Vista	CA	92081	**800-358-8292**	760-597-2155	75
Living Spa at El Monte Sagrado 317 Kit Carson Rd	Taos	NM	87571	**855-846-8267**	575-758-3502	705
Living Spaces Furniture LLC 14501 Artesia Blvd	La Mirada	CA	90638	**877-266-7300**		322
Livingston County Chamber of Commerce 4635 Millennium Dr	Geneseo	NY	14454	**800-538-7365**	585-243-2222	138
Livingston County Daily Press & Argus 323 E Grand River Ave	Howell	MI	48843	**888-999-1288**	517-548-2000	634-8
Livingston Memorial Visiting Nurse Assn Hospice 1996 Eastman Ave Ste 101	Ventura	CA	93003	**800-830-8881**	805-642-1608	371
Livingston Pipe & Tube Inc 1612 Rt 4 N	Staunton	IL	62088	**800-548-7473**	618-635-8700	491
Livingstone College 701 W Monroe St	Salisbury	NC	28144	**800-835-3435**	704-216-6963	167
LJ Gonzer Assoc Inc 14 Commerce Dr Ste 305	Cranford	NJ	07016	**866-692-4538**	908-709-9494	719
LJB Inc 2500 Newmark Dr	Miamisburg	OH	45342	**866-552-3536**	937-259-5000	263
LK Industries 1357 W Beaver St	Jacksonville	FL	32209	**800-531-4975**	904-354-8882	299
LKQ Corp 500 W Madison St Ste 2800 *NASDAQ: LKQX*	Chicago	IL	60661	**877-557-2677**	312-621-1950	60
LL Bean Inc 15 Casco St	Freeport	ME	04033	**800-341-4341**	207-552-3080	458
Ll Roberts Group 7475 Skillman St Ste 102c	Dallas	TX	75231	**877-878-6463**	214-221-6463	262
LLAMA (Library Leadership & Management Assn) 50 E Huron St	Chicago	IL	60611	**800-545-2433**		48-11
Llano Estacado Winery 3426 E FM 1585	Lubbock	TX	79404	**800-634-3854**	806-745-2258	49-6
LLEC (Lyon-Lincoln Electric Co-op Inc) 205 W Hwy 14 PO Box 639	Tyler	MN	56178	**800-927-6276**	507-247-5505	247
Llewellyn Worldwide Inc 2143 Wooddale Dr	Woodbury	MN	55125	**800-843-6666**	651-291-1970	634-2
LLLI (La Leche League International Inc) 957 N Plum Grove Rd	Schaumburg	IL	60173	**800-525-3243**	847-519-7730	47-17
Lloyd & McDaniel PLC 11405 Park Rd Ste 200	Louisville	KY	40223	**866-548-2486**	502-585-1880	428
Lloyd Gray Whitehead & Monroe PC 2501 20th Pl S Ste 300	Birmingham	AL	35223	**800-967-7299**	205-967-8822	428
Lloyd Inc 604 W Thomas Ave PO Box 130	Shenandoah	IA	51601	**800-831-0004**	712-246-4000	581
Lloyd Laboratories Inc 24 Fitch Ct	Wakefield	MA	01880	**800-361-6766**	781-224-0083	144
Lloyd Schuh Advertising Inc 2207 Cantrell Rd	Little Rock	AR	72202	**866-572-6584**	501-374-2332	197
Lloyd's Florist 9216 Preston Hwy	Louisville	KY	40229	**800-264-1825**	502-968-5428	294
LMA (Livestock Marketing Assn) 10510 N Ambassador Dr	Kansas City	MO	64153	**800-821-2048**	816-891-0502	47-2
LMG Inc PO Box 770429	Orlando	FL	32877	**888-226-3100**	407-850-0505	266-2
LMH (Lawrence Memorial Hospital) 325 Maine St	Lawrence	KS	66044	**800-749-4144**	785-505-5000	374-3
LMI (Legg Mason Inc) 100 International Dr *NYSE: LM*	Baltimore	MD	21202	**800-822-5544**	410-539-0000	688
LMS Reinforcing Steel Group Inc 6320 148th St	Surrey	BC	V3S3C4	**888-698-2008**	604-598-9930	491
Lmt USA Inc 1081 S Northpoint Blvd	Waukegan	IL	60085	**800-225-0852**		386
LN Curtis & Sons 1800 Peralta St	Oakland	CA	94607	**800-443-3556**	510-839-5111	677

Company / Address	City	State	Zip	Toll-Free	Phone	Class
LNB Bancorp Inc 457 Broadway *NASDAQ: LNBB*	Lorain	OH	44052	**800-860-1007**	440-989-3348	360-2
LNC (Lincoln National Corp) 150 N Radnor-Chester Rd *NYSE: LNC*	Radnor	PA	19087	**877-275-5462**	484-583-1400	360-4
LNI Custom Manufacturing Inc 12536 Chadron Ave	Hawthorne	CA	90250	**800-338-3387**	310-978-2000	699
Load Rite Trailers Inc 265 Lincoln Hwy	Fairless Hills	PA	19030	**800-562-3783**	215-949-0500	761
Loan Science 9600 Great Hills Trail E Ste 200	Austin	TX	78759	**866-311-9450**		219
loanDepot 26642 Towne Centre Dr	Foothill Ranch	CA	92610	**888-337-6888**		508
Loanio Inc 25 Smith St Ste 301	Nanuet	NY	10954	**800-624-8830**		393
Loblaw Cos Ltd 1 President's Choice Cir	Brampton	ON	L6Y5S5	**888-495-5111**	905-459-2500	345
Lobster Sports Inc 7340 Fulton Ave	North Hollywood	CA	91605	**800-210-5992**	818-764-6000	708
LoBue & Majdalany Management Group 572B Ruger St PO Box 29920	San Francisco	CA	94129	**800-820-4690**	415-561-6110	46
LOC Enterprises LLC 7575 E Kemper Rd	Cincinnati	OH	45249	**888-963-6320**		197
Local Government Federal Credit Union 323 W Jones St Ste 600	Raleigh	NC	27603	**888-732-8562**	919-857-2150	221
LocBox 400 Second St Ste 400	San Francisco	CA	94107	**855-256-2269**		197
Lochinvar Corp 300 Maddox Simpson Pkwy	Lebanon	TN	37090	**800-722-2101**	615-889-8900	35
Lochmueller Group 6200 Vogel Rd	Evansville	IN	47715	**800-423-7411**	812-479-6200	258
Lochsa Engineering Inc 6345 S Jones Blvd Ste 100	Las Vegas	NV	89118	**866-606-9784**	702-365-9312	263
Lock Haven University 401 N Fairview St	Lock Haven	PA	17745	**800-233-8978**	570-484-2011	167
Lock Joint Tube Inc 515 W Ireland Rd	South Bend	IN	46614	**800-257-6859**	574-299-5326	489
Lockheed Federal Credit Union (LFCU) 2340 Hollywood Way	Burbank	CA	91505	**800-328-5328**	818-565-2020	221
Lockheed Martin Corp 6801 Rockledge Dr *NYSE: LMT*	Bethesda	MD	20817	**866-562-2363**	301-897-6000	20
Lockheed Martin Space Systems Co Michoud Operations 13800 Old Gentilly Rd	New Orleans	LA	70129	**866-562-2363**	504-257-3311	503
Lockheed Window Corp Rt 100 PO Box 166	Pascoag	RI	02859	**800-537-3061**	401-568-3061	236
Lockmasters Security Institute 2101 John C Watts Dr	Nicholasville	KY	40356	**800-654-0637**	859-885-6041	350
Lockwood Advisors Inc 760 Moore Rd	King Of Prussia	PA	19406	**800-200-3033**		68
Lockwood Products Inc 5615 Willow Ln	Lake Oswego	OR	97035	**800-423-1625**	503-635-8113	370
Lodal Inc 620 N Hooper St PO Box 2315	Kingsford	MI	49802	**800-435-3500**	906-779-1700	515
LoDan Electronics Inc 3311 N Kennicott Ave	Arlington Heights	IL	60004	**800-401-4995**	847-398-5311	814
Lodge & Club at Ponte Vedra Beach 607 Ponte Vedra Blvd	Ponte Vedra Beach	FL	32082	**800-243-4304**	888-839-9145	667
Lodge & Spa at Cordillera 2205 Cordillera Way	Edwards	CO	81632	**800-877-3529**	970-926-2200	379
Lodge At Breckenridge, The 112 Overlook Dr	Breckenridge	CO	80424	**800-736-1607**	970-453-9300	379
Lodge at Pebble Beach 1700 17-Mile Dr	Pebble Beach	CA	93953	**800-654-9300**	831-624-3811	667
Lodge at Sonoma - A Renaissance Resort & Spa 1325 Broadway	Sonoma	CA	95476	**866-263-0758**	707-935-6600	667
Lodge at the Mountain Village 1415 Lowell Ave	Park City	UT	84060	**800-453-1360**	435-649-0800	379
Lodge at Ventana Canyon - A Wyndham Luxury Resort 6200 N Clubhouse Ln	Tucson	AZ	85750	**800-828-5701**	520-577-1400	667
Lodge of Four Seasons 315 Four Seasons Dr PO Box 215 *Resv	Lake Ozark	MO	65049	**888-265-5500***	573-365-3000	667
Lodge on the Desert 306 N Alvernon Way	Tucson	AZ	85711	**877-498-6776**	520-320-2000	379
Lodging Magazine 385 Oxford Vly Rd Ste 420	Yardley	PA	19067	**800-394-5157**	215-321-9662	456-5
Lodi Conference & Visitors Bureau 115 S School St	Lodi	CA	95240	**800-798-1810**	209-365-1195	208
Lodi Irrigation 1301 E Armstrong Rd	Lodi	CA	95242	**800-634-7272**		429
Lodi Memorial Hospital 975 S Fairmont Ave	Lodi	CA	95240	**800-323-3360**	209-334-3411	374-3
Lodi News-Sentinel 125 N Church St	Lodi	CA	95240	**877-333-4507**	209-369-2761	531-2
Loeb Equipment & Appraisal Co 4131 S State St	Chicago	IL	60609	**800-560-5632**	773-548-4131	40
Loeber Motors Inc 4255 W Touhy Ave	Lincolnwood	IL	60712	**888-211-4485**	847-675-1000	56
Loesel Schaaf Insurance Agency Inc 3537 W 12th St	Erie	PA	16505	**877-718-9935**	814-833-5433	390
Loews Coronado Bay Resort 4000 Coronado Bay Rd	Coronado	CA	92118	**800-815-6397**	619-424-4000	667
LOEWS HOTELS 667 Madison Ave	New York	NY	10065	**800-235-6397**	615-340-2000	669
Loews Madison Hotel 1177 15th St NW	Washington	DC	20005	**888-825-2436**	202-862-1600	669
Loews Ventana Canyon Resort 7000 N Resort Dr	Tucson	AZ	85750	**800-234-5117**	520-299-2020	667
Loftin Equipment Company Inc 12 N 45th Ave	Phoenix	AZ	85043	**800-437-4376**	602-272-9466	535
Loftness Specialized Farm Equipment Inc 650 S Main St PO Box 337	Hector	MN	55342	**800-828-7624**	320-848-6266	275
Lofton Label Inc 6290 Claude Way	Inver Grove Heights	MN	55076	**877-447-8118**	651-552-6257	551-1
Lofts Hotel & Suites 55 E Nationwide Blvd *General	Columbus	OH	43215	**877-902-9022***	614-461-2663	379
Logan Capital Management Inc 6 Coulter Ave Ste 2000	Ardmore	PA	19003	**800-215-1100**		401
Logan Clay Products Co 201 S Walnut St	Logan	OH	43138	**800-848-2141**		149
Logan Corp 555 Seventh Ave	Huntington	WV	25701	**888-853-4751**	304-526-4700	385
Logan County Chamber of Commerce 100 S Main St	Bellefontaine	OH	43311	**877-360-3608**	937-599-5121	138
Logan Farms Honey Glazed Hams 10560 Westheimer Rd	Houston	TX	77042	**800-833-4267**	713-781-4335	336
Logan Regional Medical Ctr 20 Hospital Dr	Logan	WV	25601	**888-982-9144**	304-831-1101	374-3
Logan Trucking Inc 3224 Navarre Rd SW	Canton	OH	44706	**800-683-0142**	330-478-1404	188
LoganBritton Inc 1700 Park St Ste 111	Naperville	IL	60563	**800-362-4352**		227
Logansport Financial Corp 723 E Broadway *OTC: LOGN*	Logansport	IN	46947	**800-541-9154**	574-722-3855	360-2
Logansport Juvenile Correctional Facility 1118 S St Rd 25	Logansport	IN	46947	**800-800-5556**	574-753-7571	412
Logees Greenhouses Ltd 141 N St	Danielson	CT	06239	**888-330-8038**	860-774-8038	194
Logic Devices Inc 1375 Geneva Dr *OTC: LOGC*	Sunnyvale	CA	94089	**800-233-2518**	408-542-5400	694
Logic PD Inc 6201 Bury Dr	Eden Prairie	MN	55346	**855-461-3802**	952-941-8071	393
Logicease Solutions Inc 1 Bay Plaza Ste 520	Burlingame	CA	94010	**866-212-3273**	650-373-1111	182
Logility Inc 470 E Paces Ferry Rd	Atlanta	GA	30305	**800-762-5207**	404-261-9777	180-1
Logistics Plus Inc 1406 Peach St	Erie	PA	16501	**866-564-7587**	814-461-7600	312
Logitech Inc 6505 Kaiser Dr *Sales	Fremont	CA	94555	**800-231-7717***	510-795-8500	175-2
Logitek Electronic Systems Inc 5622 Edgemoor Dr	Houston	TX	77081	**877-231-5870**	713-664-4470	645
LogoNation Inc PO Box 3847 Ste 102	Mooresville	NC	28117	**800-955-7375**	704-799-0612	626
Logos Christian College 6620 Southpoint Dr S Ste 200	Jacksonville	FL	32216	**800-776-0127**	904-745-3311	167
Loki Systems Inc 1258-13351 Commerce Pkwy	Richmond	BC	V6V2X7	**800-378-5654**	604-249-5050	181
LOKRING Technology LLC 38376 Apollo Pkwy	Willoughby	OH	44094	**800-876-2323**	440-942-0880	721
LOMA 2300 Windy Ridge Pkwy Ste 600	Atlanta	GA	30339	**800-275-5662**	770-951-1770	48-9
Loma Linda University Medical Ctr 11234 Anderson St	Loma Linda	CA	92354	**877-558-6248**	909-558-4000	374-3
Loma Linda University School of Medicine 11175 Campus St	Loma Linda	CA	92350	**800-422-4558**	909-558-4467	168-2
Lomanco Inc 2101 W Main St	Jacksonville	AR	72076	**800-643-5596**	501-982-6511	14
Lombardi's 401 Biscayne Blvd	Miami	FL	33132	**888-286-3792**		669
Lompoc Valley Chamber of Commerce & Visitors Bureau PO Box 626	Lompoc	CA	93438	**800-240-0999**	805-736-4567	138
London Computer Services 1007 Cottonwood Dr	Loveland	OH	45140	**800-669-0871**	513-583-1482	181
London Drugs Ltd 12251 Horseshoe Way	Richmond	BC	V7A4X5	**888-991-2299**	604-272-7400	240
London Fog 1615 Kellogg Dr	Douglas	GA	31535	**877-588-8189**	912-384-8189	154-5
London Free Press 369 York St PO Box 2280	London	ON	N6A4G1	**866-541-6757**	519-679-1111	531-1
London Life Insurance Co 255 Dufferin Ave	London	ON	N6A4K1	**800-990-6654**	519-432-5281	391-2
London Machinery Inc 15790 Robin's Hill Rd	London	ON	N5V0A4	**800-265-1098**	519-963-2500	60
London West Hollywood Hotel 1020 N San Vicente Blvd	West Hollywood	CA	90069	**866-282-4560**		378
London/Laurel County Tourist Commission 140 Faith Assembly Church Rd	London	KY	40741	**800-348-0095**	606-878-6900	208
Lone Mountain Ranch 750 Lone Mtn Ranch Rd PO Box 160069	Big Sky	MT	59716	**800-514-4644**	406-995-4644	241
Lone Oak Lodge 2221 N Fremont St *General	Monterey	CA	93940	**800-283-5663***	831-372-4924	379
Lone Star Circuits 901 Hensley Ln	Wylie	TX	75098	**800-303-9266**	214-291-1427	624
Lone Star Container Corp 700 N Wildwood Dr	Irving	TX	75061	**800-552-6937**		99
Lone Star Flight Museum 2002 Terminal Dr	Galveston	TX	77554	**888-359-5736**	409-740-7722	519
Lone Star Lions Eye Bank 102 E Wheeler St PO Box 347	Manor	TX	78653	**800-977-3937**	512-457-0638	271
Lone Star Percussion 10611 Control Pl	Dallas	TX	75238	**866-792-0143**	214-340-0835	525
Lonely Planet Online 150 Linden St	Oakland	CA	94607	**800-275-8555**	510-250-6400	771
Lonely Planet Publications 50 Linden St	Oakland	CA	94607	**800-275-8555**	510-893-8555	634-2
Long & Foster Realtors 14501 George Carter Way	Chantilly	VA	20151	**800-237-8800**	703-653-8500	650
Long Beach Airport LGB 4100 Donald Douglas Dr	Long Beach	CA	90808	**800-331-1212**	562-570-2600	27
Long Beach City College 4901 E Carson St	Long Beach	CA	90808	**888-442-4551**	562-938-4111	161
Long Beach Convention & Visitors Bureau 301 E Ocean Blvd	Long Beach	CA	90802	**800-452-7829**	562-436-3645	208
Long Hollow Ranch 71105 Holmes Rd	Sisters	OR	97759	**877-923-1901**	541-923-1901	241

Name	Address	City	State	Zip	Toll-Free	Phone	Class
Long House Alaskan Hotel	4335 Wisconsin St	Anchorage	AK	99517	**888-243-2133**	907-243-2133	379
Long Island College Hospital (LICH)	339 Hicks St	Brooklyn	NY	11201	**800-227-8922**	718-780-1000	374-3
Long Island Convention & Visitors Bureau & Sports Commission	330 Motor Pkwy Ste 203	Hauppauge	NY	11788	**877-386-6654**		208
Long Island MacArthur Airport	100 Arrival Ave Ste 100	Ronkonkoma	NY	11779	**888-542-4776**	631-467-3300	27
Long Island Power Authority	333 Earle Ovington Blvd Ste 403 *Cust Svc	Uniondale	NY	11553	**877-275-5472***	516-222-7700	785
Long Island Press	575 Underhill Blvd Ste 210	Syosset	NY	11791	**800-545-6683**	516-284-3300	531-5
Long Island University	*Brooklyn* 1 University Plz	Brooklyn	NY	11201	**800-548-7526**	718-488-1011	167
Long Painting Co	21414 68th Ave S	Kent	WA	98032	**800-678-5664**	253-234-8050	191-8
Long Prairie Packing Co	10 Riverside Dr	Long Prairie	MN	56347	**800-996-6440**	320-732-2171	472
Long View Systems Corp	3100 255 Fifth Ave SW	Calgary	AB	T2P3G6	**866-515-6900**	403-515-6900	176
Long Wharf Theatre	222 Sargent Dr	New Haven	CT	06511	**800-782-8497**	203-787-4282	571
Longacre Theatre	220 W 48th St	New York	NY	10036	**800-447-7400**	212-239-6200	744
Longboat Key Club	220 Sands Point Rd	Longboat Key	FL	34228	**800-237-8821**	941-383-8821	667
Longfellow-Evangeline State Historic Site	1200 N Main St	Saint Martinville	LA	70582	**888-677-2900**	337-394-3754	564
Longhorn Imports Inc	2202 E Union Bower	Irving	TX	75061	**800-641-8348**	972-721-9102	312
LongHorn Steakhouse	1000 Darden Ctr Dr	Orlando	FL	32837	**888-221-0642**		668
Longistics Transportation Inc	10900 World Trade Blvd	Raleigh	NC	27617	**800-289-0082**	919-872-7626	801-1
Longust Distributing Inc	2432 W Birchwood Ave	Mesa	AZ	85202	**800-352-0521**	480-820-6244	361
Longview News-Journal	320 E Methvin St	Longview	TX	75601	**800-825-9799**	903-757-3311	531-2
Longview Partnership	410 N Ctr St	Longview	TX	75601	**800-338-7232**	903-237-4000	138
Longview School District	2715 Lilac St	Longview	WA	98632	**800-533-7881**	360-575-7000	683
Longview Solutions	100 Matsonford Rd Ste 230	Radnor	PA	19087	**888-454-2549**	610-977-0995	180-1
Longwood Gardens	PO Box 501	Kennett Square	PA	19348	**800-737-5500**	610-388-1000	96
Longwood University	201 High St	Farmville	VA	23909	**800-281-4677**	434-395-2060	167
Lonsdale Quay Hotel	123 Carrie Cates Ct	North Vancouver	BC	V7M3K7	**800-836-6111**	604-986-6111	379
Lonseal Inc	928 E 238th St	Carson	CA	90745	**800-832-7111**	310-830-7111	361
Look Cycle Usa	6300 San Ignacio Ave Ste G	San Jose	CA	95119	**866-430-5665**	408-363-1406	709
Lookout Inn	6901 Lookout Rd	Boulder	CO	80301	**800-530-1513**	877-234-4779	379
Loomis Armored US Inc	2500 Citywest Blvd Ste 900	Houston	TX	77042	**866-383-5069**	713-435-6700	691
Loomis Co	850 N Pk Rd	Wyomissing	PA	19610	**800-782-0392**	610-374-4040	390
Loomis Communities	246 N Main St	South Hadley	MA	01075	**800-865-7655**	413-532-5325	670
Loomis Fargo & Co	2500 Citywest Blvd Ste 900	Houston	TX	77042	**866-383-5069**	713-435-6700	690
Loomis Sayles & Company Inc LP	PO Box 219594	Kansas City	MO	64121	**800-343-2029**	800-633-3330	401
Loomis Sayles Funds	1 Financial Ctr	Boston	MA	02111	**800-633-3330**	617-482-2450	527
Loop Capital Markets LLC	111 W Jackson Blvd Ste 1901	Chicago	IL	60604	**888-294-8898**	312-913-4900	688
Loop-Loc Ltd	390 Motor Pkwy	Hauppauge	NY	11788	**800-562-5667**	631-582-2626	730
LOPA (Louisiana Organ Procurement Agency)	3545 N I-10 Service Rd Ste 300	Metairie	LA	70002	**800-521-4483**		544
Lopez Mchugh LLP	1123 Admiral Peary Way	Philadelphia	PA	19112	**877-703-7070**	215-952-6910	428
Lorain Correctional Institution	2075 Avon Belden Rd	Grafton	OH	44044	**888-988-4768**	440-748-1049	215
Lorain County Community College	1005 N Abbe Rd	Elyria	OH	44035	**800-995-5222**	440-365-5222	161
Lorain County Visitors Bureau	8025 Leavitt Rd	Amherst	OH	44001	**800-334-1673**	440-984-5282	208
Lorain Public Library System	351 W Sixth St	Lorain	OH	44052	**800-322-7323**	440-244-1192	434-3
Lorain-Medina Rural Electric Co-op Inc	22898 W Rd	Wellington	OH	44090	**800-222-5673**	440-647-2133	247
Loram Maintenance of Way	3900 Arrowhead Dr PO Box 188	Hamel	MN	55340	**800-328-1466**	763-478-6014	648
Lorann Oils	4518 Aurelius Rd	Lansing	MI	48910	**800-862-8620**	517-882-0215	345
Loras College	1450 Alta Vista St	Dubuque	IA	52001	**800-245-6727**	563-588-7100	167
Lorber Greenfield & Polito LLP	13985 Stowe Dr	Poway	CA	92064	**800-659-8821**	858-513-1020	428
Lord & Taylor	424 Fifth Ave	New York	NY	10018	**800-223-7440**	212-391-3344	231
Lord Abbett & Co	90 Hudson St	Jersey City	NJ	07302	**888-522-2388**	201-827-2000	401
Lord Corp	111 Lord Dr	Cary	NC	27511	**877-275-5673**	919-468-5979	3
Lord Elgin Hotel	100 Elgin St	Ottawa	ON	K1P5K8	**800-267-4298**	613-235-3333	379
Lord Fairfax Community College	*Middletown* 173 Skirmisher Ln	Middletown	VA	22645	**800-906-5322**	540-868-7000	161
Lord Nelson Hotel & Suites	1515 S Pk St	Halifax	NS	B3J2L2	**800-565-2020**	902-423-6331	379
Lord Stanley Suites on the Park	1889 Alberni St	Vancouver	BC	V6G3G7	**888-767-7829**	604-688-9299	379
Lordco Parts Ltd	22866 Dewdney Trunk Rd	Maple Ridge	BC	V2X3K6	**877-591-1581**	604-467-1581	56
Lorenz Corp	501 E Third St	Dayton	OH	45402	**800-444-1144**	937-228-6118	634-7
Lorge & Lorge Law Firm	501 W Willow St	Bear Creek	WI	54922	**800-529-2946**	715-752-3304	428
Lori Bonn Jewelery	114 Linden St	Oakland	CA	94607	**877-507-4206**		410
Lorin Industries	1960 S Roberts St	Muskegon	MI	49443	**800-654-1159**	231-722-1631	480
Loroco Industries Inc	5000 Creek Rd	Cincinnati	OH	45242	**800-215-9474**	513-891-9544	554
Lorraine Travel Bureau Inc	377 Alhambra Cir	Coral Gables	FL	33134	**800-666-8911**	305-446-4433	769
Los Abrigados Resort	160 Portal Ln	Sedona	AZ	86336	**877-374-2582**	928-282-1777	667
Los Adaes State Historic Site	6354 Hwy 485	Robeline	LA	71469	**888-677-5378**	318-472-9449	564
Los Alamos National Laboratory (LANL)	PO Box 1663	Los Alamos	NM	87545	**877-723-4101**	505-667-7000	666
Los Alamos Technical Assoc Inc	999 Central Ave Ste 300	Los Alamos	NM	87544	**800-888-1745**	505-662-9080	194
Los Angeles Athletic Club	431 W Seventh St	Los Angeles	CA	90014	**800-421-8777**	213-625-2211	379
Los Angeles Biomedical Research Institute	1124 W Carson St	Torrance	CA	90502	**877-452-2674**		666
Los Angeles City College	855 N Vermont Ave	Los Angeles	CA	90029	**800-207-1710**	323-953-4000	161
Los Angeles Clippers	Staples Ctr 1111 S Figueroa St Ste 1100	Los Angeles	CA	90015	**855-895-0872**	213-742-7100	712-1
Los Angeles Confidential Magazine	717 N Highland Ave Unit 10	Los Angeles	CA	90038	**866-891-3144**	310-289-7300	456-22
Los Angeles County Metropolitan Transportation Authority	1 Gateway Plz	Los Angeles	CA	90012	**800-621-7828**	213-922-6000	467
Los Angeles County Public Library	7400 E Imperial Hwy	Downey	CA	90242	**888-794-9466**	562-940-8462	434-3
Los Angeles Downtown News	1264 W First St	Los Angeles	CA	90026	**877-338-1010**	213-481-1448	531-4
Los Angeles Federal Credit Union	PO Box 53032	Los Angeles	CA	90053	**877-695-2328**	818-242-8640	221
Los Angeles Galaxy	Home Depot Ctr 18400 Avalon Blvd Ste 200	Carson	CA	90746	**877-342-5299**	310-630-2200	715
Los Angeles Kings	Staples Ctr 1111 S Figueroa St	Los Angeles	CA	90015	**888-546-4752**	213-742-7100	714
Los Angeles Lakers	555 N Nash St	El Segundo	CA	90245	**866-648-4668**	310-426-6000	712-1
Los Angeles Magazine	5900 Wilshire Blvd 10th Fl *Cust Svc	Los Angeles	CA	90036	**800-876-5222***	323-801-0100	456-22
Los Angeles Police Federal Credit Union	PO Box 10188	Van Nuys	CA	91410	**877-695-2732**	818-787-6520	221
Los Angeles Smoking & Curing Co (LASCCO)	1100 W Ewing St	Seattle	WA	98119	**800-365-8950**	206-285-6800	297-13
Los Angeles Sparks	865 S Figueroa St Ste 104	Los Angeles	CA	90017	**888-694-3278**	213-929-1300	712-2
Los Angeles Times	202 W First St	Los Angeles	CA	90012	**800-528-4637**	213-237-5000	531-2
Los Angeles Times Festival of Books	Los Angeles Times 202 W First St	Los Angeles	CA	90012	**800-528-4637**	213-237-2335	283
Los Angeles Times-Washington Post News Service Inc	1150 15th St NW	Washington	DC	20071	**800-627-1150**	202-334-6000	529
Los Angeles Unified School District (LAUSD)	333 S Beaudry Ave	Los Angeles	CA	90017	**877-772-6273**	213-241-1000	683
Los Medanos College	2700 E Leland Rd	Pittsburg	CA	94565	**800-677-6337**	925-439-2181	161
LOSFA (Louisiana Office of Student Financial Assistance)	602 N Fifth St PO Box 91202	Baton Rouge	LA	70802	**800-259-5626**	225-219-1012	723
Losi	4710 E Guasti Rd	Ontario	CA	91761	**888-899-5674**	909-390-9595	760
Lost Recovery Network Lrni	406 dixon st	Vidalia	GA	30474	**877-693-1456**	912-537-3901	462
Lost River Caverns	726 Durham St PO Box M	Hellertown	PA	18055	**888-529-1907**	610-838-8767	49-4
Lotus Cars USA Inc	2402 Tech Ctr Pkwy NE *Cust Svc	Lawrenceville	GA	30043	**800-245-6887***	770-476-6540	58
Lou Bachrodt Auto Group	7070 Cherryvale N Blvd	Rockford	IL	61112	**866-635-2349**	815-332-3000	56
LOUD Technologies Inc	16220 Wood Red Rd NE *OTC: LTEC*	Woodinville	WA	98072	**866-858-5832**	425-892-6500	51
Loudoun House	209 Castlewood Dr	Lexington	KY	40505	**866-945-7920**	859-254-7024	49-2
Loudoun Times-Mirror	PO Box 359	Leesburg	VA	20178	**888-351-1660**	703-777-1111	531-4
Louhelen Baha'i School	3208 S State Rd	Davison	MI	48423	**800-894-9716**	810-653-5033	671
Louis A Johnson Veterans Affairs Medical Ctr	1 Medical Ctr Dr	Clarksburg	WV	26301	**800-733-0512**	304-623-3461	374-8
Louis Ferre Inc	302 Fifth Ave Ste 10	New York	NY	10001	**800-695-1061**	212-239-1600	348
Louis M Gerson Company Inc	16 Commerce Blvd	Middleboro	MA	02346	**800-225-8623**	508-947-4000	575
Louis M Martini Winery	254 S St Helena Hwy	Saint Helena	CA	94574	**866-549-2582**		79-3
Louis Padnos Iron & Metal Co	PO Box 1979	Holland	MI	49422	**800-442-3509**	616-396-6521	684
Louis Stokes Cleveland Veterans Affairs Medical Ctr	10701 E Blvd	Cleveland	OH	44106	**888-838-6446**	216-791-3800	374-8
Louis Vuitton NA Inc	1 E 57th St *Cust Svc	New York	NY	10022	**866-884-8866***	212-758-8877	156-6

Name / Address	City	State	ZIP	Toll-Free	Phone	Class
Louisburg College						
501 N Main St	Louisburg	NC	27549	**800-775-0208**	919-496-2521	161
Louisiana						
Community Services Office						
627 N 4th St	Baton Rouge	LA	70802	**888-524-3578**		339-19
Consumer Protection Office						
PO Box 94095	Baton Rouge	LA	70804	**800-351-4889**		339-19
Education Dept						
PO Box 94064	Baton Rouge	LA	70804	**877-453-2721**		339-19
Environmental Quality Dept						
602 N Fifth St	Baton Rouge	LA	70802	**866-896-5337**	225-219-5337	339-19
Housing Finance Agency						
2415 Quail Dr	Baton Rouge	LA	70808	**888-454-2001**	225-763-8700	339-19
Insurance Dept						
PO Box 94214	Baton Rouge	LA	70804	**800-259-5300**	225-342-5900	339-19
Legislature						
PO Box 94062	Baton Rouge	LA	70804	**800-256-3793**	225-342-2456	339-19
Office of the Governor						
PO Box 94004	Baton Rouge	LA	70804	**866-366-1121**	225-342-7015	339-19
Public Service Commission						
PO Box 91154	Baton Rouge	LA	70821	**800-256-2397**	225-342-4404	339-19
Real Estate Commission						
PO Box 14785	Baton Rouge	LA	70898	**800-821-4529**	225-765-0191	339-19
Revenue Dept						
617 N Third St PO Box 201	Baton Rouge	LA	70801	**855-307-3893**		339-19
State Parks Office						
PO Box 44426	Baton Rouge	LA	70804	**888-677-1400**	225-342-8111	339-19
Veterans Affairs Dept						
PO Box 94095	Baton Rouge	LA	70804	**877-432-8982**	225-219-5000	339-19
Wildlife & Fisheries Dept						
PO Box 98000	Baton Rouge	LA	70898	**800-442-2511**	225-765-2800	339-19
Louisiana Assn For, The Blind, The						
1750 Claiborne Ave	Shreveport	LA	71103	**877-913-6471**	318-635-6471	551-2
Louisiana Assn of Business & Industry						
3113 Vly Creek Dr						
PO Box 80258	Baton Rouge	LA	70898	**888-816-5224**	225-928-5388	139
Louisiana Association of Educators						
8322 One Kalais Ave	Baton Rouge	LA	70809	**800-256-4523**	225-343-9243	456-8
Louisiana Banker						
PO Box 2871	Baton Rouge	LA	70821	**888-249-3050**	225-387-3282	530-1
Louisiana Baptist Children's Home Inc (LBCH)						
7200 DeSiard St	Monroe	LA	71203	**877-345-7411**	318-343-2244	47-15
Louisiana College						
1140 College Dr	Pineville	LA	71359	**800-487-1906**	318-487-7011	167
Louisiana Culinary Institute						
10550 Airline Hwy	Baton Rouge	LA	70816	**877-533-3198**		162
Louisiana Delta Community College						
7500 Millhaven Rd	Monroe	LA	71203	**866-500-5322**	318-345-9000	161
Louisiana Dental Assn						
7833 Office Pk Blvd	Baton Rouge	LA	70809	**800-388-6642**	225-926-1986	229
Louisiana Ethics Board						
617 N Third St						
LaSalle Bldg Ste 10-36	Baton Rouge	LA	70802	**800-842-6630**	225-219-5600	339-19
Louisiana Medical Mutual Insurance Co						
1 Galleria Blvd Ste 700	Metairie	LA	70001	**800-452-2120**		391-5
Louisiana Office of Student Financial Assistance (LOSFA)						
602 N Fifth St PO Box 91202	Baton Rouge	LA	70802	**800-259-5626**	225-219-1012	723
Louisiana Organ Procurement Agency (LOPA)						
3545 N I-10 Service Rd Ste 300	Metairie	LA	70002	**800-521-4483**		544
Louisiana Pharmacists Assn						
450 Laurel St Ste 1400	Baton Rouge	LA	70801	**877-252-5100**	225-346-6883	584
Louisiana Public Broadcasting						
7733 Perkins Rd	Baton Rouge	LA	70810	**800-973-7246**	225-767-5660	629
Louisiana State Arboretum						
4213 Chicot Pk Rd	Ville Platte	LA	70586	**888-677-6100**	337-363-6289	564
Louisiana State Bar Assn (LSBA)						
601 St Charles Ave	New Orleans	LA	70130	**800-421-5722**	504-566-1600	71
Louisiana State Medical Society						
6767 Perkins Rd Ste 100	Baton Rouge	LA	70808	**800-375-9508**	225-763-8500	473
Louisiana State Museum						
751 Chartres St	New Orleans	LA	70116	**800-568-6968**	504-568-6968	519
Louisiana State Nurses Assn, The (LSNA)						
5713 Superior Dr Ste A-6	Baton Rouge	LA	70816	**800-457-6378**	225-201-0993	532
Louisiana State University						
Alexandria						
8100 US Hwy 71 S	Alexandria	LA	71302	**888-473-6417***	318-445-3672	167
*Admissions						
Baton Rouge						
110 Thomas Boyd Hall	Baton Rouge	LA	70803	**888-846-6810**	225-578-3202	167
Eunice PO Box 1129	Eunice	LA	70535	**888-367-5783**	337-457-7311	161
Louisiana State University School of Medicine in New Orleans						
433 Bolivar St	New Orleans	LA	70112	**844-503-7283**	504-568-6262	168-2
Louisiana State University School of Medicine in Shreveport						
1501 Kings Hwy PO Box 33932	Shreveport	LA	71130	**800-337-3627**	318-675-5069	168-2
Louisiana State University System						
125 E Boyd Dr	Baton Rouge	LA	70803	**800-227-3002**	225-578-3357	784
Louisiana Tech University						
305 Wisteria St	Ruston	LA	71272	**800-528-3241***	318-257-2000	167
*Admissions						
Louisiana Tech University Prescott Memorial Library						
PO Box 10408	Ruston	LA	71272	**877-557-2575**	318-257-3555	434-6
Louisiana Veterinary Medical Assn						
8550 United Plz Blvd						
Ste 1001	Baton Rouge	LA	70809	**800-524-2996**	225-928-5862	793
Louisiana Workforce Commission						
1001 N 23rd St	Baton Rouge	LA	70802	**877-529-6757**	225-342-3111	261
Louisiana-Pacific Corp						
414 Union St Ste 2000	Nashville	TN	37219	**888-820-0325**	615-986-5600	681
NYSE: LPX						
Louisville & Jefferson County Convention & Visitors Bureau						
401 W Main St Ste 2300	Louisville	KY	40202	**800-626-5646**	502-584-2121	208
Louisville Golf Club Co						
2320 Watterson Trail	Louisville	KY	40299	**800-456-1631**	502-491-5490	708
Louisville Magazine						
137 W Muhammad Ali Blvd						
Ste 102	Louisville	KY	40202	**866-832-0011**	502-625-0100	456-22
Louisville Presbyterian Theological Seminary						
1044 Alta Vista Rd	Louisville	KY	40205	**800-264-1839**	502-895-3411	168-3

Name / Address	City	State	ZIP	Toll-Free	Phone	Class
Louisville Science Ctr						
727 W Main St	Louisville	KY	40202	**800-591-2203**	502-561-6100	519
Louisville Slugger Museum						
800 W Main St	Louisville	KY	40202	**877-775-8443**	502-585-5226	521
Louisville Technical Institute						
Sullivan College of Technology & Design						
3901 Atkinson Sq Dr	Louisville	KY	40218	**800-844-6528**	502-456-6509	798
Louisville Zoo						
1100 Trevilian Way	Louisville	KY	40213	**866-229-0502**	502-459-2181	821
Loup Public Power District (LPPD)						
2404 15th St PO Box 988	Columbus	NE	68602	**866-869-2087**	402-564-3171	247
Lourdes College						
6832 Convent Blvd	Sylvania	OH	43560	**800-878-3210**	419-885-5291	167
Lourdes Homecare & Hospice						
2855 Jackson St	Paducah	KY	42003	**800-870-7460**	270-444-2262	371
Lou-Rich Machine Tool Inc						
505 W Front St	Albert Lea	MN	56007	**800-893-3235**	507-377-8910	755
Love & Quiches Desserts						
178 Hanse Ave	Freeport	NY	11520	**800-525-5251**	516-623-8800	298-11
Love Envelopes Inc						
10733 E Ute St	Tulsa	OK	74116	**800-532-9747**	918-836-3535	265
Love's Travel Stops & Country Stores Inc						
10601 N Pennsylvania Ave	Oklahoma City	OK	73120	**800-388-0983**		206
Lovegreen Industrial Services Inc						
2280 Sibley Ct	Eagan	MN	55122	**800-262-8284**	651-890-1166	469
Lovejoy Hospice						
939 SE Eigth St	Grants Pass	OR	97526	**888-758-8569**	541-474-1193	371
Lovejoy Tool Company Inc						
133 Main St	Springfield	VT	05156	**800-843-8376**	802-885-2194	492
Lovelace Medical Ctr						
5400 Gibson Blvd SE	Albuquerque	NM	87108	**888-281-6531**	505-262-7000	374-3
Lovelace Respiratory Research Institute (LRRI)						
2425 Ridgecrest Dr SE	Albuquerque	NM	87108	**800-700-1016**	505-348-9400	666
Loveland Chamber of Commerce						
5400 Stone Creek Cir Ste 200	Loveland	CO	80538	**800-216-0680**	970-667-6311	138
Loveland Daily Reporter-Herald						
201 E Fifth St	Loveland	CO	80537	**800-244-5613**	970-669-5050	531-2
Loveman Steel Corp						
5455 Perkins Rd	Bedford Heights	OH	44146	**800-568-3626**		491
Lovers Key State Park						
8700 Estero Blvd	Fort Myers Beach	FL	33931	**800-326-3521**	239-463-4588	564
Loveshaw Corp						
2206 Easton Tpke	South Canaan	PA	18459	**800-747-1586***	570-937-4921	546
*Cust Svc						
Lovitt & Touche Inc						
7202 E Rosewood St Ste 200						
PO Box 32702	Tucson	AZ	85710	**800-426-2756**	520-722-3000	390
Lowe Boats						
2900 Industrial Dr	Lebanon	MO	65536	**800-641-4372**	417-532-9101	89
Lowe Electric Supply Co						
1525 Forsyth St PO Box 4767	Macon	GA	31208	**800-868-8661**	478-743-8661	248
Lowe's Cos Inc						
1000 Lowe's Blvd	Mooresville	NC	28117	**800-445-6937**	704-758-1000	364
NYSE: LOW						
Lowe's Home Centers Inc						
PO Box 1111	North Wilkesboro	NC	28656	**800-445-6937**		364
Lowell Manufacturing Co						
100 Integram Dr	Pacific	MO	63069	**800-325-9660**	636-257-3400	51
Lowell Sun Publishing Co						
491 Dutton St	Lowell	MA	01854	**800-359-1300***	978-458-7100	634-8
*Cust Svc						
Lowe-Martin Company Inc						
400 Hunt Club Rd	Ottawa	ON	K1V1C1	**866-521-9871**	613-741-0962	227
Lowen Corp						
PO Box 1528	Hutchinson	KS	67504	**800-835-2365**	620-663-2161	626
Lower Bucks County Chamber of Commerce						
409 Hood Blvd	Fairless Hills	PA	19030	**800-786-2234**	215-943-7400	138
Lower Cape Fear Hospice & Life Care						
1414 Physicians Dr	Wilmington	NC	28401	**800-733-1476**	910-796-7900	371
Lower Columbia College						
1600 Maple St PO Box 3010	Longview	WA	98632	**866-900-2311**	360-442-2301	161
Lower Keys Chamber of Commerce						
31020 Overseas Hwy	Big Pine Key	FL	33043	**800-872-3722**	305-872-2411	138
Lower Keys Medical Ctr						
5900 College Rd	Key West	FL	33040	**800-355-2470**	305-294-5531	374-3
Lower Valley Energy						
236 N Washington PO Box 188	Afton	WY	83110	**800-882-5875**	307-885-3175	247
Lower Wekiva River Preserve State Park						
1800 Wekiwa Cir	Apopka	FL	32712	**800-326-3521**	407-884-2008	564
Lower Yellowstone Rural Electric Assn Inc						
3200 W Holly St PO Box 1047	Sidney	MT	59270	**844-441-5627**	406-488-1602	247
Lowes Food Stores Inc						
1381 Old Mill Cir Ste 200	Winston-Salem	NC	27103	**800-669-5693**	336-659-0180	345
Lowrance Electronics Inc						
12000 E Skelly Dr	Tulsa	OK	74128	**800-628-4487**	918-437-6881	528
Lowrey Organ Co						
989 AEC Dr	Wood Dale	IL	60191	**800-451-5939**		526
Loxcreen Co Inc, The						
1630 Old Dunbar Rd						
PO Box 4004	West Columbia	SC	29172	**800-330-5699**	803-822-8200	484
Loyal American Life Insurance Co						
Great American Financial Resources Inc						
PO Box 26580	Austin	TX	78755	**800-315-5522**	800-545-4269	391-2
Loyd's Aviation Services Inc						
1601 Skyway Dr Ste 100						
PO Box 80958	Bakersfield	CA	93308	**800-284-1334**	661-393-1334	62
Loyd's Electric Supply Inc (LES)						
838 Stonetree Dr	Branson	MO	65616	**800-492-4030**	417-334-2171	248
Loyola College						
4501 N Charles St	Baltimore	MD	21210	**800-221-9107**	410-617-5012	167
Loyola Marymount University						
1 LMU Dr	Los Angeles	CA	90045	**800-568-4636**	310-338-2700	167
Loyola University						
New Orleans						
6363 St Charles Ave	New Orleans	LA	70118	**800-456-9652***	504-865-3240	167
*Admissions						
Loyola University Chicago						
Lake Shore						
6525 N Sheridan Rd	Chicago	IL	60626	**800-262-2373**	773-508-3075	167

Name / Address	City	State	Zip	Toll-Free	Phone	Class
School of Law						
25 E Pearson St	Chicago	IL	60611	**866-596-7890**	312-915-7120	168-1
Water Tower						
820 N Michigan Ave	Chicago	IL	60611	**800-262-2373***	312-915-6500	167
*Admissions						
Loyola University Medical Ctr						
2160 S First Ave	Maywood	IL	60153	**888-584-7888**		374-3
Lozier Corp						
6336 John J Pershing Dr	Omaha	NE	68110	**800-228-9882**	402-457-8000	288
Lozier's Box R Ranch						
552 Willow Creek Rd PO Box 100	Cora	WY	82925	**800-822-8466**	307-367-4868	241
LP (Lakeland Plastics Inc)						
1550 McCormick Blvd	Mundelein	IL	60060	**800-454-4006**	847-680-1550	598
LPCH (Lucile Packard Children's Hospital)						
725 Welch Rd	Palo Alto	CA	94304	**800-995-5724**	650-497-8000	374-1
LPH (La Porte Hospital)						
1007 Lincolnway PO Box 250	La Porte	IN	46350	**800-235-6204**	219-326-1234	374-3
LPI (Life Partners Inc)						
204 Woodhew Dr	Waco	TX	76712	**800-368-5569**	254-751-7797	794
LPL Financial Services						
75 State St 24th Fl	Boston	MA	02109	**800-877-7210**		688
LPPD (Loup Public Power District)						
2404 15th St PO Box 988	Columbus	NE	68602	**866-869-2087**	402-564-3171	247
LPS Industries Inc						
10 Caesar Pl	Moonachie	NJ	07074	**800-275-6577***	201-438-3515	547
*Sales						
LQ Management LLC						
909 Hidden Ridge Ste 600	Irving	TX	75038	**800-753-3757**	214-492-6600	379
La Quinta Inn & Suites						
909 Hidden Ridge Ste 600	Irving	TX	75038	**800-753-3757**	214-492-6600	379
LQMT (Liquidmetal Technologies Inc)						
30452 Esperanza	Rancho Santa Margarita	CA	92688	**888-203-1112**	949-635-2100	481
OTC: LQMT						
LR Services						
602 Hayden Cir	Allentown	PA	18109	**888-675-9650**	610-266-2500	13
LRCC (Lakes Region Community College)						
379 Belmont Rd	Laconia	NH	03246	**800-357-2992**	603-524-3207	161
LRDC (Learning Research & Development Ctr)						
University of Pittsburgh						
3939 O'Hara St	Pittsburgh	PA	15260	**800-397-0071**	412-624-7020	666
LRECI (Little River Electric Co-op Inc)						
PO Box 220	Abbeville	SC	29620	**800-459-2141**	864-366-2141	247
LRF (Lymphoma Research Foundation)						
115 Broadway Ste 1301	New York	NY	10006	**800-500-9976**	212-349-2910	47-17
LRP Publications						
360 Hiatt Dr	Palm Beach Gardens	FL	33418	**800-621-5463**	561-622-6520	634-2
LRRI (Lovelace Respiratory Research Institute)						
2425 Ridgecrest Dr SE	Albuquerque	NM	87108	**800-700-1016**	505-348-9400	666
LS Starrett Co						
121 Crescent St	Athol	MA	01331	**800-482-8710**	978-249-3551	680
NYSE: SCX						
LSBA (Louisiana State Bar Assn)						
601 St Charles Ave	New Orleans	LA	70130	**800-421-5722**	504-566-1600	71
LSI (Lake Shore Industries Inc)						
1817 Poplar St PO BOX 3427	Erie	PA	16508	**800-458-0463**		699
LSNA (Louisiana State Nurses Assn, The)						
5713 Superior Dr Ste A-6	Baton Rouge	LA	70816	**800-457-6378**	225-201-0993	532
LSP Products Group Inc						
3689 Arrowhead Dr	Carson City	NV	89706	**800-854-3215**		607
LSQ Funding Group LC						
2600 Lucien Way Ste 100	Maitland	FL	32751	**800-474-7606**		274
Lti Printing Inc						
518 N Centerville Rd	Sturgis	MI	49091	**800-592-6990**	269-651-7574	626
LTI Trucking Services Inc						
411 N 10th St Ste 500	St. Louis	MO	63101	**800-642-7222**		315
LTS (Lawrence Companies)						
872 Lee Hwy PO Box 7667	Roanoke	VA	24019	**800-336-9626**	540-966-4000	778
LTS Wireless Inc						
311 S LHS Dr	Lumberton	TX	77657	**800-255-5471**	409-755-4038	172
LUA (Lumbermen's Underwriting Alliance)						
1905 NW Corporate Blvd						
PO Box 3061	Boca Raton	FL	33431	**800-327-0630**	561-994-1900	391-4
Lubbock Avalanche-Journal						
710 Ave J	Lubbock	TX	79401	**800-692-4021**	806-762-8844	531-2
Lubbock Christian University						
5601 19th St	Lubbock	TX	79407	**800-933-7601**	806-720-7151	167
Lubbock Convention & Visitors Bureau						
1500 Broadway St 6th Fl	Lubbock	TX	79401	**800-692-4035**	806-747-5232	208
Lubbock Municipal Auditorium/Coliseum						
1625 13th St	Lubbock	TX	79415	**800-735-2989**	806-775-2242	718
Lubbock Regional Mental Health Mental Retardation Center						
1602 10th St	Lubbock	TX	79401	**800-687-7581**	806-766-0310	371
Luberski Inc						
310 N Harbor Blvd Ste 205	Fullerton	CA	92832	**800-326-3220**	714-680-3447	298-4
Lubrication Engineers Inc						
300 Bailey Ave	Fort Worth	TX	76107	**800-537-7683**	817-834-6321	540
Lubrication Technologies Inc						
900 Mendelssohn Ave N	Golden Valley	MN	55427	**800-328-5573**	763-545-0707	540
Lubrizol Corp						
29400 Lakeland Blvd	Wickliffe	OH	44092	**800-380-5397**	440-943-4200	144
NYSE: LZ						
Luby's Inc						
13111 NW Fwy Ste 600	Houston	TX	77040	**800-886-4600**	713-329-6800	668
NYSE: LUB						
Luca International Group LLC						
39650 Liberty St Ste 410	Fremont	CA	94538	**877-988-6688**	510-498-8829	535
Lucas Assoc Inc						
3384 Peachtree Rd Ste 900	Atlanta	GA	30326	**800-515-0819**	800-466-4489	719
Lucas Color Card						
4900 N Santa Fe Ave	Oklahoma City	OK	73118	**888-845-8227**	405-524-1811	344
Lucasey Manufacturing Corp						
2744 E 11th St PO Box 14023	Oakland	CA	94601	**800-582-2739**	510-534-1435	481
Lucas-Milhaupt Inc						
5656 S Pennsylvania Ave	Cudahy	WI	53110	**800-558-3856**	414-769-6000	484
Lucchese Boot Co						
20 ZANE GREY	El Paso	TX	79906	**800-637-6888**	888-582-1883	302
Luce, Schwab & Kase Inc						
9 Gloria Ln	Fairfield	NJ	07007	**800-458-7329**	973-227-4840	663

Name / Address	City	State	Zip	Toll-Free	Phone	Class
Lucidview LLC						
80 Rolling Links Blvd	Oak Ridge	TN	37830	**888-582-4384**	865-220-8440	198
Lucile Packard Children's Hospital (LPCH)						
725 Welch Rd	Palo Alto	CA	94304	**800-995-5724**	650-497-8000	374-1
Lucks Co, The						
3003 S Pine St	Tacoma	WA	98409	**800-426-9778**	253-383-4815	297-8
Lucky Eagle Casino						
12888 188th Ave SW	Rochester	WA	98579	**800-720-1788**	360-273-2000	132
Lucky Inc 4 Times Sq	New York	NY	10036	**888-959-5203**	614-277-0827	456-11
Lucy Robbins Welles Library						
95 Cedar St	Newington	CT	06111	**800-842-1423**	860-665-8700	434-3
Ludlow Composites Corp						
2100 Commerce Dr	Fremont	OH	43420	**800-628-5463**		674
Ludlum Measurements Inc						
501 Oak St	Sweetwater	TX	79556	**800-622-0828**	325-235-5494	471
Ludowici Roof Tile Inc						
4757 Tile Plant Rd						
PO Box 69	New Lexington	OH	43764	**800-945-8453***	740-342-1995	149
*Cust Svc						
Lufkin Daily News						
300 Ellis Ave	Lufkin	TX	75904	**888-664-8792**	936-632-6631	531-2
Lufkin/Angelina County Chamber of Commerce						
1615 S Chestnut St	Lufkin	TX	75901	**800-409-5659**	936-634-6644	138
Luitpold Pharmaceuticals Inc						
1 Luitpold Dr PO Box 9001	Shirley	NY	11967	**800-645-1706**	631-924-4000	581
Luke Air Force Base						
14185 W Falcon St	Luke AFB	AZ	85309	**800-321-1080**	623-856-5853	496-1
Lumbee River Electric Membership Corp						
PO Box 830	Red Springs	NC	28377	**800-683-5571**	910-843-4131	247
Lumber Liquidators Inc						
1455 VFW Pkwy	West Roxbury	MA	02132	**800-227-0332**	617-327-1222	292
Lumbermen's Underwriting Alliance (LUA)						
1905 NW Corporate Blvd						
PO Box 3061	Boca Raton	FL	33431	**800-327-0630**	561-994-1900	391-4
Lumberton Area Visitors Bureau						
3431 Lackey St	Lumberton	NC	28360	**800-359-6971**	910-739-9999	208
Lumberton Honda Mitsubishi Inc						
301 Wintergreen Dr	Lumberton	NC	28358	**855-712-9438**	910-739-9871	515
Lumedx Corp						
555 12th St Ste 2060	Oakland	CA	94607	**800-966-0699**	510-419-1000	180-10
Lumen Legal						
1025 N Campbell Rd	Royal Oak	MI	48067	**877-933-1330**	248-597-0400	719
Lumenis Ltd						
2033 Gateway Pl Ste 200	San Jose	CA	95110	**877-586-3647**	408-764-3000	424
Lumens Light & Living						
2028 K St	Sacramento	CA	95811	**877-445-4486**	916-444-5585	813
Lumension Security Inc						
8660 E Hartford Dr Ste 300	Scottsdale	AZ	85255	**888-725-7828**		227
Lumex Inc						
290 E Helen Rd	Palatine	IL	60067	**800-278-5666**	847-359-2790	255
Lumina Foundation for Education						
30 S Meridian St Ste 700	Indianapolis	IN	46204	**800-834-5756**	317-951-5300	306
Luminator 900 Klein Rd	Plano	TX	75074	**800-388-8205**	972-424-6511	438
Luminex Corp						
12212 Technology Blvd	Austin	TX	78727	**888-219-8020**	512-219-8020	419
NASDAQ: LMNX						
Luminex Software Inc						
871 Marlborough Ave	Riverside	CA	92507	**888-586-4639***	951-781-4100	180-12
*Sales						
Luminite Products Corp						
148 Commerce Dr	Bradford	PA	16701	**888-545-2270**	814-817-1420	779
Lumitex Inc						
8443 Dow Cir	Strongsville	OH	44136	**800-969-5483**	440-243-8401	727
Lummis Cynthia M (Rep R - WY)						
2433 Rayburn HOB	Washington	DC	20515	**888-879-3599**	202-225-2311	342-2
Lummus Corp						
225 Bourne Blvd PO Box 929	Savannah	GA	31408	**800-458-6687**	912-447-9000	741
Lumos & Assoc Inc						
800 E College Pkwy	Carson City	NV	89706	**800-621-7155**	775-883-7077	263
Luna Community College						
366 Luna Dr	Las Vegas	NM	87701	**800-588-7232**	505-454-2500	161
Luna Garcia						
201 San Juan Ave	Venice	CA	90291	**800-905-9975**	310-396-8026	728
Lund International Holdings Inc						
4325 Hamilton Mill Rd Ste 400	Buford	GA	30518	**800-241-7219**	678-804-3912	59
Lunday-Thagard Co						
9302 Garfield Ave	South Gate	CA	90280	**800-266-6551**	562-928-7000	45
Lupus Foundation of America Inc (LFA)						
2000 L St NW Ste 410	Washington	DC	20036	**800-558-0121**	202-349-1155	47-17
Lurleen B Wallace Community College						
Andalusia						
1000 Dannelly Blvd						
PO Box 1418	Andalusia	AL	36420	**877-382-4357**	334-222-6591	161
MacAurthur						
1708 N Main St PO Box 910	Opp	AL	36467	**877-382-4357**	334-493-3573	798
Luster Products Inc						
1104 W 43rd St	Chicago	IL	60609	**800-621-4255**	773-579-1800	217
Luther Brookdale Chevrolet						
6701 Brooklyn Blvd	Brooklyn Center	MN	55429	**800-716-1271**		515
Luther Burbank Savings						
804 Fourth St	Santa Rosa	CA	95404	**888-205-6005**	707-578-9216	69
Luther College						
700 College Dr	Decorah	IA	52101	**800-458-8437**	563-387-2000	167
Luther Consulting LLC						
10435 Commerce Dr Ste 140	Carmel	IN	46032	**866-517-6570**	317-636-0282	198
Luther Luckett Correctional Complex						
Dawkins Rd PO Box 6	LaGrange	KY	40031	**800-511-1670**	502-222-0363	215
Luther Seminary						
2481 Como Ave	Saint Paul	MN	55108	**800-588-4373**	651-641-3456	168-3
Lutheran Church Missouri Synod (LCMS)						
1333 S Kirkwood Rd	Saint Louis	MO	63122	**888-843-5267**	314-965-9000	47-20
Lutheran Community at Telford						
12 Lutheran Home Dr	Telford	PA	18969	**877-343-7518**	215-723-9819	670
Lutheran Community Foundation						
625 Fourth Ave S Ste 200	Minneapolis	MN	55415	**800-365-4172**	612-340-4110	305
Lutheran Disaster Response						
8765 W Higgins Rd	Chicago	IL	60631	**800-638-3522**		47-5

Name	Address	City	State	ZIP	Toll-Free	Phone	Class
Lutheran Home at Hollidaysburg, The	916 Hickory St	Hollidaysburg	PA	16648	**800-400-2285**	814-696-4527	47-20
Lutheran Homes Society Inc	2021 N McCord Rd	Toledo	OH	43615	**877-646-4050**	419-861-4990	47-15
Lutheran Hospital of Indiana	7950 W Jefferson Blvd	Fort Wayne	IN	46804	**800-444-2001**	260-435-7001	374-3
Lutheran Magazine	8765 W Higgins Rd	Chicago	IL	60631	**800-638-3522**		456-18
Lutheran School of Theology at Chicago	1100 E 55th St	Chicago	IL	60615	**800-635-1116**	773-256-0700	168-3
Lutheran Social Services of Illinois	1001 E Touhy Ave Ste 50	Des Plaines	IL	60018	**888-671-0300**	847-635-4600	47-15
Lutheran Theological Seminary at Gettysburg	61 Seminary Ridge	Gettysburg	PA	17325	**800-658-8437**	717-334-6286	168-3
Lutheran Theological Seminary at Philadelphia	7301 Germantown Ave	Philadelphia	PA	19119	**800-286-4616**	215-248-4616	168-3
Lutron Electronics Company Inc	7200 Suter Rd *Tech Supp	Coopersburg	PA	18036	**800-523-9466***	610-282-6280	205
Lutsen Resort	5700 W Hwy 61 PO Box 9	Lutsen	MN	55612	**800-258-8736**	218-663-7212	667
Lutz Frey Corp	1195 Ivy Dr	Lancaster	PA	17601	**800-280-6794**	717-898-6808	191-10
Luv N' Care Ltd	3030 Aurora Ave	Monroe	LA	71201	**800-588-6227**		260
Luvata Appleton LLC	553 Carter Ct	Kimberly	WI	54136	**866-488-0217**	920-749-3820	484
Luvata Ohio Inc	1376 Pittsburgh Dr	Delaware	OH	43015	**800-749-5510**	740-363-1981	484
Lux Bond & Green Inc	46 Lasalle Rd	West Hartford	CT	06107	**800-524-7336**		410
Luxe Hotel Rodeo Drive	360 N Rodeo Dr	Beverly Hills	CA	90210	**800-468-3541**	310-273-0300	379
Luxe Hotel Sunset Blvd	11461 Sunset Blvd	Los Angeles	CA	90049	**800-468-3541**	310-476-6571	379
Luxe Worldwide Hotels	11461 W Sunset Blvd	Los Angeles	CA	90049	**888-336-3745**	310-440-3090	379
Luxfer Gas Cylinders	3016 Kansas Ave	Riverside	CA	92507	**800-764-0366**	951-684-5110	225
Luxo Corp	5 Westchester Plz	Elmsford	NY	10523	**800-222-5896**	914-345-0067	439
Luxor Div EBSCO Industries Inc	2245 Delany Rd	Waukegan	IL	60087	**800-323-4656**	847-244-1800	320-1
Luxor Hotel & Casino	3900 Las Vegas Blvd S *Resv	Las Vegas	NV	89119	**800-288-1000***	702-262-4000	132
Luxury Link LLC	5200 W Century Blvd Ste 410	Los Angeles	CA	90045	**888-297-3299**	310-215-8060	770
Luxury Retreats International Inc	5530 St Patrick St Ste 2210	Montreal	QC	H4E1A8	**877-993-0100**	514-393-8844	504
Luzerne County Community College	1333 S Prospect St	Nanticoke	PA	18634	**800-377-5222**		161
LV Lomas Ltd	99 Summerlea Rd	Brampton	ON	L6T4V2	**800-575-3382**	905-458-1555	145
LW Robbins Assoc	201 Summer St	Holliston	MA	01746	**800-229-5972**		318
LWS (Laminated Wood Systems Inc)	1327 285th Rd PO Box 386	Seward	NE	68434	**800-949-3526**		815
LXE Inc	125 Technology Pkwy	Norcross	GA	30092	**800-664-4593**	770-447-4224	175-1
Lyceum Theatre	149 W 45th St	New York	NY	10036	**800-432-7780**	212-239-6200	744
Lycoming College	700 College Pl	Williamsport	PA	17701	**800-345-3920**	570-321-4000	167
Lycoming Engines	652 Oliver St	Williamsport	PA	17701	**800-258-3279**	570-323-6181	528
Lycon Inc	1110 Harding St PO Box 427	Janesville	WI	53547	**800-955-8758**	608-754-7701	184
LycoRed Corp	377 Crane St	Orange	NJ	07051	**877-592-6733**	973-882-0322	478
Lyman Products Corp	475 Smith St	Middletown	CT	06457	**800-225-9626**	860-632-2020	286
Lymphoma Research Foundation (LRF)	115 Broadway Ste 1301	New York	NY	10006	**800-500-9976**	212-349-2910	47-17
Lyna Manufacturing Inc	1125 15th St W	North Vancouver	BC	V7P1M7	**800-993-4007**	604-990-0988	752
Lynch Livestock Co	331 Third St NW	Waucoma	IA	52171	**800-468-3178**	563-776-3311	445
Lynch Metals Inc	1075 Lousons Rd	Union	NJ	07083	**888-272-9464**	908-686-8401	789
Lynch, Traub, Keefe & Errante A Professional Corp	52 Trumbull St	New Haven	CT	06506	**888-692-7403**	203-787-0275	428
Lynchburg College	1501 Lakeside Dr	Lynchburg	VA	24501	**800-426-8101**	434-544-8100	167
Lynches River Electric Co-op Inc	1104 W McGregor St	Pageland	SC	29728	**800-922-3486**	843-672-6111	247
Lynda.com Inc	6410 Via Real	Carpinteria	CA	93013	**888-335-9632**	805-477-3900	196
Lynden Air Cargo LLC	6441 S Airpark Pl	Anchorage	AK	99502	**888-243-7248**	907-243-7248	12
Lynden Inc	18000 International Blvd Ste 800	Seattle	WA	98188	**888-596-3361**	206-241-8778	312
Lynden Transport Inc	3027 Rampart Dr	Anchorage	AK	99501	**800-327-9390**		778
Lynde-Ordway Company Inc	3308 W Warner Ave	Santa Ana	CA	92704	**800-762-7057**	714-957-1311	110
Lyndon State College	1001 College Rd PO Box 919	Lyndonville	VT	05851	**800-225-1998**	802-626-6413	167
Lynn Ladder & Scaffolding Company Inc	20 Boston St	Lynn	MA	01904	**800-225-2510**	781-598-6010	421
Lynn University	3601 N Military Trl *Admissions	Boca Raton	FL	33431	**800-888-5966***	561-237-7900	167
Lyntegar Electric Co-op Inc	PO Box 970	Tahoka	TX	79373	**877-218-2308**	806-561-4588	247
LynuxWorks Inc	855 Embedded Way	San Jose	CA	95138	**800-255-5969**	408-979-3900	180-10
Lynx Brand Fence Products	4330 76 Ave SE	Calgary	AB	T2C2J2	**800-665-5969**	403-273-4821	193-1
Lynx Computer Technologies Inc	7 Bristol Ct	Wyomissing	PA	19610	**800-331-5969**	610-678-8131	182
Lynx Grills Inc	5895 Rickenbacker Rd	Commerce	CA	90040	**888-289-5969**	323-838-1770	362
Lynx Media Inc	12501 Chandler Blvd Ste 202	Valley Village	CA	91607	**800-451-5969**	818-761-5859	179
Lyon & Healy Harps Inc	168 N Ogden Ave	Chicago	IL	60607	**800-621-3881**	312-786-1881	526
Lyon Rural Electric Co-op	116 S Marshall St	Rock Rapids	IA	51246	**800-658-3976**	712-472-2506	247
Lyon Work Space Products	420 N Main St	Montgomery	IL	60538	**800-433-8488**	630-892-8941	288
Lyon-Coffey Electric Co-op Inc	1013 N 4th PO Box 229	Burlington	KS	66839	**800-748-7395**	620-364-2116	247
Lyon-Lincoln Electric Co-op Inc (LLEC)	205 W Hwy 14 PO Box 639	Tyler	MN	56178	**800-927-6276**	507-247-5505	247
Lyons Magnus Inc	3158 E Hamilton Ave	Fresno	CA	93702	**800-344-7130**		297-20
Lyric Opera House	110 W Mt Royal Ave	Baltimore	MD	21201	**800-872-7245**	410-685-5086	571
Lyric Optical Company Wholsle	3533 Cardiff Ave	Cincinnati	OH	45209	**800-543-7376**	513-321-2456	543
LZ Truck Equipment Inc	1881 Rice St	Saint Paul	MN	55113	**800-247-1082**	651-488-2571	515

M

Name	Address	City	State	ZIP	Toll-Free	Phone	Class
M & A Technology Inc	2045 Chenault Dr	Carrollton	TX	75006	**800-225-1452**	972-490-5803	176
M & C Specialties Co	90 James Way *Cust Svc	SouthHampton	PA	18966	**800-441-6996***	215-322-1600	729
M & J Transportation	3536 Nicholson Ave	Kansas City	MO	64120	**866-298-3858**	816-231-6733	448
M & K CPAs PLLC	4100 Nsam Houston Pkwy	Houston	TX	77086	**866-770-5931**	832-242-9950	2
M & L Industries Inc	1210 St Charles St *General	Houma	LA	70360	**800-969-0068***	985-876-2280	385
M & M Designs Inc	1981 Quality Blvd	Huntsville	TX	77320	**800-627-0656**		685
M & M Innovations	7424 Blythe Island Hwy	Brunswick	GA	31523	**800-688-3384**	912-265-7110	230
M & M Supply Co	909 W Peach Ave PO Box 548	Duncan	OK	73534	**800-424-9300**	580-252-7879	536
M & R Sales & Service Inc	1n 372 Main St	Glen Ellyn	IL	60137	**800-736-6431**	630-858-6101	626
M at Miranova	2 Miranova PL Ste 100	Columbus	OH	43215	**877-491-1267**	614-629-0000	669
M Block & Sons Inc	5020 W 73rd St	Bedford Park	IL	60638	**800-621-8845**	708-728-8400	361
M Conley Co	1312 Fourth St SE	Canton	OH	44707	**800-362-6001**	330-456-8243	558
M Davis & Sons Inc	19 Germay Dr	Wilmington	DE	19804	**800-913-2847**	302-998-3385	609
M Floyd John & Assoc Inc (JMFA)	125 N Burnett Dr	Baytown	TX	77520	**800-809-2307**		196
M G Credit Inc	5115 San Juan Ave	Jacksonville	FL	32210	**800-387-6503**		159
M Holland Co	400 Skokie Blvd Ste 600	Northbrook	IL	60062	**877-578-4000**	847-272-7370	602
M K Products Inc	16882 Armstrong Ave	Irvine	CA	92606	**800-787-9707**	949-863-1234	809
M K Specialty Metal Fabricators	725 W Wintergreen Rd	Hutchins	TX	75141	**866-814-4617**	972-225-6562	695
M R L Equipment Company Inc	PO Box 31154	Billings	MT	59107	**877-788-2907**	406-869-9900	358
M. H. Eby Inc	PO Box 127	Blue Bell	PA	17506	**800-292-4752**	717-354-4971	515
M. Lee Smith Publishers LLC	PO Box 5094	Brentwood	TN	37024	**800-274-6774**	615-373-7517	626
M.d.m. Commercial Enterprises Inc	1102 A1a N Ste 205	Ponte Vedra	FL	32082	**800-359-6741**		37
M.E.G. LLC	502 S Green St PO Box 240 *Cust Svc	Cambridge City	IN	47327	**800-645-3315***		288
M.G. Newell Corp	301 Citation Ct	Greensboro	NC	27409	**800-334-0231**	336-393-0100	358
M.H. Equipment Co	2001 E Hartman Rd	Chillicothe	IL	61523	**888-564-2191**	309-579-8020	358
M/A/R/C Research	1660 Westridge Cir	Irving	TX	75038	**800-884-6272**	972-983-0400	465
M/A-COM Technology Solutions Inc	100 Chelmsford St	Lowell	MA	01851	**800-366-2266**	978-656-2500	694
M/I Homes Inc	3 Easton Oval *NYSE: MHO*	Columbus	OH	43219	**888-644-4111**	614-418-8700	651
M2 Logistics Inc	2413 Hazelwood Ln	Green Bay	WI	54304	**800-391-5121**	920-569-8800	462
M2 Technology Inc	21702 Hardy Oak Ste 100	San Antonio	TX	78258	**800-267-1760**	210-566-3773	180-1
M&A Advisor LLC, The	108-18 Queens Blvd 2nd Fl	Forest Hills	NY	11375	**877-996-3743**	718-997-7900	556
MA Gedney Co	2100 Stoughton Ave	Chaska	MN	55318	**888-244-0653**	952-448-2612	297-19
MAA (Mathematical Assn of America)	1529 18th St NW	Washington	DC	20036	**800-331-1622**	202-387-5200	48-19

Name / Address	City	State	ZIP	Toll-Free	Phone	Class
MAA FOCUS 1529 18th St NW	Washington	DC	20036	**800-741-9415**	202-387-5200	456-8
MAAC (Mid-America Apartment Communities Inc) 6584 Poplar Ave Ste 300 *NYSE: MAA*	Memphis	TN	38138	**866-620-1130**	901-682-6600	653
MAAC Machinery Corp 590 Tower Blvd	Carol Stream	IL	60188	**800-588-6222**	630-665-1700	110
Maaco LLC 440 S Church St Ste 700	Charlotte	NC	28202	**800-523-1180**	704-377-8855	61-4
Maas-Hansen Steel Corp 2435 E 37th St PO Box 58364	Vernon	CA	90058	**800-647-8335**	323-586-0171	491
Maas-Rowe Carillons Inc 2255 Meyers Ave	Escondido	CA	92029	**800-854-2023**		526
Maax Corp 160 St Joseph Blvd	Lachine	QC	H8S2L3	**888-957-7816**	877-438-6229	609
Mabis Healthcare Inc 1931 Norman Dr	Waukegan	IL	60085	**800-526-4753**		474
Mac Haik Auto Group 11711 Katy Fwy	Houston	TX	77079	**866-721-8619**		56
Mac Papers 3300 Phillips Hwy PO Box 5369	Jacksonville	FL	32207	**800-622-2968**	904-348-3300	552
Mac Tools Inc 505 N Cleveland Ave	Westerville	OH	43082	**800-622-8665**	614-755-7000	756
Mac Trailer Mfg Inc 14599 Commerce St NE	Alliance	OH	44601	**800-795-8454**	330-823-9900	777
Mac Valves Inc 30569 Beck Rd	Wixom	MI	48393	**800-622-8587**	248-624-7700	787
Mac's Convenience Stores Inc 305 Milner Ave Ste 400 4th Fl	Toronto	ON	M1B3V4	**800-268-5574**		206
Macadamian Technologies Inc 165 Rue Wellington	Gatineau	QC	J8X2J3	**877-779-6336**	819-772-0300	462
Macalester College 1600 Grand Ave *Admissions	Saint Paul	MN	55105	**800-231-7974***	651-696-6357	167
Macally USA Mace Group Inc 4601 E Airport Dr	Ontario	CA	91761	**800-644-1132**	909-230-6888	175-2
MacArthur Co 2400 Wycliff St	Saint Paul	MN	55114	**800-777-7507**	651-646-2773	193-4
MacArthur Place 29 E MacArthur St	Sonoma	CA	95476	**800-722-1866**	707-938-2929	379
Macatawa Bank Corp 10753 Macatawa Dr PO Box 3119 *NASDAQ: MCBC*	Holland	MI	49424	**877-820-2265**	616-820-1444	360-2
Macaulay-Brown Inc 4021 Executive Dr	Dayton	OH	45430	**800-669-4000**	937-426-3421	263
Macdac Engineering 27 Quality Ave	Somers	CT	06071	**866-529-5078**	860-749-5544	179
Macdonald Realty 203 5188 Wminster Hwy	Richmond	BC	V7C5S7	**877-278-3888**	604-279-9822	650
MacDonald-Miller Facility Solutions Inc 7717 Detroit Ave SE	Seattle	WA	98106	**800-962-5979**	206-763-9400	191-10
MacEwan College 10045 156 St NW	Edmonton	AB	T5P2P7	**888-497-4622**		161
MACFS (Mid-America College of Funeral Science) 3111 Hamburg Pk	Jeffersonville	IN	47130	**800-221-6158**	812-288-8878	798
Mac-Gray Corp 404 Wyman St Ste 400 *NYSE: TUC*	Waltham	MA	02451	**888-622-4729**	781-487-7600	385
Machias Savings Bank 4 Ctr St PO Box 318	Machias	ME	04654	**800-982-7179**	207-255-3347	69
Machine Maintenance Inc 2300 Cassens Dr	Fenton	MO	63026	**800-325-3322**	636-343-9970	192
Machine Specialty & Manufacturing Inc 215 Rousseau Rd	Youngsville	LA	70592	**800-256-1292**	337-837-0020	482
Machinery & Equipment Company Inc 3401 Bayshore Blvd	Brisbane	CA	94005	**800-227-4544**	415-467-3400	358
Machinery Dealers NA (MDNA) 315 S Patrick St	Alexandria	VA	22314	**800-872-7807**	703-836-9300	48-18
Machinery Sales Co 17253 Chestnut St	City of Industry	CA	91748	**800-588-8111**	626-581-9211	385
Machinery Systems Inc 614 E State Pkwy	Schaumburg	IL	60173	**866-428-1502**	847-882-8085	385
Mackay Communications Inc 3691 Trust Dr	Raleigh	NC	27616	**888-798-7979**	281-478-6245	528
Mackay Envelope Corp 2100 Elm St SE	Minneapolis	MN	55414	**800-622-5299**		265
Mack-Cali Realty Corp 343 Thornall St *NYSE: CLI*	Edison	NJ	08837	**800-317-4445**	732-590-1000	653
Mackenzie Eason & Associates 3023 S University Dr Ste 230	Fort Worth	TX	76109	**866-392-3139**	817-922-9152	363
Mackenzie Financial Corp 180 Queen St W	Toronto	ON	M5V3K1	**888-653-7070**	416-922-5322	401
MacKenzie-Childs LLC 3260 SR- 90	Aurora	NY	13152	**888-665-1999**	315-364-7123	322
Mackie Group 933 Bloor St W	Oshawa	ON	L1J5Y7	**800-565-4646**	905-728-2400	315
Mackie Research Capital Corp 110 Nineth Ave SW 9th Fl.	Calgary	AB	T2P0T1	**888-292-0980**	403-218-6375	688
Mackinaw Area Visitors Bureau 10800 US 23	Mackinaw City	MI	49701	**800-666-0160**	231-436-5664	208
Mackinnon Transport Inc 405 Laird Rd	Guelph	ON	N1G4P7	**800-265-9394**	519-821-2311	801-1
MacKissic Inc PO Box 111	Parker Ford	PA	19457	**800-348-1117**	610-495-7181	429
MacLean Power Systems 11411 Addison St	Franklin Park	IL	60131	**855-677-7447**	847-455-0014	814
Maclean's Magazine 1 Mt Pleasant Rd 11th Fl	Toronto	ON	M4Y2Y5	**800-268-9119**	416-764-1300	456-17
MacLean-Fogg Co 1000 Allanson Rd	Mundelein	IL	60060	**800-323-4536**	847-566-0010	59
MacMurray College 447 E College Ave	Jacksonville	IL	62650	**800-252-7485**	217-479-7056	167
MacNeal Hospital 3249 S Oak Pk Ave	Berwyn	IL	60402	**888-622-6325**	708-783-9100	374-3
MacNeill Engineering Company Inc 140 Locke Dr PO Box 735	Marlborough	MA	01752	**800-652-4267**	508-481-8830	708
Macnica Americas Inc 380 Stevens Ave Ste 206	Solana Beach	CA	92075	**888-399-4937**	760-707-0120	248
Macomb Community College *Center* 44575 Garfield Rd	Clinton Township	MI	48038	**866-622-6621**	586-445-7999	161
South 14500 E 12-Mile Rd	Warren	MI	48088	**866-622-6621**	586-445-7000	161
Macomb County Chamber 28 First St Ste B	Mount Clemens	MI	48043	**800-564-3136**	586-493-7600	138
Macomb Journal 203 N Randolph St	Macomb	IL	61455	**800-747-5401**	309-833-2114	531-2
Macon Centreplex Coliseum 200 Coliseum Dr	Macon	GA	31217	**877-532-6144**	478-751-9152	718
Macon City Auditorium 415 First St	Macon	GA	31201	**877-532-6144**	478-751-9152	571
Macon Electric Co-op 31571 Bus Hwy 36 E PO Box 157	Macon	MO	63552	**800-553-6901**	660-385-3157	247
Macon State College 100 College Stn Dr	Macon	GA	31206	**800-272-7619**	478-471-2700	167
Macon Telegraph 120 Broadway	Macon	GA	31201	**800-679-6397**	478-744-4200	531-2
Macon-Bibb County Convention/Visitors Bureau 450 Martin Luther King Jr Blvd	Macon	GA	31201	**800-768-3401**	478-743-1074	208
MacPherson's Property Management Inc 18551 Aurora Ave N Ste 301	Shoreline	WA	98133	**800-962-6473**	206-542-6363	650
MacPractice Inc 233 N Eighth St Ste 300	Lincoln	NE	68508	**877-220-8418**	402-420-2430	176
MACS (Mobile Air Conditioning Society Worldwide) 225 S Broad St	Lansdale	PA	19446	**800-641-1133**	215-631-7020	48-21
Macula Foundation Inc 210 E 64th St	New York	NY	10065	**800-622-8524**	212-605-3777	47-17
Macworld Magazine 501 Second St Ste 600 *Cust Svc	San Francisco	CA	94107	**800-288-6848***	415-243-0505	456-7
Macy's 400 Fifth Ave	Pittsburgh	PA	15219	**877-884-3751**	513-573-7912	231
Macy's Inc 7 W 7th St *NYSE: M*	Cincinnati	OH	45202	**800-261-5385**	513-579-7000	231
Macy's Travel 700 Nicollet Mall	Minneapolis	MN	55402	**800-316-6166**		758
Mad Catz Interactive Inc 7480 Mission Vly Rd Ste 101 *NYSE: MCZ*	San Diego	CA	92108	**800-659-2287**	619-683-9830	175-2
Mad Inc Dba Century 21 Salvadori Realty 3500 N G St	Merced	CA	95340	**800-557-6033**	209-383-6475	650
Mad Science Group 8360 Bougainville St Ste 201	Montreal	QC	H4P2G1	**800-586-5231**	514-344-4181	311
Mada Medical Products Inc 625 Washington Ave	Carlstadt	NJ	07072	**800-526-6370**	201-460-0454	474
MADD (Mothers Against Drunk Driving) 511 E John Carpenter Fwy Ste 700	Irving	TX	75062	**877-275-6233**	214-744-6233	47-6
Madden Manufacturing Inc PO Box 387	Elkhart	IN	46515	**800-369-6233**	574-295-4292	638
Madden's on Gull Lake 11266 Pine Beach Peninsula	Brainerd	MN	56401	**800-642-5363**	218-829-2811	667
Madelaine Chocolate Novelties Inc 9603 Beach Ch Dr	Rockaway Beach	NY	11693	**800-322-1505**	718-945-1500	297-8
Madera District Chamber of Commerce 120 NE St	Madera	CA	93638	**866-382-7822**	559-673-3563	138
Madera Unified School District 1902 HowaRd Rd	Madera	CA	93637	**800-322-6384**	559-675-4500	683
MadgeTech Inc 6 Warner Rd	Warner	NH	03278	**877-671-2885**	603-456-2011	258
Madico Inc 64 Industrial Pkwy	Woburn	MA	01801	**800-456-4331**	781-935-7850	598
Madison Area Technical College 1701 Wright St	Madison	WI	53704	**800-322-6282**	608-246-6100	798
Madison Cable Corp 125 Goddard Memorial Dr	Worcester	MA	01603	**877-623-4766**	508-752-2884	812
Madison Chemical Company Inc 3141 Clifty Dr	Madison	IN	47250	**800-345-1915**	812-273-6000	150
Madison Concourse Hotel & Governors Club 1 W Dayton St	Madison	WI	53703	**800-356-8293**	608-257-6000	379
Madison County 248 SW Range Ave PO Box 237	Madison	FL	32340	**877-272-3642**	850-973-2788	338
Madison Cutting Die Inc 2547 Progress Rd	Madison	WI	53716	**800-395-9405**	608-221-3422	554
Madison Gas & Electric Co 133 S Blair St	Madison	WI	53703	**800-245-1125**	608-252-7000	785
Madison Hotel, The 1 Convent Rd	Morristown	NJ	07960	**800-526-0729**	973-285-1800	379
Madison Investment Advisors Inc 550 Science Dr	Madison	WI	53711	**800-767-0300**	608-274-0300	401
Madison National Life Insurance Company Inc PO Box 5008	Madison	WI	53705	**800-356-9601**	608-830-2000	391-2
Madison Newspapers Inc 1901 Fish Hatchery Rd *Sales	Madison	WI	53713	**800-252-7723***	608-252-6200	634-8
Madison the - A Loews Hotel 667 Madison Ave	New York	NY	10065	**800-235-6397**	212-521-2000	379
Madison-Kipp Corp 201 Waubesa St	Madison	WI	53704	**800-356-6148**		309
Madisonville Community College 2000 College Dr	Madisonville	KY	42431	**866-227-4812**	270-821-2250	161
Madonna Rehabilitation Hospital 5401 S St	Lincoln	NE	68506	**800-676-5448**	402-489-7102	374-6
Madonna University 36600 Schoolcraft Rd	Livonia	MI	48150	**800-852-4951**	734-432-5339	167
MAF (Mission Aviation Fellowship) 112 N Pilatus Ln	Nampa	ID	83687	**800-359-7623**	208-498-0800	47-20
MAG (Medical Assn of Georgia) 1849 The Exchange Ste 200	Atlanta	GA	30339	**800-282-0224**	678-303-9290	473
Mag Instrument Inc 2001 S Hillman Ave	Ontario	CA	91761	**800-289-6241**	909-947-1006	439
Maga Ltd 2610 Lk Cook Rd	Riverwoods	IL	60015	**800-533-6242**	847-940-8866	390

Name	Address	City	State	ZIP	Toll-Free	Phone	Class
Magazine Publishers of America (MPA)	810 Seventh Ave 24th Fl	New York	NY	10019	**800-234-3368**	212-872-3700	48-16
Magee Rehabilitation Hospital	1513 Race St	Philadelphia	PA	19102	**800-966-2433**	215-587-3000	374-6
Magellan Health Services Inc (*NASDAQ: MGLN*)	55 Nod Rd	Avon	CT	06001	**800-424-4399**	860-507-1900	461
Magellan Midstream Partners LP (*NYSE: MMP*)	1 Williams Ctr	Tulsa	OK	74172	**800-574-6671**	918-574-7000	596
Maggie Valley Resort & Country Club	1819 Country Club Dr	Maggie Valley	NC	28751	**800-438-3861**	828-926-1616	667
Magic Plastics Inc	25215 Ave Stanford	Valencia	CA	91355	**800-369-0303**	661-257-4485	607
Magic Valley Newspapers	132 Fairfield St W	Twin Falls	ID	83301	**800-658-3883**	208-733-0931	634-8
Magid Glove & Safety Manufacturing Co	2060 N Kolmar Ave	Chicago	IL	60639	**800-444-8010**	773-384-2070	154-7
Magline Inc	1205 W Cedar St	Standish	MI	48658	**800-624-5463**		469
Magna Chek Inc	32701 Edward Ave	Madison Heights	MI	48071	**800-582-8947**	248-597-0089	740
Magna Design Inc	26246 Twelve Trees Ln NW	Poulsbo	WA	98370	**800-426-1202**	360-394-1300	320-1
Magna IV	2401 Commercial Ln	Little Rock	AR	72206	**800-946-2462**	501-376-2397	626
Magna Visual Inc	9400 Watson Rd	Sappington	MO	63126	**800-843-3399**		533
Magnatech International Inc	17 E Meadow Ave	Robesonia	PA	19551	**800-523-8193**	610-693-8866	110
Magnetech Industrial Services Inc	800 Nave Rd SE	Massillon	OH	44646	**800-837-1614*** (*General)	330-830-3500	484
MagneTek Inc (*NASDAQ: MAG*)	N49 W13650 Campbell Dr	Menomonee Falls	WI	53051	**800-288-8178**		255
Magnetic Analysis Corp	103 Fairview Park Dr	Elmsford	NY	10523	**800-463-8622**	914-699-9450	471
Magnetic Component Engineering Inc	2830 Lomita Blvd	Torrance	CA	90505	**800-989-5656**		457
Magnetic Metals Corp	1900 Hayes Ave	Camden	NJ	08105	**800-257-8174**	856-964-7842	480
Magnetic Springs Water Co	1917 Joyce Ave	Columbus	OH	43219	**800-572-2990**	614-421-1780	298-8
Magnetrol International Inc	5300 Belmont Rd	Downers Grove	IL	60515	**800-624-8765**	630-969-4000	203
Magnets Usa	817 Connecticut Ave NE	Roanoke	VA	24012	**800-869-7562**		197
Magnets.com	51 Pacific Ave Ste 4	Jersey City	NJ	07304	**866-229-8237**		366
Magnetsigns Adv Inc	4225 38th St	Camrose	AB	T4V3Z3	**800-219-8977**	780-672-8720	311
Mag-Nif Inc	8820 E Ave	Mentor	OH	44060	**800-869-5463**		760
Magnifying Ctr	10086 W McNab Rd	Tamarac	FL	33321	**800-364-1612**	954-722-1580	542
Magnolia Brush Mfg Ltd	1000 N Cedar PO Box 932	Clarksville	TX	75426	**800-248-2261**	903-427-2261	102
Magnolia Consulting LLC	5135 Blenheim Rd	Charlottesville	VA	22902	**855-984-5540**	434-984-5540	198
Magnolia Financial Inc	187 W Broad St	Spartanburg	SC	29306	**866-573-0611**	864-573-9900	274
Magnolia Forest Products Inc	13252 I- 55 S PO Box 99	Terry	MS	39170	**800-366-6374**		193-3
Magnolia Hotel & Spa, The	623 Courtney St	Victoria	BC	V8W1B8	**877-624-6654**	250-381-0999	379
Magnolia Hotel Dallas	1401 Commerce St	Dallas	TX	75201	**888-915-1110**	214-915-6500	379
Magnolia Hotel Denver	818 17th St	Denver	CO	80202	**888-915-1110**	303-607-9000	379
Magnolia Hotel Houston	1100 Texas Ave	Houston	TX	77002	**888-915-1110**	713-221-0011	379
Magnolia Metal Corp	10675 Bedford Ave Ste 200	Omaha	NE	68134	**800-228-4043**	402-455-8760	309
Magnolia Plantation & Gardens	3550 Ashley River Rd	Charleston	SC	29414	**800-367-3517**	843-571-1266	96
Magnotta Winery Corp	271 Chrislea Rd	Vaughan	ON	L4L8N6	**800-461-9463**	905-738-9463	79-3
Magnum Integrated Technologies Inc	200 First Gulf Blvd	Brampton	ON	L6W4T5	**800-830-0642**	905-595-1998	672
Magnum Magnetics Corp	801 Masonic Pk Rd	Marietta	OH	45750	**800-258-0991**	740-373-7770	457
Magnus Equipment	4500 Beidler Rd	Willoughby	OH	44094	**800-394-8964**	440-942-8488	358
Magtech Industries Corp	5625-A S Arville St	Las Vegas	NV	89119	**888-954-4481**	702-364-9998	255
Magtrol Inc	70 Gardenville Pkwy W	Buffalo	NY	14224	**800-828-7844**	716-668-5555	619
Magyar Bank	400 Somerset St	New Brunswick	NJ	08901	**800-472-3272**	732-342-7600	69
Mahaffey Theater for the Performing Arts	400 First St S	Saint Petersburg	FL	33701	**800-435-7352**	727-892-5798	571
Mahar Tool Supply Co Inc	112 Williams St	Saginaw	MI	48605	**800-456-2427**	989-799-5530	385
Maharishi University of Management	1000 N Fourth St	Fairfield	IA	52557	**800-369-6480**	641-472-1110	167
MAHLE Industries Inc	2020 Sanford St	Muskegon	MI	49444	**888-255-1942**	231-722-1300	127
Mahoning County Convention & Visitors Bureau	21 W Boardman St	Youngstown	OH	44503	**800-447-8201**	330-740-2130	208
Mahr Federal Inc	1144 Eddy St	Providence	RI	02905	**800-343-2050*** (*Orders)	401-784-3100	203
Mahuta Tool Corp	N118W19137 Bunsen Dr	Germantown	WI	53022	**888-686-4940**	262-502-4100	755
MAI (Medical Action Industries Inc) (*NASDAQ: MDCI*)	500 Expy Dr S	Brentwood	NY	11717	**800-645-7042**	631-231-4600	476
Maibec Inc	1984, 5e Rue	Levis	QC	G6W5M6	**800-363-1930**	418-659-3323	681

Name	Address	City	State	ZIP	Toll-Free	Phone	Class
Maid Brigade USA/Minimaid Canada	4 Concourse Pkwy Ste 200	Atlanta	GA	30328	**866-800-7470**	770-551-9630	151
MaidPro Corp	180 Canal St	Boston	MA	02114	**888-624-3776**	617-742-8787	311
Maid-Rite Steak Company Inc	105 Keystone Industrial Pk	Dunmore	PA	18512	**800-233-4259**	570-343-4748	297-26
Maids International	9394 W Dodge Rd Ste 140	Omaha	NE	68114	**800-843-6243**	402-558-8600	151
Mail Dispatch LLC	9710 Distribution Ave	San Diego	CA	92121	**800-275-0450**		318
Mail Shark	4125 New Holland Rd	Mohnton	PA	19540	**888-457-4275**		366
Mailender Inc	9500 Glades Dr	Hamilton	OH	45011	**800-998-5453**	513-942-5453	688
Mailing Systems Inc	2431 Mercantile Dr Ste A	Rancho Cordova	CA	95742	**877-577-2647**	916-674-2035	5
Mailings Unlimited	116 Riverside Industrial Pkwy	Portland	ME	04103	**800-773-7417**	207-347-5000	5
Mailman Research Ctr – *McLean Hospital*	115 Mill St	Belmont	MA	02478	**800-333-0338**	617-855-2000	666
Mail-Marketing Systems Inc	9420 Gerwig Ln	Columbia	MD	21046	**800-878-9537**		5
Main Source Bank	201 N Broadway	Greensburg	IN	47240	**800-713-6083**		69
Main Street America Group	55 W St	Keene	NH	03431	**800-258-5310**	603-352-4000	391-4
Main Street Capital Corp (*NYSE: MAIN*)	1300 Post Oak Blvd	Houston	TX	77056	**800-966-1559**	713-350-6000	405
Main Street Gourmet Inc	170 Muffin Ln	Cuyahoga Falls	OH	44223	**800-678-6246**	330-929-0000	297-2
Main Street Station Hotel & Casino	200 N Main St	Las Vegas	NV	89101	**800-713-8933**	702-387-1896	379
Main-Care Energy	PO Box 11029	Albany	NY	12211	**800-542-5552**		578
Maine							
Consumer Protection Unit	6 State House Stn	Augusta	ME	04333	**800-436-2131**	207-626-8849	339-20
Economic & Community Development Dept	59 State House Stn	Augusta	ME	04333	**800-541-5872**	207-624-9800	339-20
Elder Services Office	11 Statehouse Stn	Augusta	ME	04333	**800-624-8404**		339-20
Environmental Protection Dept	17 State House Stn	Augusta	ME	04333	**800-452-1942**	207-287-7688	339-20
Financial Institutions Bureau	35 Anthony Ave 11 State House Stn	Augusta	ME	04333	**800-452-1926**	207-624-8090	339-20
Governor	1 State House Stn	Augusta	ME	04333	**888-577-6690**	207-287-3531	339-20
Insurance Bureau	34 State House Stn	Augusta	ME	04333	**800-300-5000**	207-624-8475	339-20
Rehabilitation Services Bureau	150 State House Stn	Augusta	ME	04333	**800-698-4440**		339-20
State Government Information	26 Edison Dr	Augusta	ME	04330	**888-577-6690**	207-624-9494	339-20
Tourism Office	59 State House Stn	Augusta	ME	04333	**888-624-6345**		339-20
Maine Bar Journal	124 State St PO Box 788	Augusta	ME	04332	**800-475-7523**	207-622-7523	456-15
Maine Biotechnology Services Inc	1037 R Forest Ave	Portland	ME	04103	**800-925-9476**	207-797-5454	233
Maine Bucket Co	21 Fireslate Pl	Lewiston	ME	04240	**800-231-7072**	207-784-6700	202
Maine College of Art	522 Congress St	Portland	ME	04101	**800-639-4808**	207-775-3052	163
Maine Educator Magazine	35 Community Dr	Augusta	ME	04330	**800-332-8529**	207-622-5866	456-8
Maine Finance Authority of Maine (FAME)	5 Community Dr PO Box 949	Augusta	ME	04332	**800-228-3734**	207-623-3263	723
Maine Instrument Flight Inc	215 Winthrop St	Augusta	ME	04330	**888-643-3597**	207-622-1211	62
Maine Lobster Direct	48 Union Wharf	Portland	ME	04101	**800-556-2783**		298-5
Maine Maritime Academy	66 Pleasant St	Castine	ME	04420	**800-464-6565*** (*Admissions)	207-326-4311	167
Maine Medical Assn	30 Assn Dr	Manchester	ME	04351	**800-772-0815**	207-622-3374	473
Maine Medical Ctr (MMC)	22 Bramhall St	Portland	ME	04102	**877-339-3107**	207-662-0111	374-3
Maine Oxy	22 Albiston Way	Auburn	ME	04210	**800-639-1108**	207-784-5788	809
Maine Public Broadcasting Network (MPBN)	65 Texas Ave	Bangor	ME	04401	**800-884-1717**	207-941-1010	629
Maine State Bar Assn	124 State St	Augusta	ME	04330	**800-475-7523**	207-622-7523	71
Maine Veterans Home-Augusta	310 Cony Rd	Augusta	ME	04330	**888-684-4664**		791
Maine Veterans Home-Bangor	44 Hogan Rd	Bangor	ME	04401	**888-684-4665**	207-942-2333	791
Maine Veterans Home-Caribou	163 Van Buren Rd Ste 2	Caribou	ME	04736	**888-684-4667**	207-498-6074	791
Maine Veterans Home-Scarborough	290 US Rt 1	Scarborough	ME	04074	**888-684-4666**	207-883-7184	791
Maine Veterans Home-South Paris	477 High St	South Paris	ME	04281	**888-684-4668**	207-743-6300	791
Maine Veterinary Medical Assn (MVMA)	97A Exchange St Ste 305	Portland	ME	04101	**800-448-2772**		793
Maine Windjammer Cruises	PO Box 617	Camden	ME	04843	**800-736-7981**	207-236-2938	222
Maines Paper & Food Service Co	101 Broome Corporate Pkwy	Conklin	NY	13748	**800-366-3669**	607-779-1200	298-8
Mainline Information Systems Inc	1700 Summit Lk Dr	Tallahassee	FL	32317	**866-490-6246**	850-219-5000	182
Mains'l Services Inc	7000 78th Ave N	Brooklyn Park	MN	55445	**800-441-6525**		363
Mainship Corp	255 Diesel Rd	St Augustine	FL	32084	**800-771-5556**	904-827-2007	89

Alphabetical Section

Name / Address	City	State	ZIP	Toll-Free	Phone	Class
Maintenx 2202 N Howard Ave	Tampa	FL	33607	**855-751-0075**		609
Mairs & Power Funds 332 Minnesota St Ste W-1520	Saint Paul	MN	55101	**800-304-7404**	651-222-8478	527
Maison Dupuy Hotel 1001 Toulouse St	New Orleans	LA	70112	**800-535-9177**	504-586-8000	379
Maitland Art Ctr 231 W Packwood Ave	Maitland	FL	32751	**800-435-7352**	407-539-2181	49-1
Majestic Star Casino & Hotel 1 Buffington Harbor Dr	Gary	IN	46406	**800-522-4700**	219-977-7777	132
Majestic Steel USA 5300 Majestic Pkwy	Cleveland	OH	44146	**800-321-5590**	440-786-2666	491
Majestic Theatre 245 W 44th St	New York	NY	10036	**800-447-7400**	212-239-6200	744
Major Custom Cable Inc 281 Lotus Dr	Jackson	MO	63755	**800-455-6224**		811
Major Pharmaceutical Co 31778 Enterprise Dr	Livonia	MI	48150	**800-875-0123**	734-743-6161	582
Make-A-Wish Foundation of America 4742 N 24th St Ste 400	Phoenix	AZ	85016	**800-722-9474**	602-279-9474	47-5
MakeMusic! Inc 7615 Golden Triangle Dr Ste M *NASDAQ: MMUS*	Eden Prairie	MN	55344	**800-843-2066**	952-937-9611	180-6
Makino 7680 Innovation Way	Mason	OH	45040	**888-625-4661**	513-573-7200	454
Makita USA Inc 14930 Northam St	La Mirada	CA	90638	**800-462-5482**	714-522-8088	757
Malaco Music Group Inc 3023 W Northside Dr *Cust Svc	Jackson	MS	39213	**800-272-7936***	601-982-4522	655
Malaga Financial Corp 2514 Via Tejon *OTC: MLGF*	Palos Verdes Estates	CA	90274	**866-275-2677**	310-375-9000	360-2
Malaga Inn 359 Church St	Mobile	AL	36602	**800-235-1586**	251-438-4701	379
Malarkey Roofing Products PO Box 17217	Portland	OR	97217	**800-545-1191**	503-283-1191	45
Malaysia Airlines 100 N Sepulveda Blvd Ste 1710 *Resv	El Segundo	CA	90245	**800-552-9264***	310-535-9288	25
Malco Products Inc 14080 State Hwy 55 NW PO Box 400	Annandale	MN	55302	**800-328-3530**	320-274-8246	756
Malcolm Drilling Co Inc 3503 Breakwater Ct	Hayward	CA	94545	**800-523-2200**	510-780-9181	190-2
Malcolm Wiener Ctr for Social Policy John F Kennedy School of Government Harvard University 79 John F Kennedy St	Cambridge	MA	02138	**866-845-6596**	617-496-4082	631
Malcolm X College 1900 W Jackson	Chicago	IL	60612	**877-542-0285**	312-850-7000	161
Malcom Randall VAMC NF/SGVHS 1601 SW Archer Rd	Gainesville	FL	32608	**800-324-8387**	352-376-1611	374-8
Male Survivor 4768 BRdway Ste 527	New York	NY	10034	**800-738-4181**		47-17
Malema Engineering Corp 1060 S Rogers Cir	Boca Raton	FL	33487	**800-637-6418**	561-995-0595	203
Malibu Chamber of Commerce 23805 Stuart Ranch Rd Ste 210	Malibu	CA	90265	**800-442-4988**	310-456-9025	138
Mallet & Company Inc 51 Arch St Ext	Carnegie	PA	15106	**800-245-2757**	412-276-9000	297-23
Malleys Chocolates 13400 Brookpark Rd	Cleveland	OH	44135	**800-835-5684**	216-362-8700	297-8
Mallilo & Grossman 16309 Northern Blvd	Flushing	NY	11358	**866-593-6274**	718-461-6633	428
Mallin Casual Furniture 1 Minson Way	Montebello	CA	90640	**800-251-6537**		320-4
Mallinckrodt Inc 675 McDonnell Blvd	Hazelwood	MO	63042	**800-778-7898**	314-654-2000	233
Malloy Dan (D) 210 Capitol Avey	Hartford	CT	06106	**800-406-1527**		343
Malmstrom Air Force Base 7410 Flightline Dr Bldg 300	Malmstrom AFB	MT	59402	**866-731-4633**	406-731-1110	496-1
Malnati Organization Inc 3685 Woodhead Dr	Northbrook	IL	60062	**800-568-8646**	847-562-1814	668
Malnove Inc 13434 F St	Omaha	NE	68137	**800-228-9877**	402-330-1100	100
Malone College 515 25th St NW	Canton	OH	44709	**800-521-1146**	330-471-8100	167
Maloney Technical Products 1300 E Berry St	Fort Worth	TX	76119	**800-231-7236**	817-923-3344	595
Malt Products Corp 88 Market St	Saddle Brook	NJ	07663	**800-526-0180**	201-845-4420	101
Maltby Electric Supply Company Inc 336 Seventh St	San Francisco	CA	94103	**800-339-0668**	415-863-5000	248
Maltz Jupiter Theatre 1001 E Indiantown Rd	Jupiter	FL	33477	**800-445-1666**	561-743-2666	746
Maltz Sales Company Inc 67 Green St	Foxboro	MA	02035	**800-370-0439**	508-203-2400	358
Malvern Institute 940 W King Rd	Malvern	PA	19355	**888-643-3869**	610-647-0330	724
Malvern Systems Inc 81 Lancaster Ave Ste 219	Malvern	PA	19355	**800-296-9642**		180-1
MAMAC Systems Inc 8189 Century Blvd	Minneapolis	MN	55317	**800-843-5116**	952-556-4900	203
Mammography Reporting System Inc 19000 33rd Ave W Ste 130	Seattle	WA	98115	**800-253-4827**	206-633-6145	179
Mammoth Mountain Resort 10001 Minaret Rd	Mammoth Lakes	CA	93546	**800-626-6684**	760-934-2571	667
Mammoth Times, The PO Box 3929	Mammoth Lakes	CA	93546	**800-427-7623**	760-934-3929	531-4
Managed Care of America Inc 1910 Cochran Rd Ste 605	Pittsburgh	PA	15220	**800-922-4966**	412-922-2803	390
Managed Health Network Inc 1600 Los Gamos Dr Ste 300	San Rafael	CA	94903	**800-327-2133**		461
Managed HealthCare Northwest Inc 422 East Burnside St Suite 215 PO Box 4629	Portland	OR	97208	**800-648-6356**	503-413-5800	390
Management Consulting Inc 1961 Diamond Springs Rd	Virginia Beach	VA	23455	**888-892-0787**	757-460-0879	263
Management Information Control Systems Inc (MICS) 2025 Ninth St	Los Osos	CA	93402	**800-838-6427**	805-543-7000	180-10
Management Recruiters International Worldwide Inc 1717 Arch St 36th Fl	Philadelphia	PA	19103	**800-875-4000**		268
Manager's Intelligence Report (MIR) 316 N Michigan Ave Ste 400	Chicago	IL	60601	**800-878-5331**		530-2
Manarin Investment Counsel Ltd 505 N 210th St	Omaha	NE	68022	**800-397-1167**	402-330-1166	401
Manatee Convention Ctr 1 Haben Blvd	Palmetto	FL	34221	**800-822-2017**	941-722-3244	207
Manatee Memorial Hospital 206 Second St E	Bradenton	FL	34208	**844-854-9613**	941-746-5111	374-3
Manatron Inc 510 E Milham Ave *Cust Svc	Portage	MI	49002	**866-471-2900***	269-567-2900	180-11
Manatt's Inc 1775 Old 6 Rd	Brooklyn	IA	52211	**800-532-1121**	641-522-9206	190-4
Manchester College 604 E College Ave *Admissions	North Manchester	IN	46962	**800-852-3648***	260-982-5000	167
Manchester Community College 1066 Front St	Manchester	NH	03102	**800-924-3445**	603-206-8000	161
Manchester Financial Inc 2815 Townsgate Rd Ste 100	Westlake Village	CA	91361	**800-492-1107**	805-495-4405	401
Manchester Tank 1000 Corp Centre Dr Ste 300	Franklin	TN	37067	**800-399-5628**	615-370-6300	174
Mancini Foods PO Box 157	Zolfo Springs	FL	33890	**800-741-1778**		297-36
Manda Fine Meats 2445 Sorrel Ave	Baton Rouge	LA	70802	**800-343-2642**	225-344-7636	298-9
Mandalay Bay Resort & Casino 3950 Las Vegas Blvd S	Las Vegas	NV	89119	**877-632-7800**	702-632-7777	667
Mandarin Oriental Hotel Group (USA) 345 California St Ste 1250	San Francisco	CA	94104	**800-526-6566**	415-772-8800	379
Mandarin Oriental Miami 500 Brickell Key Dr	Miami	FL	33131	**800-526-6566**	305-913-8288	379
Mandarin Oriental New York 80 Columbus Cir	New York	NY	10023	**866-801-8880**	212-805-8800	379
Mandarin Oriental San Francisco 222 Sansome St	San Francisco	CA	94104	**800-526-6566**	415-276-9888	379
Mandarin Oriental Washington DC 1330 Maryland Ave SW	Washington	DC	20024	**888-888-1778**	202-554-8588	379
Mandee Shop 12 Vreeland Ave *Cust Svc	Totowa	NJ	07512	**877-756-1958***	973-890-0021	156-6
Mandel Scientific Company Inc 2 Admiral Pl	Guelph	ON	N1G4N4	**888-883-3636**	519-763-9292	419
Mandli Communications Inc 4801 Tradewinds Pkwy	Madison	WI	53718	**888-545-2214**	608-835-3500	182
Manex Resource Group Inc 1100 - 1199 W Hastings St	Vancouver	BC	V6E3T5	**888-456-1112**	604-684-9384	196
Manhasset Specialty Co 3505 Fruitvale Blvd	Yakima	WA	98902	**800-795-0965**	509-248-3810	526
Manhattan Area Chamber of Commerce 501 Poyntz Ave	Manhattan	KS	66502	**800-759-0134**	785-776-8829	138
Manhattan Area Technical College 3136 Dickens	Manhattan	KS	66503	**800-352-7575**	785-587-2800	161
Manhattan Assoc Inc 2300 Windy Ridge Pkwy 10th Fl *NASDAQ: MANH*	Atlanta	GA	30339	**877-756-7435**	770-955-7070	180-10
Manhattan Bagel Co Inc 555 Zang St Ste 300	Lakewood	CO	80228	**800-224-3563**	303-568-8000	67
Manhattan Beach State Recreation Site 725 Summer St NE Ste C	Salem	OR	97301	**800-551-6949**	503-986-0707	564
Manhattan Christian College 1415 Anderson Ave	Manhattan	KS	66502	**877-246-4622**	785-539-3571	160
Manhattan College 4513 Manhattan College Pkwy	Bronx	NY	10471	**800-622-9235**	718-862-8000	167
Manhattan Convention & Visitors Bureau 501 Poyntz Ave	Manhattan	KS	66502	**800-759-0134**	785-776-8829	208
Manhattan Public Library 629 Poyntz Ave	Manhattan	KS	66502	**800-432-2796**	785-776-4741	434-3
Manhattan Toy 300 First Ave N Ste 200	Minneapolis	MN	55401	**800-541-1345**		63
Manhattanville College 2900 Purchase St	Purchase	NY	10577	**800-328-4553**	914-323-5464	167
Manildra Group USA 4210 Shawnee Mission Pkwy Ste 312A	Shawnee Mission	KS	66205	**800-323-8435**	913-362-0777	297-23
Manitex Inc 3000 S Austin Ave	Georgetown	TX	78626	**877-314-3390**	512-942-3000	469
Manitou Cliff Dwellings Museum 10 Cliff Rd	Manitou Springs	CO	80829	**800-354-9971**	719-685-5242	519
Manitowoc Area Visitor & Convention Bureau 4221 Calumet Ave	Manitowoc	WI	54221	**800-627-4896**		208
Manitowoc Beverage Equipment 2100 Future Dr	Sellersburg	IN	47172	**800-367-4233**	812-246-7000	299
Manitowoc Ice 2110 S 26th St	Manitowoc	WI	54220	**800-545-5720**	920-682-0161	662
Manitowoc-Two Rivers Area Chamber of Commerce 1515 Memorial Dr	Manitowoc	WI	54220	**866-727-5575**	920-684-5575	138
Manke Lumber Company Inc 1717 Marine View Dr	Tacoma	WA	98422	**800-426-8488**	253-572-6252	681
Manko Window Systems Inc 800 Hayes Dr	Manhattan	KS	66502	**800-642-1488**	785-776-9643	479
Mann & Parker Lumber Company Inc, The 335 N Constitution Ave	New Freedom	PA	17349	**800-632-9098**	717-235-4834	498
Mann Packing Company Inc PO Box 690	Salinas	CA	93902	**800-285-1002**	831-422-7405	11-1
Manna Pro Corp 707 Spirit 40 Pk Dr Ste 150	Chesterfield	MO	63005	**800-690-9908**		446
Mannik & Smith Group Inc 1800 Indian Wood Cir	Maumee	OH	43537	**888-891-6321**	419-891-2222	263

Name / Address	City	State	ZIP	Toll-Free	Phone	Class
Mannington Mills Inc 75 Mannington Mills Rd	Salem	NJ	08079	**800-356-6787***	856-935-3000	293
*Cust Svc						
Manns Bait Co 1111 State Docks Rd	Eufaula	AL	36027	**800-841-8435**		708
Manoir du Lac Delage 40 Ave du Lac	Lac Delage	QC	G3C5C4	**888-202-3242**	418-848-2551	667
Manor House Inn 106 W St	Bar Harbor	ME	04609	**800-437-0088**	207-288-3759	379
Manor Park Inc 2208 N Loop 250 W	Midland	TX	79707	**800-523-9898**	432-689-9898	670
Manor Vail Lodge 595 E Vail Vly Dr	Vail	CO	81657	**800-950-8245**	970-476-5000	667
ManorCare Health Services - Mountainside 1180 Rt 22 W	Mountainside	NJ	07092	**800-366-1232**	908-654-0020	449
Manpower Demonstration Research Corp 16 E 34th St 19th Fl	New York	NY	10016	**800-221-3165**	212-532-3200	631
Manpower Inc. 8170 W Sahara Ave Ste 207	Las Vegas	NV	89101	**888-333-1597**	702-363-2626	630
Mansfield Oil Co 1025 Airport Pkwy SW	Gainesville	GA	30501	**800-695-6626**		538
Mansfield Plumbing Products Inc 150 E First St	Perrysville	OH	44864	**877-850-3060**	419-938-5211	610
Mansfield State Historic Site 15149 Hwy 175	Mansfield	LA	71052	**888-677-6267**	318-872-1474	564
Mansfield University Alumni Hall	Mansfield	PA	16933	**800-577-6826***	570-662-4000	167
*Admissions						
Mansfield, The 12 W 44th St	New York	NY	10036	**800-255-5167**	212-277-8700	379
Mansfield/Richland County Convention & Visitors Bureau 124 N Main St	Mansfield	OH	44902	**800-642-8282**	419-525-1300	208
Mansfield-Richland County Public Library 43 W Third St	Mansfield	OH	44902	**877-795-2111**	419-521-3100	434-3
Mansion on Forsyth Park 700 Drayton St	Savannah	GA	31401	**888-213-3671**	912-238-5158	379
Mansion View Inn & Suites 529 S Fourth St	Springfield	IL	62701	**800-252-1083**	217-544-7411	379
Manta Group Ltd, The 1300-350 Bay St	Toronto	ON	M5H2S6	**866-626-8247**	416-483-5166	364
MantelsDirect 217 N Seminary St	Florence	AL	35630	**888-493-8898**		185
Manton Industrial Cork Products Inc 415 Oser Ave Unit U	Hauppauge	NY	11788	**800-663-1921**	631-273-0700	211
Mantros-Haeuser & Company Inc 1175 Post Rd E	Westport	CT	06880	**800-344-4229***	203-454-1800	549
*General						
Mantua Mfg Co 7900 Northfield Rd	Walton Hills	OH	44146	**800-333-8333***		320-2
*Orders						
Manual Woodworkers & Weavers Inc 3737 HowaRd Gap Rd	Hendersonville	NC	28792	**800-542-3139**	828-692-7333	743
Manufactured Housing Enterprises Inc 09302 St Rt 6 Rt 6	Bryan	OH	43506	**800-821-0220**	419-636-4511	504
Manufactured Housing Institute (MHI) 2101 Wilson Blvd Ste 610	Arlington	VA	22201	**800-505-5500**	703-558-0400	48-3
Manufactured Housing Institute PAC (MHI PAC) 1655 N Ft Myer Dr Ste 104	Arlington	VA	22209	**800-505-5500**	703-558-0400	614
Manufacturing Jewelers & Suppliers of America Inc (MJSA) 57 John L Dietsch Sq	Attleboro	MA	02763	**800-444-6572**	401-274-3840	48-4
Manulife Financial Corp 200 Bloor St E	Toronto	ON	M4W1E5	**800-795-9767**	416-926-3000	360-4
NYSE: MFC						
MAP (Mississippi Action For Progress Inc) 1751 Morson Rd	Jackson	MS	39209	**800-924-4615**	601-923-4100	146
MAP International 4700 Glynco Pkwy	Brunswick	GA	31525	**800-225-8550**	912-265-6010	47-5
MAPEI Corp 1144 E Newport Ctr Dr	Deerfield Beach	FL	33442	**800-426-2734**	954-246-8888	3
Mapes Panels LLC 2929 Cornhusker Hwy PO Box 80069	Lincoln	NE	68504	**800-228-2391**		695
MAPFRE USA Corp 211 Main St	Webster	MA	01570	**800-922-8276**		391-4
Maple City Ice Co Inc 371 Cleveland Rd	Norwalk	OH	44857	**877-762-9119***	419-668-2531	80-1
*Cust Svc						
Maple City Rubber Co 55 Newton St PO Box 587	Norwalk	OH	44857	**800-841-9434**	419-668-8261	760
Maple Donuts Inc 3455 E Market St	York	PA	17402	**800-627-5348**	717-757-7826	67
Maple Grove Farms of Vermont 1052 Portland St	Saint Johnsbury	VT	05819	**800-525-2540**	802-748-5141	297-39
Maple Grove Raceway 30 Stauffer Pk Ln	Mohnton	PA	19540	**877-814-2538**	610-856-7812	514
Maple Hill Farm Bed & Breakfast Inn 11 Inn Rd	Hallowell	ME	04347	**800-622-2708**	207-622-2708	379
Maple Island Inc 2497 Seventh Ave E Ste 105	St Paul	MN	55109	**800-369-1022**	651-773-1000	297-10
Maple Knoll Communities Inc 11100 Springfield Pk	Cincinnati	OH	45246	**800-272-3900**	513-782-2400	670
Maple Leaf Farms Inc PO Box 308	Milford	IN	46542	**800-348-2812**	574-658-4121	10-7
Maplehurst Inc 50 Maplehurst Dr	Brownsburg	IN	46112	**800-344-4235**	317-858-9000	297-2
Maples Industries Inc 2210 Moody Ridge Rd	Scottsboro	AL	35768	**800-537-5447***	256-259-1327	130
*Hum Res						
MAQUET Cardiac Assist 15 Law Dr	Fairfield	NJ	07004	**800-777-4222**	973-244-6100	252
Maquet-Dynamed Inc 235 Shields Ct	Markham	ON	L3R8V2	**800-227-7215**	905-752-3300	474
Maquoketa Valley Rural Electric Co-op 109 N Huber St	Anamosa	IA	52205	**800-927-6068**	319-462-3542	247
MARAD (Maritime Administration) 1200 New Jersey Ave SE	Washington	DC	20590	**800-996-2723***	202-366-5807	340-15
*Hotline						
Maradyne Corp 4540 W 160th St	Cleveland	OH	44135	**800-537-7444**	216-362-0755	14
Maranatha Baptist Bible College 745 W Main St	Watertown	WI	53094	**800-622-2947**	920-206-2330	167
Marathon Coach 91333 Coburg Industrial Way	Coburg	OR	97408	**800-234-9991**	541-343-9991	61-7
Marathon Digital Services 716 W Pennway St	Kansas City	MO	64108	**877-568-1122**	816-221-7881	179
Marathon Electric Inc 100 E Randolf St PO Box 8003	Wausau	WI	54402	**800-616-7077**	715-675-3311	517
Marathon Enterprises Inc 9 Smith St	Englewood	NJ	07631	**800-722-7388**	201-935-3330	297-26
Marathon Equipment Co PO Box 1798	Vernon	AL	35592	**800-633-8974**	205-695-9105	386
Marathon Petroleum LLC PO Box 1	Findlay	OH	45839	**866-462-7284**	419-422-2121	45
MarathonFoto 3490 Martin Hurst Rd	Tallahassee	FL	32312	**800-424-3686**	972-330-7656	589
Maravia Corp of Idaho 602 E 45th St	Boise	ID	83714	**800-223-7238**	208-322-4949	708
Marble Institute of America (MIA) 28901 Clemens Rd Ste 100	Westlake	OH	44145	**800-433-4903**	440-250-9222	48-3
Marbles Kids Museum 201 E Hargett St	Raleigh	NC	27601	**800-745-3000**	919-834-4040	519
Marborg Industries 728 E Yanonali St	Santa Barbara	CA	93103	**800-798-1852**	805-963-1852	658
Marburger Farm Dairy Inc 1506 Mars Evans City Rd	Evans City	PA	16033	**800-331-1295**	724-538-4800	10-2
Marc Jacobs International 72 Spring St	New York	NY	10012	**877-707-6272**		279
Marc Publishing Co 600 Germantown Pk	Lafayette Hill	PA	19444	**800-432-5478**	610-834-8585	634-6
Marchex Inc 520 Pike St Ste 2000	Seattle	WA	98101	**800-840-1012**	206-331-3300	7
NASDAQ: MCHX						
Marco Beach Ocean Resort 480 S Collier Blvd	Marco Island	FL	34145	**800-715-8517**	239-393-1400	667
Marco Crane & Rigging Co 221 S 35th Ave	Phoenix	AZ	85009	**800-668-2671**	602-272-2671	266-3
MARCO Global 4259 22nd Ave W	Seattle	WA	98199	**866-966-2726**	206-285-3200	696
Marco Island Chamber of Commerce 1102 N Collier Blvd	Marco Island	FL	34145	**800-788-6272**	239-394-7549	138
Marco Promotional Products 2640 Commerce Dr	Harrisburg	PA	17110	**877-545-9322**		9
Marco Rubber 35 Woodworkers Way	Seabrook	NH	03874	**800-775-6525**	603-468-3600	327
MARCOA Publishing Inc 9955 Black Mtn Rd	San Diego	CA	92126	**800-854-2935**	858-695-9600	634-1
Marcus Bros Textiles Inc 980 Ave of the Americas	New York	NY	10018	**800-548-8295**	212-354-8700	593
Marcus Ctr for the Performing Arts 929 N Water St	Milwaukee	WI	53202	**888-612-3500**	414-273-7206	571
Marcus Dairy Inc 4 Eagle Rd	Danbury	CT	06810	**800-243-2511**	203-748-5611	297-27
Marcus Theatres Corp 100 E Wisconsin Ave Ste 2000	Milwaukee	WI	53202	**800-274-0099***	414-905-1000	745
*Cust Svc						
Maren Engineering 111 W Taft Dr	South Holland	IL	60473	**800-875-1038**	708-333-6250	263
Mares America Corp 1 Selleck St	Norwalk	CT	06855	**800-874-3236**	203-855-0631	708
Margaret Chase Smith Policy Ctr University of Maine York Complex Ste 4	Orono	ME	04469	**877-486-2364**	207-581-1648	631
Margaret Mary Community Hospital Inc 321 Mitchell Ave PO Box 226	Batesville	IN	47006	**800-562-5698**	812-934-6624	374-3
Marian Heath Greeting Cards Inc 9 Kendrick Rd	Wareham	MA	02571	**800-688-9998***	508-291-0766	129
*Sales						
Marian Koshland Science Museum 6th & E Sts NW	Washington	DC	20001	**888-567-4526**	202-334-1201	519
Marian University 3200 Cold Spring Rd	Indianapolis	IN	46222	**800-772-7264***	317-955-6038	167
*Admissions						
Mariani Packing Company Inc 500 Crocker Dr	Vacaville	CA	95688	**800-231-1287**	707-452-2800	11-1
Marianjoy Rehabilitation Hospital 26 W 171 Roosevelt Rd	Wheaton	IL	60187	**800-462-2366**	630-462-4000	374-6
Marianna Industries Inc 11222 "I" St	Omaha	NE	68137	**800-228-9060**	402-593-0211	233
Maricopa Medical Ctr 2601 E Roosevelt St	Phoenix	AZ	85008	**866-749-2876**	602-344-5011	374-3
Marie Callender Restaurant & Bakery 27101 Puerta Real Ste 260	Mission Viejo	CA	92691	**800-776-7437**		668
Marie Claire Magazine 300 W 57th St 34th Fl	New York	NY	10019	**800-777-3287**	515-282-1607	456-11
Marietta College 215 Fifth St	Marietta	OH	45750	**800-331-7896***	740-376-4000	167
*Admissions						
Marietta Conference Ctr & Resort 500 Powder Springs St	Marietta	GA	30064	**888-685-2500**	770-427-2500	377
Marietta Drapery & Window Coverings Company Inc 22 Trammel St PO Box 569	Marietta	GA	30064	**800-762-4774***	770-428-3335	743
*Mktg						
Marietta Hospitality 37 Huntington St	Cortland	NY	13045	**800-950-7772**	607-753-6746	9
Marietta Memorial Hospital 401 Matthew St	Marietta	OH	45750	**800-523-3977**	740-374-1400	374-3
Marietta National Cemetery 500 Washington Ave	Marietta	GA	30060	**866-236-8159**		135
Marijuana Anonymous World Services (MAWS) PO Box 7807	Torrance	CA	90504	**800-766-6779**		47-21
Marimba One Inc 901 O St Ste D	Arcata	CA	95521	**888-990-6663**	707-822-9570	526
Marin Convention & Visitors Bureau 1 Mitchell Blvd Ste B	San Rafael	CA	94903	**866-925-2060**	415-925-2060	208
Marin General Hospital 250 Bon Air Rd	Greenbrae	CA	94904	**888-996-9644**	415-925-7000	374-3
Marin Independent Journal 150 Alameda Del Prado	Novato	CA	94949	**877-229-8655**	415-883-8600	531-2

Name / Address	City	State	ZIP	Toll-Free	Phone	Class
Marina Del Rey Hospital 4650 Lincoln Blvd	Marina del Rey	CA	90292	**888-600-5600**	310-823-8911	374-3
Marina Graphic Center 12901 Cerise Ave	Hawthorne	CA	90250	**800-974-5777**	310-970-1777	626
Marina Inn at Grande Dunes 8121 Amalfi Pl *Resv	Myrtle Beach	SC	29572	**877-913-1333***	843-913-1333	379
Marinco 2655 Napa Valley Corp Dr	Napa	CA	94558	**800-307-6702**	707-226-9600	813
Marine Biological Laboratory (MBL) 7 MBL St	Woods Hole	MA	02543	**800-222-1222**	508-548-3705	666
Marine Corps Assn (MCA) PO Box 1775	Quantico	VA	22134	**800-336-0291**	703-640-6161	47-19
Marine Depot 14271 Corporate Dr	Garden Grove	CA	92843	**800-566-3474**		768
Marine Petroleum Trust 2911 Turtle Creek Blvd Ste 850 *NASDAQ: MARPS*	Dallas	TX	75219	**800-758-4672**		673
Marine Room, The 2000 Spindrift Dr	La Jolla	CA	92037	**866-644-2351**	858-459-7222	669
Marineland of Florida 9600 Ocean Shore Blvd	Saint Augustine	FL	32080	**877-933-3402**	904-460-1275	39
Marinelife Ctr of Juno Beach 14200 US Hwy 1 Loggerhead Pk	Juno Beach	FL	33408	**800-843-5451**	561-627-8280	39
Mariner Wealth Advisors 1 Giralda Farms Ste 130	Madison	NJ	07940	**800-364-2468**		196
Mariners' Museum 100 Museum Dr	Newport News	VA	23606	**800-581-7245**	757-596-2222	519
Mario Pastega Guest House 3505 NW Samaritan Dr	Corvallis	OR	97330	**800-863-5241**	541-768-4650	372
Marion Ceramics Inc PO Box 1134	Marion	SC	29571	**800-845-4010**	843-423-1311	149
Marion County 100 S Main St	Palmyra	MO	63461	**888-870-5943**	573-769-2549	338
Marion Military Institute 1101 Washington St	Marion	AL	36756	**800-664-1842**	334-683-2322	161
Marion Star, The 163 E Center St	Marion	OH	43302	**877-987-2782**	740-387-0400	531-2
Marion Technical College 1467 Mt Vernon Ave	Marion	OH	43302	**800-772-1213**	740-389-4636	798
Marion-Grant County Convention & Visitors Bureau 428 S Washington St Ste 261	Marion	IN	46953	**800-662-9474**	765-668-5435	208
Marist College 3399 N Rd	Poughkeepsie	NY	12601	**800-436-5483**	845-575-3000	167
Maritime Administration (MARAD) 1200 New Jersey Ave SE *Hotline	Washington	DC	20590	**800-996-2723***	202-366-5807	340-15
Maritime Administration *US Merchant Marine Academy* 300 Steamboat Rd	Kings Point	NY	11024	**866-546-4778**	516-773-5387	340-15
Maritime Energy Inc 234 Pk St PO Box 485	Rockland	ME	04841	**800-333-4489**	207-594-4487	578
Maritz Research Inc 1355 N Hwy Dr	Fenton	MO	63099	**877-462-7489**	385-695-2940	465
Marjorie Barrick Museum 4505 S Maryland Pkwy	Las Vegas	NV	89154	**877-895-0334**	702-895-3381	519
Mark Andy Inc 18081 Chesterfield Airport Rd	Chesterfield	MO	63005	**800-700-6275**	636-532-4433	628
Mark Cerrone Inc 2368 Maryland Ave	Niagara Falls	NY	14305	**855-250-7739**	716-282-5244	188
Mark Hershey Farms Inc 479 Horseshoe Pk	Lebanon	PA	17042	**888-801-3301**	717-867-4624	446
Mark Morris Dance Group 3 Lafayette Ave	Brooklyn	NY	11217	**800-957-1046**	718-624-8400	572-1
Mark Sand & Gravel Co 525 Kennedy Pk Rd PO Box 458	Fergus Falls	MN	56537	**800-427-8316**	218-736-7523	502-4
Mark Spencer Hotel 409 SW 11th Ave	Portland	OR	97205	**800-548-3934**	503-224-3293	379
Mark Twain Hotel 225 NE Adams St	Peoria	IL	61602	**866-325-6351**	309-676-3600	379
Mark's Work Warehouse 30-1035 64th Ave SE	Calgary	AB	T2H2J7	**800-663-6275**	403-255-9220	156-5
Markel Corp 4521 Highwoods Pkwy *NYSE: MKL*	Glen Allen	VA	23060	**877-566-6323**	800-431-1270	360-4
Markel Specialty Commercial 4600 Cox Rd	Glen Allen	VA	23060	**800-416-4364**		391-4
Markem-Imaje Inc 5448 Timberlea Blvd	Mississauga	ON	L4W2T7	**800-267-5108**		358
Marker, The 2544 Executive Dr	Indianapolis	IN	46241	**877-999-3223**		669
Market America Inc 1302 Pleasant Ridge Rd	Greensboro	NC	27409	**866-420-1709**	336-605-0040	113
Market Contractors Ltd of Oregon 10250 NE Marx St	Portland	OR	97220	**800-793-1448**	503-255-0977	188
Market Data Retrieval 6 Armstrong Rd	Shelton	CT	06484	**800-333-8802**	203-926-4800	5
Market Decisions LLC 75 Washington Ave Ste 206	Portland	ME	04101	**800-293-1538**	207-767-6440	465
Market Forge Industries Inc 35 Garvey St	Everett	MA	02149	**866-698-3188**	617-387-4100	299
Market Pavilion Hotel 225 E Bay St	Charleston	SC	29401	**877-440-2250**	843-723-0500	379
Market Scan Information Systems Inc 811 Camarillo Springs Ste B	Camarillo	CA	93012	**800-658-7226**		180-10
Market Traders Institute 400 Colonial Ctr Pkwy Ste 350	Lake Mary	FL	32746	**800-866-7431**	407-740-0900	527
Market Transport Ltd 110 N Marine Dr	Portland	OR	97217	**800-547-0781**	503-283-2405	778
Market Wire Inc 100 N Sepulveda Blvd Ste 325 *General	El Segundo	CA	90245	**800-774-9473***	310-765-3200	529
MarketBridge Inc 4350 East-West Hwy 6th Fl	Bethesda	MD	20814	**888-468-6658**	240-752-1800	197
Marketing Innovators International Inc 9701 W Higgins Rd	Rosemont	IL	60018	**800-543-7373**		384
Marketing Library Services 143 Old Marlton Pk	Medford	NJ	08055	**800-300-9868**	609-654-6266	530-10
Marketing News 311 S Wacker Dr Ste 5800	Chicago	IL	60606	**800-262-1150**	312-542-9000	456-5
MarketingProfs LLC 419 N Larchmont Blvd #295	Los Angeles	CA	90004	**866-557-9625**		197
Marketlab Inc 6850 Southbelt Dr	Caledonia	MI	49316	**866-237-3722**		474
MarketLauncher Inc 1800 Pembroke Dr Ste 300	Orlando	FL	32810	**800-901-3803**		7
Marketocracy Inc 1208 W Magnolia Ste 236	Fort Worth	TX	76104	**877-462-4180**		401
MarketVision Research Inc 10300 Alliance Rd Ste 200	Cincinnati	OH	45242	**800-232-4250**	513-791-3100	465
Markey Machinery Company Inc 7266 Eigth Ave S	Seattle	WA	98108	**800-637-3430**	206-622-4697	768
Markley Motors 3325 S College Ave	Fort Collins	CO	80525	**888-480-5167**	970-226-2214	56
Marksville State Historic Site 837 ML King Dr	Marksville	LA	71351	**888-253-8954**	318-253-8954	564
MarkWest Energy Partners LP 1515 Arapahoe St Tower 1 Ste 1600 *NYSE: MWE*	Denver	CO	80202	**800-730-8388**	303-925-9200	596
Marland Clutch 2032 VALLEYDALE Rd	Birmingham	AL	35244	**800-216-3515**		619
Marlboro College 2582 S Rd PO Box A	Marlboro	VT	05344	**800-343-0049**	802-257-4333	167
Marlen International Inc 4780 NW 41st St Ste 100	Riverside	MO	64150	**800-862-7536**		299
Marley Engineered Products 470 Beauty Spot Rd E	Bennettsville	SC	29512	**800-452-4179**	843-479-4006	36
Marlin Business Services Inc 300 Fellowship Rd *NASDAQ: MRLN*	Mount Laurel	NJ	08054	**888-479-9111**		266-2
Marlin Central Monitoring LLC 3600 Commerce Pl Ste 201	Kissimmee	FL	34742	**866-383-0333**		691
Marlin Firearms Co PO Box 1871 *Cust Svc	Madison	NC	27025	**800-544-8892***		286
Marlow Industries Inc 10451 Vista Pk Rd	Dallas	TX	75238	**877-627-5691**	214-340-4900	255
Marmon/Keystone Corp PO Box 992	Butler	PA	16003	**800-544-1748**	724-283-3000	491
Marmon-Herrington Co 13001 Magisterial Dr	Louisville	KY	40223	**800-227-0727**	502-253-0277	59
Maroon Inc 1390 Jaycox Rd *General	Avon	OH	44011	**877-627-6661***	440-937-1000	145
Marotta Controls Inc 78 Boonton Ave PO Box 427	Montville	NJ	07045	**888-627-6882**	973-334-7800	787
Marposs Corp 3300 Cross Creek Pkwy	Auburn Hills	MI	48326	**888-627-7677**	248-370-0404	471
Marq Packaging Systems Inc 3801 W Washington Ave	Yakima	WA	98903	**800-998-4301**	509-966-4300	556
Marquesa Hotel 600 Fleming St	Key West	FL	33040	**800-869-4631**	305-292-1919	379
Marquette Asset Management 60 S Sixth St Ste 3900	Minneapolis	MN	55402	**866-661-3770**	612-661-3770	401
Marquette Bank 10000 W 151st St	Orland Park	IL	60462	**888-254-9500**	708-226-8026	69
Marquette Country Convention & Visitors Bureau 337 W Washington St	Marquette	MI	49855	**800-544-4321**	906-228-7749	208
Marquette Hotel, The 710 Marquette Ave	Minneapolis	MN	55402	**800-328-4782**	612-333-4545	379
Marquette Savings Bank 920 Peach St	Erie	PA	16501	**866-672-3743**	814-455-4481	69
Marquette Transportation Company LLC 5525 Mounes St	New Orleans	LA	70123	**800-735-5845**	504-733-5845	464
Marquette University 1217 W Wisconsin Ave *Admissions	Milwaukee	WI	53233	**800-222-6544***	414-288-7302	167
Marquette University Raynor Memorial Library 1355 W Wisconsin Ave	Milwaukee	WI	53233	**800-876-1715**	414-288-7556	434-6
Marquis Spas Corp 596 Hoffman Rd	Independence	OR	97351	**800-275-0888**	503-838-0888	375
Marquis Who's Who 300 Connell Dr Ste 2000	Berkeley Heights	NJ	07922	**800-473-7020**	908-673-1000	634-2
Marriott Charleston Hotel 170 Lockwood Blvd	Charleston	SC	29403	**888-236-2427**	843-723-3000	379
Marriott Columbus 800 Front Ave	Columbus	GA	31901	**800-455-9261**	706-324-1800	379
Marriott International Inc 11966 El Camino Real	San Diego	CA	92130	**888-236-2427**		669
ExecuStay Corp 2222 Corinth Ave	Los Angeles	CA	90064	**800-990-9292**		212
Ritz-Carlton Hotel Co LLC 4445 Willard Ave Ste 800	Chevy Chase	MD	20815	**800-241-3333**	301-547-4700	379
Marriott Kaua'i Resort & Beach Club 3610 Rice St Kalapaki Beach	Lihue	HI	96766	**800-220-2925**	808-245-5050	667
Marriott Montgomery Prattville at Capitol Hill 2500 Legends Cir *Resv	Prattville	AL	36066	**800-593-6429***	334-290-1235	377
Marriott Vacation Club International 6649 Westwood Blvd Ste 500	Orlando	FL	32821	**800-307-7312**	407-206-6000	751
Mars Electric Co 38868 Mentor Ave	Willoughby	OH	44094	**877-229-7227**	440-946-2250	248
Mars Stout Inc 4500 Majestic Dr	Missoula	MT	59808	**800-451-6277**	406-721-6280	734
Marsh & Mclennan Agency 250 Pehle Ave	Saddle Brook	NJ	07663	**800-669-6330**	201-845-6600	390
Marsh & McLennan Cos Inc 1166 Ave of the Americas *NYSE: MMC*	New York	NY	10036	**866-374-2662**	212-345-5000	360-3
Marsh Bellofram Corp 8019 Ohio River Blvd	Newell	WV	26050	**800-727-5646**	304-387-1200	203
Marsh Berry & Company Inc 4420 Sherwin Rd	Willoughby	OH	44094	**800-426-2774**	440-354-3230	196

Name / Address	City	State	ZIP	Toll-Free	Phone	Class
Marsh Electronics Inc						
1563 S 101st St	Milwaukee	WI	53214	**800-926-2774***	414-475-6000	248
*Cust Svc						
Marsh Furniture Co						
PO Box 870	High Point	NC	27261	**800-696-2774**	336-884-7363	114
Marshal Mize Ford Inc						
5348 Hwy 153	Chattanooga	TN	37343	**888-633-5038**		56
Marshall & Sterling Inc						
110 Main St	Poughkeepsie	NY	12601	**800-333-3766**	845-454-0800	390
Marshall & Stevens Inc						
355 S Grand Ave Ste 1750	Los Angeles	CA	90071	**800-950-9588**	213-612-8000	196
Marshall & Sullivan Inc						
1109 First Ave Ste 200	Seattle	WA	98101	**800-735-7290**	206-621-9014	401
Marshall & Swift						
777 S Figueroa St 12th Fl	Los Angeles	CA	90017	**800-544-2678**	213-683-9000	180-10
Marshall Durbin Co						
2830 Commerce Blvd	Birmingham	AL	35210	**800-245-8204***	205-380-3251	618
*Sales						
Marshall Independent						
508 W Main St PO Box 411	Marshall	MN	56258	**877-276-6070**	507-537-1551	634-8
Marshall Pottery						
4901 Elysian Fields Rd	Marshall	TX	75672	**888-768-8721**	903-927-5400	334
Marshall Screw Products Co						
3820 Chandler Dr Ne	Minneapolis	MN	55421	**800-321-6727**		453
Marshall University						
1 John Marshall Dr	Huntington	WV	25755	**800-642-3463**	304-696-3170	167
Marshalls Inc						
770 Cochituate Rd	Framingham	MA	01701	**800-627-7425**		156-2
Marshalltown Area Chamber of Commerce						
709 S Ctr St PO Box 1000	Marshalltown	IA	50158	**800-725-5301**	641-753-6645	138
Marshalltown Co						
104 S Eigth Ave	Marshalltown	IA	50158	**800-888-0127**	641-753-5999	756
Marshalltown Community College						
3700 S Ctr St	Marshalltown	IA	50158	**866-622-4748**	641-752-7106	161
Marshfield Convention & Visitors Bureau						
700 S Central Ave PO Box 868	Marshfield	WI	54449	**800-422-4541**	715-384-3454	208
Martec Group Inc, The						
105 W Adams St Ste 2125	Chicago	IL	60603	**888-811-5755**	312-606-9690	666
Marten Transport Ltd						
129 Marten St	Mondovi	WI	54755	**800-395-3000**	715-926-4216	778
NASDAQ: MRTN						
Martha Jefferson Hospital (MJH)						
500 Martha Jefferson Dr						
	Charlottesville	VA	22902	**888-652-6663**	434-654-7000	374-3
Martha Stewart Living Magazine						
601 W 26th St 25th Fl	New York	NY	10001	**800-999-6518**		456-11
Martha Washington Hotel & Spa, The						
150 W Main St	Abingdon	VA	24210	**888-999-8078**	276-628-3161	379
Martin & Bayley Inc						
1311 A W Main	Carmi	IL	62821	**800-876-2511**	618-382-2334	345
Martin Asphalt Co						
3 Riverway Ste 400	South Houston	TX	77056	**800-662-0987**	713-350-6800	45
Martin County Travel & Tourism Authority						
100 E Church St PO Box 382	Williamston	NC	27892	**800-776-8566**	252-792-6605	208
Martin Door Manufacturing Inc						
2828 South 900 West	Salt Lake City	UT	84119	**800-388-9310**	801-973-9310	364
Martin Eagle Oil Company Inc						
2700 James St	Denton	TX	76205	**800-316-6148**	940-383-2351	578
Martin Engineering						
1 Martin Pl	Neponset	IL	61345	**800-544-2947**	309-594-2384	209
Martin Furniture						
2345 Britannia Blvd	San Diego	CA	92154	**800-268-5669***		320-1
*Cust Svc						
Martin Glass Co						
25 Ctr Plz	Belleville	IL	62220	**800-325-1946**	618-277-1946	61-2
Martin Luther College						
1995 Luther Ct	New Ulm	MN	56073	**877-652-1995**	507-354-8221	167
Martin Marietta Magnesia Specialties Inc						
8140 Corporate Dr Ste 220	Baltimore	MD	21236	**800-648-7400**	410-780-5500	142
Martin Memorial Health Systems (MMHS)						
200 SE Hospital Ave PO Box 9010	Stuart	FL	34994	**800-368-3375**	772-287-5200	374-3
Martin Methodist College						
433 W Madison St	Pulaski	TN	38478	**800-467-1273**	931-363-9804	167
Martin Midstream Partners LP						
4200 Stone Rd	Kilgore	TX	75662	**800-256-6644**	903-983-6200	578
NASDAQ: MMLP						
Martin Resource Management Corp (MRMC)						
PO Box 191	Kilgore	TX	75663	**888-334-7473**	903-983-6200	317
Martin Supply Co						
200 Appleton Ave	Sheffield	AL	35660	**800-828-8116**	256-383-3131	385
Martin Wells Industries						
5886 Compton Ave	Los Angeles	CA	90001	**800-421-6000**	323-581-6266	127
Martin Wheel Company Inc						
342 W Ave	Tallmadge	OH	44278	**800-462-7846**	330-633-3278	752
Martin Yale Industries Inc						
251 Wedcor Ave	Wabash	IN	46992	**800-225-5644**	260-563-0641	110
Martin's Famous Pastry Shoppe Inc						
1000 Potato Roll Ln	Chambersburg	PA	17201	**800-548-1200***	717-263-9580	297-1
*Cust Svc						
Martin/F Weber Co						
2727 Southampton Rd	Philadelphia	PA	19154	**800-876-8076**	215-677-5600	42
Martina's Flowers & Gifts						
3830 Washington Rd	Augusta	GA	30907	**800-927-1204**	706-863-7172	294
MartinAire Aviation LLC						
4553 Glenn Curtiss Dr	Addison	TX	75001	**866-557-1861**	972-349-5700	12
Martindale Electric Co						
1375 Hird Ave	Cleveland	OH	44107	**800-344-9191**	216-521-8567	517
Martinez Area Chamber of Commerce						
603 Marina Vista	Martinez	CA	94553	**877-855-5506**	925-228-2345	138
Martinizing Dry Cleaning						
8944 Columbia Rd Ste J	Loveland	OH	45140	**800-827-0207**		311
Martinsburg-Berkeley County Chamber of Commerce						
198 Viking Way	Martinsburg	WV	25401	**800-332-9007**	304-267-4841	138
Martinsville Bulletin						
PO Box 3711	Martinsville	VA	24115	**800-234-6575**	276-638-8801	531-2
Martinsville Speedway						
340 Speedway Rd	Martinsville	VA	24112	**877-722-3849**		514
Martinsville-Henry County Chamber of Commerce						
115 Broad St	Martinsville	VA	24112	**800-811-6302**	276-632-6401	138

Name / Address	City	State	ZIP	Toll-Free	Phone	Class
Martin-Williams Adv						
150 S 5th st Ste 900	Minneapolis	MN	55402	**800-632-1388**	612-340-0800	4
Martrex Inc						
1107 Hazeltine Blvd Ste 535	Minnetonka	MN	55345	**800-328-3627**	952-933-5000	278
Martronic Engineering Inc						
80 W Cochran St Ste B	Simi Valley	CA	93065	**800-960-0808**	805-583-0808	263
Marts & Lundy Inc						
1200 Wall St W	Lyndhurst	NJ	07071	**800-526-9005**	201-460-1660	785
Marty's Shoe Outlet Inc						
121 Carver Ave	Westwood	NJ	07675	**888-662-7897***	201-497-6637	302
*General						
Martz First Class Coach Company Inc						
4783 37th St N	Saint Petersburg	FL	33714	**800-282-8020**	727-526-9086	106
Maruka USA Inc						
400 Commons Way	Rockaway	NJ	07866	**800-631-0426**	973-983-1000	386
Maruson Technology Corp						
18557 Gale Ave	City Of Industry	CA	91748	**888-627-8766**	626-912-8388	765
Marvel Abrasive Products Inc						
6230 S Oak Pk Ave	Chicago	IL	60638	**800-621-0673**		1
Marvel Consultants Inc						
28601 Chagrin Blvd Ste 210	Cleveland	OH	44122	**800-338-1257**	216-292-2855	630
Marvel Group Inc						
3843 W 43rd St	Chicago	IL	60632	**800-621-8846***		320-1
*Cust Svc						
Marvel Mfg Company Inc						
3501 Marvel Dr	Oshkosh	WI	54902	**800-472-9464**	920-236-7200	680
Marvell Semiconductor Inc						
5488 Marvell Ln	Santa Clara	CA	95054	**855-627-8355***	408-222-2500	178
*Cust Svc						
Marvin Huffaker Consulting Inc						
1311 W Chandler Blvd Ste 160	Chandler	AZ	85224	**888-690-0013**	480-988-7215	198
Marvin Windows & Doors						
PO Box 100	Warroad	MN	56763	**888-537-7828**	218-386-1430	238
Mary Ann Liebert Publishers Inc						
140 Huguenot St 3rd Fl	New Rochelle	NY	10801	**800-654-3237**	914-740-2100	634-9
Mary Baldwin College						
318 Prospect St PO Box 1500	Staunton	VA	24401	**800-468-2262***	540-887-7019	167
*Admissions						
Mary Bridge Children's Hospital & Health Ctr						
317 Martin Luther King Jr Way	Tacoma	WA	98405	**800-552-1419**	253-403-1400	374-1
Mary Free Bed Rehabilitation Hospital						
235 Wealthy St SE	Grand Rapids	MI	49503	**800-528-8989**	616-242-0300	374-6
Mary Jane Thurston State Park						
1466 State Rt 65	McClure	OH	43534	**866-644-6727**	419-832-7662	564
Mary Kay Inc						
PO Box 799045	Dallas	TX	75379	**800-627-9529***	972-687-6300	217
*Cust Svc						
Mary Maxim Inc						
2001 Holland Ave PO Box 5019	Port Huron	MI	48061	**800-962-9504**	810-987-2000	458
Mary Maxim Ltd						
75 Scott Ave	Paris	ON	N3L3G5	**888-442-2266**		759
Mary Washington Hospice						
5012 Southpoint Pkwy	Fredericksburg	VA	22407	**800-257-1667**	540-741-1667	371
Mary Washington Hospital						
1001 Sam Perry Blvd	Fredericksburg	VA	22401	**800-395-2455**	540-741-1100	374-3
Marygrove College						
8425 W McNichols Rd	Detroit	MI	48221	**866-313-1927***	313-927-1200	167
*Admissions						
Maryland						
Assessments & Taxation Dept						
301 W Preston St 8th Fl	Baltimore	MD	21201	**888-246-5941**	410-767-1184	339-21
Court of Appeals						
361 Rowe Blvd 4th Fl	Annapolis	MD	21401	**800-926-2583**	410-260-1500	339-21
Criminal Injuries Compensation Board						
6776 Reisterstown Rd Ste 206	Baltimore	MD	21215	**888-679-9347**	410-585-3010	339-21
Department of Budget & Management						
45 Calvert St	Annapolis	MD	21401	**800-705-3493**		339-21
Education Dept						
200 W Baltimore St	Baltimore	MD	21201	**888-246-0016**	410-767-0100	339-21
Emergency Management Agency						
5401 Rue St Lo Dr	Reisterstown	MD	21136	**877-636-2872**	410-517-3600	339-21
Environment Dept						
1800 Washington Blvd	Baltimore	MD	21230	**800-633-6101**	410-537-3000	339-21
Higher Education Commision						
839 Bestgate Rd Ste 400	Annapolis	MD	21401	**800-974-0203**	410-260-4500	339-21
Housing & Community Development Dept						
100 Community Pl	Crownsville	MD	21032	**800-756-0119**		339-21
Insurance Administration						
525 St Paul Pl	Baltimore	MD	21202	**800-492-6116**	410-468-2000	339-21
Natural Resources Dept						
580 Taylor Ave	Annapolis	MD	21401	**877-620-8367**	410-260-8021	339-21
Parole & Probation Div						
6776 Reisterstown Rd	Baltimore	MD	21215	**877-227-8031**	410-585-3500	339-21
Physician Quality Assurance Board						
4201 Patterson Ave	Baltimore	MD	21215	**800-492-6836**	410-764-4777	339-21
Public Service Commission						
6 St Paul St 16th Fl	Baltimore	MD	21202	**800-492-0474**	410-767-8000	339-21
State Forest & Park Service						
580 Taylor Ave Rm E-3	Annapolis	MD	21401	**877-620-8367***	410-260-8186	339-21
*Campground Resv						
State Government Information						
State House	Annapolis	MD	21401	**800-811-8336**	410-974-3901	339-21
State Police						
1201 Reisterstown Rd	Pikesville	MD	21208	**800-525-5555**	410-653-4200	339-21
Teacher Certification & Accreditation Div						
200 W Baltimore St	Baltimore	MD	21201	**866-772-8922**	410-767-0412	339-21
Tourism Development Office						
217 E Redwood St 9th Fl	Baltimore	MD	21202	**800-543-1036**	410-767-3400	339-21
Treasurer						
80 Calvert St Rm 109	Annapolis	MD	21401	**800-974-0468**	410-260-7533	339-21
Veterans Affairs Dept						
31 Hopkins Plaza Rm 1231	Baltimore	MD	21201	**800-446-4926**	410-230-4444	339-21
Vital Records Div						
6550 Reisterstown Rd	Baltimore	MD	21215	**800-832-3277**	410-764-3038	339-21
Maryland & Virginia Milk Producers Co-op Assn Inc						
1985 Isaac Newton Sq W	Reston	VA	20190	**800-552-1976**	703-742-6800	298-4
Maryland Assn of Realtors						
2594 Riva Rd	Annapolis	MD	21401	**800-638-6425**	410-841-6080	654

Name	Address	City	State	ZIP	Toll-Free	Phone	Class
Maryland Bar Journal	520 W Fayette St	Baltimore	MD	21201	**800-492-1964**	410-685-7878	456-15
Maryland Cork Co Inc	505 Blue Ball Rd PO Box 126	Elkton	MD	21922	**800-662-2675**	410-398-2955	211
Maryland Dept of Legislative Services	90 State Cir	Annapolis	MD	21401	**800-492-7122**	410-946-5400	433
Maryland Ethics Commission	45 Calvert St 3rd Fl	Annapolis	MD	21401	**877-669-6085**	410-260-7770	267
Maryland Hall for the Creative Arts	801 Chase St	Annapolis	MD	21401	**866-438-3808**	410-263-5544	571
Maryland Historical Society Museum & Library	201 W Monument St	Baltimore	MD	21201	**800-537-5487**	410-685-3750	519
Maryland Inn	16 Church Cir	Annapolis	MD	21401	**800-847-8882**	410-263-2641	379
Maryland Match Corp	605 Alluvion St	Baltimore	MD	21230	**800-423-0013**	410-752-8164	468
Maryland Municipal League Insurance Agency Inc	1212 W St Ste 100	Annapolis	MD	21401	**800-492-7121**	410-268-5514	532
Maryland Pharmacists Assn	9115 Guilford Rd Ste 200	Columbia	MD	21046	**877-463-3464**	410-727-0746	584
Maryland Plastics Inc	251 E Central Ave *Cust Svc	Federalsburg	MD	21632	**800-544-5582***	410-754-5566	606
Maryland Public Television (MPT)	11767 Owings Mills Blvd	Owings Mills	MD	21117	**800-223-3678**	410-581-4201	629
Maryland Renaissance Festival	PO Box 315	Crownsville	MD	21032	**800-296-7304**	410-266-7304	148
Maryland State Bar Assn Inc	520 W Fayette St	Baltimore	MD	21201	**800-492-1964**	410-685-7878	71
Maryland State Medical Society	1211 Cathedral St	Baltimore	MD	21201	**800-492-1056**	410-539-0872	473
Maryland Student Financial Assistance Office	839 Bestgate Rd Ste 400	Annapolis	MD	21401	**800-974-0203**	410-260-4565	723
Maryland Veterinary Medical Assn	8015 Corporate Dr Ste A	Baltimore	MD	21236	**888-884-6862**	410-931-3332	793
Marylhurst University	17600 Pacific Hwy 43 PO Box 261	Marylhurst	OR	97036	**800-634-9982**	503-636-8141	167
Marymount Hospital	12300 McCracken Rd	Garfield Heights	OH	44125	**800-801-2273**	216-581-0500	374-3
Marymount Manhattan College	221 E 71st St	New York	NY	10021	**866-667-6572**	212-517-0400	167
Marymount University	2807 N Glebe Rd	Arlington	VA	22207	**800-548-7638**	703-522-5600	167
Maryville College	502 E Lamar Alexander Pkwy	Maryville	TN	37804	**800-597-2687**	865-981-8000	167
Marywood University Arboretum	2300 Adams Ave	Scranton	PA	18509	**866-279-9663**	570-348-6218	96
MAS Capital Inc	2715 Coney Island Ave	Brooklyn	NY	11235	**866-553-7493**		689
Masco Cabinetry LLC	5353 W US 223	Adrian	MI	49221	**866-850-8557**	517-263-0771	114
Masco Corp	21001 Van Born Rd *NYSE: MAS*	Taylor	MI	48180	**888-627-6397**	313-274-7400	608
Masergy Communications Inc	2740 N Dallas Pkwy Ste 260	Plano	TX	75093	**866-588-5885**	214-442-5700	226
Masimo Corp	40 Parker	Irvine	CA	92618	**800-326-4890**	949-297-7000	252
Masland Carpets Inc	716 Bill Myles Dr	Saraland	AL	36571	**800-633-0468**		130
Mason City Convention & Visitors Bureau	2021 Fourth St SW Hwy 122 W	Mason City	IA	50401	**800-423-5724**	641-422-1663	208
Mason Contractors Assn of America (MCAA)	1481 Merchant Dr	Algonquin	IL	60193	**800-536-2225**	224-678-9709	48-3
Mason Corp	123 W Oxmoor Rd	Birmingham	AL	35209	**800-868-4100**	205-942-4100	479
Mason Structural Steel Inc	7500 Northfield Rd	Walton Hills	OH	44146	**800-686-1223**	440-439-1040	362
Masonic Service Assn of North America (MSANA)	8120 Fenton St Ste 203	Silver Spring	MD	20910	**855-476-4010**	301-588-4010	47-15
Masonite International Corp	201 N Franklin St Ste 300	Tampa	FL	33602	**800-895-2723**	813-877-2726	238
Maspeth Federal Savings	56-18 69th St	Maspeth	NY	11378	**888-558-1300**	718-335-1300	69
Massa Products Corp	280 Lincoln St	Hingham	MA	02043	**800-962-7543**	781-749-4800	666
Massachusetts							
Banks Div	1000 Washington St Ste 710	Boston	MA	02118	**800-495-2265**	617-956-1501	339-22
Child Support Enforcement Div	51 Sleeper St 4th Fl	Boston	MA	02205	**800-332-2733**	617-660-1234	339-22
Executive Office of Transportation	10 Pk Plaza Ste 3170	Boston	MA	02116	**800-219-9936**	617-973-7000	339-22
Insurance Div	1000 Washington St Ste 810	Boston	MA	02118	**877-563-4467**	617-521-7794	339-22
Parole Board	12 Mercer Rd	Natick	MA	01760	**888-298-6272**	508-650-4500	339-22
Revenue Dept	PO Box 7010	Boston	MA	02204	**800-392-6089**	617-626-2201	339-22
Travel & Tourism Office	10 Pk Plaza Ste 4510	Boston	MA	02116	**800-227-6277**	617-973-8500	339-22
Massachusetts Assn of Realtors	256 Second Ave	Waltham	MA	02451	**800-725-6272**	781-890-3700	654
Massachusetts Bay Community College	*Wellesley Hills* 50 Oakland St	Wellesley Hills	MA	02481	**800-233-3182**	781-239-3000	161
Massachusetts Bill Status	1 Ashburton Pl Rm 1611	Boston	MA	02108	**800-392-6090**	617-727-7030	433
Massachusetts Board of Library Commissioners	98 N Washington St	Boston	MA	02114	**800-952-7403**	617-725-1860	434-5
Massachusetts College of Art	621 Huntington Ave	Boston	MA	02115	**800-834-3242**	617-879-7222	167
Massachusetts College of Pharmacy & Health Sciences	179 Longwood Ave	Boston	MA	02115	**800-225-5506**	617-732-2850	167
Massachusetts Correctional Industries	1 Industries Dr Bldg A PO Box 188	Norfolk	MA	02056	**800-222-2211**	508-850-1070	629
Massachusetts Dental Society	2 Willow St Ste 200	Southborough	MA	01745	**800-342-8747**	508-480-9797	229
Massachusetts Maritime Academy	101 Academy Dr *Admissions	Buzzards Bay	MA	02532	**800-544-3411***	508-830-5000	167
Massachusetts Medical Society (MMS)	860 Winter St	Waltham	MA	02451	**800-322-2303**	781-893-4610	473
Massachusetts National Cemetery	Conery Rd	Bourne	MA	02532	**800-827-1000**	508-563-7113	135
Massachusetts Nurses Assn (MNA)	340 Tpke St	Canton	MA	02021	**800-882-2056**	781-821-4625	532
Massachusetts Pharmacists Assn	500 W Cummings Pk Ste 3475	Woburn	MA	01801	**888-772-7227**	781-933-1107	584
Massachusetts Society of Certified Public Accountants	105 Chauncy St 10th Fl	Boston	MA	02111	**800-392-6145**	617-556-4000	2
Massage Ctr at Mohonk Mountain House	1000 Mtn Rest Rd	New Paltz	NY	12561	**800-772-6646**	845-255-1000	705
Massanutten Military Academy	614 S Main St	Woodstock	VA	22664	**877-466-6222**	540-459-2167	621
massAV	80 Cambridge St	Burlington	MA	01803	**800-423-7830**		234
Massey Cancer Ctr	*Virginia Commonwealth University* 401 College St PO Box 980037	Richmond	VA	23298	**877-462-7739**	804-828-0450	666
Massey Services Inc	315 Groveland St E	Orlando	FL	32804	**888-262-7739**	407-645-2500	576
MassMutual PAC	1295 State St	Springfield	MA	01111	**800-272-2216**	413-788-8411	614
Massoud Furniture Manufacturing Inc	8351 Moberly Ln	Dallas	TX	75227	**800-762-2797**	214-388-8655	322
MAST Vacation Partners Inc	635 Butterfield Rd Ste 150	Oakbrook Terrace	IL	60181	**855-824-9288**	630-889-9817	770
MasTec Inc	800 Douglas Rd 12th Fl *NYSE: MTZ*	Coral Gables	FL	33134	**800-531-5000**	305-599-1800	190-1
Master Appliance Corp	2420 18th St	Racine	WI	53403	**800-558-9413**	262-633-7791	757
Master Brewers Assn of the Americas (MBAA)	3340 Pilot Knob Rd	Saint Paul	MN	55121	**800-328-7560**	651-454-7250	48-6
Master Cutlery Inc	700 Penhorn Ave	Secaucus	NJ	07094	**888-271-7229**	201-271-7600	224
Master Finish Co	2020 Nelson SE PO Box 7505	Grand Rapids	MI	49510	**877-590-5819**		480
Master Halco Inc	1321 Greenway Dr	Irving	TX	75038	**800-883-8384**	972-714-7300	281
Master Lock Company LLC	137 W Forest Hill Ave PO Box 927	Oak Creek	WI	53154	**800-464-2088**		350
Master Mark Plastics	210 Ampe Dr *Cust Svc	Paynesville	MN	56362	**800-535-4838***	320-243-7318	429
Master Mfg Co	747 N Yale Ave	Villa Park	IL	60181	**800-864-1649**	630-833-7060	174
Master Package Corp	200 Madson St	Owen	WI	54460	**800-396-8425**	715-229-2156	124
Master Spas Inc	6927 Lincoln Pkwy	Fort Wayne	IN	46804	**800-860-7727**	260-436-9100	375
MASTER Teacher Inc, The	2600 Leadership Ln	Manhattan	KS	66505	**800-669-9633**		527
Master's College	21726 Placerita Canyon Rd	Santa Clarita	CA	91321	**800-568-6248**	661-259-3540	167
Master-Bilt Products	908 Hwy 15 N	New Albany	MS	38652	**800-647-1284**	662-534-9061	14
MasterCard Inc	2000 Purchase St *NYSE: MA*	Purchase	NY	10577	**800-100-1087**	914-249-2000	219
Masterchem Industries LLC	3135 Old Hwy M	Imperial	MO	63052	**866-774-6371**		549
MasterCraft Boat Co	100 Cherokee Cove Dr	Vonore	TN	37885	**800-443-8774**	423-884-2221	89
Mastercraft Industries Inc	777 S St	Newburgh	NY	12550	**800-835-7812**	845-565-8850	114
Masterfile Corp	3 Concorde Gate 4th Fl	Toronto	ON	M3C3N7	**800-387-9010**	416-929-3000	588
MasterGraphics Inc	2979 Triverton Pike Dr	Madison	WI	53711	**800-873-7238**	608-256-4884	176
Master-Lee Energy Services Corp	5631 Route 981	Latrobe	PA	15650	**800-662-4493**	724-539-8060	103
Masters Gallery Foods Inc	328 County Hwy PP PO Box 170 *General	Plymouth	WI	53073	**800-236-8431***	920-893-8431	298-4
Masters Gallery Ltd	2115 Fourth St SW	Calgary	AB	T2S1W8	**866-245-0616**	403-245-2064	41
Masters Inc	5741 NW Cornelius Pass Rd	Hillsboro	OR	97124	**877-652-5656**	503-531-3308	231
Masters' Supply Inc	4505 Bishop Ln	Louisville	KY	40218	**800-388-6353**		611
Masterword Services, International Inc	303 Stafford St	Houston	TX	77079	**866-716-4999**	281-589-0810	766
Mastodon State Historic Site	1050 Charles J Becker Dr	Imperial	MO	63052	**800-334-6946**	636-464-2976	564
Matanuska Telephone Assn Inc	1740 S Chugach St	Palmer	AK	99645	**800-478-3211**	907-745-3211	733
Matasano Security LLC	39 W 14th St Ste 202	New York	NY	10011	**888-677-0666**		198
Matco Tools	4403 Allen Rd	Stow	OH	44224	**866-289-8665**	330-926-5332	756
Matco-Norca Inc	Rt 22	Brewster	NY	10509	**800-431-2082**	845-278-7570	609
Mate Precision Tooling Inc	1295 Lund Blvd	Anoka	MN	55303	**800-328-4492**	763-421-0230	755
Matenaer Corp	810 Schoenhaar Dr	West Bend	WI	53090	**800-254-0873**	262-338-0700	491
Material & Contract Services LLC	5820 Stoneridge Mall Rd	Pleasanton	CA	94588	**866-772-9250**	925-460-0397	462
Material Handling Industry of America (MHIA)	8720 Red Oak Blvd Ste 201	Charlotte	NC	28217	**800-345-1815**	704-676-1190	48-13
Material Handling Products Corp	6601 Joy Rd	East Syracuse	NY	13057	**866-980-4788**	315-437-2891	768

Name / Address	City	State	ZIP	Toll-Free	Phone	Class
Materials Transportation Co (MTC)						
1408 S Commerce PO Box 1358	Temple	TX	76503	**800-433-3110**	254-298-2900	386
Materion Corp						
6070 Parkland Blvd	Mayfield Heights	OH	44124	**800-321-2076**	216-486-4200	501
NYSE: MTRN						
Mathematical Assn of America (MAA)						
1529 18th St NW	Washington	DC	20036	**800-331-1622**	202-387-5200	48-19
Matheson Trucking Inc						
9785 Goethe Rd	Sacramento	CA	95827	**800-455-7678**	916-685-2330	778
Matheus Lumber Company Inc						
15800 Woodinville-Redmond Rd NE						
PO Box 2260	Woodinville	WA	98072	**800-284-7501**	425-489-3000	193-3
Mathews Assoc Inc						
220 Power Ct	Sanford	FL	32771	**800-871-5262**	407-323-3390	73
Mathews Bros Co						
22 Perkins Rd	Belfast	ME	04915	**800-615-2004**	207-338-6490	238
Mathews Co						
500 Industrial Ave	Crystal Lake	IL	60012	**800-323-7045**	815-459-2210	275
Mathias Ham House Historic Site						
2241 Lincoln Ave	Dubuque	IA	52001	**800-226-3369**	563-557-9545	49-2
Mathis Bros Furniture Inc						
6611 S 101 St E Ave	Tulsa	OK	74133	**800-329-3434***	918-461-7785	322
*Cust Svc						
Mathnasium LLC						
5120 W Goldleaf Cir Ste 300	Los Angeles	CA	90056	**877-601-6284**	323-421-8000	311
Mathy Construction Co Inc						
920 Tenth Ave N	Onalaska	WI	54650	**800-822-5246**	608-783-6411	190-4
Matich Corp						
1596 Harry Sheppard Blvd	San Bernardino	CA	92408	**800-404-4975**	909-382-7400	190-4
Matik Inc						
33 Brook St	West Hartford	CT	06110	**800-245-1628**	860-232-2323	534
Matot Inc						
2501 Van Buren St	Bellwood	IL	60104	**800-369-1070**	708-547-1888	258
Matricis Informatique Inc						
1425 Rene-Levesque Blvd W						
Ste 240	Montreal	QC	H3G1T7	**866-394-0011**	514-394-0011	182
Matrix Companies, The						
7162 Reading Rd Ste 250	Cincinnati	OH	45237	**877-550-7973**	513-351-1222	393
Matrix Energy Services Inc						
3221 Ramos Cir	Sacramento	CA	95827	**800-556-2123**	916-363-9283	258
Matrix Hotel						
10640-100 Ave	Edmonton	AB	T5J3N8	**866-465-8150**	780-429-2861	379
Matrix LLC						
19 Ave D	Johnson City	NY	13790	**800-338-5603**	607-766-0700	258
Matrix Service Co						
5100 E Skelly Dr 74135	Tulsa	OK	74135	**866-367-6879**		538
NASDAQ: MTRX						
Matrix Systems Inc						
1041 Byers Rd	Miamisburg	OH	45342	**800-562-8749**	937-438-9033	690
Matrox Electronic Systems Ltd						
1055 St Regis Blvd	Dorval	QC	H9P2T4	**800-361-1408**	514-822-6000	175-5
Matson Logistics Inc						
555 12th St	Oakland	CA	94607	**800-762-8766**	510-628-4000	448
Matson Navigation Co						
555 12th St	Oakland	CA	94607	**800-462-8766***	510-628-4000	313
*Cust Svc						
Matsui International Company Inc						
1501 W 178th St	Gardena	CA	90248	**800-359-5679**	310-767-7812	388
Matsui Nursery Inc						
1645 Old Stage Rd	Salinas	CA	93908	**800-793-6433**	831-422-6433	369
Matt Blatt Inc						
501 Delsea Dr N	Glassboro	NJ	08028	**877-462-5288**	856-881-0444	56
Matt Castrucci Auto Mall of Dayton						
3013 Mall Pk Dr	Dayton	OH	45459	**855-204-5293**		515
Mattel Inc						
333 Continental Blvd	El Segundo	CA	90245	**800-524-8697**	310-252-2000	760
NASDAQ: MAT						
Mattersight Corp						
200 S Wacker Ste 3100	Chicago	IL	60606	**877-235-6925**		462
Matthaei Botanical Gardens						
1800 N Dixboro Rd	Ann Arbor	MI	48105	**800-666-8693**	734-647-7600	96
Matthews Book Co						
11559 Rock Island Ct	Maryland Heights	MO	63043	**800-633-2665**	314-432-1400	95
Matthews Currie Ford Company Inc						
130 N Tamiami Trl	Nokomis	FL	34275	**855-491-3131**	941-488-6787	56
Matthews International Corp Marking Products Div						
6515 Penn Ave	Pittsburgh	PA	15206	**800-775-7775**	412-665-2500	466
Matthews Studio Equipment Group						
2405 W Empire Ave	Burbank	CA	91504	**800-237-8263**	818-843-6715	590
Matthijssen Inc						
14 Rt 10	East Hanover	NJ	07936	**800-845-2200**	973-887-1100	177
Mattracks Systems						
202 Cleveland Ave E	Karlstad	MN	56732	**877-436-7800**	218-436-7000	370
Mattress Firm Inc						
5815 Gulf Fwy	Houston	TX	77023	**800-821-6621**	713-923-1090	362
Mattson Spray Equipment						
230 W Coleman St	Rice Lake	WI	54868	**800-877-4857**	715-234-1617	174
Mattson Technology Inc						
47131 Bayside Pkwy	Fremont	CA	94538	**800-315-6607**	510-657-5900	693
NASDAQ: MTSN						
Maui Community College						
310 W Kaahumanu Ave	Kahului	HI	96732	**800-479-6692**	808-984-3267	161
Maui Divers of Hawaii						
1520 Liona St	Honolulu	HI	96814	**800-462-4454**	808-946-7979	409
Maui Jim Inc						
721 Wainee St	Lahaina	HI	96761	**888-352-2001**	808-661-8841	541
Maui Memorial Hospital						
221 Mahalani St	Wailuku	HI	96793	**800-427-5940**	808-244-9056	374-3
Maui News						
100 Mahalani St	Wailuku	HI	96793	**888-683-1115**	808-244-3981	531-2
Maui Ocean Ctr						
192 Maalaea Rd	Wailuku	HI	96793	**800-350-5634**	808-270-7000	39
Maui Tacos International Inc						
2001 Palmer Ave. Ste 105	Larchmont	NY	10538	**866-388-3758**		668
Mauldin & Jenkins Certified Public Accountants LLC						
200 Galleria Pkwy SE	Atlanta	GA	30339	**800-277-0080**	770-955-8600	2
Maumee Bay Lodge & Conference Ctr						
1750 Pk Rd Ste 2	Oregon	OH	43616	**800-282-7275**	419-836-1466	379
Mauna Kea Beach Hotel						
62-100 Maunakea Beach Dr						
	Island of Hawaii	HI	96743	**866-977-4589**	808-882-7222	667
Mauna Lani Bay Hotel & Bungalows						
68-1400 Mauna Lani Dr	Kohala Coast	HI	96743	**800-367-2323**	808-885-6622	667
Mauna Loa Macadamia Nut Corp						
16-701 Macadamia Rd	Keaau	HI	96749	**888-628-6256***	808-966-8618	10-8
*Cust Svc						
Maupin Travel Inc						
2501 Blue Ridge Rd	Raleigh	NC	27607	**800-786-2738**	919-821-2146	769
Maupintour Inc						
2690 Weston Rd Ste 200	Weston	FL	33331	**800-255-4266**	954-653-3820	758
Maurer Mfg						
1300 38th Ave W PO Box 160	Spencer	IA	51301	**888-274-6010**	712-262-2992	777
Maurey Manufacturing Corp						
410 Industrial Pk Rd	Holly Springs	MS	38635	**800-284-2161**		619
Maurice's Gourmet Barbeque						
PO Box 6847	West Columbia	SC	29171	**800-628-7423**	803-791-5887	297-19
Maurices Inc						
105 W Superior St	Duluth	MN	55802	**866-977-1542**	218-727-8431	156-4
Mautino Distributing Co						
500 N Richards St	Spring Valley	IL	61362	**800-851-2756***	815-664-4311	80-1
*Cust Svc						
MavenWire LLC						
630 Freedom Business Ctr						
3rd Fl	King Of Prussia	PA	19406	**866-343-4870**		462
Maverick Directional Services						
25615 Oakhurst Dr	Spring	TX	77386	**866-459-0233**	281-364-1212	539
Maverick Technologies						
265 Admiral Trost Rd						
PO Box 470	Columbia	IL	62236	**888-917-9109**	618-281-9100	180-1
Maverick USA Inc						
13301 Valentine Rd	North Little Rock	AR	72117	**800-289-6600**	501-955-1255	778
Maverik Inc						
880 W Center St	North Salt Lake	UT	84054	**800-789-4455***	801-936-5557	206
*Cust Svc						
MAWS (Marijuana Anonymous World Services)						
PO Box 7807	Torrance	CA	90504	**800-766-6779**		47-21
Mawson & Mawson Inc						
1800 Old Lincoln Hwy						
PO Box 248	Langhorne	PA	19047	**800-262-9766**	215-750-1100	778
Max Credit Union						
400 Eastdale Cir	Montgomery	AL	36117	**800-776-6776**	334-260-2600	69
Max Environmental Technologies Inc						
1815 Washington Rd	Pittsburgh	PA	15241	**800-851-7845**	412-343-4900	198
Max Group Corp						
17011 Green Dr	City of Industry	CA	91745	**800-256-9040**	626-935-0050	176
Max International Converters Inc						
2360 Dairy Rd	Lancaster	PA	17601	**800-233-0222**		553
Max Levy Autograph Inc						
2710 Commerce Way	Philadelphia	PA	19154	**800-798-3675**	215-842-3675	480
Max Technical Training						
4900 Pkwy Dr Ste 160	Mason	OH	45040	**866-595-6863**	513-322-8888	198
MAX Technologies Inc						
2051 Victoria Ave 3rd Fl	Saint-Lambert	QC	J4S1H1	**800-361-1629**	450-443-3332	666
Max Tool Inc						
119b Citation Ct	Birmingham	AL	35209	**800-783-6298**	205-942-2466	351
Maxcess International, Inc.						
222 W Memorial Rd						
PO Box 26508	Oklahoma City	OK	73114	**800-333-3433**	405-755-1600	205
Maxim Crane Works						
1225 Washington Pk	Bridgeville	PA	15017	**877-629-5438**	412-504-0200	266-3
Maxim Integrated Products Inc						
120 San Gabriel Dr	Sunnyvale	CA	94086	**888-629-4642**	408-737-7600	694
NASDAQ: MXIM						
Maxim Technologies Inc						
1607 Derwent Way	Delta	BC	V3M6K8	**800-663-9925**		150
Maxima Technologies Stewart Warner						
1811 Rohrerstown Rd	Lancaster	PA	17601	**800-676-1837**	717-581-1000	494
Maximum Human Performance Inc (MHP Inc)						
21 Dwight Pl	Fairfield	NJ	07004	**888-783-8844**	973-785-9055	797
MAXIMUS Inc						
11419 Sunset Hills Rd	Reston	VA	20190	**800-629-4687**	703-251-8500	196
NYSE: MMS						
Maxium Financial Services Inc						
30 Vogell Rd Ste 1	Richmond Hill	ON	L4B3K6	**800-379-5888**	905-780-6150	568
MaxLinear Inc						
2051 Palomar Airport Rd						
Ste 100	Carlsbad	CA	92011	**888-505-4369**	760-692-0711	693
NYSE: MXL						
MAXON COMPUTER Inc						
2640 Lavery Ct Ste A	Newbury Park	CA	91320	**877-264-6283**	805-376-3333	179
Maxon Furniture Inc						
660 SW 39th St Ste 150	Renton	WA	98057	**800-876-4274***		320-1
*Cust Svc						
Maxon Industries Inc						
11921 Slauson Ave	Santa Fe Springs	CA	90670	**800-227-4116**	562-464-0099	469
Maxor National Pharmacy Services Corp						
320 S Polk St Ste 100	Amarillo	TX	79101	**800-658-6146**	806-324-5400	585
MaxPoint Interactive Inc						
3020 Carrington Mill Blvd						
Ste 300	Morrisville	NC	27560	**800-916-9960**		179
Maxsys						
173 Dalhousie St	Ottawa	ON	K1N7C7	**800-429-5177**	613-562-9943	262
Maxtex Inc						
3620 Francis Cir	Alpharetta	GA	30004	**800-241-1836**	770-772-6757	361
MaxVision Corp						
495 Production Ave	Madison	AL	35758	**800-533-5805**	256-772-3058	175-1
Maxwell Air Force Base						
55 Le May Plaza S	Maxwell AFB	AL	36112	**877-353-6807**	334-953-2014	496-1
Maxwell Technologies Inc						
5271 Viewridge Ct Ste 100	San Diego	CA	92123	**877-511-4324**	858-503-3300	255
NASDAQ: MXWL						
Maxxam Analytics Inc						
335 LaiRd Rd Ste 2	Guelph	ON	N1G4P7	**877-706-7678**		417
Maxxon Corp						
920 Hamel Rd	Hamel	MN	55340	**800-356-7887**	763-478-9600	134
MaxYield Co-op						
313 Third Ave NE PO Box 49	West Bend	IA	50597	**800-383-0003**	515-887-7211	277

Name / Address	City	State	ZIP	Toll-Free	Phone	Class
May Institute Inc 41 Pacella Pk Dr	Randolph	MA	02368	**800-778-7601**	781-440-0400	47-6
May Supply Company Inc 1775 Erickson Ave	Harrisonburg	VA	22801	**800-296-9997**	540-433-2611	611
May Trucking Co 4185 Brooklake Rd PO Box 9039	Salem	OR	97305	**800-547-9169**		778
May, Adam, Gerdes & Thompson LLP 503 S Pierre St	Pierre	SD	57501	**800-636-8803**	605-224-8803	428
Maybelline New York 575 Fifth Ave PO Box 1010	New York	NY	10017	**800-944-0730**		217
Mayberry Fine Art Inc 212 Mcdermot Ave	Winnipeg	MB	R3B0S3	**877-871-9261**	204-255-5690	41
Mayco Industries LLC 18 W Oxmoor Rd	Birmingham	AL	35209	**800-749-6061**	205-942-4242	695
Mayer Electric Supply Co 3405 Fourth Ave S PO Box 1328	Birmingham	AL	35222	**866-637-1255**	205-583-3500	248
Mayesh Wholesale Florist Inc 5401 W 104th St	Los Angeles	CA	90045	**888-462-9374**	310-348-4921	294
Mayfair Hotel & Spa 3000 Florida Ave	Coconut Grove	FL	33133	**800-433-4555**	305-441-0000	379
Mayfield Paper Co 1115 S Hill St	San Angelo	TX	76903	**800-725-1441**	325-653-1444	558
Mayfield Transfer Company Inc 3200 W Lake St	Melrose Park	IL	60160	**800-222-2959**	708-681-4440	778
Mayflower Inn 118 Woodbury Rd	Washington	CT	06793	**800-585-7198**	860-868-9466	379
Mayflower Park Hotel 405 Olive Way	Seattle	WA	98101	**800-426-5100**	206-623-8700	379
Mayflower Retirement Community 1620 Mayflower Ct	Winter Park	FL	32792	**800-228-6518**	407-672-1620	670
Mayflower Tours Inc 1225 Warren Ave PO Box 490	Downers Grove	IL	60515	**800-323-7604**	630-435-8500	758
Mayflower Transit LLC 1 Mayflower Dr	Fenton	MO	63026	**800-325-3924**	636-305-4000	518
Mayhew Steel Products Inc 199 Industrial Blvd	Turners Falls	MA	01376	**800-872-0037**	413-863-4860	756
Mayland Community College 200 Mayland Dr PO Box 547	Spruce Pine	NC	28777	**800-462-9526**	828-765-7351	161
Mayline Group 619 N Commerce St PO Box 728	Sheboygan	WI	53082	**800-822-8037**	920-457-5537	320-1
Maynard Furniture Company Inc 725 Anderson St	Belton	SC	29627	**866-420-5249**	864-338-7751	322
Mayo Aviation Inc 7735 S Peoria St	Englewood	CO	80112	**800-525-0194**	303-792-4020	13
Mayo Civic Ctr 30 Civic Ctr Dr SE	Rochester	MN	55904	**800-422-2199**	507-328-2220	207
Mayo Clinic 4500 San Pablo Rd	Jacksonville	FL	32224	**888-255-4458**	904-992-9992	379
Mayo Clinic Health Letter 200 First St NW	Rochester	MN	55905	**800-291-1128**		530-8
Mayo Clinic Health System Austin 1000 First Dr NW	Austin	MN	55912	**888-609-4065**	507-433-7351	374-3
Mayo Clinic Health System Southwest Minnesota 1025 Marsh St	Mankato	MN	56001	**800-327-3721**	507-625-4031	374-3
Mayo Clinic Hospital 5777 E Mayo Blvd	Phoenix	AZ	85054	**888-266-0440**	480-342-2000	374-3
Mayo Clinic Proceedings Magazine 200 First St SW Siebens Bldg 7-70 *Cust Svc	Rochester	MN	55905	**800-654-2452***	507-284-2094	456-16
Maysville Community & Technical College 1755 US 68	Maysville	KY	41056	**888-452-7322**	606-759-7141	161
Maytag Appliances 403 W Fourth St N *Cust Svc	Newton	IA	50208	**800-344-1274***		35
Mayville Products Corp 403 Degner Ave	Mayville	WI	53050	**800-558-7297**	920-387-3000	695
Mayville State University 330 Third St NE	Mayville	ND	58257	**800-437-4104**		167
Mazda North American Operations 7755 Irvine Ctr Dr PO Box 19734 *Cust Svc	Irvine	CA	92618	**800-222-5500***	949-727-1990	58
Mazel & Company Inc 4300 W Ferdinand St	Chicago	IL	60624	**800-525-4023**	773-533-1600	491
Mazon Assoc Inc 800 W Airport Fwy Ste 900	Irving	TX	75062	**800-442-2740**	972-554-6967	274
Mazza Vineyards 11815 E Lake Rd	North East	PA	16428	**800-796-9463**	814-725-8695	49-6
Mazzella Lifting Technologies 21000 Aerospace Pkwy	Cleveland	OH	44142	**800-362-4601**	440-239-7000	469
MB Financial Inc 6111 N River Rd *NASDAQ: MBFI*	Rosemont	IL	60018	**888-422-6562**		360-2
MBA (Military Benefit Assn) 14605 Avion Pkwy PO Box 221110	Chantilly	VA	20153	**800-336-0100**	703-968-6200	47-19
MBA (Mortgage Bankers Assn) 1919 M St NW 5th Fl	Washington	DC	20036	**800-793-6222**	202-557-2700	48-2
MBAA (Master Brewers Assn of the Americas) 3340 Pilot Knob Rd	Saint Paul	MN	55121	**800-328-7560**	651-454-7250	48-6
MBC (Memorial Blood Centers) 737 Pelham Blvd *Cust Svc	Saint Paul	MN	55114	**888-448-3253***	651-332-7000	88
MBL (Marine Biological Laboratory) 7 MBL St	Woods Hole	MA	02543	**800-222-1222**	508-548-3705	666
MBL International Corp 4 H Constitution Way	Woburn	MA	01801	**800-200-5459**	781-939-6964	196
MBM (MBM Corp) 3134 Industry Dr *Cust Svc	North Charleston	SC	29418	**800-223-2508***	843-552-2700	110
MBM Corp (MBM) 3134 Industry Dr *Cust Svc	North Charleston	SC	29418	**800-223-2508***	843-552-2700	110
MBNA (Monument Builders of North America) 136 S Keowee St	Dayton	OH	45402	**800-233-4472**		48-3
MBP (McDonough Bolyard Peck Inc) 3040 Williams Dr Williams Plz 1 Ste 300	Fairfax	VA	22031	**800-898-9088**	703-641-9088	263
MBS Assoc Inc 7800 E Kemper Rd Ste 160	Cincinnati	OH	45249	**888-469-9301**	513-645-1600	263
MBS Textbook Exchange Inc 2711 W Ash St *Cust Svc	Columbia	MO	65203	**800-325-0530***	573-445-2243	94
MBT Financial Corp 102 E Front St *NASDAQ: MBTF*	Monroe	MI	48161	**800-321-0032**	734-241-3431	360-2
MBTC (Mifflinburg Bank & Trust Co) 250 E Chestnut St PO Box 186	Mifflinburg	PA	17844	**888-966-3131**	570-966-1041	69
MC & A Inc 615 Piikoi St Ste 1000 *General	Honolulu	HI	96814	**877-589-5589***	808-589-5500	769
MC Healthcare Products Inc 4658 Ontario St	Beamsville	ON	L0R1B4	**800-268-8671**		474
MC Sign Company Inc 8959 Tyler Blvd	Mentor	OH	44060	**800-627-4460**	440-953-2280	699
MC Sports 3070 Shaffer Ave SE	Grand Rapids	MI	49512	**800-626-1762**	616-942-2600	709
MCA (Marine Corps Assn) PO Box 1775	Quantico	VA	22134	**800-336-0291**	703-640-6161	47-19
MCAA (Mason Contractors Assn of America) 1481 Merchant Dr	Algonquin	IL	60193	**800-536-2225**	224-678-9709	48-3
MCAA (Mechanical Contractors Assn of America) 1385 Piccard Dr	Rockville	MD	20850	**800-556-3653**	301-869-5800	48-3
McAfee & Taft A Professional Corp 2 Leadership Sq 211 N Robinson Ste 1000	Oklahoma City	OK	73102	**800-235-9621**	405-235-9621	428
McAfee Inc 2821 Mission College Blvd *Cust Svc	Santa Clara	CA	95054	**888-847-8766***	408-988-3832	180-12
McAllister Towing & Transportation Co Inc 17 Battery Pl Ste 1200	New York	NY	10004	**888-774-0400**	212-269-3200	464
MCAP Financial Corp 1140 W Pender St Ste 1400	Vancouver	BC	V6E4G1	**800-977-5877**	604-681-8805	216
MCAP Service Corp 400-200 King St W	Toronto	ON	M5H3T4	**800-387-4405**	416-598-2665	650
McBee Assoc Inc 997 Old Eagle School Rd Ste 205	Wayne	PA	19087	**800-767-6203**	610-964-9680	196
MCC (Mennonite Central Committee) 21 S 12th St PO Box 500	Akron	PA	17501	**888-563-4676**	717-859-1151	47-5
McCabe Software Inc 3300 N Ridge Rd	Ellicott City	MD	21043	**800-638-6316**	410-381-3710	180-12
McCain Foods Ltd 181 Bay St Ste 3600	Toronto	ON	M5J2T3	**800-938-7799**	416-955-1700	297-21
McCain Foods USA Inc 2275 Cabot Dr	Lisle	IL	60532	**800-938-7799**		297-21
McCall Aviation 300 Deinhard Ln	McCall	ID	83638	**800-992-6559**	208-634-7137	62
McCall Handling Co 8801 Wise Ave	Dundalk	MD	21222	**888-870-0685**	410-388-2600	385
McCall Oil & Chemical Corp 5480 NW Front Ave	Portland	OR	97210	**800-622-2558**	503-221-6400	578
McCall Pattern Co 615 McCall Rd	Manhattan	KS	66502	**800-255-2762**		567
McCall Patterns Magazine 120 Broadway	New York	NY	10271	**800-782-0323**		456-14
McCall Service Inc 2861 College St	Jacksonville	FL	32205	**800-342-6948**	904-389-5561	576
McCall's Quilting Magazine 741 Corporate Cir Ste A	Golden	CO	80401	**800-944-0736**	303-215-5600	456-14
McCallie School 500 Dodds Ave	Chattanooga	TN	37404	**800-234-2163**	423-624-8300	621
McCallum Theatre 73000 Fred Waring Dr	Palm Desert	CA	92260	**866-889-2787**	760-340-2787	571
Mccallum, Hoaglund, Cook & Irby LLP 905 Montgomery Hwy Ste 201	Vestavia	AL	35216	**866-974-8145**	205-824-7767	428
McCann's Engineering & Manufacturing Co 4570 W Colorado Blvd	Los Angeles	CA	90039	**800-423-2429**	818-637-7200	662
McCarran International Airport 5757 Wayne Newton Blvd PO Box 11005	Las Vegas	NV	89119	**888-261-4414**	702-261-5211	27
McClancy Seasoning Co 1 Spice Rd	Fort Mill	SC	29707	**800-843-1968**	803-548-2366	345
McClard's Bar-B-Q 505 Albert Pike Rd	Hot Springs	AR	71901	**866-622-5273**	501-623-9665	669
McClarin Plastics Inc 15 Industrial Dr	Hanover	PA	17331	**800-233-3189**	717-637-2241	605
McClatchy Newspapers 2100 Q St	Sacramento	CA	95816	**866-807-2200**	916-321-1000	634-8
McClelland Oilfield Rentals Limited Patnership 8720-110 St	Grande Prairie	AB	T8V8K1	**866-539-3656**	780-539-3656	539
McCloskey Motors Inc 6710 N Academy Blvd	Colorado Springs	CO	80918	**877-389-6671**	719-594-9400	56
McClure Co 4101 N Sixth St	Harrisburg	PA	17110	**800-382-1319**	717-232-9743	191-10
McClure-Johnston Co 201 Corey Ave	Braddock	PA	15104	**800-232-0018**	412-351-4300	193-4
McCollister's Transportation Group Inc 1800 Rt 130 N PO Box 9	Burlington	NJ	08016	**800-257-9595**	609-386-0600	518
McCone Electric Co-op Inc 110 Main St	Circle	MT	59215	**800-684-3605**	406-485-3430	247
McConkey Co 1615 Puyallup St PO Box 1690	Sumner	WA	98390	**800-426-8124**	253-863-8111	201
McConnell Air Force Base 57837 Coffeyville St Ste 271	McConnell AFB	KS	67221	**877-272-7337**	316-759-6100	496-1
McConnell Jones Lanier & Murphy LLP The Lakes On Post Oak 3040 Post Oak Blvd Ste 1600	Houston	TX	77056	**866-908-4650**	713-968-1600	2
McCook Community College 1205 E Third St	McCook	NE	69001	**800-658-4348**	308-345-8100	161
McCook Public Power District 1510 N Hwy 83	McCook	NE	69001	**800-658-4285**	308-345-2500	247

Name / Address	City	State	ZIP	Toll-Free	Phone	Class
McCormick & Company Inc McCormick Flavor Div 226 Schilling Cir	Hunt Valley	MD	21031	**800-322-7742**	410-771-7500	297-37
McCormick & Schmick's 200 S Tryon St	Charlotte	NC	28202	**800-552-6379**	704-377-0201	669
McCormick & Schmick's Harborside 0309 SW Montgomery *Resv	Portland	OR	97201	**888-262-4386***	503-220-1865	669
McCormick Ingredients 18 Loveton Cir	Sparks	MD	21152	**800-632-5847**	410-771-7301	297-37
McCormick Theological Seminary 5460 S University Ave	Chicago	IL	60615	**800-228-4687**	773-947-6300	168-3
McCorvey Sheet Metal Works LP 8610 Wallisvile Rd	Houston	TX	77029	**800-580-7545**	713-672-7545	695
McCourt Label Co 20 Egbert Ln	Lewis Run	PA	16738	**800-458-2390**	814-362-3851	413
McCowan Design & Mfg Ltd 1760 Birchmount Rd	Toronto	ON	M1P2H7	**888-782-5189**	416-291-7111	534
Mc-Coy-Mills 700 W Commonwealth *Sales	Fullerton	CA	92832	**888-434-3145***		515
McCracken County Public Library 555 Washington St	Paducah	KY	42003	**866-829-7532**	270-442-2510	434-3
McCrea Equipment Company Inc 4463 Beech Rd	Temple Hills	MD	20748	**800-597-0091**	301-423-4585	191-10
McCreary County Tourist Commission PO Box 699	Whitley City	KY	42653	**877-209-1012**	606-376-3008	338
McCrometer Inc 3255 W Stetson Ave	Hemet	CA	92545	**800-220-2279**	951-652-6811	203
McCullagh Coffee 245 Swan St	Buffalo	NY	14204	**800-753-3473**		297-7
McCullough & Assoc 1746 NE Expy PO Box 29803	Atlanta	GA	30329	**800-969-1606**	404-325-1606	145
McDaniel College 2 College Hill *Admissions	Westminster	MD	21157	**800-638-5005***	410-857-2230	167
McDaniel Motor Co 1111 Mt Vernon Ave	Marion	OH	43302	**877-362-0288**	740-389-2355	515
Mcdaniels Marketing Communications 11 Olt Ave	Pekin	IL	61554	**866-431-4230**	309-346-4230	197
McDevitt Trucks Inc 1 Mack Ave PO Box 4640	Manchester	NH	03108	**800-370-6225**	603-668-1700	56
McDonald Publishing 567 Hanley Industrial Ct	Saint Louis	MO	63144	**800-722-8080**	314-781-7400	245
McDonald Wholesale Co 2350 W Broadway St	Eugene	OR	97402	**877-722-5503**	541-345-8421	298-3
McDonald's Corp 1 McDonald's Plz *NYSE: MCD*	Oak Brook	IL	60523	**800-244-6227**	630-623-3000	668
McDonald's Restaurants of Canada Ltd 1 McDonald's Pl	Toronto	ON	M3C3L4	**888-424-4622**	416-443-1000	668
McDonough Bolyard Peck Inc (MBP) 3040 Williams Dr Williams Plz 1 Ste 300	Fairfax	VA	22031	**800-898-9088**	703-641-9088	263
McDowell County Tourism Development Authority 91 S Catawba Ave	Old Fort	NC	28762	**888-233-6111**	828-668-4282	208
MCE (Medical Ctr Enterprise) 400 N Edwards St	Enterprise	AL	36330	**800-994-6610**	334-347-0584	374-3
McElroy Metal Inc 1500 Hamilton Rd	Bossier City	LA	71111	**800-562-3576**	318-747-8097	479
McElroy Truck Lines Inc 111 80 Spur PO Box 104	Cuba	AL	36907	**800-992-7863**	205-392-5579	448
Mcenearney Assoc Inc 109 S Pitt St	Alexandria	VA	22314	**877-624-9322**	703-549-9292	650
McEntire Produce Inc 2040 American Italian Way	Columbia	SC	29209	**800-845-2334**	803-799-3388	10-9
MCF Systems Atlanta Inc 5353 Snapfinger Woods Dr	Decatur	GA	30035	**800-828-3240**	770-593-9434	658
McFarland & Company Inc 960 NC Hwy 88 W PO Box 611	Jefferson	NC	28640	**800-253-2187**	336-246-4460	634-2
McFarland Cascade 1640 E Marc St PO Box 1496 *Cust Svc	Tacoma	WA	98421	**800-426-8430***	253-572-3033	816
McFarlane Mfg Company Inc 1259 Water St PO Box 100	Sauk City	WI	53583	**800-627-8569**	608-643-3321	278
McGard LLC 3875 California Rd	Orchard Park	NY	14127	**800-444-5847**	716-662-8980	60
McGean-Rohco Inc 2910 Harvard Ave *Orders	Cleveland	OH	44105	**800-932-7006***	216-441-4900	144
MCGG (Morrow County Grain Growers Inc) 350 N Main St	Lexington	OR	97839	**800-452-7396**	541-989-8221	10-4
McGill Electrical Product Group 9377 W Higgins Rd	Rosemont	IL	60018	**800-621-1506**	847-268-6000	813
McGill Hose & Coupling Inc 41 Benton Dr PO Box 408	East Longmeadow	MA	01028	**800-669-1467**	413-525-3977	385
McGill Smith Punshon Inc 3700 Park 42 Dr Ste 190B	Cincinnati	OH	45241	**800-759-8065**	513-759-0004	263
McGough Construction Co Inc 2737 Fairview Ave N	Saint Paul	MN	55113	**800-552-7670**	651-633-5050	188
McGrath Auto Group 4610 Ctr Pt Rd NE	Cedar Rapids	IA	52402	**888-902-8414**		56
McGrath RentCorp 5700 Las Positas Rd *NASDAQ: MGRC*	Livermore	CA	94551	**800-962-4284**	925-606-9200	504
McGraw-Hill Cos Inc CTB/McGraw-Hill Div 20 Ryan Ranch Rd	Monterey	CA	93940	**800-538-9547**	831-393-0700	246
McGraw-Hill Education 8787 Orion Pl	Columbus	OH	43240	**800-334-7344**		245
McGraw-Hill Higher Education Group 1333 Burr Ridge Pkwy	Burr Ridge	IL	60527	**800-634-3963**	630-789-4000	634-2
McGraw-Hill Professional Publishing Group 2 Penn Plz 11th Fl	New York	NY	10121	**877-833-5524**		634-2
McGriff Seibels & Williams Inc 2211 Seventh Ave S	Birmingham	AL	35233	**800-476-2211**	205-252-9871	390
McGuire W194 N11481 McCormick Dr PO Box 309	Germantown	WI	53022	**800-624-8473**	518-828-7652	469
McGuire Cadillac Inc 910 Rt 1 N	Woodbridge	NJ	07095	**866-552-4208**		515
McGuire Furniture Co 1201 Bryant St	San Francisco	CA	94103	**800-662-4847**	415-626-1414	320-2
McGuire Manufacturing 60 Grandview Ct	Cheshire	CT	06410	**800-676-1832**	203-699-1801	611
McGuireWoods LLP 901 E Cary St 1 James Ctr	Richmond	VA	23219	**877-712-8778**	804-775-1000	428
McHenry County College 8900 US Hwy 14	Crystal Lake	IL	60012	**888-977-4847**	815-455-3700	161
McIlhenny Co Hwy 329 *Orders	Avery Island	LA	70513	**800-634-9599***	337-365-8173	297-19
McIntire Co 745 Clark Ave	Bristol	CT	06010	**800-437-9247**	860-585-0050	18
McIntosh Laboratory Inc 2 Chambers St	Binghamton	NY	13903	**800-538-6576**	607-723-3512	51
McKay Nursery Company Inc 750 S Monroe St PO Box 185	Waterloo	WI	53594	**800-236-4242**	920-478-2121	324
McKean County 500 W Main St	Smethport	PA	16749	**800-482-1280**	814-887-5571	338
McKee Foods Corp PO Box 750 *Cust Svc	Collegedale	TN	37315	**800-522-4499***	423-238-7111	297-1
McKee Surfaces PO Box 230 *Cust Svc	Muscatine	IA	52761	**800-553-9662***	563-263-2421	593
McKeil Marine Ltd 208 Hillyard St	Hamilton	ON	L8L6B6	**800-454-4780**	905-528-4780	314
McKendree College 701 College Rd	Lebanon	IL	62254	**800-232-7228**	618-537-4481	167
McKenna Pro Imaging 2800 Falls Ave *General	Waterloo	IA	50701	**800-238-3456***	319-235-6265	587
McKenney's Inc 1056 Moreland Industrial Blvd SE	Atlanta	GA	30316	**877-440-4204**	404-622-5000	191-10
McKenzie County PO Box 699	Watford City	ND	58854	**800-701-2804**	701-444-2804	338
McKenzie Tank Lines Inc 1966 Commonwealth Ln	Tallahassee	FL	32303	**800-828-6495**	850-576-1221	778
McKeon Door Co 44 Sawgrass Dr	Bellport	NY	11713	**800-266-9392**	631-803-3000	236
McKesson Corp 1 Post St *NYSE: MCK*	San Francisco	CA	94104	**800-482-3784**	415-983-8300	360-3
McKesson Information Solutions 5995 Windward Pkwy	Alpharetta	GA	30005	**800-981-8601**	404-338-6000	180-10
McKesson Medical Group Extended Care 8121 Tenth Ave N	Golden Valley	MN	55427	**800-328-8111**		474
McKesson Medical-Surgical 8741 Landmark Rd	Richmond	VA	23228	**800-446-3008**	415-983-8300	474
McKesson Pharmaceutical 1 Post St	San Francisco	CA	94104	**800-571-2889**	415-983-8300	586
McKinley Air Transport Inc 5430 Lauby Rd *General	North Canton	OH	44720	**800-225-6446***	330-499-3316	24
McKinley Equipment Corp 17611 Armstrong Ave	Irvine	CA	92614	**800-770-6094**	949-261-9222	385
McKinley Grand Hotel 320 Market Ave S	Canton	OH	44702	**844-378-9476**	330-454-5000	379
Mckinney Petroleum Equipment Inc 3926 Halls Mill Rd	Mobile	AL	36693	**800-476-7867**	251-661-8800	358
McKinstry Co 5005 Third Ave S	Seattle	WA	98134	**800-669-6223**	206-762-3311	191-10
McKnight's Long-Term Care News 1 Northfield Plz Ste 521	Northfield	IL	60093	**800-558-1703**	847-784-8706	634-9
MCL Inc 501 S Woodcreek Rd *Support	Bolingbrook	IL	60440	**800-743-4625***	630-759-9500	645
McLane Company Inc 4747 McLane Pkwy	Temple	TX	76504	**800-299-1401**	254-771-7500	298-8
McLane Foodservice Inc 2085 Midway Rd	Carrollton	TX	75006	**800-299-1401**	972-364-2000	298-8
McLaughlin & Moran Inc 40 Slater Rd	Cranston	RI	02920	**800-423-0156**	401-463-5454	80-1
McLaughlin Research Corp 132 Johnnycake Hill Rd	Middletown	RI	02842	**800-556-7154**	401-849-4010	263
McLaughlin Youth Ctr 2600 Providence Dr	Anchorage	AK	99508	**800-478-2221**	907-261-4399	412
McLean Electric Co-op Inc 4031 Hwy 37 Bypass NW	Garrison	ND	58540	**800-263-4922**	701-463-2291	247
McLean Hospital 115 Mill St	Belmont	MA	02478	**800-333-0338**	617-855-2000	374-5
Mclean Implement Inc 793 Illinois Rte 130	Albion	IL	62806	**888-720-4440**	618-445-3676	56
McLean Inc 3409 E Miraloma Ave *Cust Svc	Anaheim	CA	92806	**800-451-2424***	714-996-5451	454
McLellan Botanicals 2352 San Juan Rd	Aromas	CA	95004	**800-467-2443**		369
McLellan Equipment Inc 251 Shaw Rd	South San Francisco	CA	94080	**800-848-8449**	650-873-8100	192
McLennan Community College 1400 College Dr	Waco	TX	76708	**866-339-5555**	254-299-8000	161
McLennan County Electric Co-op 1111 Johnson Dr PO Box 357	McGregor	TX	76657	**800-840-2957**	254-840-2871	247
McLennan Ross LLP 600 W Chambers 12220 Stony Plain Rd	Edmonton	AB	T5N3Y4	**800-567-9200**	780-482-9200	428
McLeod Co-op Power Assn 1231 Ford Ave N	Glencoe	MN	55336	**800-494-6272**	320-864-3148	247
McLeod Express LLC 5002 Cundiff Ct *General	Decatur	IL	62526	**800-709-3936***		683
McLeod Hospice 1203 E Cheves St	Florence	SC	29506	**800-768-4556**	843-777-2564	371
McLoone 75 Sumner St	La Crosse	WI	54603	**800-624-6641**	608-784-1260	699
MCM Elegante Suites 4250 Ridgemont Dr	Abilene	TX	79606	**888-897-9644**	325-698-1234	379

Company / Address	City	State	ZIP	Toll-Free	Phone	Class
MCM Services Group 1300 Corporate Ctr Curve	Eagan	MN	55121	**888-507-6262**		198
McMenamins 430 N Killingsworth	Portland	OR	97217	**800-669-8610**	503-223-0109	101
McMurry University 1 McMurry University 1400 Sayles Blvd	Abilene	TX	79697	**800-460-2392**	325-793-4700	167
McNally Industries LLC 340 W Benson Ave	Grantsburg	WI	54840	**800-366-1410**	715-463-8300	638
McNally Robinson Booksellers Inc 1120 Grant Ave	Winnipeg	MB	R3M2A6	**800-561-1833**	204-475-0483	95
McNally Smith College of Music Foundation 19 Exchange St E	Saint Paul	MN	55101	**800-594-9500**	651-361-3320	167
McNaughton-McKay Electric Company Inc 1357 E Lincoln Ave	Madison Heights	MI	48071	**888-626-2785**	248-399-7500	248
MCNB Bank & Trust Co PO Box 549	Welch	WV	24801	**800-532-9553**	304-436-4112	69
McNeal Enterprises Inc 2031 Ringwood Ave	San Jose	CA	95131	**800-562-6325**	408-922-7290	601
McNear Brick & Block 1 McNear BrickyaRd Rd PO Box 151380	San Rafael	CA	94901	**888-442-6811**	415-453-7702	149
McNeece Brothers Oil Company Inc 691 E Heil Ave	El Centro	CA	92243	**877-782-6543**	760-352-4721	578
McNeely Pigott & Fox 611 Commerce St Ste 2800	Nashville	TN	37203	**800-818-6953**	615-259-4000	633
McNeese State University 4205 Ryan St	Lake Charles	LA	70609	**800-622-3352**	337-475-5000	167
McNeil & NRM Inc 96 E Crosier St	Akron	OH	44311	**800-669-2525**	330-253-2525	386
McNeilus Cos Inc 524 County Rd 34 E PO Box 70	Dodge Center	MN	55927	**800-265-1098**	507-374-6321	515
McNichols Co 9401 Corporate Lake Dr	Tampa	FL	33634	**877-884-4653**		491
McNulty's Tea & Coffee Company Inc 109 Christopher St	New York	NY	10014	**800-356-5200**	212-242-5351	158
M-CON Products Inc 2150 Richardson Side Rd	Carp	ON	K0A1L0	**800-267-5515**	613-831-1736	185
McPherson College PO Box 1402	McPherson	KS	67460	**800-365-7402**	620-242-0400	167
McQ Inc 1551 Forbes St	Fredericksburg	VA	22405	**866-373-2374**	540-373-2374	258
MCR Safety 5321 E Shelby Dr	Memphis	TN	38118	**800-955-6887**	901-795-5810	154-7
McRoberts Protective Agency Inc 87 Nassau St	New York	NY	10038	**800-866-7233**	212-425-6500	691
McShan Lumber Company Inc PO Box 27	McShan	AL	35471	**800-882-3712**	205-375-6277	750
Mcswain & Co PS 612 Woodland Sq Loop SE Ste 300	Lacey	WA	98503	**800-282-1301**	360-357-9304	2
MCT Industries Inc 7451 Pan American Fwy	Albuquerque	NM	87109	**800-876-8651**	505-345-8651	777
MCT Transportation LLC 1600 E Benson Rd *Cust Svc	Sioux Falls	SD	57104	**800-843-9904***	605-339-8400	778
MCVB (Merced Conference & Visitors Bureau) 710 W 16th St	Merced	CA	95340	**800-446-5353**	209-384-2791	208
McVean Trading & Investments LLC 850 Ridge Lk Blvd Ste One	Memphis	TN	38120	**800-374-1937**	901-761-8400	789
MCW Energy Group Ltd 344 Mira Loma Ave	Glendale	CA	91204	**800-979-1897**		535
MD Anderson Cancer Ctr 1515 Holcombe Blvd	Houston	TX	77030	**800-889-2094**	713-792-2121	374-7
M-D Bldg Products Inc 4041 N Santa Fe Ave *Cust Svc	Oklahoma City	OK	73118	**800-654-8454***	405-528-4411	236
MD Physician Services Inc 1870 Alta Vista Dr	Ottawa	ON	K1G6R7	**800-267-4022**	613-731-4552	527
M&D Printing 515 University Ave	Henry	IL	61537	**888-242-7552**	309-364-3957	626
MDA (Muscular Dystrophy Assn) 3300 E Sunrise Dr	Tucson	AZ	85718	**800-572-1717**	520-529-2000	47-17
MDA Information Systems Inc 6011 Executive Blvd	Rockville	MD	20852	**800-642-1687**	240-833-8200	263
MDC Holdings Inc 4350 S Monaco St Ste 500 *NYSE: MDC*	Denver	CO	80237	**888-500-7060**	303-773-1100	360-3
MDC Systems Inc 37 N Vly Rd 3 Sta Sq Ste 100	Paoli	PA	19301	**888-632-9977**	610-640-9600	188
MDI (Molecular Devices Inc) 1311 Orleans Dr	Sunnyvale	CA	94089	**800-635-5577**	408-747-1700	419
MDI Achieve 10900 Hampshire Ave South Ste 100	Bloomington	MN	55438	**800-869-1322**	952-995-9800	180-10
MDI Security Systems Inc 12500 Network Dr Ste 303	San Antonio	TX	78249	**866-435-7634**	210-477-5400	690
MDI Worldwide 38271 W 12-Mile Rd *Sales	Farmington Hills	MI	48331	**800-228-8925***	248-553-1900	235
Mdl Enterprise Inc 9888 Southwest Fwy	Houston	TX	77074	**800-879-0840**	713-771-6350	182
MDMA Equipment Dealers Inc N6291 State Hwy 25	Durand	WI	54736	**888-672-8864**	715-672-8915	276
MDNA (Machinery Dealers NA) 315 S Patrick St	Alexandria	VA	22314	**800-872-7807**	703-836-9300	48-18
Mdr Fitness Corp 14101 Nw Fourth St	Sunrise	FL	33325	**866-521-7337**	954-845-9500	354
MDRT (Million Dollar Round Table) 325 W Touhy Ave *General	Park Ridge	IL	60068	**877-883-4865***	847-692-6378	48-9
MDS (Mennonite Disaster Service) 583 Airport Rd	Lititz	PA	17543	**800-241-8111**	717-735-3536	47-5
MDS N30 W22377 Green Rd Ste C	Waukesha	WI	53186	**888-523-2611**		361
MDT Advisors Inc 125 High St Oliver St Tower Ste 2100	Boston	MA	02110	**800-685-4277**	617-235-7100	790

Company / Address	City	State	ZIP	Toll-Free	Phone	Class
MDT Labor LLC 2325 Paxton Church Rd Ste B	Harrisburg	PA	17110	**888-454-9202**		262
MDU (Montana-Dakota Utilities Co) 400 N Fourth St	Bismarck	ND	58501	**800-638-3278**	701-222-7900	785
MDU Communications International Inc 60 D Commerce Way *OTC: MDTV*	Totowa	NJ	07512	**866-286-9638**	973-237-9499	679
MDU Resources Group Inc 1200 W Century Ave PO Box 5650 *NYSE: MDU*	Bismarck	ND	58506	**866-760-4852**	701-530-1000	187
ME Heuck Co 1600 Beech St *Cust Svc	Terre Haute	IN	47804	**866-634-3825***	812-238-5000	485
ME Tile 447 Atlas Dr	Nashville	TN	37211	**888-348-8453**		749
MEA Voice Magazine 1216 Kendale Blvd PO Box 2573	East Lansing	MI	48826	**800-292-1934**	517-332-6551	456-8
Mead Clark Lumber Co Hearn Ave & Dowd Dr PO Box 529	Santa Rosa	CA	95402	**800-585-9663**	707-576-3333	193-3
Mead Fluid Dynamics Inc 4114 N Knox Ave *Cust Svc	Chicago	IL	60641	**877-632-3872***	773-685-6800	788
Meade Instruments Corp 27 Hubble *NASDAQ: MEAD*	Irvine	CA	92618	**800-626-3233**	949-451-1450	543
Meadow Lake Resort 100 St Andrews Dr	Columbia Falls	MT	59912	**800-321-4653**	406-892-8700	667
Meadowbrook Insurance Group Inc 26255 American Dr *NYSE: MIG*	Southfield	MI	48034	**800-482-2726**	248-358-1100	360-4
Meadowmere Resort 74 Main St	Ogunquit	ME	03907	**800-633-8718**	207-646-9661	378
Meadowood Napa Valley 900 Meadowood Ln	Saint Helena	CA	94574	**800-458-8080**	707-963-3646	667
Meadows Foundation Inc 3003 Swiss Ave	Dallas	TX	75204	**800-826-9431**	214-826-9431	306
Meadows Museum of Art at Centenary College 2911 Centenary Blvd	Shreveport	LA	71104	**800-234-4448**	318-869-5169	519
Meadows Psychiatric Ctr 132 The Meadows Dr	Centre Hall	PA	16828	**800-641-7529**	814-364-2161	374-5
Meadville Lombard Theological School 5701 S Woodlawn Ave	Chicago	IL	60637	**800-848-0979**	773-256-3000	168-3
Meadville Medical Ctr (MMC) 751 Liberty St	Meadville	PA	16335	**800-254-5164**	814-333-5000	374-3
Meadville Tribune 947 Federal Ct	Meadville	PA	16335	**800-879-0006**	814-724-6370	531-2
MEAG Power 1470 Riveredge Pkwy NW	Atlanta	GA	30328	**800-333-6324**	770-563-0300	785
Meaher State Park 5200 Battleship Pkwy	Spanish Fort	AL	36577	**800-252-7275**	251-626-5529	564
Mears Group Inc 4500 N Mission Rd	Rosebush	MI	48878	**800-632-7727**	989-433-2929	190-10
Mears Transportation Group 324 W Gore St	Orlando	FL	32806	**800-759-5219**	407-422-4561	441
Measurement Specialties Inc 1000 Lucas Way *NASDAQ: MEAS*	Hampton	VA	23666	**800-745-8008**	757-766-1500	682
MECA Sportswear 1120 Townline Rd	Tomah	WI	54660	**800-729-6322**	608-374-6450	154-5
Mechanical Contractors Assn of America (MCAA) 1385 Piccard Dr	Rockville	MD	20850	**800-556-3653**	301-869-5800	48-3
Mechanical Design Systems Inc 6302 Aaron Ln	Clinton	MD	20735	**877-960-0301**	301-877-9600	609
Mechanical Servants Inc 2755 Thomas St	Melrose Park	IL	60160	**800-351-2000**	708-615-9439	240
Mechanical Systems of Dayton 4401 Springfield St	Dayton	OH	45431	**800-254-9455**	937-254-3235	609
Mechanical Technology Inc 325 Washington Sq Ste 3 *NASDAQ: MKTY*	Albany	NY	12205	**800-937-5449**	518-533-2200	666
Mechanics Savings Bank 100 Minot Ave PO Box 400	Auburn	ME	04210	**877-886-1020**	207-786-5700	69
Mechanicsville Local 6400 Mechanicsville Tpke	Mechanicsville	VA	23111	**800-468-3382**	804-746-1235	531-4
Mecklenburg Electric Co-op 11633 Hwy Ninety Two	Chase City	VA	23924	**800-989-4161**	434-372-6100	247
Meckley Services Inc 5701 General Washington Dr Ste O	Alexandria	VA	22312	**877-632-5539**	703-333-2040	609
Meclabs LLC 1300 Marsh Landing Pkwy Ste 106	Jacksonville Beach	FL	32250	**800-517-5531**		136
Meco Corp 1500 Industrial Rd	Greeneville	TN	37745	**800-251-7558**		320-3
Mecosta-Osceola Intermediate School District 15760 190th Ave	Big Rapids	MI	49307	**877-211-5253**	231-796-3543	683
Med Shield Inc 2424 E 55th St	Indianapolis	IN	46220	**800-272-5454**	317-613-3700	159
Med Team Home Health Care 131 S Beckham Ave	Tyler	TX	75702	**800-825-2873**	903-592-9747	363
Meda Ltd 1575 Lauzon Rd	Windsor	ON	N8S3N4	**888-518-6332**	519-944-7221	258
Medaille College 18 Agassiz Cir	Buffalo	NY	14214	**800-292-1582**	716-880-2200	167
Medallion Athletic Products Inc 150 River Park Rd	Mooresville	NC	28117	**888-600-3412**	704-660-3000	709
Medallion Cabinetry 2222 Camden Ct	Oak Brook	IL	60523	**800-543-4074**	952-442-5171	114
Medallion Financial Corp 437 Madison Ave 38th Fl *NASDAQ: TAXI*	New York	NY	10022	**877-633-2554**	212-328-2100	218
Medallion Laboratories 9000 Plymouth Ave N	Minneapolis	MN	55427	**800-245-5615**	763-764-4453	194
Medart Inc 124 Manufacturers Dr *Cust Svc	Arnold	MO	63010	**800-888-7181***	636-282-2300	385

Name / Address	City	State	ZIP	Toll-Free	Phone	Class
MedCath Inc 10720 Sikes Pl Ste 300 *NASDAQ: MDTH*	Charlotte	NC	28277	**800-461-9330**	704-708-6600	353
Medcenter One Hospital 300 N Seventh St	Bismarck	ND	58501	**800-932-8758**	701-323-6000	374-3
Medcom Inc 6060 Phyllis Dr	Cypress	CA	90630	**800-541-0253**		33
Medcom Trainex 6060 Phyllis Dr *Cust Svc	Cypress	CA	90630	**800-877-1443***		512
Medcor Inc 4805 W Prime Pkwy	McHenry	IL	60050	**877-696-6775**	815-363-9500	462
Medeco Security Locks Inc 3625 Alleghany Dr	Salem	VA	24153	**800-839-3157**	540-380-5000	350
Medexcel USA Inc 484 Temple Hill Rd	New Windsor	NY	12553	**800-563-6384**	845-565-3700	462
Medford Leas 1 Medford Leas Way	Medford	NJ	08055	**800-331-4302**	609-654-3000	670
Medford Mail Tribune PO Box 1108	Medford	OR	97501	**800-452-4011**	541-776-4411	531-2
Medgar Evers College 1650 Bedford Ave	Brooklyn	NY	11225	**866-277-5719**	718-270-4900	167
MedGyn Products Inc 100 W Industrial Rd	Addison	IL	60101	**800-451-9667**	630-627-4105	607
Media 100 Inc 450 Donald Lynch Blvd	Marlborough	MA	02210	**888-772-6747**	508-460-1600	180-8
Media Buying Services Inc 4545 E Shea Blvd Ste 162	Phoenix	AZ	85028	**888-996-2232**	602-996-2232	4
Media Cybernetics Inc 4340 E W Hwy Ste 400 *Sales	Bethesda	MD	20814	**800-263-2088***	301-495-3305	180-10
Media General Broadcast Group 333 E Franklin St	Richmond	VA	23219	**800-937-5449**	804-649-6000	735
Media Industry Newsletter (MIN) 110 William St 11th Fl	New York	NY	10038	**888-707-5814**	212-621-4880	530-11
Media Law Reporter 1801 S Bell St	Arlington	VA	22202	**800-372-1033**		530-11
Media Logic USA LLC 59 Wolf Rd	Albany	NY	12205	**866-353-3011**	518-456-3015	4
Media Relations Report 316 N Michigan Ave Ste 400	Chicago	IL	60601	**800-878-5331**	312-960-4100	530-11
Media Services 500 S Sepulveda Blvd 4th Fl	Los Angeles	CA	90049	**800-738-0409**	310-440-9600	569
Media Space Solutions 904 MainSt	Hopkins	MN	55343	**888-672-2100**	612-253-3900	6
Media Temple Inc 8520 National Blvd Bldg A	Culver City	CA	90232	**877-578-4000**		395
Media Watch PO Box 618	Santa Cruz	CA	95061	**800-631-6355**	831-423-6355	47-8
Media/Professional Insurance Inc 1201 Walnut Ste 1800	Kansas City	MO	64106	**866-282-0565**	816-471-6118	391-5
Media3 Technologies LLC 33 Riverside Dr N River Commerce Pk	Pembroke	MA	02359	**800-903-9327**	781-826-1213	806
Mediacom Communications Corp 100 Crystal Run Rd *General	Middletown	NY	10941	**800-479-2082***	845-695-2600	115
MediaCore Inc 26 Bastion Sq Ste 205	Victoria	BC	V8W1H9	**877-682-6655**	250-590-9394	226
Mediagrif Interactive Technologies Inc 1111 St-Charles St W E Tower Ste 255 *TSE: MDF*	Longueuil	QC	J4K5G4	**877-677-9088**	450-449-0102	180-1
Mediatech Institute of Austin 4719 s congress ave	Austin	TX	78745	**866-498-1122**	512-447-2002	161
MEDICA 401 Carlson Pkwy *Cust Svc	Minnetonka	MN	55305	**800-952-3455***	952-992-2900	391-3
Medica Corp 5 Oak Park Dr	Bedford	MA	01730	**800-777-5983**	781-275-4892	475
Medical Action Industries Inc (MAI) 500 Expy Dr S *NASDAQ: MDCI*	Brentwood	NY	11717	**800-645-7042**	631-231-4600	476
Medical Analysis Systems Inc 46360 Fremont Blvd	Fremont	CA	94538	**800-232-3342**	510-979-5000	233
Medical Assn of Georgia (MAG) 1849 The Exchange Ste 200	Atlanta	GA	30339	**800-282-0224**	678-303-9290	473
Medical Assurance Inc 100 Brookwood Pl Ste 300 *Cust Svc	Birmingham	AL	35209	**800-282-6242***	205-877-4400	391-5
Medical Benefits Mutual Life Insurance Co 1975 Tamarack Rd	Newark	OH	43058	**800-423-3151**	740-522-8425	391-3
Medical Center Pharmacy 2401 N Ocoee St	Cleveland	TN	37311	**877-753-9555**	423-476-5548	239
Medical Ctr at Princeton Home Care 905 Herrontown Rd	Princeton	NJ	08540	**877-932-8395**	609-497-4900	363
Medical Ctr Enterprise (MCE) 400 N Edwards St	Enterprise	AL	36330	**800-994-6610**	334-347-0584	374-3
Medical Ctr for Federal Prisoners Springfield 1900 W Sunshine St	Springfield	MO	65807	**877-623-8426**	417-862-7041	214
Medical Diagnostic Laboratories LLC 2439 Kuser Rd	Hamilton	NJ	08690	**877-269-0090**	609-570-1000	418
Medical Doctor Assoc Inc 145 Technology Pkwy NW	Norcross	GA	30092	**800-780-3500**		196
Medical Education Technologies Inc (METI) 6300 Edgelake Dr	Sarasota	FL	34240	**866-462-7920**	941-377-5562	252
Medical Eye Bank of Maryland 815 Pk Ave	Baltimore	MD	21201	**800-756-4824**	410-752-2020	271
Medical Genetics Consultants 819 DeSoto St	Ocean Springs	MS	39564	**800-362-4363**		417
Medical Graphics Corp 350 Oak Grove Pkwy *NASDAQ: ANGN*	Saint Paul	MN	55127	**800-950-5597**	651-484-4874	252
Medical Group Management Assn (MGMA) 104 Inverness Terr E	Englewood	CO	80112	**877-275-6462**	303-799-1111	48-8
Medical Library Assn (MLA) 65 E Wacker Pl Ste 1900	Chicago	IL	60601	**800-523-1850**	312-419-9094	48-11
Medical Management Specialists 4100 Embassy Dr SE Ste 200	Grand Rapids	MI	49546	**888-707-2684**	616-975-1845	2
Medical Mutual Group 700 Spring Forest Rd	Raleigh	NC	27609	**800-662-7917**	919-872-7117	391-5
Medical Mutual Insurance Company of Maine 1 City Ctr Ste 9	Portland	ME	04112	**800-942-2791**	207-775-2791	391-5
Medical Mutual Liability Insurance Society of Maryland 225 International Cir PO Box 8016	Hunt Valley	MD	21030	**800-492-0193**	410-785-0050	391-5
Medical Mutual of Ohio 2060 E Ninth St	Cleveland	OH	44115	**800-700-2583**	216-687-7000	391-3
Medical Products Laboratories Inc 9990 Global Rd	Philadelphia	PA	19115	**800-523-0191**	215-677-2700	582
Medical Protective Co 5814 Reed Rd	Fort Wayne	IN	46835	**800-463-3776**	260-485-9622	391-5
Medical Research Law & Policy Report 1801 S Bell St	Arlington	VA	22202	**800-372-1033**		530-7
Medical Resources Inc 1455 Broad St	Bloomfield	NJ	07003	**800-537-7272**	973-707-1100	383
Medical Services of America Inc (MSA) 171 Monroe Ln	Lexington	SC	29072	**800-845-5850**	803-957-0500	363
Medical Staffing Assoc Inc 6731 Whittier Ave 3rd Fl	McLean	VA	22101	**800-235-5105**		719
Medical Staffing Network Holdings Inc 901 Yamato Rd Ste 110	Boca Raton	FL	33431	**800-676-8326**		719
Medical Teams International (MTI) PO Box 10	Portland	OR	97207	**800-959-4325**	503-624-1000	47-5
Medical University of South Carolina 41 Bee St MSC 203	Charleston	SC	29425	**800-424-6872**	843-792-3281	167
MedicAlert Foundation International 2323 Colorado Ave *Cust Svc	Turlock	CA	95382	**800-432-5378***	209-668-3333	47-17
Medicap Pharmacies Inc 1 Rider Trail Plaza Dr	Earth City	MO	63045	**800-407-8055**	314-993-6000	239
Medicare Compliance Alert 11300 Rockville Pk Ste 1100	Rockville	MD	20852	**800-929-4824**	301-287-2700	530-7
Medicare Rights Ctr (MRC) 520 Eigth Ave N Wing 3rd Fl *Hotline	New York	NY	10018	**800-333-4114***	212-869-3850	47-17
Medicines Co 8 Sylvan Way *NASDAQ: MDCO*	Parsippany	NJ	07054	**800-388-1183**	973-290-6000	84
Medicis Pharmaceutical Corp 7720 N Dobson Rd *Cust Svc	Scottsdale	AZ	85256	**866-246-8245***	800-321-4576	582
Medico Group 1515 S 75th St	Omaha	NE	68124	**800-228-6080**	402-391-6900	391-2
Medico Industries Inc 1500 Hwy 315	Wilkes-Barre	PA	18711	**800-633-0027**	570-825-7711	266-3
Medicomp Inc 7845 Ellis Rd	Melbourne	FL	32904	**800-234-3278**	321-794-3811	636
Medicus Healthcare Solutions LLC 7 Industrial Way Unit 5	Salem	NH	03079	**855-301-0563**		195
Medifast Inc 11445 Cronhill Dr *NYSE: MED*	Owings Mills	MD	21117	**800-209-0878**		297-11
Medifit Corporate Services Inc 25 Hanover Rd	Florham Park	NJ	07932	**866-848-5577**	973-593-9000	196
MediGrafix Inc 9 Fairway Ln Ste C	Blythewood	SC	29016	**888-744-1301**	803-261-6387	477
MedImpact Healthcare Systems Inc 10680 Treena St Ste 500	San Diego	CA	92131	**800-788-2949**	858-566-2727	585
Medina Electric Co-op Inc PO Box 370	Hondo	TX	78861	**866-632-3532**		247
Medina Gazette 885 W Liberty St	Medina	OH	44256	**800-633-4623**	330-725-4166	531-2
Medi-Nuclear Corp Inc 4610 Littlejohn St	Baldwin Park	CA	91706	**800-321-5981**	626-960-9822	475
MediRevv Inc 2600 University Pkwy	Coralville	IA	52241	**888-665-6310**		198
Medivo Inc 55 Broad St 16th Fl	New York	NY	10004	**888-362-4321**		179
Mediware Information Systems Inc 11711 W 79th St *NASDAQ: MEDW*	Lenexa	KS	66214	**800-255-0026**	913-307-1000	180-11
MedjetAssist 3500 Colonnade Pkwy Ste 500 PO Box 43099	Birmingham	AL	35243	**800-527-7478**	205-595-6626	30
Medler Eelectric Company Inc 2155 Redman Dr	Alma	MI	48801	**800-229-5740**		251
Medline Industries Inc 1 Medline Pl *Cust Svc	Mundelein	IL	60060	**800-351-1512***	847-949-5500	575
MedlinePlus National Library of Medicine 8600 Rockville Pk	Bethesda	MD	20894	**888-346-3656**	301-594-5983	356
Medmart Inc 10780 Reading Rd	Cincinnati	OH	45241	**888-260-4430**		198
Medone Surgical Inc 670 Tallevast Rd	Sarasota	FL	34243	**866-633-6631**	941-359-3129	475
Medovations Inc 102 E Keefe Ave	Milwaukee	WI	53212	**800-558-6408**	414-265-7620	475
MedPlus Inc 4690 Pkwy Dr	Mason	OH	45040	**800-444-6235**	513-229-5500	180-10
Med-Plus Medical Supplies 17 Vanderbilt Ave	Brooklyn	NY	11205	**888-433-2300**	718-222-4416	419
MedRx Inc 1200 Starkey Rd Ste 105	Largo	FL	33771	**888-392-1234**	727-584-9600	475
MedStar Health 5565 Sterrett Pl 5th Fl	Columbia	MD	21044	**877-772-6505**	410-772-6500	353
Med-Tech Resource Inc 29485 Airport Rd	Eugene	OR	97402	**888-627-7779**		524
MEDTOX Diagnostics Inc 1238 Anthony Rd	Burlington	NC	27215	**800-334-1116**	336-226-6311	233
MEDTOX Scientific Inc 402 W County Rd D *NASDAQ: MTOX*	Saint Paul	MN	55112	**800-832-3244**	651-636-7466	416
Medtronic Inc 710 Medtronic Pkwy NE *NYSE: MDT* ■ *Cust Svc	Minneapolis	MN	55432	**800-328-2518***	763-514-4000	252

Company	Address	City	State	ZIP	Toll-Free	Phone	Class
Medtronic MiniMed Inc	18000 Devonshire St	Northridge	CA	91325	**800-646-4633**		476
Medtronic Neurosurgery	125 Cremona Dr (*Cust Svc)	Goleta	CA	93117	**800-468-9710***	800-633-8766	475
Medtronic of Canada Ltd	6733 Kitimat Rd	Mississauga	ON	L5N1W3	**800-268-5346**	905-826-6020	252
Medtronic Perfusion Systems	7611 Northland Dr	Brooklyn Park	MN	55428	**800-328-3320**	763-391-9000	252
Medtronic Powered Surgical Solutions	4620 N Beach St	Fort Worth	TX	76137	**800-643-2773**	817-788-6400	476
Medtronic Surgical Technologies	6743 Southpoint Dr N	Jacksonville	FL	32216	**800-874-5797**	904-296-9600	476
Medvantx Inc	5626 Oberlin Dr Ste 110	San Diego	CA	92121	**866-744-0621**	858-625-2990	719
Meeder Equipment Co	12323 Sixth St	Rancho Cucamonga	CA	91739	**800-423-3711**	909-463-0600	357
Meeker Co-op Light & Power Assn	1725 E US Hwy 12 PO Box 68	Litchfield	MN	55355	**800-232-6257**	320-693-3231	247
Meet Minneapolis	250 Marquette Ave Ste 1300	Minneapolis	MN	55401	**800-445-7412**	612-767-8000	208
Meeting Connection Inc, The	6373 Meadow Glen Dr N	Westerville	OH	43082	**800-398-2568**	614-888-2568	186
Meeting Professionals International (MPI)	3030 LBJ Fwy Ste 1700	Dallas	TX	75234	**866-748-9561**	972-702-3000	48-12
Meeting Street Inn	173 Meeting St	Charleston	SC	29401	**800-842-8022**	843-723-1882	379
Mega Manufacturing Inc	PO Box 457	Hutchinson	KS	67504	**800-338-5471**	620-663-1127	455
Megadyne Medical Products Inc	11506 S State St	Draper	UT	84020	**800-747-6110**	801-576-9669	475
MEGA-FM 94.9 (Span CHR)	7601 Riviera Blvd	Miramar	FL	33023	**877-599-2946**	954-862-2000	643
Mega-Pro International Inc	251 W Hilton Dr	Saint George	UT	84770	**800-541-9469**	435-673-1001	797
Megawatt Daily	2 Penn Plz 25th Fl	New York	NY	10121	**800-752-8878**	212-904-3070	530-5
Megger	4271 Bronze Way	Dallas	TX	75237	**800-723-2861**	214-333-3201	250
Meggitt Training Systems Inc	296 Brogdon Rd	Suwanee	GA	30024	**800-813-9046**	678-288-1090	701
MEGTEC Systems Inc	830 Prosper Rd (*Cust Svc)	De Pere	WI	54115	**800-558-5535***	920-336-5715	386
Meguiar's Inc	17991 Mitchell S (*Cust Svc)	Irvine	CA	92614	**800-347-5700***	949-752-8000	150
Meherrin Agricultural & Chemical Co Inc	413 Main St	Severn	NC	27877	**800-775-0333**	252-585-1744	278
Meier Enterprises Inc	12 W. Kennewick Ave	Kennewick	WA	99336	**800-239-7589**	509-735-1589	263
Meier Supply Company Inc	530 Bloomingburg Rd	Middletown	NY	10940	**800-418-3216**	845-733-5666	609
Meijer Inc	2929 Walker Ave NW	Grand Rapids	MI	49544	**800-543-3704**	616-453-6711	345
Meijer Stores Inc	2929 Walker Ave NW	Grand Rapids	MI	49544	**800-543-3704**	616-453-6711	345
Meisel Visual Imaging	2019 McKenzie Dr	Carrollton	TX	75006	**800-527-5186**	214-688-4950	587
Meisner & Associates Pc	30200 Telegraph Rd Ste 467	Bingham Farms	MI	48025	**800-470-4433**	248-644-4433	428
Meister Media Worldwide	37733 Euclid Ave (*Orders)	Willoughby	OH	44094	**800-572-7740***	440-942-2000	634-9
Mel Bay Publications Inc	1734 Gilsinn Ln	Fenton	MO	63026	**800-863-5229**	636-257-3970	634-2
Mel Rapton Inc	3630 Fulton Ave	Sacramento	CA	95821	**800-529-3053**	916-482-5400	515
Melaleuca Inc	3910 S Yellowstone Hwy (*Sales)	Idaho Falls	ID	83402	**800-282-3000***	208-522-0700	366
Mele & Co	2007 Beechgrove Pl	Utica	NY	13501	**800-635-6353**	315-733-4600	202
Melin Tool Co	5565 Venture Dr Unit C	Cleveland	OH	44130	**800-521-1078**	216-362-4230	492
Melissa's/World Variety Produce Inc	5325 S Soto St	Vernon	CA	90058	**800-588-0151**		298-7
Melitta Canada Inc	50 Ronson Dr Unit 150	Toronto	ON	M9W1B3	**800-565-4882**		297-7
Mellano & Co	766 Wall St	Los Angeles	CA	90014	**888-635-5266**	213-622-0796	294
Melnor Inc	109 Tyson Dr	Winchester	VA	22603	**877-283-0697**	540-722-5600	429
Melting Pot of Annapolis, The	2348 Solomons Island Rd	Annapolis	MD	21401	**800-783-0867**	410-266-8004	669
Melting Pot of Charlotte, The	901 S Kings Dr Ste 140B	Charlotte	NC	28204	**800-783-0867**	704-334-4400	669
Melting Pot of Columbia, The	1410 Colonial Life Blvd	Columbia	SC	29210	**800-783-0867**	803-731-8500	669
Melting Pot of Indianapolis, The	5650 E 86th St Ste A	Indianapolis	IN	46250	**800-783-0867**	317-841-3601	669
Melting Pot of Pensacola, The	418 Gregory St Ste 500	Pensacola	FL	32501	**800-783-0867**	850-438-4030	669
Melting Pot of San Antonio, The	14855 Blanco Rd Ste 110	San Antonio	TX	78216	**800-783-0867**	210-479-6358	669
Melting Pot of Tampa, The	13164 N Dale Mabry Hwy	Tampa	FL	33618	**800-783-0867**	813-962-6936	669
Melting Pot Restaurants Inc	8810 Twin Lakes Blvd	Tampa	FL	33614	**800-783-0867**	813-881-0055	668
Melting Pot, The	1601 Concord Pike Ste 43-47 Independence Mall	Wilmington	DE	19803	**800-783-0867**	302-652-6358	669
Members Group Inc, The	1500 NW 118th St	Des Moines	IA	50325	**800-268-1884**		221
Members Trust Co	14025 Riveredge Dr Ste 280	Tampa	FL	33637	**888-727-9191**	813-631-9191	69
Memorial Blood Centers (MBC)	737 Pelham Blvd (*Cust Svc)	Saint Paul	MN	55114	**888-448-3253***	651-332-7000	88
Memorial Health Partners	4700 Waters Ave	Savannah	GA	31404	**800-537-0690**	912-350-8000	391-3
Memorial Health System (MHS) *Central*	1400 E Boulder St	Colorado Springs	CO	80909	**877-422-3648**	719-365-5000	374-3
Memorial Healthcare Ctr	826 W King St	Owosso	MI	48867	**800-206-8706**	989-723-5211	374-3
Memorial Hermann Memorial City Hospital	921 Gessner Rd	Houston	TX	77024	**800-526-2121**	713-242-3000	374-3
Memorial Hermann Prevention & Recovery Ctr (MHPARC)	3043 Gessner	Houston	TX	77080	**800-464-7272**	713-939-7272	374-5
Memorial Hospital	325 S Belmont St	York	PA	17405	**800-436-4326**	717-843-8623	374-3
Memorial Hospital & Health Care Ctr	800 W Ninth St	Jasper	IN	47546	**800-852-7279**	812-996-2345	374-3
Memorial Hospital of Rhode Island (MHRI)	111 Brewster St	Pawtucket	RI	02860	**800-647-4362**	401-729-2000	374-3
Memorial Hospital of South Bend	615 N Michigan St	South Bend	IN	46601	**800-850-7913**	574-647-1000	374-3
Memorial Hospital of Sweetwater County	1200 College Dr (*General)	Rock Springs	WY	82901	**866-571-0944***	307-362-3711	374-3
Memorial Medical Ctr	1615 Maple Ln	Ashland	WI	54806	**877-611-1988**	715-685-5500	374-3
Memorial Sloan-Kettering Cancer Ctr	1275 York Ave	New York	NY	10065	**800-525-2225**	212-639-2000	374-7
Memphis Botanic Garden	750 Cherry Rd	Memphis	TN	38117	**877-829-5500**	901-576-4100	96
Memphis College of Art	1930 Poplar Ave	Memphis	TN	38104	**800-727-1088**	901-272-5100	163
Memphis Convention & Visitors Bureau	47 Union Ave	Memphis	TN	38103	**888-633-9099**	901-543-5300	208
Memphis Flyer	460 Tennessee St	Memphis	TN	38103	**877-292-3804**	901-521-9000	531-5
Memphis Machinery & Supply Co Inc	2881 Directors Cove	Memphis	TN	38131	**800-932-8376**	901-527-4443	819
Memphis Magazine	460 Tennessee St Ste 200	Memphis	TN	38103	**800-288-9999**	901-521-9000	456-22
Memphis Publishing Co	495 Union Ave (*Cust Svc)	Memphis	TN	38103	**800-444-6397***	901-529-2666	634-8
Memphis Regional Chamber of Commerce	22 N Front St Ste 200	Memphis	TN	38103	**800-829-1040**	901-543-3500	138
Memry Corp	3 Berkshire Blvd	Bethel	CT	06801	**866-466-3679**	203-739-1100	484
Men's Health Magazine	400 S Tenth St	Emmaus	PA	18098	**800-666-2303**	610-967-5171	456-13
Men's Journal LLC	1290 Ave of the Americas 2nd Fl	New York	NY	10104	**800-677-6367**		456-11
Men's Wearhouse Inc	6380 Rogerdale Rd *NYSE: MW*	Houston	TX	77072	**877-986-9669**	281-776-7000	156-3
Mena Hospital Commission	311 Morrow St N	Mena	AR	71953	**800-394-6185**	479-394-2534	363
Menard Electric Co-op	14300 State Hwy 97 PO Box 200	Petersburg	IL	62675	**800-872-1203**	217-632-7746	247
Menardi	1 Maxwell Dr	Trenton	SC	29847	**800-321-3218**	803-663-6551	66
Menasha Corp	1645 Bergstrom Rd	Neenah	WI	54956	**800-558-5073**	920-751-1000	99
Menasha Packaging Co	1645 Bergstrom Rd	Neenah	WI	54956	**800-558-5073**	920-751-1000	99
MENC: NA for Music Education	1806 Robert Fulton Dr	Reston	VA	20191	**800-336-3768**	703-860-4000	48-5
Menches Tool & Die Inc	30995 San Benito St	Hayward	CA	94544	**877-592-2328**	510-476-1160	695
Mended Hearts Inc, The	8150 N Central Expy M2075	Dallas	TX	75206	**888-432-7899**	214-296-9252	47-17
Mendocino Coast Chamber of Commerce	217 S Main St PO Box 1141	Fort Bragg	CA	95437	**800-382-7244**	707-961-6300	138
Mendocino Wine Co	501 PaRducci Rd	Ukiah	CA	95482	**800-362-9463**	707-463-5350	79-3
Menger Hotel	204 Alamo Plz	San Antonio	TX	78205	**800-345-9285**	210-223-4361	379
Menke Marking Devices	13253 Alondra Blvd	Santa Fe Springs	CA	90670	**800-231-6023**	562-921-1380	466
Menlo College	1000 El Camino Real	Atherton	CA	94027	**800-556-3656**	650-543-3753	167
Mennel Milling Co	128 W Crocker St	Fostoria	OH	44830	**800-688-8151**	419-435-8151	297-23
Menninger Clinic	12301 S Main St PO Box 809045	Houston	TX	77035	**800-351-9058**	713-275-5000	374-5
Mennonite Brethren Biblical Seminary	4824 E Butler Ave	Fresno	CA	93727	**800-251-6227**	559-453-2000	168-3
Mennonite Central Committee (MCC)	21 S 12th St PO Box 500	Akron	PA	17501	**888-563-4676**	717-859-1151	47-5
Mennonite Disaster Service (MDS)	583 Airport Rd	Lititz	PA	17543	**800-241-8111**	717-735-3536	47-5
Mennonite Village	5353 Columbus St SE	Albany	OR	97322	**866-453-4930**	541-928-7232	670
Menominee Hotel	PO Box 760	Keshena	WI	54135	**800-343-7778**	715-799-3600	378
Mental Health America (MHA)	2000 N Beauregard St 6th Fl (*Help Line)	Alexandria	VA	22311	**800-969-6642***	703-684-7722	47-17
Mentholatum Company Inc	707 Sterling Dr	Orchard Park	NY	14127	**800-688-7660**	716-677-2500	582
Mentor Chamber of Commerce	6972 Spinach Dr	Mentor	OH	44060	**800-292-5707**	440-255-1616	138
Mentor Corp	201 Mentor Dr *NASDAQ: MENT*	Santa Barbara	CA	93111	**800-525-0245**	805-879-6000	476
Mentor Graphics Corp	8005 SW Boeckman Rd *NASDAQ: MENT*	Wilsonville	OR	97070	**800-592-2210**	503-685-7000	180-5
MENTOR Network, The	313 Congress St 5th Fl	Boston	MA	02210	**800-388-5150**	617-790-4800	461

				Toll-Free	Phone	Class
MENTOR/National Mentoring Partnership						
201 South St Ste 615	Boston	MA	02111	877-333-2464	703-224-2200	47-6
Menzner Lumber & Supply Co						
PO Box 217	Marathon	WI	54448	800-257-1284		498
Meow Inc						
307 W 36th St 16th Fl	New York	NY	10018	888-485-6738		593
Mera Pharmaceuticals Inc						
73-4460 Queen Kaahumanu Hwy						
Ste 110	Kailua-Kona	HI	96740	800-480-6515	808-326-9301	84
Meramec Valley R-3 School District						
126 N Payne St	Pacific	MO	63069	866-632-9992	636-271-1400	683
Mercantile Bank						
200 N 33rd St PO Box 3455	Quincy	IL	62305	800-405-6372	217-223-7300	360-2
NYSE: MBCR						
Mercantile Bank Corp						
310 Leonard St NW	Grand Rapids	MI	49504	888-345-6296	616-406-3000	360-2
NASDAQ: MBWM						
Merced College						
3600 M St	Merced	CA	95348	800-784-2433	209-384-6000	161
Merced Conference & Visitors Bureau (MCVB)						
710 W 18th St	Merced	CA	95340	800-446-5353	209-384-2791	208
Merced County Library						
2100 O St	Merced	CA	95340	866-249-0773	209-385-7643	434-3
Merced Irrigation District						
PO Box 2288	Merced	CA	95344	855-800-2267	209-722-5761	188
Mercedes-Benz Financial Services USA LLC						
PO Box 685	Roanoke	TX	76262	800-654-6222		216
Mercedes-Benz of San Francisco						
500 Eigth St	San Francisco	CA	94103	877-554-6016	415-673-2000	56
Mercedes-Benz U.S. International Inc						
1 Mercedes Dr	Vance	AL	35490	888-286-8762	205-507-2252	58
Mercedes-Benz USA LLC						
1 Mercedes Dr	Montvale	NJ	07645	800-367-6372*	201-573-0600	58
*Cust Svc						
Mercer Arboretum & Botanic Gardens						
22306 Aldine Westfield Rd	Humble	TX	77338	877-321-2652	281-443-8731	96
Mercer County						
621 Commerce St PO Box 4088	Bluefield	WV	24701	800-221-3206	304-325-8438	338
Mercer County Community College						
PO Box B	Trenton	NJ	08690	800-982-9491	609-586-4800	161
Kerney Ctr						
N Broad & Academy St	Trenton	NJ	08608	800-982-9491	609-586-4800	161
West Windsor						
1200 Old Trenton Rd	West Windsor	NJ	08550	800-982-9491	609-586-4800	161
Mercer County Convention & Visitors Bureau						
621 Commerce St	Bluefield	WV	24701	800-221-3206	304-325-8438	208
Mercer County Joint Township Community Hospital						
800 W Main St	Coldwater	OH	45828	888-844-2341	419-678-2341	374-3
Mercer Engineering & Research						
135 Osigian Blvd	Warner Robins	GA	31088	877-650-6372	478-953-6800	136
Mercer Forge Corp						
200 Brown St	Mercer	PA	16137	800-558-5075	724-662-2750	482
Mercer Global Advisors Inc						
1801 E Cabrillo Blvd	Santa Barbara	CA	93108	800-258-1559	800-898-4642	401
Mercer Hotel						
147 Mercer St	New York	NY	10012	888-918-6060	212-966-6060	379
Mercer Insurance Group Inc						
10 N Hwy 31 PO Box 278	Pennington	NJ	08534	800-223-0534	609-737-0426	391-4
Mercer LLC						
400 W Market St	Louisville	KY	40202	800-333-3070	502-561-4500	195
Mercer Transportation Co						
1128 W Main St PO Box 35610	Louisville	KY	40232	800-626-5375	502-584-2301	778
Mercer University						
1400 Coleman Ave	Macon	GA	31207	800-637-2378	478-301-2650	167
Cecil B Day						
3001 Mercer University Dr	Atlanta	GA	30341	800-840-8577	678-547-6089	167
Mercersburg Academy						
300 E Seminary St	Mercersburg	PA	17236	800-588-2550	717-328-6173	621
Mercersburg Printing						
9964 Buchanan Trl W	Mercersburg	PA	17236	800-955-3902	717-328-3902	626
Merchandise Mart						
222 Merchandise Mart Plz						
Ste 470	Chicago	IL	60654	800-677-6278	312-527-4141	207
Merchant & Evans Inc						
308 Connecticut Dr	Burlington	NJ	08016	800-257-6215	609-387-3033	479
Merchant Law Group LLP						
2401 Saskatchewan Dr Saskatchewan Dr Plz						
	Regina	SK	S4P4H8	888-567-7777	306-359-7777	40
Merchant One Payment Systems Inc						
524 Arthur Godfrey Rd						
3rd Fl	Miami Beach	FL	33140	800-610-4189		95
Merchants Bancshares Inc						
PO Box 1009	Burlington	VT	05402	800-322-5222	802-658-3400	360-2
NASDAQ: MBVT						
Merchants Building Maintenance LLC						
606 Monterey Pass Rd	Monterey Park	CA	91754	800-560-6700		691
Merchants Co						
1100 Edwards St	Hattiesburg	MS	39401	800-451-8346	601-583-4351	298-8
Merchants Credit Bureau						
955 Green St	Augusta	GA	30901	800-426-5265	706-823-6246	220
Merchants Grocery Co						
800 Maddox Dr PO Box 1268	Culpeper	VA	22701	877-897-9893	540-825-0786	345
Merchants Insurance Group						
250 Main St	Buffalo	NY	14202	800-462-1077	716-849-3333	391-4
Merchants Metals Inc						
900 Ashwood Pkwy Ste 600	Atlanta	GA	30338	800-272-6171	770-960-2880	281
Merchants National Bank of Bangor Inc						
25 Broadway PO Box 227	Bangor	PA	18013	877-678-6622	610-588-0981	69
Merchants Paper Co						
4625 SE 24th Ave	Portland	OR	97202	800-605-6301	503-235-2171	556
Merchants Solutions Co						
19252 S Blackhawk Pkwy Unit 75	Mokena	IL	60448	800-486-3214	708-449-6650	111
Merck & Company Inc						
1 Merck Dr						
PO Box 100	Whitehouse Station	NJ	08889	800-672-6372*	908-423-1000	582
NYSE: MRK ■ *Cust Svc						
Mercom Inc						
313 Commerce Dr	Pawleys Island	SC	29585	877-223-8330	843-979-9957	182
Merco-Savory Inc						
1111 N Hadley Rd	Fort Wayne	IN	46804	800-547-2513*	260-459-8200	299
*Cust Svc						
Mercury Insurance Group						
4484 Wilshire Blvd	Los Angeles	CA	90010	800-956-3728	323-937-1060	391-4
NYSE: MCY						
Mercury Lighting Products Company Inc						
20 Audrey Pl	Fairfield	NJ	07004	800-637-2584	973-244-9444	439
Mercury Luggage Manufacturing Co						
4843 Victor St	Jacksonville	FL	32207	800-874-1885	904-334-8801	452
Mercury Medical						
11300 49th St N	Clearwater	FL	33762	800-237-6418	727-573-0088	475
Mercury Press Inc						
1910 S Nicklas St	Oklahoma City	OK	73128	800-423-5984	405-682-3468	626
Mercury Wireless LLC						
2825 se california ave	Topeka	KS	66605	800-354-4915		733
Mercury Z						
1150 Se Maynard Rd Ste 140	Cary	NC	27511	877-548-4052		198
Mercy						
1235 E Cherokee	Springfield	MO	65804	800-909-8326	417-820-2000	374-3
Mercy College						
555 Broadway	Dobbs Ferry	NY	10522	800-637-2969	914-693-4500	167
Manhattan						
66 W 35th St	New York	NY	10001	800-637-2969	212-615-3300	167
White Plains						
277 Martine Ave Ste 201	White Plains	NY	10601	888-464-6737	914-948-3666	167
Yorktown Heights						
2651 Strang Blvd	Yorktown Heights	NY	10598	877-637-2946	914-245-6100	167
Mercy College of Ohio						
2221 Madison Ave	Toledo	OH	43604	888-806-3729	419-251-1313	506
Mercy Flights Inc						
2020 Milligan Way	Medford	OR	97504	800-903-9000	541-858-2600	30
Mercy General Health Partners						
Muskegon Campus						
1500 E Sherman Blvd	Muskegon	MI	49444	800-368-4125	231-672-2000	374-3
Mercy Hospital						
144 State St	Portland	ME	04101	800-293-6583	207-879-3000	374-3
Mercy Hospital & Trauma Ctr						
1000 Mineral Pt Ave	Janesville	WI	53548	800-756-4147	608-756-6000	374-3
Mercy Housing Inc						
1999 Broadway Ste 1000	Denver	CO	80202	866-338-0557	303-830-3300	189
Mercy Iowa City						
500 E Market St	Iowa City	IA	52245	800-637-2942	319-339-0300	374-3
Mercy Medical Center North Iowa						
1000 4th St SW	Mason City	IA	50401	800-297-4719	641-428-6208	371
Mercy Medical Ctr (MMC)						
345 St Paul Pl	Baltimore	MD	21202	800-636-3729	410-332-9000	374-3
Mercy Medical Ctr North Iowa						
1000 Fourth St SW	Mason City	IA	50401	800-433-3883	641-428-7000	374-3
Mercy Memorial Health Ctr (MMHC)						
1011 14th Ave NW	Ardmore	OK	73401	888-637-2937	580-223-5400	374-3
Mercyhurst College						
501 E 38th St	Erie	PA	16546	800-825-1926	814-824-2202	167
Mercy-USA for Aid & Development Inc (M-USA)						
44450 Pinetree Dr Ste 201	Plymouth	MI	48170	800-556-3729	734-454-0011	47-5
Meredith Collection						
1201 Millerton St SE	Canton	OH	44707	888-325-3945	330-484-1656	749
Meredith College						
3800 Hillsborough St	Raleigh	NC	27607	800-637-3348*	919-760-8581	167
*All						
Meredith Village Savings Bank (MVSB)						
24 State Rt 25 PO Box 177	Meredith	NH	03253	800-922-6872	603-279-7986	69
Mereen-Johnson Machine Co						
4401 Lyndale Ave N	Minneapolis	MN	55412	888-465-7297	612-529-7791	819
Merfish Pipe & Supply Co						
PO Box 15879	Houston	TX	77220	800-869-5731	713-869-5731	491
Merge Helathcare						
350 N Orleans St 1st Fl	Chicago	IL	60654	877-446-3743	312-565-6868	382
Mergent FIS Inc						
580 Kingsley Pk Dr	Fort Mill	SC	29715	800-342-5647		634-10
Mergent Inc						
477 Madison Ave Ste 410	New York	NY	10022	800-937-1398	212-413-7700	634-9
Mergenthaler Transfer & Storage						
1414 N Montana Ave	Helena	MT	59601	800-826-5463*	406-442-9470	778
*General						
Mergers & Acquisitions Law Report						
1801 S Bell St	Arlington	VA	22202	800-372-1033		530-7
Mergers & Acquisitions Magazine						
1 State St Plz	New York	NY	10004	888-807-8667*	212-803-6051	456-5
*Cust Svc						
Meri Meri						
63 Leonard St	Belmont	MA	02478	800-638-2881	617-484-5571	129
Merial Ltd						
3239 Satellite Blvd Bldg 500	Duluth	GA	30096	888-637-4251	678-638-3000	581
Mericon Industries Inc						
8819 N Pioneer Rd	Peoria	IL	61615	800-242-6464	309-693-2150	583
Meriden Public Library						
105 Miller St	Meriden	CT	06450	800-567-0902	203-238-2344	434-3
Meridian Auto Parts						
10211 Pacific Mesa Blvd						
Ste 404	San Diego	CA	92121	800-874-1974		53
Meridian Bioscience Inc						
3471 River Hills Dr	Cincinnati	OH	45244	800-543-1980*	513-271-3700	233
NASDAQ: VIVO ■ *Cust Svc						
Meridian Chamber of Commerce						
215 E Franklin Rd	Meridian	ID	83642	866-833-3330	208-888-2817	138
Meridian Community College						
910 Hwy 19 N	Meridian	MS	39307	800-622-8431	601-483-8241	161
Meridian Display & Merchandising Inc						
162 York Ave E	St Paul	MN	55117	800-786-2501	651-227-3020	5
Meridian Health System Inc						
1967 Hwy 34, Bldg C, Ste 104	Wall	NJ	07719	800-560-9990		363
Meridian IQ						
11501 Outlook St Ste 500	Overland Park	KS	66211	877-246-4909		448
Meridian Medical Technologies Inc						
6350 Stevens Forest Rd Ste 301	Columbia	MD	21046	800-638-8093	443-259-7800	475
Meridian Plaza Resort						
2310 N Ocean Blvd	Myrtle Beach	SC	29577	800-323-3011	843-626-4734	379

	City	State	ZIP	Toll-Free	Phone	Class
Meridian Star Inc						
814 22nd Ave	Meridian	MS	39301	**800-232-2525***	601-693-1551	634-8
*Cust Svc						
Meridian Star, The						
PO Box 1591	Meridian	MS	39302	**800-232-2525**	601-693-1551	531-2
Meridian Systems						
1720 Prairie City Rd Ste 120	Folsom	CA	95630	**800-850-2660**	916-294-2000	180-1
Meridian Technology Group Inc						
12909 SW 68th Pkwy Ste 340	Portland	OR	97223	**800-755-1038**	503-697-1600	179
Meridian Title Corp						
202 S Michigan St	South Bend	IN	46601	**800-777-1574**	574-232-5845	391-6
Meridian/Lauderdale County Tourism Bureau						
212 Constitution Ave	Meridian	MS	39301	**888-868-7720**	601-482-8001	208
Meridian-Lauderdale County Public Library						
2517 Seventh St	Meridian	MS	39301	**800-318-2596**	601-693-6771	434-3
Merion Publications Inc						
2900 Horizon Dr	King of Prussia	PA	19406	**800-355-1088**	610-278-1400	634-9
Merit Electric Company Inc						
6520 125th Ave N	Largo	FL	33773	**800-330-5945**	727-536-5945	191-4
Merit Medical Systems Inc						
1600 W Merit Pkwy	South Jordan	UT	84095	**800-356-3748**	801-253-1600	475
NASDAQ: MMSI						
Merit Systems Protection Board (MSPB)						
1615 M St NW	Washington	DC	20419	**800-209-8960**	202-653-7200	340-18
Merit Systems Protection Board Regional Offices (MSPB)						
Atlanta Region						
401 W Peachtree St NW 10th Fl	Atlanta	GA	30308	**800-209-8960**	404-730-2755	340-18
Denver Field Office						
165 S Union Blvd Ste 318	Lakewood	CO	80228	**800-209-8960**	303-969-5101	340-18
Merit Travel Group Inc						
111 Peter St Ste 200	Toronto	ON	M5V2H1	**800-268-5940**	416-364-3775	769
Merit USA						
620 Clark Ave	Pittsburg	CA	94565	**800-445-6374**		491
Meritus Health						
11116 Medical Campus Rd	Hagerstown	MD	21742	**800-735-2258**	301-790-8000	374-3
Meriwest Credit Union						
PO Box 530953	San Jose	CA	95153	**877-637-4937**		221
Merix Financial Inc						
390 Bay St 18th Fl Ste 500	Toronto	ON	M5H2Y2	**877-637-4914**		508
Merkle Wildlife Sanctuary						
580 Taylor Ave	Annapolis	MD	21401	**877-620-8367**		564
Merle Norman Cosmetics Inc						
9130 Bellanca Ave	Los Angeles	CA	90045	**800-421-6648**	310-641-3000	217
Merle's Automotive Supply Inc						
33 W University Blvd	Tucson	AZ	85705	**800-546-6040**	520-622-3526	53
Merlin Corp						
3815 E Main St	Saint Charles	IL	60174	**800-652-9910**	630-513-8200	311
Mermaid Manufacturing						
2651 Park Windsor Dr Ste 203	Fort Myers	FL	33901	**800-330-3553**	239-418-0535	14
Merrell Footwear						
9341 Courtland Dr NE	Rockford	MI	49351	**800-288-3124***	616-866-5500	302
*Cust Svc						
Merrick & Co						
2450 S Peoria St	Aurora	CO	80014	**800-544-1714**	303-751-0741	263
Merrick's Inc						
2415 Parview Rd PO Box 620307	Middleton	WI	53562	**800-637-7425**	608-831-3440	446
Merrill Area Chamber of Commerce						
705 N Ctr Ave	Merrill	WI	54452	**877-907-2757**	715-536-9474	138
Merrill Corp						
1 Merrill Cir	Saint Paul	MN	55108	**800-688-4400**	651-646-4501	626
Merrill DataSite						
225 Varick St	New York	NY	10014	**866-399-3770**		387
Merrill Mfg Corp						
236 S Genesee St	Merrill	WI	54452	**888-662-9473**	715-536-5533	809
Merrimack Valley Chamber of Commerce						
264 Essex St	Lawrence	MA	01840	**800-966-3375**	978-686-0900	138
Merrimack Valley Hospice						
360 Merrimack St Bldg 9	Lawrence	MA	01843	**800-933-5593**		371
Merrithew Corp						
2200 Yonge St Ste 500	Toronto	ON	M4S2C6	**800-910-0001**	416-482-4050	785
Merritt Equipment Co						
9339 Hwy 85	Henderson	CO	80640	**800-634-3036**	303-289-2286	777
Merritt Interpreting Services						
3626 N Hall St Ste 504	Dallas	TX	75219	**866-761-2585**	214-969-5585	766
Merriweather Post Pavilion (MPP)						
10475 Little Patuxent Pkwy	Columbia	MD	21044	**877-435-9849**	410-715-5550	571
Merry Maids						
3839 Forrest Hill-Irene Rd	Memphis	TN	38125	**800-798-8000**		151
Mersen USA BN Corp						
400 Myrtle Ave	Boonton	NJ	07005	**800-526-0877***		126
*General						
Mertz Mfg LLC						
1701 N Waverly St	Ponca City	OK	74601	**800-654-6433**	580-762-5646	275
Mervis Industries Inc						
3295 E Main St	Danville	IL	61834	**800-637-3016**	217-442-5300	684
MERX Networks Inc						
6 Antares Dr Phase II Unit 103	Ottawa	ON	K2E8A9	**800-964-6379**	613-727-4900	387
Mesa Arizona Temple						
101 S LeSueur	Mesa	AZ	85204	**855-537-4357**	480-833-1211	49
Mesa Community College						
1833 W Southern Ave	Mesa	AZ	85202	**866-532-4983**	480-461-7000	161
Red Mountain						
7110 E McKellips Rd	Mesa	AZ	85207	**866-532-4983**	480-654-7200	161
Mesa Laboratories Inc						
12100 W Sixth Ave	Lakewood	CO	80228	**800-992-6372***	303-987-8000	474
NASDAQ: MLAB ■ *Sales						
Mesa State College						
1100 N Ave	Grand Junction	CO	81501	**800-982-6372**	970-248-1020	167
Mesa Systems Inc						
681 Railroad Blvd	Grand Junction	CO	81505	**800-654-3225**	970-241-6450	360-2
Mesabi Range Community & Technical College						
1100 Industrial Pk Dr						
PO Box 648	Eveleth	MN	55734	**800-657-3860**	218-741-3095	161
Mesco Bldg Solutions						
5244 Bear Creek Ct	Irving	TX	75061	**800-556-3726**	214-687-9999	104
MESDA (Museum of Early Southern Decorative Arts)						
924 S Main St	Winston-Salem	NC	27101	**800-441-5303**	336-721-7360	519
Mesirow Financial Inc						
350 N Clark St	Chicago	IL	60610	**888-681-0082**	312-595-6000	688
Mesirow Financial Insurance Services Div						
353 N Clark St	Chicago	IL	60654	**800-453-0600**	312-595-6200	390
Mesirow Financial Private Equity						
350 N Clark St	Chicago	IL	60610	**800-453-0600**	312-595-6000	790
Meskwaki Bingo Hotel Casino						
1504 305th St	Tama	IA	52339	**800-728-4263**		132
MessageBank LLC						
250 W 57Th St Ste 1001	New York	NY	10107	**800-989-8001**	212-333-9300	387
Messaging Architects						
180 Peel St Ste 333	Montreal	QC	H3C2G7	**866-497-0101**	514-392-9220	181
Messenger, The						
713 Central Ave	Fort Dodge	IA	50501	**800-622-6613**	515-573-2141	531-2
Messiah College						
PO Box 3005	Grantham	PA	17027	**800-233-4220**	717-691-6000	167
Mesta Electronics Inc						
11020 Parker Dr	North Huntingdon	PA	15642	**800-535-6798**	412-754-3000	765
MET (Michigan Education Trust)						
PO Box 30198	Lansing	MI	48909	**800-638-4543***	517-335-4767	723
*General						
Metafile Information Systems Inc						
2900 43rd St NW	Rochester	MN	55901	**800-638-2445***	507-286-9232	180-11
*Sales						
Metal Cladding Inc						
230 S Niagara St	Lockport	NY	14094	**800-432-5513**		480
Metal Marketplace International (MMI)						
718 Sansom St	Philadelphia	PA	19106	**800-523-9191**	215-592-8777	411
Metal Masters Inc						
3825 Crater Lk Hwy	Medford	OR	97504	**800-866-9437**	541-779-1049	188
Metal Supermarkets IP Inc						
520 Abilene Dr 2nd Fl	Mississauga	ON	L5T2H7	**866-867-9344**	905-362-8226	491
Metalex Corp						
1530 Artaius Pkwy						
PO Box 399	Libertyville	IL	60048	**800-323-0792**	847-362-8300	721
Metal-Fab Inc						
3025 May St	Wichita	KS	67213	**800-835-2830**	316-943-2351	695
Metalico Annaco Inc						
943 Hazel St	Akron	OH	44305	**800-966-1499**	330-376-1400	684
Metalink Technologies Inc						
417 Wayne Ave PO Box 1124	Defiance	OH	43512	**888-999-8002**	419-782-3472	226
Metallic Arts Inc						
914 N Lake Rd	Spokane	WA	99212	**800-541-3200**	509-489-7173	775
Metals Week						
2 Penn Plaza	New York	NY	10121	**800-752-8878**		530-13
Metalworking Group Inc						
9070 Pippin Rd	Cincinnati	OH	45251	**800-476-9409**	513-521-4114	486
Metalworking Lubricants Co						
25 Silverdome Industrial Park	Pontiac	MI	48342	**800-394-5494**	248-332-3500	540
Metcam Inc						
305 Tidwell Cir	Alpharetta	GA	30004	**888-394-9633**	770-475-9633	695
Metcut Research Inc						
3980 Rosslyn Dr	Cincinnati	OH	45209	**877-847-1985**	513-271-5100	740
Meteor Crater & Museum of Astrogeology						
Exit 233 Off I-40						
Meteor Crater Rd	Winslow	AZ	86047	**800-289-5898**		519
Metex Inc						
789 Don Mills Rd Ste 218	North York	ON	M3C1T5	**866-817-8137**	416-203-8388	762
Metglas Inc						
440 Allied Dr	Conway	SC	29526	**800-581-7654**	843-349-7319	484
Methanex Corp						
1800 Waterfront Centre 200 Burrard St	Vancouver	BC	V6C3M1	**800-661-8851**	604-661-2600	143
TSE: MX						
Methapharm Inc						
11772 W Sample Rd	Coral Springs	FL	33065	**800-287-7686**	954-341-0795	240
Methode Electronics Inc						
7401 W Wilson Ave	Chicago	IL	60706	**877-316-7700**	708-867-6777	255
NYSE: MEI						
Methodist Alliance Hospice						
6400 Shelby View Dr Ste 101	Memphis	TN	38134	**800-541-8277**	901-516-1999	371
Methodist Country House						
4830 Kennett Pk	Wilmington	DE	19807	**800-976-7610**	302-654-5101	670
Methodist ElderCare Services						
5155 N High St	Columbus	OH	43214	**855-636-2225**	614-396-4990	670
Methodist Health Care System						
6565 Fannin St	Houston	TX	77030	**877-726-9362**	713-790-3311	353
Methodist Healthcare Ministries of South Texas Inc						
4507 Medical Dr	San Antonio	TX	78229	**800-959-6673**	210-692-0234	353
Methodist Hospital						
1701 N Senate Blvd						
PO Box 1367	Indianapolis	IN	46202	**800-899-8448**	317-962-2000	374-3
Methodist Hospital of Southern California						
300 W Huntington Dr	Arcadia	CA	91007	**888-388-2838**	626-898-8000	374-3
Methodist Hospitals of Dallas						
1441 N Beckley Ave	Dallas	TX	75203	**800-725-9664**	214-947-8181	353
Methodist Manor House						
1001 Middleford Rd	Seaford	DE	19973	**800-775-4593**	302-629-4593	670
Methodist Rehabilitation Ctr						
1350 E Woodrow Wilson Dr	Jackson	MS	39216	**800-223-6672**	601-981-2611	374-6
Methodist Theological School in Ohio						
3081 Columbus Pk	Delaware	OH	43015	**800-333-6876**	740-363-1146	168-3
Methodist University						
5400 Ramsey St	Fayetteville	NC	28311	**800-488-7110**	910-630-7000	167
Methods Machine Tools Inc						
65 Union Ave	Sudbury	MA	01776	**877-668-4262**	978-443-5388	358
METI (Medical Education Technologies Inc)						
6300 Edgelake Dr	Sarasota	FL	34240	**866-462-7920**	941-377-5562	252
MetLife Inc						
200 Pk Ave	New York	NY	10166	**800-638-5433**	212-578-2211	391-2
NYSE: MET						
MetLife Investors Insurance Co						
5 Pk Plz Ste 1900	Irvine	CA	92614	**800-848-3854**		391-2
Metl-Span LLC						
1720 Lakepointe Dr Ste 101	Lewisville	TX	75057	**877-585-9969**	972-221-6656	104
Met-Pro Corp Fybroc Div						
700 Emlen Way	Telford	PA	18969	**800-392-7621**	215-723-8155	638
Met-Pro Corp Sethco Div						
800 Emlen Way	Telford	PA	18969	**800-645-0500**	215-799-2577	638

Name / Address	City	State	ZIP	Toll-Free	Phone	Class
Metra Electronics Corp 460 Walker St	Holly Hill	FL	32117	800-221-0932*	386-257-1186	51
*Sales						
MetraPark 308 6th Ave N	Billings	MT	59101	800-366-8538	406-256-2400	207
MetraPark Arena 308 Sixth Ave N	Billings	MT	59101	800-366-8538	406-256-2400	718
Metric Machining Co 1425 S Vineyard Ave	Ontario	CA	91761	800-937-9311	909-947-9222	620
Metrix Instrument Co 8824 Fallbrook Dr	Houston	TX	77064	800-638-7494	713-461-2131	471
Metro - Sales Inc 1640 E 78th St	Minneapolis	MN	55423	800-862-7414	612-861-4000	111
Metro Creative Graphics Inc 519 Eigth Ave	New York	NY	10018	800-223-1600	212-947-5100	344
Metro Energy Group 1011 Hudson Ave	Ridgefield	NJ	07657	800-951-2941	201-941-3470	317
Metro Express Transportation Services Inc 875 Fee Fee Rd	St. Louis	MO	63043	800-805-0073	314-993-1511	312
Metro Ford Inc 9000 NW Seventh Ave	Miami	FL	33150	877-811-9402		56
Metro Health Hospital 5900 Byron Ctr Ave	Wyoming	MI	49519	800-968-0051	616-252-7200	374-3
Metro Jackson Convention & Visitors Bureau 111 E Capitol St Ste 102	Jackson	MS	39202	800-354-7695	601-960-1891	208
Metro Label Group Inc 999 Progress Ave	Toronto	ON	M1B6J1	800-668-4405	416-292-6600	87
Metro Mailing Service Inc 4251 Gateway Park Blvd	Sacramento	CA	95834	877-269-7055	916-928-0801	5
Metro Metals Northwest 5611 NE Columbia Blvd	Portland	OR	97218	800-610-5680	503-287-8861	684
Metro North Chamber of Commerce 14583 Orchard Pkwy Ste 300	Westminster	CO	80023	877-888-8811	303-288-1000	138
Metro Pavia Health System Inc MaraMar Plz Bldg Avenida San Patricio Ste 950-960	Guaynabo	PR	00968	888-882-0882		363
Metro Pulse 602 S Gay St Ste Mezzanine	Knoxville	TN	37902	800-686-4208	865-522-5399	531-5
Metro South Chamber of Commerce 60 School St	Brockton	MA	02301	877-777-4414	508-586-0500	138
Metro Times 733 St Antoine St	Detroit	MI	48226	866-501-3627	313-961-4060	531-5
Metro West Chamber of Commerce 1671 Worcester Rd Ste 201	Framingham	MA	01701	866-709-9401	508-879-5600	138
Metro Wire & Cable Co 6636 Metropolitan Pkwy	Sterling Heights	MI	48312	800-633-1432	586-264-3050	248
MetroHealth Medical Ctr 2500 MetroHealth Dr	Cleveland	OH	44109	800-554-5251	216-778-7800	374-3
Metrolina Greenhouses Inc 16400 Huntersville-Concord Rd	Huntersville	NC	28078	800-543-3915	704-875-1371	369
Metromont Corp PO Box 2486	Greenville	SC	29602	888-295-0383	864-295-0295	185
Metroplex Hospital 2201 S Clear Creek Rd	Killeen	TX	76549	800-926-7664	254-526-7523	374-3
Metropolis Magazine 205 Lexington Ave 17th Fl	New York	NY	10016	800-344-3046	212-627-9977	456-2
Metropolitan Ceramics 1201 Millerton St SE	Canton	OH	44707	800-325-3945		749
Metropolitan Community College PO Box 3777	Omaha	NE	68103	800-228-9553	402-457-2400	161
Metropolitan Community College Penn Valley 3201 SW Trafficway	Kansas City	MO	64111	866-676-6224	816-759-4000	161
Metropolitan Correctional Ctr *Chicago* 71 W Van Buren St	Chicago	IL	60605	877-623-8426	312-322-0567	214
Metropolitan Health Networks Inc 777 Yamato Rd Ste 510	Boca Raton	FL	33431	800-221-5487	561-805-8500	462
NYSE: MDF						
Metropolitan Hotel Vancouver 645 Howe St	Vancouver	BC	V6C2Y9	800-667-2300	604-687-1122	379
Metropolitan Milwaukee Assn of Commerce 756 N Milwaukee St	Milwaukee	WI	53202	800-362-9472	414-287-4100	138
Metropolitan Museum of Art 1000 Fifth Ave	New York	NY	10028	800-468-7386	212-879-5500	519
Metropolitan Nashville Public Schools (MNPS) 2601 Bransford Ave	Nashville	TN	37204	800-848-0298	615-259-8531	683
Metropolitan Plant & Flower Exchange 2125 Fletcher Ave	Fort Lee	NJ	07024	800-638-7613	201-944-1050	294
Metropolitan Poultry & Seafood Co 1920 Stanford Ct	Landover	MD	20785	800-522-0060	301-772-0060	298-10
Metropolitan State University 700 E Seventh St	Saint Paul	MN	55106	888-234-2690	651-793-1300	167
Metropolitan Trucking Inc (MRTK) 299 Market St	Saddle Brook	NJ	07663	800-967-3278		448
Metropolitan Tucson Convention & Visitors Bureau 100 S Church Ave	Tucson	AZ	85701	800-638-8350	520-624-1817	208
Metropolitan Vacuum Cleaner Co Inc 1 Ramapo Ave PO Box 149	Suffern	NY	10901	800-822-1602	845-357-1600	786
Metrosonics 1060 Corporate Ctr Dr	Oconomowoc	WI	53066	800-245-0779	262-567-9157	471
Metrotech Corp 3251 Olcott St	Santa Clara	CA	95054	800-446-3392	408-734-1400	471
Metro-Tel Corp 290 NE 68 St	Miami	FL	33138	888-998-8300	402-498-2964	732
MetroWest Medical Ctr 115 Lincoln St	Framingham	MA	01702	800-357-6060	508-383-1000	374-3
Metterra Hotel on Whyte 10454 82nd Ave	Edmonton	AB	T6E4Z7	866-465-8150	780-465-8150	379
Mettler Electronics Corp 1333 S Claudina St	Anaheim	CA	92805	800-854-9305	714-533-2221	476
Mettler-Toledo International Inc 5 Barr Rd	Ithaca	NY	14850	800-836-0836		682
Metzgar Conveyor Co Inc 901 Metzgar Dr NW	Comstock Park	MI	49321	888-266-8390	616-784-0930	209
Mexico 2 UN Plaza 28th Fl	New York	NY	10017	800-553-3210	212-752-0220	782
Consulate General 4506 Carolinas St	Houston	TX	77004	877-639-4835	713-271-6800	259
Mexico Plastics Company (Inc) 2000 W Blvd	Mexico	MO	65265	800-325-0216		65
Mexico Tourism Board (CSTM) 225 N Michigan Ave Ste 1800	Chicago	IL	60601	800-446-3942*		773
*General						
Meyer & Najem Inc 11787 Lantern Rd Ste 100	Fishers	IN	46038	888-578-5131	317-577-0007	188
Meyer Assoc Inc 14 Seventh Ave N	Saint Cloud	MN	56303	800-676-9233	320-259-4000	734
Meyer Corp 1 Meyer Pl	Vallejo	CA	94590	800-888-3883*	707-551-2800	485
*Cust Svc						
Meyer Jabara Hotels 1601 Belvedere Rd Ste 407 S	West Palm Beach	FL	33406	877-696-8671	561-689-6602	379
Meyer Plastics Inc 5167 E 65th St	Indianapolis	IN	46220	800-968-4131	317-259-4131	601
Meyerland Plaza 420 Meyerland Plaza	Houston	TX	77096	888-675-2275	713-349-0245	459
Meziere Enterprises Inc 220 S Hale Ave	Escondido	CA	92029	800-208-1755	760-746-3273	480
MFA Oil Co 1 Ray Young Dr	Columbia	MO	65205	800-366-0200	573-442-0171	580
MFJ Enterprises Inc 300 Industrial Pk Rd	Starkville	MS	39759	800-647-1800	662-323-5869	645
MFS Investment Management 500 Boylston St	Boston	MA	02116	877-960-6077	617-954-5000	401
Mg Scientific Inc 8500 107th St	Pleasant Prairie	WI	53158	800-343-8338	262-947-7000	534
MGA Entertainment Inc 16300 Roscoe Blvd Ste 150	Van Nuys	CA	91406	800-222-4685	818-894-2525	759
MGBW (Mitchell Gold & Bob Williams Co) 135 One Comfortable Pl	Taylorsville	NC	28681	800-789-5401	828-632-9200	320-2
MGM Grand Detroit 1777 Third St	Detroit	MI	48226	877-888-2121	313-465-1400	132
MGM Grand Hotel & Casino 3799 Las Vegas Blvd S	Las Vegas	NV	89109	877-880-0880	702-891-1111	667
MGM Industries Inc 287 Freehill Rd	Hendersonville	TN	37075	800-476-5584	615-824-6572	390
MGM Mirage Design Group Inc 3260 Industrial Rd	Las Vegas	NV	89109	800-929-1111	866-761-7111	188
MGM Transformer Co 5701 Smithway St	Commerce	CA	90040	800-423-4366	323-726-0888	765
MGMA (Medical Group Management Assn) 104 Inverness Terr E	Englewood	CO	80112	877-275-6462	303-799-1111	48-8
MGP Ingredients Inc 100 Commercial St PO Box 130	Atchison	KS	66002	800-255-0302	913-367-1480	297-23
NASDAQ: MGPI						
Mgs Inc 178 Muddy Creek Church Rd	Denver	PA	17517	800-952-4228	717-336-7528	90
MGS Services LLC 18775 N Frederick Ave Ste E	Gaithersburg	MD	20879	877-647-4255	301-330-9793	538
MHA (Mental Health America) 2000 N Beauregard St 6th Fl	Alexandria	VA	22311	800-969-6642*	703-684-7722	47-17
*Help Line						
Mha an Association of Montana Health Care Providers 1720 Ninth Ave	Helena	MT	59601	800-351-3551	406-442-1911	532
MHC Kenworth 1524 N Corrington Ave	Kansas City	MO	64120	888-259-4826	816-483-7035	776
MHI (Manufactured Housing Institute) 2101 Wilson Blvd Ste 610	Arlington	VA	22201	800-505-5500	703-558-0400	48-3
MHI PAC (Manufactured Housing Institute PAC) 1655 N Ft Myer Dr Ste 104	Arlington	VA	22209	800-505-5500	703-558-0400	614
MHIA (Material Handling Industry of America) 8720 Red Oak Blvd Ste 201	Charlotte	NC	28217	800-345-1815	704-676-1190	48-13
MHM Services Inc 1593 Spring Hill Rd Ste 600	Vienna	VA	22182	800-416-3649	703-749-4600	462
MHNet Behavioral Health 9606 N MoPac Exwy Ste 600	Austin	TX	78759	888-646-6889		461
MHP Inc (Maximum Human Performance Inc) 21 Dwight Pl	Fairfield	NJ	07004	888-783-8844	973-785-9055	797
MHPARC (Memorial Hermann Prevention & Recovery Ctr) 3043 Gessner	Houston	TX	77080	800-464-7272	713-939-7272	374-5
MHRI (Memorial Hospital of Rhode Island) 111 Brewster St	Pawtucket	RI	02860	800-647-4362	401-729-2000	374-3
MHS (Memorial Health System) *Central* 1400 E Boulder St	Colorado Springs	CO	80909	877-422-3648	719-365-5000	374-3
MIA (Marble Institute of America) 28901 Clemens Rd Ste 100	Westlake	OH	44145	800-433-4903	440-250-9222	48-3
Miami Beach Chamber of Commerce 1920 Meridian Ave 3rd Fl	Miami Beach	FL	33139	800-501-0401	305-672-1270	138
Miami Beach Resort & Spa 4833 Collins Ave	Miami Beach	FL	33140	866-765-9090	305-532-3600	667
Miami Children's Hospital 3100 SW 62nd Ave	Miami	FL	33155	800-432-6837	305-666-6511	374-1
Miami City Ballet 2200 Liberty Ave	Miami Beach	FL	33139	877-929-7010	305-929-7000	572-1
Miami Corp, The 720 Anderson Ferry Rd	Cincinnati	OH	45238	800-543-0448	513-451-6700	593
Miami County Chamber of Commerce 13 E Main St	Peru	IN	46970	800-521-9945	765-472-1923	138
Miami International Airport 2261 NW 66th Ave Bldg 702 Ste 217	Miami	FL	33122	800-825-5642	305-876-7000	27
Miami International Airport Hotel NW 20th St & Le Jeune Rd	Miami	FL	33122	800-327-1276	305-871-4100	379
Miami International University of Art & Design 1501 Biscayne Blvd	Miami	FL	33132	800-225-9023	305-428-5700	163
Miami Project to Cure Paralysis 1095 NW 14th Terr Lois Pope LIFE Ctr	Miami	FL	33136	800-782-6387*	305-243-6001	666
*General						
Miami Today 710 Brickell Ave	Miami	FL	33131	800-283-2707	305-358-2663	531-4
Miami University 501 E High St	Oxford	OH	45056	866-426-4643	513-529-1809	167

	City	State	Zip	Toll-Free	Phone	Class
Middletown						
4200 E University Blvd	Middletown	OH	45042	**877-898-4656**	513-727-3200	167
Miami Valley Hospital						
1 Wyoming St	Dayton	OH	45409	**800-544-0630***	937-208-8000	374-3
*All						
Miami-Cass County Rural Electric Membership Corp						
3086 W 100 N PO Box 168	Peru	IN	46970	**800-844-6668***	765-473-6668	247
*General						
MIBRO Group						
111 Sinnott Rd	Toronto	ON	M1L4S6	**866-941-9006**	416-285-9000	756
MIC (Micro Instrument Corp)						
1199 Emerson St PO Box 60619	Rochester	NY	14606	**800-200-3150**	585-458-3150	453
MIC Services Insurance Inc						
170 Kinnelon Rd - Ste 11	Kinnelon	NJ	07405	**800-355-2662**	973-492-2828	390
Micah Group						
389 Waller Ave Ste 210	Lexington	KY	40504	**877-260-7760**	859-260-7760	194
Micato Safaris						
15 W 26th St 11th Fl	New York	NY	10010	**800-642-2861**	212-545-7111	758
Michael Angelo's Gourmet Foods Inc						
200 Michael Angelo Way	Austin	TX	78728	**877-482-5426**	512-218-3500	297-36
Michael Baker Corp						
100 Airsite Dr						
Airsite Business Pk	Moon Township	PA	15108	**800-553-1153**	412-269-6300	263
NYSE: BKR						
Michael Brandman Associates						
220 Commerce Ste 200	Irvine	CA	92602	**888-826-5814**	714-508-4100	198
Michael C Fina Inc						
545 Fifth Ave	New York	NY	10022	**800-289-3462**	212-557-2500	362
Michael C. Fina Corporate Sales						
3301 Hunters Point Ave	Long Island	NY	11101	**800-999-3462**		195
Michael Foods Inc						
301 Carlson Pkwy Ste 400	Minnetonka	MN	55305	**800-328-5474**	952-258-4000	618
Michael Gibson Gallery						
157 Carling St	London	ON	N6A1H5	**866-644-2766**	519-439-0451	41
Michael J Fox Foundation for Parkinson's Research						
Grand Central Stn PO Box 4777	New York	NY	10163	**800-708-7644**		306
Michael J Liccar & Co						
231 s la salle st	Chicago	IL	60604	**800-922-6604**	312-702-1861	2
Michael R Rubenstein & Assoc						
12527 New Brittany Blvd	Fort Myers	FL	33907	**888-616-1222**	239-489-4443	2
Michael Ramey & Assoc Inc						
PO Box 744	Danville	CA	94526	**800-321-0505**		400
Michael Weining Inc						
124 Crosslake Pk Dr						
PO Box 3158	Mooresville	NC	28117	**877-548-0929**	704-799-0100	819
Michael's						
9777 Las Vegas Blvd S	Las Vegas	NV	89183	**866-796-7111**	702-796-7111	669
Michael's Finer Meats & Seafoods						
3775 Zane Trace Dr	Columbus	OH	43228	**800-282-0518**	614-527-4900	298-9
Michael's Transportation Service Inc						
140 Yolano Dr	Vallejo	CA	94589	**800-295-2448***	707-643-2099	108
*Cust Svc						
Michael-David Winery						
4580 W Hwy 12	Lodi	CA	95242	**888-707-9463**	209-368-7384	49-6
Michaels Stores Inc						
8000 Bent Branch Dr	Irving	TX	75063	**800-642-4235***	972-409-1300	44
*Cust Svc						
Michbi Doors Inc						
75 Emjay Blvd	Brentwood	NY	11717	**800-854-4541**	631-231-9050	498
Michelin North America Inc						
1 PkwyS PO Box 19001	Greenville	SC	29602	**800-847-3435***	864-458-5000	752
*Cust Svc						
Michell Consulting Group Inc						
8240 NW 52nd Ter Ste 410	Doral	FL	33166	**800-442-5011**	305-592-5433	198
Michels Corp						
817 W Main St	Brownsville	WI	53006	**877-297-8663**	920-583-3132	190-10
Michel-Schlumberger Partners LP						
4155 Wine Creek Rd	Healdsburg	CA	95448	**800-447-3060**	707-433-7427	79-3
Michener Institute for Applied						
222 Saint Patrick St	Toronto	ON	M5T1V4	**800-387-9066**	416-596-3101	683
Michigan						
Attorney General						
525 W Ottawa St	Lansing	MI	48933	**877-765-8388**	517-373-1110	339-23
Child Support Office						
235 S Grand Ave PO Box 30037	Lansing	MI	48933	**866-661-0005**		339-23
Civil Service Dept						
Capitol Commons Ctr						
400 S Pine St	Lansing	MI	48913	**800-788-1766**	517-373-3030	339-23
Community Health Dept						
Capitol View Bldg						
201 Townsend St	Lansing	MI	48913	**800-649-3777**	517-373-3740	339-23
Crime Victims Services Commission						
320 S Walnut St Garden Level						
Lewis Cass Bldg	Lansing	MI	48913	**877-251-7373**		339-23
Economic Development Corp (MEDC)						
300 N Washington Sq	Lansing	MI	48913	**888-522-0103**	517-373-9808	339-23
eLibrary Information						
702 W Kalamazoo St PO Box 30007	Lansing	MI	48909	**877-479-0021**	517-373-4331	339-23
Financial & Insurance Regulation						
PO Box 30220	Lansing	MI	48909	**877-999-6442**	517-373-0220	339-23
Parks & Recreation Div						
PO Box 30257	Lansing	MI	48909	**800-447-2757***	517-373-9900	339-23
*Campground Resv						
Travel Michigan						
300 N Washington Sq	Lansing	MI	48913	**888-784-7328**	517-373-0670	339-23
Michigan Assn of Realtors						
720 N Washington Ave	Lansing	MI	48906	**800-454-7842**	517-372-8890	654
Michigan Bar Journal						
306 Townsend St	Lansing	MI	48933	**888-726-3678**	517-346-6300	456-15
Michigan Career Education & Workforce Programs						
201 N Washington Sq						
Victor Office Center	Lansing	MI	48913	**888-253-6855**	517-335-5858	339-23
Michigan Chamber of Commerce						
600 S Walnut St	Lansing	MI	48933	**800-748-0266**	517-371-2100	139
Michigan Community Blood Centers						
4005 Orchard Dr	Midland	MI	48670	**866-642-5663**	989-839-3490	88
Michigan Community Blood Centers Northwest						
2575 Aero Pk Dr	Traverse City	MI	49686	**866-642-5663***	231-935-3030	88
*General						
Michigan Dental Assn						
3657 Okemos Rd Ste 200	Okemos	MI	48864	**800-589-2632**	517-372-9070	229
Michigan Education Trust (MET)						
PO Box 30198	Lansing	MI	48909	**800-638-4543***	517-335-4767	723
*General						
Michigan Fluid Power Inc						
4556 Spartan Industrial Dr SW						
	Grandville	MI	49418	**800-635-0289**	616-538-5700	386
Michigan Insurance Co						
1700 E Beltline Ne						
PO Box 152120, Ste 100	Grand Rapids	MI	49515	**888-606-6426**	616-447-3600	390
Michigan International Speedway						
12626 US 12	Brooklyn	MI	49230	**800-354-1010**	517-592-6666	514
Michigan Jewish Institute						
25401 Coolidge Hwy	Oak Park	MI	48237	**888-463-6654**	248-414-6900	167
Michigan Mfg Technology Ctr						
47911 Halyard Dr	Plymouth	MI	48170	**888-414-6682**		666
Michigan Millers Mutual Insurance Co						
2425 E Grand River Ave						
PO Box 30060	Lansing	MI	48912	**800-888-1914**		391-4
Michigan Municipal League						
1675 Green Rd PO Box 1487	Ann Arbor	MI	48105	**800-653-2483**	734-662-3246	47-5
Michigan Nurses Assn (MNA)						
2310 Jolly Oak Rd	Okemos	MI	48864	**888-646-8773**	517-349-5640	532
Michigan Out-of-Doors Magazine (MOOD)						
2101 Wood St PO Box 30235	Lansing	MI	48912	**800-777-6720**	517-371-1041	456-22
Michigan Pharmacists Assn						
408 Kalamazoo Plz	Lansing	MI	48933	**800-227-2345**	517-484-1466	584
Michigan Stadium						
1201 S Main St						
University of Michigan	Ann Arbor	MI	48104	**866-296-6849**	734-647-2583	718
Michigan State University College of Law						
368 Law College Bldg	East Lansing	MI	48824	**800-844-9352**	517-432-6810	168-1
Michigan State University Library						
100 Library	East Lansing	MI	48824	**800-500-1554**	517-353-8700	434-6
Michigan Student Financial Services Bureau						
Austin Bldg 430 W Allegan	Lansing	MI	48922	**800-642-5626***	888-447-2687	723
*General						
Michigan Technological University						
1400 Townsend Dr	Houghton	MI	49931	**888-688-1885**	906-487-2335	167
Michigan Theater						
603 E Liberty St	Ann Arbor	MI	48104	**800-745-3000**	734-668-8397	571
Michigan Theological Seminary						
41550 E Ann Arbor Trail	Plymouth	MI	48170	**800-356-6639**	734-207-9581	168-3
Michigan Wheel Corp						
1501 Buchanan Ave SW	Grand Rapids	MI	49507	**800-369-4335**	616-452-6941	386
Mickey Thompson Tires						
4600 Prosper Dr	Stow	OH	44224	**800-222-9092**	330-928-9092	752
Mickey Truck Bodies Inc						
1305 Trinity Ave PO Box 2044	High Point	NC	27261	**800-334-9061**	336-882-6806	777
Mico Inc						
1911 Lee Blvd	North Mankato	MN	56003	**800-477-6426**	507-625-6426	386
Micrel Inc						
2180 Fortune Dr	San Jose	CA	95131	**800-282-9855**	408-944-0800	694
NASDAQ: MCRL						
Micro 100 Tool Corp						
1410 E Pine Ave	Meridian	ID	83642	**800-421-8065**	208-888-7310	492
Micro Care Corp						
595 John Downey Dr	New Britain	CT	06051	**800-638-0125**	860-827-0626	150
Micro Control Co						
7956 Main St NE	Minneapolis	MN	55432	**800-328-9923**	763-786-8750	250
Micro Electronics, Inc.						
2701 Charter St Ste A	Columbus	OH	43228	**877-636-9793**	614-326-8500	175-1
Micro Express Inc						
8 Hammond Dr Ste 105	Irvine	CA	92618	**800-989-9900**	949-460-9911	175-1
Micro Instrument Corp (MIC)						
1199 Emerson St PO Box 60619	Rochester	NY	14606	**800-200-3150**	585-458-3150	453
Micro Matic USA Inc						
10726 N Second St	Machesney Park	IL	61115	**866-291-5756**	815-968-7557	662
Micro Motion Inc						
7070 Winchester Cir	Boulder	CO	80301	**800-522-6277**	303-530-8400	203
Micro Plastics Inc						
11 Industry Ln Hwy 178 N						
PO Box 149	Flippin	AR	72634	**800-466-1467**	870-453-2261	607
Micro Solutions Enterprises (MSE)						
8201 Woodley Ave	Van Nuys	CA	91406	**800-673-4968**	818-407-7500	627
Micro Surface Engr Inc						
1550 E Slauson Ave	Los Angeles	CA	90011	**800-322-5832**	323-582-7348	484
Micro Surface Finishing Products Inc						
1217 W Third St	Wilton	IA	52778	**800-225-3006**	563-732-3240	1
MicroAire Surgical Instruments Inc						
3590 Grand Forks Blvd	Charlottesville	VA	22911	**800-722-0822**		475
MicroBilt Corp						
1640 Airport Rd Ste 115	Kennesaw	GA	30144	**800-884-4747**		180-10
MicroBiz Corp						
655 Oak Grove Ave Ste 493						
Ste 493	Menlo Park	CA	94025	**800-937-2289**	702-749-5353	180-1
Microboards Technology LLC						
8150 Mallory Ct PO Box 846	Chanhassen	MN	55317	**800-646-8881**	952-556-1600	175-8
Microchip Technology Inc						
2355 W Chandler Blvd	Chandler	AZ	85224	**800-437-2767**	480-792-7200	694
NASDAQ: MCHP						
Micro-Clean Inc						
177 N Commerce Way	Bethlehem	PA	18017	**800-523-9852**	610-867-5302	740
Micro-coax Inc						
206 Jones Blvd	Pottstown	PA	19464	**800-223-2629**	610-495-0110	255
MicroFinancial Inc						
16 New England Executive Pk						
Ste 200	Burlington	MA	01803	**877-868-3800**	781-994-4800	218
NASDAQ: MFI						
Microfluidics International Corp						
90 Glacier Dr Ste 1000	Westwood	MA	02090	**800-370-5452**	617-969-5452	299
MicroGroup Inc						
7 Industrial Pk Rd	Medway	MA	02053	**800-255-8823**	508-533-4925	594
Microlife USA Inc						
1617 Gulf to Bay Blvd Second Fl						
Ste B	Clearwater	FL	33755	**888-314-2599**	727-451-0484	475
Microlink Enterprise Inc						
20955 Pathfinder Rd Ste 100	Diamond Bar	CA	91765	**800-829-3688**	562-205-1888	180-1

Company / Address	City	State	ZIP	Toll-Free	Phone	Class
Microlynx Systems Ltd 1925 18 Ave Ne Ste 107	Calgary	AB	T2E7T8	**866-835-4332**	403-275-7346	263
Micromatic LLC 525 Berne St	Berne	IN	46711	**800-333-5752**	260-589-2136	225
Micromeritics Instrument Corp 1 Micromeritics Dr	Norcross	GA	30093	**800-229-5052**	770-662-3620	419
MicroMetl Corp 3035 N Shadeland Ave Ste 300	Indianapolis	IN	46226	**800-662-4822**		662
MicroMod Automation Inc 75 Town Centre Dr	Rochester	NY	14623	**800-480-1975**	585-321-9200	203
Micron Technology Inc 8000 S Federal Way *NASDAQ: MU*	Boise	ID	83707	**888-363-2589**	208-368-4000	624
Micronesia 300 E 42nd St Ste 1600	New York	NY	10017	**800-469-4828**	212-697-8370	782
Consulate 1725 N St NW Ste 910	Washington	DC	20036	**877-730-9753**	202-223-4383	259
Microphor Inc 452 E Hill Rd *Orders	Willits	CA	95490	**800-358-8280***	707-459-5563	610
Micro-Poise Measurment Systems LLC 1624 Englewood Ave	Akron	OH	44305	**800-428-3812**	330-784-1251	386
Microprocessor Report 355 Chesley Ave	Mountain View	CA	94040	**800-413-2881**	408-270-3772	530-3
Micropump Inc 1402 NE 136th Ave *Sales	Vancouver	WA	98684	**800-222-9565***	360-253-2008	638
Micros Systems Inc 7031 Columbia Gateway Dr *NASDAQ: MCRS*	Columbia	MD	21046	**800-937-2211**	443-285-6000	613
Microsemi Corp 2381 Morse Ave *NASDAQ: MSCC*	Irvine	CA	92614	**800-713-4113**	949-221-7100	694
Microserv Computer Techs Inc 1808 E 17th St	Idaho Falls	ID	83404	**866-988-7164**		182
Microsoft Great Plains Business Solutions 3900 Great Plains Dr S	Fargo	ND	58104	**888-477-7877**	701-281-6500	180-1
MicroStrategy 1850 Towers Crescent Plz *NASDAQ: MSTR*	Tysons Corner	VA	22182	**888-266-0321**	703-848-8600	180-11
Micro-Tech Consultants Inc 1686 Jessica Pl	Santa Rosa	CA	95403	**800-752-8878**	707-575-4820	465
Microtek Medical Holdings Inc 13000 Deerfield Pkwy Ste 300	Alpharetta	GA	30004	**800-777-7977**	678-896-4400	476
Microtek Medical Inc 512 N Lehmberg Rd	Columbus	MS	39702	**800-824-3027**	662-327-1863	476
MicroVention Inc 1311 Valencia Ave	Tustin	CA	92780	**800-990-8368**	714-247-8000	476
MicroVision Development Inc 5541 Fermi Ct Ste 120	Carlsbad	CA	92008	**800-998-4555**	760-438-7781	180-8
MicroVote General Corp 6366 Guilford Ave	Indianapolis	IN	46220	**800-257-4901**	317-257-4900	799
Microwave Filter Company Inc 6743 Kinne St	East Syracuse	NY	13057	**800-448-1666**	315-438-4700	255
Microworks 359 Kent St Ste 301	Ottawa	ON	K2P0R6	**877-232-3859**	613-232-3859	182
MICS (Management Information Control Systems Inc) 2025 Ninth St	Los Osos	CA	93402	**800-838-6427**	805-543-7000	180-10
Mid America Computer Corp PO Box 700	Blair	NE	68008	**800-622-2502**	402-426-6222	227
Mid America Motorworks 17082 N Us Hwy 45 PO Box 1368	Effingham	IL	62401	**866-350-4543**	217-540-4200	60
Mid Atlantic Center for The Arts 1048 Washington St	Cape May	NJ	08204	**800-275-4278**	609-884-5404	519
Mid Coast Hospital 123 Medical Ctr Dr	Brunswick	ME	04011	**800-994-6610**	207-729-0181	374-3
Mid Ohio Energy Co-op Inc 555 W Franklin St	Kenton	OH	43326	**888-382-6732**	419-673-7289	247
Mid Ohio Regional Planning Commission 111 Liberty St Ste 100	Columbus	OH	43215	**800-750-0750**	614-228-2663	462
Mid Penn Bancorp Inc 349 Union St *NASDAQ: MPB*	Millersburg	PA	17061	**866-642-7736**	717-692-2133	360-2
Mid Pines Inn & Golf Club 1010 Midland Rd	Southern Pines	NC	28387	**800-747-7272**	910-692-2114	667
Mid Wisconsin Federated Library System 112 Clinton St	Horicon	WI	53032	**800-660-6899**	920-485-0833	434-3
MID-AM Bldg Supply Inc 1615 Omar Bradley Dr PO Box 645	Moberly	MO	65270	**800-892-5850**	660-263-2140	193-3
Midamar Corp PO Box 218	Cedar Rapids	IA	52406	**800-362-3711**	319-362-3711	298-9
Mid-America Apartment Communities Inc (MAAC) 6584 Poplar Ave Ste 300 *NYSE: MAA*	Memphis	TN	38138	**866-620-1130**	901-682-6600	653
Mid-America Charter Lines 2513 E Higgins Rd	Elk Grove Village	IL	60007	**800-323-0312**	847-437-3779	106
Mid-America Christian University 3500 SW 119th St	Oklahoma City	OK	73170	**888-888-2341**	405-691-3800	167
Mid-America College of Funeral Science (MACFS) 3111 Hamburg Pk	Jeffersonville	IN	47130	**800-221-6158**	812-288-8878	798
Mid-America Merchandising Inc 204 W Third St	Kansas City	MO	64105	**800-333-6737**	816-471-5600	9
Midamerica National Bancshares 100 W Elm St	Canton	IL	61520	**877-647-5050**	309-647-5000	69
MidAmerica Nazarene University 2030 E College Way	Olathe	KS	66062	**800-800-8887**	913-782-3750	167
Mid-America Publishing Corp 9 Second St NW	Hampton	IA	50441	**800-558-1244**	641-456-2585	634-8
Mid-America Reformed Seminary 229 Seminary Dr	Dyer	IN	46311	**888-440-6277**	219-864-2400	168-3
Mid-America Transplant Services (MTS) 1110 Highlands Plz Dr E Ste 100	Saint Louis	MO	63110	**888-376-4854**	314-735-8200	544
Mid-American Coaches Inc 4530 Hwy 47	Washington	MO	63090	**866-944-8687**		758
MidAmerican Energy Holdings Co 666 Grand Ave PO Box 657	Des Moines	IA	50303	**800-329-6261**		360-5

Company / Address	City	State	ZIP	Toll-Free	Phone	Class
Midas International Corp 1300 Arlington Heights Rd	Itasca	IL	60143	**800-621-8545**	630-438-3000	61-3
Mid-Atlantic Christian Universit 715 N Poindexter St	Elizabeth City	NC	27909	**866-996-6228**	252-334-2070	160
Mid-Atlantic PenFed Realty Berkshire Hathaway HomeServices (PCR) 3050 Chain Bridge Rd	Fairfax	VA	22030	**866-225-5778**	703-691-7653	653
Mid-Carolina Electric Co-op Inc PO Box 669 *Cust Svc	Lexington	SC	29071	**888-813-8000***	803-749-6555	247
Midcontinent Communications PO Box 5010	Sioux Falls	SD	57117	**800-888-1300**	605-274-9810	115
Mid-Continent Group 1437 S Boulder Ave W PO Box 1409	Tulsa	OK	74119	**800-722-4994**	918-587-7221	391-4
Mid-Continent Public Library 15616 E 24 Hwy	Independence	MO	64050	**800-318-2596**	816-836-5200	434-3
Mid-Continent Safety 8225 E 35th St N *General	Wichita	KS	67226	**800-776-0956***	316-522-0900	677
Mid-Continent University 99 Powell Rd E	Mayfield	KY	42066	**888-628-4723**	270-247-8521	167
Mid-Continental Restoration Company Inc 401 E Hudson Rd PO Box 429	Fort Scott	KS	66701	**800-835-3700**	620-223-3700	191-7
Middle Bass Island State Park 1719 Fox Rd	Middle Bass Island	OH	43446	**866-644-6727**	419-285-0311	564
Middle Georgia Electric Membership Corp 600 Tippettville Rd	Vienna	GA	31092	**800-342-0144**	229-268-2671	247
Middle River Aircraft Systems (MRAS) 103 Chesapeake Pk Plaza	Baltimore	MD	21220	**877-432-3272**	410-682-1500	22
Middle Tennessee Mental Health Institute 221 Stewarts Ferry Pike	Nashville	TN	37214	**800-770-8277**	615-902-7400	374-5
Middle Tennessee Natural Gas Utility District (MTNG) 1036 W Broad St PO Box 670	Smithville	TN	37166	**800-880-6373**	615-597-4300	785
Middle Tennessee State University 1301 E Main St *Admissions	Murfreesboro	TN	37132	**800-433-6878***	615-898-2111	167
Middlebury College 131 S Main St	Middlebury	VT	05753	**877-214-3330**	802-443-3000	167
Middlebury College Library 110 Storrs Ave	Middlebury	VT	05753	**800-829-1040**	802-443-5494	434-6
Middlebury Community Schools 57853 Northridge Dr	Middlebury	IN	46540	**866-632-9992**	574-825-9425	683
Middleby Corp 1400 Toastmaster Dr *NASDAQ: MIDD*	Elgin	IL	60120	**800-331-5842**	847-741-3300	299
Middlesboro Coca-Cola Bottling Works Inc 1324 Cumberland Ave	Middlesboro	KY	40965	**800-442-0102**	877-692-4679	79-2
Middlesex Community College 100 Training Hill Rd	Middletown	CT	06457	**800-818-5501**	860-343-5800	161
Middlesex County College 2600 Woodbridge Ave PO Box 3050	Edison	NJ	08818	**888-442-4551**	732-548-6000	161
Middlesex Hospital 28 Crescent St	Middletown	CT	06457	**800-548-2394**	860-358-6000	374-3
Middlesex Mutual Assurance Co 213 Ct St PO Box 891	Middletown	CT	06457	**800-622-3780**		391-4
Middlesex Research Mfg Company Inc 27 Apsley St	Hudson	MA	01749	**800-424-5188**	978-562-3697	742-2
Middlesex Savings Bank 120 Flanders Rd	Westborough	MA	01581	**877-463-6287**	508-653-0300	69
Middlesex Water Co 1500 Ronson Rd PO Box 1500 *NASDAQ: MSEX*	Iselin	NJ	08830	**800-549-3802**	732-634-1500	785
Middlesex West Chamber of Commerce 179 Great Rd Ste 104B	Acton	MA	01720	**800-439-0183**	978-263-0010	138
Middleton & Company Inc 600 Atlantic Ave 18th Fl	Boston	MA	02210	**800-357-5101**	617-357-5101	40
Middleton Place 4300 Ashley River Rd	Charleston	SC	29414	**800-782-3608**	843-556-6020	669
MidFirst Bank PO Box 76149	Oklahoma City	OK	73147	**888-643-3477**	405-943-8002	69
Mid-Island Electrical Supply 59 Mall Dr	Commack	NY	11725	**877-324-2636**	631-864-4242	248
Mid-Kansas Co-op Assn (MKC) PO Box D	Moundridge	KS	67107	**800-864-4428**	620-345-6361	47-2
Mid-Lakes Distributing Inc 1029 W Adams St	Chicago	IL	60607	**888-733-2700**	312-733-1033	611
Midland Area Chamber of Commerce 300 Rodd St Ste 101	Midland	MI	48640	**800-715-0074**	989-839-9901	138
Midland Chamber of Commerce 109 N Main St	Midland	TX	79701	**800-624-6435**	432-683-3381	138
Midland Co 7000 Midland Blvd	Amelia	OH	45102	**800-759-9008**	800-543-2644	360-4
Midland College 3600 N Garfield St	Midland	TX	79705	**800-474-7164**	432-685-4500	161
Midland County Convention & Visitors Bureau 300 Rodd St Ste 101	Midland	MI	48640	**800-444-9979**	989-839-0340	208
Midland Credit Management Inc 8875 Aero Dr Ste 200	San Diego	CA	92123	**800-265-8825**		140
Midland Daily News 124 McDonald St	Midland	MI	48640	**877-411-2762**	989-835-7171	531-2
Midland High School 615 W Missouri Ave	Midland	TX	79701	**866-632-9992**	989-923-5181	683
Midland Hospice Care 200 SW Frazier Cir	Topeka	KS	66606	**800-491-3691**	785-232-2044	371
Midland Industries Inc 1424 N Halsted St	Chicago	IL	60642	**800-662-8228**	312-664-7300	484
Midland Information Resources Co 5440 Corporate Pk Dr	Davenport	IA	52807	**800-232-3696**	563-359-3696	626
Midland Memorial Hospital 2200 W Illinois Ave	Midland	TX	79701	**800-833-2916**	432-685-1111	374-3
Midland Mortgage Co PO Box 26648	Oklahoma City	OK	73126	**800-654-4566**		508
Midland National Bank 527 N Main	Newton	KS	67114	**800-810-9457**	316-283-1700	69
Midland National Life Insurance Co 1 Sammons Plz	Sioux Falls	SD	57193	**800-923-3223**	605-335-5700	391-2
Midland Paper 101 E Palatine Rd	Wheeling	IL	60090	**800-323-8522**	847-777-2700	552

Name / Address	City	State	ZIP	Toll-Free	Phone	Class
Midland Power Co-op 1005 E Lincolnway PO Box 420	Jefferson	IA	50129	**800-833-8876**	515-386-4111	247
Midland Reporter-Telegram PO Box 1650	Midland	TX	79702	**800-542-3952**	432-682-5311	531-2
Midland University 900 N Clarkson St	Fremont	NE	68025	**800-642-8382**	402-941-6270	167
Midlands Community Hospital 11111 S 84th St	Papillion	NE	68046	**855-524-4001**	402-593-3000	374-3
Midlands Technical College PO Box 2408	Columbia	SC	29202	**800-922-8038**	803-738-1400	161
Midmark Corp 60 Vista Dr	Versailles	OH	45380	**800-643-6275**	937-526-3662	475
MidMichigan Home Care 3007 N Saginaw Rd	Midland	MI	48640	**800-852-9350**	989-633-1400	371
Midnight Rose Hotel & Casino 256 E Bennett Ave	Cripple Creek	CO	80813	**800-635-5825**	719-689-2446	132
Midnight Sun Adventure Travel 1027 Pandora Ave	Victoria	BC	V8V3P6	**800-255-5057**	250-480-9409	758
Mid-Ohio Aviation 6250 N Honeytown Rd	Smithville	OH	44677	**800-669-4243**	330-669-2671	62
Mid-Ohio Sports Car Course 7721 Steam Corners Rd PO Box 3108	Lexington	OH	44904	**800-643-6446**	419-884-4000	514
Midrange Software Inc 12716 Riverside Dr	Studio City	CA	91607	**800-737-6766**	818-762-8539	180-10
MidSouth Bancorp Inc 102 Versailles Blvd *NYSE: MSL*	Lafayette	LA	70501	**800-213-2265**	337-237-8343	360-2
Mid-South Community College 2000 W Broadway	West Memphis	AR	72301	**866-733-6722**	870-733-6722	161
Mid-South Wire Company Inc 1070 Visco Dr	Nashville	TN	37210	**800-714-7800**	615-743-2850	811
Midstate College 411 W Northmoor Rd	Peoria	IL	61614	**800-251-4299**	309-692-4092	798
Midstate Electric Co-op Inc 16755 Finley Butte Rd	La Pine	OR	97739	**800-722-7219**	541-536-2126	247
Mid-State Equipment Inc W 1115 Bristol Rd	Columbus	WI	53925	**877-677-4020**	920-623-4020	276
Mid-State Machine Products Inc 83 Verti Dr	Winslow	ME	04901	**800-341-4672**	207-873-6136	755
Mid-States Bolt & Screw Co 4126 Somers Dr	Burton	MI	48529	**800-482-0867**	810-744-0123	280
Mid-States Screw Corp 1817 18th Ave	Rockford	IL	61104	**888-354-6772**	815-397-2440	280
Mid-States Supply Co 1716 Guinotte Ave	Kansas City	MO	64120	**800-825-1410**	816-842-4290	611
Midtown Hotel 220 Huntington Ave	Boston	MA	02115	**800-343-1177**	617-262-1000	379
Midway College 512 E Stephens St	Midway	KY	40347	**800-755-0031**	859-846-5346	167
Midwesco Filter Resources Inc 385 Battaile Dr	Winchester	VA	22601	**800-336-7300**	540-667-8500	18
Midwest America Federal Credit Union 1104 Medical Pk Dr	Fort Wayne	IN	46825	**800-348-4738**	260-482-3334	221
Midwest Bank 105 E Soo St PO Box 40	Parkers Prairie	MN	56361	**877-365-5155**	218-338-6054	69
Midwest Bio-systems Inc 28933 35 E St	Tampico	IL	61283	**877-649-2114**	815-438-7200	429
Midwest Communications Inc 904 Grand Ave	Wausau	WI	54403	**877-945-4236**	715-842-1437	640
Midwest Corporate Aviation 3512 N Webb Rd	Wichita	KS	67226	**800-435-9622**	316-636-9700	62
Midwest Dental Equipment Services & Supplies 2700 Commerce St	Wichita Falls	TX	76301	**800-766-2025**		230
Midwest Elastomers Inc 700 Industrial Dr PO Box 412	Wapakoneta	OH	45895	**800-786-3539**	419-738-8844	604-3
Midwest Electric Co-op Corp 104 Washington Ave	Grant	NE	69140	**800-451-3691**	308-352-4356	247
Midwest Employers Casualty Co 14755 N Outer 40 Dr Ste 300	Chesterfield	MO	63017	**877-975-2667**	636-449-7000	391-4
Midwest Energy Co-op 901 E State St	Cassopolis	MI	49031	**800-492-5989**		247
Midwest Energy Inc 1330 Canterbury Dr	Hays	KS	67601	**800-222-3121**	785-625-3437	247
Midwest Eye Banks 4889 Venture Dr	Ann Arbor	MI	48108	**800-247-7250**	734-780-2100	271
Midwest Folding Products Inc 1414 S Western Ave	Chicago	IL	60608	**800-621-4716**	312-666-3366	320-3
Midwest Helicopter Airways Inc 525 Executive Dr	Willowbrook	IL	60527	**800-323-7609**	630-325-7860	359
MIDWEST Homes for Pets 3142 S Cowan Rd PO Box 1031	Muncie	IN	47302	**800-428-8560**	765-289-3355	577
Midwest Industries Inc 122 E State Hwy 175	Ida Grove	IA	51445	**800-859-3028**	712-364-3365	761
Midwest Library Service Inc 11443 St Charles Rock Rd	Bridgeton	MO	63044	**800-325-8833**	314-739-3100	94
Midwest Living Magazine 1716 Locust St	Des Moines	IA	50309	**800-678-8093**	515-247-2982	456-22
Midwest Mechanical Group 801 Parkview Blvd	Lombard	IL	60148	**800-214-3680**	630-850-2300	191-10
Midwest Metal Products Co 2100 W Mt Pleasant Rd	Muncie	IN	47302	**888-741-1044**		479
Midwest Motor Express Inc 5015 E Main Ave	Bismarck	ND	58502	**800-741-4097**	701-223-1880	778
Midwest Plan Service 122 Davidson Hall ISU	Ames	IA	50011	**800-562-3618**	515-294-4337	634-2
Midwest Pro Painting Inc 12845 Farmington Rd	Livonia	MI	48150	**800-860-6757**	734-427-1040	191-8
Midwest Products Company Inc 400 S Indiana St *Orders	Hobart	IN	46342	**800-348-3497***	219-942-1134	760
Midwest Quality Gloves Inc 835 Industrial Rd	Chillicothe	MO	64601	**800-821-3028**	660-646-2165	154-7
Midwest Sales & Service Inc 917 S Chapin St	South Bend	IN	46601	**800-772-7262**	574-287-3365	37
Midwest Specialized Transportation Inc PO Box 6418	Rochester	MN	55903	**800-927-8007**	507-424-4838	448

Name / Address	City	State	ZIP	Toll-Free	Phone	Class
Midwest Sports Supply Inc 11613 Reading Rd	Cincinnati	OH	45241	**800-334-4580**	513-956-4900	709
Mid-West Spring & Stamping Co 1404 Joliet Rd Unit C	Romeoville	IL	60446	**800-619-0909**	630-739-3800	717
Mid-West Steel Bldg Co 7301 Fairview	Houston	TX	77041	**800-777-9378**	713-466-7788	104
Midwest Systems 5911 Hall St	Saint Louis	MO	63147	**800-383-6281**	314-389-6280	777
Midwest Tool & Cutlery Co Inc 1210 Progress St PO Box 160	Sturgis	MI	49091	**800-782-4659**	269-651-7964	224
Midwest Towers Inc 1156 Hwy 19 East	Chickasha	OK	73018	**800-900-2190**	405-224-4622	14
Midwest Trading Horticultural Supplies Inc 48w805 Il Rt 64	Maple Park	IL	60151	**800-546-9522**	630-365-1990	294
Midwest Truck & Auto Parts Inc 1001 W Exchange	Chicago	IL	60609	**800-934-2727**	773-247-3400	60
Midwest Walnut Co 1914 Postevin St	Council Bluffs	IA	51503	**800-592-5688**	712-325-9191	447
Midwest Wire Products Inc 800 Woodward Heights	Ferndale	MI	48220	**800-989-9881**	248-399-5100	72
Midwest Wire Products LLC 649 S Lansing Ave PO Box 770	Sturgeon Bay	WI	54235	**800-445-0225**	920-743-6591	487
Midwestern Baptist Theological Seminary 5001 N Oak Trafficway	Kansas City	MO	64118	**800-944-6287**	816-414-3700	168-3
Midwestern Industries Inc 915 Oberlin Rd SW *Cust Svc	Massillon	OH	44647	**877-474-9464***	330-837-4203	192
Midwestern Intermediate Unit Iv 453 Maple St	Grove City	PA	16127	**800-942-8035**	724-458-6700	683
Midwestern Regional Medical Ctr (MRMC) 2520 Elisha Ave	Zion	IL	60099	**800-615-3055**	847-872-4561	374-7
Midwestern State University 3410 Taft Blvd *Admissions	Wichita Falls	TX	76308	**800-842-1922***	940-397-4000	167
MidWestOne Financial Group Inc 102 S Clinton St PO Box 1700 *NASDAQ: MOFG* ■ *Cust Svc	Iowa City	IA	52240	**800-247-4418***	319-356-5800	360-2
Miele Inc 9 Independence Way	Princeton	NJ	08540	**800-843-7231**	609-419-9898	35
MIF (Milk Industry Foundation) 1250 H St NW Ste 900	Washington	DC	20005	**866-225-4821**	202-737-4332	47-2
Mifflinburg Bank & Trust Co (MBTC) 250 E Chestnut St PO Box 186	Mifflinburg	PA	17844	**888-966-3131**	570-966-1041	69
Mighty Distributing System of America Inc 650 Engineering Dr	Norcross	GA	30092	**800-829-3900**	770-448-3900	60
Mii Amo at Enchantment Resort 525 Boynton Canyon Rd	Sedona	AZ	86336	**888-749-2137**	928-203-8500	705
Mijac Alarm 9339 Charles Smith Ave Ste 100	Rancho Cucamonga	CA	91730	**800-982-7612**	909-982-7612	691
Mikan Associates Consulting 141 W Jackson Blvd Ste 1520	Chicago	IL	60604	**888-902-1970**	847-613-6010	462
Mikart Inc 1750 Chattahoochee Ave NW	Atlanta	GA	30318	**888-464-5278**	404-351-4510	582
Mike Castrucci Ford Sales Inc 1020 SR- 28	Milford	OH	45150	**855-902-6741**	513-831-7010	515
Mike Davis & Associates Inc 15505 Long Vista Dr # 200	Austin	TX	78728	**888-836-8442**	512-836-8442	344
Mike Durfee State Prison 1412 Wood St	Springfield	SD	57062	**800-537-0025**	605-369-2201	215
Mike Moss Agency Inc 803 S Dogwood	Siloam Springs	AR	72761	**800-447-0163**	479-524-5111	390
Mike Murach & Assoc Inc 4340 N Knoll	Fresno	CA	93722	**800-221-5528**	559-440-9071	634-2
Mike Reed Chevrolet 1559 E Oglethorpe	Hinesville	GA	31313	**877-228-3943**		56
Mike Rose's Auto Body Inc 2260 Via de Marcardos	Concord	CA	94520	**855-340-1739**	925-689-1739	61-4
Miken Builders Inc 32782 Cedar Dr Unit 1	Millville	DE	19967	**800-888-7501**	302-537-4444	683
Mike-Sell's Potato Chip Co 333 Leo St PO Box 115	Dayton	OH	45404	**800-257-4742**	937-228-9400	297-35
Mikimoto (America) Company Ltd 680 Fifth Ave 4th Fl	New York	NY	10019	**844-341-0579**	212-457-4500	411
Mikros Engineering Inc 8755 Wyoming Ave N	Brooklyn Park	MN	55445	**800-394-5499**	763-424-4642	263
Mil Corp 4000 Mitchellville Rd	Bowie	MD	20716	**800-875-0867**	301-805-8500	179
Mila Displays Inc 1315B Broadway Ste 108	Hewlett	NY	11557	**800-295-6452**	516-791-2643	5
Milaeger's Inc 4838 Douglas Ave	Racine	WI	53402	**800-669-1229**	262-639-2040	324
Milan Express Company Inc 1091 Kefauver Dr	Milan	TN	38358	**800-231-7303**	731-686-7428	778
Milbank Tweed Hadley & McCloy LLP 1 Chase Manhattan Plaza	New York	NY	10005	**800-229-0543**	212-530-5000	428
Milbar Hydro-Test Inc 651 Aero Dr	Shreveport	LA	71107	**800-259-8210**	318-227-8210	538
Mile High Shooting Accessories LLC 3731 Monarch St	Erie	CO	80516	**877-871-9990**	303-255-9999	227
Mile Marker International Inc 2121 BLOUNT Rd	Pompano Beach	FL	33069	**800-886-8647**		60
Miles & More PO Box 946	Santa Clarita	CA	91380	**800-581-6400**		26
Miles College 5500 Myron Massey Blvd *Admissions	Fairfield	AL	35064	**800-445-0708***	205-929-1000	167
Miles Community College 2715 Dickinson St	Miles City	MT	59301	**800-541-9281**	406-874-6100	161
Miles Kimball Co 250 City Ctr Bldg *Cust Svc	Oshkosh	WI	54906	**855-202-7394***	920-231-3800	458
Miles Media Group Inc 6751 Professional Pkwy W Ste 200	Sarasota	FL	34240	**888-232-2499**	941-342-2300	634-9
Miles Technologies Inc 300 W Route 38	Moorestown	NJ	08057	**800-496-8001**	856-439-0999	182

Name / Address	City	State	ZIP	Toll-Free	Phone	Class
MilesTek Corp 1506 Interstate 35 W	Denton	TX	76207	**800-958-5173**	940-484-9400	196
Milestone Contractors LP 3410 S 650 E	Elizabethtown	IN	47232	**800-377-7727**	812-579-5248	190-4
Milestone Scientific Inc 220 S Orange Ave *OTC: MLSS*	Livingston	NJ	07039	**800-862-1125**	973-535-2717	476
Milford Bank 33 Broad St	Milford	CT	06460	**800-340-4862**	203-783-5700	69
Milford Daily News Co 197 Main St	Milford	MA	01757	**800-281-6498**	508-634-7522	634-8
Milford Federal Savings & Loan Assn PO Box 210	Milford	MA	01757	**800-478-6990**	508-634-2500	70
Milford Mirror 1000 Bridgeport Ave *Advestisement	Shelton	CT	06484	**800-372-2790***	203-402-2315	531-4
Milford-Miami Township Chamber of Commerce 983 Lila Ave	Milford	OH	45150	**877-723-0513**	513-831-2411	138
Milgram & Company Ltd 400 - 645 Wellington	Montreal	QC	H3C0L1	**800-879-6144**	514-288-2161	315
Military Benefit Assn (MBA) 14605 Avion Pkwy PO Box 221110	Chantilly	VA	20153	**800-336-0100**	703-968-6200	47-19
Military Officers Assn of America (MOAA) 201 N Washington St	Alexandria	VA	22314	**800-234-6622**	703-549-2311	47-19
Military Sealift Command 914 Charles Morris Ct SE Washington Navy Yard	Washington	DC	20398	**800-793-5784**		340-5
Milk Industry Foundation (MIF) 1250 H St NW Ste 900	Washington	DC	20005	**866-225-4821**	202-737-4332	47-2
Milk Products LLC PO Box 150	Chilton	WI	53014	**800-657-0793**	920-849-2348	297-10
Milk Specialties Co 7500 Flying Cloud Dr Ste 500	Eden Prairie	MN	55344	**800-323-4274**	952-942-7310	446
Milkco Inc 220 Deaverview Rd	Asheville	NC	28806	**800-842-8021**	828-254-9560	297-27
Mill City Museum 704 S Second St	Minneapolis	MN	55401	**800-657-3773**	612-341-7555	519
Mill Creek Mall 654 Millcreek Mall	Erie	PA	16565	**800-615-3535**	814-868-9000	459
Mill Ridge Farm 2800 Bowman Mill Rd	Lexington	KY	40513	**800-950-6397**	859-231-0606	368
Mill Steel Co 5116 36th St SE	Grand Rapids	MI	49512	**800-247-6455**		721
Mill Street Inn 75 Mill St	Newport	RI	02840	**800-392-1316**	401-849-9500	379
Mill Supply Div 266 Morse St *General	Hamden	CT	06517	**888-585-9354***	203-777-7668	86
Mill Valley Inn 165 Throckmorton Ave	Mill Valley	CA	94941	**855-334-7946**	415-389-6608	379
Mill33 Inc 848 Elm St Ste 301	Manchester	NH	03101	**888-603-2336**		197
Millard Lumber Inc 12900 I St PO Box 45445	Omaha	NE	68145	**800-228-9260**	402-896-2800	193-3
Millcraft Paper Co 6800 Grant Ave	Cleveland	OH	44105	**800-860-2482**	216-441-5500	552
Mille Lacs Band of Ojibwe 43408 Oodena Dr	Onamia	MN	56359	**800-709-6445**	320-532-4181	131
Mille Lacs Electric Co-op PO Box 230	Aitkin	MN	56431	**800-450-2191**	218-927-2191	247
Mille Lacs Health System 200 Elm St N	Onamia	MN	56359	**877-535-3154**	320-532-3154	374-3
Millennium Broadway Hotel New York 145 W 44th St	New York	NY	10036	**800-622-5569**	212-768-4400	377
Millennium Resort Scottsdale McCormick Ranch 7401 N Scottsdale Rd	Scottsdale	AZ	85253	**800-243-1332**	716-681-2400	667
Miller & Chevalier Chartered 655 15th St NW Ste 900	Washington	DC	20005	**866-628-4282**	202-626-5800	428
Miller & Co LLC 9700 W Higgins Rd Ste 1000	Rosemont	IL	60018	**800-727-9847**	847-696-2400	499
Miller Chemical & Fertilizer Corp 120 Radio Rd PO Box 333	Hanover	PA	17331	**800-233-2040**	717-632-8921	282
Miller Consolidated Industries Inc 2221 Arbor Blvd	Dayton	OH	45439	**800-589-4133**	937-294-2681	483
Miller Electric Co 2251 Rosselle St *Sales	Jacksonville	FL	32204	**877-540-2160***	904-513-2818	191-4
Miller Electric Mfg Co 1635 W Spencer St	Appleton	WI	54914	**888-843-7693**	920-734-9821	809
Miller Engineers & Scientists 5308 S 12th St	Sheboygan	WI	53081	**800-969-7013**	920-458-6164	263
Miller Industries Inc 8503 Hilltop Dr *NYSE: MLR*	Ooltewah	TN	37363	**800-292-0330**	423-238-4171	515
Miller Johnson Snell & Cummiskey PLC 250 Monroe Ave NW Ste 800 PO Box 306	Grand Rapids	MI	49503	**800-772-1213**	616-831-1700	428
Miller Packing Co 1122 Industrial Way PO Box 1390	Lodi	CA	95241	**800-624-2328**	209-339-2310	297-26
Miller Pipeline Corp 8850 Crawfordsville Rd	Indianapolis	IN	46234	**800-428-3742**	317-293-0278	190-10
Miller Products Company Inc 2511 S Tricenter Blvd	Durham	NC	27713	**800-782-7437**	919-313-2100	575
Miller Saint Nazianz Inc 511 E Main St	Saint Nazianz	WI	54232	**800-247-5557**	920-773-2121	275
Miller Studio 734 Fair Ave NW	New Philadelphia	OH	44663	**800-332-0050**	330-339-1100	499
Miller Thomson LLP Scotia Plz 40 King St W Ste 5800	Toronto	ON	M5H3S1	**888-762-5559**	416-595-8500	40
Miller Transporters Inc 5500 Hwy 80 W *Cust Svc	Jackson	MS	39209	**800-645-5378***	601-922-8331	778
Miller Travel Services Inc 4380 W 12th St	Erie	PA	16505	**800-989-8747**	814-833-8888	769
Miller Valentine Group 4000 Miller Valentine Ct	Dayton	OH	45439	**877-684-7687**	937-293-0900	653

Name / Address	City	State	ZIP	Toll-Free	Phone	Class
Miller-Eads Company Inc 4125 N Keystone Ave	Indianapolis	IN	46205	**800-530-0684**	317-545-7101	785
Miller-Leaman 800 Orange Ave	Daytona Beach	FL	32114	**800-881-0320**	386-248-0500	695
Miller-Lewis Benefit Consultants 121 E Sixth Ave	Lancaster	OH	43130	**800-734-3198**	740-654-4055	390
Millers First Insurance Co 111 E Fourth St	Alton	IL	62002	**800-558-0500**	618-463-3636	391-4
Miller-Stephenson Chemical Co 55 Backus Ave *Tech Supp	Danbury	CT	06810	**800-992-2424***	203-743-4447	144
Millersville University of Pennsylvania PO Box 1002 PO Box 1002	Millersville	PA	17551	**800-682-3648**	717-872-3011	167
Milligan College PO Box 500	Milligan College	TN	37682	**800-262-8337**	423-461-8730	167
Milliken & Co KEX Div PO Box 1926 MS 801	Spartanburg	SC	29304	**800-241-4826**	706-880-5511	130
Milliken Millwork Inc 6361 Sterling Dr N	Sterling Heights	MI	48312	**800-686-9218**	586-264-0950	498
Millikin University 1184 W Main St	Decatur	IL	62522	**800-373-7733**	217-424-6211	167
Million Air 4300 Westgrove Dr	Addison	TX	75001	**800-248-1602**	972-248-1600	62
Million Air Interlink Inc 8501 Telephone Rd	Houston	TX	77061	**888-589-9059**	713-640-4000	24
Million Dollar Round Table (MDRT) 325 W Touhy Ave *General	Park Ridge	IL	60068	**877-883-4865***	847-692-6378	48-9
Mill-Max Mfg Corp 190 Pine Hollow Rd	Oyster Bay	NY	11771	**800-333-4237**	516-922-6000	813
Mill-Rose Co 7995 Tyler Blvd	Mentor	OH	44060	**800-321-3533**	440-255-9171	102
Mills at Jersey Gardens, The 651 Kapkowski Rd	Elizabeth	NJ	07201	**877-789-2327**	908-354-5900	459
Mills College 5000 MacArthur Blvd *Admissions	Oakland	CA	94613	**877-746-4557***	510-430-2135	167
Mills House Hotel 115 Meeting St	Charleston	SC	29401	**800-874-9600**	843-577-2400	379
Mills Iron Works Inc 14834 Maple Ave	Gardena	CA	90248	**800-421-2281**	323-321-6520	594
Millsaps College 1701 N State St *Admissions	Jackson	MS	39210	**800-352-1050***	601-974-1000	167
Millsite State Park Ferron Canyon Rd PO Box 1343	Huntington	UT	84528	**800-322-3770**	435-384-2552	564
Milner Hotel Boston 78 Charles St S	Boston	MA	02116	**877-645-6377**	617-426-6220	379
Milner Hotels Inc 1538 Centre St	Detroit	MI	48226	**877-645-6377**	313-963-3950	379
Milner Technologies Inc 5125 Peachtree Industrial Blvd	Norcross	GA	30092	**800-592-3766**	770-734-5300	180-1
Milpitas Post 59 Marylinn Dr	Milpitas	CA	95035	**800-870-6397**	408-262-2454	531-4
Milsco Mfg Co 9009 N 51st St	Milwaukee	WI	53223	**800-255-0337**	414-354-0500	687
Milton Hershey School PO Box 830	Hershey	PA	17033	**800-322-3248**	717-520-2100	621
Miltons Inc 250 Granite St	Braintree	MA	02184	**888-645-8667**	781-848-1880	156-3
Milwaukee Area Technical College 700 W State St	Milwaukee	WI	53233	**866-211-3380**	414-297-6600	798
Milwaukee Art Museum 700 N Art Museum Dr	Milwaukee	WI	53202	**888-322-3326**	414-224-3200	519
Milwaukee Ballet 504 W National Ave	Milwaukee	WI	53204	**888-612-3500**	414-643-7677	572-1
Milwaukee Brewers Miller Pk 1 Brewers Way	Milwaukee	WI	53214	**877-722-6458**	414-902-4452	711
Milwaukee Coast Guard Base 2420 S Lincoln Memorial Dr	Milwaukee	WI	53207	**866-772-8724**	414-747-7100	157
Milwaukee Electric Tool Corp 13135 W Lisbon Rd	Brookfield	WI	53005	**800-729-3878**	262-781-3600	757
Milwaukee Institute of Art & Design 273 E Erie St	Milwaukee	WI	53202	**888-749-6423**	414-276-7889	167
Milwaukee Journal Sentinel 333 W State St	Milwaukee	WI	53201	**800-456-5943**	414-224-2000	531-2
Milwaukee Magazine 126 N Jefferson St	Milwaukee	WI	53202	**800-662-4818**	414-273-1101	456-22
Milwaukee Public Library 814 W Wisconsin Ave	Milwaukee	WI	53233	**866-947-7363**	414-286-3000	434-3
Milwaukee School of Engineering 1025 N Broadway St	Milwaukee	WI	53202	**800-332-6763**	414-277-6763	167
Milwaukee Symphony Orchestra 1101 N Market St STE 100	Milwaukee	WI	53202	**888-367-8101**	414-273-7121	572-3
Milwaukee Valve Company Inc 16550 W Stratton Dr	New Berlin	WI	53151	**800-348-6544**	262-432-2800	787
Milwaukee Wave LLC 510 W Kilbourn Ave	Milwaukee	WI	53203	**800-745-3000**	414-224-9283	715
Milwhite Inc 5487 S Padre Island Hwy	Brownsville	TX	78521	**800-442-0082**	956-547-1970	502-2
MiMedx Group Inc 1775 W Oak Commons Ct Ne	Marietta	GA	30062	**888-543-1917**		475
MIN (Media Industry Newsletter) 110 William St 11th Fl	New York	NY	10038	**888-707-5814**	212-621-4880	530-11
Mind Your Business Inc (myb) 305 Eighth Ave E	Hendersonville	NC	28792	**888-869-2462**		262
Mindbody Online 4051 Broad St Ste 220	Sn Luis Obisp	CA	93401	**877-755-4279**		396
Mindgrub Technologies LLC 1215 E Ft Ave Ste 200	Baltimore	MD	21230	**855-646-3472**	410-988-2444	4
Mindjet Corp 1160 Battery St E 4th Fl	San Francisco	CA	94111	**877-646-3538**	415-229-4200	180-12
MindLeaders.com Inc 5500 Glendon Ct Ste 200	Dublin	OH	43016	**800-223-3732**	614-781-7300	762
MindPlay Educational Software 440 S Williams Blvd Ste 206	Tucson	AZ	85711	**800-221-7911**	520-888-1800	180-3

Name / Address	City	State	ZIP	Toll-Free	Phone	Class
MindSpark International Inc						
1205 Peachtree Pkwy Ste 1204	Cumming	GA	30041	**888-820-3616**		198
Mine & Mill Industrial Supply Company Inc						
2500 S Combee Rd	Lakeland	FL	33801	**800-282-8489**	863-665-5601	188
Mine Safety & Health Administration (MSHA)						
1100 Wilson Blvd	Arlington	VA	22209	**800-746-1553**	202-693-9400	340-13
Miner Enterprises Inc						
1200 E State St	Geneva	IL	60134	**888-822-5334**	630-232-3000	648
Mineral Resources International						
1990 W 3300 S	Ogden	UT	84401	**800-731-7866**	801-731-7040	298-8
Mineral Wells Area Chamber of Commerce						
511 E Hubbard St	Mineral Wells	TX	76067	**800-252-6989**	940-325-2557	138
Minerals Metals & Materials Society (TMS)						
184 Thorn Hill Rd	Warrendale	PA	15086	**800-759-4867**	724-776-9000	48-13
Minerva Networks Inc						
2150 Gold St	Santa Clara	CA	95002	**800-806-9594**	408-567-9400	645
Mines Press Inc, The						
231 Croton Ave	Cortlandt Manor	NY	10567	**800-447-6788**	914-788-1698	626
Mingan Archipelago National Park Reserve of Canada						
1340 de la Digue St	Havre-Saint-Pierre	QC	G0G1P0	**877-737-3783**	418-538-3331	562
Mini-Circuits Laboratories Inc						
13 Neptune Ave	Brooklyn	NY	11235	**800-654-7949**	718-934-4500	694
Ministry of Tourism of Dominican Republic						
848 Brickell Ave	Miami	FL	33131	**888-358-9594**	305-358-2899	773
Minitab Inc						
Quality Plz 1829 Pine Hall Rd	State College	PA	16801	**800-448-3555**	814-238-3280	180-10
Minka Group						
1151 W Bradford Ct	Corona	CA	92882	**800-221-7977**	951-735-9220	439
Minn-Dak Yeast Company Inc						
18175 Red River Rd W	Wahpeton	ND	58075	**800-348-0991**	701-642-3300	297-42
Minneapolis College of Art & Design						
2501 Stevens Ave	Minneapolis	MN	55404	**800-874-6223**	612-874-3760	163
Minneapolis Community & Technical College						
1501 Hennepin Ave	Minneapolis	MN	55403	**800-247-0911**	612-659-6200	161
Minneapolis Foundation						
80 S Eigth St 800 IDS Ctr	Minneapolis	MN	55402	**866-305-0543**	612-672-3878	304
Minneapolis Grain Exchange						
400 S Fourth St 130 Grain Exchange Bldg	Minneapolis	MN	55415	**800-827-4746**	612-321-7101	689
Minneapolis Institute of Arts						
2400 Third Ave S	Minneapolis	MN	55404	**888-642-2787**	612-870-3000	519
Minneapolis Northwest						
6200 Shingle Creek Pkwy Ste 130	Brooklyn Center	MN	55430	**800-541-4364**	763-852-7500	208
Minneapolis Public Schools						
3345 Chicago Ave	Minneapolis	MN	55407	**800-543-7709**	612-668-0000	683
Minneapolis/St. Paul City Pages						
401 N Third St Ste 550	Minneapolis	MN	55401	**844-387-6962**	612-375-1015	531-5
Minneapolis-Saint Paul Magazine						
220 S Sixth St Ste 500	Minneapolis	MN	55402	**800-999-5589**	612-339-7571	456-22
Minnesota						
Aging Board 540 Cedar St	Saint Paul	MN	55155	**800-882-6262**	651-431-2500	339-24
Arts Board 400 Sibley St Ste 200	Saint Paul	MN	55101	**800-866-2787**	651-215-1600	339-24
Attorney General 1400 Bremer Tower 445 Minnesota St	Saint Paul	MN	55101	**800-657-3787**	651-296-3353	339-24
Attorney General's Office 445 Minnesota St Ste 1400	Saint Paul	MN	55101	**800-657-3787**	651-296-3353	339-24
Employment & Economic Development Dept (DEED) 1st National Bank Bldg 332 Minnesota St Ste E200	Saint Paul	MN	55101	**800-657-3858**	651-259-7114	339-24
Finance Dept 658 Cedar St Ste 400	Saint Paul	MN	55155	**800-627-3529**	651-201-8000	339-24
Governor 130 State Capitol 75 Rev Dr Martin Luther King Jr Blvd.	Saint Paul	MN	55155	**800-657-3717**	651-201-3400	339-24
Health Dept PO Box 64975	Saint Paul	MN	55164	**888-345-0823**	651-201-5000	339-24
Historical Society 345 Kellogg Blvd W	Saint Paul	MN	55102	**800-657-3773**	651-259-3000	339-24
Housing Finance Authority 400 Sibley St Ste 300	Saint Paul	MN	55101	**800-657-3769**	651-296-7608	339-24
Labor & Industry Dept 443 Lafayette Rd N	Saint Paul	MN	55155	**800-342-5354**	651-284-5005	339-24
Legislature 75 Constitution Ave State Capitol	Saint Paul	MN	55155	**800-657-3550**	651-296-2146	339-24
Medical Practice Board 2829 University Ave SE Ste 500	Minneapolis	MN	55414	**800-657-3709**	612-617-2130	339-24
Natural Resources Dept 500 Lafayette Rd	Saint Paul	MN	55155	**888-646-6367**	651-296-6157	339-24
Parks & Recreation Div 500 Lafayette Rd	Saint Paul	MN	55155	**888-646-6367**	651-296-6157	339-24
Public Utilities Commission 121 Seventh Pl E Ste 350	Saint Paul	MN	55101	**800-657-3782**	651-296-7124	339-24
Revenue Dept 600 N Roberts St	Saint Paul	MN	55101	**800-652-9094**	651-296-3403	339-24
Transportation Dept 395 John Ireland Blvd	Saint Paul	MN	55155	**800-657-3774**	651-296-3000	339-24
Workers" Compensation Div 443 Lafayette Rd	Saint Paul	MN	55155	**800-342-5354**	651-284-5005	339-24
Minnesota Assn of Realtors						
5750 Lincoln Dr	Minneapolis	MN	55436	**800-862-6097**	952-935-8313	654
Minnesota Ballet						
301 W First St Ste 800	Duluth	MN	55802	**800-627-3529**	218-529-3742	572-1
Minnesota Campaign Finance & Public Disclosure Board						
658 Cedar St Ste 190	Saint Paul	MN	55155	**800-657-3889**	651-296-5148	267
Minnesota Chamber of Commerce						
400 Robert St N Ste 1500	Saint Paul	MN	55101	**800-821-2230**	651-292-4650	139
Minnesota Chemical Co						
2285 Hampden Ave	Saint Paul	MN	55114	**800-328-5689**	651-646-7521	427
Minnesota Correctional Facility-Fairbault						
1101 Linden Ln	Faribault	MN	55021	**800-657-3830**	507-334-0700	215
Minnesota Dental Assn						
1335 Industrial Blvd Ste 200	Minneapolis	MN	55413	**800-950-3368**	612-767-8400	229
Minnesota Discovery Ctr						
1005 Discovery Dr	Chisholm	MN	55719	**800-372-6437**	218-254-7959	519
Minnesota Educator Magazine						
41 Sherburne Ave	Saint Paul	MN	55103	**800-652-9073**	651-227-9541	456-8
Minnesota Eye Consultants PA						
710 E 24th St Ste 100	Minneapolis	MN	55404	**800-526-7632**	612-813-3600	796
Minnesota Historical Society History Ctr Museum						
345 Kellogg Blvd W	Saint Paul	MN	55102	**800-657-3773**	651-259-3001	519
Minnesota Lawyers Mutual Insurance Co						
333 S Seventh St Ste 2200	Minneapolis	MN	55402	**800-422-1370**		390
Minnesota Lions Eye Bank						
1000 Westgate Dr Ste 260 *Cust Svc	Saint paul	MN	55114	**866-887-4448***	612-625-5159	271
Minnesota Nurses Assn (MNA)						
345 Randolph Ave Ste 200	Saint Paul	MN	55102	**800-536-4662**	651-646-4807	532
Minnesota Office of Higher Education						
1450 Energy Pk Dr Ste 350	Saint Paul	MN	55108	**800-657-3866**	651-642-0567	723
Minnesota Opera						
620 N First St	Minneapolis	MN	55401	**800-676-6737**	612-333-2700	572-2
Minnesota Orchestra						
1111 Nicollet Mall Orchestra Hall	Minneapolis	MN	55403	**800-292-4141**	612-371-5600	572-3
Minnesota Pharmacists Assn (MPhA)						
1935 W County Rd B2	Roseville	MN	55113	**800-451-8349**	651-697-1771	584
Minnesota Power						
30 W Superior St	Duluth	MN	55802	**800-228-4966**	218-722-2625	785
Minnesota Public Radio (MPR)						
480 Cedar St	Saint Paul	MN	55101	**800-228-7123**	651-290-1212	629
Minnesota State Bar Assn						
600 Nicollet Mall Ste 380	Minneapolis	MN	55402	**800-882-6722**	612-333-1183	71
Minnesota State Community & Technical College						
Detroit Lakes 900 Hwy 34E	Detroit Lakes	MN	56501	**800-492-4836**	218-846-3700	161
Fergus Falls 1414 College Way	Fergus Falls	MN	56537	**877-450-3322**	218-736-1500	161
Moorhead 1900 28th Ave S	Moorhead	MN	56560	**800-426-5603**	218-299-6500	161
Minnesota State University						
Mankato 122 Taylor Ctr *Admissions	Mankato	MN	56001	**800-722-0544***	507-389-1822	167
Moorhead 1104 Seventh Ave S	Moorhead	MN	56563	**800-593-7246**	218-477-2161	167
Minnesota State University Mankato						
Memorial Library PO Box 8419	Mankato	MN	56002	**800-722-0544**	507-389-5952	434-6
Minnesota State University Moorhead Regional Science Ctr						
1104 Seventh Ave S	Moorhead	MN	56563	**800-593-7246**	218-477-2920	519
Minnesota Supply Company Inc						
6470 Flying Cloud Dr	Eden Prairie	MN	55344	**800-869-1028**	952-828-7300	385
Minnesota Timberwolves						
Target Ctr 600 First Ave N	Minneapolis	MN	55403	**855-895-0872**	612-673-1600	712-1
Minnesota Twins						
Metrodome 34 Kirby Puckett Pl	Minneapolis	MN	55415	**800-338-9467**	612-375-1366	711
Minnesota Valley Co-op Light & Power Assn						
501 S First St	Montevideo	MN	56265	**800-247-5051**	320-269-2163	247
Minnesota Valley Electric Co-op						
125 Minnesota Vly Electric Dr PO Box 77024	Jordan	MN	55352	**800-282-6832**	952-492-2313	247
Minnesota Veterans Home-Minneapolis						
5101 Minnehaha Ave S	Minneapolis	MN	55407	**877-838-6757**	612-721-0600	791
Minnesota Veterans Home-Silver Bay						
45 Banks Blvd	Silver Bay	MN	55614	**877-729-8387**	218-226-6300	791
Minnesota Veterinary Medical Assn						
101 Bridgepoint Way Ste 100	South Saint Paul	MN	55075	**888-933-5363**	651-645-7533	793
Minnesota Vikings						
9520 Viking Dr	Eden Prairie	MN	55344	**877-722-6458**	952-828-6500	713-3
Minnesota West Community & Technical College						
1450 Collegeway	Worthington	MN	56187	**800-657-3966**	507-372-3400	161
Minnesota Wild						
317 Washington St	Saint Paul	MN	55102	**866-242-5006**	651-602-6000	714
Minnesota Wire & Cable Co						
1835 Energy Pk Dr	Saint Paul	MN	55108	**800-258-6922**	651-642-1800	813
Minnesota Zoo						
13000 Zoo Blvd	Apple Valley	MN	55124	**800-366-7811**	952-431-9200	821
Minntech Corp						
14605 28th Ave N	Minneapolis	MN	55447	**800-328-3345**	763-553-3300	475
Minor Rubber Company Inc						
49 Ackerman St	Bloomfield	NJ	07003	**800-433-6886**	973-338-6800	675
Minority Business Development Agency Regional Offices						
Chicago Region 105 W Adams St Ste 2300	Chicago	IL	60603	**888-324-1551**	312-353-0182	340-2
Minot Convention & Visitors Bureau						
1020 S Broadway	Minot	ND	58701	**800-264-2626**	701-857-8206	208
Minot State University						
500 University Ave W	Minot	ND	58707	**800-777-0750**	701-858-3000	167
Minot State University Bottineau						
105 Simrall Blvd	Bottineau	ND	58318	**800-542-6866**	701-228-5451	161
Minova USA Inc						
150 Carley Ct	Georgetown	KY	40324	**800-626-2948**	502-863-6800	604-2
Minskoff Theatre						
200 W 45th St	New York	NY	10036	**800-714-8452**	212-869-0550	744
Minson Corp						
1 Minson Way	Montebello	CA	90640	**800-251-6537**	323-513-1041	320-4
Mintie Corp						
1114 San Fernando Rd	Los Angeles	CA	90065	**800-964-6843**	323-225-4111	34
Minto Place Suite Hotel						
185 Lyons St N	Ottawa	ON	K1R7Y4	**800-267-3377**	613-232-2200	379
Minus Forty Technologies Corp						
30 Armstrong Ave	Georgetown	ON	L7G4R9	**800-800-5706**	905-702-1441	663
Minute Maid Park						
501 Crawford St	Houston	TX	77002	**877-927-8767**	713-259-8000	718
Minute Men Staffing Services						
3740 Carnegie Ave	Cleveland	OH	44115	**877-873-8856**	216-426-9675	719

Name / Address	City	State	ZIP	Toll-Free	Phone	Class
Minuteman International Inc						
111 S Rohlwing Rd	Addison	IL	60101	**800-323-9420**	630-627-6900	386
Minuteman Press International Inc						
61 Executive Blvd	Farmingdale	NY	11735	**800-645-3006**	631-249-1370	311
Minuteman Trucks Inc						
2181 Providence Hwy	Walpole	MA	02081	**800-231-8458**	508-668-3112	778
Minvalco Inc						
3340 Gorham Ave	Minneapolis	MN	55426	**800-642-9090**	952-920-0131	611
Minwax Co						
10 Mountainview Rd	Upper Saddle River	NJ	07458	**800-523-9299**		549
Mio 2930 Arbutus St	Vancouver	BC	V6J3Y9	**877-770-1116**	604-224-9184	474
MIR (Manager's Intelligence Report)						
316 N Michigan Ave Ste 400	Chicago	IL	60601	**800-878-5331**		530-2
Mira Monte Inn & Suites						
69 Mt Desert St	Bar Harbor	ME	04609	**800-553-5109**		379
Mirabeau Park Hotel						
1100 N Sullivan Rd	Spokane Valley	WA	99037	**866-584-4674**	509-924-9000	379
Mirabito Fuel Group Inc						
49 Ct St PO Box 5306	Binghamton	NY	13902	**800-934-9480**	607-352-2800	317
Miracle Method US Corp						
4239 N Nevada Ave Ste 115	Colorado Springs	CO	80907	**800-444-8827**	719-594-9091	191-11
Miracle Mile Shops at Planet Hollywood						
3663 Las Vegas Blvd S	Las Vegas	NV	89109	**888-800-8284**	702-866-0703	49-5
Miracle Recreation Equipment Co						
878 Hwy 60	Monett	MO	65708	**800-523-4202**	417-235-6917	346
Miracle-Ear Inc						
5000 Cheshire Pkwy N	Minneapolis	MN	55446	**800-464-8002**		476
MiraCosta College						
Oceanside						
1 Barnard Dr Ste 7	Oceanside	CA	92056	**888-201-8480**	760-757-2121	161
San Elijo						
3333 Manchester Ave	Cardiff	CA	92007	**888-201-8480**	760-944-4449	161
Mirage, The						
3400 Las Vegas Blvd S	Las Vegas	NV	89109	**800-627-6667**	702-791-7111	667
Miramar Federal Credit Union						
9494 Miramar Rd	San Diego	CA	92196	**800-640-1228**	858-695-9494	221
Miramont Castle Museum						
9 Capitol Hill Ave	Manitou Springs	CO	80829	**888-685-1011**	719-685-1011	519
Miramonte Resort & Spa						
45000 Indian Wells Ln	Indian Wells	CA	92210	**800-237-2926**	760-341-2200	667
Miratel Solutions Inc						
2501 Steeles Ave W	North York	ON	M3J2P1	**866-647-2835**	416-650-7850	734
Miraval AZ Resort & Spa						
5000 E Via Estancia Miraval	Tucson	AZ	85739	**800-232-3969**		704
Mirbeau Inn & Spa						
851 W Genesee St	Skaneateles	NY	13152	**877-647-2328**	315-685-5006	379
Mircom Technologies Ltd						
25 Interchange Way	Vaughan	ON	L4K5W3	**888-660-4655**	905-660-4655	691
Mirror Image Internet Inc						
2 Highwood Dr	Tewksbury	MA	01876	**800-353-2923**	781-376-1100	180-7
Mirrotek International LLC						
90 Dayton Ave	Passaic	NJ	07055	**888-659-3030**	973-472-1400	543
Mirus International Inc						
31 Sun Pac Blvd	Brampton	ON	L6S5P6	**888-866-4787**	905-494-1120	765
Misericordia University						
301 Lake St	Dallas	PA	18612	**866-262-6363**	570-674-6400	167
Miskelly Furniture						
101 Airport Rd	Jackson	MS	39208	**888-939-6288**	601-939-6288	322
Misonix Inc						
1938 NEW Hwy	Farmingdale	NY	11735	**800-694-9612**	631-694-9555	252
Miss Elaine Inc						
8430 Valcour Ave	Saint Louis	MO	63123	**800-458-1422**	314-631-1900	154-14
MISS Foundation						
PO Box 5333	Peoria	AZ	85385	**888-455-6477**	623-979-1000	47-21
Mission Ambulance						
1055 E Third St	Corona	CA	92879	**800-899-9100**		30
Mission Aviation Fellowship (MAF)						
112 N Pilatus Ln	Nampa	ID	83687	**800-359-7623**	208-498-0800	47-20
Mission Essential Personnel LLC						
4343 Easton Commons Ste 100	Columbus	OH	43219	**888-542-3447**	614-416-2345	764
Mission Federal Credit Union						
PO Box 919023	San Diego	CA	92121	**800-500-6328**	858-524-2850	221
Mission Foods						
1159 Cottonwood Ln Ste 200	Irving	TX	75038	**800-443-7994**	972-232-5000	297-35
Mission Golf Cars						
18865 Redland Rd	San Antonio	TX	78259	**800-324-7868**	210-545-7868	56
Mission Inn						
3649 Mission Inn Ave	Riverside	CA	92501	**800-843-7755**	951-784-0300	379
Mission Inn Resort & Club						
10400 County Rd 48	Howey in the Hills	FL	34737	**800-874-9053**	352-324-3101	667
Mission Landscape Services Inc						
536 E Dyer Rd	Santa Ana	CA	92707	**800-545-9963**		422
Mission of Nombre de Dios & Shrine of Our Lady of La Leche						
27 Ocean Ave	Saint Augustine	FL	32084	**800-342-6529**	904-824-2809	49
Mission Petroleum Carriers Inc						
8450 Mosley	Houston	TX	77075	**800-737-9911**	713-943-8250	467
Mission Pharmacal						
PO Box 786099	San Antonio	TX	78278	**800-531-3333**	210-696-8400	582
Mission Pharmacy Services LLC						
201 N Jefferson St Ste 300	Kittanning	PA	16201	**877-758-2039**		239
Mission Point Resort						
6633 Main St	Mackinac Island	MI	49757	**800-833-7711**		667
Mission Valley Ford Truck Sales Inc						
780 E Brokaw Rd	San Jose	CA	95112	**888-284-7471**	408-933-2300	56
Mission Wealth Management LLC						
1123 Chapala St 3rd Fl	Santa Barbara	CA	93101	**888-642-7221**	805-882-2360	401
Mississippi						
Banking & Consumer Finance Dept						
PO Box 23729	Jackson	MS	39225	**800-844-2499**	601-359-1031	339-25
Child Support Enforcement Div						
750 N State St	Jackson	MS	39202	**800-345-6347**	601-359-4929	339-25
Consumer Protection Div						
PO Box 22947	Jackson	MS	39225	**800-281-4418**	601-359-4230	339-25
Contractors Board						
215 Woodline Dr Ste B	Jackson	MS	39232	**800-880-6161**	601-354-6161	339-25
Emergency Management Agency						
PO Box 5644	Pearl	MS	39288	**800-222-6362**	601-933-6362	339-25
Family & Children Services Div						
750 N State St	Jackson	MS	39202	**800-345-6347**	601-359-4570	339-25
Higher Learning Institutions Board of Trustees						
3825 Ridgewood Rd Ste 915	Jackson	MS	39211	**800-327-2980**	601-432-6198	339-25
Insurance Dept						
1001 Woolfolk State Office Bldg 501 NW St PO Box 79	Jackson	MS	39201	**800-562-2957**	601-359-3569	339-25
Rehabilitation Services Dept						
1281 Highway 51 PO Box 1698	Madison	MS	39110	**800-443-1000**		339-25
State Government Information						
200 S Lamar Ste 800	Jackson	MS	39201	**877-290-9487**	601-351-5023	339-25
Mississippi Action For Progress Inc (MAP)						
1751 Morson Rd	Jackson	MS	39209	**800-924-4615**	601-923-4100	146
Mississippi Agriculture & Forestry Museum/National Agricultural Aviation Museum						
1150 Lakeland Dr	Jackson	MS	39216	**800-844-8687**	601-359-1100	519
Mississippi Assn of Realtors						
4274 Lakeland Dr PO Box 321000	Jackson	MS	39232	**800-747-1103**	601-932-9325	654
Mississippi Authority for Educational Television						
3825 Ridgewood Rd	Jackson	MS	39211	**800-850-4406**	601-432-6565	629
Mississippi Blood Services						
115 Tree St	Flowood	MS	39232	**888-902-5663**	601-981-3232	88
Mississippi Business Journal						
200 N Congress St	Jackson	MS	39201	**800-283-4625**	601-364-1000	456-5
Mississippi Coast Coliseum & Convention Ctr						
2350 Beach Blvd	Biloxi	MS	39531	**800-726-2781**	228-594-3700	207
Mississippi College						
200 S Capitol St	Clinton	MS	39056	**800-738-1236**	601-925-3000	167
Mississippi County Electric Co-op						
510 N Broadway St	Blytheville	AR	72315	**800-439-4563**	870-763-4563	247
Mississippi Dental Assn						
439 B katherine Dr Ste C	Flowood	MS	39232	**866-982-0442**	601-664-9691	229
Mississippi Economic Council						
PO Box 23276	Jackson	MS	39225	**800-748-7626**	601-969-0022	139
Mississippi Employment Security Commission						
1235 Echelon Pkwy PO Box 1699	Jackson	MS	39215	**888-844-3577**	601-321-6000	261
Mississippi Gulf Coast Community College						
51 Main St PO Box 548	Perkinston	MS	39573	**866-735-1122**	601-928-5211	161
Jackson County						
2300 Hwy 90 PO Box 100	Gautier	MS	39553	**866-735-1122**	228-497-9602	161
Jefferson Davis						
2226 Switzer Rd	Gulfport	MS	39507	**866-735-1122**	228-896-3355	161
Mississippi Gulf Coast Convention & Visitors Bureau						
2350 Beach Blvd Ste A	Biloxi	MS	39531	**888-467-4853**	228-896-6699	208
Mississippi Museum of Art						
380 S Lamar St	Jackson	MS	39201	**866-843-9278**	601-960-1515	519
Mississippi Museum of Natural Science						
2148 Riverside Dr	Jackson	MS	39202	**800-467-2757**	601-576-6000	519
Mississippi Music Inc						
222 N Main St	Hattiesburg	MS	39401	**800-844-5821**	601-544-5821	524
Mississippi Pharmacists Assn						
341 Edgewood Terr Dr	Jackson	MS	39206	**800-421-2408**	601-981-0416	584
Mississippi River Museum						
125 N Front St	Memphis	TN	38103	**800-507-6507**	901-576-7241	519
Mississippi Sports Hall of Fame & Museum						
1152 Lakeland Dr	Jackson	MS	39216	**800-280-3263**	601-982-8264	521
Mississippi State Penitentiary						
Hwy 49 W PO Box 1057	Parchman	MS	38738	**800-844-0898**	662-745-6611	215
Mississippi State Port Authority at Gulfport						
2510 14th St Ste 1450	Gulfport	MS	39501	**877-881-4367**	228-865-4300	617
Mississippi State Veterans' Home Collins						
3261 Hwy 49 S	Collins	MS	39428	**877-203-5632**	601-765-0403	791
Mississippi State Veterans' Home Kosciusko						
310 Autumn Ridge Dr	Kosciusko	MS	39090	**877-203-5632**	662-289-7044	791
Mississippi Student Financial Aid Office						
3825 Ridgewood Rd	Jackson	MS	39211	**800-327-2980**	601-432-6997	723
Mississippi University for Women						
1100 College St MUW-1613	Columbus	MS	39701	**877-462-8439**	662-329-4750	167
Mississippi Valley Equipment Company Inc						
1198 Pershall Rd	Saint Louis	MO	63137	**800-325-8001**	314-869-8600	358
Mississippi Valley Regional Blood Ctr						
5500 Lakeview Pkwy	Davenport	IA	52807	**800-747-5401**	563-359-5401	88
Mississippi Valley State University						
14000 Hwy 82	Itta Bena	MS	38941	**800-844-6885**	662-254-9041	167
Mississippi Valley Title Insurance Co						
315 Tom Bigbee St	Jackson	MS	39201	**800-647-2124**	601-969-0222	391-6
Mississippi Welders Supply Co						
5150 W Sixth St	Winona	MN	55987	**800-657-4422**	507-454-5231	386
Missman Inc						
1011 27th Ave PO Box 6040	Rock Island	IL	61201	**800-969-3029**	309-788-7644	263
Missoula Area Chamber of Commerce						
825 E Front St	Missoula	MT	59802	**800-814-2342**	406-543-6623	138
Missoula Electric Co-op Inc						
1700 W Broadway	Missoula	MT	59808	**800-352-5200**	406-541-4433	247
Missoulian						
PO Box 8029	Missoula	MT	59807	**800-366-7102**	406-523-5200	531-2
Missouri						
Child Support Enforcement Div						
PO Box 109002	Jefferson City	MO	65102	**800-859-7999**		339-26
Consumer Protection Div						
207 W High St PO Box 899	Jefferson City	MO	65102	**800-392-8222**	573-751-3321	339-26
Elementary & Secondary Education Dept						
205 Jefferson St PO Box 480	Jefferson City	MO	65101	**800-735-2966**	573-751-4212	339-26
Finance Div						
PO Box 716	Jefferson City	MO	65102	**888-246-7225**	573-751-3242	339-26
Higher Education Dept						
3515 Amazonas Dr	Jefferson City	MO	65109	**800-473-6757**	573-751-2361	339-26
Natural Resources Dept						
PO Box 176	Jefferson City	MO	65102	**800-361-4827***	573-751-3443	339-26
*Cust Svc						
Professional Registration Div						
3605 Missouri Blvd PO Box 1335	Jefferson City	MO	65102	**800-735-2966**	573-751-0293	339-26
Public Service Commission						
200 Madison St PO Box 360	Jefferson City	MO	65102	**800-819-3180**	573-751-3234	339-26
Securities Div						
600 W Main St PO Box 1276	Jefferson City	MO	65102	**800-721-7996**	573-751-4704	339-26

	City	State	ZIP	Toll-Free	Phone	Class
State Courts Administrator						
PO Box 104480	Jefferson City	MO	65110	**888-541-4894**		339-26
State Parks Div						
PO Box 176	Jefferson City	MO	65102	**800-334-6946**	573-751-2479	339-26
Supreme Court						
207 W High St	Jefferson City	MO	65101	**888-541-4894**	573-751-4144	339-26
Tourism Div						
PO Box 1055	Jefferson City	MO	65102	**800-519-2100**	573-751-4133	339-26
Transportation Dept						
105 W Capitol Ave	Jefferson City	MO	65102	**888-275-6636**	573-751-2551	339-26
Vocational & Adult Education Div						
3024 Dupont Cir						
PO Box 480	Jefferson City	MO	65109	**877-222-8963**	573-751-3251	339-26
Workers Compensation Div						
PO Box 58	Jefferson City	MO	65102	**800-775-2667**	573-751-4231	339-26
Missouri Assn of Realtors						
2601 Bernadette Pl	Columbia	MO	65203	**800-403-0101**	573-445-8400	654
Missouri Baptist Hospital of Sullivan						
751 Sappington Bridge Rd	Sullivan	MO	63080	**800-939-2273**	573-468-4186	374-3
Missouri Baptist Medical Ctr						
3015 N Ballas Rd	Saint Louis	MO	63131	**800-392-0936**	314-996-5000	374-3
Missouri Baptist University						
1 College Pk Dr	Saint Louis	MO	63141	**877-434-1115**	314-434-1115	167
Missouri Bar, The						
326 Monroe St PO Box 119	Jefferson City	MO	65102	**888-253-6013**	573-635-4128	71
Missouri Botanical Garden						
4344 Shaw Blvd	Saint Louis	MO	63110	**800-642-8842**	314-577-5100	96
Missouri Dental Assn						
3340 American Ave	Jefferson City	MO	65109	**800-688-1907**	573-634-3436	229
Missouri Enterprise						
1706 E 10th St	Rolla	MO	65401	**800-956-2682**		197
Missouri Fox Trotting Horse Breed Assn Inc						
PO Box 1027	Ava	MO	65608	**877-663-4203**	417-683-2468	47-3
Missouri Gas Energy						
3420 Broadway	Kansas City	MO	64111	**800-582-1234**	816-756-5252	785
Missouri Lawyers Media						
319 N Fourth St	Saint Louis	MO	63102	**800-635-5297**	314-421-1880	634-8
Missouri Medicine Magazine						
PO Box 1028	Jefferson City	MO	65102	**800-869-6762**	573-636-5151	456-16
Missouri Pharmacy Assn						
211 E Capitol Ave	Jefferson City	MO	65101	**800-468-4672**	573-636-7522	584
Missouri River Regional Library						
214 Adams St	Jefferson City	MO	65101	**800-949-7323**	573-634-2464	434-3
Missouri School Boards Association						
2100 I-70 Dr SW	Columbia	MO	65203	**800-221-6722**	573-445-9920	683
Missouri Southern State University						
3950 Newman Rd	Joplin	MO	64801	**866-818-6778**	417-625-9300	167
Missouri Sports Hall of Fame						
3861 E Stan Musial Dr	Springfield	MO	65809	**800-498-5678**	417-889-3100	521
Missouri State Employees' Retirement System						
907 Wildwood Dr	Jefferson City	MO	65109	**800-827-1063**	573-632-6100	527
Missouri State Medical Assn						
113 Madison St	Jefferson City	MO	65101	**800-869-6762**	573-636-5151	473
Missouri State Parks						
PO Box 176	Jefferson City	MO	65102	**800-334-6946**		564
Missouri State Teachers Assn						
407 S Sixth St	Columbia	MO	65201	**800-392-0532***	573-442-3127	456-8
*General						
Missouri State University (MSU)						
901 S National Ave	Springfield	MO	65897	**800-492-7900**	417-836-5000	167
Missouri University of Science & Technology						
Rolla						
1870 Miner Cir G2 Parker Hall	Rolla	MO	65409	**800-522-0938**	573-341-4111	167
Missouri Valley College						
500 E College St	Marshall	MO	65340	**800-999-8219**	660-831-4000	167
Missouri Veterans Home-Cape Girardeau						
2400 Veterans Memorial Dr	Cape Girardeau	MO	63701	**800-392-0210**	573-290-5870	791
Missouri Veterinary Medical Assn						
2500 Country Club Dr	Jefferson City	MO	65109	**800-632-6900**	573-636-8612	793
Missouri Vocational Enterprises						
1717 Industrial Dr						
PO Box 1898	Jefferson City	MO	65102	**800-392-8486***	573-751-6663	629
*Sales						
Missouri Western State University						
4525 Downs Dr	Saint Joseph	MO	64507	**800-662-7041**	816-271-4266	167
Missourian Publishing Co						
14 W Main St	Washington	MO	63090	**888-239-7701**	636-239-7701	634-8
Mister Car Wash						
3101 E Speedway Blvd	Tucson	AZ	85718	**866-254-3229***	520-615-4000	61-1
*Cust Svc						
Mister Money Investment						
2057 Vermont Dr	Fort Collins	CO	80525	**888-336-0403**	800-290-4598	140
Mister Safety Shoes Inc						
6-2300 Finch Ave W	Toronto	ON	M9M2Y3	**800-707-0051**	416-746-3000	358
Misty Harbor & Barefoot Beach Resort						
118 Weirs Rd	Gilford	NH	03249	**800-336-4789**	603-293-4500	379
MIT International						
77 Massachusetts Ave	Cambridge	TX	02139	**800-228-9290***	617-253-1000	389
*General						
MIT Museum						
265 Massachusetts Ave	Cambridge	MA	02139	**800-228-9000**	617-253-4444	519
Mitchell 1						
14145 Danielson St	Poway	CA	92064	**888-724-6742**	858-391-5000	634-11
Mitchell College						
437 Pequot Ave	New London	CT	06320	**800-443-2811***	860-701-5000	167
*Admitting						
Mitchell Electric Membership Corp						
475 Cairo Rd	Camilla	GA	31730	**800-479-6034**	229-336-5221	247
Mitchell Furniture Systems Inc						
1700 W St Paul Ave	Milwaukee	WI	53233	**800-290-5960**	414-342-3111	320-3
Mitchell Gold & Bob Williams Co (MGBW)						
135 One Comfortable Pl	Taylorsville	NC	28681	**800-789-5401**	828-632-9200	320-2
Mitchell Industrial Tire Co						
2915 Eigth Ave PO Box 71839	Chattanooga	TN	37407	**800-251-7226**	423-698-4442	752
Mitchell International Inc						
6220 Greenwich Dr	San Diego	CA	92122	**800-854-7030**	858-368-7000	634-11
Mitchell Metal Products Inc						
19250 Hwy 12 E PO Box 789	Kosciusko	MS	39090	**800-258-6137**	662-289-7110	695
Mitchell Rubber Products Inc						
10220 San Sevaine Way	Mira Loma	CA	91752	**800-453-7526**		674
Mitchell Selling Dynamics						
1360 Puritan Ave	Birmingham	MI	48009	**800-328-9696**	248-644-8092	462
Mitchell Supreme Fuel Co						
532 Freeman St	Orange	NJ	07050	**800-832-7090**	973-678-1800	317
Mitchell Technical Institute						
821 N Capital St	Mitchell	SD	57301	**800-684-1969**		161
MiTek Industries Inc						
14515 N Outer 40 Rd						
Ste 300	Chesterfield	MO	63017	**800-325-8075**	314-434-1200	90
Mitel Networks Corp						
350 Legget Dr PO Box 13089	Kanata	ON	K2K2W7	**800-722-1301**	613-592-2122	732
Mitem Corp						
640 Menlo Ave	Menlo Park	CA	94025	**800-648-3660***	650-323-1500	180-12
*Sales						
Mitographers Inc, The						
4720 N Fourth Ave	Sioux Falls	SD	57104	**800-221-6486**	605-336-1818	685
Mitsubishi Digital Electronics America Inc						
9351 Jeronimo Rd	Irvine	CA	92618	**800-332-2119**	949-465-6000	51
Mitsubishi Polyester Film LLC						
2001 Hood Rd	Greer	SC	29650	**800-334-1934**	864-879-5000	599
Mitsubishi Power Systems Inc						
100 Colonial Ctr Pkwy	Lake Mary	FL	32746	**800-445-9723**	407-688-6201	196
Mitsui & Co (USA) Inc						
200 Pk Ave	New York	NY	10166	**877-248-4237**	212-878-4000	448
Mitsui Chemicals America Inc						
800 Westchester Ave	Rye Brook	NY	10573	**800-972-7252**	914-253-0777	143
Mity-Lite Inc						
1301 West 400 North	Orem	UT	84057	**800-909-8034**	801-224-0589	320-3
MIX 93.1						
1331 Main St 4th Fl	Springfield	MA	01103	**888-293-9310**	413-781-1011	642-117
Mix Software Inc						
1203 Berkeley Dr	Richardson	TX	75081	**800-333-0330**	972-231-0949	180-2
Miyako Hotel Los Angeles						
328 E First St	Los Angeles	CA	90012	**800-228-6596**	213-617-2000	379
Mizkan Americas Inc						
1661 Feehanville Dr						
Ste 300	Mount Prospect	IL	60056	**800-323-4358**	847-590-0059	297-41
Mizuno USA						
4925 Avalon Ridge Pkwy	Norcross	GA	30071	**800-966-1211**	770-441-5553	708
MJ Soffe Co						
1 Soffe Dr	Fayetteville	NC	28312	**888-257-8673**		154-1
MJH (Martha Jefferson Hospital)						
500 Martha Jefferson Dr	Charlottesville	VA	22902	**888-652-6663**	434-654-7000	374-3
MJM Electric Co-op Inc (MJMEC)						
264 NE St PO Box 80	Carlinville	IL	62626	**800-648-4729**	217-854-3137	247
MJMEC (MJM Electric Co-op Inc)						
264 NE St PO Box 80	Carlinville	IL	62626	**800-648-4729**	217-854-3137	247
MJSA (Manufacturing Jewelers & Suppliers of America Inc)						
57 John L Dietsch Sq	Attleboro	MA	02763	**800-444-6572**	401-274-3840	48-4
MK Diamond Products Inc						
1315 Storm Pkwy	Torrance	CA	90501	**800-421-5830**	310-539-5221	680
MK Morse Co						
1101 11th St SE	Canton	OH	44707	**800-733-3377**	330-453-8187	680
MKC (Mid-Kansas Co-op Assn)						
PO Box D	Moundridge	KS	67107	**800-864-4428**	620-345-6361	47-2
MKS Instruments Inc						
2 Tech Dr Ste 201	Andover	MA	01810	**800-428-9401**	978-645-5500	203
ML McDonald LLC						
50 Oakland St PO Box 315	Watertown	MA	02471	**800-733-6243**	617-923-0900	191-8
MLA (Medical Library Assn)						
65 E Wacker Pl Ste 1900	Chicago	IL	60601	**800-523-1850**	312-419-9094	48-11
MLA (Modern Language Assn)						
26 Broadway 3rd Fl	New York	NY	10004	**800-323-4900**	646-576-5000	48-5
MLP Seating Corp						
950 Pratt Blvd	Elk Grove Village	IL	60007	**800-723-3030**	847-956-1700	320-3
MLQ Attorney Services						
2000 River Edge Pkwy Ste 885	Atlanta	GA	30328	**800-446-8794**	770-984-7007	632
M&M Manufacturing Co						
4001 Mark IV Pkwy	Fort Worth	TX	76106	**866-706-3999**	817-336-2311	695
M&M Pump & Supply Inc						
1125 Olivette Executive Pkwy						
Ste 110	St. Louis	MO	63132	**800-369-1450**	314-395-8122	358
MM Systems Corp						
50 MM Way	Pendergrass	GA	30567	**800-241-3460**	706-824-7500	236
MMA Capital Management LLC (MuniMae)						
621 E Pratt St Ste 600	Baltimore	MD	21202	**855-650-6932**	443-263-2900	508
OTC: MMAB						
MMC (Maine Medical Ctr)						
22 Bramhall St	Portland	ME	04102	**877-339-3107**	207-662-0111	374-3
MMC (Mercy Medical Ctr)						
345 St Paul Pl	Baltimore	MD	21202	**800-636-3729**	410-332-9000	374-3
MMC (Meadville Medical Ctr)						
751 Liberty St	Meadville	PA	16335	**800-254-5164**	814-333-5000	374-3
MMD Equipment						
121 High Hill Rd	Swedesboro	NJ	08085	**800-433-1382**	856-467-3200	482
MMF Industries						
1111 S Wheeling Rd	Wheeling	IL	60090	**800-323-8181**		690
MMG Works/Status Promotions						
4601 Madison Ave	Kansas City	MO	64112	**800-945-4044**		9
MMHC (Mercy Memorial Health Ctr)						
1011 14th Ave NW	Ardmore	OK	73401	**888-637-2937**	580-223-5400	374-3
MMHS (Martin Memorial Health Systems)						
200 SE Hospital Ave PO Box 9010	Stuart	FL	34994	**800-368-3375**	772-287-5200	374-3
MMI (Metal Marketplace International)						
718 Sansom St	Philadelphia	PA	19106	**800-523-9191**	215-592-8777	411
MMR Group Inc						
15961 Airline Hwy	Baton Rouge	LA	70817	**800-880-5090**	225-756-5090	191-4
MMS (Massachusetts Medical Society)						
860 Winter St	Waltham	MA	02451	**800-322-2303**	781-893-4610	473
MNA (Massachusetts Nurses Assn)						
340 Tpke St	Canton	MA	02021	**800-882-2056**	781-821-4625	532
MNA (Michigan Nurses Assn)						
2310 Jolly Oak Rd	Okemos	MI	48864	**888-646-8773**	517-349-5640	532
MNA (Minnesota Nurses Assn)						
345 Randolph Ave Ste 200	Saint Paul	MN	55102	**800-536-4662**	651-646-4807	532

Name / Address	City	State	ZIP	Toll-Free	Phone	Class
MNPS (Metropolitan Nashville Public Schools) 2601 Bransford Ave	Nashville	TN	37204	**800-848-0298**	615-259-8531	683
MOAA (Military Officers Assn of America) 201 N Washington St	Alexandria	VA	22314	**800-234-6622**	703-549-2311	47-19
Moai Technologies Inc 100 First Ave 9th Fl	Pittsburgh	PA	15222	**800-814-1548**	412-454-5550	180-7
Moberly Area Community College 101 College Ave	Moberly	MO	65270	**800-622-2070**	660-263-4110	161
MOBI Wireless Management LLC 6100 W 96th St Ste 150	Indianapolis	IN	46278	**855-259-6624**		198
Mobile Air Conditioning Society Worldwide (MACS) 225 S Broad St	Lansdale	PA	19446	**800-641-1133**	215-631-7020	48-21
Mobile Area Chamber of Commerce 451 Government St	Mobile	AL	36602	**800-422-6951**	251-433-6951	138
Mobile Climate Control Corp 17103 State Rd 4 E	Goshen	IN	46528	**800-450-2211**	574-534-1516	14
Mobile County Public Schools 1 Magnum Pass PO Box 180069	Mobile	AL	36618	**800-605-1033**	251-221-4000	683
Mobile National Cemetery 1202 Virginia St	Mobile	AL	36604	**800-827-1000**	850-453-4108	135
Mobile Nations 3151 E Thomas St	Inverness	FL	34453	**888-599-8998**	352-400-4400	156-5
Mobile Paint Manufacturing Co 4775 Hamilton Blvd	Theodore	AL	36582	**800-621-6952**	251-443-6110	549
Mobile Parts Inc 2472 Evans Rd PO Box 327	Val Caron	ON	P3N1P5	**800-461-4055**	705-897-4955	358
Mobile Public Library 701 Government St	Mobile	AL	36602	**877-322-8228**	251-208-7073	434-3
Mobile Regional Airport 8400 Airport Blvd	Mobile	AL	36608	**800-357-5373**	251-633-4510	27
Mobile Smith 5400 Trinity Rd Ste 320	Raleigh	NC	27607	**800-578-9000**		38
MobileIQ Inc 4800 Baseline Rd Ste E104-247	Boulder	CO	80303	**866-261-8600**		387
Mobilicity 101 Exchange Ave	Vaughan	ON	L4K5R6	**877-866-2458**		226
Mobility Center Inc 6693 Dixie Hwy	Bridgeport	MI	48722	**866-361-7559**	989-777-0910	479
Mobivity Inc 58 W Buffalo Ste 200	Chandler	AZ	85225	**877-282-7660**		5
MOCAP Inc 409 Parkway Dr	Park Hills	MO	63601	**800-633-6775**	314-543-4000	607
MODA Hotel 900 Seymour St	Vancouver	BC	V6B3L9	**877-683-5522**	604-683-4251	379
Modal Shop Inc, The 1776 Mentor Ave	Cincinnati	OH	45212	**800-860-4867**	513-351-9919	419
Model Airplane News 20 Westport Rd	Wilton	CT	06897	**800-988-6488**	203-431-9000	456-14
Model Coverall Service Inc 100 28th St SE	Grand Rapids	MI	49548	**800-968-6491**	616-241-6491	442
Modell's Sporting Goods 498 Seventh Ave 20th Fl	New York	NY	10018	**888-645-8667**	800-275-6633	156-5
Modern Aire Manufacturing Corp 7319 Lankershim Blvd	North Hollywood	CA	91605	**866-731-2007**	818-765-9870	200
Modern Art Museum of Fort Worth 3200 Darnell St	Fort Worth	TX	76107	**866-824-5566**	817-738-9215	519
Modern Automation Inc 134 Tennsco Dr	Dickson	TN	37055	**800-921-9705**	615-446-1990	358
Modern Chevrolet of Winston-Salem 5955 University Pkwy *General	Winston-Salem	NC	27105	**888-306-0825***	336-722-4191	56
Modern Corp 4746 Model City Rd	Model City	NY	14107	**800-662-0012**	716-754-8226	802
Modern Dental Laboratory USA LLC 13228 SE 30th St Ste C-6	Bellevue	WA	98005	**877-711-8778**		415
Modern Distributors Inc 817 W Columbia St	Somerset	KY	42501	**800-880-5543**	606-679-1178	754
Modern Earth 449 Provencher Blvd	Winnipeg	MB	R2J0B8	**866-766-7640**	204-885-2469	227
Modern Group Ltd 2501 Durham Rd	Bristol	PA	19007	**800-223-3827**	215-943-9100	385
Modern Ice Equipment & Supply Co 5709 Harrison Ave	Cincinnati	OH	45248	**800-543-1581**	513-367-2101	663
Modern Inc/Environmental & Wastewater 210 Durham Rd	Ottsville	PA	18942	**888-965-3227**	610-847-5112	185
Modern Language Assn (MLA) 26 Broadway 3rd Fl	New York	NY	10004	**800-323-4900**	646-576-5000	48-5
Modern Machine & Tool Company Inc 11844 Jefferson Ave	Newport News	VA	23606	**800-482-1835**	757-873-1212	407
Modern Machine Shop Magazine 6915 Valley Ave	Cincinnati	OH	45244	**800-950-8020**	513-527-8800	456-21
Modern Management Inc 253 Commerce Dr Ste 105	Grayslake	IL	60030	**800-323-1331**	847-945-7400	195
Modern Way Printing & Fulfillment 8817 Production Ln	Ooltewah	TN	37363	**800-603-5135**	423-238-4500	626
Modern Welding Company Inc 2880 New Hartford Rd	Owensboro	KY	42303	**800-922-1932**	270-685-4400	90
Modern Woodmen of America 1701 First Ave	Rock Island	IL	61201	**800-447-9811**	309-786-6481	391-2
Modernfold Inc 215 W New Rd	Greenfield	IN	46140	**800-869-9685**		288
Modesto Bee 1325 H St	Modesto	CA	95354	**800-776-4233**	209-578-2000	531-2
Modesto City Schools 426 Locust St	Modesto	CA	95351	**800-942-3767**	209-576-4011	683
Modesto Convention & Visitors Bureau 1150 Ninth St Ste C	Modesto	CA	95354	**888-640-8467**	209-526-5588	208
Modesto Symphony Orchestra 911 13th St	Modesto	CA	95354	**877-488-3380**	209-523-4156	572-3
Modine Manufacturing Co 1500 De Koven Ave *NYSE: MOD*	Racine	WI	53403	**800-828-4328**	262-636-1200	15
Modis Inc 10201 Centurion Pkwy N Ste 400	Jacksonville	FL	32256	**800-372-2788**	904-360-2300	462
Modjeski & Masters Inc 100 Sterling Pkwy Ste 302	Mechanicsburg	PA	17050	**888-663-5375**	717-790-9565	263
MOD-PAC Corp 1801 Elmwood Ave *NASDAQ: MPAC* ■ *Cust Svc	Buffalo	NY	14207	**866-216-6193***	716-873-0640	100
Modular Connections LLC 1090 Industrial Blvd	Bessemer	AL	35022	**877-903-6335**	205-980-4565	188
Modular Genius Inc 1201 S Mountain Rd	Joppa	MD	21085	**888-420-1113**		188
Moeller Mfg Company Inc Punch & Die Div 43938 Plymouth Oaks Blvd	Plymouth	MI	48170	**800-521-7613**	734-416-0000	755
Moen Inc 25300 Al Moen Dr *Cust Svc	North Olmsted	OH	44070	**800-289-6636***	440-962-2000	608
Moen Inc CSI Bath Accessories Div 25300 Al Moen Dr	North Olmsted	OH	44070	**800-289-6636**	440-962-2000	608
Moews Seed Co Inc 9821 IL Hwy 89	Granville	IL	60640	**800-663-9795**	815-339-2201	10-4
Moffatt & Nichol Engineers 3780 Kilroy Airport Way # 750	Long Beach	CA	90806	**888-399-6609**	562-590-6500	263
Moffitt Corp Inc 1351 13th Ave S Ste 130	Jacksonville Beach	FL	32250	**800-474-3267**	904-241-9944	258
MOGL Loyalty Services Inc 9645 Scranton Rd Ste 110	San Diego	CA	92121	**888-664-5669**		387
Mohair Council of America 233 W Twohig Rd	San Angelo	TX	76903	**800-583-3161**	325-655-3161	47-2
Mohave Community College						
Bullhead City 3400 Hwy 95	Bullhead City	AZ	86442	**866-664-2832**	928-758-3926	161
Lake Havasu 1977 W Acoma Blvd	Lake Havasu City	AZ	86403	**866-664-2832**	928-855-7812	161
North Mohave PO Box 980	Colorado City	AZ	86021	**800-678-3992**	928-875-2799	161
Mohave Educational Services Cooperative Inc 625 E Beale St	Kingman	AZ	86401	**800-742-2437**	928-753-6945	434-3
Mohave Mental Health Clinic Inc 3505 Western Ave	Kingman	AZ	86409	**888-757-8111**	928-757-8111	724
Mohawk Council of Akwesasne Stn Main Po Box 579	Cornwall	ON	K6H5T3	**888-632-6273**	613-575-2250	683
Mohawk Fine Papers Inc 465 Saratoga St	Cohoes	NY	12047	**800-843-6455**	518-237-1740	551-2
Mohawk Industries Inc 160 S Industrial Blvd *NYSE: MHK*	Calhoun	GA	30703	**800-241-4494**	706-629-7721	130
Mohawk Industries Inc Karastan Div 508 E Morris St	Dalton	GA	30721	**800-234-1120**		130
Mohawk Industries Inc Lees Carpets Div 160 S Industrial Blvd	Calhoun	GA	30701	**800-241-4494**	706-629-7721	130
Mohawk Valley Community College 1101 Sherman Dr	Utica	NY	13501	**800-733-6822**	315-792-5400	161
Mohawk Valley Psychiatric Ctr 1400 Noyes St	Utica	NY	13502	**800-597-8481**	315-738-3800	374-5
Mohegan Sun 1 Mohegan Sun Blvd	Uncasville	CT	06382	**877-962-2849**	860-862-4000	712-2
Mohegan Sun Resort & Casino 1 Mohegan Sun Blvd	Uncasville	CT	06382	**888-226-7711**	860-862-8150	132
Mohegan Tribal Gaming Authority 1 Mohegan Sun Blvd	Uncasville	CT	06382	**888-226-7711**		76
Mohonk Mountain House 1000 Mtn Rest Rd	New Paltz	NY	12561	**800-772-6646**	845-255-1000	667
Mohr Corp PO Box 1600	Brighton	MI	48114	**800-223-6647**	810-225-9494	457
Mohr Power Solar Inc 1452 Pomona Rd	Corona	CA	92882	**800-637-6527**	951-736-2000	609
Mojave A Desert Resort 73721 Shadow Mtn Dr *Resv	Palm Desert	CA	92260	**800-391-1104***	760-346-6121	379
Mojio Inc 1080 Howe St 9th Fl	Vancouver	BC	V6Z2T1	**855-556-6546**		226
Mokara Hotel & Spa 212 W Crockett St	San Antonio	TX	78205	**866-605-1212**	210-396-5800	705
Molalla Communications Co 211 Robbins St PO Box 360	Molalla	OR	97038	**800-332-2344**	503-829-1100	733
Mold Base Industries Inc 7501 Derry St	Harrisburg	PA	17111	**800-241-6656**		755
Mold-A-Matic Corp 147 River St	Oneonta	NY	13820	**866-886-2626**	607-433-2121	755
Molded Fiber Glass Cos 2925 MFG Pl PO Box 675	Ashtabula	OH	44005	**800-860-0196**	440-997-5851	603
Molded Fiber Glass Tray Co 6175 US Hwy 6 *Sales	Linesville	PA	16424	**800-458-6050***	814-683-4500	201
Moldex Metric Inc 10111 W Jefferson Blvd	Culver City	CA	90232	**800-421-0668**	310-837-6500	575
Molding Corp of America 10349 Norris Ave	Pacoima	CA	91331	**800-423-2747**	818-890-7877	603
Mold-Masters Injectioneering LLC 103 Peyerk Ct Ste E	Romeo	MI	48065	**800-387-2483**	586-752-6551	620
Mold-Rite Plastics LLC 1 Plant St	Plattsburgh	NY	12901	**800-432-5277**	518-561-1812	607
Mole Hollow Candles Ltd 208 Charlton Rd Rt 20 PO Box 223 *Cust Svc	Sturbridge	MA	01566	**800-445-6653***		328
Molecular Devices Inc (MDI) 1311 Orleans Dr	Sunnyvale	CA	94089	**800-635-5577**	408-747-1700	419
Molecular Imaging Services Inc 10 Whitaker Ct	Bear	DE	19701	**866-937-8855**		415
Molecular Pathology Laboratory Network Inc 250 E Broadway	Maryville	TN	37804	**800-932-2943**	865-380-9746	417
Molex Inc 2222 Wellington Ct *NASDAQ: MOLX* ■ *Cust Svc	Lisle	IL	60532	**800-786-6539***	630-969-4550	255
Molex Premise Networks 2222 Wellington Ct	Lisle	IL	60532	**866-733-6659**	630-969-4550	732
Molin Concrete Products Co 415 Lilac St	Lino Lakes	MN	55014	**800-336-6546**	651-786-7722	185

Alphabetical Section

Name / Address	City	State	ZIP	Toll-Free	Phone	Class
Molina Healthcare Inc 200 Oceangate Ste 100 *NYSE: MOH*	Long Beach	CA	90802	**888-562-5442**	562-435-3666	391-3
Moline Dispatch Publishing Co 1720 Fifth Ave	Moline	IL	61265	**800-660-2472**	309-764-4344	634-8
Molle Toyota Inc 601 W 103rd St	Kansas City	MO	64114	**888-510-7705**	816-942-5200	56
Molloy College 1000 Hempstead Ave PO Box 5002 *Admissions	Rockville Centre	NY	11571	**888-466-5569***	516-678-5000	167
Molly Pitcher Inn 88 Riverside Ave	Red Bank	NJ	07701	**800-221-1372**	732-747-2500	379
Molo Oil Company Inc 123 Southern Ave	Dubuque	IA	52003	**877-983-3761**	563-557-7540	580
Molok North America Ltd 179 Norpark Ave	Mount Forest	ON	N0G2L0	**877-558-5576**	519-323-9909	37
Molon Motor & Coil Corp 300 N Ridge Ave	Arlington Heights	IL	60005	**800-526-6867**	847-253-6000	517
Molpus Co, The 502 Vly View Dr PO Box 59	Philadelphia	MS	39350	**800-535-5434**	601-656-3373	815
Molson Coors Brewing Co 1225 17th St Ste 3200 *NYSE: TAP*	Denver	CO	80202	**800-645-5376**	303-927-2337	101
Momar Inc 1830 Ellsworth Industrial Dr	Atlanta	GA	30318	**800-556-3967**	404-355-4580	144
Moment Magazine 4115 Wisconsin Ave NW Ste 10	Washington	DC	20016	**800-777-1005**	202-363-6422	456-18
Momentum Bmw Ltd 10002 SW Fwy	Houston	TX	77074	**800-731-8114**		515
Momentum Systems Ltd 41 Twosome Dr Ste 9	Moorestown	NJ	08057	**800-279-1384**	856-727-0777	180-7
Momentum Technologies Inc (MTI) 1507 Boettler Rd	Uniontown	OH	44685	**800-720-0261**	330-896-5900	602
Momo Automotive Accessories Inc 20512 Crescent Bay Ste 104	Lake Forest	CA	92630	**800-749-6666**	949-380-7556	53
Monaco Coach Corp 1031 US 224 E	Decatur	IN	46733	**877-466-6226**		119
Monaco Government Tourist Office 565 Fifth Ave 23rd Fl	New York	NY	10017	**800-753-9696**	212-286-3330	773
Monadnock Paper Mills Inc 117 Antrim Rd *Orders	Bennington	NH	03442	**800-221-2159***	603-588-3311	556
Monaghan Medical Corp 5 Latour Ave Ste 1600	Plattsburgh	NY	12901	**800-833-9653**	518-561-7330	476
Monarch Hotel & Conference Ctr 12566 SE 93rd Ave	Clackamas	OR	97015	**800-492-8700**	503-652-1515	379
Monarch Textile Rental Services Inc 2810 Foundation Dr	South Bend	IN	46628	**800-589-9434**	574-233-9433	260
Mondrian Hotel 8440 Sunset Blvd	West Hollywood	CA	90069	**800-525-8029**	323-650-8999	379
Monell Chemical Senses Ctr 3500 Market St	Philadelphia	PA	19104	**800-732-0999**	267-519-4700	666
Monetta Family of Mutual Funds 1776A S Naperville Rd Ste 100	Wheaton	IL	60189	**800-241-9772**	630-462-9800	527
Money & Politics Report 1801 S Bell St	Arlington	VA	22202	**800-372-1033**		530-7
Money Mailer LLC 12131 Western Ave	Garden Grove	CA	92841	**800-468-5865**	714-889-3800	5
Money Movers Inc PO Box 241	Sebastopol	CA	95473	**800-861-5029**	707-829-5557	253
Money Tree Software Ltd 2430 NW Professional Wy	Corvallis	OR	97330	**877-421-9815**	541-754-3701	179
MoneyGram International Inc 2828 N Harwood Fl 15 *NASDAQ: MGI*	Dallas	TX	75201	**800-666-3947**		68
Moneytree Inc 6720 Ft Dent Way	Seattle	WA	98188	**877-613-6669**	206-246-3500	68
Monical Pizza Corp 530 N Kinzie Ave	Bradley	IL	60915	**800-929-3227**	815-937-1890	668
Monigle Associates Inc 150 Adams St	Denver	CO	80206	**800-346-4710**	303-388-9358	5
Moniker Online Services LLC 20 SW 27th Ave Ste 201	Pompano Beach	FL	33069	**800-688-6311**		396
Monitor Elevator Products Inc 125 Ricefield Ln	Hauppauge	NY	11788	**800-527-9156**		258
Monitor, The 1400 E Nolana Loop	McAllen	TX	78504	**800-366-4343**	956-683-4000	531-2
Monitronics International Inc 2350 Valley View Ln Ste 100 *Cust Svc	Dallas	TX	75234	**800-290-0709***	972-243-7443	690
Monmouth College 700 E Broadway Ave	Monmouth	IL	61462	**888-827-8268**	309-457-2311	167
Monmouth Medical Ctr 300 Second Ave	Long Branch	NJ	07740	**888-724-7123**	732-222-5200	374-3
Monmouth Plantation 36 Melrose Ave	Natchez	MS	39120	**800-828-4531**	601-442-5852	379
Monmouth University 400 Cedar Ave	West Long Branch	NJ	07764	**800-543-9671**	732-571-3456	167
Monogram Biosciences Inc 345 Oyster Pt Blvd	South San Francisco	CA	94080	**800-777-0177**	650-635-1100	419
Monograms 5301 S Federal Cir	Littleton	CO	80123	**866-270-9841**		758
Monro Muffler Brake Inc 200 Holleder Pkwy *NASDAQ: MNRO*	Rochester	NY	14615	**800-876-6676**	585-647-6400	61-3
Monroe Bank & Trust 102 E Front St	Monroe	MI	48161	**800-321-0032**	734-241-3431	69
Monroe Chamber of Commerce 212 Walnut St Ste 100	Monroe	LA	71201	**888-677-5200**	318-323-3461	138
Monroe Clinic Hospital 515 22nd Ave	Monroe	WI	53566	**800-338-0568**	608-324-2000	374-3
Monroe College 2501 Jerome Ave	Bronx	NY	10468	**800-556-6676**	718-933-6700	798
Monroe County Chamber of Commerce 1645 N Dixie Hwy Ste 20	Monroe	MI	48162	**855-386-1280**	734-384-3366	138
Monroe County Community College 1555 S Raisinville Rd	Monroe	MI	48161	**877-937-6222**	734-242-7300	161
Monroe County Electric Power Assn 601 N Main St	Amory	MS	38821	**866-656-2962**	662-256-2962	247
Monroe County Library System 3700 S Custer Rd	Monroe	MI	48161	**800-462-2050**	734-241-5277	434-3
Monroe County Public Library System 700 Fleming St	Key West	FL	33040	**877-772-8346**	305-292-3595	434-3
Monroe County Tourist Development Council 1201 White St Ste 102	Key West	FL	33040	**800-242-5229**	305-296-1552	208
Monroe County Water Authority 475 Norris Dr PO Box 10999	Rochester	NY	14610	**866-426-6292**	585-442-2000	785
Monroe Electronics Inc 100 Housel Ave	Lyndonville	NY	14098	**800-821-6001**	585-765-2254	250
Monroe Environmental Corp 810 W Front St	Monroe	MI	48161	**800-992-7707**	734-242-7654	386
Monroe Financial Partners Inc 100 N Riverside Plz Ste 1620	Chicago	IL	60606	**800-766-5560**	312-327-2530	196
Monroe Fluid Technology Inc 36 Draffin Rd	Hilton	NY	14468	**800-828-6351**	585-392-3434	144
Monroe Hardware Co 101 N Sutherland Ave	Monroe	NC	28110	**800-222-1974**	704-289-3121	351
Monroe Oil Co 519 E Franklin St *General	Monroe	NC	28112	**800-452-2717***	704-289-5438	325
Monroe Title Insurance Corp 47 W Main St	Rochester	NY	14614	**800-966-6763**	585-232-4950	391-6
Monroe Tractor & Implement Company Inc 1001 Lehigh Stn Rd	Henrietta	NY	14467	**866-683-5338**	585-334-3867	358
Monroe Truck Equipment Inc 1051 W Seventh St	Monroe	WI	53566	**800-356-8134**	608-328-8127	515
Monroeville Area Chamber of Commerce 4268 Northern Pike	Monroeville	PA	15146	**800-527-8941**	412-856-0622	138
Monroe-West Monroe Convention & Visitors Bureau 601 Constitution Dr PO Box 1436	West Monroe	LA	71292	**800-843-1872**	318-387-5691	208
Monrovia Public Library 321 S Myrtle Ave	Monrovia	CA	91016	**888-620-1749**	626-256-8274	434-3
Monsoon Commerce Solutions Inc 1250 45th St Ste 100	Emeryville	CA	94608	**800-520-2294**	510-594-4500	801-1
Monster Cable Products Inc 455 Valley Dr	Brisbane	CA	94005	**877-800-8989**	415-840-2000	51
MonsterTRAK 11845 W Olympic Blvd Ste 500	Los Angeles	CA	90064	**800-999-8725**		262
Montage Resort & Spa 30801 S Coast Hwy	Laguna Beach	CA	92651	**866-271-6953**	949-715-6000	667
Montana						
Arts Council PO Box 202201	Helena	MT	59620	**800-282-3092**	406-444-6430	339-27
Banking & Financial Institutions Div Rm 155 Mitchell Bldg 125 N Roberts St PO Box 200101	Helena	MT	59620	**800-914-8423**	406-841-2920	339-27
Child & Family Services Div PO Box 8005	Helena	MT	59604	**866-820-5437**	406-841-2400	339-27
Consumer Protection Office PO Box 200151	Helena	MT	59620	**800-481-6896**	406-444-4500	339-27
Information Technology Services Div 125 N Roberts St	Helena	MT	59601	**800-628-4917**	406-444-2700	339-27
Revenue Dept PO Box 5805	Helena	MT	59604	**866-859-2254**	406-444-6900	339-27
Securities Dept 840 Helena Ave	Helena	MT	59601	**800-332-6148**	406-444-2040	339-27
Victim Services Office 2225 11th Ave PO Box 201410	Helena	MT	59620	**800-498-6455**	406-444-1907	339-27
Vital Records Bureau 111 N Sanders St	Helena	MT	59604	**888-877-1946**	406-444-4228	339-27
Montana Assn of Realtors 1 S Montana Ave Ste M1	Helena	MT	59601	**800-477-1864**	406-443-4032	654
Montana Chamber of Commerce 900 Gibbon St PO Box 1730	Helena	MT	59624	**888-442-6668**	406-442-2405	139
Montana Coffee Traders Inc 5810 Hwy 93 S	Whitefish	MT	59937	**800-345-5282**	406-862-7633	158
Montana Dental Assn 17 1/2 S Last Chance Gulch PO Box 1154	Helena	MT	59624	**800-257-4988**	406-443-2061	229
Montana Higher Education Board of Regents 2500 Broadway St PO Box 203201	Helena	MT	59620	**877-501-1722**	406-444-6570	723
Montana Historical Society Museum 225 N Roberts St	Helena	MT	59620	**800-243-9900**	406-444-2694	519
Montana Idaho Log & Timber 1069 Us Hwy 93 N	Victor	MT	59875	**800-600-8604**	406-961-3092	105
Montana Lawyer Magazine 7 W Sixth Ave Ste 2B	Helena	MT	59601	**888-385-9119**	406-442-7660	456-15
Montana Lottery 2525 N Montana Ave	Helena	MT	59601	**800-425-1435**	406-444-5825	451
Montana Medical Assn 2021 11th Ave Ste 1	Helena	MT	59601	**877-443-4000**	406-443-4000	473
Montana Public Radio 32 Campus Dr University of Montana	Missoula	MT	59812	**800-325-1565**	406-243-4931	629
Montana Public Television 183 Visual Communications Bldg	Bozeman	MT	59717	**800-426-8243**	866-832-0829	629
Montana Rail Link Inc 101 International Way	Missoula	MT	59808	**800-338-4750**	406-523-1500	646
Montana River Outfitters 923 Tenth Ave N	Great Falls	MT	59401	**800-800-8218**	406-761-1677	758
Montana Standard 25 W Granite St	Butte	MT	59701	**800-877-1074**	406-496-5500	531-2
Montana State Prison 400 Conley Lk Rd	Deer Lodge	MT	59722	**888-739-9122**	406-846-1320	215
Montana State University						
Billings 1500 University Dr	Billings	MT	59101	**800-565-6782**	406-657-2011	167
Bozeman PO Box 172190 *Admissions	Bozeman	MT	59717	**888-678-2287***	406-994-2452	167
Northern PO Box 7751	Havre	MT	59501	**800-662-6132**	406-994-2452	167
Montana Tech of the University of Montana 1300 W Pk St *Admissions	Butte	MT	59701	**800-445-8324***	406-496-4101	167

Name	Address	City	State	Zip	Toll-Free	Phone	Class
Montana Veterans Home	400 Veterans Dr	Columbia Falls	MT	59912	**888-279-7532**	406-892-3256	791
Montana-Dakota Utilities Co (MDU)	400 N Fourth St	Bismarck	ND	58501	**800-638-3278**	701-222-7900	785
Montauk Yacht Club Resort & Marina	32 Star Island Rd	Montauk	NY	11954	**888-692-8668**	631-668-3100	667
MontaVista Software Inc	2929 Patrick Henry Dr	Santa Clara	CA	95054	**888-624-4846**	408-572-8000	176
Montclair State University	1 Normal Ave *Admissions	Montclair	NJ	07043	**800-331-9205***	973-655-4000	167
Monte Carlo Inn-Airport Suites	7035 Edwards Blvd	Mississauga	ON	L5T2H8	**800-363-6400**	905-564-8500	379
Monte Carlo Resort & Casino	3770 Las Vegas Blvd S	Las Vegas	NV	89109	**800-311-8999**	702-730-7777	667
Monte Package Company Inc	3752 Riverside Rd	Riverside	MI	49084	**800-653-2807**	269-849-1722	202
Monte Sano State Park	5105 Nolen Ave	Huntsville	AL	35801	**800-252-7275**	256-534-3757	564
Montecito Inn Inc	1295 Coast Village Rd	Santa Barbara	CA	93108	**800-843-2017**	805-969-7854	705
Montello Inc	6106 E 32nd Pl Ste 100	Tulsa	OK	74135	**800-331-4628**		144
Monterey Bay Aquarium	886 Cannery Row	Monterey	CA	93940	**866-963-9645**	831-648-4800	39
Monterey Bay Inn	242 Cannery Row	Monterey	CA	93940	**800-424-6242**	831-373-6242	379
Monterey Conference Ctr	1 Portola Plz *Sales	Monterey	CA	93940	**800-742-8091***	831-646-3770	207
Monterey County Convention & Visitors Bureau	PO Box 1770	Monterey	CA	93942	**888-221-1010**	831-657-6400	208
Monterey County Herald	2200 Garden Rd	Monterey	CA	93940	**800-688-1808**	831-372-3311	531-2
Monterey Hotel	406 Alvarado St	Monterey	CA	93940	**800-966-6490**	831-375-3184	379
Monterey Inn Resort & Conference Centre	2259 Prince of Wales Dr	Ottawa	ON	K2E6Z8	**800-565-1311**	613-288-3500	379
Monterey Jet Center LLC	300 Skypark Dr	Monterey	CA	93940	**800-679-2992**	831-373-0100	62
Monterey Mills Inc	1725 E Delavan Dr	Janesville	WI	53546	**800-255-9665**	608-754-2866	742-4
Monterey Mushrooms Inc	260 Westgate Dr	Watsonville	CA	95076	**800-333-6874**	831-763-5300	10-6
Monterey Pasta Co	2315 Moore Ave	Fullerton	CA	92833	**800-588-7782**		297-31
Monterey Peninsula College	980 Fremont St	Monterey	CA	93940	**877-663-5433**	831-646-4000	161
Monterey Plaza Hotel & Spa	400 Cannery Row	Monterey	CA	93940	**800-334-3999**	831-646-1700	379
Monterey Public Library	625 Pacific St	Monterey	CA	93940	**800-338-0505**	831-646-3932	434-3
Montesi Motors Inc	444 State St	North Haven	CT	06473	**844-282-1115**		56
Montesquieu Winery	8221 Arjons Dr	San Diego	CA	92126	**800-860-2378**		633
Montfort Bros Inc	44 Elm St	Fishkill	NY	12524	**800-724-1777**	845-896-6225	185
Montfort Group, The	44 Elm St	Fishkill	NY	12524	**800-724-1777**	845-896-6225	185
Montfort Hospital	713 Montreal Rd	Ottawa	ON	K1K0T2	**866-670-4621**	613-746-4621	374-2
Montgomery Advertiser	425 Molton St	Montgomery	AL	36104	**877-424-0007**	334-262-1611	531-2
Montgomery Area Chamber of Commerce Convention & Visitor Bureau	300 Water St	Montgomery	AL	36104	**800-240-9452**	334-261-1100	208
Montgomery Aviation Corp	4525 Selma Hwy	Montgomery	AL	36108	**800-392-8044**	334-288-7334	62
Montgomery Bank	1 Montgomery Bank Plaza PO Box 948	Sikeston	MO	63801	**800-455-2275**	573-471-2275	69
Montgomery Bell State Resort Park	1020 Jackson Hill Rd	Burns	TN	37029	**800-250-8613**	615-797-9052	564
Montgomery Botanical Ctr	11901 Old Cutler Rd	Miami	FL	33156	**800-435-7352**	305-667-3800	96
Montgomery County Visitors & Convention Bureau	218 E Pike St	Crawfordsville	IN	47933	**800-866-3973**	765-362-5200	208
Montgomery Hospice	1355 Piccard Dr Ste 100	Rockville	MD	20850	**800-994-6610**	301-921-4400	371
Montgomery Mutual Insurance Co	13830 Ballantyne Corporate Pl Ste 300	Charlotte	NC	28277	**800-561-0178**	704-759-7661	391-4
Montgomery Truss & Panel Inc	803 W Main St	Grove City	PA	16127	**800-942-8010**	724-458-7500	815
Monticello	931 Thomas Jefferson Pkwy PO Box 316	Charlottesville	VA	22902	**800-243-1743**	434-984-9822	49-2
Monticello Central School District	237 Forestburgh Rd	Monticello	NY	12701	**866-805-0990**	845-794-7700	683
Montpelier Glove Co Inc	129 N Main St	Montpelier	IN	47359	**800-645-3931**	765-728-2481	154-7
Montreal Canadiens	Bell Centre 1260 de la Gauchetiere St W	Montreal	QC	H3B5E8	**800-363-8162**	514-989-2841	714
Montreal Exchange	800 Victoria Sq Third Fl PO Box 61	Montreal	QC	H4Z1A9	**800-361-5353**	514-871-2424	689
Montreal Heart Institute	5000 Belanger St E	Montreal	QC	H1T1C8	**855-922-6387**	514-376-3330	374-2
Montreal Inn	Beach Dr & Madison Ave	Cape May	NJ	08204	**800-525-7011**	609-884-7011	667
Montreat College	310 Gaither Cir PO Box 1267	Montreat	NC	28757	**800-622-6968**	828-669-8011	167
Montrose Chamber of Commerce	1519 E Main St	Montrose	CO	81401	**800-923-5515**	970-249-5000	138
Montrose Travel	2355 Honolulu Ave	Montrose	CA	91020	**800-766-4687**		769
Montrose Visitor & Convention Bureau	107 S Cascade Ave	Montrose	CO	81401	**888-212-8294**	970-249-5000	208
Montserrat College of Art	23 Essex St PO Box 26	Beverly	MA	01915	**800-836-0487**	978-921-4242	167
Monument Builders of North America (MBNA)	136 S Keowee St	Dayton	OH	45402	**800-233-4472**		48-3
Monument Security Inc	5844 Price Ave	Sacramento	CA	95652	**877-506-1755**	916-564-4234	691
Monumental Sales Inc	537 22nd Ave N PO Box 667	Saint Cloud	MN	56302	**800-442-1660**	320-251-6585	722
MOOD (Michigan Out-of-Doors Magazine)	2101 Wood St PO Box 30235	Lansing	MI	48912	**800-777-6720**	517-371-1041	456-22
Moodie Implement Co	80335 US Hwy 87 W	Lewistown	MT	59457	**877-278-5531**	406-538-5433	358
Moody Bible Institute	820 N La Salle St	Chicago	IL	60610	**800-967-4624**	312-329-4400	160
Moody Dunbar Inc	2000 Waters Edge Dr Ste 21	Johnson City	TN	37604	**800-251-8202**	423-952-0100	297-20
Moody Gardens Convention Ctr	7 Hope Blvd	Galveston	TX	77554	**888-388-8484**	409-741-8484	207
Moody Medical Library	914 Market st	Galveston	TX	77555	**866-235-5223**	409-772-2372	434-1
Moody-Price LLC	18320 Petroleum Dr	Baton Rouge	LA	70809	**800-272-9832**		386
Moog Inc	Jamison Rd *NYSE: MOG/A*	East Aurora	NY	14052	**800-336-2112**	716-652-2000	205
Mooney Aircraft Corp	165 Al Mooney Rd	Kerrville	TX	78028	**800-456-3033**		20
Mooney General Paper Co	1451 Chestnut Ave PO Box 3800	Hillside	NJ	07205	**800-882-8846**	973-926-3800	546
Moonstruck Chocolate Co	6600 N Baltimore Ave	Portland	OR	97203	**800-557-6666**	503-247-3448	297-8
Moonworks	1137 Park E Dr	Woonsocket	RI	02895	**800-975-6666**		750
Moore & Neidenthal Inc	3034 N Wooster Ave	Dover	OH	44622	**866-364-7774**	330-364-7774	2
Moore College of Art & Design	20th St & the Pkwy	Philadelphia	PA	19103	**800-523-2025**	215-965-4000	163
Moore Erection LP	19921 Fm 2252	San Antonio	TX	78266	**800-656-6673**	210-648-7461	721
Moore Food Distributors Co	9910 Page Ave	Saint Louis	MO	63132	**800-467-7878**	314-426-1300	298-7
Moore Industries International Inc	16650 Schoenborn St	North Hills	CA	91343	**800-999-2900**	818-894-7111	203
Moore Medical Corp	389 John Downey Dr *Sales	New Britain	CT	06050	**800-234-1464***	860-826-3600	474
Moore Oil Company Inc	4033 W Custer Ave	Milwaukee	WI	53209	**800-279-2976**	414-462-3200	181
Moore Regional Hospital	155 Memorial Dr PO Box 3000	Pinehurst	NC	28374	**866-415-2778**	910-715-1000	374-3
Moore State Park	Mill St	Paxton	MA	01612	**800-437-5922**	508-792-3969	564
Moore Stephens Lovelace PA	1201 S Orlando Ave Ste 400	Winter Park	FL	32789	**800-683-5401**	407-740-5400	2
Moores Electrical & Mechanical	PO Box 119	Altavista	VA	24517	**888-722-2712**	434-369-4374	188
Mooresville Graded School District	305 N Main St	Mooresville	NC	28115	**800-222-1222**	704-658-2530	683
Moorings Park	120 Moorings Pk Dr	Naples	FL	34105	**866-802-4302**	239-643-9111	670
Moors & Cabot Inc	111 Devonshire St	Boston	MA	02109	**800-426-0501**	617-426-0500	405
Moose Travel Network	192 Spadina Ave Unit 408	Toronto	ON	M5T2C2	**888-244-6673**	604-297-0255	758
MOPS International	2370 S Trenton Way *General	Denver	CO	80231	**888-910-6677***	303-733-5353	47-6
Morabito Baking Company Inc	757 Kohn St	Norristown	PA	19401	**800-525-7747**	610-275-5419	297-1
Moraine Park Technical College	235 N National Ave	Fond du Lac	WI	54935	**800-472-4554**	920-922-8611	798
Moran Printing Inc	5425 Florida Blvd	Baton Rouge	LA	70806	**800-211-8335**	225-923-2550	625
Moran Technology Consulting Llc	1215 Hamilton Ln Ste 200	Naperville	IL	60540	**888-699-4440**		198
Mora-San Miguel Electric Co-op	PO Box 240	Mora	NM	87732	**800-421-6773**	575-387-2205	247
Moravian College	1200 Main St	Bethlehem	PA	18018	**800-441-3191**	610-861-1300	167
Moravian Theological Seminary	1200 Main St	Bethlehem	PA	18018	**800-843-6541**	610-861-1516	168-3
More Hawaii for Less Inc	11 Ash Tree Ln Ste 290	Irvine	CA	92660	**800-967-6687**	949-724-5050	769
More Space Place Inc	5040 140th Ave N	Clearwater	FL	33760	**888-731-3051**		361
Moreau-Grand Electric Co-op Inc	405 Ninth St	Timber Lake	SD	57656	**800-952-3158**	605-865-3511	247
Morehead State University	100 Admissions Ctr	Morehead	KY	40351	**800-585-6781**	606-783-2000	167
Moretz Inc	514 W 21st St	Newton	NC	28658	**866-714-8486**	828-464-0751	154-9
Morey's Seafood International LLC	1218 Hwy 10 S	Motley	MN	56466	**800-808-3474**	218-352-6345	297-14
Morgan & Co	1131 Glendon Ave	Los Angeles	CA	90024	**800-458-4367**	310-208-3377	410
Morgan & Weisbrod	6800 W Loop S Ste 450	Bellaire	TX	77401	**877-898-1581**	713-838-0003	428
Morgan Adhesives Co	4560 Darrow Rd	Stow	OH	44224	**866-262-2822**	330-688-1111	3
Morgan Bldg Systems Inc	2800 McCree Rd	Garland	TX	75041	**800-935-0321**	972-864-7300	105
Morgan Community College	920 Barlow Rd	Fort Morgan	CO	80701	**800-622-0216**	970-542-3100	161
Morgan Corp	111 Morgan Way PO Box 588	Morgantown	PA	19543	**800-666-7426**	610-286-5025	515
Morgan County	1226 Knoxville Hwy	Wartburg	TN	37887	**888-205-5017**		338

Name / Address	City	State	Zip	Toll-Free	Phone	Class
Morgan County Rural Electric Assn 20169 US Hwy 34	Fort Morgan	CO	80701	**877-495-6487**	970-867-5688	247
Morgan Foods Inc 90 W Morgan St	Austin	IN	47102	**888-430-1780**	812-794-1170	297-20
Morgan Lewis & Bockius LLP 1701 Market St	Philadelphia	PA	19103	**866-963-7137**	215-963-5000	428
Morgan Meighen & Associates Ltd 10 Toronto St	Toronto	ON	M5C2B7	**866-443-6097**	416-366-2931	527
Morgan Olson Corp 1801 S Nottawa Rd	Sturgis	MI	49091	**800-233-4823**	269-659-0200	515
Morgan Run Natural Environment Area Benros Ln	Eldersburg	MD	21784	**800-830-3974**	410-461-5005	564
Morgan Run Resort & Club 5690 Cancha de Golf *Resv	Rancho Santa Fe	CA	92091	**800-378-4653***	858-756-2471	667
Morgan Services Inc 323 N Michigan Ave	Chicago	IL	60601	**888-966-7426**	312-346-3181	442
Morgan Stanley 1585 Broadway *NYSE: MS* ■ *General	New York	NY	10036	**800-223-2440***	212-761-4000	688
Morgan Stanley Investment Management 1221 Ave of the Americas 5th Fl *General	New York	NY	10020	**800-223-2440***	212-296-6600	688
Morgan Stanley Venture Partners 1585 Broadway 38th Fl	New York	NY	10036	**866-722-7310**	212-761-4000	790
Morgan State University 1700 E Cold Spring Ln	Baltimore	MD	21251	**800-319-4678**	443-885-3333	167
Morgan-Keller Inc 70 Thomas Johnson Dr Ste 200	Frederick	MD	21702	**800-725-5051**	301-663-0626	263
Morgans Hotel 237 Madison Ave	New York	NY	10016	**800-606-6090**	212-686-0300	379
Morgans Hotel Group Co 475 Tenth Ave *NASDAQ: MHGC*	New York	NY	10018	**800-606-6090**	212-277-4100	379
Morgantown Area Chamber of Commerce 1029 University Ave Ste 101 *General	Morgantown	WV	26505	**800-618-2525***	304-292-3311	138
Mor-Gran-Sou Electric Co-op Inc 202 Sixth Ave W	Flasher	ND	58535	**800-750-8212**	701-597-3301	247
Moritz Embroidery Works Inc Pocono Mtn Business Park 405 Industrial Park Dr PO Box 187	Mount Pocono	PA	18344	**800-533-4183**	570-839-9600	260
Morley Candy Makers Inc 23770 Hall Rd	Clinton Township	MI	48036	**800-651-7263**	586-468-4300	297-8
Morley Company Inc 2717 Schust	Saginaw	MI	48603	**800-323-1492**	989-791-2565	196
Morley Financial Services Inc 1300 SW Fifth Ave Ste 3300	Portland	OR	97201	**800-548-4806**	503-484-9300	401
Morley Pedals 325 Cary Pt Dr	Cary	IL	60013	**800-284-5172**	847-639-4646	526
Morley-Murphy Co 200 S Washington St Ste 305	Green Bay	WI	54301	**877-499-3171**	920-499-3171	611
Morning Call PO Box 1260	Allentown	PA	18105	**800-666-5492**	610-820-6500	531-2
Morning Call Inc 101 N Sixth St	Allentown	PA	18101	**800-666-5492**	610-820-6500	634-8
Morning Journal 1657 Broadway Ave	Lorain	OH	44052	**888-757-0727**	440-245-6901	531-2
Morning Sentinel 31 Front St	Waterville	ME	04901	**800-287-1945**	207-873-3341	531-2
Morningside College 1501 Morningside Ave	Sioux City	IA	51106	**800-831-0806**	712-274-5000	167
Morningside of Fullerton 800 Morningside Dr	Fullerton	CA	92835	**800-803-7597**	714-256-8000	670
Morningstar Inc 22 W Washington St *NASDAQ: MORN* ■ *Orders	Chicago	IL	60606	**800-735-0700***	312-696-6000	401
Moro Bay State Park 6071 US Hwy 600	Jersey	AR	71651	**888-742-8701**	870-463-8555	564
Morongo Casino Resort & Spa 49500 Seminole Dr	Cabazon	CA	92230	**800-252-4499**	951-849-3080	667
MORPACE International Inc 31700 Middlebelt Rd Ste 200 *General	Farmington Hills	MI	48334	**800-881-1723***	248-737-5300	465
Morphix Business Consulting PO Box 5217 Stn A	Calgary	AB	T2H1X3	**866-680-2503**	403-520-7710	198
MorphoTrak Inc 113 S Columbus St 4th Fl	Alexandria	VA	22314	**800-601-6790**	703-797-2600	82
MorphoTrust USA Inc 296 Concord Rd	Billerica	MA	01821	**888-245-1114**	978-215-2400	690
Morrill Motors Inc 229 S Main Ave	Erwin	TN	37650	**888-743-7001**		517
Morrilton Packing Company Inc 51 Blue Diamond Dr	Morrilton	AR	72110	**800-264-2475**	501-354-2474	472
Morris & Dickson Co Ltd 410 Kay Ln	Shreveport	LA	71115	**800-388-3833**	318-797-7900	240
Morris College 100 W College St *Admissions	Sumter	SC	29150	**866-853-1345***	803-934-3200	167
Morris Communications Company LLC 725 Broad St	Augusta	GA	30901	**800-622-6358**	706-724-0851	634-8
Morris Coupling Co 2240 W 15th St	Erie	PA	16505	**800-426-1579**	814-459-1741	489
Morris Furniture Co Inc 2377 Commerce Ctr Dr	Fairborn	OH	45324	**800-243-0000**	937-874-7100	322
Morris Hospital 150 W High St	Morris	IL	60450	**877-743-3123**	815-942-2932	374-3
Morris Industries Inc 777 Rt 23	Pompton Plains	NJ	07444	**800-835-0777**	973-835-6600	536
Morris Material Handling Inc 315 W Forest Hill Ave	Oak Creek	WI	53154	**800-933-3001**	414-764-6200	469
Morris Performing Arts Ctr 211 N Michigan St	South Bend	IN	46601	**800-537-6415**	574-235-9190	571
Morris Printing Group 3212 Hwy 30 E	Kearney	NE	68847	**800-445-6621**	308-236-7888	626
Morris Products Inc 53 Carey Rd	Queensbury	NY	12804	**888-777-6678**	518-743-0523	785
Morrisette Paper Company Inc 5925 Summit Ave PO Box 20768	Browns Summit	NC	27214	**800-822-8882**	336-375-1515	552
Morrison Bros Co 570 E Seventh St	Dubuque	IA	52001	**800-553-4840**	563-583-5701	536
Morrison Brown Argiz & Farra LLP 1001 Brickell Bay Dr 9th Fl	Miami	FL	33131	**800-239-3843**	305-373-5500	2
Morrison County 213 SE First Ave	Little Falls	MN	56345	**866-401-1111**	320-632-2941	338
Morrison County Record 216 SE First St	Little Falls	MN	56345	**888-637-2345**	320-632-2345	531-4
Morrison Hershfield Group Inc 125 Commerce Valley Dr W Ste 300	Markham	ON	L3T7W4	**888-649-4730**	416-499-3110	263
Morrison House 116 S Alfred St	Alexandria	VA	22314	**866-834-6628**	703-838-8000	669
Morrison Management Specialists Inc 5801 Peachtree Dunwoody Rd *General	Atlanta	GA	30342	**800-225-4368***		300
Morrison Milling Co 319 E Prairie St	Denton	TX	76201	**800-531-7912**	940-387-6111	297-23
Morrison Scott Alan Law Offices of pa 141 W Patrick St Ste 300	Frederick	MD	21701	**866-220-5185**	301-694-6262	428
Morrison Supply Company Inc 311 E Vickery Blvd	Fort Worth	TX	76104	**800-451-9343**	817-870-2227	611
Morrison-Clark Historic Inn & Restaurant 1015 L St NW	Washington	DC	20001	**800-332-7898**	202-898-1200	379
Morristown Medical Ctr 100 Madison Ave	Morristown	NJ	07960	**877-310-7226**	973-971-5000	374-3
Morrisville State College 80 Eaton St PO Box 901 *Admissions	Morrisville	NY	13408	**800-258-0111***	315-684-6000	167
Morro Bay State Park 60 State Pk Rd Morro Bay State Pk Rd	Morro Bay	CA	93442	**800-777-0369**		564
Morrow & Co LLC 470 W Ave	Stamford	CT	06902	**800-662-5200**	203-658-9400	401
Morrow Control & Supply Co 810 Marion Motley Ave Ne	Canton	OH	44705	**800-362-9830**	330-452-9791	611
Morrow County Grain Growers Inc (MCGG) 350 N Main St	Lexington	OR	97839	**800-452-7396**	541-989-8221	10-4
Morse Industries Inc 25811 74th Ave S	Kent	WA	98032	**800-325-7513**		695
Morse Operations Inc 3790 W Blue Herron Blvd	Riviera Beach	FL	33404	**800-755-2593**		515
Mortara Instrument Inc 7865 N 86th St	Milwaukee	WI	53224	**800-231-7437**	414-354-1600	252
Mortgage Bankers Assn (MBA) 1919 M St NW 5th Fl	Washington	DC	20036	**800-793-6222**	202-557-2700	48-2
Mortgage Builders Software 24370 NW Hwy Ste 200	Southfield	MI	48075	**800-850-8060**		180-10
Mortgage Guaranty Insurance Corp 270 E Kilbourn Ave	Milwaukee	WI	53202	**800-558-9900**	414-347-6480	391-5
Mortgage Investors Group 8320 E Walker Springs Ln	Knoxville	TN	37923	**800-489-8910**	865-691-8910	508
Mortgage Resources Inc (MRI) 425 S Woods Mill Rd Ste 100	Chesterfield	MO	63017	**800-965-9910**	314-576-5577	508
Mortgageflex Systems Inc 1200 Riverplace Blvd Ste 650 *General	Jacksonville	FL	32207	**800-326-3539***	904-356-2490	179
Morton Buildings Inc 252 W Adams St PO Box 399	Morton	IL	61550	**800-447-7436**	309-263-7474	104
Morton Grove Pharmaceuticals Inc 6451 Main St	Morton Grove	IL	60053	**800-346-6854**	847-967-5600	583
Morton Plant Hospital 300 Pinellas St	Clearwater	FL	33756	**800-229-2273**	727-462-7000	374-3
Morton Salt Inc 123 N Wacker Dr	Chicago	IL	60606	**800-725-8847**	312-807-2000	678
Morton's The Steakhouse 618 Church St	Nashville	TN	37219	**800-297-3276**	615-259-4558	669
Mosaic Hotel 125 S Spalding Dr	Beverly Hills	CA	90212	**800-463-4466**	310-278-0303	379
Moscow Chamber of Commerce 411 S Main St	Moscow	ID	83843	**866-770-2020**	208-882-1800	138
Moser Corp 601 N 13th St	Rogers	AR	72756	**800-632-4564**	479-636-3481	322
Moses H Cone Memorial Hospital 1200 N Elm St	Greensboro	NC	27401	**866-391-2734**	336-832-7000	374-3
Moses Lake Area Chamber of Commerce 324 S Pioneer Way	Moses Lake	WA	98837	**800-992-6234**	509-765-7888	138
Moss Inc PO Box 189	Pasadena	MD	21123	**800-932-6677**	410-768-3442	233
Moss Supply Company Inc 5001 N Graham St	Charlotte	NC	28269	**800-438-0770**	704-596-8717	236
Mossberg & Company Inc 301 E Sample St	South Bend	IN	46601	**800-428-3340**	574-289-9253	625
Mosser Hotel 54 Fourth St	San Francisco	CA	94103	**800-227-3804**	415-986-4400	379
Motel 6 Wichita 465 S Webb Rd	Wichita	KS	67207	**800-466-8356**	316-684-6363	379
Mother Jones Magazine 222 Sutter St Ste 600	San Francisco	CA	94108	**800-438-6656**	415-321-1700	456-17
Mother Murphy's Labs Inc 2826 S Elm St PO Box 16846	Greensboro	NC	27416	**800-849-1277**	336-273-1737	297-15
Mother's Market & Kitchen 1890 Newport Blvd	Costa Mesa	CA	92627	**800-595-6667**	949-631-4741	345
Mother's Polishes Waxes & Cleaners 5456 Industrial Dr	Huntington Beach	CA	92649	**800-221-8257**	714-891-3364	150
Motherhood Maternity 456 N Fifth St	Philadelphia	PA	19123	**800-291-7800**	215-873-2200	156-6
Mothers Against Drunk Driving (MADD) 511 E John Carpenter Fwy Ste 700	Irving	TX	75062	**877-275-6233**	214-744-6233	47-6
Motion Control Engineering Inc 11380 White Rock Rd	Rancho Cordova	CA	95742	**800-444-7442**	916-463-9200	258
Motion Industries Inc 1605 Alton Rd	Birmingham	AL	35210	**800-526-9328**	205-956-1122	385
Motion Picture & Television Fund 23388 Mulholland Dr	Woodland Hills	CA	91364	**855-760-6783**		47-4

Name / Address	City	State	ZIP	Toll-Free	Phone	Class
Mo-Tires Ltd 2830 5 Ave N	Lethbridge	AB	T1H0P1	**800-774-3888**	403-329-4533	393
Motiva Enterprises LLC 700 Milam St	Houston	TX	77002	**877-668-4825**	713-277-8000	579
Motivano Inc 5810 W Cypress St Ste H	Tampa	FL	33607	**866-664-4621**		196
Motivation Through Incentives Inc 10400 W 103 St Ste 10	Overland Park	KS	66214	**800-826-3464**		384
Motlow State Community College PO Box 8500	Lynchburg	TN	37352	**800-654-4877**	931-393-1500	161
Motor Appliance Corp 601 International Ave	Washington	DC	63090	**800-622-3406**	636-532-3406	517
Motor City Interactive Inc 49145 Wixom Tech Dr	Wixom	MI	48393	**888-340-4638**		5
Motor Coach Industries International Co 1700 E Golf Rd Ste 300	Schaumburg	IL	60173	**800-743-3624**	847-285-2000	515
Motor Products Owosso Corp 201 S Delaney Rd	Owosso	MI	48867	**800-248-3841**		517
Motor Service Inc 130 Byassee Dr	Hazelwood	MO	63042	**800-966-5080**	314-731-4111	188
Motor State Distributing 8300 Lane Dr	Watervliet	MI	49098	**800-772-2678**	269-463-4113	53
Motor Trend Magazine 6420 Wilshire Blvd 7th Fl	Los Angeles	CA	90048	**800-800-6848**	323-782-2000	456-3
Motorcar Parts & Accessories 2929 California St	Torrance	CA	90503	**800-890-9988**	310-212-7910	249
Motorcars International 3015 E Cairo St	Springfield	MO	65802	**866-970-6800**	417-831-9999	56
MotorCity Casino Hotel 2901 Grand River Ave	Detroit	MI	48201	**866-752-9622**	313-237-7711	132
Motorcycle Consumer News Magazine 3 Burroughs	Irvine	CA	92618	**888-333-0354**	949-855-8822	456-3
Motorcycle Hall of Fame Museum 13515 Yarmouth Dr	Pickerington	OH	43147	**800-262-5646**	614-856-2222	521
MotorHome Magazine 2750 Park View Ct Ste 240 *Cust Svc	Oxnard	CA	93036	**800-678-1201***	805-667-4100	456-22
Motorlease Corp 1506 New Britain Ave	Farmington	CT	06032	**800-243-0182**	860-677-9711	291
Motorola Inc IDEN Group 8000 W Sunrise Blvd	Plantation	FL	33322	**800-102-2344**		732
Motorola PAC 600 N US Hwy 45	Libertyville	IL	60048	**800-102-2344**		614
Motson Graphics Inc 1717 Bethlehem Pk	Flourtown	PA	19031	**800-972-1986**	215-233-0500	685
Mott Corp 84 Spring Ln	Farmington	CT	06032	**800-289-6688**	860-747-6333	475
Mott's LLP PO Box 869077 *Consumer Info	Plano	TX	75086	**800-426-4891***		297-20
Moultrie Feeders 150 Industrial Rd	Alabaster	AL	35007	**800-653-3334**	205-664-6700	708
Moultrie-Colquitt County Chamber of Commerce 116 First Ave SE	Moultrie	GA	31768	**888-408-4748**	229-985-2131	138
Mount Aloysius College 7373 Admiral Perry Hwy	Cresson	PA	16630	**888-823-2220**	814-886-6383	167
Mount Angel Seminary 1 Abbey Dr	Saint Benedict	OR	97373	**800-845-8272**	503-845-3951	168-3
Mount Bachelor Village Resort & Conference Ctr 19717 Mt Bachelor Dr	Bend	OR	97702	**800-547-5204**	541-389-5900	667
Mount Carmel Public Utility Co 316 Market St PO Box 220	Mount Carmel	IL	62863	**877-262-7036**	618-262-5151	785
Mount Carmel West Hospital 793 W State St	Columbus	OH	43222	**800-346-1009**	614-234-5000	374-3
Mount Holyoke College 50 College St	South Hadley	MA	01075	**800-642-4483**	413-538-2000	167
Mount Joy Wire Corp 1000 E Main St	Mount Joy	PA	17552	**800-321-2305**	717-653-1461	811
Mount Laurel Library 100 Walt Whitman Ave	Mount Laurel	NJ	08054	**888-576-5529**	856-234-7319	434-3
Mount Marty College 1105 W Eigth St *Admissions	Yankton	SD	57078	**800-658-4552***	605-668-1545	167
Mount Mary College 2900 N Menomonee River Pkwy *Admissions	Milwaukee	WI	53222	**800-321-6265***	414-256-1219	167
Mount Mercy College 1330 Elmhurst Dr NE	Cedar Rapids	IA	52402	**800-248-4504**	319-368-6460	167
Mount Nittany Medical Ctr 1800 E Pk Ave	State College	PA	16803	**866-686-6171**	814-231-7000	374-3
Mount Olive College 634 Henderson St	Mount Olive	NC	28365	**800-653-0854**	919-658-2502	167
Mount Prospect Chamber of Commerce 662 E NW Hwy	Mount Prospect	IL	60056	**800-584-4452**	847-398-6616	138
Mount Regis Ctr 405 Kimball Ave	Salem	VA	24153	**877-217-3447**		724
Mount Revelstoke National Park of Canada PO Box 350	Revelstoke	BC	V0E2S0	**866-787-6221**	250-837-7500	562
Mount Royal College 4825 Mt Royal Gate SW	Calgary	AB	T3E6K6	**877-440-5001**	403-440-6111	783
Mount Saint Mary College 330 Powell Ave	Newburgh	NY	12550	**888-937-6762**	845-569-3248	167
Mount Saint Mary' s University 12001 Chalon Rd *Admissions	Los Angeles	CA	90049	**800-999-9893***	310-954-4250	167
Mount Saint Mary's University 16300 Old Emmitsburg Rd *Admissions	Emmitsburg	MD	21727	**800-448-4347***	301-447-5214	167
Mount Saint Vincent University 166 Bedford Hwy	Halifax	NS	B3M2J6	**877-733-6788**	902-457-6117	783
Mount San Jacinto College 1499 N State St	San Jacinto	CA	92583	**800-624-5561**	951-487-6752	161
Mount Shasta Resort 1000 Siskiyou Lk Blvd	Mount Shasta	CA	96067	**800-958-3363**	530-926-3030	667
Mount Sinai Hospital Bone Marrow Transplant Program 19 E 98th St	New York	NY	10029	**866-682-9380**	212-241-6021	767
Mount Sinai Hospital Medical Ctr of Chicago California Ave 15th St	Chicago	IL	60608	**877-448-7848**	773-542-2000	374-3
Mount Sinai Medical Ctr, The 1 Gustave L Levy Pl	New York	NY	10029	**800-637-4627**	212-241-6500	374-3
Mount Sinai Memorial Park 5950 Forest Lawn Dr	Los Angeles	CA	90068	**800-600-0076**	323-469-6000	509
Mount Sinai of Queens 25-10 30th Ave	Astoria	NY	11102	**800-968-7637**	718-932-1000	374-3
Mount Union College 1972 Clark Ave *Admissions	Alliance	OH	44601	**800-334-6682***	330-823-2590	167
Mount Vernon Convention & Visitors Bureau 1100 Main St	Mount Vernon	IL	62864	**800-252-5464**	618-242-3151	208
Mount Vernon Nazarene University 800 Martinsburg Rd *Admissions	Mount Vernon	OH	43050	**800-766-8206***	740-392-6868	167
Mount View Hotel & Spa 1457 Lincoln Ave	Calistoga	CA	94515	**800-816-6877**	707-942-6877	379
Mount Washington Hotel & Resort Rt 302	Bretton Woods	NH	03575	**800-314-1752**	603-278-1000	667
Mountain America Credit Union PO Box 9001	West Jordan	UT	84084	**800-748-4302**	801-325-6228	221
Mountain Electric Co-op Inc PO Box 180 *Cust Svc	Mountain City	TN	37683	**800-638-3788***	423-727-1800	247
Mountain Haus 292 E Meadow Dr	Vail	CO	81657	**800-237-0922**	970-476-2434	379
Mountain Home Air Force Base 366 Gunfighter Ave Ste 314	Mountain Home AFB	ID	83648	**855-366-0140**	208-828-6800	496-1
Mountain Home Area Chamber of Commerce 1023 Hwy 62	Mountain Home	AR	72653	**800-822-3536**	870-425-5111	138
Mountain Home National Cemetery PO Box 8	Mountain Home	TN	37684	**800-827-1000**	423-979-3535	135
Mountain Lake Hotel 115 Hotel Cir	Pembroke	VA	24136	**800-346-3334**	540-626-7121	379
Mountain Laurel Resort & Spa Rt 940 PO Box 9	White Haven	PA	18661	**888-243-9300**	570-443-8411	667
Mountain Laurel Spa at Stonewall Resort 940 Resort Dr	Roanoke	WV	26447	**888-278-8150**	304-269-8881	705
Mountain Lion Foundation PO Box 1896	Sacramento	CA	95812	**800-319-7621**	916-442-2666	47-3
Mountain Lodge at Telluride 457 Mtn Village Blvd	Telluride	CO	81435	**866-368-6867**	970-369-5000	667
Mountain Ltd 19 Yarmouth Dr Ste 301	New Gloucester	ME	04260	**800-322-8627**	207-688-6200	630
Mountain Manor Treatment Ctr 9701 Keysville Rd	Emmitsburg	MD	21727	**800-537-3422**	301-447-2361	724
Mountain Parks Electric Inc 321 W Agate Ave	Granby	CO	80446	**877-887-3378**	970-887-3378	247
Mountain Research LLC 825 25th St	Altoona	PA	16601	**800-837-4674**	814-949-2034	740
Mountain States Pipe & Supply Co 111 W Las Vegas St	Colorado Springs	CO	80903	**800-777-7173**	719-634-5555	611
Mountain Supply Co 2101 Mullan Rd	Missoula	MT	59808	**800-821-1646**	406-543-8255	611
Mountain Telephone Co 405 Main St	West Liberty	KY	41472	**800-939-3121**	606-743-3121	387
Mountain Travel Sobek 1266 66th St Ste 4	Emeryville	CA	94608	**888-831-7526**	510-594-6000	758
Mountain Valley Bank 317 DAVIS Ave	Elkins	WV	26241	**800-555-3503**	304-637-2265	69
Mountain View Electric Assn Inc 1655 Fifth St	Limon	CO	80828	**800-388-9881**	719-775-2861	247
Mountain View Hospital 1000 East 100 North	Payson	UT	84651	**877-865-9738**	801-465-7000	374-3
Mountain Villas 9525 W Skyline Pkwy	Duluth	MN	55810	**866-688-4552**	218-624-5784	379
Mountaineers Books 1001 Sw Klickitat Way Ste 201	Seattle	WA	98134	**800-553-4453**	206-223-6303	95
Mountaineers, The 7700 Sand Pt Way NE	Seattle	WA	98115	**800-573-8484**	206-521-6000	47-23
Mountaire Corp PO Box 1320	Millsboro	DE	19966	**877-887-1490**	302-934-1100	446
Mountaire Farms 17269 NC Hwy 71 N	Lumber Bridge	NC	28357	**877-887-1490**	910-843-5942	618
Mountrail-Williams Electric Co-op 218 58th St W PO Box 1346	Williston	ND	58802	**800-279-2667**	701-577-3765	247
Mountz Inc 1080 N 11th St	San Jose	CA	95112	**888-925-2763**	408-292-2214	350
Mouser Custom Cabinetry 2112 N Hwy 31 W	Elizabethtown	KY	42701	**800-345-7537**	270-737-7477	114
Mouser Electronics Corp 1000 N Main St	Mansfield	TX	76063	**800-346-6873**	817-804-3888	248
Movies Unlimited Inc 3015 Darnell Rd	Philadelphia	PA	19154	**800-668-4344**	215-637-4444	458
Moyer & Son Inc 113 E Reliance Rd	Souderton	PA	18964	**866-669-3747**	215-799-2000	446
Moyno Inc 1895 W Jefferson St	Springfield	OH	45506	**877-486-6966**	937-327-3111	638
MP Biomedicals LLC 3 Hutton Ctr Dr Ste 100	Santa Ana	CA	92707	**800-633-1352**	949-833-2500	476
MP Global Products Inc 2500 Old Hadar Rd	Norfolk	NE	68701	**888-379-9695**	402-379-9695	260
MP Husky Corp 204 Old Piedmont Hwy PO Box 16749	Greenville	SC	29605	**800-277-4810**	864-234-4800	814
MP Metal Products Inc W1250 Elmwood Ave	Ixonia	WI	53036	**800-824-6744**	920-261-9650	481
MP Pumps Inc 34800 Bennett Dr	Fraser	MI	48026	**800-563-8006**	586-293-8240	638
MPA (Magazine Publishers of America) 810 Seventh Ave 24th Fl	New York	NY	10019	**800-234-3368**	212-872-3700	48-16
MPBN (Maine Public Broadcasting Network) 65 Texas Ave	Bangor	ME	04401	**800-884-1717**	207-941-1010	629
MPC Promotions 4300 Produce Rd PO Box 34336	Louisville	KY	40232	**800-331-0989**	502-451-4900	154-8
MPD Inc 316 E Ninth St	Owensboro	KY	42303	**866-225-5673**	270-685-6200	419

Name	Address	City	State	ZIP	Toll-Free	Phone	Class
MPhA (Minnesota Pharmacists Assn)	1935 W County Rd B2	Roseville	MN	55113	**800-451-8349**	651-697-1771	584
mphoria LLC	1245 Rosemont Dr	Indian Land	SC	29707	**888-415-4933**		5
MPI (Meeting Professionals International)	3030 LBJ Fwy Ste 1700	Dallas	TX	75234	**866-748-9561**	972-702-3000	48-12
MPI Label Systems Inc	450 Courtney Rd	Sebring	OH	44672	**800-423-0442**	330-938-2134	413
MPI Technologies	37 E St	Winchester	MA	01890	**888-674-8088**	781-729-8300	599
MPM Capital Offices	200 Clarendon St 54th Fl	Boston	MA	02116	**888-286-8010**	617-425-9200	790
MPM Medical Inc	2301 Crown Ct	Irving	TX	75038	**800-232-5512**	972-893-4090	475
MPP (Merriweather Post Pavilion)	10475 Little Patuxent Pkwy	Columbia	MD	21044	**877-435-9849**	410-715-5550	571
MPR (Minnesota Public Radio)	480 Cedar St	Saint Paul	MN	55101	**800-228-7123**	651-290-1212	629
MPT (Maryland Public Television)	11767 Owings Mills Blvd	Owings Mills	MD	21117	**800-223-3678**	410-581-4201	629
MPW Industrial Services Group Inc	9711 Lancaster Rd SE	Hebron	OH	43025	**800-827-8790**	740-929-1614	151
Mr Appliance Corp	304 E Church Ave	Killeen	TX	76541	**888-998-2011**		311
Mr Crane Inc	647 N Hariton St	Orange	CA	92868	**800-598-3465**	714-633-2100	192
Mr Goodcents Franchise Systems Inc	8997 Commerce Dr	DeSoto	KS	66018	**800-648-2368**		668
Mr Handyman International LLC	3948 Ranchero Dr Ste 1C *Cust Svc	Ann Arbor	MI	48108	**855-632-2126***	800-289-4600	311
Mr Hero Restaurants	7010 Engle Rd Ste 100	Middleburg Heights	OH	44130	**888-860-5082**	440-625-3080	668
Mr Jim's Pizza Inc	*Franchise Service Ctr* 2521 Pepperwood St	Farmers Branch	TX	75234	**800-583-5960**	972-267-5467	668
MR Label Inc	5018 Gray Rd	Cincinnati	OH	45232	**888-522-3526**	513-681-2088	626
Mr Rooter Corp	1010 N University Parks Dr	Waco	TX	76707	**877-766-8305**	800-583-8003	191-10
M-R Sign Company Inc	1706 First Ave N	Fergus Falls	MN	56537	**800-231-5564**	218-736-5681	699
Mr Tire Auto Service Centers Inc	200 Holleder Pkwy	Rochester	NY	14615	**800-876-6676**		61-5
Mr Transmission	9675 Yonge St 2nd Fl	Richmond Hill	ON	L4C1V7	**800-373-8432**	905-884-1511	61-6
MRAS (Middle River Aircraft Systems)	103 Chesapeake Pk Plaza	Baltimore	MD	21220	**877-432-3272**	410-682-1500	22
MRC (Medicare Rights Ctr)	520 Eigth Ave N Wing 3rd Fl *Hotline	New York	NY	10018	**800-333-4114***	212-869-3850	47-17
MRC Global Inc	2 Houston Ctr	Houston	TX	77010	**877-294-7574**		785
MRI (Mortgage Resources Inc)	425 S Woods Mill Rd Ste 100	Chesterfield	MO	63017	**800-965-9910**	314-576-5577	508
MRI Group	2100 Harrisburg Pk	Lancaster	PA	17601	**888-674-1377**	717-291-1016	415
MRMC (Midwestern Regional Medical Ctr)	2520 Elisha Ave	Zion	IL	60099	**800-615-3055**	847-872-4561	374-7
MRMC (Martin Resource Management Corp)	PO Box 191	Kilgore	TX	75663	**888-334-7473**	903-983-6200	317
MRN Inc	5353 South 960 East Ste 200	Salt Lake City	UT	84117	**888-674-6741**		77
Mrs Clark's Foods	740 SE Dalbey Dr	Ankeny	IA	50021	**800-736-5674**	515-299-6400	297-21
Mrs Nelsons Library Service	1650 W Orange Grove Ave	Pomona	CA	91768	**800-875-9911**	909-397-7820	95
MRTK (Metropolitan Trucking Inc)	299 Market St	Saddle Brook	NJ	07663	**800-967-3278**		448
MRV Communications Inc	20415 Nordhoff St *OTC: MRVC* ■ *Sales	Chatsworth	CA	91311	**800-338-5316***	818-773-0900	790
Ms Aerospace Inc	13928 Balboa Blvd	Sylmar	CA	91342	**866-487-2365**	818-833-9095	280
Ms Magazine	1600 Wilson Blvd Ste 801	Arlington	VA	22209	**866-672-6363**	703-522-4201	456-11
MSA (Medical Services of America Inc)	171 Monroe Ln	Lexington	SC	29072	**800-845-5850**	803-957-0500	363
MSA Security	9 Murray St 2nd Fl	New York	NY	10007	**800-286-2000**	212-509-1336	690
MSANA (Masonic Service Assn of North America)	8120 Fenton St Ste 203	Silver Spring	MD	20910	**855-476-4010**	301-588-4010	47-15
MSB Financial Corp (MSBF)	1902 Long Hill Rd *NASDAQ: MSBF*	Millington	NJ	07946	**844-265-9680**	908-647-4000	69
MSBF (MSB Financial Corp)	1902 Long Hill Rd *NASDAQ: MSBF*	Millington	NJ	07946	**844-265-9680**	908-647-4000	69
MSC Filtration Technologies	198 Freshwater Blvd *Cust Svc	Enfield	CT	06082	**800-237-7359***	860-745-7475	804
MSC Industrial Direct Co	75 Maxess Rd *NYSE: MSM*	Melville	NY	11747	**800-645-7270**	516-812-2000	385
MSE (Micro Solutions Enterprises)	8201 Woodley Ave	Van Nuys	CA	91406	**800-673-4968**	818-407-7500	627
MSF (Multiple Sclerosis Foundation)	6520 N Andrews Ave	Fort Lauderdale	FL	33309	**800-225-6495**	954-776-6805	47-17
Msf Electric Inc	10455 Fountaingate Dr	Stafford	TX	77477	**866-366-7943**	281-494-4700	191-4
MSHA (Mine Safety & Health Administration)	1100 Wilson Blvd	Arlington	VA	22209	**800-746-1553**	202-693-9400	340-13
MSI Benefits Group Inc	245 Townpark Dr Ste 100	Kennesaw	GA	30144	**800-580-1629**	770-425-1231	390
MSI Inventory Service Corp	PO Box 320129	Flowood	MS	39232	**800-820-1460**	601-939-0130	399
Msights Inc	9935 Rea Rd Ste D-301	Charlotte	NC	28277	**877-267-4448**		807
MSK Precision Products Inc	10101 NW 67th St	Tamarac	FL	33321	**800-992-5018**	954-776-0770	620
MSM Industries Inc	802 Swan Dr	Smyrna	TN	37167	**800-648-6648**	615-355-4355	674
MSM Transportation Inc	124 Commercial Rd	Bolton	ON	L7E1K4	**800-667-4175**	905-951-6800	312
MSPB (Merit Systems Protection Board)	1615 M St NW	Washington	DC	20419	**800-209-8960**	202-653-7200	340-18
MSPB (Merit Systems Protection Board Regional Offices)	*Atlanta Region* 401 W Peachtree St NW 10th Fl	Atlanta	GA	30308	**800-209-8960**	404-730-2755	340-18
MSR Communications	832 Sansome St 2nd Fl	San Francisco	CA	94111	**866-247-6172**	415-989-9000	633
MSRB (Municipal Securities Rulemaking Board)	1900 Duke St Ste 600	Alexandria	VA	22314	**888-475-8376**	703-797-6600	48-2
MSU (Missouri State University)	901 S National Ave	Springfield	MO	65897	**800-492-7900**	417-836-5000	167
MSU-DOE Plant Research Laboratory	612 Wilson Rd	East Lansing	MI	48824	**800-875-5090**	517-353-2270	666
M&T Bank	1 M & T Plz 13th Fl *NYSE: MTB*	Buffalo	NY	14203	**800-724-2440**	716-842-4470	69
Mt Shasta Spring Water Company Inc	1878 Twin View Blvd	Redding	CA	96003	**800-922-6227**	530-246-8800	366
Mt. Lebanon School District	7 Horsman Dr	Pittsburgh	PA	15228	**800-222-3353**	412-344-2000	683
MTA Today Magazine	20 Ashburton Pl	Boston	MA	02108	**800-392-6175**	617-878-8000	456-8
MTC (Materials Transportation Co)	1408 S Commerce PO Box 1358	Temple	TX	76503	**800-433-3110**	254-298-2900	386
MTD Products Inc	5965 Grafton Rd	Valley City	OH	44280	**800-800-7310**	330-225-2600	429
MTE Corp	PO Box 9013	Menomonee Falls	WI	53051	**800-455-4683**	262-253-8200	765
MTI (Momentum Technologies Inc)	1507 Boettler Rd	Uniontown	OH	44685	**800-720-0261**	330-896-5900	602
MTI (Medical Teams International)	PO Box 10	Portland	OR	97207	**800-959-4325**	503-624-1000	47-5
MTI America	PO Box 667140	Pompano Beach	FL	33066	**800-553-2155**		393
MTI Inc	1050 NW 229th Ave	Hillsboro	OR	97124	**800-426-6844**	503-648-6500	613
MTI Systems Inc	59 Interstate D	West Springfield	MA	01089	**800-644-4318**	413-733-1972	180-12
Mtm Recognition Corp	3201 SE 29th St	Oklahoma City	OK	73115	**877-686-7464**	405-670-4545	409
MTNA (Music Teachers NA)	441 Vine St Ste 3100	Cincinnati	OH	45202	**888-512-5278**	513-421-1420	48-5
MTNG (Middle Tennessee Natural Gas Utility District)	1036 W Broad St PO Box 670	Smithville	TN	37166	**800-880-6373**	615-597-4300	785
MtronPTI	1703 E Hwy 50	Yankton	SD	57078	**800-762-8800**	605-665-9321	255
MTS (Mid-America Transplant Services)	1110 Highlands Plz Dr E Ste 100	Saint Louis	MO	63110	**888-376-4854**	314-735-8200	544
MTS (MTS Safety Products Inc)	PO Box 204 *General	Golden	MS	38847	**800-647-8168***		575
MTS Ambulance	2431 Greenup Ave	Ashland	KY	41101	**800-598-3458**	606-324-3286	30
MTS Medication Technologies Inc	2003 Gandy Blvd N Ste 800 *General	Saint Petersburg	FL	33702	**800-845-0053***		546
MTS Safety Products Inc (MTS)	PO Box 204 *General	Golden	MS	38847	**800-647-8168***		575
MTS Systems Corp	14000 Technology Dr *NASDAQ: MTSC* ■ *Cust Svc	Eden Prairie	MN	55344	**800-328-2255***	952-937-4000	471
MTT-S (IEEE Microwave Theory & Techniques Society)	5829 Bellanca Dr	Elkridge	MD	21075	**800-678-4333**	410-796-5866	48-19
MTU Onsite Energy Corp	100 Power Dr	Mankato	MN	56001	**800-325-5450**	507-625-7973	517
MTV Networks On Campus Inc (MTVU)	1540 Broadway 33rd Fl	New York	NY	10036	**877-800-4483**		736
MTVU (MTV Networks On Campus Inc)	1540 Broadway 33rd Fl	New York	NY	10036	**877-800-4483**		736
Mu Phi Epsilon International Music Fraternity	PO Box 1369	Fort Collins	CO	80522	**888-259-1471**		47-16
Mud Hole Custom Tackle Inc	400 Kane Ct	Oviedo	FL	32765	**866-790-7637**	407-447-7637	709
Mudiam Inc	7100 regency Sq blvd	Houston	TX	77036	**888-306-2062**	713-484-7266	227
Mueller Brass Co	2199 Lapeer Ave	Port Huron	MI	48060	**800-553-3336**	810-987-7770	484
Mueller Co	500 W Eldorado St	Decatur	IL	62522	**800-423-1323**	217-423-4471	787
Mueller Inc	1913 Hutchins Ave	Ballinger	TX	76821	**877-268-3553**	325-365-3555	104
Mueller Industries Inc	8285 Tournament Dr Ste 150 *NYSE: MLI*	Memphis	TN	38125	**800-348-8464**	901-753-3200	484
Mueller Plastics Corp	3070 E Cedar	Ontario	CA	91761	**800-348-8464**	909-930-2060	595
Mueller Refrigeration Co Inc	121 Rogers St *Cust Svc	Hartsville	TN	37074	**866-566-7233***	615-374-2124	787
Mueller Steam Specialty	1491 NC Hwy 20 W	Saint Pauls	NC	28384	**800-334-6259**	910-865-8241	386
Mui Scientific	145 Traders Blvd E	Mississauga	ON	L4Z3L3	**800-303-6611**	905-890-5525	475
Muir Enterprises Inc	3575 West 900 South PO Box 26775	Salt Lake City	UT	84104	**877-268-2002**	801-363-7695	298-7
Muir Glen Organic Tomato Products	PO Box 9452	Minneapolis	MN	55440	**800-624-4123**	800-248-7310	297-20

Name / Address	City	State	Zip	Toll-Free	Phone	Class
Mule Creek State Prison 4001 Hwy 104	Ione	CA	95640	**877-256-6877**	209-274-4911	215
Mule Lighting Inc 46 Baker St	Providence	RI	02905	**800-556-7690**	401-941-4446	439
Mulhern Belting Inc 148 Bauer Dr	Oakland	NJ	07436	**800-253-6300**	201-337-5700	370
MultAlloy Inc 8511 Monroe St	Houston	TX	77061	**800-568-9551**		491
Multax Systems Inc 505 N Sepulveda Blvd Ste 7	Manhattan Beach	CA	90266	**800-888-0199**	310-379-8398	263
Multi-Ad Inc 1720 W Detweiller Dr	Peoria	IL	61615	**800-348-6485**	309-692-1530	180-1
Multichannel News 28 E 28th St 12th Fl *Cust Svc	New York	NY	10016	**888-343-5563***	917-281-4700	456-9
Multicoat Corp 23331 Antonio Pkwy	Rancho Santa Margarita	CA	92688	**877-685-8426**	949-888-7100	499
Multigon Industries Inc 525 Executive Boulevard	Yonkers	NY	10701	**800-289-6858**		188
Multimatic Products Inc 390 Oser Ave	Hauppauge	NY	11788	**800-767-7633**	631-231-1515	620
MultiMedia Schools Magazine 143 Old Marlton Pk	Medford	NJ	08055	**800-300-9868**	609-654-6266	456-7
Multipet International Inc 265 W Commercial Ave	Moonachie	NJ	07074	**800-900-6738**	201-438-6600	577
Multiplan inc 115 Fifth Ave	New York	NY	10003	**800-922-4362**	212-780-2000	390
Multiple Sclerosis Foundation (MSF) 6520 N Andrews Ave	Fort Lauderdale	FL	33309	**800-225-6495**	954-776-6805	47-17
Multiquip Inc 18910 Wilmington Ave	Carson	CA	90746	**800-421-1244**	310-537-3700	385
Multisoft Corp 1723 SE 47th Ter	Cape Coral	FL	33904	**888-415-0554**	239-945-6433	179
Multi-Tech Systems 2205 Woodale Dr *Cust Svc	Mounds View	MN	55112	**800-328-9717***	763-785-3500	175-3
Multnomah University 8435 NE Glisan St	Portland	OR	97220	**800-275-4672**	503-255-0332	168-3
Muncie Star-Press 345 S High St	Muncie	IN	47305	**800-783-7827**	765-747-5700	531-2
Muncie Visitors Bureau 3700 S Madison St	Muncie	IN	47302	**800-568-6862**	765-284-2700	208
Muncie-Delaware County Chamber of Commerce 401 S High St	Muncie	IN	47305	**800-336-1373**	765-288-6681	138
Municipal Auditorium Arena 1321 Baltimore Ave	Kansas City	MO	64105	**800-767-7700**	816-691-3800	718
Municipal Credit Union PO Box 3205	New York	NY	10007	**866-512-6109**	212-693-4900	221
Municipal Litigation Reporter 590 Dutch Vly Rd NE	Atlanta	GA	30324	**800-926-7926**	404-881-1141	530-7
Municipal Securities Rulemaking Board (MSRB) 1900 Duke St Ste 600	Alexandria	VA	22314	**888-475-8376**	703-797-6600	48-2
MuniMae (MMA Capital Management LLC) 621 E Pratt St Ste 600 *OTC: MMAB*	Baltimore	MD	21202	**855-650-6932**	443-263-2900	508
Munro & Co Inc 3770 Malvern Rd 71901 PO Box 6048	Hot Springs	AR	71902	**800-819-1901**	501-262-6000	302
Munsch Hardt Kopf Harr Pc 500 N Akard St	Dallas	TX	75201	**800-321-6742**	214-855-7500	428
Munson Healthcare 1105 Sixth St	Traverse City	MI	49684	**800-468-6766**	231-935-5000	371
Munson's Candy Kitchen Inc 174 Hop River Rd	Bolton	CT	06043	**888-686-7667**	860-649-4332	297-8
Munters Corp 210 Sixth St PO Box 6428	Fort Myers	FL	33907	**800-843-5360**	239-936-1555	14
Munters Corp DHI 79 Monroe St *Sales	Amesbury	MA	01913	**800-843-5360***	978-241-1100	14
Muralo Company Inc 148 E Fifth St	Bayonne	NJ	07002	**800-631-3440**	201-437-0770	549
Murata Electronics North America Inc 2200 Lake Pk Dr	Smyrna	GA	30080	**800-704-6079**	770-436-1300	255
Murata Machinery USA Inc 2120 Queen City Dr	Charlotte	NC	28208	**800-428-8469**		455
Murdock Industrial Supply 1111 E 1st	Wichita	KS	67202	**800-362-2422**	316-262-4476	248
Murdock Webbing Co 27 Foundry St	Central Falls	RI	02863	**800-375-2052**	401-724-3000	742-5
Murnane Paper Corp 345 W Fischer Farm Rd	Elmhurst	IL	60126	**855-632-8191**	630-530-8222	552
Murphy & Nolan Inc 340 Peat St PO Box 6689	Syracuse	NY	13217	**800-836-6385**	315-474-8203	491
Murphy Co Mechanical Contractors & Engineers 1233 N Price Rd	Saint Louis	MO	63132	**888-838-4038**	314-997-6600	191-10
Murphy Hardwood Plywood 2350 Prairie Rd	Eugene	OR	97402	**888-461-4545**	541-461-4545	612
Murphy Oil Corp 200 Peach St	El Dorado	AR	71730	**888-289-9314**	870-862-6411	579
Murphy Plywood Co 2350 Prairie Rd	Eugene	OR	97402	**888-461-4545**	541-461-4545	612
Murray Bank, The 405 S 12th St	Murray	KY	42071	**877-965-1122**	270-753-5626	69
Murray Co 1215 Fern Ridge Pkwy Ste 213	Saint Louis	MO	63141	**888-323-5560**	314-576-2818	683
Murray Guard Inc 58 Murray Guard Dr	Jackson	TN	38305	**800-238-3830**	731-668-3400	691
Murray Sheet Metal Co Inc 3112 Seventh St	Parkersburg	WV	26104	**800-464-8801**	304-422-5431	695
Murray State College 1 Murray Campus	Tishomingo	OK	73460	**800-342-0698**	580-371-2371	161
Murray State University 102 Curris Ctr	Murray	KY	42071	**800-272-4678**	270-809-3741	167
Hopkinsville 5305 Ft Campbell Blvd	Hopkinsville	KY	42240	**800-669-7654**	270-707-1525	167
Murrays Ford Inc 3007 Blinker Pkwy	Du Bois	PA	15801	**800-371-6601**	814-371-6600	515
Murrey International Inc 14150 S Figueroa St	Los Angeles	CA	90061	**800-421-1022**	310-532-6091	708
Murrows Transfer Inc PO Box 4095 *Cust Svc	High Point	NC	27263	**800-669-2928***	336-475-6101	778
M-USA (Mercy-USA for Aid & Development Inc) 44450 Pinetree Dr Ste 201	Plymouth	MI	48170	**800-556-3729**	734-454-0011	47-5
Muscatine Community College 152 Colorado St	Muscatine	IA	52761	**888-336-3907**	563-288-6001	161
Muscle & Fitness Hers Magazine 21100 Erwin St	Woodland Hills	CA	91367	**800-340-8954**		456-13
Musco Sports Lighting LLC 100 First Ave W PO Box 808	Oskaloosa	IA	52577	**800-825-6020**	641-673-0411	439
Muscular Dystrophy Assn (MDA) 3300 E Sunrise Dr	Tucson	AZ	85718	**800-572-1717**	520-529-2000	47-17
Musculoskeletal Transplant Foundation 125 May St Ste 300	Edison	NJ	08837	**800-946-9008**	732-661-0202	544
Muse, The 130 W 46th St	New York	NY	10036	**877-692-6873**	212-485-2400	379
Museum Facsimiles 117 Fourth St	Pittsfield	MA	01201	**877-499-0020**	413-499-0020	129
Museum of Anthropology Wake Forest University Wingate Rd PO Box 7267	Winston-Salem	NC	27109	**888-925-3622**	336-758-5282	519
Museum of Art & Archaeology 1 Pickard Hall	Columbia	MO	65211	**866-447-9821**	573-882-3591	519
Museum of Arts & Sciences 352 S Nova Rd	Daytona Beach	FL	32114	**866-439-4769**	386-255-0285	519
Museum of Contemporary Religious Art 221 N Grand Blvd	Saint Louis	MO	63103	**800-442-1142**	314-977-7170	519
Museum of Early Southern Decorative Arts (MESDA) 924 S Main St	Winston-Salem	NC	27101	**800-441-5303**	336-721-7360	519
Museum of Geology 501 E St Joseph St S Dakota School of Mines & Technology	Rapid City	SD	57701	**800-544-8162**	605-394-2467	519
Museum of Glass 1801 Dock St *General	Tacoma	WA	98402	**866-468-7386***	253-284-4750	519
Museum of History & Art 1100 Orange Ave	Coronado	CA	92118	**866-599-7242**	619-435-7242	519
Museum of Making Music 5790 Armada Dr	Carlsbad	CA	92008	**877-551-9976**	760-438-5996	519
Museum of Missouri Military History 2302 Militia Dr	Jefferson City	MO	65101	**888-526-6664**	573-638-9603	519
Museum of Natural History & Science 1301 Western Ave Cincinnati Museum Ctr	Cincinnati	OH	45203	**800-733-2077**	513-287-7000	519
Museum of Nebraska History 15th & P St PO Box 82554	Lincoln	NE	68508	**800-833-6747**	402-471-4754	519
Museum of Northern Arizona 3101 N Ft Valley Rd	Flagstaff	AZ	86001	**800-423-1069**	928-774-5211	519
Museum of Science & Industry 5700 S Lk Shore Dr	Chicago	IL	60637	**800-468-6674**	773-684-1414	519
Museum of the Mountain Man 700 E Hennick St	Pinedale	WY	82941	**877-686-6266**	307-367-4101	519
Museum of Tolerance 9786 W Pico Blvd	Los Angeles	CA	90035	**800-900-9036**	310-553-8403	519
Museum of World Treasures 835 E First St	Wichita	KS	67202	**888-700-1311**	316-263-1311	519
Museums at 18th & Vine 1616 E 18th St	Kansas City	MO	64108	**800-734-3447**	816-474-8463	519
Museums of Oglebay Institute 1330 National Rd	Wheeling	WV	26003	**800-624-6988**	304-242-7272	519
Musgrave Pencil Company Inc 701 W Ln St	Shelbyville	TN	37160	**800-736-2450**	931-684-3611	570
Music & Arts Centers Inc 4626 Wedgewood Blvd	Frederick	MD	21703	**888-731-5396**		525
Music Box Dinner Playhouse 196 Hughes St	Swoyersville	PA	18704	**800-698-7529**	570-283-2195	571
Music Celebrations International 1440 S Priest Dr Ste 102	Tempe	AZ	85281	**800-395-2036**	480-894-3330	770
Music for All 39 W Jackson Pl Ste 150	Indianapolis	IN	46225	**800-848-2263**	317-636-2263	47-11
Music People Inc 154 Woodlawn Rd Ste C	Berlin	CT	06037	**800-289-8889**		248
Music Teachers NA (MTNA) 441 Vine St Ste 3100	Cincinnati	OH	45202	**888-512-5278**	513-421-1420	48-5
Musician's Friend Inc PO Box 7479	Westlake Village	CA	91359	**800-391-8762**	801-501-8110	525
Musiciansbuy.com Inc 7830 Byron Dr Ste 1	West Palm Beach	FL	33404	**877-778-7845**	561-842-7451	525
Muskegon Area Chamber of Commerce 380 W Western Ste 202	Muskegon	MI	49440	**800-659-2955**	231-722-3751	138
Muskegon Area District Library 4845 Airline Rd	Muskegon	MI	49444	**877-569-4801**	231-737-6248	434-3
Muskegon Chronicle 981 Third St	Muskegon	MI	49440	**800-783-3161**	231-722-3161	531-2
Muskegon Community College 221 S Quarterline Rd	Muskegon	MI	49442	**866-711-4622**	231-773-9131	161
Muskegon County Convention & Visitors Bureau 610 W Western Ave	Muskegon	MI	49440	**800-250-9283**	231-724-3100	208
Muskingum College 163 Stormont St *Admissions	New Concord	OH	43762	**800-752-6082***	740-826-8211	167
Musselman & Hall Contractors LLC 4922 E Blue Banks PO Box 300858	Kansas City	MO	64130	**800-257-4255**	816-861-1234	191-3
Musson Rubber Company Inc 1320 E Archwood Ave *Cust Svc	Akron	OH	44306	**800-321-2381***	330-773-7651	674
Musson Theatrical Inc 890 Walsh Ave	Santa Clara	CA	95050	**800-843-2837**	408-986-0210	720
Mustang Dynamometer 2300 Pinnacle Pkwy	Twinsburg	OH	44087	**888-468-7826**	330-963-5400	471
Mustang Fuel Corp 9800 N Oklahoma Ave	Oklahoma City	OK	73114	**800-332-9400**	405-748-9400	537

Name	Address	City	State	ZIP	Toll-Free	Phone	Class
Mustang Tractor & Equipment Co	12800 NW Fwy	Houston	TX	77040	**800-256-1001**	713-460-2000	358
Muth Electric Inc	1717 N Sanborn PO Box 1400	Mitchell	SD	57301	**800-888-1597**	605-996-3983	191-4
Mutiny Hotel	2951 S Bayshore Dr	Miami	FL	33133	**888-868-8469**	305-441-2100	379
Mutoh America Inc	2602 S 47th St Ste 102	Phoenix	AZ	85034	**800-996-8864**	480-968-7772	175-6
Mutual Benefit Group	409 Penn St PO Box 577	Huntingdon	PA	16652	**800-283-3531**	814-643-3000	527
Mutual Fund Store LLC, The	11095 Metcalf Ave Ste 220	Overland Park	KS	66210	**800-375-3000**		462
Mutual Industries Inc	707 W Grange St	Philadelphia	PA	19120	**800-523-0888**	215-927-6000	742-3
Mutual Insurance Company of Arizona	PO Box 33180	Phoenix	AZ	85067	**800-352-0402**	602-956-5276	391-2
Mutual Liquid Gas & Equipment Co Inc	17117 S Broadway St	Gardena	CA	90248	**800-633-3574**	323-321-3771	317
Mutual Materials Co	605 119th Ave NE	Bellevue	WA	98005	**800-477-3008**	425-452-2300	149
Mutual Mobile Inc	206 E Ninth St Ste 1400	Austin	TX	78701	**800-208-3563**	512-615-1800	179
Mutual of America Life Insurance Co	320 Pk Ave	New York	NY	10022	**800-468-3785**	212-224-1600	391-2
Mutual of Enumclaw Insurance Co	1460 Wells St	Enumclaw	WA	98022	**800-366-5551**	360-825-2591	391-4
Mutual of Omaha Bank	3333 Farnam St	Omaha	NE	68131	**866-351-5646**	877-471-7896	69
Mutual of Omaha Co	3300 Mutual of Omaha Plz	Omaha	NE	68175	**800-775-6000**	402-342-7600	360-4
Mutual of Omaha Insurance Co	Mutual of Omaha Plaza	Omaha	NE	68175	**800-775-6000**	402-342-7600	391-2
Mutual Telecom Services Inc	250 First Ave Ste 301	Needham	MA	02494	**800-687-2848**		191-4
Mutual Trust Life Insurance Co	1200 Jorie Blvd	Oak Brook	IL	60522	**800-323-7320**	630-990-1000	391-2
Mutual Wheel Co Inc	2345 Fourth Ave	Moline	IL	61265	**800-798-6926**	309-757-1200	60
MutualFirst Financial Inc	110 E Charles St *NASDAQ: MFSF*	Muncie	IN	47305	**800-382-8031**	765-747-2800	360-2
Muzak LLC	3318 Lakemont Blvd	Fort Mill	SC	29708	**888-689-2559**	770-246-3941	523
MVC Capital Inc	287 Bowman Ave 2nd Fl *NYSE: MVC*	Purchase	NY	10577	**800-322-2885**	914-510-9400	790
MVM Products LLC	940 Calle Amanecer Ste K	San Clemente	CA	92673	**888-246-5832**	949-366-1470	590
MVMA (Maine Veterinary Medical Assn)	97A Exchange St Ste 305	Portland	ME	04101	**800-448-2772**		793
MVP Health Care	625 State St	Schenectady	NY	12305	**800-777-4793**	518-370-4793	391-3
MVP Laboratories Inc	4805 G St	Omaha	NE	68117	**800-856-4648**	402-331-5106	581
MVRBC	5500 Lakeview Pkwy	Davenport	IA	52501	**800-747-5401**	641-682-8149	88
MVSB (Meredith Village Savings Bank)	24 State Rt 25 PO Box 177	Meredith	NH	03253	**800-922-6872**	603-279-7986	69
Mwh Global Inc	380 Interlocken Crescent Ste 200	Broomfield	CO	80021	**866-257-5984**	303-533-1900	194
Mx Group, The	7020 High Grove Blvd	Burr Ridge	IL	60527	**800-827-0170**		196
MXL Industries Inc	1764 Rohrerstown Rd	Lancaster	PA	17601	**800-233-0159**	717-569-8711	603
My Alarm Center LLC	3803 W Chester Pike Ste 100	Newtown Square	PA	19073	**866-484-4800**		691
My Favorite Muffin	500 Lk Cook Rd Ste 475	Deerfield	IL	60015	**800-251-6101**	847-948-7520	311
My Receptionist	800 Wisconsin St Ste 410	Eau Claire	WI	54703	**800-686-0162**		734
My Service Depot	8774 Cotter St	Lewis Center	OH	43035	**888-518-0818**		762
Myakka River State Park	13208 SR 72	Sarasota	FL	34241	**800-326-3521**	941-361-6511	564
Myers Brothers of Kansas City Inc	1210 W 28th St	Kansas City	MO	64108	**800-264-2404**	816-931-5501	53
Myers Container Corp	8435 NE Killingsworth	Portland	OR	97220	**800-406-9377**	503-501-5830	200
myFreightWorld LLC	7133 W 95th St	Overland Park	KS	66212	**877-549-9438**		393
Mylan	1000 Mylan Blvd	Canonsburg	PA	15317	**800-527-4278**	724-514-1800	582
Mylan Pharmaceuticals Inc	781 Chestnut Ridge Rd	Morgantown	WV	26505	**800-796-9526**		582
Mylan Pharmaceuticals ULC	85 Advance Rd	Etobicoke	ON	M8Z2S6	**800-575-1379**	416-236-2631	583
Mylan Technologies Inc	1000 Mylan Blvd	Canonsburg	PA	15317	**800-294-1322**	724-514-1800	607
MyLLC.com Inc	5716 Corsa Ave Ste 110	Westlake Village	CA	91362	**888-886-9552**		462
Mynelle Gardens	4736 Clinton Blvd	Jackson	MS	39209	**800-354-7695**	601-960-1894	96
MyOpenJobs LLC	203 Main St Ste 100	Lake Dallas	TX	75065	**800-396-4822**		262
Myotronics-noromed Inc	5870 S 194th St	Kent	WA	98032	**800-426-0316**	206-243-4214	230
Myre-Big Island State Park	19499 780th Ave	Albert Lea	MN	56007	**888-646-6367**	507-379-3403	564
Myriad Genetics Inc	320 Wakara Way *NASDAQ: MYGN*	Salt Lake City	UT	84108	**800-469-7423**	801-584-3600	84
Myron Corp	205 Maywood Ave	Maywood	NJ	07607	**877-803-3358**		9
Myrtle Beach Area Chamber of Commerce	1200 N Oak St	Myrtle Beach	SC	29577	**800-356-3016**	843-626-7444	138
Myrtle Beach Convention Ctr	2101 N Oak St	Myrtle Beach	SC	29577	**800-537-1690**	843-918-5000	207
Myrtle Beach Resort Vacations	5905 S Kings Hwy PO Box 3936	Myrtle Beach	SC	29578	**888-627-3767**	843-238-1559	667
Mystic Chamber of Commerce	12 Roosevelt Ave,2nd Fl PO Box 143	Mystic	CT	06355	**866-572-9578**	860-572-9578	138
Mystic Lake Casino Hotel	2400 Mystic Lk Blvd	Prior Lake	MN	55372	**800-262-7799**	952-445-9000	132
Mystic Sea Resort	2105 S Ocean Blvd	Myrtle Beach	SC	29577	**800-443-7050**	843-448-8446	667
Mystic Seaport -- The Museum of America & the Sea	75 Greenmanville Ave PO Box 6000	Mystic	CT	06355	**888-973-2767**	860-572-0711	519
Mystic Stamp Co	9700 Mill St	Camden	NY	13316	**866-660-7147**	315-245-2690	458
Mystique Casino	1855 Greyhound Pk Dr	Dubuque	IA	52001	**800-373-3647**	563-582-3647	639
MySupplyChainGroup LLC	1500 First Ave N Ste A111	Birmingham	AL	35203	**888-444-7786**	205-706-4300	448
MyUSACorporation.com Inc	1 Radisson Plz Ste 800	New Rochelle	NY	10801	**877-330-2677**		318
Mzinga	10 Burlington Mall Rd Ste 111	Burlington	MA	01803	**888-694-6428**		196
Mzinga Inc	230 Third Ave	Waltham	MA	02451	**888-694-6428**	781-577-8948	180-10

N

Name	Address	City	State	ZIP	Toll-Free	Phone	Class
N J R Corp	125 Nicholson Ln	San Jose	CA	95134	**800-800-5441**	408-321-0200	693
N o a Medical Industries Inc	801 Terry Ln	Washington	MO	63090	**800-633-6068**	636-239-7600	322
N R S I	179 Lafayette Dr	Syosset	NY	11791	**800-331-3117**	516-921-5500	244
N Tepperman Ltd	2595 Ouellette Ave	Windsor	ON	N8X4V8	**800-265-5062**	519-969-9700	322
N Wasserstrom & Sons Inc	2300 Lockbourne Rd	Columbus	OH	43207	**800-444-4697**	614-228-5550	301
N.b.c. Truck Equipment Inc	28130 Groesbeck Hwy	Roseville	MI	48066	**800-778-8207**	586-774-4900	60
N.E.T. Inc	5651 Palmer Way Ste C	Carlsbad	CA	92010	**800-888-4638**	760-929-5980	84
NA for the Advancement of Colored People (NAACP)	4805 Mt Hope Dr	Baltimore	MD	21215	**877-622-2798**	410-580-5777	47-8
NA for the Exchange of Industrial Resources (NAEIR)	560 McClure St	Galesburg	IL	61401	**800-562-0955**	309-343-0704	47-5
NA for Uniformed Services (NAUS)	5535 Hempstead Way	Springfield	VA	22151	**800-842-3451**	703-750-1342	47-19
Na Ho'ola Spa at Hyatt Regency Waikiki Resort	2424 Kalakaua Ave	Honolulu	HI	96815	**800-233-1234**	808-923-1234	705
NA of Chain Drug Stores (NACDS)	413 N Lee St	Alexandria	VA	22314	**800-678-6223**	703-549-3001	48-18
NA of Clean Water Agencies (NACWA)	1816 Jefferson Pl NW	Washington	DC	20036	**888-267-9505**	202-833-2672	48-7
NA of College Stores (NACS)	500 E Lorain St	Oberlin	OH	44074	**800-622-7498**	440-775-7777	48-18
NA of Colleges & Employers (NACE)	62 Highland Ave	Bethlehem	PA	18017	**800-544-5272**	610-868-1421	48-5
NA of Collegiate Directors of Athletics (NACDA)	24651 Detroit Rd	Westlake	OH	44145	**877-887-2261**	440-892-4000	47-22
NA of Congregational Christian Churches (NACCC)	8473 S Howell Ave	Oak Creek	WI	53154	**800-262-1620**	414-764-1620	47-20
NA of Conservation Districts (NACD)	509 Capitol Ct NE	Washington	DC	20002	**888-695-2433**	202-547-6223	48-7
NA of Convenience Stores (NACS)	1600 Duke St *Cust Svc	Alexandria	VA	22314	**800-966-6227***	703-684-3600	48-18
NA of Credit Management (NACM)	8840 Columbia 100 Pkwy	Columbia	MD	21045	**800-955-8815**	410-740-5560	48-2
NA of Electrical Distributors Inc (NAED)	1181 Corporate Lk Dr	Saint Louis	MO	63132	**888-791-2512**	314-991-9000	48-18
NA of Elementary School Principals (NAESP)	1615 Duke St	Alexandria	VA	22314	**800-386-2377**	703-684-3345	48-5
NA of Federal Credit Unions (NAFCU)	3138 Tenth St N	Arlington	VA	22201	**800-336-4644**	703-522-4770	48-2
NA of Free Will Baptists (NAFWB)	5233 Mt View Rd	Antioch	TN	37013	**877-767-7659**	615-731-6812	47-20
NA of Home Builders PAC	1201 15th St NW	Washington	DC	20005	**800-368-5242**	202-266-8200	614
NA of Housing & Redevelopment Officials (NAHRO)	630 'I' St NW	Washington	DC	20001	**877-866-2476**	202-289-3500	48-7
NA of Insurance & Financial Advisors (NAIFA)	2901 Telestar Ct *Sales	Falls Church	VA	22042	**877-866-2432***	703-770-8100	48-9
NA of Neonatal Nurses (NANN)	4700 W Lk Ave	Glenview	IL	60025	**800-451-3795**	847-375-3660	48-8
NA of Parliamentarians (NAP)	213 S Main St	Independence	MO	64050	**888-627-2929**	816-833-3892	48-12
NA of People with AIDS (NAPWA)	8401 Colesville Rd Ste 505	Silver Spring	MD	20910	**866-846-9366**	240-247-0880	47-17
NA of REALTORS	430 N Michigan Ave	Chicago	IL	60611	**800-874-6500**	312-329-8200	48-17
NA of Retired Federal Employees	606 N Washington St	Alexandria	VA	22314	**800-627-3394**	703-838-7760	614
NA of Town Watch (NATW)	308 E Lancaster Ave Ste 115	Wynnewood	PA	19096	**800-648-3688**		47-7
NA of Women in Construction (NAWIC)	327 S Adams St	Fort Worth	TX	76104	**800-552-3506**	817-877-5551	48-3

Name	Address	City	State	ZIP	Toll-Free	Phone	Class
NAA (National Apartment Assn)	4300 Wilson Blvd Ste 400	Arlington	VA	22203	800-632-3007	703-518-6141	48-17
NAA (National Auctioneers Assn)	8880 Ballentine St	Overland Park	KS	66214	877-657-1990	913-541-8084	48-18
NAAA (National Auto Auction Assn)	5320 Spectrum Dr Ste D	Frederick	MD	21703	800-232-5411	301-696-0400	48-18
NAACP (NA for the Advancement of Colored People)	4805 Mt Hope Dr	Baltimore	MD	21215	877-622-2798	410-580-5777	47-8
NAADAC PAC	44 Canal Center Plz Ste 301	Alexandria	VA	22314	800-377-1136	703-741-7686	614
Nabco Entrances Inc	S82W18717 Gemini Dr	Muskego	WI	53150	888-679-3319	262-679-0045	479
Nabors Drilling International Ltd	515 W Greens Rd Ste 1000	Houston	TX	77067	877-344-7529	281-874-0035	539
NACAC (North American Council on Adoptable Children)	970 Raymond Ave Ste 106	Saint Paul	MN	55114	877-823-2237	651-644-3036	47-6
Nacarato GMC Truck Inc	519 New Paul Rd	La Vergne	TN	37086	888-392-8486	615-280-2800	515
NACB Group Inc	10 Starwood Dr	Hampstead	NH	03841	800-370-2737	603-329-4551	248
NACCAS (National Accrediting Commission of Cosmetology Arts & Sciences)	4401 Ford Ave Ste 1300	Alexandria	VA	22302	877-212-5752	703-600-7600	47-1
NACCC (NA of Congregational Christian Churches)	8473 S Howell Ave	Oak Creek	WI	53154	800-262-1620	414-764-1620	47-20
NACCO Industries Inc	5875 Landerbrook Dr Ste 300 *NYSE: NC*	Cleveland	OH	44124	877-756-5118	440-229-5151	187
NACD (NA of Conservation Districts)	509 Capitol Ct NE	Washington	DC	20002	888-695-2433	202-547-6223	48-7
NACDA (NA of Collegiate Directors of Athletics)	24651 Detroit Rd	Westlake	OH	44145	877-887-2261	440-892-4000	47-22
NACDS (NA of Chain Drug Stores)	413 N Lee St	Alexandria	VA	22314	800-678-6223	703-549-3001	48-18
NACE (NA of Colleges & Employers)	62 Highland Ave	Bethlehem	PA	18017	800-544-5272	610-868-1421	48-5
NACE International: Corrosion Society	1440 S Creek Dr	Houston	TX	77084	800-797-6223	281-228-6200	48-13
NACHA - Electronic Payments Assn	13665 Dulles Technology Dr Ste 300	Herndon	VA	20171	800-487-9180	703-561-1100	48-2
Nachi America Inc	715 Pushville Rd	Greenwood	IN	46143	888-340-2747	317-530-1001	74
Na-Churs/Alpine Solutions	421 Leader St	Marion	OH	43302	800-622-4877	740-382-5701	282
NACM (NA of Credit Management)	8840 Columbia 100 Pkwy	Columbia	MD	21045	800-955-8815	410-740-5560	48-2
NACM South Texas Inc	10887 S Wilcrest Dr	Houston	TX	77099	866-252-6226	281-228-6100	220
Nacogdoches Convention & Visitors Bureau	200 E Main St	Nacogdoches	TX	75961	888-653-3788	936-564-7351	208
Nacogdoches Medical Ctr	4920 NE Stallings Dr	Nacogdoches	TX	75965	866-898-8446	936-569-9481	374-3
Nacogdoches Public Library	1112 N St	Nacogdoches	TX	75961	800-252-5400	936-559-2970	434-3
NACS (NA of College Stores)	500 E Lorain St	Oberlin	OH	44074	800-622-7498	440-775-7777	48-18
NACS (NA of Convenience Stores)	1600 Duke St	Alexandria	VA	22314	800-966-6227* *Cust Svc	703-684-3600	48-18
NACWA (NA of Clean Water Agencies)	1816 Jefferson Pl NW	Washington	DC	20036	888-267-9505	202-833-2672	48-7
NADA (National Automobile Dealers Assn)	8400 Westpark Dr	McLean	VA	22102	800-252-6232	703-821-7000	48-18
NAEA (National Art Education Assn)	1806 Robert Fulton Dr	Reston	VA	20191	800-299-8321	703-860-8000	48-5
NAED (NA of Electrical Distributors Inc)	1181 Corporate Lk Dr	Saint Louis	MO	63132	888-791-2512	314-991-9000	48-18
NAEIR (NA for the Exchange of Industrial Resources)	560 McClure St	Galesburg	IL	61401	800-562-0955	309-343-0704	47-5
NAESP (NA of Elementary School Principals)	1615 Duke St	Alexandria	VA	22314	800-386-2377	703-684-3345	48-5
NAF (National Abortion Federation)	1755 Massachusetts Ave NW	Washington	DC	20036	800-772-9100	202-667-5881	48-8
NAFCU (NA of Federal Credit Unions)	3138 Tenth St N	Arlington	VA	22201	800-336-4644	703-522-4770	48-2
NAFEM (North American Assn of Food Equipment Manufacturers)	161 N Clark St Ste 2020	Chicago	IL	60601	888-493-5961	312-821-0201	48-13
NAFWB (NA of Free Will Baptists)	5233 Mt View Rd	Antioch	TN	37013	877-767-7659	615-731-6812	47-20
Nagel Chase Inc	2323 Delaney Rd	Gurnee	IL	60031	800-323-4552		350
NAHB Research Ctr	400 Prince Georges Blvd	Upper Marlboro	MD	20774	800-638-8556	301-249-4000	666
Nahon, Saharovich & Trotz PLC	488 S Menhenhall Rd	Memphis	TN	38117	800-529-4004	901-683-7000	428
NAHRO (NA of Housing & Redevelopment Officials)	630 'I' St NW	Washington	DC	20001	877-866-2476	202-289-3500	48-7
NAICS (North American Industry Classification System)	US Census Bureau, 4600 Silver Hill Rd	Washington	DC	20233	800-923-8282	301-763-4636	340-2
NAIFA (NA of Insurance & Financial Advisors)	2901 Telestar Ct	Falls Church	VA	22042	877-866-2432* *Sales	703-770-8100	48-9
NAIHC (National American Indian Housing Council)	122 C S NW Ste 350	Washington	DC	20001	800-284-9165	202-789-1754	48-7
Nailpro Magazine	7628 Densmore Ave	Van Nuys	CA	91406	800-442-5667	818-782-7328	456-21
Nails Magazine	3520 Challenger St	Torrance	CA	90503	888-624-5744	310-533-2400	456-21
Naismith Memorial Basketball Hall of Fame	1000 W Columbus Ave	Springfield	MA	01105	877-446-6752	413-781-6500	521
Najarian Furniture Company Inc	17560 Rowland St	City of Industry	CA	91748	888-781-3088	626-839-8700	321
Nakase Bros Wholesale Nursery	9441 Krepp Dr	Huntington Beach	CA	92646	800-747-4388	714-962-6604	294
Nakina Systems Inc	80 Hines Rd Ste 200	Ottawa	ON	K2K2T8	877-625-4627	613-254-7351	227

Name	Address	City	State	ZIP	Toll-Free	Phone	Class
Nal Property Inspection	10416 Investment Cir	Rancho Cordova	CA	95670	800-774-9555	916-361-0555	194
Nalco Co	1601 W Diehl Rd	Naperville	IL	60563	800-288-0879	630-305-1000	144
NALF (North American Limousin Foundation)	7383 S Alton Way Ste 100	Englewood	CO	80112	888-320-8747	303-220-1693	47-2
Nalge Nunc International	75 Panorama Creek Dr	Rochester	NY	14625	800-625-4327	585-586-8800	420
Nalley Lexus Smyrna	2750 Cobb Pkwy SE	Smyrna	GA	30080	877-454-4206		56
Nalpro Business Solutions LLC	Brier Hill Ct Bldg C	East Brunswick	NJ	08816	888-868-6360	732-390-1400	263
NAMA (National Agri-Marketing Assn)	11020 King St Ste 205	Overland Park	KS	66210	800-530-5646	913-491-6500	48-18
Name Maker Inc	4450 Commerce Cir PO Box 43821	Atlanta	GA	30336	800-241-2890	404-691-2237	742-5
Name.com LLC	2500 E Second Ave 2nd Fl	Denver	CO	80206	800-365-0006	720-249-2374	396
Nameplate & Panel Technology	387 Gundersen Dr	Carol Stream	IL	60188	800-833-8397	630-690-9360	626
NAMI (National Alliance on Mental Illness)	3803 N Fairfax Dr Ste 100	Arlington	VA	22203	800-950-6264	703-524-7600	47-17
NAMM - International Music Products Assn	5790 Armada Dr	Carlsbad	CA	92008	800-767-6266	760-438-8001	48-18
NANA Regional Corporation Inc	1001 E Benson Blvd	Kotzebue	AK	99752	800-478-3301	907-442-3301	538
Nana Wall Systems Inc	707 Redwood Hwy	Mill Valley	CA	94941	800-873-5673	415-383-3148	498
Nance International Inc	2915 Milam St	Beaumont	TX	77701	877-626-2322	409-838-6127	662
NANN (NA of Neonatal Nurses)	4700 W Lk Ave	Glenview	IL	60025	800-451-3795	847-375-3660	48-8
NanoHorizons Inc	270 Rolling Ridge Dr Ste 100	Bellefonte	PA	16823	866-584-6235	814-355-4700	161
Nanonation Inc	301 S 13th St Ste 700	Lincoln	NE	68508	866-843-6266	402-323-6266	179
Nanotechnology Research Ctr	*Georgia Institute of Technology* 791 Atlantic Dr	Atlanta	GA	30332	800-424-9300	404-894-5100	666
Nantucket Accommodations	2 Windy Way	Nantucket	MA	02554	866-743-3330	508-228-9559	376
Nantucket Bank	104 Pleasant St	Nantucket	MA	02554	800-533-9313	508-228-0580	69
Nanz & Kraft Florists Inc	141 Breckenridge Ln	Louisville	KY	40207	800-897-6551	502-897-6551	294
NAO Inc	1284 E Sedgley Ave	Philadelphia	PA	19134	800-523-3495* *Cust Svc	215-743-5300	18
NAP (NA of Parliamentarians)	213 S Main St	Independence	MO	64050	888-627-2929	816-833-3892	48-12
NAP Windows & Doors Ltd	2150 Enterprise Way	Kelowna	BC	V1Y6H7	888-762-5311	250-762-5343	600
NAPA (National Automotive Parts Assn)	2999 Circle 75 Pkwy	Atlanta	GA	30339	800-538-6272	770-953-1700	60
Napa Chamber of Commerce	1556 First St	Napa	CA	94559	877-807-2249	707-226-7455	138
Napa City-County Library	580 Coombs St	Napa	CA	94559	877-848-7030	707-253-4241	434-3
Napa County	1195 Third St Ste 310	Napa	CA	94559	877-279-2976	707-253-4421	338
Napa Networks Inc	245 Stafford Rd West Ste 202	Ottawa	ON	K2H9E8	888-641-1113	613-248-3417	462
Napa River Inn	500 Main St	Napa	CA	94559	877-251-8500	707-251-8500	379
Napa State Hospital	2100 Napa-Vallejo Hwy	Napa	CA	94558	866-762-0972	707-253-5000	374-5
Napa Valley College	2277 Napa-Vallejo Hwy	Napa	CA	94558	800-826-1077	707-256-7000	161
Napa Valley Conference & Visitors Bureau	600 Main St	Napa	CA	94559	855-847-6272	707-251-5895	208
NAPCO (North American Publishing Co)	1500 Springarden St 12th Fl	Philadelphia	PA	19130	800-627-2689	215-238-5300	634-9
NAPCO Inc	120 Trojan Ave	Sparta	NC	28675	800-854-8621	336-372-5228	85
Napco Ply Gem Inc	5020 Weston Pkwy Ste 400	Cary	MO	27153	800-786-2726	888-975-9436	695
NAPCO Security Systems Inc	333 Bayview Ave *NASDAQ: NSSC*	Amityville	NY	11701	800-645-9445	631-842-9400	690
Napco Steel Inc	1800 Arthur Dr	West Chicago	IL	60185	800-292-8010	630-293-1900	491
Napili Kai Beach Club	5900 Honoapiilani Rd	Lahaina	HI	96761	800-367-5030	808-669-6271	667
Naples Bay Resort	1500 Fifth Ave S	Naples	FL	34102	866-605-1199	239-530-1199	667
Naples Beach Hotel & Golf Club	851 Gulf Shore Blvd N	Naples	FL	34102	800-237-7600	239-261-2222	667
Naples Botanical Garden	4820 Bayshore Dr	Naples	FL	34112	877-433-1874	239-643-7275	96
Naples Daily News	1100 Immokalee Rd	Naples	FL	34102	800-404-7343	239-213-6000	531-2
Naples Museum of Art	5833 Pelican Bay Blvd	Naples	FL	34108	800-597-1900	239-597-1111	519
Napoleon/Henry County Chamber of Commerce	611 N Perry St	Napoleon	OH	43545	800-322-6849	419-592-1786	138
NAPWA (NA of People with AIDS)	8401 Colesville Rd Ste 505	Silver Spring	MD	20910	866-846-9366	240-247-0880	47-17
NARBHA (Northern Arizona Regional Behavioral Health Authority Inc)	1300 S Yale St	Flagstaff	AZ	86001	877-923-1400	928-774-7128	48-15
Narcolepsy Network Inc	46 Union Dr Ste A212	North Kingstown	RI	02852	888-292-6522	401-667-2523	47-17
Nardini Fire Equipment Company Inc	405 County Rd E W	Saint Paul	MN	55126	888-627-3464	651-483-6631	677
Nardone Bros Baking Company Inc	420 New Commerce Blvd	Wilkes-Barre	PA	18706	800-822-5320	570-823-0141	297-36

Listing	Toll-Free	Phone	Class
NARF (Native American Rights Fund)			
1506 Broadway .... Boulder CO 80302	**888-280-0726**	303-447-8760	48-10
NARIC (National Rehabilitation Information Ctr)			
8400 Corporate Dr Ste 500.......... Landover MD 20785	**800-346-2742**	301-459-5900	47-17
Naropa University			
2130 Arapahoe Ave .... Boulder CO 80302	**800-772-6951**	303-444-0202	167
Narrow Fabric Industries Corp			
701 Reading Ave .... Reading PA 19611	**877-523-6373**	610-376-2891	742-5
NAS (National Audubon Society)			
225 Varick St .... New York NY 10014	**800-274-4201**	212-979-3000	47-13
NAS Recruitment Communications			
9700 Rockside Rd Ste 170.......... Cleveland OH 44125	**866-627-7327**		4
NASA TV			
300 E St SW .... Washington DC 20546	**877-546-1574**	202-358-0000	736
NASAA (North American Securities Administrators Assn)			
750 First St NE Ste 1140 .... Washington DC 20002	**800-222-1253**	202-737-0900	48-2
NASB (North American Savings Bank)			
12520 S 71 Hwy .... Grandview MO 64030	**800-677-6272**	816-765-2200	69
NASB Financial Inc			
12520 S 71 Hwy .... Grandview MO 64030	**800-677-6272**	816-765-2200	360-2
NASDAQ: NASB			
NASBIC PAC			
1100 H St NW Ste 610.......... Washington DC 20005	**800-471-6153**	202-628-5055	614
NASCO International Inc			
901 Janesville Ave .... Fort Atkinson WI 53538	**800-558-9595***	920-563-2446	458
*Orders			
NASFAA (National Assn of Student Financial Aid Administrators)			
1101 Connecticut Ave			
Ste 1100.......... Washington DC 20036	**800-877-8339**	202-785-0453	48-5
Nash Produce Co			
6160 S N Carolina 58 .... Nashville NC 27856	**800-334-3032**	252-443-6011	10-9
Nashoba Valley Chamber of Commerce			
100 Sherman Ave .... Devens MA 01434	**877-322-8228**	978-772-6976	138
Nashua Corp			
11 Trafalgar Sq 2nd Fl .... Nashua NH 03063	**800-430-7488**	603-880-2323	551-1
Nashua Homes of Idaho Inc			
PO Box 170008 .... Boise ID 83717	**855-766-0222**	208-345-0222	504
Nashville Convention & Visitors Bureau (NCVB)			
150 Fourth Ave N Ste G250 .... Nashville TN 37219	**800-657-6910**	615-259-4730	208
Nashville Display			
306 Hartmann Dr .... Lebanon TN 37087	**800-251-1150**	615-743-2900	235
Nashville General Hospital			
1818 Albion St .... Nashville TN 37208	**800-318-2596**	615-341-4000	374-3
Nashville Office Interiors			
1621 Church St .... Nashville TN 37203	**877-342-0294**	615-329-1811	322
Nashville State Community College (NSCC)			
120 White Bridge Rd .... Nashville TN 37209	**800-272-7363**	615-353-3333	798
Nashville Wire Products Manufacturing Co			
199 Polk Ave .... Nashville TN 37210	**800-448-2125**	615-743-2500	72
Nasiff Associates			
841 County Rt 37 .... Central Square NY 13036	**866-627-4332**	315-676-2346	475
NASS (National Agricultural Statistics Service)			
1400 Independence Ave SW .... Washington DC 20250	**800-727-9540**	202-720-2707	340-1
NASS (North American Spine Society)			
7075 Veterans Blvd .... Burr Ridge IL 60527	**877-774-6337**	630-230-3600	48-8
Nassau County			
PO Box 870 .... Fernandina Beach FL 32035	**888-615-4398**	904-491-7300	338
Nassau Financial Federal Credit Union			
1325 Franklin Ave Ste 500.......... Garden City NY 11530	**800-216-2328**	516-742-4900	221
Nassau Library System			
900 Jerusalem Ave .... Uniondale NY 11553	**800-662-1220**	516-292-8920	434-3
Nassau Valley Vineyards			
32165 Winery Way .... Lewes DE 19958	**800-425-2355**	302-645-9463	49-6
Nassau Veterans Memorial Coliseum			
1255 Hempstead Tpke .... Uniondale NY 11553	**800-745-3000**	516-794-9300	718
NASW News			
750 First St NE Ste 700 .... Washington DC 20002	**800-227-3590**	202-408-8600	456-16
NATA (National Air Transportation Assn)			
4226 King St .... Alexandria VA 22302	**800-808-6282**	703-845-9000	48-21
NATA (National Athletic Trainers Assn)			
2952 N Stemmons Fwy Ste 200.......... Dallas TX 75247	**800-879-6282**	214-637-6282	47-22
NATCA (National Air Traffic Controllers Assn)			
1325 Massachusetts Ave NW .... Washington DC 20005	**800-266-0895**	202-628-5451	414
Natchez Convention & Visitors Bureau			
640 S Canal St.......... Natchez MS 39120	**800-647-6724**	601-446-6345	208
Natchez Convention Ctr			
211 Main St .... Natchez MS 39120	**888-475-9144**	601-442-5880	207
Natchez Trace National Scenic Trail			
2680 Natchez Trace Pkwy .... Tupelo MS 38804	**800-305-7417**	662-680-4025	563
Natchitoches Area Chamber of Commerce			
780 Front St Ste 101.......... Natchitoches LA 71457	**877-646-6689**	318-352-6894	138
Natchitoches Parish Hospital			
501 Keyser Ave .... Natchitoches LA 71457	**888-728-8383**	318-214-4200	374-3
NATE (National Association of Tower Erectors)			
8 Second St SE .... Watertown SD 57201	**888-882-5865**	605-882-5865	48-3
Natel Engineering Co Inc			
9340 Owensmouth Ave .... Chatsworth CA 91311	**800-590-5774**	818-734-6500	624
Nation Magazine			
33 Irving Pl 8th Fl.......... New York NY 10003	**800-333-8536***	212-209-5400	456-17
*Cust Svc			
National Abortion Federation (NAF)			
1755 Massachusetts Ave NW .... Washington DC 20036	**800-772-9100**	202-667-5881	48-8
National Academies			
500 Fifth St NW .... Washington DC 20001	**800-624-6242**	202-334-2138	48-19
National Academy of Public Administration			
1600 K St Ste 400.......... Washington DC 20006	**800-883-3190**	202-347-3190	48-7
National Academy of Recording Arts & Sciences			
3030 Olympic Blvd .... Santa Monica CA 90404	**800-423-2017**	310-392-3777	47-4
National Academy Press			
500 Fifth St NW PO Box 285 .... Washington DC 20055	**800-624-6242**	202-334-3313	634-2
National Accrediting Commission of Cosmetology Arts & Sciences (NACCAS)			
4401 Ford Ave Ste 1300.......... Alexandria VA 22302	**877-212-5752**	703-600-7600	47-1
National Aeronautic Assn			
Hanger 7 1 S Smith Blvd			
Ste 202.......... Washington DC 20001	**800-644-9777**	703-416-4888	47-22
National Afro-American Museum & Cultural Ctr			
1350 Brush Row Rd			
PO Box 578.......... Wilberforce OH 45384	**800-752-2603**	937-376-4944	519
National Agricultural Statistics Service (NASS)			
1400 Independence Ave SW .... Washington DC 20250	**800-727-9540**	202-720-2707	340-1
National Agri-Marketing Assn (NAMA)			
11020 King St Ste 205 .... Overland Park KS 66210	**800-530-5646**	913-491-6500	48-18
National Air Traffic Controllers Assn (NATCA)			
1325 Massachusetts Ave NW .... Washington DC 20005	**800-266-0895**	202-628-5451	414
National Air Transportation Assn (NATA)			
4226 King St .... Alexandria VA 22302	**800-808-6282**	703-845-9000	48-21
National Alliance for Youth Sports			
2050 Vista Pkwy .... West Palm Beach FL 33411	**800-729-2057**	561-684-1141	47-22
National Alliance on Mental Illness (NAMI)			
3803 N Fairfax Dr Ste 100 .... Arlington VA 22203	**800-950-6264**	703-524-7600	47-17
National Alliance to End Homelessness			
1518 K St NW Ste 410 .... Washington DC 20005	**800-657-3769**	202-638-1526	47-5
National Alpha Lambda Delta			
328 Orange St .... Macon GA 31201	**800-925-7421**	478-744-9595	47-16
National AMBUCS Inc (AMBUCS)			
4285 Regency Ct PO Box 5127.......... High Point NC 27265	**800-838-1845**	336-852-0052	47-5
National American Indian Housing Council (NAIHC)			
122 C S NW Ste 350.......... Washington DC 20001	**800-284-9165**	202-789-1754	48-7
National American University			
321 Kansas City St .... Rapid City SD 57701	**800-843-8892**	605-394-4800	167
Sioux Falls			
5801 S Kiwanis Ave .... Sioux Falls SD 57108	**800-388-5430**	605-336-4600	167
National American University Colorado Springs			
1915 Jamboree Dr			
Ste 185.......... Colorado Springs CO 80920	**855-448-2318**	316-448-5400	167
National American University Independence			
3620 Arrowhead Ave .... Independence MO 64057	**866-628-1288**	816-412-7700	167
National Anti-Vivisection Society (NAVS)			
53 W Jackson Blvd Ste 1552 .... Chicago IL 60604	**800-888-6287**	312-427-6065	47-3
National Apartment Assn (NAA)			
4300 Wilson Blvd Ste 400 .... Arlington VA 22203	**800-632-3007**	703-518-6141	48-17
National Arbitration & Mediation			
990 Stewart Ave .... Garden City NY 11530	**800-358-2550**	516-794-8950	40
National Arbor Day Foundation			
100 Arbor Ave .... Nebraska City NE 68410	**888-448-7337**	402-474-5655	47-13
National Archives & Records Administration			
Archival Research Catalog			
8601 Adelphi Rd .... College Park MD 20740	**866-272-6272**		340-18
Office of the Federal Register			
800 N Capitol St NW			
Ste 700-K.......... Washington DC 20002	**877-684-6448**	202-741-6000	340-18
Northeast Region			
380 Trapelo Rd .... Waltham MA 02452	**866-406-2379**	781-663-0130	340-18
Pacific Alaska Region			
6125 Sand Pt Way NE .... Seattle WA 98115	**866-325-7208**	206-336-5115	340-18
National Art Education Assn (NAEA)			
1806 Robert Fulton Dr .... Reston VA 20191	**800-299-8321**	703-860-8000	48-5
National Art Materials Trade Assn			
20200 Zion Ave .... Cornelius NC 28031	**800-349-1039**	704-892-6244	48-18
National Artcraft Supply Co			
300 Campus Dr .... Aurora OH 44202	**888-937-2723**	330-562-3500	42
National Assn of Credit Management			
8840 Columbia 100 Pkwy .... Columbia MD 21045	**800-955-8815**	410-740-5560	456-5
National Assn of Student Financial Aid Administrators (NASFAA)			
1101 Connecticut Ave			
Ste 1100.......... Washington DC 20036	**800-877-8339**	202-785-0453	48-5
National Association of Housing and Redevelopment Officials			
630 'I' St NW .... Washington DC 20001	**877-866-2476**	202-289-3500	456-5
National Association of Landscape Professionals Inc (PLANET)			
950 Herndon Pkwy Ste 450 .... Herndon VA 20170	**800-395-2522**	703-736-9666	47-2
National Association of Nonprofit Accountants & Consultants (NSA)			
624 Grassmere Park Dr Ste 15 .... Nashville TN 37211	**800-231-2524**	615-373-9880	48-1
National Association of Theatre Owners. (NATO)			
1705 N St NW Ste 1130.......... Washington DC 20036	**800-365-5701***	202-962-0054	47-4
*General			
National Association of Tower Erectors (NATE)			
8 Second St SE .... Watertown SD 57201	**888-882-5865**	605-882-5865	48-3
National Athletic Trainers Assn (NATA)			
2952 N Stemmons Fwy Ste 200 .... Dallas TX 75247	**800-879-6282**	214-637-6282	47-22
National Auctioneers Assn (NAA)			
8880 Ballentine St .... Overland Park KS 66214	**877-657-1990**	913-541-8084	48-18
National Audubon Society (NAS)			
225 Varick St .... New York NY 10014	**800-274-4201**	212-979-3000	47-13
National Australia Bank Americas			
245 Pk Ave 28th Fl.......... New York NY 10167	**866-706-0509**	212-916-9500	69
National Auto Auction Assn (NAAA)			
5320 Spectrum Dr Ste D.......... Frederick MD 21703	**800-232-5411**	301-696-0400	48-18
National Automatic Sprinkler Industries			
8000 Corporate Dr .... Landover MD 20785	**800-638-2603**	301-577-1700	191-13
National Automobile Dealers Assn (NADA)			
8400 Westpark Dr .... McLean VA 22102	**800-252-6232**	703-821-7000	48-18
National Automotive Parts Assn (NAPA)			
2999 Circle 75 Pkwy .... Atlanta GA 30339	**800-538-6272**	770-953-1700	60
National Aviation Academy			
150 Hanscom Dr .... Bedford MA 01730	**800-659-2080**	727-535-8727	798
National Bank of Arizona			
335 N Wilmot Rd Ste 100.......... Tucson AZ 85711	**800-497-8168**	520-571-1500	69
National Bank of Blacksburg			
PO Box 90002 .... Blacksburg VA 24062	**800-552-4123**	540-552-2011	69
National Bank of Gatesville			
PO Box 779 .... Gatesville TX 76528	**877-628-2265**	254-865-2211	69
National Bank, The			
852 Middle Rd .... Bettendorf IA 52722	**877-321-4347**	563-344-3935	69
National Bankshares Inc			
101 Hubbard St .... Blacksburg VA 24060	**800-552-4123**	540-951-6300	360-2
NASDAQ: NKSH			
National Banner Co			
11938 Harry Hines Blvd .... Dallas TX 75234	**800-527-0860**	972-241-2131	289
National Baptist Convention USA Inc			
1700 Baptist World Ctr Dr .... Nashville TN 37207	**866-531-3054**	615-228-6292	47-20
National Baseball Hall of Fame & Museum			
25 Main St .... Cooperstown NY 13326	**888-425-5633**	607-547-7200	521
National Beef Packing Co LLC			
12200 Ambassador Dr Ste 500			
PO Box 20046.......... Kansas City MO 64163	**800-449-2333**		472
National Beer Wholesalers Assn (NBWA)			
1101 King St Ste 600 .... Alexandria VA 22314	**800-300-6417**	703-683-4300	48-6

Name / Address	City	State	Zip	Toll-Free	Phone	Class
National Billiard Manufacturing Co 3315 Eugenia Ave	Covington	KY	41015	**800-543-0880**	859-431-4129	708
National Biodynamics Laboratory (NBDL) *University of New Orleans College of Engineering* 2000 Lakeshore Dr	New Orleans	LA	70148	**888-514-4275**		666
National Board of Boiler & Pressure Vessel Inspectors 1055 Crupper Ave	Columbus	OH	43229	**877-682-8772**	614-888-8320	48-7
National Book Festival Library of Congress 101 Independence Ave SE	Washington	DC	20540	**888-714-4696**	202-707-2777	283
National Border Patrol Museum 4315 Woodrow Bean TransMtn Rd	El Paso	TX	79924	**877-276-8738**	915-759-6060	519
National Braille Press Inc 88 St Stephen St	Boston	MA	02115	**888-965-8965**	617-266-6160	634-2
National Breast Cancer Coalition (NBCC) 1101 17th St NW Ste 1300	Washington	DC	20036	**800-622-2838**	202-296-7477	47-17
National Bureau of Economic Research 1050 Massachusetts Ave	Cambridge	MA	02138	**800-621-8476**	617-868-3900	666
National Business Assn (NBA) 5151 Beltline Rd Ste 1150	Dallas	TX	75254	**800-456-0440**	972-458-0900	48-12
National Business Aviation Assn (NBAA) 1200 18th St NW Ste 400	Washington	DC	20036	**800-394-6222**	202-783-9000	48-21
National Business Coalition on Health (NBCH) 1015 18th St NW Ste 730	Washington	DC	20036	**800-223-4139**	202-775-9300	48-12
National Business Furniture Inc 735 N Water St Ste 440 *Sales	Milwaukee	WI	53202	**800-558-1010***	414-276-8511	321
National Businesswomen's Leadership Assn PO Box 419107	Kansas City	MO	64141	**800-258-7246**	913-432-7755	763
National Cable Television Co-op Inc (NCTC) 11200 Corporate Ave	Lenexa	KS	66219	**800-720-5850**	913-599-5900	48-14
National Cancer Registrars Assn (NCRA) 1340 Braddock Pl Ste 203	Alexandria	VA	22314	**800-621-4111**	703-299-6640	47-17
National Captioning Institute (NCI) 3725 Concorde Pkwy Ste 100	Chantilly	VA	20151	**800-825-6758**	703-917-7600	629
National Caregiving Foundation 801 N Pitt St	Alexandria	VA	22314	**800-930-1357**	703-299-9300	47-6
National Carriers Inc 1501 E Eigth St	Liberal	KS	67901	**800-835-9180**	620-624-1621	778
National Catholic Educational Assn (NCEA) 1077 30th St NW Ste 100	Washington	DC	20007	**800-711-6232**	202-337-6232	48-5
National Catholic Reporter Publishing Co 115 E Armour Blvd	Kansas City	MO	64111	**800-333-7373**	816-531-0538	634-9
National Cattlemen's Beef Assn (NCBA) 9110 E Nichols Ave Ste 300	Centennial	CO	80112	**866-233-3872**	303-694-0305	47-2
National Chemical Laboratories Inc 401 N Tenth St	Philadelphia	PA	19123	**800-628-2436**	215-922-1200	150
National Chemicals Inc 105 Liberty St PO Box 32 *Cust Svc	Winona	MN	55987	**800-533-0027***	507-454-5640	150
National Child Care Assn (NCCA) 1325 G St NW Ste 500	Washington	DC	20005	**866-536-1945**		47-6
National Child Care Information & Technical Assistance Ctr (NCCIC) 9300 Lee Hwy	Fairfax	VA	22031	**877-296-2250**		340-8
National Children's Ctr Inc 6200 Second St NW	Washington	DC	20011	**866-632-9992**	202-722-2300	683
National Church Residences Inc 2335 N Bank Dr	Columbus	OH	43220	**800-388-2151**		650
National Church Supply Co, The PO Box 269	Chester	WV	26034	**800-627-9900**	304-387-5200	265
National Citizens' Coalition for Nursing Home Reform (NCCNHR) *National Consumer Voice for Quality Long-Term Care, The* 1828 L St NW Ste 801	Washington	DC	20036	**866-992-3668**	202-332-2275	47-17
National Cleaners Assn 252 W 29th St 2nd Fl *General	New York	NY	10001	**800-888-1622***	212-967-3002	48-4
National Clearinghouse for Alcohol & Drug Information 11426 Rockville Pk PO Box 2345	Rockville	MD	20847	**800-729-6686**		340-8
National Club Assn (NCA) 1201 15th St NW Ste 450	Washington	DC	20005	**800-625-6221**	202-822-9822	47-23
National Coalition Against Domestic Violence (NCADV) 1 Broadway Ste B210	Denver	CO	80203	**800-799-7233**	303-839-1852	47-6
National Coalition for Cancer Survivorship (NCCS) 1010 Wayne Ave Ste 315	Silver Spring	MD	20910	**877-622-7937**		47-17
National Coalition for the Homeless (NCH) 2201 P St NW	Washington	DC	20037	**877-243-1576**	202-462-4822	47-5
National Coalition of Black Meeting Planners (NCBMP) 700 N. Fairfax St Ste 510	Alexandria	VA	22314	**800-551-9369**	571-527-3110	48-12
National Coatings Inc 3520 Rennie School Rd	Traverse City	MI	49685	**888-947-2557**	231-943-2557	480
National Coil Coating Assn (NCCA) 1300 Sumner Ave	Cleveland	OH	44115	**800-532-0500**	216-241-7333	48-13
National College *Lexington* 2376 Sir Barton Way	Lexington	KY	40509	**877-540-3494**	859-253-0621	798
National College of Business & Technology *Roanoke Valley* 1813 E Main St	Salem	VA	24153	**800-664-1886**	540-986-1800	798
National College of Business & Technology Bristol 1328 Hwy 11 W	Bristol	TN	37620	**888-956-2732**	423-878-4440	798
National College of Business & Technology Florence 8095 Connector Dr	Florence	KY	41042	**888-956-2732**	859-525-6510	798
National College of Business & Technology Nashville 1638 Bell Rd	Nashville	TN	37211	**855-800-1715**	615-333-3344	798
National College of Business & Technology Pikeville 50 National College Blvd	Pikeville	KY	41501	**800-664-1886**	606-478-7200	798
National Commerce Bank Services Inc 80 Monroe Ave Ste 250	Memphis	TN	38103	**800-264-2609**		688
National Committee for Employer Support of the Guard & Reserve (ESGR) 1555 Wilson Blvd Ste 319	Arlington	VA	22209	**800-336-4590**	703-696-1386	47-19
National Committee for Quality Assurance (NCQA) 1100 13th St	Washington	DC	20005	**888-275-7585**	202-955-3500	47-10
National Committee to Preserve Social Security & Medicare (NCPSSM) 10 G St NE Ste 600	Washington	DC	20002	**800-966-1935**	202-216-0420	47-7
National Community Pharmacists Assn (NCPA) 100 Daingerfield Rd	Alexandria	VA	22314	**800-544-7447**	703-683-8200	48-8
National Concrete Masonry Assn 13750 Sunrise Vly Dr	Herndon	VA	20171	**877-343-6268**	703-713-1900	48-3
National Confectioners Assn (NCA) 1101 30th St NW Ste 200	Washington	DC	20007	**800-433-1200**	202-534-1440	48-6
National Confectioners Assn PAC (NCA) 8320 Old Courthouse Rd Ste 300	Vienna	VA	22182	**800-433-1200**	202-534-1440	614
National Conference of State Legislatures 7700 E First Pl	Denver	CO	80230	**866-229-2386**	303-364-7700	48-7
National Conference on Citizenship (NCOC) 1875 K St NW 5th Fl	Washington	DC	20006	**800-745-7275**	202-729-8038	47-8
National Construction Rentals Inc 15319 Chatsworth St	Mission Hills	CA	91345	**800-352-5675**	818-221-6000	266-3
National Consumers League (NCL) 1701 K St NW Ste 1200	Washington	DC	20006	**800-388-2227**	202-835-3323	47-10
National Contract Management Assn (NCMA) 21740 Beaumeade Cir Ste 125	Ashburn	VA	20147	**800-344-8096**	571-382-0082	48-12
National Co-op Business Assn (NCBA) 1401 New York Ave NW Ste 1100	Washington	DC	20005	**800-356-9655**	202-638-6222	48-12
National Corporate Housing 365 Herndon Pkwy Ste 111	Herndon	VA	20170	**866-229-4720**		376
National Corvette Museum 350 Corvette Dr	Bowling Green	KY	42101	**800-538-3883**	270-781-7973	519
National Cotton Council of America 7193 Goodlett Farms Pkwy	Memphis	TN	38016	**888-232-1738**	901-274-9030	48-18
National Council for Accreditation of Teacher Education (NCATE) 2010 Massachusetts Ave NW Ste 500	Washington	DC	20036	**800-255-8664**	202-466-7496	47-1
National Council for Air & Stream Improvement Inc (NCASI) PO Box 13318	Research Triangle Park	NC	27709	**888-448-2473**	919-941-6400	47-13
National Council for Prescription Drug Programs (NCPDP) 9240 E Raintree Dr	Scottsdale	AZ	85260	**888-665-2600**	480-477-1000	48-9
National Council for the Social Studies (NCSS) 8555 16th St Ste 500 *Orders	Silver Spring	MD	20910	**800-683-0812***	301-588-1800	48-5
National Council of Examiners for Engineering & Surveying (NCEES) 280 Seneca Creek Rd	Seneca	SC	29678	**800-250-3196**	864-654-6824	48-3
National Council of Jewish Women (NCJW) 475 Riverside Dr Ste 1901	New York	NY	10115	**800-829-6259**	212-645-4048	47-24
National Council of Juvenile & Family Court Judges (NCJFCJ) Univ of Nevada PO Box 8970	Reno	NV	89507	**800-527-3223**	775-784-6012	48-10
National Council of Negro Women Inc (NCNW) 633 Pennsylvania Ave NW	Washington	DC	20004	**800-462-6420**	202-737-0120	47-24
National Council of State Boards of Nursing (NCSBN) 111 E Wacker Dr Ste 2900	Chicago	IL	60601	**866-293-9600**	312-525-3600	48-8
National Council of Teachers of English (NCTE) 1111 W Kenyon Rd	Urbana	IL	61801	**877-369-6283**	217-328-3870	48-5
National Council of Teachers of Mathematics (NCTM) 1906 Assn Dr *Orders	Reston	VA	20191	**800-235-7566***	703-620-9840	48-5
National Council of Textile Organizations (NCTO) 910 17th St NW	Washington	DC	20006	**800-238-7192**	202-822-8028	48-13
National Council on Alcoholism & Drug Dependence Inc (NCADD) 217 Broadway Ste 712	New York	NY	10007	**800-622-2255**	212-269-7797	47-17
National Council on Crime & Delinquency (NCCD) 1970 Broadway Ste 500	Oakland	CA	94612	**800-306-6223**	510-208-0500	47-8
National Council on Economic Education (NCEE) 122 E 42nd St Ste 2600	New York	NY	10168	**800-338-1192**	212-730-7007	48-5
National Council on Family Relations (NCFR) 1201 W River Pkwy Ste 200	Minneapolis	MN	55454	**888-781-9331**		47-6
National Council on Problem Gambling Inc 730 11th St NW Ste 601	Washington	DC	20001	**800-522-4700**	202-547-9204	48-8
National Council on Public History (NCPH) 425 University Blvd 327 Cavanaugh Hall	Indianapolis	IN	46202	**800-554-5542**	317-274-2716	47-7
National Council on Radiation Protection & Measurements (NCRP) 7910 Woodmont Ave Ste 400	Bethesda	MD	20814	**800-462-3683**	301-657-2652	48-19
National Council on the Aging (NCOA) 1901 L St NW 4th Fl	Washington	DC	20036	**800-677-1116**	202-479-1200	47-6
National Court Appointed Special Advocate Assn (CASA) 100 W Harrison St N Twr Ste 500	Seattle	WA	98119	**800-628-3233**	206-270-0072	47-6
National Court Reporters Assn (NCRA) 8224 Old Courthouse Rd	Vienna	VA	22182	**800-272-6272**	703-556-6272	48-10
National Cowgirl Museum & Hall of Fame 1720 Gendy St	Fort Worth	TX	76107	**800-476-3263**	817-336-4475	519
National CPA Health Care Advisors Assn (HCAA) 1801 W End Ave Ste 800	Nashville	TN	37203	**800-231-2524**	615-373-9880	48-1
National Credit Union Administration 1775 Duke St *Fraud Hotline	Alexandria	VA	22314	**800-827-9650***	703-518-6300	340-18
National Criminal Justice Reference Service PO Box 6000	Rockville	MD	20849	**800-851-3420**	301-240-7760	340-12
National Crop Insurance Services (NCIS) 8900 Indian Creek Pkwy Ste 600	Overland Park	KS	66210	**800-951-6247**	913-685-2767	47-2
National Ctr for Employee Development (NCED) 2701 E Imhoff Rd	Norman	OK	73071	**866-438-6233**	405-366-4420	377
National Ctr for Family Literacy (NCFL) 325 W Main St Ste 300	Louisville	KY	40202	**855-937-5668**	502-584-1133	47-11
National Ctr for Genome Resources 2935 Rodeo Pk Dr E	Santa Fe	NM	87505	**800-450-4854**	505-995-4400	666
National Ctr for Homeopathy (NCH) 101 S Whiting St Ste 16	Alexandria	VA	22304	**877-624-0613**	703-548-7790	47-17
National Ctr for Mfg Sciences (NCMS) 3025 Boardwalk	Ann Arbor	MI	48108	**800-222-6267**	734-995-0300	666
National Ctr for Missing & Exploited Children (NCMEC) 699 Prince St	Alexandria	VA	22314	**800-843-5678**	703-274-3900	47-6
National Ctr for Neighborhood Enterprise (NCNE) 1625 K St Ste 1200	Washington	DC	20006	**866-518-1263**	202-518-6500	47-7
National Ctr for Retirement Benefits Inc 666 Dundee Rd Ste 1200	Northbrook	IL	60062	**800-666-1000**		195
National Ctr for State Courts (NCSC) 300 Newport Ave	Williamsburg	VA	23185	**800-616-6164**	757-259-1525	48-7
National Ctr for Victims of Crime, The 2000 M St NW Ste 480	Washington	DC	20036	**800-394-2255**	202-467-8700	47-8
National Cycle Inc 2200 Maywood Dr	Maywood	IL	60153	**877-972-7336**	708-343-0400	516
National Diagnostics Inc 305 Patton Dr	Atlanta	GA	30336	**800-526-3867**	404-699-2121	233
National Disaster Search Dog Foundation 501 E Ojai Ave	Ojai	CA	93023	**888-459-4376**	805-646-1015	47-3

Name / Address	City	State	Zip	Toll-Free	Phone	Class
National Discount Cruise Co 1401 N Cedar Crest Blvd Ste 110	Allentown	PA	18104	**800-788-8108**	610-439-4883	769
National Disease Research Interchange (NDRI) 1628 John F Kennedy Blvd 8 Penn Ctr 8th Fl	Philadelphia	PA	19103	**800-222-6374**	215-557-7361	271
National Distributors Inc 1517 Avco Blvd	Sellersburg	IN	47172	**800-334-9677**	812-246-6306	448
National District Attorneys Assn (NDAA) 99 Canal Ctr Plaza Ste 510	Alexandria	VA	22314	**888-325-9943**	703-549-9222	48-7
National Diversity Newspaper Job Bank *c/o Morris Communications* 725 Broad St	Augusta	GA	30901	**800-622-6358**	706-724-0851	262
National Domestic Violence Hotline (NDVH) PO Box 161810	Austin	TX	78716	**800-799-7233**	512-794-1133	47-6
National Down Syndrome Congress (NDSC) 1370 Ctr Dr Ste 102	Atlanta	GA	30338	**800-232-6372**	770-604-9500	47-17
National Down Syndrome Society (NDSS) 666 Broadway 8th Fl	New York	NY	10012	**800-221-4602**		47-17
National Eating Disorders Assn 603 Stewart St Ste 803	Seattle	WA	98101	**800-931-2237**		47-17
National Education Assn (NEA) 1201 16th St NW	Washington	DC	20036	**888-552-0624**	202-833-4000	48-5
National Educational Telecommunications Assn (NETA) 939 S Stadium Rd	Columbia	SC	29201	**866-270-5141**	803-799-5517	629
National Electrical Carbon 251 Forrester Dr	Greenville	SC	29607	**800-471-7842**	864-284-9728	126
National Electrical Contractors Assn (NECA) 3 Bethesda Metro Ctr Ste 1100	Bethesda	MD	20814	**800-214-0585**	301-657-3110	48-3
National Electrical Manufacturers Assn (NEMA) 1300 N 17th St Ste 1752	Rosslyn	VA	22209	**800-699-9277**	703-841-3200	48-13
National Electrical Manufacturers Representatives Assn (NEMRA) 28 Deer St Ste 302	Portsmouth	NH	03801	**800-446-3672**	914-524-8650	48-18
National Electronic Attachment Inc 3577 Pkwy Ln Ste 250	Norcross	GA	30092	**800-782-5150**	770-441-3203	390
National Electronics Service Dealers Assn (NESDA) 3608 Pershing Ave	Fort Worth	TX	76107	**800-946-0201**	817-921-9061	48-18
National Emblem Inc 17036 S Avalon Blvd	Carson	CA	90746	**800-877-6185**	310-515-5055	260
National Employee Assistance Services Inc N 17 W 24100 Riverwood Dr Ste 300	Waukesha	WI	53188	**800-634-6433**	262-574-2500	461
National Endowment for the Humanities (NEH) 400 7th St SW	Washington	DC	20506	**800-634-1121**	202-606-8400	340-18
National Energy Research Scientific Computing Ctr (NERSC) Lawrence Berkeley National Laboratory	Berkeley	CA	94720	**800-666-3772**	510-486-5849	666
National Energy Technology Laboratory (NETL) 3610 Collins Ferry Rd	Morgantown	WV	26505	**800-432-8330**	304-285-4764	666
National Engineering Service Corp 72 Mirona Rd	Portsmouth	NH	03801	**800-562-3463**	603-431-9740	719
National Environmental Balancing Bureau (NEBB) 8575 Grovemont Cir	Gaithersburg	MD	20877	**866-497-4447**	301-977-3698	48-19
National Environmental Health Assn (NEHA) 720 S Colorado Blvd Ste 1000-N	Denver	CO	80246	**866-956-2258**	303-756-9090	48-7
National Environmental Satellite Data & Information Service *National Coastal Data Development Ctr* Bldg 1100 Ste 101	Stennis Space Center	MS	39529	**866-732-2382**	228-688-2936	340-2
National Enzyme Co Inc 15366 US Hwy 160	Forsyth	MO	65653	**800-825-8545**	417-546-4796	143
National Excelsior Co 1999 N Ruby St	Melrose Park	IL	60160	**855-373-9235**	708-343-4225	594
National Exchange Club 3050 W Central Ave	Toledo	OH	43606	**800-924-2643**	419-535-3232	47-15
National Fallen Firefighters Foundation PO Box 498	Emmitsburg	MD	21727	**888-744-6513**	301-447-1365	47-19
National Family Caregivers Assn (NFCA) 10400 Connecticut Ave Ste 500	Kensington	MD	20895	**800-896-3650**	301-942-6430	47-6
National Farm Life Insurance Co 6001 Bridge St	Fort Worth	TX	76112	**800-772-7557**	817-451-9550	390
National Farm Toy Museum 1110 16th Ave SE	Dyersville	IA	52040	**877-475-2727**	563-875-2727	519
National Farmers Organization (NFO) 528 Billy Sunday Rd Ste 100 PO Box 2508	Ames	IA	50010	**800-247-2110**	515-292-2000	47-2
National Farmers Union Property & Casualty Co 5619 DTC Pkwy Ste 300	Greenwood Village	CO	80111	**800-347-1961**	303-337-5500	391-4
National Federation of Community Development Credit Unions (NFCDCU) 39 Broadway Ste 2140	New York	NY	10006	**800-437-8711**	212-809-1850	48-2
National Federation of Republican Women (NFRW) 124 N Alfred St	Alexandria	VA	22314	**800-373-9688**	703-548-9688	47-7
National Federation of State High School Assn (NFHS) PO Box 690	Indianapolis	IN	46206	**800-776-3462***	317-972-6900	47-22
*Cust Svc						
National Federation of the Blind (NFB) 1800 Johnson St	Baltimore	MD	21230	**800-392-5671**	410-659-9314	47-17
National FFA Organization 6060 FFA Dr	Indianapolis	IN	46268	**800-772-0939**	317-802-6060	47-2
National Fiber Technology LLC 300 Canal St	Lawrence	MA	01840	**800-842-2751***	978-686-2964	348
*Cust Svc						
National Fibromyalgia Partnership Inc (NFP) 140 Zinn Way	Linden	VA	22642	**866-725-4404**		47-17
National Film Board of Canada Stn Centre-Ville PO Box 6100	Montreal	QC	H3C3H5	**800-267-7710**	514-283-9000	512
National Filter Media Corp 691 North 400 West	Salt Lake City	UT	84103	**800-777-4248**	801-363-6736	18
National Fingerprint Inc 6999 Dolan Rd	Glouster	OH	45732	**888-823-7873**	740-767-3853	690
National Fire & Marine Insurance Co 3024 Harney St	Omaha	NE	68131	**866-720-7861**	402-536-3000	391-4
National Fire Protection Assn (NFPA) 1 Batterymarch Pk	Quincy	MA	02169	**800-344-3555**	617-770-3000	47-17
National Fisherman Magazine 121 Free St	Portland	ME	04101	**800-959-5073**	207-842-5600	456-21
National Fitness Trade Journal PO Box 2490	White City	OR	97503	**877-867-7835**	541-830-0400	456-21
National Floral Supply Inc 3825 LeonaRdtown Rd Ste 4	Waldorf	MD	20601	**800-932-2772**	301-932-7600	294
National Forest Recreation Assn (NFRA) PO Box 488	Woodlake	CA	93286	**800-282-2444**	559-564-2365	47-23
National Foundation for Cancer Research (NFCR) 4600 E W Hwy Ste 525	Bethesda	MD	20814	**800-321-2873**	301-654-1250	306
National Frame Builders Assn (NFBA) 8735 W Higgins Rd Ste 300	Chicago	IL	60631	**800-557-6957**		48-3
National Fraternity of Kappa Delta Rho (KDR) 331 S Main St	Greensburg	PA	15601	**800-536-5371**	724-838-7100	47-16
National Fraud Information Ctr (NFIC) 1701 K St NW Ste 1200	Washington	DC	20006	**800-333-4636**	202-835-3323	47-10
National Freedom of Information Coalition Univ of Missouri	Columbia	MO	65211	**866-682-6663**	573-882-4856	47-8
National Freight Inc (NFI) 1515 Burnt Mill Rd	Cherry Hill	NJ	08003	**877-634-3777***		448
*General						
National Fresh Water Fishing Hall of Fame 10360 Hall of Fame Dr PO Box 690	Hayward	WI	54843	**866-268-4333**	715-634-4440	521
National Fruit Product Co Inc 701 Fairmont Ave	Winchester	VA	22601	**800-655-4022**	540-723-9614	316-3
National Fuel Gas Co 6363 Main St	Williamsville	NY	14221	**800-365-3234***	716-857-7000	360-5
NYSE: NFG ■ *Cust Svc						
National Fuel Gas Supply Corp 6363 Main St	Williamsville	NY	14221	**800-365-3234***	716-857-7000	785
*Cust Svc						
National Fuel Resources Inc 165 Lawrence Bell Dr Ste 120	Williamsville	NY	14221	**800-839-9993**	716-630-6778	785
National Funeral Directors & Morticians Assn (NFDMA) 6290 Shannon Pkwy	Union City	GA	30291	**800-434-0958**	770-969-0064	48-4
National Funeral Directors Assn (NFDA) 13625 Bishop's Dr	Brookfield	WI	53005	**800-228-6332**	262-789-1880	48-4
National Futures Assn (NFA) 300 S Riverside Plz Ste 1800	Chicago	IL	60606	**800-621-3570**	312-781-1300	48-2
National Garden Clubs Inc (NGC) 4401 Magnolia Ave	Saint Louis	MO	63110	**800-550-6007**	314-776-7574	47-18
National Gardening Assn (NGA) 1100 Dorset St	South Burlington	VT	05403	**800-538-7476**	802-863-5251	47-18
National Gaucher Foundation (NGF) 5410 Edson Ln Ste 220	Rockville	MD	30084	**800-504-3189**	770-934-2910	47-17
National Genealogical Society (NGS) 3108 Columbia Pk Ste 300	Arlington	VA	22204	**800-473-0060**	703-525-0050	47-18
National Genetics Institute 2440 S Blvd Ste 235	Los Angeles	CA	90064	**800-352-7788**	310-996-0036	418
National Geographic Society 1145 17th St NW	Washington	DC	20036	**800-647-5463**	202-857-7000	48-19
National Geographic Society Explorers Hall 1145 17th St NW	Washington	DC	20036	**800-647-5463**		519
National Geographic Traveler Magazine 1145 17th St NW	Washington	DC	20036	**800-647-5463**	202-857-7000	456-22
National Glass Assn (NGA) 8200 Greensboro Dr Ste 302	McLean	VA	22102	**866-342-5642**	703-442-4890	48-13
National Glass Ltd 5744 198th St	Langley	BC	V3A7J2	**800-663-8168**	604-530-2311	361
National Golf Course Owners Assn (NGCOA) 291 Seven Farms Dr 2nd Fl	Charleston	SC	29492	**800-933-4262**	843-881-9956	47-23
National Golf Foundation (NGF) 1150 S US Hwy 1 Ste 401	Jupiter	FL	33477	**800-733-6006**	561-744-6006	47-22
National Graduate School of Quality Management Inc, The 186 Jones Rd	Falmouth	MA	02540	**800-838-2580**	508-457-1313	167
National Grange 1616 H St NW	Washington	DC	20006	**888-447-2643**	202-628-3507	47-2
National Grange Mutual Insurance Co 55 W St	Keene	NH	03431	**800-258-5310**	603-352-4000	391-4
National Grid USA Service Company Inc 25 Research Dr	Westborough	MA	01582	**800-548-8000**	508-389-2000	360-5
National Ground Water Assn (NGWA) 601 Dempsey Rd	Westerville	OH	43081	**800-551-7379**	614-898-7791	47-12
National Guard Assn of the US (NGAUS) 1 Massachusetts Ave NW Ste 200	Washington	DC	20001	**888-226-4287**	202-789-0031	47-19
National Guard Products Inc 4985 E Raines Rd	Memphis	TN	38118	**800-647-7874**		236
National Guardian Life Insurance Co (NGL) 2 E Gilman St	Madison	WI	53703	**800-548-2962**	608-257-5611	391-2
National Gypsum Co 2001 Rexford Rd	Charlotte	NC	28211	**800-628-4662**	704-365-7300	347
National Hansen's Disease Program (NHDP) 1770 Physicians Pk Dr	Baton Rouge	LA	70816	**800-221-9393**		666
National Hardwood Lumber Assn (NHLA) 6830 Raleigh-LaGrange Rd	Memphis	TN	38134	**800-933-0318**	901-377-1818	48-3
National Head Start Assn (NHSA) 1651 Prince St	Alexandria	VA	22314	**866-677-8724**	703-739-0875	47-11
National Headache Foundation (NHF) 820 N Orleans St Ste 217	Chicago	IL	60610	**888-643-5552**		47-17
National Hearing Conservation Assn (NHCA) 3030 W 81st Ave	Westminster	CO	80031	**877-766-6629**	303-224-9022	47-17
National Hemophilia Foundation (NHF) 116 W 32nd St 11th Fl	New York	NY	10001	**800-424-2634**	212-328-3700	47-17
National Heritage Academies 3850 Broadmoor Ave SE Ste 201	Grand Rapids	MI	49512	**877-223-6402***		244
*General						
National Highway Express Co 971 Old Henderson St PO Box 20262	Columbus	OH	43220	**800-837-5700**	614-459-4900	778
National Highway Traffic Safety Administration (NHTSA) 1200 New Jersey Ave SE	Washington	DC	20590	**888-327-4236**	202-366-9550	340-15
National Center for Statistics & Analysis 1200 New Jersey Ave SE	Washington	DC	20590	**800-934-8517**	202-366-1503	340-15
Vehicle Research & Test Ctr 10820 SR 347 PO Box B37	East Liberty	OH	43319	**800-262-8309**	937-666-4511	340-15
National Highway Traffic Safety Administration Regional Offices *NHTSA Region 3* 1200 New Jersey Ave Ste 6700	Washington	DC	20590	**888-327-4236**		340-15

	Toll-Free	Phone	Class
National Hispanic Council on Aging (NHCOA) 734 15th St NW Ste 1050 .... Washington DC 20005	800-633-4227	202-347-9733	47-6
National Hispanic University 14271 Story Rd .... San Jose CA 95127	877-762-9801	408-254-6900	167
National Home Furnishings Assn (NHFA) 500 Giuseppe Ct Ste 6 .... Roseville CA 95678	800-422-3778	336-886-6100	48-4
National Home Health Care Corp 700 White Plains Rd Ste 275 .... Scarsdale NY 10583	800-422-4661	914-722-9000	363
National Homeland Security Research Ctr US Environmental Protection Agency 26 W Martin Luther King Dr .... Cincinnati OH 45268	888-372-7341	513-569-7907	666
National Honor Society (NHS) 1904 Assn Dr .... Reston VA 20191	800-253-7746	703-860-0200	47-11
National Hospice & Palliative Care Organization (NHPCO) 1700 Diagonal Rd Ste 625 .... Alexandria VA 22314 *Help Line	800-658-8898*	703-837-1500	48-8
National Hotel 1677 Collins Ave .... Miami Beach FL 33139	800-327-8370	305-532-2311	379
National HVAC Service Ltd 101 Bradford Rd Ste 340 .... Wexford PA 15090	800-281-3608	724-935-9390	191-10
National Independent Automobile Dealers Assn (NIADA) 2521 Brown Blvd .... Arlington TX 76006	800-682-3837	817-640-3838	48-18
National Industrial Lumber Co 1 Chicago Ave .... Elizabeth PA 15037	800-289-9352		193-3
National Industries for the Blind (NIB) 1310 Braddock Pl .... Alexandria VA 22314 *Cust Svc	800-433-2304*	703-310-0500	47-17
National Information Standards Organization (NISO) 3600 Clipper Mill Rd Ste 302 .... Baltimore MD 21211	877-375-2160	301-654-2512	48-16
National Inhalant Prevention Coalition (NIPC) 318 Lindsay St .... Chattanooga TN 37405	800-269-4237	423-265-4662	47-17
National Institute for Literacy (NIFL) 1775 'I' St NW Ste 730 .... Washington DC 20006	800-228-8813	202-233-2025	340-6
National Institute of Governmental Purchasing Inc (NIGP) 151 Spring St .... Herndon VA 20170	800-367-6447	703-736-8900	48-7
National Institute of Standards & Technology (NIST) 100 Bureau Dr Sp 1070 .... Gaithersburg MD 20899	800-877-8339	301-975-6478	340-2
National Institutes of Health			
National Cancer Institute Public Inquiries Office 6116 Executive Blvd Rm 3036A .... Bethesda MD 20892	800-422-6237	301-435-3848	666
National Center for Complementary & Alternative Medicine National Institutes of Health 31 Ctr Dr Bldg 31 .... Bethesda MD 20892	888-644-6226	301-594-7103	340-8
National Institute of Mental Health 6001 Executive Blvd Rm 8184 MSC 9663 .... Bethesda MD 20892	866-615-6464	301-443-4513	340-8
National Institute of Neurological Disorders & Stroke PO Box 5801 .... Bethesda MD 20824	800-352-9424	301-496-5751	340-8
National Institute on Deafness & Other Communication Disorders 31 Ctr Dr Bldg 31 Rm 3C35 .... Bethesda MD 20892	800-241-1044	301-496-7243	666
National Library of Medicine National Institutes of Health 8600 Rockville Pike Bldg 38 .... Bethesda MD 20894	888-346-3656	301-594-5983	340-8
National Instrument LLC 4119 Fordleigh Rd .... Baltimore MD 21215	866-258-1914	410-764-0900	546
National Instruments Corp 11500 N Mopac Expy .... Austin TX 78759 NASDAQ: NATI ■ *Cust Svc	800-433-3488*	512-794-0100	180-5
National Insulation Assn (NIA) 99 Canal Ctr Plz Ste 222 .... Alexandria VA 22314	877-968-7642	703-683-6422	48-3
National Insurance Crime Bureau (NICB) 1111 E Touhy Ave Ste 400 .... Des Plaines IL 60018	800-447-6282	847-544-7002	48-9
National Interagency Fire Ctr 3833 S Development Ave .... Boise ID 83705	877-471-2262	208-387-5512	340-11
National International Roofing Corp 11317 Smith Dr .... Huntley IL 60142	800-221-7663	847-669-3444	191-12
National Interstate Corp 3250 I- Dr .... Richfield OH 44286 NASDAQ: NATL	800-929-1500	330-659-8900	391-4
National Inventors Hall of Fame 3701 Highland Park NW .... North Canton OH 44720	800-968-4332		519
National Investment Co Service Assn (NICSA) 8400 Westpark Dr 2nd Fl .... McLean VA 22102	800-426-1122	508-485-1500	48-2
National Jets 3495 SW Ninth Ave .... Fort Lauderdale FL 33315	800-327-3710	954-359-9900	62
National Jewish Medical & Research Ctr 1400 Jackson St PO Box 17169 .... Denver CO 80206	877-225-5654	303-388-4461	374-7
National Journal 600 New Hampshire Ave NW .... Washington DC 20037	800-613-6701	202-739-8400	456-17
National Kappa Kappa Iota Inc 1875 E 15th St .... Tulsa OK 74104	800-678-0389	918-744-0389	47-16
National Kidney Foundation (NKF) 30 E 33rd St 8th Fl .... New York NY 10016	800-622-9010	212-889-2210	47-17
National Kitchen & Bath Assn (NKBA) 687 Willow Grove St .... Hackettstown NJ 07840	800-843-6522		48-3
National Labor College 10000 New Hampshire Ave .... Silver Spring MD 20903	888-427-8100	301-431-6400	798
National Labor Relations Board (NLRB) 1099 14th St NW .... Washington DC 20570	866-667-6572	202-273-1991	340-18
National Labor Relations Board Regional Offices			
Region 1 10 Cswy St 6th Fl .... Boston MA 02222	866-667-6572	617-565-6700	340-18
Region 3 Niagara Ctr Bldg 130 S Elmwood Ave Ste 630 .... Buffalo NY 14202	866-667-6572	716-551-4931	340-18
Region 8 1240 E Ninth St Rm 1695 .... Cleveland OH 44199	866-667-6572	216-522-3715	340-18
Region 9 550 Main St Rm 3003 .... Cincinnati OH 45202	866-667-6572	513-684-3686	340-18
Region 11 4035 University Pkwy Ste 200 .... Winston-Salem NC 27106	866-667-6572	336-631-5201	340-18
Region 14 1222 Spruce St Rm 8.302 .... Saint Louis MO 63103	866-667-6572	314-539-7770	340-18
Region 16 Federal Bldg 819 Taylor St Rm 8A24 .... Fort Worth TX 76102	866-667-6572	817-978-2921	340-18
Region 18 330 Second Ave S Ste 790 .... Minneapolis MN 55401	866-667-6572	612-348-1757	340-18
Region 20 901 Market St Ste 400 .... San Francisco CA 94103	866-667-6572	415-356-5130	340-18
Region 25 575 N Pennsylvania St Ste 238 .... Indianapolis IN 46204	866-667-6572	317-226-7381	340-18
Region 31 11150 W Olympic Blvd Ste 700 .... Los Angeles CA 90064	866-667-6572	310-235-7352	340-18
National League for Nursing (NLN) 61 Broadway 33rd Fl .... New York NY 10006	800-669-1656	212-363-5555	48-8
National Legal Aid & Defender Assn (NLADA) 1140 Connecticut Ave NW Ste 900 .... Washington DC 20036	800-725-4513	202-452-0620	48-10
National Little Britches Rodeo Assn (NLBRA) 5050 Edison Ave Ste 105 .... Colorado Springs CO 80915	800-763-3694	719-389-0333	47-22
National Lumber 71 Maple St .... Mansfield MA 02048	800-370-9663	508-339-8020	364
National Mail Order Assn LLC (NMOA) 2807 Polk St NE .... Minneapolis MN 55418	800-992-1377	612-788-1673	48-18
National Marfan Foundation (NMF) 22 Manhasset Ave .... Port Washington NY 11050	800-862-7326	516-883-8712	47-17
National Marine Electronics Assn (NMEA) 7 Riggs Ave .... Severna Park MD 21146	800-808-6632	410-975-9425	48-13
National Marine Fisheries Service Regional Offices			
Pacific Islands Region 1601 Kapiolani Blvd Rm 1110 .... Honolulu HI 96814	888-674-7411	808-944-2200	340-2
National Marine Representatives Assn (NMRA) PO Box 360 .... Gurnee IL 60031	800-890-3819	847-662-3167	48-18
National Marrow Donor Program (NMDP) 3001 Broadway St NE Ste 100 .... Minneapolis MN 55413	800-526-7809	612-627-5800	47-17
National Medical Assn (NMA) 8403 Colesville Rd Ste 920 .... Silver Spring MD 20910	800-662-0554	202-347-1895	48-8
National Mental Health Information Ctr PO Box 42557 .... Washington DC 20015	800-487-4889		340-8
National Metal Fabricators 2395 Greenleaf Ave .... Elk Grove Village IL 60007	800-323-8849	847-439-5321	695
National Meter & Automation 7220 S Fraser St .... Centennial CO 80112	877-212-8340	303-339-9100	609
National Middle School Assn (NMSA) 4151 Executive Pkwy Ste 300 .... Westerville OH 43081	800-528-6672	614-895-4730	48-5
National Mississippi River Museum & Aquarium 350 E Third St .... Dubuque IA 52001	800-226-3369	563-557-9545	519
National Model Railroad Assn (NMRA) 4121 Cromwell Rd .... Chattanooga TN 37421	800-654-2256	423-892-2846	47-18
National Monitoring Center 26800 Aliso Viejo Pkwy Ste 250 .... Aliso Viejo CA 92656	800-662-1711		691
National Motor Club of America Inc (NMC) 130 E John Carpenter Fwy .... Irving TX 75062	800-523-4582	972-999-1099	52
National Motor Freight Traffic Assn (NMFTA) 1001 N Fairfax St Ste 600 .... Alexandria VA 22314	866-411-6632	703-838-1810	48-21
National Motorists Assn (NMA) 402 W Second St .... Waunakee WI 53597	800-882-2785	608-849-6000	48-21
National Multi Housing Council PAC 1850 M St NW Ste 540 .... Washington DC 20036	866-987-7367	202-974-2300	614
National Multiple Sclerosis Society 733 Third Ave 3rd Fl .... New York NY 10017	800-344-4867	212-986-3240	47-17
National Museum of Dentistry 31 S Greene St .... Baltimore MD 21201	866-787-8637	410-706-0600	519
National Museum of Natural History (Smithsonian Institution) 10th St & Constitution Ave NW .... Washington DC 20560	866-868-7774	202-633-1000	519
National Museum of Naval Aviation 1750 Radford Blvd Ste C .... Pensacola FL 32508 *General	800-247-6289*	850-452-3604	519
National Museum of Racing & Hall of Fame 191 Union Ave .... Saratoga Springs NY 12866	800-562-5394	518-584-0400	521
National Museum of the American Indian (Smithsonian Institution) 1 Bowling Green .... New York NY 10004	800-242-6624	212-514-3700	519
National Museum of Wildlife Art 2820 Rungius Rd PO Box 6825 .... Jackson WY 83002	800-313-9553	307-733-5771	519
National Museum of Women in the Arts 1250 New York Ave NW .... Washington DC 20005	866-875-4627	202-783-5000	519
National Music Museum 414 E Clark St .... Vermillion SD 57069	877-225-0027	605-677-5306	519
National Mutual Benefit 6522 Grand Teton Plaza .... Madison WI 53719	800-779-1936	608-833-1936	391-2
National NeedleArts Assn, The (TNNA) 1100-H Brandywine Blvd .... Zanesville OH 43701	800-889-8662	740-455-6773	47-18
National Newspaper Assn (NNA) PO Box 7540 .... Columbia MO 65205	800-829-4662	573-777-4980	48-14
National Niemann-Pick Disease Foundation Inc (NNPDF) 401 Madison Ave Ste B PO Box 49 .... Fort Atkinson WI 53538	877-287-3672	920-563-0930	47-17
National Nonwovens PO Box 150 .... EastHampton MA 01027	800-333-3469	413-527-3445	742-6
National Notary Assn (NNA) 9350 DeSoto Ave .... Chatsworth CA 91313	800-876-6827	818-739-4000	48-12
National Nursing Staff Development Organization (NNSDO) 330 N Wabash Ave Ste 2000 .... Chicago IL 60611	800-489-1995	312-321-5135	48-8
National Ocean Industries Assn (NOIA) 1120 G St NW Ste 900 .... Washington DC 20005	800-558-9994	202-347-6900	47-12
National Office Furniture 1205 Kimball Blvd .... Jasper IN 47549	800-482-1717		320-1
National Oil & Gas Inc 409 N Main St .... Bluffton IN 46714	800-322-8454	260-824-2220	578
National Oilwell Varco (NOV) 7909 Parkwood Cir Dr .... Houston TX 77036 NYSE: NOV	888-262-8645	713-375-3700	185
National Optical Astronomy Observatories 950 N Cherry Ave .... Tucson AZ 85719	888-809-4012	520-318-8163	666
National Oral Health Information Clearinghouse (NIDCR) 1 NOHIC Way .... Bethesda MD 20892	866-232-4528	301-496-4261	47-17
National Organization for Albinism & Hypopigmentation (NOAH) PO Box 959 .... East Hampstead NH 03826	800-648-2310	603-887-2310	47-17

Name / Address	City	State	Zip	Toll-Free	Phone	Class
National Organization for Rare Disorders (NORD) 55 Kenosia Ave PO Box 1968	Danbury	CT	06813	**800-999-6673**	203-744-0100	47-17
National Organization for the Reform of Marijuana Laws (NORML) 1600 K St NW Ste 501	Washington	DC	20006	**888-676-6765**	202-483-5500	47-8
National Organization for Victim Assistance (NOVA) 510 King St Ste 424	Alexandria	VA	22314	**800-879-6682**	703-535-6682	47-8
National Organization for Women (NOW) 1100 H St NW 3rd Fl	Washington	DC	20005	**855-212-0212**	202-628-8669	47-24
National Organization of Circumcision Information Resource Centers (NOCIRC) PO Box 2512	San Anselmo	CA	94979	**800-727-8622**	415-488-9883	47-17
National Ornamental Metal Museum 374 Metal Museum Dr	Memphis	TN	38106	**877-881-2326**	901-774-6380	519
National Osteoporosis Foundation (NOF) 251 18th St S Ste 630	Arlington	VA	22202	**800-231-4222**	202-223-2226	47-17
National Outdoor Leadership School 284 Lincoln St	Lander	WY	82520	**800-710-6657**	307-332-5300	683
National Ovarian Cancer Coalition (NOCC) 2501 Oak Lawn Ave Ste 435	Dallas	TX	75219	**888-682-7426**		47-17
National Paint & Coatings Assn (NPCA) 1500 Rhode Island Ave NW	Washington	DC	20005	**800-647-5527**	202-462-6272	48-13
National Paper & Sanitary Supply 2511 S 156th Cir	Omaha	NE	68130	**800-647-2737**	402-330-5507	558
National Parking Assn (NPA) 1112 16th St NW Ste 840	Washington	DC	20036	**800-647-7275**	202-296-4336	48-3
National Parks Conservation Assn (NPCA) 1300 19th St NW Ste 300	Washington	DC	20036	**800-628-7275**	202-223-6722	47-13
National Parks Magazine 777 Sixth St NW Ste 700 *General	Washington	DC	20001	**800-628-7275***	202-223-6722	456-19
National Partitions 10300 Goldenfern Ln	Knoxville	TN	37931	**888-818-5749**	865-670-2100	288
National Peace Corps Assn (NPCA) 1900 L St NW Ste 610	Washington	DC	20036	**800-424-8580**	202-293-7728	47-5
National Pen Corp (NPC) 12121 Scripps Summit Dr Ste 200	San Diego	CA	92131	**800-854-1000**	858-675-3000	9
National Penn Bancshares Inc PO Box 547 *NASDAQ: NPBC*	Boyertown	PA	19512	**800-822-3321**		360-2
National Pesticide Information Ctr (NPIC) 333 Weniger Hall	Corvallis	OR	97331	**800-858-7378**		47-17
National Pipe & Plastics Inc 3421 Old Vestal Rd	Vestal	NY	13850	**800-836-4350**		595
National Pork Producers Council PAC 122 C St NW Ste 875	Washington	DC	20001	**866-844-9416**	202-347-3600	614
National Post 1450 Don Mills Rd Ste 300	Toronto	ON	M3B3R5	**800-267-6568**	416-383-2300	531-1
National Precast Concrete Assn (NPCA) 10333 N Meridian St Ste 272	Indianapolis	IN	46290	**800-366-7731**	317-571-9500	48-3
National Presto Industries Inc 3925 N Hastings Way *NYSE: NPK*	Eau Claire	WI	54703	**800-877-0441**	715-839-2121	36
National Printing Converters Inc 18 S Murphy Ave	Brazil	IN	47834	**800-877-6724**		413
National Processing Co 5100 Interchange Way *General	Louisville	KY	40229	**877-300-7757***	800-683-2289	257
National Property Inspections Inc (NPI) 9375 Burt St Ste 201	Omaha	NE	68114	**800-333-9807**	402-333-9807	365
National Psoriasis Foundation (NPF) 6600 SW 92nd Ave Ste 300	Portland	OR	97223	**800-723-9166**	503-244-7404	47-17
National Psychological Assn for Psychoanalysis (NPAP) 40 W 13th St Ste 1	New York	NY	10011	**800-365-7006**	212-924-7440	48-15
National PTA 1250 N Pitt St	Alexandria	VA	22314	**800-307-4782**	703-518-1200	306
National Pump Company LLC 7706 N 71st Ave	Glendale	AZ	85303	**800-966-5240**	623-979-3560	638
National Railroad Museum 2285 S Broadway St	Green Bay	WI	54304	**866-468-7630**	920-437-7623	519
National Railroad Passenger Corp 60 Massachusetts Ave NE	Washington	DC	20002	**800-872-7245**	202-906-3741	647
National Railway Equipment Co (NREC) 14400 Robey St	Dixmoor	IL	60426	**800-253-2905**	708-388-6002	648
National Ready Mixed Concrete Assn (NRMCA) 900 Spring St	Silver Spring	MD	20910	**888-846-7622**	301-587-1400	48-3
National Recreation & Park Assn 22377 Belmont Ridge Rd	Ashburn	VA	20148	**800-626-6772**	703-858-0784	47-1
National Recreation and Park Association (NSPR) 22377 Belmont Ridge Rd 22377 Belmont Ridge Rd	Ashburn	VA	20148	**800-626-6772**	703-858-0784	47-23
National Recreation Reservation Service (NRRS) PO Box 140	Ballston Spa	NY	12020	**877-444-6777**	518-885-3639	771
National Register Publishing Co 430 Mountain Ave Ste 400	New Providence	NJ	07974	**800-473-7020**		634-2
National Rehabilitation Assn (NRA) 633 S Washington St	Alexandria	VA	22314	**888-258-4295**	703-836-0850	47-17
National Rehabilitation Information Ctr (NARIC) 8400 Corporate Dr Ste 500	Landover	MD	20785	**800-346-2742**	301-459-5900	47-17
National Research Corp 1245 Q St *NASDAQ: NRCI*	Lincoln	NE	68508	**800-388-4264**	402-475-2525	465
National Research Ctr for Coal & Energy (NRCCE) *West Virginia University* 385 Evansdale Dr PO Box 6064	Morgantown	WV	26506	**800-624-8301**	304-293-2867	666
National Resource Ctr on Domestic Violence (NRCDV) 6400 Flank Dr Ste 1300	Harrisburg	PA	17112	**800-799-7233**		47-6
National Resource Ctr on Native American Aging (NRCNAA) 501 N Columbia Rd Rm 4535	Grand Forks	ND	58202	**800-896-7628**	701-777-6780	47-6
National Restaurant Assn (NRA) 2055 L St NW Ste 700	Washington	DC	20036	**800-424-5156**	202-331-5900	48-6
National Retail Federation (NRF) 1101 New York Ave NW	Washington	DC	20005	**800-673-4692**	202-783-7971	48-18
National Retail Hardware Assn (NRHA) 5822 W 74th St *Cust Svc	Indianapolis	IN	46278	**800-772-4424***	317-290-0338	48-18
National Reye's Syndrome Foundation (NRSF) 426 N Lewis St	Bryan	OH	43506	**800-233-7393**	419-924-9000	47-17
National Right to Work Committee (NRTWC) 8001 Braddock Rd Ste 500	Springfield	VA	22160	**800-325-7892**	703-321-8510	48-12
National Rivet & Manufacturing Co 21 E Jefferson St	Waupun	WI	53963	**888-324-5511**	920-324-5511	280
National Roofing Contractors Assn (NRCA) 10255 W Higgins Rd Ste 600 *Cust Svc	Rosemont	IL	60018	**800-323-9545***	847-299-9070	48-3
National Rosacea Society 800 S NW Hwy Ste 200	Barrington	IL	60010	**888-662-5874**	847-382-8971	47-17
National Rubber Technologies Corp 35 Cawthra Ave	Toronto	ON	M6N5B3	**800-387-8501**	416-657-1111	674
National Runaway Switchboard (NRS) 3141 N Lincoln Ave	Chicago	IL	60657	**800-786-2929**	773-880-9860	47-6
National Rural Electric Co-op Assn (NRECA) 4301 Wilson Blvd	Arlington	VA	22203	**866-759-2619**	703-907-5939	47-12
National Rural Utilities Co-op Finance Corp 2201 Co-op Way	Herndon	VA	20171	**800-424-2954**	703-709-6700	508
National Safety Apparel Inc (NSA) 15825 Industrial Pkwy	Cleveland	OH	44135	**800-553-0672**		575
National Safety Council (NSC) 1121 Spring Lk Dr	Itasca	IL	60143	**800-621-7615**	630-285-1121	47-17
National Salon Resources Inc 3109 Louisiana Ave N	Minneapolis	MN	55427	**800-622-0003**	763-541-1000	75
National School Products 1523 Old Niles Ferry Rd	Maryville	TN	37803	**800-627-9393**	865-984-3960	245
National School Supply & Equipment Assn (NSSEA) 8380 Colesville Rd Ste 250	Silver Spring	MD	20910	**800-395-5550**	301-495-0240	48-18
National Science Foundation (NSF) 4201 Wilson Blvd	Arlington	VA	22230	**800-877-8339**	703-292-5111	340-18
National Science Teachers Assn (NSTA) 1840 Wilson Blvd *Sales	Arlington	VA	22201	**800-722-6782***	703-243-7100	48-5
National Scouting Museum 1329 W Walnut Hill Ln	Irving	TX	75038	**800-303-3047**	972-580-2100	519
National Securities Corp 410 Park Ave 14th Fl	New York	NY	10022	**800-742-7730**	212-417-8000	688
National Seminars Training 6900 Squibb Rd	Shawnee Mission	KS	66202	**800-258-7246**	913-432-7755	763
National Senior Golf Assn (NSGA) 200 Perrine Rd Ste 201	Old Bridge	NJ	08857	**800-282-6772**		47-22
National Serv-All Inc 6231 McBeth Rd	Fort Wayne	IN	46809	**800-876-9001**	260-747-4117	802
National Services Group Inc 1682 Langley Ave	Irvine	CA	92614	**800-394-6000**	714-564-7900	191-8
National Sheriffs' Assn (NSA) 1450 Duke St	Alexandria	VA	22314	**800-424-7827**	703-836-7827	48-7
National Shoe Retailers Assn (NSRA) 7386 N La Cholla Blvd	Tucson	AZ	85741	**800-673-8446**	520-209-1710	48-18
National Shrine of Our Lady of the Snows 442 S De Mazenod Dr	Belleville	IL	62223	**800-682-2879**	618-397-6700	49
National Slovak Society of the USA (NSS) 351 Vly Brook Rd	McMurray	PA	15317	**800-488-1890**	724-731-0094	47-14
National Small Business Assn (NSBA) 1156 15th St NW Ste 1100	Washington	DC	20005	**800-345-6728**	202-293-8830	48-12
National Soccer Coaches Assn of America (NSCAA) 800 Ann Ave	Kansas City	KS	66101	**800-458-0678**	913-362-1747	47-22
National Society of Accountants (NSA) 1010 N Fairfax St	Alexandria	VA	22314	**800-966-6679**	703-549-6400	48-1
National Society of Professional Engineers (NSPE) 1420 King St	Alexandria	VA	22314	**888-285-6773**	703-684-2800	48-19
National Softball Hall of Fame & Museum 2801 NE 50th St	Oklahoma City	OK	73111	**800-654-8337**	405-424-5266	521
National Speakers Bureau 1177 W Bdwy Ste 300	Vancouver	BC	V6H1G3	**800-661-4110**	604-734-3663	706
National Speakers Bureau Inc 14047 W Petronalla Dr Ste 102	Libertyville	IL	60048	**800-323-9442**	847-295-1122	706
National Specialty Alloys LLC 18250 Keith Harrow Blvd *General	Houston	TX	77084	**800-847-5653***	281-345-2115	491
National Speed Sport News Magazine 142 F S Cardigan Way	Mooresville	NC	28117	**866-455-2531**	704-489-5231	456-3
National Spinal Cord Injury Assn (NSCIA) 75-20 Astoria Blvd Ste 120	East Elmhurst	NY	11370	**800-962-9629**	718-512-0010	47-17
National Sporting Goods Assn (NSGA) 1601 Feehanville Dr Ste 300	Mount Prospect	IL	60056	**800-815-5422**	847-296-6742	48-4
National Sprint Car Hall of Fame & Museum 1 Sprint Capital Pl	Knoxville	IA	50138	**800-874-4488**	641-842-6176	521
National Staff Development Council (NSDC) 504 S Locust St	Oxford	OH	45056	**800-727-7288**	513-523-6029	48-5
National Standard Parts Assoc Inc 4400 Mobile Hwy	Pensacola	FL	32506	**800-874-6813**	850-456-5771	56
National Stock Exchange (NSX) 101 Hudson St Ste 1200	Jersey City	NJ	07302	**800-843-3924**	201-499-3700	689
National Stock Sign Co 1040 El Dorado Ave	Santa Cruz	CA	95062	**800-462-7726**	831-476-2020	699
National Stone Sand & Gravel Assn (NSSGA) 1605 King St	Alexandria	VA	22314	**800-342-1415**	703-525-8788	48-3
National Strength & Conditioning Assn (NSCA) 1885 Bob Johnson Dr	Colorado Springs	CO	80906	**800-815-6826**	719-632-6722	47-22
National Stroke Assn (NSA) 9707 E Easter Ln *Cust Svc	Centennial	CO	80112	**800-787-6537***		47-17
National Stuttering Assn (NSA) 119 W 40th St 14th Fl	New York	NY	10018	**800-937-8888**	212-944-4050	47-17
National Sunflower Assn PAC 2401 46th Ave SE Ste 206	Mandan	ND	58554	**888-718-7033**	701-328-5100	614
National Super Service Company Inc 3115 Frenchman Rd *Cust Svc	Toledo	OH	43607	**800-677-1663***	419-531-2121	386
National Symphony Orchestra 2700 F St NW	Washington	DC	20566	**800-444-1324**	202-416-8000	572-3
National System of Garage Ventilation Inc 714 N Church St PO Box 1186	Decatur	IL	62525	**800-728-8368**	217-423-7314	15
National Taxpayers Union (NTU) 108 N Alfred St	Alexandria	VA	22314	**800-680-7289**	703-683-5700	47-7

Name / Address	City	State	ZIP	Toll-Free	Phone	Class
National Tay-Sachs & Allied Diseases Assn (NTSAD)						
2001 Beacon St Ste 204	Brighton	MA	02135	800-906-8723	617-277-4463	47-17
National Technical Information Service (NTIS)						
5285 Port Royal Rd	Springfield	VA	22161	800-553-6847*	703-605-6000	666
*Orders						
National Technical Systems Inc						
24007 Ventura Blvd Ste 200	Calabasas	CA	91302	800-879-9225	818-591-0776	740
NASDAQ: NTSC						
National Thoroughbred Racing Assn (NTRA)						
2525 Harrodsburg Rd Ste 510	Lexington	KY	40504	800-792-6872		47-22
National Tire & Wheel						
5 Garden Ct	Wheeling	WV	26003	800-847-3287		56
National Tobacco Company LP						
5201 Interchange Way	Louisville	KY	40229	800-579-0975*	502-778-4421	754
*Cust Svc						
National Tooling & Machining Assn (NTMA)						
6363 Oak Tree Blvd	Independence	OH	44131	800-248-6862		48-13
National Tour Assn (NTA)						
546 E Main St	Lexington	KY	40508	800-682-8886	859-226-4444	47-23
National Trade Productions Inc						
313 S Patrick St	Alexandria	VA	22314	800-687-7469	703-683-8500	186
National Truck Equipment Assn (NTEA)						
37400 Hills Tech Dr	Farmington Hills	MI	48331	800-441-6832	248-489-7090	48-21
National Truck Leasing System						
450 S Summit Ave	Oakbrook	IL	60181	800-729-6857	630-953-8878	776
National Trust for Historic Preservation						
1785 Massachusetts Ave NW	Washington	DC	20036	800-944-6847	202-588-6000	47-13
National Tube Supply Co						
925 Central Ave	University Park	IL	60466	800-229-6872	708-534-2700	491
National Turkey Federation (NTF)						
1225 New York Ave NW Ste 400	Washington	DC	20005	866-536-7593	202-898-0100	47-2
National Undersea Research Ctr for Hawaii & the Western Pacific						
University of Hawaii at Manoa						
41-305 Kalanianaole Hwy	Waimanalo	HI	96795	888-800-0460	808-956-6335	666
National Undersea Research Ctr for the Mid-Atlantic Bight						
Institute of Marine & Coastal Sciences						
Rutgers University 71 Dudley Rd	New Brunswick	NJ	08901	888-776-6537	732-932-6555	666
National Underwriter Co						
5081 Olympic Blvd	Erlanger	KY	41018	800-543-0874		634-2
National University						
11255 N Torrey Pines Rd	La Jolla	CA	92037	800-628-8648	858-642-8000	167
National University of Health Sciences						
200 E Roosevelt Rd	Lombard	IL	60148	800-826-6285	630-629-2000	167
National Urban Technology Ctr						
80 Maiden Ln Ste 606	New York	NY	10038	800-998-3212	212-528-7350	47-6
National Van Lines Inc						
2800 W Roosevelt Rd	Broadview	IL	60155	877-590-2810	708-450-2900	518
National Veterinary Associates Inc						
29229 Canwood St Ste 100	Agoura Hills	CA	91301	888-767-7755	805-777-7722	792
National Vinyl LLC						
7 Coburn St	Chicopee	MA	01013	800-424-5300	413-420-0548	238
National Vision Inc						
296 Grayson Hwy	Lawrenceville	GA	30045	800-637-3597*	770-822-3600	542
*Cust Svc						
National Volunteer Fire Council (NVFC)						
7852 Walker Dr Ste 450	Greenbelt	MD	20770	888-275-6832	202-887-5700	48-4
National Watch & Clock Museum						
514 Poplar St	Columbia	PA	17512	800-368-6511	717-684-8261	519
National Water Resources Assn (NWRA)						
3800 Fairfax Dr # 4	Arlington	VA	22203	800-468-3533	703-524-1544	47-12
National Waterways Conference Inc (NWC)						
4650 Washington Blvd Ste 608	Arlington	VA	22201	866-371-1390	703-243-4090	48-21
National Wellness Institute (NWI)						
1300 College Ct						
PO Box 827	Stevens Point	WI	54481	877-800-2729	715-342-2969	47-17
National Western Life Insurance Co						
850 E Anderson Ln	Austin	TX	78752	800-531-5442	512-836-1010	391-2
NASDAQ: NWLI						
National Wholesale Company Inc						
400 National Blvd	Lexington	NC	27292	800-480-4673		458
National WIC Assn (NWA)						
2001 S St NW Ste 580	Washington	DC	20009	866-782-6246	202-232-5492	47-6
National Wild Turkey Federation (NWTF)						
770 Augusta Rd PO Box 530	Edgefield	SC	29824	800-843-6983*	803-637-3106	47-3
*Cust Svc						
National Wildlife Federation (NWF)						
11100 Wildlife Ctr Dr	Reston	VA	20190	800-822-9919	703-438-6000	47-3
National Wildlife Health Ctr						
6006 Schroeder Rd	Madison	WI	53711	800-232-4636	608-270-2400	666
National Wildlife Magazine						
11100 Wildlife Ctr Dr	Reston	VA	20190	800-822-9919*	703-438-6000	456-19
*Cust Svc						
National Women's Health Information Ctr						
200 Independence Ave S.W	Washington	DC	20201	800-994-9662		340-8
National Wood Flooring Assn (NWFA)						
111 Chesterfield Industrial Blvd						
	Chesterfield	MO	63005	800-422-4556	636-519-9663	48-3
National Woodland Owners Assn (NWOA)						
374 Maple Ave E Ste 310	Vienna	VA	22180	800-476-8733	703-255-2700	47-2
National Youth Sports Coaches Assn (NYSCA)						
2050 Vista Pkwy	West Palm Beach	FL	33411	800-729-2057	561-684-1141	47-22
National/AZON						
1148 Rochester Rd	Troy	MI	48083	800-325-5939		551-1
National-Louis University						
1000 Capitol Dr	Wheeling	IL	60090	800-443-5522	847-947-5718	167
Chicago						
122 S Michigan Ave	Chicago	IL	60603	800-443-5522	888-658-8632	167
NationJob Inc						
920 Morgan St Ste T	Des Moines	IA	50309	800-292-7731		262
Nationwide Biweekly Administration Inc						
855 Lower Bellbrook Rd	Xenia	OH	45385	888-802-1296		5
Nationwide Credit Inc (NCI)						
PO Box 26314 Ste 600	Atlanta	GA	30319	800-456-4729		159
Nationwide Custom Homes						
1100 Rives Rd	Martinsville	VA	24115	800-216-7001		105
Nationwide Life & Annuity Insurance Co						
1 Nationwide Pl	Columbus	OH	43215	800-882-2822	614-249-7111	391-2
Nationwide Lift Trucks Inc						
3900 N 28th Terr	Hollywood	FL	33020	800-327-4431	954-922-4645	56
Nationwide Magazine & Book Distributors Inc						
3000 E Grauwyler Rd						
PO Box 170427	Irving	TX	75017	800-777-9068*	972-438-7852	683
*General						
Nationwide Mutual Fire Insurance Co						
1 Nationwide Plaza	Columbus	OH	43215	877-669-6877	614-249-7111	391-4
Nationwide Mutual Insurance Co						
1 Nationwide Plaza	Columbus	OH	43215	877-669-6877	614-249-7111	391-4
Nationwide Mutual Insurance Co						
5100 Rings Rd	Dublin	OH	43017	800-543-3747	877-669-6877	391-2
Nationwide Recovery Systems Inc (NRS)						
4635 McEwen Rd	Dallas	TX	75244	800-458-6357	972-798-1000	159
Nationwide Truck Brokers Inc (NTB)						
4203 Roger B Chaffee Memorial Blvd SE						
Ste 2	Grand Rapids	MI	49548	800-446-0682	616-878-5554	778
Nationwide Van Lines Inc						
1421 NW 65th Ave	Plantation	FL	33313	800-310-0056	954-585-3945	518
Native American Rights Fund (NARF)						
1506 Broadway	Boulder	CO	80302	888-280-0726	303-447-8760	48-10
Native American Times						
PO Box 411	Tahlequah	OK	74465	800-367-5390	918-708-5838	634-8
Native Eyewear Inc						
1444 Wazee St Ste 215	Denver	CO	80202	888-776-2848		542
Native Seeds-search						
3584 E River Rd	Tucson	AZ	85718	866-622-5561	520-622-0830	198
Nativo Lodge Hotel						
6000 Pan American Fwy NE	Albuquerque	NM	87109	888-628-4861	505-798-4300	379
NATO (National Association of Theatre Owners.)						
1705 N St NW Ste 1130	Washington	DC	20036	800-365-5701*	202-962-0054	47-4
*General						
Natrol Inc						
21411 Prairie St	Chatsworth	CA	91311	800-262-8765	818-739-6000	797
NATSO Inc						
1737 King St Ste 200	Alexandria	VA	22314	800-956-9160	703-549-2100	48-21
Naturade Products Inc						
2030 Main St Ste 630	Irvine	CA	92614	800-421-1830		797
Natural Alternatives International Inc						
1185 Linda Vista Dr	San Marcos	CA	92078	800-848-2646	760-744-7340	797
NASDAQ: NAII						
Natural Bridge Battlefield Historic State Park						
7502 Natural Bridge Rd	Tallahassee	FL	32305	800-326-3521	850-922-6007	564
Natural Bridge State Resort Park						
2135 Natural Bridge Rd	Slade	KY	40376	800-325-1710		564
Natural Casing Co						
410 E Railroad St PO Box A	Peshtigo	WI	54157	877-515-0270		297-26
Natural Factors Nutritional Products Ltd						
1550 United Blvd	Coquitlam	BC	V3K6Y2	800-663-8900	604-777-1757	797
Natural Habitat Adventures						
PO Box 3065	Boulder	CO	80307	800-543-8917	303-449-3711	758
Natural Healthy Concepts						
310 N Westhill Blvd	Appleton	WI	54914	866-505-7501	920-968-2350	345
Natural Life Pet Products Inc						
205 E 29th St	Pittsburg	KS	66762	800-367-2391	620-230-0888	577
Natural Organics Inc						
548 Broadhollow Rd	Melville	NY	11747	800-645-9500		797
Natural Resource Partners LP						
601 Jefferson St Ste 3600	Houston	TX	77002	888-334-7102	713-751-7507	500
NYSE: NRP						
Natural Resources Research Institute (NRRI)						
University of Minnesota Duluth						
5013 Miller Trunk Hwy	Duluth	MN	55811	800-234-0054	218-720-4294	666
NaturaLawn of America Inc						
1 E Church St	Frederick	MD	21701	800-989-5444	301-694-5440	576
Naturally Vitamins						
4404 E Elwood St	Phoenix	AZ	85040	800-899-4499	480-991-0200	797
Nature						
National Press Bldg 529 14th St NW						
Ste 968	Washington	DC	20045	800-524-0384	202-737-2355	456-19
Nature Conservancy						
4245 N Fairfax Dr Ste 100	Arlington	VA	22203	800-628-6860*	703-841-5300	47-13
*Cust Svc						
Nature Conservancy of Canada						
36 Eglinton Ave W Ste 400	Toronto	ON	M4R1A1	800-465-8005	416-932-3202	47-13
Nature's Best						
6 Pt Dr Ste 300	Brea	CA	92821	800-800-7799	714-255-4600	345
Nature's Way Products Inc						
3051 W Maple Loop Dr Ste 125	Lehi	UT	84043	800-962-8873		797
Natus Medical Inc						
1501 Industrial Rd	San Carlos	CA	94070	800-255-3901	650-802-0400	252
NASDAQ: BABY						
Natvar						
8720 US Hwy 70 W	Clayton	NC	27520	800-395-6288	909-594-3660	599
NATW (NA of Town Watch)						
308 E Lancaster Ave Ste 115	Wynnewood	PA	19096	800-648-3688		47-7
Naugatuck Savings Bank						
87 Church St	Naugatuck	CT	06770	877-729-4442	203-729-5291	70
NAUS (NA for Uniformed Services)						
5535 Hempstead Way	Springfield	VA	22151	800-842-3451	703-750-1342	47-19
Nautel Ltd						
10089 Peggy'S Cove Rd	Hackett'S Cove	NS	B3Z3J4	877-662-8835	902-823-3900	645
NAUTICUS the National Maritime Ctr						
1 Waterside Dr	Norfolk	VA	23510	800-664-1080	757-664-1000	519
Nautilus Inc						
16400 SE Nautilus Dr	Vancouver	WA	98684	800-628-8458	360-694-7722	269
NYSE: NLS						
Nautilus Insurance Group LLC						
7233 E Butherus Dr	Scottsdale	AZ	85260	800-842-8972	480-951-0905	391-4
NAV CANADA						
77 Metcalfe St PO Box 3411 Stn D	Ottawa	ON	K1P5L6	800-876-4693	613-563-5588	19
NAV Canada Training & Conference Ctr						
1950 Montreal Rd	Cornwall	ON	K6H6L2	877-832-6416	613-936-5800	377
Navajo Express Inc						
1400 W 64 Ave	Denver	CO	80221	800-525-1969	303-287-3800	778
Naval Air Station Jacksonville						
6801 Roosevelt Blvd	Jacksonville	FL	32212	800-849-6024	904-542-2338	496-3
Naval Air Station Joint Reserve Base New Orleans						
301 Russell Ave	New Orleans	LA	70143	800-729-7327	504-678-3254	496-3

Name	Address	City	State	ZIP	Toll-Free	Phone	Class
Naval Air Station Patuxent River	22268 Cedar Point Road Bldg 409	Patuxent River	MD	20670	**877-995-5247**	301-342-3000	496-3
Naval Air Station Pensacola	190 Radford Blvd	Pensacola	FL	32508	**800-628-9466**		496-3
Naval Base San Diego	3455 Senn Rd	San Diego	CA	92136	**877-995-5247**	619-556-1011	496-3
Naval Enlisted Reserve Assn (NERA)	6703 Farragut Ave	Falls Church	VA	22042	**800-776-9020**	703-534-1329	47-19
Naval Hospital Bremerton	1 Bo1 Rd	Bremerton	WA	98312	**800-422-1383**	360-475-4000	331-4
Naval Institute Press	291 Wood Rd	Annapolis	MD	21402	**800-233-8764**	410-268-6110	634-4
Naval Reserve Assn (NRA)	1619 King St	Alexandria	VA	22314	**877-628-9411**	703-548-5800	47-19
Naval Station Mayport	PO Box 280032	Mayport	FL	32228	**800-872-7245**	904-270-5401	496-3
Naval Surface Warfare Ctr *Dahlgren Div*	6149 Welsh Rd Ste 203	Dahlgren	VA	22448	**877-845-5656**		666
Navarro College	3200 W Seventh Ave	Corsicana	TX	75110	**800-628-2776**	903-874-6501	161
Navarro County Electric Co-op Inc	3800 Texas 22 PO Box 616	Corsicana	TX	75110	**800-771-9095**	903-874-7411	247
Navarro Discount Pharmacies	9400	Miami	FL	33178	**866-628-2776**		239
Navarro Research & Engineering Inc	669 Emory Valley Rd	Oak Ridge	TN	37830	**866-681-5265**	865-220-9650	194
Navasota Valley Electric Co-op Inc	2281 E US Hwy 79 PO Box 848	Franklin	TX	77856	**800-443-9462**	979-828-3232	247
Navellier Securities Corp	1 E Liberty St Ste 504	Reno	NV	89501	**800-887-8671**	775-785-2300	401
Navhouse Corp	10 Loring Dr	Bolton	ON	L7E1J9	**877-628-6667**	905-857-8102	21
Navigant Consulting Inc *NYSE: NCI*	30 S Wacker Dr Ste 3100	Chicago	IL	60606	**800-621-8390**	312-583-5700	196
Navigate Power LLC	2211 N Elston Ave Ste 309	Chicago	IL	60614	**888-601-1789**		462
Navigators Group Inc *NASDAQ: NAVG*	1 Penn Plz 32nd Fl	New York	NY	10119	**866-408-1922**	212-244-2333	360-4
Navigators of Canada	11 St John'S Dr	Arva	ON	N0M1C0	**866-202-6287**	519-660-8300	47-20
Navigators, The	3820 N 30th St PO Box 6000	Colorado Springs	CO	80934	**866-568-7827**	719-598-1212	47-20
Navis Logistics Network	6551 S Revere Pkwy Ste 250	Centennial	CO	80111	**800-344-3528**		548
Navis Pack & Ship Centers	6551 S Revere Pkwy Ste 250	Centennial	CO	80111	**800-344-3528**		112
Navitaire Inc	333 S Seventh St Ste 500	Minneapolis	MN	55402	**877-216-6787**	612-317-7000	196
Navitar Inc *Cust Svc	200 Commerce Dr	Rochester	NY	14623	**800-828-6778***	585-359-4000	590
Navopache Electric Co-op Inc	1878 W White Mtn Blvd	Lakeside	AZ	85929	**800-543-6324**	928-368-5118	247
NavPress	3820 N 30th St	Colorado Springs	CO	80904	**800-323-9400**		634-3
NAVS (National Anti-Vivisection Society)	53 W Jackson Blvd Ste 1552	Chicago	IL	60604	**800-888-6287**	312-427-6065	47-3
Navtech Seminars & Gps Supply	5501 Backlick Rd Ste 230	Springfield	VA	22151	**800-628-0885**	703-256-8900	462
Navy Exchange Service Command (NEXCOM)	3280 Virginia Beach Blvd	Virginia Beach	VA	23452	**800-628-3924**	757-463-6200	789
Navy League of the US	2300 Wilson Blvd	Arlington	VA	22201	**800-356-5760**	703-528-1775	47-19
Navy Personnel Command (NPC)	5720 Integrity Dr	Millington	TN	38055	**866-827-5672**	901-874-3165	340-5
Navy Pier	600 E Grand Ave	Chicago	IL	60611	**800-595-7437**	312-595-7437	207
Navy Times Magazine *Cust Svc	6883 Commercial Dr	Springfield	VA	22159	**800-368-5718***	703-750-7400	456-12
Navy-Marine Corps Relief Society (NMCRS)	875 N Randolph St Ste 225	Arlington	VA	22203	**800-654-8364**	703-696-4904	47-19
NAWIC (NA of Women in Construction)	327 S Adams St	Fort Worth	TX	76104	**800-552-3506**	817-877-5551	48-3
Naxos of America Inc	1810 Columbia Ave	Franklin	TN	37064	**877-629-6723**	615-771-9393	655
Nazarene Theological Seminary	1700 E Meyer Blvd	Kansas City	MO	64131	**800-831-3011**	816-333-6254	168-3
Nazareth Area Chamber of Commerce	201 N Main St PO Box 173	Nazareth	PA	18064	**866-776-8240**	610-759-9188	138
Nazareth College of Rochester	4245 E Ave	Rochester	NY	14618	**800-860-6942**	585-389-2525	167
Nazcare Inc	599 White Spar Rd	Prescott	AZ	86303	**877-756-4090**	928-442-9205	136
Nazdar	8501 Hedge Ln Terr	Shawnee	KS	66227	**800-767-9942**	913-422-1888	388
NBA (National Business Assn)	5151 Beltline Rd Ste 1150	Dallas	TX	75254	**800-456-0440**	972-458-0900	48-12
NBA Entertainment	450 Harmon Meadow Blvd	Secaucus	NJ	07094	**866-648-4668**	201-865-1500	513
NBAA (National Business Aviation Assn)	1200 18th St NW Ste 400	Washington	DC	20036	**800-394-6222**	202-783-9000	48-21
NBCC (National Breast Cancer Coalition)	1101 17th St NW Ste 1300	Washington	DC	20036	**800-622-2838**	202-296-7477	47-17
NBCH (National Business Coalition on Health)	1015 18th St NW Ste 730	Washington	DC	20036	**800-223-4139**	202-775-9300	48-12
NBDL (National Biodynamics Laboratory) *University of New Orleans College of Engineering*	2000 Lakeshore Dr	New Orleans	LA	70148	**888-514-4275**		666
NBFPL (New Bedford Free Public Library)	613 Pleasant St	New Bedford	MA	02740	**877-336-2627**	508-991-6275	434-3
NBMDA (North American Bldg Material Distribution Assn)	330 N Wabash Ave Ste 2000	Chicago	IL	60611	**888-747-7862**	312-321-6845	48-18
NBT Bancorp Inc *NASDAQ: NBTB*	52 S Broad St	Norwich	NY	13815	**800-628-2265**	607-337-2265	360-2
NBT Bank NA	PO Box 351	Norwich	NY	13815	**800-628-2265**	607-337-2265	69
NBWA (National Beer Wholesalers Assn)	1101 King St Ste 600	Alexandria	VA	22314	**800-300-6417**	703-683-4300	48-6
NC Machinery Co	17025 W Valley Hwy	Tukwila	WA	98188	**800-562-4735**	425-251-9800	385
NC Products Corp	920 Withers Rd PO Box 27077	Raleigh	NC	27603	**888-965-3227**	919-772-6301	185
NCA (National Club Assn)	1201 15th St NW Ste 450	Washington	DC	20005	**800-625-6221**	202-822-9822	47-23
NCA (National Confectioners Assn PAC)	8320 Old Courthouse Rd Ste 300	Vienna	VA	22182	**800-433-1200**	202-534-1440	614
NCA (National Confectioners Assn)	1101 30th St NW Ste 200	Washington	DC	20007	**800-433-1200**	202-534-1440	48-6
NCA CASI (North Central Assn Commission on Accreditation & School Improvement)	9115 Westside Pkwy	Alpharetta	GA	30009	**888-413-3669**		47-1
NCADD (National Council on Alcoholism & Drug Dependence Inc)	217 Broadway Ste 712	New York	NY	10007	**800-622-2255**	212-269-7797	47-17
NCADV (National Coalition Against Domestic Violence)	1 Broadway Ste B210	Denver	CO	80203	**800-799-7233**	303-839-1852	47-6
NCAE News Bulletin	PO Box 27347	Raleigh	NC	27611	**800-662-7924**	919-832-3000	456-8
NCASI (National Council for Air & Stream Improvement Inc)	PO Box 13318	Research Triangle Park	NC	27709	**888-448-2473**	919-941-6400	47-13
NCATE (National Council for Accreditation of Teacher Education)	2010 Massachusetts Ave NW Ste 500	Washington	DC	20036	**800-255-8664**	202-466-7496	47-1
NCBA (National Cattlemen's Beef Assn)	9110 E Nichols Ave Ste 300	Centennial	CO	80112	**866-233-3872**	303-694-0305	47-2
NCBA (National Co-op Business Assn)	1401 New York Ave NW Ste 1100	Washington	DC	20005	**800-356-9655**	202-638-6222	48-12
NCBMP (National Coalition of Black Meeting Planners)	700 N. Fairfax St Ste 510	Alexandria	VA	22314	**800-551-9369**	571-527-3110	48-12
NCCA (National Child Care Assn)	1325 G St NW Ste 500	Washington	DC	20005	**866-536-1945**		47-6
NCCA (National Coil Coating Assn)	1300 Sumner Ave	Cleveland	OH	44115	**800-532-0500**	216-241-7333	48-13
NCCD (National Council on Crime & Delinquency)	1970 Broadway Ste 500	Oakland	CA	94612	**800-306-6223**	510-208-0500	47-8
NCCI Holdings Inc *Cust Svc	901 Peninsula Corporate Cir	Boca Raton	FL	33487	**800-622-4123***	561-893-1000	390
NCCIC (National Child Care Information & Technical Assistance Ctr)	9300 Lee Hwy	Fairfax	VA	22031	**877-296-2250**		340-8
NCCNHR (National Citizens' Coalition for Nursing Home Reform) *National Consumer Voice for Quality Long-Term Care, The*	1828 L St NW Ste 801	Washington	DC	20036	**866-992-3668**	202-332-2275	47-17
NCCS (National Coalition for Cancer Survivorship)	1010 Wayne Ave Ste 315	Silver Spring	MD	20910	**877-622-7937**		47-17
NCEA (National Catholic Educational Assn)	1077 30th St NW Ste 100	Washington	DC	20007	**800-711-6232**	202-337-6232	48-5
NCED (National Ctr for Employee Development)	2701 E Imhoff Rd	Norman	OK	73071	**866-438-6233**	405-366-4420	377
NCEE (National Council on Economic Education)	122 E 42nd St Ste 2600	New York	NY	10168	**800-338-1192**	212-730-7007	48-5
NCEES (National Council of Examiners for Engineering & Surveying)	280 Seneca Creek Rd	Seneca	SC	29678	**800-250-3196**	864-654-6824	48-3
NCFL (National Ctr for Family Literacy)	325 W Main St Ste 300	Louisville	KY	40202	**855-937-5668**	502-584-1133	47-11
NCFR (National Council on Family Relations)	1201 W River Pkwy Ste 200	Minneapolis	MN	55454	**888-781-9331**		47-6
NCH (National Coalition for the Homeless)	2201 P St NW	Washington	DC	20037	**877-243-1576**	202-462-4822	47-5
NCH (National Ctr for Homeopathy)	101 S Whiting St Ste 16	Alexandria	VA	22304	**877-624-0613**	703-548-7790	47-17
NCH Corp	2727 Chemsearch Blvd	Irving	TX	75062	**800-527-9919**	972-438-0211	150
NCI (Nissan Canada Inc)	5290 Orbitor Dr	Mississauga	ON	L4W4Z5	**800-387-0122**		58
NCI (Nationwide Credit Inc)	PO Box 26314 Ste 600	Atlanta	GA	30319	**800-456-4729**		159
NCI (National Captioning Institute)	3725 Concorde Pkwy Ste 100	Chantilly	VA	20151	**800-825-6758**	703-917-7600	629
NCI Bldg Systems Inc *NYSE: NCS*	10943 N Sam Houston PkwyWest	Houston	TX	77064	**888-624-8677**	281-897-7788	104
NCIC (Network Communications International Corp)	PO Box 551	Longview	TX	75601	**800-382-2887**	903-757-4455	733
nCircle Network Security Inc	101 Second St Ste 400	San Francisco	CA	94105	**866-897-8776**	503-276-7500	179
NCIS (National Crop Insurance Services)	8900 Indian Creek Pkwy Ste 600	Overland Park	KS	66210	**800-951-6247**	913-685-2767	47-2
NCJFCJ (National Council of Juvenile & Family Court Judges)	Univ of Nevada PO Box 8970	Reno	NV	89507	**800-527-3223**	775-784-6012	48-10
NCJW (National Council of Jewish Women)	475 Riverside Dr Ste 1901	New York	NY	10115	**800-829-6259**	212-645-4048	47-24
NCL (National Consumers League)	1701 K St NW Ste 1200	Washington	DC	20006	**800-388-2227**	202-835-3323	47-10
NCM	404 N Berry St	Brea	CA	92821	**800-283-2933**	714-672-3500	191-16
NCMA (National Contract Management Assn)	21740 Beaumeade Cir Ste 125	Ashburn	VA	20147	**800-344-8096**	571-382-0082	48-12
NCMEC (National Ctr for Missing & Exploited Children)	699 Prince St	Alexandria	VA	22314	**800-843-5678**	703-274-3900	47-6
NCMIC Insurance Co	14001 University Ave	Clive	IA	50325	**800-769-2000**	515-313-4500	391-5
NCMS (National Ctr for Mfg Sciences)	3025 Boardwalk	Ann Arbor	MI	48108	**800-222-6267**	734-995-0300	666
NCNA (North Carolina Nurses Assn)	103 Enterprise St PO Box 12025	Raleigh	NC	27605	**800-626-2153**	919-821-4250	532
NCNE (National Ctr for Neighborhood Enterprise)	1625 K St Ste 1200	Washington	DC	20006	**866-518-1263**	202-518-6500	47-7
NCNW (National Council of Negro Women Inc)	633 Pennsylvania Ave NW	Washington	DC	20004	**800-462-6420**	202-737-0120	47-24

Name / Address	City	State	Zip	Toll-Free	Phone	Class
NCOA (National Council on the Aging) 1901 L St NW 4th Fl	Washington	DC	20036	**800-677-1116**	202-479-1200	47-6
NCOA (Non Commissioned Officers Assn) 9330 Corporate Dr Ste 701	Selma	TX	78154	**800-662-2620**	210-653-6161	47-19
NCOC (National Conference on Citizenship) 1875 K St NW 5th Fl	Washington	DC	20006	**800-745-7275**	202-729-8038	47-8
NCPA (National Community Pharmacists Assn) 100 Daingerfield Rd	Alexandria	VA	22314	**800-544-7447**	703-683-8200	48-8
NCPDP (National Council for Prescription Drug Programs) 9240 E Raintree Dr	Scottsdale	AZ	85260	**888-665-2600**	480-477-1000	48-9
NCPH (National Council on Public History) 425 University Blvd 327 Cavanaugh Hall	Indianapolis	IN	46202	**800-554-5542**	317-274-2716	47-7
NCPSSM (National Committee to Preserve Social Security & Medicare) 10 G St NE Ste 600	Washington	DC	20002	**800-966-1935**	202-216-0420	47-7
NCQA (National Committee for Quality Assurance) 1100 13th St	Washington	DC	20005	**888-275-7585**	202-955-3500	47-10
NCRA (National Cancer Registrars Assn) 1340 Braddock Pl Ste 203	Alexandria	VA	22314	**800-621-4111**	703-299-6640	47-17
NCRA (National Court Reporters Assn) 8224 Old Courthouse Rd	Vienna	VA	22182	**800-272-6272**	703-556-6272	48-10
NCRP (National Council on Radiation Protection & Measurements) 7910 Woodmont Ave Ste 400	Bethesda	MD	20814	**800-462-3683**	301-657-2652	48-19
NCSBN (National Council of State Boards of Nursing) 111 E Wacker Dr Ste 2900	Chicago	IL	60601	**866-293-9600**	312-525-3600	48-8
NCSC (National Ctr for State Courts) 300 Newport Ave	Williamsburg	VA	23185	**800-616-6164**	757-259-1525	48-7
NCSD (Nye County School District Inc) PO Box 113	Tonopah	NV	89049	**800-796-6273**	775-482-6258	683
NCSD (Niskayuna Central School District) 1239 Van Antwerp Rd	Schenectady	NY	12309	**866-893-6337**	518-377-4666	683
NCSEAA (North Carolina State Education Assistance Authority) PO Box 14103	Research Triangle Park	NC	27709	**800-700-1775**	919-549-8614	723
NCSS (National Council for the Social Studies) 8555 16th St Ste 500 *Orders	Silver Spring	MD	20910	**800-683-0812***	301-588-1800	48-5
NCTC (National Cable Television Co-op Inc) 11200 Corporate Ave	Lenexa	KS	66219	**800-720-5850**	913-599-5900	48-14
NCTE (National Council of Teachers of English) 1111 W Kenyon Rd	Urbana	IL	61801	**877-369-6283**	217-328-3870	48-5
NCTM (National Council of Teachers of Mathematics) 1906 Assn Dr *Orders	Reston	VA	20191	**800-235-7566***	703-620-9840	48-5
NCTM News Bulletin 1906 Assn Dr	Reston	VA	20191	**800-235-7566**	703-620-9840	456-8
NCTO (National Council of Textile Organizations) 910 17th St NW	Washington	DC	20006	**800-238-7192**	202-822-8028	48-13
NCVB (Nashville Convention & Visitors Bureau) 150 Fourth Ave N Ste G250	Nashville	TN	37219	**800-657-6910**	615-259-4730	208
NCVMA (North Carolina Veterinary Medical Assn) 1611 Jones Franklin Rd Ste 108	Raleigh	NC	27606	**800-446-2862**	919-851-5850	793
ND Graphic Product Ltd 55 Interchange Way Unit 1	Concord	ON	L4K5W3	**800-811-0194**	416-663-6416	626
Nd Industries Inc 1000 N Crooks Rd	Clawson	MI	48017	**800-471-5000**	248-288-0000	480
NDA (AMOA-National Dart Assn) 9100 PuRdue Rd Ste 200	Indianapolis	IN	46268	**800-808-9884**	317-387-1299	47-22
NDAA (National District Attorneys Assn) 99 Canal Ctr Plaza Ste 510	Alexandria	VA	22314	**888-325-9943**	703-549-9222	48-7
N-Dimension Solutions Inc 9030 Leslie St Unit 300	Richmond Hill	ON	L4B1G2	**866-837-8884**	905-707-8884	227
NDRI (National Disease Research Interchange) 1628 John F Kennedy Blvd 8 Penn Ctr 8th Fl	Philadelphia	PA	19103	**800-222-6374**	215-557-7361	271
NDS Americas 3500 Highland Ave	Costa Mesa	CA	92626	**866-398-8749**	714-434-2100	732
NDSC (National Down Syndrome Congress) 1370 Ctr Dr Ste 102	Atlanta	GA	30338	**800-232-6372**	770-604-9500	47-17
NDSL (North Dakota State Library) 604 E Blvd Ave Dept 250	Bismarck	ND	58505	**800-472-2104**	701-328-4622	434-5
NDSS (National Down Syndrome Society) 666 Broadway 8th Fl	New York	NY	10012	**800-221-4602**		47-17
NDVH (National Domestic Violence Hotline) PO Box 161810	Austin	TX	78716	**800-799-7233**	512-794-1133	47-6
NEA (National Education Assn) 1201 16th St NW	Washington	DC	20036	**888-552-0624**	202-833-4000	48-5
Neace Lukens Inc 2305 River Rd	Louisville	KY	40206	**888-499-8092**	502-894-2100	196
Neal Mast & Son Inc Greenhouses 1780 4 Mile Rd Nw	Grand Rapids	MI	49544	**800-311-6278**	616-784-3323	194
Neapco Inc 6735 Haggerty Rd PO Box 399	Belleville	MI	48111	**800-821-2374**	734-447-1380	59
Near-Cal Corp 512 Chaney St	Lake Elsinore	CA	92530	**800-969-3578**	951-245-5400	188
Nearfield Systems Inc 19730 Magellan Dr	Torrance	CA	90502	**800-334-7384**	310-525-7000	203
Nearly Me Technologies Po Box 21475	Waco	TX	76702	**800-887-3370**	254-662-1752	476
Nearman Maynard Vallez CPAs & Consultants pa 205 Brandywine Blvd Ste 200	Fayetteville	GA	30214	**800-288-0293**	770-461-5706	2
NEBB (National Environmental Balancing Bureau) 8575 Grovemont Cir	Gaithersburg	MD	20877	**866-497-4447**	301-977-3698	48-19
Nebraska						
Arts Council 1004 Farnam St	Omaha	NE	68131	**800-341-4067**	402-595-2122	339-28
Child Support Enforcement Div PO Box 95026	Lincoln	NE	68509	**877-631-9973**	402-471-3121	339-28
Economic Development Dept 301 Centennial Mall S PO Box 94666	Lincoln	NE	68509	**800-426-6505**	402-471-3747	339-28
Emergency Management Agency 1300 Military Rd	Lincoln	NE	68508	**877-297-2368**	402-471-7421	339-28
Environmental Quality Dept 1200 N St Ste 400	Lincoln	NE	68508	**877-253-2603**	402-471-2186	339-28
Health & Human Services Dept 301 Centennial Mall S	Lincoln	NE	68508	**800-430-3244**	402-471-3121	339-28
Historical Society 1500 R St	Lincoln	NE	68501	**800-833-6747**	402-471-3270	339-28
Insurance Dept 941 O St Ste 400	Lincoln	NE	68508	**877-564-7323**	402-471-2201	339-28
Investment Finance Authority 1230 'O' St Ste 200	Lincoln	NE	68508	**800-204-6432**	402-434-3900	339-28
Public Service Commission 1200 N St Ste 300	Lincoln	NE	68508	**800-526-0017**	402-471-3101	339-28
Travel & Tourism Div PO Box 98907	Lincoln	NE	68509	**877-632-7275**	402-471-3796	339-28
Vocational Rehabilitation Services Div 3901 N 27th St Ste 6	Lincoln	NE	68521	**800-472-3382**	402-471-3231	339-28
Workers' Compensation Court 1010 Lincoln Mall Ste 100	Lincoln	NE	68508	**800-599-5155**	402-471-6468	339-28
Nebraska Beef Council 1319 Central Ave	Kearney	NE	68848	**800-421-5326**	308-236-7551	136
Nebraska Book Co 4700 S 19th St	Lincoln	NE	68512	**800-869-0366**	402-421-7300	94
Nebraska College of Technical Agriculture 404 E 7th	Curtis	NE	69025	**800-328-7847**	308-367-4124	798
Nebraska Community Blood Bank 100 N 84th St	Lincoln	NE	68505	**877-486-9414**	402-486-9414	88
Nebraska Correctional Ctr for Women 1107 Recharge Rd	York	NE	68467	**877-634-8463**	402-362-3317	215
Nebraska Dental Assn 7160 S 29th St Ste 1	Lincoln	NE	68516	**888-789-2614**	402-476-1704	229
Nebraska Educational Telecommunications (NET) 1800 N 33rd St	Lincoln	NE	68503	**800-868-1868**		629
Nebraska Furniture Mart Inc 700 S 72nd St	Omaha	NE	68114	**800-336-9136**	402-397-6100	322
Nebraska House 983285 Nebraska Medical Ctr	Omaha	NE	68198	**800-401-4444**	402-559-5000	372
Nebraska Indian Community College PO Box 428	Macy	NE	68039	**844-440-6422**	402-837-5078	164
Nebraska Lablinc LLC 5440 S St Ste 100	Lincoln	NE	68506	**866-886-5462**	402-484-5462	418
Nebraska Library Commission 1200 N St Ste 120	Lincoln	NE	68508	**800-307-2665**	402-471-2045	434-5
Nebraska Lottery 1800 "O" St PO Box 98901	Lincoln	NE	68509	**800-587-5200**	402-471-6100	451
Nebraska Machinery Co Inc 3501 S Jeffers St	North Platte	NE	69101	**800-494-9560**	308-532-3100	385
Nebraska Medical Ctr, The 4350 Dewey Ave	Omaha	NE	68105	**800-922-0000**	402-552-2000	374-3
Nebraska Nurses Assn (NNA) PO Box 3107	Kearney	NE	68848	**800-582-3014**	402-475-3859	532
Nebraska Pharmacists Assn 6221 S 58th St Ste A	Lincoln	NE	68516	**866-365-7472**	402-420-1500	584
Nebraska Plastics Inc PO Box 45	Cozad	NE	69130	**800-445-2887**	308-784-2500	595
Nebraska Public Power District 1414 15th St PO Box 499	Columbus	NE	68602	**877-275-6773**	402-564-8561	247
Nebraska Realtors Assn 800 S 13th St Ste 200	Lincoln	NE	68508	**800-777-5231**	402-323-6500	654
Nebraska Repertory Theatre PO Box 880201	Lincoln	NE	68588	**800-432-3231**	402-472-2072	572-4
Nebraska State Bar Assn 635 S 14th St Ste 200	Lincoln	NE	68501	**800-927-0117**	402-475-7091	71
Nebraska State Penitentiary 4201 S 14th St	Lincoln	NE	68502	**877-634-8463**	402-471-3161	215
Nebraska Synod Evangelical Lutheran Church in America 4980 S 118th St Ste D	Omaha	NE	68137	**877-366-7242**	402-896-5311	47-20
Nebraska Wesleyan University 5000 St Paul Ave	Lincoln	NE	68504	**800-541-3818**		167
NEC (Nueces Electric Co-op) 709 E Main St PO Box 260970	Robstown	TX	78380	**800-632-9288**	361-387-2581	247
NEC America Inc 6555 N State Hwy 161 *Cust Svc	Irving	TX	75039	**866-632-3226***	214-262-2000	732
NEC Corp of America 10850 Gold Ctr Dr Ste 200	Rancho Cordova	CA	95670	**800-632-4636**	916-463-7000	175-4
NEC Display Solutions of America Inc 500 Pk Blvd Ste 1100 *Cust Svc	Itasca	IL	60143	**800-632-4662***	630-467-3000	175-4
NECA (National Electrical Contractors Assn) 3 Bethesda Metro Ctr Ste 1100	Bethesda	MD	20814	**800-214-0585**	301-657-3110	48-3
Neci 334 Hecla St	Lake Linden	MI	49945	**888-648-7283**	906-296-1000	233
NED Corp 31 Town Forest Rd	Oxford	MA	01540	**800-343-6086**		492
Nedco Electronics 594 American Way	Payson	UT	84651	**800-605-2323**	801-465-1790	248
Needham & Co Inc 445 Pk Ave 3rd Fl	New York	NY	10022	**800-903-3268**	212-371-8300	688
Needham Capital Partners 445 Pk Ave	New York	NY	10022	**800-625-7071**	212-371-8300	790
Neenah Foundry Co 2121 Brooks Ave	Neenah	WI	54956	**800-558-5075**	920-725-7000	308
NEH (National Endowment for the Humanities) 400 7th St SW	Washington	DC	20506	**800-634-1121**	202-606-8400	340-18
NEHA (National Environmental Health Assn) 720 S Colorado Blvd Ste 1000-N	Denver	CO	80246	**866-956-2258**	303-756-9090	48-7
Nehring Electric Works Inc 1005 E Locust St	DeKalb	IL	60115	**800-435-4481**	815-756-2741	812
Neighbors Federal Credit Union PO Box 2831	Baton Rouge	LA	70821	**866-819-2178**	225-819-2178	221
Neil Enterprises Inc 450 E Bunker Ct	Vernon Hills	IL	60061	**800-621-5584**	847-549-7627	607
Neil Medical Group Inc 2545 Jetport Rd	Kinston	NC	28504	**800-735-9111**		240
Neiman Funds Management LLC 6631 Main St	Williamsville	NY	14221	**877-385-2720**		401
NELCO Inc 3 Gill St Unit D	Woburn	MA	01801	**800-635-2613**	781-933-1940	476
NELLA Oil Co 2360 Lindbergh St	Auburn	CA	95602	**800-995-0401**	530-885-0401	325
Nellie Mae Education Foundation 1250 Hancock St Ste 205N	Quincy	MA	02169	**877-635-5436**	781-348-4200	306
Nello Capital Inc 211 W Washington St Ste 2000	South Bend	IN	46601	**800-806-3556**	574-288-3632	479

Alphabetical Section

Name	Address	City	State	ZIP	Toll-Free	Phone	Class
Nelnet Inc	121 S 13th St Ste 204 *NYSE: NNI*	Lincoln	NE	68508	**888-486-4722**	402-458-2370	216
Nelrod Co	3109 Lubbock Ave	Fort Worth	TX	76109	**866-448-0961**	817-922-9000	198
Nelson & Kennard	2180 Harvard St Ste 160 PO Box 13807	Sacramento	CA	95815	**866-920-2295**		428
Nelson & Small Inc	212 Canco Rd	Portland	ME	04103	**800-341-0780**	207-775-5666	37
Nelson County	210 B Ave W Ste 203	Lakota	ND	58344	**800-472-2286**	701-247-2462	338
Nelson Crab Inc	3088 Kindred Ave	Tokeland	WA	98590	**800-262-0069**		297-13
Nelson Dewey State Park	PO Box 658	Cassville	WI	53806	**888-936-7463**	608-725-5374	564
Nelson Electric Supply Co Inc	926 State St	Racine	WI	53404	**800-806-3576**	262-635-5050	248
Nelson Jit Packaging Supplies Inc	4022 W Turney Ave Ste 3	Phoenix	AZ	85019	**800-939-3647**	623-939-3365	556
Nelson Mullins Riley & Scarborough LLP	1320 Main St 17th Fl	Columbia	SC	29201	**800-237-2000**	803-799-2000	428
Nelson Packaging Company Inc	1801 Reservoir Rd	Lima	OH	45804	**888-229-3471**	419-229-3471	87
Nelson Publishing	2500 Tamiami Trl N	Nokomis	FL	34275	**800-226-6113**	941-966-9521	634-9
Nelson Tree Service Inc	3300 Office Pk Dr Ste 205	Dayton	OH	45439	**800-522-4311**	937-294-1313	774
Nelson Westerberg Inc	1500 Arthur Ave	Elk Grove Village	IL	60007	**800-245-2080**	847-437-2080	518
Nelson-Jameson Inc	2400 E Fifth St PO Box 647	Marshfield	WI	54449	**800-826-8302**	715-387-1151	385
Neltner Billing & Consulting Services inc	6463 Taylor Mill Rd	Independence	KY	41051	**888-635-8637**		198
NEMA (National Electrical Manufacturers Assn)	1300 N 17th St Ste 1752	Rosslyn	VA	22209	**800-699-9277**	703-841-3200	48-13
Nemacolin Woodlands Resort & Spa	1001 Lafayette Dr	Farmington	PA	15437	**800-422-2736**	724-329-8555	667
Nemetschek North America	7150 Riverwood Dr	Columbia	MD	21046	**888-646-4223**	410-290-5114	180-8
NEMRA (National Electrical Manufacturers Representatives Assn)	28 Deer St Ste 302	Portsmouth	NH	03801	**800-446-3672**	914-524-8650	48-18
Nemschoff Healthcare Furniture and Clinic Furniture	909 N Eigth St *Cust Svc	Sheboygan	WI	53081	**800-203-8916***		320-3
Neo Corp	289 Silkwood Dr	Canton	NC	28716	**800-822-1247**		194
Neogard Div Jones-blair Co	2728 Empire Central St	Dallas	TX	75235	**800-492-9400**	214-353-1600	549
Neogen Corp	620 Lesher Pl *NASDAQ: NEOG*	Lansing	MI	48912	**800-234-5333**	517-372-9200	233
NeoMedia Technologies Inc	1515 Walnut St Ste 100	Boulder	CO	80302	**800-413-4559**	678-638-0460	38
Neopost Inc Canada	150 Steelcase Rd W	Markham	ON	L3R3J9	**800-636-7678**	905-475-3722	110
Neos Therapeutics	2940 N Hwy 360 Ste 100	Grand Prairie	TX	75050	**844-375-8324**	972-408-1300	582
Neosho County Community College	*Ottawa* 226 S Beech St	Ottawa	KS	66067	**888-466-2588**	785-242-2067	161
NEP Electronics Inc	805 Mittel Dr	Wood Dale	IL	60191	**800-284-7470**	630-595-8500	248
Nephron Pharmaceuticals Corp	4121 SW 34th St	Orlando	FL	32811	**800-443-4313**	407-999-2225	583
Neptco Inc	30 Hamlet St	Pawtucket	RI	02861	**800-354-5445**	401-722-5500	729
Neptune Chemical Pump Co	PO Box 247	Lansdale	PA	19446	**800-255-4017**	215-699-8700	638
Neptune Society	4312 Woodman Ave 3rd Fl	Sherman Oaks	CA	91423	**888-637-8863**		509
Neptune-Benson Inc	6 Jefferson Dr	Coventry	RI	02816	**800-832-8002**	401-821-2200	638
NER Data Products Inc	307 S Delsea Dr	Glassboro	NJ	08028	**888-637-3282**		627
NERA (Naval Enlisted Reserve Assn)	6703 Farragut Ave	Falls Church	VA	22042	**800-776-9020**	703-534-1329	47-19
NERSC (National Energy Research Scientific Computing Ctr)	Lawrence Berkeley National Laboratory	Berkeley	CA	94720	**800-666-3772**	510-486-5849	666
Nesco/American Harvest	1700 Monroe St PO Box 237 *Cust Svc	Two Rivers	WI	54241	**800-288-4545***	920-793-1368	36
NESDA (National Electronics Service Dealers Assn)	3608 Pershing Ave	Fort Worth	TX	76107	**800-946-0201**	817-921-9061	48-18
Neskowin Beach State Recreation Site	198 NE 123rd St	Neskowin	OR	97149	**800-551-6949**		564
Nespelem Valley Electric Co-op Inc	1009 F St	Nespelem	WA	99155	**866-377-8642**	509-634-4571	247
NestFamily	1461 S Beltline Rd Ste 500	Coppell	TX	75019	**800-634-4298**	972-402-7100	33
Nestle Purina PetCare Co	801 Chouteau Ave	Saint Louis	MO	63102	**800-778-7462**	314-982-1000	577
NET (Nebraska Educational Telecommunications)	1800 N 33rd St	Lincoln	NE	68503	**800-868-1868**		629
Net Access Corp	2300 15th St Ste 300	Denver	CO	80202	**800-638-6336**	973-590-5000	733
NET Radio	1800 N 33rd St	Lincoln	NE	68503	**800-868-1868**		738-43
Net2Phone Inc	520 Broad St	Newark	NJ	07102	**800-386-6438**	973-438-3111	733
Net32 Inc	250 Towne Village Dr	Cary	NC	27513	**800-517-1997**	919-468-1177	230
NETA (National Educational Telecommunications Assn)	939 S Stadium Rd	Columbia	SC	29201	**866-270-5141**	803-799-5517	629
Netcellent System Inc	4030 Valley Blvd	Walnut	CA	91789	**888-595-3818**	909-598-9019	179
Netchannel Inc	8310 Rio Grande Blvd NW	Albuquerque	NM	87114	**888-843-8282**	505-843-8282	130
Netcracker Technology Corp	95 Sawyer Rd University Ofc Pk III	Waltham	MA	02453	**800-477-5785**	781-419-3300	462
NetFlix Inc	100 Winchester Cir *NASDAQ: NFLX*	Los Gatos	CA	95032	**800-290-8191**	408-540-3700	795
Netgain Information Systems Co	220 Reynolds Ave	Bellefontaine	OH	43311	**855-651-7001**	937-593-7177	182
Netgain Networks Inc	8378 Attica Dr	Riverside	CA	92508	**855-667-2364**	951-656-0194	181
Netherland Rubber Co	2931 Exon Ave	Cincinnati	OH	45241	**800-582-1877**	513-733-0883	327
Netherlands							
Consulate General	666 Third Ave 19th Fl	New York	NY	10017	**877-388-2443**		259
Embassy	4200 Linnean Ave NW	Washington	DC	20008	**877-388-2443**		259
NetIQ Corp	1233 W Loop S *Sales	Houston	TX	77027	**888-323-6768***	713-548-1700	180-12
NETL (National Energy Technology Laboratory)	3610 Collins Ferry Rd	Morgantown	WV	26505	**800-432-8330**	304-285-4764	666
Netlink Software Group America Inc	999 Tech Row	Madison Heights	MI	48071	**800-485-4462**		198
Netmark.com	1930 N Woodruff Ave	Idaho Falls	ID	83401	**800-935-5133**		197
NetMotion Wireless Inc	701 N 34th St Ste 250	Seattle	WA	98103	**877-818-7626**	206-691-5500	180-1
NetNation Communications Inc	550 Burrard St Ste 200	Vancouver	BC	V6C2B5	**888-277-0000**	604-688-8946	806
Neto Sausage Co Inc	288 Brokaw Rd	Santa Clara	CA	95050	**888-482-6386**	408-296-0818	297-26
Netplanner Systems Inc	3145 Northwoods Pkwy Ste 800	Norcross	GA	30071	**800-795-1975**	770-662-5482	178
Netrition Inc	25 Corporate Cir Ste 118	Albany	NY	12203	**888-817-2411**	518-464-0765	355
NetScout Systems Inc	310 Littleton Rd *NASDAQ: NTCT*	Westford	MA	01886	**800-357-7666**	978-614-4000	180-7
Netsertive Inc	2400 Perimeter Park Dr Ste 100	Research Triangle Region	NC	27560	**800-940-4351**		197
Netsmart Technologies Inc	3500 Sunrise Hwy Ste D-122	Great River	NY	11739	**800-421-7503**	631-968-2000	180-11
Netspeed Learning Solutions	3016 Ne Blakeley St Ste 100	Seattle	WA	98105	**877-517-5271**	206-517-5271	196
Netsville Inc	72 Cascade Dr	Rochester	NY	14614	**888-638-7845**	585-232-5670	191-4
Net-Temps Inc	55 Middlesex St Ste 220	North Chelmsford	MA	01863	**800-307-0062**	978-251-7272	262
Network America Inc	118 107th Ave	Treasure Island	FL	33706	**877-624-8311**		182
Network Appliance Inc	495 E Java Dr *NASDAQ: NTAP* ■ *Sales	Sunnyvale	CA	94089	**800-443-4537***	408-822-6000	178
Network Communications International Corp (NCIC)	PO Box 551	Longview	TX	75601	**800-382-2887**	903-757-4455	733
Network Dynamics Inc	640 Brooker Creek Blvd Ste 410	Oldsmar	FL	34677	**877-818-8597**	813-818-8597	178
Network Earth Inc	14 Cambridge Ct	Wappingers Falls	NY	12590	**888-201-5160**		226
Network Global Logistics (NGL)	320 Interlocken Pkwy Ste 100	Broomfield	CO	80021	**866-938-1870**		545
Network Infrastructure Corp	8945 S Harl Ave Ste 102	Tempe	AZ	85284	**866-456-4422**	480-850-5050	191-4
Network Innovations Inc	4424 Manilla Rd SE	Calgary	AB	T2G4B7	**888-466-2772**	403-287-5000	196
Network Journal, The	39 Broadway Rm 2120	New York	NY	10006	**866-259-1465**	212-962-3791	4
Network Multi-Family Security Corp	4221 W John Carpenter Fwy	Irving	TX	75063	**800-541-3138**	214-277-7000	691
Network Performance Inc	85 Green Mtn Dr	South Burlington	VT	05403	**800-639-6091**	802-859-0808	182
Network Solutions LLC	13861 Sunrise Valley Dr Ste 300	Herndon	VA	20171	**800-361-5712**	703-668-4600	396
Network Telephone Services Inc	21135 Erwin St	Woodland Hills	CA	91367	**800-742-5687**	818-992-4300	254
Network World Magazine	492 Old Connecticut Path Ste 200 PO Box 9208	Framingham	MA	01701	**800-622-1108**		456-7
Networld Inc	300 Lanidex Plz Ste 1	Parsippany	NJ	07054	**800-992-3411**	973-884-7474	758
Networld Media Group LLC	13100 Eastpoint Park Blvd Ste 100	Louisville	KY	40223	**877-441-7545**		393
NetZero Inc	21301 Burbank Blvd	Woodland Hills	CA	91367	**800-638-9376**	818-287-3000	398
Neuberger Berman Funds	PO Box 8403	Boston	MA	02266	**800-877-9700**	212-476-8800	527
Neuberger Berman LLC	605 Third Ave	New York	NY	10158	**800-223-6448**		401
Neudesic LLC	8105 Irvine Ctr Dr	Irvine	CA	92618	**800-805-1805**	949-754-4500	179
Neuisys LLC	1500 Pinecroft Rd Ste 212	Greensboro	NC	27407	**877-299-9052**		740
Neumann College	1 Neumann Dr	Aston	PA	19014	**800-963-8626**	610-459-0905	167
Neumayer Equipment Company Inc	5060 Arsenal St	Saint Louis	MO	63139	**800-843-4563**	314-772-4501	386
NeuroMetrix	62 Fourth Ave *NASDAQ: NURO*	Waltham	MA	02451	**888-786-7287**	781-890-9989	252
Neuromonics Inc	PO Box 351886	Westminster	CO	80035	**866-606-3876**		252
NeuroScience Inc	373 280th St	Osceola	WI	54020	**888-342-7272**	715-294-2144	418
Neuro-Tec Inc	975 Cobb Pl Blvd Ste 301	Kennesaw	GA	30144	**800-554-3407**		474

Name	Address	City	State	Zip	Toll-Free	Phone	Class
NeuStar Inc	21575 Ridgetop Cir	Sterling	VA	20166	**855-638-2677**	571-434-5400	46
Neutral Posture Inc	3904 N Texas Ave	Bryan	TX	77803	**800-446-3746**	979-778-0502	320-1
Neutrogena Corp	5760 W 96th St	Los Angeles	CA	90045	**800-582-4048**	310-642-1150	217
Neutron Inc	220 Reese Rd	State College	PA	16801	**800-813-4218**	814-237-0902	198
Nevada							
Child Support Enforcement Office	1470 College Pkwy	Carson City	NV	89706	**800-992-0900**	775-684-0500	339-29
Economic Development Commission	808 W Nye Ln	Carson City	NV	89703	**800-336-1600**	775-687-9900	339-29
Motor Vehicles Dept	555 Wright Way	Carson City	NV	89711	**877-368-7828**	775-684-4368	339-29
Secretary of State	101 N Carson St Ste 3	Carson City	NV	89701	**800-450-8594**	775-684-5708	339-29
Tourism Commission	401 N Carson St	Carson City	NV	89701	**800-237-0774**	775-687-4322	339-29
Welfare Div	1470 College Pkwy	Carson City	NV	89706	**800-992-0900**	775-684-0500	339-29
Nevada Appeal	580 Mallory Way *General	Carson City	NV	89701	**877-689-3249***	775-882-2111	531-2
Nevada Assn of Realtors	760 Margrave Dr Ste 200	Reno	NV	89502	**800-748-5526**	775-829-5911	654
Nevada Bill Status	401 S Carson St	Carson City	NV	89701	**800-978-2878**	775-684-3360	433
Nevada Dental Assn	8863 W Flamingo Rd Ste 102	Las Vegas	NV	89147	**800-962-6710**	702-255-4211	229
Nevada Donor Network Inc	2061 E Sahara Ave	Las Vegas	NV	89104	**855-683-6667**	702-796-9600	544
Nevada Irrigation District (NID)	1036 W Main St	Grass Valley	CA	95945	**800-222-4102**	530-273-6185	785
Nevada Magazine	401 N Carson St	Carson City	NV	89701	**855-729-7117**	775-687-5416	456-22
Nevada Power Co	6226 W Sahara Ave *NYSE: NVE* ■ *Cust Svc	Las Vegas	NV	89146	**800-331-3103***	702-402-5555	785
Nevada State Bank	PO Box 990	Las Vegas	NV	89125	**800-727-4743**	702-383-0009	69
Nevada State Library & Archives (NSLA)	100 N Stewart St	Carson City	NV	89701	**800-922-2880**	775-684-3360	434-5
Nevers Industries Inc	14125 21st Ave N	Minneapolis	MN	55447	**800-258-5591**	763-210-4206	321
Neville Chemical Co	2800 Neville Rd *Cust Svc	Pittsburgh	PA	15225	**877-704-4200***	412-331-4200	604-2
New Accountant Magazine	3525 W Peterson Ave	Chicago	IL	60659	**888-641-3169**	773-866-9900	456-5
New Acton Mobile Industries LLC	809 Gleneagles Ct	Baltimore	MD	21286	**800-251-1600**		105
New Balance Athletic Shoe Inc	20 Guest St Brighton Landing	Brighton	MA	02135	**800-595-9138**	617-783-4000	302
New Bedford Free Public Library (NBFPL)	613 Pleasant St	New Bedford	MA	02740	**877-336-2627**	508-991-6275	434-3
New Bern Area Chamber of Commerce	316 S Front St	New Bern	NC	28560	**877-811-1776**	252-637-3111	138
New Bern National Cemetery	1711 National Ave	New Bern	NC	28560	**800-827-1000**	252-637-2912	135
New Braunfels Chamber of Commerce	390 S Seguin St	New Braunfels	TX	78130	**800-572-2626**	830-625-2385	138
New Braunfels Public Library	700 E Common St	New Braunfels	TX	78130	**800-434-8013**	830-221-4300	434-3
New Brunswick Museum	1 Market Sq	Saint John	NB	E2L4Z6	**888-268-9595**	506-643-2300	519
New Brunswick Theological Seminary	35 Seminary Pl	New Brunswick	NJ	08901	**800-445-6287**	732-247-5241	168-3
New Canaan Library	151 Main St	New Canaan	CT	06840	**800-545-2433**	203-594-5000	434-3
New Castle County Detention Ctr	963 Centre Rd	Wilmington	DE	19805	**800-969-4357**	302-633-3100	412
New Castle County Library	750 Library Ave	Newark	DE	19711	**877-225-7351**	302-731-7550	434-3
New Castle Hotels & Resorts	2 Corporate Dr	Shelton	CT	06484	**800-321-2211**	203-925-8370	379
New Castle Industries Inc	1399 Countyline Rd	New Castle	PA	16101	**800-897-2830**	724-656-5620	620
New Castle Public Library	424 Delaware St	New Castle	DE	19720	**877-225-7351**	302-328-1995	434-3
New Castle Refractories Co Inc	915 Industrial St	New Castle	PA	16102	**888-396-3566**	724-654-7711	661
New Century Education Foundation	PO Box 43052	Upper Montclair	NJ	07043	**866-326-1133**		180-1
New Choices Inc	2501 18th St Ste 201	Bettendorf	IA	52722	**888-355-5502**	563-355-5502	363
New College of Florida	5800 Bay Shore Rd	Sarasota	FL	34243	**800-435-7352**	941-487-5000	167
NEW Co-op Inc	2626 First Ave S	Fort Dodge	IA	50501	**800-362-2233**	515-955-2040	277
New Country Volkswagen of Greenwich	200 W Putnam Ave	Greenwich	CT	06830	**866-584-6747**		56
New Dimensions Research Corp	260 Spagnoli Rd	Melville	NY	11747	**800-637-8870**	631-694-1356	235
New Directions Behavioral Health LLC	PO Box 6729	Leawood	KS	66206	**800-624-5544**		461
New Directions Inc	30800 Chagrin Blvd	Cleveland	OH	44124	**800-750-6709**	216-591-0324	724
New Edge Networks	3000 Columbia House Blvd Ste 106	Vancouver	WA	98661	**877-725-3343**	360-693-9009	398
New England Airlines Inc	56 Airport Rd	Westerly	RI	02891	**800-243-2460**		25
New England Baptist Hospital	125 Parker Hill Ave	Boston	MA	02120	**855-370-6324**	617-754-5000	374-3
New England Coffee Co	100 Charles St	Malden	MA	02148	**800-225-3537**		297-7
New England College	98 Bridge St *Admissions	Henniker	NH	03242	**800-521-7642***	603-428-2223	167
New England College of Business & Finance	10 High St Ste 204	Boston	MA	02110	**888-357-7332**	617-951-2350	798
New England Computer Services Inc	168 Boston Post Rd Stes 6 & 7 *Sales	Madison	CT	06443	**800-766-6327***	203-245-3999	180-10
New England Culinary Institute	56 College St	Montpelier	VT	05602	**877-223-6324**	802-223-6324	162
New England Federal Credit Union	PO Box 527	Williston	VT	05495	**800-400-8790**	802-879-8790	221
New England Garage Door	15 Campanelli Cir	Canton	MA	02021	**800-676-7734**	781-821-2737	498
New England Homes	270 Ocean Rd	Greenland	NH	03840	**800-800-8831**	603-436-8830	105
New England Institute of Art	10 Brookline Pl W	Brookline	MA	02445	**800-903-4425**	617-582-4460	163
New England Institute of Technology	2500 Post Rd	Warwick	RI	02886	**800-736-7744**	401-467-7744	798
New England Journal of Medicine	10 Shattuck St	Boston	MA	02115	**800-843-6356**	617-734-9800	456-16
New England Life Flight Inc	1727 Robins St Hangar	Bedford	MA	01730	**800-233-8998**	781-863-2213	13
New England Natural Bakers	74 Fairview St E	Greenfield	MA	01301	**800-910-2884**	413-772-2239	297-4
New England Organ Bank	60 First Ave	Waltham	MA	02451	**800-446-6362**	617-244-8000	544
New England Revolution	Gillette Stadium 1 Patriot Pl	Foxboro	MA	02035	**877-438-7387**		715
New England Ropes Inc	848 Airport Rd	Fall River	MA	02720	**800-333-6679**	508-678-8200	210
New England Security Inc	10 Industrial Dr	Westerly	RI	02891	**800-556-7395**	401-596-0660	690
New England Wild Flower Society	180 Hemenway Rd	Framingham	MA	01701	**888-636-0033**	508-877-7630	47-13
New England Wooden Ware Corp	205 School St Ste 201	Gardner	MA	01440	**800-252-9214**	978-632-3600	99
New Enterprise Rural Electric Co-op Inc	3596 Brumbaugh Rd	New Enterprise	PA	16664	**800-270-3177**	814-766-3221	247
New Era Cap Company Inc	160 Delaware Ave *General	Buffalo	NY	14202	**877-632-5950***	716-604-9000	154-8
New Era Life Insurance Co	PO Box 4884	Houston	TX	77210	**800-552-7879**		391-4
New Fairfield Free Public Library	2 Brush Hill Rd	New Fairfield	CT	06812	**877-227-7487**	203-312-5679	434-3
New Generation Research Inc	225 Friend St Ste 801	Boston	MA	02114	**800-468-3810**	617-573-9550	634-2
New Germany State Park	349 Headquarters Ln	Grantsville	MD	21536	**800-830-3974**	301-895-5453	564
New Hampshire							
Banking Dept	53 Regional Dr Ste 200	Concord	NH	03301	**800-437-5991**	603-271-3561	339-30
Child Support Services	129 Pleasant St	Concord	NH	03301	**800-852-3345**	603-271-4427	339-30
Division of Vital Records Administration	71 S Fruit St	Concord	NH	03301	**800-735-2964**	603-271-4650	339-30
Environmental Services Dept	29 Hazen Dr PO Box 95	Concord	NH	03301	**800-735-2964**	603-271-3503	339-30
Housing Finance Authority	PO Box 5087	Manchester	NH	03108	**800-439-7247**	603-472-8623	339-30
Public Utilities Commission	21 S Fruit St Ste 10 *Consumer Assistance	Concord	NH	03301	**800-852-3793***	603-271-2431	339-30
Travel & Tourism Development Office	PO Box 1856	Concord	NH	03302	**800-262-6660**	603-271-2665	339-30
Victims' Assistance Commission	33 Capitol St	Concord	NH	03301	**800-300-4500**	603-271-1284	339-30
Vocational Rehabilitation Office	21 S Fruit St Ste 20	Concord	NH	03301	**800-299-1647**	603-271-3471	339-30
New Hampshire Assn of Realtors	115A Airport Rd	Concord	NH	03301	**800-335-4862**	603-225-5549	654
New Hampshire Catholic Charities Inc	215 Myrtle St	Manchester	NH	03104	**800-562-5249**	603-669-3030	47-20
New Hampshire Div of Travel & Tourism Development	172 Pembroke Rd PO Box 1856	Concord	NH	03302	**800-262-6660**	603-271-2665	208
New Hampshire Educator Magazine	9 S Spring St	Concord	NH	03301	**866-556-3264**	603-224-7751	456-8
New Hampshire Electric Co-op	579 Tenney Mtn Hwy	Plymouth	NH	03264	**800-698-2007**	603-536-1800	247
New Hampshire Employment Security (NHES)	32 S Main St	Concord	NH	03301	**800-852-3400**	603-224-3311	261
New Hampshire Institute of Art	148 Concord St	Manchester	NH	03104	**866-241-4918**	603-623-0313	519
New Hampshire Lottery Commission	14 Integra Dr	Concord	NH	03301	**800-852-3324**	603-271-3391	451
New Hampshire Medical Society	7 N State St	Concord	NH	03301	**800-564-1909**	603-224-1909	473
New Hampshire Plastics Inc	1 Bouchard St	Manchester	NH	03103	**800-258-3036**	603-669-8523	599
New Hampshire Postsecondary Education Commission	64 South St Ste 300	Concord	NH	03301	**800-735-2964**	603-271-2555	723
New Hampshire Public Television (NHPTV)	268 Mast Rd	Durham	NH	03824	**800-639-8408**	603-868-1100	629
New Hampshire State Prison for Women	317 Mast Rd	Goffstown	NH	03045	**800-639-1122**	603-668-6137	215
New Hampshire Veterans Home	139 Winter St	Tilton	NH	03276	**800-735-2964**	603-527-4400	791
New Hanover Regional Medical Ctr	2131 S 17th St	Wilmington	NC	28401	**877-228-8135**	910-343-7000	374-3
New Haven Hotel	229 George St	New Haven	CT	06510	**800-644-6835**	203-498-3100	379
New Haven Legal Assistance Association Inc	426 State St	New Haven	CT	06510	**877-829-5500**	203-946-4811	428
New Haven Register	40 Sargent Dr	New Haven	CT	06511	**800-925-2509**	203-789-5200	531-2
New Holland Church Furniture	313 Prospect St PO Box 217	New Holland	PA	17557	**800-648-9663**		320-3

Listing	Toll-Free	Phone	Class
New Horizon Kids Quest Inc 3405 Annapolis Ln N Ste 100 . . . . Plymouth MN 55447	800-941-1007		147
New Horizons Computer Learning Centers Inc 1900 S State College Blvd Ste 450 . . . . Anaheim CA 92806	888-236-3625	714-940-8000	762
New Horizons Diagnostics Corp 9110 Red Branch Rd . . . . Columbia MD 21045	800-888-5015	410-992-9357	233
New Horizons RV Corp 2401 Lacy Dr . . . . Junction City KS 66441	800-235-3140	785-238-7575	119
New Horizons Worldwide Inc 1900 S State College Blvd Ste 450 . . . . Anaheim CA 92806	888-236-3625		762
New ICM LP PO Box 1060 . . . . El Campo TX 77437	800-987-9008	979-578-0543	154-4
New Idea Engineering Inc 2784 Homestead Rd Ste 173 . . . . Santa Clara CA 95051	866-433-2364	408-446-3460	5
New Jersey			
Banking & Insurance Dept 20 W State St PO Box 325 . . . . Trenton NJ 08625	800-446-7467	609-292-7272	339-31
Child Support Office 175 S Broad St PO Box 8068 . . . . Trenton NJ 08650	877-655-4371		339-31
Mental Health Services Div PO Box 272 . . . . Trenton NJ 08625	800-382-6717	609-777-0700	339-31
Military & Veterans' Affairs Dept 101 Eggert Crossing Rd . . . . Lawrenceville NJ 08648	800-624-0508	609-530-4600	339-31
Motor Vehicle Commission 225 E State St PO Box 160 . . . . Trenton NJ 08666	888-486-3339	609-292-6500	339-31
Securities Bureau 153 Halsey St Sixth Fl PO Box 47029 . . . . Newark NJ 07101	866-446-8378	973-504-3600	339-31
Travel & Tourism Div 225 W State St PO Box 460 . . . . Trenton NJ 08625	800-847-4865	609-599-6540	339-31
Victims of Crime Compensation Board 50 Pk Pl . . . . Newark NJ 07102	877-658-2221	973-648-2107	339-31
New Jersey Bill Status State House Annex PO Box 068 . . . . Trenton NJ 08625	800-792-8630	609-292-4840	433
New Jersey Bureau of State Use Industries 163 N Olden Ave PO Box 867 . . . . Trenton NJ 08625	800-321-6524		629
New Jersey Business Forms Manufacturing Co 55 W Sheffield Ave . . . . Englewood NJ 07631	800-466-6523	201-569-4500	109
New Jersey City University 2039 JFK Blvd . . . . Jersey City NJ 07305	888-441-6528	201-200-2000	167
New Jersey Convention & Exposition Ctr 97 Sunfield Ave . . . . Edison NJ 08837	800-367-0070	732-417-1400	207
New Jersey Herald 2 Spring St . . . . Newton NJ 07860	800-423-3725	973-383-1500	531-2
New Jersey Higher Education Student Assistance Authority 4 Quakerbridge Plaza PO Box 540 . . . . Trenton NJ 08625	800-792-8670	609-584-4480	723
New Jersey Institute of Technology University Heights . . . . Newark NJ 07102	800-925-6548	973-596-3000	167
New Jersey Legal Copy Inc 501 King Ave . . . . Cherry Hill NJ 08002	800-426-7965	856-910-0202	112
New Jersey Machine Inc 56 Etna Rd . . . . Lebanon NH 03766 *Sales	800-432-2990*	603-448-0300	546
New Jersey Manufacturers Insurance Co 301 Sullivan Way . . . . West Trenton NJ 08628	800-232-6600	609-883-1300	391-4
New Jersey Medical Society 2 Princess Rd . . . . Lawrenceville NJ 08648	800-706-7893	609-896-1766	473
New Jersey Monthly Magazine 55 Pk Pl PO Box 920 . . . . Morristown NJ 07963	888-419-0419	973-539-8230	456-22
New Jersey Natural Gas Co 1415 Wyckoff Rd . . . . Wall NJ 07719	800-221-0051	732-938-1480	537
New Jersey Nets Nets Champion Ctr 390 Murray Hill Pkwy . . . . East Rutherford NJ 07073	800-346-6387	201-935-8888	712-1
New Jersey Performing Arts Ctr 1 Ctr St . . . . Newark NJ 07102	888-466-5722	973-642-8989	571
New Jersey Resources Corp 1415 Wyckoff Rd . . . . Wall NJ 07719 *NYSE: NJR*	800-221-0051	732-938-1000	360-5
New Jersey State Nurses Assn (NJSNA) 1479 Pennington Rd . . . . Trenton NJ 08618	800-662-0108	609-883-5335	532
New Jersey Transit Corp 1 Penn Plz E . . . . Newark NJ 07105 *Cust Svc	800-772-3606*	973-491-7000	467
New Leaf Publishing Group PO Box 726 . . . . Green Forest AR 72638	800-999-3777	870-438-5288	634-3
New Method Steel Stamps Inc 31313 Kendall Ave . . . . Fraser MI 48026	800-582-0199	586-293-0200	466
New Mexico			
Children Youth & Families Dept PO Box 5160 . . . . Santa Fe NM 87502	800-610-7610	800-432-2075	339-32
Crime Victims Reparation Commission 8100 Mountain Rd NE Ste 106 . . . . Albuquerque NM 87110	800-306-6262	505-841-9432	339-32
Department of Veterans Services 490 Old SF Trail . . . . Santa Fe NM 87504	866-433-8387	505-827-6300	339-32
Economic Development Dept PO Box 20003 . . . . Santa Fe NM 87504	800-374-3061	505-827-0300	339-32
Environment Dept 1190 St Francis Dr Ste 4050 . . . . Santa Fe NM 87502	800-219-6157	505-827-2855	339-32
Highway & Transportation Dept (NMDOT) 1120 Cerrillos Rd PO Box 1149 . . . . Santa Fe NM 87504 *General	800-432-4269*	505-827-5100	339-32
Lieutenant Governor 490 Old Santa Fe Trail Rm 417 . . . . Santa Fe NM 87501	800-432-4406	505-476-2250	339-32
Mortgage Finance Authority 344 Fourth St SW . . . . Albuquerque NM 87102	800-444-6880	505-843-6880	339-32
Secretary of State 325 Don Gaspar Ave Ste 300 . . . . Santa Fe NM 87503	800-477-3632	505-827-3600	339-32
Tourism Dept 491 Old Santa Fe Trail . . . . Santa Fe NM 87503	800-545-2070		339-32
Vital Records & Health Statistics Bureau 1105 S St Francis Dr . . . . Santa Fe NM 87502	866-534-0051	505-827-0121	339-32
Vocational Rehabilitation Div 435 St Michaels Dr Bldg D . . . . Santa Fe NM 87505	800-224-7005	505-954-8500	339-32
Workers' Compensation Admin 2410 Ctr Ave SE PO Box 27198 . . . . Albuquerque NM 87125	800-255-7965	505-841-6000	339-32

Listing	Toll-Free	Phone	Class
New Mexico Behavioral Health Institute 3695 Hot Springs Blvd . . . . Las Vegas NM 87701	800-446-5970	505-454-2100	374-5
New Mexico Democratic Party (DPNM) 8214 Second St NW ste A . . . . Albuquerque NM 87114	800-624-2457	505-830-3650	615-1
New Mexico Dental Assn 9201 Montgomery Blvd NE Ste 601 . . . . Albuquerque NM 87111	888-787-1722	505-294-1368	229
New Mexico Educational Retirement Board 701 Camino de Los Marquez PO Box 26129 . . . . Santa Fe NM 87502	866-691-2345	505-827-8030	527
New Mexico Ethics Administration 325 Don Gaspar St Ste 300 . . . . Santa Fe NM 87501	800-477-3632	505-827-3600	267
New Mexico Higher Education Dept 2048 Galisteo St . . . . Santa Fe NM 87505	800-279-9777	505-476-8400	339-32
New Mexico Highlands University 901 University Ave . . . . Las Vegas NM 87701	877-850-9064	505-425-7511	167
New Mexico Institute of Mining & Technology (NMT) 801 Leroy Pl . . . . Socorro NM 87801 *Admissions	800-428-8324*	505-835-5434	167
New Mexico Junior College 1 Thunderbird Cir . . . . Hobbs NM 88240	800-657-6260	505-392-4510	161
New Mexico Lions Eye Bank 2501 Yale Blvd SE Ste 100 . . . . Albuquerque NM 87106	888-616-3937	505-266-3937	271
New Mexico Magazine PO Box 12002 . . . . Santa Fe NM 87504	800-898-6639		456-22
New Mexico Medical Society (NMMS) 316 Osuna Rd NE Ste 501 . . . . Albuquerque NM 87107	800-748-1596	505-828-0237	473
New Mexico Museum of Art 107 W Palace Ave . . . . Santa Fe NM 87501	877-567-7380	505-476-5072	519
New Mexico Museum of Space History Top of Hwy 2001 . . . . Alamogordo NM 88311	877-333-6589	575-437-2840	519
New Mexico Mutual Casualty Co PO Box 27825 . . . . Albuquerque NM 87125	800-788-8851	505-345-7260	391-4
New Mexico State University (NMSU) MSC-3A PO Box 30001 . . . . Las Cruces NM 88003 *Admissions	800-662-6678*	575-646-3121	167
Carlsbad 1500 University Dr . . . . Carlsbad NM 88220	888-888-2199	505-234-9200	161
New Mexico State Veterans Ctr 992 S Broadway St . . . . Truth or Consequences NM 87901	800-964-3976	575-894-4200	791
New Milford Block & Supply 574 Danbury Rd . . . . New Milford CT 06776	800-724-1888	860-355-1101	185
New Moon Magazine PO Box 161287 . . . . Duluth MN 55816	800-381-4743	218-878-9673	456-6
New Objective Inc 2 Constitution Way . . . . Woburn MA 01801	888-220-2998	781-933-9560	419
New Orleans Baptist Theological Seminary 3939 Gentilly Blvd . . . . New Orleans LA 70126	800-662-8701	504-282-4455	168-3
New Orleans Firemens Federal Credit Union PO Box 689 . . . . Metairie LA 70004	800-647-1689	504-889-9090	221
New Orleans Jazz National Historical Park 419 Decatur St . . . . New Orleans LA 70130	877-520-0677	504-589-4806	563
New Orleans Magazine 110 Veterans Blvd Ste 123 . . . . Metairie LA 70005 *Edit	877-221-3512*	504-828-1380	456-22
New Orleans Metropolitan Convention & Visitors Bureau 2020 St Charles Ave . . . . New Orleans LA 70130	800-672-6124	504-566-5011	208
New Otani Kaimana Beach Hotel 2863 Kalakaua Ave . . . . Honolulu HI 96815	800-356-8264	808-923-1555	379
New Otani North America Reservation Ctr 120 S Los Angeles St . . . . Los Angeles CA 90012 *Cust Svc	800-421-8795*	213-629-1200	376
New Penn Motor Express Inc 625 S Fifth Ave . . . . Lebanon PA 17042 *Cust Svc	800-285-5000*	717-274-2521	778
New Pig Corp 1 Pork Ave . . . . Tipton PA 16684	800-468-4647	814-684-0101	150
NEW Plastics Corp 112 Fourth St . . . . Luxemburg WI 54217	800-666-5207	920-845-2326	97
New Process Steel Corp 5800 Westview Dr . . . . Houston TX 77055	800-392-4989	713-686-9631	491
New Pros Data Inc 155 Hidden Ravines Dr . . . . Powell OH 43065	800-837-5478	740-201-0410	387
New Readers Press 104 Marcellus St . . . . Syracuse NY 13204	800-448-8878	315-422-9121	634-2
New Republic, The 1620 L St NW Ste 300C . . . . Washington DC 20036	800-827-1289	202-508-4444	456-17
New River Community College 5251 College PO Box 1127 . . . . Dublin VA 24084	866-462-6722	540-674-3600	161
New Riverside Ochre Co 75 Old River Rd SE . . . . Cartersville GA 30121 *Orders	800-248-0176*	770-382-4568	502-1
New Seabury Resort 20 Red Brook Rd . . . . Mashpee MA 02649	877-687-3228	508-539-8200	667
New Tech Network 1250 Main St Ste 100 . . . . Napa CA 94559	800-856-7038	707-253-6951	136
New Tribes Mission (NTM) 1000 E First St . . . . Sanford FL 32771	800-321-5375	407-323-3430	47-20
New Ulm Telecom Inc 27 N Minnesota St . . . . New Ulm MN 56073 *OTC: NULM*	888-873-6853	507-354-4111	733
New Venture Communications 218 Commercial Ave SE PO Box 157 . . . . Highmore SD 57345	800-932-0637	650-343-2735	48-17
New Ventures West PO Box 591525 . . . . San Francisco CA 94159	800-332-4618		462
New Vitality 260 Smith St . . . . Farmingdale NY 11735	888-997-2941		789
New Washington State Bank 402 E Main St PO Box 10 . . . . New Washington IN 47162	800-883-0131	812-293-3321	69
New Wave Travel 1075 Bay St . . . . Toronto ON M5S2B1	800-463-1512	416-928-3113	770
New Way Packaging Machinery Inc 210 Blettner Ave . . . . Hanover PA 17331	844-801-3711	717-637-2133	546
New West Health Services 130 Neill Ave . . . . Helena MT 59601	888-500-3355	406-457-2200	47-17
New World Library 14 Pamaron Way . . . . Novato CA 94949	800-972-6657	415-884-2100	634-3

	City	State	Zip	Toll-Free	Phone	Class
New World Pasta Co						
85 Shannon Rd	Harrisburg	PA	17112	**800-730-5957***	717-526-2200	297-31
*Sales						
New World Symphony						
500 17th St	Miami Beach	FL	33139	**800-597-3331**	305-673-3330	572-3
New Year Tech Inc						
12330 Pinecrest Rd Ste 100	Reston	VA	20191	**800-525-7767**	703-564-0290	180-12
New York						
Aging Office						
2 Empire State Plaza	Albany	NY	12223	**800-342-9871**		339-33
Banking Dept						
1 State St	New York	NY	10004	**877-226-5697**	800-342-3736	339-33
Division of Consumer Protection						
5 Empire State Plaza Ste 2101	Albany	NY	12223	**800-697-1220**	518-474-3514	339-33
Empire State Development						
30 S Pearl St	Albany	NY	12245	**800-782-8369**	518-292-5100	339-33
Health Dept						
Empire State Plaza						
Corning II Tower	Albany	NY	12237	**866-881-2809**		339-33
Historic Preservation Div						
PO Box 189	Waterford	NY	12188	**800-456-2267**	518-237-8643	339-33
Mental Health Office						
44 Holland Ave	Albany	NY	12229	**800-597-8481**	518-474-4403	339-33
Motor Vehicles Dept						
6 Empire State Plaza	Albany	NY	12228	**800-368-1186**	518-473-5595	339-33
Office of Court Admin						
25 Beaver St Rm 852	New York	NY	10004	**800-268-7869**	212-428-2100	339-33
Parks Recreation & Historic Preservation Office						
1 Empire State Plaza	Albany	NY	12238	**800-456-2267***	518-474-0456	339-33
*Campground Resv						
Taxation & Finance Dept						
WA Harriman Campus Bldg 9	Albany	NY	12227	**800-225-5829**	518-457-5149	339-33
Temporary & Disability Assistance Office						
40 N Pearl St 16th Fl	Albany	NY	12243	**800-342-3009**	518-473-1090	339-33
Tourism Div						
PO Box 2603	Albany	NY	12223	**800-225-5697**	518-473-1064	339-33
Veterans' Affairs Div						
333 E Washington St Ste 430	Albany	NY	12223	**888-838-7697**	315-428-4046	339-33
Vital Records Office						
PO Box 2602	Albany	NY	12220	**877-854-4481**	518-474-3077	339-33
Workers' Compensation Board						
328 State St	Schenectady	NY	12305	**877-632-4996**	518-462-8880	339-33
New York & Co						
330 W 34th St	New York	NY	10001	**800-961-9906**		156-6
New York Academy of Sciences						
250 Greenwich St 40th Fl	New York	NY	10007	**800-843-6927**	212-298-8600	48-19
New York Air Brake Co						
748 Starbuck Ave	Watertown	NY	13601	**888-836-6922**	315-786-5200	648
New York Athletic Commission						
123 William St 20th Fl	New York	NY	10038	**866-269-3769**	212-417-5700	710
New York Barbells						
160 Home St	Elmira	NY	14904	**800-446-1833**	607-733-8038	269
New York Bill Status						
202 Legislative Office Bldg	Albany	NY	12248	**800-342-9860**	518-455-4218	433
New York Business Development Corp (NYBDC)						
50 Beaver St Ste 500	Albany	NY	12207	**800-923-2504**	518-463-2268	218
New York Central Art Supply						
62 Third Ave	New York	NY	10003	**800-950-6111**		44
New York Central Mutual Fire Insurance Co (NYCM)						
1899 Central Plz E	Edmeston	NY	13335	**800-234-6926**		391-4
New York City Children's Ctr-Queens Campus (NYCCC)						
74-03 Commonwealth Blvd	Bellerose	NY	11426	**800-597-8481**	718-264-4500	374-1
New York City College of Technology						
300 Jay St	Brooklyn	NY	11201	**855-492-3633**	718-260-5000	167
New York Community Bank						
615 Merrick Ave	Westbury	NY	11590	**877-786-6560**		69
New York Community Trust						
909 Third Ave 22nd Fl	New York	NY	10022	**877-829-5500**	212-686-0010	304
New York Correctional Industries						
550 Broadway	Albany	NY	12204	**800-436-6321**	518-436-6321	629
New York Cryo						
900 Northern Blvd Ste 230	Great Neck	NY	11021	**877-769-2796**	516-487-2700	544
New York Daily News						
450 W 33rd St 3rd Fl	New York	NY	10001	**800-692-6397**	212-210-2100	531-2
New York Education Law Report						
360 Hiatt Dr	Palm Beach	FL	33418	**800-341-7874**	561-622-6520	530-4
New York Eye & Ear Infirmary						
310 E 14th St	New York	NY	10003	**800-522-4582**	212-979-4000	374-7
New York Graphic Society Ltd						
129 Glover Ave	Norwalk	CT	06850	**800-221-1032**	800-677-6947	634-10
New York Health Care Inc						
33 W Hawthorne Ave 3rd Fl	Valley Stream	NY	11580	**888-978-6942**	718-375-6700	363
OTC: BBAL						
New York Higher Education Services Corp						
99 Washington Ave	Albany	NY	12255	**888-697-4372**	518-473-1574	723
New York Institute of Technology						
New York Institute of Technology Northern Blvd						
PO Box 8000	Old Westbury	NY	11568	**800-345-6948**	516-686-1000	167
Islip						
PO Box 9029	Central Islip	NY	11722	**800-345-6948**	516-686-1000	167
Manhattan						
1855 Broadway	New York	NY	10023	**800-345-6948**	212-261-1500	167
New York Islanders						
1255 Hempstead Tpke	Uniondale	NY	11553	**800-843-5678**	516-501-6700	713-1
New York Labor Dept						
WA Harriman Campus Bldg 12	Albany	NY	12240	**888-469-7365**	518-457-9000	261
New York Law Journal						
120 Broadway 5th Fl	New York	NY	10271	**877-256-2472**		456-15
New York Law School						
185 W Broadway	New York	NY	10013	**877-937-6957**	212-431-2100	168-1
New York Library Assn (NYLA)						
6021 State Farm Rd	Guilderland	NY	12084	**800-252-6952***	518-432-6952	435
*General						
New York Life Insurance & Annuity Corp						
51 Madison Ave	New York	NY	10010	**800-598-2019**	212-576-7000	391-2
New York Magazine						
75 Varick St	New York	NY	10013	**800-678-0900**	212-508-0700	456-22
New York Merchants Protective Company Inc						
75 W Merrick Rd	Freeport	NY	11520	**888-696-7911**	516-561-5210	691

	City	State	Zip	Toll-Free	Phone	Class
New York Mets						
Shea Stadium 123-01 Roosevelt Ave	Flushing	NY	11368	**888-652-7467**	718-507-6387	711
New York Military Academy						
78 Academy Ave	Cornwall On Hudson	NY	12520	**888-275-6962**	845-534-3710	621
New York Mortgage Trust Inc (NYMT)						
52 Vanderbilt Ave Ste 403	New York	NY	10017	**800-937-5449**	212-792-0107	652
NASDAQ: NYMT						
New York New York Hotel & Casino						
3790 Las Vegas Blvd S	Las Vegas	NV	89109	**800-689-1797**	702-740-6969	132
New York Palace Hotel						
455 Madison Ave	New York	NY	10022	**800-697-2522**	212-888-7000	379
New York Post						
1211 Ave of the Americas	New York	NY	10036	**800-552-7678**	212-930-8000	531-2
New York Presbyterian Hospital						
525 E 68th St	New York	NY	10021	**888-694-5700**	212-746-5454	374-3
New York Public Interest Research Group (NYPIRG)						
9 Murray St	New York	NY	10007	**800-342-3377**	212-349-6460	630
New York Red Bulls						
600 Cape May St	Harrison	NJ	07029	**877-727-6223**		715
New York Replacement Parts Corp						
19 School St	Yonkers	NY	10701	**800-228-4718**	914-965-0122	611
New York Review of Books						
435 Hudson St 3rd Fl	New York	NY	10014	**800-354-0050**	212-757-8070	456-11
New York School of Interior Design						
170 E 70th St	New York	NY	10021	**800-336-9743**	212-472-1500	167
New York State Assn of Realtors						
130 Washington Ave	Albany	NY	12210	**800-462-7585**	518-463-0300	654
New York State Bar Assn						
1 Elk St	Albany	NY	12207	**800-342-3661**	518-463-3200	71
New York State Bar News						
1 Elk St	Albany	NY	12207	**800-442-3863**	518-463-3200	456-15
New York State Bridge Authority						
PO Box 1010	Highland	NY	12528	**800-333-8655**	845-691-7245	273
New York State Canal Corp						
200 Southern Blvd PO Box 189	Albany	NY	12201	**800-422-6254**	518-436-2700	464
New York State Dental Assn						
20 Corporate Woods Blvd #602	Albany	NY	12211	**800-255-2100**	518-465-0044	229
New York State Electric & Gas Corp						
Corporate Dr PO Box 5240	Binghamton	NY	13902	**800-572-1111**		785
New York State Medical Society						
865 Merrick Ave PO Box 5404	Westbury	NY	11590	**800-523-4405**	516-488-6100	473
New York State Nurses Assn (NYSNA)						
11 Cornell Rd	Latham	NY	12110	**800-724-6976**	518-782-9400	532
New York State Office of Parks Recreation & Historic Preservation						
Empire State Plaza Agency Bldg 1	Albany	NY	12238	**800-456-2267**	716-354-9101	49-4
New York State Society of Certified Public Accountant (FAE)						
14 Wall St 19th Fl	New York	NY	10005	**800-537-3635***	212-719-8300	48-1
*General						
New York State Veterinary Medical Society						
100 Great Oaks Blvd Ste 127	Albany	NY	12203	**800-876-9867**	518-869-7867	793
New York Susquehanna & Western Railway Corp (NYSW)						
1 Railroad Ave	Cooperstown	NY	13326	**800-366-6979***	607-547-2555	646
*General						
New York Teacher Magazine						
800 Troy-Schenectady Rd	Latham	NY	12110	**800-342-9810**	518-213-6000	456-8
New York Times News Service Div						
620 Eigth Ave 9th Fl	New York	NY	10018	**800-698-4637**	212-556-7652	529
New York University						
22 Washington Sq N	New York	NY	10011	**888-243-2358**	212-998-4500	167
New York University School of Law						
110 W Third St	New York	NY	10012	**800-522-0925**	212-998-6100	168-1
New York University School of Medicine						
560 First Ave	New York	NY	10016	**855-698-2220**	212-263-7300	168-2
New York's Hotel Pennsylvania						
401 Seventh Ave	New York	NY	10001	**800-223-8585**	212-736-5000	379
New Zealand						
Embassy						
37 Observatory Cir NW	Washington	DC	20008	**855-844-2835**	202-328-4800	259
NewAge Industries Inc						
145 James Way	SouthHampton	PA	18966	**800-506-3924**	215-526-2300	370
NewAgeSys Inc						
231 Clarksville Rd						
Ste 200	Princeton Junction	NJ	08550	**888-863-9243**	609-919-9800	182
Newark Chamber of Commerce						
37101 Newark Blvd	Newark	CA	94560	**844-245-8925**	510-744-1000	138
Newark Liberty International Airport						
1 Hotel Rd	Newark	NJ	07114	**888-397-4636**	973-961-6007	27
Newark Museum						
49 Washington St	Newark	NJ	07102	**888-370-6765**	973-596-6550	519
Newark Regional Business Partnership						
744 Broad St 26th Fl	Newark	NJ	07102	**888-337-3339**	973-522-0099	138
Newark School District						
100 E Miller St 4th Fl	Newark	NY	14513	**877-789-2613**	315-332-3230	778
Neway Packaging Corp						
1973 E Via Arado	Rancho Dominguez	CA	90220	**800-456-3929**	310-898-3400	94
Newberry Area Tourism Assn, The						
PO Box 308	Newberry	MI	49868	**800-831-7292**	906-293-5562	208
Newberry College						
2100 College St	Newberry	SC	29108	**800-845-4955**	803-276-5010	167
Newberry Electric Co-op Inc						
882 Wilson Rd	Newberry	SC	29108	**800-479-8838**	803-276-1121	247
Newbold Corp						
450 Weaver St	Rocky Mount	VA	24151	**800-552-3282**	540-489-4400	110
Newbridge Securities Corp						
1451 W Cypress Creek Rd	Fort Lauderdale	FL	33309	**877-447-9625**	954-334-3450	688
Newbury College						
129 Fisher Ave	Brookline	MA	02445	**800-499-0143**	617-730-7000	167
Newbury Corp						
222 Ames St	Dedham	MA	02026	**800-688-1825**		390
Newburyport Five Cents Savings Bank Inc, The						
63 State St PO Box 350	Newburyport	MA	01950	**877-462-3136**	978-462-3136	69
NewCloud Networks						
160 Inverness Dr W	Englewood	CO	80112	**855-255-5001**		387
Newcomb Spring Corp						
235 Spring St	Southington	CT	06489	**888-579-3051**	860-621-0111	717

Name / Address	City	State	Zip	Toll-Free	Phone	Class
NewComLink Inc 3900 N Capital Of Texas Hwy Ste 150	Austin	TX	78746	888-988-0603		255
Newcon Optik 105 Sparks Ave	North York	ON	M2H2S5	877-368-6666	416-663-6963	528
Newdell Co, The 13750 Hollister Rd	Houston	TX	77086	877-510-7853	713-590-1312	787
Newegg Inc 16839 E Gale Ave	City of Industry	CA	91745	800-390-1119	626-271-9700	181
Newell Coach Corp 3900 N Main St	Miami	OK	74354	888-363-9355	918-542-3344	119
Newell Paper Co 1212 Grand Ave	Meridian	MS	39301	800-844-8894		552
Newell Rubbermaid Inc 3 Glenlake Pkwy *NYSE: NWL*	Atlanta	GA	30328	800-752-9677	770-418-7000	187
Newell Rubbermaid Inc Irwin Tools Div 8935 Northpointe Executive Dr	Huntersville	NC	28078	800-866-5740	704-987-4555	756
Newfield Exploration Co 363 N Sam Houston Pkwy E Ste 100 *NYSE: NFX*	Houston	TX	77060	866-902-0562	281-847-6000	535
Newhall Klein Inc 6109 W KI Ave	Kalamazoo	MI	49009	866-639-4255	269-544-0844	344
Newjac Inc 415 S Grant St	Lebanon	IN	46052	800-827-3259	765-483-2190	695
Newkirk Products Inc 15 Corporate Cir	Albany	NY	12203	800-525-4237	518-862-3200	634-2
Newlands Systems Inc 602-30731 Simpson Rd	Abbotsford	BC	V2T6Y7	877-855-4890	604-855-4890	79-3
NewlineNoosh Inc 625 Ellis St Ste 300	Mountain View	CA	94043	888-286-6674	650-637-6000	180-1
Newly Weds Foods Inc 4140 W Fullerton Ave	Chicago	IL	60639	800-621-7521	773-489-7000	297-37
Newman & Company Inc 6101 Tacony St	Philadelphia	PA	19135	800-523-3256	215-333-8700	560
Newman Theological College (NTC) 10012-84 St	Edmonton	AB	T6A0B2	844-392-2450	780-392-2450	168-3
Newman University 3100 McCormick Ave	Wichita	KS	67213	877-639-6268	316-942-4291	167
Newman's Inc 3003 Texas 225	Pasadena	TX	77503	800-231-3505	713-675-8631	385
Newmar Corp 355 Delaware St	Nappanee	IN	46550	800-731-8300	574-773-7791	119
NewMarket Corp 330 S Fourth St *NYSE: NEU*	Richmond	VA	23219	800-625-5191	804-788-5000	360-3
Newmarket International Inc 75 New Hampshire Ave	Portsmouth	NH	03801	888-829-8871	603-436-7500	180-11
Newpark Mats & Integrated Services LLC 2700 Research Forest Dr Ste 100	The Woodlands	TX	77381	877-628-7623	281-362-6800	538
Newport Aquarium 1 Aquarium Way	Newport	KY	41071	800-406-3474	859-261-7444	39
Newport Beach Conference & Visitors Bureau 1200 Newport Ctr Dr Ste 120	Newport Beach	CA	92660	800-216-1598	949-719-6100	208
Newport Beach Hotel & Suites 1 Wave Ave	Middletown	RI	02842	800-655-1778	401-846-0310	379
Newport Beachside Hotel & Resort 16701 Collins Ave	Miami Beach	FL	33160	800-327-5476	305-949-1300	379
Newport Corp 1791 Deere Ave *NASDAQ: NEWP* ■ *Sales	Irvine	CA	92606	800-222-6440*	949-863-3144	543
Newport Electronics Inc 2229 S Yale St *Cust Svc	Santa Ana	CA	92704	800-639-7678*	714-540-4914	250
Newport Harbor Hotel & Marina 49 America's Cup Ave	Newport	RI	02840	800-955-2558	401-847-9000	379
Newport Hospital (NH) 11 Friendship St	Newport	RI	02840	866-401-0002	401-845-1646	374-3
Newport Leasing Inc 4750 Von Karman Ave *Cust Svc	Newport Beach	CA	92660	800-274-0042*	949-476-8476	266-1
Newport News Industrial Corp 182 Enterprise Dr	Newport News	VA	23603	800-627-0353	757-380-7053	787
Newport News Tourism Development Office 700 Town Ctr Dr Ste 320	Newport News	VA	23606	888-493-7386	757-926-1400	208
Newport Partners LLC 3760 Tanglewood Ln	Davidsonville	MD	21035	866-302-0017	301-889-0017	740
Newport State Park 475 County Rd NP	Ellison Bay	WI	54210	800-847-9367	920-854-2500	564
Newport Utilities PO Box 519	Newport	TN	37822	877-779-8581	423-625-2800	247
NewRetirement LLC 100 Pine St Ste 590	San Francisco	CA	94111	866-441-0246	415-738-2435	529
News & Advance PO Box 10129	Lynchburg	VA	24506	800-275-8830	434-385-5555	531-2
News & Observer 215 S McDowell St	Raleigh	NC	27602	800-522-4205	919-829-4500	531-2
News & Record 200 E Market St	Greensboro	NC	27401	800-553-6880	336-373-7000	531-2
News America Marketing 1185 Ave of the Americas 27	New York	NY	10036	800-462-0852	212-782-8000	5
News Journal 70 W Fourth St	Mansfield	OH	44903	800-472-5547	419-522-3311	531-2
News Leader 11 N Central Ave	Staunton	VA	24401	800-793-2459	540-885-7281	531-2
NEWS TALK 98.7 4711 Old Kingston Pike	Knoxville	TN	37919	800-951-8255	865-588-6511	642-63
News Tribune 1950 S State St	Tacoma	WA	98405	800-388-8742	253-597-8742	531-2
Newsbank Inc 5801 Pelican Bay Blvd Ste 600	Naples	FL	34108	800-243-7694	239-263-6004	387
News-banner Publications Inc 125 N Johnson St	Bluffton	IN	46714	800-579-7476	260-824-0224	531-3
Newsday Inc 235 Pinelawn Rd	Melville	NY	11747	888-280-4719	631-843-2700	531-2
News-Enterprise 408 W Dixie Ave	Elizabethtown	KY	42701	877-246-2322	270-769-1200	531-2
News-Herald 7085 Mentor Ave	Willoughby	OH	44094	800-947-2737	440-951-0000	531-2
NewsHub 100 Lombard St Ste 203	Toronto	ON	M5C1M3	800-889-9487	416-536-4827	397
Newsome House Museum & Cultural Ctr 2803 Oak Ave	Newport News	VA	23607	888-493-7386	757-247-2360	519
News-Review 345 NE Winchester St	Roseburg	OR	97470	800-863-3321	541-672-3321	531-2
News-Star 411 N Fourth St	Monroe	LA	71201	888-677-2524	318-322-5161	531-2
NewStar Fresh Foods LLC 900 Work St	Salinas	CA	93901	888-782-7220	831-758-7800	297-19
News-Times 333 Main St	Danbury	CT	06810	877-542-6057	203-744-5100	531-2
News-Tribune 426 Second St	La Salle	IL	61301	800-892-6452	815-223-3200	531-2
Newsweek Magazine 7 Hanover Sq *Cust Svc	New York	NY	10004	800-631-1040*		456-17
Newtek Business Services Inc 1440 Broadway 17th Fl *NASDAQ: NEWT* ■ *Sales	New York	NY	10018	866-820-8902*	212-356-9500	790
NewTek Inc 5131 Beckwith Blvd *Cust Svc	San Antonio	TX	78249	800-862-7837*	210-370-8000	180-8
Newtex Industries Inc 8050 Victor Mendon Rd	Victor	NY	14564	800-836-1001	585-924-9135	742-3
Newton Convention & Visitor Bureau 300 E 17th St S Ste 400	Newton	IA	50208	800-798-0299	641-792-0299	208
Newton County 201 N 3rd St	Kentland	IN	47951	888-663-9866	219-474-6081	338
Newton Distributing Company Inc 966 Watertown St	Newton	MA	02465	877-837-7745	617-969-4002	611
Newtown Savings Bank Foundation Inc 39 Main St PO Box 497	Newtown	CT	06470	800-461-0672	203-426-2563	69
Nexcess.net LLC 21700 Melrose Ave	Southfield	MI	48075	866-639-2377		227
NEXCOM (Navy Exchange Service Command) 3280 Virginia Beach Blvd	Virginia Beach	VA	23452	800-628-3924	757-463-6200	789
Nexen Group Inc 560 Oak Grove Pkwy	Vadnais Heights	MN	55127	800-843-7445	651-484-5900	386
Nexion 6225 N State Hwy 161 Ste 450	Irving	TX	75038	800-949-6410	408-280-6410	770
Nexlan 28 W N St	Danville	IL	61832	877-263-9526	217-431-7236	179
Next Day Flyers 18711 S Broadwick St	Rancho Dominguez	CA	90220	800-251-9948		5
Next Net Media LLC 316 California Ave Ste 804	Reno	NV	89509	800-737-5820		387
NextEra Energy Resources LLC *NextEra Energy Resources LLC* 700 Universe Blvd PO Box 14000	Juno Beach	FL	33408	888-867-3050	561-691-7171	785
NextG Networks Inc 890 Tasman Dr	Milpitas	CA	95035	877-486-9377		613
Nextgen Networks Inc 200 Katonah Ave Ste A	Katonah	NY	10536	866-639-8436		263
nextPoint Inc 4043 N Ravenswood Ave	Chicago	IL	60613	888-929-6398		179
Nextran Corp 1986 W Beaver St	Jacksonville	FL	32209	800-347-6225	904-354-3721	56
NextWave Wireless Inc 10350 Science Ctr Dr Ste 210 *OTC: WAVE*	San Diego	CA	92121	800-461-9330	858-731-5300	360-3
Nexus Corp 10983 Leroy Dr	Northglenn	CO	80233	800-228-9639	303-457-9199	105
Nexxtworks Inc 30798 Us Hwy 19 N	Palm Harbor	FL	34684	888-533-8353		387
Ney Oil Company Inc 145 S Water St	Ney	OH	43549	800-962-9839	419-658-2324	325
Neyra Industries 10700 Evendale Dr	Cincinnati	OH	45241	800-543-7077	513-733-1000	45
NF Smith & Assoc LP 5306 Hollister Rd	Houston	TX	77040	800-468-7866	713-430-3000	248
NFA (National Futures Assn) 300 S Riverside Plz Ste 1800	Chicago	IL	60606	800-621-3570	312-781-1300	48-2
NFB (National Federation of the Blind) 1800 Johnson St	Baltimore	MD	21230	800-392-5671	410-659-9314	47-17
NFBA (National Frame Builders Assn) 8735 W Higgins Rd Ste 300	Chicago	IL	60631	800-557-6957		48-3
NFCA (National Family Caregivers Assn) 10400 Connecticut Ave Ste 500	Kensington	MD	20895	800-896-3650	301-942-6430	47-6
NFCDCU (National Federation of Community Development Credit Unions) 39 Broadway Ste 2140	New York	NY	10006	800-437-8711	212-809-1850	48-2
NFCR (National Foundation for Cancer Research) 4600 E W Hwy Ste 525	Bethesda	MD	20814	800-321-2873	301-654-1250	306
NFDA (National Funeral Directors Assn) 13625 Bishop's Dr	Brookfield	WI	53005	800-228-6332	262-789-1880	48-4
NFDMA (National Funeral Directors & Morticians Assn) 6290 Shannon Pkwy	Union City	GA	30291	800-434-0958	770-969-0064	48-4
NFHS (National Federation of State High School Assn) PO Box 690 *Cust Svc	Indianapolis	IN	46206	800-776-3462*	317-972-6900	47-22
NFI (National Freight Inc) 1515 Burnt Mill Rd *General	Cherry Hill	NJ	08003	877-634-3777*		448
NFIC (National Fraud Information Ctr) 1701 K St NW Ste 1200	Washington	DC	20006	800-333-4636	202-835-3323	47-10
NFL Network 345 Park Avenue	New York	NY	10154	800-724-3377	212-450-2000	736
NFO (National Farmers Organization) 528 Billy Sunday Rd Ste 100 PO Box 2508	Ames	IA	50010	800-247-2110	515-292-2000	47-2
NFP (National Fibromyalgia Partnership Inc) 140 Zinn Way	Linden	VA	22642	866-725-4404		47-17

Name / Address	City	State	Zip	Toll-Free	Phone	Class
NFPA (National Fire Protection Assn) 1 Batterymarch Pk	Quincy	MA	02169	**800-344-3555**	617-770-3000	47-17
NFR (North Fork Ranch) 55395 Hwy 285 PO Box B	Shawnee	CO	80475	**800-843-7895**	303-838-9873	241
NFRA (National Forest Recreation Assn) PO Box 488	Woodlake	CA	93286	**800-282-2444**	559-564-2365	47-23
nFrame Inc 701 Congressional Blvd Ste 100	Carmel	IN	46032	**877-570-7827**	317-805-3759	394
NFRW (National Federation of Republican Women) 124 N Alfred St	Alexandria	VA	22314	**800-373-9688**	703-548-9688	47-7
NGA (National Gardening Assn) 1100 Dorset St	South Burlington	VT	05403	**800-538-7476**	802-863-5251	47-18
NGA (National Glass Assn) 8200 Greensboro Dr Ste 302	McLean	VA	22102	**866-342-5642**	703-442-4890	48-13
NGAUS (National Guard Assn of the US) 1 Massachusetts Ave NW Ste 200	Washington	DC	20001	**888-226-4287**	202-789-0031	47-19
NGC (National Garden Clubs Inc) 4401 Magnolia Ave	Saint Louis	MO	63110	**800-550-6007**	314-776-7574	47-18
NGCOA (National Golf Course Owners Assn) 291 Seven Farms Dr 2nd Fl	Charleston	SC	29492	**800-933-4262**	843-881-9956	47-23
NGF (National Gaucher Foundation) 5410 Edson Ln Ste 220	Rockville	MD	30084	**800-504-3189**	770-934-2910	47-17
NGF (National Golf Foundation) 1150 S US Hwy 1 Ste 401	Jupiter	FL	33477	**800-733-6006**	561-744-6006	47-22
NGK Metals Corp 917 Hwy 11 S	Sweetwater	TN	37874	**800-523-8268**	423-337-5500	309
NGK Spark Plugs Inc 46929 Magellan	Wixom	MI	48393	**877-473-6767**	248-926-6900	249
NGL (National Guardian Life Insurance Co) 2 E Gilman St	Madison	WI	53703	**800-548-2962**	608-257-5611	391-2
NGL (Network Global Logistics) 320 Interlocken Pkwy Ste 100	Broomfield	CO	80021	**866-938-1870**		545
NGS (National Genealogical Society) 3108 Columbia Pk Ste 300	Arlington	VA	22204	**800-473-0060**	703-525-0050	47-18
NGWA (National Ground Water Assn) 601 Dempsey Rd	Westerville	OH	43081	**800-551-7379**	614-898-7791	47-12
NH (Newport Hospital) 11 Friendship St	Newport	RI	02840	**866-401-0002**	401-845-1646	374-3
NH Yates & Company Inc 117 Church Ln # C	Cockeysville	MD	21030	**800-878-8181**		638
NHCA (National Hearing Conservation Assn) 3030 W 81st Ave	Westminster	CO	80031	**877-766-6629**	303-224-9022	47-17
NHCOA (National Hispanic Council on Aging) 734 15th St NW Ste 1050	Washington	DC	20005	**800-633-4227**	202-347-9733	47-6
NHDP (National Hansen's Disease Program) 1770 Physicians Pk Dr	Baton Rouge	LA	70816	**800-221-9393**		666
NHES (New Hampshire Employment Security) 32 S Main St	Concord	NH	03301	**800-852-3400**	603-224-3311	261
NHF (National Headache Foundation) 820 N Orleans St Ste 217	Chicago	IL	60610	**888-643-5552**		47-17
NHF (National Hemophilia Foundation) 116 W 32nd St 11th Fl	New York	NY	10001	**800-424-2634**	212-328-3700	47-17
NHFA (National Home Furnishings Assn) 500 Giuseppe Ct Ste 6	Roseville	CA	95678	**800-422-3778**	336-886-6100	48-4
NHK Laboratories Inc 12230 E Florience Ave	Santa Fe Springs	CA	90670	**866-645-5227**	562-944-5400	478
NHLA (National Hardwood Lumber Assn) 6830 Raleigh-LaGrange Rd	Memphis	TN	38134	**800-933-0318**	901-377-1818	48-3
NHPCO (National Hospice & Palliative Care Organization) 1700 Diagonal Rd Ste 625 *Help Line	Alexandria	VA	22314	**800-658-8898***	703-837-1500	48-8
NHPTV (New Hampshire Public Television) 268 Mast Rd	Durham	NH	03824	**800-639-8408**	603-868-1100	629
NHS (National Honor Society) 1904 Assn Dr	Reston	VA	20191	**800-253-7746**	703-860-0200	47-11
NHSA (National Head Start Assn) 1651 Prince St	Alexandria	VA	22314	**866-677-8724**	703-739-0875	47-11
NHTI Concord's Community College 31 College Dr	Concord	NH	03301	**800-247-0179**	603-271-6484	161
NHTSA (National Highway Traffic Safety Administration) 1200 New Jersey Ave SE	Washington	DC	20590	**888-327-4236**	202-366-9550	340-15
NIA (National Insulation Assn) 99 Canal Ctr Plz Ste 222	Alexandria	VA	22314	**877-968-7642**	703-683-6422	48-3
Niacet Corp 400 47th St	Niagara Falls	NY	14304	**800-828-1207**	716-285-1474	143
NIADA (National Independent Automobile Dealers Assn) 2521 Brown Blvd	Arlington	TX	76006	**800-682-3837**	817-640-3838	48-18
Niagara Blower Co Inc 673 Ontario St	Buffalo	NY	14207	**800-426-5169**	716-875-2000	14
Niagara Conservation Corp 45 Horsehill Rd	Cedar Knolls	NJ	07927	**800-831-8383**	973-829-0800	611
Niagara Corp 667 Madison Ave	New York	NY	10021	**877-289-2277**	212-317-1000	721
Niagara County Community College 3111 Saunders Settlement Rd	Sanborn	NY	14132	**800-875-6269**	716-614-6222	161
Niagara Cutter Inc 2805 Bellingham Dr	Troy	MI	48083	**800-832-8326**	716-689-8400	492
Niagara Duty Free Shop 5726 Falls Ave	Niagara Falls	ON	L2G7T5	**877-642-4337**	905-374-3700	243
Niagara Frontier Transit Metro System Inc 181 Ellicott St Ste 1	Buffalo	NY	14203	**877-294-9434**	716-855-7300	467
Niagara Helicopters Ltd 3731 Victoria Ave	Niagara Falls	ON	L2E6V5	**800-281-8034**	905-357-5672	294
Niagara Hospice 4675 Sunset Dr	Lockport	NY	14094	**800-662-1220**	716-439-4417	371
Niagara Parks Botanical Gardens 2565 Niagara Pkwy N PO Box 150	Niagara Falls	ON	L2E6T2	**877-642-7275**	905-356-8554	96
Niagara Tourism & Convention Corp 10 Rainbow Blvd	Niagara Falls	NY	14303	**877-325-5787**	716-282-8992	208
Niagara Transformer Corp 1747 Dale Rd	Buffalo	NY	14225	**800-817-5652**	716-896-6500	765
Niagara University 5795 Lewiston Rd PO Box 2011	Niagara University	NY	14109	**800-462-2111**	716-286-8700	167
NIB (National Industries for the Blind) 1310 Braddock Pl *Cust Svc	Alexandria	VA	22314	**800-433-2304***	703-310-0500	47-17
NIBCO Inc 1516 Middlebury St	Elkhart	IN	46515	**800-234-0227**	574-295-3000	594
NIC Inc 25501 W Valley Pkwy Ste 300 *NASDAQ: EGOV*	Olathe	KS	66061	**877-234-3468**		180-10
NICB (National Insurance Crime Bureau) 1111 E Touhy Ave Ste 400	Des Plaines	IL	60018	**800-447-6282**	847-544-7002	48-9
NICE Systems Inc 301 Rt 17 N 10th Fl	Rutherford	NJ	07070	**800-994-4498**	201-964-2600	732
Nice-Pak Products Inc 2 Nice-Pak Pk	Orangeburg	NY	10962	**800-444-6725**	845-365-1700	557
Niche Directories LLC 909 N Sepulveda Blvd 11th Fl	El Segundo	CA	90026	**877-242-9330**		387
Nicholas Family of Funds 700 N Water St Ste 1010	Milwaukee	WI	53202	**800-227-5987**	414-272-6133	527
Nicholas Financial Inc 2454 McMullen Booth Rd Bldg C *NASDAQ: NICK*	Clearwater	FL	33759	**800-237-2721**	727-726-0763	216
Nicholls State University 906 E First St *Admissions	Thibodaux	LA	70310	**877-642-4655***	985-446-0561	167
Nichols College 124 Ctr Rd	Dudley	MA	01571	**800-470-3379**	508-213-1560	167
Nichols Paper & Supply Company Inc PO Box 291	Muskegon	MI	49443	**800-442-0213**	231-799-2120	558
Nichols Wire 1547 Helton Dr	Florence	AL	35630	**800-633-3156**	800-873-2011	811
Nicholson Construction Co 12 McClane St	Cuddy	PA	15031	**800-388-2340**	412-221-4500	191-5
Nick Strimbu Inc 3500 PkwyRd	Brookfield	OH	44403	**800-446-8785**	330-448-4046	778
Nickell Moulding Company Inc 3015 Mobile Dr	Elkhart	IN	46515	**800-838-2151**	574-264-3129	498
Nickelodeon Family Suites by Holiday Inn 14500 Continental Gateway	Orlando	FL	32821	**877-642-5111**	407-387-5437	667
Nickers International Ltd PO Box 50066	Staten Island	NY	10305	**800-642-5377**	718-448-6283	797
Nickerson Business Supplies 876A Lebanon St	Monroe	OH	45050	**888-385-9922**	513-539-6600	322
Nicola Wealth Management Ltd 1508 W Broadway 5th Fl	Vancouver	BC	V6J1W8	**800-219-8032**	604-739-6450	794
Nicor Gas 1844 Ferry Rd	Naperville	IL	60563	**888-642-6748**		785
Nicros Inc 845 Phalen Blvd	Saint Paul	MN	55106	**800-699-1975**	651-778-1975	709
NICSA (National Investment Co Service Assn) 8400 Westpark Dr 2nd Fl	McLean	VA	22102	**800-426-1122**	508-485-1500	48-2
NID (Nevada Irrigation District) 1036 W Main St	Grass Valley	CA	95945	**800-222-4102**	530-273-6185	785
Nida Corp 300 S John Rodes Blvd	Melbourne	FL	32904	**800-327-6432**	321-727-2265	701
NIDCR (National Oral Health Information Clearinghouse) 1 NOHIC Way	Bethesda	MD	20892	**866-232-4528**	301-496-4261	47-17
Nidec Motor Corp 8050 W Florissant Ave	Saint Louis	MO	63136	**888-637-7333**		517
Niedner, Bodeux, Carmichael, Huff, Lenox & Pashos LLP 131 Jefferson St	Saint Charles	MO	63301	**888-572-2192**	636-949-9300	428
Nielsen-Massey Vanillas Inc 1550 S Shields Dr	Waukegan	IL	60085	**800-525-7873**	847-578-1550	297-15
Nietzke & Faupel PC 7274 Hartley St	Pigeon	MI	48755	**855-999-3122**	989-453-3122	2
NIFL (National Institute for Literacy) 1775 'I' St NW Ste 730	Washington	DC	20006	**800-228-8813**	202-233-2025	340-6
Night Optics USA Inc 15182 Triton Ln Ste 101	Huntington Beach	CA	92649	**800-306-4448**	714-899-4475	541
Nightingale-Conant Corp 6245 W Howard St *Cust Svc	Niles	IL	60714	**800-557-1660***		512
NIGP (National Institute of Governmental Purchasing Inc) 151 Spring St	Herndon	VA	20170	**800-367-6447**	703-736-8900	48-7
NIH Osteoporosis & Related Bone Diseases-National Resource Ctr 2 AMS Cir	Bethesda	MD	20892	**800-624-2663**	202-223-0344	340-8
Nihon Kohden America Inc 90 Icon	Foothill Ranch	CA	92610	**800-325-0283**	949-580-1555	474
Nike Inc 1 Bowerman Dr *NYSE: NKE* ■ *Cust Svc	Beaverton	OR	97005	**800-344-6453***	503-671-6453	302
Nik-O-Lok Co 3130 N Mitthoeffer Rd	Indianapolis	IN	46235	**800-428-4348**	317-899-6955	350
Nikon Inc 1300 Walt Whitman Rd *Cust Svc	Melville	NY	11747	**800-645-6687***	631-547-4200	590
Niles Audio Corp 1969 Kellog Ave	Carlsbad	CA	92008	**800-289-4434**	760-710-0992	255
Niles Community School 111 Spruce St	Niles	MI	49120	**877-622-2321**	269-683-0732	683
Nilfisk-Advance Inc 14600 21st Ave N *Cust Svc	Plymouth	MN	55447	**800-989-2235***		386
Nill Bros Sports 2814 S 44th St	Kansas City	KS	66106	**800-748-7221**	913-384-4242	709
Nims & Associates 1445 Technology Ln Ste A8	Petaluma	CA	94954	**877-454-3200**	707-781-6300	179
Nine Zero Hotel 90 Tremont St	Boston	MA	02108	**866-906-9090**	617-772-5800	379
Nines Hotel, The 525 SW Morrison	Portland	OR	97204	**877-229-9995**		40
Ninety-Nines Inc 4300 Amelia Earhart Rd	Oklahoma City	OK	73159	**800-994-1929**	405-685-7969	47-24
Nintendo of America Inc 4820 150th Ave NE *Cust Svc	Redmond	WA	98052	**800-255-3700***	425-882-2040	760
Ninyo & Moore 5710 Ruffin Rd	San Diego	CA	92123	**800-427-0401**	858-576-1000	263

Name / Address	Toll-Free	Phone	Class
NIPC (National Inhalant Prevention Coalition) 318 Lindsay St Chattanooga TN 37405	800-269-4237	423-265-4662	47-17
Nipissing University 100 College Dr PO Box 5002 North Bay ON P1B8L7	800-655-5154	705-474-3450	783
Nippon Kodo Inc 2771 Plz Del Amo Ste 805 Torrance CA 90503	888-775-5487	310-320-8881	785
Nishnabotna Valley Rural Electric Co-op 1317 Chatburn Ave Harlan IA 51537	800-234-5122	712-755-2166	247
Niskayuna Central School District (NCSD) 1239 Van Antwerp Rd Schenectady NY 12309	866-893-6337	518-377-4666	683
NISO (National Information Standards Organization) 3600 Clipper Mill Rd Ste 302 Baltimore MD 21211	877-375-2160	301-654-2512	48-16
Nissan Canada Inc (NCI) 5290 Orbitor Dr Mississauga ON L4W4Z5	800-387-0122		58
Nissan Motor Corp USA Infiniti Div 1 Nissan Way PO Box 685003 Franklin TN 37067	800-662-6200		58
Nissan North America Inc 25 Vantage way Nashville TN 37228	800-647-7261		58
NIST (National Institute of Standards & Technology) 100 Bureau Dr Sp 1070 Gaithersburg MD 20899	800-877-8339	301-975-6478	340-2
Nitel Inc 1101 W Lk St 6th Fl Chicago IL 60607	888-450-2100		226
Nitelines USA Inc 3065 Peachtree Industrial Blvd Ste 210 Duluth GA 30097	877-337-2563		393
Nitrex Metal Inc 3474 Poirier Blvd Saint-Laurent QC H4R2J5	877-335-7191	514-335-7191	483
Nitrous Express Inc 5411 Seymour Hwy Wichita Falls TX 76310	888-463-2781	940-767-7694	56
Nitta Casings Inc 141 Southside Ave Bridgewater NJ 08807 *Cust Svc	800-526-3970*	908-218-4400	299
Nitta Gelatin Inc 598 Airport Blvd Ste 900 Morrisville NC 27560	888-648-8287	919-238-3300	297-22
Nittany Lion Inn 200 W Pk Ave State College PA 16803	800-233-7505	814-865-8500	379
Niver Western Wear Inc PO Box 101224 Fort Worth TX 76185 *Orders	800-433-5752*	817-924-4299	154-19
NJHCS (East Orange Campus of the VA New Jersey Health Care System) 385 Tremont Ave East Orange NJ 07018 *General	844-872-4681*		374-8
NJSNA (New Jersey State Nurses Assn) 1479 Pennington Rd Trenton NJ 08618	800-662-0108	609-883-5335	532
NJTV 825 Eighth Avenue New York NY 10019	800-882-6622	609-777-0031	642-125
NKBA (National Kitchen & Bath Assn) 687 Willow Grove St Hackettstown NJ 07840	800-843-6522		48-3
NKF (National Kidney Foundation) 30 E 33rd St 8th Fl New York NY 10016	800-622-9010	212-889-2210	47-17
NKP Medical Marketing Inc 10220 Culver Blvd Ste 208 Culver City CA 90232	888-274-8383		197
NKS Distributors Inc 399 Churchmans Rd New Castle DE 19720	800-310-5099	302-322-1811	80-3
NKTelco Inc 301 W S St PO Box 219 New Knoxville OH 45871	888-658-3526	419-753-2457	226
NKYCVB (Northern Kentucky Convention & Visitors Bureau) 50 E RiverCenter Blvd Ste 200 Covington KY 41011	877-659-8474	859-261-4677	208
NL Industries 16801 Greenspoint Pk Dr Houston TX 77060 *NYSE: NL*	800-866-5600	281-423-3300	142
NLADA (National Legal Aid & Defender Assn) 1140 Connecticut Ave NW Ste 900 Washington DC 20036	800-725-4513	202-452-0620	48-10
NLBRA (National Little Britches Rodeo Assn) 5050 Edison Ave Ste 105 Colorado Springs CO 80915	800-763-3694	719-389-0333	47-22
NLC Inc 319 W Main St Jackson MO 63755 *Sales	800-594-3958*	573-243-3141	809
NLN (National League for Nursing) 61 Broadway 33rd Fl New York NY 10006	800-669-1656	212-363-5555	48-8
NLRB (National Labor Relations Board) 1099 14th St NW Washington DC 20570	866-667-6572	202-273-1991	340-18
NMA (National Motorists Assn) 402 W Second St Waunakee WI 53597	800-882-2785	608-849-6000	48-21
NMA (National Medical Assn) 8403 Colesville Rd Ste 920 Silver Spring MD 20910	800-662-0554	202-347-1895	48-8
NMC (National Motor Club of America Inc) 130 E John Carpenter Fwy Irving TX 75062	800-523-4582	972-999-1099	52
NMCRS (Navy-Marine Corps Relief Society) 875 N Randolph St Ste 225 Arlington VA 22203	800-654-8364	703-696-4904	47-19
NMC-Wollard Inc 2021 Truax Blvd Eau Claire WI 54703	800-656-6867	715-835-3151	469
NMDP (National Marrow Donor Program) 3001 Broadway St NE Ste 100 Minneapolis MN 55413	800-526-7809	612-627-5800	47-17
NMEA (National Marine Electronics Assn) 7 Riggs Ave Severna Park MD 21146	800-808-6632	410-975-9425	48-13
NMF (National Marfan Foundation) 22 Manhasset Ave Port Washington NY 11050	800-862-7326	516-883-8712	47-17
NMFTA (National Motor Freight Traffic Assn) 1001 N Fairfax St Ste 600 Alexandria VA 22314	866-411-6632	703-838-1810	48-21
NMMS (New Mexico Medical Society) 316 Osuna Rd NE Ste 501 Albuquerque NM 87107	800-748-1596	505-828-0237	473
NMOA (National Mail Order Assn LLC) 2807 Polk St NE Minneapolis MN 55418	800-992-1377	612-788-1673	48-18
NMRA (National Marine Representatives Assn) PO Box 360 Gurnee IL 60031	800-890-3819	847-662-3167	48-18
NMRA (National Model Railroad Assn) 4121 Cromwell Rd Chattanooga TN 37421	800-654-2256	423-892-2846	47-18
NMS (North Milwaukee State Bank) 5630 W Fond Du Lac Ave Milwaukee WI 53216	800-799-5630	414-466-2344	69
NMS Capital Group LLC 433 N Camden Dr 4th Fl Beverly Hills CA 90210	800-716-2080		689
NMS Labs 3701 Welsh Rd Willow Grove PA 19090	800-522-6671	215-657-4900	418
NMSA (National Middle School Assn) 4151 Executive Pkwy Ste 300 Westerville OH 43081	800-528-6672	614-895-4730	48-5
NMSU (New Mexico State University) MSC-3A PO Box 30001 Las Cruces NM 88003 *Admissions	800-662-6678*	575-646-3121	167
NMT (New Mexico Institute of Mining & Technology) 801 Leroy Pl Socorro NM 87801 *Admissions	800-428-8324*	505-835-5434	167
NN Inc 2000 Waters Edge Dr Bldg 3 Ste 12 Johnson City TN 37604 *NASDAQ: NNBR*	877-888-0002	423-743-9151	484
NNA (Nebraska Nurses Assn) PO Box 3107 Kearney NE 68848	800-582-3014	402-475-3859	532
NNA (National Newspaper Assn) PO Box 7540 Columbia MO 65205	800-829-4662	573-777-4980	48-14
NNA (National Notary Assn) 9350 DeSoto Ave Chatsworth CA 91313	800-876-6827	818-739-4000	48-12
NNM Peterson Manufacturing Co 24133 W 143rd St Plainfield IL 60544	800-826-9086	815-436-9201	288
NNPDF (National Niemann-Pick Disease Foundation Inc) 401 Madison Ave Ste B PO Box 49 Fort Atkinson WI 53538	877-287-3672	920-563-0930	47-17
NNSDO (National Nursing Staff Development Organization) 330 N Wabash Ave Ste 2000 Chicago IL 60611	800-489-1995	312-321-5135	48-8
NNT Corp 1320 Norwood Ave Itasca IL 60143	800-556-9999	630-875-9600	454
No Fault Sports Products 2101 Briarglen Dr Houston TX 77027	800-462-7766	713-683-7101	709
No Starch Press Inc 38 Ringold St San Francisco CA 94103	800-420-7240	415-863-9900	634-2
NOAH (National Organization for Albinism & Hypopigmentation) PO Box 959 East Hampstead NH 03826	800-648-2310	603-887-2310	47-17
Nob Hill 3799 Las Vegas Blvd S MGM Grand Hotel Las Vegas NV 89109 *Resv	800-929-1111*	702-891-1111	669
Nobel Biocare USA Inc 22715 Savi Ranch Pkwy Yorba Linda CA 92887	800-993-8100	714-282-4800	230
Nobility Homes Inc 3741 SW Seventh St Ocala FL 34474 *OTC: NOBH*	800-476-6624	352-732-5157	504
Noble Corp 13135 S Dairy Ashford Rd Ste 800 Sugar Land TX 77478 *NYSE: NE*	877-285-4162	281-276-6100	539
Noble Energy Inc 100 Glenborough Dr Ste 100 Houston TX 77067 *NYSE: NBL*	800-220-5824	281-872-3100	535
Noble Ford Mercury Inc 2406 N Jefferson Way Indianola IA 50125	800-496-9984	515-961-8151	515
Noble REMC 300 Weber Rd PO Box 137 Albion IN 46701	800-933-7362	260-636-2113	247
Noble Trade Inc 7171 Jane St Concord ON L4K1A7	800-529-9805	416-754-5533	110
Nobles Co-op Electric 22636 US Hwy 59 PO Box 788 Worthington MN 56187	800-776-0517	507-372-7331	247
NobleWorks Inc 500 Paterson Plank Rd Union City NJ 07087	800-346-6253	201-420-0095	129
NOCC (National Ovarian Cancer Coalition) 2501 Oak Lawn Ave Ste 435 Dallas TX 75219	888-682-7426		47-17
NOCIRC (National Organization of Circumcision Information Resource Centers) PO Box 2512 San Anselmo CA 94979	800-727-8622	415-488-9883	47-17
NOCO Energy Corp 2440 Sheridan Dr Tonawanda NY 14150	800-500-6626	716-833-6626	578
Nodak Electric Co-op Inc 4000 32nd Ave S Grand Forks ND 58201	800-732-4373	701-746-4461	247
Noe Restaurant & Bar 4 Riverway Houston TX 77056	800-809-6664	713-871-8181	669
Noetix Corp 5010 148th Ave NE Ste 100 Redmond WA 98052	866-466-3849	425-372-2699	179
Noevir USA Inc 1095 Main St Irvine CA 92614	800-872-8817	949-660-1111	366
NOF (National Osteoporosis Foundation) 251 18th St S Ste 630 Arlington VA 22202	800-231-4222	202-223-2226	47-17
NOIA (National Ocean Industries Assn) 1120 G St NW Ste 900 Washington DC 20005	800-558-9994	202-347-6900	47-12
Nolan Co 1016 Ninth St SW Canton OH 44707	800-297-1383	330-453-7922	648
Nolin Rural Electric Co-op Corp 411 Ring Rd Elizabethtown KY 42701	888-637-4247	270-765-6153	247
Nolo.com 950 Parker St Berkeley CA 94710	800-728-3555		180-9
Nomad Energy Inc 22762 Westheimer Pkwy Ste 515 Houston TX 77450	866-387-0287		535
Nomadic Display Capitol Inc 5617 Industrial Dr Springfield VA 22151	800-336-5019	703-912-4700	318
Nomadix Inc 30851 Agoura Rd Ste 102 Agoura Hills CA 91301	800-666-2349	818-597-1500	179
Nomanco Inc 501 Nmc Dr Zebulon NC 27597	800-345-7279	919-269-6500	320-1
Non Commissioned Officers Assn (NCOA) 9330 Corporate Dr Ste 701 Selma TX 78154	800-662-2620	210-653-6161	47-19
non-linear creations Inc 987 Wellington St Ste 201 Ottawa ON K1Y2Y1	866-915-2997	613-241-2067	7
Nook Industries 4950 E 49th St Cleveland OH 44125	800-321-7800	216-271-7900	619
Noon Hour Food Products Inc 215 N Des Plaines Chicago IL 60661 *Cust Svc	888-463-6332*	312-382-1177	297-13
Nora Lighting Inc 6505 Gayhart St Commerce CA 90040	800-686-6672	323-767-2600	248
NorAm Capital Holdings Inc 15303 N Dallas Pkwy Ste 1030 Addison TX 75001	888-886-6726		318
Noranda Aluminum Inc 801 Crescent Ctr Dr Ste 600 Franklin TN 37067	800-325-8112	615-771-5700	484
Norberg-ies 4237 S 74th E Ave Tulsa OK 74145	800-739-9145	918-665-6888	727
Norbest Inc PO Box 890 Moroni UT 84646	800-453-5327		298-10

Company	Address	City	State	Zip	Toll-Free	Phone	Class
Norbord Inc	1 Toronto St Ste 600 *TSE: NBD*	Toronto	ON	M5C2W4	**888-667-2673**	416-365-0705	612
Norcal Mutual Insurance Company Inc	560 Davis St	San Francisco	CA	94111	**800-652-1051**	415-397-9700	391-5
Nor-Cal Products Inc	1967 S Oregon St	Yreka	CA	96097	**800-824-4166**	530-842-4457	594
Norcal Rental Group LLC	318 Stealth Ct	Livermore	CA	94551	**800-649-6629**	925-961-0130	266-3
Norchem Drug Testing Laboratory	1760 E Route 66	Flagstaff	AZ	86004	**844-284-1843**	928-526-1011	740
Nor-Cote International Inc	506 Lafayette Ave	Crawfordsville	IN	47933	**800-488-9180**	765-362-9180	388
Norcraft cabinetry	3020 Denmark Ave	Eagan	MN	55121	**877-888-0002**	651-234-3300	114
NORD (National Organization for Rare Disorders)	55 Kenosia Ave PO Box 1968	Danbury	CT	06813	**800-999-6673**	203-744-0100	47-17
NORD Drivesystems	800 Nord Dr	Waunakee	WI	53597	**888-314-6673**		53
Nordaas American Homes Company Inc	10091 State Hwy 22	Minnesota Lake	MN	56068	**800-658-7076**	507-462-3331	189
Nordic Ware	5005 Hwy 7	Minneapolis	MN	55416	**877-466-7342**	952-920-2888	485
Nordion	447 March Rd *NYSE: NDZ*	Ottawa	ON	K2K1X8	**800-465-3666**	613-592-2790	84
Nordisk Systems Inc	13475 SE Johnson Rd	Milwaukie	OR	97222	**800-676-2777**	503-353-7555	198
Nordson Corp	28601 Clemens Rd *NASDAQ: NDSN*	Westlake	OH	44145	**800-321-2881**	440-892-1580	386
Nordson MEDICAL	3325 S Timberline Rd	Fort Collins	CO	80525	**888-404-5837**	970-267-5200	607
Norduyn Inc	6200 Henri-Bourassa W	Montreal	QC	H4R1C3	**877-332-3210**	514-334-3210	56
Nordyne Inc	8000 Phoenix Pkwy	O'Fallon	MO	63368	**800-422-4328**	636-561-7300	14
Nor-Ell Inc	851 Hubbard Ave	Saint Paul	MN	55104	**877-276-4075**	651-487-1441	480
Norfolk Convention & Visitors Bureau	232 E Main St	Norfolk	VA	23510	**800-368-3097**	757-664-6620	208
Norfolk Daily News	PO Box 977	Norfolk	NE	68702	**877-371-1020**	402-371-1020	531-2
Norfolk Public Schools	800 E City Hall Ave	Norfolk	VA	23510	**800-846-4464**	757-628-3843	683
Norfolk Scope Arena	201 E Brambleton Ave	Norfolk	VA	23510	**800-745-3000**	757-664-6464	718
Norfolk Southern Corp	800 Princeton Ave	Bluefield	WV	24701	**800-453-2530**	304-324-2400	653
Norfolk Southern Railway Co	3 Commercial Pl	Norfolk	VA	23510	**800-635-5768**	800-453-2530	646
Norfolk State University	700 Pk Ave	Norfolk	VA	23504	**800-274-1821**	757-823-8600	167
Norforge & Machining Inc	195 N Dean St	Bushnell	IL	61422	**800-839-3706**	309-772-3124	482
Norgen Biotek Corp	3430 Schmon Pkwy	Thorold	ON	L2V4Y6	**866-667-4362**	905-227-8848	418
Norgren	5400 S Delaware St	Littleton	CO	80120	**800-514-0129**	303-794-5000	788
Noritsu Technical Services	6900 Noritsu Ave	Buena Park	CA	90620	**888-435-7448**		393
Nor-Lake Inc	727 Second St PO Box 248	Hudson	WI	54016	**800-388-5253**	715-386-2323	662
Norlift of Oregon Inc	7373 Se Milwaukie Expy	Portland	OR	97222	**888-716-2478**	503-659-5438	768
Norm Thompson Outfitters Inc	3188 NW Aloclek Dr	Hillsboro	OR	97124	**800-547-1160**	877-718-7899	458
Norm's Refrigeration & Ice Equipment Inc	1175 N Knollwood Cir	Anaheim	CA	92801	**800-933-4423**	714-236-3600	663
Norman Convention & Visitors Bureau	309 E Main St	Norman	OK	73069	**800-767-7260**	405-366-8095	208
Norman Frede Chevrolet Co	16801 Feather Craft Ln	Houston	TX	77058	**888-307-1703**	281-486-2200	56
Normand's	11639 A Jasper Ave	Edmonton	AB	T5K2S7	**866-308-4438**	780-482-2600	669
Normandale Community College	9700 France Ave S	Bloomington	MN	55431	**866-880-8740**	952-487-8200	161
NorMed	4310 S 131 Pl Ste 160	Seattle	WA	98168	**800-288-8200**		476
Norment Security Group Inc	2511 Midpark Dr	Montgomery	AL	36109	**800-466-3007**	334-281-8440	690
NORML (National Organization for the Reform of Marijuana Laws)	1600 K St NW Ste 501	Washington	DC	20006	**888-676-6765**	202-483-5500	47-8
NORPAC Foods Inc	930 W Washington St	Stayton	OR	97383	**800-733-9311**	503-769-2101	297-21
Norris Cylinder Co	4818 W Loop 281	Longview	TX	75603	**800-527-8418**	903-757-7633	225
Norris Ford	901 Merritt Blvd *Sales	Baltimore	MD	21222	**866-460-5275***	410-285-0200	56
Norris Public Power District	606 Irving St PO Box 399	Beatrice	NE	68310	**800-858-4707**	402-223-4038	247
Norris School District	6940 Calloway Dr	Bakersfield	CA	93312	**800-877-8339**	661-387-7000	190-5
Norris, Perne & French LLP	40 Pearl St N W Ste 300	Grand Rapids	MI	49503	**800-748-0544**	616-459-3421	527
Norsask Farm Equipment Ltd	Box 49	North Battleford	SK	S9A2X6	**888-446-8128**	306-445-8128	110
Norsat International Inc	110-4020 Viking Way *TSE: NII*	Richmond	BC	V6V2N2	**800-644-4562**	604-821-2800	732
Norscot Group Inc	1000 W Donges Bay Rd PO Box 998	Mequon	WI	53092	**800-653-3313**	262-241-3313	9
Norse Dairy Systems	1740 Joyce Ave	Columbus	OH	43219	**800-637-2663**	614-294-4931	297-9
Norshield Corp	3232 Mobile Hwy	Montgomery	AL	36108	**855-859-3716**	334-551-0650	350
Nor-Son Inc	7900 Hastings Rd	Baxter	MN	56425	**800-858-1722**	218-828-1722	188

Company	Address	City	State	Zip	Toll-Free	Phone	Class
Nortech Systems Inc	7550 Meridian Cir N Ste 150 *NASDAQ: NSYS*	Maple Grove	MN	55369	**800-237-9576**	952-345-2244	255
Nortek Security & Control LLC	1950 Camino Vida Roble Ste 150 *Cust Svc	Carlsbad	CA	92008	**800-421-1587***	760-438-7000	690
North Adams Common Nursing Home	175 Franklin St	North Adams	MA	01247	**800-445-4560**	413-664-4041	449
North Alabama Electric Co-op	41103 US Hwy 72	Stevenson	AL	35772	**800-572-2900**	256-437-2281	247
North American Arms Inc	2150 South 950 East	Provo	UT	84606	**800-821-5783**	801-374-9990	805
North American Assn of Food Equipment Manufacturers (NAFEM)	161 N Clark St Ste 2020	Chicago	IL	60601	**888-493-5961**	312-821-0201	48-13
North American Bldg Material Distribution Assn (NBMDA)	330 N Wabash Ave Ste 2000	Chicago	IL	60611	**888-747-7862**	312-321-6845	48-18
North American Container Corp	1811 W Oak Pkwy Ste D	Marietta	GA	30062	**800-929-0610**	770-431-4858	99
North American Council on Adoptable Children (NACAC)	970 Raymond Ave Ste 106	Saint Paul	MN	55114	**877-823-2237**	651-644-3036	47-6
North American Development Bank	203 S St Mary'S Ste 300	San Antonio	TX	78205	**800-499-6232**	210-231-8000	69
North American Enclosures Inc	65 Jetson Ln	Central Islip	NY	11722	**800-645-9209**	631-234-9500	310
North American Industries Inc	80 Holton St	Woburn	MA	01801	**800-847-8470**	781-897-4100	469
North American Industry Classification System (NAICS)	US Census Bureau 4600 Silver Hill Rd	Washington	DC	20233	**800-923-8282**	301-763-4636	340-2
North American Limousin Foundation (NALF)	7383 S Alton Way Ste 100	Englewood	CO	80112	**888-320-8747**	303-220-1693	47-2
North American Mission Board SBC	4200 N Pt Pkwy	Alpharetta	GA	30022	**800-634-2462**	770-410-6000	47-5
North American Palladium Ltd	1 University Ave Ste 402 *TSE: PDL*	Toronto	ON	M5J2J2	**888-360-7590**	416-360-7590	501
North American Pipe Corp	2801 Post Oak Blvd Ste 600	Houston	TX	77056	**855-624-7473**	713-840-7473	595
North American Plywood Corp	12343 Hawkins St *Sales	Santa Fe Springs	CA	90670	**800-421-1372***	562-941-7575	612
North American Products Corp	1180 Wernsing Rd *Cust Svc	Jasper	IN	47546	**800-457-7468***	812-482-2000	454
North American Publishing Co (NAPCO)	1500 Springarden St 12th Fl	Philadelphia	PA	19130	**800-627-2689**	215-238-5300	634-9
North American Roofing Services Inc	41 Dogwood Rd	Asheville	NC	28806	**800-551-5602**	828-687-7767	191-12
North American Savings Bank (NASB)	12520 S 71 Hwy	Grandview	MO	64030	**800-677-6272**	816-765-2200	69
North American Science Assoc Inc	6750 Wales Rd	Northwood	OH	43619	**866-666-9455**	419-666-9455	666
North American Securities Administrators Assn (NASAA)	750 First St NE Ste 1140	Washington	DC	20002	**800-222-1253**	202-737-0900	48-2
North American Specialty Glass	2175 Kumry Rd PO Box 70	Trumbauersville	PA	18970	**888-785-5962**	215-536-0333	332
North American Specialty Insurance Co	650 Elm St Ste 600	Manchester	NH	03101	**800-542-9200**	603-644-6600	391-4
North American Spine Society (NASS)	7075 Veterans Blvd	Burr Ridge	IL	60527	**877-774-6337**	630-230-3600	48-8
North American Stainless Inc	6870 Hwy 42 East	Ghent	KY	41045	**800-499-7833**	502-347-6000	360-3
North American Steel Co	18300 Miles Ave	Cleveland	OH	44128	**800-321-9310**	216-475-7300	491
North American Title Co	1855 Gateway Blvd Ste 600	Concord	CA	94520	**800-566-0370**	925-935-5599	391-6
North American Tool Corp	215 Elmwood Ave	South Beloit	IL	61080	**800-872-8277**	815-389-2300	492
North Arkansas College	1515 Pioneer Dr	Harrison	AR	72601	**800-679-6622**	870-743-3000	161
North Atlantic Refining Ltd	29 Pippy Pl PO Box 40	St. John's	NL	A1B3X2	**877-635-3645**	709-463-8811	535
North Bay & District Chamber of Commerce	1375 Seymour St	North Bay	ON	P1B8J8	**888-249-8998**	705-472-8480	137
North Bay Nissan Inc	1250 Auto Ctr Dr	Petaluma	CA	94952	**877-818-6866**	707-769-7700	56
North Bay Produce Inc	PO Box 988	Traverse City	MI	49685	**800-678-1941**		298-7
North Beach Bar & Grill	3107 Atlantic Ave	Virginia Beach	VA	23451	**800-292-3297**	757-491-1800	669
North Carolina							
Marine Fisheries Div	PO Box 769	Morehead City	NC	28557	**800-682-2632**	252-726-7021	339-34
Parks & Recreation Div	217 W Jones St 1615 MSC	Raleigh	NC	27604	**877-722-6762**	919-707-9300	339-34
Tourism Div	301 N Wilmington St	Raleigh	NC	27601	**800-847-4862**	919-733-4171	339-34
Transportation Dept	1 S Wilmington St	Raleigh	NC	27611	**877-368-4968**		339-34
Utilities Commission	4325 Mail Service Ctr	Raleigh	NC	27699	**866-380-9816**	919-733-7328	339-34
Victims Compensation Services Div	4232 Mail Service Ctr	Raleigh	NC	27699	**800-826-6200**	919-733-7974	339-34
North Carolina A & T State University	1601 E Market St *Admissions	Greensboro	NC	27411	**800-443-8964***	336-334-7946	167
North Carolina Aquarium at Fort Fisher	900 Loggerhead Rd	Kure Beach	NC	28449	**800-832-3474**	910-458-8257	39
North Carolina Aquarium on Roanoke Island	374 Airport Rd PO Box 967	Manteo	NC	27954	**800-832-3474**	252-475-2300	39
North Carolina Assn of Realtors Inc	4511 Weybridge Ln	Greensboro	NC	27407	**800-443-9956**	336-294-1415	654
North Carolina Central University	1801 Fayetteville St *Admissions	Durham	NC	27707	**877-667-7533***	919-530-6100	167
North Carolina Dental Society	1600 Evans Rd	Cary	NC	27513	**800-662-8754**	919-677-1396	229

				Toll-Free	Phone	Class
North Carolina Eye Bank Inc						
3900 Westpoint Blvd Ste F	Winston-Salem	NC	27103	**800-552-9956**	336-765-0932	271
North Carolina Foam Industries Inc						
1515 Carter St	Mount Airy	NC	27030	**800-346-8229**	336-789-9161	193-4
North Carolina Granite Corp						
151 Granite Quarry Trl						
PO Box 151	Mount Airy	NC	27030	**800-227-6242**	336-786-5141	722
North Carolina High Country Host						
1700 Blowing Rock Rd	Boone	NC	28607	**800-438-7500**	828-264-1299	208
North Carolina Medical Society						
222 N Person St	Raleigh	NC	27601	**800-722-1350**	919-833-3836	473
North Carolina Museum of Natural Sciences						
11 W Jones St	Raleigh	NC	27601	**877-462-8724**	919-733-7450	519
North Carolina Mutual Life Insurance Co						
411 W Chapel Hill St	Durham	NC	27701	**800-626-1899**	919-682-9201	391-2
North Carolina Mutual Wholesale Drug Co						
816 Ellis Rd	Durham	NC	27703	**800-800-8551**	919-596-2151	240
North Carolina Nurses Assn (NCNA)						
103 Enterprise St PO Box 12025	Raleigh	NC	27605	**800-626-2153**	919-821-4250	532
North Carolina Sports Hall of Fame						
5 E Edenton St						
NC Museum of History	Raleigh	NC	27601	**877-627-6724**	919-807-7900	521
North Carolina State Bar						
217 E Edenton St PO Box 25996	Raleigh	NC	27601	**800-662-7407**	919-828-4620	71
North Carolina State Education Assistance Authority (NCSEAA)						
PO Box 14103	Research Triangle Park	NC	27709	**800-700-1775**	919-549-8614	723
North Carolina State Ports Authority						
2202 Burnett Blvd						
PO Box 9002	Wilmington	NC	28402	**800-334-0682**	910-763-1621	617
North Carolina State University						
2200 Hillsborough St	Raleigh	NC	27695	**800-662-7301**	919-515-2011	167
North Carolina State University Libraries						
CB 7111	Raleigh	NC	27695	**877-601-0590**	919-515-2843	434-6
North Carolina Veterinary Medical Assn (NCVMA)						
1611 Jones Franklin Rd Ste 108	Raleigh	NC	27606	**800-446-2862**	919-851-5850	793
North Carolina Wesleyan College						
3400 N Wesleyan Blvd	Rocky Mount	NC	27804	**800-488-6292***	252-985-5100	167
*Admissions						
North Carolina Zoological Park						
4401 Zoo Pkwy	Asheboro	NC	27205	**800-488-0444**	336-879-7000	821
North Central Assn Commission on Accreditation & School Improvement (NCA CASI)						
9115 Westside Pkwy	Alpharetta	GA	30009	**888-413-3669**		47-1
North Central Assn Higher Learning Commission						
230 S LaSalle St	Chicago	IL	60604	**800-621-7440**	312-263-0456	48-5
North Central Bronx Hospital						
3424 Kossuth Ave	Bronx	NY	10467	**877-207-2134**	718-519-5000	374-3
North Central College						
30 N Brainard St	Naperville	IL	60540	**800-411-1861**	630-637-5800	167
North Central Electric Co-op Inc						
13978 E County Rd 56	Attica	OH	44807	**800-426-3072**	419-426-3072	247
North Central Michigan College						
1515 Howard St	Petoskey	MI	49770	**888-298-6605**	231-348-6605	161
North Central Missouri College						
1301 Main St	Trenton	MO	64683	**800-880-6180**	660-359-3948	161
North Central Pennsylvania Regional Planning & Development Commission						
651 Montmorenci Rd	Ridgway	PA	15853	**800-942-9467**	814-773-3162	196
North Central Public Power District						
1409 Main St PO Box 90	Creighton	NE	68729	**800-578-1060**	402-358-5112	247
North Central State College						
2441 Kenwood Cir	Mansfield	OH	44906	**888-755-4899**	419-755-4800	798
North Central Telephone Co-op Corp						
PO Box 70	Lafayette	TN	37083	**800-795-3272**	615-666-2151	733
North Central University						
910 Elliot Ave S	Minneapolis	MN	55404	**800-289-6222***	612-343-4460	167
*Admissions						
North Coast Clinical Laboratory Inc						
2215 Cleveland Rd	Sandusky	OH	44870	**800-325-5737**	419-626-6012	418
North Country Business Products Inc						
1112 S Railroad St SE	Bemidji	MN	56601	**800-937-4140**	218-751-4140	321
North Country Community College						
23 Santanoni Ave	Saranac Lake	NY	12983	**888-879-6222**	518-891-2915	161
North Country Federal Credit Union Inc						
69 Swift St Ste 100	South Burlington	VT	05403	**800-660-3258**	802-657-6847	221
North Country Trail Assn						
229 E Main St	Lowell	MI	49331	**866-445-3628**	616-897-5987	47-23
North Dakota						
Accountancy Board						
2701 S Columbia Rd	Grand Forks	ND	58201	**800-532-5904**	701-775-7100	339-35
Agriculture Dept						
600 E Blvd Ave Dept 602	Bismarck	ND	58505	**800-242-7535**	701-328-2231	339-35
Attorney General						
600 E Blvd Ave Dept 125	Bismarck	ND	58505	**800-366-6888**	701-328-2210	339-35
Child Support Enforcement Div						
1600 E Century Ave Ste 7	Bismarck	ND	58501	**800-231-4255**	701-328-3582	339-35
Consumer Protection Div						
1050 E Interstate Ave Ste 200	Bismarck	ND	58503	**800-472-2600**	701-328-3404	339-35
Crime Victims Compensation Program						
PO Box 5521	Bismarck	ND	58506	**800-445-2322**	701-328-6195	339-35
Economic Development & Finance Div						
1600 E Century Ave Ste 200-B	Bismarck	ND	58503	**866-432-5682**	701-328-5300	339-35
Financial Institutions Dept						
2000 Schafer St Ste G	Bismarck	ND	58501	**800-366-6888**	701-328-9933	339-35
Housing Finance Agency						
PO Box 1535	Bismarck	ND	58502	**800-292-8621**	701-328-8080	339-35
Insurance Dept						
600 E Blvd Ave Dept 401	Bismarck	ND	58505	**800-247-0560**	701-328-2440	339-35
Parks & Recreation Dept						
1600 E Century Ave Ste 3	Bismarck	ND	58503	**800-807-4723**	701-328-5357	339-35
Secretary of State						
600 E Blvd Ave Dept 108	Bismarck	ND	58505	**800-352-0867**	701-328-2900	339-35
Tourism Div						
1600 Eentury Ave Ste 200S	Bismarck	ND	58502	**800-435-5663**	701-328-2525	339-35
Veterans Affairs Dept						
4201 38th St S Ste 104	Fargo	ND	58104	**866-634-8387**	701-239-7165	339-35
Vocational Rehabilitation Div						
1237 W Divide Ave Ste 2	Bismarck	ND	58501	**800-755-2745**	701-328-8800	339-35
Workers Compensation						
1600 E Century Ave Ste 1000	Bismarck	ND	58503	**800-777-5033**	701-328-3800	339-35

				Toll-Free	Phone	Class
North Dakota Assn of Realtors						
318 W Apollo Ave	Bismarck	ND	58503	**800-279-2361**	701-355-1010	654
North Dakota Chamber of Commerce						
2000 Schafer St PO Box 2639	Bismarck	ND	58502	**800-382-1405**	701-222-0929	139
North Dakota Dental Assn						
PO Box 1332	Bismarck	ND	58501	**800-444-1330**	701-223-8870	229
North Dakota Game & Fish Dept						
100 N Bismarck Expy	Bismarck	ND	58501	**800-406-6409**	701-328-6300	519
North Dakota Legislative Council Services						
State Capitol Bldg						
600 E Blvd Ave	Bismarck	ND	58505	**800-366-6888**	701-328-2916	433
North Dakota Mill & Elevator						
1823 Mill Rd	Grand Forks	ND	58203	**800-538-7721**	701-795-7000	297-23
North Dakota State College of Science						
800 Sixth St N	Wahpeton	ND	58076	**800-342-4325**	701-671-2401	161
North Dakota State Hospital						
2605 Cir Dr	Jamestown	ND	58401	**888-862-7342**	701-253-3650	374-5
North Dakota State Library (NDSL)						
604 E Blvd Ave Dept 250	Bismarck	ND	58505	**800-472-2104**	701-328-4622	434-5
North Dakota State University						
1301 12th Ave N	Fargo	ND	58105	**800-488-6378**	701-231-8643	167
North East Mall						
1101 Melbourne St Ste 1000	Hurst	TX	76053	**877-746-6642**	817-284-3427	459
North East MS EPA						
10 PR 2050 PO Box 1037	Oxford	MS	38655	**877-234-6331**	662-234-6331	247
North European Oil Royalty Trust						
43 W Front St Ste 19A	Red Bank	NJ	07701	**800-368-5948**	732-741-4008	673
NYSE: NRT						
North Face, The						
14450 Doolittle Dr	San Leandro	CA	94577	**855-500-8639**	877-992-0111	708
North Florida Community College						
325 NW Turner Davis Dr	Madison	FL	32340	**877-501-0956**	850-973-2288	161
North Florida Lincoln Mercury						
4620 Southside Blvd	Jacksonville	FL	32216	**888-457-1949**	877-941-1435	515
North Fork Ranch (NFR)						
55395 Hwy 285 PO Box B	Shawnee	CO	80475	**800-843-7895**	303-838-9873	241
North Fulton Hospital						
3000 Hospital Blvd	Roswell	GA	30076	**877-228-3638**	770-751-2500	374-3
North Greenville University						
7801 N Tigerville Rd						
PO Box 1892	Tigerville	SC	29688	**800-468-6642**	864-977-7000	161
North Hennepin Community College						
7411 85th Ave N	Brooklyn Park	MN	55445	**800-818-0395**	763-424-0702	161
North Idaho College						
1000 W Garden Ave	Coeur d'Alene	ID	83814	**877-404-4536**	208-769-3300	161
North Iowa Area Community College						
500 College Dr	Mason City	IA	50401	**888-466-4222**	641-423-1264	161
North Island Credit Union						
5898 Copley Dr	San Diego	CA	92111	**800-848-5654***	619-656-6525	221
*Cust Svc						
North Itasca Electric Co-op Inc						
301 Main Ave PO Box 227	Bigfork	MN	56628	**800-762-4048**	218-743-3131	247
North Lake Tahoe Resort Assn						
100 N Lake Blvd	Tahoe City	CA	96145	**800-468-2463**	530-581-6900	208
North Lake Tahoe Visitors & Convention Bureau						
PO Box 1757	Tahoe City	CA	96145	**800-462-5196**	530-581-6900	208
North Los Angel County Regional Ctr						
15400 Sherman Way Ste 170	Van Nuys	CA	91406	**800-430-4263**	818-778-1900	363
North Middlesex Savings Bank Inc						
7 Main St PO Box 469	Ayer	MA	01432	**800-762-3306**	978-772-3306	69
North Milwaukee State Bank (NMS)						
5630 W Fond Du Lac Ave	Milwaukee	WI	53216	**800-799-5630**	414-466-2344	69
North Museum of Natural History & Science						
400 College Ave	Lancaster	PA	17603	**800-732-0999**	717-291-3941	519
North Olympic Peninsula Visitor & Convention Bureau						
338 W First St Ste 104						
PO Box 670	Port Angeles	WA	98362	**800-942-4042**	360-452-8552	208
North Ontario Library Service						
334 Regent St	Sudbury	ON	P3C4E2	**800-461-6348**	705-675-6467	436
North Park Lincoln						
9207 San Pedro St	San Antonio	TX	78216	**888-696-5480**	210-341-8841	56
North Park Theological Seminary						
3225 W Foster Ave	Chicago	IL	60625	**800-964-0101**	773-244-6210	168-3
North Park University						
3225 W Foster Ave	Chicago	IL	60625	**800-888-6728**	773-244-5500	167
North Plains Electric Co-op Inc						
14585 Hwy 83 N PO Box 1008	Perryton	TX	79070	**800-272-5482**	806-435-5482	247
North Platte Community College						
North						
1101 Halligan Dr	North Platte	NE	69101	**800-658-4308**	308-535-3601	161
South						
601 W State Farm Rd	North Platte	NE	69101	**800-658-4348**		161
North Ridgeville City School District						
5490 Mills Creek Ln	North Ridgeville	OH	44039	**877-644-6457**	440-327-4444	683
North San Antonio Chamber of Commerce						
12930 Country Pkwy	San Antonio	TX	78216	**877-495-5888**	210-344-4848	138
North Santiam State Recreation Area						
PO Box 549	Detroit	OR	97342	**800-551-6949**		564
North Seattle Community College						
9600 College Way N	Seattle	WA	98103	**866-427-4747**	206-527-3600	161
North Shore Bank FSB						
15700 W Bluemound Rd	Brookfield	WI	53005	**800-236-4672**	262-797-3858	69
North Shore Gas Co						
3001 Grand Ave	Waukegan	IL	60085	**866-556-6004**	847-263-3200	785
North Shore Medical Ctr						
1100 NW 95th St	Miami	FL	33150	**800-984-3434**	305-835-6000	374-3
North Shore Recycled Fibers Inc						
53 Jefferson Ave	Salem	MA	01970	**800-225-2369**	978-744-4330	658
North Shore University Hospital						
300 Community Dr	Manhasset	NY	11030	**888-214-4065**	516-562-0100	374-3
North Shore-Long Island Jewish Health System						
Bone Marrow & Blood Cell Transplant Program						
300 Community Dr	Manhasset	NY	11030	**888-321-3627**	516-562-8973	767
North Star Electric Co-op						
441 State Hwy 172 NW						
PO Box 719	Baudette	MN	56623	**888-634-2202**	218-634-2202	247
North Star Glove Co						
2916 S Steele St	Tacoma	WA	98409	**800-423-1616**	253-627-7107	154-7

Name / Address	City	State	ZIP	Toll-Free	Phone	Class
North Star Lighting Inc 2150 Parkes Dr	Broadview	IL	60155	**800-229-4330**	708-681-4330	439
North State Bank Inc 6204 Falls of Neuse Rd	Raleigh	NC	27609	**877-357-2265**	919-787-9696	360-2
North States Industries Inc 1507 92nd Ln NE	Blaine	MN	55449	**800-848-8421**	763-486-1756	577
North Suburban Medical Ctr (NSMC) 9191 Grant St	Thornton	CO	80229	**877-647-7440**	303-451-7800	374-3
North Toledo Bend State Park 2907 N Toledo Pk Rd	Zwolle	LA	71486	**888-677-6400**	318-645-4715	564
North West REC 1505 Albany Pl SE PO Box 435	Orange City	IA	51041	**800-383-0476**	712-707-4935	247
North Western Electric Co-op Inc 04125 State Rt 576 PO Box 391	Bryan	OH	43506	**800-647-6932**	419-636-5051	247
North Winds Investigations Inc 119 S Second St PO Box 1654	Rogers	AR	72756	**800-530-4514**	479-925-1612	400
Northampton Community College 3835 Green Pond Rd	Bethlehem	PA	18020	**877-543-0998**	610-861-5300	161
Monroe 3 Old Mill Rd	Tannersville	PA	18372	**877-543-0998**	570-620-9221	161
Northbridge Financial Corp 105 Adelaide St W Ste 700	Toronto	ON	M5H1P9	**855-620-6262**	416-350-4400	360-2
Northbrook Chamber of Commerce & Industry 2002 Walters Ave	Northbrook	IL	60062	**855-354-3337**	847-498-5555	138
Northcentral Technical College 1000 W Campus Dr	Wausau	WI	54401	**888-682-7144**	715-675-3331	798
NorthCoast Asset Management LLC 1 Greenwich Office Park	Greenwich	CT	06831	**800-274-5448**	203-532-7000	401
Northeast Airmotive Inc 1011 Westbrook St	Portland	ME	04102	**877-354-7881**	207-774-6318	62
Northeast Bancorp 500 Canal St *NASDAQ: NBN*	Lewiston	ME	04240	**800-284-5989**	207-786-3245	360-2
Northeast Battery & Alternator Inc 240 Washington St	Auburn	MA	01501	**800-441-8824**	508-832-2700	60
Northeast Community College 801 E Benjamin Ave PO Box 469	Norfolk	NE	68702	**800-348-9033**	402-371-2020	161
Northeast Indiana Bancorp Inc 648 N Jefferson St *OTC: NIDB*	Huntington	IN	46750	**800-550-3372**	260-356-3311	360-2
Northeast Iowa Community College *Calmar* 1625 Hwy 150 S PO Box 400	Calmar	IA	52132	**800-728-2256**	563-562-3263	161
Peosta 10250 Sundown Rd	Peosta	IA	52068	**800-728-7367**	563-556-5110	161
Northeast Mississippi Community College 101 Cunningham Blvd	Booneville	MS	38829	**800-555-2154**	662-728-7751	161
Northeast Mississippi Daily Journal 1242 S Green St	Tupelo	MS	38804	**800-264-6397**	662-842-2611	531-2
Northeast Nebraska Public Power District 1410 W Seventh St PO Box 350	Wayne	NE	68787	**800-750-9277**	402-375-1360	247
Northeast Ohio Medical University 4209 State Rt 44 PO Box 95	Rootstown	OH	44272	**800-686-2511**	330-325-2511	168-2
Northeast Oklahoma Electric Co-op Inc 443857 E Hwy 60 PO Box 948	Vinita	OK	74301	**800-256-6405**	918-256-6405	247
Northeast Pennsylvania Lions Eye Bank Inc *Lehigh Valley Hospital* 2346 Jacksonville Rd	Bethlehem	PA	18017	**800-637-2393**	610-625-3800	271
Northeast Power Report 2 Penn Plz 25th Fl	New York	NY	10121	**800-752-8878**		530-5
Northeast Rehabilitation Hospital 70 Butler St	Salem	NH	03079	**800-439-2370**	603-893-2900	374-6
Northeast Remsco Construction Inc 1433 Hwy 34 S Bldg B1	Farmingdale	NJ	07727	**800-879-8204**	732-557-6100	190-7
Northeast State Technical Community College 2425 Hwy 75 PO Box 246	Blountville	TN	37617	**800-836-7822**	423-323-3191	798
Northeast Texas Community College 1735 Chapel Hill Rd	Mount Pleasant	TX	75455	**800-870-0142**	903-572-1911	161
Northeast Wisconsin Technical College PO Box 19042	Green Bay	WI	54307	**800-422-6982**	920-498-5400	798
Northeastern Illinois University 5500 N St Louis Ave	Chicago	IL	60625	**800-393-0865**	773-442-4050	167
Northeastern Illinois University Williams Library 5500 N St Louis Ave	Chicago	IL	60625	**800-393-0865**	773-442-4470	434-6
Northeastern Junior College 100 College Ave	Sterling	CO	80751	**800-626-4637**	970-521-6600	161
Northeastern Log Homes Inc 10 Ames Rd	Kenduskeag	ME	04450	**800-624-2797**	207-884-7000	105
Northeastern State University *Muskogee* 2400 W Shawnee	Muskogee	OK	74401	**800-722-9614**	918-683-0040	167
Tahlequah 600 N Grand Ave	Tahlequah	OK	74464	**800-722-9614**	918-456-5511	167
Northeastern Technical College 1201 Chesterfield Hwy	Cheraw	SC	29520	**800-921-7399**	843-921-6900	161
Northeastern University 360 Huntington Ave	Boston	MA	02115	**855-476-3391**	617-373-2000	167
Northeastern University School of Law 400 Huntington Ave	Boston	MA	02115	**800-732-3400**	617-373-2395	168-1
Northeastern Wisconsin Zoo 305 E Walnut St Rm 102 PO Box 23600	Green Bay	WI	54301	**888-844-8070**	920-448-6242	821
Northern Arizona Regional Behavioral Health Authority Inc (NARBHA) 1300 S Yale St	Flagstaff	AZ	86001	**877-923-1400**	928-774-7128	48-15
Northern Arizona University PO Box 4084 *Admissions	Flagstaff	AZ	86011	**888-628-2968***	928-523-5511	167
Northern Arizona VA Health Care System 500 Hwy 89 N	Prescott	AZ	86313	**800-949-1005**	928-445-4860	374-8
Northern Business Products Inc PO Box 16127	Duluth	MN	55816	**800-647-8775**	218-726-0167	534
Northern California World Trade Ctr 1 Capitol Mall Ste 300	Sacramento	CA	95814	**855-667-2259**		820
Northern Contours Inc 1355 Mendota Heights Rd Ste 100	Mendota Heights	MN	55120	**866-344-8132**	651-695-1698	114
Northern Digital Inc 103 Randall Dr	Waterloo	ON	N2V1C5	**877-634-6340**	519-884-5142	407
Northern Electric Co-op Inc 39456 133nd St	Bath	SD	57427	**800-529-0310**	605-225-0310	247
Northern Electric Inc 1275 W 124th Ave	Denver	CO	80234	**877-265-0794**	303-428-6969	785
Northern Essex Community College 100 Elliott St	Haverhill	MA	01830	**800-422-4453**	978-556-3000	161
Northern Exposure Greeting Cards 2301 Circadian Way Ste 300	Santa Rosa	CA	95407	**800-237-3524**	707-546-2153	129
Northern Factory Sales Inc PO Box 660	Willmar	MN	56201	**800-328-8900**	320-235-2288	60
Northern Funds PO Box 75986	Chicago	IL	60675	**800-595-9111**		527
Northern Highland - American Legion State Forest 4125 County Hwy M	Boulder Junction	WI	54512	**800-847-9367**	715-385-2727	564
Northern Illinois University 1425 W Lincoln Hwy	DeKalb	IL	60115	**800-892-3050**	815-753-1000	167
Northern Illinois University College of Law Swen Parson Hall	DeKalb	IL	60115	**800-892-3050**	815-753-9655	168-1
Northern Indiana Commuter Transportation District 33 E US Hwy 12	Chesterton	IN	46304	**800-743-3333**	219-926-5744	467
Northern Industrial Sales Ltd 3526 Opie Cres	Prince George	BC	V2N2P9	**800-668-3317**	250-562-4435	688
Northern Institutional Funds 801 S Canal St C5S	Chicago	IL	60607	**800-637-1380**		527
Northern Jet Management 5500 44th St SE	Grand Rapids	MI	49512	**800-462-7709**	616-336-4800	23
Northern Kentucky Convention & Visitors Bureau (NKYCVB) 50 E RiverCenter Blvd Ste 200	Covington	KY	41011	**877-659-8474**	859-261-4677	208
Northern Kentucky University Nunn Dr *Admissions	Highland Heights	KY	41099	**800-637-9948***	859-572-5220	167
Northern Kentucky Water District 2835 Crescent Springs Rd	Erlanger	KY	41018	**800-772-4636**	859-578-9898	785
Northern Lights Inc 4420 14th Ave NW	Seattle	WA	98107	**800-762-0165**	206-789-3880	264
Northern Michigan University 1401 Presque Isle Ave	Marquette	MI	49855	**800-682-9797**	906-227-2650	167
Northern Natural Gas Co 1111 S 103rd St	Omaha	NE	68124	**877-654-0646**	402-398-7000	326
Northern Neck Electric Co-op Inc 85 St Johns St PO Box 288	Warsaw	VA	22572	**800-243-2860**	804-333-3621	247
Northern New Mexico College 921 Paseo de Onate	Espanola	NM	87532	**800-477-3632**	505-747-2100	161
Northern New York Library Network 6721 Us Hwy 11	Potsdam	NY	13676	**877-833-1674**	315-265-1119	434-3
Northern Oak Capital Management Inc 555 E Wells St Ste 1625	Milwaukee	WI	53202	**888-283-1884**	414-278-0590	196
Northern Ohio Printing Inc 4721 Hinckley Indus Pkwy	Cleveland	OH	44109	**800-407-7284**	216-398-0000	626
Northern Plains Electric Co-op 1515 W Main St	Carrington	ND	58421	**800-882-2500**	701-652-3156	247
Northern Power Systems Inc 29 Pitman Rd	Barre	VT	05641	**877-906-6784**	802-461-2955	666
Northern Quest Casino 100 N Hayford Rd	Airway Heights	WA	99001	**877-871-6772**	509-242-7000	132
Northern Regional Correctional Facility 112 Northern Regional Correctional Dr	Moundsville	WV	26041	**866-984-8463**	304-843-4067	215
Northern Security Insurance Co PO Box 188	Montpelier	VT	05601	**800-451-5000**	802-223-2341	391-4
Northern State University 1200 S Jay St	Aberdeen	SD	57401	**800-678-5330**	605-626-3011	167
Northern States Financial Corp 1601 N Lewis Ave *OTC: NSFC*	Waukegan	IL	60085	**800-339-4432**	847-244-6000	360-2
Northern Tool & Equipment Co 2800 Southcross Dr W *Cust Svc	Burnsville	MN	55306	**800-222-5381***	952-894-9510	364
Northern Transportation Co Ltd 42003 Mackenzie Hwy	Hay River	NT	X0E0R9	**866-935-6825**	867-587-2442	314
Northern Trust Co 50 S LaSalle St *NASDAQ: NTRS*	Chicago	IL	60603	**888-289-6542**	312-630-6000	69
Northern Trust Company of Connecticut 300 Atlantic St Ste 400	Stamford	CT	06901	**866-876-9944**	312-630-0779	401
Northern Video Systems Inc 3625 Cincinnati Ave	Rocklin	CA	95765	**800-366-4472**	916-543-4000	248
Northern Virginia Community College *Alexandria* 3001 N Beauregard St	Alexandria	VA	22311	**855-259-1019**	703-845-6200	161
Annandale 8333 Little River Tpke	Annandale	VA	22003	**877-408-2028**	703-323-3000	161
Manassas 6901 Sudley Rd	Manassas	VA	20109	**855-259-1019**	703-257-6600	161
Northern Virginia Electric Co-op PO Box 2710	Manassas	VA	20108	**888-335-0500**	703-335-0500	247
Northern Waters Library Service 3200 E Lakeshore Dr	Ashland	WI	54806	**800-228-5684**	715-682-2365	434-3
Northern Westchester Hospital 400 E Main St	Mount Kisco	NY	10549	**877-469-4362**	914-666-1200	374-3
Northern Wholesale Supply Inc 6800 Otter Lk Rd	Lino Lakes	MN	55038	**800-333-7777**	651-429-1515	709
Northfield an Oldcastle Co 2200 S Main St	West Bend	WI	53095	**800-227-6512**	262-338-5700	185
Northfield Block Co 1 Hunt Ct	Mundelein	IL	60060	**800-358-3003**	847-949-3600	722
Northfield Lines Inc 32611 Northfield Blvd	Northfield	MN	55057	**888-670-8068**	507-645-5267	106
Northfield Mount Hermon School 1 Lamplighter Way	Gill	MA	01354	**866-664-4483**	413-498-3227	621
Northfield Savings Bank (NSB) PO Box 347	Northfield	VT	05663	**800-672-2274**	802-485-5871	69
Northland Auto & Truck Accessories 1106 S 29th St W	Billings	MT	59102	**800-736-5302**	406-245-0595	53
Northland College 1411 Ellis Ave	Ashland	WI	54806	**800-753-1840**	715-682-1224	167
Northland Community & Technical College 1101 US Hwy 1 E	Thief River Falls	MN	56701	**800-959-6282**	218-681-0701	161

Name	Address	City	State	ZIP	Toll-Free	Phone	Class
East Grand Forks	2022 Central Ave NE	East Grand Forks	MN	56721	**800-451-3441**	218-773-3441	161
Northland Corp	1260 E Van Deinse St	Greenville	MI	48838	**800-223-3900**		35
Northland Fishing Tackle LLC	1001 Naylor Dr Se	Bemidji	MN	56601	**800-786-3474**	218-751-6723	709
Northland Insurance Co	385 Washington St	Saint Paul	MN	55102	**800-237-9334**		391-4
Northland Pioneer College	PO Box 610	Holbrook	AZ	86025	**800-266-7845**	928-532-6111	161
Northland Plastics Inc	1420 S 16th St PO Box 290	Sheboygan	WI	53081	**800-776-7163**		599
Northland Services Inc	6700 W Marginal Way SW	Seattle	WA	98106	**800-426-3113**	206-763-3000	313
Northland Trucking Inc	1515 S 22nd Ave	Phoenix	AZ	85009	**800-214-5564**	602-254-0007	778
Northleaf Capital Partners	79 Wellington St W Sixth Fl PO Box 120	Toronto	ON	M5K1N9	**866-964-4141**		790
Northpoint Escrow & Title LLC	10800 NE Eighth St Ste 200	Bellevue	WA	98004	**877-678-1678**	425-453-8880	391-6
Northport Medical Ctr	2700 Hospital Dr	Northport	AL	35476	**866-840-0750**	205-333-4500	374-3
Northrim BanCorp Inc	3111 C St *NASDAQ: NRIM*	Anchorage	AK	99503	**800-478-3311**	907-562-0062	69
Northrop Grumman Newport News	13560 Jefferson Ave	Newport News	VA	23603	**888-493-7386**	757-886-7777	696
Northshire Information Inc	4869 Main St	Manchester Center	VT	05255	**800-437-3700**	802-362-2200	95
Northspan Group Inc, The	221 W First St	Duluth	MN	55802	**800-232-0707**	218-722-5545	198
Northstar Cruises	80 Bloomfield Ave Ste 102	Caldwell	NJ	07006	**800-249-9360**		769
Northstar Investment Advisors LLC	700 17th St Ste 2350	Denver	CO	80202	**800-204-6199**	303-832-2300	527
NorthStar Moving Corp	9120 Mason Ave	Chatsworth	CA	91311	**800-275-7767**	818-727-0128	518
Northstar-at-Tahoe	PO Box 129	Truckee	CA	96160	**800-466-6784**		667
Northtown Products Inc	5202 Argosy Ave	Huntington Beach	CA	92649	**800-972-7274**	714-897-0700	540
Northumberland County	201 Market St 2nd Fl	Sunbury	PA	17801	**800-692-4332**	570-988-4167	338
Northview Public School	4451 Hunsberger NE	Grand Rapids	MI	49525	**866-632-9992**	616-363-4857	683
Northville Downs	301 S Ctr St	Northville	MI	48167	**888-349-7100**	248-349-1000	639
Northway Toyota	727 New Loudon Rd	Latham	NY	12110	**877-525-3488**	877-800-5098	56
Northwest Administrators Inc	2323 Eastlake Ave E	Seattle	WA	98102	**877-304-6702**	206-329-4900	390
Northwest Aluminum Specialties Inc	2929 W Second St	The Dalles	OR	97058	**800-626-2241**	541-296-6161	491
Northwest Arctic Borough	PO Box 1110	Kotzebue	AK	99752	**800-478-1110**	907-442-2500	338
NorthWest Arkansas Community College	1 College Dr	Bentonville	AR	72712	**800-995-6922**	479-636-9222	161
Northwest Arkansas Regional Airport	1 Airport Blvd Ste 100	Bentonville	AR	72712	**800-433-7300**	479-205-1000	27
Northwest Bancorp Inc	PO Box 128	Warren	PA	16365	**800-859-1000**	814-728-7263	360-2
Northwest Bedding	6102 S Hayford Rd	Spokane	WA	99224	**800-456-7686**	509-244-3000	470
Northwest Christian College	828 E 11th Ave	Eugene	OR	97401	**877-463-6622**	541-343-1641	167
Northwest College	231 W Sixth St	Powell	WY	82435	**800-560-4692**	307-754-6000	161
Northwest Community Bank	86 Main St PO Box 1019	Winsted	CT	06098	**800-455-6668**	860-379-7561	69
Northwest Data Solutions LLC	2627 C St	Anchorage	AK	99503	**800-544-0786**	907-227-1676	179
Northwest Designs Ink Inc	13456 SE 27th Pl Ste 200	Bellevue	WA	98005	**800-925-9327**		156-5
Northwest Florida Daily News	PO Box 2949	Fort Walton Beach	FL	32549	**800-755-1185**	850-863-1111	531-2
Northwest Grain Growers Inc	850 N Fourth Ave	Walla Walla	WA	99362	**800-994-4290**	509-525-6510	277
Northwest Herald Inc	PO Box 250	Crystal Lake	IL	60039	**800-589-8910**	815-459-4040	634-8
Northwest Hospital & Medical Ctr	1550 N 115th St	Seattle	WA	98133	**877-694-4677**	206-364-0500	374-3
Northwest Hospital Ctr	5401 Old Ct Rd	Randallstown	MD	21133	**800-876-1175**	410-521-2200	374-3
Northwest Indian College	2522 Kwina Rd	Bellingham	WA	98226	**866-676-2772**	360-676-2772	164
Northwest Iowa Community College	603 W Pk St	Sheldon	IA	51201	**800-352-4907**	712-324-5061	161
Northwest Missouri Psychiatric Rehabilitation Ctr	3505 Frederick Ave	Saint Joseph	MO	64506	**800-273-8255**	816-387-2300	374-5
Northwest Missouri State University	800 University Dr	Maryville	MO	64468	**800-633-1175**	660-562-1148	167
Northwest Natural Gas Co	220 NW Second Ave *NYSE: NWN*	Portland	OR	97209	**800-422-4012**	503-226-4211	785
Northwest Nazarene University	623 Holly St *Admissions	Nampa	ID	83686	**877-668-4968***	208-467-8000	167
Northwest Outlet	1814 Belknap St	Superior	WI	54880	**800-569-8142**	715-392-9838	709
Northwest Pennsylvania's Great Outdoors Visitors Bureau	2801 Maplevale Rd	Brookville	PA	15825	**800-348-9393**	814-849-5197	208
Northwest Pipe Co	12005 N Burgard *NASDAQ: NWPX*	Portland	OR	97203	**800-989-9631**	503-285-1400	489
Northwest Pipe Fittings Inc	33 S Eigth St W	Billings	MT	59101	**800-937-4737**	406-252-0142	611
Northwest Print Strategies Inc	8175 Sw Nimbus Ave	Beaverton	OR	97008	**800-648-5156**	503-641-5156	588
Northwest Rural Public Power District	5613 State Hwy 87 PO Box 249	Hay Springs	NE	69347	**800-847-0492**	308-638-4445	247
Northwest Savings Bank	100 Liberty St PO Box 128	Warren	PA	16365	**800-822-2009**	814-726-2140	69
Northwest Texas Hospital	1501 S Coulter	Amarillo	TX	79106	**800-887-1114**	806-354-1000	374-3
Northwest University	5520 108th Ave NE *Admissions	Kirkland	WA	98033	**800-669-3781***	425-822-8266	167
Northwest Wholesale Inc	1567 N Wenatchee Ave	Wenatchee	WA	98801	**800-874-6607**	509-662-2141	278
Northwestern College	101 Seventh St SW	Orange City	IA	51041	**800-747-4757**	712-707-7000	167
Northwestern College Chicago Campus	4829 N Lipps Ave	Chicago	IL	60630	**888-205-2283**	773-777-4220	798
Northwestern Corp	PO Box 490	Morris	IL	60450	**800-942-1316**	815-942-1300	54
Northwestern Counseling & Support Services Inc	107 Fisher Pond Rd	Saint Albans	VT	05478	**800-834-7793**	802-524-6554	353
Northwestern Electric Co-op Inc	2925 William Ave	Woodward	OK	73802	**800-375-7423**	580-256-7425	247
Northwestern Industries Inc	2500 W Jameson St	Seattle	WA	98199	**800-426-2771**	206-285-3140	330
Northwestern Michigan College	1701 E Front St	Traverse City	MI	49686	**800-748-0566**	231-995-1000	161
Northwestern Mutual Investment Services LLC	611 E Wisconsin Ave Ste 300	Milwaukee	WI	53202	**866-664-7737**		401
Northwestern Ohio Security Systems Inc	121 E High St	Lima	OH	45801	**800-833-6416**	614-527-7037	691
Northwestern Pacific Indemnity Co	15 Mtn View Rd *Claims	Warren	NJ	07059	**800-252-4670***	908-903-2000	391-4
Northwestern Polytechnic University	47671 Westinghouse Dr	Fremont	CA	94539	**877-878-8883**	510-592-9688	167
Northwestern Publishing House	1250 N 113th St *Orders	Milwaukee	WI	53226	**800-662-6022***	414-475-6600	634-3
Northwestern Rural Electric Co-op Assn Inc	22534 State Rte Ste 86	Cambridge Springs	PA	16403	**800-352-0014**	800-472-7910	247
Northwestern State University	175 Sam Sibley Dr	Natchitoches	LA	71497	**800-767-8115**	318-357-4078	167
Northwestern State University Watson Memorial Library	913 University Pkwy	Natchitoches	LA	71497	**888-540-9657**	318-357-4477	434-6
Northwestern Tools Inc	3130 Valleywood Dr	Dayton	OH	45429	**800-236-3956**	937-298-9994	755
Northwestern University	1801 Hinman Ave	Evanston	IL	60208	**800-227-7368**	847-491-7271	167
Northwestern University School of Law	357 E Chicago Ave	Chicago	IL	60611	**800-229-2032**	312-503-3100	168-1
Northwest-Shoals Community College							
Muscle Shoals	800 George Wallace Blvd	Muscle Shoals	AL	35661	**800-645-8967**	256-331-5200	161
Phil Campbell	2080 College Rd	Phil Campbell	AL	35581	**800-645-8967**	256-331-6200	161
Northwood University							
Texas	1114 W FM 1382	Cedar Hill	TX	75104	**800-927-9663**	972-291-1541	167
Northwood University Florida	2600 N Military Trl *Admissions	West Palm Beach	FL	33409	**800-458-8325***	561-478-5500	167
Northwood University Michigan	4000 Whiting Dr	Midland	MI	48640	**800-622-9000**	989-837-4200	167
Norton Sandblasting Equipment	1006 Executive Blvd	Chesapeake	VA	23320	**800-366-4341**	757-548-4842	1
Norton's Flowers & Gifts	2900 Washtenaw Ave	Ypsilanti	MI	48197	**800-682-8667**	734-434-2700	294
Norwalk Chamber of Commerce	12040 Foster Rd	Norwalk	CA	90650	**800-427-2200**	562-864-7785	138
Norwalk Community College	188 Richards Ave	Norwalk	CT	06854	**800-565-3036**	203-857-7060	161
Norwalk Compressor Co	1650 Stratford Ave	Stratford	CT	06615	**800-556-5001**	203-386-1234	174
Norwalk Concert Hall	125 E Ave	Norwalk	CT	06851	**800-357-9577**	203-854-7900	571
Norwalk Concrete Industries Inc	80 Commerce Dr	Norwalk	OH	44857	**800-733-3624**	419-668-8167	185
Norwalk Public Library	1 Belden Ave	Norwalk	CT	06850	**800-382-9463**	203-899-2780	434-3
Norwegian-American Hospital	1044 N Francisco St	Chicago	IL	60622	**877-624-9333**	773-292-8200	374-3
Norwell Manufacturing Inc	82 Stevens St	East Taunton	MA	02718	**800-822-2831**	508-823-1751	439
Norwich University	158 Harmon Dr	Northfield	VT	05663	**800-468-6679**	802-485-2001	167
Norwin Chamber of Commerce	321 Main St	Irwin	PA	15642	**800-395-5665**	724-863-0888	138
Norwood Hotel	112 Marion St	Winnipeg	MB	R2H0T1	**888-888-1878**	204-233-4475	379
Norwood Marking Systems	2538 Wisconsin Ave	Downers Grove	IL	60515	**800-626-3464**	630-968-0646	466
Norwood Promotional Products Inc	14421 Myerlake Cir	Clearwater	IN	33760	**877-555-2223**	727-538-3527	9
Nossi College of Art	590 Cheron Rd	Madison	TN	37115	**888-986-2787**	615-514-2787	167
Not Rocket Science Inc	251 Hwy 21	Madisonville	LA	70447	**888-785-8896**	985-845-2334	179
Notre Dame de Namur University	1500 Ralston Ave	Belmont	CA	94002	**800-263-0545**	650-508-3600	167
Nottawaseppi Huron Band of Potawatomi's FireKeepers Development Authority	11177 E Michigan Ave	Battle Creek	MI	49014	**877-353-8777**		294
Nottoway Plantation	31025 Louisiana Hwy 1	White Castle	LA	70788	**866-527-6884**	225-545-2730	519
Notus Career Management	5 Centerpointe Dr Ste 400	Lake Oswego	OR	97035	**800-431-1990**		40

Name / Address	City	State	Zip	Toll-Free	Phone	Class
Nouvelles Images Inc						
68 Morgan Ave	Danbury	CT	06810	**800-345-1383**	203-730-1004	129
NOV (National Oilwell Varco)						
7909 Parkwood Cir Dr	Houston	TX	77036	**888-262-8645**	713-375-3700	185
NYSE: NOV						
NOVA (National Organization for Victim Assistance)						
510 King St Ste 424	Alexandria	VA	22314	**800-879-6682**	703-535-6682	47-8
Nova Biomedical Corp						
200 Prospect St	Waltham	MA	02454	**800-458-5813***	781-894-0800	419
*Sales						
NOVA Chemicals Corp						
1000 Seventh Ave SW PO Box 2518	Calgary	AB	T2P5C6	**866-289-6682**	403-750-3600	604-2
Nova Express Millennium Inc						
105 - 14271 Knox Way	Richmond	BC	V6V2Z4	**877-566-6839**	604-278-8044	318
Nova Fisheries						
2532 Yale Ave E	Seattle	WA	98102	**888-458-6682**	206-781-2000	287
Nova Fitness Equipment						
4511 S 119th Cir	Omaha	NE	68137	**800-949-6682**	402-343-0552	709
Nova Libra Inc						
8609 W Bryn Mawr Ave Ste 208	Chicago	IL	60631	**866-724-1807**	773-714-1441	179
Nova Pole International Inc						
19433 96th Ave Ste 102	Surrey	BC	V4N4C4	**866-874-8889**	604-881-0090	263
Nova Power Solutions						
23020 Eaglewood Ct Ste 100	Sterling	VA	20166	**800-999-6682**		765
Nova Scotia Dept of Tourism & Culture						
1800 Argyle St PO Box 456	Halifax	NS	B3J2R5	**800-565-0000**	902-425-5781	772
Nova Scotia Power Inc						
PO Box 910	Halifax	NS	B3J2W5	**800-428-6230**	902-428-6230	785
Nova Solutions Inc						
421 Industrial Ave	Effingham	IL	62401	**800-730-6682**	217-342-7070	320-1
Nova Southeastern University						
3301 College Ave	Fort Lauderdale	FL	33314	**800-541-6682**	954-262-8000	167
Nova Southeastern University Shepard Broad Law Ctr						
3305 College Ave	Fort Lauderdale	FL	33314	**800-986-6529**	954-262-6100	168-1
Nova Tours & Travel Inc						
504 Vine St	Liverpool	NY	13088	**800-543-6682**	315-451-0260	773
Nova Voice & Data Systems Inc						
3909 Oceanic Dr Ste 401	Oceanside	CA	92056	**800-558-6744**	760-439-5200	181
Novacel 21 Third St	Palmer	MA	01069	**877-668-2235**	413-283-3468	547
Novacoast Inc						
1505 Chapala St	Santa Barbara	CA	93101	**800-949-9933**		182
Novacopy Inc						
7251 Appling Farms Pkwy	Memphis	TN	38133	**800-264-0637**	901-388-3399	534
Novagard Solutions Inc						
5109 Hamilton Ave	Cleveland	OH	44114	**800-380-0138**	216-881-8111	327
NovaGold Resources Inc						
789 W Pender St Ste 720	Vancouver	BC	V6C1H2	**866-699-6227**	604-669-6227	501
NYSE: NG						
Novar Controls Corp						
6060 Rockside Woods Blvd Ste 400	Cleveland	OH	44131	**800-348-1235**		204
Novare Capital Management						
521 E Morehead St The Morehead Bldg Ste 510	Charlotte	NC	28202	**877-334-3698**	704-334-3698	527
Novartis Pharmaceuticals Canada Inc						
385 boul Bouchard	Dorval	QC	H9S1A9	**800-465-2244**	514-631-6775	582
Novartis Pharmaceuticals Co						
10401 Cornhusker Hwy	Waverly	NE	68462	**888-669-6682**	862-778-2100	582
Novastar Financial Inc						
2114 Central Ste 600	Kansas City	MO	64108	**800-591-1137**	816-237-7000	652
Novatec Inc						
222 Thomas Ave	Baltimore	MD	21225	**800-237-8379**	410-789-4811	319
Novatech Group Inc						
160 Murano St	Sainte-julie	QC	J3E0C6	**844-986-8001**		331
Novatel Wireless Inc						
9645 Scranton Rd Ste 205	San Diego	CA	92121	**888-888-9231**		175-3
NASDAQ: NVTL						
Novato Chamber of Commerce						
807 DeLong Ave	Novato	CA	94945	**800-897-1164**	415-897-1164	138
Novavax Inc						
9920 Belward Campus Dr	Rockville	MD	20850	**800-642-1687**	240-268-2000	84
NASDAQ: NVAX						
Novelis North America						
3560 Lenox Rd Ste 2000	Atlanta	GA	30326	**800-892-1819**	404-760-4000	484
Novell Design Studio						
2100 Felver Ct	Rahway	NJ	07065	**888-668-3551**		409
Novell Inc						
1800 S Novell Pl	Provo	UT	84606	**800-529-3400**	801-861-4272	180-1
Noveo Technologies Inc						
9655 A Ignace St	Brossard	QC	J4Y2P3	**877-314-2044**	450-444-2044	609
Novex Software Developments Inc						
8743 Commercial St	New Minas	NS	B4N3C4	**888-542-1813**	902-542-1813	179
Novi Chamber of Commerce, The						
41875 W 11 Mile Rd Ste 201	Novi	MI	48375	**888-440-7325**	248-349-3743	138
NOVIPRO Inc						
2055 Peel St Ste 701	Montreal	QC	H3A1V4	**866-726-5353**	514-744-5353	182
Novo Nordisk of North America Inc						
100 College Rd W	Princeton	NJ	08540	**800-727-6500**	609-987-5800	582
Novo Nordisk Pharmaceuticals Inc						
800 Scudders Mill Rd	Princeton	NJ	08536	**800-727-6500***	609-987-5800	582
*Cust Svc						
Novo Solutions Inc						
516 S Independence Blvd	Virginia Beach	VA	23452	**888-316-4559**	757-687-6590	182
novoGI Inc						
PO Box 12363	Atlanta	GA	30355	**866-295-7125**		474
Novosci						
2021 Airport Rd	Conroe	TX	77301	**800-854-0567**	281-363-4949	475
Novotus LLC						
5508 Parkcrest Dr Ste 100	Austin	TX	78731	**800-856-0143**	512-733-2244	196
Novus Inc						
655 Calle Cubitas	Guaynabo	PR	00969	**888-530-4546**	787-272-4546	302
Novus Law LLC						
8770 W Bryn Mawr Ave	Chicago	IL	60631	**877-668-8752**		444
NOVX Systems Inc						
9133 Leslie St Ste 110	Richmond Hill	ON	L4B4N1	**877-879-6689**	905-474-5051	740
NOW (National Organization for Women)						
1100 H St NW 3rd Fl	Washington	DC	20005	**855-212-0212**	202-628-8669	47-24
Now Courier Inc						
PO Box 6066	Indianapolis	IN	46206	**800-543-6066**		458
NOW Inc						
7402 N Eldridge Pkwy	Houston	TX	77041	**800-228-2893**	281-823-4700	538
NowDocs International Inc						
1985 Lookout Dr	North Mankato	MN	56003	**888-669-3627**		179
Nowhirecom						
21220 Kelly Rd	Eastpointe	MI	48021	**800-724-8546**	586-778-8491	262
Nox-Crete Inc						
1444 S 20th St	Omaha	NE	68108	**800-669-2738**	402-341-2080	144
Noxent Inc						
6400 Boul Taschereau Bur 220	Brossard	QC	J4W3J2	**800-268-4364**		198
Noxubee County						
503 S Washington St PO Box 308	Macon	MS	39341	**800-487-0165**		338
NP Dodge Real Estate						
8701 W Dodge Rd Ste 300	Omaha	NE	68114	**800-642-5008**	402-397-4900	650
NPA (National Parking Assn)						
1112 16th St NW Ste 840	Washington	DC	20036	**800-647-7275**	202-296-4336	48-3
Npa Computers Inc						
751 Coates Ave	Holbrook	NY	11741	**800-873-6724**	631-467-2500	177
NPAP (National Psychological Assn for Psychoanalysis)						
40 W 13th St Ste 1	New York	NY	10011	**800-365-7006**	212-924-7440	48-15
NPC (Navy Personnel Command)						
5720 Integrity Dr	Millington	TN	38055	**866-827-5672**	901-874-3165	340-5
NPC (National Pen Corp)						
12121 Scripps Summit Dr Ste 200	San Diego	CA	92131	**800-854-1000**	858-675-3000	9
NPC International Inc						
7300 W 129th St	Overland Park	KS	66213	**866-299-1148**	913-327-5555	668
NPCA (National Precast Concrete Assn)						
10333 N Meridian St Ste 272	Indianapolis	IN	46290	**800-366-7731**	317-571-9500	48-3
NPCA (National Paint & Coatings Assn)						
1500 Rhode Island Ave NW	Washington	DC	20005	**800-647-5527**	202-462-6272	48-13
NPCA (National Parks Conservation Assn)						
1300 19th St NW Ste 300	Washington	DC	20036	**800-628-7275**	202-223-6722	47-13
NPCA (National Peace Corps Assn)						
1900 L St NW Ste 610	Washington	DC	20036	**800-424-8580**	202-293-7728	47-5
NPD Group Inc						
900 W Shore Rd	Port Washington	NY	11050	**866-444-1411**	516-625-0700	465
NPES: Assn for Suppliers of Printing Publishing & Converting Technologies						
1899 Preston White Dr	Reston	VA	20191	**866-381-9839**	703-264-7200	48-16
NPF (National Psoriasis Foundation)						
6600 SW 92nd Ave Ste 300	Portland	OR	97223	**800-723-9166**	503-244-7404	47-17
NPI (National Property Inspections Inc)						
9375 Burt St Ste 201	Omaha	NE	68114	**800-333-9807**	402-333-9807	365
NPIC (National Pesticide Information Ctr)						
333 Weniger Hall	Corvallis	OR	97331	**800-858-7378**		47-17
NPSS (IEEE Nuclear & Plasma Sciences Society)						
445 Hoes Ln	Piscataway	NJ	08854	**800-678-4333**	732-562-5501	48-19
NPTA Alliance						
330 N Wabash Ave Ste 2000	Chicago	IL	60611	**800-355-6782**	312-321-4092	48-18
nQueue Inc						
7890 S Hardy Dr Ste 105	Tempe	AZ	85284	**800-299-5933**		182
NRA (National Rehabilitation Assn)						
633 S Washington St	Alexandria	VA	22314	**888-258-4295**	703-836-0850	47-17
NRA (National Restaurant Assn)						
2055 L St NW Ste 700	Washington	DC	20036	**800-424-5156**	202-331-5900	48-6
NRA (Naval Reserve Assn)						
1619 King St	Alexandria	VA	22314	**877-628-9411**	703-548-5800	47-19
NRA Institute for Legislative Action						
11250 Waples Mill Rd	Fairfax	VA	22030	**800-392-8683**		614
NRC Sports Inc						
603 Pleasant St	Paxton	MA	01612	**800-243-5033**		458
NRCA (National Roofing Contractors Assn)						
10255 W Higgins Rd Ste 600	Rosemont	IL	60018	**800-323-9545***	847-299-9070	48-3
*Cust Svc						
NRCCE (National Research Ctr for Coal & Energy)						
West Virginia University						
385 Evansdale Dr PO Box 6064	Morgantown	WV	26506	**800-624-8301**	304-293-2867	666
NRCDV (National Resource Ctr on Domestic Violence)						
6400 Flank Dr Ste 1300	Harrisburg	PA	17112	**800-799-7233**		47-6
NRCNAA (National Resource Ctr on Native American Aging)						
501 N Columbia Rd Rm 4535	Grand Forks	ND	58202	**800-896-7628**	701-777-6780	47-6
NRD LLC						
2937 Alt Blvd PO Box 310	Grand Island	NY	14072	**800-525-8076**	716-773-7634	203
NREC (National Railway Equipment Co)						
14400 Robey St	Dixmoor	IL	60426	**800-253-2905**	708-388-6002	648
NREC Power Systems						
5222 Hwy 311	Houma	LA	70360	**800-851-6732**	985-872-5480	264
NRECA (National Rural Electric Co-op Assn)						
4301 Wilson Blvd	Arlington	VA	22203	**866-759-2619**	703-907-5939	47-12
NRF (National Retail Federation)						
1101 New York Ave NW	Washington	DC	20005	**800-673-4692**	202-783-7971	48-18
NRHA (National Retail Hardware Assn)						
5822 W 74th St	Indianapolis	IN	46278	**800-772-4424***	317-290-0338	48-18
*Cust Svc						
NRMCA (National Ready Mixed Concrete Assn)						
900 Spring St	Silver Spring	MD	20910	**888-846-7622**	301-587-1400	48-3
NRRI (Natural Resources Research Institute)						
University of Minnesota Duluth						
5013 Miller Trunk Hwy	Duluth	MN	55811	**800-234-0054**	218-720-4294	666
NRRS (National Recreation Reservation Service)						
PO Box 140	Ballston Spa	NY	12020	**877-444-6777**	518-885-3639	771
NRS (National Runaway Switchboard)						
3141 N Lincoln Ave	Chicago	IL	60657	**800-786-2929**	773-880-9860	47-6
NRS (Nationwide Recovery Systems Inc)						
4635 McEwen Rd	Dallas	TX	75244	**800-458-6357**	972-798-1000	159
NRSF (National Reye's Syndrome Foundation)						
426 N Lewis St	Bryan	OH	43506	**800-233-7393**	419-924-9000	47-17
NRTA/AARP Bulletin						
601 E St NW	Washington	DC	20049	**888-867-2277**	202-434-2277	530-6
NRTWC (National Right to Work Committee)						
8001 Braddock Rd Ste 500	Springfield	VA	22160	**800-325-7892**	703-321-8510	48-12
NRV Inc						
N8155 American St	Ixonia	WI	53036	**800-558-0002**	920-261-7000	446
NSA (National Stroke Assn)						
9707 E Easter Ln	Centennial	CO	80112	**800-787-6537***		47-17
*Cust Svc						
NSA (National Association of Nonprofit Accountants & Consultants)						
624 Grassmere Park Dr Ste 15	Nashville	TN	37211	**800-231-2524**	615-373-9880	48-1

	Toll-Free	Phone	Class
NSA (National Safety Apparel Inc) 15825 Industrial Pkwy Cleveland OH 44135	800-553-0672		575
NSA (National Stuttering Assn) 119 W 40th St 14th Fl New York NY 10018	800-937-8888	212-944-4050	47-17
NSA (National Sheriffs' Assn) 1450 Duke St Alexandria VA 22314	800-424-7827	703-836-7827	48-7
NSA (National Society of Accountants) 1010 N Fairfax St Alexandria VA 22314	800-966-6679	703-549-6400	48-1
NSB (Northfield Savings Bank) PO Box 347 Northfield VT 05663	800-672-2274	802-485-5871	69
NSBA (National Small Business Assn) 1156 15th St NW Ste 1100 Washington DC 20005	800-345-6728	202-293-8830	48-12
NSC (National Safety Council) 1121 Spring Lk Dr Itasca IL 60143	800-621-7615	630-285-1121	47-17
NSC Communications 6820 Power Line Dr Florence KY 41042	800-543-1584	859-727-6640	645
NSCA (National Strength & Conditioning Assn) 1885 Bob Johnson Dr Colorado Springs CO 80906	800-815-6826	719-632-6722	47-22
NSCAA (National Soccer Coaches Assn of America) 800 Ann Ave Kansas City KS 66101	800-458-0678	913-362-1747	47-22
NSCC (Nashville State Community College) 120 White Bridge Rd Nashville TN 37209	800-272-7363	615-353-3333	798
NSCIA (National Spinal Cord Injury Assn) 75-20 Astoria Blvd Ste 120 East Elmhurst NY 11370	800-962-9629	718-512-0010	47-17
NSDC (National Staff Development Council) 504 S Locust St Oxford OH 45056	800-727-7288	513-523-6029	48-5
NSEA Voice Magazine 605 S 14th St Ste 200 Lincoln NE 68508	800-742-0047	402-475-7611	456-8
NSF (National Science Foundation) 4201 Wilson Blvd Arlington VA 22230	800-877-8339	703-292-5111	340-18
NSF-GFTC 88 McGilvray St Guelph ON N1G2W1	800-673-6275	519-821-1246	2
NSGA (National Senior Golf Assn) 200 Perrine Rd Ste 201 Old Bridge NJ 08857	800-282-6772		47-22
NSGA (National Sporting Goods Assn) 1601 Feehanville Dr Ste 300 Mount Prospect IL 60056	800-815-5422	847-296-6742	48-4
NSK America Corp 1800 Global Pkwy Hoffman Estates IL 60192	800-585-4675	847-843-7664	490
NSK Corp 4200 Goss Rd Ann Arbor MI 48105	888-446-5675	800-675-9930	619
Nsl Analytical 4450 Cranwood Pkwy Cleveland OH 44128	877-560-3943	216-447-1550	740
NSLA (Nevada State Library & Archives) 100 N Stewart St Carson City NV 89701	800-922-2880	775-684-3360	434-5
NSMC (North Suburban Medical Ctr) 9191 Grant St Thornton CO 80229	877-647-7440	303-451-7800	374-3
NSPE (National Society of Professional Engineers) 1420 King St Alexandria VA 22314	888-285-6773	703-684-2800	48-19
Nspire Health Inc 1830 Lefthand Cir Longmont CO 80501	800-574-7374	303-666-5555	475
NSPR (National Recreation and Park Association) 22377 Belmont Ridge Rd 22377 Belmont Ridge Rd Ashburn VA 20148	800-626-6772	703-858-0784	47-23
NSRA (National Shoe Retailers Assn) 7386 N La Cholla Blvd Tucson AZ 85741	800-673-8446	520-209-1710	48-18
NSS (National Slovak Society of the USA) 351 Vly Brook Rd McMurray PA 15317	800-488-1890	724-731-0094	47-14
NSSEA (National School Supply & Equipment Assn) 8380 Colesville Rd Ste 250 Silver Spring MD 20910	800-395-5550	301-495-0240	48-18
NSSGA (National Stone Sand & Gravel Assn) 1605 King St Alexandria VA 22314	800-342-1415	703-525-8788	48-3
NSTA (National Science Teachers Assn) 1840 Wilson Blvd Arlington VA 22201 *Sales	800-722-6782*	703-243-7100	48-5
NSTAR 800 Boylston St Boston MA 02199 *NYSE: NST*	800-592-2000	617-424-2000	360-5
NSTAR Gas 1 N Star Way Westwood MA 02090	800-592-2000		785
NSTAR Global Services Inc 120 Partlo St Garner NC 27529	877-678-2766		262
NSX (National Stock Exchange) 101 Hudson St Ste 1200 Jersey City NJ 07302	800-843-3924	201-499-3700	689
Nsync Services Inc 850 Greenview Dr Grand Prairie TX 75050	866-706-7962	972-641-7426	248
NTA (National Tour Assn) 546 E Main St Lexington KY 40508	800-682-8886	859-226-4444	47-23
Nta Graphics South Inc 501 Republic Cir Birmingham AL 35214	888-798-2123	205-798-2123	626
NTB (Nationwide Truck Brokers Inc) 4203 Roger B Chaffee Memorial Blvd SE Ste 2 Grand Rapids MI 49548	800-446-0682	616-878-5554	778
NTC (Newman Theological College) 10012-84 St Edmonton AB T6A0B2	844-392-2450	780-392-2450	168-3
NTEA (National Truck Equipment Assn) 37400 Hills Tech Dr Farmington Hills MI 48331	800-441-6832	248-489-7090	48-21
NTELOS Holdings Corp 1154 Shenandoah Village Dr Waynesboro VA 22980 *NASDAQ: NTLS*	877-468-3567	540-946-3500	733
NTF (National Turkey Federation) 1225 New York Ave NW Ste 400 Washington DC 20005	866-536-7593	202-898-0100	47-2
NTIS (National Technical Information Service) 5285 Port Royal Rd Springfield VA 22161 *Orders	800-553-6847*	703-605-6000	666
NTM (New Tribes Mission) 1000 E First St Sanford FL 32771	800-321-5375	407-323-3430	47-20
NTMA (National Tooling & Machining Assn) 6363 Oak Tree Blvd Independence OH 44131	800-248-6862		48-13
NTN Bearing Corp of America 1600 E Bishop Ct Mount Prospect IL 60056	800-323-2358	847-298-7500	619
NTP Distribution Inc 27150 SW Kinsman Rd Wilsonville OR 97070	800-242-6987	503-570-0171	60
NTP Software 20A NW Blvd Ste 136 Nashua NH 03063	800-226-2755	603-622-4400	180-12
NTRA (National Thoroughbred Racing Assn) 2525 Harrodsburg Rd Ste 510 Lexington KY 40504	800-792-6872		47-22
NTSAD (National Tay-Sachs & Allied Diseases Assn) 2001 Beacon St Ste 204 Brighton MA 02135	800-906-8723	617-277-4463	47-17
NTT DATA, Inc 100 City Sq Boston MA 02129	800-745-3263		182
NTT DoCoMo USA Inc 757 Third Ave 16th Fl New York NY 10017	888-362-6661		733
NTU (National Taxpayers Union) 108 N Alfred St Alexandria VA 22314	800-680-7289	703-683-5700	47-7
Nu Horizons Electronics Corp 70 Maxess Rd Melville NY 11747	855-326-4757	631-396-5000	248
Nu Way Co-op Inc PO Box Q Trimont MN 56176	800-445-4118	507-639-2311	278
Nuance Communications Inc 1 Wayside Rd Burlington MA 01803 *NASDAQ: NUAN*	800-654-1187	781-565-5000	180-7
NUBE Inc 16238 Ranch Rd Ste F-108 Austin TX 78717	888-400-3133		198
Nubenco Medical 1 Kalisa Way Ste 207 Paramus NJ 07652	800-633-1322	201-967-9000	475
Nucara Pharmacy 209 E San Marnan Dr Waterloo IA 50702	800-359-2357	319-236-8891	239
NuCare Pharmaceuticals Inc 622 W Katella Ave Orange CA 92867	888-482-9545		583
Nuclear Regulatory Commission Regional Offices			
Region 1 2100 Renaissance Blvd King of Prussia PA 19406	800-432-1156	610-337-5000	340-18
Region 2 61 Forsyth St SW Ste 23T85 Atlanta GA 30303	800-577-8510	404-562-4400	340-18
Region 3 2443 Warrenville Rd Ste 210 Lisle IL 60532	800-522-3025	630-829-9500	340-18
Region 4 1600 E Lamar Blvd Arlington TX 76011	800-952-9677	817-860-8100	340-18
NuclearFuel 1200 G St NW Ste 1000 Washington DC 20005	800-228-9290	202-383-2000	530-5
Nucleonics Week 2 Penn Plaza 25th Fl New York NY 10121	800-752-8878	212-904-3070	530-5
NuCo2 Inc 2800 SE Marketplace Stuart FL 34997	800-472-2855	772-221-1754	145
Nucor Corp 1915 Rexford Rd Charlotte NC 28211 *NYSE: NUE*	800-294-1322	704-366-7000	479
Nucor Corp Cold Finish Div 2800 N Governor Williams Hwy Darlington SC 29540	800-333-0590	704-366-7000	721
Nucor-Yamato Steel Co 5929 E State Hwy 18 Blytheville AR 72315	800-289-6977	870-762-5500	721
Nucraft Furniture Co 5151 W River Dr Comstock Park MI 49321	877-682-7238	616-784-6016	322
Nudo Products Inc 1500 Taylor Ave Springfield IL 62703	800-826-4132	217-528-5636	749
Nueces Electric Co-op (NEC) 709 E Main St PO Box 260970 Robstown TX 78380	800-632-9288	361-387-2581	247
Nuherbs co 3820 Penniman Ave Oakland CA 94619	800-233-4307	510-534-4372	298-8
Nu-Hope Laboratories Inc 12640 Branford St Pacoima CA 91331	800-899-5017	818-899-7711	476
Nujak Development Inc 711 N Kentucky Ave Lakeland FL 33801	888-685-2526	863-686-1565	188
Nu-Life Environmental Inc PO Box 1527 Easley SC 29641	800-654-1752	864-855-5155	385
Nu-Lite Electrical Wholesalers 850 Edwards Ave Harahan LA 70123	800-256-1603	504-733-3300	248
Numara Software Inc 2202 NW Shore Blvd Ste 650 Tampa FL 33607 *Sales	855-834-7487*	813-227-4500	180-12
Numark Laboratories Inc 164 Northfield Ave Edison NJ 08837	800-338-8079		582
Numerex Corp 1600 Parkwood Cir 5th Fl Atlanta GA 30339 *NASDAQ: NMRX*	800-665-5686	770-693-5950	732
Numeridex Inc 632 S Wheeling Rd Wheeling IL 60090	800-323-7737		111
Numonics Corp 101 Commerce Dr PO Box 1005 Montgomeryville PA 18936	800-523-6716	215-362-2766	175-2
Nunhems USA Inc 1200 Anderson Corner Rd Parma ID 83660 *Cust Svc	800-733-9505*	208-674-4000	692
Nuo Therapeutics Inc 207A Perry Pkwy Ste 1 Gaithersburg MD 20877 *OTC: NUOT*	866-298-6633		84
Nupla Corp 11912 Sheldon St Sun Valley CA 91352	800-872-7661	818-768-6800	609
Nursefinders Inc 12400 High Bluff Dr San Diego CA 92130	800-445-0459	877-214-4105	719
Nurserymen's Exchange 2651 N Cabrillo Hwy Half Moon Bay CA 94019 *General	800-227-5229*	650-712-4195	369
Nursing Ctr 323 Norristown Rd Ste 200 Ambler PA 19002	800-346-7844	800-787-8985	397
Nursing Spectrum Greater New York/New Jersey Metro Magazine 1721 Moon Lk Blvd Ste 540 Hoffman Estates IL 60169	800-770-0866		456-16
Nushagak Electric & Telephone Co-op Inc 557 Kenny Wren Rd Dillingham AK 99576	800-478-5296	907-842-5251	247
Nussbaum Trucking Inc 19336 N 1425 East Rd Normal IL 61748	800-322-7305	309-452-4426	778
Nustar GP Holdings LLC PO Box 781609 San Antonio TX 78248 *NYSE: NSH*	800-866-9060	210-918-2000	360-3
Nutra Pharma Corp 12502 W Atlantic Blvd Coral Springs FL 33071	877-895-5647	954-509-0911	478
Nutra-Blend Inc 3200 Second St Neosho MO 64850	800-657-5657		581
Nutraceutical International Corp 1400 Kearns Blvd Park City UT 84060 *NASDAQ: NUTR*	800-669-8877	435-655-6000	797
Nutraceutix Inc 9609 153rd Ave NE Redmond WA 98052	800-548-3222	425-883-9518	478

Company / Address	City	State	ZIP	Toll-Free	Phone	Class
Nutramax Laboratories Inc 2208 Lakeside Blvd	Edgewood	MD	21040	**800-925-5187**	410-776-4000	217
NutriCorp International 4025 Rhodes Dr	Windsor	ON	N8W5B5	**888-446-8874**		740
Nutrifaster Inc 209 S Bennett St	Seattle	WA	98108	**800-800-2641**	206-767-5054	97
NutriSystem Inc 600 Office Center Dr Bldg 1 *NASDAQ: NTRI*	Fort Washington	PA	19034	**800-585-5483**	215-706-5300	808
Nuts & Volts Magazine 430 Princeland Ct *Orders	Corona	CA	92879	**800-783-4624***	951-371-8497	456-14
Nuttall Gear LLC 2221 Niagra Falls Blvd	Niagara Falls	NY	14304	**800-724-6710**	716-298-4100	707
Nutting 450 Pheasant Ridge Dr	Watertown	SD	57201	**800-533-0337**	605-882-3000	469
NuUnion Credit Union 501 S Capitol Ave	Lansing	MI	48933	**888-267-7200**	517-267-7200	221
NuVasive Inc 7475 Lusk Blvd *NASDAQ: NUVA*	San Diego	CA	92121	**800-475-9131**	858-909-1800	475
Nuveen Investments Inc 333 W Wacker Dr	Chicago	IL	60606	**800-257-8787**	312-917-7700	688
NuView Life Sciences Inc 1389 Center Dr Ste 250	Park City	UT	84098	**888-902-7779**		740
Nuvite Chemical Compounds Corp 213 Freeman St	Brooklyn	NY	11222	**800-394-8351**	718-383-8351	150
Nu-Wa Industries Inc 3701 Johnson Rd	Chanute	KS	66720	**800-835-0676**	620-431-2088	119
Nu-Way Industries Inc 555 Howard Ave	Des Plaines	IL	60018	**888-488-5631**	847-298-7710	695
Nu-Wool Company Inc 2472 Port Sheldon Rd	Jenison	MI	49428	**800-748-0128**	616-669-0100	389
Nu-Yale Cleaners 6300 Hwy 62	Jeffersonville	IN	47130	**888-644-7400**	812-285-7400	426
NV5 2525 Natomas Pk Dr Ste 300	Sacramento	CA	95833	**877-941-2068**	916-641-9100	263
NVE Corp 11409 Vly View Rd *NASDAQ: NVEC*	Eden Prairie	MN	55344	**800-467-7141**	952-829-9217	694
NVFC (National Volunteer Fire Council) 7852 Walker Dr Ste 450	Greenbelt	MD	20770	**888-275-6832**	202-887-5700	48-4
N-Viro International Corp 2254 Centennial Rd *OTC: NVIC*	Toledo	OH	43606	**800-336-2225**	419-535-6374	802
NW Natural 220 NW Second Ave PO Box 6017	Portland	OR	97209	**800-422-4012**	503-226-4211	535
NWA (National WIC Assn) 2001 S St NW Ste 580	Washington	DC	20009	**866-782-6246**	202-232-5492	47-6
NWC (National Waterways Conference Inc) 4650 Washington Blvd Ste 608	Arlington	VA	22201	**866-371-1390**	703-243-4090	48-21
NWF (National Wildlife Federation) 11100 Wildlife Ctr Dr	Reston	VA	20190	**800-822-9919**	703-438-6000	47-3
NWFA (National Wood Flooring Assn) 111 Chesterfield Industrial Blvd	Chesterfield	MO	63005	**800-422-4556**	636-519-9663	48-3
NWI (National Wellness Institute) 1300 College Ct PO Box 827	Stevens Point	WI	54481	**877-800-2729**	715-342-2969	47-17
NWL Transformers Inc 312 Rising Sun Rd	Bordentown	NJ	08505	**800-742-5695**	609-298-7300	255
NWOA (National Woodland Owners Assn) 374 Maple Ave E Ste 310	Vienna	VA	22180	**800-476-8733**	703-255-2700	47-2
NWRA (National Water Resources Assn) 3800 Fairfax Dr # 4	Arlington	VA	22203	**800-468-3533**	703-524-1544	47-12
NWT Tourism PO Box 610	Yellowknife	NT	X1A2N5	**800-661-0788**	867-873-7200	772
NWTF (National Wild Turkey Federation) 770 Augusta Rd PO Box 530 *Cust Svc	Edgefield	SC	29824	**800-843-6983***	803-637-3106	47-3
NxStage Medical Inc 439 S Union St 5th Fl *NASDAQ: NXTM*	Lawrence	MA	01843	**866-697-8243**	978-687-4700	475
NYACK 350 N Highland Ave	Nyack	NY	10960	**800-541-6891**	845-353-2020	168-3
Nyack College 1 S Blvd *Admissions	Nyack	NY	10960	**800-336-9225***	845-358-1710	167
NYBDC (New York Business Development Corp) 50 Beaver St Ste 500	Albany	NY	12207	**800-923-2504**	518-463-2268	218
NYCCC (New York City Children's Ctr-Queens Campus) 74-03 Commonwealth Blvd	Bellerose	NY	11426	**800-597-8481**	718-264-4500	374-1
NYCE Corp 400 Plaza Dr	Secaucus	NJ	07094	**888-323-0310**	904-438-6000	68
NYCM (New York Central Mutual Fire Insurance Co) 1899 Central Plz E	Edmeston	NY	13335	**800-234-6926**		391-4
NYDJ Apparel LLC 5401 S Soto St	Vernon	CA	90058	**800-407-6001**	323-581-9040	156-6
Nye County School District Inc (NCSD) PO Box 113	Tonopah	NV	89049	**800-796-6273**	775-482-6258	683
NYLA (New York Library Assn) 6021 State Farm Rd *General	Guilderland	NY	12084	**800-252-6952***	518-432-6952	435
NYLIFE Securities Inc 51 Madison Ave Rm 251	New York	NY	10010	**800-695-4785**		688
Nylok Corp 15260 Hallmark Dr	Macomb	MI	48042	**800-826-5161**	586-786-0100	3
Nylon Corp of America 333 Sundial Ave	Manchester	NH	03103	**800-851-2001**	603-627-5150	604-1
NYMT (New York Mortgage Trust Inc) 52 Vanderbilt Ave Ste 403 *NASDAQ: NYMT*	New York	NY	10017	**800-937-5449**	212-792-0107	652
NYP Corp 805 E Grand St	Elizabeth	NJ	07201	**800-524-1052**	908-351-6550	66
NYPIRG (New York Public Interest Research Group) 9 Murray St	New York	NY	10007	**800-342-3377**	212-349-6460	630
Nysarc Inc 393 Delaware Ave	Delmar	NY	12054	**800-735-8924**	518-439-8311	428
NYSCA (National Youth Sports Coaches Assn) 2050 Vista Pkwy	West Palm Beach	FL	33411	**800-729-2057**	561-684-1141	47-22
NYSE Arca 115 Samsone St	San Francisco	CA	94104	**877-729-7291**		689
NYSE Euronext 11 Wall St *NYSE: NYX*	New York	NY	10005	**866-873-7422**	212-656-3000	689
NYSNA (New York State Nurses Assn) 11 Cornell Rd	Latham	NY	12110	**800-724-6976**	518-782-9400	532
Nystrom Inc 9300 73rd Ave N	Minneapolis	MN	55428	**800-547-2635**	763-488-9200	236
NYSW (New York Susquehanna & Western Railway Corp) 1 Railroad Ave *General	Cooperstown	NY	13326	**800-366-6979***	607-547-2555	646
Nytef Plastics Ltd Inc 6643 42nd Terr N	West Palm Beach	FL	33407	**800-646-9833**	561-840-9499	602

O

Company / Address	City	State	ZIP	Toll-Free	Phone	Class
O & S Trucking Inc 3769 E Evergreen St	Springfield	MO	65803	**855-861-9571**	417-864-4780	778
O Berk Co 3 Milltown Ct	Union	NJ	07083	**800-631-7392**	908-851-9500	385
O E C Graphics Inc 555 W Waukau Ave PO Box 2443	Oshkosh	WI	54902	**800-388-7770**	920-235-7770	480
O Henry Hotel 624 Green Vly Rd	Greensboro	NC	27408	**800-965-8259**	336-854-2000	379
O P T 918 Mission Ave	Oceanside	CA	92054	**800-483-6287**	760-722-3348	181
O S F Flavors Inc 40 Baker Hollow Rd	Windsor	CT	06095	**800-466-6015**	860-298-8350	298-11
O'Brien Dental Lab Inc 4311 SW Research Way	Corvallis	OR	97333	**800-445-5941**	541-754-1238	415
O'Brien International 14615 NE 91st St	Redmond	WA	98052	**800-662-7436**	425-202-2100	708
O'Connell Oil Assoc Inc 545 Merrill Rd	Pittsfield	MA	01201	**800-464-4894**	413-499-4800	325
O'Connor Woods 3400 Wagner Heights Rd	Stockton	CA	95209	**800-957-3308**	209-956-3400	670
O'Day Equipment Inc 1301 40th St NW	Fargo	ND	58102	**800-654-6329**	701-282-9260	636
O'Fallon Chamber of Commerce 2145 Bryan Vly Commercial Dr	O'Fallon	MO	63366	**888-349-1897**	636-240-1818	138
O'Gara Coach Company LLC 8833 W Olympic Blvd	Beverly Hills	CA	90211	**888-291-5533**		56
O'Halloran Adv Inc 270 Saugatuck Ave	Westport	CT	06880	**877-466-6616**	203-341-9400	5
O'halloran International Inc 3311 Adventureland Dr	Altoona	IA	50009	**800-800-6503**	515-967-3300	768
O'Hare International Airport *Dept of Aviation* PO Box 66142	Chicago	IL	60666	**800-832-6352**	773-686-3700	27
O'keefe Elevator Company Inc 1402 Jones St	Omaha	NE	68102	**800-369-6317**	402-345-4056	358
O'Keeffe's Inc 325 Newhall St	San Francisco	CA	94124	**888-653-3333**	415-822-4222	236
O'Leary Paint 300 E Oakland Ave	Lansing	MI	48906	**800-477-2066**	517-487-2066	549
O'More College of Design 423 S Margin St	Franklin	TN	37064	**888-662-1970**	615-794-4254	167
O'neal Flat Rolled Metals 1229 S Fulton Ave	Brighton	CO	80601	**800-336-3365**	303-654-0300	491
O'Neal Steel Inc 744 41st St N	Birmingham	AL	35222	**800-861-8272**	205-599-8000	491
O'Neill & Assoc LLC 31 New Chardon St	Boston	MA	02114	**866-989-4321**	617-646-1000	196
O'Neill Wetsuits USA 1071 41st Ave PO Box 6300	Santa Cruz	CA	95063	**800-538-0764**		708
O'Reilly & Assoc Inc 1005 Gravenstein Hwy N	Sebastopol	CA	95472	**800-998-9938**	707-829-0515	634-11
O'Reilly Automotive Inc 233 S Patterson *NASDAQ: ORLY*	Springfield	MO	65802	**888-327-7153**	417-862-6708	53
O'Reilly Rancilio PC Sterling Town Ctr 12900 Hall Rd Ste 350	Sterling Heights	MI	48313	**800-708-3528**	586-726-1000	428
O'Rourke Wrecking Co 660 Lunken Pk Dr	Cincinnati	OH	45226	**800-354-9850**	513-871-1400	191-16
O'Ryan Group Inc 4010 Pilot Ste 108	Memphis	TN	38118	**800-253-0750**	901-794-4610	699
O.E.M. Systems LLC PO Box 473	Okarche	OK	73762	**800-810-7252**	405-263-7488	60
01 Communications Inc 4359 town ctr blvd Ste 217	El Dorado hills	CA	95762	**888-444-1111**		733
OA (Overeaters Anonymous Inc) PO Box 44020	Rio Rancho	NM	87174	**866-505-4966**	505-891-2664	47-21
OAAA (Outdoor Adv Assn of America Inc) 1850 M St NW Ste 1040	Washington	DC	20036	**800-325-3694**	202-833-5566	614
OABA-PAC (Outdoor Amusement Business Assn PAC) 1035 S Semoran Blvd Ste 1045A	Winter Park	FL	32792	**800-517-6222**	407-681-9444	614
OAG Worldwide 3025 Highland Pkwy Ste 200	Downers Grove	IL	60515	**800-342-5624**	630-515-3230	634-10
OAGI (Open Applications Group Inc) PO Box 4897	Marietta	GA	30061	**800-236-4600**	404-402-1962	48-13

Name	Address	City	State	Zip	Toll-Free	Phone	Class
OAH (Organization of American Historians)	112 N Bryan Ave	Bloomington	IN	47408	**888-737-7006**	812-855-7311	48-5
Oahe Electric Co-op Inc	102 S Cranford St PO Box 216	Blunt	SD	57522	**800-640-6243**	605-962-6243	247
Oak Assoc Funds	PO Box 8233	Denver	CO	80201	**888-462-5386**		527
Oak Brook Hills Marriott Resort	3500 Midwest Rd	Oak Brook	IL	60523	**800-228-9290**	630-850-5555	377
Oak Hall Inc	6150 Poplar Ave Ste 146	Memphis	TN	38119	**844-625-4255**	901-761-3580	156-4
Oak Hall Industries	840 Union St	Salem	VA	24153	**800-223-0429**	540-387-0000	154-13
Oak Hills Christian College	1600 Oak Hills Rd SW	Bemidji	MN	56601	**888-751-8670**	218-751-8670	160
Oak Mountain State Park	200 Terr Dr PO Box 278	Pelham	AL	35124	**800-252-7275**	205-620-2520	564
Oak Park Area Convention & Visitors Bureau	1118 Westgate	Oak Park	IL	60301	**888-625-7275**	708-524-7800	208
Oak Plantation Resort & Suites Condominium Association Inc	4090 Enchanted Oaks Cir	Kissimmee	FL	34741	**888-411-4141**		378
Oak Ridge Financial	701 Xenia Ave S Ste 100	Minneapolis	MN	55416	**800-231-8364**	763-923-2200	68
Oak Ridge Hotel & Conference Ctr	1 Oak Ridge Dr *Sales	Chaska	MN	55318	**800-737-9588***	952-368-3100	377
Oakdale Electric Co-op	PO Box 128	Oakdale	WI	54649	**800-241-2468**	608-372-4131	247
Oakgrove Construction Inc	6900 Seneca St	Elma	NY	14059	**866-435-1499**	716-652-2200	190-4
Oakhill Hospital	11375 Cortez Blvd	Brooksville	FL	34613	**877-442-2362**	352-596-6632	374-3
Oakhurst Dairy	364 Forest Ave	Portland	ME	04101	**800-482-0718**	207-772-7468	297-27
Oakland Ballet Co	2201 Broadway Ste 206	Oakland	CA	94612	**866-711-6037**	510-893-3132	572-1
Oakland City University	138 N Lucretia St	Oakland City	IN	47660	**800-737-5125**	812-749-4781	167
Oakland Community College	2480 Opdyke Rd	Bloomfield Hills	MI	48304	**800-829-1040**	248-341-2000	161
Highland Lakes	7350 Cooley Lake Rd	Waterford	MI	48327	**800-829-1040**	248-942-3100	161
Southfield	2480 Opdyke Rd	Bloomfield Hills	MI	48304	**800-829-1040**	248-341-2000	161
Oakland Convention Ctr	1001 Broadway	Oakland	CA	94607	**800-228-9290**	510-451-4000	207
Oakland Museum of California	1000 Oak St *General	Oakland	CA	94607	**888-625-6873***	510-238-2200	519
Oakland Press	48 W Huron St	Pontiac	MI	48342	**888-977-3677**	248-332-8181	634-8
Oakland Raiders	1220 Harbor Bay Pkwy	Alameda	CA	94502	**800-724-3377**	510-864-5000	713-3
Oakland Unified School District	1025 Second Ave	Oakland	CA	94606	**888-604-4636**	510-879-8582	683
Oakland University	2200 Squirrel Rd *Admissions	Rochester	MI	48309	**800-625-8648***	248-370-2100	167
Oaklawn Park	2705 Central Ave *General	Hot Springs	AR	71901	**800-625-5296***	501-623-4411	639
Oakleaf Waste Management LLC	415 Day Hill Rd	Windsor	CT	06095	**888-625-5323**	713-512-6200	802
Oakley Inc	1 Icon *Cust Svc	Foothill Ranch	CA	92610	**800-403-7449***	949-951-0991	541
Oakley Transport Inc	101 ABC Rd	Lake Wales	FL	33859	**800-969-8265**	863-638-1435	448
Oakley-Lindsay Ctr	300 Civic Ctr Plaza Ste 237	Quincy	IL	62301	**800-978-4748**	217-223-1000	207
Oakmark Family of Funds	330 W nineth St	Kansas City	MO	64105	**800-625-6275**	617-483-8327	527
Oak-Mitsui Inc	80 First St	Hoosick Falls	NY	12090	**800-424-8802**	518-686-4961	296
Oaks at Ojai	122 E Ojai Ave	Ojai	CA	93023	**800-753-6257**	805-646-5573	704
Oakwood Annapolis Hospital	33155 Annapolis Rd	Wayne	MI	48184	**800-543-9355**	734-467-4000	374-3
Oakwood Capital Management LLC	12121 Wilshire Blvd Ste 1250	Los Angeles	CA	90025	**800-586-0600**	310-772-2600	196
Oakwood College	7000 Adventist Blvd	Huntsville	AL	35896	**800-824-5312**	256-726-7356	167
Oakwood Crystal City	400 15th St S	Arlington	VA	22202	**877-902-0832**	703-920-9550	212
Oakwood Heritage Hospital	10000 Telegraph Rd	Taylor	MI	48180	**800-543-9355**	313-295-5000	374-3
Oakwood Hospital & Medical Ctr	18101 Oakwood Blvd	Dearborn	MI	48124	**800-543-9355**	313-593-7000	374-3
Oakwood Products Inc	1741 Old Dunbar Rd	West Columbia	SC	29172	**800-467-3386**	803-739-8800	143
Oakwood Southshore Medical Ctr	5450 Fort St	Trenton	MI	48183	**800-543-9355**	734-671-3800	374-3
Oakwood Worldwide	2222 Corinth Ave	Los Angeles	CA	90064	**800-888-0808**	310-478-1021	212
Oakworks Inc	923 E Wellspring Rd	New Freedom	PA	17349	**800-558-8850**	717-235-6807	474
OANDA Corp	140 Broadway 46th Fl	New York	NY	10005	**800-826-8164**	416-593-9436	68
Oar Net	1224 Kinnear Rd	Columbus	OH	43212	**800-627-6420**	614-292-1956	182
OAS (Organization of American States)	1889 F St NW	Washington	DC	20006	**888-442-4887**	202-458-3000	47-7
Oasis Outsourcing	4511 Woodland Corporate Blvd	Tampa	FL	33614	**866-709-9401**	813-864-8429	630
Oasis Outsourcing Inc	2054 Vista Pkwy Ste 300 *General	West Palm Beach	FL	33411	**888-627-4735***		630
Oasis Stage Werks Inc	249 S Rio Grande St	Salt Lake City	UT	84101	**800-952-6865**	801-363-0364	351
Oatey Co	4700 W 160th St *Cust Svc	Cleveland	OH	44135	**800-321-9532***	216-267-7100	608
O-AT-KA Milk Products Co-op Inc	700 Ellicott St	Batavia	NY	14020	**800-828-8152**	585-343-0536	297-3
OATSystems Inc	309 Waverley Oaks Rd Ste 306	Waltham	MA	02452	**877-628-7877**	781-907-6100	180-10
OB Macaroni Co	PO Box 53 *Orders	Fort Worth	TX	76101	**800-553-4336***	817-335-4629	297-31
Obagi Medical Products Inc	3760 Kilroy Airport Way Ste 500	Long Beach	CA	90806	**800-636-7546**	562-628-1007	217
OBCI (Ocean Bio-Chem Inc)	4041 SW 47th Ave *NASDAQ: OBCI*	Fort Lauderdale	FL	33314	**800-327-8583**	954-587-6280	150
Oberbeck Grain Co	700 Walnut St	Highland	IL	62249	**800-632-2012**	618-654-2387	446
Oberfields LLC	1165 Alum Creek Dr	Columbus	OH	43209	**800-845-7644**	614-252-0955	193-4
Oberg Industries Inc	2301 Silverville Rd PO Box 368	Freeport	PA	16229	**866-487-2365**	724-295-2121	755
oberoSPM	7560 Airport Rd Unit 12	Mississauga	ON	L4T4H4	**888-815-2996**		318
Oberto Sausage Co	7060 S 238th St	Kent	WA	98032	**877-453-7591**	253-854-7056	297-26
OBI (Ocean Breeze International)	3910 Via Real	Carpinteria	CA	93013	**888-715-8888**	805-684-1747	369
OBI (Oklahoma Blood Institute)	1001 N Lincoln Blvd	Oklahoma City	OK	73104	**866-708-4995**	405-278-3100	88
Objectivity Inc	3099 N First St Ste 200	San Jose	CA	95134	**800-767-6259**	408-992-7100	180-1
Obs Inc	1324 WTuscarawas St PO Box 6210	Canton	OH	44706	**800-362-9592**	330-453-3725	515
Observer & Eccentric Newspapers	615 W Lafayette Second Level	Detroit	MI	48226	**866-887-2737**		634-8
Observer Publishing Co	122 S Main St	Washington	PA	15301	**800-222-6397**	724-222-2200	634-8
Observer, The	140 S Front St	Sarnia	ON	N7T7M8	**866-541-6757**	519-344-3641	531-1
Observer-Reporter	122 S Main St	Washington	PA	15301	**800-222-6397**	724-222-2200	531-2
OC Tanner Co	1930 S State St	Salt Lake City	UT	84115	**800-453-7490**		409
Ocala-Marion County Chamber of Commerce	310 SE Third St	Ocala	FL	34471	**800-466-5055**	352-629-8051	138
OCC (Optical Cable Corp)	5290 Concourse Dr *NASDAQ: OCC*	Roanoke	VA	24019	**800-622-7711**	540-265-0690	812
OCCC (Orange County Convention Ctr)	9800 International Dr	Orlando	FL	32819	**800-345-9845**	407-685-9800	207
Occidental College	1600 Campus Rd *Admissions	Los Angeles	CA	90041	**800-825-5262***	323-259-2700	167
Occk Inc	1710 W Schilling Rd	Salina	KS	67401	**800-526-9731**	785-827-9383	475
Occoneechee State Park	1192 Occoneechee Pk Rd	Clarksville	VA	23927	**800-933-7275**	434-374-2210	564
Occupational Safety & Health Administration (OSHA)	200 Constitution Ave NW	Washington	DC	20210	**800-321-6742**	202-693-1999	340-13
Occupational Safety & Health Administration Regional Offices							
Region 1	JFK Federal Bldg Rm E-340	Boston	MA	02203	**800-321-6742**	617-565-9860	340-13
Region 2	201 Varick St Ste 670	New York	NY	10014	**800-321-6742**	212-337-2378	340-13
Region 3	Curtis Ctr 170 S Independence Mall W Ste 740W	Philadelphia	PA	19106	**800-321-6742**	215-861-4900	340-13
Region 10	300 Fifth Ave Ste 1280 *Help Line	Seattle	WA	98104	**800-321-6742***	206-757-6700	340-13
Occupational Safety & Health Review Commission Regional Offices							
Atlanta Region	100 Alabama St SW Rm 2R90	Atlanta	GA	30303	**800-321-6742**	404-562-1640	340-18
OC&E Woods Line State Trail	46000 Hwy 97 N 46000 Hwy 97 N	Chiloquin	OR	97624	**800-551-6949**	541-883-5558	564
Ocean Bank	780 NW 42nd Ave	Miami	FL	33126	**877-688-2265**	305-442-2660	69
Ocean Beauty Seafoods Inc	1100 W Ewing St	Seattle	WA	98119	**800-365-8950**	206-285-6800	297-14
Ocean Bio-Chem Inc (OBCI)	4041 SW 47th Ave *NASDAQ: OBCI*	Fort Lauderdale	FL	33314	**800-327-8583**	954-587-6280	150
Ocean Breeze International (OBI)	3910 Via Real	Carpinteria	CA	93013	**888-715-8888**	805-684-1747	369
Ocean City City Hall	301 Baltimore Ave	Ocean City	MD	21842	**800-626-2326**	410-289-8931	337
Ocean City Convention & Visitors Bureau	4001 Coastal Hwy	Ocean City	MD	21842	**800-626-2326**	410-289-8181	208
Ocean City Hotel-Motel-Restaurant Assn	PO Box 340	Ocean City	MD	21843	**800-626-2326**	410-289-6733	376

Name / Address	City	State	ZIP	Toll-Free	Phone	Class
Ocean City Maryland Hotels 6600 Coastal Hwy	Ocean City	MD	21842	**800-837-3588**	410-524-5252	669
Ocean Conservancy 1300 19th St NW 8th Fl	Washington	DC	20036	**800-519-1541**	202-429-5609	47-13
Ocean Ctr 101 N Atlantic Ave	Daytona Beach	FL	32118	**800-858-6444**	386-254-4500	207
Ocean Edge Resort & Golf Club 2907 Main St	Brewster	MA	02631	**800-343-6074**	508-896-9000	667
Ocean Forest Plaza 5523 N Ocean Blvd *General	Myrtle Beach	SC	29577	**800-845-6701***	843-497-0044	379
Ocean Futures Society 325 Chapala St	Santa Barbara	CA	93101	**800-477-7500**	805-899-8899	47-13
Ocean Kayak 125 Gilman Falls Ave Bldg B	Old Town	ME	04468	**800-852-9257**		708
Ocean Key Resort 424 Atlantic Ave	Virginia Beach	VA	23451	**800-955-9700**	757-425-2200	379
Ocean Key Resort & Spa 0 Duval St	Key West	FL	33040	**800-328-9815**	305-296-7701	667
Ocean Manor Resort 4040 Galt Ocean Dr	Fort Lauderdale	FL	33308	**800-955-0444**	954-566-7500	667
Ocean Medical Ctr (OMC) 425 Jack Martin Blvd	Brick	NJ	08724	**800-560-9990**	732-840-2200	374-3
Ocean Mist Resort 97 S Shore Dr	South Yarmouth	MA	02664	**800-655-1972**	508-398-2633	667
Ocean One Cruise Outlet 3264 Marilynn St	Lancaster	CA	93536	**888-353-1922**	661-949-2873	769
Ocean Pointe Suites at Key Largo 500 Burton Dr	Tavernier	FL	33070	**800-882-9464**	305-853-3000	379
Ocean Reef Club 35 Ocean Reef Dr Ste 200	Key Largo	FL	33037	**888-422-9944**	305-367-2611	379
Ocean Reef Resort 7100 N Ocean Blvd	Myrtle Beach	SC	29572	**888-322-6411**	843-449-4441	667
Ocean Resort Hotel Waikiki 175 Paoakalani Ave	Honolulu	HI	96815	**877-367-1912**	808-922-3861	379
Ocean Sands Resort & Spa 1350 N Ocean Blvd	Pompano Beach	FL	33062	**800-721-7033**	954-590-1000	667
Ocean Shores Convention Ctr 120 W Chance a La Mer Ave	Ocean Shores	WA	98569	**800-874-6737**	360-289-4411	207
Ocean Sky Hotel & Resort 4060 Galt Ocean Dr	Fort Lauderdale	FL	33308	**800-678-9022**	954-565-6611	379
Ocean Spray Cranberries Inc 1 Ocean Spray Dr	Lakeville-Middleboro	MA	02349	**800-662-3263**	508-946-1000	297-20
Ocean Walk Resort 300 N Atlantic	Daytona Beach	FL	32118	**888-743-2561**	386-323-4800	379
Ocean Waters Spa 600 N Atlantic Ave	Daytona Beach	FL	32118	**844-284-2685**	386-267-1660	704
Oceane Marine Shipping Inc 407 E Maple St	Cumming	GA	30040	**888-262-3263**	770-888-5941	312
Oceaneering International Inc 11911 FM 529 *NYSE: OII*	Houston	TX	77041	**877-680-5478**	713-329-4500	538
OceanFirst Bank 975 Hooper Ave PO Box 2009	Toms River	NJ	08753	**888-623-2633**	732-240-4500	69
Oceania Cruises Inc 8300 NW 33rd St Ste 308	Miami	FL	33122	**800-531-5619**	305-514-2300	222
Oceanic USA 2002 Davis St	San Leandro	CA	94577	**800-435-3483**	510-562-0500	708
Oceanside Beach State Recreation Site 13000 Whiskey Creek Rd W	Tillamook	OR	97141	**800-551-6949**		564
Oceanus Partners 16540 Pointe Village Dr Ste 208	Lutz	FL	33558	**888-496-1117**		198
Oceus Networks Inc 1895 Preston White Dr Ste 300	Reston	VA	20191	**877-816-2599**	703-234-9200	387
Oce-USA Inc 5450 N Cumberland Ave	Chicago	IL	60656	**800-877-6232**	773-714-8500	588
OCF (Omaha Community Foundation) 302 S 36th St Ste 100	Omaha	NE	68131	**800-794-3458**	402-342-3458	304
Ochsner Clinic Foundation Hospital 1514 Jefferson Hwy	New Orleans	LA	70121	**800-343-0269**	504-842-3000	374-3
Ochsner Medical Ctr West Bank 2500 Belle Chasse Hwy	Gretna	LA	70056	**800-231-5257**	504-391-5454	374-3
OCLC (Online Computer Library Ctr Inc) 6565 Kilgour Pl	Dublin	OH	43017	**800-848-5878**		48-11
OCM (One Call Medical Inc) 20 Waterview Blvd PO Box 614	Parsippany	NJ	07054	**800-872-2875**	973-257-1000	382
OCMC (Ouachita County Medical Ctr) PO Box 797	Camden	AR	71711	**877-836-2472**	870-836-1000	374-3
OCMMC (Orange Coast Memorial Medical Ctr) 9920 Talbert Ave	Fountain Valley	CA	92708	**877-597-4777**	714-378-7000	374-3
Ocmulgee Electric Membership Corp 5722 Eastman St	Eastman	GA	31023	**800-342-5509**	478-374-7001	247
Oconee Electric Membership Corp 3445 US Hwy 80 W	Dudley	GA	31022	**800-522-2930**	478-676-3191	247
Oconee State Park 624 State Pk Rd	Mountain Rest	SC	29664	**888-803-0844**	864-638-5353	564
Oconomowoc Convention & Visitors Bureau 174 E Wisconsin Ave	Oconomowoc	WI	53066	**888-936-7463**	262-569-2186	208
Oconomowoc Memorial Hospital 791 Summit Ave	Oconomowoc	WI	53066	**800-242-0313**	262-569-9400	374-3
Oconto Electric Co-op PO Box 168 PO Box 168	Oconto Falls	WI	54154	**800-472-8410**	920-846-2816	247
OCP (Oregon Catholic Press) 5536 NE Hassalo St	Portland	OR	97213	**877-596-1653**	503-281-1191	634-3
Ocsea-Afscme Local 390 Worthington Rd Ste A	Westerville	OH	43082	**800-969-4702**	614-865-4700	414
October Company Inc 51 Ferry St	EastHampton	MA	01027	**800-628-9346**	413-527-9380	296
Ocwen Federal Bank FSB 1661 Worthington Rd Ste 100	West Palm Beach	FL	33409	**800-746-2936**	561-682-8000	69

Name / Address	City	State	ZIP	Toll-Free	Phone	Class
Ocwen Financial Corp 1661 Worthington Rd Ste 100 PO Box 24737 *NYSE: OCN*	West Palm Beach	FL	33409	**800-746-2936**	561-681-8000	360-2
Odan Laboratories Ltd 325 Stillview Ave	Pointe-Claire	QC	H9R2Y6	**800-387-9342**	514-428-1628	233
Odebrecht Construction Inc 201 Alhambra Cir Ste 1000	Coral Gables	FL	33134	**800-771-0001**	305-341-8800	188
ODEF (Old Dominion Eye Bank) 9200 Arboretum Pkwy Ste 104	Richmond	VA	23236	**800-832-0728**	804-560-7540	271
Odessa American PO Box 2952	Odessa	TX	79760	**800-592-4433**	432-337-4661	531-2
Odessa Chamber of Commerce 700 N Grant St Ste 200	Odessa	TX	79761	**800-780-4678**	432-332-9111	138
Odessa College 201 W University Blvd	Odessa	TX	79764	**866-968-2862**	432-335-6400	161
Odessa Convention & Visitors Bureau 700 N Grant Ave Ste 200	Odessa	TX	79761	**800-780-4678**	432-333-7871	208
Odessa Regional Medical Ctr 520 E Sixth St	Odessa	TX	79761	**877-898-6080**	432-582-8000	374-7
ODG (Ontario Drive & Gear Ltd) 220 Bergey Ct	New Hamburg	ON	N3A2J5	**877-274-6288**	519-662-2840	29
ODL Inc 215 E Roosevelt Ave	Zeeland	MI	49464	**800-253-3900**	616-772-9111	330
Odlum Brown Ltd 250 Howe St Ste 1100	Vancouver	BC	V6C3S9	**866-636-8222**	604-669-1600	401
Odom's Tennessee Pride Sausage Inc 1201 Neelys Bend Rd	Madison	TN	37115	**866-484-8641**	615-868-1360	297-26
Odon Wagner Gallery 196 Davenport Rd	Toronto	ON	M5R1J2	**800-551-2465**	416-962-0438	41
Odor Management Inc 18-6 E Dundee Rd Ste 101	Barrington	IL	60010	**800-662-6367**	847-304-9111	582
ODS Cos 601 SW Second Ave	Portland	OR	97204	**888-221-0802**	503-228-6554	391-3
ODW Logistics Inc 1580 Williams Rd	Columbus	OH	43207	**800-743-7062**	614-497-1660	448
Odwalla Inc 1625 North Market Blvd	Sacramento	CA	95834	**800-952-5210**		297-20
Odyssey HealthCare Inc 717 N Harwood St	Dallas	TX	75201	**855-865-5894**	214-922-9711	450
Odyssey Healthcare of Kansas City 4911 S Arrowhead Dr	Independence	MO	64055	**800-944-4357**	816-795-1333	371
Odyssey Magazine 30 Grove St Ste C	Peterborough	NH	03458	**800-821-0115**	603-924-7209	456-6
Odyssey Marine Exploration Inc 5215 W Laurel St *NASDAQ: OMEX*	Tampa	FL	33607	**800-458-4646**	813-876-1776	464
Odyssey Re Holdings Corp 300 First Stamford Pl	Stamford	CT	06902	**866-745-4440**	203-977-8000	391-4
OEA (Ohio Education Assn) 225 E Broad St PO Box 2550	Columbus	OH	43216	**800-282-1500**	614-228-4526	456-8
OEA (Oregon Education Magazine) 6900 SW Atlanta St Bldg 1	Portland	OR	97223	**800-858-5505**	503-684-3300	456-8
Oeconnection LLC 4205 Highlander Pkwy	Richfield	OH	44286	**888-776-5792**	330-523-1830	179
OF Mossberg & Sons Inc 7 Grasso Ave	North Haven	CT	06473	**800-363-3555**	203-230-5300	286
OFA (Orphan Foundation of America) 21351 Gentry Dr Ste 130	Sterling	VA	20166	**800-950-4673**	571-203-0270	47-6
Off the Beaten Path 7 E Beall St	Bozeman	MT	59715	**800-445-2995**	406-586-1311	758
Offen Petroleum Inc 5100 E 78th Ave	Commerce	CO	80022	**866-657-3835**	303-297-3835	578
Office Chairs Inc 14815 Radburn Ave	Santa Fe Springs	CA	90670	**866-624-4968**	562-802-0464	320-1
Office Depot Inc 2200 Old Germantown Rd *NASDAQ: ODP*	Delray Beach	FL	33445	**800-937-3600**	561-438-4800	534
Office Environments Inc 11407 Granite St	Charlotte	NC	28273	**888-861-2525**	704-714-7200	321
Office Movers Inc 6500 Kane Way	Elkridge	MD	21075	**800-331-4025**	410-799-7704	467
Office of Disability Employment Policy 200 Constitution Ave NW Ste S1303	Washington	DC	20210	**866-633-7365**	202-693-7880	340-13
Office of General Services Corning Tower 41st Fl Empire State Plz	Albany	NY	12242	**877-426-6006**	518-474-3899	207
Office of Justice Programs						
Bureau of Justice Assistance 810 Seventh St NW	Washington	DC	20531	**888-744-6513**	202-616-6500	340-12
Office for Victims of Crime 810 Seventh St NW 8th Fl	Washington	DC	20531	**800-363-0441**	202-307-5983	340-12
Office of Public Health & Science 200 Independence Ave SW Rm 716G	Washington	DC	20201	**877-696-6775**	202-690-7694	340-8
Office of Special Counsel 1730 M St NW Ste 218	Washington	DC	20036	**800-872-9855**	202-254-3600	340-18
Office of Special Counsel for Immigration-Related Unfair Employment Practices 950 Pennsylvania Ave NW	Washington	DC	20038	**800-255-7688**	202-616-5594	340-12
Office of Special Counsel Regional Offices						
Dallas Field Office 525 Griffin St Rm 824 PO Box 103	Dallas	TX	75202	**800-872-9855**	214-747-1519	340-18
San Francisco Bay Area Field Office Federal Bldg 1301 Clay St Ste 1220-N	Oakland	CA	94612	**800-872-9855**	510-637-3460	340-18
Office Playground Inc 715 Southpoint Blvd Ste 100	Petaluma	CA	94954	**800-458-1948**	415-483-1196	294
Office Solutions Inc 217 Mount Horeb Rd	Warren	NJ	07059	**800-677-1778**		181
Office Star Products 1901 S Archibald PO Box 3520	Ontario	CA	91761	**800-950-7262**	909-930-2000	321
Official Payments Corp 3550 Engineering Dr	Norcross	GA	30092	**877-754-4413**	770-325-3100	182

Name / Address	Toll-Free	Phone	Class
Off-Road Magazine 2400 E Katella Ave 7th fl. Anaheim CA 92806	877-462-6752	714-848-8880	456-3
Offwhite 521 Ft St Marietta OH 45750	800-606-1610	740-373-9010	344
OG & E Electric Services PO Box 24990 Oklahoma City OK 73124	800-272-9741	405-553-3000	785
Ogden Eccles Conference Ctr 2415 Washington Blvd Ogden UT 84401	866-472-4627	801-689-8600	207
Ogden Regional Medical Ctr 5475 Adams Ave Pkwy Ogden UT 84405	877-870-3745	801-479-2111	374-3
Ogden/Weber Convention & Visitors Bureau 2438 Washington Blvd Ogden UT 84401	800-255-8824	801-778-6250	208
OGE Energy Corp 321 N Harvey St Oklahoma City OK 73102 *NYSE: OGE*	800-272-9741	405-553-3000	360-5
Oglebay Institute's Stifel Fine Arts Ctr 1330 National Rd Wheeling WV 26003	800-624-6988	304-242-7700	49-1
Oglebay Resort & Conference Ctr 465 Lodge Dr Oglebay Pk. Wheeling WV 26003	800-624-6988	304-243-4000	667
Oglethorpe University 4484 Peachtree Rd,N.E Atlanta GA 30319	800-428-4484	404-364-8307	167
Ogontz Corp 2835 Terwood Rd Willow Grove PA 19090	800-523-2478	215-657-4770	787
OGR (International Order of the Golden Rule) 3520 Executive Ctr Dr Ste 300 Austin TX 78731	800-637-8030	512-334-5504	48-4
OHANA Waikiki Beachcomber Hotel 2300 Kalakaua Ave Honolulu HI 96815	866-956-4262	808-922-4646	379
Ohaus Corp 19-A Chapin Rd PO Box 2033 Pine Brook NJ 07058	800-672-7722	973-377-9000	682
Ohel Children's Home & Family Services Inc 4510 16th Ave Brooklyn NY 11204	800-603-6435	718-851-6300	363
Ohio			
Agriculture Dept 8995 E Main St Reynoldsburg OH 43068	800-282-1955	614-728-6201	339-36
Consumer Protection Section 30 E Broad St 14th Fl Columbus OH 43215	800-282-0515	614-466-8831	339-36
Education Dept 25 S Front St Columbus OH 43215	877-644-6338	614-995-1545	339-36
Financial Institutions Div 77 S High St 21st Fl Columbus OH 43266	866-278-0003	614-728-8400	339-36
Highway Patrol (OSHP) 1970 W Broad St PO Box 182074 Columbus OH 43223	877-772-8765	614-466-2660	339-36
Insurance Dept 50 W Town St Third Fl Ste 300 Columbus OH 43215	800-686-1526	614-644-2658	339-36
Mental Health Dept 30 E Broad St 8th Fl Columbus OH 43215	888-636-4889	614-466-2596	339-36
Parks & Recreation Div 2045 Morse Rd Bldg C-3 Columbus OH 43229	800-282-7275	614-265-6561	339-36
Taxation Dept 30 E Broad St 22nd Fl PO Box 530 Columbus OH 43215	888-405-4089	614-466-2166	339-36
Travel & Tourism Div PO Box 1001 Columbus OH 43216	800-282-5393	614-466-8844	339-36
Wildlife Div 2045 Morse Rd Bldg G Columbus OH 43229	800-945-3543	614-265-6300	339-36
Workers' Compensation Bureau 30 W Spring St Columbus OH 43215	800-644-6292	614-644-6292	339-36
Ohio a C e p 3510 Snouffer Rd Ste 100 Columbus OH 43235	888-642-2374	614-792-6506	532
Ohio Art Co 1 Toy St Bryan OH 43506 *OTC: OART*	800-800-3141	419-636-3141	760
Ohio Associated Enterprises LLC 1382 W Jackson St Painesville OH 44077	888-637-4832	440-354-3148	813
Ohio Casualty Insurance Co 9450 SewaRd Rd Fairfield OH 45014	800-843-6446	513-603-2400	391-4
Ohio Chamber of Commerce 230 E Town St PO Box 15159 Columbus OH 43215	800-533-2794	614-228-4201	139
Ohio Contractors Association 1313 Dublin Rd Columbus OH 43215	800-229-1388	614-488-0724	136
Ohio Dental Assn 1370 Dublin Rd Columbus OH 43215	800-497-6076	614-486-2700	229
Ohio Dominican University 1216 Sunbury Rd Columbus OH 43219	800-955-6446	614-251-4500	167
Ohio Edison Co 76 S Main St PO Box 3637 Akron OH 44308	800-736-3402		785
Ohio Education Assn (OEA) 225 E Broad St PO Box 2550 Columbus OH 43216	800-282-1500	614-228-4526	456-8
Ohio Gas Co PO Box 528 Bryan OH 43506	800-331-7396	419-636-1117	535
Ohio Gasket & Shim Company Inc 976 Evans Ave Akron OH 44305	800-321-2438	330-630-2030	327
Ohio Historical Society 1982 Velma Ave Columbus OH 43211	800-686-6124	614-297-2300	519
Ohio House Motel 600 N La Salle Dr Chicago IL 60654	866-601-6446	312-943-6000	705
Ohio Indemnity Co 250 E Broad St 7th Fl Columbus OH 43215	800-628-8581	614-228-2800	391-4
Ohio Legal Assistance Foundation 10 W Broad St Ste 950 Columbus OH 43215	800-877-9772	614-715-8560	428
Ohio Lottery Commission 615 W Superior Ave Cleveland OH 44113	800-686-4208	216-787-3200	451
Ohio Machinery Co 3993 E Royalton Rd Broadview Heights OH 44147	800-837-6200	440-526-6200	358
Ohio Magazine 1422 Euclid Ave Ste 730 Cleveland OH 44115	800-210-7293	216-771-2833	456-22
Ohio Magnetics Inc 5400 Dunham Rd Maple Heights OH 44137	800-486-6446	216-662-8484	469
Ohio Manufacturers' Association 33 N High St Columbus OH 43215	800-662-4463	614-224-5111	136
Ohio Medical Transportation Inc 2827 W Dblin Granville Rd Columbus OH 43235	877-633-3598	614-734-8001	13
Ohio Medicine Magazine 3401 Mill Run Dr Hilliard OH 43026	800-766-6762	614-527-6762	456-16
Ohio Northern University 525 S Main St Ada OH 45810 *Admissions	888-408-4668*	419-772-2000	167
Ohio Northern University Claude W Pettit College of Law 525 S Main St Ada OH 45810	877-452-9668	419-772-2211	168-1
Ohio Northern University Heterick Memorial Library 525 S Main St Ada OH 45810	866-943-5787	419-772-2181	434-6
Ohio Nurses Assn (ONA) 4000 E Main St Columbus OH 43213	800-735-0056	614-237-5414	532
Ohio Nut & Bolt Co 5250 W 164th St Brook Park OH 44142	800-362-0291	216-267-2240	280
Ohio Penal Industries (OPI) 1221 McKinley Ave Columbus OH 43222	800-237-3454	614-752-0287	629
Ohio State Bar Assn (OSBA) 1700 Lk Shore Dr Columbus OH 43204	800-282-6556	614-487-2050	71
Ohio State Life Insurance Co PO Box 410288 Kansas City MO 64141	800-752-1387		391-2
Ohio State Medical Assn 3401 Mill Run Dr Hilliard OH 43026	800-766-6762	614-527-6762	473
Ohio State University 154 W 12th Ave Columbus OH 43210	800-426-5046	614-292-3980	167
Libraries 1858 Neil Ave Mall Columbus OH 43210	800-555-1212	614-292-6175	434-6
Lima 4240 Campus Dr Lima OH 45804	800-228-1102	419-995-8391	167
Newark 1179 University Dr Newark OH 43055	800-963-9275	740-366-3321	167
Ohio State University Police, The 1680 Madison Ave Wooster OH 44691	800-358-4678	330-287-0111	666
Ohio Travel Association 130 E Chestnut St Ste 301 Columbus OH 43215	800-896-4682	614-572-1931	770
Ohio Tuition Trust Authority 580 S High St Ste 208 Columbus OH 43215 *Cust Svc	800-233-6734*	614-752-9400	723
Ohio University 120 Chubb Hall Athens OH 45710	800-858-6843	740-593-1000	167
Chillicothe 101 University Dr Chillicothe OH 45601	877-462-6824	740-774-7200	167
Eastern 45425 National Rd Saint Clairsville OH 43950	800-648-3331	740-695-1720	167
Lancaster 1570 Granville Pike Lancaster OH 43130	800-444-2910	740-654-6711	167
Southern 1804 Liberty Ave Ironton OH 45638	800-626-0513	740-533-4600	167
Ohio University Press 19 Cir Dr The Ridges Athens OH 45701 *Sales	800-621-2736*	740-593-1154	634-4
Ohio Valley Banc Corp 420 Third Ave Gallipolis OH 45631 *NASDAQ: OVBC*	800-468-6682	740-446-2631	360-2
Ohio Valley Supply Co 3512 Spring Grove Ave Cincinnati OH 45223	800-696-5608	513-681-8300	193-3
Ohio Veterans Home 3416 Columbus Ave Sandusky OH 44870 *Admissions	800-572-7934*	419-625-2454	791
Ohio Veterinary Medical Assn (OVMA) 3168 Riverside Dr Columbus OH 43221	800-662-6862	614-486-7253	793
Ohio Wesleyan University 61 S Sandusky St Slocum Hall Delaware OH 43015	800-922-8953	740-368-2000	167
Ohio Workforce Developement Office 4020 E Fifth Ave PO Box 1618 Columbus OH 43219	888-296-7541		339-36
Ohly Americas 3388 Bacon St Rhinelander WI 54501	800-321-2689	320-587-2481	297-42
OHM (Orchard Hiltz & McCliment Inc) 34000 Plymouth Rd Livonia MI 48150	888-522-6711	734-522-6711	263
Ohm Systems Inc 10250 Chester Rd Cincinnati OH 45215	800-878-0646	513-771-0008	462
Ohmart/VEGA Corp 4241 Allendorf Dr Cincinnati OH 45209	800-367-5383	513-272-0131	471
Ohmite Manufacturing Co 1600 Golf Rd Ste 850 Rolling Meadows IL 60008	866-964-6483	847-258-0300	255
Ohmstede 895 N Main St Beaumont TX 77704	800-568-2328	409-833-6375	90
OI Corp 151 Graham Rd PO Box 9010 College Station TX 77842	800-653-1711	979-690-1711	419
Oil & Gas Equipment Corp 8 Rd 350 Flora Vista NM 87415	800-868-9624	505-333-2300	386
Oil & Gas Journal PO Box 2002 Tulsa OK 74101	800-633-1656	918-831-9423	456-21
Oil Creek Plastics Inc 45619 State Hwy 27 PO Box 385 Titusville PA 16354	800-537-3661	814-827-3661	595
Oil Ctr Research LLC 106 Montrose Ave Lafayette LA 70503	800-256-8977	337-993-3559	540
Oil Price Information Service 3349 Hwy 138 Bldg D Ste D Wall NJ 07719 *Cust Svc	888-301-2645*	732-901-8800	530-5
Oil-Dri Corp of America 410 N Michigan Ave Ste 400 Chicago IL 60611 *NYSE: ODC*	800-645-3747	312-321-1515	499
Oil-Law Records Corp 8 N W 65th St Oklahoma City OK 73116	888-464-5529	405-840-1631	226
Ojai Valley Inn & Spa 905 Country Club Rd Ojai CA 93023	800-422-6524	805-640-2068	667
Ojo Caliente Mineral Springs Resort 50 Los Banos Dr PO Box 68 Ojo Caliente NM 87549	800-222-9162	505-583-2233	704
OK Foods Inc PO Box 1787 Fort Smith AR 72902	800-635-9441		618
Okeechobee Correctional Institution 3420 NE 168th St Okeechobee FL 34972	800-574-5729	863-462-5400	215
Okefenoke Rural Electric Membership Corp (REMC) 14384 Cleveland St PO Box 602 Nahunta GA 31553	800-262-5131	912-462-5131	247
Oki Data Americas Inc 2000 Bishops Gate Blvd Mount Laurel NJ 08054 *Cust Svc	800-654-3282*	856-235-2600	175-6

Name / Address	City	State	ZIP	Toll-Free	Phone	Class
OKI Developments Inc 1416 112th Ave NE	Bellevue	WA	98004	**877-465-3654**	425-454-2800	360-3
Oklahoma						
Child Support Enforcement Div PO Box 248822	Oklahoma City	OK	73124	**800-522-2922**	405-522-2273	339-37
Commerce Dept 900 N Stiles Ave	Oklahoma City	OK	73104	**800-879-6552**	405-815-6552	339-37
Environmental Quality Dept 707 N Robinson Ave PO Box 1677	Oklahoma City	OK	73101	**800-869-1400**	405-702-1000	339-37
Housing Finance Agency 100 NW 63rd St Ste 200	Oklahoma City	OK	73116	**800-256-1489**	405-848-1144	339-37
Insurance Dept (OID) 3625 NW 56th Ste 100	Oklahoma City	OK	73152	**800-522-0071**	405-521-2828	339-37
Parks Div PO Box 52002	Oklahoma City	OK	73152	**800-654-8240**	405-230-8300	339-37
Rehabilitative Services Dept 5501 N Portland Ave	Oklahoma City	OK	73112	**800-845-8476**	405-951-3400	339-37
Wildlife Conservation Dept (ODWC) PO Box 53465	Oklahoma City	OK	73152	**800-522-8039**	405-521-4660	339-37
Oklahoma Assn of Realtors 9807 N Broadway	Oklahoma City	OK	73114	**800-375-9944**	405-848-9944	654
Oklahoma Baptist University 500 W University St	Shawnee	OK	74804	**800-654-3285**	405-275-2850	167
Oklahoma Bar Assn 1901 N Lincoln Blvd PO Box 53036	Oklahoma City	OK	73105	**800-522-8065**	405-416-7000	71
Oklahoma Blood Institute (OBI) 1001 N Lincoln Blvd	Oklahoma City	OK	73104	**866-708-4995**	405-278-3100	88
Oklahoma Christian University PO Box 11000	Oklahoma City	OK	73136	**800-877-5010**	405-425-5000	167
Oklahoma City Convention & Visitors Bureau 123 Pk Ave	Oklahoma City	OK	73102	**800-225-5652**	405-297-8912	208
Oklahoma City Museum of Art 415 Couch Dr	Oklahoma City	OK	73102	**800-579-9278**	405-236-3100	519
Oklahoma City National Memorial & Memorial Ctr Museum 620 N Harvey Ave	Oklahoma City	OK	73102	**888-542-4673**	405-235-3313	519
Oklahoma City University 2501 N Blackwelder Ave *Admissions	Oklahoma City	OK	73106	**800-633-7242***	405-208-5050	167
Oklahoma City University School of Law 2501 N Blackwelder Ave	Oklahoma City	OK	73106	**800-230-3012**	405-208-5000	168-1
Oklahoma City Zoological Park & Botanical Gardens 2101 NE 50th St	Oklahoma City	OK	73111	**800-891-2917**	405-424-3344	821
Oklahoma Correctional Industries 3402 N Martin Luther King Ave	Oklahoma City	OK	73111	**800-522-3565**	405-425-7500	629
Oklahoma Democratic Party 4100 N Lincoln Blvd	Oklahoma City	OK	73105	**800-547-5600**	405-427-3366	615-1
Oklahoma Dental Assn 317 NE 13th St	Oklahoma City	OK	73104	**800-876-8890**	405-848-8873	229
Oklahoma Dept of Libraries 200 NE 18th St	Oklahoma City	OK	73105	**800-522-8116**	405-521-2502	434-5
Oklahoma Education Association 323 E Madison PO Box 18485	Oklahoma City	OK	73154	**800-522-8091**	405-528-7785	456-8
Oklahoma Federal Credit Union 517 NE 36th St	Oklahoma City	OK	73105	**800-522-8510**	405-524-6467	221
Oklahoma Medical Research Foundation (OMRF) 825 NE 13th St	Oklahoma City	OK	73104	**800-522-0211**	405-271-6673	666
Oklahoma Natural Gas Co 401 N Harvey PO Box 401	Oklahoma City	OK	73101	**800-664-5463**		785
Oklahoma Panhandle State University 323 Eagle Blvd	Goodwell	OK	73939	**800-664-6778**	580-349-2611	167
Oklahoma Press Service Inc 3601 N Lincoln Blvd	Oklahoma City	OK	73105	**888-815-2672**	405-524-4421	623
Oklahoma State University 219 Student Union Bldg	Stillwater	OK	74078	**800-852-1255**	405-744-5000	167
Oklahoma City 900 N Portland Ave	Oklahoma City	OK	73107	**800-560-4099**	405-947-4421	161
Okmulgee 1801 E Fourth St	Okmulgee	OK	74447	**800-722-4471**	918-293-4678	798
Tulsa 700 N Greenwood Ave	Tulsa	OK	74106	**800-522-4002**	918-594-8000	167
Oklahoma Telephone & Telegraph Inc 26 N Otis Ave	Dustin	OK	74839	**800-869-1989**		387
Oklahoma Veterans Ctr Ardmore 1015 S Commerce	Ardmore	OK	73401	**800-941-2160**	580-223-2266	791
Oklahoma Veterans Ctr Norman 1776 E Robinson St	Norman	OK	73071	**800-782-5218**	405-360-5600	449
Oklahoma Veterans Ctr Talihina 10014 SE 1138th Ave PO Box 1168	Talihina	OK	74571	**800-941-2160**	918-567-2251	791
Oklahoma Veterinary Medical Assn PO Box 14521	Oklahoma City	OK	73113	**800-248-2862**	405-478-1002	793
Oklahoman, The 9000 N Broadway	Oklahoma City	OK	73114	**800-375-6397**	405-475-3311	531-2
OLCC (Orange Lake Country Club Inc) 8505 W Irlo Bronson Memorial Hwy	Kissimmee	FL	34747	**800-877-6522**	407-239-0000	667
Old Alabama Town 301 Columbus St	Montgomery	AL	36104	**888-240-1850**	334-240-4500	49-2
Old American Insurance Co 3520 Broadway	Kansas City	MO	64111	**800-733-6242**	816-753-7000	391-2
Old Bridge Chemicals Inc PO Box 175	Old Bridge	NJ	08857	**800-275-3924**	732-727-2225	142
Old Bridge Public Library 1 Old Bridge Plz	Old Bridge	NJ	08857	**800-829-1040**	732-721-5600	434-3
Old Colony Hospice 1 Credit Union Way	Randolph	MA	02368	**800-370-1322**	781-341-4145	371
Old Dominion Capital Management Inc 815 E Jefferson St	Charlottesville	VA	22902	**800-446-2029**	434-977-1550	527
Old Dominion Eye Bank (ODEF) 9200 Arboretum Pkwy Ste 104	Richmond	VA	23236	**800-832-0728**	804-560-7540	271
Old Dominion Freight Line Inc 500 Old Dominion Way *NASDAQ: ODFL*	Thomasville	NC	27360	**800-432-6335**	336-889-5000	778
Old Dominion Insurance Co 4601 Touchton Rd E Ste 330 Ste 3400	Jacksonville	FL	32246	**800-226-0875**	904-642-3000	391-4
Old Dominion University Rollins Hall	Norfolk	VA	23529	**800-348-7926**	757-683-3685	167
Old Exchange & Provost Dungeon 122 E Bay St	Charleston	SC	29401	**888-763-0448**	843-727-2165	49-2
Old Florida Museum 259 San Marco Ave	Saint Augustine	FL	32084	**800-813-3208**	904-824-8874	519
Old House 309 W San Francisco St	Santa Fe	NM	87501	**800-955-4455**	505-988-4455	669
Old Idaho Penitentiary State Historic Site 2445 Old Penitentiary Rd	Boise	ID	83712	**877-653-4367**	208-334-2844	49-2
Old Line Bank 1525 Pointer Ridge Pl *NASDAQ: WSB*	Bowie	MD	20716	**800-416-6373**	301-430-2500	69
Old Mansion Foods 3811 Corporate Rd PO Box 1838	Petersburg	VA	23805	**800-476-1877**	804-862-9889	297-7
Old Mill Toronto 21 Old Mill Rd	Toronto	ON	M8X1G5	**866-653-6455**	416-236-2641	379
Old Mill Winery 403 S Broadway	Geneva	OH	44041	**800-227-6972**		79-3
Old National Bank 1 Main St PO Box 718	Evansville	IN	47705	**800-731-2265**		69
Old Newbury Crafters 36 Main St Ste 2	Amesbury	MA	01913	**800-343-1388**		700
Old Point Financial Corp 1 W Mellen St PO Box 3392 *NASDAQ: OPOF*	Hampton	VA	23663	**800-952-0051**	757-728-1200	360-2
Old Republic Insured Automotive Services Inc 8282 S Memorial Dr	Tulsa	OK	74133	**800-331-3780**	918-307-1000	391-5
Old Republic National Title Insurance Co (ORTIG) 400 Second Ave S	Minneapolis	MN	55401	**800-328-4441**	612-371-1111	391-6
Old Republic Surety 445 S Moorlands Rd Ste 200	Brookfield	WI	53005	**800-217-1792**	262-797-2640	391-5
Old Saint Ferdinand's Shrine 1 Rue St Francois	Florissant	MO	63031	**800-366-2427**	314-837-2110	49
Old Salem 600 S Main St	Winston-Salem	NC	27101	**800-441-5305**	336-721-7300	519
Old Second Bancorp Inc 37 S River St *NASDAQ: OSBC*	Aurora	IL	60506	**877-866-0202**	630-892-0202	360-2
Old Town Canoe Co 125 Gilman Falls Ave Bldg B	Old Town	ME	04468	**800-343-1555**	207-827-5513	708
Old Town San Diego State Historic Park 4002 Wallace St	San Diego	CA	92110	**800-777-0369**	619-220-5422	564
Old Virginia Brick Co 2500 W Main St	Salem	VA	24153	**800-879-8227**	540-389-2357	149
Old Wisconsin Sausage Co 5030 PlaybiRd Rd	Sheboygan	WI	53083	**877-451-7988**		297-26
Oldcastle BuildingEnvelope 5005 Lyndon B Johnson Fwy Ste 1050	Dallas	TX	75244	**866-653-2278**		330
Oldcastle Precast Bldg Systems Div 1401 Trimble Rd	Edgewood	MD	21040	**800-523-9144**		191-3
Oldcastle Precast Inc 7921 Southpark Pl Ste 200	Folsom	NJ	08037	**800-642-3755**		185
Olde Country Reproductions Inc 722 W Market St *Cust Svc	York	PA	17405	**800-358-3997***	717-848-1859	700
Olde Pink House 23 Abercorn St	Savannah	GA	31401	**800-554-1187**	912-232-4286	669
Olds College 4500-50 St	Olds	AB	T4H1R6	**800-661-6537**	403-556-8281	161
Olds Products Co 10700 88th Ave	Pleasant Prairie	WI	53158	**800-233-8064**	262-947-3500	297-19
Olean Times-Herald 639 Norton Dr	Olean	NY	14760	**800-722-8812**	716-372-3121	531-2
Olean Wholesale Grocery Co-op Inc 1587 Haskell Rd PO Box 1070	Olean	NY	14760	**888-835-3026**	716-372-2020	298-8
Oleco Inc 18683 Trimble Ct	Spring Lake	MI	49456	**800-575-3282**	616-842-6790	812
Olesky Associates Inc 865 Washington St Ste 3	Newtonville	MA	02460	**800-486-4330**	781-235-4330	262
Oleta River State Park 3400 NE 163rd St	North Miami Beach	FL	33160	**800-326-3521**	305-919-1846	564
Oley Foundation 214 Hun Memorial MC-28 Albany Medical Ctr	Albany	NY	12208	**800-776-6539**	518-262-5079	47-17
Olgoonik Development LLC 3201 C St Ste 700	Anchorage	AK	99503	**855-763-2613**	907-562-8728	189
Olin Corp Winchester Div 427 N Shamrock St	East Alton	IL	62024	**800-356-2666**	618-258-2000	286
Olis Inc 130 Conway Dr Ste A B & C	Bogart	GA	30622	**800-852-3504**	706-353-6547	419
Oliver Inlet State Marine Park 400 Willoughby Ave PO Box 111071	Juneau	AK	99801	**855-277-4491**	907-465-4563	564
Oliver M Dean Inc 125 Brooks St	Worcester	MA	01606	**800-648-3326**	508-856-9100	429
Oliver Machinery Co 6902 S 194th St	Kent	WA	98032	**800-559-5065**	253-867-0334	819
Oliver of Adrian Inc 1111 E Beecher St PO Box 189	Adrian	MI	49221	**877-668-0885**	517-263-2132	454
Oliver Products Co 445 Sixth St NW	Grand Rapids	MI	49504	**800-253-3893**	616-456-7711	299
Oliver Trucking Corp 1101 Harding Ct	Indianapolis	IN	46217	**888-561-4449**	317-787-1101	778

Name / Address	City	State	Zip	Toll-Free	Phone	Class
Oliver Winery 8024 N SR-37	Bloomington	IN	47404	**800-258-2783**	812-876-5800	49-6
Olivet College 320 S Main St	Olivet	MI	49076	**800-456-7189**	269-749-7000	167
Olivet Nazarene University 1 University Ave	Bourbonnais	IL	60914	**800-648-1463**	815-939-5011	167
Olivia Cruises & Resorts 434 Brannan St	San Francisco	CA	94107	**800-631-6277**	415-962-5700	758
OLM LLC 4 Trefoil Dr	Trumbull	CT	06611	**877-265-6638**	203-445-7700	806
Olney Central College 305 NW St	Olney	IL	62450	**866-622-4322**	618-395-7777	161
Olney Friends School 61830 Sandy Ridge Rd	Barnesville	OH	43713	**800-303-4291**	740-425-3655	621
Olon Industries Inc 42 Armstrong Ave	Georgetown	ON	L7G4R9	**800-387-2319**	905-877-7300	598
Olson Precast Co (OPC) 2750 Marion Dr	Las Vegas	NV	89115	**800-876-8374**	702-643-4371	185
Olson Research Assoc Inc 10290 Old Columbia Rd	Columbia	MD	21046	**888-657-6680**	410-290-6999	180-10
Olsson Assoc 1111 Lincoln Mall Ste 111	Lincoln	NE	68508	**877-831-6389**	402-474-6311	263
Olsun Electrics Corp 10901 Commercial St	Richmond	IL	60071	**800-336-5786**		765
Olum's of Binghamton Inc 3701 Vestal Pkwy E *Cust Svc	Vestal	NY	13850	**855-264-8674***	607-729-5775	322
Olymel LP 2200 Pratte Ave Pratte	Saint-Hyacinthe	QC	J2S4B6	**800-361-7990**	450-771-0400	618
Olympia Financial Group Inc Ste 2300 125 - 9 Ave SE	Calgary	AB	T2G0P6	**888-668-8384**	403-261-0900	785
Olympia Lacey Tumwater Visitor & Convention Bureau 103 Sid Snyder Ave SW	Olympia	WA	98501	**877-704-7500**	360-704-7544	208
Olympia Media Group LLC 5201 W 86th St	Indianapolis	IN	46268	**888-272-2595**		5
Olympia Promotions & Distribution 226 E Jericho Tpke	Mineola	NY	11501	**800-846-7874**	516-775-4500	328
Olympia Resort & Spa 1350 Royale Mile Rd	Oconomowoc	WI	53066	**800-558-9573**	262-369-4999	667
Olympia School District 1113 Legion Way SE	Olympia	WA	98501	**855-846-8376**	360-596-6100	683
Olympia Tile International Inc 1000 Lawrence Ave W	Toronto	ON	M6A1C6	**800-268-1613**	416-785-6666	193-4
Olympic College 1600 Chester Ave	Bremerton	WA	98337	**800-259-6718**	360-792-6050	161
Shelton 937 W Alpine Way	Shelton	WA	98584	**800-259-6718**	360-427-2119	161
Olympic Ctr Arena 2634 Main St	Lake Placid	NY	12946	**800-462-6236**	518-523-1655	718
Olympic Medical Ctr 939 Caroline St	Port Angeles	WA	98362	**888-362-6260**	360-417-7000	374-3
Olympic Steel Inc 5096 Richmond Rd *NASDAQ: ZEUS*	Bedford Heights	OH	44146	**800-321-6290**	216-292-3800	491
Olympique Expert Building Care 26232 Enterprise Ct	Lake Forest	CA	92630	**866-659-6747**	949-455-0796	462
Olympus Flag & Banner 9000 W Heather Ave	Milwaukee	WI	53224	**800-558-9620**	414-355-2010	289
OM Group Inc 811 Sharon Dr *NYSE: OMG*	Westlake	OH	44145	**800-519-0083**	440-899-2950	144
OMA (Oregon Medical Assn) 11740 SW 68th Pkwy Ste 100	Portland	OR	97223	**877-605-3229**	503-619-8000	473
Omaha Bedding Co 4011 S 60th St	Omaha	NE	68117	**800-279-9018**	402-733-8600	470
Omaha Community Foundation (OCF) 302 S 36th St Ste 100	Omaha	NE	68131	**800-794-3458**	402-342-3458	304
Omaha Community Playhouse 6915 Cass St	Omaha	NE	68132	**888-782-4338**	402-553-0800	572-4
Omaha Paper Co 6936 L St	Omaha	NE	68117	**800-288-7026**	402-331-3243	635
Omaha Standard Inc 3501 S 11th St Ste 1	Council Bluffs	IA	51501	**800-279-2201**	712-328-7444	515
Omaha Truck Center Inc 10710 I St PO Box 27379	Omaha	NE	68127	**800-866-2204**	402-592-2440	125
Omaha Wholesale Hardware Co PO Box 3628	Omaha	NE	68102	**800-238-4566**	402-444-1673	351
Omaha World-Herald 1314 Douglas St	Omaha	NE	68102	**800-284-6397**	402-444-1000	531-2
Oman Systems Inc 3334 Powell Ave	Nashville	TN	37204	**800-541-0803**	615-385-2500	190
OMAX Corp 21409 72nd Ave S	Kent	WA	98032	**800-838-0343**	253-872-2300	695
OMB Watch 1742 Connecticut Ave NW	Washington	DC	20009	**866-544-7573**	202-234-8494	47-7
OMC (Ocean Medical Ctr) 425 Jack Martin Blvd	Brick	NJ	08724	**800-560-9990**	732-840-2200	374-3
OMCO Inc 214 E Mill St	Odon	IN	47562	**800-525-0272**	812-636-7362	446
OMD Corp 3705 Missouri Blvd	Jefferson City	MO	65109	**866-440-8664**	573-893-8930	180-1
Omedix Inc 15849 N 71st St Ste 100	Scottsdale	AZ	85254	**877-866-3349**		396
Omega Engineering Inc 1 Omega Dr PO Box 4047	Stamford	CT	06907	**800-826-6342**	203-359-1660	203
Omega Flex Inc 451 Creamery Way *NASDAQ: OFLX*	Exton	PA	19341	**800-355-1039**	610-524-7272	788
Omega Healthcare Investors Inc 200 International Cir Ste 3500 *NYSE: OHI*	Hunt Valley	MD	21030	**877-511-2891**	410-427-1700	653
Omega Institute for Holistic Studies 150 Lake Dr	Rhinebeck	NY	12572	**800-944-1001**	845-266-4444	671
Omega International Inc 1937 NE Loop 410 Ste 200	San Antonio	TX	78217	**888-558-0701**	210-805-8808	360-3
Omega Medical Health Systems Inc 1200 E High St Ste 106	Pottstown	PA	19464	**866-716-6342**		474
Omega Moulding Company Ltd 1 Saw Grass Dr	Bellport	NY	11713	**800-289-6634**		361
Omega Products International 1681 California Ave	Corona	CA	92881	**800-600-6634**	951-737-7447	193-3
Omega Shielding Products Inc 1384 Pompton Ave	Cedar Grove	NJ	07009	**800-828-5784**	973-890-7455	327
Omega World Travel Inc 3102 Omega Office Pk Dr	Fairfax	VA	22031	**800-756-6342**	703-359-0200	769
Omegachem Inc 480 rue Perreault	St-romuald	QC	G6W7V6	**800-661-6342**	418-837-4444	240
Omgeo LLC 55 Thomson Pl	Boston	MA	02210	**866-496-6436**		197
OMHS (Owensboro Medical Health Systems) 811 E Parish Ave PO Box 20007	Owensboro	KY	42303	**877-888-6647**	270-688-2000	374-3
Omicron Architecture Engineering Construction Ltd 595 Burrard St Three Bentall Centre Fifth Fl PO Box 49369	Vancouver	BC	V7X1L4	**877-632-3350**	604-632-3350	258
Omnetics Connector Corp 7260 Commerce Cir E *Cust Svc	Minneapolis	MN	55432	**800-343-0025***	763-572-0656	813
Omni Barton Creek Resort & Spa 8212 Barton Club Dr	Austin	TX	78735	**800-336-6158**	512-329-4000	667
Omni Cable Corp 2 Hagerty Blvd	West Chester	PA	19382	**888-292-6664**	610-701-0100	248
Omni Cubed Inc 1390 Broadway Ste B155	Placerville	CA	95667	**877-311-1976**		228
Omni Hotels 4001 Maple Ave	Dallas	TX	75219	**800-843-6664**	402-952-6664	379
Omni Hotels Select Guest Loyalty Program 11819 Miami St 3rd Fl *Cust Svc	Omaha	NE	68164	**800-843-6664***		378
Omni Interlocken Resort 500 Interlocken Blvd	Broomfield	CO	80021	**800-843-6664**	303-438-6600	667
Omni La Mansion del Rio 112 College St	San Antonio	TX	78205	**800-292-7300**	210-518-1000	379
Omni Optical Lab 3255 Executive Blvd Ste 100	Beaumont	TX	77705	**800-364-6664**		542
Omni Orlando Resort at Championsgate 1500 Masters Blvd	Champions Gate	FL	33896	**800-843-6664**	407-390-6664	667
Omni Rancho Las Palmas Resort & Spa 41000 Bob Hope Dr	Rancho Mirage	CA	92270	**866-423-1195**	760-568-2727	705
Omnicare Inc 201 E 4th St *NYSE: OCR*	Cincinnati	OH	45202	**800-342-5627**	800-990-6664	586
Omnicell Inc 1201 Charleston Rd *NASDAQ: OMCL*	Mountain View	CA	94043	**800-850-6664**	650-251-6100	420
Omnigraphics Inc PO Box 31-1640	Detroit	MI	48231	**800-234-1340**		634-2
Omni-Lite Industries Canada Inc 17210 Edwards Rd	Cerritos	CA	90703	**800-577-6664**	562-404-8510	620
OMNIPLEX World Services Corp 14151 Pk Meadow Dr Ste 300	Chantilly	VA	20151	**800-356-3406**	703-652-3100	273
OmniSource Corp 7575 W Jefferson Blvd	Fort Wayne	IN	46804	**800-666-4789**	260-422-5541	684
Omnitracs LLC 10290 Campus Point Dr	San Diego	CA	92121	**888-627-2716**	800-647-3325	733
Omnitronics LLC 6573 Cochran Rd	Solon	OH	44139	**800-762-9266**	440-349-4900	51
Omnivex Corp 3300 Hwy 7 Ste 501	Concord	ON	L4K4M3	**800-745-8223**	905-761-6640	181
Omnni Associates Inc 1 Systems Dr	Appleton	WI	54914	**800-571-6677**	920-735-6900	263
OMNOVA Solutions Inc Performance Chemicals Div 165 S Cleveland Ave	Mogadore	OH	44260	**888-253-5454**	330-628-6536	144
OMRF (Oklahoma Medical Research Foundation) 825 NE 13th St	Oklahoma City	OK	73104	**800-522-0211**	405-271-6673	666
OMRON Corp 1 Commerce Dr	Schaumburg	IL	60173	**800-556-6766**	847-843-7900	205
Omron Healthcare Inc 1925 W Field Ct	Lake Forest	IL	60045	**877-216-1333**	847-680-6200	474
OMRON Scientific Technologies Inc 6550 Dumbarton Cir	Fremont	CA	94555	**888-510-4357**	510-608-3400	205
OMT Inc 1-1717 Dublin Ave	Winnipeg	MB	R3H0H2	**888-665-0501**	204-786-3994	395
OmTool Ltd 6 Riverside Dr *OTC: OMTL*	Andover	MA	01810	**800-886-7845**	978-327-5700	180-7
OMYA Inc 39 Main St	Proctor	VT	05765	**800-451-4468**	802-459-3311	142
On Event Services LLC 6550 McDonough Dr	Norcross	GA	30093	**800-967-2419**	770-457-0966	735
ON Semiconductor Corp 5005 E McDowell Rd *NASDAQ: ON*	Phoenix	AZ	85008	**800-282-9855**	602-244-6600	694
On Time Staffing LLC 2 Aquarium Dr Ferry Terminal Bldg Ste 150	Camden	NJ	08103	**866-333-3007**		262
ONA (Ohio Nurses Assn) 4000 E Main St	Columbus	OH	43213	**800-735-0056**	614-237-5414	532
ONA (Oregon Nurses Assn) 18765 SW Boones Ferry Rd	Tualatin	OR	97062	**800-634-3552**	503-293-0011	532
Ona Beach State Park 5580 S Coast Hwy	Newport	OR	97366	**800-551-6949**		564
Onboard Systems International 13915 NW Third Ct	Vancouver	WA	98685	**800-275-0883**	360-546-3072	528
OnCard Marketing Inc 276 Fifth Ave Ste 608	New York	NY	10001	**866-996-8729**		465
Oncenter Complex 800 S State St	Syracuse	NY	13202	**800-776-7548**	315-435-8000	207

Name / Address	City	State	ZIP	Toll-Free	Phone	Class
Oncology Nursing Society (ONS) 125 Enterprise Dr	Pittsburgh	PA	15275	**866-257-4667**	412-859-6100	48-8
Oncology Plus Inc 1070 E Brandon Blvd	Brandon	FL	33511	**877-410-0779**		239
Oncolytics Biotech Inc 1167 Kensington Crescent NW Ste 210 *TSE: ONC*	Calgary	AB	T2N1X7	**800-731-5319**	403-670-7377	84
Oncor 1616 Woodall Rodgers Fwy Ste 2M-012	Dallas	TX	75202	**888-313-6862**	214-486-2000	785
OnCorp Direct Inc 1033 Bay St Ste 313	Toronto	ON	M5S3A5	**800-461-7772**	416-964-2677	318
Ondine Biomedical Inc 1100 Melville St	Vancouver	BC	V6E4A6	**800-564-6253**	604-669-0555	233
Onduline North America Inc 4900 Ondura Dr	Fredericksburg	VA	22407	**800-777-7663**	540-898-7000	193-4
One Call Medical Inc (OCM) 20 Waterview Blvd PO Box 614	Parsippany	NJ	07054	**800-872-2875**	973-257-1000	382
One Lambda Inc 21001 Kittridge St	Canoga Park	CA	91303	**800-822-8824**	818-702-0042	478
One Liberty Properties Inc 60 Cutter Mill Rd Ste 303 *NYSE: OLP*	Great Neck	NY	11021	**800-937-5449**	516-466-3100	653
One Link Wireless 7321 Broadway Ext	Oklahoma City	OK	73116	**800-259-2929**	405-840-2345	248
One Source Industries LLC 185 Technology Dr	Irvine	CA	92618	**800-899-4990**		545
One Southern Indiana 4100 Charlestown Rd	New Albany	IN	47150	**800-521-2232**	812-945-0266	138
One Technologies LP 8144 Walnut Hill Ln Ste 600	Dallas	TX	75231	**888-550-8471**		227
One Touch Systems Inc 2528 Qume Dr Unit 14	San Jose	CA	95131	**800-227-8862**	408-436-4600	180-7
One Washington Cir Hotel 1 Washington Cir NW	Washington	DC	20037	**800-424-9671**	202-872-1680	379
One World Theatre 7701 Bee Caves Rd	Austin	TX	78746	**888-616-0522**	512-330-9500	571
OneAmerica Financial Partners Inc (PML) PO Box 368	Indianapolis	IN	46206	**800-249-6269**	317-285-1877	391-2
OneBeacon Insurance Group N 605 US-169 Ste 800	Plymouth	MN	55441	**800-662-0156**	781-332-7000	391-4
OneClass 65 Bloor St E Unit 1902	Toronto	ON	M4W3L4	**855-392-6946**		387
OneCoast Network LLC 230 Spring St Ste 1800	Atlanta	GA	30303	**866-592-5514**		361
Oneida County Convention & Visitors Bureau PO Box 551	Utica	NY	13503	**800-426-3132**	315-724-7221	208
OneLegacy Transplant Donor Network 221 S Figueroa St Ste 500	Los Angeles	CA	90012	**800-786-4077**	213-229-5600	544
OneMorePallet.com 9891 Montgomery Rd Ste 122	Cincinnati	OH	45242	**855-438-1667**		387
OneSCM 6805 Capital of Texas Hwy Ste 370	Austin	TX	78731	**800-324-5143**	512-231-8191	180-1
OneSource Information Services Inc 300 Baker Ave	Concord	MA	01742	**800-433-0287**	978-318-4300	634-10
ONESPRING LLC 980 Birmingham Rd Ste 501-165	Alpharetta	GA	30004	**888-472-1840**		182
OneTouch Direct LLC 4902 W Sligh Ave	Tampa	FL	33634	**866-948-4005**		40
OneUnited Bank 3683 Crenshaw Blvd	Los Angeles	CA	90016	**877-663-8648**	323-290-4848	69
ONGUARD Industries 1850 Clark Rd	Havre de Grace	MD	21078	**800-365-2282**	410-272-2000	302
Onity Inc 2232 Northmont Pkwy Ste 100	Duluth	GA	30096	**800-424-1433**		351
Onix Networking Corp 18519 Detroit Ave	Lakewood	OH	44107	**800-664-9638**		176
Online Computer Library Ctr Inc (OCLC) 6565 Kilgour Pl	Dublin	OH	43017	**800-848-5878**		48-11
Online Copy Corp 48815 Kato Rd	Fremont	CA	94539	**800-833-4460**		242
On-Line Strategies Inc 7920 Belt Line Rd Ste 1150	Dallas	TX	75254	**866-237-4900**	214-466-1000	255
Online Transport System Inc 6311 W Stoner Dr	Greenfield	IN	46140	**866-543-1235**	317-894-2159	778
OnlineMetals.com 1138 W Ewing	Seattle	WA	98119	**800-533-6350**		491
Onondaga Cave State Park 7556 Hwy H	Leasburg	MO	65535	**877-422-6766**	573-245-6576	564
Onondaga Coach Corp PO Box 277	Auburn	NY	13021	**800-451-1570**	315-255-2216	106
Onondaga Community College 4941 Onondaga Rd	Syracuse	NY	13215	**800-827-1000**	315-498-2622	161
onProject Inc PO Box 104	Franklin Lakes	NJ	07417	**877-936-6776**	973-971-9970	38
ONS (Oncology Nursing Society) 125 Enterprise Dr	Pittsburgh	PA	15275	**866-257-4667**	412-859-6100	48-8
Onset Computer Corp PO Box 3450	Pocasset	MA	02559	**800-564-4377**	508-759-9500	203
Onsite Management Group 4400 Bishop Ln Ste 214	Louisville	KY	40218	**800-207-4807**	502-583-1664	5
Onslow County Public Library 58 Doris Ave E	Jacksonville	NC	28540	**800-351-1697**	910-455-7350	434-3
Onslow County Tourism 1099 Gum Branch Rd	Jacksonville	NC	28540	**800-932-2144**		208
Onsrud Cutter LP 800 Liberty Dr	Libertyville	IL	60048	**800-234-1560**	847-362-1560	492
Ontario Area Chamber of Commerce 251 SW 9th St	Ontario	OR	97914	**866-989-8012**	541-889-8012	208
Ontario Centres of Excellence Inc 156 Front St W Ste 200	Toronto	ON	M5J2L6	**866-759-6014**	416-861-1092	216
Ontario Clean Water Agency 1 Yonge St	Toronto	ON	M5E1E5	**800-515-2759**	416-314-5600	194
Ontario Convention & Visitors Bureau 2000 E Convention Ctr Way	Ontario	CA	91764	**800-455-5755**	909-937-3000	208
Ontario Convention Ctr 2000 E Convention Ctr Way	Ontario	CA	91764	**800-455-5755**	909-937-3000	207
Ontario Dental Nurses & Assistants Association 869 Dundas St	London	ON	N5W2Z8	**800-461-4348**	519-679-2566	136
Ontario Drive & Gear Ltd (ODG) 220 Bergey Ct	New Hamburg	ON	N3A2J5	**877-274-6288**	519-662-2840	29
Ontario Knife Co 26 Empire St	Franklinville	NY	14737	**800-222-5233**	716-676-5527	224
Ontario Lottery & Gaming Corp 70 Foster Dr Ste 800	Sault Sainte Marie	ON	P6A6V2	**800-563-5357**	705-946-6464	639
Ontario Medical Supply Ltd 1100 Algoma Rd	Ottawa	ON	K1B0A3	**800-804-1112**	613-244-8620	363
Ontario Nurses Association 85 Grenville St Ste 400	Toronto	ON	M5S3A2	**800-387-5580**	416-964-8833	414
Ontario Pc Party 19 Duncan St	Toronto	ON	M5H3H1	**800-903-6453**	416-861-9593	614
Ontario Real Estate Assn 99 Duncan Mill Rd	Don Mills	ON	M3B1Z2	**866-444-5557**	416-445-9910	650
Ontario Science Centre 770 Don Mills Rd	Toronto	ON	M3C1T3	**888-696-1110**	416-696-1000	519
Ontario State Recreation Site 23751 Old Hwy 30	Huntington	OR	97907	**800-551-6949**		564
Ontario Tourism Marketing Partnership Corp 10 Dundas St E Ste 900	Toronto	ON	M7A2A1	**800-668-2746**	905-282-1721	772
Ontor Ltd 12 Leswyn Rd	Toronto	ON	M6A1K3	**800-567-1631**	416-781-5286	662
Onyx EMS LLC 2920 Kelly Ave	Watertown	SD	57201	**800-772-7866**	605-886-2519	255
Onyx Hotel 155 Portland St	Boston	MA	02114	**866-660-6699**	617-557-9955	379
OOIDA (Owner-Operator Independent Drivers Assn Inc) 1 NW OOIDA Dr	Grain Valley	MO	64029	**800-444-5791**	816-229-5791	48-21
OPC (Olson Precast Co) 2750 Marion Dr	Las Vegas	NV	89115	**800-876-8374**	702-643-4371	185
OPCMIA (Operative Plasterers' & Cement Masons' International Assn of the US & Canada) 11720 Beltsville Dr Ste 700	Beltsville	MD	20705	**888-379-1558**	301-623-1000	48-3
Open Applications Group Inc (OAGI) PO Box 4897	Marietta	GA	30061	**800-236-4600**	404-402-1962	48-13
Open Arms Hospice 1836 W Georgia Rd	Simpsonville	SC	29680	**866-473-6276**	864-688-1700	371
Open Automation Software 5077 Bear Mtn Dr	Evergreen	CO	80439	**800-533-4994**	303-679-0898	181
Open Court Publishing Co 70 E Lake St Ste 800	Chicago	IL	60601	**800-815-2280**		634-2
Open Dental Software Ste 110 3995 Fairview Industrial Dr SE	Salem	OR	97302	**866-239-0469**	503-363-5432	179
Open Group 44 Montgomery St Ste 960	San Francisco	CA	94104	**800-433-6611**	415-374-8280	47-9
Open Kitchen Inc 1161 W 21st St	Chicago	IL	60608	**800-339-5334**	312-666-5335	300
Open Minds 163 York St	Gettysburg	PA	17325	**877-350-6463**	717-334-1329	465
Open Pantry Food Marts 10505 Corporate Dr Ste 101	Pleasant Prairie	WI	53158	**800-242-3358**	262-857-1156	206
Open Plan Systems Inc 4700 Deepwater Terminal Rd	Richmond	VA	23234	**844-677-6771**	804-275-2468	320-1
Open Spatial Inc 13575 58th St N Ste 180	Clearwater	FL	33760	**800-696-1238**		198
Open Storage Solutions Inc 2 Castleview Dr	Toronto	ON	L6T5S9	**800-387-3419**	905-790-0660	176
Open Systems Inc 4301 Dean Lakes Blvd *Sales	Shakopee	MN	55379	**800-328-2276***		180-1
Open Systems of Cleveland Inc 22999 Forbes Rd Ste A	Cleveland	OH	44146	**888-881-6660**	440-439-2332	176
Open Text Corp 275 Frank Tompa Dr *TSE: OTC* ■ *General	Waterloo	ON	N2L0A1	**800-499-6544***	519-888-7111	180-7
Open Text Corp (USA) 100 Tri-State International Pkwy 3rd Fl *TSE: OTC* ■ *Sales	Lincolnshire	IL	60069	**800-499-6544***	847-267-9330	180-7
OpenConnect Systems Inc 2711 LBJ Fwy Ste 700	Dallas	TX	75234	**800-551-5881**	972-484-5200	180-7
Openface Inc 3445 Park Ave	Montreal	QC	H2X2H6	**800-865-8585**	514-281-8585	227
Openjar Concepts Inc 27710 jefferson ave	Temecula	CA	92590	**877-673-6527**		7
OPENonline 1650 Lk Shore Dr Ste 350	Columbus	OH	43204	**888-381-5656**	614-481-6999	632
OpenTable Inc 1 Montgomery St 4th Fl *NASDAQ: OPEN*	San Francisco	CA	94103	**800-673-6822**	415-344-4200	180-10
OpenText Corp 275 Frank Tompa Dr Ste 710 N	Waterloo	ON	N2L0A1	**800-499-6544**	773-632-1400	180-1
OpenWorks 4742 N 24th St Ste 450	Phoenix	AZ	85016	**800-777-6736**	602-224-0440	311
Opera Omaha 1625 Farnam St Ste 100	Omaha	NE	68102	**877-346-7372**	402-346-4398	572-2
Opera San Jose 2149 Paragon Dr	San Jose	CA	95131	**800-745-3000**	408-437-4450	572-2
Operation USA 3617 Hayden Ave Ste A	Culver City	CA	90232	**800-678-7255**	310-838-3455	47-5
Operational Technologies Corp 4100 NW Loop 410 Ste 230	San Antonio	TX	78229	**855-276-6136**	210-731-0000	263
Operative Plasterers' & Cement Masons' International Assn of the US & Canada (OPCMIA) 11720 Beltsville Dr Ste 700	Beltsville	MD	20705	**888-379-1558**	301-623-1000	48-3

Alphabetical Section

Name / Address	City	State	ZIP	Toll-Free	Phone	Class
Opex Corp 305 Commerce Dr	Moorestown	NJ	08057	**800-673-9288**	856-727-1100	180-10
OPGI (Original Parts Group Inc) 1770 Saturn Way	Seal Beach	CA	90740	**800-243-8355**	562-594-1000	53
OPI (Ohio Penal Industries) 1221 McKinley Ave	Columbus	OH	43222	**800-237-3454**	614-752-0287	629
Opinion Access Corp 47-10 32nd Pl	Long Island	NY	11101	**888-489-3282**	718-729-2622	227
Opinion Research Corp (ORC) 902 Carnegie Ctr Ste 220	Princeton	NJ	08540	**800-444-4672**		465
OPIS 9737 Washingtonian Blvd Ste 200	Gaithersburg	MD	20878	**888-301-2645**	301-287-2645	530-5
Opmedic Group Inc 1361 Beaumont Ave Ste 301	Mount-royal	QC	H3P2W3	**888-776-2732**	514-345-8535	418
Oppenheimer Cos Inc 877 W Main Ste 700	Boise	ID	83702	**800-727-9939**	208-343-4883	298-8
OppenheimerFunds Inc 225 Liberty St	New York	NY	10281	**800-525-7048**		527
Opsol Integrators Inc 1566 La Pradera Dr	Campbell	CA	95008	**800-996-7765**	408-364-9915	182
Opsource Inc 5201 Great America Pkwy Ste 120	Santa Clara	CA	95054	**800-664-9973**	408-567-2000	806
Optek Technology Inc 1645 Wallace Dr	Carrollton	TX	75006	**800-341-4747**	972-323-2200	694
Optex Inc 13661 Benson Ave Bldg C	Chino	CA	91710	**800-966-7839**	909-993-5770	690
Opti Care Eye Health Center 87 Grandview Ave	Waterbury	CT	06708	**800-334-3937**	203-574-2020	542
Optical Cable Corp (OCC) 5290 Concourse Dr *NASDAQ: OCC*	Roanoke	VA	24019	**800-622-7711**	540-265-0690	812
Optical Distributor Group LLC 12301 NW 39th St	Coral Springs	FL	33065	**800-852-8089**	914-347-7400	542
Optical Gaging Products Inc 850 Hudson Ave	Rochester	NY	14621	**800-647-4243**	585-544-0450	543
Optical Society of America (OSA) 2010 Massachusetts Ave NW	Washington	DC	20036	**800-766-4672**	202-223-8130	48-8
Opti-Com Mfg Network Co Inc 259 Plauche St	New Orleans	LA	70123	**800-345-8774**	504-736-0331	814
Optimal Engineering Systems 6901 Woodley Ave	Van Nuys	CA	91406	**888-777-1826**	818-222-9200	358
Optimetra Inc 1710 Chapel Hills Dr	Colorado Springs	CO	80920	**800-758-9710**		227
Optimist International 4494 Lindell Blvd	Saint Louis	MO	63108	**800-500-8130**	314-371-6000	47-15
Optimum Health Institute 6970 Central Ave	Lemon Grove	CA	91945	**800-993-4325**	619-464-3346	704
Optimum Solutions Corp 170 Earle Ave	Lynbrook	NY	11563	**800-227-0672**	516-247-5300	179
Optimum Talent Inc 25 York St Ste 1802	Toronto	ON	M5J2V5	**877-364-2605**	416-364-2605	762
OPTIO LLC 390 Spaulding Ave SE	Ada	MI	49301	**888-981-3282**		198
Option Advisor 5151 Pfeiffer Rd Ste 250	Cincinnati	OH	45242	**800-448-2080**	513-589-3800	530-9
OptionsXpress Inc 311 W Monroe Ste 1000	Chicago	IL	60606	**888-280-8020**	312-630-3300	171
Optonol Inc P.O. Box 2367	Kansas City	KS	66110	**877-707-3937**		474
Opus Bank 19900 MacArthur Blvd 12th Fl	Irvine	CA	92612	**855-678-7226**	949-250-9800	360-2
Opus Framing Ltd 3445 Cornett Rd	Vancouver	BC	V5M2H3	**800-663-6953**	604-435-9991	534
Opus Hotel 322 Davie St	Vancouver	BC	V6B5Z6	**866-642-6787**		379
OPW Engineered Systems 2726 Henkle Dr *Cust Svc	Lebanon	OH	45036	**800-547-9393***	513-932-9114	619
OPW Fuel Management Systems 6900 Santa Fe Dr	Hodgkins	IL	60525	**800-547-9393**	708-485-4200	203
Oracle Corp 500 Oracle Pkwy *NYSE: ORCL* ■ *Sales	Redwood Shores	CA	94065	**800-392-2999***	650-506-7000	180-1
Oracle Magazine 500 Oracle Pkwy	Redwood Shores	CA	94065	**800-392-2999**	650-506-7000	456-7
Oracle USA 500 Oracle Pkwy	Redwood Shores	CA	94065	**800-392-2999**	650-506-7000	180-1
Oral Health America 410 N Michigan Ave Ste 352	Chicago	IL	60611	**800-523-3438**	312-836-9900	47-17
Oral Roberts University 7777 S Lewis Ave	Tulsa	OK	74171	**800-678-8876**	918-495-6161	167
Oral Roberts University Library 7777 S Lewis Ave	Tulsa	OK	74171	**800-678-8876**	918-495-6723	434-6
Oral-B Laboratories 600 Clipper Dr Ste 200	Belmont	CA	94002	**800-566-7252**		474
Orange & Rockland Utilities Inc 390 W Rte 59 *Cust Svc	Spring Valley	NY	10977	**877-434-4100***		785
Orange Belt Stages PO Box 949	Visalia	CA	93279	**800-266-7433**	559-733-4408	758
Orange Chamber of Commerce 1940 N Tustin St	Orange	CA	92865	**888-676-1040**	714-538-3581	138
Orange City Area Health System 1000 Lincoln Cir SE	Orange City	IA	51041	**800-808-6264**	712-737-4984	374-3
Orange Coast Magazine 3701 Birch St Ste 100	Newport Beach	CA	92660	**800-397-8179**	949-862-1133	456-22
Orange Coast Memorial Medical Ctr (OCMMC) 9920 Talbert Ave	Fountain Valley	CA	92708	**877-597-4777**	714-378-7000	374-3
Orange County 200 Dailey Dr	Orange	VA	22960	**866-803-8641**	540-661-4550	338
Orange County Convention Ctr (OCCC) 9800 International Dr	Orlando	FL	32819	**800-345-9845**	407-685-9800	207
Orange County Industrial Plastics Inc 4811 E La Palma Ave	Anaheim	CA	92807	**800-974-6247**	714-632-9450	602
Orange County Public Schools 445 W Amelia St	Orlando	FL	32801	**800-378-9264**	407-317-3200	683
Orange County Regional History Ctr 65 E Central Blvd	Orlando	FL	32801	**800-965-2030**	407-836-8500	519
Orange County Register 625 N Grand Ave	Santa Ana	CA	92701	**877-469-7344**	714-796-7000	531-2
Orange County Rural Electric Membership Corp 7133 N State Rd 337 PO Box 208	Orleans	IN	47452	**888-337-5900**	812-865-2229	247
Orange County's Credit Union PO Box 11777	Santa Ana	CA	92711	**888-354-6228**	714-755-5900	221
Orange Julius of America 7505 Metro Blvd	Minneapolis	MN	55439	**866-793-7582**	952-830-0200	668
Orange Lake Country Club Inc (OLCC) 8505 W Irlo Bronson Memorial Hwy	Kissimmee	FL	34747	**800-877-6522**	407-239-0000	667
Orange Line Oil Company Inc 404 E Commercial St	Pomona	CA	91767	**800-492-6864**	909-623-0533	578
Orange Motors Company Inc 799 Central Ave	Albany	NY	12206	**888-912-5958**	518-489-5414	56
Orange Regional Medical Ctr 60 Prospect Ave	Middletown	NY	10940	**888-321-6762**	845-343-2424	374-3
Orange Research Inc 140 Cascade Blvd	Milford	CT	06460	**800-989-5657**	203-877-5657	203
Orange Tree Employment Screening 7275 Ohms Ln	Minneapolis	MN	55439	**800-886-4777**	952-941-9040	632
Orange Tree Golf & Conference Resort 10601 N 56th St	Scottsdale	AZ	85254	**866-729-7159**	480-948-6100	667
Orangeburg County Chamber of Commerce 155 Riverside Dr SW PO Box 328	Orangeburg	SC	29116	**800-545-6153**	803-534-6821	138
Orangeburg Pecan Company Inc 761 Russell St	Orangeburg	SC	29115	**800-845-6970**	803-534-4277	278
Orangevale Chamber of Commerce 9267 Greenback Ln Ste B-91	Orangevale	CA	95662	**800-962-1106**	916-988-0175	138
OraSure Technologies Inc 220 E First St *NASDAQ: OSUR*	Bethlehem	PA	18015	**800-869-3538**	610-882-1820	233
ORBCOMM 22970 Indian Creek Dr Ste 300 *Cust Svc	Sterling	VA	20166	**800-607-0088***	703-433-6300	679
ORBIS Corp 1055 Corporate Ctr Dr	Oconomowoc	WI	53066	**800-999-8683**	262-560-5000	201
ORBIS International Inc 520 Eigth Ave 11th Fl	New York	NY	10018	**800-672-4787**	646-674-5500	47-5
Orbit Medical Enterprises Inc 716 East 4500 South Ste 260 S	Salt Lake City	UT	84107	**800-430-0539**	801-713-2020	44
ORC (Opinion Research Corp) 902 Carnegie Ctr Ste 220	Princeton	NJ	08540	**800-444-4672**		465
Orchard Garden Hotel 466 Bush St	San Francisco	CA	94108	**888-717-2881**	415-399-9807	379
Orchard Hiltz & McCliment Inc (OHM) 34000 Plymouth Rd	Livonia	MI	48150	**888-522-6711**	734-522-6711	263
Orchard Hotel 665 Bush St	San Francisco	CA	94108	**888-717-2881**	415-362-8878	379
Orchard Software Corp 701 Congressional Blvd Ste 360	Carmel	IN	46032	**800-856-1948**	317-573-2633	179
Orchards Inn of Sedona 254 Hwy N 89 A	Sedona	AZ	86336	**855-474-7719**		379
Orchestra Hall 1111 Nicollet Mall	Minneapolis	MN	55403	**800-292-4141**	612-371-5600	571
Orchestra New England PO Box 200123	New Haven	CT	06520	**800-595-4849**	203-777-4690	572-3
Orchestre Symphonique de Montreal 260 de Maisonneuve Blvd W 2nd Fl	Montreal	QC	H2X1Y9	**888-842-9951**	514-842-9951	572-3
Orchid Suites Inc 1309 Emerson St NW	Washington	DC	20011	**877-255-4300**		227
Orcon Corp 1570 Atlantic St *General	Union City	CA	94587	**800-227-0505***	510-489-8100	599
Orcutt/Winslow 3003 N Central Ave	Phoenix	AZ	85012	**800-331-5842**	602-257-1764	188
Order Sons of Italy in America (OSIA) 219 E St NE	Washington	DC	20002	**800-552-6742**	202-547-2900	47-14
Oreck Corp 1400 Salem Rd	Cookeville	TN	38506	**800-289-5888**		786
Oregon						
Crime Victims Service Div 1162 Ct St NE	Salem	OR	97301	**877-877-9392**	503-378-4400	339-38
Dept of Transportation 355 Capitol St NE Ste 135 Rm 222	Salem	OR	97301	**888-275-6368**	503-986-4000	339-38
Financial Fraud/Consumer Protection Section 1162 Ct St NE	Salem	OR	97301	**877-877-9392**	503-378-4400	339-38
Fish & Wildlife Dept (ODFW) 3406 Cherry Ave NE	Salem	OR	97303	**800-720-6339**	503-947-6000	339-38
Legislative Assembly 900 Ct St NE	Salem	OR	97301	**800-332-2313**		339-38
Oregon Business Development Dept (OBDD) 775 Summer St NE Ste 200 *General	Salem	OR	97301	**800-735-2900***	503-986-0123	339-38
Parks & Recreation Dept (OPRD) 725 Summer St NE Ste C	Salem	OR	97301	**800-551-6949**	503-986-0707	339-38
Vocational Rehabilitation Services Office (OVRS) 700 Summer St NE E-87	Salem	OR	97301	**877-277-0513**	800-692-9666	339-38
Oregon Aero Inc 34020 Skyway Dr	Scappoose	OR	97056	**800-888-6910**	503-543-7399	528
Oregon Assn of Realtors 2110 Mission St SE	Salem	OR	97306	**800-252-9115**	503-362-3645	654
Oregon Catholic Press (OCP) 5536 NE Hassalo St	Portland	OR	97213	**877-596-1653**	503-281-1191	634-3
Oregon Caves National Monument 19000 Caves Hwy	Cave Junction	OR	97523	**877-245-9022**	541-592-2100	563

Name / Address	City	State	ZIP	Toll-Free	Phone	Class
Oregon Cherry Growers Inc 1520 Woodrow NE	Salem	OR	97301	**800-367-2536**	503-364-8421	316-3
Oregon Coast Aquarium 2820 SE Ferry Slip Rd	Newport	OR	97365	**800-452-7888**	541-867-3474	39
Oregon Coast Magazine 88906 Highway 101 N Ste 2B	Florence	OR	97439	**800-348-8401**	541-997-8401	456-22
Oregon Connection 1125 S First St	Coos Bay	OR	97420	**800-255-5318**	541-267-7804	328
Oregon Convention Ctr 777 NE Martin Luther King Jr Blvd	Portland	OR	97232	**800-791-2250**	503-235-7575	207
Oregon Dental Assn PO Box 3710	Wilsonville	OR	97070	**800-452-5628**	503-218-2010	229
Oregon Education Magazine (OEA) 6900 SW Atlanta St Bldg 1	Portland	OR	97223	**800-858-5505**	503-684-3300	456-8
Oregon Employment Dept 875 Union St NE	Salem	OR	97311	**877-345-3484**	503-451-2400	261
Oregon Food Bank Inc 7900 NE 33rd Dr	Portland	OR	97211	**888-398-8702**	503-282-0555	47-5
Oregon Garden, The 879 W Main St PO Box 155	Silverton	OR	97381	**877-674-2733**	503-874-8100	96
Oregon Health & Science University *Bone Marrow Transplant Program (OHSU)* 3181 SW Sam Jackson Pk Rd	Portland	OR	97239	**800-222-1222**	503-494-1617	767
School of Medicine 3181 SW Sam Jackson Pk Rd L-109	Portland	OR	97239	**800-775-5460**	503-494-7800	168-2
Oregon Health & Science University Hospital 3181 SW Sam Jackson Pk Rd	Portland	OR	97239	**800-292-4466**	503-494-8311	167
Oregon Institute of Technology 3201 Campus Dr	Klamath Falls	OR	97601	**800-422-2017**	541-885-1150	167
Oregon International Port of Coos Bay 125 Central Ave Ste 300 PO Box 1215	Coos Bay	OR	97420	**800-463-3339**	541-267-7678	617
Oregon Lions Sight & Hearing Foundation 1010 NW 22nd Ave Ste 144	Portland	OR	97210	**800-635-4667**	503-413-7399	271
Oregon Medical Assn (OMA) 11740 SW 68th Pkwy Ste 100	Portland	OR	97223	**877-605-3229**	503-619-8000	473
Oregon Museum of Science & Industry 1945 SE Water Ave	Portland	OR	97214	**800-955-6674**	503-797-4000	519
Oregon Mutual Insurance Co PO Box 808	McMinnville	OR	97128	**800-888-2141**	503-472-2141	391-4
Oregon Nurses Assn (ONA) 18765 SW Boones Ferry Rd	Tualatin	OR	97062	**800-634-3552**	503-293-0011	532
Oregon Potato Co PO Box 3110	Pasco	WA	99302	**800-336-6311**	509-545-4545	297-18
Oregon Shakespeare Festival 15 S Pioneer St	Ashland	OR	97520	**800-219-8161**	541-482-2111	746
Oregon State Bar Assn 16037 SW Upper Boones Ferry Rd	Tigard	OR	97224	**800-452-8260**	503-620-0222	71
Oregon State Bar Bulletin, The 16037 SW Upper Boones Ferry Rd PO Box 231935	Tigard	OR	97281	**800-452-8260**	503-620-0222	456-15
Oregon State Hospital 2600 Ctr St NE	Salem	OR	97301	**800-544-7078**	503-945-2800	374-5
Oregon State University 104 Kerr Admin Bldg	Corvallis	OR	97331	**800-291-4192**	541-737-4411	167
Oregon State University Press 1500 Jefferson St *Orders	Corvallis	OR	97331	**800-426-3797***	541-737-3166	634-4
Oregon Symphony Orchestra 921 SW Washington St Ste 200	Portland	OR	97205	**800-228-7343**	503-228-4294	572-3
Oregon Veterans' Home 700 Veterans Dr	The Dalles	OR	97058	**800-846-8460**	541-296-7190	791
Oregon Veterinary Medical Assn 1880 Lancaster Dr NE Ste 118	Salem	OR	97305	**800-235-3502**	503-399-0311	793
Oregon-California Trails Assn 524 S Osage St PO Box 1019	Independence	MO	64051	**888-811-6282**	816-252-2276	47-23
Oregonian 1320 SW Broadway *News Rm	Portland	OR	97201	**800-723-3638***	503-221-8100	531-2
Orelube Corp, The 20 Sawgrass Dr	Bellport	NY	11713	**800-645-9124**	631-205-9700	540
Organ Supply Industries Inc 2320 W 50th St	Erie	PA	16506	**800-458-0289**	814-835-2244	526
Organic Milling Co 505 W Allen Ave	San Dimas	CA	91773	**800-638-8686**	909-599-0961	297-4
Organic Valley Family of Farms 1 Organic Way	LaFarge	WI	54639	**888-444-6455**		298-7
Organization for Tropical Studies (OTS) 410 Swift Ave	Durham	NC	27705	**877-572-4484**	919-684-5774	48-5
Organization of American Historians (OAH) 112 N Bryan Ave	Bloomington	IN	47408	**888-737-7006**	812-855-7311	48-5
Organization of American States (OAS) 1889 F St NW	Washington	DC	20006	**888-442-4887**	202-458-3000	47-7
Organizational Dynamics Inc 790 Boston Rd Ste 201	Billerica	MA	01821	**800-634-4636**	978-671-5454	196
Organo Gold International Inc 5505 hovander rd	Ferndale	WA	98248	**877-674-2661**		462
Orgill Inc 3742 Tyndale Dr	Memphis	TN	38125	**800-347-2860**	901-754-8850	351
Orgill Singer 8360 W Sahara Ave Ste 110	Las Vegas	NV	89117	**800-745-3065**	702-796-9100	47-20
Orient Express Hotels Inc 1155 Ave of the Americas *NYSE: OEH*	New York	NY	10036	**800-237-1236**	212-302-5055	379
Oriental Institute Museum 1155 E 58th St University of Chicago	Chicago	IL	60637	**800-791-9354**	773-702-9514	519
Oriental Trading Company Inc 5455 S 90th St	Omaha	NE	68127	**800-875-8480**	402-596-1200	458
Original Cake Candle Co, The 102 Sundale Rd	Norwich	OH	43767	**888-444-2253**	740-872-3248	121
Original Lincoln Logs Ltd 5 Riverside Dr PO Box 135	Chestertown	NY	12817	**800-833-2461**		105
Original Parts Group Inc (OPGI) 1770 Saturn Way	Seal Beach	CA	90740	**800-243-8355**	562-594-1000	53
OriginClear Inc 5645 W Adams Blvd	Los Angeles	CA	90016	**877-999-6645**	323-939-6645	535
Origins Natural Resources Inc 767 Fifth Ave *Cust Svc	New York	NY	10153	**800-674-4467***		217
Oriole Park at Camden Yards 333 Camden St	Baltimore	MD	21201	**888-848-2473**	410-547-6100	718
Orion Instruments LLC 2105 Oak Villa Blvd	Baton Rouge	LA	70815	**866-556-7466**	225-906-2343	203
Orion International Consulting Group Inc 912 Capital of Texas Hwy S Ste 220	Austin	TX	78746	**800-336-7466**	512-327-7111	719
Orion Magazine 187 Main St	Great Barrington	MA	01230	**888-909-6568**	413-528-4422	456-19
Orion Mobility LLC 4 Mountainview Terrace Ste 101	Danbury	CT	06810	**800-476-7787**	203-762-0365	196
Orion Registrar Inc 7850 vance dr	Arvada	CO	80003	**800-446-0674**	303-456-6010	462
Orion Township Public Library 825 Joslyn Rd	Lake Orion	MI	48362	**877-924-7467**	248-693-3000	434-3
Oritani Financial Corp 370 Pascack Rd PO Box 1329 *NASDAQ: ORIT*	Washington Township	NJ	07676	**888-674-8264**	201-664-5400	69
Orkin Exterminating Co Inc 2170 Piedmont Rd NE	Atlanta	GA	30324	**844-499-3453**	877-250-1652	576
Orland Square 288 Orland Sq	Orland Park	IL	60462	**877-746-6642**	708-349-1646	459
Orlando Baking Company Inc 7777 Grand Ave	Cleveland	OH	44104	**800-362-5504**	216-361-1872	297-1
Orlando Magazine 801 N Magnolia Ave Ste 201	Orlando	FL	32803	**866-356-3075**	407-423-0618	456-22
Orlando Museum of Art 2416 N Mills Ave	Orlando	FL	32803	**800-435-7352**	407-896-4231	519
Orlando Regional Medical Ctr (ORMC) 1414 Kuhl Ave	Orlando	FL	32806	**800-424-6998**	321-841-5111	374-3
Orlando Science Ctr 777 E Princeton St	Orlando	FL	32803	**888-672-4386**	407-514-2000	519
Orlando Sentinel 633 N Orange Ave	Orlando	FL	32801	**800-974-7488**	407-420-5000	531-2
Orlando Weekly 1505 E Colonial Dr St Ste 200	Orlando	FL	32803	**800-474-7576**	407-377-0400	531-5
Orlando, The 8384 W Third St	Los Angeles	CA	90048	**800-624-6835**	323-658-6600	379
Orlando/Orange County Convention & Visitors Bureau Inc 6700 Forum Dr Ste 100	Orlando	FL	32821	**800-972-3304**	407-363-5872	208
Orleans Las Vegas Hotel & Casino 4500 W Tropicana Ave	Las Vegas	NV	89103	**800-675-3267**	702-365-7111	132
ORMC (Orlando Regional Medical Ctr) 1414 Kuhl Ave	Orlando	FL	32806	**800-424-6998**	321-841-5111	374-3
ORMCO Corp 1717 W Collins Ave *Cust Svc	Orange	CA	92867	**800-854-1741***	714-516-7400	230
Ormec Systems Corp 19 Linden Pk	Rochester	NY	14625	**800-656-7632**	585-385-3520	205
Oroville Area Chamber of Commerce 1789 Montgomery St	Oroville	CA	95965	**800-655-4653**	530-538-2542	138
Orphan Foundation of America (OFA) 21351 Gentry Dr Ste 130	Sterling	VA	20166	**800-950-4673**	571-203-0270	47-6
Orpheum Theatre 409 S 16th St	Omaha	NE	68102	**866-434-8587**	402-345-0202	571
Orr Safety Corp 11601 Interchange Dr	Louisville	KY	40229	**800-726-6789**	502-774-5791	677
Orrco Inc 515 Collins Blvd PO Box 147	Orrville	OH	44667	**800-321-3085**	330-683-5015	577
Orrick Herrington & Sutcliffe LLP 666 Fifth Ave	New York	NY	10103	**866-342-5259**	212-506-5000	428
Orscheln Farm & Home LLC 1800 Overcenter Dr PO Box 698	Moberly	MO	65270	**800-498-5090**	660-263-4377	278
ORT American Inc 75 Maiden Ln 10th Fl	New York	NY	10038	**800-519-2678**	212-505-7700	47-5
Orthman Manufacturing Inc 75765 Rd 435 PO Box B	Lexington	NE	68850	**800-658-3270**	308-324-4654	275
Ortho Development Corp 12187 S Business Pk Dr	Draper	UT	84020	**800-429-8339**	801-553-9991	476
Ortho Technology Inc 17401 Commerce Park Blvd	Tampa	FL	33647	**800-999-3161**	813-991-5896	475
Ortho-Clinical Diagnostics Inc 1001 US Rt 202 N PO Box 350	Raritan	NJ	08869	**800-828-6316**		475
ORTHOCON Inc 1 Bridge St Ste 121	Irvington	NY	10533	**888-445-6784**	914-357-2600	475
Orthodox Union (OU) 11 Broadway	New York	NY	10004	**855-505-7500**	212-563-4000	47-20
Orthofix Inc 1720 Bray Central Dr	McKinney	TX	75069	**800-527-0404**	469-742-2500	476
Orthopedic Designs North America Inc 5912 Breckenridge Pkwy Ste F	Tampa	FL	33610	**888-635-8535**		474
OrthoPro LLC 3939 S Wasatch Blvd Ste 19	Salt Lake City	UT	84124	**866-746-0208**		476
ORTIG (Old Republic National Title Insurance Co) 400 Second Ave S	Minneapolis	MN	55401	**800-328-4441**	612-371-1111	391-6
Orvis International Travel 178 Conservation Way	Sunderland	VT	05250	**800-547-4322**	802-362-8790	708

Name / Address	City	State	ZIP	Toll-Free	Phone	Class
OSA (Optical Society of America) 2010 Massachusetts Ave NW	Washington	DC	20036	800-766-4672	202-223-8130	48-8
Osage Hills State Park 2131 Osage Hills State Pk Rd	Pawhuska	OK	74056	800-622-6317	918-336-4141	564
Osage Valley Electric Co-op Assn 1321 N Orange St	Butler	MO	64730	800-889-6832	660-679-3131	247
OSBA (Ohio State Bar Assn) 1700 Lk Shore Dr	Columbus	OH	43204	800-282-6556	614-487-2050	71
Osborn International 5401 Hamilton Ave *Cust Svc	Cleveland	OH	44114	800-720-3358*	216-361-1900	102
Osborn Transportation Inc 1245 West Grand Ave	Rainbow City	AL	35906	866-215-3659	256-442-2514	778
Osborne Industries Inc 120 N Industrial Ave	Osborne	KS	67473	800-255-0316	785-346-2192	275
Osborne Partners Capital Management LLC 580 California St Ste 1900	San Francisco	CA	94104	800-362-7734	415-362-5637	401
Oscar Scherer State Park 1843 S Tamiami Trail	Osprey	FL	34229	800-326-3521	941-483-5956	564
Oscar Wilson Engines & Parts Inc 826 Lone Star Dr	O Fallon	MO	63366	800-233-3723	636-978-1313	386
Osceola Electric Co-op Inc 1102 Egret Dr PO Box 127	Sibley	IA	51249	888-754-2519	712-754-2519	247
Osceola News-Gazette 108 Church St	Kissimmee	FL	34741	866-354-2637	407-846-7600	531-4
Oscor Inc 3816 DeSoto Blvd *Cust Svc	Palm Harbor	FL	34683	800-726-7267*	727-937-2511	252
OSF Global Services Inc 6655 Blvd Pierre Bertrand, 204-14	Quebec City	QC	G2K1M1	888-548-4344		630
OSF Hospice 2265 W Altorfer Dr	Peoria	IL	61615	800-673-5288		371
OSF Saint Anthony Medical Ctr 5666 E State St	Rockford	IL	61108	800-343-3185	815-226-2000	374-3
OSF Saint Francis Medical Ctr 530 NE Glen Oak Ave	Peoria	IL	61637	888-627-5673	309-655-2000	374-3
OSF Saint Mary Medical Ctr 3333 N Seminary St	Galesburg	IL	61401	877-795-0416	309-344-3161	374-3
OSG Tap & Die Inc 676 E Fullerton Ave	Glendale Heights	IL	60139	800-837-2223	630-790-1400	492
Osgood Textile Company Inc 333 Park St	West Springfield	MA	01089	888-674-6638	413-737-6488	260
OSHA (Occupational Safety & Health Administration) 200 Constitution Ave NW	Washington	DC	20210	800-321-6742	202-693-1999	340-13
OSHA Up-to-Date Newsletter 1121 Spring Lk Dr *Cust Svc	Itasca	IL	60143	800-621-7615*	630-285-1121	530-8
Oshkosh Convention & Visitors Bureau 2401 W Waukau Ave	Oshkosh	WI	54904	877-303-9200	920-303-9200	47-20
Oshkosh Northwestern Co 224 State St	Oshkosh	WI	54901	800-924-6168	920-235-7700	634-8
Oshkosh Truck Corp 2307 Oregon St	Oshkosh	WI	54903	800-392-9921	920-235-9150	515
OSI Security Devices Inc 1580 Jayken Way	Chula Vista	CA	91911	800-711-6814	619-628-1000	691
OSIA (Order Sons of Italy in America) 219 E St NE	Washington	DC	20002	800-552-6742	202-547-2900	47-14
Osmose Inc 980 Ellicott St	Buffalo	NY	14209	800-877-7653	716-882-5905	816
Osprey Medical Inc 7600 Executive Dr	Eden Prairie	MN	55344	855-860-7584	952-955-8230	252
Osprey Valley Resorts 18821 Main St	Alton	ON	L7K1R1	800-833-1561	519-927-9034	705
OSRAM Sylvania Glass Technologies 131 Portsmouth Ave	Exeter	NH	03833	800-258-8290	603-772-4331	437
Ossid Corp 4000 College Rd	Battleboro	NC	27809	800-334-8369	252-446-6177	546
Ossining Union Free School District 190 Croton Ave	Ossining	NY	10562	877-769-7447	914-941-7700	683
Ossur 27412 Aliso Viejo Pkwy	Aliso Viejo	CA	92656	800-233-6263		110
Ostbye & Anderson Inc 10055 51st Ave N	Minneapolis	MN	55442	866-553-1515	763-553-1515	409
Osteomed Corp 3885 Arapaho Rd *Cust Svc	Addison	TX	75001	800-456-7779*	972-677-4600	475
Osteotech Inc 710 Medtronic Pkwy	Minneapolis	MN	55432	800-633-8766	763-514-4000	84
Osteria Del Circo 3600 Las Vegas Blvd S	Las Vegas	NV	89109	866-259-7111	888-987-6667	669
Osterman & Company Inc 726 S Main St	Cheshire	CT	06410	800-914-4437	203-272-2233	604-2
Osterman Jewelers 375 Ghent Rd	Akron	OH	44333	800-844-7130	330-668-5000	410
Osthoff Resort, The 101 Osthoff Ave PO Box 151	Elkhart Lake	WI	53020	800-876-3399	920-876-3366	667
Oswald Cos 1100 Superior Ave Ste 1500	Cleveland	OH	44114	855-467-9253	216-367-8787	390
Oswego County Opportunities Inc 239 Oneida St	Fulton	NY	13069	877-342-7618	315-598-4717	47-15
Otc Global Holdings 5151 San Felipe Ste 2200	Houston	TX	77056	877-737-8511	713-358-5450	360-3
Otelco Inc 505 Third Ave E *NASDAQ: OTT*	Oneonta	AL	35121	866-471-7888	205-625-3574	733
Otero County Electric Co-op Inc 202 Burro Ave PO Box 227	Cloudcroft	NM	88317	800-548-4660	575-682-2521	247
Otesaga, The 60 Lake St	Cooperstown	NY	13326	800-348-6222	607-547-9931	667
Otis College of Art & Design 9045 Lincoln Blvd	Los Angeles	CA	90045	800-527-6847	310-665-6820	163
Otis-Magie Insurance Agency Inc 332 W Superior St Ste 700	Duluth	MN	55802	800-241-2425	218-722-7753	390
Otomix Inc 747 Glasgow Ave	Inglewood	CA	90301	800-701-7867	310-215-6100	302
OTS (Organization for Tropical Studies) 410 Swift Ave	Durham	NC	27705	877-572-4484	919-684-5774	48-5
OTS 3924 Clock Pointe Trl	Stow	OH	44224	877-445-2058		40
Otsego Club 696 M-32 E Main St PO Box 556	Gaylord	MI	49734	800-752-5510	989-732-5181	667
Ottawa Citizen 1101 Baxter Rd PO Box 5020	Ottawa	ON	K2C3M4	800-267-6100	613-829-9100	531-1
Ottawa City Hall 110 Laurier Ave W	Ottawa	ON	K1P1J1	866-261-9799	613-580-2400	337
Ottawa Herald Inc 104 S Cedar St	Ottawa	KS	66067	800-467-8383	785-242-4700	531-3
Ottawa Macdonald-Cartier International Airport 1000 Airport PkwyPrivate Ste 2500	Ottawa	ON	K1V9B4	888-901-6222	613-248-2000	27
Ottawa Regional Cancer Foundation The 1500 Alta Vista Dr	Ottawa	ON	K1G3Y9	855-247-3527	613-247-3527	306
Ottawa Senators 1000 Palladium Dr Scotia Bank Pl	Kanata	ON	K2V1A5	800-444-7367	613-599-0100	714
Ottawa Sun PO Box 9729	Ottawa	ON	K1G5H7	877-624-1463	613-739-7000	531-1
Ottawa Tourism & Convention Authority 150 Elgin St Ste 1405	Ottawa	ON	K2P1L4	800-363-4465	613-237-5150	208
Ottawa University 1001 S Cedar St *Admissions	Ottawa	KS	66067	800-755-5200*	785-242-5200	167
Ottawa University Phoenix 10020 N 25th Ave	Phoenix	AZ	85021	800-235-9586	602-371-1188	167
Ottawa Visitors Ctr 106 W Lafayette St	Ottawa	IL	61350	888-688-2924	815-434-2737	208
Ottawa-AM 1200 (Sports) 87 George St	Ottawa	ON	K1N9H7	877-670-1200	613-789-2486	642-86
Otter Point State Recreation Site PO Box 1345	Gold Beach	OR	97444	800-551-6949		564
Otter Tail Corp 4334 18th Ave SW PO Box 9156 *NASDAQ: OTTR*	Fargo	ND	58106	866-410-8780	218-739-8479	360-3
Otter Tail Power Co 215 S Cascade St	Fergus Falls	MN	56537	800-257-4044	218-739-8200	785
Otter Tail Telcom 230 W Lincoln Ave	Fergus Falls	MN	56537	800-247-2706	218-826-6161	115
Otterbein College 1 S Grove St *Admissions	Westerville	OH	43081	800-488-8144*	614-823-1500	167
Otterbein Retirement Living Communities 580 N SR 741	Lebanon	OH	45036	888-513-9131	513-933-5400	670
Otterbine Barebo Inc 3840 Main Rd E	Emmaus	PA	18049	800-237-8837	610-965-6018	322
Otto Bock Healthcare North America Inc 2 Carlson Pkwy N Ste 100	Minneapolis	MN	55447	800-328-4058	763-553-9464	474
Otto Brehm Inc PO Box 249	Yonkers	NY	10710	800-272-6886	914-968-6100	298-11
Otto Engineering Inc 2 E Main St	Carpentersville	IL	60110	888-234-6886	847-428-7171	727
Ottumwa Courier 213 E Second St	Ottumwa	IA	52501	800-532-1504	641-684-4611	531-2
Ottumwa Regional Health Ctr 1001 Pennsylvania Ave	Ottumwa	IA	52501	800-933-6742	641-684-2300	374-3
O-two Medical Technologies Inc 7575 Kimbel St	Mississauga	ON	L5S1C8	800-387-3405	905-677-9410	252
OTZ Telephone Co-op Inc PO Box 324	Kotzebue	AK	99752	800-478-3111	907-442-3114	733
OU (Orthodox Union) 11 Broadway	New York	NY	10004	855-505-7500	212-563-4000	47-20
Ouachita Baptist University 410 Ouachita St *Admissions	Arkadelphia	AR	71998	800-342-5628*	870-245-5000	167
Ouachita County Medical Ctr (OCMC) PO Box 797	Camden	AR	71711	877-836-2472	870-836-1000	374-3
Ouachita Electric Co-op Corp 700 Bradley Ferry Rd PO Box 877	Camden	AR	71711	877-252-4538	870-836-5791	247
Ouachita Technical College 1 College Cir	Malvern	AR	72104	800-337-0266	501-337-5000	161
Our Lady of Fatima Retreat House 5353 E 56th St	Indianapolis	IN	46226	800-382-9836	317-545-7681	671
Our Lady of Holy Cross College 4123 Woodland Dr	New Orleans	LA	70131	800-259-7744	504-394-7744	167
Our Lady of Lourdes Medical Ctr 1600 Haddon Ave	Camden	NJ	08103	888-568-7337	856-757-3500	374-3
Our Lady of the Lake College 7434 Perkins Rd *Admissions	Baton Rouge	LA	70808	877-242-3509*	225-768-1700	167
Our Lady of the Lake University 411 SW 24th St	San Antonio	TX	78207	800-436-6558	210-434-6711	167
Our Sunday Visitor Inc 200 Noll Plaza	Huntington	IN	46750	800-348-2440	260-356-8400	634-8
OurParents Inc 8521 Leesburg Pk Ste 310	Vienna	VA	22182	866-629-1634		387
OutboundEngine Inc 200 E 6th, Ste 205	Austin	TX	78701	800-562-7315		197
Outdoor Adv Assn of America Inc (OAAA) 1850 M St NW Ste 1040	Washington	DC	20036	800-325-3694	202-833-5566	614
Outdoor Amusement Business Assn PAC (OABA-PAC) 1035 S Semoran Blvd Ste 1045A	Winter Park	FL	32792	800-517-6222	407-681-9444	614
Outdoor Ch 43445 Business Pk Dr Ste 103 *NASDAQ: OUTD*	Temecula	CA	92590	800-770-5750	951-699-6991	736

Name / Address	City	State	ZIP	Toll-Free	Phone	Class
Outdoor Photographer Magazine 12121 Wilshire Blvd 12th Fl *Cust Svc	Los Angeles	CA	90025	**800-283-4410***	310-820-1500	456-14
Outdoor Ventures 10579 S Main St	Hayward	WI	54843	**866-710-2846**	715-634-4447	709
Outer Banks Visitors Bureau 1 Visitor Ctr Cir	Manteo	NC	27954	**877-629-4386**	252-473-2138	208
Outerlink Corp 187 Ballardvale St Ste A260	Wilmington	MA	01887	**877-688-3770**	978-284-6070	679
Out-fit 25 W Easy St Ste 304	Simi Valley	CA	93065	**800-376-3339**	805-584-1500	709
OUTFRONT Media Inc 405 Lexington Ave	New York	NY	10174	**800-926-8834**	212-297-6400	8
Outlets at Anthem 4250 W Anthem Way	Phoenix	AZ	85086	**888-482-5834**	623-465-9500	459
Outokumpu Stainless Pipe Inc 1101 N Main St	Wildwood	FL	34785	**800-731-7473**	352-748-1313	489
Outreach Communications 2801 Glenda St	Haltom City	TX	76117	**800-982-3760**	817-288-7200	226
Outreach International 129 W Lexington PO Box 210	Independence	MO	64050	**888-833-1235**	816-833-0883	47-5
Outrigger Enterprises Group 2375 Kuhio Ave	Honolulu	HI	96815	**800-462-6262**	808-921-6941	379
Outrigger Hotels & Resorts 2375 Kuhio Ave	Honolulu	HI	96815	**800-688-7444**	808-921-6941	379
Outrigger Kanaloa at Kona 78-261 Manukai St	Kailua-Kona	HI	96740	**800-688-7444**	808-322-9625	667
Outrigger Reef on the Beach 2169 Kalia Rd	Honolulu	HI	96815	**800-688-7444**	808-923-3111	667
Outrigger Waikiki on the Beach 2335 Kalakaua Ave	Honolulu	HI	96815	**800-688-7444**	808-923-0711	379
Outside Magazine 400 Market St *General	Santa Fe	NM	87501	**888-909-2382***	505-989-7100	456-14
Outstart Inc 745 Atlantic Ave 4th Fl	Boston	MA	02111	**877-971-9171**	617-897-6800	38
Outward Bound 910 Jackson St	Golden	CO	80401	**866-467-7651**	207-510-7533	764
Ovation Instore 57-13 49th Pl	Maspeth	NY	11378	**800-553-2202**	718-628-2600	235
Overcomers in Christ PO Box 34460	Omaha	NE	68134	**866-573-0966**	402-573-0966	47-21
Overcomers Outreach PO Box 922950	Sylmar	CA	91392	**800-310-3001**	818-833-1803	47-21
Overeaters Anonymous Inc (OA) PO Box 44020	Rio Rancho	NM	87174	**866-505-4966**	505-891-2664	47-21
Overhead Door Company of Sacramento Inc 6756 Franklin Blvd	Sacramento	CA	95823	**800-929-3667**	916-421-3747	191-2
Overhead Door Corp 2501 S State Hwy 121 Bus Ste 200	Lewisville	TX	75067	**800-275-3290**	469-549-7100	236
Overhill Farms Inc 2727 E Vernon Ave *NYSE: OFI*	Vernon	CA	90058	**800-859-6406**	323-582-9977	297-36
Overland Express Co 5539 Harvey Wilson PO Box 262322	Houston	TX	77207	**800-929-7402**	713-672-6161	778
Overland Park Convention & Visitors Bureau 9001 W 110th St Ste 100	Overland Park	KS	66210	**800-262-7275**	913-491-0123	208
Overland Sheepskin Company Inc 2096 Nutmeg Ave	Fairfield	IA	52556	**800-683-7526**	641-472-8434	156-5
Overland Storage Inc 4820 Overland Ave *NASDAQ: OVRL*	San Diego	CA	92123	**800-729-8725**	858-571-5555	178
Overlook Press 141 Wooster St	New York	NY	10012	**800-527-9703**	212-673-2210	634-2
Overly Manufacturing Co 574 W Otterman St	Greensburg	PA	15601	**800-979-7300**	724-834-7300	490
Overseas Adventure Travel 347 Congress St	Boston	MA	02210	**800-221-0814**		758
Overseas Shipholding Group Inc 666 Third Ave	New York	NY	10017	**800-851-9677**	212-953-4100	314
Overstock.com Inc 6350 South 3000 East *NASDAQ: OSTK* ■ *Cust Svc	Salt Lake City	UT	84121	**800-843-2446***	801-947-3100	789
Overton Brooks Veterans Affairs Medical Ctr 510 E Stoner Ave	Shreveport	LA	71101	**800-863-7441**	318-221-8411	374-8
Overwaitea Food Group 19855 92A Ave	Langley	BC	V1M3B6	**800-242-9229**	604-888-1213	345
Overwatch Geospatial Operations 21660 Ridgetop Cir Ste 110	Sterling	VA	20166	**800-937-6881**	703-437-7651	180-8
Ovid Technologies Inc 333 Seventh Ave 20th Fl	New York	NY	10001	**800-950-2035**	646-674-6300	387
OVMA (Ohio Veterinary Medical Assn) 3168 Riverside Dr	Columbus	OH	43221	**800-662-6862**	614-486-7253	793
OW Lee Company Inc 1822 E Francis St	Ontario	CA	91761	**800-776-9533**	909-947-3771	320-4
Owatonna Area Chamber of Commerce & Tourism 320 Hoffman Dr	Owatonna	MN	55060	**800-423-6466**	507-451-7970	138
Owatonna Public Library 105 N Elm St	Owatonna	MN	55060	**800-657-3864**	507-444-2460	434-3
Owen Community Bank 279 E Morgan St	Spencer	IN	47460	**800-690-2095**	812-829-2095	360-2
Owen Electric Co-op Inc 8205 Hwy 127 N PO Box 400	Owenton	KY	40359	**800-372-7612**	502-484-3471	247
Owen Industries Inc 501 Ave H	Carter Lake	IA	51510	**800-831-9252**	712-347-5500	491
Owens & Assoc Investigations 8765 Aero Dr Ste 306	San Diego	CA	92123	**800-297-1343**		400
Owens Community College						
Findlay 3200 Bright Rd	Findlay	OH	45840	**800-466-9367**		161
Toledo 30335 Oregon Rd	Perrysburg	OH	43551	**800-466-9367**	419-661-7000	161
Owensboro Community & Technical College 4800 New Hartford Rd	Owensboro	KY	42303	**866-755-6282**	270-686-4400	798
Owensboro Federal Credit Union 717 Harvard Dr PO Box 1189	Owensboro	KY	42302	**800-264-1054**	270-683-1054	221
Owensboro Grain Co 822 E Second St	Owensboro	KY	42303	**800-874-0305**	270-926-2032	297-29
Owensboro Medical Health Systems (OMHS) 811 E Parish Ave PO Box 20007	Owensboro	KY	42303	**877-888-6647**	270-688-2000	374-3
Owensboro-Davies County Tourist Commission 215 E Second St	Owensboro	KY	42303	**800-489-1131**	270-926-1100	208
Owl Magazine 10 Lower Spadina Ave Ste 400	Toronto	ON	M5V2Z2	**800-551-6957**	416-340-2700	456-6
Owl Wire & Cable Inc 3127 Seneca Tpke	Canastota	NY	13032	**800-765-9473**	315-697-2011	811
Owner-Operator Independent Drivers Assn Inc (OOIDA) 1 NW OOIDA Dr	Grain Valley	MO	64029	**800-444-5791**	816-229-5791	48-21
OX Paper Tube & Core Inc 331 Maple Ave	Hanover	PA	17331	**800-414-2476**		124
Oxbow Meadows Environmental Learning Ctr 3535 S Lumpkin Rd	Columbus	GA	31903	**866-264-2035**	706-507-8550	49-4
Oxfam America 226 Cswy St 5th Fl	Boston	MA	02114	**800-776-9326**	617-482-1211	47-5
Oxford Alloys Inc 2632 Tee Dr	Baton Rouge	LA	70814	**800-562-3355**	225-273-4800	358
Oxford Bank PO Box 129	Addison	IL	60101	**800-236-2442**	630-629-5000	69
Oxford Biomedical Research Inc 2165 Avon Industrial Dr	Rochester Hills	MI	48309	**800-692-4633**	248-852-8815	233
Oxford Convention & Visitors Bureau 102 Ed Perry Blvd	Oxford	MS	38655	**800-758-9177**	662-232-2367	208
Oxford Global Resources Inc 100 Cummings Ctr Ste 206L	Beverly	MA	01915	**800-426-9196**	978-236-1182	719
Oxford Graduate School Inc 500 Oxford Dr	Dayton	TN	37321	**800-933-6188**	423-775-6596	167
Oxford Health Plans LLC 48 Monroe Tpke	Trumbull	CT	06611	**800-444-6222**	203-459-9100	391-3
Oxford Health Plans (NJ) Inc 111 Wood Ave S Ste 2	Iselin	NJ	08830	**800-201-6920**	732-623-1000	391-3
Oxford Hotel 1600 17th St	Denver	CO	80202	**800-228-5838**	303-628-5400	379
Oxford Instruments Measurement Systems 300 Bake Ave Ste 150	Concord	MA	01742	**800-447-4717**		471
Oxford Life Insurance Co 2721 N Central Ave *Cust Svc	Phoenix	AZ	85004	**800-308-2318***	602-263-6666	391-2
Oxford Suites Boise 1426 S Entertainment Ave *General	Boise	ID	83709	**888-322-8001***	208-322-8000	379
Oxford Suites Spokane Valley 15015 E Indiana Ave	Spokane Valley	WA	99216	**866-668-7848**	509-847-1000	379
Oxford Suites Spokane-Downtown 115 W N River Dr	Spokane	WA	99201	**800-774-1877**	509-353-9000	379
Oxford University Press 198 Madison Ave *Orders	New York	NY	10016	**800-445-9714***	212-726-6000	634-2
Oxford-Lafayette County Chamber of Commerce 299 W Jackson Ave	Oxford	MS	38655	**800-880-6967**	662-234-4651	138
Oxnard Convention & Visitors Bureau 1000 Town Ctr Dr Ste 130	Oxnard	CA	93036	**800-269-6273**	805-385-7545	208
Oxus America Inc 1685 Northfield Dr	Rochester Hills	MI	48309	**888-475-1568**		475
Oyster Point Hotel, The 146 Bodman Pl	Red Bank	NJ	07701	**800-345-3484**	732-530-8200	379
O-Z/Gedney 9377 W Higgins Rd	Rosemont	IL	60018	**800-621-1506**	847-268-6000	814
Ozark Area Chamber of Commerce 294 Painter Ave	Ozark	AL	36360	**800-582-8497**	334-774-9321	138
Ozark Border Electric Co-op 3281 S Westwood	Poplar Bluff	MO	63901	**800-392-0567**	573-785-4631	247
Ozark Christian College 1111 N Main St	Joplin	MO	64801	**800-299-4622**	417-624-2518	160
Ozark Folk Ctr State Park 1032 Pk Ave	Mountain View	AR	72560	**800-264-3655**	870-269-3851	564
Ozark Motor Lines Inc 3934 Homewood Rd	Memphis	TN	38118	**800-264-4100**	901-251-9711	778
Ozark National Scenic Riverways 404 Watercress Dr PO Box 490	Van Buren	MO	63965	**877-444-6777**	573-323-4236	563
Ozark Regional Transit 2423 E Robinson Ave	Springdale	AR	72764	**800-865-5901**	479-756-5901	107
Ozarka College 218 College Dr	Melbourne	AR	72556	**800-821-4335**	870-368-7371	161
Ozarks Coca-Cola Dr Pepper Bottling Co 1777 N Packer Rd	Springfield	MO	65803	**866-223-4498**	417-865-9900	97
Ozarks Electric Co-op Corp 3641 W Wedington Dr	Fayetteville	AR	72704	**800-521-6144**	479-521-2900	247

P

Name / Address	City	State	ZIP	Toll-Free	Phone	Class
P & F Industries Inc						
445 Broadhollow Rd	Melville	NY	11747	**800-327-9403**	631-694-9800	757
NASDAQ: PFIN						
P A Landers Inc						
351 Winter St	Hanover	MA	02339	**800-660-6404**	781-826-8818	188
P E La Moreaux & Assoc Inc						
PO Box 2310	Tuscaloosa	AL	35403	**800-682-6338**	205-752-5543	194
P J Noyes Company Inc						
89 Bridge St	Lancaster	NH	03584	**800-522-2469**	603-788-4952	298-8
P K W Associates Inc						
705 E Ordnance Rd Ste 108	Baltimore	MD	21226	**888-358-3900**	443-773-1000	227
P M Industrial Supply Co						
9613 Canoga Ave	Chatsworth	CA	91311	**800-382-3684**	818-341-9180	350
P V Rentals Ltd						
5810 S Rice Ave	Houston	TX	77081	**800-275-7878**	713-667-0665	125
P. T. M. Corp						
6560 Bethuy Rd	Fair Haven	MI	48023	**800-486-2212**	586-725-2211	59
P1 Group Inc						
2151 Haskell Ave Bldg 1	Lawrence	KS	66046	**800-376-2911**	785-843-2910	191-10
P4 Performance Management Inc						
105 Brooks Ave	Raleigh	NC	27607	**800-431-0648**		197
Paasche Airbrush Co						
4311 N Normandy	Chicago	IL	60634	**800-621-1907***	773-867-9191	42
*Sales						
PABCO Gypsum						
37851 Cherry St	Newark	CA	94560	**877-449-7786**	510-792-9555	347
Pabst Brewing Co, The						
10635 Santa Monica Blvd Ste 350	Los Angeles	CA	90025	**800-947-2278**		101
Pabst Theater						
144 E Wells St	Milwaukee	WI	53202	**866-948-6483**	414-286-3205	571
Pac Tec						
12365 Haynes St	Clinton	LA	70722	**877-554-2544**		607
PACCAR Leasing Corp						
777 106th Ave NE	Bellevue	WA	98004	**800-759-2979**	425-468-7877	776
Pace Mechanical Services Inc						
301 Merritt Seven	Norwalk	CT	06851	**866-890-7794**	203-849-7800	191-10
Pace Products Inc						
4510 W 89th St Ste 110	Prairie Village	KS	66207	**888-389-8203**		45
Pace University						
1 Pace Plz	New York	NY	10038	**866-722-3338**	212-346-1200	167
Pleasantville/Briarcliff						
861 Bedford Rd	Pleasantville	NY	10570	**866-722-3338**	914-773-3200	167
Pace-Edwards						
2400 Commercial Rd	Centralia	WA	98531	**800-338-3697**	360-736-9991	119
Pacesetter Claims Service Inc						
2871 N Hwy 167	Catoosa	Ok	74015	**888-218-4880**	918-665-8887	390
Pacesetter Steel Service Inc						
1045 Big Shanty Rd	Kennesaw	GA	30144	**800-749-6505**	770-919-8000	491
Pacific Aerospace & Electronics Inc						
434 Olds Stn Rd	Wenatchee	WA	98801	**855-285-5200**	509-667-9600	620
Pacific Bag Inc						
15300 Woodinville Redmond Rd NE Ste A	Woodinville	WA	98072	**800-562-2247**	425-455-1128	64
Pacific Beach Hotel						
2490 Kalakaua Ave	Honolulu	HI	96815	**800-367-6060**	808-922-1233	379
Pacific Biometrics Inc						
645 Elliott Ave W Ste 300	Seattle	WA	98119	**800-767-9151**	206-298-0068	233
Pacific Building Systems (PBS)						
2100 N Pacific Hwy	Woodburn	OR	97071	**800-727-7844***	503-981-9581	104
*General						
Pacific Cataract & Laser Institute						
2517 NE Kresky Ave	Chehalis	WA	98532	**800-888-9903**	360-748-8632	796
Pacific Coast Container Inc						
432 Estudillo Ave	San Leandro	CA	94577	**800-458-4788**	510-346-6100	648
Pacific Coast Feather Co						
1964 Fourth Ave S	Seattle	WA	98134	**888-297-1778**	206-624-1057	743
Pacific Coast Fruit Co						
201 NE Second Ave Ste 100	Portland	OR	97232	**800-423-4945**	503-234-6411	298-7
Pacific Coast Jet Charter Inc						
10600 White Rock Rd	Rancho Cordova	CA	95670	**800-655-3599**	916-631-6507	13
Pacific Coast Lighting						
20238 Plummer St	Chatsworth	CA	91311	**800-709-9004**	818-886-9751	439
Pacific Coast Producers						
631 N Cluff Ave	Lodi	CA	95240	**877-618-4776**	209-367-8800	297-20
Pacific Coast Valuations						
740 Corporate Ctr Dr Ste 200	Pomona	CA	91768	**888-623-4001**	909-623-4001	650
Pacific College Oriental Med Inc						
7445 Mission Vly Rd Ste 105	San Diego	CA	92108	**800-729-0941**	619-574-6909	167
Pacific Color Graphics						
440 Boulder Ct 100d	Pleasanton	CA	94566	**888-551-1482**	925-600-3006	626
Pacific Combustion Engineering Co						
2107 Border Ave	Torrance	CA	90501	**800-342-4442**	310-212-6300	420
Pacific Continental Corp						
111 W Seventh Ave PO Box 10727	Eugene	OR	97440	**877-231-2265**	541-686-8685	69
NASDAQ: PCBK						
Pacific Crest Securities Inc						
111 SW Fifth Ave 42nd Fl	Portland	OR	97204	**800-314-9837**	503-248-0721	688
Pacific Crest Trail Assn (PCTA)						
1331 Garden Hwy	Sacramento	CA	95833	**888-728-7245**	916-285-1846	47-23
Pacific Disaster Ctr						
1305 N Holopono St Ste 2	Kihei	HI	96753	**888-808-6688**	808-891-0525	666
Pacific Ethanol Corp						
400 Capitol Mall Ste 2060	Sacramento	CA	95814	**866-508-4969**	916-403-2123	144
NASDAQ: PEIX						
Pacific Fibre & Rope Company Inc						
903 Flint St	Wilmington	CA	90744	**800-825-7673**	310-834-4567	210
Pacific Fisherman Inc						
5351 24th Ave NW	Seattle	WA	98107	**877-644-6148**	206-784-2562	696
Pacific Fixture Company Inc						
12860 San Fernando Rd Unit B	Sylmar	CA	91342	**800-272-2349**	818-362-2130	288
Pacific Gas & Electric Co						
77 Beale St	San Francisco	CA	94105	**800-743-5000***	415-973-7000	785
*Cust Svc						
Pacific Grain Products International Inc						
351 Hanson Way PO Box 2060	Woodland	CA	95776	**800-333-0110***	530-662-5056	297-23
*Cust Svc						
Pacific Guardian Life Insurance Company Ltd						
1440 Kapiolani Blvd Ste 1700	Honolulu	HI	96814	**800-367-5354**	808-955-2236	391-2
Pacific Handy Cutter Inc						
17819 Gillette Ave	Irvine	CA	92614	**800-229-2233***	714-662-1033	224
*Cust Svc						
Pacific Health Laboratories Inc						
100 Matawan Rd Ste 150	Matawan	NJ	07747	**877-363-8769***	732-739-2900	797
*General						
Pacific Inn						
600 Marina Dr	Seal Beach	CA	90740	**866-466-0300**	562-493-7501	379
Pacific Inn Resort & Conference Centre						
1160 King George Hwy	Surrey	BC	V4A4Z2	**800-667-2248**	604-535-1432	379
Pacific Institute						
1709 Harbor Ave SW	Seattle	WA	98126	**800-426-3660**	206-628-4800	763
Pacific International Rice Mills Inc						
845 Kentucky Ave	Woodland	CA	95695	**800-747-4764**	530-661-6028	297-23
Pacific Internet						
105 W Clay St	Ukiah	CA	95482	**888-722-8638**	707-468-1005	806
Pacific Investment Management Company LLC						
840 Newport Ctr Dr	Newport Beach	CA	92660	**800-387-4626**	949-720-6000	401
Pacific Island Ecosystems Research Ctr (PIERC)						
12201 Sunrise Valley Dr Ste 615	Reston	VA	20192	**888-275-8747**		666
Pacific Life Insurance Co						
700 Newport Ctr Dr	Newport Beach	CA	92660	**800-800-7646**	949-219-3011	391-2
Pacific Lutheran Theological Seminary						
2770 Marin Ave	Berkeley	CA	94708	**800-235-7587**	510-524-5264	168-3
Pacific Lutheran University						
1010 122nd St S	Tacoma	WA	98444	**800-274-6758**	253-531-6900	167
Pacific Marine Credit Union						
M C X Complex	Camp Pendleton	CA	92055	**800-736-4500**	760-430-7511	221
Pacific Medical Inc						
1700 N Chrisman Rd	Tracy	CA	95304	**800-726-9180**		476
Pacific Mercantile Bancorp						
949 S Coast Dr Ste 105	Costa Mesa	CA	92626	**877-450-2265***	714-438-2600	360-2
NASDAQ: PMBC ■ *General						
Pacific Modern Homes Inc (PMHI)						
9723 Railroad St	Elk Grove	CA	95624	**800-395-1011**	916-685-9514	105
Pacific Mutual Holding Co						
700 Newport Ctr Dr	Newport Beach	CA	92660	**800-347-7787**	949-219-3011	360-4
Pacific Northwest College of Art						
1241 NW Johnson St	Portland	OR	97209	**888-390-7499**	503-226-4391	167
Pacific Northwest Inlander						
9 S Washington St	Spokane	WA	99201	**888-431-9911**	509-325-0634	531-5
Pacific Northwest National Laboratory (PNNL)						
902 Battelle Blvd PO Box 999	Richland	WA	99352	**888-375-7665**	509-375-2121	666
Pacific NW Federal Credit Union (PNWFCU)						
12106 NE Marx St	Portland	OR	97220	**866-692-8669**	503-256-5858	221
Pacific Oaks College						
5 Westmoreland Pl	Pasadena	CA	91103	**877-314-2380**		167
Pacific Packaging Products Inc						
24 Industrial Way	Wilmington	MA	01887	**800-777-0300**	978-657-9100	558
Pacific Palms Conference Resort						
1 Industry Hills Pkwy	City of Industry	CA	91744	**800-524-4557***	626-810-4455	667
*Cust Svc						
Pacific Paper Tube Inc						
1025 98th Ave	Oakland	CA	94603	**888-377-8823**	510-562-8823	124
Pacific Polymers Inc						
12271 Monarch St	Garden Grove	CA	92841	**800-888-8340**	714-898-0025	3
Pacific Power & Light						
825 NE Multnomah St	Portland	OR	97232	**888-221-7070***	503-813-6666	785
*Cust Svc						
Pacific Power Group						
600 S 56th Pl	Ridgefield	WA	98642	**800-882-3860**	360-887-7400	385
Pacific Premier Bancorp Inc						
1600 Sunflower Ave	Costa Mesa	CA	92626	**888-388-5433**	714-431-4000	360-2
NASDAQ: PPBI						
Pacific Press						
1350 N Kings Rd	Nampa	ID	83687	**800-765-6955***	208-465-2500	634-9
*Cust Svc						
Pacific Press Technologies						
714 Walnut St	Mount Carmel	IL	62863	**800-851-3586**	618-262-8666	455
Pacific Repertory Theater						
PO Box 222035	Carmel	CA	93922	**866-622-0709**	831-622-0700	572-4
Pacific Resources for Education & Learning						
900 Ft St Mall Ste 1300	Honolulu	HI	96813	**800-377-4773**	808-441-1300	244
Pacific Rim Mechanical						
7655 Convoy Ct	San Diego	CA	92111	**800-891-4822**	858-974-6500	14
Pacific Rim Mining Corp						
625 Howe St Ste 1050	Vancouver	BC	V6C2T6	**888-775-7097**	604-689-1976	501
OTC: PFRMF						
Pacific School of Religion						
1798 Scenic Ave	Berkeley	CA	94709	**800-999-0528**	510-848-0528	168-3
Pacific Science Ctr						
200 Second Ave N	Seattle	WA	98109	**800-664-8775**	206-443-2001	519
Pacific Service Federal Credit Union						
PO Box 8191	Walnut Creek	CA	94596	**888-858-6878**	925-296-6200	221
Pacific Shores Inn						
4802 Mission Blvd	San Diego	CA	92109	**888-478-7829**	858-483-6300	379
Pacific Source Inc						
PO Box 2323	Woodinville	WA	98072	**888-343-1515**		193-3
Pacific Specialty Insurance Co						
3601 Haven Ave	Menlo Park	CA	94025	**800-962-1172**		391-4
Pacific States Felt & Mfg Company Inc						
23850 Clawiter Rd	Hayward	CA	94545	**800-566-8866**	510-783-0277	327
Pacific States University						
1516 S Western Ave	Los Angeles	CA	90006	**888-200-0383**	323-731-2383	167
Pacific Steel & Recycling						
1401 Third St NW	Great Falls	MT	59404	**800-889-6264**	406-771-7222	491
Pacific Storage Co						
PO Box 334	Stockton	CA	95201	**888-823-5467**	209-320-6600	801-1
Pacific Sunwear of California Inc						
3450 E Miraloma Ave	Anaheim	CA	92806	**800-444-6770**	714-414-4000	156-4
NASDAQ: PSUN						

Alphabetical Section

	City	State	ZIP	Toll-Free	Phone	Class
Pacific Terrace Hotel 610 Diamond St	San Diego	CA	92109	**800-344-3370**	858-581-3500	379
Pacific Title Archives 10717 Vanowen St	North Hollywood	CA	91605	**800-968-9111**	818-760-4223	513
Pacific Transit System 216 N Second St	Raymond	WA	98577	**800-833-6388**	360-875-9418	107
Pacific Union College 1 Angwin Ave	Angwin	CA	94508	**800-862-7080**	707-965-6336	167
Pacific University 2043 College Way *Admissions	Forest Grove	OR	97116	**800-677-6712***	503-352-2007	167
Pacific University Library 2043 College Way	Forest Grove	OR	97116	**800-677-6712**	503-352-1400	434-6
Pacific Western Transportation Ltd 6999 ordan Dr	Mississauga	ON	L5T1K6	**800-387-6787**	905-564-3232	106
Pacific Wings 1 Keolani Pl Ste 30	Kahului	HI	96732	**888-575-4546**	808-873-0877	25
Pacificare of Texas 6200 NW Pkwy	San Antonio	TX	78249	**800-624-7272**	210-474-5000	391-3
PacifiCorp 825 NE Multnomah St	Portland	OR	97232	**888-221-7070**	503-813-5000	785
Package Industries Inc 15 Harback Rd	Sutton	MA	01590	**800-225-7242**	508-865-5871	104
Package Pavement Company Inc PO Box 408	Stormville	NY	12582	**800-724-8193**	845-221-2224	45
Packaging Corp of America 1955 W Field Ct *NYSE: PKG*	Lake Forest	IL	60045	**800-456-4725**		99
Packaging Distribution Services Inc (PDS) 2308 Sunset Rd	Des Moines	IA	50321	**800-747-2699**	515-243-3156	558
Packaging Machinery Manufacturers Institute (PMMI) 4350 N Fairfax Dr Ste 600	Arlington	VA	22203	**888-275-7664**	703-243-8555	48-13
Packaging Services of Maryland Inc 16461 Elliott Pkwy	Williamsport	MD	21795	**800-223-6255**	301-223-6200	548
Packaging Specialties Inc 300 Lake Rd	Medina	OH	44256	**800-344-9271**	330-723-6000	200
Packaging Systems International Inc 4990 Acoma St	Denver	CO	80216	**800-525-6110**	303-296-4445	546
Packard Industries Inc 1515 US 31 N	Niles	MI	49120	**800-253-0866**	269-684-2550	288
Packard Transport Inc 24021 S Municipal Dr PO Box 380	Channahon	IL	60410	**800-467-9260**	815-467-9260	467
Packer Country Visitor & Convention Bureau 1901 S Oneida St	Green Bay	WI	54304	**888-867-3342**	920-494-9507	208
Packer Thomas 6601 Westford Pl Ste 101	Canfield	OH	44406	**800-943-4278**	330-533-9777	2
Packerland Rent-a-mat Inc 12580 W Rohr Ave	Butler	WI	53007	**800-472-9339**	262-781-5321	130
Packing House 900 E Layton Ave	Milwaukee	WI	53207	**800-727-9477**	414-483-5054	669
PackLate.com Inc 100 Four Falls Corporate Ctr Ste 104	West Conshohocken	PA	19428	**877-472-2552**		387
Packless Metal Hose Inc PO Box 20668	Waco	TX	76702	**800-347-4859**	254-666-7700	14
PACO Pumps Inc 902 Koomey Rd	Brookshire	TX	77423	**800-955-5847**	281-994-2700	638
Paco Steel & Engineering Corp 19818 S Alameda St	Rancho Dominguez	CA	90221	**800-421-1473**	310-537-6375	491
Pacon Corp 2525 N Casaloma Dr	Appleton	WI	54912	**800-333-2545**		553
Pacrim Hospitality Services Inc 30 Damascus Rd	Bedford	NS	B4A0C1	**877-680-7666**	902-404-7474	196
Pactiv Corp 1900 W Field Ct	Lake Forest	IL	60045	**888-828-2850**	847-482-2000	560
Pact-One Solutions Inc 8215 S Eastern Ave Ste 101	Las Vegas	NV	89123	**866-722-8663**		176
Pad Print Machinery of Vermont Inc 201 Tennis Way	East Dorset	VT	05253	**800-272-7764**	802-362-0844	627
Padco Inc 2220 Elm St SE	Minneapolis	MN	55414	**800-328-5513**	612-378-7270	102
PADF (Pan American Development Foundation) 1889 F St NW 2nd Fl	Washington	DC	20006	**877-572-4484**	202-458-3969	47-5
Padgett Business Services 160 Hawthorne Pk	Athens	GA	30606	**800-723-4388**		2
PADI (Professional Assn of Diving Instructors International) 30151 Tomas St *Sales	Rancho Santa Margarita	CA	92688	**800-729-7234***	949-858-7234	47-22
PADI Americas 30151 Tomas St	Rancho Santa Margarita	CA	92688	**800-527-8378**	949-858-7234	512
PAFA (Pennsylvania Academy of the Fine Arts Museum) 118 N Broad St	Philadelphia	PA	19102	**800-799-7233**	215-972-7600	519
Page & Assoc Inc 1979 Lakeside Pkwy Ste 200	Tucker	GA	30084	**800-252-5282**		794
Page International Communications 2748 Bingle Rd	Houston	TX	77055	**888-464-8484**	713-464-8484	626
Pa-Go Mobile Inc 150 NE 95th St Ste 307	Seattle	WA	98115	**877-425-2196**		226
Paige Electric Company LP 1160 Springfield Rd	Union	NJ	07083	**800-327-2443**	908-687-7810	248
PAII (Professional Assn of Innkeepers International) 108 S Cleveland St	Merrill	WI	54452	**800-468-7244**	856-310-1102	48-4
Pain Enterprises Inc 101 Daniels Way	Bloomington	IN	47404	**800-245-8583**		145
Pain.com *Dannemiller Memorial Educational Foundation* 5711 NW Pkwy	San Antonio	TX	78246	**800-328-2308**	210-572-2512	356
Paine College 1235 15th St	Augusta	GA	30901	**800-476-7703**	706-821-8200	167
Paint & Decorating Retailers Assn (PDRA) 1401 Triad Ctr Dr	Saint Peters	MO	63376	**800-737-0107**	636-326-2636	48-18
Paint Creek State Park 280 Taylor Rd	Bainbridge	OH	45612	**866-644-6727**	937-981-7061	564
Painted Buffalo Inn 400 W Broadway PO Box 2547	Jackson	WY	83001	**800-288-3866**	307-733-4340	379
Painters Supply & Equipment Co 25195 Brest Rd	Taylor	MI	48180	**800-589-8100**	734-946-8119	549

	City	State	ZIP	Toll-Free	Phone	Class
Painting & Decorating Contractors of America (PDCA) 2316 Millpark Dr *Cust Svc	Maryland Heights	MO	63043	**800-332-7322***	314-514-7322	48-3
Paisano Publications LLC 28210 Dorothy Dr	Agoura Hills	CA	91301	**800-323-3484**	818-889-8740	634-9
Pak Mail Centers of America Inc 7173 S Havana St Ste 600 *Cust Svc	Centennial	CO	80112	**800-778-6665***	303-957-1000	112
Pak West Paper & Packaging 4042 W Garry Ave	Santa Ana	CA	92704	**800-927-7299**	714-557-7420	547
Pakistan International Airlines Corp (PIA) 1200 New Jersey Ave SE	Washington	DC	20590	**800-578-6786**		25
PakSense Inc 6223 N Discovery Pl	Boise	ID	83713	**877-832-0720**	208-489-9010	203
Pala Casino Resort & Spa 35008 Pala-Temecula Rd	Pala	CA	92059	**877-946-7252**	760-510-5100	667
Pala Mesa Resort 2001 Old Hwy 395	Fallbrook	CA	92028	**800-722-4700**	760-728-5881	667
Palace Casino 158 Howard Ave	Biloxi	MS	39530	**800-725-2239**	228-432-8888	131
Palace Hotel 2 New Montgomery St	San Francisco	CA	94105	**866-716-8136**	415-512-1111	379
Palace Printing & Design 100 N Maple Ave	Greensburg	PA	15601	**800-247-0108**	415-526-1370	93
Palace Station Hotel & Casino 2411 W Sahara Ave *Resv	Las Vegas	NV	89102	**800-634-3101***	702-367-2411	132
Palace, The 601 Vine St	Cincinnati	OH	45202	**800-942-9000**	513-381-6006	669
Palace, Theatre, The 1420 Celebrity Cir Broadway at the Beach	Myrtle Beach	SC	29577	**888-841-2787**	843-448-9224	571
Paladin Data Systems Corp 19362 Powder Hill Pl NE	Poulsbo	WA	98370	**800-532-8448**	360-779-2400	179
Paladin Labs Inc 100 Blvd Alexis Nihon Ste 600 *TSE: PLB*	St-Laurent	QC	H4M2P2	**888-376-7830**	514-340-1112	84
Palais Royal 10201 S Main St	Houston	TX	77025	**800-743-8730**	713-667-5601	156-2
Palestine Regional Medical Ctr 2900 S Loop 256	Palestine	TX	75801	**800-222-1222**	903-731-1000	374-3
PALHACC (President Abraham Lincoln Hotel & Conference Ctr) 701 E Adams St	Springfield	IL	62701	**855-610-8733**	217-544-8800	379
Palisade Corp 798 Cascadilla St	Ithaca	NY	14850	**800-432-7475**	607-277-8000	180-1
Pall Corp 2200 Northern Blvd *NYSE: PLL*	East Hills	NY	11548	**800-645-6532**	516-484-5400	386
Pall Life Sciences 600 S Wagner Rd	Ann Arbor	MI	48103	**800-521-1520**	734-665-0651	419
PALLAB (Physician's Automated Laboratory Inc) 9830 Brimhall Rd	Bakersfield	CA	93312	**800-675-2271**	661-829-2260	418
Palladium Group Inc 55 Old Bedford Rd Ste 100	Lincoln	MA	01773	**800-773-2399**	781-259-3737	196
Pallet Consultants Corp PO Box 1692	Pompano Beach	FL	33061	**888-782-2909**	954-946-2212	550
Pallet Masters Inc 655 E Florence Ave	Los Angeles	CA	90001	**800-675-2579**	323-758-6559	550
Pallet Services Inc 12926 Farm to Market Rd	Mount Vernon	WA	98273	**800-769-2245**		202
PalletOne Inc 1470 US Hwy 17 S	Bartow	FL	33830	**800-771-1148**	863-533-1147	550
Pallett Valo LLP 77 City Ctr Dr Ste 300	Mississauga	ON	L5B1M5	**800-323-3781**	905-273-3300	428
Palliser Furniture Upholstery Ltd 70 Lexington Park	Winnipeg	MB	R2G4H2	**866-444-0777**	204-988-5600	470
Palm 5800 Universal Blvd Hard Rock Hotel	Orlando	FL	32819	**866-333-7256**	407-503-7256	669
Palm Automotive Group 1801 Tamiami Trail *General	Punta Gorda	FL	33950	**800-643-2112***	941-639-1155	56
Palm Beach Atlantic University PO Box 24708	West Palm Beach	FL	33416	**888-468-6722**	561-803-2000	167
Palm Beach Community College *Lake Worth* 4200 Congress Ave	Lake Worth	FL	33461	**866-576-7222**	561-868-3350	161
Palm Beach Gardens 3160 PGA Blvd	Palm Beach Gardens	FL	33410	**866-576-7222**	561-207-5340	161
Palm Beach County Convention & Visitors Bureau 1555 Palm Beach Lakes Blvd Ste 800	West Palm Beach	FL	33401	**800-554-7256**	561-233-3000	208
Palm Beach County School District, The 3300 Forest Hill Blvd	West Palm Beach	FL	33406	**866-930-8402**	561-434-8000	683
Palm Beach Daily Business Review 324 Datura St Ste 140	West Palm Beach	FL	33401	**800-777-7300**	561-820-2060	456-5
Palm Beach Illustrated Magazine 1000 N Dixie Hwy Ste C	West Palm Beach	FL	33401	**800-308-7346**	561-659-6160	456-22
Palm Beach Newspapers Inc PO Box 24700	West Palm Beach	FL	33416	**800-432-7595**	561-820-4100	634-8
Palm Beach Opera 415 S Olive Ave	West Palm Beach	FL	33401	**800-435-7352**	561-833-7888	572-2
Palm Beach Post 2751 S Dixie Hwy	West Palm Beach	FL	33405	**800-432-7595**	561-820-4100	531-2
Palm Management Corp 1730 Rhode Island Ave NW Ste 900	Washington	DC	20036	**800-388-7256**	202-775-7256	668
Palm Mountain Resort & Spa 155 S BelaRdo Rd	Palm Springs	CA	92262	**800-622-9451**	760-325-1301	667
Palm Restaurant 6100 Westheimer Rd	Houston	TX	77057	**866-333-7256**	713-977-2544	669
Palm Springs Convention Ctr 277 N Avenida Caballeros	Palm Springs	CA	92262	**800-898-7256**	760-325-6611	207
Palm Springs Desert Resorts Convention & Visitors Authority 70-100 Hwy 111	Rancho Mirage	CA	92270	**800-967-3767**	760-770-9000	208
Palm Springs International Airport 3200 E Tahquitz Canyon Way	Palm Springs	CA	92262	**800-847-4389**	760-318-3800	27

Name / Address	City	State	ZIP	Toll-Free	Phone	Class
Palm, The 200 Dartmouth St	Boston	MA	02116	**866-333-7256**	617-867-9292	669
Palmer Asphalt Co 196 W Fifth St PO Box 58	Bayonne	NJ	07002	**800-352-9898**	201-339-0855	45
Palmer Correctional Ctr PO Box 919	Palmer	AK	99645	**877-741-0741**	907-745-5054	215
Palmer Holland Inc 25000 Country Club Blvd Ste 444	North Olmsted	OH	44070	**800-635-4822**		145
Palmer House Hilton 17 E Monroe St	Chicago	IL	60603	**800-445-8667**	312-726-7500	379
Palmer Investigative Services 624 W Gurley St Ste A	Prescott	AZ	86304	**800-280-2951**	928-778-2951	400
Palmer Manufacturing 18 N Bechtle Ave	Springfield	OH	45504	**800-457-5456**	937-323-6339	491
Palmer Moving & Storage 24660 Dequindre Rd	Warren	MI	48091	**800-521-3954**	586-436-3804	518
Palmer Paving Corp 25 Blanchard St	Palmer	MA	01069	**800-244-8354**	413-283-8354	190-4
Palmer Theological Seminary 588 N Gulph Rd	King Of Prussia	PA	19406	**800-220-3287**	610-896-5000	168-3
Palmer-Donavin Manufacturing Co 1200 Steelwood Rd	Columbus	OH	43212	**800-589-4412**	614-486-9657	193-3
Palmerton Area School District 680 Fourth St	Palmerton	PA	18071	**800-732-0999**	610-826-7101	683
Palmetto Brick Co 3501 BrickyaRd Rd	Wallace	SC	29596	**800-922-4423**	843-537-7861	149
Palmetto Dunes Resort 4 Queen Folly Rd	Hilton Head Island	SC	29928	**866-380-1778**		667
Palmetto Health Home Care & Hospice 1400 Pickens St	Columbia	SC	29202	**800-238-1884**	803-296-3100	371
Palmetto Island State Park 19501 Pleasant Rd	Abbeville	LA	70510	**888-677-3668**	337-893-3930	564
Palmetto State Transportation Company Inc 1050 Pk W Blvd	Greenville	SC	29611	**800-269-0175**	864-672-3800	778
Palms Casino Resort 4321 W Flamingo Rd	Las Vegas	NV	89103	**866-942-7777**	702-942-7777	132
Palms Resort 2500 N Ocean Blvd	Myrtle Beach	SC	29577	**800-300-1198**	843-626-8334	667
Palms West Hospital (PWH) 13001 Southern Blvd	Loxahatchee	FL	33470	**877-549-9337**	561-798-3300	374-3
Palms, The 3025 Collins Ave	Miami Beach	FL	33140	**800-550-0505**	305-534-0505	667
Palmyra Bologna Company Inc 230 N College St	Palmyra	PA	17078	**800-282-6336**	717-838-6336	297-26
Palomar Pomerado Health 15615 Pomerado Rd	Poway	CA	92064	**800-628-2880**	858-613-4000	353
Palomar Technologies 2728 Loker Ave W	Carlsbad	CA	92010	**800-854-3467**	760-931-3600	809
Palomino RV 1200 New Jersey Ave	Washington	MI	20590	**888-327-4236**	269-432-3271	119
Palomino System Innovations Inc 533 College St Ste 404	Toronto	ON	M6G1A8	**866-360-0360**	416-964-7333	181
Palos Sports Inc 11711 S Austin Ave	Alsip	IL	60803	**800-233-5484**	708-396-2555	709
Paltech Enterprises Inc 2560 Bing Miller Ln	Urbana	IA	52345	**800-949-1006**	319-443-2700	498
PAM Transportation Services Inc 297 W Henri De Tonti Blvd *NASDAQ: PTSI*	Tontitown	AR	72770	**800-879-7261**	479-361-9111	778
Pamarco 171 E Marquardt Dr *Sales	Wheeling	IL	60090	**800-323-7735***	847-459-6000	675
Pamarco Global Graphics 235 E 11th Ave	Roselle	NJ	07203	**800-365-6510**	908-241-1200	628
Pamlab LLC 4099 Hwy 190 E Service Rd	Covington	LA	70433	**844-639-9725**	985-893-4097	240
Pampered Chef Ltd 1 Pampered Chef Ln	Addison	IL	60101	**888-687-2433**		366
Pan Abode Cedar Homes Inc 1100 Maple Ave SW	Renton	WA	98057	**800-782-2633**	425-255-8260	105
Pan American Development Foundation (PADF) 1889 F St NW 2nd Fl	Washington	DC	20006	**877-572-4484**	202-458-3969	47-5
Pan American Screw Inc 630 Reese Dr SW *Cust Svc	Conover	NC	28613	**800-951-2222***	828-466-0060	280
Pan American Travel Services 320 East 900 South	Salt Lake City	UT	84111	**800-364-4359**	801-364-4300	770
Pan Pacific Hotel Vancouver 999 Canada Pl Ste 300	Vancouver	BC	V6C3B5	**800-937-1515**	604-662-8111	379
Pan Pacific Seattle 2125 Terry Ave	Seattle	WA	98121	**877-324-4856**	206-264-8111	379
Pan Pacific Whistler Mountainside 4320 Sundial Crescent	Whistler	BC	V0N1B4	**888-905-9995**	604-905-2999	667
Panama City Beach Convention & Visitors Bureau 17001 Panama City Beach Pkwy	Panama City Beach	FL	32413	**800-722-3224**	850-233-5070	208
Panamax Inc 1690 Corporate Cir	Petaluma	CA	94954	**800-472-5555**	707-283-5900	255
Pan-American Life Insurance Co 601 Poydras St *Life Ins	New Orleans	LA	70130	**877-939-4550***		391-2
Panasas Inc 969 W Maude Ave	Sunnyvale	CA	94085	**800-726-2727**	408-215-6800	179
Panasonic Avionics Corp 26200 Enterprise Way	Lake Forest	CA	92630	**877-627-2300**	949-672-2000	51
Panasonic Consumer Electronics Co 1 Panasonic Way *NYSE: PC*	Secaucus	NJ	07094	**800-103-1333**	888-762-2097	51
Panasonic Corp of North America 1 Panasonic Way *Cust Svc	Secaucus	NJ	07094	**800-211-7262***	888-762-2097	51
Panasonic Corporation of North America 2 Riverfront Plaza	Newark	NJ	07102	**888-223-1012**		175-1
Panasonic Electric Works Corp of America 629 Central Ave	New Providence	NJ	07974	**800-276-6289**	908-464-3550	205
Panavise Products Inc 7540 Colbert Dr	Reno	NV	89511	**800-759-7535**	775-850-2900	695

Name / Address	City	State	ZIP	Toll-Free	Phone	Class
Panavision Inc 6219 DeSoto Ave	Woodland Hills	CA	91367	**800-260-1846**	818-316-1000	590
Panda Express 1717 Walnut Grove Ave	Rosemead	CA	91770	**800-877-8988**	626-312-5401	668
Panda Restaurant Group Inc 1683 Walnut Grove Ave	Rosemead	CA	91770	**800-877-8988**	626-799-9898	668
Panda Travel 1017 Kapahulu Ave Fl 2	Honolulu	HI	96816	**800-303-6702**	808-734-1961	770
Pandel Inc 21 River Dr	Cartersville	GA	30120	**800-537-3868**	770-382-1034	364
Panduit Corp 17301 Ridgeland Ave	Tinley Park	IL	60477	**888-506-5400**	708-532-1800	813
Panel Processing Inc 120 N Industrial Hwy	Alpena	MI	49707	**800-433-7142**	989-356-9007	817
Panelfold Inc 10700 NW 36th Ave	Miami	FL	33167	**800-433-3222**	305-688-3501	288
Paneloc Corp PO Box 547	Farmington	CT	06034	**800-394-6711**	860-677-6711	350
Panera Bread Co 3630 S Geyer Rd *NASDAQ: PNRA*	Saint Louis	MO	63127	**800-301-5566**	314-984-1000	67
Panhandle Co-op Assn 401 S Beltline Hwy W *Cust Svc	Scottsbluff	NE	69361	**800-732-4546***	308-632-5301	278
Panhandle Royalty Co 5400 N Grand Blvd Grand Ctr Bldg Ste 300	Oklahoma City	OK	73112	**800-884-4225**	405-948-1560	537
Panhandle Telecommunication Systems Inc (PTSI) 2222 NW Hwy	Guymon	OK	73942	**800-562-2556**	580-338-2556	733
Pannell Kerr Forster Of Texas Pc 5847 San Felipe St	Houston	TX	77057	**800-829-3676**	713-860-1400	2
Pannier Corp 207 Sandusky St	Pittsburgh	PA	15212	**877-726-6437**	412-323-4900	493
Pannier Graphics 345 Oak Rd	Gibsonia	PA	15044	**800-544-8428**	724-265-4900	699
Pan-O-Gold Baking Co 444 E St Germain	Saint Cloud	MN	56304	**800-444-7005**	320-251-9361	297-1
Panola Partnership Inc 150-A Public Sq	Batesville	MS	38606	**888-872-6652**	662-563-3126	138
Panola-Harrison Electric Co-op 410 E Houston St	Marshall	TX	75670	**800-972-1093**	903-935-7936	247
Panolam Industries International Inc 20 Progress Dr	Shelton	CT	06484	**877-391-4130**	203-925-1556	817
Panorama Balloon Tours 2683 Via De La Valle 625G	Del Mar	CA	92014	**800-455-3592**		758
Panorama City 1751 Cir Ln SE	Lacey	WA	98503	**800-999-9807**	360-456-0111	670
Panoramic Corp 4321 Goshen Rd	Fort Wayne	IN	46818	**800-654-2027**		755
Panoramic Inc 1500 N Parker Dr	Janesville	WI	53545	**800-333-1394**	608-754-8850	100
Pan-Osten Co 6944 Louisville Rd	Bowling Green	KY	42101	**800-472-6678**	270-783-3900	288
Pantages Hotel 200 Victoria St	Toronto	ON	M5B1V8	**866-852-1777**	416-362-1777	379
Pantages Theater 901 Broadway	Tacoma	WA	98402	**800-291-7593**	253-591-5890	571
Pantages Theatre 6233 Hollywood Blvd	Los Angeles	CA	90028	**800-430-8903**		571
Pantagraph PO Box 2907	Bloomington	IL	61702	**800-747-7323**	309-829-9000	531-2
Panther State Forest HC 63 PO Box Box 923	Panther	WV	24872	**800-225-5982**	304-938-2252	564
Panzer Nursery Inc 17980 W Baseline Rd	Beaverton	OR	97006	**888-212-5327**	503-645-1185	369
Paoli Inc 201 E Martin St	Orleans	IN	47452	**800-472-8669**		320-1
Papa Gino's Inc 600 Providence Hwy	Dedham	MA	02026	**800-727-2446**	781-461-1200	668
Papa John's International Inc PO Box 99900 *NASDAQ: PZZA*	Louisville	KY	40269	**877-547-7272**		297-36
Paper Crafts Magazine 14512 S Ctr Point Way Ste 600	Bluffdale	UT	84065	**800-727-2387**	801-816-8300	456-14
Paper Machine Components 11 Old Sugar Hollow Rd	Danbury	CT	06810	**800-869-5747**	203-792-8686	203
Paper Pak Industries (PPI) 1941 N White Ave	La Verne	CA	91750	**888-293-6529**	909-392-1750	298-9
Paper Store Inc 20 Main St	Acton	MA	01720	**844-480-7100**		565
Paper Systems Inc 185 S Pioneer Blvd	Springboro	OH	45066	**888-564-6774**	937-746-6841	553
Paper Tigers, The 2201 Waukegan Rd Ste 180	Bannockburn	IL	60015	**800-621-1774**	847-919-6500	658
Paper Transport Inc 2701 Executive Dr	Green Bay	WI	54304	**800-317-3650**		778
Paperclip Software Inc 1 University Plz	Hackensack	NJ	07601	**800-929-3503**	201-525-1221	180-1
Papercone Corp 3200 Fern Vly Rd	Louisville	KY	40213	**800-626-5308**	502-961-9493	265
PaperDirect Inc 1005 E Woodmen Rd	Colorado Springs	CO	80920	**800-272-7377**		552
Paperdoll Co 4944 Encino Ave	Encino	CA	91316	**866-223-1145**	818-906-8411	129
Papers Inc 206 S Main St	Milford	IN	46542	**800-733-4111**	574-658-4111	634-8
Papers, The 206 S Main St PO Box 188	Milford	IN	46542	**800-733-4111**	574-658-4111	531-4
Pappas Restaurants Inc 13939 NW Fwy	Houston	TX	77040	**877-277-2748**	713-869-0151	668
Pappas Seafood House 13939 NW Fwy	Houston	TX	77040	**877-277-2748**	713-869-0151	668
Papyrus Franchise Corp 500 Chadbourne Rd	Fairfield	CA	94533	**800-789-1649**		128
Par Pharmaceutical Cos Inc 6 Ram Ridge Rd *NYSE: PRX*	Chestnut Ridge	NY	10977	**800-828-9393**	201-802-4000	583

Name / Address	City	State	ZIP	Toll-Free	Phone	Class
Par Pharmaceutical Inc 1 Ram Ridge Rd	Spring Valley	NY	10977	**800-828-9393**	201-802-4000	583
PAR Technology Corp 8383 Seneca Tpke *NYSE: PAR*	New Hartford	NY	13413	**800-448-6505**	315-738-0600	613
Para Plate 15910 Shoemaker Ave	Cerritos	CA	90703	**800-788-1556**	562-404-3434	779
Para Systems Inc *Minuteman UPS* 1455 LeMay Dr	Carrollton	TX	75007	**800-238-7272**	972-446-7363	255
Para-Chem Southern Inc 863 SE Main St PO Box 127	Simpsonville	SC	29681	**800-763-7272**	864-967-7691	3
Par-A-Dice Hotel 21 Blackjack Blvd	East Peoria	IL	61611	**800-727-2342**	309-699-7711	379
Paradigm Equity Strategies LLC 1611 - A Akron Peninsula Rd	Akron	OH	44313	**888-249-5727**	330-475-1690	390
Paradigm Imaging Group 1590 Metro Dr Ste 116	Costa Mesa	CA	92626	**888-221-7226**	714-432-7226	626
Paradigm Medical Industries Inc 4273 South 590 West *OTC: PDMI*	Salt Lake City	UT	84123	**800-742-0671**	801-977-8970	252
Paradise Chamber of Commerce 5550 Sky Way Ste 1	Paradise	CA	95969	**800-838-3006**	530-877-9356	138
Paradise Inc 1200 W MLK Jr Blvd *OTC: PARF*	Plant City	FL	33563	**800-330-8952**		297-8
Paradise Island Vacations 1000 S Pine Island Rd Ste 800 *Resv	Plantation	FL	33324	**888-877-7525***	954-809-2000	769
Paradise Point Resort & Spa 1404 W Vacation Rd	San Diego	CA	92109	**800-344-2626**	858-274-4630	667
Paradise Point State Recreation Site PO Box 1345	Port Orford	OR	97465	**800-551-6949**		564
Parady Financial Group Inc 340 Heald Way Ste 226	The Villages	FL	32163	**855-701-4351**	352-751-3016	401
Paragon Casino Resort 711 Paragon Pl	Marksville	LA	71351	**800-946-1946**		132
Paragon Development Systems Inc 1823 Executive Dr	Oconomowoc	WI	53066	**800-966-6090**		176
Paragon Furniture Management Inc 2224 E Randol Mill Rd	Arlington	TX	76011	**800-451-8546**	817-633-3242	321
Paragon Industries Inc 2011 S Town E Blvd	Mesquite	TX	75149	**800-876-4328**	972-288-7557	319
Paragon Laboratories 20433 Earl St	Torrance	CA	90503	**800-231-3670**	310-370-1563	797
Paragon Packaging Inc 7700 Centerville Rd	Ferndale	CA	95536	**888-615-0065**	707-786-4004	100
Paragon Sporting Goods Corp 867 Broadway 18th St	New York	NY	10003	**800-961-3030**	212-255-8889	709
Paragon Steel Enterprises LLC 4211 County Rd 61	Butler	IN	46721	**800-411-5677**	260-868-1100	491
Parallax Inc 599 Menlo Dr Ste 100	Rocklin	CA	95765	**888-512-1024**	916-624-8333	624
Parametric Technology Corp (PTC) 140 Kendrick St *NASDAQ: PTC*	Needham	MA	02494	**800-613-7535**	781-370-5000	180-5
Paramount Apparel International Inc 1 Paramount Dr	Bourbon	MO	65441	**866-274-4287**	573-732-4411	154-8
Paramount Builders Inc 501 Central Dr	Virginia Beach	VA	23454	**888-340-9002**	757-340-9000	364
Paramount Chemical Specialties Inc 14750 NE 95th St	Redmond	WA	98052	**877-846-7826**	425-882-2673	150
Paramount Cosmetics Inc 93 Entin Rd Ste 4	Clifton	NJ	07014	**800-522-9880**	973-472-2323	217
Paramount Health Care 1901 Indian Wood Cir	Maumee	OH	43537	**800-462-3589**	419-887-2525	391-3
Paramount Hotel 724 Pine St	Seattle	WA	98101	**877-821-2011**	206-292-9500	379
Paramount Industries Inc 304 N Howard St	Croswell	MI	48422	**800-521-5405**	810-679-2551	439
Paramount Technologies Inc 1374 EW Maple Rd	Walled Lake	MI	48390	**800-725-4408**	248-960-0909	38
Paramount Theatre 123 Third Ave SE	Cedar Rapids	IA	52401	**800-369-8863**	319-398-5226	571
Paramount's Kings Dominion 16000 Theme Pkwy	Doswell	VA	23047	**800-367-7623**	804-876-5000	32
Parasec Inc 2804 Gateway Oaks Dr Ste 200 PO Box 160568 *General	Sacramento	CA	95833	**800-533-7272***		632
Parc Aquarium du Quebec 1675 des Hotels Ave	Quebec	QC	G1W4S3	**866-659-5264**	418-659-5264	39
Parchem Trading Ltd 415 Huguenot St	New Rochelle	NY	10801	**800-282-3982**	914-654-6800	233
Parents Helping Parents (PHP) 1400 Parkmoor Ave Ste 100	San jose	CA	95126	**855-727-5775**	408-727-5775	47-6
Parents of Murdered Children (POMC) 4960 Ridge Ave Ste 2	Cincinnati	OH	45209	**888-818-7662**	513-721-5683	47-6
Parenty Reitmeier Inc 605 Des Meurons St	Winnipeg	MB	R2H2R1	**877-445-3737**	204-237-3737	318
PAREXEL International Corp 195 W St *NASDAQ: PRXL*	Waltham	MA	02451	**800-301-5033**	781-487-9900	666
Paris Business Products 800 Highland Dr *Cust Svc	Westampton	NJ	08060	**800-523-6454***	609-265-9200	109
Paris Farmers' Union PO Box D	South Paris	ME	04281	**800-639-3603**	207-743-8976	278
Paris Gourmet of New York Inc 145 Grand St	Carlstadt	NJ	07072	**800-727-8791**		298-8
Paris Junior College 2400 Clarksville St	Paris	TX	75460	**800-232-5804**	903-785-7661	161
Paris Las Vegas 3655 Las Vegas Blvd S	Las Vegas	NV	89109	**800-342-7724**	800-522-4700	379
Paris Mountain State Park 2401 State Pk Rd	Greenville	SC	29609	**866-345-7275**	864-244-5565	564
Paris-Henry County Chamber of Commerce 2508 Eastwood St	Paris	TN	38242	**800-345-1103**	731-642-3431	138
Park 'N Fly 2060 Mt Paran Rd Ste 207 *Cust Svc	Atlanta	GA	30327	**800-325-4863***		561
Park 100 Foods Inc 326 E Adams St	Tipton	IN	46072	**800-854-6504**	765-675-3480	297-26
Park Bancorp Inc 5400 S Pulaski Rd *OTC: PFED*	Chicago	IL	60632	**888-727-5333**	773-582-8616	360-2
Park Cities Limousine 7129 Harry Hines Blvd	Dallas	TX	75235	**888-559-0708**	214-824-0011	441
Park City Chamber of Commerce/Convention & Visitors Bureau 1850 Sidewinder Dr Ste 320	Park City	UT	84060	**800-453-1360**	435-649-6100	208
Park City Mountain Resort (PCMR) 1345 Lowell Ave PO Box 39	Park City	UT	84060	**800-222-7275**	435-649-8111	667
Park Community Federal Credit Union PO Box 18630	Louisville	KY	40261	**800-626-2870**	502-968-3681	218
Park County 1002 Sheridan Ave	Cody	WY	82414	**800-786-2844**	307-527-8510	338
Park County Travel Council (PCTC) 836 Sheridan Ave PO Box 2454	Cody	WY	82414	**800-393-2639**	307-587-2297	208
Park Electric Co-op Inc 5706 US Hwy 89 S PO Box 1119	Livingston	MT	59047	**888-298-0657**	406-222-3100	247
Park Hyatt Beaver Creek Resort & Spa 136 E Thomas Pl *Cust Svc	Avon	CO	81620	**800-233-1234***	970-949-1234	667
Park National Bank 50 N Third St PO Box 3500 *NYSE: PRK*	Newark	OH	43058	**888-791-8633**	740-349-8451	360-2
Park Place Technologies Inc 5910 Landerbrook Dr	Cleveland	OH	44124	**877-778-8707**		179
Park Seed Co 1 Parkton Ave *Orders	Greenwood	SC	29647	**800-845-3369***		692
Park Shore Resort 600 Neapolitan Way	Naples	FL	34103	**800-548-2077**	239-263-2222	667
Park Shore Waikiki Hotel 2586 Kalakaua Ave	Honolulu	HI	96815	**866-536-7975**	808-954-7426	379
Park South Hotel 124 E 28th St	New York	NY	10016	**800-315-4642**	212-448-0888	379
Park To Fly Inc 7800 Narcoossee Rd	Orlando	FL	32822	**888-851-8875**	407-851-8875	561
Park University 8700 NW River Pk Dr	Parkville	MO	64152	**800-745-7275**	816-741-2000	167
Park Vista Resort Hotel 705 Cherokee OrchaRd Rd PO Box 30 *Sales	Gatlinburg	TN	37738	**800-227-5622***	865-436-9211	379
Park Water Co 9750 Washburn Rd	Downey	CA	90241	**800-727-5987**	562-923-0711	785
Parkdale Mills Inc 531 Cotton Blossom Cir	Gastonia	NC	28054	**800-331-1843**	704-874-5000	742-9
Parke County Rural Electric Membership Corp 119 W High St	Rockville	IN	47872	**800-537-3913**	765-569-3133	247
Parke-Bell Ltd Inc 709 W 12th St	Huntingburg	IN	47542	**800-457-7456**	812-683-3707	113
Parker Drilling Co 1401 Enclave Pkwy Ste 600 *NYSE: PKD*	Houston	TX	77077	**800-468-9716**	281-406-2000	539
Parker Fluid Connectors Group 6035 Parkland Blvd *General	Cleveland	OH	44124	**800-272-7537***	216-896-3000	370
Parker Furniture 10375 SW Beaverton-Hillsdale Hwy	Beaverton	OR	97005	**866-515-9673**	503-644-0155	322
Parker Hannifin Corp Automation Actuator Div 135 Quadral Dr	Wadsworth	OH	44281	**800-272-7537**	330-336-3511	225
Parker Hannifin Corp Brass Products Div 100 Parker Dr	Otsego	MI	49078	**800-272-7537**	269-694-9411	788
Parker Hannifin Corp Cylinder Div 500 S Wolf Rd	Des Plaines	IL	60016	**800-272-7537**	847-298-2400	225
Parker Hannifin Corp Daedal Div 1140 Sandy Hill Rd	Irwin	PA	15642	**800-245-6903**	724-861-8200	543
Parker Hannifin Corp Electromechanical Automation Div 5500 Business Pk Dr	Rohnert Park	CA	94928	**800-358-9068**	707-584-7558	205
Parker Hannifin Corp Finite Filtratio & Separation Div 500 Glaspie St	Oxford	MI	48371	**800-521-4357**	248-628-6400	18
Parker Hannifin Corp General Valve Div 26 Clinton Dr Unit 103	Hollis	NH	03049	**800-272-7537**		788
Parker Hannifin Corp Hydraulic Valve Div 520 Ternes Ave	Elyria	OH	44035	**800-272-7537**	440-366-5200	787
Parker Hannifin Corp Pneumatic Div 8676 E M 89	Richland	MI	49083	**877-321-4736**	269-629-5000	788
Parker Hannifin Corp Skinner Valve Div 95 Edgewood Ave	New Britain	CT	06051	**800-825-8305**	860-827-2300	788
Parker Hannifin Corp Veriflo Div 250 Canal Blvd	Richmond	CA	94804	**800-272-7537**	510-235-9590	203
Parker Instrumentation Group 6035 Parkland Blvd	Cleveland	OH	44124	**800-272-7537**	216-896-3000	225
Parker Lumber Co of Port Arthur Inc 2948 Gulfway Dr	Port Arthur	TX	77642	**855-828-9792**	409-983-2745	193-3
Parker Majestic Inc 300 N Pike Rd	Sarver	PA	16055	**866-572-7537**	724-352-1551	454
Parker McCrory Manufacturing Co 2000 Forest Ave	Kansas City	MO	64108	**800-662-1038**	816-221-2000	205
Parker Paint Mfg Co Inc 3003 S Tacoma Way	Tacoma	WA	98409	**855-862-6639**		549
Parker Poe Adams & Bernstein LLP 3 Wachovia Ctr 401 S Tryon St Ste 3000	Charlotte	NC	28202	**866-602-5893**	704-372-9000	428
Parker Powis Inc 775 Heinz Ave	Berkeley	CA	94710	**800-321-2463**	510-848-2463	91
Parker Rose Design Inc 10075 Mesa Rim Rd Ste A	San Diego	CA	92121	**800-403-2711**		40
Parker Smith & Feek Inc 2233 112th Ave NE *Cust Svc	Bellevue	WA	98004	**800-457-0220***	425-709-3600	390
Parker Steel Co PO Box 2883	Toledo	OH	43606	**800-333-4140**	419-473-2481	491

	City	State	ZIP	Toll-Free	Phone	Class
Parker University						
2540 Walnut Hill Ln	Dallas	TX	75229	**800-637-8337**	972-438-6932	762
Parker-Hannifin Corp						
1160 Ctr Rd	Avon	OH	44011	**800-272-5464**	440-937-6211	768
Parkersburg & Wood County Public Library						
3100 Emerson Ave	Parkersburg	WV	26104	**800-642-8674**	304-420-4587	434-3
ParkerVision Inc						
7915 Baymeadows Way	Jacksonville	FL	32256	**800-532-8034**	904-737-1367	645
NASDAQ: PRKR						
Parkhill Smith & Cooper Inc						
4222 85th St	Lubbock	TX	79423	**800-400-6646**	806-473-2200	263
Parkhurst Manufacturing Co						
18999 Hwy Y	Sedalia	MO	65301	**800-821-7380**	660-826-8685	515
Parking Panda Corp						
3422 Fait Ave	Baltimore	MD	21224	**800-232-6415**		561
Parkinson's Disease Foundation (PDF)						
1359 Broadway	New York	NY	10018	**800-457-6676**	212-923-4700	47-17
Parkland College						
2400 W Bradley Ave	Champaign	IL	61821	**888-467-6065**	217-351-2200	161
Parkland College Theatre						
2400 W Bradley Ave	Champaign	IL	61821	**800-346-8089**	217-351-2528	571
Parkland Health Ctr						
1101 W Liberty St	Farmington	MO	63640	**800-734-3944**	573-756-6451	374-3
Parkland Plastics Inc						
104 Yoder Dr PO Box 339	Middlebury	IN	46540	**800-835-4110**	574-825-4336	659
Parkline Inc						
PO Box 65	Winfield	WV	25213	**800-786-4855**	304-586-2113	104
Parkridge East Hospital						
941 Spring Creek Rd	Chattanooga	TN	37412	**800-605-1527**	423-894-7870	374-3
Parks Assoc Inc						
15950 N Dallas Pkwy Ste 575	Dallas	TX	75248	**800-727-5711**	972-490-1113	666
Parks Bros Farm Inc						
6733 Parks Rd	Van Buren	AR	72956	**800-334-5770**	479-474-1125	369
Parks Canada						
25-7-N Eddy St	Gatineau	QC	K1A0M5	**888-773-8888**	613-860-1251	562
Parksite Inc						
1563 Hubbard Ave	Batavia	IL	60510	**800-338-3355**	630-761-9490	193-3
Parkson Corp						
1401 W Cyperess Creek Rd						
	Fort Lauderdale	FL	33309	**888-727-5766**		386
Parkview Hospital						
2200 Randallia Dr	Fort Wayne	IN	46805	**888-737-9311**	260-373-4000	374-3
Parkview Medical Ctr						
400 W 16th St	Pueblo	CO	81003	**800-543-4046**	719-584-4000	374-3
Parkville Insurances Services Inc						
15242 E Whittier Blvd						
PO Box 1275	Whittier	CA	90603	**800-350-2702**	562-945-2702	390
Parkway Clinical Laboratories Inc						
3494 Progress Dr	Bensalem	PA	19020	**800-327-2764**	215-245-5112	418
Parkway Electric Inc						
11952 James St	Holland	MI	49424	**800-574-9553**	616-392-2788	785
Parkway Inn						
125 N Jackson St PO Box 494	Jackson	WY	83001	**800-247-8390**		379
Parkway Properties Inc						
188 E Capitol St Ste 1000	Jackson	MS	39201	**800-748-1667**	601-948-4091	653
NYSE: PKY						
Parmalat Canada Ltd						
405 the W Mall 10th Fl	Toronto	ON	M9C5J1	**800-563-1515**		297-27
Parmed Pharmaceuticals Inc						
4220 Hyde Pk Blvd	Niagara Falls	NY	14305	**800-727-6331**	716-284-5666	240
Parnell & Crum PA						
641 S Lawrence St	Montgomery	AL	36104	**866-629-0912**	334-832-4200	40
Parr Instrument Co						
211 53rd St	Moline	IL	61265	**800-872-7720**	309-762-7716	420
Parr Richey Obremsky & Morton						
201 N Illinois St Ste 300	Indianapolis	IN	46204	**888-337-7766**	317-269-2500	428
Parrish & Heimbecker Ltd (P&H)						
201 Portage Ave Ste 1400	Winnipeg	MB	R3B3K6	**800-665-8937**	204-956-2030	277
Parrish Tire Company Inc						
5130 Indiana Ave	Winston-Salem	NC	27106	**800-849-8473**	336-767-0202	61-5
Parsec Financial Management Inc						
6 Wall St	Asheville	NC	28801	**888-877-1012**	828-255-0271	196
Parsons Buick Co, The						
151 E St	Plainville	CT	06062	**877-274-2613**	860-747-1693	56
Parsons Capital Management Inc						
10 Weybosset St Ste 1000	Providence	RI	02903	**888-521-2440**	401-521-2440	401
Parsons Child & Family Ctr						
60 Academy Rd	Albany	NY	12208	**800-342-3009**	518-426-2600	47-6
Parsons Electric LLC						
5960 Main St NE	Minneapolis	MN	55432	**800-403-4832**	763-571-8000	191-4
Parsons New School for Design						
65 Fifth Ave	New York	NY	10011	**800-252-0852***	212-229-8989	167
*Admissions						
Parter Medical Products Inc						
17015 Kingsview Ave	Carson	CA	90746	**800-666-8282**	310-327-4417	420
Particle Dynamics International LLC						
2629 S Hanley Rd	Saint Louis	MO	63144	**800-452-4682**	314-968-2376	582
Particle Measuring Systems Inc						
5475 Airport Blvd	Boulder	CO	80301	**800-238-1801***	303-443-7100	419
*Cust Svc						
Partner Assessment Corp						
2154 Torrance Blvd Ste 200	Torrance	CA	90501	**800-419-4923**		194
Partner Reinsurance Co of the US						
1 Greenwich Plaza	Greenwich	CT	06830	**800-831-9146**	203-485-4200	391-2
PARTNERS A Tasteful Choice Co						
20232 72nd Ave	South Kent	WA	98032	**800-632-7477**	253-867-1580	67
Partnership for a Drug-Free America						
405 Lexington Ave Ste 1601	New York	NY	10174	**855-378-4373**	212-922-1560	47-17
Partnerships In Community Living Inc						
480 Main St E PO Box 129	Monmouth	OR	97361	**800-222-1222**	503-838-2403	47-15
Parton Lumber Company Inc						
251 Parton Rd	Rutherfordton	NC	28139	**800-624-1501**	828-287-4257	681
Parts Assoc Inc						
12420 Plz Dr	Parma	OH	44130	**800-321-1128**	216-433-7700	351
Parts Central Inc						
3243 Whitfield St	Macon	GA	31204	**800-226-9396**	478-745-0878	60
PartsBase Inc						
905 Clint Moore Rd	Boca Raton	FL	33487	**888-322-6896***	561-953-0700	768
*Cust Svc						

	City	State	ZIP	Toll-Free	Phone	Class
PartsRiver Inc						
3155 Kearney St Ste 210	Fremont	CA	94538	**855-700-7278**		180-7
Party City Corp						
25 Green Pond Rd Ste 1	Rockaway	NJ	07866	**800-727-8924**	973-453-8600	565
Partylite Gifts Inc						
59 Armstrong Rd	Plymouth	MA	02360	**888-999-5706**	508-830-3100	366
Par-Way Tryson Co						
107 Bolte Ln	Saint Clair	MO	63077	**800-844-4554**	636-629-4545	297-30
PAS (Percussive Arts Society)						
110 W Washington St	Indianapolis	IN	46204	**888-990-6663**	317-974-4488	47-4
Pasadena Convention & Visitors Bureau						
300 E Green St	Pasadena	CA	91101	**800-307-7977**	626-795-9311	208
Pasadena Playhouse, The						
39 S El Molino Ave	Pasadena	CA	91101	**800-733-2767**	626-356-7529	746
Pasadena Star-News						
911 E Colorado Blvd	Pasadena	CA	91106	**800-788-1200**	626-578-6300	531-2
Pasco-Hernando Community College						
10230 Ridge Rd	New Port Richey	FL	34654	**877-879-7422**	727-847-2727	161
North						
11415 Ponce de Leon Blvd	Brooksville	FL	34601	**877-879-7422**	352-796-6726	161
Pasek Corp						
9 W Third St	South Boston	MA	02127	**800-628-2822**	617-269-7110	691
Paslode						
888 Forest Edge Dr	Vernon Hills	IL	60061	**800-682-3428***	847-634-1900	757
*Cust Svc						
PASNAP (Pennsylvania Assn of Staff Nurses & Allied Professionals)						
1 Fayette St Ste 475	Conshohocken	PA	19428	**800-500-7850**	610-567-2907	532
Paso Robles Inn						
1103 Spring St	Paso Robles	CA	93446	**800-676-1713**	805-238-2660	379
Pason Systems Inc						
6130 Third St SE	Calgary	AB	T2H1K4	**877-255-3158**	403-301-3400	180-10
TSE: PSI						
Passaic Valley Water Commission						
1525 Main Ave	Clifton	NJ	07011	**877-772-7077**	973-340-4300	785
Passavant Retirement Community						
401 S Main St	Zelienople	PA	16063	**888-498-7753**	724-452-5400	670
Passenger Vessel Assn (PVA)						
103 Oronoco St Ste 200	Alexandria	VA	22314	**800-807-8360**	703-518-5005	48-21
Passero Associates						
242 W Main St Ste 100	Rochester	NY	14614	**800-836-0365**	585-325-1000	263
Passport Corp						
85 Chestnut Ridge Rd	Montvale	NJ	07645	**800-926-6736**	201-573-0038	180-1
Passport Health Communications Inc						
720 Cool Springs Blvd Ste 200	Franklin	TN	37067	**888-661-5657**	615-661-5657	180-10
Passport Program-western						
925 Euclid Ave Ste 600	Cleveland	OH	44115	**800-626-7277**	216-621-0303	363
Passport Services Regional Offices						
Boston Agency						
10 Cswy St Rm 247						
Tip O'Neill Federal Bldg	Boston	MA	02222	**877-487-2778**		340-14
Chicago Agency						
Kluczynski Federal Bldg						
230 S Dearborn St 18th Fl	Chicago	IL	60604	**877-487-2778**		340-14
Connecticut Agency						
850 Canal St	Stamford	CT	06902	**877-487-2778**		340-14
Honolulu Agency						
300 Ala Moana Bldg Ste 1-330	Honolulu	HI	96850	**877-487-2778**		340-14
Los Angeles Agency						
11000 Wilshire Blvd						
Ste 1000	Los Angeles	CA	90024	**877-487-2778**		340-14
New Orleans Agency						
365 Canal St Ste 1300	New Orleans	LA	70130	**877-487-2778**		340-14
New York Agency						
376 Hudson St 10th Fl	New York	NY	10014	**877-487-2778**		340-14
Philadelphia Agency						
US Custom House						
200 Chesnut St Rm 103	Philadelphia	PA	19106	**877-487-2778**		340-14
San Francisco Agency						
95 Hawthorne St 5th Fl	San Francisco	CA	94105	**877-487-2778**		340-14
Washington (DC) Agency						
600 19th St NW						
1st Floor Sidewalk Level	Washington	DC	20006	**877-487-2778**		340-14
Passy-Muir Inc						
4521 Campus Dr Pmb 273	Irvine	CA	92612	**800-634-5397**	949-833-8255	476
Pastel Journal						
4700 E Galbraith Rd	Cincinnati	OH	45236	**800-422-2550**	513-531-2222	456-2
Pastorelli Food Products Inc						
162 N Sangamon St	Chicago	IL	60607	**800-767-2829**	312-666-2041	297-36
Pat O'Brien's International Inc						
718 St Peter St	New Orleans	LA	70116	**800-597-4823**	504-525-4823	668
Patagonia Inc						
259 W Santa Clara St PO Box 150	Ventura	CA	93001	**800-638-6464***	805-643-8616	156-4
*Cust Svc						
Patene Building Supplies Ltd						
641 Speedvale Ave W	Guelph	ON	N1K1E6	**800-265-8319**	519-822-1890	193-1
Patent Trademark & Copyright Law Daily						
1801 S Bell St	Arlington	VA	22202	**800-372-1033**		530-7
Paternity Testing Corp (PTC)						
300 Portland St	Columbia	MO	65201	**888-837-8323**	573-442-9948	417
Paterson Pacific Parchment Co						
625 Greg St	Sparks	NV	89431	**800-678-8104**	775-353-3000	558
Path Logic Inc						
950 Riverside Pkwy						
Ste 90	West Sacramento	CA	95605	**855-291-4528**		418
Path Master Inc						
1960 Midway Dr	Twinsburg	OH	44087	**855-738-2722**	330-425-4994	248
Path-2 Ventures LLC						
223 E Blvd	Charlotte	NC	28203	**888-692-1057**		462
Pathfinder Bancorp Inc						
214 W First St	Oswego	NY	13126	**800-811-5620**	315-343-0057	360-2
NASDAQ: PBHC						
PathGroup Inc						
5301 Virginia Way	Brentwood	TN	37027	**877-456-6706**	615-221-4500	196
Pathology & Cytology Laboratories Inc						
290 Big Run Rd	Lexington	KY	40503	**800-264-0514**	859-278-9513	415
Patient Advocate Foundation Inc						
700 Thimble Shoals Blvd						
Ste 200	Newport News	VA	23606	**800-532-5274**		306

Name / Address	City	State	Zip	Toll-Free	Phone	Class
Patients Rights Council (PRC) PO Box 760	Steubenville	OH	43952	800-958-5678	740-282-3810	47-8
Patina Group 12700 Center Ct Dr S 9th Fl	Cerritos	CA	90703	866-972-8462		668
Patioshoppers Inc 41188 Sandalwood Cir	Murrieta	CA	92562	800-940-6123	951-696-1700	322
Patricia Grand Resort 2710 N Ocean Blvd	Myrtle Beach	SC	29577	800-255-4763	843-448-8453	667
Patricia Seybold Group 210 Commercial St	Boston	MA	02109	855-310-0101	617-742-5200	462
Patrick Engineering Inc 4970 Varsity Dr	Lisle	IL	60532	800-799-7050	630-795-7200	263
Patrick Henry Community College 645 Patriot Ave PO Box 5311	Martinsville	VA	24112	855-874-6692	276-638-8777	161
Patrick Industries Inc 107 W Franklin St PO Box 638 *NASDAQ: PATK*	Elkhart	IN	46515	800-331-2151	574-294-7511	114
Patrick Industries Inc Patrick Metals Div 5020 Lincolnway E	Mishawaka	IN	46544	800-922-9692	574-255-9692	484
Patrick James Inc 780 W Shaw Ave	Fresno	CA	93704	888-427-6003	559-224-5500	156-3
Patrick Mcguire Certified Public Accountant 314 W 18th St	Cheyenne	WY	82001	800-544-2151	307-634-2151	2
Patriot Flooring Supply Inc 110 Commerce Way	Woburn	MA	01801	866-444-4433		688
Patriot Ledger 400 Crown Colony Dr PO Box 699159	Quincy	MA	02269	888-782-2267	617-786-7000	531-2
Patriot National Bancorp Inc 900 Bedford St *NASDAQ: PNBK*	Stamford	CT	06901	888-728-7468	203-251-7200	360-2
Patriot Staffing & Services Llc 47 Eggert Ave	Metuchen	NJ	08840	888-412-6999		569
Patriot Technologies Inc 5108 Pegasus Ct Ste F	Frederick	MD	21704	888-417-9899	301-695-7500	179
Patriot Transportation Holding Inc 501 Riverside Ave Ste 500 *NASDAQ: PATI*	Jacksonville	FL	32202	877-704-1776	904-396-5733	778
Patriot-News 812 Market St	Harrisburg	PA	17101	800-692-7207	717-255-8100	531-2
Patriots Point Naval & Maritime Museum 40 Patriots Pt Rd	Mount Pleasant	SC	29464	800-248-3508	803-771-0131	519
Patriots Theater Memorial Dr	Trenton	NJ	08608	866-847-7682	609-984-8484	571
Patten & Patten Inc 520 Lookout St	Chattanooga	TN	37403	800-757-3480	423-756-3480	196
Patten Industries Inc 635 W Lake St	Elmhurst	IL	60126	877-688-6812	630-279-4400	358
Patten University 2433 Coolidge Ave	Oakland	CA	94601	888-370-7589	510-261-8500	167
Pattern Insight Inc 465 Fairchild Dr Ste 209	Mountain View	CA	94043	866-582-2655		179
Patterson Cos Inc 1031 Mendota Heights Rd *NASDAQ: PDCO*	Saint Paul	MN	55120	800-328-5536	651-686-1600	474
Patterson Office Supplies 3310 N Duncan Rd	Champaign	IL	61822	800-637-1140	317-733-4900	109
Patterson-Schwartz & Assoc Inc 7234 Lancaster Pike Ste 100A	Hockessin	DE	19707	877-456-4663	302-234-5270	650
Patterson-UTI Energy Inc 450 Gears Rd Ste 500 *NASDAQ: PTEN*	Houston	TX	77067	866-387-1933	281-765-7100	539
Pattison Sign Group 555 Ellesmere Rd	Scarborough	ON	M1R4E8	800-268-6536	416-759-1111	699
Patton-Kiehl Group Inc 17026 Bull Church Rd	Woodford	VA	22580	888-388-0725		5
Patuxent Cos 2124 Priest Bridge Dr Ste 18	Crofton	MD	21114	800-628-4942	410-793-0181	191-16
Patz & Hall Wine Co 851 Napa Vly Corporate Way Ste A	Napa	CA	94558	877-265-6700	707-265-7700	443
Paul Brown Stadium 1 Paul Brown Stadium	Cincinnati	OH	45202	866-621-8383	513-621-3550	718
Paul C Buff Inc 2725 Bransford Ave	Nashville	TN	37204	800-443-5542	615-383-3982	439
Paul Casket Co 505 S Green St	Cambridge City	IN	47327	800-521-8202	765-478-3991	133
Paul D Camp Community College 100 N College Dr PO Box 737	Franklin	VA	23851	855-877-3918	757-569-6700	161
Hobbs Suffolk 271 Kenyon Rd	Suffolk	VA	23434	855-877-3918	757-925-6300	161
Paul deLima Co Inc 7546 Morgan Rd	Liverpool	NY	13090	800-962-8864	315-457-3725	297-7
Paul Fredrick Menstyle 223 W Poplar St	Fleetwood	PA	19522	800-247-1417	610-944-0909	156-3
Paul H Gesswein & Co 255 Hancock Ave	Bridgeport	CT	06605	800-544-2043	203-366-5400	407
Paul Heuring Motors Inc 720 N Hobart Rd	Hobart	IN	46342	888-851-9702	219-942-3673	56
Paul Laurence Dunbar House 219 N Paul Laurence Dunbar St	Dayton	OH	45402	800-860-0148	937-224-7061	49-2
Paul M. Grist State Park 1546 Grist Rd	Selma	AL	36701	800-252-7275	334-872-5846	564
Paul Mueller Co 1600 W Phelps St *OTC: MUEL*	Springfield	MO	65802	800-683-5537	417-831-3000	386
Paul Quinn College 3837 Simpson Stuart Rd	Dallas	TX	75241	800-433-3243	214-376-1000	167
Paul Sawyier Public Library 319 Wapping St	Frankfort	KY	40601	800-829-3676	502-352-2665	434-3
Paul Smith's College 7833 New York 30 PO Box 265 *Admissions	Paul Smiths	NY	12970	800-421-2605*	518-327-6227	167
Paul Stuart Inc Madison Ave & 45th St *Orders	New York	NY	10017	800-678-8278*	212-682-0320	156-4
Paul W Bryant Museum 300 Paul W Bryant Dr *General	Tuscaloosa	AL	35487	866-772-2327*	205-348-4668	521
Paulding-Putman Electric Co-op 910 N Williams St	Paulding	OH	45879	800-686-2357	419-399-5015	247
Pauline Books & Media 50 St Paul's Ave *Sales	Boston	MA	02130	800-876-4463*	617-522-8911	634-3
Pavco Inc 1935 John Crosland Jr Dr *Orders	Charlotte	NC	28208	800-321-7735*	704-496-6800	144
Pavilion Financial Corp 1001 Corydon Ave Ste 300	Winnipeg	MB	R3M0B6	866-954-5101	204-954-5101	689
Pavliks Com 80 Bell Farm Rd	Barrie	ON	L4M5K5	877-728-5457	705-726-2966	182
Pawleys Plantation 70 Tanglewood Dr	Pawleys Island	SC	29585	800-367-9959	843-237-6000	667
Pawling Corp 32 Nelson Hill Rd PO Box 200	Wassaic	NY	12592	800-431-3456		674
PAWS (Performing Animal Welfare Society) 11435 Simmerhorn Rd	Galt	CA	95632	800-513-6560	209-745-2606	47-3
Pawtucket Public Library 13 Summer St	Pawtucket	RI	02860	800-359-3090	401-725-3714	434-3
Pax World Fund Family 30 Penhallow St Ste 400	Portsmouth	NH	03801	800-767-1729	603-431-8022	527
Paxton & Vierling Steel Co 500 Ave H Carter Lake	Carter Lake	IA	51510	800-831-9252		479
Paxton Co 1111 Ingleside Rd	Norfolk	VA	23502	800-234-7290	757-853-6781	768
Paxton Van Lines Inc 5300 Port Royal Rd	Springfield	VA	22151	800-336-4536	703-321-7600	518
Pay Plus Benefits Inc 1110 N Ctr Pkwy Ste B	Kennewick	WA	99336	888-531-5781	509-735-1143	630
Paychex Inc 911 Panorama Trl S *NASDAQ: PAYX*	Rochester	NY	14625	800-828-4411	585-385-6666	569
Paychex Major Market Services 12647 Alcosta Blvd Ste 200	San Ramon	CA	94583	888-243-9329	925-242-0700	569
Paycom 7501 W Memorial Rd	Oklahoma City	OK	73142	800-580-4505		731
Payden & Rygel 333 S Grand Ave	Los Angeles	CA	90071	800-572-9336	213-625-1900	401
Payless Drug Stores Inc 16100 SW 72nd Ave PO Box 230969	Portland	OR	97224	800-330-3665	503-626-9436	583
Payless ShoeSource Inc 3231 SE Sixth Ave	Topeka	KS	66607	877-452-7500	785-233-5171	302
Payment Services Corp Inc 360 Albert St Ste 1220	Ottawa	ON	K1R7X7	866-972-0616		318
Paymetric Inc 1225 Northmeadow Pkwy Ste 110	Roswell	GA	30076	888-445-4901	678-242-5281	2
Payne Engineering Co Rt 29 PO Box 70 *Orders	Scott Depot	WV	25560	800-331-1345*	304-757-7353	205
Payne Theological Seminary 1230 Wilberforce Clifton Rd	Wilberforce	OH	45384	888-816-8933	937-376-2946	168-3
Paynes Creek Historic State Park 888 Lake Branch Rd	Bowling Green	FL	33834	800-326-3521	863-375-4717	564
Pay-O-Matic Corp 160 Oak Dr	Syosset	NY	11791	888-545-6311	516-496-4900	140
PayReel Inc 24928 Genesee Trl Rd	Golden	CO	80401	800-352-7397	303-526-4900	513
Payroll Practitioner's Monthly 3 Bethesda Metro Ctr Ste 250	Bethesda	MD	20814	800-372-1033		530-2
Payscape Advisors 729 Lambert Dr Ne	Atlanta	GA	30324	888-351-6565		508
Payson Casters Inc 2323 N Delaney Rd	Gurnee	IL	60031	800-323-4552	847-336-6200	350
Payspan Inc 7751 Belfort Pkwy Ste 200	Jacksonville	FL	32256	877-331-7154		180-1
Payworks Inc 1565 Willson Pl	Winnipeg	MB	R3T4H1	866-788-3500		731
Pazazz Printing Inc 5584 Cote-de-Liesse	Montreal	QC	H4P1A9	866-449-4417	514-856-3330	626
PBA (Professional Bowlers Assn) 719 Second Ave Ste 701	Seattle	WA	98104	877-910-2695	206-332-9688	47-22
PBA (Professional Beauty Assn) 15825 N 71st St Ste 100	Scottsdale	AZ	85254	800-468-2274	480-281-0424	48-18
PBA Health 6300 Enterprise Rd	Kansas City	MO	64120	800-333-8097	816-245-5700	233
PBCVB (Pine Bluff Convention & Visitors Bureau) 1 Convention Ctr Plz	Pine Bluff	AR	71601	800-536-7660	870-536-7600	208
PBEC (Polk-Burnett Electric Co-op) 1001 State Rd 35	Centuria	WI	54824	800-421-0283	715-646-2191	247
PBI Market Equipment Inc 2667 Gundry Ave	Signal Hill	CA	90755	800-421-3753	562-595-4785	301
PBI/Gordon Corp 1217 W 12th St PO Box 014090	Kansas City	MO	64101	800-821-7925	816-421-4070	282
PBK Bank Inc 120 Frontier Blvd	Stanford	KY	40484	877-230-3711	606-365-7098	69
PBM Corp 20600 Chagrin Blvd Ste 450	Cleveland	OH	44122	800-341-5809	216-283-7999	38
PBM Graphics Inc 3700 S Miami Blvd	Durham	NC	27703	800-849-8100	919-544-6222	626
PBM Inc 1070 Sandy Hill Rd	Irwin	PA	15642	800-967-4726	724-863-0550	788
PBR (Professional Bull Riders Inc) 101 W Riverwalk	Pueblo	CO	81003	800-366-8538	719-242-2800	47-15
PBS (Public Broadcasting Service) 2100 Crystal Dr	Arlington	VA	22202	866-864-0828	703-739-5000	737
PBS (Pacific Building Systems) 2100 N Pacific Hwy *General	Woodburn	OR	97071	800-727-7844*	503-981-9581	104
PBS Supply Company Inc 7013 S 216th St	Kent	WA	98032	877-727-7515	253-395-5550	533
PBSP (Pelican Bay State Prison) 5905 Lake Earl Dr PO Box 7000	Crescent City	CA	95531	877-256-6877	707-465-1000	215

Listing	Toll-Free	Phone	Class
PC Connection Inc 730 Milford Rd Rt 101A . . . . Merrimack NH 03054 *NASDAQ: PCCC*	**888-213-0607**	603-683-2000	181
PC Connection Inc MacConnection Div 730 Milford Rd Rt 101A . . . . Merrimack NH 03054	**888-213-0260**		181
PC Gamer Magazine 4000 Shoreline Ct Ste 400 . . . . South San Francisco CA 94080	**877-404-1337**	650-238-2505	456-14
PC Mall Inc 2555 W 190th St . . . . Torrance CA 90504 *NASDAQ: PCMI*	**800-555-6255**	310-354-5600	181
PC Richard & Son Inc 150 Price Pkwy . . . . Farmingdale NY 11735	**800-696-2000**	631-773-4900	34
PC/Nametag 124 Horizon Dr . . . . Verona WI 53593	**877-626-3824**		180-8
PCA Engineering Inc 57 Cannonball Rd PO Box 196. . . . Pompton Lakes NJ 07442	**800-666-7221**	973-616-4501	263
PCB Group Inc 3425 Walden Ave . . . . Depew NY 14043	**800-828-8840**	716-684-0001	255
PCBE Inc PO Box 1575 . . . . Tacoma WA 98401	**800-540-8322**	253-404-0891	456-5
PCF (Prevent Cancer Foundation) 1600 Duke St Ste 500. . . . Alexandria VA 22314	**800-227-2732**	703-836-4412	47-17
PCGH (UH Parma Medical Center) 7007 Powers Blvd . . . . Parma OH 44129	**855-292-4292**	440-743-3000	374-3
PCI (Project Concern International) 5151 Murphy Canyon Rd Ste 320. . . . San Diego CA 92123	**877-724-4673**	858-279-9690	47-5
PCMA (Professional Convention Management Assn) 35 E Wacker Dr Ste 500 . . . . Chicago IL 60601	**877-827-7262**	312-423-7262	48-12
PCMR (Park City Mountain Resort) 1345 Lowell Ave PO Box 39. . . . Park City UT 84060	**800-222-7275**	435-649-8111	667
PCOM (Philadelphia College of Osteopathic Medicine) 4170 City Ave . . . . Philadelphia PA 19131 *Admissions	**800-999-6998***	215-871-6100	798
PCR (Mid-Atlantic PenFed Realty Berkshire Hathaway HomeServices) 3050 Chain Bridge Rd . . . . Fairfax VA 22030	**866-225-5778**	703-691-7653	653
PCRM (Physicians Committee for Responsible Medicine) 5100 Wisconsin Ave NW Ste 400. . . . Washington DC 20016	**866-416-7276**	202-686-2210	48-8
PCS (Precision Computer Services Inc) 175 Constitution Blvd S . . . . Shelton CT 06484	**800-340-9890**	203-929-0000	177
PCS Co 34488 Doreka Dr . . . . Fraser MI 48026	**800-521-0546**	586-294-7780	755
PCTA (Pacific Crest Trail Assn) 1331 Garden Hwy . . . . Sacramento CA 95833	**888-728-7245**	916-285-1846	47-23
PCTC (Park County Travel Council) 836 Sheridan Ave PO Box 2454 . . . . Cody WY 82414	**800-393-2639**	307-587-2297	208
PDA (Presbyterian Disaster Assistance) 100 Witherspoon St . . . . Louisville KY 40202	**800-728-7228**		47-5
PDA (Property Damage Appraisers Inc) 6100 SW Blvd Ste 200. . . . Fort Worth TX 76109	**800-749-7324**		311
PDC (Petroleum Development Corp) 120 Genesis Blvd PO Box 26 . . . . Bridgeport WV 26330 *NASDAQ: PDCE*	**800-624-3821**	303-860-5800	535
PDC Facilities Inc 700 Walnut Ridge Dr . . . . Hartland WI 53029	**800-545-5998**	262-367-7700	188
PDCA (Painting & Decorating Contractors of America) 2316 Millpark Dr . . . . Maryland Heights MO 63043 *Cust Svc	**800-332-7322***	314-514-7322	48-3
PDEMC (Pee Dee Electric Membership Corp) 575 US Hwy 52 S . . . . Wadesboro NC 28170	**800-992-1626**	704-694-2114	247
PDF (Parkinson's Disease Foundation) 1359 Broadway . . . . New York NY 10018	**800-457-6676**	212-923-4700	47-17
PDI (Pearlstine Distributors Inc) 1600 Chrlston Rgonal Pkwy . . . . Charleston SC 29492	**800-922-1048**	843-388-6800	443
PDI Financial Group 601 N Lynndale Dr. . . . Appleton WI 54914	**800-234-7341**	920-739-2303	688
PDI Inc 300 Interpace Pkwy Morris Corp Ctr 1 Bldg A . . . . Parsippany NJ 07054 *NASDAQ: PDII*	**800-242-7494**		197
PDK (Phi Delta Kappa International) 408 N Union St . . . . Bloomington IN 47407	**800-766-1156**	812-339-1156	47-16
PDMA (Product Development & Management Assn) 330 N Wabash Ave Ste 2000 . . . . Chicago IL 60611	**800-232-5241**	312-321-5145	48-12
PdMA Corp 5909-C Hampton Oaks Pkwy . . . . Tampa FL 33610	**800-476-6463**	813-621-6463	203
PDQ Manufacturing 2754 Creek Hill Rd . . . . Leola PA 17540	**800-441-9692**	717-656-4281	350
PDQ Manufacturing Inc 1698 Scheuring Rd . . . . De Pere WI 54115	**800-227-3373**	920-983-8333	386
PDRA (Paint & Decorating Retailers Assn) 1401 Triad Ctr Dr. . . . Saint Peters MO 63376	**800-737-0107**	636-326-2636	48-18
PDS (Personnel Data Systems Inc) 470 Norritown Rd Ste 202. . . . Blue Bell PA 19422	**800-243-8737**	610-238-4600	180-1
PDS (Packaging Distribution Services Inc) 2308 Sunset Rd . . . . Des Moines IA 50321	**800-747-2699**	515-243-3156	558
PDS Gaming Corp 6280 Annie Oakley Dr . . . . Las Vegas NV 89120	**800-479-3612**	702-736-0700	218
Pea River Electric Co-op 1311 W Roy Parker Rd PO Box 969 . . . . Ozark AL 36361	**800-264-7732**	334-774-2545	247
Peabody Energy Corp Peabody Plz 701 Market St. . . . St. Louis MO 63101	**866-470-4500**	314-342-3400	500
Peabody Essex Museum 161 Essex St . . . . Salem MA 01970	**866-745-1876**	978-745-1876	519
Peabody Institute of the Johns Hopkins University *Peabody Conservatory of Music* 1 E Mt Vernon Pl . . . . Baltimore MD 21202	**800-368-2521**	410-659-8110	167
Peabody Memphis 149 Union Ave . . . . Memphis TN 38103	**800-732-2639**	901-529-4000	379
Peabody Supply Co Inc PO Box 669 . . . . Peabody MA 01960	**800-445-5816**	978-532-2200	611
Peace Bridge Duty Free Inc 1 Peace Bridge Plz . . . . Buffalo NY 14213	**800-361-1302**		243
Peace Corps 1111 20th St NW . . . . Washington DC 20526	**800-424-8580**	202-692-1040	340-18
Peace Corps Regional Offices *Atlanta Regional Office* 1111 20th St NW . . . . Washington DC 20526	**855-855-1961**	404-562-3456	340-18
Chicago Regional Office 55 W Monroe St Ste 450 . . . . Chicago IL 60603	**800-424-8580**	312-353-4990	340-18
Dallas Regional Office 1100 Commerce St Ste 427 . . . . Dallas TX 75242	**855-855-1961**		340-18
Denver Regional Office 1999 Broadway Ste 2205 . . . . Denver CO 80202	**855-855-1961**		340-18
Los Angeles Regional Office 2361 Rosecrans Ave Ste 155 . . . . El Segundo CA 90245	**800-424-8580**	310-356-1100	340-18
Mid-Atlantic Regional Office 1525 Wilson Blvd Ste 100 . . . . Arlington VA 22209	**800-424-8580**	202-692-1040	340-18
New York Regional Office 201 Varick St Ste 1025. . . . New York NY 10014	**800-424-8580**	212-352-5440	340-18
Northwest Regional Office 1601 Fifth Ave Ste 605. . . . Seattle WA 98101	**800-424-8580**	206-553-5490	340-18
San Francisco Regional Office 1301 Clay St Ste 620-N . . . . Oakland CA 94612	**800-424-8580**	510-452-8444	340-18
Peace River Chamber of Commerce 9309-100 St PO Box 6599 . . . . Peace River AB T8S1S4	**888-525-4423**	780-624-4166	137
Peace River Electric Co-op Inc 210 Metheny Rd PO Box 1310 . . . . Wauchula FL 33873	**800-282-3824**		247
Peace River Regional Medical Ctr 2500 Harbor Blvd . . . . Port Charlotte FL 33952	**888-941-2495**	941-766-4122	374-3
Peaceable Kingdom Press 950 Gilman St Ste 200 . . . . Berkeley CA 94710	**877-444-5195**		129
Peaceful Valley Ranch 475 Peaceful Vly Rd . . . . Lyons CO 80540	**800-955-6343**	303-747-2881	241
PeaceHealth St Joseph Medical Ctr 2901 Squalicum Pkwy . . . . Bellingham WA 98225	**800-541-7209**	360-734-5400	374-3
Peach County School District Inc 523 Vineville St . . . . Fort Valley GA 31030	**866-632-9992**	478-825-5933	683
Peach State Integrated Technologies Inc 3005 Business Pk Dr . . . . Norcross GA 30071	**800-998-6517**	678-327-2000	386
Peach State Labs Inc (PSL) 180 Burlington Rd PO Box 1087. . . . Rome GA 30162	**800-634-1653**	706-291-8743	144
Peach Trader Inc 6286 Dawson Blvd . . . . Norcross GA 30093	**888-949-9613**	404-752-6715	789
Peachtree Planning Corp 5040 Roswell Rd NE . . . . Atlanta GA 30342	**800-366-0839**	404-260-1600	112
Peacock Suites 1745 S Anaheim Blvd . . . . Anaheim CA 92805	**800-522-6401**	714-535-8255	379
Peak 10 752 Barret Ave . . . . Louisville KY 40204	**866-732-5836**	502-315-6015	178
Peak Financial Management Inc 281 Winter St Ste 160. . . . Waltham MA 02451	**877-567-9500**	781-487-9500	401
Peak Nutrition Inc 1097 11th St PO Box 87 . . . . Syracuse NE 68446 *Sales	**800-600-2069***	402-269-2825	797
Peak Technical Services Inc 583 Epsilon Dr . . . . Pittsburgh PA 15238	**888-888-7325**	412-696-1080	719
Peak Technologies Inc 10330 Old Columbia Rd . . . . Columbia MD 21046	**800-926-9212**		176
Peake DeLancey Printers LLC 2500 Schuster Dr . . . . Cheverly MD 20781	**800-521-7325**	301-341-4600	626
Peaks Resort & Golden Door Spa 136 Country Club Dr . . . . Telluride CO 81435	**800-789-2220**		667
Peapack-Gladstone Bank 500 Hills Dr Ste 300 PO Box 700. . . . Bedminster NJ 07921 *NASDAQ: PGC*	**800-742-7595**	908-234-0700	360-2
Peapod LLC 9933 Woods Dr . . . . Skokie IL 60077	**800-573-2763**	847-583-9400	345
Pearl Harbor Federal Credit Union (PHFCU) 94-449 Ukee St . . . . Waipahu HI 96797	**800-987-5583**		221
Pearl Meat Packing Company Inc 27 York Ave . . . . Randolph MA 02368	**800-462-3022**	781-228-5100	472
Pearl River Community College 101 Hwy 11 N . . . . Poplarville MS 39470	**877-772-2338**	601-403-1000	161
Pearl River Valley Electric Power Assn 1422 Hwy 13 N PO Box 1217. . . . Columbia MS 39429	**855-277-8372**	601-736-2666	247
Pearland Area Chamber of Commerce 6117 Broadway St . . . . Pearland TX 77581	**888-604-5888**	281-485-3634	138
Pearlstine Distributors Inc (PDI) 1600 Chrlston Rgonal Pkwy . . . . Charleston SC 29492	**800-922-1048**	843-388-6800	443
Pearpoint Inc 72055 Corporate Way . . . . Thousand Palms CA 92276	**800-688-8094**	760-343-7350	203
Pearson Co 1420 Progress Ave . . . . High Point NC 27260	**800-225-0265**	336-882-8135	320-2
Pearson Dental Supplies Inc 13161 Telfair Ave . . . . Sylmar CA 91342	**800-535-4535**	818-362-2600	474
Pearson Education Inc 1 Lake St . . . . Upper Saddle River NJ 07458 *Cust Svc	**800-922-0579***	201-236-6716	634-2
Pearson Education School Div 1900 E Lk Ave Ofc Ste B-110A. . . . Glenview IL 60025	**800-348-4474**		634-2
Pearson Engineering Associates Inc 8825 N 23rd Ave Ste 11 . . . . Phoenix AZ 85021	**866-747-9754**	602-264-0807	263
Pearson Packaging Systems 8120 W Sunset Hwy . . . . Spokane WA 99224	**800-732-7766**	509-838-6226	546
Pearson's Candy Co 2140 W Seventh St . . . . Saint Paul MN 55116 *Cust Svc	**800-328-6507***	651-698-0356	297-8
Peavey Electronics Corp 5022 Hartley Peavey Dr . . . . Meridian MS 39305	**877-732-8391**	601-483-5365	51
Pechanga Resort & Casino 45000 Pechanga Pkwy . . . . Temecula CA 92592	**877-711-2946**	951-693-1819	667
Pecora Corp 165 Wambold Rd . . . . Harleysville PA 19438	**800-523-6688**	215-723-6051	3
Pedal Valves Inc 13625 River Rd . . . . Luling LA 70070	**800-431-3668**	985-785-9997	609
Peddinghaus Corp 300 N Washington Ave . . . . Bradley IL 60915	**800-786-2448**	815-937-3800	454
Pedernales Electric Co-op Inc PO Box 1 . . . . Johnson City TX 78636	**888-554-4732**	830-868-7155	247
Pediatric Services of America Inc 310 Technology Pkwy . . . . Norcross GA 30092	**800-408-4442**	770-441-1580	363
Pediatric Special Care Inc 17040 W 12 Mile Rd Ste 200 . . . . Southfield MI 48076	**800-282-7337**	248-557-4800	371
Pediatrix Medical Group Inc 1301 Concord Terr . . . . Sunrise FL 33323	**800-243-3839**	954-384-0175	462

Name / Address	City	State	Zip	Toll-Free	Phone	Class
Pedorthic Footwear Assn (PFA) 2025 M St NW Ste 800	Washington	DC	20036	800-673-8447	202-367-1145	47-17
Pedowitz Group, The 810 Mayfield Rd	Milton	GA	30009	855-738-6584		197
Pee Dee Electric Co-op Inc PO Box 491	Darlington	SC	29540	866-747-0060	843-665-4070	247
Pee Dee Electric Membership Corp (PDEMC) 575 US Hwy 52 S	Wadesboro	NC	28170	800-992-1626	704-694-2114	247
Peebles Inc 1 Peebles St	South Hill	VA	23970	800-723-4548	800-743-8730	231
Peeco 7050 W Ridge Rd	Fairview	PA	16415	800-235-9382	814-474-5561	453
Peelle Co 373 Nesconset Hwy Ste 311	Hauppauge	NY	11788	800-787-5020	905-846-4545	236
Peer Bearing Co 2200 Norman Dr S	Waukegan	IL	60085	800-433-7337	847-578-1000	74
Peer Foods Group Inc 1200 W 35th St 3rd Fl	Chicago	IL	60609	800-365-5644	773-927-1440	297-26
Peerless Chain Co 1416 E Sanborn St	Winona	MN	55987	800-533-8056	507-457-9100	676
Peerless Cleaners Inc 519 N Monroe St	Decatur	IL	62522	800-879-7056	217-423-7703	83
Peerless Electronics Inc 700 Hicksville Rd	Bethpage	NY	11714	800-285-2121	516-594-3500	248
Peerless Food Equipment 500 S Vandemark Rd	Sidney	OH	45365	800-999-3327	937-492-4158	299
Peerless Industrial Group PO Box 949	Clackamas	OR	97015	800-547-6806	800-873-1916	676
Peerless Insurance Co 62 Maple Ave	Keene	NH	03431	800-542-5385	603-352-3221	391-4
Peerless Machinery Corp 500 S Vandenmark Rd PO Box 769	Sidney	OH	45365	877-795-7377	937-492-4158	299
Peerless Manufacturing Co 14651 N Dallas Pkwy Ste 500 *NASDAQ: PMFG*	Dallas	TX	75254	877-879-7634	214-357-6181	386
Peerless Pottery Inc 319 S Fifth St	Rockport	IN	47635	866-457-5785	800-457-5785	610
Peerless Premier Appliance Co 119 S 14th St	Belleville	IL	62222	800-858-5844	941-763-3915	35
Peerless Products Inc 2403 S Main St	Fort Scott	KS	66701	800-279-9999	620-223-4610	236
Peerless Pump Co 2005 ML King Jr St PO Box 7026	Indianapolis	IN	46207	800-879-0182	317-925-9661	638
Peerless Steel Corp 2450 Austin	Troy	MI	48083	800-482-3947	248-528-3200	491
Peerless Tire Co 5000 Kingston St	Denver	CO	80239	800-999-7810	303-371-4300	53
Peery Hotel 110 West 300 South	Salt Lake City	UT	84101	800-331-0073	801-521-4300	379
Peet Frate Line Inc 650 S Eastwood Dr PO Box 1129	Woodstock	IL	60098	800-435-6909	815-338-5500	778
Peet's Coffee & Tea Inc 1400 Pk Ave *NASDAQ: GMCR* ■ *Orders	Emeryville	CA	94608	800-999-2132*	510-594-2100	158
Pegasus International Hotel 501 Southard St	Key West	FL	33040	800-397-8148	305-294-9323	379
Pegasus Logistics Group Inc 306 Airline Dr Ste 100	Coppell	TX	75019	800-997-7226	469-671-0300	448
Pegasus Solutions Inc 5430 LBJ Fwy Ste 1100	Dallas	TX	75240	800-843-4343	214-234-4000	335
Pegasus Sustainability Solutions Inc 2693 Research Park Dr Ste 201	Fitchburg	WI	53711	888-681-9616		194
Peggy Knight Solutions Inc 1750 Bridgeway	Sausalito	CA	94965	800-997-7753	415-289-1777	348
Peg-Perego USA Inc 3625 Independence Dr *Cust Svc	Fort Wayne	IN	46808	800-671-1701*	260-482-8191	63
PEI-Genesis 2180 Hornig Rd	Philadelphia	PA	19116	800-675-1214	215-673-0400	248
Peirce College 1420 Pine St	Philadelphia	PA	19102	888-467-3472	215-545-6400	167
Peirce-Phelps Inc 2000 N 59th St	Philadelphia	PA	19131	800-222-2742	215-879-7000	37
Pekin Insurance (FAIA) 2505 Ct St	Pekin	IL	61558	800-322-0160	309-346-1161	391-4
Pekin Life Insurance Co 2505 Ct St *OTC: PKIN*	Pekin	IL	61558	800-322-0160	309-346-1161	391-2
Peking Noodle Co Inc 1514 N San Fernando Rd	Los Angeles	CA	90065	877-735-4648	323-223-2023	297-31
Pelco 3500 Pelco Way	Clovis	CA	93612	800-289-9100	559-292-1981	645
Pelham Hotel 444 Common St	New Orleans	LA	70130	888-856-4486	504-522-4444	379
Pelican Bay State Prison (PBSP) 5905 Lake Earl Dr PO Box 7000	Crescent City	CA	95531	877-256-6877	707-465-1000	215
Pelican Grand Beach Resort Condominium Associati 2000 N Ocean Blvd	Fort Lauderdale	FL	33305	800-525-6232	954-568-9431	379
Pelican Products Inc 147 N Main St	South Deerfield	MA	01373	800-542-7344	413-665-2163	201
Pelican Rope Works Inc 4001 W Carriage Dr	Santa Ana	CA	92704	800-464-7673	714-545-0116	210
Pelivan Transit 333 S Oak St PO Box B	Big Cabin	OK	74332	800-482-4594	918-783-5793	107
Pella Co-op Electric Assn 2615 Washington St	Pella	IA	50219	800-619-1040	641-628-1040	247
Pella Corp 102 Main St *Cust Svc	Pella	IA	50219	877-473-5527*	641-621-1000	238
Pellettieri Rabstein & Altman 100 Nassau Pk Blvd	Princeton	NJ	08540	800-432-5297	609-520-0900	428
Pembina Pipeline Corp 585 Eighth Ave SW *TSE: PPL*	Calgary	AB	T2P1G1	888-428-3222	403-231-7500	405
Pembroke Hospital 199 Oak St	Pembroke	MA	02359	800-222-2237	781-829-7000	374-5
Pembroke Management Ltd 1002 Sherbrooke St W Ste 1700	Montreal	QC	H3A3S4	800-667-0716	514-848-1991	794
Pembroke Regional Hospital 705 MacKay St	Pembroke	ON	K8A1G8	866-996-0991	613-732-2811	374-2
Pemco Inc 3333 Crocker Ave	Sheboygan	WI	53082	888-310-1898	920-458-2500	555
Pemex Procurement International Inc 10344 sam houston park dr	Houston	TX	77064	888-254-1487	713-430-3100	535
Pemiscot-Dunklin Electric Co-op Hwy 412 W PO Box 509	Hayti	MO	63851	800-558-6641	573-757-6641	247
Pemko Mfg Company Inc 4226 Transport St	Ventura	CA	93003	800-283-9988	805-642-2600	327
PEN Products 2010 E New York St	Indianapolis	IN	46201	800-736-2550	317-955-6800	629
Penasco Valley Telecommunications (PVT) 4011 W Main St	Artesia	NM	88210	800-505-4844		733
Pencco Inc 831 Bartlett Rd PO Box 600	San Felipe	TX	77473	800-864-1742	979-885-0005	143
Penco Products Inc 1820 Stonehenge Dr	Oaks	PA	19456	800-562-1000		320-1
Penda Corp PO Box 449	Portage	WI	53901	800-356-7704		59
Pender Memorial Hospital 507 E Fremont St	Burgaw	NC	28425	888-815-5188	910-259-5451	374-3
Pendle Hill 338 Plush Mill Rd	Wallingford	PA	19086	800-742-3150	610-566-4507	671
Pendleton Grain Growers Inc 1000 SW Dorian St PO Box 1248	Pendleton	OR	97801	800-422-7611	541-278-5035	277
Pendleton Woolen Mills Inc 220 NW Broadway	Portland	OR	97209	800-760-4844	503-226-4801	154-5
PendoPharm Inc 6111 Royalmount *Cust Svc	Montreal	QC	H4P2T4	866-926-7653*	514-340-5045	478
Pendu Manufacturing Inc 718 N Shirk Rd	New Holland	PA	17557	800-233-0471	717-354-4348	819
Pengo Corp 500 E Hwy 10 *Cust Svc	Laurens	IA	50554	800-599-0211*	712-845-2540	192
Pengrowth Energy Trust 222 Third Ave SW Ste 2100 *NYSE: PGH*	Calgary	AB	T2P0B4	800-223-4122	403-233-0224	673
Penguin Group (USA) Inc 375 Hudson St *Sales	New York	NY	10014	800-847-5515*	212-366-2000	634-2
Penguin Hotel 1418 Ocean Dr	Miami Beach	FL	33139	800-499-7964	305-534-9334	379
Penguin Point Franchise Systems Inc 2691 E US 30	Warsaw	IN	46580	800-577-5755	574-267-3107	668
Penguin Random House 1745 Broadway	New York	NY	10019	800-733-3000	212-782-9000	634-2
Penguin Random House Inc *Bantam Dell Publishing Group* 1745 Broadway 10th Fl	New York	NY	10019	888-523-9292	212-782-9000	634-2
Peninsula Airways Inc 6100 Boeing Ave	Anchorage	AK	99502	800-448-4226	907-771-2500	25
Peninsula Asset Management Inc 1111 Third Ave W Ste 340	Bradenton	FL	34205	800-269-6417		401
Peninsula Beverly Hills 9882 S Santa Monica Blvd	Beverly Hills	CA	90212	800-462-7899	310-551-2888	379
Peninsula Chicago 108 E Superior St	Chicago	IL	60611	866-288-8889	312-337-2888	379
Peninsula Daily News 305 W First St PO Box 1330	Port Angeles	WA	98362	800-826-7714	360-452-2345	531-2
Peninsula Light Co 13315 Goodnough Dr NW	Gig Harbor	WA	98332	888-809-8021	253-857-5950	247
Peninsula New York 700 Fifth Ave	New York	NY	10019	800-262-9467	212-956-2888	379
Peninsula Regional Medical Ctr 100 E Carroll St	Salisbury	MD	21801	800-543-7780	410-546-6400	374-3
Penn Air & Hydraulics Corp 1750 Industrial Hwy	York	PA	17402	888-631-7638	717-840-8100	638
Penn Color Inc 400 Old Dublin Pk	Doylestown	PA	18901	866-617-7366	215-345-6550	549
Penn Commercial Inc 242 Oak Spring Rd	Washington	PA	15301	888-309-7484	724-222-5330	798
Penn Emblem Co 10909 Dutton Rd	Philadelphia	PA	19154	800-793-7366		260
Penn Fibre Plastics 2434 Bristol Rd *Cust Svc	Bensalem	PA	19020	800-662-7366*		599
Penn Foster Career School 925 Oak St	Scranton	PA	18515	800-275-4410	570-342-7701	798
Penn Inc 306 S 45th Ave	Phoenix	AZ	85043	800-289-7366		708
Penn Insurance & Annuity Co 600 Dresher Rd *Cust Svc	Horsham	PA	19044	800-523-0650*	215-956-8000	391-2
Penn Machine Co 106 Stn St	Johnstown	PA	15905	800-736-6872	814-288-1547	594
Penn Mutual Life Insurance Co 600 Dresher Rd *Cust Svc	Horsham	PA	19044	800-523-0650*	215-956-8000	391-2
Penn National Gaming Inc 825 Berkshire Blvd Ste 200 *NASDAQ: PENN*	Wyomissing	PA	19610	877-565-2112		639
Penn National Insurance Co 2 N Second St PO Box 2361	Harrisburg	PA	17101	800-388-4764	717-234-4941	391-4
Penn Presbyterian Medical Ctr (PPMC) 39th & Market Sts	Philadelphia	PA	19104	800-789-7366	215-662-8000	374-3
Penn State Milton S Hershey Medical Ctr 500 University Dr	Hershey	PA	17033	800-731-3032	717-531-8521	374-3
Penn State Milton S Hershey Medical Ctr Bone Marrow Transplantation Program 500 University Dr	Hershey	PA	17033	800-243-1455	717-531-1657	767
Penn Stater Conference Ctr Hotel 215 Innovation Blvd	State College	PA	16803	800-233-7505	814-863-5000	377
Penn Treaty Network America Insurance Co 3440 Lehigh St	Allentown	PA	18103	800-362-0700		391-2
Penn United Technology Inc 799 N Pike Rd	Cabot	PA	16023	866-572-7537	724-352-1507	755
Penn Veterinary Supply Inc 53 Industrial Cir	Lancaster	PA	17601	800-233-0210	717-656-4121	792

Listing	Toll-Free	Phone	Class
Penn Virginia Corp 100 Matsonford Rd Ste 200 ... Radnor PA 19087	877-316-5288	610-687-8900	535
NYSE: PVA			
Penn West Energy Trust Penn W Plz 207 - 9th Ave SW Ste 200 ... Calgary AB T2P1K3	866-693-2707	403-777-2500	673
Penn West Petroleum Ltd Ninth Ave SW Ste 200 ... Calgary AB T2P1K3	866-693-2707	403-777-2500	535
TSE: PWT			
Penn's Best Inc PO Box 128 ... Meshoppen PA 18630	800-852-3243		778
Penn's View Hotel 14 N Front St ... Philadelphia PA 19106	800-331-7634	215-922-7600	379
Pennco Tech 3815 Otter St ... Bristol PA 19007	844-226-0975*	215-785-0111	798
*General			
Penncorp Servicegroup Inc 600 N Second St Ste 401 ... Harrisburg PA 17101	800-544-9050	717-234-2300	632
PennEngineering & Manufacturing Corp 5190 Old Easton Rd ... Danboro PA 18916	800-237-4736	215-766-8853	280
Pennichuck Corp 25 Manchester St ... Merrimack NH 03054	800-553-5191	603-882-5191	785
NASDAQ: PNNW			
Penns Grove-Carneys Point Regional Board of Education 100 Iona Ave ... Penns Grove NJ 08069	877-652-7624	856-299-4250	683
Pennswood Village 1382 Newtown-Langhorne Rd ... Newtown PA 18940	888-454-1122	215-968-9110	670
Pennsylvania			
Banking Dept 17 N Second St Market Square Plz ... Harrisburg PA 17101	800-722-2657	717-783-4721	339-39
Insurance Dept 1326 Strawberry Sq ... Harrisburg PA 17120	877-881-6388		339-39
Public Utility Commission 400 N St Keystone Bldg PO Box 3265 ... Harrisburg PA 17120	800-692-7380	717-783-1740	339-39
State Parks Bureau PO Box 8551 ... Harrisburg PA 17105	888-727-2757	717-787-6640	339-39
Transportation Dept 400 N St ... Harrisburg PA 17120	800-932-4600	717-787-2838	339-39
Vocational Rehabilitation Office (OVR) 1521 N Sixth St ... Harrisburg PA 17102	800-442-6351	717-787-5244	339-39
Workers Compensation Bureau 1171 S Cameron St Rm 324 ... Harrisburg PA 17104	800-482-2383	717-783-5421	339-39
Pennsylvania Academy of the Fine Arts			
School of Fine Arts 118 128 N Broad St ... Philadelphia PA 19102	800-799-7233	215-972-7600	163
Pennsylvania Academy of the Fine Arts Museum (PAFA) 118 N Broad St ... Philadelphia PA 19102	800-799-7233	215-972-7600	519
Pennsylvania Anthracite Heritage Museum Bald Mountain Rd Ste 1 ... Scranton PA 18504	800-732-0999	570-963-4804	519
Pennsylvania Assn of Realtors 500 N Twelfth St ... Lemoyne PA 17043	800-555-3390	717-561-1303	654
Pennsylvania Assn of Staff Nurses & Allied Professionals (PASNAP) 1 Fayette St Ste 475 ... Conshohocken PA 19428	800-500-7850	610-567-2907	532
Pennsylvania Ballet 1819 John F Kennedy Blvd ... Philadelphia PA 19103	800-732-0999	215-551-7000	572-1
Pennsylvania Bar Assn 100 S St ... Harrisburg PA 17101	800-932-0311	717-238-6715	71
Pennsylvania Chamber of Business & Industry 417 Walnut St ... Harrisburg PA 17101	800-225-7224	717-255-3252	139
Pennsylvania College of Technology 1 College Ave ... Williamsport PA 17701	800-367-9222*	570-326-3761	798
*Admissions			
Pennsylvania Convention Ctr 1101 Arch St ... Philadelphia PA 19107	800-428-9000	215-418-4700	207
Pennsylvania Correctional Industries PO Box 47 ... Camp Hill PA 17001	877-673-3724*	717-425-7292	629
*General			
Pennsylvania Dutch Candies 1250 Slate Hill Rd ... Camp Hill PA 17011	800-233-7082	717-761-5440	297-8
Pennsylvania Higher Education Assistance Agency 1200 N Seventh St ... Harrisburg PA 17102	800-233-0557		723
Pennsylvania Highlands Community College 881 Hills Plz Dr Ste 450 ... Ebensburg PA 15931	888-385-7325	814-262-6446	161
Pennsylvania Hospital 800 Spruce St ... Philadelphia PA 19107	800-789-7366	215-829-3000	374-3
Pennsylvania Institute of Technology (PIT) 800 Manchester Ave ... Media PA 19063	800-422-0025*	610-892-1500	798
*Admissions			
Pennsylvania Manufacturers Assn Co 380 Sentry Pkwy ... Blue Bell PA 19422	800-222-2749		391-4
Pennsylvania Medical Society 777 E Pk Dr ... Harrisburg PA 17111	800-228-7823	717-558-7750	473
Pennsylvania Medical Society Liability Insurance Co (PMSLIC) 1700 Bent Creek Blvd PO Box 2080 ... Mechanicsburg PA 17050	800-445-1212	844-466-7225	391-5
Pennsylvania Real Estate Investment Trust 200 S Broad St 3rd Fl ... Philadelphia PA 19102	866-875-0700	215-875-0700	653
NYSE: PEI			
Pennsylvania State Employees Credit Union 1 Credit Union Pl ... Harrisburg PA 17110	800-237-7328	717-234-8484	221
Pennsylvania State Ethics Commission 309 Finance Bldg PO Box 11470 ... Harrisburg PA 17108	800-932-0936	717-783-1610	267
Pennsylvania State System of Higher Education 2986 N Second St ... Harrisburg PA 17110	800-732-0999	717-720-4000	339-39
Pennsylvania State University			
Altoona 3000 Ivyside Pk ... Altoona PA 16601	800-848-9843	814-949-5466	167
Beaver 100 University Dr ... Monaca PA 15061	877-564-6778	724-773-3500	161
DuBois 1 College Pl ... Du Bois PA 15801	800-346-7627	814-375-4700	161
Fayette 2201 University Dr ... Lemont Furnace PA 15456	877-568-4130	724-430-4100	161
Harrisburg 777 W Harrisburg Pk ... Middletown PA 17057	800-222-2056	717-948-6250	167
Hazleton 76 University Dr ... Hazleton PA 18202	800-279-8495	570-450-3000	161
Mont Alto 1 Campus Dr ... Mont Alto PA 17237	800-392-6173	717-749-6000	161
Schuylkill 200 University Dr ... Schuylkill Haven PA 17972	800-243-2374	570-385-6000	161
Shenango 147 Shenango Ave ... Sharon PA 16146	888-275-7009	724-983-2803	161
York 1031 Edgecomb Ave ... York PA 17403	800-778-6227	717-771-4000	161
Pennsylvania State University at Erie			
Behrend College 4701 College Dr ... Erie PA 16563	866-374-3378	814-898-6000	167
Pennsylvania State University Dickinson School of Law 150 S College St ... Carlisle PA 17013	800-840-1122	717-240-5000	168-1
Pennsylvania State University Press 820 N University Dr USB1 Ste C ... University Park PA 16802	800-326-9180	814-865-1327	634-4
Pennsylvania Tool & Gages Inc PO Box 534 ... Meadville PA 16335	877-827-8285	814-336-3136	755
Pennsylvania Trust Co 5 Radnor Corp Ctr Ste 450 ... Radnor PA 19087	800-975-4316	610-975-4300	688
Penny Laine Papers 2211 Century Ctr Blvd Ste 110 ... Irving TX 75062	800-456-6484	972-812-3000	129
Pennyrile Forest State Resort Park 20781 Pennyrile Lodge Rd ... Dawson Springs KY 42408	800-325-1711		564
Pennyrile Rural Electric Co-op Corp 2000 Harrison St PO Box 2900 ... Hopkinsville KY 42241	800-297-4710*	270-886-2555	247
*Cust Svc			
Penobscot Marine Museum 5 Church St PO Box 498 ... Searsport ME 04974	800-268-8030	207-548-2529	519
Penobscot McCrum LLC 28 Pierce St ... Belfast ME 04915	800-435-4456	207-338-4360	297-21
Penray Cos Inc 440 Denniston Ct ... Wheeling IL 60090	800-373-6729	847-459-5000	144
Penrod Co 2809 S Lynnhaven Rd Ste 350 ... Virginia Beach VA 23452	800-537-3497	757-498-0186	193-2
Penrose Hospital 2222 N Nevada Ave ... Colorado Springs CO 80907	800-398-2045	719-776-5000	374-3
Pensacola Christian College 250 Brent Ln ... Pensacola FL 32503	800-722-4636	850-478-8496	167
Pensacola Convention & Visitors Bureau 1401 E Gregory St ... Pensacola FL 32502	800-874-1234	850-434-1234	208
Pensacola Greyhound Track 951 Dog Track Rd ... Pensacola FL 32506	800-345-3997	850-455-8595	639
Pensacola Gulf Coast Regional Airport 2430 Airport Blvd Ste 225 ... Pensacola FL 32504	800-874-6580	850-436-5000	27
Pensacola Junior College			
Warrington 5555 W Hwy 98 ... Pensacola FL 32507	888-897-3605	850-484-2200	161
Pension Benefit Guaranty Corp 1200 K St NW ... Washington DC 20005	800-400-7242*	202-326-4000	340-18
*Cust Svc			
Pension Rights Ctr 1350 Connecticut Ave NW Ste 206 ... Washington DC 20036	866-735-7737	202-296-3776	47-6
Pensions & Investments Magazine 711 Third Ave ... New York NY 10017	888-446-1422*	212-210-0100	456-5
*Cust Svc			
Penske Vehicle Services Inc 1225 E Maple Rd ... Troy MI 48083	877-210-5290	248-729-5400	196
Pentagon 2000 Software Inc 15 W 34th St 5th Fl ... New York NY 10001	800-643-1806	212-629-7521	180-1
Pentagon Federal Credit Union 2930 Eisenhower Ave ... Alexandria VA 22314	800-247-5626		221
Pentagroup Financial LLC 5959 Corp Dr Ste 1400 ... Houston TX 77036	800-385-9060	832-615-2100	159
Pentair 7433 Harwin Dr ... Houston TX 77036	800-545-6258		203
Pentair Ltd 1351 Rt 55 ... Lagrangeville NY 12540	888-711-7487	845-463-7200	708
Pentair Residential Filtration LLC 20580 Enterprise Ave ... Brookfield WI 53008	888-784-9065	262-784-4490	90
Pentair Water Pool & Spa 1620 Hawkins Ave ... Sanford NC 27330	800-831-7133		638
Pentastar Aviation 7310 Highland Rd ... Waterford MI 48327	800-662-9612	248-666-3630	13
Pentax Imaging Co 633 17th St Ste 2600 ... Denver CO 80202	800-877-0155	303-799-8000	175-6
Pentecostal Assemblies 3214 S Service Rd ... Burlington ON L7N3J2	800-295-6368	905-637-7558	47-20
Pentecostal Theological Seminary 900 Walker St NE ... Cleveland TN 37311	800-228-9126	423-478-1131	168-3
PenTeleData 540 Delaware Ave PO Box 197 ... Palmerton PA 18071	800-281-3564		227
Penticton & Wine Country Chamber of Commerce 553 Railway St ... Penticton BC V2A8S3	800-663-5052	250-492-4103	137
Pentron Clinical Technologies LLC 53 N Plains Industrial Rd ... Wallingford CT 06492	800-243-3969		230
Pentwater Wire Products Inc (PWP) 474 Carroll St PO Box 947 ... Pentwater MI 49449	877-869-6911	231-869-6911	288
Pentz Design Pattern & Foundry 14823 Main St Ne ... Duvall WA 98019	800-411-6555	425-788-6490	491
People for the American Way (PFAW) 2000 M St NW Ste 400 ... Washington DC 20036	800-326-7329	202-467-4999	47-7
People for the Ethical Treatment of Animals (PETA) 501 Front St ... Norfolk VA 23510	800-566-9768	757-622-7382	47-3
People Lease Inc 689 Town Ctr Blvd Ste B ... Ridgeland MS 39157	800-723-3025	601-987-3025	630
People Magazine Rockefeller Ctr Time & Life Bldg ... New York NY 10020	800-541-9000	212-522-3347	456-11
People Plus Industrial Inc 1095 Nebo Rd ... Madisonville KY 42431	888-825-1500	270-825-8939	262
People's Energy Co-op 1775 Lk Shady Ave S ... Oronoco MN 55960	800-214-2694	507-367-7000	247
People's Light & Theatre Co 39 Conestoga Rd ... Malvern PA 19355	800-732-0999	610-647-1900	746

Name	Address	City	State	ZIP	Toll-Free	Phone	Class
People's Securities Inc	850 Main St	Bridgeport	CT	06601	**800-772-4400**	203-338-0800	688
People's United Bank	850 Main St Bridgeport Ctr.	Bridgeport	CT	06604	**800-772-1090**	203-338-7171	69
Peoplecomm Inc	148 Woodbine Ave	Northport	NY	11768	**800-735-1629**		262
Peoplefit Health & Fitness Center	237 Lexington St Ste 110	Woburn	MA	01801	**855-784-4663**	781-932-9332	354
Peoples Bancorp Inc	138 Putnam St *NASDAQ: PEBO*	Marietta	OH	45750	**800-374-6123**	740-373-3155	360-2
Peoples Bancorp of North Carolina Inc	518 W 'C' St *NASDAQ: PEBK*	Newton	NC	28658	**800-948-7195**	828-464-5620	360-2
Peoples Financial Services Corp	82 Franklin Ave *NASDAQ: PFIS*	Hallstead	PA	18822	**888-868-3858**	570-879-2175	69
Peoples Gas Light & Coke Co	130 E Randolph Dr *Cust Svc	Chicago	IL	60601	**866-556-6001***	312-240-4000	785
Peoples National Bank	5175 N Academy Blvd	Colorado Springs	CO	80918	**800-862-6696**	719-528-4000	69
Peoples Savings Bank (PSB)	414 N Adams PO Box 248	Wellsburg	IA	50680	**877-493-3799**	641-869-3721	69
PeopleStrategy Inc	5883 Glenridge Dr Ste 200	Atlanta	GA	30328	**855-488-4100**		180-1
People-to-People Health Foundation	255 Carter Hall Ln	Millwood	VA	22646	**800-544-4673**	540-837-2100	47-5
PeopleWorks Inc	6158 10th Ave	Aurelia	IA	51005	**888-404-3646**		462
Peoria Area Chamber of Commerce	100 SW Water St	Peoria	IL	61602	**888-681-6561**	309-676-0755	138
Peoria Area Convention & Visitors Bureau	456 Fulton St Ste 300	Peoria	IL	61602	**800-747-0302**	309-676-0303	208
Peoria Journal Star	1 News Plz	Peoria	IL	61643	**800-225-5757**	309-686-3000	531-2
PEP Filters Inc	322 Rolling Hill Rd	Mooresville	NC	28117	**800-243-4583**	704-662-3133	804
PEPCO (Professional Electric Products Co)	33210 Lakeland Blvd	Eastlake	OH	44095	**800-872-7000**	440-946-3790	248
Pepco Energy Services Inc	1300 N 17th St Ste 1600	Arlington	VA	22209	**800-424-8028**	703-253-1800	785
Pepco Sales of Dallas Inc	11310 Gemini Ln	Dallas	TX	75229	**877-737-2699**	972-823-8700	611
Pepose Vision Institute PC	1815 Clarkson Rd	Chesterfield	MO	63017	**877-862-2020**	636-728-0111	475
Pepperball Technologies Inc	6540 Lusk Blvd Ste C137	San Diego	CA	92121	**877-887-3773**	858-638-0236	760
Pepperidge Farm Inc	595 Westport Ave *PR	Norwalk	CT	06851	**888-737-7374***	203-846-7000	297-1
Peppermill Hotel & Casino	2707 S Virginia St	Reno	NV	89502	**800-648-6992**	775-826-2121	132
Pepsi Bottling Ventures LLC	4141 Parklake Ave Ste 600	Raleigh	NC	27612	**800-662-8792**	919-865-2300	297-37
PepsiCo Inc	700 Anderson Hill Rd *NYSE: PEP* ■ *PR	Purchase	NY	10577	**800-433-2652***	914-253-2000	187
Peptides International Inc	11621 Electron Dr	Louisville	KY	40299	**800-777-4779**	502-266-8787	233
Per Mar Security	1910 E Kimberly Rd	Davenport	IA	52807	**800-473-7627**	563-359-3200	690
Perceptics Corp	9737 Cogdill Rd Ste 200	Knoxville	TN	37932	**800-448-8544**		180-12
Percival Scientific Inc	505 Research Dr	Perry	IA	50220	**800-695-2743**	515-465-9363	420
Percussion Software Inc	600 Unicorn Pk Dr	Woburn	MA	01801	**800-283-0800**	781-438-9900	180-1
Percussive Arts Society (PAS)	110 W Washington St	Indianapolis	IN	46204	**888-990-6663**	317-974-4488	47-4
Perdido Beach Resort	27200 Perdido Beach Blvd	Orange Beach	AL	36561	**800-634-8001**	251-981-9811	667
Perdue Farms Inc	31149 Old Ocean City Rd	Salisbury	MD	21804	**800-473-7383**	410-543-3000	618
Peregrine Pharmaceuticals Inc	14282 Franklin Ave Ste 100 *NASDAQ: PPHM*	Tustin	CA	92780	**800-987-8256**	714-508-6000	84
Peregrine Surgical Ltd	51 Britain Dr	New Britain	PA	18901	**877-348-0456**	215-348-0456	475
Perennial Public Power District	2122 S Lincoln Ave	York	NE	68467	**800-289-0288**	402-362-3355	247
Perfect Commerce Inc	1 Compass Way Ste 120 *Sales	Newport News	VA	23606	**877-871-3788***	757-766-8211	38
Perfect Shutters Inc	12213 Rte 173	Hebron	IL	60034	**800-548-3336**	815-648-2401	697
Perfect Turf Inc	622 Sandpebble Dr	Schaumburg	IL	60193	**888-796-8873**		600
PerfectData Corp	1323 Conshohocken Rd	Plymouth Meeting	PA	19462	**800-973-7332**		533
Perfection Clutch Co	100 Perfection Way	Timmonsville	SC	29161	**800-258-8312**	843-326-5544	59
Perf-O-Log Inc	101 Bolton St	Lafayette	LA	70508	**888-892-8276**		535
Perforated Tubes Inc	4850 Fulton St E	Ada	MI	49301	**888-869-5736**	616-942-4550	491
Performance Contracting Group Inc	16400 College Blvd	Lenexa	KS	66219	**800-255-6886**	913-888-8600	191-10
Performance Foodservice	12500 W Creek Pkwy	Richmond	VA	23238	**800-535-5053**	804-484-7700	298-8
Performance Inc	1 Performance Way *Cust Svc	Chapel Hill	NC	27514	**800-727-2453***		709
Performance Office Papers	21565 Hamburg Ave	Lakeville	MN	55044	**800-458-7189**		109
Performance Stamping Company Inc	20 Lk Marian Rd	Carpentersville	IL	60110	**800-935-0393**	847-426-2233	482
Performing Animal Welfare Society (PAWS)	11435 Simmerhorn Rd	Galt	CA	95632	**800-513-6560**	209-745-2606	47-3
Pergo Inc	3128 Highwoods Blvd Ste 100	Raleigh	NC	27604	**800-337-3746**		293
Pericom Semiconductor Corp	3545 N First St *NASDAQ: PSEM*	San Jose	CA	95134	**800-435-2336**	408-435-0800	694
Peridrome Corp	284 Park Pl	Brooklyn	NY	11238	**877-363-7770**		462
Perillo Tours	577 Chestnut Ridge Rd	Woodcliff Lake	NJ	07677	**800-431-1515**	201-307-1234	758
Peripheral Dynamics Inc	5150 Campus Dr	Plymouth Meeting	PA	19462	**800-523-0253**	610-825-7090	175-7
Peripheral Manufacturing Inc	4775 Paris St	Denver	CO	80239	**800-468-6888**	303-371-8651	656
Perkasie Industries Corp	PO Box 179 *Sales	Perkasie	PA	18944	**800-523-6747***	215-257-6581	601
Perkins Coie LLP	1201 Third Ave Ste 4800	Seattle	WA	98101	**888-720-8382**	206-359-8000	428
Perkins Equipment Div	630 John Hancock Rd	Taunton	MA	02780	**800-733-5708**	508-824-2800	301
Perkins Oil Company Inc	4707 Pflaum Rd	Madison	WI	53718	**800-634-9937**	608-221-4736	540
Perkins Restaurant & Bakery	6075 Poplar Ave Ste 800	Memphis	TN	38119	**800-877-7375**	901-766-6400	668
Perkinson Reprographics Inc	735 E Brill St	Phoenix	AZ	85006	**888-330-8782**	602-393-3131	626
Perkiomen School	200 Seminary St PO Box 130	Pennsburg	PA	18073	**866-966-9998**	215-679-9511	621
Perley-Halladay Assn Inc	1037 Andrew Dr	West Chester	PA	19380	**800-248-5800**	610-296-5800	801-2
Perlick Corp	8300 W Good Hope Rd	Milwaukee	WI	53223	**800-558-5592**	414-353-7060	662
Perma-Bound	617 E Vandalia Rd	Jacksonville	IL	62650	**800-637-6581**	217-243-5451	91
Permadur Industries Inc	186 Rt 206 S	Hillsborough	NJ	08844	**800-392-0146**	908-359-9767	386
Perma-Fix Environmental Services Inc	8302 Dunwoody Pl Ste 250 *NASDAQ: PESI*	Atlanta	GA	30350	**800-365-6066**	770-587-9898	665
Perma-Glaze Inc	1638 Research Loop Rd Ste 160	Tucson	AZ	85710	**800-332-7397**	520-722-9718	191-11
Perma-Seal Waterproofing	513 Rogers St	Downers Grove	IL	60515	**800-421-7325**	630-512-0002	188
Permatile Concrete Products Co	100 Beacon Rd	Bristol	VA	24203	**800-662-5332**	276-669-5332	134
Permatron Group	2020 Touhy Ave	Elk Grove Village	IL	60007	**800-882-8012**	847-434-1421	17
Permco Inc	1500 Frost Rd	Streetsboro	OH	44241	**800-628-2801**	330-626-2801	637
Permobil Inc	6961 Eastgate Blvd	Lebanon	TN	37090	**800-736-0925**	615-443-2839	474
Perrigo Co	515 Eastern Ave *NYSE: PRGO*	Allegan	MI	49010	**800-719-9260**	269-673-8451	583
Perry County	333 7th St	Tell City	IN	47586	**888-343-6262**	812-547-7933	338
Perry Group International	1 Market Plz Ste 3600	San Francisco	CA	94105	**800-580-3950**	415-434-0135	378
Perry Homes	PO Box 34306	Houston	TX	77234	**800-247-3779**	713-948-7700	189
Perry Technical Institute	2011 W Washington Ave	Yakima	WA	98903	**888-528-8586**	509-453-0374	161
Perry's Ice Cream Company Inc	1 Ice Cream Plz	Akron	NY	14001	**800-873-7797**	716-542-5492	297-25
Perseus Books Group, The	210 American Dr	Jackson	TN	38301	**800-343-4499**	731-426-6061	634-2
Perseverance Theatre	914 Third St	Douglas	AK	99824	**855-462-8497**	907-364-2421	572-4
Persimmon Press	PO Box 297	Belmont	CA	94002	**800-910-5080**	650-802-8325	129
Person & Covey Inc	616 Allen Ave	Glendale	CA	91201	**800-423-2341**		217
Person County Public Schools	304 S Morgan St	Roxboro	NC	27573	**866-724-6650**	336-599-2191	683
Personal Capital Corp	726 Main St	Redwood City	CA	94063	**855-855-8005**		401
Personal Finance Newsletter	7600A Leesburg Pk W Bldg Ste 300	Falls Church	VA	22043	**800-832-2330**	703-394-4931	530-9
PersonalizeDx	2980 Scott St	Vista	CA	92081	**877-429-6643**		415
Personal-Touch Home Care Inc	186-18 Hillside Ave	Jamaica	NY	11432	**888-275-4147**	718-468-2500	363
Personnel Data Systems Inc (PDS)	470 Norritown Rd Ste 202	Blue Bell	PA	19422	**800-243-8737**	610-238-4600	180-1
Personnel Management Inc	PO Box 6657	Shreveport	LA	71136	**800-259-4126**	318-869-4555	630
Persons Majestic Mfg Co	PO Box 370	Huron	OH	44839	**800-772-2453**	419-433-9057	516
Perspectives Ltd	20 N Clark St Ste 2650	Chicago	IL	60602	**800-866-7556**	312-558-5318	461
Perstorp Polyols Inc	600 Matzinger Rd *Cust Svc	Toledo	OH	43612	**800-537-0280***	419-729-5448	143
PerSys Medical Co	5310 Elm St	Houston	TX	77081	**888-737-7978**		474
Perteet Inc	2707 Colby Ave Ste 900 Ste900	Everett	WA	98201	**800-615-9900**	425-252-7700	263
Peru							
Consulate General	180 N Michigan Ave Ste 1830	Chicago	IL	60601	**877-714-7378**	312-782-1599	259
Consulate General	870 Market St Ste 1067	San Francisco	CA	94102	**877-714-7378**	415-362-7136	259
Consulate General	100 Hamilton Plaza	Paterson	NJ	07505	**877-714-7378**	973-278-3324	259
Consulate General	5177 Richmond Ave Ste 695	Houston	TX	77056	**877-714-7378**	713-355-9517	259
Consulate General	3450 Wilshire Blvd Ste 800	Los Angeles	CA	90010	**877-714-7378**	213-252-5910	259

Name / Address	City	State	ZIP	Toll-Free	Phone	Class
Consulate General 444 Brickell Ave Ste M135	Miami	FL	33131	**877-714-7378**		259
Peru State College 600 Hoyt St PO Box 10	Peru	NE	68421	**800-742-4412**	402-872-3815	167
Peru State College Library 600 Hoyt St PO Box 10	Peru	NE	68421	**800-742-4412**	402-872-3815	434-6
Pervasive Software Inc 12365 Riata Trace Pkwy Bldg B *NASDAQ: PVSW*	Austin	TX	78727	**800-287-4383**	512-231-6000	180-12
Peryam & Kroll Research Corp 6323 N Avondale Ave	Chicago	IL	60631	**800-747-5522**	800-281-3155	666
PES (IEEE Power Engineering Society) IEEE Operations Ctr 445 Hoes Ln	Piscataway	NJ	08854	**800-678-4333**	732-562-3883	48-19
Pest Shield Pest Control Inc 15329 Tradesman	San Antonio	TX	78249	**888-728-8237**	210-525-8823	576
Pet Health Pharmacy 12012 N 111th Ave	Youngtown	AZ	85363	**800-742-0516**	623-214-2791	239
Pet Industry Joint Advisory Council (PIJAC) 1220 19th St NW Ste 400	Washington	DC	20036	**800-553-7387**	202-452-1525	48-4
Pet Safe International 10427 Electric Ave *Cust Svc	Knoxville	TN	37932	**800-732-2677***	865-777-5404	577
Pet Sitters International (PSI) 201 E King St	King	NC	27021	**800-576-4229**	336-983-9222	47-3
Pet Supermarket Inc 1100 International Pkwy	Sunrise	FL	33323	**866-434-1990**	954-351-0834	577
Pet Supplies Inc Customer Service Return Ctr 1 Maplewood Dr	Hazleton	PA	18202	**800-738-7877**		789
Pet Valu Canada Inc 225 Royal Crest Crt	Markham	ON	L3R9X6	**800-845-4759**	905-946-1200	577
Pet's Health Plan 3840 Greentree Ave SW	Canton	OH	44706	**800-807-6724**		391-1
PETA (People for the Ethical Treatment of Animals) 501 Front St	Norfolk	VA	23510	**800-566-9768**	757-622-7382	47-3
PETCO Animal Supplies Inc 9125 Rehco Rd	San Diego	CA	92121	**877-738-6742**	858-453-7845	577
Petco Park 100 Pk Blvd	San Diego	CA	92101	**866-800-1275**	619-795-5000	718
Peter Dag Portfolio Strategy & Management, The 65 Lk Front Dr	Akron	OH	44319	**800-833-2782**	330-644-2782	530-9
Peter Gillhams Natural Vitality 4879 Fountain Ave	Los Angeles	CA	90029	**888-324-9904**		298-8
Peter Glenn Ski & Sports 2901 W Oakland Pk Blvd	Fort Lauderdale	FL	33311	**800-818-0946**	954-484-3606	709
Peter Lang Publishing Inc 29 Broadway	New York	NY	10006	**800-770-5264**	212-647-7706	634-2
Peter Pan Bus Lines PO Box 1776	Springfield	MA	01102	**800-343-9999**		106
Peter Pan Bus Lines Inc 1776 Main St	Springfield	MA	01103	**800-343-9999**		107
Peter Pan Seafoods Inc 2200 Sixth Ave Ste 1000	Seattle	WA	98121	**800-331-3522**	206-728-6000	297-13
Peter Paul Electronics Co Inc 480 John Downey Dr	New Britain	CT	06051	**800-825-8377**	860-229-4884	787
Peter Pepper Products Inc 17929 S Susana Rd	Compton	CA	90221	**800-496-0204**	310-639-0390	590
Peter White Public Library 217 N Front St	Marquette	MI	49855	**800-992-9012**	906-228-9510	434-3
Petersburg Fisheries PO Box 1147	Petersburg	AK	99833	**877-772-4294**	907-772-4294	297-13
Petersen Aluminum Corp 1005 Tonne Rd	Elk Grove Village	IL	60007	**800-323-1960**	847-228-7150	695
Petersen Inc 1527 North 2000 West	Ogden	UT	84404	**800-410-6789**	801-732-2000	358
PetersenDean Roofing and Solar 39300 Civic Center Dr Ste 300	Fremont	CA	94538	**877-552-4418**		45
Peterson Machine Tool Inc 1100 N Union St	Council Grove	KS	66846	**800-835-3528**		386
Peterson Manufacturing Co 4200 E 135th St	Grandview	MO	64030	**800-821-3490**	816-765-2000	438
Peterson Steel Corp 61 W Mountain St	Worcester	MA	01606	**800-325-3245**	508-853-3630	491
Peterson Tractor Co 955 Marina Blvd	San Leandro	CA	94577	**800-590-5945**	510-357-6200	276
Peterson's Nelnet LLC 121 S 13th St Ste 201	Lincoln	NE	68508	**877-338-7772**	609-896-8669	262
PetFoodDirect.com 189 Main St *Cust Svc	Harleysville	PA	19438	**877-738-3663***	215-513-1999	577
Petit Jean Electric Co-op 270 Quality Dr PO Box 37	Clinton	AR	72031	**800-786-7618**	501-745-2493	247
Petland Inc 250 Riverside St	Chillicothe	OH	45601	**800-221-5935**	740-775-2464	577
PetMed Express Inc 1441 SW 29th Ave *NASDAQ: PETS*	Pompano Beach	FL	33069	**800-738-6337**	954-979-5995	577
Petoskey Area Visitors Bureau 401 E Mitchell St	Petoskey	MI	49770	**800-845-2828**	231-348-2755	208
Petra 3602 W Lake Rd	Erie	PA	16505	**866-906-2931**	814-838-7197	669
Petra Manufacturing Co 6600 W Armitage Ave	Chicago	IL	60707	**800-888-7387**	773-622-1475	685
Petro Plastics Company Inc 450 S Ave	Garwood	NJ	07027	**800-486-4738**	908-789-1200	598
Petrocco Farms 14110 Brighton Rd	Brighton	CO	80601	**888-876-2207**	303-659-6498	10-9
Petroleum Development Corp (PDC) 120 Genesis Blvd PO Box 26 *NASDAQ: PDCE*	Bridgeport	WV	26330	**800-624-3821**	303-860-5800	535
Petroleum Marketers Assn of America's Small Business Community 1901 N Fort Myer Dr Ste 500	Arlington	VA	22209	**888-372-7341**	703-351-8000	614
PetroLiance LLC 739 N State St	Elgin	IL	60123	**800-628-7231**	877-738-7699	578
Petrotech Inc 151 Brookhollow Esplanade	New Orleans	LA	70123	**800-486-8850**	504-620-6600	517
PETsMART Inc 19601 N 27th Ave *NASDAQ: PETM* ■ *Cust Svc	Phoenix	AZ	85027	**800-738-1385***	623-580-6100	577
Pettibone Michigan 1100 Superior Ave	Baraga	MI	49908	**800-467-3884**	906-353-4800	469
Pevco Sys Intl Inc 1401 Tangier Dr	Baltimore	MD	21220	**800-296-7382**	410-931-8800	594
Pew Charitable Trusts 2005 Market St 1 Commerce Sq Ste 1700	Philadelphia	PA	19103	**800-351-6801**	215-575-9050	306
PF Chang's China Bistro Inc 7676 E Pinnacle Peak Rd *NASDAQ: PFCB*	Scottsdale	AZ	85255	**866-732-4264**	480-888-3000	668
PFA (Pedorthic Footwear Assn) 2025 M St NW Ste 800	Washington	DC	20036	**800-673-8447**	202-367-1145	47-17
Pfaltzgraff Co PO Box 21769	York	PA	17402	**800-999-2811**		728
PFAW (People for the American Way) 2000 M St NW Ste 400	Washington	DC	20036	**800-326-7329**	202-467-4999	47-7
Pfeiffer University 48380 Hwy 52 N	Misenheimer	NC	28109	**800-338-2060**	704-463-1360	167
Pfenex Inc 10790 Roselle St	San Diego	CA	92121	**844-240-0005**	858-352-4400	666
PFERD Milwaukee Brush Company Inc 30 Jytek Dr	Leominster	MA	01453	**800-342-9015**	978-840-6420	102
Pfister Hotel 424 E Wisconsin Ave	Milwaukee	WI	53202	**800-558-8222**	414-273-8222	379
Pfizer Animal Health 5 Giralda Farms	Madison	NJ	07940	**888-963-8471**		582
Pfizer Canada Inc 17300 TransCanada Hwy	Kirkland	QC	H9J2M5	**800-463-6001**	514-695-0500	582
Pfizer Inc 235 E 42nd St *NYSE: PFE*	New York	NY	10017	**800-879-3477**	212-733-2323	582
Pfizer Inc Animal Health Group 235 E 42nd St	New York	NY	10017	**800-879-3477**	212-733-2323	581
PFSweb Inc 505 Millennium Dr Ste 500 *NASDAQ: PFSW*	Allen	TX	75013	**888-330-5504**	972-881-2900	462
PG & E Corp 77 Beale St 24th Fl *NYSE: PCG*	San Francisco	CA	94105	**800-743-5000**	415-267-7000	360-5
PG Life Link Inc 167 Gap Way	Erlanger	KY	41018	**800-287-4123**	859-283-5900	255
PG Publishing Co 34 Blvd of the Allies *Cust Svc	Pittsburgh	PA	15222	**800-228-6397***	412-263-1100	634-8
PGA National Resort & Spa 400 Ave of the Champions	Palm Beach Gardens	FL	33418	**800-633-9150**	561-627-2000	667
PGA of America 100 Ave of the Champions	Palm Beach Gardens	FL	33418	**800-477-6465**	561-624-8400	47-22
PGi (Premiere Global Services Inc) 3280 Peachtree Rd NE Ste 1000 *NYSE: PGI*	Atlanta	GA	30305	**866-548-3203**	719-457-6901	38
PGT Industries 1070 Technology Dr	Nokomis	FL	34275	**800-282-6019**	941-480-1600	236
P&H (Parrish & Heimbecker Ltd) 201 Portage Ave Ste 1400	Winnipeg	MB	R3B3K6	**800-665-8937**	204-956-2030	277
Phadia US Inc 4169 Commercial Ave	Portage	MI	49002	**800-346-4364**	269-492-1940	233
Phantom Laboratory Inc, The 2727 SR-29	Greenwich	NY	12834	**800-525-1190**	518-692-1190	666
Pharmaceutical Assoc Inc 1700 Perimeter Rd	Greenville	SC	29605	**888-233-2334**	864-277-7282	233
Pharmaceutical Calibrations & Instrumentation LLC 8100 Brownleigh Dr Ste 100-A	Raleigh	NC	27617	**877-724-2257**		583
Pharmaceutical Law & Industry Report 1801 S Bell St	Arlington	VA	22202	**800-372-1033**		530-7
Pharmacists Mutual Insurance Co 808 Hwy 18 W PO Box 370 *General	Algona	IA	50511	**800-247-5930***		391-4
Pharmacists Society of the State of New York 210 Washington Ave Ext	Albany	NY	12203	**800-632-8822**	518-869-6595	584
Pharmacommunications Group Inc 100 Renfrew Dr	Markham	ON	L3R9R6	**800-267-5409**	905-477-3100	240
Pharmacy Today Magazine 2215 Constitution Ave NW	Washington	DC	20037	**800-237-2742**	202-628-4410	456-16
Pharmacyclics Inc 995 E Arques Ave *NASDAQ: PCYC*	Sunnyvale	CA	94085	**855-859-2056**	408-774-0330	84
Pharmalucence Inc 29 Dunham Rd	Billerica	MA	01821	**800-221-7554**	781-275-7120	233
Pharmasave Drugs (National) Ltd 8411 - 200th St Ste 201	Langley	BC	V2Y0E7	**800-661-6106**	604-455-2400	233
Pharmascience Inc 6111 Royalmount Ave Ste 100	Montreal	QC	H4P2T4	**866-853-1178**	514-340-9800	233
Pharmetics Inc 3695 AutoRt Des Laurentides	Laval	QC	H7L3H7	**877-472-4433**	450-682-8580	233
Phase Matrix Inc 109 Bonaventura Dr	San Jose	CA	95134	**877-447-2736**	408-428-1000	250
Phase One Inc 200 Broadhollow Rd Ste 312	Melville	NY	11747	**888-742-7366**	631-757-0400	590
Phase Technology 6400 Youngerman Cir	Jacksonville	FL	32244	**888-742-7385**	904-777-0700	51
PHCC (Plumbing-Heating-Cooling Contractors NA) 180 S Washington St	Falls Church	VA	22040	**800-533-7694**	703-237-8100	48-3
PHD Inc 9009 Clubridge Dr	Fort Wayne	IN	46809	**800-624-8511**	260-747-6151	225
PhDx Systems Inc 1001 University Blvd SE Ste 103	Albuquerque	NM	87106	**888-999-7439**	505-764-0174	38
Phelps School 583 Sugartown Rd	Malvern	PA	19355	**800-344-8328**	610-644-1754	621
Phelps Sungas Inc 224 Cross Rd	Geneva	NY	14456	**800-458-1085**	315-789-3285	317
Phenix City-Russell County Chamber of Commerce 1107 Broad St	Phenix City	AL	36867	**800-892-2248**	334-298-3639	138
Phenopath Laboratories PLLC 551 N 34th St Ste 100	Seattle	WA	98103	**888-927-4366**	206-374-9000	415

Name / Address	City	State	Zip	Toll-Free	Phone	Class
PHF (Phoenix House Foundation Inc) 164 W 74th St 4th Fl.	New York	NY	10023	**888-671-9392**		724
PHFCU (Pearl Harbor Federal Credit Union) 94-449 Ukee St	Waipahu	HI	96797	**800-987-5583**		221
PHH (Port Huron Hospital) 1221 Pine Grove Ave	Port Huron	MI	48060	**888-327-0671**	810-987-5000	374-3
PHH Mortgage Corp 3000 Leadenhall Rd	Mount Laurel	NJ	08054	**800-210-8849**		508
Phi Alpha Theta *National History Honor Society* 4202 E Fowler Ave SOC 107	Tampa	FL	33620	**800-394-8195**		47-16
Phi Delta Kappa International (PDK) 408 N Union St	Bloomington	IN	47407	**800-766-1156**	812-339-1156	47-16
Phi Delta Phi International Legal Fraternity 1426 21st St NW	Washington	DC	20036	**800-368-5606**	202-223-6801	47-16
Phi Delta Theta 2 S Campus Ave	Oxford	OH	45056	**888-373-9855**	513-523-6345	47-16
PHI Inc 2001 SE Evangeline Thwy PO Box 90808	Lafayette	LA	70508	**866-815-7101**	337-235-2452	359
NASDAQ: PHII						
Phi Kappa Phi Foundation 7576 Goodwood Blvd	Baton Rouge	LA	70806	**800-804-9880**	225-388-4917	306
Phi Kappa Psi 5395 Emerson Way	Indianapolis	IN	46226	**800-486-1852**	317-632-1852	47-16
Phi Kappa Tau 5221 Morning Sun Rd	Oxford	OH	45056	**800-758-1906**	513-523-4193	47-16
Phi Mu Alpha Sinfonia Fraternity of America Inc 10600 Old State Rd	Evansville	IN	47711	**800-473-2649**	812-867-2433	47-16
Phi Mu Fraternity 400 Westpark Dr	Peachtree City	GA	30269	**888-744-6824**	770-632-2090	47-16
Phi Sigma Kappa International 2925 E 96th St	Indianapolis	IN	46240	**888-846-6851**	317-573-5420	47-16
Phi Sigma Pi National Honor Fraternity Inc 2119 Ambassador Cir	Lancaster	PA	17603	**800-366-1916**	717-299-4710	47-16
Phi Theta Kappa International Honor Society 1625 Eastover Dr	Jackson	MS	39211	**800-946-9995**	601-984-3504	47-16
Phibro Animal Health Corp 300 Frank W Burr Blvd Ste 21	Teaneck	NJ	07660	**800-223-0434**	201-329-7300	142
Phifer Inc 4400 Kauloosa Ave PO Box 1700	Tuscaloosa	AL	35401	**800-633-5955**	205-345-2120	413
Phil Long Dealerships 1212 Motor City Dr	Colorado Springs	CO	80905	**866-644-1378**		56
Phil Smart Inc 600 E Pike St	Seattle	WA	98122	**877-241-4528**	206-324-5959	56
Philadelphia College of Osteopathic Medicine (PCOM) 4170 City Ave	Philadelphia	PA	19131	**800-999-6998***	215-871-6100	798
*Admissions						
Philadelphia Consolidated Holding Corp 231 Saint Asaph's Rd Ste 100	Bala Cynwyd	PA	19004	**888-647-8639**	610-617-7900	391-4
Philadelphia Contributionship Insurance Co 212 S Fourth St	Philadelphia	PA	19106	**888-627-1752***	215-627-1752	391-4
*Cust Svc						
Philadelphia Inquirer 801 Market St Ste 300 PO Box 8263	Philadelphia	PA	19107	**800-341-3413**	215-854-2000	531-2
Philadelphia International Airport 8000 Essington Ave	Philadelphia	PA	19153	**800-514-0301**	215-937-6937	27
Philadelphia Museum of Art 2600 Benjamin Franklin Pkwy	Philadelphia	PA	19130	**800-732-0999**	215-763-8100	519
Philadelphia Reserve Supply Co 200 Mack Dr	Croydon	PA	19021	**800-347-7726**	215-785-3141	193-4
Philadelphia University 4201 Henry Ave	Philadelphia	PA	19144	**800-951-7287***	215-951-2800	167
*Admissions						
Philander Smith College 900 Daisy Bates Dr	Little Rock	AR	72202	**800-446-6772**	501-370-5221	167
Philharmonic Ctr for the Arts 5833 Pelican Bay Blvd	Naples	FL	34108	**800-597-1900**	239-597-1111	571
Philip Crosby Assoc 306 Dartmouth St	Boston	MA	02116	**877-276-7295**		196
Philip Morris USA 2325 Bells Rd	Richmond	VA	23234	**800-343-0975**	804-274-2000	754
Philippi-Hagenbuch Inc 7424 W Plank Rd	Peoria	IL	61604	**800-447-6464**	309-697-9200	488
Philippines *Consulate General* 30 N Michigan Ave Ste 2100	Chicago	IL	60602	**888-259-7838**	312-332-6458	259
Consulate General 447 Sutter St 6th Fl Philippine Ctr Bldg.	San Francisco	CA	94108	**877-700-0669**	415-433-6666	259
Consulate General 556 Fifth Ave	New York	NY	10036	**866-589-1878**	212-764-1330	259
Embassy 1600 Massachusetts Ave NW	Washington	DC	20036	**800-527-2820**	202-467-9300	259
Philips 5000 Marina Blvd Ste 100	Brisbane	CA	94005	**877-328-2808***	650-228-5555	382
*Cust Svc						
Philips Advance Light Elctro 10275 W Higgins Rd	Rosemont	IL	60018	**800-322-2086**	847-390-5000	765
Philips Canlyte, Inc 3015 Louis Amos	Lachine	QC	H8T1C4	**800-668-2770***	514-636-0670	439
*All						
Philips Holding USA Inc 1251 Ave of the Americas	New York	NY	10020	**800-453-6860**	212-536-0500	439
Philips Lighting Co 200 Franklin Sq Dr	Somerset	NJ	08873	**800-555-0050**		437
Philips Luminaire 776 S Green St	Tupelo	MS	38804	**800-234-1890**		439
Philips Medical Systems 3000 Minuteman Rd	Andover	MA	01810	**800-934-7372**	978-659-3000	382
Phillip's Flower Shops Inc 524 N Cass Ave	Westmont	IL	60559	**800-356-7257**	630-719-5200	294
Phillips & Company Securities Inc 1300 Sw Fifth Ave Ste 2100	Portland	OR	97201	**800-572-4765**	503-224-0858	688

Name / Address	City	State	Zip	Toll-Free	Phone	Class
Phillips & Johnston Inc 21w179 Hill Ave	Glen Ellyn	IL	60137	**877-411-8823**	630-469-8150	491
Phillips & Jordan Inc 6621 Wilbanks Rd	Knoxville	TN	37912	**800-955-0876**	865-688-8342	191-5
Phillips & Temro Industries 9700 W 74th St	Eden Prairie	MN	55344	**800-328-6108**	952-941-9700	59
Phillips Academy 180 Main St	Andover	MA	01810	**877-445-5477**	978-749-4000	621
Phillips Beach Plaza Hotel 1301 Atlantic Ave	Ocean City	MD	21842	**800-492-5834**	410-289-9121	379
Phillips Bros Electrical Contractors Inc 235 Sweet Spring Rd	Glenmoore	PA	19343	**800-220-5051**	610-458-8578	191-4
Phillips Buick-Pontiac-Gmc Truck Inc 2160 US Hwy 441	Fruitland Park	FL	34731	**888-664-7454**	352-728-1212	56
Phillips Corp 7390 Coca Cola Dr	Hanover	MD	21076	**800-878-4242**	410-564-2929	492
Phillips Distributing Corp 3010 Nob Hill Rd	Madison	WI	53713	**800-236-7269**	608-222-9177	80-3
Phillips Distribution Inc 3000 E Houston St	San Antonio	TX	78220	**800-580-2397**	210-227-2397	558
Phillips Exeter Academy 20 Main St	Exeter	NH	03833	**800-245-2525**	603-772-4311	621
Phillips Gold & Company LLP 1430 Broadway Rm 1200	New York	NY	10018	**800-772-1213**	212-730-1112	2
Phillips Group 501 Fulling Mill Rd	Middletown	PA	17057	**800-538-7500**	717-944-0400	534
Phillips Machine Service Inc 367 George St	Beckley	WV	25801	**800-733-1521**	304-255-0537	386
Phillips Mushroom Farms Inc 1011 Kaolin Rd	Kennett Square	PA	19348	**800-722-8818**	610-925-0520	10-6
Phillips Plywood Company Inc 13599 Desmond St	Pacoima	CA	91331	**800-649-6410***	818-897-7736	612
*Cust Svc						
Phillips Syrup Corp 28025 Ranney Pkwy	Westlake	OH	44145	**800-350-8443**	440-835-8001	297-15
Phillips Theological Seminary 901 N Mingo Rd	Tulsa	OK	74116	**800-843-4675**	918-610-8303	168-3
Phillips, Hager & North Investment Management Ltd 200 Burrard St 20th Fl	Vancouver	BC	V6C3N5	**800-661-6141**	604-408-6100	527
Phillips-Van Heusen Corp 200 Madison Ave	New York	NY	10016	**888-203-1112**	212-381-3500	154-11
NYSE: PVH						
Philosophy Inc 3809 E Watkins	Phoenix	AZ	85034	**800-568-3151**		217
Philotechnics Ltd 201 Renovare Blvd	Oak Ridge	TN	37830	**888-723-9278**	865-483-1551	273
PhishLabs PO Box 20877	Charleston	SC	29413	**877-227-0790**	843-628-3368	198
Phoebe Putney Memorial Hospital 417 W Third Ave PO Box 3770	Albany	GA	31706	**877-312-1167**	229-312-1000	374-3
Phoenician, The 6000 E Camelback Rd	Scottsdale	AZ	85251	**800-888-8234**	480-941-8200	667
Phoenix American Inc 2401 Kerner Blvd	San Rafael	CA	94901	**866-895-5050**		218
Phoenix Children's Hospital 1919 E Thomas Rd	Phoenix	AZ	85016	**888-908-5437**	602-546-1000	374-1
Phoenix Convention Ctr 100 N Third St	Phoenix	AZ	85004	**800-282-4842**	602-262-6225	207
Phoenix Cos Inc, The 1 American Row PO Box 5056	Hartford	CT	06102	**800-628-1936**	860-403-5000	360-4
NYSE: PNX						
Phoenix Coyotes 6751 N Sunset Blvd Ste 200	Glendale	AZ	85305	**877-448-4483**	623-772-3200	714
Phoenix Flower Shops 5733 E Thomas Rd Ste 4	Scottsdale	AZ	85251	**888-311-0404**	480-289-4000	294
Phoenix Footwear Group Inc 5937 Darwin Ct Ste 109	Carlsbad	CA	92008	**888-218-7275**	760-602-9688	302
OTC: PXFG						
Phoenix Forging Company Inc 800 Front St	Catasauqua	PA	18032	**800-444-3674**	610-264-2861	482
Phoenix Grand Hotel Salem 201 Liberty St SE	Salem	OR	97301	**877-540-7800**	503-540-7800	379
Phoenix Growth Capital Corp 2401 Kerner Blvd	San Rafael	CA	94901	**866-895-5050**		218
Phoenix Hotel 601 Eddy St	San Francisco	CA	94109	**800-248-9466**	415-776-1380	379
Phoenix House Foundation Inc (PHF) 164 W 74th St 4th Fl.	New York	NY	10023	**888-671-9392**		724
Phoenix International Freight Services Ltd 14701 Charlson Rd	Eden Prairie	MN	55347	**855-229-6128**	952-937-6761	312
Phoenix Leasing Inc 2401 Kerner Blvd	San Rafael	CA	94901	**866-895-5050**		218
Phoenix Magazine 15169 N Scottsdale Ste 310	Scottsdale	AZ	85254	**866-481-6970**	480-664-3960	456-22
Phoenix Manufacturing Inc 3655 E Roeser Rd	Phoenix	AZ	85040	**800-325-6952***	602-437-1034	14
*Cust Svc						
Phoenix Media Communications Group 126 Brookline Ave	Boston	MA	02215	**888-536-7464**	617-536-5390	634-8
Phoenix Metals Co 4685 Buford Hwy	Norcross	GA	30071	**800-241-2290**	770-447-4211	491
Phoenix Park 'n Swap 3801 E Washington St	Phoenix	AZ	85034	**800-772-0852**	602-273-1250	273
Phoenix Park Hotel 520 N Capitol St	Washington	DC	20001	**800-824-5419**	202-638-6900	379
Phoenix Pharmaceuticals Inc 330 Beach Rd	Burlingame	CA	94010	**800-988-1205**	650-558-8898	233
Phoenix Seminary 4222 E Thomas Rd Ste 400	Phoenix	AZ	85018	**888-443-1020**	602-850-8000	168-3
Phoenix Society for Burn Survivors Inc 1835 RW Berends Dr SW	Grand Rapids	MI	49519	**800-888-2876**	616-458-2773	47-17
Phoenix Suns US Airways Ctr 201 E Jefferson St	Phoenix	AZ	85004	**866-648-4668**	602-379-7900	712-1
Phoenix Symphony 1 N First St Ste 200	Phoenix	AZ	85004	**800-776-9080**	602-495-1117	572-3
Phoenix Technologies Ltd 915 Murphy Ranch Rd	Milpitas	CA	95035	**800-677-7305**	408-570-1000	180-12

Company / Address	City	State	ZIP	Toll-Free	Phone	Class
Phoenix Transportation Services LLC 335 E Yusen Dr	Georgetown	KY	40324	**800-860-0889**	502-863-0108	778
Phone Ware Inc 8902 Activity Rd	San Diego	CA	92126	**800-243-8329**	858-459-3000	318
Phonic Ear Inc 2080 Lakeville Hwy	Petaluma	CA	94954	**800-227-0735**	707-769-1110	476
Photo Marketing Assn International (PMA) 3000 Picture Pl	Jackson	MI	49201	**800-762-9287**	517-788-8100	48-18
Photo Research Inc 9731 Topanga Canyon Pl	Chatsworth	CA	91311	**877-424-6423**	818-341-5151	419
Photo Researchers Inc 307 Fifth Ave 3rd Fl	New York	NY	10016	**800-833-9033**	212-758-3420	592
Photo USA 2140 Colonial Ave	Roanoke	VA	24015	**888-234-6320**	540-344-0961	587
PhotoMedex Inc 40 Ramland Rd S, 2nd Fl Ste 200 *NASDAQ: PHMD*	Orangeburg	NY	10962	**888-966-1010**	215-619-3600	424
Photon Technology International Inc 300 Birmingham Rd PO Box 272	Birmingham	NJ	08011	**877-784-4349**	609-894-4420	543
PhotoSource 5106 Louetta Rd	Spring	TX	77379	**800-786-6277**	281-370-2220	530-13
Photosource International 1910 35th Rd	Osceola	WI	54020	**800-786-6277**	715-248-3800	634-9
Photronics Inc 15 Secor Rd *NASDAQ: PLAB*	Brookfield	CT	06804	**800-292-9396**	203-775-9000	694
PHP (Parents Helping Parents) 1400 Parkmoor Ave Ste 100	San jose	CA	95126	**855-727-5775**	408-727-5775	47-6
Phunware Inc 7800 Shoal Creek Blvd	Austin	TX	78757	**855-521-8485**		179
Phybridge Inc 3495 Laird Rd Ste 12	Mississauga	ON	L5L5S5	**888-901-3633**	905-901-3633	609
Phygen LLC 2301 Dupont Ave Ste 510	Irvine	CA	92612	**800-939-7008**		476
Physician's Automated Laboratory Inc (PALLAB) 9830 Brimhall Rd	Bakersfield	CA	93312	**800-675-2271**	661-829-2260	418
Physicians Committee for Responsible Medicine (PCRM) 5100 Wisconsin Ave NW Ste 400	Washington	DC	20016	**866-416-7276**	202-686-2210	48-8
Physicians for Social Responsibility (PSR) 1875 Connecticut Ave NW Ste 1012	Washington	DC	20009	**800-459-1887**	202-667-4260	48-8
Physicians Life Insurance Co 2600 Dodge St	Omaha	NE	68131	**800-228-9100**	402-633-1000	391-2
Physicians Mutual Insurance Co 2600 Dodge St	Omaha	NE	68131	**800-228-9100**	402-633-1000	391-2
Physicians Plus Insurance Corp 2650 Novation Pkwy Ste 200	Madison	WI	53713	**800-545-5015**	608-282-8900	391-3
Physicians Weight Loss Centers of America Inc 395 Springside Dr	Akron	OH	44333	**800-205-7887**	330-666-7952	808
Physics Today Magazine 1 Physics Ellipse	College Park	MD	20740	**800-344-6902**	301-209-3040	456-19
Physio-Control Inc 11811 Willows Rd NE	Redmond	WA	98052	**800-442-1142**	425-867-4000	252
Physmark Inc 101 E Pk Blvd Ste 600	Plano	TX	75074	**800-922-7060**	972-231-8000	181
Pi Sigma Epsilon (PSE) 3747 S Howell Ave	Milwaukee	WI	53207	**800-761-9350**	414-328-1952	47-16
PIA (Pakistan International Airlines Corp) 1200 New Jersey Ave SE	Washington	DC	20590	**800-578-6786**		25
PIA (Pittsburgh Institute of Aeronautics) 5 Allegheny County Airport	West Mifflin	PA	15122	**800-444-1440**	412-346-2100	798
PIA/GATF (Printing Industries of America/Graphic Arts Technical Foundation) 200 Deer Run Rd	Sewickley	PA	15143	**800-910-4283**	412-741-6860	48-16
Piad Precision Casting Corp 112 Industrial Pk Rd	Greensburg	PA	15601	**800-441-9858**	724-838-5500	309
PianoDisc 4111 N Fwy Blvd	Sacramento	CA	95834	**800-566-3472**	916-567-9999	526
Piantedosi Baking Company Inc 240 Commercial St	Malden	MA	02148	**800-339-0080**	781-321-3400	297-1
Pibbs Industries 133-15 32nd Ave	Flushing	NY	11354	**800-551-5020**	718-445-8046	75
PIC Business Systems Inc 5119 Beckwith Blvd Ste 106	San Antonio	TX	78249	**800-742-7378**	210-690-9106	179
Pic Design Corp 86 Benson Rd PO Box 1004	Middlebury	CT	06762	**800-243-6125**	203-758-8272	619
PIC Skate 22 Village Dr	Riverside	RI	02915	**800-882-3448**	401-490-9334	708
PIC USA 100 Bluegrass Commons Blvd Ste 2200	Hendersonville	TN	37075	**800-325-3398**	615-265-2700	10-5
Picacho State Recreation Area 1416 Ninth St PO Box 942896	Sacramento	CA	95814	**800-777-0369**	916-653-6995	564
Piccadilly Circus Pizza 1007 Okoboji Ave PO Box 188	Milford	IA	51351	**800-338-4340**		668
Picco Engineering 350 Caldari Rd	Concord	ON	L4K4J4	**888-772-0773**	905-760-9688	263
Pickaway County Visitors Bureau 325 W Main St	Circleville	OH	43113	**800-283-4678**	740-474-3636	208
Pickens Snodgrass Koch & Company PC 3001 Medlin Dr Ste 100	Arlington	TX	76015	**800-424-5790**	817-664-3000	2
Pickens-Kane Moving Co 410 N Milwaukee Ave	Chicago	IL	60610	**888-871-9998**	312-942-0330	518
Pickett County 1 Courthouse Sq Ste 200	Byrdstown	TN	38549	**888-406-4704**	931-864-3798	338
Pickett State Park 4605 Pickett Pk Hwy	Jamestown	TN	38556	**877-260-0010**	931-879-5821	564
Pickwick Electric Co-op 530 Mulberry Ave	Selmer	TN	38375	**800-372-8258**	731-645-3411	247
PICO Holdings Inc 7979 Ivanhoe Ave Ste 301 *NASDAQ: PICO*	La Jolla	CA	92037	**888-389-3222**	858-456-6022	360-4
Pico Macom Inc 8880 Rehco Rd	San Diego	CA	92121	**800-421-6511**	858-546-5050	645
Pics Telecom International Corp 1920 Lyell Ave	Rochester	NY	14606	**800-521-7427**	585-295-2000	732
Pidilite USA Inc 401 Maplewood Dr Ste 18	Jupiter	FL	33458	**800-843-7813**	561-775-9600	145
Piedmont Baptist College 420 S Broad St *Admissions	Winston-Salem	NC	27101	**800-937-5097***	336-725-8344	167
Piedmont College 165 Central Ave	Demorest	GA	30535	**800-277-7020**	706-776-0103	167
Piedmont Community Health Plan Inc 2512 Langhorne Rd	Lynchburg	VA	24501	**800-400-7247**	434-947-4463	390
Piedmont Gardens 110 41st St	Oakland	CA	94611	**800-496-8126**	510-596-2600	670
Piedmont Medical Ctr 222 S Herlong Ave	Rock Hill	SC	29732	**800-222-4218**	803-329-1234	374-3
Piedmont Natural Gas 4720 Piedmont Row Dr PO Box 33068 *NYSE: PNY*	Charlotte	NC	28233	**800-752-7504**	704-364-3120	785
Piedmont Technical College 620 N Emerald Rd	Greenwood	SC	29646	**800-868-5528**	864-941-8324	798
Piedmont Truck Tires Inc PO Box 18228	Greensboro	NC	27419	**800-274-8473**	336-668-0091	753
Pieper Electric Inc 5070 N 35th St	Milwaukee	WI	53209	**800-424-8802**	414-462-7700	191-4
Pier 1 Imports Inc 100 Pier 1 Pl *NYSE: PIR*	Fort Worth	TX	76102	**800-245-4595**	817-252-8000	362
Pier 1 Kids 100 Pier 1 Pl	Fort Worth	TX	76102	**800-433-4035**	817-252-8000	322
Pier 5 Hotel 711 Eastern Ave	Baltimore	MD	21202	**866-583-4162**	410-539-2000	379
Pier House Resort Caribbean Spa 1 Duval St	Key West	FL	33040	**800-723-2791**	305-296-4600	667
Pieratt's 110 Mt Tabor Rd	Lexington	KY	40517	**855-743-7288**	859-268-6000	34
PIERC (Pacific Island Ecosystems Research Ctr) 12201 Sunrise Valley Dr Ste 615	Reston	VA	20192	**888-275-8747**		666
Pierce College *Puyallup* 1601 39th Ave SE	Puyallup	WA	98374	**877-353-6763**	253-840-8400	161
Pierce County Library System 3005 112th St E	Tacoma	WA	98446	**800-346-0995**	253-536-6500	434-3
Pierce County Security Inc 2002 99th St E	Tacoma	WA	98445	**800-773-4432**	253-535-4433	691
Pierce Distribution Services Co PO Box 15600	Loves Park	IL	61132	**800-466-7397**		448
Pierce Mfg Inc 2600 American Dr PO Box 2017 *Cust Svc	Appleton	WI	54912	**888-974-3723***	920-832-3000	515
Pierce Pacific Manufacturing Inc 4424 NE 158th PO Box 30509	Portland	OR	97294	**800-760-3270**	503-808-9110	192
Pierce Pepin Co-op Services W7725 US Hwy 10 PO Box 420	Ellsworth	WI	54011	**800-924-2133**	715-273-4355	247
Pierce Transit 3701 96th St SW PO Box 99070	Lakewood	WA	98499	**800-562-8109**	253-581-8000	467
Pierre Area Chamber of Commerce 800 W Dakota Ave	Pierre	SD	57501	**800-962-2034**	605-224-7361	138
Pigeon Forge Dept of Tourism PO Box 1390	Pigeon Forge	TN	37868	**800-251-9100**	865-453-8574	208
Piggly Wiggly Carolina Company Inc PO Box 118047	Charleston	SC	29423	**800-243-9880**	843-554-9880	345
PIIRS (Princeton Institute for International & Regional Studies) Princeton University Bendheim Hall	Princeton	NJ	08544	**888-486-3339**	609-258-4852	631
PIJAC (Pet Industry Joint Advisory Council) 1220 19th St NW Ste 400	Washington	DC	20036	**800-553-7387**	202-452-1525	48-4
Pike County 506 Broad St	Milford	PA	18337	**866-681-4947**	570-296-7613	338
Pike County Chamber of Commerce & Economic Development District PO Box 5302	Summit	MS	39666	**800-844-2653**	601-684-2291	138
Pike Electric Corp 100 Pike Way PO Box 868 *NYSE: PIKE*	Mount Airy	NC	27030	**800-424-7453**	336-789-2171	191-4
Pike Industries Inc 3 Eastgate Pk Rd	Belmont	NH	03220	**800-283-0803**	603-527-5100	190-4
Pike Lumber Company Inc PO Box 247	Akron	IN	46910	**800-356-4554**	574-893-4511	681
Pikes Peak Community College *Centennial* 5675 S Academy Blvd	Colorado Springs	CO	80906	**800-456-6847**	719-502-2000	161
Downtown Studio 100 W Pikes Peak Ave	Colorado Springs	CO	80903	**800-456-6847**	719-502-2000	161
Rampart Range 11195 Hwy 83	Colorado Springs	CO	80921	**800-456-6847**	719-502-2000	161
Pikes Peak Ctr 190 S Cascade Ave	Colorado Springs	CO	80903	**866-464-2626**	719-477-2100	571
Pikeville College 147 Sycamore St	Pikeville	KY	41501	**866-232-7700**	606-218-5250	167
Pilgrim BanCorp 2401 S Jefferson Ave	Mount Pleasant	TX	75455	**877-303-3111**	903-575-2150	69
Pilgrim Psychiatric Ctr 998 Crooked Hill Rd	West Brentwood	NY	11717	**800-597-8481**	631-761-3500	374-5
Pilgrim Tours & Travel Inc 3071 Main St PO Box 268	Morgantown	PA	19543	**800-322-0788**	610-286-0788	758
Pilgrim's Corp 1770 Promontory Cir *NASDAQ: PPC*	Greeley	CO	80634	**800-321-1470**		618
Pillar Induction Co 21905 Gateway Rd	Brookfield	WI	53045	**800-558-7733**	262-317-5300	319
Pillars Hotel at New River Sound 111 N Birch Rd	Fort Lauderdale	FL	33304	**800-241-3333**	954-467-9639	379
Piller Inc 45 Turner Rd	Middletown	NY	10941	**800-597-6937**		517
Pilling Surgical 2917 Weck Dr *Cust Svc	Research Triangle Park	NC	27709	**866-246-6990***	919-544-8000	475
Pilot Travel Centers LLC 5508 Lonas Dr	Knoxville	TN	37939	**800-562-6210**	865-938-1439	325
Pilot Tribune PO Box 1187	Storm Lake	IA	50588	**800-447-1985**	712-732-3130	531-2

Name / Address	City	State	Zip	Toll-Free	Phone	Class
Pima Community College						
401 N Bonita Ave	Tucson	AZ	85709	**800-860-7462**	520-206-2733	161
West 2202 W Anklam Rd	Tucson	AZ	85709	**800-860-7462**	520-206-6600	161
Pima County Public Library						
101 N Stone Ave	Tucson	AZ	85701	**877-705-5437**	520-594-5600	434-3
Pima Medical Institute						
3350 E Grant Rd Ste 200	Tucson	AZ	85716	**888-556-7334**	520-326-1600	506
PIMCO Institutional Funds						
PO Box 219024	Kansas City	MO	64121	**800-927-4648**		527
Pimlico Race Course						
5201 Park Heights Ave	Baltimore	MD	21215	**800-638-1859**	410-542-9400	132
Pindler & Pindler Inc						
11910 Poindexter Ave	Moorpark	CA	93021	**800-669-6002**	805-531-9090	196
Pine Bluff Convention & Visitors Bureau (PBCVB)						
1 Convention Ctr Plz	Pine Bluff	AR	71601	**800-536-7660**	870-536-7600	208
Pine Bluff Cotton Belt Federal Credit Union						
1703 River Pines Blvd	Pine Bluff	AR	71601	**888-249-1904**	870-535-6365	221
Pine Butte Guest Ranch						
351 S Fork Rd	Choteau	MT	59422	**877-812-3698**	406-466-2158	241
Pine Cone Hill Inc						
125 Pecks Rd	Pittsfield	MA	01201	**877-586-4771**		593
Pine County						
635 Northridge Dr NW	Pine City	MN	55063	**800-450-7463**	320-591-1400	338
Pine Crest Inn						
85 Pine Crest Ln	Tryon	NC	28782	**800-633-3001**	828-859-9135	379
Pine Grove Furnace State Park						
1100 Pine Grove Rd	Gardners	PA	17324	**888-727-2757**	717-486-7174	564
Pine Hall Brick Co						
2701 Shorefair Dr	Winston-Salem	NC	27116	**800-334-8689**		149
Pine Manor College						
400 Heath St	Chestnut Hill	MA	02467	**800-762-1357**	617-731-7104	167
Pine Mountain State Resort Park						
1050 State Pk Rd	Pineville	KY	40977	**800-325-1712**		564
Pine Needles Lodge & Golf Club						
PO Box 88	Southern Pines	NC	28388	**800-747-7272**	910-692-7111	667
Pine Pointe Hospice & Palliative Care						
6261 Peak Rd	Macon	GA	31210	**800-211-1084**	478-633-5660	371
Pine Rest Christian Mental Health Services						
300 68th St SE PO Box 165	Grand Rapids	MI	49501	**800-678-5500**	616-455-5000	374-5
Pine Ridge Winery LLC						
5901 Silverado Trail	Napa	CA	94558	**800-575-9777**		79-3
Pine Run Community						
777 Ferry Rd	Doylestown	PA	18901	**888-992-8992**	215-345-9000	670
Pine State Trading Co						
8 Ellis Ave	Augusta	ME	04330	**800-873-3825**	207-622-3741	80-1
Pinehurst Resort & Country Club						
80 Carolina Vista Dr	Pinehurst	NC	28374	**800-487-4653**	910-295-6811	667
Pines at Davidson						
400 Avinger Ln	Davidson	NC	28036	**877-574-8203**	704-896-1100	670
Pines Lodge						
141 Scott Hill Rd	Beaver Creek	CO	81620	**800-859-8242***	970-429-5043	379
*Resv						
Pines Resort, The						
103 Shore Rd	Digby	NS	B0V1A0	**800-667-4637**	902-245-2511	667
Pines Technology						
30505 Clemens Rd	Westlake	OH	44145	**800-207-2840**	440-835-5553	493
Pinestone Resort						
4252 County Rd Ste 21	Haliburton	ON	K0M1S0	**800-461-0357**	705-457-1800	667
Ping Inc						
2201 W Desert Cove Ave						
PO Box 82000	Phoenix	AZ	85071	**800-474-6434**		708
Pink Jeep Tours Las Vegas Inc						
3629 W Hacienda Ave	Las Vegas	NV	89118	**800-873-3662**	702-895-6777	758
Pinnacle Business Finance Inc						
615 Commerce St Ste 101	Tacoma	WA	98402	**800-566-1993**	253-284-5600	218
Pinnacle Business Systems Inc						
3824 S Blvd St Ste 200	Edmond	OK	73013	**800-311-0757**		227
Pinnacle Communications Corp						
19821 Executive Park Cir	Germantown	MD	20874	**800-644-9101**	301-601-0777	387
Pinnacle Data Systems Inc						
6600 Port Rd Ste 100	Groveport	OH	43125	**800-882-8282**	614-748-1150	175-1
Pinnacle Entertainment Inc						
3980 Howard Hughes Pkwy	Las Vegas	NV	89169	**877-764-8750**	702-541-7777	131
NYSE: PNK						
Pinnacle Foods Corp						
399 Jefferson Rd	Parsippany	NJ	07054	**866-266-7596**	973-541-6620	297-39
Pinnacle Health Hospital at Community General						
4300 Londonderry Rd	Harrisburg	PA	17109	**888-782-5678**	717-652-3000	374-3
Pinnacle Inn Resort						
301 Pinnacle Inn Rd	Beech Mountain	NC	28604	**800-405-7888**	828-387-2231	667
Pinnacle Management Systems Inc						
8500 North Stemmons Freeway						
Ste 6010	Dallas	TX	75247	**888-975-1119**	703-382-9161	196
Pinnacle Motor Club						
510 N Topeka St	Wichita	KS	67214	**800-446-1289**		52
Pinnacle Performance Improvement Worldwide (PPIW)						
101 Main St	Pepperell	MA	01463	**800-368-3408**	978-925-9797	196
Pinnacle West Capital Corp						
400 N Fifth St	Phoenix	AZ	85004	**800-457-2983**	602-250-1000	360-5
NYSE: PNW						
Pinnacles National Monument						
5000 Hwy 146	Paicines	CA	95043	**877-444-6777**	831-389-4485	563
Pinnacol Assurance						
7501 E Lowry Blvd	Denver	CO	80230	**800-873-7242**	303-361-4000	391-4
Pinova Holdings Inc						
2801 Cook St	Brunswick	GA	31520	**888-807-2958**		600
Pinpoint Data						
339 Somerset St	North Plainfield	NJ	07060	**866-974-6764**	908-756-9400	227
Pinpoint Technologies						
17802 Irvine Blvd Ste 215	Tustin	CA	92780	**866-603-7770**	714-505-7600	462
Pintoresco Advisors LLC						
466 Foothill Blvd						
Ste 333	La Canada Flintridge	CA	91011	**866-217-1140**	213-223-2070	69
Pinyon Environmental Engineering Resources						
9100 W Jewell Ave Ste 200	Denver	CO	80232	**888-641-7337**	303-980-5200	462
Pioneer Bank						
21 Second St PO Box 1048	Troy	NY	12181	**866-873-9573**	518-274-4800	70
Pioneer Broach Co						
6434 Telegraph Rd	Los Angeles	CA	90040	**800-621-1945**	323-728-1263	454
Pioneer Clubs						
123 E Elk	Carol Stream	IL	60188	**800-694-2582**		147
Pioneer Electric Co-op						
300 Herbert St	Greenville	AL	36037	**800-239-3092**	334-382-6636	247
Pioneer Electric Co-op Inc						
1850 W Oklahoma St PO Box 368	Ulysses	KS	67880	**800-794-9302**	620-356-1211	247
Pioneer Electronics (USA) Inc						
1925 E Dominguez St	Long Beach	CA	90810	**800-421-1404**	310-952-2000	51
Pioneer Funds						
60 State St	Boston	MA	02109	**800-225-6292**	617-742-7825	527
Pioneer Golf Inc						
609 Castle Ridge Rd. Ste 335	Austin	TX	78746	**800-262-5725**	512-327-2680	758
Pioneer Hi-Bred International Inc						
PO Box 1000	Johnston	IA	50131	**800-247-6803**	515-535-3200	10-4
Pioneer Long Distance Inc						
PO Box 539	Kingfisher	OK	73750	**888-782-2667**		733
Pioneer Magnetics						
1745 Berkeley St	Santa Monica	CA	90404	**800-269-6426**	310-829-6751	393
Pioneer Metal Finishing LLC						
486 Globe Ave	Green Bay	WI	54304	**877-721-1100**		480
Pioneer Mfg						
4529 Industrial Pkwy	Cleveland	OH	44135	**800-877-1500**	216-671-5500	549
Pioneer Millworks						
1180 Commercial Dr	Farmington	NY	14425	**800-951-9663**	585-924-9970	750
Pioneer National Latex Co						
5000 E 29th St N	Wichita	KS	67220	**800-386-4438**	316-685-2266	760
Pioneer Natural Resources Co						
5205 N O'Connor Blvd Ste 200	Irving	TX	75039	**888-234-6372**	972-444-9001	535
NYSE: PXD						
Pioneer Paper Stock						
155 Irving Ave N	Minneapolis	MN	55405	**800-821-8512**	612-374-2280	658
Pioneer Steel Corp						
7447 Intervale St	Detroit	MI	48238	**800-999-9440**	313-933-9400	491
Pioneer Telephone Assn Inc						
PO Box 707	Ulysses	KS	67880	**800-308-7536**	620-356-3211	733
Pioneer Tool & Forge Inc						
101 Sixth St	New Kensington	PA	15068	**800-359-6408**	724-337-4700	757
Pioneer Transfer LLC						
2034 S St Aubin St						
PO Box 2567	Sioux City	IA	51106	**800-325-4650**		312
Pioneer Wholesale Co						
500 W Bagley Rd	Berea	OH	44017	**888-234-5400**	440-234-5400	43
Pioneer/Eclipse Corp						
1 Eclipse Rd	Sparta	NC	28675	**800-367-3550***	336-372-8080	386
*Cust Svc						
Pioneers						
10123 William Carey Dr	Orlando	FL	32832	**800-359-9297**	407-382-6000	47-20
Pipe & Tube Supply Inc						
1407 N Cypress	North Little Rock	AR	72114	**800-770-8823**	501-372-6556	386
Pipeline & Hazardous Materials Safety Administration						
Office of Hazardous Materials Safety						
1200 New Jersey Ave SE	Washington	DC	20590	**800-467-4922**	202-366-4433	340-15
Piper Jaffray Cos						
800 Nicollet Mall Ste 800	Minneapolis	MN	55402	**800-333-6000**	612-303-6000	688
NYSE: PJC						
Piper Products Inc						
300 S 84th Ave	Wausau	WI	54401	**800-544-3057**	715-842-2724	299
Pipestem Resort State Park						
PO Box 150	Pipestem	WV	25979	**800-225-5982**	304-466-1800	564
Pipestone Publishing Co						
PO Box 277	Pipestone	MN	56164	**800-325-6440**	507-825-3333	634-8
Pipestone Veterinary Clinic LLC						
1300 Hwy 75 S PO Box 188	Pipestone	MN	56164	**800-658-2523**	507-825-4211	792
Piping & Equipment Inc						
9100 Canniff St	Houston	TX	77017	**888-889-9683**	713-947-9393	385
Piping Technology & Products Inc						
3701 Holmes Rd PO Box 34506	Houston	TX	77051	**866-746-9172**	713-422-2271	594
Piraeus Consulting LLC						
1408 4th Ave, Ste 400	Seattle	WA	98101	**866-747-2387**		396
PIREL Inc						
1250 Nobel Ste 190	Boucherville	QC	J4B5H1	**800-449-7196**	450-449-5199	182
Piscataway Park						
c/o Ft Washington Pk						
13551 Ft Washington Rd	Fort Washington	MD	20744	**866-705-5711**	301-763-4600	563
Pistachio Consulting Inc						
67 Maple St	Milton	MA	02186	**800-747-1941**		198
PIT (Pennsylvania Institute of Technology)						
800 Manchester Ave	Media	PA	19063	**800-422-0025***	610-892-1500	798
*Admissions						
Pitco Frialator Inc						
PO Box 501	Concord	NH	03302	**800-258-3708**	603-225-6684	299
Pitmar Tours						
7549 140th St Ste 9	Surrey	BC	V3W5J9	**877-596-9670**	604-596-9670	758
Pitney Bowes Group 1 Software						
4200 Parliament Pl Ste 600	Lanham	MD	20706	**800-367-6950**	301-731-2300	180-1
Pitney Bowes Inc						
1 Elmcroft Rd	Stamford	CT	06926	**800-672-6937**	203-356-5000	110
NYSE: PBI						
Pitney Bowes Management Services						
90 Pk Ave	New York	NY	10016	**800-322-8000**	212-808-3800	462
Pitt Ohio Express						
15 27th St	Pittsburgh	PA	15222	**800-366-7488***	412-232-3015	778
*Cust Svc						
Pitt Plastics Inc						
1400 Atkinson Ave	Pittsburg	KS	66762	**800-835-0366**		65
Pittcon						
300 Penn Ctr Blvd Ste 332	Pittsburgh	PA	15235	**800-825-3221**	412-825-3220	186
Pittenger & Anderson Inc						
5533 S 27th St Ste 201	Lincoln	NE	68512	**800-897-1588**	402-328-8800	401
Pitts Toyota Inc						
210 N Jeffreson St	Dublin	GA	31021	**888-561-8030**	478-272-3244	56
Pittsburg Area Chamber of Commerce						
117 W Fourth St	Pittsburg	KS	66762	**800-794-4780**	620-231-1000	138
Pittsburg State University						
1701 S Broadway St	Pittsburg	KS	66762	**800-854-7488**	620-235-4251	167
Pittsburg Tank & Tower Co Inc						
1 Watertank Pl	Henderson	KY	42420	**800-222-5555**	270-826-9000	191-14

Name / Address	City	State	ZIP	Toll-Free	Phone	Class
Pittsburgh Ballet Theatre 2900 Liberty Ave	Pittsburgh	PA	15201	**800-441-1414**	412-281-0360	572-1
Pittsburgh Cut Flower Co 1901 Liberty Ave	Pittsburgh	PA	15222	**800-837-2837**	412-355-7000	295
Pittsburgh Institute of Aeronautics (PIA) 5 Allegheny County Airport	West Mifflin	PA	15122	**800-444-1440**	412-346-2100	798
Pittsburgh Institute of Mortuary Science Inc 5808 Baum Blvd	Pittsburgh	PA	15206	**800-933-5808**	412-362-8500	798
Pittsburgh International Airport Landside Terminal Fourth Fl Mezz PO Box 12370	Pittsburgh	PA	15231	**888-429-5377**	412-472-3525	27
Pittsburgh Penguins 1001 Fifth Avenue	Pittsburgh	PA	15219	**800-642-7367**	412-642-1300	714
Pittsburgh Pirates 115 Federal St PO Box 7000	Pittsburgh	PA	15212	**800-289-2827**	412-321-2827	711
Pittsburgh Plumbing Heating & Industrial (PPHI) 434 Melwood Ave	Pittsburgh	PA	15213	**800-445-4155**	412-622-8100	14
Pittsburgh Public Theater 621 Penn Ave	Pittsburgh	PA	15222	**800-732-0999**	412-316-8200	572-4
Pittsburgh Supercomputing Ctr 300 S Craig St	Pittsburgh	PA	15213	**800-221-1641**	412-268-4960	666
Pittsburgh Symphony Orchestra 600 Penn Ave Heinz Hall for the Performing Arts	Pittsburgh	PA	15222	**800-743-8560**	412-566-7366	572-3
Pittsburgh Technical Institute (PTI) 1111 McKee Rd	Oakdale	PA	15071	**800-784-9675**	412-809-5100	798
Pittsburgh Theological Seminary 616 N Highland Ave	Pittsburgh	PA	15206	**800-451-4194**	412-362-5610	168-3
Pittsburgh Tribune-Review 503 Martindale St 3rd Fl	Pittsburgh	PA	15212	**800-909-8742**	412-321-6460	531-2
Pittsburgh Zoo & PPG Aquarium 1 Wild Pl	Pittsburgh	PA	15206	**800-732-0999**	412-665-3640	821
Pittsylvania County School Board 39 Bank St SE PO Box 232	Chatham	VA	24531	**888-440-6520**	434-432-2761	683
Pitzer College 1050 N Mills Ave	Claremont	CA	91711	**800-748-9371**	909-621-8129	167
Pizza Factory Inc 49430 Rd 426	Oakhurst	CA	93644	**800-654-4840**	559-683-3377	668
Pizza Inn Inc 3551 Plano Pkwy *NASDAQ: RAVE*	The Colony	TX	75056	**877-574-9924**		668
Pizza Pro Inc 2107 N Second St PO Box 1285	Cabot	AR	72023	**800-777-7554**	501-605-1175	668
Pizza Ranch Inc 204 19th St SE	Orange City	IA	51041	**800-321-3401**		668
PJ Keating Co 998 Reservoir Rd	Lunenburg	MA	01462	**800-441-4119**	978-582-5200	190-4
PK (Promise Keepers) PO Box 11798	Denver	CO	80211	**866-776-6473**		47-20
PK Safety Supply 1829 Clement Ave Ste 200	Alameda	CA	94501	**800-829-9580**	510-337-8880	677
PK4 Media Inc 1600 E Franklin Ave Ste C	El Segundo	CA	90245	**888-320-6281**		387
PKC Corp 1 Mill St C13 Ste 355	Burlington	VT	05401	**800-752-5351**	802-658-5351	180-10
PKM Electric Co-op Inc 406 N Minnesota St	Warren	MN	56762	**800-552-7366**	218-745-4711	247
PL Porter Co 3000 Winona Ave	Burbank	CA	91504	**888-236-5165**	818-526-2600	350
PLA (Public Library Assn) 50 E Huron St	Chicago	IL	60611	**800-545-2433**	312-280-5752	48-11
Place D'Armes Hotel 625 St Ann St	New Orleans	LA	70116	**800-366-2743**	504-524-4531	379
Place Louis Riel All-Suite Hotel 190 Smith St	Winnipeg	MB	R3C1J8	**800-665-0569**	204-947-6961	379
Placement Strategies Inc 6965 El Camino Real Ste 105-200	Carlsbad	CA	92009	**866-445-0710**	909-597-0668	262
Placentia Chamber of Commerce 201 E Yorba Linda Blvd Ste C	Placentia	CA	92870	**844-730-0418**	714-528-1873	138
Placentia-Linda Hospital 1301 N Rose Dr	Placentia	CA	92870	**888-754-9729**	714-993-2000	374-3
Placer County Library 350 Nevada St	Auburn	CA	95603	**800-488-4308**	530-886-4500	434-3
Placon Corp 6096 McKee Rd	Madison	WI	53719	**800-541-1535**	608-271-5634	601
Plaid Enterprises Inc 3225 Westech Dr	Norcross	GA	30092	**800-842-4197**	678-291-8100	42
Plaid Pantries Inc 10025 SW Allen Blvd	Beaverton	OR	97005	**800-677-5243**	503-646-4246	206
Plain Dealer 1801 Superior Ave	Cleveland	OH	44114	**800-362-0727**	216-999-5000	531-2
Plains All American Pipeline LP 333 Clay St Ste 1600 *NYSE: PAA* ■ *Mktg	Houston	TX	77002	**866-753-3619***	713-646-4100	596
Plains Cotton Co-op Assn 3301 E 50th St PO Box 2827	Lubbock	TX	79408	**800-333-8011**	806-763-8011	277
Plains Dairy Products 300 N Taylor St	Amarillo	TX	79107	**800-365-5608**	806-374-0385	298-4
Plains Grain & Agronomy LLC 109 Third Ave	Enderlin	ND	58027	**800-950-2219**	701-437-2400	10-3
Plains Regional Medical Ctr 2100 N ML King Blvd	Clovis	NM	88101	**800-923-6980**	505-769-2141	374-3
Plains Reporter PO Box 1447	Williston	ND	58802	**800-950-2165**	701-572-2165	531-4
PlainsCapital Corp 2323 Victory Ave Ste 1400	Dallas	TX	75219	**866-762-8392**	214-252-4100	360-2
Plainview Milk Products Co-Op 130 Second St SW	Plainview	MN	55964	**800-356-5606**	507-534-3872	297-3
Plan B Technologies Inc 16701 Melford Blvd Ste 150	Annapolis	MD	21401	**888-925-1602**	301-860-1006	179
Plan USA 155 Plan Way	Warwick	RI	02886	**800-556-7918**	401-738-5600	47-6
Planar Systems Inc 1195 NW Compton Dr *NASDAQ: PLNR*	Beaverton	OR	97006	**866-475-2627**	503-748-1100	175-4
Planemasters Ltd 32 W 611 Tower Rd DuPage Airport	West Chicago	IL	60185	**800-994-6400**	630-513-2100	13
Planesmart! Aviation LLC Addison Airport 15841 Addison Rd	Addison	TX	75001	**888-228-4283**	972-380-8004	688
PLANET (National Association of Landscape Professionals Inc) 950 Herndon Pkwy Ste 450	Herndon	VA	20170	**800-395-2522**	703-736-9666	47-2
Planet Bike 2402 Vondron Rd	Madison	WI	53718	**866-256-8510**	608-256-8510	709
Planet Hollywood Resort & Casino 3667 Las Vegas Blvd S	Las Vegas	NV	89109	**866-919-7472**	702-785-5555	667
Planit Solutions Inc 3800 Palisades Dr	Tuscaloosa	AL	35405	**800-280-6932**	205-556-9199	180-5
Planned Parenthood Action Fund Inc 1110 Vermont Ave NW	Washington	DC	20005	**800-430-4907**	202-973-4800	614
Planned Parenthood Federation of America 434 W 33rd St	New York	NY	10001	**800-230-7526**	212-541-7800	47-6
Planned Systems International Inc 10632 Little Patuxent Pkwy	Columbia	MD	21044	**800-275-7749**	410-964-8000	182
Plano Centre 2000 E Springcreek Pkwy	Plano	TX	75074	**800-613-3222**	972-422-0296	207
Plano Convention & Visitors Bureau 2000 E Spring Creek Pkwy	Plano	TX	75074	**800-817-5266**	972-941-5840	208
Plano Molding Co 431 E S St	Plano	IL	60545	**800-226-9868**	630-552-3111	201
Plant Services Magazine 555 W Pierce Rd Ste 301	Itasca	IL	60143	**800-872-9141**	630-467-1300	456-21
Plantation Inn & Golf Resort 9301 W Ft Island Trl	Crystal River	FL	34429	**800-632-6262**	352-795-4211	667
Plante & Moran PLLC 27400 NW Hwy	Southfield	MI	48034	**866-639-9991**	248-352-2500	2
Planters Cotton Oil Mill Inc 2901 Planters Dr	Pine Bluff	AR	71601	**800-264-7070**	870-534-3631	297-29
Planters Electric Membership Corp 1740 Hwy 25 N PO Box 979	Millen	GA	30442	**888-397-3742**	478-982-4722	247
Planters Inn 112 N Market St	Charleston	SC	29401	**800-845-7082**	843-722-2345	379
Plantronics Inc 345 Encinal St *NYSE: PLT*	Santa Cruz	CA	95060	**800-544-4660**	831-426-5858	732
Plants of the Southwest 3095 Agua Fria Rd	Santa Fe	NM	87507	**800-788-7333**	505-438-8888	324
Planview Inc 12301 Research BlvdResearch Park Plz Ste 101	Austin	TX	78759	**800-856-8600**	512-346-8600	180-1
Plaquemine Lock State Historic Site 57730 Main St	Plaquemine	LA	70764	**877-987-7158**	225-687-7158	519
Plaquemines Parish School Board 557 F Edward Hebert Blvd	Belle Chasse	LA	70037	**877-453-2721**	504-595-6400	683
Plascore Inc 615 N Fairview St	Zeeland	MI	49464	**800-630-9257**	616-772-1220	694
Plaskolite Inc 1770 Joyce Ave	Columbus	OH	43219	**800-848-9124**	614-294-3281	599
Plasma Ruggedized Solutions Inc 2284 Ringwood Ave Ste A	San Jose	CA	95131	**800-994-7527**	408-954-8405	480
Plaspros Inc 1143 Ridgeview Dr	McHenry	IL	60050	**800-752-7776**	815-430-2300	603
Plas-Tanks Industries Inc 39 Standen Dr	Hamilton	OH	45015	**800-247-6709**	513-942-3800	201
Plastatech Engineering Ltd 725 Morley Dr	Saginaw	MI	48601	**800-892-9358**	989-754-6500	193-4
Plasteak Inc 3563 Copley Rd	Copley	OH	44321	**800-320-1841**	330-668-2587	188
Plastic & Steel Supply Company Inc 50 Tannery Rd Readington Industrial Ctr Bldg 3	Branchburg	NJ	08876	**800-407-3726**	908-534-6111	600
Plastic Card Systems Inc 31 Pierce St	Northborough	MA	01532	**800-742-2273**	508-351-6210	175-6
Plastic Components Inc N 116 W 18271 Morse Dr	Germantown	WI	53022	**877-253-1496**		603
Plastic Development Co Inc 75 Palmer Industrial Rd PO Box 4007	Williamsport	PA	17701	**800-451-1420**		375
Plastic Film Corporation of America Inc 1287 Naperville Dr	Romeoville	IL	60446	**800-654-6589**	630-887-0800	602
Plastic Forming Company Inc 20 S Bradley Rd	Woodbridge	CT	06525	**800-732-2060**	203-397-1338	201
Plastic Recycling of Iowa Falls Inc 10252 Hwy 65	Iowa Falls	IA	50126	**800-338-1438**	641-648-5073	659
Plastic Safety Systems Inc 2444 Baldwin Rd	Cleveland	OH	44104	**800-662-6338**		676
Plasticolors Inc 2600 Michigan Ave PO Box 816	Ashtabula	OH	44005	**888-661-7675**	440-997-5137	142
Plasticrest Products Inc 4519 W Harrison St	Chicago	IL	60624	**800-828-2163**	773-826-2163	288
Plastics Color & Compounding Inc 14201 Paxton Ave	Calumet City	IL	60409	**800-922-9936**		604-2
Plastics International Inc 7600 Anagram Dr	Eden Prairie	MN	55344	**800-776-7769**	952-934-2303	602
Plastikon Industries Inc 688 Sandoval Way	Hayward	CA	94544	**800-370-0858**	510-400-1010	607
Plastipak Industries Inc 150 Industriel Blvd	Boucherville	QC	J4B2X3	**800-387-7452**	450-650-2200	600
Plast-O-Matic Valves Inc 1384 Pompton Ave	Cedar Grove	NJ	07009	**800-323-2710**	973-256-3000	787
Plastpro Inc 5200 W Century Blvd 9F	Los Angeles	CA	90045	**800-779-0561**	310-693-8600	607
Plastronics Socket Co Inc 2601 Texas Dr *Cust Svc	Irving	TX	75062	**800-582-5822***	972-258-2580	255
Platform Computing Inc 3760 14th Ave	Markham	ON	L3R3T7	**877-528-3676**	905-948-8448	180-1
Platinum Control Technologies Corp 2822 W Fifth St	Fort Worth	TX	76107	**877-374-1115**	817-529-6485	538
Platinum Hotel 211 E Flamingo Rd *General	Las Vegas	NV	89169	**877-211-9211***	702-365-5000	379
Platinum Medical Imaging LLC 1027 SW 30th Ave	Deerfield Beach	FL	33442	**888-673-5151**		474
Platinum Personnel 1475 Ellis St	Kelowna	BC	V1Y2A3	**800-652-1511**	250-979-7200	262

Name / Address	City	State	Zip	Toll-Free	Phone	Class
Platinum Vault Inc 10554 Norwalk Blvd	Santa Fe Springs	CA	90670	**888-671-2888**	562-903-1494	198
Plato Woodwork Inc 200 Third St SW	Plato	MN	55370	**800-328-5924**	320-238-2193	114
Plato's Closet 23021 Outer Dr	Allen Park	MI	48101	**800-592-8049**	313-278-2300	311
Platou Digital Graphics 136 Oregon St	El Segundo	CA	90245	**800-499-0292**		626
Platt & Labonia Co 70 Stoddard Ave	North Haven	CT	06473	**800-505-9099**	203-239-5681	695
Platt Electric Supply 10605 SW Allen Blvd	Beaverton	OR	97005	**800-257-5288**	503-641-6121	248
Platt Luggage Inc 4051 W 51st St	Chicago	IL	60632	**800-222-1555**	773-838-2000	452
Plattco Corp 7 White St	Plattsburgh	NY	12901	**800-352-1731**	518-563-4640	787
Platte-Clay Electric Co-op Inc 1000 W Hwy 92 PO Box 100	Kearney	MO	64060	**800-431-2131**	816-628-3121	247
Platts 2 Penn Plz 25th Fl	New York	NY	10121	**800-752-8878**	212-904-3070	634-9
Playback Now Inc 3139 Campus Dr Ste 700	Norcross	GA	30071	**800-241-7785**	770-447-0616	462
Playbill Magazine 525 Seventh Ave Ste 1801	New York	NY	10018	**800-533-4330**	212-557-5757	456-9
PlayCore Inc 401 Chestnut St Ste 410	Chattanooga	TN	37402	**877-762-7563**		346
Player's Club Resort 35 Deallyon Ave	Hilton Head Island	SC	29928	**800-497-7529**	843-785-3355	667
Playhouse Square 1501 Euclid Ave Ste 200	Cleveland	OH	44115	**866-546-1353**	216-771-4444	571
Playscripts 7 Penn Plz Ste 904	New York	NY	10001	**866-639-7529**		789
Playwell Group, The 4743 Iberia Ave Ste C	Dallas	TX	75207	**800-726-1816**		709
Playworld Systems Inc 1000 Buffalo Rd	Lewisburg	PA	17837	**800-233-8404**	570-522-9800	346
Plaza Art 633 Middleton St	Nashville	TN	37203	**866-668-6714**	615-254-3368	44
Plaza Artists Materials of the MidAtlantic Inc 1990 K Str NW	Washington	DC	20006	**866-668-6714**	202-331-7090	44
Plaza Bank 7460 W Irving Pk Rd *General	Norridge	IL	60706	**877-714-9599***	708-456-3440	69
Plaza Fleet Parts Inc 1520 S Broadway	Saint Louis	MO	63104	**800-325-7618**	314-231-5047	60
Plaza Group Inc 10375 Richmond Ave Ste 1620	Houston	TX	77042	**800-876-3738**	713-266-0707	145
Plaza Home Mortgage Inc 5090 Shoreham Pl Ste 206	San Diego	CA	92122	**866-260-2529**	858-346-1208	508
Plaza Hotel & Casino 1 Main St PO Box 760	Las Vegas	NV	89101	**800-634-6575**	702-386-2110	379
Plaza Hotel, The 5th Ave at Central Park S	New York	NY	10019	**888-850-0909**	212-759-3000	378
Plaza Live, The 425 N Bumby Ave	Orlando	FL	32803	**877-435-9849**	407-228-1220	571
Plaza on the River Resort Club Hotel 121 W St	Reno	NV	89501	**800-628-5974**	775-786-2200	379
Plaza Suite Hotel Resort 620 S Peters St	New Orleans	LA	70130	**800-770-6721**		379
Plaza Suites Silicon Valley 3100 Lakeside Dr	Santa Clara	CA	95054	**800-345-1554**	408-748-9800	379
Plaza Tire Service 2075 Corporate Cr PO Box 2048	Cape Girardeau	MO	63702	**877-787-1691**		61-5
Plaza Travel 16530 Ventura Blvd Ste 106	Encino	CA	91436	**800-347-4447**	818-990-4053	773
Plaza View 245 N Wildwood Dr	Branson	MO	65616	**800-850-6646**	417-335-2798	669
Pleasant Holidays LLC 2404 Townsgate Rd	Westlake Village	CA	91361	**800-742-9244**	818-991-3390	769
Pleasant Trucking Inc 2250 Industrial Dr PO Box 778	Connellsville	PA	15425	**800-245-2402**		778
Pleasant Valley State Prison 24863 W Jayne Ave PO Box 8500	Coalinga	CA	93210	**877-256-6877**	559-935-4900	215
Pleasant View Gardens Inc 7316 Pleasant St	Loudon	NH	03307	**866-862-2974**	603-435-8361	324
Pleasanton Chamber of Commerce 777 Peters Ave	Pleasanton	CA	94566	**877-807-2249**	925-846-5858	138
Please Touch Museum Memorial Hall Fairmount Pk 4231 Ave of the Republic	Philadelphia	PA	19131	**800-732-0999**	215-963-0667	520
Pleiger Plastics Co PO Box 1271	Washington	PA	15301	**800-753-4437**	724-228-2244	607
Pleora Technologies Inc 340 Terry Fox Dr Ste 300	Kanata	ON	K2K3A2	**888-687-6877**	613-270-0625	666
Plexus Corp 1 Plexus Way PO Box 156 *NASDAQ: PLXS*	Neenah	WI	54957	**877-733-7260**	920-722-3451	624
PLF (Public Lands Foundation) PO Box 7226	Arlington	VA	22207	**866-985-9636**	703-790-1988	47-13
PLH Products Inc 6655 Knott Ave	Buena Park	CA	90620	**800-946-6001**	714-739-6600	789
PLI (Practising Law Institute) 810 Seventh Ave 26th Fl	New York	NY	10019	**800-260-4754**	212-824-5700	48-10
Plitek LLC 69 Rawls Rd	Des Plaines	IL	60018	**800-966-1250**		607
PLRB (Property Loss Research Bureau) 3025 Highland Pkwy Ste 800	Downers Grove	IL	60515	**888-711-7572**	630-724-2200	48-9
Plug Power Inc 968 Albany-Shaker Rd *NASDAQ: PLUG*	Latham	NY	12110	**877-474-1993**	518-782-7700	255
Plumas County Visitors Bureau 550 Crescent St	Quincy	CA	95971	**800-326-2247**	530-283-6345	208
Plumas-Sierra Rural Electric Co-op 73233 SR 70	Portola	CA	96122	**800-555-2207**	530-832-4261	247
Plumb Supply Co 1622 NE 51st Ave	Des Moines	IA	50313	**800-483-9511**	515-262-9511	611
Plumbers Supply Co 1000 E Main St	Louisville	KY	40206	**800-626-5133**	502-582-2261	611
Plumbing Distributors Inc 1025 Old Norcross Rd	Lawrenceville	GA	30046	**800-262-9231**	770-963-9231	611
Plumbing-Heating-Cooling Contractors NA (PHCC) 180 S Washington St	Falls Church	VA	22040	**800-533-7694**	703-237-8100	48-3
Plump Jack's Squaw Valley Inn 1920 Squaw Vly Rd PO Box 2407	Olympic Valley	CA	96146	**800-323-7666**	530-583-1576	379
Plumrose USA Inc 1901 Butterfield Rd Ste 305	Downers Grove	IL	60515	**800-526-4909**	732-624-4040	472
Plunkett's Pest Control 40 NE 52nd Way	Fridley	MN	55421	**866-906-1780**	218-723-8464	576
PlusOne Solutions Inc 3501 Quadrangle Blvd Ste 120	Orlando	FL	32817	**877-943-0100**	407-359-5929	198
PlymKraft Inc 479 Export Cir	Newport News	VA	23601	**800-992-0854**	757-595-0364	210
Plymold 615 Centennial Dr	Kenyon	MN	55946	**800-759-6653**		320-1
Plymouth State University 17 High St	Plymouth	NH	03264	**800-842-6900**	603-535-2237	167
Plymouth Tube Co 29 W 150 Warrenville Rd *Mktg	Warrenville	IL	60555	**800-323-9506***	630-393-3550	489
Plymouth Village 900 Salem Dr	Redlands	CA	92373	**800-391-4552**	909-793-9195	670
Plywood Supply Inc 7036 NE 175th St	Kenmore	WA	98028	**888-774-9663**	425-485-8585	612
PM Beef Group LLC 2850 Hwy 60 E	Windom	MN	56101	**800-622-5213**	507-831-2761	10-1
PM Co 9220 Glades Dr	Fairfield	OH	45011	**800-327-4359**	513-825-7626	553
PM Construction Co Inc PO Box 728	Saco	ME	04072	**800-646-0068**	207-282-7697	188
PMA (Photo Marketing Assn International) 3000 Picture Pl	Jackson	MI	49201	**800-762-9287**	517-788-8100	48-18
PMA (Produce Marketing Assn) 1500 Casho Mill Rd	Newark	DE	19711	**800-660-4287**	302-738-7100	48-6
Pmalliance Inc 2075 Spencers Way Ste 201	Stone Mountain	GA	30087	**866-808-3735**	770-938-4947	462
PMC Commercial Trust 17950 Preston Rd Ste 600 *NASDAQ: CMCT*	Dallas	TX	75252	**800-486-3223**	972-349-3200	218
PMC Specialties Group Inc 501 Murray Rd	Cincinnati	OH	45217	**800-543-2466**	513-242-3300	143
PMCS-ICAP 829 W Genesee St	Syracuse	NY	13204	**800-245-7627**	315-423-7962	650
PMHI (Pacific Modern Homes Inc) 9723 Railroad St	Elk Grove	CA	95624	**800-395-1011**	916-685-9514	105
PMI (Project Management Institute) 14 Campus Blvd	Newtown Square	PA	19073	**866-276-4764**	610-356-4600	48-12
PMI Group Inc 3003 Oak Rd *OTC: PMI*	Walnut Creek	CA	94597	**800-288-1970**		360-4
PML (OneAmerica Financial Partners Inc) PO Box 368	Indianapolis	IN	46206	**800-249-6269**	317-285-1877	391-2
PMMI (Packaging Machinery Manufacturers Institute) 4350 N Fairfax Dr Ste 600	Arlington	VA	22203	**888-275-7664**	703-243-8555	48-13
PMP Corp 25 Security Dr *Cust Svc	Avon	CT	06001	**800-243-6628***	860-677-9656	494
PMPA (Precision Machined Products Assn) 6700 W Snowville Rd	Brecksville	OH	44141	**800-233-1234**	440-526-0300	48-13
PMS Systems Corp 2800 28th St Ste 109	Santa Monica	CA	90405	**800-755-3968**	310-450-2566	180-5
PMSLIC (Pennsylvania Medical Society Liability Insurance Co) 1700 Bent Creek Blvd PO Box 2080	Mechanicsburg	PA	17050	**800-445-1212**	844-466-7225	391-5
PNBC (Progressive National Baptist Convention Inc) 601 50th St NE	Washington	DC	20019	**800-876-7622**	202-396-0558	47-20
PNC Arena 1400 EdwaRds Mill Rd	Raleigh	NC	27607	**800-745-3000**	919-861-2300	718
PNC Bank 1 PNC Plaza 249 Fifth Ave	Pittsburgh	PA	15222	**888-762-2265**	412-762-2000	69
PNC Bank Delaware 300 Delaware Ave	Wilmington	DE	19899	**888-762-2265**	302-429-1361	69
PNC Bank NA 249 Fifth Ave 1 PNC Plaza	Pittsburgh	PA	15222	**888-762-2265**	412-762-2000	69
PNC Financial Services Group Inc 249 Fifth Ave 1 PNC Plz *NYSE: PNC*	Pittsburgh	PA	15222	**877-762-2000**	412-762-2000	360-2
PNC Park 115 Federal St	Pittsburgh	PA	15212	**866-800-1275**	412-321-2827	718
Pneumatic & Hydraulic Systems Company Inc 1338 Petroleum Pkwy	Broussard	LA	70518	**877-836-1999**	337-839-1999	358
Pneumech Systems Mfg LLC 201 Pneu Mech Dr	Statesville	NC	28625	**800-358-7374**	704-873-2475	18
Pneutek 17 Friars Dr	Hudson	NH	03051	**800-431-8665**	603-883-1660	757
PNK (River City) LLC 777 River City Casino Blvd	Saint Louis	MO	63125	**888-578-7289**		377
PNM Resources Inc Alvarado Sq *NYSE: PNM*	Albuquerque	NM	87158	**888-342-5766**	505-241-2700	360-5
PNNL (Pacific Northwest National Laboratory) 902 Battelle Blvd PO Box 999	Richland	WA	99352	**888-375-7665**	509-375-2121	666
PNWFCU (Pacific NW Federal Credit Union) 12106 NE Marx St	Portland	OR	97220	**866-692-8669**	503-256-5858	221
PNY Technologies Inc 299 Webro Rd	Parsippany	NJ	07054	**800-769-7079**	973-515-9700	290
Poblocki Sign Company LLC 922 S 70th St	West Allis	WI	53214	**800-776-7064**	414-453-4010	699
Pocahontas County PO Box 275	Marlinton	WV	24954	**800-336-7009**		338
Pocahontas State Park 10301 State Pk Rd	Chesterfield	VA	23832	**800-933-7275**	804-796-4255	564
Pocino Foods Co 14250 Lomitas Ave	City of Industry	CA	91746	**800-345-0150**	626-968-8000	297-26

Name / Address	City	State	Zip	Toll-Free	Phone	Class
Pocock Racing Shells 615 80Th St Sw	Everett	WA	98203	**888-762-6251**	425-438-9048	696
Pocomoke River State Park 3461 Worcester Hwy	Snow Hill	MD	21863	**877-620-8367**	410-632-2566	564
Pocomoke State Forest 580 Taylor Ave	Annapolis	MD	21401	**877-620-8367**		564
Pocono Manor Golf Resort & Spa 1 Manor Dr Rt 314	Pocono Manor	PA	18349	**800-233-8150**	570-839-7111	667
Pocono Mountains Vacation Bureau 1004 Main St	Stroudsburg	PA	18360	**800-722-9199**	570-421-5791	208
Pocono Raceway Long Pond Rd PO Box 500	Long Pond	PA	18334	**800-722-3929**	570-646-2300	514
Pocono Record 511 Lenox St	Stroudsburg	PA	18360	**800-530-6310**	570-421-3000	531-2
Podiatry Insurance Company of America 3000 Meridian Blvd Ste 400	Franklin	TN	37067	**800-251-5727**	615-984-2005	391-5
POH Regional Medical Ctr 50 N Perry St	Pontiac	MI	48342	**888-327-0671**	248-338-5000	374-3
Pohly Co 867 Boylston St 5th Fl	Boston	MA	02116	**800-383-0888**	617-451-1700	634-9
Point Alliance Inc 20 Adelaide St E Ste 500	Toronto	ON	M5C2T6	**855-947-6468**	416-943-0001	182
Point Loma Nazarene University 3900 Lomaland Dr *Admissions	San Diego	CA	92106	**800-733-7770***	619-849-2200	167
Point Park University 201 Wood St *Admissions	Pittsburgh	PA	15222	**800-321-0129***	412-391-4100	167
Point Pelee National Park of Canada 407 Monarch Ln RR 1	Leamington	ON	N8H3V4	**888-773-8888**	519-322-2365	562
Point Plaza Suites & Conference Hotel 950 J Clyde Morris Blvd	Newport News	VA	23601	**800-841-1112**	757-599-4460	379
Point Reyes National Seashore 1 Bear Valley Rd	Point Reyes Station	CA	94956	**877-874-2478**	415-464-5100	563
Point, The PO Box 1327	Saranac Lake	NY	12983	**800-255-3530**	518-891-5674	667
Pointe Coupee Electric Membership Corp 2506 False River Dr PO Box 160	New Roads	LA	70760	**800-738-7232**	225-638-3751	247
Pointe Hilton at Squaw Peak Resort 7677 N 16th St	Phoenix	AZ	85020	**800-685-0550**	602-997-2626	667
Pointe Hilton Resort at Tapatio Cliffs 11111 N Seventh St	Phoenix	AZ	85020	**800-947-9784**	602-866-7500	667
Pointe Scientific Inc 5449 Research Dr PO Box 87188	Canton	MI	48188	**800-445-9853**	734-487-8300	233
Points of Light Foundation & Volunteer Ctr National Network 1400 'I' St NW Ste 800	Washington	DC	20005	**866-269-0510**	202-729-8000	47-5
Poisoned Pen Bookstore 4014 N Goldwater Blvd	Scottsdale	AZ	85251	**888-560-9919**	480-947-2974	95
Polar Beverages Inc 1001 Southbridge St *Cust Svc	Worcester	MA	01610	**800-734-9800***	508-753-4300	79-2
Polar Service Centers 7600 E Sam Houston Pkwy N	Houston	TX	77049	**800-955-8558**	281-459-6400	777
Polar Tank Trailer Inc 12810 County Rd 17	Holdingford	MN	56340	**800-826-6589**	320-746-2255	777
Polar ware 502 Hgwy 67 PO Box 366	Kiel	WI	53402	**800-237-3655**		488
Polar Ware Co 502 Hwy 67 *Cust Svc	Kiel	WI	53042	**800-237-3655***		486
Polaris Pool Systems Inc 2620 Commerce Way	Vista	CA	92081	**800-822-7933**	760-599-9600	804
Police & Fire Federal Credit Union 901 Arch St	Philadelphia	PA	19107	**800-228-8801**	215-931-0300	221
Policemen's Annuity & Benefit Fund of Chicago 221 N LaSalle St Ste 1626	Chicago	IL	60601	**800-656-6606**	312-744-3891	390
Policy Research Associates Inc 345 Delaware Ave	Delmar	NY	12054	**800-311-4246**	518-439-7415	140
Politics & Prose Bookstore 5015 Connecticut Ave NW	Washington	DC	20008	**800-722-0790**	202-364-1919	95
Polk Audio Inc 5601 Metro Dr	Baltimore	MD	21215	**800-377-7655**	410-358-3600	51
Polk County Rural Public Power District 115 W 3rd St PO Box 465	Stromsburg	NE	68666	**888-242-5265**	402-764-4381	247
Polk County Travel & Tourism 20 E Mills St PO Box 308	Columbus	NC	28722	**800-440-7848**	828-894-2324	208
Polk-Burnett Electric Co-op (PBEC) 1001 State Rd 35	Centuria	WI	54824	**800-421-0283**	715-646-2191	247
Pollock Paper & Packaging 1 Pollock Pl *Cust Svc	Grand Prairie	TX	75050	**800-843-7320***	972-263-2126	558
Pollock Printing Company Inc 928 Sixth Ave South	Nashville	TN	37203	**800-349-1205**	615-255-0526	626
Pollstar 4697 W Jacquelyn Ave	Fresno	CA	93722	**800-344-7383**	559-271-7900	456-9
Pollution Control Corp 500 W Country Club Rd	Chickasha	OK	73018	**800-966-1265**		198
Pollution Probe 150 Ferrand Dr Ste 208	Toronto	ON	M3C3E5	**877-926-1907**	416-926-1907	47-13
Polsinelli Shalton Flanigan Suelthaus PC 700 W 47th St Ste 1000	Kansas City	MO	64112	**800-422-0893**	816-753-1000	428
POLY (POLY Languages Institute Inc) 5757 Wilshire Blvd Ste 510	Los Angeles	CA	90036	**877-738-5787**	323-933-9399	423
Poly Cycle Inc 5501 Campbells Run Rd	Pittsburgh	PA	15205	**800-394-4333**	412-747-1101	453
Poly Expert Inc 850 ave Munck	Laval	QC	H7S1B1	**877-384-5060**	514-384-5060	366
POLY Languages Institute Inc (POLY) 5757 Wilshire Blvd Ste 510	Los Angeles	CA	90036	**877-738-5787**	323-933-9399	423
Poly Molding LLC 96 Fourth Ave	Haskell	NJ	07420	**800-229-7161**	973-835-7161	600
Poly-America Inc 2000 W Marshall Dr	Grand Prairie	TX	75051	**800-527-3322**	972-337-7100	65
Polycom Inc 4750 Willow Rd	Pleasanton	CA	94588	**800-765-9266**		732
PolyConversions Inc 505 Condit Dr	Rantoul	IL	61866	**888-893-3330**	217-893-3330	575
Polyengineering Inc 1935 Headland Ave	Dothan	AL	36303	**888-793-4700**	334-793-4700	263
Polyfil 74 Green Pond Rd	Rockaway	NJ	07866	**866-765-9345**	973-627-4070	599
Polygon Co 103 Industrial Pk Dr PO Box 176	Walkerton	IN	46574	**800-918-9261**	574-586-3145	601
Polygon Network PO Box 4806	Dillon	CO	80435	**800-221-4435**		393
Polyguard Products Inc PO Box 755	Ennis	TX	75120	**800-541-4994**	972-875-8421	742-2
Polymedco Inc 510 Furnace Dock Rd	Cortlandt Manor	NY	10567	**800-431-2123**	914-739-5400	233
Polymer Industries LLC 10526 Alabama Hwy 40 PO Box 32	Henagar	AL	35978	**877-489-0039**	256-657-5197	600
Polynesian Adventure Tours Inc 2880 Kilihau St	Honolulu	HI	96819	**800-622-3011**	808-833-3000	758
Polynesian Cultural Ctr 55-370 Kamehameha Hwy	Laie	HI	96762	**800-367-7060**	808-293-3005	519
Polynesian Resort, The 615 Ocean Shores Blvd NW	Ocean Shores	WA	98569	**800-562-4836**	360-289-3361	667
PolyOne Corp 33587 Walker Rd *NYSE: POL*	Avon Lake	OH	44012	**866-765-9663**	440-930-1000	604-2
Poly-Pak Industries Inc 125 Spagnoli Rd	Melville	NY	11747	**800-969-1993**		65
PolyPeptide Laboratories Inc 365 Maple Ave	Torrance	CA	90503	**800-338-4965**	310-782-3569	233
Polysciences Inc 400 Valley Rd *Cust Svc	Warrington	PA	18976	**800-523-2575***	215-343-6484	233
Polyspede Electronics Company Inc 6770 Twin Hills Ave	Dallas	TX	75231	**888-476-5944**	214-363-7245	517
Polytechnic University *Long Island* 105 Maxess Rd *Admissions	Melville	NY	11747	**877-503-7659***	631-755-4300	167
Polytron Corp 4400 Wyland Dr	Elkhart	IN	46516	**888-228-0246**	574-522-0246	205
Polyvinyl Films Inc PO Box 753	Sutton	MA	01590	**800-343-6134**	508-865-3558	599
PolyVision Corp 10700 Abbotts Bridge Rd Ste 100	Johns Creek	GA	30097	**888-325-6351**	678-542-3100	175-2
POM Inc 200 S Elmira Ave PO Box 430	Russellville	AR	72802	**800-331-7275**	479-968-2880	494
POMC (Parents of Murdered Children) 4960 Ridge Ave Ste 2	Cincinnati	OH	45209	**888-818-7662**	513-721-5683	47-6
POMCO 2425 James St	Syracuse	NY	13206	**800-934-2459**	315-432-9171	390
Pomeroy IT Solutions Inc 1020 Petersburg Rd	Hebron	KY	41048	**800-846-8727**	859-586-0600	182
Pompanoosuc Mills Corp Route 5 PO Box 238	East Thetford	VT	05043	**800-757-4061**		361
Pomperaug Woods 80 Heritage Rd	Southbury	CT	06488	**866-817-8935**	203-262-6555	670
Pomps Tire Service Inc 1123 Cedar St	Green Bay	WI	54301	**800-236-8911**	920-435-8301	753
Ponca City Area Chamber of Commerce 420 E Grand Ave	Ponca City	OK	74601	**866-763-8092**	580-765-4400	138
Ponca City Library 515 E Grand Ave	Ponca City	OK	74601	**800-522-8165**	580-767-0345	434-3
Ponca City Publishing Inc PO Box 191	Ponca City	OK	74602	**866-765-3311**	580-765-3311	634-8
Ponca City Tourism 420 E Grand Ave PO Box 1109	Ponca City	OK	74602	**866-763-8092**	580-765-4400	208
Ponce de Leon's Fountain of Youth 11 Magnolia Ave	Saint Augustine	FL	32084	**800-356-8222**	904-829-3168	49-2
Pontarelli Limousine Service 2225 W Hubbard St	Chicago	IL	60612	**800-322-5466**	312-226-5466	441
Pontchartrain Ctr 4545 Williams Blvd	Kenner	LA	70065	**800-745-3000**	504-465-9985	207
Pontchartrain Hotel 2031 St Charles Ave	New Orleans	LA	70130	**800-708-6652**	504-524-0581	379
Ponte Vedra Inn & Club 200 Ponte Vedra Blvd	Ponte Vedra Beach	FL	32082	**800-234-7842**	904-285-1111	667
Pontifical College Josephinum 7625 N High St	Columbus	OH	43235	**888-252-5812**	614-885-5585	168-3
Ponvia Technology Inc 49-T Sherwood Ter	Lake Bluff	IL	60045	**877-217-0875**		448
PONY Baseball/Softball Inc 1951 Pony Pl PO Box 225	Washington	PA	15301	**800-853-2414**	724-225-1060	47-22
Pony Express National Museum 914 Penn St	Saint Joseph	MO	64503	**800-530-5930**	816-279-5059	519
Poolmaster Inc 770 Del Paso Rd	Sacramento	CA	95834	**800-854-1492**	916-567-9800	708
Pop Warner Little Scholars Inc 586 Middletown Blvd Ste C-100	Langhorne	PA	19047	**800-257-4268**	215-752-2691	47-22
Poplar Bluff Regional Medical Ctr 2620 N Westwood Blvd	Poplar Bluff	MO	63901	**855-444-7276**	573-785-7721	374-3
Poplar Bluff Regional Medical Ctr South Campus 3100 Oak Grove Rd	Poplar Bluff	MO	63901	**855-444-7276**		374-3
Poplar Springs Hospital 350 Poplar Dr	Petersburg	VA	23805	**866-546-2229**	804-733-6874	374-5
Popular Woodworking Magazine 4700 E Galbraith Rd *Cust Svc	Cincinnati	OH	45236	**877-860-9140***	513-531-2690	456-14
Population Connection 2120 L St NW Ste 500	Washington	DC	20037	**800-767-1956**	202-332-2200	47-5
Population Reference Bureau (PRB) 1875 Connecticut Ave NW Ste 520	Washington	DC	20009	**800-877-9881**	202-483-1100	47-7
Population-Environment Balance Inc 2000 P St NW Ste 600	Washington	DC	20036	**800-866-6269**	202-955-5700	47-7
Porex Technologies Corp 500 Bohannon Rd *Cust Svc	Fairburn	GA	30213	**800-241-0195***	770-964-1421	607
Pork Report 1776 NW 114th St PO Box 9114	Des Moines	IA	50325	**800-456-7675**	515-223-2600	456-1

Name / Address	City	State	Zip	Toll-Free	Phone	Class
Porky Products Corp 400 Port Carteret Dr *General	Carteret	NJ	07008	**800-952-0265***	732-541-0200	298-9
Porsche Cars North America Inc 980 Hammond Dr Ste 1000	Atlanta	GA	30328	**800-505-1041**	770-290-3500	58
Porsche of Maplewood 2780 Maplewood Dr	Maplewood	MN	55109	**888-852-8937**	888-679-1698	56
Port Arthur Convention & Visitors Bureau 3401 Cultural Ctr Dr	Port Arthur	TX	77642	**800-235-7822**	409-985-7822	208
Port Canaveral 445 Challanger Rd	Cape Canaveral	FL	32920	**888-767-8226**	321-783-7831	617
Port Everglades 1850 Eller Dr	Fort Lauderdale	FL	33316	**800-421-0188**	954-523-3404	617
Port Freeport 1001 N Gulf Blvd	Freeport	TX	77541	**800-362-5743**	979-233-2667	617
Port Hudson State Historic Site 236 Hwy 61	Jackson	LA	70748	**888-677-3400**	225-654-3775	564
Port Huron Hospital (PHH) 1221 Pine Grove Ave	Port Huron	MI	48060	**888-327-0671**	810-987-5000	374-3
Port Metro Vancouver 999 Canada Pl	Vancouver	BC	V6C3T4	**888-767-8826**	604-665-9000	617
Port of Anchorage 2000 Anchorage Port Rd	Anchorage	AK	99501	**877-650-8400**	907-343-6200	617
Port of Astoria 422 Gateway Ave	Astoria	OR	97103	**800-860-4093**	503-325-4521	617
Port of Baltimore *Maryland Port Administration* 401 E Pratt St *General	Baltimore	MD	21202	**800-638-7519***		617
Port of Brownsville 1000 Foust Rd	Brownsville	TX	78521	**800-378-5395**	956-831-4592	617
Port of Corpus Christi 222 Power St	Corpus Christi	TX	78401	**800-580-7110**	361-882-5633	617
Port of Duluth *Duluth Seaway Port Authority* 1200 Port Terminal Dr	Duluth	MN	55802	**800-232-0703**	218-727-8525	617
Port of Everett 2911 Bond St Ste 202	Everett	WA	98201	**800-729-7678**	425-259-3164	617
Port of Milwaukee 2323 S Lincoln Memorial Dr	Milwaukee	WI	53207	**800-367-5690**	414-286-3511	617
Port of New Orleans 1350 Port of New Orleans Pl	New Orleans	LA	70130	**800-776-6652**	504-522-2551	617
Port of Orange *Orange County Navigation Port District* 1201 Childers Rd	Orange	TX	77630	**800-368-3749**	409-883-4363	617
Port of Palm Beach 1 E 11th St Ste 600	Riviera Beach	FL	33404	**877-377-1737**	561-842-4201	617
Port of Pensacola 700 S Barracks St	Pensacola	FL	32502	**800-711-1712**	850-436-5070	617
Port of Port Lavaca-Point Comfort *Calhoun Port Authority* PO Box 397	Point Comfort	TX	77978	**800-933-3643**	361-987-2813	617
Port of Portland 7200 NE Airport Way	Portland	OR	97218	**800-547-8411**	503-415-6000	617
Port of Richmond Commission 900 E Broad St	Richmond	VA	23219	**800-467-4943**	804-646-6335	617
Port of San Diego 3165 Pacific Hwy	San Diego	CA	92101	**800-854-2757**	619-686-6200	617
Port of San Francisco Pier 1 The Embarcadero	San Francisco	CA	94111	**800-479-5314**	415-274-0400	617
Port of Seattle PO Box 1209	Seattle	WA	98111	**800-426-7817**	206-728-3000	617
Port of Seward PO Box 167	Seward	AK	99664	**855-445-7131**	907-224-3138	617
Port of South Louisiana 171 Belle Terre Blvd PO Box 909	LaPlace	LA	70068	**866-536-8300**	985-652-9278	617
Port of Stockton 2201 W Washington St	Stockton	CA	95203	**800-344-3213**	209-946-0246	617
Port of Vancouver 3103 NW Lower River Rd	Vancouver	WA	98660	**800-475-8012**	360-693-3611	617
Port Plastics Inc 15325 Fairfield Ranch Rd Ste 150	Chino Hills	CA	91709	**800-800-0039**	480-813-6118	602
Port Townsend Marine Science Ctr 532 Battery Way	Port Townsend	WA	98368	**800-566-3932**	360-385-5582	519
Portable Buildings Inc 3235 Bay Rd	Milford	DE	19963	**800-205-5030**	302-335-1300	188
Portable Church Industries Inc 1923 Ring Dr	Troy	MI	48083	**800-939-7722**	248-585-9540	198
Portable Technology Solutions LLC 221 David Ct	Calverton	NY	11933	**877-640-4152**		179
Porta-Bote International 1074 Independence Ave	Mountain View	CA	94043	**800-227-8882**	650-961-5334	89
Porta-Fab Corp 18080 Chesterfield Airport Rd	Chesterfield	MO	63005	**800-325-3781**	636-537-5555	104
Portage County 449 S Meridian St 7th Fl	Ravenna	OH	44266	**800-772-3799**	330-297-3600	338
Portage County Business Council 5501 Vern Holmes Dr	Stevens Point	WI	54481	**800-333-6668**	715-344-1940	138
Portage County District Library 10482 S St	Garrettsville	OH	44231	**800-500-5179**	330-527-4378	434-3
Portage Electric Products Inc 7700 Freedom Ave NW	North Canton	OH	44720	**888-464-7374**	330-499-2727	204
Porta-King Building Systems 4133 Shoreline Dr	Earth City	MO	63045	**800-284-5346**		188
Porter Capital Corp 2112 First Ave N	Birmingham	AL	35203	**800-737-7344**	205-322-5442	274
Porter Consulting Engineers PC 552 State St	Meadville	PA	16335	**800-541-5941**	814-337-4447	263
Porter Inc 2200 W Monroe St	Decatur	IN	46733	**800-736-7685**	260-724-9111	89
Porter Instrument Company Inc 245 Township Line Rd PO Box 907	Hatfield	PA	19440	**888-723-4001**	215-723-4000	203
Porter Medical Ctr Inc 115 Porter Dr	Middlebury	VT	05753	**800-994-6610**	802-388-4701	462
Porter Precision Products Inc 2734 Banning Rd	Cincinnati	OH	45239	**800-543-7041**	513-923-3777	755
Porter Truck Sales LP 135 McCarty St	Houston	TX	77029	**800-956-2408**	713-672-2400	515
PorterCorp 4240 136th Ave	Holland	MI	49424	**800-354-7721**	616-399-1963	104
Porters of Racine 301 Sixth St	Racine	WI	53403	**800-558-3245**	262-633-6363	322
Portfolio Recovery Assoc LLC 120 Corporate Blvd Ste 100 Reverside Commerce Ctr *NASDAQ: PRAA*	Norfolk	VA	23502	**888-772-7326**		159
Portico Healthnet 2610 University Ave W	Saint Paul	MN	55114	**866-489-4899**	651-603-5100	462
Portland Business Alliance 200 SW Market St Ste 150	Portland	OR	97201	**800-224-1180**	503-224-8684	138
Portland General Electric 121 SW Salmon St *NYSE: POR*	Portland	OR	97204	**800-542-8818**	503-464-8000	785
Portland Harbor Hotel 468 Fore St	Portland	ME	04101	**888-798-9090**	207-775-9090	379
Portland International Airport 7000 NE Airport Way	Portland	OR	97218	**800-547-8411**	503-460-4234	27
Portland Opera 211 SE Caruthers St	Portland	OR	97214	**866-739-6737**	503-241-1407	572-2
Portland Public Schools 501 N Dixon St	Portland	OR	97227	**800-766-8206**	503-916-2000	683
Portland Regency Hotel 20 Milk St	Portland	ME	04101	**800-727-3436**	207-774-4200	379
Portland State University 1825 SW Broadway PO Box 751	Portland	OR	97201	**800-547-8887**	503-725-3000	167
Portland Teachers Credit Union PO Box 3750	Portland	OR	97208	**800-527-3932**	503-228-7077	221
Portnoff Law Associates Ltd 1000 Sandy Hill Rd Ste 1	Norristown	PA	19401	**866-211-9466**	484-690-9300	428
Port-O-Call Hotel 1510 Boardwalk	Ocean City	NJ	08226	**800-334-4546**	609-399-8812	379
Portofino Bay Hotel at Universal Orlando - A Loews Hotel 5601 Universal Blvd	Orlando	FL	32819	**800-235-6397**	407-503-1000	667
Portofino Hotel & Yacht Club 260 Portofino Way	Redondo Beach	CA	90277	**800-468-4292**	310-379-8481	379
Portofino Inn & Suites Anaheim 1831 S Harbor Blvd *Resv	Anaheim	CA	92802	**800-398-3963***	714-782-7600	379
Portofino Spa at Portofino Island Resort 10 Portofino Dr	Pensacola	FL	32561	**866-849-0223**	850-916-5000	705
Portola Plaza Hotel 2 Portola Plaza	Monterey	CA	93940	**888-222-5851**	831-649-4511	379
Portrait Express 441 N Water St	Silverton	OR	97381	**800-228-3759**	503-873-6365	589
Portraits International 10835 Rockley Rd	Houston	TX	77099	**888-838-1495**	281-879-8444	589
Portsmouth Area Chamber of Commerce 342 Second St PO Box 509	Portsmouth	OH	45662	**800-648-2574**	740-353-7647	138
Portsmouth Daily Times 637 Sixth St	Portsmouth	OH	45662	**800-582-7277**	740-353-3101	531-2
Portsmouth Regional Hospital 333 Borthwick Ave	Portsmouth	NH	03801	**800-685-8282**	603-436-5110	374-3
Pos Source 535 Harrison Ave	Panama City	FL	32401	**800-232-1626**	850-747-0581	179
Posca Bros Dental Laboratory Inc 641 W Willow St	Long Beach	CA	90806	**800-537-6722**	562-427-1811	415
Posey Co 5635 Peck Rd	Arcadia	CA	91006	**800-447-6739**	626-443-3143	476
Positech Corp 191 N Rush Lk Rd	Laurens	IA	50554	**800-831-6026**	712-841-4548	469
Positively Cleveland Visitors Ctr 2207 Forest Hills Rd Ste 100	Harrisburg	PA	17112	**800-321-1001**	216-875-6680	208
Positron Corp 530 Oakmont Ln	Westmont	IL	60559	**866-613-7587**	317-576-0183	252
Positronic Industries Inc 423 N Campbell Ave PO Box 8247	Springfield	MO	65801	**800-641-4054**	417-866-2322	255
Posner Industries Inc 8641 Edgeworth Dr	Capitol Heights	MD	20743	**888-767-6377**	301-350-1000	491
Post & Nickel 144 N 14th St	Lincoln	NE	68508	**877-667-6107**	402-476-3432	156-5
Post Gardens Inc 21189 Huron River Dr	Rockwood	MI	48173	**800-834-4630**	734-379-9688	369
Post Glover Resistors Inc 1369 Cox Rd *Cust Svc	Erlanger	KY	41018	**800-537-6144***	859-283-0778	255
Post Hotel, The 200 Pipestone Rd PO Box 69	Lake Louise	AB	T0L1E0	**800-661-1586**	403-522-3989	379
Post University 800 Country Club Rd	Waterbury	CT	06723	**800-345-2562**	203-596-4500	167
Postal Connections of America 6136 Frisco Sq Blvd Ste 400	Frisco	TX	75034	**800-767-8257**		311
PostalAnnex+ Inc 7580 Metropolitan Dr Ste 200	San Diego	CA	92108	**800-456-1525**	619-563-4800	112
PostcardMania 2145 Sunnydale Blvd Bldg 101	Clearwater	FL	33765	**800-628-1804**		366
Post-Journal 15 W Second St	Jamestown	NY	14701	**866-756-9600**	716-487-1111	531-2
Postler & Jaeckle Corp 615 S Ave	Rochester	NY	14620	**800-724-4252**	585-546-7450	191-10
PostNet International Franchise Corp 1819 Wazee St	Denver	CO	80202	**800-841-7171**	303-771-7100	112
Postpartum Support International 2200 Pacific Coast Hwy Ste 304A	Hermosa Beach	CA	90254	**800-944-4773**		47-17
Post-Register PO Box 1800	Idaho Falls	ID	83403	**800-574-6397**	208-522-1800	531-2
Post-Standard PO Box 4915	Syracuse	NY	13221	**866-447-3787**	315-470-0011	531-2
Post-Star 76 Lawrence St	Glens Falls	NY	12801	**800-724-2543**	518-792-3131	531-2
Posty Cards 1600 Olive St	Kansas City	MO	64127	**800-821-7968**	816-231-2323	129

Company / Address	City	State	ZIP	Toll-Free	Phone	Class
Potamkin Automotive Group Inc						
6200 NW 167th Ste B	Miami Lakes	FL	33014	**855-799-9965**		56
Potash Corp						
1101 Skokie Blvd	Northbrook	IL	60062	**800-667-0403**	847-849-4200	282
Potash Corp of Saskatchewan Inc						
122 First Ave S Ste 500	Saskatoon	SK	S7K7G3	**800-667-3930**	306-933-8500	282
NYSE: POT						
Potawatomi Bingo Casino						
1721 W Canal St	Milwaukee	WI	53233	**800-729-7244**	414-645-6888	132
Potawatomi Inn						
Pokagan State Pk 6 Ln 100A						
Lk James	Angola	IN	46703	**877-768-2928**	260-833-1077	667
Potawatomi State Park						
3740 County Rd PD	Sturgeon Bay	WI	54235	**800-847-9367**	920-746-2890	564
Poteet Strawberry Festival Association						
9199 N State Hwy 16	Poteet	TX	78065	**888-742-8144**	830-742-8144	136
Potomac Conference Corp of Seventh Day Adventists						
606 Greenville Ave	Staunton	VA	24401	**800-732-1844**	540-886-0771	47-20
Potomac Mills						
2700 Potomac Mills Cir	Woodbridge	VA	22192	**877-746-6642**	703-496-9301	459
Potomac State College						
101 Ft Ave	Keyser	WV	26726	**800-262-7332**	304-788-6800	161
Potomac Supply Corp						
1398 Kinsale Rd	Kinsale	VA	22488	**800-365-3900***	804-472-2527	550
*Sales						
Potter Distributing Inc						
4037 Roger B Chaffee Blvd	Grand Rapids	MI	49548	**800-748-0568**	616-531-6860	37
Potter Electric Signal Company Inc						
5757 Phantom Dr Ste 125	Hazelwood	MO	63042	**800-325-3936**	314-878-4321	285
5757 Phantom Dr Ste 125	Hazelwood	MO	63042	**800-325-3936**	314-878-4321	747
Potter-Roemer						
17451 Hurley St	City of Industry	CA	91744	**800-366-3473**	626-855-4890	676
Poudre Valley Hospital						
1024 S Lemay Ave	Fort Collins	CO	80524	**800-994-6610**	970-495-7000	374-3
Poudre Valley Rural Electric Assn Inc						
7649 Rea Pkwy	Fort Collins	CO	80528	**800-432-1012**	970-226-1234	247
Poughkeepsie Journal						
85 Civic Ctr Plz	Poughkeepsie	NY	12601	**800-765-1120**	845-437-4800	531-2
Pounding Mill Quarry Corp						
171 St Clair S Crossing	Bluefield	VA	24605	**888-661-7625**	276-326-1145	502-5
Poverty Point National Monument						
c/o Poverty Pt State Historic Site						
PO Box 276	Epps	LA	71237	**888-926-5492**	318-926-5492	563
Poverty Point Reservoir State Park						
1500 Poverty Pt Pkwy	Delhi	LA	71232	**800-474-0392**	318-878-7536	564
Poverty Point State Historic Site						
6859 Hwy 577	Pioneer	LA	71266	**888-926-5492**	318-926-5492	564
Powder River Energy Corp (PRE)						
221 Main St PO Box 930	Sundance	WY	82729	**800-442-3630**		247
Powder River Transportation						
1700 U S 14	Gillette	WY	82716	**888-970-7233**	307-682-0960	107
Powel House						
244 S Third St	Philadelphia	PA	19106	**877-426-8056**	215-627-0364	49-2
Powell Electronics Inc						
200 Commodore Dr	Swedesboro	NJ	08085	**800-235-7880**	856-241-8000	248
Powell Industries Inc						
8550 Mosely Dr	Houston	TX	77075	**800-480-7273**	713-944-6900	727
NASDAQ: POWL						
Powell Skate One Corp						
30 S La Patera Ln	Santa Barbara	CA	93117	**800-288-7528**	805-964-1330	708
Powell's Books Inc						
7 NW Ninth Ave	Portland	OR	97209	**800-878-7323**	503-228-0540	95
Powell's City of Books						
1005 W Burnside St	Portland	OR	97209	**800-878-7323**	503-228-4651	95
Power & Motoryacht Magazine						
260 Madison Ave 4th Fl	New York	NY	10016	**800-284-8036**	860-767-3200	456-4
Power & Telephone Supply Company Inc						
2673 Yale Ave	Memphis	TN	38112	**800-238-7514***	901-866-3300	248
*Cust Svc						
Power Distribution Inc						
4200 Oakleys Ct	Richmond	VA	23223	**800-225-4838**	804-737-9880	727
Power Engineering Corp						
PO Box 766	Wilkes-Barre	PA	18703	**800-626-0903**	570-823-8822	263
Power Grid Engineering LLC						
5744 Canton Cove Ste 110	Winter Springs	FL	32708	**877-819-1171**	321-244-0170	190
Power Marketing Administrations						
Bonneville Power Administration						
905 NE 11th Ave	Portland	OR	97232	**800-282-3713**	503-230-3000	340-7
Power Motive Corp						
5000 Vasquez Blvd	Denver	CO	80216	**800-627-0087**	303-355-5900	358
Power Organics						
301 S Old Stage Rd	Mount Shasta	CA	96067	**877-769-3795**	530-926-6684	797
Power Service Products Inc						
PO Box 1089	Weatherford	TX	76086	**800-643-9089**	817-599-9486	537
Power Wellness						
2055 W Army Trl Rd Ste 124	Addison	IL	60101	**877-888-2988**	630-570-2600	462
Power Worker's Union, The						
244 Eglinton Ave E	Toronto	ON	M4P1K2	**800-958-8798**	416-481-4491	414
Powercon Corp						
PO Box 477	Severn	MD	21144	**800-638-5055**	410-551-6500	727
Powered By Search Inc						
505 Consumers Rd Ste 507	Toronto	ON	M2J4V8	**866-611-5535**	416-840-9044	226
Powerex Inc						
173 Pavilion Ln	Youngwood	PA	15697	**800-451-1415**	724-925-7272	694
Powerfilm Inc						
2337 230th St	Ames	IA	50014	**888-354-7773**	515-292-7606	694
Powernail Co						
1300 Rose Rd	Lake Zurich	IL	60047	**800-323-1653**	847-634-3000	757
Powers Fasteners Inc						
2 Powers Ln	Brewster	NY	10509	**800-524-3244**	914-235-6300	492
PowerScore Inc						
57 Hasell St	Charleston	SC	29401	**800-545-1750**		762
PowerSecure International Inc						
1609 Heritage Commerce Ct	Wake Forest	NC	27587	**866-347-5455**	919-556-3056	785
NYSE: POWR						
Powersmiths International Corp						
10 Devon Rd	Brampton	ON	L6T5B5	**800-747-9627**	905-791-1493	765
Powersteering Software Inc						
401 Congress Ave Ste 1850	Austin	TX	78701	**866-390-9088**	617-492-0707	180-7
Powrmatic Inc						
2906 Baltimore Blvd						
PO Box 439	Finksburg	MD	21048	**800-966-9100**	410-833-9100	357
Pozas Bros Trucking Company Inc						
8130 Enterprise Dr	Newark	CA	94560	**800-874-8383**	510-742-9939	778
PP Systems International Inc						
110 Haverhill Rd Ste 301	Amesbury	MA	01913	**866-211-9346**	978-834-0505	252
PPA (Professional Photographers of America Inc)						
229 Peachtree St NE Ste 2200	Atlanta	GA	30303	**800-786-6277**	404-522-8600	47-4
PPAI (Promotional Products Assn International)						
3125 Skyway Cir N	Irving	TX	75038	**888-426-7724**	972-252-0404	48-18
PPC Mechanical Seals						
2769 Mission Dr	Baton Rouge	LA	70805	**800-731-7325**	225-356-4333	327
PPFA (Professional Picture Framers Assn)						
2282 Springport Rd Ste F	Jackson	MI	49202	**800-762-9287**	517-788-8100	47-4
PPG Industries Inc						
17451 Von Karman Ave	Irvine	CA	92614	**800-544-3338**	949-474-0400	549
PPHI (Pittsburgh Plumbing Heating & Industrial)						
434 Melwood Ave	Pittsburgh	PA	15213	**800-445-4155**	412-622-8100	14
PPI (Paper Pak Industries)						
1941 N White Ave	La Verne	CA	91750	**888-293-6529**	909-392-1750	298-9
PPIW (Pinnacle Performance Improvement Worldwide)						
101 Main St	Pepperell	MA	01463	**800-368-3408**	978-925-9797	196
PPL Corp						
2 N Ninth St	Allentown	PA	18101	**800-342-5775**	610-774-5151	360-5
NYSE: PPL						
PPL Electric Utilities Corp						
2 N Ninth St	Allentown	PA	18101	**800-342-5775***	610-774-5151	785
*Cust Svc						
PPL Global LLC						
2 N Ninth St	Allentown	PA	18101	**800-345-3085**	610-774-5151	785
NYSE: PPL						
PPM Consultants Inc						
2508 Ticheli Rd	Monroe	LA	71202	**800-761-8675**	318-323-7270	263
PPMC (Penn Presbyterian Medical Ctr)						
39th & Market Sts	Philadelphia	PA	19104	**800-789-7366**	215-662-8000	374-3
PPPL (Princeton Plasma Physics Laboratory)						
James Forrestal Campus Princeton University						
PO Box 451	Princeton	NJ	08543	**800-772-2222**	609-243-2750	666
PR Photos						
4521 Pga Blvd	Palm Beach Gardens	FL	33418	**866-551-7827**		529
Prab Inc						
5944 E Kilgore Rd	Kalamazoo	MI	49048	**800-968-7722**	269-382-8200	209
Practice Concepts						
2706 Harbor Blvd	Costa Mesa	CA	92626	**877-778-2020**	714-545-5110	318
Practicon Inc						
1112 Sugg Pkwy	Greenville	NC	27834	**800-959-9505**	252-752-5183	230
Practising Law Institute (PLI)						
810 Seventh Ave 26th Fl	New York	NY	10019	**800-260-4754**	212-824-5700	48-10
Prader-Willi Syndrome Assn (USA)						
8588 Potter Pk Dr Ste 500	Sarasota	FL	34238	**800-926-4797**	941-312-0400	47-17
Pragma Systems Inc						
13809 Research Blvd Ste 675	Austin	TX	78750	**800-224-1675**	512-219-7270	180-12
Pragmatek Consulting Group						
8500 Normandale Lake Blvd						
Ste 1060	Bloomington	MN	55437	**800-833-3164**	612-333-3164	196
Prairie Band Casino & Resort						
12305 150th Rd	Mayetta	KS	66509	**888-727-4946**	785-966-7777	132
Prairie Bible Institute						
330 Fifth Ave NE						
PO Box 4000	Three Hills	AB	T0M2N0	**800-661-2425**	403-443-5511	783
Prairie Farms Dairy Inc						
1100 N Broadway St	Carlinville	IL	62626	**800-654-2547**	217-854-2547	297-27
Prairie Group Inc						
7601 W 79th St	Bridgeview	IL	60455	**800-649-3690***	708-458-0400	184
*Sales						
Prairie Knights Casino & Resort						
7932 Hwy 24	Fort Yates	ND	58538	**800-425-8277**	701-854-7777	132
Prairie Lakes Hospital & Care Ctr						
401 Ninth Ave NW	Watertown	SD	57201	**877-917-7547**	605-882-7000	374-3
Prairie Land Electric Co-op Inc						
14935 US Hwy 36	Norton	KS	67654	**800-577-3323**	785-877-3323	247
Prairie Lights Bookstore						
15 S Dubuque St	Iowa City	IA	52240	**800-295-2665**	319-337-2681	95
Prairie Livestock LLC						
2139 Barton Ferry Rd						
PO Box 636	West Point	MS	39773	**800-647-6350**	662-494-5651	445
Prairie Meadows Racetrack & Casino						
1 Prairie Meadows Dr						
PO Box 1000	Altoona	IA	50009	**800-325-9015**	515-967-1000	132
Prairie Public Broadcasting Inc						
207 N Fifth St	Fargo	ND	58102	**800-359-6900**	701-241-6900	629
Prairie State College						
202 S Halsted St	Chicago Heights	IL	60411	**866-255-5437**	708-709-3500	161
Prairie View A & M University						
PO Box 519	Prairie View	TX	77446	**877-241-1752**	936-857-2626	167
Prasco LLC						
6125 Commerce Ct	Mason	OH	45040	**866-469-1414**	513-618-3333	233
Pratt & Whitney Canada Inc						
1000 Marie-Victorin Blvd	Longueuil	QC	J4G1A1	**800-268-8000**	450-677-9411	21
Pratt Communications						
2913 Tech Ctr	Santa Ana	CA	92705	**800-980-2323***	714-540-6840	785
*General						
Pratt Community College						
348 NE SR-61	Pratt	KS	67124	**800-794-3091**	620-672-5641	161
Pratt Industries USA						
1800C Sarasota Pkwy	Conyers	GA	30013	**800-835-2088**	770-918-5678	547
Pratt Institute						
200 Willoughby Ave	Brooklyn	NY	11205	**800-331-0834**	718-636-3669	167
Pratt Regional Medical Ctr Corp						
200 Commodore St	Pratt	KS	67124	**877-572-2787**	620-672-7451	374-3
Praxair Inc						
39 Old Ridgebury Rd	Danbury	CT	06810	**800-772-9247**	203-837-2000	142
NYSE: PX						
Praxis Series Online Educational Testing Service Teaching & Learning Div (ETS)						
PO Box 6051	Princeton	NJ	08541	**800-772-9476**	609-771-7395	246
PRB (Population Reference Bureau)						
1875 Connecticut Ave NW						
Ste 520	Washington	DC	20009	**800-877-9881**	202-483-1100	47-7

Name / Address	City	State	ZIP	Toll-Free	Phone	Class
PRC (Patients Rights Council) PO Box 760	Steubenville	OH	43952	**800-958-5678**	740-282-3810	47-8
PRE (Powder River Energy Corp) 221 Main St PO Box 930	Sundance	WY	82729	**800-442-3630**		247
PreCash Inc 5120 Woodway Dr Ste 6001	Houston	TX	77056	**800-773-2274**	713-600-2267	216
Precept Medical Products Inc 370 Airport Rd PO Box 2400	Arden	NC	28704	**800-851-4431**	828-681-0209	575
PreCheck Inc 2500 E T C Jester Blvd Ste	Houston	TX	77008	**800-999-9861**		363
Precision Assoc Inc 3800 N Washington Ave	Minneapolis	MN	55412	**800-394-6590**	612-333-7464	675
Precision Auto Care Inc 748 Miller Dr SE *OTC: PACI*	Leesburg	VA	20175	**866-944-8863**		61-5
Precision BioLogic Inc 140 Eileen Stubbs Ave	Dartmouth	NS	B3B0A9	**800-267-2796**	902-468-6422	474
Precision Computer Services Inc (PCS) 175 Constitution Blvd S	Shelton	CT	06484	**800-340-9890**	203-929-0000	177
Precision Dynamics Corp 13880 Del Sur St	San Fernando	CA	91340	**800-847-0670**	818-897-1111	476
Precision Electronic Glass Inc 1013 Hendee Rd	Vineland	NJ	08360	**800-982-4734**	856-691-2234	332
Precision Fabrics Group Inc 301 N Elm St Ste 600	Greensboro	NC	27401	**800-284-8001**	336-510-8000	742-1
Precision Foods Inc 11457 Olde Cabin Rd Ste 100	Saint Louis	MO	63141	**800-442-5242**	314-567-7400	297-37
Precision H2O Inc 6328 E Utah Ave	Spokane	WA	99212	**800-425-2098**	509-536-9214	1
Precision Hose 2200 Centre Park Ct	Stone Mountain	GA	30087	**877-850-2662**	770-413-5680	296
Precision IBC Inc 8054 Mcgowin Dr	Fairhope	AL	36532	**800-544-7069**	251-990-6789	688
Precision Interconnect Corp 10025 SW Freeman Ct	Wilsonville	OR	97070	**800-522-6752**	503-685-9300	255
Precision Laboratories Inc 1429 S Shields Dr	Waukegan	IL	60085	**800-323-6280**	847-596-3001	144
Precision Machined Products Assn (PMPA) 6700 W Snowville Rd	Brecksville	OH	44141	**800-233-1234**	440-526-0300	48-13
Precision Optics Corp Inc 22 E Broadway *OTC: PEYE*	Gardner	MA	01440	**800-447-2812**	978-630-1800	382
Precision Parts & Remanufacturing Co 4411 SW 19th St	Oklahoma City	OK	73108	**800-654-3846**	405-681-2592	249
Precision Products Inc 316 Limit St *Cust Svc	Lincoln	IL	62656	**800-225-5891***	217-735-1590	429
Precision Shooting Equipment Inc 2727 N Fairview Ave	Tucson	AZ	85705	**800-477-7789**	520-884-9065	708
Precision Solar Controls Inc 2985 Market St	Garland	TX	75041	**800-686-7414**	972-278-0553	699
Precision Specialties Co 1201 East Pecan St	Sherman	TX	75090	**800-527-3295**		407
Precision Steel Warehouse Inc 3500 Wolf Rd	Franklin Park	IL	60131	**800-323-0740**	847-455-7000	491
Precision Tank & Equipment Company Inc 3503 Conover Rd	Virginia	IL	62691	**800-258-4197**	217-452-7228	275
Precision Thermoplastic Components Inc PO Box 1296	Lima	OH	45802	**800-860-4505**	419-227-4500	607
Precision Tool Die & Machine Co Inc 6901 Preston Hwy	Louisville	KY	40219	**877-511-9695**		755
Precision Valve Corp 800 Westchester Ave	Rye Brook	NY	10573	**866-686-8464**	914-969-6500	486
Precision Walls Inc 1230 NE MaynaRd Rd	Cary	NC	27513	**800-849-9255**	919-832-0380	191-9
Precisionform Inc 148 W Airport Rd	Lititz	PA	17543	**800-233-3821**	717-560-7610	620
Precix Inc 744 Bellville Ave	New Bedford	MA	02745	**800-225-8505**	508-998-4000	675
Preco Electronics Inc 10335 W Emerald St	Boise	ID	83704	**866-977-7326**	208-323-1000	471
Precor Inc 20031 142nd Ave NE	Woodinville	WA	98072	**800-786-8404**	425-486-9292	269
Predator Trucking Co 3181 Trumbull Ave	McDonald	OH	44437	**888-773-3875**		778
Preferred Bank Los Angeles 601 S Figueroa St 29th Fl *NASDAQ: PFBC*	Los Angeles	CA	90017	**888-673-1808**	213-891-1188	69
Preferred CommunityChoice PPO 218 W Sixth St	Tulsa	OK	74119	**800-884-4776**	918-594-5200	391-3
Preferred Employers Insurance Co PO Box 85478 *Cust Svc	San Diego	CA	92186	**888-472-9001***	866-472-9602	391-4
Preferred Health Systems Inc 8535 E 21st St N	Wichita	KS	67206	**800-990-0345**	316-609-2345	391-3
Preferred Hotel Group *Preferred Hotels & Resorts Worldwide Inc* 311 S Wacker Dr Ste 1900	Chicago	IL	60606	**800-650-1281**	312-913-0400	379
Summit Hotels & Resorts 311 S Wacker Dr Ste 1900	Chicago	IL	60606	**800-650-1281**	312-913-0400	379
Preferred Meal Systems Inc 5240 St Charles Rd *Cust Svc	Berkeley	IL	60163	**800-886-6325***	708-318-2500	297-36
Preferred Medical Marketing Corp 15720 Brixham Hill Ave Ste 460	Charlotte	NC	28277	**800-543-8176**	704-543-8103	179
Preferred Mutual Insurance Co 1 Preferred Way	New Berlin	NY	13411	**800-333-7642**	607-847-6161	391-4
Preferred Systems Solutions Inc 1945 Old Gallows Rd Ste 450	Vienna	VA	22182	**877-422-7149**	703-663-2777	182
Preferred Traveler 4501 Forbes Blvd	Lanham	MD	20706	**866-679-8655**		530-6
Preformed Line Products 660 Beta Dr *NASDAQ: PLPC*	Cleveland	OH	44143	**800-622-6757**	440-461-5200	813
Prelco Inc 94 Blvd Cartier	Rivi Re-Du-Loup	QC	G5R2M9	**800-463-1325**	418-862-2274	330

Name / Address	City	State	ZIP	Toll-Free	Phone	Class
Premera Blue Cross 7001 220th St SW *Cust Svc	Mountlake Terrace	WA	98043	**800-722-1471***	425-918-4000	391-3
Premera Blue Cross Blue Shield of Alaska 2550 Denali St Ste 1404 *Cust Svc	Anchorage	AK	99503	**800-508-4722***	907-258-5065	391-3
Premier & Curzons Fitness Clubs 5100 Dixie Rd	Mississauga	ON	L4W1C9	**866-371-7307**	905-602-9912	354
Premier Alaska Tours Inc 1900 Premier Ct	Anchorage	AK	99502	**888-486-8725**	907-279-0001	758
Premier America Credit Union 19867 Prairie St PO Box 2178	Chatsworth	CA	91313	**800-772-4000**	818-772-4000	221
Premier Bank & Trust 600 S Main St	North Canton	OH	44720	**855-728-6010**	330-499-1900	69
Premier Coach Company Inc 946 Rte 7 S	Milton	VT	05468	**800-532-1811**	802-655-4456	106
Premier Colors Inc 100 Industrial Dr	Union	SC	29379	**800-245-6944**	864-427-0338	144
Premier Dental Products Co 1710 Romano Dr PO Box 4500	Plymouth Meeting	PA	19462	**888-773-6872**	610-239-6000	230
Premier Die Casting Co 1177 Rahway Ave	Avenel	NJ	07001	**800-394-3006**	732-634-3000	309
Premier Direct Marketing Inc 7725 National Tpke Unit 100	Louisville	KY	40214	**800-737-0205**	502-367-6441	197
Premier Equipment LLC 2025 US Hwy 14 W	Huron	SD	57350	**800-627-5469**	605-352-7100	276
Premier Golf 4355 River Green Pkwy	Duluth	GA	30096	**866-260-4409**	770-291-4202	769
Premier Graphics LLC 1248 W Fourth St	Mansfield	OH	44906	**800-511-4881**	203-378-6200	626
Premier Inc 12255 El Camino Real	San Diego	CA	92130	**877-777-1552**	858-481-2727	353
Premier Jets 2140 NE 25th Ave	Hillsboro	OR	97124	**800-635-8583**	503-640-2927	13
Premier Malt Products Inc 25760 Groesbeck Hwy Ste 103 *Cust Svc	Warren	MI	48089	**800-521-1057***	586-443-3355	460
Premier Members Federal Credit Union 5495 Arapahoe Ave	Boulder	CO	80303	**800-468-0634**	303-657-7000	221
Premier Pyrotechnics Inc 25255 Hwy K	Richland	MO	65556	**888-647-6863**		44
Premier Realty Group 2 N Sewalls Point Rd	Stuart	FL	34996	**800-915-8517**	772-287-1777	650
Premier Safety & Service Inc 2 Industrial Pk Dr	Oakdale	PA	15071	**800-828-1080**	724-693-8699	386
Premier Subaru LLC 150 N Main St	Branford	CT	06405	**888-690-6710**	203-481-0687	56
Premier Tech Industrial Equipment Group 1 Premier Ave	Rivere-du-Loup	QC	G5R6C1	**866-571-7354**	418-867-8884	682
Premier Tool & Die Cast Corp 9886 N Tudor Rd	Berrien Springs	MI	49103	**800-417-8717**	269-471-7715	309
Premier Tours 21 S 12th St 9th Fl	Philadelphia	PA	19107	**800-545-1910**		758
Premier Valley Bank 255 E River Pk Cir Ste 180	Fresno	CA	93720	**877-438-2002**	559-438-2002	69
Premiere Global Services Inc (PGI) 3280 Peachtree Rd NE Ste 1000 *NYSE: PGI*	Atlanta	GA	30305	**866-548-3203**	719-457-6901	38
Premiere Travel Services Inc 7900 Westpark Dr Ste A60	Mclean	VA	22102	**800-458-8670**	703-893-2288	770
PremierGarage Systems LLC 21405 N 15th Ln	Phoenix	AZ	85027	**866-590-9411**	480-483-3030	311
Prentex Alloy Fabricators Inc 3108 Sylvan Ave	Dallas	TX	75212	**877-773-6839**	214-748-7837	296
Prentice-Hall Inc 1 Lake St	Upper Saddle River	NJ	07458	**800-328-5999**		634-2
Prentke Romich Co 1022 Heyl Rd	Wooster	OH	44691	**800-848-8008**	330-262-1984	204
Pre-Paid Legal Services Inc 1 Pre-Paid Way	Ada	OK	74820	**800-654-7757**	580-436-1234	391-5
Presagis 1301 W George Bush Fwy Ste 120	Richardson	TX	75080	**800-361-6424**		180-8
Presby's Inspired Life 2000 Joshua Rd	Lafayette Hill	PA	19444	**877-977-3729**	610-834-1001	47-20
Presbyterian Childrens Services Inc 1220 N Lindbergh Blvd	St. Louis	MO	63132	**800-383-8147**	314-989-9727	47-20
Presbyterian Church (USA) 100 Witherspoon St	Louisville	KY	40202	**888-728-7228**	502-569-5000	47-20
Presbyterian College 503 S Broad St	Clinton	SC	29325	**800-476-7272**	864-833-2820	167
Presbyterian Disaster Assistance (PDA) 100 Witherspoon St	Louisville	KY	40202	**800-728-7228**		47-5
Presbyterian Homes Inc, The 2109 Sandy Ridge Rd	Colfax	NC	27235	**800-225-9573**	336-886-6553	47-15
Presbyterian Homes of SC 2817 Ashland Rd	Columbia	SC	29210	**888-842-4855**	803-772-5885	670
Presbyterian Hospital 1100 Central Ave SE	Albuquerque	NM	87106	**888-977-2333**	505-841-1234	374-3
Presbyterian Kaseman Hospital 8300 Constitution Ave NE	Albuquerque	NM	87110	**800-356-2219**	505-291-2000	374-3
Presbyterian SeniorCare-Westminster Place 1215 Hulton Rd	Oakmont	PA	15139	**877-772-6500**	412-828-5600	449
Presbyterians Today Magazine 100 Witherspoon St	Louisville	KY	40202	**800-728-7228**	800-872-3283	456-18
Prescolite Inc 701 Millennium Blvd	Greenville	SC	29607	**888-777-4832**	864-678-1000	439
Prescott Chamber of Commerce 117 W Goodwin St	Prescott	AZ	86303	**800-266-7534**	928-445-2000	138
Prescott College 220 Grove Ave	Prescott	AZ	86301	**877-350-2100**		167
Prescott National Cemetery 500 Hwy 89 N	Prescott	AZ	86301	**800-827-1000**	928-717-7569	135
Prescott Valley Chamber of Commerce 3001 N Main St Ste 2A	Prescott Valley	AZ	86314	**800-355-0843**	928-772-8857	138
Prescription Solutions 3515 Harbor Blvd	Costa Mesa	CA	92626	**800-788-4863**		585

Alphabetical Section

Name / Address	City	State	ZIP	Toll-Free	Phone	Class
Prescriptives Inc 767 Fifth Ave	New York	NY	10153	866-290-6471		217
Presentation College 1500 N Main St	Aberdeen	SD	57401	800-437-6060	605-225-1634	167
Preservation Technologies LP 111 Thomson Park Dr	Cranberry Township	PA	16066	800-416-2665	724-779-2111	322
President Abraham Lincoln Hotel & Conference Ctr (PALHACC) 701 E Adams St	Springfield	IL	62701	855-610-8733	217-544-8800	379
Presidential Online Bank 4520 East-West Hwy	Bethesda	MD	20814	800-383-6266	301-652-0700	69
Presidio Group Inc, The 5295 South 300 West Ste 550	Salt Lake City	UT	84107	800-924-1404	801-924-1400	196
Presidio Networked Solutions Inc 7601 Ora Glen Dr Ste 100	Greenbelt	MD	20770	800-452-6926	301-313-2000	182
Presley Tours Inc 16 Presley Pk Dr PO Box 58	Makanda	IL	62958	800-621-6100	618-549-0704	758
Presque Isle Electric & Gas Co-op PO Box 308	Onaway	MI	49765	800-423-6634	989-733-8515	247
Presque Isle State Park 301 Peninsula Dr Ste 1	Erie	PA	16505	888-727-2757	814-833-7424	564
Press Democrat 427 Mendocino Ave	Santa Rosa	CA	95401	800-675-5056	707-546-2020	531-2
Press Ganey Associates Inc 404 Columbia Pl	South Bend	IN	46601	800-232-8032		196
Presscut Industries Inc 1730 Briercroft Ct	Carrollton	TX	75006	800-442-4924	972-389-0615	327
Pressed4Time Inc 8 Clock Tower Pl Ste 110	Maynard	MA	01754	800-423-8711		426
Press-Enterprise 3450 14th St	Riverside	CA	92501	877-473-6397	951-684-1200	531-2
Press-Enterprise Co PO Box 792	Riverside	CA	92502	800-794-6397	951-684-1200	634-8
Press-Enterprise Inc 3185 Lackawanna Ave	Bloomsburg	PA	17815	888-484-6345	570-784-2121	634-8
Presses Inc 6360 W 73rd St	Chicago	IL	60638	800-927-9393	708-496-7400	455
Pressley Ridge 5500 Corporate Dr Ste 400	Pittsburgh	PA	15237	800-718-0356	412-872-9400	47-6
Pressman Toy Corp 121 New England Ave *Cust Svc	Piscataway	NJ	08854	800-800-0298*	732-562-1590	760
Press-Republican 170 Margaret St PO Box 459	Plattsburgh	NY	12901	800-288-7323	518-561-2300	531-2
Press-Seal Gasket Corp 2424 W State Blvd	Fort Wayne	IN	46808	800-348-7325	260-436-0521	327
Presstek Inc 55 Executive Dr *NASDAQ: PRST*	Hudson	NH	03051	800-422-3616	603-595-7000	779
Pressure Profile Systems Inc 5757 Century Blvd Ste 600	Los Angeles	CA	90045	888-249-2464	310-641-8100	203
Prestera Trucking 19129 US Rt 52	South Point	OH	45680	855-761-7943	740-894-4770	778
Prestige Accommodations International 1231 E Dyer Rd Ste 240	Santa Ana	CA	92705	800-321-6338	714-957-9100	186
Prestige Chrysler Dodge Inc 200 Alpine St	Longmont	CO	80501	866-439-1926	303-651-3000	56
Prestige Financial Services Inc 1420 S 500 W	Salt Lake City	UT	84115	888-822-7422	801-844-2100	216
Prestige Graphics Inc 9630 Ridgehaven Ct Ste B	San Diego	CA	92123	800-383-9361	858-560-8213	534
Prestige Harbourfront Resort & Convention Centre 251 Harbourfront Dr Ne	Salmon Arm	BC	V1E2W7	877-737-8443	250-833-5800	379
Prestige Medical Corporation International 8600 Wilbur Ave	Northridge	CA	91324	800-762-3333	818-993-3030	474
Prestige Security 5721 W Slauson Ave Ste 120	Culver City	CA	90230	800-482-7303	310-670-5999	691
Prestige Travel & Cruises Inc 6175 Spring Mountain Rd	Las Vegas	NV	89146	800-758-5693	702-251-5552	769
Prestini Musical Instruments Inc 2020 N Aurora Dr *General	Nogales	AZ	85628	800-528-6569*	520-287-4931	526
Presto Products Co 670 N Perkins St PO Box 2399	Appleton	WI	54912	800-558-3525	920-739-9471	65
Presto Tape Inc 1626 Bridgewater Rd	Bensalem	PA	19020	800-331-1373	215-245-8555	729
Prestolite Wire Corp 200 Galleria Officentre Ste 212	Southfield	MI	48034	800-498-3132	248-355-4422	812
Preston Industries Inc 6600 W Touhy Ave	Niles	IL	60714	800-229-7569	847-647-0611	420
Presto-X Co 1221 S Saddle Creek Rd Ste 101	Omaha	NE	68106	800-759-1942		576
Pretzelmaker 1346 Oakbrook Dr Ste 170	Norcross	GA	30093	877-639-2361		668
Pretzels Inc 123 Harvest Rd PO Box 503	Bluffton	IN	46714	800-456-4838	260-824-4838	297-9
Prevent Blindness America 211 W Wacker Dr Ste 1700	Chicago	IL	60606	800-331-2020		47-17
Prevent Cancer Foundation (PCF) 1600 Duke St Ste 500	Alexandria	VA	22314	800-227-2732	703-836-4412	47-17
Prevention Magazine 733 Third Ave	Emmaus	PA	10017	800-813-8070		456-13
Preverco Inc 285 Rue De Rotterdam	Saint-augustin-de-desmaures	QC	G3A2E5	877-667-2725	418-878-8930	364
PreviMed Inc 1164 Malibu Dr	San Jose	CA	95157	800-565-3901		462
Prevost Car Inc 35 boul Gagnon	Sainte-Claire	QC	G0R2V0	877-773-8678	418-883-3391	515
Prevue Pet Products Inc 224 N Maplewood Ave	Chicago	IL	60612	800-243-3624	312-243-3624	577
PRG-Schultz International Inc 600 Galleria Pkwy Ste 100	Atlanta	GA	30339	800-752-5894	770-779-3900	2
Price Books & Forms Inc 531 E Sierra Madre Ave	Glendora	CA	91741	800-423-8961		634-2
Price Canyon Ranch PO Box 39	Rodeo	NM	88056	800-727-0065	520-558-2383	241
Price Electric Co-op 508 N Lake Ave PO Box 110	Phillips	WI	54555	800-884-0881	715-339-2155	247
Price Pfister Inc 19701 Da Vinci St	Lake Forest	CA	92610	800-732-8238	949-672-4000	608
Price Point Mail Order Ltd 1490 W Walnut Pkwy	Rancho Dominguez	CA	90220	800-774-2376		709
Price Steel Ltd 13500 156 St	Edmonton	AB	T5V1L3	800-661-6789	780-447-9999	479
Priceline.com LLC 800 Connecticut Ave *NASDAQ: PCLN*	Norwalk	CT	06854	800-774-2354		50
PriceWaiter LLC 426 Market St	Chattanooga	TN	37421	855-671-9889		387
PricewaterhouseCoopers LLP 300 Madison Ave	New York	NY	10017	800-993-9971	646-471-4000	2
Pride International Inc 5847 San Felipe St Ste 3300	Houston	TX	77057	877-736-3772	713-789-1400	538
Pride Mobility Products Corp 182 Susquehanna Ave	Exeter	PA	18643	800-800-8586		476
Pride Products Corp 4333 Veterans Memorial Hwy	Ronkonkoma	NY	11779	800-898-5550	631-737-4444	789
Pride Solvents & Chemical Co of New York Inc 6 Long Island Ave	Holtsville	NY	11742	800-424-8802	631-758-0200	145
Pride Transport Inc 5499 W 2455 S	Salt Lake City	UT	84120	800-877-1320	801-972-8890	778
Prier Products Inc 4515 E 139th St	Grandview	MO	64030	800-362-1463	816-763-4100	609
Priest Lake State Park 314 Indian Creek Pk Rd *Resv	Coolin	ID	83821	888-922-6743*	208-443-2200	564
Priester Aviation 1061 S Wolf Rd	Wheeling	IL	60090	888-323-7887	847-537-1133	24
Priester Pecan Company Inc PO Box 381	Fort Deposit	AL	36032	800-277-3226	334-227-4301	297-28
Prima Supply Inc 4603 Poplar Level Rd Ste 1	Louisville	KY	40213	888-810-5043	502-966-4578	611
Prima Tech USA 277 Faison McGowan Rd Ste 2	Kenansville	NC	28349	800-458-7454	910-296-6116	474
Primary Color Inc 9239 Premier Row	Dallas	TX	75247	800-581-9555	214-630-8800	685
Primary Freight Services Inc 6545 Caballero Blvd	Buena Park	CA	90620	800-635-0013	310-635-3000	312
Primary Global Research LLC 1975 W El Camino Real Ste 300	Mountain View	CA	94040	888-893-1688		401
Primary Packaging Inc 10810 Industrial Pkwy NW	Bolivar	OH	44612	800-774-2247	330-874-3131	87
Prime Adv & Design Inc 7351 Kirkwood Ln N Ste 144	Maple Grove	MN	55369	800-275-8777	763-424-9406	4
Prime Concepts Group Inc 1807 S Eisenhower St	Wichita	KS	67209	800-946-7804	316-942-1111	197
Prime Inc PO Box 4208 *Cust Svc	Springfield	MO	65808	800-848-4560*	417-866-0001	778
Prime Management Services 3416 Primm Ln	Birmingham	AL	35216	866-609-1599	205-823-6106	46
Prime Outlets San Marcos 3939 S IH-35	San Marcos	TX	78666	800-331-5479	512-396-2200	459
Prime Rate Premium Finance Corp 2141 Enterprise Dr PO Box 100507 *Cust Svc	Florence	SC	29501	800-777-7458*	843-669-0937	216
Prime Resources Corp 1100 Boston Ave	Bridgeport	CT	06610	800-621-5463	203-331-9100	9
Prime Therapeutics Inc 1305 Corporate Ctr Dr	Eagan	MN	55121	800-858-0723	612-777-4000	585
PrimeArray Systems Inc 127 Riverneck Rd	Chelmsford	MA	01824	800-433-5133	978-654-6250	178
PrimeConnections Contact Solutions LLC 301 Brazos St Ste 615	Austin	TX	78701	866-976-2747		396
PrimeGenesis LLC 200 W Hill Rd	Stamford	CT	06902	866-805-7777	203-323-8501	462
PrimeNet Direct Mktg Solutions LLC 7320 Bryan Dairy Rd	Largo	FL	33777	800-826-2869	727-447-6245	5
Primera Technology Inc 2 Carlson Pkwy N Ste 375	Plymouth	MN	55447	800-797-2772	763-475-6676	175-6
Primerica Financial Services 3120 Breckinridge Blvd	Duluth	GA	30099	800-257-4725	770-381-1000	401
Primeritus Financial Services Inc 440 Metroplex Dr	Nashville	TN	37211	888-833-4238		393
Primex Plastics Corp 1235 N 'F' St	Richmond	IN	47374	800-222-5116	765-966-7774	599
Primexx Energy Partners Ltd 4849 Greenville Ave Two Energy Sq Ste 1600	Dallas	TX	75206	800-754-5908	214-369-5909	535
Primitives by Kathy Inc 1817 William Penn Way	Lancaster	PA	17601	866-295-2849		294
Primm Valley Resort & Casino 31900 S Las Vegas Blvd	Primm	NV	89019	800-926-4455		667
Primo Microphones Inc 1805 Couch Dr	McKinney	TX	75069	800-767-7466	972-548-9807	51
Primorigen Biosciences Inc 510 Charmany Dr	Madison	WI	53719	866-372-7442	608-441-8332	84
Primrose Oil Company Inc 11444 Denton Dr	Dallas	TX	75229	800-275-2772	972-241-1100	540
Primrose School Franchising Co 3660 Cedarcrest Rd	Acworth	GA	30101	800-745-0677	770-529-4100	147
Primus Telecommunications (PTGi) 7901 Jones Ranch Dr Ste 900 *NYSE: PTGI*	McLean	VA	22102	866-385-3360	703-902-2800	733
Prince Albert National Park of Canada Northern Prairies Field Unit PO Box 100 *Campground Resv	Waskesiu Lake	SK	S0J2Y0	877-737-3783*	306-663-4522	562
Prince Castle Inc 355 E Kehoe Blvd	Carol Stream	IL	60188	800-722-7853	630-462-8800	299
Prince Conti Hotel 830 Conti St	New Orleans	LA	70112	800-366-2743	504-529-4172	379

Name / Address	City	State	ZIP	Toll-Free	Phone	Class
Prince Corp 8351 County Rd H	Marshfield	WI	54449	**800-777-2486**	715-384-3105	577
Prince Edward Island National Park of Canada 2 Palmers Ln *Campground Resv	Charlottetown	PE	C1A5V8	**800-663-7192***	902-672-6350	562
Prince Edward Island Tourism PO Box 2000	Charlottetown	PE	C1A7N8	**800-463-4734**	902-368-4000	772
Prince George Hotel, The 1725 Market St	Halifax	NS	B3J3N9	**800-565-1567**	902-425-1986	379
Prince Global Sports LLC 1 Advantage Ct *All	Bordentown	NJ	08505	**800-283-6647***	609-291-5800	708
Prince Lionheart Inc 2421 Westgate Rd	Santa Maria	CA	93455	**800-544-1132**	805-922-2250	63
Prince Preferred Guest Program 100 Holomoana St	Honolulu	HI	96815	**800-774-6234**		378
Prince Resorts Hawaii 100 Holomoana St	Honolulu	HI	96815	**888-977-4623**	808-956-1111	667
Prince William County-Greater Manassas Chamber of Commerce 9720 Capital Ct Ste 203	Manassas	VA	20110	**877-867-3853**	703-368-6600	138
Prince William Regional Chamber of Commerce 9720 Capital Ct Ste 203	Manassas	VA	20110	**877-867-3853**	703-368-6600	138
Princess Bayside Beach Hotel & Golf Ctr 4801 Coastal Hwy *General	Ocean City	MD	21842	**888-622-9743***	410-723-2900	379
Princess Cruises 24844 Rockefeller Ave	Santa Clarita	CA	91355	**800-774-6237**	661-753-0000	222
Princess House Inc 470 Miles Standish Blvd *Sales	Taunton	MA	02780	**800-622-0039***	508-823-0711	366
Princess Royale Oceanfront Hotel & Conference Ctr 9100 Coastal Hwy	Ocean City	MD	21842	**800-476-9253**	410-524-7777	379
Princeton Excess & Surplus Lines Insurance Co 555 College Rd E	Princeton	NJ	08543	**800-544-2378**	609-243-4200	391-4
Princeton Institute for International & Regional Studies (PIIRS) Princeton University Bendheim Hall	Princeton	NJ	08544	**888-486-3339**	609-258-4852	631
Princeton Insurance Co 746 Alexander Rd PO Box 5322	Princeton	NJ	08540	**800-334-0588**	609-452-9404	391-4
Princeton National Bancorp Inc 606 S Main St *OTC: PNBC*	Princeton	IL	61356	**888-897-2276**	309-662-4444	360-2
Princeton Packet, The 300 Witherspoon St PO Box 350	Princeton	NJ	08542	**888-747-1122**	609-924-3244	634-8
Princeton Plasma Physics Laboratory (PPPL) James Forrestal Campus Princeton University PO Box 451	Princeton	NJ	08543	**800-772-2222**	609-243-2750	666
Princeton Regional School District 25 Valley Rd Administration Bldg	Princeton	NJ	08540	**877-652-2873**	609-806-4200	683
Princeton Theological Seminary 64 Mercer St	Princeton	NJ	08540	**800-622-6767**	609-921-8300	168-3
Princeton University 33 Washington Rd	Princeton	NJ	08544	**877-609-2273**	609-258-3000	167
Princeton University Press 41 William St	Princeton	NJ	08540	**800-777-4726**	609-258-4900	634-4
Principal Financial Group Foundation Inc 711 High St	Des Moines	IA	50392	**800-986-3343**	502-855-3673	305
Principal Technical Services Inc 9960 Research Dr Ste 200	Irvine	CA	92618	**888-787-3711**		719
Principia College 13201 Clayton Rd	St. Louis	MO	63131	**800-277-4648**	618-374-2131	167
Principia Partners 604 Gordon Dr	Exton	PA	19341	**800-378-8330**		195
Principle Business Enterprises Inc PO Box 129	Dunbridge	OH	43414	**800-467-3224**	419-352-1551	557
Prinsco Inc 108 W Hwy 7 PO Box 265	Prinsburg	MN	56281	**800-992-1725**	320-222-6800	599
Print Direction Inc 1600 Indian Brook Way	Norcross	GA	30093	**877-435-1672**	770-446-6446	626
Print Magazine 10151 Carver Rd Ste 200	Blue Ash	OH	45242	**877-860-9145**	513-531-2690	456-5
Print Papa 1920 Lafayette St Ste L	Santa Clara	CA	95050	**800-657-7181**	408-567-9553	626
Print Services & Distribution Assn (PSDA) 330 N. Wabash Ave Ste 2000	Chicago	IL	60611	**800-336-4641**	800-230-0175	47-9
Print Works 3850 98 St Nw	Edmonton	AB	T6E3L2	**888-452-8921**	780-452-8921	626
Printco Graphics Inc 14112 Industrial Rd	Omaha	NE	68144	**888-593-1080**	402-593-1080	227
Printed Systems 1265 Gillingham Rd *Sales	Neenah	WI	54956	**800-352-2332***		413
PrintEdd Products of North America 2641 N Forum Dr	Grand Prairie	TX	75052	**800-367-6728**	972-660-3800	109
Printek Inc 1517 Townline Rd	Benton Harbor	MI	49022	**800-368-4636**	269-925-3200	175-6
Printers & Stationers Inc 113 N Ct St	Florence	AL	35630	**800-624-5334**	256-764-8061	534
Printfection LLC 3700 Quebec St Unit 100-136	Denver	CO	80207	**866-459-7990**		197
Printing House Ltd, The 1403 Bathurst St	Toronto	ON	M5R3H8	**800-874-0870**	416-536-6113	344
Printing Images Inc 12266 Wilkins Ave A	Rockville	MD	20852	**866-685-4356**	301-984-1140	626
Printing Industries of America/Graphic Arts Technical Foundation (PIA/GATF) 200 Deer Run Rd	Sewickley	PA	15143	**800-910-4283**	412-741-6860	48-16
Printing Prep Inc 12 E Tupper St	Buffalo	NY	14203	**877-878-7114**	716-852-5011	779
PrintingForLess.com Inc 100 PFL Way	Livingston	MT	59047	**800-930-6040**		626
Printmail Systems Inc 23 Friends Ln	Newtown	PA	18940	**800-910-4844**	215-860-4250	227
Print-O-Stat Inc 1011 W Market St	York	PA	17404	**800-711-8014**	717-854-7821	725
Print-O-Tape Inc 755 Tower Rd	Mundelein	IL	60060	**800-346-6311**	847-362-1476	413
Printpack Inc 2800 Overlook PkwyNE	Atlanta	GA	30339	**800-669-6820**	404-460-7000	547
PrintPlace.com 1130 Ave H E	Arlington	TX	76011	**877-405-3949**	817-701-3555	626
Printronix Inc 14600 Myford Rd	Irvine	CA	92606	**800-665-6210**	714-368-2300	175-6
Prior Lake-Savage Area Public School District 719 4540 Tower St SE	Prior Lake	MN	55372	**855-346-1650**	952-226-0000	683
Priority Capital Inc 174 Green St	Melrose	MA	02176	**800-761-2118**	781-321-8778	218
Priority Chevrolet of Chesapeake 1495 S Military Hwy	Chesapeake	VA	23320	**855-315-0212**	757-424-1811	56
Priority Express Courier 5 Chelsea Pkwy	Boothwyn	PA	19061	**800-526-4646**	610-364-3300	545
Priority Health 1231 E Beltline NE	Grand Rapids	MI	49525	**800-942-0954**	616-942-0954	391-3
Priority Management Systems Inc 11160 Silversmith Pl	Richmond	BC	V7A5E4	**800-437-1032**	604-214-7772	763
Priority Wire & Cable Inc PO Box 398 *General	North Little Rock	AR	72115	**800-945-5542***	501-372-5444	248
Prism Medical Ltd Unit 2 485 Millway Ave	Concord	ON	L4K3V4	**877-304-5438**	416-260-2145	475
Prism Plastics Inc 1544 Hwy 65	New Richmond	WI	54017	**877-246-7535**	715-246-7535	607
Prisma Graphic Corp 2937 E Broadway Rd	Phoenix	AZ	85040	**800-379-5777**	602-243-5777	626
PRISMHR 50 Resnik Rd Ste 200	Plymouth	MA	02360	**877-837-4311**	508-747-7261	227
Pritchett Controls Inc 6980 Muirkirk Meadows Dr	Beltsville	MD	20705	**877-743-2363**	301-470-7300	191-10
Pritchett LLC 8150 N Central Expy Ste 1350	Dallas	TX	75206	**800-992-5922**	214-239-9600	196
Pritchett Trucking Inc 1050 SE Sixth St PO Box 311	Lake Butler	FL	32054	**800-486-7504**	386-496-2630	778
Pritikin Longevity Ctr & Spa 8755 NW 36th St	Doral	FL	33178	**800-327-4914**	305-935-7131	704
Privacy & Data Security Law Resource Center 1801 S Bell St	Arlington	VA	22202	**800-372-1033**		530-7
Private Capital Management 8889 Pelican Bay Blvd Ste 500	Naples	FL	34108	**800-763-0337**	239-254-2500	790
Private Citizen Inc PO Box 233	Naperville	IL	60566	**888-382-1222**	630-393-1555	47-10
PrivateBancorp Inc 120 S LaSalle St *NASDAQ: PVTB*	Chicago	IL	60603	**800-662-7748**		360-2
Priviti Capital Corp 850 444 Fifth Ave S W	Calgary	AB	T2P2T8	**855-333-9943**	403-263-9943	527
PRL Glass Systems Inc 251 Mason Way	City Of Industry	CA	91746	**800-433-7044**	626-961-5890	193-1
PRN Health Services Inc 4321 W College Ave Ste 200	Appleton	WI	54914	**888-830-8811**		262
Pro Assurance Corp 1250 23rd St NW Ste 250	Washington	DC	20037	**800-613-3615**	202-969-1866	391-2
Pro Farmer 6612 Chancellor Dr Ste 300 *Cust Svc	Cedar Falls	IA	50613	**800-772-0023***	319-277-1278	530-13
Pro Lights & Staging News Magazine 6000 S Eastern Ste 14-J *General	Las Vegas	NV	89119	**888-667-7438***	702-932-5585	456-21
Pro Orthopedic Devices Inc 2884 E Ganley Rd	Tucson	AZ	85706	**800-523-5611**	520-294-4401	476
Pro Performance Sports LLC 2081 Faraday Ave	Carlsbad	CA	92008	**877-225-7275**		709
Pro Petroleum Inc 4985 N Sloan Ln	Las Vegas	NV	89115	**877-791-4900**		578
Pro Products LLC 7201 Engle Rd	Fort Wayne	IN	46804	**866-357-5063**	260-490-5970	804
Pro Security Group 301B S Robinson Dr	Robinson	TX	76706	**855-753-7766**	254-753-7766	691
Pro Sports Memorabilia Inc 725 Landwehr Rd	Northbrook	IL	60062	**888-950-5399**		709
Pro Star Sports Inc 1133 Winchester Ave	Kansas City	MO	64126	**800-821-8482**	816-241-9737	269
Pro Tapes & Specialties PO Box 53026	Newark	NJ	07101	**800-345-0234**	732-346-0900	729
PrO Unlimited Inc 301 Yamato Rd Ste3199	Boca Raton	FL	33431	**800-291-1099**		731
Proactive Management Consulting LLC 2700 Cumberland Pkwy SE	Atlanta	GA	30339	**877-319-2198**	770-319-7468	198
Proactive Networking 229 Marshall Rd	Platte City	MO	64079	**800-255-6863**	816-587-7878	182
Proactive Sports Inc 1200 SE Second Ave	Canby	OR	97013	**800-369-8642**	503-263-8583	709
Proair LLC 28731 County Rd 6	Elkhart	IN	46514	**800-338-8544**	574-264-5494	14
ProAssurance 20 Allen Ave Ste 430	Saint Louis	MO	63119	**800-282-6242**	314-961-7700	391-5
ProAssurance Corp 100 Brookwood Pl Ste 300 *NYSE: PRA*	Birmingham	AL	35209	**800-282-6242**	205-877-4400	360-4
Pro-cad Software Ltd 12 Elbow River Rd	Calgary	AB	T3Z2V2	**888-477-6223**	403-216-3375	179
ProCard Inc 1819 Denver W Dr Bldg 26 Ste 300	Lakewood	CO	80401	**800-469-6578**	303-279-2255	180-10
ProCare Pharmacy Benefit Manager Inc 1267 Professional Pkwy Ste 100	Gainesville	GA	30507	**888-821-5516**		807
Proceedings of the IEEE Magazine 445 Hoes Ln	Piscataway	NJ	08855	**800-678-4333**	732-562-5478	456-21
Procel Temporary Services 2447 Pacific Coast Hwy Ste 207	Hermosa Beach	CA	90254	**800-338-9905**	310-372-0560	262
Process Equipment Inc 2770 Welborn St PO Box 1607	Pelham	AL	35124	**888-663-2028**	205-663-5330	18
Process Software Corp 959 Concord St	Framingham	MA	01701	**800-722-7770**	508-879-6994	180-12
Processed Metals Innovators LLC 600 21st Ave	Bloomer	WI	54724	**888-877-7277**	715-568-1700	479

Company	Address	City	State	ZIP	Toll-Free	Phone	Class
Proco Products Inc	PO Box 590	Stockton	CA	95201	**800-344-3246**	209-943-6088	674
ProCom Inc	28838 US Hwy 69 PO Box 27	Lamoni	IA	50140	**800-433-9893**	641-784-8841	734
Procor Ltd	2001 Speers Rd	Oakville	ON	L6L2X9	**888-977-6267**	905-827-4111	266-5
Procter & Gamble Pharmaceuticals Canada Inc	PO Box 355 Stn A	Toronto	ON	M5W1C5	**800-668-0150**	416-730-4711	582
Proctor Academy	204 Main St PO Box 500	Andover	NH	03216	**800-626-4907**	603-735-6000	621
Pro-data Computer Services Inc	2809 S 160th St Ste 401	Omaha	NE	68130	**800-228-6318**	402-697-7575	177
Prodata Systems Inc	11007 Slater Ave NE	Kirkland	WA	98033	**866-582-7485**	425-296-4168	38
Prodco International Inc	9408 Boul du Golf	Montreal	QC	H1J3A1	**888-577-6326**	514-324-9796	691
Pro-Dex Inc	2361 McGaw Ave *NASDAQ: PDEX*	Irvine	CA	92614	**800-562-6204**		360-3
Prodigy Diabetes Care LLC	2701-A Hutchison McDonald Rd PO Box 481928	Charlotte	NC	28269	**800-366-5901**		475
Produce Marketing Assn (PMA)	1500 Casho Mill Rd	Newark	DE	19711	**800-660-4287**	302-738-7100	48-6
Produce Source Partners	13167 Telcourt Rd	Ashland	VA	23005	**800-344-4728**	804-262-8300	298-7
Producers Co-op Assoc	300 E Buffalo St	Girard	KS	66743	**800-442-2809**	620-724-8241	446
Producers Dairy Foods Inc	250 E Belmont Ave	Fresno	CA	93701	**800-660-1171**	559-264-6583	297-27
Producers Financial	5350 Tomah Dr Ste 3800	Colorado Springs	CO	80918	**800-985-5549**	719-535-0739	401
Producers Livestock Marketing Assn	4809 S 114th St	Omaha	NE	68137	**800-257-4046**	402-597-9189	445
Producers Peanut Company Inc	PO Box 250	Suffolk	VA	23434	**800-847-5491**	757-539-7496	297-32
Producers Rice Mill Inc	PO Box 1248	Stuttgart	AR	72160	**800-369-7675**	870-673-4444	297-23
Product Development & Management Assn (PDMA)	330 N Wabash Ave Ste 2000	Chicago	IL	60611	**800-232-5241**	312-321-5145	48-12
Product Development Corp	20 Ragsdale Dr Ste 100	Monterey	CA	93940	**800-819-6910**	831-333-1100	94
Product Safety Consulting Inc	605 Country Club Dr Ste I	Bensenville	IL	60106	**877-804-3066**	630-238-0188	198
Production Equipment Co	401 Liberty St	Meriden	CT	06450	**800-758-5697**	203-235-5795	469
Production Management Industries LLC	9761 Hwy 90 E	Morgan City	LA	70380	**888-229-3837**	985-631-3837	538
Production Press Inc	307 E Morgan St	Jacksonville	IL	62650	**800-231-3880**	217-243-3353	626
Production Products Co	6176 E Molloy Rd	East Syracuse	NY	13057	**800-800-6652**	315-431-7200	620
Production Tool Supply	8655 E Eight Mile Rd	Warren	MI	48089	**800-366-3600**	586-755-7770	385
Productive Alternatives Inc	1205 N Tower Rd	Fergus Falls	MN	56537	**800-627-3529**	218-998-5630	232
Productivity Inc	375 Bridgeport Ave 3rd Fl	Shelton	CT	06484	**800-966-5423**	203-225-0451	763
Producto Machine Co	800 Union Ave *Cust Svc	Bridgeport	CT	06607	**800-722-2606***	203-367-8675	755
Professional Assn of Diving Instructors International (PADI)	30151 Tomas St *Sales	Rancho Santa Margarita	CA	92688	**800-729-7234***	949-858-7234	47-22
Professional Assn of Innkeepers International (PAII)	108 S Cleveland St	Merrill	WI	54452	**800-468-7244**	856-310-1102	48-4
Professional Bank Services Inc	6200 Dutchmans Ln Ste 305	Louisville	KY	40205	**800-523-4778**	502-451-6633	196
Professional Beauty Assn (PBA)	15825 N 71st St Ste 100	Scottsdale	AZ	85254	**800-468-2274**	480-281-0424	48-18
Professional Bowlers Assn (PBA)	719 Second Ave Ste 701	Seattle	WA	98104	**877-910-2695**	206-332-9688	47-22
Professional Bull Riders Inc (PBR)	101 W Riverwalk	Pueblo	CO	81003	**800-366-8538**	719-242-2800	47-15
Professional Coaters Inc	100 Commerce Park Dr	Cabot	AR	72023	**800-962-0344**	501-843-7509	816
Professional Community Management Inc	23726 Birtcher Dr	Lake Forest	CA	92630	**800-369-7260**		653
Professional Convention Management Assn (PCMA)	35 E Wacker Dr Ste 500	Chicago	IL	60601	**877-827-7262**	312-423-7262	48-12
Professional Cutlery Direct LLC	242 Branford Rd	North Branford	CT	06471	**800-792-6650**		224
Professional Electric Products Co (PEPCO)	33210 Lakeland Blvd	Eastlake	OH	44095	**800-872-7000**	440-946-3790	248
Professional Liability Underwriting Society	5353 Wayzata Blvd Ste 600	Minneapolis	MN	55416	**800-845-0778**	952-746-2580	48-9
Professional Photographers of America Inc (PPA)	229 Peachtree St NE Ste 2200	Atlanta	GA	30303	**800-786-6277**	404-522-8600	47-4
Professional Picture Framers Assn (PPFA)	2282 Springport Rd Ste F	Jackson	MI	49202	**800-762-9287**	517-788-8100	47-4
Professional Research Consultants Inc	11326 P St	Omaha	NE	68137	**800-428-7455**	402-592-5656	196
Professional Service Industries Inc (PSI)	1901 S Meyers Rd Ste 400	Oakbrook Terrace	IL	60181	**800-548-7901**	630-691-1490	263
Professional Services Council (PSC)	4401 Wilson Blvd Ste 1110	Arlington	VA	22203	**800-353-9118**	703-875-8059	48-12
Professional Shorthand Reporters Inc (PSR)	601 Poydras St Ste 1615	New Orleans	LA	70130	**800-536-5255**	504-529-5255	444
Professional Software Engineering Inc	780 Lynnhaven Pkwy Ste 350	Virginia Beach	VA	23452	**800-924-1091**	757-431-2400	182
Professional Staff Management Inc	6801 Lake Plaza Dr Ste D-405	Indianapolis	IN	46220	**800-967-5515**	317-816-7007	630
Professional Tennis Registry	PO Box 4739	Hilton Head Island	SC	29938	**800-421-6289**	843-785-7244	47-22
Professional Travel Inc	25000 Great Northern Corporate Ctr Ste 170	Cleveland	OH	44070	**800-247-0060**	440-734-8800	769
Proffitt & Goodson Inc	Old Kingston Pl 4800 Old Kingston Pk Ste 200	Knoxville	TN	37919	**866-776-3355**	865-584-1850	231
Profile Bank	45 Wakefield St PO Box 1808	Rochester	NH	03866	**800-554-8969**	603-332-2610	69
Profile Food Ingredients LLC	1151 Timber Dr	Elgin	IL	60123	**877-632-1700**	847-622-1700	358
Profiles International Inc	5205 Lk Shore Dr	Waco	TX	76710	**866-751-1644**	254-751-1644	719
Profit Sharing/401(k) Council of America (PSCA)	20 N Wacker Dr Ste 3700	Chicago	IL	60606	**866-614-8407**	312-419-1863	48-12
Profitable Investing	9201 Corporate Blvd	Rockville	MD	20850	**800-219-8592**	301-250-2200	530-9
Profitsword LLC	9355 Cypress Cove Dr	Orlando	FL	32819	**866-930-6543**	407-909-8822	179
Proflowers.com	4840 Eastgate Mall	San Diego	CA	92121	**800-580-2913**		294
ProForma	8800 E Pleasant Vly Rd	Independence	OH	44131	**800-825-1525**	216-520-8400	626
Progenics Pharmaceuticals Inc	777 Old Saw Mill River Rd *NASDAQ: PGNX*	Tarrytown	NY	10591	**866-644-7188**	914-789-2800	84
Progesys Inc	4020 Blvd le Corbusier Ste 201	Laval	QC	H7L5R2	**877-274-8815**	450-667-7646	462
Program Planning Professionals	1340 Eisenhower Pl	Ann Arbor	MI	48108	**877-728-2331**	734-741-7770	196
Programmer's Paradise Inc	1157 Shrewsbury Ave Ste C	Shrewsbury	NJ	07702	**800-441-1511**	732-389-8950	176
Progress Energy Inc	410 S Wilmington St *NYSE: PGN*	Raleigh	NC	27601	**800-452-2777**	919-546-6111	360-5
Progress Instruments Inc	807 NW Commerce Dr	Lees Summit	MO	64086	**800-580-9881**	816-524-4442	624
Progress Printing Co	2677 Waterlick Rd	Lynchburg	VA	24502	**800-572-7804**		626
Progress Rail Services	1600 Progress Dr PO Box 1037	Albertville	AL	35950	**800-476-8769**	256-505-6600	684
Progress Software Corp	14 Oak Pk *NASDAQ: PRGS*	Bedford	MA	01730	**800-477-6473**	781-280-4000	180-1
Progressive Bank NA	1090 E Bethlehem Blvd	Wheeling	WV	26003	**866-235-1923**	304-238-0040	69
Progressive Casualty Insurance Co	6300 Wilson Mills Rd Campus E	Mayfield Village	OH	44143	**800-776-4737**	440-461-5000	391-4
Progressive Communications Corp	18 E Vine St PO Box 791	Mount Vernon	OH	43050	**800-772-5333**	740-397-5333	634-8
Progressive Employer Services	6407 Parkland Dr	Sarasota	FL	34243	**888-925-2990**	941-925-2990	630
Progressive Impressions	1 Hardman Dr	Bloomington	IL	61701	**800-644-0444**	309-664-0444	634-9
Progressive Mktg Products Inc	3130 E Miraloma Ave	Anaheim	CA	92806	**800-368-9700**	714-632-7100	196
Progressive National Baptist Convention Inc (PNBC)	601 50th St NE	Washington	DC	20019	**800-876-7622**	202-396-0558	47-20
Progressive Plastics Inc	14801 Emery Ave	Cleveland	OH	44135	**800-252-0053**	216-252-5595	97
Progressive Produce Co	5790 Peachtree St	Los Angeles	CA	90040	**800-900-0757**	323-890-8100	298-7
Project Concern International (PCI)	5151 Murphy Canyon Rd Ste 320	San Diego	CA	92123	**877-724-4673**	858-279-9690	47-5
Project Consulting Services Inc	3300 W Esplanade Ave S Ste 500	Metairie	LA	70002	**855-468-7473**	504-833-5321	198
Project Inform	273 Ninth St	San Francisco	CA	94103	**877-435-7443**	415-558-8669	47-17
Project Lifesaver International Headquarters	815 Battlefield Blvd S	Chesapeake	VA	23322	**877-580-5433**	757-546-5502	136
Project Management Institute (PMI)	14 Campus Blvd	Newtown Square	PA	19073	**866-276-4764**	610-356-4600	48-12
Project Safe Neighborhoods *Office of Justice Programs*	810 Seventh St NW	Washington	DC	20531	**888-744-6513**	202-616-6500	199
Project Vote	1350 I St NW Ste 1250	Washington	DC	20005	**888-546-4173**	202-546-4173	47-7
Projection Presentation Technology	5803 Rolling Rd	Springfield	VA	22152	**800-377-7650**	703-912-1334	266-2
Projections Unlimited Inc	15311 Varrenca Pkwy *Cust Svc	Irvine	CA	92618	**800-551-4405***	714-544-2700	248
Prolab Nutrition	21411 Prairie St	Chatsworth	CA	91311	**800-776-5221**	818-739-6000	797
Prolamina Corp	840 S Waukegan Rd Ste 208	Lake Forest	IL	60045	**877-536-2628**		600
Prolifics	5 Hanover Sqr Ste 2001	New York	NY	10004	**800-458-3313**	212-267-7722	180-2
ProLiteracy Worldwide	1320 Jamesville Ave	Syracuse	NY	13210	**800-448-8878**	315-422-9121	47-5
ProLogis	4545 Airport Way *NYSE: PLD*	Denver	CO	80239	**800-566-2706**	303-375-9292	653
Prolon Inc	305 Industrial Ave	Port Gibson	MS	39150	**800-628-7749**	601-437-4211	606
Pro-mail Associates Inc	22404 66th Ave S	Kent	WA	98032	**855-867-5081**	206-282-2400	197
Promark Technology Inc	10900 Pump House Rd Ste B	Annapolis Junction	MD	20701	**800-634-0255**	240-280-8030	176
ProMedica	2142 N Cove Blvd	Toledo	OH	43606	**866-865-4677**	419-291-5437	374-3
Promedica Inc	114 Douglas Rd E	Oldsmar	FL	34677	**800-899-5278**	813-854-1905	475
Promega Corp	2800 Woods Hollow Rd	Madison	WI	53711	**800-356-9526**	608-274-4330	233
Promera Health	61 accord park dr	Norwell	MA	02061	**888-878-9058**		363

Company / Address	City	State	ZIP	Toll-Free	Phone	Class
Prometheus Laboratories Inc 9410 Carroll Pk Dr	San Diego	CA	92121	888-892-8391		582
Prometric 1501 S Clinton St	Baltimore	MD	21224	866-776-6387	443-455-8000	246
Promiles Software Development 1900 Texas Ave	Bridge City	TX	77611	800-324-8588		179
Promise Keepers (PK) PO Box 11798	Denver	CO	80211	866-776-6473		47-20
Promise Technology Inc 580 Cottonwood Dr *Sales	Milpitas	CA	95035	800-888-0245*	408-228-1400	624
Promium LLC 3350 Monte Villa Pkwy Ste 220	Bothell	WA	98021	877-776-6486	425-286-9200	179
Promodel Corp 3400 Bath Pike Ste 200	Bethlehem	PA	18017	888-900-3090	801-223-4600	180-10
Promotional Products Assn International (PPAI) 3125 Skyway Cir N	Irving	TX	75038	888-426-7724	972-252-0404	48-18
Promotions Unlimited 7601 Durand Ave	Sturtevant	WI	53177	800-992-9307	262-681-7000	5
Prompton State Park c/o Lackawanna	North Abington Township	PA	18414	888-727-2757	570-945-3239	564
ProMutual Group 13th Fl 4th Fl	Boston	MA	02111	800-225-6168		391-5
Pronk Technologies Inc 8933 Lankershim Blvd	Sun Valley	CA	91352	800-609-9802	818-768-5600	475
ProPacificfresh 70 Pepsi Way PO Box 1069	Durham	CA	95938	888-232-0908	530-893-0596	298-7
Propak Systems Ltd 440 East Lk Rd NE	Airdrie	AB	T4A2J8	800-408-4434	403-912-7000	263
Property Damage Appraisers Inc (PDA) 6100 SW Blvd Ste 200	Fort Worth	TX	76109	800-749-7324		311
Property Loss Research Bureau (PLRB) 3025 Highland Pkwy Ste 800	Downers Grove	IL	60515	888-711-7572	630-724-2200	48-9
Property Owners Exchange Inc 6630 Baltimore National Pk Ste 208	Catonsville	MD	21228	800-869-3200	410-719-0100	632
Property Panorama Inc 9475 Pinecone Dr	Mentor	OH	44060	877-299-6306	440-290-2200	179
Property-Owners Insurance Co PO Box 30660	Lansing	MI	48909	800-288-8740	517-323-1200	391-2
Propet USA Inc 2415 W Valley Hwy N	Auburn	WA	98001	800-877-6738	253-854-7600	302
ProPhase Labs Inc 621 Shady Retreat Rd *NASDAQ: PRPH*	Doylestown	PA	18901	800-505-2653	215-345-0919	582
ProPhotonix Inc 32 Hampshire Rd *OTC: STKR*	Salem	NH	03079	877-941-8631	603-893-8778	543
Propper Mfg Company Inc 36-04 Skillman Ave *Cust Svc	Long Island	NY	11101	800-832-4300*	718-392-6650	475
Proserv Anchor Crane Group 455 Aldine Bender PO Box 670965	Houston	TX	77060	800-835-2223	281-405-9048	469
Proshot Concrete Inc 4158 Musgrove Dr	Florence	AL	35630	800-633-3141	256-764-5941	191-3
Proskauer Rose LLP 1585 Broadway	New York	NY	10036	866-444-3272	212-969-3000	428
Prosoco Inc 3741 Greenway Cir	Lawrence	KS	66046	800-255-4255		150
Prosource Fitness Equipment 6503 Hilburn Dr	Raleigh	NC	27613	877-781-8077	919-781-8077	626
ProSource Solutions LLC 4199 Kinross Lakes Pkwy Ste 150	Richfield	OH	44286	866-549-0279		198
Prospect Medical Holdings Inc 10780 Santa Monica Blvd Ste 400	Los Angeles	CA	90025	800-708-3230	310-943-4500	462
Prospectr Marketing 3508 W 22nd St	Minneapolis	MN	55416	800-908-3523		5
Prospects Influential Inc 3888 Sound Way	Bellingham	WA	98227	888-982-0766		7
Prosperity Bancshares Inc 1301 N Mechanic *NYSE: PB*	El Campo	TX	77437	800-862-9098	979-543-1426	360-2
Prostar Computer Inc 837 Lawson St	City of Industry	CA	91748	888-576-4742	626-839-6472	176
Prosthetic Design Inc 700 Harco Dr	Clayton	OH	45315	800-459-0177	937-836-1464	476
Prostrollo Motor Sales Inc 500 Fourth St NE	Huron	SD	57350	866-466-4515		56
Prosum technology services 2201 Park Pl Ste 102	El Segundo	CA	90245	888-477-6786	310-426-0600	38
Pro-tech Security Sales 1313 W Bagley Rd	Berea	OH	44017	800-888-4002	440-239-0100	239
Protech Systems Group 3350 Players Club Pkwy	Memphis	TN	38125	800-459-5100	901-767-7550	179
Protect-All Inc 109 Badger Pkwy	Darien	WI	53114	888-432-8526		553
Protected Investors of America Inc 235 Montgomery St Ste 1050	San Francisco	CA	94104	800-786-2559		196
protection One Alarm Monitoring 1035 N Third St Ste 101	Lawrence	KS	66044	800-438-4357	877-776-1911	690
Protection Services Inc 635 Lucknow Rd	Harrisburg	PA	17110	866-489-1234	717-236-9307	699
Protective Insurance Co 111 Congressional Blvd Ste 500	Carmel	IN	46032	800-644-5501		391-5
Protective Life Corp 2801 Hwy 280 S *NYSE: PL*	Birmingham	AL	35223	800-333-3418	205-268-1000	360-4
Protectoseal Co 225 W Foster Ave	Bensenville	IL	60106	800-323-2268	630-595-0800	123
Protein Sciences Corp 1000 Research Pkwy	Meriden	CT	06450	800-488-7099	203-686-0800	84
Protek Cargo 1568 Airport Blvd.	Napa	CA	94558	800-439-1426	707-254-9627	709
Protel Inc 4150 Kidron Rd	Lakeland	FL	33811	800-925-8882	863-644-5558	732
Protestant Episcopal Theological Seminary in Virginia 3737 Seminary Rd	Alexandria	VA	22304	800-941-0083	703-370-6600	168-3
Proteus Inc 1830 N Dinuba Blvd	Visalia	CA	93291	888-776-9998	559-733-5423	683
Protide Pharmaceuticals Inc 505 Oakwood Rd Ste 200	Lake Zurich	IL	60047	800-552-3569	847-726-3100	582
Protocol Driven Healthcare Inc 40 Morristown Rd Ste 2D	Bernardsville	NJ	07924	888-816-4006	515-277-1376	462
Protocol Networks Inc 15 Shore Dr	Johnston	RI	02919	877-676-0146		182
Protogate Inc 12225 World Trade Dr	San Diego	CA	92128	877-473-0190	858-451-0865	227
ProtoSource Network 2511 W Shaw Ave Ste 102	Fresno	CA	93711	866-490-8600		398
Protravel International Inc 515 Madison Ave 10th Fl	New York	NY	10022	800-227-1059	212-755-4550	769
Provantage Corp 7249 Whipple Ave NW	North Canton	OH	44720	800-336-1166	330-494-8715	176
Provell Inc 855 Village Center Drive Ste 116	North Oaks	MN	55127	800-624-2946	952-258-2000	462
Provia Door Inc 2150 SR- 39 *General	Sugarcreek	OH	44681	800-669-4711*	330-852-4711	237
Provide Commerce Inc 4840 Eastgate Mall *Cust Svc	San Diego	CA	92121	800-776-3569*	858-729-2800	294
Providence & Worcester Railroad Co 75 Hammond St *NASDAQ: PWX*	Worcester	MA	01610	877-373-6374	508-755-4000	646
Providence Biltmore Hotel 11 Dorrance St	Providence	RI	02903	800-294-7709		379
Providence Centralia Hospital 914 S Scheuber Rd *Help Line	Centralia	WA	98531	877-736-2803*	360-736-2803	374-3
Providence College 1 Cunningham Sq *Admissions	Providence	RI	02918	800-721-6444*	401-865-1000	167
Providence College & Seminary 10 College Crescent	Otterburne	MB	R0A1G0	800-668-7768	204-433-7488	168-3
Providence Health & Services (JWCI) 2200 Santa Monica Blvd	Santa Monica	CA	90404	800-262-6259	310-582-7450	666
Providence Homes Inc 4901 Belfort Rd Ste 140	Jacksonville	FL	32256	866-836-0981	904-262-9898	189
Providence Hospice of Seattle 425 Pontius Ave N Ste 300	Seattle	WA	98109	888-782-4445	206-320-4000	371
Providence Hospitals 2435 Forest Dr	Columbia	SC	29204	877-256-5381	803-256-5300	374-3
Providence Journal 75 Fountain St	Providence	RI	02902	888-697-7656	401-277-7303	531-2
Providence Life Services 18601 N Creek Dr	Tinley Park	IL	60477	800-509-2800	708-342-8100	670
Providence Medford Medical Ctr 1111 Crater Lk Ave	Medford	OR	97504	877-541-0588	541-732-5000	374-3
Providence Medical Ctr 8929 Parallel Pkwy	Kansas City	KS	66112	800-281-7777	913-596-4000	374-3
Providence Mountains State Recreation Area 1416 Ninth St	Sacramento	CA	95814	800-777-0369		564
Providence Mutual Fire Insurance Co 340 E Ave	Warwick	RI	02886	877-763-1800	401-827-1800	391-4
Providence Portland Medical Ctr 4805 NE Glisan St	Portland	OR	97213	800-833-8899	503-215-1111	374-3
Providence Sacred Heart Medical Ctr 101 W Eigth Ave	Spokane	WA	99204	800-442-8534	509-474-3170	374-3
Providence Saint Peter Hospital (PSPH) 413 Lilly Rd NE	Olympia	WA	98506	888-492-9480	360-491-9480	374-3
Providence Saint Vincent Medical Ctr 9205 SW Barnes Rd Ste 20	Portland	OR	97225	800-677-6752	503-216-2401	374-3
Providence Service Corp 64 E Broadway *NASDAQ: PRSC*	Tucson	AZ	85701	800-747-6950	520-748-7108	461
Providence Sound Home Care & Hospice 3432 S Bay Rd NE	Olympia	WA	98506	800-869-7062	360-459-8311	371
Providence St Mary Medical Ctr 401 W Poplar St PO Box 1477	Walla Walla	WA	99362	877-215-7833	509-525-3320	374-3
Providence Warwick Convention & Visitors Bureau 10 Memorial Blvd	Providence	RI	02903	800-233-1636	401-456-0200	208
Provident Bank 3756 Central Ave *NASDAQ: PROV*	Riverside	CA	92506	800-442-5201	951-686-6060	360-2
Provident Central Credit Union 303 Twin Dolphin Dr	Redwood City	CA	94065	800-632-4600	650-508-0300	221
Provident Savings Bank FSB 3756 Central Ave	Riverside	CA	92506	800-442-5201	951-686-6060	69
Provident Travel 11309 Montgomery Rd	Cincinnati	OH	45249	800-354-8108	513-247-1100	384
Providge Consulting LLC 2207 Concord Pike Ste 537	Wilimington	DE	19803	888-927-6583		179
Provimi North America Inc 10 Collective Way	Brookville	OH	45309	888-522-2420	937-770-2400	446
Provision Ministry Group PO Box 19700	Irvine	CA	92623	800-233-3880		683
Provista Diagnostics Inc 17301 N Perimeter Dr	Scottsdale	AZ	85255	855-552-7439		740
Provo City Library 550 N University Ave	Provo	UT	84601	800-914-8931	801-852-6650	434-3
Proxim Wireless Corp 1561 Buckeye Dr *OTC: PRXM*	Milpitas	CA	95035	800-229-1630	408-383-7600	732
Proximity Hotel 704 Green Vly Rd	Greensboro	NC	27408	800-379-8200	336-379-8200	131
Proximo Consulting Services Inc 2500 Plz Five	Jersey City	NJ	07311	800-236-9250		179
Prozyme Inc 3832 Bay Ctr Pl	Hayward	CA	94545	800-457-9444	510-638-6900	233
PRSA (Public Relations Society of America) 33 Maiden Ln 11th Fl	New York	NY	10038	800-350-0111	212-460-1400	48-18

Name / Address	City	State	ZIP	Toll-Free	Phone	Class
Prudential Financial Inc						
751 Broad St	Newark	NJ	07102	**800-843-7625**	973-802-6000	401
NYSE: PRU						
Prudential Overall Supply						
PO Box 11210	Santa Ana	CA	92711	**800-767-5536**	949-250-4855	442
Prudential Savings Bank						
1834 W Oregon Ave	Philadelphia	PA	19145	**800-554-8969**	215-755-1500	69
Prym-Dritz Corp						
950 Brisack Rd	Spartanburg	SC	29303	**800-255-7796***	864-576-5050	593
*Cust Svc						
Pryor Products						
1819 Peacock Blvd	Oceanside	CA	92056	**800-854-2280**	760-724-8244	475
PS Business Parks Inc						
701 Western Ave	Glendale	CA	91201	**888-782-6110***	818-244-8080	653
NYSE: PSB ■ *Cust Svc						
PS Energy Group Inc						
2987 Clairmont Rd Ste 500	Atlanta	GA	30329	**800-334-7548**	404-321-5711	785
PSA Airlines Inc						
3400 Terminal Dr	Vandalia	OH	45377	**800-235-0986***	937-665-2876	25
*Resv						
PSB (Peoples Savings Bank)						
414 N Adams PO Box 248	Wellsburg	IA	50680	**877-493-3799**	641-869-3721	69
PSB Industries Inc						
PO Box 1318	Erie	PA	16512	**800-829-1119**	814-453-3651	386
PSC (Professional Services Council)						
4401 Wilson Blvd Ste 1110	Arlington	VA	22203	**800-353-9118**	703-875-8059	48-12
PSC						
5151 San Felipe Ste 1100	Houston	TX	77056	**800-726-1300**		194
PSCA (Profit Sharing/401(k) Council of America)						
20 N Wacker Dr Ste 3700	Chicago	IL	60606	**866-614-8407**	312-419-1863	48-12
PSDA (Print Services & Distribution Assn)						
330 N. Wabash Ave Ste 2000	Chicago	IL	60611	**800-336-4641**	800-230-0175	47-9
PSE (Pi Sigma Epsilon)						
3747 S Howell Ave	Milwaukee	WI	53207	**800-761-9350**	414-328-1952	47-16
PSEG Power LLC						
80 Pk Plz	Newark	NJ	07101	**800-436-7734**	973-430-7000	785
PSF Industries Inc						
65 S Horton St	Seattle	WA	98134	**800-426-1204***	206-622-1252	191-10
*General						
PSI (Pet Sitters International)						
201 E King St	King	NC	27021	**800-576-4229**	336-983-9222	47-3
PSI (Professional Service Industries Inc)						
1901 S Meyers Rd						
Ste 400	Oakbrook Terrace	IL	60181	**800-548-7901**	630-691-1490	263
PSI Upsilon Fraternity						
3003 E 96th St	Indianapolis	IN	46240	**800-394-1833**	317-571-1833	47-16
PSL (Peach State Labs Inc)						
180 Burlington Rd PO Box 1087	Rome	GA	30162	**800-634-1653**	706-291-8743	144
PSPH (Providence Saint Peter Hospital)						
413 Lilly Rd NE	Olympia	WA	98506	**888-492-9480**	360-491-9480	374-3
PSR (Physicians for Social Responsibility)						
1875 Connecticut Ave NW						
Ste 1012	Washington	DC	20009	**800-459-1887**	202-667-4260	48-8
PSR (Professional Shorthand Reporters Inc)						
601 Poydras St Ste 1615	New Orleans	LA	70130	**800-536-5255**	504-529-5255	444
Psychemedics Corp						
125 Nagog Pk Ste 200	Acton	MA	01720	**800-628-8073**	978-206-8220	84
NASDAQ: PMD						
Psychiatric Institute of Washington						
4228 Wisconsin Ave NW	Washington	DC	20016	**800-369-2273**	202-885-5600	374-5
Psychology Today Magazine						
115 E 23 St 9th Fl	New York	NY	10010	**800-931-2237**	212-260-7210	456-11
Psychotherapy Networker						
5135 MacArthur Blvd NW	Washington	DC	20016	**888-851-9498**	202-537-8950	456-16
PsyMax Solutions LLC						
25550 Chagrin Blvd Ste 100	Cleveland	OH	44122	**866-774-2273**	216-896-9991	196
PTC (Paternity Testing Corp)						
300 Portland St	Columbia	MO	65201	**888-837-8323**	573-442-9948	417
PTC (Parametric Technology Corp)						
140 Kendrick St	Needham	MA	02494	**800-613-7535**	781-370-5000	180-5
NASDAQ: PTC						
Ptc Select LLC						
2450 N Knoxville Ave	Peoria	IL	61604	**800-225-2320**	309-685-8400	177
PTGi (Primus Telecommunications)						
7901 Jones Ranch Dr Ste 900	McLean	VA	22102	**866-385-3360**	703-902-2800	733
NYSE: PTGI						
PTI (Pittsburgh Technical Institute)						
1111 McKee Rd	Oakdale	PA	15071	**800-784-9675**	412-809-5100	798
PTI Technologies Inc						
501 Del Norte Blvd	Oxnard	CA	93030	**800-331-2701**	805-604-3700	386
PTR Baler & Compactor Co						
2207 E Ontario St	Philadelphia	PA	19134	**800-523-3654**	215-533-5100	469
PTSI (Panhandle Telecommunication Systems Inc)						
2222 NW Hwy	Guymon	OK	73942	**800-562-2556**	580-338-2556	733
Pubco Corp						
3830 Kelley Ave	Cleveland	OH	44114	**800-878-3399**	216-881-5300	110
Public Agenda						
6 E 39th St	New York	NY	10016	**800-659-4044**	212-686-6610	631
Public Belt Railroad Commission						
4822 Tchoupitulas St	New Orleans	LA	70115	**800-524-3421***	504-896-7410	649
*Cust Svc						
Public Broadcasting Council of Central New York						
506 Old Liverpool Rd						
PO Box 2400	Syracuse	NY	13220	**800-451-9269**	315-453-2424	629
Public Broadcasting Northwest Pennsylvania						
8425 Peach St	Erie	PA	16509	**800-727-8854**	814-864-3001	629
Public Broadcasting Service (PBS)						
2100 Crystal Dr	Arlington	VA	22202	**866-864-0828**	703-739-5000	737
Public Consulting Group Inc						
148 State St	Boston	MA	02109	**800-210-6113**		196
Public Employee Magazine						
1625 L St NW	Washington	DC	20036	**800-792-0045**	202-429-1130	456-12
Public Health Institute						
555 12th St 10th Fl	Oakland	CA	94607	**866-632-9992**	510-285-5500	47-17
Public Lands Foundation (PLF)						
PO Box 7226	Arlington	VA	22207	**866-985-9636**	703-790-1988	47-13
Public Library Assn (PLA)						
50 E Huron St	Chicago	IL	60611	**800-545-2433**	312-280-5752	48-11
Public Radio 89.5						
800 Tucker Dr	Tulsa	OK	74104	**888-594-5947**	918-631-2577	642-126
Public Relations Society of America (PRSA)						
33 Maiden Ln 11th Fl	New York	NY	10038	**800-350-0111**	212-460-1400	48-18
Public Service Enterprise Group Inc						
80 Pk Plz	Newark	NJ	07102	**800-436-7734***	973-430-7000	360-5
NYSE: PEG ■ *Cust Svc						
Public Service of New Hampshire						
780 N Commercial St	Manchester	NH	03105	**800-662-7764**	603-669-4000	785
Public Storage Inc						
701 Western Ave	Glendale	CA	91201	**800-567-0759***	818-244-8080	801-3
NYSE: PSA ■ *Cust Svc						
Public Technology Inc						
1420 Prince St Ste 200	Alexandria	VA	22314	**866-664-6368**	202-626-2400	48-7
Public Welfare Foundation						
1200 U St NW	Washington	DC	20009	**800-275-7934**	202-965-1800	306
Public Works Commission of The City of Fayetteville North Carolina						
955 Old Wilmington Rd						
PO Box 1089	Fayetteville	NC	28301	**877-687-7921**	910-483-1382	785
Publication Printers Corp						
2001 S Platte River Dr	Denver	CO	80223	**888-824-0303**	303-936-0303	626
Publications & Communications Inc						
13552 Hwy 183 N Ste A	Austin	TX	78750	**800-678-9724**	512-250-9023	634-9
Publications International Ltd						
7373 N Cicero Ave	Lincolnwood	IL	60712	**800-777-5582***	847-676-3470	634-2
*General						
Publick House Historic Resort						
277 Main St Rt 131	Sturbridge	MA	01566	**800-782-5425***	508-347-3313	379
*Cust Svc						
Publishers Press Inc						
100 Frank E Simon Ave	Shepherdsville	KY	40165	**800-627-5801**	502-955-6526	625
Publishers' Warehouse						
2700 Crestwood Blvd	Irondale	AL	35210	**800-653-2726**	205-956-2078	94
Publix Super Markets Inc						
3300 Publix Corporate Pkwy	Lakeland	FL	33811	**800-242-1227***	863-688-1188	345
*PR						
PubMed						
US National Library of Medicine						
8600 Rockville Pike	Bethesda	MD	20894	**888-346-3656**		356
Pucel Enterprises Inc						
1440 E 36th St	Cleveland	OH	44114	**800-336-4986**	216-881-4604	469
Pueblo Bonito Hotels & Resorts						
4350 La Jolla Village Dr	San Diego	CA	92122	**800-990-8250**	858-642-2050	378
Pueblo Chieftain						
825 W Sixth St PO Box 440	Pueblo	CO	81003	**800-279-6397**	719-544-3520	531-2
Pueblo Community College						
900 W Orman Ave	Pueblo	CO	81004	**888-642-6017**	719-549-3200	161
Pueblo Grande Museum & Archaeological Park						
4619 E Washington St	Phoenix	AZ	85034	**877-706-4408**	602-495-0901	519
Puerto Rico Convention Bureau						
100 Convention Blvd	San Juan	PR	00907	**800-875-4765**	787-725-2110	208
Puerto Rico Farm Credit Aca						
PO Box 363649	San Juan	PR	00936	**800-981-3323**	787-753-0579	218
Puerto Rico Tourism Co						
Paseo La Princesa	Old San Juan	PR	00902	**800-866-7827**	787-721-2400	773
Puffin Inn						
4400 SpenaRd Rd	Anchorage	AK	99517	**800-478-3346**	907-243-4044	379
Puget Sound Blood Ctr						
921 Terry Ave	Seattle	WA	98104	**800-366-2831**	206-292-6500	88
Puget Sound Educational Service District						
800 Oakesdale Ave SW	Renton	WA	98057	**800-664-4549**	425-917-7600	683
Puget Sound Energy Inc						
10885 NE Fourth St	Bellevue	WA	98004	**888-225-5773**	425-452-1234	785
Puget Sound Rope Corp						
1012 Second St	Anacortes	WA	98221	**888-525-8488**	360-293-8488	210
Pulaski County						
100 N Main St Ste 202	Somerset	KY	42501	**877-655-7154**	606-678-4853	338
Pulaski County Chamber of Commerce						
4440 Cleburne Blvd Ste B	Dublin	VA	24084	**866-256-8864**	540-674-1991	138
Pulaski Financial Corp						
12300 Olive Blvd	Saint Louis	MO	63141	**888-649-3320**	314-878-2210	360-2
NASDAQ: PULB						
Pullman Chamber of Commerce						
415 N Grand Ave	Pullman	WA	99163	**800-365-6948**	509-334-3565	138
PULSE						
1301 McKinney St Ste 2500	Houston	TX	77010	**800-420-2122**	713-223-1400	68
Pulse Communications Inc						
2900 Towerview Rd	Herndon	VA	20171	**800-381-1997***	703-471-2900	732
*Cust Svc						
Puma North America Inc						
10 Lyberty Way	Westford	MA	01886	**888-565-7862***	978-698-1000	302
*General						
Punch & Associates Inc						
3601 W 76th St Ste 225	Edina	MN	55435	**800-241-5552**	952-224-4350	527
Punchbowl Inc						
50 Speen St Ste 202	Framingham	MA	01701	**877-570-4340**	508-589-4486	106
Purafil Inc						
2654 Weaver Way	Doraville	GA	30340	**800-222-6367**	770-662-8545	18
Purchase College						
735 Anderson Hill Rd	Purchase	NY	10577	**800-553-8118**	914-251-6000	167
Purchasing Magazine						
225 Wyman St	Waltham	MA	02451	**888-393-5000**		456-5
Purdue Pharma						
575 Granite Ct	Pickering	ON	L1W3W8	**800-387-5349**	905-420-6400	233
Purdue University						
Calumet 2200 169th St	Hammond	IN	46323	**800-447-8738**	219-989-2400	167
Purdue University Press						
504 W State St Stewart Ctr 370	West Lafayette	IN	47907	**800-247-6553***	765-494-2038	634-4
*Orders						
Purdy Corp						
101 Prospect Ave	Cleveland	OH	44115	**800-547-0780**		350
Pure & Secure LLC						
4120 NW 44th St	Lincoln	NE	68524	**800-875-5915***	402-467-9300	804
*Cust Svc						
Pure Auto LLC						
164 Market St Ste 250	Charleston	SC	29401	**877-860-7873**		387
PURE Storage Inc						
650 Castro St Ste 400	Mountain View	CA	94041	**800-379-7873**	650-290-6088	175-8

Company / Address	City	State	ZIP	Toll-Free	Phone	Class
Pure-Flo Water Co 7737 Mission Gorge Rd *Cust Svc	Santee	CA	92071	800-787-3356*	619-448-5120	803
Puregas LLC 226 Commerce St	Broomfield	CO	80020	800-521-5351	303-427-3700	110
PureWorks Inc 5000 Meridian Blvd Ste 600	Franklin	TN	37067	888-202-3016	615-367-4404	38
Puritan of Cape Cod 408 Main St	Hyannis	MA	02601	800-924-0606	508-775-2400	156-2
PuriTec 4705 S Durango Dr Ste 100-102	Las Vegas	NV	89147	888-491-4100	610-268-5420	17
Purity Wholesale Grocers Inc 5400 Broken Sound Blvd NW	Boca Raton	FL	33487	800-323-6838	561-994-9360	298-8
Purnell School 51 Pottersville Rd PO Box 500	Pottersville	NJ	07979	800-228-9290	908-439-2154	621
Purolator Inc 5995 Avebury Rd	Mississauga	ON	L5R3T8	888-744-7123	905-712-8101	545
Purple Communications Inc 595 Menlo Dr	Rocklin	CA	95765	800-900-9478		387
Pursuit Boats 3901 St Lucie Blvd	Fort Pierce	FL	34946	800-947-8778	772-465-6006	89
Pursuit Group, The 2528 Wembley Ter N	Toledo	OH	43617	866-478-7783		197
Purves & Assoc Insurance 500 Fourth St	Davis	CA	95616	800-681-2025	530-756-5561	390
Putman Media Inc 555 W Pierce Rd	Itasca	IL	60143	866-666-6033	630-467-1301	634-9
Putnam Bank 40 Main St PO Box 151	Putnam	CT	06260	877-275-3342	860-928-6501	69
Putnam County 130 Orie Griffin Blvd PO Box 1578	Palatka	FL	32177	800-426-9975	386-329-0800	338
Putnam Family of Funds PO Box 41203	Providence	RI	02940	800-225-1581		527
Putnam Investments 30 Dan Rd PO Box 8383	Canton	MA	02021	888-478-8626	617-292-1000	401
Putnam Lexus 390 Convention Way	Redwood City	CA	94063	888-231-8005	650-363-8500	56
Putnam Valley School District Inc 146 Peekskill Hollow Rd	Putnam Valley	NY	10579	800-666-5327	845-528-8143	683
Putney Inc 1 Monument Sq Ste 400	Portland	ME	04101	866-683-0660	207-828-0880	240
Putney School 418 Houghton Brook Rd	Putney	VT	05346	800-999-9080	802-387-5566	621
Putzmeister America 1733 90th St	Sturtevant	WI	53177	800-553-3414		192
Puyallup Public Library 324 S Meridian	Puyallup	WA	98371	866-862-4232	253-841-5454	434-3
PVA (Passenger Vessel Assn) 103 Oronoco St Ste 200	Alexandria	VA	22314	800-807-8360	703-518-5005	48-21
PVA Consulting Group Inc 20865 Ch de la Cote Nord Ste 200	Boisbriand	QC	J7E4H5	877-970-1970	450-970-1970	462
PVA Tepla America Inc 251 Corporate Terr *Sales	Corona	CA	92879	800-527-5667*	951-371-2500	205
PVG Asset Management Corp 24918 Genesee Trl Rd	Golden	CO	80401	800-777-0818	303-526-0548	401
PVI Industries LLC 3209 Galvez Ave PO Box 7124	Fort Worth	TX	76111	800-784-8326	817-335-9531	90
PVS Chemicals Inc 10900 Harper Ave	Detroit	MI	48213	800-932-8860	313-921-1200	144
PVT (Penasco Valley Telecommunications) 4011 W Main St	Artesia	NM	88210	800-505-4844		733
PW Minor & Son Inc 3 Tread Easy Ave	Batavia	NY	14020	800-333-4067	585-343-1500	302
PW Stephens Inc 15201 Pipeline Ln Unit B	Huntington Beach	CA	92649	800-750-7733	714-892-2028	665
PWH (Palms West Hospital) 13001 Southern Blvd	Loxahatchee	FL	33470	877-549-9337	561-798-3300	374-3
PWP (Pentwater Wire Products Inc) 474 Carroll St PO Box 947	Pentwater	MI	49449	877-869-6911	231-869-6911	288
PWR LLC 6402 Deere Rd	Syracuse	NY	13206	800-342-0878	315-701-0210	765
Pybus Point Lodge PO Box 33497	Juneau	AK	99803	800-947-9287	907-790-4866	667
Pyramid Consulting Inc 11100 Atlantis Pl	Alpharetta	GA	30022	877-248-0024	678-514-3500	227
Pyramid Interiors Distributors Inc PO Box 181058	Memphis	TN	38181	800-456-0592	901-375-4197	193-3
Pyramid Point Post-Acute Rehabilitation Ctr 8530 Township Line Rd	Indianapolis	IN	46260	800-861-0086	317-876-9955	449
Pyronics Inc 17700 Miles Rd	Cleveland	OH	44128	800-883-9218	216-662-8800	319

Q

Company / Address	City	State	ZIP	Toll-Free	Phone	Class
Q Center 1405 N Fifth Ave	Saint Charles	IL	60174	877-774-4627	630-377-3100	31
QACVB (Quincy Area Convention & Visitors Bureau) 532 Gardner Expy	Quincy	IL	62301	800-978-4748	217-214-3700	208
Qantas Airways Cargo 6555 W Imperial Hwy *General	Los Angeles	CA	90045	800-227-0290*	310-665-2280	12
Qantas Airways Ltd 6080 Ctr Dr Ste 400	Los Angeles	CA	90045	800-227-4500	310-726-1400	25
QBE Holdings Inc Wall St Plz 88 Pine St	New York	NY	10005	800-362-5448	212-422-1212	391-4
QC Holdings Inc 9401 Indian Creek Pkwy Ste 1500 *NASDAQ: QCCO*	Overland Park	KS	66210	866-660-2243		140
QCI Asset Management 40A Grove St	Pittsford	NY	14534	800-836-3960	585-218-2060	401
QCSS Inc 21925 Field Pkwy Ste 210	Deer Park	IL	60010	888-229-7046	847-229-7046	318
QED Inc 1661 W Third Ave	Denver	CO	80223	800-700-5011	303-825-5011	248
QEP Co Inc 1001 Broken Sound Pkwy NW Ste A *OTC: QEPC* ■ *Sales	Boca Raton	FL	33487	800-777-8665*	561-994-5550	756
QHR Corp 1620 Dickson Ave Ste 300	Kelowna	BC	V1Y9Y2	855-550-5004	250-448-7095	179
Qivana 5255 Edgewood Dr	Provo	UT	84604	888-874-8262		366
QlikTech International AB 150 N Radnor Chester Rd Ste E220 *NASDAQ: QLIK*	Radnor	PA	19087	888-828-9768		180-10
QLogic Corp 26650 Aliso Viejo Pkwy *NASDAQ: QLGC*	Aliso Viejo	CA	92656	800-662-4471	949-389-6000	694
QLT Inc 887 Great Northern Way Ste 101 *NASDAQ: QLT*	Vancouver	BC	V5T4T5	800-663-5486	604-707-7000	84
QLT USA Inc 887 Great Northern Way Ste 250	Vancouver	CO	80525	877-764-3131	970-482-5868	582
QMI (Quality Mfg Company Inc) PO Box 616	Winchester	KY	40392	866-460-6459	859-744-0420	453
QNB Corp 15 N Third St PO Box 9005 *OTC: QNBC*	Quakertown	PA	18951	800-491-9070	215-538-5600	69
QSA ToolWorks LLC 3100 47th Ave	Long Island	NY	11101	800-784-7018	516-935-9151	180-7
QSC Audio Products LLC 1675 MacArthur Blvd	Costa Mesa	CA	92626	800-854-4079	714-754-6175	51
QSI (Quality Systems Inc) 18111 Von Karman Ave Ste 600 *NASDAQ: QSII* ■ *Cust Svc	Irvine	CA	92612	800-888-7955*	949-255-2600	180-10
Qst Consultations Ltd 11275 Edgewater Dr	Allendale	MI	49401	866-757-4751	616-895-5461	233
QST Magazine 225 Main St	Newington	CT	06111	888-277-5289	860-594-0200	456-14
Quad Cities Convention & Visitors Bureau 1601 River Dr Ste 110	Moline	IL	61265	800-747-7800	309-277-0937	208
Quad Cities Realty 1053 Ripon Ave	Lewiston	ID	83501	877-798-7798	208-798-7798	650
Quad City Bank & Trust 3551 Seventh St *NASDAQ: QCRH*	Moline	IL	61265	866-676-0551	309-736-3580	360-2
Quad-City Peterbilt Inc 8100 N Fairmount St	Davenport	IA	52806	866-601-8607		515
Quad-City Times 500 E Third St	Davenport	IA	52801	800-437-4641	563-383-2200	531-2
Quadel Consulting 1200 G St NW Ste 700	Washington	DC	20005	866-640-1019	202-789-2500	196
Quadlogic Controls Corp 3300 Northern Blvd Fl 2 Fl 2	Long Island	NY	11101	877-797-6347	212-930-9300	198
Quadra Chemicals Ltd 3901 Fixtessier	Vaudreuil-Dorion	QC	J7V5V5	800-665-6553	450-424-0161	145
Quadrant Engineering Plastic Products USA 2120 Fairmont Ave PO Box 14235	Reading	PA	19612	800-366-0300	610-320-6600	601
Quadrel Labeling Systems 7670 Jenther Dr	Mentor	OH	44060	800-321-8509	440-602-4700	546
Quadrex Corp PO Box 3881 *Sales	Woodbridge	CT	06525	800-275-7033*	203-393-3112	333
QuadriSpace Corp 705 N Greenville Ave Ste 800	Allen	TX	75002	866-337-7223		807
QuadSystems LLC N61 W23044 Harry's Way	Sussex	WI	53089	866-246-7693		344
Quail Lodge Resort & Golf Club 8205 Valley Greens Dr	Carmel	CA	93923	866-675-1101	831-624-2888	667
Quaker Chemical Corp 901 Hector St *NYSE: KWR*	Conshohocken	PA	19428	800-523-7010	610-832-4000	144
Quaker Heights Nursing Home Inc 514 High St	Waynesville	OH	45068	800-319-1317	513-897-6050	371
Quaker Oats Co 555 W Monroe St	Chicago	IL	60661	800-367-6287	312-821-1000	297-36
Quaker Window Products Inc 504 S Hwy 63 PO Box 128	Freeburg	MO	65035	800-347-0438		236
Qualcomm Stadium 9449 Friars Rd	San Diego	CA	92108	800-400-7115	619-641-3100	718
Qual-Craft Industries PO Box 559	Stoughton	MA	02072	800-231-5647	781-344-1000	350
Qualex Consulting Services Inc 4300 Biscayne Blvd	Miami	FL	33137	877-887-4727		182
Quali Tech Inc 318 Lake Hazeltine Dr	Chaska	MN	55318	800-328-5870	952-448-5151	446
Qualicaps Inc 6505 Franz Warner Pkwy	Whitsett	NC	27377	800-227-7853	336-449-3900	582
Qualico Steel Co Inc PO Box 149	Webb	AL	36376	866-234-5382	334-793-1290	479
Qualified Remodeler Magazine 1233 Janesville Ave	Fort Atkinson	WI	53538	800-547-7377	732-372-7668	456-21
Qualis Health PO Box 33400	Seattle	WA	98133	800-949-7536	206-364-9700	374-3
QualiTest Ltd 1139 Post Rd	Fairfield	CT	06824	877-882-9540		393
Qualitest Pharmaceuticals 130 Vintage Dr	Huntsville	AL	35811	800-444-4011		582
Quality Bioresources Inc 1015 N Austin St	Seguin	TX	78155	888-674-7224	830-372-4797	415

Name / Address	City	State	ZIP	Toll-Free	Phone	Class
Quality Books Inc 1003 W Pines Rd *Cust Svc	Oregon	IL	61061	**800-323-4241***	815-732-4450	94
Quality Containers of New England 247 Portland St	Yarmouth	ME	04096	**800-639-1550**	207-846-5420	97
Quality Craft Ltd 17750-65A Ave Ste 301	Surrey	BC	V3S5N4	**800-663-2252**	604-575-5550	292
Quality Customs Broker Inc 4464 S Whitnall Ave	Saint Francis	WI	53235	**888-813-4647**	414-482-9447	312
Quality Dining Inc 4220 Edison Lakes Pkwy	Mishawaka	IN	46545	**800-589-3820**	574-271-4600	668
Quality Distribution Inc 4041 Pk Oaks Blvd Ste 200 *NASDAQ: QLTY*	Tampa	FL	33610	**800-282-2031**		778
Quality Edge Inc 2712 Walkent Dr NW	Walker	MI	49544	**888-784-0878**		489
Quality Forms 4317 W US Rt 36	Piqua	OH	45356	**866-773-4595**	937-773-4595	109
Quality Hotel-airport 7228 Wminster Hwy	Richmond	BC	V6X1A1	**877-244-3051**	604-244-3051	379
Quality Inn & Suites Naples Golf Resort 4100 Golden Gate Pkwy	Naples	FL	34116	**800-277-0017**	239-455-1010	667
Quality Inn Halifax Airport Hotel 60 Sky Blvd Halifax International Airport	Goffs	NS	B2T1K3	**800-667-3333**	902-873-3000	379
Quality Liquid Feeds Inc PO Box 240	Dodgeville	WI	53533	**800-236-2345**	608-935-2345	278
Quality Management Solutions LLC 146 Lowell St Ste 300B	Wakefield	MA	01889	**800-645-6430**		198
Quality Manufacturing Inc 969 Labore Industrial Ct	Saint Paul	MN	55110	**800-243-5473**	651-483-5473	699
Quality Mat Co 6550 Tram Rd	Beaumont	TX	77713	**800-227-8159**	409-722-4594	130
Quality Meats & Seafoods 700 Ctr St	West Fargo	ND	58078	**800-342-4250**	701-282-0202	472
Quality Media Resources Inc 10929 Se 23rd St	Bellevue	WA	98004	**800-800-5129**	425-455-0558	462
Quality Metal Products Inc Orange Rd PO Box 273	Dallas	PA	18612	**888-251-2805**	570-333-4248	695
Quality Mfg Company Inc (QMI) PO Box 616	Winchester	KY	40392	**866-460-6459**	859-744-0420	453
Quality of Life Health Services Inc 1411 Piedmont Cutoff PO Box 97	Gadsden	AL	35902	**888-490-0131**	256-492-0131	374-3
Quality Perforating Inc 166 Dundaff St	Carbondale	PA	18407	**800-872-7373**	570-282-4344	487
Quality Plywood Specialties Inc 4500 110th Ave N	Clearwater	FL	33762	**888-722-1181**	727-572-0500	193-3
Quality Progress Magazine 600 N Plankinton Ave PO Box 3005 *Cust Svc	Milwaukee	WI	53201	**800-248-1946***	414-272-8575	456-21
Quality Solutions Inc 128 N First St	Colwich	KS	67030	**888-328-2454**	316-721-3656	263
Quality Systems Inc (QSI) 18111 Von Karman Ave Ste 600 *NASDAQ: QSII* ■ *Cust Svc	Irvine	CA	92612	**800-888-7955***	949-255-2600	180-10
Quality Transportation 36-40 37th St Ste 201	Long Island	NY	11101	**800-677-2838**	212-308-6333	312
Qualstar Corp 3990-B Heritage Oak Ct *NASDAQ: QBAK*	Simi Valley	CA	93063	**800-468-0680**	805-583-7744	175-8
Qualys Inc 1600 Bridge Pkwy	Redwood Shores	CA	94065	**866-801-6161**	650-801-6100	690
Quam-Nichols Company Inc 234 E Marquette Rd	Chicago	IL	60637	**800-633-3669**	773-488-5800	51
Quanex Building Products 2270 Woodale Dr	Mounds View	MN	55112	**800-233-4383**	763-231-4000	498
Quanex Building Products Corp 1900 W Loop S Ste 1500 *Cust Svc	Houston	TX	77027	**888-475-0633***	713-961-4600	237
Quantiam Technologies Inc 1651 - 94 St NW	Edmonton	AB	T6N1E6	**877-461-0707**	780-462-0707	666
Quantimetrix Corp 2005 Manhattan Beach Blvd	Redondo Beach	CA	90278	**800-624-8380**	310-536-0006	233
Quantum Analytics 3400 East Third Ave	Foster City	CA	94404	**800-992-4199**	650-312-0900	266-3
Quantum Audio Designs Inc 6408 State Hwy 77	Benton	MO	63736	**888-545-4404**	573-545-4404	525
Quantum Corp 11431 Willows Rd NE	Redmond	WA	98052	**800-284-5101**	425-881-8004	178
Quantum Corporate Funding Ltd 1140 Ave of the Americas 16th Fl	New York	NY	10036	**800-352-2535**	212-768-1200	274
Quantum Dental Technologies Inc 748 Briar Hill Ave	Toronto	ON	M6B1L3	**866-993-9910**		230
Quantum Inc PO Box 2791	Eugene	OR	97402	**800-448-1448**	541-345-5556	298
Quantum Management Services Ltd 2000 McGill College Ave Ste 1800	Montreal	QC	H3A3H3	**800-978-2688**	514-842-5555	731
Quantum/ATL 141 Innovation Dr	Irvine	CA	92617	**800-677-6268**	949-856-7800	175-8
Quantum3D Inc 5225 Hellyer Ave Ste 220	Milpitas	CA	95138	**888-747-1020**	408-600-2500	175-1
Quantus Software 32-62 Scurfield Blvd	Winnipeg	MB	R3Y1M5	**866-478-1308**		195
Quark Inc 1800 Grant St *Cust Svc	Denver	CO	80203	**800-676-4575***		180-8
Quarles & Brady LLP 411 E Wisconsin Ave Ste 2400	Milwaukee	WI	53202	**800-654-2200**	414-277-5000	428
Quartz Mountain Resort & Conference Ctr 22469 Lodge Rd	Lone Wolf	OK	73655	**877-999-5567**	580-563-2424	667
Quatech Inc 5675 Hudson Industrial Pkwy	Hudson	OH	44236	**800-553-1170**	330-655-9000	624
Quatred LLC 532 Fourth Range Rd	Pembroke	NH	03275	**888-395-8534**		40
Quebec Inn 7175 Blvd Hamel Ouest	Quebec	QC	G2G1B6	**800-567-5276**	418-872-9831	379
Queen Anne Hotel 1590 Sutter St	San Francisco	CA	94109	**800-227-3970**	415-441-2828	379
Queen City TV & Appliance Company Inc 2430 Queen City Dr *All	Charlotte	NC	28208	**800-365-6665***	704-391-6000	34
Queen Cutlery Co 507 Chestnut St *Sales	Titusville	PA	16354	**800-222-5233***	814-827-3673	224
Queen Wilhelmina State Park 3877 Arkansas 88	Mena	AR	71953	**888-287-2757**	479-394-2863	564
Queen's College Faculty of Theology 210 Prince Philip Dr Ste 3000	Saint John's	NL	A1B3R6	**877-753-0116**	709-753-0116	168-3
Queens Chamber of Commerce 75-20 Astoria Blvd Ste 140	Jackson Heights	NY	11370	**800-931-2297**	718-898-8500	138
Queens College 65-30 Kissena Blvd	Flushing	NY	11367	**888-888-0606**	718-997-5000	167
Queens Courier 38-15 Bell Blvd	Bayside	NY	11361	**800-275-8777**	718-224-5863	531-4
Queens Hospital Ctr 82-68 164th St	Jamaica	NY	11432	**888-692-6116**	718-883-3000	374-3
Queens Museum of Art New York City Bldg	Queens	NY	11368	**866-867-9665**	718-592-9700	519
Queens University of Charlotte 1900 Selwyn Ave	Charlotte	NC	28274	**800-849-0202**	704-337-2212	167
Queensboro Co 113 E Broad St PO Box 467	Louisville	GA	30434	**800-236-2442**	478-625-2000	778
Queensborough Community College 222-05 56th Ave	Bayside	NY	11364	**877-253-7122**	718-631-6262	161
Queenstown Bank of Maryland 7101 Main St PO Box 120	Queenstown	MD	21658	**888-827-4300**	410-827-8881	69
Quest Companies Inc 8011 N Point Blvd Ste 201	Winston-salem	NC	27106	**800-467-9409**		7
Quest Convergence Systems Inc 43 Metcalf Dr	Belleville	IL	62223	**877-933-8776**	618-398-3311	263
Quest Diagnostics at Nichols Institute 33608 Ortega Hwy	San Juan Capistrano	CA	92675	**800-642-4657**	949-728-4000	418
Quest Diagnostics Inc 3 Giralda Farms *NYSE: DGX*	Madison	NJ	07940	**800-222-0446**	201-393-5000	418
Quest Engineering Inc 2300 Edgewood Ave South	Minneapolis	MN	55426	**800-328-4853**	952-546-4441	358
Quest Software Inc 5 Polaris Way *NASDAQ: QSFT*	Aliso Viejo	CA	92656	**800-306-9329**	949-754-8000	180-1
Questar Assessment Inc 5550 Upper 147th St W *OTC: QUSA* ■ *Cust Svc	Apple Valley	MN	55124	**800-800-2598***	952-997-2700	245
Questar Capital Corp 5701 Golden Hills Dr	Minneapolis	MN	55416	**888-446-5872**		688
Questar Corp 333 S State St PO Box 45433 *NYSE: STR*	Salt Lake City	UT	84145	**800-323-5517**	801-324-5000	360-5
Questar Gas Co PO Box 45841	Salt Lake City	UT	84139	**800-323-5517**	801-324-5111	785
Questar Gas Management Co PO Box 45360	Salt Lake City	UT	84145	**800-323-5517**	801-324-5111	326
Questar InfoComm Inc 180 East 100 South PO Box 45433	Salt Lake City	UT	84145	**800-729-6790**	801-324-5856	733
Questel Orbit 1725 Duke St Ste 625	Alexandria	VA	22314	**800-456-7248**	703-519-1820	632
Questex LLC 275 Grove St Ste 2-130	Newton	MA	02466	**888-552-4346**	617-219-8300	530-13
Questia Media America Inc 1 N State St Ste 900	Chicago	IL	60602	**800-759-4726**	800-889-0097	387
Questica Inc 980 Fraser Dr Ste 105	Burlington	ON	L7L5P5	**877-707-7755**		181
Questor Technology Inc 1121 940 - Sixth Ave SW	Calgary	AB	T2P3T1	**844-477-8669**	403-571-1530	538
Queue Inc 703 Post Rd	Fairfield	CT	06824	**800-232-2224**		180-3
Quick Color Solutions Inc 829 Knox Rd	Mc Leansville	NC	27301	**877-698-0951**	336-698-0951	626
Quick Crete Products 731 Parkridge Ave	Norco	CA	92860	**866-703-3434**		193-1
Quick Tab Ii Inc 241 Heritage Dr	Tiffin	OH	44883	**800-332-5081**	419-448-6622	626
Quicken Loans Arena 1 Ctr Ct	Cleveland	OH	44115	**888-894-9424**	216-420-2000	718
Quickmill Inc 760 Rye St	Peterborough	ON	K9J6W9	**800-295-0509**	705-745-2961	490
Quicksilver Resources Inc 777 W Rosedale St Ste 300 *OTC: KWKAQ*	Fort Worth	TX	76104	**877-665-8600**	817-665-5000	537
QuickStart Intelligence Inc 16815 Von Karman Ave Ste 100	Irvine	CA	92606	**866-991-3924**	800-326-1044	179
Quidel Corp 10165 McKellar Ct *NASDAQ: QDEL*	San Diego	CA	92121	**800-874-1517**	858-552-1100	233
Quikbook 381 Pk Ave S 3rd Fl	New York	NY	10016	**800-789-9887**	212-779-7666	376
QUIKRETE Cos 3490 Piedmont Rd Ste 1300	Atlanta	GA	30305	**800-282-5828**	404-634-9100	185
Quikstik Labels 220 Broadway	Everett	MA	02149	**800-225-3496**	617-389-7570	413
QuikTrip Corp 4705 S 129th E Ave	Tulsa	OK	74134	**800-441-0253**	918-615-7700	206
Quilter's Newsletter Magazine 741 Corporate Cir Ste A	Golden	CO	80401	**800-477-6089**	303-215-5600	456-14
Quiltmaker Magazine 741 Corporate Cir Ste A	Golden	CO	80401	**800-388-7023**	800-881-6634	456-14
Quimby House Inn 109 Cottage St	Bar Harbor	ME	04609	**800-344-5811**	207-288-5811	379

Name / Address	City	State	Zip	Toll-Free	Phone	Class
Quincy Area Convention & Visitors Bureau (QACVB) 532 Gardner Expy	Quincy	IL	62301	**800-978-4748**	217-214-3700	208
Quincy College 1250 Hancock St	Quincy	MA	02169	**800-698-1700**	617-984-1700	161
Quincy Herald-Whig 130 S Fifth St	Quincy	IL	62301	**800-373-9444**	217-223-5100	531-2
Quincy Mutual Fire Insurance Co 57 Washington St	Quincy	MA	02169	**800-899-1116**		391-4
Quincy Newspapers Inc 130 S Fifth St	Quincy	IL	62301	**800-373-9444**	217-223-5100	634-8
Quincy Ortman Cylinders 3501 Wismann Ln PO Box C-2	Quincy	IL	62305	**844-759-4922**	217-277-0321	225
Quincy Street Inc 13350 Quincy St	Holland	MI	49424	**800-784-6290**	616-399-3330	472
Quincy University 1800 College Ave	Quincy	IL	62301	**866-703-4004**	217-222-8020	167
Quinnipiac University 275 Mt Carmel Ave *Admissions	Hamden	CT	06518	**800-462-1944***	203-582-8600	167
Quinnipiac University School of Law 275 Mt Carmel Ave	Hamden	CT	06518	**800-462-1944**	203-582-3400	168-1
Quintessence Publishing Co 4350 Chandler Dr	Hanover Park	IL	60133	**800-621-0387**	630-736-3600	779
Quintiles Canada Inc 18 Rue Elderidge *General	Dollard-des-Ormeaux	QC	H9A2P4	**866-267-4479***	514-855-0888	582
Quintiles Transnational Corp 4820 Emperor Blvd	Durham	NC	27703	**866-267-4479**	919-998-2000	582
Quippi Corp 444 S Cedros Ave Ste 410	La Jolla	CA	92037	**888-978-4774**		393
Quirch Foods Co 7600 NW 82nd Pl	Miami	FL	33166	**800-458-5252**	305-691-3535	298-9
Quiznos Corp 7595 Technology Way Ste 200	Denver	CO	80237	**866-486-2783**	720-359-3300	668
QUMAS 66 York St *Sales	Jersey City	NJ	07302	**800-577-1545***	973-805-8600	180-10
QVC Inc 1200 Wilson Dr	West Chester	PA	19380	**800-367-9444**	484-701-1000	736
Qvidian Corp 175 Cabot St Ste 210	Lowell	MA	01854	**800-272-0047**	513-631-1155	180-10

R

Name / Address	City	State	Zip	Toll-Free	Phone	Class
R & B Car Company Inc 3811 S Michigan St	South Bend	IN	46614	**800-260-1833**		515
R & B Wagner Inc PO Box 423	Butler	WI	53007	**888-243-6914**	414-214-0444	594
R & B Wholesale Distributors Inc 2350 S Milliken Ave	Ontario	CA	91761	**800-627-7539**	909-230-5400	37
R & D Batteries Inc 3300 Corporate Ctr Dr PO Box 5007	Burnsville	MN	55306	**800-950-1945**	952-890-0629	73
R & D Computers 6767 Peachtree Industrial Blvd Ste B	Atlanta	GA	30092	**800-350-3071**	770-416-0103	588
R & D Systems Inc 614 McKinley Pl NE	Minneapolis	MN	55413	**800-343-7475**	612-379-2956	233
R & D Transportation Services Inc 4036 Adolfo Rd	Camarillo	CA	93012	**800-966-7114**	805-529-7511	312
R & K Industrial Products Co 1945 Seventh St	Richmond	CA	94801	**800-842-7655**	510-234-7212	674
R & M Energy Systems 301 Premier Rd *Sales	Borger	TX	79007	**888-262-8645***	806-274-5293	385
R & M Office Furniture 9615 Oates Dr	Sacramento	CA	95827	**800-660-1756**	916-362-1756	321
R & R Limousine 4403 Kiln Ct	Louisville	KY	40218	**800-582-5576**	502-458-1862	441
R & R Trucking Inc 302 Thunder Rd PO Box 545	Duenweg	MO	64841	**800-625-6885**	417-623-6885	778
R & S/Godwin Truck Body Co LLC 5168 S US Hwy 23 PO Box 420	Ivel	KY	41642	**800-826-7413**	606-874-2151	515
R B M Co 2700 Texas Ave	Knoxville	TN	37921	**800-521-5656**	865-524-8621	385
R E I Consultants Inc PO Box 286	Beaver	WV	25813	**800-999-0105**	304-255-2500	194
R J Schinner Company Inc 16950 W Lincoln Ave	New Berlin	WI	53151	**800-234-1460**	262-797-7180	789
R K Allen Oil Inc 36002 AL Hwy 21	Talladega	AL	35161	**800-445-5823**	256-362-4261	578
R K Electric Inc 42021 Osgood Rd	Fremont	CA	94539	**800-400-4418**	510-770-5660	191-4
R Kidd Fuels Corp 1172 Twinney Dr	Newmarket	ON	L3Y9E2	**866-274-2315**		578
R N Croft Financial Group Inc 218 Steeles Ave E	Thornhill	ON	L3T1A6	**877-249-2884**	905-695-7777	401
R O I Media Solutions LLC 11500 W Olympic Blvd Ste 400	Los Angeles	CA	90064	**866-211-2580**		5
R R Floody Co 5065 27th Ave	Rockford	IL	61109	**800-678-6639**	815-399-1931	358
R Seelaus & Company Inc 25 Deforest Ave Ste 304	Summit	NJ	07901	**800-922-0584**		688
R W Mercer Co 2322 Brooklyn Rd PO Box 180	Jackson	MI	49204	**877-763-7237**	517-787-2960	188
R W Rog & Company Inc 630 Johnson Ave Ste 103	Bohemia	NY	11716	**877-218-0085**	631-218-0077	196
R.W. Lynch Company Inc 2333 San Ramon Vly Blvd	San Ramon	CA	94583	**800-594-8940**	925-837-3877	5
R2 Unified Technologies 980 N Federal Hwy Ste 410	Boca Raton	FL	33432	**866-464-7381**	561-515-6800	198

Name / Address	City	State	Zip	Toll-Free	Phone	Class
RA (Ruotolo Assoc Inc) 29 Broadway Ste 210	Cresskill	NJ	07626	**800-786-8656**	201-568-3898	318
RA Miller Industries Inc 14500 168th Ave PO Box 858	Grand Haven	MI	49417	**888-845-9450**	616-842-9450	645
RAB (Radio Adv Bureau) 125 W 55th St 21st Fl	New York	NY	10019	**800-232-3131**	212-681-7200	48-18
RAB Lighting 170 Ludlow Ave	Northvale	NJ	07647	**888-722-1000**	201-784-8600	439
Raba-Kistner Consultants Inc 12821 W Golden Ln	San Antonio	TX	78249	**866-722-2547**	210-699-9090	191-15
Rabbit Air 9242 1/2 Hall Rd	Downey	CA	90241	**888-866-8862**	562-861-4688	44
Rabbit Hill Inn 48 Lower Waterford Rd PO Box 55	Lower Waterford	VT	05848	**800-626-3215**	802-748-5168	379
Rabo Bank 1026 E Grand Ave	Arroyo Grande	CA	93420	**800-942-6222**	805-473-7710	69
Rabun County School District 963 Tiger Connector	Tiger	GA	30576	**866-632-9992**	706-212-4350	683
Rabun Gap-Nacoochee School 339 Nacoochee Dr	Rabun Gap	GA	30568	**800-543-7467**	706-746-7467	621
Raccoon Mountain Caverns 319 W Hills Dr	Chattanooga	TN	37419	**800-823-2267**	423-821-9403	49-4
Raccoon Valley Electric Co-op 28725 Hwy 30 PO Box 486	Glidden	IA	51443	**800-253-6211**	712-659-3649	247
Race Face Components Inc 100 Braid St	New Westminster	BC	V3L3P4	**800-527-9244**	604-527-9996	154-1
RaceTrac Petroleum Inc 3225 Cumberland Blvd Ste 100	Atlanta	GA	30339	**888-636-5589**	770-431-7600	325
Racine County Convention & Visitors Bureau 14015 Washington Ave	Sturtevant	WI	53177	**800-272-2463**	262-884-6400	208
Racine Public Library 75 Seventh St	Racine	WI	53403	**888-529-0061**	262-636-9241	434-3
Racks Inc PO Box 530840	San Diego	CA	92153	**877-920-7225**	619-661-0987	288
RACVB (Ridgecrest Area Convention & Visitors Bureau) 643 N China Lake Blvd Ste C	Ridgecrest	CA	93555	**800-847-4830**	760-375-8202	208
RAD Data Communications Ltd 900 Corporate Dr	Mahwah	NJ	07430	**800-444-7234**	201-529-1100	732
Rad Law Firm 2001 Beach St Ste 600	Fort Worth	TX	76103	**800-598-1090**	817-465-8733	428
Rada Manufacturing Co PO Box 838	Waverly	IA	50677	**800-311-9691**	319-352-5454	224
Radar Industries 27101 Grosbeck Hwy	Warren	MI	48089	**800-779-0301**	248-358-3570	488
Radford University 801 E Main St *Admissions	Radford	VA	24142	**800-890-4265***	540-831-5371	167
Radiac Abrasives Inc 1015 S College Ave	Salem	IL	62881	**800-851-1095**	618-548-4200	1
Radialpoint 2050 Bleury St Ste 300	Montreal	QC	H3A2J5	**866-286-2636**	514-286-2636	180-9
Radian Asset Assurance Inc *Radian Group Inc, The* 335 Madison Ave 25th Fl	New York	NY	10017	**877-723-4261**	212-983-3100	391-5
Radian Group Inc 1601 Market St *NYSE: RDN*	Philadelphia	PA	19103	**800-523-1988**	215-564-6600	391-5
Radiancy Inc 40 Ramland Rd S Ste 200	Orangeburg	NY	10962	**888-661-2220**	845-398-1647	474
Radiant Communications Corp 1600-1050 W Pender St *CVE: RCN*	Vancouver	BC	V6E4T3	**888-219-2111**		806
Radiant Electric Co-op Inc PO Box 390	Fredonia	KS	66736	**800-821-0956**	620-378-2161	247
Radiant Logistics Inc Third Fl 405 114Th Ave Se	Bellevue	WA	98004	**800-843-4784**	425-943-4599	448
Radiant Pools Div Trojan Leisure Products LLC 440 N Pearl St	Albany	NY	12207	**866-697-5870**	518-434-4161	726
Radiant Research Inc 11500 Northlake Dr Ste 320	Cincinnati	OH	45249	**855-427-8839**	513-247-5500	666
Radiant Technologies Inc 2835 Pan American Fwy Ne	Albuquerque	NM	87107	**800-289-7176**	505-842-8007	258
Radianta Inc 2154 Michelson Dr Ste A	Irvine	CA	92612	**866-467-9695**		807
Radiation Therapy Services Inc 2270 Colonial Blvd	Fort Myers	FL	33907	**800-437-1619**	239-931-7275	352
Radiator Specialty Co 1900 Wilkinson Blvd	Charlotte	NC	28208	**877-464-4865**	704-688-2405	144
Radio Adv Bureau (RAB) 125 W 55th St 21st Fl	New York	NY	10019	**800-232-3131**	212-681-7200	48-18
Radio America 1100 N Glebe Rd Ste 900	Arlington	VA	22201	**800-807-4703**	703-302-1000	641
Radio Communications Co 8035 Chapel Hill Rd	Cary	NC	27513	**800-508-7580**	919-467-2421	196
Radio Control Boat Modeler 88 Danbury Rd	Wilton	CT	06897	**888-235-2021**	203-431-9000	456-14
Radio Flyer Inc 6515 W Grand Ave	Chicago	IL	60707	**800-621-7613**	773-637-7100	760
Radio Kansas 815 N Walnut St Ste 300	Hutchinson	KS	67501	**800-723-4657**	620-662-6646	643
Radiocat 32-A Mellor Ave	Baltimore	MD	21228	**800-323-9729**		792
Radiodetection Corp 154 Portland Rd	Bridgton	ME	04009	**877-247-3797**	207-647-9495	250
Radiological Society of North America (RSNA) 820 Jorie Blvd	Oak Brook	IL	60523	**800-381-6660**	630-571-2670	48-8
Radiology Business Management Assn (RBMA) 10300 Eaton Pl Ste 460	Fairfax	VA	22030	**888-224-7262**	703-621-3355	48-8
Radiophone Engineering Inc 534 W Walnut St	Springfield	MO	65806	**800-369-2929**	417-862-6653	248
RadioShack Corp 300 RadioShack Cir *NYSE: RSH*	Fort Worth	TX	76102	**800-843-7422**	817-882-9380	34
Radio-Television News Directors Assn (RTNDA) 1600 K St NW Ste 700	Washington	DC	20006	**800-807-8632**	202-659-6510	48-14
RadioU PO Box 1887	Westerville	OH	43086	**877-272-3468**		643

Name / Address	City	State	ZIP	Toll-Free	Phone	Class
Radisson Butler Blvd 4700 Salisbury Rd	Jacksonville	FL	32256	888-201-1718	904-281-9700	379
Radisson Chicago-O'Hare Hotel 1450 E Touhy Ave	Des Plaines	IL	60018	888-201-1718	847-296-8866	379
Radisson Hotel Bloomington Mall of America 1700 American Blvd E *Resv	Bloomington	MN	55425	800-967-9033*	952-854-8700	379
Radisson Milwaukee North Shore 7065 N Port Washington Rd	Milwaukee	WI	53217	800-395-7046	414-351-6960	379
Radisson Palm Beach Shores Resort & Vacation Villas 11340 Blondo S Ste 100	Omaha	NE	68164	800-615-7253		667
Radisson Resort Parkway 2900 PkwyBlvd	Kissimmee	FL	34747	800-333-3333	407-396-7000	667
RadiSys Corp 5445 NE Dawson Creek Dr *NASDAQ: RSYS*	Hillsboro	OR	97124	800-950-0044	503-615-1100	624
RADIUS 7700 Wisconsin Ave Ste 400	Bethesda	MD	20814	800-989-3059	301-718-9500	770
Radius Professional HDD Tools 1614 N Main St	Weatherford	TX	76086	800-892-9114		537
Radnor Financial Advisors Inc 485 Devon Park Dr Ste 119	Wayne	PA	19087	888-271-9922	610-975-0280	401
RadView Software Inc 991 Hgwy 22 W Ste 200	Bridgewater	NJ	08807	888-723-8439	908-526-7756	180-12
Radware Inc 575 Corporate Dr Lobby 2	Mahwah	NJ	07430	888-234-5763	201-512-9771	180-11
Rady Children's Hospital (RCH) 3020 Children's Way MC 5101	San Diego	CA	92123	800-788-9029	858-576-1700	374-1
Radyne Corp 211 W Boden St	Milwaukee	WI	53207	800-236-8360	414-481-8360	319
RAE Corp 4615 Prime Pkwy	McHenry	IL	60050	800-323-7049	815-385-3500	517
RAE Systems 3775 N First St	San Jose	CA	95134	877-723-2878	408-952-8200	203
Raf Technologies Inc 200 Lexington Ave	Deland	FL	32724	888-876-6424	386-736-1698	765
Raffaello Hotel 201 E Delaware Pl	Chicago	IL	60611	800-916-4339	312-943-5000	379
Raft River Rural Electric Co-op Inc 155 N Main St PO Box 617	Malta	ID	83342	800-342-7732	208-645-2211	247
Ragan Communications Inc 316 N Michigan Ave Ste 400	Chicago	IL	60601	800-878-5331	312-960-4100	530-2
Rail Car Service Co 584 Fairground Rd	Mercer	PA	16137	800-521-2151	724-662-3660	648
Rail Europe Inc 44 S Broadway 11th Fl	White Plains	NY	10601	800-361-7245	914-682-2999	773
Rail Link Inc 13901 Sutton Pk Dr S Ste 125	Jacksonville	FL	32224	877-777-4778	904-223-1110	649
Railhead Corp 12549 S Laramie Ave	Alsip	IL	60803	800-235-1782	708-844-5500	768
Railroad Pass Hotel & Casino 2800 S Boulder Hwy	Henderson	NV	89002	800-654-0877	702-294-5000	132
Railroad Retirement Board 844 N Rush St	Chicago	IL	60611	877-772-5772	312-751-4300	340-18
Rails Co 101 Newark Way	Maplewood	NJ	07040	800-217-2457	973-763-4320	768
Railserve Inc 1691 Phoenix Blvd Ste 110	Atlanta	GA	30349	800-345-7245	770-996-6838	649
Railtech Ltd 325 Lee Ave	Montreal	QC	H9X3S3	877-759-3653	514-457-4760	768
Rain Creek Baking Co, The 2401 W Almond Ave	Madera	CA	93637	800-530-0505	559-674-4445	298-11
Rainbow Advertising Lp 3904 W Vickery Blvd	Fort Worth	TX	76107	800-646-3477	817-738-3838	7
Rainbow Art Glass Inc 1761 Rt 34 S	Farmingdale	NJ	07727	800-526-2356	732-681-6003	330
Rainbow Grocery Co-op Inc 1745 Folsom St	San Francisco	CA	94103	877-720-2667	415-863-0620	345
Rainbow International 1010 N University Pk Dr	Waco	TX	76707	855-724-6269	254-756-5463	151
Rainbow Light Nutritional Sys Inc 100 Ave Tea	Santa Cruz	CA	95060	800-635-1233		478
Rainbow Lodge 2011 Ella Blvd	Houston	TX	77008	866-861-8666	713-861-8666	669
Rainbow Trout Ranch (RTR) 1484 FDR 250 PO Box 458	Antonito	CO	81120	800-633-3397	719-376-5659	241
Raindance Spa at the Lodge at Sonoma Renaissance Resort 1325 Broadway	Sonoma	CA	95476	866-263-0758	707-935-6600	705
Rainforest Action Network (RAN) 221 Pine St 5th Fl	San Francisco	CA	94104	800-368-1819	415-398-4404	47-13
Rainier Group Investment Advisory LLC 500 108th Ave N E Ste 2000	Bellevue	WA	98004	800-800-8974	425-463-3000	654
Rainier Industries Ltd 18375 Olympic Ave S	Tukwila	WA	98188	800-869-7162	425-251-1800	730
Rainier Investment Management Mutual Funds 601 Union St Ste 2801	Seattle	WA	98101	800-536-4640		527
RainMaker Software Inc 1777 Sentry Pkwy W	Blue Bell	PA	19422	800-336-0339	610-567-3400	180-10
RAINN (Rape Abuse & Incest National Network) 2000 L St NW Ste 406	Washington	DC	20036	800-656-4673	202-544-1034	47-6
Raintree Resorts Management Company LLC PO Box 350	Teton Village	WY	83025	866-352-9777	307-734-9777	378
Rainwater, Holt & Sexton PA 6315 Ranch Dr	Little Rock	AR	72223	800-434-4800		428
Rainwise Inc 25 Federal St	Bar Harbor	ME	04609	800-762-5723	207-288-5169	407
Rainy River Community College 1501 Hwy 71	International Falls	MN	56649	800-456-3996	218-285-7722	161
Raj, The 1734 Jasmine Ave	Fairfield	IA	52556	800-248-9050	641-472-9580	704
Rakuten Marketing LLC 215 Pk Ave S 9th Fl	New York	NY	10003	888-880-8430	646-943-8200	7
Ralco Nutrition Inc 1600 Hahn Rd	Marshall	MN	56258	800-533-5306		446
Raleigh America Inc 6004 S 190th St Ste 101	Kent	WA	98032	800-222-5527		81
Raleigh County 215 Main St	Beckley	WV	25801	800-509-6568	304-255-9178	338
Raleigh Studios Worldwide 5300 Melrose Ave	Hollywood	CA	90038	888-960-3456	323-466-3111	511
Raleigh USA 6004 S 190th St Ste 101	Kent	WA	98032	800-222-5527	253-395-1100	81
Raleigh-Durham International Airport PO Box 80001	Raleigh	NC	27623	800-252-7522	919-840-2123	27
Raley's 500 W Capitol Ave PO Box 15618	Sacramento	CA	95852	800-925-9989	916-373-3333	345
Ralls County Electric Co-op 17594 Hwy 19 PO Box 157	New London	MO	63459	877-985-8711	573-985-8711	247
Rally House & Kansas Sampler 9750 Quivira Rd	Lenexa	KS	66215	800-645-5394		789
Rallyorg 995 Market St 2nd Fl	San Francisco	CA	94105	888-648-2220		387
Ralph Friedland & Bros 17 Industrial Dr	Keyport	NJ	07735	800-631-2162	732-290-9800	86
Ralph Pill Electrical Supply Co 50 Von Hillern St	Boston	MA	02125	800-897-1769	617-265-8800	248
Ralph Rosenberg Court Reporters Inc 1001 Bishop St Ste 2460	Honolulu	HI	96813	888-524-5888		444
Ralph Wilson Stadium 1 Bills Dr	Orchard Park	NY	14127	877-228-4257	716-648-1800	718
Ralphs Grocery Co 1014 Vine St *Cust Svc	Cincinnati	OH	45202	800-576-4377*		345
Ralston Metal Products Ltd 50 Watson Rd S	Guelph	ON	N1L1E2	800-265-7611		479
Ram Graphics Inc 2408 S Pk Ave	Alexandria	IN	46001	800-531-4656		685
Rama Corp 600 W Esplanade Ave	San Jacinto	CA	92583	800-472-5670	951-654-7351	14
Ramada Middletown 425 E Main Rd	Middletown	RI	02842	800-854-9517	401-846-3555	379
Ramada Plaza & Conference Ctr 4900 Sinclair Rd	Columbus	OH	43229	800-272-6232	614-846-0300	379
Ramada Plaza Beach Resort 1500 Miracle Strip Pkwy Se	Fort Walton Beach	FL	32548	800-874-8962	850-243-9161	378
Ramapo Catskill Library System 619 Rt 17-M	Middletown	NY	10940	800-327-7343	845-343-1131	434-3
Ramapo Sales & Marketing Inc 4760 Goer Dr Ste F	North Charleston	SC	29406	800-866-9173		197
Ramco Systems Corp 3150 Brunswick Pk Ste 130	Lawrenceville	NJ	08648	800-472-6261	609-620-4800	227
Ramona Chamber of Commerce 960 Main St	Ramona	CA	92065	800-411-7343	760-789-1311	138
Ramos Oil Company Inc 1515 S River Rd *Cust Svc	West Sacramento	CA	95691	800-477-7266*	916-371-2570	578
Rampart Brokerage Corp 1983 Marcus Ave Ste C130	New Hyde Park	NY	11042	800-772-6727	516-538-7000	390
Rampart Supply Inc 1801 N Union Blvd	Colorado Springs	CO	80909	800-748-1837	719-482-7333	611
Ramsey County 15 W Kellogg Blvd	Saint Paul	MN	55102	866-520-7225	651-266-8000	338
Ramsey County Public Library 4570 N Victoria St	Shoreview	MN	55126	888-335-9632	651-486-2200	434-3
Ramsey Winch Company Inc 1600 N Garnett Rd	Tulsa	OK	74116	800-777-2760	918-438-2760	192
Ramtech Bldg Systems Inc 1400 Hwy 287 S	Mansfield	TX	76063	855-887-1888	800-568-9376	188
Ramtron International Corp 1850 Ramtron Dr *NASDAQ: RMTR*	Colorado Springs	CO	80921	800-541-4736	719-481-7000	694
RAN (Rainforest Action Network) 221 Pine St 5th Fl	San Francisco	CA	94104	800-368-1819	415-398-4404	47-13
Ranac Computer Corp 4181 E 96th St Ste 280	Indianapolis	IN	46240	800-844-0141	317-844-0141	182
Ranch at Steamboat 1800 Ranch Rd	Steamboat Springs	CO	80487	888-686-8075	970-879-3000	379
Ranch Inn 45 E Pearl St	Jackson	WY	83001	800-348-5599	307-733-6363	379
Rancho Cucamonga Chamber of Commerce 9047 Arrow Route Ste 180	Rancho Cucamonga	CA	91730	800-677-5434	909-987-1012	138
Rancho Cucamonga Public Library 7368 Archibald Ave	Rancho Cucamonga	CA	91730	800-655-4555	909-477-2720	434-3
Rancho de la Osa Guest Ranch PO Box 1	Sasabe	AZ	85633	800-872-6240	520-240-3797	241
Rancho de los Caballeros 1551 S Vulture Mine Rd	Wickenburg	AZ	85390	800-684-5030	928-684-5484	667
Rancho Los Amigos National Rehabilitation Ctr 7601 E Imperial Hwy	Downey	CA	90242	877-726-2461	562-401-7111	374-6
Rancho Santa Fe Protective Services Inc 1991 Vlg Pk Way Ste 100	Encinitas	CA	92024	800-303-8877	760-942-0688	691
Rancho Valencia Resort 5921 Valencia Cir PO Box 9126	Rancho Santa Fe	CA	92067	800-548-3664	858-756-1123	667
Rancho Viejo Resort & Country Club 1 Rancho Viejo Dr	Rancho Viejo	TX	78575	800-531-7400	956-350-4000	667
Rancocas Metals Corp 35 Indel Ave	Rancocas	NJ	08073	800-762-6382	609-267-4120	491
RAND Corp 1776 Main St	Santa Monica	CA	90401	877-584-8642	310-393-0411	631
Rand Graphics Inc 500 S Florence St	Wichita	KS	67209	800-435-7263	316-942-1218	626
Rand McNally 9855 Woods Dr PO Box 7600	Skokie	IL	60077	800-275-7263		634-1
Randall Bearings Inc 1046 Greenlawn Ave PO Box 1258	Lima	OH	45802	800-626-7071	419-223-1075	482
Randall Bros Inc 665 Marietta St NW *Cust Svc	Atlanta	GA	30313	800-476-4539*	404-892-6666	498
Randall Mfg LLC 722 Church Rd	Elmhurst	IL	60126	800-323-7424	630-782-0001	607

				Toll-Free	Phone	Class
Randall Museum						
199 Museum Way	San Francisco	CA	94114	866-807-7148	415-554-9600	519
Randall S Miller & Associates PC						
43252 Woodward Ave						
Ste 180	Bloomfield Hills	MI	48302	844-322-6558	248-335-9200	40
Randall-Reilly Publishing Co						
3200 Rice Mine Rd NE	Tuscaloosa	AL	35406	800-633-5953*		634-9
*Cust Svc						
Randolph College						
2500 Rivermont Ave	Lynchburg	VA	24503	800-745-7692*	434-947-8000	167
*Admissions						
Randolph Community College						
629 Industrial Pk Ave	Asheboro	NC	27205	800-433-3243	336-633-0200	161
Randolph County						
110 S Main St	Huntsville	MO	65259	844-277-6555	660-277-5822	338
Randolph Electric Membership Corp						
879 McDowell Rd PO Box 40	Asheboro	NC	27204	800-672-8212	336-625-5177	247
Randolph Packing Co						
275 Roma Jean Pkwy	Streamwood	IL	60107	800-451-1607	630-830-3100	297-26
Randolph Savings Bank						
129 N Main St	Randolph	MA	02368	877-963-2100	781-963-2100	69
Randolph-Brooks Federal Credit Union						
PO Box 2097	Universal City	TX	78148	800-580-3300	210-945-3300	221
Randolph-Macon Academy						
200 Academy Dr	Front Royal	VA	22630	800-272-1172	540-636-5200	621
Randolph-Macon College						
PO Box 5005	Ashland	VA	23005	800-888-1762	804-752-7200	167
Randstad US L P						
2015 S Park Pl	Atlanta	GA	30339	800-382-7297		262
Rane Corp						
10802 47th Ave W	Mukilteo	WA	98275	877-764-0093	425-355-6000	51
R-Anell Custom Homes Inc						
235 Anthony Grave Rd	Crouse	NC	28033	800-951-5511*	704-483-5511	504
*Cust Svc						
Rangam Consultants Inc						
370 Campus Dr Ste 103	Somerset	NJ	08873	877-583-7054	908-704-8843	227
Rangen Inc						
115 13th Ave S	Buhl	ID	83316	800-657-6446*	208-543-6421	446
*Cust Svc						
Ranger College						
1100 College Cir	Ranger	TX	76470	800-772-1213	254-647-3234	161
Ranger Construction Industries Inc						
101 Sansbury's Way	West Palm Beach	FL	33411	800-969-9402	561-793-9400	190-4
Rangers Die Casting Co						
10828 S Alameda St	Lynwood	CA	90262	877-386-9969	310-764-1800	491
Rangeview Library District						
5877 E 120th Ave	Thornton	CO	80602	800-222-3937	303-288-2001	434-3
Rankin County Chamber of Commerce						
101 Service Dr	Brandon	MS	39043	800-987-8280	601-825-2268	138
Ransom & Randolph Co						
3535 Briarfield Blvd	Maumee	OH	43537	800-800-7496	419-865-9497	661
Rapat Corp						
919 Odonnel St	Hawley	MN	56549	800-325-6377	218-483-3344	209
Rape Abuse & Incest National Network (RAINN)						
2000 L St NW Ste 406	Washington	DC	20036	800-656-4673	202-544-1034	47-6
Raphael Kansas City						
325 Ward Pkwy	Kansas City	MO	64112	800-821-5343	816-756-3800	379
Rapid Chevrolet Company Inc						
2323 E Mall Dr	Rapid City	SD	57701	800-456-2105	605-343-1282	515
Rapid City Convention & Visitors Bureau						
444 Mt Rushmore Rd N	Rapid City	SD	57701	800-487-3223	605-718-8484	208
Rapid City Journal						
507 Main St	Rapid City	SD	57701	800-843-2300	605-394-8300	531-2
Rapid City Regional Airport						
4550 Terminal Rd Ste 102	Rapid City	SD	57703	888-279-2135	605-393-9924	27
Rapid Displays						
4300 W 47th St	Chicago	IL	60632	800-356-5775	773-927-1091	235
Rapid Engineering Inc						
1100 7-Mile Rd NW	Comstock Park	MI	49321	800-536-3461	616-784-0500	319
Rapid Focus Security LLC						
253 Summer St Ste 303	Boston	MA	02210	855-793-1337		691
Rapid Industries						
4003 Oaklawn Dr	Louisville	KY	40219	800-727-4381	502-968-3645	209
Rapid Insight Inc						
53 Technology Ln Ste 112	Conway	NH	03818	888-585-6511		179
Rapid Line Industries Inc						
455 N Ottawa St	Joliet	IL	60432	877-444-9955	815-727-4362	110
Rapid Response Monitoring Services Inc						
400 W Division St	Syracuse	NY	13204	800-558-7767		691
RAPIDS Wholesale Equipment Co						
6201 S Gateway Dr	Marion	IA	52302	800-472-7431	319-447-1670	301
Rappahannock Community College						
Glenns						
12745 College Dr	Glenns	VA	23149	800-836-9381	804-758-6700	161
Warsaw 52 Campus Dr	Warsaw	VA	22572	800-836-9381	804-333-6700	161
Raptim Humanitarian Travel						
6420 Inducon Dr W Ste A	Sanborn	NY	14132	800-272-7846	716-754-9232	770
Raritan Computer Inc						
400 Cottontail Ln	Somerset	NJ	08873	800-724-8090	732-764-8886	255
Raritan Valley Community College						
PO Box 3300	Somerville	NJ	08876	888-326-4058	908-526-1200	161
Rasansky Law Firm						
2525 McKinnon Ave Ste 625	Dallas	TX	75201	800-288-6763		634-6
OTC: ATTY						
Rasmussen Equipment Co						
3333 West 2100 South	Salt Lake City	UT	84119	800-453-8032	801-972-5588	358
Rasmussen Iron Works Inc						
12028 E Philadelphia St	Whittier	CA	90601	888-301-0440	562-696-8718	357
RateHub.ca						
411 Richmond St E Ste 208	Toronto	ON	M5A3S5	800-679-9622		465
Rath & Strong Inc						
1666 Massachusetts Ave						
PO Box 170	Lexington	MA	02420	800-622-2025	781-861-1700	196
Raulerson Hospital						
1796 Hwy 441 N	Okeechobee	FL	34972	877-549-9337	863-763-2151	374-3
Ravalli County Fair						
100 Old Corvallis Rd	Hamilton	MT	59840	800-225-6779	406-363-3411	639
Rave Computer Assn Inc						
7171 Sterling Ponds Ct						
	Sterling Heights	MI	48312	800-966-7283	586-939-8230	176
Raven Industries Inc						
205 E Sixth St	Sioux Falls	SD	57104	800-243-5435	605-336-2750	599
NASDAQ: RAVN						
Raven One to One Marketing						
1020 Airport Rd	Allentown	PA	18109	866-577-4121	484-240-6500	197
Ravenswood Winery Inc						
18701 Gehricke Rd	Sonoma	CA	95476	888-669-4679		79-3
Ravine Gardens State Park						
1600 Twigg St	Palatka	FL	32177	800-326-3521	386-329-3721	564
Rawah Ranch						
11447 N County Rd 103	Glendevey	CO	82063	800-820-3152		241
Rawson Inc						
2010 McAllister	Houston	TX	77092	800-779-1414		248
Raxco Software Inc						
6 Montgomery Village Ave						
Ste 500	Gaithersburg	MD	20879	800-546-9728*	301-527-0803	180-12
*Tech Supp						
Ray Products Company Inc						
1700 Chablis Ave	Ontario	CA	91761	800-423-7859	909-390-9906	601
Raybestos Powertrain LLC						
711 Tech Dr	Crawfordsville	IN	47933	800-729-7763		59
Raybourn Group International						
9100 PuRdue Rd Ste 200	Indianapolis	IN	46268	800-362-2546	317-328-4636	46
Rayco Industries Inc						
1502 Valley Rd	Richmond	VA	23222	800-505-7111	804-321-7111	491
Raymarine Inc						
21 Manchester St	Merrimack	NH	03054	800-539-5539	603-881-5200	528
Raymon H Mulford Library						
Medical College of Ohio Toledo						
3000 Arlington Ave	Toledo	OH	43614	800-321-8383	419-383-4225	434-1
Raymond Bldg Supply Corp						
7751 Bayshore Rd	North Fort Myers	FL	33917	877-731-7272	239-731-8300	193-3
Raymond Corp						
22 S Canal St	Greene	NY	13778	800-235-7200*	607-656-2311	469
*General						
Raymond Excavating Co Inc						
800 Gratiot Blvd	Marysville	MI	48040	800-837-6770	810-364-6881	191-5
Raymond F Kravis Ctr for the Performing Arts						
701 Okeechobee Blvd	West Palm Beach	FL	33401	800-572-8471	561-832-7469	571
Raymond Gary State Park						
Hwy 70	Fort Towson	OK	74735	800-622-6317	580-873-2307	564
Raymond Handling Concepts Corp						
41400 Boyce Rd	Fremont	CA	94538	800-675-2500	510-745-7500	266-3
Raymond James Financial Inc						
880 Carillon Pkwy	Saint Petersburg	FL	33716	800-248-8863	727-567-1000	688
NYSE: RJF						
Raymond James Ltd						
2200-925 W Georgia St Cathedral Pl						
	Vancouver	BC	V6C3L2	888-545-6624	604-659-8000	401
Raymond James (USA) Ltd						
2200 - 925 W Georgia St	Vancouver	BC	V6C3L2	877-570-7558		689
Raymond R Andy Guest Jr Shenandoah River State Park						
350 Daughter of Stars Dr	Bentonville	VA	22610	800-933-7275	540-622-6840	564
Raymond Vineyard						
849 Zinfandel Ln	Saint Helena	CA	94574	800-525-2659	707-963-6941	79-3
Rayner Covering Systems Inc						
665 Schneider Dr	South Elgin	IL	60177	800-648-0757	847-695-2264	607
Raynor Garage Doors						
1101 E River Rd	Dixon	IL	61021	800-472-9667	815-288-1431	236
Raypak Inc						
2151 Eastman Ave	Oxnard	CA	93030	800-438-4328	805-278-5300	357
Raytech Industries						
475 Smith St	Middletown	CT	06457	800-243-7163*	860-632-2020	1
*Cust Svc						
Raytek Inc						
1201 Shaffer Rd	Santa Cruz	CA	95061	800-227-8074	831-458-3900	694
Raytheon Co						
10 Moulton St	Cambridge	MA	02138	866-230-1307	617-873-8000	180-10
Rayven Inc						
431 Griggs St N	Saint Paul	MN	55104	800-878-3776*	651-642-1112	627
*Cust Svc						
RB Royal Industries Inc						
1350 S Hickory St						
PO Box 1168	Fond du Lac	WI	54936	800-892-1550	920-921-1550	620
RBB Innovations						
2-258 Queen St E	Sault Sainte Marie	ON	P6A1Y7	800-796-7864	705-942-9053	179
RBC Bearings Inc						
3131 W Segerstrom Ave						
PO Box 1953	Santa Ana	CA	92704	866-722-2376	714-546-3131	619
RBC Capital Markets						
1 Liberty Plaza	New York	NY	10006	800-387-1122	212-428-6200	688
RBC Centura Banks Inc						
PO Box 1220	Rocky Mount	NC	27802	800-769-2553		360-2
RBC Dain Rauscher Inc						
60 S Sixth St						
Dain Rauscher Plz	Minneapolis	MN	55402	800-933-9946		688
RBC Liberty Insurance						
PO Box 789	Greenville	SC	29602	800-551-8354	864-609-8111	391-2
RBC Royal Bank						
1127 Blvd D,carie	Montreal	QC	H4L3M8	800-769-2599		69
RBC Trust Company (Delaware) Ltd						
4550 New Linden Hill Rd						
Ste 200	Wilmington	DE	19808	800-441-7698	302-892-6976	69
RBCM (Royal British Columbia Museum)						
675 Belleville St	Victoria	BC	V8W9W2	888-447-7977	250-356-7226	519
RBG (Royal Botanical Gardens)						
680 Plains Rd W	Burlington	ON	L7T4H4	800-694-4769	905-527-1158	96
RBI Corp						
10201 Cedar Ridge Dr	Ashland	VA	23005	800-444-7370		358
RBMA (Radiology Business Management Assn)						
10300 Eaton Pl Ste 460	Fairfax	VA	22030	888-224-7262	703-621-3355	48-8
RBN Energy LLC						
2323 S Shepherd Dr Ste 1010	Houston	TX	77019	888-400-9838		462
Rbx Inc						
PO Box 2118	Springfield	MO	65802	877-450-2200	800-245-5507	778

Name / Address	City	State	ZIP	Toll-Free	Phone	Class
RC Fine Foods PO Box 236	Belle Mead	NJ	08502	800-526-3953	908-359-5500	297-11
RC Smith Co 14200 Southcross Dr W	Burnsville	MN	55306	800-747-7648	952-854-0711	288
RCA Rubber Co 1833 E Market St	Akron	OH	44305	800-321-2340	330-784-1291	293
RCH (Rady Children's Hospital) 3020 Children's Way MC 5101	San Diego	CA	92123	800-788-9029	858-576-1700	374-1
RCI (Resort Condominiums International) 9998 N Michigan Rd	Carmel	IN	46032	800-338-7777	317-805-8000	751
RCI (Retail Confectioners International) 2053 S Waverly Ste C	Springfield	MO	65804	800-545-5381	417-883-2775	48-6
RCI Custom Products 801 NE St Ste 2A	Frederick	MD	21701	800-546-4724	301-620-9130	205
RCM Technologies Inc 2500 McClellan Ave Ste 350 *NASDAQ: RCMT*	Pennsauken	NJ	08109	800-322-2885	856-356-4500	719
RCMA (Religious Conference Management Assn Inc) 7702 Woodland Dr Ste 120	Indianapolis	IN	46278	800-221-8235	317-632-1888	48-12
RCMC (Rush-Copley Medical Ctr) 2000 Ogden Ave	Aurora	IL	60504	866-426-7539	630-978-6200	374-3
RCMP Heritage Ctr 5907 Dewdney Ave	Regina	SK	S4T0P4	866-567-7267	306-522-7333	519
RCP (Rubbermaid Commercial Products) 3124 Valley Ave	Winchester	VA	22601	800-347-9800	540-667-8700	607
RCP Block & Brick Inc 8240 Broadway	Lemon Grove	CA	91945	800-794-4727	619-460-7250	185
RCS Enterprises Inc 7075 W Parkland Ct	Milwaukee	WI	53223	800-373-6873	414-354-6900	8
RDA Corp 303 International Cir Ste 340	Hunt Valley	MD	21030	888-441-1278	410-308-9300	179
RDA Group 450 Enterprise Ct	Bloomfield Hills	MI	48302	800-669-7324	248-332-5000	465
RDC (Roche Diagnostics Corp) 9115 Hague Rd PO Box 50457 *Cust Svc	Indianapolis	IN	46250	800-428-5076*	317-521-2000	233
RDI Marketing Services 4350 Glendale Milford Rd Ste 250	Cincinnati	OH	45242	800-388-7636	513-984-5927	5
Rdk Truck Sales Inc 3214 E Adamo Dr	Tampa	FL	33605	877-735-4636	813-241-0711	515
RDO Equipment Co 700 Seventh St S	Fargo	ND	58103	800-726-5391	877-444-7363	10-9
RDS Solutions LLC 99 Grayrock Rd	Clinton	NJ	08809	888-473-7435		198
RE Lewis Refrigeration Inc 803 S Lincoln St PO Box 92 *Cust Svc	Creston	IA	50801	800-264-0767*	641-782-8183	663
RE/MAX International Inc 5075 S Syracuse St *Cust Svc	Denver	CO	80237	800-525-7452*	303-770-5531	650
RE/MAX LLC 5075 S Syracuse St	Denver	CO	80237	800-525-7452		664
RE/MAX of Western Canada Inc 1060 Manhattan Dr Ste 340	Kelowna	BC	V1Y9X9	800-563-3622	250-860-3628	650
RE/MAX Ontario-Atlantic 7101 Syntex Dr	Mississauga	ON	L5N6H5	888-542-2499	905-542-2400	650
RE/MAX Quebec Inc 1500 Cunard St	Laval	QC	H7S2B7	800-361-9325	450-668-7743	650
REA Energy Co-op Inc 75 Airport Rd	Indiana	PA	15701	800-211-5667	724-349-4800	247
Rea Magnet Wire Company Inc 3600 E Pontiac St	Fort Wayne	IN	46803	800-732-9473	260-421-7321	811
Reach Resort 1435 Simonton St	Key West	FL	33040	888-318-4317	305-296-5000	667
Readerlink Distribution Services LLC 1420 Kensington Rd Ste 300	Oak Brook	IL	60523	800-549-5389	708-547-4400	94
Reading & Berks County Visitors Bureau 2525 N 12th St Ste 101	Reading	PA	19605	800-443-6610	610-375-4085	208
Reading Area Community College 10 S Second St PO Box 1706	Reading	PA	19603	800-626-1665	610-372-4721	161
Reading Is Fundamental Inc (RIF) 1825 Connecticut Ave NW Ste 400	Washington	DC	20009	877-743-7323	202-536-3400	47-11
Reading Precast Inc 5494 Pottsville Pike	Leesport	PA	19533	800-724-4881	610-926-5000	185
Reading Rock Inc 4600 Devitt Dr	Cincinnati	OH	45246	800-482-6466	513-874-2345	185
Reading Truck Body Inc 201 Hancock Blvd *All	Reading	PA	19611	800-458-2226*		515
Ready Pac Produce Inc 4401 Foxdale Ave	Irwindale	CA	91706	800-800-7822		297-33
Ready Technologies Inc 101 Capitol Way N Ste 301	Olympia	WA	98501	877-892-9104	360-413-9800	263
ReadyPulse 1600 A El Camino Real	San Carlos	CA	94070	888-998-7412		5
Reagan Wireless Corp 720 S Powerline Rd Ste D	Deerfield Beach	FL	33442	877-724-3266	954-596-2355	248
Reagent Chemical & Research Inc 115 Rt 202	Ringoes	NJ	08551	800-231-1807	908-284-2800	145
Real Estate Buyer's Agent Council (REBAC) 430 N Michigan Ave	Chicago	IL	60611	800-648-6224		48-17
Real Estate Institute of Bc 1750 - 355 Burrard St	Vancouver	BC	V6C2G8	800-667-2166	604-685-3702	650
Real Estate Institute of Canada, The 5407 Eglinton Ave W Ste 208	Toronto	ON	M9C5K6	800-542-7342	416-695-9000	654
Real Estate Law Report 610 Opperman Dr *Cust Svc	Eagan	MN	55123	800-328-4880*	651-687-7000	530-7
Real Estate One Inc 25800 NW Hwy Ste 100	Southfield	MI	48075	800-521-0508	248-304-6700	650
Real Goods Solar 833 W S Boulder Rd *NASDAQ: RSGE*	Louisville	CO	80027	888-567-6527		619
Real Living First Service Realty 13155 SW 42nd St Ste 200	Miami	FL	33175	800-899-8477	305-551-9400	650

Name / Address	City	State	ZIP	Toll-Free	Phone	Class
Realestateexpresscom 12977 N 40 Dr Ste 108	Saint Louis	MO	63141	866-739-7277		650
RealNetworks Inc 2601 Elliott Ave Ste 1000 *NASDAQ: RNWK* ■ *Cust Svc	Seattle	WA	98121	888-484-8256*	206-674-2700	180-8
Realstreet Staffing 2500 Wallington Way Ste 208	Marriottsville	MD	21104	877-480-8002	410-480-8002	462
RealTechNetwork Corp 75A Lk Rd Ste 150	Congers	NY	10920	877-279-4904		5
Realtime Software Corp 24 Deane Rd	Bernardston	MA	01337	800-323-1143	847-803-1100	180-1
Realtor Magazine 430 N Michigan Ave 9th Fl	Chicago	IL	60611	800-874-6500	312-329-8458	456-5
Realtors Assn of New Mexico 2201 Bros Rd	Santa Fe	NM	87505	800-224-2282	505-982-2442	654
Realty Executives International Inc 7600 N 16th St Ste 100	Phoenix	AZ	85020	800-252-3366	602-957-0747	650
Realty Income Corp 11995 El Camino Real *NYSE: O*	San Diego	CA	92130	877-924-6266	858-284-5000	653
RealtyBid International Inc 3225 Rainbow Dr Ste 248	Rainbow City	AL	35906	877-518-5600		393
RealtyShares Inc 637 Natoma St Ste 5	San Francisco	CA	94103	855-880-6050	415-450-6234	387
Reasio Inc 5214F Diamond Heights Blvd Ste 217	San Francisco	CA	94131	888-870-7889		387
Reason Magazine 3415 S Sepulveda Blvd Ste 400 *Cust Svc	Los Angeles	CA	90034	888-732-7668*	310-391-2245	456-17
Reason Public Policy Institute 3415 S Sepulveda Blvd Ste 400	Los Angeles	CA	90034	888-732-7668	310-391-2245	631
Reaxis Inc 941 Robinson Hwy	Mcdonald	PA	15057	800-426-7273		388
REBAC (Real Estate Buyer's Agent Council) 430 N Michigan Ave	Chicago	IL	60611	800-648-6224		48-17
Re-Bath LLC 16879 N 75th Ave Ste 101	Peoria	AZ	85382	800-426-4573		191-11
Rebco Inc 1171-1225 Madison Ave	Paterson	NJ	07509	800-777-0787	973-684-0200	236
Rebel State Historic Site 1260 Hwy 1221	Marthaville	LA	71450	888-677-3600	318-472-6255	564
Reborn Cabinets 2981 E La Palma Ave	Anaheim	CA	92806	888-273-2676	714-630-2220	322
Rebuilding Together Inc 1899 L St NW Ste 1000	Washington	DC	20036	800-473-4229		47-5
REC (Rural Electric Co-op Inc) 801 N Industrial Heights PO Box 609	Lindsay	OK	73052	800-259-3504	405-756-3104	247
Reciprocal of America 4200 Innslake Dr Ste 102	Glen Allen	VA	23060	800-284-8847	804-747-8600	391-5
Reco Equipment Inc 41245 Reco Rd	Belmont	OH	41245	800-686-7326	740-782-1314	192
RECON Dynamics LLC 2300 Carillon Point	Kirkland	WA	98033	877-480-3551		691
Recon Logistics LLC 10205 Queens Way Ste 5	Chagrin Falls	OH	44023	866-424-7153	440-708-2306	312
Recon Management Services Inc 3649 S Beglis Pkwy	Sulphur	LA	70665	888-301-4662	337-583-4662	630
Reconditioned Systems Inc (RSI) 2636 S Wilson St Ste 105	Tempe	AZ	85282	800-280-5000	480-968-1772	320-1
Record Play Tek Inc 110 E Vistula St	Bristol	IN	46507	800-809-5233	574-848-5233	51
Record Searchlight PO Box 492397	Redding	CA	96049	800-666-1331	530-243-2424	531-2
Record USA 4324 Phil Hargett Ct PO Box 3099 *Sales	Monroe	NC	28111	800-438-1937*	704-289-9212	255
Record, The PO Box 900	Stockton	CA	95201	800-606-9741	209-943-6397	531-2
Record-Courier 1050 W Main St PO Box 5199	Kent	OH	44240	800-560-9657	330-541-9400	531-2
Recordflow 1751 e garry ave	Santa Ana	CA	92705	877-896-7350		462
Recording for the Blind & Dyslexic (RFB&D) 20 Roszel Rd	Princeton	NJ	08540	800-221-4792		47-17
Record-Journal 11 Crown St	Meriden	CT	06450	800-228-6915	203-235-1661	531-2
Recreation Vehicle Dealers Assn (RVDA) 3930 University Dr 3rd Fl	Fairfax	VA	22030	800-336-0355	703-591-7130	48-18
Recreation Vehicle Industry Assn (RVIA) 1896 Preston White Dr	Reston	VA	20191	800-336-0154	703-620-6003	48-21
Recreation.gov 1849 C St NW	Washington	DC	20240	877-444-6777	202-208-4743	199
Recreational Equipment Inc (REI) 6750 S 228th St *Orders	Kent	WA	98032	800-426-4840*	253-395-3780	709
Recreatives Industries Inc 60 Depot St	Buffalo	NY	14206	800-255-2511	716-855-2226	29
Recruiting Toolbox PO Box 2573	Redmond	WA	98073	888-823-2030	425-557-2100	393
Recursion Software Inc 2591 Dallas Pkwy Ste 200	Frisco	TX	75034	800-727-8674	972-731-8800	181
Recycled Paper Greetings Inc 111 N Canal St Ste 700	Chicago	IL	60606	800-777-3331		129
Red Ball Oxygen Co Inc 609 N Market	Shreveport	LA	71107	800-551-8150	318-425-3211	385
Red Bud Industries 200 B & E Industrial Dr *Cust Svc	Red Bud	IL	62278	800-851-4612*	618-282-3801	493
Red Carpet Charters 4820 SW 20th	Oklahoma City	OK	73128	888-878-5100	405-672-5100	106
Red Clay Interactive 22 Buford Village Way Ste 221	Buford	GA	30518	866-251-2800	770-297-2430	227
Red Devil Inc 1437 S Boulder	Tulsa	OK	74119	800-423-3845		3

Name / Address	City	State	Zip	Toll-Free	Phone	Class
Red Diamond Inc 400 Park Ave	Moody	AL	35004	**800-292-4651**	205-577-4000	297-7
Red Dot Corp 1209 W Corsicana St *Cust Svc	Athens	TX	75751	**800-657-2234***		104
Red Ewald Inc 2669 US 181	Karnes City	TX	78118	**800-242-3524**	830-780-3304	605
Red Fleet State Park 8750 North Hwy 191	Vernal	UT	84078	**800-322-3770**	435-789-4432	564
Red Foundry Inc 1608 S Ashland Ave	Chicago	IL	60608	**888-406-1099**		630
Red Hat Inc 1801 Varsity Dr *NYSE: RHT*	Raleigh	NC	27606	**888-733-4281**	919-754-3700	180-12
Red Hat Society Store 431 S Acacia Ave	Fullerton	CA	92831	**866-386-2850**	714-738-0001	532
Red Hill Patrick Henry National Memorial 1250 Red Hill Rd	Brookneal	VA	24528	**800-514-7463**	434-376-2044	563
Red Hot & Blue Restaurants Inc 200 Old Mill Bottom Rd S	Annapolis	MD	21401	**888-509-7100**	410-626-7427	669
Red Inn 15 Commercial St	Provincetown	MA	02657	**866-473-3466**	508-487-7334	669
Red Jacket Beach Resort 39 Todd Rd	South Yarmouth	MA	02664	**800-227-3263**	508-398-6941	379
Red Label Vacations Inc 5450 Explorer Dr Ste 100	Mississauga	ON	L4W5N1	**866-573-3824**	905-283-6020	770
Red Lake Electric Co-op Inc 412 International Dr PO Box 430	Red Lake Falls	MN	56750	**800-245-6068**	218-253-2168	247
Red Lake Gaming Enterprises Inc PO Box 543	Red Lake	MN	56671	**888-679-2501**	218-679-2111	131
Red Lion Hotel 621 21St St	Lewiston	ID	83501	**800-232-6730**	208-799-1000	378
Red Lion Hotels Corp 201 W N River Dr Ste 100 *NYSE: RLH* ■ *Resv	Spokane	WA	99201	**800-733-5466***		379
Red Lion Templin's Hotel on the River 414 E First Ave	Post Falls	ID	83854	**800-733-5466**	208-773-1611	667
Red Peacock International Inc 1945 Gardena Ave	Glendale	CA	91204	**877-774-0037**	818-265-7722	248
Red River Commodities Inc 501 42nd St N	Fargo	ND	58102	**800-437-5539**	701-282-2600	692
Red River Specialties Inc 1324 N Hearne Ave Ste 120	Shreveport	LA	71107	**800-256-3344**	318-425-5944	278
Red River Valley Co-op Power Assn 109 Second Ave E	Halstad	MN	56548	**800-788-7784**	218-456-2139	247
Red Rock Distributing Co 1 NW 50th St	Oklahoma City	OK	73118	**800-323-7109**	405-677-3373	448
Red Rock Resort Spa & Casino 11011 W Charleston Blvd	Las Vegas	NV	89135	**866-767-7773**	702-797-7777	379
Red Spot Interactive 1001 jupiter park dr	Jupiter	FL	33458	**800-401-7931**		462
Red Spot Paint & Varnish Co Inc 1107 E Louisiana St	Evansville	IN	47711	**877-777-4778**	812-428-9100	549
Red Star Oil 802 Purser Dr	Raleigh	NC	27603	**800-774-6033**	919-772-1944	448
Red Wind Casino 12819 Yelm Hwy	Olympia	WA	98513	**866-946-2444**	360-412-5000	132
Red Wing Shoe Company Inc 314 Main St *Cust Svc	Red Wing	MN	55066	**800-733-9464***	651-388-8211	302
Red Wing Software Inc 491 Hwy 19	Red Wing	MN	55066	**800-732-9464**	651-388-1106	180-1
Redco Foods Inc 1 Hansen Island	Little Falls	NY	13365	**800-556-6674**	315-823-1300	297-40
Redd Paper Co 3851 Ctr Loop	Orlando	FL	32808	**800-961-6656**	407-299-6656	552
Redden Marine Supply Inc 1411 Roeder Ave	Bellingham	WA	98225	**800-426-9284**	360-733-0250	709
Reddy Ice Holdings Inc 8750 N Central Expy Ste 1800 *OTC: RDDYQ*	Dallas	TX	75231	**800-683-4423**	214-526-6740	380
Redeemer University College 777 Garner Rd E	Ancaster	ON	L9K1J4	**877-779-0913**	905-648-2131	783
Redemptorist, The 1 Liguori Dr	Liguori	MO	63057	**800-325-9521**	636-464-2500	47-20
Redemtech Inc 4115 Leap Rd	Hilliard	OH	43026	**800-393-7627**	614-850-3366	180-1
Redfin 9890 S Maryland Pkwy Ste 200	Las Vegas	NV	89183	**800-561-5463**	877-973-3346	5
Redi Bag USA 135 Fulton Ave	New Hyde Park	NY	11040	**800-517-2247**	516-746-0600	97
Redico Inc 1850 S Lee Ct	Buford	GA	30518	**800-242-3920**		663
Rediker Software Inc 2 Wilbraham Rd	Hampden	MA	01036	**800-213-9860**	413-566-3463	179
Redland Brick Inc 15718 Clear Spring Rd	Williamsport	MD	21795	**800-366-2742**	301-223-7700	149
Redlands Chamber of Commerce 1 E Redlands Blvd	Redlands	CA	92373	**800-966-6428**	909-793-2546	138
Redlands Community College 1300 S Country Club Rd	El Reno	OK	73036	**866-415-6367**	405-262-2552	161
Redlands Community Hospital Foundation PO Box 3391	Redlands	CA	92373	**888-397-4999**	909-335-5500	374-3
RedLegg 100 Illinois St Ste 200	St. Charles	IL	60174	**877-811-5040**		198
Redline Communications Inc 302 Town Centre Blvd 3rd Fl	Markham	ON	L3R0E8	**866-633-6669**	905-479-8344	226
Redman Equipment & Mfg Co 19800 Normandie Ave	Torrance	CA	90502	**888-733-2602**	310-329-1134	90
Redmonk LLC 93 S Jackson St	Seattle	WA	98104	**866-733-6665**		462
Redneck Trailer Supplies 2100 NW By-Pass	Springfield	MO	65803	**877-973-3632**	417-864-5210	777
Red-Ray Mfg Co Inc 10-22 County Line Rd	Branchburg	NJ	08876	**800-883-9218**	908-722-0040	319
RedRick Technologies Inc 21624 Adelaide Rd	Mount Brydges	ON	N0L1W0	**800-340-9511**	519-264-2400	474
Redstone College *Denver* 10851 W 120th Ave	Broomfield	CO	80021	**800-888-3995**	303-466-1714	798
Redstone Federal Credit Union 220 Wynn Dr NW	Huntsville	AL	35893	**800-234-1234**	256-837-6110	221
Redstone Highlands Health Care Ctr 6 Garden Ctr Dr	Greensburg	PA	15601	**800-732-0999**	724-832-8400	449
RedTail Solutions Inc 69 Milk St Ste 100	Westborough	MA	01581	**866-764-7601**	508-983-1900	227
Redwood Asset Management Inc Richmond Adelaide Centre 120 Adelaide St W Ste 2400	Toronto	ON	M5H1T1	**877-313-7011**	416-368-8898	527
Redwood Credit Union PO Box 6104	Santa Rosa	CA	95406	**800-479-7928**	707-545-4000	216
Redwood Trust Inc 1 Belvedere Pl Ste 300 *NYSE: RWT*	Mill Valley	CA	94941	**866-269-4976**	415-389-7373	508
Reeb Millwork Corp 7475 Henry Clay Blvd	Liverpool	NY	13088	**800-862-8622**	315-451-6699	498
Reebok International Ltd 1895 JW Foster Blvd	Canton	MA	02021	**866-870-1743**	781-401-5000	302
Reed 28 Sword St	Auburn	MA	01501	**800-343-6068**	508-753-6530	455
Reed Brennan Media Associates Inc 628 Virginia Dr	Orlando	FL	32803	**800-708-7311**	407-894-7300	318
Reed College 3203 SE Woodstock Blvd *Admissions	Portland	OR	97202	**800-547-4750***	503-777-7511	167
Reed Gold Mine State Historic Site 9621 Reed Mine Rd	Midland	NC	28107	**877-628-6386**	704-721-4653	49-2
Reed Manufacturing Co 1425 W Eigth St	Erie	PA	16502	**800-456-1697**	814-452-3691	756
Reed Mfg Co Inc 1321 S Veterans Blvd	Tupelo	MS	38804	**800-466-1154**	662-842-4472	154-10
Reeder Distributors Inc 5450 Wilbarger St	Fort Worth	TX	76119	**800-722-3103**	817-429-5957	578
Reedley College 995 N Reed Ave	Reedley	CA	93654	**877-253-7122**	559-638-3641	161
Reeds Family Outdoor Outfitters 522 Minnesota Ave NW	Walker	MN	56484	**800-346-0019**		709
Reeds Jewelers Inc PO Box 2229 *Orders	Wilmington	NC	28402	**877-406-3266***	910-350-3100	410
Reedsville Co-op Assn Inc PO Box 460	Reedsville	WI	54230	**800-236-4047**	920-754-4321	278
Reef Industries Inc 9209 Almeda Genoa Rd	Houston	TX	77075	**800-231-6074**	713-507-4200	598
Reef Resort 2101 S Ocean Blvd *Cust Svc	Myrtle Beach	SC	29577	**800-845-1212***	843-448-1765	667
Reese Enterprises Inc 16350 Asher Ave	Rosemount	MN	55068	**800-328-0953**	651-423-1126	236
Reese Pharmaceutical Co 10617 Frank Ave	Cleveland	OH	44106	**800-321-7178**		240
Reeve Store Equipment Co 9131 Bermudez St PO Box 276	Pico Rivera	CA	90660	**800-927-3383**	562-949-2535	288
Reeves Construction Co Inc 101 Sheraton Ct	Macon	GA	31210	**800-743-0593**	478-474-9092	190-4
Reeves-Wiedeman Co Inc 14861 W 100th St	Lenexa	KS	66215	**800-365-0024**	913-492-7100	611
Reference & User Services Assn (RUSA) 50 E Huron St	Chicago	IL	60611	**800-545-2433**	312-280-4398	48-11
Reflexite Corp 120 Darling Dr	Avon	CT	06001	**800-654-7570**	860-676-7100	742-2
Reflexite North America 315 S St	New Britain	CT	06051	**800-654-7570**	860-223-9297	676
Reformed Church in America 475 Riverside Dr 18th Fl	New York	NY	10115	**800-722-9977**	212-870-3071	47-20
Reformed Theological Seminary 5422 Clinton Blvd	Jackson	MS	39209	**800-543-2703**	601-923-1600	168-3
Refrigerated Food Express Inc 57 Littlefield St	Avon	MA	02322	**800-342-8822**	508-587-4600	778
Refrigeration Sales Corp 9450 Allen Dr Ste A	Valley View	OH	44125	**866-894-8200**	216-881-7800	611
Refrigeration Service Engineers Society (RSES) 1666 Rand Rd	Des Plaines	IL	60016	**800-297-5660**	847-297-6464	48-3
RefrigiWear Inc 54 Breakstone Dr *Cust Svc	Dahlonega	GA	30533	**800-645-3744***	706-864-5757	154-5
Refugees International (RI) 2001 S St NW Ste 700-K	Washington	DC	20009	**800-733-8433**	202-828-0110	47-5
RefWorks LLC 7200 Wisconsin Ave Ste 601	Bethesda	MD	20814	**800-843-7751**	301-961-6700	387
Regal Entertainment Group 7132 Regal Ln *NYSE: RGC* ■ *Cust Svc	Knoxville	TN	37918	**877-835-5734***	865-922-1123	745
Regal Marine Industries Inc 2300 Jetport Dr	Orlando	FL	32809	**800-877-3425**	407-851-4360	89
Regal Plastic Supply Co 111 E Tenth Ave	North Kansas City	MO	64116	**800-627-2102**	816-421-6290	602
Regal Press Inc, The 129 Guild St	Norwood	MA	02062	**800-447-3425**	781-769-3900	626
Regal Travel 615 Piikoi St Ste 104	Honolulu	HI	96814	**800-799-0865**	808-566-7620	769
Regal-Beloit Corp 200 State St *NYSE: RBC*	Beloit	WI	53511	**800-672-6495**	608-364-8800	619
Regal-Beloit Corp Durst Div PO Box 298	Beloit	WI	53512	**800-356-0775**	608-365-2563	707
Regalia Manufacturing Co 2018 Fourth Ave	Rock Island	IL	61201	**800-798-7471**	309-788-7471	775
Regatta Travel Solutions Inc 325 Winding River Ln Ste 201B	Charlottesville	VA	22911	**800-605-5093**		393
Regence Blue Cross Blue Shield of Oregon PO Box 1071	Portland	OR	97207	**888-734-3623**	888-675-6570	391-3
Regence BlueCross BlueShield of Utah 2890 E Cottonwood Pkwy *Cust Svc	Salt Lake City	UT	84121	**800-624-6519***	801-333-2100	391-3

Name / Address	City	State	ZIP	Toll-Free	Phone	Class
Regency Centers						
1 Independent Dr Ste 114	Jacksonville	FL	32202	**800-950-6333**	904-598-7000	653
NYSE: REG						
Regency Fairbanks Hotel						
95 Tenth Ave	Fairbanks	AK	99701	**800-478-1320**	907-459-2700	379
Regency Infographics Inc (SED)						
2867 E Allegheny Ave	Philadelphia	PA	19134	**800-829-0020**	215-425-8800	779
Regency Lighting Co						
9261 Jordan Ave	Chatsworth	CA	91311	**800-284-2024**		248
Regency Limousine International						
83-03 24th Ave	East Elmhurst	NY	11370	**866-302-2201**	718-507-4000	441
Regency Seating Inc						
2375 Romig Rd	Akron	OH	44320	**866-816-9822**	330-848-3700	322
Regency Suites Calgary						
610 Fourth Ave SW	Calgary	AB	T2P0K1	**800-468-4044**	403-231-1000	379
Regency Suites Hotel Midtown Atlanta						
975 W Peachtree St	Atlanta	GA	30309	**800-642-3629**	404-876-5003	379
Regent College						
5800 University Blvd	Vancouver	BC	V6T2E4	**800-663-8664**	604-224-3245	168-3
Regent Products Corp						
8999 Palmer St	River Grove	IL	60171	**800-583-1002**	708-583-1000	361
Regent University						
Library						
1000 Regent University Dr	Virginia Beach	VA	23464	**888-249-1822**	757-352-4916	434-6
Regents Point						
19191 Harvard Ave	Irvine	CA	92612	**800-347-3735***	949-988-0849	670
*General						
Regina Leader Post						
1964 Pk St	Regina	SK	S4P3G4	**800-667-9999**	306-781-5211	531-1
Regional Acceptance Corp						
1424 E Fire Tower Rd	Greenville	NC	27858	**877-722-7299**	252-321-7700	216
Regional International Corp						
1007 Lehigh Stn Rd	Henrietta	NY	14467	**800-836-0409**	585-359-2011	60
Regional Medical Ctr, The						
3000 St Matthews Rd	Orangeburg	SC	29118	**800-476-3377**	803-395-2200	374-3
Regional Occupational Programs						
300 Dana St	Fort Bragg	CA	95437	**800-451-9999**	707-964-9000	506
Regional Tissue Bank QEII Health Sciences Centre						
5788 University Ave						
Rm 431 MacKenzie Bldg	Halifax	NS	B3H1V7	**800-314-6515**	902-473-4171	544
Regional Transportation Commission of Southern Nevada (RTC)						
600 S Grand Central Pkwy						
Ste 350	Las Vegas	NV	89106	**800-228-3911**	702-676-1500	467
Regional Transportation District (RTD)						
1600 Blake St	Denver	CO	80202	**800-366-7433**	303-628-9000	467
Regions Bank						
1900 Fifth Ave N	Birmingham	AL	35203	**800-734-4667**		69
Regions Financial Corp						
1900 Fifth Ave N	Birmingham	AL	35203	**866-688-0658**		360-2
NYSE: RF						
Regions Mortgage Inc						
215 Forrest St	Hattiesburg	MS	39401	**800-986-2462**		508
Regis College						
235 Wellesley St	Weston	MA	02493	**866-438-7344**	781-768-7000	167
Regis Corp						
7201 Metro Blvd	Minneapolis	MN	55439	**888-888-7778**	952-947-7777	76
NYSE: RGS						
Regis Corp MasterCuts Div						
7201 Metro Blvd	Minneapolis	MN	55439	**877-857-2070**	952-947-7777	76
Regis Corp Pro-Cuts Div						
7201 Metro Blvd	Minneapolis	MN	55439	**877-857-2070**	952-947-7777	76
Regis Corp Regis Hairstylists Div						
7201 Metro Blvd	Minneapolis	MN	55439	**877-857-2070**	952-947-7777	76
Regis Corp SmartStyle Div						
7201 Metro Blvd	Minneapolis	MN	55439	**877-857-2070**	952-947-7777	76
Regis Technologies Inc						
8210 Austin Ave	Morton Grove	IL	60053	**800-323-8144**	847-967-6000	582
Regis University						
3333 Regis Blvd	Denver	CO	80221	**800-388-2366***	303-458-4100	167
*Admissions						
Colorado Springs						
7450 Campus Dr Ste 100	Colorado Springs	CO	80920	**800-568-8932**		167
Register Tapes Unlimited Inc						
1445 Langham Creek	Houston	TX	77084	**800-247-4793**	281-206-2500	4
Register.com Inc						
575 Eigth Ave 8th Fl	New York	NY	10018	**888-734-4783**		396
Register-Herald						
801 N Kanawha St	Beckley	WV	25801	**800-950-0250**	304-255-4400	531-2
Register-Star						
364 Warren St	Hudson	NY	12534	**800-836-4069**	518-828-1616	531-2
Regitar USA Inc						
2575 Container Dr	Montgomery	AL	36109	**877-734-4827**	334-244-1885	351
Regupol America						
33 Keystone Dr	Lebanon	PA	17042	**800-537-8737**		293
Rehabilitation Hospital of Indiana						
4141 Shore Dr	Indianapolis	IN	46254	**866-510-2273**	317-329-2000	374-6
Rehabilitation Institute of Chicago						
345 E Superior St	Chicago	IL	60611	**800-354-7342***	312-238-1000	374-6
*Admitting						
Rehau Inc						
1501 EdwaRds Ferry Rd NE	Leesburg	VA	20176	**800-247-9445**	703-777-5255	237
Rehmann Group						
5800 Gratiot St Ste 201	Saginaw	MI	48638	**866-799-9580**	989-799-9580	2
Rehoboth Beach Convention Ctr						
229 Rehoboth Ave	Rehoboth Beach	DE	19971	**888-743-3628**	302-227-4641	208
Rehoboth Beach-Dewey Beach Chamber of Commerce						
501 Rehoboth Ave	Rehoboth Beach	DE	19971	**800-441-1329**	302-227-2233	138
Rehrig Pacific Co						
4010 E 26th St	Los Angeles	CA	90023	**800-421-6244**	323-262-5145	201
REI 1700 45th St E	Sumner	WA	98352	**800-426-4840**	253-891-2500	63
REI (Recreational Equipment Inc)						
6750 S 228th St	Kent	WA	98032	**800-426-4840***	253-395-3780	709
*Orders						
REI Adventures						
PO Box 1938	Sumner	WA	98390	**800-622-2236**	253-437-1100	758
Reichhold Inc						
2400 Ellis Rd	Durham	NC	27703	**800-448-3482**	919-990-7500	604-2
Reid Jones McRorie & Williams Inc						
2200 Executive St						
PO Box 669248	Charlotte	NC	28208	**800-785-2604**	704-537-0012	390
Reidler Decal Corp						
264 Industrial Pk Rd						
PO Box 8	Saint Clair	PA	17970	**800-628-7770**		413
Reiff & Nestor Co						
50 Reiff St	Lykens	PA	17048	**800-521-3422**	717-453-7113	492
Reiko Wireless						
1218 flushing ave	Brooklyn	NY	11237	**888-797-3456**	212-213-1102	733
Reily Foods Co						
640 Magazine St	New Orleans	LA	70130	**800-535-1961**	504-524-6131	297-7
Reimers Electra Steam Inc						
4407 Martinsburg Pk						
PO Box 37	Clear Brook	VA	22624	**800-872-7562**	540-662-3811	357
Reindl Bindery Company Inc						
W194 N11381 McCormick Dr	Germantown	WI	53022	**800-878-1121**	262-293-1444	91
Reindl Printing Inc						
1300 Johnson St	Merrill	WI	54452	**800-236-9637**	715-536-9537	626
Reinhardt College						
7300 Reinhardt College Cir	Waleska	GA	30183	**877-346-4273**	770-720-5526	167
Reinke Mfg Co Inc						
5325 Reinke Rd	Deshler	NE	68340	**866-365-7381**	402-365-7251	275
Reinsurance Group of America Inc						
1370 Timberlake Manor Pkwy	Chesterfield	MO	63017	**800-985-4326**	636-736-7000	360-4
NYSE: RGA						
Reis Inc						
530 Fifth Ave 5th Fl	New York	NY	10036	**800-366-7347**	212-921-1122	465
NASDAQ: REIS						
Reisterstown Lumber Co, The						
PO Box 337	Reisterstown	MD	21136	**800-289-8739**	410-833-1300	364
REITPAC						
1875 'I' St NW Ste 600	Washington	DC	20006	**800-362-7348**	202-739-9400	614
Rejuvenation Inc						
2550 NW Nicolai St	Portland	OR	97210	**888-401-1900**	503-231-1900	439
Relais & Chateaux Assn						
10 E 53rd St	New York	NY	10022	**800-735-2478**	212-319-4880	47-23
Relais International						
1690 Woodward Dr Ste 215	Ottawa	ON	K2C3R8	**888-294-5244**	613-226-5571	180-12
Relate Corp						
900 Avenida Acaso Ste K	Camarillo	CA	93012	**800-428-3708**	805-482-7381	182
Relay Specialties Inc						
17 Raritan Rd	Oakland	NJ	07436	**800-526-5376**	201-337-1000	205
Relco Systems Inc						
7310 Chestnut Ridge Rd	Lockport	NY	14094	**800-262-1020**	716-434-8100	778
Relevancy Group LLC, The						
1010 Shenandoah Dr	Spring Lake	NJ	07762	**877-972-6886**		465
Relevant Radio						
1496 Bellevue St Ste 202						
PO Box 10707	Green Bay	WI	54311	**877-291-0123**		641
Reliability Center						
501 Westover Ave	Hopewell	VA	23860	**800-457-0645**	804-458-0645	263
Reliable Carriers Inc						
41555 Koppernick Rd	Canton	MI	48187	**800-521-6393**	734-453-6677	467
Reliable Castings Corp						
3530 Spring Grove Ave	Cincinnati	OH	45223	**866-722-2278**	513-541-2627	309
Reliable Contracting Co Inc						
2410 Evergreen Rd Ste 200	Gambrills	MD	21054	**800-492-4357**	410-987-0313	190-4
Reliable Life Insurance Co						
100 King St W PO Box 557	Hamilton	ON	L8N3K9	**800-465-0661**	905-523-5587	391-2
Reliable Racing Supply Inc						
643 Glen St	Queensbury	NY	12804	**800-223-4448**	518-793-5677	709
Reliable Tire Co						
805 N Blackhorse Pk	Blackwood	NJ	08012	**800-342-3426***		753
*All						
Reliable Wholesale Lumber Inc						
7600 Redondo Cir	Huntington Beach	CA	92648	**877-795-4638**	714-848-8222	193-3
Reliance Controls Corp						
2001 Young Ct	Racine	WI	53404	**800-634-6155**	262-634-6155	727
Reliance Parts Corp						
2535 Business Pkwy	Minden	NV	89423	**800-776-3113**		789
Reliance Standard Life Insurance						
2001 Market St Ste 1500	Philadelphia	PA	19103	**800-351-7500**	267-256-3500	391-2
Reliant Energy Retail Services LLC						
1201 Fannin St	Houston	TX	77002	**866-660-4900**	866-222-7100	785
Religion News Service (RNS)						
529 14th St NW Ste 425	Washington	DC	20045	**800-767-6781**	202-463-8777	529
Religious Conference Management Assn Inc (RCMA)						
7702 Woodland Dr Ste 120	Indianapolis	IN	46278	**800-221-8235**	317-632-1888	48-12
Relin, Goldstein & Crane LLP						
28 E Main St Ste 1800	Rochester	NY	14614	**888-984-2351**	585-325-6202	428
Relios Inc						
6815 Academy Pkwy W NE	Albuquerque	NM	87109	**800-827-6543**	505-345-5304	409
Reliv International Inc						
136 Chesterfield Industrial Blvd	Chesterfield	MO	63005	**800-735-4887**	636-537-9715	366
NASDAQ: RELV						
RELM Wireless Corp						
7100 Technology Dr	West Melbourne	FL	32904	**800-648-0947***	321-984-1414	645
NYSE: RWC ■ *Cust Svc						
RELO Direct Inc						
161 N Clark St Ste 1250	Chicago	IL	60601	**800-621-7356**	312-384-5900	664
Relocation America						
25800 NW Hwy Ste 210	Southfield	MI	48075	**877-500-4466**		664
Relocation Center Inc, The						
1042 E Juneau Ave	Milwaukee	WI	53202	**800-783-5337**	414-226-4200	650
Relton Corp						
317 Rolyn Dr PO Box 60019	Arcadia	CA	91066	**800-423-1505***	323-681-2551	756
*Cust Svc						
Rely Services Inc						
2354 Hassell Rd Ste B	Hoffman Estates	IL	60169	**866-735-9328**	847-310-8750	197
Rem Sales Inc						
910 Gay Hill Rd	Windsor	CT	06095	**877-689-1860**	860-687-3400	385
REMC (Okefenoke Rural Electric Membership Corp)						
14384 Cleveland St PO Box 602	Nahunta	GA	31553	**800-262-5131**	912-462-5131	247
Remco Products Corp						
4735 W 106th St	Zionsville	IN	46077	**800-585-8619**	317-876-9856	297

	City	State	Zip	Toll-Free	Phone	Class
Remedy Temp Inc						
3820 State St	Santa Barbara	CA	93105	**800-688-6162**	805-882-2200	719
Remet Corp						
210 Commons Rd	Utica	NY	13502	**877-939-0171**	315-797-8700	307
Reminder Press Inc						
130 Old Town Rd PO Box 27	Vernon	CT	06066	**888-456-2211**	860-875-3366	634-8
Reminder, The						
PO Box 210	Vernon	CT	06066	**888-456-2211**	860-875-3366	531-4
Reminger & Reminger Company LPa						
101 W Prospect Ave	Cleveland	OH	44115	**800-486-1311**	216-687-1311	428
Remington Arms Company Inc						
870 Remington Dr PO Box 700	Madison	NC	27025	**800-243-9700**	336-548-8700	286
Remington College						
Little Rock						
10600 Colonel Glenn Rd Ste 100	Little Rock	AR	72204	**800-323-8122**	501-312-0007	798
Remington College Largo						
6302 E Dr Martin Luther King Jr Blvd Ste 400	Tampa	FL	33619	**800-323-8122**		798
Remington College Tampa						
6302 E MLK Blvd Ste 400	Tampa	FL	33619	**800-323-8122***	813-935-5700	798
*General						
Remington Park Race Track						
1 Remington Pl	Oklahoma City	OK	73111	**866-456-9880**	405-424-1000	639
Remington Suite Hotel						
220 Travis St	Shreveport	LA	71101	**800-444-6750**	318-425-5000	379
Reminisce Magazine						
1610 N 2nd St Ste 102	Milwaukee	NY	53212	**888-859-7838**	414-423-0100	456-11
Remo Inc						
28101 Industry Dr	Valencia	CA	91355	**800-525-5134**	661-294-5600	526
Remote Access Technology Inc						
61 Atlantic St	Dartmouth	NS	B2Y4P4	**877-356-2728**	902-434-4405	365
Remstar International Inc						
41 Eisenhower Dr	Westbrook	ME	04092	**800-639-5805**		385
Remy International Inc						
600 Corp Dr	Pendleton	IN	46064	**800-372-3555**	765-778-6499	59
NYSE: REMY						
Renaissance Esmeralda Resort						
44-400 Indian Wells Ln	Indian Wells	CA	92210	**888-236-2427**	760-773-4444	667
Renaissance Group						
981 Worcester St	Wellesley	MA	02482	**800-514-2667**		390
Renaissance Learning Inc						
2911 Peach St	Wisconsin Rapids	WI	54494	**800-338-4204**	715-424-3636	180-3
Renaissance Orlando Resort at SeaWorld						
6677 Sea Harbor Dr	Orlando	FL	32821	**800-327-6677**	407-351-5555	667
Renaissance Portsmouth Hotel & Waterfront Conference Ctr						
425 Water St	Portsmouth	VA	23704	**888-839-1775**	757-673-3000	377
Renaissance Resort at World Golf Village						
500 S Legacy Trl	Saint Augustine	FL	32092	**888-740-7020**	904-940-8000	667
Renaissance Vinoy Resort & Golf Club						
501 Fifth Ave NE	Saint Petersburg	FL	33701	**800-468-3571**	727-894-1000	667
Renasant Corp						
209 Troy St PO Box 709	Tupelo	MS	38802	**800-680-1601***	662-680-1001	360-2
NASDAQ: RNST ■ *Cust Svc						
Renbor Sales Solutions Inc						
256 Thornway Ave	Thornhill	ON	L4J7X8	**855-257-2537**	416-671-3555	393
Renco Corp						
116 Third Ave N	Minneapolis	MN	55401	**800-359-8181**	612-338-6124	581
Renco Electronics Inc						
595 International Pl	Rockledge	FL	32955	**800-645-5828**	321-637-1000	248
Rencor Controls Inc						
21 Sullivan Pkwy	Fort Edward	NY	12828	**866-472-7030**	518-747-4171	358
Rend Lake College						
468 N Ken Gray Pkwy	Ina	IL	62846	**800-369-5321**	618-437-5321	161
Rendigs, Fry, Kiely & Dennis LLP						
600 Vine St Ste 2650	Cincinnati	OH	45202	**800-274-2330**	513-381-9200	428
Rene Of Paris						
9135 Independence Ave 9th Fl	Chatsworth	CA	90212	**800-353-7363***		348
*Sales						
Renee's Garden Seeds Inc						
7389 W Zayante Rd	Felton	CA	95018	**888-880-7228**	831-335-7228	692
Renegade/Kibbi LLC						
52216 State Rd 15	Bristol	IN	46507	**888-522-1126**	574-848-1126	119
Renew Data Corp						
9500 Arboretum Blvd	Austin	TX	78759	**888-811-3789**	512-276-5500	227
ReNew Life Formulas Inc						
2076 Sunnydale Blvd	Clearwater	FL	33765	**800-830-1800**	727-450-1061	298-11
Renew Plastics						
PO Box 480 PO Box 480	Luxemburg	WI	54217	**800-666-5207**	920-845-2326	659
Renfro Corp						
661 Linville Rd	Mount Airy	NC	27030	**800-334-9091**	336-719-8000	154-9
Renfrow Bros Inc						
855 Gossett Rd	Spartanburg	SC	29307	**800-260-8412**	864-579-0558	188
Reni Publishing Inc						
150 Third St SW	Winter Haven	FL	33880	**800-274-2812**		626
Renkus-heinz Inc						
19201 Cook St	Foothill Ranch	CA	92610	**855-411-2364**	949-588-9997	51
Rennco LLC 300 Elm St	Homer	MI	49245	**800-409-5225**		789
Rennoc Corp						
645 Pine St	Greenville	OH	45331	**800-372-7100**		154-5
Reno Gazette-Journal						
955 Kuenzli St	Reno	NV	89502	**800-970-7366**	775-788-6397	531-2
Reno News & Review						
708 N Ctr St	Reno	NV	89501	**866-703-3873**	916-498-1234	531-5
RENO Refractories Inc						
601 Reno Dr	Morris	AL	35116	**800-741-7366**	205-647-0240	661
RENO Refractories Inc Reftech Div						
601 Reno Dr	Morris	AL	35116	**800-741-7366***		661
*General						
Renodis Inc						
476 Robert St N	Saint Paul	MN	55101	**866-200-8986**	651-556-1200	448
Renoir Staffing Services Inc						
1301 Marina Vlg Pkwy Ste 350	Alameda	CA	94501	**866-672-3709**		262
Renold Ajax Inc						
100 Bourne St	Westfield	NY	14787	**800-251-9012**	716-326-3121	619
Renold Jeffrey						
2307 Maden Dr	Morristown	TN	37813	**800-251-9012**	423-586-1951	209
Reno-Sparks Convention & Visitors Authority						
PO Box 837	Reno	NV	89504	**800-443-1482**	775-827-7600	208
Reno-Sparks Convention Ctr						
4590 S Virginia St	Reno	NV	89502	**800-367-7366**	775-827-7600	207
Reno-Tahoe International Airport						
2001 E Plumb Ln	Reno	NV	89502	**877-736-6359**	775-328-6400	27
Renova Lighting Systems Inc						
20 Middlesex Rd	Mansfield	MA	02048	**800-635-6682**	401-682-1850	439
Renovator's Supply Inc						
Renovators Old ML	Millers Falls	MA	01349	**800-659-2211**	413-423-3300	350
RenoWorks Software Inc						
2816 21 St NE	Calgary	AB	T2E6Z2	**877-980-3880**	403-296-3880	179
Rent-A-Center Inc						
5501 Headquarters Dr	Plano	TX	75024	**800-422-8186**		266-2
NASDAQ: RCII						
Rental Research Services Inc						
7525 Mitchell Rd Ste 301	Eden Prairie	MN	55344	**800-328-0333**	952-935-5700	632
Rentals Inc						
3585 Engineering Dr	Norcross	GA	30092	**888-501-7368**		387
Rent-A-PC Inc						
265 Oser Ave	Hauppauge	NY	11788	**800-800-8686**	631-273-8888	266-1
RentPath Inc						
950 E Paces Ferry Rd NE Ste 2600	Norcross	GA	30092	**800-216-1423**	678-421-3000	634-9
RentPath, LLC						
950 East Paces Ferry Rd NE Ste 2600	Atlanta	GA	30326	**800-216-1423**	678-421-3000	634-9
Rentrak Corp						
7700 NE Ambassador Pl 3rd Fl	Portland	OR	97220	**800-929-0070**	503-284-7581	180-1
NASDAQ: RENT						
Renville-Sibley Co-op Power Assn						
103 Oak St PO Box 68	Danube	MN	56230	**800-826-2593**	320-826-2593	247
RenWeb School Management Software						
101 E Renfro St Ste A	Burleson	TX	76028	**866-800-6593**		622
Repairclinic.com Inc						
48600 Michigan Ave	Canton	MI	48188	**800-269-2609**	734-495-3079	351
Repligen Corp						
41 Seyon St	Waltham	MA	02453	**800-622-2259***	781-250-0111	84
NASDAQ: RGEN ■ *Sales						
Reporter						
12247 S Harlem Ave	Palos Heights	IL	60463	**800-633-4227**	708-448-6161	531-2
Reproduction Enterprises Inc						
908 N Prairie Rd	Stillwater	OK	74075	**866-734-2855**	405-377-8037	11-2
Republic Bancorp Inc						
601 W Market St	Louisville	KY	40202	**888-540-5363**	502-584-3600	360-2
NASDAQ: RBCAA						
Republic Financial Corp						
5251 DTC Pkwy Ste 300	Greenwood Village	CO	80111	**800-596-3608**	303-751-3501	218
Republic First Bancorp Inc						
50 S 16th St Ste 2400	Philadelphia	PA	19102	**888-875-2265**	215-735-4422	360-2
NASDAQ: FRBK						
Republic Industries Inc						
1400 Warren Dr	Marshall	TX	75672	**866-284-0941**	903-935-3680	114
Republic Mortgage Insurance Co						
101 N Cherry St Ste 101	Winston-Salem	NC	27101	**800-999-7642**		391-5
Republic Plumbing Supply Company Inc						
890 Providence Hwy	Norwood	MA	02062	**800-696-3900**		611
Republic Powdered Metals Inc						
2628 Pearl Rd	Medina	OH	44256	**800-382-1218**		549
Republic Services						
1131 N Blue Gum St	Anaheim	CA	92806	**866-238-2444**	714-238-3300	802
Republic Services of Southern Nevada						
770 E Sahara Ave	Las Vegas	NV	89193	**800-752-4092**	702-735-5151	802
Republic Storage Systems LLC						
1038 Belden Ave NE	Canton	OH	44705	**800-477-1255***	330-438-5800	288
*Sales						
Republic Western Insurance Co						
2721 N Central Ave	Phoenix	AZ	85004	**800-528-7134***		391-4
*Claims						
Republic, The						
333 Second St	Columbus	IN	47201	**800-876-7811**	812-372-7811	531-2
Republican Co						
1860 Main St	Springfield	MA	01103	**800-828-5597**	413-788-1000	634-8
Republican National Committee (RNC)						
310 First St SE	Washington	DC	20003	**800-445-5768**	202-863-8500	615
Republican-American Inc						
389 Meadow St	Waterbury	CT	06702	**800-992-3232**	203-574-3636	634-8
Reputation Rhino LLC						
711 Third Ave 12th Fl	New York	NY	10017	**888-975-3331**		387
ReQuest Inc						
100 Saratoga Village Blvd Ste 45	Ballston Spa	NY	12020	**800-236-2812***	518-899-1254	51
*Sales						
RES Exhibit Services LLC						
435 Smith St	Rochester	NY	14608	**800-482-4049**	585-546-2040	7
Rescar Inc						
1101 31st St Ste 250	Downers Grove	IL	60515	**800-851-5196**	630-963-1114	649
Resco Plastics Inc						
93783 Newport Ln	Coos Bay	OR	97420	**800-266-5097**	541-269-5485	659
Resco Products Inc						
2 Penn Ctr W Ste 430	Pittsburgh	PA	15276	**888-283-5505**	412-494-4491	660
Rescuecom Corp						
2560 Burnet Ave	Syracuse	NY	13206	**800-737-2837**		311
Research & Diagnostic Antibodies						
2645 W Cheyenne Ave	North Las Vegas	NV	89032	**800-858-7322**	702-638-7800	233
Research & Innovative Technology Administration (RITA)						
1200 New Jersey Ave SE	Washington	DC	20590	**800-853-1351**	202-366-7582	340-15
Bureau of Transportation Statistics						
1200 New Jersey Ave SE	Washington	DC	20590	**800-853-1351**	202-366-1270	340-15
Office of Research Development & Technology						
1200 New Jersey Ave SE	Washington	DC	20590	**800-853-1351**		340-15
Research Assoc Inc						
27999 Clemens Rd	Cleveland	OH	44145	**800-255-9693**	440-892-9439	400
Research into Action Inc						
3934 Ne Mlking Jr Blvd Ste 300	Portland	OR	97212	**888-492-9100**	503-287-9136	198
Research Products Corp						
1015 E Washington Ave	Madison	WI	53703	**800-334-6011**	608-257-8801	17
Research Technology International Inc						
4700 W Chase Ave	Lincolnwood	IL	60712	**800-323-7520***	847-677-3000	590
*Sales						

Name / Address	City	State	ZIP	Toll-Free	Phone	Class
Research to Prevent Blindness Inc (RPB) 645 Madison Ave 21st Fl	New York	NY	10022	**800-621-0026**	212-752-4333	47-17
Research Triangle Institute 3040 Cornwallis Rd PO Box 12194	Research Triangle Park	NC	27709	**800-334-8571**	919-541-6000	666
Research!America 1101 King St Ste 520	Alexandria	VA	22314	**800-366-2873**	703-739-2577	47-5
Reser's Fine Foods Inc 15570 SW Jenkins Rd	Beaverton	OR	97006	**800-333-6431**	503-643-6431	297-33
Reserve Casino Hotel 321 Gregory St	Central City	CO	80427	**800-924-6646**	303-582-0800	132
Reserve Officers Assn of the US (ROA) 1 Constitution Ave NE	Washington	DC	20002	**800-809-9448**	202-479-2200	47-19
Reserve Telephone Company Inc PO Box T	Reserve	LA	70084	**888-611-6111**	985-536-1111	733
ReserveAmerica Holdings Inc 2480 Meadowvale Blvd Ste 120	Mississauga	ON	L5N8M6	**877-444-6777**		771
Reserves Network, The 22021 Brookpark Rd	Cleveland	OH	44126	**866-876-2020**	440-779-6681	630
Reshape Medical 100 Calle Iglesia	San Clemente	CA	92672	**844-937-7374**		474
Residence & Conference Centre - Toronto 1760 Finch Ave E	Toronto	ON	M2J5G3	**877-225-8664**	416-491-8811	379
Residence Inn Mystic 40 Whitehall Ave	Mystic	CT	06355	**888-268-7222**	860-536-5150	705
Residential Control Systems 11481 Sunrise Gold Cir Ste 1	Rancho Cordova	CA	95742	**888-727-4822**	916-635-6784	204
Residential Mortgage LLC 100 Calais Dr	Anchorage	AK	99503	**888-357-2707**	907-222-8800	508
Resilite Sports Products PO Box 764	Sunbury	PA	17801	**800-843-6287**	570-473-3529	708
Resinall Corp PO Box 195	Severn	NC	27877	**800-421-0561**		604-2
ResMed Inc 9001 Spectrum Ctr Blvd *NYSE: RMD*	San Diego	CA	92123	**800-424-0737**	858-836-5000	475
Resolute Systems Inc 1550 N Prospect Ave	Milwaukee	WI	53202	**800-776-6060**	414-276-4774	40
RESOLVE: National Infertility Assn 1760 Old Meadow Rd Ste 500	McLean	VA	22102	**888-592-4449**	703-556-7172	47-17
Resort 2 Me 975 Cass St	Monterey	CA	93940	**800-757-5646**	831-642-6622	376
Resort at Port Arrowhead, The 3080 Bagnell Dam Blvd PO Box 1930	Lake Ozark	MO	65049	**800-532-3575**	573-365-2334	667
Resort at Singer Island 3800 N Ocean Dr	Riviera Beach	FL	33404	**800-721-7033**	561-340-1700	667
Resort at Squaw Creek 400 Squaw Creek Rd PO Box 3333	Olympic Valley	CA	96146	**800-327-3353**	530-583-6300	667
Resort Condominiums International (RCI) 9998 N Michigan Rd	Carmel	IN	46032	**800-338-7777**	317-805-8000	751
Resort Data Processing Inc 211 Eagle Rd	Avon	CO	81620	**877-779-3717**	970-845-1140	179
Resort Semiahmoo 9565 Semiahmoo Pkwy	Blaine	WA	98230	**855-917-3767**	360-318-2000	667
Resort Sports Network *Outside Television* 33 Riverside Ave 4th Fl	Westport	CT	06880	**888-795-9488**	203-221-9240	736
Resorts Casino Hotel 1133 Boardwalk	Atlantic City	NJ	08401	**800-334-6378**		667
Resorts of the Canadian Rockies Inc 1505 17th Ave SW	Calgary	AB	T2T0E2	**800-258-7669**	403-254-7669	378
Resource & Financial Management Systems Inc 3073 Palisades Ct	Tuscaloosa	AL	35405	**800-701-7367**		179
Resource Connection Inc 161 S Main St	Middleton	MA	01949	**800-649-5228**	978-777-9333	186
Resource Development Corp 280 Daines St Ste 200	Birmingham	MI	48009	**800-360-7222**	248-646-2300	38
Resource Management Inc 281 Main St Ste 5 *Cust Svc	Fitchburg	MA	01420	**800-508-0048***		630
Resource Management Service LLC 31 Inverness Ctr Pkwy Ste 360	Birmingham	AL	35242	**800-995-9516**		303
Resource Plus 9636 Heckscher Dr	Jacksonville	FL	32226	**888-678-8966**		345
Resources Global Professionals 17101 Armstrong Ave *NASDAQ: RECN*	Irvine	CA	92614	**800-900-1131**	714-430-6400	719
Respironics Novametrix LLC 5 Technology Dr	Wallingford	CT	06492	**800-345-6443**	724-387-4000	252
Response Biomedical Corp 1781 75th Ave W *TSE: RBM*	Vancouver	BC	V6P6P2	**888-591-5577**	604-456-6010	419
Response Design Corp 5541 Simpson Ave	Ocean City	NJ	08226	**888-204-3833**		198
Response Envelope Inc 1340 S Baker Ave	Ontario	CA	91761	**800-750-0046**	909-923-5855	265
Rest Haven-York 1050 S George St	York	PA	17403	**800-368-1019**	717-843-9866	449
Restaurant Developers Corp 7010 Engle Rd Ste 100	Cleveland	OH	44130	**888-860-5082**	440-625-3080	668
Restaurant School at Walnut Hill College 4207 Walnut St	Philadelphia	PA	19104	**877-925-6884**	215-222-4200	162
Restaurant Technologies Inc 2250 Pilot Knob Rd Ste 100	Mendota Heights	MN	55120	**888-796-4997**	651-796-1600	301
Restaurants Unlimited Inc 411 First Ave S Ste 200	Seattle	WA	98104	**877-855-6106**	206-634-0550	668
Restless Legs Syndrome Foundation Inc 1610 14th St NW Ste 300	Rochester	MN	55901	**877-463-6757**	507-287-6465	47-17
Reston Hospital Ctr 1850 Town Ctr Pkwy *General	Reston	VA	20190	**888-327-8882***	703-689-9000	374-3
Restonic Mattress 201 James E Casey Dr	Buffalo	NY	14206	**800-898-6075**	716-895-1414	470
Restonic Mattress Corp 737 Main St	Buffalo	NY	14203	**800-898-6075**		470
Restoration Hardware Inc 2900 N MacArthur Dr Ste 100	Tracy	CA	95376	**800-910-9836**		362
Results Travel 701 Carlson Pkwy	Minnetonka	MN	55305	**800-456-4000**	763-212-5000	311
RESUMate Inc 2500 Packard St Ste 200 *Cust Svc	Ann Arbor	MI	48104	**800-530-9310***	734-477-9402	180-10
Resume Solutions 1033 Bay St	Toronto	ON	M5S3A5	**866-361-1290**	416-361-1290	40
Resurgent Capital Services L P 15 S Main St Ste 600	Greenville	SC	29601	**888-665-0374**		568
Retail Benefits Inc 9403 Caserta St	Lake Worth	FL	33467	**866-904-6044**		5
Retail Confectioners International (RCI) 2053 S Waverly Ste C	Springfield	MO	65804	**800-545-5381**	417-883-2775	48-6
Retail Pro International LLC 400 Plz Dr Ste 200 *OTC: RTPRQ*	Folsom	CA	95630	**800-738-2457**	916-605-7200	180-10
Retail Solutions Providers Assn (RSPA) 10130 Perimeter Pkwy Ste 420	Charlotte	NC	28216	**800-782-2693**	704-357-3124	48-18
Retif Oil & Fuel Inc 527 Destrehan Ave	Harvey	LA	70058	**800-349-9000**	504-349-9000	578
Retired & Senior Volunteer Program (RSVP) 1201 New York Ave NW	Washington	DC	20525	**800-833-3722**	202-606-5000	199
Retirement Advantage Inc, The 47 Park Pl Ste 850	Appleton	WI	54914	**888-872-2364**		462
Retirement System Group Inc 108 Corporate Park Dr	White Plains	NY	10604	**855-549-6689**	212-503-0100	401
Retractable Technologies Inc 511 Lobo Ln *NYSE: RVP*	Little Elm	TX	75068	**888-806-2626**	972-294-1010	476
Retreat Hospital 2621 Grove Ave	Richmond	VA	23220	**800-888-3627**	804-254-5100	374-3
Rettew Assoc Inc 3020 Columbia Ave	Lancaster	PA	17603	**800-738-8395**	717-394-3721	263
Rev.com Inc 251 Kearny St 8th Fl	San Francisco	CA	94108	**888-369-0701**		393
Revcor Inc 251 E Edwards Ave	Carpentersville	IL	60110	**800-323-8261**		18
Revelation Software 99 Kinderkamack Rd	Westwood	NJ	07675	**800-262-4747**	201-594-1422	180-2
Revels Tractor Company Inc 2217 N Main St	Fuquay Varina	NC	27526	**800-849-5469**	919-552-5697	276
Revent Inc 100 Ethel Rd W	Piscataway	NJ	08854	**800-822-9642**	732-777-9433	297
Revention Inc 1315 W Sam Houston Pkwy North Ste 100	Houston	TX	77043	**877-738-7444**		198
Revere Control Systems Inc 2240 Rocky Ridge Rd	Birmingham	AL	35216	**800-536-2525**	205-824-0004	727
Revere Copper Products Inc 1 Revere Pk	Rome	NY	13440	**800-448-1776**	315-338-2022	484
Revere Group, The 325 N LaSalle Ste 325	Chicago	IL	60654	**800-745-3263**	213-228-2500	196
Revere Hotel Boston Common 200 Stuart St	Boston	MA	02116	**855-673-8373**	617-482-1800	705
Review & Herald Publishing Assn 55 W Oak Ridge Dr	Hagerstown	MD	21740	**800-456-3991**	301-393-3000	634-9
Revive Spa at the JW Marriott Desert Ridge Resort Phoenix 5350 E Marriott Dr	Phoenix	AZ	85054	**800-845-5279**	480-293-3700	705
Revlon Consumer Products Corp 1501 Williamsboro St	Oxford	NC	27565	**800-473-8566**	212-527-4000	217
Revlon Foundation Inc 237 Pk Ave *Cust Svc	New York	NY	10017	**800-473-8566***		305
Revlon Inc 237 Pk Ave *NYSE: REV*	New York	NY	10017	**800-473-8566**	212-527-4000	360-3
Revolution Eyewear Inc 997 Flower Glen St	Simi Valley	CA	93065	**800-986-0010**		239
Revue & News, The 319 N Main St	Alpharetta	GA	30004	**800-342-9819**	770-442-3278	531-4
Rewards Network 2 N Riverside Plaza Ste 200	Chicago	IL	60606	**866-844-3753**	866-559-3463	219
Rex Artist Supplies 3160 SW 22 St	Miami	FL	33145	**800-739-2782**	305-445-1413	44
Rex Black Consulting Services Inc 31520 Beck Rd	Bulverde	TX	78163	**866-438-4830**	830-438-4830	182
Rex Heat Treat 951 W Eigth St PO Box 270	Lansdale	PA	19446	**800-220-4739**	215-855-1131	483
Rex Lumber Co 840 Main St	Acton	MA	01720	**800-343-0567**	978-263-0055	817
Rex Moore Electrical Contractors & Engineers 6001 Outfall Cir	Sacramento	CA	95828	**800-266-1922**	916-372-1300	191-4
Rex Oil Co Inc 814 & 1000 Lexington Ave	Thomasville	NC	27360	**800-843-0572**	336-472-3368	578
Rex Supply Co 3715 Harrisburg Blvd	Houston	TX	77003	**800-369-0669**	713-222-2251	385
Rexarc Inc PO Box 7	West Alexandria	OH	45381	**877-739-2721**	937-839-4604	788
Rexel Inc 14951 Dallas Pkwy PO Box 9085	Dallas	TX	75254	**888-739-3577**	972-387-3600	248
Rexel Ryall Electrical Supplies 11775 E 45th Ave	Denver	CO	80239	**888-739-3577**	303-629-7721	248
Rexhall Industries Inc 46147 Seventh St W *OTC: REXLQ*	Lancaster	CA	93534	**800-765-7500**	661-726-0565	119
Reynolda House Museum of American Art 2250 Reynolda Rd	Winston-Salem	NC	27106	**888-663-1149**	336-758-5150	519
Reynolds & Reynolds Co 1 Reynolds Way	Dayton	OH	45430	**800-767-0080**	937-485-2000	180-10
Reynolds American Inc 401 N Main St PO Box 2990 *NYSE: LO*	Winston-Salem	NC	27101	**877-390-5533**	336-741-2000	754
Reynolds Plantation 100 Linger Longer Rd	Greensboro	GA	30642	**800-800-5250**	706-467-0600	667

Name / Address	City	State	ZIP	Toll-Free	Phone	Class
Reynolds Smith & Hills Inc						
10748 Deerwood Pk Blvd	Jacksonville	FL	32256	**800-741-2014**	904-256-2500	263
Reynolds, Mirth, Richards & Farmer LLP						
Manulife Pl 10180-101 St						
Ste 3200	Edmonton	AB	T5J3W8	**800-661-7673**	780-425-9510	428
Reynolds-Alberta Museum						
6426 40 Ave PO Box 6360	Wetaskiwin	AB	T9A2G1	**800-661-4726**	780-361-1351	519
Reynoldsburg This Week						
7801 N Central Dr	Lewis Center	OH	43035	**888-837-4342**	740-888-6100	531-4
RF Industries						
7610 Miramar Rd Bldg 6000	San Diego	CA	92126	**800-233-1728**	858-549-6340	255
NASDAQ: RFIL						
RF Micro Devices Inc						
7628 Thorndike Rd	Greensboro	NC	27409	**800-937-5449**	336-664-1233	694
NASDAQ: RFMD						
RFB&D (Recording for the Blind & Dyslexic)						
20 Roszel Rd	Princeton	NJ	08540	**800-221-4792**		47-17
RFI Communications & Security Systems						
360 Turtle Creek Ct	San Jose	CA	95125	**800-341-9292**	408-298-5400	191-4
RG Barry Corp						
13405 Yarmouth Dr NW	Pickerington	OH	43147	**800-848-7560**	614-864-6400	302
NASDAQ: DFZ						
RG Shakour Inc						
254 Tpke Rd	Westborough	MA	01581	**800-661-2030**		240
Rgen Solutions						
4156 148th Ave Ne Bldg I	Redmond	WA	98052	**800-745-0615**	425-867-1350	182
RGFCC Corp						
627 Cady Dr	Fort Washington	MD	20744	**888-389-1230**		462
Rgh Enterprises Inc						
1810 Summit Commerce Pk	Twinsburg	OH	44087	**800-307-5930**	330-963-6998	474
RGHS (Rochester General Health System)						
1425 Portland Ave	Rochester	NY	14621	**877-922-5465**	585-922-4000	374-3
RGS (Ruffed Grouse Society)						
451 McCormick Rd	Coraopolis	PA	15108	**888-564-6747**	412-262-4044	47-3
R&H Motor Cars Ltd						
9727 Reisterstown Rd	Owings Mills	MD	21117	**844-233-2593**		515
RHA Health Services Inc						
17 Church St	Asheville	NC	28801	**866-742-2428**	828-232-6844	462
RheTech Inc						
1500 E N Territorial Rd	Whitmore Lake	MI	48189	**800-869-1230**	734-769-0585	604-2
Rhett House Inn						
1009 Craven St	Beaufort	SC	29902	**888-480-9530**	843-524-9030	379
Rhinehart Oil Company Inc						
585 E State Rd	American Fork	UT	84003	**801-756-5233**	801-756-9681	578
Rhino Foods Inc						
79 Industrial Pkwy	Burlington	VT	05401	**800-639-3350**	802-862-0252	297-2
Rhino Medical Staffing						
2000 E Lamar Blvd Ste 250	Arlington	TX	76006	**866-267-4466**	817-795-2295	506
Rhino Records						
3400 W Olive Ave	Burbank	CA	91505	**800-827-4466**	800-546-3670	655
Rhode Island						
Higher Education Assistance Authority (RIHEAA)						
560 Jefferson Blvd	Warwick	RI	02886	**800-922-9855**	401-736-1100	723
Tourism Div						
315 Iron Horse Way Ste 101	Providence	RI	02908	**800-556-2484**		339-40
Rhode Island Airport Corp						
2000 Post Rd Warwick	Warwick	RI	02886	**888-268-7222**	401-691-2000	27
Rhode Island Assn of Realtors						
100 Bignall St	Warwick	RI	02888	**866-438-8345**	401-785-9898	654
Rhode Island Bar Assn						
115 Cedar St	Providence	RI	02903	**877-659-0801**	401-421-5740	71
Rhode Island Blood Ctr						
405 Promenade St	Providence	RI	02908	**800-283-8385**	401-453-8360	88
Rhode Island College						
600 Mt Pleasant Ave	Providence	RI	02908	**800-669-5760**	401-456-8000	167
Rhode Island Medical Society						
235 Promenade St Ste 500	Providence	RI	02908	**800-343-7776**	401-331-3207	473
Rhode Island School of Design						
2 College St	Providence	RI	02903	**800-364-7473**	401-454-6100	163
Rhode Island State Employees Credit Union						
160 Francis St	Providence	RI	02903	**855-322-7428**	401-751-7440	221
Rhode Island Textile Co						
211 Columbus Ave	Pawtucket	RI	02862	**800-556-6488**	401-722-3700	742-5
Rhoden Auto Ctr Inc						
3400 S Expy St	Council Bluffs	IA	51501	**866-562-6248**	712-309-4000	56
Rhodes College						
2000 N Pkwy	Memphis	TN	38112	**800-844-5969**	901-843-3700	167
Rhodes College Barret Library						
2000 N Pkwy	Memphis	TN	38112	**800-844-5969**	901-843-3000	434-6
Rhodes International Inc						
PO Box 25487	Salt Lake City	UT	84125	**800-876-7333***	801-972-0122	297-16
*Cust Svc						
Rhododendron Species Botanical Garden						
2525 S 336th St PO Box 3798	Federal Way	WA	98063	**877-242-2528**	253-838-4646	96
Rhythm City Casino						
7077 Elmore Ave	Davenport	IA	52807	**844-852-4386**	563-328-8000	132
Rhythm Tech						
29 Beechwood Ave	New Rochelle	NY	10801	**800-726-2279**	914-636-6900	526
RI (Refugees International)						
2001 S St NW Ste 700-K	Washington	DC	20009	**800-733-8433**	202-828-0110	47-5
Rialto Chamber of Commerce						
120 N Riverside Ave	Rialto	CA	92376	**800-597-4955**	909-875-5364	138
Rialto Theater						
310 S Ninth St	Tacoma	WA	98402	**800-291-7593**	253-591-5890	571
Rib Crib Corp						
4535 S Harvard Ave	Tulsa	OK	74135	**800-275-9677**	918-712-7427	668
Ribbon Technology Corp						
825 Taylor Stn Rd	Gahanna	OH	43230	**800-848-0477**	614-864-5444	811
Ribelin Sales Inc						
3857 Miller Pk Dr	Garland	TX	75042	**800-374-1594**	972-272-1594	145
Ricart Automotive Group						
4255 S Hamilton Rd	Columbus	OH	43125	**888-225-6783**	614-836-5321	56
Rice Fruit Co						
2760 Carlisle Rd	Gardners	PA	17324	**800-627-3359**	717-677-8131	316-3
Rice Lake Weighing Systems Inc						
230 W Coleman St	Rice Lake	WI	54868	**800-472-6703**		636
Rice Packaging Inc						
356 Somers Rd	Ellington	CT	06029	**800-367-6725**	860-872-8341	100
Rice University						
6100 Main St	Houston	TX	77005	**866-294-4633**	713-348-0000	167
Ricerca Biosciences LLC						
7528 Auburn Rd	Concord	OH	44077	**888-742-3722**	440-357-3300	666
RiceTec Inc						
1925 FM 2917 PO Box 1305	Alvin	TX	77511	**877-580-7423**	281-393-3532	297-23
Rich Mountain Electric Co-op Inc						
515 Janssen PO Box 897	Mena	AR	71953	**877-828-4074**	479-394-4140	247
Rich Ranch						
939 Cottonwood Lakes Rd	Seeley Lake	MT	59868	**800-532-4350**	406-677-2317	241
Rich Worldwide Travel Inc						
500 Mamaroneck Ave	Harrison	NY	10528	**800-431-1130**	914-835-7600	769
Richard H Hutchings Psychiatric Ctr						
620 Madison St	Syracuse	NY	13210	**800-690-6639**		374-5
Richard Harrison Bailey Inc						
121 S Niles Ave	South Bend	IN	46617	**866-404-8333**	574-287-8333	4
Richard King Mellon Foundation						
500 Grant St Ste 4106	Pittsburgh	PA	15219	**800-424-9836**	412-392-2800	306
Richard L. Roudebush VA Medical Ctr						
1481 W Tenth St	Indianapolis	IN	46202	**888-878-6889**	317-988-4498	374-8
Richard Rodgers Theatre						
226 W 46th St	New York	NY	10036	**866-755-3075**	212-221-1211	744
Richard Wolf Medical Instruments Corp						
353 Corporate Woods Pkwy	Vernon Hills	IL	60061	**800-323-9653**	847-913-1113	252
Richard Young's Intelligence Report						
700 Indian Springs Dr	Lancaster	PA	17601	**800-219-8592***		530-9
*Cust Svc						
Richards Graphic Communications Inc						
2700 Van Buren St	Bellwood	IL	60104	**866-827-3686**	708-547-6000	779
Richards Industries Inc						
3170 Wasson Rd	Cincinnati	OH	45209	**800-543-7311***	513-533-5600	594
*Cust Svc						
Richards Maple Products Inc						
545 Water St	Chardon	OH	44024	**800-352-4052**		297-39
Richardson Convention & Visitors Bureau						
411 W Arapaho Rd Ste 105	Richardson	TX	75080	**888-690-7287**	972-744-4034	208
Richardson Electronics Ltd						
40 W 267 Keslinger Rd PO Box 393	LaFox	IL	60147	**800-348-5580***	630-208-2200	248
NASDAQ: RELL ■ *Sales						
Richardson Pennington & Skinner Psc						
513 S Second St	Louisville	KY	40202	**800-654-3699**	502-583-9587	2
Richardson Public Library						
900 Civic Ctr Dr	Richardson	TX	75080	**800-735-2989**	972-744-4350	434-3
Richards-Wilcox Inc						
600 S Lake St	Aurora	IL	60506	**800-253-5668**		209
Richland Electric Co-op						
1027 N Jefferson St	Richland Center	WI	53581	**800-242-8511**	608-647-3173	247
Richland Glass Company Inc						
1640 SW Blvd	Vineland	NJ	08360	**800-959-0312**	856-691-1697	332
Richland Hospital Inc, The						
333 E Second St	Richland Center	WI	53581	**888-467-7485**	608-647-6321	374-3
Richline Group Inc						
6701 Nob Hill Rd	Tamarac	FL	33321	**800-327-1808**		360-2
Richmond American Homes Inc						
4350 S Monaco St	Denver	CO	80237	**888-402-4663**	303-773-1100	651
Richmond Chamber of Commerce						
3925 Macdonald Ave	Richmond	CA	94805	**866-568-4642**	510-234-3512	138
Richmond Coliseum						
601 E Leigh St	Richmond	VA	23219	**800-228-9290**	804-780-4970	718
Richmond Community College						
PO Box 1189	Hamlet	NC	28345	**800-908-9946**	910-410-1700	161
Richmond County Hospice						
1119 N US Hwy 1	Rockingham	NC	28379	**800-322-2997**	910-997-4464	371
Richmond Gear						
PO Box 238	Liberty	SC	29657	**800-934-2727***	864-843-9231	707
*Sales						
Richmond International Forest Products Inc						
4050 Innslake Dr Ste 100	Glen Allen	VA	23060	**800-767-0111**	804-747-0111	193-3
Richmond Metropolitan Convention & Visitors Bureau						
401 N Third St	Richmond	VA	23219	**800-370-9004**	804-782-2777	208
Richmond National Battlefield Park						
3215 E Broad St	Richmond	VA	23223	**866-733-7768**	804-226-1981	519
Richmond Public Library						
325 Civic Ctr Plaza	Richmond	CA	94804	**800-833-2900**	510-620-6555	434-3
Richmond Times-Dispatch						
PO Box 85333	Richmond	VA	23293	**800-468-3382**	804-649-6000	634-8
Richmond Tours						
1828 Hylan Blvd	Staten Island	NY	10305	**800-766-3868**	718-979-3111	758
Richmond, The						
1757 Collins Ave	Miami Beach	FL	33139	**855-627-3767**	305-538-2331	379
Richmond/Wayne County Convention & Tourism Bureau						
5701 National Rd E	Richmond	IN	47374	**800-828-8414**	765-935-8687	208
Richmor Aviation Inc						
1142 Rt 9 H						
Columbia County Airport	Hudson	NY	12534	**800-331-6101**	518-828-9461	62
Rick Johnson & Assoc of Colorado						
1649 Downing St	Denver	CO	80218	**800-530-2300**	303-296-2200	400
Rickard Circular Folding Co						
325 N Ashland Ave	Chicago	IL	60607	**800-747-1389**	312-243-6300	91
Ricklin-Echikson Assoc						
374 Millburn Ave	Millburn	NJ	07041	**800-544-2317**	973-376-2020	195
Ricks Barbecue Inc						
2367 Hwy 43 S	Leoma	TN	38468	**800-544-5864**	931-852-2324	188
Rickwood Caverns State Park						
370 Rickwood Pk Rd	Warrior	AL	35180	**800-252-7275**	205-647-9692	564
Ricoh Americas Corp						
5 Dedrick Pl	West Caldwell	NJ	07006	**800-727-1885**	973-882-2000	111
Ricon Corp						
7900 Nelson Rd	Panorama City	CA	91402	**800-322-2884**	818-267-3000	258
Riddle Memorial Hospital						
1068 W Baltimore Pike	Media	PA	19063	**866-225-5654**	484-227-9400	374-3
Rideau Inc						
473 Deslauriers	Montreal	QC	H4N1W2	**800-363-6464**		462
Rideout Memorial Hospital						
726 Fourth St	Marysville	CA	95901	**888-923-3800**	530-749-4300	374-3
Rider University						
2083 Lawrenceville Rd	Lawrenceville	NJ	08648	**800-257-9026**	609-896-5000	167

Name / Address	City	State	Zip	Toll-Free	Phone	Class
Westminster Choir College 101 Walnut Ln	Princeton	NJ	08540	**800-962-4647**	609-921-7100	167
Ridewell Corp PO Box 4586	Springfield	MO	65808	**877-434-8088**	417-833-4565	59
Ridge Behavioral Health System 3050 Rio Dosa Dr	Lexington	KY	40509	**800-753-4673**	859-269-2325	374-5
Ridge Tahoe 400 Ridge Club Dr PO Box 5790	Stateline	NV	89449	**800-334-1600**	775-588-3553	667
Ridgecrest Area Convention & Visitors Bureau (RACVB) 643 N China Lake Blvd Ste C	Ridgecrest	CA	93555	**800-847-4830**	760-375-8202	208
Ridgeview Medical Ctr (RMC) 500 S Maple St	Waconia	MN	55387	**800-967-4620**	952-442-2191	374-3
Ridgewater College *Hutchinson* 2 Century Ave SE	Hutchinson	MN	55350	**800-722-1151**	320-234-8500	798
Willmar 2101 15th Ave NW PO Box 1097	Willmar	MN	56201	**800-722-1151**	320-222-5200	798
Ridgewood Savings Bank 71-02 Forest Ave	Ridgewood	NY	11385	**800-250-4832**	718-240-4800	69
RidgeWorth Funds 50 Hurt Plaza Ste 1400	Atlanta	GA	30305	**866-595-2470**		527
Ridg-U-Rak Inc 120 S Lake St	North East	PA	16428	**866-479-7225**	814-725-8751	288
Riechmann Transport Inc 3328 W Chain of Rocks Rd	Granite City	IL	62040	**800-844-4225**	618-797-6700	778
Riedell Shoes Inc 122 Cannon River Ave	Red Wing	MN	55066	**800-698-6893**	651-388-8251	708
Riegel Consumer Products 51 Riegel Rd	Johnston	SC	29832	**800-845-3251**	803-275-2541	743
Riekes Equipment Co PO Box 3392	Omaha	NE	68103	**800-856-0931**	402-593-1181	385
Riel House National Historic Site of Canada 330 River Rd	Winnipeg	MB	R2M3Z8	**877-852-3100**	204-257-1783	562
RIF (Reading Is Fundamental Inc) 1825 Connecticut Ave NW Ste 400	Washington	DC	20009	**877-743-7323**	202-536-3400	47-11
Rife Resources Ltd 400 144 - Fourth Ave SW	Calgary	AB	T2P3N4	**888-257-1873**	403-221-0800	535
Rig-Chem Inc 132 Thompson Rd	Houma	LA	70363	**800-375-7208**	985-873-7208	538
Right at Home Inc 6464 Crt St Ste 150	Omaha	NE	68106	**877-697-7537**	402-697-7537	311
Right Management Consultants Inc 1600 John F Kennedy Blvd Ste 610	Philadelphia	PA	19103	**800-237-4448**	215-972-7277	195
Right Systems Inc 2600 Willamette Dr NE Ste C	Lacey	WA	98516	**800-571-1717**	360-956-0414	227
Righteous Babe Records 341 Delaware Ave PO Box 95	Buffalo	NY	14202	**800-664-3769**	716-852-8020	655
Rigid Hitch Inc 3301 W Burnsville Pkwy *Cust Svc	Burnsville	MN	55337	**800-624-7630***	952-895-5001	761
Rim Country Regional Chamber of Commerce 100 W Main St	Payson	AZ	85547	**800-249-2678**	928-474-4515	138
RIM Logistics Ltd 200 N Gary Ave	Roselle	IL	60172	**888-275-0937**	630-595-0610	448
Rimage Corp 7725 Washington Ave S	Minneapolis	MN	55439	**800-553-8312**	952-944-8144	175-8
Rimex Supply Ltd 9726 186th St	Surrey	BC	V4N3N7	**800-663-9883**	604-888-0025	110
Rimrock Foundation 1231 N 29th St	Billings	MT	59101	**800-227-3953**	406-248-3175	724
Rimrock Resort Hotel, The 300 Mountain Ave PO Box 1110	Banff	AB	T1L1J2	**888-746-7625**	403-762-3356	667
Rinaldi Printing Co 4514 E Adamo Dr	Tampa	FL	33605	**800-766-3224**	813-247-3921	626
Rinchem Company Inc 6133 Edith Blvd NE	Albuquerque	NM	87107	**888-375-2436**	505-345-3655	448
Ring Container Technology 1 Industrial Park Rd	Oakland	TN	38060	**800-280-6333**		123
Ringdale Inc 101 Halmar Cove	Georgetown	TX	78628	**888-288-9080**	512-288-9080	178
Ringling College of Art & Design 2700 N Tamiami Trl	Sarasota	FL	34234	**800-255-7695**	941-351-5100	163
Rink Systems Inc 1103 Hershey St	Albert Lea	MN	56007	**800-944-7930**	507-373-9175	14
Rinker Materials Corp Concrete Pipe Div 8311 W Carder Ct	Littleton	CO	80125	**800-909-7763**	303-791-1600	185
Rio Grande Electric Co-op Inc Hwy 90 & State Hwy 131 PO Box 1509	Brackettville	TX	78832	**800-749-1509**	830-563-2444	247
Rio Grande Valley Chamber of Commerce 322 S Missouri St	Weslaco	TX	78596	**800-628-5115**	956-968-3141	138
Rio Salado College 2323 W 14th St	Tempe	AZ	85281	**855-622-2332**	480-517-8000	161
Rio Verde Development Inc 25609 N Danny Ln	Rio Verde	AZ	85263	**800-233-7103**	480-471-1962	189
RioCan Real Estate Investment Trust 2300 Yonge St Ste 500 PO Box 2386 *TSE: REI.UN.CA*	Toronto	ON	M4P1E4	**800-465-2733**	416-866-3033	652
Rip Griffin Truck Travel Ctr Inc 4710 Fourth St	Lubbock	TX	79416	**800-333-9330**	806-795-8785	325
Ripcho Studio 7630 Lorain Ave	Cleveland	OH	44102	**800-686-7427**	216-631-0664	589
Ripley Co 46 Nooks Hill Rd	Cromwell	CT	06416	**800-528-8665**	860-635-2200	756
Ripley's Aquarium 1110 Celebrity Cir	Myrtle Beach	SC	29577	**800-734-8888**	843-916-0888	39
Ripley's Believe It or Not! Museum 19 San Marco Ave	Saint Augustine	FL	32084	**800-226-6545**	904-824-1606	519
Ripon College 300 Seward St PO Box 248 *Admissions	Ripon	WI	54971	**800-947-4766***		167
RIS Media Inc 69 E Ave	Norwalk	CT	06851	**800-724-6000**	203-855-1234	650
RISC Networks Inc 1 Rankin Ave Second Fl	Asheville	NC	28801	**866-808-1227**		198
Risdall Adv Agency 550 Main St	New Brighton	MN	55112	**888-747-3255**	651-286-6700	4
Rishi Tea LLC 185 S 33rd Ct	Milwaukee	WI	53208	**866-747-4483**	414-747-4001	298-8
Rising Star Casino Resort 777 Rising Star Dr	Rising Sun	IN	47040	**800-472-6311**	812-438-1234	132
Risk Management Assn (RMA) 1801 Market St Ste 300 *Cust Svc	Philadelphia	PA	19103	**800-677-7621***	215-446-4000	48-2
RiskWatch (RWI) 1237 N Gulfstream Ave	Sarasota	Fl	34236	**800-360-1898**		180-10
RISO Inc 800 District Ave Ste 390 *General	Burlington	MA	01803	**800-942-7476***	978-777-7377	175-6
RITA (Research & Innovative Technology Administration) 1200 New Jersey Ave SE	Washington	DC	20590	**800-853-1351**	202-366-7582	340-15
Ritchie Tractor 1746 W Lmar Alxander Pkwy	Maryville	TN	37801	**888-319-0282**	865-981-3199	324
Rite Aid Corp 30 Hunter Ln *NYSE: RAD*	Camp Hill	PA	17011	**800-748-3243**	717-761-2633	239
Rite-Hite Corp 8900 N Arbon Dr	Milwaukee	WI	53224	**800-456-0600**	414-355-2600	676
Rite-Style Optical Co 12240 Emmet St	Omaha	NE	68164	**800-373-3200**	612-520-6058	542
Riteway Bus Service Inc Motorcoach Div W201 N13900 Fond du Lac Ave	Richfield	WI	53076	**800-776-7026**	262-677-3282	106
Ritrama 800 Kasota Ave SE	Minneapolis	MN	55414	**800-328-5071**	612-378-2277	3
Rittal Corp 1 Rittal Pl	Springfield	OH	45504	**800-477-4000**	937-399-0500	814
Rittenhouse Book Distributors Inc 511 Feheley Dr *Cust Svc	King of Prussia	PA	19406	**800-345-6425***		94
Rittenhouse Hotel 210 W Rittenhouse Sq	Philadelphia	PA	19103	**800-635-1042**	215-546-9000	379
Ritz Camera & Image 2 Bergen Turnpike *Cust Svc	Ridgefield Park	NJ	07660	**855-622-7489***		118
Ritz-Carlton Amelia Island 4750 Amelia Island Pkwy	Amelia Island	FL	32034	**800-241-3333**	904-277-1100	667
Ritz-Carlton Bachelor Gulch 0130 Daybreak Ridge	Avon	CO	81620	**800-241-3333**	970-748-6200	667
Ritz-Carlton Dallas 2121 McKinney Ave *Resv	Dallas	TX	75201	**800-960-7082***	214-922-0200	379
Ritz-Carlton Half Moon Bay 1 Miramontes Pt Rd *General	Half Moon Bay	CA	94019	**800-241-3333***	650-712-7000	667
Ritz-Carlton Hotel Co LLC, The 4445 Willard Ave Ste 800	Chevy Chase	MD	20815	**800-241-3333**	301-547-4700	667
Ritz-Carlton Hotel Company, The 4445 Willard Ave Ste 800	Chevy Chase	MD	20815	**800-876-7280**	301-547-4700	705
Ritz-Carlton Huntington Hotel & Spa 4445 Willard Ave Ste 800	Chevy Chase	MD	20815	**800-241-3333**	301-547-4700	667
Ritz-Carlton Kapalua 1 Ritz-Carlton Dr Kapalua *Resv	Maui	HI	96761	**800-262-8440***	808-669-6200	667
Ritz-Carlton Key Biscayne 455 Grand Bay Dr	Key Biscayne	FL	33149	**800-241-3333**	305-365-4500	667
Ritz-Carlton Laguna Niguel, The 1 Ritz Carlton Dr	Dana Point	CA	92629	**800-542-8680**	949-240-2000	667
Ritz-Carlton Lodge Reynolds Plantation 1 Lk Oc1e Trl	Greensboro	GA	30642	**877-231-7916**	706-467-0600	667
Ritz-Carlton Naples Golf Resort 2600 Tiburon Dr *Resv	Naples	FL	34109	**877-231-7916***	239-593-2000	667
Ritz-Carlton Orlando Grande Lakes 4012 Central Florida Pkwy	Orlando	FL	32837	**866-922-6882**	407-206-2400	667
Ritz-Carlton San Juan, The 6961 Ave of the Governors Isla Verde	Carolina	PR	00979	**800-241-3333**	787-253-1700	667
Ritz-Carlton Sarasota 1111 Ritz-Carlton Dr	Sarasota	FL	34236	**800-241-3333**	941-309-2000	667
Ritz-Carlton Tysons Corner, The 1700 Tysons Blvd	McLean	VA	22102	**800-241-3333**	703-506-4300	705
Ritz-Craft Corp of Pennsylvania Inc 15 Industrial Pk Rd	Mifflinburg	PA	17844	**800-326-9836**	570-966-1053	504
Riu Hotel Florida Beach 3101 Collins Ave	Miami	FL	33140	**888-666-8816**	305-673-5333	379
Rivco Products Inc 440 S Pine St	Burlington	WI	53105	**888-801-8222**	262-763-8222	516
River Bend Industries 2421 16th Ave S	Moorhead	MN	56560	**800-365-3070**	218-236-1818	201
River Birch Homes Inc 400 River Birch Dr	Hackleburg	AL	35564	**888-760-3314**	205-935-1997	504
River City Bank PO Box 15247 *OTC: RCBC* ■ *Cust Svc	Sacramento	CA	95851	**800-564-7144***	916-567-2899	69
River City Brass Band Inc 500 Grant St Ste 2720	Pittsburgh	PA	15219	**800-292-7222**	412-434-7222	572-3
River Country Tourism Bureau PO Box 214	Three Rivers	MI	49093	**800-447-2821**		208
River Garden Hebrew Home for the Aged 11401 Old St Augustine Rd	Jacksonville	FL	32258	**800-468-3571**	904-260-1818	449
River Oaks Ctr 96 River Oaks Ctr Dr	Calumet City	IL	60409	**877-746-6642**	708-868-0600	459
River Oaks Hospital 1525 River Oaks Rd W	New Orleans	LA	70123	**800-366-1740**	504-734-1740	374-3
River Parishes Hospital 500 Rue De Sante	Laplace	LA	70068	**800-231-5275**	985-652-7000	374-3
River Park Hospital 1230 Sixth Ave	Huntington	WV	25701	**800-621-2673**	304-526-9111	374-5
River Ranch Fresh Foods 1156 Abbott St	Salinas	CA	93901	**800-538-5868**	831-758-1390	11-1
River Rock Casino Resort 8811 River Rd	Richmond	BC	V6X3P8	**866-748-3718**	604-247-8900	667
River Rock Entertainment Authority 3250 Hwy 128 E	Geyserville	CA	95441	**877-883-7777**	707-857-2777	451

Name	Address	City	State	ZIP	Toll-Free	Phone	Class
River Walk	110 Broadway Ste 500	San Antonio	TX	78204	**800-417-4139**	210-227-4262	49-5
River West Meeting Associates Inc	3616 N Lincoln Ave	Chicago	IL	60613	**888-534-5292**	773-755-3000	462
River's Edge Resort Cottages	4200 Boat St	Fairbanks	AK	99709	**800-770-3343**	907-474-0286	379
Riverbend Maximum Security Institution	7475 Cockrill Bend Blvd	Nashville	TN	37243	**800-770-8277**	615-350-3100	215
Riverdale Mills Corp	130 Riverdale St	Northbridge	MA	01534	**800-762-6374**	508-234-8715	281
Riveredge Nature Ctr	4458 W Hawthorne Dr PO Box 26	Newburg	WI	53060	**800-287-8098**	262-375-2715	49-4
Riveredge Resort Hotel	17 Holland St	Alexandria Bay	NY	13607	**800-365-6987**	315-482-9917	379
Riverfront Investment Group LLC	1214 E Cary St	Richmond	VA	23219	**866-583-0744**	804-549-4800	401
Riverhead Bldg Supply Corp	1093 Pulaski St	Riverhead	NY	11901	**800-378-3650**	631-727-3650	193-3
Riverland Community College	1900 Eigth Ave NW	Austin	MN	55912	**800-247-5039**	507-433-0600	161
Riverland Energy Co-op	N28988 State Rd 93 PO Box 277	Arcadia	WI	54612	**800-411-9115**	608-323-3381	247
RiverMead Retirement Community	150 RiverMead Rd	Peterborough	NH	03458	**800-200-5433**	603-924-0062	670
RiverPoint Group LLC	2200 E Devon Ave Ste 385	Des Plaines	IL	60018	**800-297-5601**	847-233-9600	182
Rivers Oceans & Mountains Adventures Inc (ROAM)	2485 Hwy 3A	Nelson	BC	V1L6K7	**888-639-1114**		758
Riverside City Public Library	3581 Mission Inn Ave	Riverside	CA	92501	**888-225-7377**	951-826-5201	434-3
Riverside Clay Co Inc	201 Truss Ferry Rd	Pell City	AL	35128	**800-924-0637**	205-338-3366	502-2
Riverside Convention & Visitors Bureau	3750 University Ave Ste 175	Riverside	CA	92501	**888-748-7733**	951-222-4700	208
Riverside Foods Inc	2520 Wilson St	Two Rivers	WI	54241	**800-678-4511**	920-793-4511	297-14
Riverside Ford	2625 Ludington St	Escanaba	MI	49829	**877-774-3171**	906-786-1130	56
Riverside Ford Inc	2089 Riverside Dr *Sales	Macon	GA	31204	**800-395-6210***	478-464-2900	56
Riverside Forest Products Inc	2912 Professional Pkwy	Augusta	GA	30907	**888-855-8733**	706-855-5500	193-3
Riverside Group	655 Driving Pk Ave	Rochester	NY	14613	**800-777-2463**	585-458-2090	91
Riverside Hotel	620 E Las Olas Blvd	Fort Lauderdale	FL	33301	**800-325-3280**	954-467-0671	379
Riverside Manufacturing Co	301 Riverside Dr	Moultrie	GA	31768	**800-841-8677**	229-985-5210	154-18
Riverside Marine Inc	600 Riverside Dr	Essex	MD	21221	**800-448-6872**	410-335-1500	89
Riverside Mattress Co	225 Dunn Rd	Fayetteville	NC	28312	**888-288-5195**	910-483-0461	470
Riverside Methodist Hospital	3535 Olentangy River Rd	Columbus	OH	43214	**800-837-7555**	614-566-5000	374-3
Riverside Military Academy	2001 Riverside Dr	Gainesville	GA	30501	**800-462-2338**	770-532-6251	621
Riverside Refractories Inc	201 Truss Ferry Rd	Pell City	AL	35128	**800-924-0637**	205-338-3366	660
Riverside Transit Agency (RTA)	1825 Third St PO Box 59968	Riverside	CA	92517	**800-800-7821**	951-565-5000	467
Riverside-San Bernardino County Indian Health Inc (RSBCIH)	11555 1/2 Potrero Rd	Banning	CA	92220	**800-732-8805**	951-849-4761	353
Riverstone Billings Inn	880 N 29th St	Billings	MT	59101	**800-231-7782**	406-252-6800	379
RiverStone Group Inc	1701 Fifth Ave	Moline	IL	61265	**800-906-2489**	309-757-8250	184
Riverton Memorial Hospital LLC	2100 W Sunset Dr	Riverton	WY	82501	**888-982-9144**	307-856-4161	374-3
Rivertown Newspaper Group	2760 N Service Dr PO Box 15	Red Wing	MN	55066	**800-535-1660**	651-388-8235	634-8
Rivervalley Behavioral Health Hospital	1100 Walnut St PO Box 1637	Owensboro	KY	42302	**800-755-8477**	270-689-6800	724
Riverview Hospital	395 Westfield Rd	Noblesville	IN	46060	**800-523-6001**	317-773-0760	374-3
Riverview Psychiatric Ctr	250 Arsenal St 11 State House Stn	Augusta	ME	04330	**888-261-6684**	207-624-4600	374-5
Riverwalk Casino Hotel	1046 Warrenton Rd	Vicksburg	MS	39180	**866-615-9125**	601-634-0100	451
Rivier College	420 S Main St	Nashua	NH	03060	**800-447-4843**	603-888-1311	167
Riviera Advisors Inc	P.O. Box 41446	Long Beach	CA	90853	**800-635-9063**		195
Riviera Cellular & Telecommunicat	PO Box 997	Riviera	TX	78379	**877-296-3232**	361-296-3232	387
Riviera Finance	220 Ave I	Redondo Beach	CA	90277	**800-872-7484**		274
Riviera Hotel	1431 Robson St	Vancouver	BC	V6G1C1	**888-699-5222**	604-685-1301	379
RJ Donovan Correctional Facility at Rock Mountain	480 Alta Rd	San Diego	CA	92179	**877-256-6877**	619-661-6500	215
RJ Marshall Co	26776 W 12-Mile Rd *Cust Svc	Southfield	MI	48034	**888-514-8600***	248-353-4100	722
RJ O'Brien & Assoc	222 S Riverside Plz Ste 900	Chicago	IL	60606	**866-438-7564**	312-373-5000	171
RJ Thomas Mfg Company Inc	PO Box 946	Cherokee	IA	51012	**800-762-5002**	712-225-5115	320-4
RJM Sales Inc	454 Park Ave	Scotch Plains	NJ	07076	**800-752-9055**	908-322-7880	358
RJN Group Inc	200 W Front St	Wheaton	IL	60187	**800-227-7838**	630-682-4700	194
RJR Fashion Fabrics	2203 Dominguez Way	Torrance	CA	90501	**800-422-5426**	310-222-8782	709
Rk Controls	5901 Corvette St	Commerce	CA	90040	**877-305-8451**	323-887-7066	358
RK Mechanical Inc	3800 Xanthia St	Denver	CO	80238	**877-576-9696**	303-355-9696	191-10
RKI Inc	2301 Central Pkwy	Houston	TX	77092	**800-346-8988**	713-688-4414	469
RL Adams Plastics Inc	5955 Crossroads Commerce	Wyoming	MI	49519	**800-968-2241**	616-261-4400	600
RL Drake Co	9900 Springboro Pike	Miamisburg	OH	45342	**800-777-8876**	937-746-4556	645
RLI Corp	9025 N Lindbergh Dr *NYSE: RLI* ■ *Cust Svc	Peoria	IL	61615	**800-331-4929***	309-692-1000	360-4
RLI Insurance Co	9025 N Lindbergh Dr	Peoria	IL	61615	**800-331-4929**	309-692-1000	391-4
Rlj Financial Services Inc	1788 Mitchell Rd Ste 102	Ceres	CA	95307	**800-240-1050**	209-538-7758	136
RLM Communications Inc	1027 E Manchester Rd	Spring Lake	NC	28390	**877-223-1345**	910-223-1350	181
RLTV	5525 Research Park Dr	Baltimore	MD	21228	**800-754-8464**		115
R&M Materials Handling Inc	4501 Gateway Blvd	Springfield	OH	45502	**800-955-9967**	937-328-5100	358
RMA (Risk Management Assn)	1801 Market St Ste 300 *Cust Svc	Philadelphia	PA	19103	**800-677-7621***	215-446-4000	48-2
RMA (Rubber Manufacturers Assn)	1400 K St NW Ste 900	Washington	DC	20005	**800-220-7622**	202-682-4800	48-13
RMC (Ridgeview Medical Ctr)	500 S Maple St	Waconia	MN	55387	**800-967-4620**	952-442-2191	374-3
RMCF (Rocky Mountain Chocolate Factory Inc)	265 Turner Dr *NASDAQ: RMCF* ■ *Cust Svc	Durango	CO	81303	**888-525-2462***	970-259-0554	122
RME360	4805 Independence Pkwy Ste 250	Tampa	FL	33634	**888-383-8770**		5
RMF Engineering Inc	5520 Research Pk Dr Ste 300	Baltimore	MD	21228	**800-938-5760**	410-576-0505	263
RMF Printing Technologies Inc	50 Pearl St	Lancaster	NY	14086	**800-828-7999**	716-683-7500	626
RMH (Ross Memorial Hospital)	10 Angeline St N	Lindsay	ON	K9V4M8	**800-510-7365**	705-324-6111	374-2
RMHC (Ronald McDonald House Charities)	1 Kroc Dr	Oak Brook	IL	60523	**855-670-4787**	630-623-7048	47-5
RMLEB (Rocky Mountain Lions Eye Bank)	1675 Aurora Crt Ste EI2049 PO Box 6026	Aurora	CO	80045	**800-444-7479**	720-848-3937	271
RMO Inc (Rocky Mountain Orthodontics Inc)	650 W Colfax Ave	Denver	CO	80204	**800-525-6375**	303-592-8200	230
RMPB (Rocky Mountain Public Broadcasting Network)	1089 Bannock St	Denver	CO	80204	**800-274-6666**	303-892-6666	629
RMPersonnel Inc	4707 Montana Ave	El Paso	TX	79903	**866-333-7176**	915-565-7674	630
Rmx Global Logistics	35715 US Hwy 40 Bldg B	Evergreen	CO	80439	**888-824-7365**		312
RNC (Republican National Committee)	310 First St SE	Washington	DC	20003	**800-445-5768**	202-863-8500	615
RNC Genter Capital Management	11601 Wilshire Blvd 25th Fl	Los Angeles	CA	90025	**800-877-7624**	310-477-6543	401
Rnk Inc	333 Elm St Ste 310	Dedham	MA	02026	**877-323-2486**	781-613-6000	733
RnR RV Ctr	23203 E Knox Ave	Liberty Lake	WA	99019	**866-386-4875**		56
RNS (Religion News Service)	529 14th St NW Ste 425	Washington	DC	20045	**800-767-6781**	202-463-8777	529
ROA (Reserve Officers Assn of the US)	1 Constitution Ave NE	Washington	DC	20002	**800-809-9448**	202-479-2200	47-19
Road & Track Magazine	1499 Monrovia Ave	Newport Beach	CA	92663	**800-835-6422**	949-720-5300	456-3
Road America	N 7390 Hwy 67	Elkhart Lake	WI	53020	**800-365-7223**	920-892-4576	514
Road Atlanta Raceway	5300 Winder Hwy	Braselton	GA	30517	**800-849-7223**	770-967-6143	514
Road King Inn Columbia Mall	3300 30th Ave S	Grand Forks	ND	58201	**800-707-1391**		379
Road Runner Group	60 Columbus Cir 60 Columbus Cir	New York	NY	10023	**866-689-3678**	703-345-3422	398
Roadrunner Transportation Systems Inc	4900 S Pennsylvania Ave *NYSE: RRTS*	Cudahy	WI	53110	**800-831-4394**	414-615-1500	649
Roadtec Inc	800 Manufacturers Rd PO Box 180515	Chattanooga	TN	37405	**800-272-7100**	423-265-0600	192
Roadtex Transportation Corp	13 Jensen Dr	Somerset	NJ	08873	**800-762-3839**		778
ROAM (Rivers Oceans & Mountains Adventures Inc)	2485 Hwy 3A	Nelson	BC	V1L6K7	**888-639-1114**		758
Roam Mobility Inc	400 - 311 Water St	Vancouver	BC	V6B1B8	**888-762-6487**		226
Roaman's	2300 SE Ave	Indianapolis	IN	46283	**800-677-0229**		458
Roane County	1209 N Kentucky St	Kingston	TN	37763	**888-483-1377**	865-376-5556	338
Roane State Community College	276 Patton Ln	Harriman	TN	37748	**800-343-9104**	865-354-3000	161
Roanoke College	221 College Ln *Admissions	Salem	VA	24153	**800-388-2276***	540-375-2270	167
Roanoke Electric Co-op	518 NC 561 W	Aulander	NC	27805	**800-433-2236**	252-539-4600	247
Roanoke Regional Chamber of Commerce	210 S Jefferson St	Roanoke	VA	24011	**800-924-3543**	540-983-0700	138
Roanoke Times	201 W Campbell Ave SW	Roanoke	VA	24011	**800-346-1234**	540-981-3340	531-2
Roanoke Valley Convention & Visitors Bureau	101 Shenandoah Ave NE	Roanoke	VA	24016	**800-635-5535**	540-342-6025	208
Roanoke Valley Wine Co	1250 Intervale	Salem	VA	24153	**877-478-9463**	540-444-4440	79-3
Roaring Brook Ranch & Tennis Resort	Rte 9N S	Lake George	NY	12845	**800-882-7665**	518-668-5767	667

	Toll-Free	Phone	Class
Roaring Spring Blank Book Co 740 Spang St ... Roaring Spring PA 16673	800-441-1653	814-224-5141	85
Roasterie Inc, The 1204 W 27th St ... Kansas City MO 64108	800-376-0245	816-931-4000	345
Robbers Cave State Park Hwy 2 N ... Wilburton OK 74578	800-654-8240	918-465-2565	564
Robbie Manufacturing Inc 10810 Mid America Ave ... Lenexa KS 66219	800-255-6328	913-492-3400	600
Robbins Inc 4777 Eastern Ave ... Cincinnati OH 45226	800-543-1913	513-871-8988	681
Robbins LLC 3415 Thompson St ... Muscle Shoals AL 35661	800-633-3312	256-383-5441	752
Robbins Mfg Co 13001 N Nebraska Ave ... Tampa FL 33612	888-558-8199	813-971-3030	816
Robern Inc 701 N Wilson Ave ... Bristol PA 19007	800-877-2376	215-826-9800	320-2
Roberson Motors Inc 3100 Ryan Dr SE ... Salem OR 97301	888-281-6220	503-363-4117	56
Roberson Museum & Science Ctr 30 Front St ... Binghamton NY 13905	888-269-5325	607-772-0660	519
Robert Allen Fabrics Inc 225 Foxboro Blvd ... Foxboro MA 02035	800-333-3777		593
Robert Bearden Inc 2601 Industrial Pk Dr PO Box 870 ... Cairo GA 39828	888-298-6928	229-377-6928	778
Robert Bosch LLC 38000 Hills Tech Dr ... Farmington Hills MI 48331 *Sales	800-893-6342*	248-876-1000	51
Robert Bosch Tool Corp 1800 W Central Rd ... Mount Prospect IL 60056	877-267-2499	224-232-2000	757
Robert Dietrick Co Inc PO Box 605 ... Fishers IN 46038	866-767-1888	317-842-1991	385
Robert E Nolan Company Inc 92 Hopmeadow St ... Weatogue CT 06089	800-653-1941	860-658-1941	196
Robert e Webber Institute for Worship Studies, The 151 Kingsley Ave ... Orange Park FL 32073	800-282-2977	904-264-2172	683
Robert Ferrilli LLC 41 S Haddon Ave Ste 7 ... Haddonfield NJ 08033	888-864-3282		462
Robert H Wager Co 570 Montroyal Rd ... Rural Hall NC 27045	800-562-7024	336-969-6909	787
Robert Half International Inc Accountemps Div 2884 Sand Hill Rd Ste 200 ... Menlo Park CA 94025	855-396-4598		719
Robert Hull Fleming Museum 61 Colchester Ave University of Vermont ... Burlington VT 05405	888-382-1222	802-656-0750	519
Robert J Dole VA Medical Center 5500 E Kellogg St ... Wichita KS 67218	888-878-6881	316-685-2221	374-3
Robert Kaufman Company Inc PO Box 59266 ... Los Angeles CA 90059	800-877-2066	310-538-3482	593
Robert Mondavi Co 7801 St Helena Hwy ... Oakville CA 94562	888-766-6328	707-226-1395	79-3
Robert Morris College			
Chicago 401 S State St ... Chicago IL 60605	800-762-5960	312-935-6800	167
DuPage 905 Meridian Lk Dr ... Aurora IL 60504 *Admissions	800-762-5960*	630-375-8100	167
Orland Park 43 Orland Sq Dr ... Orland Park IL 60462	800-225-1520	708-226-3800	167
Springfield 3101 Montvale Dr ... Springfield IL 62704	800-762-5960	217-793-2500	167
Robert Morris University 6001 University Blvd ... Moon Township PA 15108	800-762-0097	412-262-8200	167
Robert Morris University Institute of Culinary Arts 401 S State St ... Chicago IL 60605	800-762-5960	312-935-4100	162
Robert N Karpp Company Inc 480 E First St ... Boston MA 02127	800-244-5886	617-269-5880	193-2
Robert Packer Hospital 1 Guthrie Sq ... Sayre PA 18840	888-448-8474	570-888-6666	374-3
Robert R McCormick Tribune Foundation 205 N Michigan Ave Ste 4300 ... Chicago IL 60611	800-435-7352	312-445-5000	306
Robert S Fisher & Company Inc 280 Sheffield St ... Mountainside NJ 07092	800-526-8052	908-928-0002	409
Robert Treat Hotel 50 Pk Pl ... Newark NJ 07102	800-569-2300	973-622-1000	379
Robert W Baird & Company Inc PO Box 672 ... Milwaukee WI 53201	800-792-2473	414-765-3500	688
Robert Wood Johnson Foundation PO Box 2316 ... Princeton NJ 08543	877-843-7953		306
Robert Wood Johnson University Hospital 1 Robert Wood Johnson Pl ... New Brunswick NJ 08901	888-637-9584	732-828-3000	374-3
Roberts Automatic Products Inc 880 Lake Dr ... Chanhassen MN 55317	800-879-9837	952-949-1000	620
Roberts Dairy Co 2901 Cuming St ... Omaha NE 68131	800-779-4321	402-344-4321	298-4
Roberts Hawaii Inc 680 Iwilei Rd Ste 700 ... Honolulu HI 96817	800-831-5541	808-523-7750	758
Roberts John G Jr US Supreme Ct Bldg 1 1st St NE ... Washington DC 20543	800-772-1213	202-479-3000	341-3
Roberts Wesleyan College 2301 Westside Dr ... Rochester NY 14624 *Admissions	800-777-4792*	585-594-6000	167
Roberts-Gordon Inc 1250 William St PO Box 44 ... Buffalo NY 14240	800-828-7450	716-852-4400	357
Roberts-Hamilton 6601 Pkwy Cir Ste A ... Brooklyn Center MN 55430	800-888-2222	763-315-0100	611
Robertshaw Industrial Products 1602 Mustang Dr ... Maryville TN 37801	800-228-7429	865-981-3100	203
Robertson Furniture Company Inc 890 Elberton St ... Toccoa GA 30577	800-241-0713	706-886-1494	320-1
Robertson Heating Supply Co 2155 W Main St ... Alliance OH 44601	800-433-9532	330-821-9180	611
Robertson Inc 97 Bronte St N ... Milton ON L9T2N8	800-268-5090	905-878-2861	280
Robertson Manufacturing Inc 112 Woodland Ave ... West Grove PA 19390	800-260-5423	610-869-9600	730
Robertson Transformer Co 13611 Thornton Rd ... Blue Island IL 60406	800-323-5633	708-388-2315	192
Robinson Ctr 101 S. Spring St PO Box 3232 ... Little Rock AR 72201	800-844-4781	501-376-4781	571
Robinson Helicopter Co 2901 Airport Dr ... Torrance CA 90505	800-905-0655	310-539-0508	20
Robinson Industries Inc 3051 W Curtis Rd ... Coleman MI 48618	877-465-4055	989-465-6111	547
Robinson Mfg Company Inc 798 Market St PO Box 338 ... Dayton TN 37321	800-251-7286	423-775-2212	154-17
Robishaw Engineering Inc 10106 Mathewson Ln ... Houston TX 77043	800-877-1706	713-468-1706	696
Robotics Institute Carnegie Mellon University 5000 Forbes Ave ... Pittsburgh PA 15213	800-767-8483	412-268-3818	666
Robson Communities 9532 E Riggs Rd ... Sun Lakes AZ 85248	800-732-9949		651
Robson Forensic Inc 354 N Prince St ... Lancaster PA 17603	800-813-6736	717-293-9050	196
Robstown High School 609 W Hwy 44 ... Robstown TX 78380	800-446-3142	361-387-5999	683
Robyn Inc 7717 W Britton Rd ... Oklahoma City OK 73132	877-211-9711		626
ROC (Rutgers Organics Corp) 201 Struble Rd ... State College PA 16801	888-469-2188	814-238-2424	142
Roche Diagnostics Corp (RDC) 9115 Hague Rd PO Box 50457 ... Indianapolis IN 46250 *Cust Svc	800-428-5076*	317-521-2000	233
Roche Palo Alto LLC 4300 Hacienda Dr ... Pleasanton CA 94588	888-545-2443	925-730-8000	84
Rochester College 800 W Avon Rd ... Rochester Hills MI 48307	800-521-6010	248-218-2011	167
Rochester Community & Technical College 851 30th Ave SE ... Rochester MN 55904	800-247-1296	507-285-7210	161
Rochester Convention & Visitors Bureau 30 Civic Ctr Dr SE Ste 200 ... Rochester MN 55904	800-634-8277	507-288-4331	208
Rochester Eye & Tissue Bank 524 White Spruce Blvd ... Rochester NY 14623	800-568-4321	585-272-7890	271
Rochester Gas & Electric Corp 89 E Ave ... Rochester NY 14649	800-743-2110		785
Rochester Gauges Inc of Texas 11616 Harry Hines Blvd ... Dallas TX 75229	800-821-1829	972-241-2161	203
Rochester General Health System (RGHS) 1425 Portland Ave ... Rochester NY 14621	877-922-5465	585-922-4000	374-3
Rochester Midland Corp 333 Hollenbeck St ... Rochester NY 14621	800-836-1627	585-336-2200	144
Rock & Gem Magazine 290 Maple Ct Ste 232 ... Ventura CA 93003	866-377-4666	805-644-3824	456-14
Rock 'N Learn Inc 105 Commercial Cir ... Conroe TX 77304	800-348-8445	936-539-2731	245
Rock Bridge Memorial State Park 5901 S Hwy 163 ... Columbia MO 65203	800-334-6946	573-449-7402	564
Rock City Gardens 1400 Patten Rd ... Lookout Mountain GA 30750	800-854-0675	706-820-2531	49-4
Rock Creek Resort 6380 US Hwy 212 ... Red Lodge MT 59068	800-667-1119	406-446-1111	667
Rock Island Argus 1724 Fourth Ave ... Rock Island IL 61201	800-660-2472	309-786-6441	531-2
Rock Island State Park 82 Beach Rd ... Rock Island TN 38581	800-250-8614	931-686-2471	564
Rock of Ages Corp 560 Graniteville Rd ... Graniteville VT 05654	800-421-0166	802-476-3119	722
Rock River Lumber & Grain Co 5502 Lyndon Rd PO Box 68 ... Prophetstown IL 61277	800-605-4333	815-537-5131	297-23
Rock River Valley Blood Ctr 3065 N Perryville Rd Ste 105 ... Rockford IL 61114 *General	877-778-2299*	815-965-8751	88
Rock Springs Chamber of Commerce 1897 Dewar Dr ... Rock Springs WY 82901	800-463-8637	307-362-3771	138
Rock Springs National Bank 200 Second St PO Box 880 ... Rock Springs WY 82902	800-469-8801	307-362-8801	68
Rock Springs Run State Reserve 30601 CR 433 ... Sorrento FL 32776	800-326-3521	407-884-2008	564
Rock Valley College 3301 N Mulford Rd ... Rockford IL 61114	800-973-7821	815-921-7821	161
Rock View Resort 1049 Parkview Dr ... Hollister MO 65672	800-375-9530	417-334-4678	379
Rock Wool Manufacturing Co 1400 Seventh Ct PO Box 506 ... Leeds AL 35094 *Sales	800-874-7625*	205-699-6121	389
Rockbestos-Surprenant Cable Corp 20 Bradley Pk Rd ... East Granby CT 06026	800-327-7625	860-653-8300	812
Rocket Box Inc 125 E 144th St ... Bronx NY 10451	800-762-5521	718-292-5370	201
Rocket Supply Corp 404 N Rt 115 PO Box 98 ... Roberts IL 60962	800-252-6871		515
Rockford Area Convention & Visitors Bureau 102 N Main St ... Rockford IL 61101	800-521-0849	815-963-8111	208
Rockford Art Museum 711 N Main St ... Rockford IL 61103	800-521-0849	815-968-2787	519
Rockford Chamber of Commerce 308 W State St Ste 190 ... Rockford IL 61101	866-767-2629	815-987-8100	138
Rockford College 5050 E State St ... Rockford IL 61108	800-892-2984	815-226-4000	167
Rockford Corp 600 S Rockford Dr ... Tempe AZ 85281 *OTC: ROFO*	800-903-2897	480-967-3565	51
Rockford Industrial Welding Supply Inc 4646 Linden Rd ... Rockford IL 61109	800-226-1904	815-226-1900	386
Rockford Institute 928 N Main St ... Rockford IL 61103	800-383-0680	815-964-5053	631
Rockford MetroCentre 300 Elm St ... Rockford IL 61101	800-745-3000	815-968-5600	718
Rockford Process Control Inc 2020 Seventh St ... Rockford IL 61104	800-228-3779	815-966-2000	350
Rockford Systems Inc 4620 Hydraulic Rd ... Rockford IL 61109 *Cust Svc	800-922-7533*	815-874-7891	205
Rockhill-York County Convention & Visitors Bureau 452 S Anderson Rd ... Rock Hill SC 29730	888-702-1320	803-329-5200	208

Name	Address	City	State	ZIP	Toll-Free	Phone	Class
Rockhurst University	1100 Rockhurst Rd	Kansas City	MO	64110	**800-842-6776**	816-501-4000	167
Rockhurst University Continuing Education Ctr Inc	PO Box 419107	Kansas City	MO	64141	**800-258-7246**	913-432-7755	763
Rocking Horse Ranch Resort	600 Rt 44-55	Highland	NY	12528	**800-647-2624**	845-691-2927	667
Rock-It Cargo USA Inc	5432 W 104th St	Los Angeles	CA	90045	**800-973-1727**	310-410-0935	312
Rockland Community College	145 College Rd	Suffern	NY	10901	**800-722-7666**	845-574-4000	161
Rockland Federal Credit Union	241 Union St	Rockland	MA	02370	**800-562-7328**	781-878-0232	221
Rockland Immunochemicals Inc	PO Box 326	Gilbertsville	PA	19525	**800-656-7625**	610-369-1008	233
Rocklin Area Chamber of Commerce	3700 Rocklin Rd	Rocklin	CA	95677	**800-228-3380**	916-624-2548	138
Rocklin Park Hotel	5450 China Garden Rd	Rocklin	CA	95677	**888-630-9400**	916-630-9400	379
Rockmount Ranch Wear Manufacturing Co	1626 Wazee St	Denver	CO	80202	**800-776-2566**	303-629-7777	154-19
Rockport Company Inc	1895 JW Foster Blvd	Canton	MA	02021	**800-828-0545**	781-401-5000	302
Rockport Schooner Cruises	PO Box 272	Belfast	ME	04915	**866-732-2473**	207-338-3088	222
Rockview Dairies Inc	7011 Stewart & Gray Rd	Downey	CA	90241	**800-423-2479**	562-927-5511	298-4
Rockwell Collins Inc	400 Collins Rd NE *NYSE: COL*	Cedar Rapids	IA	52498	**888-721-3094**	319-295-1000	528
Rockwell Farms Inc	332 Rockwell Farms Rd	Rockwell	NC	28138	**800-635-6576**		369
Rockwell Medical Inc	30142 Wixom Rd *NASDAQ: RMTI*	Wixom	MI	48393	**800-449-3353**	248-960-9009	252
Rockwood Retaining Walls Inc	7200 Hwy 63 N	Rochester	MN	55906	**800-535-2375**	888-288-4045	185
Rockwood Retirement Community	2903 E 25th Ave	Spokane	WA	99223	**800-727-6650**	509-536-6650	670
Rocky Mount Area Chamber of Commerce	100 Coastline St Ste 200	Rocky Mount	NC	27804	**800-682-6746**	252-446-0323	138
Rocky Mount Cord Co	381 N Grace St *Orders	Rocky Mount	NC	27804	**800-342-9130***	252-977-9130	210
Rocky Mount Museum	200 Hyder Hill Rd PO Box 160	Piney Flats	TN	37686	**888-538-1791**	423-538-7396	519
Rocky Mountain Chocolate Factory Inc (RMCF)	265 Turner Dr *NASDAQ: RMCF* ■ *Cust Svc	Durango	CO	81303	**888-525-2462***	970-259-0554	122
Rocky Mountain College	1511 Poly Dr	Billings	MT	59102	**800-877-6259**	406-657-1000	167
Rocky Mountain Fabrication Inc	PO Box 16409	Salt Lake City	UT	84116	**888-763-5307**	801-596-2400	90
Rocky Mountain Hardware Inc	1020 Airport Way PO Box 4108	Hailey	ID	83333	**888-788-2013**	208-788-2013	350
Rocky Mountain Health Plans	2775 Crossroads Blvd PO Box 10600	Grand Junction	CO	81502	**800-843-0719**	970-244-7760	391-3
Rocky Mountain Lions Eye Bank (RMLEB)	1675 Aurora Crt Ste El2049 PO Box 6026	Aurora	CO	80045	**800-444-7479**	720-848-3937	271
Rocky Mountain Orthodontics Inc (RMO Inc)	650 W Colfax Ave	Denver	CO	80204	**800-525-6375**	303-592-8200	230
Rocky Mountain Public Broadcasting Network (RMPB)	1089 Bannock St	Denver	CO	80204	**800-274-6666**	303-892-6666	629
Rocky Mountain Tissue Bank	2993 S Peoria St Ste 390	Aurora	CO	80014	**800-424-5169**	303-337-3330	544
Rocky Rococo	105 E Wisconsin Ave	Oconomowoc	WI	53066	**800-888-7625**	262-569-5580	668
Rocky Shoes & Boots Inc	39 E Canal St *NASDAQ: RCKY*	Nelsonville	OH	45764	**877-795-2410**	740-753-3130	302
Rocky Top Furniture Inc	8957 Lexington Rd	Lancaster	KY	40444	**800-332-1143**	859-548-2828	322
Roco Rescue	7077 Exchequer Dr	Baton Rouge	LA	70809	**800-647-7626**	225-755-7626	462
Rodbat Security Services	8125 Somerset Blvd	Paramount	CA	90723	**877-676-3228**	562-806-9098	691
Rodda Paint Co	6107 N Marine Dr	Portland	OR	97203	**800-452-2315**	503-521-4300	549
Rodey Dickason Sloan Akin & Robb P A	201 Third St NW Ste 2200	Albuquerque	NM	87102	**800-226-2935**	505-765-5900	428
Rodgers & Hammerstein Organization, The	229 W 28th St 11th Fl	New York	NY	10001	**800-400-8160**	212-541-6600	513
Rodney Hunt Co	46 Mill St	Orange	MA	01364	**800-448-8860**	978-544-2511	479
Rodney Strong Vineyards	11455 Old Redwood Hwy	Healdsburg	CA	95448	**800-678-4763**	707-431-1533	79-3
Roe Dental Laboratory Inc	9565 Midwest Ave	Garfield Heights	OH	44125	**800-228-6663**	216-663-2233	415
Roeder Implement Inc	2550 Rockdale Rd	Dubuque	IA	52003	**800-557-1184**	563-557-1184	276
Roeder Travel Ltd	9805 York Rd	Cockeysville	MD	21030	**800-379-9887**	410-667-6090	769
Roehl & Yi Investment Advisors LLC	450 Country Club Rd Ste 160	Eugene	OR	97401	**888-683-4343**	541-683-2085	688
Roehl Transport Inc	1916 E 29th St PO Box 750	Marshfield	WI	54449	**800-826-8367**	715-591-3795	778
Roesch Inc	100 N 24th St	Belleville	IL	62222	**800-423-6243**		480
Roffman Miller Assoc Inc	1835 Market St Ste 500	Philadelphia	PA	19103	**800-995-1030**	215-981-1030	401
Rogan Corp	3455 Woodhead Dr	Northbrook	IL	60062	**800-584-5662**	847-498-2300	607
Roger Dean Chevrolet Inc	2235 Okeechobee Blvd	West Palm Beach	FL	33409	**877-827-4705**	561-683-8100	56
Roger Sipe CPA Firm LLC	5742 Coventry Ln	Fort Wayne	IN	46804	**888-747-3272**	260-432-9996	2
Roger Smith Hotel	501 Lexington Ave	New York	NY	10017	**800-445-0277**	212-755-1400	379
Roger Ward Inc	17275 Green Mtn Rd *General	San Antonio	TX	78247	**888-909-3147***	210-655-8623	778
Roger Williams University	1 Old Ferry Rd	Bristol	RI	02809	**800-458-7144**	401-254-3500	167
Roger Williams University Ralph R Papitto School of Law	10 Metacom Ave	Bristol	RI	02809	**800-633-2727**	401-254-4500	168-1
Rogers & Brown Custom Brokers Inc	2 Cumberland St	Charleston	SC	29401	**866-738-8197**	843-577-3630	312
Rogers Bros Corp	100 Orchard St	Albion	PA	16401	**800-441-9880**	814-756-4121	777
Rogers Corp	1 Technology Dr	Rogers	CT	06263	**800-237-2267**	860-774-9605	604-2
Rogers Jewelry Co	PO Box 3151	Modesto	CA	95353	**800-877-4221**		410
Rogers Memorial Hospital Inc	34700 Valley Rd	Oconomowoc	WI	53066	**800-767-4411**	262-646-4411	374-5
Rogers Printing Inc	PO Box 215	Ravenna	MI	49451	**800-622-5591**	231-853-2244	626
Rogers State University	1701 W Will Rogers Blvd	Claremore	OK	74017	**800-256-7511**	918-343-7546	167
Rogers State University Pryor	421 S Elliott St	Pryor	OK	74361	**800-256-7511**	918-825-6117	161
Rogers Supply Company Inc	PO Box 740	Champaign	IL	61824	**800-252-0406**	217-356-0166	663
Rogers Wireless Communications Inc	333 Bloor St. E, 4th Fl	Toronto	ON	M4W1G9	**800-575-9090**	888-764-3771	733
Rogers-Lowell Area Chamber of Commerce	317 W Walnut St	Rogers	AR	72756	**800-364-1240**	479-636-1240	138
Rogue Community College	3345 Redwood Hwy	Grants Pass	OR	97527	**800-411-6508**	541-956-7500	161
Rogue Valley Manor	1200 Mira Mar Ave	Medford	OR	97504	**800-848-7868**	541-857-7214	670
Rogue Wave Software Inc	5500 Flatiron Pkwy	Boulder	CO	80301	**800-487-3217**	303-473-9118	180-2
Rohn Industries Inc	862 Hersey St	St. Paul	MN	55114	**800-289-8580**	651-647-1300	552
Rohnert Park Chamber of Commerce	101 Golf Course Dr Ste C-7	Rohnert Park	CA	94928	**888-364-7379**	707-584-1415	138
Rohrer Corp	717 Seville Rd PO Box 1009	Wadsworth	OH	44282	**800-243-6640**	330-335-1541	607
Roi Consulting Ll Llc	176 Logan St	Noblesville	IN	46060	**866-465-6470**		198
Roka Bioscience Inc	20 Independence Blvd 4th Fl	Warren	NJ	07059	**855-765-2246**	908-605-4700	474
Ro-Lab American Rubber Co Inc	8830 W Linne Rd	Tracy	CA	95304	**800-678-0726**	209-836-0965	370
Roland Cooper State Park	285 Deer Run Dr	Camden	AL	36726	**800-252-7275**	334-682-4838	564
Roland DGA Corp	15363 Barranca Pkwy	Irvine	CA	92618	**800-542-2307**	949-727-2100	175-6
Roland Machinery Co	816 N Dirksen Pkwy	Springfield	IL	62702	**800-252-2926**	217-789-7711	358
Roland's Electric Inc	307 Suburban Ave	Deer Park	NY	11729	**800-981-8010**	631-242-8080	785
Rolf C. Hagen Corp	305 Forbes Blvd *Cust Svc	Mansfield	MA	02048	**800-724-2436***	508-339-9531	577
Rolf Institute of Structural Integration	5055 Chaparral Ct Ste 103	Boulder	CO	80301	**800-530-8875**	303-449-5903	47-17
Roll Call	77 K St NE	Washington	DC	20002	**800-432-2250**	202-650-6500	530-7
Roll Shutter Systems Inc	21633 N 14th Ave	Phoenix	AZ	85027	**800-551-7655**	623-869-7057	697
Rolla Area Chamber of Commerce	1311 KingsHwy	Rolla	MO	65401	**888-809-3817**	573-364-3577	138
Roll-A-Way Conveyor Inc	2335 N Delaney Rd	Gurnee	IL	60031	**800-747-9024**	847-336-5033	209
Roll-A-Way Inc	1661 Glenlake Ave	Itasca	IL	60143	**866-749-5424**		697
Rolled Alloys Inc	125 W Sterns Rd	Temperance	MI	48182	**800-521-0332**	734-847-0561	491
Rolled Steel Products Corp	2187 Garfield Ave	Los Angeles	CA	90040	**800-400-7833**	323-723-8836	491
Roller Bearing Company of America	400 Sullivan Way	West Trenton	NJ	08628	**800-390-3300**	609-882-5050	74
Rollex Corp	800 Chasa Ave *Cust Svc	Elk Grove Village	IL	60007	**800-251-3300***	847-437-3000	695
Rolling Hills Electric Co-op Inc	122 W Main St PO Box 307	Mankato	KS	66956	**877-906-5903**	785-378-3151	247
Rolling Oaks Mall	6909 N Loop 1604 E	San Antonio	TX	78247	**877-746-6642**	210-651-5513	459
Rolling Shield Inc	2500 NW 74th Ave	Miami	FL	33122	**800-474-9404**		697
Rolling Stone Magazine	1290 Ave of the Americas 2nd Fl	New York	NY	10104	**800-639-3865**	800-283-1549	456-9
Rollins College	1000 Holt Ave	Winter Park	FL	32789	**800-799-2586**	407-646-2000	167
Rollprint Packaging Products Inc	320 S Stewart Ave	Addison	IL	60101	**800-276-7629**	630-628-1700	547
Rolls-Royce Engine Services Inc	7200 Earhart Rd	Oakland	CA	94621	**888-255-4766**	510-613-1000	24
Rolls-Royce North America	1875 Explorer St Ste 200	Reston	VA	20190	**888-269-2377**	703-834-1700	21
Rollstock Inc	5720 Brighton Ave	Kansas City	MO	64130	**800-295-2949**	616-570-0430	546
Rollx Vans	6591 Hwy 13 W	Savage	MN	55378	**800-956-6668**	952-890-7851	61-7
Rolta Tusc Inc	333 E Butterfield Rd Ste 900	Lombard	IL	60148	**800-755-8872**	630-960-2909	182
Romac Industries Inc	21919 20th Ave SE	Bothell	WA	98021	**800-426-9341**	425-951-6200	594
Roman Research Inc	800 Franklin St	Hanson	MA	02341	**800-225-8652**		415

Name / Address	City	State	ZIP	Toll-Free	Phone	Class
Romanoff International Supply Corp						
9 Deforest St	Amityville	NY	11701	**800-221-7448***	631-842-2400	407
*Cust Svc						
Romanza						
2707 S Virginia St						
Peppermill Hotel Casino	Reno	NV	89502	**866-821-9996**	775-826-2121	669
Romar Transportation Systems Inc						
3500 S Kedzie Ave	Chicago	IL	60632	**800-621-5416**	773-376-8800	312
Rome Specialty Company Inc Rosco Div						
501 W Embargo St	Rome	NY	13440	**800-794-8357**	315-337-8200	708
Rome Tool & Die Company Inc						
113 Hemlock St	Rome	GA	30161	**800-241-3369**	706-234-6743	755
Romeo Community School District						
316 N Main St	Romeo	MI	48065	**888-427-6818**	586-752-0200	683
Romero Mazda						
1307 Kettering Dr	Ontario	CA	91761	**888-317-2233**	909-390-8484	56
Romet Ltd						
1080 Matheson Blvd East	Mississauga	ON	L4W2V2	**800-387-3201**	905-624-1591	407
Romika USA LLC						
3405 Del Webb Ave NE	Salem	OR	97301	**888-777-4174**	503-588-8117	302
Ron Jon Surf Shop						
3850 S Banana River Blvd	Cocoa Beach	FL	32931	**888-757-8737**	321-799-8888	709
Ron Kendall Masonry Inc						
101 Benoist Farms Rd	West Palm Beach	FL	33411	**866-844-1404**	561-793-5924	191-7
Ron Tonkin Dealerships						
122 NE 122nd Ave	Portland	OR	97230	**855-890-1823**	503-255-4100	56
RONA Inc						
220 Ch du Tremblay	Boucherville	QC	J4B8H7	**877-599-5900**	514-599-5100	364
TSE: RON						
Ronald Blue & Company LLC						
300 Colonial Ctr Pkwy Ste 300	Roswell	GA	30076	**800-841-0362**	770-280-6000	401
Akron 245 Locust St	Akron	OH	44302	**800-262-0333**	330-253-5400	373
Albany 139 S Lake Ave	Albany	NY	12208	**866-244-8464**	518-438-2655	373
Albuquerque						
1011 Yale Ave NE	Albuquerque	NM	87106	**877-842-8960**	505-842-8960	373
Ann Arbor						
1600 Washington Heights	Ann Arbor	MI	48104	**800-544-8684**	734-994-4442	373
Chattanooga						
200 Central Ave	Chattanooga	TN	37403	**855-670-4787**	423-778-4300	373
Cleveland						
10415 Euclid Ave	Cleveland	OH	44106	**800-223-2273**	216-229-5758	373
Durham						
506 Alexander Ave	Durham	NC	27705	**866-244-8464**	919-286-9305	373
Falls Church						
3312 Gallows Rd	Falls Church	VA	22042	**855-227-7435**	703-698-7080	373
Fort Myers						
16100 Roserush Ct	Fort Myers	FL	33908	**800-435-7352**	239-437-0202	373
Galveston						
301 14th St	Galveston	TX	77550	**800-275-2946**	409-762-8770	373
Hershey						
745 W Governor Rd	Hershey	PA	17033	**800-732-0999**	717-533-4001	373
Huntington						
1500 17th St	Huntington	WV	25701	**855-227-7435**	304-529-1122	373
Kansas City						
2502 Cherry St	Kansas City	MO	64108	**888-353-4537**	816-842-8321	373
Las Vegas						
2323 Potosi St	Las Vegas	NV	89146	**888-248-1561**	702-252-4663	373
Philadelphia						
3925 Chestnut St	Philadelphia	PA	19104	**800-723-0999**	215-387-8406	373
Phoenix						
501 E Roanoke Ave	Phoenix	AZ	85004	**877-333-2978**	602-264-2654	373
Providence						
45 Gay St	Providence	RI	02905	**888-353-4537**	401-274-4447	373
Seattle						
5130 40th Ave NE	Seattle	WA	98105	**866-987-9330**	206-838-0600	373
Wilmington						
1901 Rockland Rd	Wilmington	DE	19803	**888-656-4847**	302-656-4847	373
Winston-Salem						
419 S Hawthorne Rd	Winston-Salem	NC	27103	**855-227-7435**	336-723-0228	373
Ronald McDonald House Charities (RMHC)						
1 Kroc Dr	Oak Brook	IL	60523	**855-670-4787**	630-623-7048	47-5
Gainesville						
1600 SW 14th St	Gainesville	FL	32608	**800-435-7352**	352-374-4404	373
Ronald Reagan Presidential Library & Museum						
40 Presidential Dr	Simi Valley	CA	93065	**800-410-8354**	805-522-2977	434-2
Ronan Engineering Co						
21200 Oxnard St	Woodland Hills	CA	91367	**800-327-6626**		203
Roofing Wholesale Co Inc						
1918 W Grant St	Phoenix	AZ	85009	**800-528-4532***	602-258-3794	193-4
*Cust Svc						
Rooftop Media Inc						
188 Spear St Ste 250	San Francisco	CA	94105	**800-860-0293**		115
Rook Consulting						
5537 Makati Cir	San Jose	CA	95123	**888-712-9531**		198
Room & Board Inc						
4600 Olson Memorial Hwy	Golden Valley	MN	55422	**800-301-9720**	763-521-4431	320-2
Room 214 Inc						
3390 Valmont Rd Ste 214	Boulder	CO	80301	**866-624-1851**		7
Roosevelt & Cross Inc						
1 Exchange Plz 55 Broadway						
22nd Fl	New York	NY	10006	**800-348-3426**	212-344-2500	688
Roosevelt Field Mall						
630 Old Country Rd	Garden City	NY	11530	**877-746-6642**	516-742-8001	459
Roosevelt Hotel						
45 E 45th St	New York	NY	10017	**888-833-3969**	212-661-9600	379
Roosevelt Paper Co						
1 Roosevelt Dr	Mount Laurel	NJ	08054	**800-523-3470**	856-303-4100	552
Roosevelt University						
430 S Michigan Ave	Chicago	IL	60605	**877-277-5978***	312-341-3500	167
*Admissions						
Albert A Robin						
1400 N Roosevelt Blvd	Schaumburg	IL	60173	**877-277-5978***	847-619-8600	167
*Admissions						
Root Candles Co						
623 W Liberty St	Medina	OH	44256	**800-289-7668**	330-725-6677	121
Root Inc						
5470 Main St	Sylvania	OH	43560	**800-852-1315**		198
Root-Lowell Manufacturing Co						
1000 Foreman Rd PO Box 289	Lowell	MI	49331	**800-748-0098**	616-897-9211	275
RootsWeb.com						
360 W 4800 N	Provo	UT	84604	**800-262-3787**	801-705-7000	397
Roper Pump Co						
3475 Old Maysville Rd	Commerce	GA	30529	**800-944-6769***	706-335-5551	638
*Sales						
Roplast Industries Inc						
3155 S Fifth Ave	Oroville	CA	95965	**800-767-5278**	530-532-9500	65
Roppe Corp						
1602 N Union St	Fostoria	OH	44830	**800-537-9527**	419-435-8546	293
Rorke Data Inc						
7626 Golden Triangle Dr	Eden Prairie	MN	55344	**800-328-8147**	952-829-0300	176
Rosamond Gifford Zoo at Burnet Park						
1 Conservation Pl	Syracuse	NY	13204	**800-724-5006**	315-435-8511	821
Rosario Resort & Spa						
1400 Rosario Rd	Eastsound	WA	98245	**800-562-8820**	360-376-2222	667
Rosback Co						
125 Hawthorne Ave	Saint Joseph	MI	49085	**800-542-2420**	269-983-2582	628
Rosco Laboratories Inc						
52 Harbor View Ave	Stamford	CT	06902	**800-767-2669**	203-708-8900	720
Roscoe Co						
3535 W Harrison St	Chicago	IL	60624	**888-476-7263***	773-722-5000	442
*Cust Svc						
Roscoe Village						
600 N Whitewoman St	Coshocton	OH	43812	**800-877-1830**	740-622-7644	519
Rose & Kiernan Inc						
99 Troy Rd	East Greenbush	NY	12061	**866-488-6582**	518-244-4245	391-5
Rose Assoc Inc						
200 Madison Ave	New York	NY	10016	**888-475-8860**	212-210-6666	650
Rose Displays Ltd						
35 Congress St	Salem	MA	01970	**800-631-9707**	978-219-8100	196
Rose Hotel						
807 Main St	Pleasanton	CA	94566	**800-843-9540**	925-846-8802	379
Rose Medical Ctr						
4567 E Ninth Ave	Denver	CO	80220	**866-746-4282**	303-320-2121	374-3
Rose Packing Company Inc						
65 S Barrington Rd	South Barrington	IL	60010	**800-323-7363**	847-381-5700	472
Rose Printing Company Inc						
2503 Jackson Bluff Rd	Tallahassee	FL	32304	**800-227-3725**	850-576-4151	625
Rose Products & Services Inc						
545 Stimmel Rd	Columbus	OH	43223	**800-264-1568**	614-443-7647	406
Rose Radiology Boot Ranch						
4133 Woodlands Pkwy	Palm Harbor	FL	34685	**877-674-7673**	727-781-3888	415
Rose State College						
6420 SE 15th St	Midwest City	OK	73110	**866-621-0987**	405-733-7372	161
Roseau Electric Co-op Inc						
1107 Third St NE	Roseau	MN	56751	**888-847-8840**	218-463-1543	247
Rosebud Electric Co-op Inc						
512 Rosebud Ave PO Box 439	Gregory	SD	57533	**888-464-9304**	605-835-9624	247
Rosebud Mfg Co Inc						
701 SE 12th St	Madison	SD	57042	**800-256-4561**	605-256-4561	114
Roseburg Forest Products Co						
PO Box 1088	Roseburg	OR	97470	**800-245-1115**	541-679-3311	681
Roseburg National Cemetery						
1770 Harvard Blvd	Roseburg	OR	97470	**800-535-1117**	541-826-2511	135
Rosedale on Robson Suite Hotel						
838 Hamilton St	Vancouver	BC	V6B6A2	**800-661-8870**	604-689-8033	379
Rosedale Technical Institute						
215 Beecham Dr Ste 2	Pittsburgh	PA	15205	**800-521-6262**	412-521-6200	147
Rosedown Plantation State Historic Site						
12501 Hwy 10	Saint Francisville	LA	70775	**888-376-1867**	225-635-3332	49-2
Rose-Hulman Institute of Technology						
5500 Wabash Ave	Terre Haute	IN	47803	**800-248-7448***	812-877-1511	167
*Admissions						
Rosellen Suites at Stanley Park						
2030 Barclay St	Vancouver	BC	V6G1L5	**888-317-6648**	604-689-4807	379
Rosemont College						
1400 Montgomery Ave	Rosemont	PA	19010	**888-521-0983***	610-527-0200	167
*Admissions						
Rosemount Analytical Inc Process Analytical Div						
6565 P Davis Industrial Pkwy	Solon	OH	44139	**800-433-6076**	440-914-1261	203
Rosen Centre Hotel						
9840 International Dr	Orlando	FL	32819	**800-204-7234**	407-996-9840	379
Rosen Hotels & Resorts Inc						
9840 International Dr	Orlando	FL	32819	**800-204-7234**	407-996-9840	379
Rosen Plaza Hotel						
9700 International Dr	Orlando	FL	32819	**800-366-9700**	407-996-9700	379
Rosen Publishing Group Inc, The						
29 E 21st St	New York	NY	10010	**800-237-9932**		634-2
Rosen Shingle Creek						
9939 Universal Blvd	Orlando	FL	32819	**866-996-9939**	407-996-9939	379
Rosenbaum Family House						
30 Family House Dr						
PO Box 8228	Morgantown	WV	26506	**855-988-2273**	304-598-6094	372
Rosenberg-Richmond Area Chamber of Commerce						
4120 Ave H	Rosenberg	TX	77471	**877-382-7414**	281-342-5464	138
Rosencrantz-Bemis Water Well Co						
1105 Hwy 281 Bypass	Great Bend	KS	67530	**800-466-2467**	620-793-5512	191-15
Rosetta Stone Ltd						
1919 N Lynn St 7th Fl	Arlington	VA	22209	**800-788-0822**		683
NYSE: RST						
Rosewood Hotels & Resorts						
500 Crescent Ct Ste 300	Dallas	TX	75201	**888-767-3966**	214-880-4200	379
Rosewood Industries Inc						
1203 E Central Ter	Stigler	OK	74462	**800-228-3306**		322
Rosewood Retirement Community						
1301 New Stine Rd	Bakersfield	CA	93309	**800-984-4216**	661-834-0620	670
Roslyn Claremont Hotel						
1221 Old Northern Blvd	Roslyn	NY	11576	**800-626-9005**	516-625-2700	379
Rosner Auto Group						
3507 Jefferson Davis Hwy						
	Fredericksburg	VA	22408	**855-270-6270***	540-907-4900	56
*Sales						
Ross & Matthews PC						
3650 Lovell Ave	Fort Worth	TX	76107	**800-458-6982**	817-255-2000	428
Ross & Wallace Paper Products Inc						
204 Old Covington Hwy	Hammond	LA	70403	**800-854-2300**		64
Ross Controls						
1250 Stephenson Hwy	Troy	MI	48083	**800-438-7677**	248-764-1800	788

Name / Address	City	State	Zip	Toll-Free	Phone	Class
Ross Industries Inc						
5321 Midland Rd	Midland	VA	22728	**800-336-6010**	540-439-3271	299
Ross Lake National Recreation Area						
810 State Rt 20	Sedro Woolley	WA	98284	**866-705-5711**	360-854-7200	563
Ross Matthews Mills Inc						
657 Quarry St	Fall River	MA	02723	**800-753-7677**	508-677-0601	742-5
Ross Memorial Hospital (RMH)						
10 Angeline St N	Lindsay	ON	K9V4M8	**800-510-7365**	705-324-6111	374-2
Ross Metals Corp						
27 W 47th St	New York	NY	10036	**800-334-7191**		484
Ross Optical Industries Inc						
1410 Gail Borden Pl	El Paso	TX	79935	**800-880-5417**	915-595-5417	543
Ross Realty Investments Inc						
3325 S University Dr Ste 210	Davie	FL	33328	**800-370-4202**	954-452-5000	650
Ross Simons Jewelers Inc						
9 Ross Simons Dr	Cranston	RI	02920	**800-835-0919**		410
Ross Smith Asset Management Inc						
407 - 8th Avenue S.W Ste 305	Calgary	AB	T2P1E5	**888-494-6893**		527
Ross Technology Corp						
104 N Maple Ave	Leola	PA	17540	**800-345-8170**	717-656-2200	90
Ross Valley School District						
110 Shaw Dr	San Anselmo	CA	94960	**800-322-6384**	415-454-2162	683
Ross, Banks, May, Cron & Cavin PC						
7700 San Felipe Ste 550	Houston	TX	77063	**866-896-1492**	713-626-1200	428
Rostra Precision Controls Inc						
2519 Dana Dr	Laurinburg	NC	28352	**800-782-3379***	910-276-4853	528
*Cust Svc						
Roswell Bookbinding Co						
2614 N 29th Ave	Phoenix	AZ	85009	**888-803-8883**	602-272-9338	91
Roswell Chamber of Commerce						
131 W Second St	Roswell	NM	88202	**877-849-7679**	575-623-5695	138
Roswell Livestock Auction Sales Inc						
900 N Garden PO Box 2041	Roswell	NM	88202	**800-748-1541**	575-622-5580	445
Roswell Park Cancer Institute						
Elm and Carlton St	Buffalo	NY	14263	**877-275-7724**	716-845-2300	374-7
Roswell Park Cancer Institute Blood & Marrow Transplantation Program						
Elm & Carlton Sts	Buffalo	NY	14263	**800-685-6825**	716-845-3516	767
Rotary Forms Press Inc						
835 S High St	Hillsboro	OH	45133	**800-654-2876**	937-393-3426	109
Rotary Foundation, The						
1560 Sherman Ave	Evanston	IL	60201	**800-435-7352**	847-866-3000	47-5
Rotary Lift						
2700 Lanier Dr	Madison	IN	47250	**800-445-5438**	812-273-1622	386
Rotary Multiforms Inc						
1340 E 11 Mile Rd	Madison Heights	MI	48071	**800-762-5644**	586-558-7960	626
Rotek Inc						
1400 S Chillicothe Rd PO Box 312	Aurora	OH	44202	**800-221-8043**	330-562-4000	74
Roth Bros Inc						
PO Box 4209	Youngstown	OH	44515	**800-872-7684**	330-793-5571	191-10
Roth Distributing Co						
11300 W 47th St	Minnetonka	MN	55343	**800-363-3818**	952-933-4428	37
Roth Pump Co						
PO Box 4330	Rock Island	IL	61204	**888-444-7684**	309-787-1791	638
Rothbury Farms						
PO Box 202	Grand Rapids	MI	49501	**877-684-2879**		297-1
Rothenberger USA						
4455 Boeing Dr	Rockford	IL	61109	**800-545-7698**	815-397-7617	454
Rothschild North America Inc						
1251 Ave of the Americas						
51st Fl	New York	NY	10020	**844-726-3863**	212-403-3500	401
Rotmans Furniture & Carpet						
725 Southbridge St	Worcester	MA	01610	**800-768-6267**	508-755-5276	322
RotoMetrics Group						
800 Howerton Ln	Eureka	MO	63025	**800-325-3851**	636-587-3600	755
Rotor Clip Company Inc						
187 Davidson Ave	Somerset	NJ	08873	**800-557-6867***	732-469-7333	327
*Cust Svc						
Roto-Rooter Inc						
255 E Fifth St						
2500 Chemed Ctr	Cincinnati	OH	45202	**800-768-6911**	513-762-6690	191-10
Rottler Mfg						
8029 S 200th St	Kent	WA	98032	**800-452-0534**	253-872-7050	454
Rouge Valley Ajax & Pickering						
580 Harwood Ave S	Ajax	ON	L1S2J4	**866-752-6989**	905-683-2320	374-2
Rough Creek Lodge						
5165 County Rd 2013	Glen Rose	TX	76043	**877-907-0754**	254-965-3700	379
Rough Notes Company Inc, The						
11690 Technology Dr	Carmel	IN	46032	**800-428-4384**	317-582-1600	456-5
Rough Rider Industries						
3303 E Main Ave	Bismarck	ND	58506	**800-732-0557**	701-328-6161	629
Rough River Dam State Resort Park						
450 Lodge Rd	Falls of Rough	KY	40119	**800-325-1713**		564
Round Butte Seed Growers Inc						
505 C St	Culver	OR	97734	**866-385-7001**	541-546-5222	324
Round Lake Area Chamber of Commerce & Industry						
2007 Civic Ctr Way	Round Lake Beach	IL	60073	**800-334-7661**	847-546-2002	138
Round Sky Inc						
848 N Rainbow Blvd Ste 326	Las Vegas	NV	89107	**855-450-3618**		318
Rountree Transport & Rigging Inc						
2640 N Ln Ave	Jacksonville	FL	32254	**800-342-5036**	904-781-1033	778
Rouse-sirine Associates Ltd						
333 Office Sq Ln	Virginia Beach	VA	23462	**800-276-2023**	757-490-2300	725
Roush Manufacturing Inc						
12068 Market St	Livonia	MI	48150	**800-215-9658**	734-779-7006	59
Rousseau Metal Inc						
105 Ave De Gasp Ouest						
	St Jean-Port-Joli	QC	G0R3G0	**866-463-4270**	418-598-3381	350
Route 66 Casino Hotel						
14500 Central Ave	Albuquerque	NM	87121	**866-352-7866**	505-352-7866	132
Roux Assoc Inc						
209 Shafter St	Islandia	NY	11749	**800-322-7689**	631-232-2600	195
Rovi Corporation						
1990 Post Oak Blvd Ste 2300	Houston	TX	77056	**877-745-6591**	713-963-1200	642-56
Rowan County Convention & Visitors Bureau						
204 E Innes St Ste 120	Salisbury	NC	28144	**800-332-2343**	704-638-3100	208
Rowan Regional Medical Ctr (RRMC)						
612 Mocksville Ave	Salisbury	NC	28144	**888-844-0080**	704-210-5000	374-3

Name / Address	City	State	Zip	Toll-Free	Phone	Class
Rowan University						
201 Mullica Hill Rd	Glassboro	NJ	08028	**877-787-6926***	856-256-4200	167
*Admissions						
Rowe Machinery & Automation Inc						
76 Hinckley Rd	Clinton	ME	04927	**800-247-2645**	207-426-2351	493
Rowell Chemical Corp						
15 Salt Creek Ln Ste 205	Hinsdale	IL	60521	**888-261-7963**	630-920-8833	145
Rowley Chapman & Barney Ltd						
63 E Main St Ste 501	Mesa	AZ	85201	**888-476-8411**	480-833-1113	428
Rowman & Littlefield Publishers Inc						
4501 Forbes Blvd Ste 200	Lanham	MD	20706	**800-462-6420**	301-459-3366	634-2
Rowmark Inc						
2040 Industrial Dr	Findlay	OH	45840	**800-243-3339**	419-425-2407	598
Roy Anderson Corp						
11400 Reichold Rd	Gulfport	MS	39503	**800-688-4003**	228-896-4000	188
Roy Bros Inc						
764 Boston Rd	Billerica	MA	01821	**800-225-0830***	978-667-1921	778
*Cust Svc						
Roy E Hanson Jr Mfg						
1600 E Washington Blvd	Los Angeles	CA	90021	**800-421-9395**	213-747-7514	90
Roy J Carver Biotechnology Ctr						
1206 W Gregory	Urbana	IL	61801	**800-550-3033**	217-333-1695	666
Roy Miller Freight Lines LLC						
3165 E Coronado St	Anaheim	CA	92806	**800-336-5673**	714-632-5511	315
Roy's Wood Products Inc						
329 Thrush Ln	Lugoff	SC	29078	**800-727-1590**	803-438-1590	114
Royal & SunAlliance Insurance Co of Canada (RSA)						
18 York St Ste 800	Toronto	ON	M5J2T8	**800-268-8406**	416-366-7511	391-4
Royal Alliance Assoc Inc						
1 World Financial Ctr 14th Fl	New York	NY	10281	**800-821-5100**		688
Royal Aloha Vacation Club						
1505 Dillingham Blvd Ste 212	Honolulu	HI	96817	**800-367-5212**	808-847-8050	751
Royal Bank of Canada						
200 Bay St 9th Fl S Twr	Toronto	ON	M5J2J5	**800-769-2599**	416-955-7806	69
TSE: RY						
Royal Baths Manufacturing Co						
14635 Chrisman Rd	Houston	TX	77039	**800-826-0074**	281-442-3400	375
Royal Botanical Gardens (RBG)						
680 Plains Rd W	Burlington	ON	L7T4H4	**800-694-4769**	905-527-1158	96
Royal British Columbia Museum (RBCM)						
675 Belleville St	Victoria	BC	V8W9W2	**888-447-7977**	250-356-7226	519
Royal Business Forms Inc						
3301 Ave E E	Arlington	TX	76011	**800-255-9303**	817-640-5248	109
Royal Camp Services Ltd						
7111 - 67 St	Edmonton	AB	T6B3L7	**877-884-2267**	780-463-8000	777
Royal Canadian Military Institute						
426 University Ave	Toronto	ON	M5G1S9	**800-585-1072**	416-597-0286	519
Royal Caribbean International						
1050 Caribbean Way	Miami	FL	33132	**800-327-6700**	305-539-6000	222
Royal Coach Tours						
630 Stockton Ave	San Jose	CA	95126	**800-927-6925**	408-279-4801	758
Royal Coachman Worldwide						
88 Ford Rd Ste 26	Denville	NJ	07834	**800-472-7433**	973-400-3200	441
Royal College of Dental Surgeons of Ontario						
6 Crescent Rd	Toronto	ON	M4W1T1	**800-565-4591**	416-961-6555	164
Royal Consumer Information Products Inc						
379 Campus Dr 2nd Fl	Somerset	NJ	08873	**888-261-4555***	732-627-9977	110
*Sales						
Royal Crest Dairy Inc						
350 S Pearl St	Denver	CO	80209	**888-226-6455**	303-777-2227	297-27
Royal Cup Coffee						
160 Cleage Dr	Birmingham	AL	35217	**800-366-5836***		297-7
*Cust Svc						
Royal Cup Coffee and Tea						
160 Cleage Dr	Birmingham	AL	35217	**800-366-5836**		498
Royal Garden at Waikiki Hotel						
440 Olohana St	Honolulu	HI	96815	**800-989-0971**	808-943-0202	379
Royal Group, The						
71 Royal Group Crescent	Woodbridge	ON	L4H1X9	**800-263-2353**	905-264-0701	237
Royal Holiday Beach Resort						
1988 Beach Blvd	Biloxi	MS	39531	**800-874-0402***	228-388-7553	379
*Resv						
Royal Lahaina Resort						
2780 Kekaa Dr	Lahaina	HI	96761	**800-222-5642**	808-661-3611	667
Royal Mouldings Ltd						
135 Bearcreek Rd PO Box 610	Marion	VA	24354	**800-368-3117**	276-783-8161	310
Royal Neighbor Magazine						
230 16th St	Rock Island	IL	61201	**800-627-4762**	309-788-4561	456-10
Royal Oak Foundation, The						
35 W 35th St Ste 1200	New York	NY	10001	**800-913-6565**	212-480-2889	47-13
Royal Pacific Resort at Universal Orlando - A Loews Hotel						
6300 Hollywood Way	Orlando	FL	32819	**800-235-6397**	407-503-3000	667
Royal Palms Resort & Spa						
5200 E Camelback Rd	Phoenix	AZ	85018	**800-672-6011**	602-840-3610	667
Royal Park Hotel-brookshire & The Commons						
600 E University Dr	Rochester	MI	48307	**800-339-2761**	248-652-2600	379
Royal Regency Hotel						
165 Tuckahoe Rd	Yonkers	NY	10710	**800-215-3858**	914-476-6200	379
Royal Roads University						
2005 Sooke Rd	Victoria	BC	V9B5Y2	**800-788-8028**	250-391-2511	783
Royal Saskatchewan Museum						
2445 Albert St	Regina	SK	S4P4W7	**866-984-4964**	306-787-2815	519
Royal Securities Co						
4095 Chicago Dr SW Ste 120	Grandville	MI	49418	**800-421-3518**	616-538-2550	688
Royal Sonesta Hotel Boston						
40 Edwin H Land Blvd	Cambridge	MA	02142	**800-766-3782**	617-806-4200	379
Royal Sonesta Hotel New Orleans						
300 Bourbon St	New Orleans	LA	70130	**800-766-3782**	504-586-0300	379
Royal Sun Inn						
1700 S Palm Canyon Dr	Palm Springs	CA	92264	**800-619-4786**	760-327-1564	379
Royal Textile Mills Inc						
929 Firetower Rd	Yanceyville	NC	27379	**800-334-9361**		154-1
Royal Tractor Co Inc						
109 Overland Pk Pl	New Century	KS	66031	**888-782-7278**	913-782-2598	469
Royal Trucking Co						
1323 Eshman Ave N PO Box 387	West Point	MS	39773	**800-321-1293**	662-494-1637	778
Royal Tyrrell Museum of Palaeontology						
Hwy 838						
Midland Provincial Pk	Drumheller	AB	T0J0Y0	**888-440-4240**	403-823-7707	519

Name	Address	City	State	ZIP	Toll-Free	Phone	Class
Royalton Hotel	44 W 44th St	New York	NY	10036	**800-606-6090**	212-869-4400	379
Royalty Carpet Mills Inc	17111 Red Hill Ave	Irvine	CA	92614	**800-854-8331**	949-474-4000	130
Royce & Assoc LLC	745 Fifth Ave	New York	NY	10151	**800-221-4268**		401
Royer Corp	805 East St	Madison	IN	47250	**800-457-8997**	812-265-3133	709
Roylco Inc	3251 Abbeville Hwy PO Box 13409	Anderson	SC	29624	**800-362-8656**	864-296-0043	245
Roysons Corp	40 Vanderhoof Ave	Rockaway	NJ	07866	**888-769-7667**	973-625-7923	292
Rozelle Cosmetics	4260 Loop Rd	Westfield	VT	05874	**800-451-4216**	802-744-2270	217
RP Design Web Services	17 Meriden Ave Ste 2A	Southington	CT	06489	**800-847-3475**	203-271-7991	179
RP International	PO Box 900	Woodland Hills	CA	91365	**877-999-8322**	818-992-0500	47-17
RPB (Research to Prevent Blindness Inc)	645 Madison Ave 21st Fl	New York	NY	10022	**800-621-0026**	212-752-4333	47-17
Rpl Supplies Inc	141 Lanza Ave Bldg 3A	Garfield	NJ	07026	**800-524-0914**	973-767-0880	176
RPM Industries Inc	26 Aurelius Ave	Auburn	NY	13021	**800-669-3676**	315-255-1105	201
RPM International Inc	2628 Pearl Rd *NYSE: RPM*	Medina	OH	44256	**800-776-4488**	330-273-5090	549
RR Bowker LLC	630 Central Ave	New Providence	NJ	07974	**888-269-5372**	908-286-1090	634-2
R&R Contracting Inc	5201 N Washington St	Grand Forks	ND	58203	**800-872-5975**	701-772-7667	190
RR Donnelley	111 S Wacker Dr	Chicago	IL	60606	**800-742-4455**		625
RR Donnelley Logistics	1000 Windham Pkwy	Bolingbrook	IL	60490	**888-744-7773**	630-226-6100	5
RR Donnelley Response Marketing Services	4101 Winfield Rd	Warrenville	IL	60555	**800-722-9001**	630-963-9494	5
R&R Products Inc	3334 E Milber St	Tucson	AZ	85714	**800-528-3446**	520-889-3593	386
RRMC (Rowan Regional Medical Ctr)	612 Mocksville Ave	Salisbury	NC	28144	**888-844-0080**	704-210-5000	374-3
RS (IEEE Reliability Society)	IEEE Operations Ctr 445 Hoes Ln	Piscataway	NJ	08854	**800-678-4333**	732-981-0060	48-19
RS Corcoran Co	500 N Vine St	New Lenox	IL	60451	**800-637-1067**	815-485-2156	638
RS Electronics Inc	34443 Schoolcraft Rd	Livonia	MI	48150	**866-600-6040**	734-525-1155	248
RS Hughes Company Inc	1162 Sonora Ct	Sunnyvale	CA	94086	**877-774-8443**	818-686-9111	385
RSA (Royal & SunAlliance Insurance Co of Canada)	18 York St Ste 800	Toronto	ON	M5J2T8	**800-268-8406**	416-366-7511	391-4
RSA Security Inc	174 Middlesex Tpke	Bedford	MA	01730	**800-995-5095**	781-515-5000	180-12
RSBCIH (Riverside-San Bernardino County Indian Health Inc)	11555 1/2 Potrero Rd	Banning	CA	92220	**800-732-8805**	951-849-4761	353
RSDC of Michigan LLC	1775 Holloway Dr	Holt	MI	48842	**877-881-7732**		479
RSES (Refrigeration Service Engineers Society)	1666 Rand Rd	Des Plaines	IL	60016	**800-297-5660**	847-297-6464	48-3
R-S-H Engineering Inc	909 N 18th St Ste 200	Monroe	LA	71201	**888-340-4884**	318-323-4009	263
RSI (Reconditioned Systems Inc)	2636 S Wilson St Ste 105	Tempe	AZ	85282	**800-280-5000**	480-968-1772	320-1
Rsi Corp	543 Main St	Kiowa	KS	67070	**888-830-5648**	620-825-4600	198
RSI Home Products Inc	400 E Orangethorpe Ave	Anaheim	CA	92801	**888-774-8062**	714-449-2200	114
RSI Insurance Brokers Inc	2801 Bristol St Ste 200	Costa Mesa	CA	92626	**800-828-5273**	714-546-6616	390
RSNA (Radiological Society of North America)	820 Jorie Blvd	Oak Brook	IL	60523	**800-381-6660**	630-571-2670	48-8
RSPA (Retail Solutions Providers Assn)	10130 Perimeter Pkwy Ste 420	Charlotte	NC	28216	**800-782-2693**	704-357-3124	48-18
RSR Group Inc	4405 Metric Dr	Winter Park	FL	32792	**800-541-4867**	407-677-1000	708
RSVP (Retired & Senior Volunteer Program)	1201 New York Ave NW	Washington	DC	20525	**800-833-3722**	202-606-5000	199
RSVP Publications	6730 W Linebaugh Ave Ste 201	Tampa	FL	33625	**800-360-7787**	813-960-7787	311
RSVP Vacations	2535 25th Ave S	Minneapolis	MN	55406	**800-328-7787**	310-432-2300	758
RT Vanderbilt Company Inc	30 Winfield St *Cust Svc	Norwalk	CT	06855	**800-243-6064***	203-853-1400	143
RTA (Riverside Transit Agency)	1825 Third St PO Box 59968	Riverside	CA	92517	**800-800-7821**	951-565-5000	467
RTC (Regional Transportation Commission of Southern Nevada)	600 S Grand Central Pkwy Ste 350	Las Vegas	NV	89106	**800-228-3911**	702-676-1500	467
RTD (Regional Transportation District)	1600 Blake St	Denver	CO	80202	**800-366-7433**	303-628-9000	467
RTEA (Cloud Peak Energy Inc)	505 S Gillette Ave PO Box 3009	Gillette	WY	82717	**866-470-4300**	307-687-6000	500
RTEC (Rural Transit Enterprises Coordinated Inc)	100 E Main St	Mount Vernon	KY	40456	**800-321-7832**	606-256-9835	107
RTI Biologics Inc	11621 Research Cir *NASDAQ: RTIX*	Alachua	FL	32615	**877-343-6832**	386-418-8888	84
RTN Federal Credit Union	600 Main St	Waltham	MA	02452	**800-338-0221**	781-736-9900	221
RTNDA (Radio-Television News Directors Assn)	1600 K St NW Ste 700	Washington	DC	20006	**800-807-8632**	202-659-6510	48-14
RTP Co	580 E Front St	Winona	MN	55987	**800-433-4787**	507-454-6900	604-2
RTR (Rainbow Trout Ranch)	1484 FDR 250 PO Box 458	Antonito	CO	81120	**800-633-3397**	719-376-5659	241
RTS Financial Service	9300 Metcalf Ste 301	Overland Park	KS	66212	**877-242-4390**		274

Name	Address	City	State	ZIP	Toll-Free	Phone	Class
RTS Packaging LLC	504 Thrasher St	Norcross	GA	30071	**800-558-6984**		100
RTW Inc	8500 Normandale Lk Blvd Ste 1400 PO Box 390327 *Sales	Bloomington	MN	55437	**800-789-2242***	952-893-0403	391-4
RUAN Transportation Management Systems	666 Grand Ave 3200 Ruan Ctr	Des Moines	IA	50309	**866-782-6669**	515-245-2500	291
Ruane Cunniff & Goldfarb Inc	9 W 57th St Ste 5000	New York	NY	10019	**800-686-6884**	212-832-5280	401
RubbAir Door Div Eckel Industries Inc	100 Groton Shirley Rd	Ayer	MA	01432	**800-966-7822**	978-772-0480	237
Rubber Manufacturers Assn (RMA)	1400 K St NW Ste 900	Washington	DC	20005	**800-220-7622**	202-682-4800	48-13
Rubbermaid Commercial Products (RCP)	3124 Valley Ave	Winchester	VA	22601	**800-347-9800**	540-667-8700	607
Rubberset Co	101 W Prospect Ave	Cleveland	OH	44115	**800-345-4939**		102
Rubenstein Bros Inc	102 St Charles Ave	New Orleans	LA	70130	**800-725-7823**	504-581-6666	156-3
Rubicon Minerals Corp	44 Victoria St Ste 400 *NYSE: RBY*	Toronto	ON	M5C1Y2	**866-365-4706**	604-623-3333	501
Rubio's Restaurants Inc	1902 Wright Pl Ste 300	Carlsbad	CA	92008	**800-354-4199**	760-929-8226	668
Ruby Falls	1720 S Scenic Hwy	Chattanooga	TN	37409	**800-755-7105**	423-821-2544	49-4
Ruby Stein Wagner	300 Rue Leo-pariseau Ste 1900	Montreal	QC	H2X4B5	**866-842-3911**	514-842-3911	2
Rudd Equipment Co	4344 Poplar Level Rd	Louisville	KY	40213	**800-527-2282**	502-456-4050	358
Rudolph Brothers	6550 Oley Speaks Way	Canal Winchester	OH	43110	**800-600-9508**	614-833-0707	709
Rudolph Foods Company Inc	6575 Bellefontaine Rd	Lima	OH	45804	**800-241-7675**	419-648-3611	297-9
Rudolph Technologies Inc	1 Rudolph Rd PO Box 1000 *NASDAQ: RTEC*	Flanders	NJ	07836	**877-467-8365**	973-691-1300	471
Ruf Strategic Solutions	1533 E Spruce St	Olathe	KS	66061	**800-829-8544**		465
Ruffed Grouse Society (RGS)	451 McCormick Rd	Coraopolis	PA	15108	**888-564-6747**	412-262-4044	47-3
Ruffin Bldg Systems Inc	6914 Louisiana 2	Oak Grove	LA	71263	**800-421-4232**	318-428-2305	104
Rug Doctor LP	4701 Old Shepard Pl	Plano	TX	75093	**800-784-3628**	972-673-1400	266-2
Rug Hooking Magazine	5067 Ritter Rd	Mechanicsburg	PA	17055	**866-375-8626**	717-796-0411	456-14
Rugg Mfg Company Inc	105 Newton St	Greenfield	MA	01302	**800-633-8772**	413-773-5471	429
Rugged Systems Inc	13000 Danielson St Q	Poway	CA	92064	**888-584-2673**	858-391-1006	227
Ruggie Wealth Management	2100 Lk Eustis Dr	Tavares	FL	32778	**888-343-2711**	352-343-2700	462
Ruiz Foods Inc	PO Box 37	Dinuba	CA	93618	**800-477-6474**	559-591-5510	297-36
Rules-based Medicine Inc	3300 Duval Rd	Austin	TX	78759	**866-726-6277**	512-835-8026	582
Rumble Tuff Inc	865 North 1430 West	Orem	UT	84057	**855-228-8388**	801-609-8168	320-2
Rumpke	10795 Hughes Rd	Cincinnati	OH	45251	**800-582-3107**		802
Rumsey Electric Co	15 Colwell Ln	Conshohocken	PA	19428	**800-462-2402**	610-832-9000	248
Run Consultants LLC	925 N Point Pkwy Ste 160	Alpharetta	GA	30005	**866-457-2193**		262
Rundle-Spence Manufacturing Co	PO Box 510008	New Berlin	WI	53151	**800-783-6060**	262-782-3000	611
Runge Conservation Nature Ctr	2901 W Truman Blvd	Jefferson City	MO	65109	**800-392-1111**	573-751-4115	49-4
Runner's Edge Inc, The	3195 N Federal Hwy	Boca Raton	FL	33431	**888-361-1950**	561-361-1950	709
Runzheimer International	Runzheimer Pk	Rochester	WI	53167	**800-558-1702**	262-971-2200	195
Ruotolo Assoc Inc (RA)	29 Broadway Ste 210	Cresskill	NJ	07626	**800-786-8656**	201-568-3898	318
Rupe's Hydraulics Sales & Service	725 N Twin Oaks Vly Rd	San Marcos	CA	92069	**800-354-7873**	760-744-9350	788
Rural Electric Convenience Co-op Co	3973 W SR 104 PO Box 19	Auburn	IL	62615	**800-245-7322**	217-438-6197	247
Rural Electric Co-op Inc (REC)	801 N Industrial Heights PO Box 609	Lindsay	OK	73052	**800-259-3504**	405-756-3104	247
Rural Health Resource Center	525 S Lake Ave Ste 320	Duluth	MN	55802	**800-997-6685**	218-727-9390	448
Rural Mutual Insurance Company Inc	1241 John Q Hammons Dr PO Box 5555	Madison	WI	53705	**800-362-7881**	608-836-5525	391-4
Rural Resources Community Action	956 S Main St	Colville	WA	99114	**800-538-7659**	509-684-8421	147
Rural Telephone Service Company Inc	PO Box 158	Lenora	KS	67645	**877-625-7872**	785-567-4281	733
Rural Transit Enterprises Coordinated Inc (RTEC)	100 E Main St	Mount Vernon	KY	40456	**800-321-7832**	606-256-9835	107
Rural/Metro Corp	9221 E Via de Ventura	Scottsdale	AZ	85258	**800-352-2309**		30
Ruritan National	5451 Lyons Rd PO Box 487	Dublin	VA	24084	**877-787-8727**	540-674-5431	47-15
RUSA (Reference & User Services Assn)	50 E Huron St	Chicago	IL	60611	**800-545-2433**	312-280-4398	48-11
Rusch Inc	2917 Weck Dr PO Box 12600	Research Triangle Park	NC	27709	**866-246-6990**	919-544-8000	476
Rush Enterprises Inc	555 IH 35 S Ste 500 *NASDAQ: RUSHA*	New Braunfels	TX	78130	**800-973-7874**	830-626-5200	266-3
Rush Gears Inc	550 Virginia Dr	Fort Washington	PA	19034	**800-523-2576**		707

Name / Address	City	State	Zip	Toll-Free	Phone	Class
Rush Industries Inc 118 N Wrenn St	High Point	NC	27260	**800-524-0258**	336-886-7700	320-2
Rush Medical College of Rush University 600 S Paulina St	Chicago	IL	60612	**888-352-7874**		168-2
Rush Shelby Energy Inc 2777 S 840 W PO Box 55 *General	Manilla	IN	46150	**800-706-7362***	765-544-2600	247
Rush Truck Center - Lubbock 4515 Ave A	Lubbock	TX	79404	**888-987-2458**	806-747-2579	515
Rush Truck Center - Whittier 2450 Kella Ave	Whittier	CA	90601	**877-605-7623**	562-551-5000	56
Rush-Copley Medical Ctr (RCMC) 2000 Ogden Ave	Aurora	IL	60504	**866-426-7539**	630-978-6200	374-3
Rushmore Forest Products 23848 Hwy 385 PO Box 619	Hill City	SD	57745	**866-466-5254**	605-574-2512	681
Rushmore Plaza Civic Ctr 444 Mt Rushmore Rd N	Rapid City	SD	57701	**800-468-6463**	605-394-4115	207
Rusken Packaging Inc PO Box 2100	Cullman	AL	35056	**800-232-8108**	256-734-0092	100
Russ Bassett Co 8189 Byron Rd	Whittier	CA	90606	**800-350-2445**	562-945-2445	288
Russ' Restaurants Inc 390 E Eigth St	Holland	MI	49423	**800-521-1778**	616-396-6571	668
Russel Metals Inc 6600 Financial Dr *TSE: RUS*	Mississauga	ON	L5N7J6	**800-268-0750**	905-819-7777	491
Russelectric Inc 99 Industrial Pk Rd	Hingham	MA	02043	**800-225-5250**	781-749-6000	727
Russell Cave National Monument 3729 County Rd 98	Bridgeport	AL	35740	**866-705-5711**	256-495-2672	563
Russell Food Equipment Ltd 1255 Venables St	Vancouver	BC	V6A3X6	**800-663-0707**	604-253-6611	14
Russell Investment Group 1301 Second Ave Ste 18	Seattle	WA	98101	**800-787-7354**		401
Russell Investments 1301 Second Ave 18th Fl	Seattle	WA	98101	**800-426-7969**	206-505-7877	401
Russell Karting Specialties Inc PO Box 1220	Raymore	MO	64083	**800-821-3359**	816-322-3330	56
Russell Reynolds Assoc Inc 200 Pk Ave 23rd Fl	New York	NY	10166	**800-259-0470**	212-351-2000	268
Russell Sage College 45 Ferry St *Admissions	Troy	NY	12180	**888-837-9724***	518-244-2217	167
Russell Standard Corp 285 Kappa Dr Ste 300 *General	Pittsburgh	PA	15238	**800-323-3053***		45
Russell Stover Candies Inc 4900 Oak St	Kansas City	MO	64112	**800-477-8683**	816-842-9240	297-8
Russellville Area Chamber of Commerce 708 W Main St	Russellville	AR	72801	**855-678-2447**	479-968-2530	138
Russian National Tourist Office 224 W 30th St Ste 701	New York	NY	10001	**877-221-7120**	646-473-2233	773
Russin Lumber Corp 21 Leonards Dr	Montgomery	NY	12549	**800-724-0010**	845-457-4000	193-3
Rust College 150 Rust Ave	Holly Springs	MS	38635	**888-886-8492**	662-252-8000	167
Rustler Lodge 10380 East Hwy 210 PO Box 8030	Alta	UT	84092	**888-532-2582**	801-742-2200	667
Rust-Oleum Corp 11 E Hawthorn Pkwy	Vernon Hills	IL	60061	**800-323-3584**	847-367-7700	549
Ruston/Lincoln Chamber of Commerce 2111 N Trenton St	Ruston	LA	71270	**800-392-9032**	318-255-2031	138
Rusty Parrot Lodge & Spa PO Box 1657	Jackson	WY	83001	**800-458-2004**	307-733-2000	667
Rutan Poly Industries Inc 39 Siding Pl	Mahwah	NJ	07430	**800-872-1474**	201-529-1474	298-8
Rutgers Organics Corp (ROC) 201 Struble Rd	State College	PA	16801	**888-469-2188**	814-238-2424	142
Rutgers the State University of New Jersey *School of Law Camden* 217 N Fifth St	Camden	NJ	08102	**800-466-7561**	856-225-6375	168-1
Rutgers University Press 106 Somerset St 3rd Fl	New Brunswick	NJ	08901	**800-272-6817**	732-745-4935	634-4
Ruth Eckerd Hall 1111 McMullen Booth Rd	Clearwater	FL	33759	**800-875-8682**	727-791-7060	571
Ruth Lilly Medical Library 975 W Walnut St IB 100	Indianapolis	IN	46202	**877-952-1988**	317-274-7182	434-1
Ruth's Hospitality Group Inc 1030 W Canton Ave Ste 100 *NASDAQ: RUTH* ■ *Sales	Winter Park	FL	32789	**800-544-0808***	407-333-7440	668
Rutherford B Hayes Presidential Ctr Spiegel Grove	Fremont	OH	43420	**800-998-7737**	419-332-2081	434-2
Rutherford Controls Int'l Corp 210 Shearson Crescent	Cambridge	ON	N1T1J6	**800-265-6630**	519-621-7651	350
Rutherford County Chamber of Commerce 501 Memorial Blvd	Murfreesboro	TN	37129	**800-716-7560**	615-893-6565	138
Rutherford Electric Membership Corp 186 Hudlow Rd PO Box 1569	Forest City	NC	28043	**800-521-0920**	828-245-1621	247
Rutherford Institute PO Box 7482	Charlottesville	VA	22906	**800-225-1791**	434-978-3888	47-8
Rutland Herald PO Box 668	Rutland	VT	05702	**800-498-4296**		531-2
Rutland Plastic Technologies 10021 Rodney St	Pineville	NC	28134	**800-438-5134**	704-553-0046	604-2
Rutland Region Chamber of Commerce 50 Merchants Row	Rutland	VT	05701	**800-756-8880**	802-773-2747	338
Ruttger's Bay Lake Lodge 25039 Tame Fish Lk Rd PO Box 400	Deerwood	MN	56444	**800-450-4545**	218-678-2885	667
RV World Inc of Nokomis 2110 Tamiami Trl N	Nokomis	FL	34275	**800-262-2182**	941-966-2182	56
RVDA (Recreation Vehicle Dealers Assn) 3930 University Dr 3rd Fl	Fairfax	VA	22030	**800-336-0355**	703-591-7130	48-18
RVIA (Recreation Vehicle Industry Assn) 1896 Preston White Dr	Reston	VA	20191	**800-336-0154**	703-620-6003	48-21
RVing Women (RVW) 879 N Plaza Dr Ste B103	Apache Junction	AZ	85120	**888-557-8464**	480-671-6226	47-23
RVW (RVing Women) 879 N Plaza Dr Ste B103	Apache Junction	AZ	85120	**888-557-8464**	480-671-6226	47-23
RW Beckett Corp PO Box 1289	Elyria	OH	44036	**800-645-2876**	440-327-1060	357
RW Screw Products Inc 999 Oberlin Rd SW	Massillon	OH	44647	**866-797-2739**	330-837-9211	620
RWH Trucking Inc 2970 Old Oakwood Rd	Oakwood	GA	30566	**800-256-8119**		778
RWI (RiskWatch) 1237 N Gulfstream Ave	Sarasota	Fl	34236	**800-360-1898**		180-10
RWM Casters Co PO Box 668	Gastonia	NC	28053	**800-634-7704**		350
Rx Optical 1700 S Pk St	Kalamazoo	MI	49001	**800-792-2737**	269-342-0003	542
Rx Scan 2478 Lackey Old State Rd	Delaware	OH	43015	**800-572-2648**	740-548-1725	240
RX Worldwide Meetings Inc 3060 Communications Pkwy Ste 200	Plano	TX	75093	**800-562-1713**	214-291-2920	186
Rxusa Inc 81 Seaview Blvd	Port Washington	NY	11050	**800-764-3648**	516-467-2500	239
Ryan Herco Products Corp 3010 N San Fernando Blvd	Burbank	CA	91504	**800-848-1141**	818-841-1141	602
Rycon Construction Inc 2525 Liberty Ave	Pittsburgh	PA	15222	**800-883-1901**	412-392-2525	188
Rydell Chevrolet Inc 18600 Devonshire St	Northridge	CA	91324	**866-697-5167**	319-234-4601	515
Ryder System Inc 11690 NW 105th St *NYSE: R*	Miami	FL	33178	**800-297-9337**	305-500-3726	776
Rydex Funds 805 King Farm Blvd Ste 600 *Cust Svc	Rockville	MD	20850	**800-820-0888***	301-296-5100	527
Ryerson University 350 Victoria St	Toronto	ON	M5B2K3	**866-592-8882**	416-979-5000	783
Ryman Auditorium 116 Fifth Ave N	Nashville	TN	37219	**800-733-6779**	615-458-8700	571
Rynone Mfg Corp PO Box 128	Sayre	PA	18840	**800-839-1654**	570-888-5272	114
Ryobi Technologies Inc 1428 Pearman Dairy Rd	Anderson	SC	29625	**800-525-2579**		351
Ryokan College 11965 Venice Blvd Ste 304	Los Angeles	CA	90066	**866-796-5261**	310-390-7560	167

S

Name / Address	City	State	Zip	Toll-Free	Phone	Class
S & C Electric Co 6601 N Ridge Blvd	Chicago	IL	60626	**800-621-5546**	773-338-1000	727
S & D Coffee Inc 300 Concord Pkwy PO Box 1628 *Cust Svc	Concord	NC	28026	**800-933-2210***	704-782-3121	297-7
S & H Express Inc 400 Mulberry St	York	PA	17403	**800-637-9782**	717-848-5015	448
S & M Machine Service Inc 109 E Highland Dr	Oconto Falls	WI	54154	**800-323-1579**	920-846-8130	454
S & M Moving Systems Inc 12128 Burke St	Santa Fe Springs	CA	90670	**800-528-4561**	562-567-2100	518
S & ME Inc 3201 Spring Forest Rd *Cust Svc	Raleigh	NC	27616	**800-849-2517***	919-872-2660	194
S & s Industrial Equipment & Supply Company Inc 7 Chelten Way	Trenton	NJ	08638	**800-282-3506**	609-695-3800	358
S & S Mills Inc 414 C N Pk Dr	Dalton	GA	30720	**800-241-4013**	706-277-3677	130
S & S Technology 10625 Telge Rd	Houston	TX	77095	**800-231-1747**	281-815-1300	382
S & S Tire & Auto Service Center 1475 Jingle Bell Ln	Lexington	KY	40509	**800-685-6794**		53
S & S Transport Inc PO Box 12579	Grand Forks	ND	58208	**800-726-8022**		778
S & S Worldwide Inc 75 Mill St *Orders	Colchester	CT	06415	**800-243-9232***	860-537-3451	458
S & S X-Ray Products Inc 10625 Telge Rd	Houston	TX	77095	**800-231-1747**	281-815-1300	695
S Abraham & Sons Inc PO Box 1768 *General	Grand Rapids	MI	49501	**866-248-3163***	616-453-6358	298-8
S Central Library Syst 4610 S Biltmore Ln	Madison	WI	53718	**855-516-7257**	608-246-7970	434-3
S Howes Company Inc 25 Howard St	Silver Creek	NY	14136	**888-255-2611**	716-934-2611	299
S K C Communication Products Inc 8320 Hedge Ln Terr	Shawnee Mission	KS	66227	**800-882-7779**	913-422-4222	248
S Parker Hardware Manufacturing Corp PO Box 9882	Englewood	NJ	07631	**800-772-7537**	201-569-1600	350
S R C Corp PO Box 30676	Salt Lake City	UT	84130	**800-888-4545**	801-268-4500	278
S R C Refrigeration 6615 19 Mile Rd	Sterling Heights	MI	48314	**800-521-0398**	586-254-0610	609
S R Snodgrass AC 2100 Corporate Dr	Wexford	PA	15090	**800-580-7738**	724-934-0344	2
S T Bunn Construction 1904 University Blvd PO Box 20109	Tuscaloosa	AL	35401	**800-297-6302**	205-752-8195	778
S. Freedman & Sons Inc 3322 Pennsy Dr	Landover	MD	20785	**800-545-7277**	301-322-5000	558
S.I.c. Meter Service Inc 10375 Dixie Hwy	Davisburg	MI	48350	**800-433-4332**	248-625-0667	385
SA (Sexaholics Anonymous) PO Box 3565	Brentwood	TN	37024	**866-424-8777**	615-370-6062	47-21
SA Comunale Company Inc 2900 Newpark Dr	Barberton	OH	44203	**800-776-7181**	330-706-3040	191-13
SA Day Mfg Co Inc 1489 Niagara St	Buffalo	NY	14213	**800-747-0030**	716-881-3030	144

Name / Address	City	State	Zip	Toll-Free	Phone	Class
SA Recycling LLC 2411 N Glassell St	Orange	CA	92865	800-468-7272	714-632-2000	684
SAA (Society of American Archivists) 17 N State St Ste 1425	Chicago	IL	60602	866-722-7858	312-606-0722	47-4
SAA (Sex Addicts Anonymous) PO Box 70949	Houston	TX	77270	800-477-8191	713-869-4902	47-21
SAA (Society for American Archaeology) 900 Second St NE Ste 12	Washington	DC	20002	800-759-5219	202-789-8200	48-5
Saba Software Inc 2400 Bridge Pkwy *OTC: SABA*	Redwood Shores	CA	94065	877-722-2101	650-581-2500	180-3
Sabert Corp 2288 Main St Ext	Sayreville	NJ	08872	800-722-3781		547
Sabian Ltd 219 Main St.	Meductic	NB	E6H2L5	800-817-2242	506-272-2019	526
Sabin Corp 3800 Constitution Ave PO Box 788	Bloomington	IN	47403	800-457-4500	812-339-2235	598
Sablan Gregorio (Rep D - MP) 423 Cannon Bldg	Washington	DC	20515	877-446-3465	202-225-2646	342-2
Sable Systems International Inc 6000 S Ea Ste 1	Las Vegas	NV	89119	800-330-0465	702-269-4445	203
Sabra Dipping Co LLC 2420 49th St	Astoria	NY	11103	888-957-2272		297-37
Sabre Healthdirect Inc 590 Alden Rd	Markham	ON	L3R8N2	800-314-3346	905-305-9900	391-2
Sabre Industries Inc 8653 E Hwy 67	Alvarado	TX	76009	866-254-3707	817-852-1700	263
Sabre Solution, The 200 East 31st St	Savannah	OK	31401	888-494-7200	912-355-7200	182
Sabretech Consulting LLC 154 Lewis St	Hillsdale	MI	49242	800-267-1715	517-437-7150	198
Sabrient Systems LLC 115 S La Cumbre Ln Ste 100	Santa Barbara	CA	93105	888-502-3605	805-730-7777	666
SAC (Smith Affiliated Capital) 800 Third Ave 12th Fl	New York	NY	10022	888-387-3298	212-644-9440	403
SAC Federal Credit Union (SAFCU) 11515 S 39th St	Bellevue	NE	68123	800-228-0392	402-292-8000	221
Sac Osage Electric Co-op Inc 4815 E Hwy 54 PO Box 111	El Dorado Springs	MO	64744	800-876-2701	417-876-2721	247
Sachs Waldman Pc 1000 Farmer St	Detroit	MI	48226	800-638-6722	313-965-3464	428
Sackett & Associates 1055 Lincoln Ave	San Jose	CA	95125	800-913-3000	408-295-7755	428
Sacor Financial Inc 1911 Douglas Blvd 85-126	Roseville	CA	95661	866-556-0231		393
Sacramento Bag Manufacturing Co 440 N Pioneer Ave Ste 300	Woodland	CA	95776	800-287-2247	530-662-6130	66
Sacramento Ballet 1631 K St	Sacramento	CA	95814	800-925-9989	916-552-5800	572-1
Sacramento Bee PO Box 15779 *Cust Svc	Sacramento	CA	95852	800-284-3233*	916-321-1000	531-2
Sacramento Convention & Visitors Bureau 1608 'I' St	Sacramento	CA	95814	800-292-2334	916-808-7777	208
Sacramento Kings ARCO Arena 1 Sports Pkwy	Sacramento	CA	95834	866-746-7622	916-928-0000	712-1
Sacramento Zoo 3930 W Land Pk Dr	Sacramento	CA	95822	866-570-7318	916-808-5888	821
Sacred Heart HealthCare System 421 Chew St	Allentown	PA	18102	800-994-6610	610-776-4500	374-3
Sacred Heart Hospital 900 W Clairemont Ave	Eau Claire	WI	54701	888-445-4554	715-717-4121	374-3
Sacred Heart Hospital of Pensacola 5151 N Ninth Ave	Pensacola	FL	32504	800-874-1026	850-416-7000	374-3
Sacred Heart Medical Ctr 1255 Hilyard St	Eugene	OR	97401	800-288-7444	541-686-7300	374-3
SADD (Students Against Destructive Decisions) 255 Main St	Marlborough	MA	01752	877-723-3462	508-481-3568	47-6
Sadler's Smokehouse Ltd PO Box 1088	Henderson	TX	75653	800-777-5581	903-655-7265	297-26
Sadoff & Rudoy Industries LLP 240 W Arndt St *General	Fond du Lac	WI	54936	877-972-3633*	920-921-2070	684
SAE (Sigma Alpha Epsilon Fraternity) 1856 Sheridan Rd	Evanston	IL	60201	800-233-1856	847-475-1856	47-16
SAE (Society of Automotive Engineers Inc) 400 Commonwealth Dr	Warrendale	PA	15096	877-606-7323	724-776-4841	48-21
SAE Circuits Colorado Inc 4820 N 63rd St	Boulder	CO	80301	800-234-9001	303-530-1900	624
Saebo Inc 2725 Water Ridge Pkwy Ste 320 Six LakePointe Plaza	Charlotte	NC	28217	888-284-5433		474
SAEC (South Alabama Electric Co-op) PO Box 449	Troy	AL	36081	800-556-2060	334-566-2060	247
Saepio Technologies Inc 4601 Madison Ave 4th Fl	Kansas City	MO	64112	877-468-7613	816-777-2100	227
SAF (Santa Fe Municipal Airport) 121 Aviation Dr PO Box 909	Santa Fe	NM	87504	866-773-2587	505-955-2900	27
SAF (Society of American Florists) 1601 Duke St	Alexandria	VA	22314	800-336-4743	703-836-8700	48-4
SAF (Society of American Foresters) 5400 Grosvenor Ln	Bethesda	MD	20814	866-897-8720	301-897-8720	47-2
Safari Circuits Inc 411 Washington St	Otsego	MI	49078	888-694-7230	269-694-9471	178
Safari Micro Inc 2185 W Pecos Rd	Chandler	AZ	85224	888-446-4770		198
Safari West Wildlife Preserve & Tent Camp 3115 Porter Creek Rd	Santa Rosa	CA	95404	800-616-2695	707-579-2551	821
Safariland LLC 13386 International Pkwy	Jacksonville	FL	32218	800-347-1200	904-741-5400	575
Safco Products Co 9300 W Research Ctr Rd *Cust Svc	New Hope	MN	55428	800-328-3020*	763-536-6700	320-1
SAFCU (SAC Federal Credit Union) 11515 S 39th St	Bellevue	NE	68123	800-228-0392	402-292-8000	221

Name / Address	City	State	Zip	Toll-Free	Phone	Class
Safe & Civil Schools 2451 Willamette St	Eugene	OR	97405	800-323-8819	541-345-1442	244
Safe 1 Credit Union PO Box 2203	Bakersfield	CA	93303	800-322-4529	661-327-3818	221
Safe Auto Insurance Co 4 Easton Oval PO Box 182109	Columbus	OH	43219	800-723-3288	614-231-0200	391-4
SAFE Credit Union 3720 Madison Ave	North Highlands	CA	95660	800-733-7233	916-979-7233	221
Safeamerica Credit Union 6001 Gibraltar Dr	Pleasanton	CA	94588	800-972-0999	925-734-4111	221
Safeguard Business Systems Inc 8585 N Stemmons Fwy Ste 600 N	Dallas	TX	75247	800-523-2422		141
Safeguard Chemical Corp 411 Wales Ave	Bronx	NY	10454	800-536-3170	718-585-3170	282
SafeGuard Health Enterprises Inc 95 Enterprise Ste 100	Aliso Viejo	CA	92656	800-880-1800	949-425-4300	391-3
Safeguard Properties Inc 7887 Safeguard Cir	Valley View	OH	44125	800-852-8306	216-739-2900	508
Safeguard Security & Communications Inc 8454 N 90th St	Scottsdale	AZ	85258	800-426-6060	480-609-6200	691
Safelite Group Inc 2400 Farmers Dr	Columbus	OH	43235	877-664-8931		61-2
SafeNet Inc 4690 Millennium Dr *Sales	Belcamp	MD	21017	800-533-3958*	410-931-7500	178
Safetec of America Inc 887 Kensington Ave	Buffalo	NY	14215	800-456-7077	716-895-1822	150
Safe-T-Gard Corp 12105 W Cedar Dr *Cust Svc	Lakewood	CO	80228	800-356-9026*	303-763-8900	575
Safety Analysis & Forensic Engineering 5665 Hollister Ave	Goleta	CA	93117	800-426-7866	805-964-0676	666
Safety Components International Inc 40 Emery St	Greenville	SC	29605	800-896-6926	864-240-2692	676
Safety Harbor Resort & Spa 105 N Bayshore Dr	Safety Harbor	FL	34695	888-237-8772	727-726-1161	667
Safety Products Inc 3517 Craftsman Blvd	Lakeland	FL	33803	800-248-6860	863-665-3601	677
Safety Sam Inc 2626 S Roosevelt St Ste 2	Tempe	AZ	85282	866-478-6980		763
Safety Seal Piston Ring Co 4000 Airport Rd *Sales	Marshall	TX	75672	800-962-3631*	903-938-9241	127
Safety Speed Cut Mfg Co Inc 13943 Lincoln St NE	Ham Lake	MN	55304	800-772-2327	763-755-1600	819
Safety Supply South Inc 100 Centrum Dr *Cust Svc	Irmo	SC	29063	800-522-8344*		677
Safety Technology International Inc 2306 Airport Rd	Waterford	MI	48327	800-888-4784	248-673-9898	607
Safety-Kleen Corp 2600 N Central Expwy Ste 400	Richardson	TX	75080	800-669-5740	800-323-5040	665
Safeware Inc 3200 HubbaRd Rd *Cust Svc	Landover	MD	20785	800-331-6707*	301-683-1234	677
Safeway Insurance Group 790 Pasquinelli Dr	Westmont	IL	60559	800-273-0300	630-887-8300	391-4
Safeway Sign Co 9875 Yucca Rd	Adelanto	CA	92301	800-637-7233	760-246-7070	699
SAFH (Sutter Auburn Faith Community Hospital) 11815 Education St	Auburn	CA	95602	800-478-8837	530-888-4500	374-3
Saf-T-Cab Inc PO Box 2587	Fresno	CA	93745	800-344-7491	559-268-5541	515
Saf-T-Gard International Inc 205 Huehl Rd	Northbrook	IL	60062	800-548-4273	847-291-1600	677
Safway Services Inc N 19 W 24200 Riverwood Dr	Waukesha	WI	53188	800-558-4772	262-523-6500	266-3
SAG (Screen Actors Guild) 5757 Wilshire Blvd	Los Angeles	CA	90036	800-724-0767	323-954-1600	414
Sag Harbor Industries Inc 1668 Sag Harbor Tpke	Sag Harbor	NY	11963	800-724-5952	631-725-0440	517
Saga Communications Inc 73 Kercheval Ave *NYSE: SGA*	Grosse Pointe Farms	MI	48236	800-777-3674	313-886-7070	640
Sagamore Health Network 11555 N Meridian St Ste 400	Carmel	IN	46032	800-364-3469	317-573-2886	391-3
Sagamore Insurance Co 111 Congressional Blvd Ste 500	Carmel	IN	46032	800-317-9402		391-4
Sagamore, The 110 Sagamore Rd	Bolton Landing	NY	12814	866-384-1944	518-644-9400	667
Sage College of Albany 140 New Scotland Ave *Admissions	Albany	NY	12208	888-837-9724*	518-292-1730	167
Sage Fixed Assets 2325 Dulles Corner Blvd Ste 700	Herndon	VA	20171	800-368-2405	866-520-2519	180-1
Sage Publications Inc 2455 Teller Rd	Thousand Oaks	CA	91320	800-818-7243	805-499-9774	634-2
Sagebrush Steakhouse 129 Fast Ln	Mooresville	NC	28117	877-704-5939	704-660-5939	668
SagePoint Financial Inc 2800 N Central Ave Ste 2100	Phoenix	AZ	85004	800-552-3319		688
Sager Electronics Inc 19 Lorena Dr	Middleboro	MA	02346	800-724-3780	508-947-8888	248
Sager's Seafood Plus Inc 4802 Bridal Wreath Dr	Richmond	TX	77406	800-929-3474	281-342-8833	298-5
Sagestone Spa & Salon *Red Mountain Resort* 1275 East Red Mtn Cir	Ivins	UT	84738	877-246-4453	435-673-4905	704
Saginaw Chippewa Tribal College 2274 Enterprise Dr	Mount Pleasant	MI	48858	800-225-8172	989-775-4123	164
Saginaw Control & Engineering Inc 95 Midland Rd	Saginaw	MI	48638	800-234-6871	989-799-6871	814
Saginaw County Chamber of Commerce 515 N Washington Ave 2nd Fl	Saginaw	MI	48607	866-657-9357	989-752-7161	138
Saginaw News 203 S Washington Ave	Saginaw	MI	48607	877-611-6397	989-752-7171	531-2
Saginaw Pipe Company Inc 1980 Hwy 31 S PO Box 8	Saginaw	AL	35137	800-433-1374	205-664-3670	491

Name / Address	City	State	Zip	Toll-Free	Phone	Class
Saginaw Valley State University						
7400 Bay Rd	University Center	MI	48710	**800-968-9500**	989-964-4200	167
Saginaw Valley State University Zahnow Library						
7400 Bay Rd	University Center	MI	48710	**800-968-9500**	989-964-4240	434-6
Saguaro Resources Ltd						
3000 500 - Fourth Ave SW	Calgary	AB	T2P2V6	**855-835-4434**	403-453-3040	535
Sahlen Packing Company Inc						
318 Howard St	Buffalo	NY	14206	**800-466-8165**	716-852-8677	297-26
Sahouri Insurance & Associates Inc						
8200 Grnsburg Dr Ste 1550	Mclean	VA	22102	**855-242-6660**	703-883-0500	390
SAIC Inc (Science Application International Corp Inc)						
1710 SAIC Dr	McLean	VA	22102	**866-400-7242**	703-676-4300	180-5
SAIL Magazine						
98 N Washington St Ste 107	Boston	MA	02114	**877-388-7761**	617-720-8600	456-4
Sailing World Magazine						
55 Hammarlund Way	Middletown	RI	02842	**866-436-2460***	401-845-5100	456-4
*Cust Svc						
Saint Agnes HealthCare						
900 S Caton Ave	Baltimore	MD	21229	**800-875-8750**	410-368-6000	374-3
Saint Albert Chamber of Commerce						
71 St Albert Rd	Saint Albert	AB	T8N6L5	**800-243-2378**	780-458-2833	137
Saint Alexius Hospital						
Broadway Campus						
3933 S Broadway	Saint Louis	MO	63118	**800-245-1431**	314-865-7000	374-3
Saint Alphonsus Regional Medical Ctr						
1055 N Curtis Rd	Boise	ID	83706	**877-401-3627**	208-367-2121	374-3
Saint Ambrose University						
518 W Locust St	Davenport	IA	52803	**800-383-2627***	563-333-6000	167
*Admissions						
Saint Andrew's College						
15800 Yonge St	Aurora	ON	L4G3H7	**877-378-1899**	905-727-3178	621
Saint Andrew's School						
3900 Jog Rd	Boca Raton	FL	33434	**888-357-7332**	561-210-2000	621
Saint Andrews Estates						
6152 Verde Trail N	Boca Raton	FL	33433	**866-897-3490***	561-487-4728	670
*Mktg						
Saint Andrews Presbyterian College						
1700 Dogwood Mile	Laurinburg	NC	28352	**800-763-0198**	910-277-5555	167
Saint Anselm College						
100 St Anselm Dr	Manchester	NH	03102	**888-426-7356**	603-641-7500	167
Saint Anthony Hospital						
1000 N Lee St	Oklahoma City	OK	73101	**800-227-6964**	405-272-7000	374-3
Saint Anthony the - A Wyndham Historic Hotel						
300 E Travis St	San Antonio	TX	78205	**800-996-3426**	210-227-4392	379
Saint Anthony's Hospice						
2410 S Green St	Henderson	KY	42420	**866-380-2326**	270-826-2326	371
Saint Anthony's Medical Ctr						
10010 Kennerly Rd	Saint Louis	MO	63128	**800-554-9550**	314-525-1000	374-3
Saint Augustine National Cemetery						
104 Marine St	Saint Augustine	FL	32084	**800-273-8255**	352-793-7740	135
Saint Augustine's College						
1315 Oakwood Ave	Raleigh	NC	27610	**800-948-1126***	919-516-4016	167
*Admissions						
Saint Barnabas Medical Ctr						
94 Old Short Hills Rd	West Orange	NJ	07052	**888-724-7123**	973-322-5000	374-3
Saint Bernard Preparatory School						
1600 St Bernard Dr SE	Cullman	AL	35055	**800-722-0999**	256-739-6682	621
Saint Bernard State Park						
501 St Bernard Pkwy	Braithwaite	LA	70040	**888-677-7823**	504-682-2101	564
Saint Catherine's School						
6001 Grove Ave	Richmond	VA	23226	**800-648-4982**	804-288-2804	621
Saint Charles Mercy Hospital						
2600 Navarre Ave	Oregon	OH	43616	**888-987-6372**	419-696-7200	374-3
Saint Clair County Library System						
210 McMorran Blvd	Port Huron	MI	48060	**877-987-7323**	810-987-7323	434-3
Saint Cloud Area Convention & Visitors Bureau						
525 Hwy 10 S Ste 1	Saint Cloud	MN	56304	**800-264-2940**	320-251-4170	208
Saint Cloud Hospital						
1406 Sixth Ave	Saint Cloud	MN	56303	**800-835-6652**	320-251-2700	374-3
Saint Cloud Technical & Community College						
1540 Northway Dr	Saint Cloud	MN	56303	**800-222-1009**	320-308-5089	798
Saint Cloud Times						
3000 Seventh St N						
PO Box 768	Saint Cloud	MN	56303	**855-336-0360**	320-255-8700	531-2
Saint Croix Electric Co-op						
1925 Ridgeway St	Hammond	WI	54015	**800-924-3407**	715-796-7000	247
Saint Croix Forge Inc						
5195 Scandia Trl	Forest Lake	MN	55025	**866-668-7642**	651-464-8967	482
Saint Croix Press Inc						
1185 S Knowles Ave	New Richmond	WI	54017	**800-826-6622**	715-246-5811	634-9
Saint Croix State Park						
30065 St Croix Pk Rd	Hinckley	MN	55037	**888-646-6367**	320-384-6591	564
Saint Elizabeth Hospital						
1506 S Oneida St	Appleton	WI	54915	**800-223-7332**	920-738-2000	374-3
Saint Francis Health Ctr						
1700 SW Seventh St	Topeka	KS	66606	**855-578-3726**	785-295-8000	374-3
Saint Francis Hospital & Medical Ctr						
114 Woodland St	Hartford	CT	06105	**800-993-4312**	860-714-4000	374-3
Saint Francis Medical Ctr						
601 Hamilton Ave	Trenton	NJ	08629	**888-216-3293**	609-599-5000	374-3
Saint Francis Xavier University						
PO Box 5000	Antigonish	NS	B2G2W5	**877-867-7839***	902-863-3300	783
*Admissions						
Saint George Library Ctr						
5 Central Ave	Staten Island	NY	10301	**800-342-3688**	718-442-8560	434-3
Saint Gregory's University						
1900 W MacArthur St	Shawnee	OK	74804	**888-784-7347***	405-878-5100	167
*Admissions						
Saint John's Hospital						
800 E Carpenter St	Springfield	IL	62702	**855-228-4438**	217-544-6464	374-3
Saint John's Northwestern Military Academy						
1101 N Genesee St	Delafield	WI	53018	**800-752-2338**	262-646-7115	621
Saint John's Preparatory School						
1857 Watertower Rd						
PO Box 4000	Collegeville	MN	56321	**800-525-7737**	320-363-3321	621
Saint John's University						
PO Box 2000	Collegeville	MN	56321	**800-544-1489***	320-363-2196	167
*Admissions						
Saint John's University Alcuin Library						
2835 Abbey Plaza	Collegeville	MN	56321	**800-544-1489**	320-363-2122	434-6
Saint John's-Ravenscourt School						
400 S Dr	Winnipeg	MB	R3T3K5	**800-437-0040**	204-477-2400	621
Saint Johns River Community College						
5001 St Johns Ave	Palatka	FL	32177	**888-757-2293**	386-312-4200	161
Saint Joseph Area Chamber of Commerce						
3003 Frederick Ave	Saint Joseph	MO	64506	**800-748-7856**	816-232-4461	138
Saint Joseph Convention & Visitors Bureau						
109 S Fourth St	Saint Joseph	MO	64501	**800-785-0360**	816-233-6688	208
Saint Joseph Hospital						
700 Broadway	Fort Wayne	IN	46802	**800-258-0974**	260-425-3000	374-3
Saint Joseph Medical Ctr (SJMC)						
1717 S J St	Tacoma	WA	98405	**888-825-3227**		374-3
Saint Joseph Mercy Ann Arbor						
5301 McAuley Dr	Ypsilanti	MI	48197	**866-522-8268**	734-712-3456	374-3
Saint Joseph Mercy Oakland						
44405 Woodward Ave	Pontiac	MI	48341	**800-396-1313**	248-858-3000	374-3
Saint Joseph's College of Maine						
278 Whites Bridge Rd	Standish	ME	04084	**800-338-7057***	207-893-7746	167
*Admissions						
Saint Joseph's Hospital						
2661 County Hwy I	Chippewa Falls	WI	54729	**877-723-1811**	715-723-1811	374-3
Saint Joseph's Hospital Health Ctr						
301 Prospect Ave	Syracuse	NY	13203	**888-785-6371**	315-448-5111	374-3
Saint Joseph's Lifecare Centre						
99 Wayne Gretzky Pkwy	Brantford	ON	N3S6T6	**888-699-7817**	519-751-7096	374-2
Saint Joseph's University						
5600 City Ave	Philadelphia	PA	19131	**888-232-4295**	610-660-1000	167
Saint Jude Children's Research Hospital Stem Cell Transplantation Div						
262 Danny Thomas Pl	Memphis	TN	38105	**800-822-6344**	901-595-3300	767
Saint Jude Medical						
St Jude Medical Inc	St Paul	MN	55117	**800-328-9634**	651-756-2000	475
NYSE: STJ						
Saint Lawrence Seaway Development Corp						
1200 New Jersey Ave SE	Washington	DC	20590	**800-785-2779**	202-366-0091	340-15
Saint Lawrence University						
23 Romoda Dr	Canton	NY	13617	**800-285-1856***	315-229-5261	167
*Admissions						
Saint Leo University						
33701 State Rd 52	Saint Leo	FL	33574	**800-334-5532**	352-588-8200	167
Palatka Ctr						
33701 State Rd 52 PO Box 6665	Saint Leo	FL	33574	**800-334-5532**	352-588-8200	167
Saint Louis Children's Hospital						
1 Children's Pl	Saint Louis	MO	63110	**800-427-4626**	314-454-6000	374-1
Saint Louis Christian College						
1360 Grandview Dr	Florissant	MO	63033	**800-887-7522***	314-837-6777	160
*Admissions						
Saint Louis College of Pharmacy						
4588 Parkview Pl	Saint Louis	MO	63110	**800-278-5267**	314-367-8700	167
Saint Louis Embroidery						
1759 Scherer Pkwy	Saint Charles	MO	63303	**800-457-6676**	636-724-2200	260
Saint Louis Executive Conference Ctr						
701 Convention Plz	Saint Louis	MO	63101	**800-325-7962**	314-342-5050	207
Saint Louis Music Inc						
1400 Ferguson Ave	Saint Louis	MO	63133	**800-727-4512**	314-727-4512	526
Saint Louis Paper & Box Co						
3843 Garfield Ave	Saint Louis	MO	63113	**800-779-7901**	314-531-7900	558
Saint Louis Science Ctr						
5050 Oakland Ave	Saint Louis	MO	63110	**800-456-7572**	314-289-4400	519
Saint Louis Symphony Orchestra						
718 N Grand Blvd	Saint Louis	MO	63103	**800-232-1880**	314-533-2500	572-3
Saint Louis University						
221 N Grand Blvd	Saint Louis	MO	63103	**800-758-3678**	314-977-7288	167
Saint Louis University School of Law						
3700 Lindell Blvd	Saint Louis	MO	63108	**800-758-3678**	314-977-2766	168-1
Saint Louis University School of Medicine						
1 North Grand	Saint Louis	MO	63103	**800-758-3678**		168-2
Saint Louis Zoological Park						
1 Government Dr	Saint Louis	MO	63110	**800-966-8877**	314-781-0900	821
Saint Lucia						
Embassy						
3216 New Mexico Ave NW	Washington	DC	20016	**800-456-3984**	202-364-6792	259
Saint Lucia Tourist Board						
800 Second Ave Ste 910	New York	NY	10017	**800-456-3984**	212-867-2950	773
Saint Luke's Home Care & Hospice						
3100 Broadway St Ste 1000	Kansas City	MO	64111	**888-303-7576**	816-756-1160	371
Saint Luke's Hospital & Regional Trauma Ctr						
915 E First St	Duluth	MN	55805	**866-261-5915**	218-249-5555	374-3
Saint Luke's Hospital of New Bedford						
101 Page St	New Bedford	MA	02740	**800-497-1727**	508-997-1515	374-3
Saint Luke's Regional Medical Ctr						
2720 Stone Pk Blvd	Sioux City	IA	51104	**800-352-4660**	712-279-3500	374-3
Saint Martin's University						
5300 Pacific Ave SE	Lacey	WA	98503	**800-368-8803***	360-438-4311	167
*Admissions						
Saint Mary Mercy Hospital						
36475 Five-Mile Rd	Livonia	MI	48154	**800-464-7492**	734-655-4800	374-3
Saint Mary's College						
Le Mans Hall	Notre Dame	IN	46556	**800-551-7621***	574-284-4587	167
*Admissions						
Saint Mary's College of California						
1928 St Mary's Rd	Moraga	CA	94556	**800-800-4762***	925-631-4000	167
*Admissions						
Saint Mary's College of Maryland						
47645 College Dr	Saint Marys City	MD	20686	**800-492-7181***	240-895-2000	167
*Admissions						
Saint Mary's Health Care System						
1230 Baxter St	Athens	GA	30606	**800-233-7864**	706-389-3000	374-3
Saint Mary's Hospital						
2251 N Shore Dr	Rhinelander	WI	54501	**800-578-0840***	715-361-2000	374-3
*Cust Svc						
Saint Mary's Hospital & Regional Medical Ctr						
2635 N Seventh St	Grand Junction	CO	81502	**800-458-3888**		374-3
Saint Mary's Hospital Medical Ctr						
1726 Shawano Ave	Green Bay	WI	54303	**800-666-5606**	920-498-4200	374-3
Saint Mary's River State Park						
c/o Pt Lookout State Pk						
11175 Pt Lookout Rd	Scotland	MD	20687	**800-830-3974**	301-872-5688	564

Name / Address	City	State	ZIP	Toll-Free	Phone	Class
Saint Mary's School 900 Hillsborough St	Raleigh	NC	27603	800-948-2557	919-424-4000	621
Saint Mary's University 1 Camino Santa Maria	San Antonio	TX	78228	800-367-7868*	210-436-3126	167
*Admissions						
Saint Mary's University of Minnesota 700 Terr Heights	Winona	MN	55987	800-635-5987	507-452-4430	167
Saint Mary-Corwin Medical Ctr 1008 Minnequa Ave	Pueblo	CO	81004	800-228-4039	719-557-4000	374-3
Saint Mary-of-the-Woods College 3301 St Mary Rd	Saint Mary Of The Woods	IN	47876	800-926-7692	812-535-5106	167
Saint Meinrad Archabbey 200 Hill Dr	Saint Meinrad	IN	47577	800-682-0988	812-357-6585	671
Saint Michael's College 1 Winooski Pk	Colchester	VT	05439	800-762-8000	802-654-2000	167
Saint Michael's Hospital 30 Bond St	Toronto	ON	M5B1W8	866-797-0000	416-360-4000	374-2
Saint Michael's University School 3400 Richmond Rd	Victoria	BC	V8P4P5	800-661-5199	250-592-2411	621
Saint Michaels Harbour Inn & Marina 101 N Harbor Rd	Saint Michaels	MD	21663	800-955-9001	410-745-9001	379
Saint Norbert College 100 Grant St	De Pere	WI	54115	800-236-4878*	920-403-3005	167
*Admissions						
Saint Paul College 235 Marshall Ave	Saint Paul	MN	55102	800-227-6029	651-846-1600	798
Saint Paul Foundation, The 101 Fifth St E Ste 2400	Saint Paul	MN	55101	800-875-6167	651-224-5463	304
Saint Paul Hotel 350 Market St	Saint Paul	MN	55102	800-292-9292	651-292-9292	379
Saint Paul Public Library 90 W Fourth St	Saint Paul	MN	55102	888-335-9632	651-266-7000	434-3
Saint Paul School of Theology 4370 W 109th St Ste 300	Overland Park	KS	66211	800-825-0378		168-3
Saint Paul University 223 Main St	Ottawa	ON	K1S1C4	800-637-6859	613-236-1393	783
Saint Paul's Church National Historic Site 897 S Columbus Ave	Mount Vernon	NY	10550	866-705-5711	914-667-4116	563
Saint Peter's Seminary 1040 Waterloo St N	London	ON	N6A3Y1	888-548-9649	519-432-1824	168-3
Saint Regis Aspen 315 E Dean St	Aspen	CO	81611	888-627-7198*	970-920-3300	705
*General						
Saint Regis Culvert Inc 202 Morrell St	Charlotte	MI	48813	800-527-4604	517-543-3430	695
Saint Regis Hotel 602 Dunsmuir St	Vancouver	BC	V6B1Y6	800-770-7929	604-681-1135	379
Saint Regis Hotel Winnipeg 285 Smith St	Winnipeg	MB	R3C1K9	800-663-7344	204-942-0171	379
Saint Regis Monarch Beach Resort & Spa 1 Monarch Beach Resort	Dana Point	CA	92629	800-722-1543	949-234-3200	667
Saint Regis Resort Aspen 315 E Dean St	Aspen	CO	81611	888-627-7198	970-920-3300	667
Saint Rita's Medical Ctr (SRMC) 730 W Market St	Lima	OH	45801	800-232-7762	419-227-3361	374-3
Saint Tammany Parish Tourist & Convention Commission 68099 Hwy 59	Mandeville	LA	70471	800-634-9443	985-892-0520	208
Saint Thomas Hospital 4220 HaRding Rd	Nashville	TN	37205	800-400-5800	615-222-2111	374-3
Saint Thomas University 51 Dineen Dr	Fredericton	NB	E3B5G3	877-788-4443	506-452-0640	783
Saint Thomas University School of Law 16401 NW 37th Ave	Miami Gardens	FL	33054	800-245-4569	305-623-2310	168-1
Saint Vincent & the Grenadines Tourist Information Office 801 Second Ave 21st Fl	New York	NY	10017	800-729-1726	212-687-4981	773
Saint Vincent Charity Hospital (SVCH) 2351 E 22nd St	Cleveland	OH	44115	800-750-0750	216-861-6200	374-3
Saint Vincent College 300 Fraser Purchase Rd	Latrobe	PA	15650	800-782-5549	724-532-6600	167
Saint Vincent Hospital 835 S Van Buren St	Green Bay	WI	54301	800-236-3030	920-433-0111	374-3
Saint Vincent Hospital-Worcester Medical Ctr 123 Summer St	Worcester	MA	01608	877-633-2368	508-363-5000	374-3
Saint Vincent Women's Hospital 8111 Township Line Rd	Indianapolis	IN	46260	800-582-8258	317-415-8111	374-7
Saint Vincent's Medical Ctr 2800 Main St	Bridgeport	CT	06606	877-255-7847	203-576-6000	374-3
Saint Xavier University 3700 W 103rd St	Chicago	IL	60655	800-462-9288	773-298-3000	167
Saint-Gobain Advanced Ceramics Latrobe 4702 Rt 982	Latrobe	PA	15650	800-438-7237	724-539-6000	251
SAISD (San Antonio Independent School District) 141 Lavaca St	San Antonio	TX	78210	866-632-9992	210-554-2200	683
Sakatah Lake State Park 50499 Sakatah Lake State Pk Rd	Waterville	MN	56096	888-646-6367	507-362-4438	564
Sakura Finetek USA Inc 1750 W 214th St	Torrance	CA	90501	800-725-8723	310-972-7800	419
Saladmaster Inc 230 Westway Pl Ste 101	Arlington	TX	76018	800-765-5795	817-633-3555	485
Saleen Automotive Inc 2735 Wardlow Rd	Corona	CA	92882	800-888-8945		58
Salem College 601 S Church St	Winston-Salem	NC	27101	800-327-2536*	336-721-2600	167
*Admissions						
Salem Conference Ctr 200 Commercial St SE	Salem	OR	97301	877-589-1700*	503-589-1700	207
*Sales						
Salem Convention & Visitors Assn 181 High St NE	Salem	OR	97301	800-874-7012	503-581-4325	208
Salem County 94 Market St	Salem	NJ	08079	877-222-3737	856-935-7510	338
Salem Five & Savings Bank 210 Essex St	Salem	MA	01970	800-850-5000*	978-745-5555	69
*Cust Svc						
Salem Group, The 2 TransAm Plz Dr Ste 170	Oakbrook Terrace	IL	60181	877-768-7141	630-932-7000	719
Salem Hospital 665 Winter St SE	Salem	OR	97301	800-876-1718		374-3
Salem International University 223 W Main St	Salem	WV	26426	800-283-4562	304-326-1109	167
Salem Tools Inc 1602 Midland Rd	Salem	VA	24153	800-390-4348	540-389-0233	386
Salem Veterans Affairs Medical Ctr 1970 Roanoke Blvd	Salem	VA	24153	888-982-2463	540-982-2463	374-8
Salem Witch Museum 19 1/2 Washington Sq N	Salem	MA	01970	800-392-6100	978-744-1692	519
Salem-Keizer Public Schools 2450 Lancaster Dr NE	Salem	OR	97305	877-293-1090	503-399-3000	683
Salem-Republic Rubber Co 475 W California Ave	Sebring	OH	44672	800-686-4199	330-938-9801	370
Sales Benchmark Index 1595 Peachtree Pkwy Ste 204-328	Cumming	GA	30041	888-556-7338		5
Sales Gauge 1186 Old Marlborough Rd	Concord	MA	01742	877-406-0493	781-910-0077	393
Sales Leader 2222 Sedwick Dr	Durham	NC	27713	800-223-8720		530-10
Sales Readiness Group Inc 8015 SE 28th St Ste 206	Mercer Island	WA	98040	800-490-0715		197
Salesforce.Com Foundation The Landmark @ One Market Ste 300	San Francisco	CA	94105	800-667-6389		306
Salesnet 6340 Sugarloaf Pkwy Ste 200	Duluth	GA	30097	866-732-8632		38
Salice America Inc 2123 Crown Centre Dr	Charlotte	NC	28227	800-222-9652	704-841-7810	350
Salin Bank 8455 Keystone Xing	Indianapolis	IN	46240	800-320-7536	317-452-8000	683
Salina Area Chamber of Commerce 120 W Ash St	Salina	KS	67401	877-725-4625	785-827-9301	138
Salina Journal PO Box 740	Salina	KS	67402	800-827-6363	785-823-6363	531-2
Salinas Valley Chamber of Commerce 119 E Alisal St	Salinas	CA	93901	888-678-2871	831-751-7725	138
Salinas Valley Memorial Hospital (SVMH) 450 E Romie Ln	Salinas	CA	93901	800-813-4673	831-757-4333	374-3
Saline County Public Library 1800 Smithers	Benton	AR	72015	800-476-4466	501-778-4766	434-3
Salisbury Bancorp Inc 5 Bissell St PO Box 1868	Lakeville	CT	06039	800-222-9801	860-435-9801	360-2
NASDAQ: SAL						
Salisbury Hotel 123 W 57th St	New York	NY	10019	888-692-5757	212-246-1300	379
Salisbury Inc 29085 Airpark Dr	Easton	MD	21601	855-255-5309	410-770-4901	700
Salisbury Post 131 W Innes St	Salisbury	NC	28144	800-546-5664	704-633-8950	634-8
Salisbury University 1200 Camden Ave	Salisbury	MD	21801	888-543-0148	410-543-6000	167
Salisbury University Blackwell Library 1101 Camden Ave	Salisbury	MD	21801	888-543-0148	410-543-6130	434-6
Salish Kootenai College PO Box 70	Pablo	MT	59855	877-752-6553	406-275-4800	164
Salish Lodge & Spa 6501 Railroad Ave DE	Snoqualmie	WA	98065	800-272-5474	425-888-2556	667
Salishan Lodge & Golf Resort PO Box 118	Gleneden Beach	OR	97388	800-452-2300		667
Salit Steel Ltd 7771 Stanley Ave	Niagara Falls	ON	L2E6V6	800-263-7110	905-354-5691	491
Salix Pharmaceuticals Inc 8510 Colonnade Ctr Dr	Raleigh	NC	27615	800-508-0024	919-862-1000	582
NASDAQ: SLXP						
Salk Institute for Biological Studies PO Box 85800	San Diego	CA	92186	866-358-4354	858-453-4100	666
Sallie Mae 12061 Bluemont Way	Reston	VA	20190	888-272-5543*	703-810-3000	216
*Cust Svc						
Sally Beauty Company Inc 3001 Colorado Blvd	Denton	TX	76210	800-777-5706	940-898-7500	75
Salmon River Electric Co-op Inc 1130 Main St PO Box 384	Challis	ID	83226	877-806-2283	208-879-2283	247
Salon Service Group Inc 1859 W Arbor Ct	Springfield	MO	65807	800-933-5733		76
Salsbury Industries Inc 1010 E 62nd St	Los Angeles	CA	90001	800-624-5299	323-846-6700	288
SALT Group, The 1845 Sidney Baker St	Kerrville	TX	78028	888-257-1266	830-257-1290	731
Salt Lake City International Airport 776 N Terminal Dr PO Box 145550	Salt Lake City	UT	84116	800-595-2442	801-575-2400	27
Salt Lake Temple 50 W N Temple St	Salt Lake City	UT	84150	800-453-3860	801-240-2640	49
Salt River Bay National Historical Park & Ecological Preserve c/o Christiansted National Historic Site 2100 Church St Ste 100	Christiansted	VI	00820	866-705-5711	340-773-1460	563
Salt River Electric Co-op Corp 111 W Brashear Ave	Bardstown	KY	40004	800-221-7465	502-348-3931	247
Salt River Project (SRP) 1521 N Project Dr	Tempe	AZ	85281	800-258-4777	602-236-5900	785
Salt Springs State Park c/o Lackawanna	North Abington Township	PA	18414	888-727-2757	570-945-3239	564
Salt Water Sportsman Magazine 460 N Orlando Ave Ste 200	Winter Park	FL	32789	800-759-2127	407-628-4802	456-20
Salter Bus Lines Inc 212 Hudson Ave	Jonesboro	LA	71251	800-223-8056	318-259-2522	106
Salter Labs 100 Sycamore Rd	Arvin	CA	93203	800-421-0024	661-854-3166	475
Salty Dog Cafe, The 232 S Sea Pines Dr	Hilton Head Island	SC	29928	877-725-8936	843-671-5199	669
Salus Group Benefits Inc 37525 Mound Rd	Sterling Heights	MI	48310	866-991-9907		262
Salvatore's Italian Gardens 6461 Transit Rd	Depew	NY	14043	877-456-4097	716-683-7990	669
Salve Regina University 100 Ochre Pt Ave	Newport	RI	02840	800-829-1040	401-847-6650	167

Name / Address	City	State	ZIP	Toll-Free	Phone	Class
Sam Clar Office Furniture Inc 1221 Diamond Way	Concord	CA	94520	**800-726-2527**	925-602-3900	322
Sam Hatfield Realty Inc 4470 Mansford Rd	Winchester	TN	37398	**866-959-7474**	931-968-0500	650
Sam Hausman Meat Packer Inc 4261 Beacon	Corpus Christi	TX	78403	**800-364-5521**	361-883-5521	472
Sam Houston Electric Co-op Inc 1157 E Church St	Livingston	TX	77351	**800-458-0381**	936-327-5711	247
Sam Houston Jones State Park 107 Sutherland Rd	Lake Charles	LA	70611	**888-677-7264**	337-855-2665	564
Sam Houston State University 1903 University Ave	Huntsville	TX	77340	**866-232-7528**	936-294-1111	167
Sam's Town Hotel & Casino Shreveport 315 Clyde Fant Pkwy	Shreveport	LA	71101	**877-770-7867**		132
Sam's Town Hotel & Gambling Hall 5111 Boulder Hwy	Las Vegas	NV	89122	**800-897-8696**	702-456-7777	132
Samaritan Hospice 5 Eves Dr Ste 300	Marlton	NJ	08053	**800-229-8183**	856-596-1600	371
Samaritan Medical Ctr 830 Washington St	Watertown	NY	13601	**877-888-6138**	315-785-4000	374-3
Samaritan Village 138-02 Queens Blvd	Briarwood	NY	11435	**800-532-4357**	718-206-2000	724
Sambazon Inc 1160 Calle Cordillera	San Clemente	CA	92673	**877-726-2296**	949-498-8618	298-7
SameDay Security Inc 133 S Church St	Las Cruces	NM	88001	**866-572-3274**		474
Samford University 800 Lakeshore Dr *Admissions	Birmingham	AL	35229	**800-888-7218***	205-726-3673	167
SAMHSA (Substance Abuse & Mental Health Services Administration) 1 Choke Cherry Rd	Rockville	MD	20857	**877-726-4727**	240-276-2000	340-8
Sammons Trucking 3665 W Broadway	Missoula	MT	59808	**800-548-9276**	406-728-2600	778
Samoset Resort 220 Warrenton St	Rockport	ME	04856	**800-341-1650**	207-594-2511	667
Sampco Inc 651 W Washington Blvd Ste 300	Chicago	IL	60661	**800-767-0689**	312-346-1506	298-9
SAMPE (Society for the Advancement of Material & Process Engineering) 1161 Pk View Dr Ste 200	Covina	CA	91724	**800-562-7360**	626-331-0616	48-19
Sampson-Bladen Oil Co Inc 510 Commerce St PO Box 469	Clinton	NC	28329	**800-849-4177**	910-592-4177	325
SAMS (Society of Accredited Marine Surveyors Inc) 7855 Argyle Forest Blvd Ste 203	Jacksonville	FL	32244	**800-344-9077**	904-384-1494	47-1
Sams Technical Publishing 9850 E 30th St *Cust Svc	Indianapolis	IN	46229	**800-428-7267***		634-2
Samsill Corp 5740 Hartman Rd	Fort Worth	TX	76119	**800-255-1100**	817-536-1906	85
Samson Rope Technologies Inc 2090 Thornton Rd *Cust Svc	Ferndale	WA	98248	**800-227-7673***	360-384-4669	210
Samson Technologies Inc 45 Gilpin Ave	Hauppauge	NY	11788	**800-372-6766**	631-784-2200	513
Samsung Semiconductors Inc 3655 N First St *General	San Jose	CA	95134	**800-726-7864***	408-544-4000	694
Samsung Telecommunications America LLP 1301 E Lookout Dr	Richardson	TX	75082	**800-726-7864**	972-761-7000	732
Samtec Inc 520 Parkeast Blvd	New Albany	IN	47150	**800-726-8329**	812-944-6733	255
Samuel A Ramirez & Co Inc 61 Broadway Ste 2924	New York	NY	10006	**800-888-4086**		688
Samuel Cabot Inc 100 Hale St	Newburyport	MA	01950	**800-877-8246**	978-465-1900	549
Samuel Mahelona Memorial Hospital 4800 Kawaihau Rd	Kapaa	HI	96746	**800-845-6733**	808-822-4961	374-7
Samuel Merritt College 370 Hawthorne Ave *Admissions	Oakland	CA	94609	**800-607-6377***	510-869-6576	167
Samuels Jewelers 9607 Research Blvd Ste 100 Bldg F	Austin	TX	78759	**877-202-2870**	512-369-1400	410
Samy's Camera Inc 431 S Fairfax Ave	Los Angeles	CA	90036	**800-321-4726**	323-938-2420	118
San Angelo Chamber of Commerce 418 W Ave B	San Angelo	TX	76903	**800-252-1381**	325-655-4136	208
San Angelo Standard Times Inc PO Box 5111	San Angelo	TX	76902	**800-588-1884**	325-653-1221	634-8
San Angelo Standard-Times 34 W Harris Ave	San Angelo	TX	76903	**800-588-1884**	325-659-8200	531-2
San Antonio Convention & Visitors Bureau 203 S St Marys St Ste 200	San Antonio	TX	78205	**800-447-3372**	210-207-6700	208
San Antonio Express-News Ave E & Third St	San Antonio	TX	78205	**800-555-1551**	210-250-3000	531-2
San Antonio Federal Credit Union PO Box 1356	San Antonio	TX	78295	**800-234-7228**	210-258-1234	221
San Antonio Independent School District (SAISD) 141 Lavaca St	San Antonio	TX	78210	**866-632-9992**	210-554-2200	683
San Antonio International Airport (SAT) 9800 Airport Blvd Rm 2041	San Antonio	TX	78216	**800-237-6639**	210-207-3411	27
San Antonio Missions National Historical Park 2202 Roosevelt Ave	San Antonio	TX	78210	**866-945-7920**	210-534-8833	563
San Antonio Municipal Auditorium 200 E Market St PO Box 1809	San Antonio	TX	78205	**877-504-8895**	210-207-8500	571
San Benito Public Library 101 W Rose St	San Benito	TX	78586	**800-444-1187**	956-361-3860	434-3
San Bernard Electric Co-op Inc 309 W Main St	Bellville	TX	77418	**800-364-3171**	979-865-3171	247
San Bernardino Area Chamber of Commerce PO Box 658	San Bernardino	CA	92402	**800-928-5091**	909-885-7515	138
San Bernardino County 385 N Arrowhead Ave	San Bernardino	CA	92415	**888-818-8988**	909-387-8306	338
San Carlos Hotel 150 E 50th St	New York	NY	10022	**800-722-2012**	212-755-1800	379
San Clemente Chamber of Commerce 1100 N El Camino Real	San Clemente	CA	92672	**877-411-3662**	949-492-1131	138
San Diego Chargers 4020 Murphy Canyon Rd	San Diego	CA	92123	**877-242-7437**	858-874-4500	713-3
San Diego Christian College 2100 Greenfield Dr	El Cajon	CA	92019	**800-676-2242**	619-441-2200	167
San Diego City Hall 202 C St	San Diego	CA	92101	**866-470-1308**	619-533-4000	337
San Diego Concierge 4379 30th St Ste 4	San Diego	CA	92104	**800-979-9091**	619-280-4121	376
San Diego Convention Ctr 111 W Harbor Dr	San Diego	CA	92101	**800-525-7322**	619-525-5000	207
San Diego County Credit Union 6545 Sequence Dr	San Diego	CA	92121	**877-732-2848**		221
San Diego Daily Transcript 2131 Third Ave	San Diego	CA	92101	**800-697-6397**	619-232-4381	531-2
San Diego Eye Bank (SDEB) 9246 Lightwave Ave Ste 120	San Diego	CA	92123	**800-393-2265**	858-694-0400	271
San Diego Gas & Electric Co 101 Ash St	San Diego	CA	92101	**800-411-7343**	619-696-2000	785
San Diego Natural History Museum 1788 El Prado PO Box 121390	San Diego	CA	92101	**877-946-7797**	619-232-3821	519
San Diego Plastics Inc 2220 Mckinley Ave	National City	CA	91950	**800-925-4855**	619-477-4855	602
San Diego Public Library 820 E St	San Diego	CA	92101	**866-470-1308**	619-236-5800	434-3
San Diego Union-Tribune 350 Camino De La Reina	San Diego	CA	92108	**800-244-6397**	619-299-3131	531-2
San Diego Zoo Safari Park 15500 San Pasqual Valley Rd *Cust Svc	Escondido	CA	92027	**877-363-6237***	760-747-8702	821
San Felipe's Casino Hollywood 25 Hagon Rd	Algodones	NM	87001	**877-529-2946**	505-867-6700	451
San Francisco Art Institute 800 Chestnut St	San Francisco	CA	94133	**800-345-7324**	415-771-7020	163
San Francisco Ballet 455 Franklin St	San Francisco	CA	94102	**888-622-2108**	415-865-2000	572-1
San Francisco Chamber of Commerce 235 Montgomery St 12th Fl	San Francisco	CA	94104	**855-808-2387**	415-392-4520	138
San Francisco Chronicle 901 Mission St	San Francisco	CA	94103	**866-732-4766**	415-777-1111	531-2
San Francisco Conservatory of Music 50 Oak St	San Francisco	CA	94102	**800-999-8219**	415-864-7326	167
San Francisco Convention & Visitors Bureau 201 Third St Ste 900	San Francisco	CA	94103	**855-847-6272**	415-974-6900	208
San Francisco Federal Credit Union 770 Golden Gate Ave	San Francisco	CA	94102	**800-852-7598**	415-775-5377	221
San Francisco General Hospital Medical Ctr 1001 Potrero Ave Ste 1E21	San Francisco	CA	94110	**800-723-7140**	415-206-8426	374-3
San Francisco International Airport PO Box 8097	San Francisco	CA	94128	**800-435-9736**	650-821-8211	27
San Francisco Magazine 243 Vallejo St	San Francisco	CA	94111	**866-736-2499**	415-398-2800	456-22
San Francisco Music Box Co 5370 W 95th St	Prairie Village	KS	66207	**800-227-2190**		328
San Francisco Theological Seminary 105 Seminary Rd	San Anselmo	CA	94960	**800-447-8820**	415-451-2800	168-3
San Francisco VA Medical Ctr 4150 Clement St	San Francisco	CA	94121	**877-487-2838**	415-221-4810	374-8
San Isabel Electric 893 E Enterprise Dr	Pueblo West	CO	81007	**800-279-7432**	719-547-2160	247
San Jamar Inc 555 Koopman Ln	Elkhorn	WI	53121	**800-248-9826**	262-723-6133	14
San Jose Convention & Visitors Bureau 408 Almaden Blvd	San Jose	CA	95110	**800-726-5673**	408-295-9600	208
San Jose Convention Center (SJC) 150 W San Carlos St	San Jose	CA	95110	**800-726-5673**	408-792-4194	207
San Jose Ctr for the Performing Arts 255 Almaden Blvd	San Jose	CA	95113	**800-726-5673**	408-792-4111	571
San Jose Sharks HP Pavilion at San Jose 525 W Santa Clara St	San Jose	CA	95113	**800-755-5050**	408-287-7070	714
San Jose State University 1 Washington Sq	San Jose	CA	95192	**800-273-8255**	408-924-1000	167
San Jose Unified School District 855 Lenzen Ave	San Jose	CA	95126	**800-433-3243**	408-535-6000	683
San Juan Airlines Co 4000 Airport Rd Ste A	Anacortes	WA	98221	**800-874-4434**	360-293-4691	13
San Juan College 4601 College Blvd	Farmington	NM	87402	**866-426-1233**	505-326-3311	161
San Luis Obispo New Times 505 Higuera St	San Luis Obispo	CA	93401	**800-546-4219**	805-546-8208	531-5
San Luis Resort Spa & Conference Ctr 5222 Seawall Blvd *Cust Svc	Galveston Island	TX	77551	**800-445-0090***	409-744-1500	667
San Luis Valley Rural Electric Co-op 3625 US Hwy 160 W	Monte Vista	CO	81144	**800-332-7634**	719-852-3538	247
San Manuel Indian Bingo & Casino 777 San Manuel Blvd	Highland	CA	92346	**800-359-2464**		132
San Marcos Academy 2801 Ranch to Market 12 *Admissions	San Marcos	TX	78666	**800-428-5120***	512-353-2400	621
San Marcos Area Chamber of Commerce 202 N CM Allen Pkwy	San Marcos	TX	78666	**888-200-5620**	512-393-5900	138
San Marcos Chamber of Commerce 904 W San Marcos Blvd	San Marcos	CA	92078	**800-814-7241**	760-744-1270	138
San Mateo County Convention & Visitors Bureau 111 Anza Blvd Ste 410	Burlingame	CA	94010	**800-288-4748**	650-348-7600	208
San Mateo County Times 477 Ninth Ave Ste 110	San Mateo	CA	94402	**800-870-6397**	650-348-4321	531-2
San Mateo County Transit District 1250 San Carlos Ave PO Box 3006	San Carlos	CA	94070	**800-660-4287**	650-508-6200	467
San Miguel Power Assn Inc 170 W Tenth Ave	Nucla	CO	81424	**800-864-7256**	970-864-7311	247
San Patricio Electric Co-op Inc 402 E Sinton St	Sinton	TX	78387	**888-740-2220**	361-364-2220	247
San Rafael Chamber of Commerce 817 Mission Ave	San Rafael	CA	94901	**888-378-0777**	415-454-4163	138
San Sebastian Winery 157 King St	Saint Augustine	FL	32084	**888-352-9463**	904-826-1594	49-6

Name / Address	City	State	ZIP	Toll-Free	Phone	Class
San Vicente Inn & Golf Course 24157 San Vicente Rd	Ramona	CA	92065	**800-776-1289**	760-789-3788	667
Sancap Abrasives 16123 Armour St NE	Alliance	OH	44601	**800-433-6663**	330-821-3510	1
Sanctuary Beach Resort Monterey Bay 3295 Dunes Rd	Marina	CA	93933	**855-693-6583**	831-883-9478	705
Sanctuary on Camelback Mountain 5700 E McDonald Dr	Paradise Valley	AZ	85253	**800-245-2051**	480-948-2100	667
Sand Dunes Resort Hotel 201 74th Ave N	Myrtle Beach	SC	29572	**800-726-3783**		667
Sand Mountain Electric Co-op 402 Main St W	Rainsville	AL	35986	**877-843-2512**	256-638-2153	247
Sand Seed Service Inc 4765 Hwy 143	Marcus	IA	51035	**800-352-2228**	712-376-4135	692
Sand Technology Inc 8 Ave SW *NYSE: SNDTF*	Westmount	QC	H3Z1B1	**877-468-2538**	403-218-2010	180-1
Sandals Resorts International 4950 SW 72nd Ave	Miami	FL	33155	**888-726-3257**	305-284-1300	667
Sandata Technologies Inc 26 Harbor Pk Dr *Sales	Port Washington	NY	11050	**800-544-7263***	516-484-4400	180-11
Sandel Avionics Inc 2401 Dogwood Way	Vista	CA	92081	**877-726-3357**	760-727-4900	21
Sandelman & Assoc Inc 257 La Paloma Ste 1	San Clemente	CA	92672	**888-897-7881**	949-388-5600	666
Sanderling Resort & Spa 1461 Duck Rd	Duck	NC	27949	**800-701-4111**	252-261-4111	667
Sanders Ford Inc 1135 Lejeune Blvd *General	Jacksonville	NC	28540	**888-897-8527***	910-455-1911	515
Sanderson-MacLeod Inc 1199 S Main St PO Box 50	Palmer	MA	01069	**866-522-3481**	413-283-3481	102
Sandestin Golf & Beach Resort 9300 Emerald Coast Pkwy W	Sandestin	FL	32550	**800-277-0800**	850-267-8000	667
Sandhills Community College 3395 Airport Rd	Pinehurst	NC	28374	**800-338-3944**	910-692-6185	161
Sandhills Publishing 120 W Harvest Dr	Lincoln	NE	68521	**800-331-1978**	402-479-2181	634-9
Sandia Resort & Casino 30 Rainbow Rd NE	Albuquerque	NM	87113	**800-526-9366**	505-796-7500	132
SanDisk Corp 601 McCarthy Blvd *NASDAQ: SNDK*	Milpitas	CA	95035	**866-726-3475**	408-801-1000	290
Sandler O'Neill + Partners LP 1251 Avenue of the Americas 6th Fl	New York	NY	10020	**800-635-6851**	212-466-7800	688
Sandmeyer Steel Co 1 Sandmeyer Ln	Philadelphia	PA	19116	**800-523-3663**	215-464-7100	721
Sandridge Food Corp (SFC) 133 Commerce Dr	Medina	OH	44256	**800-672-2523**	330-725-2348	297-33
Sands Casino Resort Bethlehem 77 Sands Blvd	Bethlehem	PA	18015	**877-726-3777**		379
Sands Ocean Club Resort 9550 Shore Dr *General	Myrtle Beach	SC	29572	**888-999-8485***		379
Sands Regency Casino Hotel 345 N Arlington Ave *Resv	Reno	NV	89501	**800-233-4939***	775-348-2200	379
Sandstone Asset Management Inc 115 101 - Sixth St SW	Calgary	AB	T2P5K7	**866-318-6140**	403-218-6125	527
Sandusky Cabinets Inc 16125 Widmere Rd PO Box 517 *Cust Svc	Arvin	CA	93203	**800-886-8688***	661-854-5551	288
Sandusky Electric Inc 1513 Sycamore Line	Sandusky	OH	44870	**800-356-1243**	419-625-4915	248
Sandusky Register 314 W Market St	Sandusky	OH	44870	**800-466-1243**	419-625-5500	531-2
Sandvik Inc 1702 Nevins Rd	Fair Lawn	NJ	07410	**800-726-3845**	201-794-5000	360-3
Sandwich Lodge & Resort 54 Rt 6A - Old King's Hwy	Sandwich	MA	02563	**800-282-5353**	508-888-2275	379
Sandy Point State Park 1100 E College Pkwy	Annapolis	MD	21409	**877-620-8836**	410-974-2149	564
Sandy Sansing Chevrolet 6200 N Pensacola Blvd *Sales	Pensacola	FL	32505	**888-885-1844***	850-476-2480	56
Sandy Spring Bancorp Inc 17801 Georgia Ave *NASDAQ: SASR*	Olney	MD	20832	**800-399-5919**	301-774-6400	360-2
Sanford-Brown College *Boston* 126 Newbury St	Boston	MA	02116	**877-809-2444**	617-578-7100	798
Sangre de Cristo Electric Assn 29780 US Hwy 24	Buena Vista	CO	81211	**800-933-3823**	719-395-2412	247
Sanibel Harbour Marriott Resort & Spa 17260 Harbour Pt Dr	Fort Myers	FL	33908	**800-767-7777**	239-466-4000	667
Sanibel Inn 937 E Gulf Dr	Sanibel	FL	33957	**866-565-5480**	239-472-3181	379
SaniServ Inc 451 E County Line Rd	Mooresville	IN	46158	**800-733-8073**	317-831-7030	299
Sanitary Services Co Inc 21 Bellwether Way Ste 404	Bellingham	WA	98225	**888-333-9882**	360-734-3490	802
Sanofi Pasteur Inc Discovery Dr *Orders	Swiftwater	PA	18370	**800-822-2463***	570-839-7187	84
Sanofi-Aventis Canada 2150 St Elzear Blvd W	Laval	QC	H7L4A8	**800-363-6364**	514-331-9220	84
S-Anon International Family Groups Inc PO Box 111242	Nashville	TN	37222	**800-210-8141**	615-833-3152	47-21
Sanrio Inc 570 Eccles Ave	South San Francisco	CA	94080	**800-759-6454**	650-952-2880	329
Santa Barbara City College 721 Cliff Dr	Santa Barbara	CA	93109	**877-232-3919**	805-965-0581	161
Santa Barbara Inn 901 E Cabrillo Blvd	Santa Barbara	CA	93103	**800-231-0431**	805-966-2285	379
Santa Barbara News-Press Publishing Co 715 Anacapa St	Santa Barbara	CA	93101	**800-654-3292**	805-564-5200	634-8
Santa Barbara Visitors Bureau & Film Commission 1601 Anacapa St	Santa Barbara	CA	93101	**800-676-1266**	805-966-9222	208
Santa Clara Convention/Visitors Bureau 1850 Warburton Ave	Santa Clara	CA	95050	**800-272-6822**	408-244-9660	208
Santa Clara County Library 14600 Winchester Blvd	Los Gatos	CA	95032	**800-286-1991**	408-293-2326	434-3
Santa Clara Valley Transportation Authority (VTA) 3331 N First St	San Jose	CA	95134	**800-894-9908**	408-321-5555	467
Santa Cruz Chamber of Commerce 611 Ocean St Ste 1	Santa Cruz	CA	95060	**866-282-5900**	831-457-3713	138
Santa Cruz County Conference & Visitors Council 303 Water St Ste 100	Santa Cruz	CA	95060	**800-833-3494**	831-425-1234	208
Santa Fe Convention Ctr 201 W Marcy St	Santa Fe	NM	87501	**800-777-2489**	505-955-6200	208
Santa Fe County 102 Grant Ave	Santa Fe	NM	87504	**877-607-0741**	505-986-6200	338
Santa Fe Municipal Airport (SAF) 121 Aviation Dr PO Box 909	Santa Fe	NM	87504	**866-773-2587**	505-955-2900	27
Santa Fe Opera, The 301 Opera Dr	Santa Fe	NM	87506	**800-280-4654**	505-986-5900	572-2
Santa Fe Station 4949 N Rancho Dr *Resv	Las Vegas	NV	89130	**888-786-7389***	702-658-4900	132
Santa Fe Symphony Orchestra & Chorus Inc 551 W Cordova Rd Ste D Ste D	Santa Fe	NM	87505	**800-480-1319**	505-983-3530	572-3
Santa Fe University of Art & Design 1600 St Michaels Dr	Santa Fe	NM	87505	**800-456-2673**		167
Santa Maria Inn 801 S Broadway	Santa Maria	CA	93454	**800-462-4276**	805-928-7777	379
Santa Maria Valley Chamber of Commerce 614 S Broadway	Santa Maria	CA	93454	**800-331-3779**	805-925-2403	138
Santa Monica Civic Auditorium 1855 Main St	Santa Monica	CA	90401	**866-728-3229**	310-458-8551	207
Santa Monica Convention & Visitors Bureau 1920 Main St Ste B	Santa Monica	CA	90405	**800-544-5319**	310-319-6263	208
Santa Monica Mountains National Recreation Area 401 W Hillcrest Dr	Thousand Oaks	CA	91360	**888-275-8747**	805-370-2300	563
Santa Rosa County Chamber of Commerce 5247 Stewart St	Milton	FL	32570	**800-239-8732**	850-623-2339	138
Santa Rosa Junior College 1501 Mendocino Ave	Santa Rosa	CA	95401	**800-564-7752**	707-527-4011	161
Santana Row 3055 Olin Ave Ste 2100	San Jose	CA	95128	**888-509-7303**	408-551-4611	49-5
Sante Restaurant 45 Rideau St 2nd Fl	Ottawa	ON	K1N5W8	**877-241-8889**	613-241-7113	669
Santec Inc 3501 Challenger St	Torrance	CA	90503	**800-284-4050**	310-542-0063	361
Santee Electric Co-op Inc 424 Sumter Hwy	Kingstree	SC	29556	**800-922-1604**	843-355-6187	247
Santie Oil Co 126 Larcel Dr	Sikeston	MO	63801	**800-748-7788**	314-436-3569	136
Santillana USA Publishing Co 2023 NW 84th Ave	Doral	FL	33122	**800-245-8584**	305-591-9522	634-2
Santinelli International Inc 325 Oser Ave	Hauppauge	NY	11788	**800-644-3343**	631-435-3343	453
Santora CPA Group 220 Continental Dr Ste 112 Christiana Executive Campus	Newark	DE	19713	**800-347-0116**	302-737-6200	2
SAP 100 Consilium Pl	Scarborough	ON	M1H3E3	**888-777-1727**	416-791-7100	180-1
SAP America Inc 1721 Moon Lake Blvd Ste 300	Hoffman Estates	IL	60169	**800-872-1727**	847-230-3800	179
Sapa Inc 7933 NE 21st Ave	Portland	OR	97211	**800-547-0790**	503-802-3000	480
Sapiens International Corp 4000 CentreGreen Way Ste 150 *NASDAQ: SPNS*	Cary	NC	27513	**888-281-1167**	919-405-1500	180-10
Sapient Corp 131 Dartmouth St 3rd Fl *NASDAQ: SAPE*	Boston	MA	02116	**866-796-6860**	617-621-0200	807
Sarah Bush Lincoln Health Ctr (SBLHC) 1000 Health Ctr Dr PO Box 372	Mattoon	IL	61938	**800-345-3191**	217-258-2525	374-3
Sarah Lawrence College 1 Meadway	Bronxville	NY	10708	**800-888-2858**		167
Saranac Glove Co 999 LOmbardi Ave	Green Bay	WI	54304	**800-727-2622**	920-435-3737	154-7
Sarasota Film Festival 332 Cocoanut Ave	Sarasota	FL	34236	**800-435-7352**	941-364-9514	284
Sarasota Herald-Tribune 1741 Main St	Sarasota	FL	34236	**866-284-7102**	941-953-7755	531-2
Sarasota Jungle Gardens 3701 Bay Shore Rd	Sarasota	FL	34234	**877-681-6547**	941-355-5305	821
Sarasota Memorial Hospital 1700 S Tamiami Trl	Sarasota	FL	34239	**800-764-8255**	941-917-9000	374-3
Sarasota Opera 61 N Pineapple Ave	Sarasota	FL	34236	**866-951-0111**	941-366-8450	572-2
Sarasota Orchestra 709 N Tamiami Trl	Sarasota	FL	34236	**866-508-0611**	941-953-4252	572-3
Sarasota-Bradenton International Airport 6000 Airport Cir	Sarasota	FL	34243	**800-711-1712**	941-359-5200	27
Saratoga Convention & Tourism Bureau 60 Railroad Pl Ste 301	Saratoga Springs	NY	12866	**855-424-6073**	518-584-1531	208
Saratoga County Chamber of Commerce 28 Clinton St	Saratoga Springs	NY	12866	**855-765-7873**	518-584-3255	138
Saratoga Eagle Sales & Service Inc 45 Duplainville Rd	Saratoga Springs	NY	12866	**800-310-5099**	518-581-7377	80-1
Saratoga Hilton 534 Broadway	Saratoga Springs	NY	12866	**800-445-8667**	518-584-4000	379
Saratoga Honda 3402 Rt 9	Saratoga Springs	NY	12866	**888-658-2303**		56
Saratoga Liquor Company Inc 3215 James Day Ave	Superior	WI	54880	**800-472-6923**	715-394-4487	443
SARCOM Inc AEP Colloids Div 6299 Rt 9N	Hadley	NY	12835	**800-848-0658**	518-696-9900	145
Sargent & Greenleaf Inc 1 Security Dr	Nicholasville	KY	40356	**800-826-7652**	859-885-9411	350
Sargent Art Inc 100 E Diamond Ave	Hazleton	PA	18201	**800-424-3596**	570-454-3596	42

	Toll-Free	Phone	Class
Sargent Controls & Aerospace 5675 W Burlingame Rd ... Tucson AZ 85743	**800-230-0359**	520-744-1000	225
Sargent Corp 378 Bennoch Rd ... Stillwater ME 04489	**800-533-1812**	207-827-4435	190-4
Sargent County 355 Main St ... Forman ND 58032	**866-634-8387**	701-724-6241	338
Sargent Manufacturing Co 100 Sargent Dr ... New Haven CT 06511	**800-727-5477**		350
Sargento Foods Inc 1 Persnickety Pl ... Plymouth WI 53073	**800-243-3737**	920-893-8484	297-5
Sartomer Co 502 Thomas Jones Way ... Exton PA 19341	**800-345-8247**	610-363-4100	604-2
Sartori Food Corp 107 Pleasant View Rd ... Plymouth WI 53073 *Cust Svc	**800-558-5888***	920-893-6061	297-5
SAS (Scandinavian Airlines System) 301 Route 17 N Ste 500 ... Rutherford NJ 07070	**800-221-2350**	800-437-5807	25
SAS Institute Inc 100 SAS Campus Dr ... Cary NC 27513	**800-727-0025**	919-677-8000	180-1
Sas Safety Corp 3031 Gardenia Ave ... Long Beach CA 90807	**800-262-0200**	562-427-2775	476
SAS Shoemakers 1717 SAS Dr ... San Antonio TX 78224	**877-782-7463**		302
Sashco Inc 720 S Rochester Ave Ste D ... Ontario CA 91761	**800-600-3232**	909-937-8222	191-6
Saskatchewan Health Research Foundation 253-111 Research Dr ... Saskatoon SK S7N3R2	**800-975-1699**	306-975-1680	233
Saskatchewan Indian Gaming Authority 250 - 103 C Packham Ave ... Saskatoon SK S7N4K4	**800-306-6789**	306-477-7777	132
Saskatchewan Roughriders 1910 Piffles Taylor Way PO Box 1966 ... Regina SK S4P3E1	**888-474-3377**	306-569-2323	713-2
Saskatoon Business College Ltd 221 Third Ave N ... Saskatoon SK S7K2H7	**800-679-7711**	306-244-6333	161
Saskatoon City Hospital 701 Queen St ... Saskatoon SK S7K0M7	**855-655-7612**	306-655-8000	374-2
Sassy Inc 2305 Breton Industrial Pk Dr ... Kentwood MI 49508	**800-323-6336**	616-243-0767	63
SAT (San Antonio International Airport) 9800 Airport Blvd Rm 2041 ... San Antonio TX 78216	**800-237-6639**	210-207-3411	27
Satchidananda Ashram Yogaville (SAYVA) 108 Yogaville Way ... Buckingham VA 23921 *Resv	**800-858-9642***	434-969-3121	671
Satellite Broadcasting & Communications Assn (SBCA) 1730 M St NW Ste 600 ... Washington DC 20036	**800-541-5981**	202-349-3620	48-14
Satellite Hotel 411 Lakewood Cir ... Colorado Springs CO 80910	**800-423-8409**	719-596-6800	379
Satellite Industries Inc 2530 Xenium Ln N ... Minneapolis MN 55441	**800-328-3332**		504
Satellite Logistics Group Inc 12621 Featherwood Ste 390 ... Houston TX 77034	**877-795-7540**	281-902-5500	312
Satellite Management Services Inc 4529 E Bwy Rd ... Phoenix AZ 85040	**800-788-8388**	602-386-4444	226
Satin American Corp 40 Oliver Terr ... Shelton CT 06484	**877-356-5050**		727
SatisfYd 47 E Chicago Ave Ste 310 ... Naperville IL 60540	**800-562-9557**		198
Satmetrix Systems Inc 1100 Pk Pl ... San Mateo CA 94403	**866-697-2103**		179
Sato America Inc 10350A Nations Ford Rd ... Charlotte NC 28273	**888-871-8741**	704-644-1650	175-6
Satori Software Inc 1301 5th Ave Ste 2200 ... Seattle WA 98101	**800-553-6477**	206-357-2900	180-1
Saturday Evening Post, The 1100 Waterway Blvd ... Indianapolis IN 46202	**800-829-5576**	317-634-1100	456-11
Saturn Fasteners Inc 425 S Varney St ... Burbank CA 91502	**800-947-9414**	818-846-7145	350
Saturn Industries Inc 157 Union Tpke ... Hudson NY 12534	**800-775-1651**	518-828-9956	126
Saturn Systems Inc 314 W Superior St Ste 1015 ... Duluth MN 55802	**888-638-4335**	218-623-7200	179
Saturna Capital Corp 1300 N State St ... Bellingham WA 98225	**888-732-6262**	360-734-9900	401
Saucon Valley School District 2097 Polk Vly Rd ... Hellertown PA 18055	**866-632-9992**	610-838-7026	683
Saucony Inc 191 Spring St ... Lexington MA 02420	**800-282-6575**		302
Sauder Village 22611 SR 2 ... Archbold OH 43502	**800-590-9755**	419-446-2541	519
Sauder Woodworking Co 502 Middle St PO Box 156 ... Archbold OH 43502 *Cust Svc	**800-523-3987***	419-446-2711	320-2
Sault College of Applied Arts & Technology, The 443 Northern Ave ... Sault Sainte Marie ON P6A5L3	**800-461-2260**	705-759-6700	161
Sault Sainte Marie Convention & Visitors Bureau 225 E Portage Ave ... Sault Sainte Marie MI 49783	**800-647-2858**	906-632-3366	208
Saunders Archery Co 1874 14th Ave PO Box 1707 ... Columbus NE 68601 *Cust Svc	**800-228-1408***	402-564-7176	708
Saunders Manufacturing Co 65 Nickerson Hill Rd ... Readfield ME 04355	**800-341-4674**	207-685-9860	487
Sause Bros 3710 NW Front Ave ... Portland OR 97210	**800-488-4167**	503-222-1811	464
Savage Arms Inc 100 Springdale Rd ... Westfield MA 01085	**800-243-3220**	413-568-7001	286
Savanna Portage State Park 55626 Lake Pl ... McGregor MN 55760	**888-646-6367**	218-426-3271	564
Savannah Civic Ctr 301 W Oglethorp Ave ... Savannah GA 31401	**800-337-1101**	912-651-6550	571
Savannah College of Art & Design 342 Bull St PO Box 2072 ... Savannah GA 31402	**800-869-7223**	912-525-5100	163
Atlanta 1600 Peachtree St PO Box 77300 ... Atlanta GA 30357	**877-722-3285**	404-253-2700	163
Savannah Distributing Co Inc 2425 W Gwinnett St ... Savannah GA 31415 *General	**800-551-0777***	912-233-1167	80-1
Savannah International Trade & Convention Ctr 1 International Dr ... Savannah GA 31421	**888-644-6822**	912-447-4000	207
Savannah Technical College 5717 White Bluff Rd ... Savannah GA 31405	**800-769-6362**	912-443-5700	798
Savant Manufacturing Inc 2930 Hwy 383 PO Box 520 ... Kinder LA 70648	**800-326-6880**	337-738-5896	350
SAVE - Suicide Awareness Voices of Education 8120 Penn Ave S Ste 470 ... Bloomington MN 55431	**888-511-7283**	952-946-7998	48-15
Save America's Forests 4 Library Ct SE ... Washington DC 20003	**800-729-1363**	202-544-9219	47-13
Save the Manatee Club (SMC) 500 N Maitland Ave Ste 210 ... Maitland FL 32751	**800-432-5646**	407-539-0990	47-3
Savers Property & Casualty Insurance Co 11880 College Blvd Ste 500 ... Overland Park KS 66210	**800-482-2726**	800-351-1411	391-4
Savoy Suites Georgetown 2505 Wisconsin Ave NW ... Washington DC 20007	**877-301-0002**	202-337-9700	379
Savoy Technical Services Inc 4301 Hwy 27 South ... Sulphur LA 70665	**877-703-3235**	337-558-6071	474
Sawgrass Marriott Resort & Beach Club 1000 PGA Tour Blvd ... Ponte Vedra Beach FL 32082	**800-228-9290**	904-285-7777	667
Sawmill Creek Resort 400 Sawmill Creek Dr ... Huron OH 44839	**800-729-6455**	419-433-3800	667
Sawyer County 10610 Main St Ste 10 ... Hayward WI 54843	**877-699-4110**	715-634-4866	338
Sawyer Nursery Inc 5401 Port Sheldon St ... Hudsonville MI 49426	**888-378-7800**	616-669-9094	294
Saxon Shoes Inc 11800 W Broad St Ste 2750 ... Richmond VA 23233 *General	**800-686-5616***	804-285-3473	302
Saybrook Point Inn & Spa 2 Bridge St ... Old Saybrook CT 06475	**800-243-0212**	860-395-2000	667
Sayers Group LLC 825 Corporate Woods Pkwy ... Vernon Hills IL 60061	**800-323-5357**		182
Saylor Beall Mfg Company Inc 400 N Kibbee St ... Saint Johns MI 48879	**800-248-9001**	989-224-2371	174
SAYVA (Satchidananda Ashram Yogaville) 108 Yogaville Way ... Buckingham VA 23921 *Resv	**800-858-9642***	434-969-3121	671
SB Whistler & Sons Inc PO Box 270 ... Medina NY 14103	**800-828-1010**	585-318-4630	755
Sb1 Federal Credit Union PO Box 7480 ... Philadelphia PA 19101	**800-806-9465**	215-569-3700	221
SBA (Small Business Administration) 409 Third St SW ... Washington DC 20416	**800-827-5722**	202-205-6600	340-18
SBA Communications Corp 5900 Broken Sound Pkwy NW ... Boca Raton FL 33487 *NASDAQ: SBAC*	**800-487-7483**	561-995-7670	172
SBAA (Spina Bifida Assn) 4590 MacArthur Blvd NW Ste 250 ... Washington DC 20007	**877-686-6444**	202-944-3285	47-17
Sbar's Inc 14 Sbar Blvd ... Moorestown NJ 08057	**800-989-7227**	856-234-8220	43
SBC (Southern Baptist Convention) 901 Commerce St ... Nashville TN 37203	**866-722-5433**	615-244-2355	47-20
SBC Foundation 130 E Travis St Ste 350 ... San Antonio TX 78205	**800-591-9663**		305
SBCA (Satellite Broadcasting & Communications Assn) 1730 M St NW Ste 600 ... Washington DC 20036	**800-541-5981**	202-349-3620	48-14
SBCC (South Baldwin Chamber of Commerce) 112 W Laurel Ave PO Box 1117 ... Foley AL 36535	**877-461-3712**	251-943-3291	138
SBE (Society of Broadcast Engineers Inc) 9102 N Meridian St Ste 150 ... Indianapolis IN 46260	**800-237-1776**	317-846-9000	48-14
SBL (Society of Biblical Literature) The Luce Ctr 825 Houston Mill Rd ... Atlanta GA 30329	**866-727-9955**	404-727-3100	47-20
SBLHC (Sarah Bush Lincoln Health Ctr) 1000 Health Ctr Dr PO Box 372 ... Mattoon IL 61938	**800-345-3191**	217-258-2525	374-3
SBM (Society of Behavioral Medicine) 555 E Wells St Ste 1100 ... Milwaukee WI 53202	**800-784-8669**	414-918-3156	48-15
SBS (Storage Battery Systems Inc) N56 W16665 Ridgewood Dr ... Menomonee Falls WI 53051	**800-554-2243**	262-703-5800	248
SBSO (South Bend Symphony Orchestra) 127 N Michigan St ... South Bend IN 46601	**800-537-6415**	574-232-6343	572-3
SCA (Student Conservation Assn) 689 River Rd PO Box 550 ... Charlestown NH 03603	**888-722-9675**	603-543-1700	47-13
SCA Americas 2929 Arch St Ste 2600 ... Philadelphia PA 19104 *Cust Svc	**800-328-9043***	610-499-3700	557
SCAA (Specialty Coffee Assn of America) 117 W 4th St Ste 300 ... Santa Ana CA 92701	**800-995-9019**	562-624-4100	48-6
Scalamandre Silks Inc 350 Wireless Blvd ... Hauppauge NY 11788	**800-932-4361**	631-467-8800	742-1
Scale Auto Magazine 21027 Crossroads Cir ... Waukesha WI 53186 *Cust Svc	**800-533-6644***	262-796-8776	456-14
Scales Air Compressor Corp 110 Voice Rd ... Carle Place NY 11514	**877-798-0454**	516-248-9096	174
Scalia Antonin US Supreme Ct Bldg 1 1st St NE ... Washington DC 20543	**800-772-1213**	202-479-3000	341-3
SCAN (Sports Cardiovascular & Wellness Nutritionists) 1450 Western Ave Ste 101 ... Albany NY 12203 *General	**800-249-2875***	518-254-6730	48-8
SCAN Health Plan 3800 Kilroy Airport Way Ste 100 ... Long Beach CA 90806	**800-247-5091**	562-989-5100	352
SCANA Corp 220 Operation Way ... Cayce SC 29033 *NYSE: SCG*	**800-251-7234**	803-217-9000	360-5
SCANA Energy Marketing Inc 220 Operation Way ... Cayce SC 29033	**800-472-1051**	803-217-9000	785
Scandinavian Airlines System (SAS) 301 Route 17 N Ste 500 ... Rutherford NJ 07070	**800-221-2350**	800-437-5807	25
Scania USA Inc 121 Interpark Blvd Ste 601 ... San Antonio TX 78216	**800-272-2642**	210-403-0007	515
Scan-Optics Inc 169 Progress Dr ... Manchester CT 06042	**800-543-8681**	860-645-7878	180-8

Name / Address	City	State	ZIP	Toll-Free	Phone	Class
ScanSource Inc 6 Logue Ct *NASDAQ: SCSC*	Greenville	SC	29615	800-944-2432	864-288-2432	176
Scantron Corp 34 Parker	Irvine	CA	92618	800-722-6876	949-639-7500	175-7
Scarsdale Union Free School District 2 Brewster Rd	Scarsdale	NY	10583	888-837-6437	914-721-2410	683
Scattergood Friends School 1951 Delta Ave	West Branch	IA	52358	888-737-4636	319-643-7628	621
SCB (Shipowners Claims Bureau) 1 Battery Pk Plaza 31st Fl	New York	NY	10004	800-774-8724	212-847-4500	48-21
SCB Bancorp Inc 1501 E Eldorado St	Decatur	IL	62521	888-769-2265	217-428-7781	69
SCB Distributors 15608 New Century Dr	Gardena	CA	90248	800-729-6423	310-532-9400	94
SCBT Financial Corp 950 John C Calhoun Dr *NASDAQ: SCBT*	Orangeburg	SC	29115	800-277-2175	803-534-2175	360-2
SCC Soft Computer Inc 5400 Tech Data Dr	Clearwater	FL	33760	800-763-8352	727-789-0100	182
SCCA (Sports Car Club of America) 6700 SW Topeka Blvd Ste 300	Topeka	KS	66619	800-770-2055	785-357-7222	47-18
SCDAA (Sickle Cell Disease Assn of America) 3700 Koppers St Ste 570	Baltimore	MD	21202	800-421-8453	410-528-1555	47-17
Scelzi Equipment Inc 1030 W Gladstone St	Azusa	CA	91702	866-972-3594	626-334-0573	515
Scene 1468 W Ninth St Ste 805	Cleveland	OH	44113	877-598-8703	216-241-7550	531-5
Scenic Airlines Inc 3900 Paradise Rd Ste 223	Las Vegas	NV	89169	866-235-9422	702-638-3300	758
Scenic Rivers Energy Co-op 231 N Sheridan St	Lancaster	WI	53813	800-236-2141	608-723-2121	247
SCG (Southern Connecticut Gas) 60 Marsh Hill Rd	Orange	CT	06477	866-268-2887		785
SC&H Group LLC 910 Ridgebrook Rd	Sparks	MD	21152	800-832-3008	410-403-1500	2
Schaefer Systems International Inc 10021 Westlake Dr	Charlotte	NC	28241	800-876-6000	704-944-4500	201
Schaeffer Mfg Company Inc 102 Barton St *Cust Svc	Saint Louis	MO	63104	800-325-9962*	314-865-4100	540
Schaeffer's Investment Research Inc 5151 Pfeiffer Rd Ste 250	Cincinnati	OH	45242	800-448-2080	513-589-3800	634-9
Schaeffler Group USA Inc 308 Springhill Farm Rd	Fort Mill	SC	29715	800-361-5841	803-548-8500	74
Schaff Piano Supply Co 451 Oakwood Rd	Lake Zurich	IL	60047	800-747-4266	847-438-4556	526
Schaller & Weber Inc 22-35 46th St *Orders	Astoria	NY	11105	800-847-4115*	718-721-5480	297-26
Scharine Group, The 4213 N Scharine Rd	Whitewater	WI	53190	800-472-2880	608-883-2880	188
Schatten Properties Management Company Inc 1514 S St	Nashville	TN	37212	800-892-1315	615-329-3011	651
Schatz Bearing Corp 10 Fairview Ave	Poughkeepsie	NY	12601	800-554-1406	845-452-6000	74
Schaumburg Specialties Co 550 Albion Ave Unit 30	Schaumburg	IL	60193	800-834-8125		110
Schawbel Corp 26 Crosby Dr	Bedford	MA	01730	866-753-3837	781-541-6900	36
Schecter Guitar Research Inc 10953 Pendleton St	Sun Valley	CA	91352	800-660-6621		526
Scheirer Machine Company Inc 3200 Industrial Blvd	Bethel Park	PA	15102	800-448-4590	412-833-6500	453
Schenck Business Solutions 200 E Washington St	Appleton	WI	54911	800-236-2246	920-731-8111	2
Schenck Trebel Corp 535 Acorn St	Deer Park	NY	11729	800-873-2357	631-242-4010	682
Schendel Pest Services 1035 SE Quincy St	Topeka	KS	66612	800-591-7378	785-232-9357	576
Schenker of Canada Ltd 5935 Airport Rd 10th Fl	Mississauga	ON	L4V1W5	800-461-3686	905-676-0676	312
Schetky Northwest Sales Inc 8430 NE Killingsworth St	Portland	OR	97220	800-255-8341	503-287-4141	515
Scheurer Hospital Inc 170 N Caseville Rd	Pigeon	MI	48755	800-690-9972	989-453-3223	374-3
Schick Shadel Hospital 12101 Ambaum Blvd SW	Seattle	WA	98146	800-500-6395		724
Schindler Elevator Corp 20 Whippany Rd	Morristown	NJ	07960	800-225-3123	973-397-6500	258
Schlager Group Inc 325 N Saint Paul Ste 3425	Dallas	TX	75201	888-416-5727		93
Schlegel Systems Inc 1555 Jefferson Rd	Rochester	NY	14623	888-924-7694	585-427-7200	327
Schlenner Wenner & Co 630 Roosevelt Rd	Saint Cloud	MN	56301	877-616-0286	320-251-0286	2
Schlessman Seed Co 11513 US Rt 250	Milan	OH	44846	888-534-7333	419-499-2572	692
Schleuniger Inc 87 Colin Dr *Tech Supp	Manchester	NH	03103	877-902-1470*	603-668-8117	455
Schlichter, Bogard & Denton 100 S Fourth St Ste 900	St. Louis	MO	63102	800-873-5297	314-621-6115	428
Schlueter Co 310 N Main St	Janesville	WI	53545	800-359-1700	608-755-5444	299
Schlumberger Wireline & Testing 210 Schlumberger Dr	Sugar Land	TX	77478	800-272-7328	281-285-4551	538
Schmidt Bros. Inc 420 N Hallett Ave	Swanton	OH	43558	800-200-7318	419-826-3671	188
Schmidt Machine Co 7013 Ohio 199	Upper Sandusky	OH	43351	866-368-3814	419-294-3814	276
Schmidt-Goodman Office Products 1920 N Broadway	Rochester	MN	55906	800-247-0663	507-282-3870	322
Schmiede Corp 1865 Riley Creek Rd PO Box 1630	Tullahoma	TN	37388	800-535-1851	931-455-4801	453
Schnadig International Corp 4200 Tudor Ln	Greensboro	NC	27410	800-468-8730		320-2
Schneck Medical Ctr 411 W Tipton St	Seymour	IN	47274	800-234-9222	812-522-2349	374-3
Schneider Corp 8901 Otis Ave	Indianapolis	IN	46216	866-973-7100	317-826-7100	263
Schneider Electric Buildings LLC 1354 Clifford Ave	Loves Park	IL	61111	888-444-1311		188
Schneider Laboratories Inc 2512 W Cary St	Richmond	VA	23220	800-785-5227	804-353-6778	740
Schneider National Inc 3101 S Packerland Dr PO Box 2545	Green Bay	WI	54306	800-558-6767	920-592-2000	448
Schneider Optics Century Div 7701 Haskell Ave	Van Nuys	CA	91406	800-228-1254	818-766-3715	590
Schneiderman & Sherman 23938 Research Dr Ste 300	Farmington Hills	MI	48335	866-867-7688	248-539-7400	428
Schnuck Markets Inc 11420 Lackland Rd	Saint Louis	MO	63146	800-264-4400	314-994-4400	345
Schoepfle Garden 12882 Diagonal Rd	La Grange	OH	44050	800-526-7275	440-458-5121	96
Schofield Brothers of New England Inc 1071 Worcester Rd	Framingham	MA	01701	800-696-2874	508-879-0030	263
Schoharie Crossing State Historic Site 129 Schoharie St PO Box 140	Fort Hunter	NY	12069	800-456-2267	518-829-7516	564
Scholars Inn Gourmet Cafe 717 N College Ave	Bloomington	IN	47404	800-765-3466	812-332-1892	669
Scholarship America 1 Scholarship Way PO Box 297	Saint Peter	MN	56082	800-537-4180	507-931-1682	47-11
Scholastic Book Fairs Inc 1080 Greenwood Blvd	Lake Mary	FL	32746	800-874-4809	573-632-1687	94
Scholastic Coach & Athletic Director Magazine 557 Broadway *General	New York	NY	10012	800-724-6527*	212-343-6100	456-8
Schonbek Worldwide Lighting Inc 61 Industrial Blvd	Plattsburgh	NY	12901	800-836-1892	518-563-7500	439
School Annual Publishing Co 2568 Park Ctr Blvd	State College	PA	16801	800-436-6030		634-2
School Board of Highlands County Florida PO Box 9300	Sebring	FL	33871	877-357-7456	863-471-5555	683
School District of The Chathams 58 Meyersville Rd	Chatham	NJ	07928	800-225-5425	973-457-2500	683
School Employees Retirement System of Ohio 300 E Broad St Ste 100	Columbus	OH	43215	800-878-5853	614-222-5853	527
School Innovations & Advocacy Inc 11130 Sun Ctr Dr Ste 100	Rancho Cordova	CA	95670	877-954-4357		462
School Law News 360 Hiatt Dr	Palm Beach Gardens	FL	33418	800-341-7874		530-4
School Nurse Supply Co 1690 Wright Blvd	Schaumburg	IL	60193	800-485-2737		683
School Nutrition Assn (SNA) 700 S Washington St Ste 300	Alexandria	VA	22314	800-877-8822	703-739-3900	48-6
School of the Art Institute of Chicago 36 S Wabash Ave *Admissions	Chicago	IL	60603	800-232-7242*	312-629-6100	167
School of the Museum of Fine Arts 230 The Fenway *Admissions	Boston	MA	02115	800-643-6078*	617-369-3626	167
School of Visual Arts 209 E 23rd St	New York	NY	10010	800-436-4204	212-592-2000	163
School Photo Marketing 35 Vanderburg Rd	Marlboro	NJ	07746	877-543-9745	732-431-0440	197
School Specialty Inc PO Box 1579 *NASDAQ: SCHS*	Appleton	WI	54912	888-388-3224	920-734-5712	245
School Webmasters 2846 E Nora St	Mesa	AZ	85213	888-750-4556	602-750-4556	179
SchoolDocs LLC 5944 Luther Ln Ste 600	Dallas	TX	75225	866-311-2293		387
Schools Financial Credit Union 1485 Response Rd Ste 126	Sacramento	CA	95815	800-962-0990	916-569-5400	221
School-Tech Inc 745 State Cir	Ann Arbor	MI	48108	800-521-2832		346
Schoolwires Inc 330 Innovation Blvd Ste 301	State College	PA	16803	877-427-9413		244
Schott International Inc 2850 Gilchrist Rd	Akron	OH	44305	877-661-2121	330-794-2121	593
Schramm Inc 800 E Virginia Ave	West Chester	PA	19380	888-737-9438	610-696-2500	536
Schreiber Corp 29945 Beck Rd	Wixom	MI	48393	800-558-2706	248-926-1500	191-12
Schreiber Foods International Inc 600 E Crescent Ave Ste 103	Upper Saddle River	NJ	07458	800-631-7070	201-327-3535	298-11
Schreiner University 2100 Memorial Blvd	Kerrville	TX	78028	800-343-4919	830-792-7217	167
Schreiner's Iris Gardens 3625 Quinaby Rd NE	Salem	OR	97303	800-525-2367	503-393-3232	96
Schroder Investment Management North America Inc (SIMNA) 875 Third Ave 22nd Fl	New York	NY	10022	800-730-2932		688
Schroeder America 5620 Business Park	San Antonio	TX	78218	877-404-2488	210-662-8200	663
Schroeder Group, The 20800 Swenson Dr Ste 475	Waukesha	WI	53186	800-372-3020	262-798-8220	428
Schroeder Industries LLC 580 W Pk Rd	Leetsdale	PA	15056	800-722-4810	724-318-1100	209
Schroeder's Flowerland Inc 1530 S Webster Ave	Green Bay	WI	54301	800-236-4769	920-436-6363	294
Schroer Manufacturing Co 511 Osage Ave	Kansas City	KS	66105	800-444-1579	913-281-1500	419
Schuff Steel Co 420 S 19th Ave	Phoenix	AZ	85009	800-435-8528	602-252-7787	191-14
Schuff Steel Inc 1920 Ledo Rd	Albany	GA	31707	866-252-4628	678-821-7061	479
Schukei Chevrolet Inc 721 S Monroe	Mason City	IA	50401	866-918-6497	641-423-5402	56
Schulmerich Carillons Inc Carillon Hill	Sellersville	PA	18960	800-772-3557	215-257-2771	526

Company / Address	City	State	ZIP	Toll-Free	Phone	Class
Schulte Building Systems Inc 17600 Badtke Rd	Hockley	TX	77447	**877-257-2534**	281-304-6111	105
Schultz Collins Lawson Chambers Inc 455 Market St Ste 1250	San Francisco	CA	94105	**877-291-2205**	415-291-3000	401
Schultz Lubricants Inc 164 Shrewsbury St	West Boylston	MA	01583	**800-262-3962**	508-835-4446	540
Schumacher & Seiler Inc 10 W Aylesbury Rd	Timonium	MD	21093	**800-992-9356**	410-465-7000	611
Schumacher Electric Corp 801 E Business Ctr Dr	Mount Prospect	IL	60056	**800-621-5485**		255
Schumacher Elevator Co 1 Schumacher Way PO Box 393	Denver	IA	50622	**800-779-5438**	319-984-5676	258
Schumacher Group 200 Corporate Blvd Ste 201	Lafayette	LA	70508	**800-893-9698**		353
Schurman Fine Papers 500 Chadbourne Rd *Sales	Fairfield	CA	94533	**800-789-1649***		551-2
Schust Engineering Inc 701 North St	Auburn	IN	46706	**800-686-9297**		191-12
Schuster Electronics Inc 11320 Grooms Rd	Cincinnati	OH	45242	**800-521-1358**		248
Schuyler Mansion State Historic Site 32 Catherine St	Albany	NY	12202	**800-456-2267**	518-434-0834	564
Schuylkill Chamber of Commerce 91 S Progress Ave	Pottsville	PA	17901	**800-755-1942**	570-622-1942	138
Schwaab Inc 11415 W Burleigh St	Milwaukee	WI	53222	**800-935-9877**	414-771-4150	466
Schwan Food Co 115 W College Dr	Marshall	MN	56258	**800-533-5290**	507-532-3274	297-36
Schwank Inc 2 Schwank Way at Hwy 56N	Waynesboro	GA	30830	**877-446-3727**		357
Schwarz 8338 Austin Ave	Morton Grove	IL	60053	**800-323-4903**		558
Schwebel Baking Co PO Box 6018	Youngstown	OH	44501	**800-860-2867**	330-783-2860	297-1
Schweitzer E O Mfg Company Inc 450 Enterprise Pkwy	Lake Zurich	IL	60047	**888-870-7350**	847-362-8304	250
Schweitzer-Mauduit International Inc 100 N Pt Ctr E Ste 600 *NYSE: SWM*	Alpharetta	GA	30022	**800-514-0186**	770-569-4271	556
Schweizer Emblem Co 1022 Busse Hwy *Cust Svc	Park Ridge	IL	60068	**800-942-5215***	847-292-1022	260
Schwend Inc 28945 Johnston Rd	Dade City	FL	33523	**800-243-7757**	352-588-2220	777
Schwerdtle Stamp Co 166 Elm St	Bridgeport	CT	06604	**800-535-0004**	203-330-2750	466
SCI Logistics Ltd 180 Attwell Dr Ste 600	Toronto	ON	M9W6A9	**866-773-7735**	416-401-3011	315
SciClone Pharmaceuticals Inc 950 Tower Ln Ste 900 *NASDAQ: SCLN*	Foster City	CA	94404	**800-724-2566**	650-358-3456	582
SCI-Coal Township 1 Kelley Dr	Coal Township	PA	17866	**800-322-4472**	570-644-7890	215
Scicom Data Services Ltd 10101 Bren Rd E	Minnetonka	MN	55343	**800-488-9087**	952-933-4200	227
Sciemetric Instruments Inc 359 Terry Fox Dr Ste 100	Ottawa	ON	K2K2E7	**877-931-9200**	613-254-7054	248
Science Application International Corp Inc (SAIC Inc) 1710 SAIC Dr	McLean	VA	22102	**866-400-7242**	703-676-4300	180-5
Science Central 1950 N Clinton St	Fort Wayne	IN	46805	**888-240-7268**	260-424-2400	519
Science Magazine 1200 New York Ave NW	Washington	DC	20005	**866-434-2227**	202-326-6500	456-19
Science Museum of Minnesota 120 W Kellogg Blvd	Saint Paul	MN	55102	**800-221-9444**	651-221-9444	519
Science Museum Oklahoma 2100 NE 52nd St	Oklahoma City	OK	73111	**800-532-7652**	405-602-6664	519
Science News 1719 N St NW *Cust Svc	Washington	DC	20036	**800-552-4412***	202-785-2255	456-19
ScienceCare Inc 21410 N 19th Ave Ste 126	Phoenix	AZ	85027	**800-417-3747**	602-331-3641	544
Scientech Inc 5649 Arapahoe Ave	Boulder	CO	80303	**800-525-0522**	303-444-1361	682
Scientific Drilling Controls Inc 16701 Greenspoint Pk Dr Ste 200	Houston	TX	77060	**800-514-8949**	281-443-3300	539
Scientific Equipment & Furniture Assn (SEFA) 65 Hilton Avenue	Garden City	NY	11530	**877-294-5424**	516-294-5424	48-19
Scientific Games Corp 750 Lexington Ave 25th Fl *NASDAQ: SGMS*	New York	NY	10022	**800-827-2946**	212-754-2233	323
Scientific Industries Inc 70 Orville Dr	Bohemia	NY	11716	**888-850-6208**	631-567-4700	419
Scientific Learning Corp 300 Frank H Ogawa Plz Ste 600 *OTC: SCIL*	Oakland	CA	94612	**888-665-9707**	510-444-3500	180-3
Scientific Protein Laboratories Inc 700 E Main St PO Box 158	Waunakee	WI	53597	**800-334-4775**	608-849-5944	478
Sciforma Corp 985 University Ave Ste 5 *Sales	Los Gatos	CA	95032	**800-533-9876***	408-354-0144	180-1
SCIMEDX Corp 100 Ford Rd	Denville	NJ	07834	**800-221-5598**	973-625-8822	233
Scion Medical Technologies LLC 90 Oak St	Newton	MA	02464	**888-582-6211**		740
Scion Steel Inc 21555 Mullin Ave	Warren	MI	48089	**800-288-2127**	586-755-4000	721
Scioto Downs Inc 6000 S High St	Columbus	OH	43207	**800-514-3849**	614-295-4700	639
Scioto Sign Company Inc 6047 US Rt 68 N	Kenton	OH	43326	**800-572-4686**	419-673-1261	699
Scioto Trail State Park 144 Lake Rd	Chillicothe	OH	45601	**866-644-6727**		564
Sci-Port Discovery Ctr 820 Clyde Fant Pkwy	Shreveport	LA	71101	**877-724-7678**	318-424-3466	519
SciQuest Inc 6501 Weston Pkwy Ste 200	Cary	NC	27513	**888-638-7322**	919-659-2100	180-4
Scivantage Inc 499 Washington Blvd 11th Fl	Jersey City	NJ	07310	**866-724-8268**	646-452-0050	176
Scleroderma Foundation 300 Rosewood Dr Ste 105	Danvers	MA	01923	**800-722-4673**	978-463-5843	47-17
Scoot & Doodle Inc 2625 Middlefield Rd Ste 223	Palo Alto	CA	94306	**888-563-9224**		387
SCORE American Soccer Company Inc 726 E Anaheim St	Wilmington	CA	90744	**800-626-7774**		154-18
SCORE Assn 1175 Herndon Pkwy Ste 900	Herndon	VA	20170	**800-634-0245**		48-12
Scorpion Design Inc 28480 Ave Stanford Ste 100	Valencia	CA	91355	**866-622-5648**		182
Scosche Industries Inc PO Box 2901	Oxnard	CA	93034	**800-363-4490**	805-486-4450	255
Scot Forge Co 8001 Winn Rd PO Box 8	Spring Grove	IL	60081	**800-435-6621**	847-587-1000	482
Scot Pump 6437 Pioneer Rd PO Box 286	Cedarburg	WI	53012	**888-835-0600**	262-377-7000	638
Scotch Gulf Lumber 1850 Conception St Rd	Mobile	AL	36610	**800-496-3307**	251-457-6872	681
Scotch Lumber Co 119 W Main St PO Box 38	Fulton	AL	36446	**800-936-4424**	334-636-4424	681
Scotch Malt Whiskey Society 10210 Nw 50th St	Sunrise	FL	33351	**800-990-1991**	954-749-2440	354
Scotchman Industries Inc 180 E Hwy 14	Philip	SD	57567	**800-843-8844**	605-859-2542	492
Scotia Capital Markets 1 Liberty Plz	New York	NY	10006	**877-294-3435**	212-225-5000	688
Scotsman Ice Systems 775 Corporate Woods Pkwy *Cust Svc	Vernon Hills	IL	60061	**800-726-8762***	847-215-4500	662
Scotsman Inn West 5922 W Kellogg St	Wichita	KS	67209	**800-950-7268**	316-943-3800	379
Scott & White Health Plan 2401 S 31st St	Temple	TX	76508	**800-321-7947**	254-298-3000	391-3
Scott & White Memorial Hospital 2401 S 31st St	Temple	TX	76508	**800-792-3710**	254-724-2111	374-3
Scott Community College 500 Belmont Rd	Bettendorf	IA	52722	**888-336-3907**	563-441-4001	161
Scott Construction Inc 560 Munroe Ave	Lake Delton	WI	53940	**800-843-1556**	608-254-2555	190-4
Scott County Library System 13090 Alabama Ave S	Savage	MN	55378	**877-772-8346**	952-707-1770	434-3
Scott Danahy Naylon Company Inc (SDN) 300 Spindrift Dr	Williamsville	NY	14221	**800-728-6362**	716-633-3400	390
Scott Electric 1000 S Main St PO Box S	Greensburg	PA	15601	**800-442-8045**	724-834-4321	248
Scott Enterprises Inc 2225 Downs Dr 6th Fl Exce Stes	Erie	PA	16509	**877-866-3445**	814-868-9500	387
Scott Family of Dealerships 3333 Lehigh St	Allentown	PA	18103	**800-274-1039**		56
Scott Fetzer Company Scot Laboratories Div 16841 Pk Cir Dr	Chagrin Falls	OH	44023	**800-486-7268**	440-543-3033	150
Scott Fly Rod Co 2355 Air Pk Way	Montrose	CO	81401	**800-728-7208**		708
Scott Health & Safety 4320 Goldmine Rd PO Box 569	Monroe	NC	28110	**800-247-7257**	704-291-8300	575
Scott Industrial Systems Inc 4433 Interpoint Blvd PO Box 1387	Dayton	OH	45401	**800-416-6023**	937-233-8146	469
Scott Industries Inc 1573 Hwy 136 W PO Box 7	Henderson	KY	42419	**800-951-9276**	270-831-2037	389
Scott Logistics Corp PO Box 391	Rome	GA	30162	**800-893-6689**	706-234-1184	312
Scott Madden & Assoc Inc 2626 Glenwood Ave Ste 480	Raleigh	NC	27608	**888-473-6748**	919-781-4191	196
Scott Sheldon LLC 3985 Medina Rd Ste 220	Medina	OH	44256	**877-467-7552**	330-952-1671	462
Scott Tim (Sen R - SC) 520 Hart Senate Office Bldg	Washington	DC	20510	**855-425-6324**	202-224-6121	342-2
Scott USA Inc PO Box 2030	Sun Valley	ID	83353	**800-292-5874**	208-622-1000	708
Scott's Liquid Gold Inc 4880 Havana St *OTC: SLGD*	Denver	CO	80239	**800-447-1919**	303-373-4860	150
Scottdel Inc 400 Church St	Swanton	OH	43558	**800-446-2341**	419-825-2341	130
Scott-Gross Company Inc 664 Magnolia Ave	Lexington	KY	40505	**800-967-6874**		325
Scotts Miracle Gro Products Inc 14111 Scottslawn Rd	Marysville	OH	43041	**888-270-3714**	937-644-0011	282
Scotts Miracle-Gro Co 14111 Scottslawn Rd *NYSE: SMG* ■ *Cust Svc	Marysville	OH	43041	**800-543-8873***	937-644-0011	282
Scottsdale Camelback Resort 6302 E Camelback Rd	Scottsdale	AZ	85251	**800-891-8585**	480-947-3300	667
Scottsdale Community College 9000 E Chaparral Rd	Scottsdale	AZ	85256	**800-784-2433**	480-423-6000	161
Scottsdale Convention & Visitors Bureau 4343 N Scottsdale Rd Ste 170	Scottsdale	AZ	85251	**800-782-1117**	480-421-1004	208
Scottsdale Ctr for the Performing Arts 7380 E Second St	Scottsdale	AZ	85251	**800-309-8532**	480-994-2787	571
Scottsdale Culinary Institute 8100 E Camelback Rd Ste 1001	Scottsdale	AZ	85251	**888-557-4222**	480-990-3773	162
Scottsdale Insurance Co 8877 N Gainey Ctr Dr	Scottsdale	AZ	85258	**800-423-7675**	480-365-4000	391-4
Scottsdale Plaza Resort 7200 N Scottsdale Rd	Scottsdale	AZ	85253	**800-832-2025**	480-948-5000	667
Scottsdale Stadium 7408 E Osborn Rd	Scottsdale	AZ	85251	**877-229-5042**	480-312-2856	718
Scoular Co 2027 Dodge St	Omaha	NE	68102	**800-488-3500**	402-342-3500	277
Scout Stuff PO Box 7143	Charlotte	NC	28241	**800-323-0736**		789
Scovill Fasteners Inc 1802 Scovill Dr *Cust Svc	Clarkesville	GA	30523	**888-726-8455***	706-754-1000	593
SCPPD (South Central Public Power District) 275 S Main St PO Box 406	Nelson	NE	68961	**800-557-5254**	402-225-2351	247

Name	Address	City	State	ZIP	Toll-Free	Phone	Class
Scranton Mfg Company Inc	101 State St PO Box 336	Scranton	IA	51462	**800-831-1858**	712-652-3396	275
Scranton Times-Tribune	149 Penn Ave	Scranton	PA	18503	**800-228-4637**	570-348-9100	531-2
SCREC (Sullivan County Rural Electric Co-op Inc)	5675 Rt 87 PO Box 65	Forksville	PA	18616	**800-570-5081**	570-924-3381	247
Screen Actors Guild (SAG)	5757 Wilshire Blvd	Los Angeles	CA	90036	**800-724-0767**	323-954-1600	414
Screen Graphics of Florida Inc	1801 N Andrews Ave	Pompano Beach	FL	33069	**800-346-4420**		685
Screen Works	2201 W Fulton St *Cust Svc	Chicago	IL	60612	**800-294-8111***	312-243-8265	720
Screen Works Inc	3970 Image Dr	Dayton	OH	45414	**800-536-9111**	937-264-9111	344
Screeningone Inc	2233 W 190th St	Torrance	CA	90504	**888-327-6511**		220
Scribner Cohen & Company SC	400 E Mason St Ste 300	Milwaukee	WI	53202	**888-730-0045**	414-271-1700	2
ScripNet	10050 Banburry Cross Dr Ste 290	Las Vegas	NV	89144	**888-880-8562**	702-248-2692	585
Scripps College	1030 Columbia Ave	Claremont	CA	91711	**800-770-1333**	909-621-8149	167
Scripps Green Hospital	10666 N Torrey Pines Rd	La Jolla	CA	92037	**800-727-4777**	858-455-9100	374-3
Scripps Health	4275 Campus Pt Ct	San Diego	CA	92121	**800-727-4777**		353
Scripps Howard Foundation	312 Walnut St PO Box 5380	Cincinnati	OH	45201	**800-888-3000**	513-977-3035	305
Scripps Howard Inc	PO Box 5380	Cincinnati	OH	45202	**800-888-3000**	513-977-3000	634-8
Scripps Memorial Hospital-La Jolla	9888 Genesee Ave	La Jolla	CA	92037	**800-727-4777**		374-3
Script Care Inc	6380 Folsom Dr	Beaumont	TX	77706	**800-880-9988**		585
Scripted Inc	135 Stillman St	San Francisco	CA	94107	**800-797-4470**		387
ScriptLogic Corp	6000 Broken Sound Pkwy NW	Boca Raton	FL	33487	**800-306-9329**	561-886-2400	180-12
ScriptSave	4911 E Broadway Blvd Ste 200	Tucson	AZ	85711	**800-347-5985**		585
Scruggs Company Inc	PO Box 2065	Valdosta	GA	31604	**800-230-7263**	229-242-2388	190-4
SCS (Structural Component Systems Inc)	1255 Front St	Fremont	NE	68026	**800-844-5622**	402-721-5622	189
SCS Engineers	3900 Kilroy Airport Way Ste 100	Long Beach	CA	90806	**800-326-9544**	562-426-9544	263
SCSD (Sweetwater County School District 1)	3550 Foothill Blvd PO Box 1089	Rock Springs	WY	82901	**888-503-7562**	307-352-3400	778
SCTE (Society of Cable Telecommunications Engineers)	140 Philips Rd	Exton	PA	19341	**800-542-5040**	610-363-6888	48-19
Scuba Com Inc	1752 Langley Ave	Irvine	CA	92614	**800-347-2822**	949-221-9300	709
Scully Signal Co	70 Industrial Way	Wilmington	MA	01887	**800-272-8559**	617-692-8600	203
SD Ireland Co	193 Industrial Ave	Williston	VT	05495	**800-339-4565**	802-863-6222	185
Sda Consulting Inc	3011 183rd St # 377	Homewood	IL	60430	**800-823-2990**		182
SDEB (San Diego Eye Bank)	9246 Lightwave Ave Ste 120	San Diego	CA	92123	**800-393-2265**	858-694-0400	271
SDI Chicago	33 West Monroe Ste 400	Chicago	IL	60603	**888-968-7734**	312-580-7500	691
SDI Technologies Inc	1299 Main St	Rahway	NJ	07065	**800-333-3092**		51
SDMS (Society of Diagnostic Medical Sonography)	2745 Dallas Pkwy	Plano	TX	75093	**800-229-9506**	214-473-8057	48-8
SDN (Scott Danahy Naylon Company Inc)	300 Spindrift Dr	Williamsville	NY	14221	**800-728-6362**	716-633-3400	390
SDNA (South Dakota Nurses Assn)	PO Box 1015	Pierre	SD	57501	**888-425-3032**	605-945-4265	532
SDPB (South Dakota Public Broadcasting)	555 N Dakota St PO Box 5000	Vermillion	SD	57069	**800-456-0766**	605-677-5861	629
SDT North America Inc	PO Box 682	Cobourg	ON	K9A4R5	**800-667-5325**	905-377-1313	358
SEA (Software Engineering of America Inc)	1230 Hempstead Tpke	Franklin Square	NY	11010	**800-272-7322**	516-328-7000	180-12
Sea Blue	1 Borgata Way *Cust Svc	Atlantic City	NJ	08401	**877-786-9900***	609-317-1000	669
Sea Breeze Inc	441 Rt 202	Towaco	NJ	07082	**800-732-2733**	973-334-7777	297-15
Sea Cloud Cruises Inc	282 Grand Ave Ste 3	Englewood	NJ	07631	**888-732-2568**	201-227-9404	222
Sea Crest Resort & Conference Ctr	350 Quaker Rd	North Falmouth	MA	02556	**800-225-3110**	508-540-9400	667
Sea Eagle Boats Inc	19 N Columbia St Ste 1	Port Jefferson	NY	11777	**800-748-8066**	631-791-1799	708
Sea Gull Lighting Products LLC A Generations Brands Co	301 W Washington St	Riverside	NJ	08075	**800-347-5483**	856-764-0500	439
Sea Harvest Packing Co	PO Box 818	Brunswick	GA	31521	**800-627-4300**	912-264-3212	297-14
Sea Island Co	PO Box 30351	Sea Island	GA	31561	**800-732-4752**	912-638-3611	653
SEA Ltd	7349 Worthington-Galena Rd	Columbus	OH	43085	**800-782-6851**		462
Sea Magazine	17782 Cowan St Ste C	Irvine	CA	92614	**800-873-7327**	949-660-6150	456-4
Sea Mar Community Health Ctr	1040 S Henderson St	Seattle	WA	98108	**855-289-4503**	206-763-5277	353
Sea Mist Resort	1200 S Ocean Blvd	Myrtle Beach	SC	29577	**800-793-6507**	843-448-1551	667
Sea Palms Golf & Tennis Resort	5445 Frederica Rd	Saint Simons Island	GA	31522	**800-841-6268**	912-638-3351	667
Sea Pearl Seafood Company Inc	14120 Shell Belt Rd	Bayou La Batre	AL	36509	**800-872-8804**	251-824-2129	393
Sea Pines Resort, The	32 Greenwood Dr	Hilton Head Island	SC	29928	**866-561-8802**	843-785-3333	651
Sea Ranch Lodge	60 Sea Walk Dr PO Box 44	The Sea Ranch	CA	95497	**800-732-7262**	707-785-2371	379
Sea Spa at Loews Coronado Bay Resort	4000 Loews Coronado Bay Rd	Coronado	CA	92118	**800-815-6397**	619-424-4000	705
Sea Tow Services International Inc	1560 Youngs Ave PO Box 1178	Southold	NY	11971	**800-473-2869**	631-765-3660	464
Sea Trail Corp	75A Clubhouse Rd	Sunset Beach	NC	28468	**888-321-9048**	910-287-1100	651
Sea Venture Resort	100 Ocean View Ave	Pismo Beach	CA	93449	**800-443-7778**	805-773-4994	667
Sea View Hotel	9909 Collins Ave	Bal Harbour	FL	33154	**800-447-1010**	305-866-4441	379
Seaboard Asphalt Products Co	3601 Fairfield Rd	Baltimore	MD	21226	**800-536-0332**	410-355-0330	45
Seaboard Corp	9000 W 67th St *NYSE: SEB*	Shawnee Mission	KS	66202	**866-676-8886**	913-676-8800	187
Seaboard Folding Box Co Inc	35 Daniels St	Fitchburg	MA	01420	**800-225-6313**	978-342-8921	100
Seaboard Foods	9000 W 67th St Ste 200	Shawnee Mission	KS	66202	**800-262-7907**	913-261-2600	10-5
Seaboard International Forest Products LLC	22F Cotton Rd	Nashua	NH	03063	**800-669-6800**	603-881-3700	193-3
Seaboard Marine	8001 NW 79th Ave	Miami	FL	33166	**866-676-8886**	305-863-4444	314
Seacoast Banking Corp of Florida	PO Box 9012 PO Box 9012 *NASDAQ: SBCF* ■ *All	Stuart	FL	34995	**800-706-9991***	772-287-4000	360-2
SEACOR Holdings Inc	2200 Eller Dr PO Box 13038 *NYSE: CKH*	Fort Lauderdale	FL	33316	**800-516-6203**	954-523-2200	665
Seacrest Oceanfront Resort on the South Beach	803 S Ocean Blvd	Myrtle Beach	SC	29577	**888-889-8113**		667
SeaDream Yacht Club	601 Brickell Key Dr Ste 1050	Miami	FL	33131	**800-707-4911**	305-631-6110	222
Seafarers International Union	5201 Auth Way	Camp Springs	MD	20746	**800-252-4674**	301-899-0675	414
Seagull Book & Tape Inc	1720 S Redwood Rd	Salt Lake City	UT	84104	**800-999-6257**		95
Seal Methods Inc	11915 Shoemaker Ave	Santa Fe Springs	CA	90670	**800-423-4777**	562-944-0291	327
Sealed Air Corp Packaging Products Div	301 Mayhill St	Saddle Brook	NJ	07663	**800-648-9093**	201-712-7000	547
Sealed Unit Parts Company Inc	2230 Landmark Pl	Allenwood	NJ	08720	**800-333-9125**	732-223-6644	14
Sealing Devices Inc	4400 Walden Ave *Cust Svc	Lancaster	NY	14086	**800-727-3257***	716-684-7600	327
Sealing Equipment Products Co Inc	123 Airpark Industrial Rd *Cust Svc	Alabaster	AL	35007	**800-633-4770***		327
Seaman Corp	1000 Venture Blvd	Wooster	OH	44691	**800-927-8578**	330-262-1111	742-2
SEAMARK Asset Management Ltd	1801 Hollis St Ste 810	Halifax	NS	B3J3N4	**888-303-5055**	902-423-9367	527
Seamen's Bank	221 Commercial St PO Box 659	Provincetown	MA	02657	**855-227-5347**	508-487-0035	69
Seaport Hotel & World Trade Ctr	1 Seaport Ln	Boston	MA	02210	**877-732-7678**	617-385-4000	379
Seaport World Trade Ctr Boston	200 Seaport Blvd	Boston	MA	02210	**800-440-3318**	617-385-4212	820
SEARAC (Southeast Asia Resource Action Ctr)	1628 16th St NW 3rd Fl	Washington	DC	20009	**888-907-1485**	202-667-4690	47-5
Search Company International	1535 Grant St Ste 140	Denver	CO	80203	**800-727-2120**	303-863-1800	632
Search Network Ltd	1503 42nd St Ste 210	West Des Moines	IA	50266	**800-383-5050**	515-223-1153	632
Searcher: The Magazine for Database Professionals	143 Old Marlton Pk	Medford	NJ	08055	**800-300-9868**	609-654-6266	456-7
Searchwide Inc	320 Myrtle St W	Stillwater	MN	55082	**888-386-6390**	651-275-1370	195
Searcy Denney Scarola Barnhart	Po Box 3626	West Palm Beach	FL	33402	**800-780-8607**	561-686-6300	428
Searles Valley Minerals	9401 Indian Creek Pkwy Ste 1000	Overland Park	KS	66210	**800-637-2775**	913-344-9500	502-1
Sears Canada Inc	290 Yonge St Ste 700 *TSE: SCC*	Toronto	ON	M5B2C3	**877-987-3277**	416-362-1711	231
Sears Imported Autos Inc	13500 Wayzata Blvd *Sales	Minnetonka	MN	55305	**800-493-1720***	952-546-5301	56
Sears Manufacturing Co	1718 S Concord St PO Box 3667 *Cust Svc	Davenport	IA	52808	**800-553-3013***	563-383-2800	687
Sears Tower	233 S Wacker Dr	Chicago	IL	60606	**877-759-3325**	312-875-9447	49-2
Seaside Civic & Convention Ctr	415 First Ave	Seaside	OR	97138	**800-394-3303**	503-738-8585	207
Seaside Golf Vacations	218 Main St	North Myrtle Beach	SC	29582	**877-732-6999**		769
Seaside Inn	541 E Gulf Dr	Sanibel Island	FL	33957	**866-565-5092**	239-472-1400	379
Seasons Hospice & Palliative Care of California-Orange	750 The City Dr	Orange	CA	92868	**877-508-0644**	714-980-0900	371
Seasons Restaurant at Highland Lake Inn	86 Lilly Pad Ln	Flat Rock	NC	28731	**800-635-5101**	828-696-9094	705
Seasons-4 Inc	4500 Industrial Access Rd	Douglasville	GA	30134	**800-888-9900**	770-489-0716	14
Seastrom Mfg Company Inc	456 Seastrom St	Twin Falls	ID	83301	**800-634-2356**	208-737-4300	350
Seat of the Soul Foundation	PO Box 3310	Ashland	OR	97520	**877-733-4279**	541-482-1515	47-20

	Toll-Free	Phone	Class
Seats Inc 1515 Industrial St Reedsburg WI 53959	800-443-0615	608-524-8261	687
Seattle Cancer Care Alliance 825 Eastlake Ave E PO Box 19023 Seattle WA 98109	800-804-8824	206-288-1024	767
Seattle Children's Hospital 4800 Sand Pt Way NE Seattle WA 98105	866-987-2000	206-987-2000	374-1
Seattle Convention Ctr Pike Street 1011 Pike St Seattle WA 98101	800-225-5466	206-682-8282	379
Seattle Lighting Fixture Co 222 Second Ave Ext S Seattle WA 98104 *Cust Svc	800-689-1000*	206-622-4736	362
Seattle Manufacturing Corp 6930 Salashan Pkwy Ferndale WA 98248	800-426-6251	360-366-5534	575
Seattle Mariners Safeco Field 1250 First Ave S Seattle WA 98134	800-255-7932	206-346-4000	711
Seattle Opera PO Box 9248 Seattle WA 98109 *Sales	800-426-1619*	206-389-7600	572-2
Seattle Pacific University 3307 Third Ave W Seattle WA 98119	800-366-3344	206-281-2000	167
Seattle Post-Intelligencer 101 Elliott Ave W 2nd Fl Seattle WA 98119	800-542-0820	206-448-8000	531-2
Seattle Repertory Theatre (SRT) 155 Mercer St PO Box 900923 Seattle WA 98109	877-900-9285	206-443-2210	572-4
Seattle Seahawks 12 Seahawks Way Renton WA 98056	888-635-4295		713-3
Seattle SuperSonics 1201 Third Ave Ste 1000 Seattle WA 98101	800-743-7021	206-281-5800	712-1
Seattle Symphony 200 University St Seattle WA 98101	866-833-4747	206-215-4700	572-3
Seattle Theatre Group 911 Pine St Seattle WA 98101	877-784-4849	206-467-5510	718
Seattle University 901 12th Ave Seattle WA 98122	800-426-7123	206-296-6000	167
Seattle University Lemieux Library 901 12th Ave Seattle WA 98122	800-426-7123	206-296-6210	434-6
Seattle's Best Coffee Co PO Box 3717 Seattle WA 98124	800-611-7793		158
Seattle's Convention & Visitors Bureau 701 Pike St Ste 800 Seattle WA 98101	866-732-2695	206-461-5800	208
SeaWorld Orlando 7007 Sea World Dr Orlando FL 32821	800-327-2424	407-351-3600	32
SeaWorld San Diego 500 SeaWorld Dr San Diego CA 92109	800-257-4268	619-226-3901	32
Sebacia Inc 2905 Premiere Pkwy Ste 150 Duluth GA 30097	888-935-4411		474
Sebago Inc 9341 Courtland Dr Rockford MI 49351	866-699-7367	616-866-5500	302
Sebasco Harbor Resort 29 Keynon Rd Phippsburg ME 04562	800-225-3819	207-389-1161	667
Sebastiani Vineyards Inc 389 Fourth St E Sonoma CA 95476	855-232-2338	707-933-3230	79-3
Sebesta Blomberg & Assoc Inc 1450 Energy Park Dr Ste 300 St Paul MN 55108	877-706-6858	651-634-0775	263
Sebewaing Tool & Engineering Co 415 Union St Sebewaing MI 48759	800-453-2207	989-883-2000	350
Sebring International Raceway 113 Midway Dr Sebring FL 33870	800-626-7223	863-655-1442	514
SEC (Shelby Electric Co-op) 1355 IL-128 state PO Box 560 Shelbyville IL 62565	800-677-2612	217-774-3986	247
Secap USA Inc 10 Clipper Rd Conshohocken PA 19428	800-523-0320	610-825-6205	111
Sechrist Industries Inc 4225 E La Palma Ave Anaheim CA 92807	800-732-4747	714-579-8400	475
SECO (Southeast Electric Co-op Inc) 110 S Main St Ekalaka MT 59324	888-485-8762	406-775-8762	247
Seco Tools 2805 Bellingham Dr Troy MI 48083	800-832-8326	248-528-5200	492
Secoa Inc 8650 109th Ave N Champlin MN 55316	800-328-5519	763-506-8800	720
Seco-Larm USA Inc 16842 Millikan Ave Irvine CA 92606	800-662-0800	949-261-2999	690
Second Amendment Foundation 12500 NE Tenth Pl Bellevue WA 98005	800-426-4302	425-454-7012	47-8
Second Cup Ltd 6303 Airport Rd Mississauga ON L4V1R8	877-212-1818		158
Second Street Grill 200 E Fremont St Las Vegas NV 89101	800-634-6460	702-385-3232	669
Secova Inc 5000 Birch St W Tower Ste 1400 Newport Beach CA 92660	800-257-0011	714-384-0530	196
SECPA (Southeast Colorado Power Assn) 901 W 3rd La Junta CO 81050	800-332-8634	719-384-2551	247
Secret Garden Spa at the Prince of Wales Hotel 6 Picton St Niagara-on-the-Lake ON L0S1J0	888-669-5566	905-468-3246	705
Secretary of Education 400 Maryland Ave SW Washington DC 20202	800-872-5327	202-401-3000	340-6
Secretary of Labor 200 Constitution Ave NW Rm S2018 Washington DC 20210	866-487-2365	202-693-6000	340-13
Secretary of Transportation 1200 New Jersey Ave SE Washington DC 20590	855-368-4200		340-15
Secretary of Veterans Affairs *Board of Veterans' Appeals* 810 Vermont Ave NW Washington DC 20420	800-923-8387		340-17
Center for Women Veterans 810 Vermont Ave NW Washington DC 20420	800-827-1000		340-17
SECU (State Employees' Credit Union) PO Box 29606 Raleigh NC 27626	888-732-8562	919-857-2150	221
Secura Insurance Cos PO Box 819 Appleton WI 54912	800-558-3405	920-739-3161	391-4
Securance LLC 6922 W Linebaugh Ave Ste 101 Tampa FL 33625	877-578-0215		182
Secure First Credit Union 3000 Winewood Rd Birmingham AL 35215	877-520-2115	205-520-2115	221
SecureInfo Corp 211 N Loop 1604 E Ste 200 San Antonio TX 78232	888-677-9351	210-403-5600	182
Securitas Security Services USA Inc 2 Campus Dr Parsippany NJ 07054	800-555-0906	973-267-5300	690
Securitech Inc 8230 E Broadway Blvd Tucson AZ 85710	888-792-4473	520-721-0305	632
Securities Center Inc, The 245 E St Chula Vista CA 91910	800-244-1718	619-426-3550	688
Securities Industry & Financial Markets Assn (SIFMAA) 120 Broadway 35th Fl New York NY 10271	888-367-7966	212-313-1200	48-2
Securities Law Daily 1801 S Bell St Arlington VA 22202	800-372-1033		530-7
Securities Service Network Inc 9729 Cogdill Rd Ste 301 Knoxville TN 37932	866-843-4635		688
Securitron Magnalock Corp 10027 S 51st St Ste 102 Phoenix AZ 85044 *Sales	800-624-5625*	623-582-4626	350
Security 101 LLC 2465 Mercer Ave Ste 101 West Palm Beach FL 33401	888-909-4101		691
Security Benefit Group of Cos 1 Security Benefit Pl Topeka KS 66636	800-888-2461	785-438-3000	360-4
Security Corp 22325 Roethel Dr Novi MI 48375	877-374-5700		690
Security Credit Services LLC 2653 W Oxford Loop Ste 108 Oxford MS 38655	866-699-7889	662-281-7220	403
Security Defense Systems Corp 160 Pk Ave Nutley NJ 07110	800-325-6339		690
Security Engineered Machinery Company Inc 5 Walkup Dr PO Box 1045 Westborough MA 01581 *Sales	800-225-9293*	508-366-1488	110
Security Escrow & Title Insurance Agency 337 South Main Ste 110 Cedar City UT 84720	855-319-9820	435-867-0402	390
Security Federal Bank (SFB) 238 Richland Ave W Aiken SC 29801	866-851-3000	803-641-3000	70
Security Finance Corp 181 Security Plc Spartanburg SC 29307 *All	800-395-8195*	864-582-8193	216
Security Fire Protection Co Inc 4495 Mendenhall Rd S Memphis TN 38141	888-274-8595	901-362-6250	191-13
Security First Corp 29811 Santa Margarita Pkwy Ste 600 Rancho Santa Margarita CA 92688	888-884-7152	949-858-7525	82
Security Funds 1 Security Benefit Pl Topeka KS 66636	800-888-2461	785-438-3000	527
Security Industry Assn (SIA) 8405 Colesville Rd Ste 500 Silver Spring MD 20910	866-817-8888	703-683-2075	48-4
Security Life Insurance Co of America 10901 Red Cir Dr Minnetonka MN 55343	800-328-4667	952-544-2121	391-2
Security Mutual Life Insurance Co of New York 100 Court St PO Box 1625 Binghamton NY 13901	800-927-8846	607-723-3551	391-2
Security National Financial Corp (SNFC) 5300 South 360 West Ste 250 PO Box 57250 Salt Lake City UT 84123 *NASDAQ: SNFCA*	800-574-7117	801-264-1060	391-2
Security Service Federal Credit Union 16211 La Cantera Pkwy San Antonio TX 78256	800-527-7328	210-476-4000	221
Security Signal Devices Inc 1740 N Lemon St Anaheim CA 92801	800-888-0444		690
Security Storage Co 1701 Florida Ave NW Washington DC 20009	888-903-7695	202-234-5600	518
Security Supply Corp 196 Maple Ave Selkirk NY 12158	800-333-2226	518-767-2226	611
Security Van Lines LLC 100 W Airline Dr Kenner LA 70062	800-218-6915	800-794-5961	778
Securus Technologies Inc 14651 Dallas Pkwy Dallas TX 75254	800-844-6591	972-277-0300	733
SED (Regency Infographics Inc) 2867 E Allegheny Ave Philadelphia PA 19134	800-829-0020	215-425-8800	779
Seda France Inc 8301 Springdale Rd Ste 800 Austin TX 78724	800-474-0854	512-206-0105	94
SEDL 4700 Mueller Blvd Austin TX 78723	800-476-6861	512-476-6861	666
Sedlak Interiors Inc 34300 Solon Rd Solon OH 44139	800-260-2949	440-248-2424	322
Sedona Rouge Hotel & Spa 2250 W SR- 89A Sedona AZ 86336	866-312-4111	928-203-4111	379
See Water Inc 121 N Dillon St San Jacinto CA 92583	888-733-9283	951-487-8073	203
See's Candies Inc 210 El Camino Real South San Francisco CA 94080 *Cust Svc	800-877-7337*	650-761-2490	297-8
Seedway LLC 1734 Railroad Pl Hall NY 14463	800-836-3710	585-526-6391	692
Seelbach Hilton Louisville 500 S Fourth St Louisville KY 40202	800-333-3399	502-585-3200	379
Seelye Plastics Inc 9700 Newton Ave S Bloomington MN 55431	800-328-2728		602
SeePoint Technology LLC 2619 Manhattan Beach Blvd Redondo Beach CA 90278	888-587-1777	310-725-9660	613
SEER Technology Inc 2681 Parleys Way Ste 201 Salt Lake City UT 84109	877-505-7337	801-746-7888	419
SEFA (Scientific Equipment & Furniture Assn) 65 Hilton Avenue Garden City NY 11530	877-294-5424	516-294-5424	48-19
Sefar Printing Solutions Inc 111 Calumet St Depew NY 14043	800-995-0531	716-683-4050	742-3
Segall Bryant & Hamill 540 W Madison St Ste 1900 Chicago IL 60606	800-836-4265	312-474-1222	401
Seguin Area Chamber of Commerce 116 N Camp St Seguin TX 78155	888-674-7224	830-379-6382	138
Seguin Independent School District 1221 E Kingsbury St Seguin TX 78155	866-632-9992	830-372-5771	683
Segway Inc 14 Technology Dr Bedford NH 03110	866-473-4929	603-222-6000	515
SEI 1 Freedom Vly Dr Oaks PA 19456 *NASDAQ: SEIC*	800-342-5734	610-676-1000	527
SEI (Software Engineering Institute) 4500 Fifth Ave Pittsburgh PA 15213	888-201-4479	412-268-5800	666
SEI (Stephenson Equipment Inc) 7201 Paxton St Harrisburg PA 17111	800-325-6455	717-564-3434	266-3

Name / Address	City	State	ZIP	Toll-Free	Phone	Class
SEI (System Engineering International Inc) 5115 Pegasus Ct Ste Q	Frederick	MD	21704	800-765-4734	301-694-9601	785
Seico Security Systems 132 Court St	Pekin	IL	61554	800-272-0316	309-347-3200	691
Seiko Corp of America 1111 MacArthur Blvd *Cust Svc	Mahwah	NJ	07430	800-545-2783*	201-529-5730	152
Seiko Instruments USA Inc 21221 S Western Ave Ste 250 *Sales	Torrance	CA	90501	800-688-0817*	310-517-7700	152
Seiko Instruments USA Inc Micro Printer Div 2990 Lomita Blvd	Torrance	CA	90505	800-688-0817	310-517-7778	175-6
Seiler Instrument & Mfg Company Inc 3433 Tree Court Industrial Blvd	Saint Louis	MO	63122	800-489-2282	314-968-2282	543
Seitz LLC 212 Industrial Ln	Torrington	CT	06790	800-261-2011	860-489-0476	603
Seize The Deal LLC 1851 N Greenville Ave Ste 100	Richardson	TX	75081	866-210-0881		387
SEJ (Society of Environmental Journalists) 115 W Ave	Jenkintown	PA	19046	866-208-3372	215-884-8174	48-14
SEK Genetics 9525 70th Rd	Galesburg	KS	66740	800-443-6389		11-2
Sekisui America Corp 333 Meadowlands Pkwy *General	Secaucus	NJ	07094	866-260-5851*	201-423-7960	602
Sekisui Voltek LLC 100 Shepard St	Lawrence	MA	01843	800-225-0668	978-685-2557	600
Seko Worldwide Inc 1100 Arlington Heights Rd Ste 600	Itasca	IL	60143	800-323-1235	630-919-4800	448
Selas Heat Technology Company LLC 130 Keystone Dr	Montgomeryville	PA	18936	800-523-6500	215-646-6600	319
Selbysoft Inc 8326 Woodland Ave E	Puyallup	WA	98371	800-454-4434	253-770-2993	179
Selco Community Credit Union 299 E 11th Ave	Eugene	OR	97401	800-445-4483	541-686-8000	221
Selden's Home Furnishings 1802 62nd Ave E	Tacoma	WA	98424	800-870-7880	253-922-5700	322
Select Engineered Systems 7991 W 26th Ave	Hialeah	FL	33016	800-342-5737	305-823-5410	691
Select Medical Corp 4714 Gettysburg Rd	Mechanicsburg	PA	17055	888-735-6332	717-972-1100	462
Select Portfolio Management Inc 120 Vantis	Aliso Viejo	CA	92656	800-445-9822	949-975-7900	401
Select Portfolio Servicing Inc 3815 SW Temple	Salt Lake City	UT	84115	800-258-8602		216
Select Staffing 3820 State St	Santa Barbara	CA	93105	800-688-6162	805-882-2200	719
Select-A-Ticket Inc 25 Rt 23 S	Riverdale	NJ	07457	800-735-3288	973-839-6100	748
Selected Funds PO Box 8243	Boston	MA	02266	800-243-1575		527
Selected Independent Funeral Homes 500 Lake Cook Rd Ste 205	Deerfield	IL	60015	800-323-4219	847-236-9401	48-4
Selectica Inc 2121 S. El Camino Rl 10th Fl *NASDAQ: SLTC*	San Mateo	CA	94403	877-712-9560	650-532-1500	180-1
Selective Enterprises Inc 10701 Texland Blvd	Charlotte	NC	28273	800-334-1207	704-588-3310	361
Selective Insurance Group Inc 40 Wantage Ave *NASDAQ: SIGI*	Branchville	NJ	07890	800-777-9656	973-948-3000	360-4
Selective Service System 1515 Wilson Blvd	Arlington	VA	22209	888-655-1825	847-688-6888	340-18
Selective Service System Regional Offices						
Region 1 PO Box 94638	Palatine	IL	60094	888-655-1825	847-688-6888	340-18
Region 2 PO Box 94638	Palatine	IL	60094	888-655-1825	847-688-6888	340-18
Select-O-Hits Inc 1981 Fletcher Creek Dr	Memphis	TN	38133	800-346-0723	901-388-1190	522
Selectpath Benefits & Financial Inc 310-700 Richmond St	London	ON	N6A5C7	888-327-5777	519-675-1177	390
Selectquote Insurance Services 595 Market St 10th Fl	San Francisco	CA	94105	800-670-3213	415-543-7338	390
Selee Corp 700 Shepherd St	Hendersonville	NC	28792	800-842-3818	828-697-2411	143
SELEX Inc 11300 W 89th St	Overland Park	KS	66214	800-765-0861	913-495-2600	528
Self Magazine 4 Times Sq	New York	NY	10036	800-274-6111	212-286-2860	456-11
Self Opportunity Inc 808 Office Park Cir	Lewisville	TX	75057	800-594-7036	214-222-1500	196
Self Storage Assn (SSA) 1900 N Beauregard St Ste 450	Alexandria	VA	22311	888-735-3784	703-575-8000	48-21
Self-Employed America Magazine PO Box 241	Annapolis Junction	MD	20701	800-649-6273		456-5
Selfhelp Community Services Inc 520 Eigth Ave 5th Fl	New York	NY	10018	866-735-1234		363
Self-Seal Container Corp 401 E Fourth St	Bridgeport	PA	19405	800-334-1428	610-275-2300	124
Selkirk College 301 Frank Beinder Way	Castlegar	BC	V1N4L3	888-953-1133	250-365-7292	167
Sell My Timeshare Now LLC 383 Central Ave Ste 260	Dover	NH	03820	877-815-4227	603-516-0200	387
Sellars 6565 N 60th St	Milwaukee	WI	53223	800-237-8454	414-353-5650	742-6
Selling Power Magazine 1140 International Pkwy	Fredericksburg	VA	22406	800-752-7355	540-752-7000	456-5
Selling Source LLC 325 E Warm Springs Rd Ste 200	Las Vegas	NV	89119	800-251-6147	702-407-0707	196
Sellstrom Manufacturing Co 2050 Hammond Dr	Schaumburg	IL	60173	800-323-7402	847-358-2000	575
Selma-Dallas County Chamber of Commerce 912 Selma Ave	Selma	AL	36701	800-457-3562	334-875-7241	138
SEM (Society for Experimental Mechanics Inc) 7 School St	Bethel	CT	06801	800-627-8258	203-790-6373	48-19
SEM (Society for Ethnomusicology) Indiana University 1165 E 3rd St Morrison Hall 005	Bloomington	IN	47405	800-933-9330	812-855-6672	47-4
SEMA Equipment Inc 11555 Hwy 60 Blvd	Wanamingo	MN	55983	800-569-1377	507-824-2256	276
Semasys Inc 702 Ashland St *Cust Svc	Houston	TX	77007	800-231-1425*	713-869-8331	288
SEMCO ENERGY Gas Co 1411 Third St Ste A	Port Huron	MI	48060	800-624-2019		579
Semiconductor Equipment & Materials International 3081 Zenker Rd	San Jose	CA	95134	877-746-7788	408-943-6900	48-19
Seminole Casino Hollywood 4150 N State Rd 7	Hollywood	FL	33021	866-222-7466	954-961-3220	132
Seminole Casino Immokalee 506 S First St	Immokalee	FL	34142	800-218-0007		132
Seminole County Convention & Visitors Bureau 1515 International Pkwy Ste 1013	Lake Mary	FL	32746	800-800-7832	407-665-2900	208
Seminole Feed 335 NE Watula Ave PO Box 940	Ocala	FL	34470	800-683-1881	352-732-4143	446
Seminole Hard Rock Hotel & Casino Hollywood 1 Seminole Way	Hollywood	FL	33314	888-236-4848	866-502-7529	667
Seminole Hard Rock Hotel & Casino Tampa (SHRH & C) 5223 N Orient Rd *General	Tampa	FL	33610	866-388-4263*	813-627-7625	132
Seminole Herald PO Box 1667	Sanford	FL	32772	800-955-8770	407-322-2611	531-2
Seminole State College 2701 Boren Blvd PO Box 351	Sanford	FL	32773	877-738-6365	405-382-9950	161
Seminole Towne Ctr 200 Towne Ctr Cir	Sanford	FL	32771	877-746-6642	407-323-2262	459
Semling-Menke Company Inc PO Box 378	Merrill	WI	54452	800-333-2206	715-536-9411	238
Semonin Realtors 4967 US Hwy 42 Ste 200	Louisville	KY	40222	800-548-1650	502-425-4760	650
Sempra Energy Corp 101 Ash St *NYSE: SRE*	San Diego	CA	92101	800-411-7343	619-696-2000	360-5
Senate House State Historic Site 296 Fair St	Kingston	NY	12401	800-456-2267	845-338-2786	564
Senate Luxury Suites 900 SW Tyler St	Topeka	KS	66612	800-488-3188	785-233-5050	379
Senator Inn & Spa of Augusta 284 Western Ave	Augusta	ME	04330	877-772-2224	207-622-8800	705
SENCO Products Inc 4270 Ivy Pt Blvd *Tech Supp	Cincinnati	OH	45245	800-543-4596*		757
Sendec Corp 72 Perinton Pkwy	Fairport	NY	14450	800-295-8000	585-425-3390	205
Sendmail Inc 6475 Christie Ave Ste 350	Emeryville	CA	94608	888-594-3150	510-594-5400	180-7
Sen-Dure Products Inc 6785 NW 17th Ave	Fort Lauderdale	FL	33309	800-394-5112	954-973-1260	90
Seneca Consulting Group Inc 111 Smithtown Byp Ste 112	Hauppauge	NY	11788	866-442-2472	631-577-4092	465
Seneca Fouts Memorial State Natural Area Wygant Trail	Hood River	OR	97014	800-551-6949		564
Seneca Niagara Casino 310 Fourth St	Niagara Falls	NY	14303	877-873-6322	716-299-1100	132
Seneca Resources Corp 1201 Louisiana St Ste 400	Houston	TX	77002	800-365-3234	713-654-2600	535
Seneca Tank Inc 5585 NE 16th St	Des Moines	IA	50313	800-362-2910	515-262-5900	56
Senergy Petroleum LLC 622 S 56th Ave	Phoenix	AZ	85043	800-964-0076	602-272-6795	578
Senga Engineering 1525 E Warner Ave	Santa Ana	CA	92705	877-878-8159	714-549-8011	263
Senior Aerospace Ketema Div 790 Greenfield Dr	El Cajon	CA	92021	800-669-6820	619-442-3451	21
Senior Alternatives For Living 26211 Central Park Blvd	Southfield	MI	48076	800-350-0770		5
Senior Corps 1201 New York Ave NW	Washington	DC	20525	800-833-3722	202-606-5000	199
Senior Housing Properties Trust 255 Washington St *NYSE: SNH*	Newton	MA	02458	866-511-5038	617-796-8350	653
Senior Market Sales Inc (SMS) 8420 W Dodge Rd 5th Fl	Omaha	NE	68114	800-786-5566	402-397-3311	390
Senior Marketing Specialist 801 Gray Oak Dr	Columbia	MO	65201	800-689-2800		197
Senior Settlements LLC 1000 S Lenola Rd Bldg 1 Ste 202	Maple Shade	NJ	08052	800-834-0628	856-235-2133	794
Senior Softball USA 2701 K St Ste 101A	Sacramento	CA	95816	888-244-9499	916-326-5303	47-22
Senior Whole Health LLC (SWH) 58 Charles St	Cambridge	MA	02141	888-794-7268	617-494-5353	353
Senior-Living.com Inc 8521 Leesburg Pk Ste 310	Vienna	VA	22182	866-342-4297		387
Seniorsplus 8 Falcon Rd	Lewiston	ME	04243	800-427-1241	207-795-4010	670
Sennheiser Electronics Corp 1 Enterprise Dr	Old Lyme	CT	06371	877-736-6434	860-434-9190	248
Seno Jewelry LLC 259 W 30th St 10th Fl	New York	NY	10001	888-468-0888		411
Sensidyne Inc 16333 Bay Vista Dr	Clearwater	FL	33760	800-451-9444	727-530-3602	203
Sensient Technologies Corp 777 E Wisconsin Ave *NYSE: SXT*	Milwaukee	WI	53202	800-558-9892	414-271-6755	297-15
Sensitech Inc 800 Cummings Ctr Ste 258x	Beverly	MA	01915	800-843-8367	978-927-7033	173
Sensormatic Electronics Corp 6600 Congress Ave	Boca Raton	FL	33487	800-327-1765	561-912-6000	690
SensorMedics Corp 22745 Savi Ranch Pkwy	Yorba Linda	CA	92887	800-231-2466	714-283-2228	252
SensoryEffects Flavor Co 231 Rock Industrial Park Dr	Bridgeton	MO	63044	800-422-5444	314-291-5444	297-37

Name / Address	City	State	Zip	Toll-Free	Phone	Class
Sensus USA Inc 8601 Six Forks Rd Stes 300 & 700	Raleigh	NC	27615	**800-638-3748**	919-845-4000	203
Sentara Careplex Hospital 3000 Coliseum Dr	Hampton	VA	23666	**800-736-8272**	757-736-1000	374-3
Sentara Obici Hospital 2800 Godwin Blvd	Suffolk	VA	23434	**800-736-8272**	757-934-4000	374-3
Sentara Virginia Beach General Hospital 1060 First Colonial Rd	Virginia Beach	VA	23454	**800-736-8272**	757-395-8000	374-3
Sentient Jet LLC 100 Grossman Dr Ste 400	Braintree	MA	02184	**866-602-0044**	781-763-0200	13
Sentinel Bldg Systems Inc 237 S Fourth St PO Box 348	Albion	NE	68620	**800-327-0790**	402-395-5076	308
Sentinel Hotel 614 SW 11th Ave	Portland	OR	97205	**888-246-5631**	503-224-3400	379
Sentinel Power Services Inc 7517 E Pine St	Tulsa	OK	74115	**800-831-9550**	918-359-0350	531-3
Sentinel Process 3265 Sunset Ln	Hatboro	PA	19040	**800-345-3569**	919-462-7108	331
Sentinel Systems Corp 1620 Kipling St	Lakewood	CO	80215	**800-456-9955**	303-242-2000	531-3
Sentinel, The 300 W Sixth St	Hanford	CA	93230	**800-582-0471**	559-582-0471	531-2
Senton Printing & Packaging Inc 1669 Oxford St E	London	ON	N5V2Z5	**800-445-9808**	519-455-5500	626
Sentran LLC 4355 E Lowell St Ste F	Ontario	CA	91761	**888-545-8988**	909-605-1544	362
Sentry Alarm Systems of America Inc 8 Thomas Owens Way	Monterey	CA	93940	**800-424-7773**	831-375-2727	691
Sentry Group 900 Linden Ave *Cust Svc	Rochester	NY	14625	**800-828-1438***	585-381-4900	690
Sentry Insurance Co 2 Technology Park Dr	Westford	MA	01886	**800-373-6879**		391-4
Sentry Life Insurance Co 1800 N Pt Dr	Stevens Point	WI	54481	**800-373-6879**	715-346-6000	391-2
Sentry Security LLC 339 Egidi Dr	Wheeling	IL	60090	**888-272-7080**	847-353-7200	691
Sentry Technology Corp 1881 Lakeland Ave *OTC: SKVY*	Ronkonkoma	NY	11779	**800-645-4224**		690
Sentry Watch Inc 1705 Holbrook St	Greensboro	NC	27403	**800-632-4961**	336-292-6468	691
Senvoy LLC 115 SE Yamhill St	Portland	OR	97214	**866-373-6869**	503-234-7722	312
SEOP Inc 1720 E Garry St Ste 103	Santa Ana	CA	92705	**877-231-1557**		7
sephora.com Inc 525 Market St 1st Market Twr 32nd Fl *Cust Svc	San Francisco	CA	94105	**877-737-4672***	415-284-3300	217
SEPLSO (Southeastern Library System of Oklahoma) 401 N Second St	McAlester	OK	74501	**800-215-6494**	918-426-0456	434-3
SEPM (Society for Sedimentary Geology) 4111 S Darlington Ste 100	Tulsa	OK	74135	**800-865-9765**	918-610-3361	48-19
Sepp Leaf Products Inc 381 Pk Ave S Ste 1301	New York	NY	10016	**800-971-7377**	212-683-2840	43
Septagon Construction 113 E Third St	Sedalia	MO	65301	**800-733-5999**	660-827-2115	188
Sequachee Valley Electric Co-op 512 Cedar Ave PO Box 31	South Pittsburg	TN	37380	**800-923-2203**	423-837-8605	247
Sequatchie Concrete Service Inc 406 Cedar Ave	South Pittsburg	TN	37380	**800-824-0824**	423-837-7913	185
Sequence Controls Inc 150 Rosamond St	Carleton	ON	K7C1V2	**800-663-1833**	613-257-7356	205
Sequenom Inc 3595 John Hopkins Ct *NASDAQ: SQNM*	San Diego	CA	92121	**877-821-7266**	858-202-9000	84
Sequoia Fund Inc 767 Fifth Ave Ste 4701	New York	NY	10153	**800-686-6884**	212-832-5280	527
Sequoyah Bay State Park 6237 E 100th St N	Wagoner	OK	74467	**800-622-6317**	918-683-0878	564
SeraCare Life Sciences Inc 37 Birch St *NASDAQ: SRLS*	Milford	MA	01757	**800-676-1881**	508-244-6400	88
Serapid Inc 34100 Mound Rd	Sterling Heights	MI	48310	**800-663-4514**	586-274-0774	755
Serco Inc 1818 Library St Ste 1000	Reston	VA	20190	**866-628-6458**	703-939-6000	24
SERENA Software Inc 2345 NW Amberbrook Dr Ste 200	Hillsboro	OR	97006	**800-457-3736**	650-481-3400	180-1
Serengeti Eyewear Inc 9200 Cody St *Cust Svc	Overland Park	KS	66214	**800-423-3537***	913-752-3400	541
Serengeti Systems Inc 1108 Lavaca St Ste 120 PO Box 431	Austin	TX	78701	**800-634-3122**	512-345-2211	180-12
Serenity Lane 616 E 16th Ave	Eugene	OR	97401	**800-543-9905**	541-687-1110	724
Sererra Consulting Group LLC 5430 Trabuco Rd Ste 150	Irvine	CA	92620	**877-276-3774**		198
Serfilco Ltd 2900 MacArthur Blvd	Northbrook	IL	60062	**800-323-5431**	847-559-1777	638
SERI (Society for Ecological Restoration International) 1017 O St NW	Washington	DC	20001	**866-895-4735**	202-299-9518	47-13
Sericol Inc 1101 W Cambridge Dr	Kansas City	KS	66103	**800-737-4265**	913-342-4060	388
Serrano Hotel 405 Taylor St	San Francisco	CA	94102	**866-575-9941**	415-885-2500	379
Serta Mattress/AW Inc 8415 ARdmore Rd	Landover	MD	20785	**888-557-3782**	301-322-1000	470
Serti Informatique Inc 7555 Beclard St	Montreal	QC	H1J2S5	**800-361-6615**	514-493-1909	198
Sertoma International 1912 E Meyer Blvd	Kansas City	MO	64132	**800-593-5646**	816-333-8300	47-5
Serv-a-lite Products Inc 3451 Morton Dr	East Moline	IL	61244	**800-800-4900**		351
Servall Co 6761 E Ten Mile Rd	Center Line	MI	48015	**800-856-9874**	586-754-9985	37
SERVE 5900 Summit Ave Ste 201	Browns Summit	NC	27214	**800-755-3277**	336-315-7400	666
Serve You Custom Prescription Management 10201 Innovation Dr Ste 600	Milwaukee	WI	53226	**888-243-6890**	414-410-8100	585
Server Products Inc 3601 Pleasant Hill Rd PO Box 98	Richfield	WI	53076	**800-558-8722**	262-628-5600	299
Server Technology Inc 1040 Sandhill Dr	Reno	NV	89521	**800-835-1515**	775-284-2000	178
Service by Air Inc 222 Crossways Pk Dr	Woodbury	NY	11797	**800-243-5545**		12
Service Communications Inc 10675 Willows Rd NE Ste 100	Redmond	WA	98052	**800-488-0468**		181
Service Construction Supply Inc PO Box 13405	Birmingham	AL	35202	**866-729-4968**	205-252-3158	193-3
Service Electric Cable TV & Communications 2260 Ave A	Bethlehem	PA	18017	**800-232-9100**	610-865-9100	115
Service Employees International Union 1800 Massachusetts Ave NW	Washington	DC	20036	**800-424-8592**	202-730-7000	414
Service Graphics LLC 8350 Allison Ave	Indianapolis	IN	46268	**800-884-9876**	317-471-8246	685
Service Ideas Inc 2354 Ventura Dr	Woodbury	MN	55125	**800-328-4493**	651-730-8800	301
Service Intelligence Inc 1061 Red Venture Dr Ste 175	Fort Mill	SC	29707	**800-263-2980**		462
Service King Collision Repair Centers 808 S Central Expy	Richardson	TX	75080	**866-730-5464**	972-960-7595	61-4
Service Spring Corp 4370 Moline Martin Rd	Millbury	OH	43447	**800-752-8522**	419-838-6081	716
Service Steel Aerospace Corp 4609 70th St E	Fife	WA	98424	**800-426-9794**		491
ServiceMaster Clean 3839 Forrest Hill Irene Rd *General	Memphis	TN	38125	**844-319-5401***	800-245-4622	151
Servo Products Co 34940 Lakeland Blvd	Eastlake	OH	44095	**800-521-7359**	440-942-9999	454
Servpro Industries Inc 801 Industrial Blvd	Gallatin	TN	37066	**800-826-9586**	615-451-0600	151
SESAC Inc 55 Music Sq E	Nashville	TN	37203	**800-826-9996**	615-320-0055	47-4
Sesame Software Inc File 74625 P.O. Box 60000	San Francisco	CA	94160	**866-474-7575**		262
Sesquicentennial State Park 9564 Two Notch Rd	Columbia	SC	29223	**888-245-9300**	803-788-2706	564
SESRC (Social & Economic Sciences Research Ctr) *Washington State University* Wilson Hall Rm 133 PO Box 644014	Pullman	WA	99164	**800-932-5393**	509-335-1511	666
SETEL UC 720 Cool Springs Blvd Ste 520	Franklin	TN	37067	**800-743-1340**	615-874-6000	785
Sethness Products Co 3422 W Touhy Ave	Lincolnwood	IL	60712	**888-772-1880**	847-329-2080	297-15
Setina Manufacturing Company Inc 2926 Yelm Hwy Se	Olympia	WA	98501	**800-426-2627**		393
Seton Hall University 400 S Orange Ave	South Orange	NJ	07079	**800-992-4723**	973-761-9332	167
Seton Hall University Immaculate Conception Seminary 400 S Orange Ave	South Orange	NJ	07079	**800-843-4255**	973-761-9575	168-3
Seton Hill University 1 Seton Hill Dr	Greensburg	PA	15601	**800-826-6234**	724-838-4255	167
Seton Hotel 144 E 40th St	New York	NY	10016	**866-697-3866**	212-889-5301	462
Seton Medical Ctr 1900 Sullivan Ave	Daly City	CA	94015	**800-371-2176**	650-992-4000	374-3
Setra Systems Inc 159 Swanson Rd	Boxborough	MA	01719	**800-257-3872**	978-263-1400	471
Settle & Pou PC 3333 Lee Pkwy 8th Fl	Dallas	TX	75219	**800-538-4661**	214-520-3300	428
Settlers Life Insurance Co 1969 Lee Hwy	Bristol	VA	24201	**800-523-2650**	276-645-4300	391-2
Seva Foundation 1786 Fifth St	Berkeley	CA	94710	**877-764-7382**	510-845-7382	306
Seven Falls Co 2850 S Cheyenne Canyon Rd	Colorado Springs	CO	80906	**855-923-7272**		49-4
Seven Oaks Capital Assoc LLC 7854 Anselmo Ln PO Box 82360	Baton Rouge	LA	70810	**800-511-4588**	225-757-1919	274
Seven Pines National Cemetery 400 E Williamsburg Rd	Sandston	VA	23150	**800-535-1117**	804-795-2031	135
Seven Springs Mountain Resort 777 Waterwheel Dr	Champion	PA	15622	**800-452-2223**	814-352-7777	667
Seventh Generation Inc 60 Lake St	Burlington	VT	05401	**800-456-1191**	802-658-3773	150
Seventh-day Adventist World Church 12501 Old Columbia Pike	Silver Spring	MD	20904	**800-226-1119**	301-680-6000	47-20
Severance Hall 11001 Euclid Ave	Cleveland	OH	44106	**800-686-1141**	216-231-7300	571
Severn Bancorp Inc 200 Westgate Cir Ste 200 *NASDAQ: SVBI*	Annapolis	MD	21401	**800-752-5854**	410-260-2000	69
Seward County Community College 1801 N Campus Ave PO Box 1137	Liberal	KS	67905	**800-373-9951**	620-624-1951	161
Seward Motor Freight Inc PO Box 126	Seward	NE	68434	**800-786-4468**	402-643-4503	778
Sewing Source Inc, The PO Box 639	Spring Hope	NC	27882	**800-849-6945**	252-478-3900	361
Sex Addicts Anonymous (SAA) PO Box 70949	Houston	TX	77270	**800-477-8191**	713-869-4902	47-21
Sexaholics Anonymous (SA) PO Box 3565	Brentwood	TN	37024	**866-424-8777**	615-370-6062	47-21
Seyferth & Associates Inc 40 Monroe Ctr NW	Grand Rapids	MI	49503	**800-435-9539**	616-776-3511	633
Seymour Johnson Air Force Base 1510 Wright Bros Ave	Seymour Johnson AFB	NC	27531	**800-525-0102**	919-722-0027	496-1
Seymour Mfg Co Inc PO Box 248	Seymour	IN	47274	**800-815-7253**	812-522-2900	756

Name / Address	City	State	ZIP	Toll-Free	Phone	Class
Seymour of Sycamore Inc 917 Crosby Ave	Sycamore	IL	60178	**800-435-4482**	815-895-9101	549
Seyon Lodge State Park 1 National Life Dr	Vermont	VT	05620	**888-409-7579**	802-584-3829	564
SFB (Security Federal Bank) 238 Richland Ave W	Aiken	SC	29801	**866-851-3000**	803-641-3000	70
SFC (Sandridge Food Corp) 133 Commerce Dr	Medina	OH	44256	**800-672-2523**	330-725-2348	297-33
SFC Graphics 110 E Woodruff Ave	Toledo	OH	43604	**800-537-1130**	419-255-1283	699
SFE Investment Counsel Inc 801 S Figueroa St Ste 2100	Los Angeles	CA	90017	**800-445-6320**	213-612-0220	688
SFPA (Southern Forest Products Assn) 6660 Riverside Dr Ste 212	Metairie	LA	70065	**866-574-4155**	504-443-4464	47-2
SFS intec Inc Spring St & Van Reed Rd	Wyomissing	PA	19610	**800-234-4533**	610-376-5751	620
SFSP (Society of Financial Service Professionals) 19 Campus Blvd Ste 100	Newtown Square	PA	19073	**800-392-6900**	610-526-2500	48-9
SGH (Sharp Grossmont Hospital) 5555 Grossmont Ctr Dr	La Mesa	CA	91942	**800-827-4277**	619-740-6000	374-3
SGH (Southwest General Hospital) 7400 Barlite Blvd	San Antonio	TX	78224	**877-898-6080**	210-921-2000	374-3
SGH Golf Inc 6805 Mt Vernon Ave	Cincinnati	OH	45227	**800-284-8884**	513-984-0414	769
SGIA (Specialty Graphic Imaging Assn) 10015 Main St	Fairfax	VA	22031	**888-385-3588**	703-385-1335	48-16
SGL Carbon LLC 307 Jamestown Rd	Morganton	NC	28655	**800-828-6601**	828-437-3221	126
SGNA (Society of Gastroenterology Nurses & Assoc Inc) 401 N Michigan Ave	Chicago	IL	60611	**800-245-7462**	312-321-5165	48-8
SGS Canada Inc 6490 Vipond Dr *General	Mississauga	ON	L5T1W8	**877-747-7658***	905-364-3757	740
SGS North America Inc 201 State Rt 17 N	Rutherford	NJ	07070	**800-645-5227**	201-508-3000	360-3
SH (Shive-Hattery Inc) 316 Second St SE Ste 500 PO Box 1599	Cedar Rapids	IA	52406	**800-798-0227**	319-362-0313	263
Shackford Head State Park 106 Hogan Ave	Bangor	ME	04401	**800-400-6856**	207-941-4014	564
Shade Systems Inc 4150 Sw 19th St	Ocala	FL	34474	**800-609-6066**	352-237-0135	296
Shades of Green on Walt Disney World Resort 1950 W Magnolia Palm Dr	Lake Buena Vista	FL	32830	**888-593-2242**	407-824-3400	379
Shadin LP 6831 Oxford St	St Louis Park	MN	55426	**800-328-0584**	952-927-6500	528
Shadow Mountain Resort & Club 45-750 San Luis Rey	Palm Desert	CA	92260	**800-472-3713**	760-346-6123	667
Shadyside Nursing & Rehabilitation Ctr 5609 Fifth Ave	Pittsburgh	PA	15232	**800-366-1232**	412-362-3500	374-6
Shafer's Tour & Charter 500 N St	Endicott	NY	13760	**800-287-8986**	607-797-2006	106
Shaffer Trucking Inc 49 E Main St PO Box 418 *Cust Svc	New Kingstown	PA	17072	**800-742-3337***	402-475-9521	778
Shaffstall Corp 8531 Bash St	Indianapolis	IN	46250	**800-357-6250**	317-842-2077	175-8
Shaker Consulting Group Inc 3201 Entp Pkwy Ste 360	Cleveland	OH	44122	**888-485-7633**		462
Shaker Group Inc, The 862 Albany Shaker Rd	Latham	NY	12110	**800-267-0314**	518-786-9286	448
Shaker Recruitment Adv & Communications 1100 Lake St 3rd Fl	Oak Park	IL	60301	**800-323-5170**	708-383-5320	4
Shaker Village of Pleasant Hill 3501 Lexington Rd	Harrodsburg	KY	40330	**800-734-5611**	859-734-5411	519
Shakespeare Fishing Tackle Co 7 Science Ct *Cust Svc	Columbia	SC	29203	**800-466-5643***	803-754-7000	708
Shakespeare Monofilaments & Specialty Polymers 6111 Shakespeare Rd	Columbia	SC	29223	**800-845-2110**	803-754-7011	607
Shakespeare Theatre 516 Eigth St SE	Washington	DC	20003	**877-487-8849**	202-547-3230	572-4
Shaklee Corp 4747 Willow Rd	Pleasanton	CA	94588	**800-742-5533**	925-924-2000	366
Shambaugh & Son LP 7614 Opportunity Dr	Fort Wayne	IN	46825	**866-890-7794**	260-487-7777	191-10
Shambhala Mountain Ctr 151 Shambhala Wy	Red Feather Lakes	CO	80545	**888-788-7221**	970-881-2184	671
Shamokin Filler Company Inc PO Box 568	Shamokin	PA	17872	**800-577-8008**	570-644-0437	192
Shamrock Communications Inc 149 Penn Ave	Scranton	PA	18503	**800-228-4637**	570-348-9100	640
Shamrock Foods 3900 E Camelback Rd Ste 300	Phoenix	AZ	85018	**800-289-3663**	602-477-2500	297-27
Shamrock Scientific Specialty Systems Inc 34 Davis Dr	Bellwood	IL	60104	**800-323-0249**	708-547-9005	413
Shamrock Steel Sales Inc 238 W County Rd S	Odessa	TX	79763	**800-299-2317**	432-337-2317	491
Shamrock Technologies Inc Foot Of Pacific St	Newark	NJ	07114	**800-349-1822**	973-242-2999	145
Shanahan's LP 8400-124 St	Surrey	BC	V3W6K1	**888-591-5999**	604-591-5111	498
Shands Hospital at the University of Florida 1600 SW Archer Rd	Gainesville	FL	32610	**855-483-7546**	352-265-0111	374-3
Shane Co 9790 E Arapahoe Rd	Greenwood Village	CO	80112	**866-467-4263**		410
Shank Wealth Management LLC 2627 Chestnut Ridge Dr Ste 110	Kingwood	TX	77339	**888-359-3133**	281-359-3133	688
Shanks Extracts Inc 350 Richardson Dr	Lancaster	PA	17603	**800-346-3135**	717-393-4441	298-8
Shannon Diversified Inc 1190 N Del Rio Pl	Ontario	CA	91764	**800-794-2345**		103
Shannon Medical Ctr (SMC) 120 E Harris Ave	San Angelo	TX	76903	**800-368-1019**	325-653-6741	374-3
Shanty Creek Resort 5780 Shanty Creek Rd	Bellaire	MI	49615	**800-678-4111**	231-533-8621	667
Shape LLC 2105 Corporate Dr	Addison	IL	60101	**800-367-5811**	630-620-8394	765
Share Corp 7821 N Faulkner Rd	Milwaukee	WI	53224	**800-776-7192**	414-355-4000	150
Share Our Strength 1730 M St NW Ste 700	Washington	DC	20036	**800-969-4767**	202-393-2925	47-5
SHARE Pregnancy & Infant Loss Support Inc 402 Jackson St	Saint Charles	MO	63301	**800-821-6819**	636-947-6164	47-21
shared logic group inc, The 6904 Spring Vly Dr Ste 305	Holland	OH	43528	**877-865-0083**	419-865-0083	179
ShareSquared Inc 2155 Verdugo Blvd Ste 33	Montrose	CA	91020	**800-445-1279**		182
Sharetracker LLC 1480 E Hwy MM	Ashland	MO	65010	**866-977-7171**		465
Sharf Woodward & Associates Inc 5900 Sepulveda Blvd	Sherman Oaks	CA	91411	**877-482-6687**	818-989-2200	262
Shari's Restaurant & Pies 9400 SW Gemini Dr	Beaverton	OR	97008	**800-433-5334**	503-605-4299	668
Sharkey Howes & Javer Inc 720 S Colorado Blvd Ste 600 S Twr	Denver	CO	80246	**800-557-9380**	303-639-5100	196
Sharon Coating LLC 277 Sharpsville Ave	Sharon	PA	16146	**800-456-1794**	724-983-6464	308
Sharonville Convention Ctr 11355 Chester Rd	Sharonville	OH	45246	**800-294-3179**	513-771-7744	207
Sharp Bros Seed Co 1005 S Sycamore	Healy	KS	67850	**800-462-8483**	620-398-2231	692
Sharp Decisions Inc 1040 Ave of the A	New York	NY	10018	**800-742-7792**	212-481-5533	112
Sharp Electronics Corp 1 Sharp Plz	Mahwah	NJ	07430	**800-237-4277**	201-529-8200	51
Sharp Energy Inc 648 Ocean Hwy	Pocomoke City	MD	21851	**888-742-7740**		317
Sharp Grossmont Hospital (SGH) 5555 Grossmont Ctr Dr	La Mesa	CA	91942	**800-827-4277**	619-740-6000	374-3
Sharp Health Plan 4305 University Ave Ste 200	San Diego	CA	92105	**800-359-2002**	619-228-2300	391-3
Sharprint Silkscreen & Graphics Inc 4200 W Wrightwood Ave	Chicago	IL	60639	**888-800-5646**	773-862-9300	626
Shasta Beverages Inc 26901 Industrial Blvd	Hayward	CA	94545	**800-834-9980**	510-783-3200	79-2
Shattuck-Saint Mary's School 1000 Shumway Ave PO Box 218	Faribault	MN	55021	**800-421-2724**	507-333-1616	621
Shaw Air Force Base 517 Lance Ave Ste 106	Shaw AFB	SC	29152	**800-235-7776**	803-895-2019	496-1
Shaw Communications Inc 630 Third Ave SW *TSE: SJR/B*	Calgary	AB	T2P4L4	**888-472-2222**	403-750-4500	115
Shaw Industries Inc 616 E Walnut Ave	Dalton	GA	30722	**800-441-7429**		130
Shaw Pipeline Services Inc 4250 N Sam Houston Pkwy E Ste 180	Houston	TX	77032	**866-912-5314**	832-601-0850	538
Shaw University 118 E S St *Admissions	Raleigh	NC	27601	**800-214-6683***	919-546-8275	167
Shawano Country Chamber of Commerce 1263 S Main St	Shawano	WI	54166	**800-235-8528**	715-524-2139	138
ShawCor Ltd 25 Bethridge Rd *TSE: SCL/A*	Toronto	ON	M9W1M7	**855-744-5789**	416-743-7111	536
Shawnee Community College 8364 Shawnee College Rd	Ullin	IL	62992	**800-481-2242**	618-634-3200	161
Shawnee Milling Company Inc 201 S Broadway PO Box 1567	Shawnee	OK	74802	**800-654-2600**	405-273-7000	297-23
Shawnee State University 940 Second St	Portsmouth	OH	45662	**800-959-2778**	740-351-3221	167
Shawnee Telephone Co PO Box 69	Equality	IL	62934	**800-461-3956**	618-276-4211	733
SHDR (Stanley Hunt DuPree & Rhine Inc) 7701 Airport Ctr Dr	Greensboro	NC	27409	**888-999-4701**	800-768-4873	195
Shea's Performing Arts Ctr 646 Main St	Buffalo	NY	14202	**866-341-5945**	716-847-1410	571
Sheaff Brock Investment Advisors LLC 10401 N Meridian St Ste 100	Indianapolis	IN	46290	**866-575-5700**	317-705-5700	401
Shealy Electrical Wholesalers Inc 422 Fairforest Way	Greenville	SC	29607	**800-868-5980**	864-242-6880	248
Shealy's Truck Ctr Inc 1340 Bluff Rd	Columbia	SC	29201	**800-951-8580**	803-771-0176	515
Shean Law Offices 1114 N College Ave	Bloomington	IN	47404	**877-743-2652**	812-332-3643	428
Sheboygan County Chamber of Commerce 621 S Eigth St	Sheboygan	WI	53081	**800-457-9497**	920-457-9491	138
Sheboygan Paint Company Inc 1439 N 25th St PO Box 417	Sheboygan	WI	53082	**800-773-7801**	920-458-2157	549
Sheboygan Press 632 Center Ave PO Box 358	Sheboygan	WI	53081	**800-686-3900**	920-457-7711	531-2
Shee Atika Inc 315 Lincoln St Ste 300	Sitka	AK	99835	**800-478-3534**	907-747-3534	112
Sheely's Furniture & Appliance Company Inc 11450 S Ave	North Lima	OH	44452	**877-549-9144**	330-549-3901	322
SheerVision Inc(NDA) 4030 Palos Verdes Dr N Ste 104	Rolling Hills Estates	CA	90274	**877-678-4274**	310-265-8918	543
Sheet Metal Workers International Assn (SMWIA) 1750 New York Ave NW 6th Fl	Washington	DC	20006	**800-251-7045**	202-783-5880	48-3
Sheetz Inc 5700 Sixth Ave	Altoona	PA	16602	**800-487-5444**	814-941-5106	206
Sheffield Metals International Inc 5467 Evergreen Pkwy	Sheffield Village	OH	44054	**800-283-5262**	440-934-8500	491
Shelburne Farms 1611 Harbor Rd	Shelburne	VT	05482	**800-286-6022**	802-985-8686	47-13
Shelburne Murray Hill 303 Lexington Ave	New York	NY	10016	**866-233-4642**	212-689-5200	379
Shelby County 612 Ct St	Harlan	IA	51537	**800-735-3942**	712-755-3831	338
Shelby County Chamber of Commerce 501 N Harrison St	Shelbyville	IN	46176	**800-318-4083**	317-398-6647	138

Name / Address	City	State	ZIP	Toll-Free	Phone	Class
Shelby County Office of Tourism 315 E Main St	Shelbyville	IL	62565	**800-874-3529**	217-774-2244	208
Shelby Elastics Inc 639 N Post Rd PO Box 2405	Shelby	NC	28150	**800-562-4507**	704-487-4301	742-5
Shelby Electric Co-op (SEC) 1355 IL-128 state PO Box 560	Shelbyville	IL	62565	**800-677-2612**	217-774-3986	247
Shelby Energy Co-op Inc 620 Old Finchville Rd	Shelbyville	KY	40065	**800-292-6585**	502-633-4420	247
Shelby Materials 157 E Rampart St PO Box 242	Shelbyville	IN	46176	**800-548-9516**		184
Shelby Williams Industries Inc 810 W Hwy 25/70 *General	Newport	TN	37821	**800-873-3252***	423-623-0031	320-3
Shelbyville Daily Union 100 W Main St	Shelbyville	IL	62565	**800-772-1213**	217-774-2161	531-2
Shelbyville-Bedford County Chamber of Commerce 100 N Cannon Blvd	Shelbyville	TN	37160	**888-662-2525**	931-684-3482	138
Shelbyville-Shelby County Public Library 57 W Broadway	Shelbyville	IN	46176	**866-466-4438**	317-398-7121	434-3
Sheldahl Inc 1150 Sheldahl Rd	Northfield	MN	55057	**800-927-3580**	507-663-8000	694
Sheldon Jackson Museum 104 College Dr	Sitka	AK	99835	**800-587-0430**	907-747-8981	519
Sheldon Laboratory Systems Inc 102 Kirk St PO Box 836	Crystal Springs	MS	39059	**800-531-7604**	601-892-2731	419
Shell Canada Ltd 400 Fourth Ave SW	Calgary	AB	T2P0J4	**877-656-3111**	403-691-3111	535
Shell Island Ocean Front Suites 2700 N Lumina Ave	Wrightsville Beach	NC	28480	**800-689-6765**	910-256-8696	705
Shell Lubricants 1000 Main 12th Fl *Cust Svc	Houston	TX	77002	**888-743-5586***	713-241-6161	540
Shell Oil Co 910 Louisanna St	Houston	TX	77002	**888-467-4355**	713-241-6161	535
Shell Point Village 15101 Shell Pt Blvd *Mktg	Fort Myers	FL	33908	**800-780-1131***	239-466-1131	670
Shelly Automotive Group *Irvine BMW* 9881 Research Dr	Irvine	CA	92618	**888-853-7429**		56
SheltAir Aviation Services Fort Lauderdale 4860 NE 12th Ave	Fort Lauderdale	FL	33334	**800-700-2210**	954-771-2210	62
ShelterLogic Corp 150 Callendar Rd	Watertown	CT	06795	**800-932-9344**	860-945-6442	104
Shelton State Community College 9500 Old Greensboro Rd	Tuscaloosa	AL	35405	**877-211-7722**	205-391-2211	161
Shelton-Mason County Chamber of Commerce 215 W Railroad Ave PO Box 2389	Shelton	WA	98584	**800-576-2021**	360-426-2021	138
Shelving Inc 32 S Squirrel Rd	Auburn Hills	MI	48326	**800-637-9508**	248-852-8600	361
Shenandoah Life Insurance Co 2301 Brambleton Ave	Roanoke	VA	24015	**800-848-5433**	540-985-4400	391-2
Shenandoah National Park 3655 US Hwy 211E	Luray	VA	22835	**800-732-0911**	540-999-3500	563
Shenandoah Telecommunications Co 500 Shentel Way *NASDAQ: SHEN*	Edinburg	VA	22824	**800-743-6835**	540-984-5224	360-3
Shenandoah University 1460 University Dr	Winchester	VA	22601	**800-432-2266**	540-665-4581	167
Shenandoah Valley Westminster-Canterbury 300 Westminster-Canterbury Dr	Winchester	VA	22603	**800-492-9463**	540-665-5914	670
Shenango Valley Chamber of Commerce 41 Chestnut St	Sharon	PA	16146	**800-732-0993**	724-981-5880	138
Shenvalee Golf Resort 9660 Fairway Dr	New Market	VA	22844	**888-339-3181**	540-740-3181	667
Shepard Niles 220 N Genesee St	Montour Falls	NY	14865	**800-481-2260**	607-535-7111	469
Shephard's Beach Resort 619 S Gulfview Blvd	Clearwater Beach	FL	33767	**800-237-8477**	727-441-6875	379
Shepherd Caster Corp 203 Kerth St	Saint Joseph	MI	49085	**800-253-0868**	269-983-7351	350
Shepherd CE Company Inc 2221 Canada Dry St	Houston	TX	77023	**800-324-6733**	713-924-4300	599
Shepherd Electric Supply 7401 Pulaski Hwy *Sales	Baltimore	MD	21237	**800-253-1777***	410-866-6000	248
Shepherd of the Hills Homestead & Outdoor Theatre 5586 W Hwy 76	Branson	MO	65616	**800-653-6288**	417-334-4191	571
Shepherd University 301 N King St	Shepherdstown	WV	25443	**800-344-5231**	304-876-5000	167
Shepherdsville-Bullitt County Tourist & Convention Commission 395 Paroquet Springs Dr	Shepherdsville	KY	40165	**800-526-2068**	502-543-8687	208
Sheplers Inc 6501 W Kellogg Dr	Wichita	KS	67209	**888-835-4004**		156-5
Sheppard Air Force Base 419 G Ave Ste 3	Sheppard AFB	TX	76311	**877-676-1847**	940-676-2511	496-1
Sheppard Motors 2300 W Seventh Ave *Sales	Eugene	OR	97402	**877-362-1865***	541-343-8811	56
Sheppard Pratt Health System (SPHS) 6501 N Charles St	Baltimore	MD	21285	**800-627-0330**	410-938-3000	374-5
Sheraton Agoura Hills Hotel 30100 Agoura Rd	Agoura Hills	CA	91301	**866-716-8134**	818-707-1220	705
Sheraton Delfina Santa Monica 530 W Pico Blvd	Santa Monica	CA	90405	**888-625-4988**	310-399-9344	379
Sheraton Fishermans Wharf (San Francisco, CA) 2500 Mason St	San Francisco	CA	94133	**866-716-8134**	415-362-5500	705
Sheraton Gateway Hotel Los Angeles 6101 W Century Blvd	Los Angeles	CA	90045	**888-627-7104**	310-642-1111	379
Sheraton Gunter Hotel 205 E Houston St	San Antonio	TX	78205	**866-716-8134**	210-227-3241	705
Sheraton Kauai Resort 2440 Hoonani Rd *Resv	Koloa	HI	96756	**800-325-3535***	808-742-1661	667
Sheraton Maui Resort 2605 Kaanapali Pkwy	Lahaina	HI	96761	**866-716-8109**	808-661-0031	667
Sheraton Phoenix Downtown Hotel 340 N Third St	Phoenix	AZ	85004	**866-716-8134**	602-262-2500	705
Sheraton Raleigh Hotel 421 S Salisbury St	Raleigh	NC	27601	**866-716-8134**	919-834-9900	705
Sheraton Safari Hotel & Suites 12205 S Apopka Vineland Rd	Orlando	FL	32836	**800-325-3535**	407-239-0444	705
Sheraton Sand Key Resort 1160 Gulf Blvd	Clearwater Beach	FL	33767	**800-456-7263**	727-595-1611	667
Sheraton Suites Calgary Eau Claire 255 Barclay Parade SW	Calgary	AB	T2P5C2	**866-716-8134**	403-266-7200	379
Sheraton Waikiki 2255 Kalakaua Ave	Honolulu	HI	96815	**800-325-3535**	808-922-4422	667
Sheraton Washington North Hotel 4095 Powder Mill Rd	Beltsville	MD	20705	**866-716-8134**	301-937-4422	705
Sheraton Wild Horse Pass Resort & Spa 5594 W Wild Horse Pass Blvd	Chandler	AZ	85226	**800-325-3535**	602-225-0100	667
Shercon Inc 6262 Katella Ave	Cypress	CA	90630	**888-227-5847**	714-548-3999	674
Sheridan College 3059 Coffeen Ave PO Box 1500	Sheridan	WY	82801	**800-913-9139**	307-674-6446	161
Gillette 300 W Sinclair St	Gillette	WY	82718	**800-913-9139**	307-686-0254	161
Sheridan County Chamber of Commerce 1517 E Fifth St	Sheridan	WY	82801	**800-453-3650**	307-672-2485	138
Sheridan Electric Co-op Inc PO Box 227	Medicine Lake	MT	59247	**888-472-1533**	406-789-2231	247
Sheridan Group 11311 McCormick Rd Ste 260	Hunt Valley	MD	21031	**800-352-2210**	410-785-7277	625
Sheridan Healthcare Inc 1613 NW 136th Ave Ste 200	Sunrise	FL	33323	**800-437-2672**		462
Sherman & Reilly Inc 400 W 33rd St *Sales	Chattanooga	TN	37401	**800-251-7780***	423-756-5300	469
Sherman Bros Trucking 32921 Diamond Hill Dr PO Box 706	Harrisburg	OR	97446	**800-547-8980**	541-995-7751	778
Sherpa Adventure Gear Inc 7857 S 180th St	Kent	WA	98032	**877-724-8735**	425-251-0760	156-6
Sherpa Digital Media Inc 509 Seaport Ct	Redwood City	CA	94063	**877-989-7794**		5
Sherritt International Corp 1133 Yonge St *TSE: S*	Toronto	ON	M4T2Y7	**800-704-6698**	416-924-4551	501
Sherrod Vans Inc 3151 Industrial Blvd	Waycross	GA	31503	**800-824-6333**		61-7
Sherry Matthews Inc 200 S Congress Ave	Austin	TX	78704	**877-478-4397**	512-478-4397	4
Sherry Mfg 3287 NW 65th St	Miami	FL	33147	**800-741-4750**	305-693-7000	154-3
Sherry-Netherland Hotel 781 Fifth Ave	New York	NY	10022	**877-743-7710**	212-355-2800	379
Sherwin-Williams Automotive Finishes 4440 Warrensville Ctr Rd	Warrensville Heights	OH	44128	**800-798-5872**	216-332-8330	549
Sherwood 2200 North Main St	Washington	PA	15301	**888-508-2583**	724-225-8000	787
Sherwood Oaks 100 Norman Dr	Cranberry Township	PA	16066	**800-642-2217**	724-776-8100	670
Sherwood Windows Ltd 37 Iron St	Toronto	ON	M9W5E3	**800-770-5256**	416-675-3262	350
Shetler Moving & Storage Inc 1253 E Diamond Ave	Evansville	IN	47711	**800-321-5069**	812-421-7750	778
SHI (Software House International) 290 Davidson Ave	Somerset	NJ	08873	**888-764-8888**		176
SHI Corp 35W Broadway Ste 104	Salt Lake City	UT	84101	**888-764-8888**		176
Shibuya Hoppmann Corp 13129 Airpark Dr Ste 120 *Cust Svc	Elkwood	VA	22718	**800-368-3582***	540-829-2564	546
Shick Tube Veyor Corp 4346 Clary Blvd	Kansas City	MO	64130	**877-744-2587**	816-861-7224	209
Shield Air Solutions Inc 3708 Greenhouse Rd	Houston	TX	77084	**800-237-2095**	281-944-4300	14
Shield Pack LLC 411 Downing Pines Rd	West Monroe	LA	71292	**800-551-5185**	318-387-4743	599
Shields Bag & Printing Co 1009 Rock Ave	Yakima	WA	98902	**800-541-8630**	509-248-7500	65
SHIFT Communications LLC 275 Washington St Ste 410	Newton	MA	02458	**800-494-8477**	617-779-1800	633
ShiftCentral Inc 210 John St Ste 100	Moncton	NB	E1C0B8	**866-551-5533**		5
Shilo Inn Hotel Salt Lake City 206 SW Temple	Salt Lake City	UT	84101	**800-222-2244**		379
Shilo Inn Suites Hotel Portland Airport 117707 NE Airport Way	Portland	OR	97220	**800-222-2244**	503-252-7500	379
Shilo Inn Suites Salem 3304 Market St	Salem	OR	97301	**800-222-2244**	503-581-4001	379
Shilo Inns Suites Hotels 11600 SW Shilo Ln	Portland	OR	97225	**800-222-2244**	503-641-6565	379
Shimadzu Medical Systems 20101 S Vermont Ave *General	Torrance	CA	90502	**800-477-1227***	310-217-8855	382
Shimadzu Scientific Instruments Inc 7102 Riverwood Dr	Columbia	MD	21046	**800-477-1227**	410-381-1227	419
Shimento 1350 Hayes St	Benicia	CA	94510	**877-211-8708**		719
Shimer College 3424 S State St	Chicago	IL	60616	**800-215-7173**	312-235-3506	167
Shimpo 1701 Glenlake Ave	Itasca	IL	60143	**800-842-1479**	630-924-7138	192
Shinano Kenshi Corp 5737 Mesmer Ave	Culver City	CA	90230	**800-755-0752**	818-889-5028	517
Shin-Etsu Silicones of America 1150 Damar Dr	Akron	OH	44305	**800-544-1745**	330-630-9860	143
Shipley Energy 415 Norway St	York	PA	17403	**800-839-1849**	717-848-4100	317
Shipowners Claims Bureau (SCB) 1 Battery Pk Plaza 31st Fl	New York	NY	10004	**800-774-8724**	212-847-4500	48-21

Name / Address	Toll-Free	Phone	Class
Shippensburg University 1871 Old Main Dr ... Shippensburg PA 17257	800-822-8028	717-477-1231	167
Shippers Express Co 1651 Kerr Dr ... Jackson MS 39204	800-647-2480	601-948-4251	778
Shipshewana/LaGrange County Convention & Visitors Bureau 350 S Van Buren St Ste H ... Shipshewana IN 46565	800-254-8090	260-768-4008	208
Shirtcliff Oil Co PO Box 6003 ... Myrtle Creek OR 97457	800-422-0536	541-863-5268	325
Shive-Hattery Inc (SH) 316 Second St SE Ste 500 PO Box 1599 ... Cedar Rapids IA 52406	800-798-0227	319-362-0313	263
Shively Bros Inc 2919 S Grand Travers St PO Box 1520 ... Flint MI 48501	800-530-9352	810-232-7401	385
Shively Labs 188 Harrison Rd PO Box 389 ... Bridgton ME 04009	888-744-8359	207-647-3327	645
Shivvers Inc 614 W English St ... Corydon IA 50060	800-245-9093	641-872-1005	275
Sho-Air International 5401 Argosy Ave ... Huntington Beach CA 92649	800-227-9111	949-476-9111	312
Shoalwater Bay Casino 4112 State Hwy 105 ... Tokeland WA 98590	866-992-3675	360-267-2048	131
Shockoe Commerce Group LLC 11 S 12th St 4th Fl ... Richmond VA 23219	866-570-0498	804-343-3441	354
Shoe Carnival Inc 7500 E Columbia St ... Evansville IN 47715 *NASDAQ: SCVL* ■ *Cust Svc	800-430-7463*	812-867-6471	302
Shoe Show of Rocky Mountain Inc 2201 Trinity Church Rd ... Concord NC 28027 *Cust Svc	888-557-4637*	704-782-4143	302
Shofu Dental Corp 1225 Stone Dr ... San Marcos CA 92078	800-827-4638	760-736-3277	475
Shoney's Restaurants Inc 1717 Elm Hill Pk Ste B1 ... Nashville TN 37210	800-708-3558	615-231-2333	668
Shook & Fletcher Insulation Co 4625 Valleydale Rd ... Birmingham AL 35242	888-829-2575	205-991-7606	193-4
Shook Hardy & Bacon LLP 2555 Grand Blvd ... Kansas City MO 64108	855-380-7584	816-474-6550	428
Shooting Star Casino Hotel & Event Center 777 Se Casino Rd ... Mahnomen MN 56557	800-453-7827	218-935-2711	451
Shop 'n Save 10461 Manchester Rd ... Kirkwood MO 63122	800-428-6974	314-984-0900	345
Shop Floor Automations Inc 5360 Jackson Dr ... La Mesa CA 91942	877-611-5825	619-461-4000	227
Shop Hobby Lobby 7717 SW 44th St ... Oklahoma City OK 73179	800-888-0321	405-745-1275	43
Shoplet.com 39 Broadway Ste 2030 ... New York NY 10006	800-757-3015	212-619-3353	789
Shopper Local 2222 Sedwick Rd # 102 ... Durham NC 27713	877-251-4592		414
Shoppers Food & Pharmacy 10501 Martin Luther King Jr Hwy ... Bowie MD 20720	800-866-0514	240-544-0180	345
Shopping Centers Today 1221 Ave of the Americas ... New York NY 10020	888-427-2885	646-728-3800	530-13
Shopping Ch, The *Credit Card Dept* 59 Ambassador Dr ... Mississauga ON L5T2P9	888-202-0888		736
ShopRite PO Box 7812 ... Edison NJ 08818	800-746-7748		345
ShopRite Supermarkets Inc 600 York St ... Elizabeth NJ 07207	800-746-7748	908-527-3300	345
Shops at Carolina Furniture of Williamsburg 5425 Richmond Rd ... Williamsburg VA 23188	800-582-8916	757-565-3000	322
Shops at Woodlake 725 Woodlake Rd ... Kohler WI 53044	855-444-2838	920-459-1713	459
Shopsmith Inc 6530 Poe Ave ... Dayton OH 45414 *OTC: SSMH* ■ *Cust Svc	800-543-7586*	937-898-6070	757
Shop-Vac Corp 2323 Reach Rd ... Williamsport PA 17701	800-347-5096	570-326-0502	386
ShopVisible LLC 945 East Paces Ferry Rd Ste 1475 ... Atlanta GA 30326	866-493-7037		387
Shore Memorial Hospital 9507 Hospital Ave PO Box 17 ... Nassawadox VA 23413	800-834-7035	757-414-8000	374-3
Shore Morgan Young 300 W Wilson Bridge Rd ... Worthington OH 43085	800-288-2117	614-888-2117	688
Shoreline Community College 16101 Greenwood Ave N ... Shoreline WA 98133	866-427-4747	206-546-4101	161
Shoreline Container Inc 4450 N 136th Ave PO Box 1993 ... Holland MI 49422	800-968-2088	616-399-2088	99
Shorewest Realtors Inc 17450 W N Ave ... Brookfield WI 53008	800-434-7350	262-827-4200	650
Shorr Packaging Inc 800 N Commerce St ... Aurora IL 60504	888-885-0055	630-978-1000	558
Short Freight Lines Inc 459 S River Rd PO Box 357 ... Bay City MI 48707	800-248-0625	989-893-3505	778
Short Hills Tours 46 Chatham Rd Ste 1 ... Short Hills NJ 07078	800-348-6871	973-467-2113	758
Short-Elliott-Hendrickson Inc 3535 Vadnais Ctr Dr ... Saint Paul MN 55110	800-325-2055	651-490-2000	263
Shorter University 315 Shorter Ave ... Rome GA 30165	800-868-6980	706-233-7319	167
Showa Best Glove Inc 579 Edison St ... Menlo GA 30731	800-241-0323		432
Showplace Wood Products Inc 1 Enterprise St ... Harrisburg SD 57032	877-512-2500	605-743-2200	114
SHPTV (Smoky Hills Public Television) 604 Elm St ... Bunker Hill KS 67626	800-337-4788	785-483-6990	629
Shreve Crump & Low Inc 39 Newbury St ... Boston MA 02116	800-328-4326	617-267-9100	410
Shreve Memorial Library 424 Texas St ... Shreveport LA 71101	866-783-5462	318-226-5897	434-3
Shreveport-Bossier Convention & Tourist Bureau 629 Spring St ... Shreveport LA 71101	800-551-8682	318-222-9391	208
SHRH & C (Seminole Hard Rock Hotel & Casino Tampa) 5223 N Orient Rd ... Tampa FL 33610 *General	866-388-4263*	813-627-7625	132
Shriners Hospitals for Children 2900 N Rocky Pt Dr ... Tampa FL 33607	800-237-5055	813-281-0300	353
Shriners Hospitals for Children Boston 51 Blossom St ... Boston MA 02114	800-255-1916	617-722-3000	374-1
Shriners Hospitals for Children Canada 1529 Cedar Ave ... Montreal QC H3G1A6	800-361-7256	514-842-4464	374-1
Shriners Hospitals for Children Cincinnati 3229 Burnet Ave ... Cincinnati OH 45229	800-875-8580	513-872-6000	374-1
Shriners Hospitals for Children Erie 1645 W Eigth St ... Erie PA 16505	800-873-5437	814-875-8700	374-1
Shriners Hospitals for Children Galveston 2900 Rocky Pt Dr ... Tampa Fl 33607	844-739-0849	813-281-0300	374-1
Shriners Hospitals for Children Greenville 950 W Faris Rd ... Greenville SC 29605	800-361-7256	864-271-3444	374-1
Shriners Hospitals for Children Lexington 1900 Richmond Rd ... Lexington KY 40502	800-668-4634	859-266-2101	374-1
Shriners Hospitals for Children Los Angeles 3160 Geneva St ... Los Angeles CA 90020	888-486-5437	213-388-3151	374-1
Shriners Hospitals for Children Philadelphia 3551 N Broad St ... Philadelphia PA 19140	800-281-4050	215-430-4000	374-1
Shriners Hospitals for Children Salt Lake City Fairfax Rd & Virginia St ... Salt Lake City UT 84103	800-313-3745	801-536-3500	374-1
Shriners Hospitals for Children Tampa 12502 N Pine Dr ... Tampa FL 33612	800-237-5055	813-972-2250	374-1
SHRM (Society for Human Resource Management) 1800 Duke St ... Alexandria VA 22314	800-283-7476	703-548-3440	48-12
SHRM Global Forum 1800 Duke St ... Alexandria VA 22314	800-283-7476	703-548-3440	173
SHSMD (Society for Healthcare Strategy & Market Development) 155 N Wacker Dr Ste 400 ... Chicago IL 60606	800-242-2626	312-422-3888	48-8
Shui Spa at Crowne Pointe Historic Inn 82 Bradford St ... Provincetown MA 02657	877-276-9631	508-487-6767	705
Shumsky Enterprises Inc 811 E Fourth St ... Dayton OH 45402	800-223-2203	937-223-2203	4
Shur-Co Inc 2309 Shur-Lok St PO Box 713 ... Yankton SD 57078	800-474-8756	605-665-6000	730
Shure Inc 5800 W Touhy Ave ... Niles IL 60714	800-257-4873	847-866-2200	51
Shure Manufacturing Corp 1901 W Main St ... Washington MO 63090	800-227-4873	636-390-7100	320-1
SHURflo Pump Mfg Company Inc 5900 Katella Ave ... Cypress CA 90630	800-854-3218	562-795-5200	638
Shurtape Technologies LLC 1712 Eigth St Dr SE ... Hickory NC 28602	888-442-8273	828-322-2700	729
ShurTech Brands 32150 Just Imagine Dr ... Avon OH 44011	800-321-0253	440-937-7000	534
Shuster's Bldg Components 2920 Clay Pk ... Irwin PA 15642	800-676-0640	724-446-7000	498
Shutter Mill Inc 8517 S Perkins Rd ... Stillwater OK 74074	800-416-6455	405-377-6455	697
Shutterbug Magazine 1419 Chaffee Dr Ste 1 ... Titusville FL 32780	800-829-3340	321-269-3212	456-14
Shuttleworth Inc 10 Commercial Rd ... Huntington IN 46750	800-444-7412	260-356-8500	209
SI Holdings 3267 Bee Caves Rd Ste 107 ... Austin TX 78746	866-551-4646		396
SIA (Security Industry Assn) 8405 Colesville Rd Ste 500 ... Silver Spring MD 20910	866-817-8888	703-683-2075	48-4
SIAM (Society for Industrial & Applied Mathematics) 3600 Market St 6th Fl ... Philadelphia PA 19104	800-447-7426	215-382-9800	48-19
Siano Appliance Distributors Inc 5372 Pleasant View Rd ... Memphis TN 38134	800-742-6699	901-382-5833	37
Sibley State Park 800 Sibley Pk Rd ... New London MN 56273	888-646-6367	320-354-2055	564
SICB (Society for Integrative & Comparative Biology) 1313 Dolley Madison Blvd Ste 402 ... McLean VA 22101	800-955-1236	703-790-1745	48-19
Sickle Cell Disease Assn of America (SCDAA) 3700 Koppers St Ste 570 ... Baltimore MD 21202	800-421-8453	410-528-1555	47-17
Sico North America Inc 7525 Cahill Rd ... Minneapolis MN 55439	800-328-6138	952-941-1700	320-3
Side Effects Software Inc 123 Front St W Ste 1401 ... Toronto ON M5J2M2	888-504-9876	416-504-9876	181
Sidel Systems Usa Inc 12500 El Camino Real ... Atascadero CA 93422	800-668-5003	805-462-1250	358
Sidewinder Conversions 44658 Yale Rd W ... Chilliwack BC V2R0G5	888-266-2299	604-792-2082	61-7
Sidley Austin LLP 787 Seventh Ave ... New York NY 10019	800-306-5230	312-853-7000	428
Sidney Transportation Services 777 W Russell Rd PO Box 946 ... Sidney OH 45365	800-743-6391	937-498-2323	683
Sidran Inc 1050 Venture Ct Ste 100 ... Carrollton TX 75006	800-969-5015	214-352-7979	154-19
Sidwell Co Inc 675 Sidwell Ct ... Saint Charles IL 60174	877-743-9355	630-549-1000	725
SIE Computing Solutions Inc 10 Mupac Dr ... Brockton MA 02301	800-926-8722	508-588-6110	407
Sieben Polk PA 1640 S Frontage Rd Ste 200 ... Hastings MN 55033	800-620-1829	651-437-3148	428
Siebert Brandford Shank & Co LLC 100 Wall St 18th Fl ... New York NY 10005	800-334-6800	646-775-4850	688
Siebert Financial Corp 885 Third Ave ... New York NY 10022 *NASDAQ: SIEB*	877-327-8379	212-644-2400	360-3
Siegel & Stockman USA 126 W 25th St ... New York NY 10001	888-515-8949	212-633-0138	463
Siegel Display Products 300 Sixth Ave N ... Minneapolis MN 55401	800-626-0322	612-340-1493	234
Siegers Seed Co 13031 Reflections Dr ... Holland MI 49424	800-962-4999	616-786-4999	278
Siegfried USA LLC 33 Industrial Pk Rd ... Pennsville NJ 08070 *Cust Svc	877-763-8630*	856-678-3601	478
Siegwerk USA Co 3535 SW 56th St ... Des Moines IA 50321	800-728-8200	515-471-2100	388
Sielox LLC 170 E Ninth Ave ... Runnemede NJ 08078	800-424-2126	856-939-9300	690

	City	State	ZIP	Toll-Free	Phone	Class
Siemens Bldg Technologies Inc						
1000 Deerfield Pkwy	Buffalo Grove	IL	60089	**800-877-7545***	847-215-1000	204
*General						
Siemens Bldg Technologies Inc Fire Safety Div						
8 Fernwood Rd	Florham Park	NJ	07932	**888-303-3353**	973-593-2600	285
8 Fernwood Rd	Florham Park	NJ	07932	**888-303-3353**	973-593-2600	747
Siemens Corp						
527 Madison Ave 8th Fl	New York	NY	10022	**800-743-6367**	212-258-4000	187
Siemens Financial Services Inc						
170 Wood Ave S	Iselin	NJ	08830	**800-327-4443**	732-590-6500	218
Siemens Hearing Instruments Inc						
10 Constitution Ave						
PO Box 1397	Piscataway	NJ	08855	**800-766-4500**		476
Siemens Medical Solutions Inc						
51 Valley Stream Pkwy	Malvern	PA	19355	**800-888-7436**	888-826-9702	382
Siemens Product Lifecycle Management Software Inc						
5800 Granite Pkwy Ste 600	Plano	TX	75024	**800-498-5351**	972-987-3000	180-10
Siemens Water Technologies						
181 Thorn Hill Rd	Warrendale	PA	15086	**800-424-9300**	724-772-0044	804
Siemer Milling Co						
111 W Main St PO Box 670	Teutopolis	IL	62467	**800-826-1065**	217-857-3131	297-23
Siemon Co						
101 Siemon Co Dr	Watertown	CT	06795	**866-548-5814**	860-945-4200	812
Siena College						
515 Loudon Rd	Loudonville	NY	12211	**888-287-4362***	518-783-2300	167
*Admissions						
Siena Heights University						
1247 E Siena Heights Dr	Adrian	MI	49221	**800-521-0009**	517-263-0731	167
Siena Hotel						
1505 E Franklin St	Chapel Hill	NC	27514	**800-223-7379**	919-929-4000	379
Sierra Bancorp						
86 N Main St PO Box 1930	Porterville	CA	93257	**888-454-2265**	559-782-4900	360-2
NASDAQ: BSRR						
Sierra Club Canada						
412-1 Nicholas St	Ottawa	ON	K1N7B7	**888-810-4204**	613-241-4611	47-13
Sierra College						
Nevada County						
250 Sierra College Dr	Grass Valley	CA	95945	**800-242-4004**	530-274-5300	161
Sierra Community College						
5000 Rocklin Rd	Rocklin	CA	95677	**800-242-4004**	916-624-3333	161
Sierra Donor Services						
1760 Creekside Oak Dr						
Ste 220	Sacramento	CA	95833	**877-401-2546**	916-567-1600	544
Sierra Energy						
1020 Winding Creek Rd Ste 100	Roseville	CA	95678	**800-576-2264**	916-218-1600	578
Sierra Industries Ltd						
122 Howard Langford Dr	Uvalde	TX	78801	**888-835-9377**	830-278-4481	24
Sierra Instruments Inc						
5 Harris Ct Bldg L	Monterey	CA	93940	**800-866-0200**	831-373-0200	203
Sierra Magazine						
85 Second St 2nd Fl	San Francisco	CA	94105	**866-338-1015**	415-977-5500	456-19
Sierra Monitor Corp						
1991 Tarob Ct	Milpitas	CA	95035	**888-509-1970**	408-262-6611	471
OTC: SRMC						
Sierra Nevada College						
999 Tahoe Blvd	Incline Village	NV	89451	**866-412-4636**	775-831-1314	167
Sierra NV Healthcare Systems (VA Medical Ctr)						
975 Kirman Ave	Reno	NV	89502	**888-838-6256**	775-786-7200	374-8
Sierra Tucson Inc						
39580 S Lago Del Oro Pkwy	Tucson	AZ	85739	**800-842-4487**	520-624-4000	724
Sierra Vista Regional Medical Ctr (SVRMC)						
1010 Murray Ave	San Luis Obispo	CA	93405	**866-904-6871**	805-546-7600	374-3
Sierra Volkswagen Inc						
510 E Norris Dr	Ottawa	IL	61350	**877-854-2771**	866-374-5828	56
SIFMAA (Securities Industry & Financial Markets Assn)						
120 Broadway 35th Fl	New York	NY	10271	**888-367-7966**	212-313-1200	48-2
SIG Mfg Company Inc						
401 S Front St	Montezuma	IA	50171	**800-247-5008***	641-623-5154	760
*Sales						
SIG SAUER Inc						
18 Industrial Dr	Exeter	NH	03833	**866-345-6744**	603-772-2302	286
SightLife						
221 Yale Ave N Ste 450	Seattle	WA	98109	**800-847-5786**	206-682-8500	271
Sigma Alpha Epsilon Fraternity (SAE)						
1856 Sheridan Rd	Evanston	IL	60201	**800-233-1856**	847-475-1856	47-16
Sigma Business Solutions Inc						
55 York St	Toronto	ON	M5J1R7	**855-594-1991**		807
Sigma Chi Fraternity						
1714 Hinman Ave	Evanston	IL	60201	**877-829-5500**	847-869-3655	47-16
Sigma Corp of America						
15 Fleetwood Ct	Ronkonkoma	NY	11779	**800-896-6858**	631-585-1144	541
Sigma Design						
5521 Jackson St	Alexandria	LA	71303	**888-990-0900***	318-449-9900	180-8
*Sales						
Sigma Electronics Inc						
1027 Commercial Ave	East Petersburg	PA	17520	**866-569-2681**	717-569-2926	255
Sigma Phi Epsilon Fraternity						
310 S Blvd	Richmond	VA	23220	**800-767-1901**	804-353-1901	47-16
Sigma Pi Fraternity						
106 N Castle Heights Ave	Lebanon	TN	37087	**800-332-1897**	615-373-5728	47-16
Sigma Solutions Inc						
422 E Ramsey Rd	San Antonio	TX	78216	**800-567-5964**	210-348-9876	227
Sigma Systems Canada Inc						
55 York St Ste 1100	Toronto	ON	M5J1R7	**888-782-6468**	416-943-9696	179
Sigma Theta Tau International						
550 W N St	Indianapolis	IN	46202	**888-634-7575**	317-634-8171	47-16
Sigma Xi Scientific Research Society						
3106 E NC Hwy 54						
PO Box 13975	Research Triangle Park	NC	27709	**800-243-6534**	919-549-4691	47-16
Sigma-Aldrich Corp						
3050 Spruce St	Saint Louis	MO	63103	**800-325-3010**	314-771-5765	144
NASDAQ: SIAL						
Sigma-Tau Pharmaceutical Inc						
9841 Washingtonian Blvd						
Ste 500	Gaithersburg	MD	20878	**800-447-0169**	301-948-1041	582
SigmaTron International Inc						
2201 Landmeier Rd	Elk Grove Village	IL	60007	**800-700-9095**	847-956-8000	624
NASDAQ: SGMA						
Sign Biz Inc						
24681 La Plz Ste 270	Dana Point	CA	92629	**800-633-5580**	949-234-0408	198
Sign Builders Inc						
4800 Jefferson Ave						
PO Box 28380	Birmingham	AL	35228	**800-222-7330**		699
Sign Designs Inc						
204 Campus Way	Modesto	CA	95352	**800-421-7446**	209-524-4484	699
Signal Industrial Products Corp						
1601 Cowart St	Chattanooga	TN	37408	**800-728-1326**	423-756-4980	351
Signal Magazine						
4400 Fair Lakes Ct	Fairfax	VA	22033	**800-336-4583**	703-631-6100	456-5
Signal Transformer Company Inc						
500 Bayview Ave	Inwood	NY	11096	**866-239-5777**	516-239-5777	255
Signal Travel & Tours Inc						
219 E Main St	Niles	MI	49120	**800-811-1522**	269-684-2880	770
Signalert Corp						
150 Great Neck Rd Ste 301	Great Neck	NY	11021	**800-829-6229**	516-829-6444	401
Signalink Technologies Inc						
Units 13 & 14 2550 Acland Rd	Kelowna	BC	V1X7L4	**888-491-3883**	250-491-3883	248
Signalisation Ver-Mac Inc						
1781 Bresse	Quebec	QC	G2G2V2	**888-488-7446**	418-654-1303	407
SignalPoint Communications Corp						
433 Hackensack Ave						
Continental Plz 6th Fl	Hackensack	NJ	07601	**877-928-3292**	201-968-9797	733
Signal-Tech						
4985 Pittsburgh Ave	Erie	PA	16509	**877-547-9900**	814-835-3000	198
Sign-A-Rama						
2121 Vista Pkwy	West Palm Beach	FL	33411	**800-776-8105***	561-640-5570	699
*All						
Signator Investors Inc						
197 Clarendon St C-8	Boston	MA	02116	**800-543-6611**		401
Signature Bank						
565 Fifth Ave 12th Fl	New York	NY	10017	**866-744-5463**	646-822-1500	69
NASDAQ: SBNY						
Signature Breads Inc						
100 Justin Dr	Chelsea	MA	02150	**888-602-6533**		297-1
Signature Eyewear Inc						
498 N Oak St	Inglewood	CA	90302	**800-765-3937**	310-330-2700	541
OTC: SEYE						
Signature Graphics Inc						
1000 Signature Dr	Porter	IN	46304	**800-356-3235**	219-926-4994	344
Signature Hardware						
2700 Crescent Springs Pike	Erlanger	KY	41017	**866-855-2284**	859-647-7564	350
Signature Homes Inc						
4670 Willow Rd Ste 200	Pleasanton	CA	94588	**888-673-0200**	925-463-1122	654
Signature Inc						
5115 Parkcenter Ave	Dublin	OH	43017	**800-398-0518**	614-766-5101	196
Signature Services Corp						
2705 Hawes Ave	Dallas	TX	75235	**800-929-5519**	214-353-2661	300
Signe's Bakery & Cafe						
93 Arrow Rd	Hilton Head Island	SC	29928	**866-807-4463**	843-785-9118	669
Signet Inc						
1801 Shelby Oaks Dr N Ste 12	Memphis	TN	38134	**800-654-3889**	901-387-5555	197
Signet Marking Devices						
3121 Red Hill Ave	Costa Mesa	CA	92626	**800-421-5150**	714-549-0341	466
Signifi Solutions Inc						
2100 Matheson Blvd E						
Ste 100	Mississauga	ON	L4W5E1	**877-744-6434**	905-602-7707	179
Signs by Tomorrow USA Inc						
8681 Robert Fulton Dr	Columbia	MD	21046	**800-765-7446**	410-312-3600	699
Signs Now						
5368 Dixie Hwy Ste 1	Waterford	MI	48329	**800-356-3373**	248-596-8600	699
Signtech Electrical Adv Inc						
4444 Federal Blvd	San Diego	CA	92102	**877-885-1135**	619-527-6100	699
Signtronix						
1445 W Sepulveda Blvd	Torrance	CA	90501	**800-729-4853**		699
Sign-ups & Banners Corp						
2764 W T C Jester Blvd	Houston	TX	77018	**877-682-7979**	713-682-7979	626
SII (Steel Industries Inc)						
12600 Beech-Daly Rd	Redford Township	MI	48239	**877-783-3599**		482
Sika Corp						
201 Polito Ave	Lyndhurst	NJ	07071	**800-933-7452**	201-933-8800	144
Sika Sarnafil Inc						
100 Dan Rd	Canton	MA	02021	**800-451-2504**	781-828-5400	45
Sikich LLP						
1415 W Diehl Rd Ste 400	Naperville	IL	60563	**877-279-1900**	630-566-8400	2
Silberline Mfg Company Inc						
130 Lincoln Dr PO Box B	Tamaqua	PA	18252	**800-348-4824**	570-668-6050	142
Silbrico Corp						
6300 River Rd	Hodgkins	IL	60525	**800-323-4287**	708-354-3350	499
Silent Knight						
7550 Meridian Cir Ste 100	Maple Grove	MN	55369	**800-328-0103**	763-493-6400	285
7550 Meridian Cir Ste 100	Maple Grove	MN	55369	**800-328-0103**	763-493-6400	747
Silgan Plastics Corp						
14515 N Outer Forty						
Ste 210	Chesterfield	MO	63017	**800-274-5426**		97
Silicon Laboratories Inc						
400 W Cesar Chavez	Austin	TX	78701	**877-444-3032**	512-416-8500	694
NASDAQ: SLAB						
Silicon Valley Assn of Realtors						
19400 Stevens Creek Blvd						
Ste 100	Cupertino	CA	95014	**877-699-6787**	408-200-0100	650
Silicon Valley Staffing						
2336 Harrison St	Oakland	CA	94612	**877-660-6000**	510-923-9898	719
Silicone Specialties Inc						
430 S Rockford Ave	Tulsa	OK	74120	**888-243-0672**	918-587-5567	351
Silipos Inc						
7049 Williams Rd	Niagara Falls	NY	14304	**800-229-4404**	716-283-0700	582
Silks						
222 Sansome St	San Francisco	CA	94104	**800-526-6566**	415-986-2020	669
Silkworm Inc						
102 S Sezmore Dr	Murphysboro	IL	62966	**800-826-0577**	618-687-4077	685
Silver & Archibald LLP						
997 S Milledge Ave	Athens	GA	30605	**877-526-6281**	706-548-8122	428
Silver Airways Corp						
1100 Lee Wagener Blvd						
Ste 201	Fort Lauderdale	FL	33315	**844-674-5837**	954-985-1500	25
Silver City-Grant County Chamber of Commerce						
201 N Hudson St	Silver City	NM	88061	**800-548-9378**	575-538-3785	138

Name / Address	City	State	Zip	Toll-Free	Phone	Class
Silver Cloud Hotel Seattle Broadway						
1100 Broadway	Seattle	WA	98122	**800-590-1801**	206-325-1400	379
Silver Cloud Inn Seattle-Lake Union						
1150 Fairview Ave N	Seattle	WA	98109	**800-330-5812***	206-447-9500	379
*General						
Silver Cloud Inn University District						
5036 25th Ave NE	Seattle	WA	98105	**800-205-6940**	206-526-5200	379
Silver Creek Financial ServicesInc						
175 Hwy 82	Lostine	OR	97857	**866-569-0020**	541-569-2272	731
Silver Diner Inc						
12276 Rockville Pk	Rockville	MD	20852	**866-561-0518**	301-770-0333	668
Silver Eagle Distributors LP						
7777 Washington Ave	Houston	TX	77007	**855-332-2110**	713-869-4361	80-1
Silver Edge Co-op						
39999 Hilton Rd	Edgewood	IA	52042	**800-632-5953**	563-928-6419	278
Silver Fox Tours & Motorcoaches						
3 Silver Fox Dr	Millbury	MA	01527	**800-342-5998**	508-865-6000	758
Silver King Hotel						
1485 Empire Ave	Park City	UT	84060	**888-667-2775**	435-649-5500	379
Silver King Refrigeration Inc						
1600 Xenium Ln N	Minneapolis	MN	55441	**800-328-3329**	763-923-2441	662
Silver Lake College						
2406 S Alverno Rd	Manitowoc	WI	54220	**800-236-4752**	920-686-6175	167
Silver Lake Cookie Company Inc						
141 Freeman Ave	Islip	NY	11751	**800-645-9048**	631-581-4000	297-9
Silver Legacy Capital Corp						
407 N Virginia St	Reno	NV	89501	**800-687-8733**		688
Silver Legacy Resort & Casino						
407 N Virginia St	Reno	NV	89501	**800-687-8733**	775-325-7401	132
Silver Reef Casino						
4876 Haxton Way	Ferndale	WA	98248	**866-383-0777**	360-383-0777	131
Silver Saddle Ranch & Club Inc						
20751 Aristotle Dr	California City	CA	93505	**888-430-8728**	760-373-8617	651
Silver Smith Hotel & Suites						
10 S Wabash Ave	Chicago	IL	60603	**800-979-0084**	312-372-7696	379
Silver Springs Bottled Water Company Inc						
PO Box 926	Silver Springs	FL	34489	**800-556-0334**		298-11
Silver Standard Resources Inc						
999 W Hastings St Ste 1180	Vancouver	BC	V6C2W2	**888-338-0046**	604-689-3846	501
TSE: SSO						
Silver Star Automotive Group						
Lotus of Thousand Oaks						
3601 Auto Mall Dr	Thousand Oaks	CA	91362	**800-472-5450**		56
Silver Star Meats Inc						
1720 Middletown Rd						
PO Box 393	McKees Rocks	PA	15136	**800-548-1321**	412-771-5539	297-26
Silver Towne LP						
120 E Union City Pike						
PO Box 424	Winchester	IN	47394	**800-788-7481**	765-584-7481	328
Silverado Resort & Spa						
1600 Atlas Peak Rd	Napa	CA	94558	**800-532-0500**	707-257-0200	667
Silverado Stages Inc						
241 Prado Rd	San Luis Obispo	CA	93401	**888-383-8109**	805-545-8400	758
SilverBirch Hotels & Resorts						
1600 - 1030 W Georgia St	Vancouver	BC	V6E2Y3	**800-661-1232**	604-646-2447	379
Silverbow Honey Company Inc						
1120 E Wheeler Rd	Moses Lake	WA	98837	**866-444-6639**	509-765-6616	297-24
Silverdale Beach Hotel						
3073 NW Bucklin Hill Rd	Silverdale	WA	98383	**800-544-9799**	360-698-1000	379
Silvergate Bank						
4275 Executive Sq Ste 800	La Jolla	CA	92037	**800-595-5856**	858-362-6300	69
Silverleaf Resorts Inc						
1221 Riverbend Dr Ste 120	Dallas	TX	75247	**800-613-0310**	214-631-1166	751
SilverStone Group						
11516 Miracle Hills Dr Ste 100	Omaha	NE	68154	**800-288-5501**	402-964-5400	390
Silverton Hotel & Casino						
3333 Blue Diamond Rd	Las Vegas	NV	89139	**866-722-4608**	702-263-7777	132
Silvestri Studio Inc						
8125 Beach St	Los Angeles	CA	90001	**800-647-8874**	323-277-4420	463
Silvi Concrete Products Inc						
355 Newbold Rd	Fairless Hills	PA	19030	**800-426-6273**	215-295-0777	184
Silvon Software Inc						
900 Oakmont Ln Ste 400	Westmont	IL	60559	**800-874-5866**	630-655-3313	180-1
SIM (Society for Information Management)						
15000 Commerce Pkwy Ste C	Mount Laurel	NJ	08054	**800-387-9746**	312-527-6734	47-9
Sim USA Inc						
PO Box 7900	Charlotte	NC	28241	**800-521-6449**		47-20
Sima Products Corp						
120 Pennsylvania Ave	Oakmont	PA	15139	**800-345-7462**	412-828-3700	51
Simacor LLC						
10700 Hwy 55 Ste 170	Plymouth	MN	55441	**888-284-4415**	763-544-4415	182
Simage LLC						
300 N Elizabeth St Ste 100C	Chicago	IL	60607	**888-729-7796**		5
Simark Controls Ltd						
10509-46 St S E Ste 10509	Calgary	AB	T2C5C2	**800-565-7431**	403-236-0580	358
Simba Information						
60 Long Ridge Rd Ste 300	Stamford	CT	06902	**888-297-4622**	203-325-8193	634-9
Simco Drilling Equipment Inc						
PO Box 448	Osceola	IA	50213	**855-222-8570**	641-342-2166	192
Simco Electronics						
1178 Bordeaux Dr	Sunnyvale	CA	94089	**866-299-6029**	408-734-9750	740
Simflo Pumps Inc						
754 E Maley St PO Box 849	Willcox	AZ	85644	**800-232-4142**	520-384-2273	638
SIMKAR Corp						
700 Ramona Ave	Philadelphia	PA	19120	**800-523-3602**	215-831-7700	439
Simmons College						
300 The Fenway	Boston	MA	02115	**800-345-8468**	617-521-2000	167
Simmons College Beatley Library						
300 The Fenway	Boston	MA	02115	**800-831-4284**	617-521-2780	434-6
Simmons Engineering Corp						
400 Regency Dr	Glendale Heights	IL	60139	**800-252-3381**	630-912-2880	263
Simmons First National Corp						
501 Main St	Pine Bluff	AR	71601	**866-246-2400**	870-541-1000	360-2
NASDAQ: SFNC						
Simmons-Boardman Publishing Corp						
55 Broad St 26th fl 12th Fl	New York	NY	10004	**800-895-4389**	212-620-7200	634-9
Simmons-rockwell Inc						
784 County Rd 64	Elmira	NY	14903	**888-520-2213**	607-796-5555	56

Name / Address	City	State	Zip	Toll-Free	Phone	Class
Simms Fishing Products Corp						
101 Evergreen Dr	Bozeman	MT	59715	**800-217-4667**	406-585-3557	708
SIMNA (Schroder Investment Management North America Inc)						
875 Third Ave 22nd Fl	New York	NY	10022	**800-730-2932**		688
Simon & Assoc Inc						
3200 Commerce St	Blacksburg	VA	24060	**800-763-4234**	540-951-4234	263
Simon & Schuster Interactive						
1230 Ave of the Americas	New York	NY	10020	**800-223-2336**	212-698-7000	634-1
Simon Metals LLC						
2202 E River St	Tacoma	WA	98421	**800-562-8464**	253-272-9364	684
Simon Roofing & Sheet Metal Corp						
70 Karago Ave	Youngstown	OH	44512	**800-523-7714**	330-629-7663	45
Simon Wiesenthal Ctr						
1399 Roxbury Dr Ste 100	Los Angeles	CA	90035	**800-900-9036**	310-553-9036	47-8
Simonds International						
135 Intervale Rd	Fitchburg	MA	01420	**800-343-1616**		680
Simoniz USA						
201 Boston Tpke	Bolton	CT	06043	**800-227-5536**		150
Simons Bitzer & Assoc PC						
8350 S Emerson Ave Ste 100	Indianapolis	IN	46237	**866-702-5090**	317-782-3070	2
Simons Trucking Inc						
920 Simon Dr PO Box 8	Farley	IA	52046	**800-373-2580**	563-744-3304	778
Simonsen Industries Inc						
500 Iowa 31	Quimby	IA	51049	**800-831-4860**	712-445-2211	275
Simonson Properties Co						
535 1st St NE	Saint Cloud	MN	56304	**888-843-8789**	320-252-9385	364
Simonton Court Historic Inn & Cottages						
320 Simonton St	Key West	FL	33040	**800-944-2687**		379
Simple & Delicious						
5400 S 60th St	Greendale	WI	53129	**800-344-6913**	414-423-0100	456-11
Simplex Inc						
5300 Rising Moon Rd	Springfield	IL	62711	**800-637-8603**	217-483-1600	255
Simplicity Consulting Inc						
11250 Kirkland Way Ste 203	Kirkland	WA	98033	**888-252-0385**		198
Simplicity Manufacturing Inc						
PO Box 702	Milwaukee	WI	53201	**800-837-6836**		429
Simplifile LC						
4844 North 300 West Ste 202	Provo	UT	84604	**800-460-5657**	801-373-0151	227
Simply Healthcare Plans Inc						
1701 Ponce De Leon Blvd						
Ste 300	Coral Gables	FL	33134	**877-577-9042**	305-408-5890	196
Simply Orange Juice Co						
2659 Orange Ave	Apopka	FL	32703	**800-871-2653**		297-20
Simpson College						
701 N 'C' St	Indianola	IA	50125	**800-362-2454**	515-961-6251	167
Simpson Dura-Vent Inc						
877 Cotting Ct	Vacaville	CA	95688	**800-835-4429**	707-446-1786	695
Simpson Gumpertz & Heger Inc						
41 Seyon St Bldg 1 Ste 500	Waltham	MA	02453	**800-729-7429**	781-907-9000	263
Simpson Mfg Company Inc						
5956 W Las Positas Blvd	Pleasanton	CA	94588	**800-925-5099**	925-560-9000	15
NYSE: SSD						
Simpson Norton Corp						
4144 S Bullard Ave	Goodyear	AZ	85338	**877-859-8676**	623-932-5116	276
Simpson Strong-Tie Company Inc						
5956 W Las Positas Blvd	Pleasanton	CA	94588	**800-925-5099**	925-560-9000	350
Simpson University						
2211 College View Dr	Redding	CA	96003	**888-974-6776**	530-226-4606	167
Simpson's Eggs Inc						
5015 Hwy 218 E	Monroe	NC	28110	**800-726-1330**	704-753-1478	10-7
Sims Bros Inc						
1011 S Prospect St PO Box 1170	Marion	OH	43301	**800-536-7465**	740-387-9041	684
Sims Cab Depot						
200 Moulinette Rd	Long Sault	ON	K0C1P0	**800-225-7290**	613-534-2289	479
Simulations Plus Inc						
42505 Tenth St W	Lancaster	CA	93534	**888-266-9294**	661-723-7723	180-10
NASDAQ: SLP						
Sinai Grace Hospital						
6071 W Outer Dr	Detroit	MI	48235	**888-362-2500**	313-966-3300	374-3
Sinclair Community College						
444 W Third St	Dayton	OH	45402	**800-315-3000**	937-512-3000	161
Sindel, Sindel & Noble PC						
8008 Carondelet Ave Ste 301	Saint Louis	MO	63105	**866-489-5504**	314-721-6040	428
Singapore Airlines KrisFlyer						
380 World Way Ste 336B	Los Angeles	CA	90045	**800-742-3333**	310-646-6221	26
Singapore Airlines Ltd						
222 N Sepulveda Blvd						
Ste 1600	El Segundo	CA	90245	**800-742-3333**	310-647-1922	25
Singer Lewak Greenbaum & Goldstein LLP						
10960 Wilshire Blvd 7th Fl	Los Angeles	CA	90024	**877-754-4557**	310-477-3924	2
Singer Sewing Co						
1224 Hill Quaker Blvd						
PO Box 7017	La Vergne	TN	37086	**877-738-9869**	615-213-0880	36
Singing Machine Company Inc, The						
6601 Lyons Rd Bldg A-7	Coconut Creek	FL	33073	**866-670-6888**	954-596-1000	248
OTC: SMDM						
Sinopec Daylight Energy Ltd						
112-4th Ave SW Sun Life Plz E Tower						
Ste 2700	Calgary	AB	T2P0H3	**877-266-6901**	403-266-6900	535
Sinton Dairy Foods Co LLC						
3801 Sinton Rd	Colorado Springs	CO	80907	**800-388-4970**	719-633-3821	297-10
SinuSys Corp						
4030 Fabian Way	Palo Alto	CA	94303	**855-474-6879**	650-213-9988	474
Sioux Automation Ctr Inc						
877 First Ave NW	Sioux Center	IA	51250	**866-722-1488**	712-722-1488	276
Sioux City Convention Ctr						
801 Fourth St	Sioux City	IA	51101	**800-593-2228**	712-279-4800	207
Sioux City Foundry Co						
801 Div St	Sioux City	IA	51102	**800-831-0874**	712-252-4181	308
Sioux City Journal						
515 Pavonia St	Sioux City	IA	51101	**800-397-3530**	712-293-4300	531-2
Sioux City Tourism Bureau						
801 Fourth St	Sioux City	IA	51101	**800-593-2228**	712-279-4800	208
Sioux Falls Arena						
1201 NW Ave	Sioux Falls	SD	57104	**800-338-3177**	605-367-7288	718
Sioux Falls Convention & Visitors Bureau						
200 N Phillips Ave Ste 102	Sioux Falls	SD	57104	**800-333-2072**	605-336-1620	208
Sioux Falls Seminary						
2100 S Summit	Sioux Falls	SD	57105	**800-440-6227**	605-336-6588	168-3

Name / Address	City	State	ZIP	Toll-Free	Phone	Class
Sioux Steel Co 196 1/2 E Sixth St	Sioux Falls	SD	57104	**800-557-4689**	605-336-1750	275
Sioux Tools Inc 250 Snap-on Dr *Orders	Murphy	NC	28906	**800-722-7290***	828-835-9765	757
Sioux Valley-Southwestern Electric Co-op Inc 47092 SD Hwy 34 PO Box 216	Colman	SD	57017	**800-234-1960**	605-534-3535	247
Siouxland Chamber of Commerce 101 Pierce St	Sioux City	IA	51101	**800-228-7903**	712-255-7903	138
Sioux-Preme Packing Co 4241 US 75th Ave *General	Sioux Center	IA	51250	**800-735-7675***		472
SIPA (Specialized Information Publishers Assn) 8229 Boone Blvd Ste 260	Vienna	VA	22182	**800-356-9302**	703-992-9339	48-14
SIR (Society of Interventional Radiology) 3975 Fair Ridge Dr Ste 400 N	Fairfax	VA	22033	**800-488-7284**	703-691-1805	48-8
Sir Francis Drake Hotel 450 Powell St	San Francisco	CA	94102	**800-795-7129**	415-392-7755	379
Sir Speedy Inc 26722 Plaza Dr	Mission Viejo	CA	92691	**800-854-8297**	949-348-5000	626
Sir Winston's Restaurant & Lounge 1126 Queens Hwy	Long Beach	CA	90802	**877-342-0738**	562-435-3511	669
SIRCHIE Finger Print Laboratories Inc 100 Hunter Pl	Youngsville	NC	27596	**800-356-7311**	919-554-2244	82
Sirius Canada Inc 135 Liberty St	Toronto	ON	M6K1A7	**888-539-7474**		733
Sirona Dental Systems LLC 4835 Sirona Dr Ste 100	Charlotte	NC	28273	**800-659-5977**	704-587-0453	230
Sirsi Corp 3300 N Ashton Blvd Ste 500	Lehi	UT	84043	**800-288-8020**		179
SIRVA Inc 700 Oakmont Ln	Terrace	IL	60181	**888-444-4765**	630-570-8900	664
SIS (Software Information Systems Inc) 165 Barr St	Lexington	KY	40507	**800-337-6914**	859-977-4747	182
Sisbarro Dealerships 425 W Boutz Rd	Las Cruces	NM	88005	**800-215-8021**	575-524-7707	56
Siskin Steel & Supply Co Inc 1901 Riverfront Pkwy	Chattanooga	TN	37408	**800-756-3671**	423-756-3671	491
Siskinds LLP 680 Waterloo St PO Box 2520	London	ON	N6A3V8	**877-672-2121**	519-672-2121	428
Siskiyou Corp 110 Sw Booth St	Grants Pass	OR	97526	**877-313-6418**	541-479-8697	419
Sisters Network Inc 2922 Rosedale St	Houston	TX	77004	**866-781-1808**	713-781-0255	47-21
SISU Inc 7635 N Fraser Way Ste 102	Burnaby	BC	V5J0B8	**800-663-4163**	604-420-6610	582
Sit 'n Sleep 14300 S Main St	Gardena	CA	90248	**877-262-4006**	310-604-8903	322
Sita World Travel Inc 16250 Ventura Blvd	Encino	CA	91436	**800-421-5643**	818-990-9530	769
SITEL Corp 2 American Ctr Ste 900	Nashville	TN	37203	**866-957-4835**	615-301-7100	734
Siteman Cancer Ctr 4921 Parkview Pl	Saint Louis	MO	63110	**800-600-3606**	314-362-5196	666
Sitex Corp 1300 Commonwealth Dr	Henderson	KY	42420	**800-278-3537**	270-827-3537	442
Sitka Convention & Visitors Bureau 303 Lincoln St Ste 4	Sitka	AK	99835	**800-557-4852**	907-747-5940	208
Sitka Harbor 617 Katlian St	Sitka	AK	99835	**866-948-8683**	907-747-3439	617
Sitka National Cemetery 803 Sawmill Creek Rd	Sitka	AK	99835	**800-273-8255**	907-384-7075	135
Sitrick & Co 1840 Century Pk E Ste 800	Los Angeles	CA	90067	**800-288-8809**	310-788-2850	633
Sitton Buick GMC 2640 Laurens Rd	Greenville	SC	29607	**888-484-8009**	864-990-3600	56
Sivaco Wire Group 800 Rue Ouellette	Marieville	QC	J3M1P5	**800-876-9473**	450-658-8741	811
Six Flags Fiesta Texas 17000 IH-10 W	San Antonio	TX	78257	**800-370-7488**	210-697-5000	32
Six Flags Great Adventure 1 Six Flags Blvd	Jackson	NJ	08527	**800-772-2287**	732-928-1821	32
Six Flags New England 1623 Main St	Agawam	MA	01001	**800-370-7488**	413-786-9300	32
Six Flags Wild Safari 1 Six Flags Blvd	Jackson	NJ	08527	**800-772-2287**	732-928-1821	32
Six Robblees' Inc 11010 Tukwila International Blvd	Tukwila	WA	98168	**800-275-7499**	206-767-7970	60
Six States Distributors Inc 247 West 1700 South *Cust Svc	Salt Lake City	UT	84115	**800-453-5703***	801-488-4666	60
Sixth Floor Museum 411 Elm St Ste 120 Dealey Plz	Dallas	TX	75202	**888-485-4854**	214-747-6660	519
Sixty Hotels 54 Thompson St	New York	NY	10012	**877-431-0400**		705
Sizemore Inc 2116 Walton Way	Augusta	GA	30904	**800-445-1748**	706-736-1456	690
Sizzler Restaurants 25910 Acero Rd Ste 350	Mission Viejo	CA	92691	**855-895-9703**		668
S-j Transportation Co Inc PO Box 169	Woodstown	NJ	08098	**800-524-2552**	856-769-2741	778
SJC (San Jose Convention Center) 150 W San Carlos St	San Jose	CA	95110	**800-726-5673**	408-792-4194	207
SJE-Rhombus 22650 County Hwy 6 PO Box 1708	Detroit Lakes	MN	56502	**800-746-6287**	218-847-1317	203
SJF Material Handling Equipment 211 Baker Ave	Winsted	MN	55395	**800-598-5532**	320-485-2824	386
SJH Regional Medical Ctr (SJHRMC) 1505 W Sheman Ave	Vineland	NJ	08360	**800-770-7547**	856-641-8000	374-3
SJHRMC (SJH Regional Medical Ctr) 1505 W Sheman Ave	Vineland	NJ	08360	**800-770-7547**	856-641-8000	374-3
SJMC (Saint Joseph Medical Ctr) 1717 S J St	Tacoma	WA	98405	**888-825-3227**		374-3
SJMH (Stonewall Jackson Memorial Hospital) 230 Hospital Plaza	Weston	WV	26452	**866-637-0471**	304-269-8000	374-3
SK Food Group Inc 4600 37th Ave SW	Seattle	WA	98126	**800-722-6290**	206-935-8100	366
Skaggs Community Health Ctr 545 Branson Landing Blvd PO Box 650	Branson	MO	65615	**800-994-6610**	417-335-7000	374-3
Skagit Valley Casino Resort 5984 N Darrk Ln	Bow	WA	98232	**877-275-2448**	360-724-7777	132
Skagit Valley College 2405 E College Way	Mount Vernon	WA	98273	**877-385-5360**	360-416-7600	161
Skagit Valley Herald 1000 E College Way PO Box 578	Mount Vernon	WA	98273	**800-683-3300**	360-424-3251	531-2
Skagway Visitor Information 245 Broadway PO Box 1029	Skagway	AK	99840	**888-762-1898**	907-983-2855	208
Skamania Lodge 1131 SW Skamania Lodge Way PO Box 189	Stevenson	WA	98648	**800-221-7117**	509-427-7700	377
SKB Corp 434 W Levers Pl *Sales	Orange	CA	92867	**800-410-2024***	714-637-1252	452
Skechers USA Inc 228 Manhattan Beach Blvd *NYSE: SKX* ■ *Cust Svc	Manhattan Beach	CA	90266	**800-746-3411***	310-318-3100	302
Skelton, Brumwell & Associates Inc 93 Bell Farm Rd Ste 107	Barrie	ON	L4M5G1	**877-726-1141**	705-726-1141	263
Ski Bromont 150 Champlain	Bromont	QC	J2L1A2	**866-276-6668**	450-534-2200	379
Ski Magazine 5720 Flatiron Pkwy	Boulder	CO	80301	**888-444-8151**	303-253-6300	456-20
Ski Shawnee Inc 339 Hollow Rd	Shawnee On Delaware	PA	18356	**800-233-4218**	570-421-7231	31
Skidmore College 815 N Broadway	Saratoga Springs	NY	12866	**800-867-6007**	518-580-5000	167
Skier's Choice Inc 1717 Henry G Ln St	Maryville	TN	37801	**800-970-3744**	865-856-3035	89
Skilled Care Pharmacy Inc 6175 Hl Tek Ct	Mason	OH	45040	**800-334-1624**	513-459-7455	583
Skillforce Inc 405 Williams Court Ste 100	Baltimore	MD	21220	**866-581-8989**		262
SkillSoft PLC 107 NE Blvd	Nashua	NH	03062	**877-545-5763**	603-324-3000	763
SkillsUSA 14001 James Monroe Hwy	Leesburg	VA	20176	**800-321-8422**	703-777-8810	47-11
Skinner Transfer Corp PO Box 438	Reedsburg	WI	53959	**800-356-9350**	608-524-2326	778
Skolnik Industries Inc 4900 S Kilbourn Ave	Chicago	IL	60632	**800-441-8780**	773-735-0700	200
Skuttle Manufacturing Co 101 Margaret St	Marietta	OH	45750	**800-848-9786**	740-373-9169	14
Sky & Telescope Magazine 90 Sherman St	Cambridge	MA	02140	**800-253-0245**	617-864-7360	456-19
Sky Bird Travel & Tours Inc 24701 Swanson	Southfield	MI	48033	**888-759-2473**	248-372-4800	16
Sky Bright 65 Aviation Dr	Gilford	NH	03249	**800-639-6012**	603-528-6818	62
Sky High Marketing 6000 S Eastern Ave Ste 5D	Las Vegas	NV	89119	**800-246-7447**		197
Sky Hotel 709 E Durant Ave	Aspen	CO	81611	**800-882-2582**	970-925-6760	379
Sky I T Group LLC 330 Seventh Ave	New York	NY	10001	**866-641-6017**	212-868-7800	198
Sky Lodge, The 201 Heber Ave Main St	Park City	UT	84068	**888-876-2525**	435-658-2500	378
Sky Publishing Corp 90 Sherman St	Cambridge	MA	02140	**800-253-0245**	617-864-7360	634-9
Sky Ranch 24657 CR 448	Van	TX	75790	**800-962-2267**	903-266-3300	147
Sky Sox Stadium 4385 Tutt Blvd Security Service Field	Colorado Springs	CO	80922	**866-698-4253**	719-597-1449	718
Sky Ute Casino 14324 US Hwy 172 N	Ignacio	CO	81137	**888-842-4180**	970-563-7777	132
Skybank Financial Services Corp 1444 Biscayne Blvd Ste 309	Miami	FL	33132	**800-617-9980**		227
SkyBlox LLC 244 Peters St Ste 7	Atlanta	GA	30313	**866-632-9685**		387
Skybooks Inc 1310 Tradeport Dr	Jacksonville	FL	32218	**866-929-8700**	904-741-8700	56
Skycom Avionics Inc 2441 Aviation Rd	Waukesha	WI	53188	**800-443-4490**	262-521-8180	56
Skyemed Pharmacy 1332 N Federal Hwy	Pompano Beach	FL	33062	**866-778-8255**		239
Skygone Inc 1000 New York St Ste 107	Redlands	CA	92374	**888-759-4471**		198
Skyline Corp 2520 By-Pass Rd *NYSE: SKY*	Elkhart	IN	46514	**800-348-7469**	574-294-6521	119
Skyline Medical Ctr 3441 Dickerson Pike	Nashville	TN	37207	**800-242-5662**	615-769-2000	374-3
Skyline Properties South Inc 50 116th Ave SE Ste 120	Bellevue	WA	98004	**800-753-6156**	425-455-2065	650
Skyline Steel LLC 8 Woodhollow Rd Ste 102	Parsippany	NJ	07054	**866-875-9546**		491
Skyline Telephone Membership Corp PO Box 759	West Jefferson	NC	28694	**877-475-9546**	336-877-3111	733
Skylink Travel 980 Ave of the Americas	New York	NY	10018	**800-247-6659**	212-573-8980	16
SkyMall Inc 1520 E Pima St	Phoenix	AZ	85034	**800-759-6255**		458
Skyservice Airlines Inc 9785 Ryan Ave	Dorval	QC	H9P1A2	**888-985-1402**	514-636-3300	13
SkyTech Inc 550 Airport Rd	Rock Hill	SC	29732	**888-386-3596**	803-366-5108	62
SkyTel Corp PO Box 2469 *Cust Svc	Jackson	MS	39225	**800-759-8737***		733
Skytop Lodge 1 Skytop	Skytop	PA	18357	**800-345-7759**	570-595-7401	667
Skywalker Communications Inc 9390 Veterans Memorial Pkwy	O'Fallon	MO	63366	**800-844-9555**	636-272-8025	248

Name / Address	City	State	Zip	Toll-Free	Phone	Class
Skyward Inc 5233 Coye Dr	Stevens Point	WI	54481	800-236-0001	715-341-9406	180-12
Skyweb Networks 2710 State St	Saginaw	MI	48602	866-575-9932	989-792-8681	182
Skyworks LLC 100 Thielman Dr	Buffalo	NY	14206	877-601-5438	716-822-5438	266-3
SL Power Electronics Inc 6050 King Dr Bldg A	Ventura	CA	93003	800-235-5929	805-486-4565	255
SLA (Special Libraries Assn) 331 S Patrick St	Alexandria	VA	22314	866-446-6069	703-647-4900	48-11
Slack & Davis LLP 2705 Bee Caves Rd Ste 220	Austin	TX	78746	800-455-8686	512-795-8686	428
Slack Inc 6900 Grove Rd	Thorofare	NJ	08086	800-257-8290	856-848-1000	634-9
Slade Gorton Company Inc 225 Southampton St	Boston	MA	02118	800-225-1573	617-442-5800	298-5
Slay Industries Inc 1441 Hampton Ave	Saint Louis	MO	63139	800-852-7529	314-647-7529	448
SLB (South Louisiana Bank) 1362 W Tunnel Blvd PO Box 1718	Houma	LA	70361	877-275-3342	985-851-3434	69
Sleep Train Inc 2205 Plz Dr	Rocklin	CA	95765	800-919-2337		470
SLH (Solheim Lutheran Home) 2236 Merton Ave	Los Angeles	CA	90041	888-257-7518	323-257-7518	670
SlickEdit Inc 3000 Aerial Ctr Pkwy Ste 120	Morrisville	NC	27560	800-934-3348	919-473-0070	180-2
S-Line Cargo Control & Safety Products 11414 Mathis	Dallas	TX	75234	800-687-9900		768
Slippery Rock University 1 Morrow Way	Slippery Rock	PA	16057	800-929-4778	724-738-9000	167
SLM Corp 12061 Bluemont Way *NASDAQ: SLM* ■ *Cust Svc	Reston	VA	20190	888-272-5543*	703-810-3000	216
SLM Manufacturing Corp 215 Davidson Ave	Somerset	NJ	08873	800-526-3708	732-469-7500	599
Sloan Implement Co 120 N Business 51	Assumption	IL	62510	800-745-4020	217-226-4411	276
Sloan Management Review 77 Massachusetts Ave E60-100	Cambridge	MA	02139	800-876-5764	617-253-7170	456-5
Sloan Valve Co 10500 Seymour Ave	Franklin Park	IL	60131	800-982-5839	847-671-4300	608
Slomin's Inc 125 Lauman Ln	Hicksville	NY	11801	800-252-7663	516-932-7000	690
Slope Electric Co-op Inc 116 E 12th St PO Box 338	New England	ND	58647	800-559-4191	701-579-4191	247
Slovene National Benefit Society 247 W Allegheny Rd	Imperial	PA	15126	800-843-7675	724-695-1100	391-2
Slumberland Inc 3060 Centerville Rd	Little Canada	MN	55117	888-957-7586	651-482-7500	322
Sly Inc 8300 Dow Cir	Strongsville	OH	44136	800-334-2957	440-891-3200	18
SM Arnold Inc 7901 Michigan Ave *Cust Svc	Saint Louis	MO	63111	800-325-7865*	314-544-4103	102
SMA (Southern Medical Assn) 35 W Lakeshore Dr	Birmingham	AL	35209	800-423-4992	205-945-1840	48-8
Small Business Administration (SBA) 409 Third St SW	Washington	DC	20416	800-827-5722	202-205-6600	340-18
Small Business Administration Regional Offices *Region 6* 1301 Young St	Dallas	TX	75202	800-772-1213	214-767-9401	340-18
Region 10 701 Fifth Ave Ste 2900	Seattle	WA	98104	800-772-1213	206-615-2236	340-18
Small Planet Foods Inc 106 Woodworth St	Sedro Woolley	WA	98284	800-624-4123	360-855-0100	297-18
Small Station Assn KRWG-TV PO Box 30001	Las Cruces	NM	88003	877-308-2408	575-646-2222	629
SMART (Special Military Active Retired Travel Club) 600 University Office Blvd Ste 1A	Pensacola	FL	32504	800-354-7681	850-478-1986	47-23
SMART (Suburban Mobility Authority for Regional Transportation) 535 Griswold St Ste 600 Buhl Bldg	Detroit	MI	48226	866-962-5515	313-223-2100	467
Smart & Final Inc 600 Citadel Dr	Commerce	CA	90040	800-894-0511	323-869-7500	345
Smart Cabling Solutions Inc 1250 N Winchester St	Olathe	KS	66061	877-390-9501	913-390-9501	226
Smart Card Alliance Inc 191 Clarkville Rd	Princeton Junction	NJ	08550	800-556-6828	609-799-5654	48-2
Smart City Networks 5795 W Badura Ave Ste 110	Las Vegas	NV	89118	888-446-6911	702-943-6000	733
Smart Furniture Inc 430 Market St	Chattanooga	TN	37402	888-467-6278	423-267-7007	322
Smart Imaging Technologies Inc 1770 Saint James Pl Ste 414	Houston	TX	77056	877-280-1100	713-589-3500	419
Smart Industries Corp 1626 Delaware Ave	Des Moines	IA	50317	800-553-2442	515-265-9900	323
Smart LLC Smart TuitionOne Woodbridge Ctr Ste 800	Woodbridge	NJ	07095	866-395-2986		393
SMART Modular Technologies Inc 39870 Eureka Dr *NASDAQ: SMOD*	Newark	CA	94560	800-956-7627	510-623-1231	175-2
Smart Power Systems Inc 1760 Stebbins Dr	Houston	TX	77043	800-882-8285	713-464-8000	255
SMART Recovery 7304 Mentor Ave Ste F	Mentor	OH	44060	866-951-5357	440-951-5357	47-21
Smart Safety Group 2535 Camino Del Rio S Ste 125	San Diego	CA	92108	877-345-7627	619-491-3099	198
SMART Technologies Inc 3636 Research Rd NW *TSE: SMA*	Calgary	AB	T2L1Y1	888-427-6278	403-245-0333	175-2
SmartBargains Inc 101 S State Rd 7 Ste 201	Hollywood	FL	33023	877-222-6660		231
SmarTire Systems Inc 6900 Graybar Rd Ste 2110	Richmond	BC	V3W0A5	800-247-2725	604-276-9884	59
Smartpak Equine LLC 40 Grissom Rd Ste 500	Plymouth	MA	02360	888-752-5171	774-773-1000	366
Smartronix Inc 44150 Smartronix Way	Hollywood	MD	20636	866-442-7767	301-373-6000	179
SmartScrubs LLC 3400 E Mcdowell Rd	Phoenix	AZ	85008	800-800-5788		474
Smarty Ants Inc 1400 Rollins Rd	Burlingame	CA	94010	877-905-2687		387
SMC (Somerset Medical Ctr) 110 Rehill Ave	Somerville	NJ	08876	888-637-9584	908-685-2200	374-3
SMC (Southwestern Michigan College) 58900 Cherry Grove Rd	Dowagiac	MI	49047	800-456-8675	269-782-1000	161
SMC (Shannon Medical Ctr) 120 E Harris Ave	San Angelo	TX	76903	800-368-1019	325-653-6741	374-3
SMC (Save the Manatee Club) 500 N Maitland Ave Ste 210	Maitland	FL	32751	800-432-5646	407-539-0990	47-3
SMC Business Councils 600 Cranberry Woods Dr Ste 190	Cranberry Township	PA	16066	800-553-3260	412-371-1500	136
SMCC (Southern Maine Community College) 2 Ft Rd	South Portland	ME	04106	877-282-2182	207-741-5500	798
SMD (Surface Mount Distribution Inc) 1 Oldfield	Irvine	CA	92618	800-820-7634	949-470-7700	248
SME (Society of Mfg Engineers) 1 SME Dr *Cust Svc	Dearborn	MI	48128	800-733-4763*	313-425-3000	48-13
SME (Society for Mining Metallurgy & Exploration Inc) 8307 Shaffer Pkwy	Littleton	CO	80127	800-763-3132	303-973-9550	48-13
SMH (Southeast Missouri Hospital) 1701 Lacey St	Cape Girardeau	MO	63701	800-800-5123	573-334-4822	374-3
SMI (Spring Manufacturers Institute) 2001 Midwest Rd Ste 106	Oak Brook	IL	60523	866-482-5569	630-495-8588	48-13
Smile Train Inc 41 Madison Ave Ste 28	New York	NY	10010	877-543-7645	212-689-9199	47-5
Smith & Butterfield Co Inc 2800 Lynch Rd	Evansville	IN	47711	800-321-6543	812-422-3261	534
Smith & Greene Co 19015 66th Ave S	Kent	WA	98032	800-232-8050	425-656-8000	301
Smith & Nephew Inc 1450 E Brooks Rd *Cust Svc	Memphis	TN	38116	800-238-7538*	901-396-2121	476
Smith & Nephew Inc Endoscopy Div 150 Minuteman Rd	Andover	MA	01810	800-343-5717	978-749-1000	475
Smith & Richardson Manufacturing Co PO Box 589	Geneva	IL	60134	800-426-0876	630-232-2581	620
Smith & Wesson Corp 2100 Roosevelt Ave *Cust Svc	Springfield	MA	01104	800-331-0852*	413-781-8300	286
Smith & Wesson Holding Corp 2100 Roosevelt Ave *NASDAQ: SWHC*	Springfield	MA	01104	800-372-6454	413-781-8300	286
Smith Affiliated Capital (SAC) 800 Third Ave 12th Fl	New York	NY	10022	888-387-3298	212-644-9440	403
Smith Bros Co 3501 W 48th Pl	Chicago	IL	60632	800-621-0225	773-927-3737	297-35
Smith College 7 College Ln	NorthHampton	MA	01063	800-383-3232	413-584-2700	167
Smith Dairy 1381 Dairy Ln	Orrville	OH	44667	800-776-7076	330-683-8710	297-27
Smith Dray Line 320 Frontage Rd	Greenville	SC	29611	866-642-6389		518
Smith Equipment Mfg Co 2601 Lockheed Ave *Cust Svc	Watertown	SD	57201	866-931-9730*	605-882-3200	809
Smith Fork Ranch 45362 Needle Rock Rd	Crawford	CO	81415	855-539-1492	970-921-3454	241
Smith Gardens Inc 4164 Meridian St Ste 400	Bellingham	WA	98226	800-755-6256	360-733-4671	369
Smith Graham & Co 600 Travis St Ste 6900	Houston	TX	77002	800-739-4470	713-227-1100	401
Smith Hartvigsen PLLC The Walker Ctr 175 South Main St Ste 300	Salt Lake City	UT	84111	877-825-2064	801-413-1600	428
Smith McDonald Corp 1270 Niagara St	Buffalo	NY	14213	800-753-8548		607
SMITH Mfg Company Inc 1610 S Dixie Hwy	Pompano Beach	FL	33060	800-653-9311	954-941-9744	81
Smith Motors Inc of Hammond 6405 Indianapolis Blvd	Hammond	IN	46320	877-392-2689	219-845-4000	56
Smith Power Products Inc 3065 W California Ave	Salt Lake City	UT	84104	800-658-5352	801-415-5000	385
Smith Ranch Homes 400 Deer Vly Rd Ste L	San Rafael	CA	94903	800-772-6264	415-491-4918	670
Smith Robertson Museum & Cultural Ctr 528 Bloom St	Jackson	MS	39202	800-354-7695	601-960-1457	519
Smith Southwestern Inc 1850 N Rosemont	Mesa	AZ	85205	800-783-3909	480-854-9545	294
Smith System Driver Improvement Institute Inc 2301 E Lamar Blvd Ste 250	Arlington	TX	76006	800-777-7648	817-652-6969	161
Smith Systems Transportation Inc 417 Ninth Ave	Scottsbluff	NE	69361	800-897-5571		312
Smith Village Home Furnishings 34 N Main St	Jacobus	PA	17407	800-242-1921	717-428-1921	322
Smith, Sovik, Kendrick & Sugnet PC 250 S Clinton St Ste 600	Syracuse	NY	13202	800-675-0011	315-474-2911	428
Smithco Inc 34 W Ave	Wayne	PA	19087	877-833-7648	610-688-4009	429
Smith-Edwards-Dunlap Co 2867 E Allegheny Ave	Philadelphia	PA	19134	800-829-0020	215-425-8800	625
Smithereen Exterminators Inc 7400 N Melvina Ave	Niles	IL	60714	800-336-3500	847-647-0010	576
Smithgall Woods Conservation Area & Lodge 61 Tsalaki Trl	Helen	GA	30545	800-864-7275	706-878-3087	564
Smiths Detection 2202 Lakeside Blvd	Edgewood	MD	21040	800-297-0955	410-510-9100	471
Smiths Medical ASD Inc 160 Weymouth St	Rockland	MA	02370	800-258-5361	781-878-8011	476
Smiths Medical MD Inc 1265 Grey Fox Rd	Saint Paul	MN	55112	800-258-5361	651-633-2556	476
Smiths Medical Respiratory Support Products 5200 Upper Metro Pl Ste 200	Dublin	OH	43017	800-258-5361	214-618-0218	476

Name / Address	City	State	Zip	Toll-Free	Phone	Class
Smithsonian Air & Space Magazine PO Box 37012 *Cust Svc	Washington	DC	20013	**800-766-2149***	202-633-6070	456-19
Smithsonian Folkways Recordings 600 Maryland Ave SW Ste 200	Washington	DC	20024	**800-410-9815**	202-633-6450	655
Smithsonian Institution Business Ventures Div 600 Maryland Ave SW Ste 6000	Washington	DC	20024	**800-521-5330**	202-633-6080	634-9
Smithsonian Magazine 600 Maryland Ave Ste 6001	Washington	DC	20024	**800-766-2149**	202-633-6090	456-11
Smitty's Supply Inc 63399 Hwy 51 N PO Box 530	Roseland	LA	70456	**800-256-7575**	985-748-9687	540
SMO (Southern Maryland Oil Co Inc) 109 N Maple Ave	La Plata	MD	20646	**888-222-3720**		578
Smoke Magazine 26 Broadway	New York	NY	10004	**800-766-2633**	212-391-2060	456-14
Smoker Craft PO Box 65	New Paris	IN	46553	**866-719-7873**		89
Smoker Smith & Associates Pc 339 W Governor Rd Ste 202	Hershey	PA	17033	**888-277-1040**	717-533-5154	2
Smoky Hills Public Television (SHPTV) 604 Elm St	Bunker Hill	KS	67626	**800-337-4788**	785-483-6990	629
Smoky Mountain Truck Ctr LLC 841 Eastern Star Rd	Kingsport	TN	37663	**800-451-1508**		56
Smoky Mountain Visitors Bureau 7906 E Lamar Alexander Pkwy	Townsend	TN	37882	**800-525-6834**	865-448-6134	208
Smoll & Banning CPAs LLC 2410 Central Ave	Dodge City	KS	67801	**800-499-8881**	620-225-6100	2
Smooth-On Inc 2000 St John St	Easton	PA	18042	**800-762-0744**	610-252-5800	42
Smp Communications Corp 7626 E Greenway Rd Ste 100	Scottsdale	AZ	85260	**888-796-3342**	480-905-4100	513
SMPS (Society for Marketing Professional Services) 99 Canal Ctr Plz	Alexandria	VA	22314	**800-292-7677**	703-549-6117	48-18
SMR Technologies Inc 93 Nettie Fenwick Rd	Fenwick	WV	26202	**800-767-6899**	304-846-6636	674
SMS (Systems Maintenance Services Inc) 10420 Harris Oaks Blvd Ste C	Charlotte	NC	28269	**877-405-0330**		177
SMS (Senior Market Sales Inc) 8420 W Dodge Rd 5th Fl	Omaha	NE	68114	**800-786-5566**	402-397-3311	390
SMS Data Products Group Inc 1751 Pinnacle Dr 12th Fl	McLean	VA	22102	**800-331-1767**		182
SMS Productions Inc 10555 Guilford Rd Ste 114	Jessup	MD	20794	**800-289-7671**	301-953-0011	626
SMT Inc 7300 ACC Blvd	Raleigh	NC	27617	**888-214-4804**	919-782-4804	695
Smugglers' Notch Resort 4323 Vermont Rt 108 S	Jeffersonville	VT	05464	**800-451-8752**	802-644-8851	667
SMWIA (Sheet Metal Workers International Assn) 1750 New York Ave NW 6th Fl	Washington	DC	20006	**800-251-7045**	202-783-5880	48-3
Smyrna Air Ctr 300 Doug Warpoole Rd	Smyrna	TN	37167	**888-863-9996**		62
Smyth Cos Inc 1085 Snelling Ave N	Saint Paul	MN	55108	**800-473-3464**	651-646-4544	413
SNA (School Nutrition Assn) 700 S Washington St Ste 300	Alexandria	VA	22314	**800-877-8822**	703-739-3900	48-6
Snack Food Assn 1600 Wilson Blvd Ste 650	Arlington	VA	22209	**800-628-1334**	703-836-4500	48-6
Snacks Unlimited 1 General Mills Blvd	Minneapolis	MN	55426	**800-248-7310**	763-764-7600	297-35
SNAME (Society of Naval Architects & Marine Engineers) 601 Pavonia Ave Ste 400	Jersey City	NJ	07306	**800-798-2188**	201-798-4800	48-21
SNAP (Survivors Network of Those Abused by Priests) PO Box 6416	Chicago	IL	60680	**877-762-7432**	312-455-1499	47-21
Snap Inc 4080 Lafayette Ctr Dr Ste 340	Chantilly	VA	20151	**866-234-7627**	703-393-6400	182
Snap-on Credit LLC 950 Technology Way Ste 301	Libertyville	IL	60048	**877-777-8455**		218
Snap-on Diagnostics 420 Barclay Blvd	Lincolnshire	IL	60069	**800-424-7226**	847-478-0700	250
Snap-on Inc 2801 80th St *NYSE: SNA*	Kenosha	WI	53143	**877-762-7664**	262-656-5200	756
Snapping Shoals Electric Membership Corp 14750 Brown Bridge Rd	Covington	GA	30016	**888-999-1416**	770-786-3484	247
Snappy Tomato Pizza Co 6111 A Burgundy Hill Dr	Burlington	KY	41005	**888-463-7627**	859-525-4680	668
Snap-Tite Autoclave Engineers Div 8325 Hessinger Dr	Erie	PA	16509	**800-458-0409**	814-838-5700	90
SNBC (Sun Bancorp Inc) 226 Landis Ave *NASDAQ: SNBC*	Vineland	NJ	08360	**800-786-9066**		360-2
SNC Mfg Company Inc 101 W Waukau Ave	Oshkosh	WI	54902	**800-558-3325**	920-231-7370	255
SNC-Lavalin Operations & Maintenance Inc 304 The E Mall Ste 900	Toronto	ON	M9B6E2	**800-397-2458**	416-207-4700	194
SNE Enterprises Inc 880 Southview Dr	Mosinee	WI	54455	**800-826-5509**	715-693-7000	238
Snell & Wilmer LLP 1 Arizona Ctr 400 E Van Buren St Ste 1900	Phoenix	AZ	85004	**800-322-0430**	602-382-6000	428
Snell House 21 Atlantic Ave	Bar Harbor	ME	04609	**866-763-5524**	207-288-8004	379
Snethkamp Chrysler Dodge Jeep Ram 11600 Telegraph Rd	Redford	MI	48239	**888-455-6146**	313-255-2700	515
SNFC (Security National Financial Corp) 5300 South 360 West Ste 250 PO Box 57250 *NASDAQ: SNFCA*	Salt Lake City	UT	84123	**800-574-7117**	801-264-1060	391-2
SNK America Inc 1150 Feehanville Dr	Mount Prospect	IL	60056	**888-765-6224**	847-364-0801	454
SNM (Society of Nuclear Medicine) 1850 Samuel Morse Dr	Reston	VA	20190	**888-633-5343**	703-708-9000	48-8
SNMP Research International Inc 3001 Kimberlin Heights Rd	Knoxville	TN	37920	**877-644-5866**	865-579-3311	180-12
Snohomish Flying Service Inc 9900 Airport Way	Snohomish	WA	98296	**800-827-1000**	360-568-1541	62
Snow College 150 College Ave PO Box 1037	Ephraim	UT	84627	**800-848-3399**	435-283-7000	161
Snow Goer Magazine 10405 6th Ave N Ste 210	Plymouth	MN	55441	**800-710-5249**		456-20
Snow King Resort 400 E Snow King Ave Jackson Hole	Jackson	WY	83001	**800-522-5464**	307-733-5200	667
Snow Valley Mountain Resort 35100 State Hwy 18 PO Box 2337	Running Springs	CA	92382	**800-680-7669**	909-867-2751	667
Snowbasin Ski Resort 3925 E Snowbasin Rd	Huntsville	UT	84317	**888-437-5488**	801-620-1100	667
Snowbird Mountain Lodge 4633 Santeetlah Rd	Robbinsville	NC	28771	**800-941-9290**	828-479-3433	379
Snowbird Ski & Summer Resort Hwy 210 PO Box 929000	Snowbird	UT	84092	**800-453-3000**	801-742-2222	667
Snowdale State Park 501 S 439	Salina	OK	74361	**800-622-6317**	918-434-2651	564
Snowfire 100 Us Rt 2	Waterbury	VT	05676	**800-287-5606**	802-244-5606	56
Snowline Engineering 4261 Business Dr	Cameron Park	CA	95682	**800-361-6083**	530-677-2675	263
Snowshoe Mountain Resort 10 Snowshoe Dr	Snowshoe	WV	26209	**877-441-4386**	304-572-1000	667
Snowy Owl Inn 41 Village Rd	Waterville Valley	NH	03215	**800-766-9969**	603-236-8383	379
Snyder & Assoc Inc PO Box 1159 *General	Ankeny	IA	50023	**888-964-2020***	515-964-2020	263
Snyder Chevrolet 524 N Perry St	Napoleon	OH	43545	**800-569-3957**	567-341-4132	56
Snyder of Berlin 1313 Stadium Dr	Berlin	PA	15530	**800-374-7949**	814-267-4641	297-35
Snyder Paper Corp 250 26th St Dr SE PO Box 758	Hickory	NC	28603	**800-222-8562**	828-328-2501	558
Snyder Tire 401 Cadiz Rd	Steubenville	OH	43953	**800-967-8473**	740-264-5543	753
Snyder's of Hanover 1250 York St PO Box 6917	Hanover	PA	17331	**800-233-7125**	717-632-4477	297-9
SOAR (Soar Corp) 5200 Constitution Ave NE	Albuquerque	NM	87110	**866-616-4450**	505-268-6110	655
Soar Corp (SOAR) 5200 Constitution Ave NE	Albuquerque	NM	87110	**866-616-4450**	505-268-6110	655
Soaring Eagle Casino & Resort 6800 E Soaring Eagle Blvd	Mount Pleasant	MI	48858	**888-732-4537**		132
Sobel & Company LLC 293 Eisenhower Pkwy Ste 290	Livingston	NJ	07039	**800-471-2468**	973-994-9494	2
Sobel Westex Inc 2670 Western Ave	Las Vegas	NV	89109	**888-887-6235**		361
Soboba Casino 23333 Soboba Rd	San Jacinto	CA	92583	**866-476-2622**	951-665-1000	451
SOCAN 41 Valleybrook Dr	Toronto	ON	M3B2S6	**800-557-6226**	416-445-8700	136
Social & Economic Sciences Research Ctr (SESRC) *Washington State University* Wilson Hall Rm 133 PO Box 644014	Pullman	WA	99164	**800-932-5393**	509-335-1511	666
Region 4 61 Forsyth St SW Ste 23T30	Atlanta	GA	30303	**800-772-1213**		340-18
Region 5 600 W Madison St PO Box 8280	Chicago	IL	60680	**800-772-1213**	312-575-4050	340-18
Social Strategy1 5000 Sawgrass Village Cir Ste 30	Ponte Vedra Beach	FL	32082	**877-771-3366**		387
Social Studies School Service 10200 Jefferson Blvd PO Box 802	Culver City	CA	90232	**800-421-4246**	310-839-2436	95
Social Work Magazine 750 First St NE Ste 700	Washington	DC	20002	**800-227-3590**	202-408-8600	456-16
Society for American Archaeology (SAA) 900 Second St NE Ste 12	Washington	DC	20002	**800-759-5219**	202-789-8200	48-5
Society for Biomaterials 1120 Rte 73 Ste 200	Mount Laurel	NJ	08054	**800-337-9255**	856-439-0826	48-19
Society for Ecological Restoration International (SERI) 1017 O St NW	Washington	DC	20001	**866-895-4735**	202-299-9518	47-13
Society for Ethnomusicology (SEM) Indiana University 1165 E 3rd St Morrison Hall 005	Bloomington	IN	47405	**800-933-9330**	812-855-6672	47-4
Society for Experimental Mechanics Inc (SEM) 7 School St	Bethel	CT	06801	**800-627-8258**	203-790-6373	48-19
Society for Healthcare Strategy & Market Development (SHSMD) 155 N Wacker Dr Ste 400	Chicago	IL	60606	**800-242-2626**	312-422-3888	48-8
Society for Human Resource Management (SHRM) 1800 Duke St	Alexandria	VA	22314	**800-283-7476**	703-548-3440	48-12
Society for Industrial & Applied Mathematics (SIAM) 3600 Market St 6th Fl	Philadelphia	PA	19104	**800-447-7426**	215-382-9800	48-19
Society for Information Management (SIM) 15000 Commerce Pkwy Ste C	Mount Laurel	NJ	08054	**800-387-9746**	312-527-6734	47-9
Society for Integrative & Comparative Biology (SICB) 1313 Dolley Madison Blvd Ste 402	McLean	VA	22101	**800-955-1236**	703-790-1745	48-19
Society for Marketing Professional Services (SMPS) 99 Canal Ctr Plz	Alexandria	VA	22314	**800-292-7677**	703-549-6117	48-18
Society for Mining Metallurgy & Exploration Inc (SME) 8307 Shaffer Pkwy	Littleton	CO	80127	**800-763-3132**	303-973-9550	48-13
Society for Protective Coatings (SSPC) 40 24th St 6th Fl	Pittsburgh	PA	15222	**877-281-7772**	412-281-2331	48-13
Society for Risk Analysis (SRA) 1313 Dolley Madison Blvd Ste 402	McLean	VA	22101	**800-364-5800**	703-790-1745	48-19
Society for Sedimentary Geology (SEPM) 4111 S Darlington Ste 100	Tulsa	OK	74135	**800-865-9765**	918-610-3361	48-19
Society for Social Work Leadership in Health Care 100 N 20th St 4th Fl	Philadelphia	PA	19103	**866-237-9542**	215-599-6134	48-15
Society for Surgery of the Alimentary Tract (SSAT) 900 Cummings Ctr Ste 221-U	Beverly	MA	01915	**866-849-5866**	978-927-8330	48-8
Society for the Advancement of Material & Process Engineering (SAMPE) 1161 Pk View Dr Ste 200	Covina	CA	91724	**800-562-7360**	626-331-0616	48-19
Society for Vascular Surgery (SVS) 633 N St Clair St 22nd Fl	Chicago	IL	60611	**800-258-7188**	312-334-2300	48-8

Name	Address	City	State	Zip	Toll-Free	Phone	Class
Society of Accredited Marine Surveyors Inc (SAMS)	7855 Argyle Forest Blvd Ste 203	Jacksonville	FL	32244	**800-344-9077**	904-384-1494	47-1
Society of American Archivists (SAA)	17 N State St Ste 1425	Chicago	IL	60602	**866-722-7858**	312-606-0722	47-4
Society of American Florists (SAF)	1601 Duke St	Alexandria	VA	22314	**800-336-4743**	703-836-8700	48-4
Society of American Foresters (SAF)	5400 Grosvenor Ln	Bethesda	MD	20814	**866-897-8720**	301-897-8720	47-2
Society of Automotive Engineers Inc (SAE)	400 Commonwealth Dr	Warrendale	PA	15096	**877-606-7323**	724-776-4841	48-21
Society of Behavioral Medicine (SBM)	555 E Wells St Ste 1100	Milwaukee	WI	53202	**800-784-8669**	414-918-3156	48-15
Society of Biblical Literature (SBL)	The Luce Ctr 825 Houston Mill Rd	Atlanta	GA	30329	**866-727-9955**	404-727-3100	47-20
Society of Broadcast Engineers Inc (SBE)	9102 N Meridian St Ste 150	Indianapolis	IN	46260	**800-237-1776**	317-846-9000	48-14
Society of Cable Telecommunications Engineers (SCTE)	140 Philips Rd	Exton	PA	19341	**800-542-5040**	610-363-6888	48-19
Society of Diagnostic Medical Sonography (SDMS)	2745 Dallas Pkwy	Plano	TX	75093	**800-229-9506**	214-473-8057	48-8
Society of Environmental Journalists (SEJ)	115 W Ave	Jenkintown	PA	19046	**866-208-3372**	215-884-8174	48-14
Society of Financial Service Professionals (SFSP)	19 Campus Blvd Ste 100	Newtown Square	PA	19073	**800-392-6900**	610-526-2500	48-9
Society of Gastroenterology Nurses & Assoc Inc (SGNA)	401 N Michigan Ave	Chicago	IL	60611	**800-245-7462**	312-321-5165	48-8
Society of Interventional Radiology (SIR)	3975 Fair Rdige Dr Ste 400 N	Fairfax	VA	22033	**800-488-7284**	703-691-1805	48-8
Society of Mfg Engineers (SME)	1 SME Dr *Cust Svc	Dearborn	MI	48128	**800-733-4763***	313-425-3000	48-13
Society of Naval Architects & Marine Engineers (SNAME)	601 Pavonia Ave Ste 400	Jersey City	NJ	07306	**800-798-2188**	201-798-4800	48-21
Society of Nuclear Medicine (SNM)	1850 Samuel Morse Dr	Reston	VA	20190	**888-633-5343**	703-708-9000	48-8
Society of Petroleum Engineers (SPE)	222 Palisades Creek Dr	Richardson	TX	75080	**800-456-6863**	972-952-9393	47-12
Society of Professional Journalists (SPJ)	3909 N Meridian St	Indianapolis	IN	46208	**800-331-1212**	317-927-8000	48-14
Society of Saint Andrew (SoSA)	3383 Sweet Hollow Rd	Big Island	VA	24526	**800-333-4597**	434-299-5956	47-5
Society of Teachers of Family Medicine (STFM)	11400 Tomahawk Creek Pkwy Ste 540	Leawood	KS	66211	**800-274-7928**	913-906-6000	48-8
Society of Telecommunications Consultants (STC)	13275 California 89	Old Station	CA	96071	**800-782-7670**	530-335-7313	48-20
Society of Thoracic Surgeons (STS)	633 N St Clair St Ste 2320	Chicago	IL	60611	**877-865-5321**	312-202-5800	48-8
Society of Toxicology (SOT)	1821 Michael Faraday Dr Ste 300	Reston	VA	20190	**800-826-6762**	703-438-3115	48-8
Society of Vacuum Coaters (SVC)	71 Pinon Hill Pl NE	Albuquerque	NM	87122	**800-443-8817**	505-856-7188	48-13
Society of Women Engineers (SWE)	120 S La Salle St Ste 1515	Chicago	IL	60603	**877-793-4636**	312-596-5223	48-19
Society'S Assets Inc	5200 Washington Ave Ste 225	Racine	WI	53406	**800-378-9128**	262-637-9128	363
Socorro Electric Co-op Inc	215 Manzanares Ave PO Box H	Socorro	NM	87801	**800-351-7575**	575-835-0560	247
Socratic Technologies Inc	2505 Mariposa St	San Francisco	CA	94110	**800-576-2728**	415-430-2200	666
Sodexo Inc	9801 Washingtonian Blvd	Gaithersburg	MD	20878	**800-763-3946**		300
Sof Tec Solutions Inc	384 Inverness Pkwy # 211	Englewood	CO	80112	**888-376-3832**	303-662-1010	227
Softfront Software Inc	45437 Warm Springs Blvd	Fremont	CA	94539	**800-763-3766**	510-413-9000	180-1
Sofia Hotel	150 W Broadway	San Diego	CA	92101	**800-826-0009**	619-234-9200	379
Sofradir EC Inc	373 Rt 46W	Fairfield	NJ	07004	**800-759-9577**	973-882-0211	690
Softchalk LLC	22 S Auburn Ave	Richmond	VA	23221	**877-638-2425**		179
Softech & Associates Inc	1570 Corporate Dr Ste B	Costa Mesa	CA	92626	**877-638-3241**	714-427-1122	182
Softerware Inc	132 Welsh Rd Ste 140	Horsham	PA	19044	**800-220-8111**	215-628-0400	179
Softgate Systems Inc	330 Passaic Ave	Fairfield	NJ	07004	**888-477-7297**	973-830-1575	508
Softlayer Technologies Inc	4849 Alpha Rd *Sales	Dallas	TX	75244	**866-398-7638***	214-442-0600	227
Soft-Lite LLC	10250 Philipp Pkwy	Streetsboro	OH	44241	**800-551-1953**	330-528-3400	237
Softmart Inc	450 Acorn Ln *Cust Svc	Downingtown	PA	19335	**800-328-1319***	610-518-4000	176
Softomate LLC	901 N Pitt St Ste 325	Alexandria	VA	22314	**877-243-8735**		529
Softplan Systems Inc	8118 Isabella Ln	Brentwood	TN	37027	**800-248-0164**	615-370-1121	179
SoftPress Systems Inc	3020 Bridgeway Ste 408	Sausalito	CA	94965	**800-853-6454**	415-331-4820	180-8
Softrock-FM 98.9 (AC)	83 E Shaw Ave Ste 150	Fresno	CA	93710	**800-423-5870**	559-230-4300	642-48
Software AG USA	11700 Plz America Dr Ste 700	Reston	VA	20190	**877-724-4965**	703-860-5050	180-1
Software Engineering Institute (SEI)	4500 Fifth Ave	Pittsburgh	PA	15213	**888-201-4479**	412-268-5800	666
Software Engineering of America Inc (SEA)	1230 Hempstead Tpke	Franklin Square	NY	11010	**800-272-7322**	516-328-7000	180-12
Software Engineering Services Corp	1311 Ft Crook Rd S	Bellevue	NE	68005	**800-244-1278**	402-292-8660	666
Software House International (SHI)	290 Davidson Ave	Somerset	NJ	08873	**888-764-8888**		176
Software Information Systems Inc (SIS)	165 Barr St	Lexington	KY	40507	**800-337-6914**	859-977-4747	182
Software Pursuits Inc	1900 S Norfolk St	San Mateo	CA	94403	**800-367-4823**	650-372-0900	180-12
Software Technology Group	555 S 300 E	Salt Lake City	UT	84111	**888-595-1001**	801-595-1000	182
Softworld Inc	281 Winter St Ste 301	Waltham	MA	02451	**877-899-1166**	781-466-8882	719
SOG Specialty Knives & Tools LLC	6521 212th St SW	Lynnwood	WA	98036	**888-405-6433**	425-771-6230	361
Sogetel Inc	111, rue du 12-Novembre	Nicolet	QC	J3T1S3	**866-764-3835**		387
SoHo Grand Hotel	310 W Broadway	New York	NY	10013	**800-965-3000**	212-965-3000	379
SoHo Metropolitan Hotel	318 Wellington St W	Toronto	ON	M5V3T4	**866-764-6638**	416-599-8800	379
SOHOware Inc	1250 Oakmead Pkwy Ste 210	Sunnyvale	CA	94085	**800-632-1118**	408-565-9888	178
Soil & Water Conservation Society (SWCS)	945 SW Ankeny Rd	Ankeny	IA	50023	**800-843-7645**	515-289-2331	47-13
Soilmoisture Equipment Corp	801 S Kellogg Ave	Goleta	CA	93117	**888-964-0040**	805-964-3525	419
Sojourner-Douglass College	200 N Central Ave	Baltimore	MD	21202	**800-732-2630**	410-276-0306	167
Sokol & Co	5315 Dansher Rd *Cust Svc	Countryside	IL	60525	**800-328-7656***	708-482-8250	297-1
Sol Jewelry Designs Inc	550 S Hill St Ste 1020	Los Angeles	CA	90013	**888-323-7772**	213-622-7772	410
Solano Coalition for Bett	1 Harbor Ctr Ste 270	Suisun City	CA	94585	**800-978-7547**	707-863-4440	363
Solano County Fair	900 Fairgrounds Dr	Vallejo	CA	94589	**800-700-2482**	707-551-2000	639
Solano County Library	1150 Kentucky St	Fairfield	CA	94533	**866-572-7587**		435
Solar Industries Inc	PO Box 27337	Tucson	AZ	85726	**800-449-2323**	520-519-8258	193-3
Solar Solutions & Distribution LLC	2500 W Fifth Ave	Denver	CO	80204	**855-765-3478**	303-948-6300	694
Solar Store LLC, The	2833 N Country Club Rd	Tucson	AZ	85716	**877-264-6374**	520-322-5180	609
Solar Tours	1629 K St NW Ste 604	Washington	DC	20006	**800-388-7652**	202-861-5864	16
Solarus	440 E Grand Ave	Wisconsin Rapids	WI	54494	**800-421-9282**	715-421-8111	733
Solatube International Inc	2210 Oak Ridge Way	Vista	CA	92081	**888-765-2882**	760-477-1120	694
Solazyme Inc	225 Gateway Blvd *NASDAQ: SZYM*	South San Francisco	CA	94080	**877-917-9075**	650-780-4777	469
Soldier of Fortune Magazine	2135 11th St	Boulder	CO	80302	**800-377-2789**	303-449-3750	456-12
Soldiers + Sailors Memorial Hospital	32-36 Central Ave	Wellsboro	PA	16901	**800-808-5287**	570-723-7764	374-3
Soldiers Delight Natural Environment Area	5100 Deer Park Rd	Owings Mills	MD	21117	**800-830-3974**	410-461-5005	564
Solebury School	6832 Phillips Mill Rd	New Hope	PA	18938	**800-675-6900**	215-862-5261	621
Solectek Corp	6370 Nancy Ridge Dr Ste 109	San Diego	CA	92121	**888-299-8057**	858-450-1220	178
Soleno Inc	1160 Rt 133 CP 837	Saint-jean-sur-richelieu	QC	J2X4J5	**877-633-7473**	450-347-7855	491
Solex Academy Inc	350 E Dundee Rd Ste 200	Wheeling	IL	60090	**866-797-6539**	847-229-9595	683
Solheim Lutheran Home (SLH)	2236 Merton Ave	Los Angeles	CA	90041	**888-257-7518**	323-257-7518	670
Soliant LLC	1872 Hwy 9 Bypass	Lancaster	SC	29720	**800-288-9401**	803-285-9401	599
Solid Concepts Inc	28309 Ave Crocker	Valencia	CA	91355	**888-311-1017**	661-295-4400	453
Solid Waste Assn of North America (SWANA)	1100 Wayne Ave Ste 700	Silver Spring	MD	20910	**800-467-9262**	301-585-2898	530-5
SolidBoss Worldwide Inc	200 Veterans Blvd	South Haven	MI	49090	**888-258-7252**	269-637-6356	752
SolidWorks Corp	300 Baker Ave	Concord	MA	01742	**800-693-9000**	978-371-5011	180-10
Solisco Inc	120 10e Rue	Scott	QC	G0S3G0	**800-463-4188**	418-387-8908	626
Solitude Ski Resort	12000 Big Cottonwood Canyon	Solitude	UT	84121	**800-748-4754**	801-534-1400	667
Solix Inc	30 Lanidex Plz W PO Box 685	Parsippany	NJ	07054	**800-200-0818**	973-581-6700	706
Solmax International Inc	2801 Marie-Victorin Blvd	Varennes	QC	J3X1P7	**800-571-3904**	450-929-1234	145
Solo Printing Inc	7860 NW 66th St	Miami	FL	33166	**800-325-0118**	305-594-8699	626
Soloflex Inc	22590 NW Badertscher Rd	Hillsboro	OR	97124	**800-547-8802**		269
Solomon Corp	103 W Main	Solomon	KS	67480	**800-234-2867**	785-655-2191	619
Solomon Pond Mall	601 Donald Lynch Blvd	Marlborough	MA	01752	**877-746-6642**	508-303-6255	459
Solomon R Guggenheim Museum	1071 Fifth Ave	New York	NY	10128	**800-329-6109**	212-423-3500	519
Solon Manufacturing Co	425 Center St	Chardon	OH	44024	**800-323-9717**	440-286-7149	491
Solta Medical Inc	25881 Industrial Blvd	Hayward	CA	94545	**877-782-2286**		252
Solutek Corp	94 Shirley St	Boston	MA	02119	**800-403-0770**	617-445-5335	144
Solutioninc Technologies Ltd	5692 Bloomfield St	Halifax	NS	B3K1T2	**888-496-2221**	902-420-0077	364
Solutions 21	152 Wabash St	Pittsburgh	PA	15220	**866-765-2121**		462
Solutions AE Inc	236 Auburn Ave	Atlanta	GA	30303	**888-562-4441**		462
Solvay America Inc	3333 Richmond Ave *General	Houston	TX	77098	**800-365-6565***	713-525-6000	582

	City	State	Zip	Toll-Free	Phone	Class
Solvay Chemicals Inc						
3333 Richmond Ave	Houston	TX	77098	**800-765-8292**	713-525-6800	502-1
Solvents & Chemicals Inc						
1904 Mykawa Rd	Pearland	TX	77581	**800-622-3990**	281-485-5377	145
Somagen Diagnostics Inc						
9220 25th Ave	Edmonton	AB	T6N1E1	**800-661-9993**	780-702-9500	474
Somers Cove Marina						
715 Broadway PO Box 67	Crisfield	MD	21817	**800-967-3474**	410-968-0925	564
Somerset Capital Group Ltd						
612 Wheelers Farms Rd	Milford	CT	06461	**877-282-9922**	203-701-5100	266-2
Somerset Community College						
808 Monticello St	Somerset	KY	42501	**877-629-9722**	606-679-8501	161
Somerset County Library						
1 Vogt Dr	Bridgewater	NJ	08807	**888-313-3532**	908-526-4016	434-3
Somerset Door & Column Co						
174 Sagamore St	Somerset	PA	15501	**800-242-7916**	814-444-9427	498
Somerset Fine Arts						
PO Box 869	Fulshear	TX	77441	**800-444-2540***		634-10
*Sales						
Somerset Inn						
2601 W Big Beaver Rd	Troy	MI	48084	**800-228-8769**	248-643-7800	379
Somerset Medical Ctr (SMC)						
110 Rehill Ave	Somerville	NJ	08876	**888-637-9584**	908-685-2200	374-3
Somerset Rural Electric Co-op						
223 Industrial Pk Rd	Somerset	PA	15501	**800-443-4255**	814-445-4106	247
Somerset Trust Co						
151 W Main St PO Box 777	Somerset	PA	15501	**800-972-1651**	814-443-9200	69
Somerset Welding & Steel Inc						
10558 Somerset Pk	Somerset	PA	15501	**800-777-2671**	814-444-3400	515
Somerset-Pulaski County Chamber of Commerce						
445 S Hwy 27 Ste 101	Somerset	KY	42501	**877-629-9722**	606-679-7323	138
Sommer Electric Corp						
818 Third St NE	Canton	OH	44704	**800-766-6373**	330-455-9454	248
Sommer Metalcraft Corp						
315 Poston Dr	Crawfordsville	IN	47933	**888-876-6637**	765-362-6201	481
Sommer's Automotive						
7211 W Meq	Mequon	WI	53092	**888-494-4193**	262-242-0100	56
Sompo Japan Insurance Co of America						
777 Third Ave 28th Fl	New York	NY	10017	**800-208-3614**	212-416-1200	391-4
Sonalysts Inc						
215 Waterford Pkwy N	Waterford	CT	06385	**800-526-8091**	860-442-4355	263
Sonesta Hotel & Suites Coconut Grove						
2889 McFarlane Rd	Miami	FL	33133	**800-766-3782**	305-529-2828	379
Sonetics Corp						
7340 Sw Durham Rd	Portland	OR	97224	**800-833-4558**		645
Soniat House						
1133 Chartres St	New Orleans	LA	70116	**800-544-8808**	504-522-0570	379
Sonic Air Systems Inc						
1050 Beacon St	Brea	CA	92821	**800-827-6642**	714-255-0124	18
Sonic Corp						
1 Research Dr	Stratford	CT	06615	**866-493-1378**	203-375-0063	299
Sonic Drive-in Restaurants						
300 Johnny Bench Dr	Oklahoma City	OK	73104	**877-828-7868**	405-225-5000	668
Sonic Innovations Inc						
2501 Cottontail Ln	Somerset	NJ	08873	**888-678-4327**	888-423-7834	476
Sonicor Inc						
82 Otis St	West Babylon	NY	11704	**800-864-5022**	631-920-6555	780
Sonics & Materials Inc						
53 Church Hill Rd	Newtown	CT	06470	**800-745-1105**	203-270-4600	780
OTC: SIMA						
SonicWALL Inc						
2001 Logic Dr	San Jose	CA	95124	**888-557-6642**	408-745-9600	178
Sonit Systems LLC						
130 W Field Dr	Archbold	OH	43502	**800-296-0018**	419-446-2151	182
Sonnenalp Resort of Vail						
20 Vail Rd	Vail	CO	81657	**800-654-8312**	970-476-5656	667
Sonobond Ultrasonics Inc						
1191 McDermott Dr	West Chester	PA	19380	**800-323-1269**	610-696-4710	809
Sonoco						
1 N Second St	Hartsville	SC	29550	**800-377-2692**		600
NYSE: SON						
Sonoma County Transit						
355 W Robles Ave	Santa Rosa	CA	95407	**800-345-7433**	707-585-7516	467
Sonoma Developmental Ctr						
15000 Arnold Dr	Eldridge	CA	95431	**800-862-0007**	707-938-6000	232
Sonoma Outfitters						
2412 Magowan Dr	Santa Rosa	CA	95405	**800-290-1920**	707-528-1920	709
Sonoma Raceway						
Hwy S 37 & 121	Sonoma	CA	95476	**800-870-7223**	707-938-8448	514
Sonoma Technical Support Services						
8840 210th St Ste 342	Langley	BC	V1M2Y2	**866-898-3123**		198
Sonora Regional Medical Ctr (SRMC)						
1000 Greenly Rd	Sonora	CA	95370	**877-336-3566***	209-536-5000	374-3
*Compliance						
SonoSite Inc						
21919 30th Dr SE	Bothell	WA	98021	**888-482-9449**	425-951-1200	382
NASDAQ: SONO						
Sons of Norway						
1455 W Lake St 2nd Fl	Minneapolis	MN	55408	**800-945-8851**	612-827-3611	47-14
Sonstegard Foods Co						
5005 S Bur Oak Pl Ste 102	Sioux Falls	SD	57108	**800-533-3184**		618
Sony Corp of America						
550 Madison Ave	New York	NY	10022	**800-282-2848**	212-833-6800	51
Sony Creative Software						
1617 Sherman Ave	Madison	WI	53704	**800-577-6642**	608-256-3133	180-9
Sony Electronics Inc						
1 Sony Dr	Park Ridge	NJ	07656	**800-222-7669***	201-930-1000	51
*Cust Svc						
Sony Pictures Entertainment Inc						
10202 W Washington Blvd	Culver City	CA	90232	**855-327-7669**	310-244-4000	513
Sony Pictures Television						
10202 W Washington Blvd	Culver City	CA	90232	**800-327-3325**	310-244-4000	513
Sooner Lift Inc						
3401 S Purdue St	Oklahoma City	OK	73179	**800-593-2830**	405-682-1400	768
Sooner Pipe LLC						
1331 Lamar St						
Ste 970 4 Houston Ctr	Houston	TX	77010	**800-888-9161**	713-759-1200	385
Sopark Corp						
3300 S Pk Ave	Buffalo	NY	14218	**866-576-7275**	716-822-0434	624

	City	State	Zip	Toll-Free	Phone	Class
Sophie Station Suites						
1717 University Ave	Fairbanks	AK	99709	**800-528-4916**		379
Sophos Inc						
3 Van de Graaff Dr 2nd Fl	Burlington	MA	01803	**866-866-2802**		180-1
SOR Inc						
14685 W 105th St	Lenexa	KS	66215	**800-676-6794**	913-888-2630	203
Sorbee International Ltd						
9990 Global Rd	Philadelphia	PA	19115	**800-654-3997**	215-645-1111	297-8
Sorbothane Inc						
2144 State Rt 59	Kent	OH	44240	**800-838-3906**	330-678-9444	327
Sorenson Media Inc						
13961 Minuteman Dr Ste 100	Draper	UT	84020	**888-767-3676**	801-501-8650	543
Sorin Group USA Inc						
14401 W 65th Way	Arvada	CO	80004	**800-289-5759**	303-424-0129	475
Sorrento Electronics Inc						
4949 Greencraig Ln	San Diego	CA	92123	**800-252-1180**	858-522-8300	471
Sorrento Hotel						
900 Madison St	Seattle	WA	98104	**800-426-1265**	206-622-6400	669
SOS (Store Opening Solutions)						
800 Middle Tennessee Blvd	Murfreesboro	TN	37129	**877-388-9262**		448
SOS Children's Villages-USA						
1001 Connecticut Ave NW						
Ste 1250	Washington	DC	20036	**888-767-4543***	202-347-7920	47-6
*General						
SoSA (Society of Saint Andrew)						
3383 Sweet Hollow Rd	Big Island	VA	24526	**800-333-4597**	434-299-5956	47-5
SOT (Society of Toxicology)						
1821 Michael Faraday Dr Ste 300	Reston	VA	20190	**800-826-6762**	703-438-3115	48-8
Sotech Nitram Inc						
1695 Boul Laval	Laval	QC	H7S2M2	**877-664-8726**	450-975-2100	312
Sotheby's International Realty						
38 E 61st St	New York	NY	10065	**866-899-4747**	212-606-7660	650
Sothys USA Inc						
1500 NW 94th Ave	Miami	FL	33172	**800-325-0503**	305-594-4222	240
Soudan Underground Mine State Park						
1302 McKinley Park Rd	Soudan	MN	55782	**888-646-6367**	218-753-2245	564
Sound & Cellular Inc						
824 W Yellowstone Hwy	Casper	WY	82601	**800-689-7256**	307-234-7256	538
Sound Com Corp						
227 Depot St	Berea	OH	44017	**800-628-8739**	440-234-2604	51
Sound Glass Sales Inc						
5501 75th St W	Tacoma	WA	98499	**800-468-9949**	253-473-7477	191-6
Sound Impressions Music Marketing L.L.C						
14290 Gillis Rd Ste A	Dallas	TX	75244	**888-512-9119**		197
Sound Shore Fund						
3 Canal Plz	Portland	ME	04101	**800-754-8758**		527
Sound Shore Management Inc						
8 Sound Shore Dr Ste 180	Greenwich	CT	06830	**800-551-1980**	203-629-1980	401
SoundBite Communications Inc						
22 Crosby Dr	Bedford	MA	01730	**888-436-3797**	650-466-1100	733
NASDAQ: SDBT						
Soundcoat Co						
1 Burt Dr	Deer Park	NY	11729	**800-394-8913**	631-242-2200	389
Source Data Products Inc						
18350 Mount Langley St	Fountain Valley	CA	92708	**800-333-2669**	714-593-0387	198
Source Intelligence LLC						
1921 Palomar Oaks Way Ste 205	Carlsbad	CA	92008	**877-916-6337**		194
Source Media Inc						
1 State St Plz 27th Fl	New York	NY	10004	**800-221-1809**	212-803-8200	634-9
Source One Distribution Services						
1220 Morse Ave	Royal Oak	MI	48067	**877-763-3976**	248-399-5060	5
Source Technologies						
2910 Whitehall Pk Dr	Charlotte	NC	28273	**800-922-8501**	704-969-7500	180-1
Sourcebooks Inc						
1935 Brookdale Rd Ste 139	Naperville	IL	60563	**800-432-7444**	630-961-3900	634-2
SourceGas						
655 E Millsap Dr	Fayetteville	AR	72703	**800-563-0012**		785
SourceLink Inc						
500 Pk Blvd Ste 415	Itasca	IL	60143	**866-947-6872**		5
SourceMedical Solutions Inc						
100 Grandview Pl Ste 400	Birmingham	AL	35243	**866-245-8093**		227
South African Airways						
1200 S Pine Island Rd						
Ste 650	Plantation	FL	33324	**800-722-9675**	954-769-5000	25
South Alabama Electric Co-op (SAEC)						
PO Box 449	Troy	AL	36081	**800-556-2060**	334-566-2060	247
South Arkansas Arboretum						
PO Box 7010	El Dorado	AR	71731	**888-287-2757**		564
South Arkansas Community College						
PO Box 7010	El Dorado	AR	71731	**800-955-2289**	870-862-8131	161
South Baldwin Chamber of Commerce (SBCC)						
112 W Laurel Ave PO Box 1117	Foley	AL	36535	**877-461-3712**	251-943-3291	138
South Bay Correctional Facility						
600 US Hwy 27 S	South Bay	FL	33493	**800-574-5729**	561-992-9505	215
South Baylo University						
1126 N Brookhurst St	Anaheim	CA	92801	**888-642-2956**	714-533-1495	167
South Beach Marina Inn & Vacation Rentals						
232 S Sea Pines Dr	Hilton Head Island	SC	29928	**800-367-3909**	843-671-6498	379
South Beach State Park						
5580 S Coast Hwy	Newport	OR	97366	**800-452-5687**	541-867-4715	564
South Bend Medical Foundation						
530 N Lafayette Blvd	South Bend	IN	46601	**800-544-0925**	574-234-4176	418
South Bend Symphony Orchestra (SBSO)						
127 N Michigan St	South Bend	IN	46601	**800-537-6415**	574-232-6343	572-3
South Bend Tribune						
225 W Colfax Ave	South Bend	IN	46626	**800-220-7378**	574-235-6464	531-2
South Bend/Mishawaka Convention & Visitors Bureau						
401 E Colfax Ave Ste 310	South Bend	IN	46617	**800-519-0577**		208
South Boston Speedway						
1188 James D Hagood Hwy						
PO Box 1066	South Boston	VA	24592	**877-440-1540**	434-572-4947	514
South Broadway Cultural Ctr						
1025 Broadway Blvd SE	Albuquerque	NM	87102	**866-441-6075**	505-848-1320	49-1
South Carolina						
Child Support Enforcement Office						
3150 Harden St Ext	Columbia	SC	29203	**800-768-5858**	803-898-9210	339-41
Commerce Dept						
1201 Main St Ste 1600	Columbia	SC	29201	**800-868-7232**	803-737-0400	339-41

Listing	Toll-Free	Phone	Class
State Government Information			
1301 Gervais St Ste 710............Columbia SC 29201	**866-340-7105**	803-771-0131	339-41
Veterans Affairs Div			
1205 Pendleton St Ste 463..........Columbia SC 29201	**800-827-1000**	803-734-0200	339-41
Vocational Rehabilitation Dept			
1410 Boston Ave PO Box 15 ... West Columbia SC 29171	**800-832-7526**	803-896-6500	339-41
South Carolina Aquarium			
100 Aquarium Wharf ....Charleston SC 29401	**800-722-6455**	843-577-3474	39
South Carolina Assn of Realtors			
3780 Fernandina Rd ....Columbia SC 29210	**800-233-6381**	803-772-5206	654
South Carolina Assn of Veterinarians			
PO Box 11766 ....Columbia SC 29211	**800-441-7228**	803-254-1027	793
South Carolina Bar			
950 Taylor St ....Columbia SC 29201	**877-797-2227**	803-799-6653	71
South Carolina Chamber of Commerce			
1201 Main St Ste1100 ....Columbia SC 29201	**800-799-4601**	803-799-4601	139
South Carolina Democratic Party			
915 Lady St Ste 111 ....Columbia SC 29250	**800-841-1817**	803-799-7798	615-1
South Carolina Dental Assn			
120 Stonemark Ln ....Columbia SC 29210	**800-327-2598**	803-750-2277	229
South Carolina Education Association, The			
421 Zimalcrest Dr ....Columbia SC 29210	**800-422-7232**	803-772-6553	532
South Carolina Elastic Co			
201 S Carolina Elastic Rd ....Landrum SC 29356	**800-845-6700**	864-457-3388	742-5
South Carolina Electric & Gas Co			
PO Box 100255 ....Columbia SC 29202	**800-251-7234**	803-635-4444	785
South Carolina Federal Credit Union			
PO Box 190012 ....North Charleston SC 29419	**800-845-0432**	843-797-8300	221
South Carolina Higher Education Tuition Grants Commission			
115 Atrium Wy Ste 102..............Columbia SC 29203	**877-382-4357**	803-896-1120	723
South Carolina Medical Assn			
132 W Pk Blvd ....Columbia SC 29210	**800-327-1021**	803-798-6207	473
South Carolina Press Services Inc			
106 Outlet Pointe Blvd			
PO Box 11429.......................Columbia SC 29210	**888-727-7377**	803-750-9561	623
South Carolina State Ports Authority			
176 Concord St ....Charleston SC 29401	**800-845-7106**	843-723-8651	617
South Carolina State University			
300 College St NE			
PO Box 7127.....................Orangeburg SC 29117	**800-260-5956***	803-536-7000	167
*Admissions			
South Central Arkansas Electric Co-op			
4818 Highway 8 W PO Box 476 ......Arkadelphia AR 71923	**800-814-2931**	870-246-6701	247
South Central College			
Faribault			
1225 Third St ....Faribault MN 55021	**800-422-0391**	507-332-5800	161
Mankato			
1920 Lee Blvd ....North Mankato MN 56003	**800-722-9359**	507-389-7200	161
South Central Electric Assn			
71176 Tiell Dr PO Box 150..........Saint James MN 56081	**888-805-7232**	507-375-3164	247
South Central Indiana Rural Electric Membership Corp			
300 Morton Ave ....Martinsville IN 46151	**800-264-7362**	765-342-3344	247
South Central Power Company Inc			
2780 Coon Path Rd ....Lancaster OH 43130	**800-282-5064**	740-653-4422	247
South Central Public Power District (SCPPD)			
275 S Main St PO Box 406..............Nelson NE 68961	**800-557-5254**	402-225-2351	247
South Charlotte Nissan			
9215 S Blvd ....Charlotte NC 28273	**888-411-1423**	704-552-9191	56
South Coast Plaza			
3333 Bristol St...................Costa Mesa CA 92626	**800-782-8888**		459
South College			
3904 Lonas Dr ....Knoxville TN 37909	**877-557-2575**	865-251-1800	798
South Dakota			
Child Support Div			
700 Governors Dr ....Pierre SD 57501	**800-286-9145**	605-773-3641	339-42
Crime Victims' Compensation Program			
700 Governors Dr ....Pierre SD 57501	**800-696-9476**	605-773-6317	339-42
DEPARTMENT OF HEALTH			
600 E Capitol Ave ....Pierre SD 57501	**800-738-2301**	605-773-4961	339-42
Economic Development Office			
711 E Wells Ave ....Pierre SD 57501	**800-872-6190**	605-773-3301	339-42
Parks & Recreation Div			
523 E Capitol Ave ....Pierre SD 57501	**800-710-2267***	605-773-3391	339-42
*Campground Resv			
Rehabilitation Services Div			
500 E Capitol Ave ....Pierre SD 57501	**800-265-9684**	605-773-3195	339-42
Tourism Office			
711 E Wells Ave ....Pierre SD 57501	**800-952-3625**	605-773-3301	339-42
South Dakota Assn of Realtors			
204 N Euclid Ave ....Pierre SD 57501	**800-227-5877**	605-224-0554	654
South Dakota Chamber of Commerce & Industry			
108 N Euclid Ave ....Pierre SD 57501	**800-742-8112**	605-224-6161	139
South Dakota Dental Assn			
804 N Euclid Ave Ste 103.............Pierre SD 57501	**866-551-8023**	605-224-9133	229
South Dakota Lions Eye Bank			
4501 W 61st St N ....Sioux Falls SD 57107	**800-245-7846**	605-373-1008	271
South Dakota Newspaper Services			
1125 32nd Ave ....Brookings SD 57006	**800-658-3697**	605-692-4300	623
South Dakota Nurses Assn (SDNA)			
PO Box 1015 ....Pierre SD 57501	**888-425-3032**	605-945-4265	532
South Dakota Public Broadcasting (SDPB)			
555 N Dakota St PO Box 5000 ....Vermillion SD 57069	**800-456-0766**	605-677-5861	629
South Dakota School of Mines & Technology			
501 E St Joseph St ....Rapid City SD 57701	**800-544-8162**	605-394-2414	167
South Dakota State Library			
800 Governors Dr ....Pierre SD 57501	**800-423-6665**	605-773-3131	434-5
South Dakota State University			
PO Box 2201 ....Brookings SD 57007	**800-952-3541**	605-688-4121	167
South Dakota State University Briggs Library			
N Campus Dr PO Box 2115 ....Brookings SD 57007	**800-786-2038**	605-688-5106	434-6
South Dakota Wheat Growers Assn			
908 Lamont St SE ....Aberdeen SD 57401	**888-429-4902**	605-225-5500	277
South Florida Sun-Sentinel			
200 E Las Olas Blvd ....Fort Lauderdale FL 33301	**800-548-6397***	954-356-4000	531-2
*Cust Svc			
South Georgia Pecan Co			
309 S Lee St ....Valdosta GA 31601	**800-627-6630**	229-244-1321	297-28
South Jersey Healthcare HospiceCare			
2848 S Delsea Dr Bldg 1 ....Vineland NJ 08360	**800-770-7547**		371
South Kentucky Rural Electrical Co-op			
925 N Main St PO Box 910............Somerset KY 42502	**800-264-5112**	606-678-4121	247
South Louisiana Bank (SLB)			
1362 W Tunnel Blvd PO Box 1718........Houma LA 70361	**877-275-3342**	985-851-3434	69
South Mountain Community College			
7050 S 24th St ....Phoenix AZ 85042	**855-622-2332**	602-243-8000	161
South Nassau Communities Hospital			
1 Healthy Way ....Oceanside NY 11572	**877-768-8462**	516-632-3000	374-3
South Padre Island Convention & Visitors Bureau			
7355 Padre Blvd ....South Padre Island TX 78597	**800-767-2373**	956-761-6433	208
South Padre Island Convention Centre			
7355 Padre Blvd ....South Padre Island TX 78597	**800-657-2373**	956-761-3000	207
South Pier Inn on the Canal			
701 Lake Ave S ....Duluth MN 55802	**800-430-7437**	218-786-9007	379
South Plains Electric Co-op Inc			
PO Box 1830 ....Lubbock TX 79408	**800-658-2655**	806-775-7766	247
South Point Hotel & Casino			
9777 Las Vegas Blvd S ....Las Vegas NV 89183	**866-796-7111**	702-796-7111	379
South River Electric Membership Corp			
17494 US 421 S PO Box 931.............Dunn NC 28335	**800-338-5530**	910-892-8071	247
South Seas Island Resort			
5400 Plantation Rd ....Captiva FL 33924	**866-565-5089**	239-472-5111	667
South Shore Harbour Resort & Conference Ctr			
2500 S Shore Blvd ....League City TX 77573	**800-442-5005***	281-334-1000	667
*Resv			
South Shore Hospital			
55 Fogg Rd ....South Weymouth MA 02190	**800-439-2370**	781-340-8000	374-3
South Shore Plaza			
250 Granite St ....Braintree MA 02184	**877-746-6642**	781-843-8200	459
South Shore Transportation Inc			
4010 Columbus Ave ....Sandusky OH 44870	**888-428-0879**	419-626-6267	778
South Sioux City Convention & Visitors Bureau			
4401 Dakota Ave ....South Sioux City NE 68776	**866-494-1307**	402-494-1307	208
South Tacoma Honda			
7802 S Tacoma Way ....Tacoma WA 98409	**888-497-2416**	253-472-2300	56
South Texas Blood & Tissue Ctr			
6211 IH-10 W ....San Antonio TX 78201	**800-292-5534**	210-731-5555	88
South Texas Money Management Ltd			
700 N Saint Mary's Ste 100 ....San Antonio TX 78205	**800-805-1385**	210-824-8916	401
South Toledo Bend State Park			
120 Bald Eaglel Rd ....Anacoco LA 71403	**888-398-4770**	337-286-9075	564
South University			
Montgomery			
5355 Vaughn Rd ....Montgomery AL 36116	**866-629-2962**	334-395-8800	167
South University Columbia			
9 Science Ct ....Columbia SC 29203	**800-688-0932**	803-799-9082	167
South University Savannah			
709 Mall Blvd ....Savannah GA 31406	**800-688-0932**	912-201-8000	167
South University West Palm Beach			
9801 Belvedere Rd			
University Ctr ....West Palm Beach FL 33411	**800-688-0932**	561-273-6500	167
Southampton Inn			
91 Hill St ....SoutHampton NY 11968	**800-832-6500**	631-283-6500	379
Southbend Inc			
1100 Old Honeycutt Rd ....Fuquay Varina NC 27526	**800-755-4777**	919-762-1000	299
Southbridge Savings Bank Inc			
253-257 Main St PO Box 370........Southbridge MA 01550	**800-939-9103**	508-765-9103	69
Southco Distributing Co			
2201 S John St ....Goldsboro NC 27530	**800-969-3172**	919-735-8012	298-8
Southdale Ctr			
10 Southdale Ctr ....Edina MN 55435	**877-746-6642**	952-925-7874	459
Southeast Arkansas College			
1900 Hazel St ....Pine Bluff AR 71603	**888-732-7582**	870-543-5900	161
Southeast Asia Resource Action Ctr (SEARAC)			
1628 16th St NW 3rd Fl ....Washington DC 20009	**888-907-1485**	202-667-4690	47-5
Southeast Colorado Power Assn (SECPA)			
901 W 3rd ....La Junta CO 81050	**800-332-8634**	719-384-2551	247
Southeast Community College			
Beatrice			
4771 W Scott Rd ....Beatrice NE 68310	**800-233-5027**	402-228-3468	161
Lincoln 8800 'O' St ....Lincoln NE 68520	**800-642-4075**	402-471-3333	161
Milford 600 State St ....Milford NE 68405	**800-933-7223**	402-761-2131	798
Southeast Electric Co-op Inc (SECO)			
110 S Main St ....Ekalaka MT 59324	**888-485-8762**	406-775-8762	247
Southeast Georgia Health System Brunswick Campus			
2415 Parkwood Dr ....Brunswick GA 31520	**844-882-7227**	912-466-7000	374-3
Southeast Industrial Equipment Inc			
12200 Steele Creek Rd ....Charlotte NC 28273	**866-696-9125**	704-399-9700	469
Southeast Kentucky Community & Technical College			
Cumberland			
700 College Rd ....Cumberland KY 40823	**888-274-7322**	606-589-2145	161
Middlesboro			
1300 Chichester Ave ....Middlesboro KY 40965	**888-274-7322**	606-242-2145	161
Whitesburg			
2 Long Ave ....Whitesburg KY 41858	**888-274-7322**	606-633-0279	161
Southeast Milk Inc			
1950 SE Hwy 484 PO Box 3790........Belleview FL 34420	**800-598-7866**		297-27
Southeast Missouri Hospital (SMH)			
1701 Lacey St ....Cape Girardeau MO 63701	**800-800-5123**	573-334-4822	374-3
Southeast Missouri State University			
1 University Plaza ....Cape Girardeau MO 63701	**866-562-6801**	573-651-2000	167
Southeast Missourian			
301 Broadway St ....Cape Girardeau MO 63701	**800-879-1210**	573-335-6611	531-2
Southeast Technical Institute			
2320 N Career Ave ....Sioux Falls SD 57107	**800-247-0789**	605-367-8355	798
Southeast Tissue Alliance (SETA)			
6241 NW 23rd St Ste 400............Gainesville FL 32653	**866-432-1164**	352-248-2114	544
Southeastern Aluminum Products Inc			
6701 Suemac Pl ....Jacksonville FL 32254	**800-243-8200***	904-781-8200	236
*Sales			
Southeastern Baptist Theological Seminary			
120 S Wingate St ....Wake Forest NC 27587	**800-284-6317**	919-556-3101	168-3
Southeastern Community College North			
1500 W Agency Rd ....West Burlington IA 52655	**866-722-4692**	319-752-2731	161
Southeastern Community College South			
335 Messenger Rd ....Keokuk IA 52632	**866-722-4692**	319-524-3221	161
Southeastern Electric Co-op Inc			
1514 E Hwy 70 PO Box 1370............Durant OK 74702	**866-924-1315**	580-924-2170	247

Name / Address	City	State	ZIP	Toll-Free	Phone	Class
Southeastern Equipment Company Inc 10874 E Pike Rd	Cambridge	OH	43725	**800-798-5438**	740-432-6303	358
Southeastern Freight Lines Inc 420 Davega Rd	Lexington	SC	29073	**800-637-7335**	803-794-7300	778
Southeastern Illinois College 3575 College Rd	Harrisburg	IL	62946	**866-338-2742**	618-252-6376	161
SouthEastern Illinois Electric Co-op 585 Hwy 142 S PO Box 251	Eldorado	IL	62930	**800-833-2611**	618-273-2611	247
Southeastern Indiana Rural Electric Membership Corp 712 S Buckeye St	Osgood	IN	47037	**800-737-4111**	812-689-4111	247
Southeastern Library System of Oklahoma (SEPLSO) 401 N Second St	McAlester	OK	74501	**800-215-6494**	918-426-0456	434-3
Southeastern Louisiana University 500 Western Ave	Hammond	LA	70402	**800-222-7358**	985-549-2062	167
Southeastern Metals Mfg Company Inc 11801 Industry Dr	Jacksonville	FL	32218	**800-874-0335**	904-757-4200	236
Southeastern Oklahoma State University 1405 N Fourth St	Durant	OK	74701	**800-435-1327**	580-745-2000	167
Southeastern University 1000 Longfellow Blvd	Lakeland	FL	33801	**800-500-8760**	863-667-5000	167
Southeastern Wholesale Tire Co 4721 Trademark Dr *General	Raleigh	NC	27610	**800-849-9215***	919-832-3900	753
Southerland Inc 1973 Southerland Dr *Cust Svc	Nashville	TN	37207	**800-443-1183***	615-226-9650	470
Southern Accents Magazine 2100 Lakeshore Dr	Birmingham	AL	35209	**877-262-5866**	205-445-6000	456-22
Southern Adventist University 4881 Taylor Cir	Collegedale	TN	37315	**800-768-8437**	423-236-2000	167
Southern Air Inc 2655 Lakeside Dr	Lynchburg	VA	24501	**800-743-1214**	434-385-6200	191-10
Southern Arizona Veterans Healthcare System 3601 S Sixth Ave	Tucson	AZ	85723	**800-470-8262**	520-792-1450	374-8
Southern Arkansas University 100 E University St	Magnolia	AR	71753	**800-332-7286**	870-235-4000	167
Southern Assn of Colleges & Schools 1866 Southern Ln	Decatur	GA	30033	**888-413-3669**	404-679-4500	48-5
Southern Audio Services 14763 Florida Blvd *Cust Svc	Baton Rouge	LA	70819	**800-843-8823***	225-272-7135	51
Southern Baptist Convention (SBC) 901 Commerce St	Nashville	TN	37203	**866-722-5433**	615-244-2355	47-20
Southern Baptist Theological Seminary 2825 Lexington Rd	Louisville	KY	40280	**800-626-5525**	502-897-4011	168-3
Southern Biotechnology Assoc Inc 160A Oxmoor Blvd	Birmingham	AL	35209	**800-722-2255**	205-945-1774	233
Southern California Boiler Inc 5331 Business Dr	Huntington Beach	CA	92649	**800-775-2645**	714-891-0701	189
Southern California Edison Co 2244 Walnut Grove Ave	Rosemead	CA	91770	**800-655-4555**	626-302-1212	785
Southern California Gas Co 555 W Fifth St	Los Angeles	CA	90013	**800-427-2200**	909-305-8261	785
Southern California Regional Rail Authority 700 S Flower St Ste 2600	Los Angeles	CA	90017	**800-371-5465**	213-452-0200	467
Southern California Seminary 2075 E Madison Ave	El Cajon	CA	92019	**888-389-7244**		167
Southern Chester County Chamber of Commerce 217 W State St	Kennett Square	PA	19348	**800-343-6583**	610-444-0774	138
Southern Communications Services Inc 5555 Glenridge Connector Ste 500	Atlanta	GA	30342	**800-818-5462**		733
Southern Company Inc 3101 Carrier St	Memphis	TN	38116	**800-264-7626**	901-345-2531	536
Southern Components Inc 7360 Julie Frances Dr	Shreveport	LA	71129	**800-256-2144**	318-687-3330	815
Southern Connecticut Gas (SCG) 60 Marsh Hill Rd	Orange	CT	06477	**866-268-2887**		785
Southern Connecticut State University 501 Crescent St	New Haven	CT	06515	**888-500-7278**	203-392-5200	167
Southern Controls Inc 3511 Wetumpka Hwy	Montgomery	AL	36110	**800-392-5770**		248
Southern Copper & Supply Company Inc 875 Yeager Pkwy	Pelham	AL	35124	**800-289-2728**	205-664-9440	491
Southern Data Systems Inc 1245 Land O Lakes Dr	Roswell	GA	30075	**888-425-6151**	770-993-7103	227
Southern Film Extruders Inc 2319 English Rd	High Point	NC	27262	**800-334-6101**	336-885-8091	599
Southern Folger Detention Equipment Co 4634 S Presa St	San Antonio	TX	78223	**888-745-0530**	210-533-1231	690
Southern Forest Products Assn (SFPA) 6660 Riverside Dr Ste 212	Metairie	LA	70065	**866-574-4155**	504-443-4464	47-2
Southern FS Inc 2002 E Main St PO Box 728	Marion	IL	62959	**800-492-7684**	618-993-2833	278
Southern Glove Mfg Company Inc 749 AC Little Dr *Cust Svc	Newton	NC	28658	**800-222-1113***	828-464-4884	154-7
Southern Graphic Systems Inc 502 N Willow Ave	Tampa	FL	33606	**800-777-6789**	813-253-3427	779
Southern Graphics Systems 7435 Empire Dr	Florence	KY	41042	**800-777-6789**	859-525-1190	779
Southern Grouts & Mortars Inc 1502 SW Second Pl	Pompano Beach	FL	33069	**800-641-9247**	954-943-2288	3
Southern Healthcare Agency Inc PO Box 320999	Flowood	MS	39232	**800-880-2772**	601-933-0037	262
Southern Illinois Electric Co-op 7420 US Hwy 51 S	Dongola	IL	62926	**800-762-1400**	618-827-3555	247
Southern Illinois Healthcare 1239 E Main St	Carbondale	IL	62902	**866-744-2468**	618-457-5200	353
Southern Illinois University *Edwardsville* SR 157	Edwardsville	IL	62026	**888-328-5168**	618-650-2000	167
Southern Illinois University Edwardsville *Lovejoy Library* 30 Hairpin Dr PO Box 1063	Edwardsville	IL	62026	**888-328-5168**	618-650-4636	434-6
Southern Illinois University School of Law 1209 W Chautauqua Rd	Carbondale	IL	62901	**800-739-9187**	618-453-8858	168-1
Southern Illinois University School of Medicine 520 N Fourth St PO Box 19670	Springfield	IL	62702	**800-342-5748**	217-545-8000	168-2
Southern Illinoisan 710 N Illinois Ave PO Box 2108	Carbondale	IL	62902	**800-228-0429**	618-529-5454	531-2
Southern Imperial Inc 1400 Eddy Ave *Cust Svc	Rockford	IL	61103	**800-747-4665***	815-877-7041	288
Southern Implants Inc 5 Holland Bldg 209	Irvine	CA	92618	**866-700-2100**	949-273-8505	230
Southern Indiana Rehabilitation Hospital 3104 Blackiston Blvd	New Albany	IN	47150	**800-737-7090**	812-941-8300	374-6
Southern Indiana Rural Electric Co-op Inc 1776 Tenth St PO Box 219	Tell City	IN	47586	**800-323-2316**	812-547-2316	247
Southern Industrial Constructors Inc 6101 Triangle Dr	Raleigh	NC	27617	**866-890-7794**	919-782-4600	191-10
Southern Ionics Inc 201 Commerce St	West Point	MS	39773	**800-953-3585**	662-494-3055	142
Southern Iowa Electric Co-op Inc 22458 Hwy 2 PO Box 70	Bloomfield	IA	52537	**800-607-2027**	641-664-2277	247
Southern Lehigh School District 5775 Main St	Center Valley	PA	18034	**800-360-8989**	610-282-3121	683
Southern Living Magazine 2100 Lakeshore Dr	Birmingham	AL	35209	**800-366-4712**	205-445-6000	456-22
Southern Maine Community College (SMCC) 2 Ft Rd	South Portland	ME	04106	**877-282-2182**	207-741-5500	798
Southern Maryland Oil Co Inc (SMO) 109 N Maple Ave	La Plata	MD	20646	**888-222-3720**		578
Southern Medical Assn (SMA) 35 W Lakeshore Dr	Birmingham	AL	35209	**800-423-4992**	205-945-1840	48-8
Southern Methodist University 6425 Boaz Ln	Dallas	TX	75205	**800-323-0672**	214-768-2000	167
Southern Methodist University Dedman School of Law 3300 University Blvd Ste 331	Dallas	TX	75205	**888-768-5291**	214-768-2550	168-1
Southern Michigan Bank & Trust 51 W Pearl St PO Box 309	Coldwater	MI	49036	**800-379-7628**	517-279-5500	69
Southern Midcoast Maine Chamber 2 Main St Border Trust Business Ctr	Topsham	ME	04086	**877-725-8797**	207-725-8797	138
Southern Missouri Bancorp Inc 531 Vine St *NASDAQ: SMBC*	Poplar Bluff	MO	63901	**855-452-7272**	573-778-1800	360-2
Southern Nazarene University 6729 NW 39th Expy	Bethany	OK	73008	**800-648-9899**	405-789-6400	167
Southern New Hampshire University 2500 N River Rd	Manchester	NH	03106	**800-668-1249**	603-668-2211	167
Southern Ocean County Chamber of Commerce 265 W Ninth St	Ship Bottom	NJ	08008	**800-292-6372**	609-494-7211	138
Southern Oregon University 1250 Siskiyou Blvd Britt Hall	Ashland	OR	97520	**800-482-7672**	541-552-6411	167
Southern Park Mall 7401 Market St	Youngstown	OH	44512	**877-746-6642**	330-758-4511	459
Southern Petroleum Lab Inc 8850 Interchange Dr	Houston	TX	77054	**877-775-5227**	713-660-0901	740
Southern Pine Electric Power Assn 110 Risher St PO Box 60	Taylorsville	MS	39168	**800-231-5240**	601-785-6511	247
Southern Poverty Law Ctr (SPLC) 400 Washington Ave	Montgomery	AL	36104	**888-414-7752**	334-956-8200	47-8
Southern Public Power District (SPPD) 4550 W Husker Hwy PO Box 1687	Grand Island	NE	68803	**800-652-2013**	308-384-2350	247
Southern Pump & Tank Co 4800 N Graham St *Cust Svc	Charlotte	NC	28269	**800-477-2826***	704-596-4373	385
Southern Refrigeration Corp 3140 Shenandoah Ave	Roanoke	VA	24017	**800-763-4433**	540-342-3493	663
Southern Regional High School District Board of Education 600 North Main St	Manahawkin	NJ	08050	**866-850-0511**	609-597-9481	683
Southern Research Company Inc 2850 Centenary Blvd	Shreveport	LA	71104	**888-772-6952**	318-227-9700	400
Southern Research Institute 2000 Ninth Ave S	Birmingham	AL	35205	**800-967-6774**	205-581-2000	666
Southern Solutions Group Inc 4305 Poplar Creek Ln	High Point	NC	27265	**866-581-6055**		462
Southern Spring & Stamping Inc 401 Sub Stn Rd	Venice	FL	34285	**800-450-5882**	941-488-2276	716
Southern Staircase Inc 6025 Shiloh Rd Ste E	Alpharetta	GA	30005	**800-874-8408**	770-888-7333	498
Southern State Community College *North* 1850 Davids Dr	Wilmington	OH	45177	**877-644-6562**	937-382-6645	161
South 12681 US Rt 62	Sardinia	OH	45171	**877-644-6562**	937-695-0307	161
Southern States Chemical Co 1600 E President St	Savannah	GA	31404	**888-337-8922**	912-232-1101	282
Southern States Co-op Inc 6606 W Broad St	Richmond	VA	23230	**866-372-8272**	804-281-1000	278
Southern States Frederick Co-op Inc 500 E South St	Frederick	MD	21701	**866-633-5747**	301-663-6164	278
Southern States Packaging Co PO Box 650	Spartanburg	SC	29304	**800-621-2051**		548
Southern Tile Distributors Inc 4590 Village Ave	Norfolk	VA	23502	**800-333-8970**	757-855-8041	361
Southern Union State Community College *Opelika* 1701 Lafayette Pkwy	Opelika	AL	36801	**800-707-0057**	334-745-6437	161
Valley 321 Fob James Dr	Valley	AL	36854	**800-707-0057**	334-756-4151	161
Southern University & A & M College 156 Elton C Harrison Dr PO Box 9757 *Admissions	Baton Rouge	LA	70813	**800-256-1531***	225-771-5180	167
Southern University Law Ctr 2 Roosevelt Steptoe Dr	Baton Rouge	LA	70813	**800-537-1135**	225-771-6297	168-1
Southern University Museum of Art (SUSLA) 3050 Martin Luther King Jr Dr	Shreveport	LA	71107	**800-458-1472**	318-670-6000	519
Southern Vermont Cable Co PO Box 166	Bondville	VT	05340	**800-544-5931**		115

Name / Address	City	State	Zip	Toll-Free	Phone	Class
Southern Vermont College 982 Manison Dr	Bennington	VT	05201	**800-378-2782**	802-442-5427	167
Southern Virginia University 1 University Hill Dr	Buena Vista	VA	24416	**800-229-8420**	540-261-8400	167
Southern Weaving Co 1005 W Bramlett Rd	Greenville	SC	29611	**800-849-8962**	864-233-1635	742-5
Southern Wesleyan University 907 Wesleyan Dr	Central	SC	29630	**800-282-8798**	864-644-5000	167
Southern West Virginia Convention & Visitors Bureau 1406 Harper Rd	Beckley	WV	25801	**800-847-4898**	304-252-2244	208
Southern Wholesale Flooring Company Inc 955B Cobb Pl Blvd	Kennesaw	GA	30144	**800-282-7590**	770-514-7110	362
Southern Wine & Spirits of America Inc 1600 NW 163rd St	Miami	FL	33169	**800-776-0180**	305-625-4171	80-3
Southern Wine & Spirits of Colorado 5270 Fox St PO Box 5603	Denver	CO	80216	**800-776-0180**	303-292-1711	80-3
Southern Wine & Spirits of Illinois 300 E Crossroads Pkwy Bolingbrook Corp Ctr	Bolingbrook	IL	60440	**800-776-0180**	630-685-3000	80-3
Southern Wire Corp 8045 Metro Rd	Olive Branch	MS	38654	**800-238-0333**	662-890-4873	491
Southernmost Illinois Tourism Bureau PO Box 378	Anna	IL	62906	**800-248-4373**	618-833-9928	208
Southernmost On the Beach 508 S St	Key West	FL	33040	**800-354-4455**	305-296-6577	379
Southfield Dodge Chrysler Jeep Ram 28100 Telegraph Rd *Sales	Southfield	MI	48034	**888-388-0451***	248-354-2950	56
SouthFirst Bancshares Inc 126 N Norton Ave PO Box 167 *OTC: SZBI*	Sylacauga	AL	35150	**800-239-1492**	256-245-4365	360-2
Southfork Hotel 1600 N Central Expy	Plano	TX	75074	**877-386-4383**	972-578-8555	379
Southgate Community School District 14600 Dix Toledo Rd	Southgate	MI	48195	**888-263-5897**	734-246-4600	683
Southgroup & Financial Services Inc 795 Woodlands Pkwy Ste 101	Ridgeland	MS	39157	**855-744-6777**	601-914-3220	218
Southland Printing Company Inc 213 Airport Dr	Shreveport	LA	71107	**800-241-8662**	318-221-8662	626
Southland Safety LLC 1409 Kilgore Dr	Henderson	TX	75652	**866-723-3719**	903-657-8669	198
Southland Steel Fabricators Inc 251 Greensburg St	Greensburg	LA	70441	**800-738-7734**	225-222-4141	479
Southland Tube Inc 3525 Richard Arrington Blvd N	Birmingham	AL	35234	**800-543-9024**	205-251-1884	489
Southmedic Inc 50 Alliance Blvd	Barrie	ON	L4M5K3	**800-463-7146**	705-726-9383	476
SouthPark Mall 4400 Sharon Rd	Charlotte	NC	28211	**888-726-5930**	704-364-4411	459
SouthPointe Pavilions 2910 Pine Lake Rd Ste Q	Lincoln	NE	68516	**800-733-2767**	402-421-2114	459
Southside Bancshares Inc 1201 S Beckham Ave *NASDAQ: SBSI*	Tyler	TX	75701	**877-639-3511**	903-531-7111	360-2
Southside Electric Co-op Inc 2000 W Virgina Ave	Crewe	VA	23930	**800-552-2118**	434-645-7721	247
Southside Virginia Community College 109 Campus Dr	Alberta	VA	23821	**888-220-7822**	434-949-1000	161
Southwark Metal Mfg Company Inc 2800 Red Lion Rd	Philadelphia	PA	19114	**800-523-1052**	215-735-3401	695
Southway Inn 2431 Bank St	Ottawa	ON	K1V8R9	**877-688-4929**	613-737-0811	379
Southwest Airlines Air Cargo 2702 Love Field Dr	Dallas	TX	75235	**800-533-1222**		12
Southwest Airlines Co 2702 Love Field Dr PO Box 36611 *NYSE: LUV*	Dallas	TX	75235	**800-435-9792**	214-792-4000	25
Southwest Airport Services Inc 11811 N Brantly Ave Ste 500	Houston	TX	77034	**888-362-6738**	281-484-6551	62
Southwest Art Magazine 10901 W 120th Ave Ste 350	Broomfield	CO	80021	**877-212-1938**	303-442-0427	456-2
Southwest Bancorp Inc 608 S Main St PO Box 1988 *NASDAQ: OKSB*	Stillwater	OK	74076	**888-762-4762**		360-2
Southwest Baptist University 1600 University Ave	Bolivar	MO	65613	**800-526-5859**		167
SouthWest Capital Bank 622 Douglas Ave	Las Vegas	NM	87701	**800-748-2406**	505-425-7565	69
Southwest Communications Inc 4100 N Mulberry Dr Ste 160	Kansas City	MO	64116	**800-383-5533**	816-298-4100	387
Southwest Florida International Airport 11000 Terminal Access Rd Ste 8671	Fort Myers	FL	33913	**800-359-6786**	239-590-4800	27
Southwest Freightlines 11991 Transpark Dr *General	El Paso	TX	79927	**800-776-5799***	915-860-8592	778
Southwest Gas Corp 5241 Spring Mtn Rd PO Box 98510 *NYSE: SWX*	Las Vegas	NV	89193	**877-860-6020**	702-876-7237	785
Southwest Gas Corp Northern Nevada Div 400 Eagle Stn Ln	Carson City	NV	89701	**877-860-6020**		785
Southwest Gas Corp Southern Arizona Div PO Box 98512	Las Vegas	NV	89193	**877-860-6020**		785
Southwest Gas Corp Southern California Div 13471 Mariposa Rd	Victorville	CA	92395	**877-860-6020**		785
Southwest Gas Corp Southern Nevada Div 5241 Spring Mtn Rd	Las Vegas	NV	89150	**877-860-6020**	702-876-7011	785
Southwest General Hospital (SGH) 7400 Barlite Blvd	San Antonio	TX	78224	**877-898-6080**	210-921-2000	374-3
Southwest Georgia Financial Corp 201 First St SE *NYSE: SGB*	Moultrie	GA	31768	**888-683-2265**	229-985-1120	360-2
Southwest Institute of Healing Arts 1100 E Apache Blvd	Tempe	AZ	85281	**888-504-9106**	480-994-9244	798
Southwest Iowa Rural Electric Co-op 1801 Grove Ave	Corning	IA	50841	**888-591-1261**	641-322-3165	247
Southwest King County Chamber of Commerce 14220 Interurban Ave S Ste 134	Tukwila	WA	98168	**800-638-8613**	206-575-1633	138
Southwest Louisiana Convention & Visitors Bureau 1205 N Lakeshore Dr	Lake Charles	LA	70601	**800-456-7952**	337-436-9588	208
Southwest Louisiana Electric Membership Corp 3420 NE Evangeline Thruway	Lafayette	LA	70509	**888-275-3626**	337-896-5384	247
Southwest Materials Handling Company Inc 4719 Almond St	Dallas	TX	75247	**866-674-6067**	214-630-1375	358
Southwest Medical Assoc Inc 638 E Market St PO Box 2168	Rockport	TX	78382	**800-929-4854**		719
Southwest Minnesota State University 1501 State St	Marshall	MN	56258	**800-642-0684**		167
Southwest Mississippi Electric Power Assn 18671 Hwy 61 PO Box 5	Lorman	MS	39096	**800-287-8564**		247
Southwest Missouri Bank 2417 S Grand Ave	Carthage	MO	64836	**800-943-8488**	417-358-1770	69
Southwest Plastic Binding Co 109 Millwell Ct	Maryland Heights	MO	63043	**800-325-3628**	314-739-4400	85
Southwest Public Power District 221 S Main St PO Box 289	Palisade	NE	69040	**800-379-7977**	308-285-3295	247
Southwest Rural Electric Assn 700 N Broadway PO Box 310	Tipton	OK	73570	**800-256-7973**	580-667-5281	247
Southwest Tennessee Community College PO Box 780	Memphis	TN	38101	**877-717-7822**	901-333-5000	161
Southwest Tennessee Electric Membership Corp 1009 E Main St	Brownsville	TN	38012	**800-772-0472**	731-772-1322	247
Southwest Texas Electric Co-op Inc 101 E Gillis St PO Box 677	Eldorado	TX	76936	**800-643-3980**	325-853-2544	247
Southwest Texas Junior College 2401 Garner Field Rd	Uvalde	TX	78801	**888-886-8490**	830-278-4401	161
Southwest Virginia Community College 724 Community College Rd	Cedar Bluff	VA	24609	**855-877-3944**	276-964-2555	161
Southwest Washington Convention & Visitors Bureau 1220 Main S Ste 220	Vancouver	WA	98660	**877-600-0800**	360-750-1553	208
Southwest Wisconsin Library System 1775 Fourth St	Fennimore	WI	53809	**866-866-3393**	608-822-3393	434-3
Southwest Wisconsin Technical College (SWTC) 1800 Bronson Blvd	Fennimore	WI	53809	**800-362-3322**	608-822-3262	798
Southwestern Adventist University 100 W Hillcrest Dr PO Box 567 *Admissions	Keene	TX	76059	**888-732-7928***	817-645-3921	167
Southwestern Assemblies of God University 1200 Sycamore St	Waxahachie	TX	75165	**888-937-7248**	972-937-4010	167
Southwestern Baptist Theological Seminary PO Box 22740	Fort Worth	TX	76122	**877-467-9287**	817-923-1921	168-3
Southwestern Christian College PO Box 10	Terrell	TX	75160	**800-925-9357**	972-524-3341	167
Southwestern College 900 Otay Lakes Rd	Chula Vista	CA	91910	**866-262-9881**	619-421-6700	161
Southwestern Community College 1501 W Townline St	Creston	IA	50801	**800-247-4023**	641-782-7081	161
Southwestern Electric Co-op Inc 525 US Rt 40 PO Box 549	Greenville	IL	62246	**800-637-8667**		247
Southwestern Energy Co 2350 N Sam Houston Pkwy E Ste 300 *NYSE: SWN*	Houston	TX	77032	**866-322-0801**	832-796-1000	785
Southwestern Eye Ctr 2610 E University Dr *General	Mesa	AZ	85213	**800-224-3339***	480-892-8400	796
Southwestern Illinois College 2500 Carlyle Ave	Belleville	IL	62221	**800-222-5131**	618-235-2700	161
Southwestern Indian Polytechnic Institute 9169 Coors Blvd NW PO Box 10146	Albuquerque	NM	87120	**800-586-7474**	505-346-2306	164
Southwestern Industries Inc 2615 Homestead Pl	Rancho Dominguez	CA	90220	**800-421-6875**	310-608-4422	454
Southwestern Michigan College (SMC) 58900 Cherry Grove Rd	Dowagiac	MI	49047	**800-456-8675**	269-782-1000	161
Niles Area 2229 US 12	Niles	MI	49120	**800-456-8675**	269-782-1233	161
Southwestern Oregon Community College 1988 Newmark Ave	Coos Bay	OR	97420	**800-962-2838**	541-888-2525	161
Southwestern Petroleum Corp PO Box 961005	Fort Worth	TX	76161	**800-877-9372**	817-332-2336	540
Southwestern University PO Box 770	Georgetown	TX	78627	**800-252-3166**	512-863-1200	167
Southwestern Vermont Medical Ctr 100 Hospital Dr	Bennington	VT	05201	**800-422-6237**	802-442-6361	374-3
Southwestern Wire Inc PO Box CC	Norman	OK	73070	**800-348-9473**	405-447-6900	811
Southwestern/Great American 2451 Atrium Way *Cust Svc	Nashville	TN	37214	**888-602-7867***		94
Southwick Inc 2400 Shattuck Ave	Berkeley	CA	94704	**888-686-0046**	510-845-2530	56
Southwire Co 1 Southwire Dr	Carrollton	GA	30119	**800-444-1700**	770-832-4242	484
Southworth Co 265 Main St	Agawam	MA	01001	**800-225-1839**	413-789-1200	551-2
Southworth Products Corp PO Box 1380	Portland	ME	04104	**800-743-1000**	207-878-0700	469
Sovereign Bank FSB PO Box 12646 *Cust Svc	Reading	PA	19612	**877-768-2265***		69
Sovereign Pharmaceuticals Ltd 7590 Sand St	Fort Worth	TX	76118	**877-248-0228**	817-284-0429	582
Sovereign Society, The 98 S E Sixth Ave Ste 2	Delray Beach	FL	33483	**866-584-4096**	888-358-8125	401
Sovran Self Storage Inc 6467 Main St *NYSE: SSS*	Buffalo	NY	14221	**800-242-1715**	716-633-1850	801-3
Soybean Digest 7900 International Dr Ste 300 *Cust Svc	Minneapolis	MN	55425	**800-722-5334***	952-851-4667	456-1
Sp Mount 1306 E 55th St	Cleveland	OH	44103	**800-503-5022**	216-881-3316	626
SP Systems Inc 7500 Greenway Ctr Dr Ste 850	Greenbelt	MD	20770	**877-327-8732**	301-614-1322	180-1

Name / Address	City	State	ZIP	Toll-Free	Phone	Class
Spa & Fitness Club at the Four Seasons Hotel Washington 2800 Pennsylvania Ave NW	Washington	DC	20007	**800-819-5053**	202-944-2022	705
Spa at Big Cedar Lodge 612 Devil's Pool Rd	Ridgedale	MO	65739	**800-225-6343**	417-339-5201	705
Spa at Coeur d'Alene 115 S Second St	Coeur d'Alene	ID	83814	**800-684-0514**	208-765-4000	704
Spa at Eagle Crest Resort 1522 Cline Falls Hwy	Redmond	OR	97756	**800-682-4786**	541-923-9647	705
Spa at Kingsmill Resort 1010 Kingsmill Rd	Williamsburg	VA	23185	**800-965-4772**	757-253-8230	705
Spa at Le Merigot JW Marriott Beach Hotel Santa Monica 1740 Ocean Ave	Santa Monica	CA	90401	**888-236-2427**	310-395-9700	705
Spa at Pebble Beach 1518 Cypress Dr	Pebble Beach	CA	93953	**800-654-9300**	831-649-7615	705
Spa at Peninsula Beverly Hills 9882 S Santa Monica Blvd	Beverly Hills	CA	90212	**800-462-7899**	310-551-2888	704
Spa at Pinehurst Resort 80 Carolina Vista Dr PO Box 4000	Pinehurst	NC	28374	**800-487-4653**	910-235-8320	705
Spa at the Beverly Wilshire, The 9500 Wilshire Blvd	Beverly Hills	CA	90212	**800-545-4000**	310-385-7023	705
Spa at the Bodega Bay Lodge 103 Coast Hwy 1	Bodega Bay	CA	94923	**888-875-2250**	707-875-3525	705
Spa at the Breakers 1 S County Rd	Palm Beach	FL	33480	**888-273-2537**	561-653-6656	705
Spa at the Broadmoor 1 Lake Ave	Colorado Springs	CO	80906	**800-634-7711**	719-634-7711	705
Spa at the Buena Vista Palace Resort in the Walt Disney World Resort 1900 Buena Vista Dr	Lake Buena Vista	FL	32830	**866-397-6516**	407-827-3200	705
Spa at the Camelback Inn JW Marriott Resort Golf Club & Spa 5402 E Lincoln Dr	Scottsdale	AZ	85253	**800-922-2635**	480-596-7040	705
Spa at the Chattanoogan 1201 S Broad St	Chattanooga	TN	37402	**800-619-0018**	423-756-3400	705
Spa at the Equinox Resort 3567 Main St	Manchester Village	VT	05254	**800-362-4747**		705
Spa at the Fairmont Inn Sonoma Mission Inn 100 Boyes Blvd	Sonoma	CA	95476	**877-289-7354**	707-938-9000	705
Spa at the Hotel Hershey 100 Hotel Rd	Hershey	PA	17033	**877-772-9988**	717-520-5888	705
Spa at the JW Marriott Desert Springs Resort Palm Desert 74855 Country Club Dr	Palm Desert	CA	92260	**800-845-5279**	760-341-2211	705
Spa at the Norwich Inn 607 W Thames St	Norwich	CT	06360	**800-275-4772**	860-886-2401	705
Spa at the PGA National Resort 450 Ave of the Champions	Palm Beach Gardens	FL	33418	**800-633-9150**	561-627-3111	705
Spa at the Ritz-Carlton Amelia Island 4750 Amelia Island Pkwy	Amelia Island	FL	32034	**800-241-3333**	904-277-1087	705
Spa at the Ritz-Carlton Bachelor Gulch 0130 Daybreak Ridge	Avon	CO	81620	**800-241-3333**	970-748-6200	705
Spa at the Ritz-Carlton Half Moon Bay 1 Miramontes Pt Rd	Half Moon Bay	CA	94019	**800-241-3333**	650-712-7040	705
Spa at the Ritz-Carlton New Orleans 921 Canal St	New Orleans	LA	70112	**800-241-3333**	504-670-2929	705
Spa at the Saddlebrook Resort 5700 Saddlebrook Way	Wesley Chapel	FL	33543	**800-729-8383**	813-907-4419	705
Spa at the Sagamore 110 Sagamore Rd	Bolton Landing	NY	12814	**866-384-1944**	518-743-6081	705
Spa at the Sanderling Resort 1461 Duck Rd	Duck	NC	27949	**855-412-7866**	252-261-7744	705
Spa at The Setai 2001 Collins Ave	Miami Beach	FL	33139	**888-625-7500**		704
Spa at the Vail Marriott Mountain Resort 715 W Lionshead Cir	Vail	CO	81657	**800-648-0720**	970-479-5004	705
Spa at the Villagio Inn 6481 Washington St	Yountville	CA	94599	**800-351-1133**	707-948-5050	705
Spa at White Oaks Conference Resort 253 Taylor Rd	Niagara-on-the-Lake	ON	L0S1J0	**800-263-5766**	905-641-2599	705
Spa Esmeralda at the Renaissance Esmeralda Resort 44400 Indian Wells Ln	Indian Wells	CA	92210	**800-845-5279**	760-836-1265	705
Spa Gaucin at the Saint Regis Monarch Beach 1 Monarch Beach Resort	Dana Point	CA	92629	**800-722-1543**	949-234-3367	705
Spa Grande at the Grand Wailea Resort Maui 3850 Wailea Alanui Dr	Wailea	HI	96753	**800-772-1933**	808-875-1234	705
Spa La Quinta at La Quinta Resort 49499 Eisenhower Dr	La Quinta	CA	92253	**877-527-7721**	760-777-4800	705
Spa Manufacturers 6060 Ulmerton Rd	Clearwater	FL	33760	**877-530-9493**	727-530-9493	375
Spa Moana at the Hyatt Regency Maui Resort & Spa 200 Nohea Kai Dr	Lahaina	HI	96761	**800-233-1234**	808-667-4725	705
Spa Resort Casino 401 E Amado Rd	Palm Springs	CA	92262	**888-999-1995**		132
Spa Resort, The 401 E Amado Rd	Palm Springs	CA	92262	**800-854-1279**		667
Spa Shiki at the Lodge of Four Seasons 315 Horseshoe Bend Pkwy	Lake Ozark	MO	65049	**800-843-5253**	573-365-8108	705
Spa Suites at Kahala Hotel & Resort 5000 Kahala Ave	Honolulu	HI	96816	**800-367-2525**	808-739-8938	705
Spa Terre at LaPlaya Beach & Golf Resort 9891 Gulf Shore Dr	Naples	FL	34108	**800-237-6883**	239-597-3123	705
Spa Terre at Paradise Point Resort 1404 Vacation Rd	San Diego	CA	92109	**800-344-2626**	858-581-5998	705
Spa Terre at the Hotel Viking 1 Bellevue Ave	Newport	RI	02840	**800-556-7126**	401-847-3300	705
Spa Terre at the Inn & Spa at Loretto 211 Old Santa Fe Trl	Santa Fe	NM	87501	**800-727-5531**	505-984-7997	705
Spa Toccare at Borgata Hotel Casino 1 Borgata Way	Atlantic City	NJ	08401	**877-448-5833**	609-317-7555	705
Space Coast Credit Union 8045 N Wickham Rd PO Box 419001	Melbourne	FL	32941	**800-447-7228**	321-752-2222	221
Space Coast Jet Ctr 7003 Challenger Ave	Titusville	FL	32780	**800-559-5473**	321-267-8355	62
Space Dynamics Laboratory 1695 N Research Pkwy	North Logan	UT	84341	**866-487-2365**	435-797-4600	666
Space Needle LLC 203 Sixth Ave N	Seattle	WA	98109	**800-937-9582**	206-905-2200	49-3

Name / Address	City	State	ZIP	Toll-Free	Phone	Class
Space Optics Research Labs LLC 7 Stuart Rd	Chelmsford	MA	01824	**800-552-7675**	978-250-8640	407
Space Science & Engineering Ctr University of Wisconsin 1225 W Dayton St	Madison	WI	53706	**866-391-1753**	608-262-0544	666
Space Systems/Loral 3825 Fabian Way	Palo Alto	CA	94303	**800-332-6490**	650-852-4000	645
Space Transit Planetarium 3280 S Miami Ave	Miami	FL	33129	**866-268-0250**	305-646-4200	597
SPACECONNECTION Inc, The 10530 Victory Blvd	North Hollywood	CA	91606	**800-537-7223**	818-754-1100	387
SpaceGuard Products Inc 711 S Commerce Dr	Seymour	IN	47274	**800-841-0680**	812-523-3044	288
Spacelabs Health Care 35301 SE Center St	Snoqualmie	WA	98065	**800-522-7025**	425-396-3300	252
SpaceNet Inc 1750 Old Meadow Rd	McLean	VA	22102	**800-237-3513**	703-848-1000	679
Spacesaver Corp 1450 Janesville Ave	Fort Atkinson	WI	53538	**800-492-3434**	800-255-8170	288
Spader Business Management 2101 W 41st St Ste 49	Sioux Falls	SD	57105	**800-772-3377**		198
Spago 3500 Las Vegas Blvd S Ste G1	Las Vegas	NV	89109	**800-241-3333**	702-369-6300	669
SpaHalekulani at the Halekulani Hotel 2199 Kalia Rd	Honolulu	HI	96815	**800-367-2343**	808-931-5322	705
Spalding PO Box 90015	Bowling Green	KY	42103	**855-253-4533**		708
Spalding Hardware Ltd 1616 10 Ave SW	Calgary	AB	T3C0J5	**800-837-0850**		350
Spalding Rehabilitation Hospital 900 Potomac St	Aurora	CO	80011	**800-367-3309**	303-367-1166	374-6
Spalding University 851 S Fourth St	Louisville	KY	40203	**800-896-8941**	502-585-9911	167
Span-America Medical Systems Inc 70 Commerce Ctr *NASDAQ: SPAN*	Greenville	SC	29615	**800-888-6752**	864-288-8877	476
Spancrete Industries Inc N 16 W 23415 Stone Ridge Dr PO Box 828	Waukesha	WI	53187	**855-900-7726**	414-290-9000	185
Spangler Candy Co 400 N Portland St PO Box 71 *Sales	Bryan	OH	43506	**888-636-4221***	419-636-4221	297-8
Spanish Cove 11 Palm Ave	Yukon	OK	73099	**800-965-2683**		670
Spanish-American Translating 330 Eagle Ave	West Hempstead	NY	11552	**800-870-5790**	516-481-3339	766
Spansion Inc 915 DeGuigne Dr *NYSE: CODE*	Sunnyvale	CA	94085	**866-772-6746**	408-962-2500	290
Spark Energy Gas LP 2105 Citywest Blvd	Houston	TX	77042	**877-547-7275**		326
Sparkhound Inc 11207 Proverbs Ave	Baton Rouge	LA	70816	**866-217-1500**	225-216-1500	182
Sparkle Solutions LP 2700 Steeles Ave W Unit 4	Concord	ON	L4K3C8	**866-660-2282**	905-660-2282	34
Sparks Belting Co 3800 Stahl Dr SE	Grand Rapids	MI	49546	**800-451-4537**	616-949-2750	370
Sparks Marketing Group Inc 2828 Charter Rd	Philadelphia	PA	19154	**800-925-7727**	215-676-1100	288
Sparling Instruments Company Inc 4097 N Temple City Blvd *Sales	El Monte	CA	91731	**800-800-3569***	626-444-0571	494
Sparrow Health System 1215 E Michigan Ave	Lansing	MI	48912	**800-772-7769**	517-364-1000	374-3
Sparta Systems Inc 2000 Waterview Dr Ste 300	Holmdel	NJ	07733	**888-261-5948**	609-807-5100	179
Spartan Chemical Company Inc 1110 Spartan Dr	Maumee	OH	43537	**800-537-8990**	419-531-5551	144
Spartan College of Aeronautics & Technology 8820 E Pine St PO Box 582833 *Admissions	Tulsa	OK	74115	**800-331-1204***	918-836-6886	798
Spartan Distributors Inc 487 W Div St	Sparta	MI	49345	**800-822-2216**	616-887-7301	276
Spartan Graphics Inc 200 Applewood Dr	Sparta	MI	49345	**800-747-4477**	616-887-8243	626
Spartan Motors Inc 1541 Reynolds Rd *NASDAQ: SPAR*	Charlotte	MI	48813	**800-937-5449**	517-543-6400	515
Spartanburg Community College 800 Brisack Rd PO Box 4386	Spartanburg	SC	29305	**866-591-3700**	864-592-4800	798
Spartanburg Herald-Journal 189 W Main St	Spartanburg	SC	29306	**800-922-4158**	864-582-4511	531-2
Spartanburg Methodist College 1000 Powell Mill Rd	Spartanburg	SC	29301	**800-772-7286**	864-587-4000	161
Spartanburg Regional Medical Ctr (SRMC) 101 E Wood St	Spartanburg	SC	29303	**800-318-2596**	864-560-6000	374-3
Spartanburg Steel Products Inc 1290 New Cut Rd PO Box 6428	Spartanburg	SC	29304	**888-974-7500**	864-585-5211	488
Sparton 27 Hale Spring Rd	Plaistow	NH	03865	**800-443-4132**	603-382-3840	205
Sparton Corp 425 N Martingale Rd Ste 2050	Schaumburg	IL	60173	**800-772-7866**	847-762-5800	419
Spaulding Composites Co 55 Nadeau Dr	Rochester	NH	03867	**800-801-0560**	603-332-0555	598
Spaulding Rehabilitation Hospital 125 Nashua St	Boston	MA	02114	**888-774-0055**	617-573-7000	374-6
Spavinaw State Park 555 S Main	Spavinaw	OK	74366	**800-622-6317**	918-589-2651	564
SpawGlass Construction Corp 13800 W Rd	Houston	TX	77041	**800-771-0422**	281-970-5300	462
SPE (Society of Petroleum Engineers) 222 Palisades Creek Dr	Richardson	TX	75080	**800-456-6863**	972-952-9393	47-12
Speak Inc Speakers Bureau 10680 Treena St Ste 230	San Diego	CA	92131	**800-677-3324**	858-228-3771	706
SpeakerCraft Inc 940 Columbia Ave	Riverside	CA	92507	**800-448-0976**	951-787-0543	175-5
Speakers Unlimited PO Box 27225	Columbus	OH	43227	**888-333-6676**	614-864-3703	706

Name / Address	City	State	Zip	Toll-Free	Phone	Class
Speakman Co 400 Anchor Mill Rd	New Castle	DE	19720	800-537-2107		608
Spearfish Canyon Resort 10619 Roughlock Falls Rd	Lead	SD	57754	877-975-6343	605-584-3435	667
Spears Manufacturing Co PO Box 9203	Sylmar	CA	91392	800-862-1499	818-364-1611	607
Spec Bldg Materials Inc 4300 W Ave	San Antonio	TX	78213	800-588-3892	210-342-2727	193-4
Spec Ops Inc 319 Business Ln	Ashland	VA	23005	800-774-3854	804-752-4790	263
Spec's Wines Spirits & Finer Foods 2410 Smith St	Houston	TX	77006	888-526-8787	713-526-8787	443
Specco Industries Inc 13087 Main St	Lemont	IL	60439	800-441-6646	630-257-5060	144
Special Counsel Inc 10201 Centurion Pkwy N Ste 400	Jacksonville	FL	32256	800-737-3436	904-737-3436	719
Special Education Report 360 Hiatt Dr	Palm Beach Gardens	FL	33418	800-621-5463*	561-622-6520	530-4
*Sales						
Special Libraries Assn (SLA) 331 S Patrick St	Alexandria	VA	22314	866-446-6069	703-647-4900	48-11
Special Metals Corp 4317 Middle Settlement Rd	New Hartford	NY	13413	800-334-8351	315-798-2900	484
Special Military Active Retired Travel Club (SMART) 600 University Office Blvd Ste 1A	Pensacola	FL	32504	800-354-7681	850-478-1986	47-23
Special Olympics Inc 1133 19th St NW 11th Fl	Washington	DC	20036	800-700-8585	202-628-3630	47-22
Specialized Bicycle Components 15130 Concord Cir	Morgan Hill	CA	95037	877-808-8154	408-779-6229	81
Specialized Information Publishers Assn (SIPA) 8229 Boone Blvd Ste 260	Vienna	VA	22182	800-356-9302	703-992-9339	48-14
Specialized Printed Forms Inc 352 Ctr St	Caledonia	NY	14423	800-688-2381	585-538-2381	109
Special-Lite Inc PO Box 6	Decatur	MI	49045	800-821-6531	269-423-7068	236
Specialty Bolt & Screw Inc 235 Bowles Rd	Agawam	MA	01001	800-322-7878	413-789-6700	351
Specialty Brands Of America Inc 1400 Old Country Rd	Westbury	NY	11590	877-795-3599	516-997-6969	298-8
Specialty Catalog Corp 400 Manley St	West Bridgewater	MA	02379	800-364-9060	508-638-7000	458
Specialty Coffee Assn of America (SCAA) 117 W 4th St Ste 300	Santa Ana	CA	92701	800-995-9019	562-624-4100	48-6
Specialty Design & Mfg Co PO Box 4039	Reading	PA	19606	800-720-0867	610-779-1357	755
Specialty Graphic Imaging Assn (SGIA) 10015 Main St	Fairfax	VA	22031	888-385-3588	703-385-1335	48-16
Specialty Hearse & Ambulance Sale Corp 60 Engineers Ln E	Farmingdale	NY	11735	800-349-6102*	516-349-7700	56
*General						
Specialty Laboratories Inc 27027 Tourney Rd	Valencia	CA	91355	800-421-7110*	661-799-6543	418
*Sales						
Specialty Loose Leaf Inc 1 Cabot St	Holyoke	MA	01040	800-227-3623	413-532-0106	551-2
Specialty Merchandise Corp 996 Flower Glen St	Simi Valley	CA	93065	800-345-4762*	805-578-5500	366
*Orders						
Specialty Motors Inc 25060 Ave Tibbitts	Valencia	CA	91355	800-232-2612	661-257-7388	517
Specialty Pipe & Tube Inc PO Box 516	Mineral Ridge	OH	44440	800-842-5839	330-505-8262	491
Specialty Plastic Fabricators Inc 9658 196th St	Mokena	IL	60448	800-747-9509	708-479-5501	201
Specialty Products & Insulation Co (SPI) 1650 Manheim Pk Ste 202	Lancaster	PA	17601	800-788-7764	717-569-3900	193-4
Specialty Retailers Inc 10201 S Main St	Houston	TX	77025	800-579-2302		156-4
Specialty Silicone Fabricators 3077 Rollie Gates Dr	Paso Robles	CA	93446	800-394-4284	805-239-4284	475
Specialty Surgical Products Inc 1131 Us Hwy 93 N	Victor	MT	59875	888-878-0811	406-961-0102	474
Specialty Tires of America Inc 1600 Washington St	Indiana	PA	15701	800-622-7327	724-349-9010	752
Specialty Tools & Fasteners Distributors Assn (STAFDA) 500 Elm Grove Rd Ste 210 PO Box 44	Elm Grove	WI	53122	800-352-2981	262-784-4774	48-18
Specialty Vehicle Institute of America (SVIA) 2 Jenner St Ste 150	Irvine	CA	92618	800-887-2887	949-727-3727	48-21
Specification Rubber Products Inc 1568 First St N	Alabaster	AL	35007	800-633-3415	205-663-2521	327
Specified Technologies Inc 210 Evans Way	Somerville	NJ	08876	800-992-1180	908-526-8000	145
Specmo Auto Sound & Speed 1200 E Avis Dr	Madison Heights	MI	48529	800-545-7910		53
Speco Technologies 200 New Hwy	Amityville	NY	11701	800-645-5516	631-957-8700	37
Spectator, The 44 Frid St	Hamilton	ON	L8N3G3	800-263-6902	905-526-3333	531-1
Spectera Inc 6220 Old Dobbin Ln Liberty 6, Ste 200	Columbia	MD	21045	800-638-3120	410-265-6033	391-3
Spectra Aluminum Products Inc 95 Reagens Industrial Pkwy	Bradford	ON	L3Z2A4	866-999-2586	905-778-8093	491
Spectra Colors Corp 25 Rizzolo Rd	Kearny	NJ	07032	800-527-8588	201-997-0606	145
Spectra Energy Corp 5400 Westheimer Ct	Houston	TX	77056	800-700-8744	713-627-5400	785
Spectra Integrated Systems Inc 8100 Arrowridge Blvd	Charlotte	NC	28273	800-443-7561	704-525-7099	248
Spectra Merchandising International Inc 4230 N Normandy Ave	Chicago	IL	60634	800-777-5331	773-202-8408	248
Spectra Services Inc 6359 Dean Pkwy	Ontario	NY	14519	800-955-7732	585-265-4320	419
Spectra-Kote Corp 301 E Water St	Gettysburg	PA	17325	800-241-4626	717-334-3177	553
Spectranetics Corp 9965 Federal Dr	Colorado Springs	CO	80921	800-231-0978	719-447-2000	424
NASDAQ: SPNC						
Spectrolab Inc 12500 Gladstone Ave	Sylmar	CA	91342	800-936-4888	818-365-4611	694
Spectronics Corp 956 Brush Hollow Rd	Westbury	NY	11590	800-274-8888		203
Spectrum Analytical Inc 830 Silver St	Agawam	MA	01001	800-789-9115	413-789-9018	740
Spectrum Brands 3001 Deming Way	Middleton	WI	53711	800-566-7899	608-275-3340	282
Spectrum Corp 10048 Easthaven Blvd	Houston	TX	77075	800-392-5050	713-944-6200	699
Spectrum Data Inc 131 N Third St	Oregon	IL	61061	800-733-6567	815-732-6567	227
Spectrum Financial System Inc 163 McKenzie Rd	Mooresville	NC	28115	800-525-0555	704-663-4466	196
Spectrum Glass Co PO Box 646	Woodinville	WA	98072	800-426-3120	425-483-6699	330
Spectrum Health Blodgett Campus 100 Michigan St NE	Grand Rapids	MI	49503	866-989-7999	616-774-7444	374-3
Spectrum Health Systems Inc 10 Mechanic St Ste 302	Worcester	MA	01608	800-464-9555	508-792-5400	47-15
Spectrum Healthcare Resources Inc 12647 Olive Blvd Ste 600	Saint Louis	MO	63141	800-325-3982		462
Spectrum Industries Inc 925 First Ave	Chippewa Falls	WI	54729	800-235-1262	715-723-6750	288
Spectrum Label Corp 30803 San Clemente St	Hayward	CA	94544	800-545-2235	510-477-0707	413
Spectrum Laboratories Inc 18617 Broadwick St	Rancho Dominguez	CA	90220	800-634-3300	310-885-4600	419
Spectrum Laboratory Products Inc 14422 S San Pedro St	Gardena	CA	90248	800-772-8786*	310-516-8000	478
*General						
Spectrum Pharmaceuticals Inc 11500 S Eastern Ave Ste 240	Henderson	NV	89052	800-332-1088	702-835-6300	84
NASDAQ: SPPI						
Spectrum Signal Processing by Vecima 2700 Production Way Ste 300	Burnaby	BC	V5A4X1	800-663-8986	604-676-6700	624
Spectrum Systems Inc 3410 W Nine-Mile Rd	Pensacola	FL	32526	800-432-6119	850-944-3392	419
Speech-Language and Audiology Canada (CASLPA) 1 Nicholas St Ste 1000	Ottawa	ON	K1N7B7	800-259-8519	613-567-9968	47-1
Speechwriter's Newsletter 316 N Michigan Ave Ste 400	Chicago	IL	60601	800-878-5331	312-960-4100	530-11
Speed Skating Canada 2781 Lancaster Rd	Ottawa	ON	K1B1A7	877-572-4772	613-260-3660	136
Speedie & Assoc Inc 3331 E Wood St	Phoenix	AZ	85040	800-628-6221	602-997-6391	740
Speedling Inc 4447 Old 41 Hwy S	Ruskin	FL	33570	800-881-4769*		369
*Cust Svc						
Speedway LLC 500 Speedway Dr	Enon	OH	45323	800-643-1948*	937-864-3001	325
*Cust Svc						
Speedway Motors 340 Victory Ln PO Box 81906	Lincoln	NE	68528	800-736-3733	402-323-3200	789
Speedway Redi Mix Inc 1201 N Taylor Rd	Garrett	IN	46738	800-227-5649	260-357-6885	184
Spellman Hardwoods Inc 4645 N 43rd Ave	Phoenix	AZ	85031	800-624-5401	602-272-2313	193-3
Spelman College 350 Spelman Ln SW	Atlanta	GA	30314	800-982-2411*	404-681-3643	167
*Admissions						
Spence Law Firm LLC 15 S Jackson St	Jackson	WY	83001	800-967-2117	307-733-7290	428
Spencer Cos Inc 120 Woodson St	Huntsville	AL	35801	800-633-2910	256-533-1150	578
Spencer Fabrications Inc 29511 County Rd 561	Tavares	FL	32778	866-277-3623	352-343-0014	695
Spencer Hall Inc 11321 Terwilligerscreek Dr	Cincinnati	OH	45249	888-883-4332	513-683-9724	197
Spencer Industries Inc 19308 68th Ave S	Kent	WA	98032	800-367-5646	253-796-1100	768
Spencer Recovery Centers Inc 1316 S Coast Hwy	Laguna Beach	CA	92651	800-334-0394		724
Spencer Reed Group Inc 6900 College Blvd Ste 1	Overland Park	KS	66211	800-477-5035	913-663-4400	268
Spencer Savings Bank PO Box 912	Spencer	MA	01562	800-547-2885	508-885-5313	69
Spencer Savings Bank SLA 611 River Dr	Elmwood Park	NJ	07407	800-363-8115	973-772-6700	69
Spencer Turbine Co 600 Day Hill Rd	Windsor	CT	06095	800-232-4321	860-688-8361	18
Spenco Medical Corp PO Box 2501	Waco	TX	76702	800-877-3626		476
Spero-Smith Investment Advisers Inc 3601 Green Rd Ste 102	Cleveland	OH	44122	800-794-7545	216-464-6266	401
Sperry Automatics Company Inc 1372 New Haven Rd PO Box 717	Naugatuck	CT	06770	800-923-3709	203-729-4589	620
SPFPA (International Union Security Police & Fire Professionals of America) 25510 Kelly Rd	Roseville	MI	48066	800-228-7492	586-772-7250	414
SPG International 11230 Harland Dr	Covington	GA	30014	877-503-4774		288
Spherix Inc 6430 Rockledge Dr Ste 503	Bethesda	MD	20817	855-816-0624	301-897-2540	194
NASDAQ: SPEX						
SPHS (Sheppard Pratt Health System) 6501 N Charles St	Baltimore	MD	21285	800-627-0330	410-938-3000	374-5
SPI (Specialty Products & Insulation Co) 1650 Manheim Pk Ste 202	Lancaster	PA	17601	800-788-7764	717-569-3900	193-4
SPI Pharma Rockwood Office Park Fl 2	Wilmington	DE	19809	800-789-9755	302-576-8567	478
SPI/Mobile Pulley Works Inc 905 S Ann St	Mobile	AL	36605	866-334-6325	251-653-0606	263
Spice Hunter Inc 184 Suburban Rd PO Box 8110	San Luis Obispo	CA	93403	800-444-3061		297-37

Name	Address	City	State	ZIP	Toll-Free	Phone	Class
Spice World Inc	8101 Presidents Dr	Orlando	FL	32809	**800-433-4979**		297-37
Spiced Pear	117 Memorial Blvd	Newport	RI	02840	**866-793-5664**	401-847-2244	669
Spicers Paper Inc	12310 Slauson Ave	Santa Fe Springs	CA	90670	**800-774-2377**	562-698-1199	552
Spider Staging Corp	365 Upland Dr	Tukwila	WA	98188	**877-774-3370**	206-575-6445	490
Spillman Technologies Inc	4625 Lake Pk Blvd *General	Salt Lake City	UT	84120	**800-860-8026***	801-902-1200	180-10
Spilltech Environmental Inc	1627 Odonoghue St	Mobile	AL	36615	**800-228-3877**		607
Spilman Thomas & Battle PLLC	Spilman Cntr 300 Knwh Blv Spilman Ctr Spilman Center Ste 100	Charleston	WV	25301	**800-967-8251**	304-340-3838	428
Spin Master Ltd	450 Front St W	Toronto	ON	M5V1B6	**800-622-8339**	416-364-6002	760
Spina Bifida Assn (SBAA)	4590 MacArthur Blvd NW Ste 250	Washington	DC	20007	**877-686-6444**	202-944-3285	47-17
Spindrift Inn	652 Cannery Row	Monterey	CA	93940	**800-841-1879**	831-646-8900	379
SpinGo Solutions Inc	14193 S Minuteman Dr Ste 100	Draper	UT	84020	**877-377-4646**		387
Spinnaker Coating Inc	518 E Water St	Troy	OH	45373	**800-543-9452**	937-332-6500	553
Spiral Binding Company Inc	1 Maltese Dr	Totowa	NJ	07511	**800-631-3572**	973-256-0666	85
Spiralock Corp	25235 Dequindre Rd	Madison Heights	MI	48071	**800-521-2688**	248-543-7800	492
Spirax Sarco Inc	1150 Northpoint Blvd	Blythewood	SC	29016	**800-883-4411**	803-714-2000	203
Spire Consulting Group LLC	114 W Seventh St Ste 1300	Austin	TX	78701	**855-216-0812**	512-637-0845	198
Spire Inc	65 Bay St	Boston	MA	02125	**877-350-8837**	617-350-8837	344
Spire Investment Partners LLC	7918 Jones Branch Dr Ste 750	Mclean	VA	22102	**888-737-8907**	703-748-5800	401
Spirit Airlines Inc	2800 Executive Way *NASDAQ: SAVE*	Miramar	FL	33025	**800-772-7117**		25
Spirit Manufacturing Inc	3000 Nestle Rd	Jonesboro	AR	72401	**800-258-4555**	870-935-1107	269
Spiritual Life Ctr	7100 E 45th St N	Wichita	KS	67226	**800-348-2440**	316-744-0167	671
SPJ (Society of Professional Journalists)	3909 N Meridian St	Indianapolis	IN	46208	**800-331-1212**	317-927-8000	48-14
Splash!events Inc	210 Hillsdale Ave	San Jose	CA	95136	**866-204-6000**	408-287-8600	186
SPLC (Southern Poverty Law Ctr)	400 Washington Ave	Montgomery	AL	36104	**888-414-7752**	334-956-8200	47-8
Split Rock Creek State Park	50th Ave	Jasper	MN	56144	**888-646-6367**	507-348-7908	564
Split Rock Lighthouse State Park	3755 Split Rock Lighthouse Rd	Two Harbors	MN	55616	**800-366-8917**	218-595-7625	564
Split Rock Resort	100 Moseywood Rd	Lake Harmony	PA	18624	**800-255-7625**	570-722-9111	667
Spokane Art Supply Inc	1303 N Monroe St	Spokane	WA	99201	**800-556-5568**	509-327-6622	44
Spokane Civic Theatre	1020 N Howard St	Spokane	WA	99201	**800-325-7328**	509-325-1413	571
Spokane Community College	1810 N Greene St	Spokane	WA	99217	**800-248-5644**	509-533-7000	161
Spokane Convention & Visitors Bureau	801 W Riverside Ste 301	Spokane	WA	99201	**800-662-0084**	509-624-1341	208
Spokane Falls Community College	3410 W Ft George Wright Dr	Spokane	WA	99224	**888-509-7944**	509-533-3500	161
Spokane Hardware Supply Inc	2001 E Trent Ave	Spokane	WA	99202	**800-888-1663**	509-535-1663	350
Spokane International Airport	9000 W Airport Dr	Spokane	WA	99224	**800-776-5263**	509-455-6455	27
Spokane Public Radio	2319 N Monroe St	Spokane	WA	99205	**800-328-5729**	509-328-5729	642-115
Spokane Symphony	PO Box 365	Spokane	WA	99210	**800-899-1482**	509-624-1200	572-3
Spokane Valley Chamber of Commerce	9507 E Sprague Ave	Spokane Valley	WA	99206	**866-475-1436**	509-924-4994	138
Sponseller Group Inc	1600 Timber Wolf Dr	Holland	OH	43528	**800-776-1625**	419-861-3000	263
Spoon River College (SRC)	23235 N County Hwy 22	Canton	IL	61520	**800-334-7337**	309-647-4645	161
Spoon River Electric Co-op Inc (SREC)	930 S Fifth Ave PO Box 340	Canton	IL	61520	**877-404-2572**	309-647-2700	247
Sport Clips Inc	110 Briarwood Dr	Georgetown	TX	78628	**800-872-4247**	512-869-1201	311
Sport Fishing Magazine	460 N Orlando Ave Ste 200	Orlando	FL	32789	**800-879-0496**		456-20
Sport Obermeyer Ltd USA Inc	115 AABC	Aspen	CO	81611	**800-525-4203**	970-925-5060	154-5
Sport-Haley Inc	200 Union Blvd Ste 400	Denver	CO	80228	**800-627-9211**	303-320-8800	154-3
SportPharma Inc	3 Terminal Rd	New Brunswick	NJ	08901	**800-872-0101**	732-545-3130	797
Sports Afield Magazine	15621 Chemical Ln	Huntington Beach	CA	92649	**800-451-4788**	714-373-4910	456-20
Sports Business Daily	120 W Morehead St Ste 310	Charlotte	NC	28202	**800-829-9839**	704-973-1410	456-20
Sports Car Club of America (SCCA)	6700 SW Topeka Blvd Ste 300	Topeka	KS	66619	**800-770-2055**	785-357-7222	47-18
Sports Cardiovascular & Wellness Nutritionists (SCAN)	1450 Western Ave Ste 101 *General	Albany	NY	12203	**800-249-2875***	518-254-6730	48-8
Sports Empire	PO Box 6169	Lakewood	CA	90714	**800-255-5258**	562-920-2350	769
Sports Leisure Vacations	9812 Old Winery Pl	Sacramento	CA	95827	**800-951-5556**	916-361-2051	758
Sports Promotion Network	PO Box 200548	Arlington	TX	76006	**800-460-9989**		709
Sports Spectrum Magazine	105 Corporate Blvd Ste 2	Indian Trail	NC	28079	**866-821-2971**	704-821-2971	456-20
Sports Travel Inc	60 Main St PO Box 50	Hatfield	MA	01038	**800-662-4424**	413-247-7678	758
Sports Turf Managers Assn (STMA)	805 New Hampshire Ste E	Lawrence	KS	66044	**800-323-3875**	785-843-2549	47-22
SportsDirect Inc	211 Horseshoe Lk Dr	Halifax	NS	B3S1E1	**866-756-9771**	902-835-3320	227
Sportservice Corp	40 Fountain Plz	Buffalo	NY	14202	**800-828-7240**	716-858-5000	300
SportsPlay Equipment Inc	5642 Natural Bridge Ave	Saint Louis	MO	63120	**800-727-8180**	314-389-4140	346
Spot-Hogg Archery Products	125 Smith St	Harrisburg	OR	97446	**888-302-7768**	541-995-3702	709
Spotnails	1100 Hicks Rd	Rolling Meadows	IL	60008	**800-873-2239**	847-259-1620	811
SpotOn Inc	2350 Kerner Blvd Ste 380	San Rafael	CA	94901	**877-814-4102**		387
Spotwave Wireless Inc	500 Van Buren St Box 550	Kemptville	ON	K0G1J0	**866-704-9750**	613-591-1662	733
SPPD (Southern Public Power District)	4550 W Husker Hwy PO Box 1687	Grand Island	NE	68803	**800-652-2013**	308-384-2350	247
Spradling International Inc	200 Cahaba Vly Pkwy PO Box 1668	Pelham	AL	35124	**800-333-0955**	205-985-4206	593
Sprague Energy	185 International Dr Ste 200	Portsmouth	NH	03801	**800-225-1560**	603-431-1000	578
Sprayway Inc	1005 S Westgate Ave	Addison	IL	60101	**800-332-9000**	630-628-3000	144
Sprecher + Schuh	15910 International Plaza Dr	Houston	TX	77032	**877-721-5913**	281-442-9000	205
Spring Arbor Distributors	1 Ingram Blvd	La Vergne	TN	37086	**800-395-4340**	615-793-5000	94
Spring Arbor University	106 E Main St *Admissions	Spring Arbor	MI	49283	**800-968-9103***	517-750-1200	167
Spring Creek Barbeque	2340 W I- 20 Ste 100	Arlington	TX	76017	**888-467-0505**	817-467-0505	669
Spring Creek Ranch	1800 Spirit Dance Rd	Jackson	WY	83001	**800-443-6139**	307-733-8833	379
Spring Dynamics Inc	7378 Research Dr	Almont	MI	48003	**888-274-8432**	810-798-2622	717
Spring Engineers Inc	9740 Tanner Rd	Houston	TX	77041	**800-899-9488**	713-690-9488	717
Spring Glen Fresh Foods Inc	314 Spring Glen Dr PO Box 518	Ephrata	PA	17522	**800-641-2853**	717-733-2201	297-19
Spring Grove Cemetery	4521 Spring Grove Ave	Cincinnati	OH	45232	**888-853-2230**	513-681-7526	509
Spring Harbor Hospital	123 Andover Rd	Westbrook	ME	04092	**888-524-0080**	207-761-2200	374-5
Spring Hill College	4000 Dauphin St *Admissions	Mobile	AL	36608	**800-742-6704***	251-380-4000	167
Spring House Estates	728 Norristown Rd	Lower Gwynedd	PA	19002	**888-365-2287**	215-628-8110	670
Spring Lake Village	5555 Montgomery Dr	Santa Rosa	CA	95409	**800-795-1267**	707-538-8400	670
Spring Manufacturers Institute (SMI)	2001 Midwest Rd Ste 106	Oak Brook	IL	60523	**866-482-5569**	630-495-8588	48-13
Spring Mountain Vineyards	2805 Spring Mtn Rd	Saint Helena	CA	94574	**877-769-4637**	707-967-4188	316-5
Springboard Nonprofit Consumer Credit Management Inc	4351 Latham St	Riverside	CA	92501	**888-425-3453**		393
Springer Electric Co-op Inc	408 Maxwell Ave PO Box 698	Springer	NM	87747	**800-288-1353**	575-483-2421	247
Springfield Armory	420 W Main St	Geneseo	IL	61254	**800-680-6866**	309-944-5631	286
Springfield College	263 Alden St *Admissions	Springfield	MA	01109	**800-343-1257***	413-748-3136	167
Springfield College in Illinois - Benedictine University	1500 N Fifth St	Springfield	IL	62702	**800-635-7289**	217-525-1420	161
Springfield Conservation Nature Ctr	4600 S Chrisman Ave	Springfield	MO	65804	**800-392-1111**	417-888-4237	49-4
Springfield Convention & Visitors Bureau	109 N Seventh St	Springfield	IL	62701	**800-545-7300**	217-789-2360	208
Springfield Electric Supply Co	700 N Ninth St	Springfield	IL	62702	**800-747-2101**	217-788-2100	248
Springfield Hospital Ctr	6655 Sykesville Rd	Sykesville	MD	21784	**800-333-7564**	410-970-7000	374-5
Springfield Missouri Convention & Visitors Bureau	815 E St Louis St Ste 100	Springfield	MO	65806	**800-678-8767**	417-881-5300	208
Springfield Museums	21 Edwards St	Springfield	MA	01103	**800-625-7738**	413-263-6800	519
Springfield News Leader	651 N Boonville Ave	Springfield	MO	65806	**800-445-1059**	417-836-1100	531-2
Springfield News-Sun	202 N Limestone St	Springfield	OH	45503	**800-441-6397**	937-328-0300	531-2
Springfield Public School District #186	1900 W Monroe St	Springfield	IL	62704	**877-632-7753**	217-525-3006	683
Springfield ReManufacturing Corp	650 N Broadview Pl	Springfield	MO	65802	**800-772-7733**	417-862-3501	264
Springfield Technical Community College	1 Armory Sq PO Box 900	Springfield	MA	01102	**800-326-6142**	413-781-7822	161
Spring-Green Lawn Care Corp	11909 Spaulding School Dr	Plainfield	IL	60585	**800-435-4051**	815-436-8777	576
Springmaid Beach Resort	3200 S Ocean Blvd	Myrtle Beach	SC	29577	**866-764-8501**		705
Springs Window Fashions LP	7549 Graber Rd	Middleton	WI	53562	**877-792-0002**	608-836-1011	361
Sprocket Staffing Services	35 Colby Ave	Manasquan	NJ	08736	**800-269-1441**		262
Sprott Global Resource Investments Ltd	1910 Palomar Point Way Ste 200	Carlsbad	CA	92008	**800-477-7853**		689

Company / Address	City	State	ZIP	Toll-Free	Phone	Class
Sproule Associates Ltd 900 N Tower Sun Life Plz 140 Fourth Ave SW	Calgary	AB	T2P3N3	**877-777-6135**	403-294-5500	263
Sprout Pharmaceuticals Inc 4208 Six Forks Rd	Raleigh	NC	27609	**844-746-5745**		240
SPROUT Wellness Solutions Inc 366 Adelaide St W Ste 301	Toronto	ON	M5V1R9	**866-535-5027**		226
Spurlin Industries Inc 625 Main St	Palmetto	GA	30268	**800-749-4475**	770-463-1644	375
SPX Cooling Technologies 7401 W 129th St	Overland Park	KS	66213	**800-462-7539**	913-664-7400	90
SPX Corp 13515 Ballantyne Corporate Pl *NYSE: SPW*	Charlotte	NC	28277	**877-247-3797**	704-752-4400	187
SPX Corp OTC Div 655 Eisenhower Dr	Owatonna	MN	55060	**800-533-6127**	507-455-7000	755
SQA LABS Inc 16880 N 73rd Ave	Peoria	AZ	85382	**855-477-2522**	602-439-5500	182
Square 1 Art LLC 5470 Oakbrook Pkwy Ste E	Norcross	GA	30093	**888-332-3294**	678-906-2291	626
Square Books 160 Courthouse Sq	Oxford	MS	38655	**800-648-4001**	662-236-2262	95
Square One Mall 1201 Broadway	Saugus	MA	01906	**877-746-6642**	781-233-8787	459
Squaw Valley USA PO Box 2007	Olympic Valley	CA	96146	**800-403-0206**		667
S&R Truck Tire Center Inc 1402 Truckers Blvd	Jeffersonville	IN	47130	**800-488-2670**	812-282-4799	53
SRA (Society for Risk Analysis) 1313 Dolley Madison Blvd Ste 402	McLean	VA	22101	**800-364-5800**	703-790-1745	48-19
SRAM Corp 1333 N Kingsbury St 4th Fl	Chicago	IL	60622	**800-346-2928**	312-664-8800	81
SRC (Spoon River College) 23235 N County Hwy 22	Canton	IL	61520	**800-334-7337**	309-647-4645	161
SRC (Syracuse Research Corp) 7502 Round Pond Rd	North Syracuse	NY	13212	**800-724-0451**	315-452-8000	666
SRDS 1700 Higgins Rd	Des Plaines	IL	60018	**800-851-7737**		634-2
SREC (Spoon River Electric Co-op Inc) 930 S Fifth Ave PO Box 340	Canton	IL	61520	**877-404-2572**	309-647-2700	247
Sri Quality Sys 300 Northpointe Cir Ste 304	Seven Fields	PA	16046	**800-549-6709**	724-934-9000	198
SriLankan Airlines 379 Thornall St 6th Fl	Edison	NJ	08837	**877-915-2652**	732-205-0017	25
SRMC (Saint Rita's Medical Ctr) 730 W Market St	Lima	OH	45801	**800-232-7762**	419-227-3361	374-3
SRMC (Spartanburg Regional Medical Ctr) 101 E Wood St	Spartanburg	SC	29303	**800-318-2596**	864-560-6000	374-3
SRMC (Sonora Regional Medical Ctr) 1000 Greenly Rd *Compliance	Sonora	CA	95370	**877-336-3566***	209-536-5000	374-3
SRP (Salt River Project) 1521 N Project Dr	Tempe	AZ	85281	**800-258-4777**	602-236-5900	785
SRS Labs Inc 2909 Daimler St *NASDAQ: SRSL* ■ *General	Santa Ana	CA	92705	**800-322-2885***	949-442-1070	694
SRT (Seattle Repertory Theatre) 155 Mercer St PO Box 900923	Seattle	WA	98109	**877-900-9285**	206-443-2210	572-4
SS & C Technologies Inc 80 Lamberton Rd	Windsor	CT	06095	**800-234-0556**	860-298-4500	180-11
SS Nesbitt & Co Inc 3500 Blue Lake Dr	Birmingham	AL	35243	**800-422-3223**	205-262-2700	391-4
S&S Public Relations Inc 150 N Upper Wacker Dr Ste 2010	Chicago	IL	60606	**800-287-2279**		633
SSA (Self Storage Assn) 1900 N Beauregard St Ste 450	Alexandria	VA	22311	**888-735-3784**	703-575-8000	48-21
SSA (Social Security Administration) 6401 Security Blvd	Baltimore	MD	21235	**800-772-1213**	410-965-8904	340-18
SSA Consultants Inc 9331 Bluebonnet Blvd	Baton Rouge	LA	70810	**800-634-2758**	225-769-2676	462
SSA Marine 1131 SW Klickitat Way	Seattle	WA	98134	**800-422-3505**	206-623-0304	464
SSAT (Society for Surgery of the Alimentary Tract) 900 Cummings Ctr Ste 221-U	Beverly	MA	01915	**866-849-5866**	978-927-8330	48-8
Ssci 3065 Kent Ave	West Lafayette	IN	47906	**800-375-2179**	765-463-0112	196
SSCS (IEEE Solid State Circuits Society) 445 Hoes Ln	Piscataway	NJ	08854	**800-678-4333**	732-981-3400	48-19
SSgA Funds 1 Lincoln St	Boston	MA	02111	**800-997-7327**	617-786-3000	527
SSIT (IEEE Society on Social Implications of Technology) IEEE Operations Ctr 445 Hoes Ln	Piscataway	NJ	08854	**800-678-4333**	732-981-0060	48-19
SSJCPL (Stockton-San Joaquin County Public Library) 605 N El Dorado St	Stockton	CA	95202	**866-805-7323**	209-937-8416	434-3
SSM Health 620 E Monroe St	Mexico	MO	65265	**844-776-9355**	573-582-5000	374-3
SSM Healthy 1000 N Lee Ave	Oklahoma City	OK	73102	**866-203-5846**	618-242-4600	353
SSM Hospice 2 Harbor Bend Ct	Lake Saint Louis	MO	63367	**800-835-1212**	314-989-2700	371
SSPC (Society for Protective Coatings) 40 24th St 6th Fl	Pittsburgh	PA	15222	**877-281-7772**	412-281-2331	48-13
SSS Co 71 University Ave	Atlanta	GA	30315	**800-237-3843**	404-521-0857	582
SST Corp 635 Brighton Rd	Clifton	NJ	07012	**800-222-0921**	973-473-4300	478
SSW (Episcopal Theological Seminary of the Southwest) 501 E 32nd PO Box 2247	Austin	TX	78705	**800-252-5400**	512-472-4133	168-3
St Agnes Hospital 430 E Div St	Fond du Lac	WI	54935	**800-922-3400**	920-929-2300	374-3
St Alexius Medical Ctr 900 E Broadway Ave	Bismarck	ND	58501	**877-530-5550**	701-530-7755	374-3
S&T Bancorp Inc 800 Philadelphia St *NASDAQ: STBA*	Indiana	PA	15701	**800-325-2265**	724-349-1800	360-2
S&T Bank 800 Philadelphia St PO Box 190 *Cust Svc	Indiana	PA	15701	**800-325-2265***	724-349-1800	69
St Ignatius College Prep 2001 37th Ave	San Francisco	CA	94116	**888-225-5427**	312-421-5900	683
S-T Industries Inc 301 Armstrong Blvd N PO Box 517	Saint James	MN	56081	**800-326-2039**	507-375-3211	492
St James Hotel 406 Main St	Red Wing	MN	55066	**800-252-1875**	651-388-2846	379
St John Detroit Riverview Ctr 7733 E Jefferson Ave	Detroit	MI	48214	**866-501-3627**		374-3
St John Providence Health System 28000 Dequindre	Warren	MI	48092	**866-501-3627**		374-3
ST Johnson Co 925 Stanford Ave	Oakland	CA	94608	**800-225-1348**	510-652-6000	319
St Julien Hotel & Spa 900 Walnut St	Boulder	CO	80302	**877-303-0900**	720-406-9696	379
St Lawrence County Chamber of Commerce 101 Main St	Canton	NY	13617	**877-228-7810**	315-386-4000	138
St Mary's of Michigan (STMH) 800 S Washington Ave	Saginaw	MI	48601	**877-738-6672**	989-907-8115	374-3
St Moritz Bldg Services Inc 4616 Clairton Blvd	Pittsburgh	PA	15236	**800-218-9159**	412-885-2100	151
St Moritz Security Services Inc 4600 Clairton Blvd	Pittsburgh	PA	15236	**800-218-9156**	412-885-3144	691
St Paul Flight Ctr 270 Airport Rd Ste 5	Saint Paul	MN	55107	**800-368-0107**	651-227-8108	62
St Petersburg General Hospital 6500 38th Ave N	Saint Petersburg	FL	33710	**800-733-0610**	727-384-1414	374-3
St Renatus LLC 1000 Centre Ave	Fort Collins	CO	80526	**888-686-2314**	970-282-0156	233
St. Clair County Regional Educational Service Agency 499 Range Rd	Marysville	MI	48040	**800-294-9229**	810-364-8990	683
St. John Providence 28000 Dequindre	Warren	MI	48092	**866-501-3627**	586-573-5000	374-3
St.Vincent Health 2001 W 86th St	Indianapolis	IN	46260	**866-338-2345**	317-338-2345	449
STA (Student Transportation of America Inc) 3349 Hwy 138 Bldg B Ste D	Wall	NJ	07719	**888-942-2250**	732-280-4200	108
Sta International 1400 Old Country Rd Ste 411	Westbury	NY	11590	**866-970-9882**	516-997-2400	218
STAAR Surgical Co 1911 Walker Ave *NASDAQ: STAA*	Monrovia	CA	91016	**800-352-7842**	626-303-7902	541
Stabila Inc 332 Industrial Dr PO Box 402	South Elgin	IL	60177	**800-869-7460**		756
Stackbin Corp 29 Powderhill Rd *Sales	Lincoln	RI	02865	**800-333-1603***	401-333-1600	200
Stack-On Products Co 1360 N Old Rand Rd	Wauconda	IL	60084	**800-323-9601**	847-526-1611	487
Stafast Products Inc 505 Lk Shore Blvd	Painesville	OH	44077	**800-782-3278**	440-357-5546	280
STAFDA (Specialty Tools & Fasteners Distributors Assn) 500 Elm Grove Rd Ste 210 PO Box 44	Elm Grove	WI	53122	**800-352-2981**	262-784-4774	48-18
Staff One Inc 8111 LBJ Fwy	Dallas	TX	75251	**800-771-7823**		630
Staffing Options & Solutions Inc 6249 S E St Ste E	Indianapolis	IN	46227	**800-554-7823**	317-791-2456	262
Staffing Resource Group Inc, The 3505 E Frntage Rd Ste 320	Tampa	FL	33607	**877-774-7742**		262
Stafford Communications Group Inc 309 South St Ste 3	New Providence	NJ	07974	**877-694-7547**	908-464-7740	197
Stafford Printing Co 2707 Jefferson Davis Hwy	Stafford	VA	22554	**800-774-6831**	540-659-4554	626
Stafford-Smith Inc 3414 S Burdick St	Kalamazoo	MI	49001	**800-968-2442**	269-343-1240	663
Staffworks Group 20505 W 12 Mile Rd	Southfield	MI	48076	**877-304-9690**		262
Stage Neck Inn 8 Stage Neck Rd Rt 1A PO Box 70	York Harbor	ME	03911	**800-222-3238**	207-363-3850	667
Stageright Corp 495 Pioneer Pkwy	Clare	MI	48617	**800-438-4499**	989-386-7393	322
Stahancyk Kent & Hook P C Duniway Plz 2400 SW 4th Ave	Portland	OR	97201	**877-673-7632**		444
Stahl Peterbilt Inc 18020-118 Ave	Edmonton	AB	T5S2G2	**800-252-7981**	780-483-6666	789
Stahl Specialty Co 111 E Pacific PO Box 6	Kingsville	MO	64061	**800-821-7852**	816-597-3322	309
STAHL/A Scott Fetzer Co 3201 W Old Lincoln Way	Wooster	OH	44691	**800-277-8245**	330-264-7441	515
Sta-Home Hospice 406 Briarwood Dr Bldg 200	Jackson	MS	39206	**800-782-4663**	601-956-5100	363
Staker Parson Cos 2350 South 1900 West	Ogden	UT	84401	**888-672-7766**	801-731-1111	190-4
Staley Inc 8101 Fourche Rd	Little Rock	AR	72209	**877-616-0661**	501-565-3006	191-4
Stallings Crop Insurance Corp PO Box 6100	Lakeland	FL	33807	**800-721-7099**	863-647-2747	390
Stamats Communications Inc 615 Fifth St SE	Cedar Rapids	IA	52401	**800-553-8878**	319-364-6167	634-9
Stambaugh Auditorium 1000 Fifth Ave	Youngstown	OH	44504	**866-516-2269**	330-747-5175	571
Stamford Chamber of Commerce 733 Summer St Ste 104	Stamford	CT	06901	**866-262-4548**	203-359-4761	138
Stamford Suites 720 Bedford St	Stamford	CT	06901	**866-394-4365**	203-359-7300	379
Stampede Meat Inc 7351 S 78th Ave	Bridgeview	IL	60455	**800-353-0933**		297-26
Stamp-Rite Inc 154 S Larch St	Lansing	MI	48912	**800-328-1988**	517-487-5071	466
Stamps.com Inc 1990 E Grand Ave *NASDAQ: STMP*	El Segundo	CA	90245	**855-889-7867**		180-1

Company / Address	City	State	ZIP	Toll-Free	Phone	Class
Stan Houston Equipment Co 501 S Marion Rd	Sioux Falls	SD	57106	**800-952-3033**	605-336-3727	358
Stan Hywet Hall & Gardens 714 N Portage Path	Akron	OH	44303	**888-836-5533**	330-836-5533	519
Stan White Realty & Construction Inc 812 Ocean Trl	Corolla	NC	27927	**800-753-6200**	252-453-6131	650
Stanadyne Corp 92 Deerfield Rd	Windsor	CT	06095	**888-336-3473**	860-525-0821	59
Stanbio Laboratory LP 1261 N Main St	Boerne	TX	78006	**800-531-5535**	830-249-0772	233
Stanbury Uniforms Inc 108 Stanbury Industrial Dr PO Box 100	Brookfield	MO	64628	**800-826-2246**	660-258-2246	154-18
StanCorp Financial Group Inc 1100 SW Sixth Ave *NYSE: SFG*	Portland	OR	97204	**800-368-1135**		360-4
Standard & Poor's Corp 55 Water St	New York	NY	10041	**877-772-5436**	212-438-1000	634-2
Standard Air & Lite Corp 2406 Woodmere Dr	Pittsburgh	PA	15205	**800-472-2458**	412-920-6505	611
Standard Alloys & Mfg PO Box 969	Port Arthur	TX	77640	**800-231-8240**	409-983-3201	638
Standard Bank & Trust Co 7800 W 95th St	Hickory Hills	IL	60457	**866-499-2265**	708-598-7400	69
Standard Beverage Corp 2416 E 37th St N	Wichita	KS	67219	**800-999-8797**	316-838-7707	80-3
Standard Digital Imaging 4426 S 108th St	Omaha	NE	68137	**800-642-8062**	402-592-1292	242
Standard Duplicating Machines Corp 10 Connector Rd	Andover	MA	01810	**800-526-4774**	978-470-1920	111
Standard Electric Co 2650 Trautner Dr	Saginaw	MI	48603	**800-322-0215**	989-497-2100	248
Standard Electric Supply Co 222 N Emmber Ln PO Box 651	Milwaukee	WI	53233	**800-776-8222**	414-272-8100	248
Standard Equipment Company Inc 75 Beauregard St	Mobile	AL	36602	**800-239-3442**	251-432-1705	768
Standard Filter Corp 5928 Balfour Ct	Carlsbad	CA	92008	**800-634-5837**	760-929-8559	18
Standard Furniture Mfg Company Inc 801 Hwy 31 S *General	Bay Minette	AL	36507	**877-788-1899***	251-937-6741	320-2
Standard Imaging Inc 3120 Deming Way	Middleton	WI	53562	**800-261-4446**	608-831-0025	636
Standard Knapp Inc 63 Pickering St *Cust Svc	Portland	CT	06480	**800-628-9565***	860-342-1100	546
Standard Life Insurance Company of Indiana 10689 N Pennsylvania St	Indianapolis	IN	46280	**800-222-3216**	317-574-6201	391-2
Standard Locknut Inc 1045 E 169th St	Westfield	IN	46074	**800-783-6887**	317-867-0100	453
Standard Machine Ltd 868-60th St E	Saskatoon	SK	S7K8G8	**800-329-4327**	306-931-3343	707
Standard Meat Company LP 5105 Investment Dr	Dallas	TX	75236	**866-859-6313**	214-561-0561	297-26
Standard Motors Ltd 44 Second Ave NW	Swift Current	SK	S9H3V6	**866-334-8985**		56
Standard Office Supply 35 Sheridan St Nw	Washington	DC	20011	**888-829-4820**	202-829-4820	322
Standard Parking Corp 900 N Michigan Ave Ste 1600	Chicago	IL	60611	**888-700-7275**	312-274-2000	561
Standard Publishing Co 8805 Governors Hill Dr Ste 400 *Orders	Cincinnati	OH	45249	**800-543-1353***	513-931-4050	634-9
Standard Roofing Co 516 N McDonough St PO Box 1309	Montgomery	AL	36102	**800-239-5705**	334-265-1262	191-12
Standard Supply & Distributing Co 1431 Regal Row	Dallas	TX	75247	**800-460-7801**	214-630-7800	351
Standard Textile Company Inc 1 Knollcrest Dr	Cincinnati	OH	45237	**800-999-0400**	513-761-9255	476
Standard-Examiner 332 Standard Way	Ogden	UT	84404	**888-221-7070**	801-625-4200	531-2
Standards Council of Canada 270 Albert St Ste 200	Ottawa	ON	K1P6N7	**800-844-6790**	613-238-3222	465
Standex Electronics Inc 4538 Camberwell Rd	Cincinnati	OH	45209	**866-782-6339**	513-871-3777	255
Standex International Corp Consumer Group 11 Keewaydin Dr *NYSE: SXI*	Salem	NH	03079	**800-514-5275**	603-893-9701	634-3
Standex International Corp Custom Hoists Div 771 County Rd 30A W PO Box 98	Hayesville	OH	44838	**800-837-4668**	419-368-4721	225
Standex International Corp Food Service Equipment Group 11 Keewaydin Dr *NYSE: SXI*	Salem	NH	03079	**800-647-1284**	603-893-9701	301
Stanford Cancer Ctr 875 Lake Blake Wilbur Dr	Stanford	CA	94305	**800-422-6237**	650-498-6000	666
Stanford Federal Credit Union 1860 Embarcadero Rd	Palo Alto	CA	94303	**888-723-7328**	650-723-2509	221
Stanford University 450 Serra Mall	Stanford	CA	94305	**877-407-9529**	650-723-2091	167
Stanford University Green Library 557 Escondido Mall	Stanford	CA	94305	**800-521-0600**	650-723-2300	434-6
Stanford University Press 1450 Page Mill Rd	Palo Alto	CA	94304	**800-621-2736**	650-723-9434	634-4
Stanford University School of Medicine Blood & Marrow Transplant Program 300 Pasteur Dr Rm H-3249 MC 5623	Stanford	CA	94305	**888-275-5724**	650-723-0822	767
Stanion Wholesale Electric Co 812 S Main St PO Box F	Pratt	KS	67124	**866-782-6466**	620-672-5678	248
Stanislaus Farm Supply Co 624 E Service Rd	Modesto	CA	95358	**800-323-0725**	209-538-7070	278
Stanislaus Food Products Co 1202 D St	Modesto	CA	95354	**800-327-7201**		297-20
Stanley Access Technologies 65 Scott Swamp Rd	Farmington	CT	06032	**800-722-2377**	860-677-2861	236
Stanley Assembly Technologies Div 5335 Avion Pk Dr	Cleveland	OH	44143	**877-787-7830**	440-461-5500	757
Stanley Consultants Inc 225 Iowa Ave	Muscatine	IA	52761	**800-553-9694**	563-264-6600	263
Stanley Creations Inc 1414 Willow Ave	Melrose Park	PA	19027	**800-220-1414**	215-635-6200	409
Stanley Furniture Co Inc 200 North Hamilton St *NASDAQ: STLY*	High Point	NC	27260	**877-772-4858**		320-2
Stanley Hotel 333 Wonderview Ave	Estes Park	CO	80517	**800-976-1377**	970-586-3371	379
Stanley Hunt DuPree & Rhine Inc (SHDR) 7701 Airport Ctr Dr	Greensboro	NC	27409	**888-999-4701**	800-768-4873	195
Stanley Korshak 500 Crescent Ct Ste 100	Dallas	TX	75201	**855-749-9539**	214-871-3600	156-4
Stanley Martin Cos 11111 Sunset Hills Rd Ste 200	Reston	VA	20190	**800-446-4807**	703-964-5000	651
Stanley Mcdonald Agency of Illinois 2018 State Rd	La Crosse	WI	54601	**800-344-3948**	608-788-6160	390
Stanley Tools Inc 480 Myrtle St *Cust Svc	New Britain	CT	06053	**800-262-2161***		756
Stanley Vidmar Storage Technologies 11 Grammes Rd	Allentown	PA	18103	**800-523-9462**		288
Stanly Community College 141 College Dr	Albemarle	NC	28001	**877-275-4219**	704-982-0121	798
Stansberry & Assoc Investment Research LLC 1217 Saint Paul St	Baltimore	MD	21202	**888-261-2693**		401
Stant Corp 1620 Columbia Ave	Connersville	IN	47331	**800-822-3121**	765-825-3121	607
Stantec Inc 400 E Vine St Ste 300 *NYSE: STN*	Lexington	KY	40507	**866-782-6832**	859-233-2100	263
Stanton Carpet Corp 211 Robbins Ln	Syosset	NY	11791	**888-809-2989**	516-822-5878	364
Stanton County Public Power District 807 Douglas St	Stanton	NE	68779	**877-439-2300**	402-439-2228	247
Stanton's Sheet Music 330 S Fourth St	Columbus	OH	43215	**800-426-8742**	614-224-4257	525
Staplcotn Co-op Assn Inc 214 W Market St	Greenwood	MS	38930	**800-293-6231**	662-453-6231	277
Staples Business Advantage 500 Staples Dr	Framingham	MA	01702	**877-826-7755**		533
Staples Construction Company Inc 1501 Eastman Ave	Ventura	CA	93003	**800-881-4650**	805-658-8786	462
Staples Promotional Products 7500 W 110th St	Overland Park	KS	66210	**800-369-4669**	913-319-3100	9
Stapleton Technologies Inc 1350 W 12th St	Long Beach	CA	90813	**800-266-0541**	562-437-0541	144
Stapleton-Spence Packing Co 1530 The Alameda Ste 320	San Jose	CA	95126	**800-297-8815**	408-297-8815	297-20
Staplex Co 777 Fifth Ave *Cust Svc	Brooklyn	NY	11232	**800-221-0822***	718-768-3333	110
Star 92.9 265 Hegeman Ave	Colchester	VT	05446	**866-865-7827**	802-655-0093	643
Star Beacon PO Box 2100	Ashtabula	OH	44005	**800-554-6768**	440-998-2323	531-2
Star Bldg Systems 8600 S I-35	Oklahoma City	OK	73149	**800-879-7827**		104
Star Casualty Insurance Company Inc PO Box 451037	Miami	FL	33134	**877-782-7210**		390
Star Clippers Inc 760 NW 107th Ave *Resv	Miami	FL	33172	**800-442-0556***	305-442-0550	222
Star Cutter Co 23461 Industrial Pk Dr	Farmington	MI	48335	**877-635-3488**	248-474-8200	492
Star Democrat 29088 Airpark Dr PO Box 600	Easton	MD	21601	**888-634-4002**	410-822-1500	531-2
Star Distributors Inc 460 Frontage Rd	West Haven	CT	06516	**877-922-3501**	203-932-3636	80-1
Star Exhibits & Environments Inc 6920 93rd Ave N	Minneapolis	MN	55445	**800-419-7827**	763-561-4655	393
Star Fleet Inc 915 South Main St	Middlebury	IN	46540	**877-805-9547**	888-281-8727	778
Star Furniture Company Inc 16666 Barker Springs Rd	Houston	TX	77084	**800-364-6661**	281-492-6661	322
Star Gas Partners LP 2187 Atlantic St *NYSE: SGU*	Stamford	CT	06902	**800-960-7546**	203-328-7310	317
Star Insurance Co 26255 American Dr	Southfield	MI	48034	**800-482-2726**	248-358-4020	391-4
Star Island Resort 5000 Ave of the Stars	Kissimmee	FL	34746	**800-513-2820**	407-997-8000	379
Star Leasing Co 4080 Business Pk Dr	Columbus	OH	43204	**888-771-1004**	614-278-9999	776
Star Micronics America Inc 1150 King George's Post Rd	Edison	NJ	08837	**800-782-7636**	732-623-5500	175-6
Star Milling Co 24067 Water St	Perris	CA	92570	**800-733-6455**	951-657-3143	446
Star Multi Care Services Inc 115 Broad Hollow Rd Ste 275	Melville	NY	11747	**877-920-0600**	631-424-7827	363
Star Nail Products Inc 29120 Ave Paine	Valencia	CA	91355	**800-762-6245**	661-257-7827	217
Star of the West Milling Co 121 E Tuscola St	Frankenmuth	MI	48734	**888-281-4161**	989-652-9971	10-3
Star One Federal Credit Union PO Box 3643	Sunnyvale	CA	94088	**866-543-5202**	408-543-5202	221
Star Pipe LLC 4018 Westhollow Pkwy	Houston	TX	77082	**800-999-3009**	281-558-3000	594
Star Rentals Inc 1919 Fourth Ave S	Seattle	WA	98134	**800-825-7880**	206-622-7880	266-3
Star Sales & Distributing Corp 29 Commerce Way	Woburn	MA	01801	**800-222-8118**	781-933-8830	193-2
Star Sales Company Inc 1803 N Central St	Knoxville	TN	37917	**800-347-9494**	781-933-2145	329
Star Services 4663 Halls Mill Rd	Mobile	AL	36693	**800-661-9050**	251-661-4050	609
Star Trac by Unisen Inc 14410 Myford Rd	Irvine	CA	92606	**800-228-6635**	714-669-1660	269

Name / Address	City	State	ZIP	Toll-Free	Phone	Class
Star Transportation Inc PO Box 100925 *Cust Svc	Nashville	TN	37224	**800-333-3060***	615-256-4336	778
Star Travel Services Inc 1025 Acuff Rd	Bloomington	IN	47404	**800-542-1687**	812-336-6811	769
Star Tribune 425 Portland Ave	Minneapolis	MN	55488	**800-827-8742**	612-673-4000	531-2
Star Truck Rentals Inc 3940 Eastern Ave SE	Grand Rapids	MI	49508	**800-748-0468**	616-243-7033	776
Star West Satellite Inc 580 Prong Horn Trl	Bozeman	MT	59718	**888-814-8402**	406-522-8402	679
Star, The 404 E Martintown Rd Ste 2	North Augusta	SC	29841	**888-397-3742**	803-279-2793	531-4
Starboard Cruise Services Inc 8400 NW 36th St	Miami	FL	33166	**800-540-4785**	786-845-7300	243
Starbucks Coffee Co 2401 Utah Ave S	Seattle	WA	98134	**800-782-7282**	206-447-1575	158
Starco Impex Inc 2710 S 11th St	Beaumont	TX	77701	**866-740-9601**		345
Starcraft Marine LLC 68143 Clunette St PO Box 65	New Paris	IN	46553	**888-327-4236**	574-831-2103	89
Stardock Systems Inc 15090 N Beck Rd Ste 300	Plymouth	MI	48170	**888-782-7362**	734-927-0677	176
Star-Gazette 201 Baldwin St	Elmira	NY	14902	**800-836-8970**	607-734-5151	531-2
Stark & Stark 993 Lenox Dr Bldg 2	Lawrenceville	NJ	08648	**800-535-3425**	609-896-9060	428
Stark State College of Technology 6200 Frank Ave NW	North Canton	OH	44720	**800-797-8275**	330-494-6170	798
Starkey International Institute for Household Management Inc, The 1350 Logan St	Denver	CO	80203	**800-888-4904**	303-832-5510	148
Starkey Laboratories Inc 6700 Washington Ave S	Eden Prairie	MN	55344	**800-328-8602**	952-941-6401	476
Starkweather & Shepley Inc 60 Catamore Blvd	East Providence	RI	02914	**800-854-4625**	401-435-3600	390
Star-Ledger, The 1 Star Ledger Plz	Newark	NJ	07102	**800-501-2100**	973-877-4141	531-2
Starlight Theatre 4600 Starlight Rd Swope Pk	Kansas City	MO	64132	**800-776-1730**	816-363-7827	571
Starline Associates Inc 3901 Sw 47th Ave Ste 410	Davie	FL	33314	**866-752-6548**	954-792-1965	292
Starline Inc 1300 W Henry St	Sedalia	MO	65301	**800-280-6660**	660-827-6640	709
Starlite Limousines LLC PO Box 13542	Scottsdale	AZ	85267	**800-875-4104**	480-422-3619	441
Starmark Cabinetry 600 E 48th St N	Sioux Falls	SD	57104	**800-755-7789**	800-594-9444	114
Starmark International Inc 210 S Andrews Ave	Fort Lauderdale	FL	33301	**888-280-9630**	954-874-9000	197
Starplex Scientific Inc 50 A Steinway Blvd	Etobicoke	ON	M9W6Y3	**800-665-0954**	416-674-7474	475
Starr Bus Charter & Tours 2531 E State St	Trenton	NJ	08619	**800-782-7703**	609-587-0626	106
Starr Commonwealth 13725 Starr Commonwealth Rd	Albion	MI	49224	**800-837-5591**	517-629-5591	47-15
Starr King School for the Ministry 2441 LeConte Ave	Berkeley	CA	94709	**866-727-4894**	510-845-6232	168-3
STARR Life Sciences Corp 333 Allegheny Ave Ste 300	Oakmont	PA	15139	**866-978-2779**		419
Starrett Tru-Stone Technologies Div 1101 Prosper Dr PO Box 430	Waite Park	MN	56387	**800-959-0517**	320-251-7171	722
Starrett Webber Gage Div 24500 Detroit Rd	Cleveland	OH	44145	**800-255-3924**	440-835-0001	492
Star-Seal 6596 New Peachtree Rd	Atlanta	GA	30340	**800-779-6066**	770-455-6551	579
Starside Security & Investigation Inc 1930 S Brea Canyon Rd Ste 220	Diamond Bar	CA	91765	**888-478-2774**	909-396-9999	400
Startec Global Communications Corp 11300 Rockville Pike Ste 900	Rockville	MD	20852	**800-827-3374**	301-610-4300	733
Startech Computing Inc 1755 Old W Main St	Red Wing	MN	55066	**888-385-0607**	651-385-0607	182
Starvin' Artist Supplies 802 S Oak Pk	Oak Park	IL	60304	**800-427-8478**	708-358-3600	44
Starving Students Moving & Storage Co 1850 Sawtelle Blvd Ste 300	Los Angeles	CA	90025	**888-931-6683**		518
Starwest Botanicals Inc 11253 Trade Ctr Dr *General	Rancho Cordova	CA	95742	**888-273-4372***	916-638-8100	478
Starwood Hotels & Resorts Worldwide Inc 1111 Westchester Ave *NYSE: HOT* ■ *Cust Svc	White Plains	NY	10604	**888-625-5144***	914-640-8100	379
Saint Regis Hotels & Resorts 1111 Westchester Ave	White Plains	NY	10604	**888-625-4988**	914-640-8100	379
Westin Hotels & Resorts 1111 Westchester Ave	White Plains	NY	10604	**888-625-5144**	914-640-8100	379
Starwood Hotels Preferred Guest Program 111 Westchester Ave	White Plains	NY	10604	**888-625-4988**	512-834-2426	378
State & Federal Communications Inc 80 S Summit St	Akron	OH	44308	**888-452-9669**	330-761-9960	779
State Auto Property & Casualty Insurance Co 518 E Broad St	Columbus	OH	43215	**800-444-9950**	614-464-5000	391-4
State Bank 175 N Leroy St	Fenton	MI	48430	**800-535-0517**	810-629-2263	69
State Bank of Waterloo PO Box 148	Waterloo	IL	62298	**800-367-7576**	618-939-7194	69
State Bar Assn of North Dakota 504 N Washington St PO Box 2136	Bismarck	ND	58502	**800-472-2685**	701-255-1404	71
State Bar of Arizona 4201 N 24th St Ste 200	Phoenix	AZ	85016	**866-482-9227**	602-252-4804	71
State Bar of Georgia 104 Marietta St NW Ste 100	Atlanta	GA	30303	**800-334-6865**	404-527-8700	71
State Bar of Michigan 306 Townsend St	Lansing	MI	48933	**800-968-1442**	517-346-6300	71
State Bar of Nevada 600 E Charleston Blvd	Las Vegas	NV	89104	**800-254-2797**	702-382-2200	71

Name / Address	City	State	ZIP	Toll-Free	Phone	Class
State Bar of New Mexico 5121 Masthead St NE PO Box 92860	Albuquerque	NM	87109	**800-876-6227**	505-797-6000	71
State Bar of Texas 1414 Colorado St	Austin	TX	78701	**800-204-2222**	512-427-1463	71
State Compensation Insurance Fund PO Box 8192	Pleasanton	CA	94588	**866-721-3498**	415-565-1234	391-4
State Education Resource Center 25 Industrial Park Rd	Middletown	CT	06457	**800-842-8678**	860-632-1485	435
State Electric Supply Company Inc 2010 Second Ave *Cust Svc	Huntington	WV	25703	**800-624-3417***	304-523-7491	248
State Employees Credit Union of Maryland Inc 971 Corporate Blvd	Linthicum	MD	21090	**800-879-7328**	410-487-7328	221
State Employees Federal Credit Union 700 Patroon Creek Blvd Patroon Creek Corporate Ctr	Albany	NY	12206	**800-727-3328**	518-452-8234	221
State Employees' Credit Union (SECU) PO Box 29606	Raleigh	NC	27626	**888-732-8562**	919-857-2150	221
State Environment Daily 1801 S Bell St	Arlington	VA	22202	**800-372-1033**		530-5
State Fair & Exposition 1001 Beulah Ave	Pueblo	CO	81004	**800-876-4567**	719-404-2018	718
State Fair Community College 3201 W 16th St	Sedalia	MO	65301	**877-311-7322**	660-530-5800	161
State Farm Financial Services FSB PO Box 2316	Bloomington	IL	61702	**877-734-2265**		69
State Farm Insurance 333 First Commerce Dr	Aurora	ON	L4G8A4	**877-659-1570**		391-4
State Farm Mutual Funds PO Box 219548	Kansas City	MO	64121	**800-447-4930**		527
State Forest State Park 56750 Hwy 14	Walden	CO	80480	**866-265-6447**	970-723-8366	564
State Historical Society of Missouri, The 1020 Lowry St	Columbia	MO	65201	**800-747-6366**	573-882-1187	519
State Industrial Products 3100 Hamilton Ave	Cleveland	OH	44114	**877-747-6986**	216-861-7114	150
State Journal, The 1216 Wilkinson Blvd	Frankfort	KY	40601	**800-621-3362**	502-227-4556	531-2
State Journal-Register PO Box 219	Springfield	IL	62705	**800-397-6397**	217-788-1300	531-2
State Library of Ohio 274 E First Ave Ste 100	Columbus	OH	43201	**800-686-1532**	614-644-7061	434-5
State Life Insurance Co 1 American Sq PO Box 368 *Cust Svc	Indianapolis	IN	46206	**800-537-6442***	317-285-2300	391-2
State of the Heart Home Health & Hospice 1350 N Broadway	Greenville	OH	45331	**800-417-7535**	937-548-2999	371
State Pipe & Supply Inc 9615 S Norwalk Blvd	Santa Fe Springs	CA	90670	**800-733-6410**	562-695-5555	491
State Plaza Hotel 2117 E St NW	Washington	DC	20037	**800-424-2859**	202-861-8200	379
State Supply Co 597 Seventh St E	Saint Paul	MN	55130	**877-775-7705**	651-774-5985	609
State Teachers Retirement System of Ohio 275 E Broad St	Columbus	OH	43215	**888-227-7877**		527
State Telephone Regulation Report 2115 Ward Ct NW	Washington	DC	20037	**800-771-9202**	202-872-9200	530-11
State Training School 3211 Edgington Ave	Eldora	IA	50627	**800-362-2178**	641-858-5402	412
State Universities Retirement System of Illinois 1901 Fox Dr	Champaign	IL	61820	**800-275-7877**	217-378-8800	401
State University of New York						
Brockport 350 New Campus Dr	Brockport	NY	14420	**888-800-0029**	585-395-2751	167
Canton 34 Cornell Dr	Canton	NY	13617	**800-388-7123**	315-386-7011	161
College of Agriculture & Technology at Cobleskill Rt 7	Cobleskill	NY	12043	**800-295-8988**	518-255-5525	167
College of Environmental Science & Forestry 1 Forestry Dr *Admissions	Syracuse	NY	13210	**800-777-7373***	315-470-6500	167
College of Technology at Alfred 10 Upper College Dr	Alfred	NY	14802	**800-425-3733**	607-587-4215	161
Delhi 2 Main St	Delhi	NY	13753	**800-963-3544**	607-746-4000	161
Empire State College 1 Union Ave	Saratoga Springs	NY	12866	**800-847-3000**	518-587-2100	167
Geneseo 1 College Cir *Admitting	Geneseo	NY	14454	**866-245-5211***	585-245-5571	167
Institute of Technology PO Box 3050	Utica	NY	13504	**866-278-6948**	315-792-7500	167
Maritime College 6 Pennyfield Ave Fort Schuyler	Bronx	NY	10465	**888-800-0029**	718-409-7200	167
New Paltz 1 Hawk Dr	New Paltz	NY	12561	**877-696-7411**	845-257-3212	167
Plattsburgh 101 Broad St *Admissions	Plattsburgh	NY	12901	**888-673-0012***	518-564-2040	167
Potsdam 44 Pierrpont Ave *Admissions	Potsdam	NY	13676	**877-768-7326***	315-267-2180	167
University at Buffalo 12 Capen Hall	Buffalo	NY	14260	**888-822-3648**	716-645-2450	167
State University of New York at Buffalo						
Health Sciences Library (HSL) 3435 Main St Abbott Hall Rm 102	Buffalo	NY	14214	**866-432-5849**	716-829-3900	434-1
State University of New York Press (SUNY) 22 Corporate Woods Blvd 3rd Fl	Albany	NY	12211	**866-430-7869**	518-472-5000	634-4
State University of New York Upstate Medical University 766 Irving Ave	Syracuse	NY	13210	**800-736-2171**	315-464-4570	168-2
State University of New York Upstate Medical University Tissue Typing Laboratory 750 E Adams St	Syracuse	NY	13210	**877-464-5540**	315-464-4775	417
State University of New York, The (SUNY) State University Plz	Albany	NY	12246	**800-342-3811**	518-320-1888	784
State Volunteer Mutual Insurance Co 101 W Pk Dr Ste 300	Brentwood	TN	37027	**800-342-2239**	615-377-1999	391-5
State, The 1401 Shop Rd	Columbia	SC	29201	**800-888-5353**	803-771-6161	531-2
Statehouse Convention Ctr 426 W Markham PO Box 3232	Little Rock	AR	72203	**800-844-4781**	501-376-4781	207

Company / Address	City	ST	ZIP	Toll-Free	Phone	Class
States Industries Inc 29495 W Enid Rd	Eugene	OR	97402	**800-626-1981**	541-688-7871	612
Statesville Brick Co 391 BrickyaRd Rd	Statesville	NC	28677	**800-522-4716**	704-872-4123	149
Statewide Remodeling Inc 2450 Esters Blvd Ste 200	DFW Airport	TX	75261	**800-317-8283**	214-677-9000	237
Static Control Components Inc 3010 Lee Ave PO Box 152	Sanford	NC	27331	**800-488-2426**	919-774-3808	176
Station Casinos Inc 1505 S Pavilion Ctr Dr *Resv	Las Vegas	NV	89135	**800-634-3101***	702-495-3000	131
Stationers Inc 1945 Fifth Ave	Huntington	WV	25703	**800-862-7200**	304-528-2780	534
Staub Metals Corp 7747 E Rosecrans Ave	Paramount	CA	90723	**800-447-8282**	562-602-2200	491
Staunton National Cemetery 901 Richmond Ave	Staunton	VA	24401	**800-273-8255**	540-825-0027	135
Stavis Seafoods Inc 212 Northern Ave Ste 305	Boston	MA	02210	**800-390-5103**	617-482-6349	298-5
Stay Aspen Snowmass 425 Rio Grande Pl	Aspen	CO	81611	**888-649-5982**	970-925-9000	376
STC (Society of Telecommunications Consultants) 13275 California 89	Old Station	CA	96071	**800-782-7670**	530-335-7313	48-20
STC Network Services Inc 4904 Oak Cir Dr N	Mobile	AL	36609	**800-566-2453**	251-661-7130	182
Steadmantech 1153 Powderhouse Rd	Vestal	NY	13850	**866-772-0882**		179
Steadyhand Investment Funds Limited Partnership 1747 W Third Ave	Vancouver	BC	V6J1K7	**888-888-3147**		527
Steak N Shake Co 3810 W Washington Holt Rd	Indianapolis	IN	46241	**877-785-6745**	317-241-0483	668
Stealth Computer Corp 530 Rowntree Dairy Rd Bldg 4	Woodbridge	ON	L4L8H2	**888-783-2584**	905-264-9000	175-1
Stealth Monitoring Inc 15182 Marsh Lane	Dallas	TX	75001	**855-783-2584**	214-341-0123	691
Steam Bros Inc 2400 Vermont Ave	Bismarck	ND	58504	**800-767-5064**	701-222-1263	151
Steamboat Grand Resort Hotel & Conference Ctr 2300 Mt Werner Cir	Steamboat Springs	CO	80487	**877-269-2628**	970-871-5500	667
Steamboat Ski & Resort Corp 2305 Mt Werner Cir	Steamboat Springs	CO	80487	**877-237-2628**	970-879-6111	667
Steamtown National Historic Site 150 S Washington Ave	Scranton	PA	18503	**888-693-9391**	570-340-5200	563
Stearns ElectricAssn 900 E Kraft Dr	Melrose	MN	56352	**800-962-0655**	320-256-4241	247
Stearns Packaging Corp 4200 Sycamore Ave	Madison	WI	53714	**800-655-5008**	608-246-5150	150
Stearns Weaver Miller Weissler Alhadeff & Sitterson P.A. 150 W Flagler St Ste 2200	Miami	FL	33130	**866-293-7866**	305-789-3200	428
Steel Ceilings Inc 451 E Coshocton St	Johnstown	OH	43031	**800-848-0496**	740-967-1063	490
Steel City Corp 190 N Meridian Rd	Youngstown	OH	44501	**800-321-0350**	330-792-7663	487
Steel Dynamics Inc 7575 W Jefferson Blvd Ste 200 *NASDAQ: STLD*	Fort Wayne	IN	46804	**866-740-8700**	260-969-3500	721
Steel Grip Inc 1501 E Voorhees St	Danville	IL	61832	**800-223-1595**	217-442-6240	575
Steel House Inc 3644 Eastham Dr	Culver City	CA	90232	**888-978-3354**		5
Steel Industries Inc (SII) 12600 Beech-Daly Rd	Redford Township	MI	48239	**877-783-3599**		482
Steel King Industries Inc 2700 Chamber St	Stevens Point	WI	54481	**800-826-0203**	715-341-3120	469
Steel of West Virginia Inc 17th St & Second Ave	Huntington	WV	25703	**800-624-3492**	304-696-8200	721
Steel Service Corp 2260 Flowood Dr PO Box 321425	Jackson	MS	39232	**800-844-9222**	601-939-9222	308
Steel Supply Co, The 5101 Newport Dr	Rolling Meadows	IL	60008	**800-323-7571**		491
Steel Unlimited Inc 456 W Valley Blvd	Rialto	CA	92376	**800-544-6453**	909-873-1222	491
Steel Warehouse Company Inc 2722 W Tucker Dr	South Bend	IN	46619	**800-348-2529**	574-236-5100	491
Steelcase Inc 801 44th St SE PO Box 1967 *NYSE: SCS*	Grand Rapids	MI	49501	**888-783-3522**	616-247-2710	320-1
SteelCloud Inc 20110 Ashbrook Pl Ste 270 *OTC: SCLD*	Ashburn	VA	20147	**800-296-3866**	703-674-5500	178
Steelcraft Mfg Co 9017 Blue Ash Rd *Cust Svc	Cincinnati	OH	45242	**877-613-8766***	513-745-6400	236
Steele Canvas Basket Corp 201 William St PO Box 6267 IMCN	Chelsea	MA	02150	**800-541-8929**	617-889-0202	730
Steele Capital Management Inc 788 Main St #200	Dubuque	IA	52001	**800-397-2097**	563-588-2097	527
Steele Law Firm p C The 949 County Rt 53	Oswego	NY	13126	**877-496-2687**	315-216-4721	428
Steele Solutions Inc 9909 S 57th St	Franklin	WI	53132	**888-542-5099**	414-367-5099	479
Steele Truck Ctr Inc 2150 Rockfill Rd	Fort Myers	FL	33916	**888-806-4839**	239-334-7300	56
Steele-Waseca Co-op Electric (SWCE) 2411 W Bridge St PO Box 485	Owatonna	MN	55060	**800-526-3514**	507-451-7340	247
Steelman Industries Inc 2800 Hwy 135 N	Kilgore	TX	75662	**800-287-6633**	903-984-3061	319
Steelman Transportation 2160 N Burton	Springfield	MO	65803	**800-488-6287**	417-831-6300	778
SteelTorch Software Inc 423 Jamestown Rd	Belmont	NH	03220	**866-705-2730**		807
Steen Outdoor Advertising 3201 S 26th St	Philadelphia	PA	19145	**866-537-8336**		8
Steere Enterprises Inc 285 Commerce St	Tallmadge	OH	44278	**800-875-4926**	330-633-4926	603
Stefanini TechTeam Inc 27335 W Eleven-Mile Rd	Southfield	MI	48034	**800-522-4451**	248-357-2866	182
Steffes Corp 3050 Hwy 22 N	Dickinson	ND	58601	**888-783-3337**	701-483-5400	479
Steiff North America 24 Albion Rd Ste 220	Lincoln	RI	02865	**888-978-3433**	401-312-0080	760
Stein Eriksen Lodge 7700 Stein Way	Park City	UT	84060	**800-453-1302**	435-649-3700	667
Stein Hospice Service 1912 Hayes Ave Ste 3	Sandusky	OH	44870	**800-625-5269**	419-625-5269	371
Steinaker State Park 4335 N Hwy 191	Vernal	UT	84078	**800-322-3770**	435-789-4432	564
Steiner Electric Co 1250 Touhy Ave	Elk Grove Village	IL	60007	**800-783-4637**	847-228-0400	248
Steiner Industries 5801 N Tripp Ave	Chicago	IL	60646	**800-621-4515**	773-588-3444	575
Steinhafels W 231 N 1013 County Hwy F *Cust Svc	Waukesha	WI	53186	**866-351-4600***	262-436-4600	322
Steinwall Inc 1759 116th Ave NW	Coon Rapids	MN	55448	**800-229-9199**	763-767-7060	607
Steinway & Sons 1 Steinway Pl	Long Island	NY	11105	**800-783-4692**	718-721-2600	526
Stellar Group 2900 Hartley Rd	Jacksonville	FL	32257	**800-488-2900**	904-260-2900	188
StellArt 2012 Waltzer Rd	Santa Rosa	CA	95403	**866-621-1987**	707-569-1378	129
Stemco LP 300 Industrial Blvd PO Box 1989	Longview	TX	75606	**800-527-8492**	903-758-9981	59
Stenograph LLC 1500 Bishop Ct	Mount Prospect	IL	60056	**800-323-4247**	847-803-1400	179
Stenotype Institute of Jacksonville 3563 Phillips Hwy Bldg E Ste 501	Jacksonville	FL	32207	**800-273-5090**	904-398-4141	798
Stens Corp 2424 Cathy Ln	Jasper	IN	47546	**800-457-7444**	812-482-2526	429
Step2 Co 10010 Aurora-Hudson Rd *Cust Svc	Streetsboro	OH	44241	**800-347-8372***	330-656-0440	63
Stepan Co 22 W Frontage Rd *Cust Svc	Northfield	IL	60093	**800-745-7837***	847-446-7500	144
Stephen Miller Gallery 800 Santa Cruz Ave	Menlo Park	CA	94025	**888-566-8833**	650-327-5040	361
Stephens Inc 111 Ctr St	Little Rock	AR	72201	**800-643-9691**	501-377-2000	688
Stephenson Equipment Inc (SEI) 7201 Paxton St	Harrisburg	PA	17111	**800-325-6455**	717-564-3434	266-3
Stereotaxis Inc 4320 Forest Pk Ave *NASDAQ: STXS*	Saint Louis	MO	63108	**866-646-2346**	314-678-6100	382
Stericycle Inc 28161 N Keith Dr *NASDAQ: SRCL*	Lake Forest	IL	60045	**866-783-9816**	847-367-5910	802
Sterigenics 2015 Spring Rd Ste 650	Oak Brook	IL	60523	**800-472-4508**	630-928-1700	780
Sterilite Corp PO Box 524	Townsend	MA	01469	**800-225-1046**		606
STERIS Corp 5960 Heisley Rd *NYSE: STE*	Mentor	OH	44060	**800-548-4873**	440-354-2600	475
Sterling Bank & Trust FSB 1 Town Sq Ste 1900	Southfield	MI	48076	**877-438-4338**	248-351-3442	69
Sterling Bldg Systems PO Box 8005	Wausau	WI	54402	**800-455-0545**		105
Sterling Business Forms PO Box 2486 *Cust Svc	White City	OR	97503	**800-759-3676***		109
Sterling College PO Box 72	Craftsbury Common	VT	05827	**800-648-3591**	802-586-7711	798
Sterling Computer Corp 600 Stevens Port Dr Ste 200	Dakota Dunes	SD	57049	**877-242-4074**	605-242-4000	719
Sterling Cruises & Travel 8700 W Flagler St	Miami	FL	33174	**800-435-7967**	305-592-2522	769
Sterling Cut Glass Company Inc 5020 Olympic Blvd	Erlanger	KY	41018	**800-543-1317**	859-283-2333	361
Sterling Electric Inc 7997 Allison Ave *Cust Svc	Indianapolis	IN	46268	**800-654-6220***	317-872-0471	517
Sterling Fibers Inc 5005 Sterling Way *Cust Svc	Pace	FL	32571	**800-342-3779***	850-994-5311	604-2
Sterling Inc 2900 S 160th St *Cust Svc	New Berlin	WI	53151	**800-783-7835***	262-641-8600	203
Sterling Optical 520 Eigth Ave 23rd Fl	New York	NY	10018	**800-393-7789**	516-390-2117	542
Sterling Plumbing 444 Highland Dr *Cust Svc	Kohler	WI	53044	**888-783-7546***	920-457-4441	610
Sterling Process Engineering & Services Inc 333 McCormick Blvd	Columbus	OH	43213	**800-783-7875**	614-868-5151	755
Sterling Publishing Company Inc 387 Pk Ave S 5th Fl *Cust Svc	New York	NY	10016	**800-367-9692***	212-532-7160	634-2
Sterling Savings Bank 105 W Simpson Ave	Mccleary	WA	98557	**800-650-7141**		69
Sterling Truck Corp 12120 Telegraph Rd *Cust Svc	Redford Township	MI	48239	**800-385-4357***	800-785-4357	515
Sterling-Clark-Lurton Corp PO Box 130	Norwood	MA	02062	**800-225-9872**	781-762-5400	549
Stern Empire Dental Lab 1805 W 34th St	Houston	TX	77018	**800-229-0214**	713-688-1301	230
Stern Oil Company Inc PO Box 218	Freeman	SD	57029	**800-477-2744**	605-925-7999	578
Sterne Agee & Leach Inc 800 Shades Creek Pkwy Ste 700	Birmingham	AL	35209	**800-240-1438**	205-949-3500	688

Name	Address	City	State	ZIP	Toll-Free	Phone	Class
Stetson University	421 N Woodland Blvd Unit 8378 *Admissions	DeLand	FL	32723	**800-688-0101***	386-822-7100	167
Stetson University DuPont-Ball Library	421 N Woodland Blvd	DeLand	FL	32723	**800-688-0101**	386-822-7183	434-6
Steuben County Rural Electric Membership Corp	1212 S Wayne St	Angola	IN	46703	**888-233-9088**	260-665-3563	247
Steuben County Tourism Bureau	430 N Wayne St Ste 1B	Angola	IN	46703	**888-665-5668**	260-665-5386	208
Steuben Rural Electric Co-op Inc	9 Wilson Ave	Bath	NY	14810	**800-843-3414**	607-776-4161	247
Steuben Trust Co	1 Steuben Sq	Hornell	NY	14843	**866-783-8236**	607-324-5010	69
Steve Barry Buick Inc	16000 Detroit Ave	Lakewood	OH	44107	**866-327-5818**	216-920-0866	56
Steve Foley Cadillac	100 Skokie Blvd	Northbrook	IL	60062	**888-670-1429**		125
Steve Hopkins Inc	2499 Auto Mall Pkwy	Fairfield	CA	94533	**877-873-3913**	707-427-1000	515
Steve Landers Toyota	10825 Colonel Glenn Rd	Little Rock	AR	72204	**888-314-4350**	501-568-5800	515
Steve Millen Sportparts Inc	3176 Airway Ave	Costa Mesa	CA	92626	**866-250-5542**	714-540-5566	56
Steven Barclay Agency	12 Western Ave	Petaluma	CA	94952	**888-965-7323**	707-773-0654	706
Steven Engineering Inc	230 Ryan Way	South San Francisco	CA	94080	**800-258-9200**	650-588-9200	248
Steven Schaefer Associates Inc	10411 Medallion Dr	Cincinnati	OH	45241	**800-542-3302**	513-542-3300	263
Steven's Hope for Children Inc	1014 W Foothill Blvd Ste B	Upland	CA	91786	**866-378-3836**	909-373-0678	372
Stevens Aviation Inc	600 Delaware St	Greenville	SC	29605	**800-359-7838**	864-678-6000	62
Stevens Creek Mitsubishi	3209 Stevens Creek Blvd	San Jose	CA	95117	**888-479-0842**	408-264-9999	56
Stevens Creek Software	PO Box 2126	Cupertino	CA	95015	**800-823-4279**	408-725-0424	180-9
Stevens Henager College	1890 South 1350 West	Ogden	UT	84401	**800-622-2640**		161
Stevens Institute of Technology	Castle Pt on the Hudson	Hoboken	NJ	07030	**800-458-5323**	201-216-5194	167
Stevens John Paul	US Supreme Ct Bldg 1 1st St NE	Washington	DC	20543	**800-772-1213**	202-479-3000	341-3
Stevens Marine Inc	9180 SW Burnham St	Tigard	OR	97223	**800-225-7023**	503-620-7023	89
Stevens Transport	PO Box 279010	Dallas	TX	75227	**800-233-9369**	866-551-0337	778
Stevens Travel Management Inc	119 W 40th St 14th Fl	New York	NY	10018	**800-275-7400**	212-696-4300	769
Stevens Water Monitoring Systems	12067 NE Glenn Widing Dr Ste 106	Portland	OR	97220	**800-452-5272**	503-469-8000	543
Stevens Worldwide Van Lines	527 W Morley Dr	Saginaw	MI	48601	**888-860-4566**	800-678-3836	518
Stevenson & Vestal	2347 W Hanford Rd	Burlington	NC	27215	**800-535-3636**		197
Stewart & Assoc Inc	50 W Douglas St Ste 1200	Freeport	IL	61032	**888-310-2840**	815-235-3807	400
Stewart Directories Inc	50314 Kings Point Dr PO Box 326	Frisco	NC	27936	**800-311-0786**		634-6
Stewart EFI LLC	45 Old Waterbury Rd	Thomaston	CT	06787	**800-393-5387**	860-283-8213	488
Stewart Engineering Supply Inc	3221 E Pioneer Pkwy	Arlington	TX	76010	**800-533-1265**	817-640-1767	111
Stewart Enterprises Inc	1333 S Clearview Pkwy *NASDAQ: STEI*	New Orleans	LA	70121	**877-239-3264**	713-522-5141	509
Stewart Environmental Consultants LLC	3801 Automation Way Ste 200	Fort Collins	CO	80525	**800-373-1348**	970-226-5500	196
Stewart Filmscreen Corp	1161 W Sepulveda Blvd	Torrance	CA	90502	**800-762-4999**	310-784-5300	590
Stewart Information Services Corp	1980 Post Oak Blvd Ste 800 *NYSE: STC*	Houston	TX	77056	**800-729-1900**	713-625-8100	391-6
Stewart REI Data Inc	1980 Post Oak Blvd Ste 800	Houston	TX	77056	**800-729-1900**	212-922-0050	391-6
Stewart School of Cosmetology	604 NW Ave	Sioux Falls	SD	57104	**800-537-2625**	605-336-2775	76
Stewart Sutherland Inc	5411 E 'V' Ave	Vicksburg	MI	49097	**800-253-1034**	269-649-0530	64
Stewart Systems	808 Stewart Ave	Plano	TX	75074	**800-966-5808**	972-422-5808	209
Stewart Title Guaranty Co	1980 Post Oak Blvd Ste 800	Houston	TX	77056	**800-729-1900**	713-625-8100	391-6
Stewart Title Insurance Co	300 E 42nd St 10th Fl	New York	NY	10017	**800-913-4170**	713-625-8100	60
STFM (Society of Teachers of Family Medicine)	11400 Tomahawk Creek Pkwy Ste 540	Leawood	KS	66211	**800-274-7928**	913-906-6000	48-8
Stg International Inc	4900 Seminary Rd Ste 1100	Alexandria	VA	22311	**855-507-0660**	703-578-6030	182
STI (Superconductor Technologies Inc)	460 Ward Dr *NASDAQ: SCON*	Santa Barbara	CA	93111	**800-727-3648**	805-690-4500	255
STI Electronics Inc	261 Palmer Rd	Madison	AL	35758	**888-650-3006**	256-461-9191	386
Stickk.com LLC	39 E 30th St Ste 4	New York	NY	10016	**866-578-4255**		387
Stidham Trucking Inc	PO Box 308	Yreka	CA	96097	**800-827-9500**	530-842-4161	188
Stifel Financial Corp	501 N Broadway *NYSE: SF*	Saint Louis	MO	63102	**800-679-5446**		688
Stifel Nicolaus & Co Inc	501 N Broadway	Saint Louis	MO	63102	**800-679-5446**	314-342-2000	688
Stihl Inc	536 Viking Dr *Cust Svc	Virginia Beach	VA	23452	**800-467-8445***	757-486-9100	757
Stillman Banccorp NA	PO Box 150	Stillman Valle	IL	61084	**866-546-8273**	815-645-2000	69
Stillman College	3601 Stillman Blvd	Tuscaloosa	AL	35401	**800-841-5722**	205-349-4240	167
Stillwater Chamber of Commerce	409 S Main St	Stillwater	OK	74075	**800-593-5573**	405-372-5573	138
Stillwater Spa at the Hyatt Regency Newport	1 Goat Island	Newport	RI	02840	**800-233-1234**	401-851-3225	705
Stilson Products	15935 Sturgeon St	Roseville	MI	48066	**888-400-5978**	586-778-1100	492
Stimple & Ward Co	3400 Babcock Blvd	Pittsburgh	PA	15237	**800-792-6457**	412-364-5200	517
Stimson Lumber Co	520 SW Yamhill St Ste 700	Portland	OR	97204	**800-445-9758**	503-222-1676	681
Stimwave Technologies Inc	901 E Las Olas Blvd Ste 201	Fort Lauderdale	FL	33301	**800-965-5134**	786-565-3342	740
Stirling Properties	109 Northpark Blvd Ste 300	Covington	LA	70433	**888-261-2022**	985-898-2022	653
STMA (Sports Turf Managers Assn)	805 New Hampshire Ste E	Lawrence	KS	66044	**800-323-3875**	785-843-2549	47-22
STMH (St Mary's of Michigan)	800 S Washington Ave	Saginaw	MI	48601	**877-738-6672**	989-907-8115	374-3
STMicroelectronics NV	134 Vintage Park Blvd Ste 192	Houston	TX	77070	**888-356-1766**	844-786-4276	694
Stock & Option Solutions Inc	6399 San Ignacio Ave Ste 100	San Jose	CA	95119	**888-767-0199**	408-979-8700	462
Stock Car Racing Magazine	PO Box 420235	Palm Coast	FL	32142	**800-333-2633**		456-3
Stock Drive Products/Sterling Instrument	2101 Jericho Tpke	New Hyde Park	NY	11040	**800-737-7436**	516-328-3300	619
Stock Equipment Co	16490 Chillicothe Rd	Chagrin Falls	OH	44023	**888-742-1249**	440-543-6000	275
Stock Seed Farms	28008 Mill Rd	Murdock	NE	68407	**800-759-1520**	402-867-3771	692
Stock Transportation Ltd	128 Wellington St W Ste 201	Barrie	ON	L4N1K9	**888-952-0878**		108
Stock Yards Packing Co Inc	2457 W North Ave	Melrose Park	IL	60160	**877-785-9273**		297-26
StockCap	123 Manufacturers Dr	Arnold	MO	63010	**800-827-2277**	636-282-6800	153
Stockton-San Joaquin County Public Library (SSJCPL)	605 N El Dorado St	Stockton	CA	95202	**866-805-7323**	209-937-8416	434-3
Stockwatch	700 W Georgia St PO Box 10371	Vancouver	BC	V7Y1J6	**800-268-6397**	604-687-1500	404
Stockyards Hotel	109 E Exchange Ave	Fort Worth	TX	76164	**800-423-8471**	817-625-6427	379
Stoelting LLC	502 Hwy 67	Kiel	WI	53042	**800-558-5807**	920-894-2293	299
Stoever Glass & Company Inc	30 Wall St	New York	NY	10005	**800-223-3881**		401
Stoffel Equipment Company Inc	7764 N 81st St	Milwaukee	WI	53223	**800-354-7502**	414-354-7500	358
Stoller Fisheries	1301 18th St PO Box B	Spirit Lake	IA	51360	**800-831-5174**	712-336-1750	297-14
Stoller USA	4001 W Sam Houston Pkwy N Ste 100	Houston	TX	77043	**800-539-5283**	713-461-1493	282
Stoltzfus RV's & Marine	1335 Wilmington Pike	West Chester	PA	19382	**866-755-8858**		89
Stone Belt Freight Lines Inc	101 W Dillman Rd	Bloomington	IN	47403	**800-264-2340**	812-824-6741	315
Stone Castle Hotel & Conference Ctr, The	3050 Green Mtn Dr	Branson	MO	65616	**800-677-6906**	417-335-4700	379
Stone Mountain State Park	3042 Frank Pkwy	Roaring Gap	NC	28668	**877-722-6762**	336-957-8185	564
Stonebridge Inn	300 Carriage Way PO Box 5008	Snowmass Village	CO	81615	**800-922-7242**	970-923-2420	379
Stonebridge Press Inc	25 Elm St	Southbridge	MA	01550	**800-536-5836**	508-764-4325	634-8
Stonefield Beach State Recreation Site	725 Summer St NE 84505 Hwy 101 S	Salem	OR	97301	**800-551-6949**		564
StoneFly Inc	21353 Cabot Blvd	Hayward	CA	94545	**888-786-6335**	510-265-1616	178
Stonehenge Partners Inc	191 W Nationwide Blvd Ste 600	Columbus	OH	43215	**877-298-4409**	614-246-2500	688
Stoneridge Shopping Ctr	1 Stoneridge Mall	Pleasanton	CA	94588	**877-746-6642**	925-463-2778	459
Stonestown Galleria	3251 20th Ave	San Francisco	CA	94132	**800-326-3264**	415-564-8848	459
Stonewall Jackson Hotel & Conference Ctr	24 S Market St	Staunton	VA	24401	**866-880-0024**	540-885-4848	379
Stonewall Jackson Memorial Hospital (SJMH)	230 Hospital Plaza	Weston	WV	26452	**866-637-0471**	304-269-8000	374-3
Stonewall Resort	940 Resort Dr	Roanoke	WV	26447	**888-278-8150**	304-269-7400	667
Stoneway Electric Supply Co	402 N Perry St	Spokane	WA	99202	**800-841-1408**	509-535-2933	248
Stoney Creek Inn	101 Mariner's Way	East Peoria	IL	61611	**800-659-2220**	309-694-1300	379
Stonhard Inc	1000 E Pk Ave *Cust Svc	Maple Shade	NJ	08052	**800-854-0310***	856-779-7500	293
Stop & Shop Supermarket Co	1385 Hancock St	Quincy	MA	02169	**800-767-7772**	781-397-0006	345
Stop Hunger Now	615 Hillsborough St Ste 200	Raleigh	NC	27603	**888-501-8440**	919-839-0689	462
STOPS Inc	8855 Grissom Pkwy	Titusville	FL	32780	**866-632-2161**	321-383-4111	391-4
Stoptech Ltd	365 Industrial Dr	Harrison	OH	45030	**800-537-0102**	513-202-5500	197
Storage Battery Systems Inc (SBS)	N56 W16665 Ridgewood Dr	Menomonee Falls	WI	53051	**800-554-2243**	262-703-5800	248

Company / Address	City	State	Zip	Toll-Free	Phone	Class
Storage Engine Inc 1 Sheila Dr	Tinton Falls	NJ	07724	**866-734-8899**	732-747-6995	178
Stor-All Storage 1375 W Hillsboro Blvd	Deerfield Beach	FL	33442	**877-786-7255**	954-421-7888	801-3
Storck USA LP 325 N LaSalle St Ste 400	Chicago	IL	60654	**800-852-5542**	312-467-5700	297-8
Store Opening Solutions (SOS) 800 Middle Tennessee Blvd	Murfreesboro	TN	37129	**877-388-9262**		448
Storer Coachways 3519 McDonald Ave	Modesto	CA	95358	**800-621-3383**	209-521-8250	106
Storey Publishing LLC 210 Mass Moca Way	North Adams	MA	01247	**800-827-7444**	413-346-2100	634-2
Stork News of America Inc 1305 Hope Mills Rd Ste A	Fayetteville	NC	28304	**800-633-6395**	910-429-2229	311
Storkcraft Baby 7433 Nelson Rd	Richmond	BC	V6W1G3	**877-274-0277**	604-274-5121	320-2
Storm Internet Services Inc 1760 Courtwood Crescent	Ottawa	ON	K2C2B5	**866-257-8676**	613-567-6585	227
Storm King School 314 Mountain Rd	Cornwall On Hudson	NY	12520	**800-225-9144**	845-534-7892	621
Storm Products Inc 165 South 800 West	Brigham City	UT	84302	**800-369-4402**	435-723-0403	708
Stormont-Vail Regional Health Ctr 1500 SW Tenth Ave	Topeka	KS	66604	**800-432-2951**	785-354-6000	374-3
Stornoway Diamond Corp 980 W First St Ste 118 *TSE: SWY*	North Vancouver	BC	V7P3N4	**877-331-2232**	604-983-7750	502-3
Storopack Inc 12007 S Woodruff Ave	Downey	CA	90241	**800-829-1491**	562-803-5582	600
Storr Tractor Co 3191 Rt 22	Branchburg	NJ	08876	**800-526-3802**	908-722-9830	429
Stow Co, The 3311 Windquest Dr	Holland	MI	49424	**800-562-4257**	616-399-3311	815
Stowe Mountain Resort 5781 Mountain Rd	Stowe	VT	05672	**800-253-4754**	802-253-3000	667
Stoweflake Mountain Resort & Spa 1746 Mountain Rd PO Box 369	Stowe	VT	05672	**800-253-2232**	802-253-7355	667
Strafford Publications Inc PO Box 13729	Atlanta	GA	30324	**800-926-7926**	404-881-1141	634-9
Straight A Tours & Travel 6881 Kingspointe Pkwy Ste 18	Orlando	FL	32819	**800-237-5440**	407-896-1242	758
Straight Arrow Products Inc 2020 Highland Ave	Bethlehem	PA	18020	**800-827-9815**	610-882-9606	233
Straight North LLC 1001 W 31st St	Downers Grove	IL	60515	**866-353-3953**		7
Strait Music Co 2428 W Ben White Blvd	Austin	TX	78704	**800-725-8877**	512-476-6927	525
Straith Hospital for Special Surgery 23901 Lahser Rd	Southfield	MI	48034	**800-994-6610**	248-357-3360	374-7
Stranahan House Museum Inc 335 SE Sixth Ave	Fort Lauderdale	FL	33301	**800-435-7352**	954-524-4736	519
Stranahan Theater 4645 Heatherdowns Blvd	Toledo	OH	43614	**866-381-7469**	419-381-8851	571
Strand Lighting 10911 Petal St	Dallas	TX	75238	**800-733-0564**	214-647-7880	439
Strand Theatre 619 Louisiana Ave	Shreveport	LA	71101	**800-313-6373**	318-226-1481	571
Strange's Florist Inc 3313 Mechanicsville Pk	Richmond	VA	23223	**800-421-4070**	804-321-2200	294
Strata Oil & Gas Inc 10010 - 98 St PO Box 7770	Peace River	AB	T8S1T3	**877-237-5443**	403-237-5443	535
StrataCare Inc 17838 Gillette Ave	Irvine	CA	92614	**800-277-6512**		180-1
Stratapult Inc 2650 Pilgrim Ct	Winston-salem	NC	27106	**877-631-2900**		182
Stratasys Inc 7665 Commerce Way *NASDAQ: SSYS*	Eden Prairie	MN	55344	**800-937-3010**	952-937-3000	263
Strategic Diagnostics Inc 111 Pencader Dr *NASDAQ: SDIX*	Newark	DE	19702	**800-544-8881**	302-456-6789	233
Strategic Distribution Inc 1414 Radcliffe St Ste 300	Bristol	PA	19007	**800-322-2644**	215-633-1900	385
Strategic Finance Magazine 10 Paragon Dr Ste 1	Montvale	NJ	07645	**800-638-4427**	201-573-9000	456-5
Strategy Institute 401 Richmond St W Ste 401	Toronto	ON	M5V3A8	**866-298-9343**		465
Strater Hotel 699 Main Ave	Durango	CO	81301	**800-247-4431**	970-247-4431	379
Stratford Court 45 Katherine Blvd	Palm Harbor	FL	34684	**888-434-4648**	727-787-1500	670
Stratford General Hospital 46 General Hospital Dr	Stratford	ON	N5A2Y6	**888-275-1102**	519-272-8210	374-2
Stratford Homes LP 402 S Weber Ave	Stratford	WI	54484	**800-448-1524**	715-687-3133	105
Stratford Hotel 242 Powell St	San Francisco	CA	94102	**888-688-0038**	415-397-7080	379
Stratford Star 1000 Bridgeport Ave *Advestisement	Shelton	CT	06484	**800-372-2790***	203-402-2319	531-4
Stratford University School of Culinary Arts 7777 Leesburg Pk	Falls Church	VA	22043	**800-444-0804**	703-821-8570	162
Strathcona Hotel 60 York St	Toronto	ON	M5J1S8	**800-268-8304**	416-363-3321	379
Strathcona Hotel, The 919 Douglas St	Victoria	BC	V8W2C2	**800-663-7476**	250-383-7137	379
Stratix 4920 Avalon Ridge Pkwy	Norcross	GA	30071	**800-883-8300**	770-326-7580	175-7
Stratos Global Corp 6550 Rock Spring Dr Ste 650	Bethesda	MD	20817	**800-563-2255**	301-214-8800	679
Stratosphere Tower Hotel & Casino 2000 S Las Vegas Blvd	Las Vegas	NV	89104	**800-998-6937**	702-380-7777	132
Stratton Equity Co-op Co Inc 98 Colorado Ave PO Box 25	Stratton	CO	80836	**800-438-7070**	719-348-5326	277
Stratton Hats Inc 3200 Randolph St	Bellwood	IL	60104	**877-453-3777**	708-544-5220	154-8
Stratton Seed Co 1530 Hwy 79 S	Stuttgart	AR	72160	**800-264-4433**	870-673-4433	692
Stratton Veterans Affairs Medical Ctr 113 Holland Ave	Albany	NY	12208	**800-223-4810**	518-626-5000	374-8
Stratus Properties Inc 212 Lavaca St Ste 300 *NYSE: STRS*	Austin	TX	78701	**800-690-0315**	512-478-5788	651
Stratus Technologies 111 Powdermill Rd	Maynard	MA	01754	**800-787-2887**	978-461-7000	180-12
Straub International Inc 214 SW 40th Ave	Great Bend	KS	67530	**800-658-1706**	620-792-5256	276
Strayer University 1133 15th St NW	Washington	DC	20005	**888-311-0355**	202-408-2400	167
Takoma Park 6830 Laurel St NW	Washington	DC	20012	**888-311-0355**	202-722-8100	167
Strayer University Alexandria 2730 Eisenhower Ave	Alexandria	VA	22314	**888-311-0355**		167
Strayer University Arlington 2121 15th St N	Arlington	VA	22201	**888-478-7293**	703-892-5100	167
Strayer University Fredericksburg 150 Riverside Pkwy Ste 100	Fredericksburg	VA	22406	**888-311-0355**	540-374-4300	167
Strayer University Prince George's 4710 Auth Pl Ste 100	Suitland	MD	20746	**866-344-3297**	888-311-0355	167
Stream Gas & Electric Ltd 1950 Stemmons Fwy Ste 3000	Dallas	TX	75207	**866-447-8732**		785
Streamlight Inc 30 Eagleville Rd	Eagleville	PA	19403	**800-523-7488**	610-631-0600	439
Streamline Health Solutions Inc 10200 Alliance Rd Ste 200 *NASDAQ: STRM*	Cincinnati	OH	45242	**800-878-5269**	513-794-7100	38
StreamSend 78 York St	Sacramento	CA	95814	**877-439-4078**	916-326-5407	393
Streamwood Behavioral Health Ctr 1400 E Irving Pk Rd	Streamwood	IL	60107	**800-272-7790**	630-837-9000	374-1
Streater Inc 411 S First Ave	Albert Lea	MN	56007	**800-527-4197**		288
Streator Dependable Manufacturing Co 1705 N Shabbona St	Streator	IL	61364	**800-795-0551**	815-672-0551	469
Streck Inc 7002 S 109th St	Omaha	NE	68128	**800-228-6090**	402-333-1982	233
Streeter Assoc Inc 101 E Woodlawn Ave PO Box 118	Elmira	NY	14902	**866-493-1640**	607-734-4151	188
Streeter Printing Inc 9880 Via Pasar	San Diego	CA	92126	**866-787-3383**	858-566-0866	626
Streimer Sheet Metal Works Inc 740 N Knott St	Portland	OR	97227	**888-288-3828**	503-288-9393	695
Strem Chemicals Inc 7 Mulliken Way	Newburyport	MA	01950	**800-647-8736**	978-499-1600	145
Stretch Inc 1322 Orleans Dr	Sunnyvale	CA	94089	**800-468-6853**	408-543-2700	694
Stretch-N-Grow International Inc PO Box 7599	Seminole	FL	33775	**800-348-0166**		311
Strictly Business Computer Systems Inc 848 Fourth Ave Ste 200	Huntington	WV	25701	**888-529-0401**		178
Stride Rite Corp 191 Spring St *Cust Svc	Lexington	MA	02420	**800-299-6575***	617-824-6000	302
Stride Tool Inc Imperial Div 30333 Emerald Vly Pkwy	Glenwillow	OH	44139	**888-467-8665**	440-247-4600	756
Strider Marketing 6-6150 Hwy 7 Ste 400	Woodbridge	ON	L4H0R6	**800-314-8895**		197
StrikoDynarad 501 E Roosevelt Ave	Zeeland	MI	49464	**855-787-4561**	616-772-3705	319
Stripes Convenience Stores 4525 Ayers St *NYSE: SUSS*	Corpus Christi	TX	78415	**800-569-3585**	361-884-2464	206
Strippit Inc/LVD 12975 Clarence Ctr Rd	Akron	NY	14001	**800-828-1527**	716-542-4511	455
Strobic Air Corp 160 Cassell Rd PO Box 144	Harleysville	PA	19438	**800-722-3267**	215-723-4700	18
Strom Aviation Inc 109 S Elm St	Waconia	MN	55387	**800-356-6440**	952-544-3611	630
Strong Enterprises Inc 11236 Satellite Blvd	Orlando	FL	32837	**800-344-6319**	407-859-9317	575
Strong Memorial Hospital *University of Rochester Medical Ctr* 601 Elmwood Ave	Rochester	NY	14642	**800-999-6673**	585-275-2100	374-3
Strong Travel Services Inc 8214 Westche Ste 670	Dallas	TX	75225	**800-747-5670**	214-361-0027	770
Stronghaven Inc 5090 McDougall Dr SW	Atlanta	GA	30336	**800-331-7835**	404-699-1952	99
Strother Ventures II Inc 2929 Breezewood Ave Ste 200	Fayetteville	NC	28303	**855-753-6143**	910-864-2327	650
Strouds Run State Park 2045 Morse Rd	Columbus	OH	43229	**800-945-3543**	740-592-2302	564
Structural Component Systems Inc (SCS) 1255 Front St	Fremont	NE	68026	**800-844-5622**	402-721-5622	189
Structural Concepts Corp 888 Porter Rd	Muskegon	MI	49441	**800-433-9489**	231-798-8888	288
Structural Wood Corp 4000 Labore Rd	Saint Paul	MN	55110	**800-652-9058**	651-426-8111	815
Structure House 3017 Pickett Rd	Durham	NC	27705	**800-553-0052**	919-493-4205	704
Structures Unlimited Inc 166 River Rd	Bow	NH	03304	**800-225-3895**	603-645-6539	695
Struktol Company of America Inc PO Box 1649	Stow	OH	44224	**800-327-8649**	330-928-5188	143
Stryker Canada LP 45 Innovation Dr	Hamilton	ON	L9H7L8	**800-668-8324**		475
Stryker Corp 2825 Airview Blvd *NYSE: SYK*	Kalamazoo	MI	49002	**800-616-1406**	269-385-2600	475
Stry-Lenkoff Co Inc 1100 W Broadway	Louisville	KY	40232	**800-626-8247**	502-587-6804	109
STS (Society of Thoracic Surgeons) 633 N St Clair St Ste 2320	Chicago	IL	60611	**877-865-5321**	312-202-5800	48-8
STS Component Solutions LLC 2910 SW 42 Ave	Palm City	FL	34990	**888-777-2960**		22

Name	Address	City	State	ZIP	Toll-Free	Phone	Class
Stuart C Irby Co	815 S President St	Jackson	MS	39201	**866-687-4729**	713-476-0788	190-10
Stuart Hall School	235 W Frederick St PO Box 210	Staunton	VA	24402	**888-306-8926**	540-885-0356	621
Stuart Jet Ctr LLC	2501 Aviation Way	Stuart	FL	34996	**877-735-9538**	772-288-6700	62
Stuart Maue Mitchell & James Ltd	3850 Mckelvey Rd	St. Louis	MO	63044	**800-291-9940**	314-291-3030	197
Stuart-Martin County Chamber of Commerce	1650 S Kanner Hwy	Stuart	FL	34994	**800-962-2873**	772-287-1088	138
StubHub Inc	199 Fremont St Fl 4	San Francisco	CA	94105	**866-788-2482**	415-222-8400	458
Stuckey's Corp	8555 16th St Ste 850	Silver Spring	MD	20910	**800-423-6171**	301-585-8222	668
Studebaker National Museum	201 Chapin St	South Bend	IN	46601	**888-391-5600**	574-235-9714	519
Student Advantage LLC	280 Summer St	Boston	MA	02210	**800-333-2920**		384
Student Book Store	421 E Grand River Ave	East Lansing	MI	48823	**800-968-1111**	517-351-4210	95
Student Conservation Assn (SCA)	689 River Rd PO Box 550	Charlestown	NH	03603	**888-722-9675**	603-543-1700	47-13
Student Tours Inc	60 W Ave	Vineyard Haven	MA	02568	**800-331-7093**	508-693-5078	758
Student Transportation of America Inc (STA)	3349 Hwy 138 Bldg B Ste D	Wall	NJ	07719	**888-942-2250**	732-280-4200	108
Student Travel Services Inc	1413 Madison Pk Dr	Glen Burnie	MD	21061	**800-648-4849**		758
Student Veterans of America	PO Box 77673	Washington	DC	20013	**866-320-3826**	202-223-4710	306
Studentcity.com Inc	8 Essex Ctr Dr	Peabody	MA	01960	**888-777-4642**		769
Students Against Destructive Decisions (SADD)	255 Main St	Marlborough	MA	01752	**877-723-3462**	508-481-3568	47-6
Studio 6	PO Box 809092	Dallas	TX	75380	**855-249-0891**	614-601-4060	705
Studio y Creations Inc	1-6204 29 St Se	Calgary	AB	T2C1W3	**800-243-4024**	403-253-5447	8
Stuecker & Assoc Inc	1930 Bishop Ln Watterson Towers Ste 1001	Louisville	KY	40218	**800-799-9327**	502-452-9227	461
Stueve Siegel Hanson LLP	460 Nichols Rd Ste 200	Kansas City	MO	64112	**800-714-0360**	816-714-7100	428
Stuller Settings Inc	PO Box 87777	Lafayette	LA	70598	**800-877-7777**		407
Stupp Bros Inc	3800 Weber Rd	Saint Louis	MO	63125	**800-535-9999**	314-638-5000	479
Stupp Corp	12555 Ronaldson Rd	Baton Rouge	LA	70807	**800-535-9999**	225-775-8800	489
Sturbridge Host Hotel & Conference Ctr	366 Main St	Sturbridge	MA	01566	**800-582-3232**	508-347-7393	379
Sturdisteel Co	PO Box 2655	Waco	TX	76702	**800-433-3116**		320-3
Sturdy Corp	1822 Carolina Beach Rd	Wilmington	NC	28401	**800-721-3282**	910-763-2500	205
Sturm Foods Inc	PO Box 287	Manawa	WI	54949	**800-347-8876**	920-596-2511	298-11
Stuttering Foundation of America	3100 Walnut Grove Rd Ste 603	Memphis	TN	38111	**800-992-9392**	901-452-7343	47-17
Styer Transportation Co	7870 215th St W	Lakeville	MN	55044	**800-548-9149**	952-469-4491	778
Style Crest Inc	2450 Enterprise St	Fremont	OH	43420	**800-925-4440**	419-332-7369	103
Stylex	PO Box 5038	Delanco	NJ	08075	**800-257-5742**		320-1
Stylmark Inc	PO Box 32008	Minneapolis	MN	55432	**800-328-2495**	763-574-7474	288
Suarez Corp Industries	7800 Whipple Ave NW	North Canton	OH	44720	**800-764-0008**	330-494-5504	197
Subaru of America Inc	2235 Marlton Pike W	Cherry Hill	NJ	08002	**800-782-2783**	856-488-8500	58
Subco Foods Inc	4350 S Taylor Dr	Sheboygan	WI	53081	**800-473-0757**	920-457-7761	297-16
Subia Corp	6612 Gulton Ct NE	Albuquerque	NM	87109	**800-275-2636**	505-345-2636	344
Substance Abuse & Mental Health Services Administration (SAMHSA)	1 Choke Cherry Rd	Rockville	MD	20857	**877-726-4727**	240-276-2000	340-8
Center for Mental Health Services	1 Choke Cherry Ln	Rockville	MD	20857	**877-726-4727**		340-8
Center for Substance Abuse Prevention	1 Choke Cherry Rd	Rockville	MD	20857	**877-726-4727**	240-276-2420	340-8
Center for Substance Abuse Treatment	1 Choke Cherry Rd PO Box 2345	Rockville	MD	20857	**877-726-4727**	240-276-2130	340-8
Suburban Collection	1810 Maplelawn Dr	Troy	MI	48084	**877-471-7100**		56
Suburban Life Publications	1101 W 31st St Ste 100	Downers Grove	IL	60515	**800-397-9397**	630-368-1100	634-8
Suburban Mobility Authority for Regional Transportation (SMART)	535 Griswold St Ste 600 Buhl Bldg	Detroit	MI	48226	**866-962-5515**	313-223-2100	467
Suburban Press & Metro Press	1550 Woodville Rd	Millbury	OH	43447	**800-300-6158**	419-836-2221	531-4
Suburban Propane LP	1 Suburban Plz 240 Rt 10 W PO Box 206	Whippany	NJ	07981	**800-776-7263**	973-887-5300	317
Suburban Transit Corp	750 Somerset St	New Brunswick	NJ	08901	**800-222-0492**	732-249-1100	107
Suby Von Haden & Assoc SC	1221 John Q Hammons Dr	Madison	WI	53717	**800-279-2616**	608-831-8181	2
Sucampo Pharmaceuticals Inc	805 King Farm Blvd Ste 550 *NASDAQ: SCMP*	Rockville	MD	20850	**877-825-3327**	301-961-3400	582
Success Motivation International Inc	4567 Lakeshore Dr *Sales	Waco	TX	76710	**888-391-0050***	254-776-9966	366
Successfactors Inc	1500 Fashion Island Blvd Ste 300 *NYSE: SFSF*	San Mateo	CA	94404	**800-809-9920**	650-645-2000	180-11
Successories Inc	1040 Holland Dr	Boca Raton	FL	33487	**800-535-2773**		311
Succor Creek State Natural Area	1298 Lk Owyhee Dam Rd	Adrian	OR	97901	**800-551-6949**		564
Suddath Cos	815 S Main St	Jacksonville	FL	32207	**800-395-7100**	904-352-2577	518
Suddenlink Communications	6151 Paluxy Dr	Tyler	TX	75703	**877-694-9474**		115
Sudenga Industries Inc	2002 Kingbird Ave	George	IA	51237	**888-783-3642**	712-475-3301	275
Suffolk County Community College *Grant*	1001 Crooked Hill Rd	Brentwood	NY	11717	**800-621-3362**	631-851-6700	161
Suffolk Downs	111 Waldemar Ave	East Boston	MA	02128	**800-225-3460**	617-567-3900	132
Suffolk University	8 Ashburton Pl	Boston	MA	02108	**800-678-3365**	617-573-8460	167
Sugar Creek Foods International	301 N El Paso St	Russellville	AR	72801	**800-445-2715**		297-25
Sugar Creek Packing Co	2101 Kenskill Ave	Washington Court House	OH	43160	**800-848-8205**	740-335-7440	297-26
Sugar Creek Scrap Inc	1201 W National Ave	West Terre Haute	IN	47885	**800-466-7462**	812-533-2147	684
Sugar Foods Corp	950 Third Ave 21st Fl	New York	NY	10022	**800-732-8963**	212-753-6900	298-11
Sugarbush Resort & Inn	1840 Sugarbush Access Rd	Warren	VT	05674	**800-537-8427**	802-583-6300	667
Sugarloaf/USA	5092 Access Rd	Carrabassett Valley	ME	04947	**800-843-5623**	207-237-2000	667
Suite 66	366 Adelaide St W Ste 600	Toronto	ON	M5V1R9	**866-779-3486**	416-628-5565	8
SuiteAmerica	4970 Windplay Dr Ste C-1	El Dorado Hills	CA	95762	**800-410-4305**	916-941-7970	212
Suites at Fisherman's Wharf	2655 Hyde St	San Francisco	CA	94109	**800-227-3608**	415-771-0200	379
Suites Hotel in Canal Park, The	325 Lake Ave S	Duluth	MN	55802	**800-794-1716**	218-727-4663	379
Sukut Construction Inc	4010 W Chandler Ave	Santa Ana	CA	92704	**888-785-8801**	714-540-5351	190-4
Sul Ross State University	E Hwy 90	Alpine	TX	79832	**888-722-7778**	432-837-8011	167
Sullivan County Rural Electric Co-op Inc (SCREC)	5675 Rt 87 PO Box 65	Forksville	PA	18616	**800-570-5081**	570-924-3381	247
Sullivan Curtis Monroe	1920 Main St	Irvine	CA	92614	**800-427-3253**	949-250-7172	390
Sullivan Tire Co Inc	PO Box 370	Rockland	MA	02370	**877-855-4826**	781-871-2299	61-5
Sullivan University	3101 BaRdstown Rd	Louisville	KY	40205	**800-844-1354**	502-456-6505	167
Sullivan-Palatek Inc	1201 W US Hwy 20	Michigan City	IN	46360	**800-438-6203**	219-874-2497	174
Sulphur Springs Valley Electric Co-op Inc	350 N Haskell Ave	Willcox	AZ	85643	**877-877-6861**	520-384-2221	247
Sultana Distribution Services Inc	600 Food Ctr Dr	Bronx	NY	10474	**877-617-5500**	718-617-5500	298-3
Sulzer Metco US Inc	1101 Prospect Ave	Westbury	NY	11590	**877-280-2342**	516-334-1300	174
Sumitomo Corp of America	600 Third Ave 42nd Fl	New York	NY	10016	**877-980-3283**	212-207-0700	360-3
Sumitomo Machinery Corp of America	4200 Holland Blvd	Chesapeake	VA	23323	**800-762-9256**	757-485-3355	707
Summa Barberton Hospital	155 Fifth St NE	Barberton	OH	44203	**888-905-6071**	330-615-3000	374-3
Summer Infant Inc	1275 Park E Dr	Woonsocket	RI	02895	**800-268-6237**		785
Summerwood Corp	14 Balligomingo Rd	Conshohocken	PA	19428	**800-760-0950**	610-520-1000	668
Summit Aviation Inc	4200 Summit Bridge Rd PO Box 258	Middletown	DE	19709	**800-441-9343**	302-834-5400	24
Summit Bank	2969 Broadway	Oakland	CA	94611	**800-380-9333**	510-839-8800	69
Summit Chemical Co	235 S Kresson St	Baltimore	MD	21224	**800-227-8664**	410-522-0661	282
Summit Christian College	2025 21st St	Gering	NE	69341	**888-305-8083**	308-632-6933	167
Summit Direct Mail Inc	1655 Terre Colony Ct	Dallas	TX	75212	**877-247-0993**	469-916-5170	197
Summit Electric Supply Co	2900 Stanford NE	Albuquerque	NM	87107	**800-824-4400**	505-346-9000	248
Summit Energy Services Inc	10350 Ormsby Pk Pl Ste 400	Louisville	KY	40223	**866-907-8664**	502-429-3800	462
Summit Food Service Distributors Inc	580 Industrial Rd	London	ON	N5V1V1	**800-265-9267**	519-453-3410	300
Summit Funding Group Inc	4680 Parkway Dr Ste 300	Mason	OH	45040	**866-489-1222**	513-489-1222	266-1
Summit Golf Brands Inc	8 W 40th St 2nd Fl	New York	NY	10018	**800-926-8010**	212-302-7255	442
Summit Holding Southeast Inc	PO Box 600	Gainesville	GA	30503	**800-971-2667**	678-450-5825	360-4
Summit Hut	5045 E Speedway Blvd	Tucson	AZ	85712	**800-499-8696**	520-325-1554	709
Summit Industries Inc	PO Box 7329	Marietta	GA	30065	**800-241-6996**		150
Summit Lodge & Spa	4359 Main St	Whistler	BC	V0N1B4	**888-913-8811**	604-932-2778	379
Summit Motorsports Park	1300 Ohio 18	Norwalk	OH	44857	**800-729-6455**	419-668-5555	514
Summit Partners	222 Berkeley St 18th Fl	Boston	MA	02116	**800-503-4611**	617-824-1000	790
Summit Pet Product Distributors Inc	420 N Chimney Rock Rd	Greensboro	NC	27410	**800-323-2963**	336-294-3200	792
Summit Plastics Inc	107 S Laurel St	Summit	MS	39666	**800-790-7117**	601-276-7500	599
Summit Security Services Inc	390 Rexcorp Plz W Tower - Lobby Level	Uniondale	NY	11556	**800-615-5888**	516-240-2400	691

Name / Address	City	State	ZIP	Toll-Free	Phone	Class
Summit State Bank 500 Bicentennial Way PO Box 6188 *NASDAQ: SSBI*	Santa Rosa	CA	95406	**800-428-5008**	707-568-6000	70
Summit Technical Services Inc 355 Centerville Rd	Warwick	RI	02886	**800-643-7372**	401-736-8323	630
Summit Trailer Sales Inc 1 Summit Plz	Summit Station	PA	17979	**800-437-3729**	570-754-3511	777
Summit Travel Group 830 Menlo Ave Ste 110	Menlo Park	CA	94025	**877-232-4465**	650-373-4400	315
Summit, The 65 Steiner Ave	Akron	OH	44301	**877-411-3662**	330-761-3099	642-2
Summitt Trucking LLC 1800 Progress Way	Clarksville	IN	47129	**866-999-7799**	812-285-7777	778
Sumner School District 1202 Wood Ave	Sumner	WA	98390	**866-548-3847**	253-891-6000	683
Sumner-Cowley Electric Co-op Inc 2223 N A St PO Box 220	Wellington	KS	67152	**888-326-3356**	620-326-3356	247
Sumter Electric Co-op Inc PO Box 301	Sumterville	FL	33585	**800-732-6141**	352-793-3801	247
Sumter Electric Membership Corp 1120 Felder St	Americus	GA	31709	**800-342-6978**	229-924-8041	247
Sun & Ski Sports 10560 Bissonnet St Ste 100	Houston	TX	77099	**866-786-3869**	281-340-5000	709
Sun Bancorp Inc (SNBC) 226 Landis Ave *NASDAQ: SNBC*	Vineland	NJ	08360	**800-786-9066**		360-2
Sun Chemical Corp 35 Waterview Blvd	Parsippany	NJ	07054	**800-543-2323**	973-404-6000	388
Sun Circle Inc 286 S G St	Arcata	CA	95521	**800-458-6543**	707-822-5777	275
Sun Coast Resources Inc 6405 Cavalcade St Bldg 1	Houston	TX	77028	**800-677-3835**	713-844-9600	578
Sun Control Products Window Shades 1908 Second St SW	Rochester	MN	55902	**800-533-0010**	507-282-2620	86
Sun Country Airlines Inc 1300 Mendota Heights Rd	Mendota Heights	MN	55120	**800-359-6786**	651-681-3900	25
Sun Devil Fire Equipment Inc 2929 W Clarendon Ave	Phoenix	AZ	85017	**800-536-3845**	623-245-0636	677
Sun Devil Stadium 500 E Veterans Way Arizona State University	Tempe	AZ	85281	**888-786-3857**	480-965-3482	718
Sun Drilling Products Corp 503 Main St	Belle Chasse	LA	70037	**800-962-6490**	504-393-2778	540
Sun Engineering Services Inc 5405 Garden Grove Blvd	Westminster	CA	92683	**888-604-5888**	714-379-2300	263
Sun Ergoline Inc 1 Walter Kratz Dr	Jonesboro	AR	72401	**888-771-0996**		437
Sun Healthcare Group Inc 18831 Von Karman Ste 400 *NASDAQ: SUNH*	Irvine	CA	92612	**800-729-6600**	949-255-7100	450
SUN Home Health Services Inc 61 Duke St PO Box 232	Northumberland	PA	17857	**888-478-6227**	570-473-8320	371
Sun Life Assurance Company of Canada 1 Sun Life Executive Pk PO Box 9133	Wellesley Hills	MA	02481	**800-786-5433**	781-237-6030	391-2
Sun Life Financial Inc 150 King St W *TSE: SLF*	Toronto	ON	M5H1J9	**877-786-5433**	416-979-9966	360-4
Sun Magazine 8815 Conroy Windermere Rd Ste 130	Orlando	FL	32835	**888-218-9968**	407-477-2815	456-11
Sun Mountain Lodge 604 Patterson Lk Rd PO Box 1000	Winthrop	WA	98862	**800-572-0493**	509-996-2211	667
Sun National Bank 350 Fellowship Rd Ste. 101	Mount Laurel	NJ	08054	**800-786-9066**		69
Sun News 914 Frontage Rd E	Myrtle Beach	SC	29578	**800-568-1800**	843-626-8555	531-2
Sun Newspapers 1801 Superior Ave	Cleveland	OH	44114	**800-362-8008**	216-999-3900	634-8
Sun Orchard Inc 1198 W Fairmont Dr	Tempe	AZ	85282	**800-505-8423**		297-20
Sun River Electric Co-op Inc 310 First Ave S PO Box 309	Fairfield	MT	59436	**800-452-7516**	406-467-2527	247
Sun Valley Area Chamber of Commerce 11501 Strathern St PO Box 308	Sun Valley	CA	91352	**877-834-7064**	818-768-2014	138
Sun Valley Floral Farms Inc 3160 Upper Bay Rd	Arcata	CA	95521	**800-747-0396**		369
Sun Valley Resort 1 Sun Valley Rd	Sun Valley	ID	83353	**800-786-8259**	208-622-4111	667
Sun Valley/Ketchum Chamber & Visitors Bureau 491 Sun Vly Rd	Ketchum	ID	83340	**800-634-3347**	208-726-3423	138
Sun Viking Lodge 2411 S Atlantic Ave	Daytona Beach Shores	FL	32118	**800-874-4469**	386-252-6252	379
Sun, The 4030 N Georgia Blvd	San Bernardino	CA	92407	**800-922-0922**	909-889-9666	531-2
Sunbelt Marketing Investment Corp 3255 S Sweetwater Rd	Lithia Springs	GA	30122	**800-257-5566**	770-739-3740	611
Sunbelt Rentals Inc 2341 Deerfield Dr *General	Fort Mill	SC	29715	**800-667-9328***	704-348-2676	266-3
Sunbelt Transfomer Ltd 1922 S Martin Luther King Jr Dr	Temple	TX	76504	**800-433-3128**	254-771-3777	251
Sunburst Shutters 6480 W Flamingo Rd Ste D	Las Vegas	NV	89103	**877-786-2877**	702-367-1600	697
Sunbury Motor Co 943 N Fourth St	Sunbury	PA	17801	**800-358-8090**	570-286-7746	515
Suncast Corp 701 N Kirk Rd	Batavia	IL	60510	**800-444-3310**	630-879-2050	320-2
Sunchaser Vacation Villas 5129 Riverview Gate Rd *Resv	Fairmont Hot Springs	BC	V0B1L1	**877-451-1250***	250-345-4545	751
Sunco Carriers Inc 1025 N Chestnut Rd	Lakeland	FL	33805	**800-237-8288**	863-688-1948	778
Suncoast Communities Blood Bank 1760 Mound St	Sarasota	FL	34236	**866-972-5663**	941-954-1600	88
Suncoast Hotel & Casino 9090 Alta Dr	Las Vegas	NV	89145	**877-677-7111**	702-636-7111	379
Suncoast Post-Tension LP 509 N Sam Houston Pkwy Ste 400 E	Houston	TX	77060	**800-847-8886**	281-668-1840	191-3
Suncor Energy Inc 150 - 6 Ave SW PO Box 2844 *NYSE: SU*	Calgary	AB	T2P3E3	**800-558-9071**	403-296-8000	535
Suncor Stainless Inc 70 Armstrong Rd	Plymouth	MA	02360	**800-218-7702**	508-732-9191	350
SunCrest Healthcare Inc 9510 Ormsby Station Rd Ste 300	Louisville	KY	40223	**800-845-6987**	615-627-9267	363
Sundance Beach 59 S La Patera Ln	Goleta	CA	93117	**877-968-0036**		709
Sundance Trail Guest Ranch 17931 Red Feather Lakes Rd	Red Feather Lakes	CO	80545	**800-357-4930**	970-224-1222	241
Sunday River Ski Resort 15 S Ridge Rd PO Box 4500	Newry	ME	04261	**800-543-2754**	207-824-3500	667
Sundial Beach & Golf Resort 1451 Middle Gulf Dr	Sanibel	FL	33957	**866-717-2323**	239-472-4151	667
Sundial Boutique Hotel 4340 Sundial Crescent	Whistler	BC	V0N1B4	**800-661-2321**	604-932-2321	379
Sundog Inc 2000 44th St SW Fl 6	Fargo	ND	58103	**888-978-6364**	701-235-5525	197
Sundowner Trailers Inc 9805 S State Hwy 48	Coleman	OK	73432	**800-654-3879**	580-937-4255	761
Sundt Construction 2620 S 55th St	Tempe	AZ	85282	**800-280-3000**	480-293-3000	191-2
Sundt Construction Inc 2015 W River Rd Ste 101	Tucson	AZ	85704	**800-467-5544**	520-750-4600	188
Sunex International Inc 100 Roe Rd	Travelers Rest	SC	29690	**800-833-7869**	864-834-8759	350
SunGard Availability Services 680 E Swedesford Rd	Wayne	PA	19087	**800-468-7483**	484-582-2000	394
SunGard Data Systems Inc 680 E Swedesford Rd	Wayne	PA	19087	**866-264-4829**	416-646-5932	227
SunGard Pentamation Inc 1000 Business Ctr Dr *Cust Svc	Lake mary	FL	32746	**866-965-7732***	610-691-3616	180-11
Sun-Journal PO Box 4400	Lewiston	ME	04243	**800-482-0759**	207-784-5411	531-2
Sunland Group Inc 1033 La Posada Dr Ste 370	Austin	TX	78752	**866-732-8500**	512-494-0208	263
Sunland Park Racetrack & Casino 1200 Futurity Dr	Sunland Park	NM	88063	**800-572-1142**	575-874-5200	639
Sunnen Products Co 7910 Manchester Ave	Saint Louis	MO	63143	**800-325-3670**	314-781-2100	454
Sunny 107.9 Radio *Palm Beach Broadcasting* 701 Northpoint Pkwy Ste 500	West Palm Beach	FL	33407	**800-919-1079**	561-616-4777	642-129
Sunny Land Tours Inc 21 Old Kings Rd N Ste B-212	Palm Coast	FL	32137	**800-783-7839**	386-449-0059	758
Sunnyland Farms Inc PO Box 8200	Albany	GA	31706	**800-999-2488**		458
Sunnyland Outdoor & Casual Furniture 7879 Spring Vly Rd Ste 125	Dallas	TX	75254	**877-239-3716**	972-239-3716	322
Sunoco Chemicals 1735 Market St Ste LL	Philadelphia	PA	19103	**800-786-6261**	215-977-3000	143
Sunoco Inc 1735 Market St Ste LL *NYSE: SUN*	Philadelphia	PA	19103	**800-786-6261**	215-977-3000	535
Sunovion Pharmaceuticals Inc 84 Waterford Dr	Marlborough	MA	01752	**888-394-7377**	508-481-6700	233
SunPower Corp 77 Rio Robles *NASDAQ: SPWR*	San Jose	CA	95134	**800-786-7693**	408-240-5500	694
SunQuest Vacations 77-6435 Kuakini Hwy	Kailua-Kona	HI	96740	**800-367-5168**	808-329-6438	769
Sunrich LLC 3824 SW 93rd St PO Box 128	Hope	MN	56046	**800-297-5997**	507-451-6030	79-1
Sunrider International 1625 Abalone Ave *Orders	Torrance	CA	90501	**888-278-6743***	310-781-3808	366
Sunrise Home Health Services 3200 Broadway Blvd Ste 260	Garland	TX	75043	**800-296-7823**	972-278-1414	363
Sunrise Medical Inc 2842 Business Pk Ave	Fresno	CA	93727	**800-333-4000**		476
Sunrise Medical Laboratories Inc 250 Miller Pl *Cust Svc	Hicksville	NY	11801	**800-782-0282***	631-435-1515	418
Sunrise Mfg. Inc 2665 Mercantile Dr	Rancho Cordova	CA	95742	**800-748-6529**	916-635-6262	498
Sunrise Senior Living Inc 7902 Westpark Dr *NYSE: SRZ*	McLean	VA	22102	**800-929-4124**	703-273-7500	450
Sunrise Specialty Co 930 98th Ave	Oakland	CA	94603	**800-444-4280**	510-729-7277	610
Sunriver Resort 17600 Ctr Dr PO Box 3609	Sunriver	OR	97707	**800-547-3922**	541-593-1000	667
Sunsational Cruises 2470 E Glen Canyon Rd	Green Valley	AZ	85614	**800-239-6252**	480-491-6248	769
Sunset Beach Resort 3287 W Gulf Dr	Sanibel Island	FL	33957	**866-565-5091**	239-472-1700	667
Sunset Inn Travel Apartments 1111 Burnaby St	Vancouver	BC	V6E1P4	**800-786-1997**	604-688-2474	379
Sunset Marquis Hotel & Villas 1200 N Alta Loma Rd	West Hollywood	CA	90069	**800-858-9758**	310-657-1333	379
Sunset Publishing Corp 80 Willow Rd	Menlo Park	CA	94025	**800-227-7346**	650-321-3600	634-9
Sunset Station Hotel & Casino 1301 W Sunset Rd	Henderson	NV	89014	**888-786-7389**	702-547-7777	379
Sunset Transportation Inc 11325 Concord Village Ave	St Louis	MO	63123	**800-849-6540**		312

Company / Address	City	State	Zip	Toll-Free	Phone	Class
Sunshine Artist Magazine 4075 LB McLeod Rd Ste E	Orlando	FL	32811	**800-597-2573**	407-648-7479	456-2
Sunshine Books Inc 49 River St Ste 3	Waltham	MA	02453	**800-472-5425**	781-398-0754	95
Sunshine Business Class 150 Kingswood Dr	Mankato	MN	56001	**800-873-7681**		129
Sunshine Financial Inc 1400 E Park Ave	Tallahassee	FL	32301	**800-468-3993**	850-219-7200	360-2
Sunshine Makers Inc 15922 Pacific Coast Hwy	Huntington Harbour	CA	92649	**800-228-0709**	562-795-6000	150
Sunshine Mills Inc 500 Sixth St SW	Red Bay	AL	35582	**800-633-3349**	256-356-9541	577
Sunshine Minting Inc 7600 Mineral Dr Ste 700	Coeur d'Alene	ID	83815	**800-274-5837**	208-772-9592	409
Sunstar Americas Inc 4635 W Foster Ave	Chicago	IL	60630	**888-777-3101**		230
Sunstate Federal Credit Union (Inc) PO Box 1162	Gainesville	FL	32627	**877-786-7828**	352-381-5200	221
Sunstream Hotels & Resorts 6231 Estero Blvd	Fort Myers Beach	FL	33931	**844-652-3696**	239-765-4111	378
Sunsweet Growers Inc 901 N Walton Ave	Yuba City	CA	95993	**800-417-2253**	530-674-5010	297-18
Suntrust Bank PO Box 4418 *NYSE: STI*	Atlanta	GA	30302	**800-786-8787**		69
SunTrust Banks Inc 303 Peachtree St NE *NYSE: STI*	Atlanta	GA	30308	**800-786-8787**	404-588-7711	360-2
SunTrust Mortgage Inc 1001 Semmes Ave	Richmond	VA	23224	**800-634-7928**		508
SunTrust Robinson Humphrey Capital Markets 3333 Peachtree Rd NE	Atlanta	GA	30326	**800-634-7928**	404-926-5000	688
Sunwest Aviation Ltd 230 Aviation Pl Ne	Calgary	AB	T2E7G1	**888-291-4566**	403-275-8121	23
Sunwest Silver Company Inc 324 Lomas Blvd NW	Albuquerque	NM	87102	**800-771-3781**	505-243-3781	294
SUNY (State University of New York Press) 22 Corporate Woods Blvd 3rd Fl	Albany	NY	12211	**866-430-7869**	518-472-5000	634-4
SUNY (State University of New York, The) State University Plz	Albany	NY	12246	**800-342-3811**	518-320-1888	784
Supelco Inc 595 N Harrison Rd	Bellefonte	PA	16823	**800-247-6628**	814-359-3441	419
Super Color Digital LLC 16761 Hale Ave	Irvine	CA	92606	**800-979-4446**	949-622-0010	626
Super Glue Corp 9420 Santa Anita Ave	Rancho Cucamonga	CA	91730	**800-538-3091**	909-987-0550	3
Super H Mart Inc 2550 Pleasant Hill Rd	Duluth	GA	30096	**877-427-7386**	678-543-4000	345
Super Holiday Tours 116 Gatlin Ave	Orlando	FL	32806	**800-327-2116**		758
Super Products LLC 17000 W Cleveland Ave	New Berlin	WI	53151	**800-837-9711**	262-784-7100	386
Super Save Group 19395 Langley By-pass	Surrey	BC	V3S6K1	**800-665-2800**	604-533-4423	317
Super Shoe Stores Inc 601 Dual Hwy	Hagerstown	MD	21740	**866-842-7510**		302
Super Sky Products Inc 10301 N Enterprise Dr	Mequon	WI	53092	**800-558-0467**	262-242-2000	236
Super Store Industries 16888 McKinley Ave PO Box 549	Lathrop	CA	95330	**888-292-8004**	209-858-2010	298-8
Super Talk 1270 4303 Memorial Hwy	Mandan	ND	58554	**844-255-7886**	701-663-1270	643
Superb Internet Corp 999 Bishop St Ste 1850	Honolulu	HI	96813	**888-354-6128**	808-544-0387	806
Superbag Corp 9291 Baythrone Dr	Houston	TX	77041	**888-842-1177**	713-462-1173	65
Superchips Inc 1790 E Airport Blvd	Sanford	FL	32773	**888-227-2447**	407-585-7000	175-1
Superconductor Technologies Inc (STI) 460 Ward Dr *NASDAQ: SCON*	Santa Barbara	CA	93111	**800-727-3648**	805-690-4500	255
SuperCoups 350 Revolutionary Dr	East Taunton	MA	02718	**800-626-2620**	508-977-2000	5
Supercuts 7201 Metro Blvd	Minneapolis	MN	55439	**877-857-2070**		76
SuperFlow Technologies Group 4747 Centennial Blvd	Colorado Springs	CO	80919	**800-471-7701**	719-471-1746	471
SuperGlass Windshield Repair Inc 6101 Chancellor Dr Ste 200	Orlando	FL	32809	**866-557-7497**	407-240-1920	61-2
Superheat Fgh Services Inc 313 Garnet Dr	New Lenox	IL	60451	**888-508-3226**		226
Superior Abrasives Inc 1620 Fieldstone Way	Vandalia	OH	45377	**800-235-9123**	937-278-9123	1
Superior Air Parts Inc 621 S Royal Ln Ste 100	Coppell	TX	75019	**800-420-4727**	972-829-4600	528
Superior Aluminum Products Inc 555 E Main St PO Box 430	Russia	OH	45363	**800-548-8656**	937-526-4065	490
Superior Auto Sales Inc 5201 Camp Rd	Hamburg	NY	14075	**866-439-9637**	716-649-6695	515
Superior Boiler Works Inc 3524 E Fourth St PO Box 1527	Hutchinson	KS	67504	**800-444-6693**	620-662-6693	90
Superior Carriers Inc 711 Jory Blvd Ste 101-N	Oak Brook	IL	60523	**800-654-7707**	630-573-2555	778
Superior Clay Corp 6566 Superior Rd SE	Uhrichsville	OH	44683	**800-848-6166**	740-922-4122	149
Superior Dairy Inc 4719 Navarre Rd SW	Canton	OH	44706	**800-597-5460**	330-477-4515	297-27
Superior Die Set Corp 900 W Drexel Ave	Oak Creek	WI	53154	**800-558-6040**	414-764-4900	755
Superior Die Tool & Machine Co 2301 Fairwood Ave	Columbus	OH	43207	**800-292-2181**	614-444-2181	755
Superior Energy Services Inc 601 Poydras St Ste 2400 *NYSE: SPN*	New Orleans	LA	70130	**800-259-7774**	504-587-7374	537
Superior Environmental Corp 1128 Franklin Ct	Marne	MI	49435	**877-667-4142**	616-667-4000	195
Superior Essex Communications LP 6120 Powers Ferry Rd Ste 150	Atlanta	GA	30339	**800-551-8948**	770-657-6000	732
Superior Essex Inc 6120 Powers Ferry Rd Ste 150 *NASDAQ: SPSX*	Atlanta	GA	30339	**800-551-8948**	770-657-6000	812
Superior Essex Inc Magnet Wire/Winding Wire Div 1601 Wall St PO Box 1601	Fort Wayne	IN	46802	**800-551-8948**	260-461-4550	811
Superior Farms 1480 Drew Ave Ste 100	Davis	CA	95618	**800-228-5262**	530-758-3091	472
Superior Gearbox Co 803 W Hwy 32	Stockton	MO	65785	**800-346-5745**	417-276-5191	707
Superior Graphite 10 S Riverside Plaza Ste 1470 *Cust Svc	Chicago	IL	60606	**800-325-0337***	312-559-2999	126
Superior Industries International Inc 7800 Woodley Ave *NYSE: SUP*	Van Nuys	CA	91406	**800-322-2885**	818-781-4973	59
Superior Medical Supply Inc 11005 Dover St Unit 1100	Broomfield	CO	80021	**877-460-1411**	303-460-1411	321
Superior Mfg Group 5655 W 73rd St	Chicago	IL	60638	**800-621-2802**	708-458-4600	293
Superior Motors Inc 282 John C Calhoun Dr	Orangeburg	SC	29115	**877-375-4759**		515
Superior Oil Co Inc 1402 N Capitol Ave Ste 100	Indianapolis	IN	46202	**800-553-5480**	317-781-4400	602
Superior Packaging Solutions 26858 Almond Ave	Redlands	CA	92374	**844-792-2626**	800-680-2393	560
Superior Plus Income Fund 840-7 Ave SW Ste 1400	Calgary	AB	T2P3G2	**866-490-7587**	403-218-2970	405
Superior Press Inc 11930 Hamden Pl *Cust Svc	Santa Fe Springs	CA	90670	**888-590-7998***	562-948-1866	85
Superior Products Inc 3786 Ridge Rd	Cleveland	OH	44144	**800-651-9490**	216-651-9400	620
Superior Public Library 1530 Tower Ave	Superior	WI	54880	**866-894-4899**	715-394-8860	434-3
Superior Shores Resort 1521 Superior Shores Dr	Two Harbors	MN	55616	**800-242-1988**	218-834-5671	667
Superior Software Inc 16055 Ventura Blvd Ste 650	Encino	CA	91436	**800-421-3264**	818-990-1135	180-1
Superior Technical Resources Inc 250 International Dr	Williamsville	NY	14221	**800-568-8310**	716-929-1400	719
Superior Tire & Rubber Corp 1818 Pennsylvania Ave W PO Box 308 *Cust Svc	Warren	PA	16365	**800-289-1456***	814-723-2370	752
Superior Tool Co 100 Hayes Dr Unit C *Cust Svc	Cleveland	OH	44131	**800-533-3244***	216-398-8600	756
Superior Trailer Sales Co 501 Hwy 80	Sunnyvale	TX	75182	**800-637-0324**	972-226-3893	515
Superior Uniform Group Inc 10055Seminole Blvd *NASDAQ: SGC* ■ *Cust Svc	Seminole	FL	33772	**800-727-8643***	727-397-9611	154-18
Superior Water Light & Power 2915 Hill Ave PO Box 519	Superior	WI	54880	**800-227-7957**	715-394-2200	785
Superior/Douglas County Convention & Visitors Bureau 305 Harborview Pkwy	Superior	WI	54880	**800-942-5313**	715-392-7151	208
Superior-Douglas County Chamber of Commerce 205 Belknap St	Superior	WI	54880	**800-942-5313**	715-394-7716	138
Superlite Block Co Inc 4150 W Turney Ave	Phoenix	AZ	85019	**800-366-7877**	602-352-3500	185
Supermarket Systems Inc 6419 Bannington Rd	Charlotte	NC	28226	**800-553-1905**	704-542-6000	663
Supermercado Mi Tierra LLC 9520 International Blvd	Oakland	CA	94603	**800-225-9902**	510-567-8617	345
Superseal Mfg Co Inc PO Box 795	South Plainfield	NJ	07080	**800-433-4873**	908-561-5910	237
SuperTalk 99.7 WTN 10 Music Cir E	Nashville	TN	37203	**800-618-7445**	615-321-1067	642-81
SUPERVALU Inc 7075 Flying Cloud Dr *NYSE: SVU* ■ *Cust Svc	Eden Prairie	MN	55344	**877-322-8228***	952-828-4000	298-8
Superwinch Inc 359 Lake Rd	Dayville	CT	06241	**800-323-2031**	860-928-7787	192
Supply Room Cos Inc 14140 N Washington Hwy	Ashland	VA	23005	**800-849-7239**	804-412-1200	534
Supply Technologies LLC 6065 Parkland Blvd	Cleveland	OH	44124	**800-695-8650**	440-947-2100	351
Support Services of America Inc 12440 Firestone Blvd Ste 312	Norwalk	CA	90650	**888-564-0005**	562-868-3550	151
Support.com Inc 900 Chesapeake Dr 2nd Fl *NASDAQ: SPRT*	Redwood City	CA	94063	**877-493-2778**	650-556-9440	180-7
Supra Alloys Inc 351 Cortez Cir	Camarillo	CA	93012	**888-647-8772**	805-388-2138	491
Supreme Corp 325 Spence Rd	Conover	NC	28613	**888-604-6975**	828-322-6975	742-9
Supreme Mfg Company Inc 5 Connerty Ct	East Brunswick	NJ	08816	**800-772-7632**	732-254-0087	345
Supreme Oil Co 2109 W Monte Vista Rd	Phoenix	AZ	85009	**800-752-7888**		538
Sur La Table 5701 Sixth Ave S Ste 486	Seattle	WA	98108	**800-243-0852**		362
Sure Winner Foods Inc 2 Lehner Rd	Saco	ME	04072	**800-640-6447**	207-282-1258	298-4
Surefire LLC 18300 Mt Baldy Cir	Fountain Valley	CA	92708	**800-828-8809**	714-545-9444	73
Surefit Inc 6575 Snowdrift Rd Ste 101	Allentown	PA	18106	**888-796-0500**		743
SurePayroll 2350 Ravine Way Ste 100	Glenview	IL	60025	**877-954-7873**	847-676-8420	569
Surepoint Technologies Group Inc 744 - 4th Ave SW Ste 1000	Calgary	AB	T2P3T4	**855-777-7873**		537
Sureshred Security 3166 Diablo Ave	Hayward	CA	94545	**888-606-0008**	510-784-1150	318
Surety Group Inc 3715 Northside Pkwy NW Ste 1-315	Atlanta	GA	30327	**800-486-8211**	404-352-8211	391-5

Name / Address	City	State	ZIP	Toll-Free	Phone	Class
Surety LLC 12020 Sunrise Vly Dr Ste 250	Reston	VA	20191	800-298-3115	571-748-5800	180-7
Surf & Sand Resort 1555 S Coast Hwy	Laguna Beach	CA	92651	877-741-5908	949-497-4477	379
Surface Combustion Inc 1700 Indian Wood Cir	Maumee	OH	43537	800-537-8980	419-891-7150	319
Surface Equipment Corp 337 Cargill Rd	Kilgore	TX	75662	800-256-7732	903-984-0400	536
Surface Mount Distribution Inc (SMD) 1 Oldfield	Irvine	CA	92618	800-820-7634	949-470-7700	248
Surface Shields Inc 10457 163rd Pl	Orland Park	IL	60467	800-754-9685	708-226-9810	293
Surfsand Resort 148 W Gower Rd	Cannon Beach	OR	97110	800-547-6100	503-436-2274	379
Surfside Inn 1211 Atlantic Ave	Virginia Beach	VA	23451	800-437-2497	757-428-1183	379
Surge Resources 920 Candia Rd	Manchester	NH	03109	800-787-4387	603-623-0007	462
Surgical Appliance Industries Inc 3960 Rosslyn Dr	Cincinnati	OH	45209	800-888-0867		476
Surgical Principals Inc 1625 S Tacoma Way	Tacoma	WA	98409	888-801-9251		474
Surgical Staff Inc 120 St Matthews Ave	San Mateo	CA	94401	800-339-9599	650-558-3999	719
SurModics Inc 9924 W 74th St *NASDAQ: SRDX*	Eden Prairie	MN	55344	866-787-6639	952-829-2700	233
Surprise Valley Electric Co-op 22595 US 395	Alturas	CA	96101	866-843-2667	530-233-3511	247
Surrex Solutions Corp 300 N Sepulveda Blvd Ste 1020	El Segundo	CA	90245	866-308-2628		198
Surrey Board of Trade 14439 104th Ave Ste 101	Surrey	BC	V3R1M1	866-848-7130	604-581-7130	137
Surrey Hotel 20 E 76th St	New York	NY	10021	866-233-4642	212-288-3700	379
Surry-Yadkin Electric Membership Corp 510 S Main St	Dobson	NC	27017	800-682-5903	336-356-8241	247
Sur-Seal Gasket & Packing Inc 6156 Wesselman Rd	Cincinnati	OH	45248	800-345-8966		327
Surveillance Specialties Ltd 600 Research Dr	Wilmington	MA	01887	800-354-2616		40
Survival Systems Training Ltd 40 Mount Hope Ave	Dartmouth	NS	B2Y4K9	800-788-3888	902-465-3888	448
Survivors Network of Those Abused by Priests (SNAP) PO Box 6416	Chicago	IL	60680	877-762-7432	312-455-1499	47-21
Susan G Komen for the Cure 5005 LBJ Fwy Ste 250	Dallas	TX	75244	800-227-2345	972-855-1600	47-17
Susan Schein Automotive 3171 Pelham Pkwy	Pelham	AL	35124	800-845-1578	205-664-1491	56
SUSLA (Southern University Museum of Art) 3050 Martin Luther King Jr Dr	Shreveport	LA	71107	800-458-1472	318-670-6000	519
Susquehanna County 75 Public Ave	Montrose	PA	18801	800-932-0313	570-278-4600	338
Susquehanna University 514 University Ave	Selinsgrove	PA	17870	800-326-9672	570-374-0101	167
Suss Consulting 801 Old York Rd Noble Plz Ste 305	Jenkintown	PA	19046	888-984-5900	215-884-5900	197
Sussex Bank 200 Munsonhurst Rd *NASDAQ: SBBX*	Franklin	NJ	07416	800-511-9900	973-827-2914	360-2
Sussex County Chamber of Commerce 120 Hampton House Rd	Newton	NJ	07860	844-256-7328	973-579-1811	138
Sussex Rural Electric Co-op 64 County Rt 639 PO Box 346	Sussex	NJ	07461	877-504-6463	973-875-5101	247
Sussman Automatic Corp 43-20 34th St	Long Island	NY	11101	800-727-8326	718-937-4500	90
Suter Company Inc 258 May St	Sycamore	IL	60178	800-435-6942	815-895-9186	297-36
Sutherland Asbill & Brennan LLP 999 Peachtree St NE	Atlanta	GA	30309	855-857-9769	404-853-8000	428
Sutphen Corp PO Box 158	Amlin	OH	43002	800-726-7030	614-889-1005	515
Sutter Auburn Faith Community Hospital (SAFH) 11815 Education St	Auburn	CA	95602	800-478-8837	530-888-4500	374-3
Sutter County Library 750 Forbes Ave	Yuba City	CA	95991	800-533-2873	530-822-7137	434-3
Sutter Health 2200 River Plaza	Sacramento	CA	95833	888-888-6044	916-733-8800	353
Sutter Medical Ctr of Santa Rosa 3325 Chanate Rd	Santa Rosa	CA	95404	800-651-5111	707-576-4006	374-3
Suttle 1001 E Hwy 212	Hector	MN	55342	800-852-8662	320-848-6711	732
Sutton Alliance LLC 515 Rockaway Ave	Valley Stream	NY	11581	866-435-6600	516-837-6100	650
Sutton Ford Inc 21315 S Central Ave	Matteson	IL	60443	866-232-2966	708-720-8115	56
Suwannee Valley Electric Co-op PO Box 160	Live Oak	FL	32064	800-752-0025	386-362-2226	247
Suzuki Association of The Americas Inc 1900 Folsom St Ste 101	Boulder	CO	80302	888-378-9854	303-444-0948	136
Suzuki Musical Instrument Corp PO Box 710459 *Cust Svc	Santee	CA	92072	800-854-1594*	619-258-1896	526
Svam International Inc 233 E Shore Rd Ste 201	Great Neck	NY	11023	800-903-6716	516-466-6655	182
SVB Financial Group 3005 Tasman Dr *NASDAQ: SIVB*	Santa Clara	CA	95054	800-760-9644	408-654-7400	360-2
SVC (Society of Vacuum Coaters) 71 Pinon Hill Pl NE	Albuquerque	NM	87122	800-443-8817	505-856-7188	48-13
SVCH (Saint Vincent Charity Hospital) 2351 E 22nd St	Cleveland	OH	44115	800-750-0750	216-861-6200	374-3
SVIA (Specialty Vehicle Institute of America) 2 Jenner St Ste 150	Irvine	CA	92618	800-887-2887	949-727-3727	48-21
SVM LP 200 E Howard Ave Ste 220	Des Plaines	IL	60018	877-300-1786		228
SVMH (Salinas Valley Memorial Hospital) 450 E Romie Ln	Salinas	CA	93901	800-813-4673	831-757-4333	374-3
SVRMC (Sierra Vista Regional Medical Ctr) 1010 Murray Ave	San Luis Obispo	CA	93405	866-904-6871	805-546-7600	374-3
SVS (Society for Vascular Surgery) 633 N St Clair St 22nd Fl	Chicago	IL	60611	800-258-7188	312-334-2300	48-8
SVS Vision 140 Macomb Pl	Mount Clemens	MI	48043	800-787-4600	586-468-7612	542
SW Steakhouse 3131 Las Vegas Blvd S	Las Vegas	NV	89109	888-320-7123	702-770-7000	669
Swag, The 2300 Swag Rd	Waynesville	NC	28785	800-789-7672	828-926-0430	379
Swan & Sons-Morss Company Inc 309 E Water St	Elmira	NY	14902	877-407-1657	607-734-6283	390
Swan Corp, The 515 Olive St Ste 900	St. Louis	MO	63101	800-325-7008	314-231-8148	611
Swan Hose 1201 Delaware Ave	Marion	OH	43302	800-848-8707		370
Swan Lake Resort & Campground 17463 County Hwy 29	Fergus Falls	MN	56537	800-697-4626	218-736-4626	120
SWANA (Solid Waste Assn of North America) 1100 Wayne Ave Ste 700	Silver Spring	MD	20910	800-467-9262	301-585-2898	530-5
Swank Motion Pictures Inc 10795 Watson Rd	St Louis	MO	63127	888-248-8757	314-984-6000	513
Swans Candles 16524 Tilley Rd S	Tenino	WA	98589	888-848-7926		121
Swanson Health Products Inc PO Box 2803	Fargo	ND	58108	800-824-4491	701-356-2700	797
Swany America Corp 115 Corp Dr	Johnstown	NY	12095	888-234-5450	518-725-3333	154-7
Swarco Industries Inc PO Box 89	Columbia	TN	38402	800-216-8781	931-388-5900	674
Swarovski North America Ltd 1 Kenney Dr	Cranston	RI	02920	800-289-4900	401-463-6400	334
Swarthmore College 500 College Ave *Admissions	Swarthmore	PA	19081	800-667-3110*	610-328-8300	167
Swarthout Coaches Inc 115 Graham Rd	Ithaca	NY	14850	800-772-7267	607-257-2277	106
SWCA Inc 3033 N Central Ave Ste 145	Phoenix	AZ	85012	800-828-8517	602-274-3831	194
SWCE (Steele-Waseca Co-op Electric) 2411 W Bridge St PO Box 485	Owatonna	MN	55060	800-526-3514	507-451-7340	247
SWCS (Soil & Water Conservation Society) 945 SW Ankeny Rd	Ankeny	IA	50023	800-843-7645	515-289-2331	47-13
SWE (Society of Women Engineers) 120 S La Salle St Ste 1515	Chicago	IL	60603	877-793-4636	312-596-5223	48-19
Sweda Company LLC 17411 Vly Blvd	City of Industry	CA	91744	800-848-8417	626-357-9999	117
SwedishAmerican Hospital 1401 E State St	Rockford	IL	61104	800-322-4724	815-968-4400	374-3
Sweed Machinery Inc 653 Second Ave PO Box 228 *Sales	Gold Hill	OR	97525	800-888-1352*	541-855-1512	493
Sweeney Buick 7997 Market St	Youngstown	OH	44512	877-360-4928		515
Sweeney Law Firm 8109 Lima Rd	Fort Wayne	IN	46818	866-793-6339	260-420-3137	428
Sweepster Inc 2800 N Zeeb Rd	Dexter	MI	48130	800-456-7100	734-996-9116	102
Sweet Adelines International 9110 S Toledo Ave	Tulsa	OK	74137	800-992-7464	918-622-1444	47-18
Sweet Briar College 134 Chappel Rd *Admissions	Sweet Briar	VA	24595	800-381-6142*	434-381-6100	167
Sweet Candy Co Inc 3780 W Directors Row	Salt Lake City	UT	84104	800-669-8669	801-886-1444	297-8
Sweet Mfg Company Inc 2000 E Leffel Ln *Cust Svc	Springfield	OH	45505	800-334-7254*	937-325-1511	209
Sweetwater Authority PO Box 2328	Chula Vista	CA	91912	866-275-3772	619-420-1413	785
Sweetwater County School District 1 (SCSD) 3550 Foothill Blvd PO Box 1089	Rock Springs	WY	82901	888-503-7562	307-352-3400	778
Sweetwater Sound Inc 5501 US Hwy 30 W	Fort Wayne	IN	46818	800-222-4700	260-432-8176	525
Sweetwater Valley Oil Company Inc 1236 New Hwy 68	Sweetwater	TN	37874	800-362-4519	423-337-6671	580
Swenson Spreader Co 127 Walnut St	Lindenwood	IL	61049	888-825-7323	815-393-4455	192
SWEPCo 1 Riverside Plz 13th Fl	Columbus	OH	43215	888-216-3523		785
SWF Cos 1949 E Manning Ave	Reedley	CA	93654	800-344-8951	559-638-8484	546
SWH (Senior Whole Health LLC) 58 Charles St	Cambridge	MA	02141	888-794-7268	617-494-5353	353
SWH Supply Co 242 E Main St	Louisville	KY	40202	800-321-3598	502-589-9287	663
Swibco Inc 4810 Venture Rd	Lisle	IL	60532	877-794-2261	630-968-8900	760
Swift Energy Co 16825 Northchase Dr Ste 400 *NYSE: SFY*	Houston	TX	77060	800-777-2412	281-874-2700	535
Swift Glass Company Inc 131 W 22nd St	Elmira Heights	NY	14903	800-537-9438	607-733-7166	332
Swift Print Communication 1248 Research Blvd	Saint Louis	MO	63132	800-545-1141	314-991-4300	626
Swift Spinning Inc 16 Corporate Ridge Pkwy	Columbus	GA	31907	800-849-1252	706-323-6303	742-9
Swift Transportation Company Inc 2200 S 75th Ave *NYSE: SWFT*	Phoenix	AZ	85043	800-800-2200	602-269-9700	778

Company	Address	City	State	ZIP	Toll-Free	Phone	Class
Swiftlift Inc	820 Phillips Rd	Victor	NY	14564	**888-292-3101**	585-742-2160	23
Swiger Coils Systems Inc	4677 Mfg Rd	Cleveland	OH	44135	**800-321-3310**	216-362-7500	517
Swim 'n Sport Retail Inc	2396 NW 96th Ave	Miami	FL	33172	**800-497-2111**		156-6
Swineford National Bank	1255 N Susquehanna Trial PO Box 241	Hummels Wharf	PA	17831	**866-762-1903**	570-743-7786	69
Swintec Corp	320 W Commercial Ave	Moonachie	NJ	07074	**800-225-0867**	201-935-0115	110
Swire Coca-Cola USA	12634 S 265 W	Draper	UT	84020	**800-497-2653**	801-816-5300	80-2
Swisher County Cattle Co	Farm Market 214 Rd	Tulia	TX	79088	**800-658-6014**	806-627-4231	10-1
Swisher Electric Co-op Inc	401 SW Second St PO Box 67	Tulia	TX	79088	**800-530-4344**	806-995-3567	247
Swisher Hygiene Co	4725 Piedmont Row Dr	Charlotte	NC	28210	**800-444-4138**	704-364-7707	151
Swisher Mower & Machine Company Inc	1602 Corporate Dr	Warrensburg	MO	64093	**800-222-8183**	660-747-8183	429
Swiss Army Brands Inc	7 Victoria Dr PO Box 1212 *Cust Svc	Monroe	CT	06468	**800-442-2706***	203-929-6391	224
Swiss Knife Shop	10 Northern Blvd Ste 8	Amherst	NH	03031	**866-438-7947**	603-732-0069	197
Swiss Precision Instruments Inc	11450 Markon Dr	Garden Grove	CA	92841	**888-774-8200**	714-799-1555	386
Swiss Valley Farms	247 Research Pkwy PO Box 4493	Davenport	IA	52808	**800-747-6113**	563-468-6600	297-5
Swisslog	10825 E 47th Ave	Denver	CO	80239	**800-525-1841**	303-371-7770	209
Switzerland Tourism	608 Fifth Ave Ste 202	New York	NY	10020	**800-794-7795**	212-757-5944	773
SWTC (Southwest Wisconsin Technical College)	1800 Bronson Blvd	Fennimore	WI	53809	**800-362-3322**	608-822-3262	798
SY Bancorp Inc	1040 E Main St *NASDAQ: SYBT*	Louisville	KY	40206	**800-625-9066**	502-582-2571	360-2
Syagen Technology Inc	1411 Warner Ave	Tustin	CA	92780	**877-258-8250**	714-258-4400	740
Sycara Inc	6263 N Scottsdale Rd Ste 180	Scottsdale	AZ	85250	**855-479-2272**		630
Sycuan Casino & Resort	5469 Casino Way *General	El Cajon	CA	92019	**800-279-2826***	619-445-6002	132
Sydneys Closet	11840 Dorsett Rd	Maryland Heights	MO	63043	**888-479-3639**	314-344-5066	156-6
Sydnor Hydro Inc	2111 Magnolia St PO Box 27186	Richmond	VA	23261	**800-552-7714**	804-643-2725	804
SYGMA Network Inc	5550 Blazer Pkwy Ste 300	Dublin	OH	43017	**877-441-1144**		298-8
Sykes Enterprises Inc	400 N Ashley Dr Ste 2800 *NASDAQ: SYKE*	Tampa	FL	33602	**800-867-9537**	813-274-1000	182
Sylvan Inc	90 Glade Dr	Kittanning	PA	16201	**866-352-7520**	724-543-3900	10-6
Sylvan Learning Centers	1001 Fleet St	Baltimore	MD	21202	**888-338-2283**		244
Sylvania Steel Corp	4169 Holland Sylvania Rd *General	Toledo	OH	43623	**800-435-0986***	419-885-3838	491
Symantec Corp	350 Ellis St *NASDAQ: SYMC*	Mountain View	CA	94043	**800-441-7234**	650-527-8000	180-12
Symbolist	1090 Texan Trl	Grapevine	TX	76051	**800-498-6885**		197
Symco Group Inc	5012 Bristol Industrial Way Ste 105	Buford	GA	30518	**800-878-8002**	770-451-8002	176
SymCom Inc	222 Disk Dr	Rapid City	SD	57701	**800-843-8848**	605-348-5580	407
Symetra Life Insurance Co	777 108th Ave Ne Ste 1200	Bellevue	WA	98004	**800-574-0233**	425-256-8000	391-2
Symmetricom Inc	2300 Orchard Pkwy *NASDAQ: SYMM*	San Jose	CA	95131	**888-367-7966**	408-433-0910	732
Symmons Industries Inc	31 Brooks Dr	Braintree	MA	02184	**800-796-6667**	781-848-2250	608
Symons Capital Management Inc	650 Washington Rd Ste 800	Pittsburgh	PA	15228	**888-344-7740**	412-344-7690	239
Symphony Ctr	220 S Michigan Ave *Cust Svc	Chicago	IL	60604	**800-223-7114***	312-294-3000	571
Symphony Nova Scotia	6101 University Ave Dalhousie Arts Ctr	Halifax	NS	B3H4R2	**800-874-1669**	902-494-3820	572-3
Synagro Technologies Inc	435 Williams Ct Ste 100	Baltimore	MD	21220	**800-370-0035**	443-489-9017	802
Synalloy Corp	775 Spartan Blvd Ste 102 PO Box 5627 *NASDAQ: SYNL* ■ *Orders	Spartanburg	SC	29304	**800-937-5449***	864-585-3605	594
Synchronoss Technologies Inc	200 Crossing Blvd *NASDAQ: SNCR*	Bridgewater	NJ	08807	**866-620-3940**		226
Syndicate Sales Inc	PO Box 756	Kokomo	IN	46903	**800-428-0515**	765-457-7277	607
Syndication Networks Corp	8700 Waukegan Rd Ste 250	Morton Grove	IL	60053	**800-743-1988**	847-583-9000	644
Synergent	2 Ledgeview Dr	Westbrook	ME	04092	**800-341-0180**	207-773-5671	318
Synergetics USA Inc	3845 Corporate Ctr Dr *NASDAQ: SURG*	O'Fallon	MO	63368	**800-600-0565**	636-939-5100	475
Synergex International Corp	2330 Gold Meadow Way	Rancho Cordova	CA	95670	**800-366-3472**	916-635-7300	180-10
Synergistics Inc	9 Tech Cir Ste 2	Natick	MA	01760	**866-455-5222**	508-655-1340	180-11
Synergy Associates LLC	550 Clydesdale Trl	Medina	MN	55340	**888-763-9920**		182
Synergy Broadcast Systems	16115 Dooley Rd	Addison	TX	75001	**800-601-6991**		645
Synergy Co of Utah LLC, The	2279 S Resource Blvd	Moab	UT	84532	**800-723-0277**		666
Synergy Direct Response	130 E Alton Ave	Santa Ana	CA	92707	**888-902-6166**	714-754-5733	197
Syngenta Corp	3411 Silverside Rd Ste 100	Wilmington	DE	19810	**800-555-2470**	302-425-2000	282
Syngenta Crop Protection Inc	410 Swing Rd PO Box 18300	Greensboro	NC	27409	**800-797-5040**	336-632-6000	282
SYNNEX Canada	200 Ronson Dr	Etobicoke	ON	M9W5Z9	**800-268-1220**	416-240-7012	176
Synnex Corp	44201 Nobel Dr *NYSE: SNX* ■ *Cust Svc	Fremont	CA	94538	**800-756-1888***	510-656-3333	176
Synopsys Inc	700 E Middlefield Rd *NASDAQ: SNPS*	Mountain View	CA	94043	**800-541-7737**	650-584-5000	180-10
Synovis Life Technologies Inc	2575 University Ave *NASDAQ: SYNO*	Saint Paul	MN	55114	**800-255-4018**	651-796-7300	476
Synovus Financial Corp	1111 Bay Ave Ste 500 PO Box 120 *NYSE: SNV*	Columbus	GA	31902	**888-796-6887**	706-649-2311	360-2
Synrad Inc	4600 Campus Pl	Mukilteo	WA	98275	**800-796-7231**	425-349-3500	425
Syn-Tech Inc	3100 Ridgelake Dr Ste 101	Metairie	LA	70002	**800-535-7619**	504-835-7825	248
Synthes USA	1302 Wrights Ln E	West Chester	PA	19380	**800-523-0322**	610-719-5000	476
Syntrio	50 California St Ste 3260	San Francisco	CA	94111	**888-289-6670**	415-951-7913	38
Synutra International Inc	2275 Research Blvd Ste 500 *NASDAQ: SYUT*	Rockville	MD	20850	**866-405-2350**	301-840-3888	797
Synventive Molding Solutions Inc	10 Centennial Dr	Peabody	MA	01960	**800-367-5662**	978-750-8065	386
Synygy Pte. Ltd	2501 Seaport Dr	Chester	PA	19013	**877-883-5395**	610-494-3300	630
Sypris Electronics LLC	10901 N McKinley Dr	Tampa	FL	33612	**800-937-9220**	813-972-6000	255
Sypris Solutions Inc	101 Bullitt Ln Ste 450 *NASDAQ: SYPR*	Louisville	KY	40222	**800-588-9119**	502-329-2000	255
Syracuse Research Corp (SRC)	7502 Round Pond Rd	North Syracuse	NY	13212	**800-724-0451**	315-452-8000	666
Syracuse Scenery & Stage Lighting Company Inc	101 Monarch Dr	Liverpool	NY	13088	**800-453-7775**	315-453-8096	720
Syracuse Stamping Co	1054 S Clinton St	Syracuse	NY	13202	**800-581-5555**	315-476-5306	488
Syracuse University	900 S Crouse Ave	Syracuse	NY	13244	**800-782-5867**	315-443-3611	167
Syracuse University Bird Library	222 Waverly Ave	Syracuse	NY	13244	**866-722-7858**	315-443-2093	434-6
Syreon Corp	260 - 1401 W Eighth Ave	Vancouver	BC	V6H1C9	**866-979-7366**	604-676-5900	240
Sysazzle Inc	15815 S. 46th St Ste 116,	Phoenix	AZ	85048	**800-862-9545**		719
Sysco Central Ohio Inc	2400 Harrison Rd	Columbus	OH	43204	**800-735-3341**	614-272-0655	298-8
Sysco Denver Inc	5000 Beeler St	Denver	CO	80238	**800-366-6696**	303-585-2000	298-8
Sysco Food Services of Idaho Inc	5710 Pan Am Ave	Boise	ID	83716	**800-747-9726**	208-345-9500	298-8
Sysco Grand Rapids	3700 Sysco Ct SE	Grand Rapids	MI	49512	**800-669-6967**	616-949-3700	298-8
Sysco Hampton Roads Inc	7000 Harbour View Blvd	Suffolk	VA	23435	**800-234-2451**	757-673-4000	298-8
Sysco Indianapolis LLC	4000 W 62nd St	Indianapolis	IN	46268	**800-347-3920**	317-291-2020	298-11
Sysco Kansas City Inc	1915 E Kansas City Rd	Olathe	KS	66061	**800-735-3341**	913-829-5555	297-26
Syscon Inc	94 Mcfarland Blvd	Northport	AL	35476	**888-797-2661**	205-758-2000	182
Syska & Hennessy Group	11 W 42nd St	New York	NY	10036	**800-328-1600**	212-921-2300	263
Sysmex America Inc	1 Nelson C White Pkwy	Mundelein	IL	60060	**800-379-7639**	847-996-4500	474
SYSPRO	959 S Coast Dr Ste 100	Costa Mesa	CA	92626	**800-369-8649**	714-437-1000	180-1
Systech Corp	16510 Via Esprillo	San Diego	CA	92127	**800-800-8970**	858-674-6500	178
Systel Business Equipment Company Inc	2604 Fort Bragg Rd	Fayetteville	NC	28303	**800-849-5900**	910-321-7700	111
System Automation	7110 Samuel Morse Dr Ste 100	Columbia	MD	21046	**800-839-4729**	301-837-8000	180-10
System Concepts Inc	15900 N 78th St	Scottsdale	AZ	85260	**800-553-2438**	480-951-8011	179
System Engineering International Inc (SEI)	5115 Pegasus Ct Ste Q	Frederick	MD	21704	**800-765-4734**	301-694-9601	785

Name / Address	City	State	Zip	Toll-Free	Phone	Class
System Innovators Inc 10550 Deerwood Pk Blvd Ste 700	Jacksonville	FL	32256	**800-963-5000**		180-10
System Sensor 3825 Ohio Ave *Tech Supp	Saint Charles	IL	60174	**800-736-7672***	630-377-6580	255
Systematic Financial Management LP 300 Frank W Burr Blvd Seventh Fl Glenpoint Ctr E 7th Fl	Teaneck	NJ	07666	**800-258-0497**	201-928-1982	401
Systematics Inc 1025 Saunders Ln PO Box 2429	West Chester	PA	19380	**800-222-9353**	610-696-9040	809
Systems & Forecasts 150 Great Neck Rd Ste 301	Great Neck	NY	11021	**800-982-4372**	516-829-6444	530-9
Systems East Inc 30 Basil Sawyer Dr	Hampton	VA	23666	**800-230-8734**	757-766-8400	205
Systems Engineering Technologies Corp 6121 Lincolnia Rd Ste 200	Alexandria	VA	22312	**800-385-8977**	703-941-7887	179
Systems House, The 1033 Rte 46 East Ste A202	Clifton	NJ	07013	**800-637-5556**	973-777-8050	227
Systems Maintenance Services Inc (SMS) 10420 Harris Oaks Blvd Ste C	Charlotte	NC	28269	**877-405-0330**		177
Systems Plus Computers Inc 12 Centerra Pkwy Ste 20	Lebanon	NH	03766	**800-388-8486**	603-643-5800	198
Systemtec Inc 246 Stoneridge Dr Ste 301	Columbia	SC	29210	**888-900-1655**	803-806-8100	179
Systron Donner Inertial 355 Lennon Ln	Walnut Creek	CA	94598	**866-234-4976**	925-979-4400	528
Syvantis Technologies LLC 13822 Bluestem Ct Ste	Baxter	MN	56425	**800-450-8908**		198

T

Name / Address	City	State	Zip	Toll-Free	Phone	Class
T & A Supply Company Inc 6821 S 216th St Bldg A PO Box 927	Kent	WA	98032	**800-562-2857**	253-872-3682	361
T & C Industries Inc PO Box 629	Darien	WI	53114	**800-426-6447**	262-882-1227	695
T & E Industries Inc 215 Watchung Ave *Sales	Orange	NJ	07050	**800-245-7080***	973-672-5454	327
T & R Electric Supply Company Inc 308 SW Third St	Colman	SD	57017	**800-843-7994**	605-534-3555	765
T & S Brass & Bronze Works Inc PO Box 1088 *Cust Svc	Travelers Rest	SC	29690	**800-476-4103***	864-834-4102	608
T & t Staff Management Inc 511 Executive Ctr Blvd	El Paso	TX	79902	**800-598-1647**	915-771-0393	630
T & T Trucking Inc 11396 N Hwy 99 *Cust Svc	Lodi	CA	95240	**800-692-3457***	209-931-6000	778
T BC Corp 4770 Hickory Hill Rd	Memphis	TN	38141	**866-822-4968**		753
T Cook's 5200 E Camelback Rd	Phoenix	AZ	85018	**800-672-6011**	602-808-0766	669
T Cross Ranch LLC 82 Parque Creek Rd PO Box 638	Dubois	WY	82513	**877-827-6770**	307-455-2206	241
T G H Aviation 2389 Rickenbacker Way	Auburn	CA	95602	**800-843-4976**	530-823-6204	56
T Marzetti Co 1105 Schrock Rd	Columbus	OH	43229	**800-999-1835**	614-846-2232	297-19
T R Toppers Inc 320 Fairchild	Pueblo	CO	81001	**800-748-4635**	719-948-4902	297-8
T Rowe Price Assoc Inc 100 E Pratt St	Baltimore	MD	21202	**800-638-7890**	410-345-2000	401
T Tech Inc 510 Guthridge Ct	Norcross	GA	30092	**800-370-1530**	770-455-0676	490
T. Bruce Sales Inc 9 Carbaugh St	West Middlesex	PA	16159	**800-944-0738**	724-528-9961	479
T. Marzetti Company. PO Box 29163	Columbus	OH	43229	**800-999-1835**		297-9
T.u.c.s. Cleaning Service Inc 166 Central Ave	Orange	NJ	07050	**800-992-5998**	973-673-0700	151
T3 Expo LLC 8 Lakeville Business Park Unit 1	Lakeville	MA	02347	**888-698-3397**		186
TAB Products Co 605 Fourth St	Mayville	WI	53050	**888-466-8228**		533
Tabb Brockenbrough & Ragland LLC 4905 Dickens Rd	Richmond	VA	23230	**800-296-0531**	804-355-7984	390
TABB Inc PO Box 10	Chester	NJ	07930	**800-887-8222**		632
Taber Consultants 3911 W Capitol Ave	West Sacramento	CA	95691	**888-423-0573**	916-371-1690	263
Taber Extrusions LP 915 S Elmira Ave	Russellville	AR	72802	**800-563-6853**	479-968-1021	484
Taber Industries 455 Bryant St	North Tonawanda	NY	14120	**800-333-5300**	716-694-4000	471
Table Mountain Casino 8184 Table Mountain Rd	Friant	CA	93626	**800-541-3637**	559-822-7777	132
Taboo Resort Golf & Spa 1209 Muskoka Beach Rd	Gravenhurst	ON	P1P1R1	**800-461-0236**	705-687-2233	705
Tabor College 400 S Jefferson St *Admissions	Hillsboro	KS	67063	**800-822-6799***	620-947-3121	167
Tack Room Too Inc 201 Lee St Sw	Tumwater	WA	98501	**800-258-2581**	360-357-4268	709
Taco Cabana Inc 8918 Tesoro Dr Ste 200	San Antonio	TX	78217	**800-580-8668**	210-804-0990	668
Taco Inc 1160 Cranston St	Cranston	RI	02920	**888-778-2733**	401-942-8000	357
Taco Metals Inc 50 NE 179th St	Miami	FL	33162	**800-653-8568**	305-652-8566	491
Taco Time International Inc 9311 E Via de Venutra	Scottsdale	AZ	85258	**866-452-4252**	480-362-4800	668
Tacoma Electric Supply Inc 1311 S Tacoma Way	Tacoma	WA	98409	**800-422-0540**	253-475-0540	248
Tacoma General Hospital 315 MLK Jr Way	Tacoma	WA	98405	**800-552-1419**	253-403-1000	374-3
Tacoma Inc 328 E Church St	Martinsville	VA	24112	**800-352-9417**	276-666-9417	668
Tacoma Mall 4502 S Steele St Ste 1177	Tacoma	WA	98409	**877-746-6642**	253-475-4565	459
Tacoma Regional Convention & Visitor Bureau 1516 Commerce St	Tacoma	WA	98402	**800-272-2662**	253-627-2836	208
Tacoma Rubber Stamp & Sign 919 Market St	Tacoma	WA	98402	**800-544-7281**	253-383-5433	466
Tacoma Symphony 901 Broadway Ste 600	Tacoma	WA	98402	**800-291-7593**	253-272-7264	572-3
Taconic 136 Coonbrook Rd PO Box 69	Petersburg	NY	12138	**800-833-1805**	518-658-3202	742-2
Tadiran Batteries 2001 Marcus Ave Ste 125E	New Hyde Park	NY	11042	**800-537-1368**	516-621-4980	73
TAF (Taxpayers Against Fraud Education Fund) 1220 19th St NW Ste 501 *General	Washington	DC	20036	**800-873-2573***	202-296-4826	48-10
Taft College 29 Emmons Pk Dr	Taft	CA	93268	**800-379-6784**	661-763-7700	161
TAG (Tube Art Group) 11715 SE Fifth St	Bellevue	WA	98005	**800-562-2854**	206-223-1122	699
TAG Solutions LLC 12 Elmwood Rd	Albany	NY	12204	**800-724-0023**	518-292-6500	732
Tag-A-Long Expeditions 452 N Main St	Moab	UT	84532	**800-453-3292**	435-259-8946	758
Taglairino Advertising Group Ny Inc 75 Sw 15th Rd	Miami	FL	33129	**800-226-9988**	305-577-9988	7
Tahitian Noni International 333 W Riverpark Dr *Cust Svc	Provo	UT	84604	**800-445-2969***	801-234-1000	297-11
Tahoe Biltmore Lodge & Casino PO Box 115	Crystal Bay	NV	89402	**800-245-8667**	775-831-0660	378
Tahoe Mountain Sports 11200 Donner Pass Rd Ste 5e	Truckee	CA	96161	**866-891-9177**		709
Tahoma National Cemetery 18600 SE 240th St	Kent	WA	98042	**800-827-1000**	425-413-9614	135
Taiga Building Products Ltd 4710 Kingsway Ste 800	Burnaby	BC	V5H4M2	**800-663-1470**	604-438-1471	281
Tailhook Assn 9696 Businesspark Ave	San Diego	CA	92131	**800-322-4665**	858-689-9223	47-19
Tailored Chemical Products Inc 700 12th St Dr NW	Hickory	NC	28601	**800-627-1687**	828-322-6512	3
Tailored Living LLC 1927 N Glassell St	Orange	CA	92865	**866-675-8819**		361
Taitron Components Inc 28040 W Harrison Pkwy *NASDAQ: TAIT*	Valencia	CA	91355	**800-247-2232**	661-257-6060	248
Taiwan Semiconductor Mfg Company Ltd (TSMC) 2851 Junction Ave *NYSE: TSM*	San Jose	CA	95134	**877-248-4237**	408-382-8000	694
Taiyo Yuden (USA) Inc 1930 N Thoreau Dr Ste 190	Schaumburg	IL	60173	**800-348-2496**	847-925-0888	255
Taj Boston 15 Arlington St	Boston	MA	02116	**866-969-1825**	617-536-5700	379
Taj Campton Place 340 Stockton St	San Francisco	CA	94108	**866-969-1825**	415-781-5555	379
TAJ Technologies Inc 1168 Northland Dr	Mendota Heights	MN	55120	**877-825-2801**	651-688-2801	719
Takagi Industrial Company USA Inc 500 Wald	Irvine	CA	92618	**888-882-5244**	949-770-7171	15
Takara Belmont USA Inc 101 Belmont Dr	Somerset	NJ	08873	**877-283-1289**		75
Take 3 Trailers Inc 1808 Hwy 105	Brenham	TX	77833	**800-428-2533**	979-337-9568	761
Takeda Canada Inc 435 N Service Rd W Ste 101	Oakville	ON	L6M4X8	**888-367-3331**	905-469-9333	84
Talan Products Inc 18800 Cochran Ave	Cleveland	OH	44110	**877-419-2805**	216-458-0170	482
Talbott Recovery Campus 5448 Yorktowne Dr	Atlanta	GA	30349	**800-445-4232**	770-994-0185	724
Talent Curve 14 Bridle Path	Pittsboro	NC	27312	**866-494-0248**		462
TalentLens Inc 19500 Bulverde Rd	San Antonio	TX	78259	**888-298-6227**		262
Taleo Corp 4140 Dublin Blvd Ste 400 *NYSE: ORCL*	Dublin	CA	94568	**800-672-2531**	925-452-3000	180-1
Taliesin 5607 County Hwy C	Spring Green	WI	53588	**877-588-7900**	608-588-7090	49-2
Talisma Corp 777 Yamato Rd	Boca Raton	FL	33431	**866-397-2537**	561-923-2500	38
Talk O'Texas Brands Inc 1610 Roosevelt St	San Angelo	TX	76905	**800-749-6572**	325-655-6077	297-20
Talk Radio Network (TRN) PO Box 3755	Central Point	OR	97502	**888-383-3733**		644
TalkPoint Communications Inc 100 William St	New York	NY	10038	**866-323-8660**	212-909-2900	178
Talladega Castings & Machine Co Inc 228 N Ct St	Talladega	AL	35160	**800-766-6708**	256-362-5550	308
Talladega College 627 W Battle St	Talladega	AL	35160	**866-540-3956**	256-761-6100	167
Talladega Machinery & Supply Co Inc 301 N Johnson Ave PO Box 736 *Cust Svc	Talladega	AL	35161	**800-289-8672***	256-362-4124	308
Tallan Inc 175 Capital Blvd Ste 401	Rocky Hill	CT	06067	**800-677-3693**	860-633-3693	179
Tallapoosa River Electric Co-op 15163 US Hwy 431 S PO Box 675	Lafayette	AL	36862	**800-332-8732**	334-864-9331	247
Tallgrass Restoration LLC 2221 Hammond Dr	Schaumburg	IL	60173	**877-699-8300**	847-925-9830	198
TallyGenicom 15345 Barranca Pkwy	Irvine	CA	92618	**800-436-4266**	714-368-2300	175-6

Name / Address	City	State	Zip	Toll-Free	Phone	Class
Talquin Electric Co-op Inc 1640 W Jefferson St	Quincy	FL	32351	**888-271-8778**	850-627-7651	247
TALX Corp 11432 Lackland Dr	Saint Louis	MO	63146	**800-888-8277**	314-214-7000	38
T-A-M (Trace-A-Matic Inc) 1570 Commerce Ave	Brookfield	WI	53045	**877-375-0217**	262-797-7300	620
Tam International Inc 4620 Southerland Rd	Houston	TX	77092	**800-462-7617**	713-462-7617	536
Tamarac Inc 701 Fifth Ave 14th Fl	Seattle	WA	98104	**866-525-8811**		401
Tamarack Habilitation Technologies Inc 1670 94th Ln NE	Blaine	MN	55449	**866-795-0057**	763-795-0057	476
Tamco Inc 1466 Delberts Dr	Monongahela	PA	15063	**800-826-2672**	724-258-6622	756
Tamiment Resort & Conference Ctr Bushkill Falls Rd	Tamiment	PA	18371	**800-233-8105**	570-588-6652	667
Tampa Armature Works Inc 6312 78th St	Riverview	FL	33578	**866-465-8905**	813-621-5661	517
Tampa Bay & Co 401 E Jackson St Ste 2100	Tampa	FL	33602	**877-230-0078**	813-223-1111	208
Tampa Bay Beaches Chamber of Commerce 6990 Gulf Blvd	Saint Pete Beach	FL	33706	**866-450-9222**	727-360-6957	138
Tampa Bay Downs Inc 11225 Racetrack Rd	Tampa	FL	33626	**800-200-4434**	813-855-4401	639
Tampa Bay Fisheries Inc 3060 Gallagher Rd	Dover	FL	33527	**800-732-3663**	813-752-8883	297-14
Tampa Bay Lightning St Pete Times Forum 401 Channelside Dr	Tampa	FL	33602	**800-745-3000**	813-301-6500	714
Tampa Convention Ctr 333 S Franklin St	Tampa	FL	33602	**866-790-4111**	813-274-8511	207
Tampa International Airport 4100 George J Bean Pkwy PO Box 22287	Tampa	FL	33607	**866-289-9673**	813-870-8700	27
Tampa Marriott Waterside Hotel & Marina 700 S Florida Ave	Tampa	FL	33602	**888-268-1616**	813-204-6300	705
Tampa Museum of Art 120 W Gasparilla Plaza	Tampa	FL	33602	**866-790-4111**	813-274-8131	519
Tampa Port Authority 1101 Channelside Dr	Tampa	FL	33602	**800-741-2297**	813-905-7678	617
TAMRO Capital Partners LLC 1701 Duke St Ste 250	Alexandria	VA	22314	**888-816-2925**	703-740-1000	401
Tamwood International College 300-909 Burrard St	Vancouver	BC	V6Z2N2	**866-533-0123**	604-899-4480	423
Tandberg Data 10225 Westmoor Dr Ste 125	Westminster	CO	80021	**800-392-2983**	303-442-4333	175-8
Tandus Centiva 311 Smith Industrial Blvd PO Box 1447	Dalton	GA	30722	**800-248-2878**	706-259-9711	130
Tangent Inc 191 Airport Blvd	Burlingame	CA	94010	**800-342-9388**	650-342-9388	175-1
Tanger Factory Outlet Centers Inc 3200 Northline Ave Ste 360 *NYSE: SKT*	Greensboro	NC	27408	**800-720-6728**	336-292-3010	653
Tanger Outlet Ctr San Marcos 4015 S IH-35 Ste 319	San Marcos	TX	78666	**800-408-8424**	512-396-7446	459
Tangerine Travel Ltd 16017 Juanita Woodinville Way Ne Ste 201	Bothell	WA	98011	**800-678-8202**	425-822-2333	770
Tangible Solutions Inc 1320 Matthews Township Pkwy Ste 201	Matthews	NC	28105	**800-393-9886**	704-940-4200	182
Tanglewood Resort Hotel & Conference Ctr 290 Tanglewood Cir	Pottsboro	TX	75076	**800-833-6569**	903-786-2968	667
Tango Consulting Group LLC 31 James Vincent Dr	Clinton	CT	06413	**877-567-6045**		198
Tangoe Inc 35 Executive Blvd *NASDAQ: TNGO*	Orange	CT	06477	**877-571-4737**	203-859-9300	179
Tanimura & Antle Inc PO Box 4070	Salinas	CA	93912	**800-772-4542**		10-9
Tanita Corp of America Inc 2625 S Clearbrook Dr	Arlington Heights	IL	60005	**800-826-4828**	847-640-9241	682
Tanks-A-Lot Ltd 1810 Yellowhead Trail N.E.	Edmonton	AB	T6S1B4	**800-661-5667**	780-472-8265	768
Tanner Cos LLC 581Rock Rd	Rutherfordton	NC	28139	**877-872-4578**	828-287-4205	154-20
Tanner Electric Co 45710 SE North Bend Way	North Bend	WA	98045	**800-472-0208**	425-888-0623	247
Tanner Industries Inc 735 Davisville Rd 3rd Fl	SouthHampton	PA	18966	**800-643-6226**	215-322-1238	145
Tanner Research Inc 825 S Myrtle Ave	Monrovia	CA	91016	**877-325-2223**	626-471-9700	176
Tanner Systems Inc PO Box 488	Saint Joseph	MN	56374	**800-461-6454**	320-363-1800	142
Tanque Verde Guest Ranch 14301 E Speedway Blvd	Tucson	AZ	85748	**800-234-3833**	520-296-6275	667
Tanque Verde Ranch 14301 E Speedway	Tucson	AZ	85748	**800-234-3833**	520-296-6275	241
Tantalus Resort Lodge 4200 Whistler Way	Whistler	BC	V0N1B4	**888-806-2299**	604-932-4146	667
Tan-Tar-A Resort Golf Club & Spa 494 Tantara Dr PO Box 188TT *Resv	Osage Beach	MO	65065	**800-826-8272***	573-348-3131	667
TanTara Transportation Corp 2420 Stewart Rd	Muscatine	IA	52761	**800-650-0292**	563-262-8621	778
Tap Packaging Solutions 2160 Superior Ave	Cleveland	OH	44114	**800-827-5679**	216-781-6000	559
TAP Plastics Inc 6475 Sierra Ln	Dublin	CA	94568	**800-894-0827**	925-829-4889	606
Tapatio Springs Golf Resort & Conference Ctr 1 Resort Way	Boerne	TX	78006	**800-999-3299**	855-627-2243	667
Tapco Group 29797 Beck Rd	Wixom	MI	48393	**800-521-7567**	248-668-6400	697
Tape & Label Converters Inc 8231 Allport Ave	Santa Fe Springs	CA	90670	**888-285-2462**	562-945-3486	413
Tape Craft Corp 200 Tape Craft Dr *Cust Svc	Oxford	AL	36203	**800-521-1783***		742-5

Name / Address	City	State	Zip	Toll-Free	Phone	Class
Tapecon Inc 10 Latta Rd	Rochester	NY	14612	**800-333-2407**	585-621-8400	413
TAPEMARK Co 1685 Marthaler Ln	St Paul	MN	55118	**800-535-1998**	651-455-1611	413
Tapeswitch Corp 100 Schmitt Blvd	Farmingdale	NY	11735	**800-234-8273**	631-630-0442	727
Tapmatic Corp 802 S Clearwater Loop *General	Post Falls	ID	83854	**800-854-6019***	208-773-8048	492
TAPPI (Technical Assn of the Pulp & Paper Industry) 15 Technology Pkwy S *Sales	Norcross	GA	30092	**800-332-8686***	770-446-1400	48-13
Tapscott's 1403 E 18th St	Owensboro	KY	42303	**800-626-1922**	270-684-2308	295
TAR (Tennessee Assn of Realtors) 901 19th Ave S	Nashville	TN	37212	**877-321-1477**	615-321-1477	654
Target Corp 1000 Nicollet Mall *NYSE: TGT* ■ *Cust Svc	Minneapolis	MN	55403	**800-440-0680***	612-304-6073	231
Targeted Job Fairs Inc 4441 Glenway Ave	Cincinnati	OH	45205	**800-695-1939**		262
Targus Inc 1211 N Miller St	Anaheim	CA	92806	**877-482-7487**	714-765-5555	452
Tarkett Inc 1001 Yamaska St E	Farnham	QC	J2N1J7	**800-363-9276**	450-293-3173	293
Tarleton State University 1333 W Washington PO Box T-0030	Stephenville	TX	76402	**800-687-8236**	254-968-9000	167
Taro Pharmaceuticals Inc 130 E Dr	Brampton	ON	L6T1C1	**800-268-1975**	905-791-8276	582
Taro Pharmaceuticals USA Inc 3 Skyline Dr	Hawthorne	NY	10532	**800-544-1449**	914-345-9001	583
Tarr LLC 2429 N Borthwick St	Portland	OR	97227	**800-422-5069**		145
Tarrant County College *Northeast* 828 W Harwood Rd	Hurst	TX	76054	**800-799-7233**	817-515-8223	161
Northwest 4801 Marine Creek Pkwy	Fort Worth	TX	76179	**800-799-7233**	817-515-7100	161
Tarryall River Ranch 270015 County Rd 77	Lake George	CO	80827	**800-408-8407**	719-748-1214	241
Tarrytown House Estate & Conference Center 49 E Sunnyside Ln	Tarrytown	NY	10591	**800-553-8118**	914-591-8200	228
Tarrytown Music Hall 13 Main St PO Box 686	Tarrytown	NY	10591	**877-840-0457**	914-631-3390	571
TASC Technical Services LLC 73 Newton Rd	Plaistow	NH	03865	**877-304-8272**		197
Task Force Tips Inc 3701 Innovation Way	Valparaiso	IN	46383	**800-348-2686**	219-462-6161	285
3701 Innovation Way	Valparaiso	IN	46383	**800-348-2686**	219-462-6161	747
Taskstream LLC 71 W 23rd St	New York	NY	10010	**800-311-5656**	212-868-2700	227
TaskUs Inc 3233 Donald Douglas Loop S Ste 3	Santa Monica	CA	90405	**888-400-8275**		393
Tasler Inc 1804 Tasler Dr	Webster City	IA	50595	**800-482-7537**	515-832-5200	550
Taste of Home Magazine 5400 S 60th St	Greendale	WI	53129	**800-344-6913**	414-423-0100	456-11
Tasty Baking Co 4300 S 26th St	Philadelphia	PA	19112	**800-248-2789**	215-221-8500	297-1
Tate Access Floors Inc 7510 Montevideo Rd	Jessup	MD	20794	**800-231-7788**	410-799-4200	490
Tate Andale Inc 1941 Lansdowne Rd	Baltimore	MD	21227	**800-296-8283**	410-247-8700	594
Tatro Plumbing Company Inc 1285 Acraway Ste 300	Garden City	KS	67846	**888-828-7648**	620-277-2167	191-10
Tattered Cover Book Store Inc 1628 16th St	Denver	CO	80202	**800-833-9327**	303-436-1070	95
Tatung Company of America Inc 2850 El Presidio St	Long Beach	CA	90810	**800-827-2850**	310-637-2105	175-4
Tau Beta Pi Assn 1512 Middle Dr	Knoxville	TN	37996	**877-829-5500**	865-546-4578	47-16
Tau Beta Sigma National Honorary Band Sorority PO Box 849 *Cust Svc	Stillwater	OK	74076	**800-543-6505***	405-372-2333	47-16
Taubman Centers Inc 200 E Long Lk Rd Ste 300 *NYSE: TCO*	Bloomfield Hills	MI	48303	**800-297-6003**	248-258-6800	653
Tauck World Discovery 10 Norden Pl	Norwalk	CT	06855	**800-468-2825**	203-899-6500	758
Taurus International Mfg Inc 16175 NW 49th Ave	Miami	FL	33014	**800-327-3776**	305-624-1115	286
Tavaero Jet Charter 7930 Airport Blvd	Houston	TX	77061	**800-343-3771**	713-643-5387	13
Tavistock Restaurants LLC 4705 S Apopka Vineland Rd Ste 210	Orlando	FL	32819	**800-424-2753**	407-909-7101	668
Tax Executives Institute (TEI) 1200 G St NW Ste 300	Washington	DC	20005	**877-244-7711**	202-638-5601	48-1
Tax Management Associates Inc 2225 Coronation Blvd	Charlotte	NC	28227	**800-951-5350**	704-847-1234	227
Tax Management Inc 1801 S Bell St	Arlington	VA	22202	**800-372-1033**	703-341-3000	634-9
Taxpayers Against Fraud Education Fund (TAF) 1220 19th St NW Ste 501 *General	Washington	DC	20036	**800-873-2573***	202-296-4826	48-10
Taycom Business Solutions Inc 719 Griswold Ave Ste 820	Detroit	MI	48226	**866-482-9266**		2
Taycor LLC 6065 Bristol Pkwy	Culver City	CA	90230	**800-322-9738**	310-895-7704	218
Taylor 750 N Blackhawk Blvd	Rockton	IL	61072	**800-255-0626**	815-624-8333	299
Taylor & Francis Group 6000 Broken Sound Pkwy NW Ste 300	Boca Raton	NY	33487	**877-622-5543**	207-017-6000	634-2
Taylor & Fulton Inc 932 Fifth Ave W	Palmetto	FL	34221	**800-457-5577**	941-729-3883	10-9

Name / Address	City	State	Zip	Toll-Free	Phone	Class
Taylor & Hill Inc						
9941 Rowlett Rd	Houston	TX	77075	**800-318-0231**	713-941-2671	262
Taylor & Messick Inc						
325 Walt Messick Rd	Harrington	DE	19952	**800-237-1272**	302-398-3729	519
Taylor & Syfan Consulting Engineers Inc						
684 Clarion Ct	San Luis Obispo	CA	93401	**800-579-3881**	805-547-2000	263
Taylor Bldg Products						
631 N First St	West Branch	MI	48661	**800-248-3600**	989-345-5110	236
Taylor County RECC						
625 W Main St PO Box 100	Campbellsville	KY	42719	**800-931-4551**	270-465-4101	247
Taylor Electric Co-op						
N1831 State Hwy 13	Medford	WI	54451	**800-862-2407**	715-678-2411	247
Taylor Enterprises Inc (TEI)						
2586 Southport Rd	Spartanburg	SC	29302	**800-922-3149**	864-573-9518	578
Taylor Farms Inc						
PO Box 1649	Salinas	CA	93902	**866-675-6120**	831-676-9765	298-7
Taylor Freezer Sales Company Inc						
2032 Atlantic Ave	Chesapeake	VA	23324	**800-768-6945**		663
Taylor Freezers of California						
221 Harris Ct	South San Francisco	CA	94080	**877-978-4800**		406
Taylor Law Offices Pc						
122 E Washington Ave	Effingham	IL	62401	**800-879-2250**		428
Taylor Precision Products LLC						
2220 Entrada del Sol Ste A	Las Cruces	NM	88001	**866-843-3905**		204
Taylor Protocols Inc						
16040 Christensen Rd Ste 315	Tukwila	WA	98188	**877-355-8229**	206-283-8144	448
Taylor Technologies Inc						
31 Loveton Cir	Sparks	MD	21152	**800-837-8548***	410-472-4340	804
*Cust Svc						
Taylor Truck Line Inc						
31485 Northfield Blvd	Northfield	MN	55057	**800-962-5994**	507-645-4531	778
Taylor University						
236 W Reade Ave	Upland	IN	46989	**800-882-3456**	765-998-2751	167
Fort Wayne						
915 W Rudisill Blvd	Fort Wayne	IN	46807	**800-882-3456***	260-744-8790	167
*General						
Taylor University College & Seminary						
11525 23rd Ave	Edmonton	AB	T6J4T3	**800-567-4988**	780-431-5200	168-3
Taylor Wellons Politz & Duhe Aplc						
8550 United Plz Blvd Ste 101	Baton Rouge	LA	70809	**877-850-1047**	225-387-9888	428
Taylor-Dunn Manufacturing Co						
2114 W Ball Rd	Anaheim	CA	92804	**800-688-8680**	714-956-4040	469
TaylorMade - Adidas Golf						
5545 Fermi Ct	Carlsbad	CA	92008	**800-555-1212***	760-918-6000	708
*Cust Svc						
Tazewell Area Chamber of Commerce						
Tazewell Mall PO Box 6	Tazewell	VA	24651	**855-233-6362**	276-988-5091	138
TB Butler Publishing Co						
410 W Erwin St	Tyler	TX	75702	**800-333-9141**	903-597-8111	634-8
TB Wood's Inc						
440 N Fifth Ave	Chambersburg	PA	17201	**888-829-6637**	717-264-7161	619
TBA LLC						
6700 Enterprise Dr	Louisville	KY	40214	**800-626-3525**	502-367-0222	611
TBC (Tom Barrow Co)						
2800 Plant Atkinson Rd	Atlanta	GA	30339	**800-229-8226**	404-351-1010	14
Tbm Consulting Group Inc						
4400 Ben Franklin Blvd	Durham	NC	27704	**800-438-5535**	919-471-5535	196
TBN (Trinity Broadcasting Network)						
PO Box A	Santa Ana	CA	92711	**888-731-1000**	714-832-2950	736
TBT (Transco Business Technologies)						
34 Leighton Rd	Augusta	ME	04330	**800-322-0003**	207-622-6251	111
TCA (Truckload Carriers Assn)						
555 E Braddock Rd	Alexandria	VA	22314	**800-666-2770**	703-838-1950	48-21
TCC (Customer Communicator, The)						
712 Main St Ste 187B	Boonton	NJ	07005	**800-232-4317**	973-265-2300	530-2
TCE Capital Corp						
505 Consumers Rd Ste 707	Toronto	ON	M2J4V8	**800-465-0400**	416-497-7400	274
TCI Aluminum/North Inc						
2353 Davis Ave	Hayward	CA	94545	**800-824-6197**	510-786-3750	491
TCI College of Technology						
320 W 31st St	New York	NY	10001	**800-878-8246**	212-594-4000	798
TCI International Inc						
3541 Gateway Blvd	Fremont	CA	94538	**877-247-3797**	510-687-6100	645
TCI Scales Inc						
PO Box 1648	Snohomish	WA	98291	**800-522-2206**	425-353-4384	682
TCI Wealth Advisors Inc						
4011 E Sunrise Dr	Tucson	AZ	85718	**877-733-1859**	520-733-1477	401
TCIA (Tree Care Industry Assn)						
136 Harvey Rd Ste 101	Londonderry	NH	03053	**800-733-2622**	603-314-5380	47-13
TCK (Twin City Knitting Company Inc)						
104 Rock Barn Rd NE	Conover	NC	28613	**800-438-6884**	828-464-4830	154-9
TCM (Temp-Control Mechanical Corp)						
4800 N Ch Ave	Portland	OR	97217	**877-826-3828**	503-285-9851	14
TCR Industries						
26 Centerpointe Dr Ste 120	La Palma	CA	90623	**877-827-1444**	714-521-5222	145
Tct Computing Group Inc						
Po Box 402	Bel Air	MD	21014	**866-828-6372**	410-893-5800	195
TCT Ministries Inc						
11717 N Rt 37 PO Box 1010	Marion	IL	62959	**800-232-9855**	618-997-4700	736
TCU (Teachers Credit Union)						
PO Box 1395	South Bend	IN	46624	**800-552-4745**	574-284-6247	221
TCVB (Tyler Convention & Visitors Bureau)						
315 N Broadway	Tyler	TX	75702	**800-235-5712**	903-592-1661	208
TCW Group Inc						
865 S Figueroa St Ste 1800	Los Angeles	CA	90017	**800-386-3829**	213-244-0000	527
TD Bank NA						
1701 Rt 70 E	Cherry Hill	NJ	08034	**888-751-9000**	856-751-2739	69
TD Banknorth Massachusetts						
295 Pk Ave	Worcester	MA	01609	**800-747-7000***	508-752-2584	69
*Cust Svc						
TDECU (Texas Dow Employees Credit Union)						
1001 FM 2004	Lake Jackson	TX	77566	**800-839-1154**	979-297-1154	221
TDI-Transistor Devices Inc						
85 Horsehill Rd	Cedar Knolls	NJ	07927	**800-488-6724**	973-267-1900	255
TDS (Texas Disposal Systems Inc)						
12200 Carl Rd	Creedmoor	TX	78610	**800-375-8375**	512-421-1300	802

Name / Address	City	State	Zip	Toll-Free	Phone	Class
TDS Telecommunications Corp						
525 Junction Rd	Madison	WI	53717	**866-571-6662**	608-664-4000	733
Te21 Inc						
1184 Clements Ferry Rd Ste G	Charleston	SC	29492	**866-982-8321**	843-579-2520	198
Tea Council of the USA Inc						
362 Fifth Ave Ste 801	New York	NY	10001	**877-212-5752**	212-986-9415	48-6
Teach Away Inc						
147 Liberty St	Toronto	ON	M6K3G3	**855-483-2242**	416-628-1386	262
Teach For America						
315 W 36th St 7th Fl	New York	NY	10018	**800-832-1230**	212-279-2080	48-5
Teacher Created Resources						
6421 Industry Way	Westminster	CA	92683	**888-343-4335**		245
Teacher Magazine						
6935 Arlington Rd Ste 100	Bethesda	MD	20814	**800-346-1834**	301-280-3100	456-8
Teachers Credit Union (TCU)						
PO Box 1395	South Bend	IN	46624	**800-552-4745**	574-284-6247	221
Teachers Federal Credit Union (TFCU)						
2410 N Ocean Ave	Farmingville	NY	11738	**800-341-4333**	631-698-7000	221
Teachers of English to Speakers of Other Languages (TESOL)						
700 S Washington St Ste 200	Alexandria	VA	22314	**888-547-3369**	703-836-0774	48-5
Teachers on Reserve LLC						
604 Sonora Ave	Glendale	CA	91201	**800-457-1899**	818-502-5800	262
Teachers Protective Mutual Life Insurance Co						
116-118 N Prince St	Lancaster	PA	17603	**800-555-3122**	717-394-7156	390
Teaching & Learning Co						
1204 Buchanan St	Carthage	IL	62321	**800-444-1144**	937-228-6118	245
Teaching & Mentoring Communities (TMC)						
PO Box 2579	Laredo	TX	78044	**888-836-5151**	956-722-5174	48-5
Teal's Express Inc						
22411 Teal Dr PO Box 6010	Watertown	NY	13601	**800-836-0369**	315-788-6437	778
Teal-Jones Group, The						
17897 Triggs Rd	Surrey	BC	V4N4M8	**888-995-8325**	604-587-8700	681
Team Health Inc						
265 Brookview Ctr Way Ste 400	Knoxville	TN	37919	**800-342-2898**	865-693-1000	719
Team Inc 200 Hermann Dr	Alvin	TX	77511	**800-662-8326**	281-331-6154	538
NYSE: TISI						
Team Quality Services Inc						
4483 County Rd 19 Ste B	Auburn	IN	46706	**866-568-8326**	260-572-0060	462
Team Velocity Marketing LLC						
13825 Sunrise Valley Dr	Herndon	VA	20171	**877-832-6848**		7
Team Volkswagen of Hayward Corp						
25115 Mission Blvd	Hayward	CA	94544	**866-308-2825**		56
TeamBonding						
298 Tosca Dr	Stoughton	MA	02072	**888-398-8326**		318
TeamQuest Corp						
1 TeamQuest Way	Clear Lake	IA	50428	**800-551-8326**	641-357-2700	180-12
Teamwork Newsletter						
2222 Sedwick Dr	Durham	NC	27713	**800-223-8720**		530-2
Teaneck Public Library						
840 Teaneck Rd	Teaneck	NJ	07666	**800-245-1377**	201-837-4171	434-3
Tec Laboratories Inc						
7100 Tec Labs Way SW	Albany	OR	97321	**800-482-4464**	541-926-4577	233
Tech Allies Consulting LLC						
300 E Business Way Ste 200	Cincinnati	OH	45241	**866-321-0101**		198
Tech Briefs Media Group						
261 Fifth Ave Ste 1901	New York	NY	10016	**888-456-3398**	212-490-3999	456-19
Tech Credit Union						
10951 Broadway	Crown Point	IN	46307	**800-276-8324**	219-663-5120	221
Tech Data Corp						
5350 Tech Data Dr	Clearwater	FL	33760	**800-237-8931**	727-539-7429	176
NASDAQ: TECD						
Tech Hero Of Central Florida LLC						
4305 Vineland Rd., Ste G-12	Orlando	FL	32811	**800-900-8324**		182
Tech International						
200 E Coshocton St	Johnstown	OH	43031	**800-336-8324**	740-967-9015	752
Tech Lighting LLC						
7400 Linda Ave	Skokie	IL	60077	**800-522-5315**	847-410-4400	439
Tech Museum of Innovation						
201 S Market St	San Jose	CA	95113	**800-660-4287**	408-294-8324	519
Tech Packaging Inc						
13241 Bartram Pk Blvd Ste 601	Jacksonville	FL	32258	**866-453-8324**	904-288-6403	548
Tech Usa Inc						
8334 Veterans Hwy	Millersville	MD	21108	**888-584-8181**	410-729-4328	196
Tech West Vacuum Inc						
2625 N Argyle Ave	Fresno	CA	93727	**800-428-7139**	559-291-1650	474
Tech4Learning Inc						
10981 San Diego Mission Rd Ste 120	San Diego	CA	92108	**877-834-5453**	619-563-5348	458
Techalloy Company Inc Baltimore Wire Div						
2310 Chesapeake Ave	Baltimore	MD	21222	**800-638-1458**	410-633-9300	811
Techforce Inc						
3445 Breckinridge Blvd	Duluth	GA	30096	**866-837-3783**	678-597-2300	198
Techline USA LLC						
500 S Div St	Waunakee	WI	53597	**800-356-8400**	608-849-4181	320-1
Techne Corp						
614 McKinley Pl NE	Minneapolis	MN	55413	**800-343-7475**	612-379-8854	233
NASDAQ: TECH						
Techneal Inc						
2100 S Reservoir St	Pomona	CA	91766	**800-545-6325**	909-465-6325	534
Technetics Group						
3125 Damon Way	Burbank	CA	91505	**800-618-4701**	818-841-9667	607
Technical Assn of the Pulp & Paper Industry (TAPPI)						
15 Technology Pkwy S	Norcross	GA	30092	**800-332-8686***	770-446-1400	48-13
*Sales						
Technical Assurance Inc						
38112 Second St	Willoughby	OH	44094	**866-953-3147**	440-953-3147	198
Technical Chemical Co						
3327 Pipeline Rd	Cleburne	TX	76033	**800-527-0885**	817-645-6088	144
Technical Communications Corp						
100 Domino Dr	Concord	MA	01742	**800-952-4082**	978-287-5100	732
NASDAQ: TCCO						
Technical Communities Inc						
1000 Cherry Ave Ste 100	San Bruno	CA	94066	**888-665-2765**	650-624-0525	197
Technical Consumer Products Inc						
325 Campus Dr	Aurora	OH	44202	**800-324-1496**		437
Technical Gas Products Inc						
66 Leonardo Dr	North Haven	CT	06473	**800-847-0745**		578

Company	Address	City	State	ZIP	Toll-Free	Phone	Class
Technical Instrument San Francisco	1826 Rollins Rd	Burlingame	CA	94010	**866-800-9797**	650-651-3000	474
Technical Support Inc	11253 John Galt Blvd	Omaha	NE	68137	**800-337-0283**	402-331-4977	179
Technical Systems Integration Inc	816 Greenbrier Cir Ste 208	Chesapeake	VA	23320	**800-566-8744**	757-424-5793	258
Technical Toolboxes Ltd	3801 Kirby Dr Ste 520	Houston	TX	77098	**866-866-6766**	713-630-0505	179
Technical Transportation Inc	1701 W Northwest Hwy Ste 100	Grapevine	TX	76051	**800-852-8726**		448
Techni-Car Inc	450 Commerce Blvd	Oldsmar	FL	34677	**800-886-0022**	813-855-0022	61-5
Techni-Cast Corp	11220 Garfield Ave	South Gate	CA	90280	**800-923-4585**	562-923-4585	309
Technicote Westfield Inc	222 Mound Ave	Miamisburg	OH	45342	**800-358-4448**	937-859-4448	551-1
Technidrill Systems Inc	429 Portage Blvd	Kent	OH	44240	**844-313-7012**	330-678-9980	454
Techniform Industries Inc	2107 Hayes Ave	Fremont	OH	43420	**800-691-2816**	419-332-8484	598
Techni-Tool Inc	1547 N Trooper Rd PO Box 1117 *Cust Svc	Worcester	PA	19490	**800-832-4866***	610-941-2400	351
Techno-Aide Inc	7117 Centennial Blvd	Nashville	TN	37209	**800-251-2629**	615-350-7030	475
Technolab International Corp	2020 NE 163 St	Miami	FL	33162	**888-382-2851**	305-433-2973	198
Technology Advancement Group Inc	22355 Tag Way	Sterling	VA	20166	**800-824-7693**	703-406-3000	175-1
Technology Funding Inc	460 St Michael's Dr Ste 1000	Santa Fe	NM	87505	**800-821-5323**		790
Technology Futures Inc (TFI)	13740 Research Blvd (N Hwy 183) Ste C-1	Austin	TX	78750	**800-835-3887**	512-258-8898	198
Technology Integration Group (TIG)	7810 Trade St	San Diego	CA	92121	**800-858-0549**	858-566-1900	178
Technology Marketing Corp	1 Technology Plz *Cust Svc	Norwalk	CT	06854	**800-243-6002***	203-852-6800	634-2
Technology Partners	550 University Ave	Palo Alto	CA	94301	**800-747-3924**	650-289-9000	790
Technology Service Corp	962 Wayne Ave Ste 800	Silver Spring	MD	20910	**800-324-7700**	301-565-2970	666
Technomart RGA Inc	401 Washington Ave Ste 1101	Baltimore	MD	21204	**800-877-6555**	410-828-6555	401
TechnoServe	1 Mechanic St	Norwalk	CT	06854	**800-999-6757**	203-852-0377	47-5
TechServe Alliance	1420 King St Ste 610	Alexandria	VA	22314	**888-421-1442**	703-838-2050	47-9
TechSmith Corp	2405 Woodlake Dr	Okemos	MI	48864	**800-517-3001**	517-381-2300	180-8
TechTarget	275 Grove St Ste 800	Newton	MA	02466	**888-274-4111**	617-431-9200	634-10
Techware Distribution Inc	7720 W 78th St	Minneapolis	MN	55439	**800-295-0083**	952-944-0083	227
Teck Cominco American Inc	501 N Riverpoint Blvd Ste 300	Spokane	WA	99202	**866-225-0198**	509-747-6111	501
Tecnicard Inc	3191 Coral Way Ste 800	Miami	FL	33145	**800-317-6020**	305-442-0018	227
Tecnico Corp	831 Industrial Ave *General	Chesapeake	VA	23324	**800-786-2207***	757-545-4013	696
Teco Diagnostics	1268 N Lakeview Ave	Anaheim	CA	92807	**800-222-9880**	714-463-1111	233
Tecom Industries Inc	375 Conejo Ridge Ave	Thousand Oaks	CA	91361	**866-840-8550**	805-267-0100	645
Tecon Services Inc	515 Garden Oaks Blvd	Houston	TX	77018	**800-245-1728**	713-691-2700	190
TECO-Westinghouse Motor Co	5100 N IH-35	Round Rock	TX	78681	**800-451-8798**	512-255-4141	707
TECSYS Inc	1 Pl Alexis Nihon Ste 800	Montreal	QC	H3Z3B8	**800-922-8649**	514-866-0001	180-1
Tectonic Engineering & Surveying Consultants PC	70 Pleasant Hill Rd	Mountainville	NY	10953	**800-829-6531**	845-534-5959	263
Tectum Inc	105 S Sixth St	Newark	OH	43055	**888-977-9691**	740-345-9691	817
Teddy's Transportation System Inc	25 Van Zant St	Norwalk	CT	06855	**800-888-3339**	203-866-2231	441
Tedia Company Inc	1000 Tedia Way	Fairfield	OH	45014	**800-787-4891**	513-874-5340	143
Teeco Products Inc	16881 Armstrong Ave	Irvine	CA	92606	**800-854-3463**	949-261-6295	385
Teeter Irrigation Inc	2729 W Oklahoma	Ulysses	KS	67880	**800-524-5497**	620-353-1111	276
TEGAM Inc	10 Tegam Way	Geneva	OH	44041	**800-666-1010**	440-466-6100	250
TEI (Taylor Enterprises Inc)	2586 Southport Rd	Spartanburg	SC	29302	**800-922-3149**	864-573-9518	578
TEI (Tax Executives Institute)	1200 G St NW Ste 300	Washington	DC	20005	**877-244-7711**	202-638-5601	48-1
Teine Energy Ltd	2300 520 - Third Ave SW	Calgary	AB	T2P0R3	**866-900-2711**	403-698-8300	535
Tejas Logistics System	PO Box 1339	Waco	TX	76703	**800-535-9786**	254-753-0301	801-1
Tekelec	5200 Paramount Pkwy *NASDAQ: TKLC*	Morrisville	NC	27560	**800-633-0738**	919-460-5500	732
Tekla Inc	1075 Big Shanty Rd NW Ste 175	Kennesaw	GA	30144	**877-835-5265**	770-426-5105	176
Teknon Corp	15443 NE 95th St	Redmond	WA	98052	**800-338-6142**	425-895-8535	191-4
Teknor Apex Co	505 Central Ave	Pawtucket	RI	02861	**800-556-3864**	401-725-8000	604-3
Tekra Corp	16700 W Lincoln Ave	New Berlin	WI	53151	**800-448-3572**	262-784-5533	602
Tekran Instruments Corp	230 Tech Ctr Dr	Knoxville	TN	37912	**888-383-5726**	865-688-0688	419
Teksavers Inc	2120 Grand Ave Pkwy	Austin	TX	78728	**866-832-6188**	512-491-5304	182
TEKsystems Inc	7437 Race Rd	Hanover	MD	21076	**888-519-0776**	410-540-7700	719
Tekworks Inc	13000 Gregg St Ste B	Poway	CA	92064	**877-835-9675**		178
Tel Electronics Inc	313 S 740 E St Ste 1	American Fork	UT	84003	**800-748-5022**	801-756-9606	732
Tel Star Cablevison Inc	1295 Lourdes Rd	Metamora	IL	61548	**888-842-0258**	309-383-2677	115
TeL Systems	7235 Jackson Rd	Ann Arbor	MI	48103	**800-686-7235**	734-761-4506	248
Tel Tec Security Systems Inc	5020 Lisa Marie Ct	Bakersfield	CA	93313	**800-292-9227**	661-397-5511	198
TelAlaska Inc	201 E 56th St	Anchorage	AK	99518	**888-570-1792**	907-563-2003	733
Telax Voice Solutions	365 Evans Ave Ste 302	Toronto	ON	M8Z1K2	**888-808-3529**	416-207-0630	734
Telco Systems Inc	15 Berkshire Rd	Mansfield	MA	02048	**800-227-0937**	781-255-2120	732
Telcobuy com L L C	60 Weldon Pkwy	St. Louis	MO	63043	**877-350-0191**		248
Telcoe Federal Credit Union	820 Lousiana St	Little Rock	AR	72201	**800-482-9009**	501-375-5321	221
TelcoIQ	4300 Forbes Blvd Ste 110	Lanham	MD	20706	**877-835-2647**	202-595-1500	387
Telcom Corp	1499 W Palmetto Park Rd Ste 214	Boca Raton	FL	33486	**800-394-5448**	561-394-5448	462
Tele Business USA	1945 Techny Rd Ste 3	Northbrook	IL	60062	**877-315-8353**		734
Tel-e Technologies	7 Kodiak Crescent	Toronto	ON	M3J3E5	**800-661-2340**	416-631-1300	5
Telebyte Inc	355 Marcus Blvd	Hauppauge	NY	11788	**800-835-3298**	631-423-3232	178
Telecom AM	2115 Ward Ct NW	Washington	DC	20037	**800-771-9202**	202-872-9200	530-11
TeleCommunication Systems Inc	275 W St Ste 400 *NASDAQ: TSYS*	Annapolis	MD	21401	**800-810-0827**	410-263-7616	226
Tele-Communications Inc	5125 W 140th St	Brookpark	OH	44142	**877-841-8914**	216-267-0800	248
TelecomPioneers	1801 California St Ste 225	Denver	CO	80202	**800-872-5995**	303-571-1200	47-15
Telecon Inc	13 500 boul Metropolitain E	Montreal	QC	H1A3W1	**800-465-0349**	514-644-2333	188
Telect Inc	23321 E Knox Ave *Cust Svc	Liberty Lake	WA	99019	**800-551-4567***	509-926-6000	732
Teledyne Advanced Pollution Instrumentation	9480 Carroll Pk Dr	San Diego	CA	92121	**800-324-5190**	858-657-9800	203
Teledyne Brown Engineering Inc	300 Sparkman Dr	Huntsville	AL	35807	**800-933-2091**	256-726-1000	263
Teledyne Continental Motors Inc	2039 Broad St	Mobile	AL	36615	**800-718-3411**	251-438-3411	20
Teledyne Lighting & Display Products	12964 Panama St	Los Angeles	CA	90066	**800-563-4020**	310-823-5491	438
Teledyne Monitor Labs Inc (TML)	35 Inverness Dr E	Englewood	CO	80112	**800-422-1499**	303-792-3300	203
Teleflex Inc	155 S Limerick Rd *NYSE: TFX*	Limerick	PA	19468	**866-246-6990**	610-948-5100	187
Teleflex Medical	2917 Weck Dr PO Box 12600	Research Triangle Park	NC	27709	**866-246-6990**	919-544-8000	59
TeleflexGFI Control Systems LP	100 Hollinger Crescent	Kitchener	ON	N2K2Z3	**800-667-4275**	519-576-4270	59
Telegraph Herald	801 Bluff St	Dubuque	IA	52001	**800-553-4801**	563-588-5611	531-2
Telegraph, The	1675 Montpelier Ave Ste B	Macon	GA	31201	**800-342-5845**		531-2
Telegraph-Journal	210 Crown St PO Box 2350	Saint John	NB	E2L3V8	**888-295-8665**		531-1
Telelatino Network Inc (TLN)	5125 Steeles Ave W	Toronto	ON	M9L1R5	**800-551-8401**	416-744-8200	736
Tele-Measurements Inc	145 Main Ave	Clifton	NJ	07014	**800-223-0052**	973-473-8822	196
Tele-Media Corp	804 Jacksonville Rd PO Box 39	Bellefonte	PA	16823	**800-704-4254**	814-353-2025	115
Telepath Corp	49111 Milmont Dr	Fremont	CA	94538	**800-292-1700**	510-656-5600	645
Telephone & Data Systems Inc	30 N La Salle St Ste 4000 *NYSE: TDS*	Chicago	IL	60602	**877-337-1575**	312-630-1900	360-3
Telephone Doctor Inc	30 Hollenberg Ct	Bridgeton	MO	63044	**800-882-9911**	314-291-1012	198
Telephone Service Co	2 Willipie St	Wapakoneta	OH	45895	**800-743-5707**	419-739-2200	733
TeleProviders Inc	23461 Southpointe Dr Ste 185	Laguna Hills	CA	92653	**888-999-4244**		462
Telerent Leasing Corp	4191 Fayetteville Rd	Raleigh	NC	27603	**800-626-0682**	919-772-8604	37
Telerx	723 Dresher Rd	Horsham	PA	19044	**800-283-5379**	267-942-3300	734
Telesource Services LLC	1450 Highwood E	Pontiac	MI	48340	**800-525-4300**	248-335-3000	248
Telesouth Communications Inc	6311 Ridgewood Rd	Jackson	MS	39211	**888-808-8637**	601-957-1700	640
Telesta Therapeutics Inc	275 Labrosse Ave *TSE: TST*	Pointe-Claire	QC	H9R1A3	**800-387-0825**	514-697-6636	84
Telestream Inc	848 Gold Flat Rd Ste 1	Nevada City	CA	95959	**877-681-2088**	530-470-1300	180-8
TeleTech Holdings Inc	9197 S Peoria St *NASDAQ: TTEC* ■ *General	Englewood	CO	80112	**800-835-3832***	303-397-8100	734
Teletrac Inc	7391 Lincoln Way	Garden Grove	CA	92841	**800-500-6009**	714-897-0877	690
Tele-Track	5550 Peach Tree Pkwy Ste 600	Norcross	GA	30092	**800-729-6981**	770-449-8809	220

Name / Address	City	State	ZIP	Toll-Free	Phone	Class
Telex Communications Inc						
12000 Portland Ave S	Burnsville	MN	55337	**877-863-4169**	952-884-4051	51
Telexpertise Inc						
7790 E Arapahoe Rd Ste 240	Centennial	CO	80112	**877-767-6762**	720-200-0590	734
Telgian Corp						
10505 Sorrento Valley Rd Ste 450	San Diego	CA	92121	**877-835-4426**	858-795-1000	191-10
Teligent Inc						
105 Lincoln Ave	Buena	NJ	08310	**800-656-0793**		733
Telkonet Inc						
10200 W Innovation Dr Ste 300	Milwaukee	WI	53226	**888-703-9398***	414-223-0473	178
OTC: TKOI ■ *Sales						
Tellurex Corp						
1462 International Dr	Traverse City	MI	49686	**877-774-7468**	231-947-0110	694
Telonic Berkeley Inc						
1080 La Mirada Ct	Vista	CA	92081	**800-311-8805***	760-744-8350	255
*Sales						
Telpar Inc						
187 Crosby Rd Ste 100	Dover	NH	03820	**800-872-4886**	603-750-7237	175-6
TelSpan Inc						
101 W Washington St E Tower Ste 1200	Indianapolis	IN	46204	**800-800-1729**		387
Telus						
1000 Rue de Serigny	Longueuil	QC	J4K5B1	**888-709-8759**	450-928-6000	806
TELUS Quebec						
6 Rue Jules-A-Brillant	Rimouski	QC	G5L7E4	**866-558-2273**		226
Tembec Inc						
800 Boul Rene Levesque O Bureau 1050	Montreal	QC	H3B1X9	**800-565-3021**	514-871-0137	681
TSE: TMB						
Temecula Creek Inn						
44501 Rainbow Canyon Rd	Temecula	CA	92592	**877-517-1823**	855-685-9299	667
Temecula Valley Chamber of Commerce (TVCC)						
26790 Ynez Ct Ste A	Temecula	CA	92591	**866-676-5090**	951-676-5090	138
Temo Sunrooms Inc						
20400 Hall Rd	Clinton Township	MI	48038	**800-344-8366**		104
Tempco Electric Heater Corp						
607 N Central Ave	Wood Dale	IL	60191	**888-268-6396**	630-350-2252	319
Temp-Control Mechanical Corp (TCM)						
4800 N Ch Ave	Portland	OR	97217	**877-826-3828**	503-285-9851	14
Tempe Tourism Office						
222 South Mill Ave Ste 120	Tempe	AZ	85281	**866-914-1052**	480-894-8158	208
Temperature Systems Inc						
5001 Voges Rd	Madison	WI	53718	**800-366-0930**	608-271-7500	611
Temple College						
2600 S First St	Temple	TX	76504	**800-460-4636***	254-298-8300	161
*Admissions						
Temple Meridian						
4312 S 31st St	Temple	TX	76502	**855-444-7658**	254-598-4019	670
Temple University James E Beasley School of Law						
1719 N Broad St	Philadelphia	PA	19122	**800-560-1428**	215-204-7861	168-1
Temple University Press						
1852 N 10th St USB 305	Philadelphia	PA	19122	**800-621-2736**	215-926-2140	634-4
Templeton Unified School District						
960 Old County Rd	Templeton	CA	93465	**800-316-6142**	805-434-5800	683
Temporary Solutions Inc						
10550 Linden Lk Plz Ste 200	Manassas	VA	20109	**888-222-0457**	703-361-2220	719
Temptronic Corp						
41 Hampden Rd	Mansfield	MA	02048	**800-558-5080***	781-688-2300	419
*Tech Support						
Tempur-Pedic International Inc						
1713 Jaggie Fox Way	Lexington	KY	40511	**800-821-6621**		470
NYSE: TPX						
Tempus Resorts International						
7380 Sand Lake Rd Ste 600	Orlando	FL	32819	**877-747-4747**	407-226-1000	751
Ten-8 Fire Equipment Inc						
2904 59th Ave Dr E	Bradenton	FL	34203	**877-989-7660**	941-756-7779	515
TenCate Geosynthetics North America						
365 S Holland Dr	Pendergrass	GA	30567	**888-795-0808**	706-693-2226	742-3
TenCate Grass North America						
1131 Broadway St	Dayton	TN	37321	**800-251-1033**	423-775-0792	604-1
TenCate Protective Fabrics USA						
6501 Mall Blvd	Union City	GA	30291	**800-241-8630**		742-3
Tender Corp						
106 Burndy Rd	Littleton	NH	03561	**800-258-4696**	603-444-5464	282
Tenenbaum's Vacation Stores Inc						
300 Market St	Kingston	PA	18704	**800-545-7099**	570-288-8747	769
Tenenz Inc						
9655 Penn S Ave	Minneapolis	MN	55431	**800-888-5803**		626
Tengasco Inc						
11121 Kingston Pk Ste E	Knoxville	TN	37934	**888-669-0684**	865-675-1554	535
NYSE: TGC						
Tennant Co						
701 N Lilac Dr	Minneapolis	MN	55422	**800-553-8033***	763-540-1200	386
NYSE: TNC ■ *Cust Svc						
Tenneco Inc						
500 N Field Dr	Lake Forest	IL	60045	**866-839-3259**	847-482-5000	59
NYSE: TEN						
Tennessean						
1100 Broadway	Nashville	TN	37203	**800-342-8237**	615-257-0928	531-2
Tennessee						
Child Support Services Div						
400 Deaderick St 12th Fl	Nashville	TN	37248	**800-838-6911**	615-313-4880	339-43
Economic & Community Development Dept (ECD)						
312 Eigth Ave N 11th Fl	Nashville	TN	37243	**877-768-6374**	615-741-1888	339-43
Mental Health & Developmental Disabilities Dept						
425 Fifth Ave N 3rd Fl	Nashville	TN	37243	**800-669-1851**	615-532-6500	339-43
Real Estate Commission						
500 James Robertson Pkwy Ste 180	Nashville	TN	37243	**800-342-4031**	615-741-2273	339-43
Securities Div						
500 James Robertson Pkwy Ste 680	Nashville	TN	37243	**800-863-9117**	615-741-2947	339-43
State Parks Div						
401 Church St 7th Fl	Nashville	TN	37243	**888-867-2757**	615-532-0001	339-43
Supreme Court						
511 Union St Nashville City Ctr Ste 600	Nashville	TN	37219	**800-448-7970**	615-741-2687	339-43
Tennessee Aquarium						
1 Broad St	Chattanooga	TN	37402	**800-262-0695**	423-802-6768	39
Tennessee Assn of Realtors (TAR)						
901 19th Ave S	Nashville	TN	37212	**877-321-1477**	615-321-1477	654
Tennessee Baptist Convention						
5001 Maryland Way	Brentwood	TN	37027	**800-558-2090**	615-371-2029	47-20
Tennessee Bar Assn						
221 Fourth Ave N Ste 400	Nashville	TN	37219	**800-899-6993**	615-383-7421	71
Tennessee Commerce Bank						
381 Mallory Stn Rd Ste 207	Franklin	TN	37067	**877-275-3342**		69
Tennessee Farm Bureau News						
147 Bear Creek Pike	Columbia	TN	38401	**877-876-2222**	931-388-7872	456-1
Tennessee Farmers Co-op						
180 Old Nashville Hwy	La Vergne	TN	37086	**800-366-2667**	615-793-8011	278
Tennessee Fitness Spa						
299 Natural Bridge Pk Rd	Waynesboro	TN	38485	**800-235-8365**	931-722-5589	704
Tennessee Performing Arts Ctr						
505 Deaderick St	Nashville	TN	37219	**866-455-2823**	615-782-4000	571
Tennessee Rehabilitative Initiative in Correction (TRICOR)						
240 Great Cir Rd Ste 310	Nashville	TN	37228	**800-958-7426**	615-741-5705	629
Tennessee State Employees Association						
627 Woodland St	Nashville	TN	37206	**800-251-8732**	615-256-4533	532
Tennessee State Library & Archives						
403 Seventh Ave N	Nashville	TN	37243	**877-850-4959**	615-741-2764	434-5
Tennessee State Museum						
505 Deaderick St	Nashville	TN	37243	**800-407-4324**	615-741-2692	519
Tennessee State University						
3500 John A Merritt Blvd PO Box 9609	Nashville	TN	37209	**888-463-6878***	615-963-5000	167
*Admissions						
Tennessee Steel Haulers Inc						
PO Box 78189	Nashville	TN	37207	**800-776-4004**	615-271-2400	778
Tennessee Technological University						
1 William L J1s Dr	Cookeville	TN	38505	**800-255-8881**	931-372-3888	167
Tennessee Temple University						
1815 Union Ave	Chattanooga	TN	37404	**800-553-4050**	423-493-4100	167
Tennessee Titans						
460 Great Cir Rd	Nashville	TN	37228	**800-334-4628**	615-565-4000	713-3
Tennessee Valley Electric Co-op						
590 Florence Rd	Savannah	TN	38372	**866-925-4916**	731-925-4916	247
Tennessee Valley Printing Company Inc						
PO Box 2213	Decatur	AL	35609	**888-353-4612**	256-353-4612	634-8
Tennessee Veterinary Medical Assn						
PO Box 803	Fayetteville	TN	37334	**800-697-3587**	931-438-0070	793
Tennessee Wesleyan College						
204 E College St	Athens	TN	37371	**800-742-5892**	423-745-7504	167
Tennsco Corp						
201 Tennsco Dr PO Box 1888	Dickson	TN	37056	**866-446-8686***	615-446-8000	320-1
*Cust Svc						
Tenrox						
401 Congress Avenue	Austin	TX	78701	**855-944-7526**	450-688-3444	180-1
Tension Envelope Corp						
819 E 19th St	Kansas City	MO	64108	**800-388-5122**		265
Teo Technologies Inc						
11609 49th Pl W	Mukilteo	WA	98275	**800-524-0024**	425-349-1000	732
TEOCO Corp						
12150 Monument Dr Ste 400	Fairfax	VA	22033	**888-868-3626**	703-322-9200	790
Teradata Corp						
10000 Innovation Dr	Dayton	OH	45342	**866-548-8348**		227
NYSE: TDC						
Teradyne Inc Assembly Test Div						
600 Riverpark Dr	North Reading	MA	01864	**800-837-2396**	978-370-2700	250
Teradyne Inc Industrial/Consumer Div						
600 Riverpark Dr	North Reading	MA	01864	**800-837-2396**	978-370-2700	250
TeraGo Networks Inc						
55 Commerce Vly Dr W Ste 800	Thornhill	ON	L3T7V9	**866-837-2461**		226
Teragren Fine Bamboo Flooring Panels & Veneer						
12715 Miller Rd Ne Ste 301	Bainbridge Island	WA	98110	**800-929-6333**	206-842-9477	292
TeraMach Technologies Inc						
1130 Morrison Dr Ste 105	Ottawa	ON	K2H9N6	**877-226-6549**	613-226-7775	182
TERATECH Corp						
77-79 Terr Hall Ave	Burlington	MA	01803	**866-837-2766**	781-270-4143	475
Terex Corp Crane Div						
202 Raleigh St	Wilmington	NC	28412	**877-794-5284**	910-395-8500	469
Terex-Telelect Inc						
500 Oakwood Rd PO Box 1150	Watertown	SD	57201	**800-982-8975**	605-882-4000	469
Terlato Wine Group, The (TWG)						
900 Armour Dr	Lake Bluff	IL	60044	**800-950-7676**	847-604-8900	80-3
Terminal Corp, The						
2001 E McComas St Ste A	Baltimore	MD	21224	**800-560-7207**		312
Terminix International Company LP						
860 Ridge Lk Blvd	Memphis	TN	38120	**855-212-6399**	866-399-0453	576
Termo Co, The						
3275 Cherry Ave	Long Beach	CA	90807	**888-260-4715**		535
TernPro Inc						
1431 Washington Blvd Apt 1703	Detroit	MI	48226	**888-483-8779**		393
Terra Community College						
2830 Napoleon Rd	Fremont	OH	43420	**800-334-3886**	419-334-8400	161
Terra Dotta LLC						
501 W Franklin St Ste 105	Chapel Hill	NC	27516	**877-368-8277**		179
Terra Nova Steel & Iron (Ontario) Inc						
3595 Hawkestone Rd	Mississauga	ON	L5C2V1	**877-427-0269**	905-273-3872	491
Terracap Group						
100 Sheppard Ave E Ste 502	Toronto	ON	M2N6N5	**800-363-3207**	416-222-9345	527
Terraces at Phoenix, The						
7550 N 16th St	Phoenix	AZ	85020	**800-836-4281**	602-906-4024	670
Terraces of Los Gatos						
800 Blossom Hill Rd	Los Gatos	CA	95032	**800-673-1982**	408-356-1006	670
Terracon						
18001 W 106th St	Olathe	KS	66061	**800-593-7777**	913-599-6886	263
Terracor Business Solutions						
677 St Mary's Rd	Winnipeg	MB	R2M3M6	**877-942-0005**	204-477-5342	179
Terraine Inc						
5912-A Toole Dr	Nashville	TN	37230	**800-531-1242**		396
TERRAMAI						
8400 Agate Rd	White City	OR	97503	**800-220-9062**		40

Alphabetical Section

Name / Address	City	State	Zip	Toll-Free	Phone	Class
Terranea Resort & Spa						
100 Terranea Way	Rancho Palos Verdes	CA	90275	**866-547-3066**	310-265-2800	378
Terre Haute Convention & Visitors Bureau						
5353 E Margaret Dr	Terre Haute	IN	47803	**800-366-3043**		208
Terre Haute Regional Hospital (THRH)						
3901 S Seventh St	Terre Haute	IN	47802	**866-270-2311**	812-232-0021	374-3
Terre Hill Silo Company Inc						
PO Box 10	Terre Hill	PA	17581	**800-242-1509**	717-445-3100	185
Terrebonne General Medical Ctr (TGMC)						
8166 Main St	Houma	LA	70360	**888-850-6270**	985-873-4141	374-3
Terroco Industries Ltd						
Site 14 RR Ste 1 Box 10	Red Deer	AB	T4N5E1	**800-670-1100**	403-346-1171	538
Terry Laboratories Inc						
7005 Technology Dr	Melbourne	FL	32904	**800-367-2563**	321-259-1630	478
Terry Precision Bicycles for Women Inc						
47 Maple St	Burlington	VT	05401	**800-289-8379**		81
Terry Thompson Chevrolet Olds						
1402 Us Hwy 98	Daphne	AL	36526	**800-287-9309**	251-626-0631	56
Terry's Tire Town Inc						
2360 W Main St PO Box 2405	Alliance	OH	44601	**800-235-2921**		753
Terryberry Co						
2033 Oak Industrial Dr NE	Grand Rapids	MI	49505	**800-253-0882**	616-458-1391	409
Terry-Durin Co						
409 Seventh Ave SE	Cedar Rapids	IA	52401	**800-332-8114**	319-364-4106	248
Terumo Cardiovascular Systems Corp						
6200 Jackson Rd	Ann Arbor	MI	48103	**800-262-3304**	734-663-4145	475
Terumo Medical Corp						
2101 Cottontail Ln	Somerset	NJ	08873	**800-283-7866**	732-302-4900	475
TES (Total Energy Solutions LLC)						
100 International Dr Ste 260	Portsmouth	NH	03801	**877-436-9812**		112
Tesa Tape Inc						
5825 Carnegie Blvd	Charlotte	NC	28209	**800-426-2181**	704-554-0707	729
Tesco Industries LP						
1035 E Hacienda	Bellville	TX	77418	**800-699-5824**		320-3
Tesko Welding & Manufacturing Co						
7350 W Montrose Ave	Norridge	IL	60706	**800-621-4514**	708-452-0045	288
Tesla Motors Inc						
3500 Deer Creek Rd	Palo Alto	CA	94304	**888-518-3752**	650-681-5000	58
TESOL (Teachers of English to Speakers of Other Languages)						
700 S Washington St Ste 200	Alexandria	VA	22314	**888-547-3369**	703-836-0774	48-5
Tesoro Corp						
1225 17th St	Denver	CO	80202	**800-299-0570**		578
TESSCO Technologies Inc						
11126 McCormick Rd	Hunt Valley	MD	21031	**800-472-7373**	410-229-1000	248
NASDAQ: TESS						
Test com Inc						
1501 Euclid Ave Ste 407	Cleveland	OH	44115	**877-502-8600**		524
Test Mark Industries Inc						
995 N Market St	East Palestine	OH	44413	**800-783-3227**	330-426-2200	192
TestAmerica Laboratories Inc						
4625 E Cotton Ctr Blvd Ste 189	Phoenix	AZ	85040	**866-785-5227**	602-437-3340	740
Testcountry						
6310 Nancy Ridge Dr Ste 103	San Diego	CA	92121	**866-237-7976**	858-784-6904	740
Testing Machines Inc						
40 McCullough Dr	New Castle	DE	19720	**800-678-3221***	302-613-5600	471
*General						
Testor Corp						
440 Blackhawk Pk Ave	Rockford	IL	61104	**800-837-8677**	815-962-6654	760
Teters Floral Products Inc						
1425 S Lillian Ave	Bolivar	MO	65613	**800-999-5996**	417-326-7654	295
Teton County Public Library						
125 Virginian Ln	Jackson	WY	83001	**800-878-2167**	307-733-2164	434-3
Teton Mountain Lodge & Spa						
3385 Cody Ln	Teton Village	WY	83025	**800-631-6271**	307-201-6066	379
Tetra Corporate Services LLC						
6995 Union Park Ctr						
Ste 360	Salt Lake City	UT	84047	**800-417-0548**	801-566-2600	266-3
Tetra Medical Supply Corp						
6364 W Gross Pt Rd	Niles	IL	60714	**800-621-4041***	847-647-0590	474
*Cust Svc						
Tetra Tech Architects & Engineers						
Cornell Business & Technology Park 10 Brown Rd						
	Ithaca	NY	14850	**877-882-7241**	607-277-7100	393
TETRA Technologies Inc						
25025 I-45 N	The Woodlands	TX	77380	**800-327-7817**	281-367-1983	142
NYSE: TTI						
Tetrahedron Assoc Inc						
PO Box 710157	San Diego	CA	92171	**800-958-3872**	619-661-0552	455
Tetrault Insurance Agency Inc						
4317 Acushnet Ave	New Bedford	MA	02745	**800-696-9991**	508-995-8365	390
Tettegouche State Park						
5702 Hwy 61	Silver Bay	MN	55614	**800-366-8917**	218-226-6365	564
Teva Pharmaceutical USA						
1090 Horsham Rd	North Wales	PA	19454	**800-545-8800**	215-591-3000	583
NYSE: TEVA						
Teva Sport Sandals						
123 N Leroux St	Flagstaff	AZ	86001	**800-367-8382***	928-779-5938	302
*General						
Tevet LLC						
85 Spring St S	Mosheim	TN	37818	**866-886-8527**	678-905-1300	203
Texans Credit Union						
777 E Campbell Rd	Richardson	TX	75081	**800-843-5295**	972-348-2000	221
Texarkana Chamber of Commerce						
819 N State Line Ave	Texarkana	TX	75501	**877-275-5289**	903-792-7191	138
Texarkana College						
2500 N Robison Rd	Texarkana	TX	75599	**877-275-4377**	903-838-4541	161
Texarkana Gazette						
315 Pine St	Texarkana	TX	75501	**888-784-4747***	903-794-3311	531-2
*General						
Texas						
Aging & Disability Services						
701 W 51st St Ste W253	Austin	TX	78751	**888-388-6332**	512-438-3011	339-44
Agriculture Dept						
PO Box 12847	Austin	TX	78711	**800-835-5832***	512-463-7476	339-44
*Cust Svc						
Arts Commission						
920 Colorado Ste 501						
PO Box 13406	Austin	TX	78701	**800-252-9415**	512-463-5535	339-44

Name / Address	City	State	Zip	Toll-Free	Phone	Class
Banking Dept						
2601 N Lamar Blvd	Austin	TX	78705	**877-276-5554**	512-475-1300	339-44
Child Support Div						
300 W 15th St	Austin	TX	78701	**800-252-8014**	512-460-6000	339-44
Comptroller of Public Accounts						
111 E 17th St	Austin	TX	78774	**800-531-5441**	512-463-4600	339-44
Consumer Protection Div						
PO Box 12548	Austin	TX	78711	**800-621-0508***		339-44
*General						
Crime Victims Services Div						
PO Box 12198	Austin	TX	78711	**800-983-9933**	512-936-1200	339-44
Environmental Quality Commission (TCEQ)						
12100 Pk 35 Cir PO Box 13087	Austin	TX	78711	**800-735-2989**	512-239-1000	339-44
General Land Office						
1700 N Congress Ave Ste 935	Austin	TX	78701	**800-998-4456**	512-463-5001	339-44
Governor PO Box 12428	Austin	TX	78711	**800-843-5789**	512-463-2000	339-44
Insurance Dept						
333 Guadalupe St PO Box 149104	Austin	TX	78714	**800-252-3439**	512-463-6169	339-44
Medical Board						
PO Box 2018	Austin	TX	78768	**800-248-4062***	512-305-7010	339-44
*Cust Svc						
Motor Vehicle Div						
4000 Jackson Ave PO Box 2293	Austin	TX	78731	**888-368-4689**		339-44
Parks & Wildlife Dept						
4200 Smith School Rd	Austin	TX	78744	**800-792-1112**	512-389-4800	339-44
Public Utility Commission						
PO Box 13326	Austin	TX	78711	**888-782-8477**	512-936-7000	339-44
Railroad Commission						
PO Box 12967	Austin	TX	78711	**877-228-5740**	512-463-7131	339-44
State Government Information						
1501 N Congress Ste 4224	Austin	TX	78711	**877-452-9060**	512-936-9500	339-44
Veterans Commission						
PO Box 12277	Austin	TX	78711	**800-252-8387**	512-463-5538	339-44
Vital Statistics Bureau						
1100 W 49th St PO Box 12040	Austin	TX	78756	**888-963-7111**		339-44
Workers Compensation Commission						
7551 Metro Ctr Dr	Austin	TX	78744	**800-252-7031***	512-804-4000	339-44
*Cust Svc						
Texas A & M International University						
5201 University Blvd	Laredo	TX	78041	**888-489-2648**	956-326-2001	167
Texas A & M University						
Rudder Tower Ste 205	College Station	TX	77843	**888-890-5667**	979-845-8901	167
Texas A & M University						
Galveston						
200 Seawolf Pkwy Bldg 3026	Galveston	TX	77553	**877-322-4443**	409-740-4428	167
Kingsville						
700 University Blvd MSC 128	Kingsville	TX	78363	**800-726-8192**	361-593-2111	167
Texarkana						
7101 University Ave	Texarkana	TX	75503	**866-791-9120**	903-223-3000	167
Texas A & M University Press						
John H Lindsey Bldg 4354 TAMU						
	College Station	TX	77843	**800-826-8911***	979-845-1436	634-4
*Orders						
Texas Art Supply						
2001 Montrose Blvd	Houston	TX	77006	**800-888-9278**	713-526-5221	44
Texas Assn of Realtors						
1115 San Jacinto Blvd Ste 200	Austin	TX	78701	**800-873-9155**	512-480-8200	654
Texas Bar Journal						
1414 Colorado St Ste 902	Austin	TX	78701	**800-204-2222**	512-463-1463	456-15
Texas Basket Co						
100 Myrtle Dr	Jacksonville	TX	75766	**800-657-2200**	903-586-8014	202
Texas Book Festival						
610 Brazos St Ste 200	Austin	TX	78701	**800-222-8733**	512-477-4055	283
Texas Capital Bank						
2000 McKinney Ave Ste 700	Dallas	TX	75201	**877-839-2265**	214-932-6600	69
Texas Children's Hospital						
6621 Fannin St	Houston	TX	77030	**800-364-5437**	832-824-1000	374-1
Texas Christian University						
TCU PO Box 297043	Fort Worth	TX	76129	**800-828-3764**	817-257-7490	167
Texas Christian University Mary Couts Burnett Library						
2800 S University Dr	Fort Worth	TX	76129	**866-321-7428**	817-257-7000	434-6
Texas City-La Marque Chamber of Commerce						
9702 Emmett F Lowry Expy	Texas City	TX	77591	**877-986-8719***	409-935-1408	138
*General						
Texas Coffee Co Inc						
3297 S M L King Jr Pkwy	Beaumont	TX	77705	**800-259-3400**	409-835-3434	297-7
Texas College						
2404 N Grand Ave	Tyler	TX	75702	**800-306-6299**	903-593-8311	167
Texas Crushed Stone Co						
5300 S IH-35 PO Box 1000	Georgetown	TX	78627	**800-772-8272**	512-930-0106	502-5
Texas Ctr for Infectious Diseases						
2303 SE Military Dr	San Antonio	TX	78223	**800-839-5864**	210-534-8857	374-7
Texas Dental Assn						
1946 S IH-35 Ste 400	Austin	TX	78704	**800-832-1145**	512-443-3675	229
Texas Disposal Systems Inc (TDS)						
12200 Carl Rd	Creedmoor	TX	78610	**800-375-8375**	512-421-1300	802
Texas Dow Employees Credit Union (TDECU)						
1001 FM 2004	Lake Jackson	TX	77566	**800-839-1154**	979-297-1154	221
Texas Electric Co-ops Inc						
1122 Colorado St 24th Fl	Austin	TX	78701	**800-301-2860**	512-454-0311	247
Texas Enterprises Inc						
5005 E Seventh St	Austin	TX	78702	**800-545-4412**	512-385-2167	578
Texas Farm Bureau						
7420 Fish Pond Rd PO Box 2689	Waco	TX	76710	**800-488-7872**	254-772-3030	456-1
Texas Farm Products Co						
915 S Fredonia St	Nacogdoches	TX	75964	**800-392-3110**	936-564-3711	577
Texas Health Resources						
612 E. Lamar Blvd Ste 900	Arlington	TX	76011	**877-847-9355**		353
Texas Healthcare PLLC						
2821 Lackland Rd Ste 300	Fort Worth	TX	76116	**877-238-6200**	817-378-3640	374-3
Texas Heat Treating Inc						
155 Texas Ave	Round Rock	TX	78664	**800-580-5884**	512-255-5884	483
Texas Hospital Insurance Exchange						
8310 N Capital of Texas Hwy						
Ste 250	Austin	TX	78731	**800-792-0060**	512-451-5775	391-5
Texas Instruments Inc						
12500 TI Blvd	Dallas	TX	75243	**800-336-5236***	972-995-3773	694
NASDAQ: TXN ■ *Cust Svc						

Name / Address	City	State	Zip	Toll-Free	Phone	Class
Texas Land & Cattle Steak House 9911 W IH- 10	San Antonio	TX	78230	**855-685-1622**	210-699-8744	669
Texas Lawyers Insurance Exchange (TLIE) 1801 S MoPac Ste 300	Austin	TX	78746	**800-252-9332**	512-480-9074	391-5
Texas Legal Services Center Inc 815 Brazos St Ste 1100	Austin	TX	78701	**888-343-4414**	512-477-6000	428
Texas Life Insurance Co 900 Washington PO Box 830	Waco	TX	76703	**800-283-9233**	254-752-6521	391-2
Texas Lime Co 15865 Farm Rd 1434 PO Box 851	Cleburne	TX	76033	**800-772-8000**	817-641-4433	440
Texas Lutheran University 1000 W Ct St	Seguin	TX	78155	**800-771-8521**	830-372-8050	167
Texas Medical Assn 401 W 15th St	Austin	TX	78701	**800-880-1300**	512-370-1300	473
Texas Memorial Museum 2400 Trinity St	Austin	TX	78705	**800-687-4132**	512-471-1604	519
Texas Methodist Foundation 11709 Boulder Ln Ste 100	Austin	TX	78726	**800-933-5502**	512-331-9971	306
Texas Motorplex 7500 W Hwy 287	Ennis	TX	75119	**800-668-6775**	972-878-2641	514
Texas Mutual Insurance Co 6210 E Hwy 290	Austin	TX	78723	**888-532-5246**	512-224-3800	391-4
Texas Orthopedic Hospital 7401 Main St	Houston	TX	77030	**866-783-4549**	713-799-8600	374-7
Texas Pacific Land Trust 1700 Pacific Ave Ste 2770 *NYSE: TPL*	Dallas	TX	75201	**877-231-7500**	214-969-5530	673
Texas Pharmacy Assn 12007 Research Blvd Ste 201	Austin	TX	78759	**800-505-5463**	512-836-8350	584
Texas Pipe & Supply Co Inc 2330 Holmes Rd	Houston	TX	77051	**800-233-8736**	713-799-9235	491
Texas Pneumatics Systems Inc 2404 Superior Dr	Arlington	TX	76013	**800-211-9690**	817-794-0068	20
Texas Presbyterian Foundation 6100 Colwell Blvd Ste 250	Irving	TX	75039	**800-955-3155**	214-522-3155	47-20
Texas Process Equipment Co 5215 Ted St	Houston	TX	77040	**800-828-4114**	713-460-5555	385
Texas Public Radio (TPR) 8401 Datapoint Dr Ste 800	San Antonio	TX	78229	**800-622-8977**	210-614-8977	629
Texas Rangers Rangers Ballpark in Arlington 1000 Ballpark Way	Arlington	TX	76011	**866-800-1275**	817-273-5222	711
Texas Refinery Corp 840 N Main St	Fort Worth	TX	76164	**800-827-0711**	817-332-1161	540
Texas Republican Party 1108 Lavaca Ste 500	Austin	TX	78701	**800-525-5555**	512-477-9821	615-2
Texas Roadhouse Inc 6040 Dutchmans Ln Ste 400 *NASDAQ: TXRH*	Louisville	KY	40205	**800-839-7623**	502-426-9984	668
Texas Scottish Rite Hospital for Children 2222 Welborn St	Dallas	TX	75219	**800-421-1121**	214-559-5000	374-1
Texas Southern University 3100 Cleburne St	Houston	TX	77004	**800-252-5400**	713-313-7011	167
Texas Sports Hall of Fame 1108 S University Parks Dr	Waco	TX	76706	**800-567-9561**	254-756-1633	521
Texas Star Bank 177 E Jefferson PO Box 608	Van Alstyne	TX	75495	**866-546-8273**	903-482-5234	69
Texas State Aquarium 2710 N Shoreline Blvd *General	Corpus Christi	TX	78402	**800-477-4853***	361-881-1200	39
Texas State Cemetery 909 Navasota St	Austin	TX	78702	**877-673-6839**	512-463-0605	49-3
Texas State Technical College (TSTC) *Abilene* 650 E Hwy 80	Abilene	TX	79601	**800-852-8784**	325-672-7091	161
Waco 3801 Campus Dr	Waco	TX	76705	**800-792-8784**	254-799-3611	161
Texas State University *San Marcos* 601 University Dr *Admissions	San Marcos	TX	78666	**866-294-0987***	512-245-2340	167
Texas Station Gambling Hall & Hotel 2101 Texas Star Ln *Resv	North Las Vegas	NV	89032	**800-654-8888***	702-631-1000	132
Texas Tech University PO Box 45005	Lubbock	TX	79409	**888-270-3369**	806-742-1480	167
Texas Tech University Libraries 18th & Boston Ave PO Box 40002	Lubbock	TX	79409	**888-270-3369**	806-742-2265	434-6
Texas Tech University Press 2903 Fourth St	Lubbock	TX	79409	**800-832-4042**	806-742-2982	634-4
Texas Transplant Institute 7700 Floyd Curl Dr	San Antonio	TX	78229	**800-298-7824**	210-575-3817	767
Texas United Corp 4800 San Felipe	Houston	TX	77056	**800-554-8658**	713-877-2600	142
Texas United Pipe Inc 11627 N Houston Rosslyn Rd *Sales	Houston	TX	77086	**800-966-8741***	281-448-3276	595
Texas Vet Lab Inc 1702 N Bell St	San Angelo	TX	76903	**800-284-8403**		581
Texas Veterinary Medical Assn 8104 Exchange Dr	Austin	TX	78754	**800-711-0023**	512-452-4224	793
Texas Wesleyan University 1201 Wesleyan St	Fort Worth	TX	76105	**800-580-8980**	817-531-4444	167
Texas Wesleyan University School of Law 1515 Commerce St	Fort Worth	TX	76102	**800-733-9529**	817-212-4000	168-1
Texas Woman's University 304 Admin Dr PO Box 425589	Denton	TX	76204	**866-809-6130**	940-898-3188	167
Texas-New Mexico Power Co (TNMP) 577 N Garden Ridge Blvd	Lewisville	TX	75067	**888-866-7456**	972-420-4189	785
Texford Battery Co 2002 Milby St	Houston	TX	77003	**866-301-0125**	713-222-0125	709
Textile Care Services Inc 225 Wood Lk Dr SE	Rochester	MN	55904	**800-422-0945**		442
Textile Rental Services Assn (TRSA) 1800 Diagonal Rd Ste 200	Alexandria	VA	22314	**877-770-9274**	703-519-0029	48-4
Textile Rubber & Chemical Company Inc 1300 Tiarco Dr SW	Dalton	GA	30721	**800-727-8453**	706-277-1300	604-3
Tex-Tube Co 1503 N Post Oak Rd	Houston	TX	77055	**800-839-7473**	713-686-4351	489
Textured Coatings Of America 2422 E 15th St	Panama City	FL	32405	**800-454-0340**	850-769-0347	549
TF Kinnealey & Company Inc 1100 Pearl St	Brockton	MA	02301	**800-225-4950**	508-638-7700	297-26
TF System The Vertical ICF Inc 3030c Holmgren Way	Green Bay	WI	54304	**800-360-4634**	920-983-9960	695
TFB (Fauquier Bank, The) 10 Courthouse Sq PO Box 561	Warrenton	VA	20186	**800-638-3798**	540-347-2700	69
TFC (Franchise Co, The) 5399 Eglinton Ave W Ste 110	Etobicoke	ON	M9C5K9	**800-294-5591**	416-620-3960	462
TFC USA 150 Shoreline Dr	Redwood City	CA	94065	**800-345-2465**	650-508-6000	736
TFCU (Teachers Federal Credit Union) 2410 N Ocean Ave	Farmingville	NY	11738	**800-341-4333**	631-698-7000	221
TFI (Technology Futures Inc) 13740 Research Blvd (N Hwy 183) Ste C-1	Austin	TX	78750	**800-835-3887**	512-258-8898	198
Tforce Energy Services 6143 S Willow Ste 320	Greenwood Village	CO	80111	**877-234-1444**		683
TFS Capital LLC 10 N High St Ste 500	West Chester	PA	19380	**888-837-4446**		527
TFT (Trees for Tomorrow) 519 Sheridan St E PO Box 609	Eagle River	WI	54521	**800-838-9472**	715-479-6456	48-5
TFX Medical Inc 50 Plantation Dr	Jaffrey	NH	03452	**800-548-6600**	603-532-7706	475
TGC Industries Inc 101 E Pk Blvd Ste 955 *NASDAQ: TGE*	Plano	TX	75074	**800-223-7470**	972-881-1099	537
Tgi Direct 5365 Hill 23 Dr	Flint	MI	48507	**800-337-2237**		5
TGMC (Terrebonne General Medical Ctr) 8166 Main St	Houma	LA	70360	**888-850-6270**	985-873-4141	374-3
TH Properties 345 Main St *Sales	Harleysville	PA	19438	**800-225-5847***	215-513-4270	189
Thaddeus Stevens College of Technology (TSCT) 750 E King St	Lancaster	PA	17602	**800-842-3832**	717-299-7701	798
Thai Airways International Ltd 222 N Sepulveda Blvd Ste 100	El Segundo	CA	90245	**800-426-5204**	310-640-0097	25
Thales Communications Inc 22605 Gateway Ctr Dr	Clarksburg	MD	20871	**800-258-4420**	240-864-7000	645
Thales e-Security Inc 2200 N Commerce Pkwy Ste 200	Weston	FL	33326	**888-744-4976**	954-888-6200	180-12
Thayer Hotel 674 Thayer Rd	West Point	NY	10996	**800-247-5047**	845-446-4731	379
Thayer Scale Corp 91 Schoosett St	Pembroke	MA	02359	**855-784-2937**	781-826-8101	682
Thayers Natural Pharmaceuticals Inc PO Box 56	Westport	CT	06881	**888-842-9371**		797
Theatre Development Fund 1501 Broadway 21st Fl	New York	NY	10036	**888-424-4685**	212-221-0885	748
Theatre For A New Audience 154 Christopher St Ste 3D	New York	NY	10014	**866-811-4111**	212-229-2819	746
Theda Care at Home 3000 E College Ave	Appleton	WI	54915	**800-984-5554**	920-969-0919	371
Theda Clark Medical Ctr 130 Second St	Neenah	WI	54956	**800-236-3122**	920-729-3100	374-3
Themisonline Com Inc 11150 Commerce Dr N	Champlin	MN	55316	**866-657-6654**	763-576-8286	650
Theodore Presser Co 588 N Gulph Rd	King of Prussia	PA	19406	**800-854-6764**	610-592-1222	634-7
Theprinters.com 3500 E College Ave	State College	PA	16801	**800-359-2097**	814-237-7600	344
TheraCare 116 W 32nd St 8th Fl	New York	NY	10001	**800-505-7000**	212-564-2350	353
Therapedic International 1375 Jersey Ave	North Brunswick	NJ	08902	**800-233-7467**		470
Theriault's PO Box 151	Annapolis	MD	21404	**800-966-3655**	410-224-3655	50
Therm Air Sales Corp 1413 41st Stn	Fargo	ND	58102	**800-726-7520**	701-282-9500	611
Thermafiber Inc 3711 W Mill St	Wabash	IN	46992	**888-834-2371**	260-563-2111	389
Thermal Care Inc 7720 N Lehigh Ave	Niles	IL	60714	**888-828-7387**	847-966-2260	14
Thermal Circuits Inc 1 Technology Way	Salem	MA	01970	**800-808-4328**	978-745-1162	319
Thermal Corp 1264 Slaughter Rd	Madison	AL	35758	**800-633-2962**	256-837-1122	611
Thermal Dynamics Corp 82 Benning St	West Lebanon	NH	03784	**800-752-7621**	603-298-5711	454
Thermal Engineering Corp 2741 The Blvd	Columbia	SC	29209	**800-331-0097**	803-783-0750	319
Thermal Engineering of Arizona Inc 2250 W Wetmore Rd	Tucson	AZ	85705	**866-832-7278**	520-888-4000	427
Thermal Industries Inc 3700 Haney C	Murrysville	PA	15668	**800-245-1540**	724-733-3880	237
Thermal Product Solutions 2821 Old Rt 15 PO Box 150	New Columbia	PA	17856	**800-586-2473**	570-538-7200	420
Thermal Solutions LLC PO Box 3244	Lancaster	PA	17604	**800-860-5726**	717-239-7642	357
Therma-Tru Corp 1750 Indian Wood Cir	Maumee	OH	43537	**800-537-8827**	419-891-7400	236
Thermedx LLC 31200 Solon Rd Unit 1	Solon	OH	44139	**888-542-9276**	440-542-0883	474
Thermionics Laboratory 1842 Sabre St	Hayward	CA	94545	**800-962-2310**	510-538-3304	174
Thermo Fisher Scientific Inc 81 Wyman St *NYSE: TMO*	Waltham	MA	02454	**800-678-5599**	781-622-1000	471
Thermo Fluids Inc 4301 W Jefferson St	Phoenix	AZ	85043	**800-350-7565**	602-272-2400	684
Thermo Scientific 12076 Santa Fe Dr PO Box 14428	Lenexa	KS	66215	**800-255-6730**	913-888-0939	233
Thermo Spas Inc 155 E St	Wallingford	CT	06492	**800-876-0158**		375
Thermodyn Corp 3550 Silica Rd	Sylvania	OH	43560	**800-654-6518**	419-841-7782	675

Name / Address	City	State	ZIP	Toll-Free	Phone	Class
Thermodynetics Inc 651 Day Hill Rd; *OTC: TDYT*	Windsor	CT	06095	**800-394-1633**	860-683-2005	90
ThermoElectric Cooling America Corp 4048 W Schubert Ave	Chicago	IL	60639	**888-832-2872**	773-342-4900	14
Thermo-Fab Corp 76 Walker Rd	Shirley	MA	01464	**888-494-9777**	978-425-2311	601
ThermoGenesis Corp 2711 Citrus Rd; *NASDAQ: KOOL*	Rancho Cordova	CA	95742	**800-783-8357**	916-858-5100	420
Thermopatch Corp 2204 Erie Blvd E	Syracuse	NY	13224	**800-252-6555**	315-446-8110	741
Thermoplastic Processes Inc 1268 Valley Rd	Stirling	NJ	07980	**888-554-6400**	908-561-3000	599
Thermos Co 475 N Martingale Rd Ste 1100	Schaumburg	IL	60173	**800-243-0745**	847-439-7821	606
ThermoSafe Brands 3930 N Ventura Dr Ste 450	Arlington Heights	IL	60004	**800-323-7442**	847-398-0110	600
ThermoServ 3901 Pipestone Rd	Dallas	TX	75212	**800-635-5559**	214-631-0307	600
Thermosoft International Corp 701 corporate Woods Pkwy	Vernon Hills	IL	60061	**800-308-8057**	847-279-3800	318
Thermotron Industries Co 291 Kollen Pk Dr	Holland	MI	49423	**800-409-3449**	616-393-4580	386
Thermo-Twin Industries Inc 1155 Allegheny Ave	Oakmont	PA	15139	**800-641-2211**	412-826-1000	236
Thermwell Products Co 420 Rt 17 S	Mahwah	NJ	07430	**800-526-5265**	201-684-4400	389
Thermwood Corp 904 Buffaloville Rd; *OTC: TOOD* ■ *Mktg	Dale	IN	47523	**800-533-6901***	812-937-4476	819
Thern Inc 5712 Industrial Pk Rd PO Box 347	Winona	MN	55987	**800-843-7648**	507-454-2996	469
TheStreet.com Inc 14 Wall St 15th Fl; *NASDAQ: TST*	New York	NY	10005	**800-562-9571**	212-321-5000	404
Theta Delta Chi Inc 214 Lewis Wharf	Boston	MA	02110	**800-999-1847**	617-742-8886	47-16
Theta Tau Professional Engineering Fraternity 1011 San Jacinto Ste 205	Austin	TX	78701	**800-264-1904**	512-472-1904	47-16
Thetford Corp 7101 Jackson Ave PO Box 1285	Ann Arbor	MI	48106	**800-521-3032**	734-769-6000	609
Thetford Corp Recreational Vehicle Group 2901 E Bristol St Ste B	Elkhart	IN	46514	**800-831-1076**	574-266-7980	609
Thetubestore Inc 120 Lancing Dr	Hamilton	ON	L8W3A1	**877-570-0979**	905-570-0979	318
Thibaut Inc 480 Frelinghuysen Ave	Newark	NJ	07114	**800-223-0704**	973-643-1118	800
Thibodaux Regional Medical Ctr (TRMC) 602 N Acadia Rd	Thibodaux	LA	70301	**800-822-8442**	985-447-5500	374-3
Thief River Falls Convention & Visitors Bureau (TRFCVB) 102 Main Ave N	Thief River	MN	56701	**800-657-3700**	218-686-9785	208
Thiel College 75 College Ave	Greenville	PA	16125	**800-248-4435**	724-589-2000	167
Thiele Technologies 315 27th Ave NE	Minneapolis	MN	55418	**800-932-3647**	612-782-1200	546
Think Computer Corp 3260 Hillview Ave	Palo Alto	CA	94304	**888-815-8599**	415-670-9350	176
thinkASG 15265 Alton Pkwy Ste 300	Irvine	CA	92618	**800-991-9274**		198
ThinkTV 110 S Jefferson St	Dayton	OH	45402	**800-247-1614**	937-220-1600	629
Third Federal Savings & Loan Assn of Cleveland 7007 Broadway Ave	Cleveland	OH	44105	**888-844-7333**	216-429-5228	69
Third Millennium Ministries 316 Live Oaks Blvd	Casselberry	FL	32707	**877-443-6455**	407-830-0222	47-20
Thirstystone Resources Inc 1304 Corporate Dr	Gainesville	TX	76240	**800-829-6888**	940-668-6793	294
This Week Community Newspapers 7801 N Central Dr PO Box 608	Lewis Center	OH	43035	**800-860-1267**	740-888-6000	634-8
Thistledown Racing Club Inc 21501 Emery Rd	Cleveland	OH	44128	**800-522-4700**	216-662-8600	639
Thobe Group Inc 2727 Raintree Dr	Carrollton	TX	75006	**888-462-3477**	972-418-1163	197
Thomas Aquinas College 10000 Ojai Rd	Santa Paula	CA	93060	**800-634-9797**	805-525-4417	167
Thomas B Finan Ctr 10102 Country Club Rd SE PO Box 1722	Cumberland	MD	21502	**888-854-0035**	301-777-2405	374-5
Thomas C Wilson Inc 21-11 44th Ave	Long Island	NY	11101	**800-230-2636**	718-729-3360	757
Thomas College 180 W River Rd; *Admissions	Waterville	ME	04901	**800-339-7001***	207-859-1111	167
Thomas Conveyor Co 555 N Burleson Blvd	Burleson	TX	76028	**800-433-2217**	817-295-7151	209
Thomas Creative Apparel Inc 1 Harmony Pl	New London	OH	44851	**800-537-2575**	419-929-1506	154-13
Thomas E Creek Veterans Affairs Medical Ctr 6010 Amarillo Blvd W	Amarillo	TX	79106	**800-687-8262**	806-355-9703	374-8
Thomas Edison State College 101 W State St	Trenton	NJ	08608	**888-442-8372**		167
Thomas Engineering Inc 575 W Central Rd	Hoffman Estates	IL	60192	**800-634-9910**	847-358-5800	386
Thomas G Faria Corp 385 Norwich-New London Tpke	Uncasville	CT	06382	**800-473-2742**	860-848-9271	494
Thomas H Lee Partners 100 Federal St	Boston	MA	02110	**877-456-3427**	617-227-1050	405
Thomas Hospital 750 Morphy Ave	Fairhope	AL	36532	**800-422-2027**	251-928-2375	374-3
Thomas Jefferson Memorial c/o National Capital Parks - Central 900 Ohio Dr SW	Washington	DC	20024	**866-705-5711**	202-426-6841	563
Thomas Jefferson School of Law 1155 Island Ave	San Diego	CA	92101	**877-318-6901**	619-297-9700	168-1
Thomas Jefferson University 1020 Walnut St	Philadelphia	PA	19107	**800-533-3669**	215-955-6000	167
Thomas Jefferson University Hospital 111 S 11th St	Philadelphia	PA	19107	**800-533-3669**	215-955-6000	374-3
Thomas M Cooley Law School 300 S Capitol Ave	Lansing	MI	48933	**800-243-2586**	517-371-5140	168-1
Thomas More College 333 Thomas More Pkwy	Crestview Hills	KY	41017	**800-825-4557**	859-344-3332	167
Thomas Nelson Inc 501 Nelson Pl PO Box 141000	Nashville	TN	37214	**800-251-4000**	615-889-9000	634-3
Thomas Publishing Co 5 Penn Plaza	New York	NY	10001	**800-733-1127**	212-695-0500	634-2
Thomas Reprographics 600 N Central Expy	Richardson	TX	75080	**800-877-3776**	972-231-7227	242
Thomas Scientific 1654 High Hill Rd PO Box 99	Swedesboro	NJ	08085	**800-345-2100**	856-467-2000	420
Thomas Transcription Services Inc PO Box 26613	Jacksonville	FL	32226	**888-878-2889**	904-751-5058	477
Thomas University 1501 Millpond Rd	Thomasville	GA	31792	**800-538-9784**	229-226-1621	167
Thomas Weisel Partners Group LLC 1 Montgomery St	San Francisco	CA	94104	**888-267-3700**	415-364-2500	790
Thomaston Savings Bank 203 Main St PO Box 907; *General	Thomaston	CT	06787	**855-344-1874***	860-283-1874	69
Thomasville Medical Ctr 207 Old Lexington Rd	Thomasville	NC	27360	**888-844-0080**	336-472-2000	374-3
Thombert Inc 316 E Seventh St N	Newton	IA	50208	**800-433-3572**		607
Thompson Hine LLP 127 Public Sq 3900 Key Ctr	Cleveland	OH	44114	**877-257-3382**	216-566-5500	428
Thompson Industrial Services LLC 104 N Main	Sumter	SC	29150	**800-849-8040**	803-773-8005	609
Thompson Olde Inc 3250 Camino Del Sol	Oxnard	CA	93030	**800-827-1565**	805-983-0388	361
Thompson Packers Inc 550 Carnation St	Slidell	LA	70460	**800-989-6328**	985-641-6640	472
Thompson Publishing Group Inc 805 15th St NW 3rd Fl; *Cust Svc	Washington	DC	20005	**800-677-3789***	202-872-4000	634-9
Thompson Pump & Mfg Company Inc 4620 City Ctr Dr PO Box 291370	Port Orange	FL	32129	**800-767-7310**	386-767-7310	638
Thompson Rivers University 900 McGill Rd PO Box 3010	Kamloops	BC	V2C5N3	**800-663-1663**	250-828-5000	783
Thompson Siegel & Walmsley Inc 6806 Paragon Pl Ste 300	Richmond	VA	23230	**800-697-1056**	804-353-4500	401
Thompson Technologies Inc 114 Townpark Dr Ste 100	Kennesaw	GA	30144	**888-794-7947**	770-794-8380	719
Thompson, Ahern & Company Ltd 6299 Airport Rd Ste 506	Mississauga	ON	L4V1N3	**877-262-8226**	905-677-3471	312
Thoms Proestler Co 8001 TPC Rd	Rock Island	IL	61204	**800-747-1234**	309-787-1234	298-8
Thomsen Group LLC 1303 43rd St	Kenosha	WI	53140	**800-558-4018**		297
Thomson CenterWatch Inc 100 N Washington St Ste 301; *Cust Svc	Boston	MA	02114	**800-765-9647***	617-948-5100	634-10
Thomson CompuMark 500 Victory Rd	North Quincy	MA	02171	**800-692-8833**	617-479-1600	632
Thomson Elite 800 Corporate Pointe Ste 150; *Cust Svc	Los Angeles	CA	90230	**800-354-8337***	424-243-2100	180-10
Thomson Financial 22 Thomson Pl	Boston	MA	02210	**888-216-1929**	617-856-2000	387
Thomson ISI ResearchSoft 2141 Palomar Airport Rd Ste 350	Carlsbad	CA	92009	**800-722-1227**	760-438-5526	196
Thomson Safaris 14 Mt Auburn St	Watertown	MA	02472	**800-235-0289**	617-923-0426	633
Thomson Tax & Acctg 7322 Newman Blvd; *Cust Svc	Dexter	MI	48130	**800-968-8900***		180-1
Thomson-Hood Veterans Ctr 100 Veterans Dr	Wilmore	KY	40390	**800-928-4838**	859-858-2814	791
Thomson-Macconnell Cadillac Inc 2820 Gilbert Ave	Cincinnati	OH	45206	**877-472-0738**	513-334-4239	515
Thor Travel Services Inc 12202 Airport Way Ste 150	Broomfield	CO	80021	**800-825-1071**	303-439-4100	770
Thoratec Corp 6035 Stoneridge Dr; *NASDAQ: THOR*	Pleasanton	CA	94588	**800-528-2577**	925-847-8600	252
Thorco Industries Inc 1300 E 12th St	Lamar	MO	64759	**800-445-3375**	417-682-3375	235
Thorlabs Quantum Electronics Inc 10335 Guilford Rd	Jessup	MD	20794	**877-226-8342**	240-456-7100	694
Thor-Lo Inc 2210 Newton Dr	Statesville	NC	28677	**888-846-7567**	704-872-6522	154-9
Thornburg Investment Management Funds 2300 N Ridgetop Rd	Santa Fe	NM	87506	**800-533-9337**	505-984-0200	527
Thorndike Press 10 Water St Ste 310	Waterville	ME	04901	**800-223-1244**		634-2
Thorneloe University 935 Ramsey Lake Rd; *General	Sudbury	ON	P3E2C6	**800-461-4030***	705-673-1730	783
Thornmark Asset Management Inc 119 Spadina Ave Ste 701	Toronto	ON	M5V2L1	**877-204-6201**	416-204-6200	195
Thornton Oil Corp 10101 Linn Stn Rd Ste 200	Louisville	KY	40223	**800-928-8022**	502-425-8022	325
Thornton W Burgess Society 6 Discovery Hill Rd	East Sandwich	MA	02537	**800-844-4542**	508-888-6870	47-13
Thoro'Bred Inc 5020 E La Palma Ave	Anaheim	CA	92807	**877-585-5152**	714-779-2581	482
Thoroughbred Direct Intermodal Services 5165 Campus Dr Ste 400	Plymouth Meeting	PA	19462	**877-250-2902**	610-567-3360	448
Thoroughbred Owners & Breeders Assn (TOBA) PO Box 910668	Lexington	KY	40591	**888-606-8622**	859-276-2291	47-3
Thoroughbred Software International Inc 285 Davidson Ave Ste 302	Somerset	NJ	08873	**800-524-0430**	732-560-1377	180-2

Name / Address	City	State	Zip	Toll-Free	Phone	Class
Thorp Reed & Armstrong LLP						
301 Grant St 14th Fl	Pittsburgh	PA	15219	**800-949-3120**	412-394-7711	428
Thorpe Heating & Cooling Inc						
8402 Us Hwy 98 N	Lakeland	FL	33809	**855-858-2577**	863-858-2577	191-10
Thought Technology Ltd						
2180 Belgrave Ave	Montreal	QC	H4A2L8	**800-361-3651**	514-489-8251	740
Thousand Hills Golf Resort						
245 S Wildwood Dr	Branson	MO	65616	**877-262-0430**	417-336-5873	667
Thousand Pines Christian Camp & Conference Center						
359 Thousnd Pines Rd	Crestline	CA	92325	**888-423-2267**	909-338-2705	241
Thread Check Inc						
390 Oser Ave	Hauppauge	NY	11788	**800-767-7633**	631-231-1515	492
Thread Logic						
16775 Greystone Ln	Jordan	MN	55352	**800-347-1612**		260
Threadpoint LLC						
24881 Alicia Pkwy						
Ste E #310	Laguna Hills	CA	92653	**866-631-1595**		396
Threads Magazine						
63 S Main St PO Box 5506	Newtown	CT	06470	**866-505-4687***	203-426-8171	456-14
*General						
Three Bars Cattle & Guest Ranch						
9500 Wycliffe Perry Creek Rd	Cranbrook	BC	V1C7C7	**877-426-5230**	250-426-5230	241
Three D Graphics Inc						
11340 W Olympic Blvd						
Ste 352	Los Angeles	CA	90064	**800-913-0008**	310-231-3330	180-8
Three Hands Corp						
13259 Ralston Ave	Sylmar	CA	91342	**800-443-5443**	818-833-1200	361
Three Island Crossing State Park						
1083 S Three Island Pk Dr	Glenns Ferry	ID	83623	**888-922-6743**	208-366-2394	564
Three Lakes Information Bureau						
1704 Superior St PO Box 268	Three Lakes	WI	54562	**800-972-6103**	715-546-3344	208
Three Notch Electric Membership Corp						
PO Box 295	Donalsonville	GA	39845	**800-239-5377**	229-524-5377	247
Three Rivers Community College						
2080 Three Rivers Blvd	Poplar Bluff	MO	63901	**877-879-8722**	573-840-9600	161
Three Rivers Electric Co-op						
1324 E Main St PO Box 918	Linn	MO	65051	**800-892-2251**	573-644-9000	247
Three Rivers Planning & Development District Inc						
75 S Main St PO Box 690	Pontotoc	MS	38863	**877-489-6911**	662-489-2415	462
Threshold Communications Inc						
16541 Redmond Way Ste 245C	Redmond	WA	98052	**844-844-1382**	206-812-6200	226
Threshold Financial Technologies Inc						
3269 American Dr	Mississauga	ON	L4V1X5	**888-414-3733**	905-678-7373	255
Threshold Pharmaceuticals Inc						
170 Harbor Way						
Ste 300	South San Francisco	CA	94080	**866-276-9886**	650-474-8200	84
NASDAQ: THLD						
THRH (Terre Haute Regional Hospital)						
3901 S Seventh St	Terre Haute	IN	47802	**866-270-2311**	812-232-0021	374-3
Thrifty Car Rental						
5330 E 31st St	Tulsa	OK	74135	**888-400-8877**	918-660-7700	125
Thrifty White Stores						
6055 Nathan Lane N Ste 200	Plymouth	MN	55442	**800-642-3275**	763-513-4300	239
Thrive Networks Inc						
836 North St Bldg 300						
Ste 3201	Tewksbury	MA	01876	**866-205-2810**	978-461-3999	623
Thrivent Financial for Lutherans						
4321 N BallaRd Rd	Appleton	WI	54919	**800-847-4836**	920-684-3225	391-2
ThriveOn Inc						
210 S 20th St	New Ulm	MN	56073	**855-767-2571**		198
Thumb Cellular Ltd. Partnership						
82 S Main St	Pigeon	MI	48755	**800-443-5057**	989-453-4333	733
Thumb Correctional Facility						
3225 John Conley Dr	Lapeer	MI	48446	**855-444-3911**	810-667-2045	215
Thunder Airlines Ltd						
310 Hector Dougall Way	Thunder Bay	ON	P7E6M6	**800-803-9943**		13
Thunder Tech Inc						
3635 Perkins Ave Studio 5 SW	Cleveland	OH	44114	**888-321-8422**	216-391-2255	7
Thunder Valley Casino						
1200 Athens Ave	Lincoln	CA	95648	**877-468-8777**	916-408-7777	132
Thunderbird Rural Public Transportation System						
2801 W Loop 306 Ste A						
PO Box 60050	San Angelo	TX	76904	**877-947-8729**	325-944-9666	107
Thunderbird School of Global Management						
1 Global Pl	Glendale	AZ	85306	**800-848-9084**	602-978-7000	683
Thurgood Marshall Scholarship Fund						
901 F St NW Ste 300	Washington	DC	20004	**866-632-9992**	212-573-8888	723
Thybar Corp						
913 S Kay Ave	Addison	IL	60101	**800-666-2872**	630-543-5300	695
Thyme on the Creek						
1345 28th St	Boulder	CO	80302	**866-866-8086**	303-998-3835	669
Thyssen Krupp Hearn						
59 I- Dr	Wentzville	MO	63385	**877-854-7178**	636-332-1772	196
ThyssenKrupp Elevator						
9280 Crestwyn Hills Dr	Memphis	TN	38125	**877-230-0303**	901-261-1800	360-3
ThyssenKrupp Materials NA						
22355 W 11 Mile Rd	Southfield	MI	48033	**800-926-2600**	248-233-5600	491
TIA (Tire Industry Assn)						
1532 Pointer Ridge Pl Ste G	Bowie	MD	20716	**800-876-8372**	301-430-7280	48-4
TIA (Transportation Intermediaries Assn)						
1625 Prince St Ste 200	Alexandria	VA	22314	**888-910-4747**	703-299-5700	48-21
TIAA-CREF						
730 Third Ave	New York	NY	10017	**866-842-2442**	212-490-9000	391-2
TIAW (International Alliance for Women)						
1101 Pennsylvania Ave						
NW Fl 6	Washington	DC	20004	**888-712-5200**		47-24
TIBCO Software Inc						
1700 Westlake Ave N Ste 500	Seattle	WA	98109	**866-247-8182**	206-283-8802	180-3
Ticket Source Inc						
5516 E Mockingbird Ln Ste 100	Dallas	TX	75206	**800-557-6872**	214-821-9011	748
Tickets.com Inc						
555 Anton Blvd 11th Fl	Costa Mesa	CA	92626	**800-352-0212**	714-327-5400	748
TicketWeb Inc						
PO Box 77250	San Francisco	CA	94103	**866-777-8932***		748
*Cust Svc						
Tickfaw State Park						
27225 Patterson Rd	Springfield	LA	70462	**888-981-2020**	225-294-5020	564
Tickle Pink Inn at Carmel Highlands						
155 Highland Dr	Carmel	CA	93923	**800-635-4774**	831-624-1244	379

Name / Address	City	State	Zip	Toll-Free	Phone	Class
Ticona LLC						
8040 Dixie Hwy	Florence	KY	41042	**800-833-4882**	859-372-3244	604-2
Tidel Engineering Inc						
2025 W Belt Line Rd Ste 114	Carrollton	TX	75006	**800-678-7577**	972-484-3358	55
Tideland Electric Membership Corp						
25831 Hwy 264 E	Pantego	Nc	27860	**800-637-1079**	252-943-3046	247
Tides Canada Foundation						
400-163 W Hastings St	Vancouver	BC	V6B1H5	**866-843-3722**	604-647-6611	306
Tides Marine Inc						
3251 SW 13th Dr	Deerfield Beach	FL	33442	**800-420-0949**	954-420-0949	350
Tidewater Barge Lines Inc						
6305 NW Old Lower River Rd	Vancouver	WA	98660	**800-562-1607**	360-693-1491	315
Tidewater Community College						
Chesapeake						
1428 Cedar Rd	Chesapeake	VA	23322	**800-371-0898**	757-822-5100	161
Norfolk						
121 College Pl	Norfolk	VA	23510	**800-371-0898**	757-822-1110	161
Portsmouth						
7000 College Dr	Portsmouth	VA	23703	**800-371-0898**	757-822-2124	161
Virginia Beach						
1700 College Crescent	Virginia Beach	VA	23453	**800-371-0898**	757-822-7100	161
Tidewater Grill						
1060 Charleston Town Ctr	Charleston	WV	25389	**888-456-3463**	304-345-2620	669
Tidewater Inc						
601 Poydras St Ste 1900	New Orleans	LA	70130	**800-678-8433**	504-568-1010	464
NYSE: TDW						
Tidewater Inn & Conference Ctr						
101 E Dover St	Easton	MD	21601	**800-237-8775**	410-822-1300	379
Tidewell Hospice						
5955 Rand Blvd	Sarasota	FL	34238	**800-959-4291**	941-552-7500	371
TIDI Products LLC						
570 Enterprise Dr	Neenah	WI	54956	**800-521-1314**		476
Tie Down Engineering Inc						
255 Villanova Dr SW	Atlanta	GA	30336	**800-241-1806**	404-344-0000	479
Tier One LLC						
31 Pecks Ln	Newtown	CT	06470	**877-251-2228**	203-426-3030	453
Tier1 Inc						
2403 Sidney St Ste 225	Pittsburgh	PA	15203	**888-284-0202**	412-381-9201	179
Tierra Right of Way Services Ltd						
1575 E River Rd Ste 201	Tucson	AZ	85718	**800-887-0847**	520-319-2106	198
Tietex International						
3010 N Blackstock Rd	Spartanburg	SC	29301	**800-843-8390**	864-574-0500	742-6
Tiffany & Co						
727 Fifth Ave	New York	NY	10022	**800-526-0649***	212-755-8000	410
NYSE: TIF ■ *Orders						
Tiffen Company LLC						
90 Oser Ave	Hauppauge	NY	11788	**800-645-2522**	631-273-2500	590
Tiffin Metal Products Co						
450 Wall St	Tiffin	OH	44883	**800-537-0983**		350
Tiffin University						
155 Miami St	Tiffin	OH	44883	**800-968-6446**	419-447-6442	167
Tift Regional Medical Ctr						
1641 Madison Ave	Tifton	GA	31794	**800-648-1935**	229-382-7120	374-3
Tifton-Tift County Chamber of Commerce						
100 Central Ave	Tifton	GA	31794	**800-550-8438**	229-382-6200	138
TIG (Technology Integration Group)						
7810 Trade St	San Diego	CA	92121	**800-858-0549**	858-566-1900	178
Tiger Button Company Inc						
307 W 38th St	New York	NY	10018	**800-223-2754**	212-594-0570	593
Tiger Financial News Network						
601 Cleveland St Ste 618	Clearwater	FL	33755	**877-518-9190**	727-467-9190	641
Tiger Lines LLC Lodi						
927 Black Diamond Way	Lodi	CA	95241	**800-967-8443**	209-334-4100	778
Tiger Schulmann's Karate Ctr						
485 Blvd	Elmwood Park	NJ	07407	**800-867-1218**		147
Tiger Supplies Inc						
27 Selvage St	Irvington	NJ	07111	**888-844-3765**	973-854-8636	789
TigerDirect Inc						
7795 W Flagler St Ste 35	Miami	FL	33144	**800-800-8300**		176
TigerLead Solutions LLC						
30700 Russell Ranch Rd						
Ste 102	Westlake Village	CA	91362	**888-844-3744**		227
TigerLogic Corp						
25-A Technology Dr	Irvine	CA	92618	**800-367-7425**	949-442-4400	180-12
NASDAQ: TIGR						
Tihati Productions Ltd						
3615 Harding Ave Ste 507	Honolulu	HI	96816	**877-846-5554**	808-735-0292	572-4
TII Network Technologies Inc						
141 Rodeo Dr	Edgewood	NY	11717	**888-844-4720**	631-789-5000	637
NASDAQ: TIII						
Tilcon Connecticut Inc						
PO Box 1357	New Britain	CT	06050	**888-845-2666**	860-224-6010	45
Tilcon NY Inc						
162 Old Mill Rd	West Nyack	NY	10994	**800-872-7762**	845-358-4500	502-5
Tile Shop Holdings Inc						
14000 Carlson Pkwy	Plymouth	MN	55441	**888-398-6595**		785
Tillamook Bay Community College						
4301 Third St	Tillamook	OR	97141	**888-306-8222**	503-842-8222	161
Tillamook People's Utility District						
1115 Pacific Ave	Tillamook	OR	97141	**800-422-2535**	503-842-2535	247
Tilley Chemical Company Inc						
501 Chesapeake Pk Plz	Baltimore	MD	21220	**800-638-6968**	410-574-4500	145
Tilson HR Inc						
1530 American Way Ste 200	Greenwood	IN	46143	**800-276-3976**	317-885-3838	630
Tim Hortons Inc						
874 Sinclair Rd	Oakville	ON	L6K2Y1	**888-601-1616**	905-845-6511	668
NYSE: THI						
TimBar Packaging & Display						
148 N Penn St	Hanover	PA	17331	**800-572-6061**	717-632-4727	99
Timber Products Co						
305 S Fourth St PO Box 269	Springfield	OR	97477	**800-547-9520**	541-747-4577	193-3
Timberland Bancorp Inc						
624 Simpson Ave	Hoquiam	WA	98550	**800-562-8761**	360-533-4747	360-2
NASDAQ: TSBK						
Timberland Co, The						
200 Domain Dr	Stratham	NH	03885	**800-258-0855**	603-772-9500	302
NYSE: VFC						
Timberland Homes Inc						
1201 37th St NW	Auburn	WA	98001	**800-488-5036**	253-735-3435	105

Name / Address	City	State	ZIP	Toll-Free	Phone	Class
Timberland Regional Library 415 Tumwater Blvd SW	Tumwater	WA	98501	**877-284-6237**	360-943-5001	434-3
Timberlane Inc 150 Domorah Dr	Montgomeryville	PA	18936	**800-250-2221**	215-616-0600	362
Timberlawn Mental Health System 4600 Samuell Blvd	Dallas	TX	75228	**800-426-4944**	214-381-7181	374-5
Timberline Lodge 27500 E Timberline Rd	Government Camp	OR	97028	**800-547-1406**	503-272-3311	667
Timberwolf Tours Ltd 51404 RR 264 Ste 34	Spruce Grove	AB	T7Y1E4	**888-467-9697**	780-470-4966	758
Time Definite Services Inc 1360 Madeline Ln Ste 300	Elgin	IL	60124	**800-466-8040**		312
Time Mark Corp 11440 E Pine St	Tulsa	OK	74116	**800-862-2875**	918-438-1220	205
Time Trak Systems Inc 933 Pine Grove	Port Huron	MI	48060	**888-484-6387**	810-984-1313	179
Time Warner Inc 1 Time Warner Ctr *NYSE: TWX*	New York	NY	10019	**866-463-6899**	212-484-8000	187
Time, The 224 W 49th St	New York	NY	10019	**877-846-3692**	212-246-5252	379
Timely Inc 10241 Norris Ave	Pacoima	CA	91331	**800-247-6242**	818-492-3500	288
TimeMed Labeling Systems Inc 144 Tower Dr *Cust Svc	Burr Ridge	IL	60527	**800-323-4840***	630-986-1800	553
Time-O-Matic Inc 1015 Maple St	Danville	IL	61832	**800-637-2645**	217-442-0611	205
Times 222 Lake St	Shreveport	LA	71101	**800-551-8892**	318-459-3200	531-2
Times Fiber Communications Inc 358 Hall Ave PO Box 384	Wallingford	CT	06492	**800-677-2288**	203-265-8500	811
Times Herald 911 Military St	Port Huron	MI	48060	**800-462-4057**	810-985-7171	531-2
Times Herald Inc 410 Markley St PO Box 591	Norristown	PA	19404	**888-933-4233**	610-272-2500	634-8
Times Herald-Record 40 Mulberry St PO Box 2046	Middletown	NY	10940	**800-295-2181**	845-341-1100	531-2
Times Hotel & Suites 6515 Wilfrid-Hamel Blvd	L'Ancienne-Lorette	QC	G2E5W3	**888-902-4444**	418-877-7788	379
Times Leader 200 S Fourth St	Martins Ferry	OH	43935	**800-244-5671**	740-633-1131	531-2
Times Leader, The 15 N Main St	Wilkes-Barre	PA	18711	**800-427-8649**	570-829-7100	531-2
Times Microwave Systems Inc PO Box 5039	Wallingford	CT	06492	**800-867-2629**	203-949-8400	255
Times News Publishing Co 707 S Main St	Burlington	NC	27215	**800-488-0085**	336-227-0131	634-8
Times of Acadiana 1100 Bertrand Dr	Lafayette	LA	70506	**877-289-2216**	337-289-6300	531-4
Times Printing Company Inc 100 Industrial Dr	Random Lake	WI	53075	**800-236-4396**	920-994-4396	626
Times Record 219 S College Ave	Aledo	IL	61231	**800-784-6776**	309-582-5112	531-4
Times Record News PO Box 120	Wichita Falls	TX	76307	**800-627-1646**	940-767-8341	531-2
Times Recorder 34 S Fourth St	Zanesville	OH	43701	**888-217-2614**	740-452-4561	531-2
Times Reporter 629 Wabash Ave NW	New Philadelphia	OH	44663	**800-686-5577**	330-364-5577	531-2
Times Union 645 Albany Shaker Rd PO Box 15000	Albany	NY	12212	**877-263-7995**	518-454-5420	531-2
Times Union Ctr 51 S Pearl St	Albany	NY	12207	**866-308-3394**	518-487-2000	718
Times, The 601 W 45th Ave	Munster	IN	46321	**800-837-3232**	219-933-3200	531-2
Timesavers Inc 11123 89th Ave N	Maple Grove	MN	55369	**800-537-3611**	763-488-6600	386
Times-Citizen Communications Inc 406 Stevens St PO Box 640	Iowa Falls	IA	50126	**800-798-2691**	641-648-2521	634-8
Times-Mail 813 16th St PO Box 849	Bedford	IN	47421	**800-333-2451**	812-275-3355	531-2
Times-News PO Box 490	Hendersonville	NC	28793	**800-849-8050**	828-692-0505	531-2
Times-Picayune 3800 Howard Ave	New Orleans	LA	70125	**800-925-0000**	504-826-3279	531-2
Times-Standard 930 Sixth St	Eureka	CA	95501	**800-514-0301**	707-498-1817	531-2
Times-Tribune, The 201 N Kentucky Ave	Corbin	KY	40701	**877-629-9722**	606-528-2464	531-2
TIMET (Titanium Metals Corp) 224 Vly Creek Blvd Ste 200 *NYSE: TIE*	Exton	PA	19341	**800-753-1550**	610-968-1300	484
TimeTECH Canada Inc 7420 Airport Rd Ste 101	Mississauga	ON	L4T4E5	**877-816-8463**	905-677-7009	179
TimeValue Software 22 Mauchly *Sales	Irvine	CA	92618	**800-426-4741***	949-727-1800	180-11
Timeware Inc 9329 Ravenna Rd Ste D	Twinsburg	OH	44087	**866-936-2420**	330-963-2700	179
Timex Group USA Inc 555 Christian Rd PO Box 310	Middlebury	CT	06762	**800-448-4639**	203-346-5000	152
Timken Co 1835 Dueber Ave SW *NYSE: TKR*	Canton	OH	44706	**800-223-1954**	330-438-3000	74
Timmins & District Hospital 700 Ross Ave E	Timmins	ON	P4N8P2	**888-340-3003**	705-267-2131	374-2
Timpte Inc 1827 Industrial Dr	David City	NE	68632	**888-256-4884**	402-367-3056	777
Tims Ford State Park 570 Tims Ford Dr	Winchester	TN	37398	**800-471-5295**	931-962-1183	564
Tindall Corp 2273 Hayne St	Spartanburg	SC	29301	**800-849-4521**	864-576-3230	185
Tingley Rubber Corp 1551 S Washington Ave Ste 403 Ste 403 *Cust Svc	Piscataway	NJ	08854	**800-631-5498***		575
Tinsley Adv 2000 S Dixie Hwy	Miami	FL	33133	**800-432-2242**	305-856-6060	4
Tintri Inc 2570 W El Camino Real	Mountain View	CA	94040	**855-484-6874**	650-209-3900	175-8
Tioga County Visitors Bureau 2053 Rt 660	Wellsboro	PA	16901	**888-846-4228**	570-724-0635	208
Tioga Pipe Supply Company Inc 2450 Wheatsheaf Ln	Philadelphia	PA	19137	**800-523-3678**	215-831-0700	491
TIP Rural Electric Co-op 612 W Des Moines St PO Box 534	Brooklyn	IA	52211	**800-934-7976**	641-522-9221	247
Tip Top Canning Co 505 S Second St PO Box 126	Tipp City	OH	45371	**800-352-2635**	937-667-3713	297-20
Tip Top Poultry Inc 327 Wallace Rd	Marietta	GA	30062	**800-241-5230**	770-973-8070	618
TIPAC (Title Industry PAC) 1828 L St NW Ste 705	Washington	DC	20036	**800-787-2582**	202-296-3671	614
Tipco Punch Inc 1 Coventry Rd	Brampton	ON	L6T4B1	**800-544-8444**	905-791-9811	358
Tipmont Rural Electric Membership Corp 403 S Main St	Linden	IN	47955	**800-726-3953**		247
Tippecanoe County Public Library 627 S St	Lafayette	IN	47901	**800-542-7818**	765-429-0100	434-3
Tipper Tie Inc 2000 Lufkin Rd	Apex	NC	27502	**800-331-2905**	919-362-8811	153
Tips Inc 2402 Williams Dr	Georgetown	TX	78628	**800-242-8477**	512-863-3653	179
Tipton & Hurst Inc 1801 N Grant St	Little Rock	AR	72207	**800-666-3333**	501-666-3333	294
Tire Centers LLC 310 Inglesby Pkwy	Duncan	SC	29334	**800-603-2430**	864-329-2700	753
Tire Industry Assn (TIA) 1532 Pointer Ridge Pl Ste G	Bowie	MD	20716	**800-876-8372**	301-430-7280	48-4
Tire Rack 7101 Vorden Pkwy	South Bend	IN	46628	**888-541-1777**	574-287-2345	753
Tire Warehouse 200 Holleder Pkwy	Rochester	NY	14615	**800-876-6676**		53
Tire Warehouse Inc 7500 NW 35 Terr	Miami	FL	33122	**877-235-0102**	305-696-0096	753
Tire's Warehouse Inc 240 Teller St	Corona	CA	92879	**800-655-8851**	951-808-0111	753
Tire-Rama Inc 1429 Grand Ave	Billings	MT	59102	**800-828-1642**	406-245-4006	753
Tires Plus Total Car Care 2021 Sunnydale Blvd	Clearwater	FL	33765	**800-440-4167**	727-441-3727	61-5
TIRR Memorial Hermann Hospital 1333 Moursund St	Houston	TX	77030	**800-447-3422**	713-799-5000	374-6
Tishcon Corp 50 Sylvester St	Westbury	NY	11590	**800-848-8442**	516-333-3050	797
Titan America Inc 1151 Azalea Garden Rd	Norfolk	VA	23502	**800-468-7622**	757-858-6500	184
Titan International Inc 2701 Spruce St *NYSE: TWI*	Quincy	IL	62301	**800-872-2327**	217-228-6011	59
Titan Laboratories 1380 Zuni St PO Box 40567	Denver	CO	80204	**800-848-4826**		578
Titan Lenders Corp 5353 W Dartmouth Ave Ste 50	Denver	CO	80227	**866-412-9180**		179
Titan Logix Corp 4130 - 93 St	Edmonton	AB	T6E5P5	**877-462-4085**	780-462-4085	203
Titan Machinery 644 East Beaton Dr	West Fargo	ND	58078	**800-548-7747**	701-356-0130	358
Titan Machinery Inc 7955 179th Ave SE *NASDAQ: TITN*	Wahpeton	ND	58075	**800-654-4313**	701-642-8424	276
Titan Oil & Gas Services Inc 6809 King Ave W Bldg E	Billings	MT	59106	**800-406-5209**	406-945-5036	535
Titan Pharmaceuticals Inc 400 Oyster Pt Blvd Ste 505 *OTC: TTNP*	South San Francisco	CA	94080	**888-417-8516**	650-244-4990	84
Titan Specialties Inc 11785 Hwy 152 *Sales	Pampa	TX	79065	**800-692-4486***	806-665-3781	536
Titan Tire Co 2345 E Market St	Des Moines	IA	50317	**800-872-2327**	515-265-9200	752
Titan Wheel Corp 2701 Spruce St	Quincy	IL	62301	**800-872-2327**	217-228-6011	59
Titanium Metals Corp (TIMET) 224 Vly Creek Blvd Ste 200 *NYSE: TIE*	Exton	PA	19341	**800-753-1550**	610-968-1300	484
Titeflex Corp 603 Hendee St	Springfield	MA	01139	**800-765-2525**	413-739-5631	370
Title Guaranty of Hawaii Inc 235 Queen St	Honolulu	HI	96813	**800-222-3229**	808-533-6261	391-6
Title Industry PAC (TIPAC) 1828 L St NW Ste 705	Washington	DC	20036	**800-787-2582**	202-296-3671	614
Title Resources Guaranty Co (TRGC) 8111 LBJ Fwy Ste 1200	Dallas	TX	75251	**800-526-8018**	972-644-6500	391-6
Titonka Bancshares Inc PO Box 309	Titonka	IA	50480	**866-985-3247**	515-928-2142	360-2
Titusville Area Chamber of Commerce 2000 S Washington Ave	Titusville	FL	32780	**800-435-7352**	321-267-3036	138
TiVo Inc 2160 Gold St *NASDAQ: TIVO*	Alviso	CA	95002	**877-367-8486**	408-519-9100	115
Tivoli Lodge 386 Hanson Ranch Rd	Vail	CO	81657	**800-451-4756**	970-476-5615	379
Tizbi Inc 800 Saint Mary's St Ste 402	Raleigh	NC	27605	**888-729-0951**		179
TJ Cope Inc 11500 Norcom Rd	Philadelphia	PA	19154	**800-483-3473**	215-961-2570	814
TJ Hale Co W 139 N 9499 Hwy 145	Menomonee Falls	WI	53051	**800-236-4253**	262-255-5555	288
TJ Maxx 770 Cochituate Rd *Cust Svc	Framingham	MA	01701	**800-926-6299***	508-390-1000	156-2
TJ Samson Community Hospital 1301 N Race St	Glasgow	KY	42141	**800-651-5635**	270-651-4444	374-3
Tjernlund Products Inc 1601 Ninth St	White Bear Lake	MN	55110	**800-255-4208**	651-426-2993	18

Name	Address	City	State	ZIP	Toll-Free	Phone	Class
TJX Cos Inc NYSE: TJX	770 Cochituate Rd	Framingham	MA	01701	**800-926-6299**	508-390-1000	156-4
TK Stanley Inc	6739 Hwy 184	Waynesboro	MS	39367	**800-477-2855**		538
T-I Irrigation Co	151 E Hwy 6 AB Rd PO Box 1047	Hastings	NE	68902	**800-330-4264**	402-462-4128	275
TLC Vision Corp	50 Burnhamthorpe Rd W Ste 101	Mississauga	ON	L5B3C2	**877-852-2020**		796
TLIE (Texas Lawyers Insurance Exchange)	1801 S MoPac Ste 300	Austin	TX	78746	**800-252-9332**	512-480-9074	391-5
TLN (Telelatino Network Inc)	5125 Steeles Ave W	Toronto	ON	M9L1R5	**800-551-8401**	416-744-8200	736
TM Smith Tool International Corp	360 Hubbard Ave	Mount Clemens	MI	48043	**800-521-4894**	586-468-1465	492
TMA (Tobacco Merchants Assn)	PO Box 8019	Princeton	NJ	08543	**888-672-4991**	609-275-4900	47-2
TMA Systems LLC	5100 E Skelly Dr Ste 900	Tulsa	OK	74135	**800-862-1130**	918-858-6600	180-11
TMC (Teaching & Mentoring Communities)	PO Box 2579	Laredo	TX	78044	**888-836-5151**	956-722-5174	48-5
TMC (Tufts Medical Ctr)	800 Washington St	Boston	MA	02111	**866-220-3699**	617-636-5000	374-3
TMC (Tulane Medical Ctr)	1415 Tulane Ave	New Orleans	LA	70112	**800-588-5800**	504-988-5263	374-3
TMG Company LLC	1718 Briarcrest Dr Ste 100	Bryan	TX	77802	**800-720-1563**	979-774-4492	2
TMI Coatings Inc	3291 Terminal Dr	Saint Paul	MN	55121	**800-328-0229**	651-452-6100	191-8
TMI Hospitality Inc	4850 32nd Ave South	Fargo	ND	58104	**800-210-8223**	701-235-1060	705
TMI LLC	5350 Campbells Run Rd	Pittsburgh	PA	15205	**800-888-9750**	412-787-9750	607
TMI Systems Design Corp	50 S Third Ave W	Dickinson	ND	58601	**800-456-6716**	701-456-6716	320-3
TML (Teledyne Monitor Labs Inc)	35 Inverness Dr E	Englewood	CO	80112	**800-422-1499**	303-792-3300	203
T-Mobile USA Inc	12920 SE 38th St	Bellevue	WA	98006	**800-318-9270**	425-383-4000	733
TMP Direct	600 International Dr	Mount Olive	NJ	07828	**800-328-2439**		393
TMS (Minerals Metals & Materials Society)	184 Thorn Hill Rd	Warrendale	PA	15086	**800-759-4867**	724-776-9000	48-13
TMW Systems Inc	21111 Chagrin Blvd	Beachwood	OH	44122	**800-401-6682**	216-831-6606	180-10
TNCI (Trans National Communications International Inc)	2 Charlesgate W	Boston	MA	02215	**800-800-8400**	617-369-1000	733
Tnemec Company Inc	6800 Corporate Dr	Kansas City	MO	64120	**800-863-6321**	816-483-3400	549
TNMP (Texas-New Mexico Power Co)	577 N Garden Ridge Blvd	Lewisville	TX	75067	**888-866-7456**	972-420-4189	785
TNNA (National NeedleArts Assn, The)	1100-H Brandywine Blvd	Zanesville	OH	43701	**800-889-8662**	740-455-6773	47-18
TNR Technical Inc OTC: TNRK	301 Central Pk Dr	Sanford	FL	32771	**800-346-0601**	407-321-3011	73
TO Haas Tire Co Inc	2400 'O' St	Lincoln	NE	68510	**866-393-5204**	402-474-1525	753
TOAST.net	4841 Monroe St Ste 307	Toledo	OH	43623	**888-862-7863**	419-292-2200	398
TOBA (Thoroughbred Owners & Breeders Assn)	PO Box 910668	Lexington	KY	40591	**888-606-8622**	859-276-2291	47-3
Tobacco Merchants Assn (TMA)	PO Box 8019	Princeton	NJ	08543	**888-672-4991**	609-275-4900	47-2
Tobe Direct	9700 Park Plz Ave Ste 210	Louisville	KY	40241	**866-820-7313**		7
Tocco Financial Services Inc	6236 E Pima Ste 190	Tucson	AZ	85712	**877-881-1149**	520-881-1149	688
Toccoa Falls College *General	107 Kincaid Dr	Toccoa Falls	GA	30598	**800-868-3257***	706-886-6831	160
Today's Business Computers	213 E Black Horse Pk	Pleasantville	NJ	08232	**800-371-5132**	609-645-5132	179
Today's Christian Woman Magazine *Orders	465 Gundersen Dr	Carol Stream	IL	60188	**877-247-4787***	630-260-6200	456-18
Todd-Wadena Electric Co-op	550 Ash Ave NE PO Box 431	Wadena	MN	56482	**800-321-8932**	218-631-3120	247
TodoCast Inc	31831 Camino Capistrano Ste 301	San Juan Capistrano	CA	92675	**866-510-7889**		387
Tog Shop Inc	30 Tozer Rd	Beverly	MA	01915	**800-767-6666**	978-922-2040	458
Togus National Cemetery	VA Regional Office Ctr	Togus	ME	04330	**800-273-8255**	508-563-7113	135
Toitures GGR Inc	34 Trudel Cp 333	Amos	QC	J9T3A7	**800-043-7760**	819-727-3348	193-4
Tokatee Klootchman State Natural Site	93111 Hwy 101 N	Florence	OR	97439	**800-551-6949**		564
Tokio Marine Life	230 Pk Ave	New York	NY	10169	**800-628-2796**	212-297-6600	391-4
Tokyo Electron America Inc	2400 Grove Blvd	Austin	TX	78741	**800-828-6596**	512-424-1000	693
Toledo Edison Co	PO Box 3687	Akron	OH	44309	**800-447-3333**		785
Toledo Museum of Art	2445 Monroe St	Toledo	OH	43620	**800-644-6862**	419-255-8000	519
Toledo Opera	425 Jefferson Ave Ste 601	Toledo	OH	43604	**866-860-9048**	419-255-7464	572-2
Toledo Physical Education Supply Inc	5101 Advantage Dr	Toledo	OH	43612	**800-225-7749**	419-726-8122	709
Toledo Symphony	1838 Parkwood Ave	Toledo	OH	43604	**800-348-1253**	419-246-8000	572-3
Toledo Zoo	2700 Broadway	Toledo	OH	43609	**866-900-1146**	419-385-5721	821
Toledo-Lucas County Port Authority	1 Maritime Plaza	Toledo	OH	43604	**800-969-4700**	419-243-8251	617
Toll Bros Inc NYSE: TOL	250 Gibraltar Rd	Horsham	PA	19044	**855-897-8655**	215-938-8000	651
Toll Gas & Welding Supply	3005 Niagara Ln N	Plymouth	MN	55447	**877-865-5427**	763-551-5300	358
Tollgrade Communications Inc *Cust Svc	3120 Unionville Rd Ste 400	Cranberry Township	PA	16066	**800-878-3399***	412-820-1400	732
Tol-O-Matic Inc	3800 County Rd 116	Hamel	MN	55340	**800-328-2174**	763-478-8000	225
Tom Barrow Co (TBC)	2800 Plant Atkinson Rd	Atlanta	GA	30339	**800-229-8226**	404-351-1010	14
Tom Benson Chevrolet Co Inc	9400 San Pedro	San Antonio	TX	78216	**866-635-6971**	210-341-3311	56
Tom Duffy Co	5200 Watt Ct Ste B	Fairfield	CA	94534	**800-479-5671**		292
Tom Hassenfritz Equipment Co	1300 W Washington St	Mount Pleasant	IA	52641	**800-634-4885**	319-385-3114	276
Tom James Co	263 Seaboard Ln	Franklin	TN	37067	**800-236-9023**	615-771-0795	154-11
Tom Johnson Investment Management Inc	201 Robert S Kerr Ave	Oklahoma City	OK	73102	**888-404-8546**	405-236-2111	401
Tom Lee Music Ltd	929 Granville St	Vancouver	BC	V6Z1L3	**888-886-6533**	604-685-8471	525
Tom McCall & Assoc Inc	20180 Governors Hwy Ste 100	Olympia Fields	IL	60461	**800-715-5474**	708-747-5707	196
Tom Roush Inc	525 W David Brown Dr	Westfield	IN	46074	**800-382-4619**	317-896-5561	515
Tom Snyder Productions Inc	100 Talcott Ave	Watertown	MA	02472	**800-342-0236**	617-924-0938	180-3
Tom Stinnett Rv's	520 Marriott Dr	Clarksville	IN	47129	**800-583-5685**	812-282-7718	61-5
Tom Sturgis Pretzels Inc	2267 Lancaster Pk	Reading	PA	19607	**800-817-3834**	610-775-0335	297-9
Tom's of Maine Inc	302 Lafayette Ctr	Kennebunk	ME	04043	**800-367-8667**	800-985-3874	217
Tomah Convention & Visitors Bureau	901 Kilbourn Ave PO Box 625	Tomah	WI	54660	**800-948-6624**	608-372-2166	208
Tomah Veterans Affairs Medical Ctr	500 E Veterans St	Tomah	WI	54660	**800-872-8662**	608-372-3971	374-8
Tomball Independent School District	310 S Cherry St	Tomball	TX	77375	**877-382-4357**	281-357-3100	683
Tombigbee Electric Co-op Inc	7686 US Hwy PO Box 610	Guin	AL	35563	**800-621-8069**	205-468-3325	247
Tombigbee State Park	264 Cabin Dr	Tupelo	MS	38804	**800-467-2757**	662-842-7669	564
Tomco2 Equipment Co	3340 Rosebud Rd	Loganville	GA	30052	**800-832-4262**	770-979-8000	804
Tommy Tape	378 Four Rod Rd	Berlin	CT	06037	**888-866-8273**	860-378-0111	729
Tompkins Cortland Community College	170 N St	Dryden	NY	13053	**888-567-8211**	607-844-8211	161
Tompkins County Chamber of Commerce	904 E Shore Dr	Ithaca	NY	14850	**888-568-9816**	607-273-7080	138
Tompkins County Public Library	101 E Green St	Ithaca	NY	14850	**800-772-7267**	607-272-4557	434-3
Tompkins International	6870 Perry Creek Rd	Raleigh	NC	27616	**800-789-1257**	919-876-3667	196
Tompkins Trust Co NYSE: TMP	PO Box 460	Ithaca	NY	14851	**888-273-3210**	607-273-3210	69
Toms Truck Ctr Inc	1008 E Fourth St PO Box 88	Santa Ana	CA	92701	**800-638-1015**	714-338-6060	56
Tomson Steel Co (Inc)	PO Box 940	Middletown	OH	45042	**800-837-3001**		491
TOMY International Inc	1111 W 22nd St Ste 320	Oak Brook	IL	60523	**800-704-8697**		760
Tone Software Inc	1735 S Brookhurst St	Anaheim	CA	92804	**800-833-8663**	714-991-9460	179
Tongass Trading Co	201 Dock St	Ketchikan	AK	99901	**800-235-5102**	907-225-5101	231
Toni & Guy USA Inc	2311 Midway Rd	Carrollton	TX	75006	**800-256-9391**		76
Tonix Corp	40910 Encyclopedia Cir	Fremont	CA	94538	**800-227-2072**	510-651-8050	154-3
Tonner Doll Co	301 Wall St PO Box 4410	Kingston	NY	12402	**800-794-2107**	845-339-9537	760
Tony Packo's	1902 Front St	Toledo	OH	43605	**866-472-2567**	419-691-1953	669
Toobs Inc	347 Quintana Rd	Morro Bay	CA	93442	**800-795-8662**		708
Tool Smith Company Inc	1300 Fourth Ave S PO Box 2384	Birmingham	AL	35233	**800-317-8665**	205-323-2576	386
Tool Technology Distributors Inc	3110 Osgood Ct	Fremont	CA	94539	**800-335-8437**	510-656-8220	358
Tool-Flo Mfg Inc	7803 Hansen Rd	Houston	TX	77061	**800-345-2815**	713-941-1080	454
Tools for Bending Inc *Cust Svc	194 W Dakota Ave	Denver	CO	80223	**800-873-3305***	303-777-7170	455
Toolwire Inc	7031 Koll Ctr Pkwy Ste 220	Pleasanton	CA	94566	**866-935-8665**	925-227-8500	38
Tootsie Roll Industries Inc NYSE: TR	7401 S Cicero Ave	Chicago	IL	60629	**866-972-6879**	773-838-3400	297-8
Top Air Sprayers	601 S Broad St	Kalida	OH	45853	**800-322-6301**	419-532-3121	275
Top Flight Inc	1300 Central Ave	Chattanooga	TN	37408	**800-777-3740**	423-266-8171	265
Top Producer Magazine	1818 Market St 31st Fl	Philadelphia	PA	19103	**800-320-7992**		456-1
Top Producer Systems Inc	10651 Shellbridge Way Ste 155	Richmond	BC	V6X2W8	**800-821-3657**		181
Topa Insurance Corp	24025 Park Sorrento Ste 300	Calabasas	CA	91302	**877-353-8672**	310-201-0451	391-4

Name / Address	City	State	Zip	Toll-Free	Phone	Class
Topaz Hotel 1733 N St NW	Washington	DC	20036	**800-775-1202**	202-393-3000	379
Topaz Lighting Corp 925 Waverly Ave	Holtsville	NY	11742	**800-666-2852**	631-758-5507	362
Topco Assoc LLC 7711 Gross Pt Rd	Skokie	IL	60077	**888-423-0139**	847-676-3030	298-8
TopCoder Inc 95 Glastonbury Blvd	Glastonbury	CT	06033	**866-867-2633**	860-633-5540	179
Topcon Medical Systems Inc 111 Bauer Dr	Oakland	NJ	07436	**800-223-1130**	201-599-5100	382
Topeka Capital-Journal 616 SE Jefferson St	Topeka	KS	66607	**800-777-7171**	785-295-1111	531-2
Topeka Correctional Facility 815 SE Rice Rd	Topeka	KS	66603	**888-317-8204**	785-296-3317	215
Topica Inc 1 Post St Ste 875	San Francisco	CA	94104	**888-728-2465**	415-344-0800	7
Topnotch at Stowe Resort & Spa 4000 Mountain Rd	Stowe	VT	05672	**800-451-8686**		667
Topp Industries Inc 420 N State Rd 25 PO Box 420	Rochester	IN	46975	**800-354-4534**	574-223-3681	600
Toppenish School District 202 306 Bolin Dr	Toppenish	WA	98948	**888-730-1101**	509-865-4455	683
Topps Company Inc 1 Whitehall St	New York	NY	10004	**800-489-9149**	212-376-0300	297-6
Topps Safety Apparel Inc 2516 E State Rd 14	Rochester	IN	46975	**800-348-2990**	574-223-4311	154-18
TOPS Club Inc 4575 S Fifth St	Milwaukee	WI	53207	**800-932-8677**	414-482-4620	47-17
Toptica Photonics Inc 1286 Blossom Dr Ste 1	Victor	NY	14564	**877-277-9897**	585-657-6663	419
Torchmark Corp 3700 S Stonebridge Dr *NYSE: TMK*	McKinney	TX	75070	**877-577-3899**	972-569-4000	360-4
Torco Inc 1330 Old 41 Hwy NW	Marietta	GA	30060	**800-876-5228**	770-427-3704	620
Torian Plum Condo Resort 1855 Ski Time Sq Dr	Steamboat Springs	CO	80487	**800-228-2458**	970-879-8811	667
Torke Coffee Roasting Company Inc 3455 Paine Ave	Sheboygan	WI	53081	**800-242-7671**	920-458-4114	297-7
Tornado Alley Turbo 300 Airport Rd	Ada	OK	74820	**877-359-8284**	580-332-3510	768
Tornatech Inc 7075, Place Robert-Joncas Ste 132	Saint-laurent	QC	H4M2Z2	**800-363-8448**	514-334-0523	205
Toro Co 8111 Lyndale Ave *NYSE: TTC*	Bloomington	MN	55420	**888-384-9939**		429
Toro Co Irrigation Div 5825 Jasmine St	Riverside	CA	92504	**800-654-1882**		275
Toro Company Commercial Products Div 8111 Lyndale Ave *Cust Svc	Bloomington	MN	55420	**800-348-2424***	952-888-8801	429
Toronto Blue Jays 1 Blue Jays Way Ste 3200	Toronto	ON	M5V1J1	**888-654-6529**	416-341-1000	711
Toronto Convention & Visitors Assn 207 Queen's Quay W Ste 405 PO Box 126	Toronto	ON	M5J1A7	**800-499-2514**	416-203-2600	208
Toronto International Film Festival Inc Reitman Sq 350 King St W	Toronto	ON	M5V3X5	**888-599-8433**		284
Toronto Star 1 Yonge St	Toronto	ON	M5E1E6	**800-268-9756**	416-869-4949	531-1
Toronto Stock Exchange 130 King St W	Toronto	ON	M5X1J2	**888-873-8392**	416-947-4670	689
Toronto Sun 333 King St E	Toronto	ON	M5A3X5	**888-786-7821**	416-947-2222	531-1
Torrance Memorial Medical Ctr 3330 Lomita Blvd	Torrance	CA	90505	**866-843-2572**	310-325-9110	374-3
Torrance State Hospital 121 Longview Dr PO Box 111	Torrance	PA	15779	**866-816-9212**	724-459-8000	374-5
Torray Fund 7501 Wisconsin Ave Ste 750 W	Bethesda	MD	20814	**800-443-3036**	301-493-4600	527
Torrey Pines State Reserve c/o San Diego Coast District 4477 Pacific Hwy	San Diego	CA	92110	**866-240-4655**	858-755-2063	564
Tortoise Energy Capital Corp 11550 Ash St Ste 300 *NYSE: TYY*	Leawood	KS	66211	**866-362-9331**	913-981-1020	790
Toshiba America Inc 1251 Ave of the Americas Ste 4100	New York	NY	10020	**800-457-7777**	212-596-0600	51
Toshiba America Information Systems Inc 9740 Irvine Blvd *Cust Svc	Irvine	CA	92618	**800-457-7777***	949-583-3000	175-1
Toshiba America Medical Systems Inc 2441 Michelle Dr *Cust Svc	Tustin	CA	92780	**800-521-1968***	714-730-5000	382
Toshiba International Corp 13131 W Little York Rd	Houston	TX	77041	**800-231-1412**	713-466-0277	517
Toss Corp 1253 Worcester Rd Ste 304	Framingham	MA	01701	**888-884-8677**	508-820-2990	182
Total Energy Services Ltd 2550 300-5th Ave SW Ste 2550 *NYSE: TOT*	Calgary	AB	T2P3C4	**877-818-6825**	403-216-3939	539
Total Energy Solutions LLC (TES) 100 International Dr Ste 260	Portsmouth	NH	03801	**877-436-9812**		112
Total Lubricants USA 5 N Stiles St	Linden	NJ	07036	**800-323-3198**	908-862-9300	540
Total Management Solutions Inc 55 Harristown Rd	Glen Rock	NJ	07452	**866-544-0707**	201-447-0707	46
Total Merchant Concepts Inc 12300 NE Fourth Plain Rd A	Vancouver	WA	98682	**888-249-9919**	360-253-5934	534
Total Package Express Inc 5871 Cheviot Rd	Cincinnati	OH	45247	**800-420-5505**	513-741-5500	778
Total Plastics Inc 3316 Pagosa Ct	Indianapolis	IN	46226	**800-382-4635**	317-543-3540	601
Total Printing Systems 201 S Gregory St	Newton	IL	62448	**800-465-5200**		626
Total Quality Logistics Inc (TQL) 4289 Ivy Pointe Blvd	Cincinnati	OH	45245	**800-580-3101**	513-831-2600	312
Total Resource Management Inc 510 King St Ste 200	Alexandria	VA	22314	**877-548-5100**	703-548-4285	195
Total Seal Inc 22642 N 15th Ave	Phoenix	AZ	85027	**800-874-2753**	623-587-7400	127
Total Technologies Ltd 9710 Research Dr	Irvine	CA	92618	**800-669-4885**	949-465-0200	255
Total Telcom Inc 540 1632 Dickson Ave	Kelowna	BC	V1Y7T2	**877-860-3762**	250-860-3762	733
Totalcomp Scales & Components 13-01 Pollitt Dr Ste 2	Fair Lawn	NJ	07410	**800-631-0347**	201-797-2718	362
Totem Ocean Trailer Express Inc 32001 32nd Ave S Ste 200	Federal Way	WA	98001	**800-426-0074**	253-449-8100	313
Toter Inc PO Box 5338	Statesville	NC	28677	**800-424-0422**	704-872-8171	201
Toth Financial Advisory Corp 608 S King St Ste 300	Leesburg	VA	20175	**800-445-1880**	703-443-8684	112
Toto Tours Ltd 1326 W Albion Ave	Chicago	IL	60626	**800-565-1241**	773-274-8686	758
Toto USA Inc 1155 Southern Rd	Morrow	GA	30260	**888-295-8134**	770-282-8686	610
Touch Base 620 Sixth St Fl 3	Denver	CO	80202	**800-605-6920**	303-862-3300	115
TouchAmerica 1403 S Third St Ext	Hillsborough	NC	27278	**800-678-6824**	919-732-6968	75
TouchLogic Corp 30 Kinnear Ct Ste 602	Richmond Hill	ON	L4B1K8	**877-707-0207**		387
TouchPoint Technologies LLC 2319 Oak Myrtle Ln Ste 104	Wesley Chapel	FL	33544	**877-898-6824**		366
Touchstorm LLC 355 Lexington Ave 12th Fl	New York	NY	10017	**877-794-6101**		387
TouchSystems Corp 220 Tradesmen Dr	Hutto	TX	78634	**800-320-5944**	512-846-2424	613
Tougaloo College 500 W County Line Rd *Admissions	Tougaloo	MS	39174	**888-424-2566***	601-977-7700	167
Tough Traveler Ltd 1012 State St *Cust Svc	Schenectady	NY	12307	**800-468-6844***	518-377-8526	63
Tourette Syndrome Assn Inc 42-40 Bell Blvd Ste 205	Bayside	NY	11361	**888-486-8738**	718-224-2999	47-17
Touring & Tasting 125 S Quarantina St	Santa Barbara	CA	93103	**800-850-4370**	805-965-2813	443
Tourism Abbotsford Society 34561 Delair Rd	Abbotsford	BC	V2S2E1	**888-332-2229**	604-859-1721	342
Tourism Bureau Southwestern Illinois 4387 N. Illinois St Ste 200	Swansea	IL	62226	**800-442-1488**	618-257-1488	208
Tourism Calgary 200 238 11th Ave SE	Calgary	AB	T2G0X8	**800-661-1678**	403-263-8510	208
Tourism Council of Frederick County Inc 151 S East St	Frederick	MD	21701	**800-999-3613**	301-600-2888	208
Tourism Malaysia 818 W Seventh St Ste 970	Los Angeles	CA	90017	**800-336-6842**	213-689-9702	773
Tourism New Brunswick PO Box 6000	Fredericton	NB	E3B5H1	**800-561-0123**		772
Tourism Richmond Inc South Tower 5811 Cooney Rd Ste 205	Richmond	BC	V6X3M1	**877-247-0777**	604-821-5474	770
Tourism Saskatchewan 1621 Albert St	Regina	SK	S4P2S5	**877-237-2273**	306-787-9600	772
Tourism Saskatoon 202 Fourth Ave N	Saskatoon	SK	S7K0K1	**800-567-2444**	306-242-1206	773
Tourism Yukon PO Box 2703	Whitehorse	YT	Y1A2C6	**800-661-0494**		772
Touro College 27-33 W 23rd St	New York	NY	10010	**888-247-1387**	212-463-0400	167
Touvelle State Recreation Site Table Rock Rd 3792 N River Rd	Central Point	OR	97502	**800-551-6949**	541-983-2277	564
Tower Federal Credit Union 7901 Sandy Spring Rd	Laurel	MD	20707	**800-787-8328**	301-497-7000	221
Tower Financial Corp 116 E Berry St *NASDAQ: TOFC*	Fort Wayne	IN	46802	**800-731-2265**		360-2
Tower Group Inc 120 Broadway 14th Fl *NASDAQ: TWGP*	New York	NY	10271	**877-883-6599**	212-655-2000	391-4
Tower Innovations 3266 Tower Dr	Newburgh	IN	47630	**800-664-8222**	812-853-0595	172
Tower Travel Management 53 Ogden Ave	Clarendon Hills	IL	60514	**800-542-9700**		769
Towle Silversmiths PO Box 21379	York	PA	17402	**800-264-0758**		700
Towmaster Inc 61381 US Hwy 12	Litchfield	MN	55355	**800-462-4517**	320-693-7900	777
Town & Country Hospital 6001 Webb Rd	Tampa	FL	33615	**866-463-7449**	813-888-7060	374-3
Town & Country Inn 20 State RT 2 *General	Shelburne	NH	03581	**800-325-4386***	603-466-3315	379
Town & Country Inn & Conference Ctr 2008 Savannah Hwy	Charleston	SC	29407	**800-334-6660**	843-571-1000	379
Town & Country Resort Hotel 500 Hotel Cir N	San Diego	CA	92108	**800-772-8527**	619-291-7131	667
Town Bank 850 W N Shore Dr	Hartland	WI	53029	**800-433-3076**	262-367-1900	69
Town Fair Tire Company Inc 460 Coe Ave	East Haven	CT	06512	**800-972-2245**		53
Town Food Service Equipment Co 72 Beadel St	Brooklyn	NY	11222	**800-221-5032**	718-388-5650	299
Town Inn Suites 620 Church St	Toronto	ON	M4Y2G2	**800-387-2755**	416-964-3311	379
Town Pump Inc 600 S Main St	Butte	MT	59701	**800-823-4931**	406-497-6700	325
Town Talk Inc 6310 Cane Run Rd	Louisville	KY	40258	**800-626-2220**	502-736-2972	154-8
Towne Air Freight 24805 US 20 W	South Bend	IN	46628	**800-726-6654**	423-636-3380	312

Company / Address	City	State	ZIP	Toll-Free	Phone	Class
Towne Technologies Inc 6-10 Bell Ave PO Box 460	Somerville	NJ	08876	**800-837-2515**	908-722-9500	480
Towns County 1411 Jack Dayton Cir	Young Harris	GA	30582	**800-984-1543**	706-896-4966	338
Townsend Hotel 100 Townsend St	Birmingham	MI	48009	**800-548-4172**	248-642-7900	379
Townsend James r 150 Dufferin Ave	London	ON	N6A5N6	**888-354-0448**	519-672-5272	428
Townsend Oil Company Inc 27 Cherry St PO Box 90	Danvers	MA	01923	**800-888-2888**		318
Townsend Press 439 Kelley Dr	West Berlin	NJ	08091	**800-772-6410**	856-753-0554	634-2
Townsend Security 724 columbia st nw	Olympia	WA	98501	**800-357-1019**	360-359-4400	227
Towson University 8000 York Rd	Towson	MD	21252	**866-301-3375**	410-704-2113	167
Toxics Law Reporter 1801 S Bell St	Arlington	VA	22202	**800-372-1033**		530-5
Toxikon Corp 15 Wiggins Ave	Bedford	MA	01730	**800-458-4141**	781-275-3330	740
Toy Industry Assn 1115 Broadway Ste 400	New York	NY	10010	**800-541-1345**	212-675-1141	48-4
Toyo Ink America LLC 1225 N Michael Dr *General	Wood Dale	IL	60191	**866-969-8696***		388
Toyo Tire USA Corp 6261 Katella Ave Ste 2B	Cypress	CA	90630	**800-678-3250**		752
Toyoda Machinery USA Inc 316 W University Dr	Arlington Heights	IL	60004	**800-257-2985**	847-253-0340	454
Toyota Canada Inc 1 Toyota Pl *Cust Svc	Scarborough	ON	M1H1H9	**888-869-6828***	416-438-6320	58
Toyota Ctr 1510 Polk St	Houston	TX	77002	**866-446-8849**	713-758-7200	718
Toyota Financial Services 19001 S Western Ave *Cust Svc	Torrance	CA	90501	**800-874-8822***	212-715-7386	216
Toyota Motor North America Inc 601 Lexington Ave 49th Fl	New York	NY	10022	**800-331-4331**		360-3
Toyota Motor Sales USA Inc 19001 S Western Ave *Cust Svc	Torrance	CA	90501	**800-331-4331***	310-468-4000	58
Toyota Motor Sales USA Inc Lexus Div 19001 S Western Ave *Cust Svc	Torrance	CA	90501	**800-255-3987***		58
Toyota Sunnyvale 898 W El Camino Real	Sunnyvale	CA	94087	**888-210-0091**	408-245-6640	56
TP Orthodontics Inc 100 Ctr Plz	La Porte	IN	46350	**800-348-8856**	219-785-2591	230
TP Trucking LLC 5630 Table Rock Rd	Central Point	OR	97502	**800-292-4399**		778
TPC Advance Technology Inc 18525 Gale Ave	City Of Industry	CA	91748	**800-560-8222**	626-810-4337	474
TPI Corp PO Box 4973	Johnson City	TN	37602	**800-682-3398**		15
TPL (Trust for Public Land) 116 New Montgomery St 4th Fl	San Francisco	CA	94105	**800-714-5263**	415-495-4014	47-13
TPL Communications 3825 Foothill Blvd Unit 206	La Crescenta	CA	91214	**800-447-6937**	323-256-3000	645
TPR (Texas Public Radio) 8401 Datapoint Dr Ste 800	San Antonio	TX	78229	**800-622-8977**	210-614-8977	629
TQL (Total Quality Logistics Inc) 4289 Ivy Pointe Blvd	Cincinnati	OH	45245	**800-580-3101**	513-831-2600	312
TR Miller Mill Company Inc 215 Deer St PO Box 708	Brewton	AL	36427	**800-633-6740**	251-867-4331	681
Trabert & Hoeffer 111 E Oak St	Chicago	IL	60611	**800-539-3573**	312-787-1654	410
TRAC Media Services 2030 E Speedway Blvd Ste 210	Tucson	AZ	85719	**888-299-1866**	520-299-1866	629
Trace-A-Matic Inc (T-A-M) 1570 Commerce Ave	Brookfield	WI	53045	**877-375-0217**	262-797-7300	620
TracFone Wireless Inc 9700 NW 112th Ave	Miami	FL	33178	**800-876-5753**	305-640-2000	733
Trachte Bldg Systems Inc 314 Wilburn Rd	Sun Prairie	WI	53590	**800-356-5824**		104
Tracie Martyn Salon 59 Fifth Ave Ste 1	New York	NY	10003	**866-862-7896**	212-206-9333	704
TrackMaster 2083 Old Middlefield Way Ste 206	Mountain View	CA	94043	**800-334-3800**	650-316-1020	639
TRACO 71 Progress Ave	Cranberry Township	PA	16066	**800-992-4444**	724-776-7000	236
TRACS (TransNational Assn of Christian Colleges & Schools) 15935 Forest Rd PO Box 328	Forest	VA	24551	**800-669-4000**	434-525-9539	47-1
Tractor Supply Co 5401 Virginia Way *NASDAQ: TSCO*	Brentwood	TN	37027	**877-718-6750**		276
Tracy-Luckey Company Inc 110 N Hicks St	Harlem	GA	30814	**800-476-4796**	706-556-6216	11-1
Trada Inc 1023 Walnut St	Boulder	CO	80302	**877-871-1835**		387
Trade Manage Capital Inc 299 Market St 4th Fl	Saddle Brook	NJ	07663	**800-221-5676**		179
Trade Products Corp 12124 Popes Head Rd	Fairfax	VA	22030	**888-352-3580**	703-502-9000	321
Trade Service Company LLC 15092 Ave of Science	San Diego	CA	92128	**800-854-1527**		226
Trademark Co, The 344 Maple Ave W Ste 151	Vienna	VA	22180	**800-906-8626**		318
Trademark Transportation Inc 739 Vandalia St	Saint Paul	MN	55114	**800-646-2550**	651-646-2500	312
Trader Duke's 1117 Williston Rd	South Burlington	VT	05403	**800-445-8667**	802-660-7523	669
Tradescape Inc 520 S El Camino Real Ste 640	San Mateo	CA	94402	**800-697-6068**		198
TradeStation Group Inc 8050 SW Tenth St Ste 2000	Plantation	FL	33324	**800-871-3577**	954-652-7000	180-10
Trading Direct 160 Broadway E Bldg 7th Fl	New York	NY	10038	**800-925-8566**	212-766-0230	688
Trading Post of Kittery 301 US Rte 1 PO Box 904	Kittery	ME	03904	**800-872-4867**		393
Traditional Bank 49 W Main St PO Box 326	Mount Sterling	KY	40353	**800-498-0414**	859-498-0414	69
Traditional Door Design & Millwork Ltd 261 Regina Rd	Woodbridge	ON	L4L8M3	**877-226-9930**	416-747-1992	236
Traffic Control Service Inc 2435 Lemon Ave	Signal Hill	CA	90755	**800-763-3999**		266-3
Traffic Group Inc, The 9900 Franklin Sq Dr	Baltimore	MD	21236	**800-583-8411**	410-931-6600	462
Traffic Jam Events LLC 704 Hickory Ave	Harahan	LA	70123	**800-922-8109**		197
Trail King Industries Inc 147 Industrial Pk Rd	Brookville	PA	15825	**800-545-1549**	814-849-2342	777
Trailer Bridge Inc 10405 New Berlin Rd E *OTC: TRBRQ*	Jacksonville	FL	32226	**800-554-1589**	904-751-7100	313
Trailer Transit Inc 1130 E US 20	Porter	IN	46304	**800-423-3647**	219-926-2111	778
Trailercraft Inc 1301 E 64th Ave	Anchorage	AK	99518	**800-478-3238**	907-563-3238	515
Trailiner Corp PO Box 5270	Springfield	MO	65801	**800-833-8209**	417-866-7258	777
Trailways Transportation System Inc 3554 Chain Bridge Rd Ste 202	Fairfax	VA	22030	**877-467-3346**	703-691-3052	106
Training Advantage, The PO Box 800	Ignacio	CO	81137	**800-659-2656**	970-563-4517	107
Training Assoc Corp, The 289 Tpke Rd	Westborough	MA	01581	**800-241-8868**	508-890-8500	630
Training Industry Inc 401 Harrison Oaks Blvd Ste 300	Cary	NC	27513	**866-298-4203**		393
Training Magazine 27020 Noble Rd	Excelsior	MN	55331	**877-865-9361**	847-559-7596	456-5
Training Modernization Group Inc 9737 Peppertree Rd	Spotsylvania	VA	22553	**866-855-6449**	540-295-9313	198
Trainworld Associates LLC 751 Mcdonald Ave	Brooklyn	NY	11218	**800-541-7010**	718-436-7072	759
TRAK Microwave Corp 4726 Eisenhower Blvd	Tampa	FL	33634	**888-283-8444**	813-901-7200	255
Tramex Travel Inc 4505 Spicewood Springs Rd Ste 200	Austin	TX	78759	**800-527-3039**	512-343-2201	769
Trans Am Travel 4222 King St Ste 130	Alexandria	VA	22302	**800-822-7600**	703-998-7676	16
Trans Med USA Inc 31 Progress Ave	Tyngsboro	MA	01879	**800-442-1142**	978-649-1970	474
Trans National Communications International Inc (TNCI) 2 Charlesgate W	Boston	MA	02215	**800-800-8400**	617-369-1000	733
Trans World Corp (TWC) 545 Fifth Ave Ste 940 *OTC: TWOC*	New York	NY	10017	**877-407-9037**	212-983-3355	379
TransAct Technologies Inc 1 Hamden Ctr 2319 Whitney Ave Ste 3B *NASDAQ: TACT*	Hamden	CT	06518	**800-243-8941**	203-859-6800	175-6
Transaction Network Services Inc. 10740 Parkridge Blvd Ste 100	Reston	VA	20191	**866-523-0661**	703-453-8300	219
TransAlta Corp 110 12th Ave SW PO Box 1900 Stn M *TSE: TA*	Calgary	AB	T2P2M1	**877-700-9288**	403-267-7110	785
TransAm Trucking Inc 15910 S 169th Hwy	Olathe	KS	66062	**800-800-5945**	913-782-5300	778
Transamerica 4333 Edgewood Rd NE	Cedar Rapids	IA	52499	**800-852-4678**	319-355-8511	391-5
Transamerica Occidental Life Insurance Co 1150 S Olive St *Cust Svc	Los Angeles	CA	90015	**800-852-4678***	213-742-2111	391-2
Transat AT Inc 300 Leo-Pariseau St Ste 600 *TSE: TRZ.B*	Montreal	QC	H2X4C2	**800-387-0825**	514-987-1616	769
Trans-Border Global Freight Systems Inc 2103 Route 9	Round Lake	NY	12151	**800-493-9444**	518-785-6000	312
TransCanada Pipelines Ltd 450 First St SW	Calgary	AB	T2P5H1	**800-661-3805**	403-920-2000	326
Trans-Carriers Inc 5135 US Hwy 78	Memphis	TN	38118	**800-999-7383**	901-368-2900	778
Transcat Inc 35 Vantage Pt Dr *NASDAQ: TRNS*	Rochester	NY	14624	**800-800-5001**	585-352-9460	203
TransChemical Inc 419 De Soto Ave	Saint Louis	MO	63147	**888-873-6481**	314-231-6905	145
Transco Business Technologies (TBT) 34 Leighton Rd	Augusta	ME	04330	**800-322-0003**	207-622-6251	111
Transco Industries Inc 5534 NE 122nd Ave	Portland	OR	97230	**800-545-9991**	503-256-1955	209
Transco Railway Products Inc 820 Hopley Ave	Bucyrus	OH	44820	**800-472-4592**	419-562-1031	648
TransCon Builders Inc 25250 Rockside Rd	Cleveland	OH	44146	**800-451-2608**	440-439-2100	651
Transcontinental Inc 1100 Rene-Levesque Blvd W 24th Fl	Montreal	QC	H3B4X9	**800-361-5479**	514-392-9000	634-9
Transcontinental Insurance Co 333 S Wabash Ave CNA Ctr	Chicago	IL	60604	**800-262-2000**	312-822-5000	391-4
Transcontinental Realty Investors Inc 1603 Lyndon B Johnson Fwy Ste 800 *NYSE: TCI*	Dallas	TX	75234	**800-400-6407**	469-522-4200	652
Trans-Continental Systems Inc 10801 Evendale Dr	Cincinnati	OH	45241	**800-525-8726**	513-769-4774	646
TransCore Holdings Inc 8158 Adams Dr	Hummelstown	PA	17036	**800-923-4824**	717-561-2400	263
TransCore Link Logistics Corp 6660 Kennedy Rd Ste 205	Mississauga	ON	L5T2M9	**800-263-6149**		312
Transcript Pharmacy Inc 2506 Lakeland Dr Ste 201	Jackson	MS	39232	**866-420-4041**		239

Alphabetical Section

Name / Address	City	State	ZIP	Toll-Free	Phone	Class
Transentric 1400 Douglas St Ste 0840	Omaha	NE	68179	**800-877-0328**	402-544-6000	180-10
Transfer Express Inc 7650 Tyler Blvd	Mentor	OH	44060	**800-622-2280**	440-918-1900	626
TRANSFLO Terminal Services Inc 500 Water St Ste J975	Jacksonville	FL	32202	**866-872-6735**		448
Transforce Inc 5520 Cherokee Ave Ste 200	Alexandria	VA	22150	**800-308-6989**	703-838-5580	719
Transgenomic Inc 12325 Emmet St *OTC: TBIO*	Omaha	NE	68164	**888-233-9283**	402-452-5400	419
TRANSInternational System Inc 130 E Wilson Bridge Rd Ste 150 Ste 150	Worthington	OH	43085	**800-340-7540**	614-891-4942	312
Transit Systems Inc 999 Old Eagle School Rd Ste 114	Wayne	PA	19087	**800-626-1257**		312
Transition Networks Inc 10900 Red Cir Dr	Minnetonka	MN	55343	**800-526-9267**	952-941-7600	178
Transitions Optical Inc 9251 Belcher Rd	Pinellas Park	FL	33782	**800-533-2081**	727-545-0400	541
Translations.com Inc 3 Pk Ave 39th Fl	New York	NY	10016	**800-688-7205**	212-689-1616	181
Trans-Lux Corp 26 Pearl St *OTC: TNLX*	Norwalk	CT	06850	**800-243-5544**	203-853-4321	175-4
Trans-Lux Fair-Play Inc 1700 Delaware Ave	Des Moines	IA	50317	**800-247-0265**	515-265-5305	175-4
Transmedia 719 Battery St	San Francisco	CA	94111	**800-229-7234**	415-956-3118	644
TransNational Assn of Christian Colleges & Schools (TRACS) 15935 Forest Rd PO Box 328	Forest	VA	24551	**800-669-4000**	434-525-9539	47-1
Transocean Inc 4 Greenway Plaza *NYSE: RIG*	Houston	TX	77046	**877-440-0173**	713-232-7500	539
Transoft Solutions Inc 13575 Commerce Pkwy Ste 250	Richmond	BC	V6V2L1	**888-244-8387**	604-244-8387	176
Transource Computers Corp 2405 W Utopia Rd	Phoenix	AZ	85027	**800-486-3715**	623-879-8882	175-1
Transparent Language Inc 12 Murphy Dr	Nashua	NH	03062	**800-538-8867**		180-3
Trans-Phos Inc PO Box 9004	Bartow	FL	33831	**800-940-1575**	863-534-1575	778
Transplace 3010 Gaylord Pkwy Ste 200	Frisco	TX	75034	**866-413-9266**		448
Transpo Electronics Inc 2150 Brengle Ave	Orlando	FL	32808	**800-327-6903**		249
Transport Corp of America Inc 1715 Yankee Doodle Rd	Eagan	MN	55121	**800-328-3927**	651-686-2500	778
Transport Distribution Co PO Box 306	Joplin	MO	64802	**800-866-7709**	417-624-3814	778
Transport Inc 2225 Main Ave SE	Moorhead	MN	56560	**800-598-7267**	218-236-6300	778
Transport Workers Union of America 501 Third St NW 9th Fl	Washington	DC	20001	**888-565-6898**	202-719-3900	48-21
Transportation Communications International Union 3 Research Pl	Rockville	MD	20850	**877-772-5772**	301-948-4910	414
Transportation Insurance Co 333 S Wabash Ave	Chicago	IL	60604	**800-437-8854**	312-822-5000	391-4
Transportation Intermediaries Assn (TIA) 1625 Prince St Ste 200	Alexandria	VA	22314	**888-910-4747**	703-299-5700	48-21
Transportation Management Assoc Inc 344 Oak Grove Church Rd	Mocksville	NC	27028	**800-745-8292**		312
Transportation Research Board (TRB) 500 Fifth St NW	Washington	DC	20001	**866-233-4642**	202-334-2934	48-21
Transportation Research Ctr Inc (TRC Inc) 10820 State Rt 347 PO Box B-67	East Liberty	OH	43319	**800-837-7872**	937-666-2011	666
Transportation Security Administration (TSA) 601 S 12th St	Arlington	VA	22202	**866-289-9673**		340-9
Federal Air Marshal Service 601 S 12th St	Arlington	VA	22202	**866-289-9673**		340-9
Trans-Tel Central Inc (TTC) 2805 Broce Dr	Norman	OK	73072	**800-729-4636**	405-447-5025	785
TransUnion LLC 555 W Adams St	Chicago	IL	60661	**866-922-2100**		220
Transwest 20770 I-76 Frontage Rd	Brighton	CO	80603	**800-289-3161**	303-289-3161	56
TransWood Carriers Inc PO Box 189	Omaha	NE	68101	**888-346-8092**		778
TransWorks 9910 Dupont Cir Dr E Ste 200	Fort Wayne	IN	46825	**800-435-4691**	260-487-4400	180-10
TransWorld Business 2052 Corte Del Nogal Ste 100 *General	Carlsbad	CA	92011	**800-788-7072***	760-722-7777	634-9
Transworld Systems Inc PO Box 15618	Wilmington	DE	19850	**888-446-4733**	877-282-1250	159
TransX Group of Cos 2595 Inkster Blvd	Winnipeg	MB	R3C2E6	**877-558-9444**	204-632-6694	312
Transylvania University 300 N Broadway	Lexington	KY	40508	**800-872-6798**	859-233-8242	167
Tranter Inc 1900 Old Burk Hwy	Wichita Falls	TX	76306	**800-414-6908**	940-723-7125	90
Tranzon LLC 7204 Glen Forest Dr Ste 105	Richmond	VA	23226	**866-503-1212**	207-775-4300	40
Trapit Inc 2390 El Camino Real Ste 220	Palo Alto	CA	94306	**844-987-2748**		387
Trapp Family Lodge 700 Trapp Hill Rd PO Box 1428	Stowe	VT	05672	**800-826-7000**	802-253-8511	667
Trattoria Del Lupo 3950 Las Vegas Blvd S	Las Vegas	NV	89119	**800-275-8273**	702-740-5522	669
Traulsen & Company Inc 4401 Blue Mound Rd	Fort Worth	TX	76106	**800-825-8220**		14
Travaasa Hana 5031 Hana Hwy	Hana	HI	96713	**855-868-7282**	808-248-8211	667
Travcoa 100 N Sepulveda Blvd Ste 1700	El Segundo	CA	90245	**800-992-2003**	310-649-7104	758
Travel & Transport Inc 2120 S 72nd St	Omaha	NE	68124	**800-228-2545**	402-399-4500	769
Travel + Leisure Magazine 225 Liberty St	New York	NY	10281	**800-452-9292**	212-382-5600	456-20
Travel Agent Magazine 757 Third Ave 5th Fl	New York	NY	10017	**855-424-6247**	212-895-8200	456-22
Travel Berkley Springs 127 Fairfax St	Berkeley Springs	WV	25411	**800-447-8797**	304-258-9147	770
Travel Destinations Management Group Inc 110 Painters Mill Rd	Owings Mills	MD	21117	**800-635-7307**	410-363-3111	769
Travel Dynamics International 132 E 70th St	New York	NY	10021	**800-257-5767**	212-517-7555	222
Travel Goods Association 301 N Harrison St Ste 412	Princeton	NJ	08540	**877-842-1938**		136
Travel Impressions Ltd 465 Smith St	Farmingdale	NY	11735	**800-284-0044**	631-845-8000	769
Travel Inc 4355 River Green Pkwy	Duluth	GA	30096	**888-439-1831**	770-291-4100	769
Travel Institute 945 Concord St Ste 305	Framingham	MA	01701	**800-542-4282**	781-237-0280	47-23
Travel Insured International 855 Winding Brook Dr PO Box 280568	Glastonbury	CT	06033	**800-243-3174**		391-7
Travel Manitoba 155 Carlton St 7th Fl	Winnipeg	MB	R3C3H8	**800-665-0040**	204-927-7800	772
Travel Network Corp, The 1920 Ave Rd	Toronto	ON	M5M4A1	**888-666-8747**	416-789-3271	773
Travel One Inc 8009 34th Ave S 15th Fl	Minneapolis	MN	55425	**800-247-1311**	952-854-2551	770
Travel Portland Pioneer Courthouse Square 701 S.W. Sixth Ave.	Portland	OR	97205	**877-678-5263**	503-275-9750	208
Travel Team Inc 2495 Main St	Buffalo	NY	14214	**800-245-8326**	716-862-7600	769
TravelCenters of America 24601 Ctr Ridge Rd Ste 200	Westlake	OH	44145	**800-632-9240**	440-808-9100	325
Travelclick 7 Times Sq 38th Fl	New York	NY	10036	**866-674-4549**	212-817-4800	196
Travelennium Inc 556 Colonial Rd	Memphis	TN	38117	**800-844-4924**	901-767-0761	769
Travelers Cos Inc 385 Washington St *NYSE: TRV*	Saint Paul	MN	55102	**800-328-2189**	651-310-7911	360-4
Travelers Motor Club 720 NW 50th St	Oklahoma City	OK	73154	**800-654-9208**	405-848-1711	52
Travelers Transportation Services Inc 195 Heart Lk Rd South	Brampton	ON	L6W3N6	**800-265-8789**	905-457-8789	312
Travelex International Inc 2061 N Barrington Rd	Hoffman Estates	IL	60169	**800-882-0499**	847-882-0400	770
Travelex Worldwide Money 122 E 42nd St Ste 2800	New York	NY	10168	**800-228-9792**	212-363-6206	68
Travelhost Magazine 10701 N Stemmons Fwy	Dallas	TX	75220	**800-527-1782**	972-556-0541	456-22
Traveline Travel Agencies Inc 4074 Erie St	Willoughby	OH	44094	**888-700-8747**	440-602-8020	769
Travelodge Virginia Beach 1909 Atlantic Ave	Virginia Beach	VA	23451	**800-578-7878**	757-425-0650	379
Travelong Inc 135 W 50th St Ste 500	New York	NY	10020	**800-537-6043**	212-736-2166	769
Travelpro USA 700 Banyan Trl	Boca Raton	FL	33431	**800-741-7471**	561-998-2824	452
TravelSmith Outfitters 773 San Marin Dr Ste 2300	Novato	CA	94945	**800-770-3387**		458
TravelStore Inc 11601 Wilshire Blvd	Los Angeles	CA	90025	**800-850-3224**	310-575-5540	769
Travers Printing Inc 32 Mission St	Gardner	MA	01440	**800-696-0530**	978-632-0530	626
Travers Tool Company Inc 128-15 26th Ave *Cust Svc	Flushing	NY	11354	**800-221-0270***	718-886-7200	385
Traverse City Area Chamber of Commerce 202 E Grandview Pkwy	Traverse City	MI	49684	**844-900-0500**	231-947-5075	138
Traverse City Convention & Visitors Bureau 101 W Grandview Pkwy	Traverse City	MI	49684	**800-940-1120**	231-947-1120	208
Traverse Electric Co-op Inc 1618 Broadway PO Box 66	Wheaton	MN	56296	**800-927-5443**	320-563-8616	247
Travis & Beverly Cross Guest Housing Ctr 9320 SW Barnes Rd	Portland	OR	97225	**888-550-1575**	503-216-1575	372
Travis Body & Trailer Inc 13955 FM529	Houston	TX	77041	**800-535-4372**	713-466-5888	777
Travis Federal Credit Union 1 Travis Way	Vacaville	CA	95687	**800-877-8328**	707-449-4000	221
Travis Meats Inc 7210 Clinton Hwy PO Box 670	Powell	TN	37849	**800-247-7606**	865-938-9051	472
Travizon Meeting Management 275 Mishawum Rd Ste 300	Woburn	MA	01801	**800-423-2500**	888-781-5200	186
Trayer Engineering Corp 898 Pennsylvania Ave	San Francisco	CA	94107	**800-377-1774**	415-285-7770	263
Traylor Bros Inc 835 N Congress Ave	Evansville	IN	47715	**866-895-1491**	812-477-1542	190-4
TRB (Transportation Research Board) 500 Fifth St NW	Washington	DC	20001	**866-233-4642**	202-334-2934	48-21
TRC Holdings Inc 1300 Virginia Dr Ste 200	Fort Washington	PA	19034	**800-275-2827**	215-641-2200	465
TRC Inc (Transportation Research Ctr Inc) 10820 State Rt 347 PO Box B-67	East Liberty	OH	43319	**800-837-7872**	937-666-2011	666
Treasure Bay Casino & Hotel 1980 Beach Blvd *General	Biloxi	MS	39531	**800-747-2839***	228-385-6000	667
Treasure Chest Casino 5050 Williams Blvd	Kenner	LA	70065	**800-298-0711**	504-443-8000	132
Treasure Coast Hospice 1201 SE Indian St	Stuart	FL	34997	**800-299-4677**	772-403-4500	371
Treasure Island Hotel & Casino 3300 Las Vegas Blvd S	Las Vegas	NV	89109	**800-288-7206**	702-894-7111	667
Treasure Valley Community College 650 College Blvd	Ontario	OR	97914	**888-292-5247**	541-881-8822	161
Treats International Franchise Corp 238 Queen St S 2nd Fl	Mississauga	ON	L5M1L5	**800-461-4003**	613-563-4073	67

Name / Address	City	State	Zip	Toll-Free	Phone	Class
Tredegar Corp 1100 Boulders Pkwy *NYSE: TG*	North Chesterfield	VA	23225	**800-411-7441**	804-330-1000	360-3
Tree Care Industry Assn (TCIA) 136 Harvey Rd Ste 101	Londonderry	NH	03053	**800-733-2622**	603-314-5380	47-13
Tree Island Industries 3933 Boundary Rd	Richmond	BC	V6V1T8	**800-663-0955**	604-524-3744	484
Tree Island Steel 12459 Arrow Rt	Rancho Cucamonga	CA	91739	**800-255-6974**	909-594-7511	811
Treeline Well Services Inc 750 333 - 11th Ave SW	Calgary	AB	T2R1L9	**844-344-7447**	403-266-2868	192
Trees for Tomorrow (TFT) 519 Sheridan St E PO Box 609	Eagle River	WI	54521	**800-838-9472**	715-479-6456	48-5
Trees Inc 650 N Sam Houston Pkwy E Ste 205	Houston	TX	77060	**866-865-9617**	281-447-1327	774
Treetops Resort 3962 Wilkinson Rd	Gaylord	MI	49735	**866-348-5249**	989-732-6711	667
Trefethen Vineyards Winery Inc 1160 Oak Knoll Ave	Napa	CA	94558	**866-895-7696**	707-255-7700	79-3
Treflie Capital Management 35 Ezekills Holw	Sag Harbor	NY	11963	**866-236-3363**	631-725-2500	401
Trego County 18001 283 Hwy	WaKeeney	KS	67672	**877-962-7248**	785-743-6385	338
Trehel Corp PO Box 1707	Clemson	SC	29633	**800-319-7006**	864-654-6582	188
Trek Inc 11601 Maple Ridge Rd	Medina	NY	14103	**800-367-8735**	585-798-3140	250
Trelleborg Automotive Americas 400 Aylworth Ave	South Haven	MI	49090	**800-635-9331**	269-637-2116	59
Trelleborg Coated Systems US Inc 790 Reeves St	Spartanburg	SC	29301	**800-344-0714**		742-1
Tremco Inc Roofing Div 3735 Green Rd	Beachwood	OH	44122	**800-852-6013**	216-292-5000	3
Tremont Chicago 100 E Chestnut St	Chicago	IL	60611	**866-716-8147**	312-751-1900	379
Trempealeau County 36245 Main St	Whitehall	WI	54773	**877-538-2311**	715-538-2311	338
Trench Plate Rental Co 13217 Laureldale Ave	Downey	CA	90242	**800-821-4478**		23
Trend 660 American Ave Ste 203	King Of Prussia	PA	19406	**877-330-9900**	610-783-4650	227
TREND Enterprises Inc 300 Ninth Ave SW *Cust Svc	New Brighton	MN	55112	**800-860-6762***	651-631-2850	245
Trendex Inc 240 E Maryland Ave	Saint Paul	MN	55117	**800-328-9200**	651-489-4655	85
TrendMicro Inc 10101 N De Anza Blvd	Cupertino	CA	95014	**800-228-5651**	408-257-1500	180-12
Trends International LLC 5188 W 74th St	Indianapolis	IN	46268	**866-406-7771**	317-388-1212	329
Trendware International Inc 20675 Manhattan Pl	Torrance	CA	90501	**888-326-6061**	310-961-5500	178
Trendway Corp 13467 Quincy St PO Box 9016	Holland	MI	49422	**800-968-5344**	616-399-3900	320-1
Trenholm State Technical College 1225 Air Base Blvd	Montgomery	AL	36108	**800-917-2081**	334-420-4200	798
Trent Inc 201 Leverington Ave	Philadelphia	PA	19127	**800-544-8736**	215-482-5000	319
Trent University 1600 W Bank Dr	Peterborough	ON	K9J7B8	**888-739-8885**	705-748-1011	783
Trentonian 600 Perry St	Trenton	NJ	08618	**855-549-6525**	609-989-7800	531-2
Trevecca Nazarene University 333 Murfreesboro Rd	Nashville	TN	37210	**888-210-4868**	615-248-1200	167
Trew Industrial Wheels Inc 310 Wilhagan Rd	Nashville	TN	37217	**888-977-8739**	615-360-9100	53
Trex Enterprises Corp 10455 Pacific Ctr Ct	San Diego	CA	92121	**800-626-5885**	858-646-5300	666
TRFCVB (Thief River Falls Convention & Visitors Bureau) 102 Main Ave N	Thief River	MN	56701	**800-657-3700**	218-686-9785	208
TRGC (Title Resources Guaranty Co) 8111 LBJ Fwy Ste 1200	Dallas	TX	75251	**800-526-8018**	972-644-6500	391-6
Tri County Area Chamber of Commerce 152 E High St Ste 360	Pottstown	PA	19464	**800-223-8477**	610-326-2900	138
Tri County Ford Mercury Inc 4032 Commerce Pkwy PO Box 425	Buckner	KY	40010	**800-945-2520**	502-241-7333	56
TRI MAP International Inc 111 Val Dervin Pkwy	Stockton	CA	95206	**888-687-4627**	209-234-0100	256
Tri Star Freight System Inc 5407 Mesa Dr	Houston	TX	77028	**800-229-1095**	713-631-1095	778
Tri State Distribution Inc 600 Vista Dr	Sparta	TN	38583	**800-392-9824**		474
Tri State Wholesale Flooring Inc 3900 W 34th St N	Sioux Falls	SD	57107	**800-353-3080**	605-336-3080	130
Tri Tool Inc 3041 Sunrise Blvd	Rancho Cordova	CA	95742	**800-345-5015**	916-288-6100	620
Tri Union Express Inc 1939 N Lafayette Ct	Griffith	IN	46319	**800-228-9098**	219-838-5400	801-1
Triad Financial Services Inc 4336 Pablo Oaks Ct	Jacksonville	FL	32224	**800-522-2013**		216
Triad Guaranty Insurance Corp 101 S Stratford Rd *Cust Svc	Winston-Salem	NC	27104	**888-691-8074***	336-723-1282	391-5
Triad Isotopes Inc 4205 Vineland Rd Ste L1	Orlando	FL	32811	**866-310-0086**	407-455-6700	233
Triad Products Co 1801 W 'B' St *General	Hastings	NE	68901	**888-253-4227***	402-462-2181	607
Triad's 105.7 Man Up, The 2-B PAI Pk	Greensboro	NC	27409	**800-950-2482**	336-822-2000	643
Triangle Brick Co 6523 NC Hwy 55	Durham	NC	27713	**800-672-8547**	919-544-1796	149
Triangle Business Journal 3600 Glenwood Ave Ste 100	Raleigh	NC	27612	**800-275-9356**	919-878-0010	456-5
Triangle C Dude Ranch 3737 Hwy 26	Dubois	WY	82513	**800-661-4928**	307-455-2225	241
Triangle Fastener Corp 1925 Preble Ave *General	Pittsburgh	PA	15233	**800-486-1832***	412-321-5000	351
Triangle Orthopedic Assoc PA 120 William Penn Plz	Durham	NC	27704	**800-359-3053**	919-220-5255	374-3
Triangle Package Machinery Co 6655 W Diversey Ave	Chicago	IL	60707	**800-621-4170**	773-889-0200	546
Triangle Suspension Systems Inc 47 E Maloney Rd	Du Bois	PA	15801	**800-458-6077**	814-375-7211	59
Triangle Tech Inc *Du Bois* PO Box 551	Du Bois	PA	15801	**800-874-8324**	814-371-2090	798
Erie 2000 Liberty St	Erie	PA	16502	**800-874-8324**	814-453-6016	798
Greensburg 222 E Pittsburgh St	Greensburg	PA	15601	**800-874-8324**	724-832-1050	798
Triangle X-ray Co 4900 Thornton Rd Ste 117	Raleigh	NC	27616	**866-763-9729**	919-876-6156	474
Trianon Old Naples 955 Seventh Ave S	Naples	FL	34102	**877-482-5228**	239-435-9600	379
Triathlete Sports 186 Exchange St	Bangor	ME	04401	**800-635-0528**	207-990-2013	709
Tri-Basin Natural Resources District 1723 Burlington St	Holdrege	NE	68949	**877-995-6688**		198
Tri-boro Shelving & Partition Corp 300 Dominion Dr	Farmville	VA	23901	**800-633-3070**	434-315-5600	322
Tribridge 4830 W Kennedy Blvd Ste 890	Tampa	FL	33609	**877-744-1360**		180-1
Tribune Chronicle 240 Franklin St SE	Warren	OH	44482	**888-550-8742**	330-841-1600	531-2
Tribune Newspapers of Snohomish County 127 Ave C Ste B PO Box 499	Snohomish	WA	98291	**877-894-4663**	360-568-4121	531-4
Tribune Review Publishing Co 622 Cabin Hill Dr	Greensburg	PA	15601	**800-524-5700**	724-834-1151	634-8
Tribune, The 3825 S Higuera St	San Luis Obispo	CA	93401	**800-477-8799**	805-781-7800	531-2
Tribune-Democrat 425 Locust St	Johnstown	PA	15907	**855-255-5975**	814-532-5050	531-2
Tribune-Star PO Box 149	Terre Haute	IN	47808	**800-783-8742**	812-231-4200	531-2
Trican Well Service Ltd 645 Seventh Ave SW Ste 2900 *TSE: TCW*	Calgary	AB	T2P4G8	**877-473-2008**	403-266-0202	538
Tricerat Inc 11500 Cronridge Dr Ste 100	Owings Mills	MD	21117	**800-582-5167**	410-715-4226	181
Tri-Cities Visitor & Convention Bureau 7130 W Grandridge Blvd Ste B	Kennewick	WA	99336	**800-254-5824**	509-735-8486	208
Tri-City Electrical Contractors Inc 430 W Dr	Altamonte Springs	FL	32714	**800-768-2489**	407-788-3500	191-4
Tri-City Herald 333 W Canal Dr	Kennewick	WA	99336	**800-874-0445**	509-582-1500	531-2
Trickle Up Program Inc 104 W 27th St 12th Fl	New York	NY	10001	**866-246-9980**	212-255-9980	47-5
TriCo Bancshares 63 Constitution Dr *NASDAQ: TCBK*	Chico	CA	95973	**800-922-8742**	530-898-0300	360-2
Tricomm Services Corp 1247 N Church St Ste 8	Moorestown	NJ	08057	**800-872-2401**	856-914-9001	785
TRICOR (Tennessee Rehabilitative Initiative in Correction) 240 Great Cir Rd Ste 310	Nashville	TN	37228	**800-958-7426**	615-741-5705	629
Tri-County Electric 302 E Glaydas St PO Box 880	Hooker	OK	73945	**800-522-3315**	580-652-2418	247
Tri-County Electric Co-op 31110 Co-op Way PO Box 626	Rushford	MN	55971	**800-432-2285**	507-864-7783	247
Tri-County Electric Co-op Inc 600 NW Pkwy	Azle	TX	76020	**800-367-8232**	817-444-3201	247
Tri-County Electric Membership Corp 405 College St	Lafayette	TN	37083	**800-369-2111**	615-666-2111	247
Tri-County Mall 11700 Princeton Pike	Cincinnati	OH	45246	**866-905-4675**	513-671-0120	459
Tri-County Rural Electric Co-op Inc 22 N Main St PO Box 526	Mansfield	PA	16933	**800-343-2559**	570-662-2175	247
Tri-County Technical College 7900 Hwy 76	Pendleton	SC	29670	**866-269-5677**	864-646-8361	798
Trident Medical Ctr 9330 Medical Plz Dr	Charleston	SC	29406	**866-492-9085**	843-797-7000	374-3
Trident Steel Corp 12825 Flushing Meadows Dr Ste 110	St. Louis	MO	63131	**800-777-9687**	314-822-0500	491
Trident Technical College (TTC) 7000 Rivers Ave PO Box 118067	North Charleston	SC	29406	**877-349-7184**	843-574-6111	798
Tri-Dim Filter Corp 93 Industrial Dr	Louisa	VA	23093	**800-458-9835**	540-967-2600	18
Tri-Ed Distribution Inc 135 Crossways Pk Dr W	Woodbury	NY	11797	**888-874-3336**	516-941-2800	248
Triflo International Inc 1000 FM 830	Willis	TX	77318	**800-332-0993**	936-856-8551	358
Tri-Gas & Oil Company Inc 3941 Federalsburg Hwy PO Box 465	Federalsburg	MD	21632	**800-638-7802**	410-754-8184	326
Tri-K Industries Inc 2 Stewart Ct PO Box 10	Denville	NJ	07834	**800-526-0372**	973-298-8850	478
Tri-Land Kansas City Investors LLC 1 Wbrook Corporate Ctr Ste 520	Westchester	IL	60154	**800-441-7032**	708-531-8210	650
TriLeaf Inc 10845 Olive Blvd Ste 310	Saint Louis	MO	63141	**800-652-5552**	314-997-6111	263
Tri-line Carriers L.p 235185 Ryan Rd	Rocky View	AB	T1X0K1	**800-661-9191**		315
TriLink BioTechnologies Inc 9955 Mesa Rim Rd	San Diego	CA	92121	**800-863-6801**	858-546-0004	740
Tri-Lite Inc 1642 N Besly Ct	Chicago	IL	60642	**800-322-5250**	773-384-7765	439
Trilithic Inc 9710 Pk Davis Dr	Indianapolis	IN	46235	**800-344-2412**	317-895-3600	250
Trillium Asset Management LLC 2 Financial Ctr 60 S St Ste 1100	Boston	MA	02111	**800-548-5684**	617-423-6655	527
Trillium Community Health Plan Inc 1800 Millrace Dr	Eugene	OR	97403	**800-910-3906**	541-431-1950	391-3

Name / Address	City	State	ZIP	Toll-Free	Phone	Class
Trillium Teamologies Inc 219 S Main St Ste 300	Royal Oak	MI	48067	**866-832-6884**	248-584-2080	182
Trilogy Communications Inc 2910 Hwy 80 E	Pearl	MS	39208	**888-713-1414**	601-932-4461	812
Trimaco LLC 2300 Gateway Centre Blvd Ste 200	Morrisville	NC	27560	**800-325-7356**	919-674-3460	730
Trimark Corp PO Box 350	New Hampton	IA	50659	**800-447-0343**	641-394-3188	350
TriMark USA Inc 505 Collins St	South Attleboro	MA	02703	**800-755-5580**	508-399-2400	301
Trimble Navigation Ltd 935 Stewart Dr *NASDAQ: TRMB*	Sunnyvale	CA	94085	**800-538-7800**	408-481-8000	528
Trimco/Builders Brass Works 3528 Emery St	Los Angeles	CA	90023	**800-637-8746**	323-262-4191	350
Tri-Media Integrated Marketing Technologies Inc (Prior to the acquisition by Andromeda Media) 517 Niagara St	Welland	ON	L3C1L7	**800-367-0766**	905-732-6431	7
Trimedyne Inc 15091 Bake Pkwy *OTC: TMED*	Irvine	CA	92618	**800-733-5273**	949-559-5300	424
Trimfoot Co LLC 115 Trimfoot Terr	Farmington	MO	63640	**800-325-6116**		302
TrimMaster 4860 N Fifth St Hwy	Temple	PA	19560	**800-356-4237**	610-921-0203	741
Trim-Rite Food Corp 801 Commerce Pkwy	Carpentersville	IL	60110	**800-626-9442**	847-649-3400	298-9
TriNet Group Inc 1100 San Leandro Blvd Ste 300	San Leandro	CA	94577	**888-874-6388**	510-352-5000	630
Trinidad State Junior College 600 Prospect St	Trinidad	CO	81082	**800-621-8752**	719-846-5011	161
Trinity Bible College 50 Sixth Ave N	Ellendale	ND	58436	**800-523-1603**	701-349-3621	160
Trinity Biotech PLC 5919 Farnsworth Ct *NASDAQ: TRIB*	Carlsbad	CA	92008	**800-331-2291**	760-929-0500	233
Trinity Broadcasting Network (TBN) PO Box A	Santa Ana	CA	92711	**888-731-1000**	714-832-2950	736
Trinity Business Furniture 6089 Kennedy Rd	Trinity	NC	27370	**855-311-6660**	336-472-6660	322
Trinity College of Florida 2430 Welbilt Blvd	Trinity	FL	34655	**800-388-0869**	727-376-6911	160
Trinity Episcopal School for Ministry 311 11th St	Ambridge	PA	15003	**800-874-8754**	724-266-3838	168-3
Trinity Fiduciary Partners LLC 106 Decker Court Ste 226	Irving	TX	75062	**877-334-1283**		527
Trinity Hardwood Distributors Inc 110 East Oregon	Dallas	TX	75203	**800-492-9856**	214-948-3001	321
Trinity Hospital of Augusta 2803 Wrightsboro Rd Ste 38	Augusta	GA	30909	**800-999-6673**	706-729-6000	371
Trinity Hospital Saint Joseph's 1 W Burdick Expy	Minot	ND	58701	**800-247-1316**	701-857-5000	374-3
Trinity Industries Inc 2525 Stemmons Fwy *NYSE: TRN*	Dallas	TX	75207	**800-631-4420**	214-631-4420	187
Trinity International University 2065 Half Day Rd	Deerfield	IL	60015	**800-822-3225**	847-945-8800	167
Trinity International University South Florida 8190 W SR 84	Davie	FL	33324	**800-822-3225**	954-382-6400	167
Trinity Lutheran Seminary 2199 E Main St	Columbus	OH	43209	**866-610-8571**	614-235-4136	168-3
Trinity Marine Products Inc 2525 N Stemmons Fwy	Dallas	TX	75207	**877-876-5463**	214-589-8446	696
Trinity Medical Ctr 1 Burdick Expy W PO Box 5020	Minot	ND	58702	**800-862-0005**	701-857-5000	374-3
Trinity Medical Ctr West 4000 Johnson Rd	Steubenville	OH	43952	**877-271-4176**	740-264-8000	374-3
Trinity Mining Service 109 48th St	Pittsburgh	PA	15201	**800-264-2583**	412-682-4700	648
Trinity Rail Group LLC 2525 N Stemmons Fwy	Dallas	TX	75207	**800-631-4420**	214-631-4420	648
Trinity Systems Technologies Inc 5885 Cumming Hwy Ste 108-273	Sugar Hill	GA	30518	**888-828-5655**		198
Trinity Trailer Manufacturing Inc 8200 S Eisenman Rd	Boise	ID	83716	**800-235-6577**	208-336-3666	777
Trinity University 125 Michigan Ave NE *Admissions	Washington	DC	20017	**800-492-6882***	202-884-9000	167
Trinity Valley Community College *Athens* 100 Cardinal Dr	Athens	TX	75751	**877-392-6433**	903-675-6200	161
Palestine PO Box 2530	Palestine	TX	75802	**866-882-2937**	903-729-0256	161
Trinity Valley Electric Co-op Inc (TVEC) 1800 Hwy 243 E PO Box 888	Kaufman	TX	75142	**800-766-9576**	972-932-2214	247
Trinity Western University 7600 Glover Rd	Langley	BC	V2Y1Y1	**888-468-6898**	604-888-7511	783
Trintech Inc 15851 Dallas Pkwy Ste 900	Addison	TX	75001	**800-416-0075**	972-701-9802	180-1
Trion Industries Inc 297 Laird St	Wilkes-Barre	PA	18702	**800-444-4665**	570-824-1000	288
Triple B Forwarders Inc 1511 Glen Curtis St	Carson	CA	90746	**800-228-8465**	310-604-5840	312
Triple Creek Ranch 5551 W Fork Rd	Darby	MT	59829	**800-654-2943**	406-821-4600	667
Triple Crown Corp 5351 Jaycee Ave	Harrisburg	PA	17112	**877-822-4663**	717-657-5729	189
Triple Crown Nutrition Inc 319 Barry Ave S Ste 303	Wayzata	MN	55391	**800-451-9916**		446
Triple Crown Services 2720 Dupont Commerce Ct Ste 200	Fort Wayne	IN	46825	**800-325-6510**	260-416-3600	646
Triple J Wilderness Ranch 91 Mortimer Rd PO Box 310	Augusta	MT	59410	**800-826-1300**	406-562-3653	241
Triple Play Products LLC 904 Main St Ste 330	Hopkins	MN	55343	**800-829-1625**	952-938-0531	63
Triple/S Dynamics Inc 1031 S Haskell Ave PO Box 151027	Dallas	TX	75315	**800-527-2116**	214-828-8600	469
Tripler Army Medical Ctr 1 Jarrett White Rd Tripler AMC	Honolulu	HI	96859	**877-880-2184**	808-433-6661	331-4
Triple-S Steel Supply LLC 6000 Jensen Dr	Houston	TX	77026	**800-231-1034**	713-697-7105	491
Triplett Office Essentials Corp 3553 109th St	Urbandale	IA	50322	**800-437-5034**	515-270-9150	534
Tripos Inc 1699 S Hanley Rd	Saint Louis	MO	63144	**800-323-2960**	314-647-1099	180-5
Trippnt Inc 8830 NE 108th St	Kansas City	MO	64157	**800-874-7768**	816-792-2604	607
Tripwire Inc 101 SW Main St Ste 1500 *General	Portland	OR	97204	**800-874-7947***	503-276-7500	180-12
TriQuint Semiconductor Inc 2300 NE Brookwood Pkwy *NASDAQ: TQNT*	Hillsboro	OR	97124	**855-367-8768**	503-615-9000	694
Triseal Corp 11920 Price Rd	Hebron	IL	60034	**800-910-7325**	815-648-2473	327
Trisoft Technologies Inc 14429 Independence Dr	Plainfield	IL	60544	**866-364-7031**		462
TriSports.com 4495 S Coach Dr	Tucson	AZ	85714	**888-293-3934**		709
Tristar Southern Hills Medical Ctr 391 Wallace Rd	Nashville	TN	37211	**800-242-5662**	615-781-4000	374-3
Tri-Starr Investigations Inc 3525 Hwy 138 SW	Stockbridge	GA	30281	**800-849-9841**	770-388-9841	40
Tri-state Adjustments Inc 3439 East Ave S PO Box 3219	La Crosse	WI	54602	**800-562-3906**	608-788-8683	159
Tri-State Armature & Electrical Works Inc 330 GE Patterson PO Box 466	Memphis	TN	38126	**800-238-7654**	901-527-8412	248
Tri-State Better Business Bureau 5401 Vogel Rd Ste 410	Evansville	IN	47715	**800-359-0979**	812-473-0202	78
Tri-State Bible College 506 Margaret St	South Point	OH	45680	**800-333-3243**	740-377-2520	160
Tri-State Drilling Inc 16940 Hwy 55 W	Plymouth	MN	55446	**800-383-1033**	763-553-1234	191-15
Tri-State Electric Membership Corp (TSEMC) 2310 Blue Ridge Dr	Blue Ridge	GA	30513	**800-351-1111**	706-492-3251	247
Tri-state Fabricators Inc 1146 Ferris Rd	Amelia	OH	45102	**888-523-1488**	513-752-5005	609
Tri-state Forest Products Inc 2105 Sheridan Ave	Springfield	OH	45505	**800-949-6325**	937-323-6325	193-3
Tri-State Iron & Metal Co 1725 E Ninth St	Texarkana	AR	71854	**800-773-8409**	870-773-8409	684
Tri-State Pumps Inc 1162 Chastain Rd	Liberty	SC	29657	**800-868-4631**	864-843-8100	709
Tri-State Travel 4349 Industrial Pk Dr	Galena	IL	61036	**800-779-4869**	815-777-0820	758
Tri-State Utility Products Inc 1030 Atlanta Industrial Dr	Marietta	GA	30066	**800-282-7985**	770-427-3119	248
Tri-State Video Services Inc 1379 Pittsburgh Rd	Valencia	PA	16059	**888-382-7768**	724-898-1630	37
Triton Systems Inc 21405 B St	Long Beach	MS	39560	**866-787-4866**	228-575-3100	255
Triton-Tek Inc 445 W Erie St Ste 208	Chicago	IL	60654	**866-387-4866**	312-467-9201	227
Triumph Controls Inc 205 Church Rd	North Wales	PA	19454	**800-322-2885**	215-699-4861	205
Triumph Learning 136 Madison Ave	New York	NY	10016	**800-221-9372**		634-2
Triumph Pet Industries Inc 500 Sixth St SW	Red Bay	AL	35582	**800-633-3349**	256-356-9541	577
Triumph Twist Drill Co Inc 1 SW 7th St	Chisholm	MN	55719	**800-942-1501**	218-263-3891	756
Triumvirate Environmental 61 Innerbelt Rd	Somerville	MA	02143	**800-966-9282**	617-628-8098	802
TriZetto Corporation 501 N Broadway 3rd Fl	Sacramento	CA	95814	**800-969-3666**		179
TRMC (Thibodaux Regional Medical Ctr) 602 N Acadia Rd	Thibodaux	LA	70301	**800-822-8442**	985-447-5500	374-3
TRN (Talk Radio Network) PO Box 3755	Central Point	OR	97502	**888-383-3733**		644
Trojan Battery Co 12380 Clark St *Cust Svc	Santa Fe Springs	CA	90670	**800-423-6569***	562-236-3000	73
Trojan Inc 198 Trojan St	Mount Sterling	KY	40353	**800-264-0526**	859-498-0526	437
Trojan Professional Services Inc 14410 Cerritos Ave	Los Alamitos	CA	90720	**800-451-9723**		226
Tronair Inc 1740 Eber Rd	Holland	OH	43528	**800-426-6301**	419-866-6301	22
Trophy Nut Company Inc 320 N Second St	Tipp City	OH	45371	**800-729-6887**	937-667-8478	297-28
Trophyland USA Inc 7001 W 20th Ave	Hialeah	FL	33014	**800-327-5820**		775
Tropic Oil Company Inc 10002 NW 89th Ave	Miami	FL	33178	**866-645-3835**	305-888-4611	578
Tropical Cheese Industries Inc 450 Fayette St PO Box 1357	Perth Amboy	NJ	08861	**888-874-4928**	732-442-4898	297-5
Tropical Ford 9900 S Orange Blossom Trial *Sales	Orlando	FL	32837	**800-790-7137***	407-851-3800	56
Tropical Shipping 5 E 11th St	Riviera Beach	FL	33404	**800-367-6200**	561-881-3900	314
Tropical Winds Oceanfront Hotel 1398 N Atlantic Ave	Daytona Beach	FL	32118	**800-245-6099**	386-258-1016	379
Tropicana Entertainment 2831 Boardwalk *OTC: TPCA*	Atlantic City	NJ	08401	**800-843-8767**		667
Tropicana Express 2121 S Casino Dr	Laughlin	NV	89029	**800-243-6846**	702-298-4200	132
Tropicana Field 1 Tropicana Dr	Saint Petersburg	FL	33705	**888-326-7297**	727-825-3137	718
Tropicana Inn & Suites 1540 S Harbor Blvd	Anaheim	CA	92802	**800-828-4898**	714-635-4082	379
Tropicana Resort & Casino 3801 Las Vegas Blvd S *Resv	Las Vegas	NV	89109	**800-462-8767***	702-739-2222	667

Name / Address	City	State	ZIP	Toll-Free	Phone	Class
Trotters Restaurant 2008 Savannah Hwy	Charleston	SC	29401	**800-334-6660**	843-571-1000	669
Trout Unlimited (TU) 1300 N 17th St Ste 500	Arlington	VA	22209	**800-834-2419**	703-522-0200	47-3
Trouw Nutrition 115 Executive Dr	Highland	IL	62249	**800-365-1357**	618-654-2070	446
Troxler Electronic Laboratories Inc 3008 E Cornwallis Rd PO Box 12057	Research Triangle Park	NC	27709	**877-876-9537**	919-549-8661	203
Troy Corp 8 Vreeland Rd PO Box 955	Florham Park	NJ	07932	**800-448-2843**	973-443-4200	549
Troy Sunshade Co 607 Riffle Ave	Greenville	OH	45331	**800-833-8769**	937-548-2466	730
Troy University 600 University Ave	Troy	AL	36082	**800-551-9716**	334-670-3100	167
Montgomery 231 Montgomery St PO Box 4419	Montgomery	AL	36104	**888-357-8843**		167
Troy-CSL Lighting Inc 14508 Nelson Ave	City of Industry	CA	91744	**800-533-8769**	626-336-4511	439
Troyer Foods Inc 17141 State Rd 4	Goshen	IN	46528	**800-876-9377**	574-533-0302	298-10
Troy-Miami County Public Library 419 W Main St	Troy	OH	45373	**866-657-8556**	937-339-0502	434-3
TRSA (Textile Rental Services Assn) 1800 Diagonal Rd Ste 200	Alexandria	VA	22314	**877-770-9274**	703-519-0029	48-4
Tru Tech Corp 20 Vaughan Vly Blvd	Vaughan	ON	L4H0B1	**888-760-0099**	905-856-0096	498
TRU TECH Systems Inc 24550 N River Rd PO Box 46965	Mount Clemens	MI	48043	**877-878-8324**	586-469-2700	454
Tru Vue Inc 9400 W 55th St	McCook	IL	60525	**800-621-8339**	708-485-5080	330
Truck Equipment Service Co 800 Oak St	Lincoln	NE	68521	**800-869-0363**	402-476-3225	777
Truck Sales & Service Inc PO Box 262	Midvale	OH	44653	**800-282-6100**	740-922-3412	56
Truck Utilities Inc 2370 English St	Saint Paul	MN	55109	**800-869-1075**	651-484-3305	515
Truck Works Inc 1815 S 39th Ave	Phoenix	AZ	85009	**877-894-8757**	602-233-3713	56
Truckin Movers Corp 1031 Harvest St	Durham	NC	27704	**800-334-1651**	919-682-2300	518
Truck-Lite Company Inc 310 E Elmwood Ave *Cust Svc	Falconer	NY	14733	**800-562-5012***	716-665-6214	438
Truckload Carriers Assn (TCA) 555 E Braddock Rd	Alexandria	VA	22314	**800-666-2770**	703-838-1950	48-21
Trudell Medical Group Ltd 758 Third St	London	ON	N5V5J7	**800-757-4881**	519-685-8800	474
Trudiligence LLC 3190 S Wadsworth Blvd Ste 260	Lakewood	CO	80227	**800-580-0474**	303-692-8445	220
True Blue Inc PO Box 2910 *NYSE: TBI*	Tacoma	WA	98401	**800-610-8920**	253-383-9101	719
True Fitness Technology Inc 865 Hoff Rd	O'Fallon	MO	63366	**800-426-6570**	636-272-7100	269
True Manufacturing Co 2001 E Terra Ln	O'Fallon	MO	63366	**800-325-6152**	636-240-2400	662
True North Energy LLC 5565 Airport Hwy	Toledo	OH	43615	**888-245-9336**	419-868-6800	325
True Temper Sports 8275 Tournament Dr Ste 200	Memphis	TN	38125	**800-355-8783**	901-746-2000	708
TrueAccord Corp 148 Townsend St Ste 26	San Francisco	CA	94107	**866-611-2731**		393
TrueCloud 2147 E Baseline Rd	Tempe	AZ	85283	**866-990-8783**		198
Truett-McConnell College 100 Alumni Dr	Cleveland	GA	30528	**800-226-8621**	706-865-2134	167
Truevance Management Inc 7666 Blanding Blvd	Jacksonville	FL	32244	**800-285-2028**	904-777-9052	263
Tru-Flex Metal Hose Corp 2391 S State Rd 263 PO Box 247	West Lebanon	IN	47991	**800-255-6291**	765-893-4403	594
TruGreen ChemLawn 860 Ridge Lk Blvd	Memphis	TN	38120	**866-369-9539**		576
Truheat Inc 700 Grand St	Allegan	MI	49010	**800-879-6199**	269-673-2145	319
Truitt Bros Inc 1105 Front St NE	Salem	OR	97301	**800-547-8712**	503-362-3674	297-20
Truliant Federal Credit Union 3200 Truliant Way	Winston-Salem	NC	27103	**800-822-0382**	336-659-1955	221
Truline Corp 9390 Redwood St	Las Vegas	NV	89139	**800-634-6489**	702-362-7495	778
Tru-Link Fence Co 5440 Touhy Ave	Skokie	IL	60077	**800-568-9300**	847-568-9300	281
Trulioo Inc 300 - 420 W Hastings St	Vancouver	BC	V6B1L1	**888-773-0179**		226
Truly Nolen of America Inc 3636 E Speedway Blvd	Tucson	AZ	85716	**800-468-7859**	800-528-3442	576
Trumaker Inc 701 Sutter St Fl 5	San Francisco	CA	94109	**855-623-3878**		688
Truman State University 100 E Normal St	Kirksville	MO	63501	**800-892-7792**	660-785-4000	167
Trumbull Industries Inc 400 Dietz Rd NE	Warren	OH	44482	**800-477-1799**	330-393-6624	1
Trump International Hotel & Tower 725 Fifth Ave	New York	NY	10022	**888-448-7867**	312-588-8000	379
Trump International Sonesta Beach Resort 18001 Collins Ave	Sunny Isles Beach	FL	33160	**800-766-3782**	305-692-5600	667
Trump Soho New York 246 Spring St	New York	NY	10013	**855-878-6700**	212-842-5500	705
Trump Taj Mahal Casino Resort 1000 Boardwalk & Virginia Ave	Atlantic City	NJ	08401	**800-426-2537**	609-449-1000	667
TruSignal LLC 25 6th Ave N	St. Cloud	MN	56303	**855-569-0426**		387
Trust Bank 600 E Main St PO Box 158	Olney	IL	62450	**800-766-3451**	618-395-4311	69

Name / Address	City	State	ZIP	Toll-Free	Phone	Class
Trust for Public Land (TPL) 116 New Montgomery St 4th Fl	San Francisco	CA	94105	**800-714-5263**	415-495-4014	47-13
Trustco Bank Corp NY PO Box 1082 *NASDAQ: TRST*	Schenectady	NY	12301	**800-670-3110**	518-377-3311	360-2
Trustile Doors LLC 1780 E 66th Ave	Denver	CO	80229	**866-442-5302**	303-286-3931	238
Trustmark Insurance Co 400 Field Dr	Lake Forest	IL	60045	**888-246-9949**	847-615-1500	391-2
Trustmark National Bank 248 E Capitol St PO Box 291 *NASDAQ: TRMK* ■ *Cust Svc	Jackson	MS	39201	**800-243-2524***	601-208-5111	360-2
TruTech LLC PO Box 6849	Marietta	GA	30065	**800-842-7296**	770-977-2034	576
Truth Hardware Inc 700 W Bridge St *Cust Svc	Owatonna	MN	55060	**800-866-7884***	507-451-5620	350
Truth Publishing Company Inc 421 S Second St	Elkhart	IN	46516	**800-585-5416**	574-294-1661	634-8
Truth, The PO Box 487	Elkhart	IN	46515	**800-585-5416**	574-294-1661	531-2
TruTouch Technologies Inc 73 Carriage Way	Sudbury	MA	01776	**866-721-6221**		583
Trutrak Flight Systems Inc 1500 S Old Missouri Rd	Springdale	AR	72764	**866-878-8725**	479-751-0250	528
Truwest Credit Union PO Box 3489	Scottsdale	AZ	85271	**855-878-9378**	480-441-5900	508
Trydor Industries (Canada) Ltd 19275 - 25th Ave	Surrey	BC	V3S3X1	**800-567-8558**	604-542-4773	789
Tryiton Eyewear LLC 147 Post Rd E	Westport	CT	06880	**888-896-3885**	203-544-0770	542
Tryon Trucking Inc PO Box 68	Fairless Hills	PA	19030	**800-523-5254**	215-295-6622	778
TRYP Hotels Worldwide Inc 395 Rue De La Couronne	Quebec	QC	G1K7X4	**800-267-2002**		378
TS Distributors Inc 4404 Windfern Rd	Houston	TX	77041	**800-392-3655**	832-467-5400	350
TSA (Transportation Security Administration) 601 S 12th St	Arlington	VA	22202	**866-289-9673**		340-9
TSC Apparel LLC 12080 Mosteller Rd	Cincinnati	OH	45241	**800-543-7230**	513-771-1138	155
TSCT (Thaddeus Stevens College of Technology) 750 E King St	Lancaster	PA	17602	**800-842-3832**	717-299-7701	798
TSE Industries Inc 4370 112th Terr N	Clearwater	FL	33762	**800-237-7634**	727-573-7676	607
TSEMC (Tri-State Electric Membership Corp) 2310 Blue Ridge Dr	Blue Ridge	GA	30513	**800-351-1111**	706-492-3251	247
TSI Global Cos 700 Fountain Lakes Blvd	Saint Charles	MO	63301	**800-875-5605**	636-949-8889	732
TSI Health Sciences Inc 305 S Fourth St E Ste 101	Missoula	MT	59801	**877-549-9123**	406-549-9123	478
TSI Inc 500 CaRdigan Rd	Shoreview	MN	55126	**800-874-2811**	651-483-0900	203
TSI Power Corp 1103 W Pierce Ave	Antigo	WI	54409	**800-874-3160**	715-623-0636	255
TSMC (Taiwan Semiconductor Mfg Company Ltd) 2851 Junction Ave *NYSE: TSM*	San Jose	CA	95134	**877-248-4237**	408-382-8000	694
TSN Inc 4001 Salazar Way PO Box 679 *General	Frederick	CO	80530	**888-997-5959***	303-530-0600	558
TSO3 Inc 2505 Dalton Ave	Quebec	QC	G1P3S5	**866-715-0003**	418-651-0003	476
TSPI Inc 20 Pidgeon Hill Dr Ste 106	Sterling	VA	20165	**877-455-8774**		198
TSS Inc 110 E Old Settlers Blvd	Round Rock	TX	78664	**844-681-8158**	512-310-1000	448
TST/Impreso Inc 652 Southwestern Blvd	Coppell	TX	75019	**800-527-2878**	972-462-0100	551-1
TSTA Advocate Magazine 316 W 12th St	Austin	TX	78701	**877-275-8782**	512-476-5355	456-8
TSTC (Texas State Technical College) *Abilene* 650 E Hwy 80	Abilene	TX	79601	**800-852-8784**	325-672-7091	161
TTG Consultants 4727 Wilshire Blvd	Los Angeles	CA	90010	**800-736-8840**	323-936-6600	462
TTI Inc 2441 NE Pkwy *Sales	Fort Worth	TX	76106	**800-225-5884***	817-740-9000	248
TTSG (Twinless Twins Support Group International) PO Box 980481	Ypsilanti	MI	48198	**888-205-8962**		47-21
TTX Co 101 N Wacker Dr	Chicago	IL	60606	**800-889-4357**	312-853-3223	266-5
TU (Trout Unlimited) 1300 N 17th St Ste 500	Arlington	VA	22209	**800-834-2419**	703-522-0200	47-3
Tub Springs State Wayside 12845 Green Springs Hwy 3792 N River Rd	Ashland	OR	97520	**800-551-6949**		564
Tubbys Grilled Submarines 31920 Groesbeck Hwy	Fraser	MI	48026	**800-752-0644**		668
Tube Art Group (TAG) 11715 SE Fifth St	Bellevue	WA	98005	**800-562-2854**	206-223-1122	699
Tube City IMS Corp 1155 Business Ctr Dr Ste 200 *General	Horsham	PA	19044	**800-860-2442***	215-956-5500	684
Tube Methods Inc PO Box 460	Bridgeport	PA	19405	**800-220-2123**	610-279-7700	489
Tube Processing Corp 604 E Le Grande Ave	Indianapolis	IN	46203	**800-295-4119**	317-787-1321	489
Tubelite Inc 4878 Mackinaw Trl	Reed City	MI	49677	**800-866-2227**		236
Tube-Mac Industries Ltd 853 Arvin Ave	Stoney Creek	ON	L8E5N8	**877-643-8823**	905-643-8823	604-2
Tubular Steel Inc 1031 Executive Pkwy Dr	Saint Louis	MO	63141	**800-388-7491**	314-851-9200	491
Tucker Company Worldwide Inc 900 Dudley Ave	Cherry Hill	NJ	08002	**800-229-7780**	856-317-9600	312
Tucker County Convention & Visitors Bureau 410 William Ave	Davis	WV	26260	**800-782-2775**	304-259-5315	208

Name	Address	City	State	ZIP	Toll-Free	Phone	Class
Tucows Inc	96 Mowat Ave *TSE: TC*	Toronto	ON	M6K3M1	**800-371-6992**	416-535-0123	397
Tucson Electric Power Co	1 S Church Ave Ste 100	Tucson	AZ	85701	**800-430-4046**	520-571-4000	785
Tucson International Airport	7250 S Tucson Blvd	Tucson	AZ	85706	**800-758-1874**	520-573-8100	27
Tucson Medical Ctr	5301 E Grant Rd	Tucson	AZ	85712	**800-526-5353**	520-327-5461	374-3
Tudi Mechanical Systems of Tampa Inc	343 Munson Ave	Mc Kees Rocks	PA	15136	**877-367-8834**	412-771-4100	609
Tuesday Morning Corp	6250 LBJ Fwy *NASDAQ: TUES*	Dallas	TX	75240	**800-457-0099**	972-387-3562	328
Tufco Technologies Inc	PO Box 23500 *NASDAQ: TFCO*	Green Bay	WI	54305	**800-558-8145**	920-336-0054	553
Tuff Torq Corp	5943 Commerce Blvd	Morristown	TN	37814	**866-572-3441**	423-585-2000	429
Tuffaloy Products Inc	1400 S Batesville Rd	Greer	SC	29650	**800-521-3722**	864-879-0763	809
TuffStuff Fitness Equipment Inc	13971 Norton Ave	Chino	CA	91710	**888-884-8275**	909-629-1600	354
Tuffy Assoc Corp	7150 Granite Cir	Toledo	OH	43617	**800-228-8339**	419-865-6900	61-5
Tuffy Security Products Inc	25733 Rd H	Cortez	CO	81321	**800-348-8339**	970-564-1762	56
Tuftco Corp	2318 S Holtzclaw Ave	Chattanooga	TN	37408	**800-288-3826**	423-698-8601	741
Tuftco Finishing Systems Inc	100 W Industrial Blvd	Dalton	GA	30720	**800-288-3826**	706-277-1110	741
Tufts Associated Health Plans	705 Mt Auburn St	Watertown	MA	02472	**800-462-0224**	617-972-9400	391-3
Tufts Library	46 Broad St	Weymouth	MA	02188	**888-283-3757**	781-337-1402	434-3
Tufts Medical Ctr (TMC)	800 Washington St	Boston	MA	02111	**866-220-3699**	617-636-5000	374-3
Tufts University	4 Colby St	Medford	MA	02155	**800-326-4001**	617-628-5000	167
Tugboat Inn	80 Commercial St PO Box 267	Boothbay Harbor	ME	04538	**800-248-2628**	207-633-4434	379
Tukaiz Communications LLC	2917 N Latoria Ln	Franklin Park	IL	60131	**800-543-2674**	847-455-1588	7
Tulalip Resort Casino	10200 Quil Ceda Blvd	Tulalip	WA	98271	**888-272-1111**		705
Tulane Medical Ctr (TMC)	1415 Tulane Ave	New Orleans	LA	70112	**800-588-5800**	504-988-5263	374-3
Tulane University	6823 St Charles Ave *Admissions	New Orleans	LA	70118	**800-873-9283***	504-865-5000	167
Tulane University Law School	6329 Freret St Weinmann Hall	New Orleans	LA	70118	**800-328-6819**	504-865-5930	168-1
Tulare Joint Union High School District	426 N Blackstone Ave	Tulare	CA	93274	**800-942-3767**	559-688-2021	683
Tulco Oils Inc	5240 E Pine	Tulsa	OK	74115	**800-375-2347**	918-838-3354	578
Tulip City Air Service Inc	1581 S Washington Ave	Holland	MI	49423	**800-748-0515**	616-392-7831	13
Tulloch Engineering Inc	200 Main St	Thessalon	ON	P0R1L0	**800-797-2997**	705-842-3372	258
Tulsa Community College	*Metro* 909 S Boston Ave	Tulsa	OK	74119	**866-970-0233**	918-595-7000	161
Tulsa Convention & Visitors Bureau	1 W Third St Ste 100	Tulsa	OK	74103	**800-558-3311**		208
Tulsa Metro Chamber	1 West Third St Ste 100	Tulsa	OK	74103	**888-424-9411**	918-585-1201	138
Tulsa Opera	1610 S Boulder Ave	Tulsa	OK	74119	**866-298-2530**	918-582-4035	572-2
Tulsa Public Schools	3027 S New Haven Ave	Tulsa	OK	74114	**866-632-9992**	918-746-6800	683
Tulsa World	315 S Boulder Ave	Tulsa	OK	74103	**800-897-3557**	918-583-2161	531-2
Tulsair Beechcraft Inc	3207 N Sheridan Rd	Tulsa	OK	74115	**800-331-4071**	918-835-7651	24
Tumbleweed Inc	2301 River Rd	Louisville	KY	40206	**866-719-3892**	502-893-0323	668
Tumbling River Ranch	3715 Pk County Rd 62 PO Box 30	Grant	CO	80448	**800-654-8770**	303-838-5981	241
Tundra Lodge Resort & Waterpark	865 Lombardi Ave	Green Bay	WI	54304	**877-886-3725**	920-405-8700	667
Tundra Process Solutions Ltd	7523 Flint Rd SE	Calgary	AB	T2H1G3	**800-265-1166**	403-255-5222	110
Tunica MS	13625 Hwy 61 N	Robinsonville	MS	38664	**888-488-6422**		208
Tunnel Duty Free Shop Inc	465 Goyeau St	Windsor	ON	N9A1H1	**800-669-2105**	519-252-2713	243
Tuohy Furniture Corp	42 St Albans Pl *Cust Svc	Chatfield	MN	55923	**800-533-1696***	507-867-4280	320-1
Tuolumne County Chamber of Commerce	222 S Shepherd St	Sonora	CA	95370	**877-532-4212**	209-532-4212	138
Tupelo Buffalo Park & Zoo	2272 N Coley Rd	Tupelo	MS	38803	**866-272-4766**	662-844-8709	821
Tupelo National Battlefield	2680 Natchez Trace Pkwy	Tupelo	MS	38804	**800-305-7417**	662-680-4025	563
Tupelo Regional Airport	105 Lemons Dr	Tupelo	MS	38801	**877-777-4778**	662-823-4359	27
Tupperware Corp	14901 S Orange Blossom Trail *NYSE: TUP* ■ *Cust Svc	Orlando	FL	32837	**800-468-9716***	407-826-5050	606
Turbo 2 n 1 Grip	46460 Continental Dr	Chesterfield	MI	48047	**800-530-9878**	586-598-3948	709
Turbo Refrigerating	1000 W Ormsby Ave	Louisville	KY	40210	**800-853-8648**	502-635-3000	662
Turbomeca USA Inc	2709 N Forum Dr	Grand Prairie	TX	75052	**800-662-6322**	972-606-7600	21
Turf Paradise Racetrack	1501 W Bell Rd	Phoenix	AZ	85023	**800-639-8783**	602-942-1101	639
Turf Valley Resort & Conference Ctr	2700 Turf Vly Rd	Ellicott City	MD	21042	**888-833-8873**	410-465-1500	667
Turkey	*Consulate General* 1990 Post Oak Blvd Ste 1300	Houston	TX	77056	**888-566-7656**	713-622-5849	259
	Consulate General 6300 Wilshire Blvd Ste 2010	Los Angeles	CA	90048	**800-874-8875**	323-655-8832	259
	Embassy 2525 Massachusetts Ave NW	Washington	DC	20008	**877-367-8875**	202-612-6700	259
Turkey Hill Dairy Inc	2601 River Rd	Conestoga	PA	17516	**800-693-2479**	717-872-5461	297-25
Turks & Caicos Islands Tourism Office	225 W 35th St Ste 1200	New York	NY	10001	**800-241-0824**	646-375-8830	773
Turlock Chamber of Commerce	115 S Golden State Blvd	Turlock	CA	95380	**800-834-0401**	209-632-2221	138
Turner County	PO Box 191	Ashburn	GA	31714	**800-436-7442**	229-567-2334	338
Turner County Stockyard	1315 US Hwy 41 S	Ashburn	GA	31714	**800-344-9808**	229-567-3371	445
Turner Dairy Farms Inc	1049 Jefferson Rd	Pittsburgh	PA	15235	**800-892-1039**	412-372-2211	297-25
Turner Gas Company Inc	PO Box 26554	Salt Lake City	UT	84126	**800-932-4277**	801-973-6886	578
Turner Industries Group LLC	8687 United Plaza Blvd	Baton Rouge	LA	70809	**800-288-6503**	225-922-5050	190-9
Turner-Fairbank Highway Research Ctr	6300 Georgetown Pike	McLean	VA	22101	**800-424-9071**		666
Turning Point Hospital	3015 Veterans Pkwy PO Box 1177	Moultrie	GA	31776	**800-342-1075**	229-985-4815	724
Turning Point of Tampa	6227 Sheldon Rd	Tampa	FL	33615	**800-397-3006**	813-882-3003	724
Turning Stone Resort Casino LLC	5218 Patrick Rd	Verona	NY	13478	**800-771-7711**	315-361-7711	132
Turpin Sales & Marketing Inc	330 Cold Spring Ave	West Springfield	MA	01089	**877-377-7573**		462
Turret Steel Industries Inc	105 Pine St	Imperial	PA	15126	**800-245-4800**	724-218-1014	491
Turtle Bay Exploration Park	840 Auditorium Dr	Redding	CA	96001	**800-887-8532**	530-243-8850	519
Turtle Bay Resort	57-091 Kamehameha Hwy	Kahuku	HI	96731	**866-475-2567**	808-293-6000	667
Turtle Cay Resort	600 Atlantic Ave	Virginia Beach	VA	23451	**888-989-7788**	757-437-5565	667
Turtle Magazine	1100 Waterway Blvd	Indianapolis	IN	46202	**800-558-2376**	317-634-1100	456-6
Turtle Mountain Community College	10145 BIA Rd 7	Belcourt	ND	58316	**800-827-1100**	701-477-7862	164
Tuscaloosa News	315 28th Ave	Tuscaloosa	AL	35401	**800-888-8639**	205-345-0505	531-2
Tuscaloosa VA Medical Ctr	3701 Loop Rd E	Tuscaloosa	AL	35404	**888-269-3045**	205-554-2000	374-8
Tuscany Suites & Casino	255 E Flamingo Rd *Resv	Las Vegas	NV	89169	**877-887-2261***	702-893-8933	379
Tuscarora Yarns Inc	8760 E Franklin St	Mount Pleasant	NC	28124	**800-849-6527**	704-436-6527	742-9
Tusculum College	60 Shiloh Rd Hwy 107	Greeneville	TN	37743	**800-729-0256**	423-636-7300	167
Tuskegee University	1200 W Montgomery Rd *Admissions	Tuskegee	AL	36088	**800-622-6531***	334-727-8011	167
Tuskegee University Ford Motor Co Library/Learning Resource Ctr	Hollis Burke Frissell Library Bldg	Tuskegee	AL	36088	**800-622-6531**	334-727-8894	434-6
Tutco Inc	500 Gould Dr	Cookeville	TN	38506	**877-262-4533**	931-432-4141	14
Tuthill Corp	8500 S Madison St	Burr Ridge	IL	60527	**800-634-2695**	630-382-4900	638
Tuthill Corp Plastics Group	2050 Sunnydale Blvd	Clearwater	FL	33765	**800-634-2695**	727-446-8593	603
Tuthill Transfer Systems	8500 S Madison	Burr Ridge	IL	60527	**800-825-6937**	260-747-7529	636
Tuthill Vacuum & Blower Systems	4840 W Kearney St	Springfield	MO	65803	**800-825-6937**	417-865-8715	18
Tuthill Vacuum Systems	4840 W Kearney St	Springfield	MO	65803	**800-634-2695**	417-865-8715	174
Tuttle Law Print Inc	414 Quality Ln	Rutland	VT	05701	**800-776-7682**		626
Tuttle Publishing	364 Innovation Dr *Sales	North Clarendon	VT	05759	**800-526-2778***	802-773-8930	634-2
TV Guide Magazine LLC	11 West 42nd St 16th Fl	New York	NY	10036	**800-866-1400**	212-852-7500	456-9
TVCC (Temecula Valley Chamber of Commerce)	26790 Ynez Ct Ste A	Temecula	CA	92591	**866-676-5090**	951-676-5090	138
TVEC (Trinity Valley Electric Co-op Inc)	1800 Hwy 243 E PO Box 888	Kaufman	TX	75142	**800-766-9576**	972-932-2214	247

Name / Address	City	State	ZIP	Toll-Free	Phone	Class
Tuthill Vacuum Systems 4840 W Kearney St	Springfield	MO	65803	**800-634-2695**	417-865-8715	174
Tuttle Law Print Inc 414 Quality Ln	Rutland	VT	05701	**800-776-7682**		626
Tuttle Publishing 364 Innovation Dr *Sales	North Clarendon	VT	05759	**800-526-2778***	802-773-8930	634-2
TV Guide Magazine LLC 11 West 42nd St 16th Fl	New York	NY	10036	**800-866-1400**	212-852-7500	456-9
TVCC (Temecula Valley Chamber of Commerce) 26790 Ynez Ct Ste A	Temecula	CA	92591	**866-676-5090**	951-676-5090	138
TVEC (Trinity Valley Electric Co-op Inc) 1800 Hwy 243 E PO Box 888	Kaufman	TX	75142	**800-766-9576**	972-932-2214	247
T-w Transport Inc 7405 S Hayford Rd	Cheney	WA	99004	**800-356-4070**	509-623-4004	778
TWC (Trans World Corp) 545 Fifth Ave Ste 940 *OTC: TWOC*	New York	NY	10017	**877-407-9037**	212-983-3355	379
Tweed Museum of Art 1201 ordean Ct	Duluth	MN	55812	**866-999-6995**	218-726-8222	519
Twentieth Century Fox Home Entertainment Inc 2121 Ave of the Stars Ste 100	Los Angeles	CA	90067	**877-369-7867**	310-369-3900	510
Twenty-First Century Assoc 266 Summit Ave	Hackensack	NJ	07601	**888-760-5052**	201-678-1144	159
TWG (Terlato Wine Group, The) 900 Armour Dr	Lake Bluff	IL	60044	**800-950-7676**	847-604-8900	80-3
Twin Bridges State Park 14801 Hwy 137 S	Fairland	OK	74343	**800-622-6317**	918-540-2545	564
Twin Cities & Western Railroad 2925 12th St E	Glencoe	MN	55336	**800-290-8297**	320-864-7200	647
Twin Cities Air Service 81 Airport Dr	Auburn	ME	04210	**800-564-3882**		13
Twin Cities Public Television Inc 172 E Fourth St	Saint Paul	MN	55101	**866-229-1300**	651-222-1717	629
Twin City EDM 7940 Rancher Rd NE	Fridley	MN	55432	**800-397-0338**	763-783-7808	453
Twin City Knitting Company Inc (TCK) 104 Rock Barn Rd NE	Conover	NC	28613	**800-438-6884**	828-464-4830	154-9
Twin County Regional Hospital 200 Hospital Dr	Galax	VA	24333	**800-295-3342**	276-236-8181	374-3
Twin Falls Area Chamber of Commerce 2015 Neilsen Point Pl	Twin Falls	ID	83301	**866-734-3838**	208-733-3974	138
Twin Falls School District 411 201 Main Ave W	Twin Falls	ID	83301	**800-726-0003**	208-733-6900	683
Twin Farms 452 Royalton Tpke PO Box 115	Barnard	VT	05031	**800-894-6327**	802-234-9999	379
Twin Lakes State Park 788 Twin Lakes Rd	Green Bay	VA	23942	**800-933-7275**	434-392-3435	564
Twin Lakes Telephone Co-op 200 Telephone Ln *Cust Svc	Gainesboro	TN	38562	**800-644-8582***	931-268-2151	733
Twin Oaks Hammocks 138 Twin Oaks Rd	Louisa	VA	23093	**800-688-8946**	540-894-5125	320-4
Twin Oaks Software Development Inc 1463 Berlin Tpke	Berlin	CT	06037	**866-278-6750**	860-829-6000	179
Twin Pine Casino 22223 Hwy 29 PO Box 789	Middletown	CA	95461	**800-564-4872**	707-987-0197	378
Twin River Casino 100 Twin River Rd	Lincoln	RI	02865	**877-827-4837**	401-475-8505	639
Twin River National Bank 1507 G St	Lewiston	ID	83501	**877-743-4948**	208-746-4848	69
Twin Rivers Unified School District 3222 Winona Way	North Highlands	CA	95660	**888-674-6854**	916-566-1628	683
Twin Valley Electric Co-op Inc 501 S Huston Ave	Altamont	KS	67330	**866-784-5500**	620-784-5500	247
Twin Valleys Public Power District 1145 Nasby St	Cambridge	NE	69022	**800-658-4266**	308-697-3315	247
Twin-Boro News 210 Knickerbocker Rd	Cresskill	NJ	07626	**888-473-2673**	201-894-6715	531-4
Twinhead Corp 48303 Fremont Blvd *Sales	Fremont	CA	94538	**800-995-8946***		175-1
Twinlab 600 E Quality Dr	American Fork	UT	84003	**800-645-5626**	801-763-0700	797
Twinless Twins Support Group International (TTSG) PO Box 980481	Ypsilanti	MI	48198	**888-205-8962**		47-21
Twitchell Corp 4031 Ross Clark Cir *General	Dothan	AL	36303	**800-633-7550***	334-792-0002	742-2
Two Bunch Palms Resort & Spa 67425 Two Bunch Palms Trl	Desert Hot Springs	CA	92240	**800-472-4334**	760-329-8791	667
Two Guys Relocation Systems Inc 3571 Pacific Hwy	San Diego	CA	92101	**800-896-4897**	619-296-7995	518
Two Men & A Truck International Inc 3400 Belle Chase Way	Lansing	MI	48911	**800-345-1070**	517-394-7210	518
TWP Inc 2831 Tenth St	Berkeley	CA	94710	**800-227-1570**	510-548-4434	686
TXU Electric 1601 Bryan St	Dallas	TX	75201	**800-242-9113**	972-791-2888	785
Tyco Electronics Federal Credit Union PO Box 3449	Redwood City	CA	94064	**888-673-3288**		221
Tyco International Ltd 9 Roszel Rd *NYSE: TYC*	Princeton	NJ	08540	**800-685-4509**	609-720-4200	690
Tyco SimplexGrinnell 50 Technology Dr	Westminster	MA	01441	**800-746-7539**	978-731-2500	285
50 Technology Dr	Westminster	MA	01441	**800-746-7539**	978-731-2500	747
Tyger Scientific Inc 324 Stokes Ave	Ewing	NJ	08638	**888-329-8990**	609-434-0143	233
TYGH Capital Management Inc 1211 S W Fifth Ave Ste 2100	Portland	OR	97204	**800-972-0150**	503-972-0150	401
TYK America Inc 301 BrickyaRd Rd	Clairton	PA	15025	**800-569-9359**	412-384-4259	661
Tyler & Co 400 Northridge Rd Ste 1250	Atlanta	GA	30350	**800-989-6789**	770-396-3939	268
Tyler Area Chamber of Commerce 315 N Broadway Ave	Tyler	TX	75702	**800-235-5712**	903-592-1661	138
Tyler Convention & Visitors Bureau (TCVB) 315 N Broadway	Tyler	TX	75702	**800-235-5712**	903-592-1661	208
Tyler Equipment Corp 251 Shaker Rd	East Longmeadow	MA	01028	**800-292-6351**	413-525-6351	358
Tyler Junior College PO Box 9020	Tyler	TX	75711	**800-687-5680**	903-510-2523	161
Tyler Morning Telegraph PO Box 2030	Tyler	TX	75710	**800-772-1213**	903-597-8111	531-2
Tyler Pipe Co 11910 CR 492	Tyler	TX	75706	**800-527-8478**	903-882-5511	308
Tyler Technologies Inc 5949 Sherry Ln Ste 1400 *NYSE: TYL*	Dallas	TX	75225	**800-431-5776**		180-10
Tylok International Inc 1061 E 260th St	Euclid	OH	44132	**800-321-0466**	216-261-7310	594
Tymco Inc 225 E Industrial Blvd PO Box 2368	Waco	TX	76703	**800-258-9626**	254-799-5546	515
Tyndale House Publishers Inc 351 Executive Dr	Carol Stream	IL	60188	**800-323-9400**		634-3
Tyndale University College & Seminary 25 Ballyconnor Ct	Toronto	ON	M2M4B3	**877-896-3253**	416-226-6380	168-3
Tyndall Air Force Base 445 Suwannee Rd 101	Tyndall AFB	FL	32403	**800-356-5273**	850-283-1110	496-1
Tyndall Federal Credit Union PO Box 59760	Panama City	FL	32412	**888-896-3255**	850-769-9999	218
Tyonek Mfg Group Inc 229 Palmer Rd	Madison	AL	35758	**877-258-6200**	256-258-6200	528
TYR Sport 1790 Apollo Ct	Seal Beach	CA	90740	**800-252-7878**	714-897-0799	154-16
Tyson Events Ctr 401 Gordon Dr	Sioux City	IA	51101	**800-593-2228**	712-279-4850	207
Tyson Foods Inc 2210 W Oaklawn Dr PO Box 2020 *NYSE: TSN*	Springdale	AR	72762	**800-643-3410**	479-290-4000	618
Tyson Fresh Meats Inc 800 Stevens Port Dr	Dakota Dunes	SD	57049	**800-416-2269**	605-235-2061	472
Tyson Prepared Foods Inc 5701 McNutt Rd	Santa Teresa	NM	88008	**888-301-7304**	575-589-0100	297-26
Tysons Corner Ctr 1961 Chain Bridge Rd Ste 305	McLean	VA	22102	**877-247-5223**	703-847-7300	459

U

Name / Address	City	State	ZIP	Toll-Free	Phone	Class
U S Cavalry Inc 2855 Centennial Ave	Radcliff	KY	40160	**866-286-1359**	270-351-1164	156-5
U S Employees O C Federal Credit Union PO Box 44000	Oklahoma City	OK	73144	**800-227-6366**	405-685-6200	221
U S Monitor 86 Maple Ave	New City	NY	10956	**800-767-7967**	845-634-1331	5
U s Nameplate Company Inc Hwy 30 W	Mount Vernon	IA	52314	**800-553-8871**	319-895-8804	699
U S Risk Insurance Group Inc 10210 N Central Expy	Dallas	TX	75231	**800-926-9155**	214-265-7090	390
U W Provision Company Inc PO Box 620038	Middleton	WI	53562	**800-832-0517**	608-836-7421	298-9
U.S. Bankcard Services Inc 17171 E Gale Ave Ste 110	City Of Industry	CA	91745	**888-888-8872**		253
U.S. Department of Veterans Affairs 325 E 'H' St	Iron Mountain	MI	49801	**800-215-8262**	906-774-3300	374-8
U.S. Energy Development Corp 2350 N Forest Rd	Getzville	NY	14068	**800-636-7606**	716-636-0401	539
U.S. Facilities Inc 30 N 41 St Ste 400	Philadelphia	PA	19104	**800-236-6241**		194
U.S. Fleet Forces Command 1562 Mitscher Ave Ste 250	Norfolk	VA	23551	**800-473-3549**	757-836-3630	496-3
U.S. Kids Golf LLC 3040 Northwoods Pkwy	Norcross	GA	30071	**888-387-5437**	770-441-3077	709
U.S. National Ski Hall of Fame 610 Palms Ave	Ishpeming	MI	49849	**800-648-0720**	906-485-6323	521
UAB Comprehensive Cancer Ctr University of Alabama at Birmingham 1824 Sixth Ave S	Birmingham	AL	35294	**800-294-7780**	205-934-4011	666
UAB Medical West 995 Ninth Ave SW	Bessemer	AL	35022	**800-994-6610**	205-481-7000	374-3
UAFC (Universal American Corp) 44 S Broadway Ste 1200 *NYSE: UAM*	White Plains	NY	10601	**866-249-8668**	914-934-5200	360-4
UAMS Medical Ctr 4301 W Markham St	Little Rock	AR	72205	**877-467-6560**	501-686-7000	374-3
Ubics Inc 333 Technology Dr Ste 210 *OTC: UBIX*	Canonsburg	PA	15317	**800-441-0077**	724-746-6001	112
uBid Inc 740 Hilltop Dr	Itasca	IL	60143	**866-946-8243**		50
UBS AG 1285 Ave of the Americas	New York	NY	10019	**877-827-8001**	212-713-2000	69
UBS Financial Services Inc 1285 Ave of the Americas	New York	NY	10019	**800-221-3260**	212-713-2000	688
UBS Warburg LLC 677 Washington Blvd	Stamford	CT	06901	**800-221-3260**	203-719-3000	688
UC Davis Cancer Ctr 4501 X St	Sacramento	CA	95817	**800-362-5566**	916-734-5800	374-7
UC Irvine Healthcare 101 the City Dr S	Orange	CA	92868	**877-824-3627**	714-456-7890	374-3
UCare Minnesota 500 Stinson Blvd NE PO Box 52	Minneapolis	MN	55413	**866-457-7144**	612-676-6500	47-17
UCB Pharma Inc 1950 Lake Pk Dr	Smyrna	GA	30080	**800-477-7877**	770-970-7500	582

Name	Address	City	State	ZIP	Toll-Free	Phone	Class
UCC (United Church of Christ)	700 Prospect Ave	Cleveland	OH	44115	**866-822-8224**	216-736-2100	47-20
UCG Holdings	11300 Rockville Pike Ste 1100	Rockville	MD	20852	**800-929-4824**	301-287-2700	530-7
Uchee Pines Lifestyle Ctr	30 Uchee Pines Rd PO Box 75	Seale	AL	36875	**877-824-3374**	334-855-4764	704
UCIT Online Security	6441 Northam Dr	Mississauga	ON	L4V1J2	**866-756-7847**	905-405-9898	691
UCLA (University of California) *Berkeley*	110 Sproul Hall MC Ste 5800	Berkeley	CA	94720	**866-740-1260**	510-642-6000	167
UDASD (Upper Dauphin Area School District)	5668 State Rt 209	Lykens	PA	17048	**866-632-9992**	717-362-8134	683
UDL Laboratories Inc	1718 Northrock Ct	Rockford	IL	61103	**800-435-5272**	800-848-0462	583
UFC (United Farmers Co-op)	705 E Fourth St PO Box 461	Winthrop	MN	55396	**866-998-3266**	507-647-6600	10
UFCW (United Food & Commercial Workers International Union)	1775 K St NW	Washington	DC	20006	**800-551-4010**	202-223-3111	414
UFP Technologies Inc *NASDAQ: UFPT*	172 E Main St	Georgetown	MA	01833	**800-372-3172**	978-352-2200	600
UFPI (Universal Forest Products Inc) *NASDAQ: UFPI*	2801 E Beltline Ave NE	Grand Rapids	MI	49525	**800-598-9663**	616-364-6161	681
UGC (United Guaranty Corp)	230 N Elm St	Greensboro	NC	27401	**800-334-8966**		391-5
UGI (United-Guardian Inc) *NASDAQ: UG*	230 Marcus Blvd PO Box 18050	Hauppauge	NY	11788	**800-645-5566**	631-273-0900	478
UH Parma Medical Center (PCGH)	7007 Powers Blvd	Parma	OH	44129	**855-292-4292**	440-743-3000	374-3
U-Haul International Inc	2727 N Central Ave	Phoenix	AZ	85004	**800-528-0361**		776
Uhl Company Inc	9065 zachary ln n	Maple grove	MN	55369	**800-815-3820**	763-425-7226	393
UHMS (Undersea & Hyperbaric Medical Society)	21 W Colony Pl Ste 280	Durham	NC	27705	**877-533-8467**	919-490-5140	47-17
UIC (Universal Instruments Corp)	33 Broome Corporate Pk	Conklin	NY	13748	**800-842-9732**	607-779-7522	693
UIH (Universal Insurance Holding Inc) *NYSE: UVE*	1110 W Commerical Blvd Ste 100	Fort Lauderdale	FL	33309	**800-509-5586**		391-4
Uintah County	147 E Main St	Vernal	UT	84078	**800-966-4680**	435-781-0770	338
UK (Underwater Kinetics)	13400 Danielson St	Poway	CA	92064	**800-852-7483**	858-513-9100	708
Ukrainian NA Inc (UNA)	2200 Rt 10	Parsippany	NJ	07054	**800-253-9862**		47-14
Ukrainian National Federal Credit Union	215 Second Ave PO Box 160	New York	NY	10003	**866-859-5848**	212-533-2980	221
UL (UL LLC)	2600 NW Lk Rd	Camas	WA	98607	**877-854-3577**		740
UL LLC (UL)	2600 NW Lk Rd	Camas	WA	98607	**877-854-3577**		740
Ulbrich Stainless Steels & Special Metals Inc (USSM)	57 Dodge Ave	North Haven	CT	06473	**800-243-1676**	203-239-4481	721
ULC (Universal Lending Corp)	6775 E Evans Ave	Denver	CO	80224	**800-758-4063**		508
ULI (Urban Land Institute)	1025 Thomas Jefferson St NW Ste 500W	Washington	DC	20007	**800-321-5011*** *Orders	202-624-7000	47-8
U-line Corp	PO Box 245040	Milwaukee	WI	53224	**800-779-2547**	414-354-0300	789
ULLICO Casualty Co	1625 I St NW	Washington	DC	20006	**800-431-5425**		391-5
ULLICO Inc	1625 Eye St NW	Washington	DC	20006	**800-431-5425**		360-4
Ullman Devices Corp	664 Danbury Rd	Ridgefield	CT	06877	**800-784-7796**	203-438-6577	756
Ullman Oil Inc	PO Box 23399	Chagrin Falls	OH	44023	**800-543-5195**	440-543-5195	578
Ulster County Community College	Cottekill Rd	Stone Ridge	NY	12484	**800-724-0833**	845-687-5000	161
ULTA Beauty	1000 Remington Blvd Ste 120	Bolingbrook	IL	60440	**866-983-8582**	630-410-4800	217
Ulteig Engineers Inc	3350 38th Ave S	Fargo	ND	58104	**888-858-3441**	701-280-8500	263
Ultera Systems Inc	26081 Merit Cir Ste 125	Laguna Hills	CA	92653	**877-462-7362**	949-367-8800	178
Ultimate Software Group Inc *NASDAQ: ULTI*	2000 Ultimate Way	Weston	FL	33326	**800-432-1729**	954-331-7000	180-1
Ultimate Support Systems Inc	5836 Wright Dr	Loveland	CO	80538	**800-525-5628**		526
Ultimate Washer Inc	711 Commerce Way Ste 1	Jupiter	FL	33458	**866-858-4982**	561-741-7022	638
Ultra Electronics Flightline Systems Inc	7625 Omni Tech Pl	Victor	NY	14564	**888-959-9001**	585-924-4000	645
Ultra Electronics-DNE Technologies Inc	50 Barnes Industrial Pk N	Wallingford	CT	06492	**800-370-4485**	203-265-7151	645
UltraBac Software	15015 Main St Ste 200	Bellevue	WA	98007	**866-554-8562**	425-644-6000	180-12
Ultracraft Co	6163 Old 421 Rd	Liberty	NC	27298	**800-262-4046**		114
Ultrafabrics LLC	303 S Broadway	Tarrytown	NY	10591	**877-309-6648**	914-460-1730	742-3
Ultralife Batteries Inc *NASDAQ: ULBI*	2000 Technology Pkwy	Newark	NY	14513	**800-332-5000**	315-332-7100	73
Ultramar Travel Management International	14 E 47th St 5th Fl	New York	NY	10017	**888-856-2929**		769
Ultra-Poly Corp	102 Demi Rd PO Box 330	Portland	PA	18351	**800-932-0619**	570-897-7500	607
UltraStaff	1818 Memorial Dr Ste 200	Houston	TX	77007	**800-522-7707**	713-522-7100	719
Ultra-tech Enterprises Inc	4701 Taylor Rd	Punta Gorda	FL	33950	**800-293-2001**	941-575-2000	480
Ultratech Inc *NASDAQ: UTEK*	3050 Zanker Rd	San Jose	CA	95134	**800-222-1213**	408-321-8835	693
UMA (United Motorcoach Assn)	113 SW St 4th Fl	Alexandria	VA	22314	**800-424-8262**	703-838-2929	48-21
Uman Pharma Inc	100 De L'Industrie Blvd	Candiac	QC	J5R1J1	**877-444-9989**	450-444-9989	233
U-mark Inc	102 Iowa Ave	Belleville	IL	62220	**866-383-6275**	618-235-7500	388
UMass Hotel at the Campus Ctr	1 Campus Ctr Way	Amherst	MA	01003	**877-822-2110**	413-549-6000	379
UMB Bank NA	1010 Grand Blvd	Kansas City	MO	64106	**800-821-2171**	816-860-7000	69
UMB Capital Corp	1010 Grand Blvd	Kansas City	MO	64106	**800-821-2171**	816-860-7000	402
UMB Financial Corp *NASDAQ: UMBF*	1010 Grand Blvd	Kansas City	MO	64106	**800-821-2171**	816-860-7000	360-2
UMCES (University of Maryland Ctr for Environmental Science)	2020 Horn Pt Rd	Cambridge	MD	21613	**866-842-2520**	410-228-9250	666
UMCP (University Medical Ctr at Princeton)	253 Witherspoon St	Princeton	NJ	08540	**877-932-8935**	609-497-4304	374-3
UmeVoice Inc	20C Pimentel Ct Ste 1	Novato	CA	94949	**888-230-3300**	415-883-1500	180-7
UMF Medical	1316 Eisenhower Blvd	Johnstown	PA	15904	**800-638-5322**	814-266-8726	320-3
UMHC (University of Miami Hospital & Clinics) *Sylvester Comprehensive Cancer Ctr*	1475 NW 12th Ave	Miami	FL	33136	**800-545-2292**	305-243-1000	767
Umpqua Dairy Products Co	1686 Se N St PO Box 1306	Grants Pass	OR	97526	**800-222-6455**	541-672-2638	297-27
Umpqua Holdings Corp *NASDAQ: UMPQ*	1 SW Columbia St Ste 1200	Portland	OR	97258	**866-486-7782**	503-727-4100	360-2
Umpqua Lighthouse State Park	84505 Hwy 101 S	Florence	OR	97439	**800-551-6949**		564
UMSL (University of Missouri) *Columbia*	104 Jesse Hall	Columbia	MO	65211	**800-856-2181**	573-882-6333	167
UNA (Ukrainian NA Inc)	2200 Rt 10	Parsippany	NJ	07054	**800-253-9862**		47-14
Unaflex LLC	1350 S Dixie Hwy E	Pompano Beach	FL	33064	**800-327-1286**	954-943-5002	370
Unarco Material Handling Inc	701 16th Ave E	Springfield	TN	37172	**800-862-7261**		288
UNC Neuroscience Ctr	University of N Carolina 115 Mason Farm Rd CB 7250	Chapel Hill	NC	27599	**800-862-4938**	919-843-8536	666
Uncle Milton Industries Inc	29209 Canwood St Ste 120	Agoura	CA	91301	**800-869-7555*** *General	818-707-0800	760
Uncle Ray's LLC	14245 Birwood St	Detroit	MI	48238	**800-800-3286**	313-834-0800	297-35
UNC-TV (University of North Carolina Ctr for Public Television)	10 TW Alexander Dr PO Box 14900	Research Triangle Park	NC	27709	**800-906-5050**	919-549-7000	629
UNC-TV Ch 4 (PBS)	10 TW Alexander Dr PO Box 14900	Research Triangle Park	NC	27709	**800-906-5050**	919-549-7000	
Underground Construction Company Inc	5145 Industrial Way	Benicia	CA	94510	**800-227-2314**	707-746-8800	190-10
Undersea & Hyperbaric Medical Society (UHMS)	21 W Colony Pl Ste 280	Durham	NC	27705	**877-533-8467**	919-490-5140	47-17
Underwater Kinetics (UK)	13400 Danielson St	Poway	CA	92064	**800-852-7483**	858-513-9100	708
Underwood Transfer Company LLC	940 W Troy Ave	Indianapolis	IN	46225	**800-428-2372**	317-783-9235	778
UNFCU (United Nations Federal Credit Union)	24-01 44th Rd Ct Sq Pl	Long Island	NY	11101	**800-891-2471**	347-686-6000	221
Unger Co	12401 Berea Rd	Cleveland	OH	44111	**800-321-1418**	216-252-1400	547
Unibank For Savings	49 Church St	Whitinsville	MA	01588	**800-578-4270**	508-234-8112	69
Unibilt Industries Inc	8005 Johnson Stn Rd PO Box 373	Vandalia	OH	45377	**800-777-9942**		105
Unicell Body Co	571 Howard St	Buffalo	NY	14206	**800-628-8914*** *Cust Svc	716-853-8628	515
Unicentric Inc	3127 Penn Ave	Pittsburgh	PA	15201	**800-513-7745**	412-697-7200	179
Unicep Packaging Inc	1702 Industrial Dr	Sandpoint	ID	83864	**800-354-9396**	208-265-9696	548
Unicircuit Inc	8192 Southpark Ln	Littleton	CO	80120	**800-648-6449**	303-730-0505	624
Unico American Corp	23251 Mulholland Dr	Woodland Hills	CA	91364	**800-669-9800**	818-591-9800	391-4
Unicoi State Park & Lodge	1788 Hwy 356 Rd	Helen	GA	30545	**800-573-9659**		564
UNICOM	565 Brea Canyon Rd Ste A	Walnut	CA	91789	**800-346-6668**	626-964-7873	178
UnicornHRO	25 Hanover Rd Ste B	Florham Park	NJ	07932	**800-368-8149**	973-360-0688	38
Unicorp	291 Cleveland St	Orange	NJ	07050	**800-526-1389**	973-674-1700	350
Unicover Corp	1 Unicover Ctr	Cheyenne	WY	82008	**800-443-4225*** *Cust Svc	307-771-3000	458
Uniden America Corp	4700 Amon Carter Blvd	Fort Worth	TX	76155	**800-297-1023*** *Cust Svc	817-858-3300	732
Unifab Corp	5260 Lovers Ln	Portage	MI	49002	**800-648-9569*** *General	269-382-2803	481
Unified Brands	1055 Mendell Davis Dr	Jackson	MS	39272	**888-994-7636**		386
Unified Grocers Inc	5200 Sheila St	Commerce	CA	90040	**800-724-7762**	323-264-5200	298-8
Unified Industries Inc	6551 Loisdale Ct Ste 400	Springfield	VA	22150	**800-666-1642**	703-922-9800	263

Name / Address	City	State	ZIP	Toll-Free	Phone	Class
Unified School District of Antigo 120 S Dorr St	Antigo	WI	54409	**800-795-3272**	715-627-4355	683
Unified Systems Group Inc 1235 64th Ave SE Ste 4a	Calgary	AB	T2H2J7	**866-892-8988**	403-686-8088	176
Unifor 301 Laurier Ave W	Ottawa	ON	K1P6M6	**877-230-5201**	613-230-5200	414
Uniform & Textile Service Assn (UTSA) 1300 N 17th St Ste 750	Arlington	VA	22209	**800-996-3426**	703-247-2600	48-4
Uniform Commercial Code Law Letter 610 Opperman Dr *Cust Svc	Eagan	MN	55123	**800-328-4880***	651-687-7000	530-13
Unigen Corp 45388 Warm Springs Blvd	Fremont	CA	94539	**800-826-0808**	510-668-2088	624
UNIGLOBE Travel USA LLC 18662 MacArthur Blvd Ste 100	Irvine	CA	92612	**877-438-4338**	949-623-9000	770
UniLect Corp PO Box 3026	Danville	CA	94526	**888-864-5328**	925-833-8660	799
Unilux Inc 59 N Fifth St	Saddle Brook	NJ	07663	**800-522-0801**	201-712-1266	471
Unimark Products 9818 Pflumm Rd *Cust Svc	Lenexa	KS	66215	**800-255-6356***	913-649-2424	178
Union Bank of California NA 400 California St 1st Fl	San Francisco	CA	94104	**800-238-4486**	415-765-3434	69
Union Bankshares Inc 20 Lower Main St *NASDAQ: UNB*	Morrisville	VT	05661	**866-862-1891**	802-888-6600	360-2
Union Central Life Insurance Co, The 1876 Waycross Rd PO Box 40888	Cincinnati	OH	45240	**877-546-3863**		390
Union Church of Pocantico Hills 555 Bedford Rd	Sleepy Hollow	NY	10591	**877-325-4822**	914-631-8200	49
Union College 310 College St	Barbourville	KY	40906	**800-489-8646**	606-546-4151	167
Union County 1103 S First St	Clayton	NM	88415	**800-390-7858**	575-374-9253	338
Union County Chamber of Commerce 135 W Main St	Union	SC	29379	**877-202-8755**	864-427-9039	138
Union County College 1033 Springfield Ave	Cranford	NJ	07016	**877-468-3229**	908-709-7000	161
Union County Electric Co-op Inc 122 W Main St	Elk Point	SD	57025	**888-356-3395**	605-356-3395	247
Union Eyecare Centers 4750 Beidler Rd	Willoughby	OH	44094	**800-443-9699**	216-986-9700	542
Union FSB 1565 Mineral Spring Ave	North Providence	RI	02904	**888-226-0819**	401-353-8900	69
Union Group 649 Alden St	Fall River	MA	02722	**800-289-3523**	508-675-4545	85
Union Institute & University 440 E McMillan St	Cincinnati	OH	45206	**800-486-3116**	513-861-6400	167
Union Labor Report 1801 S Bell St	Arlington	VA	22202	**800-372-1033**		530-13
Union Leader 100 William Loeb Dr	Manchester	NH	03109	**800-562-8218**	603-668-4321	531-2
Union of American Physicians & Dentists 180 Grand Ave Ste 1380	Oakland	CA	94612	**800-622-0909**	510-839-0193	414
Union of Concerned Scientists (UCS) 2 Brattle Sq 6th Fl	Cambridge	MA	02238	**800-666-8276**	617-547-5552	47-13
Union Pacific Corp 1400 Douglas St *NYSE: UNP*	Omaha	NE	68179	**888-870-8777**	402-544-5000	360-3
Union Pacific Railroad Co 1400 Douglas St	Omaha	NE	68179	**888-870-8777**		646
Union Pacific Railroad Employees' Health Systems 1040 North 2200 West	Salt Lake City	UT	84116	**800-547-0421**	801-595-4300	391-3
Union Power Co-op 1525 N Rocky River Rd	Monroe	NC	28110	**800-922-6840**	704-289-3145	247
Union Rural Electric Co-op Inc 15461 US 36E	Marysville	OH	43040	**800-642-1826**	937-642-1826	247
Union Square Media Group 22647 Ventura Blvd No. 323	Woodland Hills	CA	91364	**800-691-1741**		7
Union Standard Equipment Co 801 E 141st St	Bronx	NY	10454	**877-282-7333**	718-585-0200	299
Union Standard Insurance Co 122 W Carpenter Fwy Ste 350	Irving	TX	75039	**800-444-0049**	972-719-2400	391-4
Union Station A Wyndham Historic Hotel PO Box 4090	Aberdeen	SD	57401	**800-996-3426**		379
Union Tank Car Co 175 W Jackson Blvd	Chicago	IL	60604	**866-535-7685**	312-431-3111	648
Union Theological Seminary 3041 Broadway	New York	NY	10027	**800-251-9489**	212-662-7100	168-3
Union Theological Seminary & Presbyterian School of Christian Education 3401 Brook Rd	Richmond	VA	23227	**800-229-2990**	804-355-0671	168-3
Union University 1050 Union University Dr	Jackson	TN	38305	**800-338-6466**	731-661-5210	167
Unipunch Products Inc 311 Fifth St NW	Clear Lake	WI	54005	**800-828-7061**		755
Unique Broadband Systems Ltd 400 Spinnaker Way Unit 1 10	Vaughan	ON	L4K5Y9	**877-669-8533**	905-669-8533	645
Unique Carpets Ltd 7360 Jurupa Ave	Riverside	CA	92504	**800-547-8266**	951-352-8125	130
Unique Communications Inc 3650 Coral Ridge Dr	Coral Springs	FL	33065	**800-881-8182**	954-735-4002	248
Unique Functional Products Corp 135 Sunshine Ln	San Marcos	CA	92069	**800-854-1905**	760-744-1610	761
Unique Industries Inc 4750 League Island Blvd	Philadelphia	PA	19112	**800-888-0559**	215-336-4300	329
Unique Lighting Systems Inc 1240 Simpson Way	Escondido	CA	92029	**800-955-4831**		765
Unique Management Services Inc 119 E Maple St	Jeffersonville	IN	47130	**800-879-5453**	812-285-0886	159
UniSea Inc 15400 NE 90th St PO Box 97019	Redmond	WA	98073	**800-535-8509**	425-881-8181	297-14
Uniseal Inc 1800 W Maryland St	Evansville	IN	47712	**800-443-9081**	812-436-4840	3
Unisearch Inc 1780 Barnes Blvd SW	Tumwater	WA	98512	**800-722-0708**	360-956-9500	632

Name / Address	City	State	ZIP	Toll-Free	Phone	Class
Unisec Inc 2555 Nicholson St	San Leandro	CA	94577	**800-982-4587**		690
Unishippers Assn Inc 746 E Winchester Ste 200	Salt Lake City	UT	84107	**800-999-8721**		545
Unisource Manufacturing Inc 8040 NE 33rd Dr	Portland	OR	97211	**800-234-2566**	503-281-4673	453
Unisource NTC 1560 Holly Court Ste 200	Thousand Oaks	CA	91360	**800-736-8470**		462
Unisource Worldwide Inc 6600 Governors Lake Pkwy	Norcross	GA	30071	**800-864-7687**	770-447-9000	552
Unist 4134 36th St SE	Grand Rapids	MI	49512	**800-253-5462**	616-949-0853	695
Unistar-Sparco Computers Inc 7089 Ryburn Dr	Millington	TN	38053	**800-840-8400**	901-872-2272	458
Unit Chemical Corp 7360 Commercial Way	Henderson	NV	89015	**800-879-8648**	702-564-6454	150
Unit Corp 7130 S Lewis Ave Ste 1000 *NYSE: UNT*	Tulsa	OK	74136	**800-722-3612**	918-493-7700	539
Unitarian Universalist Service Committee (UUSC) 689 Massachusetts Ave	Cambridge	MA	02139	**800-388-3920**	617-868-6600	47-5
Unitech Services Group 295 Parker St	Springfield	MA	01151	**800-344-3824**	413-543-6911	442
United Airlines Cargo PO Box 66100	Chicago	IL	60666	**800-822-2746**		12
United Aluminum Corp 100 United Dr	North Haven	CT	06473	**800-243-2515**	203-239-5881	491
United American Bank 101 S Ellsworth Ave *OTC: UABK*	San Mateo	CA	94401	**877-822-4822**	650-579-1500	69
United Bakery Equipment Co Inc 15815 W 110th St	Lenexa	KS	66219	**888-823-2253**	913-541-8700	299
United Bancorp Inc 201 S Fourth St *NASDAQ: UBCP*	Martins Ferry	OH	43935	**888-275-5566**	740-633-0445	360-2
United Bancshares Inc 100 S High St PO Box 67 *NASDAQ: UBOH*	Columbus Grove	OH	45830	**800-837-8111**	419-659-2141	360-2
United Bank 11185 Fairfax Blvd	Fairfax	VA	22030	**800-327-9862**	703-219-4850	69
United Behavioral Health Inc 425 Market St 27th Fl	San Francisco	CA	94105	**800-888-2998**	415-547-5000	461
United Blood Services 6210 E Oak St PO Box 1867	Scottsdale	AZ	85252	**800-288-2199**	480-946-4201	88
United Blood Services of Arizona						
Chandler 6220 E Oak St	Scottsdale	AZ	85252	**877-827-4376**		88
San Luis Obispo 4119 Broad St Ste 100	San Luis Obispo	CA	93401	**877-827-4376**	805-543-4290	88
United Blood Services of Colorado 146 Sawyer Dr	Durango	CO	81303	**800-288-2199**	970-385-4601	88
Meridian 1115 25th Ave	Meridian	MS	39301	**877-827-4376**	601-482-2482	88
United Blood Services of Mississippi						
Tupelo 4326 S Eason Blvd	Tupelo	MS	38801	**800-844-8870**	662-842-8871	88
United Blood Services of Montana						
Billings 1444 Grand Ave	Billings	MT	59102	**800-365-4450**	406-248-9168	88
United Blood Services of New Mexico 1515 University Blvd NE	Albuquerque	NM	87102	**800-333-8037**		88
Albuquerque 1515 University Blvd NE	Albuquerque	NM	87102	**800-333-8037**		88
Farmington 475 E 20th St	Farmington	NM	87401	**877-827-4376**	888-804-9913	88
Las Cruces 1515 University Blvd NE *General	Albuquerque	NM	87102	**877-827-4376***	575-527-1322	88
United Blood Services of North Dakota						
Bismarck 3231 S 11th St	Fargo	ND	58104	**800-456-6159**		88
Fargo 3231 S 11th St *General	Fargo	ND	58104	**800-288-2199***	701-293-9453	88
United Blood Services of Texas						
El Paso 424 S Mesa Hills	El Paso	TX	79912	**877-827-4376**	915-544-5422	88
Lubbock 2523 48th St	Lubbock	TX	79413	**800-333-6920**	806-797-6804	88
McAllen 1400 S Sixth St *General	McAllen	TX	78501	**888-827-4376***	956-213-7500	88
San Angelo 2020 W Beauregard Ave *General	San Angelo	TX	76901	**800-756-0024***	325-223-7500	88
United Blood Services of Wyoming						
Cheyenne 112 E Eigth Ave	Cheyenne	WY	82001	**800-955-7057**	307-638-3326	88
United Brass Works Inc 714 S Main St	Randleman	NC	27317	**800-334-3035**	336-498-2661	787
United Brotherhood of Carpenters & Joiners of America 101 Constitution Ave NW	Washington	DC	20001	**800-530-5090**	202-546-6206	414
United Chemi-Con Inc 9801 W Higgins Rd	Rosemont	IL	60018	**800-344-4539**	847-696-2000	255
United Church of Christ (UCC) 700 Prospect Ave	Cleveland	OH	44115	**866-822-8224**	216-736-2100	47-20
United Color Manufacturing Inc (UCM) PO Box 480	Newtown	PA	18940	**800-852-5942**	215-860-2165	144
United Commercial Travellers 1801 Watermark Dr Ste 100	Columbus	OH	43215	**800-848-0123**	614-228-3276	456-10
United Community Banks Inc PO Box 398 *NASDAQ: UCBI*	Blairsville	GA	30514	**866-270-7100**	706-781-2265	360-2
United Community Financial Corp PO Box 1111 *NASDAQ: UCFC*	Youngstown	OH	44501	**877-272-7661**	330-742-0500	360-2
United CoolAir Corp 491 E Princess St	York	PA	17403	**877-905-1111**	717-843-4311	14
United Country Real Estate Inc 2820 NW Barry Rd	Kansas City	MO	64154	**800-999-1020**	816-420-6200	650

Name / Address	City	State	ZIP	Toll-Free	Phone	Class
United Dairy Farmers 3955 Montgomery Rd *General	Cincinnati	OH	45212	**866-837-4833***	513-396-8700	297-27
United Dairy Inc 300 N Fifth St	Martins Ferry	OH	43935	**800-252-1542**	740-633-1451	297-27
United Displaycraft 333 E Touhy Ave *General	Des Plaines	IL	60018	**877-632-8767***	847-375-3800	235
United Drill Bushing Corp 12200 Woodruff Ave	Downey	CA	90241	**800-486-3466**	562-803-1521	492
United Electric Co-op Inc 29 United Rd	Du Bois	PA	15801	**888-581-8969**	814-371-8570	247
United Electric Supply Inc 10 Bellecor Dr	New Castle	DE	19720	**800-322-3374**	302-322-3333	785
United Electrical Sales Ltd 4496 36th St	Orlando	FL	32811	**800-432-5126**	407-246-1992	248
United Engine & Machine Company Inc 1040 Corbett St	Carson City	NV	89706	**800-648-7970**	775-882-7790	127
United Farmers Co-op (UFC) 705 E Fourth St PO Box 461	Winthrop	MN	55396	**866-998-3266**	507-647-6600	10
United Feather & Down Inc 414 E Golf Rd	Des Plaines	IL	60016	**888-297-1778**	847-296-6610	743
United Federations of Security 540 N State Rd	Briarcliff Manor	NY	10510	**800-227-4291**	914-941-4103	48-7
United Financial Bancorp Inc 95 Elm St PO Box 9020 *NASDAQ: UBNK*	West Springfield	MA	01090	**866-959-2265**	413-787-1700	69
United Fire & Casualty Co 118 Second Ave SE *NASDAQ: UFCS*	Cedar Rapids	IA	52407	**800-332-7977**	319-399-5700	391-4
United Fire Equipment Co 335 N Fourth Ave	Tucson	AZ	85705	**800-362-0150**	520-622-3639	677
United Fire Group 118 Second Ave SE PO Box 73909	Cedar Rapids	IA	52407	**800-332-7977**	319-399-5700	360-4
United Food & Commercial Workers International Union (UFCW) 1775 K St NW	Washington	DC	20006	**800-551-4010**	202-223-3111	414
United Food & Commercial Workers Union Local 555 7095 SW Sandburg St	Tigard	OR	97281	**800-452-8329**	503-684-2822	414
United Ford Parts & Distribtion Ctr Inc 12007 E 61st St	Broken Arrow	OK	74012	**800-800-9001**	918-317-6800	515
United Freezer & Storage Co 650 N Meridian Rd	Youngstown	OH	44509	**800-716-1416**	330-792-1739	801-2
United Guaranty Corp (UGC) 230 N Elm St	Greensboro	NC	27401	**800-334-8966**		391-5
United Heartland Inc PO Box 3026	Milwaukee	WI	53201	**866-206-5851**		391-4
United Heritage Life Insurance Co PO Box 7777	Meridian	ID	83680	**800-657-6351**	208-493-6100	391-2
United Hospice of Atlanta 1626 Jeurgens Ct	Norcross	GA	30093	**800-222-0321**	770-279-6200	371
United Hospital 333 N Smith Ave	Saint Paul	MN	55102	**800-869-1320**	651-241-8000	374-3
United Hospital Ctr 327 Medical pk Dr	Bridgeport	WV	26330	**800-607-8888**	304-624-2121	374-3
United Illuminating Co 157 Church St *Cust Svc	New Haven	CT	06510	**800-722-5584***	203-499-2000	785
United Insurance Holdings Corp 360 Central Ave Ste 900 *NASDAQ: UIHC*	Saint Petersburg	FL	33701	**800-861-4370**	800-295-8016	391-2
United Investors Life Insurance Co 2801 Hwy 280 S	Birmingham	AL	35223	**800-866-9933**	205-268-1000	391-2
United Laboratories Inc 320 37th Ave	Saint Charles	IL	60174	**800-323-2594**		144
United Life Insurance Co PO Box 73909	Cedar Rapids	IA	52407	**800-332-7977**	319-399-5700	391-2
United Marketing Group LLC 929 N Plum Grove Rd	Schaumburg	IL	60173	**800-513-7000**	847-240-2005	197
United Materials LLC The Woodlands Corporate Ctr E 3949 Forest Pkwy Ste 400	North Tonawanda	NY	14120	**888-918-6483**	716-213-5832	184
United Methodist News Service 810 12th Ave S	Nashville	TN	37203	**800-251-8140**	615-742-5470	529
United Methodist Publishing House 201 Eigth Ave S	Nashville	TN	37203	**800-672-1789**	615-749-6000	634-3
United Microelectronics Corp 488 De Guigne Dr *NYSE: UMC*	Sunnyvale	CA	94085	**800-990-1135**	408-523-7800	694
United Motorcoach Assn (UMA) 113 SW St 4th Fl	Alexandria	VA	22314	**800-424-8262**	703-838-2929	48-21
United National Group 3 Bala Plz E Ste 300	Bala Cynwyd	PA	19004	**800-333-0352**	610-664-1500	391-4
United National Insurance Co 3 Bala Plz E Ste 300	Bala Cynwyd	PA	19004	**800-333-0352**	610-664-1500	391-4
United Nations Federal Credit Union (UNFCU) 24-01 44th Rd Ct Sq Pl	Long Island	NY	11101	**800-891-2471**	347-686-6000	221
United Network for Organ Sharing (UNOS) 700 N Fourth St	Richmond	VA	23219	**888-894-6361**	804-782-4800	47-17
United Notions Inc 13800 Hutton St	Dallas	TX	75234	**800-527-9447**	972-484-8901	593
United of Omaha Life Insurance Co Mutual of Omaha Plaza	Omaha	NE	68175	**800-775-6000**	402-342-7600	391-2
United Pacific Pet 12060 Cabernet Dr	Fontana	CA	92337	**800-979-3333**	951-360-8550	577
United Paramount Tax Group Inc 4025 Woodland Park Blvd Ste 310	Arlington	TX	76013	**888-829-8829**	817-983-0099	2
United Parcel Service Inc (UPS) 55 Glenlake Pkwy NE *NYSE: UPS* ■ *Cust Svc	Atlanta	GA	30328	**800-742-5877***	404-828-6000	545
United Performance Metals 3475 Symmes Rd	Hamilton	OH	45015	**888-282-3292**	513-860-6500	721
United Personnel Services Inc 289 Bridge St	Springfield	MA	01103	**800-363-8200**	413-736-0800	262
United Pet Care LLC 6232 N Seventh St Ste 202	Phoenix	AZ	85014	**877-872-8800**	602-266-5303	792
United Pharmacal Company of Missouri Inc 3705 Pear St	Saint Joseph	MO	64503	**800-254-8726**	816-233-8800	577
United Pioneer Co 2777 Summer St Ste 206	Stamford	CT	06905	**800-466-9823**		575
United Plastic Fabricating Inc 165 Flagship Dr	North Andover	MA	01845	**800-638-8265**		604-1
United Plywood & Lumber Inc 1640 Mims Ave SW	Birmingham	AL	35211	**800-272-6486**	205-925-7601	612
United Power Inc 500 Co-op Way	Brighton	CO	80603	**800-468-8809**	303-659-0551	247
United Producers Inc 8351 N High St Ste 250	Columbus	OH	43235	**800-456-3276**		445
United Record Pressing LLC 453 Chestnut St	Nashville	TN	37203	**866-407-3165**	615-259-9396	625
United Recovery Systems LP 5800 N Course Dr	Houston	TX	77072	**800-568-0399**	713-977-1234	159
United Refrigeration Inc 11401 Roosevelt Blvd *General	Philadelphia	PA	19154	**888-578-9100***	215-698-9100	663
United Rentals 3266 E Washington St	Phoenix	AZ	85233	**844-873-4948**	602-267-3898	266-3
United Rentals Inc 224 Selleck St *NYSE: URI*	Stamford	CT	06902	**800-877-3687**	203-622-3131	266-3
United Road Services Inc 10701 Middlebelt Rd	Romulus	MI	48174	**800-221-5127**	734-947-7900	778
United Salt Corp 4800 San Felipe St	Houston	TX	77056	**800-554-8658**	713-877-2600	502-1
United Scenic Artists 29 W 38th St 15th Fl	New York	NY	10018	**800-456-3863**	212-581-0300	414
United Security Bancshares 2126 Inyo St *NASDAQ: UBFO*	Fresno	CA	93721	**888-683-6030**	559-248-4943	69
United Security Bancshares Inc PO Box 249 *NASDAQ: USBI*	Thomasville	AL	36784	**866-546-8273**	334-636-5424	360-2
United Services Automobile Assn (USAA) 10750 McDermott Fwy	San Antonio	TX	78288	**800-531-8722**		187
United Soybean Board (USB) 16305 Swingley Ridge Rd Ste 150	Chesterfield	MO	63017	**800-989-8721**	636-530-1777	47-2
United Space Alliance (USA) 600 Gemini Ave	Houston	TX	77058	**800-367-5690**	281-212-6200	273
United States Aviation 4141 N Memorial Dr	Tulsa	OK	74115	**800-897-5387**	918-836-7345	62
United States Brass & Copper Co Inc 1401 Brook Dr	Downers Grove	IL	60515	**800-821-2854**	630-629-9340	491
United States Endoscopy Group Inc 5976 Heisley Rd	Mentor	OH	44060	**800-769-8226**	440-639-4494	475
United States Information Systems Inc (USIS) 35 W Jefferson Ave	Pearl River	NY	10965	**866-222-3778**	845-358-7755	785
United States Steel Corp 600 Grant St *NYSE: X*	Pittsburgh	PA	15219	**866-433-4801**	412-433-1121	263
United Stationers Inc 1 PkwyN Blvd Ste 100	Deerfield	IL	60015	**855-275-6947**	847-627-7000	533
United Stations Radio Network 1065 Ave of the Americas 3rd Fl	New York	NY	10018	**866-989-1975**	212-869-1111	641
United Sugars Corp 7803 Glenroy Rd Ste 300	Bloomington	MN	55439	**800-984-3585**	952-896-0131	298-11
United Suppliers Inc 30473 260th St PO Box 538	Eldora	IA	50627	**800-782-5123**	641-858-2341	278
United Systems & Software Inc 300 Colonial Ctr Pkwy Ste 150 PO Box 958444	Lake Mary	FL	32746	**800-522-8774**	407-875-2120	179
United Textile Company Inc 751-143rd Ave *General	San Leandro	CA	94578	**800-233-0077***	510-276-2288	507
United Theological Seminary of the Twin Cities 3000 Fifth St NW	New Brighton	MN	55112	**800-937-1316**	651-633-4311	168-3
United Therapeutics Corp 1040 Spring St *NASDAQ: UTHR*	Silver Spring	MD	20910	**877-864-8437**	301-608-9292	582
United Titanium Inc 3450 Old Airport Rd	Wooster	OH	44691	**800-321-4938**	330-264-2111	309
United Tool & Die Co 1 Carney Rd	West Hartford	CT	06110	**877-262-0336**	860-246-6531	22
United Tool & Stamping Company of North Carolina Inc 2817 Enterprise Ave	Fayetteville	NC	28306	**800-883-6087**	910-323-8588	695
United Transportation Union 14600 Detroit Ave	Cleveland	OH	44107	**800-558-8842**	216-228-9400	414
United Trust Group Inc (UTGI) 5250 S Sixth St *OTC: UTGN*	Springfield	IL	62705	**800-323-0050**	217-241-6410	360-4
United Underwriters Inc PO Box 971000	Orem	UT	84097	**866-686-4833**	801-226-2662	390
United Utilities Inc 5450 A St	Anchorage	AK	99509	**800-478-2020**	907-561-1674	733
United Utility Supply Co-op Inc 4515 Bishop Ln	Louisville	KY	40218	**800-366-4887**	502-957-2568	248
United Van Lines Inc 1 United Dr	St. Louis	MO	63026	**877-740-3040**	636-343-3900	518
United Way of America 701 N Fairfax St	Alexandria	VA	22314	**800-892-2757**	703-836-7100	47-5
United Way of Central Md Inc, The 100 S Charles St PO Box 1576	Baltimore	MD	21203	**800-429-0618**	410-547-8000	195
United Window & Door Manufacturing Inc 24-36 Fadem Rd	Springfield	NJ	07081	**800-848-4550**	973-912-0600	479
United World Life Insurance Co 3300 Mutual of Omaha Plz	Omaha	NE	68175	**800-775-6000**	402-342-7600	391-2
United-Bilt Homes Inc 8500 Line Ave	Shreveport	LA	71106	**800-551-8955**	318-861-4572	189
United-Guardian Inc (UGI) 230 Marcus Blvd PO Box 18050 *NASDAQ: UG*	Hauppauge	NY	11788	**800-645-5566**	631-273-0900	478
UnitedHealth Group Inc 9900 Bren Rd E *NYSE: UNH*	Minnetonka	MN	55343	**800-328-5979**	952-936-1300	391-3

	City	State	Zip	Toll-Free	Phone	Class
Unitel Inc PO Box 165	Unity	ME	04988	**888-760-1048**	207-948-3900	733
UniteU Technologies Inc						
12 Pine Cone Dr	Pittsford	NY	14534	**866-386-4838**		226
Unitil Corp						
6 Liberty Ln W	Hampton	NH	03842	**800-852-3339**	603-772-0775	360-5
NYSE: UTL						
Unitrends Software Corp						
200 Wheeler Rd 2nd fl	Burlington	SC	01803	**866-359-5411**	803-454-0300	175-8
Unitron LP						
10925 Miller Rd PO Box 38902	Dallas	TX	75238	**800-527-1279**	214-340-8600	517
Unitus Community Credit Union						
PO Box 1937	Portland	OR	97207	**800-452-0900**	503-227-5571	221
Unity Bancorp Inc						
64 Old Hwy 22	Clinton	NJ	08809	**800-618-2265**	908-730-7630	360-2
NASDAQ: UNTY						
Unity College						
90 Quaker Hill Rd	Unity	ME	04988	**800-624-1024**	207-948-3131	167
Unity Health Insurance						
840 Carolina St	Sauk City	WI	53583	**800-362-3308**	608-643-2491	391-3
Unity Hospice						
2366 Oak Ridge Cir	De Pere	WI	54115	**800-990-9249**	920-338-1111	371
Unity Lake State Recreation Site						
725 Summer St NE Ste C	Salem	OR	97301	**800-551-6949**	541-932-4453	564
Univar Canada Ltd						
9800 Van Horne Way	Richmond	BC	V6X1W5	**855-888-8648**	604-273-1441	145
Univar USA Inc						
17425 NE Union Hill Rd	Redmond	WA	98052	**855-888-8648**	425-889-3400	145
Univenture Inc						
13311 Industrial Pkwy	Marysville	OH	43040	**800-992-8262**		607
Univera Healthcare						
205 Pk Club Ln	Buffalo	NY	14221	**877-883-9577**	716-847-1480	391-3
Universal American Corp (UAFC)						
44 S Broadway Ste 1200	White Plains	NY	10601	**866-249-8668**	914-934-5200	360-4
NYSE: UAM						
Universal American Mortgage Co						
700 NW 107th Ave	Miami	FL	33172	**800-741-8262**		508
Universal Audio Inc						
1700 Green Hills Rd	Scotts Valley	CA	95066	**877-698-2834**	831-440-1176	51
Universal Brush Manufacturing Co						
16200 Dixie Hwy	Markham	IL	60428	**800-323-3474**	708-331-1700	102
Universal Display & Fixtures Co						
726 E Hwy 121	Lewisville	TX	75057	**800-235-0701**	972-221-5022	235
Universal Enterprises Inc						
8030 SW Nimbus	Beaverton	OR	97008	**800-547-5740**	503-644-8723	360-2
Universal Fabric Structures Inc						
2200 Kumry Rd	Telford	PA	18969	**800-634-8368**	215-529-9921	730
Universal Forest Products Inc (UFPI)						
2801 E Beltline Ave NE	Grand Rapids	MI	49525	**800-598-9663**	616-364-6161	681
NASDAQ: UFPI						
Universal Health Services Inc						
367 S Gulph Rd	King of Prussia	PA	19406	**800-347-7750**	610-768-3300	353
NYSE: UHS						
Universal Hospital Services Inc						
7700 France Ave S Ste 275	Minneapolis	MN	55435	**800-847-7368**	952-893-3200	266-4
Universal Image						
PO Box 77090	Winter Garden	FL	34787	**800-553-5499**	407-352-5302	591
Universal Industries Inc						
5800 Nordic Dr	Cedar Falls	IA	50613	**800-553-4446**	319-277-7501	209
Universal Instruments Corp (UIC)						
33 Broome Corporate Pk	Conklin	NY	13748	**800-842-9732**	607-779-7522	693
Universal Insurance Holding Inc (UIH)						
1110 W Commerical Blvd						
Ste 100	Fort Lauderdale	FL	33309	**800-509-5586**		391-4
NYSE: UVE						
Universal Labeling Systems Inc						
3501 Eigth Ave S	Saint Petersburg	FL	33711	**877-236-0266**	727-327-2123	546
Universal Lending Corp (ULC)						
6775 E Evans Ave	Denver	CO	80224	**800-758-4063**		508
Universal Manufacturing Co						
405 Diagonal St PO Box 190	Algona	IA	50511	**800-651-7445**	515-295-3557	59
OTC: UFMG						
Universal Mfg Co Inc						
5030 Mackey S	Overland Park	KS	66203	**800-524-5860**	913-815-6230	760
Universal Orlando						
6000 Universal Blvd	Orlando	FL	32819	**877-801-9720**	407-363-8000	32
Universal Overall Co						
1060 W Van Buren St	Chicago	IL	60607	**800-621-3344***	312-226-3336	154-18
*Cust Svc						
Universal Plastic Mold Inc						
13245 Los Angeles St	Baldwin Park	CA	91706	**888-893-1587**		603
Universal Security Instruments Inc						
11407 Cronhill Dr	Owings Mills	MD	21117	**800-390-4321**	410-363-3000	690
TSE: UUU						
Universal Service Administrative Co (USAC)						
2000 L St NW Ste 200	Washington	DC	20036	**888-641-8722**	202-776-0200	733
Universal Service Administrative Company Schools & Libraries Div						
2000 L St NW Ste 200	Washington	DC	20036	**888-203-8100**		733
Universal Services of America Inc						
1551 N Tustin Ave Ste 650	Santa Ana	CA	92705	**866-877-1965**	714-619-9700	691
Universal Sodexho						
9801 Washingtonian Blvd	Gaithersburg	MD	20878	**888-763-3967**	301-987-4000	300
Universal Steel Co						
6600 Grant Ave	Cleveland	OH	44105	**800-669-2645**	216-883-4972	491
Universal Studios Inc						
100 Universal City Plaza	Universal City	CA	91608	**800-864-8377**		513
Universal Truckload Services Inc						
12755 E Nine Mile Rd	Warren	MI	48089	**800-233-9445**	586-920-0100	778
NASDAQ: UACL						
Universal Tube Inc						
2607 Bond St	Rochester Hills	MI	48309	**800-394-8823**	248-853-5100	594
Universal Valve Company Inc						
478 Schiller St	Elizabeth	NJ	07206	**800-223-0741**	908-351-0606	788
Universal Wilde						
26 Dartmouth St	Westwood	MA	02090	**866-825-5515**	781-251-2700	5
Universal Wire Cloth Co						
16 N Steel Rd	Morrisville	PA	19067	**800-523-0575**	215-736-8981	686
Universal's Islands of Adventure						
6000 Universal Studios Plz	Orlando	FL	32819	**877-801-9720**	407-363-8000	32
UniversalPegasus International Inc						
4848 Loop Central Dr	Houston	TX	77081	**800-966-1811***	713-977-7770	263
*General						
Universitas Foundation of Canada						
3005 Ave Maricourt	Quebec	QC	G1W4T8	**877-710-7377**	418-651-8975	306
Universite de Moncton						
Campus Shippagan						
218 Blvd JD Gauthier	Shippagan	NB	E8S1P6	**800-363-8336**	506-336-3400	783
Edmundston						
165 Blvd Hebert	Edmundston	NB	E3V2S8	**888-736-8623**	506-737-5051	783
Universite de Sherbrooke						
2500 boul de l'Universite	Sherbrooke	QC	J1K2R1	**800-267-8337**	819-821-8000	783
Universite du Quebec a Trois-Rivieres						
3351 Boul des Forges CP 500	Trois-Rivieres	QC	G9A5H7	**800-365-0922**	819-376-5011	783
Universite Sainte Anne						
1695 Rt 1	Pointe-de-l'Eglise	NS	B0W1M0	**888-338-8337**	902-769-2114	783
University & State Employees Credit Union						
10120 Pacific Heights Blvd						
Ste 100	San Diego	CA	92121	**866-873-2448**	858-795-6100	221
University at Albany						
1400 Washington Ave	Albany	NY	12222	**800-293-7869**	518-442-3300	167
University at Albany University Libraries						
1400 Washington Ave	Albany	NY	12222	**800-342-4146**	518-442-3600	434-6
University Behavioral Ctr						
2500 Discovery Dr	Orlando	FL	32826	**800-999-0807**	407-281-7000	374-5
University Galleries						
400 SW 13th St Fine Arts Bldg B						
PO Box 115803	Gainesville	FL	32611	**800-745-3000**	352-273-3000	519
University Games Corp						
2030 Harrison St	San Francisco	CA	94110	**800-347-4818**	415-503-1600	760
University Health Care System						
1350 Walton Way	Augusta	GA	30901	**866-591-2502**	706-722-9011	374-3
University Hospital						
4502 Medical Dr	San Antonio	TX	78229	**866-864-5226**	210-358-4000	374-3
University Hospital SUNY Upstate Medical University						
750 E Adams St	Syracuse	NY	13210	**877-464-5540**	315-464-5540	374-3
University Hospitals of Cleveland						
11100 Euclid Ave	Cleveland	OH	44106	**866-844-2273**	216-844-1000	374-3
University Inn Seattle						
4140 Roosevelt Way NE	Seattle	WA	98105	**800-733-3855**	206-632-5055	379
University Medical Ctr at Princeton (UMCP)						
253 Witherspoon St	Princeton	NJ	08540	**877-932-8935**	609-497-4304	374-3
University Medical Ctr Blood & Marrow Transplantation Program						
1400 Morreene Rd PO Box 24-5176	Durham	NC	27705	**800-524-5928**	520-694-0111	767
University Moving & Storage Co						
23305 Commerce Dr	Farmington Hills	MI	48335	**800-448-6683**	248-615-7000	188
University Museum						
3219 Hudson Rd						
University of Northern Iowa	Cedar Falls	IA	50614	**800-772-2736**	319-273-2188	519
University of Akron						
277 E Buchtel Ave	Akron	OH	44325	**800-655-4884***	330-972-7100	167
*Admissions						
University of Akron School of Law						
150 University Ave	Akron	OH	44325	**800-655-4884**	330-972-7331	168-1
University of Akron Wayne College						
1901 Smucker Rd	Orrville	OH	44667	**800-221-8308**	330-683-2010	161
University of Alabama						
PO Box 870132	Tuscaloosa	AL	35487	**800-933-2262***	205-348-6010	167
*Admissions						
Birmingham						
1530 Third Ave S THT 647	Birmingham	AL	35294	**800-421-8743**	205-996-6670	167
Gorgas Library						
Information Ctr First Fl	Tuscaloosa	AL	35487	**888-764-5603**	205-348-6047	434-6
Huntsville						
301 Sparkman Dr	Huntsville	AL	35899	**800-824-2255**	256-824-1000	167
University of Alabama Press, The						
200 Hackberry Ln Second Fl						
PO Box 870380	Tuscaloosa	AL	35487	**800-621-2736***	205-348-5180	634-4
*Orders						
University of Alabama System						
401 Queen City Ave	Tuscaloosa	AL	35401	**800-638-6420**	205-348-5861	784
University of Alaska Anchorage						
3211 Providence Dr	Anchorage	AK	99508	**888-822-8973**	907-786-1800	167
University of Alaska Anchorage Kenai Peninsula College						
156 College Rd	Soldotna	AK	99669	**877-262-0330**		161
University of Alaska Anchorage Kodiak College						
117 Benny Benson Dr	Kodiak	AK	99615	**800-486-7660**	907-486-4161	161
University of Alaska Fairbanks						
PO Box 757480	Fairbanks	AK	99775	**800-478-1823**	907-474-7500	167
Bristol Bay						
527 Seward St PO Box 1070	Dillingham	AK	99576	**800-478-5109**	907-842-5109	167
Northwest						
400 E Front St PO Box 400	Nome	AK	99762	**800-478-2202**	907-443-2201	161
University of Alaska Museum of the North						
907 Yukon Dr	Fairbanks	AK	99775	**866-478-2721**	907-474-7505	519
University of Alaska Press						
1760 Wwood Wy Ste 220	Fairbanks	AK	99709	**888-252-6657**	907-474-5831	634-4
University of Alaska Southeast						
11120 Glacier Hwy	Juneau	AK	99801	**877-465-4827**	907-796-6000	167
University of Alaska Southeast Ketchikan						
2600 Seventh Ave	Ketchikan	AK	99901	**877-465-6400**	907-225-6177	161
University of Alaska Southeast Sitka						
1332 Seward Ave	Sitka	AK	99835	**800-478-6653**	907-747-6653	161
University of Alberta						
Augustana						
4901-46th Ave	Camrose	AB	T4V2R3	**800-661-8714**	780-679-1100	783
University of Arizona Press, The						
1510 E University Blvd						
PO Box 210055	Tucson	AZ	85721	**800-426-3797**	520-621-1441	634-4
University of Arkansas						
232 Silas Hunt Hall	Fayetteville	AR	72701	**800-377-8632***	479-575-5346	167
*Admissions						
University of Arkansas						
Monticello						
PO Box 3600	Monticello	AR	71656	**800-844-1826**	870-460-1026	167
Pine Bluff						
1200 N University Dr	Pine Bluff	AR	71601	**800-264-6585***	870-575-8000	167
*Admissions						

	City	State	Zip	Toll-Free	Phone	Class
University of Arkansas Press						
McIlroy House 105 McIlroy	Fayetteville	AR	72701	**800-621-2736**	479-575-7258	634-4
University of Arkansas School of Law						
1045 W Maple St	Fayetteville	AR	72701	**800-295-9118**	479-575-5601	168-1
University of Baltimore						
1420 N Charles St	Baltimore	MD	21201	**877-277-5982***	410-837-4200	167
*Admitting						
University of Bridgeport						
126 Pk Ave	Bridgeport	CT	06604	**800-392-3582**	203-576-4000	167
University of British Columbia						
2016-1874 E Mall	Vancouver	BC	V6T1Z1	**877-272-1422**	604-822-9836	783
University of California (UCLA)						
Berkeley						
110 Sproul Hall MC Ste 5800	Berkeley	CA	94720	**866-740-1260**	510-642-6000	167
Santa Cruz						
1156 High St						
Hahn Bldg Rm 150	Santa Cruz	CA	95064	**800-933-7584**	831-459-2131	167
University of California Davis School of Medicine						
4610 X St	Sacramento	CA	95817	**855-221-4673**	916-734-2011	168-2
University of California Irvine						
Library PO Box 19557	Irvine	CA	92623	**800-848-4722**	949-824-6836	434-6
University of California Irvine School of Medicine						
1001 Health Sciences Rd						
252 Irvine Hall	Irvine	CA	92697	**800-824-5388**	949-824-6119	168-2
University of California Press						
2120 Berkeley Way	Berkeley	CA	94704	**800-343-4499**		634-4
University of California System						
1111 Franklin St 12th Fl	Oakland	CA	94607	**800-888-8267**	510-987-9074	784
University of Central Arkansas						
201 Donaghey Ave	Conway	AR	72035	**888-407-4747***	501-450-5000	167
*Admissions						
University of Charleston						
2300 MacCorkle Ave SE	Charleston	WV	25304	**800-995-4682***	304-357-4800	167
*Admissions						
University of Chicago Medical Ctr						
5841 S Maryland Ave	Chicago	IL	60637	**888-824-0200**	773-702-1000	374-3
University of Chicago Press						
1427 E 60th St	Chicago	IL	60637	**800-621-2736***	773-702-7700	634-4
*Sales						
University of Chicago Press Journals Div						
PO Box 37005	Chicago	IL	60637	**877-705-1878**	773-702-7700	634-9
University of Cincinnati						
2600 Clifton Ave						
PO Box 210091	Cincinnati	OH	45221	**866-397-3382**	513-556-1100	167
University of Cincinnati Clermont College						
4200 Clermont College Dr	Batavia	OH	45103	**866-446-2822**	513-732-5200	161
University of Cincinnati Langsam Library						
PO Box 210033	Cincinnati	OH	45221	**866-397-3382**	513-556-1515	434-6
University of Colorado						
Colorado Springs						
PO Box 7150	Colorado Springs	CO	80933	**800-990-8227**	719-262-3000	167
University of Colorado at Colorado Springs						
Kraemer Family Library						
1420 Austin Bluffs Pkwy						
PO Box 7150	Colorado Springs	CO	80918	**800-990-8227**	719-255-3295	434-6
University of Connecticut						
Avery Point						
1084 Shennecossett Rd	Groton	CT	06340	**888-247-5556**	860-405-9019	161
Babbidge Library						
369 Fairfield Rd Unit 2005	Storrs	CT	06269	**888-603-9635**	860-486-2219	434-6
University of Connecticut Health Ctr						
John Dempsey Hospital						
263 Farmington Ave	Farmington	CT	06030	**800-535-6232**	860-679-2000	374-3
University of Connecticut School of Law						
45 Elizabeth St	Hartford	CT	06105	**800-633-7867**	860-570-5100	168-1
University of Dallas						
1845 E Northgate Dr	Irving	TX	75062	**800-628-6999***	972-721-5266	167
*Admissions						
University of Dayton						
300 College Pk	Dayton	OH	45469	**800-837-7433**	937-229-4411	167
University of Denver						
2199 S University Blvd	Denver	CO	80210	**800-525-9495**	303-871-2036	167
University of Detroit Mercy						
4001 W McNichols Rd	Detroit	MI	48221	**800-635-5020***	313-993-1000	167
*Admissions						
University of Detroit Mercy School of Law						
651 E Jefferson Ave	Detroit	MI	48226	**888-726-6921**	313-596-0264	168-1
University of Dubuque						
2000 University Ave	Dubuque	IA	52001	**800-722-5583**	563-589-3000	167
University of Dubuque Theological Seminary						
2000 University Ave	Dubuque	IA	52001	**800-369-8387**	563-589-3122	168-3
University of Evansville						
1800 Lincoln Ave	Evansville	IN	47722	**800-423-8633**	812-488-2000	167
University of Findlay						
1000 N Main St	Findlay	OH	45840	**800-472-9502**	419-422-8313	167
University of Florida						
219 Grinter Hall						
PO Box 115500	Gainesville	FL	32611	**866-876-4472**	352-392-3261	167
University of Florida Fredric G Levin College of Law						
2500 SW Second Ave	Gainesville	FL	32611	**877-429-1297**	352-273-0890	168-1
University of Florida Libraries						
PO Box 117001	Gainesville	FL	32611	**877-351-2377**	352-392-0342	434-6
University of Georgia Library						
320 S Jackson St	Athens	GA	30602	**877-314-5560**	706-542-0621	434-6
University of Great Falls						
1301 20th St S	Great Falls	MT	59405	**800-856-9544***		167
*Admissions						
University of Guelph						
50 Stone Rd E	Guelph	ON	N1G2W1	**877-674-1610**	519-824-4120	783
University of Hartford						
200 Bloomfield Ave	West Hartford	CT	06117	**800-947-4303**	860-768-4296	167
University of Hawaii						
Hilo 200 W Kawili St	Hilo	HI	96720	**800-897-4456***	808-974-7414	167
*Admissions						
Manoa						
2600 Campus Rd Rm 001	Honolulu	HI	96822	**800-823-9771***	808-956-8975	167
*Admissions						
West Oahu						
96-129 Ala Ike	Pearl City	HI	96782	**866-299-8656**	808-454-4700	167
University of Hawaii Federal Credit Union						
PO Box 22070	Honolulu	HI	96823	**800-927-3397**	808-983-5500	221
University of Hawaii Foundation, The						
2444 Dole St Bachman Hall 105	Honolulu	HI	96822	**866-846-4262**	808-956-8849	221
University of Hawaii Press						
2840 Kolowalu St	Honolulu	HI	96822	**888-847-7377**	808-956-8255	634-4
University of Houston						
Victoria						
3007 N Ben Wilson St	Victoria	TX	77901	**877-970-4848**	361-570-4848	167
University of Houston Law Ctr						
100 Law Ctr	Houston	TX	77204	**800-252-9690**	713-743-2100	168-1
University of Idaho						
875 Perimeter Dr	Moscow	ID	83844	**888-884-3246**	208-885-6111	167
Boise						
322 E Front St Ste 190	Boise	ID	83702	**866-264-7384**	208-334-2999	167
University of Idaho College of Law						
711 S Rayburn St	Moscow	ID	83844	**888-884-3246**	208-885-4977	168-1
University of Illinois						
Springfield						
1 University Plz						
MS UHB 1080	Springfield	IL	62703	**888-977-4847**	217-206-4847	167
University of Illinois College of Law						
504 E Pennsylvania Ave	Champaign	IL	61820	**800-369-6151**	217-333-0930	168-1
University of Illinois Medical Ctr						
1740 W Taylor St	Chicago	IL	60612	**866-600-2273**	312-996-3900	374-3
University of Illinois Press						
1325 S Oak St	Champaign	IL	61820	**866-244-0626**	217-333-0950	634-4
University of Indianapolis						
1400 E Hanna Ave	Indianapolis	IN	46227	**800-232-8634**	317-788-3368	167
University of Iowa						
107 Calvin Hall	Iowa City	IA	52242	**800-553-4692**	319-335-3847	167
University of Iowa Athletics Hall of Fame						
2425 Prairie Meadow Dr	Iowa City	IA	52242	**877-462-6342**	319-384-1031	521
University of Iowa College of Law						
130 Byington Rd	Iowa City	IA	52242	**800-553-4692**	319-335-9034	168-1
University of Iowa Press						
119 W Pk Rd 100 Kuhl House	Iowa City	IA	52242	**800-621-2736**	319-335-2000	634-4
University of Iowa Roy J & Lucille A Carver College of Medicine						
200 CMAB	Iowa City	IA	52242	**800-725-8460**	319-335-6707	168-2
University of Judaism						
15600 Mulholland Dr	Los Angeles	CA	90077	**888-853-6763**	310-476-9777	167
University of Kansas School of Law						
1535 W 15th St	Lawrence	KS	66045	**877-404-5823**	785-864-4550	168-1
University of Kentucky						
800 Rose St	Lexington	KY	40536	**866-900-4685**	859-257-9000	167
University of Kentucky College of Law						
620 S Limestone St	Lexington	KY	40506	**800-888-8189**	859-257-1678	168-1
University of Kentucky College of Medicine						
Office of Medical Education						
MN 104 UKMC	Lexington	KY	40536	**800-273-8255**	859-323-6161	168-2
University of La Verne						
1950 Third St	La Verne	CA	91750	**800-876-4858***	909-593-3511	167
*Admissions						
University of Louisiana						
Lafayette						
611 McKinley St	Lafayette	LA	70504	**800-752-6553**	337-482-1000	167
Monroe						
700 University Ave	Monroe	LA	71209	**800-372-5127***	318-342-5430	167
*Admissions						
University of Louisville						
2301 S Third St	Louisville	KY	40292	**800-334-8635**	502-852-5555	167
University of Louisville Hospital						
530 S Jackson St	Louisville	KY	40202	**800-891-0947**	502-562-3000	374-3
University of Louisville School of Medicine						
323 E Chestnut St	Louisville	KY	40292	**800-334-8635**	502-852-5193	168-2
University of Maine						
5713 Chadbourne Hall	Orono	ME	04469	**877-486-2364***	207-581-1110	167
*Admissions						
Augusta						
46 University Dr	Augusta	ME	04330	**877-862-1234**	207-621-3000	167
Fort Kent						
23 University Dr	Fort Kent	ME	04743	**888-879-8635***	207-834-7500	167
*Admissions						
Machias						
116 O'Brien Ave	Machias	ME	04654	**888-468-6866***	207-255-1200	167
*Admissions						
University of Manitoba						
65 Chancellors Cir						
424 University Ctr	Winnipeg	MB	R3T2N2	**800-224-7713***	204-474-8880	783
*Admissions						
University of Mary						
7500 University Dr	Bismarck	ND	58504	**800-288-6279***	701-255-7500	167
*Admissions						
University of Mary Hardin-Baylor						
900 College St PO Box 8004	Belton	TX	76513	**800-727-8642**	254-295-8642	167
University of Mary Washington						
1301 College Ave	Fredericksburg	VA	22401	**800-468-5614***	540-654-2000	167
*Admissions						
University of Maryland						
7569 Baltimore Ave	College Park	MD	20742	**800-422-5867***	301-405-1000	167
*Admissions						
Baltimore County						
1000 Hilltop Cir	Baltimore	MD	21250	**800-810-0271**	410-455-1000	167
University of Maryland Ctr for Environmental Science (UMCES)						
2020 Horn Pt Rd	Cambridge	MD	21613	**866-842-2520**	410-228-9250	666
University of Maryland Greenebaum Cancer Ctr						
22 S Greene St Ste N9E17	Baltimore	MD	21201	**800-888-8823**	410-328-7904	767
University of Maryland Medical System						
22 S Greene St	Baltimore	MD	21201	**800-492-5538**	410-328-8667	353
University of Maryland University College Marriott Conference Ctr Hotel						
3501 University Blvd E	Adelphi	MD	20783	**800-721-7033**	301-985-7300	377
University of Massachusetts Press						
PO Box 429	Amherst	MA	01004	**800-562-0112**	413-545-2217	634-4
University of Memphis Cecil C Humphreys School of Law						
3715 Central Ave	Memphis	TN	38152	**800-872-3728**	901-678-2421	168-1
University of Memphis McWherter Library						
126 Ned R McWherter Library	Memphis	TN	38152	**866-670-6147**	901-678-2201	434-6

Listing	City	State	ZIP	Toll-Free	Phone	Class
University of Miami Hospital & Clinics (UMHC)						
Sylvester Comprehensive Cancer Ctr						
1475 NW 12th Ave	Miami	FL	33136	**800-545-2292**	305-243-1000	767
University of Michigan Press						
839 Greene St	Ann Arbor	MI	48104	**866-804-0002**	734-764-4388	634-4
University of Minnesota						
Crookston						
2900 University Ave						
170 Owen Hall	Crookston	MN	56716	**800-862-6466**	218-281-8569	167
Duluth						
1049 University Dr	Duluth	MN	55812	**800-232-1339**	218-726-8000	167
Morris 600 E Fourth St	Morris	MN	56267	**800-992-8863**	320-589-6035	167
Twin Cities						
240 Williamson Hall						
231 Pillsbury Dr SE	Minneapolis	MN	55455	**800-752-1000**	612-625-2008	167
University of Minnesota Crookston						
UMC Library						
2900 University Ave	Crookston	MN	56716	**800-862-6466**	218-281-8399	434-6
University of Minnesota Duluth						
Kathryn A. Martin Library						
416 Library Dr	Duluth	MN	55812	**866-999-6995**	218-726-8102	434-6
University of Minnesota Medical Ctr Fairview - University Campus						
500 Harvard St	Minneapolis	MN	55455	**800-688-5252**	612-273-3000	374-3
University of Minnesota Medical School Twin Cities						
420 Delaware St SE						
Mayo MC 293	Minneapolis	MN	55455	**800-752-1000**	612-624-5100	168-2
University of Mississippi						
Tupelo						
1918 Briar Ridge Rd	Tupelo	MS	38804	**888-846-5622**	662-844-5622	167
Williams Library						
1 Library Loop	University	MS	38677	**800-891-4596**	662-915-7091	434-6
University of Mississippi School of Medicine						
2500 N State St	Jackson	MS	39216	**888-815-2005**	601-984-1080	168-2
University of Missouri (UMSL)						
Columbia						
104 Jesse Hall	Columbia	MO	65211	**800-856-2181**	573-882-6333	167
University of Missouri Botanic Garden						
General Services Bldg	Columbia	MO	65211	**800-856-2181**	573-882-4240	96
University of Missouri Kansas City						
Nichols Library						
800 E 51st St	Kansas City	MO	64110	**800-775-8652**	816-235-1534	434-6
University of Missouri Press						
2910 LeMone Blvd	Columbia	MO	65201	**800-621-2736**	573-882-7641	634-4
University of Missouri System						
321 University Hall	Columbia	MO	65211	**800-225-6075**	573-882-2011	784
University of Missouri-Kansas City School of Medicine						
2411 Holmes St	Kansas City	MO	64108	**800-735-2466**	816-235-1111	168-2
University of Mobile						
5735 College Pkwy	Mobile	AL	36613	**800-946-7267**	251-675-5990	167
University of Montana						
32 Campus Dr	Missoula	MT	59812	**800-462-8636***	406-243-6266	167
*Admissions						
College of Technology						
909 S Ave W	Missoula	MT	59801	**800-542-6882**	406-243-7852	798
Helena College of Technology						
1115 N Roberts St	Helena	MT	59601	**800-827-1000**	406-444-6800	798
Western						
710 S Atlantic St	Dillon	MT	59725	**877-683-7331***	406-683-7011	167
*Admissions						
University of Montana Missoula						
Mansfield Library						
32 Campus Dr	Missoula	MT	59812	**800-240-4939**	406-243-2053	434-6
University of Nebraska						
Kearney 905 W 25th St	Kearney	NE	68849	**800-532-7639**	308-865-8441	167
Lincoln 1410 Q St	Lincoln	NE	68588	**800-742-8800**	402-472-2023	167
Omaha 6001 Dodge St	Omaha	NE	68182	**800-858-8648**	402-554-2800	167
University of Nebraska Medical Ctr						
42nd and Emile	Omaha	NE	68198	**877-726-4727**	402-559-4000	374-3
University of Nebraska Medical Ctr Bone Marrow & Stem Cell Transplantation Program (Adults)						
987400 Nebraska Medical Ctr	Omaha	NE	68198	**800-922-0000**	402-559-2000	767
University of Nebraska Medical Ctr McGoogan Library of Medicine						
986705 Nebraska Medical Ctr	Omaha	NE	68198	**866-800-5209**	402-559-4006	434-1
University of Nebraska Press						
1111 Lincoln Mall	Lincoln	NE	68508	**800-755-1105***	402-472-3581	634-4
*Orders						
University of Nebraska School of Medicine						
985527 Nebraska Medical Ctr	Omaha	NE	68198	**800-626-8431**	402-559-2259	168-2
University of Nebraska System						
3835 Holdrege St Varner Hall	Lincoln	NE	68583	**800-542-1602**	402-472-2111	784
University of Nevada						
Reno 1664 N Virginia St	Reno	NV	89557	**866-263-8232**	775-784-1110	167
University of New England						
11 Hills Beach Rd	Biddeford	ME	04005	**800-477-4863***	207-283-0171	167
*Admissions						
Westbrook College						
716 Stevens Ave	Portland	ME	04103	**800-477-4863***	207-797-7261	167
*Admissions						
University of New Hampshire						
Manchester						
400 Commercial St	Manchester	NH	03101	**800-287-9793**	603-641-4321	167
University of New Haven						
300 Boston Post Rd	West Haven	CT	06516	**800-342-5864**	203-932-7319	167
University of New Mexico (UNM)						
1 University of New Mexico	Albuquerque	NM	87131	**800-225-5866**	505-277-0111	167
Gallup 200 College Rd	Gallup	NM	87301	**800-225-5866**	505-863-7500	167
Valencia						
280 La Entrada	Los Lunas	NM	87031	**800-225-5866**	505-925-8580	161
University of New Mexico School of Medicine						
1 University of New Mexico	Albuquerque	NM	87131	**877-977-2263**	505-272-4766	168-2
University of New Orleans						
Administrative Bldg						
Rm 103 Lakefront	New Orleans	LA	70148	**800-256-5866***	504-280-6000	167
*Admissions						
University of North Alabama						
1 Harrison Plaza	Florence	AL	35632	**800-825-5862**	256-765-4608	167
University of North Carolina						
Asheville						
1 University Heights CPO 1320	Asheville	NC	28804	**800-531-9842**	828-251-6481	167
Greensboro						
1400 Spring Garden St	Greensboro	NC	27412	**877-862-4123**	336-334-5000	167
Pembroke PO Box 1510	Pembroke	NC	28372	**800-949-8627**	910-521-6000	167
Wilmington						
601 S College Rd	Wilmington	NC	28403	**800-596-2880**	910-962-3000	167
University of North Carolina Ctr for Public Television (UNC-TV)						
10 TW Alexander Dr						
PO Box 14900	Research Triangle Park	NC	27709	**800-906-5050**	919-549-7000	629
University of North Carolina Press						
116 S Boundary St	Chapel Hill	NC	27514	**800-848-6224**	919-966-3561	634-4
University of North Dakota						
PO Box 8357	Grand Forks	ND	58202	**800-225-5863**	701-777-3000	167
University of North Dakota School of Medicine & Health Sciences						
501 N Columbia Rd	Grand Forks	ND	58203	**800-225-5863**	701-777-5046	168-2
University of North Florida						
4567 St Johns Bluff Rd S	Jacksonville	FL	32224	**866-697-7150**	904-620-1000	167
University of North Texas						
PO Box 311277	Denton	TX	76203	**800-868-8211**	940-565-2681	167
University of North Texas Health Science Ctr						
3500 Camp Bowie Blvd	Fort Worth	TX	76107	**800-687-7580**	817-735-2000	417
University of North Texas Libraries						
1155 Union Cir PO Box 305190	Denton	TX	76203	**877-872-0264**	940-565-2413	434-6
University of North Texas Press						
1155 Union Cir Ste 311336	Denton	TX	76203	**800-826-8911**	940-565-2142	634-4
University of Northern Colorado						
501 20th St CB 92	Greeley	CO	80639	**888-700-4862***	970-351-2881	167
*Admissions						
University of Northern Iowa						
1222 W 27th St	Cedar Falls	IA	50614	**800-772-2037***	319-273-2281	167
*Admissions						
University of Oklahoma						
1000 Asp Ave	Norman	OK	73019	**800-234-6868**	405-325-0311	167
University of Oregon						
1585 E 13th Ave	Eugene	OR	97403	**800-232-3825***	541-346-1000	167
*Admissions						
University of Oregon Bookstore Inc						
895 E 13th Ave	Eugene	OR	97401	**800-352-1733**	541-346-4331	95
University of Ottawa						
550 Cumberland St	Ottawa	ON	K1N6N5	**877-868-8292**	613-562-5800	783
University of Ottawa Faculty of Medicine						
451 Smyth Rd	Ottawa	ON	K1H8M5	**877-868-8292**	613-562-5700	168-2
University of Pennsylvania						
3451 Walnut St	Philadelphia	PA	19104	**800-537-5487**	215-898-5000	167
University of Pennsylvania Press						
3902 Spruce St	Philadelphia	PA	19104	**800-537-5487***	215-898-6261	634-4
*Cust Svc						
University of Pennsylvania Van Pelt Library						
3420 Walnut St	Philadelphia	PA	19104	**877-784-8379**	215-898-7091	434-6
Bradford						
300 Campus Dr	Bradford	PA	16701	**800-872-1787**	814-362-7555	167
Greensburg						
150 Finoli Dr	Greensburg	PA	15601	**888-843-4563**	724-837-7040	167
Hillman Library						
3960 Forbes Ave	Pittsburgh	PA	15260	**888-465-4329**	412-648-7710	434-6
Johnstown						
157 Blackington Hall	Johnstown	PA	15904	**800-765-4875**	814-269-7050	167
Titusville						
504 E Main St	Titusville	PA	16354	**888-878-0462**		161
University of Pittsburgh Medical Ctr (UPMC)						
Horizon						
110 N Main St	Greenville	PA	16125	**888-447-1122**	724-588-2100	374-3
University of Pittsburgh Medical Ctr Health System						
200 Lothrop St	Pittsburgh	PA	15213	**800-533-8762**	412-647-2345	353
University of Pittsburgh Press						
3400 Forbes Ave 5th Fl	Pittsburgh	PA	15261	**800-621-2736***	412-383-2456	634-4
*Sales						
University of Portland						
5000 N Willamette Blvd	Portland	OR	97203	**888-627-5601**	503-943-7147	167
University of Puget Sound						
1500 N Warner St	Tacoma	WA	98416	**800-396-7191**	253-879-3100	167
University of Redlands						
1200 E Colton Ave PO Box 3080	Redlands	CA	92373	**800-455-5064**	909-793-2121	167
University of Regina						
3737 Wascana Pkwy	Regina	SK	S4S0A2	**800-644-4756**	306-585-4111	783
University of Richmond						
28 Westhampton Way	Richmond	VA	23173	**800-700-1662**	804-289-8000	167
Westhampton College						
28 Westhampton Way	University Of Richmond	VA	23173	**800-700-1662**	804-289-8000	167
University of Rio Grande						
218 N College Ave	Rio Grande	OH	45674	**800-282-7201**	740-245-5353	167
University of Rochester						
Wallace Hall PO Box 270251	Rochester	NY	14627	**888-822-2256***	585-275-2121	167
*Admissions						
University of Rochester School of Medicine & Dentistry						
601 Elmwood Ave	Rochester	NY	14642	**888-661-6162**	585-275-0017	168-2
University of Saint Francis						
180 Remsen St	Brooklyn Heights	NY	11201	**800-356-8329**	718-522-2300	167
University of Saint Mary						
4100 S Fourth St	Leavenworth	KS	66048	**800-752-7043**	913-682-5151	167
University of Saint Thomas						
3800 Montrose Blvd	Houston	TX	77006	**800-856-8565**	713-522-7911	167
University of Saint Thomas O'Shaughnessy-Frey Library						
2115 Summit Ave	Saint Paul	MN	55105	**800-328-6819**	651-962-5494	434-6
University of Saint Thomas School of Law						
1000 LaSalle Ave	Minneapolis	MN	55403	**800-328-6819**	651-962-4892	168-1
University of San Diego						
5998 Alcala Pk	San Diego	CA	92110	**800-248-4873**	619-260-4506	167
University of San Diego School of Law						
5998 Alcala Pk	San Diego	CA	92110	**800-248-4873**	619-260-4528	168-1
University of San Francisco						
2130 Fulton St	San Francisco	CA	94117	**800-854-1385***	415-422-5555	167
*Admissions						
University of Saskatchewan						
1121 College Dr	Saskatoon	SK	S7N0W3	**877-653-8501**	306-966-8970	168-3
Saint Thomas More College						
1437 College Dr	Saskatoon	SK	S7N0W6	**800-667-2019**	306-966-8900	783
University of Sciences & Arts of Oklahoma						
1727 W Alabama Ave	Chickasha	OK	73018	**800-933-8726**	405-224-3140	167

Name / Address	City	State	ZIP	Toll-Free	Phone	Class
University of Scranton						
800 Linden St St Thomas Hall	Scranton	PA	18510	**888-727-2686**	570-941-7400	167
University of Sioux Falls						
1101 W 22nd St	Sioux Falls	SD	57105	**800-888-1047**	605-331-6600	167
University of South Alabama						
2500 Meisler Hall	Mobile	AL	36688	**800-872-5247**	251-460-6141	167
University of South Carolina						
1600 Hampton St	Columbia	SC	29208	**800-868-5872**	803-777-7000	167
Aiken						
471 University Pkwy	Aiken	SC	29801	**866-254-2366**	803-648-6851	167
Beaufort						
801 Carteret St	Beaufort	SC	29902	**866-455-4753**	843-521-4100	167
Sumter 200 Miller Rd	Sumter	SC	29150	**888-872-7868**	803-775-8727	167
Union 401 E Main St	Union	SC	29379	**800-768-5566**	864-429-8728	161
Upstate						
800 University Way	Spartanburg	SC	29303	**800-277-8727**	864-503-5246	167
University of South Carolina McKissick Museum						
University of S Carolina 816 Bull St	Columbia	SC	29208	**888-825-9711**	803-777-7251	519
University of South Carolina Press						
1600 Hampton St 5th Fl	Columbia	SC	29208	**800-768-2500***	803-777-5243	634-4
*Orders						
University of South Dakota						
414 E Clark St	Vermillion	SD	57069	**877-269-6837**	605-677-5341	167
University of South Dakota Foundation						
1110 N Dakota St PO Box 5555	Vermillion	SD	57069	**800-521-3575**	605-677-6703	784
University of South Dakota School of Law						
414 E Clark St	Vermillion	SD	57069	**877-269-6837**	605-677-5443	168-1
University of South Florida						
Sarasota-Manatee						
8350 N Tamiami Trail	Sarasota	FL	34243	**866-974-1222**	941-359-4200	167
Tampa 4202 E Fowler Ave	Tampa	FL	33620	**800-299-2855**	813-974-2011	167
University of South Florida College of Medicine (USF)						
12901 Bruce B Downs Blvd	Tampa	FL	33612	**877-338-2577**	813-974-2229	168-2
University of South Florida Polytechnic						
Lakeland						
3433 Winter Lake Rd	Lakeland	FL	33803	**800-873-5636**	863-667-7000	167
University of Southern California						
Doheny Memorial Library						
3550 Trousdale Pkwy University Pk Campus	Los Angeles	CA	90089	**800-775-7330**	213-740-4039	434-6
University of Southern Indiana						
8600 University Blvd	Evansville	IN	47712	**800-467-1965**	812-464-1765	167
University of Southern Maine						
96 Falmouth St	Portland	ME	04103	**800-800-4876**	207-780-4141	167
Gorham 37 College Ave	Gorham	ME	04038	**800-800-4876**	207-780-5670	167
Lewiston-Auburn College						
51 Westminster St	Lewiston	ME	04240	**800-800-4876**	207-753-6500	167
University of Southern Maine Arboretum						
PO Box 9300	Portland	ME	04104	**800-800-4876**		96
University of Southern Mississippi						
118 College Dr	Hattiesburg	MS	39406	**800-446-0892**	601-266-1000	167
University of St Francis						
500 Wilcox St	Joliet	IL	60435	**800-735-7500**		167
University of Tennessee						
Chattanooga						
615 McCallie Ave	Chattanooga	TN	37403	**800-882-6627**	423-425-4111	167
Martin						
544 University St	Martin	TN	38238	**800-829-8861**	731-881-7020	167
University of Tennessee Health Science Ctr						
Health Sciences Library & Biocommunications Ctr						
877 Madison Ave	Memphis	TN	38103	**877-747-0004**	901-448-5634	434-1
University of Tennessee Knoxville						
Hodges Library						
1015 Volunteer Blvd	Knoxville	TN	37996	**800-426-9119**	865-974-4351	434-6
University of Texas						
Dallas						
800 W Campbell Rd Ste Be3204	Richardson	TX	75080	**800-889-2443**	972-883-2111	167
El Paso						
500 W University Ave	El Paso	TX	79968	**800-551-0294***	915-747-5000	167
*Admissions						
Pan American						
1201 W University Dr	Edinburg	TX	78539	**866-441-8872**	956-381-8872	167
Permian Basin						
4901 E University Blvd	Odessa	TX	79762	**866-552-8872***	432-552-2020	167
*Admissions						
San Antonio						
6900 N Loop 1604 W	San Antonio	TX	78249	**800-669-0919**	210-458-4011	167
Tyler						
3900 University Blvd	Tyler	TX	75799	**800-888-9537**	903-566-7000	167
University of Texas at Austin Performing Arts Ctr						
E 23rd St & E Robert Dedman Dr	Austin	TX	78713	**800-687-6010**	512-471-1444	571
University of Texas Medical Branch						
301 University Blvd	Galveston	TX	77555	**800-228-1841**	409-772-2618	168-2
University of Texas Medical Branch Hospitals						
301 University Blvd	Galveston	TX	77555	**800-201-0527**	409-772-1011	374-3
University of Texas Press						
2100 Comal St	Austin	TX	78722	**800-252-3206***	512-471-7233	634-4
*Sales						
University of Texas Southwestern Medical Ctr at Dallas Library, The						
5323 Harry Hines Blvd	Dallas	TX	75390	**866-645-6455**	214-648-2001	434-1
University of Texas Southwestern Medical Ctr Dallas						
Hematopoietic Cell Transplant Program						
2201 Inwood Rd 2nd Fl	Dallas	TX	75390	**866-645-6455**	214-645-4673	767
Southwestern Medical School						
5323 Harry Hines Blvd	Dallas	TX	75390	**866-648-2455**	214-648-3111	168-2
University of Texas System						
601 Colorado St	Austin	TX	78701	**866-882-2034**	512-499-4200	784
University of the Arts						
320 S Broad St	Philadelphia	PA	19102	**800-616-2787**	215-717-6049	163
University of the Cumberlands						
6191 College Stn Dr	Williamsburg	KY	40769	**800-343-1609**	606-539-4201	167
University of the Incarnate Word						
4301 Broadway St Ste 285	San Antonio	TX	78209	**800-749-9673***	210-829-6000	167
*Admissions						
University of the Ozarks						
415 N College Ave	Clarksville	AR	72830	**800-264-8636***	479-979-1227	167
*Admissions						

Name / Address	City	State	ZIP	Toll-Free	Phone	Class
University of the Pacific						
3601 Pacific Ave	Stockton	CA	95211	**800-959-2867**	209-946-2211	167
University of the Sciences in Philadelphia						
600 S 43rd St	Philadelphia	PA	19104	**888-857-6264**	215-596-8800	167
University of the South						
735 University Ave	Sewanee	TN	37383	**800-522-2234**	931-598-1238	167
University of Toledo						
2801 W Bancroft St	Toledo	OH	43606	**800-586-5336**	419-530-4636	167
University of Toledo Carlson Library						
2801 W Bancroft St MS 509	Toledo	OH	43606	**800-586-5336**	419-530-2324	434-6
University of Toledo Medical Center, The						
3000 Arlington Ave	Toledo	OH	43614	**800-321-8383**	419-383-4000	374-3
University of Tulsa						
800 S Tucker Rd	Tulsa	OK	74104	**800-331-3050**	918-631-2307	167
University of Utah Hospital & Clinics (UUHSC)						
Blood & Marrow Transplant Program						
50 N Medical Dr	Salt Lake City	UT	84132	**800-824-2073***	801-581-2121	767
*General						
University of Utah School of Medicine						
30 N 1900 E	Salt Lake City	UT	84132	**844-988-7284**	801-581-7201	168-2
University of Vermont						
85 S Prospect St	Burlington	VT	05405	**800-499-0113**	802-656-3131	167
University of Vermont College of Medicine						
89 Beaumont Ave E-126 Given Bldg	Burlington	VT	05405	**800-571-0668**	802-656-2156	168-2
University of Vermont Medical Center, The (FAHC)						
111 Colchester Ave	Burlington	VT	05401	**800-358-1144**	802-847-0000	374-3
University of Virginia Health System						
1215 Lee St	Charlottesville	VA	22908	**800-251-3627**	434-924-0211	374-3
University of Virginia Press						
210 Sprigg Ln PO Box 400318	Charlottesville	VA	22903	**800-831-3406***	434-924-3469	634-4
*Orders						
University of Virginia School of Law						
580 Massie Rd	Charlottesville	VA	22903	**877-307-0158**	434-924-7354	168-1
University of Virginia's College at Wise						
1 College Ave	Wise	VA	24293	**888-282-9324***	276-328-0102	167
*Admissions						
University of Washington Press						
4333 Brooklyn Ave NE	Seattle	WA	98195	**800-537-5487**	206-543-4050	634-4
University of Washington School of Law						
William H Gates Hall PO Box 353020	Seattle	WA	98195	**866-866-0158**	206-543-4078	168-1
University of West Alabama						
Station 200	Livingston	AL	35470	**800-621-8044***	205-652-3400	167
*Admissions						
University of West Florida Ctr for Fine & Performing Arts						
11000 University Pkwy Bldg 82	Pensacola	FL	32514	**800-263-1074**	850-474-2000	571
University of Western Ontario						
King's University College						
266 Epworth Ave	London	ON	N6A2M3	**800-265-4406**	519-433-3491	783
University of Wisconsin						
Baraboo/Sauk County						
1006 Connie Rd	Baraboo	WI	53913	**800-621-7440**	608-355-5200	161
Barron County						
1800 College Dr	Rice Lake	WI	54868	**800-608-4578**	715-234-8176	161
Eau Claire						
105 Garfield Ave PO Box 4004	Eau Claire	WI	54701	**800-473-2255**	715-836-2637	167
Fox Valley						
1478 Midway Rd	Menasha	WI	54952	**800-273-8255**	920-832-2600	161
Green Bay						
2420 Nicolet Dr	Green Bay	WI	54311	**800-465-4329**	920-465-2000	167
La Crosse						
1725 State St 115 Graff Main Hall	La Crosse	WI	54601	**800-382-2150**	608-785-8000	167
Manitowoc						
705 Viebahn St	Manitowoc	WI	54220	**800-657-3866**	920-683-4700	161
Marathon County						
518 S Seventh Ave	Wausau	WI	54401	**888-367-8962**	715-261-6100	161
Marshfield/Wood County						
2000 W Fifth St	Marshfield	WI	54449	**800-273-8255**	715-389-6530	161
Platteville						
1 University Plz	Platteville	WI	53818	**800-362-5515**	608-342-1125	167
Richland						
1200 Hwy 14 W	Richland Center	WI	53581	**800-947-3529**	608-647-6186	161
River Falls						
410 S Third St B3 E Hathorn Hall	River Falls	WI	54022	**800-852-5711**	715-425-3911	167
Stout						
802 S Broadway	Menomonie	WI	54751	**800-447-8688***	715-232-1232	167
*Admissions						
Superior						
Belknap & Catlin PO Box 2000	Superior	WI	54880	**800-869-5088**	715-394-8101	167
Washington County						
400 S University Dr	West Bend	WI	53095	**800-240-0276**	262-335-5200	161
University of Wisconsin Eau Claire						
McIntyre Library						
105 Garfield Ave	Eau Claire	WI	54702	**877-267-1384**	715-836-3715	434-6
University of Wisconsin Hospital & Clinics						
600 Highland Ave	Madison	WI	53792	**800-323-8942**	608-263-6400	374-3
University of Wisconsin Law School						
975 Bascom Mall	Madison	WI	53706	**866-301-1753**	608-262-2240	168-1
University of Wisconsin Stout						
Library						
315 Tenth Ave E	Menomonie	WI	54751	**866-716-6685**	715-232-1215	434-6
University of Wisconsin Superior						
Jim Dan Hill Library						
PO Box 2000	Superior	WI	54880	**877-232-1727**	715-394-8343	434-6
University of Wisconsin System						
1220 Linden Dr 1720 Van Hise Hall	Madison	WI	53706	**800-442-6461**	608-262-2321	784
University of Wyoming						
1000 E University Ave Dept 3435	Laramie	WY	82071	**800-342-5996***	307-766-5160	167
*Admissions						
University of Wyoming Libraries						
PO Box 3334	Laramie	WY	82071	**800-442-6757**	307-766-3190	434-6
University Park Mall						
6501 N Grape Rd	Mishawaka	IN	46545	**877-746-6642**	574-277-2223	459

Name	Address	City	State	ZIP	Toll-Free	Phone	Class
University Place	310 SW Lincoln St	Portland	OR	97201	**866-845-4647**	503-221-0140	379
University Press Books (UPB)	2430 Bancroft Way	Berkeley	CA	94704	**800-676-8722**	510-548-0585	95
University Press of America	4501 Forbes Blvd Ste 200	Lanham	MD	20706	**800-462-6420**	301-459-3366	634-2
University Press of Colorado	5589 Arapahoe Ave Ste 206C	Boulder	CO	80303	**800-621-2736**	720-406-8849	634-4
University Press of Florida	15 NW 15th St *Sales	Gainesville	FL	32611	**800-226-3822***	352-392-1351	634-4
University Press of Kentucky	663 S Limestone St *Sales	Lexington	KY	40508	**800-537-5487***	859-257-8400	634-4
University Press of Mississippi	3825 Ridgewood Rd	Jackson	MS	39211	**800-737-7788**	601-432-6205	634-4
University Press of New England (UPNE)	1 Ct St Ste 250 *Orders	Lebanon	NH	03766	**800-421-1561***	603-448-1533	634-4
University Products Inc	517 Main St	Holyoke	MA	01040	**800-628-1912**	413-532-3372	559
Univest Corp of Pennsylvania	14 N Main St PO Box 64197 *NASDAQ: UVSP*	Souderton	PA	18964	**877-723-5571**		360-2
Univex Corp	3 Old Rockingham Rd	Salem	NH	03079	**800-258-6358**	603-893-6191	299
Univision Television Group Inc	5999 Ctr Dr	Los Angeles	CA	90045	**800-594-5387**	310-846-2800	735
Uniweld Products Inc	2850 Ravenswood Rd	Fort Lauderdale	FL	33312	**800-323-2111**	954-584-2000	809
Uniworld	17323 Ventura Blvd	Encino	CA	91316	**800-733-7820**	818-382-7820	223
Unlimi-Tech Software Inc	1725 St Laurent Blvd Ste 205	Ottawa	ON	K1G3V4	**877-327-9387**	613-667-2439	179
Unlimited Systems Corp Inc	9530 Padgett St	San Diego	CA	92126	**800-275-6354**	858-537-5010	175-3
UNM (University of New Mexico)	1 University of New Mexico	Albuquerque	NM	87131	**800-225-5866**	505-277-0111	167
Unmetric Inc	2001 Victoria Rd	Chicago	IL	60060	**855-558-5588**		465
Uno Langmann Ltd	2117 Granville St	Vancouver	BC	V6H3E9	**800-730-8825**	604-736-8825	41
UNOS (United Network for Organ Sharing)	700 N Fourth St	Richmond	VA	23219	**888-894-6361**	804-782-4800	47-17
UnumProvident Corp	1 Fountain Sq	Chattanooga	TN	37402	**800-262-0018**	423-294-1011	360-4
Unverferth Mfg Company Inc	601 S Broad St	Kalida	OH	45853	**800-322-6301**	419-532-3121	275
UOP LLC	25 E Algonquin Rd	Des Plaines	IL	60017	**800-877-6184**	847-391-2000	142
Up With Paper	6049 Hi-Tek Ct	Mason	OH	45040	**800-852-7677**	513-759-7473	129
Up With People	6830 Broadway	Denver	CO	80221	**877-264-8856**	303-460-7100	47-15
UPAC (Imperial PFS)	8245 Nieman Rd	Lenexa	KS	66214	**800-877-7848**	913-894-6150	218
UPB (University Press Books)	2430 Bancroft Way	Berkeley	CA	94704	**800-676-8722**	510-548-0585	95
Upchurch Scientific Inc	619 Oak St	Oak Harbor	WA	98277	**800-426-0191**	360-679-2528	419
UPI Energy LP	105 Silvercreek Pkwy N Ste 200	Guelph	ON	N1H8M1	**800-396-2667**	519-821-2667	325
Upland Software Inc	Frost Tower 401 Congress Ave, Ste 2950	Austin	TX	78701	**855-944-7526**		785
UPMC (University of Pittsburgh Medical Ctr)	*Horizon* 110 N Main St	Greenville	PA	16125	**888-447-1122**	724-588-2100	374-3
Upnorth Consulting Inc	331 Second Ave S Ste 202	Minneapolis	MN	55401	**866-892-1758**		182
Upper Arlington News	7801 N Central Dr	Lewis Center	OH	43035	**800-860-1267**	740-888-6000	531-4
Upper Bucks Chamber of Commerce	2170 Portzer Rd	Quakertown	PA	18951	**888-942-8257**	215-536-3211	138
Upper Cumberland Electric Membership Corp	138 Gordonsville Hwy	South Carthage	TN	37030	**800-261-2940**	615-735-2940	247
Upper Dauphin Area School District (UDASD)	5668 State Rt 209	Lykens	PA	17048	**866-632-9992**	717-362-8134	683
Upper Deck Co LLC	5909 Sea Otter Pl *Cust Svc	Carlsbad	CA	92010	**800-873-7332***		760
Upper Iowa University	605 Washington St PO Box 1857 *Admissions	Fayette	IA	52142	**800-553-4150***	563-425-5200	167
Upper Peninsula Telephone Co	PO Box 86	Carney	MI	49812	**800-950-8506**	906-639-2111	733
Upper Room Chapel & Museum	1908 Grand Ave	Nashville	TN	37212	**800-972-0433**	615-340-7200	519
Upper Sioux Agency State Park	5908 Hwy 67	Granite Falls	MN	56241	**800-366-8917**	320-564-4777	564
Upper Valley Medical Ctr (UVMC)	3130 N County Rd 25-A	Troy	OH	45373	**866-608-3463**	937-440-4000	374-3
UPS (United Parcel Service Inc)	55 Glenlake Pkwy NE *NYSE: UPS* ■ *Cust Svc	Atlanta	GA	30328	**800-742-5877***	404-828-6000	545
UPS Capital Business Credit	35 Glenlake Pkwy NE	Atlanta	GA	30328	**877-263-8772**		69
UPS Store, The	6060 Cornerstone Ct W	San Diego	CA	92121	**800-789-4623**	858-455-8800	311
UPS Strategic Enterprise Fund	55 Glenlake Pkwy NE Bldg 1 4th Fl	Atlanta	GA	30328	**800-742-5877**		790
UPS Supply Chain Solutions	12380 Morris Rd	Alpharetta	GA	30005	**800-742-5727**	913-693-6151	448
Upsher-Smith Laboratories Inc	6701 Evenstad Dr	Maple Grove	MN	55369	**800-654-2299**	763-315-2000	582
Upstate New York Transplant Services Inc	110 Broadway	Buffalo	NY	14203	**800-227-4771**	716-853-6667	271
Upstate Shredding LLC	1 Recycle Dr Tioga Industrial Pk	Owego	NY	13827	**800-245-3133**	607-687-7777	684
Upstate Tours & Travel	207 Geyser Rd	Saratoga Springs	NY	12866	**800-237-5252**	518-584-5252	758
Upturn Solutions Inc	1396 Riverside Rd	Bigfork	MT	59911	**866-891-4363**		611
Urban Alternative	PO Box 4000	Dallas	TX	75208	**800-800-3222**	214-943-3868	47-20
Urban Barn Ltd	4085 Marine Way Ste 1	Burnaby	BC	V5J5E2	**844-456-2200**	604-456-2200	322
Urban Decay	833 W 16th St	Newport Beach	CA	92663	**800-784-8722**	949-631-4504	217
Urban Foundation/Engineering LLC	32-33 111th St	East Elmhurst	NY	11369	**877-395-5459**	718-478-3021	191-5
Urban Institute	2100 M St NW	Washington	DC	20037	**866-518-3874**	202-833-7200	631
Urban Land Institute (ULI)	1025 Thomas Jefferson St NW Ste 500W *Orders	Washington	DC	20007	**800-321-5011***	202-624-7000	47-8
Urban Outfitters Inc	30 Industrial Pk Blvd	Trenton	SC	29847	**800-282-2200**		156-4
Urban Science	400 Renaissance Ctr Ste 2900	Detroit	MI	48243	**800-321-6900**	313-259-9900	196
Urban Web Design	102-19 Dallas Rd	Victoria	BC	V8V5A6	**877-889-2573**	250-380-1296	227
Urologix Inc	14405 21st Ave N	Minneapolis	MN	55447	**800-475-1403**	763-475-1400	475
Urschel Laboratories Inc	2503 Calumet Ave PO Box 2200	Valparaiso	IN	46384	**844-877-2435**	219-464-4811	299
Ursinus College	601 E Main St PO Box 1000	Collegeville	PA	19426	**877-448-3282**	610-409-3200	167
Ursula of Switzerland Inc	31 Mohawk Ave	Waterford	NY	12188	**800-826-4041**		154-20
Ursuline College	2550 Lander Rd	Pepper Pike	OH	44124	**888-778-5463**	440-449-4200	167
Us Adventure Rv	5120 n brady st	Davenport	IA	52806	**877-768-4678**		23
US Air Force 375th Medical Group	310 W Losey St	Scott AFB	IL	62225	**866-683-2778**		331-4
US Air Force Academy (USAFA)	2304 Cadet Dr Ste 2300	Air Force Academy	CO	80840	**800-443-9266**	719-333-1110	497
US Airconditioning Distributors	16900 Chestnut St	City of Industry	CA	91748	**800-937-7222**	626-854-4500	611
US Alliance Federal Credit Union	600 Midland Ave	Rye	NY	10580	**800-431-2754**		221
US Apple Assn	8233 Old Courthouse Rd Ste 200	Vienna	VA	22182	**800-781-4443**	703-442-8850	47-2
US Army Aeromedical Research Laboratory	MCMR-UAC Bldg 6901	Fort Rucker	AL	36362	**888-386-7635**	334-255-6920	666
US Army Engineer Research & Development Ctr (ERDC)	3909 Halls Ferry Rd	Vicksburg	MS	39180	**800-522-6937**	601-634-3188	666
US Army War College	122 Forbes Ave	Carlisle	PA	17013	**800-453-0992**	717-245-3131	340-4
Us Art Company Inc	66 Pacella Park Dr	Randolph	MA	02368	**800-872-7826**	781-986-6500	521
US Balloon Mfg Company Inc	140 58th St	Brooklyn	NY	11220	**800-285-4000**	718-492-9700	329
US Bancorp	800 Nicollet Mall *NYSE: USB* ■ *Cust Svc	Minneapolis	MN	55402	**800-872-2657***	651-466-3000	360-2
US Bank NA	800 Nicollet Mall	Minneapolis	MN	55402	**800-872-2657**	651-466-3000	69
US Bankruptcy Court							
Alaska	605 W Fourth Ave Ste 138	Anchorage	AK	99501	**800-859-8059**	907-271-2655	341-1
Eastern District of Washington	904 W Riverside Ave Ste 304	Spokane	WA	99201	**800-519-2549**	509-353-2404	341-1
Minnesota	300 S Fourth St 7W US Courthouse	Minneapolis	MN	55415	**866-260-7337**	612-664-5260	341-1
Missouri Eastern	111 S Tenth St 4th Fl	Saint Louis	MO	63102	**866-803-9517**	314-244-4500	341-1
Pennsylvania Middle	197 S Main St	Wilkes-Barre	PA	18701	**877-298-2053**	570-831-2500	341-1
Texas Northern	1100 Commerce St Rm 1254	Dallas	TX	75242	**800-442-6850**	214-753-2000	341-1
Wisconsin Eastern	US Courthouse 517 E Wisconsin Ave Rm 126	Milwaukee	WI	53202	**877-781-7277**	414-297-3291	341-1
US Biathlon Assn	49 Pineland Dr Ste 301-A *General	New Gloucester	ME	04260	**800-242-8456***	207-688-6500	47-22
US Bobsled & Skeleton Federation (USBSF)	196 Old Military Rd	Lake Placid	NY	12946	**888-431-3598**	518-523-1842	47-22
US Bronze Sign Co	811 Second Ave	New Hyde Park	NY	11040	**800-872-5155**	516-352-5155	775
US Button Corp	328 Kennedy Dr	Putnam	CT	06260	**800-243-1842**	860-928-2707	593
US Catholic Magazine	205 W Monroe *Cust Svc	Chicago	IL	60606	**800-328-6515***	312-236-7782	456-18
US Cellular Corp (USCC)	8410 W Bryn Mawr Ave Ste 700 *NYSE: USM*	Chicago	IL	60631	**888-944-9400**	773-399-8900	733
US Cellular Ctr	370 First Ave E	Cedar Rapids	IA	52401	**800-745-3000**	319-398-5211	207
US Census Bureau Regional Offices							
Atlanta	101 Marietta St NW Ste 3200	Atlanta	GA	30303	**800-424-6974**	404-730-3832	340-2
Boston	4 Copley Pl Ste 301	Boston	MA	02117	**800-562-5721**	617-424-4501	340-2
Chicago	1111 W 22nd St Ste 400	Oak Brook	IL	60523	**800-865-6384**	630-288-9200	340-2
Denver	6900 W Jefferson Ave Ste 100	Denver	CO	80235	**800-852-6159**	303-264-0202	340-2
Los Angeles	15350 Sherman Way Ste 300	Van Nuys	CA	91406	**800-992-3530**	818-267-1700	340-2

Listing	City	State	Zip	Toll-Free	Phone	Class
New York						
32 Old Slip 9th Fl	New York	NY	10005	**800-991-2520**	212-584-3400	340-2
Philadelphia						
833 Chestnut St Ste 504	Philadelphia	PA	19107	**800-262-4236**	215-717-1800	340-2
US Chemical & Plastics						
600 Nova Dr SE	Massillon	OH	44646	**800-321-0672**	330-830-6000	59
US Chess Federation (USCF)						
PO Box 3967	Crossville	TN	38557	**800-903-8723**	931-787-1234	47-18
US Chrome Corp						
175 Garfield Ave	Stratford	CT	06615	**800-637-9019**		480
US Citizenship & Immigration Services Regional Offices						
Eastern Region						
70 Kimball Ave	South Burlington	VT	05403	**800-767-1833**		340-9
US Coachways Inc						
100 St Mary's Ave Ste 2B	Staten Island	NY	10305	**800-359-5991**	718-477-4242	441
US Coast Guard						
National Maritime Ctr						
100 Forbes Dr	Martinsburg	WV	25404	**888-427-5662**	304-433-3400	340-9
US Coast Guard Academy						
15 Mohegan Ave	New London	CT	06320	**800-883-8724**	860-444-8500	167
US Coast Guard Air Station Detroit						
1461 N Perimeter Rd						
Selfridge ANGB	Selfridge	MI	48045	**800-424-8802**		157
US Commission on Civil Rights Regional Offices						
Midwestern Regional Office						
55 W Monroe St Ste 410	Chicago	IL	60603	**800-552-6843**	312-353-8311	340-18
US Conference of Catholic Bishops (USCCB)						
3211 Fourth St NE	Washington	DC	20017	**866-582-0943**	202-541-3000	47-20
US Curling Assn (USCA)						
5525 Clem's Way	Stevens Point	WI	54482	**888-287-5377**	715-344-1199	47-22
US Customs & Border Protection						
1300 Pennsylvania Ave NW	Washington	DC	20229	**877-227-5511**	703-526-4200	340-9
US Data Management LLC						
1746-F S Victoria Ave	Ventura	CA	93003	**888-231-0816**		182
US Dataworks Inc						
1 Sugar Creek Ctr Blvd						
5th Fl	Sugar Land	TX	77478	**888-254-8821**	281-504-8000	180-10
OTC: UDWK						
US Dept of Education						
Region 6						
1999 Bryan St Ste 1620	Dallas	TX	75201	**877-521-2172**	214-661-9600	340-6
US Dept of Labor Women's Bureau						
200 Constitution Ave NW						
Rm S-3002	Washington	DC	20210	**800-827-5335**	202-693-6710	199
US Diamond Wheel Co						
101 Kendall Pt Dr	Oswego	IL	60543	**800-223-0457**	800-851-1095	499
US Digital Corp						
1400 NE 136th Ave	Vancouver	WA	98684	**800-736-0194**	360-260-2468	180-10
US Digital Media Inc						
1929 W Lone Cactus Dr	Phoenix	AZ	85027	**877-992-3766**	623-587-4900	546
US District Court Colorado						
901 19th St	Denver	CO	80294	**800-359-8699**	303-844-3433	341-2
US District Court for the District of Alaska						
222 W Seventh Ave Ste 4	Anchorage	AK	99513	**866-243-3814**	907-677-6100	341-2
US District Court Mississippi Southern						
PO Box 23552	Jackson	MS	39201	**866-517-7682**	601-965-4439	341-2
US District Court Nebraska						
111 S 18th Plaza Ste 1152	Omaha	NE	68102	**866-220-4381**	402-661-7350	341-2
US District Court North Carolina Western						
401 W Trade St	Charlotte	NC	28202	**866-851-1605**	704-350-7400	341-2
US District Court Oklahoma Northern						
333 W Fourth St	Tulsa	OK	74103	**866-213-1957**	918-699-4700	341-2
US District Court Vermont						
11 Elmwood Ave Rm 506						
PO Box 945	Burlington	VT	05402	**800-837-8718**	802-951-6301	341-2
US Drug Testing Laboratories Inc						
1700 S Mt Prospect Rd	Des Plaines	IL	60018	**800-235-2367**	847-375-0770	416
US Ecology						
300 E Mallard Dr Ste 300	Boise	ID	83706	**800-590-5220**	208-331-8400	665
NASDAQ: ECOL						
US Election Assistance Commission						
1201 New York Ave NW Ste 300	Washington	DC	20005	**866-747-1471**	202-566-3100	340-18
US Energy Corp						
877 N Eigth W	Riverton	WY	82501	**800-776-9271**	307-856-9271	501
NASDAQ: USEG						
US Equipment Company Inc						
8311 Sorensen Ave	Santa Fe Springs	CA	90670	**800-255-4731**		358
US Fencing Assn (USFA)						
1 Olympic Plaza	Colorado Springs	CO	80909	**888-431-3598**	719-866-4511	47-22
US Fish & Wildlife Service (USFWS)						
1849 C St NW	Washington	DC	20240	**800-344-9453**	202-208-4717	340-11
US Fish & Wildlife Service Regional Offices						
Great Lakes/Big Rivers Region						
5600 American Blvd W						
Ste 900	Bloomington	MN	55437	**800-877-8339**	612-713-5360	340-11
US Foods Culinary Equipment & Supplies						
2621 Fairview Ave N Ste 2	Roseville	MN	55113	**866-636-2338**	651-638-8993	301
US Fund for UNICEF						
125 Maiden Ln	New York	NY	10038	**800-367-5437**		47-5
US General Services Administration						
1800 F St NW	Washington	DC	20405	**800-488-3111**		340-18
US Geological Survey (USGS)						
12201 Sunrise Valley Dr	Reston	VA	20192	**888-275-8747**	703-648-6723	340-11
Ask USGS						
12201 Sunrise Valley Dr	Reston	VA	20192	**888-275-8747**	703-648-5953	340-11
US Global Investors Inc						
7900 Callaghan Rd	San Antonio	TX	78229	**800-873-8637**	210-308-1234	401
NASDAQ: GROW						
US Golf Assn (USGA)						
77 Liberty Corner Rd	Far Hills	NJ	07931	**800-336-4446***	908-234-2300	47-22
*Orders						
US Government Printing Office Bookstore (GPO)						
732 N Capitol St NW	Washington	DC	20401	**866-512-1800**	202-512-1800	342
US Grant, The						
326 Broadway	San Diego	CA	92101	**866-716-8136**	619-232-3121	379
US Health & Human Services Department						
Region 9						
90 7th St Ste 4-100	San Francisco	CA	94103	**800-368-1019**		340-8
Us Health Connect Inc						
500 Office Ctr Dr	Fort Washington	PA	19034	**800-889-4944**		161
US Immigration & Customs Enforcement (ICE)						
425 'I' St NW	Washington	DC	20536	**866-347-2423**	202-514-1900	340-9
US Industries Inc						
1701 First Ave	Evansville	IN	47710	**800-456-8721**	812-425-2428	191-12
US Ink Corp						
651 Garden St	Carlstadt	NJ	07072	**800-423-8838**	201-935-8666	388
US Junior Chamber of Commerce						
7447 S Lewis Ave	Tulsa	OK	74136	**800-905-5499**	636-681-1857	47-7
US Lawns						
4700 Millenia Blvd Ste 240	Orlando	FL	32839	**800-875-2967**		422
US Learning Inc						
516 Tennessee St Ste 219	Memphis	TN	38103	**800-647-9166**	901-767-0000	763
US Legal Support Inc						
363 N Sam Houston Pkwy E						
Ste 900	Houston	TX	77060	**800-567-8757**	713-653-7100	444
US Linen & Uniform Inc						
1106 Harding St	Richland	WA	99352	**888-875-4636**	509-946-6125	442
US Marshals Service						
401 Courthouse Square	Alexandria	VA	22314	**800-336-0102***	202-307-9100	340-12
*General						
US Merchant Marine Academy						
300 Steamboat Rd	Kings Point	NY	11024	**866-546-4778**	516-726-5800	167
Us Micro Corp						
7000 Highlnds Pkwy SE	Smyrna	GA	30082	**888-876-4276**	770-437-0706	176
US Mint						
801 Ninth St NW	Washington	DC	20220	**800-872-6468***	202-354-7462	340-16
*Cust Svc						
San Francisco						
155 Hermann St	San Francisco	CA	94102	**800-872-6468**	415-575-8000	340-16
West Point (NY)						
PO Box 37	West Point	NY	10996	**800-872-6468**		340-16
US Naval Academy						
121 Blake Rd	Annapolis	MD	21402	**888-249-7707***	410-293-1000	497
*Admissions						
US Naval Institute						
291 Wood Rd	Annapolis	MD	21402	**800-233-8764**	410-268-6110	47-19
US New Mexico Federal Credit Union (USNMFCU)						
3939 Osuna Rd NE PO Box 129	Albuquerque	NM	87109	**888-342-8766**	505-342-8888	221
US News & World Report						
1050 Thomas Jefferson St NW	Washington	DC	20007	**800-836-6397**	202-955-2000	456-17
US News University Connection LLC						
9417 Princess Palm Ave	Tampa	FL	33619	**866-442-6587**		387
US Olympic Training Ctr						
1750 E Boulder St	Colorado Springs	CO	80909	**800-775-8762**	719-866-4618	718
US PAACC (US Pan Asian American Chamber of Commerce)						
1329 18th St NW	Washington	DC	20036	**800-696-7818**	202-296-5221	47-14
US Pan Asian American Chamber of Commerce (US PAACC)						
1329 18th St NW	Washington	DC	20036	**800-696-7818**	202-296-5221	47-14
US Parole Commission						
5550 Friendship Blvd Rm 420	Chevy Chase	MD	20815	**888-585-9103**	301-492-5990	340-12
US Patent & Trademark Office						
PO Box 1450	Alexandria	VA	22313	**800-786-9199**	571-272-1000	340-2
US Penitentiary						
Atwater						
1 Federal Way PO Box 019001	Atwater	CA	95301	**877-623-8426**	209-386-0257	214
US Pharmacist Magazine						
100 Ave of the Americas	New York	NY	10013	**800-825-4696**		456-16
US Pharmacopeia (USP)						
12601 Twinbrook Pkwy	Rockville	MD	20852	**800-227-8772**	301-881-0666	48-8
US Physical Therapy						
1300 W Sam Houston Pkwy S						
Ste 300	Houston	TX	77042	**800-580-6285**	713-297-7000	352
NYSE: USPH						
US Pipe & Foundry Co						
2 Chase Corporate Drive						
Ste 200	Birmingham	AL	35244	**866-347-7473**		308
US Plastic Corp						
1390 Newbrecht Rd	Lima	OH	45801	**800-537-9724**	419-228-2242	201
US Postal Service (USPS)						
475 L'Enfant Plaza W SW	Washington	DC	20260	**800-275-8777***	202-268-2000	340-18
*Cust Svc						
US Premium Beef LLC (USPB)						
12200 N Ambassador Dr						
PO Box 20103	Kansas City	MO	64163	**866-877-2525**	816-713-8800	297-26
US Professional Tennis Assn (USPTA)						
3535 Briarpark Dr Ste 1	Houston	TX	77042	**800-877-8248**	713-978-7782	47-22
US Recordings Inc						
2925 Country Dr	Little Canada	MN	55117	**877-272-5250**	651-765-6400	391-6
US Ring Binder						
6800 Arsenal St	Saint Louis	MO	63139	**800-888-8772**	314-645-7880	85
US Robotics Corp						
1300 E Woodfield Dr Ste 506	Schaumburg	IL	60173	**877-710-0884**	847-874-2000	175-3
US Rowing Assn						
2 Wall St	Princeton	NJ	08540	**800-314-4769**	609-924-1578	47-22
US Sailing Assn						
15 Maritime Dr PO Box 1260	Portsmouth	RI	02871	**800-877-2451**	401-683-0800	47-22
US Security Assoc Inc						
200 Mansell Ct 5th Fl	Roswell	GA	30076	**800-730-9599**	770-625-1500	691
US Security Inc						
4544 NW 10th St	Oklahoma City	OK	73127	**877-917-5566**	405-947-3377	691
US Shipping Corp						
399 Thornall St 8th Fl	Edison	NJ	08837	**866-942-6592**	732-635-1500	313
US Silica Co						
8490 Progress Dr Ste 300	Frederick	MD	21701	**800-243-7500**	304-258-2500	502-4
US Soccer Federation						
1801 S Prairie Ave	Chicago	IL	60616	**800-745-3000**	312-808-1300	47-22
US Special Delivery Inc						
821 E Blvd	Kingsford	MI	49802	**800-821-6389**	906-774-1931	683
US Suites						
4970 Windplay Dr C1	El Dorado Hills	CA	95762	**800-877-8483***	916-941-7970	379
*Cust Svc						
US Synchronized Swimming						
1 Olympic Plaza	Colorado Springs	CO	80909	**800-775-8762**	317-237-5700	47-22
US Telecom Assn (USTA)						
607-14th St NW Ste 400	Washington	DC	20005	**877-869-6903**	202-326-7300	48-20
US Tool Grinding Inc						
701 S Desloge Dr	Desloge	MO	63601	**800-222-1771**	573-431-3856	454

Name / Address	City	State	Zip	Toll-Free	Phone	Class
US Travel Assn						
1100 New York Ave NW Ste 450	Washington	DC	20005	**877-212-5752**	202-408-8422	48-7
US Trotting Assn (USTA)						
750 Michigan Ave	Columbus	OH	43215	**877-800-8782**	614-224-2291	47-22
US Tsubaki Inc						
301 E Marquardt Dr	Wheeling	IL	60090	**800-323-7790**	847-459-9500	619
US Vision Inc						
1 Harmon Dr						
Glen Oaks Industrial Pk	Glendora	NJ	08029	**866-435-7111**	856-228-1000	542
US WorldMeds LLC						
4010 Dupont Cir Ste L-07	Louisville	KY	40207	**888-900-8796**	502-815-8000	240
US Xpress Enterprises Inc						
4080 Jenkins Rd	Chattanooga	TN	37421	**800-251-6291**	423-510-3000	778
USA (United Space Alliance)						
600 Gemini Ave	Houston	TX	77058	**800-367-5690**	281-212-6200	273
USA 800 Inc						
9808 E 66th Terr	Kansas City	MO	64133	**800-821-7539**	816-358-1303	734
USA Baby						
793 Springer Dr	Lombard	IL	60148	**800-767-9464**	630-652-0600	322
USA Basketball						
5465 Mark Dabling Boulevard						
	Colorado Springs	CO	80918	**888-284-5383**	719-590-4800	47-22
USA Communications Inc						
920 E 56th St Ste B	Kearney	NE	68847	**877-234-0102**		387
USA Container Company Inc						
1776 S Second St	Piscataway	NJ	08854	**888-752-7722**	732-752-7722	200
USA Datanet Corp						
109 S Warren St Ste 602	Syracuse	NY	13202	**800-566-8655**		733
USA for UNHCR						
1775 K St NW Ste 580	Washington	DC	20006	**800-770-1100**	202-296-1115	47-5
USA Freedom Corps						
1201 New York Ave NW	Washington	DC	20005	**800-833-3722**	202-606-5000	340
USA Gymnastics						
201 S Capitol Ave Ste 300	Indianapolis	IN	46225	**800-345-4719**	317-237-5050	47-22
USA Hockey						
1775 Bob Johnson Dr	Colorado Springs	CO	80906	**800-566-3288**	719-576-8724	47-22
USA Judo Inc						
1 Olympic Plaza						
Ste 505	Colorado Springs	CO	80909	**800-775-8762**	719-866-4730	47-22
USA Mobility Inc						
6677 Richmond Hwy	Alexandria	VA	22306	**800-231-2556**	703-660-6677	733
USA Student Travel						
5080 Robert J Mathews Pkwy						
	El Dorado Hills	CA	95762	**800-448-4444**	916-939-6805	758
USA Swimming						
1 Olympic Plaza	Colorado Springs	CO	80909	**800-333-3333**	719-866-4578	47-22
USA Table Tennis						
1 Olympic Plaza	Colorado Springs	CO	80909	**800-775-8762**	719-866-4583	47-22
USA Technologies Inc						
100 Deerfield Ln Ste 140	Malvern	PA	19355	**800-633-0340**		253
USA Today						
7950 Jones Branch Dr	McLean	VA	22108	**800-872-0001***	703-854-3400	531-3
*Cust Svc						
USA Track & Field (USATF)						
132 E Washington St						
Ste 800	Indianapolis	IN	46204	**800-222-8733**	317-261-0500	47-22
USA Truck Inc						
3200 Industrial Pk Rd	Van Buren	AR	72956	**800-643-9691**	479-471-2500	778
NASDAQ: USAK						
USA Water Polo						
2124 Main St Ste 210	Huntington Beach	CA	92648	**888-712-2166**	714-500-5445	47-22
USA Water Ski						
1251 Holy Cow Rd	Polk City	FL	33868	**800-533-2972**	863-324-4341	47-22
USA Weightlifting (USAW)						
1 Olympic Plaza	Colorado Springs	CO	80909	**800-775-8762**	719-866-4508	47-22
USA Workers' Injury Network						
1250 S Capital of Texas Hwy						
Bldg 3 Ste 500	Austin	TX	78746	**800-872-0020***		391-4
*Cust Svc						
USA Wrestling						
6155 Lehman Dr	Colorado Springs	CO	80918	**888-431-3598**	719-598-8181	47-22
USAA (United Services Automobile Assn)						
10750 McDermott Fwy	San Antonio	TX	78288	**800-531-8722**		187
USAA (USAA Life Insurance Co)						
9800 Fredericksburg Rd	San Antonio	TX	78288	**800-531-8000**	210-531-8722	391-2
USAA FSB (USAAFSB)						
10750 McDermott Fwy	San Antonio	TX	78288	**800-531-8722**		69
USAA Investment Management						
9800 Fredericksburg Rd						
PO Box 659453	San Antonio	TX	78288	**800-531-8722**		401
USAA Life Insurance Co (USAA)						
9800 Fredericksburg Rd	San Antonio	TX	78288	**800-531-8000**	210-531-8722	391-2
USAA Property & Casualty Insurance Group						
9800 Fredericksburg Rd	San Antonio	TX	78288	**800-531-8722**	210-531-8722	391-4
USAA Real Estate Co						
9830 Colonnade Blvd Ste 600	San Antonio	TX	78230	**800-531-8182**		653
USAAFSB (USAA FSB)						
10750 McDermott Fwy	San Antonio	TX	78288	**800-531-8722**		69
USAC (Universal Service Administrative Co)						
2000 L St NW Ste 200	Washington	DC	20036	**888-641-8722**	202-776-0200	733
USAFA (US Air Force Academy)						
2304 Cadet Dr						
Ste 2300	Air Force Academy	CO	80840	**800-443-9266**	719-333-1110	497
USANA Health Sciences Inc						
3838 West PkwyBlvd	Salt Lake City	UT	84120	**888-950-9595**	801-954-7100	797
NYSE: USNA						
US-Analytics Solutions Group LLC						
600 E Las Colinas Blvd Ste 2222	Irving	TX	75039	**877-828-8727***	214-630-0081	182
*General						
Usasia Insurance Services						
319 Union Ave	Pomona	CA	91768	**800-372-4822**	909-618-0288	390
USATF (USA Track & Field)						
132 E Washington St						
Ste 800	Indianapolis	IN	46204	**800-222-8733**	317-261-0500	47-22
U-Save Auto Rental of America Inc						
1052 Highland Colony Pkwy						
Ste 204	Ridgeland	MS	39157	**800-438-2300***	601-713-4333	125
*General						
USAW (USA Weightlifting)						
1 Olympic Plaza	Colorado Springs	CO	80909	**800-775-8762**	719-866-4508	47-22
USB (United Soybean Board)						
16305 Swingley Ridge Rd						
Ste 150	Chesterfield	MO	63017	**800-989-8721**	636-530-1777	47-2
USBSF (US Bobsled & Skeleton Federation)						
196 Old Military Rd	Lake Placid	NY	12946	**888-431-3598**	518-523-1842	47-22
USCA (US Curling Assn)						
5525 Clem's Way	Stevens Point	WI	54482	**888-287-5377**	715-344-1199	47-22
USCC (US Cellular Corp)						
8410 W Bryn Mawr Ave Ste 700	Chicago	IL	60631	**888-944-9400**	773-399-8900	733
NYSE: USM						
USCCB (US Conference of Catholic Bishops)						
3211 Fourth St NE	Washington	DC	20017	**866-582-0943**	202-541-3000	47-20
USCF (US Chess Federation)						
PO Box 3967	Crossville	TN	38557	**800-903-8723**	931-787-1234	47-18
USDA (Department of Agriculture)						
1400 Independence Ave SW	Washington	DC	20250	**844-433-2774**	202-720-3631	340-1
USF (University of South Florida College of Medicine)						
12901 Bruce B Downs Blvd	Tampa	FL	33612	**877-338-2577**	813-974-2229	168-2
USFA (US Fencing Assn)						
1 Olympic Plaza	Colorado Springs	CO	80909	**888-431-3598**	719-866-4511	47-22
USFS (Forest Service)						
1400 Independence Ave SW	Washington	DC	20050	**800-832-1355**	202-205-8333	340-1
USFWS (US Fish & Wildlife Service)						
1849 C St NW	Washington	DC	20240	**800-344-9453**	202-208-4717	340-11
USG Corp						
550 W Adams St	Chicago	IL	60661	**800-874-4968**	312-436-4000	347
NYSE: USG						
USGA (US Golf Assn)						
77 Liberty Corner Rd	Far Hills	NJ	07931	**800-336-4446***	908-234-2300	47-22
*Orders						
USGS (US Geological Survey)						
12201 Sunrise Valley Dr	Reston	VA	20192	**888-275-8747**	703-648-6723	340-11
USHEALTH Group Inc						
300 Burnett St Ste 200	Fort Worth	TX	76102	**800-387-9027**		391-6
Ushio America Inc						
5440 Cerritos Ave	Cypress	CA	90630	**800-326-1960**	714-236-8600	437
uShip Inc						
205 Brazos St	Austin	TX	78701	**800-698-7447**		387
USIS (United States Information Systems Inc)						
35 W Jefferson Ave	Pearl River	NY	10965	**866-222-3778**	845-358-7755	785
USL Pharma						
301 S Cherokee St	Denver	CO	80223	**800-654-2299**	303-607-4500	583
USM Corp						
32 Stevens St	Haverhill	MA	01830	**800-361-2056**	978-374-0303	386
USM Inc						
1880 Markley St	Norristown	PA	19401	**800-355-4000**	610-278-9000	188
US-Mexico Chamber of Commerce California Pacific Chapter						
2450 Colorado Ave Ste 400E	Santa Monica	CA	90404	**800-997-9148**	310-586-7901	136
USMotivation						
7840 Roswell Rd Bldg 100 3rd Fl	Atlanta	GA	30350	**866-885-4702**		384
USNMFCU (US New Mexico Federal Credit Union)						
3939 Osuna Rd NE PO Box 129	Albuquerque	NM	87109	**888-342-8766**	505-342-8888	221
USNR						
1981 Schurman Way PO Box 310	Woodland	WA	98674	**800-289-8767**	360-225-8267	681
USNR Inc						
558 Robinson Rd PO Box 310	Woodland	WA	98674	**800-289-8767**	360-225-8267	819
USP (US Pharmacopeia)						
12601 Twinbrook Pkwy	Rockville	MD	20852	**800-227-8772**	301-881-0666	48-8
USPB (US Premium Beef LLC)						
12200 N Ambassador Dr						
PO Box 20103	Kansas City	MO	64163	**866-877-2525**	816-713-8800	297-26
USPS (US Postal Service)						
475 L'Enfant Plaza W SW	Washington	DC	20260	**800-275-8777***	202-268-2000	340-18
*Cust Svc						
USPTA (US Professional Tennis Assn)						
3535 Briarpark Dr Ste 1	Houston	TX	77042	**800-877-8248**	713-978-7782	47-22
USS Alabama Battleship Memorial Park						
2703 Battleship Pkwy PO Box 65	Mobile	AL	36602	**888-414-4448**	251-433-2703	49-3
USS Hornet Museum						
707 W Hornet Ave Pier 3	Alameda	CA	94501	**800-555-8355**	510-521-8448	519
USS Kidd Veterans Memorial & Museum						
305 S River Rd	Baton Rouge	LA	70802	**800-638-0594**	225-342-1942	49-3
USS Lexington Museum on the Bay						
2914 N Shoreline Blvd	Corpus Christi	TX	78402	**800-523-9539**	361-888-4873	519
USS Missouri Memorial Assn Inc						
63 Cowpens St	Honolulu	HI	96818	**877-644-4896**	808-455-1600	49-3
USSM (Ulbrich Stainless Steels & Special Metals Inc)						
57 Dodge Ave	North Haven	CT	06473	**800-243-1676**	203-239-4481	721
USS-POSCO Industries						
900 Loveridge Rd	Pittsburg	CA	94565	**800-877-7672**	925-439-6000	721
USTA (US Telecom Assn)						
607-14th St NW Ste 400	Washington	DC	20005	**877-869-6903**	202-326-7300	48-20
USTA (US Trotting Assn)						
750 Michigan Ave	Columbus	OH	43215	**877-800-8782**	614-224-2291	47-22
UsTrendy INC						
1842 Beacon St Ste 404	Brookline	MA	02445	**888-535-1187**		393
USWired Inc						
2107 N First St Ste 250	San Jose	CA	95131	**877-879-4733**	408-432-1144	182
Utah						
Aging & Adult Services Div						
195 N 1950 W Rm 325	Salt Lake City	UT	84116	**877-424-4640**	801-538-3910	339-45
Child & Family Services Div						
195 N 1950 W Rm 225	Salt Lake City	UT	84116	**855-323-3237**	801-538-4100	339-45
Community & Economic Development Dept						
60 E S Temple 3rd Fl	Salt Lake City	UT	84111	**855-204-9046**	801-538-8680	339-45
Environmental Quality Dept						
195 N 1950 W	Salt Lake City	UT	84116	**800-458-0145**	801-536-4400	339-45
Governor						
350 N State St Ste 200						
PO Box 142220	Salt Lake City	UT	84114	**800-705-2464**	801-538-1000	339-45
Labor Commission						
PO Box 146600	Salt Lake City	UT	84114	**800-530-5090**	801-530-6800	339-45
Lieutenant Governor						
PO Box 142325	Salt Lake City	UT	84114	**800-705-2464**		339-45
Motor Vehicle Div						
PO Box 30412	Salt Lake City	UT	84130	**800-368-8824**	801-297-7780	339-45

Name	Address	City	State	Zip	Toll-Free	Phone	Class
Occupational & Professional Licensing Div	PO Box 146741	Salt Lake City	UT	84111	**866-275-3675**	801-530-6628	339-45
Office of Tourism	300 N State St	Salt Lake City	UT	84114	**800-200-1160**	801-538-1900	339-45
Parks & Recreation Div	1594 W N Temple Ste 116	Salt Lake City	UT	84116	**800-322-3770**	801-538-7220	339-45
Rehabilitation Office	250 E 500 S	Salt Lake City	UT	84111	**800-473-7530**	801-538-7530	339-45
Workers' Compensation Fund	100 W Towne Ridge Pkwy	Sandy	UT	84070	**800-446-2667**	385-351-8000	339-45
Utah Assn of Realtors	230 W Towne Ridge Pkwy Ste 500	Sandy	UT	84070	**800-594-8933**	801-676-5200	654
Utah Business Magazine	90 S 400 W Ste 650	Salt Lake City	UT	84101	**866-294-1660**	801-568-0114	456-5
Utah Higher Education Assistance Authority	PO Box 145112	Salt Lake City	UT	84114	**877-336-7378**	801-321-7294	723
Utah Medical Products Inc	7043 S 300 W; *NASDAQ: UTMD*	Midvale	UT	84047	**866-754-9789**	801-566-1200	475
Utah Metal Works Inc (UMW)	805 Everett Ave	Salt Lake City	UT	84116	**877-221-0099**	801-503-9153	658
Utah Nurses Assn (UNA)	4505 S Wastch Blvd Ste 330B	Salt Lake City	UT	84124	**800-338-7657**	801-272-4510	532
Utah State Bar	645 S 200 E	Salt Lake City	UT	84111	**877-752-2611**	801-531-9077	71
Utah State Library	250 N 1950 W Ste A	Salt Lake City	UT	84116	**800-662-9150**	801-715-6777	434-5
Utah State University	1600 Old Main Hill	Logan	UT	84322	**800-488-8108**	435-797-1116	167
Utah System of Higher Education	60 South 400 West	Salt Lake City	UT	84101	**800-418-8757**	801-321-7100	784
Utah Transit Authority	3600 S 700 W PO Box 30810	Salt Lake City	UT	84130	**888-743-3882**	801-262-5626	467
Utah Valley Convention & Visitors Bureau	111 S University Ave	Provo	UT	84601	**800-222-8824**	801-851-2100	208
Utah Valley State College	800 W University Pkwy	Orem	UT	84058	**800-952-8220**	801-863-4636	161
Utak Laboratories Inc	25020 Ave Tibbitts	Valencia	CA	91355	**800-235-3442**	661-294-3935	233
UTC RETAIL Inc	100 Rawson Rd	Victor	NY	14564	**800-349-0546**		613
Ute Mountain Casino	3 Weeminuche Dr	Towaoc	CO	81334	**800-258-8007**	970-565-8800	132
UTEX Industries Inc	10810 Katy Fwy Ste 100	Houston	TX	77043	**800-359-9230**	713-467-1000	327
UTGI (United Trust Group Inc)	5250 S Sixth St; *OTC: UTGN*	Springfield	IL	62705	**800-323-0050**	217-241-6410	360-4
Utica Boilers Inc	PO Box 4729	Utica	NY	13504	**800-325-5479**	866-847-6656	357
Utica College	1600 Burrstone Rd; *Admissions	Utica	NY	13502	**800-782-8884***	315-792-3111	167
Utica Community Schools (UCS)	11303 Greendale Dr	Sterling Heights	MI	48312	**800-877-8339**	586-797-1000	683
Utica First Insurance Co	5981 Airport Rd	Oriskany	NY	13424	**800-456-4556**	315-736-8211	391-4
Utica National Insurance Group	180 Genesee St	New Hartford	NY	13413	**800-274-1914**	315-734-2000	391-2
Utica School of Commerce	201 Bleecker St	Utica	NY	13501	**800-321-4872**	315-733-2307	798
Utilant LLC	475 Ellicott St Ste 5	Buffalo	NY	14203	**888-884-5268**		179
Utilimaster Holding Co	603 Earthway Blvd	Bristol	IN	46507	**800-237-7806**		53
Utility Environment Report	2 Penn Plz 25th Fl	New York	NY	10121	**800-752-8878**		530-5
Utility Forecaster	7600A Leesburg Pk W Bldg Ste 300	Falls Church	VA	22043	**800-832-2330**	703-394-4931	530-9
Utility Service Company Inc	535 Courtney Hodges Blvd	Perry	GA	31069	**855-526-4413**	478-987-0303	194
Utility Services Inc	400 N Fourth St	Bismarck	ND	58501	**800-638-3278**	701-222-7900	190-10
Utility Trailer Mfg Co	17295 E Railroad St	City of Industry	CA	91748	**800-874-6807**	626-965-1541	777
Utility/Keystone Trailer Sales Inc	1976 Auction Rd	Manheim	PA	17545	**888-327-4236**	717-653-9444	56
Utne Reader Magazine	12 N 12th St Ste 400; *Cust Svc	Minneapolis	MN	55403	**800-736-8863***	612-338-5040	456-11
Utopia Systems Inc	1172 Old Forge Rd	New Castle	DE	19720	**877-804-7421**	302-777-0772	182
Utrecht Art Supplies	PO Box 1769	Galesburg	IL	61402	**888-336-3114**	609-409-8001	42
UTSA (Uniform & Textile Service Assn)	1300 N 17th St Ste 750	Arlington	VA	22209	**800-996-3426**	703-247-2600	48-4
UTStarcom Inc	1732 North First St Ste 220; *NASDAQ: UTSI*	San Jose	CA	95112	**877-547-6340**	408-453-4557	732
UTZ Quality Foods Co	900 High St	Hanover	PA	17331	**800-367-7629**	717-637-6644	297-35
UUHSC (University of Utah Hospital & Clinics)							
Blood & Marrow Transplant Program	50 N Medical Dr; *General	Salt Lake City	UT	84132	**800-824-2073***	801-581-2121	767
Uvex Safety Inc	900 Douglas Pk; *General	Smithfield	RI	02917	**800-682-0839***		575
UVMC (Upper Valley Medical Ctr)	3130 N County Rd 25-A	Troy	OH	45373	**866-608-3463**	937-440-4000	374-3
UVP Inc	2066 W 11th St; *Cust Svc	Upland	CA	91786	**800-452-6788***	909-946-3197	437
UW Medicine Eastside Hospital & Specialty	3100 Northup Way	Bellevue	WA	98004	**877-520-5000**		374-3

V

Name	Address	City	State	Zip	Toll-Free	Phone	Class
V & S Midwest Carriers Corp	2001 Hyland Ave PO Box 107	Kaukauna	WI	54130	**800-876-4330**	920-766-9696	778
V 2 It Services Inc	2340 E Trinity Mills Rd Ste 300	Carrollton	TX	75006	**877-400-0293**		198
VA (Department of Veterans Affairs)	810 Vermont Ave NW; *Cust Svc	Washington	DC	20420	**800-827-1000***	202-461-7600	340-17
VA Hudson Valley Health Care System							
Castle Point Campus	41 Castle Pt Rd	Wappingers Falls	NY	12590	**877-222-8387**	845-831-2000	374-8
Montrose Campus	2094 Albany Post Rd PO Box 100	Montrose	NY	10548	**800-269-8749**	914-737-4400	374-8
VA Medical Ctr	2400 Hospital Rd	Tuskegee	AL	36083	**800-214-8387**	334-727-0550	374-8
VA Puget Sound Health Care System - Seattle Div	1660 S Columbian Way	Seattle	WA	98108	**800-329-8387**	206-762-1010	767
Vacation Co	42 New Orleans Rd Ste 102	Hilton Head Island	SC	29928	**800-845-7018**	843-686-6100	376
Vacation Internationale	1417 116th Ave NE	Bellevue	WA	98004	**800-444-6633**	425-454-8429	751
Vacation.com Inc	1650 King St Ste 450	Alexandria	VA	22314	**800-843-0733**		770
Vacationer RV Resort	1581 East Main St	El Cajon	CA	92021	**877-626-4409**		378
Vacudyne Inc	375 E Joe Orr Rd	Chicago Heights	IL	60411	**800-459-9591**	708-757-5200	386
VAC-U-MAX	69 William St	Belleville	NJ	07109	**800-822-8629**	973-759-4600	209
Vail Cascade Resort & Spa	1300 Westhaven Dr	Vail	CO	81657	**800-420-2424**	970-476-7111	667
Vail Mountain Lodge & Spa, The	352 E Meadow Dr	Vail	CO	81657	**888-794-0410**	970-476-0700	705
Vail Resorts Management Co	390 Interlocken Crescent Ste 1000; *NYSE: MTN*	Broomfield	CO	80021	**800-842-8062**	303-404-1800	667
Vaisala Inc	10-D Gill St	Woburn	MA	01801	**888-824-7252**	781-933-4500	471
Val Surf Inc	4810 Whitsett Ave	Valley Village	CA	91607	**888-825-7873**	818-769-6977	709
Valassis Communications Inc	19975 Victor Pkwy; *NYSE: VCI*	Livonia	MI	48152	**800-437-0479**	734-591-3000	626
Valcom Consulting Group Inc	85 Albert St	Ottawa	ON	K1P6A4	**866-561-5580**	613-594-5200	263
Valcom Inc	5614 Hollins Rd	Roanoke	VA	24019	**800-825-2661**	540-563-2000	732
Valdese General Hospital (VGH)	720 Malcolm Blvd Ste 200	Valdese	NC	28690	**800-994-6610**	828-874-2251	374-3
Valdosta Daily Times	PO Box 968	Valdosta	GA	31603	**800-600-4838**	229-244-1880	531-2
Valdosta State University	1500 N Patterson St	Valdosta	GA	31698	**800-618-1878**	229-333-5800	167
Valence Technology Inc	12303 Technology Blvd Ste 950	Austin	TX	78727	**888-825-3623**	512-527-2900	73
Valentino's	2601 S 70th St	Lincoln	NE	68506	**888-289-8257**	402-434-9350	668
Valeo Pharma Inc	16667 Hymus Blvd Kirkland	Kirkland	QC	H9H4R9	**888-694-0865**	514-694-0150	233
Valerie Wilson Travel Inc	475 Pk Ave S	New York	NY	10016	**800-776-1116**	212-532-3400	769
Valeritas Inc	750 Rt 202 S Ste 600	Bridgewater	NJ	08807	**855-384-8848**	908-927-9920	474
Valero LP	PO Box 696000	San Antonio	TX	78269	**800-333-3377**	210-345-2233	596
Valet Parking Service	1335 S Flower St	Los Angeles	CA	90015	**800-794-7275**	213-342-3388	561
Val-Fab Inc	218 Jackson St	Neenah	WI	54956	**888-482-5322**	920-722-1009	479
Valiant Corp	6555 Hawthorne Dr	Windsor	ON	N8T3G6	**888-825-4268**	519-974-5200	538
Valiant Products Corp	2727 Fifth Ave W; *Cust Svc	Denver	CO	80204	**800-347-2727***	303-892-1234	442
Valiant Steel & Equipment Inc	6455 Old Peachtree Rd	Norcross	GA	30071	**800-939-9905**	770-417-1235	491
VALIC (Variable Annuity Life Insurance Co)	2929 Allen Pkwy	Houston	TX	77019	**800-448-2542**		391-2
Valid8 .com Inc	500 W Cummings Park Ste 6550	Woburn	MA	01801	**855-482-5438**		179
Validar Inc	800 Maynard Ave S Ste 401	Seattle	WA	98134	**888-784-2929**	206-264-9151	180-1
Valin Corp	555 E California Ave	Sunnyvale	CA	94086	**800-774-5630**	408-730-9850	358
Valle Verde	900 Calle de los Amigos	Santa Barbara	CA	93105	**800-750-5089**	805-883-4000	670
Vallejo Chamber of Commerce	427 York St	Vallejo	CA	94590	**877-397-7936**	707-644-5551	138
Vallejo Convention & Visitors Bureau	289 Mare Island Way; *General	Vallejo	CA	94590	**866-921-9277***	707-642-3653	208
Vallejo Times Herald	440 Curtola Pkwy	Vallejo	CA	94590	**800-600-1141**	707-644-1141	531-2
Valley Baptist Medical Ctr Brownsville	1040 W Jefferson St	Brownsville	TX	78520	**855-720-7448**	956-698-5400	374-3
Valley Blox Inc	210 Stone Spring Rd	Harrisonburg	VA	22801	**800-648-6725**	540-434-6725	185
Valley Chevrolet Inc	601 Kidder St	Wilkes-Barre	PA	18702	**877-207-9214**	570-821-2772	515

Name / Address	City	State	ZIP	Toll-Free	Phone	Class
Valley City State University 101 College St SW	Valley City	ND	58072	**800-532-8641**	701-845-7990	167
Valley Craft 2001 S Hwy 61	Lake City	MN	55041	**800-328-1480**	651-345-3386	469
Valley Electric Assn Inc 800 E Hwy 372 PO Box 237	Pahrump	NV	89048	**800-742-3330**	775-727-5312	247
Valley Electric Supply Corp 1361 N State Rd PO Box 724	Vincennes	IN	47591	**800-825-7877**	812-882-7860	248
Valley First Credit Union PO Box 1411	Modesto	CA	95353	**877-549-4567**	209-549-8500	221
Valley Forge Christian College 1401 Charlestown Rd	Phoenixville	PA	19460	**800-432-8322**	610-935-0450	167
Valley Forge Convention & Visitors Bureau 1000 First Ave Ste 101 *General	King of Prussia	PA	19406	**888-847-4883***	610-834-1550	208
Valley Forge Medical Ctr & Hospital 1033 W Germantown Pk	Norristown	PA	19403	**888-539-8500**	610-539-8500	724
Valley Forge Military Academy & College 1001 Eagle Rd	Wayne	PA	19087	**800-234-8362**	610-989-1300	161
Valley Freightliner Inc 277 Stewart Rd SW	Pacific	WA	98047	**800-523-8014**		56
Valley Fresh Inc 3600 E Linwood Ave	Turlock	CA	95380	**800-523-4635**	209-669-5600	618
Valley Health System 223 N Van Dien Ave	Ridgewood	NJ	07450	**800-825-5391**	201-447-8000	374-3
Valley Hospice Inc 380 Summit Ave	Steubenville	OH	43952	**877-467-7423**	740-284-4440	371
Valley Internet Inc 102 Maple St East	Fayetteville	TN	37334	**888-433-1924**	931-433-1921	40
Valley Joist 3019 Gault Ave N	Fort Payne	AL	35967	**800-263-0324**	256-845-2330	695
Valley Litho Supply Inc 1047 Haugen Ave	Rice Lake	WI	54868	**800-826-6781**		358
Valley Medical Ctr 400 S 43rd St	Renton	WA	98055	**855-923-4633**	425-228-3450	374-3
Valley Morning Star PO Box 511	Harlingen	TX	78551	**877-786-7612**	956-430-6200	531-2
Valley National Bancorp 1455 Valley Rd *NYSE: VLY*	Wayne	NJ	07470	**800-522-4100**	973-305-8800	360-2
Valley National Bank 615 Main Ave	Passaic	NJ	07055	**800-522-4100**	973-777-6768	69
Valley News 24 Interchange Dr	West Lebanon	NH	03784	**800-874-2226**	603-298-8711	531-2
Valley News Dispatch 210 Fourth Ave	Tarentum	PA	15084	**877-698-2553**	800-909-8742	531-2
Valley of the Sun United Way 1515 E Osborn Rd	Phoenix	AZ	85014	**877-322-8228**	602-631-4800	47-21
Valley Offset Printing Inc 160 S Sheridan Ave	Valley Center	KS	67147	**888-895-7913**	316-755-0061	626
Valley Power Systems Inc 425 S Hacienda Blvd	City of Industry	CA	91745	**800-924-4265**	626-333-1243	768
Valley Regional Medical Ctr 100-A E Alton Gloor Blvd	Brownsville	TX	78526	**877-813-6455**	956-350-7000	374-3
Valley River Inn 1000 Vly River Way	Eugene	OR	97401	**800-543-8266**	541-743-1000	379
Valley Rural Electric Co-op Inc 10700 Fairgrounds Rd PO Box 477	Huntingdon	PA	16652	**800-432-0680**	814-643-2650	247
Valley Supply & Equipment Company Inc 1109 Middle River Rd	Baltimore	MD	21220	**800-633-5077**		23
Valley Telephone Co-op Inc 752 E Maley St	Willcox	AZ	85643	**800-421-5711**	520-384-2231	733
Valley Town Crier 1811 N 23rd St	McAllen	TX	78501	**800-621-3362**	956-682-2423	531-4
Valley View Casino Ctr 3500 Sports Arena Blvd	San Diego	CA	92110	**800-745-3000**	619-224-4171	718
Valley Yellow Pages 1850 N Gateway Blvd	Fresno	CA	93727	**800-350-8887**	559-251-8888	634-6
Valley-Dynamo 7224 Burns Rd	Richland Hills	TX	76118	**800-826-7856**	972-595-5365	323
Valmont Industries Inc 1 Valmont Plz *NYSE: VMI*	Omaha	NE	68154	**800-825-6668**	402-963-1000	275
Valor Brands LLC 960 N Point Pkwy Ste 100	Alpharetta	GA	30005	**866-949-9098**	770-346-9250	156-1
Valor Oil 1200 Alsop Ln	Owensboro	KY	42303	**800-544-5823**	844-468-2567	578
Valpak Direct Marketing Systems Inc 8605 Largo Lakes Dr	Largo	FL	33773	**800-237-6266**		5
Valparaiso University 1700 Chapel Dr	Valparaiso	IN	46383	**888-468-2576**	219-464-5011	167
Valparaiso University School of Law 651 College Ave	Valparaiso	IN	46383	**888-825-7652**	219-465-7829	168-1
Valspar Refinish Inc 210 Crosby St *Cust Svc	Picayune	MS	39466	**800-844-3691***	800-845-2500	549
Valtra Inc 7141 Paramount Blvd	Pico Rivera	CA	90660	**800-989-5244**	562-949-8625	385
Valuation Management Group LLC 1640 Powers Ferry Rd SE Bldg 15 Ste 100	Marietta	GA	30067	**866-799-7488**	678-483-4420	650
Value City Furniture 4300 E Fifth Ave	Columbus	OH	43219	**888-751-8552**	888-672-2411	322
Value Creation Inc 1100 635 - Eighth Ave SW	Calgary	AB	T2P3M3	**855-908-8800**	403-539-4500	535
Value Drug Mart Assoc Ltd 16504 - 121A Ave	Edmonton	AB	T5V1J9	**888-554-8258**	780-453-1701	240
Value Line Asset Management 220 E 42nd St	New York	NY	10017	**800-634-3583**	212-907-1500	401
ValueClick Inc 30699 Russell Ranch Rd Ste 250 *NASDAQ: VCLK*	Westlake Village	CA	91362	**877-361-3316**	818-575-4500	7
ValueClick Media 530 E Montecito St	Santa Barbara	CA	93103	**877-361-3316**	805-879-1600	7
ValueOptions Inc 12369 Sunrise Vly Dr Ste C	Reston	VA	20191	**877-334-0077**	703-390-6800	461

Name / Address	City	State	ZIP	Toll-Free	Phone	Class
Valve Manufacturers Assn of America (VMA) 1050 17th St NW Ste 280	Washington	DC	20036	**800-468-3571**	202-331-8105	48-13
Valvoline Co 3499 Blazer Pkwy PO Box 14000	Lexington	KY	40512	**800-832-6825**	859-357-7777	540
Vam USA LLC 19210 Hardy Rd	Houston	TX	77041	**888-863-5204**	713-479-3200	227
Vamac Inc 4201 Jacque St	Richmond	VA	23230	**800-768-2622**	804-353-7811	611
Van Air Systems Inc 2950 Mechanic St	Lake City	PA	16423	**800-840-9906**	814-774-2631	386
Van Ausdall & Farrar Inc 6430 E 75th St	Indianapolis	IN	46250	**800-467-7474**	317-634-2913	533
Van Bergen & Greener Inc 1818 Madison St	Maywood	IL	60153	**800-621-3889**	708-343-4700	249
Van Bortel Aircraft Inc 4912 S Collins	Arlington	TX	76018	**800-759-4295**	817-468-7788	768
Van Bortel Subaru 6327 SR- 96	Victor	NY	14564	**888-902-7961**	585-924-5230	56
Van Boxtel Rv & Auto LLC 1956 Bond St	Green Bay	WI	54303	**888-831-5267**	920-497-3072	56
Van Buren State Park 12259 Township Rd 218	Van Buren	OH	45889	**866-644-6727**	419-832-7662	564
Van Cleef & Arpels Inc 744 Fifth Ave	New York	NY	10019	**877-826-2533**	212-896-9284	410
Van Diest Supply Co 1434 220th St PO Box 610	Webster City	IA	50595	**800-779-2424**	515-832-2366	282
Van Doren Sales Inc 10 NE Cascade Ave	East Wenatchee	WA	98802	**866-886-1837**	509-886-1837	299
Van Dyk Group Inc, The 12800 Long Beach Blvd	Beach Haven	NJ	08008	**800-222-0131**	609-492-1511	390
Van Dyke Supply Co 39771 Sd Hwy 34	Woonsocket	SD	57385	**800-279-7985**	704-279-7985	458
Van Eerden Foodservice Co 650 Ionia Ave SW	Grand Rapids	MI	49503	**800-833-7374**	616-475-0900	778
Van Galder Bus Co 715 S Pearl St	Janesville	WI	53548	**800-747-0994**	608-752-5407	106
Van Horn Inc PO Box 380	Cerro Gordo	IL	61818	**800-252-1615**	217-677-2131	278
Van Meter Industrial Inc 850 32nd Ave SW	Cedar Rapids	IA	52404	**800-247-1410**	319-366-5301	248
Van Roy Coffee Co, The 4569 Spring Rd	Cleveland	OH	44131	**877-826-7669**	216-749-7069	297-7
Van Ru Credit Corp 1350 E Touhy Ave Ste 300E	Des Plaines	IL	60018	**800-468-2678**		159
Van Well Nursery 2821 Grant Rd	East Wenatchee	WA	98802	**800-572-1553**	509-886-8189	295
Van Wezel Performing Arts Ctr 777 N Tamiami Trl	Sarasota	FL	34236	**800-826-9303**	941-953-3368	571
Van Wyk Freight Lines Inc PO Box 70	Grinnell	IA	50112	**800-362-2595**	641-236-7551	778
Van Zandt Emrich & Cary Inc 12401 Plantside Dr	Louisville	KY	40299	**800-928-7355**	502-456-2001	390
Van Zyverden Inc 8079 Van Zyverden Rd	Meridian	MS	39305	**800-332-2852**	601-679-8274	295
Vanadium Group Corp 134 Three Degree Rd	Pittsburgh	PA	15237	**800-685-0354**	412-367-6060	263
Vance Air Force Base 246 Brown Pkwy	Vance AFB	OK	73705	**866-966-1020**	580-213-7476	496-1
Vance Birthplace State Historic Site 911 Reems Creek Rd	Weaverville	NC	28787	**800-767-1560**	828-645-6706	49-2
Vance Bros Inc 5201 Brighton PO Box 300107	Kansas City	MO	64130	**800-821-8549**	816-923-4325	45
Vance-Granville Community College *South* PO Box 39	Creedmoor	NC	27522	**877-823-2378**	919-528-4737	161
Warren County PO Box 207	Warrenton	NC	27536	**877-823-2378**	252-257-1900	161
Vancouver Aquarium Marine Science Ctr 845 Avison Way	Vancouver	BC	V6G3E2	**800-931-1186**	604-659-3474	39
Vancouver Canucks 800 Griffiths Way	Vancouver	BC	V6B6G1	**877-788-3937**	604-899-7400	714
Vancouver Convention & Exposition Centre (VCEC) 1055 Canada Pl	Vancouver	BC	V6C0C3	**866-785-8232**	604-689-8232	207
Vancouver Door Company Inc 203 Fifth St NW	Puyallup	WA	98371	**800-999-3667**	253-845-9581	238
Vancouver School of Theology 6040 Iona Dr	Vancouver	BC	V6T2E8	**866-822-9031**	604-822-9031	168-3
Vancouver Sun 200 Granville St Ste 1	Vancouver	BC	V6C3N3	**866-372-3707**	604-605-2000	531-1
Vander Haag's Inc 3809 Fourth Ave W	Spencer	IA	51301	**888-940-5030**	712-262-7000	60
Vanderbilt Beach Resort 9225 Gulf Shore Dr N	Naples	FL	34108	**800-243-9076**	239-597-3144	667
Vanderbilt Grace 41 Mary St	Newport	RI	02840	**888-826-4255**	401-846-6200	379
Vanderbilt Kennedy Ctr for Research on Human Development 21st Ave S	Nashville	TN	37203	**800-772-1213**	615-322-8240	666
Vanderbilt Minerals Corp 30 Winfield St	Norwalk	CT	06855	**800-243-6064**	203-853-1400	502-3
Vanderbilt Mortgage & Finance Inc 500 Alcoa Trl	Maryville	TN	37804	**800-970-7250**		508
Vanderbilt University 2201 W End Ave	Nashville	TN	37240	**800-288-0432**	615-322-7311	167
Vanderbilt University Medical Ctr 1215 21st Ave S	Nashville	TN	37232	**877-936-8422**	615-322-5000	374-3
Vanderbilt University Press 2014 Broadway Ste 320	Nashville	TN	37203	**800-627-7377**	615-322-3585	634-4
Vanderbilt University School of Medicine 215 Light Hall	Nashville	TN	37232	**866-263-8263**	615-322-2145	168-2
VanDyke Software Inc 4848 Tramway Ridge Dr NE Ste 101	Albuquerque	NM	87111	**800-952-5210**	505-332-5700	180-12
Vango Graphics Inc 1371 S Inca St	Denver	CO	80223	**877-722-6168**	303-722-6109	344
Vangold Resources Ltd 7681 Prince Edward St	Vancouver	BC	V5X3R4	**866-684-1974**	604-684-1974	535
Vanguard Brokerage Services PO Box 1110	Valley Forge	PA	19482	**800-992-8327**	610-669-1000	688

Name / Address	City	State	Zip	Toll-Free	Phone	Class
Vanguard East 1172 Azalea Garden Rd	Norfolk	VA	23502	**800-221-1264**		9
Vanguard Group 455 Devon Pk Dr	Wayne	PA	19087	**800-662-7447**	610-669-1000	401
Vanguard Integrity Professionals Inc 6625 S Eastern Ave Ste 100	Las Vegas	NV	89119	**877-794-0014**	702-794-0014	182
Vanguard Products Group Inc 720 Brooker Creek Blvd Ste 223	Oldsmar	FL	34677	**877-477-4874**	813-855-9639	691
Vanguard Trucks Centers 700 Ruskin Dr	Forest Park	GA	30297	**866-216-7925**		53
Vanguard University of Southern California 55 Fair Dr *Admissions	Costa Mesa	CA	92626	**800-722-6279***	714-556-3610	167
Vanilla Forums Inc 414 McGill St, Ste 800	Montreal	QC	H2Y1S1	**866-845-0815**		387
Vanir Construction Management Inc 4540 Duckhorn Dr Ste 300	Sacramento	CA	95834	**888-912-1201**	916-575-8887	462
Vanity Fair Magazine 4 Times Sq	New York	NY	10036	**800-365-0635**		456-11
Vanity Shop of Grand Forks Inc 2410 Great Northern Dr	Fargo	ND	58102	**866-247-7920**	701-237-3330	156-6
Van-Kam Freightways Ltd 10155 Grace Rd	Surrey	BC	V3V3V7	**800-663-2161**	604-582-7451	315
Vans Inc 15700 Shoemaker Ave	Santa Fe Springs	CA	90670	**855-909-8267**		302
Vantage Credit Union (VCU) PO Box 4433	Bridgeton	MO	63044	**800-522-6009**	314-298-0055	221
Vantage Health Plan Inc 130 Desiard St Ste 300	Monroe	LA	71201	**888-823-1910**	318-361-0900	353
Vantage Mobility International (VMI) 5202 S 28th Pl	Phoenix	AZ	85040	**800-348-8267**	602-243-2700	61-7
Vantage Sourcing LLC 328 Ross Clark Cir	Dothan	AL	36303	**866-580-4562**		318
Vantage Trailers Inc 29335 Hwy Blvd	Katy	TX	77494	**800-826-8245**	281-391-2664	777
Vanteon Corp 250 Cross Keys Office Pk Bldg 250	Fairport	NY	14450	**888-506-5677**	585-419-9555	263
VanTran Industries Inc 7711 Imperial Dr	Waco	TX	76712	**800-433-3346**	254-772-9740	765
Vapor Bus International 1010 Johnson Dr	Buffalo Grove	IL	60089	**866-375-4126**	847-777-6400	648
Varel International 1625 W Crosby Dr Ste 124	Carrollton	TX	75006	**800-827-3526**	972-242-1160	192
Varflex Corp 512 W Ct St	Rome	NY	13440	**800-648-4014**	315-336-4400	814
Variable Annuity Life Insurance Co (VALIC) 2929 Allen Pkwy	Houston	TX	77019	**800-448-2542**		391-2
Varian Medical Systems Inc 3100 Hansen Way *NYSE: VAR*	Palo Alto	CA	94304	**800-544-4636**	650-493-4000	382
Varian Semiconductor Equipment Assoc Inc 35 Dory Rd	Gloucester	MA	01930	**800-344-1111**	978-282-2000	693
Variant Microsystems 4128 Business Ctr Dr	Fremont	CA	94538	**800-827-4268**	510-440-2870	534
Variety Distributors Inc 609 Seventh St	Harlan	IA	51537	**800-274-1095**	712-755-2184	329
Variform Inc 5020 Weston Pkwy Ste 400	Cary	NC	27513	**800-800-2244**	888-975-9436	193-4
Varouh Oil Inc 970 Griswold Rd	Elyria	OH	44035	**866-482-7684**	440-324-5025	578
Varscona Hotel 8208 106th St	Edmonton	AB	T6E6R9	**866-465-8150**	780-434-6111	379
Vartek Services Inc 1785 S Metro Pkwy	Dayton	OH	45459	**800-954-2524**	937-438-3550	176
Varvid Inc 705 Sunset Pond Lane Ste 2	Bellingham	WA	98226	**855-827-8434**	360-738-7168	5
Vasamed Inc 7615 Golden Triangle Dr Ste A	Eden Prairie	MN	55344	**800-695-2737**		475
Vascular Solutions Inc 6464 Sycamore Ct *NASDAQ: VASC*	Minneapolis	MN	55369	**877-979-4300**	763-656-4300	475
Vasomedical Inc 180 Linden Ave *OTC: VASO*	Westbury	NY	11590	**800-455-3327**	516-997-4600	252
Vassar Bros Medical Ctr 45 Reade Pl	Poughkeepsie	NY	12601	**877-729-2444**	845-454-8500	374-3
Vassar College 124 Raymond Ave	Poughkeepsie	NY	12604	**800-827-7270**	845-437-7000	167
Vatterott College Berkeley 8580 Evans Ave	Berkeley	MO	63134	**888-202-2636**	314-264-1000	798
Vatterott College Joplin 809 Illinois Ave	Joplin	MO	64801	**866-200-1898**	417-781-5633	798
Vatterott College South County 12900 Maurer Industrial Dr	Saint Louis	MO	63127	**866-312-8276**	314-843-4200	798
Vatterott College Springfield 3850 S Campbell	Springfield	MO	65807	**844-244-3304**	417-831-8116	798
Vaughan & Bushnell Manufacturing Co 11414 Maple Ave	Hebron	IL	60034	**800-435-6000**	815-648-2446	756
Vaughan Chamber of Commerce 25 Edilcan Dr Ste 2	Vaughan	ON	L4K3S4	**888-943-8937**	905-761-1366	137
Vaughan Company Inc 364 Monte-Elma Rd	Montesano	WA	98563	**888-249-2467**	360-249-4042	638
Vaughan Nelson Investment Management LP 600 Travis St Ste 6300	Houston	TX	77002	**888-888-8676**	713-224-2545	527
Vaughan Regional Medical Ctr 1015 Medical Ctr Pkwy	Selma	AL	36701	**800-994-6610**	334-418-4100	374-3
Vaughn College of Aeronautics & Technology 86-01 23rd Ave	East Elmhurst	NY	11369	**866-682-8446**	718-429-6600	167
Vaughn Coltrane Pharr & Associates Inc 2060 E Exchange Pl	Tucker	GA	30084	**877-230-5315**	678-567-4513	258
Vaughn Manufacturing Corp 26 Old Elm St PO Box 5431	Salisbury	MA	01952	**800-282-8446**	978-462-6683	35
VAWC (Virginia American Water Co) 2223 Duke St	Alexandria	VA	22314	**800-452-6863**	703-706-3879	785
Vawter Financial Ltd 1161 Bethel Rd Ste 304	Columbus	OH	43220	**800-955-1575**	614-451-1002	196

Name / Address	City	State	Zip	Toll-Free	Phone	Class
VBA (Vermont Bar Assn) 35-37 Ct St PO Box 100	Montpelier	VT	05601	**800-639-7036**	802-223-2020	71
VBCVB (Virginia Beach Convention & Visitor Bureau) 2101 Parks Ave Ste 500	Virginia Beach	VA	23451	**800-700-7702**	757-385-4700	208
Vbrick Systems Inc 12 Beaumont Rd	Wallingford	CT	06492	**866-827-4251**	203-265-0044	732
VBT Bicycling & Walking Vacations 614 Monkton Rd	Bristol	VT	05443	**800-245-3868**	802-453-4811	758
VCEC (Vancouver Convention & Exposition Centre) 1055 Canada Pl	Vancouver	BC	V6C0C3	**866-785-8232**	604-689-8232	207
VCF Films Inc 1100 Sutton Ave	Howell	MI	48843	**888-905-7680**		599
VCG LLC 1805 Old Alabama Rd	Roswell	GA	30076	**800-318-4983**	770-246-2300	180-12
VCI Emergency Vehicle 43 jefferson ave	Berlin	NJ	08009	**800-394-2162**	856-768-2162	401
VCOMP Solutions 1919 S Highland Ave Ste 200D	Lombard	IL	60148	**888-978-2667**		198
VCU (Vantage Credit Union) PO Box 4433	Bridgeton	MO	63044	**800-522-6009**	314-298-0055	221
VDA (Virginia Dental Assn) 3460 Mayland Ct Ste 110	Richmond	VA	23233	**877-726-0850**	804-288-5750	229
Vdara Condo Hotel LLC 3950 Las Vegas Blvd	Las Vegas	NV	89119	**866-718-2489**		377
VDx Veterinary Diagnostics Inc 2019 Anderson Rd Ste C	Davis	CA	95616	**877-753-4285**	530-753-4285	792
Vecellio & Grogan Inc 2251 Robert C Byrd Dr	Beckley	WV	25802	**800-255-6575**	304-252-6575	190-4
Vectech Pharmaceutical Consultants Inc 12501 E Grand River Ave	Brighton	MI	48116	**800-966-8832**	248-478-5820	263
Vector Aerospace Helicopter Services Inc 22378 Billie Blackmon Rd Ste 2100	Andalusia	AL	36421	**888-729-2276**	604-276-7600	21
Vector Marketing Co 322 Houghton Ave	Olean	NY	14760	**800-828-0448**		366
Vector Planning & Services Inc 591 Camino De La Reina Ste 300	San Diego	CA	92108	**888-522-5491**	619-297-5656	179
Vector Security Inc 2000 Ericsson Dr	Warrendale	PA	15086	**800-832-8575**		690
Vectorply Corp 3500 Lakewood Dr	Phenix City	AL	36867	**800-577-4521**	334-291-7704	742-1
Vectra Bank Colorado NA 2000 S Colorado Blvd Ste 2-1200	Denver	CO	80222	**800-232-8948**	720-947-7700	69
Vectra Fitness Inc 7901 S 190th St	Kent	WA	98032	**800-283-2872**	425-291-9550	269
Vectren Corp 211 NW Riverside Dr PO Box 209 *NYSE: VVC*	Evansville	IN	47702	**800-227-1376**	812-491-4000	360-5
Vectus Inc 18685 Main St 101 PMB 360	Huntington Beach	CA	92648	**866-483-2887**		387
Vedder Transportation Group, The 400 Riverside Rd	Abbotsford	BC	V2S4P4	**866-857-1375**		315
Vee Bar Guest Ranch 38 Vee Bar Ranch Rd	Laramie	WY	82070	**800-483-3227**	307-745-7036	241
Vee Neal Aviation Inc 148 Aviation Ln Ste 109	Latrobe	PA	15650	**800-278-2710**	724-539-4533	62
Veeco Instruments Inc 1 Terminal Dr *NASDAQ: VECO*	Plainview	NY	11803	**888-724-9511**	516-677-0200	693
Veeder-Root 125 Powder Forest Dr	Simsbury	CT	06070	**888-262-7539**	860-651-2700	203
Veenstra & Kimm Inc 3000 Westown Pkwy	West Des Moines	IA	50266	**800-241-8000**	515-225-8000	263
Veetronix Inc 1311 W Pacific Ave *General	Lexington	NE	68850	**800-445-0007***	308-324-6661	813
Vegetable Juices Inc 7400 S Narragansett Ave *General	Chicago	IL	60638	**888-776-9752***	708-924-9500	297-20
Vegetarian Times 300 N Continental Blvd Ste 650	El Segundo	CA	90245	**800-573-1900**	310-356-4100	456-13
Vehicle Safety Mfg LLC 408 Central Ave *General	Newark	NJ	07107	**800-832-7233***	973-643-3000	438
VehSmart Inc 12180 Ridgecrest Rd Ste 412	Victorville	CA	92395	**855-834-7627**		645
Veka Inc 100 Veka Dr	Fombell	PA	16123	**800-654-5589**	724-452-1000	237
Velaro Inc 8174 Lark Brown Rd Ste 201	Elkridge	MD	21075	**800-983-5276**		807
Velcro USA Inc 406 Brown Ave	Manchester	NH	03103	**800-225-0180**	603-669-4880	593
Veldkamp's Flowers 9501 W Colfax Ave	Lakewood	CO	80215	**800-247-3730**	303-232-2673	294
Vellano Bros Inc 7 Hemlock St	Latham	NY	12110	**800-342-9855**	518-785-5537	385
Vellumoid Inc 54 Rockdale St	Worcester	MA	01606	**800-609-5558**	508-853-2500	327
Velsicol Chemical Corp 10400 W Higgins Rd Ste 700 *Cust Svc	Rosemont	IL	60018	**877-847-8351***	847-813-7888	143
VELUX America Inc 450 Old BrickyaRd Rd	Greenwood	SC	29648	**866-358-3589**	864-941-4700	490
Velvac Inc 2405 S Calhoun Rd	New Berlin	WI	53151	**800-783-8871**	262-786-0700	59
Velvet Cloak Inn, The 1505 Hillsborough St	Raleigh	NC	27605	**888-828-0335**	919-828-0333	379
Vendant Inc 4845 Pearl E Cir Ste 101	Bouler	CO	80301	**800-714-4900**	978-462-0737	180-12
Vendini Inc 660 Market St	San Francisco	CA	94104	**800-901-7173**		189
Vendome Group LLC 216 E 45th St 6th Fl	New York	NY	10017	**800-519-3692**		634-9
Vendors Exchange International Inc 8700 Brookpark Rd	Cleveland	OH	44129	**800-321-2311**	216-432-1800	462

Name / Address	City	State	ZIP	Toll-Free	Phone	Class
Venetian Resort Hotel & Casino 3355 Las Vegas Blvd S	Las Vegas	NV	89109	**866-659-9643**	702-414-1000	667
Vengroff Williams & Assoc Inc (VWA) 2099 S State College Bvld	Anaheim	CA	92806	**800-238-9655**	866-737-4344	159
Venkel Ltd 5900 Shepherd Mtn Cove	Austin	TX	78730	**800-950-8365**	512-794-0081	248
Venoco Inc 370 17th St Ste 3900 *NYSE: VQ*	Denver	CO	80202	**877-777-4778**	303-626-8300	151
Vensai Technologies 2450 Atlanta Hwy Ste 1002	Cumming	GA	30040	**866-849-4057**	770-888-4804	198
VENSURE Employer Services Inc 4140 E Baseline Rd Ste 201	Mesa	AZ	85206	**800-409-8958**		360-3
Ventamatic Ltd 100 Washington Rd	Mineral Wells	TX	76067	**800-433-1626**		15
Ventana Inn 48123 Hwy 1	Big Sur	CA	93920	**800-628-6500**	831-667-2331	667
Ventana Medical Systems Inc 1910 Innovation Pk Dr	Tucson	AZ	85755	**800-227-2155**	520-887-2155	475
Ventas Inc 111 S Wacker Dr Ste 4800	Chicago	IL	60606	**877-483-6827**	312-660-3800	653
Ventura County Medical Center 3291 Loma Vista Rd	Ventura	CA	93003	**800-369-7437**	805-652-6000	374-3
Ventura County Star 550 Camarillo Ctr Dr	Camarillo	CA	93010	**800-221-7827**	805-437-0000	531-2
Ventura Foods LLC 40 Pt Dr	Brea	CA	92821	**800-421-6257**	714-257-3700	297-30
Ventura Visitors & Convention Bureau 101 S California St	Ventura	CA	93001	**800-333-2989**	805-648-2075	208
Ventura Youth Correctional Facility 3100 Wright Rd	Camarillo	CA	93010	**866-232-5627**	805-485-7951	412
Venture Lighting International Inc 32000 Aurora Rd	Solon	OH	44139	**800-451-2606**	440-248-3510	437
VentureOut 575 Pierce St Ste 604	San Francisco	CA	94117	**888-431-6789**	415-626-5678	758
Venuelabs 505 Fifth Ave S Ste 300	Seattle	WA	98104	**866-333-7328**	425-633-1510	393
Venus Swimwear 11711 Marco Beach Dr	Jacksonville	FL	32224	**800-366-7946**	904-645-6000	154-16
Vera Bradley Designs 2208 Production Rd	Fort Wayne	IN	46808	**800-975-8372**	260-482-4673	349
Verant Identification Systems Inc 2496 Ridge Rd W Ste 203	Rochester	NY	14626	**866-257-4351**	585-214-2451	691
Verbatim Americas LLC 1200 W WT Harris Blvd	Charlotte	NC	28262	**800-538-8589**	704-547-6500	656
Verdigris Valley Electric Co-op 8901 E 146th St N	Collinsville	OK	74021	**800-870-5948**	918-371-2584	247
Verdin Co, The 444 Reading Rd	Cincinnati	OH	45202	**800-543-0488**		152
Verecloud Inc 555 Eldorado Blvd Ste 200	Broomfield	CO	80021	**877-300-2158**		179
Verecom Technologies Inc 61 Broadway	New York	NY	10006	**888-562-2468**		363
Verendrye Electric Co-op Inc 615 Hwy 52	Velva	ND	58790	**800-472-2141**	701-338-2855	247
Verhalen Inc 500 Pilgrim Way	Green Bay	WI	54304	**800-895-0071**	920-431-8900	193-3
Verichem Laboratories Inc 90 Narragansett Ave	Providence	RI	02907	**800-552-5859**	401-461-0180	740
Verico Capital Mortgages Inc 106-18 Deakin St	Ottawa	ON	K2E8B7	**877-459-4414**	613-228-3888	508
Vericon Resources Inc 3550 Engineering Dr Ste 225	Norcross	GA	30092	**800-795-3784**	770-457-9922	400
Veridex LLC 700 US Hwy Rt 202 S	Raritan	NJ	08869	**877-837-4339**		475
Verified Audit Circulation Inc 900 Larkspur Landing Cir	Larkspur	CA	94939	**800-775-3332**	415-461-6006	731
Verified Credentials Inc 20890 Kenbridge Ct	Lakeville	MN	55044	**800-473-4934**	952-985-7200	632
VeriFone Inc 2099 Gateway Pl Ste 600 *NYSE: PAY*	San Jose	CA	95110	**800-837-4366**	408-232-7800	613
VeriFone Systems Inc 88 W Plumeria Dr Ste 600 *NYSE: PAY*	San Jose	CA	95134	**800-837-4366**	408-232-7800	613
Veriforce LLC 19221 I-45 S Ste 200	Shenandoah	TX	77385	**800-426-1604**		763
Verigent LLC 149 Plantation Ridge Dr Ste 100	Mooresville	NC	28117	**877-637-6422**	704-658-3271	609
Verint Video Solutions 330 South Service Rd	Melville	NY	11747	**800-483-7468**		690
Verio Inc 8300 E Maplewood Ave Ste 400 *Sales	Greenwood Village	CO	80111	**800-438-8374***	561-912-2555	398
VeriSign Inc 350 Ellis St *NASDAQ: VRSN* ■ *Sales	Mountain View	CA	94043	**866-893-6565***	650-426-3100	733
Verisk Analytics 545 Washington Blvd *NASDAQ: VRSK*	Jersey City	NJ	07310	**800-888-4476**	201-469-3000	462
Veritas DGC Inc 10300 Townpark Dr	Houston	TX	77072	**800-028-1299**	832-351-8300	537
Veritas Press 1250 Belle Meade Dr	Lancaster	PA	17601	**800-922-5082**	717-519-1974	534
Veritec Inc 2445 Winnetka Ave N	Golden Valley	MN	55427	**866-546-1011**	763-253-2670	694
Veritext LLC 290 W Mt Pleasant Ave Ste 3200	Livingston	NJ	07039	**800-567-8658**		444
Verity Credit Union PO Box 75974	Seattle	WA	98175	**800-444-4589**	206-440-9000	221
Verity International Ltd 200 King St W Ste 1301	Toronto	ON	M5H3T4	**877-623-2396**	416-862-8422	196
Verizon Arena 1 Verizon Arena Way	North Little Rock	AR	72114	**800-745-3000**	501-340-5660	718

Name / Address	City	State	ZIP	Toll-Free	Phone	Class
Verizon Business 1 Verizon Way *Cust Svc	Basking Ridge	NJ	07920	**877-297-7816***	908-559-2000	733
Verizon Credit Inc 201 N Tampa St	Tampa	FL	33602	**800-483-7988**	813-229-6000	218
Verizon Wireless 180 Washington Valley Rd	Bedminster	NJ	07921	**800-922-0204**	908-306-7000	733
Vermeer Corp 1210 Vermeer Rd E PO Box 200	Pella	IA	50219	**800-829-0051**	641-628-3141	275
Vermeer Mid Atlantic Inc 10900 Carpet St	Charlotte	NC	28273	**800-768-3444**	704-588-3238	789
Vermeer Midsouth Inc 1200 Vermeer Cv	Cordova	TN	38018	**800-264-4123**	901-758-1928	386
Vermilion Community College 1900 E Camp St	Ely	MN	55731	**800-657-3608**	218-365-7200	161
Vermilion Energy Trust 3500 520 Third Ave SW *TSE: VET*	Calgary	AB	T2P0R3	**866-895-8101**	403-269-4884	539
Vermillion County 255 S Main St	Newport	IN	47966	**800-340-8155**	765-492-5345	338
Vermont Academy PO Box 500	Saxtons River	VT	05154	**800-698-8867**	802-869-6229	621
Vermont Bar Assn (VBA) 35-37 Ct St PO Box 100	Montpelier	VT	05601	**800-639-7036**	802-223-2020	71
Vermont Chamber of Commerce PO Box 37	Montpelier	VT	05601	**800-451-4279**	802-223-3443	139
Vermont Children & Families Dept 103 S Main St 2nd Fl 5 N	Waterbury	VT	05671	**800-786-3214**	802-241-2100	339-46
Vermont Consumer Assistance Program 146 University Pl	Burlington	VT	05405	**800-649-2424**	802-656-3183	339-46
Vermont Convention Bureau 60 Main St Ste 100	Burlington	VT	05401	**877-264-3503**	802-860-0606	208
Vermont Dept of Libraries 109 State St	Montpelier	VT	05609	**888-350-0950**	802-828-3261	434-5
Vermont Electric Co-op Inc 42 Wescom Rd	Johnson	VT	05656	**800-832-2667**	802-635-2331	247
Vermont Emergency Management Office 103 S Main St	Waterbury	VT	05671	**800-347-0488**	802-241-5000	339-46
Vermont Garden Park 1100 Dorset St	South Burlington	VT	05403	**800-538-7476**	802-863-5251	96
Vermont Gas Systems Inc 85 Swift St	South Burlington	VT	05403	**800-639-8081**	802-863-4511	325
Vermont Historic Preservation Div National Life Bldg 6th Fl	Montpelier	VT	05620	**800-639-1522**	802-828-3213	339-46
Vermont Law School 168 Chelsea St PO Box 96	South Royalton	VT	05068	**800-227-1395**	802-831-1239	168-1
Vermont Medical Society 134 Main St	Montpelier	VT	05601	**800-640-8767**	802-223-7898	473
Vermont Mutual Insurance Co 89 State St PO Box 188	Montpelier	VT	05601	**800-451-5000**	802-223-2341	391-4
Vermont NEA Today Magazine 10 Wheelock St	Montpelier	VT	05602	**800-649-6375**	802-223-6375	456-8
Vermont Public Television (VPT) 204 Ethan Allen Ave	Colchester	VT	05446	**800-639-7811**	802-655-4800	629
Vermont State Nurses Assn (VSNA) 100 Dorset St Ste 13	South Burlington	VT	05403	**800-540-9390**	802-651-8886	532
Vermont Structural Slate Company Inc 3 Prospect St PO Box 98	Fair Haven	VT	05743	**800-343-1900**	802-265-4933	722
Vermont Student Assistance Corp (VSAC) PO Box 2000	Winooski	VT	05404	**800-642-3177**	802-655-9602	723
Vermont Symphony Orchestra 2 Church St Ste 3B	Burlington	VT	05401	**800-876-9293**	802-864-5741	572-3
Vermont Systems Inc 12 Market Pl	Essex Junction	VT	05452	**877-883-8757**	802-879-6993	180-10
Vermont Technical College PO Box 500	Randolph Center	VT	05061	**800-442-8821**	802-728-1000	798
Vermont Teddy Bear Company Inc 6655 Shelburne Rd	Shelburne	VT	05482	**800-988-8277**	802-985-3001	760
Vermont Veterans Affairs Office 118 State St	Montpelier	VT	05602	**888-666-9844**	802-828-3379	339-46
Vermont Vocational Rehabilitation Div 103 S Main St	Waterbury	VT	05671	**866-879-6757**	802-241-2186	339-46
Vermont's North Country Chamber of Commerce 246 Cswy St	Newport	VT	05855	**800-266-2278**	802-334-7782	138
Verndale Corp, The 28 Damrell St Ste 300	Boston	MA	02127	**866-942-8376**		366
Vernon College 4400 College Dr	Vernon	TX	76384	**866-336-9371**	940-552-6291	161
Vernon Electric Co-op 110 Saugstad Rd	Westby	WI	54667	**800-447-5051**	608-634-3121	247
Vernon Parish Library 1401 Nolan Trace	Leesville	LA	71446	**800-737-2231**	337-239-2027	434-3
Vernon Tool Company Ltd 503 Jones Rd	Oceanside	CA	92054	**800-452-1542**	760-433-5860	454
Vero Beach Press-Journal PO Box 1268	Vero Beach	FL	32961	**866-894-9851**	772-562-2315	531-2
Verologix LLC 18100 Von Karman Ave	Irvine	CA	90623	**800-403-8041**		198
Veros Real Estate Solutions LLC 2333 N Broadway Ste 350	Santa Ana	CA	92706	**866-458-3767**	714-415-6300	179
Versa Press Inc 1465 Springbay Rd	East Peoria	IL	61611	**800-447-7829**		625
Versacold International Corp 2115 Commissioner St	Vancouver	BC	V5L1A6	**800-563-2653**	604-255-4656	315
Versalogic Corp 4211 W 11th Ave	Eugene	OR	97402	**800-824-3163**	541-485-8575	175-1
Versant Corp 255 Shoreline Dr Ste 450 *NASDAQ: VSNT*	Redwood City	CA	94065	**888-446-4737**	650-232-2400	180-1
Versar Inc 6850 Versar Ctr *NYSE: VSR* ■ *Cust Svc	Springfield	VA	22151	**800-283-7727***	703-750-3000	263
Versasuite 13401 Pond Springs Rd	Austin	TX	78729	**800-903-8774**	512-249-8774	227
Versatile Systems Inc 4900 Ritter Rd Ste 100 *NYSE: CVE*	Mechanicsburg	PA	17055	**800-262-1622**		227

Company	Address	City	State	Zip	Toll-Free	Phone	Class
Verso Corp	6775 Lenox Ctr Ct Ste 400 *NYSE: VRS*	Memphis	TN	38115	877-837-7606		556
Vertafore Inc	7 Waterside Crossing *General	Windsor	CT	06095	800-444-4813*		180-10
Vertellus Specialties Inc	201 N Illinois St Ste 1800	Indianapolis	IN	46204	800-777-3536	317-247-8141	144
Vertex Engineering Services Inc	400 Libbey Pkwy	Weymouth	MA	02189	888-298-5162	781-952-6000	194
Vertex Inc	1041 Old Cassatt Rd	Berwyn	PA	19312	800-355-3500	610-640-4200	180-1
Vertical Alliance Group Inc	1730 Galleria Oaks	Texarkana	TX	75503	877-792-3866	903-792-3866	244
Vertical Communications Inc	3940 Freedom Cr Ste 110 *OTC: VRCC* ■ *Sales	Santa Clara	CA	95054	800-914-9985*	408-404-1600	180-7
Vertical Management Systems Inc	7 N Fair Oaks Ave 2nd Fl	Pasadena	CA	91103	800-867-4357		179
Vertical Vision Financial Marketing LLC	145 Towne Lk Pkwy	Woodstock	GA	30188	866-984-1585		5
Vertigraph Inc	12959 Jupiter Rd Ste 252	Dallas	TX	75238	800-989-4243	214-340-9436	462
Vertisoft	990 Boul Pierre-roux E	Victoriaville	QC	G6T0K9	877-368-3241	819-751-6660	182
Vescio Threading Co	14002 Anson Ave	Santa Fe Springs	CA	90670	800-361-4218	562-802-1868	453
Vesco Oil Corp	16055 W 12-Mile Rd	Southfield	MI	48076	800-527-5358		578
Vescom Corp	705 Main Rd N	Hampden	ME	04444	800-841-1769	207-945-5051	691
Vessel Metrics LLC	3 Church Cir Ste 325	Annapolis	MD	21401	888-214-1710		387
Vested Business Brokers Inc	50 Karl Ave # 102	Smithtown	NY	11787	877-735-5224	631-265-7300	527
Vestra Resources Inc	5300 Aviation Dr	Redding	CA	96002	877-983-7872	530-223-2585	303
Veteran's Truck Line Inc	800 Black Hawk Dr	Burlington	WI	53105	800-456-9476	262-539-3400	360-2
Veterans Affairs Long Beach Medical Ctr	5901 E Seventh St	Long Beach	CA	90822	888-769-8387	562-826-8000	374-8
Veterans Affairs Medical Ctr	7180 Highland Dr	Pittsburgh	PA	15206	866-482-7488	412-365-4900	374-8
Veterans Affairs Outpatient Clinic	1515 W Pleasant St Bldg 1	Knoxville	IA	50138	800-816-8878	641-842-3101	374-8
Veterans Affairs Puget Sound Medical Ctr	1660 S Columbian Way	Seattle	WA	98108	800-329-8387	206-762-1010	374-8
Veterans Benefits Administration	810 Vermont Ave NW	Washington	DC	20420	800-827-1000		340-17
Veterans for Peace Inc (VFP)	216 S Meramec Ave	Saint Louis	MO	63105	877-429-0678	314-725-6005	47-5
Veterans Health Administration	810 Vermont Ave NW	Washington	DC	20420	800-827-1000	202-273-5400	340-17
Gulf War Veterans Information	50 Irving St NW	Washington	DC	20422	800-313-2232		340-17
Office of Research & Development	810 Vermont Ave NW MC 12	Washington	DC	20420	800-827-1000		340-17
Veterans Home of California-Barstow	100 E Veterans Pkwy	Barstow	CA	92311	800-746-0606	760-252-6200	791
Veterans Home of California-Chula Vista	700 E Naples Ct	Chula Vista	CA	91911	800-952-5626		791
Veterans Home of California-Yountville	1227 O St	Sacramento	CA	95814	800-952-5626	916-653-2573	791
Veterans Memorial Library	301 S University Ave	Mount Pleasant	MI	48858	888-520-8103	989-773-3242	434-3
Veterans of Foreign Wars of the US (VFW)	406 W 34th St	Kansas City	MO	64111	800-963-3180	816-756-3390	47-19
Veterinary Pet Insurance Inc	PO Box 2344	Brea	CA	92822	800-872-7387		391-1
Veterinary Pharmacies of America Inc	2854 Antoine Dr	Houston	TX	77092	877-838-7979		581
VetJobs Inc	PO Box 71445	Marietta	GA	30007	877-838-5627	770-993-5117	262
Vetoquinol Canada Inc	2000 Ch Georges	Lavaltrie	QC	J5T3S5	800-363-1700	450-586-2252	581
VetSelect Animal Hospital	2150 Old Novi Rd	Novi	MI	48377	800-462-8749	248-624-1100	792
VetStrategy	30 Whitmore Rd	Woodbridge	ON	L4L7Z4	866-901-6471		462
Vetstreet	780 Township Line Rd	Yardley	PA	19067	888-799-8387	215-493-0621	387
Vetter Health Services Inc	20220 Harney St	Elkhorn	NE	68022	800-388-4264	402-895-3932	462
Vetter Stone Co (VSC)	23894 Third Ave	Mankato	MN	56001	800-878-2850	507-345-4568	722
VF Corporation	PO Box 21488 *Orders	Greensboro	NC	27420	866-492-3370*	336-424-6000	154-10
VFA Inc	99 Bedford St	Boston	MA	02111	800-693-3132	617-451-5100	180-1
V-fluence Interactive Public Realtions Inc	7770 Regents Rd	San Diego	CA	92122	877-835-8362		227
VFP (Veterans for Peace Inc)	216 S Meramec Ave	Saint Louis	MO	63105	877-429-0678	314-725-6005	47-5
VFUC (Visions Federal Credit Union)	24 McKinley Ave	Endicott	NY	13760	800-242-2120	607-754-7900	221
VFW (Veterans of Foreign Wars of the US)	406 W 34th St	Kansas City	MO	64111	800-963-3180	816-756-3390	47-19
VGH (Valdese General Hospital)	720 Malcolm Blvd Ste 200	Valdese	NC	28690	800-994-6610	828-874-2251	374-3
V&H Inc	1505 S Central Ave	Marshfield	WI	54449	800-826-2308	715-486-8800	56
VH1 (Video Hits One)	1515 Broadway 20th Fl	New York	NY	10036	800-745-1892		736
Vi	71 S Wacker Dr	Chicago	IL	60606	800-421-1442	312-803-8800	670
VIA Metropolitan Transit	800 W Myrtle St	San Antonio	TX	78212	866-362-4200	210-362-2000	467
VIA Rail Canada Inc	3 Pl Ville-Marie PO Box 8116	Montreal	QC	H3C3N3	800-681-2561	514-871-6000	647
VIA Technologies Inc	940 Mission Ct	Fremont	CA	94539	888-524-9382	510-683-3300	694
Viacom Entertainment Group	1515 Broadway	New York	NY	10036	800-516-4399	212-258-6000	513
ViaSat Inc	6155 El Camino Real *NASDAQ: VSAT*	Carlsbad	CA	92009	855-463-9333	760-476-2200	679
ViaTech Publishing Solutions	1440 Fifth Ave	Bay Shore	NY	11706	800-645-8558	631-968-8500	85
Viatran Corp	3829 Forest Pkwy Ste 500	Wheatfield	NY	14120	800-688-0030	716-629-3800	255
VIBAC Canada Inc	12250 Industrial Blvd	Montreal	QC	H1B5M5	800-557-0192	514-640-0250	729
Vibro-Meter Inc	144 Harvey Rd	Londonderry	NH	03053	800-842-4291	603-669-0940	22
Viceroy Palm Springs	415 S BelaRdo Rd	Palm Springs	CA	92262	866-781-9923	760-320-4117	379
Viceroy Santa Monica	1819 Ocean Ave	Santa Monica	CA	90401	888-622-4567	310-260-7500	379
Vi-Chem Corp	55 Cottage Grove St SW	Grand Rapids	MI	49507	800-477-8501	616-247-8501	604-2
Vicon Industries Inc	89 Arkay Dr *NYSE: VII* ■ *Sales	Hauppauge	NY	11788	800-645-9116*	631-952-2288	645
Viconics Technologies Inc	9245 Langelier Blvd	Saint-Leonard	QC	H1P3K9	800-563-5660	514-321-5660	407
Vicor Corp	25 Frontage Rd *NASDAQ: VICR*	Andover	MA	01810	800-869-5300	978-470-2900	255
Victaulic Co	4901 Kesslersville Rd *Sales	Easton	PA	18040	800-742-5842*	610-559-3300	594
Victor L Phillips Co	4100 Gardner Ave	Kansas City	MO	64120	800-878-9290	816-241-9290	358
Victor Printing Inc	1 Victor Way	Sharon	PA	16146	800-443-2845	724-342-2106	109
Victor Settings Inc	25 Brook Ave	Maywood	NJ	07607	800-322-9008	201-845-4433	407
Victor Technology LLC	175 E Crossroads Pkwy	Bolingbrook	IL	60440	800-628-2420	630-754-4400	117
Victor Valley Community College	18422 Bear Valley Rd	Victorville	CA	92392	877-741-8532	760-245-4271	161
Victoria Advocate	PO Box 1518	Victoria	TX	77902	800-234-8108	361-575-1451	531-2
Victoria Cruises Inc	57-08 39th Ave *Cust Svc	Woodside	NY	11377	800-348-8084*	212-818-1680	223
Victoria Inn Winnipeg	1808 Wellington Ave	Winnipeg	MB	R3H0G3	877-842-4667	204-786-4801	379
Victoria Insurance	22901 Millcreek Blvd	Cleveland	OH	44122	800-888-8424	216-896-6990	391-4
Victoria International Airport	1962 Canso Rd	North Saanich	BC	V8L5V5	866-844-4354	250-656-3987	359
Victoria Regent Hotel, The	1234 Wharf St	Victoria	BC	V8W3H9	800-663-7472	250-386-2211	379
Victoria Theatre	138 N Main St	Dayton	OH	45402	888-228-3630	937-228-3630	571
Victoria Vaudeville Theater	1228 Market St	Wheeling	WV	26003	800-505-7464	304-233-7464	571
Victoria's Secret Stores	4 Limited Pkwy	Reynoldsburg	OH	43068	800-411-5116		156-6
Victorian Condo-Hotel & Conference Ctr	6300 Seawall Blvd	Galveston	TX	77551	800-231-6363	409-740-3555	379
Victorian Trading Co	15600 W 99th St *Cust Svc	Lenexa	KS	66219	800-700-2035*	913-438-3995	458
Victory Electric Co-op Assn Inc	3230 N 14th Ave	Dodge City	KS	67801	800-279-7915	620-227-2139	247
Victory Funds	4900 Tiedeman Rd PO Box 182593	Brooklyn	OH	44144	800-539-3863		527
Victory Furniture	9040 W Pico Blvd	Los Angeles	CA	90035	800-953-2000		322
Victory Refrigeration Inc	110 Woodcrest Rd	Cherry Hill	NJ	08003	800-523-5008	856-428-4200	662
Victory White Metal Co	6100 Roland Ave	Cleveland	OH	44127	800-635-5050	216-271-1400	484
Victorystore.Com Inc	5200 SW 30th St	Davenport	IA	52802	866-241-2295		626
Viewest Corp	1296 S Service Rd W	Oakville	ON	L6L5T7	800-265-6583	905-825-2252	490
Video Display Corp	1868 Tucker Industrial Rd *NASDAQ: VIDE* ■ *Cust Svc	Tucker	GA	30084	800-241-5005*	770-938-2080	175-4
Video Hits One (VH1)	1515 Broadway 20th Fl	New York	NY	10036	800-745-1892		736
Video King Gaming Systems (VKGS LLC)	2717 N 118 Cir Ste 210	Omaha	NE	68164	800-635-9912	402-951-2970	323
Video Symphony Entertraining Inc	266 E Magnolia Blvd	Burbank	CA	91502	888-370-7589	818-557-6500	513
Videojet Technologies Inc	1500 Mittel Blvd *Cust Svc	Wood Dale	IL	60191	800-843-3610*	630-860-7300	386
Videoland Inc	6808 Hornwood Dr	Houston	TX	77074	800-877-2900		34
Videomaker Magazine	1350 E Ninth St PO Box 4591	Chico	CA	95927	800-284-3226	530-891-8410	456-9
VideoMining Corp	403 S Allen St Ste 101	State College	PA	16801	800-898-9950		179
Videotex Systems Inc	10255 Miller Rd	Dallas	TX	75238	800-888-4336	972-231-9200	180-8
Vie de France Yamazaki Inc	2070 Chain Bridge Rd Ste 500 *General	Vienna	VA	22182	800-446-4404*	703-442-9205	67
Viejas Casino	5000 Willows Rd	Alpine	CA	91901	800-847-6537	619-445-5400	132
Viejas Outlet Ctr	5005 Willows	Alpine	CA	91901	877-303-2695	619-659-2070	459
Vienna Sausage Manufacturing Co	2501 N Damen Ave	Chicago	IL	60647	800-366-3647	773-278-7800	297-26

Name / Address	City	State	ZIP	Toll-Free	Phone	Class
Vietnam Women's Memorial Foundation Inc						
1735 Connecticut Ave NW						
3rd Fl	Washington	DC	20009	866-822-8963		49-3
ViewCentral						
900 E Hamilton Ave	Campbell	CA	95008	888-322-5169	408-626-3800	197
OTC: RMKR						
ViewSonic Corp						
381 Brea Canyon Rd	Walnut	CA	91789	800-888-8583	909-444-8888	175-4
Vigilant Insurance Co						
15 Mtn View Rd	Warren	NJ	07059	800-252-4670*	908-903-2000	391-4
*Claims						
Vignette Corp						
1301 S Mopac Expy Ste 100	Austin	TX	78746	800-540-7292	512-741-4300	180-1
VIH Logging Ltd						
1962 Canso Rd	North Saanich	BC	V8L5V5	866-844-4354	250-656-3987	359
Viking Acoustical Corp						
21480 Heath Ave	Lakeville	MN	55044	800-328-8385	952-469-3405	320-1
Viking Corp						
210 N Industrial Pk Dr	Hastings	MI	49058	800-968-9501	269-945-9501	285
210 N Industrial Pk Dr	Hastings	MI	49058	800-968-9501	269-945-9501	747
Viking Drill & Tool Inc						
355 State St	Saint Paul	MN	55107	800-328-4655	651-227-8911	492
Viking Electric Supply Inc						
451 Industrial Blvd W	Minneapolis	MN	55413	800-435-3345	612-627-1300	248
Viking Engineering & Development Inc						
5750 Main St NE	Fridley	MN	55432	800-328-2403*	763-571-2400	819
*Sales						
Viking Forest Products LLC						
7615 Smetana Ln	Eden Prairie	MN	55344	800-733-3801	952-941-6512	193-3
Viking Materials Inc						
3225 Como Ave SE	Minneapolis	MN	55414	800-682-3942*	612-617-5800	491
*General						
Viking Metal Cabinet Co						
24047 W Lockport St Ste 209	Plainfield	IL	60544	800-776-7767		288
Viking Pools Inc						
121 Crawford Rd PO Box 96	Williams	CA	95987	800-854-7665	530-473-5319	726
Viking Range Corp						
111 Front St	Greenwood	MS	38930	888-845-4641	662-455-1200	299
Viking River Cruises						
5700 Canoga Ave Ste 200	Woodland Hills	CA	91367	877-668-4546*	818-227-1234	223
*Cust Svc						
Viking Trailways						
201 Glendale Rd	Joplin	MO	64804	800-400-2779	417-781-2779	107
Viktor Incentives & Meetings						
4020 Copper View Ste 130	Traverse City	MI	49684	800-748-0478	231-947-0882	384
Villa Florence						
225 Powell St	San Francisco	CA	94102	800-553-4411	415-397-7700	379
Villa Gardens						
842 E Villa St	Pasadena	CA	91101	800-958-4552	626-463-5330	670
Villa Julie College						
1525 Green Spring Valley Rd	Stevenson	MD	21153	877-468-6852	410-486-7001	167
Villa Lighting Supply Inc						
2929 Chouteau Ave	Saint Louis	MO	63103	800-325-0963		393
Villa Marin						
100 Thorndale Dr	San Rafael	CA	94903	888-926-2030	415-492-2408	670
Villa Roma Resort & Conference Ctr						
356 Villa Roma Rd	Callicoon	NY	12723	800-533-6767	845-887-4880	667
Villa Royale Inn						
1620 Indian Trl	Palm Springs	CA	92264	800-245-2314	760-327-2314	379
Village Green Cos						
30833 NW Hwy	Farmington Hills	MI	48334	800-521-2220	248-851-9600	189
Village Inn						
400 W 48th Ave	Denver	CO	80216	800-800-3644	303-296-2121	668
Village Latch Inn						
101 Hill St PO Box 3000	SouthHampton	NY	11968	800-545-2824	631-283-2160	379
Village Nurseries						
1589 N Main St	Orange	CA	92867	800-542-0209		324
Village on the Green						
500 Village Pl	Longwood	FL	32779	888-541-3443*	407-682-0230	670
*Mktg						
Village South Inc						
3050 Biscayne Blvd 9th Fl	Miami	FL	33137	800-443-3784	305-573-3784	724
Village Super Market Inc						
733 Mountain Ave	Springfield	NJ	07081	800-746-7748	973-467-2200	345
NASDAQ: VLGEA						
Village Vacances Valcartier						
1860 Valcartier Blvd	Valcartier	QC	G0A4S0	888-384-5524	418-844-2200	32
Village, The						
2200 W Acacia Ave	Hemet	CA	92545	800-257-7888	951-658-3369	670
Villages of Lake Sumter Inc						
1000 Lk Sumter Landing	The Villages	FL	32162	800-245-1081	352-753-2270	651
Villagio Inn & Spa						
6481 Washington St	Yountville	CA	94599	800-351-1133	707-944-8877	379
Villas by the Sea Resort						
1175 N Beachview Dr	Jekyll Island	GA	31527	800-841-6262	912-635-2521	667
Villas of Grand Cypress Golf Resort						
1 N Jacaranda	Orlando	FL	32836	800-835-7377	407-239-4700	667
Villaume Industries Inc						
2926 Lone Oak Cir	Eagan	MN	55121	800-488-3610*	651-454-3610	815
*Cust Svc						
Villere's Florist						
750 Martin Behrman Ave	Metairie	LA	70005	800-845-5373	504-833-3716	294
Villeroy & Boch Tableware Ltd						
3535 Us Hwy 1	Princeton	NJ	08540	800-536-2284		362
Vimco Inc						
300 Hansen Access Rd	King Of Prussia	PA	19406	888-468-4626*	610-768-0500	193-1
*Cust Svc						
Vimich Traffic Logistics						
12201 Tecumseh Rd E	Tecumseh	ON	N8N1M3	800-284-1045		448
Vin Devers Inc						
5570 Monroe St	Sylvania	OH	43560	888-847-9535	419-885-5111	56
Vincennes University						
1002 N First St	Vincennes	IN	47591	800-742-9198	812-888-4313	161
Jasper 850 College Ave	Jasper	IN	47546	800-809-8852	812-482-3030	161
Vincent Printing Company Inc						
1512 Sholar Ave	Chattanooga	TN	37406	800-251-7262		685
Vindicator, The						
107 Vindicator Sq PO Box 780	Youngstown	OH	44501	877-700-4647	330-747-1471	531-2
Vinely						
1 Kendall Sq Bldg 400 B4202	Cambridge	MA	02139	888-294-1128		387
Vinson & Elkins LLP						
1001 Fannin St						
1st City Tower Ste 2500	Houston	TX	77002	877-610-2009	713-758-2222	428
Vinson Guard Service Inc						
955 Howard Ave	New Orleans	LA	70113	800-441-7899	504-529-2260	691
Vintage Air Inc						
18865 Goll St	San Antonio	TX	78266	800-862-6658	210-654-7171	662
Vintage Inn Napa Valley						
6541 Washington St	Yountville	CA	94599	800-351-1133*		379
*Cust Svc						
Vintners Inn						
4350 Barnes Rd	Santa Rosa	CA	95403	800-421-2584	707-575-7350	379
Vinylplex Inc						
1800 Atkinson Ave	Pittsburg	KS	66762	877-779-7473	620-231-8290	595
Vinyltech Corp						
201 S 61st Ave	Phoenix	AZ	85043	800-255-3924	602-233-0071	595
Viox Services Inc						
15 W Voorhees St	Cincinnati	OH	45215	888-846-9462	513-948-8469	273
VIP Tour & Charter Bus Co						
129-137 Fox St	Portland	ME	04101	800-231-2222*	207-772-4457	106
*General						
ViPS Inc						
1 W Pennsylvania Ave Ste 700	Towson	MD	21204	800-242-0230	410-832-8300	180-10
Viracon Inc						
800 Pk Dr	Owatonna	MN	55060	800-533-2080	507-451-9555	330
Virco Manufacturing Corp						
2027 Harpers Way	Torrance	CA	90501	800-448-4726*	310-533-0474	320-3
NASDAQ: VIRC ■ *Cust Svc						
Virgin Atlantic Airways Ltd						
747 Belden Ave	Norwalk	CT	06850	888-747-7474	800-821-5438	25
Virgin Atlantic Cargo						
JFK International Airport						
Bldg 15	Jamaica	NY	11430	800-828-6822	516-775-2600	12
Virgin Atlantic Flying Club						
747 Belden Ave	Norwalk	CT	06850	800-365-9500		26
Virgin Mobile USA Inc						
10 Independence Blvd	Warren	NJ	07059	888-322-1122	908-607-4000	733
Virginia						
Aging & Rehabilitative Services Dept						
8004 Franklin Farms Dr	Richmond	VA	23229	800-552-5019	804-662-7000	339-47
Child Support Enforcement Div						
730 E Broad St	Richmond	VA	23219	800-468-8894		339-47
Criminal Injuries Compensation Fund (CICF)						
PO Box 26927	Richmond	VA	23261	800-552-4007		339-47
Governor						
1111 E Broad St PO Box 1475	Richmond	VA	23219	800-828-1120	804-786-2211	339-47
Health Professions Dept						
9960 Mayland Dr Ste 300	Henrico	VA	23233	800-533-1560	804-367-4400	339-47
Housing Development Authority						
601 S Belvidere St	Richmond	VA	23220	800-968-7837	804-782-1986	339-47
Information Technologies Agency (VITA)						
11751 Meadowville Ln	Chester	VA	23836	866-637-8482		339-47
State Parks Div						
203 Governor St Ste 306	Richmond	VA	23219	800-933-7275*		339-47
*Resv						
Vital Records Div						
2001 Maywill St PO Box 1000	Richmond	VA	23230	877-572-6333	804-662-6200	339-47
Virginia American Water Co (VAWC)						
2223 Duke St	Alexandria	VA	22314	800-452-6863	703-706-3879	785
Virginia Assn of Realtors						
10231 Telegraph Rd	Glen Allen	VA	23059	800-755-8271	804-264-5033	654
Virginia Baptist Hospital						
3300 Rivermont Ave	Lynchburg	VA	24503	866-749-4455	434-947-4000	374-3
Virginia Beach Convention & Visitor Bureau (VBCVB)						
2101 Parks Ave Ste 500	Virginia Beach	VA	23451	800-700-7702	757-385-4700	208
Virginia Beach Resort Hotel & Conference Ctr						
2800 Shore Dr	Virginia Beach	VA	23451	800-468-2722	757-481-9000	667
Virginia Chamber of Commerce						
919 E Main St	Richmond	VA	23219	800-228-9290	804-644-1607	139
Virginia College Savings Plan						
9001 Arboretum Pkwy	Richmond	VA	23236	888-567-0540	804-786-0719	723
Virginia Commonwealth University						
910 W Franklin St	Richmond	VA	23284	800-841-3638	804-828-0100	167
Virginia Commonwealth University Cabell Library						
901 Pk Ave PO Box 842033	Richmond	VA	23284	844-352-7399	804-828-1105	434-6
Virginia Commonwealth University School of Medicine						
1101 E Marshall St						
PO Box 980565	Richmond	VA	23298	800-332-8813	804-828-9629	168-2
Virginia Credit Union						
7500 Boulders View Dr	Richmond	VA	23225	800-285-5051	804-323-6000	221
Virginia Crossings Resort						
1000 Virginia Ctr Pkwy	Glen Allen	VA	23059	888-444-6553	804-727-1400	667
Virginia Democratic Party						
1710 E Franklin St 2nd Fl	Richmond	VA	23223	800-322-1144	804-644-1966	615-1
Virginia Dental Assn (VDA)						
3460 Mayland Ct Ste 110	Richmond	VA	23233	877-726-0850	804-288-5750	229
Virginia Dept of Taxation						
1957 Westmoreland St						
PO Box 1115	Richmond	VA	23230	800-828-1120	804-367-8037	530-7
Virginia Episcopal School						
400 VES Rd	Lynchburg	VA	24503	800-937-3582	434-385-3607	621
Virginia Festival of the Book						
Virginia Foundation for the Humanities						
145 Ednam Dr.	Charlottesville	VA	22903	877-451-5098	434-924-3296	283
Virginia Intermont College						
1013 Moore St	Bristol	VA	24201	800-451-1842	276-669-6101	167
Virginia International Terminals Inc						
7737 Hampton Blvd	Norfolk	VA	23505	800-541-2431*	757-440-7000	464
*General						
Virginia Journal of Education						
116 S Third St	Richmond	VA	23219	800-552-9554	804-648-5801	456-8
Virginia Marti College of Art & Design						
11724 Detroit Ave	Lakewood	OH	44107	800-473-4350	216-221-8584	163
Virginia Medical News						
2924 Emerywood Pkwy Ste 300	Richmond	VA	23294	800-746-6768		456-16
Virginia Medical Society						
4205 Dover Rd	Richmond	VA	23221	800-746-6768	804-353-2721	473

Name / Address	City	State	ZIP	Toll-Free	Phone	Class
Virginia Military Institute 319 Letcher Ave	Lexington	VA	24450	**800-767-4207**	540-464-7211	167
Virginia Mirror Co Inc 300 Moss St S	Martinsville	VA	24112	**800-368-3011**	276-632-9816	330
Virginia Natural Gas Inc AGL Resources Inc PO Box 4569	Atlanta	GA	30302	**800-633-4236**	404-584-4000	785
Virginia Peninsula Chamber of Commerce 21 Enterprise Pkwy Ste 100	Hampton	VA	23666	**800-462-3204**	757-262-2000	138
Virginia Plastics Co Inc 3453 Aerial Way Dr PO Box 4577	Roanoke	VA	24018	**877-351-1699**	540-981-9700	814
Virginia Press Services Inc 11529 Nuckols Rd	Glen Allen	VA	23059	**800-849-8717**	804-521-7570	623
Virginia Railway Express (VRE) 1500 King St Ste 202	Alexandria	VA	22314	**800-743-3873**	703-684-1001	467
Virginia Society of Certified Public Accountants 4309 Cox Rd	Glen Allen	VA	23060	**800-733-8272**	804-270-5344	2
Virginia State Bar 707 E Main St Ste 1500	Richmond	VA	23219	**800-552-7977**	804-775-0500	71
Virginia State University 1 Hayden Dr *Admissions	Petersburg	VA	23806	**800-871-7611***	804-524-5000	167
Virginia Symphony Orchestra 861 Glenrock Rd Ste 200	Norfolk	VA	23502	**855-876-7677**	757-466-3060	572-3
Virginia Tile Co 28320 Plymouth Rd	Livonia	MI	48150	**877-356-7461**	734-762-2400	361
Virginia Transformer Corp 220 Glade View Dr	Roanoke	VA	24012	**800-882-3944**	540-345-9892	765
Virginia Union University 1500 N Lombardy St	Richmond	VA	23220	**800-368-3227**	804-342-3570	167
Virginia Veterinary Medical Assn (VVMA) 3801 Westerre Pkwy Ste D	Henrico	VA	23233	**800-937-8862**	804-346-2611	793
Virginia War Museum 9285 Warwick Blvd	Newport News	VA	23607	**888-493-7386**	757-247-8523	519
Virginia Wesleyan College 1584 Wesleyan Dr	Norfolk	VA	23502	**800-737-8684**	757-455-3200	167
Virginia West Electric Supply Co (WVES) 250 12-th St W	Huntington	WV	25704	**800-624-3433**	304-525-0361	248
Virginia Western Community College 3094 Colonial Ave PO Box 14007	Roanoke	VA	24038	**855-874-6690**	540-857-8922	161
Virginian Lodge 750 W Broadway PO Box 1052	Jackson Hole	WY	83001	**800-262-4999**	307-733-2792	379
Virginian Suites 1500 Arlington Blvd	Arlington	VA	22209	**866-371-1446**	703-522-9600	379
Virginian-Pilot 150 W Bramelton Ave	Norfolk	VA	23510	**800-446-2004**	757-446-2000	531-2
Virtela Technology Services Inc 5680 Greenwood Plz Blvd Ste 200	Greenwood Village	CO	80111	**877-803-9629**	720-475-4000	178
Virtexco Corp 977 Norfolk Sq	Norfolk	VA	23502	**800-766-1082**	757-466-1114	188
Virtual Training Company Inc 5395 Main St	Stephens City	VA	22655	**888-316-5374**	540-869-8686	179
VirtualBank 3801 PGA Blvd Ste 700 PO Box 109638	Palm Beach Gardens	FL	33410	**877-998-2265**		69
Virtuoso 505 Main St Ste 5	Fort Worth	TX	76102	**800-401-4274**	817-870-0300	770
Visa Inc PO Box 8999 *NYSE: V*	San Francisco	CA	94128	**866-765-9644**	415-932-2100	219
Visalia Convention & Visitors Bureau PO Box 2734	Visalia	CA	93279	**800-524-0303**	559-334-0141	208
Visalia Convention Ctr 303 E Acequia Ave	Visalia	CA	93291	**800-640-4888**	559-713-4000	207
Visalia Medical Lab 5400 West Hillsdale Ave	Visalia	CA	93291	**800-486-2362**	559-562-1222	418
Visara International Inc 2700 Gateway Centre Blvd Ste 600	Morrisville	NC	27560	**888-334-4380**	919-882-0200	178
Viscount Gort Hotel 1670 Portage Ave	Winnipeg	MB	R3J0C9	**800-665-1122**	204-775-0451	379
Viscount Suite Hotel 4855 E Broadway Blvd *Resv	Tucson	AZ	85711	**800-527-9666***	520-745-6500	379
Vishay Intertechnology Inc 63 Lancaster Ave *NYSE: VSH*	Malvern	PA	19355	**800-567-6098**	610-644-1300	694
Visible Systems Corp 201 Spring St *Sales	Lexington	MA	02421	**888-850-9911***	781-778-0200	180-1
Vision Council, The 225 Reinekers Ln Ste 700	Alexandria	VA	22314	**866-826-0290**	703-548-4560	48-4
Vision Financial Corp PO Box 506	Keene	NH	03431	**800-793-0223**		391-5
Vision Ford Lincoln Hyundai 1500 S White Sands Blvd	Alamogordo	NM	88310	**866-932-2441**		56
Vision Global AR Ltee 80, Queen St Ste 301	Montreal	QC	H3C2N5	**800-667-7690**	514-879-0020	513
Vision Solutions Inc 15300 Barranca Pkwy	Irvine	CA	92618	**800-683-4667**	949-253-6500	180-12
Vision Technologies Inc 530 McCormick Dr Ste G	Glen Burnie	MD	21061	**866-746-1122**	410-424-2183	179
Visionaire Inc 1502 109th St	Grand Prairie	TX	75050	**866-838-2810**	972-647-1056	56
Visionary Integration Professionals Inc 80 Iron Pt Cir Ste 100	Folsom	CA	95630	**800-434-2673**	916-985-9625	182
Vision-Ease Lens Inc 7000 Sunwood Dr NW *Cust Svc	Ramsey	MN	55303	**800-328-3449***	320-251-8140	541
Visions Federal Credit Union (VFUC) 24 McKinley Ave	Endicott	NY	13760	**800-242-2120**	607-754-7900	221
Vision-Sciences Inc 40 Ramland Rd S *NASDAQ: VSCI*	Orangeburg	NY	10962	**800-874-9975**	845-365-0600	382
Visionworks of America Inc 175 E Houston St	San Antonio	TX	78205	**800-669-1183**	210-340-3531	542
Visit Eau Claire 4319 Jeffers Rd	Eau Claire	WI	54703	**888-523-3866**	715-831-2345	208
Visit Jacksonville 208 N Laura St Ste 1	Jacksonville	FL	32202	**800-733-2668**	904-798-9111	208
Visit MercerCounty PA 50 N Water Ave	Sharon	PA	16146	**800-637-2370**	724-346-3771	208
Visit Milledgeville 200 W Hancock St	Milledgeville	GA	31061	**800-653-1804**	478-452-4687	208
Visit Rochester 45 E Ave Ste 400	Rochester	NY	14604	**800-677-7282**	585-279-8300	208
Visit Salt Lake 90 SW Temple	Salt Lake City	UT	84101	**800-541-4955**	801-534-4900	208
Visit Sarasota County 1777 Main St Ste 302	Sarasota	FL	34236	**800-522-9799**	941-955-0991	208
Visit St Petersburg Clearwater 13805 58th St N Ste 2-200	Clearwater	FL	33760	**877-352-3224**	727-464-7200	208
Visit Topeka Inc 618 S Kansas Ave	Topeka	KS	66603	**800-235-1030**	785-234-1030	208
VisitErie 208 E Bayfront Pkwy Ste 103	Erie	PA	16507	**800-524-3743**	814-454-1000	208
Visiting Nurse Assn 12565 W Ctr Rd Ste 100	Omaha	NE	68144	**800-456-8869**	402-342-5566	371
Visiting Nurse Assn of Morris County (Inc) 175 South St	Morristown	NJ	07960	**800-938-4748**	973-539-1216	363
Visiting Nurse Assn of Ohio 2500 E 22nd St	Cleveland	OH	44115	**877-698-6264**	216-931-1400	371
Visiting Nurse Assn of the Treasure Coast 1110 35th Ln	Vero Beach	FL	32960	**800-749-5760**	772-567-5551	371
Visiting Nurse Assns of America (VNAA) 900 19th St NW Ste 200	Washington	DC	20006	**888-866-8773**	202-384-1420	48-8
Viskase Cos Inc 8205 S Cass Ste 115	Darien	IL	60561	**800-323-8562**	630-874-0700	547
VIST Financial Corp PO Box 6219 PO Box 6219 *NASDAQ: VIST*	Wyomissing	PA	19610	**888-238-3330**	610-926-7632	360-2
Vista Auto 21501 Ventura Blvd	Woodland Hills	CA	91364	**888-887-6530**	888-313-4252	56
Vista del Monte 3775 Modoc Rd	Santa Barbara	CA	93105	**800-736-1333**	805-687-0793	670
Vista Electronics Inc 27525 Newhall Ranch Rd	Valencia	CA	91355	**800-847-8299**	661-294-9820	513
Vista Grande Villa 2251 Springport Rd	Jackson	MI	49202	**800-889-8499**	517-787-0222	670
Vista Host Inc 10370 Richmond Ave Ste 150	Houston	TX	77042	**800-257-3000**	713-267-5800	379
Vista Imaging Services Inc 3941 Park Dr Ste 20-463	El Dorado Hills	CA	95762	**855-972-9729**	415-272-3925	415
Vista Metals Inc 65 Ballou Blvd	Bristol	RI	02809	**800-431-4113**	401-253-1772	491
Vista Verde Guest & Ski Ranch PO Box 770465	Steamboat Springs	CO	80477	**800-526-7433**	970-879-3858	241
Vista-pro Automotive LLC 15 Century Blvd Ste 600	Nashville	TN	37214	**888-250-2676**	615-622-2200	515
Vistar Eye Center Inc 707 S Jefferson St	Roanoke	VA	24016	**866-615-5454**	540-855-5100	542
Vistar/VSA Corp 12650 E Arapahoe Rd	Centennial	CO	80112	**800-880-9900**	303-662-7100	298-8
Vistronix Inc 11091 Sunset Hills Rd Ste 700	Reston	VA	20190	**800-483-2434**	703-463-2059	182
Visual Departures Ltd 48 Sheffield Business Park Ste 195	Ashley Falls	MA	01222	**800-628-2003**		590
Visual Learning Systems Inc PO Box 8226	Missoula	MT	59807	**866-968-7857**		179
Visual Marketing Inc 154 W Erie St	Chicago	IL	60654	**800-662-8640**	312-664-9177	235
Visual Net Design Lc 212 E Ramsey Rd	San Antonio	TX	78216	**800-590-2164**	210-590-2734	177
Visual Planning Corp 71 Meadowbank Dr	Ottawa	ON	K2G0P4	**800-361-1192**	613-563-8727	486
Visualware Inc 937 Sierra Dr PO Box 668	Turlock	CA	95380	**866-847-9273**	209-262-3491	179
Vita Food Products Inc 2222 W Lake St	Chicago	IL	60612	**800-989-8482**	312-738-4500	297-13
Vita Plus Corp 2514 Fish Hatchery Rd	Madison	WI	53713	**800-362-8334**	608-256-1988	446
Vitacost.com Inc 5400 Broken Sound Blvd NW Ste 500	Boca Raton	FL	33487	**800-381-0759**		239
VitaDigest.com 20687-2 Amar Rd Ste 258	Walnut	CA	91789	**877-848-2168**		345
Vital Images Inc 5850 Opus Pkwy Ste 300	Minnetonka	MN	55343	**800-208-3005**	952-487-9500	180-10
Vital Media 508 W 5th St, Ste. 100 Ste	Charlotte	NC	28202	**866-863-3426**		7
Vital Signs Inc 20 Campus Rd	Totowa	NJ	07512	**800-932-0760**	973-790-1330	475
VitalAire Canada Inc 6990 Creditview Rd Unit 6	Mississauga	ON	L5N8R9	**888-629-0202**		475
Vitamin Shoppe Inc 2101 91st St *NYSE: VSI*	North Bergen	NJ	07047	**800-223-1216**	201-868-5959	239
Vitaminerals Inc 1815 Flower St	Glendale	CA	91201	**800-432-1856**		297-11
Vita-Mix Corp 8615 Usher Rd	Cleveland	OH	44138	**800-848-2649**	440-235-4840	36
VITAS Healthcare Corp 2675 N Mayfair Rd Ste 500	Wauwatosa	WI	53226	**866-418-4827**	414-257-2600	371
VITAS Healthcare Corp of California 990 W 190th St Ste 120	Torrance	CA	90502	**800-582-9533**	305-374-4143	371
VITAS Healthcare Corp of Pennsylvania 1787 Sentry Pk W Bldg 16 Ste 400	Blue Bell	PA	19422	**800-582-9533**	305-374-4143	371
VITAS Healthcare Corp of San Gabriel Cities 1343 N Grand Ave	Covina	CA	91724	**866-418-4827**		371
VITAS Hospice Care 201 S Biscayne Blvd Ste 400 *General	Miami	FL	33131	**800-582-9533***	305-374-4143	371
Vitasoy USA Inc 1 New England Way	Ayer	MA	01432	**800-848-2769**	978-772-6880	297-8

Name	Address	City	State	ZIP	Toll-Free	Phone	Class
Viterbo University	900 Viterbo Dr	La Crosse	WI	54601	**800-848-3726**	608-796-3000	167
Vitran Express Canada Inc (*NASDAQ: VTNC*)	1201 Creditstone Rd	Concord	ON	L4K0C2	**800-263-9588**	416-798-4965	778
Vitran Express Inc	1600 W Oliver Ave	Indianapolis	IN	46221	**800-366-0150**	317-803-4000	778
Vitria Technology Inc	945 Stewart Dr Ste 200	Sunnyvale	CA	94085	**877-365-5935**		180-1
Vitro Seating Products Inc	201 Madison St	Saint Louis	MO	63102	**800-325-7093*** (*Cust Svc)	314-241-2265	320-1
VIVA Health Inc	1222 14th Ave S	Birmingham	AL	35205	**800-633-1542**	205-939-1718	390
Viviano Flower Shop	32050 Harper Ave	Saint Clair Shores	MI	48082	**800-848-4266**	586-293-0227	294
Vivint Solar Inc	4931 North 300 West	Provo	UT	84604	**877-404-4129**		194
Vivitar Corp	195 Carter Dr	Edison	NJ	08817	**800-592-9541**	732-248-1306	590
Vivosonic Inc	120-5525 Eglinton Ave W	Toronto	ON	M9C5K5	**877-255-7685**	416-231-9997	475
Vivus Inc (*NASDAQ: VVUS*)	1172 Castro St	Mountain View	CA	94040	**800-607-0088**	650-934-5200	582
ViWo Inc	10801 National blvd 410	Los Angeles	CA	90064	**888-898-4787**	877-958-5174	198
Viziflex Seels Inc	406 N Midland Ave	Saddle Brook	NJ	07663	**800-627-7752**		607
Vizza Wash Services LLC	2208 NW Loop 410	San Antonio	TX	78230	**866-493-8822*** (*Cust Svc)	210-493-8822	61-1
VJ Technologies Inc	89 Carlough Rd	Bohemia	NY	11716	**800-858-9729**	631-589-8800	740
VJV IT	96 Linwood Plz	Fort Lee	NJ	07024	**800-614-7561**		630
VKGS LLC (Video King Gaming Systems)	2717 N 118 Cir Ste 210	Omaha	NE	68164	**800-635-9912**	402-951-2970	323
VKI Technologies Inc	3200 2e rue	Saint-hubert	QC	J3Y8Y7	**800-567-2951**	450-676-0504	158
VLN Partners LLP	1212 E Carson St	Pittsburgh	PA	15203	**877-856-3311**	412-381-0183	176
VMA (Valve Manufacturers Assn of America)	1050 17th St NW Ste 280	Washington	DC	20036	**800-468-3571**	202-331-8105	48-13
VMC Consulting Corp	11611 Willows Rd NE	Redmond	WA	98052	**877-393-8622**	425-558-7700	719
VMI (Vantage Mobility International)	5202 S 28th Pl	Phoenix	AZ	85040	**800-348-8267**	602-243-2700	61-7
VNA	154 Hindman Rd	Butler	PA	16001	**877-862-6659**	724-282-6806	371
VNA (VNA Hospice Care)	11440 Olive Blvd Ste 200	Creve Coeur	MO	63141	**800-392-4740**	314-918-7171	371
VNA & Hospice of Northern California	1900 Powell St Ste 300	Emeryville	CA	94608	**800-698-1273**	510-450-8596	371
VNA & Hospice of Southern California	150 W First St Ste 270	Claremont	CA	91711	**888-357-3574**	909-624-3574	371
VNA Hospice & Home Health of Lackawanna County	301 Delaware Ave	Olyphant	PA	18447	**800-936-7671**	570-383-5180	371
VNA Hospice Care (VNA)	11440 Olive Blvd Ste 200	Creve Coeur	MO	63141	**800-392-4740**	314-918-7171	371
VNA of Central Jersey (VNACJ)	176 Riverside Ave	Red Bank	NJ	07701	**800-862-3330**		371
VNA of Greater St Louis — *Hospice Care*	11440 Olive Blvd Ste 200	Creve Coeur	MO	63141	**800-392-4740**	314-918-7171	371
Vna of Rhode Island	475 Kilvert St	Warwick	RI	02886	**800-638-6274**	401-574-4900	363
VNAA (Visiting Nurse Assns of America)	900 19th St NW Ste 200	Washington	DC	20006	**888-866-8773**	202-384-1420	48-8
VNACJ (VNA of Central Jersey)	176 Riverside Ave	Red Bank	NJ	07701	**800-862-3330**		371
Vocalink Language Services	405 W First St Unit A	Dayton	OH	45402	**877-492-7754**	937-223-1415	766
Vocantas Inc	750 Palladium Dr Ste 200	Ottawa	ON	K2V1C7	**877-271-8853**	613-271-8853	181
Vogelsang USA	7966 State Rt 44	Ravenna	OH	44266	**800-984-9400**	330-296-3820	638
Vogt Ice	1000 W Ormsby Ave Ste 19	Louisville	KY	40210	**800-853-8648**	502-635-3000	662
Vogue Optical Inc	20 Great George St	Charlottetown	PE	C1A4J6	**866-594-3937**	902-566-3326	542
Vogue Pool Products	7050 St Patrick St	LaSalle	QC	H8N1V2	**800-363-3232**	514-363-3232	726
Voice on the Go Inc	20 Amber St Ste 207	Markham	ON	L3R5P4	**877-977-0555**	905-305-1355	181
Voice Pro Inc	2055 Lee Rd Ste 101	Cleveland	OH	44118	**800-261-0104**	216-932-8040	763
Voice, The	51180 Bedford St	New Baltimore	MI	48047	**800-561-2248**	586-716-8100	531-4
Voicecom	5900 Windward Pkwy Ste 500	Alpharetta	GA	30005	**888-468-3554**		733
Voices of September 11th	161 Cherry St	New Canaan	CT	06840	**866-505-3911**	203-966-3911	47-5
VoIP Innovations Inc	8 Penn Ctr W Ste 101	Pittsburgh	PA	15276	**877-478-6471**		387
Volcano Corp	3721 Valley Centre Dr Ste 500	San Diego	CA	92130	**800-228-4728**		476
Volk Corp	23936 Industrial Pk Dr	Farmington Hills	MI	48335	**800-521-6799*** (*Cust Svc)	248-477-6700	466
Volkswagen Canada Inc	777 Bayly St W	Ajax	ON	L1S7G7	**800-822-8987**	905-428-6700	58
Volkswagen of America Inc	3800 Hamlin Rd	Auburn Hills	MI	48326	**800-822-8987**		58
Vollrath Co LLC, The	1236 N 18th St	Sheboygan	WI	53081	**800-624-2051**	920-457-4851	301
Vollwerth & Co	200 Hancock St PO Box 239	Hancock	MI	49930	**800-562-7620**	906-482-1550	297-26
Volt VIEWtech Inc	4761 E Hunter Ave	Anaheim	CA	92807	**888-396-9927**	714-695-3377	462
Volume Transportation Inc	6575 Marshall Blvd	Lithonia	GA	30058	**800-879-5565**	770-482-1400	778
Volunteer State Community College	1480 Nashville Pk	Gallatin	TN	37066	**888-335-8722**	615-452-8600	161
Volunteers of America	1660 Duke St	Alexandria	VA	22314	**800-899-0089**	703-341-5000	47-5
Volvo Cars of North America	1 Volvo Dr	Rockleigh	NJ	07647	**800-458-1552*** (*Cust Svc)	201-768-7300	58
Volvo Honolulu	704 Ala Moana Blvd	Honolulu	HI	96813	**888-892-2456**		515
Volvo Penta of the Americas Inc	1300 Volvo Penta Dr	Chesapeake	VA	23320	**800-522-1959**	757-436-2800	264
Vomela Co, The	274 E Fillmore Ave	Saint Paul	MN	55107	**800-645-1012**	651-228-2200	699
Von Duprin Inc	2720 Tobey Dr	Indianapolis	IN	46219	**800-999-0408**		200
Von Paris Enterprises Inc	8691 Larkin Rd	Savage	MD	20763	**800-866-6355**	410-888-8500	518
Von Roll Isola USA	200 Von Roll Dr	Schenectady	NY	12306	**800-654-7652**	518-344-7100	499
Vonage Holdings Corp (*NYSE: VG*)	23 Main St	Holmdel	NJ	07733	**877-862-2562**	732-528-2600	733
Vontobel Asset Management Inc	1540 Broad Way Ave 38th Fl	New York	NY	10036	**800-445-8872*** (*General)	212-415-7000	401
Vooner Flogard Corp	4729 Stockholm Ct	Charlotte	NC	28273	**800-345-7879**	704-552-9314	296
Voorhees College	213 Wiggins Dr PO Box 678	Denmark	SC	29042	**800-446-6250*** (*Admissions)	803-780-1234	167
Voorhees Pediatric Facility	1304 Laurel Oak Rd	Voorhees	NJ	08043	**888-873-5437**	856-346-3300	449
Voorwood Co	2350 Barney St	Anderson	CA	96007	**800-826-0089**	530-365-3311	819
Vornado Air Circulation Systems Inc	415 E 13th St	Andover	KS	67002	**800-234-0604**	316-733-0035	17
Vornado Realty Trust (*NYSE: VNO*)	888 Seventh Ave	New York	NY	10019	**800-294-1322**	212-894-7000	653
Voss Lighting	PO Box 22159	Lincoln	NE	68542	**866-292-0529**	402-328-2281	248
Voto Manufacturers Sales Co	500 N Third St PO Box 1299	Steubenville	OH	43952	**800-848-4010**	740-282-3621	385
VOX Data	1155 Metcalfe St 18th Fl	Montreal	QC	H3B2V6	**800-861-9599**	514-871-1920	734
Voxtechnologies Com	301 S Sherman St	Richardson	TX	75081	**888-568-6224**	972-234-4343	177
Voya Services Co	230 Park Ave	New York	NY	10169	**855-663-8692**	860-580-4646	391-3
Voyages Groupe Ideal Inc	5415 Pare St Ste 1	Montreal	QC	H4P1P7	**800-342-9554**	514-342-9554	773
Voyageur Lakewalk Inn	333 E Superior St	Duluth	MN	55802	**800-258-3911**	218-722-3911	379
Voyageur Transportation Services	573 Admiral Ct	London	ON	N5V4L3	**855-263-7163**	519-455-4580	106
Voyageurs National Park	360 Hwy 11 E	International Falls	MN	56649	**888-381-2873**	218-283-6600	563
VPI Corp	3123 S Ninth St	Sheboygan	WI	53081	**800-874-4240*** (*Orders)	920-458-4664	599
VPOP Technologies Inc	1772J Avenida de los Arboles Ste 374	Thousand Oaks	CA	91362	**888-811-8767*** (*Sales)	805-529-9374	806
VPSI Inc	1220 Rankin Dr	Troy	MI	48083	**800-826-7433**	248-597-3500	467
VPT (Vermont Public Television)	204 Ethan Allen Ave	Colchester	VT	05446	**800-639-7811**	802-655-4800	629
VRE (Virginia Railway Express)	1500 King St Ste 202	Alexandria	VA	22314	**800-743-3873**	703-684-1001	467
Vrp Consulting Inc	268 Bush St Ste 3836	San Francisco	CA	94104	**855-545-3877**		179
VS Management of NY Inc	3281 Veterans Memorial Hwy	Ronkonkoma	NY	11779	**877-778-7648**		630
Vsa Inc	6929 Seward Ave	Lincoln	NE	68507	**800-888-2140**	402-467-3668	248
VSAC (Vermont Student Assistance Corp)	PO Box 2000	Winooski	VT	05404	**800-642-3177**	802-655-9602	723
VSC (Vetter Stone Co)	23894 Third Ave	Mankato	MN	56001	**800-878-2850**	507-345-4568	722
VSE Corp (*NASDAQ: VSEC*)	2550 Huntington Ave	Alexandria	VA	22303	**800-455-4873**	703-960-4600	263
VSM Abrasives	1012 E Wabash St	O'Fallon	MO	63366	**800-737-0176*** (*Cust Svc)	636-272-7432	1
VSNA (Vermont State Nurses Assn)	100 Dorset St Ste 13	South Burlington	VT	05403	**800-540-9390**	802-651-8886	532
V-T Industries Inc	1000 Industrial Pk	Holstein	IA	51025	**800-827-1615**	712-368-4381	598
VTA (Santa Clara Valley Transportation Authority)	3331 N First St	San Jose	CA	95134	**800-894-9908**	408-321-5555	467
VTech Communications Inc	9590 SW Gemini Dr Ste 120	Beaverton	OR	97008	**800-595-9511**	503-596-1200	732
VTech Electronics North America LLC	1155 W Dundee St Ste 130	Arlington Heights	IL	60004	**800-521-2010**	847-400-3600	760
V-Technologies LLC	675 W Johnson Ave	Cheshire	CT	06705	**800-462-4016**		524
VTS Investigations LLC	PO Box 971	Elgin	IL	60121	**800-538-4464**		400
Vulcan Corp	30 Garfield Pl Ste 1040	Cincinnati	OH	45202	**800-447-1146*** (*Sales)	513-621-2850	674
Vulcan Inc	410 E Berry Ave	Foley	AL	36535	**888-846-2728**		152

Name / Address	City	State	ZIP	Toll-Free	Phone	Class
Vulcan Industries Inc 300 Display Dr	Moody	AL	35004	888-444-4417	205-640-2400	235
Vulcan Materials Co 1200 Urban Ctr Dr PO Box 385014 *NYSE: VMC*	Birmingham	AL	35238	800-615-4331	205-298-3000	502-5
Vulcan Materials Company Western Div 3200 San Fernando Rd *NYSE: VMC*	Los Angeles	CA	90065	800-615-4331	323-258-2777	502-5
Vulcan Service 5724 Hwy 280 E	Birmingham	AL	35242	800-841-9600		94
Vutec Corp 11711 W Sample Rd	Coral Springs	FL	33065	800-770-4700	954-545-9000	590
VVMA (Virginia Veterinary Medical Assn) 3801 Westerre Pkwy Ste D	Henrico	VA	23233	800-937-8862	804-346-2611	793
VWA (Vengroff Williams & Assoc Inc) 2099 S State College Bvld	Anaheim	CA	92806	800-238-9655	866-737-4344	159
VWR International 100 Matsonford Rd Bldg 1 Ste 200	Radnorpa	PA	19087	800-932-5000	610-431-1700	474
Vystar Credit Union 1802 Kernan Blvd S	Jacksonville	FL	32246	800-445-6289	904-777-6000	221

W

Name / Address	City	State	ZIP	Toll-Free	Phone	Class
W & H Co-op Oil Co 407 13th St N	Humboldt	IA	50548	800-392-3816	515-332-2782	325
W & H Systems Inc 120 Asia Pl	Carlstadt	NJ	07072	800-966-6993	201-933-7840	209
W A Baum Company Inc 620 Oak St	Copiague	NY	11726	888-281-6061	631-226-3940	475
W a m s Inc 1800 E Lambert Ave Ste 155	Brea	CA	92821	800-421-7151	714-994-2811	179
W Atlee Burpee Co 300 Pk Ave *Cust Svc	Warminster	PA	18974	800-333-5808*	215-674-4900	692
W L Halsey Grocery Company Inc PO Box 6485	Huntsville	AL	35824	800-621-0240	256-772-9691	298-8
W M Sprinkman Corp 4234 Courtney Rd	Franksville	WI	53126	800-816-1610	262-835-2390	386
W New York- Union Square 201 Park Ave S	New York	NY	10003	877-822-0000	212-253-9119	378
W O W Logistics Co 3040 W Wisconsin Ave	Appleton	WI	54914	800-236-3565	920-734-9924	801-1
W. N. Morehouse Truck Line Inc 4010 Dahlman Ave	Omaha	NE	68107	800-228-9378	402-733-2200	683
W. R. Vernon Produce Co PO Box 4054	Winston-Salem	NC	27101	800-222-6406	336-725-9741	298-7
W.B. Nelson State Recreation Site 5580 S Coast Hwy	Newport	OR	97366	800-551-6949		564
W.F. Taylor Company Inc 11545 Pacific Ave	Fontana	CA	92337	800-397-4583	951-360-6677	3
W.H. Breshears Inc 720 B St	Modesto	CA	95354	800-637-4427	209-522-7291	580
W/M Display Group 1040 W 40th St	Chicago	IL	60609	800-443-2000	773-254-3700	288
WA Brown & Son Inc 209 Long Meadow Dr	Salisbury	NC	28147	800-438-2316	704-636-5131	662
WA Charnstrom Co 5391 12th Ave E *Cust Svc	Shakopee	MN	55379	800-328-2962*		469
WA Roosevelt Co 2727 Commerce St	La Crosse	WI	54603	800-279-2726	608-781-2000	611
WAAY-TV Ch 31 (ABC) 1000 Monte Sano Blvd SE	Huntsville	AL	35801	888-407-4747	256-533-3131	738-37
Wabash College 410 W Wabash Ave PO Box 352	Crawfordsville	IN	47933	800-345-5385	765-361-6225	167
Wabash County Rural Electric Membership Corp 350 Wedcor Ave	Wabash	IN	46992	800-563-2146	260-563-2146	247
Wabash Electric Supply Inc 1400 S Wabash St	Wabash	IN	46992	800-552-7777	260-563-4146	248
Wabash National Corp 1000 Sagamore PkwyS PO Box 6129 *NYSE: WNC* ■ *Sales	Lafayette	IN	47903	866-877-5062*	765-771-5300	777
Wabash Technologies 1375 Swan St PO Box 829	Huntington	IN	46750	800-487-6865	260-355-4100	225
Wabash Telephone Co-op Inc PO Box 299	Louisville	IL	62858	800-228-9824	618-665-3311	733
Wabash Valley Manufacturing Inc 505 E Main St	Silver Lake	IN	46982	800-253-8619	260-352-2102	320-4
Wabash Valley Service Company Inc 909 N Ct St	Grayville	IL	62844	888-869-8127	618-375-2311	278
WABCO Locomotive Products 1001 Air Brake Ave *Cust Svc	Wilmerding	PA	15148	877-922-2627*	412-825-1000	648
Wabtec Corp 1001 Air Brake Ave *NYSE: WAB* ■ *Cust Svc	Wilmerding	PA	15148	877-922-2627*	412-825-1000	648
WACG-FM 90.7 (NPR) 2500 Walton Way	Atlanta	GA	30904	800-222-4788	706-737-1661	642-10
Wachovia Bank 3800 Wilshire Blvd Ste 110e	Los Angeles	CA	90025	800-225-5935	310-477-8004	69
Wachter Inc 16001 W 99th St	Lenexa	KS	66219	800-462-9638	913-541-2500	785
Wachters' Organic Sea Products Corp 550 Sylvan St	Daly City	CA	94014	800-682-7100	650-757-9851	797
Wacker Chemical Corp 3301 Sutton Rd	Adrian	MI	49221	888-922-5374	517-264-8500	143

Name / Address	City	State	ZIP	Toll-Free	Phone	Class
Wacker Neuson N 92 W 15000 Anthony Ave	Menomonee Falls	WI	53051	800-770-0957	262-255-0500	192
Waco 2546 Gen Armistead Ave	Norristown	PA	19403	800-928-7159	610-630-4800	18
Waco Convention & Visitors Bureau 100 Washington Ave	Waco	TX	76701	800-321-9226	254-750-5810	208
Waco Tribune-Herald 900 Franklin Ave	Waco	TX	76701	800-678-8742	254-757-5757	531-2
Wacoal America 50 Polito Ave	Lyndhurst	NJ	07071	800-922-6250	201-933-8400	154-17
Wacoal Europe 65 Sprague St	Hyde Park	MA	02136	800-733-8964	617-361-7559	154-17
Wacom Technology Corp 1311 SE Cardinal Ct	Vancouver	WA	98683	800-922-6613	360-896-9833	175-2
Waco-McLennan County Library 1717 Austin Ave	Waco	TX	76701	800-433-7300	254-750-5941	434-3
Waddell & Reed Financial Inc 6300 Lamar Ave *NYSE: WDR*	Overland Park	KS	66201	888-923-3355	913-236-2000	401
Wade College 1950 N Stemmons Fwy LB 562 Ste 4080	Dallas	TX	75207	800-624-4850	214-637-3530	798
Wade Tours Inc 797 Burdeck St	Schenectady	NY	12306	800-955-9233	518-355-4500	758
Wade-Trim Group Inc 500 Griswold Ave Ste 2500	Detroit	MI	48226	800-482-2864	313-961-3650	263
WAFB-TV Ch 9 (CBS) 844 Government St	Baton Rouge	LA	70802	888-677-2900	225-215-4700	738-9
Waggoners Trucking 5220 Midland Rd	Billings	MT	59101	800-999-9097	406-248-1919	778
Wagner College 1 Campus Rd *Admissions	Staten Island	NY	10301	800-221-1010*	718-390-3400	167
Wagner Oil Co 500 Commerce St Ste 600	Fort Worth	TX	76102	800-457-5332	817-335-2222	535
Wagner Spray Tech Corp 1770 Fernbrook Ln	Plymouth	MN	55447	800-328-8251	763-553-7000	174
Wago Corp N120 W19129 Freistadt Rd	Germantown	WI	53022	800-346-7245		205
Wah Chang 1600 Old Salem Rd NE	Albany	OR	97321	888-926-4211	541-926-4211	484
Wahl Clipper Corp 2900 Locust St	Sterling	IL	61081	800-767-9245		217
Wahl Refractory Solutions LLC 767 OH-19	Fremont	OH	43420	800-837-9245	419-334-2658	661
Wahlco Inc 2722 S Fairview St	Santa Ana	CA	92704	800-423-5432	714-979-7300	453
Wahlcometroflex Inc 29 Lexington St	Lewiston	ME	04240	800-272-6652	207-784-2338	479
Wah-Sha-She State Park HC 75 Hwy 60	Copan	OK	74022	800-622-6317	918-532-4334	564
WAIglobal 411 Eagleview Blvd Ste 100	Exton	PA	19341	800-877-3340	484-875-6600	60
Waikiki Parc Hotel 2233 Helumoa Rd	Honolulu	HI	96815	800-422-0450	808-921-7272	379
Waikiki Resort Hotel 2460 Koa Ave	Honolulu	HI	96815	800-367-5116	808-922-4911	379
Wailea Beach Marriott Resort & Spa 3700 Wailea Alanui Dr	Wailea	HI	96753	800-845-5279	808-879-1922	667
WAIQ-TV Ch 26 (PBS) 1255 Madison Ave	Montgomery	AL	36107	800-239-5239	205-328-8756	738-49
Waisman Ctr University of Wisconsin 1500 Highland Ave	Madison	WI	53705	888-428-8476	608-263-5940	666
Wajax Industrial Components LP 2200 52 Nd Ave	Lachine	QC	H8T2Y3	866-546-3267	514-636-3333	358
WAKA-TV Ch 8 (CBS) 3020 Eastern Blvd	Montgomery	AL	36116	800-467-0401	334-271-8888	738-49
Wake Correctional Ctr 1000 Rock Quarry Rd	Raleigh	NC	27610	866-719-0108	919-733-7988	215
Wake Electric 100 S Franklin St PO Box 1229	Wake Forest	NC	27588	800-474-6300	919-863-6300	247
Wake Forest University School of Medicine Medical Ctr Blvd	Winston-Salem	NC	27157	800-445-2255	336-716-4264	168-2
Wakefern Food Corp 600 York St	Elizabeth	NJ	07207	800-746-7748	908-527-3300	298-8
Wakefield's Inc 3100 McClellan Blvd Quintard Ave	Anniston	AL	36201	800-333-1552	256-237-9521	156-2
Wako Chemicals USA Inc 1600 Bellwood Rd	Richmond	VA	23237	800-992-9256	804-271-7677	233
Wakunaga of America Company Ltd 23501 Madero	Mission Viejo	CA	92691	800-421-2998	949-855-2776	797
WAKW-FM 93.3 (Rel) 6275 Collegevue Pl PO Box 24126	Cincinnati	OH	45224	888-542-9393	513-542-9259	642-29
Walch Education 40 Walch Dr	Portland	ME	04103	800-558-2846	207-772-2846	634-2
Wald Relocation Services Ltd 8708 W Little York Rd Ste 190	Houston	TX	77040	800-527-1408	713-512-4800	518
Waldbaums 2 Paragon Dr	Montvale	NJ	07645	866-443-7374		345
Walden Farms 1209 W St Georges Ave	Linden	NJ	07036	800-229-1706		297-19
Walden Woods Project, The 44 Baker Farm Rd	Lincoln	MA	01773	800-554-3569	781-259-4700	47-13
Waldinger Corp 2601 Bell Ave	Des Moines	IA	50321	800-473-4934	515-284-1911	191-14
Waldoch Crafts Inc 13821 Lake Dr NE	Forest Lake	MN	55025	800-328-9259	651-464-3215	61-7
Waldon Mfg LLC 201 W Oklahoma Ave	Fiarview	OK	73737	866-283-2759	580-227-3711	469
Waldorf College 106 S Sixth St	Forest City	IA	50436	800-292-1903	641-585-2450	167
Waldorf Towers, The 100 E 50th St	New York	NY	10022	800-925-3673	212-355-3100	379

Name / Address	City	State	ZIP	Toll-Free	Phone	Class
Wale Apparatus Co Inc 400 Front St	Hellertown	PA	18055	**800-334-9253**	610-838-7047	333
Walgreen Co 200 Wilmot Rd *Cust Svc	Deerfield	IL	60015	**800-925-4733***	847-940-2500	239
Walgreens Health Services 1411 Lake Cook Rd	Deerfield	IL	60015	**800-207-2568**		585
Walker Art Ctr 1750 Hennepin Ave	Minneapolis	MN	55403	**888-339-4496**	612-375-7600	519
Walker County Board of Education 1710 Alabama Ave PO Box 311	Jasper	AL	35501	**866-276-7735**	205-387-0555	683
Walker County Chamber of Commerce 10052 N Hwy 27	Rock Spring	GA	30739	**800-321-8128**	706-375-7702	138
Walker Industries Holdings Ltd 2800 Thorold Townline Rd	Niagara Falls	ON	L2E6S4	**866-694-9360**	905-227-4142	188
Walker Information Inc 301 Pennsylvania Pkwy	Indianapolis	IN	46280	**800-334-3939**	317-843-3939	465
Walker Magnetics Group Inc 20 Rockdale St	Worcester	MA	01606	**800-962-4638**	508-853-3232	492
Walker MS Inc 20 Third Ave	Somerville	MA	02143	**800-528-2787**	617-776-6700	79-1
Walker Process Equipment 840 N Russell Ave	Aurora	IL	60506	**800-992-5537**	630-892-7921	804
Walker Tool & Die Inc 2411 Walker Ave NW	Grand Rapids	MI	49544	**877-925-5378**	616-453-5471	755
Walker's Furniture Inc 3808 N Sullivan Rd Bldg 22-C	Spokane Valley	WA	99216	**866-667-6655**	509-535-1995	322
WALK-FM 97.5 (AC) 234 Airport Plz Ste 5	Farmingdale	NY	11735	**877-263-7995**	631-475-5200	643
Walking Adventures International 14612 NE Fourth Plain Rd Ste A	Vancouver	WA	98682	**800-779-0353**		758
WalkMed Infusion LLC 6555 S Kenton St Ste 304	Centennial	CO	80111	**800-578-0555**	303-420-9569	475
Wall Street Journal, The 1211 Ave of the Americas *General	New York	NY	10036	**800-568-7625***	212-416-2000	531-3
Walla Walla Community College 500 Tausick Way	Walla Walla	WA	99362	**877-992-9922**	509-522-2500	161
Walla Walla University 204 S College Ave	College Place	WA	99324	**800-541-8900**	509-527-2327	167
Walla Walla Valley Chamber of Commerce 29 E Sumach St	Walla Walla	WA	99362	**866-826-9422**	509-525-0850	138
Wallace b e Products Corp 71 N Bacton Hill Rd	Frazer	PA	19355	**800-553-5438**	610-647-1400	358
Wallace Community College 1141 Wallace Dr	Dothan	AL	36303	**800-543-2426**	334-983-3521	161
Wallace Community College Selma 3000 Earl Goodwin Pkwy	Selma	AL	36703	**855-428-8313**	334-876-9227	798
Wallace Hardware Company Inc 5050 S Davy Crockett Pkwy PO Box 6004	Morristown	TN	37815	**800-776-0976**	423-586-5650	351
Wallace Roberts & Todd LLC 1700 Market St 28th Fl	Philadelphia	PA	19103	**800-978-4450**	215-732-5215	263
Wallace State Community College 801 Main St	Hanceville	AL	35077	**866-350-9722**	256-352-8000	161
Wallace Welch Willingham 300 First Ave S 5th Fl	Saint Petersburg	FL	33701	**800-783-5085**	727-522-7777	390
Wallach & Company Inc 107 W Federal St	Middleburg	VA	20118	**800-237-6615**	540-687-3166	391-7
Wallco Inc 53 E Jackson St # 55	Wilkes-Barre	PA	18701	**800-392-5526**	570-823-6181	694
Wallcoverings Assn 401 N Michigan Ave Ste 2200	Chicago	IL	60611	**800-575-8016**	312-644-6610	48-4
Waller County 836 Austin St	Hempstead	TX	77445	**800-901-4412**	979-826-3357	338
Waller Truck Company Inc 400 S McCleary Rd	Excelsior Springs	MO	64024	**800-821-2196**	816-629-3400	778
Wallick & Volk Mortgage 222 E 18th St	Cheyenne	WY	82001	**800-280-8655**	307-634-5941	216
Wallingford Buick GMC 1122 Old N Colony Rd *Cust Svc	Wallingford	CT	06492	**866-582-4487***		56
Wallingford Coffee Mills Inc 11401 Rockfield Ct	Cincinnati	OH	45241	**800-533-3690**	513-771-4570	79-2
Wallis Oil Co 106 E Washington St	Cuba	MO	65453	**800-467-6652**	573-885-2277	325
Walls 360 Inc 5054 Bond St	Las Vegas	NV	89118	**888-244-9969**		393
Walman Optical Company Inc 801 12th Ave N	Minneapolis	MN	55411	**800-873-9256**	612-520-6000	541
Wal-Mart Foundation 702 SW Eigth St *NYSE: WMT*	Bentonville	AR	72716	**800-438-6278**	479-273-4000	305
Wal-Mart Stores Inc 702 SW Eigth St *NYSE: WMT* ■ *Cust Svc	Bentonville	AR	72716	**800-925-6278***	479-273-4000	231
Walmart.com 1919 Davis St	San Leandro	CA	94577	**800-925-6278**		231
Walnut Hollow Farm Inc 1409 State Rd 23	Dodgeville	WI	53533	**800-395-5995**	608-935-2341	281
Walpole Co-op Bank Inc 982 Main St	Walpole	MA	02081	**877-322-8228**	508-668-1080	69
Walpole Inc PO Box 1177	Okeechobee	FL	34973	**800-741-6500**	863-763-5593	778
Walpole Woodworkers Inc 767 E St Rt 7 *Cust Svc	Walpole	MA	02081	**800-343-6948***	508-668-2800	320-4
Walsh Group Inc 929 W Adams St	Chicago	IL	60607	**800-957-1842**	312-563-5400	188
Walsh Property Management PO Box 2657	Castro Valley	CA	94546	**888-896-5510**	510-888-8965	650
Walsh University 2020 E Maple St *Admissions	North Canton	OH	44720	**800-362-9846***	330-499-7090	167
Walsworth Publishing Co 306 N Kansas Ave	Marceline	MO	64658	**800-972-4968**	660-376-3543	634-2
Walt Disney World Dolphin 1500 Epcot Resorts Blvd	Lake Buena Vista	FL	32830	**888-828-8850**	407-934-4000	667
Walt Disney World Swan 1200 Epcot Resorts Blvd	Lake Buena Vista	FL	32830	**888-828-8850**	407-934-4000	667
Walt Whitman House State Historic Site 330 Mickle Blvd	Camden	NJ	08103	**800-843-6420**		564
Waltek Inc 14310 Sunfish Lk Blvd	Ramsey	MN	55303	**800-937-9496**	763-427-3181	307
Walter B Jones Alcohol & Drug Abuse Treatment Ctr 2577 W Fifth St	Greenville	NC	27834	**800-422-1884**	252-830-3426	724
Walter E Smithe Furniture Inc 1251 W Thorndale Ave	Itasca	IL	60143	**800-948-4263**	630-285-8000	320-2
Walter Haas & Sons Inc 123 W 23rd St	Hialeah	FL	33010	**800-552-3845**	305-883-2257	699
Walter Oil & Gas Corp 1100 Louisiana St Ste 200	Houston	TX	77002	**888-756-7880**	713-659-1221	537
Walter P Moore 1301 Mckinney St Ste 1100	Houston	TX	77010	**800-364-7300**	713-630-7300	263
Walter P Reuther Psychiatric Hospital 30901 Palmer Rd	Westland	MI	48186	**877-765-8388**	734-367-8400	374-5
Walter Snyder Printer Inc 691 River St	Troy	NY	12180	**888-272-9774**	518-272-8881	626
Walter USA Inc N22 W23855 Ridgeview Pkwy W	Waukesha	WI	53188	**800-945-5554**		492
Walters State Community College 500 S Davy Crockett Pkwy	Morristown	TN	37813	**800-225-4770**	423-585-2600	161
Walters Wholesale Electric Co 2825 Temple Ave	Signal Hill	CA	90755	**800-700-5483**	562-988-3100	248
Walthall Oil Company Inc 2510 Allen Rd	Macon	GA	31216	**800-633-5685**	478-781-1234	578
Waltham Services Inc 817 Moody St	Waltham	MA	02453	**866-974-7378**	781-893-1810	576
Walton Area Chamber of Commerce 63 S Centry Trl	Santa Rosa Beach	FL	32459	**800-435-7352**	850-267-0683	138
Walton Press (WP) 402 Mayfield Dr	Monroe	GA	30655	**800-354-0235**	770-267-2596	554
Walton-De Funiak Library 3 Cir Dr	DeFuniak Springs	FL	32435	**800-342-0141**	850-892-3624	434-3
Walts Mailing Service Ltd 9610 E First Ave	Spokane Valley	WA	99206	**888-549-2006**	509-924-5939	5
WALZ Label & Mailing Systems 624 High Point Ln	East Peoria	IL	61611	**877-971-1500**	309-698-1500	534
WAMC/Northeast Public Radio 318 Central Ave	Albany	NY	12206	**800-323-9262**	518-465-5233	629
WAMC-FM 90.3 (NPR) 318 Central Ave	Albany	NY	12206	**800-323-9262**	518-465-5233	642-3
Wang Theatre 270 Tremont St	Boston	MA	02116	**800-982-2787**		571
Wanke Cascade Co 6330 N Cutter Cir	Portland	OR	97217	**800-365-5053**	503-289-8609	361
WAPE-FM 95.1 (CHR) 8000 Belfort Pkwy Ste 100	Jacksonville	FL	32256	**800-475-9595**	904-245-8500	642-60
Wapusk National Park of Canada PO Box 127	Churchill	MB	R0B0E0	**888-773-8888**	204-675-8863	562
War Resisters League 339 Lafayette St	New York	NY	10012	**800-975-9688**	212-228-0450	47-5
Ward Cedar Log Homes 37 Bangor St PO Box 72 *Cust Svc	Houlton	ME	04730	**800-341-1566***		105
Ward Manufacturing LLC 117 Gulick St	Blossburg	PA	16912	**800-248-1027**	570-638-2131	611
Ward's Food Systems Inc 5133 Lincoln Rd Ext	Hattiesburg	MS	39402	**800-748-9273**	601-268-9273	668
Ward's Marine Electric Inc 617 SW Third Ave	Fort Lauderdale	FL	33315	**800-545-9273**	954-523-2815	785
Warde Medical Laboratory 300 W Textile Rd	Ann Arbor	MI	48108	**800-876-6522**	734-214-0300	415
Ward-Kraft Inc 2401 Cooper St	Fort Scott	KS	66701	**800-821-4021**	620-223-5500	109
Ware County Board of Education 1301 Bailey St	Waycross	GA	31501	**800-419-3191**	912-283-8656	188
Warehouse Home Furnishings Distributors Inc 1851 Telfair St PO Box 1140	Dublin	GA	31021	**800-456-0424**		322
Warex Terminals Corp 1 S Water St PO Box 488	Newburgh	NY	12550	**800-724-0818**	845-561-4000	578
Warm Co 5529 186th Pl SW	Lynnwood	WA	98037	**800-234-9276**	425-248-2424	742-1
Warner Bros Entertainment Inc 4000 Warner Blvd	Burbank	CA	91522	**800-778-7879**	818-954-1853	513
Warner Electric 449 Gardner St	South Beloit	IL	61080	**800-825-6544**	815-389-3771	619
Warner Home Video 4000 Warner Blvd Bldg 168	Burbank	CA	91522	**866-373-4389**		513
Warner Manufacturing Co 13435 Industrial Pk Blvd	Plymouth	MN	55441	**800-444-0606**	763-559-4740	756
Warner Pacific College 2219 SE 68th Ave	Portland	OR	97215	**800-804-1510**	503-517-1020	167
Warner Southern College 13895 Hwy 27	Lake Wales	FL	33859	**800-309-9563**		167
Warner Vineyards Inc 706 S Kalamazoo St	Paw Paw	MI	49079	**800-756-5357**	269-657-3165	79-3
Warp Bros Flex-O-Glass Inc 4647 W Augusta Blvd	Chicago	IL	60651	**800-621-3345**	773-261-5200	547
Warrantech Corp Inc 2200 Hwy 121	Bedford	TX	76021	**800-833-8801**	817-785-6601	367
Warranty Group Inc, The 175 W Jackson 11th Fl	Chicago	IL	60604	**800-621-2130**	312-356-3000	391-5
Warranty Life Services Inc 4152 Meridian St Ste 105-29	Bellingham	WA	98226	**888-927-7269**		393
Warren Co, The 2201 Loveland Ave	Erie	PA	16506	**800-562-0357**		296
Warren Communications News Inc 2115 Ward Ct NW	Washington	DC	20037	**800-771-9202**	202-872-9200	634-9
Warren Correctional Institution 379 Collins Rd	Manson	NC	27553	**866-719-0108**	252-456-3400	215

Name / Address	City	State	Zip	Toll-Free	Phone	Class
Warren County Rural Electric Membership Corp 15 Midway St PO Box 37	Williamsport	IN	47993	**800-872-7319**	765-762-6114	247
Warren County Visitors Bureau 22045 Rt 6	Warren	PA	16365	**800-624-7802**	814-726-1222	208
Warren County-Vicksburg Public Library 700 Veto St	Vicksburg	MS	39180	**800-721-7222**	601-636-6411	434-3
Warren Electric Co-op Inc (WEC) 320 E Main St PO Box 208	Youngsville	PA	16371	**800-364-8640**	814-563-7548	247
Warren Equities Inc 27 Warren Way	Providence	RI	02905	**866-867-4075**	401-781-9900	360-3
Warren Gibson Ltd 206 Church St South PO Box 100	Alliston	ON	L9R1T9	**800-461-4374**	705-435-4342	477
Warren Oil Company Inc PO Box 1507	Dunn	NC	28335	**800-779-6456**	910-892-6456	578
Warren Printing & Mailing Inc 5000 Eagle Rock Blvd	Los Angeles	CA	90041	**888-468-6976**	323-258-2621	626
Warren Properties Inc PO Box 469114	Escondido	CA	92046	**800-831-0804**		653
Warren Resources Inc 1114 Ave of the Americas 34th Fl *NASDAQ: WRES*	New York	NY	10036	**877-587-9494**	212-697-9660	535
Warren Rural Electric Co-op Corp 951 Fairview Ave	Bowling Green	KY	42101	**866-319-3234**	270-842-6541	247
Warren Transport Inc 210 Beck Ave *General	Waterloo	IA	50701	**800-553-2007***	319-233-6113	778
Warren Wilson College 701 Warren Wilson Rd *Admissions	Swannanoa	NC	28778	**800-934-3536***	828-298-3325	167
Warrior Custom Golf Inc 15 Mason Ste A	Irvine	CA	92618	**800-600-5113**	949-699-2499	709
Warsaw Chemical Company Inc Argonne Rd PO Box 858	Warsaw	IN	46580	**800-548-3396**	574-267-3251	150
Wartburg College 100 Wartburg Blvd	Waverly	IA	50677	**800-772-2085**	319-352-8264	167
Wartburg Theological Seminary 333 Wartburg Pl	Dubuque	IA	52003	**800-225-5987**	563-589-0200	168-3
Wartsila North America Inc 16330 Air Ctr Blvd	Houston	TX	77032	**877-927-8745**	281-233-6200	264
Warwick Denver Hotel 1776 Grant St	Denver	CO	80203	**800-203-3232**	303-861-2000	379
Warwick Melrose Hotel 3015 Oak Lawn Ave	Dallas	TX	75219	**800-521-7172**	214-521-5151	379
Warwick New York Hotel 65 W 54th St	New York	NY	10019	**800-223-4099**	212-247-2700	379
Warwick Seattle Hotel 401 Lenora St	Seattle	WA	98121	**800-426-9280**	206-443-4300	379
Warwick Valley Telephone Co 47 Main St PO Box 592 *NASDAQ: WWVY* ■ *Cust Svc	Warwick	NY	10990	**800-952-7642***	845-986-8080	733
Wasatch Academy 120 South 100 West	Mount Pleasant	UT	84647	**800-634-4690**	435-462-1400	621
Wasco Electric Co-op Inc 105 E Fourth St	The Dalles	OR	97058	**800-341-8580**	541-296-2740	247
Wasco Products Inc 85 Spencer Dr Unit A	Wells	ME	04073	**800-388-0293**	207-324-8060	330
WASH Multifamily Laundry Systems 100 N Sepulveda Blvd 12th Fl *General	El Segundo	CA	90245	**800-421-6897***		37
Washburn University 1700 SW College Ave	Topeka	KS	66621	**800-736-9060**	785-670-1010	167
WASH-FM 97.1 (AC) 1801 Rockville Pk Ste 601	Rockville	MD	20852	**866-927-4361**	240-747-2700	643
Washington						
Child Support Div PO Box 11520	Olympia	WA	98411	**800-442-5437**		339-48
Financial Institutions Dept PO Box 41200	Olympia	WA	98504	**877-746-4334**	360-902-8703	339-48
Health Dept PO Box 47890	Olympia	WA	98504	**800-525-0127**	360-236-4501	339-48
Historical Society 1911 Pacific Ave	Tacoma	WA	98402	**888-238-4373**	253-272-3500	339-48
Housing Finance Commission 1000 Second Ave Ste 2700	Seattle	WA	98104	**800-767-4663**	206-464-7139	339-48
Natural Resources Dept 1111 Washington St SE PO Box 47000	Olympia	WA	98504	**800-258-5990**	360-902-1000	339-48
Revenue Dept PO Box 47478	Olympia	WA	98504	**800-647-7706**	360-705-6714	339-48
Social & Health Services Dept PO Box 45130	Olympia	WA	98504	**800-737-0617**	360-902-8400	339-48
State Parks & Recreation Commission 1111 Israel Rd SW *Campground Resv	Olympia	WA	98504	**888-226-7688***	360-902-8500	339-48
Utilities & Transportation Commission 1300 S Evergreen Pk Dr SW PO Box 47250	Olympia	WA	98504	**888-333-9882**	360-664-1160	339-48
Veterans Affairs Dept PO Box 41150	Olympia	WA	98504	**800-562-2308**	360-753-5586	339-48
Vocational Rehabilitation Div PO Box 45340	Olympia	WA	98504	**800-637-5627**	360-438-8000	339-48
Washington & Jefferson College 60 S Lincoln St	Washington	PA	15301	**888-926-3529**	724-222-4400	167
Washington & Lee University 204 W Washington St	Lexington	VA	24450	**800-221-3943**	540-458-8710	167
Washington Adventist University 7600 Flower Ave	Takoma Park	MD	20912	**800-835-4212**	301-891-4000	167
Washington Assn of Realtors 504 14th Ave SE Ste 200 *General	Olympia	WA	98501	**800-562-6024***	360-943-3100	654
Washington Bill Status PO Box 40600	Olympia	WA	98504	**800-562-6000**	360-786-7573	433
Washington Chain & Supply Inc 2901 Utah Ave S PO Box 3645	Seattle	WA	98124	**800-851-3429**	206-623-8500	768
Washington College 300 Washington Ave	Chestertown	MD	21620	**800-422-1782**	410-778-2800	167
Washington Convention Ctr Authority 801 Mt Vernon Pl NW	Washington	DC	20001	**800-368-9000**	202-249-3000	207
Washington County Chamber of Commerce 314 S Austin St	Brenham	TX	77833	**888-273-6426**	979-836-3695	138
Washington County Library 8595 Central Pk Pl	Woodbury	MN	55125	**800-657-3750**	651-275-8500	434-3
Washington County Mental Health Services Inc (WCMHS) PO Box 647	Montpelier	VT	05601	**800-649-2642**	802-229-0591	353
Washington County Tractor Inc PO Box 1619	Brenham	TX	77834	**800-256-5655**	979-836-4591	276
Washington County Visitors Assn 12725 SW Millikan Way Ste 210	Beaverton	OR	97005	**800-537-3149**	503-644-5555	208
Washington Court Hotel 525 New Jersey Ave NW	Washington	DC	20001	**800-321-3010**	202-628-2100	379
Washington DC Accommodations 2201 Wisconsin Ave NW Ste C-120	Washington	DC	20007	**800-503-3330**	202-289-2220	376
Washington DC Convention & Tourism Corp 901 Seventh St NW 4th Fl	Washington	DC	20001	**800-422-8644**	202-789-7000	208
Washington Dental Service 9706 Fourth Ave NE	Seattle	WA	98115	**800-367-4104**	206-522-1300	391-3
Washington Duke Inn & Golf Club 3001 Cameron Blvd	Durham	NC	27705	**800-443-3853**	919-490-0999	379
Washington Education Assn Inc 32032 Weyerhaeuser Way S PO Box 9100	Federal Way	WA	98001	**800-622-3393**	253-941-6700	48-5
Washington Electric Co-op 40 Church St	East Montpelier	VT	05602	**800-932-5245**	802-223-5245	247
Washington Electric Co-op Inc 406 Colegate Dr	Marietta	OH	45750	**877-594-9324**	740-373-2141	247
Washington Electric Membership Corp 258 N Harris St	Sandersville	GA	31082	**800-552-2577**	478-552-2577	247
Washington Express Service LLC 12240 Indian Creek Ct Ste 100	Beltsville	MD	20705	**800-939-5463**	301-210-0899	545
Washington Federal Inc 425 Pike St *NASDAQ: WAFD*	Seattle	WA	98101	**800-324-9375**	206-624-7930	360-2
Washington Floral Service Inc 2701 S 35th St	Tacoma	WA	98409	**800-351-5515**	253-472-8343	294
Washington Gas & Light Co 6801 Industrial Rd	Springfield	VA	22151	**800-752-7520**	703-750-4440	785
Washington Hospital Ctr 110 Irving St NW	Washington	DC	20010	**855-546-1686**	202-877-7000	374-3
Washington Internet Daily 2115 Ward Ct NW	Washington	DC	20037	**800-771-9202**	202-872-9200	530-3
Washington Jefferson LLC 318 W 51st St	New York	NY	10019	**888-567-7550**	212-246-7550	378
Washington Lawyer Magazine 1101 K St NW Ste 200	Washington	DC	20005	**877-333-2227**	202-737-4700	456-15
Washington Local Schools 3505 W Lincolnshire Blvd	Toledo	OH	43606	**800-462-3589**	419-473-8251	188
Washington Missourian 14 W Main St PO Box 336	Washington	MO	63090	**888-239-7701**	636-239-7701	531-4
Washington Mystics 627 N Glebe Rd Ste 850	Arlington	VA	22203	**877-962-2849**	202-266-2200	712-2
Washington National Insurance Co 11825 N Pennsylvania St	Carmel	IN	46032	**866-595-2255**		391-2
Washington Pavilion of Arts & Science 301 S Main PO Box 984	Sioux Falls	SD	57104	**877-927-4728**	605-367-6000	519
Washington Plaza Hotel 10 Thomas Cir NW Massachusetts Ave at 14th St	Washington	DC	20005	**800-424-1140**	202-842-1300	379
Washington Post 1301 K St NW	Washington	DC	20071	**800-627-1150**	202-334-6000	531-2
Washington Post Writers Group 1150 15th St NW	Washington	DC	20071	**800-879-9794**	202-334-6375	529
Washington Real Estate Investment Trust (WRIT) 1775 I St NW *NYSE: WRE*	Washington	DC	20006	**800-565-9748**	301-984-9400	653
Washington School District Inc 201 Allison Ave	Washington	PA	15301	**855-846-8376**	724-223-5085	683
Washington Square Hotel 103 Waverly Pl	New York	NY	10011	**800-222-0418**	212-777-9515	379
Washington State Bar Assn 1325 Fourth Ave Ste 600	Seattle	WA	98101	**800-945-9722**	206-727-8200	71
Washington State Bar News 1325 Fourth Ave Ste 600	Seattle	WA	98101	**800-945-9722**		456-15
Washington State Employees Credit Union 330 Union Ave SE	Olympia	WA	98501	**800-562-0999**	360-943-7911	221
Washington State Lottery PO Box 43000	Olympia	WA	98504	**800-732-5101**	360-664-4720	451
Washington State Medical Assn 2033 Sixth Ave Ste 1100	Seattle	WA	98121	**800-552-0612**	206-441-9762	473
Washington State Nurses Assn (WSNA) 575 Andover Pk W Ste 101	Seattle	WA	98188	**800-231-8482**	206-575-7979	532
Washington State Pharmacy Assn 411 Williams Ave S	Renton	WA	98057	**800-562-6000**	425-228-7171	584
Washington State University PO Box 641040	Pullman	WA	99164	**888-468-6978**	509-335-3564	167
Spokane 310 N Riverpoint Blvd PO Box 1495	Spokane	WA	99210	**800-233-3247**	509-358-7978	167
Washington State Veterinary Medical Assn 8024 Bracken Pl SE	Snoqualmie	WA	98065	**800-399-7862**	425-396-3191	793
Washington Trust Bancorp Inc 23 Broad St *NASDAQ: WASH*	Westerly	RI	02891	**800-475-2265**	401-348-1200	360-2
Washington University in Saint Louis Campus Box 1089	Saint Louis	MO	63130	**800-638-0700**	314-935-5000	167
Washington-Saint Tammany Electric Co-op 950 Pearl St PO Box N	Franklinton	LA	70438	**866-672-9773**	985-839-3562	247
Wasserstrom Co 477 S Front St	Columbus	OH	43215	**866-634-8927**	614-228-6525	301
Waste Industries USA Inc 3301 Benson Dr Ste 601	Raleigh	NC	27609	**800-647-9946**	919-325-3000	802
Waste Management Inc 1001 Fannin St Ste 4000 *NYSE: WM*	Houston	TX	77002	**800-633-7871**	713-512-6200	802
Wastecorp Inc PO Box 70	Grand Island	NY	14072	**888-829-2783**		638

Name / Address	City	State	Zip	Toll-Free	Phone	Class
Watanabe Floral Inc 1607 Hart St	Honolulu	HI	96817	**888-832-9360**	808-832-9360	294
WatchGuard Technologies Inc 505 Fifth Ave S Ste 500 *Sales	Seattle	WA	98104	**800-734-9905***	206-613-6600	178
Watco Companies LLC 315 W Third St	Pittsburg	KS	66762	**866-386-9321**	620-231-2230	648
Watcon Inc 2215 S Main St	South Bend	IN	46613	**800-492-8266**	574-287-3397	144
Water Country USA 176 Water Country Pkwy	Williamsburg	VA	23185	**800-343-7946**		32
Water Environment Federation (WEF) 601 Wythe St	Alexandria	VA	22314	**800-666-0206**	703-684-2400	47-13
Water Furnace International Inc 9000 Conservation Way	Fort Wayne	IN	46809	**800-222-5667**	260-478-5667	357
Water Pik Inc 1730 E Prospect Rd	Fort Collins	CO	80553	**800-525-2774**		230
Water Saver Faucet Co 701 W Erie St *Parts	Chicago	IL	60654	**800-973-7278***	312-666-5500	608
Water Street 131 N Water St	Edgartown	MA	02539	**800-225-6005**	508-627-7000	669
Water Tech Online 19 British American Blvd W	Latham	NY	12110	**888-431-2877**		530-5
Water's Edge Resort & Spa 1525 Boston Post Rd PO Box 688	Westbrook	CT	06498	**800-222-5901**	860-399-5901	667
Waterbury Button Co 1855 Peck Ln	Cheshire	CT	06410	**800-928-1812**		593
Waterco USA Inc 1864 Tobacco Rd *General	Augusta	GA	30906	**800-277-4150***	706-793-7291	804
Waterfield Technologies Inc 1 W Third St Ste 1115	Tulsa	OK	74103	**800-324-0936**	918-858-6400	140
Waterford Township Public Library 5168 Civic Ctr Dr	Waterford	MI	48329	**800-318-2596**	248-674-4831	434-3
Waterford, The 601 Universe Blvd	Juno Beach	FL	33408	**888-335-1678**	561-627-3800	670
Waterfront Hotel 10 Washington St	Oakland	CA	94607	**888-842-5333**	510-836-3800	379
Waterloo Cedar Falls Courier PO Box 540	Waterloo	IA	50701	**800-798-1730**	319-291-1421	531-2
Waterloo Convention & Visitor Bureau 500 Jefferson St	Waterloo	IA	50701	**800-728-8431**	319-233-8350	208
Waterloo Industries Inc 139 W Forest Hill Ave *Cust Svc	Oak Creek	WI	53154	**800-558-5528***		487
Watermark Learning Inc 7300 Metro Blvd Ste 207	Minneapolis	MN	55439	**800-646-9362**	952-921-0900	196
Watermark Medical LLC 1641 Worthington Rd Ste 320	West Palm Beach	FL	33409	**877-710-6999**		252
Waterous Co 125 Hardman Ave	South Saint Paul	MN	55075	**800-488-1228**	651-450-5000	638
Waters Corp 34 Maple St *NYSE: WAT*	Milford	MA	01757	**800-252-4752**	508-478-2000	419
Waters Edge Hotel 25 Main St	Tiburon	CA	94920	**888-662-9555**	415-789-5999	379
Watersaver Company Inc 5870 E 56th Ave	Commerce	CO	80022	**800-525-2424**	303-289-1818	599
Waterstone Group Inc, The 1145 W Main Ave Ste 209	De Pere	WI	54115	**800-291-3836**	920-964-0333	262
Watertech Whirlpool Bath & Spa 2507 Plymouth Rd	Johnson City	TN	37601	**800-289-8827**		375
Waterton Lakes Lodge Resort 101 Clematis Ave PO Box 4	Waterton Park	AB	T0K2M0	**888-985-6343**	403-859-2150	667
Watertown Daily Times 260 Washington St	Watertown	NY	13601	**800-642-6222**	315-782-1000	531-2
Watertown Free Public Library 123 Main St	Watertown	MA	02472	**800-829-3676**	617-972-6431	434-3
Watertown Public Library 100 S Water St	Watertown	WI	53094	**800-829-3676**	920-262-4090	434-3
Waterville Valley Resort 1 Ski Area Rd PO Box 540	Waterville Valley	NH	03215	**800-468-2553**	603-236-8311	667
Waterworks Operating Company LLC 60 Backus Ave	Danbury	CT	06810	**800-899-6757**	203-546-6000	608
Watkins College of Art & Design 2298 Rose Parks Blvd	Nashville	TN	37228	**866-877-6395**	615-383-4848	163
Watkins Mfg Corp 1280 Pk Ctr Dr	Vista	CA	92081	**800-999-4688**		375
Watlow Winona 1241 Bundy Blvd	Winona	MN	55987	**800-928-5692**	507-454-5300	204
Watrous Nursing Ctr 9 Neck Rd	Madison	CT	06443	**877-696-6775**	203-245-9483	449
Watson Foods Company Inc 301 Heffernan Dr	West Haven	CT	06516	**800-388-3481**	203-932-3000	297-16
Watson Furniture Group Inc 26246 Twelve Trees Ln NW	Poulsbo	WA	98370	**800-426-1202**	360-394-1300	320-1
Watson Label Products 10616 Trenton Ave	Saint Louis	MO	63132	**800-678-6715**	314-493-9300	626
Watson Rice & Co 301 Rt 17 N	Rutherford	NJ	07070	**800-945-5985**	201-460-4590	2
Watson SCS Inc 12157 W Linebaugh Ave Ste 381	Tampa	FL	33626	**866-805-6066**		182
Watsontown Trucking Company Inc 60 Belford Blvd	Milton	PA	17847	**800-344-0313**	570-522-9820	778
Watt Printing Co 4544 Hinckley Industrial Pkwy	Cleveland	OH	44109	**800-273-2170**	216-398-2000	626
Watts Radiant Inc 4500 E Progress Pl	Springfield	MO	65803	**800-276-2419**	417-864-6108	14
Watts Towers of Simon Rodia State Historic Park 1765 E 107th St 1925 Las Virgenes	Calabasas	CA	91302	**866-240-4655**	213-847-4646	564
WAUK-AM 540 (Sports) 310 W Wisconsin Ave Ste 100	Milwaukee	WI	53203	**800-990-3776**	414-273-3776	642-76
Waukesha Bearings Corp W 231 N 2811 Roundy Cir E Ste 200	Pewaukee	WI	53072	**888-832-3517**	262-506-3000	619
Waukesha Cherry-Burrell Corp (WCB) 611 Sugar Creek Rd	Delavan	WI	53115	**800-252-5200**	262-728-1900	638
Waukesha County Chamber of Commerce 2717 N Grandview Blvd Ste 204	Waukesha	WI	53188	**800-727-1344**	262-542-4249	138
Waukesha County Freeman 801 N Barstow St PO Box 7	Waukesha	WI	53187	**800-762-6219**	262-542-2501	531-2
Waukesha Electric Systems Inc 400 S Prairie Ave	Waukesha	WI	53186	**800-835-2732**	262-547-0121	765
Waukesha Foundry Company Inc 1300 Lincoln Ave	Waukesha	WI	53186	**800-727-0741**	262-542-0741	308
Waukesha Memorial Hospital 725 American Ave	Waukesha	WI	53188	**800-326-2011**	262-928-1000	374-3
Waupaca Elevator Co Inc 1726 N BallaRd Rd	Appleton	WI	54911	**800-238-8739**	920-991-9082	258
Waupaca Foundry 1955 Brunner Dr PO Box 249	Waupaca	WI	54981	**800-669-6820**	715-258-6611	308
Wausau Central Wisconsin Convention & Visitors Bureau (CWCVB) 219 Jefferson St Ste B	Wausau	WI	54403	**888-948-4748**	715-355-8788	208
Wausau Chemical Corp 2001 N River Dr	Wausau	WI	54403	**800-950-6656**	715-842-2285	143
Wausau Daily Herald 800 Scott St	Wausau	WI	54403	**800-477-4838**	715-842-2101	531-2
Wausau Financial Systems Inc 400 Wes2od Dr Ste 100	Wausau	WI	54455	**800-937-0017**	715-359-0427	180-10
Wausau Paper Corp 100 Paper Pl *NYSE: WPP*	Mosinee	WI	54455	**800-723-0008**	715-693-4470	551-1
Wausau Paper Corp Printing & Writing Paper Div 1 Clark's Island	Wausau	WI	54403	**800-723-0008**	715-693-4470	551-2
Wausau Paper Corp Specialty Paper Div 100 Paper Pl	Mosinee	WI	54455	**800-723-0008**	715-693-4470	551-1
Wausau Tile Inc PO Box 1520	Wausau	WI	54402	**800-388-8728**	715-359-3121	185
WaUSAu Window & Wall Systems 7800 International Dr	Wausau	WI	54401	**877-678-2983**	715-845-2161	479
Wauwinet, The 120 Wauwinet Rd PO Box 2580	Nantucket	MA	02584	**800-426-8718**	508-228-0145	379
WAV Inc 2380 Prospect Dr	Aurora	IL	60504	**800-678-2419**	630-818-1000	178
WAVA-AM 780 (Rel) 1901 N Moore St Ste 200	Arlington	VA	22209	**888-976-6924**	703-807-2266	643
WAVA-FM 105.1 (Rel) 1901 N Moore St Ste 200	Arlington	VA	22209	**888-293-9282**	703-807-2266	643
Wave Systems Corp 480 Pleasant St *NASDAQ: WAVX*	Lee	MA	01238	**800-928-3638**	413-243-1600	180-1
Wavedivision Holdings LLC 401 Kirkland Prk Pl Ste 500	Kirkland	WA	98033	**866-928-3123**	425-576-8200	733
WaveLink Corp 1011 Western Ave Ste 601 *Tech Supp	Seattle	WA	98104	**888-697-9283***	206-274-4280	180-7
Waverly Plastics Company Inc PO Box 801	Waverly	IA	50677	**800-454-6377**	319-352-3333	65
WAVE-TV Ch 3 (NBC) 725 S Floyd St PO Box 32970	Louisville	KY	40203	**800-223-2579**	502-585-2201	738-45
WAVV-FM 101.1 (AC) 11800 Tamiami Trl E	Naples	FL	34113	**866-310-9288**	239-775-9288	642-80
Wawa Inc 260 W Baltimore Pike	Media	PA	19063	**800-444-9292**	610-358-8000	206
Waxman Industries Inc 24460 Aurora Rd *OTC: WXMN*	Bedford Heights	OH	44146	**800-201-7298**	440-439-1830	611
WAXN-TV Ch 64 (ABC) 1901 N Tryon St	Charlotte	NC	28206	**855-336-0360**	704-335-4786	738-16
WAXQ-FM 104.3 (CR) 32 Ave of the Americas	New York	NY	10013	**888-872-1043**	212-377-7900	642-83
Way Station Inc 230 W Patrick St PO Box 3826	Frederick	MD	21705	**888-549-0629**	301-662-0099	47-15
Wayest Safety Inc 3750 N I-44 Service Rd	Oklahoma City	OK	73112	**800-256-1003**	405-942-7101	677
Wayland Academy 101 N University Ave	Beaver Dam	WI	53916	**800-860-7725**	920-885-3373	621
Wayland Baptist University 1900 W Seventh St	Plainview	TX	79072	**800-588-1928**	806-291-1000	167
Waymouth Farms Inc 5300 Boone Ave	New Hope	MN	55428	**800-527-0094**	763-533-5300	297-8
Wayne Bank 717 Main St	Honesdale	PA	18431	**800-598-5002**	570-253-1455	360-2
Wayne Combustion Systems 801 Glasgow Ave	Fort Wayne	IN	46803	**855-929-6327**	260-425-9200	357
Wayne Community College 3000 Wayne Memorial Dr PO Box 8002	Goldsboro	NC	27533	**866-414-5064**	919-735-5151	161
Wayne County Boot Camp PO Box 182	Clifton	TN	38425	**855-876-7283**	931-676-3345	215
Wayne County Convention & Visitors Bureau 428 W Liberty St	Wooster	OH	44691	**800-362-6474**	330-264-1800	208
Wayne Farms LLC 4110 Continental Dr	Oakwood	GA	30566	**800-392-0844**		10-7
Wayne Hummer Investments LLC 222 S Riverside Pz 28th Fl	Chicago	IL	60606	**800-621-4477**	866-943-4732	688
Wayne J Griffin Electric Inc 116 Hopping Brook Rd	Holliston	MA	01746	**800-421-0151**		191-4
Wayne Kiltz Africa Imports 240 S Main St Unit A	South Hackensack	NJ	07606	**800-500-6120**	201-457-1995	818
Wayne Mills Co Inc 130 W Berkley St	Philadelphia	PA	19144	**800-220-8053**	215-842-2134	742-5
Wayne Pipe & Supply Inc 6040 Innovation Blvd	Fort Wayne	IN	46818	**800-552-3697**	260-423-9577	611
Wayne Savings Bancshares Inc 151 N Market St *NASDAQ: WAYN*	Wooster	OH	44691	**800-414-1103**	330-264-5767	360-2
Wayne State College 1111 Main St	Wayne	NE	68787	**800-228-9972**	402-375-7000	167
Wayne State University 42 W Warren	Detroit	MI	48202	**877-978-4636**	313-577-3577	167

Name	Address	City	State	ZIP	Toll-Free	Phone	Class
Wayne-Dalton Corp	1 Door Dr PO Box 67	Mount Hope	OH	44660	**800-827-3667**	330-674-7015	236
Waynesburg College	51 W College St *Admissions	Waynesburg	PA	15370	**800-225-7393***	724-627-8191	167
Waynesville Inn Golf & Country Club, The	176 Country Club Dr	Waynesville	NC	28786	**800-627-6250**	828-456-3551	667
Wayne-White Counties Electric Co-op	1501 W Main St	Fairfield	IL	62837	**888-871-7695**	618-842-2196	247
Wayside Furniture Inc	1367 Canton Rd	Akron	OH	44312	**877-499-3968**	330-733-6221	322
WAYV-FM 95.1 (CHR)	8025 Black Horse Pike	West Atlantic City	NJ	08232	**888-966-8146**	609-484-8444	643
WAYZ-FM 104.7 (Ctry)	10960 John Wayne Dr	Greencastle	PA	17225	**888-950-1047**	717-597-9200	643
WB Bottle Supply Company Inc	3400 S Clement Ave	Milwaukee	WI	53207	**800-738-3931**	414-482-4300	333
WBAL-TV Ch 11 (NBC)	3800 Hooper Ave	Baltimore	MD	21211	**800-622-4121**	410-467-3000	738-7
WBANA (Wild Blueberry Assn of North America)	PO Box 100	Old Town	ME	04468	**800-341-1758**	207-570-3535	47-2
WBAY-TV Ch 2 (ABC)	115 S Jefferson St	Green Bay	WI	54301	**800-261-9229**	920-432-3331	738-35
WBCT-FM 93.7 (Ctry)	77 Monroe Ctr St NW Ste 1000	Grand Rapids	MI	49503	**800-633-9393**	616-459-1919	642-50
WBEN-AM 930 (N/T)	500 Corporate Pkwy Ste 200	Amherst	NY	14226	**800-616-9236**	716-843-0600	643
WBG (Wright Business Graphics)	18440 NE San Rafael St	Portland	OR	97230	**800-547-8397**		109
WBGL-FM 91.7 (Rel)	4101 Fieldstone Rd PO Box 111 *Cust Svc	Champaign	IL	61822	**800-475-9245***	217-359-8232	642-24
WBH (Baptist Health Paducah)	2501 Kentucky Ave	Paducah	KY	42003	**877-271-4176**	270-575-2100	374-3
WBHM-FM 90.3 (NPR)	650 11th St S	Birmingham	AL	35233	**800-444-9246**	205-934-2606	642-15
WBHY-FM 88.5 (Rel)	PO Box 1328	Mobile	AL	36633	**888-473-8488**	251-473-8488	642-78
WBI Energy	1250 W Century Ave	Bismarck	ND	58503	**877-924-4677**	701-530-1064	326
WBI Holdings Inc	1250 W Century Ave *General	Bismarck	ND	58503	**877-924-4677***		326
WBIG-FM 100.3 (Oldies)	1801 Rockville Pk 6th fl	Rockville	MD	20852	**800-493-1003**	240-747-2700	643
WBIQ-TV Ch 10 (PBS)	2112 11th Ave S Ste 400	Birmingham	AL	35205	**800-239-5233**	205-328-8756	738-11
WBKL-FM 92.7 (Rel)	PO Box 2098	Omaha	NE	68103	**800-525-5683**		642-13
WBNS-FM 97.1 (AC)	605 S Front St Ste 300	Columbus	OH	43215	**888-691-9710**	614-460-3850	642-34
WBNX-TV Ch 55 (CW)	2690 State Rd	Cuyahoga Falls	OH	44223	**800-282-0515**	330-922-5500	
WBRB-FM 101.3 (Ctry)	1065 Radio Pk Dr	Mount Clare	WV	26408	**877-232-7121**	304-623-6546	643
WBRE-TV Ch 28 (NBC)	62 S Franklin St	Wilkes-Barre	PA	18701	**800-367-9222**	570-823-2828	
WBUR-FM 90.9 (NPR)	890 Commonwealth Ave	Boston	MA	02215	**800-909-9287**	617-353-0909	642-18
WBZT-AM 1230 (N/T)	3071 Continental Dr	West Palm Beach	FL	33407	**800-889-0267**		642-129
WC McQuaide Inc	153 Macridge Rd	Johnstown	PA	15904	**800-456-0292**	814-269-6000	778
WCAT-FM 102.3 (Ctry)	728 N Hanover St	Carlisle	PA	17013	**888-513-5130**	717-243-1200	643
WCAU-TV Ch 10 (NBC)	10 Monument Rd	Bala Cynwyd	PA	19004	**800-847-9228**	610-668-5510	
WCB (Waukesha Cherry-Burrell Corp)	611 Sugar Creek Rd	Delavan	WI	53115	**800-252-5200**	262-728-1900	638
WCBB-TV Ch 10 (PBS)	1450 Lisbon St	Lewiston	ME	04240	**800-884-1717**	207-783-9101	
WCBU-FM 89.9 (NPR)	1501 W Bradley Ave	Peoria	IL	61625	**888-488-9228**	309-677-3690	642-88
WCEC (Wharton County Electric Co-op Inc)	1815 E Jackson St	El Campo	TX	77437	**800-460-6271**	979-543-6271	247
WCFT-TV Ch 33 (ABC)	800 Concourse Pkwy Ste 200	Birmingham	AL	35244	**800-784-8669**	205-403-3340	738-11
WCH (Women's & Children's Hospital)	4600 Ambassador Caffery Pkwy	Lafayette	LA	70508	**888-569-8331**	337-521-9100	374-7
WCHS-TV Ch 8 (ABC)	1301 Piedmont Rd	Charleston	WV	25301	**888-696-9247**	304-346-5358	738-15
WCI Communities Inc	24301 Walden Ctr Dr	Bonita Springs	FL	34134	**800-924-4005**	239-498-8200	651
WCIA-TV Ch 3 (CBS)	PO Box 20	Champaign	IL	61824	**800-676-3382**	217-356-8333	
WCIC-FM 91.5 (Rel)	3902 W Baring Trace	Peoria	IL	61615	**877-692-9242**		642-88
WCLK-FM 91.9 (Jazz)	111 James P Brawley Dr SW	Atlanta	GA	30314	**888-448-3925**	404-880-8273	642-10
WCLT-FM 100.3 (Ctry)	PO Box 5150	Newark	OH	43058	**800-837-9258**	740-345-4004	643
WCLV	1375 Euclid Ave Idea Ctr	Cleveland	OH	44115	**877-399-3307**	216-916-6301	644
WCMF-FM 96.5 (CR)	70 Commercial St	Rochester	NY	14614	**800-222-9196**	585-423-2900	642-99
WCMHS (Washington County Mental Health Services Inc)	PO Box 647	Montpelier	VT	05601	**800-649-2642**	802-229-0591	353
WCMR-AM 1270 (Rel)	PO Box 307	Elkhart	IN	46515	**800-522-9376**	574-875-5166	643
WCNY-FM 91.3 (NPR)	506 Old Liverpool Rd	Liverpool	NY	13088	**800-451-9269**	315-453-2424	643
WCNY-TV Ch 24 (PBS)	506 Old Liverpool Rd PO Box 2400	Syracuse	NY	13220	**800-638-5163**	315-453-2424	738-82
WCOL-FM 92.3 (Ctry)	2323 W Fifth Ave Ste 200	Columbus	OH	43204	**800-899-9265**	614-486-6101	642-34
WCOS-FM 97.5 (Ctry)	316 Greystone Blvd	Columbia	SC	29210	**800-570-9690**	803-343-1100	642-32
Wcp Solutions	6703 S 234th St Ste 120	Kent	WA	98032	**877-398-3030**		551-1
WCPV-FM 101.3 (CR)	265 Hegeman Ave	Colchester	VT	05446	**866-862-4267**	802-655-0093	643
WCQR-FM 88.3 (Rel)	2312 Oak St	Gray	TN	37615	**888-477-5676**	423-477-5676	643
WCQS-FM 88.1 (NPR)	73 Broadway	Asheville	NC	28801	**866-448-3881**	828-210-4800	642-9
WCR (Women's Council of REALTORS)	430 N Michigan Ave	Chicago	IL	60611	**800-245-8512**		48-17
WCSG-FM 91.3 (Rel)	1159 E Beltline Ave NE	Grand Rapids	MI	49525	**800-968-4543**	616-942-1500	642-50
WCSH-TV Ch 6 (NBC)	1 Congress Sq	Portland	ME	04101	**800-464-1213**	207-828-6666	738-62
WCTL-FM 106.3 (Rel)	10912 Peach St	Waterford	PA	16441	**800-568-8924**	814-796-6000	643
WCTV-TV Ch 6 (CBS)	1801 Halstead Blvd	Tallahassee	FL	32309	**888-297-9461**	850-893-6666	738-83
WCU (Western Carolina University)	1 University Dr	Cullowhee	NC	28723	**877-928-4968**	828-227-7211	167
WCVE-TV Ch 23 (PBS)	23 Sesame St	Richmond	VA	23235	**800-476-8440**	804-320-1301	738-66
WCWC (Western Canada Wilderness Committee)	227 Abbott St	Vancouver	BC	V6B2K7	**800-661-9453**	604-683-8220	47-13
WD-40 Co	1061 Cudahy Pl *NASDAQ: WDFC*	San Diego	CA	92110	**800-448-9340**	619-275-1400	540
WDAE-AM 620 (Sports)	4002 W Gandy Blvd	Tampa	FL	33611	**888-546-4620**	813-832-1000	642-122
WDAM-TV Ch 7 (NBC)	PO Box 16269	Hattiesburg	MS	39404	**800-844-9326**	601-544-4730	
WDAS-FM 105.3 (Urban AC)	111 Presidential Blvd Ste 100	Bala Cynwyd	PA	19004	**800-745-3000**	610-784-3333	643
WDAY-FM 93.7 (CHR)	1020 25th St S	Fargo	ND	58103	**877-478-5437**	701-237-5346	642-44
WDAZ-TV Ch 8 (ABC)	2220 S Washington St	Grand Forks	ND	58201	**877-382-4357**	701-775-2511	738-30
WDCX-FM 99.5 (Rel)	625 Delaware Ave Ste 308	Buffalo	NY	14202	**800-684-2848**	716-883-3010	642-20
WDEL-AM 1150 (N/T)	2727 Shipley Rd	Wilmington	DE	19810	**800-544-1150**	302-478-2700	642-130
WDIA-AM 1070 (Urban)	2650 Thousand Oaks Blvd Ste 4100	Memphis	TN	38118	**800-339-4673**	901-259-1300	642-74
WDIO-TV Ch 10 (ABC)	10 Observation Rd	Duluth	MN	55811	**800-477-1013**	218-727-6864	738-25
WDKS-FM 106.1 (CHR)	117 SE Fifth St	Evansville	IN	47708	**888-454-5477**	812-425-4226	642-42
WDKY-TV Ch 56 (Fox)	836 Euclid Ave Ste 201	Lexington	KY	40502	**888-404-5656**	859-269-5656	
WDL Systems	220 Chatham Business Dr *Sales	Pittsboro	NC	27312	**800-548-2319***	919-545-2500	176
WDLI-TV Ch 17 (TBN)	PO Box A	Santa Ana	CA	92711	**888-731-1000**	714-832-2950	738-18
WDMA (Window & Door Manufacturers Assn)	330 N Wabash Ave Ste 2000	Chicago	IL	60611	**800-223-2301**	847-299-5200	48-3
WDRM-FM 102.1 (Ctry)	26869 Peoples Rd	Madison	AL	35756	**866-302-0102**	256-309-2400	643
WDSC-TV	1200 W International Speedway Blvd	Daytona Beach	FL	32114	**866-273-5825**	386-506-4415	
WDSE-TV Ch 8 (PBS)	632 Niagara Ct	Duluth	MN	55811	**888-563-9373**	218-788-2831	738-25
WDSU-TV Ch 6 (NBC)	846 Howard Ave	New Orleans	LA	70113	**888-925-4127**	504-679-0600	738-52
WDUZ-AM 1400 (Sports)	810 Victoria St	Green Bay	WI	54302	**855-724-1075**	920-468-4100	642-51
WDWS-AM 1400 (N/T)	2301 S Neil St	Champaign	IL	61820	**800-223-9397**	217-351-5300	642-24
WDXB-FM 102.5 (Ctry)	600 Beacon Pkwy W Ste 400	Birmingham	AL	35209	**877-541-1966**	205-439-9600	642-15
WE Aubuchon Company Inc	95 Aubuchon Dr	Westminster	MA	01473	**800-431-2712**	978-874-0521	364
WE Donoghue & Company Inc	629 Washington St	Norwood	MA	02062	**800-642-4276**		401
We Energies	231 W Michigan St PO Box 2046	Milwaukee	WI	53203	**800-242-9137**	414-221-2345	785
WE Yoder Inc	41 S Maple St	Kutztown	PA	19530	**800-889-5149**	610-683-7383	190-8
Wealth Conservancy Inc, The	1525 Spruce St Ste 300	Boulder	CO	80302	**888-440-1919**	303-444-1919	401
WEAO-TV Ch 49 (PBS)	1750 Campus Ctr Dr	Kent	OH	44240	**800-544-4549**	330-677-4549	
WEAR-TV Ch 3 (ABC)	4990 Mobile Hwy	Pensacola	FL	32506	**800-772-1213**	850-456-3333	
Weather Ch Inc, The	300 I N Pkwy Po Box 724554	Atlanta	GA	30339	**866-843-0392**	770-226-0000	736
Weather Services International	400 Minuteman Rd	Andover	MA	01810	**800-872-2359**	978-983-6300	180-10
Weather Shield Manufacturing Inc	1 Weather Shield Plz PO Box 309	Medford	WI	54451	**800-222-2995**	715-748-2100	238
Weatherall Printing Co	1349 Cliff Gookin Blvd	Tupelo	MS	38801	**800-273-6043**	662-842-5284	626
Weatherbank Inc	1015 Waterwood Pkwy Ste J	Edmond	OK	73034	**800-687-3562**	405-359-0773	69
Weatherby Inc	1605 Commerce Way	Paso Robles	CA	93446	**800-227-2016**	805-227-2600	286
Weatherchem Corp	2222 Highland Rd	Twinsburg	OH	44087	**800-316-0072**	330-425-4206	153
Weatherford Chamber of Commerce	401 Ft Worth St	Weatherford	TX	76086	**888-594-3801**	817-596-3801	138
Weatherford College	225 College Pk Dr	Weatherford	TX	76086	**800-287-5471**	817-594-5471	161

Name / Address	City	State	ZIP	Toll-Free	Phone	Class
Weatherford International Inc						
515 Post Oak Blvd Ste 600	Houston	TX	77027	**866-398-0010**	713-693-4000	536
NYSE: WFT						
Weatherford Public Library						
1014 Charles St	Weatherford	TX	76086	**800-489-0190**	817-598-4150	434-3
Weathermatic						
3301 W Kingsley Rd	Garland	TX	75041	**888-484-3776**	972-278-6131	429
Weathers Auto Supply Inc						
23308 Airpark Dr	Petersburg	VA	23803	**888-572-2886**	804-861-1076	53
Weatherspoon Art Museum						
500 Tate St	Greensboro	NC	27402	**877-862-4123**	336-334-5770	519
Weathervane Seafood Restaurant						
306 US Rt 1	Kittery	ME	03904	**800-914-1774**	207-439-0330	668
Weaver-Bailey Contractors Inc						
PO Box 60	El Paso	AR	72045	**800-253-3385**	501-796-2301	191-3
Weavertown Environmental Group						
2 Dorrington Rd	Carnegie	PA	15106	**800-746-4850**	724-746-4850	189
Web Age Solutions Inc						
439 University Ave Ste 820	Toronto	ON	M5G1Y8	**866-206-4644**		227
Web Equipment						
464 Central Rd	Fredericksburg	VA	22401	**800-225-3858**	540-657-5855	192
Web.com						
12808 Grand Bay Pkwy W	Jacksonville	FL	32258	**800-338-1771**	904-680-6600	807
Webb Financial Group						
7900 Xerxes Ave S Ste 1920	Minneapolis	MN	55431	**800-927-9322**	952-837-3200	401
Webb Institute						
298 Crescent Beach Rd	Glen Cove	NY	11542	**866-708-9322**	516-671-2213	167
Webb School						
PO Box 488	Bell Buckle	TN	37020	**888-733-9322**	931-389-9322	621
Webb Wheel Products Inc						
2310 Industrial Dr SW	Cullman	AL	35055	**800-633-3256**	256-739-6660	59
WebBank Corp						
215 S State St Ste 1000	Salt Lake City	UT	84111	**888-881-3789**	801-456-8350	216
Webber International University						
1201 N Scenic Hwy	Babson Park	FL	33827	**800-741-1844**		167
WEBCARGO Inc						
800 Pl Victoria						
Ste 2603 Tour de la bourse CP 329	Montreal	QC	H4Z1G8	**866-905-0123**		366
WEBE-FM 108 (AC)						
2 Lafayette Sq	Bridgeport	CT	06604	**800-932-3108**	203-333-9108	642-119
Weber County Library						
2464 Jefferson Ave	Ogden	UT	84401	**866-678-5342**	801-337-2632	434-3
Weber Insurance Corp						
505 Corporate Dr W	Langhorne	PA	19047	**888-860-0400**	215-860-0400	390
Weber Logistics						
13530 Rosecrans Ave	Santa Fe Springs	CA	90670	**855-469-3237**		448
Weber Marking Systems Inc						
711 W Algonquin Rd	Arlington Heights	IL	60005	**800-843-4242***	847-364-8500	413
*Sales						
Weber State University						
3848 Harrison Blvd	Ogden	UT	84408	**800-848-7770**	801-626-6000	167
Davis						
2750 N University Pk Blvd	Layton	UT	84041	**800-848-7770**	801-395-3473	167
Stewart Library						
2901 University Cir	Ogden	UT	84408	**877-306-3140**	801-626-6403	434-6
Weber's Inn						
3050 Jackson Rd	Ann Arbor	MI	48103	**800-443-3050***	734-769-2500	379
*Resv						
Weber-Knapp Co						
441 Chandler St	Jamestown	NY	14701	**800-828-9254**	716-484-9135	350
Weber-Stephen Products Co						
200 E Daniels Rd	Palatine	IL	60067	**800-446-1071***		35
*Cust Svc						
WebEyeCare Inc						
10 Canal St Ste 302	Bristol	PA	19007	**888-536-7480**		366
WebiMax LLC						
6000 Commerce Pkwy Ste A	Mount Laurel	NJ	08054	**866-832-3638**		197
Weblink Solutions						
23950 Craftsman Rd	Calabasas	CA	91302	**866-296-1977**		226
WebNet Services Inc						
247 Rt 100	Somers	NY	10589	**866-923-4811**	914-232-6900	179
Webroot Software Inc						
2560 55th St	Boulder	CO	80301	**800-772-9383**	303-442-3813	180-12
Websense Inc						
10240 Sorrento Vly Rd	San Diego	CA	92121	**800-723-1166**	858-320-8000	180-7
NASDAQ: WBSN						
Website Magazine Inc						
999 E Touhy Ave	Des Plaines	IL	60018	**800-817-1518**	773-628-2779	529
Webster Bank Arena						
600 Main St	Bridgeport	CT	06604	**800-745-3000**	203-345-2300	718
Webster City Federal Bancorp						
820 Des Moines St	Webster City	IA	50595	**866-519-4004**	515-832-3071	360-2
NYSE: WCFB						
Webster Electric Co-op						
1240 Spur Dr	Marshfield	MO	65706	**800-643-4305**	417-859-2216	247
Webster Financial Corp						
PO Box 10305	Waterbury	CT	06726	**800-325-2424**		360-2
NYSE: WBS						
Webster First Federal Credit Union						
271 Greenwood St	Worcester	MA	01607	**800-962-4452**	508-671-5000	70
Webster Industries Inc						
95 Chestnut Ridge Rd,	Montvale	NJ	07645	**800-955-2374**	800-999-2374	65
WEC (Warren Electric Co-op Inc)						
320 E Main St PO Box 208	Youngsville	PA	16371	**800-364-8640**	814-563-7548	247
Wecsys LLC						
8825 Xylon Ave N	Minneapolis	MN	55445	**888-493-2797**	763-504-1069	74
Wedding Experience						
2307 Douglas Rd Ste 400	Coral Gables	FL	33145	**866-223-9672**	305-421-1260	228
Wedding Shoppe Inc, The						
1196 Grand Ave	Saint Paul	MN	55105	**877-294-4991**	651-298-1144	156-6
Wedge Community Co-Op Inc						
2105 Lyndale Ave S	Minneapolis	MN	55405	**800-535-4555**	612-871-3993	345
WEDGE Group Inc						
1415 Louisiana St Ste 3000	Houston	TX	77002	**888-563-5383**	713-739-6500	360-3
Wedgewood Hotel						
845 Hornby St	Vancouver	BC	V6Z1V1	**800-663-0666**	604-689-7777	379
Wedgewood Resort Hotel						
212 Wedgewood Dr	Fairbanks	AK	99701	**800-528-4916**		379

Name / Address	City	State	ZIP	Toll-Free	Phone	Class
Wedmore Place LLC						
5810 Wessex Hundred	Williamsburg	VA	23185	**866-933-6673**		378
WEDR-FM 99.1 (Urban)						
2741 N 29th Ave	Hollywood	FL	33020	**800-327-2323**	305-444-4404	643
Weecycle Environmental Consulting Inc						
5375 Western Ave Ste B	Boulder	CO	80301	**800-875-7033**	303-413-0452	740
Weed USA Inc						
5780 Harrow Glen Ct	Galena	OH	43021	**800-933-3758**	740-548-3881	708
Weeden & Company LP						
145 Mason St	Greenwich	CT	06830	**800-843-9333**	203-861-7670	196
WEEI-AM 850 (Sports)						
20 Guest St 3rd Fl	Brighton	MA	02135	**888-525-0850**	617-779-3500	643
Weekends Only Inc						
349 Marshall Ave 3rd Fl	Saint Louis	MO	63119	**855-803-5888**	314-447-1500	322
Weeks Seed Company Inc						
1050 Moye Blvd	Greenville	NC	27834	**800-322-1234**	252-757-1234	692
Weeks-Lerman Group						
58-38 Page Pl	Maspeth	NY	11378	**800-544-5959**	718-803-5000	533
Weetabix Co Inc						
300 Nickerson Rd	Marlborough	MA	01752	**800-343-0590**	978-368-0991	297-4
WEF (Water Environment Federation)						
601 Wythe St	Alexandria	VA	22314	**800-666-0206**	703-684-2400	47-13
WEG (West Essex Graphics Inc)						
305 Fairfield Ave	Fairfield	NJ	07004	**800-221-5859**		779
Wege Pretzel Co						
PO Box 334	Hanover	PA	17331	**800-888-4646**		297-9
Wegmans Food Markets Inc						
1500 Brooks Ave PO Box 30844	Rochester	NY	14603	**800-934-6267**	585-328-2550	345
WEHT-TV Ch 25 (ABC)						
800 Marywood Dr	Henderson	KY	42420	**800-879-8542**	270-826-9566	
WEI (Wieland Electric Inc)						
49 International Rd	Burgaw	NC	28425	**800-943-5263**	910-259-5050	248
Weibel Vineyards						
1 Winemaster Way	Lodi	CA	95240	**800-932-9463**	209-365-9463	79-3
Weidenhammer Systems Corp						
935 Berkshire Blvd	Reading	PA	19610	**866-497-2227**	610-378-1149	179
Weidmuller Inc						
821 Southlake Blvd	Richmond	VA	23236	**800-849-9343***	804-794-2877	813
*Cust Svc						
Weidner Ctr for the Performing Arts						
2420 Nicolet Dr						
University of Wisconsin at Green Bay	Green Bay	WI	54311	**800-895-0071**	920-465-2726	571
Weightech						
1649 Country Elite Dr	Waldron	AR	72958	**800-457-3720**	479-637-4182	361
Weiler Corp						
1 Wildwood Dr	Cresco	PA	18326	**800-835-9999***	570-595-7495	102
*Cust Svc						
Weinbrenner Shoe Co Inc						
108 S Polk St	Merrill	WI	54452	**800-569-6817***	715-536-5521	302
*General						
Weingarten Realty Investors						
2600 Citadel Plz Dr Ste 125	Houston	TX	77008	**800-688-8865**	713-866-6000	653
NYSE: WRI						
Weingartz Supply Co						
46061 Van Dyke Ave	Utica	MI	48317	**855-669-7278**	586-731-7240	324
WEIQ-TV Ch 42 (PBS)						
2112 11th Ave S Ste 400	Birmingham	AL	35205	**800-239-5233**	205-328-8756	738-11
Weirton Medical Ctr						
601 Colliers Way	Weirton	WV	26062	**800-994-6610**	304-797-6000	374-3
Weis Markets						
1000 S Second St PO Box 471	Sunbury	PA	17801	**866-999-9347**		345
NYSE: WMK						
Weiser Lock A Masco Co						
19701 Da Vinci	Lake Forest	CA	92610	**800-677-5625**		350
Weiss Research Inc						
15430 Endeavour Dr	Jupiter	FL	33478	**800-291-8545**		401
WEKU-FM 88.9 (Clas)						
521 Lancaster Ave						
102 Perkins Bldg-EKU	Richmond	KY	40475	**800-621-8890**		643
Wel Companies Inc						
1625 S Broadway PO Box 5610	De Pere	WI	54115	**800-333-4415**	920-339-0110	778
Welch & Rushe Inc						
391 Prince George's Blvd	Upper Marlboro	MD	20774	**800-683-3852**	301-430-6000	188
Welch Allyn Medical Products						
4341 State St Rd	Skaneateles Falls	NY	13152	**800-289-2500**	315-685-4100	252
Welch Allyn Monitoring Inc						
8500 SW Creekside Pl	Beaverton	OR	97008	**800-289-2500***	503-530-7500	252
*Cust Svc						
Welch Group LLC, The						
3940 Montclair Rd 5th Fl	Birmingham	AL	35213	**800-709-7100**	205-879-5001	527
Welch Packaging Group						
1020 Herman St	Elkhart	IN	46516	**800-246-2475**	574-295-2460	99
Weld Mold Co						
750 Rickett Rd	Brighton	MI	48116	**800-521-9755**	810-229-9521	809
Weldangrind Ltd						
10323 174 St NW	Edmonton	AB	T5S1H1	**866-226-2414**	780-484-3030	755
Welder Training & Testing Institute						
1144 N Graham St	Allentown	PA	18109	**800-223-9884**	610-820-9551	798
Weldmac Manufacturing Co						
1451 N Johnson Ave	El Cajon	CA	92020	**800-252-1533**	619-440-2300	453
Weldon Williams & Lick Inc						
711 N A St	Fort Smith	AR	72901	**800-242-4995**	479-783-4113	626
Welk Resort Branson						
8860 Lawrence Welk Dr	Escondido	CA	92026	**800-505-9355**	417-336-3575	667
Welk Resort San Diego						
8860 Lawrence Welk Dr	Escondido	CA	92026	**800-932-9355***	760-749-3000	667
*Resv						
Well Spa at Miramonte Resort						
45000 Indian Wells Ln	Indian Wells	CA	92210	**800-237-2926**	760-837-1652	705
Well Spouse Assn						
63 W Main St Ste H	Freehold	NJ	07728	**800-838-0879**	732-577-8899	47-6
Wella Corp						
6109 DeSoto Ave	Woodland Hills	CA	91367	**800-829-4422**	818-999-5112	217
WellCare Group Inc						
8735 Henderson Rd	Tampa	FL	33634	**866-765-4385**	813-290-6200	391-3
WellCare Health Plans Inc						
PO Box 31372	Tampa	FL	33631	**866-530-9491**		391-3

Alphabetical Section

Name	Address	City	State	ZIP	Toll-Free	Phone	Class
Welles-Turner Memorial Library	2407 Main St	Glastonbury	CT	06033	**800-411-9671**	860-652-7719	434-3
Welligent Inc	5205 Colley Ave	Norfolk	VA	23508	**888-317-5960**		179
Wellington Hotel	871 Seventh Ave	New York	NY	10019	**800-652-1212**	212-247-3900	379
Wellington Resort	551 Thames St	Newport	RI	02840	**800-228-2968**	401-849-1770	379
Wells Bloomfield Industries	10 Sunnen Dr	Saint Louis	MO	63143	**888-356-5362**		299
Wells Cargo Inc	1503 W McNaughton St	Elkhart	IN	46514	**800-348-7553**	574-264-9661	777
Wells College	170 Main St *Admissions	Aurora	NY	13026	**800-952-9355***	315-364-3266	167
Wells Concrete Products Inc	835 Hwy 109 NE PO Box 308	Wells	MN	56097	**800-658-7049**	507-553-3138	185
Wells County Public Library	200 W Washington St	Bluffton	IN	46714	**800-824-6111**	260-824-1612	434-3
Wells Enterprises Inc	1 Blue Bunny Dr *All	Le Mars	IA	51031	**888-309-1742***	712-546-4000	297-25
Wells Fargo	420 Montgomery St *NYSE: WFC*	San Francisco	CA	94104	**800-877-4833**		218
Wells Fargo Bank	5622 Third St	Katy	TX	77493	**800-869-3557**	281-391-2101	69
Wells Fargo Bank Indiana NA	111 E Wayne St	Fort Wayne	IN	46802	**800-869-3557**	260-461-6430	69
Wells Fargo Bank Iowa NA	666 Walnut St PO Box 837	Des Moines	IA	50309	**800-869-3557**		69
Wells Fargo Bank NA	420 Montgomery St	San Francisco	CA	94104	**800-869-3557**	415-222-4292	69
Wells Fargo Bank Texas NA	707 Castroville Rd	San Antonio	TX	78237	**800-869-3557**	210-856-6224	69
Wells Fargo Education Financial Services	PO Box 5185	Sioux Falls	SD	57117	**800-658-3567**		216
Wells Fargo Equipment Finance Inc	733 Marquette Ave Ste 700	Minneapolis	MN	55402	**877-322-8228**	612-667-9876	218
Wells Fargo Financial Inc	800 Walnut St	Des Moines	IA	50309	**800-735-3008**	515-280-7741	216
Wells Fargo Home Mortgage	2840 Ingersoll Ave	Des Moines	IA	50312	**800-401-1957**	515-237-5196	508
Wells Home Furnishings	101 Bowers Rd	Charleston	WV	25314	**800-249-7753**	304-343-3600	322
Wells Johnson Co	8000 S Kolb Rd	Tucson	AZ	85756	**800-528-1597**	520-298-6069	475
Wells Lamont Industry Group	6640 W Touhy Ave	Niles	IL	60714	**800-247-3295**		154-7
Wells Printing Company Inc	6030 Perimeter Pkwy	Montgomery	AL	36116	**800-264-4958**	334-281-3449	626
Wells-Gardner Electronics Corp	9500 W 55th St Ste A *NYSE: WGA*	McCook	IL	60525	**800-336-6630**	708-290-2100	175-4
Welocalize Inc	241 E Fourth St Ste 207	Frederick	MD	21701	**800-370-9515**	301-668-0330	196
Welsbach Electric Corp	111-01 14th Ave	College Point	NY	11356	**866-890-7794**	718-670-7900	191-4
WEMU-FM 89.1 (NPR)	PO Box 980350	Ypsilanti	MI	48198	**888-299-8910**	734-487-2229	643
Wenaas AGS Inc	12211 Parc Crest Dr Bldg Ste 100	Stafford	TX	77477	**888-576-2668**	281-931-4300	154-18
Wenatchee Valley Chamber of Commerce	2 S Mission St	Wenatchee	WA	98801	**800-572-7753**	509-662-2116	138
Wenatchee Valley College	1300 Fifth St	Wenatchee	WA	98801	**877-982-4968**	509-682-6800	161
Wenatchee World	14 N Mission St	Wenatchee	WA	98801	**800-572-4433**	509-663-5161	531-2
Wendell August Forge Inc	2074 Leesburg-Grove City Rd	Mercer	PA	16137	**866-354-5192**	724-748-9501	328
Wendell's Inc	6601 Bunker Lk Blvd NW PO Box 458	Ramsey	MN	55303	**800-936-3355**	763-576-8200	466
WEND-FM 106.5 (Alt)	801 Wood Ridge Ctr Dr	Charlotte	NC	28217	**800-934-1065**	704-714-9444	642-27
Wendle Motors Inc	9000 N Div	Spokane	WA	99218	**888-685-7177**		515
Wendling Printing Co	111 Beech St	Newport	KY	41071	**800-998-9553**	859-261-8300	626
Wenger Corp	555 Pk Dr PO Box 448	Owatonna	MN	55060	**800-493-6437**	507-455-4100	526
Wenger North America Inc	15 Corporate Dr *Cust Svc	Orangeburg	NY	10962	**800-431-2996***	845-365-3500	224
WENH-TV Ch 11 (PBS)	268 Mast Rd	Durham	NH	03824	**800-639-8408**	603-868-1100	
Wenner Bread Products Inc	33 Rajon Rd	Bayport	NY	11705	**800-869-6262**	631-563-6262	297-1
Wentworth Hauser & Violich (WHV)	301 Battery St	San Francisco	CA	94111	**800-204-2650**	415-981-6911	401
Wentworth Institute of Technology	550 Huntington Ave	Boston	MA	02115	**800-556-0610**	617-989-4590	167
Wentworth Mansion	149 Wentworth St	Charleston	SC	29401	**888-466-1886**	843-853-1886	379
Wentworth Printing Corp	101 N 12th St	West Columbia	SC	29169	**800-326-0784**	803-796-9990	626
Wentworth-Douglass Hospital	789 Central Ave	Dover	NH	03820	**877-201-7100**	603-742-5252	374-3
WENZ-FM 107.9 (Urban)	2510 St Clair Ave NE	Cleveland	OH	44114	**800-440-1079**	216-579-1111	642-30
Werner Co	93 Werner Rd	Greenville	PA	16125	**888-523-3371**		421
Werner Electric Supply Co	2341 Industrial Dr	Neenah	WI	54956	**800-236-5026**	920-729-4500	248
Werner Enterprises Inc	14507 Frontier Rd *NASDAQ: WERN*	Omaha	NE	68138	**800-228-2240**	402-895-6640	778
Werner G Smith Inc	1730 Train Ave *General	Cleveland	OH	44113	**800-535-8343***	216-861-3676	297-12
WERN-FM 88.7 (NPR)	821 University Ave	Madison	WI	53706	**800-747-7444**		642-72
Werres Corp	807 E S St	Frederick	MD	21701	**800-638-6563**	301-620-4000	385
Wert Bookbinding Inc	9975 Allentown Blvd *Cust Svc	Grantville	PA	17028	**800-344-9378***	717-469-0629	91
WERU-FM 89.9 (Var)	1186 Acadia Hwy	East Orland	ME	04431	**800-643-6273**	207-469-6600	643
Werzalit of America Inc	40 Holly Ave	Bradford	PA	16701	**800-999-3730**	814-362-3881	498
WesBanco Inc	1 Bank Plz *NASDAQ: WSBC*	Wheeling	WV	26003	**800-328-3369**	304-234-9000	69
Wesbury United Methodist Community	31 N Park Ave	Meadville	PA	16335	**877-937-2879**	814-332-9000	47-20
Wesco Cedar Inc	PO Box 520	Creswell	OR	97426	**800-547-2511**	541-688-5020	193-4
Wesco Fabrics Inc	4001 Forest St	Denver	CO	80216	**800-950-9372**	303-388-4101	743
Wesco Inc	1460 Whitehall Rd	Muskegon	MI	49445	**800-968-0200**		325
Wescom Credit Union	123 S Marengo Ave PO Box 7058	Pasadena	CA	91101	**888-493-7266**	626-535-1000	221
Wes-Garde Components Group Inc	190 Elliott St	Hartford	CT	06114	**800-554-8866**	860-525-6907	248
Weslaco Area Chamber of Commerce	301 W Railroad	Weslaco	TX	78596	**800-700-2443**	956-968-2102	138
Wesley Homes	815 S 216th St	Des Moines	WA	98198	**866-937-5390**	206-824-5000	670
Wesley Long Community Hospital	501 N Elam Ave	Greensboro	NC	27403	**866-391-2734**	336-832-1000	374-3
Wesley Medical Ctr	5001 Hardy St	Hattiesburg	MS	39402	**877-456-9617**	601-268-8000	374-3
Wesley Theological Seminary	4500 Massachusetts Ave NW	Washington	DC	20016	**800-882-4987**	202-885-8600	168-3
Wesley Towers	700 Monterey Pl	Hutchinson	KS	67502	**888-663-9175**	620-663-9175	670
Wesleyan College	4760 Forsyth Rd	Macon	GA	31210	**800-447-6610**	478-757-5219	167
Wesleyan University Olin Library	252 Church St	Middletown	CT	06459	**800-421-1561**	860-685-2660	434-6
Wesleyan University Press	215 Long Ln	Middletown	CT	06459	**800-421-1561**	860-685-7711	634-4
Wesspur Tree Equipment	2121 Iron St	Bellingham	WA	98225	**800-268-2141**	360-734-5242	429
West Allis Public Library	7421 W National Ave	West Allis	WI	53214	**800-877-8339**	414-302-8500	434-3
West Allis-West Milwaukee Chamber of Commerce	6737 W Washington St Ste 2141	West Allis	WI	53214	**800-554-1448**	414-302-9901	138
West Bancorp Inc	PO Box 65020 *NASDAQ: WTBA*	West Des Moines	IA	50265	**800-810-2301**	515-222-2300	360-2
West Baton Rouge Museum	845 N Jefferson Ave	Port Allen	LA	70767	**888-881-6811**	225-336-2422	519
West Bend Area Chamber of Commerce	304 S Main St	West Bend	WI	53095	**888-338-8666**	262-338-2666	138
West Bend Housewares LLC	2845 Wingate St PO Box 2780	West Bend	WI	53095	**866-290-1851**		36
West Bend Mutual Insurance Co	1900 S 18th Ave	West Bend	WI	53095	**800-236-5010**	262-334-5571	391-4
West Branch Area Chamber of Commerce	422 W Houghton Ave	West Branch	MI	48661	**800-755-9091**	989-345-2821	208
West Canadian Digital Imaging Inc	200 - 1601 Ninth Ave SE	Calgary	AB	T2G0H4	**800-267-2555**	403-245-2555	344
West Central Electric Co-op Inc	204 Main St PO Box 17	Murdo	SD	57559	**800-242-9232**	605-669-2472	247
West Central Illinois Educational Telecommunications Corp	PO Box 6248	Springfield	IL	62708	**800-232-3605**	217-483-7887	629
West Central Steel Inc	110 19th St NW PO Box 1178	Willmar	MN	56201	**800-992-8853**	320-235-4070	491
West Central Tribune	PO Box 839	Willmar	MN	56201	**800-450-1150**	320-235-1150	531-2
West Chester University	700 S High St	West Chester	PA	19383	**877-315-2165**	610-436-1000	167
West Coast Aviation Services	19711 Campus Dr Ste 150	Santa Ana	CA	92707	**800-352-6153**	949-852-8340	13
West Coast Bank	506 SW Coast Hwy *Cust Svc	Newport	OR	97365	**800-895-3345***	877-272-3678	69
West Coast Connection	1725 Main St Ste 215	Weston	FL	33326	**800-767-0227**	954-888-9780	758
West Coast Differentials	2429 Mercantile Dr Ste A	Rancho Cordova	CA	95742	**800-510-0950**	916-635-0950	53
West Coast Distributing Inc	Commerce Pl 350 Main St	Boston	MA	02148	**800-235-3730**	781-665-9393	10-9
West Coast Industries Inc	10 Jackson St	San Francisco	CA	94111	**800-243-3150**	415-621-6656	320-1
West Coast Shoe Co	52828 NW Shoe Factory Ln PO Box 607	Scappoose	OR	97056	**800-326-2711**	503-543-7114	302
West Coast Trends	17811 Jamestown Ln	Huntington Beach	CA	92647	**800-736-4568**	714-843-9288	708
West Corp	11808 Miracle Hills Dr *Sales	Omaha	NE	68154	**800-232-0900***		734
West End Gallery Ltd	12308 Jasper Ave	Edmonton	AB	T5N3K5	**855-488-4892**	780-488-4892	41
West Essex Graphics Inc (WEG)	305 Fairfield Ave	Fairfield	NJ	07004	**800-221-5859**		779
West Fargo Pioneer	101 5th St N	West Fargo	ND	58078	**888-382-1222**	701-451-5718	531-4
West Florida Electric Co-op	5282 Peanut Rd	Graceville	FL	32440	**800-342-7400**	850-263-3231	247

Name / Address	City	State	ZIP	Toll-Free	Phone	Class
West Florida Regional Library						
200 W Gregory St	Pensacola	FL	32501	**800-435-7352**	850-436-5060	434-3
West Group						
610 Opperman Dr	Eagan	MN	55123	**800-328-4880***	651-687-7000	634-2
*Cust Svc						
West Hills College						
Coalinga						
300 Cherry Ln	Coalinga	CA	93210	**800-266-1114**	559-934-2000	161
Lemoore						
555 College Ave	Lemoore	CA	93245	**800-266-1114**	559-925-3000	161
West Hollywood Convention & Visitors Bureau						
8687 Melrose Ave Ste M38	West Hollywood	CA	90069	**800-368-6020**	310-289-2525	208
West Islip Public Library						
3 Higbie Ln	West Islip	NY	11795	**866-833-1122**	631-661-7080	434-3
West Kentucky Community & Technical College						
4810 Alben Barkley Dr						
PO Box 7380	Paducah	KY	42001	**855-469-5282**	270-554-9200	161
West Kentucky Rural Electric Co-op Corp						
PO Box 589	Mayfield	KY	42066	**877-495-7322**	270-247-1321	247
West Liberty Foods LLC						
228 W Second St	West Liberty	IA	52776	**888-511-4500**	319-627-6000	618
West Linn Paper Co						
4800 Mill St	West Linn	OR	97068	**800-989-3608**	503-557-6500	556
West Marine Inc						
500 Westridge Dr	Watsonville	CA	95076	**800-262-8464**	831-728-2700	768
NASDAQ: WMAR						
West Monroe Partners LLC						
222 W Adams St	Chicago	IL	60606	**800-828-6708**	312-602-4000	196
West Music Inc						
1212 Fifth St PO Box 5521	Coralville	IA	52241	**800-373-2000**	319-351-2000	525
West Nebraska Register						
PO Box 608	Grand Island	NE	68802	**800-652-2229**	308-382-4660	531-4
West Nottingham Academy						
1079 Firetower Rd	Colora	MD	21917	**866-381-3684**	410-658-5556	621
West Orange Chamber of Commerce						
12184 W Colonial Dr	Winter Garden	FL	34787	**877-999-9981**	407-656-1304	138
West Orange Public Library						
46 Mt Pleasant Ave	West Orange	NJ	07052	**800-345-7587**	973-736-0198	434-3
West Oregon Electric Co-op Inc						
652 Rose Ave PO Box 69	Vernonia	OR	97064	**800-777-1276**	503-429-3021	247
West Palm Beach Public Library						
411 Clematis St	West Palm Beach	FL	33401	**866-472-7275**	561-868-7700	434-3
West Penetone Corp						
700 Gotham Pkwy	Carlstadt	NJ	07072	**800-631-1652**	201-567-3000	150
West Penn Allegheny Health System						
4800 Friendship Ave	Pittsburgh	PA	15224	**800-994-6610**		353
West Pharmaceutical Services Inc						
101 Gordon Dr	Lionville	PA	19341	**800-345-9800**	610-594-2900	476
NYSE: WST						
West Point Market						
1711 W Market St	Akron	OH	44313	**800-838-2156**	330-864-2151	459
West Point Underwriters LLC						
7785 66th St	Pinellas Park	FL	33781	**800-688-6213**	727-507-7565	390
West Press Printing & Copying						
1663 W Grant Rd	Tucson	AZ	85745	**888-637-0337**	520-624-4939	626
West River Co-op Telephone Co (WRCTC)						
801 Coleman Ave PO Box 39	Bison	SD	57620	**888-464-9513**	605-244-5213	733
West River Electric Assn Inc						
1200 W Fourth Ave PO Box 412	Wall	SD	57790	**888-279-2135**		247
West River Telecommunications Co-op						
PO Box 467	Hazen	ND	58545	**800-748-7220**	701-748-2211	733
West Shore Chamber of Commerce						
2830 Aldwynd Rd	Victoria	BC	V9B3S7	**888-234-3566**	250-478-1130	137
West Shore Community College						
PO Box 277	Scottville	MI	49454	**800-848-9722**	231-845-6211	161
West Side Unlimited Corp						
4201 16th Ave SW	Cedar Rapids	IA	52404	**800-373-2957**	319-390-4466	360-2
West Springfield Auto Parts						
92 Blandin Ave Ste C	Framingham	MA	01702	**800-615-2392**	508-879-6932	789
West Star Aviation Inc						
796 Heritage Way	Grand Junction	CO	81506	**800-255-4193**	970-243-7500	24
West Suburban Bank						
711 Westmore Meyers Rd	Lombard	IL	60148	**800-258-4009**	630-652-2000	69
West Suburban Chamber of Commerce						
9440 Joliet Rd Ste B	Hodgkins	IL	60525	**800-796-9696**	708-387-7550	138
West Suburban Hospital Medical Ctr						
3 Erie Ct	Oak Park	IL	60302	**866-938-7256**	708-383-6200	374-3
West Texas A & M University						
2501 Fourth Ave	Canyon	TX	79016	**877-656-2065**	806-651-2020	167
West Texas Rural TelephoneCo-op Inc						
PO Box 1737	Hereford	TX	79045	**888-440-4331**	806-364-3331	733
West Valley Construction Company Inc						
580 McGlincey Ln	Campbell	CA	95008	**800-588-5510**		190-10
West Valley Medical Ctr						
1717 Arlington Ave	Caldwell	ID	83605	**866-270-2311**	208-459-4641	374-3
West Vancouver Chamber of Commerce						
2235 Marine Dr	West Vancouver	BC	V7V1K5	**888-471-9996**	604-926-6614	137
West Virginia						
Child Support Enforcement Bureau						
231 Capitol St Ste 111	Charleston	WV	25301	**800-571-4864**	304-347-8688	339-49
Children & Families Bureau						
350 Capitol St Rm R-730	Charleston	WV	25301	**800-642-8589**	304-558-0628	339-49
Community Development Div						
1900 Kanawha Blvd E	Charleston	WV	25311	**800-982-3386**	304-558-2234	339-49
Consumer Protection Div						
812 Quarrier St 1st Fl	Charleston	WV	25301	**800-368-8808**	304-558-8986	339-49
Crime Victims Compensation Fund						
1900 Kanawha Blvd E Rm W-334	Charleston	WV	25305	**877-562-6878**	304-347-4850	339-49
Development Office						
1900 Kanawah Blvd E						
Bldg 6 Rm 525B	Charleston	WV	25305	**800-982-3386**	304-558-2234	339-49
Housing Development Fund						
814 Virginia St E	Charleston	WV	25301	**800-933-9843**	304-345-6475	339-49
Insurance Commission						
PO Box 50540	Charleston	WV	25305	**888-879-9842**	304-558-3354	339-49
Motor Vehicles Div						
5707 Maccorkle Ave SE						
Ste 400	Charleston	WV	25304	**800-642-9066**	304-558-3900	339-49
Public Service Commission						
208 Brooke St PO Box 812	Charleston	WV	25301	**800-344-5113**	304-340-0300	339-49
Rehabilitation Services Div						
107 Capitol St	Charleston	WV	25301	**800-642-8207**		339-49
Secretary of State						
1900 Kanawha Blvd E						
Bldg 1 Ste 157K	Charleston	WV	25305	**866-767-8683**	304-558-6000	339-49
Securities Div						
1900 Kanawha Blvd E						
Bldg 1 Rm W-100	Charleston	WV	25305	**877-982-9148**	304-558-2257	339-49
State Parks and Forests						
324 4th Ave	Charleston	WV	25305	**800-225-5982**	304-558-2764	339-49
Tourism Div						
90 MacCorkle Ave SW	Charleston	WV	25303	**800-225-5982**		339-49
Treasurer						
1900 Kanawha Blvd E						
Bldg 1 Ste E-145	Charleston	WV	25305	**800-422-7498**	304-558-5000	339-49
Veterans Affairs Div						
1321 Plaza E Ste 101	Charleston	WV	25301	**888-838-2332**	304-558-3661	339-49
West Virginia Assn of Realtors						
2110 Kanawha Blvd E	Charleston	WV	25311	**800-445-7600**	304-342-7600	654
West Virginia Bill Status						
State Capitol Complex						
Rm MB27 Bldg 1	Charleston	WV	25305	**877-565-3447**	304-347-4836	433
West Virginia Correctional Industries						
617 Leon Sullivan Way	Charleston	WV	25301	**800-525-5381**	304-558-6054	629
West Virginia Ethics Commission						
210 Brooks St Ste 300	Charleston	WV	25301	**866-558-0664**	304-558-0664	267
West Virginia Higher Education Policy Commission						
1018 Kanawha Blvd E Ste 700	Charleston	WV	25301	**888-825-5707**	304-558-2101	723
West Virginia Junior College						
Charleston						
1000 Virginia St E	Charleston	WV	25301	**800-924-5208**	304-345-2820	798
West Virginia Junior College - Bridgeport						
176 Thompson Dr	Bridgeport	WV	26330	**800-470-5627**	304-842-4007	798
West Virginia Library Commission						
1900 Kanawha Blvd E	Charleston	WV	25305	**800-642-9021**	304-558-2041	434-5
West Virginia Medical Journal						
PO Box 4106	Charleston	WV	25364	**800-257-4747**	304-925-0342	456-16
West Virginia National Cemetery						
42 Veterans Memorial Lane	Grafton	WV	26354	**800-273-8255**	304-265-2044	135
West Virginia Nurses Assn (WVNA)						
1007 Bigley Ave Ste 308	Charleston	WV	25302	**800-400-1226**	304-342-1169	532
West Virginia Press Association						
3422 Pennsylvania Ave	Charleston	WV	25302	**800-235-6881**	304-342-6908	623
West Virginia School Journal						
1558 Quarrier St	Charleston	WV	25311	**800-642-8261**	304-346-5315	456-8
West Virginia State Bar						
2000 Deitrick Blvd	Charleston	WV	25311	**866-989-8227**	304-553-7220	71
West Virginia State Medical Assn						
4307 MacCorkle Ave SE						
PO Box 4106	Charleston	WV	25364	**800-257-4747**	304-925-0342	473
West Virginia State Museum						
1900 Kanawha Blvd E						
The Cultural Ctr	Charleston	WV	25305	**800-946-9471**	304-558-0220	519
West Virginia State University						
117 Ferrell Hall PO Box 368	Institute	WV	25112	**800-987-2112**	304-766-3000	167
West Virginia University						
PO Box 6009	Morgantown	WV	26506	**800-344-9881**	304-293-2121	167
Institute of Technology						
405 Fayette Pk	Montgomery	WV	25136	**888-554-8324**	304-442-1000	167
Parkersburg						
300 Campus Dr	Parkersburg	WV	26104	**800-982-9887**	304-424-8000	161
West Virginia University School of Medicine						
Medical Ctr Dr						
Health Sciences Ctr N Rm 1146	Morgantown	WV	26506	**800-543-5650**	304-293-2408	168-2
West Virginia Wesleyan College						
59 College Ave	Buckhannon	WV	26201	**800-722-9933***	304-473-8000	167
*Admitting						
West Wind Inn						
3345 W Gulf Dr	Sanibel	FL	33957	**800-824-0476**	239-472-1541	667
West Window Corp						
226 Industrial Pk Dr	Martinsville	VA	24112	**800-446-4167**	276-638-2394	236
Westak Inc						
1225 Elko Dr	Sunnyvale	CA	94089	**800-387-3766**	408-734-8686	624
Westar Energy						
PO Box 758500	Topeka	KS	66675	**800-544-4857**	785-575-6300	785
Westar Energy Inc						
818 S Kansas Ave	Topeka	KS	66612	**800-383-1183**	785-575-6300	360-5
NYSE: WR						
Westat Inc						
1600 Research Blvd	Rockville	MD	20850	**800-669-6820**	301-251-1500	465
Westbend Vineyards						
5394 Williams Rd	Lewisville	NC	27023	**866-901-5032**	336-945-5032	49-6
Westbrook Engineering						
23501 Mound Rd	Warren	MI	48091	**800-899-8182**	586-759-3100	358
Westbury National Show Systems Ltd						
772 Warden Ave	Toronto	ON	M1L4T7	**855-752-1372**	416-752-1371	186
Westcare Management Inc						
3155 River Rd S Ste 100	Salem	OR	97302	**800-541-3732**		196
Westchester Community College						
75 Grasslands Rd	Valhalla	NY	10595	**800-235-7267**	914-606-6600	161
Westchester Philharmonic						
123 Main St Lobby Level	White Plains	NY	10601	**800-553-0031**	914-682-3707	572-3
Westchester Toyota Service						
75 Vredenburgh Ave	Yonkers	NY	10704	**866-232-7662**	914-968-6500	56
Westchester, The						
125 Westchester Ave	White Plains	NY	10601	**877-746-6642**	914-421-1333	459
West-Com Nurse Call Systems Inc						
2200 Cordelia Rd	Fairfield	CA	94534	**800-761-1180**	707-428-5900	176
Westcon Group Inc						
520 White Plains Rd 2nd Fl	Tarrytown	NY	10591	**800-527-9516**	914-829-7000	176
Westcon Group, Inc						
Westcon Convergence						
520 White Plains Rd Ste 100	Omaha	NE	68154	**877-642-7750**		176
WestEd						
730 Harrison St 5th Fl	San Francisco	CA	94107	**877-493-7833**	415-565-3000	666

Alphabetical Section

Name / Address	City	State	Zip	Toll-Free	Phone	Class
Westell Technologies Inc 750 N Commons Dr *NASDAQ: WSTL*	Aurora	IL	60504	**800-323-6883**	630-898-2500	732
Westerbeke Corp 150 John Hancock Rd Miles Standish Industrial Pk	Taunton	MA	02780	**800-582-7846**	508-823-7677	264
Westerly Hospital 25 Wells St	Westerly	RI	02891	**800-933-5960**	401-596-6000	374-3
Western & Southern Financial Group 400 Broadway	Cincinnati	OH	45202	**800-333-5222**	513-629-1800	360-4
Western & Southern Life Insurance Co 400 Broadway	Cincinnati	OH	45202	**800-926-1993**		391-2
Western Agcredit PO Box 95850	South Jordan	UT	84095	**800-824-9198**	801-571-9200	218
Western Aircraft Inc 4300 S Kennedy St	Boise	ID	83705	**800-333-3442**	208-338-1800	62
Western Bagel Baking Corp 7814 Sepulveda Blvd	Van Nuys	CA	91405	**800-555-0882**	818-786-5847	345
Western Bus Sales Inc 30355 SE Hwy 212	Boring	OR	97009	**800-258-2473**	503-905-0002	56
Western Canada Wilderness Committee (WCWC) 227 Abbott St	Vancouver	BC	V6B2K7	**800-661-9453**	604-683-8220	47-13
Western Cardinal Inc 205 Durley Ave	Camarillo	CA	93010	**800-882-3018**	805-482-2586	62
Western Carolina University (WCU) 1 University Dr	Cullowhee	NC	28723	**877-928-4968**	828-227-7211	167
Western Connecticut State University 181 White St	Danbury	CT	06810	**877-837-9278**	203-837-8200	167
Western Consolidated Co-op 520 Co Rd 9 PO Box 78	Holloway	MN	56249	**800-368-3310**	320-394-2171	278
Western Continental Book Co 6425 Washington St	Denver	CO	80229	**800-364-0350**	303-289-1761	95
Western Co-op Electric Assn Inc 635 S 13th St	WaKeeney	KS	67672	**800-456-6720**	785-743-5561	247
Western Co-op Transport Assn 4501 72nd St SW	Montevideo	MN	56265	**800-992-8817**	320-269-5531	778
Western Copper Corp 1040 W Georgia St FL 15	Vancouver	BC	V6E4H1	**888-966-9995**	604-684-9497	501
Western Diesel Services Inc 1100 Research Blvd	Saint Louis	MO	63132	**855-257-6937**	314-868-8620	264
Western Digital Corp 3355 Michelson Dr Ste 100 *NASDAQ: WDC*	Irvine	CA	92612	**800-832-4778**	949-672-7000	175-8
Western Enterprises Inc 875 Bassett Rd	Westlake	OH	44145	**800-783-7890**		809
Western Express Inc 7135 Centennial Pl	Nashville	TN	37209	**800-316-7160**	615-259-9920	778
Western Exterminator Co 305 N Crescent Way	Anaheim	CA	92801	**800-698-2440**	714-517-9000	576
Western Extralite Co 1470 Liberty St	Kansas City	MO	64102	**800-279-8833**	816-421-8404	248
Western Forestry & Conservation Assn 4033 SW Canyon Rd	Portland	OR	97221	**888-722-9416**	503-226-4562	47-12
Western Forge & Flange Co 687 County Rd 2201	Cleveland	TX	77327	**800-352-6433**	281-727-7060	482
Western Fraternal Life Assn (WFLA) 1900 First Ave NE	Cedar Rapids	IA	52402	**877-935-2467**	319-363-2653	391-2
Western Funding Inc PO Box 94858	Las Vegas	NV	89193	**888-434-3122**	702-434-1990	216
Western Hoist Inc 1839 Cleveland Ave	National City	CA	91950	**888-994-6478**	619-474-3361	469
Western Horizon Resorts (WHR) 103 W Tomichi Ave Ste 201A	Gunnison	CO	81230	**800-378-3709**	970-641-5387	120
Western Hydro Corp 3449 Enterprise Ave	Hayward	CA	94545	**800-972-5945**	510-783-9166	386
Western Illinois Electrical Co-op 524 N Madison St PO Box 338	Carthage	IL	62321	**800-576-3125**	217-357-3125	247
Western Illinois University 1 University Cir *Admissions	Macomb	IL	61455	**877-742-5948***	309-298-1414	167
Malpass Library 1 University Cir	Macomb	IL	61455	**800-413-6544**	309-298-2762	434-6
Quad Cities 3561 60th St	Moline	IL	61265	**877-742-5948**	309-762-9481	167
Western Implement Co Inc 2919 N Ave	Grand Junction	CO	81504	**800-338-6639**	970-242-7960	276
Western International Securities Inc 70 S Lake Ave Ste 700	Pasadena	CA	91101	**888-793-7717**		688
Western International University 9215 N Black Canyon Hwy	Phoenix	AZ	85021	**866-948-4636**	602-943-2311	167
Western Iowa Co-op 3330 Moville St PO Box 106	Hornick	IA	51026	**800-488-3201**	712-874-3211	277
Western Iowa Power Co-op 809 Iowa 39	Denison	IA	51442	**800-253-5189**	712-263-2943	247
Western Iowa Tech Community College 4647 Stone Ave	Sioux City	IA	51102	**800-352-4649**	712-274-6400	798
Western Kentucky University 1906 College Heights Blvd *Admissions	Bowling Green	KY	42101	**800-495-8463***	270-745-0111	167
Western Living Magazine 2608 Granville St Ste 560	Vancouver	BC	V6H3V3	**800-363-3272**	604-877-7732	456-11
Western Lumber Cy LLC 2240 Tower E Ste 200	Medford	OR	97504	**800-633-5554**	541-779-5121	193-3
WESTERN MASS NEWS 1300 Liberty St	Springfield	MA	01104	**877-872-2756**	413-733-4040	738-80
Western Mental Health Institute 11100 Hwy 64 W	Bolivar	TN	38008	**800-770-8277**	731-228-2000	374-5
Western Michigan University Waldo Library 1903 W Michigan Ave	Kalamazoo	MI	49008	**866-533-3438**	269-387-5202	434-6
Western Museum of Mining & Industry 225 N Gate Blvd	Colorado Springs	CO	80921	**800-752-6558**	719-488-0880	519
Western National Mutual Insurance Co 5350 W 78th St	Edina	MN	55439	**800-862-6070**	952-835-5350	391-4
Western Nebraska Community College 1601 E 27th St	Scottsbluff	NE	69361	**800-348-4435**	308-635-3606	161
Western Nevada Community College (WNC) *Douglas* 1680 Bently Pkwy S	Minden	NV	89423	**800-433-3243**	775-782-2413	161
Western Nevada Supply Co 950 S Rock Blvd	Sparks	NV	89431	**800-648-1230**	775-359-5800	611
Western New England College 1215 Wilbraham Rd	Springfield	MA	01119	**800-782-6665**	413-782-3111	167
Western New Mexico University 1000 W College St PO Box 680 *Admissions	Silver City	NM	88061	**800-872-9668***	505-538-6011	167
Western Oilfields Supply Co 3404 State Rd	Bakersfield	CA	93308	**800-742-7246**	661-399-9124	266-3
Western Oklahoma State College 2801 N Main St	Altus	OK	73521	**800-662-1113**	580-477-2000	161
Western Ophthalmics Corp 19019 36th Ave W Ste G	Lynnwood	WA	98036	**800-426-9938**	425-672-9332	543
Western Oregon University 345 Monmouth Ave N *Admissions	Monmouth	OR	97361	**877-877-1593***	503-838-8000	167
Western Oregon University Hamersly Library 345 N Monmouth Ave	Monmouth	OR	97361	**877-877-1593**	503-838-8418	434-6
Western Outdoors Magazine 185 Avenida La Pata	San Clemente	CA	92673	**800-290-2929**	949-366-0030	456-22
Western Pacific Storage Systems Inc 300 E Arrow Hwy	San Dimas	CA	91773	**800-732-9777**		288
Western Partitions Inc 8300 SW Hunziker Rd	Tigard	OR	97223	**800-783-0315**	503-620-1600	191-9
Western Petroleum Co 9531 W 78th St	Eden Prairie	MN	55344	**800-972-3835**	952-941-9090	578
Western Pioneer Inc 4601 Shilshole Ave NW	Seattle	WA	98107	**800-426-6783**	206-789-1930	313
Western Plastic Products Inc 8441 Monroe Ave	Stanton	CA	90680	**800-453-1881**		9
Western Power Sports Inc 601 E Gowen Rd	Boise	ID	83716	**800-999-3388**	208-376-8400	709
Western Reflections 261 Commerce Way *Cust Svc	Gallatin	TN	37066	**800-507-8302***	615-451-9700	439
Western Reserve Academy 115 College St	Hudson	OH	44236	**877-486-2048**	330-650-9717	621
Western Reserve Farm Co-op Inc 14961 S State Ave PO Box 339	Middlefield	OH	44062	**888-427-6672**	440-632-1192	278
Western Reserve Group, The 1685 Cleveland Rd	Wooster	OH	44691	**800-362-0426**	330-262-9060	391-4
Western Security Bank 2812 First Ave N	Billings	MT	59101	**800-983-5537**	406-371-8200	69
Western Seminary 5511 SE Hawthorne Blvd	Portland	OR	97215	**877-517-1800**	503-517-1800	168-3
Western Slope Auto Co 2264 Hwy 6 & 50	Grand Junction	CO	81505	**888-461-3493**	970-243-0843	56
Western State College of Colorado 600 N Adams St *Admissions	Gunnison	CO	81231	**800-876-5309***	970-943-2119	167
Western State Hospital 9601 Steilacoom Blvd SW	Tacoma	WA	98498	**877-501-2233**	253-582-8900	374-5
Western State University College of Law 1111 N State College Blvd	Fullerton	CA	92831	**800-978-4529**	714-459-1101	168-1
Western States Envelope & Label Co 4480 N 132nd St	Butler	WI	53007	**800-558-0514**	262-781-5540	265
Western States Petroleum Inc 450 S 15th Ave	Phoenix	AZ	85007	**800-220-1353**	602-252-4011	578
Western States Ticket Service 143 W McDowell Rd	Phoenix	AZ	85003	**800-326-0331**	602-254-3300	748
Western States Weeklies Inc PO Box 600600	San Diego	CA	92160	**800-628-9466**	619-280-2985	634-8
Western Sugar Co-op 7555 E Hampden Ave Ste 600	Denver	CO	80231	**800-523-7497**	303-830-3939	297-38
Western Syrup Co 13766 Milroy Pl	Santa Fe Springs	CA	90670	**800-521-3888**	562-921-4485	297-15
Western Technical College 400 Seventh St N	La Crosse	WI	54601	**800-322-9982**	608-785-9200	798
Western Technologies Inc 3737 E Broadway Rd	Phoenix	AZ	85040	**800-580-3737**	602-437-3737	194
Western Telematic Inc 5 Sterling	Irvine	CA	92618	**800-854-7226**	949-586-9950	175-3
Western Texas College 6200 College Ave	Snyder	TX	79549	**888-468-6982**	325-573-8511	161
Western Texas Lions Eye Bank Alliance 2030 Pullman St Ste 4	San Angelo	TX	76902	**866-226-7632**	325-653-8666	271
Western Theological Seminary 101 E 13th St	Holland	MI	49423	**800-392-8554**	616-392-8555	168-3
Western Trailer Co 251 W Gowen Rd	Boise	ID	83716	**888-344-2539**	208-344-2539	777
Western Truck Parts & Equip Co 3707 Airport Way S	Seattle	WA	98134	**800-255-7383**	206-624-7383	60
Western Union Holdings Inc 12500 E Belford Ave *NYSE: WU* ■ *Cust Svc	Englewood	CO	80112	**800-325-6000***	720-332-1000	68
Western United Life Assurance Co 929 W Sprague Ave PO Box 2290 *General	Spokane	WA	99210	**800-247-2045***	509-835-2500	391-2
Western University of Health Sciences 309 E Second St	Pomona	CA	91766	**800-346-1610**	909-623-6116	161
Western Upper Peninsula Convention & Visitor Bureau 405 N Lake St PO Box 706	Ironwood	MI	49938	**800-522-5657**	906-932-4850	208
Western Veterinary Conference 2425 E Oquendo Rd	Las Vegas	NV	89120	**866-800-7326**	702-739-6698	792
Western Village Inn & Casino 815 Nichols Blvd	Sparks	NV	89434	**800-648-1170**		132
Western Wood Preserving Co 1310 Zehnder St	Sumner	WA	98390	**800-472-7714**	253-863-8191	816
Western World Insurance Co 400 Parson's Pond Dr	Franklin Lakes	NJ	07417	**888-847-8600**	201-847-8600	391-5
Western Wyoming Community College 2500 College Dr	Rock Springs	WY	82901	**800-226-1181**	307-382-1600	161
Western-Southern Life Assurance Co 400 Broadway	Cincinnati	OH	45202	**866-832-7719**		391-2
Westerville Public Library 126 S State St	Westerville	OH	43081	**800-816-0662**	614-882-7277	434-3

Name / Address	City	State	Zip	Toll-Free	Phone	Class
Westerville This Week 7801 N Central Dr	Lewis Center	OH	43035	**888-837-4342**	740-888-6100	531-4
Westex Inc 122 W 22nd St	Oak Brook	IL	60523	**866-493-7839**	773-523-7000	742-7
Westfalia Technologies Inc 3655 Sandhurst Dr	York	PA	17406	**800-673-2522**	717-764-1115	209
Westfield Board of Education Inc 302 Elm St	Westfield	NJ	07090	**800-355-2583**	908-789-4401	683
Westfield Financial Inc 141 Elm St *NASDAQ: WFD*	Westfield	MA	01085	**800-995-5734**	413-568-1911	360-2
Westfield Industries Ltd 74 Hwy 205 E	Rosenort	MB	R0G1W0	**866-467-7207**	204-746-2396	275
Westfield Steel Inc 530 State Rd 32 W	Westfield	IN	46074	**800-622-4984**		491
Westgate Branson Woods 2201 Roark Vly Rd	Branson	MO	65616	**877-253-8572**	417-334-2324	379
Westgate Hotel, The 1055 Second Ave	San Diego	CA	92101	**800-522-1564**	619-238-1818	669
Westgate Painted Mountain Country Club 6302 E McKellips Rd	Mesa	AZ	85215	**888-433-3707**	480-654-3611	379
Westglow Resort & Spa 224 Westglow Cir	Blowing Rock	NC	28605	**800-562-0807**	828-295-4463	705
Westham Trade Co Ltd 3620 NW 114th Ave	Doral	FL	33178	**888-852-5000**	305-717-5400	176
West-Herr Automotive Group Inc 3448 McKinley Pkwy	Blasdell	NY	14219	**800-643-2112**	716-649-5640	56
Westin Automotive Products Inc 5200 N Irwindale Ave Ste 220	Irwindale	CA	91706	**800-345-8476**	626-960-6762	60
Westin Houston Downtown, The 1520 Texas Ave	Houston	TX	77002	**800-427-4697**	713-228-1520	379
Westin Key West Resort & Marina 245 Front St	Key West	FL	33040	**866-837-4250**	305-294-4000	667
Westin Kierland Resort & Spa 6902 E Greenway Pkwy	Scottsdale	AZ	85254	**800-354-5892**	480-624-1000	705
Westin Maui Resort & Spa, The 2365 Kaanapali Pkwy	Lahaina	HI	96761	**866-716-8112**	808-667-2525	705
Westin Mission Hills Resort 71333 Dinah Shore Dr	Rancho Mirage	CA	92270	**866-716-8108**	760-328-5955	705
Westin Resort & Spa 4090 Whistler Way	Whistler	BC	V0N1B4	**888-627-8979**	604-905-5000	705
WestJet Airlines Ltd 22 Aerial Pl NE *TSE: WJA*	Calgary	AB	T2E3J1	**888-293-7853**	403-444-2600	25
Westlake Chemical Corp 2801 Post Oak Blvd Ste 600 *NYSE: WLK*	Houston	TX	77056	**888-953-3623**	713-960-9111	604-2
Westlake Plastics Co PO Box 127	Lenni	PA	19052	**800-999-1700**	610-459-1000	603
Westlake Village 28550 Westlake Village Dr	Westlake	OH	44145	**855-308-2432**		670
Westland Chamber of Commerce 36900 Ford Rd	Westland	MI	48185	**800-737-4859**	734-326-7222	138
Westland Corp 1735 S Maize Rd	Wichita	KS	67209	**800-247-1144**	316-721-1144	755
Westland Sales PO Box 427	Clackamas	OR	97015	**800-356-0766**	503-655-2563	37
Westlaw Court Express 1100 13th St NW Ste 300	Washington	DC	20005	**877-362-7387**	202-423-2163	632
West-Lite Supply Company Inc 12951 166th St	Cerritos	CA	90703	**800-660-6678**		248
Westman Freightliner Inc 2200 Fourth Ave Mankato PO Box 699	Mankato	MN	56001	**866-576-6914**	507-625-4118	56
Westmark Hotels Inc 300 Elliott Ave W	Seattle	WA	98119	**800-544-0970**		379
Westminster Bradenton Manor 1700 21st Ave W	Bradenton	FL	34205	**877-382-9036**	941-748-4161	670
Westminster Chamber of Commerce 1025 Westminster Mall	Westminster	CA	92683	**800-545-5585**	714-898-2559	138
Westminster College 501 Westminster Ave *Admissions	Fulton	MO	65251	**800-475-3361***	573-592-5251	167
Westminster Oaks 4449 Meandering Way	Tallahassee	FL	32308	**800-948-1881**	850-878-1136	670
Westminster Place 3200 Grant St	Evanston	IL	60201	**888-285-3233**	847-570-3422	670
Westminster School District 14121 Cedarwood St	Westminster	CA	92683	**800-678-9133**	714-894-7311	683
Westminster Theological Seminary 2960 Church Rd	Glenside	PA	19038	**800-373-0119**	215-887-5511	168-3
Westminster Theological Seminary in California 1725 Bear Vly Pkwy	Escondido	CA	92027	**888-480-8474**	760-480-8474	168-3
Westminster Towers 1330 India Hook Rd	Rock Hill	SC	29732	**800-345-6026**	803-328-5000	670
Westminster Village 803 N Wahneta St	Allentown	PA	18109	**888-563-8147**	610-782-8300	670
Westminster-Canterbury of Lynchburg 501 VES Rd	Lynchburg	VA	24503	**800-962-3520**	434-386-3500	670
Westminster-Canterbury on Chesapeake Bay 3100 Shore Dr	Virginia Beach	VA	23451	**800-349-1722**	757-496-1785	670
Westminster-Canterbury Richmond 1600 Westbrook Ave	Richmond	VA	23227	**800-445-9904**	804-264-6000	670
Westmont College 955 La Paz Rd *Admissions	Santa Barbara	CA	93108	**800-777-9011***	805-565-6000	167
Westmoreland Chamber of Commerce 241 Tollgate Hill Rd	Greensburg	PA	15601	**866-468-1231**	724-834-2900	138
Westmoreland Coal Co 9540 S Maroon Cir Ste 200 *NASDAQ: WLB*	Englewood	CO	80112	**855-922-6463**	719-442-2600	500
Westmoreland County Community College 145 Pavilion Ln	Youngwood	PA	15697	**800-262-2103**	724-925-4000	161
Westmoreland Mall 5256 Rt 30 E	Greensburg	PA	15601	**800-333-7310**	724-836-5025	459
Weston & Sampson Inc 5 Centennial Dr	Peabody	MA	01960	**800-726-7766**	978-532-1900	263
Westpac Banking Corp Americas Div 575 Fifth Ave 39th Fl	New York	NY	10017	**888-269-2377**	212-551-1800	69
Westport Country Playhouse 25 Powers Ct	Westport	CT	06880	**888-927-7529**	203-227-4177	571
Westward Look Resort 245 E Ina Rd	Tucson	AZ	85704	**800-722-2500**	520-297-1151	667
Westward Parts Services Ltd 6517 - 67 St	Red Deer	AB	T4P1A3	**888-937-7278**	403-347-2200	110
West-Ward Pharmaceutical Corp 401 Industrial Way W *Cust Svc	Eatontown	NJ	07724	**800-631-2174***	732-542-1191	583
Westway Ford 801 W Airport Fwy	Irving	TX	75062	**844-877-9037**		56
Westwood College Atlanta Northlake 2309 Parklake Dr NE	Atlanta	GA	30345	**800-227-5695**	770-743-3000	798
Westwood College Inland Empire 20 W Seventh St	Upland	CA	91786	**866-221-5632**	909-931-7550	798
Westwood College O'Hare Airport 8501 W Higgins Rd Ste 100	Chicago	IL	60631	**866-552-7536**	773-380-6800	798
Westwood Holdings Group Inc 200 Crescent Ct Ste 1200 *NYSE: WHG*	Dallas	TX	75201	**800-687-0372**	214-756-6900	360-2
Westwood Lodge Hospital 45 Clapboardtree St	Westwood	MA	02090	**800-222-2237**	781-762-7764	374-5
Wet 'n Wild Emerald Pointe 3910 S Holden Rd	Greensboro	NC	27406	**800-555-5900**	336-852-9721	32
Wet 'n Wild Orlando 6200 International Dr *General	Orlando	FL	32819	**800-992-9453***	407-351-1800	32
Wet Seal Inc 26972 Burbank Ave *NASDAQ: WTSLA*	Foothill Ranch	CA	92610	**866-746-7938**	949-699-3900	156-6
WeTip Inc PO Box 1296	Rancho Cucamonga	CA	91729	**800-782-7463**	909-987-5005	47-8
Wetsel Inc 961 N Liberty St *Cust Svc	Harrisonburg	VA	22802	**800-572-4018***	540-434-6753	692
WETS-FM 89.5 (NPR) PO Box 70630	Johnson City	TN	37614	**888-895-9387**	423-439-6440	642-61
WEVO-FM 89.1 (N/T) 2 Pillsbury St 6th Fl	Concord	NH	03301	**800-639-4131**	603-228-8910	643
Wexler Surgical Supplies 11333 Chimney Rock Rd	Houston	TX	77035	**800-414-1076**	713-723-6900	475
Weyco Group Inc 333 W Estabrook Blvd *NASDAQ: WEYS*	Glendale	WI	53212	**866-454-0449**	414-908-1880	302
Weyerhaeuser Co 33663 Weyerhaeuser Way S *NYSE: WY*	Federal Way	WA	98003	**800-525-5440**	253-924-2345	187
WEZX-FM 106.9 (Rock) 149 Penn Ave	Scranton	PA	18503	**800-228-4637**	570-346-6555	642-110
WF Meyers Co 1008 13th St	Bedford	IN	47421	**800-457-4055**	812-275-4485	454
WF Young Inc 302 Benton Dr	East Longmeadow	MA	01028	**800-628-9653**	413-526-9999	582
WFAE-FM 90.7 (NPR) 8801 JM Keynes Dr Ste 91 *Cust Svc	Charlotte	NC	28262	**800-876-9323***	704-549-9323	642-27
WFCA (World Floor Covering Assn) 2211 Howell Ave	Anaheim	CA	92806	**800-624-6880**	714-978-6440	48-4
WFCF-FM 88.5 (Var) Flagler College PO Box 1027	Saint Augustine	FL	32085	**800-304-4208**	904-819-6449	643
WFDD-FM 88.5 (NPR) 1834 Wake Forest Rd Ste 8850	Winston-Salem	NC	27109	**800-262-8850**	336-758-8850	642-131
WFFF-TV Ch 44 (Fox) 298 Mountain View Dr	Colchester	VT	05446	**888-344-7233**	802-660-9333	
WFHN-FM 107.1 (CHR) 22 Sconticut Neck Rd	Fairhaven	MA	02719	**877-854-9467**	508-999-6690	643
WFIE-TV Ch 14 (NBC) 1115 Mt Auburn Rd	Evansville	IN	47720	**800-832-0014**	812-426-1414	738-28
WFIR-AM 960 (N/T) 3934 Electric Rd SW	Roanoke	VA	24018	**800-367-7623**	540-345-1511	642-100
WFIU-FM 103.7 Indiana University 1229 E Seventh St	Bloomington	IN	47405	**877-285-9348**	812-855-1357	643
WFLA (Western Fraternal Life Assn) 1900 First Ave NE	Cedar Rapids	IA	52402	**877-935-2467**	319-363-2653	391-2
WFLA-TV Ch 8 (NBC) PO Box 1410	Tampa	FL	33601	**800-338-0808**	813-228-8888	738-84
WFLX-TV Ch 29 (Fox) 4119 W Blue Heron Blvd	West Palm Beach	FL	33404	**844-555-1329**	561-845-2929	738-93
WFMJ-TV Ch 21 (NBC) 101 W Boardman St	Youngstown	OH	44503	**800-488-9365**	330-744-8611	738-96
WFMY-TV Ch 2 (CBS) 1615 Phillips Ave	Greensboro	NC	27405	**800-593-3692**	336-379-9369	
WFNZ-AM 610 (Sports) 1520 S Blvd Ste 300	Charlotte	NC	28203	**866-570-9610**	704-319-9369	642-27
WFP (World Food Program USA) 1725 Eye St NW Ste 510	Washington	DC	20036	**888-454-0555**	202-530-1694	47-5
WFPG-FM 96.9 (AC) 950 Tilton Rd Ste 200	Northfield	NJ	08225	**800-969-9374**	609-645-9797	643
WFSQ-FM 91.5 (Clas) 1600 Red Barber Plaza	Tallahassee	FL	32310	**866-321-9378**	850-487-3086	642-121
WFSU-FM 88.9 (NPR) 1600 Red Barber Plaza	Tallahassee	FL	32310	**800-322-9378**	850-487-3086	642-121
WFSU-TV Ch 11 (PBS) 1600 Red Barber Plz	Tallahassee	FL	32310	**800-322-9378**	850-487-3170	738-83
WFTS-TV Ch 28 (ABC) 4045 N Himes Ave	Tampa	FL	33607	**877-833-2828**	813-354-2828	738-84
WFUV-FM 90.7 (Var) 441 E Fordham Rd Fordham University	Bronx	NY	10458	**888-400-5520**	718-817-4550	643
WFWA-TV Ch 39 (PBS) 2501 E Coliseum Blvd	Fort Wayne	IN	46805	**888-484-8839**	260-484-8839	738-32
WFXT-TV Ch 25 (Fox) 25 Fox Dr	Dedham	MA	02026	**877-369-2563**	781-467-2525	
WG Bill Hefner Veterans Affairs Medical Ctr 1601 Brenner Ave	Salisbury	NC	28144	**800-469-8262**	704-638-9000	374-8

Alphabetical Section

Name / Address	City	State	ZIP	Toll-Free	Phone	Class
WGAR-FM 99.5 (Ctry) 6200 Oak Tree Blvd S 4th Fl	Independence	OH	44131	855-222-0995	216-520-2600	643
WGAw (Writers Guild of America West) 7000 W Third St	Los Angeles	CA	90048	800-421-4182	323-951-4000	414
WGBF-AM 1280 (N/T) 117 SE Fifth St	Evansville	IN	47708	877-437-5995	812-425-4226	642-42
WGBF-FM 103.1 (Rock) 117 SE Fifth St	Evansville	IN	47708	888-900-9423	812-425-4226	642-42
WGBH-TV Ch 2 (PBS) 1 Guest St	Brighton	MA	02135	800-492-1111	617-300-2000	
WGGS-TV Ch 16 (Ind) 3409 Rutherford Rd Ext *General	Taylors	SC	29687	800-849-3683*	864-244-1616	
WGGY-FM 101.3 (Ctry) 305 Hwy 315	Pittston	PA	18640	800-570-1013	570-883-1111	643
WGHP-TV Ch 8 (Fox) 2005 Francis St	High Point	NC	27263	800-808-6397	336-841-8888	
WGI Heavy Minerals Inc 810 E Sherman Ave *TSE: WG*	Coeur d'Alene	ID	83814	888-542-7638	208-666-6000	502-3
WGL Holdings Inc 101 Constitution Ave NW *NYSE: WGL*	Washington	DC	20080	800-645-3751	703-750-2000	360-5
WGM (World Gospel Mission) 3783 E State Rd 18 PO Box 948	Marion	IN	46952	800-426-0846	765-664-7331	47-20
WGMD-FM 92.7 (N/T) PO Box 530	Rehoboth Beach	DE	19971	800-518-9292	302-945-2050	643
WGNE-FM 99.9 (Ctry) 6440 Atlantic Blvd	Jacksonville	FL	32211	888-725-2345	904-727-9696	643
WG&R Furniture Co 900 Challenger Dr	Green Bay	WI	54311	888-947-7782	920-469-4880	322
WGRD-FM 97.9 (Rock) 50 Monroe Ave NW Ste 500	Grand Rapids	MI	49503	800-947-3979	616-451-4800	642-50
WGTS-FM 91.9 (Rel) 7600 Flower Ave	Takoma Park	MD	20912	800-700-1094	301-891-4200	643
WGTY-FM 107.7 (Ctry) 1560 Fairfield Rd PO Box 3179	Gettysburg	PA	17325	800-366-9489	717-334-3101	643
WGVU-FM 88.5 (NPR) 301 W Fulton St	Grand Rapids	MI	49504	800-442-2771	616-331-6666	642-50
WGVU-TV Ch 35 (PBS) 301 W Fulton St	Grand Rapids	MI	49504	800-442-2771	616-331-6666	738-34
WGY-AM 810 (N/T) 1203 Troy-Schenectady Rd	Latham	NY	12110	800-825-5949	518-452-4800	643
WH Bagshaw Company Inc 1 Pine St Ext PO Box 766	Nashua	NH	03060	800-343-7467	603-883-7758	386
WHA-AM 970 (NPR) 821 University Ave	Madison	WI	53706	800-747-7444		642-72
WHAD-FM 90.7 (NPR) 310 W Wisconsin Ave Ste 750-E	Milwaukee	WI	53203	800-486-8655	414-227-2040	642-76
WHAL-FM 95.7 (Rel) 2650 Thousand Oaks Blvd Ste 4100	Memphis	TN	38118	888-302-6222	901-259-1300	642-74
Wham-O Inc 6301 Owensmouth Ave Ste 700	Woodland Hills	CA	91367	888-942-6650		760
Wharf Resources USA Inc 10928 Wharf Rd	Lead	SD	57754	800-567-6223	605-584-1441	501
Wharton County Electric Co-op Inc (WCEC) 1815 E Jackson St	El Campo	TX	77437	800-460-6271	979-543-6271	247
Wharton County Junior College 911 Boling Hwy	Wharton	TX	77488	800-561-9252	979-532-4560	161
Sugar Land 14004 University Blvd	Sugar Land	TX	77479	800-561-9252	281-243-8447	161
Wharton County Library 1920 N Fulton St	Wharton	TX	77488	800-244-5492	979-532-8080	434-3
Wharton Ctr for the Performing Arts Michigan State University	East Lansing	MI	48824	800-942-7866	517-432-2000	571
Wharton Group 101 S Livingston Ave	Livingston	NJ	07039	800-521-2725	973-992-5775	390
Wharton Independent School District 2100 N Fulton St	Wharton	TX	77488	800-818-3453	979-532-3612	683
WHAS-AM 840 (N/T) 4000 One Radio Dr	Louisville	KY	40218	800-444-8484	502-479-2222	642-70
Whatcom Community College 237 W Kellogg Rd	Bellingham	WA	98226	855-767-9003	360-676-2170	161
WHBM (White House/Black Market) 11215 Metro Pkwy	Fort Myers	FL	33966	877-948-2525	239-277-6200	156-6
WHCF-FM 88.5 (Rel) PO Box 5000	Bangor	ME	04402	800-947-2577	207-947-2751	642-12
Wheat Belt Public Power District 2104 Illinois St	Sidney	NE	69162	800-261-7114	308-254-5871	247
Wheat Montana Farms Inc 10778 US Hwy 287	Three Forks	MT	59752	800-535-2798	406-285-3614	298-1
Wheat Ridge Ministries 1 Pierce Pl Ste 250E	Itasca	IL	60143	800-762-6748	630-766-9066	47-20
Wheatland Electric Co-op Inc 101 S Main St	Scott City	KS	67871	800-762-0436	620-872-5885	247
Wheatland Rural Electric Assn 2154 S St PO Box 1209	Wheatland	WY	82201	800-344-3351	307-322-2125	247
Wheatland Tube Co 700 S Dock St	Sharon	PA	16146	800-257-8182		489
Wheatmark Inc 1760 E River Rd Ste 145	Tucson	AZ	85718	888-934-0888	520-798-0888	634-2
Wheaton College 501 College Ave	Wheaton	IL	60187	800-222-2419	630-752-5000	167
Wheaton Franciscan Healthcare 3801 Spring St	Racine	WI	53405	877-304-6332	262-687-4011	374-3
All Saints 3801 Spring St	Racine	WI	53405	877-304-6332	262-687-4011	374-3
Wheaton Van Lines Inc 8010 Castleton Rd	Indianapolis	IN	46250	800-932-7799	317-849-7900	518
Wheaton-Kensington Chamber of Commerce 2401 Blueridge Ave Ste 101	Wheaton	MD	20902	800-927-9061	301-949-0080	138
Wheel & Sprocket Inc 5722 S 108th St	Hales Corners	WI	53130	866-995-9918	414-529-6600	709
Wheelabrator Technologies Inc 4 Liberty Ln W	Hampton	NH	03842	800-682-0026	603-929-3000	802
Wheeled Coach Industries Inc 2737 Forsyth Rd	Winter Park	FL	32792	800-342-0720	407-677-7777	515
Wheeler Lumber LLC 9330 James Ave S	Bloomington	MN	55431	800-328-3986	952-929-7854	193-3
Wheeler Mfg Co Inc 107 Main Ave PO Box 629	Lemmon	SD	57638	800-843-1937	605-374-3848	409
Wheeler Opera House 320 E Hyman St	Aspen	CO	81611	866-449-0464	970-920-5770	571
Wheeler-Rex Inc 3744 Jefferson Rd PO Box 688	Ashtabula	OH	44005	800-321-7950	440-998-2788	756
Wheeling Convention & Visitors Bureau 1401 Main St	Wheeling	WV	26003	800-828-3097	304-233-7709	208
Wheeling Island Gaming Inc 1 S St1 St	Wheeling	WV	26003	877-946-4373	304-232-5050	132
Wheeling Jesuit University 316 Washington Ave	Wheeling	WV	26003	800-624-6992	304-243-2000	167
Wheelock College 200 The Riverway	Boston	MA	02215	800-734-5212	617-879-2206	167
Wheels Etc 17521 Mesa St	Hesperia	CA	92345	800-758-4737	909-350-8200	753
Wheelwright Museum of the American Indian 704 Camino Lejo	Santa Fe	NM	87505	800-607-4636	505-982-4636	519
Whelan Security Co 1699 S Hanley Rd Ste 350	St Louis	MO	63144	888-494-3526	314-644-3227	691
Whetstone Valley Electric Co-op 1101 E Fourth Ave	Milbank	SD	57252	800-568-6631	605-432-5331	247
WHIL-FM 91.3 (NPR) 166 Reese Phifer Hall PO Box 870150	Tuscaloosa	AL	35487	800-654-4262	205-348-6644	642-78
WHIQ-TV Ch 24 (PBS) 2112 11th Ave S Ste 400	Birmingham	AL	35205	800-239-5233	205-328-8756	738-11
Whirl Air Flow Corp 20055 177th St	Big Lake	MN	55309	800-373-3461	763-262-1200	209
Whirlpool Canada 200-6750 Century Ave	Mississauga	ON	L5N0B7	800-807-6777	905-821-6400	37
Whirlpool Corp 2000 N M-63 *NYSE: WHR*	Benton Harbor	MI	49022	800-253-1301	269-923-5000	35
Whirlpool Corp KitchenAid Div 553 Benson Rd	Benton Harbor	MI	49022	800-422-1230		36
Whirlpool Corp North American Region 2000 N M-63	Benton Harbor	MI	49022	800-253-1301	269-923-5000	35
Whirlpool Foundation 2000 N M-63	Benton Harbor	MI	49022	800-952-9245	269-923-5000	305
Whirlwind Steel 8234 Hansen Rd	Houston	TX	77075	800-324-9992	713-946-7140	104
Whistler Blackcomb Mountain Ski Resort 4545 Blackcomb Way	Whistler	BC	V0N1B4	800-766-0449	604-932-3434	667
Whistler Group Inc 13016 N Walton Blvd *Cust Svc	Bentonville	AR	72712	800-531-0004*	479-273-6012	528
Whitacre Greer Fireproofing Inc 1400 S Mahoning Ave *Cust Svc	Alliance	OH	44601	800-947-2837*	330-823-1610	149
Whitaker Buick Co 131 19th St SW	Forest Lake	MN	55025	877-324-8885	651-674-3931	56
Whitaker House/Anchor Distributors 1030 Hunt Vly Cir *General	New Kensington	PA	15068	800-444-4484*	724-334-7000	634-3
Whitaker Oil Co 1557 Marietta Rd NW	Atlanta	GA	30318	888-895-3506	404-355-8220	145
WHIT-AM 1550 (Nost) 730 Rayovac Dr	Madison	WI	53711	800-422-7128	608-273-1000	642-72
White Aluminum Products LLC 2101 US Hwy 441	Leesburg	FL	34748	888-474-5884		491
White Bison Inc 5585 Erindale Dr Ste 203	Colorado Springs	CO	80918	877-871-1495	719-548-1000	47-21
White Bros Trucking Co 4N793 School Rd	Wasco	IL	60183	800-323-4762	630-584-3810	778
White Buffalo Club 160 West Gill Ave Ste 200	Jackson	WY	83001	888-256-8182	307-734-4900	428
White Cap Industries Inc 1723 S Ritchie St	Santa Ana	CA	92705	800-944-8322	714-258-3300	193-3
White Coffee Corp 18-35 Steinway Pl	Astoria	NY	11105	800-221-0140	718-204-7900	297-7
White County Chamber of Commerce 122 N Main St	Cleveland	GA	30528	800-392-8279	706-865-5356	138
White County Rural Electric Membership Corp 302 N Sixth St	Monticello	IN	47960	800-844-7161	574-583-7161	247
White Electrical Construction Co 1730 Chattahoochee Ave	Atlanta	GA	30318	888-519-4483	404-351-5740	191-4
White Elephant Inn & Cottages 50 Easton St	Nantucket	MA	02554	800-475-2637	508-228-2500	379
White Flower Farm Inc 30 Irene St *Cust Svc	Torrington	CT	06790	800-411-6159*	860-496-9624	324
White Glove Placement Inc 85 Bartlett St	Brooklyn	NY	11206	866-387-8100	718-387-8181	719
White House/Black Market (WHBM) 11215 Metro Pkwy	Fort Myers	FL	33966	877-948-2525	239-277-6200	156-6
White Knight Engineered Products 9525 Monroe Rd Ste 100	Charlotte	NC	28270	888-743-4700	704-542-6876	575
White Mountain Adventures 131 Eagle Crescent PO Box 4259	Banff	AB	T1L1A6	800-408-0005	403-760-4403	758
White Mountain Hotel & Resort 2560 W Side Rd PO Box 1828	North Conway	NH	03860	800-533-6301	603-356-7100	667
White Mountains Community College (WMCC) 2020 Riverside Dr	Berlin	NH	03570	800-445-4525	603-752-1113	161
White Mountains Insurance Group Ltd 80 S Main St *NYSE: WTM*	Hanover	NH	03755	866-295-3762	603-640-2200	360-4
White Oak Manor Inc 130 E Main St PO Box 3347	Spartanburg	SC	29304	800-826-6762	864-582-7503	670
White Oaks Conference Resort & Spa 253 Taylor Rd SS4 *Resv	Niagara-on-the-Lake	ON	L0S1J0	800-263-5766*	905-688-2550	377
White Paper Co 9990 River Way	Delta	BC	V4G1M9	888-840-7300	604-951-3900	552

Name / Address	City	State	Zip	Toll-Free	Phone	Class
White Plains Honda 344 Central Ave	White Plains	NY	10606	**877-553-9292**	914-948-3305	56
White Radio LP 5228 Everest Dr	Mississauga	ON	L4W2R4	**877-386-1956**	905-632-6894	248
White River Distributors Inc 720 Ramsey	Batesville	AR	72501	**800-548-7219**	870-793-2374	481
White River Electric Assn (WREA) PO Box 958	Meeker	CO	81641	**800-922-1987**	970-878-5041	247
White River Junction Veterans Affairs Medical Ctr 215 N Main St	White River Junction	VT	05009	**866-687-8387**	802-295-9363	374-8
White River State Park 801 W Washington St	Indianapolis	IN	46204	**800-665-9056**	317-233-2434	564
White River Valley Electric Co-op Inc 2449 State Hwy 76 E	Branson	MO	65616	**800-879-4056**	417-335-9335	247
White Rock Products Corp 141-07 20th Ave Ste 403	Whitestone	NY	11357	**800-969-7625**	718-746-3400	79-2
White Sands Federal Credit Union 2190 E Lohman Ave	Las Cruces	NM	88001	**800-658-9933**	575-647-4500	69
White Sands of La Jolla 516 Burchett St	Glendale	CA	92037	**800-347-3735**	818-247-0420	670
White Stallion Ranch 9251 W Twin Peaks Rd	Tucson	AZ	85743	**888-977-2624**	520-297-0252	241
White Star Tours 26 E Lancaster Ave	Reading	PA	19607	**800-437-2323**	610-775-5000	758
White Swan Inn 845 Bush St	San Francisco	CA	94108	**800-999-9570**	415-775-1755	379
White's Electronics Inc 1011 Pleasant Valley Rd *Sales	Sweet Home	OR	97386	**800-999-9147***	800-547-6911	471
White's Farm Supply Inc 4154 State Rt 31	Canastota	NY	13032	**800-633-4443**	315-697-2214	358
White's Inc 4614 Navigation Blvd PO Box 2344	Houston	TX	77011	**800-231-9559**	713-928-2632	276
Whitecap Resources Inc 3800 525 - 8th Ave SW	Calgary	AB	T2P1G1	**866-590-5289**	403-266-0767	535
Whitehall Printing Co 4244 Corporate Sq	Naples	FL	34104	**800-321-9290**		625
Whiteman Air Force Base 1081 Arnold Ave Bldg 59 Ste 104	Whiteman AFB	MO	65305	**866-363-8667**	660-687-6123	496-1
Whitesell Corp 2703 Avalon Ave *General	Muscle Shoals	AL	35661	**855-227-4515***	256-248-8500	485
Whitewater Grille 200 Lee St E	Charleston	WV	25301	**800-845-5279**	304-353-3636	669
Whitewater State Park 19041 Hwy 74	Altura	MN	55910	**800-366-8917**	507-932-3007	564
Whitewater Valley Rural Electric Membership Corp 101 Brownsville Ave	Liberty	IN	47353	**800-529-5557**	765-458-5171	247
WhiteWave Foods Co 12002 Airport Way	Broomfield	CO	80021	**888-820-9283**	303-635-4000	297-27
Whiting Corp 26000 Whiting Way	Monee	IL	60449	**800-861-5744**		469
Whitlam Label Company Inc 24800 Sherwood Ave	Center Line	MI	48015	**800-755-2235**	586-757-5100	413
Whitlock Group 12820 W Creekk Pkwy	Richmond	VA	23238	**800-726-9843**	804-273-9100	248
Whitman College 345 Boyer Ave *Admissions	Walla Walla	WA	99362	**877-462-9448***	509-527-5111	167
Whitmore Manufacturing Co PO Box 9300	Rockwall	TX	75087	**800-699-6318**	972-771-1000	549
Whitney Ctr 200 Leeder Hill Dr	Hamden	CT	06517	**800-237-3847**	203-848-2641	670
Whitney Museum of American Art 945 Madison Ave	New York	NY	10021	**800-944-8639**	212-570-3600	519
Whitney National Bank 228 St Charles Ave	New Orleans	LA	70130	**800-844-4450**	504-586-7456	69
Whitney the - A Wyndham Historic Hotel 610 Poydras St	New Orleans	LA	70130	**800-996-3426**	504-581-4222	379
Whitney Tool Company Inc 906 R St PO Box 545	Bedford	IN	47421	**800-536-1971**	812-275-4491	454
Whittier Hospital Medical Ctr 9080 Colima Rd	Whittier	CA	90605	**800-613-4291**	562-945-3561	374-3
Whittier Wood Products 3787 W First Ave PO Box 2827	Eugene	OR	97402	**800-653-3336**	541-687-0213	320-2
Whitworth College 300 W Hawthorne Rd *Admissions	Spokane	WA	99251	**800-533-4668***	509-777-1000	167
WHNT-TV Ch 19 (CBS) PO Box 19	Huntsville	AL	35804	**800-533-8819**	256-533-1919	738-37
WhoKnows Inc 425 BRdway St	Redwood City	CA	94063	**877-338-2763**		387
Whole Foods Market Inc 550 Bowie St *NASDAQ: WFM*	Austin	TX	78703	**888-992-6227**	512-477-4455	355
Wholeshare Inc 2431 Mission St	San Francisco	CA	94110	**800-625-4605**		387
WHO-TV Ch 13 (NBC) 1801 Grand Ave	Des Moines	IA	50309	**800-777-8398**	515-242-3500	738-24
WHP-AM 580 (N/T) 600 Corporate Cir	Harrisburg	PA	17110	**888-251-7797**	717-540-8800	642-53
WHPT-FM 102.5 (CR) 11300 Fourth St N Ste 300	Saint Petersburg	FL	33716	**800-771-1025**	727-579-2000	642-122
WHQG-FM 102.9 (Rock) 5407 W McKinley Ave	Milwaukee	WI	53208	**877-777-1029**	414-978-9000	642-76
WHR (Western Horizon Resorts) 103 W Tomichi Ave Ste 201A	Gunnison	CO	81230	**800-378-3709**	970-641-5387	120
WHTZ-FM 100.3 (CHR) 32 Ave of the Americas	New York	NY	10013	**800-242-0100**	212-377-7900	642-83
WHUR-FM 96.3 (Urban AC) 529 Bryant St NW	Washington	DC	20059	**855-787-2227**	202-806-3500	642-128
WHV (Wentworth Hauser & Violich) 301 Battery St	San Francisco	CA	94111	**800-204-2650**	415-981-6911	401
WHY (World Hunger Year Inc) 505 Eigth Ave Ste 2100	New York	NY	10018	**800-548-6479**	212-629-8850	47-5
WI (Wilderness Inquiry) 808 14th Ave SE	Minneapolis	MN	55414	**800-728-0719**	612-676-9400	47-23
WIBB-FM 97.9 (Urban) 7080 Industrial Hwy	Macon	GA	31216	**800-813-8418**	478-781-1063	642-71
WIBC-FM 93.1 (N/T) 40 Monument Cir Ste 400	Indianapolis	IN	46204	**800-571-9422**	317-266-9422	642-58
Wichita Area Technical College 301 S Grove St Bldg A	Wichita	KS	67211	**866-296-4031**	316-677-9400	798
Wichita Convention & Visitors Bureau 515 Main St Ste 115	Wichita	KS	67202	**800-288-9424**	316-265-2800	208
Wichita Eagle, The 825 E Douglas Ave	Wichita	KS	67202	**800-200-8906**	316-268-6000	531-2
Wichita Falls CVB 1000 Fifth St	Wichita Falls	TX	76301	**800-799-6732**		571
Wichita Grand Opera 225 W Douglas Ave Century II Performing Arts Ctr	Wichita	KS	67202	**855-755-7328**	316-683-3444	572-2
Wichita Kenworth Inc 5115 N Broadway	Wichita	KS	67219	**800-825-5558**	316-838-0867	515
Wichita State University 1845 Fairmount St *Admissions	Wichita	KS	67260	**800-362-2594***	316-978-3456	167
Wick Buildings 405 Walter Rd	Mazomanie	WI	53560	**855-438-9425**		504
Wickaninnish Inn 500 Osprey Ln PO Box 250	Tofino	BC	V0R2Z0	**800-333-4604**	250-725-3100	379
Wicklander Zulawski & Associates Inc 4932 Main St	Downers Grove	IL	60515	**800-222-7789**	630-852-6800	462
Wicks Pipe Organ Co 1100 Fifth St *Cust Svc	Highland	IL	62249	**877-654-2191***	618-654-2191	526
WICN-FM 90.5 (NPR) 50 Portland St	Worcester	MA	01608	**855-752-0700**	508-752-0700	642
Wicomico County Convention & Visitors Bureau 8480 Ocean Hwy	Delmar	MD	21875	**800-332-8687**	410-548-4914	208
WICU-TV Ch 12 (NBC) 3514 State St	Erie	PA	16508	**800-454-8812**	814-454-5201	738-27
WideBand Corp 401 W Grand St	Gallatin	MO	64640	**888-663-3050**	660-663-3000	178
Widener University 1 University Pl *Admissions	Chester	PA	19013	**888-943-3637***	610-499-4000	167
Widener University Commonwealth Law School 3800 Vartan Way	Harrisburg	PA	17110	**888-943-3637**	717-541-3900	168-1
Widener University School of Law Wilmington 4601 Concord Pk *General	Wilmington	DE	19803	**888-943-3637***	302-477-2100	168-1
Wider Church Ministries 700 Prospect Ave	Cleveland	OH	44115	**866-822-8224**	216-736-3200	47-20
Wiederkehr Wine Cellars Inc 3324 Swiss Family Dr	Altus	AR	72821	**800-622-9463**	479-468-3551	443
Wieland 13737 Main St PO Box 1000	Grabill	IN	46741	**888-943-5263**	260-627-3686	320-3
Wieland Electric Inc (WEI) 49 International Rd	Burgaw	NC	28425	**800-943-5263**	910-259-5050	248
Wiers Farm Inc 4465 St Rt 103 S PO Box 385	Willard	OH	44890	**800-777-6243**	419-935-0131	10-9
Wiers International Trucks Inc 2111 Jim Neu Dr	Plymouth	IN	46563	**888-889-4377**	574-936-4076	56
Wiese Industries Inc 1501 Fifth St PO Box 39	Perry	IA	50220	**800-568-4391**	515-465-9854	275
Wieser & Cawley Furniture 1301 Colegate Dr	Marietta	OH	45750	**800-339-0094**	740-373-1676	322
Wieser Concrete Products Inc W3716 US Hwy 10	Maiden Rock	WI	54750	**800-325-8456**	715-647-2311	185
Wig America Co 27317 Industrial Blvd	Hayward	CA	94545	**800-338-7600**	510-887-9579	348
Wiggins Lift Company Inc 2571 Cortez St	Oxnard	CA	93031	**800-350-7821**	805-485-7821	469
Wigwam Golf Resort & Spa 300 E Wigwam Blvd	Litchfield Park	AZ	85340	**800-327-0396**	623-935-3811	667
Wigwam Mills Inc 3402 Crocker Ave	Sheboygan	WI	53082	**800-558-7760**	920-457-5551	154-9
Wika Instrument Corp 1000 Wiegand Blvd	Lawrenceville	GA	30043	**888-945-2872**	770-513-8200	203
WIKY-FM 104.1 (AC) 1162 Mt Auburn Rd	Evansville	IN	47720	**800-866-5368**	812-424-8284	642-42
Wilbanks, Smith & Thomas Asset Management LLC 150 W Main St Ste 1700	Norfolk	VA	23510	**800-229-3677**	757-623-3676	401
Wilberforce University 1055 N Bickett Rd PO Box 1001 *Admissions	Wilberforce	OH	45384	**800-367-8568***	937-376-2911	167
Wilbraham & Monson Academy 423 Main St	Wilbraham	MA	01095	**800-616-3659**	413-596-6811	621
Wilbur Curtis Company Inc 6913 Acco St	Montebello	CA	90640	**800-421-6150**	323-837-2300	299
Wilco Farmers 200 Industrial Way	Mount Angel	OR	97362	**800-382-5339**	503-845-6122	278
Wilco Marsh Buggies & Draglines Inc 1304 Macarthur Ave	Harvey	LA	70058	**800-253-0869**	504-341-3409	192
Wilcom Inc 73 Daniel Webster Hwy PO Box 508	Belmont	NH	03220	**800-222-1898**	603-524-2622	645
Wilcox County 103 N Broad St	Abbeville	GA	31001	**866-694-5824**	229-467-2737	338
Wilcox Memorial Hospital (WMH) 3-3420 Kuhio Hwy	Lihue	HI	96766	**877-709-9355**	808-245-1100	374-3
Wilcoxon Research Inc 20511 Seneca Meadows Pkwy	Germantown	MD	20876	**800-945-2696**	301-330-8811	2
Wild 94.9 340 Townsend St Ste 5101	San Francisco	CA	94107	**888-333-9490**	415-975-5555	642-106
Wild Animal Baby Magazine 11100 Wildlife Ctr Dr	Reston	VA	20190	**800-822-9919**		456-6
Wild Animal Safari 1300 Oak Grove Rd	Pine Mountain	GA	31822	**800-367-2751**	706-663-8744	821
Wild Birds Unlimited Inc 11711 N College Ave Ste 146	Carmel	IN	46032	**800-326-4928**	317-571-7100	577

Name / Address	City	State	ZIP	Toll-Free	Phone	Class
Wild Blueberry Assn of North America (WBANA) PO Box 100	Old Town	ME	04468	800-341-1758	207-570-3535	47-2
Wild Dunes Resort 5757 Palm Blvd	Isle of Palms	SC	29451	800-845-8880	843-886-6000	667
Wild Flavors Inc 1261 Pacific Ave	Erlanger	KY	41018	800-263-5286	859-342-3600	297-15
Wild Onion Books 3441 N Ashland Ave	Chicago	IL	60657	800-621-1008	773-281-1818	95
Wild Rice Electric Co-op Inc 502 N Main PO Box 438	Mahnomen	MN	56557	800-244-5709	218-935-2517	247
Wild Wings LLC 2101 S Hwy 61	Lake City	MN	55041	800-445-4833	651-345-5355	458
Wilde Automotive Management of Wisc Onsin Inc 1710 A Hwy 164	Waukesha	WI	53186	888-379-5817	262-513-2770	56
Wilderness Inquiry (WI) 808 14th Ave SE	Minneapolis	MN	55414	800-728-0719	612-676-9400	47-23
Wilderness Press c/o Keen Communications 2204 First Ave S Ste 102	Birmingham	AL	35233	800-443-7227		634-2
Wilderness Society 1615 M St NW	Washington	DC	20036	800-843-9453	202-833-2300	47-13
Wilderness Trails Ranch 1766 County Rd 302	Durango	CO	81303	800-527-2624	970-247-0722	241
Wilderness Travel 1102 Ninth St	Berkeley	CA	94710	800-368-2794	510-558-2488	758
Wildland Adventures Inc 3516 Ne 155th St	Lake Forest Park	WA	98155	800-345-4453	206-365-0686	758
Wildlife West Nature Park 87 N Frontage Rd	Edgewood	NM	87015	877-981-9453	505-281-7655	821
Wildwoods Convention Ctr 4501 Boardwalk	Wildwood	NJ	08260	800-992-9732	609-729-9000	207
Wiley College 711 Wiley Ave *Admissions	Marshall	TX	75670	800-658-6889*	903-927-3300	167
Wiley Publishing Inc 111 River St	Hoboken	NJ	07030	800-225-5945	201-748-6000	634-2
Wiley Sanders Truck Lines Inc PO Box 707 PO Box 707	Troy	AL	36081	800-392-8017		484
Wiley Waterski and Wakeboard Pro Shop 1417 S Trenton	Seattle	WA	98108	800-962-0785	206-762-1300	708
Wilheit Packaging LLC 1527 May Dr	Gainesville	GA	30507	800-727-4421	770-532-4421	448
Wilkes & McHugh P A 1 N Dale Mabry Hwy Ste 800	Tampa	FL	33609	800-255-5070		444
Wilkes Community College 1328 S Collegiate Dr PO Box 120	Wilkesboro	NC	28697	866-222-1548	336-838-6100	161
Wilkes University 84 W S St	Wilkes-Barre	PA	18766	800-945-5378		167
Wilkes-Barre/Scranton International Airport 100 Terminal Dr Ste 1	Avoca	PA	18641	877-235-9287	570-602-2000	27
Wilkins-Rogers Inc 27 Frederick Rd *Cust Svc	Ellicott City	MD	21043	877-438-4338*	410-465-5800	297-23
Will Rogers Memorial Museum 1720 W Will Rogers Blvd	Claremore	OK	74017	800-324-9455	918-341-0719	519
Will Vision & Laser Centers 8100 NE Pkwy Dr Ste 125	Vancouver	WA	98662	877-542-3937	360-885-1327	796
Willamette Stone State Heritage Site 11321 SW Terwilliger Blvd	Portland	OR	97219	800-551-6949		564
Willamette University 900 State St	Salem	OR	97301	877-542-2787	503-370-6303	167
Willamette University College of Law 245 Winter St SE	Salem	OR	97301	844-232-7228	503-370-6282	168-1
Willamette Valley Co 1075 Arrowsmith St	Eugene	OR	97402	800-333-9826	541-484-9621	549
Willamette Valley Hospice 1015 Third St NW	Salem	OR	97304	800-555-2431	503-588-3600	371
Willamette Valley Vineyards Inc 8800 Enchanted Way SE *NASDAQ: WVVI* ■ *Sales	Turner	OR	97392	800-344-9463*	503-588-9463	79-3
Willamette View 12705 SE River Rd	Portland	OR	97222	800-446-0670	503-654-6581	670
Willard Bay State Park 900 West 650 North Ste A	Willard	UT	84340	800-322-3770	435-734-9494	564
Willbanks Metals Inc 1155 NE 28th St	Fort Worth	TX	76106	800-772-2352	817-625-6161	491
Willbros Downstream LLC 4400 Post Oak Pkwy Ste 1000	Houston	TX	77027	888-310-7712	918-556-3600	263
Willdan 2401 E Katella Ave Ste 300	Anaheim	CA	92806	800-424-9144	714-940-6300	263
Willey Honda 2215 S 500 W *Sales	Bountiful	UT	84010	888-431-4490*		56
William B Meyer Inc 255 Long Beach Blvd	Stratford	CT	06615	800-727-5985	203-375-5801	683
William Blair & Company LLC 222 W Adams St	Chicago	IL	60606	800-621-0687	312-236-1600	688
William Carey University 498 Tuscan Ave	Hattiesburg	MS	39401	800-962-5991	601-318-6051	167
William E Walter Inc 1917 Howard Ave	Flint	MI	48503	800-681-3320	810-232-7459	191-10
William F Renk & Sons Inc 6809 Wilburn Rd	Sun Prairie	WI	53590	800-289-7365		10-4
William Fox Munroe Inc 3 E Lancaster Ave	Shillington	PA	19607	800-344-2402	610-775-4521	344
William H Harvey 4334 S 67th St	Omaha	NE	68117	800-321-9532	402-331-1175	327
William H Sadlier Inc 9 Pine St *OTC: SADL*	New York	NY	10005	800-221-5175		634-2
William J Kline & Son Inc 1 Venner Rd	Amsterdam	NY	12010	800-453-6397	518-843-1100	634-8
William Jessup University 333 Sunset Blvd	Rocklin	CA	95765	800-355-7522	916-577-2200	167
William Jewell College 500 College Hill WJC	Liberty	MO	64068	888-253-9355	816-781-7700	167
William K Walthers Inc 5601 W Florist Ave	Milwaukee	WI	53218	800-877-7171	414-527-0770	760
William M. Tugman State Park 72549 Hwy 101	Lakeside	OR	97449	800-551-6949		564
William Marvy Company Inc 1540 St Clair Ave	Saint Paul	MN	55105	800-874-2651	651-698-0726	75
William Mitchell College of Law 875 Summit Ave	Saint Paul	MN	55105	888-962-5529	651-227-9171	168-1
William Morrow & Co 10 E 53rd St	New York	NY	10022	800-242-7737	212-207-7000	634-2
William Paterson University 300 Pompton Rd	Wayne	NJ	07470	877-978-3923	973-720-2000	167
William Peace University 15 E Peace St	Raleigh	NC	27604	800-732-2347	919-508-2000	167
William Penn Assn 709 Brighton Rd	Pittsburgh	PA	15233	800-848-7366	412-231-2979	390
William Penn Life Insurance Co of New York 100 Quentin Roosevelt Blvd	Garden City	NY	11530	800-346-4773	516-794-3700	391-2
William Penn University 201 Trueblood Ave	Oskaloosa	IA	52577	800-779-7366		167
William R Sharpe Jr Hospital 936 Sharpe Hospital Rd	Weston	WV	26452	866-384-5250	304-269-1210	374-5
William S Hein & Company Inc 1285 Main St	Buffalo	NY	14209	800-828-7571	716-882-2600	634-2
William V MacGill & Co 1000 N LombaRd Rd	Lombard	IL	60148	800-323-2841	630-889-0500	474
William Woods University 1 University Ave *Admissions	Fulton	MO	65251	800-995-3159*	573-592-4221	167
Williams & Williams Real Estate Auction 7120 S Lewis Ave Ste 200	Tulsa	OK	74136	800-801-8003	918-250-2012	650
Williams Baptist College 60 W Fulbright St	Walnut Ridge	AR	72476	800-722-4434	870-886-6741	167
Williams College 880 Main St	Williamstown	MA	01267	877-374-7526	413-597-3131	167
Williams Comfort Products 250 W Laurel St	Colton	CA	92324	866-677-8444	909-825-0993	357
Williams Cos Inc 1 Williams Ctr *NYSE: WMB*	Tulsa	OK	74103	800-945-5426	918-573-2000	360-3
Williams Gas Pipeline Gulfstream 1905 Intermodal Cir Ste 310	Palmetto	FL	34221	800-440-8475		326
Williams Gun Sight Co 7389 Lapeer Rd	Davison	MI	48423	800-530-9028	810-653-2131	286
Williams Nationalease Ltd 400 W Northtown Rd	Normal	IL	61761	800-779-8785	309-452-1110	56
Williams Partners LP 1 Williams Ctr *NYSE: WPZ*	Tulsa	OK	74172	800-600-3782	918-573-2000	326
Williams Performing Arts Ctr *Abilene Christian University* 1600 Campus Ct	Abilene	TX	79601	800-460-6228	325-674-2199	571
Williams Records Management 1925 E Vernon Ave *Cust Svc	Los Angeles	CA	90058	888-478-3453*	323-234-3453	227
Williams Sausage Company Inc 5132 Old Troy Hickman Rd	Union City	TN	38261	866-626-4282	731-885-5841	298-9
Williams Supply Inc 210 Seventh St	Roanoke	VA	24016	800-533-6969	540-343-9333	248
Williams White & Co 600 River Dr	Moline	IL	61265	877-797-7650		455
Williams, Turner & Holmes PC 200 N Sixth St Ste 103	Grand Junction	CO	81501	800-548-6528	970-242-6262	428
Williamsburg Area Chamber of Commerce 421 N Boundary St PO Box 3495	Williamsburg	VA	23187	800-368-6511	757-229-6511	138
Williamsburg Destination Marketing Committee 421 N Boundary St PO Box 3495	Williamsburg	VA	23187	800-368-6511	757-229-6511	208
Williamsburg Inn 136 E Francis St	Williamsburg	VA	23185	800-447-8679	757-229-1000	667
Williamsburg Landing 5700 Williamsburg Landing Dr	Williamsburg	VA	23185	800-554-5517	757-565-6505	670
Williamsburg Lodge 310 S England St *Cust Svc	Williamsburg	VA	23185	800-447-8679*	757-229-1000	379
Williamsburg Technical College 601 MLK Jr Ave	Kingstree	SC	29556	800-768-2021	843-355-4110	161
Williamson ARH Hospital 260 Hospital Dr *General	South Williamson	KY	41503	888-654-0015*	606-237-1700	374-3
Williamson Cadillac Co 7815 SW 104th St	Miami	FL	33156	877-228-6093	305-670-7100	57
Williamson County Tourism Bureau 1602 Sioux Dr *General	Marion	IL	62959	800-433-7399*	618-997-3690	208
Williamson County-Franklin Chamber of Commerce 5005 Meridian Blvd Ste 150	Franklin	TN	37067	877-811-0002	615-771-1912	138
Williamson Free School of Mechanical Trades, The 106 S New Middletown Rd	Media	PA	19063	888-565-1095	610-566-1776	798
Williamson Law Book Co 790 Canning Pkwy	Victor	NY	14564	800-733-9522	585-924-3400	180
Williamson-Dickie Mfg Co 509 W Vickery Blvd	Fort Worth	TX	76104	866-411-1501		154-18
Williamsport Area School District 201 W Third St	Williamsport	PA	17701	888-448-4642	570-327-5500	683
Williamsport Sun-Gazette 252 W Fourth St	Williamsport	PA	17701	800-339-0289	570-326-1551	531-2
Williamsport/Lycoming Chamber of Commerce 100 W Third St	Williamsport	PA	17701	800-732-2258	570-326-1971	138
Williams-Sonoma Inc 3250 Van Ness Ave *NYSE: WSM*	San Francisco	CA	94109	800-838-2589	415-421-7900	362
Williamstown Commons Nursing & Rehabilitation Ctr 25 Adams Rd	Williamstown	MA	01267	800-445-4560	413-458-2111	449
Willingboro Public Library 220 Willingboro Pkwy	Willingboro	NJ	08046	866-321-9571	609-877-6668	434-3
Willington Cos 11 Middle River Dr	Stafford Springs	CT	06076	877-967-4743	860-684-4281	480

Alphabetical Section

Name / Address	City	State	Zip	Toll-Free	Phone	Class
Willingway Hospital 311 Jones Mill Rd	Statesboro	GA	30458	**800-242-9455**	912-764-6236	724
Willis College of Business & Technology 85 O'Connor St	Ottawa	ON	K1P5M6	**877-233-1128**	613-233-1128	161
Willis Group Holdings Ltd 200 Liberty St 1 World Financial Ctr *NYSE: WSH*	New York	NY	10281	**800-234-8596**	212-915-8888	390
Willis Shaw Express Inc 201 N Elm St	Elm Springs	AR	72728	**800-843-9904**	479-248-7261	778
Williston State College 1410 University Ave PO Box 1326	Williston	ND	58802	**888-863-9455**	701-774-4200	161
Willmar Poultry Co, The (WPC) 3735 County Rd 5 SW	Willmar	MN	56201	**800-328-8849**	320-235-8850	10-7
Willougby Area Chamber of Commerce 28 Public Sq	Willoughby	OH	44094	**877-229-4361**	440-942-1632	138
Willow Creek Press Inc 9931 Hwy 70 W PO Box 147 *Cust Svc	Minocqua	WI	54548	**800-850-9453***	715-358-7010	129
Willow River State Park 1034 County Hwy A	Hudson	WI	54016	**800-847-9367**	715-386-5931	564
Willow Stream Spa at Fairmont Scottsdale Princess 7575 E Princess Dr	Scottsdale	AZ	85255	**800-908-9540**	480-585-2732	705
Willow Stream Spa at the Fairmont Banff Springs 405 Spray Ave	Banff	AB	T1L1J4	**800-404-1772**	403-762-1772	705
Willow Stream Spa at the Fairmont Empress 633 Humboldt St	Victoria	BC	V8W1A6	**866-854-7444**	250-995-4650	705
Willow Valley Lakes Manor 300 Willow Vly Lakes Dr	Willow Street	PA	17584	**800-770-5445**	717-464-0800	670
Willows Chamber of Commerce 118 W Sycamore	Willows	CA	95988	**855-233-6362**	530-934-8150	138
Willows Historic Palm Springs Inn 412 W Tahquitz Canyon Way	Palm Springs	CA	92262	**800-966-9597**	760-320-0771	379
Willows Hotel 555 W Surf St	Chicago	IL	60657	**877-207-2111**	773-528-8400	379
Willows Lodge 14580 NE 145th St	Woodinville	WA	98072	**877-424-3930**	425-424-3900	379
Willows, The 1 Lyman St	Westborough	MA	01581	**800-464-8060**	508-366-4730	670
Willsie Cap & Gown Co 1220 S 13th St	Omaha	NE	68108	**800-234-4696**	402-341-6536	154-13
Willson International Ltd 2345 Argentia Rd Ste 201	Mississauga	ON	L5N8K4	**800-754-1918**	905-363-1133	448
Willy & Jose's Mexican Cantina 5111 Boulder Hwy	Las Vegas	NV	89122	**800-897-8696**	702-456-7777	669
Wilma Theater 265 S Broad St	Philadelphia	PA	19107	**800-732-0999**	215-893-9456	571
Wilmer Service Line 515 W Sycamore St	Coldwater	OH	45828	**800-494-5637**		109
Wilmington College of Ohio 1870 Quaker Way	Wilmington	OH	45177	**800-341-9318**	937-382-6661	167
Wilmington Fibre Specialty Co 700 Washington St	New Castle	DE	19720	**800-220-5132**	302-328-7525	598
Wilmington Instrument Company Inc 332 N Fries Ave	Wilmington	CA	90744	**800-544-2843**	310-834-1133	203
Wilmington National Cemetery 2011 Market St	Wilmington	NC	28403	**800-535-1117**	910-815-4877	135
Wilmington Treatment Ctr 2520 Troy Dr	Wilmington	NC	28401	**877-762-3750**		724
Wilmington Trust Co 1100 N Market St	Wilmington	DE	19890	**800-441-7120**	302-651-1000	69
Wilmington University 320 N DuPont Hwy *Admissions	New Castle	DE	19720	**877-967-5464***	302-356-6739	167
Wilshire Assoc Inc 1299 Ocean Ave Ste 700	Santa Monica	CA	90401	**855-626-8281**	310-451-3051	401
Wilshire Enterprises Inc 100 Eagle Rock Ave Ste 100 *OTC: WLSE*	East Hanover	NJ	07936	**888-697-3962**	973-585-7770	535
Wilshire Mutual Funds Inc PO Box 219512	Kansas City	MO	64121	**888-200-6796**		527
Wilshire State Bank 3200 Wilshire Blvd Ste 1400	Los Angeles	CA	90010	**866-886-2265**	213-368-7700	69
Wilson Air Ctr 2930 Winchester Rd Memphis International Airport	Memphis	TN	38118	**800-464-2992**	901-345-2992	62
Wilson Bus Lines Inc 203 Patriots Rd PO Box 415	East Templeton	MA	01438	**800-253-5235**	978-632-3894	106
Wilson Chamber of Commerce 200 Nash St NE	Wilson	NC	27893	**855-905-0604**	252-237-0165	138
Wilson College 1015 Philadelphia Ave *Admissions	Chambersburg	PA	17201	**800-421-8402***	717-264-4141	167
Wilson County Public Library 249 W Nash St	Wilson	NC	27893	**877-321-2652**	252-237-5355	434-3
Wilson Industrial Sales Company Inc 201 S Wilson	Brook	IN	47922	**800-633-5427**	219-275-7333	145
Wilson Learning Corp 8000 W 78th St Ste 200	Edina	MN	55439	**800-328-7937**	952-944-2880	763
Wilson Lines of Minnesota Inc 2131 Second Ave *General	Newport	MN	55055	**800-525-3333***	651-459-2384	778
Wilson Manufacturing Co 4725 Green Park Rd	Saint Louis	MO	63123	**800-634-5248**	314-416-8900	695
Wilson of Wallingford Inc 221 Rogers Ln PO Box 185	Wallingford	PA	19086	**888-607-2621**	610-566-7600	317
Wilson Quarterly Magazine 1300 Pennsylvania Ave NW 1 Woodrow Wilson Plaza *Orders	Washington	DC	20004	**888-947-9018***	202-691-4000	456-11
Wilson Sporting Goods Co 8750 W Bryn Mawr Ave	Chicago	IL	60631	**800-874-5930**	773-714-6400	708
Wilson Supply Co 1302 Conti St	Houston	TX	77002	**800-874-5930**	713-237-3700	385
Wilson Tool International Inc 12912 Farnham Ave	White Bear Lake	MN	55110	**800-328-9646**	651-286-6001	695
Wilson Trailer Co 4400 S Lewis Blvd	Sioux City	IA	51106	**800-798-2002**	712-252-6500	777
Wilson Trophy Co 1724 Frienza Ave	Sacramento	CA	95815	**800-635-5005**	916-927-9733	775
Wilson Trucking Corp 137 Wilson Blvd	Fishersville	VA	22939	**866-645-7405**	540-949-3200	778
Wilson Visitors Bureau 209 Broad St	Wilson	NC	27893	**800-497-7398**	252-243-8440	208
Wilson WindowWare Inc 5421 California Ave SW	Seattle	WA	98136	**800-762-8383**	206-938-1740	180-12
Wilsonart International Inc 2400 Wilson Pl *Cust Svc	Temple	TX	76504	**800-433-3222***	254-207-7000	598
Wilsons Leather Inc 7401 Boone Ave N	Brooklyn Park	MN	55428	**800-967-6270**	763-391-4000	156-5
Wiltern Theatre 3790 Wilshire Blvd	Los Angeles	CA	90010	**800-348-8499**	213-388-1400	571
Wilton Armetale Co PO Box 600	Mount Joy	PA	17552	**800-779-4586**		485
Wilton Industries Inc 2240 W 75th St	Woodridge	IL	60517	**800-794-5866**	630-963-7100	485
WILX-TV Ch 10 (NBC) 500 American Rd	Lansing	MI	48911	**888-345-4124**	517-393-0110	738-42
Wimmer's Meat Products Inc 126 W Grant St *Cust Svc	West Point	NE	68788	**800-762-9865***	402-372-2437	297-26
WIN Energy Rural Electric Membership Corp 3981 S US Hwy 41	Vincennes	IN	47591	**800-882-5140**	812-882-5140	247
Winbco Tank Co 1200 E Main St PO Box 618	Ottumwa	IA	52501	**800-822-1855**		90
Winchester Equipment Co 121 Indian Hollow Rd	Winchester	VA	22603	**800-323-3581**		358
Winchester Star 2 N Kent St	Winchester	VA	22601	**800-296-8639**	540-667-3200	531-2
Winchester Systems Inc 101 Billerica Ave Bldg 5 *Cust Svc	North Billerica	MA	01862	**800-325-3700***	781-265-0200	178
Winchuck State Recreation Site 1655 Hwy 101 N	Brookings	OR	97415	**800-551-6949**		564
WinCo Foods Inc PO Box 5756	Boise	ID	83705	**888-674-6854**	208-377-0110	345
Winco Inc 5516 SW First Ln	Ocala	FL	34474	**800-237-3377**	352-854-2929	320-3
WinCraft Inc 1124 W Fifth St	Winona	MN	55987	**800-533-8006**	507-454-5510	329
WinCup 4640 Lewis Rd	Stone Mountain	GA	30083	**800-292-2877**	770-938-5281	600
Wind Creek State Park 4325 Al Hwy 128	Alexander City	AL	35010	**800-252-7275**	256-329-0845	564
WIND Mobile 207 Queens Quay W Ste 710 PO Box 114	Toronto	ON	M5J1A7	**877-946-3184**		226
Wind River Ranch PO Box 3410	Estes Park	CO	80517	**800-523-4212**	970-586-4212	241
Wind River Systems Inc 500 Wind River Way	Alameda	CA	94501	**800-545-9463**	510-748-4100	180-12
Windermere Relocation Inc 5424 Sand Point Way NE	Seattle	WA	98105	**866-740-9589**	206-527-3801	664
Windham Manufacturing Company Inc 8520 Forney Rd	Dallas	TX	75227	**888-965-0093**	214-388-0511	453
Windham Region Chamber of Commerce 1010 Main St	Willimantic	CT	06226	**800-683-4564**	860-423-6389	138
Windings Inc PO Box 566	New Ulm	MN	56073	**800-795-8533**	507-359-2034	453
Windmill Health Products 6 Henderson Dr	West Caldwell	NJ	07006	**800-822-4320**	973-575-6591	797
Window & Door Manufacturers Assn (WDMA) 330 N Wabash Ave Ste 2000	Chicago	IL	60611	**800-223-2301**	847-299-5200	48-3
Window Gang 405 Arendell St	Morehead City	NC	28557	**877-946-4264**	252-726-1463	151
Window Rama Enterprises Inc 71 Heartland Blvd	Edgewood	NY	11717	**800-897-7262**	631-667-8088	193-3
Windsor Arms Hotel 18 St Thomas St	Toronto	ON	M5S3E7	**877-999-2767**	416-971-9666	379
Windsor Court Hotel 300 Gravier St	New Orleans	LA	70130	**888-596-0955**	504-523-6000	379
Windsor Factory Supply Ltd 730 N Service Rd	Windsor	ON	N8X3J3	**800-387-2659**	519-966-2202	385
Windsor Foods 3355 W Alabama St Ste 730	Houston	TX	77098	**800-458-4054**	713-843-5200	297-36
Windsor Inc 4533 Pacific Blvd	Vernon	CA	90058	**888-494-6376**	323-282-9000	156-6
Windsor K„rcher Group 1351 W Stanford Ave	Englewood	CO	80110	**800-444-7654**	303-762-1800	386
Windsor Star, The 167 Ferry St	Windsor	ON	N9A4M5	**800-265-5647**	519-255-5711	531-1
Windsor Symphony Orchestra 487 Oullette Ave	Windsor	ON	N9A4J2	**888-327-8327**	519-973-1238	572-3
Windsor Vineyards 205 Concourse Blvd	Santa Rosa	CA	95403	**800-289-9463**		316-5
Windsor Windows & Doors 900 S 19th St	West Des Moines	IA	50265	**800-218-6186**	515-223-6660	238
Windsor-Bertie Area Chamber of Commerce 121 Granville St PO Box 572	Windsor	NC	27983	**800-334-5010**	252-794-4277	138
Windstar Cruises 2101 Fourth Ave Ste 210 *Resv	Seattle	WA	98121	**800-258-7245***	206-292-9606	222
Windstar Lines Inc 1903 US Hwy 71 N	Carroll	IA	51401	**888-494-6378**	712-792-4221	188
Wine & Spirits Shippers Assn Inc (WSSA) 11800 Sunrise Vly Dr *General	Reston	VA	20191	**800-368-3167***	703-860-2300	48-6
Wine Club, The 1431 S Village Way	Santa Ana	CA	92705	**800-966-5432**	714-835-6485	443
Wine Spectator Magazine 387 Pk Ave S 8th Fl *Orders	New York	NY	10016	**800-752-7799***	212-684-4224	456-14

Company / Address	City	State	ZIP	Toll-Free	Phone	Class
Wine.com Inc						
114 Sansome St 3rd Fl	San Francisco	CA	94104	**800-592-5870**	415-291-9500	443
WineAmerica						
818 Connecticut Ave Ste 1006	Washington	DC	20006	**800-824-5419**	202-783-2756	48-6
Winebow Inc						
75 Chestnut Ridge Rd	Montvale	NJ	07645	**800-859-0689**	201-445-0620	80-3
Winebrenner Theological Seminary						
950 N Main St	Findlay	OH	45840	**800-992-4987**	419-434-4200	168-3
Winegard Co						
3000 Kirkwood St	Burlington	IA	52601	**800-288-8094***	319-754-0600	645
*Cust Svc						
Winery at Wolf Creek						
2637 Cleveland Massillon Rd	Norton	OH	44203	**800-436-0426**	330-666-9285	49-6
WineShop At Home						
525 Airpark Rd	Napa	CA	94558	**800-946-3746**	707-253-0200	443
WineStyles Inc						
5515 Mills Civic Pkwy Ste 110	West Des Moines	IA	50266	**866-424-9463**		311
Winetasting Network, The						
578 Gateway Dr	Napa	CA	94558	**800-435-2225**		688
Winfield Associates Inc						
700 W St Clair Ave Ste 404	Cleveland	OH	44113	**888-322-2575**	216-241-2575	794
Winfree Marketing & Sales Institute						
1905 Arnold Palmer Blvd	Louisville	KY	40245	**800-616-9260**	502-253-0700	462
Wing Enterprises Inc						
1198 N Spring Creek	Springville	UT	84663	**866-872-5901**	801-489-3684	421
Wing Hing Foods Inc						
2539 E Philadelphia St	Ontario	CA	91761	**855-734-2742**		345
Wing Zone Franchise Corp						
900 Cir 75 Pkwy Ste 930	Atlanta	GA	30339	**877-946-4966**	404-875-5045	311
Wingate by Wyndham Calgary Hotel						
400 Midpark Way SE	Calgary	AB	T2X3S4	**800-228-1000**	403-514-0099	705
Wingate University						
220 N Camden Rd	Wingate	NC	28174	**800-755-5550**	704-233-8000	167
Wingfoot Commercial Tire Systems LLC						
1000 S 21st St	Fort Smith	AR	72901	**800-643-7330**	479-788-6400	61-5
Wingman Advertising Inc						
4061 Glencoe Ave Ste A	Marina Del Rey	CA	90292	**888-294-6462**		7
Wingra Stone Co						
2975 Kapec Rd PO Box 44284	Madison	WI	53744	**800-249-6908**	608-271-5555	185
WINGS (Wings Foundation)						
7550 W Yale Ave Ste B 201	Denver	CO	80227	**800-373-8671**	303-238-8660	47-21
Wings Financial Credit Union						
14985 Glazier Ave Ste 100	Apple Valley	MN	55124	**800-692-2274**	952-997-8000	221
Wings Foundation (WINGS)						
7550 W Yale Ave Ste B 201	Denver	CO	80227	**800-373-8671**	303-238-8660	47-21
Wings Tours Inc						
11350 McCormick Rd Ste 703	Hunt Valley	MD	21031	**800-869-4647**	410-771-0925	758
WinHolt Equipment Group						
141 Eileen Way	Syosset	NY	11791	**800-444-3595**	516-222-0335	469
Winkler Inc						
535 E Medcalf St	Dale	IN	47523	**800-621-3843**	812-937-4421	298-8
Winland Electronics Inc						
1950 Excel Dr	Mankato	MN	56001	**800-635-4269**	507-625-7231	203
NYSE: WEX						
Winmark Corp						
605Hwy 169 N Ste 400	Minneapolis	MN	55441	**877-536-1561**	763-520-8500	156-1
NASDAQ: WINA						
Winn Transportation						
1831 Westwood Ave	Richmond	VA	23227	**800-296-9466**	804-358-9466	106
Winnebago Industries Inc						
605 W Crystal Lk Rd PO Box 152	Forest City	IA	50436	**800-643-4892**	641-585-3535	119
NYSE: WGO						
Winneconne News						
908 E Main St	Winneconne	WI	54986	**800-545-5026**	920-582-4541	531-3
Winnemucca Convention & Visitors Authority						
50 W Winnemucca Blvd	Winnemucca	NV	89445	**800-962-2638**	775-623-5071	208
Winner International LLC						
32 W State St	Sharon	PA	16146	**800-258-2321**	724-981-1152	690
Winner Livestock Auction Co						
31690 Livestock Barn Rd	Winner	SD	57580	**800-201-0451**	605-842-0451	445
Winner's Cir Resort						
550 Via de la Valle	Solana Beach	CA	92075	**800-874-8770**	858-755-6666	667
Winners Sports Haven						
600 Long Wharf Dr	New Haven	CT	06511	**800-468-2260**		132
Winneshiek County						
201 W Main St	Decorah	IA	52101	**866-227-9874**	563-382-9219	338
Winnipeg Centennial Folk Festival Inc, The						
211 Bannatyne Ave Ste 203	Winnipeg	MB	R3B3P2	**866-301-3823**	204-231-0096	718
Winnipeg Free Press						
1355 Mountain Ave	Winnipeg	MB	R2X3B6	**800-542-8900**	204-697-7000	531-1
Winnipeg James Armstrong Richardson International Airport						
2000 Wellington Ave Rm 249 Administration Bldg	Winnipeg	MB	R3H1C2	**855-500-6589**	204-987-9400	27
Winnsboro State Bank & Trust Co						
3875 Front St	Winnsboro	LA	71295	**866-205-4026**	318-435-7535	69
Winona Convention & Visitors Bureau						
160 Johnson St	Winona	MN	55987	**800-657-4972**	507-452-0735	208
Winona National Bankÿÿÿ						
PO Box 499	Winona	MN	55987	**800-546-4392**	507-454-4320	360-2
Winona State University						
175 W Mark St	Winona	MN	55987	**800-342-5978**	507-457-5000	167
Winpak Ltd						
100 Salteaux Crescent	Winnipeg	MB	R3J3T3	**800-841-2600**	204-889-1015	547
TSE: WPK						
Winship Cancer Institute of Emory University						
1365 Clifton Rd NE	Atlanta	GA	30322	**888-946-7447**	404-778-1900	767
Winslow BMW						
730 N Cir Dr	Colorado Springs	CO	80909	**877-367-7357**	719-473-1373	56
Winsted Precision Ball Corp						
159 Colebrook River Rd	Winsted	CT	06098	**800-462-3075**	860-379-2788	74
Winston Bros Inc						
131 Newbury St	Boston	MA	02116	**800-457-4901**	617-541-1100	294
Winston F2S Corp						
1604 Cherokee Trace	White Oak	TX	75693	**800-527-8465**	903-757-7341	536
Winston Industries LLC						
2345 Carton Dr	Louisville	KY	40299	**800-234-5286**	502-495-5400	299
Winston-Salem Convention & Visitors Bureau						
200 Brookstown Ave	Winston-Salem	NC	27101	**866-728-4200**	336-728-4200	208
Winston-Salem Journal						
418 N Marshall St	Winston-Salem	NC	27101	**800-642-0925**	336-727-7211	531-2
Winston-Salem Southbound Railway Co						
4550 Overdale Rd	Winston-Salem	NC	27107	**888-780-7245**	336-788-9407	646
Winston-Salem State University						
601 S ML King Jr Dr 206 Thompson Ctr	Winston-Salem	NC	27110	**800-257-4052***	336-750-2000	167
*Admissions						
Wintec Industries Inc						
675 Sycamore Dr	Milpitas	CA	95035	**866-989-4683**	408-856-0500	624
Winter Gardens Quality Foods Inc						
304 Commerce St PO Box 339	New Oxford	PA	17350	**800-242-7637**	717-624-4911	297-36
Winter Hill Bank						
342 Broadway	Somerville	MA	02145	**800-444-4300**	617-666-8600	69
Winter Park Chamber of Commerce						
151 W Lyman Ave	Winter Park	FL	32789	**877-972-4262***	407-644-8281	138
*Help Line						
Winter Park Resort						
85 Parsenn Rd	Winter Park	CO	80482	**800-903-7275***	970-726-5514	376
*Resv						
Winter Quarters State Historic Site						
4929 Hwy 608	Newellton	LA	71357	**888-677-9468**	888-677-2784	564
WinterBell Co						
2018 Brevard Rd	High Point	NC	27263	**800-685-2957**	336-887-2651	560
Wintergreen Resort						
Rt 664 PO Box 706	Wintergreen	VA	22958	**855-699-1858**		705
Wintersilks Inc						
PO Box 196	Jessup	PA	18434	**800-648-7455**	800-718-3687	458
Winterthur Museum & Country Estate						
5105 Kennett Pk	Winterthur	DE	19735	**800-448-3883**	302-888-4600	519
Winthrop Realty Trust						
7 Bulfinch Pl Ste 500	Boston	MA	02114	**800-622-6757**	617-570-4614	653
NYSE: FUR						
Winward International Inc						
3089 Whipple Rd	Union City	CA	94587	**800-888-8898**	510-487-8686	294
Winware Inc						
1955 W Oak Cir	Marietta	GA	30062	**888-419-1399**	770-419-1399	179
WIOQ-FM 102.1 (CHR)						
111 Presidential Blvd Ste 100	Bala Cynwyd	PA	19004	**800-521-1021**	610-784-3333	643
Wipaire Inc						
1700 Henry Ave	South St. Paul	MN	55075	**888-947-2473**	651-451-1205	528
Wipe-Tex International Corp						
110 E 153rd St	Bronx	NY	10451	**800-643-9607**	718-665-0787	507
Wire Belt Company of America						
154 Harvey Rd	Londonderry	NH	03053	**800-922-2637***	603-644-2500	209
*Cust Svc						
Wire Rope Industries Ltd						
5501 Trans-Canada Hwy	Pointe-claire	QC	H9R1B7	**800-565-5501**	514-697-9711	491
Wired News						
Wired 520 Third St Ste 305	San Francisco	CA	94107	**800-769-4733**		397
Wireless Analytics LLC						
230 N St Ste 4	Danvers	MA	01923	**888-588-5550**		226
Wireless Toyz Ltd						
29155 NW Hwy	Southfield	MI	48034	**866-237-2624**	248-426-8200	311
Wireless Watchdogs LLC						
5800 Hannum Ave Ste B	Culver City	CA	90230	**866-522-0688**		2
Wireless Xcessories Group Inc						
1840 County Line Rd Ste 301	Huntingdon Valley	PA	19006	**800-233-0013**	215-322-4600	255
OTC: WIRX						
Wireless Zone						
34 Industrial Pk Pl	Middletown	CT	06457	**888-881-2622**	860-632-9494	34
Wiremasters Inc						
1788 N Pt Rd	Columbia	TN	38401	**800-635-5342**	615-791-0281	248
Wirerope Works Inc						
100 Maynard St	Williamsport	PA	17701	**800-541-7673***	570-326-5146	811
*Cust Svc						
WIS International						
9265 Sky Park Ct Ste 100	San Diego	CA	92123	**800-268-6848**	858-565-8111	399
Wisco Industries Inc						
736 Janesville St	Oregon	WI	53575	**800-999-4726**	608-835-3106	35
Wisco Products Inc						
109 Commercial St	Dayton	OH	45402	**800-367-6570**	937-228-2101	695
Wisco Supply Inc						
815 S Saint Vrain St	El Paso	TX	79901	**800-947-2689**	915-544-8294	609
Wiscolift Inc						
W6396 Speciality Dr	Greenville	WI	54942	**800-242-3477**	920-757-8832	491
Wisconsin						
Crime Victims Services Office						
PO Box 7951	Madison	WI	53707	**800-446-6564**	608-264-9497	339-50
Housing & Economic Development Authority						
201 W Washington Ave Ste 700	Madison	WI	53703	**800-334-6873**	608-266-7884	339-50
Insurance Commission						
PO Box 7873	Madison	WI	53707	**800-236-8517**	608-266-3585	339-50
Legislature						
State Capitol	Madison	WI	53702	**800-362-9472**	608-266-9960	339-50
Parks & Recreation Bureau						
101 S Webster St PO Box 7921	Madison	WI	53707	**888-936-7463**	608-266-2621	339-50
Public Instruction Dept						
125 S Webster St PO Box 7841	Madison	WI	53707	**800-441-4563**	608-266-3390	339-50
Teacher Education & Licensing Bureau						
125 S Webster St	Madison	WI	53703	**800-441-4563**	608-266-3390	339-50
Treasurer PO Box 2114	Madison	WI	53707	**855-375-2274**		339-50
Veterans Affairs Dept						
201 W Washington Ave PO Box 7843	Madison	WI	53703	**800-947-8387**	608-266-1311	339-50
Vocational Rehabilitation Div						
201 East Washington Avenue PO Box 7852	Madison	WI	53707	**800-442-3477**	608-261-0050	339-50
Wisconsin Aviation Inc						
1741 River Dr	Watertown	WI	53094	**800-657-0761**	920-261-4567	62
Wisconsin Bill Status						
1 E Main St	Madison	WI	53708	**800-362-9472**	608-266-9960	433
Wisconsin Box Company Inc						
929 Townline Rd	Wausau	WI	54402	**800-876-6658**	715-842-2248	202

Listing	Toll-Free	Phone	Class
Wisconsin Coach Lines Inc 1520 Arcadian Ave, Waukesha WI 53186	877-324-7767	262-542-8861	106
Wisconsin Dells Visitors & Convention Bureau 701 Superior St PO Box 390, Wisconsin Dells WI 53965	800-223-3557	608-254-8088	208
Wisconsin Dental Assn 6737 W Washington St Ste 2360, West Allis WI 53214	800-364-7646	414-276-4520	229
Wisconsin Department of Public Instruction 125 S Webster St PO Box 7841, Madison WI 53707	800-441-4563	608-266-3390	434-5
Wisconsin Educational Communications Board 3319 W Beltline Hwy, Madison WI 53713	800-422-9707	608-264-9600	629
Wisconsin Energy Corp 231 W Michigan St, Milwaukee WI 53203 *NYSE: WEC* ■ *General	800-242-9137*	414-221-2345	360-5
Wisconsin Film & Bag Inc 3100 E Richmond St, Shawano WI 54166	800-765-9224	715-524-2565	65
Wisconsin Historical Museum 30 N Carroll St, Madison WI 53703	888-748-7479	608-264-6555	519
Wisconsin Indianhead Technical College			
New Richmond Campus 1019 S Knowles Ave, New Richmond WI 54017	800-243-9482	715-246-6561	798
Rice Lake Campus 1900 College Dr, Rice Lake WI 54868	800-243-9482	715-234-7082	798
Superior Campus 600 N 21 St, Superior WI 54880	800-243-9482	715-394-6677	798
Wisconsin Machine Tool Corp 3225 Gateway Rd Ste 100, Brookfield WI 53045	800-243-3078	262-317-3048	454
Wisconsin Manufacturers & Commerce PO Box 352, Madison WI 53701	800-236-5414	608-258-3400	139
Wisconsin Maritime Museum 75 Maritime Dr, Manitowoc WI 54220	866-724-2356	920-684-0218	519
Wisconsin National Primate Research Ctr 1220 Capitol Ct, Madison WI 53715	800-833-7050	608-263-3500	666
Wisconsin Power & Light Co 4902 N Biltmore Ln PO Box 77007, Madison WI 53718	800-255-4268		785
Wisconsin Public Radio (WPR) 821 University Ave, Madison WI 53706	800-747-7444		629
Wisconsin Public Service Corp PO Box 19001, Green Bay WI 54307	800-450-7260		785
Wisconsin Public Television (WPT) 821 University Ave, Madison WI 53706	800-422-9707	608-263-2121	629
Wisconsin Realtors Assn 4801 Forest Run Rd Ste 201, Madison WI 53704	800-279-1972	608-241-2047	654
Wisconsin Reinsurance Corp 2810 City View Dr, Madison WI 53707	800-939-9473	608-242-4500	391-4
Wisconsin State Fair Park 640 S 84th St, West Allis WI 53214	800-884-3247	414-266-7033	519
Wisconsin State Journal 1901 Fish Hatchery Rd, Madison WI 53713	800-362-8333	608-252-6200	531-2
Wisconsin State Medical Society 330 E Lakeside St, Madison WI 53701	866-442-3800		473
Wisconsin Steel & Tube Corp 1555 N Mayfair Rd, Milwaukee WI 53226	800-279-8335	414-453-4441	491
Wisconsin Veterans Home N2665 County Rd QQ, King WI 54946	877-944-6667	715-258-5586	791
Wisconsin Veterinary Medical Assn (WVMA) 2801 Crossroads Dr Ste 1200, Madison WI 53718	888-254-5202	608-257-3665	793
Wise Business Forms Inc 555 McFarland 400 Dr, Alpharetta GA 30004	888-815-9473	770-442-1060	109
Wise Consulting Associates Inc 54 Scott Adam Rd Ste 206, Hunt Valley MD 21030	800-654-4550	410-628-0100	448
Wise Electric Co-op Inc 1900 N Trinity St, Decatur TX 76234	888-627-9326	940-627-2167	247
Wise Foods Inc 228 Rasely St Ste 75, Berwick PA 18603	888-759-4401	770-426-5821	297-35
Wiseco Piston Inc 7201 Industrial Pk Blvd, Mentor OH 44060	800-321-1364	440-951-6600	127
Wiseway Motor Freight Inc PO Box 838, Hudson WI 54016	800-876-1660		778
WISP (Women's Independence Scholarship Program Inc) 4900 Randall Pkwy Ste H, Wilmington NC 28403	866-255-7742	910-397-7742	306
Wist Office Products Co 107 W Julie Dr, Tempe AZ 85283	800-999-9478	480-921-2900	534
Wistar Institute 3601 Spruce St, Philadelphia PA 19104	800-724-6633	215-898-3700	666
WITF-FM 89.5 (NPR) 4801 Lindle Rd, Harrisburg PA 17111	800-366-9483	717-704-3000	642-53
WithumSmith+Brown 5 Vaughn Dr, Princeton NJ 08540	866-455-7438	609-520-1188	2
WITI (Women in Technology International) 11500 Olympic Blvd Ste 400, Los Angeles CA 90064	800-334-9484	818-788-9484	48-19
WITL-FM 100.7 (Ctry) 3420 Pine Tree Rd, Lansing MI 48911	800-968-9485	517-394-7272	642-64
Witmer's Inc 39821 SR 14, Salem OH 44460	888-427-6025	330-427-2147	276
Witt Industries Inc 4600 Mason-Montgomery Rd, Mason OH 45040	800-543-7417		659
Witt Lincoln 588 Camino Del Rio N, San Diego CA 92108	877-937-3301	619-358-5000	56
Witt Printing Company Inc 301 Oak St, El Dorado Springs MO 64744	800-641-4342	417-876-4721	109
Witt/Kieffer Ford Hadelman & Lloyd 2015 Spring Rd Ste 510, Oak Brook IL 60523	888-281-1370	630-990-1370	268
Wittek Golf Supply Co Inc 3865 N Commercial Ave, Northbrook IL 60062	800-869-1800	847-943-2399	708
Wittenberg University 200 W Ward St PO Box 720, Springfield OH 45501	800-677-7558	937-327-6314	167
WITV-TV Ch 7 (PBS) 1101 Geroge Rogers Blvd, Columbia SC 29201	800-277-3245	803-737-3200	
Witzco Trailers Inc 6101 McIntosh Rd, Sarasota FL 34238	800-462-4123	941-922-5301	777
WIVB-TV Ch 4 (CBS) 2077 Elmwood Ave, Buffalo NY 14207	800-794-3687	716-874-4410	738-13
WIVK-FM 107.7 (Ctry) 4711 Old Kingston Pike, Knoxville TN 37919	877-995-9961	865-588-6511	642-63
Wixon Inc 1390 E Bolivar Ave, Saint Francis WI 53235	800-841-5304	414-769-3000	297
Wixon Jewelers Inc 9955 Lyndale Ave S, Minneapolis MN 55420	800-853-7667	952-881-8862	410
Wizards of the Coast Inc 1600 Lind Ave SW Ste 400, Renton WA 98057	800-324-6496	425-226-6500	760
Wizcom Technologies Inc Boston Post Rd W 33 Ste 320, Marlborough MA 01752	888-777-0552	508-251-5388	175-7
WIZF-FM 101.1 (Urban) 705 Central Ave, Cincinnati OH 45202	866-236-7588	513-679-6000	642-29
WIZN-FM 106.7 (Rock) 255 S Champlain St, Burlington VT 05401	888-873-9496	802-860-2440	642-21
WJGL-FM 96.9 (CR) 8000 Belfort Pkwy, Jacksonville FL 32256	800-438-1601	904-245-8500	642-60
WJHL-TV Ch 11 (CBS) 338 E Main St, Johnson City TN 37601	800-861-5255	423-926-2151	738-39
WJHM-FM 102 (Urban) 1800 Pembrook Dr Ste 400, Orlando FL 32810	866-438-0220	407-919-1000	642-85
WJMZ-FM 107.3 (Urban) 220 N Main St Ste 402, Greenville SC 29601	800-767-1073	864-235-1073	642-52
WJQK-FM 99.3 (Rel) 425 Centerstone Ct, Zeeland MI 49464	866-931-9936	616-931-9930	643
WJSR-FM 91.1 (CR) Jefferson State Community College 2601 Carson Rd, Birmingham AL 35215	800-767-4984	205-856-7702	642-15
WKBW-TV Ch 7 (ABC) 7 Broadcast Plaza, Buffalo NY 14202	888-373-7888	716-845-6100	738-13
WKCQ-FM 98.1 (Ctry) 2000 Whittier St, Saginaw MI 48601	800-262-0098	989-752-8161	643
WKDD-FM 98.1 (AC) 7755 Freedom Ave, North Canton OH 44720	888-533-4582	330-836-4700	643
WKIS-FM 99.9 (Ctry) 194 NW 187th St, Miami FL 33169	866-978-0800	305-654-1700	642-75
WKJV-AM 1380 70 Adams Hill Rd, Asheville NC 28806	800-809-9558	828-252-1380	642-9
WKLB-FM 102.5 (Ctry) 55 Morrissey Blvd, Boston MA 02125	888-819-1025	617-822-9600	642-18
WKMG-TV Ch 6 (CBS) 4466 N John Young Pkwy, Orlando FL 32804	800-435-7352	407-521-1200	738-57
WKMJ-TV Ch 68 (PBS) 600 Cooper Dr, Lexington KY 40502	800-432-0951	859-258-7000	
WKNO-FM 91.1 (NPR) 900 Getwell Rd, Memphis TN 38111	800-766-9566	901-325-6544	642-74
WKNO-TV Ch 10 (PBS) 7151 Cherry Farms Rd, Cordova TN 38016	877-717-7822	901-729-8765	
WKPC-TV Ch 15 (PBS) 600 Cooper Dr, Lexington KY 40502	800-432-0951	859-258-7000	
WKPT-TV Ch 19 (ABC) 222 Commerce St, Kingsport TN 37660	855-646-1390	423-246-9578	
WKRC-TV Ch 12 (CBS) 1906 Highland Ave, Cincinnati OH 45219	877-889-5610	513-763-5500	738-17
WKRN-TV Ch 2 (ABC) 441 Murfreesboro Rd, Nashville TN 37210	800-222-5555	615-369-7222	738-51
WKRR-FM 92.3 (CR) 192 E Lewis St, Greensboro NC 27406	800-762-5923	336-274-8042	643
WKSF-FM 99.9 (Ctry) 13 Summerlin Rd, Asheville NC 28806	800-303-5477	828-257-2700	642-9
WKSU-FM 89.7 (NPR) 1613 E Summit St, Kent OH 44242	800-672-2132	330-672-3114	643
WKVV-FM 101.7 PO Box 2098, Omaha NE 68103	800-525-5683		643
WKXW-FM 101.5 (N/T) 109 Walters Ave, Trenton NJ 08638	800-800-7822	609-359-5300	642-125
WKYC-TV Ch 3 (NBC) 1333 Lakeside Ave E, Cleveland OH 44114	877-790-7370	216-344-3333	738-18
WKYL-FM 102.1 (NAC) 102 Perkins Bldg 521 Lancaster Ave, Richmond KY 40475	800-621-8890		642-66
WKZL-FM 107.5 (CHR) 192 E Lewis St, Greensboro NC 27406	800-682-1075	336-274-8042	643
WLAC-AM 1510 (N/T) 55 Music Sq W, Nashville TN 37203	800-688-9522	615-664-2400	642-81
WLBZ-TV Ch 2 (NBC) 329 Mt Hope Ave, Bangor ME 04401	800-244-6306	207-942-4821	738-8
WLDE-FM 101.7 (Oldies) 347 W Berry St Ste 600, Fort Wayne IN 46802	888-450-1017	260-423-3676	642-46
WLFJ-FM 89.3 (Rel) 2420 Wade Hampton Blvd, Greenville SC 29615	800-447-7234	864-292-6040	642-52
WLLL-AM 930 (Rel) PO Box 11375, Lynchburg VA 24506 *Cust Svc	888-224-9809*	434-385-9555	643
WLMB-TV Ch 40 (Ind) 825 Capital Commons Dr, Toledo OH 43615	800-218-5740	419-720-9562	
WLOS-TV Ch 13 (ABC) 110 Technology Dr, Asheville NC 28803	800-419-6356	828-684-1340	738-4
WLPB-TV Ch 27 (PBS) 7733 Perkins Rd, Baton Rouge LA 70810	800-272-8161	225-767-5660	738-9
WLRH-FM 89.3 (NPR) University of Alabama-Huntsville John Wright Dr, Huntsville AL 35899	800-239-9574	256-895-9574	642-57
WLTW-FM 106.7 (AC) 32 Ave of the Americas 2nd Fl, New York NY 10013	800-222-1067	212-377-7900	642-83
WLUK-TV Ch 11 (Fox) 787 Lombardi Ave, Green Bay WI 54304	800-242-8067	920-494-8711	738-35
WLYF-FM 101.5 (AC) 20450 NW Second Ave, Miami FL 33169	877-790-1015		642-75
WM Barr & Company Inc 2105 Ch Ave, Memphis TN 38109	800-238-2672	901-775-0100	549
WMAE-FM 89.5 (NPR) 3825 Ridgewood Rd, Jackson MS 39211	800-850-4406	601-432-6565	642-59
WMBI-FM 90.1 (Rel) 820 N LaSalle Blvd, Chicago IL 60610	877-376-2194	312-329-4300	642-28
WMBM-AM 1490 (Rel) 13242 NW Seventh Ave, North Miami FL 33168	800-721-9626	305-769-1100	642-75
WMBX-FM 102.3 (Urban) 701 Northpoint Pkwy Ste 500, West Palm Beach FL 33407	800-969-1023		642-129
WMCC (White Mountains Community College) 2020 Riverside Dr, Berlin NH 03570	800-445-4525	603-752-1113	161

Name / Address	City	State	ZIP	Toll-Free	Phone	Class
WMEB-TV Ch 12 (PBS) 63 Texas Ave	Bangor	ME	04401	**800-884-1717**	207-941-1010	738-8
WMEH-FM 90.9 (NPR) 63 Texas Ave	Bangor	ME	04401	**800-884-1717**	207-941-1010	642-12
WMF Americas Inc 3512 Faith Church Rd	Indian Trail	NC	28079	**800-966-3009**	704-882-3898	361
WMH (Wilcox Memorial Hospital) 3-3420 Kuhio Hwy	Lihue	HI	96766	**877-709-9355**	808-245-1100	374-3
WMIT-FM 106.9 (Rel) 3 Porters Cove Rd	Asheville	NC	28805	**800-330-9648**	828-285-8477	643
WMK Inc 810 Moe Dr	Akron	OH	44310	**877-275-4912**	330-633-1118	56
WMLL-FM 96.5 (CR) 500 Commercial St	Manchester	NH	03101	**800-666-0957**	603-669-5777	642-73
WMMPA (Wood Moulding & Millwork Producers Assn) 507 First St	Woodland	CA	95695	**800-550-7889**	530-661-9591	48-3
WMPI-FM 105.3 (Ctry) 22 E McClain Ave	Scottsburg	IN	47170	**800-441-1053**	812-752-3688	643
WMS Gaming Inc 800 S Northpoint Blvd	Waukegan	IL	60085	**800-522-4700**	847-785-3000	323
WMTW-TV Ch 8 (ABC) 99 Danville Corner Rd	Auburn	ME	04210	**800-248-6397**	207-782-1800	
WMU (Woman's Missionary Union) 100 Missionary Ridge	Birmingham	AL	35242	**800-968-7301**	205-991-8100	47-20
WMUM-FM 89.7 (NPR) 243 Carey Salem Rd	Cochran	GA	31014	**800-222-4788**	478-301-5760	643
WMXJ-FM 102.7 (Oldies) 20450 NW Second Ave	Miami	FL	33169	**800-924-1027**	305-521-5240	642-75
WMYD-TV Ch 20 (MNT) 2777 Franklin Rd Ste 1220	Southfield	MI	48034	**800-825-0770**	248-355-2020	
WMZQ-FM 98.7 (Ctry) 1801 Rockville Pk 5th Fl	Rockville	MD	20852	**800-505-0098**	240-747-2700	643
WN (World Neighbors Inc) 4127 NW 122nd St	Oklahoma City	OK	73120	**800-242-6387**	405-752-9700	47-5
WNC (Western Nevada Community College) *Douglas* 1680 Bently Pkwy S	Minden	NV	89423	**800-433-3243**	775-782-2413	161
WNC Supply LLC 37841 N 16th St	Phoenix	AZ	85086	**800-538-5108**	623-594-4602	627
WNCF-TV Ch 32 (ABC) 3251 Harrison Rd	Montgomery	AL	36109	**800-467-0424**	334-270-2834	738-49
WNCW-FM 88.7 (AAA) PO Box 804	Spindale	NC	28160	**800-245-8870**	828-287-8000	643
WNCY-FM 100.3 (Ctry) 1420 Bellevue St	Green Bay	WI	54311	**800-359-1003**	920-435-3771	642-51
WNDV-FM 92.9 (CHR) 3371 Cleveland Rd Ste 300	South Bend	IN	46628	**800-242-0100**	574-273-9300	642-114
WNEM-TV Ch 5 (CBS) 107 N Franklin St	Saginaw	MI	48607	**800-522-9636**	989-755-8191	
WNEP-TV Ch 16 (ABC) 16 Montage Mtn Rd	Moosic	PA	18507	**800-982-4374**	570-346-7474	
WNET PO Box 5776	Englewood	NJ	07631	**800-882-6622**	609-777-0031	
WNIN-FM 88.3 (NPR) 405 Carpenter St	Evansville	IN	47708	**855-888-9646**	812-423-2973	642-42
WNIN-TV Ch 9 (PBS) 405 Carpenter St	Evansville	IN	47708	**855-888-9646**	812-423-2973	738-28
WNIT Public Television 300 W Jefferson Blvd PO Box 7034	South Bend	IN	46601	**877-411-3662**	574-675-9648	738-78
WNJU-TV Ch 47 (Tele) 2200 Fletcher Ave 6th Fl	Fort Lee	NJ	07024	**877-478-3536**		
WNKU-FM 105.9 (Ctry) 301 Landrum Academic Ctr	Highland Heights	KY	41099	**855-897-7897**	859-572-6500	643
WNND-FM 103.5 (NAC) 4401 Carriage Hill Ln	Columbus	OH	43220	**877-984-8786**	614-451-2191	642-34
WNNL-FM 103.9 (Rel) 8001-101 Creedmoor Rd	Raleigh	NC	27613	**877-310-9665**	919-848-9736	642-95
WNSN-FM 101.5 (AC) 1301 E Douglas Rd	Mishawaka	IN	46545	**855-757-1719**	574-233-3141	643
WNYT-TV Ch 13 (NBC) 715 N Pearl St	Albany	NY	12204	**800-999-9698**	518-436-4791	738-1
WO Grubb Steel Erection Inc 5120 Jefferson Davis Hwy	Richmond	VA	23234	**866-964-7822**	804-271-9471	191-14
Wo Stinson & Son Ltd 4726 Bank St	Ottawa	ON	K1T3W7	**800-267-9714**	613-822-7400	317
WOAI-AM 1200 (N/T) 6222 NW IH-10	San Antonio	TX	78201	**800-707-5150**	210-736-9700	642-104
Woburn Public Library 45 Pleasant St	Woburn	MA	01801	**800-392-6089**	781-933-0148	434-3
WOCL-FM 105.9 (Rock) 1800 Pembrook Dr Ste 400	Orlando	FL	32810	**877-919-1059**	407-919-1000	642-85
WOCN (Wound Ostomy & Continence Nurses Society) 1120 Rt 73 Ste 200	Mount Laurel	NJ	08054	**888-224-9626**		48-8
WODE-FM 99.9 107 Paxinosa Rd W	Easton	PA	18040	**800-733-2767**	610-258-6155	643
WOGG-FM 94.9 (Ctry) 123 Blaine Rd	Brownsville	PA	15417	**866-983-9898**	724-938-2000	643
WOGL-FM 98.1 (Oldies) 2 Bala Plz Ste 800	Bala Cynwyd	PA	19004	**800-942-8998**	610-668-5900	643
WOI-TV Ch 5 (ABC) 3903 Westown Pkwy	West Des Moines	IA	50266	**800-858-5555**	515-457-9645	
Wojan Window & Door Corp 217 Stover Rd	Charlevoix	MI	49720	**800-632-9827**	231-547-2931	479
Wojanis Inc 1001 Montour W Ind Park	Coraopolis	PA	15108	**800-345-9024**	724-695-1415	358
WOKO-FM 98.9 (Ctry) 70 Joy Dr	South Burlington	VT	05403	**800-354-9890**	802-862-9890	643
WOKQ-FM 97.5 (Ctry) 292 Middle Rd PO Box 576	Dover	NH	03821	**877-975-1037**	603-749-9750	643
Wolcott Systems Group LLC 1684 Medina Rd Ste 204	Medina	OH	44256	**866-965-2688**	330-666-5900	182
Wolf Gordon Inc 33-00 47th Ave	Long Island	NY	11101	**800-347-0550**		549
Wolf Manufacturing Co 1801 W Waco Dr PO Box 3100	Waco	TX	76707	**800-437-0940**	254-753-7301	154-3
Wolf Ridge Ski Resort 578 Vly View Cir	Mars Hill	NC	28754	**800-817-4111**	828-689-4111	667
Wolf Robotics LLC 4600 Innovation Dr	Fort Collins	CO	80525	**866-965-3911**	970-225-7600	490
Wolf Trap Foundation for the Performing Arts 1645 Trap Rd	Vienna	VA	22182	**877-965-3872**	703-255-1900	571
Wolf X-Ray Corp 100 W Industry Ct *Cust Svc	Deer Park	NY	11729	**800-356-9729***	631-242-9729	382
Wolfe Industrial Auctions Inc 9801 Hansonville Rd	Frederick	MD	21702	**800-443-9580**	301-898-0340	40
Wolferman's 2500 S Pacific Hwy PO Box 9100	Medford	OR	97501	**800-999-0169**		297-1
Wolfgang Candy Co 50 E Fourth Ave	York	PA	17404	**800-248-4273**	717-843-5536	297-8
Wolfram Research Inc 100 Trade Ctr Dr	Champaign	IL	61820	**800-965-3726**	217-398-0700	179
Wolters Kluwer Financial Services Inc 100 S Fifth St Ste 700	Minneapolis	MN	55402	**800-552-9408**	612-656-7700	180-10
Wolverine Mutual Insurance Co 1 Wolverine Way	Dowagiac	MI	49047	**800-733-3320**	269-782-3451	390
Wolverine Power Systems Inc 3229 80th Ave	Zeeland	MI	49464	**800-485-8068**	616-879-0040	517
Wolverton Securities Ltd 777 Dunsmuir St 17th Fl	Vancouver	BC	V7Y1J5	**877-390-7771**	604-622-1000	688
Woman's Life Insurance Society 1338 Military St PO Box 5020	Port Huron	MI	48061	**800-521-9292**	810-985-5191	391-2
Woman's Missionary Union (WMU) 100 Missionary Ridge	Birmingham	AL	35242	**800-968-7301**	205-991-8100	47-20
Women Alive 1566 Burnside Ave	Los Angeles	CA	90019	**800-472-2321**		47-17
Women in Military Service for America Memorial Foundation Inc Dept 560	Washington	DC	20042	**800-222-2294**	703-533-1155	47-19
Women in Technology International (WITI) 11500 Olympic Blvd Ste 400	Los Angeles	CA	90064	**800-334-9484**	818-788-9484	48-19
Women Management 199 Lafayette St 7th Fl	New York	NY	10012	**800-838-3006**	212-334-7480	505
Women's & Children's Hospital (WCH) 4600 Ambassador Caffery Pkwy	Lafayette	LA	70508	**888-569-8331**	337-521-9100	374-7
Women's & Children's Hospital of Buffalo 219 Bryant St	Buffalo	NY	14222	**800-462-7653**	716-878-7000	374-1
Women's Bureau 200 Constitution Ave NW Rm S3002	Washington	DC	20210	**800-827-5335**	202-693-6710	340-13
Women's Bureau Regional Offices *Region 2* 201 Varick St Rm 602	New York	NY	10014	**800-827-5335**	212-337-2389	340-13
Region 3 200 Constitution Ave NW Ste 631E	Washington	DC	20210	**800-827-5335**	866-487-2365	340-13
Region 4 Sam Nunn Federal Ctr 61 Forsyth St SW Ste 6B75	Atlanta	GA	30303	**800-827-5335**	404-562-2336	340-13
Region 5 Federal Bldg 230 S Dearborn St Rm 1022	Chicago	IL	60604	**800-827-5335**	312-353-6985	340-13
Region 6 Federal Bldg 525 Griffin St Ste 735	Dallas	TX	75202	**800-827-5335**	972-850-4700	340-13
Region 7 2300 Main St Ste 1050	Kansas City	MO	64108	**800-827-5335**	816-285-7233	340-13
Region 8 1999 Broadway Ste 1620 PO Box 46550	Denver	CO	80201	**800-827-5335**	303-844-1286	340-13
Region 9 90 Seventh St Ste 2650	San Francisco	CA	94103	**800-827-5335**	415-625-2638	340-13
Region 10 1111 Third Ave Ste 620	Seattle	WA	98101	**800-827-5335**	206-553-1534	340-13
Women's Council of REALTORS (WCR) 430 N Michigan Ave	Chicago	IL	60611	**800-245-8512**		48-17
Women's Independence Scholarship Program Inc (WISP) 4900 Randall Pkwy Ste H	Wilmington	NC	28403	**866-255-7742**	910-397-7742	306
Women's International Pharmacy Inc PO Box 6468	Madison	WI	53716	**800-279-5708**	608-221-7800	458
Women's Sports Foundation 1899 Hempstead Tpke Ste 400 Eisenhower Pk	East Meadow	NY	11554	**800-227-3988**	516-542-4700	47-22
Women's Wear Daily Magazine 750 Third Ave 5th Fl	New York	NY	10017	**800-289-0273**	212-630-4600	456-11
WOMX-FM 105.1 (AC) 1800 Pembrook Dr Ste 400	Orlando	FL	32810	**877-919-1051**	407-919-1000	642-85
Wonder View Inn & Suites 50 Eden St PO Box 25	Bar Harbor	ME	04609	**888-439-8439**	207-288-3358	379
Wonderland Amusement Park 2601 Dumas Dr	Amarillo	TX	79107	**800-383-4712**	806-383-0832	32
Wonderlic Inc 400 Lakeview Pkwy Ste 200	Vernon Hills	IL	60061	**877-605-9496**	847-680-4900	634-10
Wonders of Wildlife 500 W Sunshine St	Springfield	MO	65807	**877-245-9453**	417-890-9453	821
Won-Door Corp 1865 South 3480 West	Salt Lake City	UT	84104	**800-453-8494**	801-973-7500	236
WONE-FM 97.5 (Rock) 1795 W Market St	Akron	OH	44313	**888-588-8436**	330-869-9800	642-2
Wong & Knowles CPA PC 340 W Butterfield Rd	Elmhurst	IL	60126	**866-966-4272**	630-993-2223	2
Wood & Tait Inc 64-5249 Kauakea Rd	Kamuela	HI	96743	**800-774-8585**	808-885-5090	400
Wood County 1 Courthouse Sq	Bowling Green	OH	43402	**866-860-4140**	419-354-9000	338
Wood County Electric Co-op Inc 501 S Main St	Quitman	TX	75783	**800-762-2203**	903-763-2203	247
Wood Moulding & Millwork Producers Assn (WMMPA) 507 First St	Woodland	CA	95695	**800-550-7889**	530-661-9591	48-3
Wood National Cemetery 5000 W National Ave Bldg 1301	Milwaukee	WI	53295	**888-878-3256**	414-382-5300	135
Wood Preservers Inc 15939 Historyland Hwy PO Box 158	Warsaw	VA	22572	**800-368-2536**	804-333-4022	816
Wood Pro Inc 421 Washington St PO Box 363	Auburn	MA	01501	**800-786-5577**	508-832-3291	749
Wood River Technologies Inc 191 Sun Valley Rd Ste 202	Ketchum	ID	83340	**888-661-4094**		76

Name / Address	City	State	Zip	Toll-Free	Phone	Class
Wood Tobe-Coburn School 8 E 40th St	New York	NY	10016	**800-394-9663**	212-686-9040	798
Woodard & Curran 41 Hutchins Dr	Portland	ME	04102	**800-426-4262**	207-774-2112	263
Woodbine Entertainment Group Inc 555 Rexdale Blvd PO Box 156	Toronto	ON	M9W5L2	**888-675-7223**	416-675-7223	639
Woodburn Nursery & Azaleas 13009 McKee School Rd NE *Sales	Woodburn	OR	97071	**888-634-2232***	503-634-2231	369
Woodbury Box Company Inc 301 McIntosh Pkwy	Thomaston	GA	30286	**800-722-2061**		350
Woodbury County Rural Electric Co-op Assn 1495 Humboldt Ave	Moville	IA	51039	**800-469-3125**	712-873-3125	247
Woodbury Pewterers Inc 860 Main St S	Woodbury	CT	06798	**800-648-2014**		700
Woodbury Technologies Inc 1725 East 1450 South	Clearfield	UT	84015	**800-408-8857**		198
Woodbury University 7500 Glenoaks Blvd	Burbank	CA	91510	**800-784-9663**	818-767-0888	167
Woodcliff Hotel & Spa 199 Woodcliff Dr	Fairport	NY	14450	**800-365-3065**	585-381-4000	667
Woodcock Washburn LLP 2929 Arch St Fl 12	Philadelphia	PA	19104	**877-843-4821**	215-568-3100	428
Woodcraft Supply LLC 1177 Rosemar Rd	Parkersburg	WV	26105	**800-535-4482**		44
Woodfield Inc 3161 Hwy 376 S	Camden	AR	71701	**800-501-6020**	870-231-6020	188
Woodford Manufacturing Co 2121 Waynoka Rd *Sales	Colorado Springs	CO	80915	**800-621-6032***		608
Woodforest Financial Group Inc PO Box 7889	Spring	TX	77387	**877-968-7962**	832-375-2000	69
Wood-Fruitticher Grocery Company Inc 2900 Alton Rd	Birmingham	AL	35210	**800-328-0026**	205-836-9663	298-8
Woodgrain Distribution 80 Shelby St	Montevallo	AL	35115	**800-756-0199**	205-665-2546	310
Woodgrain Millworks Inc 300 NW 16th St	Fruitland	ID	83619	**888-783-5485**	208-452-3801	498
Woodhill Supply Inc 4665 Beidler Rd	Willoughby	OH	44094	**800-362-6111**	440-269-1100	611
Woodland Aviation Inc 25170 Aviation Ave	Davis	CA	95616	**800-442-1333**	530-759-6037	62
Woodland Chamber of Commerce 307 First St	Woodland	CA	95695	**888-843-2636**	530-662-7327	138
Woodland Heights Medical Ctr 505 S John Redditt Dr	Lufkin	TX	75904	**800-222-1222**	936-634-8311	374-3
Woodland Hills Chamber of Commerce 20121 Ventura Blvd Ste 309	Woodland Hills	CA	91364	**888-852-9961**	818-347-4737	138
Woodland Hills Youth Development Ctr 3965 Stewarts Ln	Nashville	TN	37218	**855-418-1622**	615-532-2000	412
Woodland Public Library 250 First St	Woodland	CA	95695	**800-321-2752**	530-661-5980	434-3
Woodlands Academy of the Sacred Heart 760 E Westleigh Rd	Lake Forest	IL	60045	**888-234-3080**	847-234-4300	621
Woodlands Inn, The 1073 Hwy 315	Wilkes-Barre	PA	18702	**844-779-8472**	570-824-9831	667
Woodlands Resort & Conference Ctr, The 2301 N Millbend Dr *Resv	The Woodlands	TX	77380	**800-433-2624***	281-367-1100	377
Woodlawn Cemetery Inc, The Webster Ave & E 233rd St	Bronx	NY	10470	**877-496-6352**	718-920-0500	509
Woodlawn National Cemetery 1825 Davis St	Elmira	NY	14901	**877-907-8585**	607-732-5411	135
Woodloch Pines Inc 731 Welcome Lk Rd	Hawley	PA	18428	**800-966-3562**	570-685-8000	379
Woodmark Hotel on Lake Washington 1200 Carillon Pt	Kirkland	WA	98033	**800-822-3700**	425-822-3700	379
WOODMEN Magazine 1700 Farnam St	Omaha	NE	68102	**800-225-3108**	402-342-1890	456-10
Woodmont Investment Counsel LLC 401 Commerce St Ste 5400	Nashville	TN	37219	**800-278-8003**	615-297-6144	401
Woodridge Public Library 3 Plaza Dr	Woodridge	IL	60517	**800-279-0400**	630-964-7899	434-3
Woodrow Wilson Presidential Library 20 N Coalter St PO Box 24	Staunton	VA	24401	**888-496-6376**	540-885-0897	434-2
Woodruff Electric Co-op PO Box 1619	Forrest City	AR	72336	**888-559-6400**	870-633-2262	247
Woodruff Energy 73 Water St PO Box 777	Bridgeton	NJ	08302	**800-557-1121**	856-455-1111	317
Woods Equipment Co 2606 S Illinois Rt 2 PO Box 1000	Oregon	IL	61061	**800-319-6637**	815-732-2141	275
Woods Resort & Conference Ctr Mountain Lk Rd PO Box 5	Hedgesville	WV	25427	**800-248-2222**		667
Woodshop News 10 Bokum Rd	Essex	CT	06426	**800-444-7686**	860-767-8227	456-14
Woodsmith Magazine 2200 Grand Ave *Cust Svc	Des Moines	IA	50312	**800-333-5075***		456-14
Woodson & Bozeman Inc 3870 New Getwell Rd	Memphis	TN	38118	**800-876-4243**	901-362-1500	37
Woodstock Inn & Resort 14 The Green	Woodstock	VT	05091	**800-448-7900**	802-457-1100	667
Woodstream Corp 69 N Locust St *All	Lititz	PA	17543	**800-800-1819***	717-626-2125	282
Woodsville Guaranty Savings Bank 10 Pleasant St PO Box 266	Woodsville	NH	03785	**800-564-2735**	603-747-2735	69
WoodTrust Financial Corp 181 Second St S	Wisconsin Rapids	WI	54494	**800-716-3742**	715-423-7600	69
Woodward Communications Inc 801 Bluff St	Dubuque	IA	52001	**800-553-4801**		643
Woodward Resource Ctr 1251 334th St	Woodward	IA	50276	**888-229-9223**	515-438-2600	232
Woodway USA W229 N591 Foster Ct	Waukesha	WI	53186	**800-966-3929**	262-548-6235	269
Woodwind & Brasswind 4004 Technology Dr	South Bend	IN	46628	**800-348-5003**	574-251-3500	525
Woody Bogler Trucking Co PO Box 229	Rosebud	MO	63091	**800-899-4120**	573-764-3700	778
Woolaroc Ranch Museum & Wildlife Preserve 1925 Woolaroc Ranch Rd	Bartlesville	OK	74003	**888-966-5276**	918-336-0307	519
Woolrich Inc 2 Mill St	Woolrich	PA	17779	**800-995-1299**	570-769-6464	154-5
Woonsocket Harris Public Library 303 Clinton St	Woonsocket	RI	02895	**800-359-3090**	401-769-9044	434-3
Wooster Brush Co 604 Madison Ave	Wooster	OH	44691	**800-392-7246**	330-264-4440	102
Wooster Products Inc 1000 Spruce St PO Box 6005	Wooster	OH	44691	**800-321-4936**	330-264-2844	490
Wooster Republican Printing Co 212 E Liberty St	Wooster	OH	44691	**800-686-2958**	330-264-1125	634-8
Woot Inc 4121 International Pkwy	Carrollton	TX	75007	**866-551-6881**	972-417-3959	176
Worcester Academy 81 Providence St	Worcester	MA	01604	**800-235-6426**	508-754-5302	621
Worcester County Convention & Visitors Bureau 91 Prescott St	Worcester	MA	01605	**866-755-7439**	508-755-7400	208
Worcester Envelope Co 22 Millbury St	Auburn	MA	01501	**800-343-1398**	508-832-5394	265
Worcester Telegram & Gazette Inc 20 Franklin St PO Box 15012	Worcester	MA	01615	**800-678-6680**	508-793-9100	634-8
Word Among Us Inc 9639 Doctor Perry Rd	Ijamsville	MD	21754	**800-775-9673**	301-874-1700	95
Worden Bros Inc 4905 Pine Cone Dr	Durham	NC	27707	**800-776-4940**	919-408-0542	180-1
Worden Company Inc 199 E 17th St	Holland	MI	49423	**800-748-0561**	616-392-1848	320-3
Wordsmart Corp 10025 Mesa Rim Rd	San Diego	CA	92121	**800-858-9673**	858-565-8068	180-3
Work 'n Gear Stores 2300 Crown Colony Dr Ste 300	Quincy	MA	02169	**800-987-0218**		156-5
Work Out World 762 SR- 18	Brunswick	NJ	08816	**888-564-6969**	732-390-7390	354
WorkCare.com 300 S Harbor Blvd Ste 600	Anaheim	CA	92805	**800-455-6155**		196
Workers' Credit Union 815 Main St PO Box 900	Fitchburg	MA	01420	**800-221-4020**	978-345-1021	221
Working Machines Corp 2170 Dwight Way	Berkeley	CA	94704	**877-648-4808**	510-704-1100	182
Working Solutions 1820 Preston Pk Blvd Ste 2000	Plano	TX	75093	**866-857-4800**	972-964-4800	734
Working Together 360 Hiatt Dr	Palm Beach Gardens	FL	33418	**800-621-5463**	561-622-6520	530-2
Workman Publishing 225 Varick St	New York	NY	10014	**800-722-7202**	212-254-5900	634-2
Workmen's Circle/Arbeter Ring Inc 247 W 37th St 5th Fl	New York	NY	10018	**800-922-2558**	212-889-6800	48-9
Workplace Answers LLC 3701 Executive Ctr Dr Ste 201	Austin	TX	78731	**866-861-4410**		401
Workplace Law Report 1801 S Bell St	Arlington	VA	22202	**800-372-1033**		530-7
Workplace Resource LLC 4400 NE Loop 410 Ste 130	San Antonio	TX	78218	**800-580-3000**	512-472-7300	322
Workplace Systems Inc 562 Mammoth Rd	Londonderry	NH	03053	**800-258-9700**	603-622-3727	320-1
Works Computing Inc 1801 American Blvd E Ste 12	Bloomington	MN	55425	**866-222-4077**	952-746-1580	175-3
Worksman Trading Corp 94-15 100th St	Ozone Park	NY	11416	**800-962-2453**	718-322-2000	81
Worksoft Inc 15851 Dallas Pkwy Ste 855	Addison	TX	75001	**866-836-1773**	214-239-0400	180-10
World Book Inc 233 N Michigan Ave Ste 2000	Chicago	IL	60601	**800-967-5325**	312-729-5800	634-2
World Cat 1090 W St James St	Tarboro	NC	27886	**866-485-8899**	252-641-8000	89
World Chamber of Commerce Directory Inc 446 E 29th St	Loveland	CO	80538	**888-883-3231**	970-663-3231	634-6
World Class Lighting 14350 60th St N	Clearwater	FL	33760	**877-499-6753**	727-524-7661	362
World Class Plastics Inc 7695 SR- 708	Russells Point	OH	43348	**800-954-3140**	937-843-4927	607
World Concern 19303 Fremont Ave N	Seattle	WA	98133	**800-755-5022**	206-546-7201	47-5
World Courier Inc 1313 Fourth Ave	New Hyde Park	NY	11040	**800-221-6600**	516-354-2600	545
World Currency USA Inc 16 W Main St	Marlton	NJ	08053	**888-593-7927**		689
World Data Products Inc 121 Cheshire Ln	Minnetonka	MN	55305	**888-210-7636**	952-476-9000	178
World Dryer Corp 5700 McDermott Dr	Berkeley	IL	60163	**800-323-0701**	708-449-6950	36
World Electronics Sales & Service Inc 3000 Kutztown Rd	Reading	PA	19605	**800-523-0427**	610-939-9800	255
World Energy Alternatives LLC 2 Constitution Ctr	Boston	MA	02129	**800-829-3676**	617-889-7300	203
World Floor Covering Assn (WFCA) 2211 Howell Ave	Anaheim	CA	92806	**800-624-6880**	714-978-6440	48-4
World Food Program USA (WFP) 1725 Eye St NW Ste 510	Washington	DC	20036	**888-454-0555**	202-530-1694	47-5
World Fuel Services Corp 9800 NW 41st St Ste 400 *NYSE: INT*	Miami	FL	33178	**800-345-3818**	305-428-8000	578
World Future Society 7910 Woodmont Ave Ste 450	Bethesda	MD	20814	**800-989-8274**	301-656-8274	48-19
World Gospel Mission (WGM) 3783 E State Rd 18 PO Box 948	Marion	IN	46952	**800-426-0846**	765-664-7331	47-20
World Health 7222 Edgemont Blvd NW	Calgary	AB	T3A2X7	**866-278-4131**	403-239-4048	354
World Hunger Year Inc (WHY) 505 Eigth Ave Ste 2100	New York	NY	10018	**800-548-6479**	212-629-8850	47-5
World Inspection Network International Inc 12345 Lk City Way NE Ste 365	Seattle	WA	98125	**800-309-6753**		365
World Learning 1 Kipling Rd PO Box 676	Brattleboro	VT	05302	**800-257-7751**	802-257-7751	47-5

Name / Address	City	State	ZIP	Toll-Free	Phone	Class
World Learning International Development Programs 1015 15th St NW Ste 750	Washington	DC	20005	800-345-2929	202-408-5420	47-11
World Literature CrUSAde 640 Chapel Hills Dr	Colorado Springs	CO	80920	800-423-5054	719-260-8888	47-20
World Minerals Inc 130 Castilian Dr	Goleta	CA	93117	800-893-4445	805-562-0200	411
World Music Supply 2414 W Seventh St	Muncie	IN	47302	800-867-4611	765-213-6085	525
World Neighbors Inc (WN) 4127 NW 122nd St	Oklahoma City	OK	73120	800-242-6387	405-752-9700	47-5
World of Coca-Cola Atlanta 121 Baker St NW	Atlanta	GA	30313	888-855-5701	404-676-5151	519
World of Watches 3701 Flamingo Rd Ste 100	Miramar	FL	33027	866-961-8463	954-983-2181	152
World of Wigs 2305 E 17th St	Santa Ana	CA	92705	800-794-5572	714-547-4461	348
World Policy Institute (WPI) 220 Fifth Ave 9th Fl	New York	NY	10001	800-207-8354	212-481-5005	631
World Publishing Co 315 S Boulder Ave	Tulsa	OK	74102	800-444-6552	918-583-2161	634-8
World Relief 7 E Baltimore St	Baltimore	MD	21202	800-535-5433	443-451-1900	47-5
World Securities Law Report 1801 S Bell St	Arlington	VA	22202	800-372-1033		530-7
World Spice Inc 223 E Highland Pkwy	Roselle	NJ	07203	800-234-1060	908-245-0600	297-37
World Travel Bureau Inc 618 N Main St	Santa Ana	CA	92701	800-899-3370	714-835-8111	769
World Travel Holdings (WTH) 100 Fordham Rd Bldg C Bldg C	Wilmington	MA	01887	877-958-7447	617-424-7990	769
World Travel Inc 1724 W Schuylkill Rd	Douglassville	PA	19518	877-265-1881	610-327-9000	769
World University 107 N Ventura St PO Box 1567	Ojai	CA	93024	888-370-7589	805-646-1444	167
World Vision Inc 34834 Weyerhaeuser Way S PO Box 9716	Federal Way	WA	98001	888-511-6548	253-815-1000	47-5
World Wide Concessions Inc 1950 Old Cuthbert Rd Ste M	Cherry Hill	NJ	08034	888-377-7666	856-933-9900	699
World Wide Fittings Inc 7501 N Natchez Ave	Niles	IL	60714	800-393-9894	847-588-2200	594
World Wide Packaging LLC 15 Vreeland Rd Ste 4	Florham Park	NJ	07932	800-950-0390	973-805-6500	233
World Wildlife Fund (WWF) 1250 24th St NW PO Box 97180	Washington	DC	20090	800-225-5993	202-293-4800	47-3
World Wildlife Fund Canada (WWF) 245 Eglinton Ave E Ste 410	Toronto	ON	M4P3J1	800-267-2632	416-489-8800	47-3
World Wrestling Entertainment Inc 1241 E Main St *NYSE: WWE*	Stamford	CT	06902	866-993-7467	203-352-8600	183
World's Finest Chocolate Inc 4801 S Lawndale	Chicago	IL	60632	888-821-8452		297-8
World*Class Learning Materials PO Box 639	Candler	NC	28715	800-638-6470		245
World, The 403 US Rt 302-Berlin	Barre	VT	05641	800-639-9753	802-479-2582	531-4
Worldata 3000 N Military Trl	Boca Raton	FL	33431	800-331-8102	561-393-8200	6
WorldatWork 14040 N Northsight Blvd	Scottsdale	AZ	85260	877-951-9191	202-315-5500	48-12
WorldClass Travel Network 7831 Southtown Ctr Ste A	Bloomington	MN	55431	800-234-3576	952-835-8636	770
Worldfest Houston International Film Festival PO Box 56566	Houston	TX	77240	866-965-9955	713-629-3700	284
WorldMark the Club 9805 Willows Rd NE	Redmond	WA	98052	800-722-3487	425-498-1950	751
WorldMed Assist 1230 Mtn Side Ct	Concord	CA	94521	866-999-3848		363
WORLDPAC Inc 37137 Hickory St	Newark	CA	94560	800-888-9982	510-742-8900	60
Worlds.com Inc 11 Royal Rd	Brookline	MA	02445	800-315-2580	617-725-8900	180-8
WorldStrides 218 W Water St Ste 400 *General	Charlottesville	VA	22902	800-999-7676*		758
WorldTEK Event & Travel Management 1 Audubon Ste 400	New Haven	CT	06511	800-233-5989	203-772-0470	770
Worldtrans Services Inc 7130 Miramar Rd Ste 100a	San Diego	CA	92121	800-736-3769	858-536-7900	312
Worldwatch Institute 1776 Massachusetts Ave NW	Washington	DC	20036	877-539-9946	202-452-1999	631
Worldwide Court Reporters 3000 Weslayan St Ste 235	Houston	TX	77027	800-745-1101	713-572-2000	393
Worldwide Express 2602 McKinney Ave Ste 400	Dallas	TX	75204	800-758-7447	214-720-2400	545
Worldwide Golf Shops Inc 1421 Village Wy	Santa Ana	CA	92705	888-216-5252	714-543-8284	708
Worldwide Holidays Inc 7800 Red Rd Ste 112	South Miami	FL	33143	800-327-9854	305-665-0841	769
Worldwide Sign Systems 446 N Cecil St	Bonduel	WI	54107	800-874-3334		699
Worldwide Steel Buildings PO Box 588	Peculiar	MO	64078	800-825-0316		104
Worldwide Travel & Cruise Assoc Inc 150 S University Dr Ste E	Plantation	FL	33324	800-881-8484	954-452-8800	769
Worley & Obetz Inc 85 White Oak Rd PO Box 429	Manheim	PA	17545	800-697-6891	717-665-6891	317
Worly Plumbing Supply Inc 54 E Harrison St	Delaware	OH	43015	800-365-1175	740-363-1151	609
Wormser Corp 150 Coolidge Ave	Englewood	NJ	07631	800-546-4040		154-14
Worrell Corp 305 S Post Rd	Indianapolis	IN	46219	800-297-9599	317-895-9708	294
Worship Network PO Box 428	Safety Harbor	FL	34695	800-728-8723		736
Wort Hotel 50 N Glenwood *Cust Svc	Jackson	WY	83001	800-322-2727*	307-733-2190	379
Worth & Company Inc 6263 Kellers Church Rd	Pipersville	PA	18947	800-220-5130	267-362-1100	191-10
Worth Co, The 214 Sherman Ave PO Box 88	Stevens Point	WI	54481	800-944-1899	715-344-6081	708
Worth Higgins & Assoc Inc 8770 Park Central Dr	Richmond	VA	23227	800-883-7768	804-264-2304	176
Worthington Biochemical Corp 730 Vassar Ave	Lakewood	NJ	08701	800-445-9603	732-942-1660	233
Worthington Direct Holdings LLC 6301 Gaston Ave Ste 670	Dallas	TX	75214	800-599-6636		360-3
Worthington Industries 200 Old E Wilson Bridge Rd	Columbus	OH	43085	866-928-2657	614-438-3013	90
Worthington Steel Co 200 W Old Wilson Bridge Rd	Columbus	OH	43085	800-944-3733	614-438-3210	721
Wor-Wic Community College 32000 Campus Dr	Salisbury	MD	21804	800-735-2258	410-334-2800	161
WOUC-TV Ch 44 (PBS) 35 S College St	Athens	OH	45701	800-456-2044	740-593-1771	
Wound Ostomy & Continence Nurses Society (WOCN) 1120 Rt 73 Ste 200	Mount Laurel	NJ	08054	888-224-9626		48-8
WOWK-TV Ch 13 (CBS) 555 Fifth Ave	Huntington	WV	25701	800-333-7636	304-525-1313	
WOWO-AM 1190 (N/T) 2915 Maples Rd	Fort Wayne	IN	46816	800-333-1190	260-447-5511	642-46
WOWT-TV Ch 6 (NBC) 3501 Farnam St	Omaha	NE	68131	866-434-8587	402-346-6666	738-56
Wozniak Industries Inc Commercial Forged Products Div 5757 W 65th St	Bedford Park	IL	60638	800-637-2695	708-458-1220	482
WP (Walton Press) 402 Mayfield Dr	Monroe	GA	30655	800-354-0235	770-267-2596	554
WP Carey & Company LLC 50 Rockefeller Plz 2nd Fl *NYSE: WPC*	New York	NY	10020	800-972-2739	212-492-1100	653
WPBT-TV Ch 2 (PBS) 14901 NE 20th Ave	Miami	FL	33181	800-222-9728	305-949-8321	738-47
WPC (Willmar Poultry Co, The) 3735 County Rd 5 SW	Willmar	MN	56201	800-328-8849	320-235-8850	10-7
WPCS-FM 89.5 (Rel) PO Box 18000	Pensacola	FL	32523	800-726-1191	850-479-6570	642-87
WPCV-FM 97.5 (Ctry) 404 W Lime St	Lakeland	FL	33815	800-227-9797	863-682-8184	643
WPGC-FM 95.5 (CHR) 4200 Parliament Pl Ste 300	Lanham	MD	20706	877-955-5267		643
WPI (World Policy Institute) 220 Fifth Ave 9th Fl	New York	NY	10001	800-207-8354	212-481-5005	631
WPLM-FM 99.1 (AC) 17 Columbus Rd	Plymouth	MA	02360	877-327-9991	508-746-1390	643
WPLN-FM 90.3 (NPR) 630 Mainstream Dr	Nashville	TN	37228	877-760-2903	615-760-2903	642-81
WPMT-TV Ch 43 (Fox) 2005 S Queen St	York	PA	17403	866-976-8747	717-843-0043	
WPNE-FM 89.3 (NPR) 2420 Nicolet Dr	Green Bay	WI	54311	800-654-6228	920-465-2444	642-51
WPOC-FM 93.1 (Country) 711 W 40th St Ste 350	Baltimore	MD	21211	866-962-5487	410-366-7600	642-11
WPR (Wisconsin Public Radio) 821 University Ave	Madison	WI	53706	800-747-7444		629
WPRO-FM 92.3 (CHR) 1502 Wampanoag Trl	East Providence	RI	02915	800-638-0092	401-433-4200	643
WPST-FM 94.5 (AC) 619 Alexander Rd 3rd Fl	Princeton	NJ	08540	800-248-9778	609-419-0300	643
WPT (Wisconsin Public Television) 821 University Ave	Madison	WI	53706	800-422-9707	608-263-2121	629
WPTD-TV Ch 16 (PBS) 110 S Jefferson St	Dayton	OH	45402	800-247-1614	937-220-1600	738-22
WPTF-AM 680 (N/T) 3012 Highwoods Blvd Ste 201	Raleigh	NC	27604	800-662-7979	919-790-9392	642-95
WPX Delivery Solutions 3320 W Valley Hwy N Ste 111	Auburn	WA	98001	800-562-1091	253-876-2760	545
WPXD-TV Ch 31 (I) 3975 Varsity Dr	Ann Arbor	MI	48108	888-467-2988	734-973-7900	
WPXN-TV Ch 31 (I) 810 Seventh Ave 30th Fl	New York	NY	10019	800-987-9936	212-603-8419	738-53
WQBE-FM 97.5 (Ctry) 817 Suncrest Pl	Charleston	WV	25303	800-222-3697	304-344-9700	642-26
WQED-FM 89.3 (Clas) 4802 Fifth Ave	Pittsburgh	PA	15213	800-876-1316	412-622-1436	642-92
WQED-TV Ch 13 (PBS) 4802 Fifth Ave	Pittsburgh	PA	15213	800-876-1316	412-622-1370	738-60
WQFL-FM 100.9 (Rel) PO Box 2118	Omaha	NE	68103	888-937-2471		643
WQHT-FM 97.1 (Urban) 395 Hudson St 7th Fl	New York	NY	10014	800-223-9797	212-229-9797	642-83
WQLH-FM 98.5 (AC) 810 Victoria St	Green Bay	WI	54302	855-782-7985	920-468-4100	642-51
WQLN-FM 91.3 (NPR) 8425 Peach St	Erie	PA	16509	800-727-8854	814-864-3001	642-40
WQLN-TV Ch 54 (PBS) 8425 Peach St	Erie	PA	16509	800-727-8854	814-864-3001	738-27
WQN Inc 14911 Quorum Dr Ste 140 *OTC: WQNI*	Dallas	TX	75254	866-661-6176		733
WQUN-AM 1220 (Nost) 3085 Whitney Ave	Hamden	CT	06518	800-462-1944	203-582-8984	643
WR Case & Sons Cutlery Co 50 Owens Way PO Box 4000	Bradford	PA	16701	800-523-6350		224
WR Grace & Co 7500 Grace Dr *NYSE: GRA*	Columbia	MD	21044	800-638-6014	410-531-4000	144
WR Hambrecht & Co 909 Montgomery St 3rd Fl *Cust Svc	San Francisco	CA	94133	855-753-6484*	415-551-8600	688
Wragtime Air Freight Inc 596 W 135th St	Gardena	CA	90248	800-586-9701		778
WRAL-FM 101.5 (AC) 3100 Highwoods Blvd Ste 140	Raleigh	NC	27604	800-745-3000	919-890-6101	642-95
WRAL-TV Ch 5 (CBS) 2619 Western Blvd	Raleigh	NC	27606	800-245-9725	919-821-8555	738-64

				Toll-Free	Phone	Class
Wrangell Harbor PO Box 531	Wrangell	AK	99929	**800-347-4462**	907-874-3736	617
Wrangell-Saint Elias National Park & Preserve Mile 1068 Richardson Hwy PO Box 439	Copper Center	AK	99573	**866-705-5711**	907-822-5234	563
Wrap-On Company Inc 5550 W 70th Pl	Chicago	IL	60638	**800-621-6947**	708-496-2150	811
WRAZ-TV Ch 50 (Fox) 512 S Mangum St	Durham	NC	27701	**877-369-5050**	919-595-5050	738-64
WRBS-FM 95.1 (Rel) 3500 Commerce Dr	Baltimore	MD	21227	**800-965-9324**	410-247-4100	642-11
WRCG-AM 1420 (N/T) 1820 Wynnton Rd	Columbus	GA	31906	**844-706-7625**	706-327-1217	642-33
WRCH-FM 100.5 (AC) 10 Executive Dr	Farmington	CT	06032	**800-530-1005**	860-677-6700	643
WRCTC (West River Co-op Telephone Co) 801 Coleman Ave PO Box 39	Bison	SD	57620	**888-464-9513**	605-244-5213	733
WRDW-TV Ch 12 (CBS) PO Box 1212	Augusta	GA	30903	**866-591-2502**	803-278-1212	738-5
WREA (White River Electric Assn) PO Box 958	Meeker	CO	81641	**800-922-1987**	970-878-5041	247
Wren Assoc Ltd 124 Wren Pkwy	Jefferson City	MO	65109	**800-881-2249**	573-893-2249	607
Wright & Lato 2100 Felver Ct	Rahway	NJ	07065	**800-724-1855**	973-674-8700	409
Wright Business Graphics (WBG) 18440 NE San Rafael St	Portland	OR	97230	**800-547-8397**		109
Wright Color Graphics 9051 Sunland Blvd	Sun Valley	CA	91352	**877-246-8877**	818-246-8877	625
Wright Express Corp 97 Darling Ave *NYSE: WEX*	South Portland	ME	04106	**800-761-7181**	207-773-8171	219
Wright Global Graphics 5115 Prospect St	Thomasville	NC	27360	**800-678-9019**	336-472-4200	413
Wright Group, The 6428 Airport Rd	Crowley	LA	70526	**800-201-3096**	337-783-3096	582
Wright Investors' Service 440 Wheelers Farms Rd	Milford	CT	06461	**800-232-0013**	203-783-4400	401
Wright Line LLC 160 Gold Star Blvd	Worcester	MA	01606	**800-225-7348**	508-852-4300	320-1
Wright Medical Group Inc 5677 Airline Rd *NASDAQ: WMGI*	Arlington	TN	38002	**800-238-7188**	901-867-9971	476
Wright Medical Technology Inc 5677 Airline Rd	Arlington	TN	38002	**800-238-7188**	901-867-9971	476
Wright State University 3640 Colonel Glenn Hwy *Admissions	Dayton	OH	45435	**800-247-1770***	937-775-5740	167
Wright State University Boonshoft School of Medicine 3640 Col Glenn Hwy	Dayton	OH	45435	**800-338-4057**	937-775-2934	168-2
Wright State University Lake 7600 Lk Campus Dr	Celina	OH	45822	**800-237-1477**	419-586-0300	161
Wright Tool Company Inc 1 Wright Dr	Barberton	OH	44203	**800-321-2902**	330-848-0600	350
Wright Transportation Inc 2333 Dauphin Island Pkwy	Mobile	AL	36605	**800-342-4598**	251-432-6390	778
Wright Travel Inc 2505 21st Ave S 5th Fl	Nashville	TN	37212	**800-577-0888**	615-783-1111	769
Wright's Media 2407 Timberloch Pl Ste B	The Woodlands	TX	77380	**877-652-5295**	281-419-5725	634-9
Wright-Hennepin Co-op Electric Assn 6800 Electric Dr PO Box 330	Rockford	MN	55373	**800-943-2667**	763-477-3000	247
Wright-Patt Credit Union Inc 2455 Executive Pk Blvd PO Box 286	Fairborn	OH	45324	**800-762-0047**	937-912-7000	221
Wrightsoft Corp 131 Hartwell Ave	Lexington	MA	02421	**800-225-8697**		227
Wrigley Co, The 410 N Michigan Ave	Chicago	IL	60611	**888-985-2064**	312-644-2121	297-6
Wrigley Field 1060 W Addison St	Chicago	IL	60613	**866-800-1275**	773-404-2827	718
Wrisco Industries Inc 355 Hiatt Dr Ste B	Palm Beach Gardens	FL	33418	**800-627-2646**	561-626-5700	491
WRIT (Washington Real Estate Investment Trust) 1775 I St NW *NYSE: WRE*	Washington	DC	20006	**800-565-9748**	301-984-9400	653
Writer's Digest 4700 E Galbraith Rd *Cust Svc	Cincinnati	OH	45236	**800-283-0963***	513-531-2690	456-21
Writer's Digest Book Club 4700 E Galbraith Rd *Cust Svc	Cincinnati	OH	45236	**800-759-0963***	513-531-2690	92
Writers Guild of America West (WGAw) 7000 W Third St	Los Angeles	CA	90048	**800-421-4182**	323-951-4000	414
WRKF-FM 89.3 (NPR) 3050 Vly Creek Dr	Baton Rouge	LA	70808	**855-893-9753**	225-926-3050	642-13
WRKO-AM 680 (N/T) 20 Guest St 3rd Fl	Brighton	MA	02135	**877-469-4322**	617-779-3400	643
WRLK-TV Ch 35 (PBS) 1101 George Rogers Blvd	Columbia	SC	29201	**800-922-5437**	803-737-3200	738-19
WRNR-FM 103.1 112 Main St 3rd Fl	Annapolis	MD	21401	**877-762-1031**	410-626-0103	642-8
WROQ-FM 101.1 (CR) 25 Garlington Rd	Greenville	SC	29615	**888-257-0058**	864-271-9200	642-52
Wrought Washer Manufacturing Inc 2100 S Bay St	Milwaukee	WI	53207	**800-558-5217**	414-744-0771	482
WRQN-FM 93.5 (Oldies) 3225 Arlington Ave	Toledo	OH	43614	**866-240-1935**	419-725-5700	642-123
WRR Environmental Services 5200 Ryder Rd	Eau Claire	WI	54701	**800-727-8760**	715-834-9624	665
WRTI-FM 90.1 (NPR) 1509 Cecil B Moore Ave 3rd Fl	Philadelphia	PA	19121	**866-809-9784**	215-204-8405	642-89
WRTV-TV Ch 6 (ABC) 1330 N Meridian St	Indianapolis	IN	46202	**877-667-4265**	317-635-9788	738-38
WRVM-FM 102.7 (Rel) PO Box 212	Suring	WI	54174	**888-225-9786**	920-842-2900	643
WS Badcock Corp (WSBC) PO Box 497	Mulberry	FL	33860	**800-223-2625**		322
WS Emerson Co Inc 15 Acme Rd	Brewer	ME	04412	**800-789-6120**		155
WS Hampshire Inc 365 Keyes Ave	Hampshire	IL	60140	**800-541-0251**	847-683-4400	722
WS Packaging Group Inc 2571 S. Hemlock Rd	Green Bay	WI	54229	**800-236-3424**	800-818-5481	413
WSBC (WS Badcock Corp) PO Box 497	Mulberry	FL	33860	**800-223-2625**		322
WSBT-TV Ch 22 (CBS) 1301 E Douglas Rd	Mishawaka	IN	46545	**877-634-7181**	574-232-6397	
WSCB-FM 89.9 (Urban) 263 Alden St	Springfield	MA	01109	**800-727-0504**	413-748-3000	642-117
WSEE-TV Ch 35 (CBS) 3514 State St	Erie	PA	16508	**888-697-2217**	814-454-5201	738-27
WSET-TV Ch 13 (ABC) 2320 Langhorne Rd	Lynchburg	VA	24501	**800-639-7847**	434-528-1313	
WSF Industries Inc 7 Hackett Dr	Tonawanda	NY	14150	**800-874-8265**	716-692-4930	479
WSFS Financial Corp 500 Delaware Ave *NASDAQ: WSFS*	Wilmington	DE	19801	**888-973-7226**	302-792-6000	360-2
WSHA-FM 88.9 (Jazz) 118 E S St	Raleigh	NC	27601	**800-241-0421**	919-546-8430	642-95
WSHU-FM 91.1 (NPR) 5151 Pk Ave	Fairfield	CT	06825	**800-937-6045**	203-365-0425	643
WSI Internet 5580 Explorer Dr Ste 600	Mississauga	ON	L4W4Y1	**888-678-7588**	905-678-7588	311
WSJV-TV Ch 28 (Fox) PO Box 28	South Bend	IN	46624	**800-435-3803**	574-679-9758	738-78
WSLQ-FM 99.1 (AC) 3934 Electric Rd SW	Roanoke	VA	24018	**800-410-9936**	540-387-0234	642-100
WSLS-TV Ch 10 (NBC) PO Box 10	Roanoke	VA	24022	**855-447-7647**	540-981-9110	738-67
WSNA (Washington State Nurses Assn) 575 Andover Pk W Ste 101	Seattle	WA	98188	**800-231-8482**	206-575-7979	532
WSOC-TV Ch 9 (ABC) 1901 N Tryon St	Charlotte	NC	28206	**855-336-0360**	704-338-9999	738-16
WSOS Community Action Commission Inc 109 S Front St	Fremont	OH	43420	**800-775-9767**	419-334-8911	8
WSPA-TV Ch 7 (CBS) 250 International Dr	Spartanburg	SC	29303	**866-946-6349**	864-576-7777	738-4
WSPD-AM 1370 (N/T) 125 S Superior St	Toledo	OH	43604	**800-745-3000**	419-244-8321	642-123
WSSA (Wine & Spirits Shippers Assn Inc) 11800 Sunrise Vly Dr *General	Reston	VA	20191	**800-368-3167***	703-860-2300	48-6
WSTO-FM 96.1 (CHR) 1162 Mt Auburn Rd	Evansville	IN	47720	**888-685-1961**	812-491-9468	642-42
WSTW-FM 93.7 (CHR) 2727 Shipley Rd	Wilmington	DE	19810	**800-544-9370**	302-478-2700	642-130
WSUA-AM 1260 (Span) 2100 Coral Way Ste 201	Miami	FL	33145	**877-453-5437**	305-285-1260	642-75
WSUN-FM 97.1 (Alt) 11300 Fourth St N Ste 300	Saint Petersburg	FL	33716	**877-327-9797**	727-579-2000	642-122
WSVH-FM 91.1 (NPR) 13040 Abercorn St Ste 8	Savannah	GA	31419	**877-472-1227**	912-344-3565	642-109
WTB Financial Corp PO Box 2127	Spokane	WA	99210	**800-788-4578**		360-2
WTBC-AM 1230 (N/T) 2110 McFarland Blvd E Ste C	Tuscaloosa	AL	35404	**800-518-1977**	205-758-5523	642-127
WTFM-FM 98.5 (AC) 222 Commerce St	Kingsport	TN	37660	**888-633-5452**	423-246-9578	643
WTH (World Travel Holdings) 100 Fordham Rd Bldg C Bldg C	Wilmington	MA	01887	**877-958-7447**	617-424-7990	769
WTIU-TV Ch 30 (PBS) 1229 E Seventh St	Bloomington	IN	47405	**800-662-3311**	812-855-5900	
WTKR-TV Ch 3 (CBS) 720 Boush St	Norfolk	VA	23510	**866-347-2423**	757-446-1000	738-54
WTKS-AM 1290 (N/T) 245 Alfred St	Savannah	GA	31408	**877-263-7995**	912-964-7794	642-109
WTP Inc PO Box 937	Coloma	MI	49038	**800-521-0731**	269-468-3399	729
WTPT-FM 93.3 (Rock) 25 Garlington Rd	Greenville	SC	29615	**800-774-0093**	864-271-9200	642-52
WTSP-TV Ch 10 (CBS) 11450 Gandy Blvd N	Saint Petersburg	FL	33702	**877-248-6922**	727-577-1010	738-84
WTSU-FM 89.9 (NPR) Troy University Wallace Hall	Troy	AL	36082	**800-800-6616**		643
WTTG-TV Ch 5 (Fox) 5151 Wisconsin Ave NW	Washington	DC	20016	**866-756-3587**	202-244-5151	738-92
WTTS-FM 92.3 (AAA) 400 One City Centre	Bloomington	IN	47404	**800-923-9887**	812-332-3366	643
WTVP-TV Ch 47 (PBS) 101 State St	Peoria	IL	61602	**800-837-4747**	309-677-4747	738-58
WUAL-FM 91.5 (NPR) 920 Paul W Bryant Dr Box 870370	Tuscaloosa	AL	35487	**800-654-4262**	205-348-6644	642-127
Wuesthoff Medical Ctr Rockledge 110 Longwood Ave	Rockledge	FL	32955	**877-456-9617**	321-636-2211	374-3
WUIS-FM 91.9 (NPR) University of Illinois at Springfield 1 University Plz WUIS-130	Springfield	IL	62703	**866-206-9847**	217-206-9847	642-116
Wulftec International Inc 209 Wulftec St	Ayer's Cliff	QC	J0B1C0	**877-985-3832**	819-838-4232	546
WUMB-FM 91.9 (Folk) 100 Morrissey Blvd	Boston	MA	02125	**800-573-2100**	617-287-6900	642-18
WUMP-AM 730 (Sports) 3280 Peachtree Rd Ste 2300	Atlanta	GA	30305	**866-485-9867**	256-830-8300	643
WUNC-FM 91.5 (NPR) 120 Friday Center Dr	Chapel Hill	NC	27517	**800-962-9862**	919-445-9150	643
WUOM-FM 91.7 (NPR) 535 W William St Ste 110	Ann Arbor	MI	48103	**888-258-9866**	734-764-9210	642-7
WUOT-FM 91.9 (NPR) 209 Communications Bldg University of Tennessee	Knoxville	TN	37996	**888-266-9868**	865-974-5375	642-63
WURTH (Action Bolt & Tool Co) 2051 E Blue Heron Blvd	Riviera Beach	FL	33404	**800-423-0700**	561-845-8800	351

Name / Address	City	State	ZIP	Toll-Free	Phone	Class
Wurth Revcar Fasteners Inc						
3845 Thirlane Rd	Roanoke	VA	24019	**877-999-8784**		351
Wurth USA Inc						
93 Grant St	Ramsey	NJ	07446	**800-987-8487**	201-825-2710	60
WUSF-FM 89.7 (NPR)						
4202 E Fowler Ave TVB 100	Tampa	FL	33620	**800-741-9090**	813-974-8700	642-122
WUSF-TV Ch 16 (PBS)						
4202 E Fowler Ave	Tampa	FL	33620	**800-654-3703**	813-974-4000	738-84
WUTC-FM 88.1 (NPR)						
615 McCallie Ave						
104 Cadek Hall Dept 1151	Chattanooga	TN	37403	**800-272-3900**	423-425-4756	642-25
WUWF-FM 88.1 (NPR)						
11000 University Pkwy	Pensacola	FL	32514	**800-239-9893**	850-474-2787	642-87
WVCY-TV Ch 30 (Ind)						
3434 W Kilbourn Ave	Milwaukee	WI	53208	**800-729-9829**	414-935-3000	738-48
WVES (Virginia West Electric Supply Co)						
250 12-th St W	Huntington	WV	25704	**800-624-3433**	304-525-0361	248
WVII-TV Ch 7 (ABC)						
371 Target Industrial Cir	Bangor	ME	04401	**888-820-8458***	207-945-6457	738-8
*General						
WVIT-TV Ch 30 (NBC)						
1422 New Britain Ave	West Hartford	CT	06110	**800-523-9848**	860-521-3030	
WVMA (Wisconsin Veterinary Medical Assn)						
2801 Crossroads Dr Ste 1200	Madison	WI	53718	**888-254-5202**	608-257-3665	793
WVMA (Wyoming Veterinary Medical Assn)						
1841 W Secluded Ct	Kuna	ID	83634	**800-272-1813**	208-922-9431	793
WVNA (West Virginia Nurses Assn)						
1007 Bigley Ave Ste 308	Charleston	WV	25302	**800-400-1226**	304-342-1169	532
WVOM-FM 103.9 (N/T)						
184 Target Industrial Cir	Bangor	ME	04401	**800-966-1039**	207-947-9100	642-12
WVPE-FM 88.1 (NPR)						
2424 California Rd	Elkhart	IN	46514	**888-399-9873**	574-674-9873	643
WVPS-FM 107.9 (NPR)						
365 Troy Ave	Colchester	VT	05446	**800-639-2192**	802-655-9451	643
WVTF-FM 89.1 (NPR)						
3520 Kingsbury Ln	Roanoke	VA	24014	**800-856-8900**	540-989-8900	642-100
WVTM-TV Ch 13 (NBC)						
1732 Valley View Dr	Birmingham	AL	35209	**844-248-7698**	205-933-1313	738-11
WW Grainger Inc						
100 Grainger Pkwy	Lake Forest	IL	60045	**888-361-8649**	847-535-1000	248
NYSE: GWW						
WW Norton & Company Inc						
500 Fifth Ave 6th Fl	New York	NY	10110	**800-233-4830**	212-354-5500	634-2
WWDC-FM 101.1 (Rock)						
1801 Rockville Pk 5th Fl	Rockville	MD	20852	**866-913-2101**	240-747-2701	643
WWF (World Wildlife Fund Canada)						
245 Eglinton Ave E Ste 410	Toronto	ON	M4P3J1	**800-267-2632**	416-489-8800	47-3
WWF (World Wildlife Fund)						
1250 24th St NW PO Box 97180	Washington	DC	20090	**800-225-5993**	202-293-4800	47-3
WWGR-FM 101.9 (Ctry)						
10915 K-Nine Dr	Bonita Springs	FL	34135	**877-787-1019**	239-495-8383	643
WWKA-FM 92.3 (Ctry)						
4192 N John Young Pkwy	Orlando	FL	32804	**866-438-0220**	407-424-9236	642-85
WWMT-TV Ch 3 (CBS)						
590 W Maple St	Kalamazoo	MI	49008	**800-875-3333**		
WWNO-FM 89.9 (NPR)						
University of New Orleans						
Lake Frnt Campus	New Orleans	LA	70148	**800-286-7002**	504-280-7000	642-82
WWPR-FM 105.1 (Urban)						
32 Ave of the Americas	New York	NY	10013	**800-585-1051**	212-377-7900	642-83
WXCY-FM 103.7 (Ctry)						
707 Revolution St	Havre de Grace	MD	21078	**800-788-9929**	410-939-1100	643
WXEL-FM 90.7 (NPR)						
3401 S Congress Ave	West Palm Beach	FL	33426	**800-915-9935**	561-737-8000	642-129
WXEL-TV Ch 42 (PBS)						
PO Box 6607	West Palm Beach	FL	33405	**800-915-9935**	561-737-8000	738-93
WXGI-AM 950 (Sports)						
701 German School Rd	Richmond	VA	23225	**877-994-4950**	804-233-7666	642-97
WXGL-FM 107.3 (AC)						
11300 Fourth St N						
Ste 300	Saint Petersburg	FL	33716	**800-242-1073**	727-579-2000	642-122
WXKR-FM 94.5 (CR)						
3225 Arlington Ave	Toledo	OH	43614	**866-240-9945**	419-725-5700	642-123
WXRV-FM 92.5 (AAA)						
30 How St	Haverhill	MA	01830	**800-352-9250**	978-374-4733	643
WXXJ-FM 102.9 (AC)						
8000 Belfort Pkwy	Jacksonville	FL	32256	**800-460-6394**	904-245-8500	642-60
WXYZ-TV Ch 7 (ABC)						
20777 W 10-Mile Rd	Southfield	MI	48037	**800-825-0770**	248-827-7777	
Wyandot Inc						
135 Wyandot Ave	Marion	OH	43302	**800-992-6368**	740-383-4031	297-35
Wyandotte Nation Casino						
100 Jackpot Pl	Wyandotte	OK	74370	**866-447-4946**	918-678-4946	451
Wyatt Transfer Inc						
3035 Bells Rd PO Box 24326	Richmond	VA	23224	**800-552-5708**	804-743-3800	778
Wyatt-Quarles Seed Co						
730 US Hwy 70 W	Garner	NC	27529	**800-662-7591**	919-772-4243	276
Wycliffe Bible Translators						
11221 John Wycliffe Blvd	Orlando	FL	32832	**800-992-5433**	407-852-3600	47-20
Wyffels Hybrids Inc						
13344 US Hwy 6	Geneseo	IL	61254	**800-369-7833**	309-944-8334	10-4
WYFF-TV Ch 4 (NBC)						
505 Rutherford St	Greenville	SC	29609	**800-453-9933**	864-242-4404	738-4
WYLD-AM 940 (Rel)						
929 Howard Ave	New Orleans	LA	70113	**800-899-9265**	504-679-7300	642-82
Wylie Spray Center						
702 E 40th St	Lubbock	TX	79404	**888-249-5162**	806-763-1335	275
Wyndham ByRequest Program						
PO Box 4090	Aberdeen	SD	57401	**800-996-3426**		378
Wyndham Hotel Group						
Baymont Inn & Suites						
1023 Eighth Ave NW	Aberdeen	SD	57401	**800-337-0550**		379
Ramada						
949 Route 46	Parsippany	NJ	07054	**877-212-2733***		379
*Resv						
Travelodge						
PO Box 4090	Aberdeen	SD	57041	**800-525-4055***	312-427-8000	379
*Resv						
Wyndham Vacation Resorts						
6277 Sea Harbor Dr	Orlando	FL	32821	**800-251-8736**		379
Wyndham Lake Buena Vista						
1850 Hotel Plaza Blvd	Lake Buena Vista	FL	32830	**800-624-4109**	407-828-4444	379
Wyndham Peachtree Conference Ctr						
2443 Hwy 54 W	Peachtree City	GA	30269	**800-996-3426**	770-487-2000	377
Wyndham Vacation Rentals						
14 Sylvan Way	Vail	CO	81657	**800-467-3529**	973-753-6300	667
Wyndham Vacation Rentals						
14 Sylvan Way	Parsippany	NJ	07054	**800-467-3529**	973-753-6300	667
Wyndham Vacation Resorts King Cotton Villas						
1 King Cotton Rd	Edisto Beach	SC	29438	**800-251-8736**	843-869-2561	667
Wynfrey Hotel						
1000 Riverchase Galleria	Birmingham	AL	35244	**800-633-7313**	205-705-1234	379
Wynn Las Vegas						
3131 Las Vegas Blvd S	Las Vegas	NV	89109	**877-321-9966**	702-770-7000	379
Wynne Transport Service Inc						
2222 N 11th St	Omaha	NE	68108	**800-383-9330**	402-342-4001	778
Wyo-Ben Inc						
1345 Discovery Dr	Billings	MT	59102	**800-548-7055***	406-652-6351	502-2
*Cust Svc						
Wyoming						
Aging Div						
6101 Yellowstone Rd N Rm 259B	Cheyenne	WY	82002	**800-442-2766**	307-777-7986	339-51
Highway Patrol (WHP)						
5300 Bishop Blvd	Cheyenne	WY	82009	**800-442-9090**	307-777-4301	339-51
State Parks & Historical Sites Div						
2301 Central Ave	Cheyenne	WY	82002	**877-996-7275**	307-777-6323	339-51
Tourism Div						
1520 Etchepare Cir	Cheyenne	WY	82007	**800-225-5996**	307-777-7777	339-51
Wyoming Assn of Realtors						
777 Overland Trail Ste 220	Casper	WY	82601	**800-676-4085**	307-237-4085	654
Wyoming Legislative Service Office						
3001 E Pershing Blvd	Cheyenne	WY	82002	**800-342-9570**	307-777-7881	433
Wyoming Machinery Co						
5300 Old W Yellowstone Hwy	Casper	WY	82604	**800-244-0527**	307-472-1000	358
Wyoming Medical Ctr						
1233 E Second St	Casper	WY	82601	**800-822-7201**	307-577-7201	374-3
Wyoming Medical Society						
122 E 17th St	Cheyenne	WY	82001	**888-879-3599**	307-635-2424	473
Wyoming Public Television						
2660 Peck Ave	Riverton	WY	82501	**800-495-9788**	307-856-6944	629
Wyoming Seminary						
201 N Sprague Ave	Kingston	PA	18704	**877-996-7361**	570-270-2160	621
Wyoming State Bar						
4124 Laramie St	Cheyenne	WY	82001	**855-445-8058**	307-632-9061	71
Wyoming Tribune-Eagle						
702 W Lincolnway	Cheyenne	WY	82001	**800-561-6268**	307-634-3361	531-2
Wyoming Veterinary Medical Assn (WVMA)						
1841 W Secluded Ct	Kuna	ID	83634	**800-272-1813**	208-922-9431	793
Wyotech Sacramento						
980 Riverside Pkwy	West Sacramento	CA	95605	**888-308-7158**	916-376-8888	798
WYOU-TV Ch 22 (CBS)						
62 S Franklin St	Wilkes-Barre	PA	18701	**855-241-5144**	570-961-2222	
WYPR-FM 88.1 (NPR)						
2216 N Charles St	Baltimore	MD	21218	**866-789-8627**	410-235-1660	642-11
Wyrulec Co						
3978 US Hwy 26/85	Torrington	WY	82240	**800-628-5266**	307-837-2225	247
Wyse Meter Solutions Inc						
RPO Newmarket Court						
PO Box 95530	Newmarket	ON	L3Y8J8	**866-681-9465**		393
WYSE Technology Inc						
3471 N First St	San Jose	CA	95134	**800-800-9973**	408-473-1200	175-1
Wysong Inc						
4820 US 29 N	Greensboro	NC	27405	**800-299-7664**	336-621-3960	455
WZBT-FM 91.1 (Alt)						
300 N Washington St						
Gettysburg College	Gettysburg	PA	17325	**800-431-0803**	717-337-6300	643
WZPX-TV Ch 43 (I)						
2610 Horizon Dr SE Ste E	Grand Rapids	MI	49546	**800-987-9936**	616-222-4343	738-34
WZVN-TV Ch 26 (ABC)						
3719 Central Ave	Fort Myers	FL	33901	**888-232-8635**	239-939-2020	738-50
WZZK-FM 104.7 (Ctry)						
2700 Corporate Dr Ste 115	Birmingham	AL	35242	**866-998-1047**	205-916-1100	642-15

X

Name / Address	City	State	ZIP	Toll-Free	Phone	Class
Xactware Solutions Inc						
1100 West Traverse Pkwy	Lehi	UT	84043	**800-424-9228***	801-764-5900	180-11
*Sales						
Xaloy Inc						
1399 Countyline Rd	New Castle	PA	16101	**800-897-2830**		620
Xamax Industries Inc						
63 Silvermine Rd	Seymour	CT	06483	**888-926-2988**	203-888-7200	556
XanGo Goodness						
2889 Ashton Blvd	Lehi	UT	84043	**877-469-2646**	801-816-8000	306
Xante Corp						
2800 Dauphin St Ste 100	Mobile	AL	36606	**800-926-8839**	251-473-6502	175-6
Xantech Corp						
1969 Kellogg Ave	Carlsbad	CA	92008	**800-843-5465***	818-362-0353	51
*Sales						
Xanterra Parks & Resorts						
6312 S Fiddlers Green Cir						
Ste 600-N	Greenwood Village	CO	80111	**800-236-7916**	303-600-3400	273
Xantrex Technology Inc						
3700 Gilmore Way	Burnaby	BC	V5G4M1	**800-670-0707**	604-422-8595	255
Xavier University						
3800 Victory Pkwy	Cincinnati	OH	45207	**800-344-4698**	513-745-3000	167
Xavier University Library						
3800 Victory Pkwy	Cincinnati	OH	45207	**888-468-4509**	513-745-3881	434-6
Xcaliber LP						
5051 Fm 2920	Spring	TX	77388	**866-620-8586**	281-219-8100	192

Name / Address	City	State	Zip	Toll-Free	Phone	Class
Xcape Solutions Inc 207 Crystal Grove Blvd	Lutz	FL	33548	**866-285-4899**	813-964-9101	179
Xcel Energy Inc 414 Nicollet Mall *NYSE: XEL*	Minneapolis	MN	55401	**800-328-8226**	612-330-5500	785
X-Cel Optical Company Inc 806 S Benton Dr *General	Sauk Rapids	MN	56379	**800-747-9235***	320-251-8404	541
Xcitex Inc 25 First St Ste 105	Cambridge	MA	02141	**800-780-7836**	617-225-0080	645
X-COM Systems LLC 12345-B Sunrise Vly Dr	Reston	VA	20191	**800-342-8408**	703-390-1087	205
XE.com Inc 1145 Nicholson Rd Ste 200	Newmarket	ON	L3Y9C3	**877-932-6640**	416-214-5606	227
Xeris Pharmaceuticals Inc 3208 Red River St Ste 300	Austin	TX	78705	**888-570-4781**		233
Xerox Canada Ltd 5650 Yonge St	North York	ON	M2M4G7	**800-939-3769**		588
Xerox Corp 45 Glover Ave PO Box 4505 *NYSE: XRX*	Norwalk	CT	06856	**800-327-9753**	203-968-3000	588
Xerox Financial Services Inc 800 Long Ridge Rd	Stamford	CT	06904	**800-275-9376**	203-968-3000	218
Xerox Foundation 45 Glover Ave	Norwalk	CT	06856	**800-275-9376**		305
XETV-TV Ch 6 (CW) 8253 Ronson Rd	San Diego	CA	92111	**866-700-6397**	858-279-6666	738-73
Xfer International Inc 39201 Schoolcraft Rd Ste B 9	Livonia	MI	48150	**800-438-9337**	734-927-6666	182
X-Gen Pharmaceuticals Inc 300 Daniels Zenker Dr	Horseheads	NY	14845	**866-390-4411**		583
Xilinx Inc 2100 Logic Dr *NASDAQ: XLNX*	San Jose	CA	95124	**800-594-5469**	408-559-7778	694
Xiologix 8215 SW Tualatin Sherwood	Tualatin	OR	97062	**888-492-6843**	503-691-4364	227
XIOtech Corp 9950 Federal Dr Ste 100	Colorado Springs	CO	80921	**866-472-6764**	719-388-5500	180-12
XKS Unlimited Inc 850 Fiero Ln	San Luis Obispo	CA	93401	**800-444-5247**	805-544-7864	53
XL Brands 198 Nexus Dr	Dalton	GA	30721	**800-367-4583**	706-272-5800	144
XL Specialty Insurance Co 70 Seaview Ave	Stamford	CT	06902	**877-263-7995**	203-964-5200	391-5
Xlibris Corp 1663 Liberty Dr Ste 200	Bloomington	IN	47403	**888-795-4274**		626
XO Communications Inc 13865 Sunrise Vly Dr	Herndon	VA	20171	**866-349-0134**	703-547-2000	733
XOMA (US) LLC 2910 Seventh St *NASDAQ: XOMA*	Berkeley	CA	94710	**800-468-9716**	510-204-7200	84
XP Power 990 Benicia Ave	Sunnyvale	CA	94085	**800-253-0490**	408-732-7777	248
XPO Logistics Inc 6805 Perimeter Dr	Dublin	OH	43016	**800-837-7584**	614-923-1400	448
XRS Corporation 12900 Whitewater Dr Ste 300	Hopkins	MN	55343	**800-348-7227**		528
Xs Sight Systems Inc 2401 Ludelle St	Fort Worth	TX	76105	**888-744-4880**	817-536-0136	709
XS Smith Inc 932 Page Rd	Washington	NC	27889	**800-631-2226**	252-940-5060	104
Xtek Inc 11451 Reading Rd	Cincinnati	OH	45241	**888-332-9835**	513-733-7800	453
XTO Energy Inc 810 Houston St	Fort Worth	TX	76102	**800-299-2800**	817-870-2800	535
XTRAC LLC 245 Summer St	Boston	MA	02210	**855-975-3569**		387
Xtramart 221 Quinebaug Rd	North Grosvenordale	CT	06255	**800-243-6366**		206
Xtreme Drilling & Coil Services Corp 9805 Katy Freeway Ste 650	Houston	TX	77024	**800-564-6253**	403-262-9500	539
XtremeEDA Corp 200-25 Holland Ave	Ottawa	ON	K1Y4R9	**800-586-0280**	613-728-5912	465
Xttrium Laboratories Inc 1200 E Business Ctr Dr	Mt. Prospect	IL	60056	**800-587-3721**	773-268-5800	233
Xybernet Inc 10640 Scripps Ranch Blvd *Cust Svc	San Diego	CA	92131	**800-228-9026***	858-530-1900	180-10
Xyron Inc 8465 N 90th St Ste 6	Scottsdale	AZ	85258	**800-793-3523**	480-443-9419	484
XYZ Two Way Radio Inc 275 20th St	Brooklyn	NY	11215	**800-535-3377**	718-499-2007	441

Y

Name / Address	City	State	Zip	Toll-Free	Phone	Class
Y-12 Federal Credit Union 501 Lafayette Dr	Oak Ridge	TN	37830	**800-482-1043**	865-482-1043	221
Yachats Ocean Road State Natural Site 5580 S Coast Hwy	Newport	OR	97366	**800-551-6949**		564
Yachting Magazine 55 Hammarlund Way	Middletown	RI	02842	**800-999-0869**		456-4
Yacktman Asset Management Co 6300 Bridgepoint Pkwy Bldg 1 Ste 320	Austin	TX	78730	**800-835-3879**	512-767-6700	401
Yadkin Bank 1318 N Bridge St *NASDAQ: YDKN*	Elkin	NC	28621	**866-867-9979**	336-526-6371	69
Yadkin County Chamber of Commerce 205 S Jackson St PO Box 1840	Yadkinville	NC	27055	**877-492-3546**	336-679-2200	138
Yaffe Cos Inc, The 1200 S G St	Muskogee	OK	74403	**800-759-2333**	918-687-7543	684
Yahoo! Photos 701 First Ave	Sunnyvale	CA	94089	**888-267-7574**	408-349-3300	587
Yak Communications Corp 48 Yonge St Ste 1200	Toronto	ON	M5E1G6	**877-925-4925**		733
Yakima Bait Company Inc PO Box 310	Granger	WA	98932	**800-527-2711**	509-854-1311	708
Yakima Convention Ctr 10 N Eigth St	Yakima	WA	98901	**800-221-0751**	509-575-6062	207
Yakima Federal Savings & Loan Assn 118 E Yakima Ave	Yakima	WA	98901	**800-331-3225**	509-248-2634	69
Yakima Herald-Republic PO Box 9668	Yakima	WA	98909	**800-343-2799**	509-248-1251	531-2
Yale Appliance 296 Freeport St	Dorchester	MA	02122	**800-565-6435**	617-825-9253	34
Yale Carolinas Inc (YCI) 9839 S Tryon St	Charlotte	NC	28273	**800-844-1454**	704-588-6930	386
Yale Club of New York City, The 50 Vanderbilt Ave	New York	NY	10017	**800-335-9253**	212-716-2100	393
Yale Ctr for British Art 1080 Chapel St PO Box 208280	New Haven	CT	06510	**877-274-8278**	203-432-2800	519
Yale Divinity School Admissions Office 409 Prospect St	New Haven	CT	06511	**866-358-3806**	203-432-5360	168-3
Yale Repertory Theatre 1120 Chapel St PO Box 1257	New Haven	CT	06505	**800-973-2837**	203-432-1234	572-4
Yale Residential Security Products Inc 100 Yale Ave *Cust Svc	Lenoir City	TN	37771	**800-438-1951***		350
Yale Security Inc.ÿ 1902 Airport Rd	Monroe	NC	28110	**800-438-1951**		350
Yale University Press 302 Temple St *Sales	New Haven	CT	06511	**800-405-1619***	203-432-0960	634-4
Yale University School of Medicine 333 Cedar St	New Haven	CT	06510	**877-925-3637**	203-785-2643	168-2
YALSA (Young Adult Library Services Assn) 50 E Huron St	Chicago	IL	60611	**800-545-2433**	312-280-4390	48-11
Yamaha Electronics Corp 6660 Orangethorpe Ave	Buena Park	CA	90620	**800-292-2982**	714-522-9888	51
Yamaha Motor Corp USA 6555 Katella Ave *Cust Svc	Cypress	CA	90630	**800-656-7695***		516
Yamato Corp 1775 S Murray Blvd	Colorado Springs	CO	80916	**800-538-1762**	719-591-1500	682
Yamazen Inc 735 E Remington Rd	Schaumburg	IL	60173	**800-882-8558**	847-490-8130	385
Yampa Valley Electric Assn Inc 435 Mack Ln Ste 203	Craig	CO	81626	**888-873-9832**	970-879-1160	247
Yankee Barn Homes 131 Yankee Barn Rd	Grantham	NH	03753	**800-258-9786**		105
Yankee Candle Company Inc PO Box 110	South Deerfield	MA	01373	**877-803-6890**	413-665-8306	328
Yankee Gas Services Co 107 Selden St	Berlin	CT	06037	**800-989-0900**		785
Yankee Magazine 1121 Main St PO Box 520	Dublin	NH	03444	**800-288-4284**	603-563-8111	456-22
Yankee Publishing Inc PO Box 520	Dublin	NH	03444	**800-729-9265**	603-563-8111	634-9
Yankton Ag Service 114 Mulberry St	Yankton	SD	57078	**800-456-5528**	605-665-3691	278
Yankton Press & Dakotan 319 Walnut St PO Box 56	Yankton	SD	57078	**800-743-2968**	605-665-7811	634-8
Yarde Metals Inc 45 Newell St	Southington	CT	06489	**800-444-9494**	860-406-6061	489
Yardley Products Corp 10 W College Ave	Yardley	PA	19067	**800-457-0154**	215-493-2723	350
Yarema Die & Engineering Co Inc 300 Minnesota Rd	Troy	MI	48083	**800-937-9311**	248-585-2830	755
Yark Automotive Group Inc 6019 W Central Ave	Toledo	OH	43615	**866-390-8894**		515
Yarmouth Resort 343 Main St Rt 28	West Yarmouth	MA	02673	**877-838-3524**	508-775-5155	379
Yaskawa America Inc 2121 Norman Dr S	Waukegan	IL	60085	**800-927-5292**	847-887-7000	205
Yates County 417 Liberty St	Penn Yan	NY	14527	**866-212-5160**	315-536-5120	338
Yates-American Machine Company Inc 2880 Kennedy Dr	Beloit	WI	53511	**800-752-6377**	608-364-6333	819
Yavapai College 1100 E Sheldon St	Prescott	AZ	86301	**800-922-6787**	928-445-7300	161
Verde Valley 601 Black Hills Dr	Clarkdale	AZ	86324	**800-922-6787**	928-634-7501	161
Yavapai Regional Medical Ctr 1003 Willow Creek Rd	Prescott	AZ	86301	**877-843-9762**	928-445-2700	374-3
Yazoo County PO Box 186	Yazoo City	MS	39194	**800-381-0662**	662-746-1815	338
Yazoo County Chamber of Commerce 1615 H St NW	Washington	DC	20062	**800-638-6582**	662-746-1273	138
Yazoo Mills Inc PO Box 369 *Cust Svc	New Oxford	PA	17350	**800-242-5216***	717-624-8993	124
Yazoo Valley Electric Power Assn 2255 Gordon Ave	Yazoo City	MS	39194	**800-281-5098**	662-746-4251	247
YBP Library Services 999 Maple St	Contoocook	NH	03229	**800-258-3774**	603-746-3102	94
YCI (Yale Carolinas Inc) 9839 S Tryon St	Charlotte	NC	28273	**800-844-1454**	704-588-6930	386
Yeck Bros Co 2222 Arbor Blvd	Dayton	OH	45439	**800-417-2767**	937-294-4000	5
Yellow Book USA 398 RXR Plaza	Uniondale	NY	11556	**877-237-6120**	917-861-5858	634-6
YellowBrix Inc 200 North Glebe Rd Ste 1025	Arlington	VA	22203	**888-325-9366**	703-548-3300	180-7
Yellowhead Helicopters Ltd 3010 Selwyn Rd	Valemount	BC	V0E2Z0	**888-566-4401**	250-566-4401	359
YELLOWPAGES.com LLC 208 S Akard	Dallas	TX	75202	**866-329-7118**		397
Yellowstone Baptist College 1515 S Shiloh Rd	Billings	MT	59106	**800-487-9950**	406-656-9950	167

Name / Address	City	State	ZIP	Toll-Free	Phone	Class
Yellowstone Public Radio 1500 University Dr	Billings	MT	59101	**800-441-2941**	406-657-2941	642-14
Yellowstone Valley Electric Co-op 150 Co-op Way	Huntley	MT	59037	**800-736-5323**	406-348-3411	247
Yenkin-Majestic Paint Corp 1920 Leonard Ave	Columbus	OH	43219	**800-848-1898**	614-253-8511	549
Yesmail 421 SW Sixth Ave Ste 400	Portland	OR	97204	**877-937-6245**	503-241-4185	7
Yesterday USA Radio Networks, The 2001 Plymouth Rock Dr	Richardson	TX	75081	**800-624-2272**	972-889-9872	641
Yesware Inc 75 Kneeland St Fl 15	Boston	MA	02111	**855-937-9273**		387
Yeti Coolers 3411 Hidalgo St	Austin	TX	78702	**888-872-0227**	512-394-9384	607
Yetter Manufacturing Inc 109 S McDonough St PO Box 358	Colchester	IL	62326	**800-447-5777**	309-776-4111	275
Yingling Aircraft Inc 2010 Airport Rd	Wichita	KS	67209	**800-835-0083**	316-943-3246	768
YK International Co 3246 W Montrose Ave	Chicago	IL	60618	**800-266-5254**	773-583-5270	348
YMCA (YMCA of the USA) 101 N Wacker Dr	Chicago	IL	60606	**800-872-9622**	312-977-0031	47-6
YMCA of the USA (YMCA) 101 N Wacker Dr	Chicago	IL	60606	**800-872-9622**	312-977-0031	47-6
YoCream International Inc 5858 NE 87th Ave	Portland	OR	97220	**800-962-7326**	503-256-3754	297-25
Yodle Inc 330 W 34th St 18th Fl	New York	NY	10001	**877-276-5104**		395
Yogo Inn 211 E Main St	Lewistown	MT	59457	**800-860-9646**	406-535-8721	379
Yokogawa Corp of America 12530 W Airport Blvd	Sugar Land	TX	77478	**800-888-6400**	281-340-3800	250
Yokohama Tire Corp 601 S Acacia Ave	Fullerton	CA	92831	**800-423-4544**	714-870-3800	752
Yolo Federal Credit Union 266 W Main St	Woodland	CA	95695	**877-965-6328**	530-668-2700	221
Yonex Corp 20140 S Western Ave	Torrance	CA	90501	**800-449-6639**	310-793-3800	708
York Barbell Co Inc 3300 BoaRd Rd *Cust Svc	York	PA	17406	**800-358-9675***	717-767-6481	269
York Bldg Products Co 950 Smile Way	York	PA	17404	**800-673-2408**	717-848-2831	185
York Building Services Inc 99 Grand St Ste 3	Moonachie	NJ	07074	**855-443-9675**		258
York College 1125 E Eigth St	York	NE	68467	**800-950-9675**	402-363-5600	167
York County Community College 112 College Dr	Wells	ME	04090	**800-580-3820**	207-646-9282	161
York County Transportation Authority 1230 Roosevelt Ave	York	PA	17404	**800-632-9063**	717-846-5562	467
York Electric Co-op Inc PO Box 150	York	SC	29745	**800-582-8810**	803-684-4247	247
York Ford Inc 1481 Bwy	Saugus	MA	01906	**888-705-6229**	781-231-1945	56
York Metal Fabricators Inc 27 Ne 26th St	Oklahoma City	OK	73105	**800-255-4703**	405-528-7495	695
York Newspaper Co 1891 Loucks Rd	York	PA	17408	**800-559-3520**	717-767-6397	634-8
York Solutions LLC 1 Westbrook Corporate Ctr Ste 910	Westchester	IL	60154	**877-700-9675**	708-531-8362	719
York State Bank & Trust Co 700 N Lincoln AvE	York	NE	68467	**888-295-5540**	402-362-4411	69
York Sunday News 1891 Loucks Rd	York	PA	17408	**888-629-4095**	717-767-6397	531-4
York Technical College 452 S Anderson Rd	Rock Hill	SC	29730	**800-922-8324**	803-327-8000	161
York Telecom Corp 81 Corbett Way	Eatontown	NJ	07724	**866-836-8463**	732-413-6000	733
York University 4700 Keele St	Toronto	ON	M3J1P3	**800-426-2255**	416-736-2100	783
York Wallcoverings Inc 750 Linden Ave PO Box 5166	York	PA	17405	**800-375-9675**	717-846-4456	800
York Water Co, The 130 E Market St PO Box 15089 *NASDAQ: YORW*	York	PA	17405	**800-750-5561**	717-845-3601	785
Yorkston Oil Company Inc 2801 Roeder Ave	Bellingham	WA	98225	**800-401-2201**	360-734-2201	578
Yorktowne Hotel 48 E Market St	York	PA	17401	**800-233-9324**	717-848-1111	379
Yosemite Assn *Yosemite Conservancy* 5020 El Portal Rd PO Box 230	El Portal	CA	95318	**800-469-7275**	209-379-2317	47-13
Yoshinoya Beef Bowl 991 Knox St	Torrance	CA	90502	**800-576-8017**	310-527-6060	668
Youghiogheny River Natural Resources Management Area c/o Deep Creek Lake State Pk 898 State Pk Rd	Swanton	MD	21561	**877-620-8367**	301-387-5563	564
YouMail Inc 43 Corporate Park Ste 200	Irvine	CA	92606	**800-374-0013**		182
Young Adult Library Services Assn (YALSA) 50 E Huron St	Chicago	IL	60611	**800-545-2433**	312-280-4390	48-11
Young America Corp 10 S 5th St 7th Fl	Minneapolis	MN	55402	**800-533-4529**		734
Young America's Foundation 110 Elden St	Herndon	VA	20170	**800-292-9231**	800-872-1776	47-7
Young at Art Children's Museum 751 SW 121st Ave	Davie	FL	33325	**800-435-7352**	954-424-0085	520
Young Bros Ltd PO Box 3288	Honolulu	HI	96801	**800-572-2743**	808-543-9311	313
Young Children Magazine 1313 L St NW Ste 500 PO Box 97156	Washington	DC	20005	**800-424-2460**	202-232-8777	456-8
Young Corp 3231 Utah Ave S	Seattle	WA	98134	**800-321-9090**	206-624-1071	192
Young Electric Sign Co 2401 Foothill Dr	Salt Lake City	UT	84109	**866-779-8357**	801-464-4600	699
Young Fashions Inc 10300 Perkins Rd	Baton Rouge	LA	70810	**800-824-4154**	225-766-1010	593
Young Harris College PO Box 116	Young Harris	GA	30582	**800-241-3754**	706-379-3111	161
Young Industries Inc 16 Painter St	Muncy	PA	17756	**800-546-3165**	570-546-3165	209
Young Israel of New Rochelle 1149 N Ave	New Rochelle	NY	10804	**888-942-3638**	914-636-2215	47-20
Young Living Essential Oils 3125 Executive Pkwy	Lehi	UT	84043	**866-203-5666**	801-418-8900	797
Young Manufacturing Inc 2331 N 42nd St	Grand Forks	ND	58203	**800-451-9884**	701-772-5541	482
Young Mfg Company Inc 521 S Main St PO Box 167	Beaver Dam	KY	42320	**800-545-6595**	270-274-3306	498
Young Pecan Co 1831 W Evans St Ste 200 *All	Florence	SC	29501	**800-829-6864***	843-662-8591	297-28
Young Presidents' Organization (YPO) 600 E Las Colinas Blvd Ste 1000	Irving	TX	75039	**800-773-7976**	972-587-1500	48-12
Young Transportation & Tours 843 Riverside Dr	Asheville	NC	28804	**800-622-5444**	828-258-0084	106
Young's Commercial Transfer 2075 W Scranton Ave PO Box 871	Porterville	CA	93257	**800-289-1639**	559-784-6651	778
Young's Market Company LLC 500 S Central Ave	Los Angeles	CA	90013	**800-627-2777**	213-612-1248	80-3
Young's Plant Farm PO Box 3410	Auburn	AL	36830	**800-304-8609**		369
Younger Optics 2925 California St	Torrance	CA	90503	**800-366-5367**	310-783-1533	541
Youngsoft Inc 49197 Wixom Tech Dr	Wixom	MI	48393	**888-470-4553**	248-675-1200	179
Youngstown State University 1 University Plz *Admissions	Youngstown	OH	44555	**877-468-6978***	330-941-3000	167
Youngstown Warren Regional Chamber 11 Central Sq Ste 1600	Youngstown	OH	44503	**877-807-2249**	330-744-2131	138
Youngstown-Warren Regional Airport 1453 Youngstown-Kingsville Rd NE	Vienna	OH	44473	**800-444-1440**	330-856-1537	27
Your Big Backyard Magazine 11100 Wildlife Ctr Dr	Reston	VA	20190	**800-822-9919**		456-6
Your Church Magazine 465 Gundersen Dr	Carol Stream	IL	60188	**877-247-4787**	630-260-6200	456-5
Your Community Bank 2323 Ring Rd	Elizabethtown	KY	42701	**800-314-2265**	270-765-2131	68
Your Selling Team 100 Spectrum Ctr Dr Ste 700	Irvine	CA	92618	**888-387-8002**		734
yourDealer 420 E 55th St Ste 8H	New York	NY	10022	**866-847-7502**		197
Yourga Trucking Inc 100 Shenango St	Wheatland	PA	16161	**800-245-1722**	724-981-3600	778
Youth For Understanding USA 6400 Goldsboro Rd Ste 100	Bethesda	MD	20817	**800-424-3691**	240-235-2100	47-11
Youth Frontiers Inc 6009 Excelsior Blvd	Minneapolis	MN	55416	**888-992-0222**	952-922-0222	198
Youth Home Inc 20400 Colonel Glenn Rd	Little Rock	AR	72210	**800-728-6452**	501-821-5500	724
Youth Villages Inner Harbour 4685 Dorsett Shoals Rd	Douglasville	GA	30135	**800-255-8657**	770-852-6333	374-1
YouVisit LLC 20533 Biscayne Blvd Ste 1322	Aventura	FL	33180	**866-585-7158**		387
YPO (Young Presidents' Organization) 600 E Las Colinas Blvd Ste 1000	Irving	TX	75039	**800-773-7976**	972-587-1500	48-12
YPO-WPO 600 E Las Colinas Blvd Ste 1100	Irving	TX	75039	**800-773-7976**	972-587-1500	48-12
YRC Worldwide Inc 10990 Roe Ave *NASDAQ: YRCW*	Overland Park	KS	66211	**800-846-4300**	913-696-6100	360-3
YSI Inc 1700-1725 Brannum Ln *Cust Svc	Yellow Springs	OH	45387	**800-765-4974***	937-767-7241	203
Y-Tex Corp 1825 Big Horn Ave PO Box 1450	Cody	WY	82414	**800-443-6401**	307-587-5515	282
Yucaipa Valley Water District PO Box 730	Yucaipa	CA	92399	**800-272-8869**	909-797-5117	785
Yucca Valley Chamber of Commerce 56711 29 Palms Hwy	Yucca Valley	CA	92284	**855-568-5348**	760-365-6323	138
Yule Tree Farms LLC 8804 S Heinz Rd	Canby	OR	97013	**888-970-8733**	503-651-2114	750
Yum! Brands Inc 1441 Gardiner Ln *NYSE: YUM*	Louisville	KY	40213	**800-225-5532**	502-874-8300	668
Yuma Civic Ctr 1440 W Desert Hills Dr	Yuma	AZ	85365	**866-966-0220**	928-373-5040	207
Yuma Convention & Visitors Bureau 201 N Fourth Ave	Yuma	AZ	85364	**800-293-0071**	928-783-0071	208
Yuma County Chamber of Commerce 180 W First St Ste A	Yuma	AZ	85364	**877-782-0438**	928-782-2567	138
Y-W Electric Assn Inc 250 Main Ave PO Box Y	Akron	CO	80720	**800-660-2291**	970-345-2291	247
YWCA (YWCA USA) 2025 M St NW Ste 550	Washington	DC	20036	**888-872-9259**	202-467-0801	47-6
YWCA USA (YWCA) 2025 M St NW Ste 550	Washington	DC	20036	**888-872-9259**	202-467-0801	47-6

Z

Name / Address	City	State	ZIP	Toll-Free	Phone	Class
Z Communications Inc 14118 Stowe Dr Ste B	Poway	CA	92064	**877-808-1226**	858-621-2700	255
Z Gallerie Inc 1855 W 139th St	Gardena	CA	90249	**800-358-8288**	310-630-1200	362

Name / Address	City	State	ZIP	Toll-Free	Phone	Class
Z57 Internet Solutions						
10045 Mesa Rim Rd	San Diego	CA	92121	**800-899-8148**		227
Z92 FM						
10714 Mockingbird Dr	Omaha	NE	68127	**800-955-9230**		642-84
Zachary & Elizabeth Fisher House						
111 Rockville Pk Ste 420	Rockville	MD	20850	**888-294-8560**		372
Zachary Confections Inc						
2130 IN-28	Frankfort	IN	46041	**800-445-4222***		297-8
*Cust Svc						
Zachary Piper LLC						
1410 Spring Hill Rd Ste 300	Mclean	VA	22012	**888-487-8812**	703-649-4001	262
Zachys Wine & Liquor Inc						
16 E Pkwy	Scarsdale	NY	10583	**800-723-0241**	914-723-0241	443
Zack Electronics Inc						
1070 Hamilton Rd	Duarte	CA	91010	**800-466-0449**	626-303-0655	248
Zacky Farms						
13200 Crossroads Pkwy N Ste 250	City of Industry	CA	91746	**800-888-0235**	562-641-2020	298-10
Zacky Farms Inc						
2020 SE Ave	Fresno	CA	93721	**800-888-0235**	562-641-2020	10-7
Zadro Products Inc						
5422 Argosy Ave	Huntington Beach	CA	92649	**800-468-4348**	714-892-9200	607
ZAGG Inc						
3855 South 500 West Ste J	Salt Lake City	UT	84115	**800-700-9244**	801-263-0699	607
Zale Corp						
6201 15th Ave	Brooklyn	NY	11219	**866-249-2593***	718-921-8137	410
NYSE: ZLC ■ *Cust Svc						
Zales Jewelers Div						
901 W Walnut Hill Ln	Irving	TX	75038	**800-311-5393***	972-580-4000	410
*Cust Svc						
Zampell Cos						
9 Stanley Tucker Dr	Newburyport	MA	01950	**877-926-7355**	978-465-0055	609
Zane State College						
1555 Newark Rd	Zanesville	OH	43701	**800-686-8324**	740-454-2501	798
Zaner Group LLC						
150 S Wacker Dr Ste 2350	Chicago	IL	60606	**800-621-1414**	312-277-0050	171
Zaner-Bloser Inc						
1201 Dublin Rd	Columbus	OH	43215	**800-421-3018**	614-486-0221	634-2
Zanesville City School Board						
160 N Fourth St	Zanesville	OH	43701	**866-280-7377**	740-454-9751	683
Zanesville-Muskingum County Chamber of Commerce						
205 N Fifth St	Zanesville	OH	43701	**800-743-2303**	740-455-8282	138
ZAP 501 Fourth St	Santa Rosa	CA	95401	**800-251-4555***	707-525-8658	768
OTC: ZAAP ■ *Orders						
Zappos.com						
400 E Stewart Ave	Las Vegas	NV	89101	**800-927-7671**		458
Zasio Enterprises Inc						
401 W Front St Ste 305	Boise	ID	83702	**800-513-1000**		179
ZaZa Energy Corp						
1301 McKinney St Ste 2800	Houston	TX	77010	**866-202-3048**	713-595-1900	535
NASDAQ: ZAZA						
ZBA Inc						
94 Old Camplain Rd	Hillsborough	NJ	08844	**800-750-4239**	908-359-2070	175-7
ZE PowerGroup Inc						
130 - 5920 No Two Rd	Richmond	BC	V7C4R9	**866-944-1469**	604-244-1469	195
ZeaVision LLC						
716-I Crown Industrial Ct	Chesterfield	MO	63005	**866-833-2800**	314-628-1000	345
Zebra Books						
Kensington Publishing Corp						
119 W 40th St	New York	NY	10018	**800-221-2647**	212-407-1500	634-2
Zebra Technologies Corp						
475 Half Day Rd Ste 500	Lincolnshire	IL	60069	**800-423-0422**	847-634-6700	175-6
NASDAQ: ZBRA						
zedSuite						
210 Water St Ste 400	St. John's	NL	A1C1A9	**877-722-1177**	709-722-7213	198
Zee Medical Inc						
22 Corporate Pk	Irvine	CA	92606	**800-435-7763**		474
Zeeland Lumber & Supply Co						
146 E Washington	Zeeland	MI	49464	**888-772-2119**	616-772-2119	193-3
Zehnder America Inc						
6 Merrill Industrial Dr Ste 7	Hampton	NH	03842	**888-778-6701**	603-601-8544	609
Zeigler Beverage Co						
1513 N Broad St	Lansdale	PA	19446	**800-854-6123***	215-855-5161	297-20
*Sales						
Zeigler Bros Inc						
400 GaRdner Stn Rd	Gardners	PA	17324	**800-841-6800**	717-677-6181	446
Zeiser Wilbert Vault Inc						
750 Howard St	Elmira	NY	14904	**800-472-4335**	607-733-0568	193-1
Zeks Compressed Air Solutions						
1302 Goshen Pkwy	West Chester	PA	19380	**800-888-2323**	610-692-9100	174
Zen Ventures LLC						
3939 S 6th St Ste 201	Klamath Falls	OR	97603	**888-936-2278**		807
Zenith Cutter Co						
5200 Zenith Pkwy	Loves Park	IL	61111	**800-223-5202**	815-282-5200	492
Zenith Insurance Co						
PO Box 9055	Van Nuys	CA	91409	**800-440-5020**	818-713-1000	391-4
Zenith Products Corp						
400 Lukens Dr	New Castle	DE	19720	**800-892-3986**		320-2
Zenith Specialty Bag Company Inc						
17625 E Railroad St PO Box 8445	City of Industry	CA	91748	**800-962-2247**	626-912-2481	64
ZEP Inc						
1310 Seaboard Industrial Blvd NW	Atlanta	GA	30318	**877-428-9937**	404-352-1680	150
NYSE: ZEP						
Zephyr Egg Co Inc						
4622 Gall Blvd	Zephyrhills	FL	33542	**800-333-4415**	813-782-1521	10-7
Zephyr Environmental Corp						
2600 Via Fortuna Ste 450	Austin	TX	78746	**800-452-5558**	512-329-5544	263
Zephyr Mfg Company Inc						
201 Hindry Av	Inglewood	CA	90301	**800-624-3944**	310-410-4907	756
Zephyrhills Chamber of Commerce						
38550 Fifth Ave	Zephyrhills	FL	33542	**800-851-8754**	813-782-1913	138
Zephyr-Tec Corp						
9651 Business Ctr Dr Ste C	Rancho Cucamonga	CA	91730	**877-493-7497**	909-481-9991	179
Zepto Metrix Corp						
872 Main St	Buffalo	NY	14202	**800-274-5487***	716-882-0920	233
*Cust Svc						
Zero International Inc						
415 Concord Ave	Bronx	NY	10455	**800-635-5335**	718-585-3230	327
Zero Manufacturing Inc						
500 West 200 North	North Salt Lake	UT	84054	**800-959-5050**	801-298-5900	452
Zero-Max Inc						
13200 Sixth Ave N	Plymouth	MN	55441	**800-533-1731**	763-546-4300	619
Zerowait Corp						
707 Kirkwood Hwy	Wilmington	DE	19805	**888-811-0808**	302-996-9408	194
Zeta Phi Beta Sorority Inc						
1734 New Hampshire Ave NW	Washington	DC	20009	**800-393-2503**	202-387-3103	47-16
Zeta Psi Fraternity of North America						
15 S Henry St	Pearl River	NY	10965	**800-477-1847**	845-735-1847	47-16
Zetec Inc						
8226 Bracken Pl SE Ste 100	Snoqualmie	WA	98065	**800-643-1771**	425-974-2700	250
Zeton Inc						
740 Oval Ct	Burlington	ON	L7L6A9	**877-299-3866**	905-632-3123	263
Zhone Technologies Inc						
7001 Oakport St	Oakland	CA	94621	**877-946-6320**	510-777-7000	732
NASDAQ: ZHNE						
Ziebart International Corp						
1290 E Maple Rd	Troy	MI	48083	**800-877-1312**	248-588-4100	61-1
Zieger & Sons Inc						
6215 Ardleigh St	Philadelphia	PA	19138	**800-752-2003**	215-438-7060	295
Zierick Manufacturing Corp						
131 Radio Cr	Mount Kisco	NY	10549	**800-882-8020**	914-666-2911	813
Ziff Davis, LLC						
28 E 28th St	New York	NY	10016	**800-289-0429**	212-503-3500	456-7
Zimmer Inc						
1800 W Ctr St PO Box 708	Warsaw	IN	46580	**800-613-6131**	574-267-6131	476
Zimmer Radio Group						
3215 Lemone Industrial Blvd Ste 200	Columbia	MO	65201	**800-455-1099**	573-875-1099	640
Zimmerman Auto Center						
4001 First Ave	Cedar Rapids	IA	52402	**855-877-4223**	319-313-5086	56
Zimmerman Metals Inc						
201 E 58th Ave	Denver	CO	80216	**800-247-4202**	303-294-0180	479
Zimmet Healthcare Consulting LLC						
4006 Us Hwy 9	Morganville	NJ	07751	**877-763-2001**	732-970-0733	462
Zingle Inc						
5235 Avenida Encinas Ste A	Carlsbad	CA	92008	**877-946-4536**		226
Zinkan Enterprises Inc						
1919 Case Pkwy N	Twinsburg	OH	44087	**800-229-6801**		144
Zions First National Bank						
1 S Main St	Salt Lake City	UT	84111	**800-974-8800**	801-974-8800	69
Zipcar Inc						
35 Thomson Pl	Boston	MA	02210	**877-353-9227**		52
NASDAQ: ZIP						
Zippertubing Co						
7150 W Erie St	Chandler	AZ	85226	**855-289-1874**	480-285-3990	599
ZipRealty Inc						
2000 Powell St Ste 300	Emeryville	CA	94608	**800-225-5947**	510-735-2600	650
NASDAQ: ZIPR						
Zix Corp						
2711 N Haskell Ave Ste 2300-LB	Dallas	TX	75204	**888-771-4049**	214-370-2000	180-12
NASDAQ: ZIXI						
ZK Celltest Inc						
256 Gibraltar Dr Ste 109	Sunnyvale	CA	94089	**800-837-8235**	408-752-0449	203
Z-Law Software Inc						
80 Upton Ave PO Box 40602	Providence	RI	02940	**800-526-5588**	401-331-3002	179
ZLB Behring LLC						
1020 First Ave PO Box 61501	King of Prussia	PA	19406	**800-683-1288**	610-878-4000	582
Zodiac Pool Systems Inc						
2620 Commerce Way	Vista	CA	92081	**800-822-7933**		804
Zoeller Co						
3649 Kane Run Rd	Louisville	KY	40211	**800-928-7867**	502-778-2731	638
OTC: ZOLR						
Zogenix Inc						
12400 High Bluff Dr Ste 650	San Diego	CA	92130	**866-964-3649**	858-259-1165	582
Zolato Inc						
2801 First Ave Ste 306	Seattle	WA	98121	**866-557-6716**		465
ZOLL Medical Corp						
269 Mill Rd	Chelmsford	MA	01824	**800-348-9011**	978-421-9655	252
Zonar Systems LLC						
18200 Cascade Ave S	Seattle	WA	98188	**877-843-3847**	206-878-2459	528
Zone Alarm						
800 Bridge Pkwy	Redwood City	CA	94065	**877-966-5221**	415-633-4500	180-7
Zontec Inc						
1389 Kemper Meadow Dr	Cincinnati	OH	45240	**866-955-0088**	513-648-9695	182
Zoocheck Canada						
788 1/2 O'Connor Dr	Toronto	ON	M4B2S6	**888-801-3222**	416-285-1744	47-3
Zookbinders Inc						
151-K S Pfingsten Rd Ste	Deerfield	IL	60015	**800-810-5745**		626
Zoom Information Inc						
307 Waverley Oaks Rd	Waltham	MA	02452	**800-949-7040**	781-693-7500	112
Zortec International						
25 Century Blvd Ste 103	Nashville	TN	37214	**800-361-7005**	615-361-7000	180-2
Zotos International Inc						
100 Tokeneke Rd	Darien	CT	06820	**888-242-4247**	203-655-8911	217
ZT Group International Inc						
350 Meadowlands Pkwy	Secaucus	NJ	07094	**888-984-8899**	201-559-1000	178
ZTEST Electronics Inc						
523 Mcnicoll Ave	North York	ON	M2H2C9	**866-393-4891**	416-297-5155	624
ZTR Control Systems Inc						
8050 County Rd 101 East	Minneapolis	MN	55379	**855-724-5987**		419
Zuercher Technologies LLC						
5121 S Solberg Ave Ste 150	Sioux Falls	SD	57108	**877-229-2205**	605-274-6061	176
Zuken USA						
238 Littleton Rd Ste 100	Westford	MA	01886	**800-447-7332**	978-692-4900	180-5
Zumar Industries Inc						
9719 Santa Fe Springs Rd	Santa Fe Springs	CA	90670	**800-654-7446**	562-941-4633	699
Zumiez Inc						
6300 Merrill Creek Pkwy Ste B	Everett	WA	98203	**877-828-6929**	425-551-1500	156-2
NASDAQ: ZUMZ						

				Toll-Free	Phone	Class
Zurich North America						
1400 American Ln	Schaumburg	IL	60196	**800-382-2150**	847-605-6000	391-5
Zygo Corp						
Laurel Brook Rd	Middlefield	CT	06455	**800-994-6669**	860-347-8506	543
NASDAQ: ZIGO						
ZyLAB North America LLC						
7918 Jones Branch Dr Ste 230	McLean	VA	22102	**866-995-2262**		180-1
Zyme Solutions Inc						
240 Twin Dolphin Dr Ste D	Redwood Shores	CA	94065	**888-200-6629**	650-294-4700	226
ZymoGenetics Inc						
1201 Eastlake Ave E	Seattle	WA	98102	**800-332-2056**	206-442-6600	84
Zyng Inc						
RPO Atwater PO Box 72108	Montreal	QC	H3J2Z6	**888-328-9964**	514-288-8800	668
ZyQuest Inc						
1385 W Main Ave	De Pere	WI	54115	**800-992-0533**	920-499-0533	182
ZyXEL Communications Inc						
1130 N Miller St	Anaheim	CA	92806	**800-255-4101**	714-632-0882	175-3

Classified Section

Listings in the Classified Section are organized alphabetically under subject headings denoting a business or organization type. These headings are fully outlined in the Index to Classified Headings located at the back of this book. "See" and "See Also" references are included in this section to help locate appropriate subject categories. Alphabetizing is on a word-by-word rather than letter-by-letter basis. For a detailed explanation of the scope and arrangement of listings in Toll-Free Phone Book USA, please refer to "How To Use This Directory" at the beginning of this book. An explanation of individual page elements is also provided under the "Sample Entry" on the back inside cover of the book.

1 ABRASIVE PRODUCTS

Name	Address	City	State	Zip	Toll-Free	Phone
Basic Carbide Corp	900 Main St	Lowber	PA	15660	**800-426-4291**	724-446-1630
Bullard Abrasives Inc	6 Carol Dr	Lincoln	RI	02865	**800-227-4469**	401-333-3000
Comco Inc	2151 N Lincoln St	Burbank	CA	91504	**800-796-6626**	818-841-5500
Composition Materials Company Inc	249 Pepes Farm Rd	Milford	CT	06460	**800-262-7763**	203-874-6500
Ervin Industries Inc	3893 Research Pk Dr	Ann Arbor	MI	48108	**800-748-0055**	734-769-4600
Formax Manufacturing Corp	168 Wealthy St SW	Grand Rapids	MI	49503	**800-242-2833**	616-456-5458
Gemtex Abrasives	234 Belfield Rd	Toronto	ON	M9W1H3	**800-387-5100**	416-245-5605
Hermes Abrasives Ltd	PO Box 2389	Virginia Beach	VA	23450	**800-464-8314**	757-486-6623
Kennametal Inc	2879 Aero Pk Dr *NYSE: KMT*	Traverse City	MI	49686	**800-662-2131**	231-946-2100
Marvel Abrasive Products Inc	6230 S Oak Pk Ave	Chicago	IL	60638	**800-621-0673**	
Micro Surface Finishing Products Inc	1217 W Third St	Wilton	IA	52778	**800-225-3006**	563-732-3240
Norton Sandblasting Equipment	1006 Executive Blvd	Chesapeake	VA	23320	**800-366-4341**	757-548-4842
Precision H2O Inc	6328 E Utah Ave	Spokane	WA	99212	**800-425-2098**	509-536-9214
Radiac Abrasives Inc	1015 S College Ave	Salem	IL	62881	**800-851-1095**	618-548-4200
Raytech Industries	475 Smith St *Cust Svc	Middletown	CT	06457	**800-243-7163***	860-632-2020
Sancap Abrasives	16123 Armour St NE	Alliance	OH	44601	**800-433-6663**	330-821-3510
Superior Abrasives Inc	1620 Fieldstone Way	Vandalia	OH	45377	**800-235-9123**	937-278-9123
Trumbull Industries Inc	400 Dietz Rd NE	Warren	OH	44482	**800-477-1799**	330-393-6624
VSM Abrasives	1012 E Wabash St *Cust Svc	O'Fallon	MO	63366	**800-737-0176***	636-272-7432

2 ACCOUNTING FIRMS

Name	Address	City	State	Zip	Toll-Free	Phone
Accounts Payable Chexs Inc	1829 Ranchlands Blvd Nw	Calgary	AB	T3G2A7	**888-437-0624**	403-247-8913
Active Captive Management	16485 Laguna Canyon Rd Ste 200	Irvine	CA	92618	**800-921-0155**	949-727-0155
ACU Serve Corp	2020 Front St Ste 205	Cuyahoga Fls	OH	44221	**800-887-8965**	330-923-5258
Ahern Adcock Devlin LLP	1650 Iowa Ave Ste 200	Riverside	CA	92507	**888-226-9449**	951-683-0672
Ahola Corp, The	6820 W Snowville Rd	Brecksville	OH	44141	**800-727-2849**	440-717-7620
Altera Payroll Inc	2400 Northside Crossing	Macon	GA	31210	**877-474-6060**	478-477-6060
Andrews Hooper Pavlik Plc	5300 Gratiot Rd	Saginaw	MI	48638	**888-754-8478**	989-497-5300
Bauman Associates Ltd	PO Box 1225	Eau Claire	WI	54702	**888-952-2866**	715-834-2001
Beason & Nalley Inc	101 Monroe St Ne	Huntsville	AL	35801	**800-416-1946**	256-533-1720
BenefitMall	3450 Lakeside Dr Ste 400	Miramar	FL	33027	**877-729-6299**	954-874-4800
Berkowitz Dick Pollack & Brant LLP	200 S Biscayne Blvd 6th Fl	Miami	FL	33131	**800-999-1272**	305-379-7000
Berry Dunn Mcneil & Parker	100 Middle St 4th Fl	Portland	ME	04101	**800-908-4490**	207-775-2387
Blackman Kallick	10 S Riverside Plaza	Chicago	IL	60606	**866-939-3921**	312-207-1040
Blue & Co	12800 N Meridian St Ste 400	Carmel	IN	46032	**800-717-2583**	317-848-8920
Bolden Lipkin PC	3993 Huntingdon Pk	Huntingdon Valley	PA	19006	**888-947-3750**	215-947-3750
Bonadio Group, The	171 Sully's Trail Ste 201	Pittsford	NY	14534	**877-917-3077**	585-381-1000
Brockman Coats Gedelian & Co	1735 Merriman Rd	Akron	OH	44313	**800-968-6661**	330-864-6661
Broniec Assoc Inc	4855 Peachtree Industrial Blvd Ste 215	Norcross	GA	30092	**800-432-8348**	770-729-9664
CBIZ Tofias PC	500 Boylston St	Boston	MA	02116	**888-761-8835**	617-761-0600
Certipay	199 Ave B NW Ste 270	Winter Haven	FL	33881	**800-422-3782**	863-299-2400
Clark Nuber PS	10900 NE Fourth St Ste 1700 *General	Bellevue	WA	98004	**800-504-8747***	425-454-4919
CliftonLarsonAllen - CLA	301 SW Adams St Ste 1000	Peoria	IL	61602	**800-354-5849**	309-671-4500
Clinic Service Corp	3464 S Willow St	Denver	CO	80231	**800-929-5395**	303-755-2900
Complete Payroll Processing Inc	7488 SR- 39 Po Box 190	Perry	NY	14530	**888-237-5800**	585-237-5800
Conner Ash PC	12101 Woodcrest Exec Dr 300	Saint Louis	MO	63141	**877-366-1690**	314-205-2510
Contingent Workforce Solutions Inc	2430 Meadowpine Blvd Ste 101	Mississauga	ON	L5N6S2	**866-837-8630**	
ECS Financial Services Inc	3400 Dundee Rd	Northbrook	IL	60062	**800-826-7070**	847-291-1333
Elliott Davis Decosimo LLC	629 Market St Ste 100	Chattanooga	TN	37402	**800-782-8382**	423-756-7100
Elliott Davis LLC	200 E Broad St PO Box 6286	Greenville	SC	29606	**800-503-4721**	864-242-3370
Ernst & Young	Ernst & Young Tower 222 Bay St PO Box 251	Toronto	ON	M5K1J7	**800-291-3380**	416-864-1234
Farmers Insurance Group	6060 W Manchester Ave Ste 302	Los Angeles	CA	90045	**888-327-6335**	
Federal Management Systems Inc	462 K St NW	Washington	DC	20001	**877-637-8277**	202-842-3003
Fiducial	1370 Ave of the Americas 31st Fl	New York	NY	10019	**866-343-8242**	212-207-4700
Flex Checks Inc	PO Box 141215	Grand Rapids	MI	49514	**866-791-7900**	616-791-7900
Freyberg Hinkle Ashland Powers & Stowell Sc CPA	15420 W Capitol Dr	Brookfield	WI	53005	**800-413-8799**	262-784-6210
Friedberg Smith & Co PC	855 Main St	Bridgeport	CT	06604	**800-772-1213**	203-366-5876
Friedman LLP	1700 Broadway	New York	NY	10019	**800-372-1033**	212-842-7000
Gallina LLP	925 Highland Pointe Dr Ste 450	Roseville	CA	95678	**877-638-1188**	916-638-1188
Gompers & Assoc PLLC	117 Edgington Ln	Wheeling	WV	26003	**844-805-9844**	304-242-9300
Grant Bennett Accountants	1375 Exposition Blvd Ste 230	Sacramento	CA	95815	**888-763-7323**	916-922-5109
Gross Mendelsohn & Assoc pa	36 S Charles St 18th fl	Baltimore	MD	21201	**800-899-4623**	410-685-5512
Gumbiner Savett Inc	1723 Cloverfield Blvd	Santa Monica	CA	90404	**800-989-9798**	310-828-9798
Hacker Johnson & Smith PA	500 N Wshore Blvd Ste 1000	Tampa	FL	33609	**800-366-7126**	813-286-2424
Hill Barth & King LLC	7680 Market St	Youngstown	OH	44512	**800-733-8613**	330-758-8613
Honegger Ringger & Company Inc	1905 N Main St	Bluffton	IN	46714	**888-853-5906**	260-824-4107
Honkamp Krueger & Company PC	2345 JFK Rd PO Box 699	Dubuque	IA	52004	**888-556-0123**	563-556-0123
Huckstep & Assoc LLC	3734 S Ave Ste E	Springfield	MO	65807	**800-269-6466**	417-889-8991
Jobe Hastings & Assoc CPA's	745 S Church St Ste 105	Murfreesboro	TN	37133	**866-207-2384**	615-893-7777
Kahn Litwin Renza & Company Ltd	951 N Main St	Providence	RI	02904	**888-557-8557**	401-274-2001
Kaufman Rossin & Co PA	2699 S Bayshore Dr	Miami	FL	33133	**866-357-9634**	305-858-5600
Keystone Payroll	355 Colonnade Blvd Ste C	State College	PA	16803	**877-717-2272**	814-234-2272
Lazer Grant Inc	309 Mcdermot Ave	Winnipeg	MB	R3A1T3	**800-220-0005**	204-942-0300
Lefkowitz Garfinkel Champi & DeRienzo PC	10 Weybosset St	Providence	RI	02903	**800-927-5423**	401-421-4800
Lenning & Company Inc	13924 Seal Beach Blvd Ste C	Seal Beach	CA	90740	**800-200-4829**	562-594-9729

Company / Address	City	State	Zip	Toll-Free	Phone
Lewis & Knopf CPAs PC 5206 Gateway Centre Ste 100	Flint	MI	48507	**877-244-1787**	810-238-4617
M & K CPAs PLLC 4100 Nsam Houston Pkwy	Houston	TX	77086	**866-770-5931**	832-242-9950
Massachusetts Society of Certified Public Accountants 105 Chauncy St 10th Fl	Boston	MA	02111	**800-392-6145**	617-556-4000
Mauldin & Jenkins Certified Public Accountants LLC 200 Galleria Pkwy SE	Atlanta	GA	30339	**800-277-0080**	770-955-8600
McConnell Jones Lanier & Murphy LLP The Lakes On Post Oak 3040 Post Oak Blvd Ste 1600	Houston	TX	77056	**866-908-4650**	713-968-1600
Mcswain & Co PS 612 Woodland Sq Loop SE Ste 300	Lacey	WA	98503	**800-282-1301**	360-357-9304
Medical Management Specialists 4100 Embassy Dr SE Ste 200	Grand Rapids	MI	49546	**888-707-2684**	616-975-1845
Michael J Liccar & Co 231 s la salle st	Chicago	IL	60604	**800-922-6604**	312-702-1861
Michael R Rubenstein & Assoc 12527 New Brittany Blvd	Fort Myers	FL	33907	**888-616-1222**	239-489-4443
Moore & Neidenthal Inc 3034 N Wooster Ave	Dover	OH	44622	**866-364-7774**	330-364-7774
Moore Stephens Lovelace PA 1201 S Orlando Ave Ste 400	Winter Park	FL	32789	**800-683-5401**	407-740-5400
Morrison Brown Argiz & Farra LLP 1001 Brickell Bay Dr 9th Fl	Miami	FL	33131	**800-239-3843**	305-373-5500
Nearman Maynard Vallez CPAs & Consultants pa 205 Brandywine Blvd Ste 200	Fayetteville	GA	30214	**800-288-0293**	770-461-5706
Nietzke & Faupel PC 7274 Hartley St	Pigeon	MI	48755	**855-999-3122**	989-453-3122
NSF-GFTC 88 McGilvray St	Guelph	ON	N1G2W1	**800-673-6275**	519-821-1246
Packer Thomas 6601 Westford Pl Ste 101	Canfield	OH	44406	**800-943-4278**	330-533-9777
Padgett Business Services 160 Hawthorne Pk	Athens	GA	30606	**800-723-4388**	
Pannell Kerr Forster Of Texas Pc 5847 San Felipe St	Houston	TX	77057	**800-829-3676**	713-860-1400
Patrick Mcguire Certified Public Accountant 314 W 18th St	Cheyenne	WY	82001	**800-544-2151**	307-634-2151
Paymetric Inc 1225 Northmeadow Pkwy Ste 110	Roswell	GA	30076	**888-445-4901**	678-242-5281
Phillips Gold & Company LLP 1430 Broadway Rm 1200	New York	NY	10018	**800-772-1213**	212-730-1112
Pickens Snodgrass Koch & Company PC 3001 Medlin Dr Ste 100	Arlington	TX	76015	**800-424-5790**	817-664-3000
Plante & Moran PLLC 27400 NW Hwy	Southfield	MI	48034	**866-639-9991**	248-352-2500
PRG-Schultz International Inc 600 Galleria Pkwy Ste 100	Atlanta	GA	30339	**800-752-5894**	770-779-3900
PricewaterhouseCoopers LLP 300 Madison Ave	New York	NY	10017	**800-993-9971**	646-471-4000
Rehmann Group 5800 Gratiot St Ste 201	Saginaw	MI	48638	**866-799-9580**	989-799-9580
Richardson Pennington & Skinner Psc 513 S Second St	Louisville	KY	40202	**800-654-3699**	502-583-9587
Roger Sipe CPA Firm LLC 5742 Coventry Ln	Fort Wayne	IN	46804	**888-747-3272**	260-432-9996
Ruby Stein Wagner 300 Rue Leo-pariseau Ste 1900	Montreal	QC	H2X4B5	**866-842-3911**	514-842-3911
S R Snodgrass AC 2100 Corporate Dr	Wexford	PA	15090	**800-580-7738**	724-934-0344
Santora CPA Group 220 Continental Dr Ste 112 Christiana Executive Campus	Newark	DE	19713	**800-347-0116**	302-737-6200
SC&H Group LLC 910 Ridgebrook Rd	Sparks	MD	21152	**800-832-3008**	410-403-1500
Schenck Business Solutions 200 E Washington St	Appleton	WI	54911	**800-236-2246**	920-731-8111
Schlenner Wenner & Co 630 Roosevelt Rd	Saint Cloud	MN	56301	**877-616-0286**	320-251-0286
Scribner Cohen & Company SC 400 E Mason St Ste 300	Milwaukee	WI	53202	**888-730-0045**	414-271-1700
Sikich LLP 1415 W Diehl Rd Ste 400	Naperville	IL	60563	**877-279-1900**	630-566-8400
Simons Bitzer & Assoc PC 8350 S Emerson Ave Ste 100	Indianapolis	IN	46237	**866-702-5090**	317-782-3070
Singer Lewak Greenbaum & Goldstein LLP 10960 Wilshire Blvd 7th Fl	Los Angeles	CA	90024	**877-754-4557**	310-477-3924
Smoker Smith & Associates Pc 339 W Governor Rd Ste 202	Hershey	PA	17033	**888-277-1040**	717-533-5154
Smoll & Banning CPAs LLC 2410 Central Ave	Dodge City	KS	67801	**800-499-8881**	620-225-6100
Sobel & Company LLC 293 Eisenhower Pkwy Ste 290	Livingston	NJ	07039	**800-471-2468**	973-994-9494
Suby Von Haden & Assoc SC 1221 John Q Hammons Dr	Madison	WI	53717	**800-279-2616**	608-831-8181
Taycom Business Solutions Inc 719 Griswold Ave Ste 820	Detroit	MI	48226	**866-482-9266**	
TMG Company LLC 1718 Briarcrest Dr Ste 100	Bryan	TX	77802	**800-720-1563**	979-774-4492
United Paramount Tax Group Inc 4025 Woodland Park Blvd Ste 310	Arlington	TX	76013	**888-829-8829**	817-983-0099
Virginia Society of Certified Public Accountants 4309 Cox Rd	Glen Allen	VA	23060	**800-733-8272**	804-270-5344
Watson Rice & Co 301 Rt 17 N	Rutherford	NJ	07070	**800-945-5985**	201-460-4590
Wilcoxon Research Inc 20511 Seneca Meadows Pkwy	Germantown	MD	20876	**800-945-2696**	301-330-8811
Wireless Watchdogs LLC 5800 Hannum Ave Ste B	Culver City	CA	90230	**866-522-0688**	
WithumSmith+Brown 5 Vaughn Dr	Princeton	NJ	08540	**866-455-7438**	609-520-1188
Wong & Knowles CPA PC 340 W Butterfield Rd	Elmhurst	IL	60126	**866-966-4272**	630-993-2223

3 ADHESIVES & SEALANTS

Company / Address	City	State	Zip	Toll-Free	Phone
Adhesives Research Inc 400 Seaks Run Rd PO Box 100	Glen Rock	PA	17327	**800-445-6240**	717-235-7979
Arlon Graphics 2811 S Harbor Blvd	Santa Ana	CA	92704	**800-232-7161**	714-540-2811
Atlas Minerals & Chemicals Inc 1227 Valley Rd *Cust Svc	Mertztown	PA	19539	**800-523-8269***	610-682-7171
Avery Dennison Corp 207 Goode Ave *NYSE: AVY* ■ *Cust Svc	Glendale	CA	91203	**888-567-4387***	626-304-2000
BASF Corp/Bldg Systems 889 Valley Pk Dr *Cust Svc	Shakopee	MN	55379	**800-433-9517***	952-496-6000
Bestolife Corp 2777 Stemmons Fwy Ste 1800	Dallas	TX	75207	**855-243-9164**	214-583-0271
Bonstone Materials Corp 707 Swan Dr	Mukwonago	WI	53149	**800-425-2214**	262-363-9877
BR 111 Exotic Hardwood Flooring 1 NE 40th St	Miami	FL	33137	**800-525-2711**	
Brady Coated Products 6555 W Good Hope Rd	Milwaukee	WI	53223	**800-662-1191**	414-358-6600
CFC International Inc 500 State St	Chicago Heights	IL	60411	**800-393-4505**	708-891-3456
Colloid Environmental Technologies Co (CETCO) 2870 Forbs Ave	Hoffman Estates	IL	60192	**800-527-9948**	847-851-1899
Custom Bldg Products 13001 Seal Beach Blvd	Seal Beach	CA	90740	**800-272-8786**	562-598-8808
DAP Products Inc 2400 Boston St Ste 200 *Cust Svc	Baltimore	MD	21224	**800-543-3840***	410-675-2100
Devcon Inc 30 Endicott St	Danvers	MA	01923	**800-626-7226**	855-489-7262
Dymax Corp 318 Industrial Ln	Torrington	CT	06790	**877-396-2963**	860-482-1010
Eclectic Products Inc 1075 Arrowsmith St PO Box 2280	Eugene	OR	97402	**800-693-4667**	
Elmer's Products Inc 1 Easton Oval	Columbus	OH	43219	**888-435-6377**	
Euclid Chemical Co 19218 Redwood Rd	Cleveland	OH	44110	**800-321-7628**	216-531-9222
Foster Construction Products Inc 1105 S Frontenac St	Aurora	IL	60504	**800-231-9541**	
Fox Industries Inc 3100 Falls Cliff Rd	Baltimore	MD	21211	**888-760-0369**	410-243-8856
Franklin International 2020 Bruck St	Columbus	OH	43207	**800-877-4583**	614-443-0241
Geocel Corp PO Box 398	Elkhart	IN	46515	**800-348-7615**	574-264-0645
H B Fuller Construction Products Inc 1105 S Frontenac Rd	Aurora	IL	60504	**800-832-9002**	
HB Fuller Co 1200 Willow Lk Blvd PO Box 64683 *NYSE: FUL*	Saint Paul	MN	55164	**888-423-8553**	651-236-5900
Henkel Corp 1 Henkel Way *Cust Svc	Rocky Hill	CT	06067	**800-243-4874***	860-571-5100
Hercules Chemical Company Inc 111 S St	Passaic	NJ	07055	**800-221-9330**	973-778-5000
Houghton International Inc 945 Madison Ave PO Box 930	Valley Forge	PA	19482	**888-459-9844**	610-666-4000
Inovex Industries Inc 45681 Oakbrook Ct Ste 102	Sterling	VA	20166	**888-374-3366**	703-421-9778
IPS Corp 455 W Victoria St	Compton	CA	90220	**800-888-8312**	310-898-3300
ITW Polymers Sealants North America 111 S Nursery R *Hotline	Irving	TX	75060	**888-751-0409***	972-438-9111
Laticrete International Inc 91 Amity Rd	Bethany	CT	06524	**800-243-4788**	203-393-0010
Lord Corp 111 Lord Dr	Cary	NC	27511	**877-275-5673**	919-468-5979
MAPEI Corp 1144 E Newport Ctr Dr	Deerfield Beach	FL	33442	**800-426-2734**	954-246-8888
Morgan Adhesives Co 4560 Darrow Rd	Stow	OH	44224	**866-262-2822**	330-688-1111
Nylok Corp 15260 Hallmark Dr	Macomb	MI	48042	**800-826-5161**	586-786-0100
Pacific Polymers Inc 12271 Monarch St	Garden Grove	CA	92841	**800-888-8340**	714-898-0025
Para-Chem Southern Inc 863 SE Main St PO Box 127	Simpsonville	SC	29681	**800-763-7272**	864-967-7691
Pecora Corp 165 Wambold Rd	Harleysville	PA	19438	**800-523-6688**	215-723-6051
Red Devil Inc 1437 S Boulder	Tulsa	OK	74119	**800-423-3845**	
Ritrama 800 Kasota Ave SE	Minneapolis	MN	55414	**800-328-5071**	612-378-2277
Southern Grouts & Mortars Inc 1502 SW Second Pl	Pompano Beach	FL	33069	**800-641-9247**	954-943-2288
Super Glue Corp 9420 Santa Anita Ave	Rancho Cucamonga	CA	91730	**800-538-3091**	909-987-0550
Tailored Chemical Products Inc 700 12th St Dr NW	Hickory	NC	28601	**800-627-1687**	828-322-6512
Tremco Inc Roofing Div 3735 Green Rd	Beachwood	OH	44122	**800-852-6013**	216-292-5000
Uniseal Inc 1800 W Maryland St	Evansville	IN	47712	**800-443-9081**	812-436-4840
W.F. Taylor Company Inc 11545 Pacific Ave	Fontana	CA	92337	**800-397-4583**	951-360-6677

4 ADVERTISING AGENCIES

SEE ALSO Public Relations Firms

Company / Address	City	State	Zip	Toll-Free	Phone
A Web That Works 2733 Concession Rd 7	Bowmanville	ON	L1C3K6	**800-579-9253**	905-263-2666
Aj Ross Creative Media 1149 NY 17M	Chester	NY	10918	**800-723-4644**	845-783-5770

Company	Address	City	State	Zip	Toll-Free	Phone
Alesco Data Group LLC	5276 Summerlin Commons Way	Fort Myers	FL	33907	**800-701-6531**	239-275-5006
All-Ways Adv Co	1442 Broad St	Bloomfield	NJ	07003	**800-255-9291**	973-338-0700
Aspen Marketing Services	1240 N Ave	West Chicago	IL	60185	**800-848-0212**	630-293-9600
Beehive Specialty Co	8701 Wall St Ste 900	Austin	TX	78754	**866-898-8774**	512-912-7940
Cade & Assoc Adv Inc	1645 Metropolitan Blvd	Tallahassee	FL	32308	**800-715-2233**	850-385-0300
Commercial Mailing Accessories Inc	28220 Playmor Beach Rd	Rocky Mount	MO	65072	**800-325-7303**	
Cooper-smith Adv LLC	4444 Bennett Rd	Toledo	OH	43612	**800-215-8812**	419-470-5900
Cotton & Co	633 SE Fifth St	Stuart	FL	34994	**800-266-9076**	772-287-6612
Creative Alliance Inc	437 W Jefferson St	Louisville	KY	40202	**800-525-0294**	502-584-8787
Dastmalchi Enterprises Inc	31 East Macarthur Crescent Ste 111	Santa Ana	CA	92707	**888-358-0331**	
Dudnyk	5 Walnut Grove Dr Ste 280	Horsham	PA	19044	**800-767-3263**	215-443-9406
DW Green Co	8100 S Priest Dr	Tempe	AZ	85284	**800-253-7146**	480-491-8483
Fahlgren Inc	4030 Easton Station Ste 300	Columbus	OH	43219	**800-731-8927**	614-383-1500
Ideal Adv & Printing	116 N Winnebago St	Rockford	IL	61101	**800-208-0294**	815-965-1713
Innis Maggiore Group Inc	4715 Whipple Ave NW	Canton	OH	44718	**800-460-4111**	330-492-5500
Intermark Group Inc	101 25th St N	Birmingham	AL	35243	**800-624-9239**	205-803-0000
Iris Group Inc, The	1675 Faraday Ave	Carlsbad	CA	92008	**800-347-1103**	760-431-1103
Kuno Creative Group LLC	36901 American Wy Ste 2A	Avon	OH	44011	**800-303-0806**	
Laughlin/Constable Inc	207 E Michigan St	Milwaukee	WI	53202	**800-432-8747**	414-272-2400
Launch Agency LP	4100 Midway Rd Ste 2110	Carrollton	TX	75007	**866-427-5013**	972-818-4100
Martin-Williams Adv	150 S 5th st Ste 900	Minneapolis	MN	55402	**800-632-1388**	612-340-0800
Media Buying Services Inc	4545 E Shea Blvd Ste 162	Phoenix	AZ	85028	**888-996-2232**	602-996-2232
Media Logic USA LLC	59 Wolf Rd	Albany	NY	12205	**866-353-3011**	518-456-3015
Mindgrub Technologies LLC	1215 E Ft Ave Ste 200	Baltimore	MD	21230	**855-646-3472**	410-988-2444
NAS Recruitment Communications	9700 Rockside Rd Ste 170	Cleveland	OH	44125	**866-627-7327**	
Network Journal, The	39 Broadway Rm 2120	New York	NY	10006	**866-259-1465**	212-962-3791
Prime Adv & Design Inc	7351 Kirkwood Ln N Ste 144	Maple Grove	MN	55369	**800-275-8777**	763-424-9406
Register Tapes Unlimited Inc	1445 Langham Creek	Houston	TX	77084	**800-247-4793**	281-206-2500
Richard Harrison Bailey Inc	121 S Niles Ave	South Bend	IN	46617	**866-404-8333**	574-287-8333
Risdall Adv Agency	550 Main St	New Brighton	MN	55112	**888-747-3255**	651-286-6700
Shaker Recruitment Adv & Communications	1100 Lake St 3rd Fl	Oak Park	IL	60301	**800-323-5170**	708-383-5320
Sherry Matthews Inc	200 S Congress Ave	Austin	TX	78704	**877-478-4397**	512-478-4397
Shumsky Enterprises Inc	811 E Fourth St	Dayton	OH	45402	**800-223-2203**	937-223-2203
Tinsley Adv	2000 S Dixie Hwy	Miami	FL	33133	**800-432-2242**	305-856-6060

ADVERTISING DISPLAYS

SEE Signs ; Displays - Exhibit & Trade Show ; Displays - Point-of-Purchase

5 ADVERTISING SERVICES - DIRECT MAIL

Company	Address	City	State	Zip	Toll-Free	Phone
29 Prime Inc	9701 Jeronimo Rd	Irvine	CA	92618	**888-513-7746**	
3D Internet	633 W Fifth St US Bank Twr Fl 28	Los Angeles	CA	90071	**800-442-5299**	
Aa Temps Inc	7002 little river tpke	Annandale	VA	22003	**800-901-8367**	703-642-9050
Access Worldwide Inc	5192 Southridge Pkwy Ste 112	Atlanta	GA	30349	**877-564-8581**	404-675-0633
Accurate Mailings Inc	215 O'Neill Ave	Belmont	CA	94002	**800-732-3290**	650-508-8885
Action Mailing Corp	3165 W Heartland Dr	Liberty	MO	64068	**866-990-9001**	816-415-9000
Acxiom Corp	601 E Third St *NASDAQ: ACXM*	Little Rock	AR	72201	**888-337-7699**	501-342-7799
Adwerx Inc	307 W Main St	Durham	NC	27701	**888-746-5678**	
Adzzup LLC	8240 S Kyrene Rd Ste 101	Tempe	AZ	85284	**888-723-9987**	
Agency Revolution	698 NW	Bend	OR	97701	**800-606-0477**	
Airbrush Action Inc	PO Box 438	Allenwood	NJ	08720	**800-876-2472**	732-223-7878
AKT Enterprises	6424 Forest City Rd	Orlando	FL	32810	**877-306-3651**	
Allview Networks LLC	8303 Arlington Dr Ste 210	Fairfax	VA	22031	**888-982-8489**	
Amazing Mail-print Center	2130 S 7th Ave Ste 170	Phoenix	AZ	85007	**888-681-1214**	
Americomm	804 Greenbrier Cir	Chesapeake	VA	23320	**800-527-6757**	757-622-2724
Ameripack Inc	107 N Gold Dr	Robbinsville	NJ	08691	**800-456-7963**	609-259-7004
BlueSpire Strategic Marketing	7650 Edinborough Way Ste 500	Minneapolis	MN	55435	**800-727-6397**	
Boostability Inc	2600 West Executive Pkwy Ste 200	Lehi	UT	84043	**800-261-1537**	
Booth	4900 Nautilus Ct N Ste 220	Boulder	CO	80301	**800-332-6684**	323-805-0150
Brandpoint	850 5Th St S	Hopkins	MN	55343	**877-374-5270**	
Brierley & Partners	5465 Legacy Dr Ste 300	Plano	TX	75024	**800-899-8700**	214-760-8700
Bulldog Solutions LLC	7600 N Capital of Texas Hwy Bldg C Ste 250	Austin	TX	78731	**877-402-9199**	
Cardlytics Inc	675 Ponce de Leon Ave NE Ste 6000	Atlanta	GA	30308	**888-798-5802**	
Catalina Marketing Corp	200 Carillon Pkwy	Saint Petersburg	FL	33716	**888-322-3814**	727-579-5000
Centron Data Services Inc	1175 Devin Dr *Cust Svc	Norton Shores	MI	49441	**800-732-8787***	
Ciplex	475 Washington Blvd Ste A	Marina Del Rey	CA	90292	**866-406-8258**	310-461-0330
Comark Direct	507 S Main St	Ft. Worth	TX	76104	**888-742-0405**	
Cruising Gide Publications Inc	1130 Pinehurst Rd Ste B	Dunedin	FL	34698	**800-330-9542**	727-733-5322
DirectMailcom	201 Skipjack Rd	Prince Frederick	MD	20678	**866-284-5816**	301-855-1700
Dp Murphy Company Inc	945 Grand Blvd	Deer Park	NY	11729	**800-424-8724**	631-673-9400
Dynamicard	332 S Juniper St Ste 101	Escondido	CA	92025	**800-928-7670**	
eLocal Listing LLC	28765 Single Oak Dr Ste 250	Temecula	CA	92590	**800-285-0484**	
ELS Marketing Inc	3133 Orlando Dr	Mississauga	ON	L4V1C5	**877-612-2673**	905-612-1060
Empyre Media	1150 N Carroll Ave	Southlake	TX	76092	**866-996-9893**	
eTagz Inc	108 1st Ave S Ste 450	Seattle	WA	98104	**800-831-0399**	
EventRebels com Inc	10013 Fox Den Rd	Ellicott City	MD	21042	**877-883-1786**	
eyeReturn Marketing	110 Eglinton Ave E Ste 705	Toronto	ON	M4P2Y1	**866-878-3335**	416-929-4834
FFF Enterprises Inc	41093 County Ctr Dr	Temecula	CA	92591	**800-843-7477**	951-296-2500
Focus Direct LLC	9707 Broadway	San Antonio	TX	78217	**800-555-1551**	210-805-9185
Forthea	3355 W Alabama St Ste 1230	Houston	TX	77098	**800-882-5905**	713-568-2763
Funnel Science Internet Marketing LLC	1802 N Carson St	Carson City	NV	89701	**877-301-0001**	
Griffin Tabor Communications	8445 camino santa fe	San Diego	CA	92121	**800-795-4472**	858-625-0070
Guest Communications Corp	15009 W 101st Ter	Shawnee Mission	KS	66215	**800-637-8525**	913-888-1217
Haines & Company Inc	8050 Freedom Ave	North Canton	OH	44720	**800-843-8452**	
Harte-Hanks Inc	9601 McAllister Fwy Ste 610 *NYSE: HHS*	San Antonio	TX	78216	**800-456-9748**	210-829-9000
Haystak Digital Marketing LLC	1514 Broadway Ste 201	Fort Myers	FL	33901	**866-292-0194**	
Heritage Co, The	2402 Wildwood Ave Ste 500	North Little Rock	AR	72120	**800-643-8822**	501-835-5000
Hkm Direct Market Communications Inc	5501 Cass Ave *General	Cleveland	OH	44102	**800-860-4456***	216-651-9500
I Imagine Studio Inc	152 W Huron Ste 100	Chicago	IL	60654	**855-792-7263**	847-467-0308
Immediate Mailing Services Inc	245 Commerce Blvd	Liverpool	NY	13088	**800-466-4189**	
infoGroup Inc	1020 E First St	Papillion	NE	68046	**866-414-7848**	402-836-5290
International Delivery Solutions LLC	7340 S Howell Ave	Milwaukee	WI	53154	**877-437-8722**	
JLS Mailing Services Inc	672 Crescent St	Brockton	MA	02302	**866-557-6245**	508-313-1000
Kirk Integrated Marketing Services Ltd	11388 No 5 Rd Ste 110	Richmond	BC	V7A4E7	**888-275-5475**	604-279-8484
KnowEm LLC	58 Phoenix Ave	Morristown	NJ	07960	**800-691-5669**	
LeadRival	1207 S White Chapel Blvd Ste 250	Southlake	TX	76092	**800-332-8017**	
Lemon Peak Marketing Services	500 W Putnam Ave Ste 400	Greenwich	CT	06831	**888-253-7348**	
Level Interactive	241 Fourth Ave	Pittsburgh	PA	15222	**877-733-8625**	
Lewis Direct Marketing	325 E Oliver St	Baltimore	MD	21202	**800-533-5394**	410-539-5100
Lexinet Corp, The	701 N Union St	Council Grove	KS	66846	**800-767-1577**	620-767-7000
Mail-Marketing Systems Inc	9420 Gerwig Ln	Columbia	MD	21046	**800-878-9537**	
Mailing Systems Inc	2431 Mercantile Dr Ste A	Rancho Cordova	CA	95742	**877-577-2647**	916-674-2035
Mailings Unlimited	116 Riverside Industrial Pkwy	Portland	ME	04103	**800-773-7417**	207-347-5000
Market Data Retrieval	6 Armstrong Rd	Shelton	CT	06484	**800-333-8802**	203-926-4800
Meridian Display & Merchandising Inc	162 York Ave E	St Paul	MN	55117	**800-786-2501**	651-227-3020
Metro Mailing Service Inc	4251 Gateway Park Blvd	Sacramento	CA	95834	**877-269-7055**	916-928-0801
Mila Displays Inc	1315B Broadway Ste 108	Hewlett	NY	11557	**800-295-6452**	516-791-2643
Mobivity Inc	58 W Buffalo Ste 200	Chandler	AZ	85225	**877-282-7660**	
Money Mailer LLC	12131 Western Ave	Garden Grove	CA	92841	**800-468-5865**	714-889-3800

Classified Section

Company / Address	City	State	Zip	Toll-Free	Phone
Monigle Associates Inc 150 Adams St	Denver	CO	80206	**800-346-4710**	303-388-9358
Motor City Interactive Inc 49145 Wixom Tech Dr	Wixom	MI	48393	**888-340-4638**	
mphoria LLC 1245 Rosemont Dr	Indian Land	SC	29707	**888-415-4933**	
Nationwide Biweekly Administration Inc 855 Lower Bellbrook Rd	Xenia	OH	45385	**888-802-1296**	
New Idea Engineering Inc 2784 Homestead Rd Ste 173	Santa Clara	CA	95051	**866-433-2364**	408-446-3460
News America Marketing 1185 Ave of the Americas 27	New York	NY	10036	**800-462-0852**	212-782-8000
Next Day Flyers 18711 S Broadwick St	Rancho Dominguez	CA	90220	**800-251-9948**	
O'Halloran Adv Inc 270 Saugatuck Ave	Westport	CT	06880	**877-466-6616**	203-341-9400
Olympia Media Group LLC 5201 W 86th St	Indianapolis	IN	46268	**888-272-2595**	
Onsite Management Group 4400 Bishop Ln Ste 214	Louisville	KY	40218	**800-207-4807**	502-583-1664
Patton-Kiehl Group Inc 17026 Bull Church Rd	Woodford	VA	22580	**888-388-0725**	
PrimeNet Direct Mktg Solutions LLC 7320 Bryan Dairy Rd	Largo	FL	33777	**800-826-2869**	727-447-6245
Promotions Unlimited 7601 Durand Ave	Sturtevant	WI	53177	**800-992-9307**	262-681-7000
Prospectr Marketing 3508 W 22nd St	Minneapolis	MN	55416	**800-908-3523**	
R O I Media Solutions LLC 11500 W Olympic Blvd Ste 400	Los Angeles	CA	90064	**866-211-2580**	
R.W. Lynch Company Inc 2333 San Ramon Vly Blvd	San Ramon	CA	94583	**800-594-8940**	925-837-3877
RDI Marketing Services 4350 Glendale Milford Rd Ste 250	Cincinnati	OH	45242	**800-388-7636**	513-984-5927
ReadyPulse 1600 A El Camino Real	San Carlos	CA	94070	**888-998-7412**	
RealTechNetwork Corp 75A Lk Rd Ste 150	Congers	NY	10920	**877-279-4904**	
Redfin 9890 S Maryland Pkwy Ste 200	Las Vegas	NV	89183	**800-561-5463**	877-973-3346
Retail Benefits Inc 9403 Caserta St	Lake Worth	FL	33467	**866-904-6044**	
RME360 4805 Independence Pkwy Ste 250	Tampa	FL	33634	**888-383-8770**	
RR Donnelley Logistics 1000 Windham Pkwy	Bolingbrook	IL	60490	**888-744-7773**	630-226-6100
RR Donnelley Response Marketing Services 4101 Winfield Rd	Warrenville	IL	60555	**800-722-9001**	630-963-9494
RSVP Publications 6730 W Linebaugh Ave Ste 201	Tampa	FL	33625	**800-360-7787**	813-960-7787
Sales Benchmark Index 1595 Peachtree Pkwy Ste 204-328	Cumming	GA	30041	**888-556-7338**	
Senior Alternatives For Living 26211 Central Park Blvd	Southfield	MI	48076	**800-350-0770**	
Sherpa Digital Media Inc 509 Seaport Ct	Redwood City	CA	94063	**877-989-7794**	
ShiftCentral Inc 210 John St Ste 100	Moncton	NB	E1C0B8	**866-551-5533**	
Simage LLC 300 N Elizabeth St Ste 100C	Chicago	IL	60607	**888-729-7796**	
Source One Distribution Services 1220 Morse Ave	Royal Oak	MI	48067	**877-763-3976**	248-399-5060
SourceLink Inc 500 Pk Blvd Ste 415	Itasca	IL	60143	**866-947-6872**	
Steel House Inc 3644 Eastham Dr	Culver City	CA	90232	**888-978-3354**	
SuperCoups 350 Revolutionary Dr	East Taunton	MA	02718	**800-626-2620**	508-977-2000
Tel-e Technologies 7 Kodiak Crescent	Toronto	ON	M3J3E5	**800-661-2340**	416-631-1300
Tension Envelope Corp 819 E 19th St	Kansas City	MO	64108	**800-388-5122**	
Tgi Direct 5365 Hill 23 Dr	Flint	MI	48507	**800-337-2237**	
U S Monitor 86 Maple Ave	New City	NY	10956	**800-767-7967**	845-634-1331
Universal Wilde 26 Dartmouth St	Westwood	MA	02090	**866-825-5515**	781-251-2700
Valpak Direct Marketing Systems Inc 8605 Largo Lakes Dr	Largo	FL	33773	**800-237-6266**	
Varvid Inc 705 Sunset Pond Lane Ste 2	Bellingham	WA	98226	**855-827-8434**	360-738-7168
Vertical Vision Financial Marketing LLC 145 Towne Lk Pkwy	Woodstock	GA	30188	**866-984-1585**	
Walts Mailing Service Ltd 9610 E First Ave	Spokane Valley	WA	99206	**888-549-2006**	509-924-5939
Yeck Bros Co 2222 Arbor Blvd	Dayton	OH	45439	**800-417-2767**	937-294-4000

6 ADVERTISING SERVICES - MEDIA BUYERS

Company / Address	City	State	Zip	Toll-Free	Phone
Ektron Inc 542 Amherst St (Rt 101A)	Nashua	NH	03063	**877-383-0885**	603-594-0249
Media Space Solutions 904 MainSt	Hopkins	MN	55343	**888-672-2100**	612-253-3900
Worldata 3000 N Military Trl	Boca Raton	FL	33431	**800-331-8102**	561-393-8200

7 ADVERTISING SERVICES - ONLINE

Company / Address	City	State	Zip	Toll-Free	Phone
Access To Media 432 Front St	Chicopee	MA	01013	**866-612-0034**	
Active Network 10182 Telesis Ct Ste 100	San Diego	CA	92121	**888-543-7223**	858-964-3800
Agency Mabu 1003 Gateway Ave	Bismarck	ND	58503	**800-568-9346**	701-250-0728
Alamo Tee's & Advertising 12814 Cogburn	San Antonio	TX	78249	**888-562-3800**	210-699-3800
AMCI 4755 Alla Rd Ste 1000	Marina Del Rey	CA	90292	**855-486-5527**	
Barnes Advertising Corp 1580 Fairview Rd	Zanesville	OH	43701	**800-458-1410**	740-453-6836
Blue Cat Design Mastwoods Rd	Port Hope	ON	L1A3V5	**888-258-3228**	905-753-1017
Blue Zebra Appointment Setting 25 PEQUOT AVE Ste A	Port Washington	NY	11050	**800-755-0094**	
Bolin Marketing & Advertising 2523 Wayzata Blvd Ste 300	Minneapolis	MN	55405	**800-876-6264**	612-374-1200
Brunet-Garcia Advertising Inc 1510 Hendricks Ave	Jacksonville	FL	32207	**866-346-1977**	904-346-1977
Business Direct Inc 5620 Old Bullard Rd Ste 128	Tyler	TX	75703	**888-580-7799**	
Chrisad Inc 11 Professional Ctr Pkwy	San Rafael	CA	94903	**800-505-4150**	415-924-8575
City of Com, The 1559 S Brownlee Blvd	Corpus Christi	TX	78404	**888-785-0500**	
Commission Junction Inc 530 E Montecito St	Santa Barbara	CA	93103	**800-761-1072**	805-730-8000
Concerto Marketing Group Inc 128 Hastings St W	Vancouver	BC	V6B1G8	**877-873-2738**	604-684-8933
Confluent Translations LLC 340 Mansfield Ave	Pittsburgh	PA	15220	**888-539-9077**	412-539-1410
Conway Marketing Communications 6400 Baum Dr	Knoxville	TN	37919	**800-882-7875**	865-588-5731
Creative Outdoor Advertising 2402 Stouffville Rd	Gormley	ON	L0H1G0	**800-661-6088**	
Crouch Group Inc, The 300 N Carroll Blvd Ste 103	Denton	TX	76201	**888-211-0273**	940-383-1990
Cyphers Agency Inc, The 53 Old Solomons Is Rd Ste G	Annapolis	MD	21401	**888-412-7469**	
Dailey Marketing Group Inc 29829 Santa Margarita Pkwy Ste 100	Rancho Santa Margarita	CA	92688	**888-364-6584**	949-454-0751
Daniels & Roberts Inc 209 N Seacrest Blvd Ste 2	Boynton Beach	FL	33435	**800-488-0066**	561-241-0066
Datamine Internet Marketing Solutions Inc 330 S Lake St	Gary	IN	46403	**877-328-2646**	219-939-9987
Davco Advertising Inc 89 N Kinzer Rd PO Box 288	Kinzers	PA	17535	**800-283-2826**	717-442-4155
Dogwood Productions Inc 757 Government St	Mobile	AL	36602	**800-254-9903**	251-476-0858
Evo Exhibits 399 Wegner Dr	West Chicago	IL	60185	**888-404-4224**	630-520-0710
F p i s Inc 220 Story Rd	Ocoee	FL	34761	**800-346-5977**	407-656-8818
Faction Media LLP 1730 Blake St Ste 200	Denver	CO	80202	**866-788-5306**	
Gbsa Inc 2710 N ave	Bridgeport	CT	06604	**800-544-0005**	203-549-0060
HelloWorld 3000 Town center ste 2100	South Field	MI	48075	**877-837-7493**	
Internet Matrix Inc 10179 Huennekens St	San Diego	CA	92121	**800-462-8749**	
Jarrard Phillips Cate & Hancock Inc 219 Ward Cir	Brentwood	TN	37027	**888-844-6274**	312-419-0575
Jobelephantcom Inc 5443 Fremontia Ln	San Diego	CA	92115	**800-311-0563**	619-795-0837
JT Mega 4020 Minnetonka Blvd	Minneapolis	MN	55416	**800-923-6342**	952-929-1370
Kutoka Interactive Inc 225 Roy E Ste 100	Montreal	QC	H2W1M5	**877-858-8652**	514-849-4800
Marchex Inc 520 Pike St Ste 2000 *NASDAQ: MCHX*	Seattle	WA	98101	**800-840-1012**	206-331-3300
MarketLauncher Inc 1800 Pembroke Dr Ste 300	Orlando	FL	32810	**800-901-3803**	
non-linear creations Inc 987 Wellington St Ste 201	Ottawa	ON	K1Y2Y1	**866-915-2997**	613-241-2067
Openjar Concepts Inc 27710 jefferson ave	Temecula	CA	92590	**877-673-6527**	
Prospects Influential Inc 3888 Sound Way	Bellingham	WA	98227	**888-982-0766**	
Quest Companies Inc 8011 N Point Blvd Ste 201	Winston-salem	NC	27106	**800-467-9409**	
Rainbow Advertising Lp 3904 W Vickery Blvd	Fort Worth	TX	76107	**800-646-3477**	817-738-3838
Rakuten Marketing LLC 215 Pk Ave S 9th Fl	New York	NY	10003	**888-880-8430**	646-943-8200
RES Exhibit Services LLC 435 Smith St	Rochester	NY	14608	**800-482-4049**	585-546-2040
Room 214 Inc 3390 Valmont Rd Ste 214	Boulder	CO	80301	**866-624-1851**	
SEOP Inc 1720 E Garry St Ste 103	Santa Ana	CA	92705	**877-231-1557**	
Straight North LLC 1001 W 31st St	Downers Grove	IL	60515	**866-353-3953**	
Taglairino Advertising Group Ny Inc 75 Sw 15th Rd	Miami	FL	33129	**800-226-9988**	305-577-9988
Team Velocity Marketing LLC 13825 Sunrise Valley Dr	Herndon	VA	20171	**877-832-6848**	
Thunder Tech Inc 3635 Perkins Ave Studio 5 SW	Cleveland	OH	44114	**888-321-8422**	216-391-2255
Tobe Direct 9700 Park Plz Ave Ste 210	Louisville	KY	40241	**866-820-7313**	
Topica Inc 1 Post St Ste 875	San Francisco	CA	94104	**888-728-2465**	415-344-0800
Transcontinental Inc 1100 Rene-Levesque Blvd W 24th Fl	Montreal	QC	H3B4X9	**800-361-5479**	514-392-9000
Tri-Media Integrated Marketing Technologies Inc (Prior to the acquisition by Andromeda Media) 517 Niagara St	Welland	ON	L3C1L7	**800-367-0766**	905-732-6431
Tukaiz Communications LLC 2917 N Latoria Ln	Franklin Park	IL	60131	**800-543-2674**	847-455-1588
Union Square Media Group 22647 Ventura Blvd No. 323	Woodland Hills	CA	91364	**800-691-1741**	

Classified Section

	City	State	ZIP	Toll-Free	Phone
ValueClick Inc 30699 Russell Ranch Rd Ste 250 *NASDAQ: VCLK*	Westlake Village	CA	91362	**877-361-3316**	818-575-4500
ValueClick Media 530 E Montecito St	Santa Barbara	CA	93103	**877-361-3316**	805-879-1600
Vital Media 508 W 5th St, Ste. 100 Ste	Charlotte	NC	28202	**866-863-3426**	
Wingman Advertising Inc 4061 Glencoe Ave Ste A	Marina Del Rey	CA	90292	**888-294-6462**	
Yesmail 421 SW Sixth Ave Ste 400	Portland	OR	97204	**877-937-6245**	503-241-4185

8 ADVERTISING SERVICES - OUTDOOR ADVERTISING

	City	State	ZIP	Toll-Free	Phone
BriteVision Media LLC 50 First St Ste 600	San Francisco	CA	94105	**877-479-7777**	
Cineplex Digital Networks 369 York St Ste 2C	London	ON	N6B3R4	**866-353-8324**	519-438-0111
Compass Collective 2150 Button Gwinnett Dr	Atlanta	GA	30340	**800-492-3402**	404-875-6543
Kubin-Nicholson Corp 8440 N 87th St	Milwaukee	WI	53224	**800-858-9557**	414-586-4300
Lamar Adv Co 5321 Corporate Blvd *NASDAQ: LAMR*	Baton Rouge	LA	70808	**800-235-2627**	225-926-1000
OUTFRONT Media Inc 405 Lexington Ave	New York	NY	10174	**800-926-8834**	212-297-6400
RCS Enterprises Inc 7075 W Parkland Ct	Milwaukee	WI	53223	**800-373-6873**	414-354-6900
Steen Outdoor Advertising 3201 S 26th St	Philadelphia	PA	19145	**866-537-8336**	
Studio y Creations Inc 1-6204 29 St Se	Calgary	AB	T2C1W3	**800-243-4024**	403-253-5447
Suite 66 366 Adelaide St W Ste 600	Toronto	ON	M5V1R9	**866-779-3486**	416-628-5565
WSOS Community Action Commission Inc 109 S Front St	Fremont	OH	43420	**800-775-9767**	419-334-8911

9 ADVERTISING SPECIALTIES

SEE ALSO Signs ; Smart Cards ; Trophies, Plaques, Awards

	City	State	ZIP	Toll-Free	Phone
ADG Promotional Products 2300 Main St	Hugo	MN	55038	**800-852-5208**	
Airmate Co Inc 16280 County Rd D	Bryan	OH	43506	**800-544-3614**	419-636-3184
Alexander Mfg Co 12978 Tesson Ferry Rd *General	Sappington	MO	63128	**800-258-2743***	314-842-3344
Allen Co 712 E Main St	Blanchester	OH	45107	**800-329-2491**	937-783-2491
Americanna Co 29 Aldrin Rd *Cust Svc	Plymouth	MA	02360	**888-747-5550***	508-747-5550
Amsterdam Printing & Litho Corp 166 Wallins Corners Rd *Cust Svc	Amsterdam	NY	12010	**800-833-6231***	518-842-6000
Arthur Blank & Co Inc 225 Rivermoor St	Boston	MA	02132	**800-776-7333**	617-325-9600
Atlas Match LLC 1801 S Airport Cir	Euless	TX	76040	**800-628-2426**	817-267-1500
Belaire Products Inc 763 S Broadway St	Akron	OH	44311	**800-886-3224**	330-253-3116
Bergamot Inc 820 E Wisconsin St *Cust Svc	Delavan	WI	53115	**800-922-6733***	262-728-5572
Brown & Bigelow Inc 345 Plato Blvd E *Cust Svc	Saint Paul	MN	55107	**800-628-1755***	651-293-7000
Churchwell Co 814 S Edgewood Ave	Jacksonville	FL	32205	**877-537-6166**	904-356-5721
Dunn Manufacturing Inc 1400 Goldmine Rd	Monroe	NC	28110	**800-868-7111**	704-283-2147
EBSCO Creative Concepts 3500 Blue Lake Dr Ste 150	Birmingham	AL	35243	**800-756-7023**	205-262-2696
Hit Promotional Products Inc 7150 Bryan Dairy Rd	Largo	FL	33777	**800-237-6305**	727-541-5561
Instant Imprints 5897 Oberlin Dr Ste 200	San Diego	CA	92121	**800-542-3437**	858-642-4848
Marco Promotional Products 2640 Commerce Dr	Harrisburg	PA	17110	**877-545-9322**	
Marietta Hospitality 37 Huntington St	Cortland	NY	13045	**800-950-7772**	607-753-6746
Maryland Match Corp 605 Alluvion St	Baltimore	MD	21230	**800-423-0013**	410-752-8164
Mid-America Merchandising Inc 204 W Third St	Kansas City	MO	64105	**800-333-6737**	816-471-5600
MMG Works/Status Promotions 4601 Madison Ave	Kansas City	MO	64112	**800-945-4044**	
Myron Corp 205 Maywood Ave	Maywood	NJ	07607	**877-803-3358**	
National Pen Corp (NPC) 12121 Scripps Summit Dr Ste 200	San Diego	CA	92131	**800-854-1000**	858-675-3000
Norscot Group Inc 1000 W Donges Bay Rd PO Box 998	Mequon	WI	53092	**800-653-3313**	262-241-3313
Norwood Promotional Products Inc 14421 Myerlake Cir	Clearwater	IN	33760	**877-555-2223**	727-538-3527
Prime Resources Corp 1100 Boston Ave	Bridgeport	CT	06610	**800-621-5463**	203-331-9100
Staples Promotional Products 7500 W 110th St	Overland Park	KS	66210	**800-369-4669**	913-319-3100
Vanguard East 1172 Azalea Garden Rd	Norfolk	VA	23502	**800-221-1264**	
Western Plastic Products Inc 8441 Monroe Ave	Stanton	CA	90680	**800-453-1881**	

AGRICULTURAL CHEMICALS

AGRICULTURAL MACHINERY & EQUIPMENT

SEE Farm Machinery & Equipment - Mfr ; Farm Machinery & Equipment - Whol

10 AGRICULTURAL PRODUCTS

SEE ALSO Seed Companies ; Fruit Growers ; Horse Breeders ; Horticultural Products Growers

	City	State	ZIP	Toll-Free	Phone
United Farmers Co-op (UFC) 705 E Fourth St PO Box 461	Winthrop	MN	55396	**866-998-3266**	507-647-6600

10-1 Cattle Ranches, Farms, Feedlots (Beef Cattle)

	City	State	ZIP	Toll-Free	Phone
Agri Beef Co 1555 Shoreline Dr Ste 320	Boise	ID	83702	**800-657-6305**	208-338-2500
AzTx Cattle Co PO Box 390	Hereford	TX	79045	**800-999-5065**	806-364-8871
Boise Valley Feeders LLC 1555 Shoreline Dr Ste 320	Boise	ID	83702	**800-657-6305**	208-338-2605
Cactus Feeders Inc 2209 W Seventh Ave	Amarillo	TX	79106	**877-698-7355**	806-373-2333
Coyote Lake Feedyard Inc 1287 FM 1731	Muleshoe	TX	79347	**800-299-3321**	806-946-3321
Dean Cluck Feedyard Inc 105 Dean Cluck Ave	Gruver	TX	79040	**888-458-4787**	806-733-5021
Dinklage Feedyards PO Box 274	Sidney	NE	69162	**888-343-5940**	308-254-5940
Friona Feedyard 2370 FM 3140	Friona	TX	79035	**800-658-6014**	806-265-3574
Friona Industries LP 500 S Taylor St Ste 601	Amarillo	TX	79101	**800-658-6014**	806-374-1811
Garden City Feed Yard 1805 W Annie Scheer Rd	Garden City	KS	67846	**800-272-4191**	620-275-4191
JR Simplot Co 999 W Main St Ste 1300	Boise	ID	83702	**800-832-8893**	208-336-2110
Littlefield Feedyard Farm to Market 37	Littlefield	TX	79339	**800-658-6014**	806-385-5141
PM Beef Group LLC 2850 Hwy 60 E	Windom	MN	56101	**800-622-5213**	507-831-2761
Swisher County Cattle Co Farm Market 214 Rd	Tulia	TX	79088	**800-658-6014**	806-627-4231

10-2 Dairy Farms

	City	State	ZIP	Toll-Free	Phone
Kreider Farms 1461 Lancaster Rd	Manheim	PA	17545	**888-665-4415**	717-665-4415
Marburger Farm Dairy Inc 1506 Mars Evans City Rd	Evans City	PA	16033	**800-331-1295**	724-538-4800

10-3 General Farms

	City	State	ZIP	Toll-Free	Phone
Agrex Inc 10975 Grandview Dr St Ste 200	Overland Park	KS	66210	**800-523-8181**	913-851-6300
Amana Colonies 622 46th Ave	Amana	IA	52203	**800-579-2294**	319-622-7622
Farmers Win Coop (FFC) 110 N Jefferson	Fredericksburg	IA	50630	**800-562-8389**	563-237-5324
FarmTek 1440 Field of Dreams Way	Dyersville	IA	52040	**800-327-6835**	563-875-2288
Gold-Eagle Co-op PO Box 280 PO Box 280	Goldfield	IA	50542	**800-825-3331**	
Plains Grain & Agronomy LLC 109 Third Ave	Enderlin	ND	58027	**800-950-2219**	701-437-2400
Star of the West Milling Co 121 E Tuscola St	Frankenmuth	MI	48734	**888-281-4161**	989-652-9971

10-4 Grain Farms

	City	State	ZIP	Toll-Free	Phone
Country Pride Co-op (CPC) 201 S Monroe PO Box 529	Winner	SD	57580	**888-325-7743**	605-842-2711
Erwin-Keith Inc 1529 Hwy 193	Wynne	AR	72396	**888-535-7333**	870-238-2079
Golden Grain Energy LLC 1822 43rd St SW	Mason City	IA	50401	**888-443-2676**	641-423-8525
Hoegemeyer Hybrids Inc 1755 Hoegemeyer Rd	Hooper	NE	68031	**800-245-4631**	402-654-3399
Moews Seed Co Inc 9821 IL Hwy 89	Granville	IL	60640	**800-663-9795**	815-339-2201
Morrow County Grain Growers Inc (MCGG) 350 N Main St	Lexington	OR	97839	**800-452-7396**	541-989-8221
Pioneer Hi-Bred International Inc PO Box 1000	Johnston	IA	50131	**800-247-6803**	515-535-3200
William F Renk & Sons Inc 6809 Wilburn Rd	Sun Prairie	WI	53590	**800-289-7365**	
Wyffels Hybrids Inc 13344 US Hwy 6	Geneseo	IL	61254	**800-369-7833**	309-944-8334

10-5 Hog Farms

	City	State	ZIP	Toll-Free	Phone
Cargill Inc 15407 McGinty Rd W	Wayzata	MN	55391	**800-227-4455**	952-742-7575

Company / Address	City	State	ZIP	Toll-Free	Phone
Hog Slat Inc PO Box 300	Newton Grove	NC	28366	**800-949-4647**	910-594-0219
PIC USA 100 Bluegrass Commons Blvd Ste 2200	Hendersonville	TN	37075	**800-325-3398**	615-265-2700
Seaboard Foods 9000 W 67th St Ste 200	Shawnee Mission	KS	66202	**800-262-7907**	913-261-2600
Tyson Foods Inc 2210 W Oaklawn Dr PO Box 2020 *NYSE: TSN*	Springdale	AR	72762	**800-643-3410**	479-290-4000

10-6 Mushroom Growers

Company / Address	City	State	ZIP	Toll-Free	Phone
Monterey Mushrooms Inc 260 Westgate Dr	Watsonville	CA	95076	**800-333-6874**	831-763-5300
Phillips Mushroom Farms Inc 1011 Kaolin Rd	Kennett Square	PA	19348	**800-722-8818**	610-925-0520
Sylvan Inc 90 Glade Dr	Kittanning	PA	16201	**866-352-7520**	724-543-3900

10-7 Poultry & Eggs Production

Company / Address	City	State	ZIP	Toll-Free	Phone
Amick Farms Inc 2079 Batesburg Hwy	Batesburg	SC	29006	**800-926-4257**	803-532-1400
Aviagen Group 5015 Bradford Dr	Huntsville	AL	35805	**800-826-9685**	256-890-3800
Cobb-Vantress Inc PO Box 1030	Siloam Springs	AR	72761	**800-748-9719**	479-524-3166
Cooper Farms 22348 County Rd 140 PO Box 547	Oakwood	OH	45873	**800-423-2765**	419-594-3325
Culver Duck Farms Inc PO Box 910	Middlebury	IN	46540	**800-825-9225**	574-825-9537
Echo Lake Farm Produce Co PO Box 279	Burlington	WI	53105	**800-888-3447**	
Foster Farms Inc PO Box 306 PO Box 457	Livingston	CA	95334	**800-255-7227**	
Maple Leaf Farms Inc PO Box 308	Milford	IN	46542	**800-348-2812**	574-658-4121
Michael Foods Inc 301 Carlson Pkwy Ste 400	Minnetonka	MN	55305	**800-328-5474**	952-258-4000
Perdue Farms Inc 31149 Old Ocean City Rd	Salisbury	MD	21804	**800-473-7383**	410-543-3000
Pilgrim's Corp 1770 Promontory Cir *NASDAQ: PPC*	Greeley	CO	80634	**800-321-1470**	
Simpson's Eggs Inc 5015 Hwy 218 E	Monroe	NC	28110	**800-726-1330**	704-753-1478
Tyson Foods Inc 2210 W Oaklawn Dr PO Box 2020 *NYSE: TSN*	Springdale	AR	72762	**800-643-3410**	479-290-4000
Wayne Farms LLC 4110 Continental Dr	Oakwood	GA	30566	**800-392-0844**	
Willmar Poultry Co, The (WPC) 3735 County Rd 5 SW	Willmar	MN	56201	**800-328-8849**	320-235-8850
Zacky Farms Inc 2020 SE Ave	Fresno	CA	93721	**800-888-0235**	562-641-2020
Zephyr Egg Co Inc 4622 Gall Blvd	Zephyrhills	FL	33542	**800-333-4415**	813-782-1521

10-8 Tree Nuts Growers

Company / Address	City	State	ZIP	Toll-Free	Phone
Mauna Loa Macadamia Nut Corp 16-701 Macadamia Rd *Cust Svc	Keaau	HI	96749	**888-628-6256***	808-966-8618
Sunnyland Farms Inc PO Box 8200	Albany	GA	31706	**800-999-2488**	

10-9 Vegetable Farms

Company / Address	City	State	ZIP	Toll-Free	Phone
Barnes Farming Corp 7840 Old Bailey Hwy	Spring Hope	NC	27882	**800-367-2799**	
Bolthouse Farms 7200 E Brundage Ln	Bakersfield	CA	93307	**800-467-4683**	
Buurma Farms Inc 3909 Kok Rd	Willard	OH	44890	**888-428-8762**	419-935-6411
Caruso Inc 3465 Hauck Rd	Cincinnati	OH	45241	**800-759-7659**	513-860-9200
Christopher Ranch 305 Bloomfield Ave	Gilroy	CA	95020	**800-779-1156**	408-847-1100
CROPP Co-op 1 Organic Way	LaFarge	WI	54639	**888-444-6455**	
D'Arrigo Bros Company of California Inc PO Box 850 *Cust Svc	Salinas	CA	93902	**800-995-5939***	831-455-4500
Earthbound Farm 1721 San Juan Hwy	San Juan Bautista	CA	95045	**800-690-3200**	831-623-7880
Fresh Express Inc 4757 The Grove Rd Ste 1212 *Cust Svc	Windermere	NC	34786	**800-242-5472***	
Greenheart Farms Inc 902 Zenon Way	Arroyo Grande	CA	93420	**800-549-5531**	805-481-2234
Grimmway Farms Inc PO Box 81498	Bakersfield	CA	93380	**800-301-3101**	
Harris Farms Inc 27366 W Oakland Ave	Coalinga	CA	93210	**800-311-6211**	559-884-2859
Hartung Bros Inc 708 Heartland Trl Ste 2000	Madison	WI	53717	**800-362-2522**	608-829-6000
McEntire Produce Inc 2040 American Italian Way	Columbia	SC	29209	**800-845-2334**	803-799-3388
Nash Produce Co 6160 S N Carolina 58	Nashville	NC	27856	**800-334-3032**	252-443-6011
Petrocco Farms 14110 Brighton Rd	Brighton	CO	80601	**888-876-2207**	303-659-6498
RDO Equipment Co 700 Seventh St S	Fargo	ND	58103	**800-726-5391**	877-444-7363
Tanimura & Antle Inc PO Box 4070	Salinas	CA	93912	**800-772-4542**	
Taylor & Fulton Inc 932 Fifth Ave W	Palmetto	FL	34221	**800-457-5577**	941-729-3883
West Coast Distributing Inc Commerce Pl 350 Main St	Boston	MA	02148	**800-235-3730**	781-665-9393
Wiers Farm Inc 4465 St Rt 103 S PO Box 385	Willard	OH	44890	**800-777-6243**	419-935-0131

11 AGRICULTURAL SERVICES

11-1 Crop Preparation Services

Company / Address	City	State	ZIP	Toll-Free	Phone
Erwin-Keith Inc 1529 Hwy 193	Wynne	AR	72396	**888-535-7333**	870-238-2079
Farmers Co-op Union, The 225 S Broadway PO Box 159	Sterling	KS	67579	**800-238-1843**	620-278-2141
Fresh Express Inc 4757 The Grove Rd Ste 1212 *Cust Svc	Windermere	NC	34786	**800-242-5472***	
Gruma Corp 1159 Cottonwood L Ste 200	Irving	TX	75038	**800-147-8629**	972-232-5000
Haines City Citrus Growers Assn (HCCGA) 8 Railroad Ave PO Box 337 *Sales	Haines City	FL	33844	**800-327-6676***	863-422-1174
Hazelnut Growers of Oregon 401 N 26th Ave	Cornelius	OR	97113	**800-273-4676**	503-648-4176
Index Fresh Inc 18184 Slover Ave	Bloomington	CA	92316	**800-352-6931**	909-877-0999
Mann Packing Company Inc PO Box 690	Salinas	CA	93902	**800-285-1002**	831-422-7405
Mariani Packing Company Inc 500 Crocker Dr	Vacaville	CA	95688	**800-231-1287**	707-452-2800
River Ranch Fresh Foods 1156 Abbott St	Salinas	CA	93901	**800-538-5868**	831-758-1390
Tracy-Luckey Company Inc 110 N Hicks St	Harlem	GA	30814	**800-476-4796**	706-556-6216

11-2 Livestock Improvement Services

Company / Address	City	State	ZIP	Toll-Free	Phone
ABS Global Inc 1525 River Rd PO Box 459 *Cust Svc	DeForest	WI	53532	**800-356-5331***	608-846-3721
Accelerated Genetics E 10890 Penny Ln	Baraboo	WI	53913	**800-451-9275**	608-356-8357
Alta California N8350 High Rd	Watertown	WI	53094	**800-932-2855**	920-261-5065
COBA/Select Sires Inc 1224 Alton Darby Creek Rd	Columbus	OH	43228	**800-837-2621**	614-878-5333
Cobb-Vantress Inc PO Box 1030	Siloam Springs	AR	72761	**800-748-9719**	479-524-3166
Dairy One 730 Warren Rd	Ithaca	NY	14850	**800-344-2697**	607-257-1272
Genex Co-op Inc/CRI 117 E Green Bay St	Shawano	WI	54166	**888-333-1783**	715-526-2141
Hagyard-Davidson-McGee Assoc PSC 4250 Iron Works Pike	Lexington	KY	40511	**888-323-7798**	859-255-8741
Reproduction Enterprises Inc 908 N Prairie Rd	Stillwater	OK	74075	**866-734-2855**	405-377-8037
SEK Genetics 9525 70th Rd	Galesburg	KS	66740	**800-443-6389**	

12 AIR CARGO CARRIERS

Company / Address	City	State	ZIP	Toll-Free	Phone
ABX Air Inc 145 Hunter Dr	Wilmington	OH	45177	**800-736-3973**	937-382-5591
Aeronet Worldwide 42 Corporate Pk	Irvine	CA	92606	**800-552-3869**	949-474-3000
Air Creebec Inc 101 Fecteau St	Val-d'or	QC	J9P0G4	**800-567-6567**	819-825-8375
Air North Charter & Training Ltd 150 Condor Rd	Whitehorse	YT	Y1A6E6	**800-661-0407**	867-668-2228
Ameriflight Inc 4700 Empire Ave Hngr 1	Burbank	CA	91505	**800-800-4538**	818-847-0000
Amerijet International Inc 2800 S Andrews Ave	Fort Lauderdale	FL	33316	**800-927-6059**	954-320-5300
Atlas Air Worldwide Holdings Inc 2000 Westchester Ave *NASDAQ: AAWW*	Purchase	NY	10577	**866-434-1617**	914-701-8000
Cathay Pacific Cargo 6040 Avion Dr Ste 338	Los Angeles	CA	90045	**800-628-6960**	310-417-0052
Cayman Airways Cargo Services 6103 NW 72nd Ave	Miami	FL	33166	**800-252-2746**	305-526-3190
China Airlines Cargo Sales & Service 11201 Aviation Blvd	Los Angeles	CA	90045	**800-778-4838**	310-646-4293
Delta Air Cargo PO Box 20559 Dept 670	Atlanta	GA	30320	**800-352-2737**	
Kalitta Flying Service 818 Willow Run Airport	Ypsilanti	MI	48198	**800-521-1590**	734-484-0088
Lynden Air Cargo LLC 6441 S Airpark Pl	Anchorage	AK	99502	**888-243-7248**	907-243-7248
MartinAire Aviation LLC 4553 Glenn Curtiss Dr	Addison	TX	75001	**866-557-1861**	972-349-5700
Qantas Airways Cargo 6555 W Imperial Hwy *General	Los Angeles	CA	90045	**800-227-0290***	310-665-2280
Service by Air Inc 222 Crossways Pk Dr	Woodbury	NY	11797	**800-243-5545**	

Company / Address	City	State	Zip	Toll-Free	Phone
Southwest Airlines Air Cargo 2702 Love Field Dr	Dallas	TX	75235	**800-533-1222**	
United Airlines Cargo PO Box 66100	Chicago	IL	60666	**800-822-2746**	
Virgin Atlantic Cargo JFK International Airport Bldg 15	Jamaica	NY	11430	**800-828-6822**	516-775-2600

13 AIR CHARTER SERVICES

SEE ALSO Helicopter Transport Services ; Aviation - Fixed-Base Operations

Company / Address	City	State	Zip	Toll-Free	Phone
Active Aero Group 2068 E St *Cust Svc	Belleville	MI	48111	**800-872-5387***	734-547-7200
Aero Air LLC 2050 NE 25th Ave	Hillsboro	OR	97124	**800-448-2376**	503-640-3711
Air Charter Team 4151 N Mulberry Dr Ste 250	Kansas City	MO	64116	**800-205-6610**	816-283-3280
Air Palm Springs 145 S Gene Autry Trl Ste 14	Palm Springs	CA	92262	**800-760-7774**	760-322-1104
Airbus Helicopters Canada 1100 Gilmore Rd PO Box 250	Fort Erie	ON	L2A5M9	**800-267-4999**	905-871-7772
AirFlite Inc 3250 AirFlite Way	Long Beach	CA	90807	**800-241-3548**	562-490-6200
American Air Charter Inc 577 Bell Ave	Chesterfield	MO	63005	**888-532-2710**	636-532-2707
Avstar Aviation Ltd 12 N Haven Ln	East Northport	NY	11731	**800-575-2359**	631-499-0048
Berry Aviation Inc 1807 Airport Dr	San Marcos	TX	78666	**800-229-2379**	512-353-2379
Charter Flight Inc 1928 S Blvd	Charlotte	NC	28208	**800-521-3148**	704-359-9124
Chrysler Aviation Inc (CAI) 7120 Hayvenhurst Ave Ste 309	Van Nuys	CA	91406	**800-995-0825**	818-989-7900
Clay Lacy Aviation 7435 Valjean Ave	Van Nuys	CA	91406	**800-423-2904**	818-989-2900
CSI Aviation Services Inc 3700 Rio Grand Blvd NW	Albuquerque	NM	87107	**800-765-9464**	505-761-9000
Era Helicopters LLC 600 Airport Service Rd PO Box 6550	Lake Charles	LA	70606	**800-256-2372**	337-478-6131
Exec Air Montana Inc 2430 Airport Rd	Helena	MT	59601	**800-513-2190**	406-442-2190
Executive Jet 4556 Airport Rd	Cincinnati	OH	45226	**877-356-5387**	513-979-6600
Fair Winds Air Charter Inc 2525 SE Witham Field Hngr 7	Stuart	FL	34996	**800-989-9665**	772-288-4130
Flightstar Corp 7 Airport Rd Willard Airport	Savoy	IL	61874	**800-747-4777**	217-351-7700
Hop-A-Jet Inc 5525 NW 15th Ave Ste 150	Fort Lauderdale	FL	33309	**800-556-6633**	954-771-5779
International Jet Aviation Services 8511 Aviator Ln	Centennial	CO	80112	**800-858-5891**	303-790-0414
Jet Resource Inc 455 Wilmer Ave Lunken Airport Hngr 27	Cincinnati	OH	45226	**800-404-5387**	513-871-1554
JetSuite 18952 MacArthur Blvd	Irvine	CA	92612	**866-779-7770**	
KaiserAir Inc 8735 Earhart Rd PO Box 2626	Oakland	CA	94621	**800-538-2625**	510-569-9622
Key Air LLC 3 Juliano Dr Ste 201	Oxford	CT	06478	**888-539-2471**	203-264-0605
Life Flight Network LLC 22285 Yellow Gate Ln NE	Aurora	OR	97002	**800-232-0911**	503-678-4364
LR Services 602 Hayden Cir	Allentown	PA	18109	**888-675-9650**	610-266-2500
Mayo Aviation Inc 7735 S Peoria St	Englewood	CO	80112	**800-525-0194**	303-792-4020
Million Air Interlink Inc 8501 Telephone Rd	Houston	TX	77061	**888-589-9059**	713-640-4000
New England Life Flight Inc 1727 Robins St Hangar	Bedford	MA	01730	**800-233-8998**	781-863-2213
Ohio Medical Transportation Inc 2827 W Dblin Granville Rd	Columbus	OH	43235	**877-633-3598**	614-734-8001
Pacific Coast Jet Charter Inc 10600 White Rock Rd	Rancho Cordova	CA	95670	**800-655-3599**	916-631-6507
Pentastar Aviation 7310 Highland Rd	Waterford	MI	48327	**800-662-9612**	248-666-3630
Planemasters Ltd 32 W 611 Tower Rd DuPage Airport	West Chicago	IL	60185	**800-994-6400**	630-513-2100
Premier Jets 2140 NE 25th Ave	Hillsboro	OR	97124	**800-635-8583**	503-640-2927
Priester Aviation 1061 S Wolf Rd	Wheeling	IL	60090	**888-323-7887**	847-537-1133
San Juan Airlines Co 4000 Airport Rd Ste A	Anacortes	WA	98221	**800-874-4434**	360-293-4691
Sentient Jet LLC 100 Grossman Dr Ste 400	Braintree	MA	02184	**866-602-0044**	781-763-0200
Skyservice Airlines Inc 9785 Ryan Ave	Dorval	QC	H9P1A2	**888-985-1402**	514-636-3300
Tavaero Jet Charter 7930 Airport Blvd	Houston	TX	77061	**800-343-3771**	713-643-5387
Thunder Airlines Ltd 310 Hector Dougall Way	Thunder Bay	ON	P7E6M6	**800-803-9943**	
Tulip City Air Service Inc 1581 S Washington Ave	Holland	MI	49423	**800-748-0515**	616-392-7831
Twin Cities Air Service 81 Airport Dr	Auburn	ME	04210	**800-564-3882**	
West Coast Aviation Services 19711 Campus Dr Ste 150	Santa Ana	CA	92707	**800-352-6153**	949-852-8340

14 AIR CONDITIONING & HEATING EQUIPMENT - COMMERCIAL/INDUSTRIAL

SEE ALSO Refrigeration Equipment - Mfr ; Air Conditioning & Heating Equipment - Residential

Company / Address	City	State	Zip	Toll-Free	Phone
Absolut Aire Inc 5496 N Riverview Dr	Kalamazoo	MI	49004	**800-804-4000**	269-382-1875
ACS Group 1100 E Woodfield Rd Ste 588	Schaumburg	IL	60173	**800-783-7835**	847-273-7700
Advantage Engineering Inc 525 E S- 18 Rd	Greenwood	IN	46142	**800-669-1282**	317-887-0729
American Coolair Corp 3604 Mayflower St	Jacksonville	FL	32205	**877-250-2822**	904-389-3646
Arctic Industries Inc 9731 NW 114th Way	Miami	FL	33178	**800-325-0123**	305-883-5581
Armstrong International Inc 2081 SE Ocean Blvd 4th Fl	Stuart	FL	34996	**866-738-5125**	772-286-7175
Auer Steel & Heating Supply Co 2935 W Silver Spring Dr	Milwaukee	WI	53209	**800-242-0406**	414-463-1234
Blissfield Manufacturing Co 626 Depot St *Cust Svc	Blissfield	MI	49228	**800-626-1772***	517-486-2121
Brainerd Compressor Rebuilders Inc 3034 Sandbrook St	Memphis	TN	38116	**800-228-4138**	
Bristol Compressors Inc 15185 Industrial Pk Rd	Bristol	VA	24202	**855-601-0894**	276-466-4121
Brooks Automation Inc Polycold Systems 3800 Lakeville Hwy	Petaluma	CA	94954	**800-698-6149**	707-769-7000
Bry-Air Inc 10793 SR 37 W	Sunbury	OH	43074	**877-427-9247**	740-965-2974
Carrier Corp 1 Carrier Pl	Farmington	CT	06034	**800-227-7437**	860-674-3000
CEI Enterprises Inc 245 WoodwaRd Rd SE	Albuquerque	NM	87102	**800-545-4034**	
ClimateMaster Inc 7300 SW 44th St	Oklahoma City	OK	73179	**800-299-9747**	405-745-6000
Cold Shot Chillers 14020 InterDr W	Houston	TX	77032	**800-473-9178**	281-227-8400
Colmac Coil Manufacturing Inc 370 N Lincoln St PO Box 571	Colville	WA	99114	**800-845-6778**	509-684-2595
Cummins Northwest LLC 811 SW Grady Way	Renton	WA	98055	**800-274-0336**	425-235-3400
Dehumidification Manufacturing Gp LLC 6609 Ave U	Houston	TX	77011	**866-736-8348**	713-939-1166
DiversiTech Inc 6650 Sugarloaf Pkwy Ste 100	Duluth	GA	30097	**800-995-2222**	678-542-3600
Dometic Corp 2320 Industrial Pkwy	Elkhart	IN	46516	**800-544-4881**	574-294-2511
Doucette Industries Inc (DII) 20 Leigh Dr	York	PA	17406	**800-445-7511**	717-845-8746
Drink More Water Store 7595-A Rickenbacker Dr	Gaithersburg	MD	20879	**800-697-2070**	
DRISTEEM Corp 14949 Technology Dr	Eden Prairie	MN	55344	**800-328-4447**	952-949-2415
DRS Sustainment Systems Inc 7375 Industrial Rd	Florence	KY	41042	**800-694-5005**	859-372-8204
Duro Dyne Corp 81 Spence St	Bay Shore	NY	11706	**800-899-3876**	631-249-9000
Fidelity Engineering Corp 25 Loveton Cir PO Box 2500	Sparks	MD	21152	**800-787-6000**	410-771-9400
Friedrich 10001 Reunion Pl Ste 500	San Antonio	TX	78216	**800-541-6645**	210-546-0500
Hastings HVAC Inc 3606 Yost Ave PO Box 669 *Cust Svc	Hastings	NE	68902	**800-228-4243***	402-463-9821
Henry Technologies 701 S Main St	Chatham	IL	62629	**800-964-3679**	217-483-2406
Howden Buffalo Inc 7909 Parklane Rd Ste 300	Columbia	SC	29223	**866-757-0908**	803-741-2700
ITW Vortec 10125 Carver Rd	Cincinnati	OH	45242	**800-441-7475**	513-891-7485
Layton Manufacturing Corp 825 Remsen Ave	Brooklyn	NY	11236	**800-545-8002**	718-498-6000
Lintern Corp 8685 Stn St	Mentor	OH	44060	**800-321-3638**	440-255-9333
Lomanco Inc 2101 W Main St	Jacksonville	AR	72076	**800-643-5596**	501-982-6511
Maradyne Corp 4540 W 160th St	Cleveland	OH	44135	**800-537-7444**	216-362-0755
Master-Bilt Products 908 Hwy 15 N	New Albany	MS	38652	**800-647-1284**	662-534-9061
Mermaid Manufacturing 2651 Park Windsor Dr Ste 203	Fort Myers	FL	33901	**800-330-3553**	239-418-0535
Midwest Towers Inc 1156 Hwy 19 East	Chickasha	OK	73018	**800-900-2190**	405-224-4622
Mobile Climate Control Corp 17103 State Rd 4 E	Goshen	IN	46528	**800-450-2211**	574-534-1516
Munters Corp 210 Sixth St PO Box 6428	Fort Myers	FL	33907	**800-843-5360**	239-936-1555
Munters Corp DHI 79 Monroe St *Sales	Amesbury	MA	01913	**800-843-5360***	978-241-1100
Niagara Blower Co Inc 673 Ontario St	Buffalo	NY	14207	**800-426-5169**	716-875-2000
Nordyne Inc 8000 Phoenix Pkwy	O'Fallon	MO	63368	**800-422-4328**	636-561-7300
Pacific Rim Mechanical 7655 Convoy Ct	San Diego	CA	92111	**800-891-4822**	858-974-6500
Packless Metal Hose Inc PO Box 20668	Waco	TX	76702	**800-347-4859**	254-666-7700
Phoenix Manufacturing Inc 3655 E Roeser Rd *Cust Svc	Phoenix	AZ	85040	**800-325-6952***	602-437-1034
Pittsburgh Plumbing Heating & Industrial (PPHI) 434 Melwood Ave	Pittsburgh	PA	15213	**800-445-4155**	412-622-8100

Classified Section

Company / Address	City	State	ZIP	Toll-Free	Phone
Proair LLC 28731 County Rd 6	Elkhart	IN	46514	**800-338-8544**	574-264-5494
Rama Corp 600 W Esplanade Ave	San Jacinto	CA	92583	**800-472-5670**	951-654-7351
Rink Systems Inc 1103 Hershey St	Albert Lea	MN	56007	**800-944-7930**	507-373-9175
Russell Food Equipment Ltd 1255 Venables St	Vancouver	BC	V6A3X6	**800-663-0707**	604-253-6611
San Jamar Inc 555 Koopman Ln	Elkhorn	WI	53121	**800-248-9826**	262-723-6133
Sealed Unit Parts Company Inc 2230 Landmark Pl	Allenwood	NJ	08720	**800-333-9125**	732-223-6644
Seasons-4 Inc 4500 Industrial Access Rd	Douglasville	GA	30134	**800-888-9900**	770-489-0716
Shield Air Solutions Inc 3708 Greenhouse Rd	Houston	TX	77084	**800-237-2095**	281-944-4300
Skuttle Manufacturing Co 101 Margaret St	Marietta	OH	45750	**800-848-9786**	740-373-9169
Temp-Control Mechanical Corp (TCM) 4800 N Ch Ave	Portland	OR	97217	**877-826-3828**	503-285-9851
Thermal Care Inc 7720 N Lehigh Ave	Niles	IL	60714	**888-828-7387**	847-966-2260
ThermoElectric Cooling America Corp 4048 W Schubert Ave	Chicago	IL	60639	**888-832-2872**	773-342-4900
Tom Barrow Co (TBC) 2800 Plant Atkinson Rd	Atlanta	GA	30339	**800-229-8226**	404-351-1010
Traulsen & Company Inc 4401 Blue Mound Rd	Fort Worth	TX	76106	**800-825-8220**	
Tutco Inc 500 Gould Dr	Cookeville	TN	38506	**877-262-4533**	931-432-4141
United CoolAir Corp 491 E Princess St	York	PA	17403	**877-905-1111**	717-843-4311
Watts Radiant Inc 4500 E Progress Pl	Springfield	MO	65803	**800-276-2419**	417-864-6108

15 AIR CONDITIONING & HEATING EQUIPMENT - RESIDENTIAL

SEE ALSO Air Conditioning & Heating Equipment - Commercial/Industrial

Company / Address	City	State	ZIP	Toll-Free	Phone
Airefco Inc 18755 SW Teton Ave PO Box 1349	Tualatin	OR	97062	**800-869-1349**	503-692-3210
Allied Air Enterprises 215 Metropolitan Dr	West Columbia	SC	29170	**800-448-5872**	
Amana Appliances Inc 2800 220th Trl *Cust Svc	Amana	IA	52204	**800-843-0304***	319-622-5511
Bard Mfg Co Inc 1914 Randolph Dr	Bryan	OH	43506	**800-563-5660**	419-636-1194
Friedrich 10001 Reunion Pl Ste 500	San Antonio	TX	78216	**800-541-6645**	210-546-0500
HDT Global 30500 Aurora Rd Ste 100	Solon	OH	44139	**800-969-8527**	216-438-6111
Kim Hotstart Manufacturing Co 5723 E Alki Ave	Spokane	WA	99212	**800-224-5550**	509-536-8660
Lennox Industries Inc 2100 Lake Pk Blvd *Cust Svc	Richardson	TX	75080	**800-953-6669***	
Lennox International Inc 2140 Lake Pk Blvd *NYSE: LII*	Richardson	TX	75080	**800-953-6669**	972-497-5000
Modine Manufacturing Co 1500 De Koven Ave *NYSE: MOD*	Racine	WI	53403	**800-828-4328**	262-636-1200
National System of Garage Ventilation Inc 714 N Church St PO Box 1186	Decatur	IL	62525	**800-728-8368**	217-423-7314
Simpson Mfg Company Inc 5956 W Las Positas Blvd *NYSE: SSD*	Pleasanton	CA	94588	**800-925-5099**	925-560-9000
Takagi Industrial Company USA Inc 500 Wald	Irvine	CA	92618	**888-882-5244**	949-770-7171
TPI Corp PO Box 4973	Johnson City	TN	37602	**800-682-3398**	
Ventamatic Ltd 100 Washington Rd	Mineral Wells	TX	76067	**800-433-1626**	
Whirlpool Corp 2000 N M-63 *NYSE: WHR*	Benton Harbor	MI	49022	**800-253-1301**	269-923-5000

AIR CONDITIONING EQUIPMENT - AUTOMOTIVE

AIR CONDITIONING EQUIPMENT - WHOL

SEE Plumbing, Heating, Air Conditioning Equipment & Supplies - Whol

16 AIR FARE CONSOLIDATORS

Company / Address	City	State	ZIP	Toll-Free	Phone
Brazilian Travel Service (BTS) 16 W 46th St 2nd Fl	New York	NY	10036	**800-342-5746**	212-764-6161
C & H International 4751 Wilshire Blvd Ste 201	Los Angeles	CA	90010	**800-833-8888**	323-933-2288
Centrav Inc 511 E Travelers Trl	Burnsville	MN	55337	**800-874-2033**	952-886-7650
GTT Global 600 Data Dr Ste 101	Plano	TX	75075	**800-485-6828**	972-239-5069
International Travel Systems Inc 64 Madison Ave	Wood-Ridge	NJ	07075	**800-258-0135**	201-727-0470
Sky Bird Travel & Tours Inc 24701 Swanson	Southfield	MI	48033	**888-759-2473**	248-372-4800
Skylink Travel 980 Ave of the Americas	New York	NY	10018	**800-247-6659**	212-573-8980
Solar Tours 1629 K St NW Ste 604	Washington	DC	20006	**800-388-7652**	202-861-5864
Trans Am Travel 4222 King St Ste 130	Alexandria	VA	22302	**800-822-7600**	703-998-7676

17 AIR PURIFICATION EQUIPMENT - HOUSEHOLD

SEE ALSO Appliances - Small - Mfr

Company / Address	City	State	ZIP	Toll-Free	Phone
Air Quality Engineering Inc 7140 Northland Dr N	Brooklyn Park	MN	55428	**888-883-3273**	763-531-9823
Airguard Industries Inc 100 River Ridge Cir	Jeffersonville	IN	47130	**800-999-3458**	866-247-4827
Dayton Reliable Air Filter Inc 2294 N Moraine Dr *Orders	Dayton	OH	45439	**800-699-0747***	
Gaylord Industries Inc 10900 SW Avery St	Tualatin	OR	97062	**800-547-9696**	503-691-2010
General Filters Inc 43800 Grand River Ave	Novi	MI	48375	**866-476-5101**	
Home Care Industries Inc ALFCO Div 1 Lisbon St *Cust Svc	Clifton	NJ	07013	**800-325-1908***	973-365-1600
Indoor Purification Systems Inc *Surround Air Div* 334 N Marshall Way Ste C	Layton	UT	84041	**888-812-1516**	801-547-1162
Koch Filter Corp 625 W Hill St	Louisville	KY	40208	**800-757-5624**	502-634-4796
Permatron Group 2020 Touhy Ave	Elk Grove Village	IL	60007	**800-882-8012**	847-434-1421
PuriTec 4705 S Durango Dr Ste 100-102	Las Vegas	NV	89147	**888-491-4100**	610-268-5420
Research Products Corp 1015 E Washington Ave	Madison	WI	53703	**800-334-6011**	608-257-8801
Spencer Turbine Co 600 Day Hill Rd	Windsor	CT	06095	**800-232-4321**	860-688-8361
Tjernlund Products Inc 1601 Ninth St	White Bear Lake	MN	55110	**800-255-4208**	651-426-2993
Vornado Air Circulation Systems Inc 415 E 13th St	Andover	KS	67002	**800-234-0604**	316-733-0035

18 AIR PURIFICATION EQUIPMENT - INDUSTRIAL

Company / Address	City	State	ZIP	Toll-Free	Phone
AAF International Corp 10300 Ormsby Pk Pl Ste 600	Louisville	KY	40223	**888-223-2003**	502-637-0011
Acme Engineering & Manufacturing Corp PO Box 978	Muskogee	OK	74402	**800-382-2263**	918-682-7791
Advantec MFS Inc 6723 Sierra Ct Ste A	Dublin	CA	94568	**800-334-7132**	925-479-0625
Aget Manufacturing Co 1408 E Church St	Adrian	MI	49221	**800-832-2438**	517-263-5781
Air Quality Engineering Inc 7140 Northland Dr N	Brooklyn Park	MN	55428	**888-883-3273**	763-531-9823
Airflow Systems Inc 11221 Pagemill Rd	Dallas	TX	75243	**800-818-6185**	214-503-8008
Airguard Industries Inc 100 River Ridge Cir	Jeffersonville	IN	47130	**800-999-3458**	866-247-4827
American Fan Company Inc 2933 Symmes Rd	Fairfield	OH	45014	**866-771-6266**	513-874-2400
Anguil Environmental Systems Inc 8855 N 55th St	Milwaukee	WI	53223	**800-488-0230**	414-365-6400
Baghouse & Industrial Sheet Metal Services Inc 1731 Pomona Rd	Corona	CA	92880	**888-224-4687**	951-272-6610
Beckett Air Inc 37850 Beckett Pkwy	North Ridgeville	OH	44039	**800-831-7839**	440-327-9999
Clarcor Inc 840 Crescent Ctr Dr Ste 600 *NYSE: CLC*	Franklin	TN	37067	**800-252-7267**	615-771-3100
Cleanroom Systems 7000 Performance Dr	North Syracuse	NY	13212	**800-825-3268**	315-452-7400
Clements National Co 6650 S Narragansett Ave	Chicago	IL	60638	**800-966-0016**	708-594-5890
Columbus Industries Inc 2938 SR-752	Ashville	OH	43103	**800-766-2552**	740-983-2552
CUNO Inc 400 Research Pkwy	Meriden	CT	06450	**800-243-6894**	203-237-5541
Disa Systems Inc 150 Transit Ave	Thomasville	NC	27360	**800-845-8508**	336-889-9187
Filtration Group Inc 912 E Washington St	Joliet	IL	60433	**877-603-1003**	815-726-4600
Flanders Corp 531 Flanders Filters Rd *OTC: FLDR*	Washington	NC	27889	**800-637-2803**	252-946-8081
Fuel Tech Inc 27601 Bella Vista Pkwy *NASDAQ: FTEK* ■ *General	Warrenville	IL	60555	**800-666-9688***	630-845-4500
Gaylord Industries Inc 10900 SW Avery St	Tualatin	OR	97062	**800-547-9696**	503-691-2010
General Filters Inc 43800 Grand River Ave	Novi	MI	48375	**866-476-5101**	
Great Lakes Filters 301 Arch Ave	Hillsdale	MI	49242	**800-521-8565**	
Greenheck Fan Corp 1100 Greenheck Dr PO Box 410	Schofield	WI	54476	**800-355-5354**	715-359-6171
Hartzell Fan Inc 910 S Downing St	Piqua	OH	45356	**800-336-3267**	937-773-7411
Home Care Industries Inc ALFCO Div 1 Lisbon St *Cust Svc	Clifton	NJ	07013	**800-325-1908***	973-365-1600
Honeyville Metal Inc 4200 S 900 W	Topeka	IN	46571	**800-593-8377**	260-593-2266
Houston Service Industries Inc 7901 Hansen Rd	Houston	TX	77061	**800-725-2291**	713-947-1623
Howden Buffalo Inc 7909 Parklane Rd Ste 300	Columbia	SC	29223	**866-757-0908**	803-741-2700
King Engineering Corp 3201 S State St *Cust Svc	Ann Arbor	MI	48106	**800-242-8871***	734-662-5691

Classified Section

Company / Address	City	State	ZIP	Toll-Free	Phone
Koch Filter Corp 625 W Hill St	Louisville	KY	40208	**800-757-5624**	502-634-4796
McIntire Co 745 Clark Ave	Bristol	CT	06010	**800-437-9247**	860-585-0050
Midwesco Filter Resources Inc 385 Battaile Dr	Winchester	VA	22601	**800-336-7300**	540-667-8500
NAO Inc 1284 E Sedgley Ave *Cust Svc	Philadelphia	PA	19134	**800-523-3495***	215-743-5300
National Filter Media Corp 691 North 400 West	Salt Lake City	UT	84103	**800-777-4248**	801-363-6736
Parker Hannifin Corp Finite Filtratio & Separation Div 500 Glaspie St	Oxford	MI	48371	**800-521-4357**	248-628-6400
Pneumech Systems Mfg LLC 201 Pneu Mech Dr	Statesville	NC	28625	**800-358-7374**	704-873-2475
Process Equipment Inc 2770 Welborn St PO Box 1607	Pelham	AL	35124	**888-663-2028**	205-663-5330
Purafil Inc 2654 Weaver Way	Doraville	GA	30340	**800-222-6367**	770-662-8545
Revcor Inc 251 E Edwards Ave	Carpentersville	IL	60110	**800-323-8261**	
Sly Inc 8300 Dow Cir	Strongsville	OH	44136	**800-334-2957**	440-891-3200
Sonic Air Systems Inc 1050 Beacon St	Brea	CA	92821	**800-827-6642**	714-255-0124
Spencer Turbine Co 600 Day Hill Rd	Windsor	CT	06095	**800-232-4321**	860-688-8361
Standard Filter Corp 5928 Balfour Ct	Carlsbad	CA	92008	**800-634-5837**	760-929-8559
Strobic Air Corp 160 Cassell Rd PO Box 144	Harleysville	PA	19438	**800-722-3267**	215-723-4700
Tjernlund Products Inc 1601 Ninth St	White Bear Lake	MN	55110	**800-255-4208**	651-426-2993
Tri-Dim Filter Corp 93 Industrial Dr	Louisa	VA	23093	**800-458-9835**	540-967-2600
Tuthill Vacuum & Blower Systems 4840 W Kearney St	Springfield	MO	65803	**800-825-6937**	417-865-8715
Waco 2546 Gen Armistead Ave	Norristown	PA	19403	**800-928-7159**	610-630-4800

19 AIR TRAFFIC CONTROL SERVICES

The Federal Aviation Administration (a US government agency) and NAV CANADA (a private, not-for-profit Canadian firm) provide air traffic services nationwide in the US and Canada, respectively. The types of services provided include aircraft routing, approach and departure instruction, and weather information.

Company / Address	City	State	ZIP	Toll-Free	Phone
Federal Aviation Administration Northwest Mountain Region 1601 Lind Ave SW	Renton	WA	98057	**800-220-5715**	425-227-2001
NAV CANADA 77 Metcalfe St PO Box 3411 Stn D	Ottawa	ON	K1P5L6	**800-876-4693**	613-563-5588

20 AIRCRAFT

SEE ALSO Airships

Company / Address	City	State	ZIP	Toll-Free	Phone
AeroVironment Inc 181 W Huntington Dr Ste 202 *NASDAQ: AVAV*	Monrovia	CA	91016	**888-833-2148**	626-357-9983
Airbus Helicopters Inc 2701 Forum Dr	Grand Prairie	TX	75052	**800-873-0001**	972-641-0000
Bell Helicopter Textron Inc 600 E Hurst Blvd (State Hwy 10)	Hurst	TX	76053	**888-874-5884**	817-280-2011
Bombardier Aerospace 400 Cote-Vertu Rd W *General	Dorval	QC	H4S1Y9	**866-855-5001***	514-855-5000
Dassault Falcon Jet Corp PO Box 2000	South Hackensack	NJ	07606	**800-527-2463**	201-440-6700
Diamond Aircraft Industries Inc 1560 Crumlin Sideroad	London	ON	N5V1S2	**888-359-3220**	519-457-4000
Epic AIR LLC 22590 Nelson Rd	Bend	OR	97701	**888-359-3742**	541-318-8849
Erickson Air-Crane Co 5550 SW Macadam Ave Ste 200	Portland	OR	97239	**877-870-5176**	503-505-5800
Lockheed Martin Corp 6801 Rockledge Dr *NYSE: LMT*	Bethesda	MD	20817	**866-562-2363**	301-897-6000
Mooney Aircraft Corp 165 Al Mooney Rd	Kerrville	TX	78028	**800-456-3033**	
Robinson Helicopter Co 2901 Airport Dr	Torrance	CA	90505	**800-905-0655**	310-539-0508
Teledyne Continental Motors Inc 2039 Broad St	Mobile	AL	36615	**800-718-3411**	251-438-3411
Texas Pneumatics Systems Inc 2404 Superior Dr	Arlington	TX	76013	**800-211-9690**	817-794-0068

21 AIRCRAFT ENGINES & ENGINE PARTS

Company / Address	City	State	ZIP	Toll-Free	Phone
AAR Corp 1100 N Wood Dale Rd 1 AAR Pl *NYSE: AIR*	Wood Dale	IL	60191	**800-422-2213**	630-227-2000
Abipa Canada Inc 2000, Blvd Dagenais ouest	Laval	QC	H7L5W2	**877-963-6888**	450-963-6888
Action Aircraft Lp 10570 Olympic Dr	Dallas	TX	75220	**800-909-7616**	214-351-1284
Aviation Systems of Northwest Florida Inc 175 E Olive Rd	Pensacola	FL	32514	**800-759-0953**	
Beacon Industries Inc 12300 Old Tesson Rd	Saint Louis	MO	63128	**800-454-7159**	314-487-7600
Continental Motors Inc 2039 Broad St	Mobile	AL	36615	**800-718-3411**	251-438-3411
Dart Aerospace Ltd 1270 Aberdeen St	Hawkesbury	ON	K6A1K7	**800-556-4166**	613-632-3336
Engine Components Inc (ECI) 9503 Middlex	San Antonio	TX	78217	**800-324-2359**	210-820-8101
Flight Dimensions International Inc 4835 Cordell Ave Ste 150	Bethesda	MD	20814	**866-235-6870**	301-634-8201
Garsite LLC 539 S Tenth St	Kansas City	KS	66105	**888-427-7483**	913-342-5600
Gros-Ite Industries 1790 New Britain Ave	Farmington	CT	06032	**877-777-4778**	860-677-2603
Hartzell Engine Technologies LLC 2900 Selma Hwy	Montgomery	AL	36108	**877-359-5355**	334-386-5400
Insight Technology Inc 9 Akira Way	Londonderry	NH	03053	**866-509-2040**	603-626-4800
Institute For Natural Resources PO Box 5757	Concord	CA	94524	**877-246-6336**	925-609-2820
Kalitta Charters LLC 843 Willow Run Airport	Ypsilanti	MI	48198	**800-525-4882**	734-544-3400
Kreisler Mfg Corp 180 Van Riper Ave	Elmwood Park	NJ	07407	**888-750-5834**	201-791-0700
Navhouse Corp 10 Loring Dr	Bolton	ON	L7E1J9	**877-628-6667**	905-857-8102
Pratt & Whitney Canada Inc 1000 Marie-Victorin Blvd	Longueuil	QC	J4G1A1	**800-268-8000**	450-677-9411
Rolls-Royce North America 1875 Explorer St Ste 200	Reston	VA	20190	**888-269-2377**	703-834-1700
Sandel Avionics Inc 2401 Dogwood Way	Vista	CA	92081	**877-726-3357**	760-727-4900
Senior Aerospace Ketema Div 790 Greenfield Dr	El Cajon	CA	92021	**800-669-6820**	619-442-3451
Turbomeca USA Inc 2709 N Forum Dr	Grand Prairie	TX	75052	**800-662-6322**	972-606-7600
Vector Aerospace Helicopter Services Inc 22378 Billie Blackmon Rd Ste 2100	Andalusia	AL	36421	**888-729-2276**	604-276-7600

22 AIRCRAFT PARTS & AUXILIARY EQUIPMENT

SEE ALSO Precision Machined Products

Company / Address	City	State	ZIP	Toll-Free	Phone
AAR Composites 14201 Myerlake Cir	Clearwater	FL	33760	**800-422-2213**	727-539-8585
AAR Corp 1100 N Wood Dale Rd 1 AAR Pl *NYSE: AIR*	Wood Dale	IL	60191	**800-422-2213**	630-227-2000
Advanced Technology Co 2858 E Walnut St	Pasadena	CA	91107	**800-447-2442**	626-449-2696
Aerospace Products International (API) 3778 Distriplex Dr N	Memphis	TN	38118	**888-274-2497**	901-365-3470
Arkwin Industries Inc 686 Main St	Westbury	NY	11590	**800-284-2551**	516-333-2640
Avcorp Industries Inc 10025 River Way	Delta	BC	V4G1M7	**866-781-3111**	604-582-6677
CEF Industries Inc 320 S Church St	Addison	IL	60101	**800-888-6419**	630-628-2299
CRS Jet Spares Inc 6701 NW 12th Ave	Fort Lauderdale	FL	33309	**800-338-5387**	954-972-2807
Curtiss-Wright Corp 10 Waterview Blvd 2nd Fl *NYSE: CW*	Parsippany	NJ	07054	**855-449-0995**	973-541-3700
Esterline Interface Technologies 600 W Wilbur Ave	Coeur d'Alene	ID	83815	**800-444-5923**	208-765-8000
Fairchild Controls Corp 540 Highland St	Frederick	MD	21701	**800-695-5378**	301-228-3400
FletchAir Inc 103 Turkey Run Ln	Comfort	TX	78013	**800-329-4647**	830-995-5900
General Electrodynamics Corporation Inc 8000 Calendar Rd	Arlington	TX	76001	**800-551-6038**	817-572-0366
Global Ground Support LLC 540 Old Hwy 56	Olathe	KS	66061	**888-780-0303**	913-780-0300
Goodrich Corp Aircraft Interior Products Div 3420 S Seventh St	Phoenix	AZ	85040	**877-808-7575**	602-243-2200
Hartzell Propeller Inc 1 Propeller Pl	Piqua	OH	45356	**800-942-7767**	937-778-4200
Honeywell Aerospace 3520 Westmoor St	South Bend	IN	46628	**800-707-4555**	574-231-2000
L-3 Communications Integrated Systems 10001 Jack Finney Blvd	Greenville	TX	75402	**877-282-1168**	903-455-3450
Middle River Aircraft Systems (MRAS) 103 Chesapeake Pk Plaza	Baltimore	MD	21220	**877-432-3272**	410-682-1500
STS Component Solutions LLC 2910 SW 42 Ave	Palm City	FL	34990	**888-777-2960**	
Tronair Inc 1740 Eber Rd	Holland	OH	43528	**800-426-6301**	419-866-6301
United Tool & Die Co 1 Carney Rd	West Hartford	CT	06110	**877-262-0336**	860-246-6531
Vibro-Meter Inc 144 Harvey Rd	Londonderry	NH	03053	**800-842-4291**	603-669-0940

23 AIRCRAFT RENTAL

SEE ALSO Aviation - Fixed-Base Operations

Company / Address	City	State	ZIP	Toll-Free	Phone
Apple Discount Drugs 404 N Fruitland Blvd	Salisbury	MD	21801	**800-424-8401**	410-749-8401
Armour Transportation Systems Inc 689 Edinburgh Dr	Moncton	NB	E1E2L4	**800-561-7987**	506-857-0205
Bigrentz Inc 1063 Mcgaw Ave Ste 200	Irvine	CA	92614	**855-999-5438**	
FlexShopper Inc 2700 N Military Trl Ste 200	Boca Raton	FL	33431	**855-353-9289**	
Lease Equity Appreciation Fund I LP 110 S Poplar St Ste 101	Wilmington	DE	19801	**800-819-5556**	
Northern Jet Management 5500 44th St SE	Grand Rapids	MI	49512	**800-462-7709**	616-336-4800
Sunwest Aviation Ltd 230 Aviation Pl Ne	Calgary	AB	T2E7G1	**888-291-4566**	403-275-8121
Swiftlift Inc 820 Phillips Rd	Victor	NY	14564	**888-292-3101**	585-742-2160
Trench Plate Rental Co 13217 Laureldale Ave	Downey	CA	90242	**800-821-4478**	

Name / Address	City	State	ZIP	Toll-Free	Phone
Us Adventure Rv 5120 n brady st	Davenport	IA	52806	**877-768-4678**	
Valley Supply & Equipment Company Inc 1109 Middle River Rd	Baltimore	MD	21220	**800-633-5077**	

24 AIRCRAFT SERVICE & REPAIR

Name / Address	City	State	ZIP	Toll-Free	Phone
AAR Aircraft Component Services 747 Zeckendorf Blvd	Garden City	NY	11530	**800-422-2213**	516-222-9000
AAR Corp 1100 N Wood Dale Rd 1 AAR Pl *NYSE: AIR*	Wood Dale	IL	60191	**800-422-2213**	630-227-2000
AAR Landing Gear Services 9371 NW 100th St	Miami	FL	33178	**800-422-2213**	305-887-4027
American Avionics 7023 Perimeter Rd S *Sales	Seattle	WA	98108	**800-518-5858***	206-763-8530
Barfield Inc 4101 NW 29th St	Miami	FL	33142	**800-321-1039**	305-894-5300
Cutter Aviation 2802 E Old Tower Rd	Phoenix	AZ	85034	**800-234-5382**	602-273-1237
Duncan Aviation Inc 3701 Aviation Rd	Lincoln	NE	68524	**800-228-4277**	402-475-2611
Elliott Aviation Inc 6601 74th Ave PO Box 100	Milan	IL	61264	**800-447-6711**	309-799-3183
Emteq Inc 5349 S Emmer Dr	New Berlin	WI	53151	**888-679-6170**	262-679-6170
Honeywell Aerospace 3520 Westmoor St	South Bend	IN	46628	**800-707-4555**	574-231-2000
Jet Aviation 112 Charles A Lindbergh Dr	Teterboro	NJ	07608	**800-538-0832**	201-288-8400
Kfs Inc 1840 West Airfield Dr	Dallas	TX	75261	**800-364-4115**	817-488-4115
L-3 Communications Flight International Aviation LLC 1 Lear Dr	Newport News	VA	23602	**800-358-4685**	757-886-5500
McKinley Air Transport Inc 5430 Lauby Rd *General	North Canton	OH	44720	**800-225-6446***	330-499-3316
Million Air Interlink Inc 8501 Telephone Rd	Houston	TX	77061	**888-589-9059**	713-640-4000
Priester Aviation 1061 S Wolf Rd	Wheeling	IL	60090	**888-323-7887**	847-537-1133
Rolls-Royce Engine Services Inc 7200 Earhart Rd	Oakland	CA	94621	**888-255-4766**	510-613-1000
Serco Inc 1818 Library St Ste 1000	Reston	VA	20190	**866-628-6458**	703-939-6000
Sierra Industries Ltd 122 Howard Langford Dr	Uvalde	TX	78801	**888-835-9377**	830-278-4481
Summit Aviation Inc 4200 Summit Bridge Rd PO Box 258	Middletown	DE	19709	**800-441-9343**	302-834-5400
Tulsair Beechcraft Inc 3207 N Sheridan Rd	Tulsa	OK	74115	**800-331-4071**	918-835-7651
West Star Aviation Inc 796 Heritage Way	Grand Junction	CO	81506	**800-255-4193**	970-243-7500

25 AIRLINES - COMMERCIAL

SEE ALSO Air Cargo Carriers ; Air Charter Services ; Airlines - Frequent Flyer Programs

Name / Address	City	State	ZIP	Toll-Free	Phone
Aeroflot Russian International Airlines 10 Rockefeller Plaza Ste 1015	New York	NY	10020	**866-879-7647**	212-944-2300
Air India 570 Lexington Ave 15th Fl	New York	NY	10022	**800-223-7776**	
Air Sunshine Inc PO Box 22237	Fort Lauderdale	FL	33335	**800-435-8900**	954-434-8900
Air Tahiti Nui 1990 E Grand Ave *Cust Svc	El Segundo	CA	90245	**877-824-4846***	310-662-1860
All Nippon Airways Company Ltd 2050 W 190th St Ste 100	Torrance	CA	90504	**800-235-9262**	
American Airlines Inc 4333 Amon Carter Blvd	Fort Worth	TX	76155	**800-433-7300**	817-963-1234
Bearskin Airlines 1475 W Walsh St	Thunder Bay	ON	P7E4X6	**800-465-2327**	807-577-1141
Bering Air 1470 Sepalla Dr PO Box 1650	Nome	AK	99762	**800-478-5422**	907-443-5464
Bulloch & Bulloch Inc 309 Cash Memorial Blvd	Forest Park	GA	30297	**800-339-8177**	404-762-5063
Cape Air 660 Barnstable Rd	Hyannis	MA	02601	**800-227-3247**	508-771-6944
Cayman Airways Ltd 91 Owen Roberts Dr	Grand Cayman	KY	10092	**800-422-9626**	345-949-8200
Czech Airlines 1 Penn Plaza Ste 1416	New York	NY	10001	**855-359-2932**	
Delta Air Lines Inc 1030 Delta Blvd *NYSE: DAL*	Atlanta	GA	30354	**800-221-1212**	404-715-2600
El Al Israel Airlines Inc 15 E 26th St	New York	NY	10010	**800-223-6700**	212-852-0600
EVA Airways 200 N Sepulveda Blvd Ste 1600	El Segundo	CA	90245	**800-695-1188**	310-362-6600
Great Lakes Aviation Ltd 1022 Airport Pkwy *OTC: GLUX*	Cheyenne	WY	82001	**800-554-5111**	307-432-7000
Hawaiian Airlines Inc 3375 Koapaka St Ste G350	Honolulu	HI	96819	**800-367-5320**	808-835-3700
Kenmore Air Harbor Inc 6321 NE 175th St	Kenmore	WA	98028	**866-435-9524**	425-486-1257
Korean Air 6101 W Imperial Hwy	Los Angeles	CA	90045	**800-438-5000**	310-417-5200
Malaysia Airlines 100 N Sepulveda Blvd Ste 1710 *Resv	El Segundo	CA	90245	**800-552-9264***	310-535-9288
New England Airlines Inc 56 Airport Rd	Westerly	RI	02891	**800-243-2460**	
Pacific Wings 1 Keolani Pl Ste 30	Kahului	HI	96732	**888-575-4546**	808-873-0877
Pakistan International Airlines Corp (PIA) 1200 New Jersey Ave SE	Washington	DC	20590	**800-578-6786**	
Peninsula Airways Inc 6100 Boeing Ave	Anchorage	AK	99502	**800-448-4226**	907-771-2500
PSA Airlines Inc 3400 Terminal Dr *Resv	Vandalia	OH	45377	**800-235-0986***	937-665-2876
Qantas Airways Ltd 6080 Ctr Dr Ste 400	Los Angeles	CA	90045	**800-227-4500**	310-726-1400
Scandinavian Airlines System (SAS) 301 Route 17 N Ste 500	Rutherford	NJ	07070	**800-221-2350**	800-437-5807
Silver Airways Corp 1100 Lee Wagener Blvd Ste 201	Fort Lauderdale	FL	33315	**844-674-5837**	954-985-1500
Singapore Airlines Ltd 222 N Sepulveda Blvd Ste 1600	El Segundo	CA	90245	**800-742-3333**	310-647-1922
Skyservice Airlines Inc 9785 Ryan Ave	Dorval	QC	H9P1A2	**888-985-1402**	514-636-3300
South African Airways 1200 S Pine Island Rd Ste 650	Plantation	FL	33324	**800-722-9675**	954-769-5000
Southwest Airlines Co 2702 Love Field Dr PO Box 36611 *NYSE: LUV*	Dallas	TX	75235	**800-435-9792**	214-792-4000
Spirit Airlines Inc 2800 Executive Way *NASDAQ: SAVE*	Miramar	FL	33025	**800-772-7117**	
SriLankan Airlines 379 Thornall St 6th Fl	Edison	NJ	08837	**877-915-2652**	732-205-0017
Sun Country Airlines Inc 1300 Mendota Heights Rd	Mendota Heights	MN	55120	**800-359-6786**	651-681-3900
Thai Airways International Ltd 222 N Sepulveda Blvd Ste 100	El Segundo	CA	90245	**800-426-5204**	310-640-0097
Virgin Atlantic Airways Ltd 747 Belden Ave	Norwalk	CT	06850	**888-747-7474**	800-821-5438
WestJet Airlines Ltd 22 Aerial Pl NE *TSE: WJA*	Calgary	AB	T2E3J1	**888-293-7853**	403-444-2600

26 AIRLINES - FREQUENT FLYER PROGRAMS

Name / Address	City	State	ZIP	Toll-Free	Phone
Aer Lingus Airlines Gold Cir Club 300 Jericho Quad Ste 130	Jericho	NY	11753	**800-474-7424**	
British Airways Executive Club PO Box 300743	Jamaica	NY	11430	**800-452-1201**	
Continental Airlines Inc 900 Grand Plz Dr	Houston	TX	77067	**800-621-7467**	713-952-1630
Czech Airlines OK Plus 147 W 35th St Ste 1505	New York	NY	10001	**855-359-2932**	
Hawaiian Airlines HawaiianMiles PO Box 30008	Honolulu	HI	96820	**877-426-4537**	
Icelandair North America 1900 Crown Colony Dr	Quincy	MA	02169	**800-223-5500**	
Korean Air Skypass 1813 Wilshire Blvd Ste 300	Los Angeles	CA	90057	**800-438-5000**	213-484-1900
Kuwait Airways Oasis Club 400 Kelby St	Fort Lee	NJ	07024	**800-458-9248**	201-582-9222
Miles & More PO Box 946	Santa Clarita	CA	91380	**800-581-6400**	
Singapore Airlines KrisFlyer 380 World Way Ste 336B	Los Angeles	CA	90045	**800-742-3333**	310-646-6221
Virgin Atlantic Flying Club 747 Belden Ave	Norwalk	CT	06850	**800-365-9500**	

27 AIRPORTS

SEE ALSO Ports & Port Authorities

Listings for airports in the US and Canada are organized by states and provinces, and then by city names within those groupings.

Name / Address	City	State	ZIP	Toll-Free	Phone
Akron-Canton Airport 5400 Lauby Rd NW	North Canton	OH	44720	**888-434-2359**	330-499-4221
Asheville Regional Airport 61 Terminal Dr Ste 1	Fletcher	NC	28732	**866-719-3910**	828-684-2226
Augusta Regional Airport - Bush Field (AGS) 1501 Aviation Way	Augusta	GA	30906	**866-289-9673**	706-798-3236
Augusta State Airport 75 Airport Rd	Augusta	ME	04330	**800-654-3131**	207-626-2306
Baltimore/Washington International Thurgood Marshall Airport (BWI) PO Box 8766	Baltimore	MD	21240	**800-435-9294**	410-859-7111
Bangor International Airport 287 Godfrey Blvd	Bangor	ME	04401	**866-359-2264**	207-992-4600
Baton Rouge Metropolitan Airport 9430 Jackie Cochran Dr Ste 300	Baton Rouge	LA	70807	**877-359-2538**	225-355-0333
Bishop International Airport G-3425 W Bristol Rd	Flint	MI	48507	**800-433-7300**	810-235-6560
Blue Grass Airport 4000 Terminal Dr	Lexington	KY	40510	**800-800-4000**	859-425-3100
Buffalo Niagara International Airport 4200 Genesee St	Cheektowaga	NY	14225	**877-359-2642**	716-630-6000
Calgary International Airport 2000 Airport Rd NE	Calgary	AB	T2E6W5	**877-254-7427**	403-735-1200
Capital Region International Airport 4100 Capital City Blvd	Lansing	MI	48906	**866-841-4900**	517-321-6121
Chicago Midway Airport 5700 S Cicero Ave	Chicago	IL	60638	**800-832-6352**	773-838-0600
Dallas Love Field 8008 Cedar Springs Rd LB 16	Dallas	TX	75235	**877-359-8474**	214-670-5683
Dallas-Fort Worth International Airport (DFW) 3200 E Airfield Dr PO Box 619428	Dallas	TX	75261	**800-252-7522**	972-973-8888
Dayton International Airport 3600 Terminal Dr Ste 300	Vandalia	OH	45377	**877-359-3291**	937-454-8200
Denver International Airport 8500 Pena Blvd	Denver	CO	80249	**800-247-2336**	303-342-2000

	City	State	ZIP	Toll-Free	Phone
Des Moines International Airport 5800 Fleur Dr	Des Moines	IA	50321	**877-686-0029**	515-256-5050
Du Page Airport Authority 2700 International Dr Ste 200	West Chicago	IL	60185	**800-208-5690**	630-584-2211
Duluth International Airport 4701 Grinden Dr	Duluth	MN	55811	**855-787-2227**	218-727-2968
Edmonton International Airport 8340 Sparrow Crescent	Edmonton	AB	T9E8B7	**800-854-9517**	780-800-0622
Flagstaff Pulliam Airport 6200 S Pulliam Dr	Flagstaff	AZ	86001	**800-463-1389**	928-556-1234
Fort Lauderdale/Hollywood International Airport 100 Aviation Blvd	Fort Lauderdale	FL	33315	**866-682-2258**	954-359-1200
Fort Smith Regional Airport 6700 McKennon Blvd Ste 200	Fort Smith	AR	72903	**800-992-7433**	479-452-7000
Fresno Yosemite International Airport 5175 E Clinton Way	Fresno	CA	93727	**800-244-2359**	559-621-4500
Gerald R Ford International Airport 5500 44th St SE	Grand Rapids	MI	49512	**866-289-9673**	616-233-6000
Greater Rockford Airport 60 Airport Dr	Rockford	IL	61109	**800-517-2000**	815-969-4000
Greenville-Spartanburg Airport (GSP) 2000 GSP Dr Ste 1	Greer	SC	29651	**800-331-1212**	864-877-7426
Harrisburg International Airport 1 Terminal Dr Ste 300	Middletown	PA	17057	**888-235-9442**	717-948-3900
Hartsfield-Jackson Atlanta International Airport 6000 N Terminal Pkwy Ste 4000	Atlanta	GA	30320	**800-897-1910**	404-530-6600
Hattiesburg-Laurel Regional Airport 1002 Terminal Dr	Moselle	MS	39459	**800-433-7300**	601-649-2444
Hot Springs Memorial Field 525 Airport Rd	Hot Springs	AR	71913	**800-992-7433**	501-321-6750
Jackson International Airport 100 International Dr Ste 300	Jackson	MS	39208	**800-227-7368**	601-939-5631
Juneau International Airport 1873 Shell Simmons Dr Ste 200	Juneau	AK	99801	**800-478-4176**	907-789-7821
Kahului Airport 1 Kahului Airport Rd	Kahului	HI	96732	**800-321-3712**	808-872-3830
Kona International Airport 73-200 Kupipi St	Kailua-Kona	HI	96740	**800-321-3712**	808-327-9520
Lambert Saint Louis International Airport 10701 Lambert International Blvd PO Box 10212	Saint Louis	MO	63145	**855-787-2227**	314-426-8000
Lehigh Valley International Airport 3311 Airport Rd	Allentown	PA	18109	**800-359-5842**	610-266-6000
Long Beach Airport LGB 4100 Donald Douglas Dr	Long Beach	CA	90808	**800-331-1212**	562-570-2600
Long Island MacArthur Airport 100 Arrival Ave Ste 100	Ronkonkoma	NY	11779	**888-542-4776**	631-467-3300
McCarran International Airport 5757 Wayne Newton Blvd PO Box 11005	Las Vegas	NV	89119	**888-261-4414**	702-261-5211
Miami International Airport 2261 NW 66th Ave Bldg 702 Ste 217	Miami	FL	33122	**800-825-5642**	305-876-7000
Mobile Regional Airport 8400 Airport Blvd	Mobile	AL	36608	**800-357-5373**	251-633-4510
Newark Liberty International Airport 1 Hotel Rd	Newark	NJ	07114	**888-397-4636**	973-961-6007
Northwest Arkansas Regional Airport 1 Airport Blvd Ste 100	Bentonville	AR	72712	**800-433-7300**	479-205-1000
O'Hare International Airport *Dept of Aviation* PO Box 66142	Chicago	IL	60666	**800-832-6352**	773-686-3700
Ottawa Macdonald-Cartier International Airport 1000 Airport PkwyPrivate Ste 2500	Ottawa	ON	K1V9B4	**888-901-6222**	613-248-2000
Palm Springs International Airport 3200 E Tahquitz Canyon Way	Palm Springs	CA	92262	**800-847-4389**	760-318-3800
Pensacola Gulf Coast Regional Airport 2430 Airport Blvd Ste 225	Pensacola	FL	32504	**800-874-6580**	850-436-5000
Philadelphia International Airport 8000 Essington Ave	Philadelphia	PA	19153	**800-514-0301**	215-937-6937
Pittsburgh International Airport Landside Terminal Fourth Fl Mezz PO Box 12370	Pittsburgh	PA	15231	**888-429-5377**	412-472-3525
Portland International Airport 7000 NE Airport Way	Portland	OR	97218	**800-547-8411**	503-460-4234
Raleigh-Durham International Airport PO Box 80001	Raleigh	NC	27623	**800-252-7522**	919-840-2123
Rapid City Regional Airport 4550 Terminal Rd Ste 102	Rapid City	SD	57703	**888-279-2135**	605-393-9924
Reno-Tahoe International Airport 2001 E Plumb Ln	Reno	NV	89502	**877-736-6359**	775-328-6400
Rhode Island Airport Corp 2000 Post Rd Warwick	Warwick	RI	02886	**888-268-7222**	401-691-2000
Salt Lake City International Airport 776 N Terminal Dr PO Box 145550	Salt Lake City	UT	84116	**800-595-2442**	801-575-2400
San Antonio International Airport (SAT) 9800 Airport Blvd Rm 2041	San Antonio	TX	78216	**800-237-6639**	210-207-3411
San Francisco International Airport PO Box 8097	San Francisco	CA	94128	**800-435-9736**	650-821-8211
Santa Fe Municipal Airport (SAF) 121 Aviation Dr PO Box 909	Santa Fe	NM	87504	**866-773-2587**	505-955-2900
Sarasota-Bradenton International Airport 6000 Airport Cir	Sarasota	FL	34243	**800-711-1712**	941-359-5200
Southwest Florida International Airport 11000 Terminal Access Rd Ste 8671	Fort Myers	FL	33913	**800-359-6786**	239-590-4800
Spokane International Airport 9000 W Airport Dr	Spokane	WA	99224	**800-776-5263**	509-455-6455
Tampa International Airport 4100 George J Bean Pkwy PO Box 22287	Tampa	FL	33607	**866-289-9673**	813-870-8700
Tucson International Airport 7250 S Tucson Blvd	Tucson	AZ	85706	**800-758-1874**	520-573-8100
Tupelo Regional Airport 105 Lemons Dr	Tupelo	MS	38801	**877-777-4778**	662-823-4359
Wilkes-Barre/Scranton International Airport 100 Terminal Dr Ste 1	Avoca	PA	18641	**877-235-9287**	570-602-2000
Winnipeg James Armstrong Richardson International Airport 2000 Wellington Ave Rm 249 Administration Bldg.	Winnipeg	MB	R3H1C2	**855-500-6589**	204-987-9400
Youngstown-Warren Regional Airport 1453 Youngstown-Kingsville Rd NE	Vienna	OH	44473	**800-444-1440**	330-856-1537

28 AIRSHIPS

SEE ALSO Aircraft

	City	State	ZIP	Toll-Free	Phone
Cameron Balloons US PO Box 3672	Ann Arbor	MI	48106	**866-423-6178**	734-426-5525
ILC Dover Inc 1 Moonwalker Rd	Frederica	DE	19946	**800-631-9567**	302-335-3911

29 ALL-TERRAIN VEHICLES

SEE ALSO Sporting Goods

	City	State	ZIP	Toll-Free	Phone
American Honda Motor Company Inc 1919 Torrance Blvd	Torrance	CA	90501	**800-999-1009**	310-783-3170
Cycle Country Access Corp 205 N Depot St PO Box 107 *Sales	Fox Lake	WI	53933	**800-841-2222***	
Kawasaki Motors Corp USA PO Box 25252	Santa Ana	CA	92799	**866-802-9381**	949-770-0400
Ontario Drive & Gear Ltd (ODG) 220 Bergey Ct	New Hamburg	ON	N3A2J5	**877-274-6288**	519-662-2840
Recreatives Industries Inc 60 Depot St	Buffalo	NY	14206	**800-255-2511**	716-855-2226
Yamaha Motor Corp USA 6555 Katella Ave *Cust Svc	Cypress	CA	90630	**800-656-7695***	

30 AMBULANCE SERVICES

	City	State	ZIP	Toll-Free	Phone
Abbott Ambulance Inc 2500 Abbott Pl	Saint Louis	MO	63143	**888-974-7035**	314-768-1000
Acadian Ambulance Service Inc 300 Hopkins St	Lafayette	LA	70501	**800-259-3333**	
American Medical Response (AMR) 6200 S Syracuse Way Ste 200	Greenwood Village	CO	80111	**877-244-4890**	303-495-1200
Danville Ambulance Service Office 12 A St	Danville	PA	17821	**877-721-3671**	570-275-3031
Emergency Ambulance Service International Inc 3200 E Birch St Ste A	Brea	CA	92821	**800-400-0689**	714-990-1331
Global Air Response 5919 Approach Rd	Sarasota	FL	34238	**800-631-6565**	
Lifenet Inc 6225 St Michaels Dr	Texarkana	TX	75503	**800-832-6395**	903-832-8531
MedjetAssist 3500 Colonnade Pkwy Ste 500 PO Box 43099	Birmingham	AL	35243	**800-527-7478**	205-595-6626
Mercy Flights Inc 2020 Milligan Way	Medford	OR	97504	**800-903-9000**	541-858-2600
Mission Ambulance 1055 E Third St	Corona	CA	92879	**800-899-9100**	
MTS Ambulance 2431 Greenup Ave	Ashland	KY	41101	**800-598-3458**	606-324-3286
Rural/Metro Corp 9221 E Via de Ventura	Scottsdale	AZ	85258	**800-352-2309**	
Skyservice Airlines Inc 9785 Ryan Ave	Dorval	QC	H9P1A2	**888-985-1402**	514-636-3300

31 AMUSEMENT PARK COMPANIES

SEE ALSO Circus, Carnival, Festival Operators

	City	State	ZIP	Toll-Free	Phone
Buffalo Grove Park District 530 Bernard Dr	Buffalo Grove	IL	60089	**800-526-0844**	847-850-2100
Georgia Public Library 1800 Century Pl NE Ste 150	Atlanta	GA	30345	**800-248-6701**	404-235-7200
Hershey Entertainment & Resorts Co 100 W Hersheypark Dr	Hershey	PA	17033	**800-437-7439**	
International Training Inc 1045 Ne Industrial Blvd	Jensen Beach	FL	34957	**888-778-9073**	207-729-4201
Island Windjammers Inc 165 Shaw Dr	Acworth	GA	30102	**877-772-4549**	
Lake Quassapaug Park 2132 Middlebury Rd	Middlebury	CT	06762	**800-367-7275**	203-758-2913
Q Center 1405 N Fifth Ave	Saint Charles	IL	60174	**877-774-4627**	630-377-3100
Ski Shawnee Inc 339 Hollow Rd	Shawnee On Delaware	PA	18356	**800-233-4218**	570-421-7231

32 AMUSEMENT PARKS

	City	State	ZIP	Toll-Free	Phone
Adventuredome 2880 Las Vegas Blvd S	Las Vegas	NV	89109	**866-456-8894**	702-691-5861
Adventureland Park 305 34th Ave NW	Altoona	IA	50009	**800-532-1286**	515-266-2121
Busch Gardens Williamsburg 1 Busch Gardens Blvd	Williamsburg	VA	23185	**800-343-7946**	
Cedar Fair Parks 14523 Carowinds Blvd	Charlotte	NC	28273	**800-888-4386**	704-588-2600
Darien Lake Theme Park Resort 9993 Allegheny Rd PO Box 91	Darien Center	NY	14040	**866-640-0652**	585-599-4641
Disney's California Adventure 1313 S Disneyland Dr	Anaheim	CA	92802	**800-225-2024**	714-781-7290
Dollywood 2700 Dollywood Parks Blvd.	Pigeon Forge	TN	37863	**800-365-5996**	

Company	City	State	ZIP	Toll-Free	Phone
Dorney Park & Wildwater Kingdom 3830 Dorney Pk Rd	Allentown	PA	18104	**800-747-0561**	610-395-3724
Dutch Wonderland Family Amusement Park 2249 Lincoln Hwy E	Lancaster	PA	17602	**866-386-2839**	717-291-1888
Fun Town Splash Town USA Inc US Rt 1 774 Portland Rd	Saco	ME	04072	**800-843-5678**	207-284-5139
Grand Harbor Resort & Waterpark 350 Bell St	Dubuque	IA	52001	**866-690-4006**	563-690-4000
Hersheypark 100 Hershey Pk Dr	Hershey	PA	17033	**844-330-1813**	717-534-3900
Holiday World & Splashin' Safari 452 E Christmas Blvd	Santa Claus	IN	47579	**877-463-2645**	812-937-4401
Knoebels Amusement Resort 391 Knoebels Blvd	Elysburg	PA	17824	**800-487-4386**	570-672-2572
Knott's Berry Farm 8039 Beach Blvd	Buena Park	CA	90620	**800-742-6427**	714-220-5220
Lagoon & Pioneer Village 375 N Lagoon Dr	Farmington	UT	84025	**800-748-5246**	801-451-8000
LEGOLAND California 1 Legoland Dr	Carlsbad	CA	92008	**877-534-6526**	760-438-5346
Paramount's Kings Dominion 16000 Theme Pkwy	Doswell	VA	23047	**800-367-7623**	804-876-5000
SeaWorld Orlando 7007 Sea World Dr	Orlando	FL	32821	**800-327-2424**	407-351-3600
SeaWorld San Diego 500 SeaWorld Dr	San Diego	CA	92109	**800-257-4268**	619-226-3901
Six Flags Fiesta Texas 17000 IH-10 W	San Antonio	TX	78257	**800-370-7488**	210-697-5000
Six Flags Great Adventure 1 Six Flags Blvd	Jackson	NJ	08527	**800-772-2287**	732-928-1821
Six Flags New England 1623 Main St	Agawam	MA	01001	**800-370-7488**	413-786-9300
Six Flags Wild Safari 1 Six Flags Blvd	Jackson	NJ	08527	**800-772-2287**	732-928-1821
Universal Orlando 6000 Universal Blvd	Orlando	FL	32819	**877-801-9720**	407-363-8000
Universal's Islands of Adventure 6000 Universal Studios Plz	Orlando	FL	32819	**877-801-9720**	407-363-8000
Village Vacances Valcartier 1860 Valcartier Blvd	Valcartier	QC	G0A4S0	**888-384-5524**	418-844-2200
Water Country USA 176 Water Country Pkwy	Williamsburg	VA	23185	**800-343-7946**	
Wet 'n Wild Emerald Pointe 3910 S Holden Rd	Greensboro	NC	27406	**800-555-5900**	336-852-9721
Wet 'n Wild Orlando 6200 International Dr *General	Orlando	FL	32819	**800-992-9453***	407-351-1800
Wonderland Amusement Park 2601 Dumas Dr	Amarillo	TX	79107	**800-383-4712**	806-383-0832

33 ANIMATION COMPANIES

SEE ALSO Motion Picture Production - Special Interest ; Motion Picture & Television Production

Company	City	State	ZIP	Toll-Free	Phone
Medcom Inc 6060 Phyllis Dr	Cypress	CA	90630	**800-541-0253**	
NestFamily 1461 S Beltline Rd Ste 500	Coppell	TX	75019	**800-634-4298**	972-402-7100

34 APPLIANCE & HOME ELECTRONICS STORES

SEE ALSO Computer Stores ; Department Stores ; Furniture Stores ; Home Improvement Centers

Company	City	State	ZIP	Toll-Free	Phone
ABC Appliance Inc 1 Silverdome Industrial Pk	Pontiac	MI	48343	**800-981-3866**	248-335-4222
Air Cleaning Technologies Inc 1300 W Detroit	Broken Arrow	OK	74012	**800-351-1858**	918-251-8000
Audio Direct 2004 E Irvington Rd Ste 264 *Cust Svc	Tucson	AZ	85714	**888-628-3467***	
Best Buy Company Inc 7601 Penn Ave S *NYSE: BBY*	Minneapolis	MN	55423	**888-237-8289**	612-291-1000
BrandsMart USA Corp 3200 SW 42nd St	Fort Lauderdale	FL	33312	**800-432-8579**	
Conn's Inc 3295 College St *NASDAQ: CONN* ■ *Cust Svc	Beaumont	TX	77701	**800-511-5750***	409-832-1696
Gregg Appliances Inc 4151 E 96th St *NYSE: HGG*	Indianapolis	IN	46240	**800-284-7344**	317-848-8710
Harco Company Ltd 5915 Coopers Ave	Mississauga	ON	L4Z1R9	**800-387-9503**	905-890-1220
Interbond Corp of America 3200 SW 42nd St	Fort Lauderdale	FL	33312	**800-432-8579**	
Mintie Corp 1114 San Fernando Rd	Los Angeles	CA	90065	**800-964-6843**	323-225-4111
PC Richard & Son Inc 150 Price Pkwy	Farmingdale	NY	11735	**800-696-2000**	631-773-4900
Pieratt's 110 Mt Tabor Rd	Lexington	KY	40517	**855-743-7288**	859-268-6000
Queen City TV & Appliance Company Inc 2430 Queen City Dr *All	Charlotte	NC	28208	**800-365-6665***	704-391-6000
RadioShack Corp 300 RadioShack Cir *NYSE: RSH*	Fort Worth	TX	76102	**800-843-7422**	817-882-9380
Sparkle Solutions LP 2700 Steeles Ave W Unit 4	Concord	ON	L4K3C8	**866-660-2282**	905-660-2282
Videoland Inc 6808 Hornwood Dr	Houston	TX	77074	**800-877-2900**	
Wireless Zone 34 Industrial Pk Pl	Middletown	CT	06457	**888-881-2622**	860-632-9494
Yale Appliance 296 Freeport St	Dorchester	MA	02122	**800-565-6435**	617-825-9253

35 APPLIANCES - MAJOR - MFR

SEE ALSO Air Conditioning & Heating Equipment - Residential

Company	City	State	ZIP	Toll-Free	Phone
Anaheim Mfg Co 2680 Orbiter St PO Box 4146 *Cust Svc	Brea	CA	92821	**800-854-3229***	310-542-5259
AO Smith Corp 11270 W Pk Pl Ste 170 PO Box 245008 *NYSE: AOS*	Milwaukee	WI	53224	**800-359-4065**	414-359-4000
AO Smith Water Products Co 500 Tennessee Waltz Pkwy	Ashland City	TN	37015	**800-527-1953**	
ASKO Appliances Inc PO Box 44848	Madison	WI	53744	**800-898-1879**	
Atlanta Attachment Co Inc 362 Industrial Pk Dr	Lawrenceville	GA	30045	**877-206-5116**	770-963-7369
Bradford White Corp 725 Talamore Dr	Ambler	PA	19002	**800-523-2931**	215-641-9400
Brown Stove Works Inc 1422 Carolina Ave *All	Cleveland	TN	37320	**800-251-7485***	423-476-6544
Cemline Corp PO Box 55	Cheswick	PA	15024	**800-245-6268**	724-274-5430
Char-Broil 1442 Belfast Ave *Cust Svc	Columbus	GA	31902	**866-239-6777***	706-324-0421
CookTek LLC 156 N Jefferson St Ste 300	Chicago	IL	60661	**888-266-5835**	312-563-9600
Dwyer Products Corp 1226 Michael Dr Ste F	Wood Dale	IL	60191	**800-822-0092**	630-741-7900
Electric Heater Co 45 Seymour St	Stratford	CT	06615	**800-647-3165**	203-378-2659
Electrolux Appliances PO Box 212237	Augusta	GA	30907	**877-435-3287**	
Fisher & Paykel Appliances Inc 5900 Skylab Rd	Huntington Beach	CA	92647	**888-936-7872**	
In-Sink-Erator 4700 21st St	Racine	WI	53406	**800-558-5712**	262-554-5432
LG Electronics USA Inc 1000 Sylvan Ave *Tech Supp	Englewood Cliffs	NJ	07632	**800-243-0000***	201-816-2000
Lochinvar Corp 300 Maddox Simpson Pkwy	Lebanon	TN	37090	**800-722-2101**	615-889-8900
Maytag Appliances 403 W Fourth St N *Cust Svc	Newton	IA	50208	**800-344-1274***	
Miele Inc 9 Independence Way	Princeton	NJ	08540	**800-843-7231**	609-419-9898
Northland Corp 1260 E Van Deinse St	Greenville	MI	48838	**800-223-3900**	
Peerless Premier Appliance Co 119 S 14th St	Belleville	IL	62222	**800-858-5844**	941-763-3915
Sharp Electronics Corp 1 Sharp Plz	Mahwah	NJ	07430	**800-237-4277**	201-529-8200
Vaughn Manufacturing Corp 26 Old Elm St PO Box 5431	Salisbury	MA	01952	**800-282-8446**	978-462-6683
Weber-Stephen Products Co 200 E Daniels Rd *Cust Svc	Palatine	IL	60067	**800-446-1071***	
Whirlpool Corp 2000 N M-63 *NYSE: WHR*	Benton Harbor	MI	49022	**800-253-1301**	269-923-5000
Whirlpool Corp North American Region 2000 N M-63	Benton Harbor	MI	49022	**800-253-1301**	269-923-5000
Wisco Industries Inc 736 Janesville St	Oregon	WI	53575	**800-999-4726**	608-835-3106

36 APPLIANCES - SMALL - MFR

SEE ALSO Vacuum Cleaners - Household ; Air Purification Equipment - Household

Company	City	State	ZIP	Toll-Free	Phone
Abatement Technologies 605 Satellite Blvd Ste 300	Suwanee	GA	30024	**800-634-9091**	678-889-4200
Andis Co 1800 County Rd H	Sturtevant	WI	53177	**800-558-9441**	262-884-2600
Broan-NuTone LLC 926 W State St PO Box 140 *Cust Svc	Hartford	WI	53027	**800-558-1711***	262-673-4340
Bunn-O-Matic Corp 1400 Stevenson Dr	Springfield	IL	62703	**800-637-8606**	217-529-6601
Cadet Mfg Company Inc 2500 W Fourth Plain Blvd	Vancouver	WA	98660	**800-442-2338**	360-693-2505
Casablanca Fan Co 761 Corporate Ctr Dr	Pomona	CA	91768	**888-227-2178**	909-689-1477
City of Chula Vista 276 Fourth Ave	Chula Vista	CA	91910	**877-478-5478**	619-691-5047
Conair Corp 1 Cummings Pt Rd *OTC: CNGA*	Stamford	CT	06902	**800-326-6247**	203-351-9000
Craftmade International Inc 650 S Royal Ln *OTC: CRFT*	Coppell	TX	75019	**800-486-4892**	972-393-3800
Cuisinart 1 Cummings Pt Rd	Stamford	CT	06902	**800-726-0190**	203-975-4609
El Electronics LLC 1800 Shames Dr	Westbury	NY	11590	**877-346-3837**	516-334-0870
Fan-Tastic Vent Corp 2083 S Almont Ave	Imlay City	MI	48444	**800-521-0298**	810-724-3818
Hamilton Beach/Proctor-Silex Inc 4421 Waterfront Dr *Cust Svc	Glen Allen	VA	23060	**800-851-8900***	804-273-9777
Hunter Fan Co 7130 Goodlett Farms Pkwy Ste 400	Memphis	TN	38016	**888-830-1326**	901-743-1360
Jarden Consumer Solutions 2381 Executive Ctr Dr	Boca Raton	FL	33431	**800-777-5452**	561-912-4100
KAZ Inc 250 Tpke Rd	Southborough	MA	01772	**800-477-0457**	

Company	City	State	ZIP	Toll-Free	Phone
King Electrical Manufacturing Co 9131 Tenth Ave S	Seattle	WA	98108	**800-603-5464**	206-762-0400
Lasko Metal Products Inc 820 Lincoln Ave	West Chester	PA	19380	**800-233-0268**	610-692-7400
LG Electronics USA Inc 1000 Sylvan Ave *Tech Supp	Englewood Cliffs	NJ	07632	**800-243-0000***	201-816-2000
Marley Engineered Products 470 Beauty Spot Rd E	Bennettsville	SC	29512	**800-452-4179**	843-479-4006
National Presto Industries Inc 3925 N Hastings Way *NYSE: NPK*	Eau Claire	WI	54703	**800-877-0441**	715-839-2121
Nesco/American Harvest 1700 Monroe St PO Box 237 *Cust Svc	Two Rivers	WI	54241	**800-288-4545***	920-793-1368
Schawbel Corp 26 Crosby Dr	Bedford	MA	01730	**866-753-3837**	781-541-6900
Sharp Electronics Corp 1 Sharp Plz	Mahwah	NJ	07430	**800-237-4277**	201-529-8200
Singer Sewing Co 1224 Hill Quaker Blvd PO Box 7017	La Vergne	TN	37086	**877-738-9869**	615-213-0880
Vita-Mix Corp 8615 Usher Rd	Cleveland	OH	44138	**800-848-2649**	440-235-4840
West Bend Housewares LLC 2845 Wingate St PO Box 2780	West Bend	WI	53095	**866-290-1851**	
Whirlpool Corp KitchenAid Div 553 Benson Rd	Benton Harbor	MI	49022	**800-422-1230**	
World Dryer Corp 5700 McDermott Dr	Berkeley	IL	60163	**800-323-0701**	708-449-6950

37 APPLIANCES - WHOL

Company	City	State	ZIP	Toll-Free	Phone
All Inc 185 Plato Blvd W	Saint Paul	MN	55107	**800-829-2127**	651-227-6331
Almo Corp 2709 Commerce Way	Philadelphia	PA	19154	**800-345-2566**	215-698-4000
Aves Audio Visual Systems Inc PO Box 500	Sugar Land	TX	77487	**800-365-2837**	281-295-1300
Blodgett Supply Co Inc 100 Ave D PO Box 759	Williston	VT	05495	**888-888-3424**	802-864-9831
Brooke Distributors Inc 16250 NW 52nd Ave	Hialeah	FL	33014	**800-275-8792**	305-624-9752
Bursma Electronic Distributing Inc 2851 Buchanan Ave SW	Grand Rapids	MI	49548	**800-777-2604**	616-831-0080
C & L Supply Co PO Box 578	Vinita	OK	74301	**800-256-6411**	
DAS Inc 724 Lawn Rd	Palmyra	PA	17078	**866-622-7979**	717-964-3642
Electrical Distributing Inc 4600 NW St Helens Rd	Portland	OR	97210	**800-877-4229**	503-226-4044
Gamla Enterprises North America Inc 875 Ave of The Americas Ste 205	New York	NY	10001	**800-442-6526**	212-947-3790
HB Communications Inc 60 Dodge Ave	North Haven	CT	06473	**800-243-4414**	203-234-9246
Home Entertainment Distribution Inc 120 Shawmut Rd	Canton	MA	02021	**800-343-9619**	888-567-7557
M.d.m. Commercial Enterprises Inc 1102 A1a N Ste 205	Ponte Vedra	FL	32082	**800-359-6741**	
Midwest Sales & Service Inc 917 S Chapin St	South Bend	IN	46601	**800-772-7262**	574-287-3365
Molok North America Ltd 179 Norpark Ave	Mount Forest	ON	N0G2L0	**877-558-5576**	519-323-9909
Nelson & Small Inc 212 Canco Rd	Portland	ME	04103	**800-341-0780**	207-775-5666
Peirce-Phelps Inc 2000 N 59th St	Philadelphia	PA	19131	**800-222-2742**	215-879-7000
Potter Distributing Inc 4037 Roger B Chaffee Blvd	Grand Rapids	MI	49548	**800-748-0568**	616-531-6860
R & B Wholesale Distributors Inc 2350 S Milliken Ave	Ontario	CA	91761	**800-627-7539**	909-230-5400
Roth Distributing Co 11300 W 47th St	Minnetonka	MN	55343	**800-363-3818**	952-933-4428
Servall Co 6761 E Ten Mile Rd	Center Line	MI	48015	**800-856-9874**	586-754-9985
Siano Appliance Distributors Inc 5372 Pleasant View Rd	Memphis	TN	38134	**800-742-6699**	901-382-5833
Speco Technologies 200 New Hwy	Amityville	NY	11701	**800-645-5516**	631-957-8700
Telerent Leasing Corp 4191 Fayetteville Rd	Raleigh	NC	27603	**800-626-0682**	919-772-8604
Tri-State Video Services Inc 1379 Pittsburgh Rd	Valencia	PA	16059	**888-382-7768**	724-898-1630
WASH Multifamily Laundry Systems 100 N Sepulveda Blvd 12th Fl *General	El Segundo	CA	90245	**800-421-6897***	
Westland Sales PO Box 427	Clackamas	OR	97015	**800-356-0766**	503-655-2563
Whirlpool Canada 200-6750 Century Ave	Mississauga	ON	L5N0B7	**800-807-6777**	905-821-6400
Woodson & Bozeman Inc 3870 New Getwell Rd	Memphis	TN	38118	**800-876-4243**	901-362-1500

38 APPLICATION SERVICE PROVIDERS (ASPS)

Application Service Providers rent, deliver, license, manage, and/or host proprietary and/or third-party business software ("applications") and/or computer services to multiple users (customers). Included here are companies that host software applications as well as companies that provide the equipment necessary to do so.

Company	City	State	ZIP	Toll-Free	Phone
AllMeds Inc 151 Lafayette Dr Ste 401	Oak Ridge	TN	37830	**888-343-6337**	865-482-1999
Ariba Inc 807 11th Ave *NASDAQ: ARBA*	Sunnyvale	CA	94089	**866-772-7422**	650-390-1000
Avanade Inc 818 Stewart St	Seattle	WA	98101	**844-282-6233**	206-239-5600
Baillio's Inc 5301 Menaul Blvd NE	Albuquerque	NM	87110	**800-540-7511**	505-883-7511
BizLand Inc 70 BlanchaRd Rd	Burlington	MA	01803	**800-249-5263**	
Cayenta Canada Corp 4200 N Fraser Way Ste 201	Burnaby	BC	V5J5K7	**866-229-3682**	604-570-4300
Chemical Safety Corp 5901 Christie Ave Ste 502	Emeryville	CA	94608	**888-594-1100**	510-594-1000
Cision Inc 12051 Indian Creek Ct *NASDAQ: VOCS*	Beltsville	MD	20705	**866-639-5087**	301-459-2590
CliniComp International 9655 Towne Ctr Dr	San Diego	CA	92121	**800-350-8202**	858-546-8202
Connectria Hosting 10845 Olive Blvd Ste 300	Saint Louis	MO	63141	**800-781-7820**	314-587-7000
Crexendo Inc 1615 S 52nd St *OTC: CXDO*	Tempe	AZ	85281	**866-621-6111**	801-431-4695
Daptiv 1008 Western Ave Ste 700	Seattle	WA	98101	**888-621-8361**	206-341-9117
Digital River Inc 10380 Bren Rd W *NASDAQ: DRIV*	Minnetonka	MN	55343	**800-598-7450**	
DigitalWork Inc 14300 N Northsight Blvd Ste 206	Scottsdale	AZ	85260	**877-496-7571**	
E-Builder Inc 1800 NW 69 Ave Ste 201	Plantation	FL	33313	**800-580-9322**	954-556-6701
E-Markets Inc 807 Mountain Ave Ste 200	Berthoud	CO	80513	**877-674-7419**	
eGain Communications Corp 1252 Borregas Ave *NASDAQ: EGAN*	Mountain View	CA	94043	**888-603-4246**	408-636-4500
Electric Mail Company Inc 3999 Henning Dr Ste 300	Burnaby	BC	V5C6P9	**866-950-5333**	604-482-1111
ePlus Inc 13595 Dulles Technology Dr *NASDAQ: PLUS*	Herndon	VA	20171	**888-482-1122**	703-984-8400
FinancialCAD Corp 13450 102nd Ave Ste 1750	Surrey	BC	V3T5X3	**800-304-0702**	604-957-1200
HealthMEDX 5100 N Towne Ctr Dr	Ozark	MO	65721	**877-875-1200**	417-582-1816
Intacct Corp 300 Park Ave Ste 1400	San Jose	CA	95110	**877-437-7765**	408-878-0900
Internap Network Services Corp 250 Williams St Ste E-100 *NASDAQ: INAP*	Atlanta	GA	30303	**877-843-7627**	404-302-9700
IntraLinks Inc 150 E 42nd St Ste 8	New York	NY	10017	**888-546-5383**	212-543-7700
Journyx Inc 7600 Burnet Rd Ste. 300	Austin	TX	78757	**800-755-9878**	512-834-8888
Kleinschmidt Inc 450 Lake Cook Rd	Deerfield	IL	60015	**800-824-2330**	847-945-1000
Mobile Smith 5400 Trinity Rd Ste 320	Raleigh	NC	27607	**800-578-9000**	
NeoMedia Technologies Inc 1515 Walnut St Ste 100	Boulder	CO	80302	**800-413-4559**	678-638-0460
onProject Inc PO Box 104	Franklin Lakes	NJ	07417	**877-936-6776**	973-971-9970
Oracle Corp 500 Oracle Pkwy *NYSE: ORCL* ■ *Sales	Redwood Shores	CA	94065	**800-392-2999***	650-506-7000
Outstart Inc 745 Atlantic Ave 4th Fl	Boston	MA	02111	**877-971-9171**	617-897-6800
Paramount Technologies Inc 1374 EW Maple Rd	Walled Lake	MI	48390	**800-725-4408**	248-960-0909
PBM Corp 20600 Chagrin Blvd Ste 450	Cleveland	OH	44122	**800-341-5809**	216-283-7999
Perfect Commerce Inc 1 Compass Way Ste 120 *Sales	Newport News	VA	23606	**877-871-3788***	757-766-8211
PhDx Systems Inc 1001 University Blvd SE Ste 103	Albuquerque	NM	87106	**888-999-7439**	505-764-0174
Premiere Global Services Inc (PGI) 3280 Peachtree Rd NE Ste 1000 *NYSE: PGI*	Atlanta	GA	30305	**866-548-3203**	719-457-6901
Prodata Systems Inc 11007 Slater Ave NE	Kirkland	WA	98033	**866-582-7485**	425-296-4168
Prosum technology services 2201 Park Pl Ste 102	El Segundo	CA	90245	**888-477-6786**	310-426-0600
PureWorks Inc 5000 Meridian Blvd Ste 600	Franklin	TN	37067	**888-202-3016**	615-367-4404
Radware Inc 575 Corporate Dr Lobby 2	Mahwah	NJ	07430	**888-234-5763**	201-512-9771
Resource Development Corp 280 Daines St Ste 200	Birmingham	MI	48009	**800-360-7222**	248-646-2300
Salesnet 6340 Sugarloaf Pkwy Ste 200	Duluth	GA	30097	**866-732-8632**	
Streamline Health Solutions Inc 10200 Alliance Rd Ste 200 *NASDAQ: STRM*	Cincinnati	OH	45242	**800-878-5269**	513-794-7100
Syntrio 50 California St Ste 3260	San Francisco	CA	94111	**888-289-6670**	415-951-7913
Talisma Corp 777 Yamato Rd	Boca Raton	FL	33431	**866-397-2537**	561-923-2500
TALX Corp 11432 Lackland Dr	Saint Louis	MO	63146	**800-888-8277**	314-214-7000
Toolwire Inc 7031 Koll Ctr Pkwy Ste 220	Pleasanton	CA	94566	**866-935-8665**	925-227-8500
UnicornHRO 25 Hanover Rd Ste B	Florham Park	NJ	07932	**800-368-8149**	973-360-0688

39 AQUARIUMS - PUBLIC

SEE ALSO Zoos & Wildlife Parks ; Botanical Gardens & Arboreta

Company	City	State	ZIP	Toll-Free	Phone
Adventure Aquarium 1 Riverside Dr	Camden	NJ	08103	**800-616-5297**	856-365-3300
Florida Aquarium 701 Channelside Dr	Tampa	FL	33602	**800-353-4741**	813-273-4000
Key West Aquarium 1 Whitehead St	Key West	FL	33040	**888-544-5927**	305-296-2051

Classified Section

Name	Address	City	State	Zip	Toll-Free	Phone
Marineland of Florida	9600 Ocean Shore Blvd	Saint Augustine	FL	32080	**877-933-3402**	904-460-1275
Marinelife Ctr of Juno Beach	14200 US Hwy 1 Loggerhead Pk	Juno Beach	FL	33408	**800-843-5451**	561-627-8280
Maui Ocean Ctr	192 Maalaea Rd	Wailuku	HI	96793	**800-350-5634**	808-270-7000
Monterey Bay Aquarium	886 Cannery Row	Monterey	CA	93940	**866-963-9645**	831-648-4800
Newport Aquarium	1 Aquarium Way	Newport	KY	41071	**800-406-3474**	859-261-7444
North Carolina Aquarium at Fort Fisher	900 Loggerhead Rd	Kure Beach	NC	28449	**800-832-3474**	910-458-8257
North Carolina Aquarium on Roanoke Island	374 Airport Rd PO Box 967	Manteo	NC	27954	**800-832-3474**	252-475-2300
Oregon Coast Aquarium	2820 SE Ferry Slip Rd	Newport	OR	97365	**800-452-7888**	541-867-3474
Parc Aquarium du Quebec	1675 des Hotels Ave	Quebec	QC	G1W4S3	**866-659-5264**	418-659-5264
Pittsburgh Zoo & PPG Aquarium	1 Wild Pl	Pittsburgh	PA	15206	**800-732-0999**	412-665-3640
Ripley's Aquarium	1110 Celebrity Cir	Myrtle Beach	SC	29577	**800-734-8888**	843-916-0888
SeaWorld Orlando	7007 Sea World Dr	Orlando	FL	32821	**800-327-2424**	407-351-3600
South Carolina Aquarium	100 Aquarium Wharf	Charleston	SC	29401	**800-722-6455**	843-577-3474
Tennessee Aquarium	1 Broad St	Chattanooga	TN	37402	**800-262-0695**	423-802-6768
Texas State Aquarium	2710 N Shoreline Blvd *General	Corpus Christi	TX	78402	**800-477-4853***	361-881-1200
Vancouver Aquarium Marine Science Ctr	845 Avison Way	Vancouver	BC	V6G3E2	**800-931-1186**	604-659-3474

40 ARBITRATION SERVICES - LEGAL

Name	Address	City	State	Zip	Toll-Free	Phone
Allerair Industries Inc	9600 Rte Transcanadienne	Saint-laurent	QC	H4S1V9	**888-852-8247**	
Alliance Abroad Group LP	1221 S Mo Pac Expy Ste 250	Austin	TX	78746	**866-622-7623**	512-457-8062
Alliance Credit Counseling Inc	15720 Brixham Hill Ave Ste 575	Charlotte	NC	28277	**888-995-7856**	704-341-1010
Americall	1502 Tacoma Ave S	Tacoma	WA	98402	**800-964-3556**	253-272-4111
American Arbitration Assn Inc (AAA)	1633 Broadway 10th Fl	New York	NY	10019	**800-778-7879**	212-716-5800
Annuvia Inc	1725 Clay St Ste 100	San Francisco	CA	94109	**866-364-7940**	
Anresco Inc	1375 Van Dyke Ave	San Francisco	CA	94124	**800-359-0920**	415-822-1100
ap Services LLC, The	562 Watertown Ave Ste 3	Waterbury	CT	06708	**866-843-7270**	
Arbitration Forums Inc	3350 Buschwood Pk Dr Ste 295 *Cust Svc	Tampa	FL	33618	**800-967-8889***	813-931-4004
Arcturus Advisors	1643 Plantation Oaks Ln	Fernandina Beach	FL	32034	**866-593-2207**	
Balasa Dinverno Foltz LLC	500 Park Blvd Ste 1400	Itasca	IL	60143	**800-840-4740**	630-875-4900
Bluteau DeVenney & Company Inc	5670 Spring Garden Rd Ste 901A	Halifax	NS	B3J1H6	**877-210-9800**	902-425-0467
Brunswick School Inc	100 Maher Ave	Greenwich	CT	06830	**800-546-9425**	203-625-5800
Careerpros LLC	3392 Hillcrest Rd	Dubuque	IA	52002	**800-383-7641**	563-556-3040
CIR Law Offices LLP	8665 Gibbs Dr Ste 150	San Diego	CA	92123	**800-496-8909**	
Council of Better Business Bureaus Inc *Dispute Resolution Services & Mediation Training*	4200 Wilson Blvd Ste 800	Arlington	VA	22203	**855-748-4600**	703-276-0100
CPR Institute for Dispute Resolution	575 Lexington Ave 21st Fl	New York	NY	10022	**866-723-1781**	212-949-6490
EmpXtrack	150 Motor Parkway Ste 401	Hauppauge	NY	11788	**888-840-2682**	
Family Credit Counseling Service	111 N Wabash Ste 1408	Chicago	IL	60602	**800-994-3328**	
Farris Vaughan Wills & Murphy	700 W Georgia St Pacific Centre S 25th Fl PO Box 10026	Vancouver	BC	V7Y1B3	**877-684-9151**	604-684-9151
Fasken Martineau DuMoulin LLP	333 Bay St Bay Adelaide Centre Ste 2400 PO Box 20	Toronto	ON	M5H2T6	**800-268-8424**	416-366-8381
Florida Council Against Sexual Violence Inc	1820 E Park Ave Ste 100	Tallahassee	FL	32301	**888-956-7273**	850-297-2000
Florida Surplus Lines Service Office	1441 Maclay Commerce Dr	Tallahassee	FL	32312	**800-562-4496**	850-224-7676
Gokeyless	3646 Cargo Rd	Vandalia	OH	45377	**877-439-5377**	937-890-2333
Guidesoft Inc	5875 Castle Creek Pkwy Ste 400	Indianapolis	IN	46250	**877-256-6948**	317-578-1700
JAMS/Endispute	500 N State College Blvd 14th Fl	Orange	CA	92868	**800-352-5267**	714-939-1300
Jeffrey Byrne & Associates	4042 Central St	Kansas City	MO	64111	**800-222-9233**	
JS Paluch Company Inc	3708 River Rd Ste 400	Franklin Park	IL	60131	**800-621-5197**	847-678-9300
Judicate West	1851 E First St Ste 1600	Santa Ana	CA	92705	**800-488-8805**	714-834-1340
July Business Services	215 Mary Ave Ste 302	Waco	TX	76701	**888-333-5859**	
Kaufman Company Inc	19 Walkhill Rd	Norwood	MA	02062	**800-338-8023**	781-255-1000
Living Color Enterprises Inc	6850 NW 12th Ave	Fort Lauderdale	FL	33309	**800-878-9511**	954-970-9511
Loeb Equipment & Appraisal Co	4131 S State St	Chicago	IL	60609	**800-560-5632**	773-548-4131
Merchant Law Group LLP	2401 Saskatchewan Dr Saskatchewan Dr Plz	Regina	SK	S4P4H8	**888-567-7777**	306-359-7777
Middleton & Company Inc	600 Atlantic Ave 18th Fl	Boston	MA	02210	**800-357-5101**	617-357-5101
Miller Thomson LLP	Scotia Plz 40 King St W Ste 5800	Toronto	ON	M5H3S1	**888-762-5559**	416-595-8500
National Arbitration & Mediation	990 Stewart Ave	Garden City	NY	11530	**800-358-2550**	516-794-8950
Nines Hotel, The	525 SW Morrison	Portland	OR	97204	**877-229-9995**	
Notus Career Management	5 Centerpointe Dr Ste 400	Lake Oswego	OR	97035	**800-431-1990**	
OneTouch Direct LLC	4902 W Sligh Ave	Tampa	FL	33634	**866-948-4005**	
OTS	3924 Clock Pointe Trl	Stow	OH	44224	**877-445-2058**	
Parker Rose Design Inc	10075 Mesa Rim Rd Ste A	San Diego	CA	92121	**800-403-2711**	
Parnell & Crum PA	641 S Lawrence St	Montgomery	AL	36104	**866-629-0912**	334-832-4200
Quatred LLC	532 Fourth Range Rd	Pembroke	NH	03275	**888-395-8534**	
Randall S Miller & Associates PC	43252 Woodward Ave Ste 180	Bloomfield Hills	MI	48302	**844-322-6558**	248-335-9200
Resolute Systems Inc	1550 N Prospect Ave	Milwaukee	WI	53202	**800-776-6060**	414-276-4774
Resume Solutions	1033 Bay St	Toronto	ON	M5S3A5	**866-361-1290**	416-361-1290
Surveillance Specialties Ltd	600 Research Dr	Wilmington	MA	01887	**800-354-2616**	
TERRAMAI	8400 Agate Rd	White City	OR	97503	**800-220-9062**	
Tranzon LLC	7204 Glen Forest Dr Ste 105	Richmond	VA	23226	**866-503-1212**	207-775-4300
Tri-Starr Investigations Inc	3525 Hwy 138 SW	Stockbridge	GA	30281	**800-849-9841**	770-388-9841
Valley Internet Inc	102 Maple St East	Fayetteville	TN	37334	**888-433-1924**	931-433-1921
Wolfe Industrial Auctions Inc	9801 Hansonville Rd	Frederick	MD	21702	**800-443-9580**	301-898-0340

ARCHITECTS

SEE Engineering & Design

ART - COMMERCIAL

SEE Graphic Design

41 ART DEALERS & GALLERIES

Name	Address	City	State	Zip	Toll-Free	Phone
Abbozzo Gallery	401 Richmond Stt W Ste 128	Toronto	ON	M5V3A8	**866-844-4481**	416-260-2220
Feheley Fine Arts	65 George St	Toronto	ON	M5A4L8	**877-904-9114**	416-323-1373
Gallery 78 Inc	796 Queen St	Fredericton	NB	E3B1C6	**888-883-8322**	506-454-5192
Heffel Gallery Ltd	2247 Granville St	Vancouver	BC	V6H3G1	**800-528-9608**	604-732-6505
Inuit Gallery of Vancouver Ltd	206 Cambie St Gastown	Vancouver	BC	V6B2M9	**888-615-8399**	604-688-7323
Masters Gallery Ltd	2115 Fourth St SW	Calgary	AB	T2S1W8	**866-245-0616**	403-245-2064
Mayberry Fine Art Inc	212 Mcdermot Ave	Winnipeg	MB	R3B0S3	**877-871-9261**	204-255-5690
Michael Gibson Gallery	157 Carling St	London	ON	N6A1H5	**866-644-2766**	519-439-0451
Odon Wagner Gallery	196 Davenport Rd	Toronto	ON	M5R1J2	**800-551-2465**	416-962-0438
Uno Langmann Ltd	2117 Granville St	Vancouver	BC	V6H3E9	**800-730-8825**	604-736-8825
West End Gallery Ltd	12308 Jasper Ave	Edmonton	AB	T5N3K5	**855-488-4892**	780-488-4892

42 ART MATERIALS & SUPPLIES - MFR

SEE ALSO Pens, Pencils, Parts

Name	Address	City	State	Zip	Toll-Free	Phone
Adco Inc	PO Box 815382	Dallas	TX	75381	**800-486-4583**	972-484-6177
Alvin & Company Inc	1335 Blue Hills Ave	Bloomfield	CT	06002	**800-444-2584**	860-243-8991
American Art Clay Co (AMACO)	6060 Guion Rd	Indianapolis	IN	46254	**800-374-1600**	317-244-6871
American Metalcraft Inc	2074 George St	Melrose Park	IL	60160	**800-333-9133**	708-345-1177
Ampersand Art Supply	1235 S Loop 4 Ste 400	Buda	TX	78610	**800-822-1939**	512-322-0278
ART Studio Clay Co	9320 Michigan Ave	Sturtevant	WI	53177	**800-323-0212**	262-884-4278
Artist Brand Canvas	2448 Loma Ave *Orders	South El Monte	CA	91733	**888-579-2704***	626-579-2740
Badger Air Brush Co	9128 Belmont Ave	Franklin Park	IL	60131	**800-247-2787**	847-678-3104
Chartpak Inc	1 River Rd	Leeds	MA	01053	**800-628-1910**	413-584-5446
DecoArt Inc	49 Cotton Ave	Stanford	KY	40484	**800-367-3047**	606-365-3193
Duncan Enterprises	5673 E Shields Ave	Fresno	CA	93727	**800-438-6226**	559-291-4444
Gare Inc	165 Rosemont St	Haverhill	MA	01832	**888-289-4273**	978-373-9131
Georgie's Ceramic & Clay Company Inc	756 NE Lombard St	Portland	OR	97211	**800-999-2529**	503-283-1353
Golden Artists Colors Inc	188 Bell Rd	New Berlin	NY	13411	**800-959-6543**	607-847-6154
Jack Richeson & Company Inc	557 Marcella Dr	Kimberly	WI	54136	**800-233-2404**	920-738-0744

	City	State	ZIP	Toll-Free	Phone
Martin/F Weber Co 2727 Southampton Rd	Philadelphia	PA	19154	**800-876-8076**	215-677-5600
National Artcraft Supply Co 300 Campus Dr	Aurora	OH	44202	**888-937-2723**	330-562-3500
Paasche Airbrush Co 4311 N Normandy *Sales	Chicago	IL	60634	**800-621-1907***	773-867-9191
Plaid Enterprises Inc 3225 Westech Dr	Norcross	GA	30092	**800-842-4197**	678-291-8100
Sargent Art Inc 100 E Diamond Ave	Hazleton	PA	18201	**800-424-3596**	570-454-3596
Smooth-On Inc 2000 St John St	Easton	PA	18042	**800-762-0744**	610-252-5800
Testor Corp 440 Blackhawk Pk Ave	Rockford	IL	61104	**800-837-8677**	815-962-6654
Utrecht Art Supplies PO Box 1769	Galesburg	IL	61402	**888-336-3114**	609-409-8001

43 ART MATERIALS & SUPPLIES - WHOL

	City	State	ZIP	Toll-Free	Phone
Creative Hobbies Inc 900 Creek Rd	Bellmawr	NJ	08031	**800-843-5456**	856-933-2540
CWI Gifts & Crafts 77 Cypress St SW	Reynoldsburg	OH	43068	**800-666-5858**	740-964-6210
D&L Art Glass Supply 1440 W 52nd Ave	Denver	CO	80221	**800-525-0940**	303-449-8737
Darice Inc 13000 Darice Pkwy	Strongsville	OH	44149	**866-432-7423**	
Howell's Craftand Imports 6030 NE 112th Ave	Portland	OR	97220	**800-547-0368**	
Pioneer Wholesale Co 500 W Bagley Rd	Berea	OH	44017	**888-234-5400**	440-234-5400
Sbar's Inc 14 Sbar Blvd	Moorestown	NJ	08057	**800-989-7227**	856-234-8220
Sepp Leaf Products Inc 381 Pk Ave S Ste 1301	New York	NY	10016	**800-971-7377**	212-683-2840
Shop Hobby Lobby 7717 SW 44th St	Oklahoma City	OK	73179	**800-888-0321**	405-745-1275

44 ART SUPPLY STORES

	City	State	ZIP	Toll-Free	Phone
AC Moore Arts & Crafts Inc 130 AC Moore Dr *NASDAQ: ACMR*	Berlin	NJ	08009	**888-226-6673**	
Accord Carton 6155 W 115th St	Alsip	IL	60803	**800-648-6780**	
Al Friedman Company Inc 44 W 18th St	New York	NY	10011	**800-204-6352**	212-243-9000
Alabama Art Supply Inc 1006 23rd St S *Cust Svc	Birmingham	AL	35205	**800-749-4741***	205-322-4741
All in One Poster Co 8521 Whitaker St	Buena Park	CA	90621	**800-273-0307**	714-521-7720
All-Fab Building Components Inc 1755 Dugald Rd	Winnipeg	MB	R2J0H3	**800-665-0335**	204-661-8880
Alpina Manufacturing LLC 3418 N Knox Ave	Chicago	IL	60641	**800-915-2828**	773-202-8887
Arizona Art Supply 4025 N 16th St	Phoenix	AZ	85016	**877-264-9514**	602-264-9514
Art Supply Warehouse 6672 Westminster Blvd	Westminster	CA	92683	**800-854-6467**	714-891-3626
Asel Art Supply 2701 Cedar Springs	Dallas	TX	75201	**888-273-5278**	214-871-2425
Blaine's Art Supply 1025 Photo Ave	Anchorage	AK	99503	**866-561-4278**	907-561-5344
Dick Blick Co PO Box 1267 *Orders	Galesburg	IL	61402	**800-447-8192***	309-343-6181
Excelleris Technologies Inc 4445 Lougheed Hwy Ste 201	Burnaby	BC	V5C0E4	**866-728-4777**	
Flax Art & Design 1699 Market St	San Francisco	CA	94103	**844-352-9278**	415-552-2355
Georgie's Ceramic & Clay Company Inc 756 NE Lombard St	Portland	OR	97211	**800-999-2529**	503-283-1353
Herweck's Art & Drafting Supplies 300 Broadway St	San Antonio	TX	78205	**800-725-1349**	210-227-1349
Hobby Lobby Creative Centers 7707 SW 44th St	Oklahoma City	OK	73179	**855-329-7060**	405-745-1100
Lantana Communications Corp 1700 Tech Centre Pkwy Ste 100	Arlington	TX	76014	**800-345-4211**	
Michaels Stores Inc 8000 Bent Branch Dr *Cust Svc	Irving	TX	75063	**800-642-4235***	972-409-1300
New York Central Art Supply 62 Third Ave	New York	NY	10003	**800-950-6111**	
Orbit Medical Enterprises Inc 716 East 4500 South Ste 260 S	Salt Lake City	UT	84107	**800-430-0539**	801-713-2020
Plaza Art 633 Middleton St	Nashville	TN	37203	**866-668-6714**	615-254-3368
Plaza Artists Materials of the MidAtlantic Inc 1990 K Str NW	Washington	DC	20006	**866-668-6714**	202-331-7090
Premier Pyrotechnics Inc 25255 Hwy K	Richland	MO	65556	**888-647-6863**	
Rabbit Air 9242 1/2 Hall Rd	Downey	CA	90241	**888-866-8862**	562-861-4688
Rex Artist Supplies 3160 SW 22 St	Miami	FL	33145	**800-739-2782**	305-445-1413
Spokane Art Supply Inc 1303 N Monroe St	Spokane	WA	99201	**800-556-5568**	509-327-6622
Starvin' Artist Supplies 802 S Oak Pk	Oak Park	IL	60304	**800-427-8478**	708-358-3600
Texas Art Supply 2001 Montrose Blvd	Houston	TX	77006	**800-888-9278**	713-526-5221
Woodcraft Supply LLC 1177 Rosemar Rd	Parkersburg	WV	26105	**800-535-4482**	

45 ASPHALT PAVING & ROOFING MATERIALS

	City	State	ZIP	Toll-Free	Phone
Atlas Roofing Corp 2322 Valley Rd *Cust Svc	Meridian	MS	39307	**800-478-0258***	601-483-7111
Baker Rock Resources 21880 SW Farmington Rd	Beaverton	OR	97007	**800-340-7625**	503-642-2531
Brewer Co 1354 US Hwy 50	Milford	OH	45150	**800-394-0017**	513-576-6300
Burkholder Paving 621 Martindale Rd	Ephrata	PA	17522	**866-839-3426**	717-354-1340
Capitol Aggregates Ltd 12625 Wetmore Rd Ste 301	San Antonio	TX	78247	**800-292-5315**	210-871-6100
CertainTeed Corp 750 E Swedesford Rd *Prod Info	Valley Forge	PA	19482	**800-782-8777***	610-341-7000
Crafco Inc 420 N Roosevelt Ave	Chandler	AZ	85226	**800-528-8242**	602-276-0406
Dalton Enterprises Inc 131 Willow St	Cheshire	CT	06410	**800-851-5606**	203-272-3221
Dewitt Products Co 5860 Plumer Ave *Cust Svc	Detroit	MI	48209	**800-962-8599***	313-554-0575
Fields Company LLC 2240 Taylor Way	Tacoma	WA	98421	**800-627-4098**	
GAF Materials Corp 1361 Alps Rd	Wayne	NJ	07470	**800-365-7353**	973-628-3000
Gardner-Gibson PO Box 5449	Tampa	FL	33675	**800-237-1155**	813-248-2101
Garland Company Inc 3800 E 91st St	Cleveland	OH	44105	**800-321-9336**	216-641-7500
Glenn O Hawbaker Inc 1952 Waddle Rd Ste 203	State College	PA	16803	**800-221-1355**	814-237-1444
Heely-Brown Company Inc 1280 Chattahoochee Ave	Atlanta	GA	30318	**800-241-4628**	404-352-0022
Henry Co 909 N Sepulveda Blvd Ste 650	El Segundo	CA	90245	**800-598-7663**	310-955-9200
HRI Inc 1750 W College Ave	State College	PA	16801	**877-474-9999**	814-238-5071
Innovative Metals Company Inc (IMETCO) 4648 S Old Peachtree Rd	Norcross	GA	30084	**800-646-3826**	770-908-1030
Karnak Corp, The 330 Central Ave	Clark	NJ	07066	**800-526-4236**	732-388-0300
Koppers Inc 436 Seventh Ave *NYSE: KOP*	Pittsburgh	PA	15219	**800-385-4406**	412-227-2001
Lunday-Thagard Co 9302 Garfield Ave	South Gate	CA	90280	**800-266-6551**	562-928-7000
Malarkey Roofing Products PO Box 17217	Portland	OR	97217	**800-545-1191**	503-283-1191
Marathon Petroleum LLC PO Box 1	Findlay	OH	45839	**866-462-7284**	419-422-2121
Martin Asphalt Co 3 Riverway Ste 400	South Houston	TX	77056	**800-662-0987**	713-350-6800
Neyra Industries 10700 Evendale Dr	Cincinnati	OH	45241	**800-543-7077**	513-733-1000
Pace Products Inc 4510 W 89th St Ste 110	Prairie Village	KS	66207	**888-389-8203**	
Package Pavement Company Inc PO Box 408	Stormville	NY	12582	**800-724-8193**	845-221-2224
Palmer Asphalt Co 196 W Fifth St PO Box 58	Bayonne	NJ	07002	**800-352-9898**	201-339-0855
PetersenDean Roofing and Solar 39300 Civic Center Dr Ste 300	Fremont	CA	94538	**877-552-4418**	
Pike Industries Inc 3 Eastgate Pk Rd	Belmont	NH	03220	**800-283-0803**	603-527-5100
Russell Standard Corp 285 Kappa Dr Ste 300 *General	Pittsburgh	PA	15238	**800-323-3053***	
Seaboard Asphalt Products Co 3601 Fairfield Rd	Baltimore	MD	21226	**800-536-0332**	410-355-0330
Sika Sarnafil Inc 100 Dan Rd	Canton	MA	02021	**800-451-2504**	781-828-5400
Simon Roofing & Sheet Metal Corp 70 Karago Ave	Youngstown	OH	44512	**800-523-7714**	330-629-7663
Tilcon Connecticut Inc PO Box 1357	New Britain	CT	06050	**888-845-2666**	860-224-6010
Vance Bros Inc 5201 Brighton PO Box 300107	Kansas City	MO	64130	**800-821-8549**	816-923-4325
Vulcan Materials Co 1200 Urban Ctr Dr PO Box 385014 *NYSE: VMC*	Birmingham	AL	35238	**800-615-4331**	205-298-3000

46 ASSOCIATION MANAGEMENT COMPANIES

	City	State	ZIP	Toll-Free	Phone
Allen Press Inc 810 E Tenth St PO Box 1897	Lawrence	KS	66044	**800-627-0932**	785-843-1235
Center for Assn Growth 1926 Waukegan Rd Ste 1	Glenview	IL	60025	**800-492-6462**	847-657-6700
Center for Assn Resources Inc 1901 N Roselle Rd Ste 920	Schaumburg	IL	60195	**888-705-1434**	
CM Services Inc 800 Roosevelt Rd Bldg C Ste 312	Glen Ellyn	IL	60137	**800-613-6672**	630-858-7337
Grassley Group, The (FMCI) 409 Washington St Ste A	Cedar Falls	IA	50613	**866-619-5580**	
Hauck & Assoc Inc 1025 Thomas Jefferson St Ste 500 E	Washington	DC	20007	**800-767-7777**	202-452-8100
J Edgar Eubanks & Assoc 1 Windsor Cove Ste 305	Columbia	SC	29223	**800-445-8629**	803-252-5646
LoBue & Majdalany Management Group 572B Ruger St PO Box 29920	San Francisco	CA	94129	**800-820-4690**	415-561-6110
NeuStar Inc 21575 Ridgetop Cir	Sterling	VA	20166	**855-638-2677**	571-434-5400
Prime Management Services 3416 Primm Ln	Birmingham	AL	35216	**866-609-1599**	205-823-6106

Name / Address	City	State	ZIP	Toll-Free	Phone
Raybourn Group International 9100 PuRdue Rd Ste 200	Indianapolis	IN	46268	**800-362-2546**	317-328-4636
Total Management Solutions Inc 55 Harristown Rd	Glen Rock	NJ	07452	**866-544-0707**	201-447-0707

47 ASSOCIATIONS & ORGANIZATIONS - GENERAL

SEE ALSO Performing Arts Organizations ; Political Action Committees ; Political Parties (Major)

47-1 Accreditation & Certification Organizations

Name / Address	City	State	ZIP	Toll-Free	Phone
Accreditation Commission for Acupuncture & Oriental Medicine (ACAOM) 7501 Greenway Ctr Dr Ste 760	Greenbelt	MD	20770	**800-735-2968**	301-313-0855
Accreditation Council for Accountancy & Taxation (ACAT) 1010 N Fairfax St	Alexandria	VA	22314	**888-289-7763**	703-549-2228
Accrediting Bureau of Health Education Schools (ABHES) 7777 Leesburg Pike Ste 314 N	Falls Church	VA	22043	**800-228-9290**	703-917-9503
Accrediting Council for Independent Colleges & Schools (ACICS) 750 First St NE Ste 980	Washington	DC	20002	**800-258-3826**	202-336-6780
American Assn for Accreditation of Ambulatory Surgery Facilities Inc (AAAASF) 5101 Washington St Ste 2F PO Box 9500	Gurnee	IL	60031	**888-545-5222**	847-775-1985
American Board of Internal Medicine (ABIM) 510 Walnut St Ste 1700	Philadelphia	PA	19106	**800-441-2246**	215-446-3500
American Culinary Federation Inc (ACF) 180 Ctr Pl Way	Saint Augustine	FL	32095	**800-624-9458**	904-824-4468
American National Standards Institute (ANSI) 25 W 43rd St 4th fl	New York	NY	10036	**800-374-3818**	212-642-4900
American Osteopathic Assn (AOA) 142 E Ontario St	Chicago	IL	60611	**800-621-1773**	312-202-8000
Association for Assessment & Accreditation of Laboratory Animal Care International 5283 Corporate Dr Ste 203	Frederick	MD	21703	**800-926-0066**	301-696-9626
Canadian Assn of Occupational Therapists (CAOT) 1125 Colonel By Dr	Ottawa	ON	K1S5R1	**800-434-2268**	613-523-2268
Canadian Information Processing Society (CIPS) 5090 Explorer Dr Ste 801	Mississauga	ON	L4W4T9	**877-275-2477**	905-602-1370
Certified Financial Planner Board of Standards Inc 1425 K St NW Ste 500	Washington	DC	20005	**800-487-1497**	202-379-2200
COLA 9881 Broken Land Pkwy Ste 200	Columbia	MD	21046	**800-981-9883**	410-381-6581
Commission on Accreditation for Dietetics Education (CADE) 120 S Riverside Plz Ste 2000	Chicago	IL	60606	**800-877-1600**	312-899-0040
Commission on Accreditation for Law Enforcement Agencies (CALEA) 13575 Heathcote Blvd Ste 320	Gainesville	VA	20155	**877-789-6904**	703-352-4225
Commission on Accreditation in Physical Therapy Education (CAPTE) 1111 N Fairfax St	Alexandria	VA	22314	**800-999-2782**	703-706-3245
Commission on Accreditation of Allied Health Education Programs (CAAHEP) 1361 Pk St	Clearwater	FL	33756	**800-228-2262**	727-210-2350
Commission on Accreditation of Rehabilitation Facilities International (CARF) 6951 E Southpoint Rd	Tucson	AZ	85756	**888-281-6531**	520-325-1044
Commission on Collegiate Nursing Education 1 Dupont Cir NW Ste 530	Washington	DC	20036	**800-441-1414**	202-887-6791
Commission on Dental Accreditation of Canada 1815 Alta Vista Dr	Ottawa	ON	K1G3Y6	**866-521-2322**	613-523-7114
Community Health Accreditation Program Inc (CHAP) 1275 K St NW Ste 800	Washington	DC	20005	**800-656-9656**	202-862-3413
Continuing Care Accreditation Commission (CARF-CCAC) 1730 Rhode Island Ave NW Ste 209	Washington	DC	20036	**866-888-1122**	202-587-5001
Council of the Section of Legal Education & Admissions to the Bar 321 N Clark St 21st Fl	Chicago	IL	60654	**800-238-2667**	312-988-6738
Council on Academic Accreditation in Audiology & Speech-Language Pathology 2200 Research Blvd	Rockville	MD	20850	**800-498-2071**	301-296-5700
Council on Accreditation (COA) 45 Broadway 29th Fl	New York	NY	10006	**866-262-8088**	212-797-3000
Council on Accreditation of Nurse Anesthesia Educational Programs 222 S Prospect Ave	Park Ridge	IL	60068	**855-526-2262**	847-692-7050
Council on Aviation Accreditation (CAA) *Aviation Accreditation Board International* 3410 Skyway Dr	Auburn	AL	36830	**800-767-4767**	334-844-2431
Council on Chiropractic Education Commission on Accreditation 8049 N 85th Way	Scottsdale	AZ	85258	**888-443-3506**	480-443-8877
Council on Occupational Education 7840 Roswell Rd Bldg 300 Ste 325	Atlanta	GA	30350	**800-917-2081**	770-396-3898
Engineers Canada 180 Elgin St Ste 1100	Ottawa	ON	K2P2K3	**877-408-9273**	613-232-2474
National Accrediting Commission of Cosmetology Arts & Sciences (NACCAS) 4401 Ford Ave Ste 1300	Alexandria	VA	22302	**877-212-5752**	703-600-7600
National Council for Accreditation of Teacher Education (NCATE) 2010 Massachusetts Ave NW Ste 500	Washington	DC	20036	**800-255-8664**	202-466-7496
National Recreation & Park Assn 22377 Belmont Ridge Rd	Ashburn	VA	20148	**800-626-6772**	703-858-0784
North Central Assn Commission on Accreditation & School Improvement (NCA CASI) 9115 Westside Pkwy	Alpharetta	GA	30009	**888-413-3669**	
North Central Assn Higher Learning Commission 230 S LaSalle St	Chicago	IL	60604	**800-621-7440**	312-263-0456
Society of Accredited Marine Surveyors Inc (SAMS) 7855 Argyle Forest Blvd Ste 203	Jacksonville	FL	32244	**800-344-9077**	904-384-1494
Society of American Foresters (SAF) 5400 Grosvenor Ln	Bethesda	MD	20814	**866-897-8720**	301-897-8720
Southern Assn of Colleges & Schools 1866 Southern Ln	Decatur	GA	30033	**888-413-3669**	404-679-4500
Speech-Language and Audiology Canada (CASLPA) 1 Nicholas St Ste 1000	Ottawa	ON	K1N7B7	**800-259-8519**	613-567-9968
TransNational Assn of Christian Colleges & Schools (TRACS) 15935 Forest Rd PO Box 328	Forest	VA	24551	**800-669-4000**	434-525-9539

47-2 Agricultural Organizations

Name / Address	City	State	ZIP	Toll-Free	Phone
Agricultural Retailers Assn (ARA) 1156 15th St NW Ste 500	Washington	DC	20005	**800-535-6272**	202-457-0825
American Angus Assn (AAA) 3201 Frederick Ave	Saint Joseph	MO	64506	**800-821-5478**	816-383-5100
American Assn of Bovine Practitioners (AABP) 3320 Skyway Dr Ste 802 PO Box 3610	Auburn	AL	36831	**800-269-2227**	334-821-0442
American Dairy Science Assn (ADSA) 1111 N Dunlap Ave	Savoy	IL	61874	**888-670-2250**	217-356-5146
American Egg Board (AEB) 1460 Renaissance Dr Ste 301	Park Ridge	IL	60068	**888-549-2140**	847-296-7043
American Farmland Trust (AFT) 1200 18th St	Washington	DC	20036	**800-431-1499**	202-331-7300
American Forest & Paper Assn (AF&PA) 1111 19th St NW Ste 800	Washington	DC	20036	**800-878-8878**	202-463-2700
American Gelbvieh Assn 10900 Dover St	Westminster	CO	80021	**800-529-0900**	303-465-2333
American Royal Assn 1701 American Royal Ct	Kansas City	MO	64102	**866-844-2295**	816-221-9800
American Seed Trade Assn (ASTA) 1701 Duke St Ste 275	Alexandria	VA	22304	**888-890-7333**	703-837-8140
American Society for Horticultural Science (ASHS) 1018 Duke St	Alexandria	VA	22314	**800-331-1600**	703-836-4606
American Society of Agronomy (ASA) 5585 Guilford Rd	Madison	WI	53711	**866-359-9161**	608-273-8080
American Society of Landscape Architects (ASLA) 636 'I' St NW	Washington	DC	20001	**888-999-2752**	202-898-2444
American Soybean Assn (ASA) 12125 Woodcrest Executive Dr Ste 100	Saint Louis	MO	63141	**800-688-7692**	314-576-1770
American-International Charolais Assn (AICA) 11700 NW Plaza Cir	Kansas City	MO	64153	**800-270-7711**	816-464-5977
Association of Consulting Foresters of America (ACF) 312 Montgomery St Ste 208	Alexandria	VA	22314	**888-540-8733**	703-548-0990
Association of Farmworker Opportunity Programs (AFOP) 1120 20th St NW Ste 300	Washington	DC	20036	**866-487-9243**	202-828-6006
Association of Water Technologies (AWT) 9707 Key W Ave Ste 100	Rockville	MD	20850	**800-858-6683**	301-740-1421
Breg Inc 2885 Loker Ave E	Carlsbad	CA	92010	**800-897-2734**	760-599-3000
Cotton Inc 6399 Weston Pkwy	Cary	NC	27513	**800-334-5868**	919-678-2220
CropLife America 1156 15th St NW Ste 400	Washington	DC	20005	**800-266-9432**	202-296-1585
Dairy Management Inc (DMI) 10255 W Higgins Rd Ste 900	Rosemont	IL	60018	**800-853-2479**	
Decatur Co-op Assn 305 S York Ave	Oberlin	KS	67749	**800-886-2293**	785-475-2234
Farmer's Co-op Assn 110 S Keokuk Wash Rd	Keota	IA	52248	**877-843-4893**	641-636-3748
Golf Course Superintendents Assn of America (GCSAA) 1421 Research Pk Dr	Lawrence	KS	66049	**800-472-7878**	785-841-2240
Hohman Assoc Inc (HAI) 6951 W Little York	Houston	TX	77040	**800-324-0978**	713-896-0978
Holstein Assn USA Inc 1 Holstein Pl PO Box 808 *Orders	Brattleboro	VT	05302	**800-952-5200***	802-254-4551
International Plant Nutrition Institute (IPNI) 3500 PkwyLn Ste 550	Norcross	GA	30092	**800-521-3044**	770-447-0335
International Society of Arboriculture (ISA) PO Box 3129	Champaign	IL	61826	**888-472-8733**	217-355-9411
Livestock Marketing Assn (LMA) 10510 N Ambassador Dr	Kansas City	MO	64153	**800-821-2048**	816-891-0502
Mid-Kansas Co-op Assn (MKC) PO Box D	Moundridge	KS	67107	**800-864-4428**	620-345-6361
Milk Industry Foundation (MIF) 1250 H St NW Ste 900	Washington	DC	20005	**866-225-4821**	202-737-4332
Mohair Council of America 233 W Twohig Rd	San Angelo	TX	76903	**800-583-3161**	325-655-3161
National Agri-Marketing Assn (NAMA) 11020 King St Ste 205	Overland Park	KS	66210	**800-530-5646**	913-491-6500
National Association of Landscape Professionals Inc (PLANET) 950 Herndon Pkwy Ste 450	Herndon	VA	20170	**800-395-2522**	703-736-9666
National Cattlemen's Beef Assn (NCBA) 9110 E Nichols Ave Ste 300	Centennial	CO	80112	**866-233-3872**	303-694-0305
National Cotton Council of America 7193 Goodlett Farms Pkwy	Memphis	TN	38016	**888-232-1738**	901-274-9030
National Crop Insurance Services (NCIS) 8900 Indian Creek Pkwy Ste 600	Overland Park	KS	66210	**800-951-6247**	913-685-2767
National Farmers Organization (NFO) 528 Billy Sunday Rd Ste 100 PO Box 2508	Ames	IA	50010	**800-247-2110**	515-292-2000
National FFA Organization 6060 FFA Dr	Indianapolis	IN	46268	**800-772-0939**	317-802-6060
National Grange 1616 H St NW	Washington	DC	20006	**888-447-2643**	202-628-3507
National Turkey Federation (NTF) 1225 New York Ave NW Ste 400	Washington	DC	20005	**866-536-7593**	202-898-0100
National Woodland Owners Assn (NWOA) 374 Maple Ave E Ste 310	Vienna	VA	22180	**800-476-8733**	703-255-2700
North American Limousin Foundation (NALF) 7383 S Alton Way Ste 100	Englewood	CO	80112	**888-320-8747**	303-220-1693
Shelburne Farms 1611 Harbor Rd	Shelburne	VT	05482	**800-286-6022**	802-985-8686
Society of American Foresters (SAF) 5400 Grosvenor Ln	Bethesda	MD	20814	**866-897-8720**	301-897-8720
Southern Forest Products Assn (SFPA) 6660 Riverside Dr Ste 212	Metairie	LA	70065	**866-574-4155**	504-443-4464
Tobacco Merchants Assn (TMA) PO Box 8019	Princeton	NJ	08543	**888-672-4991**	609-275-4900
United Producers Inc 8351 N High St Ste 250	Columbus	OH	43235	**800-456-3276**	
United Soybean Board (USB) 16305 Swingley Ridge Rd Ste 150	Chesterfield	MO	63017	**800-989-8721**	636-530-1777
US Apple Assn 8233 Old Courthouse Rd Ste 200	Vienna	VA	22182	**800-781-4443**	703-442-8850
Wild Blueberry Assn of North America (WBANA) PO Box 100	Old Town	ME	04468	**800-341-1758**	207-570-3535

47-3 Animals & Animal Welfare Organizations

Name / Address	City	State	ZIP	Toll-Free	Phone
African Wildlife Foundation (AWF) 1400 16th St NW Ste 120	Washington	DC	20036	**888-494-5354**	202-939-3333

Organization	Address	City	State	ZIP	Toll-Free	Phone
American Animal Hospital Assn (AAHA)	12575 W Bayaud Ave	Lakewood	CO	80228	**800-252-2242**	303-986-2800
American Assn of Equine Practitioners (AAEP)	4075 Iron Works Pkwy	Lexington	KY	40511	**800-443-0177**	859-233-0147
American Donkey & Mule Society (ADMS)	1346 Morningside Ave	Lewisville	TX	75057	**877-752-4068**	972-219-0781
American Humane Assn (AHA)	63 Inverness Dr E	Englewood	CO	80112	**800-227-4645**	303-792-9900
American Morgan Horse Assn (AMHA)	4066 Shelburne Rd Ste 5	Shelburne	VT	05482	**888-436-3700**	802-985-4944
American Quarter Horse Assn (AQHA)	1600 Quarter Horse Dr	Amarillo	TX	79104	**800-291-7323**	806-376-4811
American Shorthorn Assn	8288 Hascall St	Omaha	NE	68124	**877-272-0686**	402-393-7200
Appaloosa Horse Club (ApHC)	2720 W Pullman Rd	Moscow	ID	83843	**888-304-7768**	208-882-5578
ASPCA Animal Poison Control Ctr	424 E 92nd St	New York	NY	10128	**888-426-4435**	212-876-7700
Association of Zoos & Aquariums (AZA)	8403 Colesville Rd Ste 710	Silver Spring	MD	20910	**800-323-6593**	301-562-0777
Atlantic Salmon Federation (ASF)	PO Box 5200	Saint Andrews	NB	E5B3S8	**800-565-5666**	506-529-1033
Bat Conservation International (BCI)	500 N Capital of Texas Hwy	Austin	TX	78746	**800-538-2287**	512-327-9721
Bird Studies Canada	115 Front St PO Box 160	Port Rowan	ON	N0E1M0	**888-448-2473**	519-586-3531
Born Free USA United with Animal Protection Institute	1122 S St	Sacramento	CA	95814	**800-348-7387**	916-447-3085
Canadian Federation of Humane Societies (CFHS)	30 Concourse Gate Ste 102	Ottawa	ON	K2E7V7	**888-678-2347**	613-224-8072
Canadian Kennel Club (CKC)	200 Ronson Dr Ste 400	Etobicoke	ON	M9W5Z9	**800-250-8040**	416-675-5511
Canadian Peregrine Foundation	1450 O'Connor Dr Bldg B Ste 214	Toronto	ON	M4B2T8	**888-709-3944**	416-481-1233
Certified Horsemanship Assn (CHA)	1795 Alysheba Way Ste 7102	Lexington	KY	40509	**800-399-0138**	859-259-3399
Defenders of Wildlife	1130 17th St NW	Washington	DC	20036	**800-385-9712**	202-682-9400
Delta Waterfowl Foundation	PO Box 3128	Bismarck	ND	58502	**888-987-3695**	701-222-8857
Dian Fossey Gorilla Fund International	800 Cherokee Ave SE	Atlanta	GA	30315	**800-851-0203**	404-624-5881
Friends of Animals Inc (FOA)	777 Post Rd Ste 205	Darien	CT	06820	**800-321-7387**	203-656-1522
In Defense of Animals (IDA)	3010 Kerner Blvd	San Rafael	CA	94901	**800-705-0425**	415-448-0048
International Fund for Animal Welfare (IFAW)	290 Summer St	Yarmouth Port	MA	02675	**800-932-4329**	508-744-2000
International Society for Animal Rights (ISAR)	PO Box F	Clarks Summit	PA	18411	**888-589-6397**	570-586-2200
Jane Goodall Institute for Wildlife Research Education & Conservation (JGI)	1595 Spring Hill Rd Ste 550	Vienna	VA	22182	**800-592-5263**	703-682-9220
Missouri Fox Trotting Horse Breed Assn Inc	PO Box 1027	Ava	MO	65608	**877-663-4203**	417-683-2468
Mountain Lion Foundation	PO Box 1896	Sacramento	CA	95812	**800-319-7621**	916-442-2666
National Anti-Vivisection Society (NAVS)	53 W Jackson Blvd Ste 1552	Chicago	IL	60604	**800-888-6287**	312-427-6065
National Disaster Search Dog Foundation	501 E Ojai Ave	Ojai	CA	93023	**888-459-4376**	805-646-1015
National Wild Turkey Federation (NWTF)	770 Augusta Rd PO Box 530	Edgefield	SC	29824	**800-843-6983*** (*Cust Svc)	803-637-3106
National Wildlife Federation (NWF)	11100 Wildlife Ctr Dr	Reston	VA	20190	**800-822-9919**	703-438-6000
People for the Ethical Treatment of Animals (PETA)	501 Front St	Norfolk	VA	23510	**800-566-9768**	757-622-7382
Performing Animal Welfare Society (PAWS)	11435 Simmerhorn Rd	Galt	CA	95632	**800-513-6560**	209-745-2606
Pet Sitters International (PSI)	201 E King St	King	NC	27021	**800-576-4229**	336-983-9222
Ruffed Grouse Society (RGS)	451 McCormick Rd	Coraopolis	PA	15108	**888-564-6747**	412-262-4044
Save the Manatee Club (SMC)	500 N Maitland Ave Ste 210	Maitland	FL	32751	**800-432-5646**	407-539-0990
Thoroughbred Owners & Breeders Assn (TOBA)	PO Box 910668	Lexington	KY	40591	**888-606-8622**	859-276-2291
Trout Unlimited (TU)	1300 N 17th St Ste 500	Arlington	VA	22209	**800-834-2419**	703-522-0200
World Wildlife Fund (WWF)	1250 24th St NW PO Box 97180	Washington	DC	20090	**800-225-5993**	202-293-4800
World Wildlife Fund Canada (WWF)	245 Eglinton Ave E Ste 410	Toronto	ON	M4P3J1	**800-267-2632**	416-489-8800
Zoocheck Canada	788 1/2 O'Connor Dr	Toronto	ON	M4B2S6	**888-801-3222**	416-285-1744

47-4 Arts & Artists Organizations

Organization	Address	City	State	ZIP	Toll-Free	Phone
American Academy of Arts & Sciences	136 Irving St	Cambridge	MA	02138	**800-666-2211**	617-576-5000
American Assn of Museums (AAM)	1575 Eye St NW Ste 400	Washington	DC	20005	**866-226-2150**	202-289-1818
American Ceramic Society (ACerS)	600 N Cleveland Ave # 210	Westerville	OH	43082	**866-721-3322**	614-890-4700
American Craft Council	72 Spring St 6th Fl	New York	NY	10012	**800-836-3470**	212-274-0630
American Federation of Musicians of the US & Canada (AFM)	1501 Broadway Ste 600	New York	NY	10036	**800-762-3444**	212-869-1330
American Film Institute (AFI)	2021 N Western Ave	Los Angeles	CA	90027	**866-234-3378**	323-856-7600
American Guild of Musical Artists (AGMA)	1430 Broadway 14th Fl	New York	NY	10018	**800-543-2462**	212-265-3687
American Guild of Organists (AGO)	475 Riverside Dr Ste 1260	New York	NY	10115	**855-631-0759**	212-870-2310
American Guild of Variety Artists (AGVA)	363 Seventh Ave 17th Fl	New York	NY	10001	**800-331-0890**	212-675-1003
American Institute of Architects (AIA)	1735 New York Ave NW	Washington	DC	20006	**800-242-3837*** (*Orders)	202-626-7300
American Institute of Graphic Arts (AIGA)	164 Fifth Ave	New York	NY	10010	**800-548-1634**	212-807-1990
American Musicological Society (AMS)	6010 College Stn	Brunswick	ME	04011	**888-421-1442**	207-798-4243
American Society of Cinematographers (ASC)	1782 N Orange Dr	Hollywood	CA	90028	**800-448-0145**	323-969-4333
Americans for the Arts	1000 Vermont Ave NW 6th Fl	Washington	DC	20005	**866-471-2787**	202-371-2830
Association of Film Commissioners International (AFCI)	109 E 17th St	Cheyenne	WY	82001	**888-765-5777**	307-637-4422
Association of Performing Arts Presenters	1211 Connecticut Ave NW Ste 200	Washington	DC	20036	**888-820-2787**	202-833-2787
Bix Beiderbecke Memorial Society	PO Box 3688	Davenport	IA	52808	**888-249-5487**	563-324-7170
Broadway League, The	729 Seventh Ave 5th Fl	New York	NY	10019	**866-442-9878**	212-764-1122
Chamber Music America (CMA)	305 Seventh Ave 5th Fl	New York	NY	10001	**888-221-9836**	212-242-2022
Choristers Guild	2834 W Kingsley Rd	Garland	TX	75041	**800-246-7478**	972-271-1521
Clowns of America International (COAI)	PO Box 122	Eustis	FL	32727	**877-816-6941**	352-357-1676
Country Music Assn Inc (CMA)	1 Music Cir S	Nashville	TN	37203	**800-788-3045**	615-244-2840
Dramatists Guild of America Inc	1501 Broadway Ste 701	New York	NY	10036	**800-289-9366**	212-398-9366
Drum Corps International (DCI)	PO Box 3129	Indianapolis	IN	46206	**800-495-7469*** (*Orders)	317-275-1212
Glass Art Society (GAS)	6512 23rd Ave NW Ste 329	Seattle	WA	98121	**800-636-2377**	206-382-1305
International Interior Design Assn (IIDA)	222 Merchandise Mart Plz Ste 567	Chicago	IL	60654	**888-799-4432**	312-467-1950
Motion Picture & Television Fund	23388 Mulholland Dr	Woodland Hills	CA	91364	**855-760-6783**	
National Academy of Recording Arts & Sciences	3030 Olympic Blvd	Santa Monica	CA	90404	**800-423-2017**	310-392-3777
National Association of Theatre Owners. (NATO)	1705 N St NW Ste 1130	Washington	DC	20036	**800-365-5701*** (*General)	202-962-0054
Percussive Arts Society (PAS)	110 W Washington St	Indianapolis	IN	46204	**888-990-6663**	317-974-4488
Professional Photographers of America Inc (PPA)	229 Peachtree St NE Ste 2200	Atlanta	GA	30303	**800-786-6277**	404-522-8600
Professional Picture Framers Assn (PPFA)	2282 Springport Rd Ste F	Jackson	MI	49202	**800-762-9287**	517-788-8100
Screen Actors Guild (SAG)	5757 Wilshire Blvd	Los Angeles	CA	90036	**800-724-0767**	323-954-1600
SESAC Inc	55 Music Sq E	Nashville	TN	37203	**800-826-9996**	615-320-0055
Society for Ethnomusicology (SEM)	Indiana University, 1165 E 3rd St Morrison Hall 005	Bloomington	IN	47405	**800-933-9330**	812-855-6672
Society of American Archivists (SAA)	17 N State St Ste 1425	Chicago	IL	60602	**866-722-7858**	312-606-0722

47-5 Charitable & Humanitarian Organizations

Organization	Address	City	State	ZIP	Toll-Free	Phone
ACDI/VOCA	50 F St NW Ste 1075	Washington	DC	20001	**800-929-8622**	202-638-4661
Action Against Hunger	247 W 37th St 10th Fl	New York	NY	10018	**877-777-1420**	212-967-7800
Adventist Community Services	12501 Old Columbia Pk	Silver Spring	MD	20904	**877-227-2702**	301-680-6438
Adventist Development & Relief Agency International (ADRA)	12501 Old Columbia Pk	Silver Spring	MD	20904	**800-424-2372**	301-680-6380
Aga Khan Foundation USA (AKF)	1825 K St NW Ste 901	Washington	DC	20006	**800-267-2532**	202-293-2537
Alan Guttmacher Institute (AGI)	125 Maiden Ln 7th Fl	New York	NY	10038	**800-355-0244**	212-248-1111
America's Second Harvest	35 E Wacker Dr Ste 2000	Chicago	IL	60601	**800-771-2303**	312-263-2303
American Anti-Slavery Group, The	198 Tremont St	Boston	MA	02116	**800-884-0719**	617-426-8161
American Jewish World Service (AJWS)	45 W 36th St	New York	NY	10018	**800-889-7146**	212-792-2900
American Lebanese Syrian Associated Charities (ALSAC)	262 Danny Thomas Pl	Memphis	TN	38105	**800-822-6344**	901-578-2000
American Red Cross	2025 E St NW	Washington	DC	20006	**800-257-7575**	202-303-4498
American Refugee Committee (ARC)	430 Oak Grove St Ste 204	Minneapolis	MN	55403	**800-875-7060**	612-872-7060
AmeriCares Foundation	88 Hamilton Ave	Stamford	CT	06902	**800-486-4357**	203-658-9500
Amigos de las Americas	1800 West Loop S Ste 1325	Houston	TX	77027	**800-231-7796**	713-782-5290
Amnesty International USA (AIUSA)	5 Penn Plaza 16th Fl	New York	NY	10001	**866-273-4466**	212-807-8400
Association of Fundraising Professionals (AFP)	4300 Wilson Blvd Ste 300	Arlington	VA	22203	**800-666-3863**	703-684-0410
Bread for the World	425 Third St SW Ste 1200	Washington	DC	20024	**800-822-7323*** (*Cust Svc)	202-639-9400
CARE USA	151 Ellis St NE	Atlanta	GA	30303	**800-521-2273**	404-681-2552
Catholic Medical Mission Board (CMMB)	10 W 17th St	New York	NY	10011	**800-678-5659**	212-242-7757
Catholic Relief Services (CRS)	228 W Lexington St	Baltimore	MD	21201	**800-235-2772**	410-625-2220
Children International	2000 E Red Bridge Rd	Kansas City	MO	64131	**800-888-3089**	816-942-2000
Christian Appalachian Project	6550 S KY Rt 321 PO Box 459	Hagerhill	KY	41222	**800-755-5322**	
Christian Blind Mission (CBM)	450 E Pk Ave	Greenville	SC	29601	**800-937-2264**	864-239-0065

Organization / Address	City	State	Zip	Toll-Free	Phone
Christian Reformed World Relief Committee (CRWRC) 2850 Kalamazoo Ave SE	Grand Rapids	MI	49560	**800-552-7972**	616-241-1691
Church World Service 28606 Phillips St PO Box 968	Elkhart	IN	46515	**800-297-1516**	574-264-3102
Church World Service Emergency Response Program 475 Riverside Dr Ste 700	New York	NY	10115	**888-297-2767**	212-870-2061
Coalition on Human Needs (CHN) 1120 Connecticut Ave NW	Washington	DC	20036	**800-822-7323**	202-223-2532
Community Food Bank of New Jersey Inc 31 Evans Terminal	Hillside	NJ	07205	**866-527-1087**	908-355-3663
Community Health Charities 200 N Glebe Rd Ste 801	Arlington	VA	22203	**800-654-0845**	703-528-1007
Compassion International 12290 Voyager Pkwy	Colorado Springs	CO	80921	**800-336-7676**	719-487-7000
Concern America 2015 N Broadway	Santa Ana	CA	92706	**800-266-2376**	714-953-8575
Council on Foundations 2121 Crystal Dr Ste 700	Arlington	VA	22202	**800-673-9036**	703-879-0600
CRISTA Ministries 19303 Fremont Ave N *Cust Svc	Seattle	WA	98133	**800-346-9140***	206-546-7200
Direct Relief International 27 S La Patera Ln	Goleta	CA	93117	**800-676-1638**	805-964-4767
Doctors Without Borders USA Inc 333 Seventh Ave 2nd Fl	New York	NY	10001	**888-392-0392**	212-679-6800
Enterprise Community Partners Inc 10227 Wincopin Cir	Columbia	MD	21044	**800-624-4298**	410-964-1230
Episcopal Migration Ministries (EMM) 815 Second Ave	New York	NY	10017	**800-334-7626**	212-716-6258
Episcopal Relief & Development 815 Second Ave	New York	NY	10017	**800-334-7626**	855-312-4325
Evangelical Council for Financial Accountability (ECFA) 440 W Jubal Early Dr Ste 130	Winchester	VA	22601	**800-323-9473**	540-535-0103
Feed the Children (FTC) PO Box 36	Oklahoma City	OK	73101	**800-627-4556**	405-942-0228
Food for the Poor Inc (FFP) 6401 Lyons Rd	Coconut Creek	FL	33073	**800-427-9104**	954-427-2222
Foundation for International Community Assistance (FINCA) 1201 15th St NW 8th fl	Washington	DC	20005	**855-903-4622**	202-682-1510
Freedom from Hunger 1460 Drew Ave Ste 300	Davis	CA	95618	**800-708-2555**	530-758-6200
Goodwill Industries International Inc 15810 Indianola Dr	Rockville	MD	20855	**800-741-0197**	301-530-6500
Habitat for Humanity International Inc 121 Habitat St	Americus	GA	31709	**800-422-4828**	229-924-6935
Healing the Children (HTC) 2624 W Beacon Ave	Spokane	WA	99208	**888-233-9527**	509-327-4281
Hebrew Immigrant Aid Society (HIAS) 333 Seventh Ave 16th Fl	New York	NY	10001	**800-442-7714**	212-967-4100
Heifer International 1 World Ave	Little Rock	AR	72202	**800-422-0474**	501-907-2600
Helen Keller International 352 Pk Ave S Ste 1200	New York	NY	10010	**877-535-5374**	212-532-0544
HELP USA 5 Hanover Sq	New York	NY	10004	**800-311-7999**	212-400-7000
Housing Assistance Council (HAC) 1025 Vermont Ave NW Ste 606	Washington	DC	20005	**866-234-2689**	202-842-8600
Hunger Project, The 5 Union Sq W	New York	NY	10003	**800-228-6691**	212-251-9100
Independent Charities of America (ICA) 1100 Larkspur Landing Cir Ste 340	Larkspur	CA	94939	**800-477-0733**	415-925-2600
Independent Order of Foresters (IOF) 789 Don Mills Rd	Toronto	ON	M3C1T9	**800-828-1540**	416-429-3000
Independent Sector 1602 L St NW Ste 900	Washington	DC	20036	**888-737-9477**	202-467-6100
Interchurch Medical Assistance Inc (IMA) 500 Main St PO Box 429	New Windsor	MD	21776	**877-241-7952**	410-635-8720
International Aid Inc 17011 W Hickory St	Spring Lake	MI	49456	**800-968-7490**	616-846-7490
International Medical Corps (IMC) 1919 Santa Monica Blvd Ste 400	Santa Monica	CA	90404	**800-481-4462**	310-826-7800
International Orthodox Christian Charities (IOCC) 110 W Rd Ste 360	Towson	MD	21204	**877-803-4622**	410-243-9820
International Planned Parenthood Federation - Western Hemisphere Region (IPPF/WHR) 125 Maiden Ln 9th Fl	New York	NY	10005	**866-477-3947**	212-248-6400
International Rescue Committee (IRC) 122 E 42nd St 12th Fl	New York	NY	10168	**800-435-7352**	212-551-3000
Lutheran Disaster Response 8765 W Higgins Rd	Chicago	IL	60631	**800-638-3522**	
Make-A-Wish Foundation of America 4742 N 24th St Ste 400	Phoenix	AZ	85016	**800-722-9474**	602-279-9474
MAP International 4700 Glynco Pkwy	Brunswick	GA	31525	**800-225-8550**	912-265-6010
Medical Teams International (MTI) PO Box 10	Portland	OR	97207	**800-959-4325**	503-624-1000
Mennonite Central Committee (MCC) 21 S 12th St PO Box 500	Akron	PA	17501	**888-563-4676**	717-859-1151
Mennonite Disaster Service (MDS) 583 Airport Rd	Lititz	PA	17543	**800-241-8111**	717-735-3536
MENTOR/National Mentoring Partnership 201 South St Ste 615	Boston	MA	02111	**877-333-2464**	703-224-2200
Mercy-USA for Aid & Development Inc (M-USA) 44450 Pinetree Dr Ste 201	Plymouth	MI	48170	**800-556-3729**	734-454-0011
Michigan Municipal League 1675 Green Rd PO Box 1487	Ann Arbor	MI	48105	**800-653-2483**	734-662-3246
NA for the Exchange of Industrial Resources (NAEIR) 560 McClure St	Galesburg	IL	61401	**800-562-0955**	309-343-0704
National Alliance to End Homelessness 1518 K St NW Ste 410	Washington	DC	20005	**800-657-3769**	202-638-1526
National AMBUCS Inc (AMBUCS) 4285 Regency Ct PO Box 5127	High Point	NC	27265	**800-838-1845**	336-852-0052
National Coalition for the Homeless (NCH) 2201 P St NW	Washington	DC	20037	**877-243-1576**	202-462-4822
National Peace Corps Assn (NPCA) 1900 L St NW Ste 610	Washington	DC	20036	**800-424-8580**	202-293-7728
North American Mission Board SBC 4200 N Pt Pkwy	Alpharetta	GA	30022	**800-634-2462**	770-410-6000
Operation USA 3617 Hayden Ave Ste A	Culver City	CA	90232	**800-678-7255**	310-838-3455

Organization / Address	City	State	Zip	Toll-Free	Phone
ORBIS International Inc 520 Eigth Ave 11th Fl	New York	NY	10018	**800-672-4787**	646-674-5500
Oregon Food Bank Inc 7900 NE 33rd Dr	Portland	OR	97211	**888-398-8702**	503-282-0555
ORT American Inc 75 Maiden Ln 10th Fl	New York	NY	10038	**800-519-2678**	212-505-7700
Outreach International 129 W Lexington PO Box 210	Independence	MO	64050	**888-833-1235**	816-833-0883
Oxfam America 226 Cswy St 5th Fl	Boston	MA	02114	**800-776-9326**	617-482-1211
Pan American Development Foundation (PADF) 1889 F St NW 2nd Fl	Washington	DC	20006	**877-572-4484**	202-458-3969
People-to-People Health Foundation 255 Carter Hall Ln	Millwood	VA	22646	**800-544-4673**	540-837-2100
Physicians for Social Responsibility (PSR) 1875 Connecticut Ave NW Ste 1012	Washington	DC	20009	**800-459-1887**	202-667-4260
Points of Light Foundation & Volunteer Ctr National Network 1400 'I' St NW Ste 800	Washington	DC	20005	**866-269-0510**	202-729-8000
Population Connection 2120 L St NW Ste 500	Washington	DC	20037	**800-767-1956**	202-332-2200
Presbyterian Disaster Assistance (PDA) 100 Witherspoon St	Louisville	KY	40202	**800-728-7228**	
Project Concern International (PCI) 5151 Murphy Canyon Rd Ste 320	San Diego	CA	92123	**877-724-4673**	858-279-9690
ProLiteracy Worldwide 1320 Jamesville Ave	Syracuse	NY	13210	**800-448-8878**	315-422-9121
Rebuilding Together Inc 1899 L St NW Ste 1000	Washington	DC	20036	**800-473-4229**	
Refugees International (RI) 2001 S St NW Ste 700-K	Washington	DC	20009	**800-733-8433**	202-828-0110
Research!America 1101 King St Ste 520	Alexandria	VA	22314	**800-366-2873**	703-739-2577
Ronald McDonald House Charities (RMHC) 1 Kroc Dr	Oak Brook	IL	60523	**855-670-4787**	630-623-7048
Rotary Foundation, The 1560 Sherman Ave	Evanston	IL	60201	**800-435-7352**	847-866-3000
Sertoma International 1912 E Meyer Blvd	Kansas City	MO	64132	**800-593-5646**	816-333-8300
Share Our Strength 1730 M St NW Ste 700	Washington	DC	20036	**800-969-4767**	202-393-2925
Smile Train Inc 41 Madison Ave Ste 28	New York	NY	10010	**877-543-7645**	212-689-9199
Society of Saint Andrew (SoSA) 3383 Sweet Hollow Rd	Big Island	VA	24526	**800-333-4597**	434-299-5956
Southeast Asia Resource Action Ctr (SEARAC) 1628 16th St NW 3rd Fl	Washington	DC	20009	**888-907-1485**	202-667-4690
TechnoServe 1 Mechanic St	Norwalk	CT	06854	**800-999-6757**	203-852-0377
Trickle Up Program Inc 104 W 27th St 12th Fl	New York	NY	10001	**866-246-9980**	212-255-9980
Unitarian Universalist Service Committee (UUSC) 689 Massachusetts Ave	Cambridge	MA	02139	**800-388-3920**	617-868-6600
United Way of America 701 N Fairfax St	Alexandria	VA	22314	**800-892-2757**	703-836-7100
US Fund for UNICEF 125 Maiden Ln	New York	NY	10038	**800-367-5437**	
USA for UNHCR 1775 K St NW Ste 580	Washington	DC	20006	**800-770-1100**	202-296-1115
Veterans for Peace Inc (VFP) 216 S Meramec Ave	Saint Louis	MO	63105	**877-429-0678**	314-725-6005
Voices of September 11th 161 Cherry St	New Canaan	CT	06840	**866-505-3911**	203-966-3911
Volunteers of America 1660 Duke St	Alexandria	VA	22314	**800-899-0089**	703-341-5000
War Resisters League 339 Lafayette St	New York	NY	10012	**800-975-9688**	212-228-0450
World Concern 19303 Fremont Ave N	Seattle	WA	98133	**800-755-5022**	206-546-7201
World Food Program USA (WFP) 1725 Eye St NW Ste 510	Washington	DC	20036	**888-454-0555**	202-530-1694
World Hunger Year Inc (WHY) 505 Eigth Ave Ste 2100	New York	NY	10018	**800-548-6479**	212-629-8850
World Learning 1 Kipling Rd PO Box 676	Brattleboro	VT	05302	**800-257-7751**	802-257-7751
World Neighbors Inc (WN) 4127 NW 122nd St	Oklahoma City	OK	73120	**800-242-6387**	405-752-9700
World Relief 7 E Baltimore St	Baltimore	MD	21202	**800-535-5433**	443-451-1900
World Vision Inc 34834 Weyerhaeuser Way S PO Box 9716	Federal Way	WA	98001	**888-511-6548**	253-815-1000

47-6 Children & Family Advocacy Organizations

Organization / Address	City	State	Zip	Toll-Free	Phone
AARP 601 E St NW	Washington	DC	20049	**888-687-2277**	202-434-2277
AARP Grandparent Information Ctr 601 E St NW	Washington	DC	20049	**888-687-2277**	202-434-3525
Adoption ARC Inc 4701 Pine St Ste J-7	Philadelphia	PA	19143	**800-884-4004**	215-748-1441
Alliance for Aging Research (AAR) 750 17th St NW Ste 1100	Washington	DC	20006	**866-840-6283**	202-293-2856
Alliance for Children & Families Inc 11700 W Lk Pk Dr	Milwaukee	WI	53224	**800-221-3726**	414-359-1040
Alliance for Retired Americans 815 16th St NW 4th Fl	Washington	DC	20006	**888-373-6497**	202-637-5399
American Academy of Pediatrics (AAP) 141 NW Pt Blvd	Elk Grove Village	IL	60007	**800-433-9016**	847-434-4000
American Coalition for Fathers & Children (ACFC) 1718 M St NW Ste 1187	Washington	DC	20036	**800-978-3237**	
American Humane Assn (AHA) 63 Inverness Dr E	Englewood	CO	80112	**800-227-4645**	303-792-9900
American Society on Aging (ASA) 575 Market St Ste 2100	San Francisco	CA	94105	**800-537-9728**	415-974-9600
Association for Couples in Marriage Enrichment (ACME) PO Box 21374	Winston-Salem	NC	27120	**800-634-8325**	336-724-1526
Believe In Tomorrow National Children's Foundation 6601 Frederick Rd	Baltimore	MD	21228	**800-933-5470**	410-744-1032

Name / Address	City	State	Zip	Toll-Free	Phone
Blue Grass Regional Mental Health-Mental Retardation Board Inc 1351 Newtown Pike Bldg 1	Lexington	KY	40511	800-928-8000	859-253-1686
Boys Town 14100 Crawford St	Boys Town	NE	68010	800-448-3000	402-498-1300
Buckner International 600 N Pearl St Ste 2000 20th Fl	Dallas	TX	75201	800-442-4800	214-758-8000
Cal Farley's Boys Ranch 600 W 11th St PO Box 1890	Amarillo	TX	79174	800-687-3722	806-372-2341
Camelot Community Care Inc 4910 D Creekside Dr	Clearwater	FL	33760	800-435-7352	727-593-0003
Child Find Canada 212-2211 McPhillips St	Winnipeg	MB	R2V3M5	800-387-7962	204-339-5584
Child Lures Prevention 5166 Shelburne Rd	Shelburne	VT	05482	800-552-2197	802-985-8458
Childhelp USA 4350 E Camelback Rd Bldg F250	Phoenix	AZ	85018	800-422-4453	480-922-8212
Children Awaiting Parents Inc (CAP) 595 Blossom Rd Ste 306	Rochester	NY	14610	888-835-8802	585-232-5110
Children Inc 4205 Dover Rd	Richmond	VA	23221	800-538-5381	804-359-4562
Children of the Night 14530 Sylvan St	Van Nuys	CA	91411	800-551-1300	818-908-4474
Children's Defense Fund (CDF) 25 E St NW	Washington	DC	20001	800-233-1200	202-628-8787
Christian Foundation for Children & Aging (CFCA) 1 Elmwood Ave	Kansas City	KS	66103	800-875-6564	913-384-6500
Connecting Generations 100 W Tenth St Ste 1115	Wilmington	DE	19801	877-202-9050	302-656-2122
Corps Network, The 1275 K St NW Ste 1050	Washington	DC	20005	800-245-5627	202-737-6272
Covenant House 5 Penn Plz Ste 2	New York	NY	10001	800-999-9999	212-727-4000
DePelchin Children's Ctr 4950 Memorial Dr	Houston	TX	77007	888-730-2335	713-730-2335
Envision Inc 610 N Main St	Wichita	KS	67203	888-425-7072	316-440-1500
Evan B Donaldson Adoption Institute 120 E 38th St	New York	NY	10016	800-837-2655	212-925-4089
Experience Works Inc 4401 Wilson Blvd Ste 1100	Arlington	VA	22203	866-397-9757	703-522-7272
Family Research Council (FRC) 801 G St NW	Washington	DC	20001	800-225-4008	202-393-2100
Find the Children 2656 29th St Ste 203	Santa Monica	CA	90405	888-477-6721	310-314-3213
First Candle 1314 Bedford Ave Ste 210	Baltimore	MD	21208	800-221-7437	410-653-8226
Focus on the Family 8605 Explorer Dr *Sales	Colorado Springs	CO	80920	800-232-6459*	719-531-3400
Generations United (GU) 1333 H St NW Ste 500-W	Washington	DC	20005	800-677-1116	202-289-3979
Girls Inc 120 Wall St 3rd Fl	New York	NY	10005	800-374-4475	212-509-2000
Human Life International (HLI) 4 Family Life Ln *Orders	Front Royal	VA	22630	800-549-5433*	540-635-7884
Jewish Board of Family & Children Services (JBFCS) 120 W 57th St	New York	NY	10019	888-523-2769	212-582-9100
Kansas Children's Service League (KCSL) 3545 SW 5th	Topeka	KS	66606	877-530-5275	785-274-3100
Leading Age 2519 Connecticut Ave NW	Washington	DC	20008	866-702-3278	202-783-2242
May Institute Inc 41 Pacella Pk Dr	Randolph	MA	02368	800-778-7601	781-440-0400
MENTOR/National Mentoring Partnership 201 South St Ste 615	Boston	MA	02111	877-333-2464	703-224-2200
MOPS International 2370 S Trenton Way *General	Denver	CO	80231	888-910-6677*	303-733-5353
Mothers Against Drunk Driving (MADD) 511 E John Carpenter Fwy Ste 700	Irving	TX	75062	877-275-6233	214-744-6233
National Caregiving Foundation 801 N Pitt St	Alexandria	VA	22314	800-930-1357	703-299-9300
National Child Care Assn (NCCA) 1325 G St NW Ste 500	Washington	DC	20005	866-536-1945	
National Coalition Against Domestic Violence (NCADV) 1 Broadway Ste B210	Denver	CO	80203	800-799-7233	303-839-1852
National Council on Family Relations (NCFR) 1201 W River Pkwy Ste 200	Minneapolis	MN	55454	888-781-9331	
National Council on the Aging (NCOA) 1901 L St NW 4th Fl	Washington	DC	20036	800-677-1116	202-479-1200
National Court Appointed Special Advocate Assn (CASA) 100 W Harrison St N Twr Ste 500	Seattle	WA	98119	800-628-3233	206-270-0072
National Ctr for Family Literacy (NCFL) 325 W Main St Ste 300	Louisville	KY	40202	855-937-5668	502-584-1133
National Ctr for Missing & Exploited Children (NCMEC) 699 Prince St	Alexandria	VA	22314	800-843-5678	703-274-3900
National Domestic Violence Hotline (NDVH) PO Box 161810	Austin	TX	78716	800-799-7233	512-794-1133
National Family Caregivers Assn (NFCA) 10400 Connecticut Ave Ste 500	Kensington	MD	20895	800-896-3650	301-942-6430
National Hispanic Council on Aging (NHCOA) 734 15th St NW Ste 1050	Washington	DC	20005	800-633-4227	202-347-9733
National Resource Ctr on Domestic Violence (NRCDV) 6400 Flank Dr Ste 1300	Harrisburg	PA	17112	800-799-7233	
National Resource Ctr on Native American Aging (NRCNAA) 501 N Columbia Rd Rm 4535	Grand Forks	ND	58202	800-896-7628	701-777-6780
National Runaway Switchboard (NRS) 3141 N Lincoln Ave	Chicago	IL	60657	800-786-2929	773-880-9860
National Urban Technology Ctr 80 Maiden Ln Ste 606	New York	NY	10038	800-998-3212	212-528-7350
National WIC Assn (NWA) 2001 S St NW Ste 580	Washington	DC	20009	866-782-6246	202-232-5492
North American Council on Adoptable Children (NACAC) 970 Raymond Ave Ste 106	Saint Paul	MN	55114	877-823-2237	651-644-3036
Orphan Foundation of America (OFA) 21351 Gentry Dr Ste 130	Sterling	VA	20166	800-950-4673	571-203-0270
Parents Helping Parents (PHP) 1400 Parkmoor Ave Ste 100	San jose	CA	95126	855-727-5775	408-727-5775
Parents of Murdered Children (POMC) 4960 Ridge Ave Ste 2	Cincinnati	OH	45209	888-818-7662	513-721-5683
Parsons Child & Family Ctr 60 Academy Rd	Albany	NY	12208	800-342-3009	518-426-2600
Pension Rights Ctr 1350 Connecticut Ave NW Ste 206	Washington	DC	20036	866-735-7737	202-296-3776
Plan USA 155 Plan Way	Warwick	RI	02886	800-556-7918	401-738-5600
Planned Parenthood Federation of America 434 W 33rd St	New York	NY	10001	800-230-7526	212-541-7800
Pressley Ridge 5500 Corporate Dr Ste 400	Pittsburgh	PA	15237	800-718-0356	412-872-9400
Promise Keepers (PK) PO Box 11798	Denver	CO	80211	866-776-6473	
Rape Abuse & Incest National Network (RAINN) 2000 L St NW Ste 406	Washington	DC	20036	800-656-4673	202-544-1034
SOS Children's Villages-USA 1001 Connecticut Ave NW Ste 1250 *General	Washington	DC	20036	888-767-4543*	202-347-7920
Students Against Destructive Decisions (SADD) 255 Main St	Marlborough	MA	01752	877-723-3462	508-481-3568
Well Spouse Assn 63 W Main St Ste H	Freehold	NJ	07728	800-838-0879	732-577-8899
YMCA of the USA (YMCA) 101 N Wacker Dr	Chicago	IL	60606	800-872-9622	312-977-0031
YWCA USA (YWCA) 2025 M St NW Ste 550	Washington	DC	20036	888-872-9259	202-467-0801

47-7 Civic & Political Organizations

Name / Address	City	State	Zip	Toll-Free	Phone
Advocates for Self-Government 1010 N Tennessee St Ste 215	Cartersville	GA	30120	800-932-1776	770-386-8372
Americans for Democratic Action (ADA) 1625 K St NW Ste 210	Washington	DC	20006	855-712-8441	202-785-5980
Americans for Peace Now (APN) 1101 14th St NW 6th Fl	Washington	DC	20005	877-429-0678	202-728-1893
Americans United for Separation of Church & State 518 C St NE	Washington	DC	20002	800-875-3707	202-466-3234
Brady Campaign to Prevent Gun Violence 1225 'I' St NW Ste 1100	Washington	DC	20005	800-732-0999	202-898-0792
Campaign Legal Ctr Media Policy Program Campaign Legal Ctr	Washington	DC	20036	877-855-5007	202-736-2200
Center for Democracy & Technology (CDT) 1634 'I' St NW 11th Fl	Washington	DC	20006	800-869-4499	202-637-9800
Christian Coalition of America PO Box 37030	Washington	DC	20013	888-999-6778	202-479-6900
Citizens Against Government Waste (CAGW) 1301 Pennsylvania Ave NW Ste 1075	Washington	DC	20004	800-435-7352	202-467-5300
Citizens Committee for the Right to Keep & Bear Arms (CCRKBA) 12500 NE Tenth Pl	Bellevue	WA	98005	800-426-4302	425-454-4911
Citizens for Tax Justice (CTJ) 1616 P St NW Ste 200-B	Washington	DC	20036	888-626-2622	202-299-1066
Close Up Foundation 1330 Braddock Pl Ste 400	Alexandria	VA	22314	800-256-7387	703-706-3300
Community Assns Institute (CAI) 6402 Arlington Blvd Ste 500	Falls Church	VA	22042	888-224-4321	703-970-9220
Concord Coalition 1011 Arlington Blvd Ste 300	Arlington	VA	22209	888-333-4248	703-894-6222
Congress Watch 215 Pennsylvania Ave SE	Washington	DC	20003	800-289-3787	202-546-4996
Constitutional Rights Foundation 601 S Kingsley Dr	Los Angeles	CA	90005	800-488-4273	213-487-5590
Council of Canadians 170 Laurier Ave W Ste 700	Ottawa	ON	K1P5V5	800-387-7177	613-233-2773
EMILY's List 1800 M St NW Ste 375N	Washington	DC	20036	800-683-6459	202-326-1400
Evangelicals for Social Action (ESA) PO Box 367	Wayne	PA	19087	800-650-6600	484-384-2990
Families USA 1201 New York Ave NW Ste 1100	Washington	DC	20005	888-392-5132	202-628-3030
Federation for American Immigration Reform (FAIR) 25 Massachusetts Ave NW Ste 330	Washington	DC	20009	877-627-3247	202-328-7004
Foreign Policy Assn (FPA) 470 Pk Ave S	New York	NY	10016	800-628-5754	212-481-8100
FreedomWorks 400 N Capitol St NW Ste 765	Washington	DC	20001	888-564-6273	202-783-3870
Global Exchange 2017 Mission St Ste 303	San Francisco	CA	94110	800-497-1994	415-255-7296
Interfaith Alliance 1212 New York Ave NW Ste 1250	Washington	DC	20005	800-510-0969	202-238-3300
Judicial Watch Inc 425 Third St SW Ste 800	Washington	DC	20024	888-593-8442	202-646-5172
Junior Chamber International (JCI) 15645 Olive Blvd	Chesterfield	MO	63017	800-905-5499	636-449-3100
NA of Town Watch (NATW) 308 E Lancaster Ave Ste 115	Wynnewood	PA	19096	800-648-3688	
National Committee to Preserve Social Security & Medicare (NCPSSM) 10 G St NE Ste 600	Washington	DC	20002	800-966-1935	202-216-0420
National Council on Public History (NCPH) 425 University Blvd 327 Cavanaugh Hall	Indianapolis	IN	46202	800-554-5542	317-274-2716
National Ctr for Neighborhood Enterprise (NCNE) 1625 K St Ste 1200	Washington	DC	20006	866-518-1263	202-518-6500
National Federation of Republican Women (NFRW) 124 N Alfred St	Alexandria	VA	22314	800-373-9688	703-548-9688
National Taxpayers Union (NTU) 108 N Alfred St	Alexandria	VA	22314	800-680-7289	703-683-5700
OMB Watch 1742 Connecticut Ave NW	Washington	DC	20009	866-544-7573	202-234-8494
Organization of American States (OAS) 1889 F St NW	Washington	DC	20006	888-442-4887	202-458-3000
People for the American Way (PFAW) 2000 M St NW Ste 400	Washington	DC	20036	800-326-7329	202-467-4999
Population Reference Bureau (PRB) 1875 Connecticut Ave NW Ste 520	Washington	DC	20009	800-877-9881	202-483-1100

Classified Section

Organization / Address	City	State	Zip	Toll-Free	Phone
Population-Environment Balance Inc 2000 P St NW Ste 600	Washington	DC	20036	**800-866-6269**	202-955-5700
Project Vote 1350 I St NW Ste 1250	Washington	DC	20005	**888-546-4173**	202-546-4173
US Junior Chamber of Commerce 7447 S Lewis Ave	Tulsa	OK	74136	**800-905-5499**	636-681-1857
Young America's Foundation 110 Elden St	Herndon	VA	20170	**800-292-9231**	800-872-1776

47-8 Civil & Human Rights Organizations

Organization / Address	City	State	Zip	Toll-Free	Phone
American Civil Liberties Union (ACLU) 125 Broad St 18th Fl	New York	NY	10004	**877-867-1025**	212-549-2500
Americans for Effective Law Enforcement (AELE) 841 W Touhy Ave	Park Ridge	IL	60068	**800-763-2802**	847-685-0700
Anti-Defamation League (ADL) 605 Third Ave	New York	NY	10158	**866-386-3235**	212-885-7700
Asian American Legal Defense & Education Fund (AALDEF) 99 Hudson St 12th Fl	New York	NY	10013	**800-966-5946**	212-966-5932
Center for Individual Rights (CIR) 1233 20th St NW Ste 300	Washington	DC	20036	**877-426-2665**	202-833-8400
Corporate Accountability International 10 Milk St Ste 610	Boston	MA	02108	**800-688-8797**	617-695-2525
Disability Rights Ctr Inc 18 Low Ave	Concord	NH	03301	**800-834-1721**	603-228-0432
Families Against Mandatory Minimums (FAMM) 1612 K St NW Ste 700	Washington	DC	20006	**800-435-7352**	202-822-6700
Human Rights Campaign 1640 Rhode Island Ave NW	Washington	DC	20036	**800-777-4723**	202-628-4160
Lambda Legal Defense & Education Fund 120 Wall St Ste 1500	New York	NY	10005	**866-542-8336**	212-809-8585
Leadership Conference on Civil Rights (LCCR) 1629 K St NW Ste 1000	Washington	DC	20006	**888-460-0813**	202-466-3311
Media Watch PO Box 618	Santa Cruz	CA	95061	**800-631-6355**	831-423-6355
Medicare Rights Ctr (MRC) 520 Eigth Ave N Wing 3rd Fl *Hotline	New York	NY	10018	**800-333-4114***	212-869-3850
NA for the Advancement of Colored People (NAACP) 4805 Mt Hope Dr	Baltimore	MD	21215	**877-622-2798**	410-580-5777
National Abortion Federation (NAF) 1755 Massachusetts Ave NW	Washington	DC	20036	**800-772-9100**	202-667-5881
National Coalition Against Domestic Violence (NCADV) 1 Broadway Ste B210	Denver	CO	80203	**800-799-7233**	303-839-1852
National Conference on Citizenship (NCOC) 1875 K St NW 5th Fl	Washington	DC	20006	**800-745-7275**	202-729-8038
National Council on Crime & Delinquency (NCCD) 1970 Broadway Ste 500	Oakland	CA	94612	**800-306-6223**	510-208-0500
National Ctr for Victims of Crime, The 2000 M St NW Ste 480	Washington	DC	20036	**800-394-2255**	202-467-8700
National Freedom of Information Coalition Univ of Missouri	Columbia	MO	65211	**866-682-6663**	573-882-4856
National Organization for the Reform of Marijuana Laws (NORML) 1600 K St NW Ste 501	Washington	DC	20006	**888-676-6765**	202-483-5500
National Organization for Victim Assistance (NOVA) 510 King St Ste 424	Alexandria	VA	22314	**800-879-6682**	703-535-6682
Patients Rights Council (PRC) PO Box 760	Steubenville	OH	43952	**800-958-5678**	740-282-3810
Rutherford Institute PO Box 7482	Charlottesville	VA	22906	**800-225-1791**	434-978-3888
Second Amendment Foundation 12500 NE Tenth Pl	Bellevue	WA	98005	**800-426-4302**	425-454-7012
Simon Wiesenthal Ctr 1399 Roxbury Dr Ste 100	Los Angeles	CA	90035	**800-900-9036**	310-553-9036
Southern Poverty Law Ctr (SPLC) 400 Washington Ave	Montgomery	AL	36104	**888-414-7752**	334-956-8200
Urban Land Institute (ULI) 1025 Thomas Jefferson St NW Ste 500W *Orders	Washington	DC	20007	**800-321-5011***	202-624-7000
WeTip Inc PO Box 1296	Rancho Cucamonga	CA	91729	**800-782-7463**	909-987-5005

47-9 Computer & Internet Organizations

Organization / Address	City	State	Zip	Toll-Free	Phone
Association for Computing Machinery (ACM) 2 Penn Plz Ste 701	New York	NY	10121	**800-342-6626**	212-626-0500
Consortium for School Networking (CoSN) 1025 Vermont Ave NW Ste 1010	Washington	DC	20005	**866-267-8747**	202-861-2676
Information Systems Audit & Control Assn (ISACA) 3701 Algonquin Rd Ste 1010	Rolling Meadows	IL	60008	**888-491-8833**	847-253-1545
Institute for Certification of Computing Professionals (ICCP) 2400 E Devon Ave Ste 281	Des Plaines	IL	60018	**800-843-8227**	847-299-4227
National Urban Technology Ctr 80 Maiden Ln Ste 606	New York	NY	10038	**800-998-3212**	212-528-7350
Open Group 44 Montgomery St Ste 960	San Francisco	CA	94104	**800-433-6611**	415-374-8280
Print Services & Distribution Assn (PSDA) 330 N. Wabash Ave Ste 2000	Chicago	IL	60611	**800-336-4641**	800-230-0175
Society for Information Management (SIM) 15000 Commerce Pkwy Ste C	Mount Laurel	NJ	08054	**800-387-9746**	312-527-6734
TechServe Alliance 1420 King St Ste 610	Alexandria	VA	22314	**888-421-1442**	703-838-2050

47-10 Consumer Interest Organizations

Organization / Address	City	State	Zip	Toll-Free	Phone
Accuracy in Media Inc (AIM) 4350 EW Hwy Ste 555	Bethesda	MD	20814	**800-787-4567**	202-364-4401
Advocates for Highway & Auto Safety 750 First St NE Ste 901	Washington	DC	20002	**877-366-0711**	202-408-1711
American Council on Science & Health (ACSH) 110 E 42nd St Ste 1300	New York	NY	10017	**866-905-2694**	212-362-7044
Consumer Federation of America (CFA) 1620 I St NW Ste 200	Washington	DC	20006	**877-382-4357**	202-387-6121
Consumers' Research Council of America (CRCA) 2020 Pennsylvania Ave NW Ste 300-A	Washington	DC	20006	**877-774-6337**	202-835-9698
Funeral Consumers Alliance 33 Patchen Rd	South Burlington	VT	05403	**800-765-0107**	802-865-8300
Insurance Information Institute Inc (III) 110 William St	New York	NY	10038	**877-263-7995**	212-346-5500
National Committee for Quality Assurance (NCQA) 1100 13th St	Washington	DC	20005	**888-275-7585**	202-955-3500
National Consumers League (NCL) 1701 K St NW Ste 1200	Washington	DC	20006	**800-388-2227**	202-835-3323
National Fraud Information Ctr (NFIC) 1701 K St NW Ste 1200	Washington	DC	20006	**800-333-4636**	202-835-3323
Private Citizen Inc PO Box 233	Naperville	IL	60566	**888-382-1222**	630-393-1555

47-11 Educational Associations & Organizations

Organization / Address	City	State	Zip	Toll-Free	Phone
A Better Chance Inc 253 W 35th St 6th Fl	New York	NY	10001	**800-562-7865**	646-346-1310
Alliance for International Educational & Cultural Exchange 1776 Massachusetts Ave NW Ste 620	Washington	DC	20036	**888-304-9023**	202-293-6141
American Indian College Fund 8333 Greenwood Blvd	Denver	CO	80221	**800-776-3863**	303-426-8900
Archaeological Institute of America (AIA) 656 Beacon St 4th Fl	Boston	MA	02215	**877-524-6300**	617-353-9361
Astronomical Society of the Pacific 390 Ashton Ave	San Francisco	CA	94112	**800-335-2624**	415-337-1100
Braille Institute of America Inc 741 N Vermont Ave	Los Angeles	CA	90029	**800-272-4553**	323-663-1111
Challenger Ctr for Space Science Education 422 First St SE 3rd Fl *General	Washington	DC	20003	**800-969-5747***	202-827-1580
Chickasaw Nation, The 520 Arlington St PO Box 1548	Ada	OK	74821	**866-466-1481**	580-436-2603
College Board 45 Columbus Ave	New York	NY	10023	**800-927-4302**	212-713-8000
College Parents of America (CPA) 2200 Wilson Blvd Ste 102-396	Arlington	VA	22201	**888-761-6702**	
Comstar Enterprises Inc PO Box 6698	Springdale	AR	72766	**800-533-2343**	479-361-2111
Education Development Ctr Inc (EDC) 55 Chapel St	Newton	MA	02458	**800-225-4276**	617-969-7100
Facing History & Ourselves 16 HuRd Rd	Brookline	MA	02445	**800-856-9039**	617-232-1595
Family Career & Community Leaders of America (FCCLA) 1910 Assn Dr	Reston	VA	20191	**800-234-4425**	703-476-4900
FIRST 200 Bedford St	Manchester	NH	03101	**800-871-8326**	603-666-3906
Foundation Ctr 79 Fifth Ave 2nd Fl	New York	NY	10003	**800-424-9836**	212-620-4230
Future Business Leaders of America-Phi Beta Lambda Inc (FBLA-PBL) 1912 Assn Dr	Reston	VA	20191	**800-325-2946**	
Graduate Management Admission Council (GMAC) 11921 Freedom Dr Ste 300	Reston	VA	20190	**866-505-6559**	703-668-9600
Great Books Foundation 35 E Wacker Dr Ste 400	Chicago	IL	60601	**800-222-5870**	312-332-5870
Institute of General Semantics (IGS) 72-11 Austin St	Forest Hills	NY	11375	**800-346-1359**	212-729-7973
Intercollegiate Studies Institute (ISI) 3901 Centerville Rd	Wilmington	DE	19807	**800-526-7022**	302-652-4600
International Montessori Council & The Montessori Foundation 19600 Florida 64 PO Box 130	Bradenton	FL	34212	**800-655-5843**	941-729-9565
Junior Achievement of Canada (JACAN) 1 Eva Rd Ste 218	Toronto	ON	M9C4Z5	**800-265-0699**	416-622-4602
Junior State of America (JSA) 400 S El Camino Real Ste 300	San Mateo	CA	94402	**800-334-5353**	650-347-1600
Music for All 39 W Jackson Pl Ste 150	Indianapolis	IN	46225	**800-848-2263**	317-636-2263
National Ctr for Family Literacy (NCFL) 325 W Main St Ste 300	Louisville	KY	40202	**855-937-5668**	502-584-1133
National Head Start Assn (NHSA) 1651 Prince St	Alexandria	VA	22314	**866-677-8724**	703-739-0875
National Honor Society (NHS) 1904 Assn Dr	Reston	VA	20191	**800-253-7746**	703-860-0200
Reading Is Fundamental Inc (RIF) 1825 Connecticut Ave NW Ste 400	Washington	DC	20009	**877-743-7323**	202-536-3400
Scholarship America 1 Scholarship Way PO Box 297	Saint Peter	MN	56082	**800-537-4180**	507-931-1682
SkillsUSA 14001 James Monroe Hwy	Leesburg	VA	20176	**800-321-8422**	703-777-8810
World Learning International Development Programs 1015 15th St NW Ste 750	Washington	DC	20005	**800-345-2929**	202-408-5420
Youth For Understanding USA 6400 Goldsboro Rd Ste 100	Bethesda	MD	20817	**800-424-3691**	240-235-2100

47-12 Energy & Natural Resources Organizations

Organization / Address	City	State	Zip	Toll-Free	Phone
Air & Waste Management Assn (A&WMA) 420 Fort Duquesne Blvd 1 Gateway Ctr 3rd Fl	Pittsburgh	PA	15222	**800-270-3444**	412-232-3444
Alliance to Save Energy (ASE) 1850 M St NW Ste 600	Washington	DC	20036	**800-862-2086**	202-857-0666
American Assn of Petroleum Geologists (AAPG) 1444 S Boulder Ave PO Box 979	Tulsa	OK	74119	**800-364-2274**	918-584-2555
American Assn of Professional Landmen (AAPL) 4100 Fossil Creek Blvd	Fort Worth	TX	76137	**888-566-2275**	817-847-7700
American Institute of Mining Metallurgical & Petroleum Engineers (AIME) 12999 E Adam Aircraft Cir	Englewood	CO	80112	**888-702-0049**	303-325-5185
American Oil Chemists Society (AOCS) 2710 S Boulder PO Box 17190	Urbana	IL	61802	**866-535-2730**	217-359-2344
American Public Gas Assn (APGA) 201 Massachusetts Ave NE Ste C-4	Washington	DC	20002	**800-927-4204**	202-464-2742

Organization / Address	City	State	Zip	Toll-Free	Phone
American Public Power Assn (APPA) 1875 Connecticut Ave Ste 1200	Washington	DC	20009	**800-369-6220**	202-467-2900
American Water Works Assn (AWWA) 6666 W Quincy Ave	Denver	CO	80235	**800-926-7337**	303-794-7711
Association of Energy Engineers (AEE) 4025 Pleasantdale Rd Ste 420	Atlanta	GA	30340	**877-407-0784**	770-447-5083
Association of Energy Service Cos (AESC) 14531 Fm 529 Ste 250	Houston	TX	77095	**800-692-0771**	713-781-0758
Edison Electric Institute (EEI) 701 Pennsylvania Ave NW	Washington	DC	20004	**800-649-1202**	202-508-5000
Environmental Industry Assn 4301 Connecticut Ave NW Ste 300	Washington	DC	20008	**800-424-2869**	202-244-4700
Independent Petroleum Assn of America (IPAA) 1201 15th St NW Ste 300	Washington	DC	20005	**800-433-2851**	202-857-4722
Institute of Clean Air Cos (ICAC) 1730 M St NW Ste 206	Washington	DC	20036	**800-631-9505**	202-457-0911
Institute of Hazardous Materials Management (IHMM) 11900 Parklawn Dr Ste 450	Rockville	MD	20852	**800-437-0137**	301-984-8969
National Ground Water Assn (NGWA) 601 Dempsey Rd	Westerville	OH	43081	**800-551-7379**	614-898-7791
National Ocean Industries Assn (NOIA) 1120 G St NW Ste 900	Washington	DC	20005	**800-558-9994**	202-347-6900
National Rural Electric Co-op Assn (NRECA) 4301 Wilson Blvd	Arlington	VA	22203	**866-759-2619**	703-907-5939
National Water Resources Assn (NWRA) 3800 Fairfax Dr # 4	Arlington	VA	22203	**800-468-3533**	703-524-1544
Society of Petroleum Engineers (SPE) 222 Palisades Creek Dr	Richardson	TX	75080	**800-456-6863**	972-952-9393
Western Forestry & Conservation Assn 4033 SW Canyon Rd	Portland	OR	97221	**888-722-9416**	503-226-4562

47-13 Environmental Organizations

Organization / Address	City	State	Zip	Toll-Free	Phone
Adirondack Council 103 Hand Ave Ste 3 Ste 3	Elizabethtown	NY	12932	**877-873-2240**	518-873-2240
American Farmland Trust (AFT) 1200 18th St	Washington	DC	20036	**800-431-1499**	202-331-7300
American Forests 1220 L St NW Ste 750	Washington	DC	20005	**800-368-5748**	202-737-1944
American Littoral Society (ALS) 18 Hartshorne Dr Ste 1	Highlands	NJ	07732	**800-424-8802**	732-291-0055
American Rivers 1101 14th St NW Ste 1400	Washington	DC	20005	**877-347-7550**	202-347-7550
American Shore & Beach Preservation Assn (ASBPA) 5460 Beaujolais Ln	Fort Myers	FL	33919	**800-331-1600**	239-489-2616
Appalachian Mountain Club (AMC) 5 Joy St	Boston	MA	02108	**800-262-4455*** *Orders	617-523-0655
Audubon Naturalist Society 8940 Jones Mill Rd	Chevy Chase	MD	20815	**888-744-4723**	301-652-9188
Beyond Pesticides 701 E St SE Ste 200	Washington	DC	20003	**866-260-6653**	202-543-5450
Canadian Parks & Wilderness Society (CPAWS) 250 City Ctr Ave Ste 506	Ottawa	ON	K1R6K7	**800-333-9453**	613-569-7226
Canadian Wildlife Federation (CWF) 350 Michael Cowpland Dr	Kanata	ON	K2M2W1	**800-563-9453**	613-599-9594
Civil War Preservation Trust (CWPT) 1331 H St NW Ste 1001	Washington	DC	20005	**888-606-1400**	202-367-1861
Clean Water Action 4455 Connecticut Ave NW	Washington	DC	20008	**800-657-3864**	202-895-0420
Co-op America 1612 K St NW Ste 600	Washington	DC	20006	**800-584-7336**	202-872-5307
Coastal Conservation Assn (CCA) 6919 Portwest Dr Ste 100	Houston	TX	77024	**800-201-3474**	713-626-4234
Conservation Fund 1655 N Fort Myer Dr Ste 1300	Arlington	VA	22209	**877-347-7550**	703-525-6300
Conservation International (CI) 2011 Crystal Dr Ste 500	Arlington	VA	22202	**800-406-2306**	703-341-2400
Earth Share 7735 Old Georgetown Rd Ste 900	Bethesda	MD	20814	**800-875-3863**	240-333-0300
EarthRights International 1612 K St NW Ste 401	Washington	DC	20006	**888-224-9043**	202-466-5188
Earthwatch Institute 114 Western Ave	Boston	MA	02134	**800-776-0188**	978-461-0081
Ecojustice Canada 131 Water St Ste 214	Vancouver	BC	V6B4M3	**800-926-7744**	604-685-5618
Environmental Defense 257 Pk Ave S	New York	NY	10010	**800-505-0703**	212-505-2100
Environmental Information Assn (EIA) 6935 Wisconsin Ave Ste 306	Chevy Chase	MD	20815	**888-343-4342**	301-961-4999
Environmental Law Institute (ELI) 2000 L St NW Ste 620	Washington	DC	20036	**800-433-5120**	202-939-3800
Forest Landowners Assn (FLA) 900 Cir 75 Pkwy Ste 205	Atlanta	GA	30339	**800-325-2954**	404-325-2954
Freshwater Society 2500 Shadywood Rd	Excelsior	MN	55331	**888-471-9773**	952-471-9773
Friends of the Earth 1717 Massachusetts Ave NW Ste 600	Washington	DC	20036	**877-843-8687**	202-783-7400
Friends of the River 1418 20th St Ste 100	Sacramento	CA	95811	**888-464-2477**	916-442-3155
Greater Yellowstone Coalition (GYC) 215 S Wallace Ave Ste 2	Bozeman	MT	59715	**800-775-1834**	406-586-1593
Greenpeace Canada 33 Cecil St	Toronto	ON	M5T1N1	**800-320-7183**	416-597-8408
Greenpeace USA 702 H St NW Ste 300	Washington	DC	20001	**800-326-0959**	202-462-1177
Heritage Canada Foundation 5 Blackburn Ave	Ottawa	ON	K1N8A2	**866-964-1066**	613-237-1066
Historic New England 141 Cambridge St	Boston	MA	02114	**800-722-2256**	617-227-3956
International Society of Tropical Foresters (ISTF) 5400 Grosvenor Ln	Bethesda	MD	20814	**866-897-8720**	301-530-4514
Izaak Walton League of America (IWLA) 707 Conservation Ln	Gaithersburg	MD	20878	**800-453-5463**	301-548-0150
League to Save Lake Tahoe 2608 Lake Tahoe Blvd	South Lake Tahoe	CA	96150	**888-844-9904**	530-541-5388
National Arbor Day Foundation 100 Arbor Ave	Nebraska City	NE	68410	**888-448-7337**	402-474-5655
National Audubon Society (NAS) 225 Varick St	New York	NY	10014	**800-274-4201**	212-979-3000
National Council for Air & Stream Improvement Inc (NCASI) PO Box 13318	Research Triangle Park	NC	27709	**888-448-2473**	919-941-6400
National Parks Conservation Assn (NPCA) 1300 19th St NW Ste 300	Washington	DC	20036	**800-628-7275**	202-223-6722
National Trust for Historic Preservation 1785 Massachusetts Ave NW	Washington	DC	20036	**800-944-6847**	202-588-6000
Nature Conservancy 4245 N Fairfax Dr Ste 100	Arlington	VA	22203	**800-628-6860*** *Cust Svc	703-841-5300
Nature Conservancy of Canada 36 Eglinton Ave W Ste 400	Toronto	ON	M4R1A1	**800-465-8005**	416-932-3202
New England Wild Flower Society 180 Hemenway Rd	Framingham	MA	01701	**888-636-0033**	508-877-7630
Ocean Conservancy 1300 19th St NW 8th Fl	Washington	DC	20036	**800-519-1541**	202-429-5609
Ocean Futures Society 325 Chapala St	Santa Barbara	CA	93101	**800-477-7500**	805-899-8899
Pollution Probe 150 Ferrand Dr Ste 208	Toronto	ON	M3C3E5	**877-926-1907**	416-926-1907
Public Lands Foundation (PLF) PO Box 7226	Arlington	VA	22207	**866-985-9636**	703-790-1988
Rainforest Action Network (RAN) 221 Pine St 5th Fl	San Francisco	CA	94104	**800-368-1819**	415-398-4404
Royal Oak Foundation, The 35 W 35th St Ste 1200	New York	NY	10001	**800-913-6565**	212-480-2889
Save America's Forests 4 Library Ct SE	Washington	DC	20003	**800-729-1363**	202-544-9219
Shelburne Farms 1611 Harbor Rd	Shelburne	VT	05482	**800-286-6022**	802-985-8686
Sierra Club Canada 412-1 Nicholas St	Ottawa	ON	K1N7B7	**888-810-4204**	613-241-4611
Society for Ecological Restoration International (SERI) 1017 O St NW	Washington	DC	20001	**866-895-4735**	202-299-9518
Soil & Water Conservation Society (SWCS) 945 SW Ankeny Rd	Ankeny	IA	50023	**800-843-7645**	515-289-2331
Student Conservation Assn (SCA) 689 River Rd PO Box 550	Charlestown	NH	03603	**888-722-9675**	603-543-1700
Thornton W Burgess Society 6 Discovery Hill Rd	East Sandwich	MA	02537	**800-844-4542**	508-888-6870
Tree Care Industry Assn (TCIA) 136 Harvey Rd Ste 101	Londonderry	NH	03053	**800-733-2622**	603-314-5380
Trust for Public Land (TPL) 116 New Montgomery St 4th Fl	San Francisco	CA	94105	**800-714-5263**	415-495-4014
Union of Concerned Scientists (UCS) 2 Brattle Sq 6th Fl	Cambridge	MA	02238	**800-666-8276**	617-547-5552
Walden Woods Project, The 44 Baker Farm Rd	Lincoln	MA	01773	**800-554-3569**	781-259-4700
Water Environment Federation (WEF) 601 Wythe St	Alexandria	VA	22314	**800-666-0206**	703-684-2400
Western Canada Wilderness Committee (WCWC) 227 Abbott St	Vancouver	BC	V6B2K7	**800-661-9453**	604-683-8220
Wilderness Society 1615 M St NW	Washington	DC	20036	**800-843-9453**	202-833-2300
Yosemite Assn *Yosemite Conservancy* 5020 El Portal Rd PO Box 230	El Portal	CA	95318	**800-469-7275**	209-379-2317

47-14 Ethnic & Nationality Organizations

Organization / Address	City	State	Zip	Toll-Free	Phone
American Folklore Society (AFS) 1501 Neil Ave 1501 Neil Ave	Columbus	OH	43201	**866-311-1200**	614-292-4715
American Hellenic Educational Progressive Assn (AHEPA) 1909 Q St NW Ste 500	Washington	DC	20009	**855-473-3512**	202-232-6300
Assembly of Turkish American Assn (ATAA) 1526 18th St NW	Washington	DC	20036	**800-627-7692**	202-483-9090
First Nations Development Institute 2217 Princess Anne St Ste 111-1	Fredericksburg	VA	22401	**888-371-3686**	540-371-5615
German-American National Congress (DANK) 4740 N Western Ave Ste 206	Chicago	IL	60625	**888-872-3265**	773-275-1100
National Slovak Society of the USA (NSS) 351 Vly Brook Rd	McMurray	PA	15317	**800-488-1890**	724-731-0094
Order Sons of Italy in America (OSIA) 219 E St NE	Washington	DC	20002	**800-552-6742**	202-547-2900
Sons of Norway 1455 W Lake St 2nd Fl	Minneapolis	MN	55408	**800-945-8851**	612-827-3611
Ukrainian NA Inc (UNA) 2200 Rt 10	Parsippany	NJ	07054	**800-253-9862**	
US Pan Asian American Chamber of Commerce (US PAACC) 1329 18th St NW	Washington	DC	20036	**800-696-7818**	202-296-5221

47-15 Fraternal & Social Organizations

Organization / Address	City	State	Zip	Toll-Free	Phone
American Mensa Ltd 1229 Corporate Dr W	Arlington	TX	76006	**800-666-3672**	817-607-0060
Association of Junior Leagues International Inc (AJLI) 80 Maiden Ln Ste 305	New York	NY	10038	**800-955-3248**	212-951-8300
Boys & Girls Clubs of America 1275 Peachtree St NE	Atlanta	GA	30309	**800-995-3579**	404-487-5700
Civitan International PO Box 130744	Birmingham	AL	35213	**800-248-4826**	205-591-8910
Cosmopolitan International 7341 W 80th St PO Box 4588	Lancaster	PA	17604	**800-648-4331**	913-648-4330
DeMolay International 10200 NW Ambassabor Dr	Kansas City	MO	64153	**800-336-6529*** *Orders	816-891-8333
Fraternal Order of Police (FOP) 701 Marriott Dr	Nashville	TN	37214	**800-451-2711**	615-399-0900
Girl Scouts of the USA 420 Fifth Ave	New York	NY	10018	**800-478-7248**	212-852-8000

Organization	Address	City	State	ZIP	Toll-Free	Phone
Goodwill Industries of Central Texas	1015 Norwood Pk Blvd	Austin	TX	78753	**800-735-2989**	512-637-7106
Grand Aerie Fraternal Order of Eagles	1623 Gateway Cir S	Grove City	OH	43123	**877-829-5500**	614-883-2200
Independent Order of Odd Fellows	422 N Trade St	Winston-Salem	NC	27101	**800-235-8358**	336-725-5955
International Assn of Lions Clubs	300 W 22nd St	Oak Brook	IL	60523	**800-710-7822**	630-571-5466
Key Club International	3636 Woodview Trace	Indianapolis	IN	46268	**800-549-2647**	317-875-8755
Klingberg Family Centers Inc	370 Linwood St	New Britain	CT	06052	**877-696-6775**	860-224-9113
Knights of Columbus	1 Columbus Plz	New Haven	CT	06510	**800-380-9995***	203-752-4000
	*Cust Svc					
Louisiana Baptist Children's Home Inc (LBCH)	7200 DeSiard St	Monroe	LA	71203	**877-345-7411**	318-343-2244
Lutheran Homes Society Inc	2021 N McCord Rd	Toledo	OH	43615	**877-646-4050**	419-861-4990
Lutheran Social Services of Illinois	1001 E Touhy Ave Ste 50	Des Plaines	IL	60018	**888-671-0300**	847-635-4600
Masonic Service Assn of North America (MSANA)	8120 Fenton St Ste 203	Silver Spring	MD	20910	**855-476-4010**	301-588-4010
National Exchange Club	3050 W Central Ave	Toledo	OH	43606	**800-924-2643**	419-535-3232
Optimist International	4494 Lindell Blvd	Saint Louis	MO	63108	**800-500-8130**	314-371-6000
Oswego County Opportunities Inc	239 Oneida St	Fulton	NY	13069	**877-342-7618**	315-598-4717
Partnerships In Community Living Inc	480 Main St E PO Box 129	Monmouth	OR	97361	**800-222-1222**	503-838-2403
Presbyterian Homes Inc, The	2109 Sandy Ridge Rd	Colfax	NC	27235	**800-225-9573**	336-886-6553
Professional Bull Riders Inc (PBR)	101 W Riverwalk	Pueblo	CO	81003	**800-366-8538**	719-242-2800
Ruritan National	5451 Lyons Rd PO Box 487	Dublin	VA	24084	**877-787-8727**	540-674-5431
Spectrum Health Systems Inc	10 Mechanic St Ste 302	Worcester	MA	01608	**800-464-9555**	508-792-5400
Starr Commonwealth	13725 Starr Commonwealth Rd	Albion	MI	49224	**800-837-5591**	517-629-5591
TelecomPioneers	1801 California St Ste 225	Denver	CO	80202	**800-872-5995**	303-571-1200
Up With People	6830 Broadway	Denver	CO	80221	**877-264-8856**	303-460-7100
Way Station Inc	230 W Patrick St PO Box 3826	Frederick	MD	21705	**888-549-0629**	301-662-0099

47-16 Greek Letter Societies

Organization	Address	City	State	ZIP	Toll-Free	Phone
Alpha Chi Omega	5939 Castle Creek Pkwy N Dr	Indianapolis	IN	46250	**800-328-0522**	317-579-5050
Alpha Chi Sigma	2141 N Franklin Rd	Indianapolis	IN	46219	**800-252-4369**	317-357-5944
Alpha Epsilon Phi Sorority (AEPhi)	11 Lake Ave Ext Ste 1-A	Danbury	CT	06811	**888-668-4293**	203-748-0029
Alpha Epsilon Pi Fraternity Inc	8815 Wesleyan Rd	Indianapolis	IN	46268	**800-684-3608**	317-876-1913
Alpha Gamma Rho	10101 NW Ambassador Dr	Kansas City	MO	64153	**888-241-4546**	816-891-9200
Alpha Omega International Dental Fraternity	50 W Edmonston Dr	Rockville	MD	20852	**877-368-6326**	301-738-6400
Alpha Omicron Pi International	5390 Virginia Way	Brentwood	TN	37027	**855-230-1183**	615-370-0920
Alpha Sigma Phi National Fraternity	710 Adams St	Carmel	IN	46032	**866-515-4747**	317-843-1911
Alpha Tau Omega Fraternity (ATO)	1 N Pennsylvania St 12th Fl	Indianapolis	IN	46204	**800-798-9286**	317-684-1865
Beta Gamma Sigma Inc (BGS)	125 Weldon Pkwy	Maryland Heights	MO	63043	**800-337-4677**	314-432-5650
Beta Theta Pi	5134 Bonham Rd	Oxford	OH	45056	**800-800-2382**	
Chi Alpha Campus Ministries USA	1445 Booneville Ave	Springfield	MO	65802	**855-700-2457**	417-862-2781
Chi Phi Fraternity	1160 Satellite Blvd	Suwanee	GA	30024	**800-849-1824**	404-231-1824
Delta Delta Delta Fraternity	2331 Brookhollow Plz Dr	Arlington	TX	76006	**877-746-7333**	817-633-8001
Delta Sigma Theta Sorority Inc	1707 New Hampshire Ave NW	Washington	DC	20009	**866-615-6464**	202-986-2400
Delta Tau Delta Fraternity	10000 Allisonville Rd	Fishers	IN	46038	**800-335-8795**	317-284-0203
Delta Theta Phi	225 Hillsborough St Ste 432	Raleigh	NC	27603	**800-783-2600**	
Eta Sigma Gamma	2000 University Ave	Muncie	IN	47306	**800-715-2559**	765-285-2258
Gamma Beta Phi Society	78 Mitchell Rd Ste A	Oak Ridge	TN	37830	**800-628-9920**	865-483-6212
International Fraternity of Phi Gamma Delta	1201 Red Mile Rd PO Box 4599	Lexington	KY	40544	**888-668-4293**	859-255-1848
Kappa Alpha Order	115 Liberty Hall Rd	Lexington	VA	24450	**888-922-6335**	540-463-1865
Kappa Alpha Theta Fraternity	8740 Founders Rd	Indianapolis	IN	46268	**800-526-1870**	317-876-1870
Kappa Delta Pi	3707 Woodview Trace	Indianapolis	IN	46268	**800-284-3167**	317-871-4900
Kappa Delta Sorority	3205 Players Ln	Memphis	TN	38125	**800-536-1897**	901-748-1897
Kappa Kappa Gamma	PO Box 38	Columbus	OH	43216	**866-554-1870**	614-228-6515
Mu Phi Epsilon International Music Fraternity	PO Box 1369	Fort Collins	CO	80522	**888-259-1471**	
National Alpha Lambda Delta	328 Orange St	Macon	GA	31201	**800-925-7421**	478-744-9595
National Fraternity of Kappa Delta Rho (KDR)	331 S Main St	Greensburg	PA	15601	**800-536-5371**	724-838-7100
National Kappa Kappa Iota Inc	1875 E 15th St	Tulsa	OK	74104	**800-678-0389**	918-744-0389
Phi Alpha Theta *National History Honor Society*	4202 E Fowler Ave SOC 107	Tampa	FL	33620	**800-394-8195**	
Phi Delta Kappa International (PDK)	408 N Union St	Bloomington	IN	47407	**800-766-1156**	812-339-1156
Phi Delta Phi International Legal Fraternity	1426 21st St NW	Washington	DC	20036	**800-368-5606**	202-223-6801
Phi Delta Theta	2 S Campus Ave	Oxford	OH	45056	**888-373-9855**	513-523-6345
Phi Kappa Psi	5395 Emerson Way	Indianapolis	IN	46226	**800-486-1852**	317-632-1852
Phi Kappa Tau	5221 Morning Sun Rd	Oxford	OH	45056	**800-758-1906**	513-523-4193
Phi Mu Alpha Sinfonia Fraternity of America Inc	10600 Old State Rd	Evansville	IN	47711	**800-473-2649**	812-867-2433
Phi Mu Fraternity	400 Westpark Dr	Peachtree City	GA	30269	**888-744-6824**	770-632-2090
Phi Sigma Kappa International	2925 E 96th St	Indianapolis	IN	46240	**888-846-6851**	317-573-5420
Phi Sigma Pi National Honor Fraternity Inc	2119 Ambassador Cir	Lancaster	PA	17603	**800-366-1916**	717-299-4710
Phi Theta Kappa International Honor Society	1625 Eastover Dr	Jackson	MS	39211	**800-946-9995**	601-984-3504
Pi Sigma Epsilon (PSE)	3747 S Howell Ave	Milwaukee	WI	53207	**800-761-9350**	414-328-1952
PSI Upsilon Fraternity	3003 E 96th St	Indianapolis	IN	46240	**800-394-1833**	317-571-1833
Sigma Alpha Epsilon Fraternity (SAE)	1856 Sheridan Rd	Evanston	IL	60201	**800-233-1856**	847-475-1856
Sigma Chi Fraternity	1714 Hinman Ave	Evanston	IL	60201	**877-829-5500**	847-869-3655
Sigma Phi Epsilon Fraternity	310 S Blvd	Richmond	VA	23220	**800-767-1901**	804-353-1901
Sigma Pi Fraternity	106 N Castle Heights Ave	Lebanon	TN	37087	**800-332-1897**	615-373-5728
Sigma Theta Tau International	550 W N St	Indianapolis	IN	46202	**888-634-7575**	317-634-8171
Sigma Xi Scientific Research Society	3106 E NC Hwy 54 PO Box 13975	Research Triangle Park	NC	27709	**800-243-6534**	919-549-4691
Tau Beta Pi Assn	1512 Middle Dr	Knoxville	TN	37996	**877-829-5500**	865-546-4578
Tau Beta Sigma National Honorary Band Sorority	PO Box 849	Stillwater	OK	74076	**800-543-6505***	405-372-2333
	*Cust Svc					
Theta Delta Chi Inc	214 Lewis Wharf	Boston	MA	02110	**800-999-1847**	617-742-8886
Theta Tau Professional Engineering Fraternity	1011 San Jacinto Ste 205	Austin	TX	78701	**800-264-1904**	512-472-1904
Zeta Phi Beta Sorority Inc	1734 New Hampshire Ave NW	Washington	DC	20009	**800-393-2503**	202-387-3103
Zeta Psi Fraternity of North America	15 S Henry St	Pearl River	NY	10965	**800-477-1847**	845-735-1847

47-17 Health & Health-Related Organizations

Organization	Address	City	State	ZIP	Toll-Free	Phone
Acoustic Neuroma Assn (ANA)	600 Peachtree Pkwy Ste 108	Cumming	GA	30041	**877-200-8211**	770-205-8211
Alliance for Aging Research (AAR)	750 17th St NW Ste 1100	Washington	DC	20006	**866-840-6283**	202-293-2856
Alliance for Lupus Research (ALA)	28 W 44th St Ste 501	New York	NY	10036	**800-867-1743**	212-218-2840
Alzheimer's Assn	225 N Michigan Ave Fl 17	Chicago	IL	60601	**800-272-3900**	312-335-8700
American Assn of Acupunture & Oriental Medicine (AAAOM)	PO Box 162340	Sacramento	CA	95816	**866-455-7999**	916-443-4770
American Assn of Drugless Practitioners (AADP)	2200 Market St Ste 803	Galveston	TX	77550	**888-764-2237**	409-621-2600
American Assn of Naturopathic Physicians (AANP)	818 18th St Ste 250	Washington	DC	20006	**866-538-2267**	202-237-8150
American Assn on Intellectual & Developmental Disabilities (AAIDD)	444 N Capitol St NW Ste 846	Washington	DC	20001	**800-424-3688**	202-387-1968
American Autoimmune Related Disease Assn (AARDA)	22100 Gratiot Ave	Eastpointe	MI	48021	**800-598-4668**	586-776-3900
American Botanical Council	6200 Manor Rd PO Box 144345	Austin	TX	78723	**800-373-7105**	512-926-4900
American Brain Tumor Assn (ABTA)	2720 River Rd	Des Plaines	IL	60018	**800-886-2282**	847-827-9910
American Cancer Society (ACS)	250 William St NW	Atlanta	GA	30303	**800-227-2345**	404-320-3333
American Chronic Pain Assn (ACPA)	PO Box 850	Rocklin	CA	95677	**800-533-3231**	916-632-0922
American Council of the Blind (ACB)	1155 15th St NW Ste 1004	Washington	DC	20005	**800-424-8666**	202-467-5081
American Council on Alcoholism (ACA)	1000 E Indian School Rd	Phoenix	AZ	85014	**800-527-5344**	
American Council on Exercise (ACE)	4851 Paramount Dr	San Diego	CA	92123	**800-825-3636**	858-576-6500
American Diabetes Assn (ADA)	1701 N Beauregard St	Alexandria	VA	22311	**800-232-3472**	703-549-1500
American Epilepsy Society (AES)	342 N Main St	West Hartford	CT	06117	**888-233-2334**	860-586-7505
American Foundation for Suicide Prevention (AFSP)	120 Wall St 22nd Fl	New York	NY	10005	**888-333-2377**	212-363-3500
American Foundation for the Blind (AFB)	2 Penn Plaza	New York	NY	10001	**800-232-5463**	212-502-7600
American Heart Assn (AHA)	7272 Greenville Ave	Dallas	TX	75231	**800-242-8721**	214-373-6300
American Holistic Nurses' Assn (AHNA)	323 N San Francisco St Ste 201	Flagstaff	AZ	86001	**800-278-2462**	928-526-2196
American Kidney Fund (AKF)	6110 Executive Blvd Ste 1010	Rockville	MD	20852	**800-638-8299**	
American Liver Foundation (ALF)	39 Broadway	New York	NY	10006	**800-465-4837**	212-668-1000
American Lung Assn (ALA)	14 Wall St	New York	NY	10005	**800-586-4872**	212-315-8700

Classified Section

Organization	Address	City	State	ZIP	Toll-Free	Phone
American Massage Therapy Assn (AMTA)	500 Davis St Ste 900	Evanston	IL	60201	**877-905-2700**	847-864-0123
American Pain Society (APS)	4700 W Lake Ave	Glenview	IL	60025	**877-752-4754**	847-375-4715
American Parkinson Disease Assn (APDA)	135 Parkinson Ave	Staten Island	NY	10305	**800-223-2732**	718-981-8001
American Sleep Apnea Assn (ASAA)	6856 Eastern Ave NW #203	Washington	DC	20012	**888-293-3650**	202-293-3650
American Social Health Assn (ASHA)	PO Box 13827	Research Triangle Park	NC	27709	**800-552-4375**	919-361-8400
American Therapeutic Recreation Assn (ATRA)	629 N Main St	Hattiesburg	MS	39401	**800-433-5255**	601-450-2872
American Tinnitus Assn (ATA)	522 SW Fifth Ave Ste 825	Portland	OR	97204	**800-634-8978**	503-248-9985
Anxiety Disorders Assn of America (ADAA)	8730 Georgia Ave Ste 600	Silver Spring	MD	20910	**800-922-8947**	240-485-1001
Arc of the US	1010 Wayne Ave Ste 650	Silver Spring	MD	20910	**800-433-5255**	301-565-3842
Arthritis Foundation	1330 W Peachtree St Ste 100	Atlanta	GA	30309	**800-283-7800**	404-872-7100
Associated Bodywork & Massage Professionals (ABMP)	25188 Genesee Trl Rd Ste 200	Golden	CO	80401	**800-458-2267**	303-674-8478
Association for Applied & Therapeutic Humor (AATH)	65 Enterprise	Aliso Viejo	CA	92656	**888-747-2284**	815-708-6587
Association for Research & Enlightenment (ARE)	215 67th St	Virginia Beach	VA	23451	**800-333-4499**	757-428-3588
Asthma & Allergy Foundation of America (AAFA)	8201 Corporate Dr Ste 1000	Landover	MD	20785	**800-727-8462**	202-466-7643
Autism Research Institute (ARI)	4182 Adams Ave	San Diego	CA	92116	**866-366-3361**	619-281-7165
Autism Society of America (ASA)	4340 EW Hwy Ste 350	Bethesda	MD	20814	**800-328-8476**	301-657-0881
BEGINNINGS	156 Wind Chime Ct Ste A	Raleigh	NC	27605	**800-541-4327**	919-715-4092
Better Hearing Institute (BHI)	1444 I St NW Ste 700	Washington	DC	20005	**800-639-3884**	202-449-1100
Better Vision Institute, The (BVI)	*Vision Council, The* 225 Reinekers Ln Ste 700	Alexandria	VA	22314	**800-372-3937**	703-548-4560
Brain Injury Assn of America	1608 Spring Hill Rd Ste 110	Vienna	VA	22182	**800-444-6443**	703-761-0750
Cancer Care Inc	275 Seventh Ave 22nd Fl	New York	NY	10001	**800-813-4673**	212-712-8400
Candlelighters Childhood Cancer Foundation	10920 Connecticut Ave Suuite A PO Box 498	Kensington	MD	20895	**800-366-2223**	301-962-3520
Canine Companions for Independence Inc (CCI)	2965 Dutton Ave PO Box 446	Santa Rosa	CA	95402	**800-572-2275**	707-577-1700
Carcinoid Cancer Foundation Inc	333 Mamaroneck Ave Ste 492	White Plains	NY	10605	**888-722-3132**	212-722-3132
Center for Practical Bioethics	1111 Main St Ste 500	Kansas City	MO	64105	**800-344-3829**	816-221-1100
Children & Adults with Attention-Deficit/Hyperactivity Disorder (CHADD)	8181 Professional Pl Ste 150	Landover	MD	20785	**800-233-4050**	301-306-7070
Children's Organ Transplant Assn (COTA)	2501 W Cota Dr	Bloomington	IN	47403	**800-366-2682**	812-336-8872
Children's Tumor Foundation	95 Pine St 16th Fl	New York	NY	10005	**800-323-7938**	212-344-6633
Children's Wish Foundation International	8615 Roswell Rd	Atlanta	GA	30350	**800-323-9474**	770-393-9474
Christopher Reeve Foundation	636 Morris Tpke Ste 3A	Short Hills	NJ	07078	**800-225-0292**	973-379-2690
Cleft Palate Foundation (CPF)	1504 E Franklin St Ste 102	Chapel Hill	NC	27514	**800-242-5338**	919-933-9044
Compassion & Choices	PO Box 101810	Denver	CO	80250	**800-247-7421**	303-639-1202
Cornelia de Lange Syndrome Foundation Inc (CdLS)	302 W Main St Ste 100	Avon	CT	06001	**800-753-2357**	860-676-8166
Creutzfeldt-Jakob Disease Foundation Inc	341 W 38th St Ste 501	New York	NY	10018	**800-659-1991**	212-719-5900
Crohn's & Colitis Foundation of America (CCFA)	386 Pk Ave S 17th Fl	New York	NY	10016	**800-932-2423**	212-685-3440
Cystic Fibrosis Foundation	6931 Arlington Rd Ste 200	Bethesda	MD	20814	**800-344-4823**	301-951-4422
Dental Lifeline Network	1800 15th St Ste 100	Denver	CO	80202	**888-471-6334**	303-534-5360
Depression & Bipolar Support Alliance (DBSA)	730 N Franklin St Ste 501	Chicago	IL	60610	**800-826-3632**	312-642-0049
Disability Rights Ctr Inc	18 Low Ave	Concord	NH	03301	**800-834-1721**	603-228-0432
Disabled & Alone/Life Services for the Handicapped	1440 Broadway 23rd Floor	New York	NY	10018	**800-995-0066**	212-532-6740
Dystonia Medical Research Foundation	1 E Wacker Dr Ste 2810 *General	Chicago	IL	60601	**800-377-3978***	312-755-0198
Easter Seals	230 W Monroe St Ste 1800	Chicago	IL	60606	**800-221-6827**	312-726-6200
ECRI Institute	5200 Butler Pike	Plymouth Meeting	PA	19462	**866-247-3004**	610-825-6000
El Paso First Health Plans Inc	1145 Westmoreland Dr	El Paso	TX	79925	**877-532-3778**	915-532-3778
Elizabeth Glaser Pediatric AIDS Foundation	1140 Connecticut Ave NW Ste 200	Washington	DC	20036	**888-499-4673**	202-296-9165
Endometriosis Assn	8585 N 76th Pl	Milwaukee	WI	53223	**800-992-3636**	414-355-2200
EngenderHealth	440 Ninth Ave 13th Fl	New York	NY	10001	**800-564-2872**	212-561-8000
Epilepsy Foundation	8301 Professional Pl E	Landover	MD	20785	**800-332-1000**	301-459-3700
FaithTrust Institute	2400 N 45th St Ste 101	Seattle	WA	98103	**877-860-2255**	206-634-1903
Family Caregiver Alliance (FCA)	180 Montgomery St Ste 900	San Francisco	CA	94104	**800-445-8106**	415-434-3388
Family of the Americas Foundation	PO Box 1170	Dunkirk	MD	20754	**800-443-3395**	301-627-3346
Feingold Assn of the US	37 Shell Rd 2nd Fl	Rocky Point	NY	11778	**800-321-3287**	631-369-9340
First Candle	1314 Bedford Ave Ste 210	Baltimore	MD	21208	**800-221-7437**	410-653-8226
Food Allergy & Anaphylaxis Network (FAAN)	11781 Lee Jackson Hwy Ste 160	Fairfax	VA	22033	**800-929-4040**	703-691-3179
Foundation Fighting Blindness	11435 Cron Hill Dr	Owings Mills	MD	21117	**800-683-5555**	410-568-0150
Gay Men's Health Crisis (GMHC)	119 W 24th St	New York	NY	10011	**800-243-7692**	212-367-1000
Gift of Life Bone Marrow Foundation	800 Yamato Rd Ste 101	Boca Raton	FL	33431	**800-962-7769**	561-982-2900
Glaucoma Research Foundation	251 Post St Ste 600	San Francisco	CA	94108	**800-826-6693**	415-986-3162
Guide Dog Foundation for the Blind Inc	371 E Jericho Tkpe	Smithtown	NY	11787	**800-548-4337**	
Guide Dogs for the Blind	350 Los Ranchitos Rd	San Rafael	CA	94903	**800-295-4050**	415-499-4000
Guide Dogs of America	13445 Glenoaks Blvd	Sylmar	CA	91342	**800-459-4843**	818-362-5834
Health Physics Society	1313 Dolley Madison Blvd Ste 402	McLean	VA	22101	**888-624-8373**	703-790-1745
Hearing Loss Assn of America	7910 Woodmont Ave Ste 1200	Bethesda	MD	20814	**800-221-6827**	301-657-2248
Hepatitis Foundation International (HFI)	504 Blick Dr	Silver Spring	MD	20904	**800-891-0707**	301-622-4200
Herb Research Foundation (HRF)	4140 15th St	Boulder	CO	80304	**800-748-2617**	303-449-2265
Herpes Resource Center, The (HRC)	PO Box 13827	Research Triangle Park	NC	27709	**877-478-5868**	919-361-8400
Hospice Education Institute	3 Unity Sq PO Box 98	Machiasport	ME	04655	**800-331-1620**	207-255-8800
Human Factors & Ergonomics Society (HFES)	1124 Montana Ave Ste B PO Box 1369	Santa Monica	CA	90406	**800-233-1234**	310-394-1811
Human Growth Foundation	997 Glen Cove Ave Ste 5	Glen Head	NY	11545	**800-451-6434**	516-671-4041
Huntington's Disease Society of America (HDSA)	505 Eigth Ave Ste 902	New York	NY	10018	**800-345-4372**	212-242-1968
Hysterectomy Educational Resources & Services Foundation (HERS)	422 Bryn Mawr Ave	Bala Cynwyd	PA	19004	**888-750-4377**	610-667-7757
Immune Deficiency Foundation (IDF)	40 W Chesapeake Ave Ste 308	Towson	MD	21204	**800-296-4433**	410-321-6647
International Assn for the Study of Pain (IASP)	111 Queen Anne Ave N Ste 501	Seattle	WA	98109	**866-574-2654**	206-283-0311
International Dyslexia Assn, The (IDA)	40 York Rd 4th Fl	Towson	MD	21204	**800-222-3123**	410-296-0232
International Hearing Society (IHS)	16880 Middlebelt Rd Ste 4	Livonia	MI	48154	**800-521-5247**	734-522-7200
Juvenile Diabetes Research Foundation International (JDRF)	120 Wall St	New York	NY	10005	**800-533-2873**	212-785-9500
Kristin Brooks Hope Ctr (KBHC)	1250 24th St NW	Washington	DC	20037	**800-784-2433**	202-536-3200
La Leche League International Inc (LLLI)	957 N Plum Grove Rd	Schaumburg	IL	60173	**800-525-3243**	847-519-7730
Lamaze International	2025 M St NW Ste 800	Washington	DC	20036	**800-368-4404**	202-367-1128
Laurent Clerc National Deaf Education Ctr	800 Florida Ave NE	Washington	DC	20002	**866-637-0102**	202-651-5050
Learning Disabilities Assn of America (LDA)	4156 Library Rd	Pittsburgh	PA	15234	**888-300-6710**	412-341-1515
Lifespire	350 Fifth Ave Ste 301	New York	NY	10118	**800-221-5594**	212-741-0100
Light for Life Foundation International	PO Box 644	Westminster	CO	80036	**800-273-8255**	303-429-3530
Living Bank	PO Box 6725	Houston	TX	77027	**800-528-2971**	713-961-9431
Lupus Foundation of America Inc (LFA)	2000 L St NW Ste 410	Washington	DC	20036	**800-558-0121**	202-349-1155
Lymphoma Research Foundation (LRF)	115 Broadway Ste 1301	New York	NY	10006	**800-500-9976**	212-349-2910
Macula Foundation Inc	210 E 64th St	New York	NY	10065	**800-622-8524**	212-605-3777
Male Survivor	4768 BRdway Ste 527	New York	NY	10034	**800-738-4181**	
MedicAlert Foundation International	2323 Colorado Ave *Cust Svc	Turlock	CA	95382	**800-432-5378***	209-668-3333
Medicare Rights Ctr (MRC)	520 Eigth Ave N Wing 3rd Fl *Hotline	New York	NY	10018	**800-333-4114***	212-869-3850
Mended Hearts Inc, The	8150 N Central Expy M2075	Dallas	TX	75206	**888-432-7899**	214-296-9252
Mental Health America (MHA)	2000 N Beauregard St 6th Fl *Help Line	Alexandria	VA	22311	**800-969-6642***	703-684-7722
Multiple Sclerosis Foundation (MSF)	6520 N Andrews Ave	Fort Lauderdale	FL	33309	**800-225-6495**	954-776-6805
Muscular Dystrophy Assn (MDA)	3300 E Sunrise Dr	Tucson	AZ	85718	**800-572-1717**	520-529-2000
NA of People with AIDS (NAPWA)	8401 Colesville Rd Ste 505	Silver Spring	MD	20910	**866-846-9366**	240-247-0880
Narcolepsy Network Inc	46 Union Dr Ste A212	North Kingstown	RI	02852	**888-292-6522**	401-667-2523
National Alliance on Mental Illness (NAMI)	3803 N Fairfax Dr Ste 100	Arlington	VA	22203	**800-950-6264**	703-524-7600
National Breast Cancer Coalition (NBCC)	1101 17th St NW Ste 1300	Washington	DC	20036	**800-622-2838**	202-296-7477
National Cancer Registrars Assn (NCRA)	1340 Braddock Pl Ste 203	Alexandria	VA	22314	**800-621-4111**	703-299-6640
National Citizens' Coalition for Nursing Home Reform (NCCNHR)	*National Consumer Voice for Quality Long-Term Care, The* 1828 L St NW Ste 801	Washington	DC	20036	**866-992-3668**	202-332-2275
National Coalition for Cancer Survivorship (NCCS)	1010 Wayne Ave Ste 315	Silver Spring	MD	20910	**877-622-7937**	
National Committee for Quality Assurance (NCQA)	1100 13th St	Washington	DC	20005	**888-275-7585**	202-955-3500
National Council on Alcoholism & Drug Dependence Inc (NCADD)	217 Broadway Ste 712	New York	NY	10007	**800-622-2255**	212-269-7797
National Ctr for Homeopathy (NCH)	101 S Whiting St Ste 16	Alexandria	VA	22304	**877-624-0613**	703-548-7790

Classified Section

Organization	City	State	ZIP	Toll-Free	Phone
National Down Syndrome Congress (NDSC) 1370 Ctr Dr Ste 102	Atlanta	GA	30338	**800-232-6372**	770-604-9500
National Down Syndrome Society (NDSS) 666 Broadway 8th Fl	New York	NY	10012	**800-221-4602**	
National Eating Disorders Assn 603 Stewart St Ste 803	Seattle	WA	98101	**800-931-2237**	
National Federation of the Blind (NFB) 1800 Johnson St	Baltimore	MD	21230	**800-392-5671**	410-659-9314
National Fibromyalgia Partnership Inc (NFP) 140 Zinn Way	Linden	VA	22642	**866-725-4404**	
National Fire Protection Assn (NFPA) 1 Batterymarch Pk	Quincy	MA	02169	**800-344-3555**	617-770-3000
National Gaucher Foundation (NGF) 5410 Edson Ln Ste 220	Rockville	MD	30084	**800-504-3189**	770-934-2910
National Headache Foundation (NHF) 820 N Orleans St Ste 217	Chicago	IL	60610	**888-643-5552**	
National Hearing Conservation Assn (NHCA) 3030 W 81st Ave	Westminster	CO	80031	**877-766-6629**	303-224-9022
National Hemophilia Foundation (NHF) 116 W 32nd St 11th Fl	New York	NY	10001	**800-424-2634**	212-328-3700
National Industries for the Blind (NIB) 1310 Braddock Pl *Cust Svc	Alexandria	VA	22314	**800-433-2304***	703-310-0500
National Inhalant Prevention Coalition (NIPC) 318 Lindsay St	Chattanooga	TN	37405	**800-269-4237**	423-265-4662
National Kidney Foundation (NKF) 30 E 33rd St 8th Fl	New York	NY	10016	**800-622-9010**	212-889-2210
National Marfan Foundation (NMF) 22 Manhasset Ave	Port Washington	NY	11050	**800-862-7326**	516-883-8712
National Marrow Donor Program (NMDP) 3001 Broadway St NE Ste 100	Minneapolis	MN	55413	**800-526-7809**	612-627-5800
National Multiple Sclerosis Society 733 Third Ave 3rd Fl	New York	NY	10017	**800-344-4867**	212-986-3240
National Niemann-Pick Disease Foundation Inc (NNPDF) 401 Madison Ave Ste B PO Box 49	Fort Atkinson	WI	53538	**877-287-3672**	920-563-0930
National Oral Health Information Clearinghouse (NIDCR) 1 NOHIC Way	Bethesda	MD	20892	**866-232-4528**	301-496-4261
National Organization for Albinism & Hypopigmentation (NOAH) PO Box 959	East Hampstead	NH	03826	**800-648-2310**	603-887-2310
National Organization for Rare Disorders (NORD) 55 Kenosia Ave PO Box 1968	Danbury	CT	06813	**800-999-6673**	203-744-0100
National Organization of Circumcision Information Resource Centers (NOCIRC) PO Box 2512	San Anselmo	CA	94979	**800-727-8622**	415-488-9883
National Osteoporosis Foundation (NOF) 251 18th St S Ste 630	Arlington	VA	22202	**800-231-4222**	202-223-2226
National Ovarian Cancer Coalition (NOCC) 2501 Oak Lawn Ave Ste 435	Dallas	TX	75219	**888-682-7426**	
National Pesticide Information Ctr (NPIC) 333 Weniger Hall	Corvallis	OR	97331	**800-858-7378**	
National Psoriasis Foundation (NPF) 6600 SW 92nd Ave Ste 300	Portland	OR	97223	**800-723-9166**	503-244-7404
National Rehabilitation Assn (NRA) 633 S Washington St	Alexandria	VA	22314	**888-258-4295**	703-836-0850
National Rehabilitation Information Ctr (NARIC) 8400 Corporate Dr Ste 500	Landover	MD	20785	**800-346-2742**	301-459-5900
National Reye's Syndrome Foundation (NRSF) 426 N Lewis St	Bryan	OH	43506	**800-233-7393**	419-924-9000
National Rosacea Society 800 S NW Hwy Ste 200	Barrington	IL	60010	**888-662-5874**	847-382-8971
National Safety Council (NSC) 1121 Spring Lk Dr	Itasca	IL	60143	**800-621-7615**	630-285-1121
National Spinal Cord Injury Assn (NSCIA) 75-20 Astoria Blvd Ste 120	East Elmhurst	NY	11370	**800-962-9629**	718-512-0010
National Stroke Assn (NSA) 9707 E Easter Ln *Cust Svc	Centennial	CO	80112	**800-787-6537***	
National Stuttering Assn (NSA) 119 W 40th St 14th Fl	New York	NY	10018	**800-937-8888**	212-944-4050
National Tay-Sachs & Allied Diseases Assn (NTSAD) 2001 Beacon St Ste 204	Brighton	MA	02135	**800-906-8723**	617-277-4463
National Wellness Institute (NWI) 1300 College Ct PO Box 827	Stevens Point	WI	54481	**877-800-2729**	715-342-2969
New West Health Services 130 Neill Ave	Helena	MT	59601	**888-500-3355**	406-457-2200
Oley Foundation 214 Hun Memorial MC-28 Albany Medical Ctr	Albany	NY	12208	**800-776-6539**	518-262-5079
Oral Health America 410 N Michigan Ave Ste 352	Chicago	IL	60611	**800-523-3438**	312-836-9900
Parkinson's Disease Foundation (PDF) 1359 Broadway	New York	NY	10018	**800-457-6676**	212-923-4700
Partnership for a Drug-Free America 405 Lexington Ave Ste 1601	New York	NY	10174	**855-378-4373**	212-922-1560
Pedorthic Footwear Assn (PFA) 2025 M St NW Ste 800	Washington	DC	20036	**800-673-8447**	202-367-1145
Phoenix Society for Burn Survivors Inc 1835 RW Berends Dr SW	Grand Rapids	MI	49519	**800-888-2876**	616-458-2773
Postpartum Support International 2200 Pacific Coast Hwy Ste 304A	Hermosa Beach	CA	90254	**800-944-4773**	
Prader-Willi Syndrome Assn (USA) 8588 Potter Pk Dr Ste 500	Sarasota	FL	34238	**800-926-4797**	941-312-0400
Prevent Blindness America 211 W Wacker Dr Ste 1700	Chicago	IL	60606	**800-331-2020**	
Prevent Cancer Foundation (PCF) 1600 Duke St Ste 500	Alexandria	VA	22314	**800-227-2732**	703-836-4412
Project Inform 273 Ninth St	San Francisco	CA	94103	**877-435-7443**	415-558-8669
Public Health Institute 555 12th St 10th Fl	Oakland	CA	94607	**866-632-9992**	510-285-5500
Recording for the Blind & Dyslexic (RFB&D) 20 Roszel Rd	Princeton	NJ	08540	**800-221-4792**	
Research to Prevent Blindness Inc (RPB) 645 Madison Ave 21st Fl	New York	NY	10022	**800-621-0026**	212-752-4333
RESOLVE: National Infertility Assn 1760 Old Meadow Rd Ste 500	McLean	VA	22102	**888-592-4449**	703-556-7172
Restless Legs Syndrome Foundation Inc 1610 14th St NW Ste 300	Rochester	MN	55901	**877-463-6757**	507-287-6465
Rolf Institute of Structural Integration 5055 Chaparral Ct Ste 103	Boulder	CO	80301	**800-530-8875**	303-449-5903
RP International PO Box 900	Woodland Hills	CA	91365	**877-999-8322**	818-992-0500
Scleroderma Foundation 300 Rosewood Dr Ste 105	Danvers	MA	01923	**800-722-4673**	978-463-5843
Sickle Cell Disease Assn of America (SCDAA) 3700 Koppers St Ste 570	Baltimore	MD	21202	**800-421-8453**	410-528-1555
Spina Bifida Assn (SBAA) 4590 MacArthur Blvd NW Ste 250	Washington	DC	20007	**877-686-6444**	202-944-3285
Stuttering Foundation of America 3100 Walnut Grove Rd Ste 603	Memphis	TN	38111	**800-992-9392**	901-452-7343
Susan G Komen for the Cure 5005 LBJ Fwy Ste 250	Dallas	TX	75244	**800-227-2345**	972-855-1600
TOPS Club Inc 4575 S Fifth St	Milwaukee	WI	53207	**800-932-8677**	414-482-4620
Tourette Syndrome Assn Inc 42-40 Bell Blvd Ste 205	Bayside	NY	11361	**888-486-8738**	718-224-2999
UCare Minnesota 500 Stinson Blvd NE PO Box 52	Minneapolis	MN	55413	**866-457-7144**	612-676-6500
Undersea & Hyperbaric Medical Society (UHMS) 21 W Colony Pl Ste 280	Durham	NC	27705	**877-533-8467**	919-490-5140
United Network for Organ Sharing (UNOS) 700 N Fourth St	Richmond	VA	23219	**888-894-6361**	804-782-4800
Well Spouse Assn 63 W Main St Ste H	Freehold	NJ	07728	**800-838-0879**	732-577-8899
Women Alive 1566 Burnside Ave	Los Angeles	CA	90019	**800-472-2321**	

47-18 Hobby Organizations

Organization	City	State	ZIP	Toll-Free	Phone
Academy of Model Aeronautics (AMA) 5161 E Memorial Dr	Muncie	IN	47302	**800-435-9262**	765-287-1256
American Contract Bridge League (ACBL) 6575 Windchase Blvd *Sales	Horn Lake	MS	38637	**800-264-2743***	662-253-3100
American Craft Council 72 Spring St 6th Fl	New York	NY	10012	**800-836-3470**	212-274-0630
American Federation of Astrologers (AFA) 6535 S Rural Rd	Tempe	AZ	85283	**888-301-7630**	480-838-1751
American Horticultural Society (AHS) 7931 E Blvd Dr	Alexandria	VA	22308	**800-777-7931**	703-768-5700
American Radio Relay League (ARRL) 225 Main St	Newington	CT	06111	**888-277-5289**	860-594-0200
American Rose Society (ARS) 8877 Jefferson Paige Rd	Shreveport	LA	71119	**800-637-6534**	318-938-5402
Barbershop Harmony Society 110 Seventh Ave N	Nashville	TN	37203	**800-876-7464**	615-823-3993
Craft & Hobby Assn (CHA) 319 E 54th St	Elmwood Park	NJ	07407	**800-822-0494**	201-835-1200
Experimental Aircraft Assn (EAA) 3000 Poberezny Rd	Oshkosh	WI	54902	**800-236-4800**	920-426-4800
National Garden Clubs Inc (NGC) 4401 Magnolia Ave	Saint Louis	MO	63110	**800-550-6007**	314-776-7574
National Gardening Assn (NGA) 1100 Dorset St	South Burlington	VT	05403	**800-538-7476**	802-863-5251
National Genealogical Society (NGS) 3108 Columbia Pk Ste 300	Arlington	VA	22204	**800-473-0060**	703-525-0050
National Model Railroad Assn (NMRA) 4121 Cromwell Rd	Chattanooga	TN	37421	**800-654-2256**	423-892-2846
National NeedleArts Assn, The (TNNA) 1100-H Brandywine Blvd	Zanesville	OH	43701	**800-889-8662**	740-455-6773
Sports Car Club of America (SCCA) 6700 SW Topeka Blvd Ste 300	Topeka	KS	66619	**800-770-2055**	785-357-7222
Sweet Adelines International 9110 S Toledo Ave	Tulsa	OK	74137	**800-992-7464**	918-622-1444
US Chess Federation (USCF) PO Box 3967	Crossville	TN	38557	**800-903-8723**	931-787-1234

47-19 Military, Veterans, Patriotic Organizations

Organization	City	State	ZIP	Toll-Free	Phone
Air Force Assn (AFA) 1501 Lee Hwy 4th Fl	Arlington	VA	22209	**800-727-3337**	703-247-5800
American Legion, The 700 N Pennsylvania St *Cust Svc	Indianapolis	IN	46204	**800-433-3318***	317-630-1200
American Logistics Assn (ALA) 1133 15th St NW Ste 640	Washington	DC	20005	**800-791-7146**	202-466-2520
American Society of Military Comptrollers (ASMC) 415 N Alfred St	Alexandria	VA	22314	**800-462-5637**	703-549-0360
AMVETS 4647 Forbes Blvd	Lanham	MD	20706	**877-726-8387**	301-459-9600
Armed Forces Communications & Electronics Assn (AFCEA) 4400 Fair Lakes Ct	Fairfax	VA	22033	**800-336-4583**	703-631-6100
Armed Services Mutual Benefit Assn (ASMBA) PO Box 160384	Nashville	TN	37216	**800-251-8434**	615-851-0800
Army Distaff Foundation 6200 Oregon Ave NW	Washington	DC	20015	**800-541-4255**	202-541-0149
Association of Old Crows (AOC) 1000 N Payne St Ste 300	Alexandria	VA	22314	**800-247-5626**	703-549-1600
Association of the US Army (AUSA) 2425 Wilson Blvd	Arlington	VA	22201	**800-336-4570**	703-841-4300
Disabled American Veterans (DAV) 3725 Alexandria Pike	Cold Spring	KY	41076	**877-426-2838**	859-441-7300
Enlisted Assn of the National Guard of the US (EANGUS) 3133 Mt Vernon Ave	Alexandria	VA	22305	**800-234-3264**	703-519-3846
Fleet Reserve Assn (FRA) 125 NW St	Alexandria	VA	22314	**800-372-1924**	703-683-1400
Marine Corps Assn (MCA) PO Box 1775	Quantico	VA	22134	**800-336-0291**	703-640-6161
Military Benefit Assn (MBA) 14605 Avion Pkwy PO Box 221110	Chantilly	VA	20153	**800-336-0100**	703-968-6200
Military Officers Assn of America (MOAA) 201 N Washington St	Alexandria	VA	22314	**800-234-6622**	703-549-2311

Classified Section

	City	State	Zip	Toll-Free	Phone
NA for Uniformed Services (NAUS) 5535 Hempstead Way	Springfield	VA	22151	**800-842-3451**	703-750-1342
National Committee for Employer Support of the Guard & Reserve (ESGR) 1555 Wilson Blvd Ste 319	Arlington	VA	22209	**800-336-4590**	703-696-1386
National Fallen Firefighters Foundation PO Box 498	Emmitsburg	MD	21727	**888-744-6513**	301-447-1365
National Guard Assn of the US (NGAUS) 1 Massachusetts Ave NW Ste 200	Washington	DC	20001	**888-226-4287**	202-789-0031
Naval Enlisted Reserve Assn (NERA) 6703 Farragut Ave	Falls Church	VA	22042	**800-776-9020**	703-534-1329
Naval Reserve Assn (NRA) 1619 King St	Alexandria	VA	22314	**877-628-9411**	703-548-5800
Navy League of the US 2300 Wilson Blvd	Arlington	VA	22201	**800-356-5760**	703-528-1775
Navy-Marine Corps Relief Society (NMCRS) 875 N Randolph St Ste 225	Arlington	VA	22203	**800-654-8364**	703-696-4904
Non Commissioned Officers Assn (NCOA) 9330 Corporate Dr Ste 701	Selma	TX	78154	**800-662-2620**	210-653-6161
Reserve Officers Assn of the US (ROA) 1 Constitution Ave NE	Washington	DC	20002	**800-809-9448**	202-479-2200
Tailhook Assn 9696 Businesspark Ave	San Diego	CA	92131	**800-322-4665**	858-689-9223
US Naval Institute 291 Wood Rd	Annapolis	MD	21402	**800-233-8764**	410-268-6110
Veterans for Peace Inc (VFP) 216 S Meramec Ave	Saint Louis	MO	63105	**877-429-0678**	314-725-6005
Veterans of Foreign Wars of the US (VFW) 406 W 34th St	Kansas City	MO	64111	**800-963-3180**	816-756-3390
Women in Military Service for America Memorial Foundation Inc Dept 560	Washington	DC	20042	**800-222-2294**	703-533-1155

47-20 Religious Organizations

	City	State	Zip	Toll-Free	Phone
American Academy of Religion (AAR) 825 Houston Mill Rd NE Ste 300	Atlanta	GA	30329	**800-282-6632**	404-727-3049
American Baptist Assn (ABA) 4605 N State Line Ave	Texarkana	TX	75503	**800-264-2482**	903-792-2783
American Baptist Churches USA PO Box 851	Valley Forge	PA	19482	**800-222-3872**	610-768-2000
American Theological Library Assn (ATLA) 300 S Wacker Dr Ste 2100	Chicago	IL	60606	**888-665-2852**	312-454-5100
Antiochian Orthodox Christian Archdiocese of North America 358 Mountain Rd	Englewood	NJ	07631	**888-421-1442**	201-871-1355
Archdiocese of Saint Paul & Minneapolis 226 Summit Ave	Saint Paul	MN	55102	**877-290-1605**	651-291-4411
Arkansas Baptist Foundation 10 Remington Dr	Little Rock	AR	72204	**800-838-2272**	501-376-0732
Assemblies of God (A/G) 1445 N Boonville Ave	Springfield	MO	65802	**800-641-4310**	417-862-2781
Avant Ministries 10000 N Oak Trafficway	Kansas City	MO	64155	**800-468-1892**	816-734-8500
B'nai B'rith International 2020 K St NW 7th Fl	Washington	DC	20006	**888-388-4224**	202-857-6600
Baptist World Alliance 405 N Washington St	Falls Church	VA	22046	**844-862-2739**	703-790-8980
Benny Hinn Ministries PO Box 162000	Irving	TX	75016	**800-433-1900**	817-722-2000
Bible League 3801 Eagle Nest Dr	Crete	IL	60417	**866-825-4636**	817-595-1664
Billy Graham Evangelistic Assn 1 Billy Graham Pkwy	Charlotte	NC	28201	**877-247-2426**	704-401-2432
Campus Crusade for Christ International 100 Lk Hart Dr	Orlando	FL	32832	**888-278-7233**	407-826-2500
Catholic Church Extension Society of the USA 150 S Wacker Dr 20th Fl	Chicago	IL	60606	**800-842-7804**	
Catholic Supply of st Louis Inc 6759 Chippewa St	Saint Louis	MO	63109	**800-325-9026**	314-644-0643
Catholic Transcript Inc, The 467 Bloomfield Ave	Bloomfield	CT	06002	**800-726-2381**	860-286-2828
Child Evangelism Fellowship Inc 17482 Hwy M	Warrenton	MO	63383	**800-748-7710**	636-456-4321
Christ in Youth Inc PO Box B	Joplin	MO	64801	**855-999-7238**	417-781-2273
Christian & Missionary Alliance 8595 Explorer Dr	Colorado Springs	CO	80920	**800-700-2651**	719-599-5999
Christian Reformed Church in North America (CRC) 2850 Kalamazoo Ave SE	Grand Rapids	MI	49560	**800-272-5125**	616-241-1691
Christophers, The 5 Hanover Sq 11th Fl	New York	NY	10004	**888-298-4050**	212-759-4050
Church of God in Christ Inc 930 Mason St	Memphis	TN	38126	**877-746-8578**	901-947-9300
Church of God Ministries 1201 E Fifth St	Anderson	IN	46012	**800-848-2464**	765-642-0256
Church of God World Missions (COGWM) 2490 Keith St PO Box 8016	Cleveland	TN	37320	**800-345-7492**	423-478-7190
Church of the Brethren 1451 Dundee Ave	Elgin	IL	60120	**800-323-8039**	847-742-5100
Church Women United (CWU) 475 Riverside Dr Ste 243	New York	NY	10115	**800-298-5551**	212-870-2347
Commons at Orlando Lutheran Towers, The 300 E Church St	Orlando	FL	32801	**800-859-1033**	407-872-7088
Community of Christ 1001 W Walnut St	Independence	MO	64050	**800-825-2806**	816-833-1000
Compassion Canada 985 Adelaide St S	London	ON	N6E4A3	**800-563-5437**	519-668-0224
Connecting Businessmen to Christ (CBMC) 5746 Marlin Rd Ste 602 Osborne Ctr	Chattanooga	TN	37411	**800-566-2262**	423-698-4444
Crossworld 306 Bala Ave	Bala Cynwyd	PA	19004	**888-785-0087**	
Dare 2 Share Ministries International PO Box 745323	Arvada	CO	80006	**800-462-8355**	303-425-1606
Diocese of Greensburg 723 E Pittsburgh St	Greensburg	PA	15601	**866-409-6455**	724-837-0901
Diocese of Rochester 1150 Buffalo Rd	Roch	NY	14624	**800-388-7177**	585-328-3210
Diocese of St. Augustine Inc 11625 Old St Augustine	Jacksonville	FL	32258	**800-775-4659**	904-262-3200
Episcopal Church USA 815 Second Ave	New York	NY	10017	**800-334-7626**	212-716-6000
Episcopal Diocese of West Texas 111 Torcido Dr	San Antonio	TX	78209	**888-824-5387**	210-824-5387
Evangelical Church Alliance (ECA) 205 W Broadway St PO Box 9	Bradley	IL	60915	**888-855-6060**	815-937-0720
Evangelical Fellowship of Canada (EFC) 600 Alden Rd Ste 300 Markham Industrial Pk	Markham	ON	L3R0E7	**866-302-3362**	905-479-5885
Evangelical Free Church of America, The 901 E 78th St	Minneapolis	MN	55420	**800-745-2202**	952-854-1300
Evangelical Lutheran Church in America (ELCA) 8765 W Higgins Rd	Chicago	IL	60631	**800-638-3522**	773-380-2700
Evangelical Training Assn (ETA) PO Box 327 *General	Wheaton	IL	60187	**800-369-8291***	
First Church of Christ Scientist 210 Massachusetts Ave P05-10	Boston	MA	02115	**800-288-7155**	617-450-2000
Franciscan Sisters of Chicago Inc 11500 Theresa Dr	Lemont	IL	60439	**800-524-6126**	
Friends General Conference 1216 Arch St Ste 2B	Philadelphia	PA	19107	**800-966-4556**	215-561-1700
General Assn of Regular Baptist Churches (GARBC) 1300 N Meacham Rd	Schaumburg	IL	60173	**888-588-1600**	847-585-0816
Greater Atlanta Christian 1575 Indian Trl Lilburn Rd	Norcross	GA	30093	**800-450-1327**	770-243-2000
Henderson Hills Baptist Church 1200 E I 35 Frontage Rd	Edmond	OK	73034	**877-901-4639**	405-341-4639
Holy Cross Family Ministries 518 Washington St	North Easton	MA	02356	**800-299-7729**	508-238-4095
IFCA International 3520 Fairlane Ave SW	Grandville	MI	49418	**800-347-1840**	616-531-1840
Interfaith Ministries for Greater Houston 3217 Montrose Blvd	Houston	TX	77006	**800-511-0999**	713-533-4900
International Bible Society (IBS) *Biblica* 1820 Jet Stream Dr *Cust Svc	Colorado Springs	CO	80921	**800-524-1588***	719-488-9200
International Church of the Foursquare Gospel (ICFG) 1910 W Sunset Blvd PO Box 26902	Los Angeles	CA	90026	**888-635-4234**	213-989-4234
International Pentecostal Holiness Church (IPHC) PO Box 12609	Oklahoma City	OK	73157	**888-474-2966**	405-787-7110
Interserve USA PO Box 418	Upper Darby	PA	19082	**800-809-4440**	610-352-0581
InterVarsity Christian Fellowship/USA 6400 Schroeder Rd	Madison	WI	53711	**866-734-4823**	608-274-9001
Jewish National Fund (JNF) 42 E 69th St	New York	NY	10021	**800-542-8733**	212-879-9300
Jewish Reconstructionist Federation (JRF) 101 Greenwood Ave	Jenkintown	PA	19046	**877-226-7573**	215-885-5601
Jewish United Fund/Jewish Federation of Metropolitan Chicago (JUF) 30 S Wells St	Chicago	IL	60606	**855-275-5237**	312-346-6700
Jews for Jesus 60 Haight St	San Francisco	CA	94102	**800-366-5521**	415-864-2600
Jimmy Swaggart Ministries (JSM) 8919 World Ministry Blvd PO Box 262550 *Orders	Baton Rouge	LA	70810	**800-288-8350***	225-768-8300
Kingsway Charities 1119 Commonwealth Ave	Bristol	VA	24201	**800-321-9234**	276-466-3014
Lake Junaluska Assembly Lake Junaluska Conference Retreat Ctr 689 N Lakeshore Dr	Lake Junaluska	NC	28745	**800-482-1442**	828-452-2881
Lutheran Church Missouri Synod (LCMS) 1333 S Kirkwood Rd	Saint Louis	MO	63122	**888-843-5267**	314-965-9000
Lutheran Home at Hollidaysburg, The 916 Hickory St	Hollidaysburg	PA	16648	**800-400-2285**	814-696-4527
Mission Aviation Fellowship (MAF) 112 N Pilatus Ln	Nampa	ID	83687	**800-359-7623**	208-498-0800
NA of Congregational Christian Churches (NACCC) 8473 S Howell Ave	Oak Creek	WI	53154	**800-262-1620**	414-764-1620
NA of Free Will Baptists (NAFWB) 5233 Mt View Rd	Antioch	TN	37013	**877-767-7659**	615-731-6812
National Baptist Convention USA Inc 1700 Baptist World Ctr Dr	Nashville	TN	37207	**866-531-3054**	615-228-6292
Navigators of Canada 11 St John'S Dr	Arva	ON	N0M1C0	**866-202-6287**	519-660-8300
Navigators, The 3820 N 30th St PO Box 6000	Colorado Springs	CO	80934	**866-568-7827**	719-598-1212
Nebraska Synod Evangelical Lutheran Church in America 4980 S 118th St Ste D	Omaha	NE	68137	**877-366-7242**	402-896-5311
New Hampshire Catholic Charities Inc 215 Myrtle St	Manchester	NH	03104	**800-562-5249**	603-669-3030
New Tribes Mission (NTM) 1000 E First St	Sanford	FL	32771	**800-321-5375**	407-323-3430
Orgill Singer 8360 W Sahara Ave Ste 110	Las Vegas	NV	89117	**800-745-3065**	702-796-9100
Orthodox Union (OU) 11 Broadway	New York	NY	10004	**855-505-7500**	212-563-4000
Oshkosh Convention & Visitors Bureau 2401 W Waukau Ave	Oshkosh	WI	54904	**877-303-9200**	920-303-9200
Pentecostal Assemblies 3214 S Service Rd	Burlington	ON	L7N3J2	**800-295-6368**	905-637-7558
Pioneers 10123 William Carey Dr	Orlando	FL	32832	**800-359-9297**	407-382-6000
Potomac Conference Corp of Seventh Day Adventists 606 Greenville Ave	Staunton	VA	24401	**800-732-1844**	540-886-0771
Presby's Inspired Life 2000 Joshua Rd	Lafayette Hill	PA	19444	**877-977-3729**	610-834-1001
Presbyterian Childrens Services Inc 1220 N Lindbergh Blvd	St. Louis	MO	63132	**800-383-8147**	314-989-9727
Presbyterian Church (USA) 100 Witherspoon St	Louisville	KY	40202	**888-728-7228**	502-569-5000
Progressive National Baptist Convention Inc (PNBC) 601 50th St NE	Washington	DC	20019	**800-876-7622**	202-396-0558
Promise Keepers (PK) PO Box 11798	Denver	CO	80211	**866-776-6473**	
Redemptorist, The 1 Liguori Dr	Liguori	MO	63057	**800-325-9521**	636-464-2500

Organization / Address	City	State	ZIP	Toll-Free	Phone
Reformed Church in America 475 Riverside Dr 18th Fl	New York	NY	10115	**800-722-9977**	212-870-3071
Seat of the Soul Foundation PO Box 3310	Ashland	OR	97520	**877-733-4279**	541-482-1515
Seventh-day Adventist World Church 12501 Old Columbia Pike	Silver Spring	MD	20904	**800-226-1119**	301-680-6000
Sim USA Inc PO Box 7900	Charlotte	NC	28241	**800-521-6449**	
Society of Biblical Literature (SBL) The Luce Ctr 825 Houston Mill Rd	Atlanta	GA	30329	**866-727-9955**	404-727-3100
Southern Baptist Convention (SBC) 901 Commerce St	Nashville	TN	37203	**866-722-5433**	615-244-2355
Tennessee Baptist Convention 5001 Maryland Way	Brentwood	TN	37027	**800-558-2090**	615-371-2029
Texas Presbyterian Foundation 6100 Colwell Blvd Ste 250	Irving	TX	75039	**800-955-3155**	214-522-3155
Third Millennium Ministries 316 Live Oaks Blvd	Casselberry	FL	32707	**877-443-6455**	407-830-0222
United Church of Christ (UCC) 700 Prospect Ave	Cleveland	OH	44115	**866-822-8224**	216-736-2100
Urban Alternative PO Box 4000	Dallas	TX	75208	**800-800-3222**	214-943-3868
US Conference of Catholic Bishops (USCCB) 3211 Fourth St NE	Washington	DC	20017	**866-582-0943**	202-541-3000
Wesbury United Methodist Community 31 N Park Ave	Meadville	PA	16335	**877-937-2879**	814-332-9000
Wheat Ridge Ministries 1 Pierce Pl Ste 250E	Itasca	IL	60143	**800-762-6748**	630-766-9066
Wider Church Ministries 700 Prospect Ave	Cleveland	OH	44115	**866-822-8224**	216-736-3200
Woman's Missionary Union (WMU) 100 Missionary Ridge	Birmingham	AL	35242	**800-968-7301**	205-991-8100
World Gospel Mission (WGM) 3783 E State Rd 18 PO Box 948	Marion	IN	46952	**800-426-0846**	765-664-7331
World Literature CrUSAde 640 Chapel Hills Dr	Colorado Springs	CO	80920	**800-423-5054**	719-260-8888
Wycliffe Bible Translators 11221 John Wycliffe Blvd	Orlando	FL	32832	**800-992-5433**	407-852-3600
Young Israel of New Rochelle 1149 N Ave	New Rochelle	NY	10804	**888-942-3638**	914-636-2215

47-21 Self-Help Organizations

Organization / Address	City	State	ZIP	Toll-Free	Phone
Al-Anon Family Group Inc 1600 Corporate Landing Pkwy	Virginia Beach	VA	23454	**888-425-2666**	757-563-1600
Calix Society, The 3881 Highland Ave Ste 201	St Paul	MN	55110	**800-398-0524**	651-773-3117
Candlelighters Childhood Cancer Foundation 10920 Connecticut Ave Suuite A PO Box 498	Kensington	MD	20895	**800-366-2223**	301-962-3520
Chemically Dependent Anonymous (CDA) PO Box 423	Severna Park	MD	21146	**888-232-4673**	
Children of Lesbians & Gays Everywhere (COLAGE) 3815 S Othello St Ste 100	Seattle	WA	98118	**800-657-3717**	415-861-5437
Co-Anon Family Groups PO Box 12722	Tucson	AZ	85732	**800-898-9985**	520-513-5028
Co-Dependents Anonymous Inc (CODA) PO Box 33577	Phoenix	AZ	85067	**888-444-2359**	602-277-7991
Cocaine Anonymous World Services Inc (CA) PO Box 492000	Los Angeles	CA	90049	**800-347-8998**	310-559-5833
Compassionate Friends PO Box 3696	Oak Brook	IL	60522	**877-969-0010**	630-990-0010
Concerned United Birthparents Inc (CUB) PO Box 503475	San Diego	CA	92150	**800-822-2777**	
Concerns of Police Survivors Inc (COPS) 846 Old S 5 PO Box 3199	Camdenton	MO	65020	**800-784-2677**	573-346-4911
Crystal Meth Anonymous General Service Organization (CMA) 4470 W Sunset Blvd Ste 107 PO Box 555	Los Angeles	CA	90027	**877-262-6691**	
Debtors Anonymous (DA) PO Box 920888	Needham	MA	02492	**800-421-2383**	781-453-2743
DignityUSA Inc PO Box 376	Medford	MA	02155	**800-877-8797**	202-861-0017
International Lawyers in Alcoholics Anonymous (ILAA) 415-1080 Mainland St	Vancouver	BC	V6B2T4	**888-685-2171**	604-685-2171
LifeRing Secular Recovery 1440 Broadway Ste 312	Oakland	CA	94612	**800-811-4142**	510-763-0779
Marijuana Anonymous World Services (MAWS) PO Box 7807	Torrance	CA	90504	**800-766-6779**	
MISS Foundation PO Box 5333	Peoria	AZ	85385	**888-455-6477**	623-979-1000
Overcomers in Christ PO Box 34460	Omaha	NE	68134	**866-573-0966**	402-573-0966
Overcomers Outreach PO Box 922950	Sylmar	CA	91392	**800-310-3001**	818-833-1803
Overeaters Anonymous Inc (OA) PO Box 44020	Rio Rancho	NM	87174	**866-505-4966**	505-891-2664
S-Anon International Family Groups Inc PO Box 111242	Nashville	TN	37222	**800-210-8141**	615-833-3152
Sex Addicts Anonymous (SAA) PO Box 70949	Houston	TX	77270	**800-477-8191**	713-869-4902
Sexaholics Anonymous (SA) PO Box 3565	Brentwood	TN	37024	**866-424-8777**	615-370-6062
SHARE Pregnancy & Infant Loss Support Inc 402 Jackson St	Saint Charles	MO	63301	**800-821-6819**	636-947-6164
Sisters Network Inc 2922 Rosedale St	Houston	TX	77004	**866-781-1808**	713-781-0255
SMART Recovery 7304 Mentor Ave Ste F	Mentor	OH	44060	**866-951-5357**	440-951-5357
Survivors Network of Those Abused by Priests (SNAP) PO Box 6416	Chicago	IL	60680	**877-762-7432**	312-455-1499
TOPS Club Inc 4575 S Fifth St	Milwaukee	WI	53207	**800-932-8677**	414-482-4620
Twinless Twins Support Group International (TTSG) PO Box 980481	Ypsilanti	MI	48198	**888-205-8962**	
Valley of the Sun United Way 1515 E Osborn Rd	Phoenix	AZ	85014	**877-322-8228**	602-631-4800
White Bison Inc 5585 Erindale Dr Ste 203	Colorado Springs	CO	80918	**877-871-1495**	719-548-1000
Wings Foundation (WINGS) 7550 W Yale Ave Ste B 201	Denver	CO	80227	**800-373-8671**	303-238-8660

47-22 Sports Organizations

Organization / Address	City	State	ZIP	Toll-Free	Phone
Adventure Cycling Assn 150 E Pine St PO Box 8308	Missoula	MT	59807	**800-755-2453**	406-721-1776
Aerobics & Fitness Assn of America (AFAA) 15250 Ventura Blvd Ste 200	Sherman Oaks	CA	91403	**877-968-7263**	818-905-0040
Amateur Athletic Union of the US (AAU) 1910 Hotel Plaza Blvd	Lake Buena Vista	FL	32830	**800-228-4872**	407-934-7200
Amateur Trapshooting Assn (ATA) 601 W National Rd	Vandalia	OH	45377	**800-671-8042**	937-898-4638
American Alliance for Health Physical Education Recreation & Dance (AAH-PERD) 1900 Assn Dr	Reston	VA	20191	**800-213-7193**	703-476-3400
American Bicycle Assn (ABA) 1645 W Sunrise Blvd	Gilbert	AZ	85233	**866-650-4867**	480-961-1903
American Canoe Assn (ACA) 503 Sophia St Ste 100	Fredericksburg	VA	22401	**888-229-3792**	540-907-4460
American Council on Exercise (ACE) 4851 Paramount Dr	San Diego	CA	92123	**800-825-3636**	858-576-6500
American Football Coaches Assn (AFCA) 100 Legends Ln	Waco	TX	76706	**877-557-5338**	254-754-9900
American Motorcyclist Assn (AMA) 13515 Yarmouth Dr	Pickerington	OH	43147	**800-262-5646**	614-856-1900
American Running Assn 4405 E W Hwy Ste 405	Bethesda	MD	20814	**800-776-2732**	301-913-9517
American Volkssport Assn (AVA) 1001 Pat Booker Rd Ste 101	Universal City	TX	78148	**855-999-5200**	210-659-2112
American Youth Soccer Organization (AYSO) 19750 S Vermont Ave Ste 200	Torrance	CA	90502	**800-872-2976**	
AMOA-National Dart Assn (NDA) 9100 PuRdue Rd Ste 200	Indianapolis	IN	46268	**800-808-9884**	317-387-1299
Babe Ruth League Inc 1770 Brunswick Pk PO Box 5000	Trenton	NJ	08638	**800-880-3142**	609-695-1434
Boat Owners Assn of the US 880 S Pickett St	Alexandria	VA	22304	**800-395-2628**	703-823-9550
Cross Country Ski Areas Assn (CCSAA) 259 Bolton Rd	Winchester	NH	03470	**877-779-2754**	603-239-4341
Disabled Sports USA (DS/USA) 451 Hungerford Dr Ste 100	Rockville	MD	20850	**800-543-2754**	301-217-0960
Fellowship of Christian Athletes (FCA) 8701 Leeds Rd	Kansas City	MO	64129	**800-289-0909**	816-921-0909
Hockey North America (HNA) 45570 Shepard Dr	Sterling	VA	20164	**800-446-2539**	703-430-8100
IDEA Inc 10455 Pacific Ctr Ct	San Diego	CA	92121	**800-999-4332**	858-535-8979
International Assn of Approved Basketball Officials (IAABO) PO Box 355	Carlisle	PA	17013	**800-526-1379**	717-713-8129
International Collegiate Licensing Assn (ICLA) 24651 Detroit Rd	Westlake	OH	44145	**877-887-2261**	440-892-4000
International Health Racquet & Sportsclub Assn (IHRSA) 70 Fargo St	Boston	MA	02210	**800-228-4772**	617-951-0055
Jockeys' Guild Inc 103 Wind Haven Dr Ste 200	Nicholasville	KY	40356	**866-465-6257**	859-305-0606
NA of Collegiate Directors of Athletics (NACDA) 24651 Detroit Rd	Westlake	OH	44145	**877-887-2261**	440-892-4000
National Aeronautic Assn Hanger 7 1 S Smith Blvd Ste 202	Washington	DC	20001	**800-644-9777**	703-416-4888
National Alliance for Youth Sports 2050 Vista Pkwy	West Palm Beach	FL	33411	**800-729-2057**	561-684-1141
National Athletic Trainers Assn (NATA) 2952 N Stemmons Fwy Ste 200	Dallas	TX	75247	**800-879-6282**	214-637-6282
National Federation of State High School Assn (NFHS) PO Box 690	Indianapolis	IN	46206	**800-776-3462***	317-972-6900
*Cust Svc					
National Golf Foundation (NGF) 1150 S US Hwy 1 Ste 401	Jupiter	FL	33477	**800-733-6006**	561-744-6006
National Little Britches Rodeo Assn (NLBRA) 5050 Edison Ave Ste 105	Colorado Springs	CO	80915	**800-763-3694**	719-389-0333
National Senior Golf Assn (NSGA) 200 Perrine Rd Ste 201	Old Bridge	NJ	08857	**800-282-6772**	
National Soccer Coaches Assn of America (NSCAA) 800 Ann Ave	Kansas City	KS	66101	**800-458-0678**	913-362-1747
National Strength & Conditioning Assn (NSCA) 1885 Bob Johnson Dr	Colorado Springs	CO	80906	**800-815-6826**	719-632-6722
National Thoroughbred Racing Assn (NTRA) 2525 Harrodsburg Rd Ste 510	Lexington	KY	40504	**800-792-6872**	
National Youth Sports Coaches Assn (NYSCA) 2050 Vista Pkwy	West Palm Beach	FL	33411	**800-729-2057**	561-684-1141
PGA of America 100 Ave of the Champions	Palm Beach Gardens	FL	33418	**800-477-6465**	561-624-8400
PONY Baseball/Softball Inc 1951 Pony Pl PO Box 225	Washington	PA	15301	**800-853-2414**	724-225-1060
Pop Warner Little Scholars Inc 586 Middletown Blvd Ste C-100	Langhorne	PA	19047	**800-257-4268**	215-752-2691
Professional Assn of Diving Instructors International (PADI) 30151 Tomas St	Rancho Santa Margarita	CA	92688	**800-729-7234***	949-858-7234
*Sales					
Professional Bowlers Assn (PBA) 719 Second Ave Ste 701	Seattle	WA	98104	**877-910-2695**	206-332-9688
Professional Tennis Registry PO Box 4739	Hilton Head Island	SC	29938	**800-421-6289**	843-785-7244
Senior Softball USA 2701 K St Ste 101A	Sacramento	CA	95816	**888-244-9499**	916-326-5303
Special Olympics Inc 1133 19th St NW 11th Fl	Washington	DC	20036	**800-700-8585**	202-628-3630
Sports Turf Managers Assn (STMA) 805 New Hampshire Ste E	Lawrence	KS	66044	**800-323-3875**	785-843-2549
US Biathlon Assn 49 Pineland Dr Ste 301-A	New Gloucester	ME	04260	**800-242-8456***	207-688-6500
*General					
US Bobsled & Skeleton Federation (USBSF) 196 Old Military Rd	Lake Placid	NY	12946	**888-431-3598**	518-523-1842
US Curling Assn (USCA) 5525 Clem's Way	Stevens Point	WI	54482	**888-287-5377**	715-344-1199

Organization	Address	City	State	Zip	Toll-Free	Phone
US Fencing Assn (USFA)	1 Olympic Plaza	Colorado Springs	CO	80909	**888-431-3598**	719-866-4511
US Golf Assn (USGA)	77 Liberty Corner Rd	Far Hills	NJ	07931	**800-336-4446***	908-234-2300
*Orders						
US Professional Tennis Assn (USPTA)	3535 Briarpark Dr Ste 1	Houston	TX	77042	**800-877-8248**	713-978-7782
US Rowing Assn	2 Wall St	Princeton	NJ	08540	**800-314-4769**	609-924-1578
US Sailing Assn	15 Maritime Dr PO Box 1260	Portsmouth	RI	02871	**800-877-2451**	401-683-0800
US Soccer Federation	1801 S Prairie Ave	Chicago	IL	60616	**800-745-3000**	312-808-1300
US Synchronized Swimming	1 Olympic Plaza	Colorado Springs	CO	80909	**800-775-8762**	317-237-5700
US Trotting Assn (USTA)	750 Michigan Ave	Columbus	OH	43215	**877-800-8782**	614-224-2291
USA Basketball	5465 Mark Dabling Boulevard	Colorado Springs	CO	80918	**888-284-5383**	719-590-4800
USA Gymnastics	201 S Capitol Ave Ste 300	Indianapolis	IN	46225	**800-345-4719**	317-237-5050
USA Hockey	1775 Bob Johnson Dr	Colorado Springs	CO	80906	**800-566-3288**	719-576-8724
USA Judo Inc	1 Olympic Plaza Ste 505	Colorado Springs	CO	80909	**800-775-8762**	719-866-4730
USA Swimming	1 Olympic Plaza	Colorado Springs	CO	80909	**800-333-3333**	719-866-4578
USA Table Tennis	1 Olympic Plaza	Colorado Springs	CO	80909	**800-775-8762**	719-866-4583
USA Track & Field (USATF)	132 E Washington St Ste 800	Indianapolis	IN	46204	**800-222-8733**	317-261-0500
USA Water Polo	2124 Main St Ste 210	Huntington Beach	CA	92648	**888-712-2166**	714-500-5445
USA Water Ski	1251 Holy Cow Rd	Polk City	FL	33868	**800-533-2972**	863-324-4341
USA Weightlifting (USAW)	1 Olympic Plaza	Colorado Springs	CO	80909	**800-775-8762**	719-866-4508
USA Wrestling	6155 Lehman Dr	Colorado Springs	CO	80918	**888-431-3598**	719-598-8181
Women's Sports Foundation	1899 Hempstead Tpke Ste 400 Eisenhower Pk	East Meadow	NY	11554	**800-227-3988**	516-542-4700

47-23 Travel & Recreation Organizations

Organization	Address	City	State	Zip	Toll-Free	Phone
Adirondack Mountain Club	814 Goggins Rd	Lake George	NY	12845	**800-395-8080***	518-668-4447
*Orders						
Alberta Hotel & Lodging Assn (AHLA)	2707 Ellwood Dr	Edmonton	AB	T6X0P7	**888-436-6112**	780-436-6112
America Outdoors	5816 Kingston Pk	Knoxville	TN	37919	**800-524-4814**	865-558-3595
American Amusement Machine Assn (AAMA)	450 E Higgins Rd Ste 201	Elk Grove Village	IL	60007	**866-372-5190**	847-290-9088
American Assn for Physical Activity & Recreation (AAPAR)	1900 Assn Dr	Reston	VA	20191	**800-213-7193**	703-476-3400
American Camp Assn (ACA)	5000 State Rd 67 N	Martinsville	IN	46151	**800-428-2267**	765-342-8456
American Hiking Society (AHS)	1422 Fenwick Ln	Silver Spring	MD	20910	**800-972-8608**	301-565-6704
American Park & Recreation Society (APRS)	22377 Belmont Ridge Rd	Ashburn	VA	20148	**800-765-3110**	703-858-0784
American Society of Travel Agents (ASTA)	1101 King St Ste 200	Alexandria	VA	22314	**800-275-2782**	703-739-2782
American Trails	PO Box 491797	Redding	CA	96049	**866-363-7226**	530-547-2060
American Whitewater (AW)	PO Box 1540	Cullowhee	NC	28723	**866-262-8429**	828-586-1930
Amusement & Music Operators Assn (AMOA)	600 Spring Hill Ring Rd Ste 111	West Dundee	IL	60118	**800-937-2662**	847-428-7699
Appalachian Mountain Club (AMC)	5 Joy St	Boston	MA	02108	**800-262-4455***	617-523-0655
*Orders						
Appalachian Trail Conservancy (ATC)	799 Washington St PO Box 807	Harpers Ferry	WV	25425	**888-287-8673***	304-535-6331
*Sales						
Back Country Horsemen of America (BCHA)	PO Box 1367	Graham	WA	98338	**888-893-5161**	360-832-2461
Bowling Proprietors' Assn of America (BPAA)	621 Six Flags Dr PO Box 5802	Arlington	TX	76011	**800-343-1329**	817-649-5105
Canadian Automobile Assn (CAA)	2151 Thurston Dr	Ottawa	ON	K1G6C9	**800-267-8713**	613-820-1890
Colorado Dude & Guest Ranch Assn (CDGRA)	PO Box D	Shawnee	CO	80475	**866-942-3472**	
Cruise Lines International Assn (CLIA)	1201 F St NW Ste 250	Washington	DC	20004	**855-444-2542**	754-224-2200
Dude Ranchers' Assn	1122 12th St PO Box 2307	Cody	WY	82414	**866-399-2339**	307-587-2339
Elderhostel Inc	11 Ave de Lafayette	Boston	MA	02111	**800-454-5768**	
Escapees RV Club	100 Rainbow Dr	Livingston	TX	77399	**800-231-9896**	936-327-8873
Family Campers & RVers (FCRV)	4804 Transit Rd Bldg 2	Depew	NY	14043	**800-245-9755**	716-668-6242
Family Motor Coach Assn (FMCA)	8291 Clough Pk	Cincinnati	OH	45244	**800-543-3622**	513-474-3622
Global Business Travel Assn, The (GBTA)	123 N Pitt St	Alexandria	VA	22314	**888-574-6447**	703-684-0836
Good Sam Club	PO Box 6888	Englewood	CO	80155	**800-234-3450**	
Hostelling International USA - American Youth Hostels (HI-AYH)	8401 Colesville Rd Ste 600	Silver Spring	MD	20910	**800-725-2331**	301-495-1240
International Airline Passengers Assn (IAPA)	PO Box 700188	Dallas	TX	75370	**800-821-4272**	972-404-9980
International Assn of Fairs & Expositions, The (IAFE)	3043 E Cairo	Springfield	MO	65802	**800-516-0313**	417-862-5771
International Gay & Lesbian Travel Assn (IGLTA)	1201 NE 26th St Ste 103	Fort Lauderdale	FL	33305	**888-789-3090**	954-630-1637
International Mountain Bicycling Assn (IMBA)	4888 Pearl E Cir Ste 200E	Boulder	CO	80301	**888-442-4622**	303-545-9011
Leave No Trace Ctr for Outdoor Ethics Inc	1830 17th St	Boulder	CO	80302	**800-332-4100**	303-442-8222
Lewis & Clark Trail Heritage Foundation	4201 Giant Springs Rd	Great Falls	MT	59405	**888-701-3434**	406-454-1234
Mountaineers, The	7700 Sand Pt Way NE	Seattle	WA	98115	**800-573-8484**	206-521-6000
National Club Assn (NCA)	1201 15th St NW Ste 450	Washington	DC	20005	**800-625-6221**	202-822-9822
National Forest Recreation Assn (NFRA)	PO Box 488	Woodlake	CA	93286	**800-282-2444**	559-564-2365
National Golf Course Owners Assn (NGCOA)	291 Seven Farms Dr 2nd Fl	Charleston	SC	29492	**800-933-4262**	843-881-9956
National Recreation and Park Association (NSPR)	22377 Belmont Ridge Rd 22377 Belmont Ridge Rd	Ashburn	VA	20148	**800-626-6772**	703-858-0784
National Tour Assn (NTA)	546 E Main St	Lexington	KY	40508	**800-682-8886**	859-226-4444
North Country Trail Assn	229 E Main St	Lowell	MI	49331	**866-445-3628**	616-897-5987
Oregon-California Trails Assn	524 S Osage St PO Box 1019	Independence	MO	64051	**888-811-6282**	816-252-2276
Pacific Crest Trail Assn (PCTA)	1331 Garden Hwy	Sacramento	CA	95833	**888-728-7245**	916-285-1846
Relais & Chateaux Assn	10 E 53rd St	New York	NY	10022	**800-735-2478**	212-319-4880
RVing Women (RVW)	879 N Plaza Dr Ste B103	Apache Junction	AZ	85120	**888-557-8464**	480-671-6226
Special Military Active Retired Travel Club (SMART)	600 University Office Blvd Ste 1A	Pensacola	FL	32504	**800-354-7681**	850-478-1986
Travel Institute	945 Concord St Ste 305	Framingham	MA	01701	**800-542-4282**	781-237-0280
Wilderness Inquiry (WI)	808 14th Ave SE	Minneapolis	MN	55414	**800-728-0719**	612-676-9400

47-24 Women's Organizations

Organization	Address	City	State	Zip	Toll-Free	Phone
Equal Rights Advocates (ERA)	1170 Market St Ste 700	San Francisco	CA	94102	**800-839-4372**	415-621-0672
General Federation of Women's Clubs (GFWC)	1734 N St NW	Washington	DC	20036	**800-443-4392**	202-347-3168
Girls Inc	120 Wall St 3rd Fl	New York	NY	10005	**800-374-4475**	212-509-2000
International Alliance for Women (TIAW)	1101 Pennsylvania Ave NW Fl 6	Washington	DC	20004	**888-712-5200**	
National Council of Jewish Women (NCJW)	475 Riverside Dr Ste 1901	New York	NY	10115	**800-829-6259**	212-645-4048
National Council of Negro Women Inc (NCNW)	633 Pennsylvania Ave NW	Washington	DC	20004	**800-462-6420**	202-737-0120
National Organization for Women (NOW)	1100 H St NW 3rd Fl	Washington	DC	20005	**855-212-0212**	202-628-8669
Ninety-Nines Inc	4300 Amelia Earhart Rd	Oklahoma City	OK	73159	**800-994-1929**	405-685-7969
Women's Sports Foundation	1899 Hempstead Tpke Ste 400 Eisenhower Pk	East Meadow	NY	11554	**800-227-3988**	516-542-4700

48 ASSOCIATIONS & ORGANIZATIONS - PROFESSIONAL & TRADE

SEE ALSO Realtor Associations - State ; Veterinary Medical Associations - State ; Dental Associations - State ; Labor Unions ; Library Associations - State & Province ; Medical Associations - State ; Nurses Associations - State ; Pharmacy Associations - State ; Bar Associations - State

48-1 Accountants Associations

Organization	Address	City	State	Zip	Toll-Free	Phone
AACE International - Assn for the Advancement of Cost Engineering	209 Prairie Ave Ste 100	Morgantown	WV	26501	**800-858-2678**	304-296-8444
AGN International-North America	2851 S Parker Rd Ste 850	Aurora	CO	80014	**800-782-2272**	303-743-7880
American Institute of Certified Public Accountants (AICPA)	1211 Ave of the Americas	New York	NY	10036	**888-777-7077**	212-596-6200
American Institute of Professional Bookkeepers (AIPB)	6001 Montrose Rd Ste 500	Rockville	MD	20852	**800-622-0121**	
Association of Certified Fraud Examiners (ACFE)	716 W Ave	Austin	TX	78701	**800-245-3321**	512-478-9000
Association of Government Accountants (AGA)	2208 Mt Vernon Ave	Alexandria	VA	22301	**800-242-7211**	703-684-6931
Association of Healthcare Internal Auditors (AHIA)	10200 W 44th Ave Ste 304	Wheat Ridge	CO	80033	**888-275-2442**	303-327-7546
BKR International	19 Fulton St Ste 401	New York	NY	10038	**800-257-4685**	212-964-2115
Construction Financial Management Assn (CFMA)	100 Village Blvd Ste 200A	Princeton	NJ	08540	**877-462-7827**	609-452-8000
CPA Auto Dealer Consultants Assn (CADCA)	1801 W End Ave Ste 800	Nashville	TN	37203	**800-231-2524**	615-373-9880
CPAmerica International	11801 Research Dr	Alachua	FL	32615	**800-992-2324**	386-418-4001
Financial Acctg Standards Board (FASB)	401 Merritt 7 PO Box 5116	Norwalk	CT	06856	**800-748-0659**	203-847-0700
Hospitality Financial & Technology Professionals (HFTP)	11709 Boulder Ln Ste 110	Austin	TX	78726	**800-646-4387**	512-249-5333
Institute of Management Accountants Inc (IMA)	10 Paragon Dr Ste 1	Montvale	NJ	07645	**800-638-4427**	201-573-9000
International Federation of Accountants	545 Fifth Ave 14th Fl	New York	NY	10017	**888-272-2001**	212-286-9344
National Association of Nonprofit Accountants & Consultants (NSA)	624 Grassmere Park Dr Ste 15	Nashville	TN	37211	**800-231-2524**	615-373-9880
National CPA Health Care Advisors Assn (HCAA)	1801 W End Ave Ste 800	Nashville	TN	37203	**800-231-2524**	615-373-9880
National Society of Accountants (NSA)	1010 N Fairfax St	Alexandria	VA	22314	**800-966-6679**	703-549-6400

Organization / Address	City	State	ZIP	Toll-Free	Phone
New York State Society of Certified Public Accountant (FAE) 14 Wall St 19th Fl	New York	NY	10005	**800-537-3635***	212-719-8300
*General					
Tax Executives Institute (TEI) 1200 G St NW Ste 300	Washington	DC	20005	**877-244-7711**	202-638-5601

48-2 Banking & Finance Professionals Associations

Organization / Address	City	State	ZIP	Toll-Free	Phone
ABA Marketing Network 1120 Connecticut Ave NW	Washington	DC	20036	**800-226-5377**	202-663-5000
ACA International - Assn of Credit & Collection Professionals 4040 W 70th St PO Box 390106	Minneapolis	MN	55439	**800-844-5654**	952-926-6547
Accuplan Benefits Services 515 East 4500 South Ste G200	Salt Lake City	UT	84107	**800-454-2649**	801-266-9900
America's Community Bankers (ACB) 1120 Connecticut Ave NW	Washington	DC	20036	**800-226-5377**	
American Assn of Daily Money Managers (AADMM) 174 Crestview Dr	Bellefonte	PA	16823	**877-326-5991**	
American Assn of Individual Investors (AAII) 625 N Michigan Ave Ste 1900	Chicago	IL	60611	**800-428-2244**	312-280-0170
American Bankers Assn (ABA) 1120 Connecticut Ave NW	Washington	DC	20036	**800-226-5377***	202-663-5000
*Cust Svc					
American Benefits Council 1501 M St NW Ste 600	Washington	DC	20005	**877-829-5500**	202-289-6700
American Finance Assn (AFA) 350 Main St	Malden	MA	02148	**800-835-6770**	781-388-8599
Bank Administration Institute (BAI) 115 S LaSalle St Ste 3300	Chicago	IL	60603	**800-224-9889***	312-683-2464
*Cust Svc					
Better Investing PO Box 220	Royal Oak	MI	48068	**877-275-6242**	248-583-6242
Certified Financial Planner Board of Standards Inc 1425 K St NW Ste 500	Washington	DC	20005	**800-487-1497**	202-379-2200
CFA Institute 915 E High St PO Box 3668	Charlottesville	VA	22903	**800-247-8132**	434-951-5499
Community Banking Advisory Network (CBAN) 1801 W End Ave Ste 800	Nashville	TN	37203	**800-231-2524**	615-373-9880
Credit Research Foundation (CRF) 8840 Columbia 100 Pkwy	Columbia	MD	21045	**866-265-3298**	410-740-5499
Credit Union Executives Society (CUES) 5510 Research Pk Dr	Madison	WI	53711	**800-252-2664**	608-271-2664
Farm Credit Council 50 F St NW Ste 900	Washington	DC	20001	**866-632-9992**	202-626-8710
Financial Managers Society (FMS) 100 W Monroe St Ste 810	Chicago	IL	60603	**800-275-4367***	312-578-1300
*Cust Svc					
Financial Planning Assn (FPA) 7535 E Hampden Ave Ste 600	Denver	CO	80231	**800-322-4237**	303-759-4900
FINRA 1735 K St NW	Washington	DC	20006	**800-289-9999**	202-728-8000
Independent Community Bankers of America (ICBA) 1615 L St NW Ste 900	Washington	DC	20036	**800-422-8439**	202-659-8111
Investment Management Consultants Assn (IMCA) 5619 DTC Pkwy Ste 500	Greenwood Village	CO	80111	**800-250-9083**	303-770-3377
Mortgage Bankers Assn (MBA) 1919 M St NW 5th Fl	Washington	DC	20036	**800-793-6222**	202-557-2700
Municipal Securities Rulemaking Board (MSRB) 1900 Duke St Ste 600	Alexandria	VA	22314	**888-475-8376**	703-797-6600
NA of Credit Management (NACM) 8840 Columbia 100 Pkwy	Columbia	MD	21045	**800-955-8815**	410-740-5560
NA of Federal Credit Unions (NAFCU) 3138 Tenth St N	Arlington	VA	22201	**800-336-4644**	703-522-4770
NACHA - Electronic Payments Assn 13665 Dulles Technology Dr Ste 300	Herndon	VA	20171	**800-487-9180**	703-561-1100
National Federation of Community Development Credit Unions (NFCDCU) 39 Broadway Ste 2140	New York	NY	10006	**800-437-8711**	212-809-1850
National Futures Assn (NFA) 300 S Riverside Plz Ste 1800	Chicago	IL	60606	**800-621-3570**	312-781-1300
National Investment Co Service Assn (NICSA) 8400 Westpark Dr 2nd Fl	McLean	VA	22102	**800-426-1122**	508-485-1500
North American Securities Administrators Assn (NASAA) 750 First St NE Ste 1140	Washington	DC	20002	**800-222-1253**	202-737-0900
Risk Management Assn (RMA) 1801 Market St Ste 300	Philadelphia	PA	19103	**800-677-7621***	215-446-4000
*Cust Svc					
Securities Industry & Financial Markets Assn (SIFMAA) 120 Broadway 35th Fl	New York	NY	10271	**888-367-7966**	212-313-1200
Smart Card Alliance Inc 191 Clarkville Rd	Princeton Junction	NJ	08550	**800-556-6828**	609-799-5654

48-3 Construction Industry Associations

Organization / Address	City	State	ZIP	Toll-Free	Phone
American Fence Assn (AFA) 800 Roosevelt Rd Bldg C-312	Glen Ellyn	IL	60137	**800-822-4342**	630-942-6598
American Road & Transportation Builders Assn (ARTBA) 1219 28th St NW	Washington	DC	20007	**800-636-2377**	202-289-4434
American Society of Heating Refrigerating & Air-Conditioning Engineers Inc (ASHRAE) 1791 Tullie Cir NE	Atlanta	GA	30329	**800-527-4723***	404-636-8400
*Cust Svc					
American Society of Home Inspectors (ASHI) 932 Lee St Ste 101	Des Plaines	IL	60016	**800-743-2744**	847-759-2820
American Society of Professional Estimators (ASPE) 2525 Perimeter Pl Dr Ste 103	Nashville	TN	37214	**888-378-6283**	615-316-9200
American Subcontractors Assn Inc (ASA) 1004 Duke St	Alexandria	VA	22314	**866-378-8866**	703-684-3450
American Welding Society (AWS) 550 NW 42nd Ave	Miami	FL	33126	**800-443-9353**	305-443-9353
Architectural Woodwork Institute (AWI) 46179 Westlake Dr Ste 120	Potomac Falls	VA	20165	**866-877-6933**	571-323-3636
Asphalt Roofing Manufacturers Assn (ARMA) 529 14th St NW Ste 750	Washington	DC	20045	**800-247-6637**	202-207-0917
Associated Builders & Contractors Inc (ABC) 4250 Fairfax Dr	Arlington	VA	22203	**877-889-5627**	703-812-2000
Associated General Contractors of America (AGC) 2300 Wilson Blvd Ste 400	Arlington	VA	22201	**800-242-1766**	703-548-3118
Associated Locksmiths of America (ALOA) 3500 Easy St	Dallas	TX	75247	**800-532-2562**	214-819-9733
Association for Retail Environment (ARE) 4651 Sheridan St Ste 470	Hollywood	FL	33021	**800-421-3483**	954-893-7300
Brick Industry Assn (BIA) 1850 Centennial Pk Dr Ste 301	Reston	VA	20191	**866-644-1293**	703-620-0010
Building Material Dealers Assn (BMDA) 1006 SE Grand Ave Ste 301	Portland	OR	97214	**888-960-6329**	503-208-3763
Ceilings & Interior Systems Construction Assn (CISCA) 1010 Jorie Blvd Ste 30	Oak Brook	IL	60523	**866-560-8537**	630-584-1919
Composite Panel Assn 19465 Deerfield Ave Ste 306	Leesburg	VA	20176	**866-426-6767**	703-724-1128
Construction Financial Management Assn (CFMA) 100 Village Blvd Ste 200A	Princeton	NJ	08540	**877-462-7827**	609-452-8000
Electronic Security Assn Inc (ESA) 2300 Vly View Ln Ste 230	Irving	TX	75062	**888-447-1689**	214-260-5970
Interlocking Concrete Pavement Institute (ICPI) 14801 Murdock St Ste 2300	Chantilly	VA	20151	**800-241-3652**	202-712-9036
International Assn of Electrical Inspectors (IAEI) 901 Waterfall Way Ste 602	Richardson	TX	75080	**800-786-4234**	972-235-1455
International Code Council (ICC) 500 New Jersey Ave NW 6th Fl	Washington	DC	20001	**888-422-7233**	202-370-1800
International Institute of Ammonia Refrigeration 1001 N Fairfax St Ste 503	Alexandria	VA	22314	**800-937-8461**	703-312-4200
International Masonry Institute (IMI) 17101 Science Dr	Bowie	MD	20715	**800-803-0295**	
International Wood Products Assn (IWPA) 4214 King St	Alexandria	VA	22302	**855-435-0005**	703-820-6696
Manufactured Housing Institute (MHI) 2101 Wilson Blvd Ste 610	Arlington	VA	22201	**800-505-5500**	703-558-0400
Marble Institute of America (MIA) 28901 Clemens Rd Ste 100	Westlake	OH	44145	**800-433-4903**	440-250-9222
Mason Contractors Assn of America (MCAA) 1481 Merchant Dr	Algonquin	IL	60193	**800-536-2225**	224-678-9709
Mechanical Contractors Assn of America (MCAA) 1385 Piccard Dr	Rockville	MD	20850	**800-556-3653**	301-869-5800
Monument Builders of North America (MBNA) 136 S Keowee St	Dayton	OH	45402	**800-233-4472**	
NA of Women in Construction (NAWIC) 327 S Adams St	Fort Worth	TX	76104	**800-552-3506**	817-877-5551
National Association of Tower Erectors (NATE) 8 Second St SE	Watertown	SD	57201	**888-882-5865**	605-882-5865
National Concrete Masonry Assn 13750 Sunrise Vly Dr	Herndon	VA	20171	**877-343-6268**	703-713-1900
National Council of Examiners for Engineering & Surveying (NCEES) 280 Seneca Creek Rd	Seneca	SC	29678	**800-250-3196**	864-654-6824
National Electrical Contractors Assn (NECA) 3 Bethesda Metro Ctr Ste 1100	Bethesda	MD	20814	**800-214-0585**	301-657-3110
National Frame Builders Assn (NFBA) 8735 W Higgins Rd Ste 300	Chicago	IL	60631	**800-557-6957**	
National Hardwood Lumber Assn (NHLA) 6830 Raleigh-LaGrange Rd	Memphis	TN	38134	**800-933-0318**	901-377-1818
National Insulation Assn (NIA) 99 Canal Ctr Plz Ste 222	Alexandria	VA	22314	**877-968-7642**	703-683-6422
National Kitchen & Bath Assn (NKBA) 687 Willow Grove St	Hackettstown	NJ	07840	**800-843-6522**	
National Parking Assn (NPA) 1112 16th St NW Ste 840	Washington	DC	20036	**800-647-7275**	202-296-4336
National Precast Concrete Assn (NPCA) 10333 N Meridian St Ste 272	Indianapolis	IN	46290	**800-366-7731**	317-571-9500
National Ready Mixed Concrete Assn (NRMCA) 900 Spring St	Silver Spring	MD	20910	**888-846-7622**	301-587-1400
National Roofing Contractors Assn (NRCA) 10255 W Higgins Rd Ste 600	Rosemont	IL	60018	**800-323-9545***	847-299-9070
*Cust Svc					
National Stone Sand & Gravel Assn (NSSGA) 1605 King St	Alexandria	VA	22314	**800-342-1415**	703-525-8788
National Wood Flooring Assn (NWFA) 111 Chesterfield Industrial Blvd	Chesterfield	MO	63005	**800-422-4556**	636-519-9663
North American Bldg Material Distribution Assn (NBMDA) 330 N Wabash Ave Ste 2000	Chicago	IL	60611	**888-747-7862**	312-321-6845
Operative Plasterers' & Cement Masons' International Assn of the US & Canada (OPCMIA) 11720 Beltsville Dr Ste 700	Beltsville	MD	20705	**888-379-1558**	301-623-1000
Painting & Decorating Contractors of America (PDCA) 2316 Millpark Dr	Maryland Heights	MO	63043	**800-332-7322***	314-514-7322
*Cust Svc					
Plumbing-Heating-Cooling Contractors NA (PHCC) 180 S Washington St	Falls Church	VA	22040	**800-533-7694**	703-237-8100
Refrigeration Service Engineers Society (RSES) 1666 Rand Rd	Des Plaines	IL	60016	**800-297-5660**	847-297-6464
Sheet Metal Workers International Assn (SMWIA) 1750 New York Ave NW 6th Fl	Washington	DC	20006	**800-251-7045**	202-783-5880
Window & Door Manufacturers Assn (WDMA) 330 N Wabash Ave Ste 2000	Chicago	IL	60611	**800-223-2301**	847-299-5200
Wood Moulding & Millwork Producers Assn (WMMPA) 507 First St	Woodland	CA	95695	**800-550-7889**	530-661-9591

48-4 Consumer Sales & Service Professionals Associations

Organization / Address	City	State	ZIP	Toll-Free	Phone
American Apparel & Footwear Assn (AAFA) 1601 N Kent St Ste 1200	Arlington	VA	22209	**800-520-2262**	703-524-1864
American Gem Society (AGS) 8881 W Sahara Ave	Las Vegas	NV	89117	**866-805-6500**	702-255-6500
American Gem Trade Assn (AGTA) 3030 LBJ Fwy Ste 840	Dallas	TX	75234	**800-972-1162**	214-742-4367
American Institute of Floral Designers (AIFD) 720 Light St	Baltimore	MD	21230	**877-865-5320**	410-752-3318
American Lighting Assn (ALA) 2050 Stemmons Fwy Ste 10046	Dallas	TX	75207	**800-605-4448**	214-698-9898
American Pet Products Manufacturers Assn (APPMA) 255 Glenville Rd	Greenwich	CT	06831	**800-452-1225**	203-532-0000
American Rental Assn (ARA) 1900 19th St	Moline	IL	61265	**800-334-2177**	309-764-2475

Organization	Address	City	State	Zip	Toll-Free	Phone
American Watchmakers-Clockmakers Institute (AWI)	701 Enterprise Dr	Harrison	OH	45030	**866-367-2924**	513-367-9800
Association for Linen Management	2161 Lexington Rd Ste 2	Richmond	KY	40475	**800-669-0863**	859-624-0177
Association of Home Appliance Manufacturers (AHAM)	1111 19th St NW Ste 402	Washington	DC	20036	**888-258-3247**	202-872-5955
Association of Pool & Spa Professionals (APSP)	2111 Eisenhower Ave Ste 500	Alexandria	VA	22314	**800-323-3996**	703-838-0083
Automotive Recyclers Assn (ARA)	3975 Fair Ridge Dr Ste 20N	Fairfax	VA	22033	**888-385-1005**	703-385-1001
Awards and Personalization Association (ARA)	8735 W Higgins Rd Ste 300	Chicago	IL	60631	**800-344-2148**	847-375-4800
Coin Laundry Assn (CLA)	1s660 Midwest Rd Ste 205	Oakbrook Terrace	IL	60181	**800-570-5629**	630-953-7920
Contact Lens Manufacturers Assn	PO Box 29398	Lincoln	NE	68529	**800-344-9060**	402-465-4122
Diamond Council of America (DCA)	3212 W End Ave Ste 202	Nashville	TN	37203	**877-283-5669**	615-385-5301
Diving Equipment & Marketing Assn (DEMA)	3750 Convoy St Ste 310	San Diego	CA	92111	**800-862-3483**	858-616-6408
Drycleaning & Laundry Institute	14700 Sweitzer Ln	Laurel	MD	20707	**800-638-2627**	301-622-1900
Gemological Institute of America (GIA)	5345 Armada Dr	Carlsbad	CA	92008	**800-421-7250**	760-603-4000
Home Furnishings Independents Assn (HFIA)	2050 Stemmons World Fwy Ste 292	Dallas	TX	75207	**800-422-3778**	
Independent Jewelers Organization (IJO)	136 Old Post Rd	Southport	CT	06890	**800-624-9252**	
International Cemetery Cremation & Funeral Assn (ICCFA)	107 Carpenter Dr Ste 100	Sterling	VA	20164	**800-645-7700**	703-391-8400
International Engraved Graphics Assn	305 Plus Pk Blvd	Nashville	TN	37217	**800-821-3138**	
International Executive Housekeepers Assn (IEHA)	1001 Eastwind Dr Ste 301	Westerville	OH	43081	**800-200-6342**	614-895-7166
International Housewares Assn (IHA)	6400 Shafer Ct Ste 650	Rosemont	IL	60018	**800-752-1052**	847-292-4200
International Order of the Golden Rule (OGR)	3520 Executive Ctr Dr Ste 300	Austin	TX	78731	**800-637-8030**	512-334-5504
International Sign Assn (ISA)	1001 N Fairfax St Ste 301	Alexandria	VA	22314	**866-949-7446**	703-836-4012
Jewelers of America (JA)	52 Vanderbilt Ave 19th Fl	New York	NY	10017	**800-223-0673**	646-658-0246
Leather Industries of America (LIA)	3050 K St NW Ste 400	Washington	DC	20007	**800-635-0617**	202-342-8497
Manufacturing Jewelers & Suppliers of America Inc (MJSA)	57 John L Dietsch Sq	Attleboro	MA	02763	**800-444-6572**	401-274-3840
National Cleaners Assn	252 W 29th St 2nd Fl *General	New York	NY	10001	**800-888-1622***	212-967-3002
National Funeral Directors & Morticians Assn (NFDMA)	6290 Shannon Pkwy	Union City	GA	30291	**800-434-0958**	770-969-0064
National Funeral Directors Assn (NFDA)	13625 Bishop's Dr	Brookfield	WI	53005	**800-228-6332**	262-789-1880
National Home Furnishings Assn (NHFA)	500 Giuseppe Ct Ste 6	Roseville	CA	95678	**800-422-3778**	336-886-6100
National Shoe Retailers Assn (NSRA)	7386 N La Cholla Blvd	Tucson	AZ	85741	**800-673-8446**	520-209-1710
National Sporting Goods Assn (NSGA)	1601 Feehanville Dr Ste 300	Mount Prospect	IL	60056	**800-815-5422**	847-296-6742
National Volunteer Fire Council (NVFC)	7852 Walker Dr Ste 450	Greenbelt	MD	20770	**888-275-6832**	202-887-5700
Pet Industry Joint Advisory Council (PIJAC)	1220 19th St NW Ste 400	Washington	DC	20036	**800-553-7387**	202-452-1525
Professional Assn of Innkeepers International (PAII)	108 S Cleveland St	Merrill	WI	54452	**800-468-7244**	856-310-1102
Recreation Vehicle Industry Assn (RVIA)	1896 Preston White Dr	Reston	VA	20191	**800-336-0154**	703-620-6003
Security Industry Assn (SIA)	8405 Colesville Rd Ste 500	Silver Spring	MD	20910	**866-817-8888**	703-683-2075
Selected Independent Funeral Homes	500 Lake Cook Rd Ste 205	Deerfield	IL	60015	**800-323-4219**	847-236-9401
Society of American Florists (SAF)	1601 Duke St	Alexandria	VA	22314	**800-336-4743**	703-836-8700
Textile Rental Services Assn (TRSA)	1800 Diagonal Rd Ste 200	Alexandria	VA	22314	**877-770-9274**	703-519-0029
Tire Industry Assn (TIA)	1532 Pointer Ridge Pl Ste G	Bowie	MD	20716	**800-876-8372**	301-430-7280
Toy Industry Assn	1115 Broadway Ste 400	New York	NY	10010	**800-541-1345**	212-675-1141
Uniform & Textile Service Assn (UTSA)	1300 N 17th St Ste 750	Arlington	VA	22209	**800-996-3426**	703-247-2600
Vision Council, The	225 Reinekers Ln Ste 700	Alexandria	VA	22314	**866-826-0290**	703-548-4560
Wallcoverings Assn	401 N Michigan Ave Ste 2200	Chicago	IL	60611	**800-575-8016**	312-644-6610
World Floor Covering Assn (WFCA)	2211 Howell Ave	Anaheim	CA	92806	**800-624-6880**	714-978-6440

48-5 Education Professionals Associations

Organization	Address	City	State	Zip	Toll-Free	Phone
American Assn of Collegiate Registrars & Admissions Officers (AACRAO)	1 Dupont Cir NW Ste 520	Washington	DC	20036	**800-222-4922**	202-293-9161
American Assn of Family & Consumer Sciences (AAFCS)	400 N Columbus St Ste 202	Alexandria	VA	22314	**800-424-8080**	703-706-4600
American Assn of School Administrators (AASA)	801 N Quincy St Ste 700	Arlington	VA	22203	**800-771-1162**	703-528-0700
American Assn of State Colleges & Universities (AASCU)	1307 New York Ave NW 5th Fl	Washington	DC	20005	**800-558-3417**	202-293-7070
American Assn of Teachers of German (AATG)	112 Haddontowne Ct Ste 104	Cherry Hill	NJ	08034	**800-835-6770**	856-795-5553
American Assn of Teachers of Spanish & Portuguese (AATSP)	900 Ladd Rd	Walled Lake	MI	48390	**877-832-2457**	248-960-2180
American Assn of University Professors (AAUP)	1133 Nineteenth St Ste 200	Washington	DC	20036	**800-424-2973**	202-737-5900
American Assn of University Women (AAUW)	1111 16th St NW	Washington	DC	20036	**800-326-2289**	202-785-7700
American Council on the Teaching of Foreign Languages (ACTFL)	1001 N Fairfax St Ste 200	Alexandria	VA	22314	**844-685-4373**	703-894-2900
American Dental Education Assn (ADEA)	1400 K St NW Ste 1100	Washington	DC	20005	**800-353-2237**	202-289-7201
American Educational Research Assn (AERA)	1430 K St NW Ste 1200	Washington	DC	20005	**800-893-7950**	202-238-3200
American Historical Assn (AHA)	400 A St SE	Washington	DC	20003	**888-444-6664**	202-544-2422
American Library Assn (ALA)	50 E Huron St	Chicago	IL	60611	**800-545-2433**	312-944-6780
American Medical Student Assn (AMSA)	1902 Assn Dr	Reston	VA	20191	**800-767-2266**	703-620-6600
American School Counselor Assn (ASCA)	1101 King St Ste 625	Alexandria	VA	22314	**800-306-4722**	703-683-2722
American Sociological Assn (ASA)	1307 New York Ave	Washington	DC	20005	**800-524-9400**	202-383-9005
American String Teachers Assn (ASTA)	4155 Chain Bridge Rd	Fairfax	VA	22030	**800-821-7303**	703-279-2113
American Studies Assn (ASA)	1120 19th St NW Ste 301	Washington	DC	20036	**800-468-3571**	202-467-4783
American Translators Assn (ATA)	225 Reinekers Ln Ste 590	Alexandria	VA	22314	**800-253-2252**	703-683-6100
Association for Advanced Training in the Behavioral Sciences (AATBS)	5126 Ralston St	Ventura	CA	93003	**800-472-1931**	805-676-3030
Association for Career & Technical Education (ACTE)	1410 King St	Alexandria	VA	22314	**800-826-9972**	703-683-3111
Association for Childhood Education International (ACEI)	1101 16th St NW Ste 300	Washington	DC	20036	**800-423-3563**	202-372-9986
Association for Continuing Higher Education (ACHE)	1700 Asp Ave	Norman	OK	73072	**800-807-2243**	
Association for Supervision & Curriculum Development (ASCD)	1703 N Beauregard St	Alexandria	VA	22311	**800-933-2723**	703-578-9600
Association for the Advancement of Computing in Education (AACE)	PO Box 1545	Chesapeake	VA	23327	**800-352-5397**	757-366-5606
Association of American Medical Colleges (AAMC)	2450 N St NW	Washington	DC	20037	**800-273-8255**	202-828-0400
Association of Christian Schools International (ACSI)	731 Chapel Hills Dr *Cust Svc	Colorado Springs	CO	80920	**800-367-0798***	719-528-6906
Association of Collegiate Schools of Architecture (ACSA)	1735 New York Ave NW 3rd Fl	Washington	DC	20006	**877-426-6323**	202-785-2324
Association of Community College Trustees (ACCT)	1101 17th St NW Ste 300	Washington	DC	20036	**866-895-2228**	202-775-4667
Association of Governing Boards of Universities & Colleges (AGB)	1133 20th St NW Ste 300	Washington	DC	20036	**800-356-6317**	202-296-8400
Association of School Business Officials International (ASBO)	11401 N Shore Dr	Reston	VA	20190	**866-682-2729**	
Association of Test Publishers	601 Pennsylvania Ave NW Ste 900	Washington	DC	20004	**866-240-7909**	
Association of Universities for Research in Astronomy (AURA)	1200 New York Ave NW Ste 350	Washington	DC	20005	**888-624-8373**	202-483-2101
Association of University Centers on Disabilities (AUCD)	1100 Wayne Avenue Ste 1000	Silver Spring	MD	20910	**888-572-2249**	301-588-8252
Broadcast Education Assn (BEA)	1771 N St NW	Washington	DC	20036	**888-326-1415**	202-429-3935
Business Professionals of America	5454 Cleveland Ave	Columbus	OH	43231	**800-334-2007**	614-895-7277
Christian Schools International (CSI)	3350 E Paris Ave SE	Grand Rapids	MI	49512	**800-635-8288**	616-957-1070
College & University Professional Assn for Hum Res (CUPA-HR)	1811 Commons Pt Dr	Knoxville	TN	37932	**877-287-2474**	865-637-7673
College Music Society (CMS)	312 E Pine St	Missoula	MT	59802	**800-729-0235**	406-721-9616
Conference on College Composition & Communication (CCCC)	1111 W Kenyon Rd	Urbana	IL	61801	**877-369-6283**	217-328-3870
Council for Advancement & Support of Education (CASE)	1307 New York Ave NW Ste 1000 *Orders	Washington	DC	20005	**800-554-8536***	202-328-5900
Council for Professional Recognition	2460 16th St NW	Washington	DC	20009	**800-424-4310**	202-265-9090
Council of Administrators of Special Education (CASE)	Osigian Office Centre 101 Katelyn Cir Ste E	Warner Robins	GA	31088	**800-585-1753**	478-333-6892
Council of the Great City Schools	1301 Pennsylvania Ave NW Ste 702	Washington	DC	20004	**888-280-7903**	202-393-2427
Council on International Educational Exchange (CIEE)	300 Fore St 2nd Fl *Cust Svc	Portland	ME	04101	**888-268-6245***	207-553-4000
Council on Social Work Education (CSWE)	1701 Duke St	Alexandria	VA	22314	**866-573-4235**	703-683-8080
Educational Housing Services Inc	55 Clark St	Brooklyn	NY	11201	**800-385-1689**	212-977-7622
Hispanic Assn of Colleges & Universities (HACU)	8415 Datapoint Dr Ste 400	San Antonio	TX	78229	**800-780-4228**	210-692-3805
International Society for Technology in Education (ISTE)	1530 Wilson Blvd Ste 730 *General	Arlington	VA	22209	**800-336-5191***	202-861-7777
MENC: NA for Music Education	1806 Robert Fulton Dr	Reston	VA	20191	**800-336-3768**	703-860-4000
Modern Language Assn (MLA)	26 Broadway 3rd Fl	New York	NY	10004	**800-323-4900**	646-576-5000
Music Teachers NA (MTNA)	441 Vine St Ste 3100	Cincinnati	OH	45202	**888-512-5278**	513-421-1420
NA of Colleges & Employers (NACE)	62 Highland Ave	Bethlehem	PA	18017	**800-544-5272**	610-868-1421
NA of Elementary School Principals (NAESP)	1615 Duke St	Alexandria	VA	22314	**800-386-2377**	703-684-3345
National Art Education Assn (NAEA)	1806 Robert Fulton Dr	Reston	VA	20191	**800-299-8321**	703-860-8000
National Assn of Student Financial Aid Administrators (NASFAA)	1101 Connecticut Ave Ste 1100	Washington	DC	20036	**800-877-8339**	202-785-0453
National Catholic Educational Assn (NCEA)	1077 30th St NW Ste 100	Washington	DC	20007	**800-711-6232**	202-337-6232
National Council for the Social Studies (NCSS)	8555 16th St Ste 500 *Orders	Silver Spring	MD	20910	**800-683-0812***	301-588-1800
National Council of Teachers of English (NCTE)	1111 W Kenyon Rd	Urbana	IL	61801	**877-369-6283**	217-328-3870

Organization / Address	City	State	Zip	Toll-Free	Phone
National Council of Teachers of Mathematics (NCTM) 1906 Assn Dr *Orders	Reston	VA	20191	**800-235-7566***	703-620-9840
National Council on Economic Education (NCEE) 122 E 42nd St Ste 2600	New York	NY	10168	**800-338-1192**	212-730-7007
National Education Assn (NEA) 1201 16th St NW	Washington	DC	20036	**888-552-0624**	202-833-4000
National Middle School Assn (NMSA) 4151 Executive Pkwy Ste 300	Westerville	OH	43081	**800-528-6672**	614-895-4730
National Science Teachers Assn (NSTA) 1840 Wilson Blvd *Sales	Arlington	VA	22201	**800-722-6782***	703-243-7100
National Staff Development Council (NSDC) 504 S Locust St	Oxford	OH	45056	**800-727-7288**	513-523-6029
North Central Assn Higher Learning Commission 230 S LaSalle St	Chicago	IL	60604	**800-621-7440**	312-263-0456
Organization for Tropical Studies (OTS) 410 Swift Ave	Durham	NC	27705	**877-572-4484**	919-684-5774
Organization of American Historians (OAH) 112 N Bryan Ave	Bloomington	IN	47408	**888-737-7006**	812-855-7311
Society for American Archaeology (SAA) 900 Second St NE Ste 12	Washington	DC	20002	**800-759-5219**	202-789-8200
Southern Assn of Colleges & Schools 1866 Southern Ln	Decatur	GA	30033	**888-413-3669**	404-679-4500
Teach For America 315 W 36th St 7th Fl	New York	NY	10018	**800-832-1230**	212-279-2080
Teachers of English to Speakers of Other Languages (TESOL) 700 S Washington St Ste 200	Alexandria	VA	22314	**888-547-3369**	703-836-0774
Teaching & Mentoring Communities (TMC) PO Box 2579	Laredo	TX	78044	**888-836-5151**	956-722-5174
Trees for Tomorrow (TFT) 519 Sheridan St E PO Box 609	Eagle River	WI	54521	**800-838-9472**	715-479-6456
Washington Education Assn Inc 32032 Weyerhaeuser Way S PO Box 9100	Federal Way	WA	98001	**800-622-3393**	253-941-6700

48-6 Food & Beverage Industries Professional Associations

Organization / Address	City	State	Zip	Toll-Free	Phone
American Assn of Cereal Chemists Inc (AACC) 3340 Pilot Knob Rd	Saint Paul	MN	55121	**800-328-7560**	651-454-7250
American Beverage Licensees (ABL) 5101 River Rd Ste 108	Bethesda	MD	20816	**800-656-3241**	301-656-1494
American Culinary Federation Inc (ACF) 180 Ctr Pl Way	Saint Augustine	FL	32095	**800-624-9458**	904-824-4468
American Society for Nutrition (ASNS) 9211 Corporate Blvd Ste 300	Rockville	MD	20850	**800-627-8723**	301-634-7050
Beer Institute 440 First St NW Ste 350	Washington	DC	20001	**800-379-2739**	202-737-2337
Biscuit & Cracker Manufacturers Assn (B&CMA) 6325 Woodside Ct Ste 125	Columbia	MD	21046	**877-701-8111**	443-545-1645
Food Marketing Institute (FMI) 2345 Crystal Dr Ste 800	Arlington	VA	22202	**800-732-2639**	202-220-0600
Institute of Food Technologists (IFT) 525 W Van Buren St Ste 1000	Chicago	IL	60607	**800-438-3663**	312-782-8424
International Assn for Food Protection (IAFP) 6200 Aurora Ave Ste 200W *General	Des Moines	IA	50322	**800-369-6337***	515-276-3344
International Assn of Culinary Professionals (IACP) 1221 Ave of the Americas 42nd fl	New York	NY	10020	**800-928-4227**	866-358-2524
International Bottled Water Assn (IBWA) 1700 Diagonal Rd Ste 650	Alexandria	VA	22314	**800-928-3711**	703-683-5213
International Dairy-Deli-Bakery Assn (IDDBA) 636 Science Dr	Madison	WI	53705	**877-399-4925**	608-238-7908
International Food Information Council Foundation (IFIC) 1100 Connecticut Ave NW Ste 430	Washington	DC	20036	**888-723-3366**	202-296-6540
Master Brewers Assn of the Americas (MBAA) 3340 Pilot Knob Rd	Saint Paul	MN	55121	**800-328-7560**	651-454-7250
National Beer Wholesalers Assn (NBWA) 1101 King St Ste 600	Alexandria	VA	22314	**800-300-6417**	703-683-4300
National Confectioners Assn (NCA) 1101 30th St NW Ste 200	Washington	DC	20007	**800-433-1200**	202-534-1440
National Restaurant Assn (NRA) 2055 L St NW Ste 700	Washington	DC	20036	**800-424-5156**	202-331-5900
Produce Marketing Assn (PMA) 1500 Casho Mill Rd	Newark	DE	19711	**800-660-4287**	302-738-7100
Retail Confectioners International (RCI) 2053 S Waverly Ste C	Springfield	MO	65804	**800-545-5381**	417-883-2775
School Nutrition Assn (SNA) 700 S Washington St Ste 300	Alexandria	VA	22314	**800-877-8822**	703-739-3900
Snack Food Assn 1600 Wilson Blvd Ste 650	Arlington	VA	22209	**800-628-1334**	703-836-4500
Specialty Coffee Assn of America (SCAA) 117 W 4th St Ste 300	Santa Ana	CA	92701	**800-995-9019**	562-624-4100
Tea Council of the USA Inc 362 Fifth Ave Ste 801	New York	NY	10001	**877-212-5752**	212-986-9415
Wine & Spirits Shippers Assn Inc (WSSA) 11800 Sunrise Vly Dr *General	Reston	VA	20191	**800-368-3167***	703-860-2300
WineAmerica 818 Connecticut Ave Ste 1006	Washington	DC	20006	**800-824-5419**	202-783-2756

48-7 Government & Public Administration Professional Associations

Organization / Address	City	State	Zip	Toll-Free	Phone
American Assn of State Highway & Transportation Officials (AASHTO) 444 N Capitol St NW Ste 249	Washington	DC	20001	**800-880-4117**	202-624-5800
American Correctional Assn (ACA) 206 N Washington St Ste 200	Alexandria	VA	22314	**800-222-5646**	703-224-0000
American Federation of Police & Concerned Citizens 6350 Horizon Dr	Titusville	FL	32780	**800-435-7352**	321-264-0911
American Foreign Service Assn (AFSA) 2101 E St NW	Washington	DC	20037	**800-704-2372**	202-338-4045
American Public Works Assn (APWA) 2345 Grand Blvd Ste 700	Kansas City	MO	64108	**800-848-2792**	816-472-6100
Association of Public Health Laboratories (APHL) 8515 Georgia Ave Ste 700	Silver Spring	MD	20910	**800-899-2278**	240-485-2745
Association of Public-Safety Communications Officials International Inc 351 N Williamson Blvd	Daytona Beach	FL	32114	**888-272-6911**	386-322-2500
Association of Social Work Boards (ASWB) 400 S Ridge Pkwy Ste B	Culpeper	VA	22701	**800-225-6880**	540-829-6880
Association of State Wetland Managers 32 Tandberg Trail Ste 2A	Windham	ME	04062	**800-451-6027**	207-892-3399
Commission on Accreditation for Law Enforcement Agencies (CALEA) 13575 Heathcote Blvd Ste 320	Gainesville	VA	20155	**877-789-6904**	703-352-4225
Conference of State Bank Supervisors (CSBS) 1129 20th St NW 5th Fl	Washington	DC	20036	**800-886-2727**	202-296-2840
Council of State & Territorial Epidemiologists (CSTE) 2872 Woodcock Blvd Ste 303	Atlanta	GA	30341	**866-577-9956**	770-458-3811
Council of State Governments (CSG) 2760 Research Pk Dr *Sales	Lexington	KY	40511	**800-800-1910***	859-244-8000
Federation of State Medical Boards of the US Inc (FSMB) 400 Fuller Wiser Rd Ste 300	Euless	TX	76039	**800-793-7939**	817-868-4000
Forest Service Employees for Environmental Ethics (FSEEE) PO Box 11615	Eugene	OR	97440	**800-270-7504**	541-484-2692
International Assn of Arson Investigators (IAAI) 2111 Baldwin Ave # 203	Crofton	MD	21114	**800-468-4224**	410-451-3473
International Assn of Assessing Officers (IAAO) 314 W Tenth St	Kansas City	MO	64105	**800-616-4226**	816-701-8100
International Assn of Chiefs of Police (IACP) 44 Canal Ctr Plz Ste 200	Alexandria	VA	22314	**800-843-4227**	703-836-6767
International Assn of Fire Chiefs (IAFC) 4025 Fair Ridge Dr Ste 300	Fairfax	VA	22033	**866-385-9110**	703-273-0911
International Assn of Plumbing & Mechanical Officials (IAPMO) 4755 E Philadelphia St	Ontario	CA	91761	**877-427-6601**	909-472-4100
International City/County Management Assn (ICMA) 777 N Capitol St NE Ste 500	Washington	DC	20002	**800-745-8780**	202-289-4262
International Conference of Funeral Service Examining Boards Inc 1885 Shelby Ln	Fayetteville	AR	72704	**800-709-0180**	479-442-7076
International Institute of Municipal Clerks (IIMC) 8331 Utica Ave Ste 200	Rancho Cucamonga	CA	91730	**800-251-1639**	909-944-4162
International Municipal Signal Assn (IMSA) 165 E Union St PO Box 539	Newark	NY	14513	**800-723-4672**	315-331-2182
International Society of Fire Service Instructors (ISFSI) 14001C St Germain Dr	Centreville	VA	20121	**800-435-0005**	
NA of Clean Water Agencies (NACWA) 1816 Jefferson Pl NW	Washington	DC	20036	**888-267-9505**	202-833-2672
NA of Conservation Districts (NACD) 509 Capitol Ct NE	Washington	DC	20002	**888-695-2433**	202-547-6223
NA of Housing & Redevelopment Officials (NAHRO) 630 'I' St NW	Washington	DC	20001	**877-866-2476**	202-289-3500
National Academy of Public Administration 1600 K St Ste 400	Washington	DC	20006	**800-883-3190**	202-347-3190
National American Indian Housing Council (NAIHC) 122 C S NW Ste 350	Washington	DC	20001	**800-284-9165**	202-789-1754
National Board of Boiler & Pressure Vessel Inspectors 1055 Crupper Ave	Columbus	OH	43229	**877-682-8772**	614-888-8320
National Conference of State Legislatures 7700 E First Pl	Denver	CO	80230	**866-229-2386**	303-364-7700
National Ctr for State Courts (NCSC) 300 Newport Ave	Williamsburg	VA	23185	**800-616-6164**	757-259-1525
National District Attorneys Assn (NDAA) 99 Canal Ctr Plaza Ste 510	Alexandria	VA	22314	**888-325-9943**	703-549-9222
National Environmental Health Assn (NEHA) 720 S Colorado Blvd Ste 1000-N	Denver	CO	80246	**866-956-2258**	303-756-9090
National Fire Protection Assn (NFPA) 1 Batterymarch Pk	Quincy	MA	02169	**800-344-3555**	617-770-3000
National Institute of Governmental Purchasing Inc (NIGP) 151 Spring St	Herndon	VA	20170	**800-367-6447**	703-736-8900
National Sheriffs' Assn (NSA) 1450 Duke St	Alexandria	VA	22314	**800-424-7827**	703-836-7827
National Volunteer Fire Council (NVFC) 7852 Walker Dr Ste 450	Greenbelt	MD	20770	**888-275-6832**	202-887-5700
Public Technology Inc 1420 Prince St Ste 200	Alexandria	VA	22314	**866-664-6368**	202-626-2400
United Federations of Security 540 N State Rd	Briarcliff Manor	NY	10510	**800-227-4291**	914-941-4103
US Travel Assn 1100 New York Ave NW Ste 450	Washington	DC	20005	**877-212-5752**	202-408-8422

48-8 Health & Medical Professionals Associations

Organization / Address	City	State	Zip	Toll-Free	Phone
Academy of General Dentistry (AGD) 211 E Chicago Ave Ste 900	Chicago	IL	60611	**888-243-3368**	312-440-4300
Academy of Managed Care Pharmacy (AMCP) 100 N Pitt St Ste 400	Alexandria	VA	22314	**800-827-2627**	703-683-8416
Academy of Osseointegration 85 W Algonquin Rd Ste 550	Arlington Heights	IL	60005	**800-656-7736**	847-439-1919
Academy of Pharmacy Practice & Management American Pharmacists Assn 1100 15th St NW Ste 400	Washington	DC	20005	**800-237-2742**	202-628-4410
Academy of Students of Pharmacy American Pharmacists Assn 1100 15th St NW Ste 400	Washington	DC	20005	**800-237-2742**	202-628-4410
America's Blood Centers (ABC) 725 15th St NW Ste 700	Washington	DC	20005	**888-872-5663**	202-393-5725
American Academy of Allergy Asthma & Immunology (AAAAI) 555 E Wells St Ste 1100	Milwaukee	WI	53202	**800-654-2452**	414-272-6071
American Academy of Audiology (AAA) 11730 Plz America Dr Ste 300	Reston	VA	20190	**800-222-2336**	703-790-8466
American Academy of Cosmetic Dentistry (AACD) 402 W Wilson St	Madison	WI	53703	**800-543-9220**	608-222-8583
American Academy of Dermatology (AAD) 930 E Woodfield Rd	Schaumburg	IL	60173	**800-868-2472**	847-330-0230
American Academy of Disability Evaluating Physicians (AADEP) 223 W Jackson Blvd Ste 1104	Chicago	IL	60606	**800-456-6095**	312-663-1171
American Academy of Family Physicians (AAFP) 11400 Tomahawk Creek Pkwy	Leawood	KS	66211	**800-274-2237**	913-906-6000
American Academy of Neurology (AAN) 1080 Montreal Ave	Saint Paul	MN	55116	**800-879-1960**	651-695-1940

Classified Section

Organization / Address	City	State	Zip	Toll-Free	Phone
American Academy of Ophthalmology 655 Beach St	San Francisco	CA	94109	**866-561-8558**	415-561-8500
American Academy of Optometry (AAO) 6110 Executive Blvd Ste 506	Rockville	MD	20852	**800-368-6263**	301-984-1441
American Academy of Orthopaedic Surgeons (AAOS) 6300 N River Rd	Rosemont	IL	60018	**800-346-2267**	847-823-7186
American Academy of Orthotists & Prosthetists (AAOP) 526 King St Ste 201	Alexandria	VA	22314	**800-669-6024**	703-836-0788
American Academy of Otolaryngology-Head & Neck Surgery (AAO-HNS) 1650 Diagonal Rd	Alexandria	VA	22314	**877-722-6467**	703-836-4444
American Academy of Pain Management (AAPM) 13947 Mono Way Ste A	Sonora	CA	95370	**888-519-9901**	209-533-9744
American Academy of Pediatric Dentistry (AAPD) 211 E Chicago Ave Ste 1600	Chicago	IL	60611	**800-974-3084**	312-337-2169
American Academy of Pediatrics (AAP) 141 NW Pt Blvd	Elk Grove Village	IL	60007	**800-433-9016**	847-434-4000
American Academy of Periodontology (AAP) 737 N Michigan Ave Ste 800	Chicago	IL	60611	**800-282-4867**	312-787-5518
American Assn for Cancer Research (AACR) 615 Chestnut St 17th Fl	Philadelphia	PA	19106	**866-423-3965**	215-440-9300
American Assn for Thoracic Surgery (AATS) 900 Cummings Ctr Ste 221-U	Beverly	MA	01915	**800-424-5249**	978-927-8330
American Assn of Bioanalysts (AAB) 906 Olive St Ste 1200	Saint Louis	MO	63101	**800-457-3332**	314-241-1445
American Assn of Clinical Endocrinologists (AACE) 245 Riverside Ave Ste 2000	Jacksonville	FL	32202	**800-435-7352**	904-353-7878
American Assn of Colleges of Osteopathic Medicine (AACOM) 5550 Friendship Blvd Ste 310	Chevy Chase	MD	20815	**800-356-7836**	301-968-4100
American Assn of Critical-Care Nurses (AACN) 101 Columbia	Aliso Viejo	CA	92656	**800-809-2273**	949-362-2000
American Assn of Endodontists (AAE) 211 E Chicago Ave Ste 1100	Chicago	IL	60611	**800-872-3636**	312-266-7255
American Assn of Gynecological Laparoscopists (AAGL) 6757 Katella Ave	Cypress	CA	90630	**800-554-2245**	714-503-6200
American Assn of Immunologists (AAI) 9650 Rockville Pike	Bethesda	MD	20814	**888-503-1050**	301-634-7178
American Assn of Integrated Healthcare Delivery Systems Inc (AAIHDS) 4435 Waterfront Dr Ste 101	Glen Allen	VA	23060	**888-491-8833**	804-747-5823
American Assn of Medical Assistants (AAMA) 20 N Wacker Dr Ste 1575	Chicago	IL	60606	**800-228-2262**	312-899-1500
American Assn of Medical Review Officers (AAMRO) PO Box 12873	Research Triangle Park	NC	27709	**800-489-1839**	919-489-5407
American Assn of Neurological Surgeons (AANS) 5550 Meadowbrook Dr	Rolling Meadows	IL	60008	**888-566-2267**	847-378-0500
American Assn of Neuromuscular & Electrodiagnostic Medicine (AANEM) 2621 Superior Dr NW	Rochester	MN	55901	**844-347-3277**	507-288-0100
American Assn of Neuroscience Nurses (AANN) 4700 W Lk Ave	Glenview	IL	60025	**888-557-2266**	847-375-4733
American Assn of Nurse Anesthetists (AANA) 222 S Prospect Ave	Park Ridge	IL	60068	**855-526-2262**	847-692-7050
American Assn of Oral & Maxillofacial Surgeons (AAOMS) 9700 W Bryn Mawr Ave	Rosemont	IL	60018	**800-822-6637**	847-678-6200
American Assn of Poison Control Centers (AAPCC) 3201 New Mexico Ave Ste 310	Washington	DC	20016	**800-222-1222**	
American Autoimmune Related Disease Assn (AARDA) 22100 Gratiot Ave	Eastpointe	MI	48021	**800-598-4668**	586-776-3900
American Cancer Society (ACS) 250 William St NW	Atlanta	GA	30303	**800-227-2345**	404-320-3333
American Chiropractic Assn (ACA) 1701 Clarendon Blvd 2nd Fl.	Arlington	VA	22209	**800-986-4636**	703-276-8800
American College of Allergy Asthma & Immunology (ACAAI) 85 W Algonquin Rd Ste 550	Arlington Heights	IL	60005	**800-466-3649**	847-427-1200
American College of Cardiology (ACC) 2400 N St NW *Cust Svc	Washington	DC	20037	**800-253-4636***	202-375-6000
American College of Chest Physicians (ACCP) 3300 Dundee Rd	Northbrook	IL	60062	**800-343-2227**	847-498-1400
American College of Emergency Physicians (ACEP) 1125 Executive Cir PO Box 619911	Dallas	TX	75261	**800-798-1822**	972-550-0911
American College of Foot & Ankle Surgeons (ACFAS) 8725 W Higgins Rd Ste 555	Chicago	IL	60631	**800-421-2237**	773-693-9300
American College of Forensic Examiners International (ACFEI) 2750 E Sunshine St	Springfield	MO	65804	**800-423-9737**	417-881-3818
American College of Managed Care Medicine (ACMCM) 4435 Waterfront Dr Ste 101	Glen Allen	VA	23060	**888-491-8833**	804-527-1905
American College of Osteopathic Family Physicians (ACOFP) 330 E Algonquin Rd Ste 1	Arlington Heights	IL	60005	**800-323-0794**	847-952-5100
American College of Physician Executives (ACPE) 400 N Ashley Dr Ste 400	Tampa	FL	33602	**800-562-8088**	813-287-2000
American College of Physicians (ACP) 190 N Independence Mall W	Philadelphia	PA	19106	**800-523-1546**	215-351-2400
American College of Radiology (ACR) 1892 Preston White Dr	Reston	VA	20191	**800-227-5463**	703-648-8900
American College of Surgeons (ACS) 633 N St Clair St	Chicago	IL	60611	**800-621-4111**	312-202-5000
American Dental Assistants Assn (ADAA) 140 N Bloomingdale Rd	Bloomingdale	IL	60108	**877-874-3785**	312-541-1550
American Dental Hygienists' Assn (ADHA) 444 N Michigan Ave Ste 3400	Chicago	IL	60611	**800-243-2342**	312-440-8900
American Diabetes Assn (ADA) 1701 N Beauregard St	Alexandria	VA	22311	**800-232-3472**	703-549-1500
American Epilepsy Society (AES) 342 N Main St	West Hartford	CT	06117	**888-233-2334**	860-586-7505
American Federation for Aging Research (AFAR) 55 W 39th St 16th Fl.	New York	NY	10018	**888-582-2327**	212-703-9977
American Federation for Medical Research (AFMR) 900 Cummings Ctr Ste 221-U	Beverly	MA	01915	**888-737-9477**	978-927-8330
American Gastroenterological Assn (AGA) 4930 Del Ray Ave	Bethesda	MD	20814	**800-227-7888**	301-654-2055
American Health Care Assn (AHCA) 1201 L St NW	Washington	DC	20005	**800-321-0343**	202-842-4444
American Health Information Management Assn (AHIMA) 233 N Michigan Ave Ste 2100	Chicago	IL	60601	**800-335-5535**	312-233-1100
American Healthcare Radiology Administrators (AHRA) 490-B Boston Post Rd Ste 200	Sudbury	MA	01776	**800-334-2472**	978-443-7591
American Hospital Assn (AHA) 155 N Wacker Dr	Chicago	IL	60606	**800-424-4301**	312-422-3000
American Institute of Ultrasound in Medicine (AIUM) 14750 Sweitzer Ln Ste 100	Laurel	MD	20707	**800-638-5352**	301-498-4100
American Lung Assn (ALA) 14 Wall St	New York	NY	10005	**800-586-4872**	212-315-8700
American Medical Assn (AMA) 515 N State St	Chicago	IL	60610	**800-621-8335**	312-464-5000
American Medical Directors Assn (AMDA) 11000 Broken Land Pkwy Ste 400	Columbia	MD	21044	**800-876-2632**	410-740-9743
American Medical Rehabilitation Providers Assn (AMRPA) 1710 N St NW	Washington	DC	20036	**888-346-4624**	202-223-1920
American Medical Technologists (AMT) 10700 W Higgins Rd Ste 150	Rosemont	IL	60018	**800-275-1268**	847-823-5169
American Nephrology Nurses Assn (ANNA) 200 E Holly Ave	Sewell	NJ	08080	**888-600-2662**	856-256-2320
American Nurses Assn (ANA) 8515 Georgia Ave Ste 400	Silver Spring	MD	20910	**800-274-4262**	301-628-5000
American Occupational Therapy Assn Inc (AOTA) 4720 Montgomery Ln PO Box 31220	Bethesda	MD	20824	**800-877-1383**	301-652-2682
American Orthopaedic Society for Sports Medicine (AOSSM) 6300 N River Rd Ste 500	Rosemont	IL	60018	**877-321-3500**	847-292-4900
American Osteopathic Assn (AOA) 142 E Ontario St	Chicago	IL	60611	**800-621-1773**	312-202-8000
American Pain Society (APS) 4700 W Lake Ave	Glenview	IL	60025	**877-752-4754**	847-375-4715
American Physical Therapy Assn (APTA) 1111 N Fairfax St	Alexandria	VA	22314	**800-999-2782**	703-684-2782
American Podiatric Medical Assn (APMA) 9312 Old Georgetown Rd	Bethesda	MD	20814	**800-275-2762**	301-581-9200
American Psychiatric Nurses Assn (APNA) 1555 Wilson Blvd Ste 530	Arlington	VA	22209	**866-243-2443**	703-243-2443
American Registry of Diagnostic Medical Sonographers (ARDMS) 1401 Rockville Pike Ste 600	Rockville	MD	20852	**800-541-9754**	301-738-8401
American Roentgen Ray Society (ARRS) 44211 Slatestone Ct	Leesburg	VA	20176	**800-438-2777**	703-729-3353
American Society for Aesthetic Plastic Surgery, The (ASAPS) 11262 Monarch St	Garden Grove	CA	92841	**800-364-2147**	562-799-2356
American Society for Clinical Pathology (ASCP) 33 W Monroe St Ste 1600 *Cust Svc	Chicago	IL	60603	**800-621-4142***	312-541-4999
American Society for Colposcopy & Cervical Pathology (ASCCP) 152 W Washington St	Hagerstown	MD	21740	**800-787-7227**	301-733-3640
American Society for Gastrointestinal Endoscopy (ASGE) 1520 Kensington Rd Ste 202	Oak Brook	IL	60523	**866-353-2743**	630-573-0600
American Society for Laser Medicine & Surgery Inc (ASLMS) 2100 Stewart Ave Ste 240	Wausau	WI	54401	**877-258-6028**	715-845-9283
American Society for Parenteral & Enteral Nutrition (ASPEN) 8630 Fenton St Ste 412	Silver Spring	MD	20910	**800-727-4567**	301-587-6315
American Society for Therapeutic Radiology & Oncology (ASTRO) 8280 Willow Oaks Corporate Dr Ste 500	Fairfax	VA	22031	**800-962-7876**	703-502-1550
American Society of Anesthesiologists (ASA) 520 N NW Hwy	Park Ridge	IL	60068	**800-331-1600**	847-825-5586
American Society of Cataract & Refractive Surgery (ASCRS) 4000 Legato Rd Ste 700	Fairfax	VA	22033	**877-996-4464**	703-591-2220
American Society of Clinical Oncology (ASCO) 2318 Mill Rd Ste 800	Alexandria	VA	22314	**888-282-2552**	571-483-1300
American Society of Consultant Pharmacists (ASCP) 1321 Duke St	Alexandria	VA	22314	**800-355-2727**	703-739-1300
American Society of Dermatopathology, The 111 Deer Lake Rd Ste 100	Deerfield	IL	60015	**800-445-8667**	847-686-2231
American Society of Health-System Pharmacists (ASHP) 7272 Wisconsin Ave	Bethesda	MD	20814	**866-279-0681**	301-664-8700
American Society of PeriAnesthesia Nurses (ASPAN) 90 Frontage Rd	Cherry Hill	NJ	08034	**877-737-9696**	856-616-9600
American Society of Plastic Surgeons (ASPS) 444 E Algonquin Rd	Arlington Heights	IL	60005	**888-475-2784**	847-228-9900
American Society of Radiologic Technologists (ASRT) 15000 Central Ave SE	Albuquerque	NM	87123	**800-444-2778**	505-298-4500
American Society of Regional Anesthesia & Pain Medicine (ASRA) 239 Fourth Ave Ste 1714	Pittsburgh	PA	15222	**855-795-2772**	412-471-2718
American Speech-Language-Hearing Assn (ASHA) 2200 Research Blvd	Rockville	MD	20850	**800-498-2071**	301-296-5700
American Thoracic Society (ATS) 61 Broadway 4th Fl.	New York	NY	10006	**866-316-2673**	212-315-8600
American Urological Assn (AUA) 1000 Corporate Blvd	Linthicum	MD	21090	**866-746-4282**	410-689-3700
American Veterinary Medical Assn (AVMA) 1931 N Meacham Rd Ste 100	Schaumburg	IL	60173	**800-248-2862**	847-925-8070
AORN Inc 2170 S Parker Rd Ste 300	Denver	CO	80231	**800-755-2676**	303-755-6300
Arthroscopy Assn of North America (AANA) 9400 W Higgins Rd Ste 200	Rosemont	IL	60018	**877-924-0305**	847-292-2262
Association for Applied Psychophysiology & Biofeedback (AAPB) 10200 W 44th Ave Ste 304	Wheat Ridge	CO	80033	**800-477-8892**	303-422-8436
Association for Healthcare Documentation Integrity (AHDI) 4230 Kiernan Ave Ste 130	Modesto	CA	95356	**800-982-2182**	209-527-9620
Association for Professionals in Infection Control & Epidemiology Inc (APIC) 1275 K St NW Ste 1000	Washington	DC	20005	**800-650-9883**	202-789-1890
Association for Research in Vision & Ophthalmology (ARVO) 12300 Twinbrook Pkwy Ste 250	Rockville	MD	20852	**888-503-1050**	240-221-2900
Association for the Advancement of Medical Instrumentation (AAMI) 4301 N Fairfax Dr Ste 301	Arlington	VA	22203	**800-332-2264**	703-525-4890
Association for Vascular Access (AVA) 5526 West 13400 South Ste 229	Herriman	UT	84096	**888-576-2826**	801-792-9079
Association of Clinical Research Professionals (ACRP) 500 Montgomery St Ste 800	Alexandria	VA	22314	**888-508-5731**	703-254-8100
Association of Military Surgeons of the United States (AMSUS) 9320 Old Georgetown Rd	Bethesda	MD	20814	**800-761-9320**	301-897-8800
Association of Nurses in AIDS Care (ANAC) 3538 Ridgewood Rd	Akron	OH	44333	**800-260-6780**	330-670-0101
Association of Osteopathic Directors & Medical Educators (AODME) 142 E Ontario St	Chicago	IL	60611	**800-621-1773**	312-202-8211
Association of Rehabilitation Nurses (ARN) 4700 W Lk Ave	Glenview	IL	60025	**800-229-7530**	847-375-4710
Association of Reproductive Health Professionals (ARHP) 1901 L St NW Ste 300	Washington	DC	20036	**877-311-8972**	202-466-3825
Association of Schools & Colleges of Optometry (ASCO) 6110 Executive Blvd Ste 420	Rockville	MD	20852	**800-397-2424**	301-231-5944

Organization	Address	City	State	ZIP	Toll-Free	Phone
Association of Staff Physician Recruiters (ASPR)	1000 Westgate Dr Ste 252	Saint Paul	MN	55114	**800-830-2777**	
Association of Surgical Technologists (AST)	6 W Dry Creek Cir Ste 200	Littleton	CO	80120	**800-637-7433**	303-694-9130
Association of University Programs in Health Administration (AUPHA)	2000 N 14th St Ste 780	Arlington	VA	22201	**877-275-6462**	703-894-0941
Association of Women's Health Obstetric & Neonatal Nurses (AWHONN)	2000 L St NW Ste 740	Washington	DC	20036	**800-673-8499**	202-261-2400
Asthma & Allergy Foundation of America (AAFA)	8201 Corporate Dr Ste 1000	Landover	MD	20785	**800-727-8462**	202-466-7643
Canadian Academy of Sport Medicine (CASM)	180 Elgin St Ste 1400	Ottawa	ON	K2P2K3	**877-585-2394**	613-748-5851
Canadian Assn of Emergency Physicians (CAEP)	1785 Alta Vista Dr Ste 104	Ottawa	ON	K1G3Y6	**800-463-1158**	613-523-3343
Canadian Medical Assn (CMA)	1867 Alta Vista Dr	Ottawa	ON	K1G5W8	**800-663-7336**	613-731-9331
Canadian Veterinary Medical Assn (CVMA)	339 Booth St	Ottawa	ON	K1R7K1	**800-567-2862**	613-236-1162
Case Management Society of America (CMSA)	6301 Ranch Dr	Little Rock	AR	72223	**800-216-2672**	501-225-2229
Christian Medical & Dental Assn (CMDA)	2604 Hwy 421 PO Box 7500	Bristol	TN	37620	**888-231-2637**	423-844-1000
COLA	9881 Broken Land Pkwy Ste 200	Columbia	MD	21046	**800-981-9883**	410-381-6581
College of American Pathologists (CAP)	325 Waukegan Rd	Northfield	IL	60093	**800-323-4040**	847-832-7000
Emergency Nurses Assn (ENA)	915 Lee St	Des Plaines	IL	60016	**800-900-9659**	847-460-4000
Endocrine Society	8401 Connecticut Ave Ste 900	Chevy Chase	MD	20815	**888-363-6274**	301-941-0200
Eye Bank Assn of America (EBAA)	1015 18th St NW Ste 1010	Washington	DC	20036	**888-491-8833**	202-775-4999
Federation of State Medical Boards of the US Inc (FSMB)	400 Fuller Wiser Rd Ste 300	Euless	TX	76039	**800-793-7939**	817-868-4000
Gerontological Society of America, The	1220 L St NW Ste 901	Washington	DC	20005	**800-677-1116**	202-842-1275
Gynecologic Oncology Group (GOG)	1600 JFK Blvd Ste 1020	Philadelphia	PA	19103	**800-225-3053**	215-854-0770
Health Industry Business Communications Council (HIBCC)	2525 E Arizona Biltmore Cir Ste 127	Phoenix	AZ	85016	**800-755-5505**	602-381-1091
Healthcare Financial Management Assn (HFMA)	2 Westbrook Corporate Ctr Ste 700	Westchester	IL	60154	**800-252-4362**	708-531-9600
Hospice Foundation of America (HFA)	1710 Rhode Island Ave NW Ste 400	Washington	DC	20036	**800-854-3402**	202-457-5811
Infectious Diseases Society of America (IDSA)	1300 Wilson Blvd Ste 300	Arlington	VA	22209	**888-844-4372**	703-299-0200
Infusion Nurses Society (INS)	315 Norwood Pk S	Norwood	MA	02062	**800-694-0298**	781-440-9408
Institute for Healthcare Improvement (IHI)	20 University Rd 7th Fl	Cambridge	MA	02138	**866-787-0831**	617-301-4800
Institute for the Advancement of Human Behavior (IAHB)	PO BOX 5527	Santa Rosa	CA	95402	**800-258-8411**	650-851-8411
International Academy of Compounding Pharmacists (IACP)	4638 Riverstone Blvd	Missouri City	TX	77459	**800-927-4227**	281-933-8400
International Chiropractors Assn (ICA)	6400 Arlington Blvd Ste 800	Falls Church	VA	22042	**800-423-4690**	703-528-5000
International College of Dentists (ICD)	51 Monroe St Ste 1400	Rockville	MD	20850	**800-533-6825**	301-251-8861
International Congress of Oral Implantologists (ICOI)	248 Lorraine Ave 3rd Fl	Upper Montclair	NJ	07043	**800-442-0525**	973-783-6300
International Society for Heart & Lung Transplantation (ISHLT)	14673 Midway Rd Ste 200	Addison	TX	75001	**888-722-2220**	972-490-9495
International Society for Magnetic Resonance in Medicine (ISMRM)	2030 Addison St Ste 700	Berkeley	CA	94704	**800-445-8667**	510-841-1899
International Society for Peritoneal Dialysis (ISPD)	66 Martin St	Milton	ON	L9T2R2	**888-834-1001**	905-875-2456
International Society for Pharmacoeconomics & Outcomes Research (ISPOR)	3100 Princeton Pk Bldg 3 Ste E	Lawrenceville	NJ	08648	**800-992-0643**	609-219-0773
International Society for Pharmacoepidemiology (ISPE)	5272 River Rd Ste 630	Bethesda	MD	20816	**888-887-7955**	301-718-6500
International Society of Refractive Surgery (ISRS)	655 Beach St PO Box 7424	San Francisco	CA	94109	**866-561-8558**	415-561-8581
International Transplant Nurses Society (ITNS)	1739 E Carson St PO Box 351	Pittsburgh	PA	15203	**800-776-8636**	412-343-4867
Lamaze International	2025 M St NW Ste 800	Washington	DC	20036	**800-368-4404**	202-367-1128
Medical Group Management Assn (MGMA)	104 Inverness Terr E	Englewood	CO	80112	**877-275-6462**	303-799-1111
NA of Neonatal Nurses (NANN)	4700 W Lk Ave	Glenview	IL	60025	**800-451-3795**	847-375-3660
National Abortion Federation (NAF)	1755 Massachusetts Ave NW	Washington	DC	20036	**800-772-9100**	202-667-5881
National Community Pharmacists Assn (NCPA)	100 Daingerfield Rd	Alexandria	VA	22314	**800-544-7447**	703-683-8200
National Council of State Boards of Nursing (NCSBN)	111 E Wacker Dr Ste 2900	Chicago	IL	60601	**866-293-9600**	312-525-3600
National Council on Problem Gambling Inc	730 11th St NW Ste 601	Washington	DC	20001	**800-522-4700**	202-547-9204
National Hospice & Palliative Care Organization (NHPCO)	1700 Diagonal Rd Ste 625	Alexandria	VA	22314	**800-658-8898*** (*Help Line)	703-837-1500
National League for Nursing (NLN)	61 Broadway 33rd Fl	New York	NY	10006	**800-669-1656**	212-363-5555
National Medical Assn (NMA)	8403 Colesville Rd Ste 920	Silver Spring	MD	20910	**800-662-0554**	202-347-1895
National Nursing Staff Development Organization (NNSDO)	330 N Wabash Ave Ste 2000	Chicago	IL	60611	**800-489-1995**	312-321-5135
National Organization for Rare Disorders (NORD)	55 Kenosia Ave PO Box 1968	Danbury	CT	06813	**800-999-6673**	203-744-0100
North American Spine Society (NASS)	7075 Veterans Blvd	Burr Ridge	IL	60527	**877-774-6337**	630-230-3600
Oncology Nursing Society (ONS)	125 Enterprise Dr	Pittsburgh	PA	15275	**866-257-4667**	412-859-6100
Optical Society of America (OSA)	2010 Massachusetts Ave NW	Washington	DC	20036	**800-766-4672**	202-223-8130
Physicians Committee for Responsible Medicine (PCRM)	5100 Wisconsin Ave NW Ste 400	Washington	DC	20016	**866-416-7276**	202-686-2210
Physicians for Social Responsibility (PSR)	1875 Connecticut Ave NW Ste 1012	Washington	DC	20009	**800-459-1887**	202-667-4260
Radiological Society of North America (RSNA)	820 Jorie Blvd	Oak Brook	IL	60523	**800-381-6660**	630-571-2670
Radiology Business Management Assn (RBMA)	10300 Eaton Pl Ste 460	Fairfax	VA	22030	**888-224-7262**	703-621-3355
Society for Healthcare Strategy & Market Development (SHSMD)	155 N Wacker Dr Ste 400	Chicago	IL	60606	**800-242-2626**	312-422-3888
Society for Surgery of the Alimentary Tract (SSAT)	900 Cummings Ctr Ste 221-U	Beverly	MA	01915	**866-849-5866**	978-927-8330
Society for Vascular Surgery (SVS)	633 N St Clair St 22nd Fl	Chicago	IL	60611	**800-258-7188**	312-334-2300
Society of Diagnostic Medical Sonography (SDMS)	2745 Dallas Pkwy	Plano	TX	75093	**800-229-9506**	214-473-8057
Society of Gastroenterology Nurses & Assoc Inc (SGNA)	401 N Michigan Ave	Chicago	IL	60611	**800-245-7462**	312-321-5165
Society of Interventional Radiology (SIR)	3975 Fair Rdige Dr Ste 400 N	Fairfax	VA	22033	**800-488-7284**	703-691-1805
Society of Nuclear Medicine (SNM)	1850 Samuel Morse Dr	Reston	VA	20190	**888-633-5343**	703-708-9000
Society of Teachers of Family Medicine (STFM)	11400 Tomahawk Creek Pkwy Ste 540	Leawood	KS	66211	**800-274-7928**	913-906-6000
Society of Thoracic Surgeons (STS)	633 N St Clair St Ste 2320	Chicago	IL	60611	**877-865-5321**	312-202-5800
Society of Toxicology (SOT)	1821 Michael Faraday Dr Ste 300	Reston	VA	20190	**800-826-6762**	703-438-3115
Southern Medical Assn (SMA)	35 W Lakeshore Dr	Birmingham	AL	35209	**800-423-4992**	205-945-1840
Sports Cardiovascular & Wellness Nutritionists (SCAN)	1450 Western Ave Ste 101	Albany	NY	12203	**800-249-2875*** (*General)	518-254-6730
US Pharmacopeia (USP)	12601 Twinbrook Pkwy	Rockville	MD	20852	**800-227-8772**	301-881-0666
Visiting Nurse Assns of America (VNAA)	900 19th St NW Ste 200	Washington	DC	20006	**888-866-8773**	202-384-1420
Wound Ostomy & Continence Nurses Society (WOCN)	1120 Rt 73 Ste 200	Mount Laurel	NJ	08054	**888-224-9626**	

48-9 Insurance Industry Associations

Organization	Address	City	State	ZIP	Toll-Free	Phone
American Academy of Actuaries	1100 17th St NW 7th Fl	Washington	DC	20036	**888-888-1778**	202-223-8196
American Assn of Insurance Services (AAIS)	1745 S Naperville Rd	Wheaton	IL	60189	**800-564-2247**	630-681-8347
American Assn of Managing General Agents (AAMGA)	610 Freedom Business Ctr Ste 110	King of Prussia	PA	19406	**800-467-8725**	610-225-1999
American Institute for CPCU & Insurance Institute of America (AICPCU/IIA)	720 Providence Rd Ste 100	Malvern	PA	19355	**800-644-2101**	610-644-2100
Associated Risk Managers (ARM)	2 Pierce Pl	Itasca	IL	60143	**800-735-5441**	630-285-4324
Association for Advanced Life Underwriting (AALU)	11921 Freedom Dr Ste 1100	Reston	VA	20190	**888-275-0092**	703-641-9400
Association for Co-op Operations Research & Development (ACORD)	1 Blue Hill Plz PO Box 1529	Pearl River	NY	10965	**800-444-3341**	845-620-1700
Blue Cross & Blue Shield Assn	225 N Michigan Ave	Chicago	IL	60601	**888-630-2583**	312-297-6000
Coalition Against Insurance Fraud	1012 14th St NW Ste 200	Washington	DC	20005	**800-835-6422**	202-393-7330
Council of Insurance Agents & Brokers	701 Pennsylvania Ave NW Ste 750	Washington	DC	20004	**877-267-9855**	202-783-4400
CPCU Society	720 Providence Rd	Malvern	PA	19355	**800-932-2728**	
GAMA International	2901 Telestar Ct	Falls Church	VA	22042	**800-345-2687*** (*Cust Svc)	
Independent Insurance Agents & Brokers of America Inc (IIABA)	127 S Peyton St	Alexandria	VA	22314	**800-221-7917**	703-683-4422
Institute for Business & Home Safety (IBHS)	4775 E Fowler Ave	Tampa	FL	33617	**866-657-4247**	813-286-3400
Insurance Information Institute Inc (III)	110 William St	New York	NY	10038	**877-263-7995**	212-346-5500
Insurance Institute for Highway Safety	1005 N Glebe Rd Ste 800	Arlington	VA	22201	**888-327-4236**	703-247-1500
Insurance Research Council (IRC)	718 Providence Rd	Malvern	PA	19355	**800-644-2101**	610-644-2212
LIMRA International Inc	300 Day Hill Rd	Windsor	CT	06095	**800-235-4672**	860-688-3358
LOMA	2300 Windy Ridge Pkwy Ste 600	Atlanta	GA	30339	**800-275-5662**	770-951-1770
Million Dollar Round Table (MDRT)	325 W Touhy Ave	Park Ridge	IL	60068	**877-883-4865*** (*General)	847-692-6378
NA of Insurance & Financial Advisors (NAIFA)	2901 Telestar Ct	Falls Church	VA	22042	**877-866-2432*** (*Sales)	703-770-8100
National Council for Prescription Drug Programs (NCPDP)	9240 E Raintree Dr	Scottsdale	AZ	85260	**888-665-2600**	480-477-1000
National Crop Insurance Services (NCIS)	8900 Indian Creek Pkwy Ste 600	Overland Park	KS	66210	**800-951-6247**	913-685-2767
National Insurance Crime Bureau (NICB)	1111 E Touhy Ave Ste 400	Des Plaines	IL	60018	**800-447-6282**	847-544-7002
Professional Liability Underwriting Society	5353 Wayzata Blvd Ste 600	Minneapolis	MN	55416	**800-845-0778**	952-746-2580
Property Loss Research Bureau (PLRB)	3025 Highland Pkwy Ste 800	Downers Grove	IL	60515	**888-711-7572**	630-724-2200
Society of Financial Service Professionals (SFSP)	19 Campus Blvd Ste 100	Newtown Square	PA	19073	**800-392-6900**	610-526-2500
Workmen's Circle/Arbeter Ring Inc	247 W 37th St 5th Fl	New York	NY	10018	**800-922-2558**	212-889-6800

48-10 Legal Professionals Associations

Organization	City	State	Zip	Toll-Free	Phone
ABA Commission on Domestic Violence 321 N Clark St 9th Fl	Chicago	IL	60654	**800-799-7233**	312-988-5000
American Academy of Psychiatry & the Law (AAPL) 1 Regency Dr PO Box 30	Bloomfield	CT	06002	**800-331-1389**	860-242-5450
American Arbitration Assn Inc (AAA) 1633 Broadway 10th Fl	New York	NY	10019	**800-778-7879**	212-716-5800
American Assn for Justice (AAJ) 777 Sixth St NW Ste 200	Washington	DC	20001	**800-424-2725**	202-965-3500
American Bar Assn (ABA) 321 N Clark St	Chicago	IL	60610	**800-285-2221**	312-988-5000
American Judicature Society (AJS) 2700 University Ave	Des Moines	IA	50311	**800-626-4089**	515-271-2281
American Land Title Assn (ALTA) 1828 L St NW Ste 705	Washington	DC	20036	**800-787-2582**	202-296-3671
American Law Institute (ALI) 4025 Chestnut St	Philadelphia	PA	19104	**800-253-6397**	215-243-1600
American Tort Reform Assn (ATRA) 1101 Connecticut Ave NW Ste 400	Washington	DC	20036	**877-333-2227**	202-682-1163
Association for Conflict Resolution (ACR) 12100 Sunset Hills Rd Ste 130	Reston	VA	20190	**800-880-7303**	703-234-4141
Association of Corporate Counsel (ACC) 1025 Connecticut Ave NW Ste 200	Washington	DC	20036	**877-647-3411**	202-293-4103
Association of Legal Administrators (ALA) 75 Tri-State International Ste 222	Lincolnshire	IL	60069	**877-675-5571**	847-267-1252
Battered Women's Justice Project 1801 Nicollet Ave S Ste 102	Minneapolis	MN	55403	**800-903-0111**	612-824-8768
Commercial Law League of America (CLLA) 70 E Lake St Ste 630	Chicago	IL	60601	**800-978-2552**	312-781-2000
Defense Research Institute (DRI) 55 W Monroe St Ste 20	Chicago	IL	60603	**866-525-6466**	312-795-1101
Environmental Law Institute (ELI) 2000 L St NW Ste 620	Washington	DC	20036	**800-433-5120**	202-939-3800
Food & Drug Law Institute (FDLI) 1155 15th St NW Ste 800	Washington	DC	20005	**800-956-6293**	202-371-1420
International Municipal Lawyers Assn (IMLA) 7910 Woodmont Ave Ste 1440	Bethesda	MD	20814	**800-942-7732**	202-466-5424
Lawyers' Committee for Civil Rights Under Law 1401 New York Ave NW Ste 400	Washington	DC	20005	**888-299-5227**	202-662-8600
National Council of Juvenile & Family Court Judges (NCJFCJ) Univ of Nevada PO Box 8970	Reno	NV	89507	**800-527-3223**	775-784-6012
National Court Reporters Assn (NCRA) 8224 Old Courthouse Rd	Vienna	VA	22182	**800-272-6272**	703-556-6272
National Legal Aid & Defender Assn (NLADA) 1140 Connecticut Ave NW Ste 900	Washington	DC	20036	**800-725-4513**	202-452-0620
Native American Rights Fund (NARF) 1506 Broadway	Boulder	CO	80302	**888-280-0726**	303-447-8760
Pension Rights Ctr 1350 Connecticut Ave NW Ste 206	Washington	DC	20036	**866-735-7737**	202-296-3776
Practising Law Institute (PLI) 810 Seventh Ave 26th Fl	New York	NY	10019	**800-260-4754**	212-824-5700
Taxpayers Against Fraud Education Fund (TAF) 1220 19th St NW Ste 501 *General	Washington	DC	20036	**800-873-2573***	202-296-4826

48-11 Library & Information Science Associations

Organization	City	State	Zip	Toll-Free	Phone
American Assn of School Librarians (AASL) 50 E Huron St	Chicago	IL	60611	**800-545-2433**	312-280-4386
American Library Assn (ALA) 50 E Huron St	Chicago	IL	60611	**800-545-2433**	312-944-6780
American Theological Library Assn (ATLA) 300 S Wacker Dr Ste 2100	Chicago	IL	60606	**888-665-2852**	312-454-5100
Association for Library & Information Science Education (ALISE) 2150 N 107th St Ste 205	Seattle	WA	98133	**877-275-7547**	206-209-5267
Association for Library Collections & Technical Services (ALCTS) 50 E Huron St	Chicago	IL	60611	**800-545-2433**	312-280-5038
Association for Library Service to Children (ALSC) 50 E Huron St	Chicago	IL	60611	**800-545-2433**	312-280-2163
Association for Library Trustees, Advocates, Friends & Foundations (ALTAFF) 50 E Huron St	Chicago	IL	60611	**800-545-2433**	
Association of College & Research Libraries (ACRL) 50 E Huron St	Chicago	IL	60611	**800-545-2433**	312-280-2519
Association of Specialized & Co-op Library Agencies (ASCLA) 50 E Huron St	Chicago	IL	60611	**800-545-2433**	312-280-4395
Library & Information Technology Assn (LITA) 50 E Huron St	Chicago	IL	60611	**800-545-2433**	312-280-4270
Library Leadership & Management Assn (LLAMA) 50 E Huron St	Chicago	IL	60611	**800-545-2433**	
Medical Library Assn (MLA) 65 E Wacker Pl Ste 1900	Chicago	IL	60601	**800-523-1850**	312-419-9094
Online Computer Library Ctr Inc (OCLC) 6565 Kilgour Pl	Dublin	OH	43017	**800-848-5878**	
Public Library Assn (PLA) 50 E Huron St	Chicago	IL	60611	**800-545-2433**	312-280-5752
Reference & User Services Assn (RUSA) 50 E Huron St	Chicago	IL	60611	**800-545-2433**	312-280-4398
Special Libraries Assn (SLA) 331 S Patrick St	Alexandria	VA	22314	**866-446-6069**	703-647-4900
Young Adult Library Services Assn (YALSA) 50 E Huron St	Chicago	IL	60611	**800-545-2433**	312-280-4390

48-12 Management & Business Professional Associations

Organization	City	State	Zip	Toll-Free	Phone
Academy of Management (AOM) 235 Elm Rd PO Box 3020	Briarcliff Manor	NY	10510	**800-633-4931**	914-923-2607
American Business Women's Assn (ABWA) 11050 Roe Ave Ste 200	Overland Park	KS	66211	**800-228-0007**	
American Chamber of Commerce Executives (ACCE) 4875 Eisenhower Ave Ste 250	Alexandria	VA	22304	**800-394-2223**	703-998-0072
American Seminar Leaders Assn (ASLA) 2405 E Washington Blvd	Pasadena	CA	91104	**800-801-1886**	626-791-1211
American Society of Assn Executives (ASAE) 1575 'I' St NW	Washington	DC	20005	**888-950-2723**	202-626-2723
American Staffing Assn (ASA) 277 S Washington St Ste 200	Alexandria	VA	22314	**800-456-4324**	703-253-2020
APQC 123 N Post Oak Ln Ste 300	Houston	TX	77024	**800-776-9676**	713-681-4020
ARMA International 11880 College Blvd Ste 450	Overland Park	KS	66210	**800-422-2762**	913-341-3808
Association for Corporate Growth (ACG) 125 S. Wacker Dr Ste 3100	Chicago	IL	60606	**877-358-2220**	312-957-4260
Association for Mfg Technology (AMT) 7901 Westpark Dr	McLean	VA	22102	**800-524-0475**	703-893-2900
Association of Fundraising Professionals (AFP) 4300 Wilson Blvd Ste 300	Arlington	VA	22203	**800-666-3863**	703-684-0410
Business Forms Management Assn (BFMA) 3800 Old Cheney Rd Ste 101-285	Lincoln	NE	68516	**888-367-3078**	402-216-0479
Christian Leadership Alliance (CLA) 635 Camino De Los Mares Ste 216	San Clemente	CA	92673	**800-263-6317**	949-487-0900
Club Managers Assn of America (CMAA) 1733 King St	Alexandria	VA	22314	**800-409-7755**	703-739-9500
ESOP Assn 1726 M St NW Ste 501	Washington	DC	20036	**866-366-3832**	202-293-2971
Executive Women International (EWI) 3860 S 2300 E	Salt Lake City	UT	84109	**877-439-4669**	801-355-2800
HR People & Strategy (HRPS) 401 N Michigan Ave Ste 2200	Chicago	IL	60611	**800-337-9517**	312-321-6805
Institute for a Drug-Free Workplace (IDFW) 10701 Parkridge Blvd Ste 300	Reston	VA	20191	**877-696-6775**	703-391-7222
Institute for Supply Management (ISM) 2055 Centennial Cir *Cust Svc	Tempe	AZ	85284	**800-888-6276***	480-752-6276
Institute of Business Appraisers (IBA) 1111 BrickyaRd Rd Ste 200	Salt Lake City	UT	84106	**800-299-4130**	
Institute of Certified Professional Managers (ICPM) James Madison University MSC 5504	Harrisonburg	VA	22807	**800-460-8013**	540-568-3247
Institute of Management Consultants USA Inc (IMC USA) 2025 M St NW Ste 800	Washington	DC	20036	**800-221-2557**	202-367-1134
International Assn for Human Resource Information Management Inc (IHRIM) PO Box 1086	Burlington	MA	01803	**800-804-3983**	
International Assn of Business Communicators (IABC) 155 Montgomery St Ste 1210	San Francisco	CA	94104	**800-766-4222**	415-544-4700
International Assn of Venue Managers Inc (IAVM) 635 Fritz Dr Ste 100	Coppell	TX	75019	**800-935-4226**	972-906-7441
International Assn of Workforce Professionals (IAPES) 1801 Louisville Rd	Frankfort	KY	40601	**888-898-9960**	502-223-4459
International Public Management Assn for Hum Res (IPMA-HR) 1617 Duke St	Alexandria	VA	22314	**800-381-8378**	703-549-7100
International Society for Performance Improvement (ISPI) PO Box 13035	Silver Spring	MD	20910	**800-825-7550**	301-587-8570
International Society of Certified Employee Benefit Specialists (ISCEBS) 18700 W Bluemond Rd PO Box 209	Brookfield	WI	53008	**888-334-3327**	262-786-8771
International Trademark Assn (INTA) 655 Third Ave 10th Fl	New York	NY	10017	**800-995-3579**	212-768-9887
Latin Business Assn (LBA) 120 S San Pedro St Ste 530	Los Angeles	CA	90012	**866-924-9757**	213-628-8510
Meeting Professionals International (MPI) 3030 LBJ Fwy Ste 1700	Dallas	TX	75234	**866-748-9561**	972-702-3000
NA of Parliamentarians (NAP) 213 S Main St	Independence	MO	64050	**888-627-2929**	816-833-3892
National Business Assn (NBA) 5151 Beltline Rd Ste 1150	Dallas	TX	75254	**800-456-0440**	972-458-0900
National Business Coalition on Health (NBCH) 1015 18th St NW Ste 730	Washington	DC	20036	**800-223-4139**	202-775-9300
National Co-op Business Assn (NCBA) 1401 New York Ave NW Ste 1100	Washington	DC	20005	**800-356-9655**	202-638-6222
National Coalition of Black Meeting Planners (NCBMP) 700 N. Fairfax St Ste 510	Alexandria	VA	22314	**800-551-9369**	571-527-3110
National Contract Management Assn (NCMA) 21740 Beaumeade Cir Ste 125	Ashburn	VA	20147	**800-344-8096**	571-382-0082
National Notary Assn (NNA) 9350 DeSoto Ave	Chatsworth	CA	91313	**800-876-6827**	818-739-4000
National Right to Work Committee (NRTWC) 8001 Braddock Rd Ste 500	Springfield	VA	22160	**800-325-7892**	703-321-8510
National Small Business Assn (NSBA) 1156 15th St NW Ste 1100	Washington	DC	20005	**800-345-6728**	202-293-8830
Product Development & Management Assn (PDMA) 330 N Wabash Ave Ste 2000	Chicago	IL	60611	**800-232-5241**	312-321-5145
Professional Convention Management Assn (PCMA) 35 E Wacker Dr Ste 500	Chicago	IL	60601	**877-827-7262**	312-423-7262
Professional Services Council (PSC) 4401 Wilson Blvd Ste 1110	Arlington	VA	22203	**800-353-9118**	703-875-8059
Profit Sharing/401(k) Council of America (PSCA) 20 N Wacker Dr Ste 3700	Chicago	IL	60606	**866-614-8407**	312-419-1863
Project Management Institute (PMI) 14 Campus Blvd	Newtown Square	PA	19073	**866-276-4764**	610-356-4600
Religious Conference Management Assn Inc (RCMA) 7702 Woodland Dr Ste 120	Indianapolis	IN	46278	**800-221-8235**	317-632-1888
SCORE Assn 1175 Herndon Pkwy Ste 900	Herndon	VA	20170	**800-634-0245**	
Society for Human Resource Management (SHRM) 1800 Duke St	Alexandria	VA	22314	**800-283-7476**	703-548-3440
WorldatWork 14040 N Northsight Blvd	Scottsdale	AZ	85260	**877-951-9191**	202-315-5500
Young Presidents' Organization (YPO) 600 E Las Colinas Blvd Ste 1000	Irving	TX	75039	**800-773-7976**	972-587-1500
YPO-WPO 600 E Las Colinas Blvd Ste 1100	Irving	TX	75039	**800-773-7976**	972-587-1500

48-13 Manufacturing Industry Professional & Trade Associations

Organization	City	State	Zip	Toll-Free	Phone

Organization / Address	City	State	ZIP	Toll-Free	Phone
American Boiler Manufacturers Assn (ABMA) 8221 Old Courthouse Rd Ste 207	Vienna	VA	22182	**800-227-1966**	703-356-7172
American Foundry Society (AFS) 1695 N Penny Ln	Schaumburg	IL	60173	**800-537-4237**	847-824-0181
American Galvanizers Assn (AGA) 6881 S Holly Cir Ste 108	Centennial	CO	80112	**800-468-7732**	720-554-0900
American Society for Quality (ASQ) 600 N Plankinton Ave	Milwaukee	WI	53203	**800-248-1946**	414-272-8575
ASM International 9639 Kinsman Rd	Materials Park	OH	44073	**800-336-5152**	440-338-5151
Association of Equipment Manufacturers (AEM) 6737 W Washington St Ste 2400	Milwaukee	WI	53214	**866-236-0442**	414-272-0943
Building Service Contractors Assn International (BSCAI) 401 N Michigan Ave Ste 2200	Chicago	IL	60611	**800-368-3414**	312-321-5167
Copper Development Assn Inc 260 Madison Ave 16th Fl	New York	NY	10016	**800-232-3282**	212-251-7200
Crane Manufacturers Assn of America (CMAA) 8720 Red Oak Blvd Ste 201	Charlotte	NC	28217	**800-345-1815**	704-676-1190
Fabricators & Manufacturers Assn International (FMA) 833 Featherstone Rd	Rockford	IL	61107	**888-394-4362**	815-399-8700
Food Processing Suppliers Assn (FPSA) 1451 Dolley Madison Blvd Ste 101	McLean	VA	22101	**855-670-4787**	703-761-2600
Glass Assn of North America (GANA) 800 SW Jackson St Ste 1500	Topeka	KS	66612	**877-275-2421**	785-271-0208
Industrial Fabrics Assn International (IFAI) 1801 County Rd 'B' W	Roseville	MN	55113	**800-225-4324**	651-222-2508
Institute of Caster & Wheel Manufacturers (ICWM) 8720 Red Oak Blvd Ste 201	Charlotte	NC	28217	**877-522-5431**	704-676-1190
Institute of Industrial Engineers (IIE) 3577 PkwyLn Ste 200 *Cust Svc	Norcross	GA	30092	**800-494-0460***	770-449-0460
Institute of Makers of Explosives (IME) 1120 19th St NW Ste 310	Washington	DC	20036	**800-461-8841**	202-429-9280
Institute of Packaging Professionals (IoPP) 1833 Centre Point Cir Ste 123	Naperville	IL	60563	**800-432-4085**	630-544-5050
International Ground Source Heat Pump Assn (IGSHPA) Oklahoma State University 374 Cordell S	Stillwater	OK	74078	**800-626-4747**	405-744-5175
Material Handling Industry of America (MHIA) 8720 Red Oak Blvd Ste 201	Charlotte	NC	28217	**800-345-1815**	704-676-1190
Minerals Metals & Materials Society (TMS) 184 Thorn Hill Rd	Warrendale	PA	15086	**800-759-4867**	724-776-9000
NACE International: Corrosion Society 1440 S Creek Dr	Houston	TX	77084	**800-797-6223**	281-228-6200
National Coil Coating Assn (NCCA) 1300 Sumner Ave	Cleveland	OH	44115	**800-532-0500**	216-241-7333
National Council of Textile Organizations (NCTO) 910 17th St NW	Washington	DC	20006	**800-238-7192**	202-822-8028
National Electrical Manufacturers Assn (NEMA) 1300 N 17th St Ste 1752	Rosslyn	VA	22209	**800-699-9277**	703-841-3200
National Glass Assn (NGA) 8200 Greensboro Dr Ste 302	McLean	VA	22102	**866-342-5642**	703-442-4890
National Marine Electronics Assn (NMEA) 7 Riggs Ave	Severna Park	MD	21146	**800-808-6632**	410-975-9425
National Paint & Coatings Assn (NPCA) 1500 Rhode Island Ave NW	Washington	DC	20005	**800-647-5527**	202-462-6272
National Tooling & Machining Assn (NTMA) 6363 Oak Tree Blvd	Independence	OH	44131	**800-248-6862**	
North American Assn of Food Equipment Manufacturers (NAFEM) 161 N Clark St Ste 2020	Chicago	IL	60601	**888-493-5961**	312-821-0201
Open Applications Group Inc (OAGI) PO Box 4897	Marietta	GA	30061	**800-236-4600**	404-402-1962
Packaging Machinery Manufacturers Institute (PMMI) 4350 N Fairfax Dr Ste 600	Arlington	VA	22203	**888-275-7664**	703-243-8555
Precision Machined Products Assn (PMPA) 6700 W Snowville Rd	Brecksville	OH	44141	**800-233-1234**	440-526-0300
Rubber Manufacturers Assn (RMA) 1400 K St NW Ste 900	Washington	DC	20005	**800-220-7622**	202-682-4800
Society for Mining Metallurgy & Exploration Inc (SME) 8307 Shaffer Pkwy	Littleton	CO	80127	**800-763-3132**	303-973-9550
Society for Protective Coatings (SSPC) 40 24th St 6th Fl	Pittsburgh	PA	15222	**877-281-7772**	412-281-2331
Society of Mfg Engineers (SME) 1 SME Dr *Cust Svc	Dearborn	MI	48128	**800-733-4763***	313-425-3000
Society of Vacuum Coaters (SVC) 71 Pinon Hill Pl NE	Albuquerque	NM	87122	**800-443-8817**	505-856-7188
Spring Manufacturers Institute (SMI) 2001 Midwest Rd Ste 106	Oak Brook	IL	60523	**866-482-5569**	630-495-8588
Technical Assn of the Pulp & Paper Industry (TAPPI) 15 Technology Pkwy S *Sales	Norcross	GA	30092	**800-332-8686***	770-446-1400
Valve Manufacturers Assn of America (VMA) 1050 17th St NW Ste 280	Washington	DC	20036	**800-468-3571**	202-331-8105

48-14 Media Professionals Associations

Organization / Address	City	State	ZIP	Toll-Free	Phone
Accuracy in Media Inc (AIM) 4350 EW Hwy Ste 555	Bethesda	MD	20814	**800-787-4567**	202-364-4401
American Radio Relay League (ARRL) 225 Main St	Newington	CT	06111	**888-277-5289**	860-594-0200
Association of Alternative Newsweeklies (AAN) 115615th St NW	Washington	DC	20005	**866-415-0704**	202-289-8484
Catholic Press Assn (CPA) 205 W Monroe St Ste 470	Chicago	IL	60606	**800-777-7432**	312-380-6789
National Cable Television Co-op Inc (NCTC) 11200 Corporate Ave	Lenexa	KS	66219	**800-720-5850**	913-599-5900
National Newspaper Assn (NNA) PO Box 7540	Columbia	MO	65205	**800-829-4662**	573-777-4980
Radio-Television News Directors Assn (RTNDA) 1600 K St NW Ste 700	Washington	DC	20006	**800-807-8632**	202-659-6510
Satellite Broadcasting & Communications Assn (SBCA) 1730 M St NW Ste 600	Washington	DC	20036	**800-541-5981**	202-349-3620
Society of Broadcast Engineers Inc (SBE) 9102 N Meridian St Ste 150	Indianapolis	IN	46260	**800-237-1776**	317-846-9000
Society of Environmental Journalists (SEJ) 115 W Ave	Jenkintown	PA	19046	**866-208-3372**	215-884-8174
Society of Professional Journalists (SPJ) 3909 N Meridian St	Indianapolis	IN	46208	**800-331-1212**	317-927-8000
Specialized Information Publishers Assn (SIPA) 8229 Boone Blvd Ste 260	Vienna	VA	22182	**800-356-9302**	703-992-9339

48-15 Mental Health Professionals Associations

Organization / Address	City	State	ZIP	Toll-Free	Phone
American Academy of Child & Adolescent Psychiatry (AACAP) 3615 Wisconsin Ave NW	Washington	DC	20016	**800-333-7636**	202-966-7300
American Academy of Psychiatry & the Law (AAPL) 1 Regency Dr PO Box 30	Bloomfield	CT	06002	**800-331-1389**	860-242-5450
American Counseling Assn (ACA) 5999 Stevenson Ave	Alexandria	VA	22304	**800-347-6647**	703-823-9800
American Group Psychotherapy Assn (AGPA) 25 E 21st St 6th Fl	New York	NY	10010	**877-668-2472**	212-477-2677
American Mental Health Counselors Assn (AMHCA) 801 N Fairfax St Ste 304	Alexandria	VA	22314	**800-326-2642**	703-548-6002
American Psychiatric Assn (APA) 1000 Wilson Blvd Ste 1825	Arlington	VA	22209	**888-357-7924**	703-907-7300
American Psychiatric Nurses Assn (APNA) 1555 Wilson Blvd Ste 530	Arlington	VA	22209	**866-243-2443**	703-243-2443
American Psychological Assn (APA) 750 First St NE	Washington	DC	20002	**800-374-2721**	202-336-5500
Arc of Stanly County, The 350 Pee Dee Ave Ste A	Albemarle	NC	28001	**800-230-7525**	704-986-1500
Association for Behavioral & Cognitive Therapies (ABCT) 305 Seventh Ave 16th Fl	New York	NY	10001	**800-685-2228**	212-647-1890
International Assn of Marriage & Family Counselors (IAMFC) 5999 Stevenson Ave	Alexandria	VA	22304	**800-347-6647**	
International Society for Traumatic Stress Studies (ISTSS) 111 Deer Lk Rd Ste 100	Deerfield	IL	60015	**877-469-7873**	847-480-9028
Lifespring Inc 460 Spring St	Jeffersonville	IN	47130	**800-456-2117**	812-280-2080
National Psychological Assn for Psychoanalysis (NPAP) 40 W 13th St Ste 1	New York	NY	10011	**800-365-7006**	212-924-7440
Northern Arizona Regional Behavioral Health Authority Inc (NARBHA) 1300 S Yale St	Flagstaff	AZ	86001	**877-923-1400**	928-774-7128
Northwestern Counseling & Support Services Inc 107 Fisher Pond Rd	Saint Albans	VT	05478	**800-834-7793**	802-524-6554
SAVE - Suicide Awareness Voices of Education 8120 Penn Ave S Ste 470	Bloomington	MN	55431	**888-511-7283**	952-946-7998
Society for Social Work Leadership in Health Care 100 N 20th St 4th Fl	Philadelphia	PA	19103	**866-237-9542**	215-599-6134
Society of Behavioral Medicine (SBM) 555 E Wells St Ste 1100	Milwaukee	WI	53202	**800-784-8669**	414-918-3156

48-16 Publishing & Printing Professional Associations

Organization / Address	City	State	ZIP	Toll-Free	Phone
Association of American Publishers Inc (AAP) 71 Fifth Ave	New York	NY	10003	**866-271-4968**	212-255-0200
Association of Directory Publishers (ADP) PO Box 209	Traverse City	MI	49685	**800-267-9002**	231-486-2182
Canadian Newspaper Assn 890 Yonge St Ste 200	Toronto	ON	M4W3P4	**877-305-2262**	416-923-3567
Copyright Clearance Ctr Inc (CCC) 222 Rosewood Dr	Danvers	MA	01923	**855-239-3415**	978-750-8400
Editorial Freelancers Assn (EFA) 71 W 23rd St 4th Fl	New York	NY	10010	**866-929-5400**	212-929-5400
Idealliance 1600 Duke St Ste 420	Alexandria	VA	22314	**800-255-8141**	952-896-1908
International Reprographic Assn (IRgA) 401 N Michigan Ave Ste 2200	Chicago	IL	60611	**800-833-4742**	312-245-1026
Magazine Publishers of America (MPA) 810 Seventh Ave 24th Fl	New York	NY	10019	**800-234-3368**	212-872-3700
National Information Standards Organization (NISO) 3600 Clipper Mill Rd Ste 302	Baltimore	MD	21211	**877-375-2160**	301-654-2512
NPES: Assn for Suppliers of Printing Publishing & Converting Technologies 1899 Preston White Dr	Reston	VA	20191	**866-381-9839**	703-264-7200
Printing Industries of America/Graphic Arts Technical Foundation (PIA/GATF) 200 Deer Run Rd	Sewickley	PA	15143	**800-910-4283**	412-741-6860
Specialty Graphic Imaging Assn (SGIA) 10015 Main St	Fairfax	VA	22031	**888-385-3588**	703-385-1335

48-17 Real Estate Professionals Associations

Organization / Address	City	State	ZIP	Toll-Free	Phone
American Society of Appraisers (ASA) 555 Herndon Pkwy Ste 125	Herndon	VA	20170	**800-272-8258**	703-478-2228
Appraisal Institute 550 W Van Buren St Ste 1000	Chicago	IL	60607	**888-756-4624**	312-335-4100
Building Owners & Managers Assn International (BOMA) 1101 15th St NW Ste 800	Washington	DC	20005	**800-426-6292**	202-408-2662
CCIM Institute 430 N Michigan Ave Ste 800	Chicago	IL	60611	**800-621-7027**	312-321-4460
CoreNet Global Inc 260 Peachtree St NW Ste 1500	Atlanta	GA	30303	**800-726-8111**	404-589-3200
Council of Real Estate Brokerage Managers (CRB) 430 N Michigan Ave	Chicago	IL	60611	**800-621-8738**	
Council of Residential Specialists 430 N Michigan Ave Ste 300	Chicago	IL	60611	**800-462-8841**	312-321-4400
Institute of Business Appraisers (IBA) 1111 BrickyaRd Rd Ste 200	Salt Lake City	UT	84106	**800-299-4130**	
Institute of Real Estate Management (IREM) 430 N Michigan Ave	Chicago	IL	60611	**800-837-0706**	312-329-6000
NA of REALTORS 430 N Michigan Ave	Chicago	IL	60611	**800-874-6500**	312-329-8200
National Apartment Assn (NAA) 4300 Wilson Blvd Ste 400	Arlington	VA	22203	**800-632-3007**	703-518-6141
New Venture Communications 218 Commercial Ave SE PO Box 157	Highmore	SD	57345	**800-932-0637**	650-343-2735

Organization / Address	City	State	Zip	Toll-Free	Phone
Real Estate Buyer's Agent Council (REBAC) 430 N Michigan Ave	Chicago	IL	60611	800-648-6224	
Women's Council of REALTORS (WCR) 430 N Michigan Ave	Chicago	IL	60611	800-245-8512	

48-18 Sales & Marketing Professional Associations

Organization / Address	City	State	Zip	Toll-Free	Phone
Advertising Council Inc 815 Second Ave 9th Fl	New York	NY	10016	888-200-4005	212-922-1500
American Adv Federation (AAF) 1101 Vermont Ave NW Ste 500	Washington	DC	20005	800-999-2231	202-898-0089
American Assn of Franchisees & Dealers (AAFD) PO Box 10158	Palm Desert	CA	92255	800-733-9858	619-209-3775
American Booksellers Assn (ABA) 200 White Plains Rd Ste 600	Tarrytown	NY	10591	800-637-0037	914-591-2665
American International Automobile Dealers Assn (AIADA) 500 Montgomery St Ste 800	Alexandria	VA	22314	800-462-4232	703-519-7800
American Marketing Assn (AMA) 311 S Wacker Dr Ste 5800	Chicago	IL	60606	800-262-1150	312-542-9000
Associated Equipment Distributors (AED) 650 E Algonquin Rd Ste 305	Schaumburg	IL	60173	800-388-0650	630-574-0650
Association of Progressive Rental Organizations (APRO) 1504 Robin Hood Trl	Austin	TX	78703	800-204-2776	512-794-0095
Audit Bureau of Circulations (ABC) 48 W Seegers Rd	Arlington Heights	IL	60005	800-759-6397	224-366-6939
Automotive Distribution Network 3085 Fountainside Dr Ste 210	Germantown	TN	38138	800-727-8112	901-682-9090
Brick Industry Assn (BIA) 1850 Centennial Pk Dr Ste 301	Reston	VA	20191	866-644-1293	703-620-0010
Business Technology Assn (BTA) 12411 Wornall Rd Ste 200	Kansas City	MO	64145	800-325-7219	816-941-3100
Chain Drug Marketing Assn (CDMA) 43157 W Nine-Mile Rd PO Box 995	Novi	MI	48376	800-935-2362	248-449-9300
Dairyamerica Inc 7815 N Palm Ave Ste 250	Fresno	CA	93711	800-722-3110	559-251-0992
Direct Marketing Assn Inc (DMA) 1120 Ave of the Americas	New York	NY	10036	855-422-0749	212-768-7277
Food Marketing Institute (FMI) 2345 Crystal Dr Ste 800	Arlington	VA	22202	800-732-2639	202-220-0600
HARDI Hydronic Heating & Cooling Council 3455 Mill Run Dr Ste 820	Hilliard	OH	43026	888-253-2128	614-345-4328
Health Industry Distributors Assn (HIDA) 310 Montgomery St	Alexandria	VA	22314	800-549-4432	703-549-4432
International Assn of Exhibitions & Events (IAEE) 12700 Park Central Dr Ste 308	Dallas	TX	75251	866-266-3378	972-458-8002
International Franchise Assn (IFA) 1501 K St NW Ste 350	Washington	DC	20005	800-543-1038	202-628-8000
International Sanitary Supply Assn (ISSA) 3300 Dundee Rd	Northbrook	IL	60062	800-225-4772	847-982-0800
Machinery Dealers NA (MDNA) 315 S Patrick St	Alexandria	VA	22314	800-872-7807	703-836-9300
NA of Chain Drug Stores (NACDS) 413 N Lee St	Alexandria	VA	22314	800-678-6223	703-549-3001
NA of College Stores (NACS) 500 E Lorain St	Oberlin	OH	44074	800-622-7498	440-775-7777
NA of Convenience Stores (NACS) 1600 Duke St *Cust Svc	Alexandria	VA	22314	800-966-6227*	703-684-3600
NA of Electrical Distributors Inc (NAED) 1181 Corporate Lk Dr	Saint Louis	MO	63132	888-791-2512	314-991-9000
NAMM - International Music Products Assn 5790 Armada Dr	Carlsbad	CA	92008	800-767-6266	760-438-8001
National Agri-Marketing Assn (NAMA) 11020 King St Ste 205	Overland Park	KS	66210	800-530-5646	913-491-6500
National Art Materials Trade Assn 20200 Zion Ave	Cornelius	NC	28031	800-349-1039	704-892-6244
National Auctioneers Assn (NAA) 8880 Ballentine St	Overland Park	KS	66214	877-657-1990	913-541-8084
National Auto Auction Assn (NAAA) 5320 Spectrum Dr Ste D	Frederick	MD	21703	800-232-5411	301-696-0400
National Automobile Dealers Assn (NADA) 8400 Westpark Dr	McLean	VA	22102	800-252-6232	703-821-7000
National Cotton Council of America 7193 Goodlett Farms Pkwy	Memphis	TN	38016	888-232-1738	901-274-9030
National Electrical Manufacturers Representatives Assn (NEMRA) 28 Deer St Ste 302	Portsmouth	NH	03801	800-446-3672	914-524-8650
National Electronics Service Dealers Assn (NESDA) 3608 Pershing Ave	Fort Worth	TX	76107	800-946-0201	817-921-9061
National Independent Automobile Dealers Assn (NIADA) 2521 Brown Blvd	Arlington	TX	76006	800-682-3837	817-640-3838
National Mail Order Assn LLC (NMOA) 2807 Polk St NE	Minneapolis	MN	55418	800-992-1377	612-788-1673
National Marine Representatives Assn (NMRA) PO Box 360	Gurnee	IL	60031	800-890-3819	847-662-3167
National Retail Federation (NRF) 1101 New York Ave NW	Washington	DC	20005	800-673-4692	202-783-7971
National Retail Hardware Assn (NRHA) 5822 W 74th St *Cust Svc	Indianapolis	IN	46278	800-772-4424*	317-290-0338
National School Supply & Equipment Assn (NSSEA) 8380 Colesville Rd Ste 250	Silver Spring	MD	20910	800-395-5550	301-495-0240
National Shoe Retailers Assn (NSRA) 7386 N La Cholla Blvd	Tucson	AZ	85741	800-673-8446	520-209-1710
North American Bldg Material Distribution Assn (NBMDA) 330 N Wabash Ave Ste 2000	Chicago	IL	60611	888-747-7862	312-321-6845
NPTA Alliance 330 N Wabash Ave Ste 2000	Chicago	IL	60611	800-355-6782	312-321-4092
Paint & Decorating Retailers Assn (PDRA) 1401 Triad Ctr Dr	Saint Peters	MO	63376	800-737-0107	636-326-2636
Photo Marketing Assn International (PMA) 3000 Picture Pl	Jackson	MI	49201	800-762-9287	517-788-8100
Professional Beauty Assn (PBA) 15825 N 71st St Ste 100	Scottsdale	AZ	85254	800-468-2274	480-281-0424
Promotional Products Assn International (PPAI) 3125 Skyway Cir N	Irving	TX	75038	888-426-7724	972-252-0404
Public Relations Society of America (PRSA) 33 Maiden Ln 11th Fl	New York	NY	10038	800-350-0111	212-460-1400
Radio Adv Bureau (RAB) 125 W 55th St 21st Fl	New York	NY	10019	800-232-3131	212-681-7200
Recreation Vehicle Dealers Assn (RVDA) 3930 University Dr 3rd Fl	Fairfax	VA	22030	800-336-0355	703-591-7130
Retail Solutions Providers Assn (RSPA) 10130 Perimeter Pkwy Ste 420	Charlotte	NC	28216	800-782-2693	704-357-3124
Society for Marketing Professional Services (SMPS) 99 Canal Ctr Plz	Alexandria	VA	22314	800-292-7677	703-549-6117
Specialty Tools & Fasteners Distributors Assn (STAFDA) 500 Elm Grove Rd Ste 210 PO Box 44	Elm Grove	WI	53122	800-352-2981	262-784-4774

48-19 Technology, Science, Engineering Professionals Associations

Organization / Address	City	State	Zip	Toll-Free	Phone
AES Electrophoresis Society 1202 Ann St	Madison	WI	53713	800-242-4363	608-258-1565
American Assn for Clinical Chemistry Inc (AACC) 1850 K St NW Ste 625 *Cust Svc	Washington	DC	20006	800-892-1400*	202-857-0717
American Assn of Engineering Societies (AAES) 1620 'I' St NW Ste 210 *Orders	Washington	DC	20006	888-400-2237*	202-296-2237
American Assn of Pharmaceutical Scientists (AAPS) 2107 Wilson Blvd Ste 700	Arlington	VA	22201	877-998-2277	703-243-2800
American Assn of Variable Star Observers (AAVSO) 49 Bay State Rd	Cambridge	MA	02138	888-802-7827	617-354-0484
American Chemical Society (ACS) 1155 16th St NW	Washington	DC	20036	800-227-5558	202-872-4600
American Council of Independent Laboratories (ACIL) 1875 I St NW Ste 500	Washington	DC	20006	800-368-1131	202-887-5872
American Council on Science & Health (ACSH) 110 E 42nd St Ste 1300	New York	NY	10017	866-905-2694	212-362-7044
American Geological Institute (AGI) 4220 King St	Alexandria	VA	22302	800-334-2564	703-379-2480
American Geophysical Union (AGU) 2000 Florida Ave NW	Washington	DC	20009	800-966-2481	202-462-6900
American Indian Science & Engineering Society (AISES) 2305 Renard SE Ste 200	Albuquerque	NM	87106	800-759-5219	505-765-1052
American Institute of Aeronautics & Astronautics Inc (AIAA) 1801 Alexander Bell Dr Ste 500	Reston	VA	20191	800-639-2422	703-264-7500
American Institute of Biological Sciences (AIBS) 1444 'I' St NW Ste 200	Washington	DC	20005	800-992-2427	202-628-1500
American Institute of Chemical Engineers (AIChE) 120 Wall St Fl 23 *Cust Svc	New York	NY	10005	800-242-4363*	203-702-7660
American Institute of Chemists (AIC) 315 Chestnut St	Philadelphia	PA	19106	800-829-0115	215-873-8224
American Mathematical Society (AMS) 201 Charles St *Cust Svc	Providence	RI	02904	800-321-4267*	401-455-4000
American Meteorological Society (AMS) 45 Beacon St	Boston	MA	02108	800-824-0405	617-227-2425
American Nuclear Society (ANS) 555 N Kensington Ave	La Grange Park	IL	60526	800-323-3044	708-352-6611
American Physical Society (APS) 1 Physics Ellipse	College Park	MD	20740	866-918-1164	301-209-3200
American Phytopathological Society, The (APS) 3340 Pilot Knob Rd	Saint Paul	MN	55121	800-328-7560	651-454-7250
American Society for Nondestructive Testing Inc (ASNT) 1711 Arlingate Ln PO Box 28518 *Orders	Columbus	OH	43228	800-222-2768*	614-274-6003
American Society of Human Genetics (ASHG) 9650 Rockville Pike	Bethesda	MD	20814	800-720-4363	301-634-7300
American Society of Limnology & Oceanography (ASLO) 5400 Bosque Blvd Ste 680	Waco	TX	76710	800-929-2756	254-399-9635
American Statistical Assn (ASA) 732 N Washington St	Alexandria	VA	22314	888-231-3473	703-684-1221
AOAC International 481 N Frederick Ave Ste 500	Gaithersburg	MD	20877	800-379-2622	301-924-7077
Association for Women in Science Inc (AWIS) 1321 Duke St Ste 210	Alexandria	VA	22314	866-736-7343	703-894-4490
Association of American Geographers (AAG) 1710 16th St NW	Washington	DC	20009	800-696-7353	202-234-1450
ASTM International 100 Barr Harbor Dr PO Box C700	West Conshohocken	PA	19428	800-814-1017	610-832-9500
Audio Engineering Society 60 E 42nd St Rm 2520	New York	NY	10165	800-541-7299	212-661-8528
Biotechnology Industry Organization 1201 Maryland Ave SW Ste 900	Washington	DC	20024	866-356-5155	202-962-9200
Center for Chemical Process Safety (CCPS) 120 Wall St	New York	NY	10005	800-242-4363	646-495-1371
Coordinating Research Council Inc (CRC) 3650 Mansell Rd Ste 140	Alpharetta	GA	30022	800-445-8667	678-795-0506
Council for Responsible Genetics (CRG) 5 Upland Rd Ste 3	Cambridge	MA	02140	888-591-3911	617-868-0870
Custom Electronic Design & Installation Assn (CEDIA) 7150 Winton Dr Ste 300	Indianapolis	IN	46268	800-669-5329	317-328-4336
Drug Chemical & Associated Technologies Assn (DCAT) 1 Washington Blvd Ste 7	Robbinsville	NJ	08691	800-640-3228	609-448-1000
Electronics Technicians Assn International (ETA) 5 Depot St	Greencastle	IN	46135	800-288-3824	765-653-8262
Entomological Society of America 10001 Derekwood Ln Ste 100	Lanham	MD	20706	800-523-8635	301-731-4535
Federation of American Societies for Experimental Biology (FASEB) 9650 Rockville Pk	Bethesda	MD	20814	800-433-2732	301-634-7000
Generic Pharmaceutical Assn (GPhA) 2300 Clarendon Blvd Ste 400	Arlington	VA	22201	800-859-8003	703-647-2480
Genetics Society of America (GSA) 9650 Rockville Pk	Bethesda	MD	20814	866-486-4363	301-634-7300
Geological Society of America, The (GSA) 3300 Penrose Pl PO Box 9140	Boulder	CO	80301	800-472-1988	303-357-1000
IEEE Broadcast Technology Society (BTS) 445 Hoes Ln	Piscataway	NJ	08854	800-678-4333	732-562-5407

Organization	Address	City	State	ZIP	Toll-Free	Phone
IEEE Computer Society	2001 L St NW Ste 700	Washington	DC	20036	**800-272-6657**	202-371-0101
IEEE Consumer Electronics Society (CES)	445 Hoes Ln	Piscataway	NJ	08854	**800-678-4333**	732-981-0060
IEEE Education Society (ES)	IEEE Operations Ctr 445 Hoes Ln	Piscataway	NJ	08854	**800-678-4333**	732-981-0060
IEEE Electromagnetic Compatibility Society (EMC)	IEEE Operations Ctr 445 Hoes Ln	Piscataway	NJ	08854	**800-678-4333**	732-981-0060
IEEE Electron Devices Society (EDS)	IEEE Operations Ctr 445 Hoes Ln	Piscataway	NJ	08854	**800-678-4333**	732-981-0060
IEEE Engineering Management Society (EMS)	IEEE Operations Ctr 445 Hoes Ln	Piscataway	NJ	08854	**800-678-4333**	732-981-0060
IEEE Geoscience & Remote Sensing Society (GRSS)	IEEE Operations Ctr 445 Hoes Ln	Piscataway	NJ	08854	**800-678-4333**	732-562-5550
IEEE Industrial Electronics Society (IES)	IEEE Operations Ctr 445 Hoes Ln	Piscataway	NJ	08854	**800-678-4333**	732-981-0060
IEEE Instrumentation & Measurement Society (IM)	445 Hoes Ln	Piscataway	NJ	08854	**800-327-6677**	732-562-3844
IEEE Magnetics Society	445 Hoes Ln PO Box 459	Piscataway	NJ	08855	**800-678-4333**	908-981-0060
IEEE Microwave Theory & Techniques Society (MTT-S)	5829 Bellanca Dr	Elkridge	MD	21075	**800-678-4333**	410-796-5866
IEEE Nuclear & Plasma Sciences Society (NPSS)	445 Hoes Ln	Piscataway	NJ	08854	**800-678-4333**	732-562-5501
IEEE Power Engineering Society (PES)	IEEE Operations Ctr 445 Hoes Ln	Piscataway	NJ	08854	**800-678-4333**	732-562-3883
IEEE Product Safety Engineering Society	IEEE Operations Ctr 445 Hoes Ln	Piscataway	NJ	08854	**800-678-4333**	732-981-0060
IEEE Reliability Society (RS)	IEEE Operations Ctr 445 Hoes Ln	Piscataway	NJ	08854	**800-678-4333**	732-981-0060
IEEE Signal Processing Society	IEEE Operations Ctr 445 Hoes Ln	Piscataway	NJ	08854	**800-678-4333**	732-981-0060
IEEE Society on Social Implications of Technology (SSIT)	IEEE Operations Ctr 445 Hoes Ln	Piscataway	NJ	08854	**800-678-4333**	732-981-0060
IEEE Solid State Circuits Society (SSCS)	445 Hoes Ln	Piscataway	NJ	08854	**800-678-4333**	732-981-3400
IEEE Ultrasonics Ferroelectrics & Frequency Control Society	IEEE Operations Ctr 445 Hoes Ln	Piscataway	NJ	08854	**800-678-4333**	732-981-0060
Institute for Operations Research & the Management Sciences (INFORMS)	7240 Pkwy Dr Ste 300	Hanover	MD	21076	**800-446-3676**	443-757-3500
International Biometric Society (IBS)	1444 'I' St NW Ste 700	Washington	DC	20005	**800-262-1171**	202-712-9049
International Society of Certified Electronics Technicians (ISCET)	3608 Pershing Ave	Fort Worth	TX	76107	**800-946-0201**	817-921-9101
Laser Institute of America (LIA)	13501 Ingenuity Dr Ste 128	Orlando	FL	32826	**800-345-2737**	407-380-1553
Mathematical Assn of America (MAA)	1529 18th St NW	Washington	DC	20036	**800-331-1622**	202-387-5200
National Academies	500 Fifth St NW	Washington	DC	20001	**800-624-6242**	202-334-2138
National Council on Radiation Protection & Measurements (NCRP)	7910 Woodmont Ave Ste 400	Bethesda	MD	20814	**800-462-3683**	301-657-2652
National Environmental Balancing Bureau (NEBB)	8575 Grovemont Cir	Gaithersburg	MD	20877	**866-497-4447**	301-977-3698
National Geographic Society	1145 17th St NW	Washington	DC	20036	**800-647-5463**	202-857-7000
National Society of Professional Engineers (NSPE)	1420 King St	Alexandria	VA	22314	**888-285-6773**	703-684-2800
New York Academy of Sciences	250 Greenwich St 40th Fl	New York	NY	10007	**800-843-6927**	212-298-8600
Scientific Equipment & Furniture Assn (SEFA)	65 Hilton Avenue	Garden City	NY	11530	**877-294-5424**	516-294-5424
Semiconductor Equipment & Materials International	3081 Zenker Rd	San Jose	CA	95134	**877-746-7788**	408-943-6900
Society for Biomaterials	1120 Rte 73 Ste 200	Mount Laurel	NJ	08054	**800-337-9255**	856-439-0826
Society for Experimental Mechanics Inc (SEM)	7 School St	Bethel	CT	06801	**800-627-8258**	203-790-6373
Society for Industrial & Applied Mathematics (SIAM)	3600 Market St 6th Fl	Philadelphia	PA	19104	**800-447-7426**	215-382-9800
Society for Integrative & Comparative Biology (SICB)	1313 Dolley Madison Blvd Ste 402	McLean	VA	22101	**800-955-1236**	703-790-1745
Society for Risk Analysis (SRA)	1313 Dolley Madison Blvd Ste 402	McLean	VA	22101	**800-364-5800**	703-790-1745
Society for Sedimentary Geology (SEPM)	4111 S Darlington Ste 100	Tulsa	OK	74135	**800-865-9765**	918-610-3361
Society for the Advancement of Material & Process Engineering (SAMPE)	1161 Pk View Dr Ste 200	Covina	CA	91724	**800-562-7360**	626-331-0616
Society of Cable Telecommunications Engineers (SCTE)	140 Philips Rd	Exton	PA	19341	**800-542-5040**	610-363-6888
Society of Women Engineers (SWE)	120 S La Salle St Ste 1515	Chicago	IL	60603	**877-793-4636**	312-596-5223
Women in Technology International (WITI)	11500 Olympic Blvd Ste 400	Los Angeles	CA	90064	**800-334-9484**	818-788-9484
World Future Society	7910 Woodmont Ave Ste 450	Bethesda	MD	20814	**800-989-8274**	301-656-8274

48-20 Telecommunications Professionals Associations

Organization	Address	City	State	ZIP	Toll-Free	Phone
Alliance for Telecommunications Industry Solutions (ATIS)	1200 G St NW Ste 500	Washington	DC	20005	**800-649-1202**	202-628-6380
American Public Communications Council Inc (APCC)	625 Slaters Ln Ste 104	Alexandria	VA	22314	**800-868-2722**	703-739-1322
Communications Supply Service Assn (CSSA)	5700 Murray St	Little Rock	AR	72209	**800-252-2772**	501-562-7666
Enterprise Wireless Alliance (EWA)	8484 Westpark Dr Ste 630	McLean	VA	22102	**800-482-8282**	703-528-5115
International Communications Industries Assn (ICIA)	11242 Waples Mill Rd Ste 200	Fairfax	VA	22030	**800-659-7469**	703-273-7200
Society of Telecommunications Consultants (STC)	13275 California 89	Old Station	CA	96071	**800-782-7670**	530-335-7313
US Telecom Assn (USTA)	607-14th St NW Ste 400	Washington	DC	20005	**877-869-6903**	202-326-7300

48-21 Transportation Industry Associations

Organization	Address	City	State	ZIP	Toll-Free	Phone
Aerospace Industries Assn of America (AIA)	1000 Wilson Blvd Ste 1700	Arlington	VA	22209	**877-229-7555**	703-358-1000
Air Traffic Control Assn (ATCA)	1101 King St Ste 300	Alexandria	VA	22314	**866-953-2189**	703-299-2430
Aircraft Owners & Pilots Assn (AOPA)	421 Aviation Way	Frederick	MD	21701	**800-872-2672**	301-695-2000
American Ambulance Assn (AAA)	8400 Wpark Dr Fl 2	McLean	VA	22102	**800-523-4447**	703-610-9018
American Assn of Airport Executives (AAAE)	601 Madison St Ste 400	Alexandria	VA	22314	**800-609-7374**	703-824-0500
American Assn of State Highway & Transportation Officials (AASHTO)	444 N Capitol St NW Ste 249	Washington	DC	20001	**800-880-4117**	202-624-5800
American Helicopter Society International (AHS)	217 N Washington St	Alexandria	VA	22314	**855-247-4685**	703-684-6777
American International Automobile Dealers Assn (AIADA)	500 Montgomery St Ste 800	Alexandria	VA	22314	**800-462-4232**	703-519-7800
American Moving & Storage Assn (AMSA)	1611 Duke St	Alexandria	VA	22314	**888-849-2672**	703-683-7410
American Traffic Safety Services Assn (ATSSA)	15 Riverside Pkwy Ste 100	Fredericksburg	VA	22406	**800-272-8772**	540-368-1701
American Trucking Assn (ATA)	950 N Glebe Rd Ste 210	Arlington	VA	22203	**800-282-5463**	703-838-1700
Automatic Transmission Rebuilders Assn (ATRA)	2400 Latigo Ave	Oxnard	CA	93030	**866-464-2872**	805-604-2000
Automotive Aftermarket Industry Assn (AAIA)	7101 Wisconsin Ave	Bethesda	MD	20814	**800-936-8906**	301-654-6664
Automotive Engine Rebuilders Assn (AERA)	500 Coventry Ln Ste 180	Crystal Lake	IL	60014	**888-326-2372**	847-541-6550
Automotive Industry Action Group (AIAG)	26200 Lahser Rd Ste 200	Southfield	MI	48033	**877-275-2424**	248-358-3570
Automotive Oil Change Assn (AOCA)	330 N. Wabash Ave Ste 2000	Chicago	IL	60611	**800-230-0702**	312-321-5132
Automotive Parts Remanufacturers Assn (APRA)	4215 Lafayette Ctr Dr Ste 3	Chantilly	VA	20151	**877-734-4827**	703-968-2772
Automotive Recyclers Assn (ARA)	3975 Fair Ridge Dr Ste 20N	Fairfax	VA	22033	**888-385-1005**	703-385-1001
Automotive Service Assn (ASA)	1901 Airport Fwy *Cust Svc	Bedford	TX	76021	**800-272-7467***	
Coalition for Auto Repair Equality (CARE)	105 Oronoco St Ste 115	Alexandria	VA	22314	**800-229-5380**	703-519-7555
Community Transportation Assn of America (CTAA)	1341 G St NW 10th Fl	Washington	DC	20005	**800-891-0590**	202-628-1480
General Aviation Manufacturers Assn (GAMA)	1400 K St NW Ste 801	Washington	DC	20005	**866-427-3287**	202-393-1500
Helicopter Assn International (HAI)	1635 Prince St	Alexandria	VA	22314	**800-435-4976**	703-683-4646
Institute of Navigation Inc (ION)	8551 Rixlew Ln Ste 360	Manassas	VA	20109	**800-696-7353**	703-366-2723
Insurance Institute for Highway Safety	1005 N Glebe Rd Ste 800	Arlington	VA	22201	**888-327-4236**	703-247-1500
Intelligent Transportation Society of America (ITS)	1100 17th St NW Ste 1200	Washington	DC	20036	**800-374-8472**	202-484-4847
Intermodal Assn of North America (IANA)	11785 Beltsville Dr Ste 1100	Calverton	MD	20705	**877-438-8442**	301-982-3400
International Air Transport Assn	800 Pl Victoria PO Box 113	Montreal	QC	H4Z1M1	**800-716-6326**	514-874-0202
International Carwash Assn	230 E Ohio St	Chicago	IL	60611	**888-422-8422**	
International Motor Coach Group Inc (IMG)	8695 College Blvd Ste 260	Overland Park	KS	66210	**888-447-3466**	913-906-0111
International Safe Transit Assn (ISTA)	1400 Abbott Rd Ste 160	East Lansing	MI	48823	**888-299-2208**	517-333-3437
Jewelers Shipping Assn (JSA)	125 Carlsbad St	Cranston	RI	02920	**800-688-4572**	401-943-6020
Mobile Air Conditioning Society Worldwide (MACS)	225 S Broad St	Lansdale	PA	19446	**800-641-1133**	215-631-7020
National Air Transportation Assn (NATA)	4226 King St	Alexandria	VA	22302	**800-808-6282**	703-845-9000
National Automobile Dealers Assn (NADA)	8400 Westpark Dr	McLean	VA	22102	**800-252-6232**	703-821-7000
National Business Aviation Assn (NBAA)	1200 18th St NW Ste 400	Washington	DC	20036	**800-394-6222**	202-783-9000
National Motor Freight Traffic Assn (NMFTA)	1001 N Fairfax St Ste 600	Alexandria	VA	22314	**866-411-6632**	703-838-1810
National Motorists Assn (NMA)	402 W Second St	Waunakee	WI	53597	**800-882-2785**	608-849-6000
National Truck Equipment Assn (NTEA)	37400 Hills Tech Dr	Farmington Hills	MI	48331	**800-441-6832**	248-489-7090
National Waterways Conference Inc (NWC)	4650 Washington Blvd Ste 608	Arlington	VA	22201	**866-371-1390**	703-243-4090
NATSO Inc	1737 King St Ste 200	Alexandria	VA	22314	**800-956-9160**	703-549-2100
Owner-Operator Independent Drivers Assn Inc (OOIDA)	1 NW OOIDA Dr	Grain Valley	MO	64029	**800-444-5791**	816-229-5791
Passenger Vessel Assn (PVA)	103 Oronoco St Ste 200	Alexandria	VA	22314	**800-807-8360**	703-518-5005
Recreation Vehicle Dealers Assn (RVDA)	3930 University Dr 3rd Fl	Fairfax	VA	22030	**800-336-0355**	703-591-7130
Recreation Vehicle Industry Assn (RVIA)	1896 Preston White Dr	Reston	VA	20191	**800-336-0154**	703-620-6003
Self Storage Assn (SSA)	1900 N Beauregard St Ste 450	Alexandria	VA	22311	**888-735-3784**	703-575-8000
Shipowners Claims Bureau (SCB)	1 Battery Pk Plaza 31st Fl	New York	NY	10004	**800-774-8724**	212-847-4500
Society of Automotive Engineers Inc (SAE)	400 Commonwealth Dr	Warrendale	PA	15096	**877-606-7323**	724-776-4841
Society of Naval Architects & Marine Engineers (SNAME)	601 Pavonia Ave Ste 400	Jersey City	NJ	07306	**800-798-2188**	201-798-4800
Specialty Vehicle Institute of America (SVIA)	2 Jenner St Ste 150	Irvine	CA	92618	**800-887-2887**	949-727-3727
Transport Workers Union of America	501 Third St NW 9th Fl	Washington	DC	20001	**888-565-6898**	202-719-3900

Name / Address	City	State	Zip	Toll-Free	Phone
Transportation Intermediaries Assn (TIA) 1625 Prince St Ste 200	Alexandria	VA	22314	**888-910-4747**	703-299-5700
Transportation Research Board (TRB) 500 Fifth St NW	Washington	DC	20001	**866-233-4642**	202-334-2934
Truckload Carriers Assn (TCA) 555 E Braddock Rd	Alexandria	VA	22314	**800-666-2770**	703-838-1950
United Motorcoach Assn (UMA) 113 SW St 4th Fl	Alexandria	VA	22314	**800-424-8262**	703-838-2929

49 ATTRACTIONS

Name / Address	City	State	Zip	Toll-Free	Phone
Cathedral of Our Lady of the Angels 555 W Temple St	Los Angeles	CA	90012	**800-838-1356**	213-680-5200
Historic Trinity Lutheran Church 1345 Gratiot Ave	Detroit	MI	48207	**800-268-3058**	313-567-3100
Mesa Arizona Temple 101 S LeSueur	Mesa	AZ	85204	**855-537-4357**	480-833-1211
Mission of Nombre de Dios & Shrine of Our Lady of La Leche 27 Ocean Ave	Saint Augustine	FL	32084	**800-342-6529**	904-824-2809
National Shrine of Our Lady of the Snows 442 S De Mazenod Dr	Belleville	IL	62223	**800-682-2879**	618-397-6700
Old Saint Ferdinand's Shrine 1 Rue St Francois	Florissant	MO	63031	**800-366-2427**	314-837-2110
Salt Lake Temple 50 W N Temple St	Salt Lake City	UT	84150	**800-453-3860**	801-240-2640
Union Church of Pocantico Hills 555 Bedford Rd	Sleepy Hollow	NY	10591	**877-325-4822**	914-631-8200

49-1 Cultural & Arts Centers

Name / Address	City	State	Zip	Toll-Free	Phone
Anderson Ranch Arts Ctr 5263 Owl Creek Rd PO Box 5598	Snowmass Village	CO	81615	**800-525-6363**	970-923-3181
Arkansas Arts Ctr 501 E Ninth St	Little Rock	AR	72202	**800-264-2787**	501-372-4000
Center for Puppetry Arts 1404 Spring St NW	Atlanta	GA	30309	**800-642-3629**	404-873-3089
Daybreak Star Ctr 3801 W Government Way PO Box 99100	Seattle	WA	98199	**800-321-4321**	206-285-4425
Dougherty Arts Ctr, The (DAC) 1110 Barton Springs Rd	Austin	TX	78704	**855-787-2227**	512-974-4000
Durango Arts Ctr 802 E Second Ave	Durango	CO	81301	**800-838-3006**	970-259-2606
Flint Cultural Ctr Corp 1310 E Kearsley St	Flint	MI	48503	**800-214-7275**	810-237-7333
Gerald R Ford Conservation Ctr 1326 S 32nd St	Omaha	NE	68105	**800-634-6932**	402-595-1180
Maitland Art Ctr 231 W Packwood Ave	Maitland	FL	32751	**800-435-7352**	407-539-2181
Oglebay Institute's Stifel Fine Arts Ctr 1330 National Rd	Wheeling	WV	26003	**800-624-6988**	304-242-7700
South Broadway Cultural Ctr 1025 Broadway Blvd SE	Albuquerque	NM	87102	**866-441-6075**	505-848-1320

49-2 Historic Homes & Buildings

Name / Address	City	State	Zip	Toll-Free	Phone
Ashland-The Henry Clay Estate 120 Sycamore Rd	Lexington	KY	40502	**800-735-5251**	859-266-8581
Corn Palace 604 N Main St	Mitchell	SD	57301	**800-289-7469**	605-995-8430
Cosanti Originals Inc 6433 Doubletree Ranch Rd	Paradise Valley	AZ	85253	**800-752-3187**	480-948-6145
Fort Meigs State Memorial 29100 W River Rd	Perrysburg	OH	43551	**800-283-8916**	419-874-4121
Frank Lloyd Wright's Martin House Complex 125 Jewett Pkwy	Buffalo	NY	14214	**877-377-3858**	716-856-3858
Gassaway Mansion 106 Dupont Dr	Greenville	SC	29607	**888-912-7469**	864-271-0188
Glensheen Mansion 3300 London Rd	Duluth	MN	55804	**888-454-4536**	218-726-8910
Greenwood Plantation 6838 Highland Rd	Saint Francisville	LA	70775	**800-259-4475**	225-655-4475
Guenther House 205 E Guenther St	San Antonio	TX	78204	**800-235-8186**	210-227-1061
Historic Rock Ford Plantation 881 Rockford Rd	Lancaster	PA	17602	**800-732-0999**	717-392-7223
Historic Roswell District 617 Atlanta St	Roswell	GA	30075	**800-776-7935**	
Houmas House Plantation & Gardens 40136 Hwy 942	Darrow	LA	70725	**800-979-3370**	225-473-7841
James J Hill House 240 Summit Ave	Saint Paul	MN	55102	**888-727-8386**	651-297-2555
Jane Addams Hull-House Museum 800 S Halsted St	Chicago	IL	60607	**800-625-2013**	312-413-5353
Loudoun House 209 Castlewood Dr	Lexington	KY	40505	**866-945-7920**	859-254-7024
Mathias Ham House Historic Site 2241 Lincoln Ave	Dubuque	IA	52001	**800-226-3369**	563-557-9545
Monticello 931 Thomas Jefferson Pkwy PO Box 316	Charlottesville	VA	22902	**800-243-1743**	434-984-9822
Old Alabama Town 301 Columbus St	Montgomery	AL	36104	**888-240-1850**	334-240-4500
Old Exchange & Provost Dungeon 122 E Bay St	Charleston	SC	29401	**888-763-0448**	843-727-2165
Old Idaho Penitentiary State Historic Site 2445 Old Penitentiary Rd	Boise	ID	83712	**877-653-4367**	208-334-2844
Paul Laurence Dunbar House 219 N Paul Laurence Dunbar St	Dayton	OH	45402	**800-860-0148**	937-224-7061
Ponce de Leon's Fountain of Youth 11 Magnolia Ave	Saint Augustine	FL	32084	**800-356-8222**	904-829-3168
Powel House 244 S Third St	Philadelphia	PA	19106	**877-426-8056**	215-627-0364
Reed Gold Mine State Historic Site 9621 Reed Mine Rd	Midland	NC	28107	**877-628-6386**	704-721-4653
Rosedown Plantation State Historic Site 12501 Hwy 10	Saint Francisville	LA	70775	**888-376-1867**	225-635-3332
Sears Tower 233 S Wacker Dr	Chicago	IL	60606	**877-759-3325**	312-875-9447
Taliesin 5607 County Hwy C	Spring Green	WI	53588	**877-588-7900**	608-588-7090
Vance Birthplace State Historic Site 911 Reems Creek Rd	Weaverville	NC	28787	**800-767-1560**	828-645-6706

49-3 Monuments, Memorials, Landmarks

Name / Address	City	State	Zip	Toll-Free	Phone
Chamizal National Memorial 800 S San Marcial St	El Paso	TX	79905	**877-642-4743**	915-532-7273
De Soto National Memorial 8300 Desoto Memorial Hwy	Bradenton	FL	34209	**888-831-7526**	941-792-0458
Empire State Bldg 350 Fifth Ave Ste 100	New York	NY	10118	**877-692-8439**	212-736-3100
Gateway Arch 50 S Leonor K Sullivan Blvd	Saint Louis	MO	63102	**877-982-1410**	
George Washington Masonic National Memorial 101 Callahan Dr	Alexandria	VA	22301	**800-435-7352**	703-683-2007
Golden Gate Bridge Golden Gate Bridge Toll Plz Presidio Stn PO Box 9000	San Francisco	CA	94129	**877-229-8655**	415-921-5858
Littleton Coin Company LLC 1309 Mt Eustis Rd	Littleton	NH	03561	**800-645-3122**	603-444-5386
Space Needle LLC 203 Sixth Ave N	Seattle	WA	98109	**800-937-9582**	206-905-2200
Texas State Cemetery 909 Navasota St	Austin	TX	78702	**877-673-6839**	512-463-0605
USS Alabama Battleship Memorial Park 2703 Battleship Pkwy PO Box 65	Mobile	AL	36602	**888-414-4448**	251-433-2703
USS Kidd Veterans Memorial & Museum 305 S River Rd	Baton Rouge	LA	70802	**800-638-0594**	225-342-1942
USS Missouri Memorial Assn Inc 63 Cowpens St	Honolulu	HI	96818	**877-644-4896**	808-455-1600
Vietnam Women's Memorial Foundation Inc 1735 Connecticut Ave NW 3rd Fl	Washington	DC	20009	**866-822-8963**	

49-4 Nature Centers, Parks, Other Natural Areas

Name / Address	City	State	Zip	Toll-Free	Phone
Black Hills Caverns 2600 Cavern Rd	Rapid City	SD	57702	**800-837-9358**	605-343-0542
Boyden Caverns 5350 Moaning Cave Rd	Vallecito	CA	95251	**866-762-2837**	209-736-2708
Butterfly House - Faust Park, The 15193 Olive Blvd	Chesterfield	MO	63017	**800-642-8842**	636-530-0076
Carson Hot Springs 1500 Hot Springs Rd	Carson City	NV	89706	**888-917-3711**	775-885-8844
DeGraaf Nature Ctr 600 Graafschap Rd	Holland	MI	49423	**888-535-5792**	616-355-1057
El Dorado Nature Ctr 7550 E Spring St	Long Beach	CA	90815	**800-662-8887**	562-570-1745
Genesee County Parks & Recreation 5045 Stanley Rd	Flint	MI	48506	**800-648-7275**	810-736-7100
Great Plains Nature Ctr 6232 E 29th St N	Wichita	KS	67220	**800-222-1222**	316-683-5499
Hanauma Bay Nature Preserve 100 Hanauma Bay Rd	Honolulu	HI	96825	**800-690-6200**	808-396-4229
Houston Arboretum & Nature Ctr 4501 Woodway Dr	Houston	TX	77024	**866-510-7219**	713-681-8433
Jefferson Barracks County Park 345 N Dr	Saint Louis	MO	63125	**800-735-2966**	314-615-8800
Katharine Ordway Preserve 4245 N Fairfax Dr Ste 100	Arlington	VA	22203	**800-628-6860**	203-226-4991
Lava Hot Springs State Foundation 430 E Main St PO Box 669	Lava Hot Springs	ID	83246	**800-423-8597**	208-776-5221
Linville Caverns Inc 19929 US 221 N	Marion	NC	28752	**800-419-0540**	
Lost River Caverns 726 Durham St PO Box M	Hellertown	PA	18055	**888-529-1907**	610-838-8767
New York State Office of Parks Recreation & Historic Preservation Empire State Plaza Agency Bldg 1	Albany	NY	12238	**800-456-2267**	716-354-9101
Oxbow Meadows Environmental Learning Ctr 3535 S Lumpkin Rd	Columbus	GA	31903	**866-264-2035**	706-507-8550
Raccoon Mountain Caverns 319 W Hills Dr	Chattanooga	TN	37419	**800-823-2267**	423-821-9403
Riveredge Nature Ctr 4458 W Hawthorne Dr PO Box 26	Newburg	WI	53060	**800-287-8098**	262-375-2715
Rock City Gardens 1400 Patten Rd	Lookout Mountain	GA	30750	**800-854-0675**	706-820-2531
Ruby Falls 1720 S Scenic Hwy	Chattanooga	TN	37409	**800-755-7105**	423-821-2544
Runge Conservation Nature Ctr 2901 W Truman Blvd	Jefferson City	MO	65109	**800-392-1111**	573-751-4115
Seven Falls Co 2850 S Cheyenne Canyon Rd	Colorado Springs	CO	80906	**855-923-7272**	
Springfield Conservation Nature Ctr 4600 S Chrisman Ave	Springfield	MO	65804	**800-392-1111**	417-888-4237

49-5 Shopping/Dining/Entertainment Districts

Name / Address	City	State	Zip	Toll-Free	Phone
Bannister's Wharf 1 Bannister's Wharf	Newport	RI	02840	**800-395-1343**	401-846-4500
Great Lakes Crossing Outlets 4000 Baldwin Rd	Auburn Hills	MI	48326	**877-746-7452**	248-454-5000
Harborplace & the Gallery 201 E Pratt St	Baltimore	MD	21202	**800-722-8614**	410-332-4191

Name / Address	City	State	Zip	Toll-Free	Phone
Hillcrest Historic District Markham & Kavanaugh	Little Rock	AR	72216	**877-637-0037**	501-371-0075
Miracle Mile Shops at Planet Hollywood 3663 Las Vegas Blvd S	Las Vegas	NV	89109	**888-800-8284**	702-866-0703
River Walk 110 Broadway Ste 500	San Antonio	TX	78204	**800-417-4139**	210-227-4262
Santana Row 3055 Olin Ave Ste 2100	San Jose	CA	95128	**888-509-7303**	408-551-4611

49-6 Wineries

The wineries listed in this category feature wine-tasting as an attraction.

Name / Address	City	State	Zip	Toll-Free	Phone
Adams County Winery 251 Peach Tree Rd	Orrtanna	PA	17353	**877-601-7936**	717-334-4631
Chateau Elan Winery 100 Tour de France	Braselton	GA	30517	**800-233-9463**	678-425-0900
Chateau Morrisette Winery 287 Winery Rd SW	Floyd	VA	24091	**866-695-2001**	540-593-2865
Chateau Ste Michelle Winery 14111 NE 145th St	Woodinville	WA	98072	**800-267-6793**	425-415-3300
Columbia Winery 14030 NE 145th St PO Box 1248	Woodinville	WA	98072	**800-488-2347**	425-488-2776
Eola Hills Wine Cellars 501 S Pacific Hwy 99 W	Rickreall	OR	97371	**800-291-6730**	503-623-2405
Forks of Cheat Winery 2811 Stewart Town Rd	Morgantown	WV	26508	**877-989-4637**	304-598-2019
Honeywood Winery 1350 Hines St SE	Salem	OR	97302	**800-726-4101**	503-362-4111
Huber's Orchard & Winery 19816 Huber Rd	Borden	IN	47106	**800-345-9463**	812-923-9463
King Estate Winery 80854 Territorial Rd	Eugene	OR	97405	**800-884-4441**	541-942-9874
Latah Creek Winery 13030 E Indiana Ave	Spokane	WA	99216	**800-528-2427**	509-926-0164
Llano Estacado Winery 3426 E FM 1585	Lubbock	TX	79404	**800-634-3854**	806-745-2258
Mazza Vineyards 11815 E Lake Rd	North East	PA	16428	**800-796-9463**	814-725-8695
Michael-David Winery 4580 W Hwy 12	Lodi	CA	95242	**888-707-9463**	209-368-7384
Nassau Valley Vineyards 32165 Winery Way	Lewes	DE	19958	**800-425-2355**	302-645-9463
Oliver Winery 8024 N SR-37	Bloomington	IN	47404	**800-258-2783**	812-876-5800
San Sebastian Winery 157 King St	Saint Augustine	FL	32084	**888-352-9463**	904-826-1594
Westbend Vineyards 5394 Williams Rd	Lewisville	NC	27023	**866-901-5032**	336-945-5032
Winery at Wolf Creek 2637 Cleveland Massillon Rd	Norton	OH	44203	**800-436-0426**	330-666-9285

50 AUCTIONS

Name / Address	City	State	Zip	Toll-Free	Phone
ADESA Inc 13085 Hamilton Crossing Blvd	Carmel	IN	46032	**800-923-3725**	317-815-1100
Akron Auto Auction Inc 2471 Ley Dr	Akron	OH	44319	**800-773-0033**	330-773-8245
American Auction Co 951 W Watkins	Phoenix	AZ	85007	**800-801-8880**	
Bonhams & Butterfields 220 San Bruno Ave	San Francisco	CA	94103	**800-223-2854**	415-861-7500
Collectors Universe Inc PO Box 6280 *NASDAQ: CLCT*	Newport Beach	CA	92658	**800-325-1121**	949-567-1234
eBay Inc 2065 Hamilton Ave *NASDAQ: EBAY*	San Jose	CA	95125	**800-322-9266**	408-376-7400
Fasig-Tipton Co Inc 2400 Newtown Pike	Lexington	KY	40511	**877-945-2020**	859-255-1555
Gallery of History Inc 3601 W Sahara Ave	Las Vegas	NV	89102	**800-425-5379**	702-364-1000
Greater Rockford Auto Auction Inc (GRAA) 5937 Sandy Hollow Rd	Rockford	IL	61109	**800-830-4722**	815-874-7800
Harry Davis & Co 1725 Blvd of Allies	Pittsburgh	PA	15219	**800-775-2289**	412-765-1170
Henderson Auctions 13340 Florida Blvd PO Box 336	Livingston	LA	70754	**800-334-7443**	225-686-2252
Heritage Place Inc 2829 S MacArthur	Oklahoma City	OK	73128	**888-343-9831**	405-682-4551
iCollector Technologies Inc 1750 Coast Meridian Rd Ste 114	Port Coquitlam	BC	V3C6R8	**866-313-0123**	604-941-2221
Insurance Auto Auctions Inc 2 Westbrook Corporate Ctr Ste 500	Westchester	IL	60154	**800-872-1501**	708-492-7000
Ironplanet Inc 3825 Hopyard Rd Ste 250 *Cust Svc	Pleasanton	CA	94588	**888-433-5426***	925-225-8600
Kennedy-Wilson Inc 9701 Wilshire Blvd Ste 700	Beverly Hills	CA	90212	**800-522-6664**	310-887-6400
Liquidity Services Inc 1920 L St NW 6th Fl *NASDAQ: LQDT*	Washington	DC	20036	**800-310-4604**	202-467-6868
Priceline.com LLC 800 Connecticut Ave *NASDAQ: PCLN*	Norwalk	CT	06854	**800-774-2354**	
Theriault's PO Box 151	Annapolis	MD	21404	**800-966-3655**	410-224-3655
uBid Inc 740 Hilltop Dr	Itasca	IL	60143	**866-946-8243**	

51 AUDIO & VIDEO EQUIPMENT

Name / Address	City	State	Zip	Toll-Free	Phone
Alpine Electronics of America 19145 Gramercy Pl	Torrance	CA	90501	**800-257-4631**	310-326-8000
AmpliVox Sound Systems LLC 3995 Commercial Ave	Northbrook	IL	60062	**800-267-5486**	847-498-9000
Applied Research & Technology 215 Tremont St	Rochester	NY	14608	**800-775-2427**	585-436-2720
Atlas Sound 1601 Jack McKay Blvd	Ennis	TX	75119	**800-876-3333**	972-875-8413
Audio Command Systems 694 Main St	Westbury	NY	11590	**800-382-2939**	516-997-5800
Audiosears Corp 2 S St	Stamford	NY	12167	**800-533-7863**	607-652-7305
Audiovox Corp 180 Marcus Blvd *NASDAQ: VOXX*	Hauppauge	NY	11788	**800-645-4994**	631-231-7750
Biamp Systems Inc 9300 SW Gemini Dr	Beaverton	OR	97008	**800-826-1457**	
Bogen Communications International Inc 50 Spring St *OTC: BOGN*	Ramsey	NJ	07446	**800-999-2809**	201-934-8500
Bose Corp The Mountain *Sales	Framingham	MA	01701	**800-379-2073***	508-766-1099
Car Toys Inc 20 W Galer St	Seattle	WA	98119	**800-997-3644**	206-443-0980
City of Chula Vista 276 Fourth Ave	Chula Vista	CA	91910	**877-478-5478**	619-691-5047
Clarion Corp of America 6200 Gateway Dr	Cypress	CA	90630	**800-347-8667**	310-327-9100
Community Professional Loudspeakers 333 E Fifth St	Chester	PA	19013	**800-523-4934**	610-876-3400
Creative Labs Inc 1901 McCarthy Blvd *Cust Svc	Milpitas	CA	95035	**800-998-1000***	408-428-6600
Crest Electronics Inc 3706 Alliance Dr	Greensboro	NC	27407	**888-502-7378**	336-855-6422
Dana Innovations 212 Avenida Fabricante	San Clemente	CA	92672	**800-582-7777**	949-492-7777
DEI Holdings Inc 1 Viper Way *OTC: DEIX*	Vista	CA	92081	**800-876-0800**	760-598-6200
Dynamic Instruments Inc 3860 Calle Fortunada	San Diego	CA	92123	**800-793-3358**	858-278-4900
Eminence Speaker LLC 838 Mulberry Pike PO Box 360	Eminence	KY	40019	**800-897-8373**	502-845-5622
Extron Electronics 1230 S Lewis St *Tech Supp	Anaheim	CA	92805	**800-633-9876***	714-491-1500
FlexHead Industries Inc 56 Lowland St	Holliston	MA	01746	**800-829-6975**	508-893-9596
Ford Audio-Video Systems Inc 4800 W I- 40	Oklahoma City	OK	73128	**800-654-6744**	405-946-9966
Fujitsu Ten Corp of America 19600 S Vermont Ave	Torrance	CA	90502	**800-233-2216**	310-327-2151
Furman Sound LLC 1690 Corporate Cir	Petaluma	CA	94954	**877-486-4738**	707-763-1010
Harman International Industries Inc 400 Atlantic St 15th Fl *NYSE: HAR*	Stamford	CT	06901	**800-473-0602**	203-328-3500
Interactive Digital Solutions Inc 14701 Cumberland Rd Ste 400	Noblesville	IN	46060	**877-880-0022**	317-770-3521
JBL Professional 8500 Balboa Blvd	Northridge	CA	91329	**800-852-5776**	818-894-8850
JVC Professional Products Co 1700 Valley Rd	Wayne	NJ	07470	**800-252-5722**	973-317-5000
Kenwood USA Corp 2201 E Dominguez St	Long Beach	CA	90810	**800-536-9663**	310-639-9000
Klipsch LLC 137 Hempstead 278	Hope	AR	71801	**888-250-8561**	
Koss Corp 4129 N Port Washington Ave *NASDAQ: KOSS*	Milwaukee	WI	53212	**800-872-5677**	414-964-5000
Law Enforcement Assoc Corp (LEA) 120 Penmarc Dr Ste 125 *OTC: LAWEQ*	Raleigh	NC	27616	**800-354-9669**	919-872-6210
Lectrosonics Inc PO Box 15900	Rio Rancho	NM	87174	**800-821-1121**	505-892-4501
LifeSize Communications Inc 1601 S Mopac Expwy Ste 100	Austin	TX	78746	**877-543-3749**	512-347-9300
Logitech Inc 6505 Kaiser Dr *Sales	Fremont	CA	94555	**800-231-7717***	510-795-8500
LOUD Technologies Inc 16220 Wood Red Rd NE *OTC: LTEC*	Woodinville	WA	98072	**866-858-5832**	425-892-6500
Lowell Manufacturing Co 100 Integram Dr	Pacific	MO	63069	**800-325-9660**	636-257-3400
McIntosh Laboratory Inc 2 Chambers St	Binghamton	NY	13903	**800-538-6576**	607-723-3512
Metra Electronics Corp 460 Walker St *Sales	Holly Hill	FL	32117	**800-221-0932***	386-257-1186
Mitsubishi Digital Electronics America Inc 9351 Jeronimo Rd	Irvine	CA	92618	**800-332-2119**	949-465-6000
Monster Cable Products Inc 455 Valley Dr	Brisbane	CA	94005	**877-800-8989**	415-840-2000
Omnitronics LLC 6573 Cochran Rd	Solon	OH	44139	**800-762-9266**	440-349-4900
Panasonic Avionics Corp 26200 Enterprise Way	Lake Forest	CA	92630	**877-627-2300**	949-672-2000
Panasonic Consumer Electronics Co 1 Panasonic Way *NYSE: PC*	Secaucus	NJ	07094	**800-103-1333**	888-762-2097
Panasonic Corp of North America 1 Panasonic Way *Cust Svc	Secaucus	NJ	07094	**800-211-7262***	888-762-2097
Peavey Electronics Corp 5022 Hartley Peavey Dr	Meridian	MS	39305	**877-732-8391**	601-483-5365
Phase Technology 6400 Youngerman Cir	Jacksonville	FL	32244	**888-742-7385**	904-777-0700
Pioneer Electronics (USA) Inc 1925 E Dominguez St	Long Beach	CA	90810	**800-421-1404**	310-952-2000
Polk Audio Inc 5601 Metro Dr	Baltimore	MD	21215	**800-377-7655**	410-358-3600
Primo Microphones Inc 1805 Couch Dr	McKinney	TX	75069	**800-767-7466**	972-548-9807

Company	Address	City	State	Zip	Toll-Free	Phone
QSC Audio Products LLC	1675 MacArthur Blvd	Costa Mesa	CA	92626	**800-854-4079**	714-754-6175
Quam-Nichols Company Inc	234 E Marquette Rd	Chicago	IL	60637	**800-633-3669**	773-488-5800
Rane Corp	10802 47th Ave W	Mukilteo	WA	98275	**877-764-0093**	425-355-6000
Record Play Tek Inc	110 E Vistula St	Bristol	IN	46507	**800-809-5233**	574-848-5233
Renkus-heinz Inc	19201 Cook St	Foothill Ranch	CA	92610	**855-411-2364**	949-588-9997
ReQuest Inc	100 Saratoga Village Blvd Ste 45 *Sales	Ballston Spa	NY	12020	**800-236-2812***	518-899-1254
Robert Bosch LLC	38000 Hills Tech Dr *Sales	Farmington Hills	MI	48331	**800-893-6342***	248-876-1000
Rockford Corp	600 S Rockford Dr *OTC: ROFO*	Tempe	AZ	85281	**800-903-2897**	480-967-3565
SDI Technologies Inc	1299 Main St	Rahway	NJ	07065	**800-333-3092**	
Sharp Electronics Corp	1 Sharp Plz	Mahwah	NJ	07430	**800-237-4277**	201-529-8200
Shure Inc	5800 W Touhy Ave	Niles	IL	60714	**800-257-4873**	847-866-2200
Sima Products Corp	120 Pennsylvania Ave	Oakmont	PA	15139	**800-345-7462**	412-828-3700
Sony Corp of America	550 Madison Ave	New York	NY	10022	**800-282-2848**	212-833-6800
Sony Electronics Inc	1 Sony Dr *Cust Svc	Park Ridge	NJ	07656	**800-222-7669***	201-930-1000
Sound Com Corp	227 Depot St	Berea	OH	44017	**800-628-8739**	440-234-2604
Southern Audio Services	14763 Florida Blvd *Cust Svc	Baton Rouge	LA	70819	**800-843-8823***	225-272-7135
Telex Communications Inc	12000 Portland Ave S	Burnsville	MN	55337	**877-863-4169**	952-884-4051
Toshiba America Inc	1251 Ave of the Americas Ste 4100	New York	NY	10020	**800-457-7777**	212-596-0600
Universal Audio Inc	1700 Green Hills Rd	Scotts Valley	CA	95066	**877-698-2834**	831-440-1176
Xantech Corp	1969 Kellogg Ave *Sales	Carlsbad	CA	92008	**800-843-5465***	818-362-0353
Yamaha Electronics Corp	6660 Orangethorpe Ave	Buena Park	CA	90620	**800-292-2982**	714-522-9888

52 AUTO CLUBS

Company	Address	City	State	Zip	Toll-Free	Phone
AAA Allied Group Inc	15 W Central Pkwy	Cincinnati	OH	45202	**800-543-2345**	513-762-3100
AAA Carolinas	6600 AAA Dr	Charlotte	NC	28212	**800-477-4222**	704-569-3600
AAA Chicago Motor Club	975 Meridian Lake Dr	Aurora	IL	60504	**866-968-7222**	
AAA Colorado	4100 E Arkansas Ave	Denver	CO	80222	**866-625-3601**	303-753-8800
AAA East Penn	1020 W Hamilton St	Allentown	PA	18101	**800-222-4357**	
AAA Hawaii	1130 N Nimitz Hwy Ste A-170	Honolulu	HI	96817	**800-736-2886**	808-593-2221
AAA Massillon Auto Club	1972 Wales Rd NE	Massillon	OH	44646	**800-222-4357**	330-833-1084
AAA Michigan	1 Auto Club Dr	Dearborn	MI	48126	**800-222-6424**	
AAA Minnesota/Iowa	600 W Travelers Trl	Burnsville	MN	55337	**800-222-1333**	952-707-4500
AAA Missouri	12901 N Forty Dr	Saint Louis	MO	63141	**800-222-4357**	314-523-7350
AAA MountainWest	2100 11th Ave	Helena	MT	59601	**800-332-6119**	406-447-8100
AAA Nebraska	910 N 96th St	Omaha	NE	68114	**800-222-6327**	402-390-1000
AAA North Penn	1035 N Washington Ave	Scranton	PA	18509	**800-222-4357**	570-348-2511
AAA Northern New England	68 Marginal Way	Portland	ME	04104	**800-222-4357**	207-780-6800
AAA Northway	112 Railroad St	Schenectady	NY	12305	**866-222-7283**	518-374-4696
AAA Northwest Ohio	7150 W Central Ave	Toledo	OH	43617	**800-428-0060**	419-843-1200
AAA Ohio Auto Club	90 E Wilson Bridge Rd	Worthington	OH	43085	**888-222-6446**	614-431-7901
AAA Oklahoma	2121 E 15th St	Tulsa	OK	74104	**800-222-2582**	918-748-1000
AAA Southern New England	110 Royal Little Dr	Providence	RI	02904	**800-222-7448**	401-868-2000
AAA Southern Pennsylvania	2840 Eastern Blvd	York	PA	17402	**800-222-1469**	717-600-8700
AAA Washington-Inland	1745 114th Ave SE	Bellevue	WA	98004	**800-222-4357**	425-646-2058
AAA Western & Central New York	100 International Dr	Williamsville	NY	14221	**800-836-2582**	716-633-9860
AAA Wisconsin	8401 Excelsior Dr	Madison	WI	53717	**800-236-1300**	608-828-2495
AARP Motoring Plan	601 E St NW	Washington	DC	20049	**888-687-2277**	800-555-1121
American Automobile Association, Inc.	321 Whittington Pkwy	Louisville	KY	40222	**800-727-2552**	502-582-3311
Auto Club Ltd	PO Box 162526	Austin	TX	78716	**866-247-3728**	
Auto Club of America Corp (ACA)	9411 N Georgia St	Oklahoma City	OK	73120	**800-411-2007**	405-751-4430
Automobile Club of Southern California	2601 S Figueroa St	Los Angeles	CA	90007	**800-400-4222**	213-741-3686
BP MotorClub	PO Box 4441	Carol Stream	IL	60197	**800-334-3300**	
Brickell Financial Services Motor Club Inc	7300 Corporate Ctr Dr Ste 601	Miami	FL	33126	**800-262-7262**	305-392-4300
British Columbia Automobile Assn (BCAA)	4567 Canada Way	Burnaby	BC	V5G4T1	**800-222-4357**	604-268-5000
CAA Central Ontario	60 Commerce Vly Dr E	Thornhill	ON	L3T7P9	**800-268-3750**	905-771-3000
CAA Manitoba	870 Empress St	Winnipeg	MB	R3C2Z3	**800-222-4357**	204-262-6166
CAA Maritimes Ltd	378 Westmorland Rd	Saint John	NB	E2J2G4	**800-471-1611**	506-634-1400
CAA North & East Ontario	PO Box 8350	Ottawa	ON	K1G3T2	**800-267-8713**	613-820-1890
CAA Quebec	444 Bouvier St	Quebec	QC	G2J1E3	**800-222-4357**	418-624-8222
CAA Stoney Creek	163 Centennial Pkwy N	Hamilton	ON	L8E1H8	**800-992-8143**	905-664-8000
California State Automobile Assn	150 Van Ness Ave *Cust Svc	San Francisco	CA	94102	**800-922-8228***	
Canadian Automobile Assn (CAA)	2151 Thurston Dr	Ottawa	ON	K1G6C9	**800-267-8713**	613-820-1890
Findlay Automobile Club	1550 Tiffin Ave	Findlay	OH	45840	**800-222-4357**	419-422-4961
National Motor Club of America Inc (NMC)	130 E John Carpenter Fwy	Irving	TX	75062	**800-523-4582**	972-999-1099
Pinnacle Motor Club	510 N Topeka St	Wichita	KS	67214	**800-446-1289**	
Travelers Motor Club	720 NW 50th St	Oklahoma City	OK	73154	**800-654-9208**	405-848-1711
Zipcar Inc	35 Thomson Pl *NASDAQ: ZIP*	Boston	MA	02210	**877-353-9227**	

53 AUTO SUPPLY STORES

Company	Address	City	State	Zip	Toll-Free	Phone
A 1 Auto Recyclers	7804 S Hwy 79	Rapid City	SD	57701	**800-456-0715**	605-348-8442
Advance Auto Parts Inc	5008 Airport Rd *NYSE: AAP*	Roanoke	VA	24012	**877-238-2623**	
Air Lift Co	2727 Snow Rd	Lansing	MI	48917	**800-248-0892**	517-322-2144
American Glass Distributors	3901 Airline Dr	Houston	TX	77022	**800-570-3303**	713-692-8522
Ats All Tire Supply Co	6600 Long Point Rd Ste 101	Houston	TX	77055	**888-339-6665**	
AutoZone Inc	123 S Front St *NYSE: AZO*	Memphis	TN	38103	**800-288-6966**	901-495-6500
BMW of Manhattan Inc	555 W 57th St	New York	NY	10019	**877-855-4607**	212-586-2269
Bond Auto Parts	45 Summer St	Barre	VT	05641	**800-639-1982**	802-476-3108
Bowditch Ford Inc	11291 Jefferson Ave	Newport News	VA	23601	**866-399-2616**	757-595-2211
Carquest Corp	2635 E Millbrook Rd	Raleigh	NC	27604	**800-876-1291**	919-573-3000
CEC Industries Ltd	599 Bond St	Lincolnshire	IL	60069	**800-572-4168**	847-821-1199
Chris Alston Chassisworks Inc	8661 Younger Creek Dr	Sacramento	CA	95828	**800-722-2269**	916-388-0288
Cumberland Truck Parts	15 Sylmar Rd	Nottingham	PA	19362	**800-364-6995**	610-932-1152
Custom Truck Accessories Inc	13408 Hwy 65 Ne	Ham Lake	MN	55304	**800-333-1282**	763-757-5326
Delco Diesel Services Inc	1100 S Agnew Ave	Oklahoma City	OK	73108	**800-256-0395**	405-232-3595
Hedahls Inc	100 East Broadway	Bismarck	ND	58502	**800-433-2457**	701-223-8393
JE Adams Industries Ltd	1025 63rd Ave Sw	Cedar Rapids	IA	52404	**800-553-8861**	319-363-0237
KOI Warehouse Inc	2701 Spring Grove Ave	Cincinnati	OH	45225	**800-354-0408**	513-357-2400
Meridian Auto Parts	10211 Pacific Mesa Blvd Ste 404	San Diego	CA	92121	**800-874-1974**	
Merle's Automotive Supply Inc	33 W University Blvd	Tucson	AZ	85705	**800-546-6040**	520-622-3526
Momo Automotive Accessories Inc	20512 Crescent Bay Ste 104	Lake Forest	CA	92630	**800-749-6666**	949-380-7556
Motor State Distributing	8300 Lane Dr	Watervliet	MI	49098	**800-772-2678**	269-463-4113
Myers Brothers of Kansas City Inc	1210 W 28th St	Kansas City	MO	64108	**800-264-2404**	816-931-5501
NORD Drivesystems	800 Nord Dr	Waunakee	WI	53597	**888-314-6673**	
Northland Auto & Truck Accessories	1106 S 29th St W	Billings	MT	59102	**800-736-5302**	406-245-0595
O'Reilly Automotive Inc	233 S Patterson *NASDAQ: ORLY*	Springfield	MO	65802	**888-327-7153**	417-862-6708
Original Parts Group Inc (OPGI)	1770 Saturn Way	Seal Beach	CA	90740	**800-243-8355**	562-594-1000
Peerless Tire Co	5000 Kingston St	Denver	CO	80239	**800-999-7810**	303-371-4300
S & S Tire & Auto Service Center	1475 Jingle Bell Ln	Lexington	KY	40509	**800-685-6794**	
S&R Truck Tire Center Inc	1402 Truckers Blvd	Jeffersonville	IN	47130	**800-488-2670**	812-282-4799
Specmo Auto Sound & Speed	1200 E Avis Dr	Madison Heights	MI	48529	**800-545-7910**	
Tire Warehouse	200 Holleder Pkwy	Rochester	NY	14615	**800-876-6676**	
Town Fair Tire Company Inc	460 Coe Ave	East Haven	CT	06512	**800-972-2245**	
Trew Industrial Wheels Inc	310 Wilhagan Rd	Nashville	TN	37217	**888-977-8739**	615-360-9100
Utilimaster Holding Co	603 Earthway Blvd	Bristol	IN	46507	**800-237-7806**	
Vanguard Trucks Centers	700 Ruskin Dr	Forest Park	GA	30297	**866-216-7925**	
Weathers Auto Supply Inc	23308 Airpark Dr	Petersburg	VA	23803	**888-572-2886**	804-861-1076
West Coast Differentials	2429 Mercantile Dr Ste A	Rancho Cordova	CA	95742	**800-510-0950**	916-635-0950

Name / Address	City	State	Zip	Toll-Free	Phone
XKS Unlimited Inc 850 Fiero Ln	San Luis Obispo	CA	93401	**800-444-5247**	805-544-7864

54 AUTOMATIC MERCHANDISING EQUIPMENT & SYSTEMS

SEE ALSO Food Service

Name / Address	City	State	Zip	Toll-Free	Phone
Affiliated Control Equipment Inc 640 Wheat Ln	Wood Dale	IL	60191	**800-942-8753**	630-595-4680
AIR-serv Group LLC 1370 Mendota Heights Rd	Mendota Heights	MN	55120	**800-247-8363**	651-454-0465
American Vending Sales Inc 750 Morse Ave	Elk Grove Village	IL	60007	**800-441-0009**	847-439-9400
Automatic Products International Ltd 165 Bridgepoint Dr	Saint Paul	MN	55075	**800-523-8363**	
Bastian Material Handling LLC (BMH) 10585 N Meridian St 3rd Fl	Indianapolis	IN	46290	**800-772-0464**	317-575-9992
Betson Enterprises Inc 303 Patterson Plank Rd	Carlstadt	NJ	07072	**800-524-2343**	201-438-1300
Birmingham Vending Co 540 Second Ave N	Birmingham	AL	35204	**800-288-7635**	205-324-7526
Coin Acceptors Inc 300 Hunter Ave	Saint Louis	MO	63124	**800-325-2646**	314-725-0100
Coinstar Inc 1800 114th Ave SE	Bellevue	WA	98004	**800-928-2274**	425-943-8000
Dixie-Narco Inc 3330 Dixie-Narco Blvd	Williston	SC	29853	**800-688-9090**	803-266-5000
Glacier Water Services Inc 1385 Pk Ctr Dr *OTC: GWSV*	Vista	CA	92081	**800-452-2437**	760-560-1111
Harcourt Outlines Inc 7765 S 175 W PO Box 128	Milroy	IN	46156	**800-428-6584**	
Northwestern Corp PO Box 490	Morris	IL	60450	**800-942-1316**	815-942-1300

55 AUTOMATIC TELLER MACHINES (ATMS)

Name / Address	City	State	Zip	Toll-Free	Phone
Accu-time Systems Inc 420 Somers Rd	Ellington	CT	06029	**800-355-4648**	860-870-5000
Diebold Inc 5995 Mayfair Rd *NYSE: DBD*	North Canton	OH	44720	**800-999-3600**	330-490-4000
Electronic Cash Systems Inc (ECS) 30352 Esperanza	Rancho Santa Margarita	CA	92688	**888-327-2860**	949-888-8580
Everi Holdings Inc (GCA) 7250 S Tenaya Way Ste 100 *NYSE: EVRI*	Las Vegas	NV	89113	**800-833-7110**	702-855-3000
Tidel Engineering Inc 2025 W Belt Line Rd Ste 114	Carrollton	TX	75006	**800-678-7577**	972-484-3358

56 AUTOMOBILE DEALERS & GROUPS

SEE ALSO Automobile Sales & Related Services - Online

Name / Address	City	State	Zip	Toll-Free	Phone
A C Nelson Rv World 11818 L St	Omaha	NE	68137	**888-655-2332**	402-333-1122
Alberic Colon Auto Sales Inc Ave John F Kennedy Carr Ste 2 KM 3.4	San Juan	PR	00920	**877-292-4610**	
Allied Toyotalift 1640 Island Home Ave	Knoxville	TN	37920	**866-538-0667**	865-573-0995
American Augers Inc 135 US Rt 42	West Salem	OH	44287	**800-324-4930**	419-869-7107
Ancira Winton Chevrolet 6111 Bandera Rd *General	San Antonio	TX	78238	**800-299-5286***	210-762-4545
Arrow Truck Sales Inc 3200 Manchester Trfy	Kansas City	MO	64129	**800-311-7144**	816-923-5000
Art Morrison Enterprises Inc 5301 Eighth St E	Fife	WA	98424	**888-640-0516**	253-922-7188
Asheville Chevrolet Inc 205 Smokey Pk Hwy	Asheville	NC	28806	**866-921-1073**	828-665-4444
Astoria Ford 710 W Marine Dr	Astoria	OR	97103	**888-760-9303**	503-325-6411
Atlantic British Ltd Halfmoon Light Industrial Pk 6 Enterprise Ave	Clifton Park	NY	12065	**800-533-2210**	518-664-6169
Auto Lenders Liquidation Center 104 Rt 73	Voorhees	NJ	08043	**888-305-5968**	
Autoland 170 Rt 22 E *Sales	Springfield	NJ	07081	**877-813-7239***	973-467-2900
Automobile Racing Club of America 8117 Lewis Ave	Temperance	MI	48182	**800-385-2503**	734-847-6726
Autorama Inc 5389 Poplar Ave	Memphis	TN	38119	**888-356-7636**	901-345-6211
AutoRevo LTD 7920 Belt Line Rd Ste 450	Dallas	TX	75254	**888-311-7386**	972-715-8600
Aviation Ground Equipment Corp 53 Hanse Ave	Freeport	NY	11520	**800-758-0044**	516-546-0003
Ball Automotive Group 1935 National City Blvd	National City	CA	91950	**888-318-6492**	619-474-6431
Barry Bunker Chevrolet Inc 1307 N Wabash Ave *Sales	Marion	IN	46952	**866-603-8625***	765-664-1275
Baskin Auto Truck & Tractor Inc 1844 Hwy 51 S	Covington	TN	38019	**877-476-2626**	901-476-2626
Bates Ford 1673 W Main St	Lebanon	TN	37087	**888-834-4671**	
Bayway Lincoln-mercury Inc 12333 Gulf Fwy	Houston	TX	77034	**888-262-9275**	
Bed Wood & Parts LLC 8345 Madisonville Rd	Hopkinsville	KY	42240	**877-205-9663**	270-424-3000
Bell Ford Inc 2401 W Bell Rd	Phoenix	AZ	85023	**800-688-1776**	602-866-1776
Bergstrom of Kaukauna 2929 Lawe St	Kaukauna	WI	54130	**866-939-0130**	
Best Chevrolet Inc 128 Derby St	Hingham	MA	02043	**866-208-7873**	
Biggers Chevrolet 1385 E Chicago St	Elgin	IL	60120	**866-431-1555**	847-742-9000
Bill Collins 4220 BaRdstown Rd	Louisville	KY	40218	**888-327-9095**	502-459-9550
Bill Snethkamp Lansing Dodge Inc 6131 S Pennsylvania Ave	Lansing	MI	48911	**800-863-6343**	517-394-1200
BMW of Darien 140 Ledge Rd	Darien	CT	06820	**855-349-6240**	203-656-1804
Bob Allen Ford 9239 Metcalf Ave	Overland Park	KS	66212	**888-573-6364**	913-381-3000
Bob Davidson Ford Lincoln 1845 E Joppa Rd	Baltimore	MD	21234	**877-885-7890**	410-661-6400
Bob Stall Chevrolet 7601 Alvarado Rd	La Mesa	CA	91942	**800-295-2695**	619-460-1311
Bommarito Automotive Group 15736 Manchester Rd	Ellisville	MO	63011	**800-367-2289**	636-391-7200
Brasher Motor Company of Weimar Inc 1700 I- 10	Weimar	TX	78962	**800-783-1746**	979-725-8515
Brighton Ford Inc 8240 W Grand River	Brighton	MI	48114	**888-644-9991**	810-227-1171
Brown Automotive Group LP 4300 S Georgia	Amarillo	TX	79110	**888-388-6728**	806-353-7211
Buchanan Automotive Group 50 Central Ave Ste 900	Sarasota	FL	34236	**888-292-4883**	941-364-9500
Buckeye Nissan Inc 3820 Pkwy Ln	Hilliard	OH	43026	**800-686-4391**	614-771-2345
Bus Andrews Truck Equipment Inc 2828 N E Ave	Springfield	MO	65803	**800-273-0733**	417-869-1541
Byerly Ford 4041 Dixie Hwy	Louisville	KY	40216	**888-436-0819**	502-448-1661
Cable-Dahmer Chevrolet Inc 1834 S Noland Rd	Independence	MO	64055	**888-738-5260**	816-521-7508
Callaway Cars Inc 3 High St	Old Lyme	CT	06371	**866-927-9400**	860-434-9002
Canfield Equipment Service 21533 Mound Rd	Warren	MI	48091	**800-637-3956**	586-757-2020
Capital Ford Inc 4900 Capital Blvd	Raleigh	NC	27616	**877-659-2496**	919-790-4600
Capitol Chevrolet Montgomery 711 Eastern Blvd *Sales	Montgomery	AL	36117	**800-410-1137***	334-272-8700
Car City Motor Company Inc 3100 S US Hwy 169	Saint Joseph	MO	64503	**800-525-7008**	816-233-9149
CarMax Inc 12800 Tuckahoe Creek Pkwy *NYSE: KMX*	Richmond	VA	23238	**888-722-7629**	804-747-0422
Carolina International Trucks Inc 1619 Bluff Rd	Columbia	SC	29201	**800-868-4923**	803-799-4923
Charles Gabus Ford Inc 4545 Merle Hay Rd *Sales	Des Moines	IA	50310	**800-934-2287***	515-270-0707
Checkered Flag Motor Car Corp 5225 Virginia Beach Blvd	Virginia Beach	VA	23462	**866-414-7820**	757-687-3486
Cherry Creek Dodge 2727 S Havana St *Sales	Denver	CO	80014	**888-891-7522***	303-751-1104
Coffman Truck Sales 1149 W Lake St Rt 31	Aurora	IL	60506	**800-255-7641**	630-892-7093
College Station Ford 1351 Earl Rudder Fwy S	College Station	TX	77845	**888-508-0241**	979-694-2022
Conant Auto Retail Group 18900 Studebaker Rd	Cerritos	CA	90703	**888-318-5001**	
Concord Road Equipment Manufacturing Inc 348 Chester St	Painesville	OH	44077	**800-942-7623**	440-357-5344
Cook Truck Equipment & Tools 3701 Harlee Ave	Charlotte	NC	28208	**800-241-4210**	704-392-4138
Cooley Motors Corp 401 N Greenbush Rd	Rensselaer	NY	12144	**888-518-0245**	518-283-2902
Cooper Motors Inc 985 York St	Hanover	PA	17331	**866-414-2809**	
Coral Springs Auto Mall 9400 W Atlantic Blvd	Coral Springs	FL	33071	**800-353-8660**	954-369-1016
Courtesy Chevrolet 1233 E Camelback Rd	Phoenix	AZ	85014	**877-295-4648**	602-235-0255
Courtesy Chrysler Jeep Dodge 9207 Adamo Dr E	Tampa	FL	33619	**866-343-9730**	813-620-4300
Crown Motors Ltd 196 Regent Blvd	Holland	MI	49423	**800-466-7000**	616-396-5268
Cumberland Chrysler Ctr 1550 Interstate Dr	Cookeville	TN	38501	**888-277-4902**	
D-Patrick Motoplex Inc 200 N Green River Rd	Evansville	IN	47715	**800-831-6870**	812-473-6500
Dan Wolf Chevrolet of Naperville 1515 W Ogden Ave	Naperville	IL	60540	**800-243-8872**	630-596-1189
Dave White Chevrolet Inc 5880 Monroe St	Sylvania	OH	43560	**800-893-5217**	419-517-6111
DCH Honda of Nanuet 10 Rt 304	Nanuet	NY	10954	**888-495-8660**	845-623-1200
Dean Team Automotive Group Inc 15121 Manchester Rd	Ballwin	MO	63011	**888-699-0663**	636-227-0100
Dearth Motors Inc 520 Eigth St	Monroe	WI	53566	**877-495-5321**	608-325-3181
Dellenbach Motors 3111 S College Ave	Fort Collins	CO	80525	**866-963-5689**	
DeMontrond 888 I- 45 S *Sales	Conroe	TX	77304	**888-843-6583***	281-443-2500
Dick Brantmeier Ford Inc 3624 Kohler Memorial Dr	Sheboygan	WI	53082	**800-498-6111**	920-458-6111
Don McGill Toyota Inc 11800 Katy Fwy	Houston	TX	77079	**877-259-6888**	281-496-2000
Dothan Chrysler-Dodge Inc 4074 Ross Clark Cir NW	Dothan	AL	36303	**877-674-9574**	
DriveTime Corp 4020 E Indian School Rd	Phoenix	AZ	85018	**888-418-1212**	
Dueck Auto Group 12100 Featherstone Way	Richmond	BC	V6W1K9	**877-993-8325**	604-273-1311

Classified Section

Name / Address	City	State	Zip	Toll-Free	Phone
Durocher Auto Sales Inc 4651 Rt 9	Plattsburgh	NY	12901	**877-215-8954**	888-635-4599
Earnhardt Auto Centers 7300 W Orchid Ln	Chandler	AZ	85226	**888-378-7711**	480-926-4000
East Bay Ford Truck Sales Inc 70 Hegenberger Loop	Oakland	CA	94621	**888-219-8551**	510-272-4400
Eastern Carolina Nissan 3315 Hwy 70 E	New Bern	NC	28564	**888-944-7822**	252-636-1000
Eckenrod Ford Lincoln Mercury of Cullman Inc 5255 Alabama Hwy 157	Cullman	AL	35058	**888-470-7346**	256-734-3361
Ed Bozarth Chevrolet Inc 2001 S Havana St	Aurora	CO	80014	**877-626-9358**	
Ed Martin Inc 3800 E 96th St	Indianapolis	IN	46240	**800-211-5410**	317-846-3800
El Cajon Motors D/B/A El Cajon Ford 1595 E Main St	El Cajon	CA	92021	**877-375-1408**	619-579-8888
El Camino Store, The 420 Athena Dr	Athens	GA	30601	**888-685-5987**	706-546-9217
Electro Enterprises Inc 3601 N I-35 Service Rd	Oklahoma City	OK	73111	**800-324-6591**	405-427-6591
Elm Chevrolet Co Inc 301 E Church St	Elmira	NY	14901	**877-265-6708**	607-734-4141
Erhard Bmw Of Bloomfield Hills 4065 W Maple Rd	Bloomfield Hills	MI	48301	**888-481-4058**	248-642-6565
F C Kerbeck & Sons 100 Rt 73 N *General	Palmyra	NJ	08065	**855-846-1500***	856-829-8200
Finish Line Ford Inc 2211 W Pioneer Pkwy	Peoria	IL	61615	**888-841-4002**	309-693-2525
First Truck Centre Inc 11313 170 St	Edmonton	AB	T5M3P5	**888-882-8530**	780-413-8800
Fitzgerald Auto Mall 10915 Georgia Ave	Wheaton	MD	20902	**855-776-0552**	
Five Star Dodge 3068 Riverside Dr	Macon	GA	31210	**877-748-9845**	478-474-3700
Fletch's Inc 825 Charlevoix Ave PO Box 265	Petoskey	MI	49770	**877-238-0816**	231-347-9651
Fletcher Jones Imports 7300 W Sahara Ave	Las Vegas	NV	89117	**888-927-3675**	702-364-2700
Folsom Lake Ford 12755 Folsom Blvd	Folsom	CA	95630	**800-730-0457**	916-353-2000
Ford of Montebello Inc 2747 Via Campo	Montebello	CA	90640	**888-313-2305**	323-838-6920
FordDirect 1740 Us Hwy 60 PO Box 700	Republic	MO	65738	**888-865-2576**	417-732-2626
Fordham Auto Sales Inc 236 W Fordham Rd	Bronx	NY	10468	**800-407-1153**	
Formula Ford Inc 265 River St	Montpelier	VT	05602	**888-872-9439**	802-223-5201
Frederick Motor Co, The 1 Waverley Dr	Frederick	MD	21702	**800-734-9118**	
Freightliner of Hartford Inc 222 Roberts St	East Hartford	CT	06108	**800-453-6967**	860-289-0201
Galpin Motors Inc 15505 Roscoe Blvd	North Hills	CA	91343	**800-256-7137**	818-787-3800
Gateway Industrial Power Inc 921 Fournie Ln	Collinsville	IL	62234	**888-865-8675**	618-345-0123
Gillman Cos 10595 W Sam Houston Pkwy S	Houston	TX	77099	**888-532-8956**	713-776-7000
Gilroy Chevrolet Cadillac Inc 6720 Bear Cat Ct	Gilroy	CA	95020	**800-201-7241**	408-842-9301
Gladstone Dodge 5610 N Oak Trafficway	Gladstone	MO	64118	**866-695-2043**	
Global Filtration Inc 9207 Emmott St	Houston	TX	77040	**888-717-0888**	713-856-9800
Globe Motors Inc 2275 Stanley Ave	Dayton	OH	45404	**800-433-5700**	937-228-3171
Graff Truck Centers Inc 1401 S Saginaw St	Flint	MI	48503	**888-870-4203**	810-239-8300
Grossinger Motors 1430 Fort Jesse Rd	Normal	IL	61761	**888-719-0095**	
Group 1 Automotive Inc 800 Gessner Ste 500 *NYSE: GPI*	Houston	TX	77024	**888-707-4094**	713-647-5700
Grubbs Infiniti Ltd 1661 Airport Fwy	Euless	TX	76040	**800-685-1111**	817-318-1200
H&R Construction Parts & Equipment Inc 20 Milburn St	Buffalo	NY	14212	**800-333-0650**	716-891-4311
Hainen Ford Inc 800 Hwy 5 S	Tipton	MO	65081	**888-526-6979**	
Hamilton Chevrolet 5800 E 14 Mile Rd	Warren	MI	48092	**888-466-7827**	586-264-1400
Harte Nissan Inc 165 W Service Rd	Hartford	CT	06120	**866-687-8971**	860-549-2800
Harvey Cadillac Co 2600 28th St SE *Sales	Grand Rapids	MI	49512	**877-845-1557***	616-949-1140
Headquarter Toyota 5895 NW 167th St	Miami	FL	33015	**800-549-0947**	305-364-9800
Hendrick Buick GMC Cadillac 1151 W 104th St	Kansas City	MO	64114	**888-255-9362**	877-584-7140
Herb Chambers I 95 Inc 107 Andover St	Danvers	MA	01923	**877-907-1965**	
Herb Gordon Nissan 3131 Automobile Blvd	Silver Spring	MD	20904	**844-249-4077**	866-399-7502
Heritage Ford Inc 2100 Sisk Rd	Modesto	CA	95350	**888-323-9990**	209-529-5110
Herson's Inc 15525 Frederick Rd	Rockville	MD	20855	**888-203-8318**	
Hines Park Lincoln Inc 40601 Ann Arbor Rd	Plymouth	MI	48170	**866-979-3919**	
Hinshaws Acura/Honda 5955 20th St E	Fife	WA	98424	**800-752-2872**	253-922-8830
Holman Cadillac Co 1200 Rt 73 S	Mount Laurel	NJ	08054	**866-865-6973**	856-778-1000
Honda of Santa Monica 1726 Santa Monica Blvd	Santa Monica	CA	90404	**800-269-2031**	310-264-4900
Honda World 10645 Studebaker Rd	Downey	CA	90241	**888-458-9404**	562-929-7000
Hoover Toyota 2686 Hwy 150	Hoover	AL	35244	**866-980-8082**	205-978-2600
Horwith Trucks Inc PO Box 7	NorthHampton	PA	18067	**800-220-8807**	610-261-2220
Island Lincoln-Mercury Inc 1850 E Merritt Island Cswy	Merritt Island	FL	32952	**800-392-3673**	321-452-9220
James Wood Motors Inc 2111 Us Hwy 287 S	Decatur	TX	76234	**888-833-7230**	940-627-2177
Joe Holland Chevrolet Inc 210 Maccorkle Ave SW	South Charleston	WV	25303	**855-468-9491**	304-744-1561
Joe Van Horn Chevrolet Inc PO Box 238	Plymouth	WI	53073	**800-236-1415**	920-893-6361
John Watson Chevrolet 3535 Wall Ave	Ogden	UT	84401	**866-647-9930**	801-394-2611
Johnson Motors Inc 1891 Blinker Pkwy	Du Bois	PA	15801	**800-537-1768**	814-371-4444
Joyce Motors Corp 3166 SR- 10	Denville	NJ	07834	**844-332-5955**	973-361-3000
Keeler Motor Car Co 1111 Troy Schenectady Rd	Latham	NY	12110	**800-474-4197**	518-785-4197
Ken Fowler Motors 1265 Airport Pk Blvd	Ukiah	CA	95482	**800-287-0107**	707-468-0101
Ken Garff Automotive Group 405 S Main St	Salt Lake City	UT	84111	**888-630-6838**	801-257-3400
Kenworth Northwest Inc 20220 International Blvd S	SeaTac	WA	98198	**800-562-0060**	206-433-5911
Kenworth of Indianapolis Inc 2929 S Holt Rd	Indianapolis	IN	46241	**800-827-8421**	317-247-8421
Knippelmier Chevrolet Inc 1811 E Hwy 62 E	Blanchard	OK	73010	**877-644-7255**	
Kolosso Toyota 3000 W Wisconsin Ave	Appleton	WI	54914	**877-756-2297**	920-738-3666
Koons Ford of Annapolis Inc 2540 Riva Rd	Annapolis	MD	21401	**888-313-5524**	410-224-2100
L & S Truck Ctr of Appleton Inc 330 N Bluemound Dr	Appleton	WI	54914	**888-617-3140**	920-749-1700
La Beau Bros Inc 295 N Harrison Ave	Kankakee	IL	60901	**800-747-9519**	815-933-5519
La Belle Dodge Chrysler Jeep Inc 501 S Main St	Labelle	FL	33935	**800-226-1193**	863-675-2701
La Mesa Rv Ctr Inc 7430 Copley Pk Pl *Sales	San Diego	CA	92111	**888-509-4199***	858-874-8000
Lafontaine Honda 2245 S Telegraph Rd	Dearborn	MI	48124	**866-567-5088**	
Lakeside International LLC 11000 W Silver Spring Rd	Milwaukee	WI	53225	**800-236-0444**	414-353-4800
Lakeside Toyota 3701 N Cswy Blvd *Sales	Metairie	LA	70002	**877-512-8274***	504-833-3311
Lancaster Toyota Inc 5270 Manheim Pk	East Petersburg	PA	17520	**888-424-1295**	
Landers Ford Inc 2082 W Poplar Ave	Collierville	TN	38017	**888-281-5266**	
Landmark Lincoln-Mercury Inc 5000 S Broadway	Englewood	CO	80113	**888-318-9692**	303-761-1560
Lankota Inc 270 Wpark Ave	Huron	SD	57350	**866-526-5682**	605-352-4550
Lawrence Hall Chevrolet Inc 1385 S Danville Dr	Abilene	TX	79605	**800-568-7158**	325-695-8800
LEKTRO Inc 1190 SE Flightline Dr	Warrenton	OR	97146	**800-535-8767**	503-861-2288
Les Stanford Chevrolet Inc 21730 Michigan Ave	Dearborn	MI	48124	**800-836-0972**	313-457-0364
Lexus of Memphis Inc 2600 Ridgeway Rd *Sales	Memphis	TN	38119	**877-876-9996***	901-362-8833
Lia Auto Group, The 1258 Central Ave PO Box 5789	Albany	NY	12205	**855-212-7985**	518-489-2111
Lithia Motors Inc 360 E Jackson St *NYSE: LAD*	Medford	OR	97501	**866-318-9660**	
Loeber Motors Inc 4255 W Touhy Ave	Lincolnwood	IL	60712	**888-211-4485**	847-675-1000
Lordco Parts Ltd 22866 Dewdney Trunk Rd	Maple Ridge	BC	V2X3K6	**877-591-1581**	604-467-1581
Lou Bachrodt Auto Group 7070 Cherryvale N Blvd	Rockford	IL	61112	**866-635-2349**	815-332-3000
Mac Haik Auto Group 11711 Katy Fwy	Houston	TX	77079	**866-721-8619**	
Markley Motors 3325 S College Ave	Fort Collins	CO	80525	**888-480-5167**	970-226-2214
Marshal Mize Ford Inc 5348 Hwy 153	Chattanooga	TN	37343	**888-633-5038**	
Matt Blatt Inc 501 Delsea Dr N	Glassboro	NJ	08028	**877-462-5288**	856-881-0444
Matthews Currie Ford Company Inc 130 N Tamiami Trl	Nokomis	FL	34275	**855-491-3131**	941-488-6787
McCloskey Motors Inc 6710 N Academy Blvd	Colorado Springs	CO	80918	**877-389-6671**	719-594-9400
McDevitt Trucks Inc 1 Mack Ave PO Box 4640	Manchester	NH	03108	**800-370-6225**	603-668-1700
McGrath Auto Group 4610 Ctr Pt Rd NE	Cedar Rapids	IA	52402	**888-902-8414**	
Mclean Implement Inc 793 Illinois Rte 130	Albion	IL	62806	**888-720-4440**	618-445-3676
Mercedes-Benz of San Francisco 500 Eigth St	San Francisco	CA	94103	**877-554-6016**	415-673-2000
Metro Ford Inc 9000 NW Seventh Ave	Miami	FL	33150	**877-811-9402**	
Mike Reed Chevrolet 1559 E Oglethorpe	Hinesville	GA	31313	**877-228-3943**	
Mission Golf Cars 18865 Redland Rd	San Antonio	TX	78259	**800-324-7868**	210-545-7868
Mission Valley Ford Truck Sales Inc 780 E Brokaw Rd	San Jose	CA	95112	**888-284-7471**	408-933-2300
Modern Chevrolet of Winston-Salem 5955 University Pkwy *General	Winston-Salem	NC	27105	**888-306-0825***	336-722-4191

Classified Section

Name	Address	City	State	ZIP	Toll-Free	Phone
Molle Toyota Inc	601 W 103rd St	Kansas City	MO	64114	**888-510-7705**	816-942-5200
Montesi Motors Inc	444 State St	North Haven	CT	06473	**844-282-1115**	
Motorcars International	3015 E Cairo St	Springfield	MO	65802	**866-970-6800**	417-831-9999
Nalley Lexus Smyrna	2750 Cobb Pkwy SE	Smyrna	GA	30080	**877-454-4206**	
National Standard Parts Assoc Inc	4400 Mobile Hwy	Pensacola	FL	32506	**800-874-6813**	850-456-5771
National Tire & Wheel	5 Garden Ct	Wheeling	WV	26003	**800-847-3287**	
Nationwide Lift Trucks Inc	3900 N 28th Terr	Hollywood	FL	33020	**800-327-4431**	954-922-4645
New Country Volkswagen of Greenwich	200 W Putnam Ave	Greenwich	CT	06830	**866-584-6747**	
Nextran Corp	1986 W Beaver St	Jacksonville	FL	32209	**800-347-6225**	904-354-3721
Nitrous Express Inc	5411 Seymour Hwy	Wichita Falls	TX	76310	**888-463-2781**	940-767-7694
Norduyn Inc	6200 Henri-Bourassa W	Montreal	QC	H4R1C3	**877-332-3210**	514-334-3210
Norman Frede Chevrolet Co	16801 Feather Craft Ln	Houston	TX	77058	**888-307-1703**	281-486-2200
Norris Ford	901 Merritt Blvd	Baltimore	MD	21222	**866-460-5275***	410-285-0200
	*Sales					
North Bay Nissan Inc	1250 Auto Ctr Dr	Petaluma	CA	94952	**877-818-6866**	707-769-7700
North Park Lincoln	9207 San Pedro St	San Antonio	TX	78216	**888-696-5480**	210-341-8841
Northway Toyota	727 New Loudon Rd	Latham	NY	12110	**877-525-3488**	877-800-5098
O'Gara Coach Company LLC	8833 W Olympic Blvd	Beverly Hills	CA	90211	**888-291-5533**	
Orange Motors Company Inc	799 Central Ave	Albany	NY	12206	**888-912-5958**	518-489-5414
Palm Automotive Group	1801 Tamiami Trail	Punta Gorda	FL	33950	**800-643-2112***	941-639-1155
	*General					
Parsons Buick Co, The	151 E St	Plainville	CT	06062	**877-274-2613**	860-747-1693
Paul Heuring Motors Inc	720 N Hobart Rd	Hobart	IN	46342	**888-851-9702**	219-942-3673
Phil Long Dealerships	1212 Motor City Dr	Colorado Springs	CO	80905	**866-644-1378**	
Phil Smart Inc	600 E Pike St	Seattle	WA	98122	**877-241-4528**	206-324-5959
Phillips Buick-Pontiac-Gmc Truck Inc	2160 US Hwy 441	Fruitland Park	FL	34731	**888-664-7454**	352-728-1212
Pitts Toyota Inc	210 N Jeffreson St	Dublin	GA	31021	**888-561-8030**	478-272-3244
Porsche of Maplewood	2780 Maplewood Dr	Maplewood	MN	55109	**888-852-8937**	888-679-1698
Potamkin Automotive Group Inc	6200 NW 167th Ste B	Miami Lakes	FL	33014	**855-799-9965**	
Premier Subaru LLC	150 N Main St	Branford	CT	06405	**888-690-6710**	203-481-0687
Prestige Chrysler Dodge Inc	200 Alpine St	Longmont	CO	80501	**866-439-1926**	303-651-3000
Priority Chevrolet of Chesapeake	1495 S Military Hwy	Chesapeake	VA	23320	**855-315-0212**	757-424-1811
Prostrollo Motor Sales Inc	500 Fourth St NE	Huron	SD	57350	**866-466-4515**	
Putnam Lexus	390 Convention Way	Redwood City	CA	94063	**888-231-8005**	650-363-8500
Rhoden Auto Ctr Inc	3400 S Expy St	Council Bluffs	IA	51501	**866-562-6248**	712-309-4000
Ricart Automotive Group	4255 S Hamilton Rd	Columbus	OH	43125	**888-225-6783**	614-836-5321
Riverside Ford	2625 Ludington St	Escanaba	MI	49829	**877-774-3171**	906-786-1130
Riverside Ford Inc	2089 Riverside Dr	Macon	GA	31204	**800-395-6210***	478-464-2900
	*Sales					
RnR RV Ctr	23203 E Knox Ave	Liberty Lake	WA	99019	**866-386-4875**	
Roberson Motors Inc	3100 Ryan Dr SE	Salem	OR	97301	**888-281-6220**	503-363-4117
Roger Dean Chevrolet Inc	2235 Okeechobee Blvd	West Palm Beach	FL	33409	**877-827-4705**	561-683-8100
Romero Mazda	1307 Kettering Dr	Ontario	CA	91761	**888-317-2233**	909-390-8484
Ron Tonkin Dealerships	122 NE 122nd Ave	Portland	OR	97230	**855-890-1823**	503-255-4100
Rosner Auto Group	3507 Jefferson Davis Hwy	Fredericksburg	VA	22408	**855-270-6270***	540-907-4900
	*Sales					
Rush Truck Center - Whittier	2450 Kella Ave	Whittier	CA	90601	**877-605-7623**	562-551-5000
Russell Karting Specialties Inc	PO Box 1220	Raymore	MO	64083	**800-821-3359**	816-322-3330
RV World Inc of Nokomis	2110 Tamiami Trl N	Nokomis	FL	34275	**800-262-2182**	941-966-2182
Sandy Sansing Chevrolet	6200 N Pensacola Blvd	Pensacola	FL	32505	**888-885-1844***	850-476-2480
	*Sales					
Saratoga Honda	3402 Rt 9	Saratoga Springs	NY	12866	**888-658-2303**	
Schukei Chevrolet Inc	721 S Monroe	Mason City	IA	50401	**866-918-6497**	641-423-5402
Scott Family of Dealerships	3333 Lehigh St	Allentown	PA	18103	**800-274-1039**	
Sears Imported Autos Inc	13500 Wayzata Blvd	Minnetonka	MN	55305	**800-493-1720***	952-546-5301
	*Sales					
Seneca Tank Inc	5585 NE 16th St	Des Moines	IA	50313	**800-362-2910**	515-262-5900
Shelly Automotive Group	*Irvine BMW* 9881 Research Dr	Irvine	CA	92618	**888-853-7429**	
Sheppard Motors	2300 W Seventh Ave	Eugene	OR	97402	**877-362-1865***	541-343-8811
	*Sales					
Sierra Volkswagen Inc	510 E Norris Dr	Ottawa	IL	61350	**877-854-2771**	866-374-5828
Silver Star Automotive Group	*Lotus of Thousand Oaks* 3601 Auto Mall Dr	Thousand Oaks	CA	91362	**800-472-5450**	
Simmons-rockwell Inc	784 County Rd 64	Elmira	NY	14903	**888-520-2213**	607-796-5555
Sisbarro Dealerships	425 W Boutz Rd	Las Cruces	NM	88005	**800-215-8021**	575-524-7707
Sitton Buick GMC	2640 Laurens Rd	Greenville	SC	29607	**888-484-8009**	864-990-3600
Skybooks Inc	1310 Tradeport Dr	Jacksonville	FL	32218	**866-929-8700**	904-741-8700
Skycom Avionics Inc	2441 Aviation Rd	Waukesha	WI	53188	**800-443-4490**	262-521-8180
Smith Motors Inc of Hammond	6405 Indianapolis Blvd	Hammond	IN	46320	**877-392-2689**	219-845-4000
Smoky Mountain Truck Ctr LLC	841 Eastern Star Rd	Kingsport	TN	37663	**800-451-1508**	
Snowfire	100 Us Rt 2	Waterbury	VT	05676	**800-287-5606**	802-244-5606
Snyder Chevrolet	524 N Perry St	Napoleon	OH	43545	**800-569-3957**	567-341-4132
Sommer's Automotive	7211 W Meq	Mequon	WI	53092	**888-494-4193**	262-242-0100
South Charlotte Nissan	9215 S Blvd	Charlotte	NC	28273	**888-411-1423**	704-552-9191
South Tacoma Honda	7802 S Tacoma Way	Tacoma	WA	98409	**888-497-2416**	253-472-2300
Southfield Dodge Chrysler Jeep Ram	28100 Telegraph Rd	Southfield	MI	48034	**888-388-0451***	248-354-2950
	*Sales					
Southwick Inc	2400 Shattuck Ave	Berkeley	CA	94704	**888-686-0046**	510-845-2530
Specialty Hearse & Ambulance Sale Corp	60 Engineers Ln E	Farmingdale	NY	11735	**800-349-6102***	516-349-7700
	*General					
Standard Motors Ltd	44 Second Ave NW	Swift Current	SK	S9H3V6	**866-334-8985**	
Steele Truck Ctr Inc	2150 Rockfill Rd	Fort Myers	FL	33916	**888-806-4839**	239-334-7300
Steve Barry Buick Inc	16000 Detroit Ave	Lakewood	OH	44107	**866-327-5818**	216-920-0866
Steve Millen Sportparts Inc	3176 Airway Ave	Costa Mesa	CA	92626	**866-250-5542**	714-540-5566
Stevens Creek Mitsubishi	3209 Stevens Creek Blvd	San Jose	CA	95117	**888-479-0842**	408-264-9999
Suburban Collection	1810 Maplelawn Dr	Troy	MI	48084	**877-471-7100**	
Susan Schein Automotive	3171 Pelham Pkwy	Pelham	AL	35124	**800-845-1578**	205-664-1491
Sutton Ford Inc	21315 S Central Ave	Matteson	IL	60443	**866-232-2966**	708-720-8115
T G H Aviation	2389 Rickenbacker Way	Auburn	CA	95602	**800-843-4976**	530-823-6204
Team Volkswagen of Hayward Corp	25115 Mission Blvd	Hayward	CA	94544	**866-308-2825**	
Terry Thompson Chevrolet Olds	1402 Us Hwy 98	Daphne	AL	36526	**800-287-9309**	251-626-0631
Tom Bensen Chevrolet Co Inc	9400 San Pedro	San Antonio	TX	78216	**866-635-6971**	210-341-3311
Toms Truck Ctr Inc	1008 E Fourth St PO Box 88	Santa Ana	CA	92701	**800-638-1015**	714-338-6060
Toyota Sunnyvale	898 W El Camino Real	Sunnyvale	CA	94087	**888-210-0091**	408-245-6640
Transwest	20770 I-76 Frontage Rd	Brighton	CO	80603	**800-289-3161**	303-289-3161
Tri County Ford Mercury Inc	4032 Commerce Pkwy PO Box 425	Buckner	KY	40010	**800-945-2520**	502-241-7333
Tropical Ford	9900 S Orange Blossom Trial	Orlando	FL	32837	**800-790-7137***	407-851-3800
	*Sales					
Truck Sales & Service Inc	PO Box 262	Midvale	OH	44653	**800-282-6100**	740-922-3412
Truck Works Inc	1815 S 39th Ave	Phoenix	AZ	85009	**877-894-8757**	602-233-3713
Tuffy Security Products Inc	25733 Rd H	Cortez	CO	81321	**800-348-8339**	970-564-1762
Utility/Keystone Trailer Sales Inc	1976 Auction Rd	Manheim	PA	17545	**888-327-4236**	717-653-9444
V&H Inc	1505 S Central Ave	Marshfield	WI	54449	**800-826-2308**	715-486-8800
Valley Freightliner Inc	277 Stewart Rd SW	Pacific	WA	98047	**800-523-8014**	
Van Bortel Subaru	6327 SR- 96	Victor	NY	14564	**888-902-7961**	585-924-5230
Van Boxtel Rv & Auto LLC	1956 Bond St	Green Bay	WI	54303	**888-831-5267**	920-497-3072
Vin Devers Inc	5570 Monroe St	Sylvania	OH	43560	**888-847-9535**	419-885-5111
Vision Ford Lincoln Hyundai	1500 S White Sands Blvd	Alamogordo	NM	88310	**866-932-2441**	
Visionaire Inc	1502 109th St	Grand Prairie	TX	75050	**866-838-2810**	972-647-1056
Vista Auto	21501 Ventura Blvd	Woodland Hills	CA	91364	**888-887-6530**	888-313-4252
Wallingford Buick GMC	1122 Old N Colony Rd	Wallingford	CT	06492	**866-582-4487***	
	*Cust Svc					
West-Herr Automotive Group Inc	3448 McKinley Pkwy	Blasdell	NY	14219	**800-643-2112**	716-649-5640
Westchester Toyota Service	75 Vredenburgh Ave	Yonkers	NY	10704	**866-232-7662**	914-968-6500

	City	State	Zip	Toll-Free	Phone
Western Bus Sales Inc 30355 SE Hwy 212	Boring	OR	97009	**800-258-2473**	503-905-0002
Western Slope Auto Co 2264 Hwy 6 & 50	Grand Junction	CO	81505	**888-461-3493**	970-243-0843
Westman Freightliner Inc 2200 Fourth Ave Mankato PO Box 699	Mankato	MN	56001	**866-576-6914**	507-625-4118
Westway Ford 801 W Airport Fwy	Irving	TX	75062	**844-877-9037**	
Whitaker Buick Co 131 19th St SW	Forest Lake	MN	55025	**877-324-8885**	651-674-3931
White Plains Honda 344 Central Ave	White Plains	NY	10606	**877-553-9292**	914-948-3305
Wiers International Trucks Inc 2111 Jim Neu Dr	Plymouth	IN	46563	**888-889-4377**	574-936-4076
Wilde Automotive Management of Wisc Onsin Inc 1710 A Hwy 164	Waukesha	WI	53186	**888-379-5817**	262-513-2770
Willey Honda 2215 S 500 W *Sales	Bountiful	UT	84010	**888-431-4490***	
Williams Nationalease Ltd 400 W Northtown Rd	Normal	IL	61761	**800-779-8785**	309-452-1110
Winslow BMW 730 N Cir Dr	Colorado Springs	CO	80909	**877-367-7357**	719-473-1373
Witt Lincoln 588 Camino Del Rio N	San Diego	CA	92108	**877-937-3301**	619-358-5000
WMK Inc 810 Moe Dr	Akron	OH	44310	**877-275-4912**	330-633-1118
York Ford Inc 1481 Bwy	Saugus	MA	01906	**888-705-6229**	781-231-1945
Zimmerman Auto Center 4001 First Ave	Cedar Rapids	IA	52402	**855-877-4223**	319-313-5086

AUTOMOBILE LEASING

SEE Credit & Financing - Consumer ; Credit & Financing - Commercial ; Fleet Leasing & Management

57 AUTOMOBILE SALES & RELATED SERVICES - ONLINE

SEE ALSO Automobile Dealers & Groups

	City	State	Zip	Toll-Free	Phone
Autobytel Inc 18872 MacArthur Blvd *NASDAQ: ABTL*	Irvine	CA	92612	**888-422-8999**	949-225-4500
Autofusion Corp 6215 Ferris Sq Ste 200	San Diego	CA	92121	**800-410-7354**	858-270-9444
Automobile Consumer Services Inc 6249 Stewart Rd	Cincinnati	OH	45227	**800-223-4882**	513-527-7700
Automotive Information Ctr 18872 MacArthur Blvd	Irvine	CA	92612	**888-422-8999**	
Cars.com 175 W Jackson Blvd Ste 800	Chicago	IL	60604	**888-246-6298**	312-601-5000
CarsDirect.com Inc 909 N Sepulveda Blvd 11th Fl *Cust Svc	El Segundo	CA	90245	**888-227-7347***	
Kelley Blue Book Company Inc 195 Technology Dr	Irvine	CA	92623	**800-258-3266**	949-770-7704
Williamson Cadillac Co 7815 SW 104th St	Miami	FL	33156	**877-228-6093**	305-670-7100

58 AUTOMOBILES - MFR

SEE ALSO Snowmobiles ; Motor Vehicles - Commercial & Special Purpose ; Motorcycles & Motorcycle Parts & Accessories ; All-Terrain Vehicles

	City	State	Zip	Toll-Free	Phone
American Honda Motor Company Inc 1919 Torrance Blvd	Torrance	CA	90501	**800-999-1009**	310-783-3170
Audi of America 3800 Hamlin Rd	Auburn Hills	MI	48326	**888-237-2834**	
BMW of North America LLC 300 Chestnut Ridge Rd	Woodcliff Lake	NJ	07677	**800-831-1117**	201-307-4000
Braun Industries Inc 1170 Production Dr	Van Wert	OH	45891	**877-344-9990**	
Chrysler Group LLC 1000 Chrysler Dr *Cust Svc	Auburn Hills	MI	48326	**800-423-6343***	
Collins Bus Corp PO Box 2946	Hutchinson	KS	67504	**800-533-1850**	620-662-9000
DaimlerChrysler Corp Jeep Div PO Box 21-8004 *Cust Svc	Auburn Hills	MI	48321	**800-992-1997***	
Eldorado National Inc 1655 Wall St	Salina	KS	67401	**800-850-1287**	909-591-9557
Ferrara Fire Apparatus Inc PO Box 249	Holden	LA	70744	**800-443-9006**	225-567-7100
Ford Motor Co PO Box 6248 *NYSE: F*	Dearborn	MI	48126	**800-392-3673**	313-845-8540
Freightliner Specialty Vehicles Inc 2300 S 13th St	Clinton	OK	73601	**800-358-7624**	580-323-4100
General Motors Corp Buick Motor Div 300 Renaissance Ctr PO Box 33136 *Cust Svc	Detroit	MI	48265	**800-521-7300***	
Glaval Bus 914 County Rd 1	Elkhart	IN	46514	**800-445-2825**	574-262-2212
Horton Emergency Vehicles 3800 McDowell Rd	Grove City	OH	43123	**800-282-5113**	614-539-8181
Hyundai Motor America 10550 Talbert Ave *Cust Svc	Fountain Valley	CA	92708	**800-633-5151***	714-965-3000
Land Rover North America Inc 555 MacArthur Blvd	Mahwah	NJ	07430	**800-637-6837**	
Lincoln-Mercury Co PO Box 6128	Dearborn	MI	48121	**800-521-4140**	
Lotus Cars USA Inc 2402 Tech Ctr Pkwy NE *Cust Svc	Lawrenceville	GA	30043	**800-245-6887***	770-476-6540
Mazda North American Operations 7755 Irvine Ctr Dr PO Box 19734 *Cust Svc	Irvine	CA	92618	**800-222-5500***	949-727-1990
Mercedes-Benz U.S. International Inc 1 Mercedes Dr	Vance	AL	35490	**888-286-8762**	205-507-2252
Mercedes-Benz USA LLC 1 Mercedes Dr *Cust Svc	Montvale	NJ	07645	**800-367-6372***	201-573-0600
Nissan Canada Inc (NCI) 5290 Orbitor Dr	Mississauga	ON	L4W4Z5	**800-387-0122**	
Nissan Motor Corp USA Infiniti Div 1 Nissan Way PO Box 685003	Franklin	TN	37067	**800-662-6200**	
Nissan North America Inc 25 Vantage way	Nashville	TN	37228	**800-647-7261**	
Porsche Cars North America Inc 980 Hammond Dr Ste 1000	Atlanta	GA	30328	**800-505-1041**	770-290-3500
Saleen Automotive Inc 2735 Wardlow Rd	Corona	CA	92882	**800-888-8945**	
Subaru of America Inc 2235 Marlton Pike W	Cherry Hill	NJ	08002	**800-782-2783**	856-488-8500
Tesla Motors Inc 3500 Deer Creek Rd	Palo Alto	CA	94304	**888-518-3752**	650-681-5000
Toyota Canada Inc 1 Toyota Pl *Cust Svc	Scarborough	ON	M1H1H9	**888-869-6828***	416-438-6320
Toyota Motor Sales USA Inc 19001 S Western Ave *Cust Svc	Torrance	CA	90501	**800-331-4331***	310-468-4000
Toyota Motor Sales USA Inc Lexus Div 19001 S Western Ave *Cust Svc	Torrance	CA	90501	**800-255-3987***	
Volkswagen Canada Inc 777 Bayly St W	Ajax	ON	L1S7G7	**800-822-8987**	905-428-6700
Volkswagen of America Inc 3800 Hamlin Rd	Auburn Hills	MI	48326	**800-822-8987**	
Volvo Cars of North America 1 Volvo Dr *Cust Svc	Rockleigh	NJ	07647	**800-458-1552***	201-768-7300

59 AUTOMOTIVE PARTS & SUPPLIES - MFR

SEE ALSO Carburetors, Pistons, Piston Rings, Valves ; Electrical Equipment for Internal Combustion Engines ; Engines & Turbines ; Gaskets, Packing, Sealing Devices ; Hose & Belting - Rubber or Plastics ; Motors (Electric) & Generators

	City	State	Zip	Toll-Free	Phone
Accuride Corp 7140 Office Cir *NYSE: ACW* ■ *Cust Svc	Evansville	IN	47715	**800-823-8332***	812-962-5000
Aer Mfg Inc PO Box 979	Carrollton	TX	75011	**800-753-5237**	972-417-2582
Airtex Products 407 W Main St	Fairfield	IL	62837	**800-880-3056**	618-842-2111
Alma Products Co 2000 Michigan Ave	Alma	MI	48801	**877-427-2624**	989-463-1151
AMBAC International Inc 910 Spears Creek Ct	Elgin	SC	29045	**800-628-6894**	803-735-1400
AP Exhaust Technologies Inc 300 Dixie Trial	Goldsboro	NC	27530	**800-277-2787**	919-580-2000
Atwood Mobile Products 1120 N Main St	Elkhart	IN	46514	**800-546-8759**	574-264-2131
Autocam Corp 4070 E Paris Ave	Kentwood	MI	49512	**800-747-6978**	616-698-0707
Baldwin Filters 4400 Hwy 30	Kearney	NE	68847	**800-822-5394**	
Beach Manufacturing Co PO Box 129	Donnelsville	OH	45319	**800-543-5942**	937-882-6372
Borla Performance Industries Inc 500 Borla Dr	Johnson City	TN	37604	**877-462-6752**	423-979-4000
Bushwacker Inc 6710 N Catlin Ave	Portland	OR	97203	**800-234-8920**	503-283-4335
Cardone Industries Inc 5501 Whitaker Ave *Cust Svc	Philadelphia	PA	19124	**800-777-4780***	215-912-3000
Carlisle Cos Inc 13925 Ballantyne Corporate Pl Ste 400 *NYSE: CSL*	Charlotte	NC	28277	**800-248-5995**	704-501-1100
Carlisle Industrial Brake 1031 E Hillside Dr	Bloomington	IN	47401	**800-873-6361**	812-336-3811
Clarcor Inc 840 Crescent Ctr Dr Ste 600 *NYSE: CLC*	Franklin	TN	37067	**800-252-7267**	615-771-3100
Competition Cams Inc 3406 Democrat Rd	Memphis	TN	38118	**800-999-0853**	901-795-2400
Consolidated Metco Inc 13940 N Rivergate Blvd *Sales	Portland	OR	97203	**800-547-9473***	
Cummins Filtration 2931 Elm Hill Pike	Nashville	TN	37214	**800-777-7064**	615-367-0040
Cummins Inc 500 Jackson St PO Box 3005 *NYSE: CMI*	Columbus	IN	47201	**800-343-7357**	812-377-5000
CWC Textron 1085 W Sherman Blvd	Muskegon	MI	49441	**800-999-0853**	231-733-1331
DACCO Transmission Parts 741 Dacco Dr PO Box 2789 *Cust Svc	Cookeville	TN	38502	**866-645-1452***	931-528-7581
Danaher Corp 2200 Pennsylvania Ave NW Ste 800 *NYSE: DHR*	Washington	DC	20037	**800-833-9200**	202-828-0850
Davco Technology LLC 1600 Woodland Dr PO Box 487	Saline	MI	48176	**800-328-2611**	734-429-5665
Dayton Parts LLC 3500 Industrial Rd PO Box 5795 *Cust Svc	Harrisburg	PA	17110	**800-225-2159***	717-255-8500
Decoma International Inc *Magna Exteriors & Interiors* 50 Casmir Ct	Concord	ON	L4K4J5	**888-348-2398**	905-669-2888
Dexter Axle 2900 Industrial Pkwy	Elkhart	IN	46516	**800-522-7291**	574-295-7888

Classified Section

Company	Address	City	State	ZIP	Toll-Free	Phone
Dorman Products Inc	3400 E Walnut St *NASDAQ: DORM*	Colmar	PA	18915	**800-523-2492**	215-997-1800
Edelbrock Corp	2700 California St	Torrance	CA	90503	**800-739-3737**	310-781-2222
Evercoat	6600 Cornell Rd	Cincinnati	OH	45242	**800-729-7600**	513-489-7600
Federal-Mogul Corp	27300 W 11 Mile Rd *NASDAQ: FDML* ■ *Cust Svc	Southfield	MI	48034	**800-325-8886***	248-354-7700
Firestone Industrial Products Co	250 W 96th St	Indianapolis	IN	46260	**800-888-0650**	317-818-8600
Flex-N-Gate Corp	1306 E University Ave	Urbana	IL	61802	**800-398-1496**	217-278-2600
Fontaine Fifth Wheel	7574 Commerce Cir	Trussville	AL	35173	**800-874-9780**	205-661-4900
Fontaine Truck Equipment Co	7574 Commerce Cir	Trussville	AL	35173	**800-874-9780**	205-661-4900
Griffin Thermal Products	100 Hurricane Creek Rd	Piedmont	SC	29673	**800-722-3723**	864-845-5000
Grote Industries Inc	2600 Lanier Dr	Madison	IN	47250	**800-628-0809**	812-273-2121
Gunite Corp	302 Peoples Ave	Rockford	IL	61104	**800-677-3786**	815-964-3301
Hastings Manufacturing Co	325 N Hanover St	Hastings	MI	49058	**800-776-1088**	269-945-2491
Hayden Automotive	1801 Waters Ridge Dr	Lewisville	TX	75057	**888-505-4567**	
Hendrickson International	800 S Frontage Rd	Woodridge	IL	60517	**855-743-3733**	630-910-2800
Hennessy Industries Inc	1601 JP Hennesey Dr	La Vergne	TN	37086	**800-688-6359**	855-876-3864
Holley Performance Products Inc	1801 Russellville Rd *Sales	Bowling Green	KY	42101	**800-638-0032***	270-782-2900
Hopkins Manufacturing Corp	428 Peyton St	Emporia	KS	66801	**800-524-1458**	620-342-7320
Hutchens Industries Inc	215 N Patterson Ave	Springfield	MO	65802	**800-654-8824**	417-862-5012
HWH Corp	2096 Moscow Rd	Moscow	IA	52760	**800-321-3494**	563-724-3396
Indian Head Industries Inc	8530 Cliff Cameron Dr	Charlotte	NC	28269	**800-527-1534**	704-547-7411
JASPER Engines & Transmissions	815 Wernsing Rd PO Box 650	Jasper	IN	47547	**800-827-7455**	812-482-1041
John Bean Co	309 Exchange Ave	Conway	AR	72032	**800-225-5786**	501-450-1500
Lund International Holdings Inc	4325 Hamilton Mill Rd Ste 400	Buford	GA	30518	**800-241-7219**	678-804-3912
MacLean-Fogg Co	1000 Allanson Rd	Mundelein	IL	60060	**800-323-4536**	847-566-0010
MAHLE Industries Inc	2020 Sanford St	Muskegon	MI	49444	**888-255-1942**	231-722-1300
Marmon-Herrington Co	13001 Magisterial Dr	Louisville	KY	40223	**800-227-0727**	502-253-0277
Neapco Inc	6735 Haggerty Rd PO Box 399	Belleville	MI	48111	**800-821-2374**	734-447-1380
P. T. M. Corp	6560 Bethuy Rd	Fair Haven	MI	48023	**800-486-2212**	586-725-2211
Penda Corp	PO Box 449	Portage	WI	53901	**800-356-7704**	
Perfection Clutch Co	100 Perfection Way	Timmonsville	SC	29161	**800-258-8312**	843-326-5544
Phillips & Temro Industries	9700 W 74th St	Eden Prairie	MN	55344	**800-328-6108**	952-941-9700
Raybestos Powertrain LLC	711 Tech Dr	Crawfordsville	IN	47933	**800-729-7763**	
Remy International Inc	600 Corp Dr *NYSE: REMY*	Pendleton	IN	46064	**800-372-3555**	765-778-6499
Ridewell Corp	PO Box 4586	Springfield	MO	65808	**877-434-8088**	417-833-4565
Roush Manufacturing Inc	12068 Market St	Livonia	MI	48150	**800-215-9658**	734-779-7006
SmarTire Systems Inc	6900 Graybar Rd Ste 2110	Richmond	BC	V3W0A5	**800-247-2725**	604-276-9884
Stanadyne Corp	92 Deerfield Rd	Windsor	CT	06095	**888-336-3473**	860-525-0821
Stemco LP	300 Industrial Blvd PO Box 1989	Longview	TX	75606	**800-527-8492**	903-758-9981
Superior Industries International Inc	7800 Woodley Ave *NYSE: SUP*	Van Nuys	CA	91406	**800-322-2885**	818-781-4973
Teleflex Medical	2917 Weck Dr PO Box 12600	Research Triangle Park	NC	27709	**866-246-6990**	919-544-8000
TeleflexGFI Control Systems LP	100 Hollinger Crescent	Kitchener	ON	N2K2Z3	**800-667-4275**	519-576-4270
Tenneco Inc	500 N Field Dr *NYSE: TEN*	Lake Forest	IL	60045	**866-839-3259**	847-482-5000
Titan International Inc	2701 Spruce St *NYSE: TWI*	Quincy	IL	62301	**800-872-2327**	217-228-6011
Titan Wheel Corp	2701 Spruce St	Quincy	IL	62301	**800-872-2327**	217-228-6011
Trelleborg Automotive Americas	400 Aylworth Ave	South Haven	MI	49090	**800-635-9331**	269-637-2116
Triangle Suspension Systems Inc	47 E Maloney Rd	Du Bois	PA	15801	**800-458-6077**	814-375-7211
Universal Manufacturing Co	405 Diagonal St PO Box 190 *OTC: UFMG*	Algona	IA	50511	**800-651-7445**	515-295-3557
US Chemical & Plastics	600 Nova Dr SE	Massillon	OH	44646	**800-321-0672**	330-830-6000
Velvac Inc	2405 S Calhoun Rd	New Berlin	WI	53151	**800-783-8871**	262-786-0700
Webb Wheel Products Inc	2310 Industrial Dr SW	Cullman	AL	35055	**800-633-3256**	256-739-6660

60 AUTOMOTIVE PARTS & SUPPLIES - WHOL

Company	Address	City	State	ZIP	Toll-Free	Phone
AA Wheel & Truck Supply Inc	717 E 16th Ave	Kansas City	MO	64116	**800-486-4335**	816-221-9556
Ace Tool Co	7337 Bryan Dairy Rd	Largo	FL	33777	**800-777-5910**	727-544-4331
Advantage Truck Accessories Inc	6535 Jacson Rd	Ann Arbor	MI	48103	**800-773-3110**	
Advantech International Inc	PO Box 6739	Somerset	NJ	08875	**800-322-6150**	
Allomatic Products Co	102 Jericho Tpke Ste 104 Floral Pk	Floral Park	NY	11001	**800-568-0330**	516-775-0330
Automotive Distributors Company Inc	2981 Morse Rd	Columbus	OH	43231	**800-421-5556**	
Automotive Parts Headquarters	2959 Clearwater Rd	Saint Cloud	MN	56301	**800-247-0339**	320-252-5411
Bell Industries Inc Recreational Products Group	580 Yankee Doodle Rd	Eagan	MN	55121	**800-866-5017**	651-203-2300
Bendix Commercial Vehicle Systems LLC	901 Cleveland St	Elyria	OH	44035	**800-247-2725**	440-329-9000
Carolina Rim & Wheel Co	1308 Upper Asbury Ave	Charlotte	NC	28206	**800-247-4337**	704-334-7276
Carolinas Auto Supply House Inc	2135 Tipton Dr	Charlotte	NC	28206	**800-438-4070**	704-334-4646
Carquest Corp	2635 E Millbrook Rd	Raleigh	NC	27604	**800-876-1291**	919-573-3000
Champion Power Equipment Inc	10006 Santa Fe Springs Rd	Santa Fe Springs	CA	90670	**877-338-0999**	562-236-9422
Coast Distribution System	350 Woodview Ave *NYSE: CRV*	Morgan Hill	CA	95037	**800-495-5858**	408-782-6686
Custom Chrome Inc	155 E Main Ave Ste 150	Morgan Hill	CA	95037	**800-729-3332**	408-778-0500
Dero Bike Racks Inc	504 Malcolm Ave SE Ste 100	Minneapolis	MN	55414	**888-337-6729**	612-359-0689
Drive Train Industries Inc	5555 Joliet St	Denver	CO	80239	**800-525-6177**	303-292-5176
Eagle Parts & Products Inc	1411 Marvin Griffin Rd	Augusta	GA	30906	**888-972-9911**	706-790-6687
Enginetech Inc	1205 W Crosby Rd	Carrollton	TX	75006	**800-869-8711**	972-245-0110
Flowers Auto Parts Co	935 Hwy 70 SE *Cust Svc	Hickory	NC	28602	**800-538-6272***	828-322-5414
General Truck Parts & Equipment Co	3835 W 42nd St	Chicago	IL	60632	**800-621-3914**	773-247-6900
GK Industries Ltd	50 Precidio Ct	Brampton	ON	L6S6E3	**800-463-8889**	905-799-1972
Harmonic Drive LLC	247 Lynnfield St	Peabody	MA	01960	**800-921-3332**	978-532-1800
Hedahls Inc	100 East Broadway	Bismarck	ND	58502	**800-433-2457**	701-223-8393
Henderson Wheel & Warehouse Supply	1825 South 300 West	Salt Lake City	UT	84115	**800-748-5111**	801-486-2073
Instrument Sales & Service Inc	16427 NE Airport Way	Portland	OR	97230	**800-333-7976**	503-239-0754
InterAmerican Motor Corp (IMC)	8901 Canoga Ave	Canoga Park	CA	91304	**800-874-8925**	818-678-1200
Interstate Batteries	12770 Merit Dr Ste 400	Dallas	TX	75251	**800-541-8419**	972-991-1444
JEGS Performance Auto Parts	101 Jeg'S Pl	Delaware	OH	43015	**800-345-4545**	614-294-5050
Johnson Industries	5944 Peachtree Corners E *Orders	Norcross	GA	30071	**800-922-8111***	770-441-1128
Kansas City Peterbilt Inc	8915 Woodend Rd	Kansas City	KS	66111	**800-489-1122**	913-441-2888
Keystone Automotive Operations Inc	44 Tunkhannock Ave	Exeter	PA	18643	**800-521-9999**	570-655-4514
L & M Radiator Inc	1414 E 37th St	Hibbing	MN	55746	**800-346-3500**	218-263-8993
Lakeshirts Inc	750 Randolph Rd	Detroit Lakes	MN	56501	**800-627-2780**	218-847-2171
LKQ Corp	500 W Madison St Ste 2800 *NASDAQ: LKQX*	Chicago	IL	60661	**877-557-2677**	312-621-1950
London Machinery Inc	15790 Robin's Hill Rd	London	ON	N5V0A4	**800-265-1098**	519-963-2500
McGard LLC	3875 California Rd	Orchard Park	NY	14127	**800-444-5847**	716-662-8980
Mid America Motorworks	17082 N Us Hwy 45 PO Box 1368	Effingham	IL	62401	**866-350-4543**	217-540-4200
Midwest Truck & Auto Parts Inc	1001 W Exchange	Chicago	IL	60609	**800-934-2727**	773-247-3400
Mighty Distributing System of America Inc	650 Engineering Dr	Norcross	GA	30092	**800-829-3900**	770-448-3900
Mile Marker International Inc	2121 BLOUNT Rd	Pompano Beach	FL	33069	**800-886-8647**	
Mutual Wheel Co Inc	2345 Fourth Ave	Moline	IL	61265	**800-798-6926**	309-757-1200
N.b.c. Truck Equipment Inc	28130 Groesbeck Hwy	Roseville	MI	48066	**800-778-8207**	586-774-4900
National Automotive Parts Assn (NAPA)	2999 Circle 75 Pkwy	Atlanta	GA	30339	**800-538-6272**	770-953-1700
Northeast Battery & Alternator Inc	240 Washington St	Auburn	MA	01501	**800-441-8824**	508-832-2700
Northern Factory Sales Inc	PO Box 660	Willmar	MN	56201	**800-328-8900**	320-235-2288
NTP Distribution Inc	27150 SW Kinsman Rd	Wilsonville	OR	97070	**800-242-6987**	503-570-0171
O.E.M. Systems LLC	PO Box 473	Okarche	OK	73762	**800-810-7252**	405-263-7488
Parts Central Inc	3243 Whitfield St	Macon	GA	31204	**800-226-9396**	478-745-0878

Name	Address	City	State	Zip	Toll-Free	Phone
Plaza Fleet Parts Inc	1520 S Broadway	Saint Louis	MO	63104	**800-325-7618**	314-231-5047
Regional International Corp	1007 Lehigh Stn Rd	Henrietta	NY	14467	**800-836-0409**	585-359-2011
Six Robblees' Inc	11010 Tukwila International Blvd	Tukwila	WA	98168	**800-275-7499**	206-767-7970
Six States Distributors Inc	247 West 1700 South *Cust Svc	Salt Lake City	UT	84115	**800-453-5703***	801-488-4666
Stewart Title Insurance Co	300 E 42nd St 10th Fl	New York	NY	10017	**800-913-4170**	713-625-8100
Vander Haag's Inc	3809 Fourth Ave W	Spencer	IA	51301	**888-940-5030**	712-262-7000
WAIglobal	411 Eagleview Blvd Ste 100	Exton	PA	19341	**800-877-3340**	484-875-6600
Western Truck Parts & Equip Co	3707 Airport Way S	Seattle	WA	98134	**800-255-7383**	206-624-7383
Westin Automotive Products Inc	5200 N Irwindale Ave Ste 220	Irwindale	CA	91706	**800-345-8476**	626-960-6762
WORLDPAC Inc	37137 Hickory St	Newark	CA	94560	**800-888-9982**	510-742-8900
Wurth USA Inc	93 Grant St	Ramsey	NJ	07446	**800-987-8487**	201-825-2710

61 AUTOMOTIVE SERVICES

SEE ALSO Gas Stations

Name	Address	City	State	Zip	Toll-Free	Phone
Boyd Group Inc, The	3570 Portage Ave	Winnipeg	MB	R3K0Z8	**800-385-5451**	204-895-1244

61-1 Appearance Care - Automotive

Name	Address	City	State	Zip	Toll-Free	Phone
Autobell Car Wash Inc	1521 E Third St	Charlotte	NC	28204	**800-582-8096**	704-527-9274
Color-Glo International	7111 Ohms Ln	Minneapolis	MN	55439	**800-333-8523**	952-835-1338
Creative Colors International Inc	19015 S Jodi Rd Ste E	Mokena	IL	60448	**800-933-2656**	708-478-1437
Dr Vinyl & Assoc Ltd	1350 SE Hamblen Rd *General	Lees Summit	MO	64081	**800-531-6600***	816-525-6060
Fleetwash Inc	PO Box 1577	West Caldwell	NJ	07007	**800-847-3735**	
Mister Car Wash	3101 E Speedway Blvd *Cust Svc	Tucson	AZ	85718	**866-254-3229***	520-615-4000
Precision Auto Care Inc	748 Miller Dr SE *OTC: PACI*	Leesburg	VA	20175	**866-944-8863**	
Vizza Wash Services LLC	2208 NW Loop 410 *Cust Svc	San Antonio	TX	78230	**866-493-8822***	210-493-8822
Ziebart International Corp	1290 E Maple Rd	Troy	MI	48083	**800-877-1312**	248-588-4100

61-2 Glass Replacement - Automotive

Name	Address	City	State	Zip	Toll-Free	Phone
All Star Glass Co Inc	1845 Morena Blvd	San Diego	CA	92110	**800-225-4184**	619-275-3343
City Auto Glass Inc	116 S Concord Exchange	South Saint Paul	MN	55075	**888-552-4272**	651-552-1000
Martin Glass Co	25 Ctr Plz	Belleville	IL	62220	**800-325-1946**	618-277-1946
Safelite Group Inc	2400 Farmers Dr	Columbus	OH	43235	**877-664-8931**	
SuperGlass Windshield Repair Inc	6101 Chancellor Dr Ste 200	Orlando	FL	32809	**866-557-7497**	407-240-1920

61-3 Mufflers & Exhaust Systems Repair - Automotive

Name	Address	City	State	Zip	Toll-Free	Phone
Midas International Corp	1300 Arlington Heights Rd	Itasca	IL	60143	**800-621-8545**	630-438-3000
Monro Muffler Brake Inc	200 Holleder Pkwy *NASDAQ: MNRO*	Rochester	NY	14615	**800-876-6676**	585-647-6400

61-4 Paint & Body Work - Automotive

Name	Address	City	State	Zip	Toll-Free	Phone
CARSTAR Quality Collision Service	8400 W 110th St Ste 200 *Cust Svc	Overland Park	KS	66210	**800-227-7827***	913-451-1294
Colors on Parade	125 Daytona St PO Box 50940 *Cust Svc	Conway	SC	29526	**866-756-4207***	843-347-8818
Dent Clinic	711 48th Ave SE	Calgary	AB	T2G2A7	**888-722-3368**	403-255-3111
Dent Wizard International	4710 Earth City Expway	Bridgeton	MO	63044	**800-267-9369**	314-592-1800
Gerber Auto Collision & Glass Centers Inc	8250 Skokie Blvd	Skokie	IL	60077	**877-743-7237**	847-679-0510
Gerber Collision & Glass	44700 Enterprise Dr *General	Clinton Township	MI	48038	**877-743-7237***	586-954-3850
Maaco LLC	440 S Church St Ste 700	Charlotte	NC	28202	**800-523-1180**	704-377-8855
Mike Rose's Auto Body Inc	2260 Via de Marcardos	Concord	CA	94520	**855-340-1739**	925-689-1739
Service King Collision Repair Centers	808 S Central Expy	Richardson	TX	75080	**866-730-5464**	972-960-7595

61-5 Repair Service (General) - Automotive

Name	Address	City	State	Zip	Toll-Free	Phone
All Tune & Lube Brakes & More Inc	8334 Veteran's Hwy	Millersville	MD	21108	**877-978-1758**	410-987-1011
All Tune & Lube International Inc *ATL International Inc*	8334 Veterans Hwy *Cust Svc	Millersville	MD	21108	**877-978-1758***	410-987-1011
Basin Tire & Auto Inc	2700 E Main St	Farmington	NM	87402	**800-832-9832**	505-326-2231
Belle Tire Inc	1000 Enterprise Dr	Allen Park	MI	48101	**888-462-3553**	313-271-9400
Bergey's Inc	462 Harleysville Pike	Souderton	PA	18964	**800-237-4397**	215-723-6071
Bridgestone Americas Holding Inc	535 Marriott Dr *Cust Svc	Nashville	TN	37214	**877-201-2373***	615-937-1000
Evans Tire & Service Centers Inc	510 N Broadway	Escondido	CA	92025	**877-338-2678**	
Express Oil Change	1880 S Pk Dr	Hoover	AL	35244	**888-945-1771**	205-945-1771
Fyda Freightliner Youngstown Inc	5260 76th Dr	Youngstown	OH	44515	**800-837-3932**	330-797-0224
Grease Monkey International	7450 E Progress Pl	Greenwood Village	CO	80111	**800-822-7706**	303-308-1660
Hunter Engineering Co	11250 Hunter Dr	Bridgeton	MO	63044	**800-448-6848**	314-731-3020
Jack Williams Tire Co Inc	PO Box 3655	Scranton	PA	18505	**800-833-5051**	
Jiffy Lube	PO Box 4427	Houston	TX	77210	**800-344-6933**	
Jubitz Corp	33 NE Middlefield Rd	Portland	OR	97211	**800-523-0600**	503-283-1111
Kansas City Peterbilt Inc	8915 Woodend Rd	Kansas City	KS	66111	**800-489-1122**	913-441-2888
Merlin Corp	3815 E Main St	Saint Charles	IL	60174	**800-652-9910**	630-513-8200
Mr Tire Auto Service Centers Inc	200 Holleder Pkwy	Rochester	NY	14615	**800-876-6676**	
Parrish Tire Company Inc	5130 Indiana Ave	Winston-Salem	NC	27106	**800-849-8473**	336-767-0202
Plaza Tire Service	2075 Corporate Cr PO Box 2048	Cape Girardeau	MO	63702	**877-787-1691**	
Precision Auto Care Inc	748 Miller Dr SE *OTC: PACI*	Leesburg	VA	20175	**866-944-8863**	
Sullivan Tire Co Inc	PO Box 370	Rockland	MA	02370	**877-855-4826**	781-871-2299
Techni-Car Inc	450 Commerce Blvd	Oldsmar	FL	34677	**800-886-0022**	813-855-0022
Tire-Rama Inc	1429 Grand Ave	Billings	MT	59102	**800-828-1642**	406-245-4006
Tires Plus Total Car Care	2021 Sunnydale Blvd	Clearwater	FL	33765	**800-440-4167**	727-441-3727
Tom Stinnett Rv's	520 Marriott Dr	Clarksville	IN	47129	**800-583-5685**	812-282-7718
Tuffy Assoc Corp	7150 Granite Cir	Toledo	OH	43617	**800-228-8339**	419-865-6900
Wingfoot Commercial Tire Systems LLC	1000 S 21st St	Fort Smith	AR	72901	**800-643-7330**	479-788-6400

61-6 Transmission Repair - Automotive

Name	Address	City	State	Zip	Toll-Free	Phone
Lee Myles Auto Group	914 Fern Ave	Reading	PA	19607	**800-533-6953**	
Mr Transmission	9675 Yonge St 2nd Fl	Richmond Hill	ON	L4C1V7	**800-373-8432**	905-884-1511

61-7 Van Conversions

Name	Address	City	State	Zip	Toll-Free	Phone
Clock Mobility	6700 Clay Ave	Grand Rapids	MI	49548	**800-732-5625**	616-698-9400
Foley Inc	855 Centennial Ave	Piscataway	NJ	08854	**888-417-6464**	732-885-5555
Marathon Coach	91333 Coburg Industrial Way	Coburg	OR	97408	**800-234-9991**	541-343-9991
Monaco Coach Corp	1031 US 224 E	Decatur	IN	46733	**877-466-6226**	
Rollx Vans	6591 Hwy 13 W	Savage	MN	55378	**800-956-6668**	952-890-7851
Sherrod Vans Inc	3151 Industrial Blvd	Waycross	GA	31503	**800-824-6333**	
Sidewinder Conversions	44658 Yale Rd W	Chilliwack	BC	V2R0G5	**888-266-2299**	604-792-2082
Vantage Mobility International (VMI)	5202 S 28th Pl	Phoenix	AZ	85040	**800-348-8267**	602-243-2700
Waldoch Crafts Inc	13821 Lake Dr NE	Forest Lake	MN	55025	**800-328-9259**	651-464-3215

62 AVIATION - FIXED-BASE OPERATIONS

SEE ALSO Air Cargo Carriers ; Air Charter Services ; Aircraft Rental ; Aircraft Service & Repair

Name	Address	City	State	Zip	Toll-Free	Phone
Banyan Air Service	5360 NW 20th Terr	Fort Lauderdale	FL	33309	**800-200-2031**	954-491-3170
Belshire Environmental Services Inc	25971 Towne Centre Dr	Foothill Ranch	CA	92610	**800-995-8220**	949-460-5200
BMG Aviation Inc	984 S Kirby Rd	Bloomington	IN	47403	**888-457-3787**	812-825-7979

Company / Address	City	State	Zip	Toll-Free	Phone
Central Flying Service Inc 1501 Bond St	Little Rock	AR	72202	**800-888-5387**	501-375-3245
Columbia Air Services 175 Tower Ave Groton-New London Airport	Groton	CT	06340	**800-787-5001**	860-449-1400
Cook Aviation Inc 970 S Kirby Rd	Bloomington	IN	47403	**800-880-3499**	812-825-2392
Corporate Air LLC 15 Allegheny County Airport	West Mifflin	PA	15122	**888-429-5377**	412-469-6800
Crow Executive Air Inc 28331 Lemoyne Rd Toledo Metcalf Airport	Millbury	OH	43447	**800-972-2769**	419-838-6921
DB Aviation Inc 3550 N McAree Rd	Waukegan	IL	60087	**888-362-6738**	847-244-8504
Dulles Aviation Inc 10501 Observation Rd Manassas Regl Airport	Manassas	VA	20110	**888-835-9324**	703-361-2171
Eagle Aviation 2861 Aviation Way Columbia Metropolitan Airport	West Columbia	SC	29170	**800-849-3245**	803-822-5555
Edwards Jet Ctr 1691 Aviation Pl	Billings	MT	59105	**866-353-8245**	406-252-0508
Epps Aviation Inc 1 Aviation Way DeKalb Peachtree Airport	Atlanta	GA	30341	**800-241-6807**	770-458-9851
Felts Field Aviation Inc 6205 E Rutter Ave	Spokane	WA	99212	**800-676-5538**	509-535-9011
Flight Light Inc 2708 47th Ave	Sacramento	CA	95822	**800-806-3548**	916-394-2800
Grand Aire Express Inc 11777 W Airport Service Rd	Swanton	OH	43558	**800-704-7263**	
Hunt Pan Am Aviation Inc 505 Amelia Earhart Dr	Brownsville	TX	78521	**800-888-7524**	956-542-9111
Interstate Aviation 62 Johnson Ave	Plainville	CT	06062	**800-573-5519**	860-747-5519
Kansas City Aviation Ctr Inc 15325 S Pflumm Rd	Olathe	KS	66062	**800-720-5222**	913-782-0530
Keystone Aviation Services Inc 288 Christian St	Oxford	CT	06478	**866-436-2177**	203-264-6525
Landmark Aviation 3501 Aviation Ave *General	Sioux Falls	SD	57104	**800-888-1646***	408-286-3832
Lane Aviation Corp 4389 International Gateway	Columbus	OH	43219	**800-848-6263**	614-237-3747
Loyd's Aviation Services Inc 1601 Skyway Dr Ste 100 PO Box 80958	Bakersfield	CA	93308	**800-284-1334**	661-393-1334
Maine Instrument Flight Inc 215 Winthrop St	Augusta	ME	04330	**888-643-3597**	207-622-1211
McCall Aviation 300 Deinhard Ln	McCall	ID	83638	**800-992-6559**	208-634-7137
Mid-Ohio Aviation 6250 N Honeytown Rd	Smithville	OH	44677	**800-669-4243**	330-669-2671
Midwest Corporate Aviation 3512 N Webb Rd	Wichita	KS	67226	**800-435-9622**	316-636-9700
Million Air 4300 Westgrove Dr	Addison	TX	75001	**800-248-1602**	972-248-1600
Monterey Jet Center LLC 300 Skypark Dr	Monterey	CA	93940	**800-679-2992**	831-373-0100
Montgomery Aviation Corp 4525 Selma Hwy	Montgomery	AL	36108	**800-392-8044**	334-288-7334
National Jets 3495 SW Ninth Ave	Fort Lauderdale	FL	33315	**800-327-3710**	954-359-9900
Northeast Airmotive Inc 1011 Westbrook St	Portland	ME	04102	**877-354-7881**	207-774-6318
Richmor Aviation Inc 1142 Rt 9 H Columbia County Airport	Hudson	NY	12534	**800-331-6101**	518-828-9461
SheltAir Aviation Services Fort Lauderdale 4860 NE 12th Ave	Fort Lauderdale	FL	33334	**800-700-2210**	954-771-2210
Sky Bright 65 Aviation Dr	Gilford	NH	03249	**800-639-6012**	603-528-6818
Skyservice Airlines Inc 9785 Ryan Ave	Dorval	QC	H9P1A2	**888-985-1402**	514-636-3300
SkyTech Inc 550 Airport Rd	Rock Hill	SC	29732	**888-386-3596**	803-366-5108
Smyrna Air Ctr 300 Doug Warpoole Rd	Smyrna	TN	37167	**888-863-9996**	
Snohomish Flying Service Inc 9900 Airport Way	Snohomish	WA	98296	**800-827-1000**	360-568-1541
Southwest Airport Services Inc 11811 N Brantly Ave Ste 500	Houston	TX	77034	**888-362-6738**	281-484-6551
Space Coast Jet Ctr 7003 Challenger Ave	Titusville	FL	32780	**800-559-5473**	321-267-8355
St Paul Flight Ctr 270 Airport Rd Ste 5	Saint Paul	MN	55107	**800-368-0107**	651-227-8108
Stevens Aviation Inc 600 Delaware St	Greenville	SC	29605	**800-359-7838**	864-678-6000
Stuart Jet Ctr LLC 2501 Aviation Way	Stuart	FL	34996	**877-735-9538**	772-288-6700
United States Aviation 4141 N Memorial Dr	Tulsa	OK	74115	**800-897-5387**	918-836-7345
Vee Neal Aviation Inc 148 Aviation Ln Ste 109	Latrobe	PA	15650	**800-278-2710**	724-539-4533
Western Aircraft Inc 4300 S Kennedy St	Boise	ID	83705	**800-333-3442**	208-338-1800
Western Cardinal Inc 205 Durley Ave	Camarillo	CA	93010	**800-882-3018**	805-482-2586
Wilson Air Ctr 2930 Winchester Rd Memphis International Airport	Memphis	TN	38118	**800-464-2992**	901-345-2992
Wisconsin Aviation Inc 1741 River Dr	Watertown	WI	53094	**800-657-0761**	920-261-4567
Woodland Aviation Inc 25170 Aviation Ave	Davis	CA	95616	**800-442-1333**	530-759-6037

63 BABY PRODUCTS

SEE ALSO Toys, Games, Hobbies ; Children's & Infants' Clothing ; Household Furniture ; Paper Products - Sanitary

Company / Address	City	State	Zip	Toll-Free	Phone
Baby Jogger Co 8575 Magellan Pkwy Ste 1000	Richmond	VA	23227	**800-241-1848**	
Baby Trend Inc 1567 S Campus Ave *Cust Svc	Ontario	CA	91761	**800-328-7363***	
Baby's Dream Furniture Inc 411 Industrial Blvd	Buena Vista	GA	31803	**800-835-2742**	229-649-4404
Ball Bounce & Sport Inc/Hedstrom Plastics 1 Hedstrom Dr	Ashland	OH	44805	**800-765-9665**	419-289-9310
Britax Child Safety Inc 4140 Pleasant Rd	Fort Mill	NC	29708	**888-427-4829**	704-409-1700
Cardinal Gates 79 Amlajack Way	Newnan	GA	30265	**800-318-3380**	770-252-4200
Central Specialties Ltd 220 Exchange Dr	Crystal Lake	IL	60014	**800-873-4370**	815-459-6000
Delta Enterprises 114 W 26th St 8th Fl	New York	NY	10001	**800-377-3777**	212-736-7000
Dorel Juvenile Group USA 2525 State St	Columbus	IN	47201	**800-544-1108**	812-372-0141
Evenflo Company Inc 1801 Commerce Dr	Piqua	OH	45356	**800-233-5921**	
Fisher-Price Inc 636 Girard Ave	East Aurora	NY	14052	**800-432-5437**	716-687-3000
Gerber Products Co 445 State St	Fremont	MI	49412	**800-284-9488**	
Infantino LLC 4920 Carroll Canyon Rd Ste 200	San Diego	CA	92121	**800-840-4916**	
Kelty 6235 Lookout Rd	Boulder	CO	80301	**800-423-2320**	800-535-3589
KidCo Inc 1013 Technology Way	Libertyville	IL	60048	**800-553-5529**	847-549-8600
Kids II 555 N Pt Ctr E Ste 600	Alpharetta	GA	30022	**800-230-8190**	770-751-0442
Kolcraft Enterprises Inc 10832 NC Hwy 211 E *Cust Svc	Aberdeen	NC	28315	**800-453-7673***	910-944-9345
Little Tikes Co, The 2180 Barlow Rd *Cust Svc	Hudson	OH	44236	**800-321-0183***	
Manhattan Toy 300 First Ave N Ste 200	Minneapolis	MN	55401	**800-541-1345**	
Peg-Perego USA Inc 3625 Independence Dr *Cust Svc	Fort Wayne	IN	46808	**800-671-1701***	260-482-8191
Prince Lionheart Inc 2421 Westgate Rd	Santa Maria	CA	93455	**800-544-1132**	805-922-2250
REI 1700 45th St E	Sumner	WA	98352	**800-426-4840**	253-891-2500
Sassy Inc 2305 Breton Industrial Pk Dr	Kentwood	MI	49508	**800-323-6336**	616-243-0767
Step2 Co 10010 Aurora-Hudson Rd *Cust Svc	Streetsboro	OH	44241	**800-347-8372***	330-656-0440
Tough Traveler Ltd 1012 State St *Cust Svc	Schenectady	NY	12307	**800-468-6844***	518-377-8526
Triple Play Products LLC 904 Main St Ste 330	Hopkins	MN	55343	**800-829-1625**	952-938-0531

64 BAGS - PAPER

Company / Address	City	State	Zip	Toll-Free	Phone
Bancroft Bag Inc 425 Bancroft Blvd	West Monroe	LA	71292	**800-551-4950**	318-387-2550
Bemis Company Inc Paper Packaging Div 2445 Deer Pk Blvd	Omaha	NE	68105	**800-541-4303**	
Bonita Pioneer Packaging Products Inc 7333 SW Bonita Rd	Portland	OR	97224	**800-677-7725**	
Colonial Bag Co 1 Ocean Pond Ave PO Box 929	Lake Park	GA	31636	**800-392-4875**	229-559-8484
Hood Packaging Corp 25 Woodgreen Pl	Madison	MS	39110	**800-321-8115**	601-853-7260
Pacific Bag Inc 15300 Woodinville Redmond Rd NE Ste A	Woodinville	WA	98072	**800-562-2247**	425-455-1128
Ross & Wallace Paper Products Inc 204 Old Covington Hwy	Hammond	LA	70403	**800-854-2300**	
Stewart Sutherland Inc 5411 E 'V' Ave	Vicksburg	MI	49097	**800-253-1034**	269-649-0530
Weyerhaeuser Co 33663 Weyerhaeuser Way S *NYSE: WY*	Federal Way	WA	98003	**800-525-5440**	253-924-2345
Zenith Specialty Bag Company Inc 17625 E Railroad St PO Box 8445	City of Industry	CA	91748	**800-962-2247**	626-912-2481

65 BAGS - PLASTICS

Company / Address	City	State	Zip	Toll-Free	Phone
Admiral Packaging Inc 10 Admiral St	Providence	RI	02908	**800-556-6454**	401-274-7000
Ampac Packaging LLC 12025 Tricon Rd	Cincinnati	OH	45246	**800-543-7030**	513-671-1777
Apco Extruders Inc 180 National Rd *Orders	Edison	NJ	08817	**800-942-8725***	732-287-3000
Armand Manufacturing Inc 2399 Silver Wolf Dr	Henderson	NV	89011	**800-669-9811**	702-565-7500
Associated Bag Co 400 W Boden St	Milwaukee	WI	53207	**800-926-6100**	

Name / Address	City	State	ZIP	Toll-Free	Phone
Bag Makers Inc 6606 S Union Rd	Union	IL	60180	**800-458-9031**	
Clear View Bag Co 5 Burdick Dr	Albany	NY	12205	**800-458-7153**	518-458-7153
Clorox Co 1221 Broadway *NYSE: CLX* ■ *Cust Svc	Oakland	CA	94612	**800-424-9300***	510-271-7000
Colonial Bag Corp 205 E Fullerton Ave	Carol Stream	IL	60188	**800-445-7496**	630-690-3999
Enviro-Tote Inc 4 Cote Ln	Bedford	NH	03110	**800-868-3224**	603-647-7171
Heritage Bags 1648 Diplomat Dr	Carrollton	TX	75006	**800-527-2247**	
International Poly Bag Inc 990 Pk Ctr Dr Ste F & G	Vista	CA	92081	**800-976-5922**	760-598-2468
Mexico Plastics Company (Inc) 2000 W Blvd	Mexico	MO	65265	**800-325-0216**	
Pacific Bag Inc 15300 Woodinville Redmond Rd NE Ste A	Woodinville	WA	98072	**800-562-2247**	425-455-1128
Pactiv Corp 1900 W Field Ct	Lake Forest	IL	60045	**888-828-2850**	847-482-2000
Pitt Plastics Inc 1400 Atkinson Ave	Pittsburg	KS	66762	**800-835-0366**	
Poly-America Inc 2000 W Marshall Dr	Grand Prairie	TX	75051	**800-527-3322**	972-337-7100
Poly-Pak Industries Inc 125 Spagnoli Rd	Melville	NY	11747	**800-969-1993**	
Presto Products Co 670 N Perkins St PO Box 2399	Appleton	WI	54912	**800-558-3525**	920-739-9471
Roplast Industries Inc 3155 S Fifth Ave	Oroville	CA	95965	**800-767-5278**	530-532-9500
Shields Bag & Printing Co 1009 Rock Ave	Yakima	WA	98902	**800-541-8630**	509-248-7500
Superbag Corp 9291 Baythrone Dr	Houston	TX	77041	**888-842-1177**	713-462-1173
Waverly Plastics Company Inc PO Box 801	Waverly	IA	50677	**800-454-6377**	319-352-3333
Webster Industries Inc 95 Chestnut Ridge Rd,	Montvale	NJ	07645	**800-955-2374**	800-999-2374
Wisconsin Film & Bag Inc 3100 E Richmond St	Shawano	WI	54166	**800-765-9224**	715-524-2565

66 BAGS - TEXTILE

SEE ALSO Handbags, Totes, Backpacks ; Luggage, Bags, Cases

Name / Address	City	State	ZIP	Toll-Free	Phone
A Rifkin Co 1400 Sans Souci Pkwy *Cust Svc	Wilkes-Barre	PA	18706	**800-458-7300***	570-825-9551
Bulk Lift International Inc (BLI) 1013 Tamarac Dr	Carpentersville	IL	60110	**800-879-2247**	847-428-6059
GEM Group 9 International Way	Lawrence	MA	01843	**800-800-3200**	978-691-2000
Halsted Corp 51 Commerce Dr Ste 3	Cranbury	NJ	08512	**800-843-5184**	201-433-3323
HBD Inc 3901 Riverdale Rd	Greensboro	NC	27406	**800-403-2247**	336-275-4800
Indian Valley Industries Inc PO Box 810	Johnson City	NY	13790	**800-659-5111**	607-729-5111
J & M Industries Inc 300 Ponchatoula Pkwy	Ponchatoula	LA	70454	**800-989-1002**	985-386-6000
Menardi 1 Maxwell Dr	Trenton	SC	29847	**800-321-3218**	803-663-6551
NYP Corp 805 E Grand St	Elizabeth	NJ	07201	**800-524-1052**	908-351-6550
Sacramento Bag Manufacturing Co 440 N Pioneer Ave Ste 300	Woodland	CA	95776	**800-287-2247**	530-662-6130

67 BAKERIES

Name / Address	City	State	ZIP	Toll-Free	Phone
Awrey Bakeries Inc 12301 Farmington Rd	Livonia	MI	48150	**800-950-2253**	734-522-1100
Big Apple Bagels 500 Lk Cook Rd Ste 475	Deerfield	IL	60015	**800-251-6101**	847-948-7520
Cheryl & Co 646 McCorkle Blvd	Westerville	OH	43082	**800-443-8124**	
Collin Street Bakery Inc 401 W Seventh Ave *Sales	Corsicana	TX	75151	**800-267-4657***	
Cookies By Design Inc 1865 Summit Ave Ste 605	Plano	TX	75074	**800-945-2665**	972-398-9536
Corner Bakery Cafe 12700 Pk Central Dr Ste 1300 *General	Dallas	TX	75251	**800-309-4642***	972-619-4100
Damascus Bakery Inc 56 Gold St	Brooklyn	NY	11201	**800-367-7482**	
Daylight Donut Flour Company LLC 11707 E 11th St	Tulsa	OK	74128	**800-331-2245**	918-438-0800
Dunkin' Donuts 130 Royall St *Cust Svc	Canton	MA	02021	**800-859-5339***	781-737-3000
East Balt Inc 1801 W 31st Pl	Chicago	IL	60608	**800-621-8555**	773-376-4444
Eleni's 75 Ninth Ave	New York	NY	10011	**888-435-3647**	
Galasso's Inc 10820 San Sevaine Way	Mira Loma	CA	91752	**800-339-7494**	951-360-1211
Gold Medal Bakery Inc 1397 Bay St	Fall River	MA	02724	**800-642-7568**	508-674-5766
Gonnella Baking Co 1001 W Chicago Ave	Chicago	IL	60642	**800-262-3442**	312-733-2020
Great American Cookie Company Inc 3300 Chambers Rd Ste 170	Horseheads	NY	14845	**877-639-2361**	
Great Harvest Bread Co 28 S Montana St	Dillon	MT	59725	**800-442-0424**	406-683-6842
Hill & Valley Inc 3915 9th St	Rock Island	IL	61201	**800-480-0055**	309-793-0161
Holsum Bakery Inc 2322 W Lincoln St	Phoenix	AZ	85009	**800-755-8167**	602-252-2351
Honey Dew Assoc Inc 2 Taunton St	Plainville	MA	02762	**800-946-6393**	508-699-3900
Hot Stuff Pizza 2930 W Maple St	Sioux Falls	SD	57107	**800-336-1320**	605-336-6961
Krispy Kreme Doughnuts Corp 370 Knollwood St Ste 500 *NYSE: KKD*	Winston-Salem	NC	27103	**800-457-4779**	336-725-2981
Manhattan Bagel Co Inc 555 Zang St Ste 300	Lakewood	CO	80228	**800-224-3563**	303-568-8000
Maple Donuts Inc 3455 E Market St	York	PA	17402	**800-627-5348**	717-757-7826
Panera Bread Co 3630 S Geyer Rd *NASDAQ: PNRA*	Saint Louis	MO	63127	**800-301-5566**	314-984-1000
PARTNERS A Tasteful Choice Co 20232 72nd Ave	South Kent	WA	98032	**800-632-7477**	253-867-1580
Treats International Franchise Corp 238 Queen St S 2nd Fl	Mississauga	ON	L5M1L5	**800-461-4003**	613-563-4073
Vie de France Yamazaki Inc 2070 Chain Bridge Rd Ste 500 *General	Vienna	VA	22182	**800-446-4404***	703-442-9205

68 BANKING-RELATED SERVICES

Name / Address	City	State	ZIP	Toll-Free	Phone
Atm Merchant Systems 1667 Helm Dr	Las Vegas	NV	89119	**888-878-8166**	702-837-8787
Automatic Funds Transfer Services 151 S Landers St Ste C	Seattle	WA	98134	**800-275-2033**	206-254-0975
Blackhawk Bank PO Box 719	Beloit	WI	53511	**888-769-2600**	608-364-4534
Bremer Financial Corp 2100 Bremer Tower 445 Minnesota St	Saint Paul	MN	55101	**800-908-2265**	651-227-7621
Capital Farm Credit Aca 7000 Woodway Dr	Waco	TX	76712	**877-944-5500**	254-776-7506
Citizens Federal Savings & Loan Assn 110 N Main St PO Box 9	Bellefontaine	OH	43311	**800-436-5177**	937-593-0015
Civista Bank 100 E Water St	Sandusky	OH	44870	**888-645-4121**	419-625-4121
Comdata Corp 5301 Maryland Way	Brentwood	TN	37027	**800-266-3282**	615-370-7000
Community Bank 505 E Colorado Blvd	Pasadena	CA	91101	**800-788-9999**	
eCivis Inc 418 N Fair Oaks Ave Ste 301	Pasadena	CA	91103	**877-232-4847**	
Emprise Financial Corp 257 N Broadway St PO Box 2970 *Cust Svc	Wichita	KS	67202	**800-201-7118***	316-383-4301
Eureka Homestead 1922 Veterans Memorial Blvd	Metairie	LA	70005	**855-858-5179**	504-834-0242
Fiserv Inc 255 Fiserv Dr PO Box 979 *NASDAQ: FISV* ■ *Sales	Brookfield	WI	53008	**800-872-7882***	262-879-5000
Hawaii National Bank 45 N King St	Honolulu	HI	96817	**800-528-2273**	808-528-7711
HomEquity Bank 1881 Yonge St Ste 300	Toronto	ON	M4S3C4	**866-522-2447**	416-925-4757
Lockwood Advisors Inc 760 Moore Rd	King Of Prussia	PA	19406	**800-200-3033**	
MoneyGram International Inc 2828 N Harwood Fl 15 *NASDAQ: MGI*	Dallas	TX	75201	**800-666-3947**	
Moneytree Inc 6720 Ft Dent Way	Seattle	WA	98188	**877-613-6669**	206-246-3500
NYCE Corp 400 Plaza Dr	Secaucus	NJ	07094	**888-323-0310**	904-438-6000
Oak Ridge Financial 701 Xenia Ave S Ste 100	Minneapolis	MN	55416	**800-231-8364**	763-923-2200
OANDA Corp 140 Broadway 46th Fl	New York	NY	10005	**800-826-8164**	416-593-9436
PULSE 1301 McKinney St Ste 2500	Houston	TX	77010	**800-420-2122**	713-223-1400
Rock Springs National Bank 200 Second St PO Box 880	Rock Springs	WY	82902	**800-469-8801**	307-362-8801
Travelex Worldwide Money 122 E 42nd St Ste 2800	New York	NY	10168	**800-228-9792**	212-363-6206
Western Union Holdings Inc 12500 E Belford Ave *NYSE: WU* ■ *Cust Svc	Englewood	CO	80112	**800-325-6000***	720-332-1000
Your Community Bank 2323 Ring Rd	Elizabethtown	KY	42701	**800-314-2265**	270-765-2131

69 BANKS - COMMERCIAL & SAVINGS

SEE ALSO Credit & Financing - Consumer ; Credit & Financing - Commercial ; Credit Unions ; Bank Holding Companies

Name / Address	City	State	ZIP	Toll-Free	Phone
1st Colonial Bancorp Inc 1040 Haddon Ave *OTC: FCOB*	Collingswood	NJ	08108	**800-500-1044**	856-858-1100
1st Source Bank 100 N Michigan St	South Bend	IN	46601	**800-513-2360**	574-235-2254
3rd Federal Bank 3 Penns Trail	Newtown	PA	18940	**800-822-3321**	215-579-4600
Alostar Bank 3680 Grandview Pkwy Ste 200	Birmingham	AL	35243	**877-738-6391**	205-298-6391
Amalgamated Bank of New York 275 Seventh Ave	New York	NY	10001	**800-662-0860**	
Amarillo National Bank 410 S Taylor St Plaza 1	Amarillo	TX	79101	**800-253-1031**	806-378-8000
Amboy National Bank 3590 US Hwy 9 S	Old Bridge	NJ	08857	**800-942-6269**	732-591-8700
Amegy Bank of Texas 4400 Post Oak Pkwy	Houston	TX	77027	**800-287-0301**	713-235-8800
American Bank of Texas NA 200 N Austin St	Seguin	TX	78155	**800-567-1817**	830-379-5236

Classified Section

Name / Address	City	State	ZIP	Toll-Free	Phone
American Exchange Bank (AEB) 510 W Main St PO Box 818	Henryetta	OK	74437	**888-652-3321**	918-652-3321
American Savings Bank FSB 1001 Bishop St PO Box 2300	Honolulu	HI	96813	**800-272-2566**	808-627-6900
Ameriserv Financial 216 Franklin St PO Box 520 *NASDAQ: ASRV*	Johnstown	PA	15907	**800-837-2265**	814-533-5300
AmTrust Bank 1801 E Ninth St	Cleveland	OH	44114	**888-696-4444**	216-736-3480
Anchor Bank 1055 Wayzata Blvd E	Wayzata	MN	55391	**800-425-5150**	952-473-4606
AnchorBank 25 W Main St PO Box 7933	Madison	WI	53703	**800-252-6246**	608-252-8827
Apple Bank for Savings 122 E 42nd St 9th Fl	New York	NY	10168	**800-824-0710**	914-902-2775
Apple Creek Banc Corp 3 W Main St PO Box 237	Apple Creek	OH	44606	**888-327-7533**	330-698-2631
Arthur State Bank 100 E Main St PO Box 769	Union	SC	29379	**877-226-5246**	864-427-1213
Artisan's Bank 2961 Centerville Rd	Wilmington	DE	19808	**800-282-8255**	302-658-6881
Asheville Savings Bank S S B PO Box 652	Asheville	NC	28802	**800-222-3230**	828-254-7411
Associated Bank 2870 Holmgren Way	Green Bay	WI	54304	**800-728-3501**	262-879-0133
Associated Bank Green Bay NA 200 N Adams St	Green Bay	WI	54301	**800-728-3501**	920-433-3200
Associated Bank Illinois NA 612 N Main St	Rockford	IL	61103	**800-236-8866**	815-987-3500
Associated Bank Milwaukee 401 E Kilbourn Ave	Milwaukee	WI	53202	**800-236-8866**	414-271-1786
Associated Bank North 303 S First Ave	Wausau	WI	54401	**800-236-8866**	715-848-4793
Athens State Bank 6530 N State Rt 29	Springfield	IL	62707	**800-367-7576**	217-487-7766
Bancorp Bank 409 Silverside Rd Ste 105 *NASDAQ: TBBK* ■ *Cust Svc	Wilmington	DE	19809	**866-255-9831***	302-385-5000
Bangor Savings Bank 99 Franklin St	Bangor	ME	04401	**877-226-4671**	207-942-5211
Bank Financial 6415 W 95th St	Chicago Ridge	IL	60415	**800-894-6900**	
Bank Leumi USA 579 Fifth Ave	New York	NY	10017	**800-892-5430**	917-542-2343
Bank of Albuquerque NA 201 3rd St NW Ste 1400	Albuquerque	NM	87102	**800-583-0709**	505-855-0855
Bank of Louisiana 300 St Charles Ave	New Orleans	LA	70130	**866-392-9952**	504-592-0600
Bank of Marin 504 Tamalpais Dr *NASDAQ: BMRC*	Corte Madera	CA	94925	**800-654-5111**	415-927-2265
Bank of McKenney 20718 First St *OTC: BOMK*	McKenney	VA	23872	**800-528-2273**	804-478-4434
Bank of Montreal 3 Times Sq	New York	NY	10036	**877-225-5266**	
Bank of Nevada 2700 W Sahara Ave	Las Vegas	NV	89102	**877-750-0010**	702-248-4200
Bank of North Dakota 1200 Memorial Hwy	Bismarck	ND	58504	**800-472-2166**	701-328-5600
Bank of Nova Scotia 1 Liberty Plaza 26th Fl *TSE: BNS*	New York	NY	10006	**800-472-6842**	212-225-5000
Bank of Oklahoma NA PO Box 2300	Tulsa	OK	74192	**800-234-6181**	918-588-6010
Bank of Springfield 2600 Adlai Stevenson Dr	Springfield	IL	62703	**877-698-3278**	217-529-5555
Bank of Stanly PO Box 338	Albemarle	NC	28002	**800-438-6864**	704-983-6181
Bank of Stockton PO Box 1110	Stockton	CA	95201	**800-941-1494**	209-929-1600
Bank of Sunset & Trust Co 863 Napoleon Ave	Sunset	LA	70584	**800-264-5578**	337-662-5222
Bank of the Carolinas 135 Boxwood Village Dr *OTC: BCAR*	Mocksville	NC	27028	**877-751-5755**	336-751-5755
Bank of the Ozarks 4328 Old Spanish Trail	Houston	TX	77021	**800-274-4482**	713-747-9000
Bank of the Sierra PO Box 1930 *Cust Svc	Porterville	CA	93258	**888-454-2265***	559-782-4900
Bank Of Utica 222 Genesee St *OTC: BKUT*	Utica	NY	13502	**800-442-1028**	315-797-2700
Bank of Virginia 11730 Hull St Rd *NASDAQ: BOVA*	Midlothian	VA	23112	**800-500-1044**	804-744-7576
BankAtlantic 200 W Second St	Winston-Salem	NC	27101	**800-226-5228**	888-628-3926
Bankers' Bank 7700 Mineral Point Rd	Madison	WI	53717	**800-388-5550**	608-833-5550
Bankwest Corporation 2050 N California Blvd	Walnut Creek	CA	94596	**888-389-8668**	925-933-7810
Bankwest Inc 420 S Pierre St PO Box 998	Pierre	SD	57501	**800-253-0362**	605-224-7391
Banterra Corp 1404 US Rt 45 S	Eldorado	IL	62930	**877-541-2265**	618-273-9346
BB & T Corp 200 W Second St *NYSE: BBT*	Winston-Salem	NC	27101	**800-226-5228**	336-733-1470
Beneficial Mutual Savings Bank 530 Walnut St	Philadelphia	PA	19106	**800-784-8490**	215-864-6000
Berkshire Bank PO Box 1308	Pittsfield	MA	01202	**800-773-5601**	413-443-5601
Blue Ridge Bank & Trust Co 4240 Blue Ridge Blvd Ste 100	Kansas City	MO	64133	**800-569-4287**	816-358-5000
Blueharbor Bank 106 Corporate Park Dr	Mooresville	NC	28117	**877-322-8228**	704-662-7700
BMO Harris Bank 111 W Monroe St	Chicago	IL	60603	**888-340-2265**	847-238-2265
BNC National Bank 322 E Main Ave	Bismarck	ND	58501	**800-262-2265**	701-250-3000
Boiling Springs Savings Bank (BSSB) 25 Orient Way	Rutherford	NJ	07070	**888-388-7459**	201-939-5000
Branch Banking & Trust Company of South Carolina 301 College St	Greenville	SC	29601	**800-226-5228**	
Brotherhood Bank & Trust 756 Minnesota Ave	Kansas City	MO	66101	**855-522-6722**	913-321-4242
Burke & Herbert Bank & Trust Co 100 S Fairfax St	Alexandria	VA	22314	**877-440-0800**	703-751-7701
Byline Bank 3639 N Broadway St	Chicago	IL	60613	**866-957-7700**	773-244-7000
California Bank & Trust 11622 El Camino Real Ste 200	San Diego	CA	92130	**800-400-6080**	858-793-7400
Cambridge Savings Bank 1374 Massachusetts Ave	Cambridge	MA	02138	**888-418-5626**	617-441-4155
Canadian Imperial Bank of Commerce (CIBC) 199 Bay St Commerce Ct W *NYSE: CM*	Toronto	ON	M5L1A2	**800-465-2422**	
Canadian Western Bank 10303 Jasper Ave Ste 3000 *TSE: CWB*	Edmonton	AB	T5J3X6	**866-317-0356**	780-423-8888
Cape Cod Five Cents Savings Bank 19 W Rd PO Box 20	Orleans	MA	02653	**800-678-1855**	508-240-0555
Capital City Bank 2111 N Monroe St PO Box 900	Tallahassee	FL	32302	**888-671-0400**	850-402-7500
Capital One Auto Finance Inc PO Box 60511	City of Industry	CA	91716	**800-946-0332**	
Capitol FSB 700 S Kansas Ave	Topeka	KS	66603	**888-822-7333**	785-235-1341
Carolina Trust Bank 901 E Main St *NASDAQ: CART*	Lincolnton	NC	28092	**877-983-5537**	704-735-1104
Casey State Bank 305-307 N Central Ave	Casey	IL	62420	**866-666-2754**	217-932-2136
Centerstate Banks Inc 42725 Us Hwy 27	Davenport	FL	33837	**855-863-2265**	
Central BanCo 238 Madison St	Jefferson City	MO	65101	**877-554-5535**	573-634-1155
Century National Bank 14 S Fifth St *Cust Svc	Zanesville	OH	43701	**800-548-3557***	740-454-2521
CFG Community Bank 1422 Clarkview Rd	Baltimore	MD	21209	**866-619-1417**	410-823-0500
CharterBank 1233 OG Skinner Dr	West Point	GA	31833	**800-763-4444**	706-645-1391
Chase Bank 1 Chase Manhattan Plz	New York	NY	10005	**800-935-9935**	
Chinatrust Bank USA 801 S Figueroa St Ste 2300	Los Angeles	CA	90017	**888-839-9000**	310-791-2828
Citibank (Delaware) 4500 New Linden Hill Rd	Wilmington	DE	19808	**800-374-9700**	302-323-3600
Citibank NA 399 Pk Ave	New York	NY	10022	**800-627-3999**	
Citibank (South Dakota) NA 701 E 60th St N	Sioux Falls	SD	57104	**800-627-3999**	605-331-2626
Citizen National Bank Of Bluffton, The 102 S Main St PO Box 88	Bluffton	OH	45817	**800-262-4663**	419-358-8040
Citizens Bank of Clovis 420 Wheeler	Texico	NM	88135	**844-657-3553**	575-482-3381
Citizens Bank of Massachusetts 28 State St	Boston	MA	02109	**800-610-7300**	
Citizens Bank of Mukwonago 301 N Rochester St PO Box 223	Mukwonago	WI	53149	**877-546-5868**	262-363-6500
Citizens Bank of Rhode Island 1 Citizens Plz *Cust Svc	Providence	RI	02903	**800-922-9999***	401-456-7000
Citizens Business Bank (CBB) 701 N Haven Ave *Cust Svc	Ontario	CA	91764	**888-222-5432***	909-980-4030
Citizens Financial Services 707 Ridge Rd	Munster	IN	46321	**866-622-1370**	219-836-5500
Citizens Trust Bank 1700 3rd Ave N	Birmingham	AL	35203	**888-214-3099**	205-328-2041
City National Bank 400 N Roxbury Dr *Cust Svc	Beverly Hills	CA	90210	**800-773-7100***	310-888-6000
City National Bank of Florida 450 E Las Olas Blvd	Fort Lauderdale	FL	33301	**800-762-2489**	954-467-6667
City National Bank of New Jersey (CNB) 900 Broad St	Newark	NJ	07102	**877-350-3524**	973-624-0865
City National Bank of West Virginia 3601 McCorckle Ave	Charleston	WV	25304	**888-816-8064**	304-926-3324
City Savings Bank & Trust 301 N Pine St	Deridder	LA	70634	**800-920-8661**	337-463-8661
Clearfield Bank & Trust Co 11 N Second St PO Box 171	Clearfield	PA	16830	**888-765-7551**	814-765-7551
Coast Capital Savings 645 Tyee Rd Ste 400	Victoria	BC	V9A6X5	**888-517-7000**	250-483-7000
College Savings Bank PO Box 3769	Princeton	NJ	08543	**800-888-2723**	
Colorado Fsb 8400 E Prentice Ave Ste 545	Greenwood Village	CO	80111	**877-484-2372**	303-793-3555
Columbia Bank, The 7168 Columbia Gateway Dr	Columbia	MD	21046	**888-822-2265**	
Columbia Savings Bank 19-01 Rt 208 *Cust Svc	Fair Lawn	NJ	07410	**800-747-4428***	800-522-4167
Columbia State Bank PO Box 2156	Tacoma	WA	98401	**800-305-1905**	253-305-1900
Columbus Bank & Trust Co 1148 Broadway	Columbus	GA	31901	**800-334-9007**	706-649-4900
Comerica Bank 411 W Lafayette	Detroit	MI	48226	**800-643-4418**	313-222-3344
Comerica Bank-California 333 W Santa Clara St	San Jose	CA	95113	**800-522-2265**	408-556-5300
Comerica Bank-Texas 1717 Main St	Dallas	TX	75201	**800-925-2160**	
Commerce Bank & Trust Co 386 Main St	Worcester	MA	01608	**800-698-2265**	508-797-6842

Name / Address	City	State	Zip	Toll-Free	Phone
Commercial Bank 301 N State St PO Box 638 *OTC: CEFC*	Alma	MI	48801	**800-547-8531**	989-463-2185
Community Bank of Raymore PO Box 200	Raymore	MO	64083	**800-322-6772**	816-322-2100
Community Trust Bank NA 346 N Mayo Trl PO Box 2947	Pikeville	KY	41501	**800-422-1090**	606-432-1414
Conneaut Savings Bank 305 Main St PO Box 740	Conneaut	OH	44030	**888-453-2311**	440-599-8121
Cornhusker Bank 1101 Cornhusker Hwy	Lincoln	NE	68521	**877-837-4481**	402-434-2265
Country Bank for Savings 75 Main St	Ware	MA	01082	**800-322-8233**	413-967-6221
Credit Union of Denver 9305 W Alameda Ave	Lakewood	CO	80226	**800-951-9014**	303-234-1700
D L Evans Bank 397 N Overland PO Box 1188	Burley	ID	83318	**888-873-9777**	208-678-9076
DBS Bank Ltd 725 S Figueroa St	Los Angeles	CA	90017	**800-209-4555**	213-627-0222
Dedham Institution For Savings 55 Elm St PO Box 9107	Dedham	MA	02026	**888-289-0342**	781-329-6700
Devon Bank 6445 N Western Ave	Chicago	IL	60645	**866-683-3866**	
Dime Bank, The 820 Church St PO Box 509	Honesdale	PA	18431	**888-469-3463**	570-253-1902
Discover Bank PO Box 30416	Salt Lake City	UT	84130	**800-347-7000**	302-323-7810
Dollar Bank FSB 225 Forbes Ave	Pittsburgh	PA	15222	**800-828-5527**	
Durant Bancorp / First United Bank 1400 W Main	Durant	OK	74701	**800-924-4427**	580-924-2211
E*Trade Bank 671 N Glebe Rd	Arlington	VA	22203	**800-387-2331**	877-800-1208
East Boston Savings Bank 10 Meridian St	Boston	MA	02128	**800-657-3272**	617-567-1500
Eastern Bank 1 Eastern Pl	Lynn	MA	01901	**800-327-8376**	781-599-2100
El Dorado Savings Bank 4040 El Dorado Rd	Placerville	CA	95667	**800-874-9779**	530-622-1492
Elmira Savings Bank 333 E Water St *NASDAQ: ESBK*	Elmira	NY	14901	**888-372-9299**	607-734-3374
Encore Bank 3003 Tamiami Trail N Ste 100	Naples	FL	34103	**800-472-3272**	239-919-5888
Enterprise Bank of SC 13497 Broxton Bridge Rd PO Box 8	Ehrhardt	SC	29081	**800-554-8969**	803-267-3191
Equitable Bank 113 N Locust St	Grand Island	NE	68802	**800-641-5046**	308-382-3136
Essex Savings Bank PO Box 950	Essex	CT	06426	**877-377-3922**	860-767-4414
Euro Pacific Capital Inc 88 Post Rd W 2nd Fl	Westport	CT	06880	**800-727-7922**	203-662-9700
Exchange State Bank 3992 Chandler St PO Box 68	Carsonville	MI	48419	**888-488-9300**	810-657-9333
F&M Bank PO Box 1130	Clarksville	TN	37041	**800-645-4199**	931-645-2400
Farm Bureau Bank 2165 Green Vista Dr Ste 204	Sparks	NV	89431	**800-492-3276**	775-673-4566
Farmers Bank, The 9 E Clinton St PO Box 129	Frankfort	IN	46041	**800-932-7368**	765-654-8731
Fauquier Bank, The (TFB) 10 Courthouse Sq PO Box 561	Warrenton	VA	20186	**800-638-3798**	540-347-2700
Fidelity Bancshares Nc Inc PO Box 8	Fuquay Varina	NC	27526	**800-816-9608**	919-552-2242
Fidelity Bank 100 E English St	Wichita	KS	67201	**800-658-1637**	
Fifth Third Bank Central Ohio 21 E State St	Columbus	OH	43215	**866-671-5353**	800-972-3030
First American Bank & Trust 2785 Hwy 20 W PO Box 550	Vacherie	LA	70090	**800-738-2265**	225-265-2265
First Bank Financial Centre (FBFC) 155 W Wisconsin Ave PO Box 1004	Oconomowoc	WI	53066	**888-569-9909**	262-569-9900
First Bank Muleshoe 202 S 1st PO Box 565	Muleshoe	TX	79347	**888-653-9558**	806-272-4515
First Business Financial Services Inc 401 Charmany Dr *NASDAQ: FBIZ*	Madison	WI	53719	**888-455-2263**	608-238-8008
First Calgary Savings 510 16th Ave NE	Calgary	AB	T2E1K4	**866-923-4778**	
First Century Bank NA 500 Federal St	Bluefield	WV	24701	**877-214-9426**	304-325-8181
First Citizens Bank & Trust Co Inc 1230 Main St	Columbia	SC	29201	**888-612-4444**	919-716-4588
First Federal Bank Fsb 6900 N Executive Dr	Kansas City	MO	64120	**888-651-4759**	816-241-7800
First Federal Lakewood 14806 Detroit Ave	Lakewood	OH	44107	**800-966-7300**	216-529-2700
First Financial Bank 1 First Financial Plz	Terre Haute	IN	47807	**800-511-0045**	812-238-6000
First Foundation Bank 18101 Von Karman Ave Ste 750	Irvine	CA	92612	**800-224-7931**	949-202-4100
First Hawaiian Bank 999 Bishop St	Honolulu	HI	96813	**888-844-4444**	808-525-6340
First Interstate Bank 401 N 31st St	Billings	MT	59101	**888-752-3341**	406-255-5000
First Jackson Bank 43243 Us Hwy 72	Stevenson	AL	35772	**888-950-2265**	256-437-2107
First Mercantile Trust Co 57 Germantown Ct 4th Fl	Cordova	TN	38018	**800-753-3682**	901-753-9080
First National Bank PO Box 578	Fort Collins	CO	80521	**800-883-8773**	970-495-9450
First National Bank Alaska 101 W 36 Ave PO Box 100720 *OTC: FBAK*	Anchorage	AK	99510	**800-856-4362**	907-777-4362
First National Bank Creston PO Box 445	Creston	IA	50801	**877-782-2195**	641-782-2195
First National Bank of Omaha 1620 Dodge St	Omaha	NE	68197	**800-462-5266**	402-341-0500
First National Bank of Oneida, The 18418 Alberta St PO Box 4699	Oneida	TN	37841	**866-546-8273**	423-569-8586
First National Bank of Santa Fe PO Box 609	Santa Fe	NM	87504	**888-912-2265**	505-992-2000
First National Bankers Bankshares Inc (FNBB) 7813 Office Pk Blvd	Baton Rouge	LA	70809	**800-421-6182**	225-924-8015
First NBC (CPB) 29092 Kretel Rd	Lacombe	LA	70445	**800-423-7503**	985-819-1200
First Niagara Financial Group 726 Exchange St Ste 618	Buffalo	NY	14210	**800-421-0004**	716-625-7500
First Palmetto Savings Bank Fsb PO Box 430	Camden	SC	29021	**800-922-7411**	803-432-2265
First Republic Bank 111 Pine St *NYSE: FRC*	San Francisco	CA	94111	**800-392-1400**	415-392-1400
First Savings Bank 2804 N Telshor Blvd	Las Cruces	NM	88011	**800-555-6895**	575-521-7931
First Security Bank of Missoula 1704 Dearborn PO Box 4506	Missoula	MT	59801	**888-782-3115**	406-728-3115
First State Bank 708 Azalea Dr PO Box 506	Waynesboro	MS	39367	**866-408-3582**	
First State Bank & Trust Co 1005 E 23rd St	Fremont	NE	68025	**888-674-4344**	402-721-2500
First State Bank of Kansas City 650 Kansas Ave	Kansas City	KS	66105	**800-883-1242**	913-371-1242
First Tennessee Bank 165 Madison Ave	Memphis	TN	38103	**800-382-5465**	901-523-4883
First Texas Bank 501 E Third St	Lampasas	TX	76550	**866-220-1598**	512-556-3691
First Western Bank & Trust PO Box 1090	Minot	ND	58702	**800-688-2584**	701-852-3711
First-Knox National Bank 1 S Main St	Mount Vernon	OH	43050	**800-837-5266**	740-399-5500
Firstrust Savings Bank 15 E Ridge Pike 4th Fl	Conshohocken	PA	19428	**800-220-2265**	610-941-9898
Flagstar Bank FSB 5151 Corporate Dr	Troy	MI	48098	**800-945-7700**	248-312-2000
Four Oaks Bank & Trust Co PO Box 309	Four Oaks	NC	27524	**877-963-6257**	919-963-2177
Fowler State Bank 300 E Fifth St PO Box 511	Fowler	IN	47944	**800-439-3951**	765-884-1200
Fremont Bank PO Box 5101	Fremont	CA	94538	**800-359-2265**	510-792-2300
Frontenac Bank 3330 Rider Trl S	Earth City	MO	63045	**877-205-5777**	314-298-8200
Garden State Community Bank (GSCB) 36 Ferry St *NYSE: NYB*	Newark	NJ	07105	**877-786-6560**	973-589-8616
Genesis Capital LLC 3414 Peachtree Rd Ne Ste 700	Atlanta	GA	30326	**800-998-8479**	404-816-7540
Giantbank.com 6300 NE First Ave	Fort Lauderdale	FL	33334	**877-446-4200**	954-958-0001
Glenwood State Bank 5 E Minnesota Ave PO Box 197	Glenwood	MN	56334	**800-207-7333**	320-634-5111
Golden Valley Bank Community Foundation 190 Cohasset Rd Ste 170	Chico	CA	95926	**800-808-2070**	530-894-1000
Grants State Bank 824 W Santa Fe Ave PO Box 1088	Grants	NM	87020	**877-285-6611**	505-285-6611
Great Western Bank 6015 NW Radial Hwy	Omaha	NE	68104	**800-952-2043**	402-952-6000
Greenfield Savings Bank 400 Main St PO Box 1537	Greenfield	MA	01302	**888-324-3191**	413-774-3191
Greenville First Bank 100 Verdae Blvd Ste 100	Greenville	SC	29072	**877-679-9646**	864-679-9000
Guaranty Bank 4000 W Brown Deer Rd	Brown Deer	WI	53209	**800-235-4636**	414-362-4000
Guaranty Bank & Trust Co PO Box 1807	Cedar Rapids	IA	52406	**800-362-2119**	319-286-6200
Guaranty State Bank & Trust Company Beloit Kansas, The 201 S Mill St	Beloit	KS	67420	**888-738-8000**	785-738-3501
Guilford Savings Bank (GSB) PO Box 369	Guilford	CT	06437	**866-878-1480**	203-453-2015
Gulf Coast Bank 4310 Johnston St	Lafayette	LA	70503	**800-722-5363**	337-989-1133
Hamler State Bank 210 Randolph St PO Box 358	Hamler	OH	43524	**888-508-3955**	419-274-3955
Heritage Group Inc 1101 12th St	Aurora	NE	68818	**888-463-6611**	402-694-3136
Hickory Point Bank & Trust FSB PO Box 2548 *Cust Svc	Decatur	IL	62525	**800-872-0081***	217-875-3131
Hills Bank & Trust Co 131 Main St PO Box 70	Hills	IA	52235	**800-445-5725**	319-679-2291
Hocking Valley Bank 7 W Stimson Ave	Athens	OH	45701	**888-482-5854**	740-592-4441
Home Federal Bank 225 S Main Ave	Sioux Falls	SD	57104	**800-244-2149**	605-336-2470
Home Savings & Loan Company of Youngstown 275 W Federal St	Youngstown	OH	44503	**888-822-4751**	330-742-0500
HomeStreet Bank 601 Union St 2 Union Sq Ste 2000	Seattle	WA	98101	**800-654-1075**	206-623-3050
Hometown Bank 245 N Peters Ave	Fond du Lac	WI	54935	**877-261-2220**	920-907-2220
Hometrust Bank, The PO Box 10	Asheville	NC	28802	**800-627-1632**	828-259-3939
Homewood FSB 3228-30 Eastern Ave	Baltimore	MD	21224	**800-554-8969**	410-327-5220
Hudson City Savings Bank W 80 Century Rd	Paramus	NJ	07652	**800-222-0194**	201-967-1900
Huntington National Bank 41 S High St Huntington Ctr	Columbus	OH	43287	**800-480-2265**	614-480-8300
Illinois National Bank 322 E Capitol	Springfield	IL	62701	**877-771-2316**	217-747-5500
InsurBanc 10 Executive Dr	Farmington	CT	06032	**866-467-2262**	860-677-9701
Inter-County Bakers Inc 1095 Long Island Ave	Deer Park	NY	11729	**800-696-1350**	631-957-1350
Investors Savings Bank 101 Wood Ave S *NASDAQ: ISBC*	Iselin	NJ	08830	**855-422-6548**	973-924-5100

Classified Section

Name / Address	City	State	ZIP	Toll-Free	Phone
Iowa State Savings Bank 401 W Adams St	Creston	IA	50801	**888-508-0142**	641-782-1000
Jeff Davis Bancshares Inc 507 N Main St PO Box 730 *OTC: JDVB*	Jennings	LA	70546	**800-789-5159**	337-824-3424
Jersey Shore State Bank 300 Market St PO Box 967	Williamsport	PA	17701	**888-412-5772**	570-322-1111
Kearny FSB 120 Passaic Ave	Fairfield	NJ	07004	**800-273-3406**	973-244-4500
Kennebec Savings Bank 150 State St PO Box 50	Augusta	ME	04332	**888-303-7788**	207-622-5801
Kentucky Bank PO Box 157	Paris	KY	40362	**877-322-8228**	859-987-1795
Key Bank 65 Dutch Hill Rd *Cust Svc	Orangeburg	NY	10962	**800-539-2968***	
Kingston National Bank 2 N Main St PO Box 613	Kingston	OH	45644	**866-642-2191**	740-642-2191
Kirkwood Bank & Trust Co 2911 N 14th St	Bismarck	ND	58503	**800-492-4955**	701-258-6550
Kish Bancorp Inc 4255 E Main St PO Box 917 *OTC: KISB*	Belleville	PA	17004	**888-554-4748**	717-935-2191
Labette Bank 4th & Huston PO Box 497	Altamont	KS	67330	**800-711-5311**	620-784-5311
Lakeside Bank 55 W Wacker Dr	Chicago	IL	60601	**866-892-1572**	312-435-5100
LaPorte Savings Bank, The 710 Indiana Ave	LaPorte	IN	46350	**866-362-7511**	219-362-7511
Laurentian Bank of Canada 1981 McGill College Ave *TSE: LB*	Montreal	QC	H3A3K3	**800-252-1846**	514-284-4500
LCNB National Bank 3209 W Galbraith Rd	Cincinnati	OH	45239	**800-344-2265**	513-932-1414
Legacy Bank 1580 E Cheyenne Mtn Blvd	Colorado Springs	CO	80906	**866-627-0800**	719-579-9150
Liberty Bank 315 Main St	Middletown	CT	06457	**800-622-6732**	800-354-8950
Liberty Bank & Trust Co PO Box 60131	New Orleans	LA	70160	**800-883-3943**	504-240-5100
Liberty Savings Bank FSB 2251 Rombach Ave	Wilmington	OH	45177	**800-436-6300**	
Little Bank Inc, The 804 Carey Rd *OTC: LTLB*	Kinston	NC	28501	**855-449-0975**	252-939-9990
Luther Burbank Savings 804 Fourth St	Santa Rosa	CA	95404	**888-205-6005**	707-578-9216
M&T Bank 1 M & T Plz 13th Fl *NYSE: MTB*	Buffalo	NY	14203	**800-724-2440**	716-842-4470
Machias Savings Bank 4 Ctr St PO Box 318	Machias	ME	04654	**800-982-7179**	207-255-3347
Magyar Bank 400 Somerset St	New Brunswick	NJ	08901	**800-472-3272**	732-342-7600
Main Source Bank 201 N Broadway	Greensburg	IN	47240	**800-713-6083**	
Marquette Bank 10000 W 151st St	Orland Park	IL	60462	**888-254-9500**	708-226-8026
Marquette Savings Bank 920 Peach St	Erie	PA	16501	**866-672-3743**	814-455-4481
Maspeth Federal Savings 56-18 69th St	Maspeth	NY	11378	**888-558-1300**	718-335-1300
Max Credit Union 400 Eastdale Cir	Montgomery	AL	36117	**800-776-6776**	334-260-2600
MCNB Bank & Trust Co PO Box 549	Welch	WV	24801	**800-532-9553**	304-436-4112
Mechanics Savings Bank 100 Minot Ave PO Box 400	Auburn	ME	04210	**877-886-1020**	207-786-5700
Members Trust Co 14025 Riveredge Dr Ste 280	Tampa	FL	33637	**888-727-9191**	813-631-9191
Merchants National Bank of Bangor Inc 25 Broadway PO Box 227	Bangor	PA	18013	**877-678-6622**	610-588-0981
Meredith Village Savings Bank (MVSB) 24 State Rt 25 PO Box 177	Meredith	NH	03253	**800-922-6872**	603-279-7986
Midamerica National Bancshares 100 W Elm St	Canton	IL	61520	**877-647-5050**	309-647-5000
Middlesex Savings Bank 120 Flanders Rd	Westborough	MA	01581	**877-463-6287**	508-653-0300
MidFirst Bank PO Box 76149	Oklahoma City	OK	73147	**888-643-3477**	405-943-8002
Midland National Bank 527 N Main	Newton	KS	67114	**800-810-9457**	316-283-1700
Midwest Bank 105 E Soo St PO Box 40	Parkers Prairie	MN	56361	**877-365-5155**	218-338-6054
Mifflinburg Bank & Trust Co (MBTC) 250 E Chestnut St PO Box 186	Mifflinburg	PA	17844	**888-966-3131**	570-966-1041
Milford Bank 33 Broad St	Milford	CT	06460	**800-340-4862**	203-783-5700
Monroe Bank & Trust 102 E Front St	Monroe	MI	48161	**800-321-0032**	734-241-3431
Montgomery Bank 1 Montgomery Bank Plaza PO Box 948	Sikeston	MO	63801	**800-455-2275**	573-471-2275
Mountain Valley Bank 317 DAVIS Ave	Elkins	WV	26241	**800-555-3503**	304-637-2265
MSB Financial Corp (MSBF) 1902 Long Hill Rd *NASDAQ: MSBF*	Millington	NJ	07946	**844-265-9680**	908-647-4000
Murray Bank, The 405 S 12th St	Murray	KY	42071	**877-965-1122**	270-753-5626
Mutual of Omaha Bank 3333 Farnam St	Omaha	NE	68131	**866-351-5646**	877-471-7896
Nantucket Bank 104 Pleasant St	Nantucket	MA	02554	**800-533-9313**	508-228-0580
National Australia Bank Americas 245 Pk Ave 28th Fl	New York	NY	10167	**866-706-0509**	212-916-9500
National Bank of Arizona 335 N Wilmot Rd Ste 100	Tucson	AZ	85711	**800-497-8168**	520-571-1500
National Bank of Blacksburg PO Box 90002	Blacksburg	VA	24062	**800-552-4123**	540-552-2011
National Bank of Gatesville PO Box 779	Gatesville	TX	76528	**877-628-2265**	254-865-2211
National Bank, The 852 Middle Rd	Bettendorf	IA	52722	**877-321-4347**	563-344-3935
NBT Bank NA PO Box 351	Norwich	NY	13815	**800-628-2265**	607-337-2265
Nevada State Bank PO Box 990	Las Vegas	NV	89125	**800-727-4743**	702-383-0009
New Washington State Bank 402 E Main St PO Box 10	New Washington	IN	47162	**800-883-0131**	812-293-3321
New York Community Bank 615 Merrick Ave	Westbury	NY	11590	**877-786-6560**	
Newburyport Five Cents Savings Bank Inc, The 63 State St PO Box 350	Newburyport	MA	01950	**877-462-3136**	978-462-3136
Newtown Savings Bank Foundation Inc 39 Main St PO Box 497	Newtown	CT	06470	**800-461-0672**	203-426-2563
North American Development Bank 203 S St Mary'S Ste 300	San Antonio	TX	78205	**800-499-6232**	210-231-8000
North American Savings Bank (NASB) 12520 S 71 Hwy	Grandview	MO	64030	**800-677-6272**	816-765-2200
North Middlesex Savings Bank Inc 7 Main St PO Box 469	Ayer	MA	01432	**800-762-3306**	978-772-3306
North Milwaukee State Bank (NMS) 5630 W Fond Du Lac Ave	Milwaukee	WI	53216	**800-799-5630**	414-466-2344
North Shore Bank FSB 15700 W Bluemound Rd	Brookfield	WI	53005	**800-236-4672**	262-797-3858
Northern Trust Co 50 S LaSalle St *NASDAQ: NTRS*	Chicago	IL	60603	**888-289-6542**	312-630-6000
Northfield Savings Bank (NSB) PO Box 347	Northfield	VT	05663	**800-672-2274**	802-485-5871
Northrim BanCorp Inc 3111 C St *NASDAQ: NRIM*	Anchorage	AK	99503	**800-478-3311**	907-562-0062
Northwest Community Bank 86 Main St PO Box 1019	Winsted	CT	06098	**800-455-6668**	860-379-7561
Northwest Savings Bank 100 Liberty St PO Box 128	Warren	PA	16365	**800-822-2009**	814-726-2140
Ocean Bank 780 NW 42nd Ave	Miami	FL	33126	**877-688-2265**	305-442-2660
OceanFirst Bank 975 Hooper Ave PO Box 2009	Toms River	NJ	08753	**888-623-2633**	732-240-4500
Ocwen Federal Bank FSB 1661 Worthington Rd Ste 100	West Palm Beach	FL	33409	**800-746-2936**	561-682-8000
Old Line Bank 1525 Pointer Ridge Pl *NASDAQ: WSB*	Bowie	MD	20716	**800-416-6373**	301-430-2500
Old National Bank 1 Main St PO Box 718	Evansville	IN	47705	**800-731-2265**	
OneUnited Bank 3683 Crenshaw Blvd	Los Angeles	CA	90016	**877-663-8648**	323-290-4848
Oritani Financial Corp 370 Pascack Rd PO Box 1329 *NASDAQ: ORIT*	Washington Township	NJ	07676	**888-674-8264**	201-664-5400
Oxford Bank PO Box 129	Addison	IL	60101	**800-236-2442**	630-629-5000
Pacific Continental Corp 111 W Seventh Ave PO Box 10727 *NASDAQ: PCBK*	Eugene	OR	97440	**877-231-2265**	541-686-8685
PBK Bank Inc 120 Frontier Blvd	Stanford	KY	40484	**877-230-3711**	606-365-7098
People's United Bank 850 Main St Bridgeport Ctr	Bridgeport	CT	06604	**800-772-1090**	203-338-7171
Peoples Financial Services Corp 82 Franklin Ave *NASDAQ: PFIS*	Hallstead	PA	18822	**888-868-3858**	570-879-2175
Peoples National Bank 5175 N Academy Blvd	Colorado Springs	CO	80918	**800-862-6696**	719-528-4000
Peoples Savings Bank (PSB) 414 N Adams PO Box 248	Wellsburg	IA	50680	**877-493-3799**	641-869-3721
Pilgrim BanCorp 2401 S Jefferson Ave	Mount Pleasant	TX	75455	**877-303-3111**	903-575-2150
Pintoresco Advisors LLC 466 Foothill Blvd Ste 333	La Canada Flintridge	CA	91011	**866-217-1140**	213-223-2070
Plaza Bank 7460 W Irving Pk Rd *General	Norridge	IL	60706	**877-714-9599***	708-456-3440
PNC Bank 1 PNC Plaza 249 Fifth Ave	Pittsburgh	PA	15222	**888-762-2265**	412-762-2000
PNC Bank Delaware 300 Delaware Ave	Wilmington	DE	19899	**888-762-2265**	302-429-1361
PNC Bank NA 249 Fifth Ave 1 PNC Plaza	Pittsburgh	PA	15222	**888-762-2265**	412-762-2000
Preferred Bank Los Angeles 601 S Figueroa St 29th Fl *NASDAQ: PFBC*	Los Angeles	CA	90017	**888-673-1808**	213-891-1188
Premier Bank & Trust 600 S Main St	North Canton	OH	44720	**855-728-6010**	330-499-1900
Premier Valley Bank 255 E River Pk Cir Ste 180	Fresno	CA	93720	**877-438-2002**	559-438-2002
Presidential Online Bank 4520 East-West Hwy	Bethesda	MD	20814	**800-383-6266**	301-652-0700
Profile Bank 45 Wakefield St PO Box 1808	Rochester	NH	03866	**800-554-8969**	603-332-2610
Progressive Bank NA 1090 E Bethlehem Blvd	Wheeling	WV	26003	**866-235-1923**	304-238-0040
Provident Savings Bank FSB 3756 Central Ave	Riverside	CA	92506	**800-442-5201**	951-686-6060
Prudential Savings Bank 1834 W Oregon Ave	Philadelphia	PA	19145	**800-554-8969**	215-755-1500
Putnam Bank 40 Main St PO Box 151	Putnam	CT	06260	**877-275-3342**	860-928-6501
QNB Corp 15 N Third St PO Box 9005 *OTC: QNBC*	Quakertown	PA	18951	**800-491-9070**	215-538-5600
Queenstown Bank of Maryland 7101 Main St PO Box 120	Queenstown	MD	21658	**888-827-4300**	410-827-8881
Rabo Bank 1026 E Grand Ave	Arroyo Grande	CA	93420	**800-942-6222**	805-473-7710
Randolph Savings Bank 129 N Main St	Randolph	MA	02368	**877-963-2100**	781-963-2100

Classified Section

	City	State	ZIP	Toll-Free	Phone
RBC Royal Bank 1127 Blvd D,carie	Montreal	QC	H4L3M8	**800-769-2599**	
RBC Trust Company (Delaware) Ltd 4550 New Linden Hill Rd Ste 200	Wilmington	DE	19808	**800-441-7698**	302-892-6976
Regions Bank 1900 Fifth Ave N	Birmingham	AL	35203	**800-734-4667**	
Ridgewood Savings Bank 71-02 Forest Ave	Ridgewood	NY	11385	**800-250-4832**	718-240-4800
River City Bank PO Box 15247 *OTC: RCBC* ■ *Cust Svc	Sacramento	CA	95851	**800-564-7144***	916-567-2899
Royal Bank of Canada 200 Bay St 9th Fl S Twr *TSE: RY*	Toronto	ON	M5J2J5	**800-769-2599**	416-955-7806
S&T Bank 800 Philadelphia St PO Box 190 *Cust Svc	Indiana	PA	15701	**800-325-2265***	724-349-1800
Salem Five & Savings Bank 210 Essex St *Cust Svc	Salem	MA	01970	**800-850-5000***	978-745-5555
SCB Bancorp Inc 1501 E Eldorado St	Decatur	IL	62521	**888-769-2265**	217-428-7781
Seamen's Bank 221 Commercial St PO Box 659	Provincetown	MA	02657	**855-227-5347**	508-487-0035
Severn Bancorp Inc 200 Westgate Cir Ste 200 *NASDAQ: SVBI*	Annapolis	MD	21401	**800-752-5854**	410-260-2000
Signature Bank 565 Fifth Ave 12th Fl *NASDAQ: SBNY*	New York	NY	10017	**866-744-5463**	646-822-1500
Silvergate Bank 4275 Executive Sq Ste 800	La Jolla	CA	92037	**800-595-5856**	858-362-6300
Somerset Trust Co 151 W Main St PO Box 777	Somerset	PA	15501	**800-972-1651**	814-443-9200
South Louisiana Bank (SLB) 1362 W Tunnel Blvd PO Box 1718	Houma	LA	70361	**877-275-3342**	985-851-3434
Southbridge Savings Bank Inc 253-257 Main St PO Box 370	Southbridge	MA	01550	**800-939-9103**	508-765-9103
Southern Michigan Bank & Trust 51 W Pearl St PO Box 309	Coldwater	MI	49036	**800-379-7628**	517-279-5500
SouthWest Capital Bank 622 Douglas Ave	Las Vegas	NM	87701	**800-748-2406**	505-425-7565
Southwest Missouri Bank 2417 S Grand Ave	Carthage	MO	64836	**800-943-8488**	417-358-1770
Sovereign Bank FSB PO Box 12646 *Cust Svc	Reading	PA	19612	**877-768-2265***	
Spencer Savings Bank PO Box 912	Spencer	MA	01562	**800-547-2885**	508-885-5313
Spencer Savings Bank SLA 611 River Dr	Elmwood Park	NJ	07407	**800-363-8115**	973-772-6700
Standard Bank & Trust Co 7800 W 95th St	Hickory Hills	IL	60457	**866-499-2265**	708-598-7400
State Bank 175 N Leroy St	Fenton	MI	48430	**800-535-0517**	810-629-2263
State Bank of Waterloo PO Box 148	Waterloo	IL	62298	**800-367-7576**	618-939-7194
State Farm Financial Services FSB PO Box 2316	Bloomington	IL	61702	**877-734-2265**	
Sterling Bank & Trust FSB 1 Town Sq Ste 1900	Southfield	MI	48076	**877-438-4338**	248-351-3442
Sterling Savings Bank 105 W Simpson Ave	Mccleary	WA	98557	**800-650-7141**	
Steuben Trust Co 1 Steuben Sq	Hornell	NY	14843	**866-783-8236**	607-324-5010
Stillman Banccorp NA PO Box 150	Stillman Valle	IL	61084	**866-546-8273**	815-645-2000
Summit Bank 2969 Broadway	Oakland	CA	94611	**800-380-9333**	510-839-8800
Sun National Bank 350 Fellowship Rd Ste. 101	Mount Laurel	NJ	08054	**800-786-9066**	
Suntrust Bank PO Box 4418 *NYSE: STI*	Atlanta	GA	30302	**800-786-8787**	
Swineford National Bank 1255 N Susquehanna Trial PO Box 241	Hummels Wharf	PA	17831	**866-762-1903**	570-743-7786
TD Bank NA 1701 Rt 70 E	Cherry Hill	NJ	08034	**888-751-9000**	856-751-2739
TD Banknorth Massachusetts 295 Pk Ave *Cust Svc	Worcester	MA	01609	**800-747-7000***	508-752-2584
Tennessee Commerce Bank 381 Mallory Stn Rd Ste 207	Franklin	TN	37067	**877-275-3342**	
Texas Capital Bank 2000 McKinney Ave Ste 700	Dallas	TX	75201	**877-839-2265**	214-932-6600
Texas Star Bank 177 E Jefferson PO Box 608	Van Alstyne	TX	75495	**866-546-8273**	903-482-5234
Third Federal Savings & Loan Assn of Cleveland 7007 Broadway Ave	Cleveland	OH	44105	**888-844-7333**	216-429-5228
Thomaston Savings Bank 203 Main St PO Box 907 *General	Thomaston	CT	06787	**855-344-1874***	860-283-1874
Tompkins Trust Co PO Box 460 *NYSE: TMP*	Ithaca	NY	14851	**888-273-3210**	607-273-3210
Town Bank 850 W N Shore Dr	Hartland	WI	53029	**800-433-3076**	262-367-1900
Traditional Bank 49 W Main St PO Box 326	Mount Sterling	KY	40353	**800-498-0414**	859-498-0414
Trust Bank 600 E Main St PO Box 158	Olney	IL	62450	**800-766-3451**	618-395-4311
Twin River National Bank 1507 G St	Lewiston	ID	83501	**877-743-4948**	208-746-4848
UBS AG 1285 Ave of the Americas	New York	NY	10019	**877-827-8001**	212-713-2000
UMB Bank NA 1010 Grand Blvd	Kansas City	MO	64106	**800-821-2171**	816-860-7000
Umpqua Bank PO Box 1820	Roseburg	OR	97470	**866-486-7782**	503-973-5945
Unibank For Savings 49 Church St	Whitinsville	MA	01588	**800-578-4270**	508-234-8112
Union Bank of California NA 400 California St 1st Fl	San Francisco	CA	94104	**800-238-4486**	415-765-3434
Union FSB 1565 Mineral Spring Ave	North Providence	RI	02904	**888-226-0819**	401-353-8900
United American Bank 101 S Ellsworth Ave *OTC: UABK*	San Mateo	CA	94401	**877-822-4822**	650-579-1500
United Bank 11185 Fairfax Blvd	Fairfax	VA	22030	**800-327-9862**	703-219-4850
United Financial Bancorp Inc 95 Elm St PO Box 9020 *NASDAQ: UBNK*	West Springfield	MA	01090	**866-959-2265**	413-787-1700
United Security Bancshares 2126 Inyo St *NASDAQ: UBFO*	Fresno	CA	93721	**888-683-6030**	559-248-4943
UPS Capital Business Credit 35 Glenlake Pkwy NE	Atlanta	GA	30328	**877-263-8772**	
US Bank NA 800 Nicollet Mall	Minneapolis	MN	55402	**800-872-2657**	651-466-3000
USAA FSB (USAAFSB) 10750 McDermott Fwy	San Antonio	TX	78288	**800-531-8722**	
Valley National Bank 615 Main Ave	Passaic	NJ	07055	**800-522-4100**	973-777-6768
Vectra Bank Colorado NA 2000 S Colorado Blvd Ste 2-1200	Denver	CO	80222	**800-232-8948**	720-947-7700
VirtualBank 3801 PGA Blvd Ste 700 PO Box 109638	Palm Beach Gardens	FL	33410	**877-998-2265**	
Wachovia Bank 3800 Wilshire Blvd Ste 110e	Los Angeles	CA	90025	**800-225-5935**	310-477-8004
Walpole Co-op Bank Inc 982 Main St	Walpole	MA	02081	**877-322-8228**	508-668-1080
Weatherbank Inc 1015 Waterwood Pkwy Ste J	Edmond	OK	73034	**800-687-3562**	405-359-0773
Wells Fargo Bank 5622 Third St	Katy	TX	77493	**800-869-3557**	281-391-2101
Wells Fargo Bank Indiana NA 111 E Wayne St	Fort Wayne	IN	46802	**800-869-3557**	260-461-6430
Wells Fargo Bank Iowa NA 666 Walnut St PO Box 837	Des Moines	IA	50309	**800-869-3557**	
Wells Fargo Bank NA 420 Montgomery St	San Francisco	CA	94104	**800-869-3557**	415-222-4292
Wells Fargo Bank Texas NA 707 Castroville Rd	San Antonio	TX	78237	**800-869-3557**	210-856-6224
WesBanco Inc 1 Bank Plz *NASDAQ: WSBC*	Wheeling	WV	26003	**800-328-3369**	304-234-9000
West Coast Bank 506 SW Coast Hwy *Cust Svc	Newport	OR	97365	**800-895-3345***	877-272-3678
West Suburban Bank 711 Westmore Meyers Rd	Lombard	IL	60148	**800-258-4009**	630-652-2000
Western Security Bank 2812 First Ave N	Billings	MT	59101	**800-983-5537**	406-371-8200
Westpac Banking Corp Americas Div 575 Fifth Ave 39th Fl	New York	NY	10017	**888-269-2377**	212-551-1800
White Sands Federal Credit Union 2190 E Lohman Ave	Las Cruces	NM	88001	**800-658-9933**	575-647-4500
Whitney National Bank 228 St Charles Ave	New Orleans	LA	70130	**800-844-4450**	504-586-7456
Wilmington Trust Co 1100 N Market St	Wilmington	DE	19890	**800-441-7120**	302-651-1000
Wilshire State Bank 3200 Wilshire Blvd Ste 1400	Los Angeles	CA	90010	**866-886-2265**	213-368-7700
Winnsboro State Bank & Trust Co 3875 Front St	Winnsboro	LA	71295	**866-205-4026**	318-435-7535
Winter Hill Bank 342 Broadway	Somerville	MA	02145	**800-444-4300**	617-666-8600
Woodforest Financial Group Inc PO Box 7889	Spring	TX	77387	**877-968-7962**	832-375-2000
Woodsville Guaranty Savings Bank 10 Pleasant St PO Box 266	Woodsville	NH	03785	**800-564-2735**	603-747-2735
WoodTrust Financial Corp 181 Second St S	Wisconsin Rapids	WI	54494	**800-716-3742**	715-423-7600
Yadkin Bank 1318 N Bridge St *NASDAQ: YDKN*	Elkin	NC	28621	**866-867-9979**	336-526-6371
Yakima Federal Savings & Loan Assn 118 E Yakima Ave	Yakima	WA	98901	**800-331-3225**	509-248-2634
York State Bank & Trust Co 700 N Lincoln AvE	York	NE	68467	**888-295-5540**	402-362-4411
Zions First National Bank 1 S Main St	Salt Lake City	UT	84111	**800-974-8800**	801-974-8800

70 BANKS - FEDERAL RESERVE

	City	State	ZIP	Toll-Free	Phone
Federal Reserve Bank of Atlanta 1000 Peachtree St NE	Atlanta	GA	30309	**888-500-7390**	404-498-8353
Birmingham Branch 524 Liberty Pkwy	Birmingham	AL	35242	**800-257-7013**	205-968-6700
New Orleans Branch 525 St Charles Ave	New Orleans	LA	70130	**877-638-7003**	504-593-3200
Federal Reserve Bank of Cleveland *Cincinnati Branch* 150 E Fourth St	Cincinnati	OH	45202	**877-372-2457**	513-721-4787
Federal Reserve Bank of Dallas 2200 N Pearl St PO Box 655906	Dallas	TX	75201	**800-333-4460**	214-922-6000
El Paso Branch 301 E Main St	El Paso	TX	79901	**800-333-4460**	915-521-5200
San Antonio Branch 402 Dwyer Ave	San Antonio	TX	78204	**800-333-4460**	210-978-1200
Federal Reserve Bank of Kansas City 1 Memorial Dr PO Box 1200	Kansas City	MO	64198	**800-333-1010**	816-881-2000
Denver Branch 1 Memorial Dr	Kansas City	MO	64198	**888-851-1920**	
Oklahoma City Branch 226 Dean A McGee Ave	Oklahoma City	OK	73102	**800-333-1030**	405-270-8400
Omaha Branch 2201 Farnam St	Omaha	NE	68102	**800-333-1040**	402-221-5500
Federal Reserve Bank of Minneapolis 90 Hennepin Ave	Minneapolis	MN	55401	**800-553-9656**	612-204-5000

Name / Address	City	State	ZIP	Toll-Free	Phone
Federal Reserve Bank of Philadelphia 10 Independence Mall	Philadelphia	PA	19106	**877-574-1776**	215-574-6000
Federal Reserve Bank of Saint Louis 701 Convention Plaza	Saint Louis	MO	63101	**800-333-0810**	314-444-8444
Little Rock Branch 111 Ctr St Ste 1000 Stephens Bldg	Little Rock	AR	72201	**877-372-2457**	501-324-8300
Federal Reserve Bank of San Francisco (FRBSF) 101 Market St	San Francisco	CA	94105	**800-227-4133**	415-974-2000
Portland Branch 1500 SW First Ave Ste 100	Portland	OR	97201	**800-227-4133**	503-276-3000
Salt Lake City Branch 101 Market St	San Francisco	CA	94105	**800-227-4133**	415-974-2000
First Federal of Northern Michigan 100 S Second Ave *NASDAQ: FFNM*	Alpena	MI	49707	**800-916-8800**	989-356-9041
First FSB 633 La Salle St	Ottawa	IL	61350	**800-443-8780**	815-434-3500
First Shore Federal 106-108 S Div St PO Box 4248	Salisbury	MD	21803	**800-634-6309**	410-546-1101
Lincoln FSB 1101 N St 68508	Lincoln	NE	68501	**800-333-2158**	402-474-1400
Milford Federal Savings & Loan Assn PO Box 210	Milford	MA	01757	**800-478-6990**	508-634-2500
Naugatuck Savings Bank 87 Church St	Naugatuck	CT	06770	**877-729-4442**	203-729-5291
Pioneer Bank 21 Second St PO Box 1048	Troy	NY	12181	**866-873-9573**	518-274-4800
Security Federal Bank (SFB) 238 Richland Ave W	Aiken	SC	29801	**866-851-3000**	803-641-3000
Summit State Bank 500 Bicentennial Way PO Box 6188 *NASDAQ: SSBI*	Santa Rosa	CA	95406	**800-428-5008**	707-568-6000
Webster First Federal Credit Union 271 Greenwood St	Worcester	MA	01607	**800-962-4452**	508-671-5000

71 BAR ASSOCIATIONS - STATE

SEE ALSO Legal Professionals Associations

Name / Address	City	State	ZIP	Toll-Free	Phone
Alabama State Bar 415 Dexter Ave	Montgomery	AL	36104	**800-392-5660**	334-269-1515
Alaska Bar Assn 550 W Seventh Ave Ste 1900 PO Box 100279	Anchorage	AK	99501	**800-478-4372**	907-272-7469
Delaware State Bar Assn 405 N King St	Wilmington	DE	19801	**855-872-5911**	302-658-5279
District of Columbia Bar, The 1101 K St NW Ste 200	Washington	DC	20005	**877-333-2227**	202-737-4700
Florida Bar 651 E Jefferson St	Tallahassee	FL	32399	**800-342-8060**	850-561-5600
Idaho State Bar 525 W Jefferson St	Boise	ID	83702	**800-221-3295**	208-334-4500
Illinois State Bar Assn 424 S Second St	Springfield	IL	62701	**800-252-8908**	217-525-1760
Indiana State Bar Assn 1 Indiana Sq Ste 530	Indianapolis	IN	46204	**800-266-2581**	317-639-5465
Kansas Bar Assn 1200 SW Harrison St	Topeka	KS	66612	**800-928-3111**	785-234-5696
Louisiana State Bar Assn (LSBA) 601 St Charles Ave	New Orleans	LA	70130	**800-421-5722**	504-566-1600
Maine State Bar Assn 124 State St	Augusta	ME	04330	**800-475-7523**	207-622-7523
Maryland State Bar Assn Inc 520 W Fayette St	Baltimore	MD	21201	**800-492-1964**	410-685-7878
Minnesota State Bar Assn 600 Nicollet Mall Ste 380	Minneapolis	MN	55402	**800-882-6722**	612-333-1183
Missouri Bar, The 326 Monroe St PO Box 119	Jefferson City	MO	65102	**888-253-6013**	573-635-4128
Nebraska State Bar Assn 635 S 14th St Ste 200	Lincoln	NE	68501	**800-927-0117**	402-475-7091
New York State Bar Assn 1 Elk St	Albany	NY	12207	**800-342-3661**	518-463-3200
North Carolina State Bar 217 E Edenton St PO Box 25996	Raleigh	NC	27601	**800-662-7407**	919-828-4620
Ohio State Bar Assn (OSBA) 1700 Lk Shore Dr	Columbus	OH	43204	**800-282-6556**	614-487-2050
Oklahoma Bar Assn 1901 N Lincoln Blvd PO Box 53036	Oklahoma City	OK	73105	**800-522-8065**	405-416-7000
Oregon State Bar Assn 16037 SW Upper Boones Ferry Rd	Tigard	OR	97224	**800-452-8260**	503-620-0222
Pennsylvania Bar Assn 100 S St	Harrisburg	PA	17101	**800-932-0311**	717-238-6715
Rhode Island Bar Assn 115 Cedar St	Providence	RI	02903	**877-659-0801**	401-421-5740
South Carolina Bar 950 Taylor St	Columbia	SC	29201	**877-797-2227**	803-799-6653
State Bar Assn of North Dakota 504 N Washington St PO Box 2136	Bismarck	ND	58502	**800-472-2685**	701-255-1404
State Bar of Arizona 4201 N 24th St Ste 200	Phoenix	AZ	85016	**866-482-9227**	602-252-4804
State Bar of Georgia 104 Marietta St NW Ste 100	Atlanta	GA	30303	**800-334-6865**	404-527-8700
State Bar of Michigan 306 Townsend St	Lansing	MI	48933	**800-968-1442**	517-346-6300
State Bar of Nevada 600 E Charleston Blvd	Las Vegas	NV	89104	**800-254-2797**	702-382-2200
State Bar of New Mexico 5121 Masthead St NE PO Box 92860	Albuquerque	NM	87109	**800-876-6227**	505-797-6000
State Bar of Texas 1414 Colorado St	Austin	TX	78701	**800-204-2222**	512-427-1463
Tennessee Bar Assn 221 Fourth Ave N Ste 400	Nashville	TN	37219	**800-899-6993**	615-383-7421
Utah State Bar 645 S 200 E	Salt Lake City	UT	84111	**877-752-2611**	801-531-9077
Vermont Bar Assn (VBA) 35-37 Ct St PO Box 100	Montpelier	VT	05601	**800-639-7036**	802-223-2020
Virginia State Bar 707 E Main St Ste 1500	Richmond	VA	23219	**800-552-7977**	804-775-0500
Washington State Bar Assn 1325 Fourth Ave Ste 600	Seattle	WA	98101	**800-945-9722**	206-727-8200
West Virginia State Bar 2000 Deitrick Blvd	Charleston	WV	25311	**866-989-8227**	304-553-7220
Wyoming State Bar 4124 Laramie St	Cheyenne	WY	82001	**855-445-8058**	307-632-9061

72 BASKETS, CAGES, RACKS, ETC - WIRE

SEE ALSO Pet Products

Name / Address	City	State	ZIP	Toll-Free	Phone
Bright Co-op Inc 803 W Seale St	Nacogdoches	TX	75964	**800-562-0730**	936-564-8378
Glamos Wire Products Company Inc 5561 N 152nd St	Hugo	MN	55038	**800-328-5062**	651-429-5386
InterMetro Industries Corp 651 N Washington St *Cust Svc	Wilkes-Barre	PA	18705	**800-992-1776***	570-825-2741
Lab Products Inc 742 Sussex Ave PO Box 639	Seaford	DE	19973	**800-526-0469**	302-628-4300
Midwest Wire Products Inc 800 Woodward Heights	Ferndale	MI	48220	**800-989-9881**	248-399-5100
Nashville Wire Products Manufacturing Co 199 Polk Ave	Nashville	TN	37210	**800-448-2125**	615-743-2500
Riverdale Mills Corp 130 Riverdale St	Northbridge	MA	01534	**800-762-6374**	508-234-8715

73 BATTERIES

Name / Address	City	State	ZIP	Toll-Free	Phone
A123 Systems Inc 200 W St	Waltham	MA	02451	**800-224-7654**	617-778-5700
Applied Energy Solutions LLC 1 Technology Pl	Caledonia	NY	14423	**800-836-2132**	585-538-4421
C & D Technologies Inc 1400 Union Meeting Rd PO Box 3053	Blue Bell	PA	19422	**800-543-8630**	215-619-2700
Cell-con Inc 305 Commerce Dr Ste 300	Exton	PA	19341	**800-771-7139**	610-280-7630
Continental Battery Corp 4919 Woodall St	Dallas	TX	75247	**800-442-0081**	214-631-5701
Crown Battery Manufacturing Co 1445 Majestic Dr	Fremont	OH	43420	**800-487-2879**	419-334-7181
Douglas Battery Manufacturing Co 500 Battery Dr	Winston-Salem	NC	27107	**800-368-4527**	
Duracell 14 Research Dr	Bethel	CT	06801	**800-551-2355**	800-544-5454
EnerSys 2366 Bernville Rd *NYSE: ENS*	Reading	PA	19605	**800-538-3627**	610-208-1991
Exide Technologies 13000 Deerfield Pkwy Bldg 200 *NASDAQ: XIDE*	Milton	GA	30004	**888-563-6300**	678-566-9000
Hawker Powersource Inc 9404 Ooltewah Industrial Dr PO Box 808	Ooltewah	TN	37363	**800-238-8658**	423-238-5700
Industrial Battery & Charger Inc 5831 Orr Rd	Charlotte	NC	28213	**800-833-8412**	704-597-7330
Mathews Assoc Inc 220 Power Ct	Sanford	FL	32771	**800-871-5262**	407-323-3390
R & D Batteries Inc 3300 Corporate Ctr Dr PO Box 5007	Burnsville	MN	55306	**800-950-1945**	952-890-0629
Surefire LLC 18300 Mt Baldy Cir	Fountain Valley	CA	92708	**800-828-8809**	714-545-9444
Tadiran Batteries 2001 Marcus Ave Ste 125E	New Hyde Park	NY	11042	**800-537-1368**	516-621-4980
TNR Technical Inc 301 Central Pk Dr *OTC: TNRK*	Sanford	FL	32771	**800-346-0601**	407-321-3011
Trojan Battery Co 12380 Clark St *Cust Svc	Santa Fe Springs	CA	90670	**800-423-6569***	562-236-3000
Ultralife Batteries Inc 2000 Technology Pkwy *NASDAQ: ULBI*	Newark	NY	14513	**800-332-5000**	315-332-7100
Valence Technology Inc 12303 Technology Blvd Ste 950	Austin	TX	78727	**888-825-3623**	512-527-2900

74 BEARINGS - BALL & ROLLER

Name / Address	City	State	ZIP	Toll-Free	Phone
Accurate Bushing Company Inc 443 N Ave *Sales	Garwood	NJ	07027	**800-932-0076***	908-789-1121
AST Bearings 115 Main Rd	Montville	NJ	07045	**800-526-1250**	973-335-2230
Bearing Inspection Inc 4500 Mount Pleasant NW *Cust Svc	North Canton	OH	44720	**800-416-8881***	234-262-3000
Bearing Service Co of Pennsylvania 630 Alpha Dr RIDC Park	Pittsburgh	PA	15238	**800-783-2327**	412-963-7710
General Bearing Corp 44 High St *Sales	West Nyack	NY	10994	**800-431-1766***	845-358-6000
JTEKT Corporation 29570 Clemens Rd *Cust Svc	Westlake	OH	44145	**800-263-5163***	440-835-1000
Nachi America Inc 715 Pushville Rd	Greenwood	IN	46143	**888-340-2747**	317-530-1001
Peer Bearing Co 2200 Norman Dr S	Waukegan	IL	60085	**800-433-7337**	847-578-1000
Roller Bearing Company of America 400 Sullivan Way	West Trenton	NJ	08628	**800-390-3300**	609-882-5050
Rotek Inc 1400 S Chillicothe Rd PO Box 312	Aurora	OH	44202	**800-221-8043**	330-562-4000
Schaeffler Group USA Inc 308 Springhill Farm Rd	Fort Mill	SC	29715	**800-361-5841**	803-548-8500
Schatz Bearing Corp 10 Fairview Ave	Poughkeepsie	NY	12601	**800-554-1406**	845-452-6000

Company	Address	City	State	ZIP	Toll-Free	Phone
Timken Co	1835 Dueber Ave SW	Canton	OH	44706	**800-223-1954**	330-438-3000
NYSE: TKR						
Wecsys LLC	8825 Xylon Ave N	Minneapolis	MN	55445	**888-493-2797**	763-504-1069
Winsted Precision Ball Corp	159 Colebrook River Rd	Winsted	CT	06098	**800-462-3075**	860-379-2788

75 BEAUTY SALON EQUIPMENT & SUPPLIES

Company	Address	City	State	ZIP	Toll-Free	Phone
Belvedere USA Corp	1 Belvedere Blvd	Belvidere	IL	61008	**800-435-5491**	815-544-3131
Betty Dain Creations Inc	9701 NW 112 Ave Ste 10	Miami	FL	33178	**800-327-5256***	305-769-3451
*General						
Burmax Co	28 Barretts Ave	Holtsville	NY	11742	**800-645-5118**	
Collins Manufacturing Co	2000 Bowser Rd	Cookeville	TN	38506	**800-292-6450**	931-528-5151
Dr Kern USA Inc	221 S Franklin Rd	Indianapolis	IN	46219	**800-908-9885**	317-472-0873
Jeunesse Global LLC	650 Douglas Ave	Altamonte Springs	FL	32714	**800-400-2676**	407-215-7414
Living Earth Crafts	3210 Executive Ridge Dr	Vista	CA	92081	**800-358-8292**	760-597-2155
National Salon Resources Inc	3109 Louisiana Ave N	Minneapolis	MN	55427	**800-622-0003**	763-541-1000
Pibbs Industries	133-15 32nd Ave	Flushing	NY	11354	**800-551-5020**	718-445-8046
Sally Beauty Company Inc	3001 Colorado Blvd	Denton	TX	76210	**800-777-5706**	940-898-7500
Takara Belmont USA Inc	101 Belmont Dr	Somerset	NJ	08873	**877-283-1289**	
TouchAmerica	1403 S Third St Ext	Hillsborough	NC	27278	**800-678-6824**	919-732-6968
William Marvy Company Inc	1540 St Clair Ave	Saint Paul	MN	55105	**800-874-2651**	651-698-0726

76 BEAUTY SALONS

Company	Address	City	State	ZIP	Toll-Free	Phone
Adam Broderick Salon & Spa	89 Danbury Rd	Ridgefield	CT	06877	**800-438-3834**	203-431-3994
Aromaland Inc	1326 Rufina Cir	Santa Fe	NM	87507	**800-933-5267**	505-438-0402
Ball Beauty Supplies	416 N Fairfax Ave	Los Angeles	CA	90036	**800-588-0244**	323-655-2330
Beauty Brands Inc	4600 Madison St Ste 400	Kansas City	MO	64112	**877-640-2248**	816-531-2266
Beauty Craft Supply & Equipment Co	11110 Bren Rd W	Minnetonka	MN	55343	**800-328-5010**	952-935-4420
Chella Professional Skin Care	507 Calle San Pablo	Camarillo	CA	93012	**877-424-3552**	805-383-7711
Genesis Biosystems Inc	1500 Eagle Ct # 75057	Lewisville	TX	75057	**888-577-7335**	972-315-7888
Gino Morena Enterprises LLC	111 Starlite St	South San Francisco	CA	94080	**800-227-6905**	
Great Clips Inc	7700 France Ave S Ste 425	Minneapolis	MN	55435	**800-999-5959**	952-893-9088
Holiday Hair	7201 Metro Blvd	Minneapolis	MN	55439	**800-345-7811**	
Mohegan Tribal Gaming Authority	1 Mohegan Sun Blvd	Uncasville	CT	06382	**888-226-7711**	
Regis Corp	7201 Metro Blvd	Minneapolis	MN	55439	**888-888-7778**	952-947-7777
NYSE: RGS						
Regis Corp MasterCuts Div	7201 Metro Blvd	Minneapolis	MN	55439	**877-857-2070**	952-947-7777
Regis Corp Pro-Cuts Div	7201 Metro Blvd	Minneapolis	MN	55439	**877-857-2070**	952-947-7777
Regis Corp Regis Hairstylists Div	7201 Metro Blvd	Minneapolis	MN	55439	**877-857-2070**	952-947-7777
Regis Corp SmartStyle Div	7201 Metro Blvd	Minneapolis	MN	55439	**877-857-2070**	952-947-7777
Salon Service Group Inc	1859 W Arbor Ct	Springfield	MO	65807	**800-933-5733**	
Sport Clips Inc	110 Briarwood Dr	Georgetown	TX	78628	**800-872-4247**	512-869-1201
Stewart School of Cosmetology	604 NW Ave	Sioux Falls	SD	57104	**800-537-2625**	605-336-2775
Supercuts	7201 Metro Blvd	Minneapolis	MN	55439	**877-857-2070**	
Toni & Guy USA Inc	2311 Midway Rd	Carrollton	TX	75006	**800-256-9391**	
Wood River Technologies Inc	191 Sun Valley Rd Ste 202	Ketchum	ID	83340	**888-661-4094**	

77 BETTER BUSINESS BUREAUS - CANADA

Company	Address	City	Province	Postal Code	Toll-Free	Phone
Better Business Bureau of Saskatchewan	980 Albert St Ste 201	Regina	SK	S4R2P7	**888-352-7601**	306-352-7601
Better Business Bureau of Vancouver Island	220-1175 Cook St Ste 220	Victoria	BC	V8V4A1	**877-826-4222**	250-386-6348
Better Business Bureau Serving Mainland British Columbia	788 Beatty St Ste 404	Vancouver	BC	V6B2M1	**888-803-1222**	604-682-2711
Better Business Bureau Serving Western Ontario	190 Wortley Rd Ste 206	London	ON	N6C4Y7	**877-283-9222**	519-673-3222
Better Business Bureau Serving Winnipeg & Manitoba	1030B Empress St	Winnipeg	MB	R3G3H4	**800-385-3074**	204-989-9010

78 BETTER BUSINESS BUREAUS - US

SEE ALSO Consumer Interest Organizations

Company	Address	City	State	ZIP	Toll-Free	Phone
Better Business Bureau Online	*Council of Better Business Bureaus, The* 4200 Wilson Blvd Ste 800	Arlington	VA	22203	**800-459-8875**	703-276-0100
Better Business Bureau Heartland	11811 P St	Omaha	NE	68137	**800-649-6814**	402-391-7612
Better Business Bureau Inc	1000 Broadway Ste 625	Oakland	CA	94607	**866-411-2221**	510-844-2000
Better Business Bureau of Ark-La-Tex	401 Edwards St Ste 135	Shreveport	LA	71101	**800-372-4222**	318-222-7575
Better Business Bureau of Asheville/Western North Carolina	112 Executive Pk	Asheville	NC	28801	**800-452-2882**	828-253-2392
Better Business Bureau of Canton Region/West Virginia	1434 Cleveland Ave NW	Canton	OH	44703	**800-362-0494**	330-454-9401
Better Business Bureau of Central & Eastern Kentucky	1460 Newtown Pk	Lexington	KY	40511	**800-866-6668**	859-259-1008
Better Business Bureau of Central East Texas	3600 Old BullaRd Rd Bldg 1	Tyler	TX	75701	**800-443-0131**	903-581-5704
Better Business Bureau of Central East Texas Longview Branch	102 Commander Ste 7	Longview	TX	75605	**800-443-0131**	903-758-3222
Better Business Bureau of Central Illinois	112 Harrison St	Peoria	IL	61602	**800-763-4222**	309-688-3741
Better Business Bureau of Central Indiana	151 N Delaware St	Indianapolis	IN	46204	**866-463-9222**	317-488-2222
Better Business Bureau of Central Louisiana & Ark-La-Tex	5220-C Rue Verdun	Alexandria	LA	71303	**800-372-4222***	318-473-4494
*General						
Better Business Bureau of Central Northeast Northwest & Southwest Arizona	4428 N 12th St	Phoenix	AZ	85014	**877-291-6222**	602-264-1721
Better Business Bureau of Central Ohio	1169 Dublin Rd	Columbus	OH	43215	**800-759-2400**	614-486-6336
Better Business Bureau of Eastern Massachusetts Maine Rhode Island & Vermont	290 Donald Lynch Blvd Ste 102	Marlborough	MA	01752	**800-422-2811**	508-652-4800
Better Business Bureau of Greater Kansas City	8080 Ward Pkwy Ste 401	Kansas City	MO	64114	**877-606-0695**	816-421-7800
Better Business Bureau of Hawaii	1132 Bishop St Ste 615	Honolulu	HI	96813	**877-222-6551**	808-536-6956
Better Business Bureau of Kansas Inc	345 N Riverview St Ste 720	Wichita	KS	67203	**800-856-2417**	316-263-3146
Better Business Bureau of Louisville Southern Indiana & Western Kentucky	844 S Fourth St	Louisville	KY	40203	**800-388-2222**	502-583-6546
Better Business Bureau of Maine	290 Donald Lynch Blvd Ste 102	Marlborough	MA	01752	**800-422-2811**	508-652-4800
Better Business Bureau of Metropolitan New York	257 Pk Ave S	New York	NY	10010	**800-684-3322**	212-533-6200
Better Business Bureau of New Jersey	1700 Whitehorse-Hamilton Sq Rd Ste D-5	Trenton	NJ	08690	**888-494-4009**	609-588-0808
Better Business Bureau of Northeast California	3075 Beacon Blvd	West Sacramento	CA	95691	**866-334-6272**	916-443-6843
Better Business Bureau of Northeast Florida & The Southeast Atlantic	4417 Beach Blvd Ste 202	Jacksonville	FL	32207	**800-713-6661**	904-721-2288
Better Business Bureau of Northeast Ohio	2800 Euclid Ave 4th Fl	Cleveland	OH	44115	**800-233-0361**	216-241-7678
Better Business Bureau of Northern Colorado & East Central Wyoming	8020 S County Rd 5 Ste 100	Fort Collins	CO	80528	**800-564-0371**	970-484-1348
Better Business Bureau of Northern Indiana	4011 Parnell Ave	Fort Wayne	IN	46805	**800-552-4631**	260-423-4433
Better Business Bureau of Northwest North Carolina	500 W Fifth St Ste 202	Winston-Salem	NC	27101	**800-777-8348**	336-725-8348
Better Business Bureau of Northwest Ohio & Southeast Michigan	7668 King's Pt Rd	Toledo	OH	43617	**800-743-4222**	419-531-3116
Better Business Bureau of Rockford	330 North Wabash Ave Ste 3120	Chicago	IL	60611	**800-955-5100**	312-832-0500
Better Business Bureau of Southeast Florida & the Caribbean	4411 Beacon Cir Ste 4	West Palm Beach	FL	33407	**866-966-7226**	561-842-1918
Better Business Bureau of Southeast Tennessee & Northwest Georgia	508 N Market St	Chattanooga	TN	37405	**800-548-4456**	423-266-6144
Better Business Bureau of Southeast Texas	550 Fannin St Ste 100	Beaumont	TX	77701	**800-685-7650**	409-835-5348
Better Business Bureau of Southwest Georgia	PO Box 2587	Columbus	GA	31902	**800-768-4222**	706-324-0712
Better Business Bureau of Southwest Idaho & Eastern Oregon	1200 N Curtis Rd PO Box 9817	Boise	ID	83706	**800-218-1001**	208-342-4649
Better Business Bureau of Southwest Louisiana Inc	2309 E Prien Lk Rd	Lake Charles	LA	70601	**800-542-7085**	337-478-6253
Better Business Bureau of the Akron Inc	222 W Market St	Akron	OH	44303	**800-825-8887**	330-253-4590
Better Business Bureau of the Bakersfield Area	1601 H St Ste 101	Bakersfield	CA	93301	**800-675-8118**	661-322-2074
Better Business Bureau of the Denver-Boulder Metro Area	1020 Cherokee St	Denver	CO	80204	**800-356-6333**	303-758-2100
Better Business Bureau of the Mid-South	3693 Tyndale Dr	Memphis	TN	38125	**800-222-8754**	901-759-1300
Better Business Bureau of Upstate New York	100 Bryant Woods S	Amherst	NY	14228	**800-828-5000**	716-881-5222
Better Business Bureau of Utah	5673 S Redwood Rd	Salt Lake City	UT	84123	**800-456-3907**	801-892-6009
Better Business Bureau of West Florida	2655 McCormick Dr	Clearwater	FL	33759	**800-525-1447**	727-535-5522
Better Business Bureau of West Georgia & East Alabama	PO Box 2587	Columbus	GA	31902	**800-768-4222**	706-324-0712
Better Business Bureau of Western Massachusetts	35 Ctr St Ste 203	Chicopee	MA	01013	**866-566-9222**	
Better Business Bureau Serving Central California	4201 W Shaw Ave Ste 107	Fresno	CA	93722	**800-675-8118**	559-222-8111
Tri-State Better Business Bureau	5401 Vogel Rd Ste 410	Evansville	IN	47715	**800-359-0979**	812-473-0202

79 BEVERAGES - MFR

SEE ALSO Water - Bottled ; Breweries

79-1 Liquor - Mfr

Company / Address	City	State	ZIP	Toll-Free	Phone
Anheuser-Busch Cos Inc 1 Busch Pl	Saint Louis	MO	63118	**800-342-5283**	314-577-2000
Laird & Co 1 LaiRd Rd	Scobeyville	NJ	07724	**877-438-5247**	732-542-0312
Sunrich LLC 3824 SW 93rd St PO Box 128	Hope	MN	56046	**800-297-5997**	507-451-6030
Walker MS Inc 20 Third Ave	Somerville	MA	02143	**800-528-2787**	617-776-6700

79-2 Soft Drinks - Mfr

Company / Address	City	State	ZIP	Toll-Free	Phone
Coca-Cola Co 1 Coca-Cola Plz PO Box 1734 *NYSE: KO*	Atlanta	GA	30313	**800-438-2653**	404-676-2121
Cott Corp 6525 Viscount Rd *NYSE: COT*	Mississauga	ON	L4V1H6	**866-732-8683**	905-672-1900
Crystal Rock Holdings Inc 1050 Buckingham St *NYSE: AMEX*	Watertown	CT	06795	**800-525-0070**	860-945-0661
Dr Pepper/Seven-Up Inc 5301 Legacy Dr	Plano	TX	75024	**800-696-5891**	972-673-7000
Fiji Water Company LLC 11444 W Olympic Blvd 2nd Fl	Los Angeles	CA	90064	**888-426-3454**	310-312-2850
Great Plains Coca-Cola Bottling Company Inc 600 N May Ave	Oklahoma City	OK	73107	**800-753-2653**	405-280-2000
Jones Soda Co 66 S Hanford St Ste 150 *OTC: JSDA*	Seattle	WA	98134	**800-690-6903**	206-624-3357
Middlesboro Coca-Cola Bottling Works Inc 1324 Cumberland Ave	Middlesboro	KY	40965	**800-442-0102**	877-692-4679
Polar Beverages Inc 1001 Southbridge St *Cust Svc	Worcester	MA	01610	**800-734-9800***	508-753-4300
Shasta Beverages Inc 26901 Industrial Blvd	Hayward	CA	94545	**800-834-9980**	510-783-3200
Wallingford Coffee Mills Inc 11401 Rockfield Ct	Cincinnati	OH	45241	**800-533-3690**	513-771-4570
White Rock Products Corp 141-07 20th Ave Ste 403	Whitestone	NY	11357	**800-969-7625**	718-746-3400

79-3 Wines - Mfr

Company / Address	City	State	ZIP	Toll-Free	Phone
Barton Brescome Inc 69 Defco Park Rd	North Haven	CT	06473	**800-922-4840**	203-239-4901
Beaulieu Vineyard 1960 St Helena Hwy	Rutherford	CA	94573	**800-373-5896**	707-967-5233
Bronco Wine Co 6342 Bystrum Rd	Ceres	CA	95307	**855-874-2394**	209-538-3131
Canandaigua Wine Company Inc 235 N Bloomfield Rd	Canandaigua	NY	14424	**888-659-7900**	585-396-7600
Clos du Bois 19410 Geyserville Ave *Sales	Geyserville	CA	95441	**800-222-3189***	707-857-1651
Columbia Crest Winery 178810 State Rt 221 PO Box 231	Paterson	WA	99345	**888-309-9463**	509-875-4227
Domaine Chandon Inc 1 California Dr	Yountville	CA	94599	**888-242-6366**	
Garvey Wholesale Beverage Inc 2542 San Gabriel Blvd	Rosemead	CA	91770	**800-287-2075**	626-280-5244
Hogue Cellars 2800 Lee Rd	Prosser	WA	99350	**800-565-9779**	
Kendall-Jackson Wine Estates Ltd 425 Aviation Blvd	Santa Rosa	CA	95403	**800-769-3649**	707-544-4000
Kysela Pere Et Fils Ltd 331 Victory Rd	Winchester	VA	22602	**877-492-7917**	540-722-9228
Laetitia Vineyards & Winery Inc 453 Laetitia Vineyard Dr	Arroyo Grande	CA	93420	**888-809-8463**	805-481-1772
Louis M Martini Winery 254 S St Helena Hwy	Saint Helena	CA	94574	**866-549-2582**	
Magnotta Winery Corp 271 Chrislea Rd	Vaughan	ON	L4L8N6	**800-461-9463**	905-738-9463
Mendocino Wine Co 501 PaRducci Rd	Ukiah	CA	95482	**800-362-9463**	707-463-5350
Michel-Schlumberger Partners LP 4155 Wine Creek Rd	Healdsburg	CA	95448	**800-447-3060**	707-433-7427
Newlands Systems Inc 602-30731 Simpson Rd	Abbotsford	BC	V2T6Y7	**877-855-4890**	604-855-4890
Old Mill Winery 403 S Broadway	Geneva	OH	44041	**800-227-6972**	
Pine Ridge Winery LLC 5901 Silverado Trail	Napa	CA	94558	**800-575-9777**	
Ravenswood Winery Inc 18701 Gehricke Rd	Sonoma	CA	95476	**888-669-4679**	
Raymond Vineyard 849 Zinfandel Ln	Saint Helena	CA	94574	**800-525-2659**	707-963-6941
Roanoke Valley Wine Co 1250 Intervale	Salem	VA	24153	**877-478-9463**	540-444-4440
Robert Mondavi Co 7801 St Helena Hwy	Oakville	CA	94562	**888-766-6328**	707-226-1395
Rodney Strong Vineyards 11455 Old Redwood Hwy	Healdsburg	CA	95448	**800-678-4763**	707-431-1533
Sebastiani Vineyards Inc 389 Fourth St E	Sonoma	CA	95476	**855-232-2338**	707-933-3230
Trefethen Vineyards Winery Inc 1160 Oak Knoll Ave	Napa	CA	94558	**866-895-7696**	707-255-7700
Warner Vineyards Inc 706 S Kalamazoo St	Paw Paw	MI	49079	**800-756-5357**	269-657-3165
Weibel Vineyards 1 Winemaster Way	Lodi	CA	95240	**800-932-9463**	209-365-9463
Willamette Valley Vineyards Inc 8800 Enchanted Way SE *NASDAQ: WVVI ■ *Sales*	Turner	OR	97392	**800-344-9463***	503-588-9463

80 BEVERAGES - WHOL

80-1 Beer & Ale - Whol

Company / Address	City	State	ZIP	Toll-Free	Phone
Arkansas Distributing Company LLC 800 E Barton Ave	West Memphis	AR	72301	**877-735-3506**	870-735-3506
Associated Distributors LLC 401 Woodlake Dr	Chesapeake	VA	23320	**800-308-2600**	757-424-6300
Atlas Distributing Corp 44 Southbridge St	Auburn	MA	01501	**800-649-6221**	508-791-6221
Banko Beverage Co 5001 Crackersport Rd *General	Allentown	PA	18104	**800-322-9295***	610-434-0147
Blach Distributing Co 131 W Main St	Elko	NV	89801	**800-310-5099**	775-738-7111
Buck Distributing Company Inc 15827 Commerce Ct *Cust Svc	Upper Marlboro	MD	20774	**800-750-2825***	301-952-0400
Columbia Distributing Co 6840 N Cutter Cir	Portland	OR	97217	**888-417-5001**	503-289-9600
Frank B Fuhrer Wholesale Co 3100 E Carson St	Pittsburgh	PA	15203	**800-837-2212**	412-488-8844
Gambrinus Co, The 14800 San Pedro Ave 3rd Fl	San Antonio	TX	78232	**800-596-6486**	210-490-9128
Georgia Crown Distributing Co 100 Georgia Crown Dr	McDonough	GA	30253	**800-342-2350**	770-302-3000
Gretz Beer Co 710 E Main St *General	Norristown	PA	19401	**800-310-5099***	610-275-0285
Iron City Distributing Co 2670 Commercial Ave *Cust Svc	Mingo Junction	OH	43938	**800-759-2671***	740-598-4171
Labatt Breweries of Canada 207 Queen's Quay W Ste 299 *Cust Svc	Toronto	ON	M5J1A7	**800-268-2337***	416-361-5050
Maple City Ice Co Inc 371 Cleveland Rd *Cust Svc	Norwalk	OH	44857	**877-762-9119***	419-668-2531
Mautino Distributing Co 500 N Richards St *Cust Svc	Spring Valley	IL	61362	**800-851-2756***	815-664-4311
McLaughlin & Moran Inc 40 Slater Rd	Cranston	RI	02920	**800-423-0156**	401-463-5454
NKS Distributors Inc 399 Churchmans Rd	New Castle	DE	19720	**800-310-5099**	302-322-1811
Pine State Trading Co 8 Ellis Ave	Augusta	ME	04330	**800-873-3825**	207-622-3741
Saratoga Eagle Sales & Service Inc 45 Duplainville Rd	Saratoga Springs	NY	12866	**800-310-5099**	518-581-7377
Savannah Distributing Co Inc 2425 W Gwinnett St *General	Savannah	GA	31415	**800-551-0777***	912-233-1167
Silver Eagle Distributors LP 7777 Washington Ave	Houston	TX	77007	**855-332-2110**	713-869-4361
Southern Wine & Spirits of Colorado 5270 Fox St PO Box 5603	Denver	CO	80216	**800-776-0180**	303-292-1711
Standard Beverage Corp 2416 E 37th St N	Wichita	KS	67219	**800-999-8797**	316-838-7707
Star Distributors Inc 460 Frontage Rd	West Haven	CT	06516	**877-922-3501**	203-932-3636

80-2 Soft Drinks - Whol

Company / Address	City	State	ZIP	Toll-Free	Phone
Atlas Distributing Corp 44 Southbridge St	Auburn	MA	01501	**800-649-6221**	508-791-6221
Buffalo Rock Co 111 Oxmoor Rd	Birmingham	AL	35209	**800-822-9799**	205-942-3435
Coca-Cola Bottling Co Consolidated 4100 Coca-Cola Plaza *NASDAQ: COKE*	Charlotte	NC	28211	**800-777-2653**	704-557-4000
Swire Coca-Cola USA 12634 S 265 W	Draper	UT	84020	**800-497-2653**	801-816-5300

80-3 Wine & Liquor - Whol

Company / Address	City	State	ZIP	Toll-Free	Phone
Alabama Crown Distributing 421 Industrial Ln	Birmingham	AL	35211	**800-548-1869**	205-941-1155
Badger Liquor Company Inc 850 S Morris St	Fond du Lac	WI	54936	**800-242-9708**	920-923-8160
Badger West Wine & Spirits LLC 5400 Old Town Hall Rd	Eau Claire	WI	54701	**800-472-6674**	715-836-8600
Ben Arnold Beverage Company LP 101 Beverage Blvd *Acctg	Ridgeway	SC	29130	**888-262-9787***	803-337-3500
Beverage Distributors Co 14200 E Moncrieff Pl *General	Aurora	CO	80011	**888-262-9787***	303-371-3421
Castle Brands Inc 122 E 42nd St Ste 4700 *NYSE: ROX*	New York	NY	10168	**800-882-8140**	646-356-0200
Charmer Sunbelt Group, The 60 E 42nd St Ste 1915	New York	NY	10165	**888-262-9787**	212-699-7000
Columbia Distributing Co 6840 N Cutter Cir	Portland	OR	97217	**888-417-5001**	503-289-9600
Constellation Brands Inc 207 High Pt Dr Bldg 100 *NYSE: STZ*	Victor	NY	14564	**888-724-2169**	

Company / Address	City	State	ZIP	Toll-Free	Phone
Frederick Wildman & Sons Ltd 307 E 53rd St *General	New York	NY	10022	**800-733-9463***	212-355-0700
Georgia Crown Distributing Co 100 Georgia Crown Dr	McDonough	GA	30253	**800-342-2350**	770-302-3000
Glazer's Wholesale Drug Company Inc 14911 Quorum Dr Ste 400	Dallas	TX	75254	**800-275-2854**	972-392-8200
NKS Distributors Inc 399 Churchmans Rd	New Castle	DE	19720	**800-310-5099**	302-322-1811
Phillips Distributing Corp 3010 Nob Hill Rd	Madison	WI	53713	**800-236-7269**	608-222-9177
Savannah Distributing Co Inc 2425 W Gwinnett St *General	Savannah	GA	31415	**800-551-0777***	912-233-1167
Southern Wine & Spirits of America Inc 1600 NW 163rd St	Miami	FL	33169	**800-776-0180**	305-625-4171
Southern Wine & Spirits of Colorado 5270 Fox St PO Box 5603	Denver	CO	80216	**800-776-0180**	303-292-1711
Southern Wine & Spirits of Illinois 300 E Crossroads Pkwy Bolingbrook Corp Ctr	Bolingbrook	IL	60440	**800-776-0180**	630-685-3000
Standard Beverage Corp 2416 E 37th St N	Wichita	KS	67219	**800-999-8797**	316-838-7707
Terlato Wine Group, The (TWG) 900 Armour Dr	Lake Bluff	IL	60044	**800-950-7676**	847-604-8900
Winebow Inc 75 Chestnut Ridge Rd	Montvale	NJ	07645	**800-859-0689**	201-445-0620
Young's Market Company LLC 500 S Central Ave	Los Angeles	CA	90013	**800-627-2777**	213-612-1248

81 BICYCLES & BICYCLE PARTS & ACCESSORIES

SEE ALSO Sporting Goods ; Toys, Games, Hobbies

Company / Address	City	State	ZIP	Toll-Free	Phone
Cane Creek Cycling Components 355 Cane Creek Rd	Fletcher	NC	28732	**800-234-2725**	828-684-3551
Huffy Bicycle Co 6551 Centerville Business Pkwy	Centerville	OH	45459	**800-872-2453**	937-865-2800
Raleigh America Inc 6004 S 190th St Ste 101	Kent	WA	98032	**800-222-5527**	
Raleigh USA 6004 S 190th St Ste 101	Kent	WA	98032	**800-222-5527**	253-395-1100
SMITH Mfg Company Inc 1610 S Dixie Hwy	Pompano Beach	FL	33060	**800-653-9311**	954-941-9744
Specialized Bicycle Components 15130 Concord Cir	Morgan Hill	CA	95037	**877-808-8154**	408-779-6229
SRAM Corp 1333 N Kingsbury St 4th Fl	Chicago	IL	60622	**800-346-2928**	312-664-8800
Terry Precision Bicycles for Women Inc 47 Maple St	Burlington	VT	05401	**800-289-8379**	
Worksman Trading Corp 94-15 100th St	Ozone Park	NY	11416	**800-962-2453**	718-322-2000

82 BIOMETRIC IDENTIFICATION EQUIPMENT & SOFTWARE

Company / Address	City	State	ZIP	Toll-Free	Phone
Bio Medic Data Systems Inc 1 Silas Rd	Seaford	DE	19973	**800-526-2637**	302-628-4100
Count Me In LLC 1530 E Dundee Ste 150	Palatine	IL	60074	**866-514-5888**	
Crossmatch 720 Bay Rd Ste 100	Redwood City	CA	94063	**866-463-7792**	650-474-4000
MorphoTrak Inc 113 S Columbus St 4th Fl	Alexandria	VA	22314	**800-601-6790**	703-797-2600
NEC Corp of America 10850 Gold Ctr Dr Ste 200	Rancho Cordova	CA	95670	**800-632-4636**	916-463-7000
Security First Corp 29811 Santa Margarita Pkwy Ste 600	Rancho Santa Margarita	CA	92688	**888-884-7152**	949-858-7525
SIRCHIE Finger Print Laboratories Inc 100 Hunter Pl	Youngsville	NC	27596	**800-356-7311**	919-554-2244

83 BIO-RECOVERY SERVICES

Companies listed here provide services for managing and eliminating biohazard dangers that may be present after a death or injury. These services include cleaning, disinfecting, and deodorizing biohazard scenes resulting from accidents, homicides, suicides, natural deaths, and similar events.

Company / Address	City	State	ZIP	Toll-Free	Phone
Bio-Recovery Corp 1863 Pond Rd Ste 4	Ronkonkoma	NY	11779	**800-556-0621**	631-676-2600
Bio-Scene Recovery 13191 Meadow St NE	Alliance	OH	44601	**877-380-5500**	330-823-5500
Grangeville Environmental Services (GES) *GES Property Pros LLC* 585 McAllister St	Hanover	PA	17331	**866-437-5151**	717-637-6152
JP Maguire Assoc Inc 266 Brookside Rd	Waterbury	CT	06708	**877-576-2484**	203-755-2297
Peerless Cleaners Inc 519 N Monroe St	Decatur	IL	62522	**800-879-7056**	217-423-7703

84 BIOTECHNOLOGY COMPANIES

SEE ALSO Diagnostic Products ; Medicinal Chemicals & Botanical Products ; Pharmaceutical Companies ; Pharmaceutical Companies - Generic Drugs

Company / Address	City	State	ZIP	Toll-Free	Phone
Alkermes Inc 852 Winter St *NASDAQ: ALKS*	Waltham	MA	02451	**800-848-4876**	781-609-6000
Alnylam Pharmaceuticals Inc 300 Third St 3rd Fl *NASDAQ: ALNY*	Cambridge	MA	02142	**866-330-0326**	617-551-8200
American Bio Medica Corp (ABMC) 122 Smith Rd *OTC: ABMC* ■ *General	Kinderhook	NY	12106	**800-227-1243***	518-758-8158
Amgen Canada Inc 6775 Financial Dr Ste 100	Mississauga	ON	L5N0A4	**800-665-4273**	905-285-3000
Amgen Inc 1 Amgen Ctr Dr	Thousand Oaks	CA	91320	**800-563-9798**	805-447-1000
AmpliPhi Biosciences Corp 3579 Valley Centre Dr Ste 100 *OTC: APHB*	San Diego	CA	92130	**877-795-3647**	804-205-5069
Antibodies Inc PO Box 1560	Davis	CA	95617	**800-824-8540**	
ArQule Inc 19 Presidential Way *NASDAQ: ARQL*	Woburn	MA	01801	**800-373-7827**	781-994-0300
Array BioPharma Inc 3200 Walnut St *NASDAQ: ARRY*	Boulder	CO	80301	**877-633-2436**	303-381-6600
Astellas Pharma US Inc 1 Astellas Way	Northbrook	IL	60062	**800-695-4321**	
AtriCure Inc 6217 Centre Pk Dr *NASDAQ: ATRC*	West Chester	OH	45069	**888-347-6403**	513-755-4100
BD Biosciences PharMingen 10975 Torreyana Rd	San Diego	CA	92121	**800-848-6227**	858-812-8800
Bellus Health Inc 275 Armand Frappier Blvd *TSE: BLU*	Laval	QC	H7V4A7	**877-680-4500**	450-680-4500
BioReliance Corp 14920 Broschart Rd	Rockville	MD	20850	**800-553-5372**	301-738-1000
Cardiome Pharma Corp 6190 Agronomy Rd 6th Fl *NASDAQ: CRME*	Vancouver	BC	V6T1Z3	**800-330-9928**	604-677-6905
CEL-SCI Corp 8229 Boone Blvd Ste 802 *NYSE: CVM*	Vienna	VA	22182	**800-422-6237**	703-506-9460
Celgene Corp 86 Morris Ave *NASDAQ: CELG*	Summit	NJ	07901	**888-771-0141**	908-673-9000
Cell Therapeutics Inc (CTI) 501 Elliott Ave W Ste 400 *NASDAQ: CTIC*	Seattle	WA	98119	**800-215-2355**	206-282-7100
Cerus Corp 2550 Stanwell Dr *NASDAQ: CERS*	Concord	CA	94520	**800-401-1957**	925-288-6000
Colorado Serum Co 4950 York St PO Box 16428 *Orders	Denver	CO	80216	**800-525-2065***	303-295-7527
CombiMatrix Corp 300 Goddard Ste 100 *NASDAQ: CBMX*	Irvine	CA	92618	**800-710-0624**	949-753-0624
Cook Biotech Inc 1425 Innovation Pl	West Lafayette	IN	47906	**888-299-4224**	765-497-3355
Covance Inc 210 Carnegie Ctr *NYSE: CVD*	Princeton	NJ	08540	**888-268-2623**	609-419-2240
Cryolife Inc 1655 Roberts Blvd NW *NYSE: CRY*	Kennesaw	GA	30144	**800-438-8285**	770-419-3355
Dendreon Corp 301 2nd Ave *OTC: DNDNQ*	Seattle	WA	98101	**877-256-4545**	206-256-4545
DexCom Inc 6340 Sequence Dr *NASDAQ: DXCM*	San Diego	CA	92121	**888-738-3646**	858-200-0200
Dow AgroSciences LLC 9330 Zionsville Rd	Indianapolis	IN	46268	**800-331-6451**	317-337-3000
DUSA Pharmaceuticals Inc 25 Upton Dr *NASDAQ: DUSA*	Wilmington	MA	01887	**877-533-3872**	978-657-7500
EMD Serono Inc 1 Technology Pl	Rockland	MA	02370	**800-283-8088**	781-982-9000
Encore Medical Corp 9800 Metric Blvd	Austin	TX	78758	**800-456-8696**	512-832-9500
Enzo Biochem Inc 527 Madison Ave *NYSE: ENZ*	New York	NY	10022	**800-522-5052**	212-583-0100
Galectin Therapeutics 4960 Peachtree Industrial Blvd Ste 240	Norcross	GA	02459	**888-286-8010**	617-559-0033
Genaera Corp 5110 Campus Dr	Plymouth Meeting	PA	19462	**800-299-9156**	610-941-4020
Generex Biotechnology Corp 555 Richmond St W Ste 202 *OTC: GNBT*	Toronto	ON	M5J2G2	**800-391-6755**	416-364-2551
Genomic Health Inc 101 Galveston Dr *NASDAQ: GHDX*	Redwood City	CA	94063	**866-662-6897**	650-556-9300
Genzyme Corp 500 Kendall St	Cambridge	MA	02142	**800-745-4447**	617-252-7500
Gilead Sciences Inc 333 Lakeside Dr *NASDAQ: GILD*	Foster City	CA	94404	**800-445-3235**	650-574-3000
Grifols USA LLC 2410 Lillyvale Ave	Los Angeles	CA	90032	**888-474-3657**	
Idenix Pharmaceuticals Inc 320 Bent St 4th fl *NYSE: MRK*	Cambridge	MA	02141	**800-770-4674**	908-423-1000
Illumina Inc 9885 Towne Centre Dr *NASDAQ: ILMN*	San Diego	CA	92121	**800-809-4566**	858-202-4500
Immunomedics Inc 300 American Rd *NASDAQ: IMMU*	Morris Plains	NJ	07950	**800-327-7211**	973-605-8200
Integra LifeSciences Holdings Corp 311 Enterprise Dr *NASDAQ: IART*	Plainsboro	NJ	08536	**800-654-2873**	609-275-0500
Irvine Scientific 2511 Daimler St	Santa Ana	CA	92705	**800-577-6097**	949-261-7800
Ivers-Lee Inc 31 Hansen S	Brampton	ON	L6W3H7	**800-265-1009**	905-451-5535
Lexicon Pharmaceuticals Inc 8800 Technology Forest Pl *NASDAQ: LXRX*	The Woodlands	TX	77381	**855-828-4651**	281-863-3000

Classified Section

Company / Address	City	State	ZIP	Toll-Free	Phone
LifeCore Biomedical LLC 3515 Lyman Blvd *Cust Svc	Chaska	MN	55318	**800-348-4368***	952-368-4300
LiphaTech Inc 3600 W Elm St	Milwaukee	WI	53209	**888-331-7900**	
Medicines Co 8 Sylvan Way *NASDAQ: MDCO*	Parsippany	NJ	07054	**800-388-1183**	973-290-6000
Mera Pharmaceuticals Inc 73-4460 Queen Kaahumanu Hwy Ste 110	Kailua-Kona	HI	96740	**800-480-6515**	808-326-9301
Myriad Genetics Inc 320 Wakara Way *NASDAQ: MYGN*	Salt Lake City	UT	84108	**800-469-7423**	801-584-3600
N.E.T. Inc 5651 Palmer Way Ste C	Carlsbad	CA	92010	**800-888-4638**	760-929-5980
Nordion 447 March Rd *NYSE: NDZ*	Ottawa	ON	K2K1X8	**800-465-3666**	613-592-2790
Novavax Inc 9920 Belward Campus Dr *NASDAQ: NVAX*	Rockville	MD	20850	**800-642-1687**	240-268-2000
Nuo Therapeutics Inc 207A Perry Pkwy Ste 1 *OTC: NUOT*	Gaithersburg	MD	20877	**866-298-6633**	
Oncolytics Biotech Inc 1167 Kensington Crescent NW Ste 210 *TSE: ONC*	Calgary	AB	T2N1X7	**800-731-5319**	403-670-7377
Osteotech Inc 710 Medtronic Pkwy	Minneapolis	MN	55432	**800-633-8766**	763-514-4000
Paladin Labs Inc 100 Blvd Alexis Nihon Ste 600 *TSE: PLB*	St-Laurent	QC	H4M2P2	**888-376-7830**	514-340-1112
Peregrine Pharmaceuticals Inc 14282 Franklin Ave Ste 100 *NASDAQ: PPHM*	Tustin	CA	92780	**800-987-8256**	714-508-6000
Pharmacyclics Inc 995 E Arques Ave *NASDAQ: PCYC*	Sunnyvale	CA	94085	**855-859-2056**	408-774-0330
Primorigen Biosciences Inc 510 Charmany Dr	Madison	WI	53719	**866-372-7442**	608-441-8332
Progenics Pharmaceuticals Inc 777 Old Saw Mill River Rd *NASDAQ: PGNX*	Tarrytown	NY	10591	**866-644-7188**	914-789-2800
Protein Sciences Corp 1000 Research Pkwy	Meriden	CT	06450	**800-488-7099**	203-686-0800
Psychemedics Corp 125 Nagog Pk Ste 200 *NASDAQ: PMD*	Acton	MA	01720	**800-628-8073**	978-206-8220
QLT Inc 887 Great Northern Way Ste 101 *NASDAQ: QLT*	Vancouver	BC	V5T4T5	**800-663-5486**	604-707-7000
Repligen Corp 41 Seyon St *NASDAQ: RGEN* ■ *Sales	Waltham	MA	02453	**800-622-2259***	781-250-0111
Roche Palo Alto LLC 4300 Hacienda Dr	Pleasanton	CA	94588	**888-545-2443**	925-730-8000
RTI Biologics Inc 11621 Research Cir *NASDAQ: RTIX*	Alachua	FL	32615	**877-343-6832**	386-418-8888
Sanofi Pasteur Inc Discovery Dr *Orders	Swiftwater	PA	18370	**800-822-2463***	570-839-7187
Sanofi-Aventis Canada 2150 St Elzear Blvd W	Laval	QC	H7L4A8	**800-363-6364**	514-331-9220
Sequenom Inc 3595 John Hopkins Ct *NASDAQ: SQNM*	San Diego	CA	92121	**877-821-7266**	858-202-9000
Spectrum Pharmaceuticals Inc 11500 S Eastern Ave Ste 240 *NASDAQ: SPPI*	Henderson	NV	89052	**800-332-1088**	702-835-6300
Takeda Canada Inc 435 N Service Rd W Ste 101	Oakville	ON	L6M4X8	**888-367-3331**	905-469-9333
Telesta Therapeutics Inc 275 Labrosse Ave *TSE: TST*	Pointe-Claire	QC	H9R1A3	**800-387-0825**	514-697-6636
Threshold Pharmaceuticals Inc 170 Harbor Way Ste 300 *NASDAQ: THLD*	South San Francisco	CA	94080	**866-276-9886**	650-474-8200
Titan Pharmaceuticals Inc 400 Oyster Pt Blvd Ste 505 *OTC: TTNP*	South San Francisco	CA	94080	**888-417-8516**	650-244-4990
XOMA (US) LLC 2910 Seventh St *NASDAQ: XOMA*	Berkeley	CA	94710	**800-468-9716**	510-204-7200
ZymoGenetics Inc 1201 Eastlake Ave E	Seattle	WA	98102	**800-332-2056**	206-442-6600

85 BLANKBOOKS & BINDERS

SEE ALSO Checks - Personal & Business

Company / Address	City	State	ZIP	Toll-Free	Phone
Abco Inc 1621 Wall St	Dallas	TX	75215	**800-969-2226**	214-565-1191
Advanced Looseleaf Technologies Inc 1424 Somerset Ave	Dighton	MA	02715	**800-339-6354**	508-669-6354
Allison Payment Systems LLC 2200 Production Dr	Indianapolis	IN	46241	**800-755-2440**	
American Thermoplastic Co (ATC) 106 Gamma Dr	Pittsburgh	PA	15238	**800-245-6600**	
Avery Dennison Corp 207 Goode Ave *NYSE: AVY* ■ *Cust Svc	Glendale	CA	91203	**888-567-4387***	626-304-2000
Blackbourn 200 Fourth Ave N	Edgerton	MN	56128	**800-842-7550**	
Blair Packaging Inc 1515 Independence St	Cape Girardeau	MO	63703	**800-624-3150**	573-334-2146
Colad Group 801 Exchange St	Buffalo	NY	14210	**800-950-1755**	716-961-1776
Continental Binder & Specialty Corp 407 W Compton Blvd	Gardena	CA	90248	**800-872-2897**	310-324-8227
Continental Loose Leaf Inc 1122 16th Ave	Minneapolis	MN	55414	**888-719-5013**	612-378-4800
Data Management Inc 537 New Britain Ave *Orders	Farmington	CT	06034	**800-243-1969***	860-677-8586
Dilley Manufacturing Co 215 E Third St	Des Moines	IA	50309	**800-247-5087**	515-288-7289
EBSCO Industries Inc Vulcan Information Packaging Div PO Box 29	Vincent	AL	35178	**800-633-4526**	
Eckhart & Company Inc 4011 W 54th St	Indianapolis	IN	46254	**800-443-3791**	317-347-2665
Federal Business Products Inc 95 Main Ave	Clifton	NJ	07014	**800-927-5123**	973-667-9800
Fey Industries Inc 200 Fourth Ave N	Edgerton	MN	56128	**800-533-5340**	507-442-4311
Formflex Inc PO Box 218	Bloomingdale	IN	47832	**800-255-7659**	
General Loose Leaf Bindery Co 3811 Hawthorn Ct	Waukegan	IL	60087	**800-621-0493**	847-244-9700
Holum & Sons Company Inc 740 Burr Oak Dr	Westmont	IL	60559	**800-447-4479**	630-654-8222
Kurtz Bros Company Inc 400 Reed St PO Box 392	Clearfield	PA	16830	**800-252-3811**	814-765-6561
Leed Selling Tools Corp 9700 Hwy 57	Evansville	IN	47725	**855-687-5333**	812-867-4340
NAPCO Inc 120 Trojan Ave	Sparta	NC	28675	**800-854-8621**	336-372-5228
Roaring Spring Blank Book Co 740 Spang St	Roaring Spring	PA	16673	**800-441-1653**	814-224-5141
Samsill Corp 5740 Hartman Rd	Fort Worth	TX	76119	**800-255-1100**	817-536-1906
Southwest Plastic Binding Co 109 Millwell Ct	Maryland Heights	MO	63043	**800-325-3628**	314-739-4400
Spiral Binding Company Inc 1 Maltese Dr	Totowa	NJ	07511	**800-631-3572**	973-256-0666
Superior Press Inc 11930 Hamden Pl *Cust Svc	Santa Fe Springs	CA	90670	**888-590-7998***	562-948-1866
Trendex Inc 240 E Maryland Ave	Saint Paul	MN	55117	**800-328-9200**	651-489-4655
Union Group 649 Alden St	Fall River	MA	02722	**800-289-3523**	508-675-4545
US Ring Binder 6800 Arsenal St	Saint Louis	MO	63139	**800-888-8772**	314-645-7880
ViaTech Publishing Solutions 1440 Fifth Ave	Bay Shore	NY	11706	**800-645-8558**	631-968-8500

86 BLINDS & SHADES

Company / Address	City	State	ZIP	Toll-Free	Phone
Aeroshade Inc 433 Oakland Ave	Waukesha	WI	53186	**800-331-7179**	262-547-2101
Beauti-Vue Products Inc 8555 194th Ave	Bristol	WI	53104	**800-558-9431**	262-857-2306
Budget Blinds Inc 1927 N Glassell St	Orange	CA	92865	**800-800-9250**	714-637-2100
Comfortex Window Fashions Inc 21 Elm St *Cust Svc	Maplewood	NY	12189	**800-843-4151***	518-273-3333
Delaine James Inc 10508C Boyer Blvd *Claims	Austin	TX	78758	**800-999-5333***	512-835-5333
Hunter Douglas Inc 1 Hunter Douglas Dr	Cumberland	MD	21502	**800-365-3399**	301-722-7700
Kenney Mfg Co 1000 Jefferson Blvd *Cust Svc	Warwick	RI	02886	**800-753-6639***	401-739-2200
Lafayette Venetian Blind Inc 3000 Klondike Rd. PO Box 2838	West Lafayette	IN	47996	**800-342-5523**	
Levolor Kirsch Window Fashions 4110 Premier Dr	High Point	NC	27265	**800-752-9677**	336-812-8181
Mill Supply Div 266 Morse St *General	Hamden	CT	06517	**888-585-9354***	203-777-7668
Ralph Friedland & Bros 17 Industrial Dr	Keyport	NJ	07735	**800-631-2162**	732-290-9800
Sun Control Products Window Shades 1908 Second St SW	Rochester	MN	55902	**800-533-0010**	507-282-2620
Warm Co 5529 186th Pl SW	Lynnwood	WA	98037	**800-234-9276**	425-248-2424

87 BLISTER PACKAGING

Company / Address	City	State	ZIP	Toll-Free	Phone
Adec Industries 2700 Industrial Pkwy	Elkhart	IN	46516	**866-730-3111**	574-295-3167
Andex Industries Inc 1911 Fourth Ave N	Escanaba	MI	49829	**800-338-9882**	
Card Pak Inc 29601 Solon Rd	Solon	OH	44139	**800-824-3342**	440-542-3100
Metro Label Group Inc 999 Progress Ave	Toronto	ON	M1B6J1	**800-668-4405**	416-292-6600
Nelson Packaging Company Inc 1801 Reservoir Rd	Lima	OH	45804	**888-229-3471**	419-229-3471
Placon Corp 6096 McKee Rd	Madison	WI	53719	**800-541-1535**	608-271-5634
Primary Packaging Inc 10810 Industrial Pkwy NW	Bolivar	OH	44612	**800-774-2247**	330-874-3131

88 BLOOD CENTERS

SEE ALSO Laboratories - Drug-Testing ; Laboratories - Genetic Testing ; Laboratories - Medical

The centers listed here are members of America's Blood Centers (ABC), the national network of non-profit, independent community blood centers. ABC members are licensed and regulated by the US Food & Drug Administration.

Company / Address	City	State	ZIP	Toll-Free	Phone
Belle Bonfils Memorial Blood Ctr 717 Yosemite St	Denver	CO	80230	**800-365-0006**	303-341-4000

Name / Address	City	State	Zip	Toll-Free	Phone
Blood Assurance Inc 705 E Fourth St	Chattanooga	TN	37403	**800-962-0628**	423-756-0966
Blood Bank of Delmarva 100 Hygeia Dr	Newark	DE	19713	**800-548-4009**	302-737-8405
Blood Bank of Hawaii 2043 Dillingham Blvd	Honolulu	HI	96819	**800-372-9966**	808-845-9966
Blood Bank of the Redwoods 2324 Bethards Dr	Santa Rosa	CA	95405	**888-393-4483**	707-545-1222
Blood Centers of the Pacific 250 Bush St Ste 136	San Francisco	CA	94104	**888-393-4483**	415-567-6400
Blood Ctr, The 2609 Canal St	New Orleans	LA	70112	**800-862-5663**	504-524-1322
BloodCenter of Wisconsin 638 N 18th St	Milwaukee	WI	53233	**877-232-4376**	414-933-5000
BloodSource 1608 Q St	Sacramento	CA	95811	**800-995-4420**	916-456-1500
Carter BloodCare 2205 Hwy 121	Bedford	TX	76021	**800-366-2834**	817-412-5000
Cascade Regional Blood Services 220 S 'I' St	Tacoma	WA	98405	**877-242-5663**	253-383-2553
Central Illinois Community Blood Ctr 1134 S Seventh St *Help Line	Springfield	IL	62703	**800-448-3253***	217-753-1530
Central Jersey Blood Ctr 494 Sycamore Ave	Shrewsbury	NJ	07702	**888-712-5663**	732-842-5750
Central Kentucky Blood Ctr 3121 Beaumont Centre Cir	Lexington	KY	40513	**800-775-2522**	859-276-2534
Central Pennsylvania Blood Bank 8167 Adams Dr	Hummelstown	PA	17036	**800-771-0059**	717-566-6161
Coastal Bend Blood Ctr 209 N Padre Island Dr	Corpus Christi	TX	78406	**800-299-4943**	361-855-4943
Community Blood Bank of Northwest Pennsylvania 2646 Peach St	Erie	PA	16508	**877-842-0631**	814-456-4206
Community Blood Ctr 349 S Main St	Dayton	OH	45402	**800-388-4483**	937-461-3450
Blue Springs Ctr 4040 Main St	Kansas City	MO	64111	**888-647-4040**	816-753-4040
Gladstone Ctr 7265 N Oak Trafficway	Gladstone	MO	64118	**877-468-6844**	816-468-9813
Community Blood Ctr Inc 4406 W Spencer St	Appleton	WI	54914	**800-280-4102**	920-738-3131
Community Blood Ctr of the Ozarks 220 W Plainview Rd	Springfield	MO	65810	**800-280-5337**	417-227-5000
Community Blood Services 970 Linwood Ave W PO Box 39	Paramus	NJ	07653	**866-228-1500**	201-444-3900
Community Blood Services of Illinois 1408 W University Ave	Urbana	IL	61801	**800-217-4483**	217-367-2202
Delta Blood Bank 65 N Commerce St	Stockton	CA	95202	**888-942-5663**	209-943-3830
Gulf Coast Regional Blood Ctr 1400 La Concha Ln	Houston	TX	77054	**888-482-5663**	713-790-1200
Heartland Blood Centers 1200 N Highland Ave	Aurora	IL	60506	**800-786-4483**	630-892-7055
Hemacare Corp 15350 Sherman Way Ste 350	Van Nuys	CA	91406	**877-310-0717**	818-226-1968
Hoxworth Blood Ctr University of Cincinnati Medical Ctr 3130 Highland Ave ML0055	Cincinnati	OH	45267	**800-265-1515**	513-558-1200
Inland Northwest Blood Ctr 210 W Cataldo Ave	Spokane	WA	99201	**800-423-0151**	509-624-0151
Lifeblood Mid-South Regional Blood Ctr 1040 Madison Ave	Memphis	TN	38104	**888-543-3256**	901-522-8585
LifeServe Blood Ctr 431 E Locust St	Des Moines	IA	50309	**800-287-4903**	
LifeShare Blood Centers 8910 Linwood Ave	Shreveport	LA	71106	**800-256-4483**	318-222-7770
LifeShare Community Blood Services 105 Cleveland St	Elyria	OH	44035	**800-317-5412**	440-322-5700
LifeSource Blood Services 2764 Aurora Ave	Naperville	IL	60540	**877-543-3768**	
LifeSouth Community Blood Centers 4039 Newberry Rd	Gainesville	FL	32607	**888-795-2707**	
LifeSouth Community Blood Centers Atlanta 4891 Ashford Dunwoody Rd	Atlanta	GA	30338	**888-795-2707**	404-329-1994
Memorial Blood Centers (MBC) 737 Pelham Blvd *Cust Svc	Saint Paul	MN	55114	**888-448-3253***	651-332-7000
Michigan Community Blood Centers 4005 Orchard Dr	Midland	MI	48670	**866-642-5663**	989-839-3490
Michigan Community Blood Centers Northwest 2575 Aero Pk Dr *General	Traverse City	MI	49686	**866-642-5663***	231-935-3030
Mississippi Blood Services 115 Tree St	Flowood	MS	39232	**888-902-5663**	601-981-3232
Mississippi Valley Regional Blood Ctr 5500 Lakeview Pkwy	Davenport	IA	52807	**800-747-5401**	563-359-5401
MVRBC 5500 Lakeview Pkwy	Davenport	IA	52501	**800-747-5401**	641-682-8149
Nebraska Community Blood Bank 100 N 84th St	Lincoln	NE	68505	**877-486-9414**	402-486-9414
Oklahoma Blood Institute (OBI) 1001 N Lincoln Blvd	Oklahoma City	OK	73104	**866-708-4995**	405-278-3100
Puget Sound Blood Ctr 921 Terry Ave	Seattle	WA	98104	**800-366-2831**	206-292-6500
Rhode Island Blood Ctr 405 Promenade St	Providence	RI	02908	**800-283-8385**	401-453-8360
Rock River Valley Blood Ctr 3065 N Perryville Rd Ste 105 *General	Rockford	IL	61114	**877-778-2299***	815-965-8751
SeraCare Life Sciences Inc 37 Birch St *NASDAQ: SRLS*	Milford	MA	01757	**800-676-1881**	508-244-6400
South Texas Blood & Tissue Ctr 6211 IH-10 W	San Antonio	TX	78201	**800-292-5534**	210-731-5555
Suncoast Communities Blood Bank 1760 Mound St	Sarasota	FL	34236	**866-972-5663**	941-954-1600
United Blood Services 6210 E Oak St PO Box 1867	Scottsdale	AZ	85252	**800-288-2199**	480-946-4201
United Blood Services of Arizona *Chandler* 6220 E Oak St	Scottsdale	AZ	85252	**877-827-4376**	
San Luis Obispo 4119 Broad St Ste 100	San Luis Obispo	CA	93401	**877-827-4376**	805-543-4290
United Blood Services of Colorado 146 Sawyer Dr	Durango	CO	81303	**800-288-2199**	970-385-4601
Meridian 1115 25th Ave	Meridian	MS	39301	**877-827-4376**	601-482-2482
United Blood Services of Mississippi *Tupelo* 4326 S Eason Blvd	Tupelo	MS	38801	**800-844-8870**	662-842-8871
United Blood Services of Montana *Billings* 1444 Grand Ave	Billings	MT	59102	**800-365-4450**	406-248-9168
United Blood Services of New Mexico 1515 University Blvd NE	Albuquerque	NM	87102	**800-333-8037**	
Albuquerque 1515 University Blvd NE	Albuquerque	NM	87102	**800-333-8037**	
Farmington 475 E 20th St	Farmington	NM	87401	**877-827-4376**	888-804-9913
Las Cruces 1515 University Blvd NE *General	Albuquerque	NM	87102	**877-827-4376***	575-527-1322
United Blood Services of North Dakota *Bismarck* 3231 S 11th St	Fargo	ND	58104	**800-456-6159**	
Fargo 3231 S 11th St *General	Fargo	ND	58104	**800-288-2199***	701-293-9453
United Blood Services of Texas *El Paso* 424 S Mesa Hills	El Paso	TX	79912	**877-827-4376**	915-544-5422
Lubbock 2523 48th St	Lubbock	TX	79413	**800-333-6920**	806-797-6804
McAllen 1400 S Sixth St *General	McAllen	TX	78501	**888-827-4376***	956-213-7500
San Angelo 2020 W Beauregard Ave *General	San Angelo	TX	76901	**800-756-0024***	325-223-7500
United Blood Services of Wyoming *Cheyenne* 112 E Eigth Ave	Cheyenne	WY	82001	**800-955-7057**	307-638-3326

89 BOATS - RECREATIONAL

Name / Address	City	State	Zip	Toll-Free	Phone
Alumaweld Boats Inc 1601 Ave F	White City	OR	97503	**800-401-2628**	541-826-7171
Boston Whaler Inc 100 Whaler Way	Edgewater	FL	32141	**877-294-5645**	
Carolina Skiff Inc 3231 Fulford Rd	Waycross	GA	31503	**800-422-7282**	912-287-0547
Chris-Craft Boats 8161 15th St E	Sarasota	FL	34243	**800-845-5255**	941-351-4900
Cobalt Boats LLC 1715 N Eigth St	Neodesha	KS	66757	**800-468-5764**	620-325-2653
Concept Boats Corp 2410 NW 147th St	Opa Locka	FL	33054	**888-635-8712**	305-635-8712
Correct Craft Inc 14700 Aerospace Pkwy	Orlando	FL	32809	**800-346-2092**	407-855-4141
Crestliner Inc 9040 Quaday Ave NE	Ostego	MN	55330	**866-301-8544**	
Donzi Marine 1653 WhichaRds Beach Rd	Washington	NC	27889	**800-624-3304**	
Ebbtide Corp 2545 Jones Creek Rd	White Bluff	TN	37187	**866-467-4010**	615-797-3193
Everglades Boats 544 Air Pk Rd	Edgewater	FL	32132	**800-368-5647**	386-409-2202
Hinckley Co, The 1 Little Harbor Landing	Portsmouth	RI	02871	**866-446-2553**	401-683-7005
Hobie Cat Co 4925 Oceanside Blvd	Oceanside	CA	92056	**800-462-4349**	760-758-9100
Johnson Outdoors Inc 555 Main St *NASDAQ: JOUT*	Racine	WI	53403	**800-468-9716**	262-631-6600
Lowe Boats 2900 Industrial Dr	Lebanon	MO	65536	**800-641-4372**	417-532-9101
Mainship Corp 255 Diesel Rd	St Augustine	FL	32084	**800-771-5556**	904-827-2007
MasterCraft Boat Co 100 Cherokee Cove Dr	Vonore	TN	37885	**800-443-8774**	423-884-2221
Porta-Bote International 1074 Independence Ave	Mountain View	CA	94043	**800-227-8882**	650-961-5334
Porter Inc 2200 W Monroe St	Decatur	IN	46733	**800-736-7685**	260-724-9111
Pursuit Boats 3901 St Lucie Blvd	Fort Pierce	FL	34946	**800-947-8778**	772-465-6006
Regal Marine Industries Inc 2300 Jetport Dr	Orlando	FL	32809	**800-877-3425**	407-851-4360
Riverside Marine Inc 600 Riverside Dr	Essex	MD	21221	**800-448-6872**	410-335-1500
Skier's Choice Inc 1717 Henry G Ln St	Maryville	TN	37801	**800-970-3744**	865-856-3035
Smoker Craft PO Box 65	New Paris	IN	46553	**866-719-7873**	
Starcraft Marine LLC 68143 Clunette St PO Box 65	New Paris	IN	46553	**888-327-4236**	574-831-2103
Stevens Marine Inc 9180 SW Burnham St	Tigard	OR	97223	**800-225-7023**	503-620-7023
Stoltzfus RV's & Marine 1335 Wilmington Pike	West Chester	PA	19382	**866-755-8858**	
World Cat 1090 W St James St	Tarboro	NC	27886	**866-485-8899**	252-641-8000

90 BOILER SHOPS

Name / Address	City	State	Zip	Toll-Free	Phone
Adamson Global Technology Corp 13101 N Eron Church Rd	Chester	VA	23836	**800-525-7703**	
Aerofin Corp 4621 Murray Pl PO Box 10819	Lynchburg	VA	24506	**800-237-6346**	434-845-7081
American Welding & Tank Co 4718 Old Gettysburg Rd Ste 300	Mechanicsburg	PA	17055	**800-345-2495**	717-763-5080
API Heat Transfer Inc 2777 Walden Ave	Buffalo	NY	14225	**877-274-4328**	716-684-6700
Arrow Tank & Engineering Co 650 N Emerson St	Cambridge	MN	55008	**888-892-7769**	763-689-3360

Company / Address	City	State	Zip	Toll-Free	Phone
AustinMohawk & Company Inc 2175 Beechgrove Pl	Utica	NY	13501	**800-765-3110**	315-793-3000
Babcock & Wilcox Co 20 S Van Buren Ave	Barberton	OH	44203	**800-222-2625**	330-753-4511
Babcock Power Inc 6 Kimball Ln Ste 210	Lynnfield	MA	01940	**800-523-0480**	978-646-3300
Chicago Boiler Co 1300 NW Ave *Cust Svc	Gurnee	IL	60031	**800-522-7343***	847-662-4000
Clawson Tank Co 4701 White Lake Rd	Clarkston	MI	48346	**800-272-1367**	248-625-8700
Cleaver Brooks Thomasville 221 Law St	Thomasville	GA	31792	**800-250-5883**	229-226-3024
Eaton Metal Products Co 4803 York St	Denver	CO	80216	**800-208-2657**	303-296-4800
Enerfab Inc 4955 Spring Grove Ave	Cincinnati	OH	45232	**800-772-5066**	513-641-0500
Engineered Storage Products Co 345 Harvestore Dr	DeKalb	IL	60115	**800-880-3663**	815-756-1551
Essick Air Products Inc 5800 Murray St	Little Rock	AR	72209	**800-643-8341**	501-562-1094
Fafco Inc 435 Otterson Dr	Chico	CA	95928	**800-994-7652**	530-332-2100
Hammersmith Mfg & Sales Inc 401 Central Ave	Horton	KS	66439	**800-375-8245**	785-486-2121
Harsco Industrial Air-X-Changers 5215 Arkansas Rd	Catoosa	OK	74015	**800-404-3904**	918-619-8000
Hurst Boiler & Welding Company Inc 100 Boilermaker Ln	Coolidge	GA	31738	**877-994-8778**	229-346-3545
ITT Standard 175 Standard Pkwy	Cheektowaga	NY	14227	**800-447-7700**	800-281-4111
Mgs Inc 178 Muddy Creek Church Rd	Denver	PA	17517	**800-952-4228**	717-336-7528
MiTek Industries Inc 14515 N Outer 40 Rd Ste 300	Chesterfield	MO	63017	**800-325-8075**	314-434-1200
Modern Welding Company Inc 2880 New Hartford Rd	Owensboro	KY	42303	**800-922-1932**	270-685-4400
Ohmstede 895 N Main St	Beaumont	TX	77704	**800-568-2328**	409-833-6375
Pentair Residential Filtration LLC 20580 Enterprise Ave	Brookfield	WI	53008	**888-784-9065**	262-784-4490
PVI Industries LLC 3209 Galvez Ave PO Box 7124	Fort Worth	TX	76111	**800-784-8326**	817-335-9531
Redman Equipment & Mfg Co 19800 Normandie Ave	Torrance	CA	90502	**888-733-2602**	310-329-1134
Rocky Mountain Fabrication Inc PO Box 16409	Salt Lake City	UT	84116	**888-763-5307**	801-596-2400
Ross Technology Corp 104 N Maple Ave	Leola	PA	17540	**800-345-8170**	717-656-2200
Roy E Hanson Jr Mfg 1600 E Washington Blvd	Los Angeles	CA	90021	**800-421-9395**	213-747-7514
Sen-Dure Products Inc 6785 NW 17th Ave	Fort Lauderdale	FL	33309	**800-394-5112**	954-973-1260
Snap-Tite Autoclave Engineers Div 8325 Hessinger Dr	Erie	PA	16509	**800-458-0409**	814-838-5700
SPX Cooling Technologies 7401 W 129th St	Overland Park	KS	66213	**800-462-7539**	913-664-7400
Superior Boiler Works Inc 3524 E Fourth St PO Box 1527	Hutchinson	KS	67504	**800-444-6693**	620-662-6693
Superior Die Set Corp 900 W Drexel Ave	Oak Creek	WI	53154	**800-558-6040**	414-764-4900
Sussman Automatic Corp 43-20 34th St	Long Island	NY	11101	**800-727-8326**	718-937-4500
Thermodynetics Inc 651 Day Hill Rd *OTC: TDYT*	Windsor	CT	06095	**800-394-1633**	860-683-2005
Tranter Inc 1900 Old Burk Hwy	Wichita Falls	TX	76306	**800-414-6908**	940-723-7125
Winbco Tank Co 1200 E Main St PO Box 618	Ottumwa	IA	52501	**800-822-1855**	
Worthington Industries 200 Old E Wilson Bridge Rd	Columbus	OH	43085	**866-928-2657**	614-438-3013

91 BOOK BINDING & RELATED WORK

SEE ALSO Printing Companies - Book Printers

Company / Address	City	State	Zip	Toll-Free	Phone
Bindagraphics Inc 2701 Wilmarco Ave	Baltimore	MD	21223	**800-326-0300**	410-362-7200
Booksource Inc 1230 Macklind Ave	Saint Louis	MO	63110	**800-444-0435**	314-647-0600
Bound to Stay Bound Books Inc (BTSB) 1880 W Morton Ave	Jacksonville	IL	62650	**800-637-6586**	217-245-5191
Library Binding Service (LBS) 1801 Thompson Ave	Des Moines	IA	50316	**800-247-5323**	515-262-3191
Parker Powis Inc 775 Heinz Ave	Berkeley	CA	94710	**800-321-2463**	510-848-2463
Perma-Bound 617 E Vandalia Rd	Jacksonville	IL	62650	**800-637-6581**	217-243-5451
Reindl Bindery Company Inc W194 N11381 McCormick Dr	Germantown	WI	53022	**800-878-1121**	262-293-1444
Rickard Circular Folding Co 325 N Ashland Ave	Chicago	IL	60607	**800-747-1389**	312-243-6300
Riverside Group 655 Driving Pk Ave	Rochester	NY	14613	**800-777-2463**	585-458-2090
Roswell Bookbinding Co 2614 N 29th Ave	Phoenix	AZ	85009	**888-803-8883**	602-272-9338
Wert Bookbinding Inc 9975 Allentown Blvd *Cust Svc	Grantville	PA	17028	**800-344-9378***	717-469-0629

92 BOOK, MUSIC, VIDEO CLUBS

Company / Address	City	State	Zip	Toll-Free	Phone
NetFlix Inc 100 Winchester Cir *NASDAQ: NFLX*	Los Gatos	CA	95032	**800-290-8191**	408-540-3700
Writer's Digest Book Club 4700 E Galbraith Rd *Cust Svc	Cincinnati	OH	45236	**800-759-0963***	513-531-2690

93 BOOK PRODUCERS

Book producers, or book packagers, work with authors, editors, printers, publishers, and others to provide all publication services except sales and order fulfillment. These publication services include editing of manuscripts, formatting of computer disks, producing books as a finished product, and helping the book publisher to develop marketing plans. Book producers listed here are members of the American Book Producers Association.

Company / Address	City	State	Zip	Toll-Free	Phone
Focus Strategic Communications Inc 2474 Waterford St	Oakville	ON	L6L5E6	**866-263-6287**	905-825-8757
Palace Printing & Design 100 N Maple Ave	Greensburg	PA	15601	**800-247-0108**	415-526-1370
Schlager Group Inc 325 N Saint Paul Ste 3425	Dallas	TX	75201	**888-416-5727**	

94 BOOKS, PERIODICALS, NEWSPAPERS - WHOL

Company / Address	City	State	Zip	Toll-Free	Phone
21st Century Christian Inc PO Box 40526	Nashville	TN	37204	**800-251-2477**	615-383-3842
Advantage Mktg Inc 14 W Main St	Ashland	OH	44805	**800-670-7479**	419-281-4762
Auto Export Shipping Inc 187 Mill Ln Ste 103	Mountainside	NJ	07092	**800-829-4933**	908-436-2150
Baker & Taylor Inc 2550 W Tyvola Rd Ste 300	Charlotte	NC	28217	**800-775-1800**	
BMI Educational Services PO Box 800	Dayton	NJ	08810	**800-222-8100**	732-329-6991
Book Depot Inc 67 Front St N	Thorold	ON	L2V1X3	**888-402-7323**	905-680-7230
Bookazine Company Inc 75 Hook Rd	Bayonne	NJ	07002	**800-221-8112**	201-339-7777
Booksource Inc 1230 Macklind Ave	Saint Louis	MO	63110	**800-444-0435**	314-647-0600
C2F Inc 6600 SW 111th Ave	Beaverton	OR	97008	**800-544-8825**	503-643-9050
Choice Books LLC 2387 Grace Chapel Rd	Harrisonburg	VA	22801	**800-224-5006**	540-434-1827
Comag Marketing Group LLC 155 Village Blvd 3rd Fl	Princeton	NJ	08540	**866-790-9353**	609-524-1800
Command Spanish Inc PO Box 1091	Petal	MS	39465	**800-250-8637**	601-582-8378
Direct Holdings Americas Inc 8280 Willow Oaks Corporate Dr	Fairfax	VA	22031	**800-950-7887**	
Directory Distributing Assoc (DDA) 1602 Pk 370 Ct *General	Hazelwood	MO	63042	**800-325-1964***	314-592-8600
EBSCO Subscription Services 110 Olmsted St Ste 100	Birmingham	AL	35242	**800-653-2726**	205-995-1596
Educational Development Corp 10302 E 55th Pl *NASDAQ: EDUC*	Tulsa	OK	74146	**800-475-4522**	918-622-4522
ePromos Promotional Products Inc 120 Broadway Ste 1360	New York	NY	10271	**877-377-6667**	212-286-8008
Follett Corp 3 Westbrook Corporate Center Ste 200	Westchester	IL	60154	**800-365-5388**	708-884-0000
Follett Educational Services 1433 International Pkwy	Woodridge	IL	60517	**800-621-4272**	630-972-5600
General Pet Supply Inc 7711 N 81st St	Milwaukee	WI	53223	**800-433-9786**	414-365-3400
Independent Publishers Group 814 N Franklin St *Orders	Chicago	IL	60610	**800-888-4741***	312-337-0747
InfraRed Imaging Systems Inc 22718 Holycross Epps Rd	Marysville	OH	43040	**888-987-5768**	
Ingram Book Group 1 Ingram Blvd	La Vergne	TN	37086	**800-937-8000**	615-793-5000
MBS Textbook Exchange Inc 2711 W Ash St *Cust Svc	Columbia	MO	65203	**800-325-0530***	573-445-2243
Midwest Library Service Inc 11443 St Charles Rock Rd	Bridgeton	MO	63044	**800-325-8833**	314-739-3100
Nebraska Book Co 4700 S 19th St	Lincoln	NE	68512	**800-869-0366**	402-421-7300
Neway Packaging Corp 1973 E Via Arado	Rancho Dominguez	CA	90220	**800-456-3929**	310-898-3400
Product Development Corp 20 Ragsdale Dr Ste 100	Monterey	CA	93940	**800-819-6910**	831-333-1100
Publishers' Warehouse 2700 Crestwood Blvd	Irondale	AL	35210	**800-653-2726**	205-956-2078
Quality Books Inc 1003 W Pines Rd *Cust Svc	Oregon	IL	61061	**800-323-4241***	815-732-4450
Readerlink Distribution Services LLC 1420 Kensington Rd Ste 300	Oak Brook	IL	60523	**800-549-5389**	708-547-4400
Rittenhouse Book Distributors Inc 511 Feheley Dr *Cust Svc	King of Prussia	PA	19406	**800-345-6425***	
SCB Distributors 15608 New Century Dr	Gardena	CA	90248	**800-729-6423**	310-532-9400
Scholastic Book Fairs Inc 1080 Greenwood Blvd	Lake Mary	FL	32746	**800-874-4809**	573-632-1687
Seda France Inc 8301 Springdale Rd Ste 800	Austin	TX	78724	**800-474-0854**	512-206-0105
Southwestern/Great American 2451 Atrium Way *Cust Svc	Nashville	TN	37214	**888-602-7867***	
Spring Arbor Distributors 1 Ingram Blvd	La Vergne	TN	37086	**800-395-4340**	615-793-5000

Name / Address	City	State	Zip	Toll-Free	Phone
Vulcan Service 5724 Hwy 280 E	Birmingham	AL	35242	**800-841-9600**	
YBP Library Services 999 Maple St	Contoocook	NH	03229	**800-258-3774**	603-746-3102

95 BOOK STORES

Name / Address	City	State	Zip	Toll-Free	Phone
Amazon.com Inc 1200 12th Ave S Ste 1200 — *NASDAQ: AMZN* ■ *Cust Svc	Seattle	WA	98144	**800-201-7575***	206-266-1000
barnesandnoble.com Inc 122 Fifth Ave	New York	NY	10011	**800-843-2665**	212-414-6000
Book Exchange Inc 152 Willey St	Morgantown	WV	26505	**800-339-7691**	304-292-7354
Book House Inc, The 208 W Chicago St	Jonesville	MI	49250	**800-248-1146**	
Book Passage 51 Tamal Vista Blvd	Corte Madera	CA	94925	**800-999-7909**	415-927-0960
BookPal LLC 18101 Von Karman Ave Ste 1240	Irvine	CA	92612	**866-522-6657**	
BookPeople 603 N Lamar	Austin	TX	78703	**800-853-9757**	512-472-5050
Books on the Square 471 Angell St	Providence	RI	02906	**888-669-9660**	401-331-9097
Books-A-Million Inc 402 Industrial Ln — *NASDAQ: BAMM*	Birmingham	AL	35211	**800-201-3550**	205-942-3737
Boston Consumers Checkbook 185 Franklin St	Boston	MA	02110	**888-382-1222**	
Boulder Book Store 1107 Pearl St	Boulder	CO	80302	**800-244-4651**	303-447-2074
Childrens Plus Inc 1387 Dutch American Way	Beecher	IL	60401	**800-230-1279**	
Daedalus Books Inc 9645 Gerwig Ln	Columbia	MD	21046	**800-395-2665**	410-309-2706
Deseret Book Co 57 W S Temple	Salt Lake City	UT	84111	**800-453-4532**	801-534-1515
Dickens Books Ltd 219 N Milwaukee St	Milwaukee	WI	53202	**800-236-7323**	
Drama Book Shop Inc 250 E 40th St Frnt 2	New York	NY	10018	**800-322-0595**	212-944-0595
Elliott Bay Book Co 101 S Main St	Seattle	WA	98104	**800-962-5311**	206-624-6600
Follett Corp 3 Westbrook Corporate Center Ste 200	Westchester	IL	60154	**800-365-5388**	708-884-0000
Follett Higher Education Group 3 Westbrook Corporate Ctr Ste 200	Westchester	IL	60154	**800-323-4506**	
Harvard Book Store Inc 1256 Massachusetts Ave	Cambridge	MA	02138	**800-542-7323**	617-661-1515
Hastings Entertainment Inc 3601 Plains Blvd — *NASDAQ: HAST* ■ *Cust Svc	Amarillo	TX	79102	**877-427-8464***	
Horizon Books 243 E Front St	Traverse City	MI	49684	**800-587-2147**	231-946-7290
Hosanna 2421 Aztec Rd Ne	Albuquerque	NM	87107	**800-545-6552**	505-881-3321
Indigo Books & Music Inc 468 King St W Ste 500 — *NYSE: IDG* ■ *Cust Svc	Toronto	ON	M5V1L8	**800-832-7569***	416-364-4499
Keyano College 8115 Franklin Ave	Fort Mcmurray	AB	T9H2H7	**800-251-1408**	780-791-4800
LibertyTree 100 Swan Way	Oakland	CA	94621	**800-927-8733**	510-632-1366
Matthews Book Co 11559 Rock Island Ct	Maryland Heights	MO	63043	**800-633-2665**	314-432-1400
McNally Robinson Booksellers Inc 1120 Grant Ave	Winnipeg	MB	R3M2A6	**800-561-1833**	204-475-0483
Merchant One Payment Systems Inc 524 Arthur Godfrey Rd 3rd Fl	Miami Beach	FL	33140	**800-610-4189**	
Mountaineers Books 1001 Sw Klickitat Way Ste 201	Seattle	WA	98134	**800-553-4453**	206-223-6303
Mrs Nelsons Library Service 1650 W Orange Grove Ave	Pomona	CA	91768	**800-875-9911**	909-397-7820
Northshire Information Inc 4869 Main St	Manchester Center	VT	05255	**800-437-3700**	802-362-2200
Poisoned Pen Bookstore 4014 N Goldwater Blvd	Scottsdale	AZ	85251	**888-560-9919**	480-947-2974
Politics & Prose Bookstore 5015 Connecticut Ave NW	Washington	DC	20008	**800-722-0790**	202-364-1919
Powell's Books Inc 7 NW Ninth Ave	Portland	OR	97209	**800-878-7323**	503-228-0540
Powell's City of Books 1005 W Burnside St	Portland	OR	97209	**800-878-7323**	503-228-4651
Prairie Lights Bookstore 15 S Dubuque St	Iowa City	IA	52240	**800-295-2665**	319-337-2681
Seagull Book & Tape Inc 1720 S Redwood Rd	Salt Lake City	UT	84104	**800-999-6257**	
Social Studies School Service 10200 Jefferson Blvd PO Box 802	Culver City	CA	90232	**800-421-4246**	310-839-2436
Square Books 160 Courthouse Sq	Oxford	MS	38655	**800-648-4001**	662-236-2262
Student Book Store 421 E Grand River Ave	East Lansing	MI	48823	**800-968-1111**	517-351-4210
Sunshine Books Inc 49 River St Ste 3	Waltham	MA	02453	**800-472-5425**	781-398-0754
Tattered Cover Book Store Inc 1628 16th St	Denver	CO	80202	**800-833-9327**	303-436-1070
University of Oregon Bookstore Inc 895 E 13th Ave	Eugene	OR	97401	**800-352-1733**	541-346-4331
University Press Books (UPB) 2430 Bancroft Way	Berkeley	CA	94704	**800-676-8722**	510-548-0585
Western Continental Book Co 6425 Washington St	Denver	CO	80229	**800-364-0350**	303-289-1761
Wild Onion Books 3441 N Ashland Ave	Chicago	IL	60657	**800-621-1008**	773-281-1818
Word Among Us Inc 9639 Doctor Perry Rd	Ijamsville	MD	21754	**800-775-9673**	301-874-1700

96 BOTANICAL GARDENS & ARBORETA

SEE ALSO Zoos & Wildlife Parks

Name / Address	City	State	Zip	Toll-Free	Phone
Arboretum, The Arboretum Rd University of Guelph	Guelph	ON	N1G2W1	**877-674-1610**	519-824-4120
Bellingrath Gardens & Home 12401 Bellingrath Garden Rd	Theodore	AL	36582	**800-247-8420**	251-973-2217
Botanical Gardens at Asheville 151 WT Weaver Blvd	Asheville	NC	28804	**888-823-4622**	828-252-5190
Boyce Thompson Arboretum 37615 US Hwy 60	Superior	AZ	85273	**877-763-5315**	520-689-2723
Brookgreen Gardens 1931 Brookgreen Dr	Murrells Inlet	SC	29576	**800-849-1931**	843-235-6000
Brookside Gardens 1800 Glenallan Ave	Wheaton	MD	20902	**800-366-2012**	301-962-1400
Butchart Gardens, The 800 Benvenuto Ave	Brentwood Bay	BC	V8M1J8	**866-652-4422**	250-652-4422
Calgary Zoo Botanical Garden & Prehistoric Park 1300 Zoo Rd NE	Calgary	AB	T2E7V6	**800-588-9993**	403-232-9300
Callaway Gardens 17800 Hwy 27	Pine Mountain	GA	31822	**800-225-5292**	706-663-2281
Cedar Crest College 100 College Dr — *Admissions	Allentown	PA	18104	**800-360-1222***	610-437-4471
Cheekwood Museum of Art & Botanical Garden 1200 Forrest Pk Dr	Nashville	TN	37205	**877-356-8150**	615-356-8000
Chicago Botanic Garden 1000 Lake Cook Rd	Glencoe	IL	60022	**877-829-5500**	847-835-5440
Chimney Rock Park 431 Main St	Chimney Rock	NC	28720	**800-277-9611**	828-625-9611
Cincinnati Zoo & Botanical Garden 3400 Vine St	Cincinnati	OH	45220	**800-944-4776**	513-281-4700
Cornell Plantations 1 Plantations Rd	Ithaca	NY	14850	**800-269-8368**	607-255-2400
Cox Arboretum MetroPark 6733 Springboro Pike	Dayton	OH	45449	**800-865-6543**	937-434-9005
Dawes Arboretum 7770 Jacksontown Rd SE	Newark	OH	43056	**800-443-2937**	740-323-2355
Desert Botanical Garden 1201 N Galvin Pkwy	Phoenix	AZ	85008	**888-314-9480**	480-941-1225
Earl Burns Miller Japanese Garden 1250 Bellflower Blvd	Long Beach	CA	90840	**800-985-8880**	562-985-8885
Edith J Carrier Arboretum & Botanical Gardens at James Madison University 780 University Blvd MSC 3705	Harrisonburg	VA	22807	**888-568-2586**	540-568-3194
Erie Zoo 423 W 38th St	Erie	PA	16508	**877-371-5422**	814-864-4091
Filoli 86 Canada Rd	Woodside	CA	94062	**866-691-9080**	650-364-8300
Flamingo Gardens 3750 S Flamingo Rd	Davie	FL	33330	**800-435-7352**	954-473-2955
Foellinger-Freimann Botanical Conservatory 1100 S Calhoun St	Fort Wayne	IN	46802	**866-220-8842**	260-427-6440
Frederik Meijer Gardens & Sculpture Park 1000 E Beltline Ave NE	Grand Rapids	MI	49525	**877-975-3171**	616-957-1580
Gardens of the American Rose Ctr 8877 Jefferson-Paige Rd	Shreveport	LA	71119	**800-637-6534**	318-938-5402
Garvan Woodland Gardens 550 Arkridge Rd PO Box 22240	Hot Springs	AR	71903	**800-366-4664**	501-262-9300
Green Bay Botanical Garden 2600 Larsen Rd	Green Bay	WI	54303	**877-355-4224**	920-490-9457
Huntsville Botanical Garden 4747 Bob Wallace Ave	Huntsville	AL	35805	**800-300-4916**	256-830-4447
Idaho Botanical Garden 2355 N Penitentiary Rd	Boise	ID	83712	**877-527-8233**	208-343-8649
JC Raulston Arboretum North Carolina State University PO Box 7522	Raleigh	NC	27695	**888-842-2442**	919-513-7457
Journey Museum 222 New York St	Rapid City	SD	57701	**877-343-8220**	605-394-6923
Kenilworth Aquatic Gardens 1550 Anacostia Ave NE	Washington	DC	20019	**877-642-4743**	202-426-6905
Lady Bird Johnson Wildflower Ctr 4801 LaCrosse Ave	Austin	TX	78739	**877-945-3357**	512-292-4200
Lakewold Gardens 12317 Gravelly Lk Dr SW	Lakewood	WA	98499	**888-858-4106**	253-584-4106
Lincoln Botanical Garden & Arboretum (BGA) University of Nebraska 1309 N 17th St	Lincoln	NE	68588	**800-742-8800**	402-472-2679
Longwood Gardens PO Box 501	Kennett Square	PA	19348	**800-737-5500**	610-388-1000
Magnolia Plantation & Gardens 3550 Ashley River Rd	Charleston	SC	29414	**800-367-3517**	843-571-1266
Marywood University Arboretum 2300 Adams Ave	Scranton	PA	18509	**866-279-9663**	570-348-6218
Matthaei Botanical Gardens 1800 N Dixboro Rd	Ann Arbor	MI	48105	**800-666-8693**	734-647-7600
Memphis Botanic Garden 750 Cherry Rd	Memphis	TN	38117	**877-829-5500**	901-576-4100
Mercer Arboretum & Botanic Gardens 22306 Aldine Westfield Rd	Humble	TX	77338	**877-321-2652**	281-443-8731
Missouri Botanical Garden 4344 Shaw Blvd	Saint Louis	MO	63110	**800-642-8842**	314-577-5100
Montgomery Botanical Ctr 11901 Old Cutler Rd	Miami	FL	33156	**800-435-7352**	305-667-3800
Monticello 931 Thomas Jefferson Pkwy PO Box 316	Charlottesville	VA	22902	**800-243-1743**	434-984-9822
Mynelle Gardens 4736 Clinton Blvd	Jackson	MS	39209	**800-354-7695**	601-960-1894
Naples Botanical Garden 4820 Bayshore Dr	Naples	FL	34112	**877-433-1874**	239-643-7275
New England Wild Flower Society 180 Hemenway Rd	Framingham	MA	01701	**888-636-0033**	508-877-7630
Niagara Parks Botanical Gardens 2565 Niagara Pkwy N PO Box 150	Niagara Falls	ON	L2E6T2	**877-642-7275**	905-356-8554
Oregon Garden, The 879 W Main St PO Box 155	Silverton	OR	97381	**877-674-2733**	503-874-8100

Classified Section

	City	State	Zip	Toll-Free	Phone
Polynesian Cultural Ctr 55-370 Kamehameha Hwy	Laie	HI	96762	**800-367-7060**	808-293-3005
Rhododendron Species Botanical Garden 2525 S 336th St PO Box 3798	Federal Way	WA	98063	**877-242-2528**	253-838-4646
Royal Botanical Gardens (RBG) 680 Plains Rd W	Burlington	ON	L7T4H4	**800-694-4769**	905-527-1158
Schoepfle Garden 12882 Diagonal Rd	La Grange	OH	44050	**800-526-7275**	440-458-5121
Schreiner's Iris Gardens 3625 Quinaby Rd NE	Salem	OR	97303	**800-525-2367**	503-393-3232
Shambhala Mountain Ctr 151 Shambhala Wy	Red Feather Lakes	CO	80545	**888-788-7221**	970-881-2184
Stan Hywet Hall & Gardens 714 N Portage Path	Akron	OH	44303	**888-836-5533**	330-836-5533
University of Missouri Botanic Garden General Services Bldg	Columbia	MO	65211	**800-856-2181**	573-882-4240
University of Southern Maine Arboretum PO Box 9300	Portland	ME	04104	**800-800-4876**	
Vanderbilt University 2201 W End Ave	Nashville	TN	37240	**800-288-0432**	615-322-7311
Vermont Garden Park 1100 Dorset St	South Burlington	VT	05403	**800-538-7476**	802-863-5251
Winterthur Museum & Country Estate 5105 Kennett Pk	Winterthur	DE	19735	**800-448-3883**	302-888-4600

97 BOTTLES - PLASTICS

	City	State	Zip	Toll-Free	Phone
Alpha Packaging 1555 Page Industrial Blvd	Saint Louis	MO	63132	**800-421-4772**	314-427-4300
Colt's Plastics Co 969 N Main St PO Box 429	Dayville	CT	06241	**800-222-2658**	860-774-2301
Comar LLC 141 N Fifth St	Saddle Brook	NJ	07663	**800-962-6627**	201-909-3400
NEW Plastics Corp 112 Fourth St	Luxemburg	WI	54217	**800-666-5207**	920-845-2326
Nutrifaster Inc 209 S Bennett St	Seattle	WA	98108	**800-800-2641**	206-767-5054
Ozarks Coca-Cola Dr Pepper Bottling Co 1777 N Packer Rd	Springfield	MO	65803	**866-223-4498**	417-865-9900
Progressive Plastics Inc 14801 Emery Ave	Cleveland	OH	44135	**800-252-0053**	216-252-5595
Quality Containers of New England 247 Portland St	Yarmouth	ME	04096	**800-639-1550**	207-846-5420
Redi Bag USA 135 Fulton Ave	New Hyde Park	NY	11040	**800-517-2247**	516-746-0600
Silgan Plastics Corp 14515 N Outer Forty Ste 210	Chesterfield	MO	63017	**800-274-5426**	

98 BOWLING CENTERS

	City	State	Zip	Toll-Free	Phone
AMF Bowling Worldwide Inc 7313 Bell Creek Rd	Mechanicsville	VA	23111	**800-342-5263**	
Collins Bowling Centers Inc 750 E New Cir Rd	Lexington	KY	40505	**866-252-2695**	859-252-3429

99 BOXES - CORRUGATED & SOLID FIBER

	City	State	Zip	Toll-Free	Phone
American Corrugated Products Inc 4700 Alkire Rd	Columbus	OH	43228	**800-248-6840**	614-870-2000
American Environmental Container Corp 2302 Lasso Ln	Lakeland	FL	33801	**800-535-7946**	863-666-3020
Arrowhead Containers Inc 4330 Clary Blvd	Kansas City	MO	64130	**888-861-9225**	816-861-8050
Artistic Carton Co 1975 Big Timber Rd	Elgin	IL	60123	**800-735-7225**	847-741-0247
Arvco Container Corp 845 Gibson St	Kalamazoo	MI	49001	**800-968-9127**	269-381-0900
Atlas Container Corp 8140 Telegraph Rd	Severn	MD	21144	**800-394-4894**	410-551-6300
Bates Container 6433 Davis Blvd	North Richland Hills	TX	76182	**888-541-0192**	817-498-3200
Beacon Container Corp 700 W First St	Birdsboro	PA	19508	**800-422-8383**	610-582-2222
Buckeye Container Inc 3350 Long Rd	Wooster	OH	44691	**800-968-6894**	330-264-6336
Bulk-pack Inc 1025 N Ninth St	Monroe	LA	71201	**800-498-4215**	318-387-3260
Capitol City Container Corp 8240 Zionsville Rd	Indianapolis	IN	46268	**800-233-5145**	317-875-0290
Carolina Container Co 909 Prospect St	High Point	NC	27260	**800-627-0825**	336-883-7146
Ferguson Supply & Box Manufacturing Co 10820 Quality Dr	Charlotte	NC	28278	**800-821-1023**	704-597-0310
Great Lakes Packaging Corp W 190 N 11393 Carnegie Dr	Germantown	WI	53022	**800-261-4572**	262-255-2100
Great Northern Corp 395 Stroebe Rd	Appleton	WI	54914	**800-236-3671**	920-739-3671
Green Bay Packaging Inc 1700 Webster Ct	Green Bay	WI	54302	**800-236-8400**	920-433-5111
Key Container Corp 21 Campbell St	Pawtucket	RI	02861	**800-343-8811**	401-723-2000
Lawrence Paper Co 2801 Lakeview Rd	Lawrence	KS	66049	**800-535-4553**	785-843-8111
Lone Star Container Corp 700 N Wildwood Dr	Irving	TX	75061	**800-552-6937**	
Menasha Corp 1645 Bergstrom Rd	Neenah	WI	54956	**800-558-5073**	920-751-1000
Menasha Packaging Co 1645 Bergstrom Rd	Neenah	WI	54956	**800-558-5073**	920-751-1000
New England Wooden Ware Corp 205 School St Ste 201	Gardner	MA	01440	**800-252-9214**	978-632-3600
North American Container Corp 1811 W Oak Pkwy Ste D	Marietta	GA	30062	**800-929-0610**	770-431-4858
Packaging Corp of America 1955 W Field Ct *NYSE: PKG*	Lake Forest	IL	60045	**800-456-4725**	
Pactiv Corp 1900 W Field Ct	Lake Forest	IL	60045	**888-828-2850**	847-482-2000
Shoreline Container Inc 4450 N 136th Ave PO Box 1993	Holland	MI	49422	**800-968-2088**	616-399-2088
Stronghaven Inc 5090 McDougall Dr SW	Atlanta	GA	30336	**800-331-7835**	404-699-1952
TimBar Packaging & Display 148 N Penn St	Hanover	PA	17331	**800-572-6061**	717-632-4727
Welch Packaging Group 1020 Herman St	Elkhart	IN	46516	**800-246-2475**	574-295-2460

100 BOXES - PAPERBOARD

Products made by these companies include setup, folding, and nonfolding boxes.

	City	State	Zip	Toll-Free	Phone
Apex Paper Box Co 5601 Walworth Ave *Cust Svc	Cleveland	OH	44102	**800-438-2269***	216-416-9475
Burd & Fletcher 3000 W Geospace Dr	Independence	MO	64056	**800-821-2776**	816-257-0291
Caraustar Industries Inc 5000 Austell-Powder Springs Rd Ste 300	Austell	GA	30106	**800-858-1438**	770-948-3100
Carton Service Inc First Quality Dr PO Box 702 *General	Shelby	OH	44875	**800-533-7744***	419-342-5010
Climax Packaging Inc 4515 Easton Rd	Saint Joseph	MO	64503	**800-225-4629**	816-233-3181
Complemar Partners 500 Lee Rd Ste 200	Rochester	NY	14606	**800-388-7254**	585-647-5800
Dee Paper Box Company Inc 100 Broomall St	Chester	PA	19013	**800-359-0041**	610-876-9285
Diamond Packaging Company Inc 111 Commerce Dr PO Box 23620	Rochester	NY	14692	**800-333-4079**	585-334-8030
Graphic Packaging International 1500 Riveredge Parkway NW Ste 100 *NYSE: GPK*	Atlanta	GA	30328	**888-548-8395**	770-240-7200
Hub Folding Box Co Inc 774 Norfolk St	Mansfield	MA	02048	**800-334-1113**	508-339-0005
Malnove Inc 13434 F St	Omaha	NE	68137	**800-228-9877**	402-330-1100
Menasha Corp 1645 Bergstrom Rd	Neenah	WI	54956	**800-558-5073**	920-751-1000
MOD-PAC Corp 1801 Elmwood Ave *NASDAQ: MPAC* ■ *Cust Svc	Buffalo	NY	14207	**866-216-6193***	716-873-0640
Pactiv Corp 1900 W Field Ct	Lake Forest	IL	60045	**888-828-2850**	847-482-2000
Panoramic Inc 1500 N Parker Dr	Janesville	WI	53545	**800-333-1394**	608-754-8850
Paragon Packaging Inc 7700 Centerville Rd	Ferndale	CA	95536	**888-615-0065**	707-786-4004
Rice Packaging Inc 356 Somers Rd	Ellington	CT	06029	**800-367-6725**	860-872-8341
RTS Packaging LLC 504 Thrasher St	Norcross	GA	30071	**800-558-6984**	
Rusken Packaging Inc PO Box 2100	Cullman	AL	35056	**800-232-8108**	256-734-0092
Seaboard Folding Box Co Inc 35 Daniels St	Fitchburg	MA	01420	**800-225-6313**	978-342-8921

101 BREWERIES

SEE ALSO Malting Products

	City	State	Zip	Toll-Free	Phone
Abita Brewing Co 21084 Hwy 36	Covington	LA	70433	**800-737-2311**	985-893-3143
Boston Beer Co 1 Design Ctr Pl Ste 850 *NYSE: SAM*	Boston	MA	02210	**888-661-2337**	617-368-5000
BridgePort Brewing Co 1318 NW Northrup St	Portland	OR	97209	**888-834-7546**	503-241-7179
Jacob Leinenkugel Brewing Co 124 E Elm St *General	Chippewa Falls	WI	54729	**888-534-6437***	715-723-5558
Keurig Inc 53 S Ave	Burlington	MA	01867	**866-901-2739**	
Labatt Breweries of Canada 207 Queen's Quay W Ste 299 *Cust Svc	Toronto	ON	M5J1A7	**800-268-2337***	416-361-5050
Malt Products Corp 88 Market St	Saddle Brook	NJ	07663	**800-526-0180**	201-845-4420
McMenamins 430 N Killingsworth	Portland	OR	97217	**800-669-8610**	503-223-0109
Molson Coors Brewing Co 1225 17th St Ste 3200 *NYSE: TAP*	Denver	CO	80202	**800-645-5376**	303-927-2337
Pabst Brewing Co, The 10635 Santa Monica Blvd Ste 350	Los Angeles	CA	90025	**800-947-2278**	

BROKERS

SEE Real Estate Agents & Brokers; Securities Brokers & Dealers; Commodity Contracts Brokers & Dealers; Electronic Communications Networks (ECNs); Insurance Agents, Brokers, Services; Mortgage Lenders & Loan Brokers

102 BRUSHES & BROOMS

SEE ALSO Art Materials & Supplies - Mfr

Company / Address	City	State	Zip	Toll-Free	Phone
Abco Cleaning Products 6800 NW 36th Ave	Miami	FL	33147	**888-694-2226**	305-694-2226
Carlisle Sanitary Maintenance Products 402 S Black River St	Sparta	WI	54656	**800-654-8210**	608-269-2151
Corona Brushes Inc 5065 Savarese Cir	Tampa	FL	33634	**800-458-3483**	813-885-2525
Crystal Lake Manufacturing Inc 2225 Alabama 14 PO Box 159	Autaugaville	AL	36003	**800-633-8720**	334-365-3342
Detroit Quality Brush Mfg 32165 Schoolcraft Rd	Livonia	MI	48150	**800-722-3037**	734-525-5660
Felton Brush Inc 7 Burton Dr	Londonderry	NH	03053	**800-258-9702**	603-425-0200
Fuller Brush Co, The PO Box 729 1 Fuller Way *Cust Svc	Great Bend	KS	67530	**800-522-0499***	620-792-1711
Gordon Brush Mfg Company Inc 6247 Randolph St	Commerce	CA	90040	**800-950-7950**	323-724-7777
Greenwood Mop & Broom Inc 312 Palmer St	Greenwood	SC	29646	**800-635-6849**	864-227-8411
Harper Brush Works Inc 400 N Second St	Fairfield	IA	52556	**800-223-7894**	641-472-5186
Industrial Brush Company Inc 105 Clinton Rd	Fairfield	NJ	07004	**800-241-9860**	973-575-0455
Industries for the Blind 445 S Curtis Rd	West Allis	WI	53214	**800-642-8778**	414-778-3040
Laitner Brush Co 1561 Laitner Dr *Cust Svc	Traverse City	MI	49686	**800-423-6805***	231-929-3300
Libman Co 220 N Sheldon St	Arcola	IL	61910	**877-818-3380**	
Magnolia Brush Mfg Ltd 1000 N Cedar PO Box 932	Clarksville	TX	75426	**800-248-2261**	903-427-2261
Mill-Rose Co 7995 Tyler Blvd	Mentor	OH	44060	**800-321-3533**	440-255-9171
Osborn International 5401 Hamilton Ave *Cust Svc	Cleveland	OH	44114	**800-720-3358***	216-361-1900
Padco Inc 2220 Elm St SE	Minneapolis	MN	55414	**800-328-5513**	612-378-7270
PFERD Milwaukee Brush Company Inc 30 Jytek Dr	Leominster	MA	01453	**800-342-9015**	978-840-6420
Rubberset Co 101 W Prospect Ave	Cleveland	OH	44115	**800-345-4939**	
Sanderson-MacLeod Inc 1199 S Main St PO Box 50	Palmer	MA	01069	**866-522-3481**	413-283-3481
SM Arnold Inc 7901 Michigan Ave *Cust Svc	Saint Louis	MO	63111	**800-325-7865***	314-544-4103
Sweepster Inc 2800 N Zeeb Rd	Dexter	MI	48130	**800-456-7100**	734-996-9116
Universal Brush Manufacturing Co 16200 Dixie Hwy	Markham	IL	60428	**800-323-3474**	708-331-1700
Weiler Corp 1 Wildwood Dr *Cust Svc	Cresco	PA	18326	**800-835-9999***	570-595-7495
Wooster Brush Co 604 Madison Ave	Wooster	OH	44691	**800-392-7246**	330-264-4440

103 BUILDING MAINTENANCE SERVICES

SEE ALSO Cleaning Services

Company / Address	City	State	Zip	Toll-Free	Phone
Aid Maintenance Co 300 Roosevelt Ave	Pawtucket	RI	02860	**800-886-6627**	401-722-6627
Calico Building Services Inc 15550-C Rockfield Blvd	Irvine	CA	92618	**800-576-7313**	
Courtesy Building Services Inc 2154 W Northwest Hwy Ste 214	Dallas	TX	75220	**800-479-3853**	972-831-1444
Cummins Facility Services 5202 Marion Waldo Rd	Prospect	OH	43342	**800-451-5629**	740-726-9800
DMS Facility Services Inc 417 East Huntington Dr	Monrovia	CA	91016	**800-443-8677**	626-305-8500
Drayton Group 2295 N Opdyke Rd Ste D	Auburn Hills	MI	48326	**888-655-4442**	
Eagle Cleaning Service Inc 525 Belview St	Bessemer	AL	35020	**877-864-5696**	205-424-5252
Ecolo Odor Control Technologies Inc 59 Penn Dr	Toronto	ON	M9L2A6	**800-667-6355**	416-740-3900
FBG Service Corp 407 S 27th Ave	Omaha	NE	68131	**800-777-8326**	402-346-4422
Griesbach Diamond Water N1022 Quality Dr	Greenville	WI	54942	**800-236-8931**	920-757-5440
Horizon Services Co 250 Governor St	East Hartford	CT	06108	**800-949-5323**	
Master-Lee Energy Services Corp 5631 Route 981	Latrobe	PA	15650	**800-662-4493**	724-539-8060
Shannon Diversified Inc 1190 N Del Rio Pl	Ontario	CA	91764	**800-794-2345**	
Style Crest Inc 2450 Enterprise St	Fremont	OH	43420	**800-925-4440**	419-332-7369
UV Pure Technologies Inc 60 Venture Dr Unit 19	Toronto	ON	M1B3S4	**888-407-9997**	416-208-9884

104 BUILDINGS - PREFABRICATED - METAL

Company / Address	City	State	Zip	Toll-Free	Phone
American Buildings Co 1150 State Docks Rd	Eufaula	AL	36027	**888-307-4338**	334-687-2032
CEMCO 263 N Covina Ln	City Of Industry	CA	91744	**800-775-2362**	
Erect-A-Tube Inc 701 W Pk St PO Box 100	Harvard	IL	60033	**800-624-9219**	815-943-4091
Four Seasons Solar Products LLC 5005 Veterans Memorial Hwy	Holbrook	NY	11741	**800-368-7732**	631-563-4000
Garco Bldg Systems 2714 S Garfield Rd	Airway Heights	WA	99001	**800-941-2291**	509-244-5611
Imperial Industries Inc 505 Industrial Pk Ave	Rothschild	WI	54474	**800-558-2945**	715-359-0200
Kirby Bldg Systems Inc 124 Kirby Dr	Portland	TN	37148	**800-348-7799**	615-325-4165
Mesco Bldg Solutions 5244 Bear Creek Ct	Irving	TX	75061	**800-556-3726**	214-687-9999
Metl-Span LLC 1720 Lakepointe Dr Ste 101	Lewisville	TX	75057	**877-585-9969**	972-221-6656
Mid-West Steel Bldg Co 7301 Fairview	Houston	TX	77041	**800-777-9378**	713-466-7788
Morton Buildings Inc 252 W Adams St PO Box 399	Morton	IL	61550	**800-447-7436**	309-263-7474
Mueller Inc 1913 Hutchins Ave	Ballinger	TX	76821	**877-268-3553**	325-365-3555
NCI Bldg Systems Inc 10943 N Sam Houston PkwyWest *NYSE: NCS*	Houston	TX	77064	**888-624-8677**	281-897-7788
Pacific Building Systems (PBS) 2100 N Pacific Hwy *General	Woodburn	OR	97071	**800-727-7844***	503-981-9581
Package Industries Inc 15 Harback Rd	Sutton	MA	01590	**800-225-7242**	508-865-5871
Parkline Inc PO Box 65	Winfield	WV	25213	**800-786-4855**	304-586-2113
Porta-Fab Corp 18080 Chesterfield Airport Rd	Chesterfield	MO	63005	**800-325-3781**	636-537-5555
PorterCorp 4240 136th Ave	Holland	MI	49424	**800-354-7721**	616-399-1963
Red Dot Corp 1209 W Corsicana St *Cust Svc	Athens	TX	75751	**800-657-2234***	
Ruffin Bldg Systems Inc 6914 Louisiana 2	Oak Grove	LA	71263	**800-421-4232**	318-428-2305
ShelterLogic Corp 150 Callendar Rd	Watertown	CT	06795	**800-932-9344**	860-945-6442
Star Bldg Systems 8600 S I-35	Oklahoma City	OK	73149	**800-879-7827**	
Temo Sunrooms Inc 20400 Hall Rd	Clinton Township	MI	48038	**800-344-8366**	
Trachte Bldg Systems Inc 314 Wilburn Rd	Sun Prairie	WI	53590	**800-356-5824**	
Whirlwind Steel 8234 Hansen Rd	Houston	TX	77075	**800-324-9992**	713-946-7140
Worldwide Steel Buildings PO Box 588	Peculiar	MO	64078	**800-825-0316**	
XS Smith Inc 932 Page Rd	Washington	NC	27889	**800-631-2226**	252-940-5060

105 BUILDINGS - PREFABRICATED - WOOD

Company / Address	City	State	Zip	Toll-Free	Phone
Acorn Deck House Co 852 Main St	Acton	MA	01720	**800-727-3325**	978-263-6800
Barden & Robeson Corp 103 Kelly Ave	Middleport	NY	14105	**800-724-0141**	716-735-3732
Blazer Industries Inc PO Box 489	Aumsville	OR	97325	**877-211-3437**	503-749-1900
Cedarstore.com 5410 Rt 8	Gibsonia	PA	15044	**888-885-3806**	724-444-5300
Deluxe Bldg Systems Inc 499 W Third St	Berwick	PA	18603	**800-843-7372**	570-752-5914
Design Homes Inc 600 N Marquette Rd	Prairie du Chien	WI	53821	**800-627-9443**	608-326-6041
Dickinson Homes Inc 404 N Stephenson Ave Hwy US-2 PO Box 2245	Iron Mountain	MI	49801	**800-438-4687**	906-774-2186
Dynamic Homes LLC 525 Roosevelt Ave	Detroit Lakes	MN	56501	**800-492-4833**	218-847-2611
Flexospan Steel Buildings Inc 253 Railroad St	Sandy Lake	PA	16145	**800-245-0396**	724-376-7221
Foremost Industries Inc 2375 Buchanan Trl W	Greencastle	PA	17225	**877-284-5334**	717-597-7166
Homes by Keystone Inc 13338 Midvale Rd PO Box 69	Waynesboro	PA	17268	**800-890-7926**	
Indaco Metal 3 American Way	Shawnee	OK	74804	**877-750-5614**	877-300-7334
International Homes of Cedar Inc (IHC) PO Box 886	Woodinville	WA	98072	**800-767-7674**	360-668-8511
Keiser Homes 56 Mechanic Falls Rd Rte 121	Oxford	ME	04270	**888-333-1748**	
KIT HomeBuilders West LLC 1124 Garber St	Caldwell	ID	83605	**800-859-0347**	208-454-5000
Lester Bldg Systems LLC 1111 Second Ave S	Lester Prairie	MN	55354	**800-826-4439**	320-395-2531
Lindal Cedar Homes Inc 4300 S 104th Pl *Prod Info	Seattle	WA	98178	**800-426-0536***	206-725-0900
Montana Idaho Log & Timber 1069 Us Hwy 93 N	Victor	MT	59875	**800-600-8604**	406-961-3092
Morgan Bldg Systems Inc 2800 McCree Rd	Garland	TX	75041	**800-935-0321**	972-864-7300
Nationwide Custom Homes 1100 Rives Rd	Martinsville	VA	24115	**800-216-7001**	
New Acton Mobile Industries LLC 809 Gleneagles Ct	Baltimore	MD	21286	**800-251-1600**	
New England Homes 270 Ocean Rd	Greenland	NH	03840	**800-800-8831**	603-436-8830
Nexus Corp 10983 Leroy Dr	Northglenn	CO	80233	**800-228-9639**	303-457-9199
Northeastern Log Homes Inc 10 Ames Rd	Kenduskeag	ME	04450	**800-624-2797**	207-884-7000
Original Lincoln Logs Ltd 5 Riverside Dr PO Box 135	Chestertown	NY	12817	**800-833-2461**	
Pacific Modern Homes Inc (PMHI) 9723 Railroad St	Elk Grove	CA	95624	**800-395-1011**	916-685-9514
Pan Abode Cedar Homes Inc 1100 Maple Ave SW	Renton	WA	98057	**800-782-2633**	425-255-8260

Name / Address	City	State	Zip	Toll-Free	Phone
Schulte Building Systems Inc 17600 Badtke Rd	Hockley	TX	77447	**877-257-2534**	281-304-6111
Sterling Bldg Systems PO Box 8005	Wausau	WI	54402	**800-455-0545**	
Stratford Homes LP 402 S Weber Ave	Stratford	WI	54484	**800-448-1524**	715-687-3133
Timberland Homes Inc 1201 37th St NW	Auburn	WA	98001	**800-488-5036**	253-735-3435
Unibilt Industries Inc 8005 Johnson Stn Rd PO Box 373	Vandalia	OH	45377	**800-777-9942**	
Ward Cedar Log Homes 37 Bangor St PO Box 72 *Cust Svc	Houlton	ME	04730	**800-341-1566***	
Yankee Barn Homes 131 Yankee Barn Rd	Grantham	NH	03753	**800-258-9786**	

106 BUS SERVICES - CHARTER

Name / Address	City	State	Zip	Toll-Free	Phone
A Yankee Line 370 W First St	Boston	MA	02127	**800-942-8890**	617-268-8890
All West Coach Lines 7701 Wilbur Way	Sacramento	CA	95828	**800-843-2121**	916-423-4000
Anderson Coach & Travel 1 Anderson Plz	Greenville	PA	16125	**800-345-3435**	724-588-8310
Arrow Stage Lines 720 E Norfolk Ave	Norfolk	NE	68701	**800-672-8302**	402-371-3850
B & C Transportation Inc 427 Continental Dr	Maryville	TN	37804	**877-812-2287**	865-983-4653
Badger Bus 5501 Femrite Dr	Madison	WI	53718	**800-442-8259**	608-255-1511
Blue Lakes Charters & Tours 12154 N Saginaw Rd	Clio	MI	48420	**800-282-4287**	810-686-4287
Boise-Winnemucca Stage Lines Inc 1105 S La Pt St	Boise	ID	83706	**800-448-5692**	208-336-3300
Brown Coach Inc 50 Venner Rd	Amsterdam	NY	12010	**800-424-4700**	518-843-4700
Butler Motor Transit Company Inc 210 S Monroe St PO Box 1602	Butler	PA	16003	**800-222-8750**	724-282-1000
Carl R Bieber Tourways Inc 320 Fair St PO Box 180	Kutztown	PA	19530	**800-243-2374**	610-683-7333
Central States Coach Repairs 3426 Gilbert Rd	Grand Prairie	TX	75050	**800-533-1939**	972-399-1059
Chippewa Trucking 510 E S Ave	Chippewa Falls	WI	54729	**866-777-1399**	715-726-2457
Citizen Auto Stage Co 3594 E Lincoln St	Tucson	AZ	85714	**800-276-1528**	520-622-8811
Coach Tours Ltd 475 Federal Rd	Brookfield	CT	06804	**800-822-6224**	203-740-1118
Colorado Charter Lines 4960 Locust St	Commerce	CO	80022	**800-821-7491**	303-287-0239
Cowtown Bus Charters Inc 5504 Forest Hill Dr	Fort Worth	TX	76119	**877-287-4897**	817-531-3287
Croswell Bus Lines Inc 975 W Main St	Williamsburg	OH	45176	**800-782-8747**	513-724-2206
CYR Bus Lines 153 Gilman Falls Ave	Old Town	ME	04468	**800-244-2335**	207-827-2335
DATTCO Inc 583 S St	New Britain	CT	06051	**800-229-4879**	860-229-4878
Elite Coach 1685 W Main St	Ephrata	PA	17522	**800-722-6206**	717-733-7710
Eyre Bus Service Inc 13600 Triadelphia Rd PO Box 239	Glenelg	MD	21737	**800-321-3973**	410-442-1330
Gold Coast Tours 105 Gemini Ave	Brea	CA	92821	**800-638-6427**	714-449-6888
Good Time Tours 455 Corday St	Pensacola	FL	32503	**800-446-0886**	850-476-0046
Gray Line Worldwide 1835 Gaylord St	Denver	CO	80206	**800-472-9546**	303-394-6920
Greyhound Canada Transportation Corp 1111 International Blvd Ste 700	Burlington	ON	L7L6W1	**800-661-8747**	
Harms Charters 532 S Vly View Rd	Sioux Falls	SD	57106	**800-678-6543**	605-336-3339
Hawkeye Stages Inc 703 Dudley St	Decorah	IA	52101	**877-464-2954**	563-382-3639
Indian Trails Inc 109 E Comstock St	Owosso	MI	48867	**800-292-3831**	989-725-5105
Kerrville Bus Co 1 S Main St	Del Rio	TX	78840	**800-474-3352**	830-775-7515
Lamers Bus Lines Inc 2407 S Pt Rd	Green Bay	WI	54313	**800-236-1240**	920-496-3600
Martz First Class Coach Company Inc 4783 37th St N	Saint Petersburg	FL	33714	**800-282-8020**	727-526-9086
Mid-America Charter Lines 2513 E Higgins Rd	Elk Grove Village	IL	60007	**800-323-0312**	847-437-3779
Northfield Lines Inc 32611 Northfield Blvd	Northfield	MN	55057	**888-670-8068**	507-645-5267
Onondaga Coach Corp PO Box 277	Auburn	NY	13021	**800-451-1570**	315-255-2216
Pacific Western Transportation Ltd 6999 ordan Dr	Mississauga	ON	L5T1K6	**800-387-6787**	905-564-3232
Peter Pan Bus Lines PO Box 1776	Springfield	MA	01102	**800-343-9999**	
Peter Pan Bus Lines Inc 1776 Main St	Springfield	MA	01103	**800-343-9999**	
Premier Coach Company Inc 946 Rte 7 S	Milton	VT	05468	**800-532-1811**	802-655-4456
Punchbowl Inc 50 Speen St Ste 202	Framingham	MA	01701	**877-570-4340**	508-589-4486
Red Carpet Charters 4820 SW 20th	Oklahoma City	OK	73128	**888-878-5100**	405-672-5100
Riteway Bus Service Inc Motorcoach Div W201 N13900 Fond du Lac Ave	Richfield	WI	53076	**800-776-7026**	262-677-3282
Salter Bus Lines Inc 212 Hudson Ave	Jonesboro	LA	71251	**800-223-8056**	318-259-2522
Shafer's Tour & Charter 500 N St	Endicott	NY	13760	**800-287-8986**	607-797-2006
Silver Fox Tours & Motorcoaches 3 Silver Fox Dr	Millbury	MA	01527	**800-342-5998**	508-865-6000
Starr Bus Charter & Tours 2531 E State St	Trenton	NJ	08619	**800-782-7703**	609-587-0626
Storer Coachways 3519 McDonald Ave	Modesto	CA	95358	**800-621-3383**	209-521-8250
Swarthout Coaches Inc 115 Graham Rd	Ithaca	NY	14850	**800-772-7267**	607-257-2277
Trailways Transportation System Inc 3554 Chain Bridge Rd Ste 202	Fairfax	VA	22030	**877-467-3346**	703-691-3052
Van Galder Bus Co 715 S Pearl St	Janesville	WI	53548	**800-747-0994**	608-752-5407
VIP Tour & Charter Bus Co 129-137 Fox St *General	Portland	ME	04101	**800-231-2222***	207-772-4457
Voyageur Transportation Services 573 Admiral Ct	London	ON	N5V4L3	**855-263-7163**	519-455-4580
Wilson Bus Lines Inc 203 Patriots Rd PO Box 415	East Templeton	MA	01438	**800-253-5235**	978-632-3894
Winn Transportation 1831 Westwood Ave	Richmond	VA	23227	**800-296-9466**	804-358-9466
Wisconsin Coach Lines Inc 1520 Arcadian Ave	Waukesha	WI	53186	**877-324-7767**	262-542-8861
Young Transportation & Tours 843 Riverside Dr	Asheville	NC	28804	**800-622-5444**	828-258-0084

107 BUS SERVICES - INTERCITY & RURAL

SEE ALSO Bus Services - School ; Mass Transportation (Local & Suburban)

Name / Address	City	State	Zip	Toll-Free	Phone
Adirondack Trailways 499 Hurley Ave	Hurley	NY	12443	**800-858-8555**	845-339-4230
Colorado Valley Transit Inc 108 Cardinal Ln PO Box 940	Columbus	TX	78934	**800-548-1068**	979-732-6281
Everything Parking Inc 1415 S Church St Ste T	Charlotte	NC	28203	**877-751-6683**	704-377-1755
GATRA 2 Oak St	Taunton	MA	02780	**800-483-2500**	508-823-8828
Geauga County Transit 12555 Merritt Rd *Cust Svc	Chardon	OH	44024	**888-287-7190***	440-279-2150
Greyhound Canada Transportation Corp 1111 International Blvd Ste 700	Burlington	ON	L7L6W1	**800-661-8747**	
Jefferson Partners LP 2100 E 26th St *Cust Svc	Minneapolis	MN	55404	**800-767-5333***	612-359-3400
Ozark Regional Transit 2423 E Robinson Ave	Springdale	AR	72764	**800-865-5901**	479-756-5901
Pacific Transit System 216 N Second St	Raymond	WA	98577	**800-833-6388**	360-875-9418
Pelivan Transit 333 S Oak St PO Box B	Big Cabin	OK	74332	**800-482-4594**	918-783-5793
Peter Pan Bus Lines Inc 1776 Main St	Springfield	MA	01103	**800-343-9999**	
Powder River Transportation 1700 U S 14	Gillette	WY	82716	**888-970-7233**	307-682-0960
Rural Transit Enterprises Coordinated Inc (RTEC) 100 E Main St	Mount Vernon	KY	40456	**800-321-7832**	606-256-9835
Suburban Transit Corp 750 Somerset St	New Brunswick	NJ	08901	**800-222-0492**	732-249-1100
Thunderbird Rural Public Transportation System 2801 W Loop 306 Ste A PO Box 60050	San Angelo	TX	76904	**877-947-8729**	325-944-9666
Training Advantage, The PO Box 800	Ignacio	CO	81137	**800-659-2656**	970-563-4517
Viking Trailways 201 Glendale Rd	Joplin	MO	64804	**800-400-2779**	417-781-2779

108 BUS SERVICES - SCHOOL

Name / Address	City	State	Zip	Toll-Free	Phone
Birnie Bus Service Inc 248 Otis St	Rome	NY	13441	**800-734-3950**	315-336-3950
Brown Bus Co 2111 E Sherman Ave	Nampa	ID	83686	**800-574-1580**	208-466-4181
Davidsmeyer Bus Service Inc 2513 E Higgins Rd	Elk Grove Village	IL	60007	**800-323-0312**	847-437-3767
Dean Transportation Inc 4812 Aurelius Rd	Lansing	MI	48910	**800-282-3326**	517-319-8300
Hastings Bus Co 425 31st St E	Hastings	MN	55033	**800-210-6362**	651-437-1888
John T Cyr & Sons Inc 153 Gilman Falls Ave	Old Town	ME	04468	**800-244-2335**	207-827-2335
Kobussen Buses Ltd W914 County Rd CE	Kaukauna	WI	54130	**800-447-0116**	920-766-0606
Michael's Transportation Service Inc 140 Yolano Dr *Cust Svc	Vallejo	CA	94589	**800-295-2448***	707-643-2099
Riteway Bus Service Inc Motorcoach Div W201 N13900 Fond du Lac Ave	Richfield	WI	53076	**800-776-7026**	262-677-3282
Stock Transportation Ltd 128 Wellington St W Ste 201	Barrie	ON	L4N1K9	**888-952-0878**	
Student Transportation of America Inc (STA) 3349 Hwy 138 Bldg B Ste D	Wall	NJ	07719	**888-942-2250**	732-280-4200

109 BUSINESS FORMS

SEE ALSO Printing Companies - Commercial Printers

Name / Address	City	State	Zip	Toll-Free	Phone
Ace Forms of Kansas Inc 2900 N Rotary Terr	Pittsburg	KS	66762	**800-223-9287**	
Allison Payment Systems LLC 2200 Production Dr	Indianapolis	IN	46241	**800-755-2440**	
Amsterdam Printing & Litho Corp 166 Wallins Corners Rd *Cust Svc	Amsterdam	NY	12010	**800-833-6231***	518-842-6000
Apex Color 200 N Lee St	Jacksonville	FL	32204	**800-367-6790**	

Company	Address	City	State	Zip	Toll-Free	Phone
Bestforms Inc	1135 Avenida Acaso	Camarillo	CA	93012	**800-350-0618**	805-383-6993
Central States Business Forms Inc	2500 Industrial Pkwy	Dewey	OK	74029	**800-331-0920**	
Champion Industries Inc	PO Box 2968 PO Box 2968 *OTC: CHMP*	Huntington	WV	25728	**800-624-3431**	304-528-2791
Curtis 1000 Inc	1725 Breckinridge Pkwy Ste 500	Duluth	GA	30096	**877-287-8715**	678-380-9095
Custom Business Forms Inc	210 Edge Pl *General	Minneapolis	MN	55418	**800-234-1221***	612-789-0002
Data Papers Inc	468 Industrial Pk Rd	Muncy	PA	17756	**800-233-3032**	
Data Source Inc	1400 Universal Ave	Kansas City	MO	64120	**877-846-9120**	816-483-3282
Datatel Resources Corp	1729 Pennsylvania Ave	Monaca	PA	15061	**800-245-2688**	724-775-5300
DFS Group	500 Main St *General	Groton	MA	01471	**800-225-9528***	
Dupli-Systems Inc	8260 Dow Cir	Strongsville	OH	44136	**800-321-1610**	440-234-9415
Eastern Business Forms Inc	PO Box 10	Mauldin	SC	29662	**800-387-2648**	
Federal Business Products Inc	95 Main Ave	Clifton	NJ	07014	**800-927-5123**	973-667-9800
FedEx	450 W First Ave	Roselle	NJ	07203	**800-463-3339**	406-252-6265
Flesh Co	2118 59th St	Saint Louis	MO	63110	**800-869-3330**	314-781-4400
Forms Manufacturers Inc	312 E Forest Ave	Girard	KS	66743	**800-835-0614**	620-724-8225
Freedom Graphic Systems Inc (FGS)	1101 S Janesville St	Milton	WI	53563	**800-334-3540**	
General Credit Forms Inc (GCF)	3595 Rider Trl S	Earth City	MO	63045	**888-423-6397**	314-216-8600
Genoa Business Forms Inc	445 Pk Ave	Sycamore	IL	60178	**800-383-2801**	
Gulf Business Forms Inc	2460 S IH-35 PO Box 1073	San Marcos	TX	78667	**800-433-4853**	512-353-8313
Highland Computer Forms Inc	1025 W Main St	Hillsboro	OH	45133	**800-669-5213**	937-393-4215
Hospital Forms & Systems Corp	8900 Ambassador Row	Dallas	TX	75247	**800-527-5081**	214-634-8900
IBS Direct	431 Yerkes Rd	King of Prussia	PA	19406	**800-220-1255**	610-265-8210
Imperial Graphics Inc	3100 Walkent Dr NW	Grand Rapids	MI	49544	**800-777-2591**	
Kaye-Smith	4101 Oakesdale Ave SW	Renton	WA	98057	**800-822-9987**	425-228-8600
New Jersey Business Forms Manufacturing Co	55 W Sheffield Ave	Englewood	NJ	07631	**800-466-6523**	201-569-4500
Paris Business Products	800 Highland Dr *Cust Svc	Westampton	NJ	08060	**800-523-6454***	609-265-9200
Patterson Office Supplies	3310 N Duncan Rd	Champaign	IL	61822	**800-637-1140**	317-733-4900
Performance Office Papers	21565 Hamburg Ave	Lakeville	MN	55044	**800-458-7189**	
PrintEdd Products of North America	2641 N Forum Dr	Grand Prairie	TX	75052	**800-367-6728**	972-660-3800
Quality Forms	4317 W US Rt 36	Piqua	OH	45356	**866-773-4595**	937-773-4595
Rotary Forms Press Inc	835 S High St	Hillsboro	OH	45133	**800-654-2876**	937-393-3426
Royal Business Forms Inc	3301 Ave E E	Arlington	TX	76011	**800-255-9303**	817-640-5248
Specialized Printed Forms Inc	352 Ctr St	Caledonia	NY	14423	**800-688-2381**	585-538-2381
Sterling Business Forms	PO Box 2486 *Cust Svc	White City	OR	97503	**800-759-3676***	
Stry-Lenkoff Co Inc	1100 W Broadway	Louisville	KY	40232	**800-626-8247**	502-587-6804
Victor Printing Inc	1 Victor Way	Sharon	PA	16146	**800-443-2845**	724-342-2106
Ward-Kraft Inc	2401 Cooper St	Fort Scott	KS	66701	**800-821-4021**	620-223-5500
Wilmer Service Line	515 W Sycamore St	Coldwater	OH	45828	**800-494-5637**	
Wise Business Forms Inc	555 McFarland 400 Dr	Alpharetta	GA	30004	**888-815-9473**	770-442-1060
Witt Printing Company Inc	301 Oak St	El Dorado Springs	MO	64744	**800-641-4342**	417-876-4721
Wright Business Graphics (WBG)	18440 NE San Rafael St	Portland	OR	97230	**800-547-8397**	

110 BUSINESS MACHINES - MFR

SEE ALSO Business Machines - Whol ; Calculators - Electronic ; Computer Equipment ; Photocopying Equipment & Supplies

Company	Address	City	State	Zip	Toll-Free	Phone
Abbott Vascular	26531 Ynez Rd	Temecula	CA	92591	**800-227-9902**	
Agissar Corp	526 Benton St	Stratford	CT	06615	**800-627-8256**	203-375-8662
Amano Cincinnati Inc	140 Harrison Ave	Roseland	NJ	07068	**800-526-2559**	973-403-1900
Better Packages Inc	255 Canal St PO Box 711	Shelton	CT	06484	**800-237-9151**	203-926-3722
Brandt Tractor Ltd	Hwy 1 E PO Box 3856	Regina	SK	S4P3R8	**888-227-2638**	306-791-7777
Brother International Corp	100 Somerset Corporate Blvd *Cust Svc	Bridgewater	NJ	08807	**877-552-6255***	908-704-1700
CCTF Corp	5407 - 53 Ave NW	Edmonton	AB	T6B3G2	**800-661-3633**	780-463-8700
Cubeit Portable Storage Canada Inc	100 Canadian Rd	Scarborough	ON	M1R4Z5	**888-428-2348**	
Cummins-Allison Corp	852 Feehanville Dr	Mount Prospect	IL	60056	**800-786-5528**	847-299-9550
Dynetics Engineering Corp	515 Bond St	Lincolnshire	IL	60069	**800-888-8110**	847-541-7300
Ecco Business Systems Inc	60 W 38th St 4th Fl	New York	NY	10018	**800-558-6777**	212-921-4545
ECRM Inc	554 Clark Rd	Tewksbury	MA	01876	**800-537-3276**	978-851-0207
Ernest Green & Son Ltd	2395 Skymark Ave	Mississauga	ON	L4W4Y6	**800-387-7577**	905-629-8999
Exocor Inc	271 Ridley Rd	St. Catharines	ON	L2R6P7	**888-317-2209**	905-704-0603
Fellowes Inc	1789 Norwood Ave	Itasca	IL	60143	**800-945-4545**	630-893-1600
Fireside Hearth & Home	7571 215th St W	Lakeville	MN	55044	**800-669-4328**	651-452-3399
Fountain Industries Co	922 E 14th St	Albert Lea	MN	56007	**800-328-3594**	507-373-2351
G & O Thermal Supply Co	5435 N Northwest Hwy	Chicago	IL	60630	**800-621-4997**	773-763-1300
GenServe Inc	80 Sweeneydale Ave	Bay Shore	NY	11706	**800-247-7215**	631-435-0437
Imaging Business Machines LLC	2750 Crestwood Blvd	Birmingham	AL	35210	**877-627-8325**	205-439-7100
International Business Machines Corp (IBM)	1 New OrchaRd Rd *NYSE: IBM*	Armonk	NY	10504	**800-426-4968**	914-499-1900
Lakeside Process Controls Ltd	2475 Hogan Dr	Mississauga	ON	L5N0E9	**800-265-1005**	905-629-9340
Lathem Time Corp	200 Selig Dr SW	Atlanta	GA	30336	**800-241-4990**	404-691-0400
Leeson Canada Inc	320 Superior Blvd	Mississauga	ON	L5T2N7	**800-563-0949**	905-670-4770
Lynde-Ordway Company Inc	3308 W Warner Ave	Santa Ana	CA	92704	**800-762-7057**	714-957-1311
MAAC Machinery Corp	590 Tower Blvd	Carol Stream	IL	60188	**800-588-6222**	630-665-1700
Magnatech International Inc	17 E Meadow Ave	Robesonia	PA	19551	**800-523-8193**	610-693-8866
Martin Yale Industries Inc	251 Wedcor Ave	Wabash	IN	46992	**800-225-5644**	260-563-0641
MBM Corp (MBM)	3134 Industry Dr *Cust Svc	North Charleston	SC	29418	**800-223-2508***	843-552-2700
Neopost Inc Canada	150 Steelcase Rd W	Markham	ON	L3R3J9	**800-636-7678**	905-475-3722
Newbold Corp	450 Weaver St	Rocky Mount	VA	24151	**800-552-3282**	540-489-4400
Noble Trade Inc	7171 Jane St	Concord	ON	L4K1A7	**800-529-9805**	416-754-5533
Norsask Farm Equipment Ltd	Box 49	North Battleford	SK	S9A2X6	**888-446-8128**	306-445-8128
Ossur	27412 Aliso Viejo Pkwy	Aliso Viejo	CA	92656	**800-233-6263**	
Pitney Bowes Inc	1 Elmcroft Rd *NYSE: PBI*	Stamford	CT	06926	**800-672-6937**	203-356-5000
Pubco Corp	3830 Kelley Ave	Cleveland	OH	44114	**800-878-3399**	216-881-5300
Puregas LLC	226 Commerce St	Broomfield	CO	80020	**800-521-5351**	303-427-3700
Rapid Line Industries Inc	455 N Ottawa St	Joliet	IL	60432	**877-444-9955**	815-727-4362
Rimex Supply Ltd	9726 186th St	Surrey	BC	V4N3N7	**800-663-9883**	604-888-0025
Royal Consumer Information Products Inc	379 Campus Dr 2nd Fl *Sales	Somerset	NJ	08873	**888-261-4555***	732-627-9977
Schaumburg Specialties Co	550 Albion Ave Unit 30	Schaumburg	IL	60193	**800-834-8125**	
Security Engineered Machinery Company Inc	5 Walkup Dr PO Box 1045 *Sales	Westborough	MA	01581	**800-225-9293***	508-366-1488
Sharp Electronics Corp	1 Sharp Plz	Mahwah	NJ	07430	**800-237-4277**	201-529-8200
Staplex Co	777 Fifth Ave *Cust Svc	Brooklyn	NY	11232	**800-221-0822***	718-768-3333
Swintec Corp	320 W Commercial Ave	Moonachie	NJ	07074	**800-225-0867**	201-935-0115
Tundra Process Solutions Ltd	7523 Flint Rd SE	Calgary	AB	T2H1G3	**800-265-1166**	403-255-5222
Westward Parts Services Ltd	6517 - 67 St	Red Deer	AB	T4P1A3	**888-937-7278**	403-347-2200

111 BUSINESS MACHINES - WHOL

SEE ALSO Business Machines - Mfr ; Computer Equipment & Software - Whol ; Photocopying Equipment & Supplies

Company	Address	City	State	Zip	Toll-Free	Phone
Adams Remco Inc	PO Box 3968	South Bend	IN	46619	**800-627-2113**	574-288-2113
Canon Business Solutions-Central	425 N Martingale Rd Ste 100	Schaumburg	IL	60173	**800-706-3303**	847-706-3400
Carr Business Systems Inc	130 Spagnoli Rd	Melville	NY	11747	**800-720-2277**	631-249-9880
Copiers Northwest Inc	601 Dexter Ave N	Seattle	WA	98109	**866-692-0700**	206-282-1200
CRS Inc	4851 White Bear Pkwy	Saint Paul	MN	55110	**800-333-4949**	651-294-2700
Daisy IT Supplies Sales & Service	8575 Red Oak Ave	Rancho Cucamonga	CA	91730	**800-266-5585**	909-989-5585
Datamax Office Systems Inc	6717 Waldemar Ave	Saint Louis	MO	63139	**800-325-9299**	314-633-1400
Dieterich-Post Co	616 Monterey Pass Rd	Monterey Park	CA	91754	**800-955-3729**	626-289-5021
El Dorado Trading Group Inc	760 San Antonio Rd	Palo Alto	CA	94303	**800-227-8292**	

Company / Address	City	State	Zip	Toll-Free	Phone
FP Mailing Solutions 140 N Mitchell Ct	Addison	IL	60101	**800-341-6052**	630-827-5500
Global Imaging Systems Inc 3820 Northdale Blvd Ste 200A	Tampa	FL	33624	**888-628-7834**	813-960-5508
Illinois Wholesale Cash Register Inc 2790 Pinnacle Dr	Elgin	IL	60124	**800-544-5493**	847-310-4200
Merchants Solutions Co 19252 S Blackhawk Pkwy Unit 75	Mokena	IL	60448	**800-486-3214**	708-449-6650
Metro - Sales Inc 1640 E 78th St	Minneapolis	MN	55423	**800-862-7414**	612-861-4000
Numeridex Inc 632 S Wheeling Rd	Wheeling	IL	60090	**800-323-7737**	
Pitney Bowes Inc 1 Elmcroft Rd *NYSE: PBI*	Stamford	CT	06926	**800-672-6937**	203-356-5000
Ricoh Americas Corp 5 Dedrick Pl	West Caldwell	NJ	07006	**800-727-1885**	973-882-2000
Secap USA Inc 10 Clipper Rd	Conshohocken	PA	19428	**800-523-0320**	610-825-6205
Standard Duplicating Machines Corp 10 Connector Rd	Andover	MA	01810	**800-526-4774**	978-470-1920
Stewart Engineering Supply Inc 3221 E Pioneer Pkwy	Arlington	TX	76010	**800-533-1265**	817-640-1767
Systel Business Equipment Company Inc 2604 Fort Bragg Rd	Fayetteville	NC	28303	**800-849-5900**	910-321-7700
Transco Business Technologies (TBT) 34 Leighton Rd	Augusta	ME	04330	**800-322-0003**	207-622-6251
UPS Store, The 6060 Cornerstone Ct W	San Diego	CA	92121	**800-789-4623**	858-455-8800
Zoom Information Inc 307 Waverley Oaks Rd	Waltham	MA	02452	**800-949-7040**	781-693-7500

BUSINESS ORGANIZATIONS

SEE Management & Business Professional Associations ; Chambers of Commerce - Canadian ; Chambers of Commerce - US - Local ; Chambers of Commerce - US - State

112 BUSINESS SERVICE CENTERS

Company / Address	City	State	Zip	Toll-Free	Phone
Allegra Network LLC 47585 Galleon Dr *General	Plymouth	MI	48170	**800-726-9050***	248-596-8600
Aloha Petroleum Ltd 1132 Bishop St Ste 1700	Honolulu	HI	96813	**800-621-4654**	808-522-9700
Alphanumeric Systems Inc 3801 Wake Forest Rd	Raleigh	NC	27609	**800-638-6556**	919-781-7575
Aminian Business Services Inc 50 Tesla	Irvine	CA	92618	**888-800-5207**	949-724-1155
Annex Brands Inc 7580 Metropolitan Dr Ste 200	San Diego	CA	92108	**877-722-5236**	619-563-4800
Asi System Integration Inc 48 W 37th St	New York	NY	10018	**866-308-3920**	
Concentrix Corp 3750 Monroe Ave	Pittsford	NY	14534	**800-747-0583**	585-218-5300
Core Bts Inc 201 W 103rd St Ste 240	Indianapolis	IN	46290	**855-267-3287**	
Corporation Service Co 2711 Centerville Rd Ste 400	Wilmington	DE	19808	**866-403-5272**	302-636-5400
Craters & Freighters 331 Corporate Cir Ste J	Golden	CO	80401	**800-736-3335**	
Duncan-Parnell Inc 900 S McDowell St	Charlotte	NC	28204	**800-849-7708**	704-372-7766
Evolve Discovery Inc 611 Mission St 4th Fl	San Francisco	CA	94105	**866-488-1032**	415-398-8600
Galaxie Coffee Services 110 Sea Ln	Farmingdale	NY	11735	**800-564-9104**	631-694-2688
Group O Inc 4905 77th Ave *Cust Svc	Milan	IL	61264	**800-752-0730***	309-736-8300
Hackworth Reprographics 1700 Liberty St	Chesapeake	VA	23324	**800-676-2424**	757-545-7675
Java Dave's Executive Coffee Service 6239 E 15th St	Tulsa	OK	74112	**800-725-7315**	918-836-5570
Juran Institute Inc 160 Main St Ste 100	Southington	CT	06489	**800-338-7726**	203-267-3445
Navis Logistics Network 6551 S Revere Pkwy Ste 250	Centennial	CO	80111	**800-344-3528**	
Navis Pack & Ship Centers 6551 S Revere Pkwy Ste 250	Centennial	CO	80111	**800-344-3528**	
New Jersey Legal Copy Inc 501 King Ave	Cherry Hill	NJ	08002	**800-426-7965**	856-910-0202
Office Depot Inc 2200 Old Germantown Rd *NASDAQ: ODP*	Delray Beach	FL	33445	**800-937-3600**	561-438-4800
Pak Mail Centers of America Inc 7173 S Havana St Ste 600 *Cust Svc	Centennial	CO	80112	**800-778-6665***	303-957-1000
Peachtree Planning Corp 5040 Roswell Rd NE	Atlanta	GA	30342	**800-366-0839**	404-260-1600
Postal Connections of America 6136 Frisco Sq Blvd Ste 400	Frisco	TX	75034	**800-767-8257**	
PostalAnnex+ Inc 7580 Metropolitan Dr Ste 200	San Diego	CA	92108	**800-456-1525**	619-563-4800
PostNet International Franchise Corp 1819 Wazee St	Denver	CO	80202	**800-841-7171**	303-771-7100
Sharp Decisions Inc 1040 Ave of the A	New York	NY	10018	**800-742-7792**	212-481-5533
Shee Atika Inc 315 Lincoln St Ste 300	Sitka	AK	99835	**800-478-3534**	907-747-3534
Sir Speedy Inc 26722 Plaza Dr	Mission Viejo	CA	92691	**800-854-8297**	949-348-5000
Total Energy Solutions LLC (TES) 100 International Dr Ste 260	Portsmouth	NH	03801	**877-436-9812**	
Toth Financial Advisory Corp 608 S King St Ste 300	Leesburg	VA	20175	**800-445-1880**	703-443-8684
Ubics Inc 333 Technology Dr Ste 210 *OTC: UBIX*	Canonsburg	PA	15317	**800-441-0077**	724-746-6001

113 BUYER'S GUIDES - ONLINE

SEE ALSO Investment Guides - Online

Company / Address	City	State	Zip	Toll-Free	Phone
Ace Mart - Downtown San Antonio 1220 S St Mary's	San Antonio	TX	78210	**888-898-8079**	210-224-0082
InsWeb Inc 11290 Pyrites Way	Gold River	CA	95670	**866-697-9085**	916-853-3300
Market America Inc 1302 Pleasant Ridge Rd	Greensboro	NC	27409	**866-420-1709**	336-605-0040
Parke-Bell Ltd Inc 709 W 12th St	Huntingburg	IN	47542	**800-457-7456**	812-683-3707

114 CABINETS - WOOD

SEE ALSO Carpentry & Flooring Contractors ; Household Furniture

Company / Address	City	State	Zip	Toll-Free	Phone
Allen Lumber Company Inc 502 N Main St	Barre	VT	05641	**800-696-2666**	802-476-4156
Cabinetry By Karman Inc 6000 Stratler St	Salt Lake City	UT	84107	**800-255-3581**	801-281-6400
Canyon Creek Cabinet Co 16726 Tye St SE	Monroe	WA	98272	**800-228-1830**	360-348-4973
Conestoga Wood Specialties Inc 245 Reading Rd	East Earl	PA	17519	**800-964-3667**	
Crystal Cabinet Works Inc 1100 Crystal Dr	Princeton	MN	55371	**800-347-5045**	763-389-4187
Decore-ative Specialties Inc 2772 S Peck Rd	Monrovia	CA	91016	**800-729-7277**	626-254-9191
Doormark Inc 430 Goolsby Blvd	Deerfield Beach	FL	33442	**888-969-0124**	954-418-4700
Grabill Cabinet Company Inc 13844 Sawmill Dr	Grabill	IN	46741	**877-472-2782**	
Grandview Products Co 1601 Superior Dr	Parsons	KS	67357	**800-247-9105**	620-421-6950
Haas Cabinet Company Inc 625 W Utica St	Sellersburg	IN	47172	**800-457-6458**	812-246-4431
Huntwood Industries 23800 E Apple Way	Liberty Lake	WA	99019	**800-873-7350**	509-924-5858
Jim Bishop Cabinets Inc 5640 Bell Rd	Montgomery	AL	36116	**800-410-2444**	
Kraftmaid Cabinetry Inc 15535 S State Ave PO Box 1055	Middlefield	OH	44062	**888-562-7744**	
Marsh Furniture Co PO Box 870	High Point	NC	27261	**800-696-2774**	336-884-7363
Masco Cabinetry LLC 5353 W US 223	Adrian	MI	49221	**866-850-8557**	517-263-0771
Masco Corp 21001 Van Born Rd *NYSE: MAS*	Taylor	MI	48180	**888-627-6397**	313-274-7400
Mastercraft Industries Inc 777 S St	Newburgh	NY	12550	**800-835-7812**	845-565-8850
Medallion Cabinetry 2222 Camden Ct	Oak Brook	IL	60523	**800-543-4074**	952-442-5171
Mouser Custom Cabinetry 2112 N Hwy 31 W	Elizabethtown	KY	42701	**800-345-7537**	270-737-7477
Norcraft cabinetry 3020 Denmark Ave	Eagan	MN	55121	**877-888-0002**	651-234-3300
Northern Contours Inc 1355 Mendota Heights Rd Ste 100	Mendota Heights	MN	55120	**866-344-8132**	651-695-1698
Patrick Industries Inc 107 W Franklin St PO Box 638 *NASDAQ: PATK*	Elkhart	IN	46515	**800-331-2151**	574-294-7511
Plato Woodwork Inc 200 Third St SW	Plato	MN	55370	**800-328-5924**	320-238-2193
Republic Industries Inc 1400 Warren Dr	Marshall	TX	75672	**866-284-0941**	903-935-3680
Rosebud Mfg Co Inc 701 SE 12th St	Madison	SD	57042	**800-256-4561**	605-256-4561
Roy's Wood Products Inc 329 Thrush Ln	Lugoff	SC	29078	**800-727-1590**	803-438-1590
RSI Home Products Inc 400 E Orangethorpe Ave	Anaheim	CA	92801	**888-774-8062**	714-449-2200
Rynone Mfg Corp PO Box 128	Sayre	PA	18840	**800-839-1654**	570-888-5272
Showplace Wood Products Inc 1 Enterprise St	Harrisburg	SD	57032	**877-512-2500**	605-743-2200
Starmark Cabinetry 600 E 48th St N	Sioux Falls	SD	57104	**800-755-7789**	800-594-9444
Ultracraft Co 6163 Old 421 Rd	Liberty	NC	27298	**800-262-4046**	

115 CABLE & OTHER PAY TELEVISION SERVICES

Company / Address	City	State	Zip	Toll-Free	Phone
Access Communications Co-operative Ltd 2250 Park St	Regina	SK	S4N7K7	**866-211-6334**	306-569-2225
All West Communications Inc 50 West 100 North	Kamas	UT	84036	**866-255-9378**	435-783-4361
Big Bend Telephone Company Inc 808 N Fifth St	Alpine	TX	79830	**800-520-0092**	432-364-1000
Broadnet Teleservices LLC 1805 Shea Ctr Dr Ste 160	Highlands Ranch	CO	80129	**877-579-4929**	
Cable Connection, The 52 Heppner Dr	Carson City	NV	89706	**800-851-2961**	775-885-1443
Cable One Inc 210 E Earll Drive	Phoenix	AZ	85012	**877-692-2253**	602-364-6000
CableAmerica Corp 7822 E Gray Rd	Scottsdale	AZ	85260	**866-871-4492**	

Classified Section

				Toll-Free	Phone
Campus Televideo Inc 100 First Stamford Pl	Stamford	CT	06902	**866-615-8674**	203-983-5400
Capitol Connection 4400 University Dr MS 1D2	Fairfax	VA	22030	**844-504-7161**	703-993-3100
Cass Cable Tv Inc 100 Redbud Rd	Virginia	IL	62691	**800-252-1799**	217-452-7725
Charter Communications Inc 12405 Powerscourt Dr Ste 100 *NASDAQ: CHTR*	Saint Louis	MO	63131	**888-438-2427**	314-965-0555
Cogeco Cable Inc 5 Pl Ville-Marie Ste 915	Montreal	QC	H3B4M7	**800-855-0511**	514-874-2600
Concierge Communications LLC 4801 S Lkshore Dr Ste 106	Tempe	AZ	85282	**888-624-2643**	
Country Cablevision Inc 9449 State Hwy 197 S	Burnsville	NC	28714	**800-722-4074**	828-682-4074
Cox Communications Inc 1400 Lake Hearn Dr	Atlanta	GA	30319	**866-961-0027**	404-843-5000
Custom Cable Corp 242 Butler St	Westbury	NY	11590	**800-832-3600**	516-334-3600
DIRECTV Inc 2230 E Imperial Hwy *Cust Svc	El Segundo	CA	90245	**800-531-5000***	310-535-5000
DISH Network LLC 9601 S Meridian Blvd *NASDAQ: DISH*	Englewood	CO	80112	**800-823-4929**	
Fibercomm Lc 1605 Ninth St	Sioux City	IA	51101	**800-836-2472**	712-224-2020
Green Earth Cleaning 51 W 135th St	Kansas City	MO	64145	**877-926-0895**	816-926-0895
Hamilton Telephone Co 1001 12th St	Aurora	NE	68818	**800-821-1831**	402-694-5101
High Power Technical Services Inc (HPTS) 2230 Ampere Dr	Louisville	KY	40299	**866-310-5377**	
Kincardine Cable TV Ltd 223 Bruce Ave	Kincardine	ON	N2Z2P2	**800-265-3064**	519-396-8880
Kmtelecom 18 Second Ave NW	Kasson	MN	55944	**888-232-3796**	507-634-2511
Ksbj 1722 Treble Dr	Humble	TX	77338	**877-644-5725**	281-446-5725
Ksby-Tv 1772 Calle Joaquin	San Luis Obispo	CA	93405	**800-583-4135**	805-541-6666
Link Electronics Inc 2137 Rust Ave	Cape Girardeau	MO	63703	**800-776-4411**	573-334-4433
Mediacom Communications Corp 100 Crystal Run Rd *General	Middletown	NY	10941	**800-479-2082***	845-695-2600
Midcontinent Communications PO Box 5010	Sioux Falls	SD	57117	**800-888-1300**	605-274-9810
National Cable Television Co-op Inc (NCTC) 11200 Corporate Ave	Lenexa	KS	66219	**800-720-5850**	913-599-5900
Otter Tail Telcom 230 W Lincoln Ave	Fergus Falls	MN	56537	**800-247-2706**	218-826-6161
RLTV 5525 Research Park Dr	Baltimore	MD	21228	**800-754-8464**	
Rooftop Media Inc 188 Spear St Ste 250	San Francisco	CA	94105	**800-860-0293**	
Service Electric Cable TV & Communications 2260 Ave A	Bethlehem	PA	18017	**800-232-9100**	610-865-9100
Shaw Communications Inc 630 Third Ave SW *TSE: SJR/B*	Calgary	AB	T2P4L4	**888-472-2222**	403-750-4500
Southern Vermont Cable Co PO Box 166	Bondville	VT	05340	**800-544-5931**	
Suddenlink Communications 6151 Paluxy Dr	Tyler	TX	75703	**877-694-9474**	
Tel Star Cablevison Inc 1295 Lourdes Rd	Metamora	IL	61548	**888-842-0258**	309-383-2677
Tele-Media Corp 804 Jacksonville Rd PO Box 39	Bellefonte	PA	16823	**800-704-4254**	814-353-2025
TiVo Inc 2160 Gold St *NASDAQ: TIVO*	Alviso	CA	95002	**877-367-8486**	408-519-9100
Touch Base 620 Sixth St Fl 3	Denver	CO	80202	**800-605-6920**	303-862-3300

116 CABLE REELS

				Toll-Free	Phone
American Reeling Devices Inc 15 Airpark Vista Blvd *Sales	Dayton	NV	89403	**800-354-7335***	
Conductix 10102 F St	Omaha	NE	68127	**800-521-4888**	402-339-9300
Gleason Reel Corp 600 S Clark St	Mayville	WI	53050	**888-504-5151**	920-387-4120
Hannay Reels Inc 553 SR 143	Westerlo	NY	12193	**877-467-3357**	518-797-3791

117 CALCULATORS - ELECTRONIC

				Toll-Free	Phone
Calculated Industries Inc 4840 Hytech Dr	Carson City	NV	89706	**800-854-8075**	775-885-4900
Sharp Electronics Corp 1 Sharp Plz	Mahwah	NJ	07430	**800-237-4277**	201-529-8200
Sweda Company LLC 17411 Vly Blvd	City of Industry	CA	91744	**800-848-8417**	626-357-9999
Texas Instruments Inc 12500 TI Blvd *NASDAQ: TXN* ■ *Cust Svc	Dallas	TX	75243	**800-336-5236***	972-995-3773
Victor Technology LLC 175 E Crossroads Pkwy	Bolingbrook	IL	60440	**800-628-2420**	630-754-4400

118 CAMERAS & RELATED SUPPLIES - RETAIL

				Toll-Free	Phone
Adorama Camera Inc 42 W 18th St	New York	NY	10011	**800-223-2500**	212-741-0052
B & H Photo-Video-Pro Audio Corp 420 Ninth Ave	New York	NY	10001	**800-947-9954**	212-444-6615
Beach Camera 203 Rt 22 E	Green Brook	NJ	08812	**800-572-3224**	732-968-6400
Black Photo Corp 200 Consilium Pl Ste 1600	Toronto	ON	M1H3J3	**800-668-3826**	416-279-0007
CambridgeWorld 34 Franklin Ave	Brooklyn	NY	11205	**800-221-2253**	718-858-5002
Camera Corner Inc PO Box 1899	Burlington	NC	27216	**800-868-2462**	336-228-0251
Dodd Camera 2077 E 30th St	Cleveland	OH	44115	**800-507-1676**	216-361-6800
Dury's 701 Ewing Ave	Nashville	TN	37203	**800-824-2379**	615-255-3456
F-11 Photographic Supplies 16 E Main St	Bozeman	MT	59715	**888-548-0203**	406-586-3281
Focus Camera Inc 905 McDonald Ave	Brooklyn	NY	11218	**800-221-0828**	718-437-8810
Kenmore Camera Inc 18031 67th Ave NE PO Box 82467	Kenmore	WA	98028	**888-485-7447**	425-485-7447
Ritz Camera & Image 2 Bergen Turnpike *Cust Svc	Ridgefield Park	NJ	07660	**855-622-7489***	
Samy's Camera Inc 431 S Fairfax Ave	Los Angeles	CA	90036	**800-321-4726**	323-938-2420

119 CAMPERS, TRAVEL TRAILERS, MOTOR HOMES

				Toll-Free	Phone
A & N Trailer Parts 6028 S 118th E Ave	Tulsa	OK	74146	**800-272-1898**	918-461-8404
Coach House Inc 3480 Technology Dr	Nokomis	FL	34275	**800-235-0984**	941-485-0984
Cruise America 11 W Hampton Ave	Mesa	AZ	85210	**800-671-8042**	480-464-7300
Custom Fiberglass Mfg Corp *Snugtop* 1711 Harbor Ave PO Box 121	Long Beach	CA	90813	**800-768-4867**	562-432-5454
Davidson-Kennedy Co 800 Industrial Park Dr	Marietta	GA	30062	**800-733-3434**	770-427-9467
Dutchmen Mfg Inc 2164 Caragana Ct PO Box 2164	Goshen	IN	46527	**866-425-4369**	574-537-0600
Exiss Aluminum Trailers Inc 900 East Trailer Blvd	El Reno	OK	73036	**877-553-9477**	
Foretravel Motorcoach Inc 1221 NW Stallings Dr	Nacogdoches	TX	75964	**800-955-6226**	936-564-8367
Four Wheel Campers 1460 Churchill Downs Ave	Woodland	CA	95776	**800-242-1442**	530-666-1442
Gulf Stream Coach Inc 503 S Oakland Ave PO Box 1005	Nappanee	IN	46550	**800-289-8787**	574-773-7761
Jayco Inc 903 S Main St *Cust Svc	Middlebury	IN	46540	**800-283-8267***	574-825-5861
Keystone RV Co 2642 Hackberry Dr PO Box 2000	Goshen	IN	46527	**866-425-4369**	574-535-2100
Monaco Coach Corp 1031 US 224 E	Decatur	IN	46733	**877-466-6226**	
New Horizons RV Corp 2401 Lacy Dr	Junction City	KS	66441	**800-235-3140**	785-238-7575
Newell Coach Corp 3900 N Main St	Miami	OK	74354	**888-363-9355**	918-542-3344
Newmar Corp 355 Delaware St	Nappanee	IN	46550	**800-731-8300**	574-773-7791
Nu-Wa Industries Inc 3701 Johnson Rd	Chanute	KS	66720	**800-835-0676**	620-431-2088
Pace-Edwards 2400 Commercial Rd	Centralia	WA	98531	**800-338-3697**	360-736-9991
Palomino RV 1200 New Jersey Ave	Washington	MI	20590	**888-327-4236**	269-432-3271
Renegade/Kibbi LLC 52216 State Rd 15	Bristol	IN	46507	**888-522-1126**	574-848-1126
Rexhall Industries Inc 46147 Seventh St W *OTC: REXLQ*	Lancaster	CA	93534	**800-765-7500**	661-726-0565
Skyline Corp 2520 By-Pass Rd *NYSE: SKY*	Elkhart	IN	46514	**800-348-7469**	574-294-6521
Winnebago Industries Inc 605 W Crystal Lk Rd PO Box 152 *NYSE: WGO*	Forest City	IA	50436	**800-643-4892**	641-585-3535

120 CAMPGROUND OPERATORS

				Toll-Free	Phone
Carson Valley Inn Inc 1627 US Hwy 395 N	Minden	NV	89423	**866-284-7766**	775-782-9711
F Visions Services 500 Greenwich St Fl 3	New York	NY	10013	**888-245-8333**	212-625-1616
Glen Eden Corp 25999 Glen Eden Rd	Corona	CA	92883	**800-843-6833**	951-277-4650
Holiday Trails Resorts (Western) Inc 53730 Bridal Falls Rd	Rosedale	BC	V0X1X1	**800-663-2265**	604-794-7876
Kampgrounds of America Inc (KOA) PO Box 30558	Billings	MT	59114	**888-562-0000**	
Leisure Systems Inc 502 TechneCenter Dr Ste D	Milford	OH	45150	**866-928-9644**	513-831-2100
Swan Lake Resort & Campground 17463 County Hwy 29	Fergus Falls	MN	56537	**800-697-4626**	218-736-4626
Western Horizon Resorts (WHR) 103 W Tomichi Ave Ste 201A	Gunnison	CO	81230	**800-378-3709**	970-641-5387

121 CANDLES

SEE ALSO Gift Shops

				Toll-Free	Phone
Dadant & Sons Inc 51 S Second St	Hamilton	IL	62341	**888-922-1293**	217-847-3324

Classified Section

Company	Address	City	State	Zip	Toll-Free	Phone
General Wax & Candle Co	6863 Beck Ave PO Box 9398	North Hollywood	CA	91605	**800-929-7867**	818-765-5800
Knorr Beeswax Products Inc	14906 Via De La Valle	Del Mar	CA	92014	**800-807-2337**	760-431-2007
Original Cake Candle Co, The	102 Sundale Rd	Norwich	OH	43767	**888-444-2253**	740-872-3248
Root Candles Co	623 W Liberty St	Medina	OH	44256	**800-289-7668**	330-725-6677
Swans Candles	16524 Tilley Rd S	Tenino	WA	98589	**888-848-7926**	

122 CANDY STORES

Company	Address	City	State	Zip	Toll-Free	Phone
Candy Bouquet International Inc	510 Mclean St	Little Rock	AR	72202	**877-226-3901**	501-375-9990
Gardners Candies Inc	2600 Adams Ave PO Box E	Tyrone	PA	16686	**800-242-2639**	814-684-3925
Gertrude Hawk Chocolates Inc	9 Keystone Pk	Dunmore	PA	18512	**866-932-4295**	800-822-2032
Kilwins Quality Confections Inc (KQC)	1050 Bay View Rd	Petoskey	MI	49770	**888-454-5946**	
Lammes Candies Since 1885 Inc	PO Box 1885	Austin	TX	78767	**800-252-1885**	512-310-2223
Provide Commerce Inc	4840 Eastgate Mall *Cust Svc	San Diego	CA	92121	**800-776-3569***	858-729-2800
Rocky Mountain Chocolate Factory Inc (RMCF)	265 Turner Dr *NASDAQ: RMCF* ■ *Cust Svc	Durango	CO	81303	**888-525-2462***	970-259-0554
See's Candies Inc	210 El Camino Real *Cust Svc	South San Francisco	CA	94080	**800-877-7337***	650-761-2490

123 CANS - METAL

SEE ALSO Containers - Metal (Barrels, Drums, Kegs)

Company	Address	City	State	Zip	Toll-Free	Phone
BWAY Corp	8607 Roberts Dr Ste 250	Atlanta	GA	30350	**800-527-2267**	770-645-4800
Crown Holdings Inc	1 Crown Way *NYSE: CCK*	Philadelphia	PA	19154	**800-523-3644**	215-698-5100
JL Clark Mfg Co	923 23rd Ave	Rockford	IL	61104	**877-482-5275**	815-962-8861
JL Clark Mfg Co Lancaster Div	303 N Plum St	Lancaster	PA	17602	**877-482-5275**	717-392-4125
KOR Water Inc	95 Enterprise Ste 310	Aliso Viejo	CA	92656	**877-708-7567**	714-708-7567
Protectoseal Co	225 W Foster Ave	Bensenville	IL	60106	**800-323-2268**	630-595-0800
Ring Container Technology	1 Industrial Park Rd	Oakland	TN	38060	**800-280-6333**	

124 CANS, TUBES, DRUMS - PAPER (FIBER)

Company	Address	City	State	Zip	Toll-Free	Phone
Acme Spirally Wound Paper Products Inc	4810 W 139th St PO Box 35320	Cleveland	OH	44135	**800-274-2797**	216-267-2950
Callenor Company Inc	N 60 W 15725 Kohler Ln	Menomonee Falls	WI	53051	**800-813-7429**	262-252-3343
Caraustar Industries Inc	5000 Austell-Powder Springs Rd Ste 300	Austell	GA	30106	**800-858-1438**	770-948-3100
Custom Paper Tubes Inc	15900 Industrial Pkwy	Cleveland	OH	44135	**800-343-8823**	216-362-2964
Greif Inc	425 Winter Rd *NYSE: GEF*	Delaware	OH	43015	**877-781-9797**	740-549-6000
Industrial Paper Tube Inc	1335 E Bay Ave	Bronx	NY	10474	**800-345-0960**	
LCH Paper Tube & Core Co	11930 Larc Industrial Blvd	Burnsville	MN	55337	**800-472-3477**	952-358-3587
Master Package Corp	200 Madson St	Owen	WI	54460	**800-396-8425**	715-229-2156
OX Paper Tube & Core Inc	331 Maple Ave	Hanover	PA	17331	**800-414-2476**	
Pacific Paper Tube Inc	1025 98th Ave	Oakland	CA	94603	**888-377-8823**	510-562-8823
Self-Seal Container Corp	401 E Fourth St	Bridgeport	PA	19405	**800-334-1428**	610-275-2300
Yazoo Mills Inc	PO Box 369 *Cust Svc	New Oxford	PA	17350	**800-242-5216***	717-624-8993

125 CAR RENTAL AGENCIES

SEE ALSO Truck Rental & Leasing ; Fleet Leasing & Management

Company	Address	City	State	Zip	Toll-Free	Phone
A Betterway Rent-a-car Inc	1110 Northchase Pkwy SE	Marietta	GA	30067	**800-527-0700**	770-240-3305
ACE Rent A Car	4529 W 96th St	Indianapolis	IN	46268	**888-261-7368**	317-248-5686
Advantage Rent-A-Car	1288 Old Bayshore Hwy *Cust Svc	Burlingame	CA	94010	**800-777-5500***	
Affiliated Car Rental	105 Hwy 36	Eatontown	NJ	07724	**800-367-5159**	
Affordable Car Rental LC	105 Hwy 36	Eatontown	NJ	07724	**800-367-5159**	732-380-0888
Auto Europe	39 Commercial St	Portland	ME	04101	**800-223-5555**	207-842-2000
Avis Rent A Car System Inc	6 Sylvan Way	Parsippany	NJ	07054	**800-331-1212**	973-496-3500
Budget Rent A Car System Inc	6 Sylvan Way	Parsippany	NJ	07054	**800-527-0700**	800-283-4382
Dewey Ford Inc	3055 SE Delaware Ave	Ankeny	IA	50021	**877-704-6793**	
Discount Car & Truck Rentals Ltd	720 Arrow Rd	North York	ON	M9M2M1	**866-742-5968**	
Dollar Rent A Car Inc	5330 E 31st St	Tulsa	OK	74135	**800-800-4000**	918-669-3000
Dollar Thrifty Automotive Group Inc	5330 E 31st St PO Box 35985	Tulsa	OK	74135	**800-334-1705**	918-660-7700
Enterprise Rent-A-Car	600 Corporate Pk Dr	Saint Louis	MO	63105	**844-377-0171**	314-512-5000
Europe by Car	40 Exchange Pl Ste 1720	New York	NY	10005	**800-223-1516**	212-581-3040
Foss National Leasing	7200 Yonge St	Thornhill	ON	L4J1V8	**800-461-3677**	905-886-4244
Hale Trailer Brake & Wheel Inc	Rt 73 & Cooper Rd	Voorhees	NJ	08043	**800-232-6535**	856-768-1330
Hertz Global Holdings Inc	225 Brae Blvd *NYSE: HTZ*	Park Ridge	NJ	07656	**800-654-3131**	201-307-2000
Kemwel Inc	39 Commercial St	Portland	ME	04112	**800-678-0678**	207-842-2285
Omaha Truck Center Inc	10710 I St PO Box 27379	Omaha	NE	68127	**800-866-2204**	402-592-2440
P V Rentals Ltd	5810 S Rice Ave	Houston	TX	77081	**800-275-7878**	713-667-0665
Steve Foley Cadillac	100 Skokie Blvd	Northbrook	IL	60062	**888-670-1429**	
Thrifty Car Rental	5330 E 31st St	Tulsa	OK	74135	**888-400-8877**	918-660-7700
U-Save Auto Rental of America Inc	1052 Highland Colony Pkwy Ste 204 *General	Ridgeland	MS	39157	**800-438-2300***	601-713-4333

126 CARBON & GRAPHITE PRODUCTS

Company	Address	City	State	Zip	Toll-Free	Phone
Advance Carbon Products Inc	2036 National Ave	Hayward	CA	94545	**800-283-1249**	510-293-5930
Helwig Carbon Products Inc	8900 W Tower Ave	Milwaukee	WI	53224	**800-365-3113**	414-354-2411
Mersen USA BN Corp	400 Myrtle Ave *General	Boonton	NJ	07005	**800-526-0877***	
National Electrical Carbon	251 Forrester Dr	Greenville	SC	29607	**800-471-7842**	864-284-9728
Saturn Industries Inc	157 Union Tpke	Hudson	NY	12534	**800-775-1651**	518-828-9956
SGL Carbon LLC	307 Jamestown Rd	Morganton	NC	28655	**800-828-6601**	828-437-3221
Superior Graphite	10 S Riverside Plaza Ste 1470 *Cust Svc	Chicago	IL	60606	**800-325-0337***	312-559-2999

127 CARBURETORS, PISTONS, PISTON RINGS, VALVES

SEE ALSO Aircraft Engines & Engine Parts ; Automotive Parts & Supplies - Mfr

Company	Address	City	State	Zip	Toll-Free	Phone
Compressor Products International	4410 Greenbriar Dr	Stafford	TX	77477	**800-675-6646**	281-207-4600
Grover Corp	2759 S 28th St	Milwaukee	WI	53234	**800-776-3602**	414-384-9472
Hastings Manufacturing Co	325 N Hanover St	Hastings	MI	49058	**800-776-1088**	269-945-2491
Holley Performance Products Inc	1801 Russellville Rd *Sales	Bowling Green	KY	42101	**800-638-0032***	270-782-2900
MAHLE Industries Inc	2020 Sanford St	Muskegon	MI	49444	**888-255-1942**	231-722-1300
Martin Wells Industries	5886 Compton Ave	Los Angeles	CA	90001	**800-421-6000**	323-581-6266
Safety Seal Piston Ring Co	4000 Airport Rd *Sales	Marshall	TX	75672	**800-962-3631***	903-938-9241
Total Seal Inc	22642 N 15th Ave	Phoenix	AZ	85027	**800-874-2753**	623-587-7400
United Engine & Machine Company Inc	1040 Corbett St	Carson City	NV	89706	**800-648-7970**	775-882-7790
Wiseco Piston Inc	7201 Industrial Pk Blvd	Mentor	OH	44060	**800-321-1364**	440-951-6600

128 CARD SHOPS

SEE ALSO Gift Shops

Company	Address	City	State	Zip	Toll-Free	Phone
Ad-venture Promotions LLC	2625 Regency Rd	Lexington	KY	40503	**800-218-5488**	859-263-4299
Design It Yourself Gift Baskets LLC	7999 Hansen Rd Ste 204	Houston	TX	77061	**800-589-7553**	713-944-3440
Future of Flight Foundation	8415 Paine Field Blvd	Mukilteo	WA	98275	**888-467-4777**	425-438-8100
Get Noticed Promotions Inc	152 Sonwil Dr	Buffalo	NY	14225	**877-296-7179**	716-688-8152
Hallmark Cards Inc	2501 McGee St	Kansas City	MO	64108	**800-425-5627**	816-274-5111
Papyrus Franchise Corp	500 Chadbourne Rd	Fairfield	CA	94533	**800-789-1649**	
Recycled Paper Greetings Inc	111 N Canal St Ste 700	Chicago	IL	60606	**800-777-3331**	

129 CARDS - GREETING - MFR

Company	City	State	Zip	Toll-Free	Phone
Amber Lotus Publishing PO Box 11329	Portland	OR	97211	**800-326-2375**	503-284-6400
American Greetings Corp 1 American Rd *NYSE: AM* ■ *Sales	Cleveland	OH	44144	**800-777-4891***	216-252-7300
AtticSalt Greetings Inc PO Box 5773	Topeka	KS	66605	**888-345-6005**	
Avanti Press Inc 155 W Congress St Ste 200	Detroit	MI	48226	**800-228-2684**	313-961-0022
Bayview Press 30 Knox St PO Box 153	Thomaston	ME	04861	**800-903-2346**	207-354-9919
Birchcraft Studios Inc 10 Railroad St	Abington	MA	02351	**800-333-0405**	781-878-5152
Blue Mountain Arts Inc PO Box 4549 *Sales	Boulder	CO	80306	**800-545-8573***	303-449-0536
Bonair Daydreams PO Box 1522	Wrightsville Beach	NC	28480	**888-226-6247**	910-617-3887
Carole Joy Creations Inc 1087 Federal Rd Unit 8 *Sales	Brookfield	CT	06804	**800-223-6945***	203-740-4490
Colors By Design 7723 Densmore Ave	Van Nuys	CA	91406	**800-832-8436**	
DaySpring Cards Inc 21154 Hwy 16 E	Siloam Springs	AR	72761	**800-944-8000**	479-524-9301
Design Design Inc 19 La Grave SE	Grand Rapids	MI	49503	**800-334-3348**	616-774-2448
Eclectik 1332 W Lake St	Chicago	IL	60607	**866-308-1231**	312-676-2442
Fantus Paper Products P.S. Greetings Inc 5730 N Tripp Ave *Sales	Chicago	IL	60646	**800-621-8823***	773-267-6069
Freedom Greeting Card Company Inc 774 American Dr *Sales	Bensalem	PA	19020	**800-359-3301***	215-604-0300
Galison Publishing LLC 28 W 44th St Ste 1411	New York	NY	10036	**800-670-7441**	212-354-8840
Gallant Greetings Corp 4300 United Pkwy	Schiller Park	IL	60176	**800-621-4279**	847-671-6500
Gina B Designs Inc 12700 Industrial Pk Blvd Ste 40	Plymouth	MN	55441	**800-228-4856**	763-559-7595
Graphique De France 9 State St *Sales	Woburn	MA	01801	**800-444-1464***	781-935-3405
Great Arrow Graphics 2495 Main St Ste 457	Buffalo	NY	14214	**800-835-0490**	716-836-0408
Hallmark Cards Inc 2501 McGee St	Kansas City	MO	64108	**800-425-5627**	816-274-5111
Hallmark International PO Box 419034	Kansas City	MO	64141	**800-425-5627**	816-274-5111
Laughing Elephant 3645 Interlake Ave N	Seattle	WA	98103	**800-354-0400**	
Laurel Ink 911 N 145th St *Cust Svc	Seattle	WA	98133	**800-850-0081***	
Marian Heath Greeting Cards Inc 9 Kendrick Rd *Sales	Wareham	MA	02571	**800-688-9998***	508-291-0766
Meri Meri 63 Leonard St	Belmont	MA	02478	**800-638-2881**	617-484-5571
Museum Facsimiles 117 Fourth St	Pittsfield	MA	01201	**877-499-0020**	413-499-0020
NobleWorks Inc 500 Paterson Plank Rd	Union City	NJ	07087	**800-346-6253**	201-420-0095
Northern Exposure Greeting Cards 2301 Circadian Way Ste 300	Santa Rosa	CA	95407	**800-237-3524**	707-546-2153
Nouvelles Images Inc 68 Morgan Ave	Danbury	CT	06810	**800-345-1383**	203-730-1004
Paperdoll Co 4944 Encino Ave	Encino	CA	91316	**866-223-1145**	818-906-8411
Peaceable Kingdom Press 950 Gilman St Ste 200	Berkeley	CA	94710	**877-444-5195**	
Penny Laine Papers 2211 Century Ctr Blvd Ste 110	Irving	TX	75062	**800-456-6484**	972-812-3000
Persimmon Press PO Box 297	Belmont	CA	94002	**800-910-5080**	650-802-8325
Posty Cards 1600 Olive St	Kansas City	MO	64127	**800-821-7968**	816-231-2323
Recycled Paper Greetings Inc 111 N Canal St Ste 700	Chicago	IL	60606	**800-777-3331**	
Schurman Fine Papers 500 Chadbourne Rd *Sales	Fairfield	CA	94533	**800-789-1649***	
StellArt 2012 Waltzer Rd	Santa Rosa	CA	95403	**866-621-1987**	707-569-1378
Sunshine Business Class 150 Kingswood Dr	Mankato	MN	56001	**800-873-7681**	
Up With Paper 6049 Hi-Tek Ct	Mason	OH	45040	**800-852-7677**	513-759-7473
Victorian Trading Co 15600 W 99th St *Cust Svc	Lenexa	KS	66219	**800-700-2035***	913-438-3995
Willow Creek Press Inc 9931 Hwy 70 W PO Box 147 *Cust Svc	Minocqua	WI	54548	**800-850-9453***	715-358-7010

130 CARPETS & RUGS

SEE ALSO Tile - Ceramic (Wall & Floor) ; Flooring - Resilient
The companies listed here include carpet finishers and makers of mats and padding.

Company	City	State	Zip	Toll-Free	Phone
Architectural Floor Systems Inc 595 Supreme Dr	Bensenville	IL	60106	**877-437-3567**	
Artisans Inc W4146 Second St PO Box 278	Glen Flora	WI	54526	**800-311-8756**	715-322-5285
Atlas Carpet Mills Inc 2200 Saybrook Ave	Los Angeles	CA	90040	**800-272-8527**	323-724-9000
Barrett Carpet Mills Inc 2216 Abutment Rd	Dalton	GA	30721	**800-241-4064**	
Beaulieu of America Inc 1502 Coronet Dr PO Box 1248	Dalton	GA	30722	**800-227-7211**	
Bentley Prince Street 14641 E Don Julian Rd	City of Industry	CA	91746	**800-423-4709**	
Bloomsburg Carpet Industries Inc 4999 Columbia Blvd	Bloomsburg	PA	17815	**800-233-8773**	570-784-9188
Camelot Carpet Mills Inc 17111 Red Hill Ave	Irvine	CA	92614	**800-854-8331**	949-474-4000
Capel Inc 831 N Main St	Troy	NC	27371	**800-334-3711**	800-382-6574
Dixie Group Inc 104 Nowlin Ln Ste 101 *NASDAQ: DXYN*	Chattanooga	TN	37421	**800-289-4811**	423-510-7000
Dorsett Industries Inc 1304 May St PO Box 805	Dalton	GA	30721	**800-241-4035**	706-278-1961
Durkan Patterned Carpet Inc 405 Virgil Dr	Dalton	GA	30721	**800-981-2009**	
Flex Foam 617 N 21st Ave	Phoenix	AZ	85009	**800-266-3626**	602-252-5819
Garland Sales Inc PO Box 1870	Dalton	GA	30720	**800-524-0361**	706-278-7880
Home Dynamix LLC 1 Carol Pl	Moonachie	NJ	07074	**800-726-9290**	201-807-0111
Indian Summer Carpet Mills Inc 601 Callahan Rd PO Box 3577	Dalton	GA	30719	**800-824-4010**	706-277-6277
J & J Industries Inc 818 J & J Dr PO Box 1287	Dalton	GA	30721	**800-241-4586**	706-529-2100
Jaipur Rugs Inc 2775 Pacific Dr	Norcross	GA	30071	**888-676-7330**	404-351-2360
Johnson Wholesale Floors Inc 1874 Defoor Ave NW	Atlanta	GA	30318	**800-345-9318**	404-352-2700
Johnsonite Inc 16910 Munn Rd	Chagrin Falls	OH	44023	**800-899-8916**	440-543-8916
Lexmark Carpet Mills Inc 285 Kraft Dr	Dalton	GA	30721	**800-871-3211**	
Maples Industries Inc 2210 Moody Ridge Rd *Hum Res	Scottsboro	AL	35768	**800-537-5447***	256-259-1327
Masland Carpets Inc 716 Bill Myles Dr	Saraland	AL	36571	**800-633-0468**	
Milliken & Co KEX Div PO Box 1926 MS 801	Spartanburg	SC	29304	**800-241-4826**	706-880-5511
Mohawk Industries Inc 160 S Industrial Blvd *NYSE: MHK*	Calhoun	GA	30703	**800-241-4494**	706-629-7721
Mohawk Industries Inc Karastan Div 508 E Morris St	Dalton	GA	30721	**800-234-1120**	
Mohawk Industries Inc Lees Carpets Div 160 S Industrial Blvd	Calhoun	GA	30701	**800-241-4494**	706-629-7721
Netchannel Inc 8310 Rio Grande Blvd NW	Albuquerque	NM	87114	**888-843-8282**	505-843-8282
Packerland Rent-a-mat Inc 12580 W Rohr Ave	Butler	WI	53007	**800-472-9339**	262-781-5321
Quality Mat Co 6550 Tram Rd	Beaumont	TX	77713	**800-227-8159**	409-722-4594
Royalty Carpet Mills Inc 17111 Red Hill Ave	Irvine	CA	92614	**800-854-8331**	949-474-4000
S & S Mills Inc 414 C N Pk Dr	Dalton	GA	30720	**800-241-4013**	706-277-3677
Scottdel Inc 400 Church St	Swanton	OH	43558	**800-446-2341**	419-825-2341
Shaw Industries Inc 616 E Walnut Ave	Dalton	GA	30722	**800-441-7429**	
Tandus Centiva 311 Smith Industrial Blvd PO Box 1447	Dalton	GA	30722	**800-248-2878**	706-259-9711
Tri State Wholesale Flooring Inc 3900 W 34th St N	Sioux Falls	SD	57107	**800-353-3080**	605-336-3080
Unique Carpets Ltd 7360 Jurupa Ave	Riverside	CA	92504	**800-547-8266**	951-352-8125

131 CASINO COMPANIES

SEE ALSO Games & Gaming

Company	City	State	Zip	Toll-Free	Phone
Ameristar Casinos Inc 3773 Howard Hughes Pkwy Ste 490-S *NASDAQ: ASCA*	Las Vegas	NV	89169	**888-708-5699**	702-567-7000
Boomtown Inc 2100 Garson Rd	Verdi	NV	89439	**800-648-3790**	775-345-6000
Boyd Gaming Corp 3883 Howard Hughes Pkwy 9th Fl *NYSE: BYD*	Las Vegas	NV	89169	**800-522-4700**	702-792-7200
Century Casinos Inc 2860 S Cir Dr Ste 350 *NASDAQ: CNTY*	Colorado Springs	CO	80906	**888-966-2257**	719-527-8300
Colony Palms Hotel 572 N Indian Canyon Dr	Palm Springs	CA	92262	**800-557-2187**	760-969-1800
Fond du Lac Band of Lake Superior Chippewa 1720 Big Lake Rd	Cloquet	MN	55720	**888-888-6007**	218-879-4593
Four Winds Casino Resort 11111 Wilson Rd	New Buffalo	MI	49117	**866-494-6371**	
Mille Lacs Band of Ojibwe 43408 Oodena Dr	Onamia	MN	56359	**800-709-6445**	320-532-4181
Palace Casino 158 Howard Ave	Biloxi	MS	39530	**800-725-2239**	228-432-8888
Pinnacle Entertainment Inc 3980 Howard Hughes Pkwy *NYSE: PNK*	Las Vegas	NV	89169	**877-764-8750**	702-541-7777
Proximity Hotel 704 Green Vly Rd	Greensboro	NC	27408	**800-379-8200**	336-379-8200
Red Lake Gaming Enterprises Inc PO Box 543	Red Lake	MN	56671	**888-679-2501**	218-679-2111
Shoalwater Bay Casino 4112 State Hwy 105	Tokeland	WA	98590	**866-992-3675**	360-267-2048
Silver Reef Casino 4876 Haxton Way	Ferndale	WA	98248	**866-383-0777**	360-383-0777
Station Casinos Inc 1505 S Pavilion Ctr Dr *Resv	Las Vegas	NV	89135	**800-634-3101***	702-495-3000

132 CASINOS

SEE ALSO Games & Gaming
Listings for casinos are alphabetized by states.

Name / Address	City	State	ZIP	Toll-Free	Phone
Birmingham Race Course 1000 John Rogers Dr	Birmingham	AL	35210	**800-998-8238**	205-838-7500
Deerfoot Inn & Casino 1000 11500 35th St SE	Calgary	AB	T2Z3W4	**877-236-5225**	403-236-7529
Apache Greyhound Park 3801 E Washington	Phoenix	AZ	85034	**800-772-0852**	480-982-2371
Casino Arizona at Salt River 524 N 92nd St *General	Scottsdale	AZ	85256	**866-877-9897***	480-850-7777
Fort McDowell Casino 10424 N Ft McDowell Rd	Fort Mcdowell	AZ	85264	**800-843-3678**	
River Rock Casino Resort 8811 River Rd	Richmond	BC	V6X3P8	**866-748-3718**	604-247-8900
Agua Caliente Casino Resort Spa 32-250 Bob Hope Dr	Rancho Mirage	CA	92270	**888-999-1995**	760-321-2000
Augustine Casino 84-001 Ave 54	Coachella	CA	92236	**888-752-9294**	760-391-9500
Barona Resort & Casino 1932 Wildcat Canyon Rd	Lakeside	CA	92040	**888-722-7662**	619-443-2300
Eagle Mountain Casino 681 S Tule Resv Rd	Porterville	CA	93257	**800-903-3353**	559-788-6220
Fantasy Springs Resort Casino 84-245 Indio Springs Pkwy *Cust Svc	Indio	CA	92203	**800-827-2946***	760-342-5000
Golden West Casino 1001 S Union Ave	Bakersfield	CA	93307	**800-267-3983**	661-324-6936
Pala Casino Resort & Spa 35008 Pala-Temecula Rd	Pala	CA	92059	**877-946-7252**	760-510-5100
Pechanga Resort & Casino 45000 Pechanga Pkwy	Temecula	CA	92592	**877-711-2946**	951-693-1819
San Manuel Indian Bingo & Casino 777 San Manuel Blvd	Highland	CA	92346	**800-359-2464**	
Spa Resort Casino 401 E Amado Rd	Palm Springs	CA	92262	**888-999-1995**	
Sycuan Casino & Resort 5469 Casino Way *General	El Cajon	CA	92019	**800-279-2826***	619-445-6002
Table Mountain Casino 8184 Table Mountain Rd	Friant	CA	93626	**800-541-3637**	559-822-7777
Thunder Valley Casino 1200 Athens Ave	Lincoln	CA	95648	**877-468-8777**	916-408-7777
Viejas Casino 5000 Willows Rd	Alpine	CA	91901	**800-847-6537**	619-445-5400
Bronco Billy's Casino 233 E Bennett Ave PO Box 590	Cripple Creek	CO	80813	**877-989-2142**	719-689-2142
Dostal Alley Casino 1 Dostal Alley	Central City	CO	80427	**888-949-2757**	303-582-1610
Double Eagle Hotel & Casino 442 E Bennett Ave	Cripple Creek	CO	80813	**800-711-7234**	719-689-5000
Midnight Rose Hotel & Casino 256 E Bennett Ave	Cripple Creek	CO	80813	**800-635-5825**	719-689-2446
Reserve Casino Hotel 321 Gregory St	Central City	CO	80427	**800-924-6646**	303-582-0800
Sky Ute Casino 14324 US Hwy 172 N	Ignacio	CO	81137	**888-842-4180**	970-563-7777
Ute Mountain Casino 3 Weeminuche Dr	Towaoc	CO	81334	**800-258-8007**	970-565-8800
Mohegan Sun Resort & Casino 1 Mohegan Sun Blvd	Uncasville	CT	06382	**888-226-7711**	860-862-8150
Winners Sports Haven 600 Long Wharf Dr	New Haven	CT	06511	**800-468-2260**	
Seminole Casino Hollywood 4150 N State Rd 7	Hollywood	FL	33021	**866-222-7466**	954-961-3220
Seminole Casino Immokalee 506 S First St	Immokalee	FL	34142	**800-218-0007**	
Seminole Hard Rock Hotel & Casino Tampa (SHRH & C) 5223 N Orient Rd *General	Tampa	FL	33610	**866-388-4263***	813-627-7625
Argosy's Alton Belle Casino 1 Piasa St	Alton	IL	62002	**800-711-4263**	
Casino Queen 200 S Front St	East Saint Louis	IL	62201	**800-777-0777**	618-874-5000
Harrah's Joliet 151 N Joliet St	Joliet	IL	60432	**800-522-4700**	815-740-7800
Hollywood Casino Joliet 777 Hollywood Blvd	Joliet	IL	60436	**800-426-2537**	
Belterra Casino Resort 777 Belterra Dr	Florence	IN	47020	**888-235-8377**	812-427-7777
Blue Chip Casino Inc 777 Blue Chip Dr	Michigan City	IN	46360	**888-879-7711**	219-879-7711
Casino Aztar 421 NW Riverside Dr	Evansville	IN	47708	**800-342-5386**	812-433-4000
Horseshoe Casino 777 Casino Ctr Dr	Hammond	IN	46320	**800-522-4700**	219-473-7000
Majestic Star Casino & Hotel 1 Buffington Harbor Dr	Gary	IN	46406	**800-522-4700**	219-977-7777
Rising Star Casino Resort 777 Rising Star Dr	Rising Sun	IN	47040	**800-472-6311**	812-438-1234
Ameristar Casino Hotel Council Bluffs 2200 River Rd	Council Bluffs	IA	51501	**866-667-3386**	712-328-8888
Harrah's Council Bluffs 1 Harrahs Blvd	Council Bluffs	IA	51501	**800-342-7724**	712-329-6000
Meskwaki Bingo Hotel Casino 1504 305th St	Tama	IA	52339	**800-728-4263**	
Prairie Meadows Racetrack & Casino 1 Prairie Meadows Dr PO Box 1000	Altoona	IA	50009	**800-325-9015**	515-967-1000
Rhythm City Casino 7077 Elmore Ave	Davenport	IA	52807	**844-852-4386**	563-328-8000
Prairie Band Casino & Resort 12305 150th Rd	Mayetta	KS	66509	**888-727-4946**	785-966-7777
Belle of Baton Rouge Casino 103 France St	Baton Rouge	LA	70802	**800-676-4847**	
Coushatta Casino Resort 777 Coushatta Dr PO Box 1510	Kinder	LA	70648	**800-584-7263**	
DiamondJacks Casino Resort 711 Diamond Jacks Blvd	Bossier City	LA	71111	**866-552-9629**	318-678-7777
Eldorado Resort Casino Shreveport 451 Clyde Fant Pkwy	Shreveport	LA	71101	**877-602-0711**	318-220-0711
Harrah's New Orleans 8 Canal St	New Orleans	LA	70130	**800-427-7247**	504-533-6000
Hollywood Casino Baton Rouge 1717 River Rd N	Baton Rouge	LA	70802	**800-447-6843**	225-709-7777
Isle of Capri Casino Hotel Lake Charles 100 W Lake Ave	Westlake	LA	70669	**800-843-4753**	
Paragon Casino Resort 711 Paragon Pl	Marksville	LA	71351	**800-946-1946**	
Sam's Town Hotel & Casino Shreveport 315 Clyde Fant Pkwy	Shreveport	LA	71101	**877-770-7867**	
Treasure Chest Casino 5050 Williams Blvd	Kenner	LA	70065	**800-298-0711**	504-443-8000
Pimlico Race Course 5201 Park Heights Ave	Baltimore	MD	21215	**800-638-1859**	410-542-9400
Suffolk Downs 111 Waldemar Ave	East Boston	MA	02128	**800-225-3460**	617-567-3900
MGM Grand Detroit 1777 Third St	Detroit	MI	48226	**877-888-2121**	313-465-1400
MotorCity Casino Hotel 2901 Grand River Ave	Detroit	MI	48201	**866-752-9622**	313-237-7711
Soaring Eagle Casino & Resort 6800 E Soaring Eagle Blvd	Mount Pleasant	MI	48858	**888-732-4537**	
Black Bear Casino Resort 1785 Hwy 210 PO Box 777	Carlton	MN	55718	**888-771-0777**	218-878-2327
Grand Casino Hinckley 777 Lady Luck Dr	Hinckley	MN	55037	**800-472-6321**	
Grand Casino Mille Lacs 777 Grand Ave PO Box 343	Onamia	MN	56359	**800-626-5825**	
Jackpot Junction Casino Hotel 39375 County Hwy 24 PO Box 420	Morton	MN	56270	**800-946-2274**	507-697-8000
Mystic Lake Casino Hotel 2400 Mystic Lk Blvd	Prior Lake	MN	55372	**800-262-7799**	952-445-9000
Bally's Casino Tunica 1450 Bally's Blvd	Robinsonville	MS	38664	**866-422-5597**	
Boomtown Casino Biloxi 676 Bayview Ave	Biloxi	MS	39530	**800-627-0777**	228-435-7000
Fitzgeralds Casino & Hotel Tunica 711 Lucky Ln	Robinsonville	MS	38664	**888-766-5825**	662-363-5825
Gold Strike Casino Resort 1010 Casino Ctr Dr *Resv	Tunica Resorts	MS	38664	**888-245-7829***	662-357-1111
Golden Nugget Hotels & Casinos 151 Beach Blvd	Biloxi	MS	39530	**800-777-7568**	228-435-5400
Hard Rock Hotel & Casino Biloxi 777 Beach Blvd	Biloxi	MS	39530	**877-877-6256**	228-374-7625
Harrah's Tunica 1021 Casino Ctr Dr	Robinsonville	MS	38664	**800-946-4946**	800-303-7463
Hollywood Casino Bay Saint Louis 711 Hollywood Blvd	Bay Saint Louis	MS	39520	**866-758-2591**	
IP Casino Resort & Spa 850 Bayview Ave *Resv	Biloxi	MS	39530	**888-946-2847***	228-436-3000
Island View Casino Resort 3300 W Beach Blvd PO Box 1600 *General	Gulfport	MS	39502	**888-777-9696***	228-314-2100
Isle of Capri Casino 1800 E Front St	Kansas City	MO	64120	**800-843-4753**	816-855-7777
Aquarius Casino Resort 1900 S Casino Dr	Laughlin	NV	89029	**888-662-5825**	702-298-5111
Arizona Charlie's Boulder Casino & Hotel 4575 Boulder Hwy	Las Vegas	NV	89121	**888-236-9066**	702-951-5800
Arizona Charlie's Decatur Casino & Hotel 740 S Decatur Blvd	Las Vegas	NV	89107	**888-236-8645**	702-258-5200
Atlantis Casino Resort 3800 S Virginia St	Reno	NV	89502	**800-723-6500**	775-825-4700
Bally's Las Vegas 3645 Las Vegas Blvd S *Resv	Las Vegas	NV	89109	**800-522-4700***	702-967-4111
Binion's Gambling Hall & Hotel 128 E Fremont St	Las Vegas	NV	89101	**800-937-6537**	702-382-1600
Boomtown Casino & Hotel Reno 2100 Garson Rd *Resv	Verdi	NV	89439	**800-648-3790***	775-345-6000
Boulder Station Hotel & Casino 4111 Boulder Hwy	Las Vegas	NV	89121	**800-683-7777**	702-432-7777
Buffalo Bill's Resort & Casino 31900 Las Vegas Blvd S	Primm	NV	89019	**888-774-6668**	702-386-7867
California Hotel & Casino 12 E Ogden Ave	Las Vegas	NV	89101	**800-634-6505**	702-385-1222
Carson City Nugget 507 N Carson St	Carson City	NV	89701	**800-426-5239**	775-882-1626
Casino Royale Hotel 3411 Las Vegas Blvd S	Las Vegas	NV	89109	**800-854-7666**	702-737-3500
Circus Circus Hotel & Casino Reno 500 N Sierra St	Reno	NV	89503	**800-648-5010**	775-329-0711
Circus Circus Hotel Casino & Theme Park Las Vegas 2880 Las Vegas Blvd S *Resv	Las Vegas	NV	89109	**800-634-3450***	702-734-0410
Colorado Belle Hotel & Casino 2100 S Casino Dr *Resv	Laughlin	NV	89029	**877-460-0777***	702-298-4000
Don Laughlin's Riverside Resort & Casino 1650 Casino Dr	Laughlin	NV	89029	**800-227-3849**	702-298-2535
Edgewater Hotel & Casino 2020 S Casino Dr *Resv	Laughlin	NV	89029	**866-352-3553***	702-298-2453
El Cortez Hotel & Casino 600 E Fremont St	Las Vegas	NV	89101	**800-634-6703**	702-385-5200
Eldorado Hotel Casino 345 N Virginia St *Resv	Reno	NV	89501	**800-879-8879***	775-786-5700

Name / Address	City	State	Zip	Toll-Free	Phone
Excalibur Hotel & Casino 3850 Las Vegas Blvd S	Las Vegas	NV	89109	**877-750-5464**	702-597-7777
Fiesta Rancho Casino Hotel 2400 N Rancho Dr *Resv	Las Vegas	NV	89130	**800-731-7333***	702-631-7000
Fremont Hotel & Casino 200 Fremont St	Las Vegas	NV	89101	**800-634-6460**	702-385-3232
Gold Coast Hotel & Casino 4000 W Flamingo Rd	Las Vegas	NV	89103	**800-331-5334**	702-367-7111
Gold Dust West Carson City 2171 E William St	Carson City	NV	89701	**877-519-5567**	775-885-9000
Gold Ranch Casino & RV Resort 350 Gold Ranch Rd	Verdi	NV	89439	**877-914-6789**	775-345-6789
Gold Strike Hotel & Gambling Hall 1 Main St	Jean	NV	89019	**800-634-1359**	702-477-5000
Golden Nugget Laughlin 2300 S Casino Dr	Laughlin	NV	89029	**800-950-7700**	702-298-7111
Grand Sierra Resort & Casino 2500 E Second St	Reno	NV	89595	**800-501-2651**	775-789-2000
Green Valley Ranch Resort Casino & Spa 2300 Paseo Verde Pkwy *Resv	Henderson	NV	89052	**866-782-9487***	702-617-7777
Harrah's Laughlin 2900 S Casino Dr	Laughlin	NV	89029	**800-427-7247**	702-298-4600
Harveys Lake Tahoe Hwy 50 at Stateline Ave PO Box 128	Lake Tahoe	NV	89449	**800-522-4700**	775-588-6611
Hooters Casino Hotel 115 E Tropicana Ave	Las Vegas	NV	89109	**866-584-6687**	702-739-9000
Hyatt Regency Lake Tahoe Resort & Casino 111 Country Club Dr	Incline Village	NV	89451	**800-233-1234**	775-832-1234
Luxor Hotel & Casino 3900 Las Vegas Blvd S *Resv	Las Vegas	NV	89119	**800-288-1000***	702-262-4000
Mandalay Bay Resort & Casino 3950 Las Vegas Blvd S	Las Vegas	NV	89119	**877-632-7800**	702-632-7777
MGM Grand Hotel & Casino 3799 Las Vegas Blvd S	Las Vegas	NV	89109	**877-880-0880**	702-891-1111
Monte Carlo Resort & Casino 3770 Las Vegas Blvd S	Las Vegas	NV	89109	**800-311-8999**	702-730-7777
New York New York Hotel & Casino 3790 Las Vegas Blvd S	Las Vegas	NV	89109	**800-689-1797**	702-740-6969
Orleans Las Vegas Hotel & Casino 4500 W Tropicana Ave	Las Vegas	NV	89103	**800-675-3267**	702-365-7111
Palace Station Hotel & Casino 2411 W Sahara Ave *Resv	Las Vegas	NV	89102	**800-634-3101***	702-367-2411
Palms Casino Resort 4321 W Flamingo Rd	Las Vegas	NV	89103	**866-942-7777**	702-942-7777
Peppermill Hotel & Casino 2707 S Virginia St	Reno	NV	89502	**800-648-6992**	775-826-2121
Railroad Pass Hotel & Casino 2800 S Boulder Hwy	Henderson	NV	89002	**800-654-0877**	702-294-5000
Red Rock Resort Spa & Casino 11011 W Charleston Blvd	Las Vegas	NV	89135	**866-767-7773**	702-797-7777
Sam's Town Hotel & Gambling Hall 5111 Boulder Hwy	Las Vegas	NV	89122	**800-897-8696**	702-456-7777
Santa Fe Station 4949 N Rancho Dr *Resv	Las Vegas	NV	89130	**888-786-7389***	702-658-4900
Silver Legacy Resort & Casino 407 N Virginia St	Reno	NV	89501	**800-687-8733**	775-325-7401
Silverton Hotel & Casino 3333 Blue Diamond Rd	Las Vegas	NV	89139	**866-722-4608**	702-263-7777
South Point Hotel & Casino 9777 Las Vegas Blvd S	Las Vegas	NV	89183	**866-796-7111**	702-796-7111
Stratosphere Tower Hotel & Casino 2000 S Las Vegas Blvd	Las Vegas	NV	89104	**800-998-6937**	702-380-7777
Suncoast Hotel & Casino 9090 Alta Dr	Las Vegas	NV	89145	**877-677-7111**	702-636-7111
Sunset Station Hotel & Casino 1301 W Sunset Rd	Henderson	NV	89014	**888-786-7389**	702-547-7777
Texas Station Gambling Hall & Hotel 2101 Texas Star Ln *Resv	North Las Vegas	NV	89032	**800-654-8888***	702-631-1000
Treasure Island Hotel & Casino 3300 Las Vegas Blvd S	Las Vegas	NV	89109	**800-288-7206**	702-894-7111
Tropicana Express 2121 S Casino Dr	Laughlin	NV	89029	**800-243-6846**	702-298-4200
Tuscany Suites & Casino 255 E Flamingo Rd *Resv	Las Vegas	NV	89169	**877-887-2261***	702-893-8933
Western Village Inn & Casino 815 Nichols Blvd	Sparks	NV	89434	**800-648-1170**	
Wynn Las Vegas 3131 Las Vegas Blvd S	Las Vegas	NV	89109	**877-321-9966**	702-770-7000
Casino New Brunswick LP 21 Casino Dr	Moncton	NB	E1G0R7	**877-859-7775**	506-859-7770
Harrah's Resort Atlantic City 777 Harrah's Blvd	Atlantic City	NJ	08401	**800-342-7724**	609-441-5000
Resorts Casino Hotel 1133 Boardwalk	Atlantic City	NJ	08401	**800-334-6378**	
Tropicana Entertainment 2831 Boardwalk *OTC: TPCA*	Atlantic City	NJ	08401	**800-843-8767**	
Trump Taj Mahal Casino Resort 1000 Boardwalk & Virginia Ave	Atlantic City	NJ	08401	**800-426-2537**	609-449-1000
Camel Rock Casino 17486A Hwy 84/285	Santa Fe	NM	87506	**800-483-1040**	505-983-2667
Cities of Gold Casino 10-B Cities of Gold Rd	Santa Fe	NM	87506	**800-455-3313**	505-455-3313
Route 66 Casino Hotel 14500 Central Ave	Albuquerque	NM	87121	**866-352-7866**	505-352-7866
Sandia Resort & Casino 30 Rainbow Rd NE	Albuquerque	NM	87113	**800-526-9366**	505-796-7500
Seneca Niagara Casino 310 Fourth St	Niagara Falls	NY	14303	**877-873-6322**	716-299-1100
Turning Stone Resort Casino LLC 5218 Patrick Rd	Verona	NY	13478	**800-771-7711**	315-361-7711
Harrah's Cherokee Casino & Hotel 777 Casino Dr *General	Cherokee	NC	28719	**877-811-0777***	828-497-7777
Prairie Knights Casino & Resort 7932 Hwy 24	Fort Yates	ND	58538	**800-425-8277**	701-854-7777
Casino Nova Scotia 1983 Upper Water St	Halifax	NS	B3J3Y5	**888-642-6376**	902-425-7777
Caesars License Company LLC 377 Riverside Dr E	Windsor	ON	N9A7H7	**800-991-7777**	519-258-7878
Casino Niagara 5705 Falls Ave	Niagara Falls	ON	L2E6T3	**888-325-5788**	
Fallsview Casino Resort 6380 Fallsview Blvd	Niagara Falls	ON	L2G7X5	**888-325-5788**	
Saskatchewan Indian Gaming Authority 250 - 103 C Packham Ave	Saskatoon	SK	S7N4K4	**800-306-6789**	306-477-7777
Emerald Downs 2300 Emerald Downs Dr PO Box 617	Auburn	WA	98001	**888-931-8400**	253-288-7000
Emerald Queen Casino (EQC) 2024 E 29th St	Tacoma	WA	98404	**888-831-7655**	253-594-7777
Lucky Eagle Casino 12888 188th Ave SW	Rochester	WA	98579	**800-720-1788**	360-273-2000
Northern Quest Casino 100 N Hayford Rd	Airway Heights	WA	99001	**877-871-6772**	509-242-7000
Red Wind Casino 12819 Yelm Hwy	Olympia	WA	98513	**866-946-2444**	360-412-5000
Skagit Valley Casino Resort 5984 N Darrk Ln	Bow	WA	98232	**877-275-2448**	360-724-7777
Wheeling Island Gaming Inc 1 S St1 St	Wheeling	WV	26003	**877-946-4373**	304-232-5050
Ho-Chunk Casino S 3214 County Rd BD	Baraboo	WI	53913	**800-746-2486**	
Lake of the Torches Resort Casino 510 Old Abe Rd	Lac du Flambeau	WI	54538	**800-258-6724**	715-588-7070
Potawatomi Bingo Casino 1721 W Canal St	Milwaukee	WI	53233	**800-729-7244**	414-645-6888

133 CASKETS & VAULTS

SEE ALSO Mortuary, Crematory, Cemetery Products & Services

Name / Address	City	State	Zip	Toll-Free	Phone
Batesville Casket Co 1 Batesville Blvd *Cust Svc	Batesville	IN	47006	**800-622-8373***	812-934-7500
Paul Casket Co 505 S Green St	Cambridge City	IN	47327	**800-521-8202**	765-478-3991

134 CEMENT

Name / Address	City	State	Zip	Toll-Free	Phone
Ash Grove Cement Co 8900 Indian Creek Pkwy *OTC: ASHG*	Overland Park	KS	66210	**800-545-1882**	913-451-8900
California Portland Cement Co 2025 E Financial Way *Cust Svc	Glendora	CA	91741	**800-272-1891***	626-852-6200
Cemex USA 840 Gessner Ste 1400 *NYSE: CX*	Houston	TX	77024	**888-292-0070**	713-650-6200
CGM Inc 1445 Ford Rd	Bensalem	PA	19020	**800-523-6570**	215-638-4400
Continental Cement Company LLC 14755 N Outer 40 Ste 514	Chesterfield	MO	63017	**800-625-1144**	636-532-7440
E Z Grout Corp 405 Watertown Rd	Waterford	OH	45786	**888-344-7688**	740-749-3512
ESSROC Materials Inc 3251 Bath Pike	Nazareth	PA	18064	**800-437-7762**	610-837-6725
Federal White Cement Ltd PO Box 1609 *Sales	Woodstock	ON	N4S0A8	**800-265-1806***	519-485-5410
Lehigh Inland Cement Ltd 12640 Inland Way *Orders	Edmonton	AB	T5V1K2	**800-252-9304***	780-420-2500
Maxxon Corp 920 Hamel Rd	Hamel	MN	55340	**800-356-7887**	763-478-9600
Permatile Concrete Products Co 100 Beacon Rd	Bristol	VA	24203	**800-662-5332**	276-669-5332
Prairie Group Inc 7601 W 79th St *Sales	Bridgeview	IL	60455	**800-649-3690***	708-458-0400
Titan America Inc 1151 Azalea Garden Rd	Norfolk	VA	23502	**800-468-7622**	757-858-6500

135 CEMETERIES - NATIONAL

SEE ALSO Historic Homes & Buildings ; Parks - National - US

Name / Address	City	State	Zip	Toll-Free	Phone
Alexandria National Cemetery 209 E Shamrock St	Pineville	LA	71360	**800-827-1000**	318-449-1793
Alton National Cemetery 600 Pearl St	Alton	IL	62003	**800-535-1117**	314-845-8320
Baltimore National Cemetery 5501 Frederick Ave	Baltimore	MD	21228	**800-535-1117**	410-644-9696
Beaufort National Cemetery 1601 Boundary St	Beaufort	SC	29902	**800-273-8255**	843-524-3925
Calverton National Cemetery 210 Princeton Blvd	Calverton	NY	11933	**800-829-1040**	631-727-5410
Camp Butler National Cemetery 5063 Camp Butler Rd	Springfield	IL	62707	**877-907-8585**	217-492-4070
Camp Nelson National Cemetery 6980 Danville Rd	Nicholasville	KY	40356	**800-827-1000**	859-885-5727
Chattanooga National Cemetery 1200 Bailey Ave	Chattanooga	TN	37404	**877-907-8585**	423-855-6590
Corinth National Cemetery 1551 Horton St	Corinth	MS	38834	**800-273-8255**	901-386-8311
Culpeper National Cemetery 305 US Ave	Culpeper	VA	22701	**800-827-1000**	540-825-0027

Classified Section

Name / Address	City	State	Zip	Toll-Free	Phone
Cypress Hills National Cemetery 625 Jamaica Ave	Brooklyn	NY	11208	800-535-1117	631-454-4949
Danville National Cemetery 1900 E Main St	Danville	IL	61832	800-827-1000	217-554-4550
Dayton National Cemetery 4100 W Third St	Dayton	OH	45428	800-273-8255	937-262-2115
Eagle Point National Cemetery 2763 Riley Rd	Eagle Point	OR	97524	800-535-1117	541-826-2511
Finn's Point National Cemetery 454 Ft. Mott Rd	Pennsville	NJ	08070	800-827-1000	215-504-5610
Florence National Cemetery 803 E National Cemetery Rd	Florence	SC	29506	877-907-8585	843-669-8783
Florida National Cemetery 6502 SW 102nd Ave	Bushnell	FL	33513	877-907-8585	352-793-7740
Fort Bliss National Cemetery PO Box 6342	El Paso	TX	79906	800-273-8255	915-564-0201
Fort Custer National Cemetery 15501 Dickman Rd	Augusta	MI	49012	800-273-8255	269-731-4164
Fort Smith National Cemetery 522 Garland Ave	Fort Smith	AR	72901	800-535-1117	479-783-5345
Grafton National Cemetery 431 Walnut St	Grafton	WV	26354	800-535-1117	304-265-2044
Jefferson Barracks National Cemetery 2900 Sheridan Rd	Saint Louis	MO	63125	800-827-1000	314-845-8320
Jefferson City National Cemetery 1024 E McCarty St	Jefferson City	MO	65101	877-907-8585	314-845-8320
Keokuk National Cemetery 1701 J St	Keokuk	IA	52632	800-273-8255	309-782-2094
Kerrville National Cemetery 3600 Memorial Blvd	Kerrville	TX	78028	800-273-8255	210-820-3891
Marietta National Cemetery 500 Washington Ave	Marietta	GA	30060	866-236-8159	
Massachusetts National Cemetery Conery Rd	Bourne	MA	02532	800-827-1000	508-563-7113
Mobile National Cemetery 1202 Virginia St	Mobile	AL	36604	800-827-1000	850-453-4108
Mountain Home National Cemetery PO Box 8	Mountain Home	TN	37684	800-827-1000	423-979-3535
New Bern National Cemetery 1711 National Ave	New Bern	NC	28560	800-827-1000	252-637-2912
Prescott National Cemetery 500 Hwy 89 N	Prescott	AZ	86301	800-827-1000	928-717-7569
Roseburg National Cemetery 1770 Harvard Blvd	Roseburg	OR	97470	800-535-1117	541-826-2511
Saint Augustine National Cemetery 104 Marine St	Saint Augustine	FL	32084	800-273-8255	352-793-7740
Seven Pines National Cemetery 400 E Williamsburg Rd	Sandston	VA	23150	800-535-1117	804-795-2031
Sitka National Cemetery 803 Sawmill Creek Rd	Sitka	AK	99835	800-273-8255	907-384-7075
Staunton National Cemetery 901 Richmond Ave	Staunton	VA	24401	800-273-8255	540-825-0027
Tahoma National Cemetery 18600 SE 240th St	Kent	WA	98042	800-827-1000	425-413-9614
Togus National Cemetery VA Regional Office Ctr	Togus	ME	04330	800-273-8255	508-563-7113
West Virginia National Cemetery 42 Veterans Memorial Lane	Grafton	WV	26354	800-273-8255	304-265-2044
Wilmington National Cemetery 2011 Market St	Wilmington	NC	28403	800-535-1117	910-815-4877
Wood National Cemetery 5000 W National Ave Bldg 1301	Milwaukee	WI	53295	888-878-3256	414-382-5300
Woodlawn National Cemetery 1825 Davis St	Elmira	NY	14901	877-907-8585	607-732-5411

137 CHAMBERS OF COMMERCE

Name / Address	City	State	Zip	Toll-Free	Phone
Alberta Soccer 9023 111 Ave Nw	Edmonton	AB	T5B0C3	866-250-2200	780-474-2200
Arizona Automobile Dealers Association 4701 N 24th St Ste B3	Phoenix	AZ	85016	800-678-3875	602-468-0888
Aski Financial Inc 419 Notre Dame Ave	Winnipeg	MB	R3B1R3	866-987-7180	204-987-7180
Association of American Chambers of Commerce in Latin America 1615 H St NW 3rd Fl	Washington	DC	20062	800-638-6582	202-463-5485
Burns Bog Conservation Society 7953 120 St	Delta	BC	V4C6P6	888-850-6264	604-572-0373
Canadian Finance & Leasing Association 15 Toronto St	Toronto	ON	M5C2E3	877-213-7373	416-860-1133
Canadian Payroll Association 250 Bloor St E	Toronto	ON	M4W1E6	800-387-4693	416-487-3380
Chinese Chamber of Commerce of Hawaii 8 S King St	Honolulu	HI	96817	877-533-2444	808-533-3181
Chinese Chamber of Commerce of Los Angeles 977 N Broadway Ground Fl Ste E	Los Angeles	CA	90012	800-400-7115	213-617-0396
Coach Canada's Health Informatics Association 250 Consumers Rd	North York	ON	M2J4V6	888-253-8554	416-494-9324
Constructors Association of Western Pennsylvania 1201 Banksville Rd	Pittsburgh	PA	15216	877-343-2297	412-343-8000
Electronic Transactions Association, The 1101 16th St NW Ste 402	Washington	DC	20036	800-695-5509	202-828-2635
Empire Building Services 1570 E Edinger Ave	Santa Ana	CA	92705	888-296-2078	714-836-7700
Flagship Fire Inc 1500 15th Ave dr e	Palmetto	FL	34221	866-242-3307	941-723-7230
Florida Venture Forum Inc, The 707 W Azeele St	Tampa	FL	33606	888-375-7136	813-335-8116
French-American Chamber of Commerce in New York 1350 Broadway Ste 2101	New York	NY	10018	800-821-2241	212-867-0123
FSNA 1052 St Laurent Blvd	Ottawa	ON	K1K3B4	855-304-4700	613-745-2559
Georgia Society of Cpa's 3353 Peachtree Rd NE Ste 400	Alpharetta	GA	30326	800-330-8889	404-231-8676
Grants Manager Network 1666 K St NW Ste 440	Washington	DC	02006	888-466-1996	504-834-9656
Hive Modern Design 820 nw glisan st	Portland	OR	97209	866-663-4483	503-242-1967
Houston Area Safety Council 1301 W 13th St	Deer Park	TX	77536	888-955-7233	281-476-9900
Ibb Design Group 5798 Genesis Ct	Frisco	TX	75034	800-355-9195	214-618-6600
Info. Quality Healthcare 385b Highland Colony Pkwy Ste 504	Ridgeland	MS	39157	800-844-0500	601-957-1575
Iowa Soybean Association 4554 114th st	Urbandale	IA	50322	800-383-1423	515-251-8640
Italy-America Chamber of Commerce Southeast Inc 2 S Biscayne Blvd Ste 1880	Miami	FL	33131	800-428-3003	305-577-9868
Kids Help Phone 300-439 University Ave	Toronto	ON	M5G1Y8	800-268-3062	416-586-5437
Labor Law Center Inc 12534 Vly view st	Garden Grove	CA	92845	800-745-9970	
Lignite Energy Council 1016 E Owens Ave	Bismarck	ND	58502	800-932-7117	701-258-7117
Meclabs LLC 1300 Marsh Landing Pkwy Ste 106	Jacksonville Beach	FL	32250	800-517-5531	
Mercer Engineering & Research 135 Osigian Blvd	Warner Robins	GA	31088	877-650-6372	478-953-6800
Nazcare Inc 599 White Spar Rd	Prescott	AZ	86303	877-756-4090	928-442-9205
Nebraska Beef Council 1319 Central Ave	Kearney	NE	68848	800-421-5326	308-236-7551
New Tech Network 1250 Main St Ste 100	Napa	CA	94559	800-856-7038	707-253-6951
Ohio Contractors Association 1313 Dublin Rd	Columbus	OH	43215	800-229-1388	614-488-0724
Ohio Manufacturers' Association 33 N High St	Columbus	OH	43215	800-662-4463	614-224-5111
Ontario Dental Nurses & Assistants Association 869 Dundas St	London	ON	N5W2Z8	800-461-4348	519-679-2566
Poteet Strawberry Festival Association 9199 N State Hwy 16	Poteet	TX	78065	888-742-8144	830-742-8144
Project Lifesaver International Headquarters 815 Battlefield Blvd S	Chesapeake	VA	23322	877-580-5433	757-546-5502
Rlj Financial Services Inc 1788 Mitchell Rd Ste 102	Ceres	CA	95307	800-240-1050	209-538-7758
Santie Oil Co 126 Larcel Dr	Sikeston	MO	63801	800-748-7788	314-436-3569
SMC Business Councils 600 Cranberry Woods Dr Ste 190	Cranberry Township	PA	16066	800-553-3260	412-371-1500
SOCAN 41 Valleybrook Dr	Toronto	ON	M3B2S6	800-557-6226	416-445-8700
Speed Skating Canada 2781 Lancaster Rd	Ottawa	ON	K1B1A7	877-572-4772	613-260-3660
Suzuki Association of The Americas Inc 1900 Folsom St Ste 101	Boulder	CO	80302	888-378-9854	303-444-0948
Travel Goods Association 301 N Harrison St Ste 412	Princeton	NJ	08540	877-842-1938	
US-Mexico Chamber of Commerce California Pacific Chapter 2450 Colorado Ave Ste 400E	Santa Monica	CA	90404	800-997-9148	310-586-7901

137 CHAMBERS OF COMMERCE - CANADIAN

Listings are organized by provinces and then are alphabetized within each province grouping according to the name of the city in which each chamber is located.

Name / Address	City	Prov.	Postal Code	Toll-Free	Phone
Alberta Chambers of Commerce 10025 - 102A Ave Edmonton Ctr Ste 1808	Edmonton	AB	T5J2Z2	800-272-8854	780-425-4180
Belleville Chamber of Commerce 5 Moira St E	Belleville	ON	K8P2S3	888-852-9992	613-962-4597
British Columbia Chamber of Commerce 750 W Pender St Ste 1201	Vancouver	BC	V6C2T8	800-669-9655	604-683-0700
Burlington Chamber of Commerce 414 Locust St Ste 201	Burlington	ON	L7S1T7	888-635-8687	905-639-0174
Cambridge Chamber of Commerce 750 Hespeler Rd *General	Cambridge	ON	N3H5L8	800-749-7560*	519-622-2221
Comox Valley Chamber of Commerce 2040 Cliffe Ave	Courtenay	BC	V9N2L3	888-357-4471	250-334-3234
Greater Peterborough Chamber of Commerce 175 George St N	Peterborough	ON	K9J3G6	877-640-4037	705-748-9771
Leamington District Chamber of Commerce 318 Erie St S	Leamington	ON	N8H3C5	800-393-3769	519-326-2721
North Bay & District Chamber of Commerce 1375 Seymour St	North Bay	ON	P1B8J8	888-249-8998	705-472-8480
Peace River Chamber of Commerce 9309-100 St PO Box 6599	Peace River	AB	T8S1S4	888-525-4423	780-624-4166
Penticton & Wine Country Chamber of Commerce 553 Railway St	Penticton	BC	V2A8S3	800-663-5052	250-492-4103
Saint Albert Chamber of Commerce 71 St Albert Rd	Saint Albert	AB	T8N6L5	800-243-2378	780-458-2833
Surrey Board of Trade 14439 104th Ave Ste 101	Surrey	BC	V3R1M1	866-848-7130	604-581-7130
Vaughan Chamber of Commerce 25 Edilcan Dr Ste 2	Vaughan	ON	L4K3S4	888-943-8937	905-761-1366
West Shore Chamber of Commerce 2830 Aldwynd Rd	Victoria	BC	V9B3S7	888-234-3566	250-478-1130
West Vancouver Chamber of Commerce 2235 Marine Dr	West Vancouver	BC	V7V1K5	888-471-9996	604-926-6614

138 CHAMBERS OF COMMERCE - US - LOCAL

SEE ALSO Civic & Political Organizations

Chambers listed here represent areas with a population of 25,000 or more. Listings are organized by states and then are alphabetized within each state grouping according to the name of the city in which each chamber is located.

Alabama

Name	Address	City	State	ZIP	Toll-Free	Phone
Greater Limestone County Chamber of Commerce	101 S Beaty St	Athens	AL	35611	**866-953-6565**	256-232-2600
Bessemer Area Chamber of Commerce	321 N 18th St	Bessemer	AL	35020	**888-423-7736**	205-425-3253
Cullman Area Chamber of Commerce	301 Second Ave SW	Cullman	AL	35055	**800-313-5114**	256-734-0454
Dothan Area Chamber of Commerce	102 Jamestown Blvd	Dothan	AL	36301	**800-221-1027**	334-792-5138
Eufaula/Barbour County Chamber of Commerce	333 E Broad St	Eufaula	AL	36027	**800-524-7529**	334-687-6664
South Baldwin Chamber of Commerce (SBCC)	112 W Laurel Ave PO Box 1117	Foley	AL	36535	**877-461-3712**	251-943-3291
Gadsden & Etowah County Chamber	1 Commerce Sq	Gadsden	AL	35901	**800-659-2955**	256-543-3472
Greenville Area Chamber of Commerce	1 Depot Sq	Greenville	AL	36037	**800-959-0717**	334-382-3251
Mobile Area Chamber of Commerce	451 Government St	Mobile	AL	36602	**800-422-6951**	251-433-6951
Ozark Area Chamber of Commerce	294 Painter Ave	Ozark	AL	36360	**800-582-8497**	334-774-9321
Phenix City-Russell County Chamber of Commerce	1107 Broad St	Phenix City	AL	36867	**800-892-2248**	334-298-3639
Greater Jackson County Chamber of Commerce	PO Box 973	Scottsboro	AL	35768	**800-259-5508**	256-259-5500
Selma-Dallas County Chamber of Commerce	912 Selma Ave	Selma	AL	36701	**800-457-3562**	334-875-7241

Alaska

Name	Address	City	State	ZIP	Toll-Free	Phone
Juneau Chamber of Commerce	9301 Glacier Hwy Ste 110	Juneau	AK	99801	**888-581-2201**	907-463-3488

Arizona

Name	Address	City	State	ZIP	Toll-Free	Phone
Bullhead Area Chamber of Commerce	1251 Hwy 95	Bullhead City	AZ	86429	**800-987-7457**	928-754-4121
Chandler Chamber of Commerce	25 S Arizona Pl Ste 201	Chandler	AZ	85225	**800-963-4571**	480-963-4571
Lake Havasu Area Chamber of Commerce	314 London Bridge Rd	Lake Havasu City	AZ	86403	**800-307-3610**	928-855-4115
Rim Country Regional Chamber of Commerce	100 W Main St	Payson	AZ	85547	**800-249-2678**	928-474-4515
Prescott Chamber of Commerce	117 W Goodwin St	Prescott	AZ	86303	**800-266-7534**	928-445-2000
Prescott Valley Chamber of Commerce	3001 N Main St Ste 2A	Prescott Valley	AZ	86314	**800-355-0843**	928-772-8857
Graham County Chamber of Commerce	1111 Thatcher Blvd	Safford	AZ	85546	**888-837-1841**	928-428-2511
Greater Sierra Vista Area Chamber of Commerce	21 E Wilcox Dr	Sierra Vista	AZ	85635	**800-288-3861**	520-458-6940
Yuma County Chamber of Commerce	180 W First St Ste A	Yuma	AZ	85364	**877-782-0438**	928-782-2567

Arkansas

Name	Address	City	State	ZIP	Toll-Free	Phone
Jacksonville Chamber of Commerce	200 Dupree Dr	Jacksonville	AR	72076	**888-857-3019**	501-982-1511
Mountain Home Area Chamber of Commerce	1023 Hwy 62	Mountain Home	AR	72653	**800-822-3536**	870-425-5111
Rogers-Lowell Area Chamber of Commerce	317 W Walnut St	Rogers	AR	72756	**800-364-1240**	479-636-1240
Russellville Area Chamber of Commerce	708 W Main St	Russellville	AR	72801	**855-678-2447**	479-968-2530

California

Name	Address	City	State	ZIP	Toll-Free	Phone
Atascadero Chamber of Commerce	6904 El Camino Real	Atascadero	CA	93422	**877-204-9830**	805-466-2044
Atwater Chamber of Commerce	1181 Third St	Atwater	CA	95301	**844-269-9688**	209-358-4251
Auburn Area Chamber of Commerce	601 Lincoln Way	Auburn	CA	95603	**800-310-2355**	530-885-5616
Kern County Board of Trade	2101 Oak St	Bakersfield	CA	93301	**800-787-9920*** *General	661-868-5376
Berkeley Chamber of Commerce	1834 University Ave	Berkeley	CA	94703	**800-847-4823**	510-549-7000
Chico Chamber of Commerce	441 Main St	Chico	CA	95928	**800-852-8570**	530-891-5556
Greater Concord Chamber of Commerce	2280 Diamond Blvd Ste 200	Concord	CA	94520	**800-427-8686**	925-685-1181
Downey Chamber of Commerce	11131 Brookshire Ave	Downey	CA	90241	**888-201-0995**	562-923-2191
Encinitas Chamber of Commerce	527 Encinitas Blvd	Encinitas	CA	92024	**800-953-6041**	760-753-6041
Greater Eureka Chamber of Commerce, The	2112 Broadway	Eureka	CA	95501	**866-267-4255**	707-442-3738
Mendocino Coast Chamber of Commerce	217 S Main St PO Box 1141	Fort Bragg	CA	95437	**800-382-7244**	707-961-6300
Garden Grove Chamber of Commerce	12866 Main St Ste 102	Garden Grove	CA	92840	**800-959-5560**	714-638-7950
Glendora Chamber of Commerce	131 E Foothill Blvd	Glendora	CA	91741	**800-926-4478**	626-963-4128
Goleta Valley Chamber of Commerce	271 N Fairview Ave Ste 104	Goleta	CA	93117	**800-646-5382**	805-967-2500
Hawthorne Chamber of Commerce	12519 Crenshaw Blvd	Hawthorne	CA	90250	**800-977-4770**	310-676-1163
Hesperia Chamber of Commerce	16816 Main St Ste D	Hesperia	CA	92345	**855-574-7337**	760-244-2135
Irvine Chamber of Commerce	2485 McCabe Way Ste 150	Irvine	CA	92614	**800-321-2211*** *General	949-660-9112
Amador County Chamber of Commerce	115 Main St PO Box 596	Jackson	CA	95642	**800-822-9466*** *General	209-223-0350
Lakeport Regional Chamber of Commerce	875 Lakeport Blvd PO Box 295	Lakeport	CA	95453	**866-525-3767**	707-263-5092
Lompoc Valley Chamber of Commerce & Visitors Bureau	PO Box 626	Lompoc	CA	93438	**800-240-0999**	805-736-4567
Century City Chamber of Commerce	2029 Century Pk E Concourse Level	Los Angeles	CA	90067	**800-462-7899**	310-553-2222
Madera District Chamber of Commerce	120 NE St	Madera	CA	93638	**866-382-7822**	559-673-3563
Malibu Chamber of Commerce	23805 Stuart Ranch Rd Ste 210	Malibu	CA	90265	**800-442-4988**	310-456-9025
Martinez Area Chamber of Commerce	603 Marina Vista	Martinez	CA	94553	**877-855-5506**	925-228-2345
Greater Merced Chamber of Commerce	1640 N St Ste 120	Merced	CA	95340	**800-877-2345**	209-384-7092
Napa Chamber of Commerce	1556 First St	Napa	CA	94559	**877-807-2249**	707-226-7455
Newark Chamber of Commerce	37101 Newark Blvd	Newark	CA	94560	**844-245-8925**	510-744-1000
Norwalk Chamber of Commerce	12040 Foster Rd	Norwalk	CA	90650	**800-427-2200**	562-864-7785
Novato Chamber of Commerce	807 DeLong Ave	Novato	CA	94945	**800-897-1164**	415-897-1164
Orange Chamber of Commerce	1940 N Tustin St	Orange	CA	92865	**888-676-1040**	714-538-3581
Orangevale Chamber of Commerce	9267 Greenback Ln Ste B-91	Orangevale	CA	95662	**800-962-1106**	916-988-0175
Oroville Area Chamber of Commerce	1789 Montgomery St	Oroville	CA	95965	**800-655-4653**	530-538-2542
Paradise Chamber of Commerce	5550 Sky Way Ste 1	Paradise	CA	95969	**800-838-3006**	530-877-9356
Placentia Chamber of Commerce	201 E Yorba Linda Blvd Ste C	Placentia	CA	92870	**844-730-0418**	714-528-1873
El Dorado County Chamber of Commerce	542 Main St	Placerville	CA	95667	**800-457-6279**	530-621-5885
Pleasanton Chamber of Commerce	777 Peters Ave	Pleasanton	CA	94566	**877-807-2249**	925-846-5858
Ramona Chamber of Commerce	960 Main St	Ramona	CA	92065	**800-411-7343**	760-789-1311
Rancho Cucamonga Chamber of Commerce	9047 Arrow Route Ste 180	Rancho Cucamonga	CA	91730	**800-677-5434**	909-987-1012
Redlands Chamber of Commerce	1 E Redlands Blvd	Redlands	CA	92373	**800-966-6428**	909-793-2546
Rialto Chamber of Commerce	120 N Riverside Ave	Rialto	CA	92376	**800-597-4955**	909-875-5364
Richmond Chamber of Commerce	3925 Macdonald Ave	Richmond	CA	94805	**866-568-4642**	510-234-3512
Rocklin Area Chamber of Commerce	3700 Rocklin Rd	Rocklin	CA	95677	**800-228-3380**	916-624-2548
Rohnert Park Chamber of Commerce	101 Golf Course Dr Ste C-7	Rohnert Park	CA	94928	**888-364-7379**	707-584-1415
Salinas Valley Chamber of Commerce	119 E Alisal St	Salinas	CA	93901	**888-678-2871**	831-751-7725
San Bernardino Area Chamber of Commerce	PO Box 658	San Bernardino	CA	92402	**800-928-5091**	909-885-7515
San Clemente Chamber of Commerce	1100 N El Camino Real	San Clemente	CA	92672	**877-411-3662**	949-492-1131
San Francisco Chamber of Commerce	235 Montgomery St 12th Fl	San Francisco	CA	94104	**855-808-2387**	415-392-4520
San Marcos Chamber of Commerce	904 W San Marcos Blvd	San Marcos	CA	92078	**800-814-7241**	760-744-1270
San Rafael Chamber of Commerce	817 Mission Ave	San Rafael	CA	94901	**888-378-0777**	415-454-4163
Santa Cruz Chamber of Commerce	611 Ocean St Ste 1	Santa Cruz	CA	95060	**866-282-5900**	831-457-3713
Santa Maria Valley Chamber of Commerce	614 S Broadway	Santa Maria	CA	93454	**800-331-3779**	805-925-2403
Tuolumne County Chamber of Commerce	222 S Shepherd St	Sonora	CA	95370	**877-532-4212**	209-532-4212
Sun Valley Area Chamber of Commerce	11501 Strathern St PO Box 308	Sun Valley	CA	91352	**877-834-7064**	818-768-2014
Lassen County Chamber of Commerce	75 N Weatherlow St	Susanville	CA	96130	**877-686-7878**	530-257-4323
Temecula Valley Chamber of Commerce (TVCC)	26790 Ynez Ct Ste A	Temecula	CA	92591	**866-676-5090**	951-676-5090
Turlock Chamber of Commerce	115 S Golden State Blvd	Turlock	CA	95380	**800-834-0401**	209-632-2221
Vallejo Chamber of Commerce	427 York St	Vallejo	CA	94590	**877-397-7936**	707-644-5551
Westminster Chamber of Commerce	1025 Westminster Mall	Westminster	CA	92683	**800-545-5585**	714-898-2559
Willows Chamber of Commerce	118 W Sycamore	Willows	CA	95988	**855-233-6362**	530-934-8150
Woodland Chamber of Commerce	307 First St	Woodland	CA	95695	**888-843-2636**	530-662-7327
Woodland Hills Chamber of Commerce	20121 Ventura Blvd Ste 309	Woodland Hills	CA	91364	**888-852-9961**	818-347-4737
Yucca Valley Chamber of Commerce	56711 29 Palms Hwy	Yucca Valley	CA	92284	**855-568-5348**	760-365-6323

Colorado

Name	Address	City	State	ZIP	Toll-Free	Phone
Aspen Chamber Resort Assn	425 Rio Grande Pl	Aspen	CO	81611	**800-670-0792**	970-925-1940
Canon City Chamber of Commerce	403 Royal Gorge Blvd	Canon City	CO	81212	**800-876-7922**	719-275-2331
Colorado Springs Regional Business Alliance	102 S Tejon St Ste 430	Colorado Springs	CO	80903	**866-804-8763**	719-471-8183
Fort Collins Area Chamber of Commerce	225 S Meldrum St	Fort Collins	CO	80521	**877-652-8607**	970-482-3746
Fort Morgan Area Chamber of Commerce	300 Main St	Fort Morgan	CO	80701	**800-354-8660**	970-867-6702

Name / Address	City	State	Zip	Toll-Free	Phone
Grand Junction Area Chamber of Commerce 360 Grand Ave	Grand Junction	CO	81501	**800-352-5286**	970-242-3214
Greeley-Weld Chamber of Commerce 902 Seventh Ave	Greeley	CO	80631	**800-449-3866**	970-352-3566
La Veta/Cuchara Chamber of Commerce 132 W Ryus Ave	La Veta	CO	81055	**866-277-5550**	719-742-3676
Loveland Chamber of Commerce 5400 Stone Creek Cir Ste 200	Loveland	CO	80538	**800-216-0680**	970-667-6311
Montrose Chamber of Commerce 1519 E Main St	Montrose	CO	81401	**800-923-5515**	970-249-5000
Greater Pueblo Chamber of Commerce 302 N Santa Fe Ave	Pueblo	CO	81003	**800-233-3446**	719-542-1704
Metro North Chamber of Commerce 14583 Orchard Pkwy Ste 300	Westminster	CO	80023	**877-888-8811**	303-288-1000

Connecticut

Name / Address	City	State	Zip	Toll-Free	Phone
Greater Bristol Chamber of Commerce 200 Main St	Bristol	CT	06010	**855-344-1874**	860-584-4718
Greater Meriden Chamber of Commerce 3 Colony St Ste 301	Meriden	CT	06451	**877-283-8158**	203-235-7901
Mystic Chamber of Commerce 12 Roosevelt Ave,2nd Fl PO Box 143	Mystic	CT	06355	**866-572-9578**	860-572-9578
Stamford Chamber of Commerce 733 Summer St Ste 104	Stamford	CT	06901	**866-262-4548**	203-359-4761
Windham Region Chamber of Commerce 1010 Main St	Willimantic	CT	06226	**800-683-4564**	860-423-6389

Delaware

Name / Address	City	State	Zip	Toll-Free	Phone
Rehoboth Beach-Dewey Beach Chamber of Commerce 501 Rehoboth Ave	Rehoboth Beach	DE	19971	**800-441-1329**	302-227-2233
Yazoo County Chamber of Commerce 1615 H St NW	Washington	DC	20062	**800-638-6582**	662-746-1273

Florida

Name / Address	City	State	Zip	Toll-Free	Phone
Apalachicola Bay Chamber of Commerce 122 Commerce St	Apalachicola	FL	32320	**866-269-3022**	850-653-9419
Lower Keys Chamber of Commerce 31020 Overseas Hwy	Big Pine Key	FL	33043	**800-872-3722**	305-872-2411
Greater Boca Raton Chamber of Commerce 1800 N Dixie Hwy	Boca Raton	FL	33432	**800-435-7352**	561-395-4433
Bonita Springs Area Chamber of Commerce 25071 Chamber of Commerce Dr	Bonita Springs	FL	34135	**800-226-2943**	239-992-2943
Clearwater Regional Chamber of Commerce 401 Cleveland St	Clearwater	FL	33755	**877-447-7356**	727-461-0011
Greater Deerfield Beach Chamber of Commerce 1601 E Hillsboro Blvd	Deerfield Beach	FL	33441	**866-551-9805**	954-427-1050
DeLand Area Chamber of Commerce 336 N Woodland Blvd	DeLand	FL	32720	**800-611-5207**	386-734-4331
Englewood-Cape Haze Area Chamber of Commerce 601 S Indiana Ave	Englewood	FL	34223	**800-603-7198**	941-474-5511
Broward County Chamber of Commerce 2425 E Commercial Blvd #103	Fort Lauderdale	FL	33308	**877-653-4752**	954-565-5750
Greater Fort Lauderdale Chamber of Commerce 512 NE Third Ave	Fort Lauderdale	FL	33301	**800-683-8338**	954-462-6000
Greater Fort Myers Chamber of Commerce 2310 Edwards Dr	Fort Myers	FL	33901	**800-366-3622**	239-332-3624
Fort Myers Beach Chamber of Commerce 17200 San Carlos Blvd	Fort Myers Beach	FL	33931	**866-998-9250**	239-454-7500
Gainesville Area Chamber of Commerce 300 E University Ave Ste 100	Gainesville	FL	32601	**888-795-2707**	352-334-7100
Islamorada Chamber of Commerce PO Box 915	Islamorada	FL	33036	**800-322-5397**	305-664-4503
Key Largo Chamber of Commerce 106000 Overseas Hwy	Key Largo	FL	33037	**800-680-9701**	305-451-1414
Greater Marathon Chamber of Commerce 12222 Overseas Hwy	Marathon	FL	33050	**800-262-7284**	305-743-5417
Marco Island Chamber of Commerce 1102 N Collier Blvd	Marco Island	FL	34145	**800-788-6272**	239-394-7549
Greater Miami Chamber of Commerce 1601 Biscayne Blvd	Miami	FL	33132	**888-660-5955**	305-350-7700
Miami Beach Chamber of Commerce 1920 Meridian Ave 3rd Fl	Miami Beach	FL	33139	**800-501-0401**	305-672-1270
Santa Rosa County Chamber of Commerce 5247 Stewart St	Milton	FL	32570	**800-239-8732**	850-623-2339
Ocala-Marion County Chamber of Commerce 310 SE Third St	Ocala	FL	34471	**800-466-5055**	352-629-8051
Clay County Chamber of Commerce 1734 Kingsley Ave	Orange Park	FL	32073	**800-435-7352**	904-264-2651
Greater Plant City Chamber of Commerce 106 N Evers St	Plant City	FL	33563	**800-760-2315**	813-754-3707
Gadsden County Chamber of Commerce 208 N Adams St	Quincy	FL	32351	**800-627-9231**	850-627-9231
Tampa Bay Beaches Chamber of Commerce 6990 Gulf Blvd	Saint Pete Beach	FL	33706	**866-450-9222**	727-360-6957
Walton Area Chamber of Commerce 63 S Centry Trl	Santa Rosa Beach	FL	32459	**800-435-7352**	850-267-0683
Chamber South 6410 SW 80th St	South Miami	FL	33143	**800-206-3715**	305-661-1621
Stuart-Martin County Chamber of Commerce 1650 S Kanner Hwy	Stuart	FL	34994	**800-962-2873**	772-287-1088
Greater Tampa Chamber of Commerce 201 N Franklin St Ste 201	Tampa	FL	33602	**800-707-8846**	813-228-7777
Titusville Area Chamber of Commerce 2000 S Washington Ave	Titusville	FL	32780	**800-435-7352**	321-267-3036
Indian River County Chamber of Commerce 1216 21st St	Vero Beach	FL	32960	**877-646-6889**	772-567-3491
West Orange Chamber of Commerce 12184 W Colonial Dr	Winter Garden	FL	34787	**877-999-9981**	407-656-1304
Winter Park Chamber of Commerce 151 W Lyman Ave *Help Line	Winter Park	FL	32789	**877-972-4262***	407-644-8281
Zephyrhills Chamber of Commerce 38550 Fifth Ave	Zephyrhills	FL	33542	**800-851-8754**	813-782-1913

Georgia

Name / Address	City	State	Zip	Toll-Free	Phone
Albany Area Chamber of Commerce 225 W Broad Ave	Albany	GA	31701	**800-475-8700**	229-434-8700
Greater North Fulton Chamber of Commerce (GNFCC) 11605 Haynes Bridge Rd Ste 100	Alpharetta	GA	30009	**866-840-5770**	770-993-8806
Cobb Chamber of Commerce 240 I- N Pkwy	Atlanta	GA	30339	**800-228-2545**	770-980-2000
Augusta Metro Chamber of Commerce 1 10th St Ste 120	Augusta	GA	30901	**888-639-8188**	706-821-1300
Brunswick-Golden Isles Chamber of Commerce 1505 Richmond St 2nd Fl	Brunswick	GA	31520	**888-453-5955**	912-265-0620
Gordon County Chamber of Commerce 300 S Wall St	Calhoun	GA	30701	**800-887-3811**	706-625-3200
Chatsworth-Murray County Chamber of Commerce PO Box 516	Chatsworth	GA	30705	**800-969-9490**	706-695-2834
White County Chamber of Commerce 122 N Main St	Cleveland	GA	30528	**800-392-8279**	706-865-5356
Greater Columbus Chamber of Commerce 1200 Sixth Ave PO Box 1200	Columbus	GA	31902	**800-360-8552**	706-327-1566
Habersham County Chamber of Commerce 668 Clarkesville St	Cornelia	GA	30531	**800-835-2559**	706-778-4654
Douglas-Coffee County Chamber of Commerce 211 S Gaskin Ave	Douglas	GA	31533	**888-426-3334**	912-384-1873
Dublin-Laurens County Chamber of Commerce 1200 Bellvue	Dublin	GA	31021	**800-829-4933**	478-272-5546
Liberty County Chamber of Commerce 425 W Oglethorpe Hwy	Hinesville	GA	31313	**855-846-3940**	912-368-4445
Jackson County Area Chamber of Commerce 270 Athens St PO Box 629	Jefferson	GA	30549	**800-243-6921**	706-387-0300
Clayton County Chamber of Commerce 2270 Mt Zion Rd	Jonesboro	GA	30236	**877-790-1831**	678-610-4021
Moultrie-Colquitt County Chamber of Commerce 116 First Ave SE	Moultrie	GA	31768	**888-408-4748**	229-985-2131
Walker County Chamber of Commerce 10052 N Hwy 27	Rock Spring	GA	30739	**800-321-8128**	706-375-7702
Camden County Chamber of Commerce 2603 Osborne Rd Unit CC	Saint Marys	GA	31558	**888-331-8226**	912-729-5840
Effingham County Chamber of Commerce 520 W Third St PO Box 1078	Springfield	GA	31329	**800-241-3333**	912-754-3301
Tifton-Tift County Chamber of Commerce 100 Central Ave	Tifton	GA	31794	**800-550-8438**	229-382-6200
DeKalb Chamber of Commerce 125 Clairemont Ave Ste 235	Tucker	GA	30084	**800-428-7337**	404-378-8000

Hawaii

Name / Address	City	State	Zip	Toll-Free	Phone
Hawaii Island Chamber of Commerce 117 Keawe St	Hilo	HI	96720	**877-482-4411**	808-935-7178
Kailua Chamber of Commerce 600 Kailua Rd Ste 107	Kailua	HI	96734	**888-261-7997**	808-261-2727

Idaho

Name / Address	City	State	Zip	Toll-Free	Phone
Caldwell Chamber of Commerce 704 Blaine St	Caldwell	ID	83605	**877-375-7382**	208-459-7493
Coeur d'Alene Area Chamber of Commerce 105 N First St Ste 100	Coeur d'Alene	ID	83814	**877-782-9232**	208-664-3194
Sun Valley/Ketchum Chamber & Visitors Bureau 491 Sun Vly Rd	Ketchum	ID	83340	**800-634-3347**	208-726-3423
Meridian Chamber of Commerce 215 E Franklin Rd	Meridian	ID	83642	**866-833-3330**	208-888-2817
Moscow Chamber of Commerce 411 S Main St	Moscow	ID	83843	**866-770-2020**	208-882-1800
Twin Falls Area Chamber of Commerce 2015 Neilsen Point Pl	Twin Falls	ID	83301	**866-734-3838**	208-733-3974

Illinois

Name / Address	City	State	Zip	Toll-Free	Phone
Aurora Chamber of Commerce 43 W Galena Blvd	Aurora	IL	60506	**866-947-8081**	630-256-3180
Champaign County Chamber of Commerce 1817 S Neil St Ste 201	Champaign	IL	61820	**800-328-1627**	217-359-1791
Crystal Lake Chamber of Commerce 427 W Virginia St	Crystal Lake	IL	60014	**800-946-2248**	815-459-1300
Elgin Area Chamber of Commerce 31 S Grove Ave	Elgin	IL	60120	**800-621-3362**	847-741-5660
Greater O'Hare Assn of Industry & Commerce PO Box 1516	Elk Grove Village	IL	60009	**877-355-4768**	630-773-2944
Glen Ellyn Chamber of Commerce 800 Roosevelt Rd Bldg D Ste 108	Glen Ellyn	IL	60137	**800-622-9000**	630-469-0907
Growth Assn of Southwestern Illinois 5800 Godfrey Rd Alden Hall	Godfrey	IL	62035	**855-852-9460**	618-467-2280
West Suburban Chamber of Commerce 9440 Joliet Rd Ste B	Hodgkins	IL	60525	**800-796-9696**	708-387-7550
Jacksonville Area Chamber of Commerce 310 E State St	Jacksonville	IL	62650	**800-593-5678**	217-243-5678
Joliet Region Chamber of Commerce & Industry 63 N Chicago St	Joliet	IL	60432	**877-499-9669**	815-727-5371
Grundy County Chamber of Commerce & Industry 909 Liberty St	Morris	IL	60450	**800-892-1412**	815-942-0113
Mount Prospect Chamber of Commerce 662 E NW Hwy	Mount Prospect	IL	60056	**800-584-4452**	847-398-6616
Northbrook Chamber of Commerce & Industry 2002 Walters Ave	Northbrook	IL	60062	**855-354-3337**	847-498-5555
Peoria Area Chamber of Commerce 100 SW Water St	Peoria	IL	61602	**888-681-6561**	309-676-0755
Rockford Chamber of Commerce 308 W State St Ste 190	Rockford	IL	61101	**866-767-2629**	815-987-8100
Round Lake Area Chamber of Commerce & Industry 2007 Civic Ctr Way	Round Lake Beach	IL	60073	**800-334-7661**	847-546-2002

Indiana

Name / Address	City	State	ZIP	Toll-Free	Phone
Goshen Chamber of Commerce 232 S Main St	Goshen	IN	46526	**800-307-4204**	574-533-2102
Greater Greenwood Chamber of Commerce 65 Airport Pkwy	Greenwood	IN	46143	**800-462-7585**	317-888-4856
Lakeshore Chamber of Commerce 5246 Hohman Ave Ste 100	Hammond	IN	46320	**855-464-6368**	219-931-1000
Greater Lawrence Township Chamber of Commerce 9120 Otis Ave Ste 100	Indianapolis	IN	46216	**800-473-2328**	317-541-9876
Dearborn County Chamber of Commerce 320 Walnut St	Lawrenceburg	IN	47025	**800-322-8198**	812-537-0814
Greater Monticello Chamber of Commerce 116 N Main St	Monticello	IN	47960	**800-541-7906**	574-583-7220
Muncie-Delaware County Chamber of Commerce 401 S High St	Muncie	IN	47305	**800-336-1373**	765-288-6681
One Southern Indiana 4100 Charlestown Rd	New Albany	IN	47150	**800-521-2232**	812-945-0266
Jennings County Chamber of Commerce 203 N State St PO Box 340	North Vernon	IN	47265	**866-382-4968**	812-346-2339
Miami County Chamber of Commerce 13 E Main St	Peru	IN	46970	**800-521-9945**	765-472-1923
Shelby County Chamber of Commerce 501 N Harrison St	Shelbyville	IN	46176	**800-318-4083**	317-398-6647

Iowa

Name / Address	City	State	ZIP	Toll-Free	Phone
Ames Chamber of Commerce 1601 Golden Aspen Dr Ste 110	Ames	IA	50010	**800-288-7470**	515-232-2310
Burlington/West Burlington Area Chamber of Commerce 610 N Fourth St Ste 200	Burlington	IA	52601	**800-827-4837**	319-752-6365
Council Bluffs Area Chamber of Commerce 149 W Bdwy	Council Bluffs	IA	51503	**800-228-6878**	712-325-1000
Greater Des Moines Partnership 700 Locust St Ste 100	Des Moines	IA	50309	**866-487-9243**	515-286-4950
Dubuque Area Chamber of Commerce 300 Main St Ste 200	Dubuque	IA	52001	**800-798-4748**	563-557-9200
Marshalltown Area Chamber of Commerce 709 S Ctr St PO Box 1000	Marshalltown	IA	50158	**800-725-5301**	641-753-6645
Siouxland Chamber of Commerce 101 Pierce St	Sioux City	IA	51101	**800-228-7903**	712-255-7903
Greater Cedar Valley Chamber of Commerce 10 W 4th St Ste 310	Waterloo	IA	50703	**800-288-1047**	319-232-1156

Kansas

Name / Address	City	State	ZIP	Toll-Free	Phone
Emporia Area Chamber of Commerce 719 Commercial St	Emporia	KS	66801	**800-279-3730**	620-342-1600
Hutchinson/Reno County Chamber of Commerce 117 N Walnut St	Hutchinson	KS	67501	**800-691-4262**	620-662-3391
Manhattan Area Chamber of Commerce 501 Poyntz Ave	Manhattan	KS	66502	**800-759-0134**	785-776-8829
Pittsburg Area Chamber of Commerce 117 W Fourth St	Pittsburg	KS	66762	**800-794-4780**	620-231-1000
Salina Area Chamber of Commerce 120 W Ash St	Salina	KS	67401	**877-725-4625**	785-827-9301

Kentucky

Name / Address	City	State	ZIP	Toll-Free	Phone
Ashland Alliance Chamber of Commerce 1733 Winchester Ave	Ashland	KY	41101	**800-233-3826**	606-324-5111
Bowling Green Area Chamber of Commerce 710 College St	Bowling Green	KY	42101	**866-330-2422**	270-781-3200
Glasgow-Barren County Chamber of Commerce 118 E Public Sq	Glasgow	KY	42141	**800-264-3161**	270-651-3161
Hopkinsville-Christian County Chamber of Commerce 2800 Port Campbell Blvd	Hopkinsville	KY	42240	**800-842-9959**	270-885-9096
Somerset-Pulaski County Chamber of Commerce 445 S Hwy 27 Ste 101	Somerset	KY	42501	**877-629-9722**	606-679-7323

Louisiana

Name / Address	City	State	ZIP	Toll-Free	Phone
Bossier Chamber of Commerce 710 Benton Rd	Bossier City	LA	71111	**800-659-2955**	318-746-0252
Monroe Chamber of Commerce 212 Walnut St Ste 100	Monroe	LA	71201	**888-677-5200**	318-323-3461
Natchitoches Area Chamber of Commerce 780 Front St Ste 101	Natchitoches	LA	71457	**877-646-6689**	318-352-6894
Iberville Parish Chamber of Commerce 23675 Church St	Plaquemine	LA	70764	**800-266-2692**	225-687-3560
Ruston/Lincoln Chamber of Commerce 2111 N Trenton St	Ruston	LA	71270	**800-392-9032**	318-255-2031
Greater Shreveport Chamber of Commerce 400 Edwards St	Shreveport	LA	71101	**800-448-5432**	318-677-2500
East St Tammany Chamber of Commerce 118 W Hall Ave	Slidell	LA	70460	**800-870-3673**	985-643-5678

Maine

Name / Address	City	State	ZIP	Toll-Free	Phone
Bar Harbor Chamber of Commerce 2 Cottage St	Bar Harbor	ME	04609	**888-540-9990**	207-288-5103
Belfast Area Chamber of Commerce 14 Main St	Belfast	ME	04915	**877-338-9015**	207-338-5900
Southern Midcoast Maine Chamber 2 Main St Border Trust Business Ctr	Topsham	ME	04086	**877-725-8797**	207-725-8797

Maryland

Name / Address	City	State	ZIP	Toll-Free	Phone
Harford County Chamber of Commerce 108 S Bond St	Bel Air	MD	21014	**800-682-8536**	410-838-2020
Greater Bethesda-Chevy Chase Chamber of Commerce 7910 Woodmont Ave Ste 1204	Bethesda	MD	20814	**800-333-6778**	301-652-4900
Charles County Chamber of Commerce 101 Centennial St Ste A	La Plata	MD	20646	**800-992-3194**	301-932-6500
Garrett County Chamber of Commerce 15 Visitors Ctr Dr	McHenry	MD	21541	**888-387-5237**	301-387-4386
Greater Ocean City Chamber of Commerce 12320 Ocean Gateway	Ocean City	MD	21842	**888-626-3386**	410-213-0144
Wheaton-Kensington Chamber of Commerce 2401 Blueridge Ave Ste 101	Wheaton	MD	20902	**800-927-9061**	301-949-0080

Massachusetts

Name / Address	City	State	ZIP	Toll-Free	Phone
Middlesex West Chamber of Commerce 179 Great Rd Ste 104B	Acton	MA	01720	**800-439-0183**	978-263-0010
Beverly Chamber of Commerce 100 Cummings Ctr Ste 107K	Beverly	MA	01915	**800-924-8167**	978-232-9559
Greater Boston Chamber of Commerce 265 Franklin St	Boston	MA	02110	**800-476-3094**	617-227-4500
Metro South Chamber of Commerce 60 School St	Brockton	MA	02301	**877-777-4414**	508-586-0500
Cape Cod Canal Regional Chamber of Commerce 70 Main St	Buzzards Bay	MA	02532	**888-332-2732**	508-759-6000
Cape Cod Chamber of Commerce 5 Shoot Flying Hill Rd	Centerville	MA	02632	**888-332-2732**	508-362-3225
Nashoba Valley Chamber of Commerce 100 Sherman Ave	Devens	MA	01434	**877-322-8228**	978-772-6976
Fall River Area Chamber of Commerce & Industry 200 Pocasset St	Fall River	MA	02721	**800-647-2824**	508-676-8226
Falmouth Chamber of Commerce 20 Academy Ln	Falmouth	MA	02540	**800-526-8532**	508-548-8500
Metro West Chamber of Commerce 1671 Worcester Rd Ste 201	Framingham	MA	01701	**866-709-9401**	508-879-5600
Merrimack Valley Chamber of Commerce 264 Essex St	Lawrence	MA	01840	**800-966-3375**	978-686-0900
Greater Lowell Chamber of Commerce 131 Merrimack St	Lowell	MA	01852	**800-338-0221**	978-459-8154
Greater Northampton Chamber of Commerce 99 Pleasant St	NorthHampton	MA	01060	**800-392-6090**	413-584-1900
Affiliated Chamber of Commerce of Greater Springfield 1441 Main St	Springfield	MA	01103	**888-283-3757**	413-787-1555
Blackstone Valley Chamber of Commerce 110 Church St	Whitinsville	MA	01588	**800-841-0919**	508-234-9090

Michigan

Name / Address	City	State	ZIP	Toll-Free	Phone
Alpena Area Chamber of Commerce 235 W Chisholm St	Alpena	MI	49707	**800-425-7362**	989-354-4181
Dearborn Chamber of Commerce 22100 Michigan Ave	Dearborn	MI	48124	**800-844-5440**	313-584-6100
Delta County Area Chamber of Commerce 230 Ludington St	Escanaba	MI	49829	**800-221-2001**	906-786-2192
Genesee Regional Chamber of Commerce 519 S Saginaw St Ste 200	Flint	MI	48502	**800-829-3676**	810-600-1404
Dickinson Area Partnership 600 S Stephenson Ave	Iron Mountain	MI	49801	**888-543-2139**	906-774-2002
Greater Jackson Chamber of Commerce 141 S Jackson St	Jackson	MI	49201	**800-366-3699**	517-782-8221
Midland Area Chamber of Commerce 300 Rodd St Ste 101	Midland	MI	48640	**800-715-0074**	989-839-9901
Monroe County Chamber of Commerce 1645 N Dixie Hwy Ste 20	Monroe	MI	48162	**855-386-1280**	734-384-3366
Macomb County Chamber 28 First St Ste B	Mount Clemens	MI	48043	**800-564-3136**	586-493-7600
Muskegon Area Chamber of Commerce 380 W Western Ste 202	Muskegon	MI	49440	**800-659-2955**	231-722-3751
Novi Chamber of Commerce, The 41875 W 11 Mile Rd Ste 201	Novi	MI	48375	**888-440-7325**	248-349-3743
Blue Water Area Chamber of Commerce 512 McMorran Blvd	Port Huron	MI	48060	**800-361-0526**	810-985-7101
Saginaw County Chamber of Commerce 515 N Washington Ave 2nd Fl	Saginaw	MI	48607	**866-657-9357**	989-752-7161
Traverse City Area Chamber of Commerce 202 E Grandview Pkwy	Traverse City	MI	49684	**844-900-0500**	231-947-5075
Westland Chamber of Commerce 36900 Ford Rd	Westland	MI	48185	**800-737-4859**	734-326-7222

Minnesota

Name / Address	City	State	ZIP	Toll-Free	Phone
Alexandria Lakes Area Chamber of Commerce 206 Broadway	Alexandria	MN	56308	**800-235-9441**	320-763-3161
Apple Valley Chamber of Commerce 14800 Galaxie Ave Ste 101	Apple Valley	MN	55124	**800-301-9435**	952-432-8422
Bemidji Area Chamber of Commerce 300 Bemidji Ave	Bemidji	MN	56601	**800-458-2223**	218-444-3541
Brainerd Lakes Area Chamber of Commerce 7393 State Hwy 371 PO Box 356	Brainerd	MN	56401	**800-450-2838**	218-829-2838
Cloquet Area Chamber of Commerce 225 Sunnyside Dr	Cloquet	MN	55720	**800-554-4350**	218-879-1551
Detroit Lakes Regional Chamber of Commerce 700 Summit Ave	Detroit Lakes	MN	56501	**800-542-3992**	218-847-9202
Duluth Area Chamber of Commerce 5 W First St Ste 101	Duluth	MN	55802	**800-385-8842**	218-722-5501
Grand Rapids Area Chamber of Commerce 1 NW Third St	Grand Rapids	MN	55744	**800-472-6366**	218-326-6619
Hastings Area Chamber of Commerce & Tourism Bureau 111 E Third St	Hastings	MN	55033	**888-612-6122**	651-437-6775
Lakeville Area Chamber of Commerce & Convention & Visitors Bureau 19950 Dodd Blvd Ste 101	Lakeville	MN	55044	**888-525-3845**	952-469-2020
Owatonna Area Chamber of Commerce & Tourism 320 Hoffman Dr	Owatonna	MN	55060	**800-423-6466**	507-451-7970
Leech Lake Area Chamber of Commerce 205 Minnesota Ave E	Walker	MN	56484	**800-833-1118**	218-547-1313

Mississippi

Organization	Address	City	State	ZIP	Toll-Free	Phone
Panola Partnership Inc	150-A Public Sq	Batesville	MS	38606	**888-872-6652**	662-563-3126
Rankin County Chamber of Commerce	101 Service Dr	Brandon	MS	39043	**800-987-8280**	601-825-2268
Brookhaven-Lincoln County Chamber of Commerce	230 S Whitworth Ave	Brookhaven	MS	39601	**800-613-4667**	601-833-1411
Clarksdale-Coahoma County Chamber of Commerce & Industrial Foundation	1540 DeSoto Ave	Clarksdale	MS	38614	**800-626-3764**	662-627-7337
Alliance, The	810 Tate St	Corinth	MS	38834	**877-347-0545**	662-287-5269
Greenwood-Leflore County Chamber of Commerce	402 Hwy 82	Greenwood	MS	38930	**800-844-7483**	662-453-4152
Area Development Partnership	1 Convention Ctr Plz	Hattiesburg	MS	39401	**800-238-4288**	601-296-7500
Oxford-Lafayette County Chamber of Commerce	299 W Jackson Ave	Oxford	MS	38655	**800-880-6967**	662-234-4651
Community Development Partnership	256 W Beacon Str 256 W Beacon	Philadelphia	MS	39350	**877-752-2643**	601-656-1000
Greater Starkville Development Partnership	200 E Main St	Starkville	MS	39759	**800-649-8687**	662-323-3322
Pike County Chamber of Commerce & Economic Development District	PO Box 5302	Summit	MS	39666	**800-844-2653**	601-684-2291

Missouri

Organization	Address	City	State	ZIP	Toll-Free	Phone
Branson/Lakes Area Chamber of Commerce	PO Box 1897	Branson	MO	65615	**800-214-3661**	417-334-4084
Chesterfield Chamber of Commerce	101 Chesterfield Business Pkwy	Chesterfield	MO	63005	**888-242-4262**	636-532-3399
Jefferson City Area Chamber of Commerce	213 Adams St	Jefferson City	MO	65101	**866-223-6535**	573-634-3616
Lebanon Area Chamber of Commerce	186 N Adams St	Lebanon	MO	65536	**888-588-5710**	417-588-3256
Lee's Summit Chamber of Commerce	220 SE Main St	Lees Summit	MO	64063	**888-816-5757**	816-524-2424
O'Fallon Chamber of Commerce	2145 Bryan Vly Commercial Dr	O'Fallon	MO	63366	**888-349-1897**	636-240-1818
Rolla Area Chamber of Commerce	1311 KingsHwy	Rolla	MO	65401	**888-809-3817**	573-364-3577
Saint Joseph Area Chamber of Commerce	3003 Frederick Ave	Saint Joseph	MO	64506	**800-748-7856**	816-232-4461

Montana

Organization	Address	City	State	ZIP	Toll-Free	Phone
Billings Area Chamber of Commerce	815 S 27th St	Billings	MT	59101	**855-328-9116**	406-245-4111
Butte-Silver Bow Chamber of Commerce	1000 George St	Butte	MT	59701	**800-735-6814**	406-723-3177
Great Falls Area Chamber of Commerce	100 First Ave N	Great Falls	MT	59401	**800-735-8535**	406-761-4434
Helena Area Chamber of Commerce	225 Cruse Ave	Helena	MT	59601	**800-743-5362**	406-442-4120
Missoula Area Chamber of Commerce	825 E Front St	Missoula	MT	59802	**800-814-2342**	406-543-6623

Nebraska

Organization	Address	City	State	ZIP	Toll-Free	Phone
Kearney Area Chamber of Commerce	1007 Second Ave PO Box 607	Kearney	NE	68848	**800-227-8340**	308-237-3101

Nevada

Organization	Address	City	State	ZIP	Toll-Free	Phone
Carson Valley Chamber of Commerce & Visitors Authority	1477 Hwy 395 N Ste A	Gardnerville	NV	89410	**800-727-7677**	775-782-8144
Las Vegas Chamber of Commerce	575 Symphony Park Ave Ste 100	Las Vegas	NV	89105	**888-635-7272**	702-641-5822

New Jersey

Organization	Address	City	State	ZIP	Toll-Free	Phone
Greater Atlantic City Chamber	12 S Virginia Ave	Atlantic City	NJ	08401	**800-123-4567**	609-345-4524
Brick Township Chamber of Commerce	270 Chambers Bridge Rd	Brick	NJ	08723	**877-539-2020**	732-477-4949
Greater Monmouth Chamber of Commerce	57 Schanck Rd Ste C-3	Freehold	NJ	07728	**800-700-6400**	732-462-3030
Newark Regional Business Partnership	744 Broad St 26th Fl	Newark	NJ	07102	**888-337-3339**	973-522-0099
Sussex County Chamber of Commerce	120 Hampton House Rd	Newton	NJ	07860	**844-256-7328**	973-579-1811
Greater Paterson Chamber of Commerce	100 Hamilton Plaza Ste 1201	Paterson	NJ	07505	**800-220-2892**	973-881-7300
Southern Ocean County Chamber of Commerce	265 W Ninth St	Ship Bottom	NJ	08008	**800-292-6372**	609-494-7211
Greater Vineland Chamber of Commerce	2115 S Delsea Dr	Vineland	NJ	08360	**800-922-1766**	856-691-7400

New Mexico

Organization	Address	City	State	ZIP	Toll-Free	Phone
Alamogordo Chamber of Commerce	1301 N White Sands Blvd	Alamogordo	NM	88310	**800-826-0294**	575-437-6120
Clovis/Curry County Chamber of Commerce	105 E Third St	Clovis	NM	88101	**800-261-7656**	575-763-3435
Grants/Cibola County Chamber of Commerce	100 N Iron Ave	Grants	NM	87020	**866-270-5110**	505-287-4802
Hobbs Chamber of Commerce	400 N Marland Blvd	Hobbs	NM	88240	**800-658-6291**	575-397-3202
Roswell Chamber of Commerce	131 W Second St	Roswell	NM	88202	**877-849-7679**	575-623-5695
Silver City-Grant County Chamber of Commerce	201 N Hudson St	Silver City	NM	88061	**800-548-9378**	575-538-3785

New York

Organization	Address	City	State	ZIP	Toll-Free	Phone
Genesee County Chamber of Commerce	210 E Main St	Batavia	NY	14020	**877-788-6846**	585-343-7440
Buffalo Niagara Partnership	665 Main St Ste 200	Buffalo	NY	14203	**844-308-9165**	716-852-7100
St Lawrence County Chamber of Commerce	101 Main St	Canton	NY	13617	**877-228-7810**	315-386-4000
Corning Area Chamber of Commerce	1 W Market St Ste 302	Corning	NY	14830	**866-463-6264**	607-936-4686
Greater East Aurora Chamber of Commerce	652 Main St	East Aurora	NY	14052	**800-441-2881**	716-652-8444
Chemung County Chamber of Commerce	400 E Church St *General	Elmira	NY	14901	**800-627-5892***	607-734-5137
Livingston County Chamber of Commerce	4635 Millennium Dr	Geneseo	NY	14454	**800-538-7365**	585-243-2222
Huntington Township Chamber of Commerce	164 Main St	Huntington	NY	11743	**888-962-9932**	631-423-6100
Tompkins County Chamber of Commerce	904 E Shore Dr	Ithaca	NY	14850	**888-568-9816**	607-273-7080
Queens Chamber of Commerce	75-20 Astoria Blvd Ste 140	Jackson Heights	NY	11370	**800-931-2297**	718-898-8500
Kenmore-Town of Tonawanda Chamber of Commerce	3411 Delaware Ave	Kenmore	NY	14217	**888-710-6626**	716-874-1202
Lewis County Chamber of Commerce	7576 S State St	Lowville	NY	13367	**800-724-0242**	315-376-2213
Herkimer County Chamber of Commerce	28 W Main St	Mohawk	NY	13407	**877-984-4636**	315-866-7820
Dutchess County Regional Chamber of Commerce	1 Civic Ctr Plaza Ste 400	Poughkeepsie	NY	12601	**800-817-2918**	845-454-1700
Saratoga County Chamber of Commerce	28 Clinton St	Saratoga Springs	NY	12866	**855-765-7873**	518-584-3255
Greater Watertown-North Country Chamber of Commerce	1241 Coffeen St	Watertown	NY	13601	**800-924-5145**	315-788-4400

North Carolina

Organization	Address	City	State	ZIP	Toll-Free	Phone
Asheville Area Chamber of Commerce	36 Montford Ave	Asheville	NC	28802	**888-314-1041**	828-258-6101
Black Mountain-Swannanoa Chamber of Commerce	201 E State St	Black Mountain	NC	28711	**800-669-2301**	828-669-2300
Blowing Rock Chamber of Commerce	7738 Vly Blvd	Blowing Rock	NC	28605	**800-295-7851**	828-295-7851
Brevard-Transylvania Chamber of Commerce	175 E Main St	Brevard	NC	28712	**800-648-4523**	828-883-3700
Chapel Hill-Carrboro Chamber of Commerce	104 S Estes Dr	Chapel Hill	NC	27515	**800-694-9784**	919-967-7075
Lake Norman Chamber of Commerce	19900 W Catawba Ave Ste 101	Cornelius	NC	28031	**800-305-2508**	704-892-1922
Gaston Chamber of Commerce	601 W Franklin Blvd	Gastonia	NC	28052	**800-933-3909**	704-864-2621
High Point Chamber of Commerce	1634 N Main St	High Point	NC	27262	**844-704-3663**	336-882-5000
Jacksonville/Onslow Chamber of Commerce	1099 Gum Branch Rd	Jacksonville	NC	28541	**800-877-8339**	910-347-3141
Carteret County Chamber of Commerce	801 Arendell St Ste 1	Morehead City	NC	28557	**800-622-6278**	252-726-6350
Greater Mount Airy Chamber of Commerce	200 N Main St	Mount Airy	NC	27030	**800-948-0949**	336-786-6116
New Bern Area Chamber of Commerce	316 S Front St	New Bern	NC	28560	**877-811-1776**	252-637-3111
Greater Raleigh Chamber of Commerce	PO Box 2978	Raleigh	NC	27602	**888-456-8535**	919-664-7000
Rocky Mount Area Chamber of Commerce	100 Coastline St Ste 200	Rocky Mount	NC	27804	**800-682-6746**	252-446-0323
Brunswick County Chamber of Commerce	4948 Main St	Shallotte	NC	28459	**800-426-6644**	910-754-6644
Jackson County Chamber of Commerce	773 W Main St	Sylva	NC	28779	**800-962-1911**	828-586-2155
Haywood County Chamber of Commerce	28 Walnut St	Waynesville	NC	28786	**877-456-3073**	828-456-3021
Greater Wilmington Chamber of Commerce	1 Estell Lee Pl	Wilmington	NC	28401	**800-829-4477**	910-762-2611
Wilson Chamber of Commerce	200 Nash St NE	Wilson	NC	27893	**855-905-0604**	252-237-0165
Windsor-Bertie Area Chamber of Commerce	121 Granville St PO Box 572	Windsor	NC	27983	**800-334-5010**	252-794-4277
Yadkin County Chamber of Commerce	205 S Jackson St PO Box 1840	Yadkinville	NC	27055	**877-492-3546**	336-679-2200

North Dakota

Organization	Address	City	State	ZIP	Toll-Free	Phone
Grand Forks Chamber of Commerce	202 N Third St	Grand Forks	ND	58203	**855-233-6362**	701-772-7271

Ohio

Organization	Address	City	State	ZIP	Toll-Free	Phone
Athens Area Chamber of Commerce	449 E State St Ste 1	Athens	OH	45701	**877-360-3608**	740-594-2251
Logan County Chamber of Commerce	100 S Main St	Bellefontaine	OH	43311	**877-360-3608**	937-599-5121
Canton Regional Chamber of Commerce	222 Market Ave N	Canton	OH	44702	**800-533-4302**	330-456-7253
Carroll County Chamber of Commerce & Economic Development	61 N Lisbon St PO Box 277	Carrollton	OH	44615	**800-956-4684**	330-627-4811
Greater Cleveland Partnership	1240 Huron Rd E Ste 300	Cleveland	OH	44115	**888-304-4769**	216-621-3300
Columbus Chamber of Commerce	150 S Front St Ste 200	Columbus	OH	43215	**877-771-5202**	614-221-1321
Dayton Area Chamber of Commerce	1 Chamber Plaza Ste 200	Dayton	OH	45402	**800-621-9131**	937-226-1444

Name / Address	City	State	ZIP	Toll-Free	Phone
Hardin County Chamber of Commerce (HCCBA) 225 S Detroit St	Kenton	OH	43326	**888-642-7346**	419-673-4131
Mentor Chamber of Commerce 6972 Spinach Dr	Mentor	OH	44060	**800-292-5707**	440-255-1616
Chamber of Commerce serving Middletown Monroe & Trenton 1500 Central Ave	Middletown	OH	45044	**800-837-3200**	513-422-4551
Milford-Miami Township Chamber of Commerce 983 Lila Ave	Milford	OH	45150	**877-723-0513**	513-831-2411
Napoleon/Henry County Chamber of Commerce 611 N Perry St	Napoleon	OH	43545	**800-322-6849**	419-592-1786
Portsmouth Area Chamber of Commerce 342 Second St PO Box 509	Portsmouth	OH	45662	**800-648-2574**	740-353-7647
Greater Lawrence County Area Chamber of Commerce 216 Collins Ave	South Point	OH	45680	**800-408-1334**	740-377-4550
Adams County Travel & Visitors Bureau 509 E Main St	West Union	OH	45693	**877-232-6764**	937-544-5639
Willougby Area Chamber of Commerce 28 Public Sq	Willoughby	OH	44094	**877-229-4361**	440-942-1632
Youngstown Warren Regional Chamber 11 Central Sq Ste 1600	Youngstown	OH	44503	**877-807-2249**	330-744-2131
Zanesville-Muskingum County Chamber of Commerce 205 N Fifth St	Zanesville	OH	43701	**800-743-2303**	740-455-8282

Oklahoma

Name / Address	City	State	ZIP	Toll-Free	Phone
Greater Enid Chamber of Commerce PO Box 907	Enid	OK	73702	**877-334-2665**	580-237-2494
Greater Muskogee Area Chamber of Commerce PO Box 797	Muskogee	OK	74402	**866-381-6543**	918-682-2401
Ponca City Area Chamber of Commerce 420 E Grand Ave	Ponca City	OK	74601	**866-763-8092**	580-765-4400
Greater Shawnee Area Chamber of Commerce 131 N Bell Ave	Shawnee	OK	74801	**800-762-7695**	405-273-6092
Stillwater Chamber of Commerce 409 S Main St	Stillwater	OK	74075	**800-593-5573**	405-372-5573
Tulsa Metro Chamber 1 West Third St Ste 100	Tulsa	OK	74103	**888-424-9411**	918-585-1201

Oregon

Name / Address	City	State	ZIP	Toll-Free	Phone
Bend Chamber of Commerce 777 NW Wall St	Bend	OR	97701	**800-905-2363**	541-382-3221
Grants Pass Chamber of Commerce 1995 NW Vine St PO Box 970	Grants Pass	OR	97526	**800-547-5927**	541-476-7717
La Grande-Union County Chamber of Commerce 102 Elm St	La Grande	OR	97850	**800-848-9969**	541-963-8588
Greater Newport Chamber of Commerce 555 SW Coast Hwy	Newport	OR	97365	**800-262-7844**	541-265-8801
Portland Business Alliance 200 SW Market St Ste 150	Portland	OR	97201	**800-224-1180**	503-224-8684

Pennsylvania

Name / Address	City	State	ZIP	Toll-Free	Phone
Greater Lehigh Valley Chamber of Commerce 840 Hamilton St Ste 205	Allentown	PA	18101	**800-845-7941**	610-841-5800
Bedford County Chamber of Commerce 137 E Pitt St	Bedford	PA	15522	**800-732-0999**	814-623-2233
Erie Regional Chamber & Growth Partnership 208 E Bayfront Pkwy	Erie	PA	16507	**888-300-3743**	814-454-7191
Lower Bucks County Chamber of Commerce 409 Hood Blvd	Fairless Hills	PA	19030	**800-786-2234**	215-943-7400
Franklin Area Chamber of Commerce (FACC) 1259 Liberty St	Franklin	PA	16323	**888-547-2377**	814-432-5823
Gettysburg-Adams County Area Chamber of Commerce 18 Carlisle St Ste 203	Gettysburg	PA	17325	**800-699-1176**	717-334-8151
Westmoreland Chamber of Commerce 241 Tollgate Hill Rd	Greensburg	PA	15601	**866-468-1231**	724-834-2900
Harrisburg Regional Chamber 3211 N Front St Ste 201	Harrisburg	PA	17110	**877-883-8339**	717-232-4099
Norwin Chamber of Commerce 321 Main St	Irwin	PA	15642	**800-395-5665**	724-863-0888
Greater Johnstown/Cambria County Chamber of Commerce 245 Market St Ste 100	Johnstown	PA	15901	**800-790-4522**	814-536-5107
Southern Chester County Chamber of Commerce 217 W State St	Kennett Square	PA	19348	**800-343-6583**	610-444-0774
Juniata Valley Area Chamber of Commerce 1 W Market St	Lewistown	PA	17044	**866-377-1234**	717-248-6713
Clinton County Economic Partnership 212 N Jay St	Lock Haven	PA	17745	**888-388-6991**	570-748-5782
Monroeville Area Chamber of Commerce 4268 Northern Pike	Monroeville	PA	15146	**800-527-8941**	412-856-0622
Nazareth Area Chamber of Commerce 201 N Main St PO Box 173	Nazareth	PA	18064	**866-776-8240**	610-759-9188
Greater Pittsburgh Chamber of Commerce 425 Sixth Ave Ste 1100	Pittsburgh	PA	15219	**877-392-1300**	412-392-4500
Tri County Area Chamber of Commerce 152 E High St Ste 360	Pottstown	PA	19464	**800-223-8477**	610-326-2900
Schuylkill Chamber of Commerce 91 S Progress Ave	Pottsville	PA	17901	**800-755-1942**	570-622-1942
Upper Bucks Chamber of Commerce 2170 Portzer Rd	Quakertown	PA	18951	**888-942-8257**	215-536-3211
Greater Susquehanna Valley Chamber of Commerce 2859 N Susquehanna Trl PO Box 10	Shamokin Dam	PA	17876	**800-410-2880**	570-743-4100
Shenango Valley Chamber of Commerce 41 Chestnut St	Sharon	PA	16146	**800-732-0993**	724-981-5880
Chamber of Business & Industry of Centre County 200 Innovation Blvd Ste 150	State College	PA	16803	**877-234-5050**	814-234-1829
Fayette Chamber of Commerce 65 W Main St	Uniontown	PA	15401	**800-916-9365**	724-437-4571
Greater Wilkes-Barre Chamber of Business & Industry 2 Public Sq PO Box 5340	Wilkes-Barre	PA	18710	**800-701-8449**	570-823-2101
Williamsport/Lycoming Chamber of Commerce 100 W Third St	Williamsport	PA	17701	**800-732-2258**	570-326-1971

Rhode Island

Name / Address	City	State	ZIP	Toll-Free	Phone
East Bay Chamber of Commerce 16 Cutler St Ste 102	Warren	RI	02885	**877-797-9790**	401-245-0750

South Carolina

Name / Address	City	State	ZIP	Toll-Free	Phone
Anderson Area Chamber of Commerce 907 N Main St Ste 200	Anderson	SC	29621	**800-922-1150**	864-226-3454
Kershaw County Chamber of Commerce 607 S Broad St	Camden	SC	29020	**800-968-4037**	803-432-2525
Laurens County Chamber of Commerce 291 Professional Pk Rd	Clinton	SC	29325	**866-548-9674**	864-833-2716
Georgetown County Chamber of Commerce 531 Front St	Georgetown	SC	29440	**800-777-7705**	843-546-8436
Greater Greenville Chamber of Commerce 24 Cleveland St	Greenville	SC	29601	**866-485-5262**	864-242-1050
Greater Hartsville Chamber of Commerce PO Box 578	Hartsville	SC	29551	**866-747-0060**	843-332-6401
Hilton Head Island-Bluffton Chamber of Commerce 1 Chamber Dr	Hilton Head Island	SC	29928	**800-523-3373**	843-785-3673
Berkeley County Chamber of Commerce PO Box 968	Moncks Corner	SC	29461	**800-882-0337**	843-761-8238
Myrtle Beach Area Chamber of Commerce 1200 N Oak St	Myrtle Beach	SC	29577	**800-356-3016**	843-626-7444
Orangeburg County Chamber of Commerce 155 Riverside Dr SW PO Box 328	Orangeburg	SC	29116	**800-545-6153**	803-534-6821
Union County Chamber of Commerce 135 W Main St	Union	SC	29379	**877-202-8755**	864-427-9039

South Dakota

Name / Address	City	State	ZIP	Toll-Free	Phone
Aberdeen Area Chamber of Commerce 516 S Main St	Aberdeen	SD	57401	**800-874-9038**	605-225-2860
Pierre Area Chamber of Commerce 800 W Dakota Ave	Pierre	SD	57501	**800-962-2034**	605-224-7361

Tennessee

Name / Address	City	State	ZIP	Toll-Free	Phone
Chattanooga Area Chamber of Commerce 811 Broad St	Chattanooga	TN	37402	**877-756-1684**	423-756-2121
Clarksville Area Chamber of Commerce 25 Jefferson St Ste 300	Clarksville	TN	37040	**800-530-2487**	931-647-2331
Cleveland/Bradley Chamber of Commerce 225 Keith St	Cleveland	TN	37311	**800-533-9930**	423-472-6587
Cookeville Area-Putnam County Chamber of Commerce 1 W First St	Cookeville	TN	38501	**800-264-5541**	931-526-2211
Crossville Cumberland County Chamber of Commerce 34 S Main St	Crossville	TN	38555	**877-465-3861**	931-484-8444
Jefferson County Chamber of Commerce 532 Patriot Dr	Dandridge	TN	37725	**877-237-3847**	865-397-9642
Dickson County Chamber of Commerce 119 Hwy 70 E	Dickson	TN	37055	**877-718-4967**	615-446-2349
Fayetteville-Lincoln County Chamber of Commerce 208 S Elk Ave	Fayetteville	TN	37334	**888-433-1238**	931-433-1234
Williamson County-Franklin Chamber of Commerce 5005 Meridian Blvd Ste 150	Franklin	TN	37067	**877-811-0002**	615-771-1912
Jackson Area Chamber of Commerce 197 Auditorium St	Jackson	TN	38301	**866-262-8867**	731-423-2200
Lawrence County Tennessee Chamber of Commerce 25B Public Sqr PO Box 86	Lawrenceburg	TN	38464	**877-388-4911**	931-762-4911
Blount County Chamber of Commerce 201 S Washington St	Maryville	TN	37804	**855-257-3964**	865-983-2241
Memphis Regional Chamber of Commerce 22 N Front St Ste 200	Memphis	TN	38103	**800-829-1040**	901-543-3500
Rutherford County Chamber of Commerce 501 Memorial Blvd	Murfreesboro	TN	37129	**800-716-7560**	615-893-6565
Donelson-Hermitage Chamber of Commerce 125 Donelson Pike PO Box 140200	Nashville	TN	37214	**800-688-9889**	615-883-7896
Paris-Henry County Chamber of Commerce 2508 Eastwood St	Paris	TN	38242	**800-345-1103**	731-642-3431
Shelbyville-Bedford County Chamber of Commerce 100 N Cannon Blvd	Shelbyville	TN	37160	**888-662-2525**	931-684-3482
Claiborne County Chamber of Commerce 1732 Main St Ste 1	Tazewell	TN	37879	**800-332-8164**	423-626-4149

Texas

Name / Address	City	State	ZIP	Toll-Free	Phone
Alvin-Manvel Area Chamber of Commerce 105 W Willis St	Alvin	TX	77511	**888-755-6864**	281-331-3944
Greater Austin Chamber of Commerce 535 E 5th St	Austin	TX	78701	**888-409-5380**	512-478-9383
Washington County Chamber of Commerce 314 S Austin St	Brenham	TX	77833	**888-273-6426**	979-836-3695
Canyon Chamber of Commerce 1518 Fifth Ave	Canyon	TX	79015	**800-999-9481**	806-655-7815
Corsicana Area Chamber of Commerce 120 N 12th St	Corsicana	TX	75110	**866-222-7100**	903-874-4731
Del Rio Chamber of Commerce (DRCoC) 1915 Veterans Blvd *General	Del Rio	TX	78840	**877-218-5117***	830-775-3551
Denton Chamber of Commerce 414 W Pkwy St	Denton	TX	76201	**800-747-2316**	940-382-9693
Eagle Pass Chamber of Commerce 400 E Garrison St	Eagle Pass	TX	78852	**888-355-3224**	830-773-3224
Edinburg Chamber of Commerce 602 W University Dr	Edinburg	TX	78540	**800-800-7214**	956-383-4974
Fort Worth Chamber of Commerce 777 Taylor St Ste 900	Fort Worth	TX	76102	**800-433-5747**	817-336-2491
Grapevine Chamber of Commerce 200 Vine St	Grapevine	TX	76051	**866-322-8667**	817-481-1522

Organization	City	State	ZIP	Toll-Free	Phone
Clear Lake Area Chamber of Commerce 1201 NASA Pkwy	Houston	TX	77058	**800-877-8339**	281-488-7676
Huntsville-Walker County Chamber of Commerce 1327 11th St	Huntsville	TX	77340	**800-289-0389**	936-295-8113
Greater Killeen Chamber of Commerce 1 Santa Fe Plz	Killeen	TX	76540	**866-790-4769**	254-526-9551
Laredo-Webb County Chamber of Commerce 2310 San Bernardo Ave	Laredo	TX	78042	**800-292-2122**	956-722-9895
Longview Partnership 410 N Ctr St	Longview	TX	75601	**800-338-7232**	903-237-4000
Lufkin/Angelina County Chamber of Commerce 1615 S Chestnut St	Lufkin	TX	75901	**800-409-5659**	936-634-6644
Greater Cedar Creek Lake Area Chamber of Commerce 604 S Third St Ste E	Mabank	TX	75147	**800-331-6844**	903-887-3152
Midland Chamber of Commerce 109 N Main St	Midland	TX	79701	**800-624-6435**	432-683-3381
Mineral Wells Area Chamber of Commerce 511 E Hubbard St	Mineral Wells	TX	76067	**800-252-6989**	940-325-2557
New Braunfels Chamber of Commerce 390 S Seguin St	New Braunfels	TX	78130	**800-572-2626**	830-625-2385
Odessa Chamber of Commerce 700 N Grant St Ste 200	Odessa	TX	79761	**800-780-4678**	432-332-9111
Lamar County Chamber of Commerce 1125 Bonham St	Paris	TX	75460	**800-727-4789**	903-784-2501
Pearland Area Chamber of Commerce 6117 Broadway St	Pearland	TX	77581	**888-604-5888**	281-485-3634
Rosenberg-Richmond Area Chamber of Commerce 4120 Ave H	Rosenberg	TX	77471	**877-382-7414**	281-342-5464
Greater San Antonio Chamber of Commerce 602 E Commerce St	San Antonio	TX	78205	**888-828-8680**	210-229-2100
North San Antonio Chamber of Commerce 12930 Country Pkwy	San Antonio	TX	78216	**877-495-5888**	210-344-4848
San Marcos Area Chamber of Commerce 202 N CM Allen Pkwy	San Marcos	TX	78666	**888-200-5620**	512-393-5900
Seguin Area Chamber of Commerce 116 N Camp St	Seguin	TX	78155	**888-674-7224**	830-379-6382
Texarkana Chamber of Commerce 819 N State Line Ave	Texarkana	TX	75501	**877-275-5289**	903-792-7191
Texas City-La Marque Chamber of Commerce 9702 Emmett F Lowry Expy *General	Texas City	TX	77591	**877-986-8719***	409-935-1408
Tyler Area Chamber of Commerce 315 N Broadway Ave	Tyler	TX	75702	**800-235-5712**	903-592-1661
Weatherford Chamber of Commerce 401 Ft Worth St	Weatherford	TX	76086	**888-594-3801**	817-596-3801
Rio Grande Valley Chamber of Commerce 322 S Missouri St	Weslaco	TX	78596	**800-628-5115**	956-968-3141
Weslaco Area Chamber of Commerce 301 W Railroad	Weslaco	TX	78596	**800-700-2443**	956-968-2102

Vermont

Organization	City	State	ZIP	Toll-Free	Phone
Bennington Area Chamber of Commerce 100 Veterans Memorial Dr	Bennington	VT	05201	**800-229-0252**	802-447-3311
Central Vermont Chamber of Commerce 33 Stewart Rd	Berlin	VT	05602	**877-887-3678**	802-229-5711
Brattleboro Area Chamber of Commerce 180 Main St	Brattleboro	VT	05301	**877-254-4565**	802-254-4565
Lake Champlain Regional Chamber of Commerce 60 Main St Ste 100	Burlington	VT	05401	**877-686-5253**	802-863-3489
Vermont's North Country Chamber of Commerce 246 Cswy St	Newport	VT	05855	**800-266-2278**	802-334-7782

Virginia

Organization	City	State	ZIP	Toll-Free	Phone
Pulaski County Chamber of Commerce 4440 Cleburne Blvd Ste B	Dublin	VA	24084	**866-256-8864**	540-674-1991
Greater Augusta Regional Chamber of Commerce 30 Ladd Rd PO Box 1107	Fishersville	VA	22939	**866-922-2514**	540-324-1133
Fredericksburg Regional Chamber of Commerce 2300 Fall Hill Ave Ste 240	Fredericksburg	VA	22401	**888-338-0252**	540-373-9400
Virginia Peninsula Chamber of Commerce 21 Enterprise Pkwy Ste 100	Hampton	VA	23666	**800-462-3204**	757-262-2000
Prince William County-Greater Manassas Chamber of Commerce 9720 Capital Ct Ste 203	Manassas	VA	20110	**877-867-3853**	703-368-6600
Prince William Regional Chamber of Commerce 9720 Capital Ct Ste 203	Manassas	VA	20110	**877-867-3853**	703-368-6600
Martinsville-Henry County Chamber of Commerce 115 Broad St	Martinsville	VA	24112	**800-811-6302**	276-632-6401
Greater Reston Chamber of Commerce 1763 Fountain Dr	Reston	VA	20190	**888-274-2912**	703-707-9045
Roanoke Regional Chamber of Commerce 210 S Jefferson St	Roanoke	VA	24011	**800-924-3543**	540-983-0700
Halifax County Chamber of Commerce PO Box 399	South Boston	VA	24592	**800-283-0098**	434-572-3085
Tazewell Area Chamber of Commerce Tazewell Mall PO Box 6	Tazewell	VA	24651	**855-233-6362**	276-988-5091
Williamsburg Area Chamber of Commerce 421 N Boundary St PO Box 3495	Williamsburg	VA	23187	**800-368-6511**	757-229-6511

Washington

Organization	City	State	ZIP	Toll-Free	Phone
Grays Harbor Chamber of Commerce 506 Duffy St	Aberdeen	WA	98520	**800-321-1924**	360-532-1924
Camas-Washougal Chamber of Commerce 422 NE Fourth Ave	Camas	WA	98607	**800-468-5865**	360-834-2472
Centralia-Chehalis Chamber of Commerce 500 NW Chamber of Commerce Way	Chehalis	WA	98532	**800-525-3323**	360-748-8885
Kent Chamber of Commerce 524 W Meeker St Ste 1	Kent	WA	98032	**800-321-2808**	253-854-1770
Moses Lake Area Chamber of Commerce 324 S Pioneer Way	Moses Lake	WA	98837	**800-992-6234**	509-765-7888
Pullman Chamber of Commerce 415 N Grand Ave	Pullman	WA	99163	**800-365-6948**	509-334-3565
Greater Renton Chamber of Commerce 625 S Fourth St	Renton	WA	98057	**877-467-3686**	425-226-4560
Greater Seattle Chamber of Commerce 1301 Fifth Ave Ste 1500	Seattle	WA	98101	**866-978-2997**	206-389-7200
Shelton-Mason County Chamber of Commerce 215 W Railroad Ave PO Box 2389	Shelton	WA	98584	**800-576-2021**	360-426-2021
Greater Spokane Inc 801 W Riverside Ave Ste 100	Spokane	WA	99201	**800-776-5263**	509-624-1393
Spokane Valley Chamber of Commerce 9507 E Sprague Ave	Spokane Valley	WA	99206	**866-475-1436**	509-924-4994
Southwest King County Chamber of Commerce 14220 Interurban Ave S Ste 134	Tukwila	WA	98168	**800-638-8613**	206-575-1633
Walla Walla Valley Chamber of Commerce 29 E Sumach St	Walla Walla	WA	99362	**866-826-9422**	509-525-0850
Wenatchee Valley Chamber of Commerce 2 S Mission St	Wenatchee	WA	98801	**800-572-7753**	509-662-2116

West Virginia

Organization	City	State	ZIP	Toll-Free	Phone
Beckley-Raleigh County Chamber of Commerce 245 N Kanawha St	Beckley	WV	25801	**877-987-3847**	304-252-7328
Charleston Regional Chamber of Commerce 1116 Smith St	Charleston	WV	25301	**800-792-4326**	304-340-4253
Martinsburg-Berkeley County Chamber of Commerce 198 Viking Way	Martinsburg	WV	25401	**800-332-9007**	304-267-4841
Morgantown Area Chamber of Commerce 1029 University Ave Ste 101 *General	Morgantown	WV	26505	**800-618-2525***	304-292-3311

Wisconsin

Organization	City	State	ZIP	Toll-Free	Phone
Fox Cities Chamber of Commerce & Industry 125 N Superior St	Appleton	WI	54911	**888-249-2587**	920-734-7101
Greater Beloit Chamber of Commerce 500 Public Ave	Beloit	WI	53511	**866-981-5969**	608-365-8835
Chippewa Falls Area Chamber of Commerce 10 S Bridge St	Chippewa Falls	WI	54729	**888-723-0024**	715-723-0331
Fond du Lac Area Assn of Commerce 207 N Main St	Fond du Lac	WI	54935	**800-279-8811**	920-921-9500
Manitowoc-Two Rivers Area Chamber of Commerce 1515 Memorial Dr	Manitowoc	WI	54220	**866-727-5575**	920-684-5575
Greater Menomonie Area Chamber of Commerce 342 E Main St	Menomonie	WI	54751	**800-283-1862**	715-235-9087
Merrill Area Chamber of Commerce 705 N Ctr Ave	Merrill	WI	54452	**877-907-2757**	715-536-9474
Metropolitan Milwaukee Assn of Commerce 756 N Milwaukee St	Milwaukee	WI	53202	**800-362-9472**	414-287-4100
Shawano Country Chamber of Commerce 1263 S Main St	Shawano	WI	54166	**800-235-8528**	715-524-2139
Sheboygan County Chamber of Commerce 621 S Eigth St	Sheboygan	WI	53081	**800-457-9497**	920-457-9491
Portage County Business Council 5501 Vern Holmes Dr	Stevens Point	WI	54481	**800-333-6668**	715-344-1940
Superior-Douglas County Chamber of Commerce 205 Belknap St	Superior	WI	54880	**800-942-5313**	715-394-7716
Waukesha County Chamber of Commerce 2717 N Grandview Blvd Ste 204	Waukesha	WI	53188	**800-727-1344**	262-542-4249
West Allis-West Milwaukee Chamber of Commerce 6737 W Washington St Ste 2141	West Allis	WI	53214	**800-554-1448**	414-302-9901
West Bend Area Chamber of Commerce 304 S Main St	West Bend	WI	53095	**888-338-8666**	262-338-2666

Wyoming

Organization	City	State	ZIP	Toll-Free	Phone
Casper Area Chamber of Commerce 500 N Ctr St	Casper	WY	82601	**866-234-5311**	307-234-5311
Campbell County Chamber of Commerce 314 S Gillette Ave	Gillette	WY	82716	**800-448-7801**	307-682-3673
Laramie Area Chamber of Commerce 800 S Third St	Laramie	WY	82070	**866-876-1012**	307-745-7339
Rock Springs Chamber of Commerce 1897 Dewar Dr	Rock Springs	WY	82901	**800-463-8637**	307-362-3771
Sheridan County Chamber of Commerce 1517 E Fifth St	Sheridan	WY	82801	**800-453-3650**	307-672-2485

139 CHAMBERS OF COMMERCE - US - STATE

Organization	City	State	ZIP	Toll-Free	Phone
Arizona Chamber of Commerce & Industry 3200 N Central Ave Ste 1125	Phoenix	AZ	85012	**866-275-5816**	602-248-9172
Arkansas State Chamber of Commerce 1200 W Capitol Ave PO Box 3645	Little Rock	AR	72203	**800-482-1127**	501-372-2222
Association of Washington Business PO Box 658	Olympia	WA	98507	**800-521-9325**	360-943-1600
Business Council of Alabama 2 N Jackson St Ste 501	Montgomery	AL	36101	**800-665-9647**	334-834-6000
Business Council of New York State Inc 152 Washington Ave	Albany	NY	12210	**800-358-1202**	518-465-7511
Delaware State Chamber of Commerce 1201 N Orange St Ste 200 PO Box 671	Wilmington	DE	19899	**800-292-9507**	302-655-7221
Florida Chamber of Commerce 136 S Bronough St PO Box 11309	Tallahassee	FL	32302	**877-521-1230**	850-521-1200
Georgia Chamber of Commerce 233 Peachtree St NE Ste 2000	Atlanta	GA	30303	**800-241-2286**	404-223-2264
Iowa Assn of Business & Industry 400 E Ct Ave Ste 100	Des Moines	IA	50309	**800-383-4224**	515-280-8000
Kentucky Chamber of Commerce 464 Chenault Rd	Frankfort	KY	40601	**800-533-0127**	502-695-4700
Louisiana Assn of Business & Industry 3113 Vly Creek Dr PO Box 80258	Baton Rouge	LA	70898	**888-816-5224**	225-928-5388
Michigan Chamber of Commerce 600 S Walnut St	Lansing	MI	48933	**800-748-0266**	517-371-2100

Classified Section

Name	Address	City	State	Zip	Toll-Free	Phone
Minnesota Chamber of Commerce	400 Robert St N Ste 1500	Saint Paul	MN	55101	**800-821-2230**	651-292-4650
Mississippi Economic Council	PO Box 23276	Jackson	MS	39225	**800-748-7626**	601-969-0022
Montana Chamber of Commerce	900 Gibbon St PO Box 1730	Helena	MT	59624	**888-442-6668**	406-442-2405
North Dakota Chamber of Commerce	2000 Schafer St PO Box 2639	Bismarck	ND	58502	**800-382-1405**	701-222-0929
Ohio Chamber of Commerce	230 E Town St PO Box 15159	Columbus	OH	43215	**800-533-2794**	614-228-4201
Pennsylvania Chamber of Business & Industry	417 Walnut St	Harrisburg	PA	17101	**800-225-7224**	717-255-3252
South Carolina Chamber of Commerce	1201 Main St Ste1100	Columbia	SC	29201	**800-799-4601**	803-799-4601
South Dakota Chamber of Commerce & Industry	108 N Euclid Ave	Pierre	SD	57501	**800-742-8112**	605-224-6161
Vermont Chamber of Commerce	PO Box 37	Montpelier	VT	05601	**800-451-4279**	802-223-3443
Virginia Chamber of Commerce	919 E Main St	Richmond	VA	23219	**800-228-9290**	804-644-1607
Wisconsin Manufacturers & Commerce	PO Box 352	Madison	WI	53701	**800-236-5414**	608-258-3400

140 CHECK CASHING SERVICES

Name	Address	City	State	Zip	Toll-Free	Phone
ACE Cash Express	1231 Greenway Dr Ste 600	Irving	TX	75038	**800-817-5106**	972-550-5000
Advance America Cash Advance Centers Inc	135 N Church St *NYSE: AEA*	Spartanburg	SC	29306	**800-538-1579**	864-342-5600
Check Cashing Store (CCS)	6340 NW Fifth Way	Fort Lauderdale	FL	33309	**800-361-1407**	
First Cash Financial Services Inc	690 E Lamar Blvd Ste 400 *NASDAQ: FCFS*	Arlington	TX	76011	**800-290-4598**	817-460-3947
Midland Credit Management Inc	8875 Aero Dr Ste 200	San Diego	CA	92123	**800-265-8825**	
Mister Money Investment	2057 Vermont Dr	Fort Collins	CO	80525	**888-336-0403**	800-290-4598
Pay-O-Matic Corp	160 Oak Dr	Syosset	NY	11791	**888-545-6311**	516-496-4900
Policy Research Associates Inc	345 Delaware Ave	Delmar	NY	12054	**800-311-4246**	518-439-7415
QC Holdings Inc	9401 Indian Creek Pkwy Ste 1500 *NASDAQ: QCCO*	Overland Park	KS	66210	**866-660-2243**	
Waterfield Technologies Inc	1 W Third St Ste 1115	Tulsa	OK	74103	**800-324-0936**	918-858-6400

141 CHECKS - PERSONAL & BUSINESS

Name	Address	City	State	Zip	Toll-Free	Phone
4checks.com	8245 N Union Blvd	Colorado Springs	CO	80920	**800-995-9925**	
Artistic Checks Inc	1809 Fashion Ct PO Box 1000	Conyers	GA	30012	**800-243-2577**	800-824-3255
Check Printers Inc	1530 Antioch Pike	Antioch	TN	37013	**800-766-1217**	
Checks In The Mail Inc	2435 Goodwin Ln	New Braunfels	TX	78135	**800-733-4443**	
Checks Unlimited	8245 N Union Blvd	Colorado Springs	CO	80920	**800-210-0468**	719-531-3900
Safeguard Business Systems Inc	8585 N Stemmons Fwy Ste 600 N	Dallas	TX	75247	**800-523-2422**	

CHEMICALS - AGRICULTURAL

SEE Fertilizers & Pesticides

142 CHEMICALS - INDUSTRIAL (INORGANIC)

Name	Address	City	State	Zip	Toll-Free	Phone
Air Liquide America LP	2700 Post Oak Blvd Ste 1800	Houston	TX	77056	**877-855-9533**	
Air Products & Chemicals Inc	7201 Hamilton Blvd *NYSE: APD* ■ *Prod Info	Allentown	PA	18195	**800-345-3148***	610-481-4911
AkzoNobel Surface Chemistry LLC	525 W Van Buren St *Cust Svc	Chicago	IL	60607	**800-937-5449***	312-544-7000
Almatis Inc	501 W Pk Rd	Leetsdale	PA	15056	**800-643-8771**	412-630-2800
Americhem Inc	2000 Americhem Way	Cuyahoga Falls	OH	44221	**800-228-3476**	330-929-4213
Ampacet Corp	660 White Plains Rd *Cust Svc	Tarrytown	NY	10591	**800-888-4267***	914-631-6600
Ashta Chemicals Inc	3509 Middle Rd *Cust Svc	Ashtabula	OH	44004	**800-492-5082***	440-997-5221
BASF Canada	100 Milverton Dr 5th Fl *Cust Svc	Mississauga	ON	L5R4H1	**866-485-2273***	289-360-1300
BASF Corp	100 Campus Dr	Florham Park	NJ	07932	**800-526-1072**	973-245-6000
Bio-Lab Inc	1725 N Brown Rd PO Box 30000	Lawrenceville	GA	30043	**800-859-7946**	678-502-4000
Cabot Corp	2 Seaport Ln Ste 1300 *NYSE: CBT*	Boston	MA	02210	**800-322-1236**	617-345-0100
Calgon Carbon Corp	3000 GSK Dr *NYSE: CCC* ■ *Cust Svc	Moon Township	PA	15108	**800-422-7266***	412-787-6700
Carus Corp	315 Fifth St	Peru	IL	61354	**800-435-6856**	815-223-1500
Centrus Energy Corp	6903 Rockledge Dr Ste 800 *NYSE: USU*	Bethesda	MD	20817	**800-273-7754**	301-564-3200
Chemical Products Corp	102 Old Mill Rd *Cust Svc	Cartersville	GA	30120	**877-210-9814***	770-382-2144
Dow Chemical Co	2030 Dow Ctr *NYSE: DOW* ■ *Cust Svc	Midland	MI	48674	**800-422-8193***	989-636-1463
DuPont Titanium Technologies	1007 Market St	Wilmington	DE	19898	**800-441-7515**	302-774-1000
Elementis Specialties Inc	469 Old Trenton Rd	East Windsor	NJ	08512	**800-866-6800**	
FMC Corp	2929 Walnut St *NYSE: FMC*	Philadelphia	PA	19104	**888-548-4486**	215-299-6000
Green Plains Renewable Energy Inc	450 Regency Pkwy Ste 400 *NASDAQ: GPRE*	Omaha	NE	68114	**877-886-2288**	402-884-8700
Hawkins Inc	3100 E Hennepin Ave *NASDAQ: HWKN*	Minneapolis	MN	55413	**800-328-5460**	612-331-6910
Horsehead Corp	4955 Steubenville Pk Ste 405	Pittsburgh	PA	15205	**800-648-8897**	724-774-1020
Interstate Chemical Co Inc	2797 Freedland Rd	Hermitage	PA	16148	**800-422-2436**	724-981-3771
Jones Hamilton Co	30354 Tracy Rd	Walbridge	OH	43465	**888-858-4425**	419-666-9838
Kanto Corp	13424 N Woodrush Way	Portland	OR	97203	**866-609-5571**	503-283-0405
Keystone Aniline Corp	2501 W Fulton St	Chicago	IL	60612	**800-522-4393**	312-666-2015
Martin Marietta Magnesia Specialties Inc	8140 Corporate Dr Ste 220	Baltimore	MD	21236	**800-648-7400**	410-780-5500
NL Industries	16801 Greenspoint Pk Dr *NYSE: NL*	Houston	TX	77060	**800-866-5600**	281-423-3300
Old Bridge Chemicals Inc	PO Box 175	Old Bridge	NJ	08857	**800-275-3924**	732-727-2225
OMYA Inc	39 Main St	Proctor	VT	05765	**800-451-4468**	802-459-3311
Phibro Animal Health Corp	300 Frank W Burr Blvd Ste 21	Teaneck	NJ	07660	**800-223-0434**	201-329-7300
Plasticolors Inc	2600 Michigan Ave PO Box 816	Ashtabula	OH	44005	**888-661-7675**	440-997-5137
Potash Corp	1101 Skokie Blvd	Northbrook	IL	60062	**800-667-0403**	847-849-4200
Praxair Inc	39 Old Ridgebury Rd *NYSE: PX*	Danbury	CT	06810	**800-772-9247**	203-837-2000
Rutgers Organics Corp (ROC)	201 Struble Rd	State College	PA	16801	**888-469-2188**	814-238-2424
Silberline Mfg Company Inc	130 Lincoln Dr PO Box B	Tamaqua	PA	18252	**800-348-4824**	570-668-6050
Solvay America Inc	3333 Richmond Ave *General	Houston	TX	77098	**800-365-6565***	713-525-6000
Southern Ionics Inc	201 Commerce St	West Point	MS	39773	**800-953-3585**	662-494-3055
Synalloy Corp	775 Spartan Blvd Ste 102 PO Box 5627 *NASDAQ: SYNL* ■ *Orders	Spartanburg	SC	29304	**800-937-5449***	864-585-3605
Tanner Systems Inc	PO Box 488	Saint Joseph	MN	56374	**800-461-6454**	320-363-1800
TETRA Technologies Inc	25025 I-45 N *NYSE: TTI*	The Woodlands	TX	77380	**800-327-7817**	281-367-1983
Texas United Corp	4800 San Felipe	Houston	TX	77056	**800-554-8658**	713-877-2600
UOP LLC	25 E Algonquin Rd	Des Plaines	IL	60017	**800-877-6184**	847-391-2000
Vulcan Materials Co	1200 Urban Ctr Dr PO Box 385014 *NYSE: VMC*	Birmingham	AL	35238	**800-615-4331**	205-298-3000
Westlake Chemical Corp	2801 Post Oak Blvd Ste 600 *NYSE: WLK*	Houston	TX	77056	**888-953-3623**	713-960-9111

143 CHEMICALS - INDUSTRIAL (ORGANIC)

Name	Address	City	State	Zip	Toll-Free	Phone
Ampacet Corp	660 White Plains Rd *Cust Svc	Tarrytown	NY	10591	**800-888-4267***	914-631-6600
Bayer Inc	77 Belfield Rd	Toronto	ON	M9W1G6	**800-622-2937**	416-248-0771
BP PLC	28100 Torch Pkwy *NYSE: BP*	Warrenville	IL	60555	**800-333-3991**	
Cambrex Corp	1 Meadowlands Plz *NYSE: CBM*	East Rutherford	NJ	07073	**866-286-9133**	201-804-3000
Cardolite Corp	500 Doremus Ave	Newark	NJ	07105	**800-322-7365**	
Chemstar Products Co	3915 Hiawatha Ave	Minneapolis	MN	55406	**800-328-5037**	612-722-0079
Chevron Phillips Chemical Company LP	10001 Six Pines Dr	The Woodlands	TX	77380	**800-231-1212**	832-813-4100
Dow Chemical Canada Inc (DCCI)	450 First St SW Ste 2100	Calgary	AB	T2P5H1	**800-447-4369**	403-267-3500
Dow Chemical Co	2030 Dow Ctr *NYSE: DOW* ■ *Cust Svc	Midland	MI	48674	**800-422-8193***	989-636-1463
Dow Corning Corp	PO Box 994 *Cust Svc	Midland	MI	48686	**800-248-2481***	989-496-4000
DSM Chemicals North America Inc	1 Columbia Nitrogen Rd	Augusta	GA	30901	**800-526-0189**	706-849-6600
Eastman Chemical Co	200 S Wilcox Dr *NYSE: EMN* ■ *Cust Svc	Kingsport	TN	37660	**800-327-8626***	423-229-2000
First Chemical Corp	1001 Industrial Rd	Pascagoula	MS	39581	**877-243-6178**	228-762-0870

Company / Address	City	State	ZIP	Toll-Free	Phone
Huntsman Corp 500 Huntsman Way *NYSE: HUN*	Salt Lake City	UT	84108	**888-490-8484**	801-584-5700
ICC Industries Inc 460 Pk Ave	New York	NY	10022	**800-422-1720**	212-521-1700
Inolex Chemical Co 2101 S Swanson St *Cust Svc	Philadelphia	PA	19148	**800-521-9891***	215-271-0800
International Specialty Products Inc (ISP) 1361 Alps Rd	Wayne	NJ	07470	**800-622-4423**	973-628-4000
Methanex Corp 1800 Waterfront Centre 200 Burrard St *TSE: MX*	Vancouver	BC	V6C3M1	**800-661-8851**	604-661-2600
Mitsui Chemicals America Inc 800 Westchester Ave	Rye Brook	NY	10573	**800-972-7252**	914-253-0777
National Enzyme Co Inc 15366 US Hwy 160	Forsyth	MO	65653	**800-825-8545**	417-546-4796
Niacet Corp 400 47th St	Niagara Falls	NY	14304	**800-828-1207**	716-285-1474
Oakwood Products Inc 1741 Old Dunbar Rd	West Columbia	SC	29172	**800-467-3386**	803-739-8800
Pencco Inc 831 Bartlett Rd PO Box 600	San Felipe	TX	77473	**800-864-1742**	979-885-0005
Perstorp Polyols Inc 600 Matzinger Rd *Cust Svc	Toledo	OH	43612	**800-537-0280***	419-729-5448
PMC Specialties Group Inc 501 Murray Rd	Cincinnati	OH	45217	**800-543-2466**	513-242-3300
RT Vanderbilt Company Inc 30 Winfield St *Cust Svc	Norwalk	CT	06855	**800-243-6064***	203-853-1400
Selee Corp 700 Shepherd St	Hendersonville	NC	28792	**800-842-3818**	828-697-2411
Shin-Etsu Silicones of America 1150 Damar Dr	Akron	OH	44305	**800-544-1745**	330-630-9860
Struktol Company of America Inc PO Box 1649	Stow	OH	44224	**800-327-8649**	330-928-5188
Sun Chemical Corp 35 Waterview Blvd	Parsippany	NJ	07054	**800-543-2323**	973-404-6000
Sunoco Chemicals 1735 Market St Ste LL	Philadelphia	PA	19103	**800-786-6261**	215-977-3000
Sunoco Inc 1735 Market St Ste LL *NYSE: SUN*	Philadelphia	PA	19103	**800-786-6261**	215-977-3000
Synalloy Corp 775 Spartan Blvd Ste 102 PO Box 5627 *NASDAQ: SYNL* ■ *Orders	Spartanburg	SC	29304	**800-937-5449***	864-585-3605
Tedia Company Inc 1000 Tedia Way	Fairfield	OH	45014	**800-787-4891**	513-874-5340
Velsicol Chemical Corp 10400 W Higgins Rd Ste 700 *Cust Svc	Rosemont	IL	60018	**877-847-8351***	847-813-7888
Vulcan Materials Co 1200 Urban Ctr Dr PO Box 385014 *NYSE: VMC*	Birmingham	AL	35238	**800-615-4331**	205-298-3000
Wacker Chemical Corp 3301 Sutton Rd	Adrian	MI	49221	**888-922-5374**	517-264-8500
Wausau Chemical Corp 2001 N River Dr	Wausau	WI	54403	**800-950-6656**	715-842-2285

144 CHEMICALS - SPECIALTY

Company / Address	City	State	ZIP	Toll-Free	Phone
ADA-ES Inc 9135 S Ridgeline Blvd Ste 200 *NASDAQ: ADES*	Highlands Ranch	CO	80129	**888-822-8617**	303-734-1727
Airosol Company Inc 1206 Illinois St	Neodesha	KS	66757	**800-633-9576**	620-325-2666
Akzo Nobel Chemicals Inc 10 Finderne Ave	Bridgewater	NJ	08807	**888-331-6212**	
Alex C Fergusson LLC (AFCO) 5000 Letterkenny Rd	Chambersburg	PA	17201	**800-345-1329**	
Alfa Aesar Co 26 Parkridge Rd	Ward Hill	MA	01835	**800-343-0660**	978-521-6300
American Polywater Corp 11222 60th St N	Stillwater	MN	55082	**800-328-9384**	651-430-2270
American Radiolabeled Chemicals Inc (ARC) 101 ARC Dr	Saint Louis	MO	63146	**800-331-6661**	314-991-4545
AMPAC Fine Chemicals (AFC) MS 1007 PO Box 1718	Rancho Cordova	CA	95741	**800-311-9668**	916-357-6880
Anderson Chemical Co 325 S Davis	Litchfield	MN	55355	**800-366-2477**	320-693-2477
Angstrom Technologies Inc 7880 Foundation Dr *Cust Svc	Florence	KY	41042	**800-543-7358***	859-282-0020
Arch Chemicals Inc 1200 Old Lower River Rd PO Box 800 *NYSE: ARJ*	Charleston	TN	37310	**800-638-8174**	423-780-2724
Athea Laboratories Inc 1900 W Cornell St	Milwaukee	WI	53209	**800-743-6417**	
Baker Hughes Inc Baker Petrolite Div 12645 W Airport Blvd	Sugar Land	TX	77478	**800-231-3606**	281-276-5400
Birchwood Laboratories Inc 7900 Fuller Rd	Eden Prairie	MN	55344	**800-328-6156**	952-937-7900
Brulin & Company Inc 2920 Dr AJ Brown Ave	Indianapolis	IN	46205	**800-776-7149**	317-923-3211
Buckman Laboratories Inc 1256 N McLean Blvd	Memphis	TN	38108	**800-282-5626**	901-278-0330
Cabot Corp 2 Seaport Ln Ste 1300 *NYSE: CBT*	Boston	MA	02210	**800-322-1236**	617-345-0100
Cabot Microelectronics Corp 870 N Commons Dr *NASDAQ: CCMP*	Aurora	IL	60504	**800-811-2756**	630-375-6631
Cabot Specialty Fluids Inc Waterway Plaza Two 10001 Woodlock Forest Dr Ste 275	The Woodlands	TX	77380	**800-322-1236**	281-298-9955
Cambridge Isotope Laboratories Inc 3 Highwood Dr	Tewksbury	MA	01876	**800-322-1174**	978-749-8000
Chemtronics Inc 8125 Cobb Centre Dr	Kennesaw	GA	30152	**800-645-5244**	770-424-4888
Claire Manufacturing Co 1005 S Westgate Ave *Sales	Addison	IL	60101	**800-252-4731***	630-543-7600
Columbian Chemicals Co 1800 W Oak Commons Ct	Marietta	GA	30062	**800-235-4003**	770-792-9400
Coral Chemical Co 1915 Industrial Ave	Zion	IL	60099	**800-228-4646**	847-246-6666
Cortec Corp 4119 White Bear Pkwy	Saint Paul	MN	55110	**800-426-7832**	651-429-1100
CPC Aeroscience Inc 2700 SW 14th St *Cust Svc	Pompano Beach	FL	33069	**800-327-1835***	
CRC Industries Inc 885 Louis Dr *Cust Svc	Warminster	PA	18974	**800-556-5074***	215-674-4300
Cytec Industries Inc 5 Garret Mtn Plz *NYSE: CYT*	West Paterson	NJ	07424	**800-652-6013**	973-357-3100
Delta Chemical Corp 2601 Cannery Ave	Baltimore	MD	21226	**800-282-5322**	410-354-0100
Diversified Chemical Technologies Inc (DCT) 15477 Woodrow Wilson St	Detroit	MI	48238	**800-243-1424**	313-867-5444
Dober Chemical Group 11230 Katherine Crossing Ste 100	Woodridge	IL	60517	**800-323-4983**	630-410-7300
Dover Chemical Corp 3676 Davis Rd NW *General	Dover	OH	44622	**800-321-8805***	330-343-7711
DSM Desotech Inc 1122 St Charles St	Elgin	IL	60120	**800-222-7189**	847-697-0400
DuPont Chemical Solutions 1007 Market St	Wilmington	DE	19898	**800-441-7515**	302-774-1000
Dynaloy LLC 6445 Olivia Ln	Indianapolis	IN	46226	**800-669-5709**	317-788-5694
Elantas PDG Inc 5200 N Second St	Saint Louis	MO	63147	**800-325-7492**	314-621-5700
Enthone Inc 350 Frontage Rd	West Haven	CT	06516	**800-431-2200**	203-934-8611
Excelda Manufacturing Co 12785 Emerson Dr	Brighton	MI	48116	**877-486-3801**	248-486-3800
Frac Tech Services LLC 301 E 18th St	Cisco	TX	76437	**866-877-1008**	817-850-1008
Fremont Industries Inc 4400 Vly Industrial Blvd N PO Box 67	Shakopee	MN	55379	**800-436-1238**	952-445-4121
GE Betz 4636 Somerton Rd *Cust Svc	Trevose	PA	19053	**866-439-2837***	215-355-3300
Genieco Inc 200 N Laflin St	Chicago	IL	60607	**800-223-8217**	312-421-2383
Gold Eagle Co 4400 S Kildare Ave	Chicago	IL	60632	**800-367-3245**	
Grace Davison 7500 Grace Dr	Columbia	MD	21044	**800-638-6014**	410-531-4000
Honeywell 101 Columbia Rd	Morristown	NJ	07960	**800-822-7673**	973-455-2000
Honeywell Fluorine Products 101 Columbia Rd	Morristown	NJ	07962	**800-951-1527**	973-455-2000
Houghton Chemical Corp 52 Cambridge St	Allston	MA	02134	**800-777-2466**	617-254-1010
International Chemical Co 2628 N Mascher St	Philadelphia	PA	19133	**888-225-5422**	215-739-2313
JM Huber Corp 499 Thornall St 8th Fl	Edison	NJ	08837	**877-418-0038**	732-549-8600
Kao Specialties Americas LLC 243 Woodbine St PO Box 2316	High Point	NC	27261	**800-727-2214**	336-884-2214
Kester Inc 800 W Thorndale Ave	Itasca	IL	60143	**800-253-7837**	630-616-4000
KIK Custom Products 2730 Middlebury St	Elkhart	IN	46516	**800-479-6603**	574-295-0000
KIK Pool Additives Inc 5160 E Airport Dr	Ontario	CA	91761	**800-745-4536**	909-390-9912
King Industries Inc 1 Science Rd	Norwalk	CT	06852	**800-431-7900**	203-866-5551
Kolene Corp 12890 Westwood Ave	Detroit	MI	48223	**800-521-4182**	313-273-9220
Koppers Inc 436 Seventh Ave *NYSE: KOP*	Pittsburgh	PA	15219	**800-385-4406**	412-227-2001
Kronos Worldwide Inc 5430 LBJ Freeway Ste 1700 *NYSE: KRO*	Houston	TX	75240	**800-866-5600**	281-423-3300
Leadership Performance Sustainability Laboratories 4647 Hugh Howell Rd	Tucker	GA	30084	**800-241-8334**	
Lloyd Laboratories Inc 24 Fitch Ct	Wakefield	MA	01880	**800-361-6766**	781-224-0083
Lubrizol Corp 29400 Lakeland Blvd *NYSE: LZ*	Wickliffe	OH	44092	**800-380-5397**	440-943-4200
McGean-Rohco Inc 2910 Harvard Ave *Orders	Cleveland	OH	44105	**800-932-7006***	216-441-4900
Miller-Stephenson Chemical Co 55 Backus Ave *Tech Supp	Danbury	CT	06810	**800-992-2424***	203-743-4447
Momar Inc 1830 Ellsworth Industrial Dr	Atlanta	GA	30318	**800-556-3967**	404-355-4580
Monroe Fluid Technology Inc 36 Draffin Rd	Hilton	NY	14468	**800-828-6351**	585-392-3434
Montello Inc 6106 E 32nd Pl Ste 100	Tulsa	OK	74135	**800-331-4628**	
Nalco Co 1601 W Diehl Rd	Naperville	IL	60563	**800-288-0879**	630-305-1000
Nox-Crete Inc 1444 S 20th St	Omaha	NE	68108	**800-669-2738**	402-341-2080

Classified Section

Company	Address	City	State	Zip	Toll-Free	Phone
OM Group Inc	811 Sharon Dr	Westlake	OH	44145	**800-519-0083**	440-899-2950
NYSE: OMG						
OMNOVA Solutions Inc Performance Chemicals Div	165 S Cleveland Ave	Mogadore	OH	44260	**888-253-5454**	330-628-6536
Pacific Ethanol Corp	400 Capitol Mall Ste 2060	Sacramento	CA	95814	**866-508-4969**	916-403-2123
NASDAQ: PEIX						
Pavco Inc	1935 John Crosland Jr Dr	Charlotte	NC	28208	**800-321-7735***	704-496-6800
*Orders						
Peach State Labs Inc (PSL)	180 Burlington Rd PO Box 1087	Rome	GA	30162	**800-634-1653**	706-291-8743
Penray Cos Inc	440 Denniston Ct	Wheeling	IL	60090	**800-373-6729**	847-459-5000
Precision Laboratories Inc	1429 S Shields Dr	Waukegan	IL	60085	**800-323-6280**	847-596-3001
Premier Colors Inc	100 Industrial Dr	Union	SC	29379	**800-245-6944**	864-427-0338
PVS Chemicals Inc	10900 Harper Ave	Detroit	MI	48213	**800-932-8860**	313-921-1200
Quaker Chemical Corp	901 Hector St	Conshohocken	PA	19428	**800-523-7010**	610-832-4000
NYSE: KWR						
Radiator Specialty Co	1900 Wilkinson Blvd	Charlotte	NC	28208	**877-464-4865**	704-688-2405
Rochester Midland Corp	333 Hollenbeck St	Rochester	NY	14621	**800-836-1627**	585-336-2200
SA Day Mfg Co Inc	1489 Niagara St	Buffalo	NY	14213	**800-747-0030**	716-881-3030
Sigma-Aldrich Corp	3050 Spruce St	Saint Louis	MO	63103	**800-325-3010**	314-771-5765
NASDAQ: SIAL						
Sika Corp	201 Polito Ave	Lyndhurst	NJ	07071	**800-933-7452**	201-933-8800
Solutek Corp	94 Shirley St	Boston	MA	02119	**800-403-0770**	617-445-5335
Spartan Chemical Company Inc	1110 Spartan Dr	Maumee	OH	43537	**800-537-8990**	419-531-5551
Specco Industries Inc	13087 Main St	Lemont	IL	60439	**800-441-6646**	630-257-5060
Sprayway Inc	1005 S Westgate Ave	Addison	IL	60101	**800-332-9000**	630-628-3000
Stapleton Technologies Inc	1350 W 12th St	Long Beach	CA	90813	**800-266-0541**	562-437-0541
Stepan Co	22 W Frontage Rd	Northfield	IL	60093	**800-745-7837***	847-446-7500
*Cust Svc						
Technical Chemical Co	3327 Pipeline Rd	Cleburne	TX	76033	**800-527-0885**	817-645-6088
United Color Manufacturing Inc (UCM)	PO Box 480	Newtown	PA	18940	**800-852-5942**	215-860-2165
United Laboratories Inc	320 37th Ave	Saint Charles	IL	60174	**800-323-2594**	
United Salt Corp	4800 San Felipe St	Houston	TX	77056	**800-554-8658**	713-877-2600
Vertellus Specialties Inc	201 N Illinois St Ste 1800	Indianapolis	IN	46204	**800-777-3536**	317-247-8141
Watcon Inc	2215 S Main St	South Bend	IN	46613	**800-492-8266**	574-287-3397
WR Grace & Co	7500 Grace Dr	Columbia	MD	21044	**800-638-6014**	410-531-4000
NYSE: GRA						
XL Brands	198 Nexus Dr	Dalton	GA	30721	**800-367-4583**	706-272-5800
Zinkan Enterprises Inc	1919 Case Pkwy N	Twinsburg	OH	44087	**800-229-6801**	

145 CHEMICALS & RELATED PRODUCTS - WHOL

Company	Address	City	State	Zip	Toll-Free	Phone
Airgas Inc	259 N Radnor-Chester Rd Ste 100	Radnor	PA	19087	**800-255-2165**	610-687-5253
NYSE: ARG						
Americas Styrenics LLC	24 Waterway Ave Ste 1200	Woodlands	TX	77380	**844-512-1212**	
Aquatic Informatics Inc	570 Granville St Ste 1100	Vancouver	BC	V6C3P1	**877-870-2782**	604-873-2782
Aramsco Inc	1480 Grandview Ave	Paulsboro	NJ	08086	**800-767-6933**	856-686-7700
Astro Chemicals Inc	126 Memorial Dr	Springfield	MA	01104	**800-223-0776**	413-781-7240
Barton Solvents Inc	1920 NE Broadway Ave	Des Moines	IA	50313	**800-728-6488**	515-265-7998
Berryman Products Inc	3800 E Randol Mill Rd	Arlington	TX	76011	**800-433-1704**	817-640-2376
Brenntag Canada Inc	35 Vulcan St	Rexdale	ON	M9W1L3	**866-516-9707**	416-243-9615
Brenntag Southwest Inc	610 Fisher Rd	Longview	TX	75604	**800-945-4528**	903-759-7151
Brown Machine LLC	330 N Ross St	Beaverton	MI	48612	**877-702-4142**	989-435-7741
Connell Bros Co Ltd	345 California St 27th Fl	San Francisco	CA	94104	**800-210-9839**	415-772-4000
Coolant Control Inc	5353 Spring Grove Ave	Cincinnati	OH	45217	**800-535-3885**	513-471-8770
Dar-tech Inc	16485 Rockside Rd	Cleveland	OH	44137	**800-228-7347**	216-663-7600
DB Becker Company Inc	46 Leigh St	Clinton	NJ	08809	**800-394-3991**	908-730-6010
Denso North America Inc	9747 Whithorn Dr	Houston	TX	77095	**888-821-2300**	281-821-3355
DM Figley Company Inc	10 Kelly Ct	Menlo Park	CA	94025	**800-292-9919**	650-329-8700
Dorsett & Jackson Inc	3800 Noakes St	Los Angeles	CA	90023	**800-871-8365**	323-268-1815
Durr Marketing Assoc Inc	PO Box 17600	Pittsburgh	PA	15235	**800-937-3877**	
Ellsworth Corp	PO Box 1002	Germantown	WI	53022	**877-454-9224**	262-253-8600
ET Horn Co	16050 Canary Ave	La Mirada	CA	90638	**800-442-4676**	714-523-8050
EW Kaufmann Co	140 Wharton Rd	Bristol	PA	19007	**800-635-5358**	215-364-0240
Gallade Chemical Inc	1230 E St Gertrude Pl	Santa Ana	CA	92707	**888-830-9092**	714-546-9901
General Air Service & Supply Company Inc	1105 Zuni St	Denver	CO	80204	**877-782-8434**	303-892-7003
George S Coyne Chemical Co	3015 State Rd	Croydon	PA	19021	**800-523-1230**	215-785-3000
Haviland Enterprises Inc	421 Ann St NW	Grand Rapids	MI	49504	**800-456-1134**	616-361-6691
Hill Bros Chemical Co	1675 N Main St	Orange	CA	92867	**800-994-8801**	714-998-8800
HM Royal Inc	689 Pennington Ave	Trenton	NJ	08618	**800-257-9452**	609-396-9176
Hubbard-Hall Inc	563 S Leonard St	Waterbury	CT	06708	**800-331-6871**	203-756-5521
Hydrite Chemical Co	300 N Patrick Blvd	Brookfield	WI	53045	**800-543-4560**	262-792-1450
ICC Chemical Corp	460 Pk Ave	New York	NY	10022	**800-422-1720**	212-521-1700
Ideal Chemical & Supply Co	4025 Air Pk St	Memphis	TN	38118	**800-232-6776**	901-363-7720
Independent Chemical Corp	79-51 Cooper Ave	Glendale	NY	11385	**800-892-2578**	718-894-0700
Industrial Chemicals Inc	2042 Montreat Dr	Vestavia	AL	35216	**800-476-2042***	205-823-7330
*Cust Svc						
John R Hess & Company Inc	400 Stn St PO Box 3615	Cranston	RI	02910	**800-828-4377**	401-785-9300
John R White Company Inc	PO Box 10043	Birmingham	AL	35202	**800-245-1183**	205-595-8381
KA Steel Chemicals Inc	15185 Main St PO Box 729	Lemont	IL	60439	**800-677-8335**	630-257-3900
Kraft Chemical Co	1975 N Hawthorne Ave	Melrose Park	IL	60160	**800-345-5200**	708-345-5200
LV Lomas Ltd	99 Summerlea Rd	Brampton	ON	L6T4V2	**800-575-3382**	905-458-1555
Maroon Inc	1390 Jaycox Rd	Avon	OH	44011	**877-627-6661***	440-937-1000
*General						
McCullough & Assoc	1746 NE Expy PO Box 29803	Atlanta	GA	30329	**800-969-1606**	404-325-1606
NuCo2 Inc	2800 SE Marketplace	Stuart	FL	34997	**800-472-2855**	772-221-1754
Pain Enterprises Inc	101 Daniels Way	Bloomington	IN	47404	**800-245-8583**	
Palmer Holland Inc	25000 Country Club Blvd Ste 444	North Olmsted	OH	44070	**800-635-4822**	
Pidilite USA Inc	401 Maplewood Dr Ste 18	Jupiter	FL	33458	**800-843-7813**	561-775-9600
Plaza Group Inc	10375 Richmond Ave Ste 1620	Houston	TX	77042	**800-876-3738**	713-266-0707
Pride Solvents & Chemical Co of New York Inc	6 Long Island Ave	Holtsville	NY	11742	**800-424-8802**	631-758-0200
Quadra Chemicals Ltd	3901 Fixtessier	Vaudreuil-Dorion	QC	J7V5V5	**800-665-6553**	450-424-0161
Reagent Chemical & Research Inc	115 Rt 202	Ringoes	NJ	08551	**800-231-1807**	908-284-2800
Ribelin Sales Inc	3857 Miller Pk Dr	Garland	TX	75042	**800-374-1594**	972-272-1594
Rowell Chemical Corp	15 Salt Creek Ln Ste 205	Hinsdale	IL	60521	**888-261-7963**	630-920-8833
SARCOM Inc AEP Colloids Div	6299 Rt 9N	Hadley	NY	12835	**800-848-0658**	518-696-9900
Shamrock Technologies Inc	Foot Of Pacific St	Newark	NJ	07114	**800-349-1822**	973-242-2999
Solmax International Inc	2801 Marie-Victorin Blvd	Varennes	QC	J3X1P7	**800-571-3904**	450-929-1234
Solvents & Chemicals Inc	1904 Mykawa Rd	Pearland	TX	77581	**800-622-3990**	281-485-5377
Specified Technologies Inc	210 Evans Way	Somerville	NJ	08876	**800-992-1180**	908-526-8000
Spectra Colors Corp	25 Rizzolo Rd	Kearny	NJ	07032	**800-527-8588**	201-997-0606
Strem Chemicals Inc	7 Mulliken Way	Newburyport	MA	01950	**800-647-8736**	978-499-1600
Tanner Industries Inc	735 Davisville Rd 3rd Fl	SouthHampton	PA	18966	**800-643-6226**	215-322-1238
Tarr LLC	2429 N Borthwick St	Portland	OR	97227	**800-422-5069**	
TCR Industries	26 Centerpointe Dr Ste 120	La Palma	CA	90623	**877-827-1444**	714-521-5222
Tilley Chemical Company Inc	501 Chesapeake Pk Plz	Baltimore	MD	21220	**800-638-6968**	410-574-4500
TransChemical Inc	419 De Soto Ave	Saint Louis	MO	63147	**888-873-6481**	314-231-6905
Univar Canada Ltd	9800 Van Horne Way	Richmond	BC	V6X1W5	**855-888-8648**	604-273-1441
Univar USA Inc	17425 NE Union Hill Rd	Redmond	WA	98052	**855-888-8648**	425-889-3400
Whitaker Oil Co	1557 Marietta Rd NW	Atlanta	GA	30318	**888-895-3506**	404-355-8220
Wilson Industrial Sales Company Inc	201 S Wilson	Brook	IN	47922	**800-633-5427**	219-275-7333

146 CHILD CARE MONITORING SYSTEMS - INTERNET

Company	Address	City	State	Zip	Toll-Free	Phone
Mississippi Action For Progress Inc (MAP)	1751 Morson Rd	Jackson	MS	39209	**800-924-4615**	601-923-4100

147 CHILDREN'S LEARNING CENTERS

Company	Address	City	State	Zip	Toll-Free	Phone
Autistic Treatment Center Inc	10503 Metric Dr	Dallas	TX	75243	**877-666-2747**	972-644-2076

Company / Address	City	State	ZIP	Toll-Free	Phone
Bright Horizons Family Solutions LLC 200 Talcott Ave S	Watertown	MA	02472	**800-324-4386**	617-673-8000
Child Development Assoc Inc 678 Third Ave Ste 201	Chula Vista	CA	91910	**888-755-2445**	619-427-4411
Childcare Network Inc 3025 University Ave Ste B-2	Columbus	GA	31907	**866-521-5437**	706-562-8600
Computer Explorers 12715 Telge Rd	Cypress	TX	77429	**800-531-5053**	
DePelchin Children's Ctr 4950 Memorial Dr	Houston	TX	77007	**888-730-2335**	713-730-2335
FasTracKids International Ltd 6900 E Belleview Ave Ste 100	Greenwood Village	CO	80111	**888-576-6888**	303-224-0200
Goddard Systems Inc 1016 W Ninth Ave	King of Prussia	PA	19406	**800-463-3273**	610-265-8510
Golflogix Inc 15685 N Greenway-Hayden Loop Ste 100A	Scottsdale	AZ	85260	**877-977-0162**	
Huntington Learning Centers Inc 496 Kinderkamack Rd	Oradell	NJ	07649	**800-653-8400**	201-261-8400
KinderCare Learning Centers Inc 650 NE Holladay St Ste 1400 PO Box 6760	Portland	OR	97232	**800-633-1488**	
Kumon North America Inc 300 Frank W Burr Blvd Glenpointe Ctr E Ste 6	Teaneck	NJ	07666	**800-222-6284**	201-928-0444
Lad Lake Inc W350s1401 Waterville Rd	Dousman	WI	53118	**877-965-2131**	262-965-2131
Learning Care Group Inc 21333 Haggerty Rd Ste 300	Novi	MI	48375	**877-817-3883**	248-697-9000
New Horizon Kids Quest Inc 3405 Annapolis Ln N Ste 100	Plymouth	MN	55447	**800-941-1007**	
Pioneer Clubs 123 E Elk	Carol Stream	IL	60188	**800-694-2582**	
Primrose School Franchising Co 3660 Cedarcrest Rd	Acworth	GA	30101	**800-745-0677**	770-529-4100
Rosedale Technical Institute 215 Beecham Dr Ste 2	Pittsburgh	PA	15205	**800-521-6262**	412-521-6200
Rural Resources Community Action 956 S Main St	Colville	WA	99114	**800-538-7659**	509-684-8421
Sky Ranch 24657 CR 448	Van	TX	75790	**800-962-2267**	903-266-3300
Tiger Schulmann's Karate Ctr 485 Blvd	Elmwood Park	NJ	07407	**800-867-1218**	

148 CIRCUS, CARNIVAL, FESTIVAL OPERATORS

Company / Address	City	State	ZIP	Toll-Free	Phone
Big Apple Circus 1 Metrotech Ctr 3rd Fl	Brooklyn	NY	11201	**800-922-3772**	212-268-2500
Chippendales USA LLC 4 ExpressWay Plz Ste 218	Roslyn Heights	NY	11577	**866-244-7999**	516-454-0981
Cirque du Soleil Inc 8400 Second Ave	Montreal	QC	H1Z4M6	**800-678-2119**	514-722-2324
Maryland Renaissance Festival PO Box 315	Crownsville	MD	21032	**800-296-7304**	410-266-7304
Starkey International Institute for Household Management Inc, The 1350 Logan St	Denver	CO	80203	**800-888-4904**	303-832-5510

149 CLAY PRODUCTS - STRUCTURAL

SEE ALSO Brick, Stone, Related Materials

Company / Address	City	State	ZIP	Toll-Free	Phone
Acme Brick Co 3024 Acme Brick Plaza	Fort Worth	TX	76109	**866-430-2263**	817-332-4101
Boral Bricks Inc 9143 Bob Williams Pkwy	Covington	GA	30014	**800-526-7255**	678-625-4051
Cherokee Brick & Tile Co Inc 3250 Waterville Rd	Macon	GA	31206	**800-277-2745**	478-781-6800
Colloid Environmental Technologies Co (CETCO) 2870 Forbs Ave	Hoffman Estates	IL	60192	**800-527-9948**	847-851-1899
Cunningham Brick Co Inc 701 N Main St	Lexington	NC	27292	**800-672-6181**	336-248-8541
General Shale Products LLC 3015 Bristol Hwy	Johnson City	TN	37601	**800-414-4661**	423-282-4661
Henry Brick Co Inc 3409 Water Ave	Selma	AL	36703	**800-218-3906**	334-875-2600
International Chimney Corp 55 S Long St	Williamsville	NY	14221	**800-828-1446**	
Kinney Brick Co 100 Prosperity Rd PO Box 1804	Albuquerque	NM	87103	**800-464-4605**	505-877-4550
Lee Brick & Tile Co 3704 Hawkins Ave PO Box 1027	Sanford	NC	27330	**800-672-7559**	919-774-4800
Logan Clay Products Co 201 S Walnut St	Logan	OH	43138	**800-848-2141**	
Ludowici Roof Tile Inc 4757 Tile Plant Rd PO Box 69 *Cust Svc	New Lexington	OH	43764	**800-945-8453***	740-342-1995
Marion Ceramics Inc PO Box 1134	Marion	SC	29571	**800-845-4010**	843-423-1311
McNear Brick & Block 1 McNear BrickyaRd Rd PO Box 151380	San Rafael	CA	94901	**888-442-6811**	415-453-7702
Mutual Materials Co 605 119th Ave NE	Bellevue	WA	98005	**800-477-3008**	425-452-2300
Old Virginia Brick Co 2500 W Main St	Salem	VA	24153	**800-879-8227**	540-389-2357
Palmetto Brick Co 3501 BrickyaRd Rd	Wallace	SC	29596	**800-922-4423**	843-537-7861
Pine Hall Brick Co 2701 Shorefair Dr	Winston-Salem	NC	27116	**800-334-8689**	
Redland Brick Inc 15718 Clear Spring Rd	Williamsport	MD	21795	**800-366-2742**	301-223-7700
Statesville Brick Co 391 BrickyaRd Rd	Statesville	NC	28677	**800-522-4716**	704-872-4123
Superior Clay Corp 6566 Superior Rd SE	Uhrichsville	OH	44683	**800-848-6166**	740-922-4122

150 CLEANING PRODUCTS

SEE ALSO Brushes & Brooms ; Mops, Sponges, Wiping Cloths

Company / Address	City	State	ZIP	Toll-Free	Phone
ABC Compounding Company Inc & Acme Wholesale 6970 Jonesboro Rd	Morrow	GA	30260	**800-795-9222**	770-968-9222
American Cleaning Solutions 39-30 Review Ave	Long Island	NY	11101	**888-929-7587**	718-392-8080
Arrow-Magnolia International 2646 Rodney Ln	Dallas	TX	75229	**800-527-2101**	972-247-7111
Aztec International Inc 3010 Henson Rd	Knoxville	TN	37921	**800-369-5357**	865-588-5357
BAF Industries Inc 1451 Edinger Ave	Tustin	CA	92780	**800-437-9893**	714-258-8055
Buckeye International Inc 2700 Wagner Pl	Maryland Heights	MO	63043	**800-321-2583**	314-291-1900
Bullen Cos 1640 Delmar Dr PO Box 37	Folcroft	PA	19032	**800-444-8900**	610-534-8900
Camco Chemical Co 8145 Holton Dr *Cust Svc	Florence	KY	41042	**800-354-1001***	859-727-3200
Canberra Corp 3610 Holland Sylvania Rd	Toledo	OH	43615	**800-832-8992**	419-841-6616
Carroll Co 2900 W Kingsley Rd	Garland	TX	75041	**800-527-5722**	972-278-1304
Cello Professional Products 1354 Old Post Rd	Havre de Grace	MD	21078	**800-638-4850**	410-939-1234
Champion Chemical Co 8319 S Greenleaf Ave	Whittier	CA	90602	**800-424-9300**	
Chemical Specialties Manufacturing Corp 901 N Newkirk St *Sales	Baltimore	MD	21205	**800-638-7370***	410-675-4800
Clorox Co 1221 Broadway *NYSE: CLX* ■ *Cust Svc	Oakland	CA	94612	**800-424-9300***	510-271-7000
Correlated Products Inc 5616 Progress Rd	Indianapolis	IN	46242	**800-428-3266**	317-243-3248
Damon Industries Inc 12435 Rockhill Ave NE	Alliance	OH	44601	**800-362-9850**	330-821-5310
Delta Carbona LP 376 Hollywood Ave Ste 208	Fairfield	NJ	07004	**888-746-5599**	973-808-6260
Dreumex USA 3445 BoaRd Rd	York	PA	17406	**800-233-9382**	717-767-6881
Dubois Chemicals 3630 E Kemper Rd	Cincinnati	OH	45241	**800-438-2647**	
Dura Wax Co 4101 W Albany St	McHenry	IL	60050	**800-435-5705**	815-385-5000
Falcon Safety Products Inc 25 Imclone Dr	Branchburg	NJ	08876	**800-332-5266**	908-707-4900
Fine Organics Corp 420 Kuller Rd PO Box 2277	Clifton	NJ	07015	**800-526-7480**	973-478-1000
Heritage-Crystal Clean Inc 2175 Pt Blvd Ste 375	Elgin	IL	60123	**877-938-7948**	847-836-5670
Hill Mfg Company Inc 1500 Jonesboro Rd SE	Atlanta	GA	30315	**800-445-5123**	404-522-8364
Hillyard Chemical Company Inc 302 N Fourth St PO Box 909	Saint Joseph	MO	64501	**800-365-1555**	816-233-1321
Impact Products LLC 2840 Centennial Rd *Cust Svc	Toledo	OH	43617	**800-333-1541***	419-841-2891
ITW Dymon 805 E Old 56 Hwy	Olathe	KS	66061	**800-443-9536**	913-829-6296
James Austin Co 115 Downieville Rd PO Box 827	Mars	PA	16046	**800-245-1942**	724-625-1535
Kay Chemical Co 8300 Capital Dr	Greensboro	NC	27409	**877-315-1115**	336-668-7290
Koger/Air Corp PO Box 2098	Martinsville	VA	24113	**800-368-2096**	276-638-8821
Leadership Performance Sustainability Laboratories 4647 Hugh Howell Rd	Tucker	GA	30084	**800-241-8334**	
Madison Chemical Company Inc 3141 Clifty Dr	Madison	IN	47250	**800-345-1915**	812-273-6000
Maxim Technologies Inc 1607 Derwent Way	Delta	BC	V3M6K8	**800-663-9925**	
Meguiar's Inc 17991 Mitchell S *Cust Svc	Irvine	CA	92614	**800-347-5700***	949-752-8000
Micro Care Corp 595 John Downey Dr	New Britain	CT	06051	**800-638-0125**	860-827-0626
Mother's Polishes Waxes & Cleaners 5456 Industrial Dr	Huntington Beach	CA	92649	**800-221-8257**	714-891-3364
National Chemical Laboratories Inc 401 N Tenth St	Philadelphia	PA	19123	**800-628-2436**	215-922-1200
National Chemicals Inc 105 Liberty St PO Box 32 *Cust Svc	Winona	MN	55987	**800-533-0027***	507-454-5640
NCH Corp 2727 Chemsearch Blvd	Irving	TX	75062	**800-527-9919**	972-438-0211
New Pig Corp 1 Pork Ave	Tipton	PA	16684	**800-468-4647**	814-684-0101
Nuvite Chemical Compounds Corp 213 Freeman St	Brooklyn	NY	11222	**800-394-8351**	718-383-8351
Ocean Bio-Chem Inc (OBCI) 4041 SW 47th Ave *NASDAQ: OBCI*	Fort Lauderdale	FL	33314	**800-327-8583**	954-587-6280
Paramount Chemical Specialties Inc 14750 NE 95th St	Redmond	WA	98052	**877-846-7826**	425-882-2673
Prosoco Inc 3741 Greenway Cir	Lawrence	KS	66046	**800-255-4255**	
Safeguard Chemical Corp 411 Wales Ave	Bronx	NY	10454	**800-536-3170**	718-585-3170
Safetec of America Inc 887 Kensington Ave	Buffalo	NY	14215	**800-456-7077**	716-895-1822
Scott Fetzer Company Scot Laboratories Div 16841 Pk Cir Dr	Chagrin Falls	OH	44023	**800-486-7268**	440-543-3033
Scott's Liquid Gold Inc 4880 Havana St *OTC: SLGD*	Denver	CO	80239	**800-447-1919**	303-373-4860
Seventh Generation Inc 60 Lake St	Burlington	VT	05401	**800-456-1191**	802-658-3773

Classified Section

	City	State	Zip	Toll-Free	Phone
Share Corp 7821 N Faulkner Rd	Milwaukee	WI	53224	**800-776-7192**	414-355-4000
Simoniz USA 201 Boston Tpke	Bolton	CT	06043	**800-227-5536**	
State Industrial Products 3100 Hamilton Ave	Cleveland	OH	44114	**877-747-6986**	216-861-7114
Stearns Packaging Corp 4200 Sycamore Ave	Madison	WI	53714	**800-655-5008**	608-246-5150
Summit Industries Inc PO Box 7329	Marietta	GA	30065	**800-241-6996**	
Sunshine Makers Inc 15922 Pacific Coast Hwy	Huntington Harbour	CA	92649	**800-228-0709**	562-795-6000
Unit Chemical Corp 7360 Commercial Way	Henderson	NV	89015	**800-879-8648**	702-564-6454
Warsaw Chemical Company Inc Argonne Rd PO Box 858	Warsaw	IN	46580	**800-548-3396**	574-267-3251
WD-40 Co 1061 Cudahy Pl *NASDAQ: WDFC*	San Diego	CA	92110	**800-448-9340**	619-275-1400
West Penetone Corp 700 Gotham Pkwy	Carlstadt	NJ	07072	**800-631-1652**	201-567-3000
ZEP Inc 1310 Seaboard Industrial Blvd NW *NYSE: ZEP*	Atlanta	GA	30318	**877-428-9937**	404-352-1680

151 CLEANING SERVICES

SEE ALSO Building Maintenance Services ; Bio-Recovery Services

	City	State	Zip	Toll-Free	Phone
1-800-Water Damage 1167 Mercer St	Seattle	WA	98109	**800-928-3732**	206-381-3041
Boston's Best Chimney Sweep 76 Bacon St *Cust Svc	Waltham	MA	02451	**800-660-6708***	781-893-6611
Clean Power LLC 124 N 121st St	Milwaukee	WI	53226	**888-566-1717**	414-302-3000
Cleaning Authority 7230 Lee DeForest Dr	Columbia	MD	21046	**888-658-0659**	410-740-1900
CleanNet USA 9861 Brokenland Pkwy Ste 208	Columbia	MD	21046	**800-735-8838**	410-720-6444
Coverall Cleaning Concepts 5201 Congress Ave Ste 275	Boca Raton	FL	33487	**800-537-3371**	866-296-8944
Diversified Maintenance Systems Inc 5110 Eisenhower Blvd Ste250	Tampa	FL	33634	**800-351-1557**	813-383-0238
Duraclean International Inc 220 W Campus Dr	Arlington Heights	IL	60004	**800-862-5326**	847-704-7100
Federal Bldg Services Inc 1641 Barclay Blvd	Buffalo Grove	IL	60089	**800-982-9234**	847-279-7360
Fish Window Cleaning Services Inc 200 Enchanted Pkwy	Manchester	MO	63021	**877-707-3474**	636-779-1500
GCA Services Group 1350 Euclid Ave Ste 1500	Cleveland	OH	44115	**800-422-8760**	
Healthcare Services Group Inc (HCSG) 3220 Tillman Dr Ste 300	Bensalem	PA	19020	**800-486-3289**	215-639-4274
Heaven's Best Carpet & Upholstery Cleaning PO Box 607	Rexburg	ID	83440	**800-359-2095**	208-359-1106
Jan-Pro International Inc (JPI) 2520 Northwinds Pkwy Ste 375	Alpharetta	GA	30009	**866-355-1064**	678-336-1780
Jani-King International Inc 16885 Dallas Pkwy	Addison	TX	75001	**800-526-4546**	972-991-0900
Maid Brigade USA/Minimaid Canada 4 Concourse Pkwy Ste 200	Atlanta	GA	30328	**866-800-7470**	770-551-9630
MaidPro Corp 180 Canal St	Boston	MA	02114	**888-624-3776**	617-742-8787
Maids International 9394 W Dodge Rd Ste 140	Omaha	NE	68114	**800-843-6243**	402-558-8600
Merry Maids 3839 Forrest Hill-Irene Rd	Memphis	TN	38125	**800-798-8000**	
MPW Industrial Services Group Inc 9711 Lancaster Rd SE	Hebron	OH	43025	**800-827-8790**	740-929-1614
Rainbow International 1010 N University Pk Dr	Waco	TX	76707	**855-724-6269**	254-756-5463
ServiceMaster Clean 3839 Forrest Hill Irene Rd *General	Memphis	TN	38125	**844-319-5401***	800-245-4622
Servpro Industries Inc 801 Industrial Blvd	Gallatin	TN	37066	**800-826-9586**	615-451-0600
St Moritz Bldg Services Inc 4616 Clairton Blvd	Pittsburgh	PA	15236	**800-218-9159**	412-885-2100
Steam Bros Inc 2400 Vermont Ave	Bismarck	ND	58504	**800-767-5064**	701-222-1263
Support Services of America Inc 12440 Firestone Blvd Ste 312	Norwalk	CA	90650	**888-564-0005**	562-868-3550
Swisher Hygiene Co 4725 Piedmont Row Dr	Charlotte	NC	28210	**800-444-4138**	704-364-7707
T.u.c.s. Cleaning Service Inc 166 Central Ave	Orange	NJ	07050	**800-992-5998**	973-673-0700
Venoco Inc 370 17th St Ste 3900 *NYSE: VQ*	Denver	CO	80202	**877-777-4778**	303-626-8300
Window Gang 405 Arendell St	Morehead City	NC	28557	**877-946-4264**	252-726-1463

152 CLOCKS, WATCHES, RELATED DEVICES, PARTS

	City	State	Zip	Toll-Free	Phone
Bulova Corp Empire State Bldg 350 Fifth Ave	Woodside	NY	10118	**800-228-5682**	718-204-3300
Canterbury International 5632 W Washington Blvd	Los Angeles	CA	90016	**800-935-7111**	323-936-7111
Citizen Watch Co of America Inc 1000 W 190th St	Torrance	CA	90502	**800-321-1023**	
E Gluck Corp 60-15 Little Neck Pkwy	Little Neck	NY	11362	**800-840-2933**	718-784-0700
Seiko Corp of America 1111 MacArthur Blvd *Cust Svc	Mahwah	NJ	07430	**800-545-2783***	201-529-5730
Seiko Instruments USA Inc 21221 S Western Ave Ste 250 *Sales	Torrance	CA	90501	**800-688-0817***	310-517-7700
Timex Group USA Inc 555 Christian Rd PO Box 310	Middlebury	CT	06762	**800-448-4639**	203-346-5000
Verdin Co, The 444 Reading Rd	Cincinnati	OH	45202	**800-543-0488**	
Vulcan Inc 410 E Berry Ave	Foley	AL	36535	**888-846-2728**	
World of Watches 3701 Flamingo Rd Ste 100	Miramar	FL	33027	**866-961-8463**	954-983-2181

153 CLOSURES - METAL OR PLASTICS

	City	State	Zip	Toll-Free	Phone
Caplugs LLC 2150 Elmwood Ave *Cust Svc	Buffalo	NY	14207	**888-227-5847***	716-876-9855
Essentra PLC 3123 Stn Rd	Erie	PA	16510	**800-847-0486**	814-899-9263
StockCap 123 Manufacturers Dr	Arnold	MO	63010	**800-827-2277**	636-282-6800
Tipper Tie Inc 2000 Lufkin Rd	Apex	NC	27502	**800-331-2905**	919-362-8811
Weatherchem Corp 2222 Highland Rd	Twinsburg	OH	44087	**800-316-0072**	330-425-4206

154 CLOTHING & ACCESSORIES - MFR

SEE ALSO Clothing & Accessories - Whol ; Fashion Design Houses ; Footwear ; Leather Goods - Personal ; Personal Protective Equipment & Clothing ; Baby Products

154-1 Athletic Apparel

	City	State	Zip	Toll-Free	Phone
Bristol Products Corp 700 Shelby St *Orders	Bristol	TN	37620	**800-336-8775***	423-968-4140
Choi Bros Inc 3401 W Div St	Chicago	IL	60651	**800-524-2464**	773-489-2800
Columbia Sportswear Co 14375 NW Science Pk Dr *NASDAQ: COLM*	Portland	OR	97229	**800-622-6953**	503-985-4125
Cutter & Buck Inc 701 N 34th St Ste 400	Seattle	WA	98103	**800-713-7810**	888-338-9944
Dodger Industries 2075 Stultz Rd PO Box 711 *Cust Svc	Martinsville	VA	24112	**800-247-7879***	
Elite Sportswear LP 2136 N 13th St *Cust Svc	Reading	PA	19604	**800-345-4087***	610-921-1469
Gear for Sports Inc 9700 Commerce Pkwy	Lenexa	KS	66219	**800-255-1065**	913-693-3200
MJ Soffe Co 1 Soffe Dr	Fayetteville	NC	28312	**888-257-8673**	
Race Face Components Inc 100 Braid St	New Westminster	BC	V3L3P4	**800-527-9244**	604-527-9996
Royal Textile Mills Inc 929 Firetower Rd	Yanceyville	NC	27379	**800-334-9361**	

154-2 Belts (Leather, Plastics, Fabric)

	City	State	Zip	Toll-Free	Phone
Gem Dandy Inc 200 W Academy St	Madison	NC	27025	**800-334-5101**	336-548-9624

154-3 Casual Wear (Men's & Women's)

	City	State	Zip	Toll-Free	Phone
Attraction Inc 672 Rue du Parc	Lac-Drolet	QC	G0Y1C0	**800-567-6095**	819-549-2477
Badger Sportswear Inc 111 Badger Ln	Statesville	NC	28625	**888-871-0990**	704-871-0990
Big Dogs 519 Lincoln County Pkwy	Lincolnton	NC	28092	**800-244-3647**	
Bobby Jones Retail Corp 1034 Windward Ridge Pkwy *Cust Svc	Alpharetta	GA	30005	**888-776-0076***	
Columbia Sportswear Co 14375 NW Science Pk Dr *NASDAQ: COLM*	Portland	OR	97229	**800-622-6953**	503-985-4125
Crazy Shirts Inc 99-969 Iwaena St	Aiea	HI	96701	**800-771-2720**	808-487-9919
Deckers Outdoor Corp 495-A S Fairview Ave *NYSE: DECK*	Goleta	CA	93117	**877-337-8333**	805-967-7611
Delta Apparel Inc 2750 Premier Pkwy Ste 100 *NYSE: DLA*	Duluth	GA	30097	**800-285-4456**	678-775-6900
Fruit of the Loom Inc 1 Fruit of the Loom Dr PO Box 90015	Bowling Green	KY	42102	**888-378-4829**	270-781-6400
Sherry Mfg 3287 NW 65th St	Miami	FL	33147	**800-741-4750**	305-693-7000
Sport-Haley Inc 200 Union Blvd Ste 400	Denver	CO	80228	**800-627-9211**	303-320-8800
Tonix Corp 40910 Encyclopedia Cir	Fremont	CA	94538	**800-227-2072**	510-651-8050
Wolf Manufacturing Co 1801 W Waco Dr PO Box 3100	Waco	TX	76707	**800-437-0940**	254-753-7301

154-4 Children's & Infants' Clothing

	City	State	Zip	Toll-Free	Phone
Byer California 66 Potrero Ave	San Francisco	CA	94103	**844-628-4498**	415-626-7844

Company / Address	City	State	Zip	Toll-Free	Phone
Florence Eiseman company LLC 1966 S Fourth St	Milwaukee	WI	53204	**800-558-9013**	
Gerber Childrenswear Inc 7005 Pelham Rd Ste D	Greenville	SC	29602	**800-642-4452**	864-987-5200
New ICM LP PO Box 1060	El Campo	TX	77437	**800-987-9008**	979-578-0543

154-5 Coats (Overcoats, Jackets, Raincoats, etc)

Company / Address	City	State	Zip	Toll-Free	Phone
Alpha Industries Inc 14200 Pk Meadow Dr Ste 110S *General	Chantilly	VA	20151	**866-631-0719***	703-378-1420
Helly Hansen US Inc 4104 C St NE Ste 200	Auburn	WA	98002	**800-435-5901**	
Holloway Sportswear Inc 2633 Campbell Rd	Sidney	OH	45365	**800-331-5156**	
London Fog 1615 Kellogg Dr	Douglas	GA	31535	**877-588-8189**	912-384-8189
MECA Sportswear 1120 Townline Rd	Tomah	WI	54660	**800-729-6322**	608-374-6450
Pendleton Woolen Mills Inc 220 NW Broadway	Portland	OR	97209	**800-760-4844**	503-226-4801
RefrigiWear Inc 54 Breakstone Dr *Cust Svc	Dahlonega	GA	30533	**800-645-3744***	706-864-5757
Rennoc Corp 645 Pine St	Greenville	OH	45331	**800-372-7100**	
Sport Obermeyer Ltd USA Inc 115 AABC	Aspen	CO	81611	**800-525-4203**	970-925-5060
Sport-Haley Inc 200 Union Blvd Ste 400	Denver	CO	80228	**800-627-9211**	303-320-8800
Woolrich Inc 2 Mill St	Woolrich	PA	17779	**800-995-1299**	570-769-6464

154-6 Costumes

Company / Address	City	State	Zip	Toll-Free	Phone
Costume Gallery 4451 Rt 130	Burlington	NJ	08016	**800-222-8125**	609-386-6601
Costume Specialists Inc 211 N Fifth St	Columbus	OH	43215	**800-596-9357**	614-464-2115
Curtain Call Costumes 333 E Seventh Ave	York	PA	17404	**888-808-0801**	717-852-6910
Disguise 12120 Kear Pl	Poway	CA	92064	**877-875-2557**	858-391-3600

154-7 Gloves & Mittens

Company / Address	City	State	Zip	Toll-Free	Phone
Carolina Glove Co 116 Mclin Creek Rd PO Box 999	Conover	NC	28613	**800-335-1918**	828-464-1132
Fownes Bros & Company Inc 16 E 34th St *All	New York	NY	10016	**800-345-6837***	212-683-0150
Gloves Inc 1950 Collins Boulevard	Austell	MA	30106	**800-476-4568**	770-944-9186
Guard-Line Inc 215 S Louise St PO Box 1030	Atlanta	TX	75551	**800-527-8822**	903-796-4111
Illinois Glove Co 3701 Commercial Ave	Northbrook	IL	60062	**800-342-5458**	847-291-1700
Kinco International 4286 NE 185th Dr *General	Portland	OR	97230	**800-547-8410***	
Magid Glove & Safety Manufacturing Co 2060 N Kolmar Ave	Chicago	IL	60639	**800-444-8010**	773-384-2070
MCR Safety 5321 E Shelby Dr	Memphis	TN	38118	**800-955-6887**	901-795-5810
Midwest Quality Gloves Inc 835 Industrial Rd	Chillicothe	MO	64601	**800-821-3028**	660-646-2165
Montpelier Glove Co Inc 129 N Main St	Montpelier	IN	47359	**800-645-3931**	765-728-2481
North Star Glove Co 2916 S Steele St	Tacoma	WA	98409	**800-423-1616**	253-627-7107
Saranac Glove Co 999 LOmbardi Ave	Green Bay	WI	54304	**800-727-2622**	920-435-3737
Southern Glove Mfg Company Inc 749 AC Little Dr *Cust Svc	Newton	NC	28658	**800-222-1113***	828-464-4884
Swany America Corp 115 Corp Dr	Johnstown	NY	12095	**888-234-5450**	518-725-3333
Wells Lamont Industry Group 6640 W Touhy Ave	Niles	IL	60714	**800-247-3295**	

154-8 Hats & Caps

Company / Address	City	State	Zip	Toll-Free	Phone
180s Inc 700 S Caroline St	Baltimore	MD	21231	**877-725-4386**	410-534-6320
Ahead LLC 270 Samuel Barnet Blvd	New Bedford	MA	02745	**800-282-2246**	508-985-9898
F & M Hat Co Inc 103 Walnut St PO Box 40	Denver	PA	17517	**800-953-4287**	717-336-5505
Greg Norman Collection 134 W 37th St Ste 4	New York	NY	10018	**888-667-6264**	
Korber Hats Inc 394 Kilburn St *Cust Svc	Fall River	MA	02724	**800-428-9911***	508-672-7033
MPC Promotions 4300 Produce Rd PO Box 34336	Louisville	KY	40232	**800-331-0989**	502-451-4900
New Era Cap Company Inc 160 Delaware Ave *General	Buffalo	NY	14202	**877-632-5950***	716-604-9000
Paramount Apparel International Inc 1 Paramount Dr	Bourbon	MO	65441	**866-274-4287**	573-732-4411
Stratton Hats Inc 3200 Randolph St	Bellwood	IL	60104	**877-453-3777**	708-544-5220
Town Talk Inc 6310 Cane Run Rd	Louisville	KY	40258	**800-626-2220**	502-736-2972

154-9 Hosiery & Socks

Company / Address	City	State	Zip	Toll-Free	Phone
Fox River Mills Inc 227 Poplar Stq PO Box 298	Osage	IA	50461	**800-247-1815**	641-732-3798
Jefferies Socks 2203 Tucker St	Burlington	NC	27215	**800-334-6831**	336-226-7315
Jockey International Inc 2300 60th St PO Box 1417	Kenosha	WI	53140	**800-562-5391**	
Moretz Inc 514 W 21st St	Newton	NC	28658	**866-714-8486**	828-464-0751
Renfro Corp 661 Linville Rd	Mount Airy	NC	27030	**800-334-9091**	336-719-8000
Thor-Lo Inc 2210 Newton Dr	Statesville	NC	28677	**888-846-7567**	704-872-6522
Twin City Knitting Company Inc (TCK) 104 Rock Barn Rd NE	Conover	NC	28613	**800-438-6884**	828-464-4830
Wigwam Mills Inc 3402 Crocker Ave	Sheboygan	WI	53082	**800-558-7760**	920-457-5551

154-10 Jeans

Company / Address	City	State	Zip	Toll-Free	Phone
Lee Jeans 9001 W 67th St *Cust Svc	Merriam	KS	66202	**800-453-3348***	913-384-4000
Levi Strauss & Co 1155 Battery St	San Francisco	CA	94111	**866-290-6064**	415-501-6000
Reed Mfg Co Inc 1321 S Veterans Blvd	Tupelo	MS	38804	**800-466-1154**	662-842-4472
VF Corporation PO Box 21488 *Orders	Greensboro	NC	27420	**866-492-3370***	336-424-6000

154-11 Men's Clothing

Company / Address	City	State	Zip	Toll-Free	Phone
After Six 118 W 20th St	New York	NY	10011	**800-444-8304**	646-638-9600
American Apparel LLC 747 Warehouse St	Los Angeles	CA	90021	**888-747-0070**	213-488-0226
Anniston Sportswear Corp PO Box 189	Anniston	AL	36201	**866-814-9253**	256-236-1551
Antigua Sportswear Inc 16651 N 84 Ave	Peoria	AZ	85382	**800-528-3133**	623-523-6000
Gitman & Co 2309 Chestnut St	Ashland	PA	17921	**800-526-3929**	570-875-3100
Gitman Bros Shirt Company Inc 2309 Chestnut St 19th Fl *General	Ashland	PA	10019	**800-526-3929***	212-581-6968
Granite Knitwear Inc 805 S Salberry Ave Hwy 52S *Cust Svc	Granite Quarry	NC	28072	**800-476-9944***	704-279-5526
Greg Norman Collection 134 W 37th St Ste 4	New York	NY	10018	**888-667-6264**	
H Freeman & Son Inc 411 N Cranberry Rd	Westminster	MD	21157	**800-876-7700**	410-857-5774
Haggar Clothing Co 11511 Luna Rd 2 Colinas Crossing	Dallas	TX	75234	**877-841-2219**	214-352-8481
Hardwick Clothes Inc 3800 Old Tasso Rd	Cleveland	TN	37312	**800-251-6392**	
Hart Schaffner Marx (HSM) 1680 E Touhy Ave	Des Plaines	IL	60018	**800-327-4466**	
Hickey Freeman 1155 N Clinton Ave *Cust Svc	Rochester	NY	14621	**844-755-7344***	585-467-7021
Jos A Bank Clothiers 500 Hanover Pk *Cust Svc	Hampstead	MD	21074	**800-999-7472***	410-239-2700
Phillips-Van Heusen Corp 200 Madison Ave *NYSE: PVH*	New York	NY	10016	**888-203-1112**	212-381-3500
Tom James Co 263 Seaboard Ln	Franklin	TN	37067	**800-236-9023**	615-771-0795

154-12 Neckwear

Company / Address	City	State	Zip	Toll-Free	Phone
Carolina Mfg 7025 Augusta Rd	Greenville	SC	29605	**800-845-2744**	864-299-0600
Echo Design Group 10 E 40th St 16th Fl *General	New York	NY	10016	**800-327-3896***	212-686-8771

154-13 Robes (Ceremonial)

Company / Address	City	State	Zip	Toll-Free	Phone
Academic Apparel 20644 Superior St	Chatsworth	CA	91311	**800-626-5000**	818-886-8697
CM Almy Inc 1 Ruth Rd	Pittsfield	ME	04967	**800-225-2569**	207-487-3232
Gaspard Inc 200 N Janacek Rd	Brookfield	WI	53045	**800-784-6868**	262-784-6800
Jostens Inc 3601 Minnesota Ave Ste 400	Minneapolis	MN	55435	**800-235-4774**	952-830-3300
Oak Hall Industries 840 Union St	Salem	VA	24153	**800-223-0429**	540-387-0000
Thomas Creative Apparel Inc 1 Harmony Pl	New London	OH	44851	**800-537-2575**	419-929-1506
Willsie Cap & Gown Co 1220 S 13th St	Omaha	NE	68108	**800-234-4696**	402-341-6536

154-14 Sleepwear

				Toll-Free	Phone
Miss Elaine Inc 8430 Valcour Ave	Saint Louis	MO	63123	**800-458-1422**	314-631-1900
Wormser Corp 150 Coolidge Ave	Englewood	NJ	07631	**800-546-4040**	

154-15 Sweaters (Knit)

				Toll-Free	Phone
Binghamton Knitting Co Inc 11 Alice St	Binghamton	NY	13904	**877-746-3368**	

154-16 Swimwear

				Toll-Free	Phone
Blue Sky Swimwear 729 E International Speedway Blvd *Orders	Daytona Beach	FL	32118	**800-799-6445***	386-255-2590
TYR Sport 1790 Apollo Ct	Seal Beach	CA	90740	**800-252-7878**	714-897-0799
Venus Swimwear 11711 Marco Beach Dr	Jacksonville	FL	32224	**800-366-7946**	904-645-6000

154-17 Undergarments

				Toll-Free	Phone
Cupid Foundations Inc 475 Pk Ave S 17th Fl	New York	NY	10016	**877-649-5283**	212-686-6224
Gelmart Industries Inc 136 Madison Ave 4th Fl *General	New York	NY	10016	**800-746-0014***	212-743-6900
Indera Mills Co 350 W Maple St PO Box 309	Yadkinville	NC	27055	**800-334-8605**	336-679-4440
Jockey International Inc 2300 60th St PO Box 1417	Kenosha	WI	53140	**800-562-5391**	
Leading Lady 24050 Commerce Pk *Cust Svc	Beachwood	OH	44122	**800-321-4804***	216-464-5490
Robinson Mfg Company Inc 798 Market St PO Box 338	Dayton	TN	37321	**800-251-7286**	423-775-2212
Wacoal America 50 Polito Ave	Lyndhurst	NJ	07071	**800-922-6250**	201-933-8400
Wacoal Europe 65 Sprague St	Hyde Park	MA	02136	**800-733-8964**	617-361-7559

154-18 Uniforms & Work Clothes

				Toll-Free	Phone
A+ School Apparel 401 Knoss Ave	Star City	AR	71667	**800-227-3215**	
Action Sports Systems Inc 617 Carbon City Rd PO Box 1442	Morganton	NC	28655	**800-631-1091**	828-584-8000
Algy Team Collection 440 NE First Ave	Hallandale	FL	33009	**800-458-2549**	954-457-8100
Barco Uniforms Inc 350 W Rosecrans Ave	Gardena	CA	90248	**800-421-1874**	310-323-7315
Berne Apparel Co 2210 Summit St	New Haven	IN	46774	**800-843-7657**	260-469-3136
Blauer Mfg Co Inc 20 Aberdeen St	Boston	MA	02215	**800-225-6715**	617-536-6606
Blue Generation Div of M Rubin & Sons Inc 34-01 38th Ave	Long Island	NY	11101	**888-336-4687**	718-361-2800
Carhartt Inc 5750 Mercury Dr	Dearborn	MI	48126	**800-833-3118**	313-271-8460
Choi Bros Inc 3401 W Div St	Chicago	IL	60651	**800-524-2464**	773-489-2800
DeMoulin Bros & Company Inc 1025 S Fourth St	Greenville	IL	62246	**800-228-8134**	618-664-2000
Dennis Uniform Mfg Company Inc 135 SE Hawthorne Blvd	Portland	OR	97214	**800-854-6951**	
Earl's Apparel Inc 908 S Fourth St	Crockett	TX	75835	**800-527-3148**	936-544-5521
Elbeco Inc 4418 Pottsville Pk	Reading	PA	19605	**800-468-4654**	610-921-0651
Encompass Group LLC 615 Macon Rd	McDonough	GA	30253	**800-284-4540**	770-957-1211
Fechheimer Bros Company Inc 4545 Malsbary Rd	Cincinnati	OH	45242	**800-543-1939**	513-793-5400
Gibson & Barnes 1900 Weld Blvd Ste 140 *Sales	El Cajon	CA	92020	**800-748-6693***	619-440-6977
Howard Uniform Co 1915 Annapolis Rd	Baltimore	MD	21230	**800-628-8299**	410-727-3086
Key Industries Inc 400 Marble Rd	Fort Scott	KS	66701	**800-835-0365**	620-223-2000
LC King Mfg Company Inc 24 Seventh St	Bristol	TN	37620	**800-826-2510**	423-764-5188
Leventhal Ltd PO Box 564 *General	Fayetteville	NC	28302	**800-847-4095***	
Lion Apparel Inc 7200 Poe Ave Ste 400	Dayton	OH	45414	**800-548-6614**	937-898-1949
Riverside Manufacturing Co 301 Riverside Dr	Moultrie	GA	31768	**800-841-8677**	229-985-5210
SCORE American Soccer Company Inc 726 E Anaheim St	Wilmington	CA	90744	**800-626-7774**	
Stanbury Uniforms Inc 108 Stanbury Industrial Dr PO Box 100	Brookfield	MO	64628	**800-826-2246**	660-258-2246
Standard Textile Company Inc 1 Knollcrest Dr	Cincinnati	OH	45237	**800-999-0400**	513-761-9255
Superior Uniform Group Inc 10055Seminole Blvd *NASDAQ: SGC* ■ *Cust Svc	Seminole	FL	33772	**800-727-8643***	727-397-9611
Topps Safety Apparel Inc 2516 E State Rd 14	Rochester	IN	46975	**800-348-2990**	574-223-4311
Universal Overall Co 1060 W Van Buren St *Cust Svc	Chicago	IL	60607	**800-621-3344***	312-226-3336
Wenaas AGS Inc 12211 Parc Crest Dr Bldg Ste 100	Stafford	TX	77477	**888-576-2668**	281-931-4300
Williamson-Dickie Mfg Co 509 W Vickery Blvd	Fort Worth	TX	76104	**866-411-1501**	

154-19 Western Wear (Except Hats & Boots)

				Toll-Free	Phone
Niver Western Wear Inc PO Box 101224 *Orders	Fort Worth	TX	76185	**800-433-5752***	817-924-4299
Rockmount Ranch Wear Manufacturing Co 1626 Wazee St	Denver	CO	80202	**800-776-2566**	303-629-7777
Sidran Inc 1050 Venture Ct Ste 100	Carrollton	TX	75006	**800-969-5015**	214-352-7979

154-20 Women's Clothing

				Toll-Free	Phone
Alfred Angelo Inc 1301 Virginia Dr	Fort Washington	PA	19034	**888-218-0044**	215-659-5300
bebe stores Inc 400 Valley Dr *NASDAQ: BEBE*	Brisbane	CA	94005	**877-232-3777**	415-715-3900
Byer California 66 Potrero Ave	San Francisco	CA	94103	**844-628-4498**	415-626-7844
Darue of California Inc 14102 S Broadway	Los Angeles	CA	90061	**877-693-2783**	310-323-1350
Donna Karan International Inc 550 Seventh Ave *General	New York	NY	10018	**877-316-0975***	212-789-1500
JLM Couture Inc 525 Seventh Ave Ste 1703	New York	NY	10018	**800-924-6475**	212-221-8203
Jones Apparel Group Inc Jones New York Collection Div 1411 Broadway	New York	NY	10018	**800-999-1877**	212-355-4449
Leon Max Inc 3100 New York Dr	Pasadena	CA	91107	**888-334-4629**	626-797-9991
Tanner Cos LLC 581Rock Rd	Rutherfordton	NC	28139	**877-872-4578**	828-287-4205
Ursula of Switzerland Inc 31 Mohawk Ave	Waterford	NY	12188	**800-826-4041**	

155 CLOTHING & ACCESSORIES - WHOL

				Toll-Free	Phone
Crew Outfitters Inc 1001 Virginia Ave	Atlanta	GA	30354	**888-345-5353**	
Herman's Inc 2820 Blackhawk Rd	Rock Island	IL	61201	**800-447-1295**	309-788-9568
TSC Apparel LLC 12080 Mosteller Rd	Cincinnati	OH	45241	**800-543-7230**	513-771-1138
WS Emerson Co Inc 15 Acme Rd	Brewer	ME	04412	**800-789-6120**	

156 CLOTHING STORES

SEE ALSO Department Stores

156-1 Children's Clothing Stores

				Toll-Free	Phone
Children's Place Retail Stores Inc 500 Plz Dr *NASDAQ: PLCE*	Secaucus	NJ	07094	**877-752-2387**	201-558-2400
Goldbug Inc 18245 E 40th Ave	Aurora	CO	80011	**800-942-9442**	303-371-2535
Gymboree Corp 500 Howard St *NASDAQ: GYMB*	San Francisco	CA	94105	**877-449-6932**	415-278-7000
Valor Brands LLC 960 N Point Pkwy Ste 100	Alpharetta	GA	30005	**866-949-9098**	770-346-9250
Winmark Corp 605Hwy 169 N Ste 400 *NASDAQ: WINA*	Minneapolis	MN	55441	**877-536-1561**	763-520-8500

156-2 Family Clothing Stores

				Toll-Free	Phone
Bob's Stores Inc 160 Corporate Ct	Meriden	CT	06450	**866-333-2627**	203-235-5775
Dawahares Inc 1845 Alexandria Dr	Lexington	KY	40504	**800-677-9108**	859-278-0422
Foursome Inc 3570 Vicksveurg Ln N Ste 100	Plymouth	MN	55447	**888-368-7766**	763-473-4667
Halston LLC 1201 W Fifth St 11th fl	Los Angeles	CA	90017	**844-425-7866**	
Kittery Trading Post 301 US 1	Kittery	ME	03904	**888-587-6246**	603-334-1157
Marshalls Inc 770 Cochituate Rd	Framingham	MA	01701	**800-627-7425**	
Palais Royal 10201 S Main St	Houston	TX	77025	**800-743-8730**	713-667-5601

Classified Section

Company / Address	City	State	Zip	Toll-Free	Phone
Puritan of Cape Cod 408 Main St	Hyannis	MA	02601	**800-924-0606**	508-775-2400
TJ Maxx 770 Cochituate Rd *Cust Svc	Framingham	MA	01701	**800-926-6299***	508-390-1000
Wakefield's Inc 3100 McClellan Blvd Quintard Ave	Anniston	AL	36201	**800-333-1552**	256-237-9521
Zumiez Inc 6300 Merrill Creek Pkwy Ste B *NASDAQ: ZUMZ*	Everett	WA	98203	**877-828-6929**	425-551-1500

156-3 Men's Clothing Stores

Company / Address	City	State	Zip	Toll-Free	Phone
Carroll & Co 425 N Canon Dr	Beverly Hills	CA	90210	**800-238-9400**	310-273-9060
Jos A Bank Clothiers 500 Hanover Pk *Cust Svc	Hampstead	MD	21074	**800-999-7472***	410-239-2700
Men's Wearhouse Inc 6380 Rogerdale Rd *NYSE: MW*	Houston	TX	77072	**877-986-9669**	281-776-7000
Miltons Inc 250 Granite St	Braintree	MA	02184	**888-645-8667**	781-848-1880
Patrick James Inc 780 W Shaw Ave	Fresno	CA	93704	**888-427-6003**	559-224-5500
Paul Fredrick Menstyle 223 W Poplar St	Fleetwood	PA	19522	**800-247-1417**	610-944-0909
Rubenstein Bros Inc 102 St Charles Ave	New Orleans	LA	70130	**800-725-7823**	504-581-6666

156-4 Men's & Women's Clothing Stores

Company / Address	City	State	Zip	Toll-Free	Phone
American Eagle Outfitters Inc 77 Hot Metal St *NYSE: AEO* ■ *Cust Svc	Pittsburgh	PA	15203	**888-232-4535***	412-432-3300
Bergdorf Goodman Inc 754 Fifth Ave *Cust Svc	New York	NY	10019	**888-774-2424***	212-753-7300
Buckle Inc 2407 W 24th St *NYSE: BKE*	Kearney	NE	68845	**800-626-1255**	308-236-8491
Eddie Bauer LLC PO Box 7001 *Orders	Groveport	OH	43125	**800-426-8020***	
Gap Inc 2 Folsom St *NYSE: GPS*	San Francisco	CA	94105	**800-333-7899**	650-952-4400
J Crew Group Inc 770 Broadway	New York	NY	10003	**800-562-0258**	212-209-2500
J McLaughlin 236250 Greenpoint Ave 2nd Fl	Brooklyn	NY	10021	**844-532-5625**	212-879-9565
Joe's Jeans Inc 2340 S Eastern Ave *NASDAQ: JOEZ*	Commerce	CA	90040	**877-528-5637**	323-837-3700
John B Malouf Inc 8201 Quaker Ave Ste 106	Lubbock	TX	79424	**800-658-9500**	806-794-9500
Maurices Inc 105 W Superior St	Duluth	MN	55802	**866-977-1542**	218-727-8431
Oak Hall Inc 6150 Poplar Ave Ste 146	Memphis	TN	38119	**844-625-4255**	901-761-3580
Pacific Sunwear of California Inc 3450 E Miraloma Ave *NASDAQ: PSUN*	Anaheim	CA	92806	**800-444-6770**	714-414-4000
Patagonia Inc 259 W Santa Clara St PO Box 150 *Cust Svc	Ventura	CA	93001	**800-638-6464***	805-643-8616
Paul Stuart Inc Madison Ave & 45th St *Orders	New York	NY	10017	**800-678-8278***	212-682-0320
Plato's Closet 23021 Outer Dr	Allen Park	MI	48101	**800-592-8049**	313-278-2300
Specialty Retailers Inc 10201 S Main St	Houston	TX	77025	**800-579-2302**	
Stanley Korshak 500 Crescent Ct Ste 100	Dallas	TX	75201	**855-749-9539**	214-871-3600
TJX Cos Inc 770 Cochituate Rd *NYSE: TJX*	Framingham	MA	01701	**800-926-6299**	508-390-1000
Urban Outfitters Inc 30 Industrial Pk Blvd	Trenton	SC	29847	**800-282-2200**	

156-5 Specialty Clothing Stores

Specialty clothing stores are those which sell a specific type of clothing, such as Western wear, uniforms, etc.

Company / Address	City	State	Zip	Toll-Free	Phone
5.11 Inc 4300 Spyres Way	Modesto	CA	95356	**866-451-1726**	209-527-4511
Country Curtains PO Box 955	Stockbridge	MA	01262	**800-937-1237**	413-243-1474
Hat World Corp 7555 Woodland Dr	Indianapolis	IN	46278	**888-564-4287**	
HorseLoverZ com 254 N Cedar St	Hazleton	PA	18201	**877-804-7810**	570-579-0054
Mark's Work Warehouse 30-1035 64th Ave SE	Calgary	AB	T2H2J7	**800-663-6275**	403-255-9220
Mobile Nations 3151 E Thomas St	Inverness	FL	34453	**888-599-8998**	352-400-4400
Modell's Sporting Goods 498 Seventh Ave 20th Fl	New York	NY	10018	**888-645-8667**	800-275-6633
Niver Western Wear Inc PO Box 101224 *Orders	Fort Worth	TX	76185	**800-433-5752***	817-924-4299
Northwest Designs Ink Inc 13456 SE 27th Pl Ste 200	Bellevue	WA	98005	**800-925-9327**	

Company / Address	City	State	Zip	Toll-Free	Phone
Overland Sheepskin Company Inc 2096 Nutmeg Ave	Fairfield	IA	52556	**800-683-7526**	641-472-8434
Post & Nickel 144 N 14th St	Lincoln	NE	68508	**877-667-6107**	402-476-3432
Sheplers Inc 6501 W Kellogg Dr	Wichita	KS	67209	**888-835-4004**	
U S Cavalry Inc 2855 Centennial Ave	Radcliff	KY	40160	**866-286-1359**	270-351-1164
Wilsons Leather Inc 7401 Boone Ave N	Brooklyn Park	MN	55428	**800-967-6270**	763-391-4000
Work 'n Gear Stores 2300 Crown Colony Dr Ste 300	Quincy	MA	02169	**800-987-0218**	

156-6 Women's Clothing Stores

Company / Address	City	State	Zip	Toll-Free	Phone
A'Gaci LLC 12460 Network Blvd Ste 106	San Antonio	TX	78249	**866-265-3036**	
Ann Inc 7 Times Sq *NYSE: ANN*	New York	NY	10036	**800-677-6788**	212-541-3300
AnnTaylor Inc 7 Times Sq	New York	NY	10036	**800-342-5266**	212-541-3300
Avenue Stores Inc 365 W Passaic St	Rochelle Park	NJ	07662	**888-843-2836**	201-845-0880
Big Girls Bras Etcetera Inc 3540 NW 56th St Ste 207	Lauderdale	FL	33309	**866-352-4494**	954-484-2701
Bluefly Inc 42 W 39th St 9th Fl *NASDAQ: BFLY* ■ *Cust Svc	New York	NY	10018	**877-258-3359***	212-944-8000
Born Into It Inc 185 New Boston St	Woburn	MA	01801	**800-560-2840**	781-491-0707
Capsmith Inc 2240 Old Lk Mary Rd	Sanford	FL	32771	**800-228-3889**	407-328-7660
Cato Corp, The 8100 Denmark Rd	Charlotte	NC	28273	**800-526-9169**	704-554-8510
Charlotte Russe Inc 5910 Pacific Center Blvd	San Diego	CA	92121	**888-211-7271**	
Chico's FAS Inc 11215 Metro Pkwy *NYSE: CHS*	Fort Myers	FL	33966	**800-690-6903**	888-855-4986
Claire's Accessories 2400 W Central Rd	Hoffman Estates	IL	60192	**800-252-4737**	847-765-1100
David's Bridal Inc 1001 Washington St	Conshohocken	PA	19428	**844-400-3222**	610-943-5000
Destination Maternity Corp 456 N Fifth St *NASDAQ: DEST*	Philadelphia	PA	19123	**800-466-6223**	215-873-2200
Drapers & Damons 9 Pasteur Ste 200	Irvine	CA	92618	**800-843-1174**	
Express 1 Limited Pkwy *NYSE: EXPR*	Columbus	OH	43230	**888-397-1980**	
Forever 21 Inc 2001 S Alameda St *Cust Svc	Los Angeles	CA	90058	**800-966-1355***	213-741-5100
Frederick's of Hollywood Inc PO Box 2949	Phoenix	AZ	85062	**855-655-2514**	800-323-9525
Henri Bendel Inc 712 Fifth Ave	New York	NY	10019	**866-875-7975**	212-247-1100
Irresistibles 7 Hawkes St	Marblehead	MA	01945	**800-555-9865**	781-631-1248
Lady Grace Stores Inc 139 Endicott St Ste 1	Denvers	MA	01923	**800-922-0504**	781-569-0727
Lane Bryant Inc 3344 Morse Crossing *Cust Svc	Columbus	OH	43215	**866-886-4731***	954-970-2205
Louis Vuitton NA Inc 1 E 57th St *Cust Svc	New York	NY	10022	**866-884-8866***	212-758-8877
Mandee Shop 12 Vreeland Ave *Cust Svc	Totowa	NJ	07512	**877-756-1958***	973-890-0021
Motherhood Maternity 456 N Fifth St	Philadelphia	PA	19123	**800-291-7800**	215-873-2200
New York & Co 330 W 34th St	New York	NY	10001	**800-961-9906**	
NYDJ Apparel LLC 5401 S Soto St	Vernon	CA	90058	**800-407-6001**	323-581-9040
Sherpa Adventure Gear Inc 7857 S 180th St	Kent	WA	98032	**877-724-8735**	425-251-0760
Swim 'n Sport Retail Inc 2396 NW 96th Ave	Miami	FL	33172	**800-497-2111**	
Sydneys Closet 11840 Dorsett Rd	Maryland Heights	MO	63043	**888-479-3639**	314-344-5066
Vanity Shop of Grand Forks Inc 2410 Great Northern Dr	Fargo	ND	58102	**866-247-7920**	701-237-3330
Victoria's Secret Stores 4 Limited Pkwy	Reynoldsburg	OH	43068	**800-411-5116**	
Wedding Shoppe Inc, The 1196 Grand Ave	Saint Paul	MN	55105	**877-294-4991**	651-298-1144
Wet Seal Inc 26972 Burbank Ave *NASDAQ: WTSLA*	Foothill Ranch	CA	92610	**866-746-7938**	949-699-3900
White House/Black Market (WHBM) 11215 Metro Pkwy	Fort Myers	FL	33966	**877-948-2525**	239-277-6200
Windsor Inc 4533 Pacific Blvd	Vernon	CA	90058	**888-494-6376**	323-282-9000

157 COAST GUARD INSTALLATIONS

Company / Address	City	State	Zip	Toll-Free	Phone
Cape Cod Coast Guard Air Station 2300 Wilson Blvd Ste 500	Arlington	VA	20598	**877-669-8724**	202-372-4620
Integrated Support Command Miami Beach 100 MacArthur Cswy	Miami Beach	FL	33139	**866-772-8724**	305-535-4300
Milwaukee Coast Guard Base 2420 S Lincoln Memorial Dr	Milwaukee	WI	53207	**866-772-8724**	414-747-7100
US Coast Guard Air Station Detroit 1461 N Perimeter Rd Selfridge ANGB	Selfridge	MI	48045	**800-424-8802**	

158 COFFEE & TEA STORES

Name / Address	City	State	Zip	Toll-Free	Phone
Caribou Coffee Company Inc 3900 Lakebreeze Ave N *NASDAQ: CBOU* ■ *Cust Svc	Minneapolis	MN	55429	**888-227-4268***	763-592-2200
Coffee Beanery Ltd, The 3429 Pierson Pl	Flushing	MI	48433	**800-441-2255**	
Dunkin' Donuts 130 Royall St *Cust Svc	Canton	MA	02021	**800-859-5339***	781-737-3000
Hawaii Coffee Company Inc 1555 Kalani St	Honolulu	HI	96817	**800-338-8353**	808-847-3600
McNulty's Tea & Coffee Company Inc 109 Christopher St	New York	NY	10014	**800-356-5200**	212-242-5351
Montana Coffee Traders Inc 5810 Hwy 93 S	Whitefish	MT	59937	**800-345-5282**	406-862-7633
Peet's Coffee & Tea Inc 1400 Pk Ave *NASDAQ: GMCR* ■ *Orders	Emeryville	CA	94608	**800-999-2132***	510-594-2100
Seattle's Best Coffee Co PO Box 3717	Seattle	WA	98124	**800-611-7793**	
Second Cup Ltd 6303 Airport Rd	Mississauga	ON	L4V1R8	**877-212-1818**	
Starbucks Coffee Co 2401 Utah Ave S	Seattle	WA	98134	**800-782-7282**	206-447-1575
VKI Technologies Inc 3200 2e rue	Saint-hubert	QC	J3Y8Y7	**800-567-2951**	450-676-0504

159 COLLECTION AGENCIES

Name / Address	City	State	Zip	Toll-Free	Phone
A.R.M. Solutions Inc PO Box 2929	Camarillo	CA	93011	**888-772-6468**	
AAA Collections Inc 3500 S First Ave Cir	Sioux Falls	SD	57105	**800-611-7371**	605-339-1333
AllianceOne Inc 4850 E St Rd Ste 300	Trevose	PA	19053	**866-405-7241**	215-354-5511
Allied International Credit Corp 16635 Young St Unit 26	Newmarket	ON	L3X1V6	**877-451-2594**	
American Accounts & Advisors PO Box 250	Cottage Grove	MN	55016	**866-714-0489**	651-287-6100
Asset Acceptance Capital Corp (AACC) 28405 Van Dyke Ave *NASDAQ: AACC*	Warren	MI	48093	**800-545-9931**	586-939-9600
Atlantic Credit & Finance Inc 2727 Franklin Rd	Roanoke	VA	24014	**800-888-9419**	540-772-7800
Bonneville Billing & Collection Inc 1186 East 4600 South Ste 100	Ogden	UT	84403	**800-660-6138**	801-621-7880
Brennan & Clark LLC 721 E Madison Ste 200	Villa Park	IL	60181	**800-858-7600**	630-279-7600
CBV Collections 1200-100 Sheppard Ave E	Toronto	ON	M2N6N5	**866-877-9323**	416-482-9323
Cc Columbia Collectors Inc 1104 Main St Ste 311	Vancouver	WA	98660	**800-694-7585**	360-694-7585
Collectcents Inc 1450 Meyerside Dr 2nd Fl	Mississauga	ON	L5T2N5	**800-256-8964**	905-670-7575
Computer Credit Inc 470 W Hanes Mill Rd Ste 200	Winston-Salem	NC	27105	**800-942-2995**	336-761-1524
Continental Service Group Inc 200 Cross Keys Office Pk	Fairport	NY	14450	**800-724-7500**	585-421-1000
Credit Control Services Inc (CCS) 2 Wells Ave Ste 1	Newton	MA	02459	**800-526-0532**	617-965-2000
Credit Management LP 4200 International Pkwy	Carrollton	TX	75007	**800-377-7713**	
Creditors Adjustment Bureau-LC Financial (CABLCF) 14226 Ventura Blvd	Sherman Oaks	CA	91423	**800-800-4523**	818-990-4800
Encore Capital Group Inc 3111 Camino Del Rio N Ste 300 *NASDAQ: ECPG*	San Diego	CA	92108	**877-445-4581**	858-560-2600
Expert Global Solutions, Inc 507 Prudential Rd	Horsham	PA	19044	**877-217-4423**	215-441-3000
FMA Alliance Ltd 80 Garden Ctr Ste 3	Broomfield	CO	80020	**800-955-5598**	281-931-5050
Focus Receivables Management LLC 1130 Northchase Pkwy Ste 150	Marietta	GA	30067	**877-362-8766**	678-305-9606
GC Services LP 6330 Gulfton St	Houston	TX	77081	**800-756-6524**	713-777-4441
General Revenue Corp 4660 Duke Dr Ste 300	Mason	OH	45040	**800-234-6258**	
Gulf Coast Collection Bureau Inc 5630 Marquesas Cir	Sarasota	FL	34233	**866-991-7358**	941-927-6999
Hospital Billing & Collection Service Ltd 118 Lukens Dr	New Castle	DE	19720	**877-254-9580**	302-552-8000
M G Credit Inc 5115 San Juan Ave	Jacksonville	FL	32210	**800-387-6503**	
Med Shield Inc 2424 E 55th St	Indianapolis	IN	46220	**800-272-5454**	317-613-3700
Nationwide Credit Inc (NCI) PO Box 26314 Ste 600	Atlanta	GA	30319	**800-456-4729**	
Nationwide Recovery Systems Inc (NRS) 4635 McEwen Rd	Dallas	TX	75244	**800-458-6357**	972-798-1000
Pentagroup Financial LLC 5959 Corp Dr Ste 1400	Houston	TX	77036	**800-385-9060**	832-615-2100
Portfolio Recovery Assoc LLC 120 Corporate Blvd Ste 100 Reverside Commerce Ctr *NASDAQ: PRAA*	Norfolk	VA	23502	**888-772-7326**	
Transworld Systems Inc PO Box 15618	Wilmington	DE	19850	**888-446-4733**	877-282-1250
Tri-state Adjustments Inc 3439 East Ave S PO Box 3219	La Crosse	WI	54602	**800-562-3906**	608-788-8683
Twenty-First Century Assoc 266 Summit Ave	Hackensack	NJ	07601	**888-760-5052**	201-678-1144
Unique Management Services Inc 119 E Maple St	Jeffersonville	IN	47130	**800-879-5453**	812-285-0886
United Recovery Systems LP 5800 N Course Dr	Houston	TX	77072	**800-568-0399**	713-977-1234
Van Ru Credit Corp 1350 E Touhy Ave Ste 300E	Des Plaines	IL	60018	**800-468-2678**	
Vengroff Williams & Assoc Inc (VWA) 2099 S State College Bvld	Anaheim	CA	92806	**800-238-9655**	866-737-4344

160 COLLEGES - BIBLE

SEE ALSO Colleges & Universities - Christian

Name / Address	City	State	Zip	Toll-Free	Phone
Alaska Bible College 248 E Elmwood Ave	Palmer	AK	99645	**800-478-7884**	907-822-3201
Allegheny Wesleyan College 2161 Woodsdale Rd	Salem	OH	44460	**800-292-3153**	330-337-6403
Baptist Bible College 628 E Kearney St	Springfield	MO	65803	**800-228-5754**	
Baptist University of the Americas 8019 S Pan Am Expy	San Antonio	TX	78224	**800-721-1396**	210-924-4338
Barclay College 607 N Kingman St	Haviland	KS	67059	**800-862-0226**	620-862-5252
Beulah Heights Bible College 892 Berne St SE PO Box 18145	Atlanta	GA	30316	**888-777-2422**	404-627-2681
Boise Bible College 8695 W Marigold St	Boise	ID	83714	**800-893-7755**	208-376-7731
Calvary Bible College & Theological Seminary 15800 Calvary Rd	Kansas City	MO	64147	**800-326-3960**	816-322-3960
Central Christian College of the Bible 911 E Urbandale Dr	Moberly	MO	65270	**888-263-3900**	660-263-3900
Cincinnati Christian University 2700 Glenway Ave	Cincinnati	OH	45204	**800-949-4228**	513-244-8100
Clear Creek Baptist Bible College 300 Clear Creek Rd	Pineville	KY	40977	**866-340-3196**	606-337-3196
College of Biblical Studies-Houston 7000 Regency Sq Blvd Ste 110	Houston	TX	77036	**844-227-9673**	713-785-5995
Columbia International University 7435 Monticello Rd	Columbia	SC	29203	**800-777-2227**	803-754-4100
Crossroads Bible College 601 N Shortridge Rd	Indianapolis	IN	46219	**800-822-3119**	317-352-8736
Crossroads College 920 Mayowood Rd SW	Rochester	MN	55902	**800-456-7651**	507-288-4563
Crown College 8700 College View Dr	Saint Bonifacius	MN	55375	**800-346-9252**	952-446-4100
Dallas Christian College 2700 Christian Pkwy	Dallas	TX	75234	**800-688-1029**	972-241-3371
Ecclesia College 9653 Nations Dr	Springdale	AR	72762	**800-735-9926**	479-248-7236
Emmaus Bible College 2570 Asbury Rd	Dubuque	IA	52001	**800-397-2425**	563-588-8000
Faith Baptist Bible College 1900 NW Fourth St	Ankeny	IA	50023	**800-409-3305**	515-964-0601
Florida Christian College 1011 Bill Beck Blvd	Kissimmee	FL	34744	**888-468-6322**	407-847-8966
Free Will Baptist Bible College 3606 W End Ave	Nashville	TN	37205	**888-979-3524**	615-844-5000
God's Bible School & College 1810 Young St	Cincinnati	OH	45202	**800-486-4637**	513-721-7944
Grace Bible College 1011 Aldon St SW PO Box 910	Grand Rapids	MI	49509	**800-968-1887**	616-538-2330
Grace University 1311 S Ninth St	Omaha	NE	68108	**800-383-1422**	402-449-2800
Great Lakes Christian College 6211 W Willow Hwy *Admissions	Lansing	MI	48917	**800-937-4522***	517-321-0242
Heritage Christian University 3625 Helton Dr PO Box HCU	Florence	AL	35630	**800-367-3565**	256-766-6610
Hobe Sound Bible College PO Box 1065	Hobe Sound	FL	33475	**800-881-5534**	772-546-5534
Johnson University 7900 Johnson Dr	Knoxville	TN	37998	**800-827-2122**	865-573-4517
Kentucky Mountain Bible College 855 Hwy 541	Jackson	KY	41339	**800-879-5622**	606-693-5000
Kuyper College 3333 E Beltline Ave NE	Grand Rapids	MI	49525	**800-511-3749**	616-222-3000
Lancaster Bible College 901 Eden Rd PO Box 83403	Lancaster	PA	17608	**800-544-7335**	717-569-7071
Laurel University 1215 Eastchester Dr	High Point	NC	27265	**855-528-7358**	336-887-3000
Life Pacific College 1100 W Covina Blvd	San Dimas	CA	91773	**877-886-5433**	909-599-5433
Lincoln Christian College Seminary 100 Campus View Dr	Lincoln	IL	62656	**888-522-5228**	217-732-3168
Manhattan Christian College 1415 Anderson Ave	Manhattan	KS	66502	**877-246-4622**	785-539-3571
Mid-Atlantic Christian Universit 715 N Poindexter St	Elizabeth City	NC	27909	**866-996-6228**	252-334-2070
Moody Bible Institute 820 N La Salle St	Chicago	IL	60610	**800-967-4624**	312-329-4400
Multnomah University 8435 NE Glisan St	Portland	OR	97220	**800-275-4672**	503-255-0332
Oak Hills Christian College 1600 Oak Hills Rd SW	Bemidji	MN	56601	**888-751-8670**	218-751-8670
Ozark Christian College 1111 N Main St	Joplin	MO	64801	**800-299-4622**	417-624-2518
Saint Louis Christian College 1360 Grandview Dr *Admissions	Florissant	MO	63033	**800-887-7522***	314-837-6777
Toccoa Falls College 107 Kincaid Dr *General	Toccoa Falls	GA	30598	**800-868-3257***	706-886-6831
Tri-State Bible College 506 Margaret St	South Point	OH	45680	**800-333-3243**	740-377-2520
Trinity Bible College 50 Sixth Ave N	Ellendale	ND	58436	**800-523-1603**	701-349-3621

	City	State	ZIP	Toll-Free	Phone
Trinity College of Florida					
2430 Welbilt Blvd	Trinity	FL	34655	**800-388-0869**	727-376-6911

161 COLLEGES - COMMUNITY & JUNIOR

SEE ALSO Vocational & Technical Schools ; Colleges - Fine Arts ; Colleges - Tribal ; Colleges & Universities - Four-Year

Institutions that offer academic degrees that can be transferred to a four-year college or university.

Alabama

	City	State	ZIP	Toll-Free	Phone
Alabama Southern Community College					
2800 S Alabama Ave	Monroeville	AL	36461	**866-901-1117**	251-575-3156
Bevill State Community College					
2631 Temple Ave N	Fayette	AL	35555	**800-648-3271**	205-932-3221
Jasper 1411 Indiana Ave	Jasper	AL	35501	**800-648-3271**	205-387-0511
Calhoun Community College					
PO Box 2216	Decatur	AL	35609	**800-626-3628**	256-306-2500
Huntsville 102B Wynn Dr	Huntsville	AL	35805	**800-626-3628**	256-890-4701
Redstone Arsenal					
6250 Hwy 31 N	Tanner	AL	35671	**800-626-3628**	256-306-2500
Central Alabama Community College					
1675 Cherokee Rd	Alexander City	AL	35010	**800-643-2657**	256-234-6346
Faulkner State Community College					
Bay Minette					
1900 Hwy 31 S	Bay Minette	AL	36507	**800-381-3722**	251-580-2111
Fairhope 440 Fairhope Ave	Fairhope	AL	36532	**800-231-3752**	251-990-0420
Gulf Shores					
3301 Gulf Shores Pkwy	Gulf Shores	AL	36542	**800-231-3752**	251-968-3101
Gadsden State Community College					
1001 George Wallace Dr PO Box 227	Gadsden	AL	35902	**800-226-5563**	256-549-8200
Jefferson State Community College					
2601 Carson Rd	Birmingham	AL	35215	**800-239-5900**	205-853-1200
Lurleen B Wallace Community College					
Andalusia					
1000 Dannelly Blvd PO Box 1418	Andalusia	AL	36420	**877-382-4357**	334-222-6591
Marion Military Institute					
1101 Washington St	Marion	AL	36756	**800-664-1842**	334-683-2322
Northwest-Shoals Community College					
Muscle Shoals					
800 George Wallace Blvd	Muscle Shoals	AL	35661	**800-645-8967**	256-331-5200
Phil Campbell					
2080 College Rd	Phil Campbell	AL	35581	**800-645-8967**	256-331-6200
Shelton State Community College					
9500 Old Greensboro Rd	Tuscaloosa	AL	35405	**877-211-7722**	205-391-2211
Southern Union State Community College					
Opelika 1701 Lafayette Pkwy	Opelika	AL	36801	**800-707-0057**	334-745-6437
Valley 321 Fob James Dr	Valley	AL	36854	**800-707-0057**	334-756-4151
Wallace Community College					
1141 Wallace Dr	Dothan	AL	36303	**800-543-2426**	334-983-3521
Wallace State Community College					
801 Main St	Hanceville	AL	35077	**866-350-9722**	256-352-8000

Alaska

	City	State	ZIP	Toll-Free	Phone
University of Alaska Anchorage Kenai Peninsula College					
156 College Rd	Soldotna	AK	99669	**877-262-0330**	
University of Alaska Anchorage Kodiak College					
117 Benny Benson Dr	Kodiak	AK	99615	**800-486-7660**	907-486-4161
University of Alaska Fairbanks					
PO Box 757480	Fairbanks	AK	99775	**800-478-1823**	907-474-7500
Northwest					
400 E Front St PO Box 400	Nome	AK	99762	**800-478-2202**	907-443-2201
University of Alaska Southeast Ketchikan					
2600 Seventh Ave	Ketchikan	AK	99901	**877-465-6400**	907-225-6177
University of Alaska Southeast Sitka					
1332 Seward Ave	Sitka	AK	99835	**800-478-6653**	907-747-6653

Arizona

	City	State	ZIP	Toll-Free	Phone
Arizona Western College					
2020 S Ave 8 E	Yuma	AZ	85366	**888-293-0392**	928-317-6000
Central Arizona College					
8470 N Overfield Rd	Coolidge	AZ	85228	**800-237-9814**	520-494-5444
Cochise College					
4190 W Hwy 80	Douglas	AZ	85607	**800-966-7943**	520-364-7943
Sierra Vista					
901 N Colombo Ave	Sierra Vista	AZ	85635	**800-966-7943**	520-515-0500
Coconino Community College					
Lonetree					
2800 S Lone Tree Rd	Flagstaff	AZ	86001	**800-350-7122**	928-527-1222
Eastern Arizona College					
615 N Stadium Ave	Thatcher	AZ	85552	**800-678-3808**	928-428-8472
GateWay Community College					
108 N 40th St	Phoenix	AZ	85034	**888-994-4433**	602-286-8000
Mesa Community College					
1833 W Southern Ave	Mesa	AZ	85202	**866-532-4983**	480-461-7000
Red Mountain					
7110 E McKellips Rd	Mesa	AZ	85207	**866-532-4983**	480-654-7200
Mohave Community College					
Bullhead City					
3400 Hwy 95	Bullhead City	AZ	86442	**866-664-2832**	928-758-3926
Lake Havasu					
1977 W Acoma Blvd	Lake Havasu City	AZ	86403	**866-664-2832**	928-855-7812
North Mohave					
PO Box 980	Colorado City	AZ	86021	**800-678-3992**	928-875-2799
Northland Pioneer College					
PO Box 610	Holbrook	AZ	86025	**800-266-7845**	928-532-6111
Pima Community College					
401 N Bonita Ave	Tucson	AZ	85709	**800-860-7462**	520-206-2733
West 2202 W Anklam Rd	Tucson	AZ	85709	**800-860-7462**	520-206-6600
Rio Salado College					
2323 W 14Th St	Tempe	AZ	85281	**855-622-2332**	480-517-8000
Scottsdale Community College					
9000 E Chaparral Rd	Scottsdale	AZ	85256	**800-784-2433**	480-423-6000
South Mountain Community College					
7050 S 24th St	Phoenix	AZ	85042	**855-622-2332**	602-243-8000
Yavapai College					
1100 E Sheldon St	Prescott	AZ	86301	**800-922-6787**	928-445-7300
Verde Valley					
601 Black Hills Dr	Clarkdale	AZ	86324	**800-922-6787**	928-634-7501

Arkansas

	City	State	ZIP	Toll-Free	Phone
Arkansas State University Newport					
7648 Victory Blvd	Newport	AR	72112	**800-976-1676**	870-512-7800
Black River Technical College					
1410 Hwy 304 E	Pocahontas	AR	72455	**866-890-6933**	870-248-4000
Crowley's Ridge College					
100 College Dr	Paragould	AR	72450	**800-264-1096**	870-236-6901
East Arkansas Community College					
1700 Newcastle Rd	Forrest City	AR	72335	**877-797-3222**	870-633-4480
Mid-South Community College					
2000 W Broadway	West Memphis	AR	72301	**866-733-6722**	870-733-6722
North Arkansas College					
1515 Pioneer Dr	Harrison	AR	72601	**800-679-6622**	870-743-3000
NorthWest Arkansas Community College					
1 College Dr	Bentonville	AR	72712	**800-995-6922**	479-636-9222
Ouachita Technical College					
1 College Cir	Malvern	AR	72104	**800-337-0266**	501-337-5000
Ozarka College					
218 College Dr	Melbourne	AR	72556	**800-821-4335**	870-368-7371
South Arkansas Community College					
PO Box 7010	El Dorado	AR	71731	**800-955-2289**	870-862-8131
Southeast Arkansas College					
1900 Hazel St	Pine Bluff	AR	71603	**888-732-7582**	870-543-5900

California

	City	State	ZIP	Toll-Free	Phone
Allan Hancock College					
800 S College Dr	Santa Maria	CA	93454	**866-342-5242**	805-922-6966
Barstow College					
2700 Barstow Rd	Barstow	CA	92311	**877-823-2378**	760-252-2411
Butte College					
3536 Butte Campus Dr	Oroville	CA	95965	**800-933-8322***	530-895-2511
*Hum Res					
Cabrillo College					
6500 Soquel Dr	Aptos	CA	95003	**888-624-1139**	831-479-6100
Cerro Coso Community College					
Bishop 4090 W Line St	Bishop	CA	93514	**888-537-6932**	760-872-1565
Indian Wells Valley					
3000 College Heights Blvd	Ridgecrest	CA	93555	**888-537-6932**	760-384-6100
Kern River Valley					
5520 Lk Isabella Blvd	Lake Isabella	CA	93240	**888-537-6932**	760-379-5501
Mammoth					
101 College Pkwy PO Box 1865	Mammoth Lakes	CA	93546	**888-537-6932**	760-934-2875
South Kern					
140 Methusa Ave	Edwards AFB	CA	93524	**888-537-6932**	661-258-8644
City College of San Francisco					
50 Phelan Ave	San Francisco	CA	94112	**800-433-3243**	415-239-3000
Coastline Community College					
11460 Warner Ave	Fountain Valley	CA	92708	**866-422-2645**	714-546-7600
College of the Redwoods					
7351 Tompkins Hill Rd	Eureka	CA	95501	**800-641-0400**	707-476-4100
Del Norte					
883 W Washington Blvd	Crescent City	CA	95531	**800-641-0400**	707-465-2300
Mendocino Coast					
440 Alger St	Fort Bragg	CA	95437	**800-641-0400**	707-962-2600
College of the Siskiyous					
800 College Ave	Weed	CA	96094	**888-397-4339**	530-938-4461
Copper Mountain College					
6162 Rotary Way	Joshua Tree	CA	92252	**866-366-3791**	760-366-3791
Cuesta College					
PO Box 8106	San Luis Obispo	CA	93403	**800-675-2526**	805-546-3100
Cuyamaca College					
900 Rancho San Diego Pkwy	El Cajon	CA	92019	**800-234-1597**	619-660-4000
Diablo Valley College					
321 Golf Club Rd	Pleasant Hill	CA	94523	**800-227-1060**	925-685-1230
El Camino College					
16007 Crenshaw Blvd	Torrance	CA	90506	**866-352-2646**	310-532-3670
Feather River College					
570 Golden Eagle Ave	Quincy	CA	95971	**800-442-9799**	530-283-0202
Foothill College					
12345 El Monte Rd	Los Altos Hills	CA	94022	**800-234-1597**	650-949-7777
Fresno City College					
1101 E University Ave	Fresno	CA	93741	**866-245-3276**	559-442-4600
Glendale Community College					
1500 N Verdugo Rd	Glendale	CA	91208	**866-251-1977**	818-240-1000
Hartnell College					
156 Homestead Ave	Salinas	CA	93901	**888-678-2871**	831-755-6700
Long Beach City College					
4901 E Carson St	Long Beach	CA	90808	**888-442-4551**	562-938-4111
Los Angeles City College					
855 N Vermont Ave	Los Angeles	CA	90029	**800-207-1710**	323-953-4000
Los Medanos College					
2700 E Leland Rd	Pittsburg	CA	94565	**800-677-6337**	925-439-2181
Merced College 3600 M St	Merced	CA	95348	**800-784-2433**	209-384-6000
MiraCosta College					
Oceanside					
1 Barnard Dr Ste 7	Oceanside	CA	92056	**888-201-8480**	760-757-2121
San Elijo					
3333 Manchester Ave	Cardiff	CA	92007	**888-201-8480**	760-944-4449
Monterey Peninsula College					
980 Fremont St	Monterey	CA	93940	**877-663-5433**	831-646-4000
Mount San Jacinto College					
1499 N State St	San Jacinto	CA	92583	**800-624-5561**	951-487-6752

	City	State	ZIP	Toll-Free	Phone
Napa Valley College					
2277 Napa-Vallejo Hwy	Napa	CA	94558	**800-826-1077**	707-256-7000
Reedley College					
995 N Reed Ave	Reedley	CA	93654	**877-253-7122**	559-638-3641
Santa Barbara City College					
721 Cliff Dr	Santa Barbara	CA	93109	**877-232-3919**	805-965-0581
Santa Rosa Junior College					
1501 Mendocino Ave	Santa Rosa	CA	95401	**800-564-7752**	707-527-4011
Sierra College					
Nevada County					
250 Sierra College Dr	Grass Valley	CA	95945	**800-242-4004**	530-274-5300
Sierra Community College					
5000 Rocklin Rd	Rocklin	CA	95677	**800-242-4004**	916-624-3333
Southwestern College					
900 Otay Lakes Rd	Chula Vista	CA	91910	**866-262-9881**	619-421-6700
Taft College 29 Emmons Pk Dr	Taft	CA	93268	**800-379-6784**	661-763-7700
Victor Valley Community College					
18422 Bear Valley Rd	Victorville	CA	92392	**877-741-8532**	760-245-4271
West Hills College					
Coalinga 300 Cherry Ln	Coalinga	CA	93210	**800-266-1114**	559-934-2000
Lemoore 555 College Ave	Lemoore	CA	93245	**800-266-1114**	559-925-3000
Western University of Health Sciences					
309 E Second St	Pomona	CA	91766	**800-346-1610**	909-623-6116

Colorado

	City	State	ZIP	Toll-Free	Phone
Aims Community College					
5401 W 20th St	Greeley	CO	80634	**800-301-5388**	970-330-8008
Arapahoe Community College					
5900 S Santa Fe Dr	Littleton	CO	80160	**888-800-9198**	303-797-0100
Colorado Mountain College					
Alpine					
1330 Bob Adams Dr	Steamboat Springs	CO	80487	**800-621-8559**	970-870-4444
Aspen 0255 Sage Way	Aspen	CO	81611	**800-621-8559**	970-925-7740
Roaring Fork-Spring Valley					
3000 County Rd 114	Glenwood Springs	CO	81601	**800-621-8559**	970-945-7481
Colorado Northwestern Community College					
500 Kennedy Dr	Rangely	CO	81648	**800-562-1105**	970-675-3335
Craig 50 College Dr	Craig	CO	81625	**800-562-1105**	
Community College of Aurora					
16000 E Centretech Pkwy	Aurora	CO	80011	**844-493-8255**	303-360-4700
Front Range Community College (FRCC)					
Boulder County					
2190 Miller Dr	Longmont	CO	80501	**888-800-9198**	303-678-3722
Larimer					
4616 S Shields St	Fort Collins	CO	80526	**888-800-9198**	970-226-2500
Lamar Community College					
2401 S Main St	Lamar	CO	81052	**800-968-6920**	719-336-2248
Morgan Community College					
920 Barlow Rd	Fort Morgan	CO	80701	**800-622-0216**	970-542-3100
Northeastern Junior College					
100 College Ave	Sterling	CO	80751	**800-626-4637**	970-521-6600
Pikes Peak Community College					
Centennial					
5675 S Academy Blvd	Colorado Springs	CO	80906	**800-456-6847**	719-502-2000
Downtown Studio					
100 W Pikes Peak Ave	Colorado Springs	CO	80903	**800-456-6847**	719-502-2000
Rampart Range					
11195 Hwy 83	Colorado Springs	CO	80921	**800-456-6847**	719-502-2000
Pueblo Community College					
900 W Orman Ave	Pueblo	CO	81004	**888-642-6017**	719-549-3200
Trinidad State Junior College					
600 Prospect St	Trinidad	CO	81082	**800-621-8752**	719-846-5011

Connecticut

	City	State	ZIP	Toll-Free	Phone
Asnuntuck Community College					
170 Elm St	Enfield	CT	06082	**800-501-3967**	860-253-3000
Capital Community College					
950 Main St	Hartford	CT	06103	**800-894-6126**	860-906-5000
Housatonic Community College					
900 Lafayette Blvd	Bridgeport	CT	06604	**866-733-2463**	203-332-5000
Middlesex Community College					
100 Training Hill Rd	Middletown	CT	06457	**800-818-5501**	860-343-5800
Norwalk Community College					
188 Richards Ave	Norwalk	CT	06854	**800-565-3036**	203-857-7060
University of Connecticut					
Avery Point					
1084 Shennecossett Rd	Groton	CT	06340	**888-247-5556**	860-405-9019

Florida

	City	State	ZIP	Toll-Free	Phone
Brevard Community College (BCC)					
Cocoa 1519 Clearlake Rd	Cocoa	FL	32922	**888-747-2802**	321-632-1111
Melbourne					
3865 N Wickham Rd	Melbourne	FL	32935	**888-747-2802**	321-632-1111
Palm Bay					
250 Community College Pkwy	Palm Bay	FL	32909	**888-747-2802**	321-632-1111
Titusville 1311 N US 1	Titusville	FL	32796	**888-747-2802**	321-632-1111
Broward Community College					
Downtown Ctr					
111 E Las Olas Blvd	Fort Lauderdale	FL	33301	**888-654-6482**	954-201-7350
North					
1000 Coconut Creek Blvd	Coconut Creek	FL	33066	**888-654-6482**	954-201-2240
Daytona Beach Community College					
1200 W International Speedway Blvd	Daytona Beach	FL	32114	**877-822-6669**	386-506-3000
Edison College					
Charlotte					
26300 Airport Rd	Punta Gorda	FL	33950	**800-749-2322**	941-637-5629
Florida Community College at Jacksonville					
Downtown					
101 State St W	Jacksonville	FL	32202	**877-633-5950**	904-633-8100
Florida Keys Community College					
5901 College Rd	Key West	FL	33040	**866-567-2665**	305-296-9081
Gulf Coast Community College					
5230 W Hwy 98	Panama City	FL	32401	**800-311-3685**	850-769-1551
Hillsborough Community College					
Dale Mabry					
4001 Tampa Bay Blvd	Tampa	FL	33614	**866-253-7077**	813-253-7000
Indian River State College (IRSC)					
3209 Virginia Ave	Fort Pierce	FL	34981	**866-792-4772**	772-462-4772
North Florida Community College					
325 NW Turner Davis Dr	Madison	FL	32340	**877-501-0956**	850-973-2288
Palm Beach Community College					
Lake Worth					
4200 Congress Ave	Lake Worth	FL	33461	**866-576-7222**	561-868-3350
Palm Beach Gardens					
3160 PGA Blvd	Palm Beach Gardens	FL	33410	**866-576-7222**	561-207-5340
Pasco-Hernando Community College					
10230 Ridge Rd	New Port Richey	FL	34654	**877-879-7422**	727-847-2727
North					
11415 Ponce de Leon Blvd	Brooksville	FL	34601	**877-879-7422**	352-796-6726
Pensacola Junior College					
Warrington 5555 W Hwy 98	Pensacola	FL	32507	**888-897-3605**	850-484-2200
Saint Johns River Community College					
5001 St Johns Ave	Palatka	FL	32177	**888-757-2293**	386-312-4200
Seminole State College					
2701 Boren Blvd PO Box 351	Sanford	FL	32773	**877-738-6365**	405-382-9950

Georgia

	City	State	ZIP	Toll-Free	Phone
Abraham Baldwin Agricultural College					
2802 Moore Hwy ABAC 3	Tifton	GA	31793	**800-733-3653**	229-391-5001
Andrew College					
501 College St	Cuthbert	GA	39840	**800-664-9250**	
Darton College					
2400 Gillionville Rd	Albany	GA	31707	**866-775-1214**	229-430-6742
East Georgia College					
131 College Cir	Swainsboro	GA	30401	**800-715-4255**	478-289-2000
Emory University Oxford College					
201 Dowman Dr PO Box 1418	Atlanta	GA	30322	**800-723-8328**	404-727-6069
Georgia Highlands College					
Cartersville					
5441 Hwy 20 NE	Cartersville	GA	30121	**800-332-2406**	678-872-8000
Floyd 3175 Cedartown Hwy	Rome	GA	30161	**800-332-2406**	706-802-5000
Georgia Military College					
201 E Green St	Milledgeville	GA	31061	**800-342-0413**	478-387-4900
Young Harris College					
PO Box 116	Young Harris	GA	30582	**800-241-3754**	706-379-3111

Hawaii

	City	State	ZIP	Toll-Free	Phone
Kauai Community College					
3-1901 Kaumualii Hwy	Lihue	HI	96766	**800-776-4816**	808-245-8311
Leeward Community College					
96-045 Ala Ike	Pearl City	HI	96782	**888-442-4551**	808-455-0011
Maui Community College					
310 W Kaahumanu Ave	Kahului	HI	96732	**800-479-6692**	808-984-3267
University of Hawaii					
Hilo 200 W Kawili St	Hilo	HI	96720	**800-897-4456***	808-974-7414
*Admissions					

Idaho

	City	State	ZIP	Toll-Free	Phone
College of Southern Idaho					
PO Box 1238	Twin Falls	ID	83303	**800-680-0274**	208-733-9554
North Idaho College					
1000 W Garden Ave	Coeur d'Alene	ID	83814	**877-404-4536**	208-769-3300

Illinois

	City	State	ZIP	Toll-Free	Phone
Black Hawk College					
East 1501 State Hwy 78	Kewanee	IL	61443	**800-233-5671**	309-852-5671
Quad Cities 6600 34th Ave	Moline	IL	61265	**800-334-1311**	309-796-5000
Carl Sandburg College					
2400 Tom L Wilson Blvd	Galesburg	IL	61401	**877-236-1862**	309-344-2518
City Colleges of Chicago					
226 W Jackson	Chicago	IL	60606	**866-908-7582**	312-553-2500
Danville Area Community College					
2000 E Main St	Danville	IL	61832	**877-342-3042**	217-443-3222
Elgin Community College					
1700 Spartan Dr	Elgin	IL	60123	**855-850-2525**	847-697-1000
Harry S Truman College					
1145 W Wilson Ave	Chicago	IL	60640	**877-863-6339**	773-878-1700
Joliet Junior College					
North 1215 Houbolt Rd	Joliet	IL	60431	**800-899-4722**	815-729-9020
Kankakee Community College					
100 College Dr	Kankakee	IL	60901	**800-526-0844**	815-802-8100
Kishwaukee College					
21193 Malta Rd	Malta	IL	60150	**888-656-7329**	815-825-2086
Lincoln College					
300 Keokuk St	Lincoln	IL	62656	**800-569-0556**	217-732-3155
Lincoln Land Community College					
5250 Shepherd Rd PO Box 19256	Springfield	IL	62794	**800-727-4161**	217-786-2200
Lincoln Trail College					
11220 State Hwy 1	Robinson	IL	62454	**866-582-4322**	618-544-8657
Malcolm X College					
1900 W Jackson	Chicago	IL	60612	**877-542-0285**	312-850-7000
McHenry County College					
8900 US Hwy 14	Crystal Lake	IL	60012	**888-977-4847**	815-455-3700
Olney Central College					
305 NW St	Olney	IL	62450	**866-622-4322**	618-395-7777
Parkland College					
2400 W Bradley Ave	Champaign	IL	61821	**888-467-6065**	217-351-2200
Prairie State College					
202 S Halsted St	Chicago Heights	IL	60411	**866-255-5437**	708-709-3500
Rend Lake College					
468 N Ken Gray Pkwy	Ina	IL	62846	**800-369-5321**	618-437-5321

	City	State	Zip	Toll-Free	Phone
Rock Valley College					
3301 N Mulford Rd	Rockford	IL	61114	**800-973-7821**	815-921-7821
Shawnee Community College					
8364 Shawnee College Rd	Ullin	IL	62992	**800-481-2242**	618-634-3200
Southeastern Illinois College					
3575 College Rd	Harrisburg	IL	62946	**866-338-2742**	618-252-6376
Southwestern Illinois College					
2500 Carlyle Ave	Belleville	IL	62221	**800-222-5131**	618-235-2700
Spoon River College (SRC)					
23235 N County Hwy 22	Canton	IL	61520	**800-334-7337**	309-647-4645
Springfield College in Illinois - Benedictine University					
1500 N Fifth St	Springfield	IL	62702	**800-635-7289**	217-525-1420

Indiana

	City	State	Zip	Toll-Free	Phone
Vincennes University					
1002 N First St	Vincennes	IN	47591	**800-742-9198**	812-888-4313
Jasper 850 College Ave	Jasper	IN	47546	**800-809-8852**	812-482-3030

Iowa

	City	State	Zip	Toll-Free	Phone
Clinton Community College					
1000 Lincoln Blvd	Clinton	IA	52732	**877-495-3320**	563-244-7001
Des Moines Area Community College					
Ankeny 2006 S Ankeny Blvd	Ankeny	IA	50021	**800-362-2127**	515-964-6200
Boone 1125 Hancock Dr	Boone	IA	50036	**800-362-2127**	515-432-7203
Carroll 906 N Grant Rd	Carroll	IA	51401	**800-622-3334**	712-792-1755
Urban/Des Moines					
1100 Seventh St	Des Moines	IA	50314	**800-622-3334**	515-244-4226
Ellsworth Community College					
1100 College Ave	Iowa Falls	IA	50126	**800-322-9235**	641-648-4611
Hawkeye Community College					
1501 E Orange Rd	Waterloo	IA	50704	**800-670-4769**	319-296-2320
Indian Hills Community College					
525 Grandview Ave	Ottumwa	IA	52501	**800-726-2585**	641-683-5111
Iowa Central Community College					
2031 Quail Ave	Fort Dodge	IA	50501	**800-362-2793**	515-576-7201
Iowa Lakes Community College					
300 S 18th St	Estherville	IA	51334	**800-242-5106**	712-362-2604
Iowa Western Community College					
Clarinda					
923 E Washington St	Clarinda	IA	51632	**800-521-2073**	712-542-5117
Kirkwood Community College					
6301 Kirkwood Blvd SW	Cedar Rapids	IA	52404	**800-332-2055**	319-398-5411
Marshalltown Community College					
3700 S Ctr St	Marshalltown	IA	50158	**866-622-4748**	641-752-7106
Muscatine Community College					
152 Colorado St	Muscatine	IA	52761	**888-336-3907**	563-288-6001
North Iowa Area Community College					
500 College Dr	Mason City	IA	50401	**888-466-4222**	641-423-1264
Northeast Iowa Community College					
Calmar					
1625 Hwy 150 S PO Box 400	Calmar	IA	52132	**800-728-2256**	563-562-3263
Peosta 10250 Sundown Rd	Peosta	IA	52068	**800-728-7367**	563-556-5110
Northwest Iowa Community College					
603 W Pk St	Sheldon	IA	51201	**800-352-4907**	712-324-5061
Scott Community College					
500 Belmont Rd	Bettendorf	IA	52722	**888-336-3907**	563-441-4001
Southeastern Community College North					
1500 W Agency Rd	West Burlington	IA	52655	**866-722-4692**	319-752-2731
Southeastern Community College South					
335 Messenger Rd	Keokuk	IA	52632	**866-722-4692**	319-524-3221
Southwestern Community College					
1501 W Townline St	Creston	IA	50801	**800-247-4023**	641-782-7081

Kansas

	City	State	Zip	Toll-Free	Phone
Allen County Community College					
1801 N Cottonwood St	Iola	KS	66749	**800-444-0535**	620-365-5116
Barton County Community College					
245 NE 30th Rd	Great Bend	KS	67530	**800-722-6842**	620-792-2701
Cloud County Community College					
2221 Campus Dr	Concordia	KS	66901	**800-729-5101**	785-243-1435
Colby Community College					
1255 S Range Ave	Colby	KS	67701	**888-634-9350**	785-462-3984
Cowley County Community College & Area Vocational-Technical School					
PO Box 1147	Arkansas City	KS	67005	**800-593-2222**	620-442-0430
Dodge City Community College					
2501 N 14th Ave	Dodge City	KS	67801	**800-367-3222**	620-225-1321
Donnelly College					
608 N 18th St	Kansas City	KS	66102	**800-908-9946**	913-621-6070
Fort Scott Community College					
2108 S Horton St	Fort Scott	KS	66701	**800-874-3722**	620-223-2700
Garden City Community College					
801 N Campus Dr	Garden City	KS	67846	**800-658-1696**	620-276-7611
Hesston College					
325 S College Dr PO Box 3000	Hesston	KS	67062	**800-995-2757**	620-327-4221
Hutchinson Community College & Area Vocational School					
1300 N Plum St	Hutchinson	KS	67501	**800-289-3501**	620-665-3500
Independence Community College					
1057 W College Ave PO Box 708	Independence	KS	67301	**800-842-6063**	620-331-4100
Johnson County Community College					
12345 College Blvd	Overland Park	KS	66210	**866-896-5893**	913-469-8500
Labette Community College					
200 S 14th St	Parsons	KS	67357	**888-522-3883**	620-421-6700
Manhattan Area Technical College					
3136 Dickens	Manhattan	KS	66503	**800-352-7575**	785-587-2800
Neosho County Community College					
Ottawa 226 S Beech St	Ottawa	KS	66067	**888-466-2588**	785-242-2067
Pratt Community College					
348 NE SR-61	Pratt	KS	67124	**800-794-3091**	620-672-5641
Seward County Community College					
1801 N Campus Ave PO Box 1137	Liberal	KS	67905	**800-373-9951**	620-624-1951

Kentucky

	City	State	Zip	Toll-Free	Phone
Ashland Community & Technical College					
1400 College Dr	Ashland	KY	41101	**800-928-4256**	606-326-2000
Big Sandy Community & Technical College					
1 Bert T Combs Dr	Prestonsburg	KY	41653	**888-641-4132**	606-886-3863
Bluegrass Community & Technical College					
Cooper Campus					
470 Cooper Dr	Lexington	KY	40506	**866-774-4872**	859-246-6200
Elizabethtown Community & Technical College					
600 College St Rd	Elizabethtown	KY	42701	**877-246-2322**	270-769-2371
Hazard Community & Technical College					
1 Community College Dr	Hazard	KY	41701	**800-246-7521**	606-436-5721
Hazard Campus 101 Vo Tech Dr	Hazard	KY	41701	**800-246-7521**	606-436-5721
Lees Campus					
601 Jefferson Ave	Jackson	KY	41339	**800-246-7521**	606-666-7521
Henderson Community College					
2660 S Green St	Henderson	KY	42420	**800-696-9958**	270-827-1867
Hopkinsville Community College					
720 N Dr	Hopkinsville	KY	42240	**866-534-2224**	270-886-3921
Jefferson Community & Technical College					
109 E Broadway	Louisville	KY	40202	**855-246-5282**	502-213-5333
Madisonville Community College					
2000 College Dr	Madisonville	KY	42431	**866-227-4812**	270-821-2250
Maysville Community & Technical College					
1755 US 68	Maysville	KY	41056	**888-452-7322**	606-759-7141
Somerset Community College					
808 Monticello St	Somerset	KY	42501	**877-629-9722**	606-679-8501
Southeast Kentucky Community & Technical College					
Cumberland					
700 College Rd	Cumberland	KY	40823	**888-274-7322**	606-589-2145
Middlesboro					
1300 Chichester Ave	Middlesboro	KY	40965	**888-274-7322**	606-242-2145
Whitesburg 2 Long Ave	Whitesburg	KY	41858	**888-274-7322**	606-633-0279
West Kentucky Community & Technical College					
4810 Alben Barkley Dr PO Box 7380	Paducah	KY	42001	**855-469-5282**	270-554-9200

Louisiana

	City	State	Zip	Toll-Free	Phone
Baton Rouge Community College (BRCC)					
201 Community College Dr	Baton Rouge	LA	70806	**866-217-9823**	225-216-8000
Elaine P Nunez Community College					
3710 Paris Rd	Chalmette	LA	70043	**866-825-1954**	504-278-7497
Louisiana Delta Community College					
7500 Millhaven Rd	Monroe	LA	71203	**866-500-5322**	318-345-9000
Louisiana State University					
Alexandria					
8100 US Hwy 71 S	Alexandria	LA	71302	**888-473-6417***	318-445-3672
*Admissions					
Eunice PO Box 1129	Eunice	LA	70535	**888-367-5783**	337-457-7311

Maine

	City	State	Zip	Toll-Free	Phone
Kennebec Valley Community College					
92 Western Ave	Fairfield	ME	04937	**800-528-5882**	207-453-5000
York County Community College					
112 College Dr	Wells	ME	04090	**800-580-3820**	207-646-9282

Maryland

	City	State	Zip	Toll-Free	Phone
Allegany College of Maryland					
12401 Willowbrook Rd SE	Cumberland	MD	21502	**800-974-0203**	301-784-5000
Baltimore City Community College					
2901 Liberty Heights Ave	Baltimore	MD	21215	**888-203-1261**	410-462-8000
Carroll Community College					
1601 Washington Rd	Westminster	MD	21157	**888-221-9748**	410-386-8000
Cecil Community College					
1 Seahawk Dr	North East	MD	21901	**866-966-1001**	410-287-6060
College of Southern Maryland					
Leonardtown					
22950 Hollywood Rd	Leonardtown	MD	20650	**800-933-9177**	240-725-5300
Prince Frederick					
115 J W Williams Rd	Prince Frederick	MD	20678	**800-933-9177**	443-550-6000
Community College of Baltimore County					
Essex 7201 Rossville Blvd	Baltimore	MD	21237	**877-557-2575**	410-682-6000
Garrett College					
687 Mosser Rd	McHenry	MD	21541	**866-554-2773**	301-387-3000
Wor-Wic Community College					
32000 Campus Dr	Salisbury	MD	21804	**800-735-2258**	410-334-2800

Massachusetts

	City	State	Zip	Toll-Free	Phone
Bunker Hill Community College					
Charlestown					
250 New Rutherford Ave	Boston	MA	02129	**877-218-8829**	617-228-2000
Cape Cod Community College					
2240 Iyanough Rd	West Barnstable	MA	02668	**877-846-3672**	508-362-2131
Dean College 99 Main St	Franklin	MA	02038	**877-879-3326**	508-541-1508
Fisher College 118 Beacon St	Boston	MA	02116	**866-266-6007**	617-236-8800
Holyoke Community College					
303 Homestead Ave	Holyoke	MA	01040	**877-442-6222**	413-538-7000
Massachusetts Bay Community College					
Wellesley Hills					
50 Oakland St	Wellesley Hills	MA	02481	**800-233-3182**	781-239-3000
Northern Essex Community College					
100 Elliott St	Haverhill	MA	01830	**800-422-4453**	978-556-3000
Quincy College					
1250 Hancock St	Quincy	MA	02169	**800-698-1700**	617-984-1700
Springfield Technical Community College					
1 Armory Sq PO Box 900	Springfield	MA	01102	**800-326-6142**	413-781-7822

Michigan

College / Address	City	State	ZIP	Toll-Free	Phone
Alpena Community College (ACC)					
665 Johnson St	Alpena	MI	49707	**888-468-6222**	989-356-9021
Bay de Noc Community College					
2001 N Lincoln Rd	Escanaba	MI	49829	**800-221-2001**	906-786-5802
Bay Mills Community College					
12214 W Lakeshore Dr	Brimley	MI	49715	**800-844-2622**	906-248-3354
Delta College					
1961 Delta Rd	University Center	MI	48710	**888-636-4211**	989-686-9000
Glen Oaks Community College					
62249 Shimmel Rd	Centreville	MI	49032	**888-994-7818**	269-467-9945
Gogebic Community College					
E 4946 Jackson Rd	Ironwood	MI	49938	**800-682-5910**	906-932-4231
Henry Ford Community College					
5101 Evergreen Rd	Dearborn	MI	48128	**800-585-4322**	313-845-9600
Jackson Community College					
2111 Emmons Rd	Jackson	MI	49201	**888-522-7344**	517-787-0800
Hillsdale 3120 W Carleton Rd PO Box 712	Hillsdale	MI	49242	**888-522-7344**	517-437-3343
Kirtland Community College					
10775 N St Helen Rd	Roscommon	MI	48653	**866-632-9992**	989-275-5000
Lake Michigan College					
Bertrand Crossing 1905 Foundation Dr	Niles	MI	49120	**800-252-1562**	269-695-1391
South Haven 125 Veterans Blvd	South Haven	MI	49090	**800-252-1562**	269-639-8442
Lansing Community College					
419 N Washington Sq	Lansing	MI	48933	**800-644-4522**	517-483-1957
Macomb Community College					
Center 44575 Garfield Rd	Clinton Township	MI	48038	**866-622-6621**	586-445-7999
South 14500 E 12-Mile Rd	Warren	MI	48088	**866-622-6621**	586-445-7000
Monroe County Community College					
1555 S Raisinville Rd	Monroe	MI	48161	**877-937-6222**	734-242-7300
Muskegon Community College					
221 S Quarterline Rd	Muskegon	MI	49442	**866-711-4622**	231-773-9131
North Central Michigan College					
1515 Howard St	Petoskey	MI	49770	**888-298-6605**	231-348-6605
Northwestern Michigan College					
1701 E Front St	Traverse City	MI	49686	**800-748-0566**	231-995-1000
Oakland Community College					
2480 Opdyke Rd	Bloomfield Hills	MI	48304	**800-829-1040**	248-341-2000
Highland Lakes 7350 Cooley Lake Rd	Waterford	MI	48327	**800-829-1040**	248-942-3100
Southfield 2480 Opdyke Rd	Bloomfield Hills	MI	48304	**800-829-1040**	248-341-2000
Saginaw Chippewa Tribal College					
2274 Enterprise Dr	Mount Pleasant	MI	48858	**800-225-8172**	989-775-4123
Southwestern Michigan College (SMC)					
58900 Cherry Grove Rd	Dowagiac	MI	49047	**800-456-8675**	269-782-1000
Niles Area 2229 US 12	Niles	MI	49120	**800-456-8675**	269-782-1233
West Shore Community College					
PO Box 277	Scottville	MI	49454	**800-848-9722**	231-845-6211

Minnesota

College / Address	City	State	ZIP	Toll-Free	Phone
Anoka-Ramsey Community College					
11200 Mississippi Blvd NW	Coon Rapids	MN	55433	**800-627-3529**	763-433-1100
Central Lakes College					
Brainerd 501 W College Dr	Brainerd	MN	56401	**800-933-0346**	218-855-8199
Staples 1830 Airport Rd	Staples	MN	56479	**800-247-6836**	218-894-5100
Century College					
3300 Century Ave N	White Bear Lake	MN	55115	**800-228-1978**	651-779-3300
Fond du Lac Tribal & Community College					
2101 14th St	Cloquet	MN	55720	**800-657-3712**	218-879-0800
Hibbing Community College					
1515 E 25th St	Hibbing	MN	55746	**800-224-4422**	218-262-7200
Inver Hills Community College					
2500 80th St E	Inver Grove Heights	MN	55076	**866-576-0689**	651-450-8500
Itasca Community College					
1851 E Us Hwy 169	Grand Rapids	MN	55744	**800-996-6422**	218-327-4460
Lake Superior College					
2101 Trinity Rd	Duluth	MN	55811	**800-432-2884**	218-733-7600
Leech Lake Tribal College					
6945 Little Wolf Rd PO Box 180	Cass Lake	MN	56633	**866-676-2772**	218-335-4200
Mesabi Range Community & Technical College					
1100 Industrial Pk Dr PO Box 648	Eveleth	MN	55734	**800-657-3860**	218-741-3095
Minneapolis Community & Technical College					
1501 Hennepin Ave	Minneapolis	MN	55403	**800-247-0911**	612-659-6200
Minnesota State Community & Technical College					
Detroit Lakes 900 Hwy 34E	Detroit Lakes	MN	56501	**800-492-4836**	218-846-3700
Fergus Falls 1414 College Way	Fergus Falls	MN	56537	**877-450-3322**	218-736-1500
Moorhead 1900 28th Ave S	Moorhead	MN	56560	**800-426-5603**	218-299-6500
Minnesota West Community & Technical College					
1450 Collegeway	Worthington	MN	56187	**800-657-3966**	507-372-3400
Normandale Community College					
9700 France Ave S	Bloomington	MN	55431	**866-880-8740**	952-487-8200
North Hennepin Community College					
7411 85th Ave N	Brooklyn Park	MN	55445	**800-818-0395**	763-424-0702
Northland Community & Technical College					
1101 US Hwy 1 E	Thief River Falls	MN	56701	**800-959-6282**	218-681-0701
East Grand Forks 2022 Central Ave NE	East Grand Forks	MN	56721	**800-451-3441**	218-773-3441
Rainy River Community College					
1501 Hwy 71	International Falls	MN	56649	**800-456-3996**	218-285-7722
Riverland Community College					
1900 Eigth Ave NW	Austin	MN	55912	**800-247-5039**	507-433-0600
Rochester Community & Technical College					
851 30th Ave SE	Rochester	MN	55904	**800-247-1296**	507-285-7210
South Central College					
Faribault 1225 Third St	Faribault	MN	55021	**800-422-0391**	507-332-5800
Mankato 1920 Lee Blvd	North Mankato	MN	56003	**800-722-9359**	507-389-7200
Vermilion Community College					
1900 E Camp St	Ely	MN	55731	**800-657-3608**	218-365-7200

Mississippi

College / Address	City	State	ZIP	Toll-Free	Phone
East Central Community College					
PO Box 129	Decatur	MS	39327	**877-462-3222**	601-635-2111
Hinds Community College					
501 E Main St PO Box 1100	Raymond	MS	39154	**800-446-3722**	601-857-5261
Holmes Community College					
PO Box 399	Goodman	MS	39079	**800-465-6374**	662-472-2312
Itawamba Community College					
Fulton 602 W Hill St	Fulton	MS	38843	**800-433-3243**	662-862-8000
Meridian Community College					
910 Hwy 19 N	Meridian	MS	39307	**800-622-8431**	601-483-8241
Mississippi Gulf Coast Community College					
51 Main St PO Box 548	Perkinston	MS	39573	**866-735-1122**	601-928-5211
Jackson County 2300 Hwy 90 PO Box 100	Gautier	MS	39553	**866-735-1122**	228-497-9602
Jefferson Davis 2226 Switzer Rd	Gulfport	MS	39507	**866-735-1122**	228-896-3355
Northeast Mississippi Community College					
101 Cunningham Blvd	Booneville	MS	38829	**800-555-2154**	662-728-7751
Pearl River Community College					
101 Hwy 11 N	Poplarville	MS	39470	**877-772-2338**	601-403-1000

Missouri

College / Address	City	State	ZIP	Toll-Free	Phone
A.T. Still University of Health Sciences					
800 W Jefferson St	Kirksville	MO	63501	**866-626-2878**	660-626-2121
Cottey College					
1000 W Austin Blvd	Nevada	MO	64772	**888-526-8839**	417-667-8181
Crowder College					
601 Laclede Ave	Neosho	MO	64850	**866-238-7788**	417-451-3223
East Central College					
1964 Prairie Dell Rd	Union	MO	63084	**800-392-6848**	636-583-5193
Metropolitan Community College Penn Valley					
3201 SW Trafficway	Kansas City	MO	64111	**866-676-6224**	816-759-4000
Moberly Area Community College					
101 College Ave	Moberly	MO	65270	**800-622-2070**	660-263-4110
North Central Missouri College					
1301 Main St	Trenton	MO	64683	**800-880-6180**	660-359-3948
State Fair Community College					
3201 W 16th St	Sedalia	MO	65301	**877-311-7322**	660-530-5800
Three Rivers Community College					
2080 Three Rivers Blvd	Poplar Bluff	MO	63901	**877-879-8722**	573-840-9600

Montana

College / Address	City	State	ZIP	Toll-Free	Phone
Dawson Community College					
300 College Dr	Glendive	MT	59330	**800-821-8320**	406-377-3396
Flathead Valley Community College					
777 Grandview Dr	Kalispell	MT	59901	**800-313-3822**	406-756-3822
Miles Community College					
2715 Dickinson St	Miles City	MT	59301	**800-541-9281**	406-874-6100
Salish Kootenai College					
PO Box 70	Pablo	MT	59855	**877-752-6553**	406-275-4800

Nebraska

College / Address	City	State	ZIP	Toll-Free	Phone
Central Community College					
Grand Island 3134 W Hwy 34 PO Box 4903	Grand Island	NE	68802	**877-222-0780**	308-398-4222
McCook Community College					
1205 E Third St	McCook	NE	69001	**800-658-4348**	308-345-8100
Metropolitan Community College					
PO Box 3777	Omaha	NE	68103	**800-228-9553**	402-457-2400
Nebraska Indian Community College					
PO Box 428	Macy	NE	68039	**844-440-6422**	402-837-5078
North Platte Community College					
North 1101 Halligan Dr	North Platte	NE	69101	**800-658-4308**	308-535-3601
South 601 W State Farm Rd	North Platte	NE	69101	**800-658-4348**	
Northeast Community College					
801 E Benjamin Ave PO Box 469	Norfolk	NE	68702	**800-348-9033**	402-371-2020
Southeast Community College					
Beatrice 4771 W Scott Rd	Beatrice	NE	68310	**800-233-5027**	402-228-3468
Lincoln 8800 'O' St	Lincoln	NE	68520	**800-642-4075**	402-471-3333
Western Nebraska Community College					
1601 E 27th St	Scottsbluff	NE	69361	**800-348-4435**	308-635-3606

Nevada

College / Address	City	State	ZIP	Toll-Free	Phone
Western Nevada Community College (WNC)					
Douglas 1680 Bently Pkwy S	Minden	NV	89423	**800-433-3243**	775-782-2413

New Hampshire

College / Address	City	State	ZIP	Toll-Free	Phone
Community College System of New Hampshire (CCSNH)					
26 College Dr	Concord	NH	03301	**866-945-2255**	603-271-2722
Lakes Region Community College (LRCC)					
379 Belmont Rd	Laconia	NH	03246	**800-357-2992**	603-524-3207
Manchester Community College					
1066 Front St	Manchester	NH	03102	**800-924-3445**	603-206-8000
NHTI Concord's Community College					
31 College Dr	Concord	NH	03301	**800-247-0179**	603-271-6484
White Mountains Community College (WMCC)					
2020 Riverside Dr	Berlin	NH	03570	**800-445-4525**	603-752-1113

New Jersey

	City	State	Zip	Toll-Free	Phone
Bergen Community College					
400 Paramus Rd	Paramus	NJ	07652	**877-612-5381**	201-447-7200
Brookdale Community College					
765 Newman Springs Rd	Lincroft	NJ	07738	**866-767-9512**	732-842-1900
Camden County College					
200 College Dr	Blackwood	NJ	08012	**888-228-2466**	856-227-7200
County College of Morris					
214 Ctr Grove Rd	Randolph	NJ	07869	**888-726-3260**	973-328-5000
Cumberland County College					
3322 College Dr	Vineland	NJ	08360	**866-367-6232**	856-691-8600
Mercer County Community College					
PO Box B	Trenton	NJ	08690	**800-982-9491**	609-586-4800
Kerney Ctr					
N Broad & Academy St	Trenton	NJ	08608	**800-982-9491**	609-586-4800
West Windsor					
1200 Old Trenton Rd	West Windsor	NJ	08550	**800-982-9491**	609-586-4800
Middlesex County College					
2600 Woodbridge Ave PO Box 3050	Edison	NJ	08818	**888-442-4551**	732-548-6000
Raritan Valley Community College					
PO Box 3300	Somerville	NJ	08876	**888-326-4058**	908-526-1200
Union County College					
1033 Springfield Ave	Cranford	NJ	07016	**877-468-3229**	908-709-7000

New Mexico

	City	State	Zip	Toll-Free	Phone
Clovis Community College (CCC)					
417 Schepps Blvd	Clovis	NM	88101	**800-769-1409**	575-769-2811
Dona Ana Branch Community College (DACC)					
2800 N Sonoma Ranch Blvd PO Box 30001	Las Cruces	NM	88011	**800-903-7503**	575-528-7000
Eastern New Mexico University Roswell					
52 University Blvd PO Box 6000	Roswell	NM	88202	**800-243-6687**	
Luna Community College					
366 Luna Dr	Las Vegas	NM	87701	**800-588-7232**	505-454-2500
New Mexico Junior College					
1 Thunderbird Cir	Hobbs	NM	88240	**800-657-6260**	505-392-4510
New Mexico State University (NMSU)					
MSC-3A PO Box 30001	Las Cruces	NM	88003	**800-662-6678***	575-646-3121
*Admissions					
Carlsbad					
1500 University Dr	Carlsbad	NM	88220	**888-888-2199**	505-234-9200
Northern New Mexico College					
921 Paseo de Onate	Espanola	NM	87532	**800-477-3632**	505-747-2100
San Juan College					
4601 College Blvd	Farmington	NM	87402	**866-426-1233**	505-326-3311
University of New Mexico (UNM)					
1 University of New Mexico	Albuquerque	NM	87131	**800-225-5866**	505-277-0111
Valencia 280 La Entrada	Los Lunas	NM	87031	**800-225-5866**	505-925-8580

New York

	City	State	Zip	Toll-Free	Phone
Adirondack Community College					
640 Bay Rd	Queensbury	NY	12804	**888-786-9235**	518-743-2200
Borough of Manhattan Community College					
199 Chambers St Rm S-300	New York	NY	10007	**877-222-8387**	212-220-1265
Bronx Community College					
2155 University Ave	Bronx	NY	10453	**866-888-8777**	718-289-5100
Broome Community College					
901 Front St	Binghamton	NY	13905	**800-836-0689**	607-778-5000
Cayuga Community College					
197 Franklin St	Auburn	NY	13021	**866-598-8883**	315-255-1743
Columbia-Greene Community College					
4400 Rt 23	Hudson	NY	12534	**888-668-4293**	518-828-4181
Genesee Community College					
1 College Rd	Batavia	NY	14020	**866-225-5422**	585-343-0068
Herkimer County Community College					
100 Reservoir Rd	Herkimer	NY	13350	**844-464-4375**	315-866-0300
Hostos Community College					
500 Grand Concourse	Bronx	NY	10451	**888-993-7650**	718-518-4444
Hudson Valley Community College					
80 Vandenburgh Ave	Troy	NY	12180	**877-325-4822**	518-629-4822
Jamestown Community College					
525 Faulkner St PO Box 20	Jamestown	NY	14702	**800-388-8557**	716-338-1000
Cattaraugus County					
260 N Union St PO Box 5901	Olean	NY	14760	**800-388-9776**	716-376-7500
Jefferson Community College					
1220 Coffeen St	Watertown	NY	13601	**888-435-6522**	315-786-2200
Mohawk Valley Community College					
1101 Sherman Dr	Utica	NY	13501	**800-733-6822**	315-792-5400
Niagara County Community College					
3111 Saunders Settlement Rd	Sanborn	NY	14132	**800-875-6269**	716-614-6222
North Country Community College					
23 Santanoni Ave	Saranac Lake	NY	12983	**888-879-6222**	518-891-2915
Onondaga Community College					
4941 Onondaga Rd	Syracuse	NY	13215	**800-827-1000**	315-498-2622
Queensborough Community College					
222-05 56th Ave	Bayside	NY	11364	**877-253-7122**	718-631-6262
Rockland Community College					
145 College Rd	Suffern	NY	10901	**800-722-7666**	845-574-4000
State University of New York					
Brockport					
350 New Campus Dr	Brockport	NY	14420	**888-800-0029**	585-395-2751
Canton 34 Cornell Dr	Canton	NY	13617	**800-388-7123**	315-386-7011
College of Technology at Alfred					
10 Upper College Dr	Alfred	NY	14802	**800-425-3733**	607-587-4215
Delhi 2 Main St	Delhi	NY	13753	**800-963-3544**	607-746-4000
Suffolk County Community College					
Grant					
1001 Crooked Hill Rd	Brentwood	NY	11717	**800-621-3362**	631-851-6700
Tompkins Cortland Community College					
170 N St	Dryden	NY	13053	**888-567-8211**	607-844-8211
Ulster County Community College					
Cottekill Rd	Stone Ridge	NY	12484	**800-724-0833**	845-687-5000
Westchester Community College					
75 Grasslands Rd	Valhalla	NY	10595	**800-235-7267**	914-606-6600

North Carolina

	City	State	Zip	Toll-Free	Phone
Alamance Community College					
PO Box 8000	Graham	NC	27253	**877-667-7533**	336-578-2002
Brunswick Community College					
50 College Rd	Bolivia	NC	28422	**800-754-1050**	910-755-7300
Cape Fear Community College					
411 N Front St	Wilmington	NC	28401	**800-487-5553**	910-362-7000
Catawba Valley Community College					
2550 US Hwy 70 SE	Hickory	NC	28602	**800-433-3243**	828-327-7000
Central Carolina Community College					
1105 Kelly Dr	Sanford	NC	27330	**800-682-8353**	919-775-5401
Central Piedmont Community College					
1201 Elizabeth Ave	Charlotte	NC	28204	**877-530-8815**	704-330-2722
College of the Albemarle					
PO Box 2327	Elizabeth City	NC	27906	**800-335-9050**	252-335-0821
Davidson County Community College					
PO Box 1287	Lexington	NC	27293	**800-233-4050**	336-249-8186
Fayetteville Technical Community College					
2201 Hull Rd	Fayetteville	NC	28303	**877-245-5520**	910-678-8400
Gaston College 201 Hwy 321-S	Dallas	NC	28034	**800-634-7854**	704-922-6200
Haywood Community College					
185 Freedlander Dr	Clyde	NC	28721	**866-468-6422**	828-627-2821
Lenoir Community College					
PO Box 188	Kinston	NC	28502	**866-866-2362**	252-527-6223
Louisburg College					
501 N Main St	Louisburg	NC	27549	**800-775-0208**	919-496-2521
Mayland Community College					
200 Mayland Dr PO Box 547	Spruce Pine	NC	28777	**800-462-9526**	828-765-7351
Randolph Community College					
629 Industrial Pk Ave	Asheboro	NC	27205	**800-433-3243**	336-633-0200
Richmond Community College					
PO Box 1189	Hamlet	NC	28345	**800-908-9946**	910-410-1700
Sandhills Community College					
3395 Airport Rd	Pinehurst	NC	28374	**800-338-3944**	910-692-6185
Vance-Granville Community College					
South PO Box 39	Creedmoor	NC	27522	**877-823-2378**	919-528-4737
Warren County PO Box 207	Warrenton	NC	27536	**877-823-2378**	252-257-1900
Wayne Community College					
3000 Wayne Memorial Dr PO Box 8002	Goldsboro	NC	27533	**866-414-5064**	919-735-5151
Wilkes Community College					
1328 S Collegiate Dr PO Box 120	Wilkesboro	NC	28697	**866-222-1548**	336-838-6100

North Dakota

	City	State	Zip	Toll-Free	Phone
Bismarck State College					
1500 Edwards Ave	Bismarck	ND	58501	**800-445-5073**	701-224-5400
Cankdeska Cikana Community College					
PO Box 269	Fort Totten	ND	58335	**888-783-1463**	701-766-4415
Lake Region State College					
1801 College Dr N	Devils Lake	ND	58301	**800-443-1313**	701-662-1514
Minot State University Bottineau					
105 Simrall Blvd	Bottineau	ND	58318	**800-542-6866**	701-228-5451
North Dakota State College of Science					
800 Sixth St N	Wahpeton	ND	58076	**800-342-4325**	701-671-2401
Turtle Mountain Community College					
10145 BIA Rd 7	Belcourt	ND	58316	**800-827-1100**	701-477-7862
Williston State College					
1410 University Ave PO Box 1326	Williston	ND	58802	**888-863-9455**	701-774-4200

Ohio

	City	State	Zip	Toll-Free	Phone
Buckeye Career Center					
545 University Dr Ne	New Philadelphia	OH	44663	**800-227-1665**	330-339-2288
Cincinnati State Technical & Community College					
3520 Central Pkwy	Cincinnati	OH	45223	**877-569-0115**	513-569-1500
Columbus State Community College					
550 E Spring St	Columbus	OH	43215	**800-621-6407**	614-287-2400
Cuyahoga Community College					
Eastern					
4250 Richmond Rd	Highland Hills	OH	44122	**800-954-8742**	216-987-2024
Metropolitan					
2900 Community College Ave	Cleveland	OH	44115	**800-954-8742**	216-987-4200
Western					
11000 Pleasant Valley Rd	Parma	OH	44130	**800-954-8742**	216-987-2800
Edison Community College					
1973 Edison Dr	Piqua	OH	45356	**888-442-4551**	937-778-8600
Kent State University					
800 E. Summit St PO Box 5190	Kent	OH	44242	**800-988-5368**	330-672-2121
Ashtabula 3300 Lake Rd W	Ashtabula	OH	44004	**800-988-5368**	440-964-3322
Lakeland Community College					
7700 Clocktower Dr	Kirtland	OH	44094	**800-589-8520**	440-525-7000
Lorain County Community College					
1005 N Abbe Rd	Elyria	OH	44035	**800-995-5222**	440-365-5222
Miami University					
501 E High St	Oxford	OH	45056	**866-426-4643**	513-529-1809
Owens Community College					
Findlay 3200 Bright Rd	Findlay	OH	45840	**800-466-9367**	
Toledo 30335 Oregon Rd	Perrysburg	OH	43551	**800-466-9367**	419-661-7000
Sinclair Community College					
444 W Third St	Dayton	OH	45402	**800-315-3000**	937-512-3000
Southern State Community College					
North 1850 Davids Dr	Wilmington	OH	45177	**877-644-6562**	937-382-6645
South 12681 US Rt 62	Sardinia	OH	45171	**877-644-6562**	937-695-0307
Terra Community College					
2830 Napoleon Rd	Fremont	OH	43420	**800-334-3886**	419-334-8400
University of Akron Wayne College					
1901 Smucker Rd	Orrville	OH	44667	**800-221-8308**	330-683-2010

				Toll-Free	Phone
University of Cincinnati Clermont College					
4200 Clermont College Dr	Batavia	OH	45103	**866-446-2822**	513-732-5200
Wright State University Lake					
7600 Lk Campus Dr	Celina	OH	45822	**800-237-1477**	419-586-0300

Oklahoma

				Toll-Free	Phone
Connors State College					
700 College Rd	Warner	OK	74469	**888-594-5171**	918-463-2931
Murray State College					
1 Murray Campus	Tishomingo	OK	73460	**800-342-0698**	580-371-2371
Oklahoma State University					
219 Student Union Bldg	Stillwater	OK	74078	**800-852-1255**	405-744-5000
Oklahoma City					
900 N Portland Ave	Oklahoma City	OK	73107	**800-560-4099**	405-947-4421
Redlands Community College					
1300 S Country Club Rd	El Reno	OK	73036	**866-415-6367**	405-262-2552
Rogers State University Pryor					
421 S Elliott St	Pryor	OK	74361	**800-256-7511**	918-825-6117
Rose State College					
6420 SE 15th St	Midwest City	OK	73110	**866-621-0987**	405-733-7372
Tulsa Community College					
Metro 909 S Boston Ave	Tulsa	OK	74119	**866-970-0233**	918-595-7000
Western Oklahoma State College					
2801 N Main St	Altus	OK	73521	**800-662-1113**	580-477-2000
College of Nurses of Ontario					
101 Davenport Rd	Toronto	ON	M5R3P1	**800-387-5526**	416-928-0900
Fleming College					
200 Albert St S	Lindsay	ON	K9V5E6	**866-353-6464**	705-324-9144
Institute of Corporate Directors					
602 - 40 University Ave	Toronto	ON	M5J1T1	**877-593-7741**	416-593-7741
Sault College of Applied Arts & Technology, The					
443 Northern Ave	Sault Sainte Marie	ON	P6A5L3	**800-461-2260**	705-759-6700
Willis College of Business & Technology					
85 O'Connor St	Ottawa	ON	K1P5M6	**877-233-1128**	613-233-1128

Oregon

				Toll-Free	Phone
Blue Mountain Community College					
2411 NW Carden Ave PO Box 100	Pendleton	OR	97801	**888-441-7232**	541-276-1260
Clatsop Community College					
1653 Jerome Ave	Astoria	OR	97103	**855-252-8767**	503-325-0910
Lane Community College					
4000 E 30th Ave	Eugene	OR	97405	**800-321-2211**	541-463-3000
Florence 3149 Oak St	Florence	OR	97439	**800-222-3290**	541-997-8444
Rogue Community College					
3345 Redwood Hwy	Grants Pass	OR	97527	**800-411-6508**	541-956-7500
Southwestern Oregon Community College					
1988 Newmark Ave	Coos Bay	OR	97420	**800-962-2838**	541-888-2525
Tillamook Bay Community College					
4301 Third St	Tillamook	OR	97141	**888-306-8222**	503-842-8222
Treasure Valley Community College					
650 College Blvd	Ontario	OR	97914	**888-292-5247**	541-881-8822
Umpqua Community College					
1140 Umpqva College Rd PO Box 967	Roseburg	OR	97470	**800-820-5161**	541-440-4600

Pennsylvania

				Toll-Free	Phone
Butler County Community College					
107 College Dr	Butler	PA	16002	**888-826-2829**	724-287-8711
Community College of Beaver County					
1 Campus Dr	Monaca	PA	15061	**800-335-0222**	724-775-8561
Delaware County Community College					
901 Media Line Rd	Media	PA	19063	**800-908-9946**	610-359-5000
Harcum College					
750 Montgomery Ave	Bryn Mawr	PA	19010	**800-650-0035**	610-525-4100
Harrisburg Area Community College					
1 HACC Dr	Harrisburg	PA	17110	**800-222-4222**	717-780-2300
Gettysburg					
731 Old Harrisburg Rd	Gettysburg	PA	17325	**800-222-4222**	717-337-3855
Lebanon 735 Cumberland St	Lebanon	PA	17042	**800-222-4222**	717-270-4222
Lackawanna College					
501 Vine St	Scranton	PA	18509	**877-346-3552**	570-961-7810
Lehigh Carbon Community College					
4525 Education Pk Dr	Schnecksville	PA	18078	**800-414-3975***	610-799-2121
*General					
Morgan Ctr 234 High St	Tamaqua	PA	18252	**800-424-2460**	570-668-6880
Luzerne County Community College					
1333 S Prospect St	Nanticoke	PA	18634	**800-377-5222**	
NanoHorizons Inc					
270 Rolling Ridge Dr Ste 100	Bellefonte	PA	16823	**866-584-6235**	814-355-4700
Northampton Community College					
3835 Green Pond Rd	Bethlehem	PA	18020	**877-543-0998**	610-861-5300
Monroe 3 Old Mill Rd	Tannersville	PA	18372	**877-543-0998**	570-620-9221
Pennsylvania Highlands Community College					
881 Hills Plz Dr Ste 450	Ebensburg	PA	15931	**888-385-7325**	814-262-6446
Beaver 100 University Dr	Monaca	PA	15061	**877-564-6778**	724-773-3500
DuBois 1 College Pl	Du Bois	PA	15801	**800-346-7627**	814-375-4700
Fayette					
2201 University Dr	Lemont Furnace	PA	15456	**877-568-4130**	724-430-4100
Hazleton 76 University Dr	Hazleton	PA	18202	**800-279-8495**	570-450-3000
Mont Alto 1 Campus Dr	Mont Alto	PA	17237	**800-392-6173**	717-749-6000
Schuylkill					
200 University Dr	Schuylkill Haven	PA	17972	**800-243-2374**	570-385-6000
Shenango 147 Shenango Ave	Sharon	PA	16146	**888-275-7009**	724-983-2803
York 1031 Edgecomb Ave	York	PA	17403	**800-778-6227**	717-771-4000
Reading Area Community College					
10 S Second St PO Box 1706	Reading	PA	19603	**800-626-1665**	610-372-4721
Titusville 504 E Main St	Titusville	PA	16354	**888-878-0462**	
Us Health Connect Inc					
500 Office Ctr Dr	Fort Washington	PA	19034	**800-889-4944**	
Valley Forge Military Academy & College					
1001 Eagle Rd	Wayne	PA	19087	**800-234-8362**	610-989-1300
Westmoreland County Community College					
145 Pavilion Ln	Youngwood	PA	15697	**800-262-2103**	724-925-4000

Quebec

				Toll-Free	Phone
College Merici					
755 Ch St-Louis	Quebec	QC	G1S1C1	**800-208-1463**	418-683-1591
Saskatoon Business College Ltd					
221 Third Ave N	Saskatoon	SK	S7K2H7	**800-679-7711**	306-244-6333

South Carolina

				Toll-Free	Phone
Clinton Junior College					
1029 Crawford Rd	Rock Hill	SC	29730	**877-837-9645**	803-327-7402
Greenville Technical College					
Barton					
506 S Pleasantburg Dr	Greenville	SC	29607	**800-723-0673***	864-250-8000
*All					
Greer 2522 Locust Hill Rd	Taylors	SC	29687	**800-723-0673**	
Midlands Technical College					
PO Box 2408	Columbia	SC	29202	**800-922-8038**	803-738-1400
North Greenville University					
7801 N Tigerville Rd PO Box 1892	Tigerville	SC	29688	**800-468-6642**	864-977-7000
Northeastern Technical College					
1201 Chesterfield Hwy	Cheraw	SC	29520	**800-921-7399**	843-921-6900
Spartanburg Methodist College					
1000 Powell Mill Rd	Spartanburg	SC	29301	**800-772-7286**	864-587-4000
University of South Carolina					
1600 Hampton St	Columbia	SC	29208	**800-868-5872**	803-777-7000
Union 401 E Main St	Union	SC	29379	**800-768-5566**	864-429-8728
Williamsburg Technical College					
601 MLK Jr Ave	Kingstree	SC	29556	**800-768-2021**	843-355-4110
York Technical College					
452 S Anderson Rd	Rock Hill	SC	29730	**800-922-8324**	803-327-8000

South Dakota

				Toll-Free	Phone
Kilian Community College					
300 E Sixth St	Sioux Falls	SD	57103	**800-888-1147**	605-221-3100
Lake Area Technical Institute					
230 11th St NE PO Box 730	Watertown	SD	57201	**800-657-4344**	605-882-5284
Mitchell Technical Institute					
821 N Capital St	Mitchell	SD	57301	**800-684-1969**	

Tennessee

				Toll-Free	Phone
Chattanooga State Technical Community College					
4501 Amnicola Hwy	Chattanooga	TN	37406	**866-547-3733**	423-697-4400
Cleveland State Community College					
3535 Adkisson Dr	Cleveland	TN	37312	**800-604-2722**	423-472-7141
Hiwassee College					
225 Hiwassee College Dr	Madisonville	TN	37354	**800-356-2187**	423-442-2001
Motlow State Community College					
PO Box 8500	Lynchburg	TN	37352	**800-654-4877**	931-393-1500
Roane State Community College					
276 Patton Ln	Harriman	TN	37748	**800-343-9104**	865-354-3000
Southwest Tennessee Community College					
PO Box 780	Memphis	TN	38101	**877-717-7822**	901-333-5000
Volunteer State Community College					
1480 Nashville Pk	Gallatin	TN	37066	**888-335-8722**	615-452-8600
Walters State Community College					
500 S Davy Crockett Pkwy	Morristown	TN	37813	**800-225-4770**	423-585-2600

Texas

				Toll-Free	Phone
Austin Community College (ACC)					
5930 Middle Fiskville Rd	Austin	TX	78752	**877-442-3522**	512-223-7000
Eastview 3401 Webberville Rd	Austin	TX	78702	**888-626-1697**	512-223-5100
Northridge					
11928 Stonehollow Dr	Austin	TX	78758	**877-990-0462**	512-223-4000
Pinnacle 7748 Hwy 290 W	Austin	TX	78736	**888-626-1697**	512-223-8001
Rio Grande					
1212 Rio Grande St	Austin	TX	78701	**877-990-0462**	512-223-3000
Riverside 1020 Grove Blvd	Austin	TX	78741	**877-990-0462**	512-223-6000
Brazosport College					
500 College Dr	Lake Jackson	TX	77566	**877-717-7873**	979-230-3000
Central Texas College					
PO Box 1800	Killeen	TX	76540	**800-792-3348**	254-526-7161
Clarendon College					
1122 College Dr PO Box 968	Clarendon	TX	79226	**800-687-9737**	806-874-3571
Coastal Bend College					
Beeville 3800 Charco Rd	Beeville	TX	78102	**866-722-2838**	361-358-2838
Del Mar College					
East					
101 Baldwin Blvd	Corpus Christi	TX	78404	**800-652-3357**	361-698-1200
Eastfield College					
3737 Motley Dr	Mesquite	TX	75150	**800-260-8000**	972-860-7100
El Paso Community College					
Valle Verde 919 Hunter Dr	El Paso	TX	79915	**800-531-8292**	915-831-2000
Galveston College					
4015 Ave Q	Galveston	TX	77550	**866-483-4242**	409-763-6551
Howard College					
1001 Birdwell Ln	Big Spring	TX	79720	**877-898-3833**	432-264-5000
Kingwood College					
20000 Kingwood Dr	Kingwood	TX	77339	**800-883-7939**	281-312-1600
Lamar State College					
Port Arthur PO Box 310	Port Arthur	TX	77641	**800-477-5872**	409-983-4921
McLennan Community College					
1400 College Dr	Waco	TX	76708	**866-339-5555**	254-299-8000
Mediatech Institute of Austin					
4719 s congress ave	Austin	TX	78745	**866-498-1122**	512-447-2002

	City	State	Zip	Toll-Free	Phone
Midland College 3600 N Garfield St	Midland	TX	79705	**800-474-7164**	432-685-4500
Navarro College 3200 W Seventh Ave	Corsicana	TX	75110	**800-628-2776**	903-874-6501
Northeast Texas Community College 1735 Chapel Hill Rd	Mount Pleasant	TX	75455	**800-870-0142**	903-572-1911
Odessa College 201 W University Blvd	Odessa	TX	79764	**866-968-2862**	432-335-6400
Paris Junior College 2400 Clarksville St	Paris	TX	75460	**800-232-5804**	903-785-7661
Ranger College 1100 College Cir	Ranger	TX	76470	**800-772-1213**	254-647-3234
Smith System Driver Improvement Institute Inc 2301 E Lamar Blvd Ste 250	Arlington	TX	76006	**800-777-7648**	817-652-6969
Southwest Texas Junior College 2401 Garner Field Rd	Uvalde	TX	78801	**888-886-8490**	830-278-4401
Tarrant County College					
Northeast 828 W Harwood Rd	Hurst	TX	76054	**800-799-7233**	817-515-8223
Northwest 4801 Marine Creek Pkwy	Fort Worth	TX	76179	**800-799-7233**	817-515-7100
Temple College 2600 S First St	Temple	TX	76504	**800-460-4636***	254-298-8300
*Admissions					
Texarkana College 2500 N Robison Rd	Texarkana	TX	75599	**877-275-4377**	903-838-4541
Texas State Technical College (TSTC)					
Abilene 650 E Hwy 80	Abilene	TX	79601	**800-852-8784**	325-672-7091
Harlingen 1902 N Loop 499	Harlingen	TX	78550	**800-852-8784**	956-364-4000
Sweetwater 300 Homer K Taylor Dr	Sweetwater	TX	79556	**877-450-3595**	325-235-7300
Waco 3801 Campus Dr	Waco	TX	76705	**800-792-8784**	254-799-3611
Trinity Valley Community College					
Athens 100 Cardinal Dr	Athens	TX	75751	**877-392-6433**	903-675-6200
Palestine PO Box 2530	Palestine	TX	75802	**866-882-2937**	903-729-0256
Tyler Junior College PO Box 9020	Tyler	TX	75711	**800-687-5680**	903-510-2523
Vernon College 4400 College Dr	Vernon	TX	76384	**866-336-9371**	940-552-6291
Weatherford College 225 College Pk Dr	Weatherford	TX	76086	**800-287-5471**	817-594-5471
Western Texas College 6200 College Ave	Snyder	TX	79549	**888-468-6982**	325-573-8511
Wharton County Junior College 911 Boling Hwy	Wharton	TX	77488	**800-561-9252**	979-532-4560
Sugar Land 14004 University Blvd	Sugar Land	TX	77479	**800-561-9252**	281-243-8447

Utah

	City	State	Zip	Toll-Free	Phone
College of Eastern Utah 451 E 400 N	Price	UT	84501	**800-336-2381**	435-613-5000
San Juan 639 West 100 South	Blanding	UT	84511	**800-395-2969**	435-678-2201
Snow College 150 College Ave PO Box 1037	Ephraim	UT	84627	**800-848-3399**	435-283-7000
Stevens Henager College 1890 South 1350 West	Ogden	UT	84401	**800-622-2640**	
Utah Valley State College 800 W University Pkwy	Orem	UT	84058	**800-952-8220**	801-863-4636

Vermont

	City	State	Zip	Toll-Free	Phone
Community College of Vermont					
Bennington 324 Main St	Bennington	VT	05201	**800-431-0025**	802-447-2361
Brattleboro 70 Landmark Hill Ste 101	Brattleboro	VT	05301	**800-431-0025**	802-254-6370
Middlebury 10 Merchants Row Ste 223	Middlebury	VT	05753	**800-431-0025**	802-388-3032
Montpelier PO Box 489	Montpelier	VT	05602	**800-228-6686**	802-828-4060
Morrisville 197 Harrell St Ste 2	Morrisville	VT	05661	**800-431-0025**	802-888-4258
Newport 100 Main St Ste 150	Newport	VT	05855	**800-431-0025**	802-334-3387
Rutland 60 W St	Rutland	VT	05701	**800-228-6686**	802-786-6996
Upper Valley 145 Billings Farm Rd	White River Junction	VT	05001	**800-431-0025**	802-295-8822

Virginia

	City	State	Zip	Toll-Free	Phone
Blue Ridge Community College 1 College Ln PO Box 80	Weyers Cave	VA	24486	**888-750-2722**	540-234-9261
Dabney S Lancaster Community College 1000 Dabney Dr PO Box 1000	Clifton Forge	VA	24422	**887-773-7522**	540-863-2800
Danville Community College 1008 S Main St	Danville	VA	24541	**800-560-4291**	434-797-2222
Lord Fairfax Community College					
Middletown 173 Skirmisher Ln	Middletown	VA	22645	**800-906-5322**	540-868-7000
New River Community College 5251 College PO Box 1127	Dublin	VA	24084	**866-462-6722**	540-674-3600
Northern Virginia Community College					
Alexandria 3001 N Beauregard St	Alexandria	VA	22311	**855-259-1019**	703-845-6200
Annandale 8333 Little River Tpke	Annandale	VA	22003	**877-408-2028**	703-323-3000
Manassas 6901 Sudley Rd	Manassas	VA	20109	**855-259-1019**	703-257-6600
Patrick Henry Community College 645 Patriot Ave PO Box 5311	Martinsville	VA	24112	**855-874-6692**	276-638-8777
Paul D Camp Community College 100 N College Dr PO Box 737	Franklin	VA	23851	**855-877-3918**	757-569-6700
Hobbs Suffolk 271 Kenyon Rd	Suffolk	VA	23434	**855-877-3918**	757-925-6300
Rappahannock Community College					
Glenns 12745 College Dr	Glenns	VA	23149	**800-836-9381**	804-758-6700
Warsaw 52 Campus Dr	Warsaw	VA	22572	**800-836-9381**	804-333-6700
Southside Virginia Community College 109 Campus Dr	Alberta	VA	23821	**888-220-7822**	434-949-1000
Southwest Virginia Community College 724 Community College Rd	Cedar Bluff	VA	24609	**855-877-3944**	276-964-2555
Tidewater Community College					
Chesapeake 1428 Cedar Rd	Chesapeake	VA	23322	**800-371-0898**	757-822-5100
Norfolk 121 College Pl	Norfolk	VA	23510	**800-371-0898**	757-822-1110
Portsmouth 7000 College Dr	Portsmouth	VA	23703	**800-371-0898**	757-822-2124
Virginia Beach 1700 College Crescent	Virginia Beach	VA	23453	**800-371-0898**	757-822-7100
Virginia Western Community College 3094 Colonial Ave PO Box 14007	Roanoke	VA	24038	**855-874-6690**	540-857-8922

Washington

	City	State	Zip	Toll-Free	Phone
Big Bend Community College 7662 Chanute St	Moses Lake	WA	98837	**877-745-1212**	509-793-2222
Edmonds Community College 20000 68th Ave W	Lynnwood	WA	98036	**866-886-4854**	425-640-1500
Everett Community College 2000 Tower St	Everett	WA	98201	**866-575-9027**	425-388-9100
Grays Harbor College 1620 Edward P Smith Dr	Aberdeen	WA	98520	**800-562-4830**	360-532-9020
Lower Columbia College 1600 Maple St PO Box 3010	Longview	WA	98632	**866-900-2311**	360-442-2301
North Seattle Community College 9600 College Way N	Seattle	WA	98103	**866-427-4747**	206-527-3600
Northwest Indian College 2522 Kwina Rd	Bellingham	WA	98226	**866-676-2772**	360-676-2772
Olympic College 1600 Chester Ave	Bremerton	WA	98337	**800-259-6718**	360-792-6050
Shelton 937 W Alpine Way	Shelton	WA	98584	**800-259-6718**	360-427-2119
Perry Technical Institute 2011 W Washington Ave	Yakima	WA	98903	**888-528-8586**	509-453-0374
Pierce College					
Puyallup 1601 39th Ave SE	Puyallup	WA	98374	**877-353-6763**	253-840-8400
Shoreline Community College 16101 Greenwood Ave N	Shoreline	WA	98133	**866-427-4747**	206-546-4101
Skagit Valley College 2405 E College Way	Mount Vernon	WA	98273	**877-385-5360**	360-416-7600
Spokane Community College 1810 N Greene St	Spokane	WA	99217	**800-248-5644**	509-533-7000
Spokane Falls Community College 3410 W Ft George Wright Dr	Spokane	WA	99224	**888-509-7944**	509-533-3500
Walla Walla Community College 500 Tausick Way	Walla Walla	WA	99362	**877-992-9922**	509-522-2500
Wenatchee Valley College 1300 Fifth St	Wenatchee	WA	98801	**877-982-4968**	509-682-6800
Whatcom Community College 237 W Kellogg Rd	Bellingham	WA	98226	**855-767-9003**	360-676-2170

West Virginia

	City	State	Zip	Toll-Free	Phone
Eastern West Virginia Community & Technical College 316 Eastern Dr	Moorefield	WV	26836	**877-982-2322**	304-434-8000
Potomac State College 101 Ft Ave	Keyser	WV	26726	**800-262-7332**	304-788-6800
West Virginia University PO Box 6009	Morgantown	WV	26506	**800-344-9881**	304-293-2121
Parkersburg 300 Campus Dr	Parkersburg	WV	26104	**800-982-9887**	304-424-8000

Wisconsin

	City	State	Zip	Toll-Free	Phone
College of Menominee Nation PO Box 1179	Keshena	WI	54135	**800-567-2344**	715-799-5600
Lac Courte Oreilles Ojibwa Community College 13466 W Trepania Rd	Hayward	WI	54843	**888-526-6221**	715-634-4790
University of Wisconsin					
Baraboo/Sauk County 1006 Connie Rd	Baraboo	WI	53913	**800-621-7440**	608-355-5200
Barron County 1800 College Dr	Rice Lake	WI	54868	**800-608-4578**	715-234-8176
Fox Valley 1478 Midway Rd	Menasha	WI	54952	**800-273-8255**	920-832-2600
Manitowoc 705 Viebahn St	Manitowoc	WI	54220	**800-657-3866**	920-683-4700
Marathon County 518 S Seventh Ave	Wausau	WI	54401	**888-367-8962**	715-261-6100
Marshfield/Wood County 2000 W Fifth St	Marshfield	WI	54449	**800-273-8255**	715-389-6530
Richland 1200 Hwy 14 W	Richland Center	WI	53581	**800-947-3529**	608-647-6186
Washington County 400 S University Dr	West Bend	WI	53095	**800-240-0276**	262-335-5200

Wyoming

	City	State	Zip	Toll-Free	Phone
Casper College 125 College Dr	Casper	WY	82601	**800-442-2963**	307-268-2100
Central Wyoming College 2660 Peck Ave	Riverton	WY	82501	**800-735-8418**	307-855-2000
Eastern Wyoming College 3200 W 'C' St	Torrington	WY	82240	**800-658-3195**	307-532-8200
Laramie County Community College 1400 E College Dr	Cheyenne	WY	82007	**800-522-2993**	307-778-5222
Albany County 1125 Boulder Dr	Laramie	WY	82070	**800-522-2993**	307-721-5138
Northwest College 231 W Sixth St	Powell	WY	82435	**800-560-4692**	307-754-6000
Sheridan College 3059 Coffeen Ave PO Box 1500	Sheridan	WY	82801	**800-913-9139**	307-674-6446
Gillette 300 W Sinclair St	Gillette	WY	82718	**800-913-9139**	307-686-0254

				Toll-Free	Phone
Western Wyoming Community College					
2500 College Dr	Rock Springs	WY	82901	**800-226-1181**	307-382-1600

162 COLLEGES - CULINARY ARTS

				Toll-Free	Phone
Arizona Culinary Institute					
10585 N 114th St Ste 401	Scottsdale	AZ	85259	**866-294-2433**	480-603-1066
Baltimore International College					
17 Commerce St	Baltimore	MD	21202	**800-624-9926**	410-752-4710
Capital Culinary Institute of Keiser College					
Melbourne					
900 S Babcock St	Melbourne	FL	32901	**877-636-3618**	321-409-4800
Cooking & Hospitality Institute of Chicago					
361 W Chestnut St	Chicago	IL	60610	**877-828-7772***	312-944-0882
*Admissions					
Culinary Institute Alain & Marie LeNotre					
7070 Allensby	Houston	TX	77022	**888-536-6873**	713-692-0077
Culinary Institute of America					
1946 Campus Dr	Hyde Park	NY	12538	**800-285-4627***	845-452-9430
*Admissions					
Culinary Institute of Charleston					
7000 Rivers Ave	Charleston	SC	29406	**877-349-7184**	843-574-6111
French Culinary Institute					
462 Broadway	New York	NY	10013	**888-324-2433**	
Institute of Culinary Education					
50 W 23rd St	New York	NY	10010	**800-522-4610**	212-847-0700
Kendall College					
900 N North Branch St	Chicago	IL	60622	**888-905-3632**	312-752-2000
Kitchen Academy					
6370 W Sunset Blvd	Hollywood	CA	90028	**866-548-2223**	
L'Academie de Cuisine Inc					
16006 Industrial Dr	Gaithersburg	MD	20877	**800-664-2433**	301-670-8670
Le Cordon Bleu College of Culinary Arts					
Atlanta 1927 Lakeside Pkwy	Tucker	GA	30084	**888-549-8222**	770-938-4711
Las Vegas					
1451 Ctr Crossing Rd	Las Vegas	NV	89144	**888-551-8222**	702-365-7690
Lincoln Educational Services					
85 Sigourney St	Hartford	CT	06105	**800-762-4337**	800-254-0547
Suffield 8 PROGRESS DR	Shelton	CT	06484	**800-254-0547**	203-929-0592
Louisiana Culinary Institute					
10550 Airline Hwy	Baton Rouge	LA	70816	**877-533-3198**	
New England Culinary Institute					
56 College St	Montpelier	VT	05602	**877-223-6324**	802-223-6324
Restaurant School at Walnut Hill College					
4207 Walnut St	Philadelphia	PA	19104	**877-925-6884**	215-222-4200
Robert Morris University Institute of Culinary Arts					
401 S State St	Chicago	IL	60605	**800-762-5960**	312-935-4100
Scottsdale Culinary Institute					
8100 E Camelback Rd Ste 1001	Scottsdale	AZ	85251	**888-557-4222**	480-990-3773
Stratford University School of Culinary Arts					
7777 Leesburg Pk	Falls Church	VA	22043	**800-444-0804**	703-821-8570

163 COLLEGES - FINE ARTS

SEE ALSO Vocational & Technical Schools ; Colleges & Universities - Four-Year

				Toll-Free	Phone
American Academy of Art					
332 S Michigan Ave 3rd Fl	Chicago	IL	60604	**888-461-0600**	312-461-0600
American Academy of Dramatic Arts					
120 Madison Ave	New York	NY	10016	**800-463-8990**	212-686-9244
Antonelli Institute					
300 Montgomery Ave	Erdenheim	PA	19038	**800-722-7871**	215-836-2222
Art Academy of Cincinnati					
1212 Jackson St	Cincinnati	OH	45202	**800-323-5692**	513-562-6262
Art Institute of Atlanta					
6600 Peachtree Dunwoody Rd NE					
100 Embassy Row	Atlanta	GA	30328	**800-275-4242**	770-394-8300
Art Institute of Boston at Lesley (AIB)					
29 Everett St	Cambridge	MA	22138	**800-773-0494**	617-585-6600
Art Institute of California					
Inland Empire					
674 E Brier Dr	San Bernardino	CA	92408	**800-353-0812**	909-915-2100
Los Angeles					
2900 31st St	Santa Monica	CA	90405	**888-646-4610**	310-752-4700
San Diego					
7650 Mission Valley Rd	San Diego	CA	92108	**888-624-0300**	858-598-1200
San Francisco					
1170 Market St	San Francisco	CA	94102	**888-493-3261**	415-865-0198
Art Institute of Charlotte					
3 Lake Pointe Plz 3 LakePointe Plz	Charlotte	NC	28217	**800-872-4417**	704-357-8020
Art Institute of Colorado					
1200 Lincoln St	Denver	CO	80203	**800-275-2420**	303-837-0825
Art Institute of Dallas					
8080 Pk Ln Ste 100	Dallas	TX	75231	**800-275-4243**	214-692-8080
Art Institute of Fort Lauderdale					
1799 SE 17th St	Fort Lauderdale	FL	33316	**800-275-7603**	954-463-3000
Art Institute of Houston					
1900 Yorktown St	Houston	TX	77056	**800-275-4244**	713-623-2040
Art Institute of Indianapolis					
3500 Depauw Blvd	Indianapolis	IN	46268	**866-441-9031**	317-613-4800
Art Institute of Las Vegas					
2350 Corporate Cir	Henderson	NV	89074	**800-833-2678**	702-369-9944
Art Institute of Ohio					
Cincinnati					
8845 Covernor's Hill Dr Ste 100	Cincinnati	OH	45249	**866-613-5184**	513-833-2400
Art Institute of Philadelphia					
1622 Chestnut St	Philadelphia	PA	19103	**800-275-2474**	215-567-7080
Art Institute of Pittsburgh					
420 Blvd of the Allies	Pittsburgh	PA	15219	**800-275-2470**	412-263-6600
Art Institute of Portland					
1122 NW Davis St	Portland	OR	97209	**888-228-6528**	503-228-6528
Art Institute of Seattle					
2323 Elliott Ave	Seattle	WA	98121	**800-275-2471**	206-448-0900
Art Institute of Tampa					
4401 N Himes Ave Ste 150	Tampa	FL	33614	**866-703-3277**	813-873-2112
Art Institute of Washington					
1820 N Ft Myer Dr	Arlington	VA	22209	**877-303-3771**	703-358-9550
Art Institutes , The					
15 S Ninth St	Minneapolis	MN	55402	**800-777-3643**	612-332-3361
California College of the Arts					
Oakland 5212 Broadway	Oakland	CA	94618	**800-447-1278**	510-594-3600
San Francisco					
1111 Eigth St	San Francisco	CA	94107	**800-447-1278**	415-703-9500
California Institute of the Arts					
24700 McBean Pkwy	Valencia	CA	91355	**800-545-2787**	661-255-1050
Cleveland Institute of Art					
11141 E Blvd	Cleveland	OH	44106	**800-223-4700**	
Columbus College of Art & Design					
60 Cleveland Ave	Columbus	OH	43215	**877-997-2223**	614-224-9101
Cornish College of the Arts					
710 E Roy St	Seattle	WA	98121	**800-726-2787**	206-323-1400
Fashion Institute of Design & Merchandising					
Los Angeles					
919 S Grand Ave	Los Angeles	CA	90015	**800-624-1200***	213-624-1200
*Admissions					
Orange County					
17590 Gillette Ave	Irvine	CA	92614	**888-974-3436**	949-851-6200
San Diego 350 Tenth Ave	San Diego	CA	92101	**800-243-3436**	619-235-2049
San Francisco					
55 Stockton St	San Francisco	CA	94108	**800-422-3436**	415-675-5200
Illinois Institute of Art					
Chicago					
350 N Orleans St Ste 136-L	Chicago	IL	60654	**800-351-3450**	312-280-3500
Schaumburg 1000 N Plz Dr	Schaumburg	IL	60173	**800-314-3450**	847-619-3450
Institute of American Indian Arts (IAIA)					
83 Avan Nu Po Rd	Santa Fe	NM	87508	**800-804-6422**	505-424-2300
International Academy of Design & Technology					
Chicago 1 N State St Ste 500	Chicago	IL	60602	**888-318-6111**	312-386-7681
Las Vegas					
2495 Village View Dr	Henderson	NV	89074	**866-400-4238**	702-990-0150
Kansas City Art Institute					
4415 Warwick Blvd	Kansas City	MO	64111	**800-522-5224**	816-474-5224
Maine College of Art					
522 Congress St	Portland	ME	04101	**800-639-4808**	207-775-3052
Memphis College of Art					
1930 Poplar Ave	Memphis	TN	38104	**800-727-1088**	901-272-5100
Miami International University of Art & Design					
1501 Biscayne Blvd	Miami	FL	33132	**800-225-9023**	305-428-5700
Minneapolis College of Art & Design					
2501 Stevens Ave	Minneapolis	MN	55404	**800-874-6223**	612-874-3760
Moore College of Art & Design					
20th St & the Pkwy	Philadelphia	PA	19103	**800-523-2025**	215-965-4000
New England Institute of Art					
10 Brookline Pl W	Brookline	MA	02445	**800-903-4425**	617-582-4460
New Hampshire Institute of Art					
148 Concord St	Manchester	NH	03104	**866-241-4918**	603-623-0313
Otis College of Art & Design					
9045 Lincoln Blvd	Los Angeles	CA	90045	**800-527-6847**	310-665-6820
Pennsylvania Academy of the Fine Arts					
School of Fine Arts					
118 128 N Broad St	Philadelphia	PA	19102	**800-799-7233**	215-972-7600
Rhode Island School of Design					
2 College St	Providence	RI	02903	**800-364-7473**	401-454-6100
Ringling College of Art & Design					
2700 N Tamiami Trl	Sarasota	FL	34234	**800-255-7695**	941-351-5100
San Francisco Art Institute					
800 Chestnut St	San Francisco	CA	94133	**800-345-7324**	415-771-7020
Savannah College of Art & Design					
342 Bull St PO Box 2072	Savannah	GA	31402	**800-869-7223**	912-525-5100
Atlanta					
1600 Peachtree St PO Box 77300	Atlanta	GA	30357	**877-722-3285**	404-253-2700
School of Visual Arts					
209 E 23rd St	New York	NY	10010	**800-436-4204**	212-592-2000
University of the Arts					
320 S Broad St	Philadelphia	PA	19102	**800-616-2787**	215-717-6049
Virginia Marti College of Art & Design					
11724 Detroit Ave	Lakewood	OH	44107	**800-473-4350**	216-221-8584
Watkins College of Art & Design					
2298 Rose Parks Blvd	Nashville	TN	37228	**866-877-6395**	615-383-4848

164 COLLEGES - TRIBAL

SEE ALSO Colleges - Community & Junior

Tribal Colleges generally serve geographically isolated American Indian populations that have no other means of accessing education beyond the high school level. They are unique institutions that combine personal attention with cultural relevance.

				Toll-Free	Phone
Anaheim University					
1240 S State College Blvd Rm 110	Anaheim	CA	92806	**800-955-6040**	714-772-3330
Bay Mills Community College					
12214 W Lakeshore Dr	Brimley	MI	49715	**800-844-2622**	906-248-3354
Briarcliffe College					
1055 Stewart Ave	Bethpage	NY	11714	**855-512-5333**	516-918-3600
Cankdeska Cikana Community College					
PO Box 269	Fort Totten	ND	58335	**888-783-1463**	701-766-4415
College of Menominee Nation					
PO Box 1179	Keshena	WI	54135	**800-567-2344**	715-799-5600
Fond du Lac Tribal & Community College					
2101 14th St	Cloquet	MN	55720	**800-657-3712**	218-879-0800
Institute of American Indian Arts (IAIA)					
83 Avan Nu Po Rd	Santa Fe	NM	87508	**800-804-6422**	505-424-2300
Lac Courte Oreilles Ojibwa Community College					
13466 W Trepania Rd	Hayward	WI	54843	**888-526-6221**	715-634-4790
Leech Lake Tribal College					
6945 Little Wolf Rd PO Box 180	Cass Lake	MN	56633	**866-676-2772**	218-335-4200
Nebraska Indian Community College					
PO Box 428	Macy	NE	68039	**844-440-6422**	402-837-5078
Northwest Indian College					
2522 Kwina Rd	Bellingham	WA	98226	**866-676-2772**	360-676-2772

Name / Address	City	State	ZIP	Toll-Free	Phone
Royal College of Dental Surgeons of Ontario 6 Crescent Rd	Toronto	ON	M4W1T1	**800-565-4591**	416-961-6555
Saginaw Chippewa Tribal College 2274 Enterprise Dr	Mount Pleasant	MI	48858	**800-225-8172**	989-775-4123
Salish Kootenai College PO Box 70	Pablo	MT	59855	**877-752-6553**	406-275-4800
Southwestern Indian Polytechnic Institute 9169 Coors Blvd NW PO Box 10146	Albuquerque	NM	87120	**800-586-7474**	505-346-2306
Turtle Mountain Community College 10145 BIA Rd 7	Belcourt	ND	58316	**800-827-1100**	701-477-7862

165 COLLEGES - WOMEN'S (FOUR-YEAR)

Name / Address	City	State	ZIP	Toll-Free	Phone
Agnes Scott College 141 E College Ave	Decatur	GA	30030	**800-868-8602**	404-471-6000
Alverno College PO Box 343922	Milwaukee	WI	53234	**800-933-3401**	414-382-6100
Bay Path College 588 Longmeadow St	Longmeadow	MA	01106	**800-782-7284**	
Bennett College 900 E Washington St — *Admissions	Greensboro	NC	27401	**800-413-5323***	336-370-8624
Blue Mountain College PO Box 160	Blue Mountain	MS	38610	**800-235-0136**	662-685-4771
Brenau University 500 Washington St	Gainesville	GA	30501	**800-252-5119**	770-534-6299
Bryn Mawr College 101 N Merion Ave — *Admissions	Bryn Mawr	PA	19010	**800-262-2586***	610-526-5000
Carlow University 3333 Fifth Ave	Pittsburgh	PA	15213	**800-333-2275**	412-578-6000
Cedar Crest College 100 College Dr — *Admissions	Allentown	PA	18104	**800-360-1222***	610-437-4471
Chatham University 1 Woodland Rd	Pittsburgh	PA	15232	**800-837-1290**	412-365-1100
College of New Rochelle 29 Castle Pl	New Rochelle	NY	10805	**800-933-5923**	914-654-5000
College of Notre Dame of Maryland 4701 N Charles St — *Admissions	Baltimore	MD	21210	**800-753-3757***	410-435-0100
College of Saint Catherine 2004 Randolph Ave	Saint Paul	MN	55105	**800-945-4599**	651-690-6000
Minneapolis 601 25th Ave S	Minneapolis	MN	55454	**800-945-4599**	651-690-7700
College of Saint Elizabeth 2 Convent Rd — *Admissions	Morristown	NJ	07960	**800-210-7900***	973-290-4700
College of Saint Mary 7000 Mercy Rd	Omaha	NE	68106	**800-926-5534**	402-399-2400
Converse College 580 E Main St — *Admissions	Spartanburg	SC	29302	**800-766-1125***	864-596-9000
Fordham University 441 E Fordham Rd	Bronx	NY	10458	**800-367-3426**	718-817-3240
Westchester 400 Westchester Ave	West Harrison	NY	10604	**800-606-6090**	914-332-8295
Georgian Court University 900 Lakewood Ave	Lakewood	NJ	08701	**800-458-8422**	
Hollins University PO BOX 9707 — *Admissions	Roanoke	VA	24020	**800-456-9595***	540-362-6401
Judson College 302 Bibb St — *Admissions	Marion	AL	36756	**800-447-9472***	334-683-5110
Mary Baldwin College 318 Prospect St PO Box 1500 — *Admissions	Staunton	VA	24401	**800-468-2262***	540-887-7019
Meredith College 3800 Hillsborough St — *All	Raleigh	NC	27607	**800-637-3348***	919-760-8581
Midway College 512 E Stephens St	Midway	KY	40347	**800-755-0031**	859-846-5346
Mills College 5000 MacArthur Blvd — *Admissions	Oakland	CA	94613	**877-746-4557***	510-430-2135
Moore College of Art & Design 20th St & the Pkwy	Philadelphia	PA	19103	**800-523-2025**	215-965-4000
Mount Holyoke College 50 College St	South Hadley	MA	01075	**800-642-4483**	413-538-2000
Mount Mary College 2900 N Menomonee River Pkwy — *Admissions	Milwaukee	WI	53222	**800-321-6265***	414-256-1219
Mount Saint Mary' s University 12001 Chalon Rd — *Admissions	Los Angeles	CA	90049	**800-999-9893***	310-954-4250
Pine Manor College 400 Heath St	Chestnut Hill	MA	02467	**800-762-1357**	617-731-7104
Randolph College 2500 Rivermont Ave — *Admissions	Lynchburg	VA	24503	**800-745-7692***	434-947-8000
Regis College 235 Wellesley St	Weston	MA	02493	**866-438-7344**	781-768-7000
Rosemont College 1400 Montgomery Ave — *Admissions	Rosemont	PA	19010	**888-521-0983***	610-527-0200
Russell Sage College 45 Ferry St — *Admissions	Troy	NY	12180	**888-837-9724***	518-244-2217
Saint Mary's College Le Mans Hall — *Admissions	Notre Dame	IN	46556	**800-551-7621***	574-284-4587
Saint Mary-of-the-Woods College 3301 St Mary Rd	Saint Mary Of The Woods	IN	47876	**800-926-7692**	812-535-5106
Salem College 601 S Church St — *Admissions	Winston-Salem	NC	27101	**800-327-2536***	336-721-2600
Scripps College 1030 Columbia Ave	Claremont	CA	91711	**800-770-1333**	909-621-8149
Simmons College 300 The Fenway	Boston	MA	02115	**800-345-8468**	617-521-2000
Smith College 7 College Ln	NorthHampton	MA	01063	**800-383-3232**	413-584-2700
Spelman College 350 Spelman Ln SW — *Admissions	Atlanta	GA	30314	**800-982-2411***	404-681-3643
Sweet Briar College 134 Chappel Rd — *Admissions	Sweet Briar	VA	24595	**800-381-6142***	434-381-6100
Texas Woman's University 304 Admin Dr PO Box 425589	Denton	TX	76204	**866-809-6130**	940-898-3188
Trinity University 125 Michigan Ave NE — *Admissions	Washington	DC	20017	**800-492-6882***	202-884-9000
Ursuline College 2550 Lander Rd	Pepper Pike	OH	44124	**888-778-5463**	440-449-4200
Wesleyan College 4760 Forsyth Rd	Macon	GA	31210	**800-447-6610**	478-757-5219
William Peace University 15 E Peace St	Raleigh	NC	27604	**800-732-2347**	919-508-2000
Wilson College 1015 Philadelphia Ave — *Admissions	Chambersburg	PA	17201	**800-421-8402***	717-264-4141

166 COLLEGES & UNIVERSITIES - CHRISTIAN

SEE ALSO Colleges - Bible ; Colleges & Universities - Jesuit

The institutions listed here are members of the Council for Christian Colleges & Universities (CCCU). Although many other colleges and universities describe themselves as "religiously affiliated," members of CCCU are intentionally Christ-centered. Among the criteria for membership in CCCU, schools must have curricular and extra-curricular programs that reflect the integration of scholarship, biblical faith, and service.

Name / Address	City	State	ZIP	Toll-Free	Phone
Anderson University 1100 E Fifth St — *Admissions	Anderson	IN	46012	**800-428-6414***	765-649-9071
Asbury College 1 Macklem Dr — *Admissions	Wilmore	KY	40390	**800-888-1818***	859-858-3511
Azusa Pacific University 901 E Alosta Ave PO Box 7000	Azusa	CA	91702	**800-825-5278**	626-969-3434
Belhaven College 1500 Peachtree St PO Box 153	Jackson	MS	39202	**800-960-5940**	601-968-5940
Biola University 13800 Biola Ave — *Admissions	La Mirada	CA	90639	**800-652-4652***	562-903-6000
Bluffton University 1 University Dr	Bluffton	OH	45817	**800-488-3257**	419-358-3000
Bryan College 721 Bryan Dr PO Box 7000	Dayton	TN	37321	**800-277-9522**	423-775-2041
California Baptist University 8432 Magnolia Ave	Riverside	CA	92504	**877-228-8866**	951-689-5771
Calvin College 3201 Burton St SE	Grand Rapids	MI	49546	**800-688-0122**	616-526-6000
Campbellsville University 1 University Dr — *Admissions	Campbellsville	KY	42718	**800-264-6014***	270-789-5000
Carson-Newman College 1646 Russell Ave	Jefferson City	TN	37760	**800-678-9061**	865-471-2000
Cedarville University 251 N Main St	Cedarville	OH	45314	**800-233-2784**	937-766-7700
College of the Ozarks 1 Industrial Dr PO Box 17 — *Admissions	Point Lookout	MO	65726	**800-222-0525***	417-334-6411
Colorado Christian University 8787 W Alameda Ave	Lakewood	CO	80226	**800-443-2484**	303-963-3200
Corban College 5000 Deer Pk Dr SE	Salem	OR	97317	**800-845-3005**	503-581-8600
Cornerstone University 1001 E Beltline Ave NE — *Admissions	Grand Rapids	MI	49525	**800-787-9778***	616-222-1426
Covenant College 14049 Scenic Hwy	Lookout Mountain	GA	30750	**888-451-2683**	706-820-1560
Crown College 8700 College View Dr	Saint Bonifacius	MN	55375	**800-346-9252**	952-446-4100
Dallas Baptist University 3000 Mtn Creek Pkwy	Dallas	TX	75211	**800-460-1328**	214-333-7100
Dordt College 498 Fourth Ave NE	Sioux Center	IA	51250	**800-343-6738**	712-722-6080
East Texas Baptist University 1209 N Grove St	Marshall	TX	75670	**800-804-3828**	903-935-7963
Eastern Mennonite University 1200 Pk Rd — *Admissions	Harrisonburg	VA	22802	**800-368-2665***	540-432-4118
Eastern Nazarene College 23 E Elm Ave	Quincy	MA	02170	**800-883-6288**	617-745-3000
Eastern University 1300 Eagle Rd — *Admissions	Wayne	PA	19087	**800-452-0996***	610-341-5800
Erskine College 2 Washington St — *Admissions	Due West	SC	29639	**888-359-4358***	
Evangel University 1111 N Glenstone Ave	Springfield	MO	65802	**800-382-6435**	417-865-2815
Geneva College 3200 College Ave	Beaver Falls	PA	15010	**800-847-8255**	724-847-6500
George Fox University 414 N Meridian St	Newberg	OR	97132	**800-765-4369**	503-538-8383
Gordon College 255 Grapevine Rd	Wenham	MA	01984	**800-343-1379**	978-927-2300
Goshen College 1700 S Main St	Goshen	IN	46526	**800-348-7422**	574-535-7000
Grace College 200 Seminary Dr	Winona Lake	IN	46590	**800-544-7223**	574-372-5100

	City	State	ZIP	Toll-Free	Phone
Greenville College 315 E College Ave	Greenville	IL	62246	**800-345-4440**	618-664-7100
Hardin-Simmons University 2200 Hickory St	Abilene	TX	79698	**877-464-7889**	325-670-1206
Hope International University 2500 E Nutwood Ave	Fullerton	CA	92831	**866-722-4673**	714-879-3901
Houghton College 1 Willard Ave PO Box 128	Houghton	NY	14744	**800-777-2556**	585-567-9200
Houston Baptist University 7502 Fondren Rd *Admissions	Houston	TX	77074	**800-969-3210***	281-649-3000
Howard Payne University 1000 Fisk Ave	Brownwood	TX	76801	**800-950-8465**	325-646-2502
Huntington University 2303 College Ave *Admissions	Huntington	IN	46750	**800-642-6493***	260-356-6000
Indiana Wesleyan University 4201 S Washington St	Marion	IN	46953	**800-332-6901**	765-677-2138
John Brown University 2000 W University St *Admissions	Siloam Springs	AR	72761	**877-528-4636***	479-524-9500
Judson College 302 Bibb St *Admissions	Marion	AL	36756	**800-447-9472***	334-683-5110
Judson University 1151 N State St *Admissions	Elgin	IL	60123	**800-879-5376***	847-628-2500
Kentucky Christian University 100 Academic Pkwy *Admissions	Grayson	KY	41143	**800-522-3181***	606-474-3000
King College 1350 King College Rd *Admissions	Bristol	TN	37620	**800-362-0014***	423-652-4861
King's University College 9125 50th St	Edmonton	AB	T6B2H3	**800-661-8582**	780-465-3500
Lee University 1120 N Ocoee St	Cleveland	TN	37311	**800-533-9930**	423-614-8000
LeTourneau University 2100 S Mobberly Ave	Longview	TX	75602	**800-759-8811**	903-233-3000
Lipscomb University 3901 Granny White Pk	Nashville	TN	37204	**800-333-4358**	615-966-1000
Louisiana College 1140 College Dr	Pineville	LA	71359	**800-487-1906**	318-487-7011
Malone College 515 25th St NW	Canton	OH	44709	**800-521-1146**	330-471-8100
Master's College 21726 Placerita Canyon Rd	Santa Clarita	CA	91321	**800-568-6248**	661-259-3540
Messiah College PO Box 3005	Grantham	PA	17027	**800-233-4220**	717-691-6000
MidAmerica Nazarene University 2030 E College Way	Olathe	KS	66062	**800-800-8887**	913-782-3750
Milligan College PO Box 500	Milligan College	TN	37682	**800-262-8337**	423-461-8730
Mississippi College 200 S Capitol St	Clinton	MS	39056	**800-738-1236**	601-925-3000
Missouri Baptist University 1 College Pk Dr	Saint Louis	MO	63141	**877-434-1115**	314-434-1115
Montreat College 310 Gaither Cir PO Box 1267	Montreat	NC	28757	**800-622-6968**	828-669-8011
Mount Vernon Nazarene University 800 Martinsburg Rd *Admissions	Mount Vernon	OH	43050	**800-766-8206***	740-392-6868
North Greenville University 7801 N Tigerville Rd PO Box 1892	Tigerville	SC	29688	**800-468-6642**	864-977-7000
North Park University 3225 W Foster Ave	Chicago	IL	60625	**800-888-6728**	773-244-5500
Northwest Christian College 828 E 11th Ave	Eugene	OR	97401	**877-463-6622**	541-343-1641
Northwest Nazarene University 623 Holly St *Admissions	Nampa	ID	83686	**877-668-4968***	208-467-8000
Northwest University 5520 108th Ave NE *Admissions	Kirkland	WA	98033	**800-669-3781***	425-822-8266
Northwestern College 101 Seventh St SW	Orange City	IA	51041	**800-747-4757**	712-707-7000
Nyack College 1 S Blvd *Admissions	Nyack	NY	10960	**800-336-9225***	845-358-1710
Oklahoma Baptist University 500 W University St	Shawnee	OK	74804	**800-654-3285**	405-275-2850
Oklahoma Christian University PO Box 11000	Oklahoma City	OK	73136	**800-877-5010**	405-425-5000
Olivet Nazarene University 1 University Ave	Bourbonnais	IL	60914	**800-648-1463**	815-939-5011
Oral Roberts University 7777 S Lewis Ave	Tulsa	OK	74171	**800-678-8876**	918-495-6161
Palm Beach Atlantic University PO Box 24708	West Palm Beach	FL	33416	**888-468-6722**	561-803-2000
Point Loma Nazarene University 3900 Lomaland Dr *Admissions	San Diego	CA	92106	**800-733-7770***	619-849-2200
Redeemer University College 777 Garner Rd E	Ancaster	ON	L9K1J4	**877-779-0913**	905-648-2131
Roberts Wesleyan College 2301 Westside Dr *Admissions	Rochester	NY	14624	**800-777-4792***	585-594-6000
Seattle Pacific University 3307 Third Ave W	Seattle	WA	98119	**800-366-3344**	206-281-2000
Simpson University 2211 College View Dr	Redding	CA	96003	**888-974-6776**	530-226-4606
Southeastern University 1000 Longfellow Blvd	Lakeland	FL	33801	**800-500-8760**	863-667-5000
Southern Nazarene University 6729 NW 39th Expy	Bethany	OK	73008	**800-648-9899**	405-789-6400
Southern Wesleyan University 907 Wesleyan Dr	Central	SC	29630	**800-282-8798**	864-644-5000
Southwest Baptist University 1600 University Ave	Bolivar	MO	65613	**800-526-5859**	
Spring Arbor University 106 E Main St *Admissions	Spring Arbor	MI	49283	**800-968-9103***	517-750-1200
Tabor College 400 S Jefferson St *Admissions	Hillsboro	KS	67063	**800-822-6799***	620-947-3121
Taylor University 236 W Reade Ave	Upland	IN	46989	**800-882-3456**	765-998-2751
Trevecca Nazarene University 333 Murfreesboro Rd	Nashville	TN	37210	**888-210-4868**	615-248-1200
Trinity International University 2065 Half Day Rd	Deerfield	IL	60015	**800-822-3225**	847-945-8800
Trinity Western University 7600 Glover Rd	Langley	BC	V2Y1Y1	**888-468-6898**	604-888-7511
Union University 1050 Union University Dr	Jackson	TN	38305	**800-338-6466**	731-661-5210
University of Sioux Falls 1101 W 22nd St	Sioux Falls	SD	57105	**800-888-1047**	605-331-6600
Vanguard University of Southern California 55 Fair Dr *Admissions	Costa Mesa	CA	92626	**800-722-6279***	714-556-3610
Warner Pacific College 2219 SE 68th Ave	Portland	OR	97215	**800-804-1510**	503-517-1020
Warner Southern College 13895 Hwy 27	Lake Wales	FL	33859	**800-309-9563**	
Wayland Baptist University 1900 W Seventh St	Plainview	TX	79072	**800-588-1928**	806-291-1000
Waynesburg College 51 W College St *Admissions	Waynesburg	PA	15370	**800-225-7393***	724-627-8191
Westmont College 955 La Paz Rd *Admissions	Santa Barbara	CA	93108	**800-777-9011***	805-565-6000
Wheaton College 501 College Ave	Wheaton	IL	60187	**800-222-2419**	630-752-5000
Whitworth College 300 W Hawthorne Rd *Admissions	Spokane	WA	99251	**800-533-4668***	509-777-1000
Williams Baptist College 60 W Fulbright St	Walnut Ridge	AR	72476	**800-722-4434**	870-886-6741

167 COLLEGES & UNIVERSITIES - FOUR-YEAR

SEE ALSO Universities - Canadian ; Vocational & Technical Schools ; Colleges - Community & Junior ; Colleges - Fine Arts ; Colleges - Women's (Four-Year) ; Colleges & Universities - Christian ; Colleges & Universities - Graduate & Professional Schools ; Colleges & Universities - Historically Black ; Colleges & Universities - Jesuit ; Military Service Academies

Alabama

	City	State	ZIP	Toll-Free	Phone
Alabama Agricultural & Mechanical University 4900 Meridian St PO Box 1087	Huntsville	AL	35810	**800-553-0816**	256-372-5000
Alabama State University 915 S Jackson St *Admissions	Montgomery	AL	36104	**800-253-5037***	334-229-4100
Amridge University 1200 Taylor Rd	Montgomery	AL	36117	**888-790-8080**	334-387-3877
Auburn University 202 Mary Martin Hall *Admissions	Auburn University	AL	36849	**866-389-6770***	334-844-6425
Montgomery 7440 E Dr	Montgomery	AL	36117	**800-227-2649**	334-244-3000
Birmingham-Southern College 900 Arkadelphia Rd	Birmingham	AL	35254	**800-523-5793**	205-226-4600
Faulkner University 5345 Atlanta Hwy	Montgomery	AL	36109	**800-879-9816**	334-272-5820
Huntingdon College 1500 E Fairview Ave *Admissions	Montgomery	AL	36106	**800-763-0313***	334-833-4497
Jacksonville State University 700 Pelham Rd N	Jacksonville	AL	36265	**800-231-5291**	256-782-5781
Judson College 302 Bibb St *Admissions	Marion	AL	36756	**800-447-9472***	334-683-5110
Miles College 5500 Myron Massey Blvd *Admissions	Fairfield	AL	35064	**800-445-0708***	205-929-1000
Oakwood College 7000 Adventist Blvd	Huntsville	AL	35896	**800-824-5312**	256-726-7356
Samford University 800 Lakeshore Dr *Admissions	Birmingham	AL	35229	**800-888-7218***	205-726-3673
South University *Montgomery* 5355 Vaughn Rd	Montgomery	AL	36116	**866-629-2962**	334-395-8800
Spring Hill College 4000 Dauphin St *Admissions	Mobile	AL	36608	**800-742-6704***	251-380-4000
Stillman College 3601 Stillman Blvd	Tuscaloosa	AL	35401	**800-841-5722**	205-349-4240
Talladega College 627 W Battle St	Talladega	AL	35160	**866-540-3956**	256-761-6100
Troy University 600 University Ave	Troy	AL	36082	**800-551-9716**	334-670-3100
Montgomery 231 Montgomery St PO Box 4419	Montgomery	AL	36104	**888-357-8843**	
Tuskegee University 1200 W Montgomery Rd *Admissions	Tuskegee	AL	36088	**800-622-6531***	334-727-8011
University of Alabama PO Box 870132 *Admissions	Tuscaloosa	AL	35487	**800-933-2262***	205-348-6010
Birmingham 1530 Third Ave S THT 647	Birmingham	AL	35294	**800-421-8743**	205-996-6670
Huntsville 301 Sparkman Dr	Huntsville	AL	35899	**800-824-2255**	256-824-1000

Classified Section

	City	State	ZIP	Toll-Free	Phone
University of Mobile					
5735 College Pkwy	Mobile	AL	36613	**800-946-7267**	251-675-5990
University of North Alabama					
1 Harrison Plaza	Florence	AL	35632	**800-825-5862**	256-765-4608
University of South Alabama					
2500 Meisler Hall	Mobile	AL	36688	**800-872-5247**	251-460-6141
University of West Alabama					
Station 200	Livingston	AL	35470	**800-621-8044***	205-652-3400
*Admissions					

Alaska

	City	State	ZIP	Toll-Free	Phone
Alaska Pacific University					
4101 University Dr	Anchorage	AK	99508	**800-252-7528**	907-564-8248
University of Alaska Anchorage					
3211 Providence Dr	Anchorage	AK	99508	**888-822-8973**	907-786-1800
University of Alaska Fairbanks					
PO Box 757480	Fairbanks	AK	99775	**800-478-1823**	907-474-7500
Bristol Bay					
527 Seward St PO Box 1070	Dillingham	AK	99576	**800-478-5109**	907-842-5109
University of Alaska Southeast					
11120 Glacier Hwy	Juneau	AK	99801	**877-465-4827**	907-796-6000

Arizona

	City	State	ZIP	Toll-Free	Phone
American Indian College of the Assemblies of God					
10020 N 15th Ave	Phoenix	AZ	85021	**800-621-7440**	602-944-3335
West PO Box 37100	Phoenix	AZ	85069	**855-278-5080**	602-543-5500
Embry-Riddle Aeronautical University Prescott					
3700 Willow Creek Rd	Prescott	AZ	86301	**800-888-3728**	928-777-3728
Grand Canyon University					
3300 W Camelback Rd	Phoenix	AZ	85017	**800-800-9776**	602-639-7500
Indian Bible College					
2918 N Aris Ave	Flagstaff	AZ	86004	**866-503-7789**	928-774-3890
International Baptist College					
2211 W Germann Rd	Chandler	AZ	85286	**800-422-4858***	480-245-7900
*General					
Northern Arizona University					
PO Box 4084	Flagstaff	AZ	86011	**888-628-2968***	928-523-5511
*Admissions					
Ottawa University Phoenix					
10020 N 25th Ave	Phoenix	AZ	85021	**800-235-9586**	602-371-1188
Prescott College					
220 Grove Ave	Prescott	AZ	86301	**877-350-2100**	
Western International University					
9215 N Black Canyon Hwy	Phoenix	AZ	85021	**866-948-4636**	602-943-2311

Arkansas

	City	State	ZIP	Toll-Free	Phone
Arkansas State University					
PO Box 1630	State University	AR	72467	**800-382-3030**	870-972-3024
Central Baptist College					
1501 College Ave	Conway	AR	72034	**800-205-6872**	501-329-6872
Harding University					
915 E. Market Ave	Searcy	AR	72149	**800-477-4407**	501-279-4000
Henderson State University					
1100 Henderson St	Arkadelphia	AR	71999	**800-228-7333**	870-230-5000
Hendrix College					
1600 Washington Ave	Conway	AR	72032	**800-277-9017**	501-329-6811
John Brown University					
2000 W University St	Siloam Springs	AR	72761	**877-528-4636***	479-524-9500
*Admissions					
Ouachita Baptist University					
410 Ouachita St	Arkadelphia	AR	71998	**800-342-5628***	870-245-5000
*Admissions					
Philander Smith College					
900 Daisy Bates Dr	Little Rock	AR	72202	**800-446-6772**	501-370-5221
Southern Arkansas University					
100 E University St	Magnolia	AR	71753	**800-332-7286**	870-235-4000
University of Arkansas					
232 Silas Hunt Hall	Fayetteville	AR	72701	**800-377-8632***	479-575-5346
*Admissions					
University of Arkansas					
Monticello PO Box 3600	Monticello	AR	71656	**800-844-1826**	870-460-1026
Pine Bluff					
1200 N University Dr	Pine Bluff	AR	71601	**800-264-6585***	870-575-8000
*Admissions					
University of Central Arkansas					
201 Donaghey Ave	Conway	AR	72035	**888-407-4747***	501-450-5000
*Admissions					
University of the Ozarks					
415 N College Ave	Clarksville	AR	72830	**800-264-8636***	479-979-1227
*Admissions					
Williams Baptist College					
60 W Fulbright St	Walnut Ridge	AR	72476	**800-722-4434**	870-886-6741
Selkirk College					
301 Frank Beinder Way	Castlegar	BC	V1N4L3	**888-953-1133**	250-365-7292

California

	City	State	ZIP	Toll-Free	Phone
Academy of Art University					
79 New Montgomery St	San Francisco	CA	94105	**800-544-2787**	415-274-2200
Alliant International University					
10455 Pomerado Rd	San Diego	CA	92131	**866-825-5426**	858-635-4772
American Career College Inc					
151 Innovation Dr	Irvine	CA	92617	**877-832-0790**	949-783-4800
Azusa Pacific University					
901 E Alosta Ave PO Box 7000	Azusa	CA	91702	**800-825-5278**	626-969-3434
Biola University					
13800 Biola Ave	La Mirada	CA	90639	**800-652-4652***	562-903-6000
*Admissions					
California Baptist University					
8432 Magnolia Ave	Riverside	CA	92504	**877-228-8866**	951-689-5771
California Institute of Technology					
1200 E California Blvd	Pasadena	CA	91125	**800-568-8324**	626-395-6811
California Lutheran University					
60 W Olsen Rd	Thousand Oaks	CA	91360	**877-258-3678**	805-493-3135
California Maritime Academy					
200 Maritime Academy Dr	Vallejo	CA	94590	**800-561-1945**	707-654-1330
California Polytechnic State University					
1 Grand Ave	San Luis Obispo	CA	93407	**800-424-6723**	805-756-1111
California State University					
Chico CSU Chico	Chico	CA	95929	**800-542-4426***	530-898-6321
*Admissions					
Dominguez Hills					
1000 E Victoria St	Carson	CA	90747	**888-545-6512**	310-243-3300
East Bay					
25800 Carlos Bee Blvd	Hayward	CA	94542	**877-829-5500**	510-885-3000
Fresno 5241 N Maple Ave	Fresno	CA	93740	**800-700-2320**	559-278-4240
Fullerton					
800 N State College Blvd	Fullerton	CA	92834	**888-433-9406**	714-278-2011
Long Beach					
1250 Bellflower Blvd	Long Beach	CA	90840	**800-663-1144**	562-985-4111
Northridge					
18111 Nordhoff St	Northridge	CA	91330	**800-399-4529**	818-677-1200
San Bernardino					
5500 University Pkwy	San Bernardino	CA	92407	**866-275-3772**	909-537-5188
San Marcos					
333 S Twin Oaks Valley Rd	San Marcos	CA	92096	**888-225-5427**	760-750-4000
Stanislaus 1 University Cir	Turlock	CA	95382	**800-235-9292**	209-667-3152
Chapman University					
1 University Dr	Orange	CA	92866	**888-282-7759**	714-997-6815
Cogswell Polytechnical College					
1175 Bordeaux Dr	Sunnyvale	CA	94089	**800-264-7955**	408-541-0100
Coleman College					
8888 Balboa Ave	San Diego	CA	92123	**800-430-2030**	858-499-0202
Columbia College Hollywood					
18618 Oxnard St	Tarzana	CA	91356	**800-785-0585**	818-345-8414
Concordia University Irvine					
1530 Concordia W	Irvine	CA	92612	**800-229-1200**	949-854-8002
Design Institute of San Diego					
8555 Commerce Ave	San Diego	CA	92121	**800-619-4337**	858-566-1200
Dominican University of California					
50 Acacia Ave	San Rafael	CA	94901	**888-323-6763***	415-457-4440
*Admissions					
Harvey Mudd College					
301 Platt Blvd Kingston Hall	Claremont	CA	91711	**877-827-5462**	909-621-8011
Hebrew Union College Los Angeles					
3077 University Ave	Los Angeles	CA	90007	**800-899-0925**	213-749-3424
Holy Names University					
3500 Mountain Blvd	Oakland	CA	94619	**800-430-1321**	510-436-1000
Hope International University					
2500 E Nutwood Ave	Fullerton	CA	92831	**866-722-4673**	714-879-3901
Humboldt State University					
1 Harpst St	Arcata	CA	95521	**866-850-9556**	707-826-3011
Humphreys College					
6650 Inglewood Ave	Stockton	CA	95207	**800-433-3243**	209-478-0800
John F Kennedy University					
100 Ellinwood Way	Pleasant Hill	CA	94523	**800-696-5358**	925-969-3300
La Sierra University					
4500 Riverwalk Pkwy	Riverside	CA	92515	**800-874-5587**	951-785-2000
Laguna College of Art & Design					
2222 Laguna Canyon Rd	Laguna Beach	CA	92651	**800-255-0762**	949-376-6000
Loyola Marymount University					
1 LMU Dr	Los Angeles	CA	90045	**800-568-4636**	310-338-2700
Master's College					
21726 Placerita Canyon Rd	Santa Clarita	CA	91321	**800-568-6248**	661-259-3540
Menlo College					
1000 El Camino Real	Atherton	CA	94027	**800-556-3656**	650-543-3753
Mills College					
5000 MacArthur Blvd	Oakland	CA	94613	**877-746-4557***	510-430-2135
*Admissions					
Mount Saint Mary' s University					
12001 Chalon Rd	Los Angeles	CA	90049	**800-999-9893***	310-954-4250
*Admissions					
National Hispanic University					
14271 Story Rd	San Jose	CA	95127	**877-762-9801**	408-254-6900
National University					
11255 N Torrey Pines Rd	La Jolla	CA	92037	**800-628-8648**	858-642-8000
Northwestern Polytechnic University					
47671 Westinghouse Dr	Fremont	CA	94539	**877-878-8883**	510-592-9688
Notre Dame de Namur University					
1500 Ralston Ave	Belmont	CA	94002	**800-263-0545**	650-508-3600
Occidental College					
1600 Campus Rd	Los Angeles	CA	90041	**800-825-5262***	323-259-2700
*Admissions					
Pacific College Oriental Med Inc					
7445 Mission Vly Rd Ste 105	San Diego	CA	92108	**800-729-0941**	619-574-6909
Pacific Oaks College					
5 Westmoreland Pl	Pasadena	CA	91103	**877-314-2380**	
Pacific States University					
1516 S Western Ave	Los Angeles	CA	90006	**888-200-0383**	323-731-2383
Pacific Union College					
1 Angwin Ave	Angwin	CA	94508	**800-862-7080**	707-965-6336
Patten University					
2433 Coolidge Ave	Oakland	CA	94601	**888-370-7589**	510-261-8500
Pitzer College					
1050 N Mills Ave	Claremont	CA	91711	**800-748-9371**	909-621-8129
Point Loma Nazarene University					
3900 Lomaland Dr	San Diego	CA	92106	**800-733-7770***	619-849-2200
*Admissions					
Ryokan College					
11965 Venice Blvd Ste 304	Los Angeles	CA	90066	**866-796-5261**	310-390-7560
Saint Mary's College of California					
1928 St Mary's Rd	Moraga	CA	94556	**800-800-4762***	925-631-4000
*Admissions					
Samuel Merritt College					
370 Hawthorne Ave	Oakland	CA	94609	**800-607-6377***	510-869-6576
*Admissions					
San Diego Christian College					
2100 Greenfield Dr	El Cajon	CA	92019	**800-676-2242**	619-441-2200

Classified Section

	City	State	Zip	Toll-Free	Phone
San Francisco Conservatory of Music 50 Oak St	San Francisco	CA	94102	**800-999-8219**	415-864-7326
San Jose State University 1 Washington Sq	San Jose	CA	95192	**800-273-8255**	408-924-1000
Scripps College 1030 Columbia Ave	Claremont	CA	91711	**800-770-1333**	909-621-8149
Simpson University 2211 College View Dr	Redding	CA	96003	**888-974-6776**	530-226-4606
South Baylo University 1126 N Brookhurst St	Anaheim	CA	92801	**888-642-2956**	714-533-1495
Southern California Seminary 2075 E Madison Ave	El Cajon	CA	92019	**888-389-7244**	
Stanford University 450 Serra Mall	Stanford	CA	94305	**877-407-9529**	650-723-2091
Thomas Aquinas College 10000 Ojai Rd	Santa Paula	CA	93060	**800-634-9797**	805-525-4417
University of California (UCLA)					
Berkeley 110 Sproul Hall MC Ste 5800	Berkeley	CA	94720	**866-740-1260**	510-642-6000
Merced PO Box 2039	Merced	CA	95344	**866-270-7301**	209-724-4400
Riverside 900 University Ave 1120 Hinderaker Hall	Riverside	CA	92521	**800-426-2586**	951-827-3411
Santa Barbara 1210 Cheadle Hall	Santa Barbara	CA	93106	**888-488-8272**	805-893-8000
Santa Cruz 1156 High St Hahn Bldg Rm 150	Santa Cruz	CA	95064	**800-933-7584**	831-459-2131
University of Judaism 15600 Mulholland Dr	Los Angeles	CA	90077	**888-853-6763**	310-476-9777
University of La Verne 1950 Third St *Admissions	La Verne	CA	91750	**800-876-4858***	909-593-3511
University of Redlands 1200 E Colton Ave PO Box 3080	Redlands	CA	92373	**800-455-5064**	909-793-2121
University of San Diego 5998 Alcala Pk	San Diego	CA	92110	**800-248-4873**	619-260-4506
University of San Francisco 2130 Fulton St *Admissions	San Francisco	CA	94117	**800-854-1385***	415-422-5555
University of the Pacific 3601 Pacific Ave	Stockton	CA	95211	**800-959-2867**	209-946-2211
Vanguard University of Southern California 55 Fair Dr *Admissions	Costa Mesa	CA	92626	**800-722-6279***	714-556-3610
Westmont College 955 La Paz Rd *Admissions	Santa Barbara	CA	93108	**800-777-9011***	805-565-6000
William Jessup University 333 Sunset Blvd	Rocklin	CA	95765	**800-355-7522**	916-577-2200
Woodbury University 7500 Glenoaks Blvd	Burbank	CA	91510	**800-784-9663**	818-767-0888
World University 107 N Ventura St PO Box 1567	Ojai	CA	93024	**888-370-7589**	805-646-1444

Colorado

	City	State	Zip	Toll-Free	Phone
Adams State College 208 Edgemont Blvd	Alamosa	CO	81102	**800-824-6494**	719-587-7712
Beth-El College of Nursing & Health Sciences 1420 Austin Bluffs Pkwy	Colorado Springs	CO	80918	**800-990-8227**	719-255-8227
Colorado Christian University 8787 W Alameda Ave	Lakewood	CO	80226	**800-443-2484**	303-963-3200
Loveland 3553 Clydesdale Pkwy Ste 300	Loveland	CO	80538	**800-443-2484**	970-669-8700
Colorado College 14 E Cache La Poudre St	Colorado Springs	CO	80903	**800-542-7214**	719-389-6344
Colorado School of Mines 1600 Maple St	Golden	CO	80401	**800-446-9488**	303-273-3000
Colorado State University *Pueblo* 2200 Bonforte Blvd	Pueblo	CO	81001	**877-307-5678**	719-549-2100
Colorado Technical University 4435 N Chestnut St	Colorado Springs	CO	80907	**855-230-0555**	719-598-0200
Fort Lewis College 1000 Rim Dr	Durango	CO	81301	**877-352-2656**	970-247-7010
Johnson & Wales University Denver 7150 E Montview Blvd	Denver	CO	80220	**877-598-3368**	303-256-9300
Mesa State College 1100 N Ave	Grand Junction	CO	81501	**800-982-6372**	970-248-1020
Naropa University 2130 Arapahoe Ave	Boulder	CO	80302	**800-772-6951**	303-444-0202
National American University Colorado Springs 1915 Jamboree Dr Ste 185	Colorado Springs	CO	80920	**855-448-2318**	316-448-5400
Regis University 3333 Regis Blvd *Admissions	Denver	CO	80221	**800-388-2366***	303-458-4100
Colorado Springs 7450 Campus Dr Ste 100	Colorado Springs	CO	80920	**800-568-8932**	
University of Colorado *Colorado Springs* PO Box 7150	Colorado Springs	CO	80933	**800-990-8227**	719-262-3000
University of Denver 2199 S University Blvd	Denver	CO	80210	**800-525-9495**	303-871-2036
University of Northern Colorado 501 20th St CB 92 *Admissions	Greeley	CO	80639	**888-700-4862***	970-351-2881
US Air Force Academy (USAFA) 2304 Cadet Dr Ste 2300	Air Force Academy	CO	80840	**800-443-9266**	719-333-1110
Western State College of Colorado 600 N Adams St *Admissions	Gunnison	CO	81231	**800-876-5309***	970-943-2119

Connecticut

	City	State	Zip	Toll-Free	Phone
Albertus Magnus College 700 Prospect St *Admissions	New Haven	CT	06511	**800-578-9160***	203-773-8550
Briarwood College 2279 Mt Vernon Rd	Southington	CT	06489	**800-952-2444**	860-628-4751
Connecticut College 270 Mohegan Ave	New London	CT	06320	**800-892-3363**	860-439-2000
Eastern Connecticut State University 83 Windham St *Admissions	Willimantic	CT	06226	**877-353-3278***	860-465-5000
Hartford Seminary 77 Sherman St	Hartford	CT	06105	**877-860-2255**	860-509-9500
Mitchell College 437 Pequot Ave *Admitting	New London	CT	06320	**800-443-2811***	860-701-5000
Post University 800 Country Club Rd	Waterbury	CT	06723	**800-345-2562**	203-596-4500
Quinnipiac University 275 Mt Carmel Ave *Admissions	Hamden	CT	06518	**800-462-1944***	203-582-8600
Southern Connecticut State University 501 Crescent St	New Haven	CT	06515	**888-500-7278**	203-392-5200
University of Bridgeport 126 Pk Ave	Bridgeport	CT	06604	**800-392-3582**	203-576-4000
University of Hartford 200 Bloomfield Ave	West Hartford	CT	06117	**800-947-4303**	860-768-4296
University of New Haven 300 Boston Post Rd	West Haven	CT	06516	**800-342-5864**	203-932-7319
US Coast Guard Academy 15 Mohegan Ave	New London	CT	06320	**800-883-8724**	860-444-8500
Western Connecticut State University 181 White St	Danbury	CT	06810	**877-837-9278**	203-837-8200

Delaware

	City	State	Zip	Toll-Free	Phone
Delaware State University 1200 N DuPont Hwy *Admissions	Dover	DE	19901	**800-845-2544***	302-857-6351
Goldey Beacom College 4701 Limestone Rd	Wilmington	DE	19808	**800-833-4877**	302-998-8814
Wilmington University 320 N DuPont Hwy *Admissions	New Castle	DE	19720	**877-967-5464***	302-356-6739

District of Columbia

	City	State	Zip	Toll-Free	Phone
American University 4400 Massachusetts Ave NW	Washington	DC	20016	**800-829-1040**	202-885-1000
Gallaudet University 800 Florida Ave NE	Washington	DC	20002	**800-995-0550**	202-651-5000
George Washington University 2121 'I' St NW	Washington	DC	20052	**866-498-3382**	202-994-1000
Mount Vernon College 2100 Foxhall Rd NW	Washington	DC	20007	**800-447-3765**	202-994-1000
Howard University 2400 Sixth St NW	Washington	DC	20059	**800-822-6363**	202-806-6100
Strayer University 1133 15th St NW	Washington	DC	20005	**888-311-0355**	202-408-2400
Takoma Park 6830 Laurel St NW	Washington	DC	20012	**888-311-0355**	202-722-8100
Trinity University 125 Michigan Ave NE *Admissions	Washington	DC	20017	**800-492-6882***	202-884-9000

Florida

	City	State	Zip	Toll-Free	Phone
American Intercontinental University South Florida 2250 N Commerce Pkwy	Weston	FL	33326	**855-377-1888**	954-446-6100
Ave Maria University 5050 Ave Maria Blvd	Naples	FL	34119	**877-283-8648**	239-280-2500
Baptist College of Florida 5400 College Dr	Graceville	FL	32440	**800-328-2660**	850-263-3261
Barry University 11300 NE Second Ave	Miami Shores	FL	33161	**800-756-6000**	305-899-3000
Orlando 1650 Sandlake Rd Ste 390	Orlando	FL	32809	**800-756-6000**	407-438-4150
Tallahassee 325 John Knox Rd Bldg A	Tallahassee	FL	32303	**800-756-6000**	850-385-2279
Bethune-Cookman College 640 Dr Mary McLeod Bethune Blvd *Admissions	Daytona Beach	FL	32114	**800-448-0228***	386-481-2900
Columbia College Orlando 2600 Technology Dr Ste 100	Orlando	FL	32804	**800-231-2391**	407-293-9911
Eckerd College 4200 54th Ave S *Admissions	Saint Petersburg	FL	33711	**800-456-9009***	727-867-1166
Embry-Riddle Aeronautical University *Daytona Beach* 600 S Clyde Morris Blvd	Daytona Beach	FL	32114	**800-862-2416**	386-226-6000
Flagler College 74 King St *Admissions	Saint Augustine	FL	32084	**800-304-4208***	904-829-6481
Florida A & M University 1700 Lee Hall Dr Rm G-7 Foote-Hilyer Administration Ctr	Tallahassee	FL	32307	**866-642-1198**	850-599-3000
Florida Atlantic University (FAU) 777 Glades Rd *Admissions	Boca Raton	FL	33431	**800-299-4328***	561-297-3000
Davie 3200 College Ave	Davie	FL	33314	**800-764-2222**	954-236-1000
Fort Lauderdale 111 E Las Olas Blvd	Fort Lauderdale	FL	33301	**800-764-2222**	954-201-7350
MacArthur 5353 Parkside Dr	Jupiter	FL	33458	**888-328-2586**	561-799-8500
Florida College 119 N Glen Arven Ave	Temple Terrace	FL	33617	**800-326-7655**	813-988-5131
Florida Institute of Technology 150 W University Blvd	Melbourne	FL	32901	**800-888-4348**	321-674-8000

Classified Section

Name / Address	City	State	Zip	Toll-Free	Phone
Florida International University 11200 SW Eigth St	Miami	FL	33199	**800-677-6337**	305-348-2000
Florida Memorial University 15800 NW 42nd Ave	Miami Gardens	FL	33054	**800-822-1362**	305-626-3600
Florida Southern College 111 Lk Hollingsworth Dr *Admissions	Lakeland	FL	33801	**800-274-4131***	863-680-4131
Hodges University 2655 Northbrooke Dr	Naples	FL	34119	**800-466-8017**	239-513-1122
Fort Myers 4501 Colonial Blvd	Fort Myers	FL	33966	**800-466-0019**	239-938-7701
Jacksonville University 2800 University Blvd N	Jacksonville	FL	32211	**800-225-2027**	904-256-8000
Johnson & Wales University North Miami 1701 NE 127th St	North Miami	FL	33181	**866-598-3567**	800-342-5598
Jones College 5353 Arlington Expy	Jacksonville	FL	32211	**800-331-0176**	904-743-1122
Logos Christian College 6620 Southpoint Dr S Ste 200	Jacksonville	FL	32216	**800-776-0127**	904-745-3311
Lynn University 3601 N Military Trl *Admissions	Boca Raton	FL	33431	**800-888-5966***	561-237-7900
New College of Florida 5800 Bay Shore Rd	Sarasota	FL	34243	**800-435-7352**	941-487-5000
Northwood University Florida 2600 N Military Trl *Admissions	West Palm Beach	FL	33409	**800-458-8325***	561-478-5500
Nova Southeastern University 3301 College Ave	Fort Lauderdale	FL	33314	**800-541-6682**	954-262-8000
Palm Beach Atlantic University PO Box 24708	West Palm Beach	FL	33416	**888-468-6722**	561-803-2000
Pensacola Christian College 250 Brent Ln	Pensacola	FL	32503	**800-722-4636**	850-478-8496
Rollins College 1000 Holt Ave	Winter Park	FL	32789	**800-799-2586**	407-646-2000
Saint Leo University 33701 State Rd 52	Saint Leo	FL	33574	**800-334-5532**	352-588-8200
Palatka Ctr 33701 State Rd 52 PO Box 6665	Saint Leo	FL	33574	**800-334-5532**	352-588-8200
South University West Palm Beach 9801 Belvedere Rd University Ctr	West Palm Beach	FL	33411	**800-688-0932**	561-273-6500
Southeastern University 1000 Longfellow Blvd	Lakeland	FL	33801	**800-500-8760**	863-667-5000
Stetson University 421 N Woodland Blvd Unit 8378 *Admissions	DeLand	FL	32723	**800-688-0101***	386-822-7100
Trinity International University South Florida 8190 W SR 84	Davie	FL	33324	**800-822-3225**	954-382-6400
University of Florida 219 Grinter Hall PO Box 115500	Gainesville	FL	32611	**866-876-4472**	352-392-3261
University of North Florida 4567 St Johns Bluff Rd S	Jacksonville	FL	32224	**866-697-7150**	904-620-1000
University of South Florida *Sarasota-Manatee* 8350 N Tamiami Trail	Sarasota	FL	34243	**866-974-1222**	941-359-4200
Tampa 4202 E Fowler Ave	Tampa	FL	33620	**800-299-2855**	813-974-2011
University of South Florida Polytechnic *Lakeland* 3433 Winter Lake Rd	Lakeland	FL	33803	**800-873-5636**	863-667-7000
Warner Southern College 13895 Hwy 27	Lake Wales	FL	33859	**800-309-9563**	
Webber International University 1201 N Scenic Hwy	Babson Park	FL	33827	**800-741-1844**	

Georgia

Name / Address	City	State	Zip	Toll-Free	Phone
Agnes Scott College 141 E College Ave	Decatur	GA	30030	**800-868-8602**	404-471-6000
American InterContinental University *Atlanta* 6600 Peachtree Dunwoody Rd 500 Embassy Row NE	Atlanta	GA	30328	**800-491-0182**	404-965-6500
Dunwoody 6600 Peachtree-Dunwoody Rd 500 Embassy Row	Atlanta	GA	30328	**855-377-1888**	404-965-6500
Armstrong Atlantic State University 11935 Abercorn St	Savannah	GA	31419	**800-633-2349**	
Augusta State University 2500 Walton Way	Augusta	GA	30904	**800-341-4373**	706-737-1632
Berry College 2277 Martha Berry Hwy PO Box 490159	Mount Berry	GA	30149	**800-237-7942**	706-232-5374
Brenau University 500 Washington St	Gainesville	GA	30501	**800-252-5119**	770-534-6299
Brewton-Parker College 201 David-Eliza Fountain Cir Hwy 280 PO Box 197	Mount Vernon	GA	30445	**800-342-1087**	912-583-2241
Clark Atlanta University 223 James P Brawley Dr SW *Admissions	Atlanta	GA	30314	**800-688-3228***	404-880-8000
Columbus State University 4225 University Ave	Columbus	GA	31907	**866-264-2035**	706-507-8800
Covenant College 14049 Scenic Hwy	Lookout Mountain	GA	30750	**888-451-2683**	706-820-1560
Dalton State College 650 N College Dr	Dalton	GA	30720	**800-829-4436**	706-272-4436
Emmanuel College 181 Spring St	Franklin Springs	GA	30639	**800-860-8800**	706-245-7226
Emory University 201 Dowman Dr *Admissions	Atlanta	GA	30322	**800-727-6036***	404-727-6036
Fort Valley State University 1005 State University Dr	Fort Valley	GA	31030	**877-462-3878**	478-825-6211
Georgia College & State University 231 W Hancock St CB 23	Milledgeville	GA	31061	**800-342-0471**	478-445-5004
Macon 433 Cherry St	Macon	GA	31206	**800-342-0471**	478-752-4278
Georgia Southwestern State University 800 Gsw State University Dr *Admissions	Americus	GA	31709	**800-338-0082***	229-928-1273
Kennesaw State University 1000 Chastain Rd	Kennesaw	GA	30144	**888-875-3697**	770-423-6000
LaGrange College 601 Broad St *Admissions	LaGrange	GA	30240	**800-593-2885***	706-880-8000
Life University 1269 Barclay Cir	Marietta	GA	30060	**800-543-3203**	770-426-2884
Macon State College 100 College Stn Dr	Macon	GA	31206	**800-272-7619**	478-471-2700
Mercer University 1400 Coleman Ave	Macon	GA	31207	**800-637-2378**	478-301-2650
Cecil B Day 3001 Mercer University Dr	Atlanta	GA	30341	**800-840-8577**	678-547-6089
Oglethorpe University 4484 Peachtree Rd,N.E	Atlanta	GA	30319	**800-428-4484**	404-364-8307
Paine College 1235 15th St	Augusta	GA	30901	**800-476-7703**	706-821-8200
Piedmont College 165 Central Ave	Demorest	GA	30535	**800-277-7020**	706-776-0103
Reinhardt College 7300 Reinhardt College Cir	Waleska	GA	30183	**877-346-4273**	770-720-5526
Shorter University 315 Shorter Ave	Rome	GA	30165	**800-868-6980**	706-233-7319
South University Savannah 709 Mall Blvd	Savannah	GA	31406	**800-688-0932**	912-201-8000
Spelman College 350 Spelman Ln SW *Admissions	Atlanta	GA	30314	**800-982-2411***	404-681-3643
Thomas University 1501 Millpond Rd	Thomasville	GA	31792	**800-538-9784**	229-226-1621
Truett-McConnell College 100 Alumni Dr	Cleveland	GA	30528	**800-226-8621**	706-865-2134
Valdosta State University 1500 N Patterson St	Valdosta	GA	31698	**800-618-1878**	229-333-5800
Wesleyan College 4760 Forsyth Rd	Macon	GA	31210	**800-447-6610**	478-757-5219

Hawaii

Name / Address	City	State	Zip	Toll-Free	Phone
Atlantic International University 900 Ft St Mall	Honolulu	HI	96813	**800-993-0066**	808-924-9567
Chaminade University 3140 Waialae Ave	Honolulu	HI	96816	**800-735-3733**	808-735-4711
Hawaii Pacific University 1164 Bishop St Ste 200	Honolulu	HI	96813	**866-225-5478**	808-544-0200
Windward Hawaii Loa 1164 Bishop St *Admissions	Honolulu	HI	96813	**866-225-5478***	808-544-0200
University of Hawaii *Hilo* 200 W Kawili St *Admissions	Hilo	HI	96720	**800-897-4456***	808-974-7414
Manoa 2600 Campus Rd Rm 001 *Admissions	Honolulu	HI	96822	**800-823-9771***	808-956-8975
West Oahu 96-129 Ala Ike	Pearl City	HI	96782	**866-299-8656**	808-454-4700

Idaho

Name / Address	City	State	Zip	Toll-Free	Phone
Boise State University 1910 University Dr	Boise	ID	83725	**800-824-7017**	208-426-1156
Brigham Young University Idaho 525 S Ctr	Rexburg	ID	83460	**866-672-2984**	
College of Idaho 2112 Cleveland Blvd *Admissions	Caldwell	ID	83605	**800-224-3246***	208-459-5011
Lewis-Clark State College 500 Eigth Ave	Lewiston	ID	83501	**800-933-5272**	208-792-5272
Northwest Nazarene University 623 Holly St *Admissions	Nampa	ID	83686	**877-668-4968***	208-467-8000
University of Idaho 875 Perimeter Dr	Moscow	ID	83844	**888-884-3246**	208-885-6111
Boise 322 E Front St Ste 190	Boise	ID	83702	**866-264-7384**	208-334-2999

Illinois

Name / Address	City	State	Zip	Toll-Free	Phone
American InterContinental University Los Angeles 231 N Martingale Rd 6th Fl	Schaumburg	IL	60173	**877-701-3800**	
Augustana College 639 38th St	Rock Island	IL	61201	**800-798-8100**	309-794-7000
Aurora University 347 S Gladstone Ave	Aurora	IL	60506	**800-742-5281**	630-844-5533
Benedictine University 5700 College Rd	Lisle	IL	60532	**888-829-6363**	630-829-6300
Blackburn College 700 College Ave	Carlinville	IL	62626	**800-233-3550**	217-854-3231
Bradley University 1501 W Bradley Ave *Admissions	Peoria	IL	61625	**800-447-6460***	309-676-7611
Columbia College 600 S Michigan Ave 3rd Fl	Chicago	IL	60605	**866-705-0200**	312-663-1600
Concordia University Chicago 7400 Augusta St	River Forest	IL	60305	**888-258-6773**	708-771-8300
Dominican University 7900 W Div St	River Forest	IL	60305	**800-828-8475**	708-366-2490
East-West University 816 S Michigan Ave	Chicago	IL	60605	**877-398-9376**	312-939-0111
Eastern Illinois University 600 Lincoln Ave *Admissions	Charleston	IL	61920	**800-252-5711***	217-581-2223
Elmhurst College 190 Prospect Ave	Elmhurst	IL	60126	**800-697-1871**	630-617-3400

				Toll-Free	Phone
Eureka College 300 E College Ave *Admissions	Eureka	IL	61530	**888-438-7352***	309-467-6350
Governors State University 1 University Pkwy	University Park	IL	06048	**800-478-8478**	708-534-5000
Greenville College 315 E College Ave	Greenville	IL	62246	**800-345-4440**	618-664-7100
Harrington College of Design 200 W Madison St	Chicago	IL	60606	**866-590-4423**	
Illinois College 1101 W College Ave *Admissions	Jacksonville	IL	62650	**866-464-5265***	217-245-3030
Illinois Institute of Technology 10 W 33rd St	Chicago	IL	60616	**800-448-2329**	312-567-3025
Illinois State University North and School Streets Hovey Hall 201 *Admissions	Normal	IL	61790	**800-366-2478***	309-438-2111
Illinois Wesleyan University 1312 Pk St *Admissions	Bloomington	IL	61701	**800-332-2498***	309-556-3031
Judson University 1151 N State St *Admissions	Elgin	IL	60123	**800-879-5376***	847-628-2500
Knox College 2 E S St *Admissions	Galesburg	IL	61401	**800-678-5669***	309-341-7000
Lake Forest College 555 N Sheridan Rd	Lake Forest	IL	60045	**800-828-4751**	847-234-3100
Lewis University 1 University Pkwy Unit 297	Romeoville	IL	60446	**800-897-9000**	815-836-5250
Loyola University Chicago					
Lake Shore 6525 N Sheridan Rd	Chicago	IL	60626	**800-262-2373**	773-508-3075
Water Tower 820 N Michigan Ave *Admissions	Chicago	IL	60611	**800-262-2373***	312-915-6500
MacMurray College 447 E College Ave	Jacksonville	IL	62650	**800-252-7485**	217-479-7056
McKendree College 701 College Rd	Lebanon	IL	62254	**800-232-7228**	618-537-4481
Millikin University 1184 W Main St	Decatur	IL	62522	**800-373-7733**	217-424-6211
Monmouth College 700 E Broadway Ave	Monmouth	IL	61462	**888-827-8268**	309-457-2311
National University of Health Sciences 200 E Roosevelt Rd	Lombard	IL	60148	**800-826-6285**	630-629-2000
National-Louis University 1000 Capitol Dr	Wheeling	IL	60090	**800-443-5522**	847-947-5718
Chicago 122 S Michigan Ave	Chicago	IL	60603	**800-443-5522**	888-658-8632
North Central College 30 N Brainard St	Naperville	IL	60540	**800-411-1861**	630-637-5800
North Park University 3225 W Foster Ave	Chicago	IL	60625	**800-888-6728**	773-244-5500
Northeastern Illinois University 5500 N St Louis Ave	Chicago	IL	60625	**800-393-0865**	773-442-4050
Northern Illinois University 1425 W Lincoln Hwy	DeKalb	IL	60115	**800-892-3050**	815-753-1000
Northwestern University 1801 Hinman Ave	Evanston	IL	60208	**800-227-7368**	847-491-7271
Olivet Nazarene University 1 University Ave	Bourbonnais	IL	60914	**800-648-1463**	815-939-5011
Quincy University 1800 College Ave	Quincy	IL	62301	**866-703-4004**	217-222-8020
Robert Morris College					
Chicago 401 S State St	Chicago	IL	60605	**800-762-5960**	312-935-6800
DuPage 905 Meridian Lk Dr *Admissions	Aurora	IL	60504	**800-762-5960***	630-375-8100
Orland Park 43 Orland Sq Dr	Orland Park	IL	60462	**800-225-1520**	708-226-3800
Springfield 3101 Montvale Dr	Springfield	IL	62704	**800-762-5960**	217-793-2500
Rockford College 5050 E State St	Rockford	IL	61108	**800-892-2984**	815-226-4000
Roosevelt University 430 S Michigan Ave *Admissions	Chicago	IL	60605	**877-277-5978***	312-341-3500
Albert A Robin 1400 N Roosevelt Blvd *Admissions	Schaumburg	IL	60173	**877-277-5978***	847-619-8600
Saint Xavier University 3700 W 103rd St	Chicago	IL	60655	**800-462-9288**	773-298-3000
School of the Art Institute of Chicago 36 S Wabash Ave *Admissions	Chicago	IL	60603	**800-232-7242***	312-629-6100
Shimer College 3424 S State St	Chicago	IL	60616	**800-215-7173**	312-235-3506
Southern Illinois University *Edwardsville* SR 157	Edwardsville	IL	62026	**888-328-5168**	618-650-2000
Trinity International University 2065 Half Day Rd	Deerfield	IL	60015	**800-822-3225**	847-945-8800
University of Illinois					
Springfield 1 University Plz MS UHB 1080	Springfield	IL	62703	**888-977-4847**	217-206-4847
University of St Francis 500 Wilcox St	Joliet	IL	60435	**800-735-7500**	
Western Illinois University 1 University Cir *Admissions	Macomb	IL	61455	**877-742-5948***	309-298-1414
Quad Cities 3561 60th St	Moline	IL	61265	**877-742-5948**	309-762-9481
Wheaton College 501 College Ave	Wheaton	IL	60187	**800-222-2419**	630-752-5000

Indiana

				Toll-Free	Phone
Anderson University 1100 E Fifth St *Admissions	Anderson	IN	46012	**800-428-6414***	765-649-9071
Ball State University 2000 W University Ave	Muncie	IN	47306	**800-382-8540**	765-289-1241
Butler University 4600 Sunset Ave	Indianapolis	IN	46208	**800-368-6852**	317-940-8100
Calumet College of Saint Joseph 2400 New York Ave	Whiting	IN	46394	**877-700-9100**	219-473-4215
DePauw University 101 E Seminary St	Greencastle	IN	46135	**800-447-2495**	765-658-4006
Earlham College 801 National Rd W	Richmond	IN	47374	**800-327-5426**	765-983-1600
Franklin College 101 Branigin Blvd	Franklin	IN	46131	**800-852-0232**	317-738-8000
Goshen College 1700 S Main St	Goshen	IN	46526	**800-348-7422**	574-535-7000
Grace College 200 Seminary Dr	Winona Lake	IN	46590	**800-544-7223**	574-372-5100
Hanover College 484 Ball Dr	Hanover	IN	47243	**800-213-2178**	812-866-7000
Huntington University 2303 College Ave *Admissions	Huntington	IN	46750	**800-642-6493***	260-356-6000
Indiana State University 200 N Seventh St	Terre Haute	IN	47809	**800-468-6478**	
Indiana Tech 1600 E Washington Blvd	Fort Wayne	IN	46803	**800-937-2448**	260-422-5561
Indiana University					
East 2325 Chester Blvd	Richmond	IN	47374	**800-959-3278**	765-973-8208
Kokomo 2300 S Washington St PO Box 9003	Kokomo	IN	46904	**888-875-4485**	765-455-9217
Northwest 3400 Broadway	Gary	IN	46408	**888-968-7486**	219-980-6500
South Bend 1700 Mishawaka Ave PO Box 7111	South Bend	IN	46634	**877-462-4872**	574-520-4870
Southeast 4201 Grant Line Rd	New Albany	IN	47150	**800-852-8835**	812-941-2212
Indiana University-Purdue University					
Fort Wayne 2101 E Coliseum Blvd	Fort Wayne	IN	46805	**800-324-4739**	260-481-6100
Indiana Wesleyan University 4201 S Washington St	Marion	IN	46953	**800-332-6901**	765-677-2138
Manchester College 604 E College Ave *Admissions	North Manchester	IN	46962	**800-852-3648***	260-982-5000
Marian University 3200 Cold Spring Rd *Admissions	Indianapolis	IN	46222	**800-772-7264***	317-955-6038
Oakland City University 138 N Lucretia St	Oakland City	IN	47660	**800-737-5125**	812-749-4781
Purdue University *Calumet* 2200 169th St	Hammond	IN	46323	**800-447-8738**	219-989-2400
Rose-Hulman Institute of Technology 5500 Wabash Ave *Admissions	Terre Haute	IN	47803	**800-248-7448***	812-877-1511
Saint Mary's College Le Mans Hall *Admissions	Notre Dame	IN	46556	**800-551-7621***	574-284-4587
Saint Mary-of-the-Woods College 3301 St Mary Rd	Saint Mary Of The Woods	IN	47876	**800-926-7692**	812-535-5106
Taylor University 236 W Reade Ave	Upland	IN	46989	**800-882-3456**	765-998-2751
Fort Wayne 915 W Rudisill Blvd *General	Fort Wayne	IN	46807	**800-882-3456***	260-744-8790
University of Evansville 1800 Lincoln Ave	Evansville	IN	47722	**800-423-8633**	812-488-2000
University of Indianapolis 1400 E Hanna Ave	Indianapolis	IN	46227	**800-232-8634**	317-788-3368
University of Southern Indiana 8600 University Blvd	Evansville	IN	47712	**800-467-1965**	812-464-1765
Valparaiso University 1700 Chapel Dr	Valparaiso	IN	46383	**888-468-2576**	219-464-5011
Wabash College 410 W Wabash Ave PO Box 352	Crawfordsville	IN	47933	**800-345-5385**	765-361-6225

Iowa

				Toll-Free	Phone
Ashford University 400 N Bluff Blvd	Clinton	IA	52732	**800-242-4153**	563-242-4023
Briar Cliff University 3303 Rebecca St	Sioux City	IA	51104	**800-662-3303**	712-279-5321
Buena Vista University 610 W Fourth St	Storm Lake	IA	50588	**800-383-9600**	712-749-2253
Central College 812 University St	Pella	IA	50219	**877-462-3687**	641-628-5285
Clarke College 1550 Clarke Dr	Dubuque	IA	52001	**888-825-2753**	563-588-6300
Coe College 1220 First Ave NE	Cedar Rapids	IA	52402	**877-225-5263**	319-399-8500
Cornell College 600 First St SW *Admissions	Mount Vernon	IA	52314	**800-747-1112***	319-895-4215
Divine Word College 102 Jacoby Dr SW	Epworth	IA	52045	**800-553-3321**	563-876-3353
Dordt College 498 Fourth Ave NE	Sioux Center	IA	51250	**800-343-6738**	712-722-6080
Drake University 2507 University Ave	Des Moines	IA	50311	**800-443-7253**	515-271-3181
Graceland University 1 University Pl	Lamoni	IA	50140	**800-859-1215**	641-784-5000
Grand View College 1200 Grandview Ave	Des Moines	IA	50316	**800-444-6083**	515-263-2800
Grinnell College 1115 8th Ave	Grinnell	IA	50112	**800-247-0113**	641-269-3600
Iowa State University 100 Alumni Hall *Admissions	Ames	IA	50011	**800-262-3810***	515-294-4111
Iowa Wesleyan College 601 N Main St	Mount Pleasant	IA	52641	**800-582-2383**	

Classified Section

Institution / Address	City	State	ZIP	Toll-Free	Phone
Loras College 1450 Alta Vista St	Dubuque	IA	52001	**800-245-6727**	563-588-7100
Luther College 700 College Dr	Decorah	IA	52101	**800-458-8437**	563-387-2000
Maharishi University of Management 1000 N Fourth St	Fairfield	IA	52557	**800-369-6480**	641-472-1110
Morningside College 1501 Morningside Ave	Sioux City	IA	51106	**800-831-0806**	712-274-5000
Mount Mercy College 1330 Elmhurst Dr NE	Cedar Rapids	IA	52402	**800-248-4504**	319-368-6460
Northwestern College 101 Seventh St SW	Orange City	IA	51041	**800-747-4757**	712-707-7000
Saint Ambrose University 518 W Locust St *Admissions	Davenport	IA	52803	**800-383-2627***	563-333-6000
Simpson College 701 N 'C' St	Indianola	IA	50125	**800-362-2454**	515-961-6251
University of Dubuque 2000 University Ave	Dubuque	IA	52001	**800-722-5583**	563-589-3000
University of Iowa 107 Calvin Hall	Iowa City	IA	52242	**800-553-4692**	319-335-3847
University of Northern Iowa 1222 W 27th St *Admissions	Cedar Falls	IA	50614	**800-772-2037***	319-273-2281
Upper Iowa University 605 Washington St PO Box 1857 *Admissions	Fayette	IA	52142	**800-553-4150***	563-425-5200
Waldorf College 106 S Sixth St	Forest City	IA	50436	**800-292-1903**	641-585-2450
Wartburg College 100 Wartburg Blvd	Waverly	IA	50677	**800-772-2085**	319-352-8264
William Penn University 201 Trueblood Ave	Oskaloosa	IA	52577	**800-779-7366**	

Kansas

Institution / Address	City	State	ZIP	Toll-Free	Phone
Benedictine College 1020 N Second St	Atchison	KS	66002	**800-467-5340**	913-367-5340
Bethel College 300 E 27th St	North Newton	KS	67117	**800-522-1887**	316-283-2500
Central Christian College PO Box 1403	McPherson	KS	67460	**800-835-0078**	620-241-0723
Emporia State University 1200 Commercial St	Emporia	KS	66801	**877-468-6378**	620-341-1200
Fort Hays State University 600 Pk St *Admissions	Hays	KS	67601	**800-628-3478***	785-628-4000
Friends University 2100 University St	Wichita	KS	67213	**800-794-6945**	316-295-5000
Kansas State University 119 Anderson Hall *Admissions	Manhattan	KS	66506	**800-432-8270***	785-532-6250
Kansas Wesleyan University 100 E Claflin Ave	Salina	KS	67401	**800-874-1154**	785-827-5541
McPherson College PO Box 1402	McPherson	KS	67460	**800-365-7402**	620-242-0400
MidAmerica Nazarene University 2030 E College Way	Olathe	KS	66062	**800-800-8887**	913-782-3750
Newman University 3100 McCormick Ave	Wichita	KS	67213	**877-639-6268**	316-942-4291
Ottawa University 1001 S Cedar St *Admissions	Ottawa	KS	66067	**800-755-5200***	785-242-5200
Pittsburg State University 1701 S Broadway St	Pittsburg	KS	66762	**800-854-7488**	620-235-4251
Tabor College 400 S Jefferson St *Admissions	Hillsboro	KS	67063	**800-822-6799***	620-947-3121
University of Saint Mary 4100 S Fourth St	Leavenworth	KS	66048	**800-752-7043**	913-682-5151
Washburn University 1700 SW College Ave	Topeka	KS	66621	**800-736-9060**	785-670-1010
Wichita State University 1845 Fairmount St *Admissions	Wichita	KS	67260	**800-362-2594***	316-978-3456

Kentucky

Institution / Address	City	State	ZIP	Toll-Free	Phone
Alice Lloyd College 100 Purpose Rd *Admissions	Pippa Passes	KY	41844	**888-280-4252***	606-368-6000
Asbury College 1 Macklem Dr *Admissions	Wilmore	KY	40390	**800-888-1818***	859-858-3511
Bellarmine University 2001 Newburg Rd	Louisville	KY	40205	**800-274-4723**	502-272-8000
Berea College 101 Chestnut St	Berea	KY	40403	**800-326-5948**	859-985-3500
Brescia University 717 Frederica St *Admissions	Owensboro	KY	42301	**877-273-7242***	270-685-3131
Campbellsville University 1 University Dr *Admissions	Campbellsville	KY	42718	**800-264-6014***	270-789-5000
Centre College 600 W Walnut St	Danville	KY	40422	**800-423-6236**	859-238-5350
Eastern Kentucky University 521 Lancaster Ave	Richmond	KY	40475	**800-465-9191**	859-622-2106
Georgetown College 400 E College St *Admissions	Georgetown	KY	40324	**800-788-9985***	502-863-8000
Kentucky Christian University 100 Academic Pkwy *Admissions	Grayson	KY	41143	**800-522-3181***	606-474-3000
Kentucky State University 400 E Main St *Admissions	Frankfort	KY	40601	**800-325-1716***	502-597-6000
Kentucky Wesleyan College 3000 Frederica St *Admissions	Owensboro	KY	42301	**800-999-0592***	270-852-3120
Lindsey Wilson College 210 Lindsey Wilson St	Columbia	KY	42728	**800-264-0138**	270-384-2126
Mid-Continent University 99 Powell Rd E	Mayfield	KY	42066	**888-628-4723**	270-247-8521
Midway College 512 E Stephens St	Midway	KY	40347	**800-755-0031**	859-846-5346
Morehead State University 100 Admissions Ctr	Morehead	KY	40351	**800-585-6781**	606-783-2000
Murray State University 102 Curris Ctr	Murray	KY	42071	**800-272-4678**	270-809-3741
Hopkinsville 5305 Ft Campbell Blvd	Hopkinsville	KY	42240	**800-669-7654**	270-707-1525
Northern Kentucky University Nunn Dr *Admissions	Highland Heights	KY	41099	**800-637-9948***	859-572-5220
Pikeville College 147 Sycamore St	Pikeville	KY	41501	**866-232-7700**	606-218-5250
Spalding University 851 S Fourth St	Louisville	KY	40203	**800-896-8941**	502-585-9911
Sullivan University 3101 BaRdstown Rd	Louisville	KY	40205	**800-844-1354**	502-456-6505
Thomas More College 333 Thomas More Pkwy	Crestview Hills	KY	41017	**800-825-4557**	859-344-3332
Transylvania University 300 N Broadway	Lexington	KY	40508	**800-872-6798**	859-233-8242
Union College 310 College St	Barbourville	KY	40906	**800-489-8646**	606-546-4151
University of Kentucky 800 Rose St	Lexington	KY	40536	**866-900-4685**	859-257-9000
University of Louisville 2301 S Third St	Louisville	KY	40292	**800-334-8635**	502-852-5555
University of the Cumberlands 6191 College Stn Dr	Williamsburg	KY	40769	**800-343-1609**	606-539-4201
Western Kentucky University 1906 College Heights Blvd *Admissions	Bowling Green	KY	42101	**800-495-8463***	270-745-0111

Louisiana

Institution / Address	City	State	ZIP	Toll-Free	Phone
Centenary College of Louisiana 2911 Centenary Blvd *Admissions	Shreveport	LA	71104	**800-234-4448***	318-869-5131
Grambling State University 403 Main St	Grambling	LA	71245	**800-569-4714**	318-247-3811
Louisiana College 1140 College Dr	Pineville	LA	71359	**800-487-1906**	318-487-7011
Louisiana State University *Alexandria* 8100 US Hwy 71 S *Admissions	Alexandria	LA	71302	**888-473-6417***	318-445-3672
Baton Rouge 110 Thomas Boyd Hall	Baton Rouge	LA	70803	**888-846-6810**	225-578-3202
Louisiana Tech University 305 Wisteria St *Admissions	Ruston	LA	71272	**800-528-3241***	318-257-2000
Loyola University *New Orleans* 6363 St Charles Ave *Admissions	New Orleans	LA	70118	**800-456-9652***	504-865-3240
McNeese State University 4205 Ryan St	Lake Charles	LA	70609	**800-622-3352**	337-475-5000
Nicholls State University 906 E First St *Admissions	Thibodaux	LA	70310	**877-642-4655***	985-446-0561
Northwestern State University 175 Sam Sibley Dr	Natchitoches	LA	71497	**800-767-8115**	318-357-4078
Our Lady of Holy Cross College 4123 Woodland Dr	New Orleans	LA	70131	**800-259-7744**	504-394-7744
Our Lady of the Lake College 7434 Perkins Rd *Admissions	Baton Rouge	LA	70808	**877-242-3509***	225-768-1700
Southeastern Louisiana University 500 Western Ave	Hammond	LA	70402	**800-222-7358**	985-549-2062
Southern University & A & M College 156 Elton C Harrison Dr PO Box 9757 *Admissions	Baton Rouge	LA	70813	**800-256-1531***	225-771-5180
Tulane University 6823 St Charles Ave *Admissions	New Orleans	LA	70118	**800-873-9283***	504-865-5000
University of Louisiana *Lafayette* 611 McKinley St	Lafayette	LA	70504	**800-752-6553**	337-482-1000
Monroe 700 University Ave *Admissions	Monroe	LA	71209	**800-372-5127***	318-342-5430
University of New Orleans Administrative Bldg Rm 103 Lakefront *Admissions	New Orleans	LA	70148	**800-256-5866***	504-280-6000

Maine

Institution / Address	City	State	ZIP	Toll-Free	Phone
Bates College 2 Andrews Rd Ln Hall Rm1	Lewiston	ME	04240	**888-522-8371**	207-786-6255
Bowdoin College 5000 College Stn	Brunswick	ME	04011	**800-829-1040**	207-725-3000
Colby College 4800 Mayflower Hill *Admissions	Waterville	ME	04901	**800-723-3032***	207-859-4800
College of the Atlantic 105 Eden St *Admissions	Bar Harbor	ME	04609	**800-528-0025***	207-288-5015
Husson College 1 College Cir	Bangor	ME	04401	**800-448-7766**	207-941-7000

Name	Address	City	State	ZIP	Toll-Free	Phone
Maine Maritime Academy	66 Pleasant St	Castine	ME	04420	**800-464-6565***	207-326-4311
	*Admissions					
Saint Joseph's College of Maine	278 Whites Bridge Rd	Standish	ME	04084	**800-338-7057***	207-893-7746
	*Admissions					
Thomas College	180 W River Rd	Waterville	ME	04901	**800-339-7001***	207-859-1111
	*Admissions					
Unity College	90 Quaker Hill Rd	Unity	ME	04988	**800-624-1024**	207-948-3131
University of Maine	5713 Chadbourne Hall	Orono	ME	04469	**877-486-2364***	207-581-1110
	*Admissions					
Augusta	46 University Dr	Augusta	ME	04330	**877-862-1234**	207-621-3000
Fort Kent	23 University Dr	Fort Kent	ME	04743	**888-879-8635***	207-834-7500
	*Admissions					
Machias	116 O'Brien Ave	Machias	ME	04654	**888-468-6866***	207-255-1200
	*Admissions					
University of New England	11 Hills Beach Rd	Biddeford	ME	04005	**800-477-4863***	207-283-0171
	*Admissions					
Westbrook College	716 Stevens Ave	Portland	ME	04103	**800-477-4863***	207-797-7261
	*Admissions					
University of Southern Maine	96 Falmouth St	Portland	ME	04103	**800-800-4876**	207-780-4141
Gorham	37 College Ave	Gorham	ME	04038	**800-800-4876**	207-780-5670
Lewiston-Auburn College	51 Westminster St	Lewiston	ME	04240	**800-800-4876**	207-753-6500

Maryland

Name	Address	City	State	ZIP	Toll-Free	Phone
Bowie State University	14000 Jericho Pk Rd	Bowie	MD	20715	**877-772-6943**	301-860-4000
Capitol Technology University	11301 Springfield Rd	Laurel	MD	20708	**800-950-1992**	301-369-2800
College of Notre Dame of Maryland	4701 N Charles St	Baltimore	MD	21210	**800-753-3757***	410-435-0100
	*Admissions					
Coppin State University	2500 W N Ave	Baltimore	MD	21216	**800-635-3674***	410-951-3600
	*Admissions					
Goucher College	1021 Dulaney Vly Rd	Towson	MD	21204	**800-468-2437**	410-337-6000
Hood College	401 Rosemont Ave	Frederick	MD	21701	**800-922-1599**	301-696-3400
Loyola College	4501 N Charles St	Baltimore	MD	21210	**800-221-9107**	410-617-5012
McDaniel College	2 College Hill	Westminster	MD	21157	**800-638-5005***	410-857-2230
	*Admissions					
Morgan State University	1700 E Cold Spring Ln	Baltimore	MD	21251	**800-319-4678**	443-885-3333
Mount Saint Mary's University	16300 Old Emmitsburg Rd	Emmitsburg	MD	21727	**800-448-4347***	301-447-5214
	*Admissions					
Peabody Institute of the Johns Hopkins University						
Peabody Conservatory of Music	1 E Mt Vernon Pl	Baltimore	MD	21202	**800-368-2521**	410-659-8110
Saint Mary's College of Maryland	47645 College Dr	Saint Marys City	MD	20686	**800-492-7181***	240-895-2000
	*Admissions					
Salisbury University	1200 Camden Ave	Salisbury	MD	21801	**888-543-0148**	410-543-6000
Sojourner-Douglass College	200 N Central Ave	Baltimore	MD	21202	**800-732-2630**	410-276-0306
Strayer University Prince George's	4710 Auth Pl Ste 100	Suitland	MD	20746	**866-344-3297**	888-311-0355
Towson University	8000 York Rd	Towson	MD	21252	**866-301-3375**	410-704-2113
University of Baltimore	1420 N Charles St	Baltimore	MD	21201	**877-277-5982***	410-837-4200
	*Admitting					
University of Maryland	7569 Baltimore Ave	College Park	MD	20742	**800-422-5867***	301-405-1000
	*Admissions					
Baltimore County	1000 Hilltop Cir	Baltimore	MD	21250	**800-810-0271**	410-455-1000
US Naval Academy	121 Blake Rd	Annapolis	MD	21402	**888-249-7707***	410-293-1000
	*Admissions					
Villa Julie College	1525 Green Spring Valley Rd	Stevenson	MD	21153	**877-468-6852**	410-486-7001
Washington Adventist University	7600 Flower Ave	Takoma Park	MD	20912	**800-835-4212**	301-891-4000
Washington College	300 Washington Ave	Chestertown	MD	21620	**800-422-1782**	410-778-2800

Massachusetts

Name	Address	City	State	ZIP	Toll-Free	Phone
American International College	1000 State St	Springfield	MA	01109	**800-242-3142***	413-205-3201
	*Admissions					
Amherst College	220 S Pleasant St	Amherst	MA	01002	**866-542-4438**	413-542-2000
Anna Maria College	50 Sunset Ln	Paxton	MA	01612	**800-344-4586**	
Assumption College	500 Salisbury St	Worcester	MA	01609	**888-882-7786**	508-767-7000
Atlantic Union College	338 Main St	South Lancaster	MA	01561	**800-282-2030**	978-368-2000
Babson College	231 Forest St	Babson Park	MA	02457	**800-488-3696***	781-235-1200
	*Admissions					
Bay Path College	588 Longmeadow St	Longmeadow	MA	01106	**800-782-7284**	
Becker College	61 Sever St	Worcester	MA	01609	**877-523-2537**	508-791-9241
Bentley College	175 Forest St	Waltham	MA	02452	**800-642-7131***	781-891-2244
	*Admissions					
Berklee College of Music	1140 Boylston St	Boston	MA	02215	**800-421-0084**	617-747-2221
Boston Baptist College	950 Metropolitan Ave	Boston	MA	02136	**888-235-2014**	617-364-3510
Boston College	140 Commonwealth Ave	Chestnut Hill	MA	02467	**800-360-2522**	617-552-3100
Brandeis University	415 S St	Waltham	MA	02454	**800-622-0622**	781-736-3500
Clark University	950 Main St	Worcester	MA	01610	**800-462-5275**	508-793-7711
College of the Holy Cross	1 College St	Worcester	MA	01610	**800-442-2421**	508-793-2011
Curry College	1071 Blue Hill Ave	Milton	MA	02186	**800-669-0686**	617-333-2210
Eastern Nazarene College	23 E Elm Ave	Quincy	MA	02170	**800-883-6288**	617-745-3000
ELMS College	291 Springfield St	Chicopee	MA	01013	**800-255-3567***	413-592-3189
	*Admissions					
Emerson College	10 Boylston Pl	Boston	MA	02116	**888-627-7115**	617-824-8500
Endicott College	376 Hale St	Beverly	MA	01915	**800-325-1114***	978-232-2021
	*Admissions					
Framingham State College	100 State St PO Box 9101	Framingham	MA	01701	**866-361-8970**	508-620-1220
Gordon College	255 Grapevine Rd	Wenham	MA	01984	**800-343-1379**	978-927-2300
Lasell College	1844 Commonwealth Ave	Newton	MA	02466	**888-527-3554***	617-243-2225
	*Admissions					
Lesley University	29 Everett St	Cambridge	MA	02138	**800-999-1959**	617-868-9600
Massachusetts College of Art	621 Huntington Ave	Boston	MA	02115	**800-834-3242**	617-879-7222
Massachusetts College of Pharmacy & Health Sciences	179 Longwood Ave	Boston	MA	02115	**800-225-5506**	617-732-2850
Massachusetts Maritime Academy	101 Academy Dr	Buzzards Bay	MA	02532	**800-544-3411***	508-830-5000
	*Admissions					
Montserrat College of Art	23 Essex St PO Box 26	Beverly	MA	01915	**800-836-0487**	978-921-4242
Mount Holyoke College	50 College St	South Hadley	MA	01075	**800-642-4483**	413-538-2000
National Graduate School of Quality Management Inc, The	186 Jones Rd	Falmouth	MA	02540	**800-838-2580**	508-457-1313
Newbury College	129 Fisher Ave	Brookline	MA	02445	**800-499-0143**	617-730-7000
Nichols College	124 Ctr Rd	Dudley	MA	01571	**800-470-3379**	508-213-1560
Northeastern University	360 Huntington Ave	Boston	MA	02115	**855-476-3391**	617-373-2000
Pine Manor College	400 Heath St	Chestnut Hill	MA	02467	**800-762-1357**	617-731-7104
Regis College	235 Wellesley St	Weston	MA	02493	**866-438-7344**	781-768-7000
School of the Museum of Fine Arts	230 The Fenway	Boston	MA	02115	**800-643-6078***	617-369-3626
	*Admissions					
Simmons College	300 The Fenway	Boston	MA	02115	**800-345-8468**	617-521-2000
Smith College	7 College Ln	NorthHampton	MA	01063	**800-383-3232**	413-584-2700
Springfield College	263 Alden St	Springfield	MA	01109	**800-343-1257***	413-748-3136
	*Admissions					
Suffolk University	8 Ashburton Pl	Boston	MA	02108	**800-678-3365**	617-573-8460
Tufts University	4 Colby St	Medford	MA	02155	**800-326-4001**	617-628-5000
Wentworth Institute of Technology	550 Huntington Ave	Boston	MA	02115	**800-556-0610**	617-989-4590
Western New England College	1215 Wilbraham Rd	Springfield	MA	01119	**800-782-6665**	413-782-3111
Wheelock College	200 The Riverway	Boston	MA	02215	**800-734-5212**	617-879-2206
Williams College	880 Main St	Williamstown	MA	01267	**877-374-7526**	413-597-3131

Michigan

Name	Address	City	State	ZIP	Toll-Free	Phone
Adrian College	110 S Madison St	Adrian	MI	49221	**800-877-2246***	517-265-5161
	*Admissions					
Albion College	611 E Porter St	Albion	MI	49224	**800-858-6770**	517-629-1000
Alma College	614 W Superior St	Alma	MI	48801	**800-321-2562**	989-463-7139
Andrews University	3976 Rose Dr	Berrien Springs	MI	49103	**800-253-2874**	269-471-7771
Baker College						
Auburn Hills	1500 University Dr	Auburn Hills	MI	48326	**888-429-0410**	248-340-0600
Cadillac	9600 E 13th St	Cadillac	MI	49601	**888-313-3463**	231-876-3100
Clinton Township	34950 Little Mack Ave	Clinton Township	MI	48035	**888-272-2842**	586-791-6610
Flint	1050 W Bristol Rd	Flint	MI	48507	**800-964-4299**	810-767-7600
Jackson	2800 Springport Rd	Jackson	MI	49202	**888-343-3683**	517-788-7800
Owosso	1020 S Washington St	Owosso	MI	48867	**800-879-3797**	989-729-3350
Port Huron	3403 Lapeer Rd	Port Huron	MI	48060	**888-262-2442**	810-985-7000
Calvin College	3201 Burton St SE	Grand Rapids	MI	49546	**800-688-0122**	616-526-6000

Classified Section

	City	State	Zip	Toll-Free	Phone
Central Michigan University					
102 Warriner Hall	Mount Pleasant	MI	48859	**888-292-5366***	989-774-4000
*Admissions					
Concordia University Ann Arbor					
4090 Geddes Rd	Ann Arbor	MI	48105	**888-282-2338**	734-995-7322
Cornerstone University					
1001 E Beltline Ave NE	Grand Rapids	MI	49525	**800-787-9778***	616-222-1426
*Admissions					
Davenport University					
Dearborn 4801 Oakman Blvd	Dearborn	MI	48126	**800-585-1479**	313-581-4400
Flint 4318 Miller Rd Ste A	Flint	MI	48507	**800-727-1443**	810-732-9977
Lansing 220 E Kalamazoo St	Lansing	MI	48933	**800-686-1600**	517-484-2600
Lettinga Campus					
6191 Kraft Ave SE	Grand Rapids	MI	49512	**866-925-3884**	616-698-7111
Saginaw 5300 Bay Rd	Saginaw	MI	48604	**800-968-8133**	989-799-7800
Warren 27650 Dequindre Rd	Warren	MI	48092	**800-724-7708**	586-558-8700
Eastern Michigan University					
1000 College Pl	Ypsilanti	MI	48197	**800-468-6368**	734-487-1849
Ferris State University					
1201 S State St	Big Rapids	MI	49307	**800-433-7747**	231-591-2000
Traverse City					
2200 Dendrinos Dr Ste 200H	Traverse City	MI	49684	**866-857-1954**	231-995-1734
Finlandia University					
601 Quincy St	Hancock	MI	49930	**800-682-7604**	906-482-5300
Grand Valley State University					
1 Campus Dr	Allendale	MI	49401	**800-748-0246**	616-331-5000
Hillsdale College					
33 E College St	Hillsdale	MI	49242	**888-886-1174**	517-437-7341
Hope College					
69 E Tenth St PO Box 9000	Holland	MI	49422	**800-968-7850***	616-395-7850
*Admissions					
Kalamazoo College					
1200 Academy St	Kalamazoo	MI	49006	**800-253-3602***	269-337-7166
*Admissions					
Kendall College of Art & Design of Ferris State University					
17 Fountain St NW	Grand Rapids	MI	49503	**800-676-2787**	616-451-2787
Kettering University					
1700 University Ave	Flint	MI	48504	**800-955-4464**	810-762-9500
Lake Superior State University					
650 W Easterday Ave	Sault Sainte Marie	MI	49783	**888-800-5778***	906-632-6841
*Admissions					
Lawrence Technological University					
21000 W 10-Mile Rd	Southfield	MI	48075	**800-225-5588**	248-204-3160
Madonna University					
36600 Schoolcraft Rd	Livonia	MI	48150	**800-852-4951**	734-432-5339
Marygrove College					
8425 W McNichols Rd	Detroit	MI	48221	**866-313-1927***	313-927-1200
*Admissions					
Michigan Jewish Institute					
25401 Coolidge Hwy	Oak Park	MI	48237	**888-463-6654**	248-414-6900
Michigan Technological University					
1400 Townsend Dr	Houghton	MI	49931	**888-688-1885**	906-487-2335
Northern Michigan University					
1401 Presque Isle Ave	Marquette	MI	49855	**800-682-9797**	906-227-2650
Northwood University Michigan					
4000 Whiting Dr	Midland	MI	48640	**800-622-9000**	989-837-4200
Oakland University					
2200 Squirrel Rd	Rochester	MI	48309	**800-625-8648***	248-370-2100
*Admissions					
Olivet College 320 S Main St	Olivet	MI	49076	**800-456-7189**	269-749-7000
Rochester College					
800 W Avon Rd	Rochester Hills	MI	48307	**800-521-6010**	248-218-2011
Saginaw Valley State University					
7400 Bay Rd	University Center	MI	48710	**800-968-9500**	989-964-4200
Siena Heights University					
1247 E Siena Heights Dr	Adrian	MI	49221	**800-521-0009**	517-263-0731
Spring Arbor University					
106 E Main St	Spring Arbor	MI	49283	**800-968-9103***	517-750-1200
*Admissions					
University of Detroit Mercy					
4001 W McNichols Rd	Detroit	MI	48221	**800-635-5020***	313-993-1000
*Admissions					
University of Michigan					
Flint 303 E Kearsley St	Flint	MI	48502	**800-942-5636**	810-762-3000
Wayne State University					
42 W Warren	Detroit	MI	48202	**877-978-4636**	313-577-3577

Minnesota

	City	State	Zip	Toll-Free	Phone
Argosy University					
1515 Central Pkwy	Eagan	MN	55121	**888-844-2004**	651-846-2882
Augsburg College					
2211 Riverside Ave	Minneapolis	MN	55454	**800-788-5678**	612-330-1000
Bemidji State University					
1500 Birchmont Dr NE	Bemidji	MN	56601	**800-475-2001***	218-755-2001
*Admissions					
Bethany Lutheran College					
700 Luther Dr	Mankato	MN	56001	**800-944-3066**	507-344-7000
Bethel University					
3900 Bethel Dr	Saint Paul	MN	55112	**800-255-8706**	651-638-6400
Carleton College					
100 S College St	Northfield	MN	55057	**800-995-2275***	507-646-4000
*Admissions					
College of Saint Catherine					
2004 Randolph Ave	Saint Paul	MN	55105	**800-945-4599**	651-690-6000
Minneapolis					
601 25th Ave S	Minneapolis	MN	55454	**800-945-4599**	651-690-7700
College of Saint Scholastica					
1200 Kenwood Ave	Duluth	MN	55811	**800-447-5444**	218-723-6046
Concordia College					
901 Eigth St S	Moorhead	MN	56562	**800-699-9897**	218-299-4000
Gustavus Adolphus College					
800 W College Ave	Saint Peter	MN	56082	**800-487-8288**	507-933-8000
Hamline University					
1536 Hewitt Ave	Saint Paul	MN	55104	**800-753-9753**	651-523-2207
Macalester College					
1600 Grand Ave	Saint Paul	MN	55105	**800-231-7974***	651-696-6357
*Admissions					
Martin Luther College					
1995 Luther Ct	New Ulm	MN	56073	**877-652-1995**	507-354-8221
McNally Smith College of Music Foundation					
19 Exchange St E	Saint Paul	MN	55101	**800-594-9500**	651-361-3320
Metropolitan State University					
700 E Seventh St	Saint Paul	MN	55106	**888-234-2690**	651-793-1300
Minnesota State University					
Mankato 122 Taylor Ctr	Mankato	MN	56001	**800-722-0544***	507-389-1822
*Admissions					
Moorhead					
1104 Seventh Ave S	Moorhead	MN	56563	**800-593-7246**	218-477-2161
North Central University					
910 Elliot Ave S	Minneapolis	MN	55404	**800-289-6222***	612-343-4460
*Admissions					
Saint John's University					
PO Box 2000	Collegeville	MN	56321	**800-544-1489***	320-363-2196
*Admissions					
Saint Mary's University of Minnesota					
700 Terr Heights	Winona	MN	55987	**800-635-5987**	507-452-4430
Southwest Minnesota State University					
1501 State St	Marshall	MN	56258	**800-642-0684**	
University of Minnesota					
Crookston					
2900 University Ave 170 Owen Hall	Crookston	MN	56716	**800-862-6466**	218-281-8569
Duluth 1049 University Dr	Duluth	MN	55812	**800-232-1339**	218-726-8000
Morris 600 E Fourth St	Morris	MN	56267	**800-992-8863**	320-589-6035
Twin Cities					
240 Williamson Hall					
231 Pillsbury Dr SE	Minneapolis	MN	55455	**800-752-1000**	612-625-2008
Winona State University					
175 W Mark St	Winona	MN	55987	**800-342-5978**	507-457-5000

Mississippi

	City	State	Zip	Toll-Free	Phone
Belhaven College					
1500 Peachtree St PO Box 153	Jackson	MS	39202	**800-960-5940**	601-968-5940
Blue Mountain College					
PO Box 160	Blue Mountain	MS	38610	**800-235-0136**	662-685-4771
Delta State University					
1003 W Sunflower Rd	Cleveland	MS	38733	**800-468-6378**	662-846-4020
Jackson State University					
1400 John R Lynch St	Jackson	MS	39217	**800-848-6817**	601-979-2121
Millsaps College					
1701 N State St	Jackson	MS	39210	**800-352-1050***	601-974-1000
*Admissions					
Mississippi College					
200 S Capitol St	Clinton	MS	39056	**800-738-1236**	601-925-3000
Mississippi University for Women					
1100 College St MUW-1613	Columbus	MS	39701	**877-462-8439**	662-329-4750
Mississippi Valley State University					
14000 Hwy 82	Itta Bena	MS	38941	**800-844-6885**	662-254-9041
Rust College					
150 Rust Ave	Holly Springs	MS	38635	**888-886-8492**	662-252-8000
Tougaloo College					
500 W County Line Rd	Tougaloo	MS	39174	**888-424-2566***	601-977-7700
*Admissions					
University of Mississippi					
Tupelo 1918 Briar Ridge Rd	Tupelo	MS	38804	**888-846-5622**	662-844-5622
University of Southern Mississippi					
118 College Dr	Hattiesburg	MS	39406	**800-446-0892**	601-266-1000
William Carey University					
498 Tuscan Ave	Hattiesburg	MS	39401	**800-962-5991**	601-318-6051

Missouri

	City	State	Zip	Toll-Free	Phone
Avila University					
11901 Wornall Rd	Kansas City	MO	64145	**866-943-5787**	816-501-2400
Central Methodist University					
411 Central Methodist Sq	Fayette	MO	65248	**877-268-1854**	660-248-3391
Chamberlain College of Nursing					
11830 Westline Industrial Ste 106	Saint Louis	MO	63146	**888-556-8226**	314-991-6200
College of the Ozarks					
1 Industrial Dr PO Box 17	Point Lookout	MO	65726	**800-222-0525***	417-334-6411
*Admissions					
Columbia College Jefferson City					
3314 Emerald Ln	Jefferson City	MO	65109	**800-231-2391**	573-634-3250
Columbia College Lake of the Ozarks					
900 College Blvd	Osage Beach	MO	65065	**800-231-2391**	573-348-6463
Drury University					
900 N Benton Ave	Springfield	MO	65802	**800-922-2274**	417-873-7879
Evangel University					
1111 N Glenstone Ave	Springfield	MO	65802	**800-382-6435**	417-865-2815
Graceland University Independence					
1401 W Truman Rd	Independence	MO	64050	**800-833-0524**	816-833-0524
Hannibal-LaGrange College					
2800 Palmyra Rd	Hannibal	MO	63401	**800-454-1119***	573-221-3675
*Admissions					
Lincoln University					
820 Chestnut St B-7 Young Hall	Jefferson City	MO	65102	**800-521-5052***	573-681-5599
*Admissions					
Lindenwood University					
209 S Kingshighway	Saint Charles	MO	63301	**877-615-8212**	636-949-2000
Missouri Baptist University					
1 College Pk Dr	Saint Louis	MO	63141	**877-434-1115**	314-434-1115
Missouri Southern State University					
3950 Newman Rd	Joplin	MO	64801	**866-818-6778**	417-625-9300
Missouri State University (MSU)					
901 S National Ave	Springfield	MO	65897	**800-492-7900**	417-836-5000
Missouri University of Science & Technology					
Rolla					
1870 Miner Cir G2 Parker Hall	Rolla	MO	65409	**800-522-0938**	573-341-4111
Missouri Valley College					
500 E College St	Marshall	MO	65340	**800-999-8219**	660-831-4000

Name / Address	City	State	Zip	Toll-Free	Phone
Missouri Western State University 4525 Downs Dr	Saint Joseph	MO	64507	**800-662-7041**	816-271-4266
National American University Independence 3620 Arrowhead Ave	Independence	MO	64057	**866-628-1288**	816-412-7700
Northwest Missouri State University 800 University Dr	Maryville	MO	64468	**800-633-1175**	660-562-1148
Park University 8700 NW River Pk Dr	Parkville	MO	64152	**800-745-7275**	816-741-2000
Principia College 13201 Clayton Rd	St. Louis	MO	63131	**800-277-4648**	618-374-2131
Rockhurst University 1100 Rockhurst Rd	Kansas City	MO	64110	**800-842-6776**	816-501-4000
Saint Louis College of Pharmacy 4588 Parkview Pl	Saint Louis	MO	63110	**800-278-5267**	314-367-8700
Saint Louis University 221 N Grand Blvd	Saint Louis	MO	63103	**800-758-3678**	314-977-7288
Southeast Missouri State University 1 University Plaza	Cape Girardeau	MO	63701	**866-562-6801**	573-651-2000
Southwest Baptist University 1600 University Ave	Bolivar	MO	65613	**800-526-5859**	
Truman State University 100 E Normal St	Kirksville	MO	63501	**800-892-7792**	660-785-4000
University of Missouri (UMSL) *Columbia* 104 Jesse Hall	Columbia	MO	65211	**800-856-2181**	573-882-6333
Kansas City 5100 Rockhill Rd	Kansas City	MO	64110	**800-775-8652**	816-235-1000
Saint Louis 1 University Blvd *Admissions	Saint Louis	MO	63121	**888-462-8675***	314-516-5000
Washington University in Saint Louis Campus Box 1089	Saint Louis	MO	63130	**800-638-0700**	314-935-5000
Westminster College 501 Westminster Ave *Admissions	Fulton	MO	65251	**800-475-3361***	573-592-5251
William Jewell College 500 College Hill WJC	Liberty	MO	64068	**888-253-9355**	816-781-7700
William Woods University 1 University Ave *Admissions	Fulton	MO	65251	**800-995-3159***	573-592-4221

Montana

Name / Address	City	State	Zip	Toll-Free	Phone
Carroll College 1601 N Benton Ave	Helena	MT	59625	**800-992-3648**	406-447-4300
Montana State University *Billings* 1500 University Dr	Billings	MT	59101	**800-565-6782**	406-657-2011
Bozeman PO Box 172190 *Admissions	Bozeman	MT	59717	**888-678-2287***	406-994-2452
Northern PO Box 7751	Havre	MT	59501	**800-662-6132**	406-994-2452
Montana Tech of the University of Montana 1300 W Pk St *Admissions	Butte	MT	59701	**800-445-8324***	406-496-4101
Rocky Mountain College 1511 Poly Dr	Billings	MT	59102	**800-877-6259**	406-657-1000
University of Great Falls 1301 20th St S *Admissions	Great Falls	MT	59405	**800-856-9544***	
University of Montana 32 Campus Dr *Admissions	Missoula	MT	59812	**800-462-8636***	406-243-6266
Western 710 S Atlantic St *Admissions	Dillon	MT	59725	**877-683-7331***	406-683-7011
Yellowstone Baptist College 1515 S Shiloh Rd	Billings	MT	59106	**800-487-9950**	406-656-9950

Nebraska

Name / Address	City	State	Zip	Toll-Free	Phone
Bellevue University 1000 Galvin Rd S	Bellevue	NE	68005	**800-756-7920**	402-293-2000
Chadron State College 1000 Main St	Chadron	NE	69337	**800-242-3766**	308-432-6000
Clarkson College 101 S 42nd St	Omaha	NE	68131	**800-647-5500**	402-552-3100
College of Saint Mary 7000 Mercy Rd	Omaha	NE	68106	**800-926-5534**	402-399-2400
Concordia University Nebraska 800 N Columbia Ave	Seward	NE	68434	**800-535-5494**	402-643-3651
Creighton University 2500 California Plz	Omaha	NE	68178	**800-282-5835**	402-280-2700
Doane College 1014 Boswell Ave	Crete	NE	68333	**800-333-6263**	402-826-2161
Grand Island 3180 W US Hwy 34	Grand Island	NE	68801	**800-333-6263**	308-398-0800
Lincoln 303 N 52nd St	Lincoln	NE	68504	**888-803-6263**	402-466-4774
Hastings College 710 N Turner Ave	Hastings	NE	68901	**800-532-7642**	402-463-2402
Midland University 900 N Clarkson St	Fremont	NE	68025	**800-642-8382**	402-941-6270
Nebraska Wesleyan University 5000 St Paul Ave	Lincoln	NE	68504	**800-541-3818**	
Peru State College 600 Hoyt St PO Box 10	Peru	NE	68421	**800-742-4412**	402-872-3815
Summit Christian College 2025 21st St	Gering	NE	69341	**888-305-8083**	308-632-6933
University of Nebraska *Kearney* 905 W 25th St	Kearney	NE	68849	**800-532-7639**	308-865-8441
Lincoln 1410 Q St	Lincoln	NE	68588	**800-742-8800**	402-472-2023
Omaha 6001 Dodge St	Omaha	NE	68182	**800-858-8648**	402-554-2800
Wayne State College 1111 Main St	Wayne	NE	68787	**800-228-9972**	402-375-7000
York College 1125 E Eigth St	York	NE	68467	**800-950-9675**	402-363-5600

Nevada

Name / Address	City	State	Zip	Toll-Free	Phone
Great Basin College 1500 College Pkwy	Elko	NV	89801	**888-590-6726**	775-738-8493
Sierra Nevada College 999 Tahoe Blvd	Incline Village	NV	89451	**866-412-4636**	775-831-1314
University of Nevada *Reno* 1664 N Virginia St	Reno	NV	89557	**866-263-8232**	775-784-1110

New Hampshire

Name / Address	City	State	Zip	Toll-Free	Phone
Colby-Sawyer College 541 Main St *Admissions	New London	NH	03257	**800-272-1015***	603-526-3700
Daniel Webster College 20 University Dr	Nashua	NH	03063	**800-325-6876**	603-577-6000
Franklin Pierce University *Concord* 5 Chenell Dr	Concord	NH	03301	**800-437-0048**	603-228-1155
Keene 17 Bradco St	Keene	NH	03431	**800-325-1090**	603-899-4000
Lebanon 24 Airport Rd Ste 19	West Lebanon	NH	03784	**800-325-1090**	603-298-5549
Manchester 670 N Commercial St *Admissions	Manchester	NH	03101	**800-437-0048***	603-626-4972
Portsmouth 73 Corporate Dr	Portsmouth	NH	03801	**800-325-1090**	603-433-2000
Rindge 40 University Dr *Admissions	Rindge	NH	03461	**800-437-0048***	603-899-4000
Granite State College 8 Old Suncook Rd	Concord	NH	03301	**888-228-3000**	603-228-3000
Berlin 25 Hall St Rm 144	Concord	NH	03301	**855-472-4255**	603-447-3970
Hesser College 3 Sundial Ave	Manchester	NH	03103	**888-971-2190**	603-668-6660
Keene State College 229 Main St	Keene	NH	03435	**800-572-1909**	603-352-1909
New England College 98 Bridge St *Admissions	Henniker	NH	03242	**800-521-7642***	603-428-2223
Plymouth State University 17 High St	Plymouth	NH	03264	**800-842-6900**	603-535-2237
Rivier College 420 S Main St	Nashua	NH	03060	**800-447-4843**	603-888-1311
Saint Anselm College 100 St Anselm Dr	Manchester	NH	03102	**888-426-7356**	603-641-7500
Southern New Hampshire University 2500 N River Rd	Manchester	NH	03106	**800-668-1249**	603-668-2211
University of New Hampshire *Manchester* 400 Commercial St	Manchester	NH	03101	**800-287-9793**	603-641-4321

New Jersey

Name / Address	City	State	Zip	Toll-Free	Phone
Bloomfield College 467 Franklin St	Bloomfield	NJ	07003	**800-848-4555**	973-748-9000
Caldwell University 120 Bloomfield Ave *Admissions	Caldwell	NJ	07006	**888-864-9516***	973-618-3500
Centenary College 400 Jefferson St *Admissions	Hackettstown	NJ	07840	**800-236-8679***	908-852-1400
College of New Jersey 2000 Pennington Rd PO Box 7718	Ewing	NJ	08628	**800-644-3562**	609-771-1855
College of Saint Elizabeth 2 Convent Rd *Admissions	Morristown	NJ	07960	**800-210-7900***	973-290-4700
Fairleigh Dickinson University 285 Madison Ave	Madison	NJ	07940	**800-338-8803**	973-443-8500
Metropolitan 1000 River Rd	Teaneck	NJ	07666	**800-338-8803**	201-692-2000
Felician College 262 S Main St	Lodi	NJ	07644	**888-442-4551**	201-559-6000
Rutherford 223 Montross Ave	Rutherford	NJ	07070	**888-442-4551**	201-559-6000
Georgian Court University 900 Lakewood Ave	Lakewood	NJ	08701	**800-458-8422**	
Kean University 1000 Morris Ave Kean Hall	Union	NJ	07083	**800-882-1037**	908-737-7100
Monmouth University 400 Cedar Ave	West Long Branch	NJ	07764	**800-543-9671**	732-571-3456
Montclair State University 1 Normal Ave *Admissions	Montclair	NJ	07043	**800-331-9205***	973-655-4000
New Jersey City University 2039 JFK Blvd	Jersey City	NJ	07305	**888-441-6528**	201-200-2000
New Jersey Institute of Technology University Heights	Newark	NJ	07102	**800-925-6548**	973-596-3000
Princeton University 33 Washington Rd	Princeton	NJ	08544	**877-609-2273**	609-258-3000
Rider University 2083 Lawrenceville Rd	Lawrenceville	NJ	08648	**800-257-9026**	609-896-5000
Westminster Choir College 101 Walnut Ln	Princeton	NJ	08540	**800-962-4647**	609-921-7100
Rowan University 201 Mullica Hill Rd *Admissions	Glassboro	NJ	08028	**877-787-6926***	856-256-4200
Seton Hall University 400 S Orange Ave	South Orange	NJ	07079	**800-992-4723**	973-761-9332
Stevens Institute of Technology Castle Pt on the Hudson	Hoboken	NJ	07030	**800-458-5323**	201-216-5194
Thomas Edison State College 101 W State St	Trenton	NJ	08608	**888-442-8372**	
William Paterson University 300 Pompton Rd	Wayne	NJ	07470	**877-978-3923**	973-720-2000

New Mexico

Name / Address	City	State	Zip	Toll-Free	Phone
College of Santa Fe 1600 St Michaels Dr	Santa Fe	NM	87505	**800-862-7759**	505-473-6011
College of the Southwest 6610 N Lovington Hwy	Hobbs	NM	88240	**800-530-4400**	575-392-6561
Eastern New Mexico University 1500 S Ave K Stn 6	Portales	NM	88130	**800-367-3668**	575-562-1011

				Toll-Free	Phone
New Mexico Highlands University					
901 University Ave	Las Vegas	NM	87701	**877-850-9064**	505-425-7511
New Mexico Institute of Mining & Technology (NMT)					
801 Leroy Pl	Socorro	NM	87801	**800-428-8324***	505-835-5434
*Admissions					
New Mexico State University (NMSU)					
MSC-3A PO Box 30001	Las Cruces	NM	88003	**800-662-6678***	575-646-3121
*Admissions					
Santa Fe University of Art & Design					
1600 St Michaels Dr	Santa Fe	NM	87505	**800-456-2673**	
University of New Mexico (UNM)					
1 University of New Mexico	Albuquerque	NM	87131	**800-225-5866**	505-277-0111
Gallup 200 College Rd	Gallup	NM	87301	**800-225-5866**	505-863-7500
Western New Mexico University					
1000 W College St PO Box 680	Silver City	NM	88061	**800-872-9668***	505-538-6011
*Admissions					

New York

				Toll-Free	Phone
Adelphi University					
PO Box 701	Garden City	NY	11530	**800-233-5744**	516-877-3050
Manhattan Ctr					
75 Varick St 2nd Fl	New York	NY	10013	**800-233-5744**	212-965-8340
Albany College of Pharmacy (ACPHS)					
106 New Scotland Ave	Albany	NY	12208	**888-203-8010***	518-694-7221
*General					
Bard College					
PO Box 5000	Annandale-on-Hudson	NY	12504	**800-872-7423**	845-758-7472
Baruch College					
55 Lexington Ave at 24th St	New York	NY	10010	**800-273-8255**	646-312-1000
Binghamton University					
4400 Vestal Pkwy E	Binghamton	NY	13902	**800-782-0289**	607-777-2000
Canisius College					
2001 Main St	Buffalo	NY	14208	**800-843-1517**	716-888-2200
Cazenovia College					
8 Sullivan St	Cazenovia	NY	13035	**800-654-3210**	315-655-7208
City College of New York					
138th St & Convent Ave	New York	NY	10031	**800-286-9937***	212-650-6448
*Admissions					
Clarkson University					
10 Clarkson Ave	Potsdam	NY	13699	**800-527-6577***	315-268-6480
*Admissions					
College of Mount Saint Vincent					
6301 Riverdale Ave	Riverdale	NY	10471	**800-722-4867**	718-405-3304
College of New Rochelle					
29 Castle Pl	New Rochelle	NY	10805	**800-933-5923**	914-654-5000
College of Saint Rose					
432 Western Ave	Albany	NY	12203	**800-637-8556**	518-454-5150
College of Staten Island					
2800 Victory Blvd	Staten Island	NY	10314	**888-442-4551**	718-982-2000
Concordia College New York					
171 White Plains Rd	Bronxville	NY	10708	**800-937-2655***	914-337-9300
*Admissions					
Cooper Union for the Advancement of Science & Art					
30 Cooper Sq	New York	NY	10003	**800-872-2777**	212-353-4100
D'Youville College					
320 Porter Ave	Buffalo	NY	14201	**800-777-3921**	716-829-7600
Daemen College 4380 Main St	Amherst	NY	14226	**800-462-7652**	716-839-8225
Dominican College					
470 Western Hwy	Orangeburg	NY	10962	**866-432-4636**	845-359-7800
Dowling College					
150 Idle Hour Blvd	Oakdale	NY	11769	**800-369-5464**	631-244-3000
Elmira College 1 Pk Pl	Elmira	NY	14901	**800-935-6472***	607-735-1724
*Admissions					
Excelsior College					
7 Columbia Cir	Albany	NY	12203	**888-647-2388**	518-464-8500
Fordham University					
441 E Fordham Rd	Bronx	NY	10458	**800-367-3426**	718-817-3240
College at Lincoln Ctr					
113 W 60th St	New York	NY	10023	**800-367-3426**	212-636-6710
Westchester					
400 Westchester Ave	West Harrison	NY	10604	**800-606-6090**	914-332-8295
Hamilton College					
198 College Hill Rd	Clinton	NY	13323	**800-843-2655***	315-859-4421
*Admissions					
Hartwick College					
1 Hartwick Dr	Oneonta	NY	13820	**888-427-8942**	607-431-4150
Hilbert College					
5200 S Pk Ave	Hamburg	NY	14075	**800-649-8003**	716-649-7900
Hobart & William Smith Colleges					
300 Pulteney St	Geneva	NY	14456	**800-852-2256***	315-781-3000
*Admissions					
Hofstra University					
1000 Fulton Ave	Hempstead	NY	11549	**800-463-7872**	516-463-6600
Houghton College					
1 Willard Ave PO Box 128	Houghton	NY	14744	**800-777-2556**	585-567-9200
Iona College 715 N Ave	New Rochelle	NY	10801	**800-264-6350**	914-633-2502
Ithaca College 953 Danby Rd	Ithaca	NY	14850	**800-429-4274***	607-274-3124
*Admissions					
Keuka College					
141 Central Ave	Keuka Park	NY	14478	**866-632-9992***	315-279-5254
*Admissions					
Laboratory Institute of Merchandising					
12 E 53rd St	New York	NY	10022	**800-677-1323**	212-752-1530
Le Moyne College					
1419 Salt Springs Rd	Syracuse	NY	13214	**800-333-4733***	315-445-4100
*Admissions					
Lehman College					
250 Bedford Pk Blvd W	Bronx	NY	10468	**800-311-5656**	718-960-8000
Long Island University					
Brooklyn 1 University Plz	Brooklyn	NY	11201	**800-548-7526**	718-488-1011
Manhattan College					
4513 Manhattan College Pkwy	Bronx	NY	10471	**800-622-9235**	718-862-8000
Manhattanville College					
2900 Purchase St	Purchase	NY	10577	**800-328-4553**	914-323-5464
Marist College					
3399 N Rd	Poughkeepsie	NY	12601	**800-436-5483**	845-575-3000
Marymount Manhattan College					
221 E 71st St	New York	NY	10021	**866-667-6572**	212-517-0400
Medaille College					
18 Agassiz Cir	Buffalo	NY	14214	**800-292-1582**	716-880-2200
Medgar Evers College					
1650 Bedford Ave	Brooklyn	NY	11225	**866-277-5719**	718-270-4900
Mercy College					
555 Broadway	Dobbs Ferry	NY	10522	**800-637-2969**	914-693-4500
Manhattan 66 W 35th St	New York	NY	10001	**800-637-2969**	212-615-3300
White Plains					
277 Martine Ave Ste 201	White Plains	NY	10601	**888-464-6737**	914-948-3666
Yorktown Heights					
2651 Strang Blvd	Yorktown Heights	NY	10598	**877-637-2946**	914-245-6100
Molloy College					
1000 Hempstead Ave					
PO Box 5002	Rockville Centre	NY	11571	**888-466-5569***	516-678-5000
*Admissions					
Morrisville State College					
80 Eaton St PO Box 901	Morrisville	NY	13408	**800-258-0111***	315-684-6000
*Admissions					
Mount Saint Mary College					
330 Powell Ave	Newburgh	NY	12550	**888-937-6762**	845-569-3248
Nazareth College of Rochester					
4245 E Ave	Rochester	NY	14618	**800-860-6942**	585-389-2525
New York City College of Technology					
300 Jay St	Brooklyn	NY	11201	**855-492-3633**	718-260-5000
New York Institute of Technology					
New York Institute of Technology Northern Blvd					
PO Box 8000	Old Westbury	NY	11568	**800-345-6948**	516-686-1000
Islip PO Box 9029	Central Islip	NY	11722	**800-345-6948**	516-686-1000
Manhattan 1855 Broadway	New York	NY	10023	**800-345-6948**	212-261-1500
New York School of Interior Design					
170 E 70th St	New York	NY	10021	**800-336-9743**	212-472-1500
New York University					
22 Washington Sq N	New York	NY	10011	**888-243-2358**	212-998-4500
Niagara University					
5795 Lewiston Rd					
PO Box 2011	Niagara University	NY	14109	**800-462-2111**	716-286-8700
Nyack College 1 S Blvd	Nyack	NY	10960	**800-336-9225***	845-358-1710
*Admissions					
Pace University 1 Pace Plz	New York	NY	10038	**866-722-3338**	212-346-1200
Pleasantville/Briarcliff					
861 Bedford Rd	Pleasantville	NY	10570	**866-722-3338**	914-773-3200
Parsons New School for Design					
65 Fifth Ave	New York	NY	10011	**800-252-0852***	212-229-8989
*Admissions					
Paul Smith's College					
7833 New York 30 PO Box 265	Paul Smiths	NY	12970	**800-421-2605***	518-327-6227
*Admissions					
Polytechnic University					
Long Island 105 Maxess Rd	Melville	NY	11747	**877-503-7659***	631-755-4300
*Admissions					
Pratt Institute					
200 Willoughby Ave	Brooklyn	NY	11205	**800-331-0834**	718-636-3669
Purchase College					
735 Anderson Hill Rd	Purchase	NY	10577	**800-553-8118**	914-251-6000
Queens College					
65-30 Kissena Blvd	Flushing	NY	11367	**888-888-0606**	718-997-5000
Roberts Wesleyan College					
2301 Westside Dr	Rochester	NY	14624	**800-777-4792***	585-594-6000
*Admissions					
Russell Sage College					
45 Ferry St	Troy	NY	12180	**888-837-9724***	518-244-2217
*Admissions					
Sage College of Albany					
140 New Scotland Ave	Albany	NY	12208	**888-837-9724***	518-292-1730
*Admissions					
Saint Lawrence University					
23 Romoda Dr	Canton	NY	13617	**800-285-1856***	315-229-5261
*Admissions					
Sarah Lawrence College					
1 Meadway	Bronxville	NY	10708	**800-888-2858**	
Siena College					
515 Loudon Rd	Loudonville	NY	12211	**888-287-4362***	518-783-2300
*Admissions					
Skidmore College					
815 N Broadway	Saratoga Springs	NY	12866	**800-867-6007**	518-580-5000
State University of New York					
Brockport					
350 New Campus Dr	Brockport	NY	14420	**888-800-0029**	585-395-2751
College of Agriculture & Technology at Cobleskill					
Rt 7	Cobleskill	NY	12043	**800-295-8988**	518-255-5525
College of Environmental Science & Forestry					
1 Forestry Dr	Syracuse	NY	13210	**800-777-7373***	315-470-6500
*Admissions					
Empire State College					
1 Union Ave	Saratoga Springs	NY	12866	**800-847-3000**	518-587-2100
Geneseo 1 College Cir	Geneseo	NY	14454	**866-245-5211***	585-245-5571
*Admitting					
Institute of Technology					
PO Box 3050	Utica	NY	13504	**866-278-6948**	315-792-7500
Maritime College					
6 Pennyfield Ave Fort Schuyler	Bronx	NY	10465	**888-800-0029**	718-409-7200
New Paltz 1 Hawk Dr	New Paltz	NY	12561	**877-696-7411**	845-257-3212
Plattsburgh					
101 Broad St	Plattsburgh	NY	12901	**888-673-0012***	518-564-2040
*Admissions					
Potsdam 44 Pierrpont Ave	Potsdam	NY	13676	**877-768-7326***	315-267-2180
*Admissions					
University at Buffalo					
12 Capen Hall	Buffalo	NY	14260	**888-822-3648**	716-645-2450
Syracuse University					
900 S Crouse Ave	Syracuse	NY	13244	**800-782-5867**	315-443-3611
Touro College					
27-33 W 23rd St	New York	NY	10010	**888-247-1387**	212-463-0400
University at Albany					
1400 Washington Ave	Albany	NY	12222	**800-293-7869**	518-442-3300

Classified Section

	City	State	Zip	Toll-Free	Phone
University of Rochester Wallace Hall PO Box 270251 *Admissions	Rochester	NY	14627	**888-822-2256***	585-275-2121
University of Saint Francis 180 Remsen St	Brooklyn Heights	NY	11201	**800-356-8329**	718-522-2300
US Merchant Marine Academy 300 Steamboat Rd	Kings Point	NY	11024	**866-546-4778**	516-726-5800
Utica College 1600 Burrstone Rd *Admissions	Utica	NY	13502	**800-782-8884***	315-792-3111
Vassar College 124 Raymond Ave	Poughkeepsie	NY	12604	**800-827-7270**	845-437-7000
Vaughn College of Aeronautics & Technology 86-01 23rd Ave	East Elmhurst	NY	11369	**866-682-8446**	718-429-6600
Wagner College 1 Campus Rd *Admissions	Staten Island	NY	10301	**800-221-1010***	718-390-3400
Webb Institute 298 Crescent Beach Rd	Glen Cove	NY	11542	**866-708-9322**	516-671-2213
Wells College 170 Main St *Admissions	Aurora	NY	13026	**800-952-9355***	315-364-3266

North Carolina

	City	State	Zip	Toll-Free	Phone
Barton College PO Box 5000	Wilson	NC	27893	**800-345-4973**	252-399-6300
Belmont Abbey College 100 Belmont-Mt Holly Rd	Belmont	NC	28012	**888-222-0110**	704-461-6748
Bennett College 900 E Washington St *Admissions	Greensboro	NC	27401	**800-413-5323***	336-370-8624
Brevard College 1 Brevard College Dr *Admissions	Brevard	NC	28712	**800-527-9090***	828-883-8292
Campbell University 450 Leslie Campbell Ave PO Box 546	Buies Creek	NC	27506	**800-334-4111**	910-893-1290
Catawba College 2300 W Innes St	Salisbury	NC	28144	**800-228-2922**	704-637-4111
Chowan University 1 University Pl *Admissions	Murfreesboro	NC	27855	**888-424-6926***	252-398-6439
Davidson College PO Box 7156	Davidson	NC	28035	**800-768-0380**	704-894-2000
Elizabeth City State University 1704 Weeksville Rd *Admissions	Elizabeth City	NC	27909	**800-347-3278***	252-335-3400
Elon University 100 Campus Dr	Elon	NC	27244	**800-334-8448**	336-278-2000
Fayetteville State University 1200 Murchison Rd *Admissions	Fayetteville	NC	28301	**800-222-2594***	910-672-1371
Gardner-Webb University PO Box 817	Boiling Springs	NC	28017	**800-253-6472**	704-406-4498
Greensboro College 815 W Market St	Greensboro	NC	27401	**800-346-8226**	336-272-7102
Guilford College 5800 W Friendly Ave *Admissions	Greensboro	NC	27410	**800-992-7759***	336-316-2000
Heritage Bible College 1747 Bud Hawkins Rd PO Box 1628	Dunn	NC	28334	**800-297-6351**	910-892-3178
High Point University 833 Montlieu Ave	High Point	NC	27262	**800-345-6993**	336-841-9216
Johnson & Wales University Charlotte 801 W Trade St	Charlotte	NC	28202	**866-598-2427**	980-598-1100
Johnson C Smith University 100 Beatties Ford Rd *Admissions	Charlotte	NC	28216	**800-782-7303***	704-378-1000
King's College Library 322 Lamar Ave	Charlotte	NC	28204	**800-768-2255**	704-372-0266
Lees-McRae College 191 Main St W	Banner Elk	NC	28604	**800-280-4562**	828-898-5241
Lenoir-Rhyne University 625 Seventh Ave NE	Hickory	NC	28601	**800-277-5721**	828-328-7300
Livingstone College 701 W Monroe St	Salisbury	NC	28144	**800-835-3435**	704-216-6963
Meredith College 3800 Hillsborough St *All	Raleigh	NC	27607	**800-637-3348***	919-760-8581
Methodist University 5400 Ramsey St	Fayetteville	NC	28311	**800-488-7110**	910-630-7000
Montreat College 310 Gaither Cir PO Box 1267	Montreat	NC	28757	**800-622-6968**	828-669-8011
Mount Olive College 634 Henderson St	Mount Olive	NC	28365	**800-653-0854**	919-658-2502
North Carolina A & T State University 1601 E Market St *Admissions	Greensboro	NC	27411	**800-443-8964***	336-334-7946
North Carolina Central University 1801 Fayetteville St *Admissions	Durham	NC	27707	**877-667-7533***	919-530-6100
North Carolina State University 2200 Hillsborough St	Raleigh	NC	27695	**800-662-7301**	919-515-2011
North Carolina Wesleyan College 3400 N Wesleyan Blvd *Admissions	Rocky Mount	NC	27804	**800-488-6292***	252-985-5100
Pfeiffer University 48380 Hwy 52 N	Misenheimer	NC	28109	**800-338-2060**	704-463-1360
Piedmont Baptist College 420 S Broad St *Admissions	Winston-Salem	NC	27101	**800-937-5097***	336-725-8344
Queens University of Charlotte 1900 Selwyn Ave	Charlotte	NC	28274	**800-849-0202**	704-337-2212
Saint Andrews Presbyterian College 1700 Dogwood Mile	Laurinburg	NC	28352	**800-763-0198**	910-277-5555
Saint Augustine's College 1315 Oakwood Ave *Admissions	Raleigh	NC	27610	**800-948-1126***	919-516-4016
Salem College 601 S Church St *Admissions	Winston-Salem	NC	27101	**800-327-2536***	336-721-2600
Shaw University 118 E S St *Admissions	Raleigh	NC	27601	**800-214-6683***	919-546-8275
University of North Carolina					
Asheville 1 University Heights CPO 1320	Asheville	NC	28804	**800-531-9842**	828-251-6481
Greensboro 1400 Spring Garden St	Greensboro	NC	27412	**877-862-4123**	336-334-5000
Pembroke PO Box 1510	Pembroke	NC	28372	**800-949-8627**	910-521-6000
Wilmington 601 S College Rd	Wilmington	NC	28403	**800-596-2880**	910-962-3000
Warren Wilson College 701 Warren Wilson Rd *Admissions	Swannanoa	NC	28778	**800-934-3536***	828-298-3325
Western Carolina University (WCU) 1 University Dr	Cullowhee	NC	28723	**877-928-4968**	828-227-7211
William Peace University 15 E Peace St	Raleigh	NC	27604	**800-732-2347**	919-508-2000
Wingate University 220 N Camden Rd	Wingate	NC	28174	**800-755-5550**	704-233-8000
Winston-Salem State University 601 S ML King Jr Dr 206 Thompson Ctr *Admissions	Winston-Salem	NC	27110	**800-257-4052***	336-750-2000

North Dakota

	City	State	Zip	Toll-Free	Phone
Dickinson State University 291 Campus Dr	Dickinson	ND	58601	**800-279-4295**	701-483-2507
Jamestown College 6000 College Ln	Jamestown	ND	58405	**800-336-2554**	701-252-3467
Mayville State University 330 Third St NE	Mayville	ND	58257	**800-437-4104**	
Minot State University 500 University Ave W	Minot	ND	58707	**800-777-0750**	701-858-3000
North Dakota State University 1301 12th Ave N	Fargo	ND	58105	**800-488-6378**	701-231-8643
University of Mary 7500 University Dr *Admissions	Bismarck	ND	58504	**800-288-6279***	701-255-7500
University of North Dakota PO Box 8357	Grand Forks	ND	58202	**800-225-5863**	701-777-3000
Valley City State University 101 College St SW	Valley City	ND	58072	**800-532-8641**	701-845-7990

Ohio

	City	State	Zip	Toll-Free	Phone
Ashland University 401 College Ave	Ashland	OH	44805	**800-882-1548**	419-289-4142
Baldwin-Wallace College 275 Eastland Rd	Berea	OH	44017	**877-292-7759**	440-826-2222
Bluffton University 1 University Dr	Bluffton	OH	45817	**800-488-3257**	419-358-3000
Bowling Green State University 1001 E Wooster St	Bowling Green	OH	43403	**866-246-6732**	419-372-2531
Capital University College & Main St	Columbus	OH	43209	**866-544-6175**	614-236-6101
Case Western Reserve University 2061 Cornell Rd	Cleveland	OH	44106	**800-967-8898**	216-368-2000
Cedarville University 251 N Main St	Cedarville	OH	45314	**800-233-2784**	937-766-7700
Central State University 1400 Brush Row Rd PO Box 1004	Wilberforce	OH	45384	**800-388-2781**	937-376-6011
Cleveland State University 2121 Euclid Ave	Cleveland	OH	44115	**888-278-6446**	216-687-2000
College of Mount Saint Joseph 5701 Delhi Rd	Cincinnati	OH	45233	**800-654-9314**	513-244-4200
College of Wooster 1189 Beall Ave	Wooster	OH	44691	**800-877-9905**	330-263-2000
Defiance College 701 N Clinton St	Defiance	OH	43512	**800-520-4632**	419-784-4010
Denison University 100 W College St	Granville	OH	43023	**800-336-4766**	740-587-6394
Franklin University 201 S Grant Ave	Columbus	OH	43215	**877-341-6300**	614-797-4700
Heidelberg University 310 E Market St	Tiffin	OH	44883	**800-434-3352**	419-448-2000
Hiram College PO Box 67 *Admissions	Hiram	OH	44234	**800-362-5280***	330-569-5169
Hondros College 4140 Executive Pkwy	Westerville	OH	43081	**888-466-3767**	
John Carroll University 20700 N Pk Blvd	Cleveland	OH	44118	**888-335-6800**	216-397-1886
Kent State University 800 E. Summit St PO Box 5190	Kent	OH	44242	**800-988-5368**	330-672-2121
Ashtabula 3300 Lake Rd W	Ashtabula	OH	44004	**800-988-5368**	440-964-3322
Stark 6000 Frank Ave NW	North Canton	OH	44720	**800-988-5368**	330-499-9600
Trumbull Campus 4314 Mahoning Ave NW	Warren	OH	44483	**800-988-5368**	330-847-0571
Tuscarawas 330 University Dr NE	New Philadelphia	OH	44663	**800-988-5368**	330-339-3391
Kenyon College 103 College Dr	Gambier	OH	43022	**800-848-2468**	740-427-5000
Lake Erie College 391 W Washington St	Painesville	OH	44077	**800-533-4996**	440-375-7050
Lourdes College 6832 Convent Blvd	Sylvania	OH	43560	**800-878-3210**	419-885-5291
Malone College 515 25th St NW	Canton	OH	44709	**800-521-1146**	330-471-8100
Marietta College 215 Fifth St *Admissions	Marietta	OH	45750	**800-331-7896***	740-376-4000

Classified Section

	City	State	ZIP	Toll-Free	Phone
Miami University					
501 E High St	Oxford	OH	45056	**866-426-4643**	513-529-1809
Middletown 4200 E University Blvd	Middletown	OH	45042	**877-898-4656**	513-727-3200
Mount Union College					
1972 Clark Ave	Alliance	OH	44601	**800-334-6682***	330-823-2590
*Admissions					
Mount Vernon Nazarene University					
800 Martinsburg Rd	Mount Vernon	OH	43050	**800-766-8206***	740-392-6868
*Admissions					
Muskingum College					
163 Stormont St	New Concord	OH	43762	**800-752-6082***	740-826-8211
*Admissions					
Ohio Dominican University					
1216 Sunbury Rd	Columbus	OH	43219	**800-955-6446**	614-251-4500
Ohio Northern University					
525 S Main St	Ada	OH	45810	**888-408-4668***	419-772-2000
*Admissions					
Ohio State University					
154 W 12th Ave	Columbus	OH	43210	**800-426-5046**	614-292-3980
Lima 4240 Campus Dr	Lima	OH	45804	**800-228-1102**	419-995-8391
Newark 1179 University Dr	Newark	OH	43055	**800-963-9275**	740-366-3321
Ohio University					
120 Chubb Hall	Athens	OH	45710	**800-858-6843**	740-593-1000
Chillicothe 101 University Dr	Chillicothe	OH	45601	**877-462-6824**	740-774-7200
Eastern 45425 National Rd	Saint Clairsville	OH	43950	**800-648-3331**	740-695-1720
Lancaster 1570 Granville Pike	Lancaster	OH	43130	**800-444-2910**	740-654-6711
Southern 1804 Liberty Ave	Ironton	OH	45638	**800-626-0513**	740-533-4600
Ohio Wesleyan University					
61 S Sandusky St Slocum Hall	Delaware	OH	43015	**800-922-8953**	740-368-2000
Otterbein College					
1 S Grove St	Westerville	OH	43081	**800-488-8144***	614-823-1500
*Admissions					
Shawnee State University					
940 Second St	Portsmouth	OH	45662	**800-959-2778**	740-351-3221
Tiffin University					
155 Miami St	Tiffin	OH	44883	**800-968-6446**	419-447-6442
Union Institute & University					
440 E McMillan St	Cincinnati	OH	45206	**800-486-3116**	513-861-6400
University of Akron					
277 E Buchtel Ave	Akron	OH	44325	**800-655-4884***	330-972-7100
*Admissions					
University of Cincinnati					
2600 Clifton Ave PO Box 210091	Cincinnati	OH	45221	**866-397-3382**	513-556-1100
University of Dayton					
300 College Pk	Dayton	OH	45469	**800-837-7433**	937-229-4411
University of Findlay					
1000 N Main St	Findlay	OH	45840	**800-472-9502**	419-422-8313
University of Rio Grande					
218 N College Ave	Rio Grande	OH	45674	**800-282-7201**	740-245-5353
University of Toledo					
2801 W Bancroft St	Toledo	OH	43606	**800-586-5336**	419-530-4636
Ursuline College					
2550 Lander Rd	Pepper Pike	OH	44124	**888-778-5463**	440-449-4200
Walsh University					
2020 E Maple St	North Canton	OH	44720	**800-362-9846***	330-499-7090
*Admissions					
Wilberforce University					
1055 N Bickett Rd PO Box 1001	Wilberforce	OH	45384	**800-367-8568***	937-376-2911
*Admissions					
Wilmington College of Ohio					
1870 Quaker Way	Wilmington	OH	45177	**800-341-9318**	937-382-6661
Wittenberg University					
200 W Ward St PO Box 720	Springfield	OH	45501	**800-677-7558**	937-327-6314
Wright State University					
3640 Colonel Glenn Hwy	Dayton	OH	45435	**800-247-1770***	937-775-5740
*Admissions					
Xavier University					
3800 Victory Pkwy	Cincinnati	OH	45207	**800-344-4698**	513-745-3000
Youngstown State University					
1 University Plz	Youngstown	OH	44555	**877-468-6978***	330-941-3000
*Admissions					

Oklahoma

	City	State	ZIP	Toll-Free	Phone
Bacone College					
2299 Old Bacone Rd	Muskogee	OK	74403	**888-682-5514***	918-683-4581
*Admissions					
Cameron University					
2800 W Gore Blvd	Lawton	OK	73505	**888-454-7600***	580-581-2289
*Admissions					
Hillsdale Free Will Baptist College					
PO Box 7208	Moore	OK	73153	**800-460-6328**	405-912-9000
Langston University					
2013 Langston University PO Box 1500	Langston	OK	73050	**877-466-2231**	
Mid-America Christian University					
3500 SW 119th St	Oklahoma City	OK	73170	**888-888-2341**	405-691-3800
Northeastern State University					
Muskogee 2400 W Shawnee	Muskogee	OK	74401	**800-722-9614**	918-683-0040
Tahlequah 600 N Grand Ave	Tahlequah	OK	74464	**800-722-9614**	918-456-5511
Oklahoma Baptist University					
500 W University St	Shawnee	OK	74804	**800-654-3285**	405-275-2850
Oklahoma Christian University					
PO Box 11000	Oklahoma City	OK	73136	**800-877-5010**	405-425-5000
Oklahoma City University					
2501 N Blackwelder Ave	Oklahoma City	OK	73106	**800-633-7242***	405-208-5050
*Admissions					
Oklahoma Panhandle State University					
323 Eagle Blvd	Goodwell	OK	73939	**800-664-6778**	580-349-2611
Oklahoma State University					
219 Student Union Bldg	Stillwater	OK	74078	**800-852-1255**	405-744-5000
Tulsa 700 N Greenwood Ave	Tulsa	OK	74106	**800-522-4002**	918-594-8000
Oral Roberts University					
7777 S Lewis Ave	Tulsa	OK	74171	**800-678-8876**	918-495-6161
Rogers State University					
1701 W Will Rogers Blvd	Claremore	OK	74017	**800-256-7511**	918-343-7546
Saint Gregory's University					
1900 W MacArthur St	Shawnee	OK	74804	**888-784-7347***	405-878-5100
*Admissions					
Southeastern Oklahoma State University					
1405 N Fourth St	Durant	OK	74701	**800-435-1327**	580-745-2000
Southern Nazarene University					
6729 NW 39th Expy	Bethany	OK	73008	**800-648-9899**	405-789-6400
University of Oklahoma					
1000 Asp Ave	Norman	OK	73019	**800-234-6868**	405-325-0311
University of Sciences & Arts of Oklahoma					
1727 W Alabama Ave	Chickasha	OK	73018	**800-933-8726**	405-224-3140
University of Tulsa					
800 S Tucker Rd	Tulsa	OK	74104	**800-331-3050**	918-631-2307

Oregon

	City	State	ZIP	Toll-Free	Phone
Concordia University Portland					
2811 NE Holman St	Portland	OR	97211	**800-321-9371**	503-288-9371
Corban College					
5000 Deer Pk Dr SE	Salem	OR	97317	**800-845-3005**	503-581-8600
Eastern Oregon University					
1 University Blvd	La Grande	OR	97850	**800-452-8639**	541-962-3393
George Fox University					
414 N Meridian St	Newberg	OR	97132	**800-765-4369**	503-538-8383
Lewis & Clark College					
0615 SW Palatine Hill Rd	Portland	OR	97219	**800-444-4111***	503-768-7040
*Admissions					
Linfield College					
900 SE Baker St	McMinnville	OR	97128	**800-640-2287***	503-883-2213
*Admissions					
Marylhurst University					
17600 Pacific Hwy 43 PO Box 261	Marylhurst	OR	97036	**800-634-9982**	503-636-8141
Northwest Christian College					
828 E 11th Ave	Eugene	OR	97401	**877-463-6622**	541-343-1641
Oregon Health & Science University Hospital					
3181 SW Sam Jackson Pk Rd	Portland	OR	97239	**800-292-4466**	503-494-8311
Oregon Institute of Technology					
3201 Campus Dr	Klamath Falls	OR	97601	**800-422-2017**	541-885-1150
Oregon State University					
104 Kerr Admin Bldg	Corvallis	OR	97331	**800-291-4192**	541-737-4411
Pacific Northwest College of Art					
1241 NW Johnson St	Portland	OR	97209	**888-390-7499**	503-226-4391
Pacific University					
2043 College Way	Forest Grove	OR	97116	**800-677-6712***	503-352-2007
*Admissions					
Portland State University					
1825 SW Broadway PO Box 751	Portland	OR	97201	**800-547-8887**	503-725-3000
Reed College					
3203 SE Woodstock Blvd	Portland	OR	97202	**800-547-4750***	503-777-7511
*Admissions					
Southern Oregon University					
1250 Siskiyou Blvd Britt Hall	Ashland	OR	97520	**800-482-7672**	541-552-6411
University of Oregon					
1585 E 13th Ave	Eugene	OR	97403	**800-232-3825***	541-346-1000
*Admissions					
University of Portland					
5000 N Willamette Blvd	Portland	OR	97203	**888-627-5601**	503-943-7147
Warner Pacific College					
2219 SE 68th Ave	Portland	OR	97215	**800-804-1510**	503-517-1020
Western Oregon University					
345 Monmouth Ave N	Monmouth	OR	97361	**877-877-1593***	503-838-8000
*Admissions					
Willamette University					
900 State St	Salem	OR	97301	**877-542-2787**	503-370-6303

Pennsylvania

	City	State	ZIP	Toll-Free	Phone
Albright College					
1621 N 13th St	Reading	PA	19604	**800-252-1856**	610-921-2381
Allegheny College					
520 N Main St	Meadville	PA	16335	**800-521-5293**	814-332-4351
Alvernia College					
540 Upland Ave	Reading	PA	19611	**888-258-3764**	610-796-8200
Arcadia University					
450 S Easton Rd	Glenside	PA	19038	**877-272-2342**	215-572-2900
Automotive Training Center-warminster pa Campus					
114 Pickering Way	Exton	PA	19341	**888-321-8992**	610-363-6716
Bloomsburg University					
400 E Second St	Bloomsburg	PA	17815	**888-651-6117**	570-389-3900
Bryn Mawr College					
101 N Merion Ave	Bryn Mawr	PA	19010	**800-262-2586***	610-526-5000
*Admissions					
Cabrini College					
610 King of Prussia Rd	Radnor	PA	19087	**800-848-1003**	610-902-8552
California University of Pennsylvania					
250 University Ave	California	PA	15419	**888-412-0479**	724-938-4000
Carlow University					
3333 Fifth Ave	Pittsburgh	PA	15213	**800-333-2275**	412-578-6000
Carnegie Mellon University					
5000 Forbes Ave	Pittsburgh	PA	15213	**844-625-4600**	412-268-2000
Cedar Crest College					
100 College Dr	Allentown	PA	18104	**800-360-1222***	610-437-4471
*Admissions					
Chatham University					
1 Woodland Rd	Pittsburgh	PA	15232	**800-837-1290**	412-365-1100
Chestnut Hill College					
9601 Germantown Ave	Philadelphia	PA	19118	**800-248-0052**	215-248-7001
Cheyney University of Pennsylvania					
1837 University Cir PO Box 200	Cheyney	PA	19319	**800-243-9639**	610-399-2275
Clarion University of Pennsylvania					
840 Wood St	Clarion	PA	16214	**800-672-7171**	814-393-2306
Venango 1801 W First St	Oil City	PA	16301	**800-672-7171**	814-676-6591
Curtis Institute of Music					
1726 Locust St	Philadelphia	PA	19103	**800-640-4155**	215-893-5252

Name / Address	City	State	Zip	Toll-Free	Phone
Delaware Valley College 700 E Butler Ave	Doylestown	PA	18901	**800-233-5825**	215-489-2211
DeSales University 2755 Stn Ave	Center Valley	PA	18034	**877-433-7253**	610-282-1100
Dickinson College PO Box 1773	Carlisle	PA	17013	**800-644-1773**	717-243-5121
Drexel University 3141 Chestnut St *Admissions	Philadelphia	PA	19104	**866-358-1010***	215-895-2000
Duquesne University 600 Forbes Ave	Pittsburgh	PA	15282	**800-456-0590**	412-396-6000
East Stroudsburg University 200 Prospect St *Admissions	East Stroudsburg	PA	18301	**877-230-5547***	570-422-3542
Eastern University 1300 Eagle Rd *Admissions	Wayne	PA	19087	**800-452-0996***	610-341-5800
Edinboro University of Pennsylvania 200 E Normal St	Edinboro	PA	16444	**888-846-2676**	814-732-2761
Franklin & Marshall College PO Box 3003	Lancaster	PA	17604	**877-678-9111**	717-291-3951
Gannon University 109 University Sq *Admissions	Erie	PA	16541	**800-426-6668***	814-871-7000
Geneva College 3200 College Ave	Beaver Falls	PA	15010	**800-847-8255**	724-847-6500
Gettysburg College 300 N Washington St	Gettysburg	PA	17325	**800-431-0803**	717-337-6000
Gratz College 7605 Old York Rd	Melrose Park	PA	19027	**800-475-4635**	215-635-7300
Great Lakes Institute of Technology Toni & Guy Hairdressing Academy 5100 Peach St	Erie	PA	16509	**800-394-4548**	814-864-6666
Gwynedd-Mercy College 1325 Sunneytown Pk PO Box 901 *Admissions	Gwynedd Valley	PA	19437	**800-342-5462***	215-646-7300
Holy Family University 9801 Frankford Ave	Philadelphia	PA	19114	**800-422-0010**	215-637-7700
Immaculata University 1145 King Rd	Immaculata	PA	19345	**877-428-6329**	610-647-4400
Indiana University of Pennsylvania 1011 S Dr Sutton Hall Ste 117	Indiana	PA	15705	**800-442-6830**	724-357-2230
Juniata College 1700 Moore St	Huntingdon	PA	16652	**877-586-4282**	814-641-3000
Keystone College 1 College Green	La Plume	PA	18440	**800-824-2764**	570-945-5141
King's College 133 N River St	Wilkes-Barre	PA	18711	**800-955-5777**	570-208-5858
Kutztown University 15200 Kutztown Rd	Kutztown	PA	19530	**877-628-1915**	610-683-4000
La Roche College 9000 Babcock Blvd *Admissions	Pittsburgh	PA	15237	**800-838-4572***	412-367-9300
La Salle University 1900 W Olney Ave	Philadelphia	PA	19141	**800-328-1910**	215-951-1500
Lebanon Valley College 101 N College Ave	Annville	PA	17003	**866-582-4236**	717-867-6181
Lock Haven University 401 N Fairview St	Lock Haven	PA	17745	**800-233-8978**	570-484-2011
Lycoming College 700 College Pl	Williamsport	PA	17701	**800-345-3920**	570-321-4000
Mansfield University Alumni Hall *Admissions	Mansfield	PA	16933	**800-577-6826***	570-662-4000
Mercyhurst College 501 E 38th St	Erie	PA	16546	**800-825-1926**	814-824-2202
Messiah College PO Box 3005	Grantham	PA	17027	**800-233-4220**	717-691-6000
Millersville University of Pennsylvania PO Box 1002 PO Box 1002	Millersville	PA	17551	**800-682-3648**	717-872-3011
Misericordia University 301 Lake St	Dallas	PA	18612	**866-262-6363**	570-674-6400
Moravian College 1200 Main St	Bethlehem	PA	18018	**800-441-3191**	610-861-1300
Mount Aloysius College 7373 Admiral Perry Hwy	Cresson	PA	16630	**888-823-2220**	814-886-6383
Neumann College 1 Neumann Dr	Aston	PA	19014	**800-963-8626**	610-459-0905
Peirce College 1420 Pine St	Philadelphia	PA	19102	**888-467-3472**	215-545-6400
Pennsylvania State University *Altoona* 3000 Ivyside Pk	Altoona	PA	16601	**800-848-9843**	814-949-5466
Harrisburg 777 W Harrisburg Pk	Middletown	PA	17057	**800-222-2056**	717-948-6250
Pennsylvania State University at Erie *Behrend College* 4701 College Dr	Erie	PA	16563	**866-374-3378**	814-898-6000
Philadelphia University 4201 Henry Ave *Admissions	Philadelphia	PA	19144	**800-951-7287***	215-951-2800
Point Park University 201 Wood St *Admissions	Pittsburgh	PA	15222	**800-321-0129***	412-391-4100
Robert Morris University 6001 University Blvd	Moon Township	PA	15108	**800-762-0097**	412-262-8200
Rosemont College 1400 Montgomery Ave *Admissions	Rosemont	PA	19010	**888-521-0983***	610-527-0200
Saint Joseph's University 5600 City Ave	Philadelphia	PA	19131	**888-232-4295**	610-660-1000
Saint Vincent College 300 Fraser Purchase Rd	Latrobe	PA	15650	**800-782-5549**	724-532-6600
Seton Hill University 1 Seton Hill Dr	Greensburg	PA	15601	**800-826-6234**	724-838-4255
Shippensburg University 1871 Old Main Dr	Shippensburg	PA	17257	**800-822-8028**	717-477-1231
Slippery Rock University 1 Morrow Way	Slippery Rock	PA	16057	**800-929-4778**	724-738-9000
Susquehanna University 514 University Ave	Selinsgrove	PA	17870	**800-326-9672**	570-374-0101
Swarthmore College 500 College Ave *Admissions	Swarthmore	PA	19081	**800-667-3110***	610-328-8300
Thiel College 75 College Ave	Greenville	PA	16125	**800-248-4435**	724-589-2000
Thomas Jefferson University 1020 Walnut St	Philadelphia	PA	19107	**800-533-3669**	215-955-6000
University of Pennsylvania 3451 Walnut St	Philadelphia	PA	19104	**800-537-5487**	215-898-5000
Bradford 300 Campus Dr	Bradford	PA	16701	**800-872-1787**	814-362-7555
Greensburg 150 Finoli Dr	Greensburg	PA	15601	**888-843-4563**	724-837-7040
Johnstown 157 Blackington Hall	Johnstown	PA	15904	**800-765-4875**	814-269-7050
University of Scranton 800 Linden St St Thomas Hall	Scranton	PA	18510	**888-727-2686**	570-941-7400
University of the Sciences in Philadelphia 600 S 43rd St	Philadelphia	PA	19104	**888-857-6264**	215-596-8800
Ursinus College 601 E Main St PO Box 1000	Collegeville	PA	19426	**877-448-3282**	610-409-3200
Valley Forge Christian College 1401 Charlestown Rd	Phoenixville	PA	19460	**800-432-8322**	610-935-0450
Washington & Jefferson College 60 S Lincoln St	Washington	PA	15301	**888-926-3529**	724-222-4400
Waynesburg College 51 W College St *Admissions	Waynesburg	PA	15370	**800-225-7393***	724-627-8191
West Chester University 700 S High St	West Chester	PA	19383	**877-315-2165**	610-436-1000
Widener University 1 University Pl *Admissions	Chester	PA	19013	**888-943-3637***	610-499-4000
Wilkes University 84 W S St	Wilkes-Barre	PA	18766	**800-945-5378**	
Wilson College 1015 Philadelphia Ave *Admissions	Chambersburg	PA	17201	**800-421-8402***	717-264-4141

Rhode Island

Name / Address	City	State	Zip	Toll-Free	Phone
Bryant University 1150 Douglas Pk *Admissions	Smithfield	RI	02917	**800-622-7001***	401-232-6000
Johnson & Wales University *Providence* 8 Abbott Pk Pl	Providence	RI	02903	**800-342-5598**	401-598-1000
Providence College 1 Cunningham Sq *Admissions	Providence	RI	02918	**800-721-6444***	401-865-1000
Rhode Island College 600 Mt Pleasant Ave	Providence	RI	02908	**800-669-5760**	401-456-8000
Roger Williams University 1 Old Ferry Rd	Bristol	RI	02809	**800-458-7144**	401-254-3500
Salve Regina University 100 Ochre Pt Ave	Newport	RI	02840	**800-829-1040**	401-847-6650

South Carolina

Name / Address	City	State	Zip	Toll-Free	Phone
Allen University 1530 Harden St	Columbia	SC	29204	**877-625-5368**	803-376-5700
Benedict College 1600 Harden St	Columbia	SC	29204	**800-868-6598**	803-253-5000
Bob Jones University 1700 Wade Hampton Blvd *Admissions	Greenville	SC	29614	**800-252-6363***	864-242-5100
Charleston Southern University 9200 University Blvd	Charleston	SC	29423	**800-947-7474**	843-863-7050
Citadel, The 171 Moultrie St	Charleston	SC	29409	**800-868-1842**	843-953-5230
Claflin University 400 Magnolia St	Orangeburg	SC	29115	**800-922-1276**	803-535-5000
Clemson University 105 Sikes Hall	Clemson	SC	29634	**800-640-2657**	864-656-3311
Coastal Carolina University PO Box 261954	Conway	SC	29528	**800-277-7000**	843-349-2170
Coker College 300 E College Ave	Hartsville	SC	29550	**800-950-1908**	843-383-8000
College of Charleston 66 George St	Charleston	SC	29424	**866-327-2400**	843-805-5507
Converse College 580 E Main St *Admissions	Spartanburg	SC	29302	**800-766-1125***	864-596-9000
Erskine College 2 Washington St *Admissions	Due West	SC	29639	**888-359-4358***	
Francis Marion University PO Box 100547	Florence	SC	29501	**800-368-7551**	843-661-1231
Lander University 320 Stanley Ave *Admissions	Greenwood	SC	29649	**800-922-1117***	864-388-8307
Limestone College 1115 College Dr	Gaffney	SC	29340	**800-795-7151**	864-489-7151
Medical University of South Carolina 41 Bee St MSC 203	Charleston	SC	29425	**800-424-6872**	843-792-3281
Morris College 100 W College St *Admissions	Sumter	SC	29150	**866-853-1345***	803-934-3200
Newberry College 2100 College St	Newberry	SC	29108	**800-845-4955**	803-276-5010
Presbyterian College 503 S Broad St	Clinton	SC	29325	**800-476-7272**	864-833-2820
South Carolina State University 300 College St NE PO Box 7127 *Admissions	Orangeburg	SC	29117	**800-260-5956***	803-536-7000
South University Columbia 9 Science Ct	Columbia	SC	29203	**800-688-0932**	803-799-9082

	City	State	Zip	Toll-Free	Phone
Southern Wesleyan University 907 Wesleyan Dr	Central	SC	29630	**800-282-8798**	864-644-5000
University of South Carolina 1600 Hampton St	Columbia	SC	29208	**800-868-5872**	803-777-7000
Aiken 471 University Pkwy	Aiken	SC	29801	**866-254-2366**	803-648-6851
Beaufort 801 Carteret St	Beaufort	SC	29902	**866-455-4753**	843-521-4100
Sumter 200 Miller Rd	Sumter	SC	29150	**888-872-7868**	803-775-8727
Upstate 800 University Way	Spartanburg	SC	29303	**800-277-8727**	864-503-5246
Voorhees College 213 Wiggins Dr PO Box 678 *Admissions	Denmark	SC	29042	**800-446-6250***	803-780-1234

South Dakota

	City	State	Zip	Toll-Free	Phone
Black Hills State University 1200 University St Unit 9502	Spearfish	SD	57799	**800-255-2478**	605-642-6343
Dakota State University 820 N Washington Ave	Madison	SD	57042	**888-378-9988**	605-256-5139
Dakota Wesleyan University 1200 W University Ave	Mitchell	SD	57301	**800-333-8506**	605-995-2600
Mount Marty College 1105 W Eigth St *Admissions	Yankton	SD	57078	**800-658-4552***	605-668-1545
National American University 321 Kansas City St	Rapid City	SD	57701	**800-843-8892**	605-394-4800
Sioux Falls 5801 S Kiwanis Ave	Sioux Falls	SD	57108	**800-388-5430**	605-336-4600
Northern State University 1200 S Jay St	Aberdeen	SD	57401	**800-678-5330**	605-626-3011
Presentation College 1500 N Main St	Aberdeen	SD	57401	**800-437-6060**	605-225-1634
South Dakota School of Mines & Technology 501 E St Joseph St	Rapid City	SD	57701	**800-544-8162**	605-394-2414
South Dakota State University PO Box 2201	Brookings	SD	57007	**800-952-3541**	605-688-4121
University of Sioux Falls 1101 W 22nd St	Sioux Falls	SD	57105	**800-888-1047**	605-331-6600
University of South Dakota 414 E Clark St	Vermillion	SD	57069	**877-269-6837**	605-677-5341

Tennessee

	City	State	Zip	Toll-Free	Phone
Aquinas College 4210 HaRding Rd *Admissions	Nashville	TN	37205	**800-649-9956***	615-297-7545
Austin Peay State University 601 College St *Admissions	Clarksville	TN	37044	**800-844-2778***	931-221-7661
Belmont University 1900 Belmont Blvd	Nashville	TN	37212	**800-563-6765**	615-460-6000
Bryan College 721 Bryan Dr PO Box 7000	Dayton	TN	37321	**800-277-9522**	423-775-2041
Carson-Newman College 1646 Russell Ave	Jefferson City	TN	37760	**800-678-9061**	865-471-2000
Christian Bros University 650 E Pkwy S *Admissions	Memphis	TN	38104	**800-288-7576***	901-321-3000
Cumberland University 1 Cumberland Sq	Lebanon	TN	37087	**800-467-0562**	615-444-2562
East Tennessee State University PO Box 70731	Johnson City	TN	37614	**800-462-3878**	423-439-4213
Fisk University 1000 17th Ave N	Nashville	TN	37208	**888-702-0022**	615-329-8500
Freed-Hardeman University 158 E Main St	Henderson	TN	38340	**800-348-3481**	731-989-6651
King College 1350 King College Rd *Admissions	Bristol	TN	37620	**800-362-0014***	423-652-4861
Lambuth University 705 Lambuth Blvd	Jackson	TN	38301	**800-526-2305**	731-427-4725
Lane College 545 Ln Ave *Admissions	Jackson	TN	38301	**800-960-7533***	731-426-7500
Lee University 1120 N Ocoee St	Cleveland	TN	37311	**800-533-9930**	423-614-8000
Lincoln Memorial University 6965 Cumberland Gap Pkwy	Harrogate	TN	37752	**800-325-0900**	423-869-3611
Lipscomb University 3901 Granny White Pk	Nashville	TN	37204	**800-333-4358**	615-966-1000
Martin Methodist College 433 W Madison St	Pulaski	TN	38478	**800-467-1273**	931-363-9804
Maryville College 502 E Lamar Alexander Pkwy	Maryville	TN	37804	**800-597-2687**	865-981-8000
Middle Tennessee State University 1301 E Main St *Admissions	Murfreesboro	TN	37132	**800-433-6878***	615-898-2111
Milligan College PO Box 500	Milligan College	TN	37682	**800-262-8337**	423-461-8730
Nossi College of Art 590 Cheron Rd	Madison	TN	37115	**888-986-2787**	615-514-2787
O'More College of Design 423 S Margin St	Franklin	TN	37064	**888-662-1970**	615-794-4254
Oxford Graduate School Inc 500 Oxford Dr	Dayton	TN	37321	**800-933-6188**	423-775-6596
Rhodes College 2000 N Pkwy	Memphis	TN	38112	**800-844-5969**	901-843-3700
Southern Adventist University 4881 Taylor Cir	Collegedale	TN	37315	**800-768-8437**	423-236-2000
Tennessee State University 3500 John A Merritt Blvd PO Box 9609 *Admissions	Nashville	TN	37209	**888-463-6878***	615-963-5000
Tennessee Technological University 1 William L J1s Dr	Cookeville	TN	38505	**800-255-8881**	931-372-3888
Tennessee Temple University 1815 Union Ave	Chattanooga	TN	37404	**800-553-4050**	423-493-4100
Tennessee Wesleyan College 204 E College St	Athens	TN	37371	**800-742-5892**	423-745-7504
Trevecca Nazarene University 333 Murfreesboro Rd	Nashville	TN	37210	**888-210-4868**	615-248-1200
Tusculum College 60 Shiloh Rd Hwy 107	Greeneville	TN	37743	**800-729-0256**	423-636-7300
Union University 1050 Union University Dr	Jackson	TN	38305	**800-338-6466**	731-661-5210
University of Tennessee *Chattanooga* 615 McCallie Ave	Chattanooga	TN	37403	**800-882-6627**	423-425-4111
Martin 544 University St	Martin	TN	38238	**800-829-8861**	731-881-7020
University of the South 735 University Ave	Sewanee	TN	37383	**800-522-2234**	931-598-1238
Vanderbilt University 2201 W End Ave	Nashville	TN	37240	**800-288-0432**	615-322-7311

Texas

	City	State	Zip	Toll-Free	Phone
Angelo State University 2601 W Ave N ASU Stn 11014	San Angelo	TX	76909	**800-946-8627**	325-942-2041
Austin College 900 N Grand Ave	Sherman	TX	75090	**866-776-0056**	903-813-3000
Austin Graduate School of Theology 7640 Guadalupe St	Austin	TX	78752	**866-287-4723**	512-476-2772
Baylor University 1301 S University Parks Dr	Waco	TX	76798	**800-229-5678**	254-710-3718
Concordia University Austin 3400 IH-35 N	Austin	TX	78705	**800-865-4282**	512-486-2000
Criswell College 4010 Gaston Ave	Dallas	TX	75246	**800-899-0012**	214-821-5433
Dallas Baptist University 3000 Mtn Creek Pkwy	Dallas	TX	75211	**800-460-1328**	214-333-7100
East Texas Baptist University 1209 N Grove St	Marshall	TX	75670	**800-804-3828**	903-935-7963
Hardin-Simmons University 2200 Hickory St	Abilene	TX	79698	**877-464-7889**	325-670-1206
Houston Baptist University 7502 Fondren Rd *Admissions	Houston	TX	77074	**800-969-3210***	281-649-3000
Howard Payne University 1000 Fisk Ave	Brownwood	TX	76801	**800-950-8465**	325-646-2502
Huston-Tillotson University 900 Chicon St	Austin	TX	78702	**877-487-8702**	512-505-3000
LeTourneau University 2100 S Mobberly Ave	Longview	TX	75602	**800-759-8811**	903-233-3000
Lubbock Christian University 5601 19th St	Lubbock	TX	79407	**800-933-7601**	806-720-7151
McMurry University 1 McMurry University 1400 Sayles Blvd	Abilene	TX	79697	**800-460-2392**	325-793-4700
Midwestern State University 3410 Taft Blvd *Admissions	Wichita Falls	TX	76308	**800-842-1922***	940-397-4000
Northwood University *Texas* 1114 W FM 1382	Cedar Hill	TX	75104	**800-927-9663**	972-291-1541
Our Lady of the Lake University 411 SW 24th St	San Antonio	TX	78207	**800-436-6558**	210-434-6711
Paul Quinn College 3837 Simpson Stuart Rd	Dallas	TX	75241	**800-433-3243**	214-376-1000
Prairie View A & M University PO Box 519	Prairie View	TX	77446	**877-241-1752**	936-857-2626
Rice University 6100 Main St	Houston	TX	77005	**866-294-4633**	713-348-0000
Saint Mary's University 1 Camino Santa Maria *Admissions	San Antonio	TX	78228	**800-367-7868***	210-436-3126
Sam Houston State University 1903 University Ave	Huntsville	TX	77340	**866-232-7528**	936-294-1111
Schreiner University 2100 Memorial Blvd	Kerrville	TX	78028	**800-343-4919**	830-792-7217
Southern Methodist University 6425 Boaz Ln	Dallas	TX	75205	**800-323-0672**	214-768-2000
Southwestern Adventist University 100 W Hillcrest Dr PO Box 567 *Admissions	Keene	TX	76059	**888-732-7928***	817-645-3921
Southwestern Assemblies of God University 1200 Sycamore St	Waxahachie	TX	75165	**888-937-7248**	972-937-4010
Southwestern Christian College PO Box 10	Terrell	TX	75160	**800-925-9357**	972-524-3341
Southwestern University PO Box 770	Georgetown	TX	78627	**800-252-3166**	512-863-1200
Sul Ross State University E Hwy 90	Alpine	TX	79832	**888-722-7778**	432-837-8011
Tarleton State University 1333 W Washington PO Box T-0030	Stephenville	TX	76402	**800-687-8236**	254-968-9000
Texas A & M International University 5201 University Blvd	Laredo	TX	78041	**888-489-2648**	956-326-2001
Texas A & M University Rudder Tower Ste 205	College Station	TX	77843	**888-890-5667**	979-845-8901
Texas A & M University *Galveston* 200 Seawolf Pkwy Bldg 3026	Galveston	TX	77553	**877-322-4443**	409-740-4428
Kingsville 700 University Blvd MSC 128	Kingsville	TX	78363	**800-726-8192**	361-593-2111
Texarkana 7101 University Ave	Texarkana	TX	75503	**866-791-9120**	903-223-3000
Texas Christian University TCU PO Box 297043	Fort Worth	TX	76129	**800-828-3764**	817-257-7490
Texas College 2404 N Grand Ave	Tyler	TX	75702	**800-306-6299**	903-593-8311
Texas Lutheran University 1000 W Ct St	Seguin	TX	78155	**800-771-8521**	830-372-8050
Texas Southern University 3100 Cleburne St	Houston	TX	77004	**800-252-5400**	713-313-7011

	City	State	ZIP	Toll-Free	Phone
Texas State University					
San Marcos					
601 University Dr	San Marcos	TX	78666	**866-294-0987***	512-245-2340
*Admissions					
Texas Tech University					
PO Box 45005	Lubbock	TX	79409	**888-270-3369**	806-742-1480
Texas Wesleyan University					
1201 Wesleyan St	Fort Worth	TX	76105	**800-580-8980**	817-531-4444
Texas Woman's University					
304 Admin Dr PO Box 425589	Denton	TX	76204	**866-809-6130**	940-898-3188
University of Dallas					
1845 E Northgate Dr	Irving	TX	75062	**800-628-6999***	972-721-5266
*Admissions					
University of Houston					
Victoria					
3007 N Ben Wilson St	Victoria	TX	77901	**877-970-4848**	361-570-4848
University of Mary Hardin-Baylor					
900 College St PO Box 8004	Belton	TX	76513	**800-727-8642**	254-295-8642
University of North Texas					
PO Box 311277	Denton	TX	76203	**800-868-8211**	940-565-2681
University of Saint Thomas					
3800 Montrose Blvd	Houston	TX	77006	**800-856-8565**	713-522-7911
University of Texas					
Dallas					
800 W Campbell Rd Ste Be3204	Richardson	TX	75080	**800-889-2443**	972-883-2111
El Paso					
500 W University Ave	El Paso	TX	79968	**800-551-0294***	915-747-5000
*Admissions					
Pan American					
1201 W University Dr	Edinburg	TX	78539	**866-441-8872**	956-381-8872
Permian Basin					
4901 E University Blvd	Odessa	TX	79762	**866-552-8872***	432-552-2020
*Admissions					
San Antonio					
6900 N Loop 1604 W	San Antonio	TX	78249	**800-669-0919**	210-458-4011
Tyler 3900 University Blvd	Tyler	TX	75799	**800-888-9537**	903-566-7000
University of the Incarnate Word					
4301 Broadway St Ste 285	San Antonio	TX	78209	**800-749-9673***	210-829-6000
*Admissions					
Wayland Baptist University					
1900 W Seventh St	Plainview	TX	79072	**800-588-1928**	806-291-1000
West Texas A & M University					
2501 Fourth Ave	Canyon	TX	79016	**877-656-2065**	806-651-2020
Wiley College					
711 Wiley Ave	Marshall	TX	75670	**800-658-6889***	903-927-3300
*Admissions					

Utah

	City	State	ZIP	Toll-Free	Phone
Dixie State University					
225 S 700 E	Saint George	UT	84770	**855-628-8140**	435-652-7500
Utah State University					
1600 Old Main Hill	Logan	UT	84322	**800-488-8108**	435-797-1116
Weber State University					
3848 Harrison Blvd	Ogden	UT	84408	**800-848-7770**	801-626-6000
Davis					
2750 N University Pk Blvd	Layton	UT	84041	**800-848-7770**	801-395-3473

Vermont

	City	State	ZIP	Toll-Free	Phone
Bennington College					
1 College Dr	Bennington	VT	05201	**800-833-6845**	802-442-5401
Burlington College					
351 N Ave	Burlington	VT	05401	**800-862-9616**	
Castleton State College					
86 Seminary St	Castleton	VT	05735	**800-639-8521**	802-468-5611
Champlain College					
163 S Willard St	Burlington	VT	05401	**800-570-5858**	802-860-2700
College of Saint Joseph in Vermont					
71 Clement Rd	Rutland	VT	05701	**877-270-9998***	802-773-5900
*Admissions					
Goddard College					
123 Pitkin Rd	Plainfield	VT	05667	**800-468-4888**	802-454-8311
Green Mountain College					
1 Brennan Cir	Poultney	VT	05764	**800-776-6675***	802-287-8000
*Admissions					
Johnson State College					
337 College Hill	Johnson	VT	05656	**800-635-2356**	802-635-2356
Lyndon State College					
1001 College Rd PO Box 919	Lyndonville	VT	05851	**800-225-1998**	802-626-6413
Marlboro College					
2582 S Rd PO Box A	Marlboro	VT	05344	**800-343-0049**	802-257-4333
Middlebury College					
131 S Main St	Middlebury	VT	05753	**877-214-3330**	802-443-3000
Norwich University					
158 Harmon Dr	Northfield	VT	05663	**800-468-6679**	802-485-2001
Saint Michael's College					
1 Winooski Pk	Colchester	VT	05439	**800-762-8000**	802-654-2000
Southern Vermont College					
982 Manison Dr	Bennington	VT	05201	**800-378-2782**	802-442-5427
University of Vermont					
85 S Prospect St	Burlington	VT	05405	**800-499-0113**	802-656-3131

Virginia

	City	State	ZIP	Toll-Free	Phone
Bluefield College					
3000 College Dr	Bluefield	VA	24605	**800-872-0175**	276-326-3682
Bridgewater College					
402 E College St	Bridgewater	VA	22812	**800-759-8328**	540-828-5375
Christendom College					
134 Christendom Dr	Front Royal	VA	22630	**800-877-5456**	540-636-2900
Christopher Newport University					
1 University Pl	Newport News	VA	23606	**800-333-4268***	757-594-7015
*Admissions					
Eastern Mennonite University					
1200 Pk Rd	Harrisonburg	VA	22802	**800-368-2665***	540-432-4118
*Admissions					
Emory & Henry College					
PO Box 10	Emory	VA	24327	**800-848-5493***	276-944-4121
*Admissions					
Ferrum College					
215 Ferrum Mtn Rd	Ferrum	VA	24088	**800-868-9797**	540-365-2121
George Mason University					
4400 University Dr	Fairfax	VA	22030	**888-627-6612**	703-993-1000
Hampden-Sydney College					
PO Box 667	Hampden Sydney	VA	23943	**800-755-0733***	434-223-6120
*Admissions					
Hampton University					
100 E Queen St	Hampton	VA	23668	**800-624-3341**	757-727-5000
Hollins University					
PO BOX 9707	Roanoke	VA	24020	**800-456-9595***	540-362-6401
*Admissions					
Liberty University					
1971 University Blvd	Lynchburg	VA	24502	**800-543-5317**	434-582-2000
Longwood University					
201 High St	Farmville	VA	23909	**800-281-4677**	434-395-2060
Lynchburg College					
1501 Lakeside Dr	Lynchburg	VA	24501	**800-426-8101**	434-544-8100
Mary Baldwin College					
318 Prospect St PO Box 1500	Staunton	VA	24401	**800-468-2262***	540-887-7019
*Admissions					
Marymount University					
2807 N Glebe Rd	Arlington	VA	22207	**800-548-7638**	703-522-5600
Norfolk State University					
700 Pk Ave	Norfolk	VA	23504	**800-274-1821**	757-823-8600
Old Dominion University					
Rollins Hall	Norfolk	VA	23529	**800-348-7926**	757-683-3685
Radford University					
801 E Main St	Radford	VA	24142	**800-890-4265***	540-831-5371
*Admissions					
Randolph College					
2500 Rivermont Ave	Lynchburg	VA	24503	**800-745-7692***	434-947-8000
*Admissions					
Randolph-Macon College					
PO Box 5005	Ashland	VA	23005	**800-888-1762**	804-752-7200
Roanoke College					
221 College Ln	Salem	VA	24153	**800-388-2276***	540-375-2270
*Admissions					
Shenandoah University					
1460 University Dr	Winchester	VA	22601	**800-432-2266**	540-665-4581
Southern Virginia University					
1 University Hill Dr	Buena Vista	VA	24416	**800-229-8420**	540-261-8400
Strayer University Alexandria					
2730 Eisenhower Ave	Alexandria	VA	22314	**888-311-0355**	
Strayer University Arlington					
2121 15th St N	Arlington	VA	22201	**888-478-7293**	703-892-5100
Strayer University Fredericksburg					
150 Riverside Pkwy Ste 100	Fredericksburg	VA	22406	**888-311-0355**	540-374-4300
Sweet Briar College					
134 Chappel Rd	Sweet Briar	VA	24595	**800-381-6142***	434-381-6100
*Admissions					
University of Mary Washington					
1301 College Ave	Fredericksburg	VA	22401	**800-468-5614***	540-654-2000
*Admissions					
University of Richmond					
28 Westhampton Way	Richmond	VA	23173	**800-700-1662**	804-289-8000
Westhampton College					
28 Westhampton Way	University Of Richmond	VA	23173	**800-700-1662**	804-289-8000
University of Virginia's College at Wise					
1 College Ave	Wise	VA	24293	**888-282-9324***	276-328-0102
*Admissions					
Virginia Commonwealth University					
910 W Franklin St	Richmond	VA	23284	**800-841-3638**	804-828-0100
Virginia Intermont College					
1013 Moore St	Bristol	VA	24201	**800-451-1842**	276-669-6101
Virginia Military Institute					
319 Letcher Ave	Lexington	VA	24450	**800-767-4207**	540-464-7211
Virginia State University					
1 Hayden Dr	Petersburg	VA	23806	**800-871-7611***	804-524-5000
*Admissions					
Virginia Union University					
1500 N Lombardy St	Richmond	VA	23220	**800-368-3227**	804-342-3570
Virginia Wesleyan College					
1584 Wesleyan Dr	Norfolk	VA	23502	**800-737-8684**	757-455-3200
Washington & Lee University					
204 W Washington St	Lexington	VA	24450	**800-221-3943**	540-458-8710

Washington

	City	State	ZIP	Toll-Free	Phone
Antioch University					
2326 Sixth Ave	Seattle	WA	98121	**888-268-4477**	206-441-5352
Central Washington University					
400 E University Way	Ellensburg	WA	98926	**866-298-4968***	509-963-1111
*Admissions					
City University					
11900 NE First St	Bellevue	WA	98005	**800-426-5596***	425-637-1010
*Admissions					
Digipen Institute of Technology					
5001 150th Ave Ne	Redmond	WA	98052	**866-478-5236**	425-558-0299
Evergreen State College					
2700 Evergreen Pkwy	Olympia	WA	98505	**888-492-9480**	360-867-6000
Gonzaga University					
502 E Boone Ave	Spokane	WA	99258	**800-986-9585**	509-323-6572
Heritage University					
3240 Ft Rd	Toppenish	WA	98948	**888-272-6190**	509-865-8500
Northwest University					
5520 108th Ave NE	Kirkland	WA	98033	**800-669-3781***	425-822-8266
*Admissions					
Pacific Lutheran University					
1010 122nd St S	Tacoma	WA	98444	**800-274-6758**	253-531-6900

				Toll-Free	Phone
Saint Martin's University					
5300 Pacific Ave SE	Lacey	WA	98503	**800-368-8803***	360-438-4311
*Admissions					
Seattle Pacific University					
3307 Third Ave W	Seattle	WA	98119	**800-366-3344**	206-281-2000
Seattle University					
901 12th Ave	Seattle	WA	98122	**800-426-7123**	206-296-6000
University of Puget Sound					
1500 N Warner St	Tacoma	WA	98416	**800-396-7191**	253-879-3100
Walla Walla University					
204 S College Ave	College Place	WA	99324	**800-541-8900**	509-527-2327
Washington State University					
PO Box 641040	Pullman	WA	99164	**888-468-6978**	509-335-3564
Spokane					
310 N Riverpoint Blvd PO Box 1495	Spokane	WA	99210	**800-233-3247**	509-358-7978
Whitman College					
345 Boyer Ave	Walla Walla	WA	99362	**877-462-9448***	509-527-5111
*Admissions					
Whitworth College					
300 W Hawthorne Rd	Spokane	WA	99251	**800-533-4668***	509-777-1000
*Admissions					

West Virginia

				Toll-Free	Phone
Alderson-Broaddus College					
101 College Hill Rd	Philippi	WV	26416	**800-263-1549***	304-457-1700
*Admissions					
Bethany College					
31 E Campus Dr	Bethany	WV	26032	**800-922-7611**	304-829-7000
Bluefield State College					
219 Rock St	Bluefield	WV	24701	**800-654-7798**	304-327-4000
Concord University					
PO Box 1000	Athens	WV	24712	**800-344-6679**	304-384-3115
Davis & Elkins College					
100 Campus Dr	Elkins	WV	26241	**800-624-3157**	304-637-1900
Fairmont State University					
1201 Locust Ave	Fairmont	WV	26554	**800-641-5678***	304-367-4892
*Admissions					
Glenville State College					
200 High St	Glenville	WV	26351	**800-924-2010***	304-462-7361
*Admissions					
Marshall University					
1 John Marshall Dr	Huntington	WV	25755	**800-642-3463**	304-696-3170
Salem International University					
223 W Main St	Salem	WV	26426	**800-283-4562**	304-326-1109
Shepherd University					
301 N King St	Shepherdstown	WV	25443	**800-344-5231**	304-876-5000
University of Charleston					
2300 MacCorkle Ave SE	Charleston	WV	25304	**800-995-4682***	304-357-4800
*Admissions					
West Virginia State University					
117 Ferrell Hall PO Box 368	Institute	WV	25112	**800-987-2112**	304-766-3000
West Virginia University					
PO Box 6009	Morgantown	WV	26506	**800-344-9881**	304-293-2121
Institute of Technology					
405 Fayette Pk	Montgomery	WV	25136	**888-554-8324**	304-442-1000
West Virginia Wesleyan College					
59 College Ave	Buckhannon	WV	26201	**800-722-9933***	304-473-8000
*Admitting					
Wheeling Jesuit University					
316 Washington Ave	Wheeling	WV	26003	**800-624-6992**	304-243-2000

Wisconsin

				Toll-Free	Phone
Alverno College					
PO Box 343922	Milwaukee	WI	53234	**800-933-3401**	414-382-6100
Bellin College of Nursing					
3201 Eaton Rd	Green Bay	WI	54311	**800-236-8707**	920-433-6699
Beloit College					
700 College St	Beloit	WI	53511	**800-331-4943***	608-363-2500
*Admissions					
Cardinal Stritch University					
6801 N Yates Rd	Milwaukee	WI	53217	**800-347-8822**	414-410-4000
Carroll University					
100 NE Ave	Waukesha	WI	53186	**800-227-7655**	262-547-1211
Carthage College					
2001 Alford Pk Dr	Kenosha	WI	53140	**800-351-4058***	262-551-8500
*Admissions					
Columbia College of Nursing (CCON)					
4425 N Port Washington Rd	Glendale	WI	53212	**800-221-5573**	414-326-2330
Concordia University Wisconsin					
12800 N Lake Shore Dr	Mequon	WI	53097	**888-628-9472***	262-243-5700
*Admissions					
Edgewood College					
1000 Edgewood College Dr	Madison	WI	53711	**800-444-4861**	608-663-2294
Lakeland College					
PO Box 359	Sheboygan	WI	53082	**800-569-2166**	920-565-2111
Lawrence University					
115 S Drew St	Appleton	WI	54911	**800-432-5427**	920-832-7000
Maranatha Baptist Bible College					
745 W Main St	Watertown	WI	53094	**800-622-2947**	920-206-2330
Marquette University					
1217 W Wisconsin Ave	Milwaukee	WI	53233	**800-222-6544***	414-288-7302
*Admissions					
Milwaukee Institute of Art & Design					
273 E Erie St	Milwaukee	WI	53202	**888-749-6423**	414-276-7889
Milwaukee School of Engineering					
1025 N Broadway St	Milwaukee	WI	53202	**800-332-6763**	414-277-6763
Mount Mary College					
2900 N Menomonee River Pkwy	Milwaukee	WI	53222	**800-321-6265***	414-256-1219
*Admissions					
Northland College					
1411 Ellis Ave	Ashland	WI	54806	**800-753-1840**	715-682-1224
Ripon College					
300 Seward St PO Box 248	Ripon	WI	54971	**800-947-4766***	
*Admissions					
Saint Norbert College					
100 Grant St	De Pere	WI	54115	**800-236-4878***	920-403-3005
*Admissions					
Silver Lake College					
2406 S Alverno Rd	Manitowoc	WI	54220	**800-236-4752**	920-686-6175
University of Wisconsin					
Baraboo/Sauk County					
1006 Connie Rd	Baraboo	WI	53913	**800-621-7440**	608-355-5200
Eau Claire					
105 Garfield Ave PO Box 4004	Eau Claire	WI	54701	**800-473-2255**	715-836-2637
Green Bay 2420 Nicolet Dr	Green Bay	WI	54311	**800-465-4329**	920-465-2000
La Crosse					
1725 State St 115 Graff Main Hall	La Crosse	WI	54601	**800-382-2150**	608-785-8000
Platteville					
1 University Plz	Platteville	WI	53818	**800-362-5515**	608-342-1125
River Falls					
410 S Third St B3 E Hathorn Hall	River Falls	WI	54022	**800-852-5711**	715-425-3911
Stout 802 S Broadway	Menomonie	WI	54751	**800-447-8688***	715-232-1232
*Admissions					
Superior					
Belknap & Catlin PO Box 2000	Superior	WI	54880	**800-869-5088**	715-394-8101
Viterbo University					
900 Viterbo Dr	La Crosse	WI	54601	**800-848-3726**	608-796-3000

Wyoming

				Toll-Free	Phone
University of Wyoming					
1000 E University Ave Dept 3435	Laramie	WY	82071	**800-342-5996***	307-766-5160
*Admissions					

168 COLLEGES & UNIVERSITIES - GRADUATE & PROFESSIONAL SCHOOLS

				Toll-Free	Phone
American Public University System (AMU)					
111 W Congress St	Charles Town	WV	25414	**877-777-9081**	304-724-3700

168-1 Law Schools

Law schools listed here are approved by the American Bar Association.

				Toll-Free	Phone
Albany Law School of Union University (ALS)					
80 New Scotland Ave	Albany	NY	12208	**800-448-3500**	518-445-2311
American University Washington College of Law					
4801 Massachusetts Ave NW	Washington	DC	20016	**800-995-6423**	202-274-4101
Appalachian School of Law					
1169 Edgewater Dr	Grundy	VA	24614	**800-895-7411**	276-935-4349
Arizona State University					
Sandra Day O'Connor College of Law					
PO Box 877906	Tempe	AZ	85287	**855-278-5080**	480-965-6181
Barry University Dwayne O Andreas School of Law					
6441 E Colonial Dr	Orlando	FL	32807	**800-756-6000**	321-206-5600
Baylor University School of Law					
1114 S University Parks Dr					
1 Bear Pl 97288	Waco	TX	76798	**800-229-5678**	254-710-1911
Benjamin N Cardozo School of Law Yeshiva University					
55 Fifth Ave Brookdale Ctr	New York	NY	10003	**800-232-5463**	212-790-0200
Boston College Law School					
885 Centre St	Newton	MA	02459	**800-321-2211**	617-552-8550
Boston University School of Law					
765 Commonwealth Ave	Boston	MA	02215	**800-321-2211**	617-353-3100
California Western School of Law					
225 Cedar St	San Diego	CA	92101	**800-255-4252**	619-239-0391
Campbell University Norman Adrian Wiggins School of Law					
113 Main St	Buies Creek	NC	27506	**800-334-4111**	919-865-5991
Capital University Law School					
303 E Broad St	Columbus	OH	43215	**800-362-2779**	614-236-6500
Case Western Reserve University School of Law					
11075 E Blvd	Cleveland	OH	44106	**800-756-0036**	216-368-3600
Cleveland State University Cleveland-Marshall College of Law					
1801 Euclid Ave LB 138	Cleveland	OH	44115	**866-687-2304**	216-687-2344
DePaul University College of Law					
25 E Jackson Blvd	Chicago	IL	60604	**800-445-8667**	312-362-8701
Drake University School of Law					
2507 University Ave	Des Moines	IA	50311	**800-443-7253**	515-271-2824
Duke University School of Law					
201 Science Dr PO Box 90362	Durham	NC	27708	**888-529-2586**	919-613-7006
Florida Coastal School of Law					
8787 Bay Pine Rd	Jacksonville	FL	32256	**877-210-2591**	904-680-7700
Golden Gate University School of Law					
536 Mission St	San Francisco	CA	94105	**800-448-4968**	415-442-6600
Gonzaga University School of Law					
721 N Cincinnati St PO Box 3528	Spokane	WA	99220	**800-793-1710***	509-313-3700
*Admissions					
Howard University School of Law					
2900 Van Ness St NW	Washington	DC	20008	**800-829-9019**	202-806-8000
John Marshall Law School					
315 S Plymouth Ct	Chicago	IL	60604	**800-285-2221**	312-427-2737
School of Law					
25 E Pearson St	Chicago	IL	60611	**866-596-7890**	312-915-7120
Michigan State University College of Law					
368 Law College Bldg	East Lansing	MI	48824	**800-844-9352**	517-432-6810
New York Law School					
185 W Broadway	New York	NY	10013	**877-937-6957**	212-431-2100
New York University School of Law					
110 W Third St	New York	NY	10012	**800-522-0925**	212-998-6100
Northeastern University School of Law					
400 Huntington Ave	Boston	MA	02115	**800-732-3400**	617-373-2395
Northern Illinois University College of Law					
Swen Parson Hall	DeKalb	IL	60115	**800-892-3050**	815-753-9655
Northwestern University School of Law					
357 E Chicago Ave	Chicago	IL	60611	**800-229-2032**	312-503-3100
Nova Southeastern University Shepard Broad Law Ctr					
3305 College Ave	Fort Lauderdale	FL	33314	**800-986-6529**	954-262-6100

Classified Section

	City	State	ZIP	Toll-Free	Phone
Ohio Northern University Claude W Pettit College of Law					
525 S Main St	Ada	OH	45810	**877-452-9668**	419-772-2211
Oklahoma City University School of Law					
2501 N Blackwelder Ave	Oklahoma City	OK	73106	**800-230-3012**	405-208-5000
Pennsylvania State University Dickinson School of Law					
150 S College St	Carlisle	PA	17013	**800-840-1122**	717-240-5000
Quinnipiac University School of Law					
275 Mt Carmel Ave	Hamden	CT	06518	**800-462-1944**	203-582-3400
Roger Williams University Ralph R Papitto School of Law					
10 Metacom Ave	Bristol	RI	02809	**800-633-2727**	401-254-4500
Rutgers the State University of New Jersey					
School of Law Camden					
217 N Fifth St	Camden	NJ	08102	**800-466-7561**	856-225-6375
Saint Louis University School of Law					
3700 Lindell Blvd	Saint Louis	MO	63108	**800-758-3678**	314-977-2766
Saint Thomas University School of Law					
16401 NW 37th Ave	Miami Gardens	FL	33054	**800-245-4569**	305-623-2310
Southern Illinois University School of Law					
1209 W Chautauqua Rd	Carbondale	IL	62901	**800-739-9187**	618-453-8858
Southern Methodist University Dedman School of Law					
3300 University Blvd Ste 331	Dallas	TX	75205	**888-768-5291**	214-768-2550
Southern University Law Ctr					
2 Roosevelt Steptoe Dr	Baton Rouge	LA	70813	**800-537-1135**	225-771-6297
Temple University James E Beasley School of Law					
1719 N Broad St	Philadelphia	PA	19122	**800-560-1428**	215-204-7861
Texas Wesleyan University School of Law					
1515 Commerce St	Fort Worth	TX	76102	**800-733-9529**	817-212-4000
Thomas Jefferson School of Law					
1155 Island Ave	San Diego	CA	92101	**877-318-6901**	619-297-9700
Thomas M Cooley Law School					
300 S Capitol Ave	Lansing	MI	48933	**800-243-2586**	517-371-5140
Tulane University Law School					
6329 Freret St Weinmann Hall	New Orleans	LA	70118	**800-328-6819**	504-865-5930
University of Akron School of Law					
150 University Ave	Akron	OH	44325	**800-655-4884**	330-972-7331
University of Alabama					
PO Box 870132	Tuscaloosa	AL	35487	**800-933-2262***	205-348-6010
*Admissions					
University of Arkansas School of Law					
1045 W Maple St	Fayetteville	AR	72701	**800-295-9118**	479-575-5601
University of Connecticut School of Law					
45 Elizabeth St	Hartford	CT	06105	**800-633-7867**	860-570-5100
University of Detroit Mercy School of Law					
651 E Jefferson Ave	Detroit	MI	48226	**888-726-6921**	313-596-0264
University of Florida Fredric G Levin College of Law					
2500 SW Second Ave	Gainesville	FL	32611	**877-429-1297**	352-273-0890
University of Houston Law Ctr					
100 Law Ctr	Houston	TX	77204	**800-252-9690**	713-743-2100
University of Idaho College of Law					
711 S Rayburn St	Moscow	ID	83844	**888-884-3246**	208-885-4977
University of Illinois College of Law					
504 E Pennsylvania Ave	Champaign	IL	61820	**800-369-6151**	217-333-0930
University of Iowa College of Law					
130 Byington Rd	Iowa City	IA	52242	**800-553-4692**	319-335-9034
University of Kansas School of Law					
1535 W 15th St	Lawrence	KS	66045	**877-404-5823**	785-864-4550
University of Kentucky College of Law					
620 S Limestone St	Lexington	KY	40506	**800-888-8189**	859-257-1678
University of Memphis Cecil C Humphreys School of Law					
3715 Central Ave	Memphis	TN	38152	**800-872-3728**	901-678-2421
University of Saint Thomas School of Law					
1000 LaSalle Ave	Minneapolis	MN	55403	**800-328-6819**	651-962-4892
University of San Diego School of Law					
5998 Alcala Pk	San Diego	CA	92110	**800-248-4873**	619-260-4528
University of South Dakota School of Law					
414 E Clark St	Vermillion	SD	57069	**877-269-6837**	605-677-5443
University of Virginia School of Law					
580 Massie Rd	Charlottesville	VA	22903	**877-307-0158**	434-924-7354
University of Washington School of Law					
William H Gates Hall PO Box 353020	Seattle	WA	98195	**866-866-0158**	206-543-4078
University of Wisconsin Law School					
975 Bascom Mall	Madison	WI	53706	**866-301-1753**	608-262-2240
Valparaiso University School of Law					
651 College Ave	Valparaiso	IN	46383	**888-825-7652**	219-465-7829
Vermont Law School					
168 Chelsea St PO Box 96	South Royalton	VT	05068	**800-227-1395**	802-831-1239
Western State University College of Law					
1111 N State College Blvd	Fullerton	CA	92831	**800-978-4529**	714-459-1101
Widener University Commonwealth Law School					
3800 Vartan Way	Harrisburg	PA	17110	**888-943-3637**	717-541-3900
Widener University School of Law Wilmington					
4601 Concord Pk	Wilmington	DE	19803	**888-943-3637***	302-477-2100
*General					
Willamette University College of Law					
245 Winter St SE	Salem	OR	97301	**844-232-7228**	503-370-6282
William Mitchell College of Law					
875 Summit Ave	Saint Paul	MN	55105	**888-962-5529**	651-227-9171

168-2 Medical Schools

Medical schools listed here are accredited, MD-granting members of the Association of American Medical Colleges. Accredited Canadian schools that do not offer classes in English are not included among these listings.

	City	State	ZIP	Toll-Free	Phone
Brody School of Medicine at East Carolina University					
600 Moye Blvd	Greenville	NC	27834	**800-722-3281**	252-744-1020
Cincinnati Children's Hospital Medical Ctr					
3333 Burnet Ave	Cincinnati	OH	45229	**800-344-2462**	513-636-4200
Duke University School of Medicine					
Office of Admissions DUMC 3710	Durham	NC	27710	**888-275-3853**	919-684-2985
George Washington University School of Medicine & Health Sciences					
2300 'I' St NW Ross Hall 716	Washington	DC	20037	**866-846-1107**	202-994-3506
Harvard Medical School					
25 Shattuck St	Boston	MA	02115	**866-606-0573**	617-432-1550
Jefferson Medical College of Thomas Jefferson University					
1015 Walnut St	Philadelphia	PA	19107	**800-533-3669**	215-955-6983
Joan & Sanford Weill Medical College of Cornell University					
445 E 69th St	New York	NY	10021	**800-422-0711**	212-746-5454
Joan C Edwards School of Medicine at Marshall University					
1600 Medical Ctr Dr	Huntington	WV	25701	**877-691-1600**	304-691-1700
Loma Linda University School of Medicine					
11175 Campus St	Loma Linda	CA	92350	**800-422-4558**	909-558-4467
Louisiana State University School of Medicine in New Orleans					
433 Bolivar St	New Orleans	LA	70112	**844-503-7283**	504-568-6262
Louisiana State University School of Medicine in Shreveport					
1501 Kings Hwy PO Box 33932	Shreveport	LA	71130	**800-337-3627**	318-675-5069
New York University School of Medicine					
560 First Ave	New York	NY	10016	**855-698-2220**	212-263-7300
Northeast Ohio Medical University					
4209 State Rt 44 PO Box 95	Rootstown	OH	44272	**800-686-2511**	330-325-2511
Oregon Health & Science University					
Bone Marrow Transplant Program (OHSU)					
3181 SW Sam Jackson Pk Rd	Portland	OR	97239	**800-222-1222**	503-494-1617
School of Medicine					
3181 SW Sam Jackson Pk Rd L-109	Portland	OR	97239	**800-775-5460**	503-494-7800
Rush Medical College of Rush University					
600 S Paulina St	Chicago	IL	60612	**888-352-7874**	
Saint Louis University School of Medicine					
1 North Grand	Saint Louis	MO	63103	**800-758-3678**	
Southern Illinois University School of Medicine					
520 N Fourth St PO Box 19670	Springfield	IL	62702	**800-342-5748**	217-545-8000
State University of New York Upstate Medical University					
766 Irving Ave	Syracuse	NY	13210	**800-736-2171**	315-464-4570
University of California Davis School of Medicine					
4610 X St	Sacramento	CA	95817	**855-221-4673**	916-734-2011
University of California Irvine School of Medicine					
1001 Health Sciences Rd					
252 Irvine Hall	Irvine	CA	92697	**800-824-5388**	949-824-6119
University of Iowa Roy J & Lucille A Carver College of Medicine					
200 CMAB	Iowa City	IA	52242	**800-725-8460**	319-335-6707
University of Kentucky College of Medicine					
Office of Medical Education					
MN 104 UKMC	Lexington	KY	40536	**800-273-8255**	859-323-6161
University of Louisville School of Medicine					
323 E Chestnut St	Louisville	KY	40292	**800-334-8635**	502-852-5193
University of Minnesota Medical School Twin Cities					
420 Delaware St SE Mayo MC 293	Minneapolis	MN	55455	**800-752-1000**	612-624-5100
University of Mississippi School of Medicine					
2500 N State St	Jackson	MS	39216	**888-815-2005**	601-984-1080
University of Missouri-Kansas City School of Medicine					
2411 Holmes St	Kansas City	MO	64108	**800-735-2466**	816-235-1111
University of Nebraska School of Medicine					
985527 Nebraska Medical Ctr	Omaha	NE	68198	**800-626-8431**	402-559-2259
University of New Mexico School of Medicine					
1 University of New Mexico	Albuquerque	NM	87131	**877-977-2263**	505-272-4766
University of North Dakota School of Medicine & Health Sciences					
501 N Columbia Rd	Grand Forks	ND	58203	**800-225-5863**	701-777-5046
University of Ottawa Faculty of Medicine					
451 Smyth Rd	Ottawa	ON	K1H8M5	**877-868-8292**	613-562-5700
University of Rochester School of Medicine & Dentistry					
601 Elmwood Ave	Rochester	NY	14642	**888-661-6162**	585-275-0017
University of South Florida College of Medicine (USF)					
12901 Bruce B Downs Blvd	Tampa	FL	33612	**877-338-2577**	813-974-2229
University of Texas Medical Branch					
301 University Blvd	Galveston	TX	77555	**800-228-1841**	409-772-2618
University of Texas Southwestern Medical Ctr Dallas					
Hematopoietic Cell Transplant Program					
2201 Inwood Rd 2nd Fl	Dallas	TX	75390	**866-645-6455**	214-645-4673
Southwestern Medical School					
5323 Harry Hines Blvd	Dallas	TX	75390	**866-648-2455**	214-648-3111
University of Utah School of Medicine					
30 N 1900 E	Salt Lake City	UT	84132	**844-988-7284**	801-581-7201
University of Vermont College of Medicine					
89 Beaumont Ave E-126 Given Bldg	Burlington	VT	05405	**800-571-0668**	802-656-2156
Vanderbilt University School of Medicine					
215 Light Hall	Nashville	TN	37232	**866-263-8263**	615-322-2145
Virginia Commonwealth University School of Medicine					
1101 E Marshall St PO Box 980565	Richmond	VA	23298	**800-332-8813**	804-828-9629
Wake Forest University School of Medicine					
Medical Ctr Blvd	Winston-Salem	NC	27157	**800-445-2255**	336-716-4264
West Virginia University School of Medicine					
Medical Ctr Dr					
Health Sciences Ctr N Rm 1146	Morgantown	WV	26506	**800-543-5650**	304-293-2408
Wright State University Boonshoft School of Medicine					
3640 Col Glenn Hwy	Dayton	OH	45435	**800-338-4057**	937-775-2934
Yale University School of Medicine					
333 Cedar St	New Haven	CT	06510	**877-925-3637**	203-785-2643

168-3 Theological Schools

Theological schools listed here are members of the Association of Theological Schools (ATS), an organization of graduate schools in the U.S. and Canada that conduct post-baccalaureate professional and academic degree programs to educate persons for the practice of ministry and for teaching and research in the theological disciplines. Listings include ATS accredited member schools, candidates for accredited membership, and associate member schools.

	City	State	ZIP	Toll-Free	Phone
Acadia Divinity College					
38 Highland Ave	Wolfville	NS	B4P2R6	**866-875-8975**	902-585-2210
American Baptist Seminary of the West					
2606 Dwight Way	Berkeley	CA	94704	**800-799-7233**	510-841-1905
Anderson University					
1100 E Fifth St	Anderson	IN	46012	**800-428-6414***	765-649-9071
*Admissions					
Andover Newton Theological School					
210 Herrick Rd	Newton Center	MA	02459	**800-964-2687**	617-964-1100
Andrews University Seventh-day Adventist Theological Seminary					
4145 E Campus Cir Dr					
Andrews University	Berrien Springs	MI	49104	**800-253-2874**	269-471-3537
Aquinas Institute of Theology					
23 S Spring Ave	Saint Louis	MO	63108	**800-977-3869**	314-256-8800

Institution	Address	City	State	Zip	Toll-Free	Phone
Asbury Theological Seminary	204 N Lexington Ave	Wilmore	KY	40390	**800-227-2879**	859-858-3581
Assemblies of God Theological Seminary	1435 N Glenstone Ave	Springfield	MO	65802	**800-467-2487**	417-268-1000
Associated Mennonite Biblical Seminary	3003 Benham Ave	Elkhart	IN	46517	**800-964-2627**	574-295-3726
Azusa Pacific University	901 E Alosta Ave PO Box 7000	Azusa	CA	91702	**800-825-5278**	626-969-3434
Bangor Theological Seminary	159 State St	Portland	ME	04101	**800-287-6781**	207-942-6781
Baptist Missionary Assn Theological Seminary	1530 E Pine St	Jacksonville	TX	75766	**800-259-5673**	903-586-2501
Baptist Theological Seminary at Richmond	8040 Villa Park Dr Ste 250	Richmond	VA	23227	**888-345-2877**	804-355-8135
Barry University	11300 NE Second Ave	Miami Shores	FL	33161	**800-756-6000**	305-899-3000
Bethany Theological Seminary	615 National Rd W	Richmond	IN	47374	**800-287-8822**	765-983-1800
Bethel Seminary	3949 Bethel Dr	Saint Paul	MN	55112	**800-255-8706**	651-638-6400
Biblical Theological Seminary	200 N Main St	Hatfield	PA	19440	**800-235-4021**	215-368-5000
Biola University	13800 Biola Ave *Admissions	La Mirada	CA	90639	**800-652-4652***	562-903-6000
Calvin Theological Seminary	3233 Burton St SE	Grand Rapids	MI	49546	**800-388-6034**	616-957-6036
Campbell University	450 Leslie Campbell Ave PO Box 546	Buies Creek	NC	27506	**800-334-4111**	910-893-1290
Canadian Southern Baptist Seminary	200 Seminary View	Cochrane	AB	T4C2G1	**877-922-2727**	403-932-6622
Carey Theological College	5920 Iona Dr	Vancouver	BC	V6T1J6	**844-862-2739**	604-224-4308
Central Baptist Theological Seminary	6601 Monticello Rd	Shawnee	KS	66226	**800-677-2287**	913-667-5700
Christian Theological Seminary	1000 W 42nd St	Indianapolis	IN	46208	**800-585-0108**	317-924-1331
Cincinnati Christian University	2700 Glenway Ave	Cincinnati	OH	45204	**800-949-4228**	513-244-8100
Claremont School of Theology	1325 N College Ave	Claremont	CA	91711	**800-733-5181**	909-447-2500
Colgate Rochester Crozer Divinity School	1100 S Goodman St	Rochester	NY	14620	**888-937-3732**	585-271-1320
Columbia International University	7435 Monticello Rd	Columbia	SC	29203	**800-777-2227**	803-754-4100
Columbia Theological Seminary	701 S Columbia Dr	Decatur	GA	30030	**888-601-8916**	404-378-8821
Concordia Seminary	801 Seminary Pl	Saint Louis	MO	63105	**800-822-9545**	314-505-7000
Concordia Theological Seminary	6600 N Clinton St	Fort Wayne	IN	46825	**800-481-2155**	260-452-2100
Cornerstone University	1001 E Beltline Ave NE *Admissions	Grand Rapids	MI	49525	**800-787-9778***	616-222-1426
Dallas Theological Seminary	3909 Swiss Ave	Dallas	TX	75204	**800-992-0998**	800-387-9673
Denver Seminary	6399 S Santa Fe Dr	Littleton	CO	80120	**800-922-3040**	303-761-2482
Dominican School of Philosophy & Theology	2301 Vine St	Berkeley	CA	94708	**888-450-3778**	510-849-2030
Duke University Divinity School	407 Chapel Drive PO Box 90968	Durham	NC	27708	**800-367-3853**	919-660-3400
Earlham School of Religion	228 College Ave	Richmond	IN	47374	**800-432-1377**	765-983-1423
Eastern Mennonite University	1200 Pk Rd *Admissions	Harrisonburg	VA	22802	**800-368-2665***	540-432-4118
Eden Theological Seminary	475 E Lockwood Ave	Saint Louis	MO	63119	**800-969-3627**	314-961-3627
Episcopal Divinity School	99 Brattle St	Cambridge	MA	02138	**866-333-8742**	617-868-3450
Episcopal Theological Seminary of the Southwest (SSW)	501 E 32nd PO Box 2247	Austin	TX	78705	**800-252-5400**	512-472-4133
Erskine Theological Seminary	2 Washington St PO Box 338	Due West	SC	29639	**888-359-4358**	864-379-8885
Evangelical School of Theology	121 S College St	Myerstown	PA	17067	**800-532-5775**	717-866-5775
Franciscan School of Theology	1712 Euclid Ave	Berkeley	CA	94709	**855-355-1550**	760-547-1800
Fuller Theological Seminary	135 N Oakland Ave	Pasadena	CA	91182	**800-235-2222**	626-584-5200
General Theological Seminary	440 W 21st St	New York	NY	10011	**888-487-5649**	212-243-5150
George Fox Evangelical Seminary	12753 SW 68th Ave	Portland	OR	97223	**800-493-4937**	503-554-6150
Golden Gate Baptist Theological Seminary	201 Seminary Dr	Mill Valley	CA	94941	**888-442-8701**	415-380-1300
Gordon-Conwell Theological Seminary	130 Essex St	South Hamilton	MA	01982	**800-428-7329**	978-468-7111
Grace Theological Seminary	200 Seminary Dr	Winona Lake	IN	46590	**800-544-7223**	574-372-5100
Graduate Theological Union	2400 Ridge Rd	Berkeley	CA	94709	**800-826-4488**	510-649-2400
Harding University Graduate School of Religion	915 E Market Ave	Searcy	AR	72143	**800-477-4407**	501-279-4407
Hartford Seminary	77 Sherman St	Hartford	CT	06105	**877-860-2255**	860-509-9500
Howard University School of Divinity	1400 Shepherd St NE	Washington	DC	20017	**800-822-6363**	202-806-0500
Iliff School of Theology	2201 S University Blvd	Denver	CO	80210	**800-678-3360**	303-744-1287
Interdenominational Theological Ctr	700 Martin Luther King Jr Dr	Atlanta	GA	30314	**800-908-9946**	404-527-7700
Jesuit School of Theology at Berkeley	1735 LeRoy Ave	Berkeley	CA	94709	**800-824-0122**	510-549-5000
La Sierra University	4500 Riverwalk Pkwy	Riverside	CA	92515	**800-874-5587**	951-785-2000
Lancaster Theological Seminary	555 W James St	Lancaster	PA	17603	**800-393-0654**	717-393-0654
Lexington Theological Seminary	631 S Limestone St	Lexington	KY	40508	**866-296-6087**	859-252-0361
Lincoln Christian College Seminary	100 Campus View Dr	Lincoln	IL	62656	**888-522-5228**	217-732-3168
Lipscomb University	3901 Granny White Pk	Nashville	TN	37204	**800-333-4358**	615-966-1000
Louisville Presbyterian Theological Seminary	1044 Alta Vista Rd	Louisville	KY	40205	**800-264-1839**	502-895-3411
Luther Seminary	2481 Como Ave	Saint Paul	MN	55108	**800-588-4373**	651-641-3456
Lutheran School of Theology at Chicago	1100 E 55th St	Chicago	IL	60615	**800-635-1116**	773-256-0700
Lutheran Theological Seminary at Gettysburg	61 Seminary Ridge	Gettysburg	PA	17325	**800-658-8437**	717-334-6286
Lutheran Theological Seminary at Philadelphia	7301 Germantown Ave	Philadelphia	PA	19119	**800-286-4616**	215-248-4616
McCormick Theological Seminary	5460 S University Ave	Chicago	IL	60615	**800-228-4687**	773-947-6300
Meadville Lombard Theological School	5701 S Woodlawn Ave	Chicago	IL	60637	**800-848-0979**	773-256-3000
Mennonite Brethren Biblical Seminary	4824 E Butler Ave	Fresno	CA	93727	**800-251-6227**	559-453-2000
Methodist Theological School in Ohio	3081 Columbus Pk	Delaware	OH	43015	**800-333-6876**	740-363-1146
Michigan Theological Seminary	41550 E Ann Arbor Trail	Plymouth	MI	48170	**800-356-6639**	734-207-9581
Mid-America Reformed Seminary	229 Seminary Dr	Dyer	IN	46311	**888-440-6277**	219-864-2400
Midwestern Baptist Theological Seminary	5001 N Oak Trafficway	Kansas City	MO	64118	**800-944-6287**	816-414-3700
Moravian Theological Seminary	1200 Main St	Bethlehem	PA	18018	**800-843-6541**	610-861-1516
Mount Angel Seminary	1 Abbey Dr	Saint Benedict	OR	97373	**800-845-8272**	503-845-3951
Mount Saint Mary's University	16300 Old Emmitsburg Rd *Admissions	Emmitsburg	MD	21727	**800-448-4347***	301-447-5214
Multnomah University	8435 NE Glisan St	Portland	OR	97220	**800-275-4672**	503-255-0332
Nazarene Theological Seminary	1700 E Meyer Blvd	Kansas City	MO	64131	**800-831-3011**	816-333-6254
New Brunswick Theological Seminary	35 Seminary Pl	New Brunswick	NJ	08901	**800-445-6287**	732-247-5241
New Orleans Baptist Theological Seminary	3939 Gentilly Blvd	New Orleans	LA	70126	**800-662-8701**	504-282-4455
Newman Theological College (NTC)	10012-84 St	Edmonton	AB	T6A0B2	**844-392-2450**	780-392-2450
North Park Theological Seminary	3225 W Foster Ave	Chicago	IL	60625	**800-964-0101**	773-244-6210
NYACK	350 N Highland Ave	Nyack	NY	10960	**800-541-6891**	845-353-2020
Oakland City University	138 N Lucretia St	Oakland City	IN	47660	**800-737-5125**	812-749-4781
Oral Roberts University	7777 S Lewis Ave	Tulsa	OK	74171	**800-678-8876**	918-495-6161
Pacific Lutheran Theological Seminary	2770 Marin Ave	Berkeley	CA	94708	**800-235-7587**	510-524-5264
Pacific School of Religion	1798 Scenic Ave	Berkeley	CA	94709	**800-999-0528**	510-848-0528
Palmer Theological Seminary	588 N Gulph Rd	King Of Prussia	PA	19406	**800-220-3287**	610-896-5000
Payne Theological Seminary	1230 Wilberforce Clifton Rd	Wilberforce	OH	45384	**888-816-8933**	937-376-2946
Pentecostal Theological Seminary	900 Walker St NE	Cleveland	TN	37311	**800-228-9126**	423-478-1131
Phillips Theological Seminary	901 N Mingo Rd	Tulsa	OK	74116	**800-843-4675**	918-610-8303
Phoenix Seminary	4222 E Thomas Rd Ste 400	Phoenix	AZ	85018	**888-443-1020**	602-850-8000
Pittsburgh Theological Seminary	616 N Highland Ave	Pittsburgh	PA	15206	**800-451-4194**	412-362-5610
Pontifical College Josephinum	7625 N High St	Columbus	OH	43235	**888-252-5812**	614-885-5585
Princeton Theological Seminary	64 Mercer St	Princeton	NJ	08540	**800-622-6767**	609-921-8300
Protestant Episcopal Theological Seminary in Virginia	3737 Seminary Rd	Alexandria	VA	22304	**800-941-0083**	703-370-6600
Providence College & Seminary	10 College Crescent	Otterburne	MB	R0A1G0	**800-668-7768**	204-433-7488
Queen's College Faculty of Theology	210 Prince Philip Dr Ste 3000	Saint John's	NL	A1B3R6	**877-753-0116**	709-753-0116
Reformed Theological Seminary	5422 Clinton Blvd	Jackson	MS	39209	**800-543-2703**	601-923-1600
Regent College	5800 University Blvd	Vancouver	BC	V6T2E4	**800-663-8664**	604-224-3245
Roberts Wesleyan College	2301 Westside Dr *Admissions	Rochester	NY	14624	**800-777-4792***	585-594-6000
Saint Paul School of Theology	4370 W 109th St Ste 300	Overland Park	KS	66211	**800-825-0378**	
Saint Peter's Seminary	1040 Waterloo St N	London	ON	N6A3Y1	**888-548-9649**	519-432-1824
Samford University	800 Lakeshore Dr *Admissions	Birmingham	AL	35229	**800-888-7218***	205-726-3673
San Francisco Theological Seminary	105 Seminary Rd	San Anselmo	CA	94960	**800-447-8820**	415-451-2800
Seton Hall University Immaculate Conception Seminary	400 S Orange Ave	South Orange	NJ	07079	**800-843-4255**	973-761-9575
Shaw University	118 E S St *Admissions	Raleigh	NC	27601	**800-214-6683***	919-546-8275
Sioux Falls Seminary	2100 S Summit	Sioux Falls	SD	57105	**800-440-6227**	605-336-6588
Southeastern Baptist Theological Seminary	120 S Wingate St	Wake Forest	NC	27587	**800-284-6317**	919-556-3101
Southern Baptist Theological Seminary	2825 Lexington Rd	Louisville	KY	40280	**800-626-5525**	502-897-4011

	City	State	Zip	Toll-Free	Phone
Southwestern Baptist Theological Seminary PO Box 22740	Fort Worth	TX	76122	**877-467-9287**	817-923-1921
Starr King School for the Ministry 2441 LeConte Ave	Berkeley	CA	94709	**866-727-4894**	510-845-6232
Taylor University College & Seminary 11525 23rd Ave	Edmonton	AB	T6J4T3	**800-567-4988**	780-431-5200
Trinity Episcopal School for Ministry 311 11th St	Ambridge	PA	15003	**800-874-8754**	724-266-3838
Trinity International University 2065 Half Day Rd	Deerfield	IL	60015	**800-822-3225**	847-945-8800
Trinity Lutheran Seminary 2199 E Main St	Columbus	OH	43209	**866-610-8571**	614-235-4136
Trinity Western University 7600 Glover Rd	Langley	BC	V2Y1Y1	**888-468-6898**	604-888-7511
Tyndale University College & Seminary 25 Ballyconnor Ct	Toronto	ON	M2M4B3	**877-896-3253**	416-226-6380
Union Theological Seminary 3041 Broadway	New York	NY	10027	**800-251-9489**	212-662-7100
Union Theological Seminary & Presbyterian School of Christian Education 3401 Brook Rd	Richmond	VA	23227	**800-229-2990**	804-355-0671
United Theological Seminary of the Twin Cities 3000 Fifth St NW	New Brighton	MN	55112	**800-937-1316**	651-633-4311
University of Dubuque Theological Seminary 2000 University Ave	Dubuque	IA	52001	**800-369-8387**	563-589-3122
University of Saskatchewan 1121 College Dr	Saskatoon	SK	S7N0W3	**877-653-8501**	306-966-8970
University of the South 735 University Ave	Sewanee	TN	37383	**800-522-2234**	931-598-1238
Vancouver School of Theology 6040 Iona Dr	Vancouver	BC	V6T2E8	**866-822-9031**	604-822-9031
Virginia Union University 1500 N Lombardy St	Richmond	VA	23220	**800-368-3227**	804-342-3570
Wartburg Theological Seminary 333 Wartburg Pl	Dubuque	IA	52003	**800-225-5987**	563-589-0200
Wesley Theological Seminary 4500 Massachusetts Ave NW	Washington	DC	20016	**800-882-4987**	202-885-8600
Western Seminary 5511 SE Hawthorne Blvd	Portland	OR	97215	**877-517-1800**	503-517-1800
Western Theological Seminary 101 E 13th St	Holland	MI	49423	**800-392-8554**	616-392-8555
Westminster Theological Seminary 2960 Church Rd	Glenside	PA	19038	**800-373-0119**	215-887-5511
Westminster Theological Seminary in California 1725 Bear Vly Pkwy	Escondido	CA	92027	**888-480-8474**	760-480-8474
Winebrenner Theological Seminary 950 N Main St	Findlay	OH	45840	**800-992-4987**	419-434-4200
Yale Divinity School Admissions Office 409 Prospect St	New Haven	CT	06511	**866-358-3806**	203-432-5360

169 COLLEGES & UNIVERSITIES - HISTORICALLY BLACK

Historically Black Colleges & Universities (HBCUs) are colleges or universities that were established before 1964 with the intention of serving the African-American community. (Prior to 1964, African-Americans were almost always excluded from higher education opportunities at the predominantly white colleges and universities.)

	City	State	Zip	Toll-Free	Phone
Allen University 1530 Harden St	Columbia	SC	29204	**877-625-5368**	803-376-5700
Benedict College 1600 Harden St	Columbia	SC	29204	**800-868-6598**	803-253-5000
Bennett College 900 E Washington St *Admissions	Greensboro	NC	27401	**800-413-5323***	336-370-8624
Bethune-Cookman College 640 Dr Mary McLeod Bethune Blvd *Admissions	Daytona Beach	FL	32114	**800-448-0228***	386-481-2900
Bluefield State College 219 Rock St	Bluefield	WV	24701	**800-654-7798**	304-327-4000
Bowie State University 14000 Jericho Pk Rd	Bowie	MD	20715	**877-772-6943**	301-860-4000
Central State University 1400 Brush Row Rd PO Box 1004	Wilberforce	OH	45384	**800-388-2781**	937-376-6011
Cheyney University of Pennsylvania 1837 University Cir PO Box 200	Cheyney	PA	19319	**800-243-9639**	610-399-2275
Claflin University 400 Magnolia St	Orangeburg	SC	29115	**800-922-1276**	803-535-5000
Clark Atlanta University 223 James P Brawley Dr SW *Admissions	Atlanta	GA	30314	**800-688-3228***	404-880-8000
Clinton Junior College 1029 Crawford Rd	Rock Hill	SC	29730	**877-837-9645**	803-327-7402
Coppin State University 2500 W N Ave *Admissions	Baltimore	MD	21216	**800-635-3674***	410-951-3600
Delaware State University 1200 N DuPont Hwy *Admissions	Dover	DE	19901	**800-845-2544***	302-857-6351
Elizabeth City State University 1704 Weeksville Rd *Admissions	Elizabeth City	NC	27909	**800-347-3278***	252-335-3400
Fayetteville State University 1200 Murchison Rd *Admissions	Fayetteville	NC	28301	**800-222-2594***	910-672-1371
Fisk University 1000 17th Ave N	Nashville	TN	37208	**888-702-0022**	615-329-8500
Florida A & M University 1700 Lee Hall Dr Rm G-7 Foote-Hilyer Administration Ctr	Tallahassee	FL	32307	**866-642-1198**	850-599-3000
Florida Memorial University 15800 NW 42nd Ave	Miami Gardens	FL	33054	**800-822-1362**	305-626-3600
Fort Valley State University 1005 State University Dr	Fort Valley	GA	31030	**877-462-3878**	478-825-6211
Grambling State University 403 Main St	Grambling	LA	71245	**800-569-4714**	318-247-3811
Hampton University 100 E Queen St	Hampton	VA	23668	**800-624-3341**	757-727-5000
Hinds Community College 501 E Main St PO Box 1100	Raymond	MS	39154	**800-446-3722**	601-857-5261
Howard University 2400 Sixth St NW	Washington	DC	20059	**800-822-6363**	202-806-6100
Huston-Tillotson University 900 Chicon St	Austin	TX	78702	**877-487-8702**	512-505-3000
Interdenominational Theological Ctr 700 Martin Luther King Jr Dr	Atlanta	GA	30314	**800-908-9946**	404-527-7700
Jackson State University 1400 John R Lynch St	Jackson	MS	39217	**800-848-6817**	601-979-2121
Johnson C Smith University 100 Beatties Ford Rd *Admissions	Charlotte	NC	28216	**800-782-7303***	704-378-1000
Kentucky State University 400 E Main St *Admissions	Frankfort	KY	40601	**800-325-1716***	502-597-6000
Lane College 545 Ln Ave *Admissions	Jackson	TN	38301	**800-960-7533***	731-426-7500
Langston University 2013 Langston University PO Box 1500	Langston	OK	73050	**877-466-2231**	
Lincoln University 820 Chestnut St B-7 Young Hall *Admissions	Jefferson City	MO	65102	**800-521-5052***	573-681-5599
Livingstone College 701 W Monroe St	Salisbury	NC	28144	**800-835-3435**	704-216-6963
Miles College 5500 Myron Massey Blvd *Admissions	Fairfield	AL	35064	**800-445-0708***	205-929-1000
Mississippi Valley State University 14000 Hwy 82	Itta Bena	MS	38941	**800-844-6885**	662-254-9041
Morgan State University 1700 E Cold Spring Ln	Baltimore	MD	21251	**800-319-4678**	443-885-3333
Morris College 100 W College St *Admissions	Sumter	SC	29150	**866-853-1345***	803-934-3200
Norfolk State University 700 Pk Ave	Norfolk	VA	23504	**800-274-1821**	757-823-8600
North Carolina A & T State University 1601 E Market St *Admissions	Greensboro	NC	27411	**800-443-8964***	336-334-7946
North Carolina Central University 1801 Fayetteville St *Admissions	Durham	NC	27707	**877-667-7533***	919-530-6100
Oakwood College 7000 Adventist Blvd	Huntsville	AL	35896	**800-824-5312**	256-726-7356
Paine College 1235 15th St	Augusta	GA	30901	**800-476-7703**	706-821-8200
Paul Quinn College 3837 Simpson Stuart Rd	Dallas	TX	75241	**800-433-3243**	214-376-1000
Prairie View A & M University PO Box 519	Prairie View	TX	77446	**877-241-1752**	936-857-2626
Rust College 150 Rust Ave	Holly Springs	MS	38635	**888-886-8492**	662-252-8000
Saint Augustine's College 1315 Oakwood Ave *Admissions	Raleigh	NC	27610	**800-948-1126***	919-516-4016
Shaw University 118 E S St *Admissions	Raleigh	NC	27601	**800-214-6683***	919-546-8275
Shelton State Community College 9500 Old Greensboro Rd	Tuscaloosa	AL	35405	**877-211-7722**	205-391-2211
South Carolina State University 300 College St NE PO Box 7127 *Admissions	Orangeburg	SC	29117	**800-260-5956***	803-536-7000
Southern University & A & M College 156 Elton C Harrison Dr PO Box 9757 *Admissions	Baton Rouge	LA	70813	**800-256-1531***	225-771-5180
Southwestern Christian College PO Box 10	Terrell	TX	75160	**800-925-9357**	972-524-3341
Spelman College 350 Spelman Ln SW *Admissions	Atlanta	GA	30314	**800-982-2411***	404-681-3643
Stillman College 3601 Stillman Blvd	Tuscaloosa	AL	35401	**800-841-5722**	205-349-4240
Tennessee State University 3500 John A Merritt Blvd PO Box 9609 *Admissions	Nashville	TN	37209	**888-463-6878***	615-963-5000
Texas College 2404 N Grand Ave	Tyler	TX	75702	**800-306-6299**	903-593-8311
Texas Southern University 3100 Cleburne St	Houston	TX	77004	**800-252-5400**	713-313-7011
Tougaloo College 500 W County Line Rd *Admissions	Tougaloo	MS	39174	**888-424-2566***	601-977-7700
Trenholm State Technical College 1225 Air Base Blvd	Montgomery	AL	36108	**800-917-2081**	334-420-4200
Tuskegee University 1200 W Montgomery Rd *Admissions	Tuskegee	AL	36088	**800-622-6531***	334-727-8011
Virginia State University 1 Hayden Dr *Admissions	Petersburg	VA	23806	**800-871-7611***	804-524-5000
Virginia Union University 1500 N Lombardy St	Richmond	VA	23220	**800-368-3227**	804-342-3570
Voorhees College 213 Wiggins Dr PO Box 678 *Admissions	Denmark	SC	29042	**800-446-6250***	803-780-1234
West Virginia State University 117 Ferrell Hall PO Box 368	Institute	WV	25112	**800-987-2112**	304-766-3000
Wilberforce University 1055 N Bickett Rd PO Box 1001 *Admissions	Wilberforce	OH	45384	**800-367-8568***	937-376-2911
Wiley College 711 Wiley Ave *Admissions	Marshall	TX	75670	**800-658-6889***	903-927-3300

	City	State	Zip	Toll-Free	Phone
Winston-Salem State University 601 S ML King Jr Dr					
206 Thompson Ctr	Winston-Salem	NC	27110	**800-257-4052***	336-750-2000
*Admissions					

170 COLLEGES & UNIVERSITIES - JESUIT

The institutions listed here are members of the Association of Jesuit Colleges & Universities.

	City	State	Zip	Toll-Free	Phone
Boston College 140 Commonwealth Ave	Chestnut Hill	MA	02467	**800-360-2522**	617-552-3100
Canisius College 2001 Main St	Buffalo	NY	14208	**800-843-1517**	716-888-2200
College of the Holy Cross 1 College St	Worcester	MA	01610	**800-442-2421**	508-793-2011
Creighton University 2500 California Plz	Omaha	NE	68178	**800-282-5835**	402-280-2700
Fordham University 441 E Fordham Rd	Bronx	NY	10458	**800-367-3426**	718-817-3240
College at Lincoln Ctr 113 W 60th St	New York	NY	10023	**800-367-3426**	212-636-6710
Gonzaga University 502 E Boone Ave	Spokane	WA	99258	**800-986-9585**	509-323-6572
John Carroll University 20700 N Pk Blvd	Cleveland	OH	44118	**888-335-6800**	216-397-1886
Le Moyne College 1419 Salt Springs Rd	Syracuse	NY	13214	**800-333-4733***	315-445-4100
*Admissions					
Loyola College 4501 N Charles St	Baltimore	MD	21210	**800-221-9107**	410-617-5012
Loyola Marymount University 1 LMU Dr	Los Angeles	CA	90045	**800-568-4636**	310-338-2700
Loyola University *New Orleans* 6363 St Charles Ave	New Orleans	LA	70118	**800-456-9652***	504-865-3240
*Admissions					
Loyola University Chicago *Lake Shore* 6525 N Sheridan Rd	Chicago	IL	60626	**800-262-2373**	773-508-3075
Water Tower 820 N Michigan Ave	Chicago	IL	60611	**800-262-2373***	312-915-6500
*Admissions					
Marquette University 1217 W Wisconsin Ave	Milwaukee	WI	53233	**800-222-6544***	414-288-7302
*Admissions					
Regis University 3333 Regis Blvd	Denver	CO	80221	**800-388-2366***	303-458-4100
*Admissions					
Rockhurst University 1100 Rockhurst Rd	Kansas City	MO	64110	**800-842-6776**	816-501-4000
Saint Joseph's University 5600 City Ave	Philadelphia	PA	19131	**888-232-4295**	610-660-1000
Saint Louis University 221 N Grand Blvd	Saint Louis	MO	63103	**800-758-3678**	314-977-7288
Seattle University 901 12th Ave	Seattle	WA	98122	**800-426-7123**	206-296-6000
Spring Hill College 4000 Dauphin St	Mobile	AL	36608	**800-742-6704***	251-380-4000
*Admissions					
University of Detroit Mercy 4001 W McNichols Rd	Detroit	MI	48221	**800-635-5020***	313-993-1000
*Admissions					
University of San Francisco 2130 Fulton St	San Francisco	CA	94117	**800-854-1385***	415-422-5555
*Admissions					
University of Scranton 800 Linden St St Thomas Hall	Scranton	PA	18510	**888-727-2686**	570-941-7400
Wheeling Jesuit University 316 Washington Ave	Wheeling	WV	26003	**800-624-6992**	304-243-2000
Xavier University 3800 Victory Pkwy	Cincinnati	OH	45207	**800-344-4698**	513-745-3000

171 COMMODITY CONTRACTS BROKERS & DEALERS

SEE ALSO Securities Brokers & Dealers ; Investment Advice & Management

	City	State	Zip	Toll-Free	Phone
Basic Commodities Inc 863 S Orlando Ave	Winter Park	FL	32789	**800-338-7006**	407-629-2000
GFI Group Inc 55 Water St	New York	NY	10041	**888-750-5884**	212-968-4100
NYSE: GFIG					
Keeley Investment Corp 401 S La Salle St Ste 1201	Chicago	IL	60605	**800-533-5344**	312-786-5000
Koch Mineral Services LLC 4111 E 37th St N	Wichita	KS	67220	**800-750-5834**	316-828-5500
OptionsXpress Inc 311 W Monroe Ste 1000	Chicago	IL	60606	**888-280-8020**	312-630-3300
RJ O'Brien & Assoc 222 S Riverside Plz Ste 900	Chicago	IL	60606	**866-438-7564**	312-373-5000
Zaner Group LLC 150 S Wacker Dr Ste 2350	Chicago	IL	60606	**800-621-1414**	312-277-0050

172 COMMUNICATIONS TOWER OPERATORS

SEE ALSO Communications Lines & Towers Construction

Listed here are companies that own, operate, lease, maintain, and/or manage towers used by telecommunications services and radio broadcast companies, including free-standing towers as well as antenna systems mounted on monopoles or rooftops. Many of these companies also build their communications towers, but companies that only do the building are classified as heavy construction contractors.

	City	State	Zip	Toll-Free	Phone
American Tower Corp 116 Huntington Ave 11th Fl	Boston	MA	02116	**877-282-7483**	617-375-7500
NYSE: AMT					
Crown Castle International Corp 1220 Augusta Dr Ste 500	Houston	TX	77057	**877-486-9377**	713-570-3000
NYSE: CCI					
Crown Castle USA Inc 2000 Corporate Dr	Canonsburg	PA	15317	**877-486-9377**	724-416-2000
LTS Wireless Inc 311 S LHS Dr	Lumberton	TX	77657	**800-255-5471**	409-755-4038
SBA Communications Corp 5900 Broken Sound Pkwy NW	Boca Raton	FL	33487	**800-487-7483**	561-995-7670
NASDAQ: SBAC					
Tower Innovations 3266 Tower Dr	Newburgh	IN	47630	**800-664-8222**	812-853-0595

173 COMMUNITIES - ONLINE

SEE ALSO Internet Service Providers (ISPs)

	City	State	Zip	Toll-Free	Phone
Beliefnet Inc 999 Waterside Dr Ste 1900	Norfolk	VA	23150	**800-311-2458**	
Lawyers.com Martindale-Hubbell 121 Chanlon Rd	New Providence	NJ	07974	**800-526-4902**	908-464-6800
Sensitech Inc 800 Cummings Ctr Ste 258x	Beverly	MA	01915	**800-843-8367**	978-927-7033
SHRM Global Forum 1800 Duke St	Alexandria	VA	22314	**800-283-7476**	703-548-3440

COMPRESSORS - AIR CONDITIONING & REFRIGERATION

SEE Air Conditioning & Heating Equipment - Commercial/Industrial

174 COMPRESSORS - AIR & GAS

	City	State	Zip	Toll-Free	Phone
Brabazon Pumps & Compressor 2484 Century Rd	Green Bay	WI	54303	**800-825-3222**	920-498-6020
Cameron Turbocompressor 3101 Broadway	Buffalo	NY	14225	**877-805-7911**	716-896-6603
Compressed Air Systems Inc 9303 Stannum St	Tampa	FL	33619	**800-626-8177**	813-626-8177
Compressor Engineering Corp (CECO) 5440 Alder Dr	Houston	TX	77081	**800-879-2326**	713-664-7333
Corken Inc 3805 NW 36th St	Oklahoma City	OK	73112	**800-631-4929**	405-946-5576
Curtis-Toledo Inc 1905 Kienlen Ave	Saint Louis	MO	63133	**800-925-5431**	314-383-1300
Elliott Group 901 N Fourth St	Jeannette	PA	15644	**800-635-2208**	724-527-2811
Federal Equipment Co 5298 River Rd	Cincinnati	OH	45233	**877-435-4723**	513-621-5260
Fountainhead Group Inc 23 Garden St	New York Mills	NY	13417	**800-311-9903**	315-736-0037
Gardner Denver Nash 1800 Gardner Expy	Quincy	IL	62305	**800-637-5729**	217-222-5400
Gas Technology Energy Concepts LLC 401 William L Gaiter Pkwy Ste 4	Buffalo	NY	14215	**800-451-8294**	
Guardair Corp 47 Veterans Dr	Chicopee	MA	01022	**800-482-7324**	413-594-4400
Ingersoll Rand Air Solutions Group 800-D Beaty St	Davidson	NC	28036	**800-866-5457**	
Manchester Tank 1000 Corp Centre Dr Ste 300	Franklin	TN	37067	**800-399-5628**	615-370-6300
Master Mfg Co 747 N Yale Ave	Villa Park	IL	60181	**800-864-1649**	630-833-7060
Mattson Spray Equipment 230 W Coleman St	Rice Lake	WI	54868	**800-877-4857**	715-234-1617
Norwalk Compressor Co 1650 Stratford Ave	Stratford	CT	06615	**800-556-5001**	203-386-1234
Saylor Beall Mfg Company Inc 400 N Kibbee St	Saint Johns	MI	48879	**800-248-9001**	989-224-2371
Scales Air Compressor Corp 110 Voice Rd	Carle Place	NY	11514	**877-798-0454**	516-248-9096
Spencer Turbine Co 600 Day Hill Rd	Windsor	CT	06095	**800-232-4321**	860-688-8361
Sullivan-Palatek Inc 1201 W US Hwy 20	Michigan City	IN	46360	**800-438-6203**	219-874-2497
Sulzer Metco US Inc 1101 Prospect Ave	Westbury	NY	11590	**877-280-2342**	516-334-1300
Thermionics Laboratory 1842 Sabre St	Hayward	CA	94545	**800-962-2310**	510-538-3304
Tuthill Vacuum Systems 4840 W Kearney St	Springfield	MO	65803	**800-634-2695**	417-865-8715
Wagner Spray Tech Corp 1770 Fernbrook Ln	Plymouth	MN	55447	**800-328-8251**	763-553-7000
Zeks Compressed Air Solutions 1302 Goshen Pkwy	West Chester	PA	19380	**800-888-2323**	610-692-9100

175 COMPUTER EQUIPMENT

SEE ALSO Modems ; Business Machines - Mfr ; Calculators - Electronic ; Computer Networking Products & Systems ; Flash Memory Devices ; Point-of-Sale (POS) & Point-of-Information (POI) Systems ; Automatic Teller Machines (ATMs)

COMPUTER & INTERNET TRAINING PROGRAMS

SEE Training & Certification Programs - Computer & Internet

175-1 Computers

	City	State	Zip	Toll-Free	Phone
Aberdeen LLC 9130 Norwalk Blvd	Santa Fe Springs	CA	90670	**800-500-9526**	562-699-6998

Company / Address	City	State	Zip	Toll-Free	Phone
Acer America Corp 333 W San Carlos St Ste 1500	San Jose	CA	95110	**800-103-3311**	408-533-7700
ACMA Computers Inc 1565 Reliance Way *Sales	Fremont	CA	94539	**800-800-6328***	510-651-8886
Amax Engineering Corp 1565 Reliance Way *Cust Svc	Fremont	CA	94539	**800-889-2629***	510-651-8886
Apple Inc 1 Infinite Loop *NASDAQ: AAPL* ■ *Cust Svc	Cupertino	CA	95014	**800-275-2273***	408-996-1010
Azul Systems Inc 1600 Plymouth St	Mountain View	CA	94043	**800-258-4199**	650-230-6500
Bytespeed LLC 3131 24th Ave S	Moorhead	MN	56560	**877-553-0777**	218-227-0445
Chem USA Corp 38507 Cherry St	Newark	CA	94560	**800-866-2436**	510-608-8818
Comark Corp 93 W St	Medfield	MA	02052	**800-280-8522**	508-359-8161
CSP Inc 43 Manning Rd *NASDAQ: CSPI*	Billerica	MA	01821	**800-325-3110**	978-663-7598
CSS Laboratories Inc 1641 McGaw Ave	Irvine	CA	92614	**800-852-2680**	949-852-8161
Datalux Corp 155 Aviation Dr	Winchester	VA	22602	**800-328-2589**	540-662-1500
Dedicated Computing N26 W23880 Commerce Cir	Waukesha	WI	53188	**877-523-3301**	262-951-7200
Dell Inc 1 Dell Way *NASDAQ: DELL*	Round Rock	TX	78682	**800-879-3355**	512-338-4400
Drive Thru Technology Inc 1755 N Main St	Los Angeles	CA	90031	**800-933-8388**	323-576-1400
Ectaco Inc 31-21 31st St	Long Island	NY	11106	**800-710-7920**	718-728-6110
Electrovaya Inc 2645 Royal Windsor Dr *TSE: EFL*	Mississauga	ON	L5J1K9	**800-388-2865**	905-855-4610
Equus Computer Systems Inc 5801 Clearwater Dr	Minnetonka	MN	55343	**866-378-8727**	612-617-6200
Fujitsu America Inc 1250 E Arques Ave	Sunnyvale	CA	94085	**800-538-8460**	408-746-6200
Gateway Inc 7565 Irvine Ctr Dr	Irvine	CA	92618	**800-846-2000**	949-471-7040
Hewlett-Packard (Canada) Ltd (HP) 5150 Spectrum Way	Mississauga	ON	L4W5G1	**888-447-4636**	905-206-4725
Hewlett-Packard Co 3000 Hanover St *NYSE: HPQ* ■ *Sales	Palo Alto	CA	94304	**800-752-0900***	650-857-1501
International Business Machines Corp (IBM) 1 New OrchaRd Rd *NYSE: IBM*	Armonk	NY	10504	**800-426-4968**	914-499-1900
Kontron Mobile Computing Inc 7631 Anagram Dr	Eden Prairie	MN	55344	**888-343-5396**	952-974-7000
LXE Inc 125 Technology Pkwy	Norcross	GA	30092	**800-664-4593**	770-447-4224
MaxVision Corp 495 Production Ave	Madison	AL	35758	**800-533-5805**	256-772-3058
Micro Electronics, Inc. 2701 Charter St Ste A	Columbus	OH	43228	**877-636-9793**	614-326-8500
Micro Express Inc 8 Hammond Dr Ste 105	Irvine	CA	92618	**800-989-9900**	949-460-9911
Panasonic Corporation of North America 2 Riverfront Plaza	Newark	NJ	07102	**888-223-1012**	
Pinnacle Data Systems Inc 6600 Port Rd Ste 100	Groveport	OH	43125	**800-882-8282**	614-748-1150
Quantum3D Inc 5225 Hellyer Ave Ste 220	Milpitas	CA	95138	**888-747-1020**	408-600-2500
Sharp Electronics Corp 1 Sharp Plz	Mahwah	NJ	07430	**800-237-4277**	201-529-8200
Sony Electronics Inc 1 Sony Dr *Cust Svc	Park Ridge	NJ	07656	**800-222-7669***	201-930-1000
Stealth Computer Corp 530 Rowntree Dairy Rd Bldg 4	Woodbridge	ON	L4L8H2	**888-783-2584**	905-264-9000
Superchips Inc 1790 E Airport Blvd	Sanford	FL	32773	**888-227-2447**	407-585-7000
Tangent Inc 191 Airport Blvd	Burlingame	CA	94010	**800-342-9388**	650-342-9388
Technology Advancement Group Inc 22355 Tag Way	Sterling	VA	20166	**800-824-7693**	703-406-3000
Toshiba America Inc 1251 Ave of the Americas Ste 4100	New York	NY	10020	**800-457-7777**	212-596-0600
Toshiba America Information Systems Inc 9740 Irvine Blvd *Cust Svc	Irvine	CA	92618	**800-457-7777***	949-583-3000
Transource Computers Corp 2405 W Utopia Rd	Phoenix	AZ	85027	**800-486-3715**	623-879-8882
Twinhead Corp 48303 Fremont Blvd *Sales	Fremont	CA	94538	**800-995-8946***	
Versalogic Corp 4211 W 11th Ave	Eugene	OR	97402	**800-824-3163**	541-485-8575
WYSE Technology Inc 3471 N First St	San Jose	CA	95134	**800-800-9973**	408-473-1200

175-2 Computer Input Devices

Company / Address	City	State	Zip	Toll-Free	Phone
3M Touch Systems 501 Griffin Brook Dr	Methuen	MA	01844	**866-407-6666**	978-659-9000
Aten Technology Inc 23 Hubble	Irvine	CA	92618	**888-999-2836**	949-428-1111
Cirque Corp 2463 South 3850 West	Salt Lake City	UT	84120	**800-454-3375**	801-467-1100
Elo TouchSystems Inc 301 Constitution Dr	Menlo Park	CA	94025	**800-557-1458**	650-361-4700
Esterline Interface Technologies 600 W Wilbur Ave	Coeur d'Alene	ID	83815	**800-444-5923**	208-765-8000
Gyration Inc 3601-B Calle Tecate	Camarillo	CA	93012	**888-340-0033**	
Kensington Computer Products Group 333 Twin Dolphin Dr 6th Fl	Redwood Shores	CA	94065	**800-535-4242**	650-572-2700
Kinesis Corp 22030 20th Ave SE Ste 102	Bothell	WA	98021	**800-454-6374**	425-402-8100
KYE Systems Corp 1301 NW 84th Ave Ste 127	Doral	FL	33126	**800-488-3111**	305-468-9250
Logitech Inc 6505 Kaiser Dr *Sales	Fremont	CA	94555	**800-231-7717***	510-795-8500
Macally USA Mace Group Inc 4601 E Airport Dr	Ontario	CA	91761	**800-644-1132**	909-230-6888
Mad Catz Interactive Inc 7480 Mission Vly Rd Ste 101 *NYSE: MCZ*	San Diego	CA	92108	**800-659-2287**	619-683-9830
Numonics Corp 101 Commerce Dr PO Box 1005	Montgomeryville	PA	18936	**800-523-6716**	215-362-2766
PolyVision Corp 10700 Abbotts Bridge Rd Ste 100	Johns Creek	GA	30097	**888-325-6351**	678-542-3100
SMART Modular Technologies Inc 39870 Eureka Dr *NASDAQ: SMOD*	Newark	CA	94560	**800-956-7627**	510-623-1231
SMART Technologies Inc 3636 Research Rd NW *TSE: SMA*	Calgary	AB	T2L1Y1	**888-427-6278**	403-245-0333
TouchSystems Corp 220 Tradesmen Dr	Hutto	TX	78634	**800-320-5944**	512-846-2424
Wacom Technology Corp 1311 SE Cardinal Ct	Vancouver	WA	98683	**800-922-6613**	360-896-9833

175-3 Modems

Company / Address	City	State	Zip	Toll-Free	Phone
ActionTec Electronics Inc 760 N Mary Ave *Tech Supp	Sunnyvale	CA	94085	**888-436-0657***	408-752-7700
Avocent Corp 4991 Corporate Dr	Huntsville	AL	35805	**866-286-2368**	256-430-4000
Biscom Inc 321 Billerica Rd	Chelmsford	MA	01824	**800-477-2472**	978-250-1800
Canoga Perkins Corp 20600 Prairie St *Tech Supp	Chatsworth	CA	91311	**800-360-6642***	818-718-6300
Cermetek Microelectronics Inc 374 Turquoise St	Milpitas	CA	95035	**800-882-6271**	408-752-5000
Copia International Ltd 1220 Iroquois Dr Ste 180 *Sales	Naperville	IL	60563	**800-689-8898***	630-778-8898
Dataforth Corp 3331 E Hemisphere Loop	Tucson	AZ	85706	**800-444-7644**	520-741-1404
FreeWave Technologies Inc 1880 S Flatiron Ct Ste F *Cust Svc	Boulder	CO	80301	**866-923-6168***	303-444-3862
GRE America Inc 425 Harbor Blvd	Belmont	CA	94002	**800-233-5973**	650-591-1400
Multi-Tech Systems 2205 Woodale Dr *Cust Svc	Mounds View	MN	55112	**800-328-9717***	763-785-3500
Novatel Wireless Inc 9645 Scranton Rd Ste 205 *NASDAQ: NVTL*	San Diego	CA	92121	**888-888-9231**	
Unlimited Systems Corp Inc 9530 Padgett St	San Diego	CA	92126	**800-275-6354**	858-537-5010
US Robotics Corp 1300 E Woodfield Dr Ste 506	Schaumburg	IL	60173	**877-710-0884**	847-874-2000
Western Telematic Inc 5 Sterling	Irvine	CA	92618	**800-854-7226**	949-586-9950
Works Computing Inc 1801 American Blvd E Ste 12	Bloomington	MN	55425	**866-222-4077**	952-746-1580
ZyXEL Communications Inc 1130 N Miller St	Anaheim	CA	92806	**800-255-4101**	714-632-0882

175-4 Monitors & Displays

Company / Address	City	State	Zip	Toll-Free	Phone
Aydin Displays Inc 1 Riga Ln	Birdsboro	PA	19508	**866-367-2934**	610-404-7400
Barco Electronic Systems Pvt Ltd 11101 Trade Ctr Dr	Rancho Cordova	CA	95670	**888-414-7226**	916-859-2500
Conrac Inc 5124 Commerce Dr	Baldwin Park	CA	91706	**800-451-5288**	626-480-0095
Daktronics Inc 201 Daktronics Dr *NASDAQ: DAKT*	Brookings	SD	57006	**800-325-8766**	605-692-0200
Dotronix Inc 160 First St SE	New Brighton	MN	55112	**800-720-7218**	651-633-1742
Eizo Nanao Technologies Inc 5710 Warland Dr	Cypress	CA	90630	**800-800-5202**	562-431-5011
Envision Peripherals Inc (EPI) 47490 Seabridge Dr *Tech Supp	Fremont	CA	94538	**888-838-6388***	510-770-9988
General Digital Corp 8 Nutmeg Rd S	South Windsor	CT	06074	**800-952-2535**	860-282-2900
LG Electronics USA Inc 1000 Sylvan Ave *Tech Supp	Englewood Cliffs	NJ	07632	**800-243-0000***	201-816-2000
NEC Corp of America 10850 Gold Ctr Dr Ste 200	Rancho Cordova	CA	95670	**800-632-4636**	916-463-7000
NEC Display Solutions of America Inc 500 Pk Blvd Ste 1100 *Cust Svc	Itasca	IL	60143	**800-632-4662***	630-467-3000
Pioneer Electronics (USA) Inc 1925 E Dominguez St	Long Beach	CA	90810	**800-421-1404**	310-952-2000
Planar Systems Inc 1195 NW Compton Dr *NASDAQ: PLNR*	Beaverton	OR	97006	**866-475-2627**	503-748-1100
Sharp Electronics Corp 1 Sharp Plz	Mahwah	NJ	07430	**800-237-4277**	201-529-8200

Company	Address	City	State	ZIP	Toll-Free	Phone
Sony Electronics Inc	1 Sony Dr *Cust Svc	Park Ridge	NJ	07656	**800-222-7669***	201-930-1000
Tatung Company of America Inc	2850 El Presidio St	Long Beach	CA	90810	**800-827-2850**	310-637-2105
Trans-Lux Corp	26 Pearl St *OTC: TNLX*	Norwalk	CT	06850	**800-243-5544**	203-853-4321
Trans-Lux Fair-Play Inc	1700 Delaware Ave	Des Moines	IA	50317	**800-247-0265**	515-265-5305
Video Display Corp	1868 Tucker Industrial Rd *NASDAQ: VIDE* ■ *Cust Svc	Tucker	GA	30084	**800-241-5005***	770-938-2080
ViewSonic Corp	381 Brea Canyon Rd	Walnut	CA	91789	**800-888-8583**	909-444-8888
Wells-Gardner Electronics Corp	9500 W 55th St Ste A *NYSE: WGA*	McCook	IL	60525	**800-336-6630**	708-290-2100

175-5 Multimedia Equipment & Supplies

Company	Address	City	State	ZIP	Toll-Free	Phone
Corsair Memory Inc	46221 Landing Pkwy	Fremont	CA	94538	**888-222-4346**	510-657-8747
Creative Labs Inc	1901 McCarthy Blvd *Cust Svc	Milpitas	CA	95035	**800-998-1000***	408-428-6600
Kinyo Company Inc	14235 Lomitas Ave	La Puente	CA	91746	**800-735-4696**	626-333-3711
Matrox Electronic Systems Ltd	1055 St Regis Blvd	Dorval	QC	H9P2T4	**800-361-1408**	514-822-6000
SpeakerCraft Inc	940 Columbia Ave	Riverside	CA	92507	**800-448-0976**	951-787-0543

175-6 Printers

Company	Address	City	State	ZIP	Toll-Free	Phone
AMT Datasouth Corp	803 Camarillo Springs Rd Ste D	Camarillo	CA	93012	**800-215-9192**	805-388-5799
Citizen Systems America Corp	363 Van Ness Way Ste 404	Torrance	CA	90501	**800-421-6516**	310-781-1460
Datamax Corp	4501 Pkwy Commerce Blvd	Orlando	FL	32808	**800-321-2233**	407-578-8007
Digital Design Inc	67 Sand Pk Rd	Cedar Grove	NJ	07009	**800-967-7746**	973-857-0900
Epson America Inc	3840 Kilroy Airport Way	Long Beach	CA	90806	**800-463-7766**	562-981-3840
Hewlett-Packard (Canada) Ltd (HP)	5150 Spectrum Way	Mississauga	ON	L4W5G1	**888-447-4636**	905-206-4725
Hewlett-Packard Co	3000 Hanover St *NYSE: HPQ* ■ *Sales	Palo Alto	CA	94304	**800-752-0900***	650-857-1501
International Business Machines Corp (IBM)	1 New OrchaRd Rd *NYSE: IBM*	Armonk	NY	10504	**800-426-4968**	914-499-1900
Kroy LLC	3830 Kelley Ave *Cust Svc	Cleveland	OH	44114	**888-888-5769***	216-426-5600
Lexmark International Inc	740 W New Cir Rd *NYSE: LXK* ■ *Cust Svc	Lexington	KY	40550	**800-539-6275***	859-232-2000
Mutoh America Inc	2602 S 47th St Ste 102	Phoenix	AZ	85034	**800-996-8864**	480-968-7772
NEC Corp of America	10850 Gold Ctr Dr Ste 200	Rancho Cordova	CA	95670	**800-632-4636**	916-463-7000
Oce-USA Inc	5450 N Cumberland Ave	Chicago	IL	60656	**800-877-6232**	773-714-8500
Oki Data Americas Inc	2000 Bishops Gate Blvd *Cust Svc	Mount Laurel	NJ	08054	**800-654-3282***	856-235-2600
Pentax Imaging Co	633 17th St Ste 2600	Denver	CO	80202	**800-877-0155**	303-799-8000
Plastic Card Systems Inc	31 Pierce St	Northborough	MA	01532	**800-742-2273**	508-351-6210
Primera Technology Inc	2 Carlson Pkwy N Ste 375	Plymouth	MN	55447	**800-797-2772**	763-475-6676
Printek Inc	1517 Townline Rd	Benton Harbor	MI	49022	**800-368-4636**	269-925-3200
Printronix Inc	14600 Myford Rd	Irvine	CA	92606	**800-665-6210**	714-368-2300
RISO Inc	800 District Ave Ste 390 *General	Burlington	MA	01803	**800-942-7476***	978-777-7377
Roland DGA Corp	15363 Barranca Pkwy	Irvine	CA	92618	**800-542-2307**	949-727-2100
Sato America Inc	10350A Nations Ford Rd	Charlotte	NC	28273	**888-871-8741**	704-644-1650
Seiko Instruments USA Inc	21221 S Western Ave Ste 250 *Sales	Torrance	CA	90501	**800-688-0817***	310-517-7700
Seiko Instruments USA Inc Micro Printer Div	2990 Lomita Blvd	Torrance	CA	90505	**800-688-0817**	310-517-7778
Sharp Electronics Corp	1 Sharp Plz	Mahwah	NJ	07430	**800-237-4277**	201-529-8200
Star Micronics America Inc	1150 King George's Post Rd	Edison	NJ	08837	**800-782-7636**	732-623-5500
Stratix	4920 Avalon Ridge Pkwy	Norcross	GA	30071	**800-883-8300**	770-326-7580
TallyGenicom	15345 Barranca Pkwy	Irvine	CA	92618	**800-436-4266**	714-368-2300
Telpar Inc	187 Crosby Rd Ste 100	Dover	NH	03820	**800-872-4886**	603-750-7237
Toshiba America Inc	1251 Ave of the Americas Ste 4100	New York	NY	10020	**800-457-7777**	212-596-0600
TransAct Technologies Inc	1 Hamden Ctr 2319 Whitney Ave Ste 3B *NASDAQ: TACT*	Hamden	CT	06518	**800-243-8941**	203-859-6800
Unimark Products	9818 Pflumm Rd *Cust Svc	Lenexa	KS	66215	**800-255-6356***	913-649-2424
Xante Corp	2800 Dauphin St Ste 100	Mobile	AL	36606	**800-926-8839**	251-473-6502
Xerox Corp	45 Glover Ave PO Box 4505 *NYSE: XRX*	Norwalk	CT	06856	**800-327-9753**	203-968-3000
Zebra Technologies Corp	475 Half Day Rd Ste 500 *NASDAQ: ZBRA*	Lincolnshire	IL	60069	**800-423-0422**	847-634-6700

175-7 Scanning Equipment

Company	Address	City	State	ZIP	Toll-Free	Phone
Accu-Sort Systems Inc	511 School House Rd	Telford	PA	18969	**800-227-2633**	215-723-0981
AirClic Inc	900 Northbrook Dr Ste 100	Trevose	PA	19053	**800-419-8495**	215-504-0560
BenQ America Corp	15375 Barranca Ste A205	Irvine	CA	92618	**866-600-2367**	949-255-9500
BOWE Bell + Howell	760 S Wolf Rd	Wheeling	IL	60090	**800-220-3030**	847-675-7600
CardScan Inc	25 First St Ste 107	Cambridge	MA	02141	**800-942-6739**	617-492-4200
Computerwise Inc	302 N Winchester Ln	Olathe	KS	66062	**800-255-3739**	913-829-0600
Datalogic Scanning	959 Terry St	Eugene	OR	97402	**800-695-5700**	541-683-5700
Hewlett-Packard Co	3000 Hanover St *NYSE: HPQ* ■ *Sales	Palo Alto	CA	94304	**800-752-0900***	650-857-1501
Hitachi Canada Ltd	5450 Explore Dr Ste 501	Mississauga	ON	L4W5N1	**877-248-4237**	905-629-9300
iCAD Inc	98 Spit Brook Rd Ste 100 *NASDAQ: ICAD*	Nashua	NH	03062	**866-280-2239**	603-882-5200
InPath Devices	3610 Dodge St Ste 200	Omaha	NE	68131	**800-988-1914**	402-345-9200
Oce-USA Inc	5450 N Cumberland Ave	Chicago	IL	60656	**800-877-6232**	773-714-8500
Peripheral Dynamics Inc	5150 Campus Dr	Plymouth Meeting	PA	19462	**800-523-0253**	610-825-7090
Roland DGA Corp	15363 Barranca Pkwy	Irvine	CA	92618	**800-542-2307**	949-727-2100
Scan-Optics Inc	169 Progress Dr	Manchester	CT	06042	**800-543-8681**	860-645-7878
Scantron Corp	34 Parker	Irvine	CA	92618	**800-722-6876**	949-639-7500
Stratix	4920 Avalon Ridge Pkwy	Norcross	GA	30071	**800-883-8300**	770-326-7580
Wizcom Technologies Inc	Boston Post Rd W 33 Ste 320	Marlborough	MA	01752	**888-777-0552**	508-251-5388
ZBA Inc	94 Old Camplain Rd	Hillsborough	NJ	08844	**800-750-4239**	908-359-2070

175-8 Storage Devices

Company	Address	City	State	ZIP	Toll-Free	Phone
Appro International Inc	901 Fifth Ave Ste 1000	Seattle	WA	98164	**800-950-2729**	206-701-2000
Apricorn Inc	12191 Kirkham Rd	Poway	CA	92064	**800-458-5448**	858-513-2000
Avere Systems Inc	5000 Mcknight Rd Ste 404	Pittsburgh	PA	15237	**888-882-8373**	412-894-2570
BridgeSTOR LLC	18060 Old Coach Dr	Poway	CA	92064	**800-280-8204**	858-375-7076
Cirrascale Corp	12140 Community Rd	Poway	CA	92064	**888-942-3800**	858-874-3800
CMS Peripherals Inc	12 Mauchly Unit E	Irvine	CA	92618	**800-327-5773**	714-424-5520
Creative Labs Inc	1901 McCarthy Blvd *Cust Svc	Milpitas	CA	95035	**800-998-1000***	408-428-6600
CRU Acquisitions Group LLC	1000 SE Tech Ctr Dr Ste 160	Vancouver	WA	98683	**800-260-9800**	360-816-1800
DataDirect Networks	9351 Deering Ave	Chatsworth	CA	91311	**800-837-2298**	818-700-7600
Datalink Corp	8170 Upland Cir *NASDAQ: DTLK*	Chanhassen	MN	55317	**800-448-6314**	952-944-3462
Digital Peripheral Solutions Inc	8015 E Crystal Dr	Anaheim	CA	92807	**877-998-3440**	
Disc Makers	7905 N Rt 130	Pennsauken	NJ	08110	**800-468-9353**	856-663-9030
Dynamic Network Factory Inc	21353 Cabot Blvd	Hayward	CA	94545	**800-947-4742**	510-265-1122
Edge Electronics Inc	75 Orville Dr	Bohemia	NY	11716	**800-647-3343**	631-471-3343
Fujitsu Computer Products of America Inc	1255 E Arques Ave	Sunnyvale	CA	94085	**800-626-4686**	408-746-7000
Gridstore Inc	1975 W El Camino Real Ste 306	Mountain View	CA	94040	**855-786-7065**	650-316-5515
H Company Computer Products Inc	16812 Hale Ave	Irvine	CA	92606	**800-726-2477**	949-833-3222
Hewlett-Packard (Canada) Ltd (HP)	5150 Spectrum Way	Mississauga	ON	L4W5G1	**888-447-4636**	905-206-4725
Hewlett-Packard Co	3000 Hanover St *NYSE: HPQ* ■ *Sales	Palo Alto	CA	94304	**800-752-0900***	650-857-1501
Hie Electronics Inc	321 N Central Expy Ste 260	Mckinney	TX	75070	**888-782-7937**	972-542-2327
Hitachi America Ltd Computer Div	2000 Sierra Pt Pkwy	Brisbane	CA	94005	**800-448-2244**	
Hitachi Data Systems Corp	750 Central Expy	Santa Clara	CA	95050	**877-437-3849**	408-970-1000
Idealstor LLC	12400 St Hwy 71 W Ste 350-364	Austin	TX	78738	**888-864-3257**	512-279-4321

Company	City	State	Zip	Toll-Free	Phone
Imation Corp 1 Imation Pl *NYSE: IMN*	Oakdale	MN	55128	**888-466-3456**	651-704-4000
International Business Machines Corp (IBM) 1 New OrchaRd Rd *NYSE: IBM*	Armonk	NY	10504	**800-426-4968**	914-499-1900
Kanguru Solutions 1360 Main St *Sales	Millis	MA	02054	**888-526-4878***	508-376-4245
LG Electronics USA Inc 1000 Sylvan Ave *Tech Supp	Englewood Cliffs	NJ	07632	**800-243-0000***	201-816-2000
Luminex Software Inc 871 Marlborough Ave *Sales	Riverside	CA	92507	**888-586-4639***	951-781-4100
Microboards Technology LLC 8150 Mallory Ct PO Box 846	Chanhassen	MN	55317	**800-646-8881**	952-556-1600
NEC Corp of America 10850 Gold Ctr Dr Ste 200	Rancho Cordova	CA	95670	**800-632-4636**	916-463-7000
Pioneer Electronics (USA) Inc 1925 E Dominguez St	Long Beach	CA	90810	**800-421-1404**	310-952-2000
PURE Storage Inc 650 Castro St Ste 400	Mountain View	CA	94041	**800-379-7873**	650-290-6088
Qualstar Corp 3990-B Heritage Oak Ct *NASDAQ: QBAK*	Simi Valley	CA	93063	**800-468-0680**	805-583-7744
Quantum/ATL 141 Innovation Dr	Irvine	CA	92617	**800-677-6268**	949-856-7800
Rimage Corp 7725 Washington Ave S	Minneapolis	MN	55439	**800-553-8312**	952-944-8144
Shaffstall Corp 8531 Bash St	Indianapolis	IN	46250	**800-357-6250**	317-842-2077
Sony Electronics Inc 1 Sony Dr *Cust Svc	Park Ridge	NJ	07656	**800-222-7669***	201-930-1000
Tandberg Data 10225 Westmoor Dr Ste 125	Westminster	CO	80021	**800-392-2983**	303-442-4333
Tintri Inc 2570 W El Camino Real	Mountain View	CA	94040	**855-484-6874**	650-209-3900
Toshiba America Inc 1251 Ave of the Americas Ste 4100	New York	NY	10020	**800-457-7777**	212-596-0600
Unitrends Software Corp 200 Wheeler Rd 2nd fl	Burlington	SC	01803	**866-359-5411**	803-454-0300
Western Digital Corp 3355 Michelson Dr Ste 100 *NASDAQ: WDC*	Irvine	CA	92612	**800-832-4778**	949-672-7000

176 COMPUTER EQUIPMENT & SOFTWARE - WHOL

SEE ALSO Business Machines - Whol ; Electrical & Electronic Equipment & Parts - Whol

Company	City	State	Zip	Toll-Free	Phone
Access Specialties International LLC 15230 Carrousel Way	Rosemount	MN	55068	**800-332-1013**	651-453-1283
Ahearn & Soper Inc 100 Woodbine Downs Blvd	Rexdale	ON	M9W5S6	**800-263-4258**	416-675-3999
Alexander Open Systems Inc 12851 Foster St	Overland Park	KS	66213	**800-473-1110**	913-307-2300
Allied Group Inc, The 25 Amflex Dr	Cranston	RI	02921	**800-556-6310**	401-946-6100
Altametrics Inc 3191 Red Hill Ave Ste 100	Costa Mesa	CA	92626	**800-676-1281**	
American Portwell Technology Inc 44200 Christy St	Fremont	CA	94538	**877-278-8899**	510-403-3399
APCON Inc 9255 SW Pioneer Ct	Wilsonville	OR	97070	**800-624-6808**	503-682-4050
ASA Tire Systems Inc 651 S Stratford Dr	Meridian	ID	83642	**800-241-8472**	208-855-0781
ASI Corp 48289 Fremont Blvd	Fremont	CA	94538	**800-200-0274**	510-226-8000
Atlantix Global Systems 1 Sun Ct	Norcross	GA	30092	**877-552-8526**	770-248-7700
Autostar Solutions Inc 1300 Summit Ave Ste 800	Fort Worth	TX	76102	**800-682-2215**	
AVAD Canada Ltd 205 Courtneypark Dr W	Mississauga	ON	L5W0A5	**866-523-2823**	
Avnet Inc 2211 S 47th St *NYSE: AVT*	Phoenix	AZ	85034	**888-822-8638**	480-643-2000
Avnet Technology Solutions 8700 S Price Rd	Tempe	AZ	85284	**800-409-1483**	480-794-6500
Axiom Memory Solutions LLC 15 Chrysler	Irvine	CA	92618	**888-658-3326**	949-581-1450
Bay Technical Assoc Inc 5239 Ave A	Long Beach Industrial Park	MS	39560	**800-523-2702**	228-563-7334
Burstek 12801 Westlinks Dr Ste 101	Fort Myers	FL	33913	**800-709-2551**	239-495-5900
Butler Technologies Inc 231 W Wayne St	Butler	PA	16001	**800-494-6656**	724-283-6656
CAD/CAM Consulting Services Inc (CCCS) 996 Lawrence Dr Ste 101	Newbury Park	CA	91320	**888-375-7676**	805-375-7676
Champion Solutions Group 791 Pk of Commerce Blvd Ste 200	Boca Raton	FL	33487	**800-771-7000**	561-997-2900
Colorfx Inc 10776 Aurora Ave	Des Moines	IA	50322	**800-348-9044**	
Columbia Ultimate Business Systems Inc 4400 NE 77th Ave Ste 100	Vancouver	WA	98662	**800-488-4420**	360-256-7358
Column Technologies Inc 1400 Opus Pl Ste 110	Downers Grove	IL	60515	**866-265-8665**	630-515-6660
Computer Aided Technology Inc 165 N Arlington Heights Rd Ste 101	Buffalo Grove	IL	60089	**888-308-2284**	
Computer Dynamics Inc 3030 Whitehall Pk Dr	Charlotte	NC	28273	**866-599-6512**	
Comstor Inc 14850 Conference Ctr Dr Ste 200	Chantilly	VA	20151	**800-955-9590**	703-345-5100
Cranel Inc 8999 Gemini Pkwy *General	Columbus	OH	43240	**800-288-3475***	614-431-8000
Crown Micro Inc 48351 Fremont Blvd	Fremont	CA	94538	**800-963-7070**	510-490-8187
D & H Distributing Company Inc 2525 N Seventh St	Harrisburg	PA	17110	**800-340-1001**	
Data Impressions 17418 Studebaker Rd	Cerritos	CA	90703	**800-777-6488**	562-207-9050
Data Sales Company Inc 3450 W Burnsville Pkwy	Burnsville	MN	55337	**800-328-2730**	952-890-8838
De Marque inc 400 Boul Jean-Lesage Bureau 540	Quebec	QC	G1K8W1	**888-458-9143**	418-658-9143
Desire2Learn Inc 151 Charles SW Ste 400	Kitchener	ON	N2G1H6	**888-772-0325**	519-772-0325
DigiLink Inc 840 S Pickett St	Alexandria	VA	22304	**877-806-3444**	703-340-1800
Digital Storage Inc 7611 Green Meadows Dr	Lewis Center	OH	43035	**800-232-3475**	740-548-7179
Dirxion LLC 1859 Bowles Ave Ste 100	Fenton	MO	63026	**888-391-0202**	636-717-2300
DLT Solutions 13861 Sunrise Valley Dr Ste 400	Herndon	VA	20171	**800-262-4358**	703-709-7172
DPC DATA Inc 103 Eisenhower Pkwy Ste 300	Roseland	NJ	07068	**800-996-4747**	201-346-0701
Dynamic Computer Corp 23400 Industrial Pk Ct	Farmington Hills	MI	48335	**866-257-2111**	248-473-2200
Electronic Environments Corp 410 Forest St	Marlborough	MA	01752	**800-342-5332**	508-229-1400
Elk River Systems Inc 777 E Main Ste 108	Bozeman	MT	59715	**888-771-0809**	406-632-4763
ESRI Canada Ltd 12 Concorde Pl Ste 900	Toronto	ON	M3C3R8	**866-625-4577**	416-441-6035
General Data Co Inc 4354 Ferguson Dr	Cincinnati	OH	45245	**800-733-5252**	513-752-7978
Genius Jones Inc 49 NE 39th St	Miami	FL	33137	**866-436-4875**	
Global Computer Supplies Inc 11 Harbor Pk Dr	Port Washington	NY	11050	**800-446-9662**	888-278-4437
Good Printers Inc 213 Dry River Rd	Bridgewater	VA	22812	**800-296-3731**	540-828-4663
Graphic Products Inc PO Box 4030	Beaverton	OR	97076	**888-326-9244**	503-644-5572
GTSI Corp 2553 Dulles View Dr Ste 100 *NASDAQ: GTSI*	Herndon	VA	20171	**800-999-4874**	703-502-2000
Helmel Engineering Products Inc 6520 Lockport Rd	Niagara Falls	NY	14305	**800-237-8266**	716-297-8644
Home Automated Living Inc 14401 Sweitzer Ln 6th Fl	Laurel	MD	20707	**800-935-5313**	301-498-6000
Horizon USA Data Supplies Inc 1595 Meadow Wood Ln Ste 1	Reno	NV	89502	**800-325-1199**	775-858-2300
Iceptstechnology Group Inc 1301 Fulling Mill Rd	Middletown	PA	17057	**888-477-7989**	717-704-1000
Ingram Micro Inc 1600 E St Andrew Pl *NYSE: IM* ■ *Sales	Santa Ana	CA	92705	**800-456-8000***	714-566-1000
Intelligent Computer Solutions Inc 9350 Eton Ave	Chatsworth	CA	91311	**888-994-4678**	818-998-5805
Journey Education Marketing Inc 13755 Hutton Dr Ste 500	Dallas	TX	75234	**800-874-9001**	972-481-2000
Laser Pros International 1 International Ln	Rhinelander	WI	54501	**888-558-5277**	715-369-5995
Leadman Electronic USA Inc 382 Laurelwood Dr	Santa Clara	CA	95054	**877-532-3626**	408-738-1751
Legacy Electronics Inc 1220 N Dakota St PO Box 348	Canton	SD	57013	**888-466-3853**	949-498-9600
Lindsey & Company Inc 2302 Llama Dr	Searcy	AR	72143	**800-890-7058**	501-268-5324
Long View Systems Corp 3100 255 Fifth Ave SW	Calgary	AB	T2P3G6	**866-515-6900**	403-515-6900
M & A Technology Inc 2045 Chenault Dr	Carrollton	TX	75006	**800-225-1452**	972-490-5803
MacPractice Inc 233 N Eighth St Ste 300	Lincoln	NE	68508	**877-220-8418**	402-420-2430
MasterGraphics Inc 2979 Triverton Pike Dr	Madison	WI	53711	**800-873-7238**	608-256-4884
Max Group Corp 17011 Green Dr	City of Industry	CA	91745	**800-256-9040**	626-935-0050
MontaVista Software Inc 2929 Patrick Henry Dr	Santa Clara	CA	95054	**888-624-4846**	408-572-8000
Onix Networking Corp 18519 Detroit Ave	Lakewood	OH	44107	**800-664-9638**	
Open Storage Solutions Inc 2 Castleview Dr	Toronto	ON	L6T5S9	**800-387-3419**	905-790-0660
Open Systems of Cleveland Inc 22999 Forbes Rd Ste A	Cleveland	OH	44146	**888-881-6660**	440-439-2332
Pact-One Solutions Inc 8215 S Eastern Ave Ste 101	Las Vegas	NV	89123	**866-722-8663**	
Paragon Development Systems Inc 1823 Executive Dr	Oconomowoc	WI	53066	**800-966-6090**	
Peak Technologies Inc 10330 Old Columbia Rd	Columbia	MD	21046	**800-926-9212**	
Programmer's Paradise Inc 1157 Shrewsbury Ave Ste C	Shrewsbury	NJ	07702	**800-441-1511**	732-389-8950
Promark Technology Inc 10900 Pump House Rd Ste B	Annapolis Junction	MD	20701	**800-634-0255**	240-280-8030
Prostar Computer Inc 837 Lawson St	City of Industry	CA	91748	**888-576-4742**	626-839-6472
Provantage Corp 7249 Whipple Ave NW	North Canton	OH	44720	**800-336-1166**	330-494-8715
Rave Computer Assn Inc 7171 Sterling Ponds Ct	Sterling Heights	MI	48312	**800-966-7283**	586-939-8230
Rorke Data Inc 7626 Golden Triangle Dr	Eden Prairie	MN	55344	**800-328-8147**	952-829-0300
Rpl Supplies Inc 141 Lanza Ave Bldg 3A	Garfield	NJ	07026	**800-524-0914**	973-767-0880
ScanSource Inc 6 Logue Ct *NASDAQ: SCSC*	Greenville	SC	29615	**800-944-2432**	864-288-2432

Company	Address	City	State	ZIP	Toll-Free	Phone
Scivantage Inc	499 Washington Blvd 11th Fl	Jersey City	NJ	07310	**866-724-8268**	646-452-0050
SHI Corp	35W Broadway Ste 104	Salt Lake City	UT	84101	**888-764-8888**	
Softmart Inc	450 Acorn Ln *Cust Svc	Downingtown	PA	19335	**800-328-1319***	610-518-4000
Software House International (SHI)	290 Davidson Ave	Somerset	NJ	08873	**888-764-8888**	
Stardock Systems Inc	15090 N Beck Rd Ste 300	Plymouth	MI	48170	**888-782-7362**	734-927-0677
Static Control Components Inc	3010 Lee Ave PO Box 152	Sanford	NC	27331	**800-488-2426**	919-774-3808
Symco Group Inc	5012 Bristol Industrial Way Ste 105	Buford	GA	30518	**800-878-8002**	770-451-8002
SYNNEX Canada	200 Ronson Dr	Etobicoke	ON	M9W5Z9	**800-268-1220**	416-240-7012
Synnex Corp	44201 Nobel Dr *NYSE: SNX* ■ *Cust Svc	Fremont	CA	94538	**800-756-1888***	510-656-3333
Tanner Research Inc	825 S Myrtle Ave	Monrovia	CA	91016	**877-325-2223**	626-471-9700
Tech Data Corp	5350 Tech Data Dr *NASDAQ: TECD*	Clearwater	FL	33760	**800-237-8931**	727-539-7429
Tekla Inc	1075 Big Shanty Rd NW Ste 175	Kennesaw	GA	30144	**877-835-5265**	770-426-5105
Think Computer Corp	3260 Hillview Ave	Palo Alto	CA	94304	**888-815-8599**	415-670-9350
TigerDirect Inc	7795 W Flagler St Ste 35	Miami	FL	33144	**800-800-8300**	
Transoft Solutions Inc	13575 Commerce Pkwy Ste 250	Richmond	BC	V6V2L1	**888-244-8387**	604-244-8387
Unified Systems Group Inc	1235 64th Ave SE Ste 4a	Calgary	AB	T2H2J7	**866-892-8988**	403-686-8088
Us Micro Corp	7000 Highlnds Pkwy SE	Smyrna	GA	30082	**888-876-4276**	770-437-0706
Vartek Services Inc	1785 S Metro Pkwy	Dayton	OH	45459	**800-954-2524**	937-438-3550
VLN Partners LLP	1212 E Carson St	Pittsburgh	PA	15203	**877-856-3311**	412-381-0183
WDL Systems	220 Chatham Business Dr *Sales	Pittsboro	NC	27312	**800-548-2319***	919-545-2500
West-Com Nurse Call Systems Inc	2200 Cordelia Rd	Fairfield	CA	94534	**800-761-1180**	707-428-5900
Westcon Group Inc	520 White Plains Rd 2nd Fl	Tarrytown	NY	10591	**800-527-9516**	914-829-7000
Westcon Group, Inc *Westcon Convergence*	520 White Plains Rd Ste 100	Omaha	NE	68154	**877-642-7750**	
Westham Trade Co Ltd	3620 NW 114th Ave	Doral	FL	33178	**888-852-5000**	305-717-5400
Wintec Industries Inc	675 Sycamore Dr	Milpitas	CA	95035	**866-989-4683**	408-856-0500
Woot Inc	4121 International Pkwy	Carrollton	TX	75007	**866-551-6881**	972-417-3959
Worth Higgins & Assoc Inc	8770 Park Central Dr	Richmond	VA	23227	**800-883-7768**	804-264-2304
Zuercher Technologies LLC	5121 S Solberg Ave Ste 150	Sioux Falls	SD	57108	**877-229-2205**	605-274-6061

177 COMPUTER MAINTENANCE & REPAIR

Company	Address	City	State	ZIP	Toll-Free	Phone
24hourtek LLC	268 Bush St	San Francisco	CA	94104	**855-378-0787**	415-294-4449
Accram Inc	2901 W Clarendon Ave	Phoenix	AZ	85017	**800-786-0288**	
Ariel Technologies	1980 E Lohman Ave	Las Cruces	NM	88001	**877-524-6860**	
Bde Computer Services LLC	399 Lakeview Ave	Clifton	NJ	07011	**877-233-4877**	973-772-8507
Brentech Inc	9340 Carmel Mtn Rd Ste C	San Diego	CA	92129	**800-709-0440**	858-484-7314
Brooks-Jeffrey Computer Store	19 Medical Plz	Mountain Home	AR	72653	**800-506-8064**	870-425-8064
C&W Enterprises Inc	2522 SE Federal Hwy	Stuart	FL	34994	**844-241-6442**	772-287-5215
CAD & Graphic Supply Inc	2410 Luna Rd Ste 114	Carrollton	TX	75006	**866-409-8211**	972-409-7333
Computer Troubleshooters USA	755 Commerce Dr Ste 605	Decatur	GA	30030	**877-704-1702**	800-877-0020
ComputerPlus Sales & Service Inc	5 Northway Ct	Greer	SC	29651	**800-849-4426**	
Comware Technical Services Inc	17922 Sky Park Cir Ste E	Irvine	CA	92614	**800-460-1970**	949-851-9600
Data Exchange Corp	3600 Via Pescador	Camarillo	CA	93012	**800-237-7911**	805-388-1711
Dataserv Corp	8625 F St	Omaha	NE	68127	**888-901-8700**	402-339-8700
DBK Concepts Inc	12905 SW 129 Ave	Miami	FL	33186	**800-725-7226**	305-596-7226
Decatur Computers Inc	1234 N Water St Ste B	Decatur	IL	62521	**800-429-7140**	217-475-0226
DecisionOne Corp	426 W Lancaster Ave	Devon	PA	19333	**800-767-2876**	610-296-6000
Desktop Consulting Services	43311 Joy Rd	Canton	MI	48187	**888-600-2731**	
Electrosonics	17150 15 Mile Rd	Fraser	MI	48026	**800-858-8448**	586-415-5555
Emf Inc	60 Foundry St	Keene	NH	03431	**800-992-3003**	603-352-8400
Essential Technologies Inc	1107 Hazeltine Blvd Ste 477	Chaska	MN	55318	**800-818-1125**	952-368-9001
Everprint International Inc	18021 Cortney Ct	City of Industry	CA	91748	**800-984-5777**	626-839-2569
IIS Group LLC	1015 Virginia Dr Ste 1 W	Fort Washington	PA	19034	**855-443-5777**	
Insight Computing LLC	448 Ignacio Blvd Ste 490	Novato	CA	94949	**800-380-8985**	415-898-5411
Integration Technologies Group Inc	2745 Hartland Rd Ste 200	Falls Church	VA	22043	**800-835-7823**	703-698-8282
Interactive Services Group Inc	600 Delran Pkwy Ste C	Delran	NJ	08075	**800-566-3310**	
Intratek Computer Inc	5431 Industrial Dr	Huntington Beach	CA	92649	**800-892-8282**	
Matthijssen Inc	14 Rt 10	East Hanover	NJ	07936	**800-845-2200**	973-887-1100
Npa Computers Inc	751 Coates Ave	Holbrook	NY	11741	**800-873-6724**	631-467-2500
Precision Computer Services Inc (PCS)	175 Constitution Blvd S	Shelton	CT	06484	**800-340-9890**	203-929-0000
Pro-data Computer Services Inc	2809 S 160th St Ste 401	Omaha	NE	68130	**800-228-6318**	402-697-7575
Ptc Select LLC	2450 N Knoxville Ave	Peoria	IL	61604	**800-225-2320**	309-685-8400
Rescuecom Corp	2560 Burnet Ave	Syracuse	NY	13206	**800-737-2837**	
Systems Maintenance Services Inc (SMS)	10420 Harris Oaks Blvd Ste C	Charlotte	NC	28269	**877-405-0330**	
Visual Net Design Lc	212 E Ramsey Rd	San Antonio	TX	78216	**800-590-2164**	210-590-2734
Voxtechnologies Com	301 S Sherman St	Richardson	TX	75081	**888-568-6224**	972-234-4343

178 COMPUTER NETWORKING PRODUCTS & SYSTEMS

SEE ALSO Telecommunications Equipment & Systems ; Modems ; Systems & Utilities Software

Company	Address	City	State	ZIP	Toll-Free	Phone
Allied Telesyn International Corp	19800 N Creek Pkwy Ste 100	Bothell	WA	98011	**800-424-4284**	425-481-3895
American Megatrends Inc (AMI)	5555 Oakbrook Pkwy Bldg 200	Norcross	GA	30093	**800-828-9264**	770-246-8600
ASA Computers Inc	645 National Ave	Mountain View	CA	94043	**800-732-5727**	650-230-8000
Avaya Inc	211 Mt Airy Rd	Basking Ridge	NJ	07920	**866-462-8292**	908-953-6000
Axis Communications Inc (ACI)	100 Apollo Dr	Chelmsford	MA	01824	**800-444-2947**	978-614-2000
Black Box Corp	1000 Pk Dr *NASDAQ: BBOX*	Lawrence	PA	15055	**877-877-2269**	724-746-5500
Blue Coat Systems Inc	420 N Mary Ave *NASDAQ: BCSI*	Sunnyvale	CA	94085	**866-302-2628**	408-220-2200
Brocade Communications Systems Inc	130 Holger Way *NASDAQ: BRCD*	San Jose	CA	95134	**800-752-8061**	408-333-8000
Cambex Corp	337 Tpke Rd *OTC: CBEX*	Southborough	MA	01772	**800-325-5565**	508-281-0209
Chatsworth Products Inc	31425 Agoura Rd	Westlake Village	CA	91361	**800-834-4969**	818-735-6100
Cisco Systems Inc	170 W Tasman Dr *NASDAQ: CSCO*	San Jose	CA	95134	**800-553-6387**	408-526-4000
Compex Inc	7918 Jones Branch Dr	Mclean	VA	22102	**800-279-8891**	503-873-0188
CompuCom Systems Inc	7171 Forest Ln *Cust Svc	Dallas	TX	75230	**800-597-0555***	972-856-3600
Comtrol Corp	100 Fifth Ave NW	Maple Grove	MN	55112	**800-926-6876**	763-494-4100
Continental Resources Inc	175 Middlesex Tpke	Bedford	MA	01730	**800-937-4688**	781-275-0850
Crossroads Systems Inc	8300 N MoPac Expy *NASDAQ: CRDS*	Austin	TX	78759	**800-643-7148**	512-349-0300
Crystal Group Inc	850 Kacena Rd	Hiawatha	IA	52233	**877-279-7863**	319-378-1636
Cubix Corp	2800 Lockheed Way *Sales	Carson City	NV	89706	**800-829-0550***	775-888-1000
Cyberdata Corp	3 Justin Ct	Monterey	CA	93940	**800-363-8010**	831-373-2601
D-Link Systems Inc	17595 Mt Herrmann St	Fountain Valley	CA	92708	**800-326-1688**	714-885-6000
Daly Computers Inc	22521 Gateway Ctr Dr	Clarksburg	MD	20871	**800-955-3259**	301-670-0381
Dell Inc	1 Dell Way *NASDAQ: DELL*	Round Rock	TX	78682	**800-879-3355**	512-338-4400
Digi International Inc	11001 Bren Rd E *NASDAQ: DGII*	Minnetonka	MN	55343	**877-912-3444**	952-912-3444
Dot Hill Systems Corp	1351 S Sunset St *NASDAQ: HILL*	Longmont	CO	80501	**800-872-2783**	303-845-3200
Echelon Corp	550 Meridian Ave *NASDAQ: ELON*	San Jose	CA	95126	**888-324-3566**	408-938-5200
Egenera Inc	80 Central St	Boxborough	MA	01719	**866-301-3117**	978-206-6300
Electronics for Imaging Inc	303 Velocity Way *NASDAQ: EFII*	Foster City	CA	94404	**888-334-8650**	650-357-3500
eSoft Inc	295 Interlocken Blvd Ste 500	Broomfield	CO	80021	**866-233-2296**	303-444-1600
Extreme Networks Inc	3585 Monroe St *NASDAQ: EXTR*	Santa Clara	CA	95051	**888-257-3000**	408-579-2800
Ezenia! Inc	14 Celina Ave Ste 17	Nashua	NH	03063	**800-966-2301**	781-505-2100
F5 Networks Inc	401 Elliott Ave W *NASDAQ: FFIV*	Seattle	WA	98119	**888-882-4447**	206-272-5555

Classified Section

Company / Address	City	State	Zip	Toll-Free	Phone
Fujitsu Computer Systems Corp 1250 E Arques Ave	Sunnyvale	CA	94085	**800-538-8460**	408-746-6000
Futurex Inc 864 Old Boerne Rd	Bulverde	TX	78163	**800-251-5112**	830-980-9782
iGo Inc 17800 N Perimeter Dr Ste 200 *NASDAQ: IGOI*	Scottsdale	AZ	85255	**888-205-0093**	480-596-0061
iLinc Communications Inc 2999 N 44th St Ste 650	Phoenix	AZ	85018	**800-767-9054**	602-952-1200
IMC Networks Corp 19772 Pauling	Foothill Ranch	CA	92610	**800-624-1070**	949-465-3000
Interphase Corp 4240 International Pkwy Ste 105 *NASDAQ: INPH*	Carrollton	TX	75007	**800-327-8638**	214-654-5000
Juniper Networks Inc 1194 N Mathilda Ave *NYSE: JNPR*	Sunnyvale	CA	94089	**888-586-4737**	408-745-2000
Marvell Semiconductor Inc 5488 Marvell Ln *Cust Svc	Santa Clara	CA	95054	**855-627-8355***	408-222-2500
NEC Corp of America 10850 Gold Ctr Dr Ste 200	Rancho Cordova	CA	95670	**800-632-4636**	916-463-7000
Netplanner Systems Inc 3145 Northwoods Pkwy Ste 800	Norcross	GA	30071	**800-795-1975**	770-662-5482
Network Appliance Inc 495 E Java Dr *NASDAQ: NTAP* ■ *Sales	Sunnyvale	CA	94089	**800-443-4537***	408-822-6000
Network Dynamics Inc 640 Brooker Creek Blvd Ste 410	Oldsmar	FL	34677	**877-818-8597**	813-818-8597
Overland Storage Inc 4820 Overland Ave *NASDAQ: OVRL*	San Diego	CA	92123	**800-729-8725**	858-571-5555
Peak 10 752 Barret Ave	Louisville	KY	40204	**866-732-5836**	502-315-6015
Polycom Inc 4750 Willow Rd	Pleasanton	CA	94588	**800-765-9266**	
PrimeArray Systems Inc 127 Riverneck Rd	Chelmsford	MA	01824	**800-433-5133**	978-654-6250
Quantum Corp 11431 Willows Rd NE	Redmond	WA	98052	**800-284-5101**	425-881-8004
Ringdale Inc 101 Halmar Cove	Georgetown	TX	78628	**888-288-9080**	512-288-9080
Safari Circuits Inc 411 Washington St	Otsego	MI	49078	**888-694-7230**	269-694-9471
SafeNet Inc 4690 Millennium Dr *Sales	Belcamp	MD	21017	**800-533-3958***	410-931-7500
Server Technology Inc 1040 Sandhill Dr	Reno	NV	89521	**800-835-1515**	775-284-2000
SOHOware Inc 1250 Oakmead Pkwy Ste 210	Sunnyvale	CA	94085	**800-632-1118**	408-565-9888
Solectek Corp 6370 Nancy Ridge Dr Ste 109	San Diego	CA	92121	**888-299-8057**	858-450-1220
SonicWALL Inc 2001 Logic Dr	San Jose	CA	95124	**888-557-6642**	408-745-9600
SteelCloud Inc 20110 Ashbrook Pl Ste 270 *OTC: SCLD*	Ashburn	VA	20147	**800-296-3866**	703-674-5500
StoneFly Inc 21353 Cabot Blvd	Hayward	CA	94545	**888-786-6335**	510-265-1616
Storage Engine Inc 1 Sheila Dr	Tinton Falls	NJ	07724	**866-734-8899**	732-747-6995
Strictly Business Computer Systems Inc 848 Fourth Ave Ste 200	Huntington	WV	25701	**888-529-0401**	
Systech Corp 16510 Via Esprillo	San Diego	CA	92127	**800-800-8970**	858-674-6500
TalkPoint Communications Inc 100 William St	New York	NY	10038	**866-323-8660**	212-909-2900
Technology Integration Group (TIG) 7810 Trade St	San Diego	CA	92121	**800-858-0549**	858-566-1900
Tekworks Inc 13000 Gregg St Ste B	Poway	CA	92064	**877-835-9675**	
Telebyte Inc 355 Marcus Blvd	Hauppauge	NY	11788	**800-835-3298**	631-423-3232
Telkonet Inc 10200 W Innovation Dr Ste 300 *OTC: TKOI* ■ *Sales	Milwaukee	WI	53226	**888-703-9398***	414-223-0473
Transition Networks Inc 10900 Red Cir Dr	Minnetonka	MN	55343	**800-526-9267**	952-941-7600
Transource Computers Corp 2405 W Utopia Rd	Phoenix	AZ	85027	**800-486-3715**	623-879-8882
Trendware International Inc 20675 Manhattan Pl	Torrance	CA	90501	**888-326-6061**	310-961-5500
Ultera Systems Inc 26081 Merit Cir Ste 125	Laguna Hills	CA	92653	**877-462-7362**	949-367-8800
UNICOM 565 Brea Canyon Rd Ste A	Walnut	CA	91789	**800-346-6668**	626-964-7873
Unimark Products 9818 Pflumm Rd *Cust Svc	Lenexa	KS	66215	**800-255-6356***	913-649-2424
US Robotics Corp 1300 E Woodfield Dr Ste 506	Schaumburg	IL	60173	**877-710-0884**	847-874-2000
Virtela Technology Services Inc 5680 Greenwood Plz Blvd Ste 200	Greenwood Village	CO	80111	**877-803-9629**	720-475-4000
Visara International Inc 2700 Gateway Centre Blvd Ste 600	Morrisville	NC	27560	**888-334-4380**	919-882-0200
WatchGuard Technologies Inc 505 Fifth Ave S Ste 500 *Sales	Seattle	WA	98104	**800-734-9905***	206-613-6600
WAV Inc 2380 Prospect Dr	Aurora	IL	60504	**800-678-2419**	630-818-1000
WideBand Corp 401 W Grand St	Gallatin	MO	64640	**888-663-3050**	660-663-3000
Winchester Systems Inc 101 Billerica Ave Bldg 5 *Cust Svc	North Billerica	MA	01862	**800-325-3700***	781-265-0200
Works Computing Inc 1801 American Blvd E Ste 12	Bloomington	MN	55425	**866-222-4077**	952-746-1580
World Data Products Inc 121 Cheshire Ln	Minnetonka	MN	55305	**888-210-7636**	952-476-9000
ZT Group International Inc 350 Meadowlands Pkwy	Secaucus	NJ	07094	**888-984-8899**	201-559-1000

179 COMPUTER PROGRAMMING SERVICES - CUSTOM

SEE ALSO Computer Software ; Computer Systems Design Services

Company / Address	City	State	Zip	Toll-Free	Phone
4th Source Inc 2400 Veterans Blvd Ste 480	Kenner	LA	70062	**855-875-4700**	
Access Innovations Inc 4725 Indian School Rd NE Ste 100	Albuquerque	NM	87110	**800-926-8328**	505-265-3591
AccuCode Inc 6886 S Yosemite St Ste 100	Centennial	CO	80112	**866-705-9879**	303-639-6111
Accumedic Computer Systems Inc 11 Grace Ave Ste 401	Great Neck	NY	11021	**800-765-9300**	516-466-6800
Accuzip 3216 El Camino Real	Atascadero	CA	93422	**800-233-0555**	805-461-7300
Actsoft Inc 8910 N Dale Mabry Hwy	Tampa	FL	33614	**888-732-6638**	813-936-2331
Advanced Chemistry Development Inc 110 Yonge St 14th Fl	Toronto	ON	M5C1T4	**800-304-3988**	416-368-3435
Advanced Digital Data Inc 6 Laurel Dr	Flanders	NJ	07836	**800-922-0972**	973-584-4026
Agilysys NV LLC 28925 Fountain Pkwy	Solon	OH	44139	**800-241-8768**	770-810-7800
Ahead Hum Res Inc/Prosoft LLC 2209 Heather Ln	Louisville	KY	40218	**888-749-1000**	502-485-1000
Alebra Technologies Inc 3810 Pheasant Ridge Dr NE Ste 100	Minneapolis	MN	55449	**888-340-2727**	651-366-6140
Alta Via Consulting LLC 127 ConKinnon Dr	Lenoir City	TN	37772	**877-258-2842**	
Altech Services Inc 1160 Parsippany Blvd Ste 202	Parsippany	NJ	07054	**888-725-8324**	
Analytical Graphics Inc 220 Vly Creek Blvd	Exton	PA	19341	**800-220-4785**	610-981-8000
Aparaa Corp 14900 Landmark Blvd Ste 630	Dallas	TX	75254	**888-441-2535**	
Applied Business Software 2847 Gundry Ave	Signal Hill	CA	90755	**800-833-3343**	562-426-2188
Applied Software Inc 3919 National Dr Ste 200	Burtonsville	MD	20866	**888-624-8439**	
AppTech Corp 2011 Palomar Airport Rd Ste 102	Carlsbad	CA	92011	**877-720-0022**	
Apriva Inc 8501 N Scottsdale Rd Ste 110	Scottsdale	AZ	85253	**877-277-0728**	480-421-1210
Archive-cd LLC 910 Beverly Way	Jacksonville	OR	97530	**800-323-1868**	541-899-5704
Aristatek Inc 710 E Garfield St Ste 220	Laramie	WY	82070	**877-912-2200**	307-721-2126
Aruba Networks Inc 1344 Crossman Ave *NASDAQ: ARUN*	Sunnyvale	CA	94089	**800-943-4526**	408-227-4500
Assist Cornerstone Technologies Inc 150 West Civic Ctr Dr Ste 601	Sandy	UT	84070	**800-732-0136**	
Atlas Systems Inc 5712 Cleveland St Ste 200	Virginia Beach	VA	23462	**800-567-7401**	757-467-7872
Avtech Software Inc 16 Cutler St Cutler Mill	Warren	RI	02885	**888-220-6700**	401-847-6700
Axcient Inc 1161 San Antonio Rd	Mountain View	CA	94043	**800-715-2339**	
Axiom Software Ltd 400 Columbus Ave	Valhalla	NY	10595	**800-588-8805**	914-769-8800
B Sharp Technologies Inc 23 Lesmill Rd Ste 404	Toronto	ON	M3B3P6	**866-994-2499**	416-445-7162
Barcontrol Systems & Services Inc 113 Edinburgh Ct	Greenville	SC	29607	**800-947-4362**	864-421-0050
Bedrock Prime 1309 N Wilson Rd Ste A	Radcliff	KY	40160	**866-334-5914**	270-351-8043
Bframe Data Systems Inc 3057 Peachtree Industrial Blvd Ste 200	Duluth	GA	30097	**800-833-1059**	678-387-0100
Billpro Management Systems Inc 30575 Euclid Ave	Wickliffe	OH	44092	**800-736-0587**	440-516-3776
Boingo Wireless Inc 10960 Wilshire Blvd Ste 800	Los Angeles	CA	90024	**800-880-4117**	310-586-5180
Boost Motor Group Inc 3080 Yonge St	Toronto	ON	M4N3N1	**877-266-7841**	416-487-7000
Bradford Technologies Inc 302 Piercy Rd	San Jose	CA	95138	**866-445-8367**	408-360-8520
Carina Technology Inc 1300 Meridian St Ste A-13	Huntsville	AL	35806	**866-915-5464**	256-704-0422
Carnegie Learning Inc 437 Grant St	Pittsburgh	PA	15219	**888-851-7094**	412-690-6284
Charles River Analytics Inc 625 Mt Auburn St Ste 3	Cambridge	MA	02138	**877-547-4600**	617-491-3474
Cherryroad Technologies Inc 301 Gibraltar Dr Ste 2C	Morris Plains	NJ	07950	**877-402-7804**	973-402-7802
Cisys Inc 8386 Six Forks Rd	Raleigh	NC	27615	**844-494-9236**	
Citizant Inc 5180 Parkstone Dr Ste 100	Chantilly	VA	20151	**877-248-4926**	703-667-9420
Claricent Inc 22 Preserve way	Sturbridge	MA	01566	**888-325-6496**	
Clients First Business Solutions LLC 670 N Beers St Bldg 4	Holmdel	NJ	07733	**866-677-6290**	
CMA Consulting Services Inc 700 Troy Schenectady Rd	Latham	NY	12110	**800-276-6101**	518-783-9003
CollabNet Inc 8000 Marina Blvd Ste 600	Brisbane	CA	94005	**888-532-6823**	650-228-2500
College Health Services LLC 144 Turnpike Rd Ste 240	Southborough	MA	01772	**866-636-8336**	
Commercial Programming Systems Inc 4400 Coldwater Canyon Ave	Studio City	CA	91604	**888-277-4562**	323-851-2681
Companion Professional Services LLC 1301 Gervais St Ste 1700	Columbia	SC	29201	**800-780-1170**	803-765-1310
Compu-data International LLC 431 Nursery Rd Ste A300	Spring	TX	77380	**866-936-6069**	281-292-1333
Compusearch Software Systems Inc 21251 Ridgetop Cir	Dulles	VA	20166	**855-817-2720**	571-449-4000

Company / Address	City	State	ZIP	Toll-Free	Phone
Computer Aid Inc (CAI) 1390 Ridgeview Dr	Allentown	PA	18104	**877-432-7228**	610-530-5000
Computer Arts Inc 320 SW Fifth Ave	Meridian	ID	83642	**800-365-9335**	208-385-9335
Computer Guidance Corp 15035 N 75th St	Scottsdale	AZ	85260	**888-361-4551**	480-444-7000
Computerworks of Chicago Inc 5153 N Clark St	Chicago	IL	60640	**800-977-8212**	773-275-4437
Computrition Inc 19808 Nordhoff Pl	Chatsworth	CA	91311	**800-222-4488**	
CoNetrix LLC 5214 68th St Ste 200	Lubbock	TX	79424	**800-356-6568**	806-687-8600
CONIX Systems Inc 7252 Main St	Manchester Center	VT	05255	**800-332-1899**	
Construx Software 11820 Northup Way Ste E-200	Bellevue	WA	98005	**866-296-6300**	425-636-0100
Consult Usa Inc 634 Alpha Dr	Pittsburgh	PA	15238	**866-963-8621**	412-963-8621
Corptax LLC 1751 Lk Cook Rd Ste 100	Deerfield	IL	60015	**800-966-1639**	
Credant Technologies Inc 15303 Dallas Pkwy Ste 1420	Addison	TX	75001	**800-929-8331**	972-458-5400
Crescendo Systems Corp 1600 Montgolfier	Laval	QC	H7T0A2	**800-724-2930**	450-973-8029
CTE Solutions Inc 11 Holland Ave Ste 100	Ottawa	ON	K1Y4S1	**800-699-4007**	613-798-5353
Culinary Software Services Inc 1900 Folsom St Ste 210	Boulder	CO	80302	**800-447-1466**	303-447-3334
Customer Service Delivery Platform Corp 15615 Alton Pkwy Ste 310	Irvine	CA	92618	**888-741-2737**	
Cutting Edge 1825 Gillespie Way Ste 100	El Cajon	CA	92020	**800-257-1666**	619-258-7800
Cyber-Ark Software Inc 60 Wells Ave	Newton	MA	02459	**888-808-9005**	617-965-1544
D-Ta Systems Inc 2500 Lancaster Rd	Ottawa	ON	K1B4S5	**877-382-3222**	613-745-8713
Data Management Marketing 3225 Jordan Blvd	Malabar	FL	32950	**888-266-4127**	321-725-8081
Datafirst Corp 5124 Departure Dr	Raleigh	NC	27616	**800-634-8504**	919-876-6650
Dataflux Corp 940 NW Cary Pkwy Ste 201	Cary	NC	27513	**800-727-0025**	919-447-3000
DecisionPoint Systems Inc 19655 Descartes *OTC: DPSI*	Foothill Ranch	CA	92610	**800-336-3670**	949-465-0065
Denim Group Ltd 1354 N Loop 1604 E Ste 110	San Antonio	TX	78232	**844-572-4400**	
Desco Dental Systems LLC 5005 W Loomis Rd Ste 100	Greenfield	WI	53220	**800-392-7610**	414-281-9192
Dh Web Inc 11377 Robinwood Dr Ste D	Hagerstown	MD	21742	**877-567-6599**	301-733-7672
Digital ChoreoGraphics PO Box 8268	Newport Beach	CA	92658	**800-548-1969**	949-548-1969
Digital I-Ollc 1424 30th St	San Diego	CA	92154	**866-423-4433**	619-423-4433
Edge Systems LLC 3S721 W Ave Ste 200 *Tech Supp	Warrenville	IL	60555	**800-352-3343***	630-810-9669
Edgenet Inc 2948 Sidco Dr	Atlanta	GA	30326	**877-334-3638**	615-371-3848
Education Management Systems Inc 4110 Shipyard Blvd	Wilmington	NC	28403	**800-541-8999**	910-799-0121
Electrocon International Inc 405 Little Lk Dr	Ann Arbor	MI	48103	**888-240-4044**	734-761-8612
Ellie Mae Inc 4155 Hopyard Rd Ste 200	Pleasanton	CA	94588	**800-848-4904**	925-227-7000
Entero Corp 1040 Seventh Ave SW Ste 500	Calgary	AB	T2P3G9	**877-261-1820**	403-261-1820
Epac Software Technologies Inc 42 Ladd St	East Greenwich	RI	02818	**888-336-3722**	
Eric A. King 301 Grant St Ste 4300	Pittsburgh	PA	15219	**888-742-2454**	281-667-4200
Execusys Inc 6767 N Wickham Rd	Melbourne	FL	32940	**800-454-3081**	321-253-0077
Extensis 1800 SW First Ave Ste 500	Portland	OR	97201	**800-796-9798**	503-274-2020
Eyefinity Inc 10875 International Dr Ste 200	Rancho Cordova	CA	95670	**877-448-0707**	
Freedom Scientific Inc 11800 31st Court N	St. Petersburg	FL	33716	**800-444-4443**	727-803-8000
FusionStorm 2 Bryant St Ste 150	San Francisco	CA	94105	**800-228-8324**	415-623-2626
Futrend Technology Inc 8605 Westwood Ctr Dr Ste 502	Vienna	VA	22182	**866-388-7363**	703-556-0016
GeBBS Healthcare Solutions Inc 560 Sylvan Ave Second Fl	Englewood Cliffs	NJ	07632	**888-539-4282**	
Gene Codes Corp 775 Technology Dr	Ann Arbor	MI	48108	**800-497-4939**	734-769-7249
Genesisfour Corp 7747 Ten Acre Rd	Andrews	SC	29510	**800-937-4364**	843-461-4117
Global Nest LLC 281 State Rt 79 N Ste 208	Morganville	NJ	07751	**866-850-5872**	732-333-5848
Global Reach Internet Productions LLC 2321 N Loop Dr Ste 101	Ames	IA	50010	**877-254-9828**	515-996-0996
Go 2 Group 138 N Hickory Ave	Bel Air	MD	21014	**877-442-4669**	410-879-8102
Great South Texas Corp 814 Arion Pkwy	San Antonio	TX	78216	**800-531-3858**	210-369-0300
Gst Information Technology Solutions 13043 166th St	Cerritos	CA	90703	**800-833-0128**	562-345-8700
H & W Computer Systems Inc 6154 N Meeker Pl Ste 100	Boise	ID	83713	**800-338-6692**	208-377-0336
Hanson Information System 2433 W White Oaks Dr	Springfield	IL	62704	**888-245-8468**	217-726-2400
Harvey Software Inc 7050 Winkler Rd Ste 104	Fort Myers	FL	33919	**800-231-0296**	
Health Care Software Inc PO Box 2430	Farmingdale	NJ	07727	**800-524-1038**	
Healthcare Automation Inc 41 Sharpe Dr	Cranston	RI	02920	**800-738-8850**	401-572-3040
Human Factors International Inc 410 W Lowe Ave	Fairfield	IA	52556	**800-242-4480**	641-472-4480
HyperDisk Marketing Inc 18251 McDurmott W Ste A	Irvine	CA	92614	**800-241-1210**	949-442-9850
I. s Outsource Inc 19119 N Creek Pkwy Ste 200	Bothell	WA	98011	**800-240-2821**	206-374-0251
Idea Works Inc, The 100 W Briarwood Ln	Columbia	MO	65203	**800-537-4866**	573-445-4554
Ideal Software Systems Inc 4909 29th Ave	Meridian	MS	39305	**800-964-3325**	601-693-1673
Ignify Inc 200 Pine Ave 4th Fl	Long Beach	CA	90802	**888-599-4332**	562-219-2000
iLookabout Corp 383 Richmond St Ste 408	London	ON	N6A3C4	**866-963-2015**	519-963-2015
Image API LLC 2002 Old St Augustine Rd Bldg D	Tallahassee	FL	32301	**877-560-4274**	850-222-1400
Imaginet Resources Corp 233 Portage Ave	Winnipeg	MB	R3B2A7	**800-989-6022**	204-989-6022
In-Touch Insight Systems Inc 400 March Rd	Ottawa	ON	K2K3H4	**800-263-2980**	
Infoaccess.net LLC 8801 E Pleasant Vly Rd	Cleveland	OH	44131	**800-255-0253**	216-328-0100
Informant Technologies Inc 19 Jenkins Ave Ste 200	Lansdale	PA	19446	**877-503-4636**	215-412-9165
Infosource Inc 1300 City View Ctr	Oviedo	FL	32765	**800-393-4636**	407-796-5200
Inmedius Inc 2247 Babcock Blvd	Pittsburgh	PA	15237	**800-697-7110**	
Innovative Data Management Systems LLC 4006 W Azeele St	Tampa	FL	33609	**866-706-4588**	813-207-2025
Innovative Systems Group Inc 799 Roosevelt Rd	Glen Ellyn	IL	60137	**800-739-2400**	630-858-8500
Insurity Inc 170 Huyshope Ave	Hartford	CT	06106	**866-476-2606**	860-616-7721
Integrity Systems & Solutions LLC 1247 Highland Ave Ste 202	Cheshire	CT	06410	**866-446-8797**	203-271-7971
Isc Sales Inc 4421 Tradition Trl	Plano	TX	75093	**800-836-7472**	972-964-2700
It Doctors 2175 Northdale Blvd Nw	Minneapolis	MN	55433	**888-472-2287**	763-267-6980
Itology.com Ltd 214 - 11 Ave SE Ste 210	Calgary	AB	T2G0X8	**877-226-7726**	403-226-3040
IV Most Consulting Inc 33 Park Dr	Mt Kisco	NY	10549	**800-448-6678**	
Ivenuecom 9925 Painter Ave Ste A	Whittier	CA	90605	**800-683-8314**	
Karpel Computer Systems Inc 770 Spirit of St	Saint Louis	MO	63005	**888-294-7886**	314-892-6300
KBACE Technologies Inc 6 Trafalgar Sq	Nashua	NH	03063	**800-334-4470**	603-821-7000
KEYW Corp 7740 Milestone Pkwy Ste 400	Hanover	MD	21076	**800-340-1001**	443-733-1600
Klein Systems Group Ltd 360-4400 Dominion St	Burnaby	BC	V5G4G3	**877-689-7117**	604-689-7117
Knowles - Mcniff 12862 Garden Grove Blvd Ste C	Garden Grove	CA	92843	**800-820-5254**	
Krillion Inc 607A W Dana St	Mountain View	CA	94041	**877-784-0805**	949-784-0800
Lancore Technologies 11211 Richmond Ave	Houston	TX	77082	**866-492-5800**	281-493-5850
Lexicon Technologies Inc 2195 Eastview Pkwy	Conyers	GA	30013	**888-250-4075**	
Lieberman Software Corp 1900 Ave of the Stars Ste 425	Los Angeles	CA	90067	**800-829-6263**	310-550-8575
Lynx Media Inc 12501 Chandler Blvd Ste 202	Valley Village	CA	91607	**800-451-5969**	818-761-5859
Macdac Engineering 27 Quality Ave	Somers	CT	06071	**866-529-5078**	860-749-5544
Mammography Reporting System Inc 19000 33rd Ave W Ste 130	Seattle	WA	98115	**800-253-4827**	206-633-6145
Marathon Digital Services 716 W Pennway St	Kansas City	MO	64108	**877-568-1122**	816-221-7881
MAXON COMPUTER Inc 2640 Lavery Ct Ste A	Newbury Park	CA	91320	**877-264-6283**	805-376-3333
MaxPoint Interactive Inc 3020 Carrington Mill Blvd Ste 300	Morrisville	NC	27560	**800-916-9960**	
Medivo Inc 55 Broad St 16th Fl	New York	NY	10004	**888-362-4321**	
Meridian Technology Group Inc 12909 SW 68th Pkwy Ste 340	Portland	OR	97223	**800-755-1038**	503-697-1600
Mil Corp 4000 Mitchellville Rd	Bowie	MD	20716	**800-875-0867**	301-805-8500
Money Tree Software Ltd 2430 NW Professional Wy	Corvallis	OR	97330	**877-421-9815**	541-754-3701
Mortgageflex Systems Inc 1200 Riverplace Blvd Ste 650 *General	Jacksonville	FL	32207	**800-326-3539***	904-356-2490
Multisoft Corp 1723 SE 47th Ter	Cape Coral	FL	33904	**888-415-0554**	239-945-6433
Mutual Mobile Inc 206 E Ninth St Ste 1400	Austin	TX	78701	**800-208-3563**	512-615-1800
Nanonation Inc 301 S 13th St Ste 700	Lincoln	NE	68508	**866-843-6266**	402-323-6266
nCircle Network Security Inc 101 Second St Ste 400	San Francisco	CA	94105	**866-897-8776**	503-276-7500
Netcellent System Inc 4030 Valley Blvd	Walnut	CA	91789	**888-595-3818**	909-598-9019
Network Dynamics Inc 640 Brooker Creek Blvd Ste 410	Oldsmar	FL	34677	**877-818-8597**	813-818-8597
Neudesic LLC 8105 Irvine Ctr Dr	Irvine	CA	92618	**800-805-1805**	949-754-4500
Nexlan 28 W N St	Danville	IL	61832	**877-263-9526**	217-431-7236
nextPoint Inc 4043 N Ravenswood Ave	Chicago	IL	60613	**888-929-6398**	
Nims & Associates 1445 Technology Ln Ste A8	Petaluma	CA	94954	**877-454-3200**	707-781-6300

Company / Address	City	State	ZIP	Toll-Free	Phone
Noetix Corp 5010 148th Ave NE Ste 100	Redmond	WA	98052	**866-466-3849**	425-372-2699
Nomadix Inc 30851 Agoura Rd Ste 102	Agoura Hills	CA	91301	**800-666-2349**	818-597-1500
Northwest Data Solutions LLC 2627 C St	Anchorage	AK	99503	**800-544-0786**	907-227-1676
Not Rocket Science Inc 251 Hwy 21	Madisonville	LA	70447	**888-785-8896**	985-845-2334
Nova Libra Inc 8609 W Bryn Mawr Ave Ste 208	Chicago	IL	60631	**866-724-1807**	773-714-1441
Novex Software Developments Inc 8743 Commercial St	New Minas	NS	B4N3C4	**888-542-1813**	902-542-1813
NowDocs International Inc 1985 Lookout Dr	North Mankato	MN	56003	**888-669-3627**	
Oeconnection LLC 4205 Highlander Pkwy	Richfield	OH	44286	**888-776-5792**	330-523-1830
Open Dental Software Ste 110 3995 Fairview Industrial Dr SE	Salem	OR	97302	**866-239-0469**	503-363-5432
Optimum Solutions Corp 170 Earle Ave	Lynbrook	NY	11563	**800-227-0672**	516-247-5300
Orchard Software Corp 701 Congressional Blvd Ste 360	Carmel	IN	46032	**800-856-1948**	317-573-2633
Paladin Data Systems Corp 19362 Powder Hill Pl NE	Poulsbo	WA	98370	**800-532-8448**	360-779-2400
Panasas Inc 969 W Maude Ave	Sunnyvale	CA	94085	**800-726-2727**	408-215-6800
Park Place Technologies Inc 5910 Landerbrook Dr	Cleveland	OH	44124	**877-778-8707**	
Patriot Technologies Inc 5108 Pegasus Ct Ste F	Frederick	MD	21704	**888-417-9899**	301-695-7500
Pattern Insight Inc 465 Fairchild Dr Ste 209	Mountain View	CA	94043	**866-582-2655**	
Phunware Inc 7800 Shoal Creek Blvd	Austin	TX	78757	**855-521-8485**	
PIC Business Systems Inc 5119 Beckwith Blvd Ste 106	San Antonio	TX	78249	**800-742-7378**	210-690-9106
Plan B Technologies Inc 16701 Melford Blvd Ste 150	Annapolis	MD	21401	**888-925-1602**	301-860-1006
Portable Technology Solutions LLC 221 David Ct	Calverton	NY	11933	**877-640-4152**	
Pos Source 535 Harrison Ave	Panama City	FL	32401	**800-232-1626**	850-747-0581
Preferred Medical Marketing Corp 15720 Brixham Hill Ave Ste 460	Charlotte	NC	28277	**800-543-8176**	704-543-8103
Pro-cad Software Ltd 12 Elbow River Rd	Calgary	AB	T3Z2V2	**888-477-6223**	403-216-3375
Profitsword LLC 9355 Cypress Cove Dr	Orlando	FL	32819	**866-930-6543**	407-909-8822
Promiles Software Development 1900 Texas Ave	Bridge City	TX	77611	**800-324-8588**	
Promium LLC 3350 Monte Villa Pkwy Ste 220	Bothell	WA	98021	**877-776-6486**	425-286-9200
Property Panorama Inc 9475 Pinecone Dr	Mentor	OH	44060	**877-299-6306**	440-290-2200
Protech Systems Group 3350 Players Club Pkwy	Memphis	TN	38125	**800-459-5100**	901-767-7550
Providge Consulting LLC 2207 Concord Pike Ste 537	Wilmington	DE	19803	**888-927-6583**	
Proximo Consulting Services Inc 2500 Plz Five	Jersey City	NJ	07311	**800-236-9250**	
QHR Corp 1620 Dickson Ave Ste 300	Kelowna	BC	V1Y9Y2	**855-550-5004**	250-448-7095
QuickStart Intelligence Inc 16815 Von Karman Ave Ste 100	Irvine	CA	92606	**866-991-3924**	800-326-1044
Rapid Insight Inc 53 Technology Ln Ste 112	Conway	NH	03818	**888-585-6511**	
RBB Innovations 2-258 Queen St E	Sault Sainte Marie	ON	P6A1Y7	**800-796-7864**	705-942-9053
RDA Corp 303 International Cir Ste 340	Hunt Valley	MD	21030	**888-441-1278**	410-308-9300
Rediker Software Inc 2 Wilbraham Rd	Hampden	MA	01036	**800-213-9860**	413-566-3463
RenoWorks Software Inc 2816 21 St NE	Calgary	AB	T2E6Z2	**877-980-3880**	403-296-3880
Resort Data Processing Inc 211 Eagle Rd	Avon	CO	81620	**877-779-3717**	970-845-1140
Resource & Financial Management Systems Inc 3073 Palisades Ct	Tuscaloosa	AL	35405	**800-701-7367**	
RP Design Web Services 17 Meriden Ave Ste 2A	Southington	CT	06489	**800-847-3475**	203-271-7991
SAP America Inc 1721 Moon Lake Blvd Ste 300	Hoffman Estates	IL	60169	**800-872-1727**	847-230-3800
Satmetrix Systems Inc 1100 Pk Pl	San Mateo	CA	94403	**866-697-2103**	
Saturn Systems Inc 314 W Superior St Ste 1015	Duluth	MN	55802	**888-638-4335**	218-623-7200
School Webmasters 2846 E Nora St	Mesa	AZ	85213	**888-750-4556**	602-750-4556
Selbysoft Inc 8326 Woodland Ave E	Puyallup	WA	98371	**800-454-4434**	253-770-2993
shared logic group inc, The 6904 Spring Vly Dr Ste 305	Holland	OH	43528	**877-865-0083**	419-865-0083
Sigma Systems Canada Inc 55 York St Ste 1100	Toronto	ON	M5J1R7	**888-782-6468**	416-943-9696
Signifi Solutions Inc 2100 Matheson Blvd E Ste 100	Mississauga	ON	L4W5E1	**877-744-6434**	905-602-7707
Sirsi Corp 3300 N Ashton Blvd Ste 500	Lehi	UT	84043	**800-288-8020**	
Smartronix Inc 44150 Smartronix Way	Hollywood	MD	20636	**866-442-7767**	301-373-6000
Softchalk LLC 22 S Auburn Ave	Richmond	VA	23221	**877-638-2425**	
Softerware Inc 132 Welsh Rd Ste 140	Horsham	PA	19044	**800-220-8111**	215-628-0400
Softplan Systems Inc 8118 Isabella Ln	Brentwood	TN	37027	**800-248-0164**	615-370-1121
Sparta Systems Inc 2000 Waterview Dr Ste 300	Holmdel	NJ	07733	**888-261-5948**	609-807-5100
Steadmantech 1153 Powderhouse Rd	Vestal	NY	13850	**866-772-0882**	
Stenograph LLC 1500 Bishop Ct	Mount Prospect	IL	60056	**800-323-4247**	847-803-1400
System Concepts Inc 15900 N 78th St	Scottsdale	AZ	85260	**800-553-2438**	480-951-8011
Systems Engineering Technologies Corp 6121 Lincolnia Rd Ste 200	Alexandria	VA	22312	**800-385-8977**	703-941-7887
Systemtec Inc 246 Stoneridge Dr Ste 301	Columbia	SC	29210	**888-900-1655**	803-806-8100
Tallan Inc 175 Capital Blvd Ste 401	Rocky Hill	CT	06067	**800-677-3693**	860-633-3693
Tangoe Inc 35 Executive Blvd *NASDAQ: TNGO*	Orange	CT	06477	**877-571-4737**	203-859-9300
Technical Support Inc 11253 John Galt Blvd	Omaha	NE	68137	**800-337-0283**	402-331-4977
Technical Toolboxes Ltd 3801 Kirby Dr Ste 520	Houston	TX	77098	**866-866-6766**	713-630-0505
Terra Dotta LLC 501 W Franklin St Ste 105	Chapel Hill	NC	27516	**877-368-8277**	
Terracor Business Solutions 677 St Mary's Rd	Winnipeg	MB	R2M3M6	**877-942-0005**	204-477-5342
Tier1 Inc 2403 Sidney St Ste 225	Pittsburgh	PA	15203	**888-284-0202**	412-381-9201
Time Trak Systems Inc 933 Pine Grove	Port Huron	MI	48060	**888-484-6387**	810-984-1313
TimeTECH Canada Inc 7420 Airport Rd Ste 101	Mississauga	ON	L4T4E5	**877-816-8463**	905-677-7009
Timeware Inc 9329 Ravenna Rd Ste D	Twinsburg	OH	44087	**866-936-2420**	330-963-2700
Tips Inc 2402 Williams Dr	Georgetown	TX	78628	**800-242-8477**	512-863-3653
Titan Lenders Corp 5353 W Dartmouth Ave Ste 50	Denver	CO	80227	**866-412-9180**	
Tizbi Inc 800 Saint Mary's St Ste 402	Raleigh	NC	27605	**888-729-0951**	
Today's Business Computers 213 E Black Horse Pk	Pleasantville	NJ	08232	**800-371-5132**	609-645-5132
Tone Software Inc 1735 S Brookhurst St	Anaheim	CA	92804	**800-833-8663**	714-991-9460
TopCoder Inc 95 Glastonbury Blvd	Glastonbury	CT	06033	**866-867-2633**	860-633-5540
Trade Manage Capital Inc 299 Market St 4th Fl	Saddle Brook	NJ	07663	**800-221-5676**	
TriZetto Corporation 501 N Broadway 3rd Fl	Sacramento	CA	95814	**800-969-3666**	
Twin Oaks Software Development Inc 1463 Berlin Tpke	Berlin	CT	06037	**866-278-6750**	860-829-6000
Unicentric Inc 3127 Penn Ave	Pittsburgh	PA	15201	**800-513-7745**	412-697-7200
United Systems & Software Inc 300 Colonial Ctr Pkwy Ste 150 PO Box 958444	Lake Mary	FL	32746	**800-522-8774**	407-875-2120
Unlimi-Tech Software Inc 1725 St Laurent Blvd Ste 205	Ottawa	ON	K1G3V4	**877-327-9387**	613-667-2439
Utilant LLC 475 Ellicott St Ste 5	Buffalo	NY	14203	**888-884-5268**	
Valid8 .com Inc 500 W Cummings Park Ste 6550	Woburn	MA	01801	**855-482-5438**	
Vector Planning & Services Inc 591 Camino De La Reina Ste 300	San Diego	CA	92108	**888-522-5491**	619-297-5656
Verecloud Inc 555 Eldorado Blvd Ste 200	Broomfield	CO	80021	**877-300-2158**	
Veros Real Estate Solutions LLC 2333 N Broadway Ste 350	Santa Ana	CA	92706	**866-458-3767**	714-415-6300
Vertical Management Systems Inc 7 N Fair Oaks Ave 2nd Fl	Pasadena	CA	91103	**800-867-4357**	
VideoMining Corp 403 S Allen St Ste 101	State College	PA	16801	**800-898-9950**	
Virtual Training Company Inc 5395 Main St	Stephens City	VA	22655	**888-316-5374**	540-869-8686
Vision Technologies Inc 530 McCormick Dr Ste G	Glen Burnie	MD	21061	**866-746-1122**	410-424-2183
Visual Learning Systems Inc PO Box 8226	Missoula	MT	59807	**866-968-7857**	
Visualware Inc 937 Sierra Dr PO Box 668	Turlock	CA	95380	**866-847-9273**	209-262-3491
Vrp Consulting Inc 268 Bush St Ste 3836	San Francisco	CA	94104	**855-545-3877**	
W a m s Inc 1800 E Lambert Ave Ste 155	Brea	CA	92821	**800-421-7151**	714-994-2811
WebNet Services Inc 247 Rt 100	Somers	NY	10589	**866-923-4811**	914-232-6900
Weidenhammer Systems Corp 935 Berkshire Blvd	Reading	PA	19610	**866-497-2227**	610-378-1149
Welligent Inc 5205 Colley Ave	Norfolk	VA	23508	**888-317-5960**	
Winware Inc 1955 W Oak Cir	Marietta	GA	30062	**888-419-1399**	770-419-1399
Wolfram Research Inc 100 Trade Ctr Dr	Champaign	IL	61820	**800-965-3726**	217-398-0700
Xcape Solutions Inc 207 Crystal Grove Blvd	Lutz	FL	33548	**866-285-4899**	813-964-9101
Youngsoft Inc 49197 Wixom Tech Dr	Wixom	MI	48393	**888-470-4553**	248-675-1200
Z-Law Software Inc 80 Upton Ave PO Box 40602	Providence	RI	02940	**800-526-5588**	401-331-3002
Zasio Enterprises Inc 401 W Front St Ste 305	Boise	ID	83702	**800-513-1000**	
Zephyr-Tec Corp 9651 Business Ctr Dr Ste C	Rancho Cucamonga	CA	91730	**877-493-7497**	909-481-9991

COMPUTER RESELLERS

SEE Computer Equipment & Software - Whol

180 COMPUTER SOFTWARE

SEE ALSO Computer Equipment & Software - Whol ; Computer Networking Products & Systems ; Computer Programming Services - Custom ; Computer Stores ; Computer Systems Design Services ; Educational Materials & Supplies ; Application Service Providers (ASPs)

Company / Address	City	State	Zip	Toll-Free	Phone
Williamson Law Book Co 790 Canning Pkwy	Victor	NY	14564	**800-733-9522**	585-924-3400

180-1 Business Software (General)

Companies listed here make general-purpose software products that are designed for use by all types of businesses, professionals, and, to some extent, personal users.

Company / Address	City	State	Zip	Toll-Free	Phone
1MAGE Software Inc 384 Inverness Pkwy Ste 206	Englewood	CO	80112	**800-844-1468**	
4D Inc 3031 Tisch Way Ste 900	San Jose	CA	95128	**800-785-3303**	408-557-4600
ACI Worldwide 4965 Preston Pk Blvd Ste 800	Plano	TX	75093	**877-238-3095**	972-599-5600
ACOM Solutions Inc 2850 E 29th St	Long Beach	CA	90806	**800-347-3638**	562-424-7899
Actuate Corp 2207 Bridgepointe Pkwy Ste 500 *NASDAQ: OTEX* ■ *Sales	San Mateo	CA	94404	**800-914-2259***	650-645-3000
Adexa Inc 5933 W Century Blvd 12th Fl	Los Angeles	CA	90045	**888-300-7692**	310-642-2100
Adobe Systems Inc 345 Pk Ave *NASDAQ: ADBE*	San Jose	CA	95110	**800-833-6687**	408-536-6000
Advent Software Inc 600 Townsend St Ste 500 5th Fl *NASDAQ: ADVS*	San Francisco	CA	94103	**800-727-0605**	415-543-7696
AgilQuest Corp 9407 Hull St Rd	Richmond	VA	23236	**888-745-7455**	804-745-0467
American Business Systems Inc 315 Littleton Rd	Chelmsford	MA	01824	**800-356-4034**	
American Software Inc 470 E Paces Ferry Rd *NASDAQ: AMSWA*	Atlanta	GA	30305	**800-726-2946**	404-261-4381
APPX Software Inc 11363 San Jose Blvd Ste 301	Jacksonville	FL	32223	**800-879-2779**	904-880-5560
Astea International Inc 240 Gibraltar Rd *NASDAQ: ATEA*	Horsham	PA	19044	**800-878-4657**	215-682-2500
athenahealth Inc 311 Arsenal St *NASDAQ: ATHN*	Watertown	MA	02472	**800-981-5084**	617-402-1000
AttachmateWRQ 1500 Dexter Ave N *Sales	Seattle	WA	98109	**800-872-2829***	206-217-7500
Attunity Inc 70 BlanchaRd Rd	Burlington	MA	01803	**866-288-8648**	781-730-4070
Baudville Inc 5380 52nd St SE *Orders	Grand Rapids	MI	49512	**800-728-0888***	616-698-0889
Blackbaud Inc 2000 Daniel Island Dr *NASDAQ: BLKB*	Charleston	SC	29492	**800-468-8996**	843-216-6200
BMC Software Inc 2101 City W Blvd *NASDAQ: BMC*	Houston	TX	77042	**800-841-2031**	713-918-8800
Bottomline Technologies 325 Corporate Dr *NASDAQ: EPAY*	Portsmouth	NH	03801	**800-243-2528**	603-436-0700
Bradmark Technologies Inc 4265 San Felipe St Ste 700	Houston	TX	77027	**800-621-2808**	713-621-2808
Brady Identification Solutions 6555 W Good Hope Rd *Cust Svc	Milwaukee	WI	53223	**800-537-8791***	414-358-6600
Brainworks Software Inc 100 S Main St	Sayville	NY	11782	**800-755-1111**	631-563-5000
CA Inc 1 CA Plz *NASDAQ: CA*	Islandia	NY	11749	**800-225-5224**	631-342-6000
CDC Trade Beam Inc 2 Waters Pk Dr Ste 100	San Mateo	CA	94403	**888-311-1415**	650-653-4800
Cicero Inc 8000 Regency Pkwy Ste 542	Cary	NC	27518	**866-538-3588**	919-380-5000
Cincom Systems Inc 55 Merchant St	Cincinnati	OH	45246	**800-224-6266**	513-612-2300
Compuware Corp 1 Campus Martius St *NASDAQ: CPWR*	Detroit	MI	48226	**800-292-7432**	313-227-7300
Current Analysis Inc 21335 Signal Hill Plz Ste 200	Sterling	VA	20164	**877-787-8947**	703-404-9200
Cyma Systems Inc 2330 W University Dr Ste 4	Tempe	AZ	85281	**800-292-2962**	
D&B Sales & Marketing Solutions 460 Totten Pond Rd	Waltham	MA	02451	**866-473-3932**	781-672-9200
Data Pro Acctg Software Inc 111 Second Ave NE Ste 1200	Saint Petersburg	FL	33701	**800-237-6377**	727-803-1500
Datamatics Management Services Inc 330 New Brunswick Ave	Fords	NJ	08863	**800-673-0366**	732-738-9600
Deltek Inc 13880 Dulles Corner Ln *NASDAQ: PROJ*	Herndon	VA	20171	**800-456-2009**	703-734-8606
Drake Software 235 E Palmer St	Franklin	NC	28734	**800-890-9500**	
E*Trade Financial Corp Corporate Services 4500 Bohannon Dr	Menlo Park	CA	94025	**800-786-2575**	650-331-6000
eCredit 777 Yamato Rd Ste 500	Boca Raton	FL	33431	**800-276-2321**	561-226-9000
Edge Technologies Inc 3702 Pender Dr Ste 250	Fairfax	VA	22030	**888-771-3343**	703-691-7900
eSignal 3955 Pt Eden Way	Hayward	CA	94545	**800-815-8256**	510-266-6000
FileMaker Inc 5201 Patrick Henry Dr *Cust Svc	Santa Clara	CA	95054	**800-325-2747***	408-987-7000
Fischer International Systems Corp 9045 Strada Stell Ct Ste 201 *Tech Supp	Naples	FL	34109	**800-776-7258***	239-643-1500
FlexiInternational Software Inc 2 Enterprise Dr *OTC: FLXI*	Shelton	CT	06484	**800-353-9492**	203-925-3040
Gemstone Systems Inc 1260 NW Waterhouse Ave Ste 200	Beaverton	OR	97006	**800-243-4772**	503-533-3000
Global Shop Solutions Inc 975 Evergreen Cir *Sales	The Woodlands	TX	77380	**800-364-5958***	281-681-1959
Global Software Inc 3201 Beechleaf Ct Ste 170	Raleigh	NC	27604	**800-326-3444**	919-872-7800
Glovia International Inc 2250 E Imperial Hwy Ste 200	El Segundo	CA	90245	**888-245-6842**	310-563-7000
Grandite Inc PO Box 47133	Quebec	QC	G1S4X1	**866-808-3932**	581-318-2018
GSE Systems Inc 1332 Londontown Blvd Ste 200 *NYSE: GVP* ■ *Cust Svc	Sykesville	MD	21784	**800-638-7912***	410-970-7800
Halogen Software 495 March Rd	Kanata	ON	K2K3G1	**866-566-7778**	613-270-1011
HarrisData 13555 Bishops Ct Ste 300	Brookfield	WI	53005	**800-225-0585**	262-784-9099
HighJump Software 5600 W 83rd St Ste 600	Minneapolis	MN	55437	**800-328-3271**	952-947-4088
HK Systems Inc 2855 S James Dr	New Berlin	WI	53151	**800-424-7365**	262-860-7000
I-many Inc 1735 Market St 37th Fl	Philadelphia	PA	19103	**877-774-2451**	215-344-1900
iCIMS Inc 90 Matawan Rd Pkwy 120 5th Fl	Matawan	NJ	07747	**800-889-4422**	732-847-1941
Iconixx Software 3420 Executive Ctr Dr Ste 250	Austin	TX	78731	**877-426-6499**	
IFS North America Inc 300 Pk Blvd Ste 555	Chicago	IL	60143	**888-437-4968**	
Informatica Corp 100 Cardinal Way *NASDAQ: INFA*	Redwood City	CA	94063	**800-653-3871**	650-385-5000
Information & Computing Services Inc (ICS) 1650 Prudential Dr Ste 300	Jacksonville	FL	32207	**800-676-4427**	904-399-8500
InfoVista Corp 12950 Worldgate Dr Ste 250	Herndon	VA	20170	**866-921-9219**	703-435-2435
Innovative Systems Inc 790 Holiday Dr Bldg 11	Pittsburgh	PA	15220	**800-622-6390**	412-937-9300
Inova Solutions Inc 110 Avon St	Charlottesville	VA	22902	**800-637-1077**	434-817-8000
Inspiration Software Inc 6443 SW Beaverton Hillsdale Hwy Ste 370	Portland	OR	97221	**800-877-4292**	503-297-3004
Integrated Business Systems & Services Inc 1601 Shop Rd Ste E	Columbia	SC	29201	**800-553-1038**	803-736-5595
International Business Machines Corp (IBM) 1 New OrchaRd Rd *NYSE: IBM*	Armonk	NY	10504	**800-426-4968**	914-499-1900
InterraTech Corp PO Box 4	Mount Ephraim	NJ	08059	**888-589-4889**	856-854-5100
ISG Novasoft (ISGN) 600 A N John Rodes Blvd	Melbourne	FL	32934	**800-462-5545**	800-939-8258
K-Systems Inc 2104 Aspen Dr	Mechanicsburg	PA	17055	**800-221-0204**	717-795-7711
Kalido 1 Wall St Ste 3	Burlington	MA	01803	**866-466-3849**	781-202-3200
Logility Inc 470 E Paces Ferry Rd	Atlanta	GA	30305	**800-762-5207**	404-261-9777
Longview Solutions 100 Matsonford Rd Ste 230	Radnor	PA	19087	**888-454-2549**	610-977-0995
M2 Technology Inc 21702 Hardy Oak Ste 100	San Antonio	TX	78258	**800-267-1760**	210-566-3773
Malvern Systems Inc 81 Lancaster Ave Ste 219	Malvern	PA	19355	**800-296-9642**	
Maverick Technologies 265 Admiral Trost Rd PO Box 470	Columbia	IL	62236	**888-917-9109**	618-281-9100
Mediagrif Interactive Technologies Inc 1111 St-Charles St W E Tower Ste 255 *TSE: MDF*	Longueuil	QC	J4K5G4	**877-677-9088**	450-449-0102
Meridian Systems 1720 Prairie City Rd Ste 120	Folsom	CA	95630	**800-850-2660**	916-294-2000
MicroBiz Corp 655 Oak Grove Ave Ste 493 Ste 493	Menlo Park	CA	94025	**800-937-2289**	702-749-5353
Microlink Enterprise Inc 20955 Pathfinder Rd Ste 100	Diamond Bar	CA	91765	**800-829-3688**	562-205-1888
Microsoft Great Plains Business Solutions 3900 Great Plains Dr S	Fargo	ND	58104	**888-477-7877**	701-281-6500
Milner Technologies Inc 5125 Peachtree Industrial Blvd	Norcross	GA	30092	**800-592-3766**	770-734-5300
Multi-Ad Inc 1720 W Detweiller Dr	Peoria	IL	61615	**800-348-6485**	309-692-1530
NetMotion Wireless Inc 701 N 34th St Ste 250	Seattle	WA	98103	**877-818-7626**	206-691-5500
New Century Education Foundation PO Box 43052	Upper Montclair	NJ	07043	**866-326-1133**	
NewlineNoosh Inc 625 Ellis St Ste 300	Mountain View	CA	94043	**888-286-6674**	650-637-6000
Novell Inc 1800 S Novell Pl	Provo	UT	84606	**800-529-3400**	801-861-4272
Objectivity Inc 3099 N First St Ste 200	San Jose	CA	95134	**800-767-6259**	408-992-7100
OMD Corp 3705 Missouri Blvd	Jefferson City	MO	65109	**866-440-8664**	573-893-8930

Company	Address	City	State	Zip	Toll-Free	Phone
OneSCM	6805 Capital of Texas Hwy Ste 370	Austin	TX	78731	**800-324-5143**	512-231-8191
Open Systems Inc	4301 Dean Lakes Blvd *Sales	Shakopee	MN	55379	**800-328-2276***	
OpenText Corp	275 Frank Tompa Dr Ste 710 N	Waterloo	ON	N2L0A1	**800-499-6544**	773-632-1400
Oracle Corp	500 Oracle Pkwy *NYSE: ORCL* ■ *Sales	Redwood Shores	CA	94065	**800-392-2999***	650-506-7000
Oracle USA	500 Oracle Pkwy	Redwood Shores	CA	94065	**800-392-2999**	650-506-7000
Palisade Corp	798 Cascadilla St	Ithaca	NY	14850	**800-432-7475**	607-277-8000
Paperclip Software Inc	1 University Plz	Hackensack	NJ	07601	**800-929-3503**	201-525-1221
Passport Corp	85 Chestnut Ridge Rd	Montvale	NJ	07645	**800-926-6736**	201-573-0038
Payspan Inc	7751 Belfort Pkwy Ste 200	Jacksonville	FL	32256	**877-331-7154**	
Pentagon 2000 Software Inc	15 W 34th St 5th Fl	New York	NY	10001	**800-643-1806**	212-629-7521
PeopleStrategy Inc	5883 Glenridge Dr Ste 200	Atlanta	GA	30328	**855-488-4100**	
Percussion Software Inc	600 Unicorn Pk Dr	Woburn	MA	01801	**800-283-0800**	781-438-9900
Personnel Data Systems Inc (PDS)	470 Norritown Rd Ste 202	Blue Bell	PA	19422	**800-243-8737**	610-238-4600
Pitney Bowes Group 1 Software	4200 Parliament Pl Ste 600	Lanham	MD	20706	**800-367-6950**	301-731-2300
Planview Inc	12301 Research BlvdResearch Park Plz Ste 101	Austin	TX	78759	**800-856-8600**	512-346-8600
Platform Computing Inc	3760 14th Ave	Markham	ON	L3R3T7	**877-528-3676**	905-948-8448
Print-O-Stat Inc	1011 W Market St	York	PA	17404	**800-711-8014**	717-854-7821
Progress Software Corp	14 Oak Pk *NASDAQ: PRGS*	Bedford	MA	01730	**800-477-6473**	781-280-4000
Quest Software Inc	5 Polaris Way *NASDAQ: QSFT*	Aliso Viejo	CA	92656	**800-306-9329**	949-754-8000
Realtime Software Corp	24 Deane Rd	Bernardston	MA	01337	**800-323-1143**	847-803-1100
Red Wing Software Inc	491 Hwy 19	Red Wing	MN	55066	**800-732-9464**	651-388-1106
Redemtech Inc	4115 Leap Rd	Hilliard	OH	43026	**800-393-7627**	614-850-3366
Rentrak Corp	7700 NE Ambassador Pl 3rd Fl *NASDAQ: RENT*	Portland	OR	97220	**800-929-0070**	503-284-7581
Sage Fixed Assets	2325 Dulles Corner Blvd Ste 700	Herndon	VA	20171	**800-368-2405**	866-520-2519
Sand Technology Inc	8 Ave SW *NYSE: SNDTF*	Westmount	QC	H3Z1B1	**877-468-2538**	403-218-2010
SAP	100 Consilium Pl	Scarborough	ON	M1H3E3	**888-777-1727**	416-791-7100
SAS Institute Inc	100 SAS Campus Dr	Cary	NC	27513	**800-727-0025**	919-677-8000
Satori Software Inc	1301 5th Ave Ste 2200	Seattle	WA	98101	**800-553-6477**	206-357-2900
Sciforma Corp	985 University Ave Ste 5 *Sales	Los Gatos	CA	95032	**800-533-9876***	408-354-0144
Selectica Inc	2121 S. El Camino Rl 10th Fl *NASDAQ: SLTC*	San Mateo	CA	94403	**877-712-9560**	650-532-1500
SERENA Software Inc	2345 NW Amberbrook Dr Ste 200	Hillsboro	OR	97006	**800-457-3736**	650-481-3400
Silvon Software Inc	900 Oakmont Ln Ste 400	Westmont	IL	60559	**800-874-5866**	630-655-3313
Soffront Software Inc	45437 Warm Springs Blvd	Fremont	CA	94539	**800-763-3766**	510-413-9000
Software AG USA	11700 Plz America Dr Ste 700	Reston	VA	20190	**877-724-4965**	703-860-5050
Sophos Inc	3 Van de Graaff Dr 2nd Fl	Burlington	MA	01803	**866-866-2802**	
Source Technologies	2910 Whitehall Pk Dr	Charlotte	NC	28273	**800-922-8501**	704-969-7500
SP Systems Inc	7500 Greenway Ctr Dr Ste 850	Greenbelt	MD	20770	**877-327-8732**	301-614-1322
Stamps.com Inc	1990 E Grand Ave *NASDAQ: STMP*	El Segundo	CA	90245	**855-889-7867**	
StrataCare Inc	17838 Gillette Ave	Irvine	CA	92614	**800-277-6512**	
Superior Software Inc	16055 Ventura Blvd Ste 650	Encino	CA	91436	**800-421-3264**	818-990-1135
SYSPRO	959 S Coast Dr Ste 100	Costa Mesa	CA	92626	**800-369-8649**	714-437-1000
Taleo Corp	4140 Dublin Blvd Ste 400 *NYSE: ORCL*	Dublin	CA	94568	**800-672-2531**	925-452-3000
TECSYS Inc	1 Pl Alexis Nihon Ste 800	Montreal	QC	H3Z3B8	**800-922-8649**	514-866-0001
Tenrox	401 Congress Avenue	Austin	TX	78701	**855-944-7526**	450-688-3444
Thomson Tax & Acctg	7322 Newman Blvd *Cust Svc	Dexter	MI	48130	**800-968-8900***	
Tribridge	4830 W Kennedy Blvd Ste 890	Tampa	FL	33609	**877-744-1360**	
Trintech Inc	15851 Dallas Pkwy Ste 900	Addison	TX	75001	**800-416-0075**	972-701-9802
Ultimate Software Group Inc	2000 Ultimate Way *NASDAQ: ULTI*	Weston	FL	33326	**800-432-1729**	954-331-7000
Validar Inc	800 Maynard Ave S Ste 401	Seattle	WA	98134	**888-784-2929**	206-264-9151
Versant Corp	255 Shoreline Dr Ste 450 *NASDAQ: VSNT*	Redwood City	CA	94065	**888-446-4737**	650-232-2400
Vertex Inc	1041 Old Cassatt Rd	Berwyn	PA	19312	**800-355-3500**	610-640-4200
VFA Inc	99 Bedford St	Boston	MA	02111	**800-693-3132**	617-451-5100
Vignette Corp	1301 S Mopac Expy Ste 100	Austin	TX	78746	**800-540-7292**	512-741-4300
Visible Systems Corp	201 Spring St *Sales	Lexington	MA	02421	**888-850-9911***	781-778-0200
Vitria Technology Inc	945 Stewart Dr Ste 200	Sunnyvale	CA	94085	**877-365-5935**	
Wave Systems Corp	480 Pleasant St *NASDAQ: WAVX*	Lee	MA	01238	**800-928-3638**	413-243-1600
Worden Bros Inc	4905 Pine Cone Dr	Durham	NC	27707	**800-776-4940**	919-408-0542
ZyLAB North America LLC	7918 Jones Branch Dr Ste 230	McLean	VA	22102	**866-995-2262**	

180-2 Computer Languages & Development Tools

Company	Address	City	State	Zip	Toll-Free	Phone
Applied Dynamics International Inc	3800 Stone School Rd	Ann Arbor	MI	48108	**888-465-4329**	734-973-1300
BSQUARE Corp	110 110th Ave NE *NASDAQ: BSQR*	Bellevue	WA	98004	**888-820-4500**	425-519-5900
Data Access Corp	14000 SW 119th Ave	Miami	FL	33186	**800-451-3539**	305-238-0012
Empress Software Inc	11785 Beltsville Dr	Beltsville	MD	20705	**866-626-8888**	301-220-1919
FMS Inc	8150 Leesburg Pk Ste 600	Vienna	VA	22182	**866-367-7801**	703-356-4700
Forth Inc	5959 W Century Blvd Ste 700	Los Angeles	CA	90045	**800-553-6784**	310-999-6784
Green Hills Software Inc	30 W Sola St	Santa Barbara	CA	93101	**800-765-4733**	805-965-6044
Instantiations Inc	Officers Row Ste 1325B	Vancouver	WA	98661	**855-476-2558**	503-649-3836
Lattice Inc	1751 S Naperville Rd Ste 100 *Sales	Wheaton	IL	60189	**800-444-4309***	630-949-3250
Mix Software Inc	1203 Berkeley Dr	Richardson	TX	75081	**800-333-0330**	972-231-0949
Numara Software Inc	2202 NW Shore Blvd Ste 650 *Sales	Tampa	FL	33607	**855-834-7487***	813-227-4500
Prolifics	5 Hanover Sqr Ste 2001	New York	NY	10004	**800-458-3313**	212-267-7722
Revelation Software	99 Kinderkamack Rd	Westwood	NJ	07675	**800-262-4747**	201-594-1422
Rogue Wave Software Inc	5500 Flatiron Pkwy	Boulder	CO	80301	**800-487-3217**	303-473-9118
SlickEdit Inc	3000 Aerial Ctr Pkwy Ste 120	Morrisville	NC	27560	**800-934-3348**	919-473-0070
Thoroughbred Software International Inc	285 Davidson Ave Ste 302	Somerset	NJ	08873	**800-524-0430**	732-560-1377
Zortec International	25 Century Blvd Ste 103	Nashville	TN	37214	**800-361-7005**	615-361-7000

180-3 Educational & Reference Software

Company	Address	City	State	Zip	Toll-Free	Phone
Allen Communication Learning Services	55 West 900 South	Salt Lake City	UT	84101	**866-310-7800**	801-537-7800
Blackboard Inc	1899 L St NW 5th Fl	Washington	DC	20036	**800-424-9299**	202-463-4860
CompassLearning Inc	203 Colorado St	Austin	TX	78701	**800-232-9556**	512-478-9600
Fuel Education LLC	2300 Corporate Park Dr	Herndon	VA	20171	**800-222-2811**	844-251-4687
Individual Software Inc	4255 HopyaRd Rd Ste 2	Pleasanton	CA	94588	**800-822-3522**	925-734-6767
Inscape Publishing Inc	6465 Wayzata Blvd Ste 800	Minneapolis	MN	55426	**877-735-8383**	763-765-2222
Inspiration Software Inc	6443 SW Beaverton Hillsdale Hwy Ste 370	Portland	OR	97221	**800-877-4292**	503-297-3004
Language Engineering Co	135 Beaver St Ste 204	Waltham	MA	02452	**888-366-4532**	781-642-8900
LDP Inc	75 Kiwanis Blvd PO Box O	West Hazleton	PA	18201	**800-522-8413**	
MindPlay Educational Software	440 S Williams Blvd Ste 206	Tucson	AZ	85711	**800-221-7911**	520-888-1800
Queue Inc	703 Post Rd	Fairfield	CT	06824	**800-232-2224**	
Renaissance Learning Inc	2911 Peach St	Wisconsin Rapids	WI	54494	**800-338-4204**	715-424-3636
Saba Software Inc	2400 Bridge Pkwy *OTC: SABA*	Redwood Shores	CA	94065	**877-722-2101**	650-581-2500
Scientific Learning Corp	300 Frank H Ogawa Plz Ste 600 *OTC: SCIL*	Oakland	CA	94612	**888-665-9707**	510-444-3500
TIBCO Software Inc	1700 Westlake Ave N Ste 500	Seattle	WA	98109	**866-247-8182**	206-283-8802
Tom Snyder Productions Inc	100 Talcott Ave	Watertown	MA	02472	**800-342-0236**	617-924-0938
Transparent Language Inc	12 Murphy Dr	Nashua	NH	03062	**800-538-8867**	
Wordsmart Corp	10025 Mesa Rim Rd	San Diego	CA	92121	**800-858-9673**	858-565-8068

180-4 Electronic Purchasing & Procurement Software

Company	City	State	ZIP	Toll-Free	Phone
Apptis Inc 4800 Westfields Blvd	Chantilly	VA	20151	**888-277-8478**	703-279-3000
Ariba Inc 807 11th Ave *NASDAQ: ARBA*	Sunnyvale	CA	94089	**866-772-7422**	650-390-1000
CA Inc 1 CA Plz *NASDAQ: CA*	Islandia	NY	11749	**800-225-5224**	631-342-6000
Covisint 1 Campus Martius Ste 700	Detroit	MI	48226	**800-229-4125**	
Elavon 2 Concourse Pkwy Ste 300	Atlanta	GA	30328	**800-725-1243**	678-731-5000
GXS Inc 9711 Washingtonian Blvd	Gaithersburg	MD	20878	**800-560-4347**	301-340-4000
International Business Machines Corp (IBM) 1 New OrchaRd Rd *NYSE: IBM*	Armonk	NY	10504	**800-426-4968**	914-499-1900
SciQuest Inc 6501 Weston Pkwy Ste 200	Cary	NC	27513	**888-638-7322**	919-659-2100

180-5 Engineering Software

Company	City	State	ZIP	Toll-Free	Phone
Accelrys Inc 10188 Telesis Ct Ste 100 *NASDAQ: ACCL*	San Diego	CA	92121	**888-249-2284**	858-799-5000
Altium Inc 2175 Salk Ave Ste 100 *Sales	Carlsbad	CA	92008	**800-544-4186***	760-231-0760
ANSYS Inc 275 Technology Dr *NASDAQ: ANSS*	Canonsburg	PA	15317	**800-937-3321**	724-746-3304
Ashlar Inc 9600 Great Hills Trl Ste 150W-1625	Austin	TX	78759	**800-877-2745**	512-250-2186
Aspen Technology Inc 200 Wheeler Rd *NASDAQ: AZPN*	Burlington	MA	01803	**888-996-7100**	781-221-6400
Autodesk Inc 111 McInnis Pkwy *NASDAQ: ADSK* ■ *Tech Supp	San Rafael	CA	94903	**800-964-6432***	415-507-5000
Bentley Systems Inc 685 Stockton Dr	Exton	PA	19341	**800-236-8539**	610-458-5000
Bohannan Huston Inc 7500 Jefferson St NE Courtyard 1	Albuquerque	NM	87109	**800-877-5332**	505-823-1000
Cadence Design Systems Inc 2655 Seely Ave *NASDAQ: CDNS* ■ *Cust Svc	San Jose	CA	95134	**800-746-6223***	408-943-1234
CambridgeSoft Corp 100 CambridgePark Dr	Cambridge	MA	02140	**800-315-7300**	617-588-9100
Direct Source Inc 8176 Mallory Ct	Chanhassen	MN	55317	**800-934-8055**	952-934-8000
DP Technology Corp 1150 Avenida Acaso	Camarillo	CA	93012	**800-627-8479**	805-388-6000
Evolution Computing 7000 N 16th St Ste 120 514	Phoenix	AZ	85020	**800-874-4028**	
Geocomp Corp 1145 Massachusetts Ave *Cust Svc	Boxborough	MA	01719	**800-822-2669***	978-635-0012
Gibbs & Assoc 323 Science Dr *Cust Svc	Moorpark	CA	93021	**800-654-9399***	805-523-0004
Infinite Graphics Inc 4611 E Lake St *OTC: INFG*	Minneapolis	MN	55406	**800-679-0676**	612-721-6283
Intergraph Corp 19 Interpro Rd	Madison	AL	35758	**800-345-4856**	256-730-2000
Kubotek USA 2 Mt Royal Ave Ste 500	Marlborough	MA	01752	**800-372-3872**	508-229-2020
LINDO Systems Inc 1415 N Dayton St *Sales	Chicago	IL	60622	**800-441-2378***	312-988-7422
Mentor Graphics Corp 8005 SW Boeckman Rd *NASDAQ: MENT*	Wilsonville	OR	97070	**800-592-2210**	503-685-7000
National Instruments Corp 11500 N Mopac Expy *NASDAQ: NATI* ■ *Cust Svc	Austin	TX	78759	**800-433-3488***	512-794-0100
Parametric Technology Corp (PTC) 140 Kendrick St *NASDAQ: PTC*	Needham	MA	02494	**800-613-7535**	781-370-5000
Planit Solutions Inc 3800 Palisades Dr	Tuscaloosa	AL	35405	**800-280-6932**	205-556-9199
PMS Systems Corp 2800 28th St Ste 109	Santa Monica	CA	90405	**800-755-3968**	310-450-2566
Science Application International Corp Inc (SAIC Inc) 1710 SAIC Dr	McLean	VA	22102	**866-400-7242**	703-676-4300
Tripos Inc 1699 S Hanley Rd	Saint Louis	MO	63144	**800-323-2960**	314-647-1099
Zuken USA 238 Littleton Rd Ste 100	Westford	MA	01886	**800-447-7332**	978-692-4900

180-6 Games & Entertainment Software

Company	City	State	ZIP	Toll-Free	Phone
Disney Consumer Products 500 S Buena Vista St *PR	Burbank	CA	91521	**855-553-4763***	818-560-1000
Her Interactive Inc 1150 114th Ave SE Ste 200 *Orders	Bellevue	WA	98004	**800-461-8787***	425-460-8787
MakeMusic! Inc 7615 Golden Triangle Dr Ste M *NASDAQ: MMUS*	Eden Prairie	MN	55344	**800-843-2066**	952-937-9611
Nintendo of America Inc 4820 150th Ave NE *Cust Svc	Redmond	WA	98052	**800-255-3700***	425-882-2040

180-7 Internet & Communications Software

Company	City	State	ZIP	Toll-Free	Phone
@Comm Corp 150 Dow St	Manchester	NH	03101	**800-641-5400**	650-375-8188
Adaptive Micro Systems Inc 7840 N 86th St	Milwaukee	WI	53224	**800-558-4187**	414-357-2020
Akamai Technologies Inc 150 Broadway *NASDAQ: AKAM*	Cambridge	MA	02142	**877-425-2624**	617-444-3000
Amcom Software Inc 10400 Yellow Cir Dr	Eden Prairie	MN	55343	**800-852-8935**	952-230-5200
Answers Corp 237 W 35th St Ste 1101	New York	NY	10001	**888-885-5008**	646-502-4778
AnyDoc Software Inc 5404 Cypress Ctr Dr Ste 140	Tampa	FL	33609	**888-495-2638**	
Apex Voice Communications Inc 21700 Oxnard St Ste 1060	Woodland Hills	CA	91367	**800-727-3970**	818-379-8400
Ariba Inc 807 11th Ave *NASDAQ: ARBA*	Sunnyvale	CA	94089	**866-772-7422**	650-390-1000
Asure Softwar 110 Wild Basin Rd *NASDAQ: ASUR*	Austin	TX	78746	**888-323-8835**	512-437-2700
AttachmateWRQ 1500 Dexter Ave N *Sales	Seattle	WA	98109	**800-872-2829***	206-217-7500
Authorize.Net Corp PO Box 8999	San Francisco	CA	94128	**877-447-3938**	801-492-6450
Avanquest Software USA 1333 W 120th Ave	Westminster	CO	80234	**800-011-2312**	
Avistar Communications Corp 1855 S Grant St 4th Fl *OTC: AVSR*	San Mateo	CA	94402	**800-803-0153**	650-525-3300
Big Sky Technologies 9325 Sky Pk Ct Ste 120	San Diego	CA	92123	**800-736-2751**	858-715-5000
Blast Inc 220 Chatham Business Dr PO Box 818	Pittsboro	NC	27312	**800-242-5278**	919-533-0143
Callware Technologies Inc 9100 S 500 W	Sandy	UT	84070	**800-888-4226**	801-988-6800
ClickSoftware Inc 35 Corporate Dr Ste 400 *NASDAQ: CKSW*	Burlington	MA	01803	**888-438-3308**	781-272-5903
Cothern Computer Systems Inc 1640 Lelia Dr Ste 200	Jackson	MS	39216	**800-844-1155**	601-969-1155
DataMotion Inc 35 Airport Rd Ste 120	Morristown	NJ	07960	**800-672-7233**	973-455-1245
DealerTrack Holdings Inc 1111 Marcus Ave Ste M04 *NASDAQ: TRAK*	Lake Success	NY	11042	**877-357-8725**	516-734-3600
Dynamic Instruments Inc 3860 Calle Fortunada	San Diego	CA	92123	**800-793-3358**	858-278-4900
eAcceleration Corp 1050 NE Hostmark St Ste 100-B *Sales	Poulsbo	WA	98370	**800-803-4588***	360-779-6301
Education Management Solutions Inc 436 Creamery Way Ste 300	Exton	PA	19341	**877-367-5050**	610-701-7002
EXTOL International Inc 529 Terry Reiley Way	Pottsville	PA	17901	**800-542-7284**	570-628-5500
FutureSoft Inc 1660 Townhurst Dr Ste E	Houston	TX	77043	**800-989-8908**	281-496-9400
GeoTrust Inc 350 Ellis St Bldg J	Mountain View	CA	94043	**866-511-4141**	650-426-5010
Hilgraeve Inc 115 E Elm Ave *Sales	Monroe	MI	48162	**800-826-2760***	734-243-0576
Hyland Software Inc 28500 Clemens Rd	Westlake	OH	44145	**888-495-2638**	440-788-5000
Imecom Group 8 Governor Wentworth Hwy	Wolfeboro	NH	03894	**800-329-9099**	603-569-0600
InfoNow Corp 1875 Lawrence St Ste 1200	Denver	CO	80202	**855-524-3282**	303-293-0212
Information Builders Inc 2 Penn Plz	New York	NY	10121	**800-969-4636**	212-736-4433
IntelliNet Technologies Inc 1990 W New Haven Ave Ste 303	Melbourne	FL	32904	**888-726-0686**	321-726-0686
Interactive Intelligence Inc 7601 Interactive Way *NASDAQ: ININ*	Indianapolis	IN	46278	**800-267-1364**	317-872-3000
InternetSafety.com Inc 3979 S Main St Ste 230	Acworth	GA	30101	**877-944-8080**	
Ion Networks Inc 120 Corporate Blvd Ste A	South Plainfield	NJ	07080	**800-722-8986**	908-546-3900
Keynote Systems Inc 777 Mariners Island Blvd *NASDAQ: KEYN*	San Mateo	CA	94404	**888-539-7978**	650-403-2400
LassoSoft LLC PO Box 33	Manchester	WA	98353	**888-286-7753**	954-302-3526
Mirror Image Internet Inc 2 Highwood Dr	Tewksbury	MA	01876	**800-353-2923**	781-376-1100
Moai Technologies Inc 100 First Ave 9th Fl	Pittsburgh	PA	15222	**800-814-1548**	412-454-5550
Momentum Systems Ltd 41 Twosome Dr Ste 9	Moorestown	NJ	08057	**800-279-1384**	856-727-0777
NetScout Systems Inc 310 Littleton Rd *NASDAQ: NTCT*	Westford	MA	01886	**800-357-7666**	978-614-4000
NICE Systems Inc 301 Rt 17 N 10th Fl	Rutherford	NJ	07070	**800-994-4498**	201-964-2600
Nuance Communications Inc 1 Wayside Rd *NASDAQ: NUAN*	Burlington	MA	01803	**800-654-1187**	781-565-5000
OmTool Ltd 6 Riverside Dr *OTC: OMTL*	Andover	MA	01810	**800-886-7845**	978-327-5700
One Touch Systems Inc 2528 Qume Dr Unit 14	San Jose	CA	95131	**800-227-8862**	408-436-4600

				Toll-Free	Phone
Open Text Corp 275 Frank Tompa Dr	Waterloo	ON	N2L0A1	**800-499-6544***	519-888-7111
TSE: OTC ■ *General					
Open Text Corp (USA) 100 Tri-State International Pkwy 3rd Fl	Lincolnshire	IL	60069	**800-499-6544***	847-267-9330
TSE: OTC ■ *Sales					
OpenConnect Systems Inc 2711 LBJ Fwy Ste 700	Dallas	TX	75234	**800-551-5881**	972-484-5200
PartsRiver Inc 3155 Kearney St Ste 210	Fremont	CA	94538	**855-700-7278**	
Powersteering Software Inc 401 Congress Ave Ste 1850	Austin	TX	78701	**866-390-9088**	617-492-0707
QSA ToolWorks LLC 3100 47th Ave	Long Island	NY	11101	**800-784-7018**	516-935-9151
Selectica Inc 2121 S. El Camino Rl 10th Fl	San Mateo	CA	94403	**877-712-9560**	650-532-1500
NASDAQ: SLTC					
Sendmail Inc 6475 Christie Ave Ste 350	Emeryville	CA	94608	**888-594-3150**	510-594-5400
Support.com Inc 900 Chesapeake Dr 2nd Fl	Redwood City	CA	94063	**877-493-2778**	650-556-9440
NASDAQ: SPRT					
Surety LLC 12020 Sunrise Vly Dr Ste 250	Reston	VA	20191	**800-298-3115**	571-748-5800
Symantec Corp 350 Ellis St	Mountain View	CA	94043	**800-441-7234**	650-527-8000
NASDAQ: SYMC					
UmeVoice Inc 20C Pimentel Ct Ste 1	Novato	CA	94949	**888-230-3300**	415-883-1500
Vertical Communications Inc 3940 Freedom Cr Ste 110	Santa Clara	CA	95054	**800-914-9985***	408-404-1600
OTC: VRCC ■ *Sales					
WaveLink Corp 1011 Western Ave Ste 601	Seattle	WA	98104	**888-697-9283***	206-274-4280
*Tech Supp					
Websense Inc 10240 Sorrento Vly Rd	San Diego	CA	92121	**800-723-1166**	858-320-8000
NASDAQ: WBSN					
YellowBrix Inc 200 North Glebe Rd Ste 1025	Arlington	VA	22203	**888-325-9366**	703-548-3300
Zone Alarm 800 Bridge Pkwy	Redwood City	CA	94065	**877-966-5221**	415-633-4500

180-8 Multimedia & Design Software

				Toll-Free	Phone
3D Systems Inc 333 Three D Systems Cir	Rock Hill	SC	29730	**800-793-3669**	803-326-3900
Adobe Systems Inc 345 Pk Ave	San Jose	CA	95110	**800-833-6687**	408-536-6000
NASDAQ: ADBE					
Apple Inc 1 Infinite Loop	Cupertino	CA	95014	**800-275-2273***	408-996-1010
NASDAQ: AAPL ■ *Cust Svc					
Auto FX Software 141 Village St Ste 2	Birmingham	AL	35242	**800-839-2008**	205-980-0056
Avid Technology Inc 65-75 Network Dri	Burlington	MA	01803	**800-949-2843**	978-640-6789
NASDAQ: AVID					
Concurrent 4375 River Green Pkwy Ste 100	Duluth	GA	30096	**877-978-7363**	678-258-4000
NASDAQ: CCUR					
Corel Corp 1600 Carling Ave	Ottawa	ON	K1Z8R7	**800-772-6735***	613-728-8200
*Orders					
DeLorme 2 DeLorme Dr PO Box 298	Yarmouth	ME	04096	**800-452-5931***	207-846-7000
*Sales					
Equilibrium Inc 100 Tamal Plz Ste 225	Corte Madera	CA	94925	**855-378-4542**	415-332-4343
eWorkplace Solutions Inc 24461 Ridge Rt Dr Ste 210	Laguna Hills	CA	92653	**888-477-7989**	949-583-1646
HydroCAD Software Solutions LLC PO Box 477	Chocorua	NH	03817	**800-927-7246**	603-323-8666
Image Labs International PO Box 1545	Belgrade	MT	59714	**800-785-5995**	406-585-7225
Media 100 Inc 450 Donald Lynch Blvd	Marlborough	MA	02210	**888-772-6747**	508-460-1600
MicroVision Development Inc 5541 Fermi Ct Ste 120	Carlsbad	CA	92008	**800-998-4555**	760-438-7781
Nemetschek North America 7150 Riverwood Dr	Columbia	MD	21046	**888-646-4223**	410-290-5114
NewTek Inc 5131 Beckwith Blvd	San Antonio	TX	78249	**800-862-7837***	210-370-8000
*Cust Svc					
Overwatch Geospatial Operations 21660 Ridgetop Cir Ste 110	Sterling	VA	20166	**800-937-6881**	703-437-7651
PC/Nametag 124 Horizon Dr	Verona	WI	53593	**877-626-3824**	
Presagis 1301 W George Bush Fwy Ste 120	Richardson	TX	75080	**800-361-6424**	
Quark Inc 1800 Grant St	Denver	CO	80203	**800-676-4575***	
*Cust Svc					
RealNetworks Inc 2601 Elliott Ave Ste 1000	Seattle	WA	98121	**888-484-8256***	206-674-2700
NASDAQ: RNWK ■ *Cust Svc					
Scan-Optics Inc 169 Progress Dr	Manchester	CT	06042	**800-543-8681**	860-645-7878
Sigma Design 5521 Jackson St	Alexandria	LA	71303	**888-990-0900***	318-449-9900
*Sales					
SoftPress Systems Inc 3020 Bridgeway Ste 408	Sausalito	CA	94965	**800-853-6454**	415-331-4820
TechSmith Corp 2405 Woodlake Dr	Okemos	MI	48864	**800-517-3001**	517-381-2300
Telestream Inc 848 Gold Flat Rd Ste 1	Nevada City	CA	95959	**877-681-2088**	530-470-1300
Three D Graphics Inc 11340 W Olympic Blvd Ste 352	Los Angeles	CA	90064	**800-913-0008**	310-231-3330
Videotex Systems Inc 10255 Miller Rd	Dallas	TX	75238	**800-888-4336**	972-231-9200
Worlds.com Inc 11 Royal Rd	Brookline	MA	02445	**800-315-2580**	617-725-8900

180-9 Personal Software

				Toll-Free	Phone
Avery Dennison Corp 207 Goode Ave	Glendale	CA	91203	**888-567-4387***	626-304-2000
NYSE: AVY ■ *Cust Svc					
Corel Corp 1600 Carling Ave	Ottawa	ON	K1Z8R7	**800-772-6735***	613-728-8200
*Orders					
Equis International 90 South 400 West Ste 620	Salt Lake City	UT	84101	**800-882-3040***	801-265-9996
*Sales					
HowardSoft 7852 Ivanhoe Ave	La Jolla	CA	92037	**800-248-2937**	858-454-0121
Intuit Inc 2632 Marine Way	Mountain View	CA	94043	**800-446-8848***	650-944-6000
NASDAQ: INTU ■ *Cust Svc					
Nolo.com 950 Parker St	Berkeley	CA	94710	**800-728-3555**	
Radialpoint 2050 Bleury St Ste 300	Montreal	QC	H3A2J5	**866-286-2636**	514-286-2636
Sony Creative Software 1617 Sherman Ave	Madison	WI	53704	**800-577-6642**	608-256-3133
Stevens Creek Software PO Box 2126	Cupertino	CA	95015	**800-823-4279**	408-725-0424
Symantec Corp 350 Ellis St	Mountain View	CA	94043	**800-441-7234**	650-527-8000
NASDAQ: SYMC					

180-10 Professional Software (Industry-Specific)

Companies listed here manufacture software designed for specific professions or business sectors (i.e., architecture, banking, investment, physical sciences, real estate, etc.).

				Toll-Free	Phone
AGFA HealthCare Corp 10 S Academy St	Greenville	SC	29601	**877-777-2432**	864-421-1600
AIMS Inc 235 Desiard St	Monroe	LA	71201	**800-729-2467**	318-323-2467
Allot Communications 300 Tradecenter Ste 4680	Woburn	MA	01801	**877-255-6826**	781-939-9300
Allscripts Healthcare Solutions 222 Merchandise Mart Plz Ste 2024	Chicago	IL	60654	**800-654-0889**	
NASDAQ: MDRX					
Amdocs Ltd 1390 Timberlake Manor Pkwy	Chesterfield	MO	63017	**866-426-8003**	314-212-7000
NYSE: DOX					
Anchor Computer Inc 1900 New Hwy	Farmingdale	NY	11735	**800-728-6262**	631-293-6100
ARI Network Services Inc 10850 W Pk Pl Ste 1200	Milwaukee	WI	53224	**877-805-0803**	414-973-4300
ASI DataMyte Inc 2800 Campus Dr Ste 60	Plymouth	MN	55441	**800-207-5631**	763-553-1040
Aspyra Inc 4360 Pk Terr Dr Ste 100	Westlake Village	CA	91361	**800-437-9000**	
OTC: APYI					
Avantus 15 W Strong St Ste 20A	Pensacola	FL	32501	**800-600-2510**	850-470-9336
Avaya Government Solutions Inc 12730 Fair Lakes Cir	Fairfax	VA	22033	**800-492-6769**	703-653-8000
BatchMaster Software Inc 24461 Ridge Rt Dr Ste 210	Laguna Hills	CA	92653	**800-359-0920**	949-583-1646
BenefitMall Inc 4851 LBJ Fwy Ste 1100	Dallas	TX	75244	**888-338-6293**	469-791-3300
Brodart Co 500 Arch St	Williamsport	PA	17701	**800-233-8467**	570-326-2461
CAM Commerce Solutions Inc 17075 Newhope St Ste A	Fountain Valley	CA	92708	**800-726-3282**	714-241-9241
CareCentric Inc 20 Church St 12th Fl	Hartford	CT	06103	**866-467-8263**	800-808-1902
Carousel Industries of North America Inc 659 S County Trl	Exeter	RI	02822	**800-401-0760**	
CCH Small Firm Services 225 Chastain Meadows Ct NW Ste 200	Kennesaw	GA	30144	**866-345-4171***	
*Sales					
Cedara Software Corp 6303 Airport Rd Ste 500	Mississauga	ON	L4V1R8	**800-724-5970**	905-364-8000
CliniComp International 9655 Towne Ctr Dr	San Diego	CA	92121	**800-350-8202**	858-546-8202
Command Alkon Inc 1800 International Pk Dr Ste 400	Birmingham	AL	35243	**800-624-1872**	205-879-3282
Computers Unlimited 2407 Montana Ave	Billings	MT	59101	**800-763-0308**	406-255-9500
Construction Software Technologies Inc 4500 W Lake Forest Drive Ste 502	Cincinnati	OH	45242	**800-364-2059**	513-645-8004
Construction Systems Software Inc 494 Covered Bridge	Schertz	TX	78154	**800-531-1035**	210-979-6494
CoStar Group Inc 2 Bethesda Metro Ctr 10th Fl	Bethesda	MD	20814	**800-613-1303**	301-215-8300
NASDAQ: CSGP					
Datatel Inc 4375 Fair Lakes Ct	Fairfax	VA	22033	**800-223-7036**	
DealerTrack Holdings Inc 1111 Marcus Ave Ste M04	Lake Success	NY	11042	**877-357-8725**	516-734-3600
NASDAQ: TRAK					
DIS Corp 1315 Cornwall Ave	Bellingham	WA	98225	**800-426-8870***	360-733-7610
*Cust Svc					
Document Security Systems Inc 200 Canal View Blvd Ste 300	Rochester	NY	14623	**877-407-8031**	585-325-3610
NYSE: DSS					
Eagle Point Software Corp 4131 Westmark Dr	Dubuque	IA	52002	**800-678-6565**	563-556-8392
Ellucian 4375 Fair Lakes Ct	Fairfax	VA	22033	**800-223-7036**	610-647-5930

Classified Section

Company / Address	City	State	Zip	Toll-Free	Phone
Enghouse Systems Ltd 80 Tiverton Ct Ste 800 *TSE: ESL*	Markham	ON	L3R0G4	**866-206-0240**	905-946-3200
Environmental Systems Research Institute Inc 380 New York St *Sales	Redlands	CA	92373	**800-447-9778***	909-793-2853
Equis International 90 South 400 West Ste 620 *Sales	Salt Lake City	UT	84101	**800-882-3040***	801-265-9996
eResearch Technology Inc 1818 Market St Ste 1000 *NASDAQ: ERT*	Philadelphia	PA	19103	**800-704-9698**	215-972-0420
Ericsson 1 Telcordia Dr	Piscataway	NJ	08854	**800-521-2673**	732-699-2000
Final Draft Inc 26707 W Agoura Rd Ste 205	Calabasas	CA	91302	**800-231-4055**	818-995-8995
Financial Engines Inc 1804 Embarcadero Rd *NASDAQ: FNGN*	Palo Alto	CA	94303	**888-443-8577**	408-498-6000
First DataBank Inc (FDB) 701 Gateway Blvd Ste 600 *General	South San Francisco	CA	94080	**800-633-3453***	
Follett Software Co 1391 Corporate Dr	McHenry	IL	60050	**800-323-3397**	815-759-1700
FXCM Inc 32 Old Slip *NYSE: FXCM*	New York	NY	10005	**888-503-6739**	212-897-7660
General Dynamics C4 Systems 400 John Quincy Adams Rd Bldg 80	Taunton	MA	02780	**877-449-0600**	
GHG Corp 960 Clear Lk City Blvd	Webster	TX	77598	**866-380-4146**	281-488-8806
Glimmerglass Networks Inc 26142 Eden Landing Rd	Hayward	CA	94545	**877-723-1900**	510-723-1900
gomembers Inc 1155 Perimeter Center West	Atlanta	GA	30338	**855-411-2783**	
Guidance Software Inc 215 N Marengo Ave 2nd Fl	Pasadena	CA	91101	**866-229-9199**	626-229-9191
IHS Energy Group 15 Inverness Way E	Englewood	CO	80112	**800-447-2273**	303-736-3000
Info Tech Inc 5700 SW 34th St Ste 1235	Gainesville	FL	32608	**888-352-2439**	352-381-4400
Infor Global Solutions 13560 Morris Rd Ste 4100	Alpharetta	GA	30004	**866-244-5479**	678-319-8000
Innovative Technologies Corp (ITC) 1020 Woodman Dr Ste 100	Dayton	OH	45432	**800-745-8050**	937-252-2145
Input 1 LLC 6200 Canoga Ave Ste 400	Woodland Hills	CA	91367	**888-882-2554**	818-713-2303
Intradiem 3650 Mansell Rd Ste 500	Alpharetta	GA	30022	**888-566-9457**	678-356-3500
Island Pacific Inc 17310 Red Hill Ave Ste 320	Irvine	CA	92614	**800-994-3847**	
iWay Software 2 Penn Plz	New York	NY	10121	**800-736-6130**	212-736-4433
Jenzabar Inc 101 Huntington Ave Ste 2200	Boston	MA	02199	**800-593-0028**	617-492-9099
Kinaxis 700 Silver Seven Rd *General	Ottawa	ON	K2V1C3	**877-546-2947***	613-592-5780
Land & Legal Solutions Inc 300 S Hamilton Ave	Greensburg	PA	15601	**800-245-7900**	724-853-8992
Lumedx Corp 555 12th St Ste 2060	Oakland	CA	94607	**800-966-0699**	510-419-1000
LynuxWorks Inc 855 Embedded Way	San Jose	CA	95138	**800-255-5969**	408-979-3900
Management Information Control Systems Inc (MICS) 2025 Ninth St	Los Osos	CA	93402	**800-838-6427**	805-543-7000
Manhattan Assoc Inc 2300 Windy Ridge Pkwy 10th Fl *NASDAQ: MANH*	Atlanta	GA	30339	**877-756-7435**	770-955-7070
Market Scan Information Systems Inc 811 Camarillo Springs Ste B	Camarillo	CA	93012	**800-658-7226**	
Marshall & Swift 777 S Figueroa St 12th Fl	Los Angeles	CA	90017	**800-544-2678**	213-683-9000
McKesson Information Solutions 5995 Windward Pkwy	Alpharetta	GA	30005	**800-981-8601**	404-338-6000
MDI Achieve 10900 Hampshire Ave South Ste 100	Bloomington	MN	55438	**800-869-1322**	952-995-9800
Media Cybernetics Inc 4340 E W Hwy Ste 400 *Sales	Bethesda	MD	20814	**800-263-2088***	301-495-3305
MedPlus Inc 4690 Pkwy Dr	Mason	OH	45040	**800-444-6235**	513-229-5500
MicroBilt Corp 1640 Airport Rd Ste 115	Kennesaw	GA	30144	**800-884-4747**	
Midrange Software Inc 12716 Riverside Dr	Studio City	CA	91607	**800-737-6766**	818-762-8539
Minitab Inc Quality Plz 1829 Pine Hall Rd	State College	PA	16801	**800-448-3555**	814-238-3280
Mortgage Builders Software 24370 NW Hwy Ste 200	Southfield	MI	48075	**800-850-8060**	
Mzinga Inc 230 Third Ave	Waltham	MA	02451	**888-694-6428**	781-577-8948
New England Computer Services Inc 168 Boston Post Rd Stes 6 & 7 *Sales	Madison	CT	06443	**800-766-6327***	203-245-3999
NIC Inc 25501 W Valley Pkwy Ste 300 *NASDAQ: EGOV*	Olathe	KS	66061	**877-234-3468**	
OATSystems Inc 309 Waverley Oaks Rd Ste 306	Waltham	MA	02452	**877-628-7877**	781-907-6100
Olson Research Assoc Inc 10290 Old Columbia Rd	Columbia	MD	21046	**888-657-6680**	410-290-6999
OpenTable Inc 1 Montgomery St 4th Fl *NASDAQ: OPEN*	San Francisco	CA	94103	**800-673-6822**	415-344-4200
Opex Corp 305 Commerce Dr	Moorestown	NJ	08057	**800-673-9288**	856-727-1100
Pason Systems Inc 6130 Third St SE *TSE: PSI*	Calgary	AB	T2H1K4	**877-255-3158**	403-301-3400
Passport Health Communications Inc 720 Cool Springs Blvd Ste 200	Franklin	TN	37067	**888-661-5657**	615-661-5657
PKC Corp 1 Mill St C13 Ste 355	Burlington	VT	05401	**800-752-5351**	802-658-5351
ProCard Inc 1819 Denver W Dr Bldg 26 Ste 300	Lakewood	CO	80401	**800-469-6578**	303-279-2255
Promodel Corp 3400 Bath Pike Ste 200	Bethlehem	PA	18017	**888-900-3090**	801-223-4600
QlikTech International AB 150 N Radnor Chester Rd Ste E220 *NASDAQ: QLIK*	Radnor	PA	19087	**888-828-9768**	
Quality Systems Inc (QSI) 18111 Von Karman Ave Ste 600 *NASDAQ: QSII* ■ *Cust Svc	Irvine	CA	92612	**800-888-7955***	949-255-2600
QUMAS 66 York St *Sales	Jersey City	NJ	07302	**800-577-1545***	973-805-8600
Qvidian Corp 175 Cabot St Ste 210	Lowell	MA	01854	**800-272-0047**	513-631-1155
RainMaker Software Inc 1777 Sentry Pkwy W	Blue Bell	PA	19422	**800-336-0339**	610-567-3400
Raytheon Co 10 Moulton St	Cambridge	MA	02138	**866-230-1307**	617-873-8000
Red Wing Software Inc 491 Hwy 19	Red Wing	MN	55066	**800-732-9464**	651-388-1106
RESUMate Inc 2500 Packard St Ste 200 *Cust Svc	Ann Arbor	MI	48104	**800-530-9310***	734-477-9402
Retail Pro International LLC 400 Plz Dr Ste 200 *OTC: RTPRQ*	Folsom	CA	95630	**800-738-2457**	916-605-7200
Reynolds & Reynolds Co 1 Reynolds Way	Dayton	OH	45430	**800-767-0080**	937-485-2000
RiskWatch (RWI) 1237 N Gulfstream Ave	Sarasota	Fl	34236	**800-360-1898**	
Sapiens International Corp 4000 CentreGreen Way Ste 150 *NASDAQ: SPNS*	Cary	NC	27513	**888-281-1167**	919-405-1500
Scantron Corp 34 Parker	Irvine	CA	92618	**800-722-6876**	949-639-7500
Siemens Product Lifecycle Management Software Inc 5800 Granite Pkwy Ste 600	Plano	TX	75024	**800-498-5351**	972-987-3000
Simulations Plus Inc 42505 Tenth St W *NASDAQ: SLP*	Lancaster	CA	93534	**888-266-9294**	661-723-7723
Snap-on Diagnostics 420 Barclay Blvd	Lincolnshire	IL	60069	**800-424-7226**	847-478-0700
SolidWorks Corp 300 Baker Ave	Concord	MA	01742	**800-693-9000**	978-371-5011
Spillman Technologies Inc 4625 Lake Pk Blvd *General	Salt Lake City	UT	84120	**800-860-8026***	801-902-1200
Synergex International Corp 2330 Gold Meadow Way	Rancho Cordova	CA	95670	**800-366-3472**	916-635-7300
Synopsys Inc 700 E Middlefield Rd *NASDAQ: SNPS*	Mountain View	CA	94043	**800-541-7737**	650-584-5000
System Automation 7110 Samuel Morse Dr Ste 100	Columbia	MD	21046	**800-839-4729**	301-837-8000
System Innovators Inc 10550 Deerwood Pk Blvd Ste 700	Jacksonville	FL	32256	**800-963-5000**	
Thomson Elite 800 Corporate Pointe Ste 150 *Cust Svc	Los Angeles	CA	90230	**800-354-8337***	424-243-2100
TMW Systems Inc 21111 Chagrin Blvd	Beachwood	OH	44122	**800-401-6682**	216-831-6606
TradeStation Group Inc 8050 SW Tenth St Ste 2000	Plantation	FL	33324	**800-871-3577**	954-652-7000
Transentric 1400 Douglas St Ste 0840	Omaha	NE	68179	**800-877-0328**	402-544-6000
TransWorks 9910 Dupont Cir Dr E Ste 200	Fort Wayne	IN	46825	**800-435-4691**	260-487-4400
Tyler Technologies Inc 5949 Sherry Ln Ste 1400 *NYSE: TYL*	Dallas	TX	75225	**800-431-5776**	
US Dataworks Inc 1 Sugar Creek Ctr Blvd 5th Fl *OTC: UDWK*	Sugar Land	TX	77478	**888-254-8821**	281-504-8000
US Digital Corp 1400 NE 136th Ave	Vancouver	WA	98684	**800-736-0194**	360-260-2468
Vermont Systems Inc 12 Market Pl	Essex Junction	VT	05452	**877-883-8757**	802-879-6993
Vertafore Inc 7 Waterside Crossing *General	Windsor	CT	06095	**800-444-4813***	
ViPS Inc 1 W Pennsylvania Ave Ste 700	Towson	MD	21204	**800-242-0230**	410-832-8300
Vital Images Inc 5850 Opus Pkwy Ste 300	Minnetonka	MN	55343	**800-208-3005**	952-487-9500
Wausau Financial Systems Inc 400 Wes2od Dr Ste 100	Wausau	WI	54455	**800-937-0017**	715-359-0427
Weather Services International 400 Minuteman Rd	Andover	MA	01810	**800-872-2359**	978-983-6300
Wolters Kluwer Financial Services Inc 100 S Fifth St Ste 700	Minneapolis	MN	55402	**800-552-9408**	612-656-7700
Worksoft Inc 15851 Dallas Pkwy Ste 855	Addison	TX	75001	**866-836-1773**	214-239-0400
Xybernet Inc 10640 Scripps Ranch Blvd *Cust Svc	San Diego	CA	92131	**800-228-9026***	858-530-1900

180-11 Service Software

Company / Address	City	State	Zip	Toll-Free	Phone
Applied Systems Inc 200 Applied Pkwy *Sales	University Park	IL	60466	**800-999-5368***	708-534-5575
Aptech Computer Systems Inc 135 Delta Dr	Pittsburgh	PA	15238	**800-245-0720**	412-963-7440
ARINC Inc 2551 Riva Rd	Annapolis	MD	21401	**866-321-6060**	410-266-4000
Aristotle Inc 205 Pennsylvania Ave SE *Sales	Washington	DC	20003	**800-296-2747***	202-543-8345

	City	State	Zip	Toll-Free	Phone
Cerner Corp					
2800 Rockcreek Pkwy	North Kansas City	MO	64117	**888-827-7220**	816-221-1024
NASDAQ: CERN					
Datamann Inc					
1994 Hartford Ave	Wilder	VT	05088	**800-451-4263**	802-295-6600
DHI Computing Service Inc					
1525 West 820 North PO Box 51427	Provo	UT	84601	**800-992-1344**	801-373-8518
Digital Solutions Inc					
955 SE Olson Dr	Waukee	IA	50263	**888-464-8770***	515-987-6227
*Cust Svc					
DPSI Inc					
1801 Stanley Rd Ste 301	Greensboro	NC	27407	**800-897-7233**	336-854-7700
Ebix Inc					
5 Concourse Pkwy Ste 3200	Atlanta	GA	30328	**800-755-2326**	678-281-2020
NASDAQ: EBIX					
Firstwave Technologies Inc					
6263 N Scottsdale Rd Ste 180	Scottsdale	AZ	85250	**800-540-6061**	678-672-3112
Galaxy Hotel Systems LLC					
15621 Red Hill Ave Ste 100	Tustin	CA	92780	**800-624-2953**	714-258-5800
IHS Inc					
321 Inverness Dr S	Englewood	CO	80112	**800-525-7052**	303-790-0600
NYSE: IHS					
Incontact Inc					
7730 S Union Pk Ave Ste 500	Salt Lake City	UT	84047	**800-363-6177**	801-320-3200
NASDAQ: SAAS					
Insurance Data Processing Inc (IDP)					
8101 Washington Ln	Wyncote	PA	19095	**800-523-6745**	215-885-2150
Jack Henry & Assoc Inc					
663 W Hwy 60 PO Box 807	Monett	MO	65708	**800-299-4222**	417-235-6652
NASDAQ: JKHY					
Jobscope Corp					
355 Woodruff Rd	Greenville	SC	29607	**800-443-5794**	
Kalibrate Technologies PLC					
25B Hanover Rd	Florham Park	NJ	07932	**800-727-6774***	973-549-1850
*Cust Svc					
Keane Care Inc					
8383 158th Ave NE Ste 100	Redmond	WA	98052	**800-426-2675**	
Key Information Systems Inc					
30077 Agoura Ct 1st fl	Agoura Hills	CA	91301	**877-442-3249**	818-992-8950
Kronos Inc					
297 Billerica Rd	Chelmsford	MA	01824	**888-293-5549**	978-250-9800
Manatron Inc					
510 E Milham Ave	Portage	MI	49002	**866-471-2900***	269-567-2900
*Cust Svc					
Mediware Information Systems Inc					
11711 W 79th St	Lenexa	KS	66214	**800-255-0026**	913-307-1000
NASDAQ: MEDW					
Metafile Information Systems Inc					
2900 43rd St NW	Rochester	MN	55901	**800-638-2445***	507-286-9232
*Sales					
MicroStrategy					
1850 Towers Crescent Plz	Tysons Corner	VA	22182	**888-266-0321**	703-848-8600
NASDAQ: MSTR					
Netsmart Technologies Inc					
3500 Sunrise Hwy Ste D-122	Great River	NY	11739	**800-421-7503**	631-968-2000
Newmarket International Inc					
75 New Hampshire Ave	Portsmouth	NH	03801	**888-829-8871**	603-436-7500
Radware Inc					
575 Corporate Dr Lobby 2	Mahwah	NJ	07430	**888-234-5763**	201-512-9771
Sandata Technologies Inc					
26 Harbor Pk Dr	Port Washington	NY	11050	**800-544-7263***	516-484-4400
*Sales					
SS & C Technologies Inc					
80 Lamberton Rd	Windsor	CT	06095	**800-234-0556**	860-298-4500
Strictly Business Computer Systems Inc					
848 Fourth Ave Ste 200	Huntington	WV	25701	**888-529-0401**	
Successfactors Inc					
1500 Fashion Island Blvd Ste 300	San Mateo	CA	94404	**800-809-9920**	650-645-2000
NYSE: SFSF					
SunGard Pentamation Inc					
1000 Business Ctr Dr	Lake mary	FL	32746	**866-965-7732***	610-691-3616
*Cust Svc					
Synergistics Inc					
9 Tech Cir Ste 2	Natick	MA	01760	**866-455-5222**	508-655-1340
TimeValue Software					
22 Mauchly	Irvine	CA	92618	**800-426-4741***	949-727-1800
*Sales					
TMA Systems LLC					
5100 E Skelly Dr Ste 900	Tulsa	OK	74135	**800-862-1130**	918-858-6600
Xactware Solutions Inc					
1100 West Traverse Pkwy	Lehi	UT	84043	**800-424-9228***	801-764-5900
*Sales					

180-12 Systems & Utilities Software

	City	State	Zip	Toll-Free	Phone
activePDF Inc					
27405 Puerta Real Ste 100	Mission Viejo	CA	92691	**866-468-6733**	949-582-9002
Allen Systems Group Inc (ASG)					
1333 Third Ave S	Naples	FL	34102	**800-932-5536**	239-435-2200
Avatier Corp					
2603 Camino Ramon Ste 110	San Ramon	CA	94583	**800-609-8610**	925-217-5170
Basis International Ltd					
5901 Jefferson St NE	Albuquerque	NM	87109	**800-423-1394***	505-345-5232
*Orders					
Blue Lance Inc					
410 Pierce St	Houston	TX	77002	**800-856-2583**	713-255-4800
CA Inc 1 CA Plz	Islandia	NY	11749	**800-225-5224**	631-342-6000
NASDAQ: CA					
CardLogix 16 Hughes Ste 100	Irvine	CA	92618	**866-392-8326**	949-380-1312
Certicom Corp					
4701 Tahoe Blvd Bldg A	Mississauga	ON	L4W0B5	**800-561-6100**	905-507-4220
Check Point Software Technologies Ltd					
800 Bridge Pkwy	Redwood City	CA	94065	**800-429-4391**	650-628-2000
NASDAQ: CHKP					
Cincom Systems Inc					
55 Merchant St	Cincinnati	OH	45246	**800-224-6266**	513-612-2300

	City	State	Zip	Toll-Free	Phone
Citrix Systems Inc					
851 W Cypress Creek Rd	Fort Lauderdale	FL	33309	**800-393-1888**	954-267-3000
NASDAQ: CTXS					
Columbia Data Products Inc					
925 Sunshine Ln Ste 1080	Altamonte Springs	FL	32714	**800-613-6288***	407-869-6700
*Sales					
CommuniGate Systems Inc					
655 Redwood Hwy Ste 275	Mill Valley	CA	94941	**800-262-4722**	415-383-7164
ComponentOne LLC					
201 S Highland Ave Third Fl 3rd Fl	Pittsburgh	PA	15206	**800-858-2739**	412-681-4343
Condusiv Technologies					
7590 N Glenoaks Blvd	Burbank	CA	91504	**800-829-6468***	818-771-1600
*Sales					
Crossmatch					
720 Bay Rd Ste 100	Redwood City	CA	94063	**866-463-7792**	650-474-4000
CSI International Inc					
8120 State Rt 138	Williamsport	OH	43164	**800-795-4914**	740-420-5400
CSP Inc 43 Manning Rd	Billerica	MA	01821	**800-325-3110**	978-663-7598
NASDAQ: CSPI					
DataViz Inc					
612 Wheelers Farms Rd	Milford	CT	06460	**800-733-0030**	203-874-0085
Datawatch Corp					
271 Mill Rd	Chelmsford	MA	01824	**800-445-3311**	978-441-2200
NASDAQ: DWCH					
Descartes Systems Group Inc					
120 Randall Dr	Waterloo	ON	N2V1C6	**800-419-8495**	519-746-8110
TSE: DSG					
Digimarc Corp					
9405 SW Gemini Dr	Beaverton	OR	97008	**800-344-4627**	503-469-4800
NASDAQ: DMRC					
eMag Solutions LLC					
1120 Sanctuary Pkwy Ste 275	Alpharetta	GA	30305	**844-252-0113**	404-995-6060
EMC Corp					
2831 Mission College Blvd	Santa Clara	CA	95054	**877-534-2867***	408-566-2000
*Tech Supp					
Entrust Inc					
5400 LBJ Fwy Ste 1340	Dallas	TX	75240	**888-690-2424***	972-728-0447
*Sales					
Esker Inc					
1212 Deming Way Ste 350	Madison	WI	53717	**800-368-5283**	608-828-6000
Expert Choice Inc					
1501 Lee Hwy Ste 302	Arlington	VA	22209	**888-259-6400**	703-243-5595
Heroix Corp					
165 Bay State Dr	Braintree	MA	02184	**800-229-6500**	781-848-1701
HID Global Corp					
611 Center Ridge Dr	Austin	TX	78753	**800-237-7769**	512-776-9000
Hitachi Data Systems Corp					
750 Central Expy	Santa Clara	CA	95050	**877-437-3849**	408-970-1000
Innodata-Isogen Inc					
3 University Plz Dr	Hackensack	NJ	07601	**877-454-8400**	201-371-8000
NASDAQ: INOD					
International Business Machines Corp (IBM)					
1 New OrchaRd Rd	Armonk	NY	10504	**800-426-4968**	914-499-1900
NYSE: IBM					
InterTrust Technologies Corp					
920 Stewart Dr Ste 100	Sunnyvale	CA	94085	**800-393-2272**	408-616-1600
Intrusion Inc					
1101 E Arapaho Rd	Richardson	TX	75081	**888-637-7770**	972-234-6400
Ipswitch Inc					
83 Hartwell Ave	Lexington	MA	02421	**800-793-4825**	781-676-5700
Kroll Ontrack Inc					
9023 Columbine Rd	Eden Prairie	MN	55347	**800-872-2599**	952-937-5161
LapLink Software Inc					
600 108th Ave NE Ste 610	Bellevue	WA	98004	**800-343-8080**	425-952-6000
Lattice Inc					
1751 S Naperville Rd Ste 100	Wheaton	IL	60189	**800-444-4309***	630-949-3250
*Sales					
Luminex Software Inc					
871 Marlborough Ave	Riverside	CA	92507	**888-586-4639***	951-781-4100
*Sales					
McAfee Inc					
2821 Mission College Blvd	Santa Clara	CA	95054	**888-847-8766***	408-988-3832
*Cust Svc					
McCabe Software Inc					
3300 N Ridge Rd	Ellicott City	MD	21043	**800-638-6316**	410-381-3710
Mindjet Corp					
1160 Battery St E 4th Fl	San Francisco	CA	94111	**877-646-3538**	415-229-4200
Mitem Corp 640 Menlo Ave	Menlo Park	CA	94025	**800-648-3660***	650-323-1500
*Sales					
MTI Systems Inc					
59 Interstate D	West Springfield	MA	01089	**800-644-4318**	413-733-1972
NetIQ Corp 1233 W Loop S	Houston	TX	77027	**888-323-6768***	713-548-1700
*Sales					
Network Appliance Inc					
495 E Java Dr	Sunnyvale	CA	94089	**800-443-4537***	408-822-6000
NASDAQ: NTAP ■ *Sales					
New Year Tech Inc					
12330 Pinecrest Rd Ste 100	Reston	VA	20191	**800-525-7767**	703-564-0290
NTP Software					
20A NW Blvd Ste 136	Nashua	NH	03063	**800-226-2755**	603-622-4400
Numara Software Inc					
2202 NW Shore Blvd Ste 650	Tampa	FL	33607	**855-834-7487***	813-227-4500
*Sales					
Oracle Corp					
500 Oracle Pkwy	Redwood Shores	CA	94065	**800-392-2999***	650-506-7000
NYSE: ORCL ■ *Sales					
Perceptics Corp					
9737 Cogdill Rd Ste 200	Knoxville	TN	37932	**800-448-8544**	
Pervasive Software Inc					
12365 Riata Trace Pkwy Bldg B	Austin	TX	78727	**800-287-4383**	512-231-6000
NASDAQ: PVSW					
Phoenix Technologies Ltd					
915 Murphy Ranch Rd	Milpitas	CA	95035	**800-677-7305**	408-570-1000
Pragma Systems Inc					
13809 Research Blvd Ste 675	Austin	TX	78750	**800-224-1675**	512-219-7270
Process Software Corp					
959 Concord St	Framingham	MA	01701	**800-722-7770**	508-879-6994
RadView Software Inc					
991 Hgwy 22 W Ste 200	Bridgewater	NJ	08807	**888-723-8439**	908-526-7756

Company / Address	City	State	ZIP	Toll-Free	Phone
Raxco Software Inc 6 Montgomery Village Ave Ste 500	Gaithersburg	MD	20879	**800-546-9728***	301-527-0803
*Tech Supp					
Red Hat Inc 1801 Varsity Dr	Raleigh	NC	27606	**888-733-4281**	919-754-3700
NYSE: RHT					
Relais International 1690 Woodward Dr Ste 215	Ottawa	ON	K2C3R8	**888-294-5244**	613-226-5571
RSA Security Inc 174 Middlesex Tpke	Bedford	MA	01730	**800-995-5095**	781-515-5000
ScriptLogic Corp 6000 Broken Sound Pkwy NW	Boca Raton	FL	33487	**800-306-9329**	561-886-2400
Serengeti Systems Inc 1108 Lavaca St Ste 120 PO Box 431	Austin	TX	78701	**800-634-3122**	512-345-2211
Skyward Inc 5233 Coye Dr	Stevens Point	WI	54481	**800-236-0001**	715-341-9406
SNMP Research International Inc 3001 Kimberlin Heights Rd	Knoxville	TN	37920	**877-644-5866**	865-579-3311
Software Engineering of America Inc (SEA) 1230 Hempstead Tpke	Franklin Square	NY	11010	**800-272-7322**	516-328-7000
Software Pursuits Inc 1900 S Norfolk St	San Mateo	CA	94403	**800-367-4823**	650-372-0900
Stratus Technologies 111 Powdermill Rd	Maynard	MA	01754	**800-787-2887**	978-461-7000
Symantec Corp 350 Ellis St	Mountain View	CA	94043	**800-441-7234**	650-527-8000
NASDAQ: SYMC					
TeamQuest Corp 1 TeamQuest Way	Clear Lake	IA	50428	**800-551-8326**	641-357-2700
TechSmith Corp 2405 Woodlake Dr	Okemos	MI	48864	**800-517-3001**	517-381-2300
Thales e-Security Inc 2200 N Commerce Pkwy Ste 200	Weston	FL	33326	**888-744-4976**	954-888-6200
TigerLogic Corp 25-A Technology Dr	Irvine	CA	92618	**800-367-7425**	949-442-4400
NASDAQ: TIGR					
TrendMicro Inc 10101 N De Anza Blvd	Cupertino	CA	95014	**800-228-5651**	408-257-1500
Tripwire Inc 101 SW Main St Ste 1500	Portland	OR	97204	**800-874-7947***	503-276-7500
*General					
UltraBac Software 15015 Main St Ste 200	Bellevue	WA	98007	**866-554-8562**	425-644-6000
VanDyke Software Inc 4848 Tramway Ridge Dr NE Ste 101	Albuquerque	NM	87111	**800-952-5210**	505-332-5700
VCG LLC 1805 Old Alabama Rd	Roswell	GA	30076	**800-318-4983**	770-246-2300
Vendant Inc 4845 Pearl E Cir Ste 101	Bouler	CO	80301	**800-714-4900**	978-462-0737
Vision Solutions Inc 15300 Barranca Pkwy	Irvine	CA	92618	**800-683-4667**	949-253-6500
Webroot Software Inc 2560 55th St	Boulder	CO	80301	**800-772-9383**	303-442-3813
Wilson WindowWare Inc 5421 California Ave SW	Seattle	WA	98136	**800-762-8383**	206-938-1740
Wind River Systems Inc 500 Wind River Way	Alameda	CA	94501	**800-545-9463**	510-748-4100
XIOtech Corp 9950 Federal Dr Ste 100	Colorado Springs	CO	80921	**866-472-6764**	719-388-5500
Zix Corp 2711 N Haskell Ave Ste 2300-LB	Dallas	TX	75204	**888-771-4049**	214-370-2000
NASDAQ: ZIXI					
Zone Alarm 800 Bridge Pkwy	Redwood City	CA	94065	**877-966-5221**	415-633-4500

181 COMPUTER STORES

SEE ALSO Appliance & Home Electronics Stores

Company / Address	City	State	ZIP	Toll-Free	Phone
A Matter of Fax 105 Harrison Ave	Harrison	NJ	07029	**800-433-3329**	973-482-3700
Aberdeen LLC 9130 Norwalk Blvd	Santa Fe Springs	CA	90670	**800-500-9526**	562-699-6998
Accordant Company LLC 365 S St Ste 100	Morristown	NJ	07960	**800-363-1002**	973-887-8900
Aim 2 Berkeley St Ste 403	Toronto	ON	M5A4J5	**866-645-2224**	416-594-9393
Answer One Inc 2216 Young Dr Ste 3	Lexington	KY	40505	**800-517-7395**	859-269-3482
Arbutus Software Inc 6450 Roberts St	Burnaby	BC	V5G4E1	**877-333-6336**	604-437-7873
Atiwa Computer Leasing Exchange 6950 Portwest Dr Ste 100	Houston	TX	77024	**800-428-2532**	713-467-9390
Automated Medical Systems Inc 2310 N Patterson St Bldg H	Valdosta	GA	31602	**800-256-3240**	
Balihoo Inc 404 S Eighth St Ste 300	Boise	ID	83702	**866-446-9914**	
Barcoding Inc 2220 Boston St	Baltimore	MD	21231	**888-412-7226**	410-385-8532
Carrillo Business Technologies Inc 750 The City Dr S Ste 225	Orange	CA	92868	**888-241-7585**	
CDW Corp 200 N Milwaukee Ave	Vernon Hills	IL	60061	**800-800-4239**	847-465-6000
Colligo Networks Inc 400-1152 Mainland St	Vancouver	BC	V6B4X2	**866-685-7962**	604-685-7962
Concepts In Data Management Inc 205 Oxford St E	London	ON	N6A5G6	**800-668-8768**	
ConnectWise Inc 4110 George Rd Ste 200	Tampa	FL	33634	**800-671-6898**	813-463-4700
Crawford Technologies Inc 45 St Clair Ave W Ste 102	Toronto	ON	M4V1K9	**866-679-0864**	416-923-0080
Ddi System LLC 75 Glen Rd Ste 204	Sandy Hook	CT	06482	**877-599-4334**	
Dehart Marine Electronics Inc 134 W Carolina Ave	Memphis	TN	38103	**800-523-4278**	901-523-0945
DOVICO Software Inc 236 St George St Ste 119	Moncton	NB	E1C1W1	**800-618-8463**	506-855-4477
DTM Systems Inc 2323 Boundary Rd Unit 130	Vancouver	BC	V5M4V8	**888-655-3282**	604-257-6700
Employee Development Systems Inc 7308 S Alton Way Ste 2J	Centennial	CO	80112	**800-282-3374**	303-221-0710
GameStop Corp 625 Westport Pkwy	Grapevine	TX	76051	**800-883-8895**	817-424-2000
NYSE: GME					
Gateway Inc 7565 Irvine Ctr Dr	Irvine	CA	92618	**800-846-2000**	949-471-7040
Govconnection Inc 7503 Standish Pl	Rockville	MD	20855	**800-998-0009**	
Gts Communications & Cabling Co 11953 Prospect Rd	Strongsville	OH	44149	**877-487-8866**	440-878-8866
ICAM Technologies Corp 21500 Nassr St	Sainte-anne-de-bellevue	QC	H9X4C1	**800-827-4226**	514-697-8033
Indigo Rose Corp 123 Bannatyne Ave Ste 200	Winnipeg	MB	R3B0R3	**800-665-9668**	204-946-0263
Innovative Information Solutions Inc 61 I- Ln	Waterbury	CT	06705	**800-343-8121**	203-756-4243
Insight Enterprises Inc 6820 S Harl Ave	Tempe	AZ	85283	**800-467-4448**	480-333-3000
NASDAQ: NSIT					
Jive Communications Inc 1275 West 1600 North Ste 100	Orem	UT	84057	**866-768-5429**	
Jonah Group Ltd, The 461 King St W 3rd Fl	Toronto	ON	M5V1K4	**888-594-6260**	416-304-0860
KLJ Computer Solutions Inc 115 Joseph Zatzman Dr	Dartmouth	NS	B3B1N3	**888-455-5669**	
Knowledge Information Solutions Inc 2877 Guardian Ln Ste 201	Virginia Beach	VA	23452	**877-547-7248**	757-463-0033
Launch Pad 18130 Jorene Rd	Odessa	FL	33556	**888-920-3450**	
Loki Systems Inc 1258-13351 Commerce Pkwy	Richmond	BC	V6V2X7	**800-378-5654**	604-249-5050
London Computer Services 1007 Cottonwood Dr	Loveland	OH	45140	**800-669-0871**	513-583-1482
Messaging Architects 180 Peel St Ste 333	Montreal	QC	H3C2G7	**866-497-0101**	514-392-9220
Moore Oil Company Inc 4033 W Custer Ave	Milwaukee	WI	53209	**800-279-2976**	414-462-3200
Netgain Networks Inc 8378 Attica Dr	Riverside	CA	92508	**855-667-2364**	951-656-0194
Newegg Inc 16839 E Gale Ave	City of Industry	CA	91745	**800-390-1119**	626-271-9700
Nova Voice & Data Systems Inc 3909 Oceanic Dr Ste 401	Oceanside	CA	92056	**800-558-6744**	760-439-5200
O P T 918 Mission Ave	Oceanside	CA	92054	**800-483-6287**	760-722-3348
Office Solutions Inc 217 Mount Horeb Rd	Warren	NJ	07059	**800-677-1778**	
Omnivex Corp 3300 Hwy 7 Ste 501	Concord	ON	L4K4M3	**800-745-8223**	905-761-6640
Open Automation Software 5077 Bear Mtn Dr	Evergreen	CO	80439	**800-533-4994**	303-679-0898
Palomino System Innovations Inc 533 College St Ste 404	Toronto	ON	M6G1A8	**866-360-0360**	416-964-7333
PC Connection Inc 730 Milford Rd Rt 101A	Merrimack	NH	03054	**888-213-0607**	603-683-2000
NASDAQ: PCCC					
PC Connection Inc MacConnection Div 730 Milford Rd Rt 101A	Merrimack	NH	03054	**888-213-0260**	
PC Mall Inc 2555 W 190th St	Torrance	CA	90504	**800-555-6255**	310-354-5600
NASDAQ: PCMI					
Physmark Inc 101 E Pk Blvd Ste 600	Plano	TX	75074	**800-922-7060**	972-231-8000
Questica Inc 980 Fraser Dr Ste 105	Burlington	ON	L7L5P5	**877-707-7755**	
Recursion Software Inc 2591 Dallas Pkwy Ste 200	Frisco	TX	75034	**800-727-8674**	972-731-8800
RLM Communications Inc 1027 E Manchester Rd	Spring Lake	NC	28390	**877-223-1345**	910-223-1350
Service Communications Inc 10675 Willows Rd NE Ste 100	Redmond	WA	98052	**800-488-0468**	
Side Effects Software Inc 123 Front St W Ste 1401	Toronto	ON	M5J2M2	**888-504-9876**	416-504-9876
Top Producer Systems Inc 10651 Shellbridge Way Ste 155	Richmond	BC	V6X2W8	**800-821-3657**	
Translations.com Inc 3 Pk Ave 39th Fl	New York	NY	10016	**800-688-7205**	212-689-1616
Tricerat Inc 11500 Cronridge Dr Ste 100	Owings Mills	MD	21117	**800-582-5167**	410-715-4226
Vocantas Inc 750 Palladium Dr Ste 200	Ottawa	ON	K2V1C7	**877-271-8853**	613-271-8853
Voice on the Go Inc 20 Amber St Ste 207	Markham	ON	L3R5P4	**877-977-0555**	905-305-1355

182 COMPUTER SYSTEMS DESIGN SERVICES

SEE ALSO Web Site Design Services

Companies that plan and design computer systems that integrate hardware, software, and communication technologies.

Company / Address	City	State	ZIP	Toll-Free	Phone
4Sight Group LLC 4001 Kennett Pk Ste 134-233	Wilmington	DE	19807	**800-490-2131**	
7strategy LLC 117 N Cooper St	Olathe	KS	66061	**888-231-3062**	913-638-2130
A Partner in Technology 105 Dresden Ave	Gardiner	ME	04345	**877-582-0888**	207-582-0888
Aasys Group 11301 N US Hwy 301 Ste 106	Thonotosassa	FL	33592	**800-852-7091**	813-246-4757
Abacus Technology Corp 5454 Wisconsin Ave Ste 1100	Chevy Chase	MD	20815	**800-225-2135**	301-907-8500
Acg Inc 7007 Corporate Way	Dayton	OH	45459	**800-890-5023**	937-433-8122
Achilles Guard Inc 4201 Spring Vly Rd Ste 1400	Dallas	TX	75244	**866-525-8680**	
Acranet 521 W Maxwell Ave Ste 209	Spokane	WA	99201	**800-304-1249**	
Advanced Information Systems Group Inc 11315 Corporate Blvd Ste 210	Orlando	FL	32817	**800-593-8359**	407-581-2929

Company / Address	City	State	ZIP	Toll-Free	Phone
AETEA Information Technology Inc 1445 Research Blvd Ste 300	Rockville	MD	20850	**888-772-3832**	301-721-4200
AGSI 3343 Peachtree Rd NE Ste 510	Atlanta	GA	30326	**800-768-2474**	404-816-7577
Alaska Computer Brokers 551 W Dimond Blvd	Anchorage	AK	99515	**866-261-4225**	907-267-4200
ALI's Database Consultants 1151 Williams Dr	Aiken	SC	29803	**866-257-8970**	803-648-5931
AlphaKOR Group Inc 7800 Twin Oaks Dr	Windsor	ON	N8N5B6	**877-944-6009**	519-944-6009
American Systems Corp 14151 Pk Meadow Dr Ste 500	Chantilly	VA	20151	**800-733-2721**	703-968-6300
Amgraf Inc 1501 Oak St	Kansas City	MO	64108	**800-304-4797**	816-474-4797
Arcane Technologies Inc 918 Monticello Ave	Charlottesville	VA	22902	**844-977-4890**	
Architel Inc 8350 N Central Expy Ste 250	Dallas	TX	75206	**866-649-7571**	214-550-2000
Arlington Computer Products Inc 851 Commerce Ct *Orders	Buffalo Grove	IL	60089	**800-548-5105***	847-541-6333
Arx Networks LLC 581 Foster City Blvd Ste 210	Foster City	CA	94404	**800-972-2175**	650-403-4279
Asi Networks Inc 19331 E Walnut Dr N	City Of Industry	CA	91748	**800-251-1336**	
Asponte Technology Inc 11523 Palmbrush Trl Ste 137	Lakewood Ranch	FL	34202	**888-926-9434**	
AVT Inc 341 Bonnie Cir Ste 102	Corona	CA	92880	**877-424-3663**	
Axyz Automation Inc 2844 E Kemper Rd	Cincinnati	OH	45241	**800-527-9670**	513-771-7444
Azure Horizons Inc 7115 N Ave Ste 185	Oak Park	IL	60302	**877-494-6070**	
B Green Innovations Inc 750 Hwy 34	Matawan	NJ	07747	**877-996-9333**	732-441-7700
Banyan Medical Systems Inc 4106 S 87th St	Omaha	NE	68127	**866-225-7790**	402-403-4400
Bazon Cox & Associates Inc 1244 Executive Blvd	Chesapeake	VA	23320	**800-769-1763**	757-410-2128
Bell Techlogix 5777 Decatur Blvd	Indianapolis	IN	46241	**866-782-2355**	317-333-7777
bitHeads Inc 1309 Carling Ave	Ottawa	ON	K1Z7L3	**855-622-3232**	613-722-3232
Blast Advanced Media 950 Reserve Dr Ste 150	Roseville	CA	95678	**888-252-7866**	916-724-6701
Bluelock LLC 6325 Morenci Trl	Indianapolis	IN	46268	**888-402-2583**	
Blytheco LLC 23161 Mill Creek Dr	Laguna Hills	CA	92653	**800-425-9843**	949-583-9500
Boxworks Technologies Inc 2065 Pkwy Blve	Salt Lake City	UT	84119	**877-495-2250**	801-214-6100
Bridgeline Digital 80 BlanchaRd Rd	Burlington	MA	01803	**800-603-9936**	781-376-5555
Broadleaf Services Inc 10 Mall Rd	Burlington	MA	01803	**866-337-7733**	
Buchanan Technologies Inc 1026 Texan Trl	Grapevine	TX	76051	**888-730-2774**	972-869-3966
CACI International Inc 1100 N Glebe Rd *NYSE: CACI*	Arlington	VA	22201	**866-606-3471**	703-841-7800
Cad Technology Center 1000 Boone Ave N Ste 200	Minneapolis	MN	55427	**866-941-1181**	952-941-1181
Cadre Computer Resources Co 201 E Fifth St Ste 1800	Cincinnati	OH	45202	**866-762-6700**	513-762-7350
Calibre Systems Inc 6354 Walker Ln Ste 300 Metro Pk	Alexandria	VA	22310	**888-225-4273**	703-797-8500
Camber Corp 670 Discovery Dr	Huntsville	AL	35806	**800-998-7988**	256-922-0200
Canweb Internet Services 1086 Modeland Rd	Sarnia	ON	N7S6L2	**877-422-6932**	519-332-6900
CARA Group Inc, The Drake Oak Brook Plz 2215 York Rd Ste 300	Oak Brook	IL	60523	**866-401-2272**	630-574-2272
Catapult Systems Inc 1221 S MoPac Expwy Ste 350	Austin	TX	78746	**800-528-6248**	512-328-8181
Cayman Technologies Inc 12954 Stonecreek Dr Ste E	Pickerington	OH	43147	**877-370-9470**	614-759-9461
CBM of America Inc 1455 W Newport Ctr Dr	Deerfield Beach	FL	33442	**800-881-8202**	954-698-9104
Cca Medical Inc 6 Southridge Ct	Greenville	SC	29607	**800-775-2556**	864-233-2700
CDMS Inc 550 Sherbrooke W West Tower Ste 250	Montreal	QC	H3A1B9	**866-337-2367**	514-286-2367
Cdo Technologies Inc 5200 Sprngfeld St Ste 320	Dayton	OH	45431	**866-307-6616**	937-258-0022
CGI Group Inc 1130 Sherbrooke St W 7th Fl *TSE: GIB/A*	Montreal	QC	H3A2M8	**800-828-8377**	514-841-3200
Chameleon Consulting Inc 89 Falmouth Rd W	Arlington	MA	02474	**866-903-7912**	781-646-2272
CIBER Inc 6363 S Fiddler's Green Cir Ste 1400 *NYSE: CBR*	Greenwood Village	CO	80111	**800-242-3799**	303-220-0100
Clarkston Consulting 2655 Meridian Pkwy Ste 400	Durham	NC	27713	**800-652-4274**	919-484-4400
Clever Devices Ltd 300 Crossways Pk Dr	Woodbury	NY	11797	**800-872-6129**	516-433-6100
Cognizant Technology Solutions Corp 500 Frank W Burr Blvd *NASDAQ: CTSH*	Teaneck	NJ	07666	**888-937-3277**	201-801-0233
Computer Analytical Systems Inc (CASI) 1418 S Third St	Louisville	KY	40208	**800-977-3475**	502-635-2019
Computer Power Solutions Inc 4644 Katella Ave	Los Alamitos	CA	90720	**800-444-1938**	562-493-4487
Computer Pundits Corp 6515 Cecilia Cir	Bloomington	MN	55439	**888-786-3487**	952-854-2422
Computer Sciences Corp 2100 E Grand Ave *NYSE: CSC*	El Segundo	CA	90245	**866-310-0950**	310-615-0311

Company / Address	City	State	ZIP	Toll-Free	Phone
Computer Task Group Inc (CTG) 800 Delaware Ave *OTC: CTG*	Buffalo	NY	14209	**800-992-5350**	716-882-8000
Connect Tech Inc 42 Arrow Rd	Guelph	ON	N1K1S6	**800-426-8979**	519-836-1291
Covansys Corp 32605 W 12 Mile Rd Ste 250	Farmington Hills	MI	48334	**866-310-0950**	248-488-2088
Creation Engine 348 E Middlefield Rd	Mountain View	CA	94043	**800-431-8713**	650-934-0176
Creative Logistics Solutions Inc 980 Mercantile Dr Ste J	Hanover	MD	21076	**800-407-0280**	410-793-0708
Custom Computer Specialists Inc (CCS) 70 Suffolk Ct	Hauppauge	NY	11788	**800-598-8989**	631-864-6699
CWPS Inc 14120 A Sullyfield Cir	Chantilly	VA	20151	**877-297-7472**	
Cypress Networks 4125 Walker Ave Ste C	Greensboro	NC	27407	**866-625-3502**	336-841-3030
Data Systems Analysts Inc (DSA) Eigth Neshaminy Interplex Ste 209	Trevose	PA	19053	**877-422-4372**	215-245-4800
DataLink Interactive Inc 1120 Benfield Blvd Ste G	Millersville	MD	21108	**888-565-3279**	410-729-0440
Datapro Solutions Inc 6336 E Utah Ave	Spokane	WA	99212	**888-658-6881**	509-532-3530
Dcs Netlink 1800 Macauley Ave	Rice Lake	WI	54868	**877-327-6385**	715-236-7424
Decision Systems Plus Inc 248 Spring Lake Dr Ste 170	Itasca	IL	60143	**800-676-7374**	
Decisive Business Systems Inc 7150 N Park Dr Ste 400	Pennsauken	NJ	08109	**866-203-8948**	856-910-0900
Delta Corporate Services Inc 129 Littleton Rd	Parsippany	NJ	07054	**800-335-8220**	973-334-6260
Denali Advance Integration (DAI) 17735 NE 65th St Ste 130	Redmond	WA	98052	**877-467-8008**	425-885-4000
Design Strategy Corp 805 Third Ave 11th Fl	New York	NY	10022	**800-331-8726**	212-370-0000
Dialogic Inc 1504 Mccarthy Blvd	Milpitas	CA	95035	**800-755-4444**	408-750-9400
Digital Celerity LLC 548 Market St Ste 22067	San Francisco	CA	94104	**888-963-8876**	
Digital Measures 301 N Broadway 4th Fl	Milwaukee	WI	53202	**866-348-5677**	
Dirks Group, The 3802 Hummingbird Rd	Wausau	WI	54401	**800-866-1486**	715-848-9865
DPE Systems Inc 425 Pontius Ave N Ste 430	Seattle	WA	98109	**800-541-6566**	206-223-3737
Dr Tax Software Inc 3333 Graham Blvd Ste 222	Montreal	QC	H3R3L5	**800-663-7829**	514-733-8355
Dyonyx LP 1235 N Loop W *General	Houston	TX	77008	**855-749-6758***	713-485-7000
Echomountain Llc 1483 Patriot Blvd	Glenview	IL	60026	**877-311-1980**	
Ecom Enterprises Inc 1230 Oakmead Pkwy Ste 318	Sunnyvale	CA	94085	**877-955-3266**	408-720-9194
Electronic Warfare Assoc Inc (EWA Inc) 13873 Pk Ctr Rd Ste 500 *General	Herndon	VA	20171	**888-392-0002***	703-904-5700
eMedia Music Corp 664 NE Northlake Way	Seattle	WA	98105	**888-363-3424**	206-329-5657
Eos Systems Inc 72 River Park St Ste 4	Needham	MA	02494	**855-453-2600**	
eVerge Group Inc 4965 Preston Pk Blvd Ste 700	Plano	TX	75093	**888-548-1973**	972-608-1803
Force 3 Inc 2151 Priest Bridge Dr	Crofton	MD	21114	**800-391-0204**	301-261-0204
Frontier Computer Corp 1275 Business Pk Dr	Traverse City	MI	49686	**866-226-6344**	231-929-1386
Frontier Consulting Inc 10101 SW Fwy Ste 202	Houston	TX	77074	**877-324-8729**	713-778-0799
Fujitsu Consulting 1250 E Arques Ave	Sunnyvale	CA	94085	**800-831-3183**	
G2 Web Services LLC 1750 112th Ave NE Ste C101	Bellevue	WA	98004	**888-788-5353**	425-749-4040
Garvin-Allen Solutions Ltd Unit 12 155 Chain Lk Dr	Halifax	NS	B3S1B3	**877-325-9062**	902-453-3554
General Dynamics Information Technology 3211 Jermantown Rd	Fairfax	VA	22030	**800-242-0230**	703-246-0200
Genesis Corp 950 Third Ave Fl 26	New York	NY	10022	**800-261-1776**	212-688-5522
GeoLogics Corp 5285 Shawnee Rd Ste 300	Alexandria	VA	22312	**800-684-3455**	703-750-4000
Geoscape International Inc 2100 W Flagler St	Miami	FL	33135	**888-211-9353**	
Global Consultants Inc 25 Airport Rd	Morristown	NJ	07960	**877-264-6424**	973-889-5200
Global Help Desk Services Inc 2080 Silas Deane Hwy	Rocky Hill	CT	06067	**800-770-1075**	
Global Technology Resources Inc 990 S Bdwy Ste 300	Denver	CO	80209	**877-603-1984**	303-455-8800
Globalspec Inc 350 Jordan Rd	Troy	NY	12180	**800-261-2052**	518-880-0200
GP Strategies Corp 11000 Broken Land Parkway Ste 200	Columbia	MD	21044	**888-843-4784**	443-367-9600
Greenpages Inc 33 Badgers Island W	Kittery	ME	03904	**888-687-4876**	207-439-7310
Gsat Inc 100 W Oak St Ste 200	Denton	TX	76201	**866-977-4728**	469-287-6771
Hartford Computer Group Inc 10440 Little Patuxent Pkwy 3rd Fl	Columbia	MD	21044	**800-370-5849**	410-740-3020
Henry A Bromelkamp & Co 106 E 24th St	Minneapolis	MN	55404	**877-767-6703**	612-870-9087
Hexaware Technologies Inc 1095 Cranbury Rd	Jamesburg	NJ	08831	**866-746-2133**	609-409-6950
Hixardt Technologies Inc 119 W Intendencia St	Pensacola	FL	32502	**866-985-3282**	850-439-3282
House of Brick Technologies LLC 9300 Underwood Ave Ste 300	Omaha	NE	68114	**877-780-7038**	402-445-0764
Howard Systems International 2777 Summer St	Stamford	CT	06905	**800-326-4860**	
HUB Technical Services 44 Norfolk Ave Ste 4	South Easton	MA	02375	**877-482-8324**	508-238-9887

Company / Address	City	State	ZIP	Toll-Free	Phone
Ibaset 27442 Portola Pkwy	Foothill Ranch	CA	92610	**877-422-7381**	949-598-5200
Ice Technologies Inc 411 SE Ninth St	Pella	IA	50219	**877-754-8420**	641-628-8724
Iconixx Software 3420 Executive Ctr Dr Ste 250	Austin	TX	78731	**877-426-6499**	
Idealogical Systems Inc 2900 John St	Markham	ON	L3R5G3	**855-554-4332**	905-474-0772
Ilan Systems 1107 Fair Oaks Ave	South Pasadena	CA	91030	**800-678-3526**	
iMakeNews Inc 200 Fifth Ave	Waltham	MA	02451	**866-964-6397**	781-890-4700
InCycle Software Inc 545 Promenade du Centropolis Ste 220	Laval	QC	H7T0A3	**800-565-0510**	450-682-4777
Indigo Dynamic Networks Llc 2413 W Algonquin Rd	Algonquin	IL	60102	**888-464-6344**	
Inetsolution 250 Monroe NW Ste 400	Grand Rapids	MI	49503	**855-728-5839**	586-726-9490
Integrated Systems Analysts Inc 2001 N Beauregard St Ste 600	Alexandria	VA	22311	**800-929-1024**	703-824-0700
Intellicom Computer Consulting 1702 Second Ave	Kearney	NE	68847	**877-501-3375**	308-237-0684
Intelligent Decisions Inc 21445 Beaumeade Cir	Ashburn	VA	20147	**800-929-8331**	703-554-1600
IntelliSoft Group LLC 61 Spit Brook Rd	Nashua	NH	03060	**888-634-4464**	
Interactive Business Systems Inc 2625 Butterfield Rd	Oak Brook	IL	60523	**800-555-5427**	630-571-9100
InterDev LLC 2650 Holcomb Bridge Rd Ste 310	Alpharetta	GA	30022	**877-841-8069**	770-643-4400
InterVision Systems Technologies Inc 2270 Martin Ave	Santa Clara	CA	95050	**800-787-6707**	408-980-8550
InterWorks Inc 1425 S Sangre Rd	Stillwater	OK	74074	**866-490-9643**	405-624-3214
Intrepid Control Systems Inc 5700 18 Mile Rd	Sterling Heights	MI	48314	**800-859-6265**	586-731-7950
IOActive Inc 701 Fifth Ave Ste 6850	Seattle	WA	98104	**866-760-0222**	206-784-4313
IQware Inc 5850 Coral Ridge Dr Ste 309	Coral Springs	FL	33076	**877-698-5151**	954-698-5151
Isis It Inc 88 Vilcom Ctr Dr Ste 180	Chapel Hill	NC	27514	**877-970-4747**	919-932-6150
Itergy International Inc 2075 University Ste 700	Montreal	QC	H3A2L1	**866-522-5881**	514-845-5881
ITSource Technology Inc 1401 Los Gamos Dr Ste 102	San Rafael	CA	94903	**866-548-4911**	415-472-5700
Kanatek Technologies Inc 535 Legget Dr Ste 400	Kanata	ON	K2K3B8	**800-526-2821**	613-591-1482
Kemtah Group Inc 7601 Jefferson St NE Ste 120	Albuquerque	NM	87109	**877-753-6824**	505-346-4900
KForce Government Soultions 2750 Prosperity Ave Ste 300	Fairfax	VA	22031	**800-200-7465**	703-245-7350
Lighthouse Computer Services Inc 6 Blackstone Valley Pl Ste 205	Lincoln	RI	02865	**888-542-8030**	401-334-0799
Logicease Solutions Inc 1 Bay Plaza Ste 520	Burlingame	CA	94010	**866-212-3273**	650-373-1111
Lynx Computer Technologies Inc 7 Bristol Ct	Wyomissing	PA	19610	**800-331-5969**	610-678-8131
Mainline Information Systems Inc 1700 Summit Lk Dr	Tallahassee	FL	32317	**866-490-6246**	850-219-5000
Mandli Communications Inc 4801 Tradewinds Pkwy	Madison	WI	53718	**888-545-2214**	608-835-3500
Matricis Informatique Inc 1425 Rene-Levesque Blvd W Ste 240	Montreal	QC	H3G1T7	**866-394-0011**	514-394-0011
Mdl Enterprise Inc 9888 Southwest Fwy	Houston	TX	77074	**800-879-0840**	713-771-6350
Mercom Inc 313 Commerce Dr	Pawleys Island	SC	29585	**877-223-8330**	843-979-9957
Microserv Computer Techs Inc 1808 E 17th St	Idaho Falls	ID	83404	**866-988-7164**	
Microworks 359 Kent St Ste 301	Ottawa	ON	K2P0R6	**877-232-3859**	613-232-3859
Miles Technologies Inc 300 W Route 38	Moorestown	NJ	08057	**800-496-8001**	856-439-0999
Netgain Information Systems Co 220 Reynolds Ave	Bellefontaine	OH	43311	**855-651-7001**	937-593-7177
Network America Inc 118 107th Ave	Treasure Island	FL	33706	**877-624-8311**	
Network Performance Inc 85 Green Mtn Dr	South Burlington	VT	05403	**800-639-6091**	802-859-0808
NewAgeSys Inc 231 Clarksville Rd Ste 200	Princeton Junction	NJ	08550	**888-863-9243**	609-919-9800
Novacoast Inc 1505 Chapala St	Santa Barbara	CA	93101	**800-949-9933**	
NOVIPRO Inc 2055 Peel St Ste 701	Montreal	QC	H3A1V4	**866-726-5353**	514-744-5353
Novo Solutions Inc 516 S Independence Blvd	Virginia Beach	VA	23452	**888-316-4559**	757-687-6590
nQueue Inc 7890 S Hardy Dr Ste 105	Tempe	AZ	85284	**800-299-5933**	
NTT DATA, Inc 100 City Sq	Boston	MA	02129	**800-745-3263**	
Oar Net 1224 Kinnear Rd	Columbus	OH	43212	**800-627-6420**	614-292-1956
Official Payments Corp 3550 Engineering Dr	Norcross	GA	30092	**877-754-4413**	770-325-3100
ONESPRING LLC 980 Birmingham Rd Ste 501-165	Alpharetta	GA	30004	**888-472-1840**	
Opsol Integrators Inc 1566 La Pradera Dr	Campbell	CA	95008	**800-996-7765**	408-364-9915
Pavliks Com 80 Bell Farm Rd	Barrie	ON	L4M5K5	**877-728-5457**	705-726-2966
PIREL Inc 1250 Nobel Ste 190	Boucherville	QC	J4B5H1	**800-449-7196**	450-449-5199
Planned Systems International Inc 10632 Lttle Patuxent Pkwy	Columbia	MD	21044	**800-275-7749**	410-964-8000
Point Alliance Inc 20 Adelaide St E Ste 500	Toronto	ON	M5C2T6	**855-947-6468**	416-943-0001
Pomeroy IT Solutions Inc 1020 Petersburg Rd	Hebron	KY	41048	**800-846-8727**	859-586-0600
Preferred Systems Solutions Inc 1945 Old Gallows Rd Ste 450	Vienna	VA	22182	**877-422-7149**	703-663-2777
Presidio Networked Solutions Inc 7601 Ora Glen Dr Ste 100	Greenbelt	MD	20770	**800-452-6926**	301-313-2000
Proactive Networking 229 Marshall Rd	Platte City	MO	64079	**800-255-6863**	816-587-7878
Professional Software Engineering Inc 780 Lynnhaven Pkwy Ste 350	Virginia Beach	VA	23452	**800-924-1091**	757-431-2400
Protocol Networks Inc 15 Shore Dr	Johnston	RI	02919	**877-676-0146**	
Qualex Consulting Services Inc 4300 Biscayne Blvd	Miami	FL	33137	**877-887-4727**	
Ranac Computer Corp 4181 E 96th St Ste 280	Indianapolis	IN	46240	**800-844-0141**	317-844-0141
Relate Corp 900 Avenida Acaso Ste K	Camarillo	CA	93012	**800-428-3708**	805-482-7381
Rex Black Consulting Services Inc 31520 Beck Rd	Bulverde	TX	78163	**866-438-4830**	830-438-4830
Rgen Solutions 4156 148th Ave Ne Bldg I	Redmond	WA	98052	**800-745-0615**	425-867-1350
RiverPoint Group LLC 2200 E Devon Ave Ste 385	Des Plaines	IL	60018	**800-297-5601**	847-233-9600
Rolta Tusc Inc 333 E Butterfield Rd Ste 900	Lombard	IL	60148	**800-755-8872**	630-960-2909
Sabre Solution, The 200 East 31st St	Savannah	OK	31401	**888-494-7200**	912-355-7200
Sayers Group LLC 825 Corporate Woods Pkwy	Vernon Hills	IL	60061	**800-323-5357**	
SCC Soft Computer Inc 5400 Tech Data Dr	Clearwater	FL	33760	**800-763-8352**	727-789-0100
Scorpion Design Inc 28480 Ave Stanford Ste 100	Valencia	CA	91355	**866-622-5648**	
Sda Consulting Inc 3011 183rd St # 377	Homewood	IL	60430	**800-823-2990**	
Securance LLC 6922 W Linebaugh Ave Ste 101	Tampa	FL	33625	**877-578-0215**	
SecureInfo Corp 211 N Loop 1604 E Ste 200	San Antonio	TX	78232	**888-677-9351**	210-403-5600
ShareSquared Inc 2155 Verdugo Blvd Ste 33	Montrose	CA	91020	**800-445-1279**	
Simacor LLC 10700 Hwy 55 Ste 170	Plymouth	MN	55441	**888-284-4415**	763-544-4415
Skyweb Networks 2710 State St	Saginaw	MI	48602	**866-575-9932**	989-792-8681
SMS Data Products Group Inc 1751 Pinnacle Dr 12th Fl	McLean	VA	22102	**800-331-1767**	
Snap Inc 4080 Lafayette Ctr Dr Ste 340	Chantilly	VA	20151	**866-234-7627**	703-393-6400
Softech & Associates Inc 1570 Corporate Dr Ste B	Costa Mesa	CA	92626	**877-638-3241**	714-427-1122
Software Information Systems Inc (SIS) 165 Barr St	Lexington	KY	40507	**800-337-6914**	859-977-4747
Software Technology Group 555 S 300 E	Salt Lake City	UT	84111	**888-595-1001**	801-595-1000
Sonit Systems LLC 130 W Field Dr	Archbold	OH	43502	**800-296-0018**	419-446-2151
Sparkhound Inc 11207 Proverbs Ave	Baton Rouge	LA	70816	**866-217-1500**	225-216-1500
SQA LABS Inc 16880 N 73rd Ave	Peoria	AZ	85382	**855-477-2522**	602-439-5500
Startech Computing Inc 1755 Old W Main St	Red Wing	MN	55066	**888-385-0607**	651-385-0607
STC Network Services Inc 4904 Oak Cir Dr N	Mobile	AL	36609	**800-566-2453**	251-661-7130
Stefanini TechTeam Inc 27335 W Eleven-Mile Rd	Southfield	MI	48034	**800-522-4451**	248-357-2866
Stg International Inc 4900 Seminary Rd Ste 1100	Alexandria	VA	22311	**855-507-0660**	703-578-6030
Stratapult Inc 2650 Pilgrim Ct	Winston-salem	NC	27106	**877-631-2900**	
Svam International Inc 233 E Shore Rd Ste 201	Great Neck	NY	11023	**800-903-6716**	516-466-6655
Sykes Enterprises Inc 400 N Ashley Dr Ste 2800 *NASDAQ: SYKE*	Tampa	FL	33602	**800-867-9537**	813-274-1000
Synergy Associates LLC 550 Clydesdale Trl	Medina	MN	55340	**888-763-9920**	
Syscon Inc 94 Mcfarland Blvd	Northport	AL	35476	**888-797-2661**	205-758-2000
Tangible Solutions Inc 1320 Matthews Township Pkwy Ste 201	Matthews	NC	28105	**800-393-9886**	704-940-4200
Tech Hero Of Central Florida LLC 4305 Vineland Rd., Ste G-12	Orlando	FL	32811	**800-900-8324**	
Teksavers Inc 2120 Grand Ave Pkwy	Austin	TX	78728	**866-832-6188**	512-491-5304
TeraMach Technologies Inc 1130 Morrison Dr Ste 105	Ottawa	ON	K2H9N6	**877-226-6549**	613-226-7775
Toss Corp 1253 Worcester Rd Ste 304	Framingham	MA	01701	**888-884-8677**	508-820-2990
Tribridge 4830 W Kennedy Blvd Ste 890	Tampa	FL	33609	**877-744-1360**	
Trillium Teamologies Inc 219 S Main St Ste 300	Royal Oak	MI	48067	**866-832-6884**	248-584-2080
Upnorth Consulting Inc 331 Second Ave S Ste 202	Minneapolis	MN	55401	**866-892-1758**	
US Data Management LLC 1746-F S Victoria Ave	Ventura	CA	93003	**888-231-0816**	
US-Analytics Solutions Group LLC 600 E Las Colinas Blvd Ste 2222 *General	Irving	TX	75039	**877-828-8727***	214-630-0081
USWired Inc 2107 N First St Ste 250	San Jose	CA	95131	**877-879-4733**	408-432-1144
Utopia Systems Inc 1172 Old Forge Rd	New Castle	DE	19720	**877-804-7421**	302-777-0772
Vanguard Integrity Professionals Inc 6625 S Eastern Ave Ste 100	Las Vegas	NV	89119	**877-794-0014**	702-794-0014
Vertisoft 990 Boul Pierre-roux E	Victoriaville	QC	G6T0K9	**877-368-3241**	819-751-6660
Visionary Integration Professionals Inc 80 Iron Pt Cir Ste 100	Folsom	CA	95630	**800-434-2673**	916-985-9625

	City	State	ZIP	Toll-Free	Phone
Vistronix Inc 11091 Sunset Hills Rd Ste 700	Reston	VA	20190	**800-483-2434**	703-463-2059
Watson SCS Inc 12157 W Linebaugh Ave Ste 381	Tampa	FL	33626	**866-805-6066**	
Wolcott Systems Group LLC 1684 Medina Rd Ste 204	Medina	OH	44256	**866-965-2688**	330-666-5900
Working Machines Corp 2170 Dwight Way	Berkeley	CA	94704	**877-648-4808**	510-704-1100
Xfer International Inc 39201 Schoolcraft Rd Ste B 9	Livonia	MI	48150	**800-438-9337**	734-927-6666
YouMail Inc 43 Corporate Park Ste 200	Irvine	CA	92606	**800-374-0013**	
Zontec Inc 1389 Kemper Meadow Dr	Cincinnati	OH	45240	**866-955-0088**	513-648-9695
ZyQuest Inc 1385 W Main Ave	De Pere	WI	54115	**800-992-0533**	920-499-0533

183 CONCERT, SPORTS, OTHER LIVE EVENT PRODUCERS & PROMOTERS

	City	State	ZIP	Toll-Free	Phone
Gilmore Entertainment Group 8901-A Business 17 N	Myrtle Beach	SC	29572	**800-843-6779**	843-913-4000
Harlem Globetrotters International Inc 400 E Van Buren St Ste 300	Phoenix	AZ	85004	**800-641-4667**	602-258-0000
World Wrestling Entertainment Inc 1241 E Main St *NYSE: WWE*	Stamford	CT	06902	**866-993-7467**	203-352-8600

184 CONCRETE - READY-MIXED

	City	State	ZIP	Toll-Free	Phone
Baccala Concrete Corp 100 Armento St	Johnston	RI	02919	**866-705-2382**	401-231-8300
Bonded Concrete Inc 303 Rt 155	Watervliet	NY	12189	**800-252-8589**	518-273-5800
Boston Sand & Gravel Company Inc 100 N Washington St *OTC: BSND*	Boston	MA	02114	**800-624-2724**	617-227-9000
Builders Redi-Mix Inc 30701 W 10 Mile Rd Ste 500 PO Box 2900	Farmington Hills	MI	48333	**888-988-4400**	
Building Products Corp 950 Freeburg Ave	Belleville	IL	62220	**800-233-1996**	618-233-4427
CalPortland Co 5975 E Marginal Way S PO Box 1730	Seattle	WA	98134	**800-750-0123**	206-764-3000
Cemex USA 840 Gessner Ste 1400 *NYSE: CX*	Houston	TX	77024	**888-292-0070**	713-650-6200
Cemstone Products Co 2025 Centre Pt Blvd Ste 300	Mendota Heights	MN	55120	**800-236-7866**	651-688-9292
Central Builders Supply Company Inc 125 Bridge Ave PO Box 152	Sunbury	PA	17801	**800-326-9361**	570-286-6461
Central Concrete Supply Company Inc 755 Stockton Ave	San Jose	CA	95126	**866-404-1000**	408-293-6272
Century Ready-Mix Corp 3250 Armand St PO Box 4420	Monroe	LA	71211	**800-732-3969**	318-322-4444
Clayton Cos, The PO Box 3015	Lakewood	NJ	08701	**800-662-3044**	
Dolese Bros Co 20 NW 13th St	Oklahoma City	OK	73103	**800-375-2311**	405-235-2311
Eastern Concrete Materials Inc 475 Market St	Elmwood Park	NJ	07407	**800-822-7242**	201-797-7979
Ernst Enterprises Inc 3361 Successful Way	Dayton	OH	45414	**800-353-1555**	937-233-5555
Geneva Rock Products Inc 302 W 5400 S Ste 200	Murray	UT	84107	**855-614-6497**	801-281-7900
Janesville Sand & Gravel Co (JSG) 1110 Harding St	Janesville	WI	53547	**800-955-7702**	608-754-7701
King's Material Inc 650 12th Ave SW	Cedar Rapids	IA	52404	**800-332-5298**	319-363-0233
Krehling Industries Inc 1399 Hagy Way	Harrisburg	PA	17110	**800-839-1654**	717-232-7936
Kuhlman Corp 1845 Indian Woods Cir	Maumee	OH	43537	**800-669-3309**	419-897-6000
L Suzio Concrete Company Inc 975 Westfield Rd	Meriden	CT	06450	**888-789-4626**	203-237-8421
Lycon Inc 1110 Harding St PO Box 427	Janesville	WI	53547	**800-955-8758**	608-754-7701
Prairie Group Inc 7601 W 79th St *Sales	Bridgeview	IL	60455	**800-649-3690***	708-458-0400
RiverStone Group Inc 1701 Fifth Ave	Moline	IL	61265	**800-906-2489**	309-757-8250
Sequatchie Concrete Service Inc 406 Cedar Ave	South Pittsburg	TN	37380	**800-824-0824**	423-837-7913
Shelby Materials 157 E Rampart St PO Box 242	Shelbyville	IN	46176	**800-548-9516**	
Silvi Concrete Products Inc 355 Newbold Rd	Fairless Hills	PA	19030	**800-426-6273**	215-295-0777
Speedway Redi Mix Inc 1201 N Taylor Rd	Garrett	IN	46738	**800-227-5649**	260-357-6885
Tilcon Connecticut Inc PO Box 1357	New Britain	CT	06050	**888-845-2666**	860-224-6010
Titan America Inc 1151 Azalea Garden Rd	Norfolk	VA	23502	**800-468-7622**	757-858-6500
United Materials LLC The Woodlands Corporate Ctr E 3949 Forest Pkwy Ste 400	North Tonawanda	NY	14120	**888-918-6483**	716-213-5832

185 CONCRETE PRODUCTS - MFR

	City	State	ZIP	Toll-Free	Phone
A Duchini Inc 2550 McKinley Ave	Erie	PA	16503	**800-937-7317**	814-456-7027
Abresist Corp PO Box 38	Urbana	IN	46990	**800-348-0717**	260-774-3327
Accord Industries 4001 Forsyth Rd *General	Winter Park	FL	32792	**800-876-6989***	407-671-6989
Adams Products Co 5701 McCrimmon Pkwy PO Box 189	Morrisville	NC	27560	**800-672-3131**	919-467-2218
American Artstone Co 2025 N Broadway St	New Ulm	MN	56073	**800-967-2076**	507-233-3700
Anvic Inc 501 McNicoll Ave	Toronto	ON	M2H2E2	**877-470-9991**	416-410-5674
Atlantic Concrete Products Inc 8900 Old Rt 13	Tullytown	PA	19007	**800-988-7837**	215-945-5600
Basalite Concrete Products LLC 605 Industrial Way	Dixon	CA	95620	**800-776-6690**	707-678-1901
BNZ Materials Inc 6901 S Pierce St Ste 260	Littleton	CO	80128	**800-999-0890**	303-978-1199
Bonsal American Inc 8201 Arrowridge Blvd	Charlotte	NC	28273	**800-424-9300**	704-525-1621
Buehner Block Co 2800 SW Temple	Salt Lake City	UT	84115	**800-999-2565**	801-467-5456
Carr Concrete Corp Waverly Rd	Waverly	WV	26184	**800-837-8918**	304-464-4013
Cast-Crete Corp 6324 County Rd 579	Seffner	FL	33584	**800-999-4641**	813-621-4641
Cement Industries Inc 2925 Hanson St PO Box 823	Fort Myers	FL	33902	**800-332-1440**	239-332-1440
Century Group Inc, The 1106 W Napoleon St PO Box 228	Sulphur	LA	70664	**800-527-5232**	337-527-5266
Chaney Enterprises 12480 Mattawoman Dr PO Box 548	Waldorf	MD	20604	**888-244-0411**	301-932-5000
Clayton Block Co PO Box 3015	Lakewood	NJ	08701	**800-662-3044**	
Clayton Cos, The PO Box 3015	Lakewood	NJ	08701	**800-662-3044**	
Con Cast Pipe LP 299 Brock Rd S RR#3	Guelph	ON	N1H6H9	**800-668-7473**	
Con Forms 777 Maritime Dr	Port Washington	WI	53074	**800-223-3676**	262-284-7800
Construction Products Inc 1631 Ashport Rd	Jackson	TN	38305	**800-238-8226**	731-668-7305
Creter Vault Corp 417 US Hwy 202	Flemington	NJ	08822	**800-352-4890**	908-782-7771
DN Tanks 351 Cypress Ln	El Cajon	CA	92020	**800-227-8181**	619-440-8181
Dolese Bros Co 20 NW 13th St	Oklahoma City	OK	73103	**800-375-2311**	405-235-2311
Dura-Stress Inc 11325 County Rd 44 *General	Leesburg	FL	34788	**800-342-9239***	352-787-1422
E Dillon & Co 2522 Swords Creek Rd PO Box 160	Swords Creek	VA	24649	**800-234-8970**	276-873-6816
EP Henry Corp 201 Pk Ave	Woodbury	NJ	08096	**800-444-3679**	856-845-6200
Ernest Maier Inc 4700 Annapolis Rd	Bladensburg	MD	20710	**888-927-8303**	301-927-8300
Fabcon Inc 6111 Hwy 13 W	Savage	MN	55378	**800-727-4444**	952-890-4444
Federal Block Corp 247 Walsh Ave	New Windsor	NY	12553	**800-724-1999**	845-561-4108
Fin Pan Inc 3255 Symmes Rd	Hamilton	OH	45015	**800-833-6444**	513-870-9200
Flexicore of Texas PO Box 450049	Houston	TX	77245	**888-359-4267**	281-437-5700
Fritz Industries Inc 180 Gordon Dr Ste 113	Exton	PA	19341	**800-345-6202**	
General Shale Products LLC 3015 Bristol Hwy	Johnson City	TN	37601	**800-414-4661**	423-282-4661
George L Throop Co 444 N Fair Oaks Ave	Pasadena	CA	91103	**800-796-0285**	626-796-0285
Grand Blanc Cement Products 10709 Ctr Rd	Grand Blanc	MI	48439	**800-875-7500**	810-694-7500
High Concrete Structures Inc 125 Denver Rd	Denver	PA	17517	**800-773-2278**	717-336-9300
Hy-Grade Precast Concrete 2411 First St	St Catharines	ON	L2R6P7	**800-229-8568**	905-684-8568
Isabel Bloom LLC 736 Federal St Ste 2100	Davenport	IA	52803	**800-273-5436**	
Jensen Precast 625 Bergin Way	Sparks	NV	89431	**800-648-1134**	775-359-6200
JW Peters Inc 500 W Market St	Burlington	WI	53105	**866-265-7888**	262-806-9009
King's Material Inc 650 12th Ave SW	Cedar Rapids	IA	52404	**800-332-5298**	319-363-0233
Kistner Concrete Products Inc 8713 Read Rd	East Pembroke	NY	14056	**800-809-2801**	585-762-8216
L M Scofield Co 6533 Bandini Blvd	Los Angeles	CA	90040	**800-800-9900**	323-720-3000
M-CON Products Inc 2150 Richardson Side Rd	Carp	ON	K0A1L0	**800-267-5515**	613-831-1736
MantelsDirect 217 N Seminary St	Florence	AL	35630	**888-493-8898**	
Metromont Corp PO Box 2486	Greenville	SC	29602	**888-295-0383**	864-295-0295
Modern Inc/Environmental & Wastewater 210 Durham Rd	Ottsville	PA	18942	**888-965-3227**	610-847-5112
Molin Concrete Products Co 415 Lilac St	Lino Lakes	MN	55014	**800-336-6546**	651-786-7722
Montfort Bros Inc 44 Elm St	Fishkill	NY	12524	**800-724-1777**	845-896-6225
Montfort Group, The 44 Elm St	Fishkill	NY	12524	**800-724-1777**	845-896-6225
Mutual Materials Co 605 119th Ave NE	Bellevue	WA	98005	**800-477-3008**	425-452-2300
National Oilwell Varco (NOV) 7909 Parkwood Cir Dr *NYSE: NOV*	Houston	TX	77036	**888-262-8645**	713-375-3700
NC Products Corp 920 Withers Rd PO Box 27077	Raleigh	NC	27603	**888-965-3227**	919-772-6301
New Milford Block & Supply 574 Danbury Rd	New Milford	CT	06776	**800-724-1888**	860-355-1101
Northfield an Oldcastle Co 2200 S Main St	West Bend	WI	53095	**800-227-6512**	262-338-5700

Classified Section

Company / Address	City	State	Zip	Toll-Free	Phone
Norwalk Concrete Industries Inc 80 Commerce Dr	Norwalk	OH	44857	**800-733-3624**	419-668-8167
Oldcastle Precast Inc 7921 Southpark Pl Ste 200	Folsom	NJ	08037	**800-642-3755**	
Olson Precast Co (OPC) 2750 Marion Dr	Las Vegas	NV	89115	**800-876-8374**	702-643-4371
QUIKRETE Cos 3490 Piedmont Rd Ste 1300	Atlanta	GA	30305	**800-282-5828**	404-634-9100
RCP Block & Brick Inc 8240 Broadway	Lemon Grove	CA	91945	**800-794-4727**	619-460-7250
Reading Precast Inc 5494 Pottsville Pike	Leesport	PA	19533	**800-724-4881**	610-926-5000
Reading Rock Inc 4600 Devitt Dr	Cincinnati	OH	45246	**800-482-6466**	513-874-2345
Rinker Materials Corp Concrete Pipe Div 8311 W Carder Ct	Littleton	CO	80125	**800-909-7763**	303-791-1600
Rockwood Retaining Walls Inc 7200 Hwy 63 N	Rochester	MN	55906	**800-535-2375**	888-288-4045
SD Ireland Co 193 Industrial Ave	Williston	VT	05495	**800-339-4565**	802-863-6222
Sequatchie Concrete Service Inc 406 Cedar Ave	South Pittsburg	TN	37380	**800-824-0824**	423-837-7913
Spancrete Industries Inc N 16 W 23415 Stone Ridge Dr PO Box 828	Waukesha	WI	53187	**855-900-7726**	414-290-9000
Superlite Block Co Inc 4150 W Turney Ave	Phoenix	AZ	85019	**800-366-7877**	602-352-3500
Terre Hill Silo Company Inc PO Box 10	Terre Hill	PA	17581	**800-242-1509**	717-445-3100
Tindall Corp 2273 Hayne St	Spartanburg	SC	29301	**800-849-4521**	864-576-3230
Valley Blox Inc 210 Stone Spring Rd	Harrisonburg	VA	22801	**800-648-6725**	540-434-6725
Wausau Tile Inc PO Box 1520	Wausau	WI	54402	**800-388-8728**	715-359-3121
Wells Concrete Products Inc 835 Hwy 109 NE PO Box 308	Wells	MN	56097	**800-658-7049**	507-553-3138
Wieser Concrete Products Inc W3716 US Hwy 10	Maiden Rock	WI	54750	**800-325-8456**	715-647-2311
Wingra Stone Co 2975 Kapec Rd PO Box 44284	Madison	WI	53744	**800-249-6908**	608-271-5555
York Bldg Products Co 950 Smile Way	York	PA	17404	**800-673-2408**	717-848-2831

186 CONFERENCE & EVENTS COORDINATORS

Company / Address	City	State	Zip	Toll-Free	Phone
ASD 6255 Sunset Blvd 19th Fl	Los Angeles	CA	90028	**800-421-4511**	323-817-2200
Bixel & Co 8721 Sunset Blvd Ste 101	Los Angeles	CA	90069	**855-854-9830**	310-854-3828
Can-do Promotions Inc 6517 Wise Ave Nw	North Canton	OH	44720	**800-325-7981**	330-494-3527
Celebritees Inc 1014 Atlantic Ave	Savannah	GA	31401	**877-831-1005**	912-233-9941
Conference & Travel 5655 Coventry Ln	Fort Wayne	IN	46804	**800-346-9807**	260-434-6600
Courtesy Assoc 2025 M St NW Ste 800	Washington	DC	20036	**800-647-4689**	
Creative Impact Group Inc 801 Skokie Blvd Ste 108	Northbrook	IL	60062	**800-445-2171**	847-945-7401
CSI Worldwide Inc 40 Regency Plz	Glen Mills	PA	19342	**800-523-7118**	610-558-4500
Destination Resources 5435 Balboa Blvd Ste 106	Encino	CA	91316	**800-422-6524**	818-995-7915
Event Planning International Corp 10900 Granite St	Charlotte	NC	28273	**800-940-2164**	980-233-3777
Exhibit Concepts Inc 700 Crossroads Ct	Vandalia	OH	45377	**800-324-5063**	
Expo Group, The 5931 W Campus Cir Dr	Irving	TX	75063	**800-736-7775**	972-580-9000
Gavel International Corp 300 Tri State International Ste 320	Lincolnshire	IL	60069	**800-544-2835**	847-945-8150
GES Exposition Services 7000 Lindell Rd	Las Vegas	NV	89118	**800-443-9767**	702-515-5500
Gls Group Inc 27850 Detroit Rd	Westlake	OH	44145	**800-955-9435**	440-899-7770
Graylyn International Conference Center Inc 1900 Reynolda Rd	Winston-Salem	NC	27106	**800-472-9596**	336-758-2600
Great Events & TEAMS Inc 2170 S Parker Rd Ste 290	Denver	CO	80231	**866-706-7814**	303-394-2022
Idegy 3990 Business Park Dr	Columbus	OH	43204	**888-421-2288**	614-545-5000
International Meeting Managers Inc 4550 Post Oak Pl Ste 342	Houston	TX	77027	**800-423-7175**	713-965-0566
Meeting Connection Inc, The 6373 Meadow Glen Dr N	Westerville	OH	43082	**800-398-2568**	614-888-2568
National Trade Productions Inc 313 S Patrick St	Alexandria	VA	22314	**800-687-7469**	703-683-8500
Pittcon 300 Penn Ctr Blvd Ste 332	Pittsburgh	PA	15235	**800-825-3221**	412-825-3220
Prestige Accommodations International 1231 E Dyer Rd Ste 240	Santa Ana	CA	92705	**800-321-6338**	714-957-9100
Resource Connection Inc 161 S Main St	Middleton	MA	01949	**800-649-5228**	978-777-9333
RX Worldwide Meetings Inc 3060 Communications Pkwy Ste 200	Plano	TX	75093	**800-562-1713**	214-291-2920
Splash!events Inc 210 Hillsdale Ave	San Jose	CA	95136	**866-204-6000**	408-287-8600
T3 Expo LLC 8 Lakeville Business Park Unit 1	Lakeville	MA	02347	**888-698-3397**	
Travizon Meeting Management 275 Mishawum Rd Ste 300	Woburn	MA	01801	**800-423-2500**	888-781-5200
Westbury National Show Systems Ltd 772 Warden Ave	Toronto	ON	M1L4T7	**855-752-1372**	416-752-1371

187 CONGLOMERATES

SEE ALSO Holding Companies

A business conglomerate is defined here as a corporation that consists of many business units in different industries.

Company / Address	City	State	Zip	Toll-Free	Phone
3M Co 3M Ctr Bldg 225-3S-06 *NYSE: MMM*	Saint Paul	MN	55144	**800-364-3577**	651-733-1110
Alexander & Baldwin Inc 822 Bishop St *NYSE: ALEX*	Honolulu	HI	96813	**866-442-6551**	808-525-6611
Andersons Inc 480 W Dussel Dr *NASDAQ: ANDE*	Maumee	OH	43537	**800-537-3370**	419-893-5050
APi Group Inc 1100 Old Hwy 8 NW	New Brighton	MN	55112	**800-223-4922**	
ARAMARK Corp 1101 Market St	Philadelphia	PA	19107	**800-388-3300**	937-660-4708
Archer Daniels Midland Co (ADM) 4666 E Faries Pkwy *NYSE: ADM*	Decatur	IL	62526	**800-637-5843**	217-424-5200
Ashland Inc 50 E River Ctr Blvd PO Box 391 *NYSE: ASH*	Covington	KY	41012	**877-546-2782**	859-815-3333
Berkshire Hathaway Inc 3555 Farnam St Ste 1440 *NYSE: BRK/A*	Omaha	NE	68131	**800-223-2064**	402-346-1400
Brown-Forman Corp 850 Dixie Hwy PO Box 1080 *NYSE: BFB*	Louisville	KY	40210	**800-831-9146**	502-585-1100
Canadian Tire Corp Ltd 2180 Yonge St PO Box 770 Stn K *TSE: CTC*	Toronto	ON	M4P2V8	**800-387-8803**	416-480-3000
Chemed Corp 255 E Fifth St Ste 2600 *NYSE: CHE* ■ *General	Cincinnati	OH	45202	**800-982-7650***	513-762-6900
Clorox Co 1221 Broadway *NYSE: CLX* ■ *Cust Svc	Oakland	CA	94612	**800-424-9300***	510-271-7000
Delaware North Cos Inc 40 Fountain Plz	Buffalo	NY	14202	**800-828-7240**	716-858-5000
EBSCO Industries Inc 5724 Hwy 280	Birmingham	AL	35242	**800-653-2726**	205-991-6600
Fortune Brands Inc 520 Lk Cook Rd *NYSE: FBHS*	Deerfield	IL	60015	**800-225-2719**	847-484-4400
Harris Teeter Inc PO Box 10100 *NYSE: HTSI*	Mathews	NC	28106	**800-432-6111**	704-844-3100
Harsco Corp 350 Poplar Church Rd *NYSE: HSC*	Camp Hill	PA	17011	**866-470-3900**	717-763-7064
Hitachi America Ltd 50 Prospect Ave	Tarrytown	NY	10591	**800-448-2244**	914-332-5800
Holiday Cos 4567 American Blvd W PO Box 1224	Bloomington	MN	55437	**800-745-7411**	952-830-8700
HT Hackney Co 502 S Gay St PO Box 238	Knoxville	TN	37901	**800-406-1291**	865-546-1291
iHeartMedia, Inc 200 E Basse Rd	San Antonio	TX	78209	**800-829-6551**	210-822-2828
Kaman Corp PO Box 1 *NYSE: KAMN*	Bloomfield	CT	06002	**866-450-3663**	860-243-7100
Kimball International Inc 1600 Royal St *NASDAQ: KBAL*	Jasper	IN	47549	**800-482-1616**	812-482-1600
Kohler Co Inc 444 Highland Dr	Kohler	WI	53044	**800-456-4537**	920-457-4441
Kraus-Anderson Co (KA) 523 S Eigth St	Minneapolis	MN	55404	**888-547-3983**	612-305-2934
MDU Resources Group Inc 1200 W Century Ave PO Box 5650 *NYSE: MDU*	Bismarck	ND	58506	**866-760-4852**	701-530-1000
NACCO Industries Inc 5875 Landerbrook Dr Ste 300 *NYSE: NC*	Cleveland	OH	44124	**877-756-5118**	440-229-5151
Newell Rubbermaid Inc 3 Glenlake Pkwy *NYSE: NWL*	Atlanta	GA	30328	**800-752-9677**	770-418-7000
PepsiCo Inc 700 Anderson Hill Rd *NYSE: PEP* ■ *PR	Purchase	NY	10577	**800-433-2652***	914-253-2000
Seaboard Corp 9000 W 67th St *NYSE: SEB*	Shawnee Mission	KS	66202	**866-676-8886**	913-676-8800
Siemens Corp 527 Madison Ave 8th Fl	New York	NY	10022	**800-743-6367**	212-258-4000
SPX Corp 13515 Ballantyne Corporate Pl *NYSE: SPW*	Charlotte	NC	28277	**877-247-3797**	704-752-4400
Teleflex Inc 155 S Limerick Rd *NYSE: TFX*	Limerick	PA	19468	**866-246-6990**	610-948-5100
Time Warner Inc 1 Time Warner Ctr *NYSE: TWX*	New York	NY	10019	**866-463-6899**	212-484-8000
Trinity Industries Inc 2525 Stemmons Fwy *NYSE: TRN*	Dallas	TX	75207	**800-631-4420**	214-631-4420
United Services Automobile Assn (USAA) 10750 McDermott Fwy	San Antonio	TX	78288	**800-531-8722**	
Weyerhaeuser Co 33663 Weyerhaeuser Way S *NYSE: WY*	Federal Way	WA	98003	**800-525-5440**	253-924-2345

188 CONSTRUCTION - BUILDING CONTRACTORS - NON-RESIDENTIAL

Company	Address	City	State	Zip	Toll-Free	Phone
1st Choice Facilities Services Corp	1941 Whitfield Park Loop	Sarasota	FL	34243	**866-241-0070**	
Advanced Industrial Services Inc	3250 Susquehanna Trial	York	PA	17406	**800-544-5080**	717-764-9811
Ameris Bank	24 Second Ave SE PO Box 3668	Moultrie	GA	31768	**866-616-6020**	
Anchor Tampa Inc	3907 W Osborne Ave	Tampa	FL	33614	**800-879-8685**	813-879-8685
Apex Homes Inc	7172 Rt 522	Middleburg	PA	17842	**800-326-9524**	570-837-2333
Bank of the Orient	233 Sansome St	San Francisco	CA	94104	**877-275-3342**	415-338-0843
Becker Arena Products Inc	6611 W Hwy 13	Savage	MN	55378	**800-234-5522**	952-890-2690
Brannan Paving Coltd	111 Elk Dr PO Box 3403	Victoria	TX	77903	**800-626-7064**	361-573-3130
Brasfield & Gorrie LLC	3021 Seventh Ave S	Birmingham	AL	35233	**800-239-8017**	205-328-4000
Bristol Construction Services LLC	111 W 16th Ave Fl 3	Anchorage	AK	99501	**877-563-0013**	907-563-0013
Budreck Truck Lines Inc	8040 S Roberts Rd	Bridgeview	IL	60455	**800-621-0013**	708-496-0522
C.a. Murren & Sons Co Inc	2275 Loganville Hwy	Grayson	GA	30017	**866-912-8906**	770-682-2940
Ca Lindman Inc	10401 Guilford Rd	Jessup	MD	20794	**877-737-8675**	301-470-4700
Cedar Grove Composting Inc	7343 E Marginal Way S	Seattle	WA	98108	**888-832-3008**	206-832-3000
CenTex House Leveling	1120 E 52nd St	Austin	TX	78723	**888-425-5438**	512-444-5438
CG Schmidt Inc	11777 W Lake Pk Dr	Milwaukee	WI	53224	**800-248-1254**	414-577-1177
Clark Construction Group LLC	7500 Old Georgetown Rd	Bethesda	MD	20814	**800-655-1330**	301-272-8100
Clark Transfer Inc	800A Paxton St	Harrisburg	PA	17104	**800-488-7585**	717-238-0801
Clarksdale Municipal School District	101 McGuire St PO Box 1088	Clarksdale	MS	38614	**877-820-7831**	662-627-8500
Conrad Schmitt Studios Inc	2405 S 162nd St	New Berlin	WI	53151	**800-969-3033**	262-786-3030
Daryl Flood Inc	450 Airline Dr Ste 100	Coppell	TX	75019	**800-325-9340**	972-471-1496
Daw Construction Group LLC	12552 South 125 West	Draper	UT	84020	**800-748-4778**	801-553-9111
Deltec Homes Inc	69 Bingham Rd	Asheville	NC	28806	**800-642-2508**	
Diffenbaugh Inc	6865 Airport Dr	Riverside	CA	92504	**800-394-5334**	951-351-6865
Duffield Assoc Inc	5400 Limestone Rd	Wilmington	DE	19808	**877-732-9633**	302-239-6634
Dyad Constructors Inc	8505 Holt St	Houston	TX	77054	**800-803-9202**	713-799-9380
Emery Air Charter Inc	1 Airport Cir	Rockford	IL	61109	**800-435-8090**	815-968-8287
Flintco LLC	1624 W 21st St	Tulsa	OK	74107	**800-947-2828**	918-587-8451
G & D Transportation Inc	50 Commerce Dr	Morton	IL	61550	**800-451-6680**	
Gaines Motor Lines Inc	2349 13th Ave SW PO Box 1549	Hickory	NC	28603	**800-438-7311**	828-322-2000
Galaxie Defense Marketing Services	5330 Napa St	San Diego	CA	92110	**888-711-3427**	619-299-9950
Gerald H Phipps	5995 Greenwood Florida Plaza Blvd Ste 100	Greenwood Village	CO	80111	**866-487-2365**	303-571-5377
Gerloff Company Inc	14955 Bulverde Rd	San Antonio	TX	78247	**800-486-3621**	210-490-2777
Gilbane Bldg Co New England Regional Office	7 Jackson Walkway	Providence	RI	02903	**800-445-2263**	401-456-5800
Gilbane Bldg Company Mid-Atlantic Regional Office	7901 Sandy Spring Rd Ste 500	Laurel	MD	20707	**800-445-2263**	410-649-1750
Gilbane Bldg Company Southwest Regional Office	1331 Lamar St Ste 1170	Houston	TX	77010	**800-445-2263**	713-209-1873
Golden Sands General Contractors Inc	2500 NW 39 St	Miami	FL	33142	**888-994-4742**	305-633-3336
Gray Construction	10 Quality St	Lexington	KY	40507	**800-814-8468**	859-281-5000
Greystone Construction Co	500 S Marschall Rd Ste 300	Shakopee	MN	55379	**888-742-6837**	952-496-2227
Harkins Builders Inc	2201 Warwick Way	Marriottsville	MD	21104	**800-227-2345**	410-750-2600
Haskell Co	111 Riverside Ave	Jacksonville	FL	32202	**800-622-4326**	904-791-4500
Holloman Corp	333 N Sam Houston Pkwy E Ste 600	Houston	TX	77060	**800-521-2461**	281-878-2600
Jaynes Corp	2906 Broadway NE	Albuquerque	NM	87107	**800-393-6343**	505-345-8591
John E Jones Oil Co Inc	1016 S Cedar PO Box 546	Stockton	KS	67669	**800-323-9821**	785-425-6746
Kiwi Ii Construction Inc	28177 Keller Rd	Murrieta	CA	92563	**877-465-4942**	951-301-8975
Kustom Fl LLC	265 Hunt Park Cv	Longwood	FL	32750	**866-679-0699**	
Lewis & Michael Inc	1827 Woodman Dr	Dayton	OH	45420	**800-543-3524**	937-252-6683
Lightner Electronics Inc	1771 Beaver Dam Rd	Claysburg	PA	16625	**866-239-3888**	814-239-8323
Logan Trucking Inc	3224 Navarre Rd SW	Canton	OH	44706	**800-683-0142**	330-478-1404
Mark Cerrone Inc	2368 Maryland Ave	Niagara Falls	NY	14305	**855-250-7739**	716-282-5244
Market Contractors Ltd of Oregon	10250 NE Marx St	Portland	OR	97220	**800-793-1448**	503-255-0977
McGough Construction Co Inc	2737 Fairview Ave N	Saint Paul	MN	55113	**800-552-7670**	651-633-5050
MDC Systems Inc	37 N Vly Rd 3 Sta Sq Ste 100	Paoli	PA	19301	**888-632-9977**	610-640-9600
Merced Irrigation District	PO Box 2288	Merced	CA	95344	**855-800-2267**	209-722-5761
Metal Masters Inc	3825 Crater Lk Hwy	Medford	OR	97504	**800-866-9437**	541-779-1049
Meyer & Najem Inc	11787 Lantern Rd Ste 100	Fishers	IN	46038	**888-578-5131**	317-577-0007
MGM Mirage Design Group Inc	3260 Industrial Rd	Las Vegas	NV	89109	**800-929-1111**	866-761-7111
Mine & Mill Industrial Supply Company Inc	2500 S Combee Rd	Lakeland	FL	33801	**800-282-8489**	863-665-5601
Modular Connections LLC	1090 Industrial Blvd	Bessemer	AL	35022	**877-903-6335**	205-980-4565
Modular Genius Inc	1201 S Mountain Rd	Joppa	MD	21085	**888-420-1113**	
Moores Electrical & Mechanical	PO Box 119	Altavista	VA	24517	**888-722-2712**	434-369-4374
Motor Service Inc	130 Byassee Dr	Hazelwood	MO	63042	**800-966-5080**	314-731-4111
Multigon Industries Inc	525 Executive Boulevard	Yonkers	NY	10701	**800-289-6858**	
Near-Cal Corp	512 Chaney St	Lake Elsinore	CA	92530	**800-969-3578**	951-245-5400
Nor-Son Inc	7900 Hastings Rd	Baxter	MN	56425	**800-858-1722**	218-828-1722
Nujak Development Inc	711 N Kentucky Ave	Lakeland	FL	33801	**888-685-2526**	863-686-1565
Odebrecht Construction Inc	201 Alhambra Cir Ste 1000	Coral Gables	FL	33134	**800-771-0001**	305-341-8800
Orcutt/Winslow	3003 N Central Ave	Phoenix	AZ	85012	**800-331-5842**	602-257-1764
P A Landers Inc	351 Winter St	Hanover	MA	02339	**800-660-6404**	781-826-8818
PDC Facilities Inc	700 Walnut Ridge Dr	Hartland	WI	53029	**800-545-5998**	262-367-7700
Perma-Seal Waterproofing	513 Rogers St	Downers Grove	IL	60515	**800-421-7325**	630-512-0002
Plasteak Inc	3563 Copley Rd	Copley	OH	44321	**800-320-1841**	330-668-2587
PM Construction Co Inc	PO Box 728	Saco	ME	04072	**800-646-0068**	207-282-7697
Porta-King Building Systems	4133 Shoreline Dr	Earth City	MO	63045	**800-284-5346**	
Portable Buildings Inc	3235 Bay Rd	Milford	DE	19963	**800-205-5030**	302-335-1300
R W Mercer Co	2322 Brooklyn Rd PO Box 180	Jackson	MI	49204	**877-763-7237**	517-787-2960
Ramtech Bldg Systems Inc	1400 Hwy 287 S	Mansfield	TX	76063	**855-887-1888**	800-568-9376
Renfrow Bros Inc	855 Gossett Rd	Spartanburg	SC	29307	**800-260-8412**	864-579-0558
Ricks Barbecue Inc	2367 Hwy 43 S	Leoma	TN	38468	**800-544-5864**	931-852-2324
Roy Anderson Corp	11400 Reichold Rd	Gulfport	MS	39503	**800-688-4003**	228-896-4000
Rycon Construction Inc	2525 Liberty Ave	Pittsburgh	PA	15222	**800-883-1901**	412-392-2525
Scharine Group, The	4213 N Scharine Rd	Whitewater	WI	53190	**800-472-2880**	608-883-2880
Schmidt Bros. Inc	420 N Hallett Ave	Swanton	OH	43558	**800-200-7318**	419-826-3671
Schneider Electric Buildings LLC	1354 Clifford Ave	Loves Park	IL	61111	**888-444-1311**	
Septagon Construction	113 E Third St	Sedalia	MO	65301	**800-733-5999**	660-827-2115
Stellar Group	2900 Hartley Rd	Jacksonville	FL	32257	**800-488-2900**	904-260-2900
Stidham Trucking Inc	PO Box 308	Yreka	CA	96097	**800-827-9500**	530-842-4161
Streeter Assoc Inc	101 E Woodlawn Ave PO Box 118	Elmira	NY	14902	**866-493-1640**	607-734-4151
Sundt Construction Inc	2015 W River Rd Ste 101	Tucson	AZ	85704	**800-467-5544**	520-750-4600
Telecon Inc	13 500 boul Metropolitain E	Montreal	QC	H1A3W1	**800-465-0349**	514-644-2333
Trehel Corp	PO Box 1707	Clemson	SC	29633	**800-319-7006**	864-654-6582
University Moving & Storage Co	23305 Commerce Dr	Farmington Hills	MI	48335	**800-448-6683**	248-615-7000
USM Inc	1880 Markley St	Norristown	PA	19401	**800-355-4000**	610-278-9000
Virtexco Corp	977 Norfolk Sq	Norfolk	VA	23502	**800-766-1082**	757-466-1114
Walker Industries Holdings Ltd	2800 Thorold Townline Rd	Niagara Falls	ON	L2E6S4	**866-694-9360**	905-227-4142
Walsh Group Inc	929 W Adams St	Chicago	IL	60607	**800-957-1842**	312-563-5400
Ware County Board of Education	1301 Bailey St	Waycross	GA	31501	**800-419-3191**	912-283-8656
Washington Local Schools	3505 W Lincolnshire Blvd	Toledo	OH	43606	**800-462-3589**	419-473-8251
Welch & Rushe Inc	391 Prince George's Blvd	Upper Marlboro	MD	20774	**800-683-3852**	301-430-6000
Windstar Lines Inc	1903 US Hwy 71 N	Carroll	IA	51401	**888-494-6378**	712-792-4221
Woodfield Inc	3161 Hwy 376 S	Camden	AR	71701	**800-501-6020**	870-231-6020

189 CONSTRUCTION - BUILDING CONTRACTORS - RESIDENTIAL

Company	Address	City	State	Zip	Toll-Free	Phone
Air Contact Transport Inc	PO Box 570	Budd Lake	NJ	07828	**800-765-2769**	
Arthur Rutenberg Homes Inc	13922 58th St N	Clearwater	FL	33760	**800-274-6637**	727-536-5900
Ball Homes LLC	3609 Walden Dr	Lexington	KY	40517	**888-268-1101**	859-268-1191

Classified Section

Name / Address	City	State	Zip	Toll-Free	Phone
Bar None Auction Inc 4751 Power Inn Rd	Sacramento	CA	95826	**866-372-1700**	
Bozzuto Group 7850 Walker Dr Ste 400 *General	Greenbelt	MD	20770	**866-698-7513***	301-220-0100
Dot-Line Transportation PO Box 8739	Fountain Valley	CA	92728	**800-423-3780**	323-780-9010
Drees Co 211 Grandview Dr	Fort Mitchell	KY	41017	**866-265-2980**	859-578-4200
Eyde Co 4660 S Hagadorn Ste 660	East Lansing	MI	48823	**800-422-3933**	517-351-2480
Grupe Co 3255 W March Ln Ste 400	Stockton	CA	95219	**877-984-7873**	209-473-6000
Harkins Builders Inc 2201 Warwick Way	Marriottsville	MD	21104	**800-227-2345**	410-750-2600
JB Sandlin Cos 5137 Davis Blvd	Fort Worth	TX	76180	**800-821-4663**	817-281-3509
Kopf Builders Inc 420 Avon Belden Rd	Avon Lake	OH	44012	**888-933-5673**	440-933-6908
LAS Enterprises Inc 2413 L & A Rd	Metairie	LA	70001	**800-264-1527**	504-887-1515
Mercy Housing Inc 1999 Broadway Ste 1000	Denver	CO	80202	**866-338-0557**	303-830-3300
Nordaas American Homes Company Inc 10091 State Hwy 22	Minnesota Lake	MN	56068	**800-658-7076**	507-462-3331
Norris School District 6940 Calloway Dr	Bakersfield	CA	93312	**800-877-8339**	661-387-7000
Olgoonik Development LLC 3201 C St Ste 700	Anchorage	AK	99503	**855-763-2613**	907-562-8728
Perry Homes PO Box 34306	Houston	TX	77234	**800-247-3779**	713-948-7700
Providence Homes Inc 4901 Belfort Rd Ste 140	Jacksonville	FL	32256	**866-836-0981**	904-262-9898
Rio Verde Development Inc 25609 N Danny Ln	Rio Verde	AZ	85263	**800-233-7103**	480-471-1962
Southern California Boiler Inc 5331 Business Dr	Huntington Beach	CA	92649	**800-775-2645**	714-891-0701
Staples Construction Company Inc 1501 Eastman Ave	Ventura	CA	93003	**800-881-4650**	805-658-8786
Structural Component Systems Inc (SCS) 1255 Front St	Fremont	NE	68026	**800-844-5622**	402-721-5622
TH Properties 345 Main St *Sales	Harleysville	PA	19438	**800-225-5847***	215-513-4270
Triple Crown Corp 5351 Jaycee Ave	Harrisburg	PA	17112	**877-822-4663**	717-657-5729
United-Bilt Homes Inc 8500 Line Ave	Shreveport	LA	71106	**800-551-8955**	318-861-4572
Vendini Inc 660 Market St	San Francisco	CA	94104	**800-901-7173**	
Village Green Cos 30833 NW Hwy	Farmington Hills	MI	48334	**800-521-2220**	248-851-9600
Walsh Group Inc 929 W Adams St	Chicago	IL	60607	**800-957-1842**	312-563-5400
Weavertown Environmental Group 2 Dorrington Rd	Carnegie	PA	15106	**800-746-4850**	724-746-4850

190 CONSTRUCTION - HEAVY CONSTRUCTION CONTRACTORS

Name / Address	City	State	Zip	Toll-Free	Phone
Bo-mac Contractors Ltd 1020 Lindbergh Dr	Beaumont	TX	77707	**800-526-6221**	409-842-2125
Gulf Engineering LLC 611 Hill St	Jefferson	LA	70121	**800-347-4749**	504-733-4868
Larkin Enterprises Inc 317 W Broadway PO Box 405	Lincoln	ME	04457	**800-990-5418**	207-794-8700
Oman Systems Inc 3334 Powell Ave	Nashville	TN	37204	**800-541-0803**	615-385-2500
Power Grid Engineering LLC 5744 Canton Cove Ste 110	Winter Springs	FL	32708	**877-819-1171**	321-244-0170
R&R Contracting Inc 5201 N Washington St	Grand Forks	ND	58203	**800-872-5975**	701-772-7667
Tecon Services Inc 515 Garden Oaks Blvd	Houston	TX	77018	**800-245-1728**	713-691-2700

190-1 Communications Lines & Towers Construction

Name / Address	City	State	Zip	Toll-Free	Phone
MasTec Inc 800 Douglas Rd 12th Fl *NYSE: MTZ*	Coral Gables	FL	33134	**800-531-5000**	305-599-1800
Utility Services Inc 400 N Fourth St	Bismarck	ND	58501	**800-638-3278**	701-222-7900

190-2 Foundation Drilling & Pile Driving

Name / Address	City	State	Zip	Toll-Free	Phone
Case Foundation Co 1325 W Lake St	Roselle	IL	60172	**800-999-4087**	630-529-2911
LG Barcus & Sons Inc 1430 State Ave	Kansas City	KS	66102	**800-255-0180**	913-621-1100
Malcolm Drilling Co Inc 3503 Breakwater Ct	Hayward	CA	94545	**800-523-2200**	510-780-9181

190-3 Golf Course Construction

Name / Address	City	State	Zip	Toll-Free	Phone
Harris Miniature Golf 141 W Burk Ave	Wildwood	NJ	08260	**888-294-6530**	609-522-4200

190-4 Highway, Street, Bridge, Tunnel Construction

Name / Address	City	State	Zip	Toll-Free	Phone
Adams Construction Co 523 Rutherford Ave NE	Roanoke	VA	24016	**800-237-6060**	540-982-2366
Ajax Paving Industries Inc 1957 Crooks Rd Ste A	Troy	MI	48084	**888-468-5489**	248-244-3300
Allan A Myers Inc 1805 Berks Rd PO Box 1340	Worcester	PA	19490	**800-596-6118**	610-222-8800
Allen Company Inc 525 Burbank St	Broomfield	CO	80020	**800-876-8600**	303-469-1857
Barriere Construction Co LLC 1 Galleria Blvd Ste 1650	Metairie	LA	70001	**866-645-3060**	504-581-7283
Boh Bros Construction Co LLC 730 S Tonti St	New Orleans	LA	70119	**800-284-3377**	504-821-2400
Cianbro Corp 335 Hunnewell Ave	Pittsfield	ME	04967	**866-242-6276**	
Clark Construction Group LLC 7500 Old Georgetown Rd	Bethesda	MD	20814	**800-655-1330**	301-272-8100
Crowder Construction Company Inc PO Box 30007	Charlotte	NC	28230	**800-849-2966**	704-372-3541
Cummins Construction Company Inc 1420 W Chestnut Ave	Enid	OK	73702	**800-375-6001**	580-233-6000
Dean Word Company Ltd 1245 River Rd PO Box 310330	New Braunfels	TX	78131	**800-683-3926**	830-625-2365
Duininck Inc 408 Sixth St PO Box 208 *General	Prinsburg	MN	56281	**800-328-8949***	
Elam Construction Inc 556 Struthers Ave	Grand Junction	CO	81501	**800-675-4598**	970-242-5370
Fred Weber Inc 2320 Creve Coeur Mill Rd	Maryland Heights	MO	63043	**866-739-8855**	314-344-0070
Gallagher Asphalt Corp 18100 S Indiana Ave	Thornton	IL	60476	**800-536-7160**	708-877-7160
Glasgow Inc 104 Willow Grove Ave	Glenside	PA	19038	**877-222-5514**	215-884-8800
Gray & Sons Inc 430 W Padonia Rd	Timonium	MD	21093	**800-254-0752**	410-771-4311
Herzog Contracting Corp 600 S Riverside Rd	Saint Joseph	MO	64507	**800-541-7846**	816-233-9001
Hoover Construction Co Inc PO Box 1007	Virginia	MN	55792	**800-741-0970**	218-741-3280
HRI Inc 1750 W College Ave	State College	PA	16801	**877-474-9999**	814-238-5071
Hunter Contracting Co 701 N Cooper Rd	Gilbert	AZ	85233	**877-992-0521**	480-892-0521
Hutchens Construction Co 1007 Main St	Cassville	MO	65625	**888-728-3482**	417-847-2489
Jack B Parson Cos 2350 South 1900 West	Ogden	UT	84401	**888-672-7766**	801-731-1111
James D Morrissey Inc 9119 Frankford Ave	Philadelphia	PA	19114	**877-536-6857**	215-357-5505
JF Shea Construction Inc 655 Brea Canyon Rd	Walnut	CA	91789	**888-779-7333**	909-594-9500
JF White Contracting Co 10 Burr St	Framingham	MA	01701	**866-539-4400**	508-879-4700
Kokosing Construction Company Inc 17531 Waterford Rd PO Box 226	Fredericktown	OH	43019	**800-800-6315**	740-694-6315
Lehigh Asphalt Paving & Construction Co Inc PO Box 549	Tamaqua	PA	18252	**877-222-5514**	570-668-4303
Manatt's Inc 1775 Old 6 Rd	Brooklyn	IA	52211	**800-532-1121**	641-522-9206
Mathy Construction Co Inc 920 Tenth Ave N	Onalaska	WI	54650	**800-822-5246**	608-783-6411
Matich Corp 1596 Harry Sheppard Blvd	San Bernardino	CA	92408	**800-404-4975**	909-382-7400
Michael Baker Corp 100 Airsite Dr Airsite Business Pk *NYSE: BKR*	Moon Township	PA	15108	**800-553-1153**	412-269-6300
Milestone Contractors LP 3410 S 650 E	Elizabethtown	IN	47232	**800-377-7727**	812-579-5248
Oakgrove Construction Inc 6900 Seneca St	Elma	NY	14059	**866-435-1499**	716-652-2200
Odebrecht Construction Inc 201 Alhambra Cir Ste 1000	Coral Gables	FL	33134	**800-771-0001**	305-341-8800
Palmer Paving Corp 25 Blanchard St	Palmer	MA	01069	**800-244-8354**	413-283-8354
Pike Industries Inc 3 Eastgate Pk Rd	Belmont	NH	03220	**800-283-0803**	603-527-5100
PJ Keating Co 998 Reservoir Rd	Lunenburg	MA	01462	**800-441-4119**	978-582-5200
Ranger Construction Industries Inc 101 Sansbury's Way	West Palm Beach	FL	33411	**800-969-9402**	561-793-9400
Reeves Construction Co Inc 101 Sheraton Ct	Macon	GA	31210	**800-743-0593**	478-474-9092
Reliable Contracting Co Inc 2410 Evergreen Rd Ste 200	Gambrills	MD	21054	**800-492-4357**	410-987-0313
Sargent Corp 378 Bennoch Rd	Stillwater	ME	04489	**800-533-1812**	207-827-4435
Scott Construction Inc 560 Munroe Ave	Lake Delton	WI	53940	**800-843-1556**	608-254-2555
Scruggs Company Inc PO Box 2065	Valdosta	GA	31604	**800-230-7263**	229-242-2388
Staker Parson Cos 2350 South 1900 West	Ogden	UT	84401	**888-672-7766**	801-731-1111
Sukut Construction Inc 4010 W Chandler Ave	Santa Ana	CA	92704	**888-785-8801**	714-540-5351
Sundt Construction Inc 2015 W River Rd Ste 101	Tucson	AZ	85704	**800-467-5544**	520-750-4600
Traylor Bros Inc 835 N Congress Ave	Evansville	IN	47715	**866-895-1491**	812-477-1542
Vecellio & Grogan Inc 2251 Robert C Byrd Dr	Beckley	WV	25802	**800-255-6575**	304-252-6575
Walsh Group Inc 929 W Adams St	Chicago	IL	60607	**800-957-1842**	312-563-5400

190-5 Marine Construction

Name / Address	City	State	ZIP	Toll-Free	Phone
Andrie Inc 561 E Western Ave	Muskegon	MI	49442	**800-722-2421**	231-728-2226
Bellingham Marine Industries Inc 1001 C St	Bellingham	WA	98225	**800-733-5679**	360-676-2800
Dot-Line Transportation PO Box 8739	Fountain Valley	CA	92728	**800-423-3780**	323-780-9010
Frontier-Kemper Constructors Inc 1695 Allen Rd	Evansville	IN	47710	**877-554-8600**	812-426-2741
JR Filanc Construction Company Inc 740 N Andreasen Dr	Escondido	CA	92029	**877-225-5428**	760-941-7130
Norris School District 6940 Calloway Dr	Bakersfield	CA	93312	**800-877-8339**	661-387-7000

190-6 Mining Construction

Name / Address	City	State	ZIP	Toll-Free	Phone
AME Inc 2467 Coltharp Rd PO Box 909	Fort Mill	SC	29716	**800-849-7766**	803-548-7766
Frontier-Kemper Constructors Inc 1695 Allen Rd	Evansville	IN	47710	**877-554-8600**	812-426-2741
Sundt Construction Inc 2015 W River Rd Ste 101	Tucson	AZ	85704	**800-467-5544**	520-750-4600

190-7 Plant Construction

Name / Address	City	State	ZIP	Toll-Free	Phone
Brasfield & Gorrie LLC 3021 Seventh Ave S	Birmingham	AL	35233	**800-239-8017**	205-328-4000
Cajun Constructors Inc 15635 Airline Hwy	Baton Rouge	LA	70817	**877-401-5911**	225-753-5857
Cianbro Corp 335 Hunnewell Ave	Pittsfield	ME	04967	**866-242-6276**	
Clark Construction Group LLC 7500 Old Georgetown Rd	Bethesda	MD	20814	**800-655-1330**	301-272-8100
Day & Zimmermann Group Inc 1818 Market St	Philadelphia	PA	19130	**877-319-0270**	215-299-8000
Gilbane Bldg Co 7 Jackson Walkway	Providence	RI	02903	**800-445-2263**	401-456-5800
Gray Construction 10 Quality St	Lexington	KY	40507	**800-814-8468**	859-281-5000
Haskell Co 111 Riverside Ave	Jacksonville	FL	32202	**800-622-4326**	904-791-4500
Hunter Contracting Co 701 N Cooper Rd	Gilbert	AZ	85233	**877-992-0521**	480-892-0521
JF White Contracting Co 10 Burr St	Framingham	MA	01701	**866-539-4400**	508-879-4700
Koch Specialty Plant Services 12221 E Sam Houston Pkwy N	Houston	TX	77044	**800-765-9177**	713-427-7700
Northeast Remsco Construction Inc 1433 Hwy 34 S Bldg B1	Farmingdale	NJ	07727	**800-879-8204**	732-557-6100
Sargent Corp 378 Bennoch Rd	Stillwater	ME	04489	**800-533-1812**	207-827-4435
Turner Industries Group LLC 8687 United Plaza Blvd	Baton Rouge	LA	70809	**800-288-6503**	225-922-5050
Walsh Group Inc 929 W Adams St	Chicago	IL	60607	**800-957-1842**	312-563-5400

190-8 Railroad Construction

Name / Address	City	State	ZIP	Toll-Free	Phone
WE Yoder Inc 41 S Maple St	Kutztown	PA	19530	**800-889-5149**	610-683-7383

190-9 Refinery (Petroleum or Oil) Construction

Name / Address	City	State	ZIP	Toll-Free	Phone
Austin Industrial Inc 2801 E 13th S PO Box 87888	La Porte	TX	77571	**866-308-2592**	713-641-3400
Turner Industries Group LLC 8687 United Plaza Blvd	Baton Rouge	LA	70809	**800-288-6503**	225-922-5050
Underground Construction Company Inc 5145 Industrial Way	Benicia	CA	94510	**800-227-2314**	707-746-8800

190-10 Water & Sewer Lines, Pipelines, Power Lines Construction

Name / Address	City	State	ZIP	Toll-Free	Phone
B Frank Joy LLC 5355 Kilmer Pl	Hyattsville	MD	20781	**800-992-3569**	301-779-9400
BRB Contractors Inc 3805 NW 25th St	Topeka	KS	66618	**800-722-3145**	785-232-1245
Cajun Constructors Inc 15635 Airline Hwy	Baton Rouge	LA	70817	**877-401-5911**	225-753-5857
Cianbro Corp 335 Hunnewell Ave	Pittsfield	ME	04967	**866-242-6276**	
Elkins Constructors Inc 6104 S Gazebo Pk	Jacksonville	FL	32257	**800-772-1213**	904-353-6500
Frontier-Kemper Constructors Inc 1695 Allen Rd	Evansville	IN	47710	**877-554-8600**	812-426-2741
Henkels & McCoy Inc 985 Jolly Rd	Blue Bell	PA	19422	**888-436-5357**	215-283-7600
Insituform Technologies Inc 17988 Edison Ave *Cust Svc	St. Louis	MO	63005	**800-234-2992***	636-530-8000
JF Shea Construction Inc 655 Brea Canyon Rd	Walnut	CA	91789	**888-779-7333**	909-594-9500
JF White Contracting Co 10 Burr St	Framingham	MA	01701	**866-539-4400**	508-879-4700
JR Filanc Construction Company Inc 740 N Andreasen Dr	Escondido	CA	92029	**877-225-5428**	760-941-7130
Koch Specialty Plant Services 12221 E Sam Houston Pkwy N	Houston	TX	77044	**800-765-9177**	713-427-7700
Landmark Structures LP 1665 Harmon Rd	Fort Worth	TX	76177	**800-888-6816**	817-439-8888
Layne 4520 N State Rd 37 *All	Orleans	IN	47452	**855-529-6301***	812-865-3232
MasTec Inc 800 Douglas Rd 12th Fl *NYSE: MTZ*	Coral Gables	FL	33134	**800-531-5000**	305-599-1800
Mears Group Inc 4500 N Mission Rd	Rosebush	MI	48878	**800-632-7727**	989-433-2929
Michels Corp 817 W Main St	Brownsville	WI	53006	**877-297-8663**	920-583-3132
Miller Pipeline Corp 8850 Crawfordsville Rd	Indianapolis	IN	46234	**800-428-3742**	317-293-0278
Northeast Remsco Construction Inc 1433 Hwy 34 S Bldg B1	Farmingdale	NJ	07727	**800-879-8204**	732-557-6100
Stuart C Irby Co 815 S President St	Jackson	MS	39201	**866-687-4729**	713-476-0788
Underground Construction Company Inc 5145 Industrial Way	Benicia	CA	94510	**800-227-2314**	707-746-8800
Utility Services Inc 400 N Fourth St	Bismarck	ND	58501	**800-638-3278**	701-222-7900
West Valley Construction Company Inc 580 McGlincey Ln	Campbell	CA	95008	**800-588-5510**	

191 CONSTRUCTION - SPECIAL TRADE CONTRACTORS

SEE ALSO Swimming Pools

191-1 Building Equipment Installation or Erection

Name / Address	City	State	ZIP	Toll-Free	Phone
AWC Commercial Window Coverings Inc 825 Williamson Ave	Fullerton	CA	92832	**800-252-2280**	714-879-3880
Baltimore Rigging Company Inc, The 6601 Tributary St	Baltimore	MD	21224	**800-626-2150**	443-696-4001
Bigge Crane & Rigging Company Inc 10700 Bigge St PO Box 1657	San Leandro	CA	94577	**888-337-2444**	510-638-8100
Columbia Elevator Products Company Inc 380 Horace St	Bridgeport	NY	06610	**888-858-1558**	
Elward Construction Co 680 Harlan St	Lakewood	CO	80214	**800-933-5339**	303-239-6303
James Machine Works LLC 1521 Adams St	Monroe	LA	71201	**800-259-6104**	318-322-6104
Schindler Elevator Corp 20 Whippany Rd	Morristown	NJ	07960	**800-225-3123**	973-397-6500
W & H Systems Inc 120 Asia Pl	Carlstadt	NJ	07072	**800-966-6993**	201-933-7840

191-2 Carpentry & Flooring Contractors

Name / Address	City	State	ZIP	Toll-Free	Phone
Archadeck 2924 Emerywood Pkwy Ste 101	Richmond	VA	23294	**800-722-4668**	804-353-6999
Associated Floors 32 Morris Ave	Springfield	NJ	07081	**800-800-4320**	
Carpenter Contractors of America Inc 3900 Ave D NW	Winter Haven	FL	33880	**800-959-8806**	863-294-6449
Cincinnati Floor Company Inc 5162 Broerman Ave	Cincinnati	OH	45217	**800-886-4501**	513-641-4500
E&K Companies 343 Carol Ln	Elmhurst	IL	60126	**800-365-5760**	630-530-9001
Kalman Floor Company Inc 1202 Bergen Pkwy Ste 110	Evergreen	CO	80439	**800-525-7840**	303-674-2290
Overhead Door Company of Sacramento Inc 6756 Franklin Blvd	Sacramento	CA	95823	**800-929-3667**	916-421-3747
Sundt Construction 2620 S 55th St	Tempe	AZ	85282	**800-280-3000**	480-293-3000

191-3 Concrete Contractors

Name / Address	City	State	ZIP	Toll-Free	Phone
Baker Concrete Construction Inc 900 N Garver Rd	Monroe	OH	45050	**800-359-3935**	513-539-4000
Culbertson Enterprises Inc (CEI) 600A Snyder Ave	West Chester	PA	19382	**800-382-2685**	610-436-6400
Dywidag Systems International 320 Marmon Dr	Bolingbrook	IL	60440	**800-457-7633**	630-739-1100
Kalman Floor Company Inc 1202 Bergen Pkwy Ste 110	Evergreen	CO	80439	**800-525-7840**	303-674-2290
Larson Contracting Inc 508 West Main St	Lake Mills	IA	50450	**800-765-1426**	641-592-5800
Musselman & Hall Contractors LLC 4922 E Blue Banks PO Box 300858	Kansas City	MO	64130	**800-257-4255**	816-861-1234
Oldcastle Precast Bldg Systems Div 1401 Trimble Rd	Edgewood	MD	21040	**800-523-9144**	
Proshot Concrete Inc 4158 Musgrove Dr	Florence	AL	35630	**800-633-3141**	256-764-5941
Suncoast Post-Tension LP 509 N Sam Houston Pkwy Ste 400 E	Houston	TX	77060	**800-847-8886**	281-668-1840
Weaver-Bailey Contractors Inc PO Box 60	El Paso	AR	72045	**800-253-3385**	501-796-2301

191-4 Electrical Contractors

Name / Address	City	State	ZIP	Toll-Free	Phone
A. M. Ortega Construction Inc 10125 Ch Rd	Lakeside	CA	92040	**800-909-1988**	619-390-1988

Classified Section

191-10 Plumbing, Heating, Air Conditioning Contractors

Company	Address	City	State	ZIP	Toll-Free	Phone
AC Corp	301 Creek Ridge Rd	Greensboro	NC	27406	**800-422-7378**	336-273-4472
ACCO Engineered Systems	6265 San Fernando Rd	Glendale	CA	91201	**800-998-2226***	818-243-1727
	*Cust Svc					
Air Comfort Corp	2550 Braga Dr	Broadview	IL	60155	**800-466-3779**	708-345-1900
Aire Serv Heating & Air Conditioning Inc	1020 N University Parks Dr Ste 101	Waco	TX	76707	**855-259-2280**	254-523-3600
Alaka'i Mechanical Corp	2655 Waiwai Loop	Honolulu	HI	96819	**800-600-1085**	808-834-1085
Allied Fire Protection LP	PO Box 2842	Pearland	TX	77588	**800-604-2600**	281-485-6803
Allied Mechanical Services Inc	145 N Plains Industrial Rd	Wallingford	CT	06492	**888-237-3017**	269-344-0191
Althoff Industries Inc	8001 S Rt 31	Crystal Lake	IL	60014	**800-225-2443**	815-455-7000
American Residential Services LLC	9010 Maier Rd Ste 105	Laurel	MD	20723	**866-399-2885**	901-271-9700
Armistead Mechanical Inc	168 Hopper Ave	Waldwick	NJ	07463	**800-587-5267**	201-447-6740
Arnold Refrigeration Inc	1122 N Cherry	San Antonio	TX	78202	**800-441-1170**	210-225-5493
B-G Mechanical Service Inc	12 Second Ave	Chicopee	MA	01020	**800-992-7386**	413-888-1500
Baker Group	4224 Hubbell Ave	Des Moines	IA	50317	**855-262-4000**	515-262-4000
Bay Mechanical Inc	2696 Reliance Dr Ste 200	Virginia Beach	VA	23452	**888-229-6324**	757-468-6700
Beutler Air Conditioning Service	855 National Dr Ste 109	Sacramento	CA	95834	**866-559-0108**	
Butters-Fetting Company Inc	1669 S First St	Milwaukee	WI	53204	**800-361-6154**	414-645-1535
C & R Mechanical	12825 Pennridge Dr	Bridgeton	MO	63044	**800-524-3828**	314-739-1800
Climate Design Air ConditioningIn	12530 47th Way N	Clearwater	FL	33762	**888-572-7245**	
Coastal Mechanical Services LLC	394 E Dr	Melbourne	FL	32904	**866-584-9528**	321-725-3061
ColonialWebb Contractors Co	2820 Ackley Ave	Richmond	VA	23228	**877-208-3894**	804-916-1400
Comfort Systems USA Inc	675 Bering Ste 400	Houston	TX	77057	**800-723-8431**	713-830-9600
	NYSE: FIX					
DeBra-Kuempel	3976 Southern Ave	Cincinnati	OH	45227	**800-395-5741**	513-271-6500
Dunbar Mechanical Inc	2806 N Reynolds Rd	Toledo	OH	43615	**800-719-2201**	419-537-1900
EMCOR Group Inc	301 Merritt 7 6th Fl	Norwalk	CT	06851	**866-890-7794**	203-849-7800
	NYSE: EME					
Fisher Container Corp	1111 Busch Pkwy	Buffalo Grove	IL	60089	**800-837-2247**	847-541-0000
Fitzgerald Contractors Inc	7103 St Vincent Ave	Shreveport	LA	71106	**800-259-3264**	318-869-3262
Fox Service Co	PO Box 19047	Austin	TX	78760	**866-668-4749**	512-442-6782
Gold Mechanical Inc	4735 W Division St	Springfield	MO	65802	**877-873-9770**	417-873-9770
Goyette Mechanical Co	3842 Gorey Ave	Flint	MI	48501	**877-469-3883**	810-743-6883
Grunau Company Inc	1100 W Anderson Ct	Oak Creek	WI	53154	**800-365-1920**	414-216-6900
Hardy Corp	350 Industrial Dr	Birmingham	AL	35211	**800-289-4822**	205-252-7191
Harold G Butzer Inc	730 Wicker Ln	Jefferson City	MO	65109	**800-769-1065**	573-636-4115
HE Neumann Inc	100 Middle Creek Rd	Triadelphia	WV	26059	**800-627-5312**	304-232-3040
Herman Goldner Co Inc	7777 Brewster Ave	Philadelphia	PA	19153	**800-355-5997**	215-365-5400
Hooper Corp	2030 Pennsylvania Ave	Madison	WI	53704	**877-630-7554**	608-249-0451
Hubbard & Drake General Mechanical Contractors Inc	PO Box 1867	Decatur	AL	35602	**800-353-9245**	256-353-9244
Hurckman Mechanical Industries Inc	PO Box 10977	Green Bay	WI	54307	**844-499-8771**	920-499-8771
IMCOR-Interstate Mechanical Corp	1841 E Washington St	Phoenix	AZ	85034	**800-628-0211**	602-257-1319
Industrial Contractors Inc	701 Ch Dr	Bismarck	ND	58501	**800-467-3089**	701-258-9908
Industrial Piping Inc	800 Culp Rd	Pineville	NC	28134	**800-951-0988**	704-588-1100
Janazzo Services Corp	140 Norton St Rt 10 PO Box 469	Milldale	CT	06467	**800-297-3931**	860-621-7381
JF Ahern Co	855 Morris St	Fond du Lac	WI	54935	**800-532-0155**	920-921-9020
John W Danforth Co	300 Colvin Woods Pkwy	Tonawanda	NY	14150	**800-888-6119**	716-832-1940
KLM Mechanical Service Inc	PO Box 35121	Louisville	KY	40232	**866-466-4438**	502-955-2062
Lutz Frey Corp	1195 Ivy Dr	Lancaster	PA	17601	**800-280-6794**	717-898-6808
MacDonald-Miller Facility Solutions Inc	7717 Detroit Ave SE	Seattle	WA	98106	**800-962-5979**	206-763-9400
McClure Co	4101 N Sixth St	Harrisburg	PA	17110	**800-382-1319**	717-232-9743
McCrea Equipment Company Inc	4463 Beech Rd	Temple Hills	MD	20748	**800-597-0091**	301-423-4585
McKenney's Inc	1056 Moreland Industrial Blvd SE	Atlanta	GA	30316	**877-440-4204**	404-622-5000
McKinstry Co	5005 Third Ave S	Seattle	WA	98134	**800-669-6223**	206-762-3311
Midwest Mechanical Group	801 Parkview Blvd	Lombard	IL	60148	**800-214-3680**	630-850-2300
Mr Rooter Corp	1010 N University Parks Dr	Waco	TX	76707	**877-766-8305**	800-583-8003
Murphy Co Mechanical Contractors & Engineers	1233 N Price Rd	Saint Louis	MO	63132	**888-838-4038**	314-997-6600
National HVAC Service Ltd	101 Bradford Rd Ste 340	Wexford	PA	15090	**800-281-3608**	724-935-9390
P1 Group Inc	2151 Haskell Ave Bldg 1	Lawrence	KS	66046	**800-376-2911**	785-843-2910
Pace Mechanical Services Inc	301 Merritt Seven	Norwalk	CT	06851	**866-890-7794**	203-849-7800
Performance Contracting Group Inc	16400 College Blvd	Lenexa	KS	66219	**800-255-6886**	913-888-8600
Postler & Jaeckle Corp	615 S Ave	Rochester	NY	14620	**800-724-4252**	585-546-7450
Pritchett Controls Inc	6980 Muirkirk Meadows Dr	Beltsville	MD	20705	**877-743-2363**	301-470-7300
PSF Industries Inc	65 S Horton St	Seattle	WA	98134	**800-426-1204***	206-622-1252
	*General					
RK Mechanical Inc	3800 Xanthia St	Denver	CO	80238	**877-576-9696**	303-355-9696
Roth Bros Inc	PO Box 4209	Youngstown	OH	44515	**800-872-7684**	330-793-5571
Roto-Rooter Inc	255 E Fifth St 2500 Chemed Ctr	Cincinnati	OH	45202	**800-768-6911**	513-762-6690
Shambaugh & Son LP	7614 Opportunity Dr	Fort Wayne	IN	46825	**866-890-7794**	260-487-7777
Southern Air Inc	2655 Lakeside Dr	Lynchburg	VA	24501	**800-743-1214**	434-385-6200
Southern Industrial Constructors Inc	6101 Triangle Dr	Raleigh	NC	27617	**866-890-7794**	919-782-4600
Tatro Plumbing Company Inc	1285 Acraway Ste 300	Garden City	KS	67846	**888-828-7648**	620-277-2167
Telgian Corp	10505 Sorrento Valley Rd Ste 450	San Diego	CA	92121	**877-835-4426**	858-795-1000
Thorpe Heating & Cooling Inc	8402 Us Hwy 98 N	Lakeland	FL	33809	**855-858-2577**	863-858-2577
William E Walter Inc	1917 Howard Ave	Flint	MI	48503	**800-681-3320**	810-232-7459
Worth & Company Inc	6263 Kellers Church Rd	Pipersville	PA	18947	**800-220-5130**	267-362-1100

191-11 Remodeling, Refinishing, Resurfacing Contractors

Company	Address	City	State	ZIP	Toll-Free	Phone
Bathcrest Inc	265E 3900 S	Salt Lake City	UT	84107	**800-826-6790**	801-957-1400
California Closet Co	610A DuBois St	San Rafael	CA	94901	**888-336-9707***	415-256-8500
	*General					
Closet Factory	12800 S Broadway	Los Angeles	CA	90061	**800-838-7995**	310-516-7000
DreamMaker Bath & Kitchen by Worldwide	510 N Valley Mills Dr Ste 304	Waco	TX	76710	**800-583-2133**	
Handyman Connection Inc	11115 Kenwood Rd	Cincinnati	OH	45242	**800-884-2639**	513-771-3003
Kitchen Tune-Up Inc	813 Cir Dr	Aberdeen	SD	57401	**800-333-6385**	605-225-4049
Miracle Method US Corp	4239 N Nevada Ave Ste 115	Colorado Springs	CO	80907	**800-444-8827**	719-594-9091
Perma-Glaze Inc	1638 Research Loop Rd Ste 160	Tucson	AZ	85710	**800-332-7397**	520-722-9718
Re-Bath LLC	16879 N 75th Ave Ste 101	Peoria	AZ	85382	**800-426-4573**	

191-12 Roofing, Siding, Sheet Metal Contractors

Company	Address	City	State	ZIP	Toll-Free	Phone
All-South Subcontractors Inc	2678 Queenstown Rd	Birmingham	AL	35210	**800-873-8110**	205-836-8111
Baker Roofing Co	517 Mercury St	Raleigh	NC	27603	**800-849-4096**	919-828-2975
Beldon Enterprises Inc	PO Box 13380	San Antonio	TX	78213	**800-688-7663**	210-341-3100
Birdair Inc	65 Lawrence Bell Dr Ste 100	Amherst	NY	14221	**800-622-2246**	716-633-9500
Bonland Industries Inc	50 Newark-Pompton Tpke	Wayne	NJ	07470	**800-232-6600**	973-694-3211
Brazos Urethane Inc	1031 Sixth St N	Texas City	TX	77590	**866-527-2967**	409-965-0011
Centimark Corp	12 Grandview Cir	Canonsburg	PA	15317	**800-558-4100**	
Commercial Siding & Maintenance Co, The	8059 Crile Rd	Painesville	OH	44077	**800-229-4276**	440-352-7800
DC Taylor Co	312 29th St NE	Cedar Rapids	IA	52402	**800-876-6346**	319-363-2073
Dee Cramer Inc	4221 E Baldwin Rd	Holly	MI	48442	**888-342-6995**	810-579-5000
Douglass Colony Group Inc	5901 E 58th Ave	Commerce	CO	80022	**877-288-0650**	303-288-2635
Heidler Roofing Services Inc	2120 Alpha Dr	York	PA	17408	**866-792-3549**	717-792-3549
IG Inc	720 S Sara Rd	Mustang	OK	73064	**800-654-8433**	405-376-9393
Jottan Inc	PO Box 166	Florence	NJ	08518	**800-364-4234**	609-447-6200
National International Roofing Corp	11317 Smith Dr	Huntley	IL	60142	**800-221-7663**	847-669-3444
North American Roofing Services Inc	41 Dogwood Rd	Asheville	NC	28806	**800-551-5602**	828-687-7767
Schreiber Corp	29945 Beck Rd	Wixom	MI	48393	**800-558-2706**	248-926-1500
Schust Engineering Inc	701 North St	Auburn	IN	46706	**800-686-9297**	
Standard Roofing Co	516 N McDonough St PO Box 1309	Montgomery	AL	36102	**800-239-5705**	334-265-1262

Company	Address	City	State	ZIP	Toll-Free	Phone
Bierschbach Equipment & Supply Co	PO Box 1444	Sioux Falls	SD	57101	**800-843-3707**	605-332-4466
Century Roof Tile	23135 Saklan Rd	Hayward	CA	94545	**888-233-7548**	510-780-9489
FAYBLOCK Materials Inc	130 Builders Blvd	Fayetteville	NC	28302	**800-326-9198**	910-323-9198
Foundation Technologies Inc	1400 Progress Industrial Blvd	Lawrenceville	GA	30043	**800-773-2368**	678-407-4640
Fullen Dock & Warehouse Inc	382 Klinke Rd	Memphis	TN	38127	**800-467-7104**	901-358-9544
Graniterock Co	350 Technology Dr PO Box 50001	Watsonville	CA	95077	**888-762-5100**	831-768-2000
Henry Products Inc	302 S 23rd Ave	Phoenix	AZ	85009	**800-525-5533**	602-253-3191
In-O-Vate Technologies Inc	810 Saturn St Ste 21	Jupiter	FL	33477	**888-443-7937**	561-743-8696
Jaeckle Wholesale Inc	4101 Owl Creek Dr	Madison	WI	53718	**800-236-7225**	608-838-5400
L Thorn Co Inc	6000 Grant Line Rd	New Albany	IN	47150	**800-662-4594**	812-246-4461
Lynx Brand Fence Products	4330 76 Ave SE	Calgary	AB	T2C2J2	**800-665-5969**	403-273-4821
Patene Building Supplies Ltd	641 Speedvale Ave W	Guelph	ON	N1K1E6	**800-265-8319**	519-822-1890
PRL Glass Systems Inc	251 Mason Way	City Of Industry	CA	91746	**800-433-7044**	626-961-5890
Quick Crete Products	731 Parkridge Ave	Norco	CA	92860	**866-703-3434**	
Vimco Inc	300 Hansen Access Rd *Cust Svc	King Of Prussia	PA	19406	**888-468-4626***	610-768-0500
Zeiser Wilbert Vault Inc	750 Howard St	Elmira	NY	14904	**800-472-4335**	607-733-0568

193-2 Construction Materials (Misc)

Company	Address	City	State	ZIP	Toll-Free	Phone
Alliance Wood Group Engineering LP	330 Barker Cypress Rd	Houston	TX	77094	**866-313-0052**	281-828-6000
American Fence Inc	2502 N 27th Ave	Phoenix	AZ	85009	**888-691-4565**	602-272-2333
Arabel Inc	16301 NW 49th Ave *Sales	Hialeah	FL	33014	**800-759-5959***	305-623-8302
Basic Components Inc	1201 S Second Ave	Mansfield	TX	76063	**800-452-1780**	817-473-7224
Chemung Supply Corp	PO Box 527	Elmira	NY	14903	**800-733-5508**	607-733-5506
CR Laurence Company Inc	2503 E Vernon Ave PO Box 58923	Los Angeles	CA	90058	**800-421-6144**	323-588-1281
DS Brown Co	300 E Cherry St	North Baltimore	OH	45872	**800-848-1730**	419-257-3561
Eastern Wholesale Fence Co Inc	274 Middle Island Rd	Medford	NY	11763	**800-339-3362**	631-698-0900
Empire Bldg Materials Inc	PO Box 220	Bozeman	MT	59771	**800-332-4577**	800-548-8201
Gossen /Corp	2030 W Bender Rd	Milwaukee	WI	53209	**800-558-8984**	414-228-9800
J O Galloup Co	3838 Clay Ave SW	Wyoming	MI	49548	**888-755-3110**	269-965-4005
Kuriyama of America Inc	360 E State Pkwy	Schaumburg	IL	60173	**800-800-0320**	847-755-0360
Penrod Co	2809 S Lynnhaven Rd Ste 350	Virginia Beach	VA	23452	**800-537-3497**	757-498-0186
Robert N Karpp Company Inc	480 E First St	Boston	MA	02127	**800-244-5886**	617-269-5880
Star Sales & Distributing Corp	29 Commerce Way	Woburn	MA	01801	**800-222-8118**	781-933-8830

193-3 Lumber & Building Supplies

Company	Address	City	State	ZIP	Toll-Free	Phone
84 Lumber Co	1019 Rt 519	Eighty Four	PA	15330	**800-664-1984**	724-228-8820
Alamo Lumber Co	10800 Sentinel Dr	San Antonio	TX	78217	**855-828-9792**	210-352-1300
Allied Bldg Products Corp	15 E Union Ave	East Rutherford	NJ	07073	**800-541-2198**	201-507-8400
Alpine Lumber Co	1120 W 122nd Ave Ste 301	Denver	CO	80234	**800-499-1634**	303-451-8001
American International Forest Products LLC (AIFP)	5560 SW 107th Ave	Beaverton	OR	97005	**800-366-1611**	503-641-1611
Arnold Lumber Co	251 Fairgrounds Rd	West Kingston	RI	02892	**800-339-0116**	401-783-2266
Auburn Corp	10490 164th Pl	Orland Park	IL	60467	**800-393-1826**	708-349-7676
Babcock Lumber Company Inc	2220 Palmer St PO Box 8348	Pittsburgh	PA	15218	**800-553-4441**	412-351-3515
Baille Lumber Co	4002 Legion Dr PO Box 6	Hamburg	NY	14075	**800-950-2850**	716-649-2850
Banner Supply Co	7195 NW 30th St	Miami	FL	33122	**888-511-4004**	305-593-2946
Beavertooth Oak Inc	401 S Fir St	Medford	OR	97501	**800-306-1942**	541-779-1942
Big C Lumber Inc	50860 Princess Way PO Box 176	Granger	IN	46530	**888-297-0010**	574-277-4550
Birmingham International Forest Products LLC	300 Riverhills Business Pk	Birmingham	AL	35242	**800-767-2437**	205-972-1500
Britton Lumber Company Inc	7 Ely Rd PO Box 389	Fairlee	VT	05045	**800-343-5300**	802-333-4388
Buckeye Pacific LLC	4386 SW Macadam Ave Ste 200	Portland	OR	97207	**800-767-9191**	503-274-2284
Builders General Supply Co	15 Sycamore Ave	Little Silver	NJ	07739	**800-570-7227**	
Chelsea Lumber Co	1 Old Barn Cir	Chelsea	MI	48118	**800-875-9126**	734-475-9126
Chicago Lumber Company of Omaha, The	1324 Pierce St PO Box 3487	Omaha	NE	68103	**800-642-8210**	402-342-0840
Cleary Millwork Company Inc	235 Dividend Rd	Rocky Hill	CT	06067	**800-486-7600**	860-721-0520
Counter Pro Inc	210 Lincoln St	Manchester	NH	03103	**800-899-2444**	603-647-2444
Coventry Lumber Inc	2030 Nooseneck Hill Rd	Coventry	RI	02816	**800-390-0919**	401-821-2800
Creative Pultrusions Inc	214 Industrial Ln	Alum Bank	PA	15521	**888-274-7855**	814-839-4186
Doka USA Ltd	214 Gates Rd	Little Ferry	NJ	07643	**877-365-2872**	201-329-7839
Door Systems Inc	PO Box 511	Framingham	MA	01704	**800-545-3667**	508-875-3508
Forest City Trading Group LLC	10250 SW Greenburg Rd Ste 300	Portland	OR	97223	**800-767-3284**	503-246-8500
Foxworth-Galbraith Lumber Co	4965 Preston Pk Blvd Ste 400	Plano	TX	75093	**800-688-8082**	972-665-2400
Frank Miller Lumber Company Inc	1690 Frank Miller Rd	Union City	IN	47390	**800-345-2643**	765-964-3196
Frank Paxton Lumber Co	7455 Dawson Rd	Cincinnati	OH	45243	**800-325-9800**	513-984-8200
Guardian Building Products (GBPD)	979 Batesville Rd	Greer	SC	29651	**800-569-4262**	864-297-6101
Hawaii Planing Mill Ltd (HPM)	16-166 Melekahiwa St	Keaau	HI	96749	**877-841-7633**	808-966-5693
Holt & Bugbee Co	1600 Shawsheen St	Tewksbury	MA	01876	**800-325-6010**	978-851-7201
Hutchison Inc	7460 Hwy 85 PO Box 1158	Adams City	CO	80022	**800-525-0121**	303-287-2826
Huttig Bldg Products Inc (HBP)	555 Maryville University Dr Ste 400 *OTC: HBPI*	Saint Louis	MO	63141	**800-325-4466**	314-216-2600
Idaho Pacific Lumber Co (IdaPac)	7255 Franklin Rd	Boise	ID	83709	**800-231-2310**	208-375-8052
Jewett-Cameron Trading Company Ltd	32275 NW Hillcrest PO Box 1010 *NASDAQ: JCTCF*	North Plains	OR	97133	**800-547-5877**	503-647-0110
Kleet Lumber Company Inc	777 Pk Ave	Huntington	NY	11743	**800-696-5533**	631-427-7060
Magnolia Forest Products Inc	13252 I- 55 S PO Box 99	Terry	MS	39170	**800-366-6374**	
Matheus Lumber Company Inc	15800 Woodinville-Redmond Rd NE PO Box 2260	Woodinville	WA	98072	**800-284-7501**	425-489-3000
Mead Clark Lumber Co	Hearn Ave & Dowd Dr PO Box 529	Santa Rosa	CA	95402	**800-585-9663**	707-576-3333
MID-AM Bldg Supply Inc	1615 Omar Bradley Dr PO Box 645	Moberly	MO	65270	**800-892-5850**	660-263-2140
Millard Lumber Inc	12900 I St PO Box 45445	Omaha	NE	68145	**800-228-9260**	402-896-2800
National Industrial Lumber Co	1 Chicago Ave	Elizabeth	PA	15037	**800-289-9352**	
Ohio Valley Supply Co	3512 Spring Grove Ave	Cincinnati	OH	45223	**800-696-5608**	513-681-8300
Omega Products International	1681 California Ave	Corona	CA	92881	**800-600-6634**	951-737-7447
Pacific Source Inc	PO Box 2323	Woodinville	WA	98072	**888-343-1515**	
Palmer-Donavin Manufacturing Co	1200 Steelwood Rd	Columbus	OH	43212	**800-589-4412**	614-486-9657
Parker Lumber Co of Port Arthur Inc	2948 Gulfway Dr	Port Arthur	TX	77642	**855-828-9792**	409-983-2745
Parksite Inc	1563 Hubbard Ave	Batavia	IL	60510	**800-338-3355**	630-761-9490
Pyramid Interiors Distributors Inc	PO Box 181058	Memphis	TN	38181	**800-456-0592**	901-375-4197
Quality Plywood Specialties Inc	4500 110th Ave N	Clearwater	FL	33762	**888-722-1181**	727-572-0500
Raymond Bldg Supply Corp	7751 Bayshore Rd	North Fort Myers	FL	33917	**877-731-7272**	239-731-8300
Reliable Wholesale Lumber Inc	7600 Redondo Cir	Huntington Beach	CA	92648	**877-795-4638**	714-848-8222
Richmond International Forest Products Inc	4050 Innslake Dr Ste 100	Glen Allen	VA	23060	**800-767-0111**	804-747-0111
Riverhead Bldg Supply Corp	1093 Pulaski St	Riverhead	NY	11901	**800-378-3650**	631-727-3650
Riverside Forest Products Inc	2912 Professional Pkwy	Augusta	GA	30907	**888-855-8733**	706-855-5500
Russin Lumber Corp	21 Leonards Dr	Montgomery	NY	12549	**800-724-0010**	845-457-4000
Seaboard International Forest Products LLC	22F Cotton Rd	Nashua	NH	03063	**800-669-6800**	603-881-3700
Service Construction Supply Inc	PO Box 13405	Birmingham	AL	35202	**866-729-4968**	205-252-3158
Solar Industries Inc	PO Box 27337	Tucson	AZ	85726	**800-449-2323**	520-519-8258
Spellman Hardwoods Inc	4645 N 43rd Ave	Phoenix	AZ	85031	**800-624-5401**	602-272-2313
Timber Products Co	305 S Fourth St PO Box 269	Springfield	OR	97477	**800-547-9520**	541-747-4577
Tri-state Forest Products Inc	2105 Sheridan Ave	Springfield	OH	45505	**800-949-6325**	937-323-6325
Verhalen Inc	500 Pilgrim Way	Green Bay	WI	54304	**800-895-0071**	920-431-8900
Viking Forest Products LLC	7615 Smetana Ln	Eden Prairie	MN	55344	**800-733-3801**	952-941-6512
Western Lumber Cy LLC	2240 Tower E Ste 200	Medford	OR	97504	**800-633-5554**	541-779-5121
Wheeler Lumber LLC	9330 James Ave S	Bloomington	MN	55431	**800-328-3986**	952-929-7854
White Cap Industries Inc	1723 S Ritchie St	Santa Ana	CA	92705	**800-944-8322**	714-258-3300
Window Rama Enterprises Inc	71 Heartland Blvd	Edgewood	NY	11717	**800-897-7262**	631-667-8088

Company / Address	City	State	Zip	Toll-Free	Phone
Floyd Browne Group 3875 Embassy Parkway *General	Akron	OH	44333	**800-362-2764***	330-375-0800
FPMI Solutions Inc 1033 N Fairfax St Ste 200	Alexandria	VA	22314	**888-644-3764**	
Gabriel Roeder Smith & Co 1 Towne Sq Ste 800	Southfield	MI	48076	**800-521-0498**	248-799-9000
Geomet Technologies LLC 20251 Century Blvd	Germantown	MD	20874	**877-407-8033**	301-428-9898
Global Search Network Inc 118 S Fremont Ave	Tampa	FL	33606	**800-254-3398**	813-832-8300
Globe Consultants Inc 3112 Porter St Ste D	Soquel	CA	95073	**800-208-0663**	
Goodwill Industries of Akron Ohio Inc, The 570 E Waterloo Rd	Akron	OH	44319	**800-989-8428**	330-724-6995
Hanley Wood Market Intelligence 555 Anton Blvd Ste 950	Costa Mesa	CA	92626	**800-938-8839**	714-540-8500
Hay Group Inc 1650 Arch St Ste 2300	Philadelphia	PA	19107	**800-716-4429**	215-861-2000
InfoMart Inc 1582 Terrell Mill Rd	Marietta	GA	30067	**800-800-3774**	770-984-2727
Insight 444 Scott Dr	Bloomingdale	IL	60108	**800-467-4448**	
Insight Global Inc (IGI) 4170 Ashford Dunwoody Rd Ste 250	Atlanta	GA	30319	**888-336-7463**	404-257-7900
ITR Group Inc 2520 Lexington Ave S Ste 500	Saint Paul	MN	55120	**866-290-3423**	
Lee Hecht Harrison LLC 50 Tice Blvd	Woodcliff Lake	NJ	07677	**800-611-4544**	
LifeCourse Associates Inc 9080 Eaton Park Rd	Great Falls	VA	22066	**866-537-4999**	
Medicus Healthcare Solutions LLC 7 Industrial Way Unit 5	Salem	NH	03079	**855-301-0563**	
Mercer LLC 400 W Market St	Louisville	KY	40202	**800-333-3070**	502-561-4500
Michael C. Fina Corporate Sales 3301 Hunters Point Ave	Long Island	NY	11101	**800-999-3462**	
Modern Management Inc 253 Commerce Dr Ste 105	Grayslake	IL	60030	**800-323-1331**	847-945-7400
National Ctr for Retirement Benefits Inc 666 Dundee Rd Ste 1200	Northbrook	IL	60062	**800-666-1000**	
Principia Partners 604 Gordon Dr	Exton	PA	19341	**800-378-8330**	
Quantus Software 32-62 Scurfield Blvd	Winnipeg	MB	R3Y1M5	**866-478-1308**	
Ricklin-Echikson Assoc 374 Millburn Ave	Millburn	NJ	07041	**800-544-2317**	973-376-2020
Right Management Consultants Inc 1600 John F Kennedy Blvd Ste 610	Philadelphia	PA	19103	**800-237-4448**	215-972-7277
Riviera Advisors Inc P.O. Box 41446	Long Beach	CA	90853	**800-635-9063**	
Roux Assoc Inc 209 Shafter St	Islandia	NY	11749	**800-322-7689**	631-232-2600
Runzheimer International Runzheimer Pk	Rochester	WI	53167	**800-558-1702**	262-971-2200
Searchwide Inc 320 Myrtle St W	Stillwater	MN	55082	**888-386-6390**	651-275-1370
Stanley Hunt DuPree & Rhine Inc (SHDR) 7701 Airport Ctr Dr	Greensboro	NC	27409	**888-999-4701**	800-768-4873
Superior Environmental Corp 1128 Franklin Ct	Marne	MI	49435	**877-667-4142**	616-667-4000
Tct Computing Group Inc Po Box 402	Bel Air	MD	21014	**866-828-6372**	410-893-5800
Thornmark Asset Management Inc 119 Spadina Ave Ste 701	Toronto	ON	M5V2L1	**877-204-6201**	416-204-6200
Total Resource Management Inc 510 King St Ste 200	Alexandria	VA	22314	**877-548-5100**	703-548-4285
United Way of Central Md Inc, The 100 S Charles St PO Box 1576	Baltimore	MD	21203	**800-429-0618**	410-547-8000
ZE PowerGroup Inc 130 - 5920 No Two Rd	Richmond	BC	V7C4R9	**866-944-1469**	604-244-1469

196 CONSULTING SERVICES - MANAGEMENT

SEE ALSO Management Services ; Association Management Companies

Company / Address	City	State	Zip	Toll-Free	Phone
1secureaudit LLC 1600 Tysons Blvd Fl 8	Mc Lean	VA	22102	**800-321-0706**	424-220-8940
360 Solutions LLC 2114 Austin Ave	Waco	TX	76701	**800-374-2879**	254-755-7000
A C e International Company Inc 85 Independence Dr	Taunton	MA	02780	**800-223-4685**	508-884-9600
Abba Technologies Inc 1501 San Pedro Dr NE	Albuquerque	NM	87110	**888-222-2832**	505-889-3337
Achievement Incentives & Meetings 64 River Rd	East Hanover	NJ	07936	**800-454-1424**	973-386-9500
Advanced Electronics 2601 Manhattan Beach Blvd	Redondo Beach	CA	90278	**800-750-7234**	310-725-0410
Advanced Energy Corp 909 Capability Dr Ste 2100	Raleigh	NC	27606	**800-869-8001**	919-857-9000
Advancement LLC 32200 Solon Rd	Solon	OH	44139	**866-364-3370**	440-248-8550
Advantage Performance Group Inc 700 Larkspur Landing Cir	Larkspur	CA	94939	**800-494-6646**	415-925-6832
AFC Industries Inc 13-16 133rd Pl	College Point	NY	11356	**800-663-3412**	718-747-0237
Affiliated Power Purchasers International LLC 224 Phillip Morris Dr Ste 402	Salisbury	MD	21804	**800-520-6685**	
Affinitas Corp 1015 N 98th St Ste 100	Omaha	NE	68114	**800-369-6495**	402-505-5000
Affinity Wealth Management Inc 1702 Lovering Ave	Wilmington	DE	19806	**800-825-8399**	302-652-6767
Agcall Inc 251 Midpark Blvd SE	Calgary	AB	T2X1S3	**877-273-4333**	403-256-1229
Ageatia Technology Consultancy Services Inc 850 E Higgins Rd Ste 125	Schaumburg	IL	60173	**855-243-4842**	847-517-8415
Airbus North America Holdings 198 Van Buren St Ste 300	Herndon	VA	20170	**888-340-2375**	703-834-3400
ALCO Sales & Service Co 6851 High Grove Blvd	Burr Ridge	IL	60527	**800-323-4282**	630-655-1900
Alego Health 24651 Center Ridge Rd., Ste 400	Westlake	OH	44145	**855-918-4570**	440-918-4570
Allant Group Inc, The 2056 Westings Ave Ste 500	Naperville	IL	60563	**800-367-7311**	
Allsup Inc 300 Allsup Pl	Belleville	IL	62223	**800-854-1418**	
Alpha & Omega Financial Management Consultants Inc 8580 La Mesa Blvd Ste 100	La Mesa	CA	91942	**800-755-5060**	
Alpine Innovations 275 North 950 East	Lehi	UT	84043	**866-489-6788**	801-766-4994
Altair Customer Intelligence 341 Cool Springs Blvd Ste 450	Franklin	TN	37067	**800-241-6631**	615-468-6800
Altair Engineering Inc 1820 E Big Beaver Rd	Troy	MI	48083	**888-222-7822**	248-614-2400
Altman Weil Inc PO Box 625	Newtown Square	PA	19073	**866-886-3600**	610-359-9900
Altoros Systems 830 Stewart Dr Ste 119	Sunnyvale	CA	94085	**855-258-6767**	650-395-7002
Ami Adini & Assoc Inc 4609 Russell Ave	Los Angeles	CA	90027	**888-400-4260**	323-913-4073
Amino Transport Inc 223 NE Loop 820 Ste 101	Hurst	TX	76053	**800-304-3360**	
Anchor Benefit Consulting Inc 2400 Maitland Ctr Pkwy Ste 111	Maitland	FL	32751	**800-845-7629**	407-667-8766
Andrews Logistics Inc 2445 E Southlake Blvd	Southlake	TX	76092	**866-536-1234**	817-527-2770
Arlington Capital Management Inc 21 S Evergreen Ave Ste 210	Arlington Heights	IL	60005	**855-471-5796**	847-670-4030
Artifex Technology Consulting Inc 614 George Washington Hwy	Lincoln	RI	02865	**888-278-4339**	401-723-6644
Atlas Brown Investment Advisors Inc 333 E Main St - 400	Louisville	KY	40202	**866-871-0334**	502-271-2900
Audio Advisor 3427 Kraft Ave SE	Grand Rapids	MI	49512	**800-942-0220**	616-254-8870
Austin Ribbon & Computer Supplies Inc (ARC) 9211 Waterford Centre Blvd Ste 202	Austin	TX	78758	**800-783-7459**	512-452-0651
Award Solutions Inc 2100 Lakeside Blvd	Richardson	TX	75082	**877-472-9273**	972-664-0727
Axiom Resource Management Inc 5203 Leesburg Pk Ste 300	Falls Church	VA	22041	**800-566-9305**	703-208-3000
Beacon Assoc Inc 900-A S Main St Ste 102	Bel Air	MD	21014	**877-846-5046**	410-638-7279
Beacon Financial Partners 25800 Science Park Dr Ste 100	Beachwood	OH	44122	**866-568-3951**	216-910-1850
Becker''s ASC Review 77 Wacker	Chicago	IL	60611	**800-417-2035**	312-750-6016
Behavioral Science Technology Inc 417 Bryant Cir	Ojai	CA	93023	**800-548-5781**	805-646-0166
Benchmark Technologies International Inc 411 Hackensack Ave Fl 8	Hackensack	NJ	07601	**800-265-8254**	201-996-0077
Benemax Inc 7 W Mill St	Medfield	MA	02052	**800-528-1530**	
Berkeley Communications Corp 1321 67th St	Emeryville	CA	94608	**877-237-5266**	510-644-1599
BIA Financial Network Inc 15120 Enterprise Ct	Chantilly	VA	20151	**800-331-5086**	703-818-2425
Blaine Tech Services Inc 1680 Rogers Ave	San Jose	CA	95112	**800-545-7558**	408-573-0555
Blanton & Assoc Inc 5 Lakeway Centre Ct Ste 200	Austin	TX	78734	**888-863-5881**	512-264-1095
Bluepoint Leadership Development Ltd 25 Whitney Dr	Milford	OH	45150	**888-221-8685**	513-683-4702
Boa Technology Inc 1760 Platte St	Denver	CO	80202	**844-203-1297**	303-455-5126
Bonanza Trade & Supply 6853 Lankershim Blvd	North Hollywood	CA	91605	**888-965-6577**	818-765-6577
Boomer Consulting 610 Humboldt St	Manhattan	KS	66502	**800-739-9998**	785-537-2358
Boomtown Internet Group Inc 111 Rosemary Ln	Glenmoore	PA	19343	**888-454-3330**	
Booz Allen Hamilton Inc 8283 Greensboro Dr	McLean	VA	22102	**866-390-3908**	703-902-5000
Brakke Consulting Inc 2735 Villa Creek Ste 140	Dallas	TX	75234	**877-399-6354**	972-243-4033
Breakthrough Management Group Inc 1200 17th St Ste 180	Denver	CO	80202	**800-467-4462**	303-827-0010
Brownlie & Braden LLC 2820 Ross Tower 500 N Akard	Dallas	TX	75201	**888-339-4650**	214-219-4650
BTS USA Inc 300 Stamford Pl Ste 425	Stamford	CT	06902	**800-445-7089**	203-316-2740
Bucher & Christian Consulting Inc 10 W Market St Ste 1300	Indianapolis	IN	46204	**866-363-1132**	317-423-8980
Building Performance Institute Inc 107 Hermes Rd Ste 210	Malta	NY	12020	**877-274-1274**	518-899-2727
Burchfield Group Inc, The 1295 Northland Dr Ste 350	St Paul	MN	55120	**800-778-1359**	651-389-5640
Business Resource Group (BRG) 10440 N Central Expy Ste 1150	Dallas	TX	75231	**888-391-9166**	214-777-5100
C Myers Corp 8222 S 48th St Ste 275	Phoenix	AZ	85044	**800-238-7475**	602-840-0606
Callisto Integration 635 Fourth Line Ste 16	Oakville	ON	L6L5B3	**800-387-0467**	905-339-0059
Calnet Inc 12359 Sunrise Vly Dr Ste 270 *General	Reston	VA	20191	**877-322-5638***	703-547-6800
Capital Advisors Ltd LLC 20600 Chagrin Blvd	Shaker Heights	OH	44122	**888-295-7908**	216-295-7900
Capital Investment Advisors Inc 200 Sandy Springs Pl Ne Ste 300	Atlanta	GA	30328	**888-531-0018**	404-531-0018
Capitol Archives & Record Storage Inc 133 Laurel St	Hartford	CT	06106	**800-381-2277**	860-951-8981
Carepro Health Services 1014 Fifth Ave SE	Cedar Rapids	IA	52403	**800-575-8810**	
Carter Express Inc 4020 W 73rd St	Anderson	IN	46011	**800-738-7705**	
CartwrightDownes Inc 950 Lee St Ste 110	Des Plaines	IL	60016	**800-323-2049**	847-685-2700

Company	Address	City	State	Zip	Toll-Free	Phone
Oakwood Capital Management LLC	12121 Wilshire Blvd Ste 1250	Los Angeles	CA	90025	**800-586-0600**	310-772-2600
Organizational Dynamics Inc	790 Boston Rd Ste 201	Billerica	MA	01821	**800-634-4636**	978-671-5454
Orion Mobility LLC	4 Mountainview Terrace Ste 101	Danbury	CT	06810	**800-476-7787**	203-762-0365
Pacrim Hospitality Services Inc	30 Damascus Rd	Bedford	NS	B4A0C1	**877-680-7666**	902-404-7474
Palladium Group Inc	55 Old Bedford Rd Ste 100	Lincoln	MA	01773	**800-773-2399**	781-259-3737
Parsec Financial Management Inc	6 Wall St	Asheville	NC	28801	**888-877-1012**	828-255-0271
PathGroup Inc	5301 Virginia Way	Brentwood	TN	37027	**877-456-6706**	615-221-4500
Patten & Patten Inc	520 Lookout St	Chattanooga	TN	37403	**800-757-3480**	423-756-3480
Penske Vehicle Services Inc	1225 E Maple Rd	Troy	MI	48083	**877-210-5290**	248-729-5400
Philip Crosby Assoc	306 Dartmouth St	Boston	MA	02116	**877-276-7295**	
Pindler & Pindler Inc	11910 Poindexter Ave	Moorpark	CA	93021	**800-669-6002**	805-531-9090
Pinnacle Management Systems Inc	8500 North Stemmons Freeway Ste 6010	Dallas	TX	75247	**888-975-1119**	703-382-9161
Pinnacle Performance Improvement Worldwide (PPIW)	101 Main St	Pepperell	MA	01463	**800-368-3408**	978-925-9797
Pragmatek Consulting Group	8500 Normandale Lake Blvd Ste 1060	Bloomington	MN	55437	**800-833-3164**	612-333-3164
Presidio Group Inc, The	5295 South 300 West Ste 550	Salt Lake City	UT	84107	**800-924-1404**	801-924-1400
Press Ganey Associates Inc	404 Columbia Pl	South Bend	IN	46601	**800-232-8032**	
Pritchett LLC	8150 N Central Expy Ste 1350	Dallas	TX	75206	**800-992-5922**	214-239-9600
Professional Bank Services Inc	6200 Dutchmans Ln Ste 305	Louisville	KY	40205	**800-523-4778**	502-451-6633
Professional Research Consultants Inc	11326 P St	Omaha	NE	68137	**800-428-7455**	402-592-5656
Program Planning Professionals	1340 Eisenhower Pl	Ann Arbor	MI	48108	**877-728-2331**	734-741-7770
Progressive Mktg Products Inc	3130 E Miraloma Ave	Anaheim	CA	92806	**800-368-9700**	714-632-7100
Protected Investors of America Inc	235 Montgomery St Ste 1050	San Francisco	CA	94104	**800-786-2559**	
PsyMax Solutions LLC	25550 Chagrin Blvd Ste 100	Cleveland	OH	44122	**866-774-2273**	216-896-9991
Public Consulting Group Inc	148 State St	Boston	MA	02109	**800-210-6113**	
Quadel Consulting	1200 G St NW Ste 700	Washington	DC	20005	**866-640-1019**	202-789-2500
R W Rog & Company Inc	630 Johnson Ave Ste 103	Bohemia	NY	11716	**877-218-0085**	631-218-0077
Radio Communications Co	8035 Chapel Hill Rd	Cary	NC	27513	**800-508-7580**	919-467-2421
Rath & Strong Inc	1666 Massachusetts Ave PO Box 170	Lexington	MA	02420	**800-622-2025**	781-861-1700
Revere Group, The	325 N LaSalle Ste 325	Chicago	IL	60654	**800-745-3263**	213-228-2500
Robert E Nolan Company Inc	92 Hopmeadow St	Weatogue	CT	06089	**800-653-1941**	860-658-1941
Robson Forensic Inc	354 N Prince St	Lancaster	PA	17603	**800-813-6736**	717-293-9050
Rose Displays Ltd	35 Congress St	Salem	MA	01970	**800-631-9707**	978-219-8100
Sapient Corp	131 Dartmouth St 3rd Fl *NASDAQ: SAPE*	Boston	MA	02116	**866-796-6860**	617-621-0200
Scott Madden & Assoc Inc	2626 Glenwood Ave Ste 480	Raleigh	NC	27608	**888-473-6748**	919-781-4191
Secova Inc	5000 Birch St W Tower Ste 1400	Newport Beach	CA	92660	**800-257-0011**	714-384-0530
Self Opportunity Inc	808 Office Park Cir	Lewisville	TX	75057	**800-594-7036**	214-222-1500
Selling Source LLC	325 E Warm Springs Rd Ste 200	Las Vegas	NV	89119	**800-251-6147**	702-407-0707
Sharkey Howes & Javer Inc	720 S Colorado Blvd Ste 600 S Twr	Denver	CO	80246	**800-557-9380**	303-639-5100
Signature Inc	5115 Parkcenter Ave	Dublin	OH	43017	**800-398-0518**	614-766-5101
Simply Healthcare Plans Inc	1701 Ponce De Leon Blvd Ste 300	Coral Gables	FL	33134	**877-577-9042**	305-408-5890
Spectrum Financial System Inc	163 McKenzie Rd	Mooresville	NC	28115	**800-525-0555**	704-663-4466
Ssci	3065 Kent Ave	West Lafayette	IN	47906	**800-375-2179**	765-463-0112
Stewart Environmental Consultants LLC	3801 Automation Way Ste 200	Fort Collins	CO	80525	**800-373-1348**	970-226-5500
Tbm Consulting Group Inc	4400 Ben Franklin Blvd	Durham	NC	27704	**800-438-5535**	919-471-5535
Tech Usa Inc	8334 Veterans Hwy	Millersville	MD	21108	**888-584-8181**	410-729-4328
Tele-Measurements Inc	145 Main Ave	Clifton	NJ	07014	**800-223-0052**	973-473-8822
Thomson ISI ResearchSoft	2141 Palomar Airport Rd Ste 350	Carlsbad	CA	92009	**800-722-1227**	760-438-5526
Thyssen Krupp Hearn	59 I- Dr	Wentzville	MO	63385	**877-854-7178**	636-332-1772
Tom McCall & Assoc Inc	20180 Governors Hwy Ste 100	Olympia Fields	IL	60461	**800-715-5474**	708-747-5707
Tompkins International	6870 Perry Creek Rd	Raleigh	NC	27616	**800-789-1257**	919-876-3667
Travelclick	7 Times Sq 38th Fl	New York	NY	10036	**866-674-4549**	212-817-4800
Urban Science	400 Renaissance Ctr Ste 2900	Detroit	MI	48243	**800-321-6900**	313-259-9900
Vawter Financial Ltd	1161 Bethel Rd Ste 304	Columbus	OH	43220	**800-955-1575**	614-451-1002
Verity International Ltd	200 King St W Ste 1301	Toronto	ON	M5H3T4	**877-623-2396**	416-862-8422
Watermark Learning Inc	7300 Metro Blvd Ste 207	Minneapolis	MN	55439	**800-646-9362**	952-921-0900
Weeden & Company LP	145 Mason St	Greenwich	CT	06830	**800-843-9333**	203-861-7670
Welocalize Inc	241 E Fourth St Ste 207	Frederick	MD	21701	**800-370-9515**	301-668-0330
West Monroe Partners LLC	222 W Adams St	Chicago	IL	60606	**800-828-6708**	312-602-4000
Westcare Management Inc	3155 River Rd S Ste 100	Salem	OR	97302	**800-541-3732**	
WorkCare.com	300 S Harbor Blvd Ste 600	Anaheim	CA	92805	**800-455-6155**	

197 CONSULTING SERVICES - MARKETING

Company	Address	City	State	Zip	Toll-Free	Phone
220 Marketing	3405 Kenyon St Ste 501	San Diego	CA	92110	**877-220-6584**	
5th Business	5100 Orbitor Dr Ste 100	Mississauga	ON	L4W4Z4	**866-875-2220**	905-275-2220
6s Marketing	1120 Hamilton St	Vancouver	BC	V6B2S2	**888-642-6765**	604-642-6765
7Summits LLC	1110 Old World Third St Ste 500	Milwaukee	WI	53203	**866-705-6372**	
Adfirmative LLC	11416 Hollister Dr Ste	Austin	TX	78739	**866-966-9968**	
Advisors Excel LLC	1300 SW Arrowhead Rd Ste 200	Topeka	KS	66604	**866-363-9595**	
AIS RealTime	4440 Bowen Blvd SE	Grand Rapids	MI	49508	**877-314-1100**	
Apex Asset Management LLC	2501 Oregon Pike Ste 201	Lancaster	PA	17601	**888-592-2149**	717-519-1780
Bellomy Research Inc	175 Sunnynoll Ct	Winston-Salem	NC	27106	**800-443-7344**	
Beverage Marketing Corp	850 Third Ave 18th Fl	New York	NY	10022	**800-275-4630**	212-688-7640
Boomers & Beyond Inc	1998 Ruffin Mill Rd	Colonial Heights	VA	23834	**800-958-8324**	804-524-9888
Boost Rewards	811 E Fourth St Ste B	Dayton	OH	45402	**800-324-9756**	
Brand Protection Agency LLC	2700 Fairmount St	Dallas	TX	75201	**866-339-5657**	
Cadmium Cd LLC	19 Newport Dr Ste 101	Forest Hill	MD	21050	**877-426-6323**	410-638-9239
Campus Special LLC, The	3575 Koger Blvd Ste 300	Duluth	GA	30096	**800-365-8520**	
Cargo Management Systems Llc	827 E Main St	Richmond	KY	40475	**855-484-9235**	
Cdr Assessment Group Inc	1644 S Denver Ave	Tulsa	OK	74119	**888-406-0100**	918-488-0722
Cheshire Marketing Inc	3209 Guess Rd Ste 108	Durham	NC	27705	**800-495-4633**	919-479-2008
Classical Marketing LLC	150 N Martingale Rd Ste 800	Schaumburg	IL	60173	**800-613-3489**	847-969-1696
ComNet Marketing Group Inc	1214 Stowe Ave	Medford	OR	97501	**877-581-2565**	
ComStar Networks LLC	1820 NE Jensen Beach Blvd Ste 564	Jensen Beach	FL	34957	**800-516-1595**	
Creor Group LLC	Po Box 110398	Campbell	CA	95011	**877-774-4312**	408-248-4822
Crossmark Inc	5100 Legacy Dr	Plano	TX	75024	**877-699-6275**	469-814-1000
Crucial Interactive Inc	21 Camden St 5th Fl	Toronto	ON	M5V1V2	**877-244-6562**	416-645-0135
Dane Media LLC	385 Sylvan Ave Ste 24	Englewood Cliffs	NJ	07632	**888-233-2863**	
Deniro Marketing LLC	6777 Embarcadero Dr Ste 3	Stockton	CA	95219	**877-752-1458**	209-477-7676
Driveline Holdings Inc	700 Freeport Pkwy Ste 100	Coppell	TX	75019	**888-123-4567**	
Eclipse Marketing Services Inc	240 Cedar Knolls Rd Ste 100	Cedar Knolls	NJ	07927	**800-837-4648**	
eGumBall Inc	8687 Research Dr Ste 200	Irvine	CA	92618	**800-890-8940**	
Environics Analytics Group Ltd	33 Bloor St E Ste 400	Toronto	ON	M4W3H1	**888-339-3304**	416-969-2733
Eze Castle Integration Inc	260 Franklin St 12th Fl	Boston	MA	02110	**800-752-1382**	617-217-3000
FarmLink Marketing Solutions Inc	Suite 110-93 Lombard Ave	Winnipeg	MB	R3B3B1	**877-376-5465**	
Frantz Group Inc, The	1245 Cheyenne Ave	Grafton	WI	53024	**800-707-0064**	262-204-6000
FuelFX LLC	5205 Spruce St	Bellaire	TX	77401	**877-255-2543**	
G3 Communications	411 State Rt 17 S Ste 410	Hasbrouck Heights	NJ	07604	**888-603-3626**	
GoalLine Solutions	3115 Harvester Rd Ste 200	Burlington	ON	L7N3H8	**866-788-4625**	
Gold Stars Speakers Bureau	7478 N La Cholla Blvd	Tucson	AZ	85741	**800-844-4384**	520-742-4384
Great Falls Marketing LLC	121 Mill St	Auburn	ME	04210	**800-221-8895**	
Hansa GCR LLC	308 SW First Ave	Portland	OR	97204	**800-755-7683**	503-241-8036
HatchBeauty Agency LLC	1715 18th St	Santa Monica	CA	90404	**877-428-2424**	
Hcpro Inc	75 Sylvan St Ste A-10	Danvers	MA	01923	**800-650-6787**	
Hollis Marketing	2130 Brenner St	Saginaw	MI	48602	**866-797-3301**	989-797-3300
Huka Productions LLC	924 Valmont St Ste 103	New Orleans	LA	70115	**888-512-7469**	
Hunter Business Group LLC	4650 N Port Washington Rd	Milwaukee	WI	53212	**800-423-4010**	
ICS Marketing Services Inc	4225 Legacy Pkwy	Lansing	MI	48911	**888-394-1890**	517-394-1890

Company	Address	City	State	ZIP	Toll-Free	Phone
Core Vision IT Solutions	1266 NW Hwy	Palatine	IL	60067	**855-788-5835**	
Corporate It Solutions Inc	661 Pleasant St	Norwood	MA	02062	**888-521-2487**	
Cost Control Associates Inc	310 Bay Rd	Queensbury	NY	12804	**800-836-3787**	518-798-4437
CRM Dynamics Inc	5800 Ambler Dr, Unit 106	Mississauga	ON	M4N2A5	**866-740-2424**	
Crystal Communications Ltd	1525 Lakeville Dr Ste 230	Kingwood	TX	77339	**888-949-6603**	281-361-5199
Cynergy Solutions LLC	543 Country Club Dr Ste 538	Simi Valley	CA	93065	**877-296-3749**	805-416-1610
Data Path	318 McHenry Ave	Modesto	CA	95354	**888-693-2827**	209-521-0055
Datashield LLC	1440 Show Berry St	Park City	UT	84098	**855-328-2744**	
DCR Workforce Inc	7815 NW Beacon Sq Blvd Ste 224	Boca Raton	FL	33487	**888-327-4867**	
DelaGet LLC	6608 Flying Cloud Dr	Eden Prairie	MN	55344	**866-264-5050**	
Dimension Consulting Inc	2620 Second Ave Ste 9D	San Diego	CA	92103	**855-222-6444**	703-636-0933
Directec Corp	1650 Lyndon Farm Ct Ste 202	Louisville	KY	40223	**800-588-7800**	502-357-5000
Donriver Inc	2633 McKinney Ave Ste 130-101	Dallas	TX	75204	**866-733-1684**	
Due North Consulting Inc	105 Owens Pkwy Ste C	Birmingham	AL	35244	**800-899-2676**	205-989-9394
Dynamics Edge Inc	2635 N First St Ste #148	San Jose	CA	95134	**800-453-5961**	
Eastex Environmental Lab Inc	1119 S University Dr PO Box 631375	Nacogdoches	TX	75961	**800-525-0508**	936-569-8879
ECS & R	3237 Us Hwy 19	Cochranton	PA	16314	**866-815-0016**	814-425-7773
Edwards Industries LLC	6085 Marshalee Dr Ste 140	Elkridge	MD	21075	**800-556-2506**	443-561-0180
ELI Inc	2675 Paces Ferry Rd Se Ste 470	Atlanta	GA	30339	**800-497-7654**	770-319-7999
Elk Environmental Services	1420 Clarion St	Reading	PA	19601	**800-851-7156**	610-372-4760
Ellis Management Services Inc	4324 N Beltine Rd	Irving	TX	75038	**888-988-3767**	972-256-3767
Ericsson	1 Telcordia Dr	Piscataway	NJ	08854	**800-521-2673**	732-699-2000
Evogi Group Inc, The	20645 N Pima Rd Bldg N Ste 130	Scottsdale	AZ	85255	**888-277-5573**	
Fortin Consulting Inc	215 Hamel Rd	Hamel	MN	55340	**844-273-3117**	763-478-3606
Frank Lynn & Associates Inc	500 Park Blvd Ste 1300	Itasca	IL	60143	**800-245-5966**	312-263-7888
Greenbusch Group Inc	1900 W Nickerson St Ste 201	Seattle	WA	98119	**855-476-2874**	206-378-0569
Greenview Data Inc	8178 Jackson Rd	Ann Arbor	MI	48103	**800-458-3348**	734-426-7500
Greenwood King Properties 2 Inc	1616 S Voss Rd Ste 900	Houston	TX	77057	**800-403-0888**	713-784-0888
HCI Group, The	6440 Southpoint Pkwy Ste 300	Jacksonville	FL	32216	**866-793-2484**	904-337-6300
Heritage Global Solutions Inc	230 N Maryland Ave	Glendale	CA	91206	**800-915-4474**	818-547-4474
HR Focal Point LLC	5151 Headquarters Dr Ste 135	Plano	TX	75024	**855-464-4737**	
Hrd Discount Book Society	2002 Renaissance Blvd	King Of Prussia	PA	19406	**800-633-4533**	610-279-2002
I.T. Blueprint Solutions Consulting Inc	170-422 Richards St	Vancouver	BC	V6B2Z4	**866-261-8981**	
IDT|RPM Consulting Services	1009 W Hawthorn Dr	Itasca	IL	60143	**877-722-6438**	630-875-1100
IeSmart Systems LLC	15200 E Hardy Rd	Houston	TX	77032	**866-437-6278**	281-447-6278
Ifocus Consulting Inc	100 39th St Ste 201	Astoria	OR	97103	**888-308-6192**	503-338-7443
iMethods LLC	10748 Deerwood Park Blvd Ste 150	Jacksonville	FL	32256	**888-306-2261**	
iMomentous	20 Gibraltar Rd Ste 109	Horsham	PA	19044	**888-985-7755**	
IMPRES Technology Solutions Inc	10330 Pioneer Blvd Ste 280	Santa Fe Springs	CA	90670	**800-652-9686**	562-298-4030
Improve Group Inc, The	1385 Mendota Heights Rd Ste 200b	Mendota Heights	MN	55120	**877-467-7847**	
Infogrow Corp	2140 Front St	Cuyahoga Falls	OH	44221	**800-897-9807**	
Intact Info Solutions LLC	1370 Vly Vista Dr Ste 265	Diamond Bar	CA	91765	**888-986-7736**	909-396-9200
Integra Information Technologies Inc	101 South 27th St	Boise	ID	83702	**800-444-8688**	208-336-2720
integraSoft Inc	2547 Tech Dr	Bettendorf	IA	52722	**877-630-7960**	563-332-5030
Iomosaic Corp	93 Stiles Rd	Salem	NH	03079	**844-466-6724**	603-893-7009
IPC Technologies Inc	7200 Glen Forest Dr Ste 100	Richmond	VA	23226	**877-947-2835**	804-622-7288
J K Consulting	990 E Ninth St	Lockport	IL	60441	**866-634-9633**	815-588-4530
Janalent Corp	7582 Las Vegas Blvd. S. Ste. 580 Ste	Las Vegas	NV	89123	**888-290-4870**	
Jdk Consulting	4924 Balboa Blvd Ste 487	Encino	CA	91316	**855-535-7877**	818-705-8050
Jones Environmental Inc	708 Milam St Ste 100	Shreveport	LA	71101	**877-345-4534**	318-226-8444
Kaseya Corp	400 Totten Pond Rd Ste 200	Waltham	MA	02451	**877-926-0001**	
KDC Technologies	27201 Tourney Rd Ste 201	Valencia	CA	91355	**877-532-1112**	
Laminar Consulting Services	424 S Olive St	Orange	CA	92866	**888-531-9995**	
Lawrence Behr Assoc Inc	3400 Tupper Dr	Greenville	NC	27834	**800-522-4464**	252-757-0279
LED Supply Co	747 Sheridan Blvd Unit 8E	Lakewood	CO	80214	**877-595-4769**	
Lucidview LLC	80 Rolling Links Blvd	Oak Ridge	TN	37830	**888-582-4384**	865-220-8440
Luther Consulting LLC	10435 Commerce Dr Ste 140	Carmel	IN	46032	**866-517-6570**	317-636-0282
Magnolia Consulting LLC	5135 Blenheim Rd	Charlottesville	VA	22902	**855-984-5540**	434-984-5540
Marvin Huffaker Consulting Inc	1311 W Chandler Blvd Ste 160	Chandler	AZ	85224	**888-690-0013**	480-988-7215
Matasano Security LLC	39 W 14th St Ste 202	New York	NY	10011	**888-677-0666**	
Max Environmental Technologies Inc	1815 Washington Rd	Pittsburgh	PA	15241	**800-851-7845**	412-343-4900
Max Technical Training	4900 Pkwy Dr Ste 160	Mason	OH	45040	**866-595-6863**	513-322-8888
MCM Services Group	1300 Corporate Ctr Curve	Eagan	MN	55121	**888-507-6262**	
MediRevv Inc	2600 University Pkwy	Coralville	IA	52241	**888-665-6310**	
Medmart Inc	10780 Reading Rd	Cincinnati	OH	45241	**888-260-4430**	
Mercury Z	1150 Se Maynard Rd Ste 140	Cary	NC	27511	**877-548-4052**	
Michael Brandman Associates	220 Commerce Ste 200	Irvine	CA	92602	**888-826-5814**	714-508-4100
Michell Consulting Group Inc	8240 NW 52nd Ter Ste 410	Doral	FL	33166	**800-442-5011**	305-592-5433
MindSpark International Inc	1205 Peachtree Pkwy Ste 1204	Cumming	GA	30041	**888-820-3616**	
MOBI Wireless Management LLC	6100 W 96th St Ste 150	Indianapolis	IN	46278	**855-259-6624**	
Moran Technology Consulting Llc	1215 Hamilton Ln Ste 200	Naperville	IL	60540	**888-699-4440**	
Morphix Business Consulting	PO Box 5217 Stn A	Calgary	AB	T2H1X3	**866-680-2503**	403-520-7710
Native Seeds-search	3584 E River Rd	Tucson	AZ	85718	**866-622-5561**	520-622-0830
Nelrod Co	3109 Lubbock Ave	Fort Worth	TX	76109	**866-448-0961**	817-922-9000
Neltner Billing & Consulting Services inc	6463 Taylor Mill Rd	Independence	KY	41051	**888-635-8637**	
Netlink Software Group America Inc	999 Tech Row	Madison Heights	MI	48071	**800-485-4462**	
Neutron Inc	220 Reese Rd	State College	PA	16801	**800-813-4218**	814-237-0902
Nordisk Systems Inc	13475 SE Johnson Rd	Milwaukie	OR	97222	**800-676-2777**	503-353-7555
Northspan Group Inc, The	221 W First St	Duluth	MN	55802	**800-232-0707**	218-722-5545
Noxent Inc	6400 Boul Taschereau Bur 220	Brossard	QC	J4W3J2	**800-268-4364**	
NUBE Inc	16238 Ranch Rd Ste F-108	Austin	TX	78717	**888-400-3133**	
Oceanus Partners	16540 Pointe Village Dr Ste 208	Lutz	FL	33558	**888-496-1117**	
Open Spatial Inc	13575 58th St N Ste 180	Clearwater	FL	33760	**800-696-1238**	
OPTIO LLC	390 Spaulding Ave SE	Ada	MI	49301	**888-981-3282**	
PhishLabs	PO Box 20877	Charleston	SC	29413	**877-227-0790**	843-628-3368
Pistachio Consulting Inc	67 Maple St	Milton	MA	02186	**800-747-1941**	
Platinum Vault Inc	10554 Norwalk Blvd	Santa Fe Springs	CA	90670	**888-671-2888**	562-903-1494
PlusOne Solutions Inc	3501 Quadrangle Blvd Ste 120	Orlando	FL	32817	**877-943-0100**	407-359-5929
Pollution Control Corp	500 W Country Club Rd	Chickasha	OK	73018	**800-966-1265**	
Portable Church Industries Inc	1923 Ring Dr	Troy	MI	48083	**800-939-7722**	248-585-9540
Proactive Management Consulting LLC	2700 Cumberland Pkwy SE	Atlanta	GA	30339	**877-319-2198**	770-319-7468
Product Safety Consulting Inc	605 Country Club Dr Ste I	Bensenville	IL	60106	**877-804-3066**	630-238-0188
Project Consulting Services Inc	3300 W Esplanade Ave S Ste 500	Metairie	LA	70002	**855-468-7473**	504-833-5321
ProSource Solutions LLC	4199 Kinross Lakes Pkwy Ste 150	Richfield	OH	44286	**866-549-0279**	
Quadlogic Controls Corp	3300 Northern Blvd Fl 2 Fl 2	Long Island	NY	11101	**877-797-6347**	212-930-9300
Quality Management Solutions LLC	146 Lowell St Ste 300B	Wakefield	MA	01889	**800-645-6430**	
R2 Unified Technologies	980 N Federal Hwy Ste 410	Boca Raton	FL	33432	**866-464-7381**	561-515-6800
RDS Solutions LLC	99 Grayrock Rd	Clinton	NJ	08809	**888-473-7435**	
RedLegg	100 Illinois St Ste 200	St. Charles	IL	60174	**877-811-5040**	
Research into Action Inc	3934 Ne Mlking Jr Blvd Ste 300	Portland	OR	97212	**888-492-9100**	503-287-9136
Response Design Corp	5541 Simpson Ave	Ocean City	NJ	08226	**888-204-3833**	
Revention Inc	1315 W Sam Houston Pkwy North Ste 100	Houston	TX	77043	**877-738-7444**	
RISC Networks Inc	1 Rankin Ave Second Fl	Asheville	NC	28801	**866-808-1227**	
Roi Consulting Ll Llc	176 Logan St	Noblesville	IN	46060	**866-465-6470**	
Rook Consulting	5537 Makati Cir	San Jose	CA	95123	**888-712-9531**	
Root Inc	5470 Main St	Sylvania	OH	43560	**800-852-1315**	
Rsi Corp	543 Main St	Kiowa	KS	67070	**888-830-5648**	620-825-4600
Sabretech Consulting LLC	154 Lewis St	Hillsdale	MI	49242	**800-267-1715**	517-437-7150
Safari Micro Inc	2185 W Pecos Rd	Chandler	AZ	85224	**888-446-4770**	
SatisfYd	47 E Chicago Ave Ste 310	Naperville	IL	60540	**800-562-9557**	

Company	Address	City	State	ZIP	Toll-Free	Phone
McConkey Co	1615 Puyallup St PO Box 1690	Sumner	WA	98390	**800-426-8124**	253-863-8111
Menasha Corp	1645 Bergstrom Rd	Neenah	WI	54956	**800-558-5073**	920-751-1000
Molded Fiber Glass Tray Co	6175 US Hwy 6	Linesville	PA	16424	**800-458-6050*** *Sales	814-683-4500
ORBIS Corp	1055 Corporate Ctr Dr	Oconomowoc	WI	53066	**800-999-8683**	262-560-5000
Pelican Products Inc	147 N Main St	South Deerfield	MA	01373	**800-542-7344**	413-665-2163
Plano Molding Co	431 E S St	Plano	IL	60545	**800-226-9868**	630-552-3111
Plas-Tanks Industries Inc	39 Standen Dr	Hamilton	OH	45015	**800-247-6709**	513-942-3800
Plastic Forming Company Inc	20 S Bradley Rd	Woodbridge	CT	06525	**800-732-2060**	203-397-1338
Rehrig Pacific Co	4010 E 26th St	Los Angeles	CA	90023	**800-421-6244**	323-262-5145
River Bend Industries	2421 16th Ave S	Moorhead	MN	56560	**800-365-3070**	218-236-1818
Rocket Box Inc	125 E 144th St	Bronx	NY	10451	**800-762-5521**	718-292-5370
RPM Industries Inc	26 Aurelius Ave	Auburn	NY	13021	**800-669-3676**	315-255-1105
Schaefer Systems International Inc	10021 Westlake Dr	Charlotte	NC	28241	**800-876-6000**	704-944-4500
Specialty Plastic Fabricators Inc	9658 196th St	Mokena	IL	60448	**800-747-9509**	708-479-5501
Stack-On Products Co	1360 N Old Rand Rd	Wauconda	IL	60084	**800-323-9601**	847-526-1611
Toter Inc	PO Box 5338	Statesville	NC	28677	**800-424-0422**	704-872-8171
US Plastic Corp	1390 Newbrecht Rd	Lima	OH	45801	**800-537-9724**	419-228-2242

202 CONTAINERS - WOOD

SEE ALSO Pallets & Skids

Company	Address	City	State	ZIP	Toll-Free	Phone
Abbot & Abbot Box Corp	37-11 Tenth St	Long Island	NY	11101	**888-525-7186**	
Commercial Lumber & Pallet Co	135 Long Ln	City Of Industry	CA	91746	**800-252-4968**	
Dove Manufacturing Plant 1	2525 N Sixth St	Vincennes	IN	47591	**866-444-3272**	812-886-4312
Greif Inc (*NYSE: GEF*)	425 Winter Rd	Delaware	OH	43015	**877-781-9797**	740-549-6000
Maine Bucket Co	21 Fireslate Pl	Lewiston	ME	04240	**800-231-7072**	207-784-6700
Mele & Co	2007 Beechgrove Pl	Utica	NY	13501	**800-635-6353**	315-733-4600
Monte Package Company Inc	3752 Riverside Rd	Riverside	MI	49084	**800-653-2807**	269-849-1722
Pallet Services Inc	12926 Farm to Market Rd	Mount Vernon	WA	98273	**800-769-2245**	
Texas Basket Co	100 Myrtle Dr	Jacksonville	TX	75766	**800-657-2200**	903-586-8014
Wisconsin Box Company Inc	929 Townline Rd	Wausau	WI	54402	**800-876-6658**	715-842-2248

203 CONTROLS - INDUSTRIAL PROCESS

Company	Address	City	State	ZIP	Toll-Free	Phone
ADA-ES Inc (*NASDAQ: ADES*)	9135 S Ridgeline Blvd Ste 200	Highlands Ranch	CO	80129	**888-822-8617**	303-734-1727
ADS Environmental Services	4940 Research Dr	Huntsville	AL	35805	**800-633-7246**	256-430-3366
ALL-TEST Pro LLC	123 Spencer Plain Rd	Old Saybrook	CT	06475	**800-952-8776**	860-399-4222
Alpha Technologies Services LLC	3030 Gilchrist Rd	Akron	OH	44305	**800-356-9886**	330-745-1641
AMETEK Automation & Process Technologies	1080 N Crooks	Clawson	MI	48017	**800-635-0289**	248-435-0700
Applied Microstructures Inc	2381 Bering Dr	San Jose	CA	95131	**877-683-2678**	408-907-2885
Arcet Equipment Company Inc	1700 Chamberlayne Ave	Richmond	VA	23222	**800-388-0302**	
ARi Industries Inc	381 Ari Ct	Addison	IL	60101	**800-237-6725**	630-953-9100
Arzel Zoning Technology Inc	4801 Commerce Pkwy	Cleveland	OH	44128	**800-611-8312**	216-831-6068
Athena Controls Inc	5145 Campus Dr	Plymouth Meeting	PA	19462	**800-782-6776**	610-828-2490
Auburn Systems LLC	8 Electronics Ave	Danvers	MA	01923	**800-255-5008**	978-777-2460
Automation Products Group Inc (APG)	1025 West 1700 North	Logan	UT	84321	**888-525-7300**	435-753-7300
Automation Service	13871 Parks Steed Dr	Earth City	MO	63045	**800-325-4808**	314-785-6600
Azonix Corp	900 Middlesex Tpke Bldg 6	Billerica	MA	01821	**800-967-5558**	978-670-6300
Bacharach Inc	621 Hunt Vly Cir	New Kensington	PA	15068	**800-736-4666**	724-334-5000
Barksdale Inc	3211 Fruitland Ave	Los Angeles	CA	90058	**800-835-1060**	323-589-6181
Brookfield Engineering Lab Inc	11 Commerce Blvd	Middleboro	MA	02346	**800-628-8139**	508-946-6200
Buhler Inc	13105 12th Ave N	Plymouth	MN	55441	**800-722-7483**	763-847-9900
Canfield Connector Div	8510 Foxwood Ct	Youngstown	OH	44514	**800-554-5071**	
Cec Controls Co Inc	14555 Barber Ave	Warren	MI	48088	**877-924-0303**	586-779-0222
Celesco Transducer Products Inc	20630 Plummer St	Chatsworth	CA	91311	**800-423-5483**	818-701-2750
Cincinnati Test Systems Inc	5555 Dry Fork Rd	Cleves	OH	45002	**800-850-3189**	513-367-6699
Conax Buffalo Technologies LLC	2300 Walden Ave	Buffalo	NY	14225	**800-223-2389**	716-684-4500
Cooper Atkins Corp	33 Reeds Gap Rd	Middlefield	CT	06455	**800-835-5011*** *Sales	860-349-3473
Crane Company Dynalco Controls Div	3690 NW 53rd St	Fort Lauderdale	FL	33309	**800-368-6666**	954-739-4300
CUES Inc	3600 Rio Vista Ave	Orlando	FL	32805	**800-327-7791**	407-849-0190
Daniel Measurement & Control Inc	5650 Brittmoore Rd	Houston	TX	77041	**800-518-1623**	713-467-6000
Del Mar Scientific Acquisition Ltd	4951 Airport Pkwy Ste 803	Addison	TX	75001	**800-722-4270**	972-661-5160
Dickson Co	930 S Westwood Ave	Addison	IL	60101	**800-757-3747**	630-543-3747
Eldridge Products Inc	2700 Garden Rd Bldg A	Monterey	CA	93940	**800-321-3569**	831-648-7777
Emulation Technology Inc	759 Flynn Rd	Camarillo	CA	93012	**800-232-7837**	805-383-8480
Encoder Products Co	464276 Hwy 95 S PO Box 249	Sagle	ID	83860	**800-366-5412**	208-263-8541
Endress+Hauser Inc	2350 Endress Pl	Greenwood	IN	46143	**888-363-7377**	317-535-7138
Enerac Inc	67 Bond St	Westbury	NY	11590	**800-695-3637**	516-997-2100
Fairchild Industrial Products Co	3920 Westpoint Blvd	Winston-Salem	NC	27103	**800-334-8422**	336-659-3400
Fast Heat Inc	776 Oaklawn Ave	Elmhurst	IL	60126	**877-747-8575**	630-833-5400
Fluid Components International	1755 La Costa Meadows Dr	San Marcos	CA	92078	**800-863-8703**	760-744-6950
Forney Corp	16479 N Dallas Pkwy Ste 600	Addison	TX	75001	**800-356-7740*** *Cust Svc	972-458-6100
Galvanic Applied Sciences USA Inc	41 Wellman St	Lowell	MA	01851	**866-252-8470**	978-848-2701
GE Infrastructure Sensing	1100 Technology Pk Dr	Billerica	MA	01821	**800-833-9438**	978-437-1000
Gefran ISI Inc	8 Lowell Ave	Winchester	MA	01890	**888-888-4474**	781-729-5249
Gems Sensors Inc	1 Cowles Rd	Plainville	CT	06062	**800-378-1600**	860-747-3000
General Devices Company Inc	1410 S Post Rd	Indianapolis	IN	46239	**800-821-3520**	317-897-7000
Geotech Environmental Equipment Inc	2650 E 40th Ave	Denver	CO	80205	**800-833-7958**	303-320-4764
GfG Instrumentation Inc	1194 Oak Vly Dr Ste 20	Ann Arbor	MI	48108	**800-959-0329**	734-769-0573
Harding Instruments	7741 Wagner Rd NW	Edmonton	AB	T6E5X7	**888-792-1171**	780-462-7100
Hart Scientific Inc	799 E Utah Vly Dr	American Fork	UT	84003	**800-438-4278**	801-763-1600
Healthspace USA Inc	4860 Cox Rd Ste 200	Glen Allen	VA	23060	**866-860-4224**	804-935-8532
HO Trerice Co	12950 W Eight-Mile Rd	Oak Park	MI	48237	**888-873-7423**	248-399-8000
HSQ Technology	26227 Research Rd	Hayward	CA	94545	**800-486-6684**	510-259-1334
Industrial Scientific Corp	7848 Steubenville Pk	Oakdale	PA	15071	**800-338-3287**	412-788-4353
ISCO Inc	4700 Superior St PO Box 82531	Lincoln	NE	68501	**800-228-4250**	402-464-0231
ITT Industries Inc (*NYSE: ITT*)	1133 Westchester Ave	White Plains	NY	10604	**800-254-2823**	914-641-2000
Kistler-Morse Corp	150 Venture Blvd	Spartanburg	SC	29306	**800-426-9010**	864-574-2763
Lake Shore Cryotronics	575 McCorkle Blvd	Westerville	OH	43082	**877-969-0010**	614-891-2243
LaMotte Co	802 Washington Ave	Chestertown	MD	21620	**800-344-3100**	410-778-3100
Linear Laboratories	42025 Osgood Rd	Fremont	CA	94539	**800-536-0262**	510-226-0488
Magnetrol International Inc	5300 Belmont Rd	Downers Grove	IL	60515	**800-624-8765**	630-969-4000
Mahr Federal Inc	1144 Eddy St	Providence	RI	02905	**800-343-2050*** *Orders	401-784-3100
Malema Engineering Corp	1060 S Rogers Cir	Boca Raton	FL	33487	**800-637-6418**	561-995-0595
MAMAC Systems Inc	8189 Century Blvd	Minneapolis	MN	55317	**800-843-5116**	952-556-4900
Marsh Bellofram Corp	8019 Ohio River Blvd	Newell	WV	26050	**800-727-5646**	304-387-1200
McCrometer Inc	3255 W Stetson Ave	Hemet	CA	92545	**800-220-2279**	951-652-6811
Micro Motion Inc	7070 Winchester Cir	Boulder	CO	80301	**800-522-6277**	303-530-8400
MicroMod Automation Inc	75 Town Centre Dr	Rochester	NY	14623	**800-480-1975**	585-321-9200
MKS Instruments Inc	2 Tech Dr Ste 201	Andover	MA	01810	**800-428-9401**	978-645-5500
Moore Industries International Inc	16650 Schoenborn St	North Hills	CA	91343	**800-999-2900**	818-894-7111
Nearfield Systems Inc	19730 Magellan Dr	Torrance	CA	90502	**800-334-7384**	310-525-7000
NRD LLC	2937 Alt Blvd PO Box 310	Grand Island	NY	14072	**800-525-8076**	716-773-7634
Omega Engineering Inc	1 Omega Dr PO Box 4047	Stamford	CT	06907	**800-826-6342**	203-359-1660
Onset Computer Corp	PO Box 3450	Pocasset	MA	02559	**800-564-4377**	508-759-9500
OPW Fuel Management Systems	6900 Santa Fe Dr	Hodgkins	IL	60525	**800-547-9393**	708-485-4200
Orange Research Inc	140 Cascade Blvd	Milford	CT	06460	**800-989-5657**	203-877-5657
Orion Instruments LLC	2105 Oak Villa Blvd	Baton Rouge	LA	70815	**866-556-7466**	225-906-2343
PakSense Inc	6223 N Discovery Pl	Boise	ID	83713	**877-832-0720**	208-489-9010

				Toll-Free	Phone
Polytron Corp 4400 Wyland Dr	Elkhart	IN	46516	**888-228-0246**	574-522-0246
PVA Tepla America Inc 251 Corporate Terr *Sales	Corona	CA	92879	**800-527-5667***	951-371-2500
RCI Custom Products 801 NE St Ste 2A	Frederick	MD	21701	**800-546-4724**	301-620-9130
Relay Specialties Inc 17 Raritan Rd	Oakland	NJ	07436	**800-526-5376**	201-337-1000
Rockford Systems Inc 4620 Hydraulic Rd *Cust Svc	Rockford	IL	61109	**800-922-7533***	815-874-7891
Sendec Corp 72 Perinton Pkwy	Fairport	NY	14450	**800-295-8000**	585-425-3390
Sequence Controls Inc 150 Rosamond St	Carleton	ON	K7C1V2	**800-663-1833**	613-257-7356
SOR Inc 14685 W 105th St	Lenexa	KS	66215	**800-676-6794**	913-888-2630
Sparton 27 Hale Spring Rd	Plaistow	NH	03865	**800-443-4132**	603-382-3840
Sprecher + Schuh 15910 International Plaza Dr	Houston	TX	77032	**877-721-5913**	281-442-9000
Sturdy Corp 1822 Carolina Beach Rd	Wilmington	NC	28401	**800-721-3282**	910-763-2500
Systems East Inc 30 Basil Sawyer Dr	Hampton	VA	23666	**800-230-8734**	757-766-8400
Time Mark Corp 11440 E Pine St	Tulsa	OK	74116	**800-862-2875**	918-438-1220
ime-O-Matic Inc 1015 Maple St		.	61832	**800-637-2645**	
ornatech Inc 7075, Place Robert-Joncas Ste 132		C	H4M2Z2	**800-363-8448**	
riumph Controls Inc 205 Church Rd		A	19454	**800-322-2885**	
Vago Corp N120 W19129 Freistadt Rd		/I	53022	**800-346-7245**	
(-COM Systems LLC 12345-B Sunrise Vly Dr		A	20191	**800-342-8408**	
'askawa America Inc 2121 Norman Dr S		.	60085	**800-927-5292**	

206 CE STORES

rocery Stores

			Toll-Free
'-Eleven Inc 1722 Routh Ste 100	X	75221	**800-255-0711**
:afepress.com Inc 1850 Gateway Dr Ste 300	A	94404	**877-809-1659**
racker Barrel Convenience S 12221 Industriplex Blvd	A	70809	**800-547-4151**
kg Oil Co 721 W Main	.	62220	**800-873-3546**
loliday Stationstores 4567 American Blvd W	IN	55437	**800-745-7411**
.ove's Travel Stops & Country 10601 N Pennsylvania Ave	K	73120	**800-388-0983**
lac's Convenience Stores Inc 305 Milner Ave Ste 400 4th Fl	N	M1B3V4	**800-268-5574**
laverik Inc 880 W Center St *Cust Svc	T	84054	**800-789-4455***
lpen Pantry Food Marts 10505 Corporate Dr Ste 101	/I	53158	**800-242-3358**
'laid Pantries Inc 10025 SW Allen Blvd	R	97005	**800-677-5243**
luikTrip Corp 4705 S 129th E Ave	K	74134	**800-441-0253**
heetz Inc 5700 Sixth Ave	A	16602	**800-487-5444**
peedway LLC 500 Speedway Dr *Cust Svc	H	45323	**800-643-1948***
tripes Convenience Stores 4525 Ayers St NYSE: SUSS	X	78415	**800-569-3585**
Vawa Inc 260 W Baltimore Pike	A	19063	**800-444-9292**
(tramart 221 Quinebaug Rd	T	06255	**800-243-6366**

207 N CENTERS

SEE ALS ... rforming Arts Facilities

Listings are alphabeti ... groupings.

				Toll-Free	Phone
Cross Insurance Center 515 Main St	Bangor	ME	04401	**800-745-3000**	207-561-8300
Dallas Convention Ctr 650 S Griffin St	Dallas	TX	75202	**877-850-2100**	214-939-2750
Dallas Market Ctr 2100 Stemmons Fwy Ste 113	Dallas	TX	75207	**800-325-6587**	214-655-6100
Duluth Entertainment Convention Ctr 350 Harbor Dr	Duluth	MN	55802	**800-628-8385**	218-722-5573
El Paso Convention & Performing Arts Ctr 1 Civic Ctr Plz	El Paso	TX	79901	**800-351-6024**	915-534-0600
Elko Convention & Visitors Authority 700 Moren Way	Elko	NV	89801	**800-248-3556**	775-738-4091
Expo Square 4145 E 21st St	Tulsa	OK	74114	**877-781-2660**	918-744-1113
Festival Plaza 101 Crockett St	Shreveport	LA	71101	**888-458-4748**	318-673-5100
Florence Events Ctr 715 Quince St	Florence	OR	97439	**888-968-4086**	541-997-1994
Fort Worth Convention Ctr 1201 Houston St	Fort Worth	TX	76102	**866-630-2588**	817-392-6338
Frontier Airlines Ctr 400 W Wisconsin Ave	Milwaukee	WI	53203	**800-745-3000**	414-908-6000
Gateway Ctr 1 Gateway Dr	Collinsville	IL	62234	**800-289-2388**	618-345-8998
George R Brown Convention Ctr 1001 Avenida de Las Americas	Houston	TX	77010	**800-427-4697**	713-853-8000
Georgia International Convention Ctr 2000 Convention Ctr Concourse	College Park	GA	30337	**888-331-4422**	770-997-3566
: Convention Ctr, The Main St			1	**866-782-7897**	817-41
olumbus Convention Ctr igh St			5	**800-626-0241**	614-82
acoma Convention & Trade Ct adway			2	**800-745-3000**	253-83
Inn Philadelphia Ctr City-Con ce St			7	**800-426-7866**	215-66
nvention Ctr lakaua Ave			5	**800-295-6603**	808-94
n Convention Ctr ater St			5	**877-775-5252**	702-26
onzalez Convention Ctr arket St			5	**877-504-8895**	210-20
onvention Ctr igh St			5	**888-288-8860**	765-28
gs Convention Ctr (HSCVB) vention Blvd PO Box 6000			2	**800-625-7576**	501-32
nal Exposition Ctr Dr			5	**855-436-8683**	216-67
nes Veterans Memorial Conv lston St			5	**800-392-6089**	617-95
ight Ctr l St			3	**800-245-4254**	330-37
ity Convention & Entertainme 3th St			5	**800-767-7700**	816-51
xpocentre entre Dr			2	**800-745-3000**	785-23
International Convention Ctr ourth St			2	**800-701-5831**	502-59
Convention Ctr Blvd			1	**800-822-2017**	941-72
ic Ctr Ctr Dr SE			4	**800-422-2199**	507-32
lise Mart chandise Mart Plz Ste 470			4	**800-677-6278**	312-52
k 308 6th Ave N			1	**800-366-8538**	406-25
pi Coast Coliseum & Conventi ach Blvd			1	**800-726-2781**	228-59
Conference Ctr a Plz			0	**800-742-8091***	831-64
rdens Convention Ctr Blvd			4	**888-388-8484**	409-74
ach Convention Ctr Oak St			7	**800-537-1690**	843-91
onvention Ctr n St			0	**888-475-9144**	601-44
600 E Grand Ave			1	**800-595-7437**	312-59
y Convention & Exposition Ct eld Ave			7	**800-367-0070**	732-41
Convention Ctr adway			7	**800-228-9290**	510-45
ndsay Ctr Ctr Plaza Ste 257			1	**800-978-4748**	2?7-22

Company	Address	City	State	ZIP	Toll-Free	Phone
McConkey Co	1615 Puyallup St PO Box 1690	Sumner	WA	98390	**800-426-8124**	253-863-8111
Menasha Corp	1645 Bergstrom Rd	Neenah	WI	54956	**800-558-5073**	920-751-1000
Molded Fiber Glass Tray Co	6175 US Hwy 6	Linesville	PA	16424	**800-458-6050***	814-683-4500
	*Sales					
ORBIS Corp	1055 Corporate Ctr Dr	Oconomowoc	WI	53066	**800-999-8683**	262-560-5000
Pelican Products Inc	147 N Main St	South Deerfield	MA	01373	**800-542-7344**	413-665-2163
Plano Molding Co	431 E S St	Plano	IL	60545	**800-226-9868**	630-552-3111
Plas-Tanks Industries Inc	39 Standen Dr	Hamilton	OH	45015	**800-247-6709**	513-942-3800
Plastic Forming Company Inc	20 S Bradley Rd	Woodbridge	CT	06525	**800-732-2060**	203-397-1338
Rehrig Pacific Co	4010 E 26th St	Los Angeles	CA	90023	**800-421-6244**	323-262-5145
River Bend Industries	2421 16th Ave S	Moorhead	MN	56560	**800-365-3070**	218-236-1818
Rocket Box Inc	125 E 144th St	Bronx	NY	10451	**800-762-5521**	718-292-5370
RPM Industries Inc	26 Aurelius Ave	Auburn	NY	13021	**800-669-3676**	315-255-1105
Schaefer Systems International Inc	10021 Westlake Dr	Charlotte	NC	28241	**800-876-6000**	704-944-4500
Specialty Plastic Fabricators Inc	9658 196th St	Mokena	IL	60448	**800-747-9509**	708-479-5501
Stack-On Products Co	1360 N Old Rand Rd	Wauconda	IL	60084	**800-323-9601**	847-526-1611
Toter Inc	PO Box 5338	Statesville	NC	28677	**800-424-0422**	704-872-8171
US Plastic Corp	1390 Newbrecht Rd	Lima	OH	45801	**800-537-9724**	419-228-2242

202 CONTAINERS - WOOD

SEE ALSO Pallets & Skids

Company	Address	City	State	ZIP	Toll-Free	Phone
Abbot & Abbot Box Corp	37-11 Tenth St	Long Island	NY	11101	**888-525-7186**	
Commercial Lumber & Pallet Co	135 Long Ln	City Of Industry	CA	91746	**800-252-4968**	
Dove Manufacturing Plant 1	2525 N Sixth St	Vincennes	IN	47591	**866-444-3272**	812-886-4312
Greif Inc	425 Winter Rd	Delaware	OH	43015	**877-781-9797**	740-549-6000
	NYSE: GEF					
Maine Bucket Co	21 Fireslate Pl	Lewiston	ME	04240	**800-231-7072**	207-784-6700
Mele & Co	2007 Beechgrove Pl	Utica	NY	13501	**800-635-6353**	315-733-4600
Monte Package Company Inc	3752 Riverside Rd	Riverside	MI	49084	**800-653-2807**	269-849-1722
Pallet Services Inc	12926 Farm to Market Rd	Mount Vernon	WA	98273	**800-769-2245**	
Texas Basket Co	100 Myrtle Dr	Jacksonville	TX	75766	**800-657-2200**	903-586-8014
Wisconsin Box Company Inc	929 Townline Rd	Wausau	WI	54402	**800-876-6658**	715-842-2248

203 CONTROLS - INDUSTRIAL PROCESS

Company	Address	City	State	ZIP	Toll-Free	Phone
ADA-ES Inc	9135 S Ridgeline Blvd Ste 200	Highlands Ranch	CO	80129	**888-822-8617**	303-734-1727
	NASDAQ: ADES					
ADS Environmental Services	4940 Research Dr	Huntsville	AL	35805	**800-633-7246**	256-430-3366
ALL-TEST Pro LLC	123 Spencer Plain Rd	Old Saybrook	CT	06475	**800-952-8776**	860-399-4222
Alpha Technologies Services LLC	3030 Gilchrist Rd	Akron	OH	44305	**800-356-9886**	330-745-1641
AMETEK Automation & Process Technologies	1080 N Crooks	Clawson	MI	48017	**800-635-0289**	248-435-0700
Applied Microstructures Inc	2381 Bering Dr	San Jose	CA	95131	**877-683-2678**	408-907-2885
Arcet Equipment Company Inc	1700 Chamberlayne Ave	Richmond	VA	23222	**800-388-0302**	
ARi Industries Inc	381 Ari Ct	Addison	IL	60101	**800-237-6725**	630-953-9100
Arzel Zoning Technology Inc	4801 Commerce Pkwy	Cleveland	OH	44128	**800-611-8312**	216-831-6068
Athena Controls Inc	5145 Campus Dr	Plymouth Meeting	PA	19462	**800-782-6776**	610-828-2490
Auburn Systems LLC	8 Electronics Ave	Danvers	MA	01923	**800-255-5008**	978-777-2460
Automation Products Group Inc (APG)	1025 West 1700 North	Logan	UT	84321	**888-525-7300**	435-753-7300
Automation Service	13871 Parks Steed Dr	Earth City	MO	63045	**800-325-4808**	314-785-6600
Azonix Corp	900 Middlesex Tpke Bldg 6	Billerica	MA	01821	**800-967-5558**	978-670-6300
Bacharach Inc	621 Hunt Vly Cir	New Kensington	PA	15068	**800-736-4666**	724-334-5000
Barksdale Inc	3211 Fruitland Ave	Los Angeles	CA	90058	**800-835-1060**	323-589-6181
Brookfield Engineering Lab Inc	11 Commerce Blvd	Middleboro	MA	02346	**800-628-8139**	508-946-6200
Buhler Inc	13105 12th Ave N	Plymouth	MN	55441	**800-722-7483**	763-847-9900
Canfield Connector Div	8510 Foxwood Ct	Youngstown	OH	44514	**800-554-5071**	
Cec Controls Co Inc	14555 Barber Ave	Warren	MI	48088	**877-924-0303**	586-779-0222
Celesco Transducer Products Inc	20630 Plummer St	Chatsworth	CA	91311	**800-423-5483**	818-701-2750
Cincinnati Test Systems Inc	5555 Dry Fork Rd	Cleves	OH	45002	**800-850-3189**	513-367-6699
Conax Buffalo Technologies LLC	2300 Walden Ave	Buffalo	NY	14225	**800-223-2389**	716-684-4500
Cooper Atkins Corp	33 Reeds Gap Rd	Middlefield	CT	06455	**800-835-5011***	860-349-3473
	*Sales					
Crane Company Dynalco Controls Div	3690 NW 53rd St	Fort Lauderdale	FL	33309	**800-368-6666**	954-739-4300
CUES Inc	3600 Rio Vista Ave	Orlando	FL	32805	**800-327-7791**	407-849-0190
Daniel Measurement & Control Inc	5650 Brittmoore Rd	Houston	TX	77041	**800-518-1623**	713-467-6000
Del Mar Scientific Acquisition Ltd	4951 Airport Pkwy Ste 803	Addison	TX	75001	**800-722-4270**	972-661-5160
Dickson Co	930 S Westwood Ave	Addison	IL	60101	**800-757-3747**	630-543-3747
Eldridge Products Inc	2700 Garden Rd Bldg A	Monterey	CA	93940	**800-321-3569**	831-648-7777
Emulation Technology Inc	759 Flynn Rd	Camarillo	CA	93012	**800-232-7837**	805-383-8480
Encoder Products Co	464276 Hwy 95 S PO Box 249	Sagle	ID	83860	**800-366-5412**	208-263-8541
Endress+Hauser Inc	2350 Endress Pl	Greenwood	IN	46143	**888-363-7377**	317-535-7138
Enerac Inc	67 Bond St	Westbury	NY	11590	**800-695-3637**	516-997-2100
Fairchild Industrial Products Co	3920 Westpoint Blvd	Winston-Salem	NC	27103	**800-334-8422**	336-659-3400
Fast Heat Inc	776 Oaklawn Ave	Elmhurst	IL	60126	**877-747-8575**	630-833-5400
Fluid Components International	1755 La Costa Meadows Dr	San Marcos	CA	92078	**800-863-8703**	760-744-6950
Forney Corp	16479 N Dallas Pkwy Ste 600	Addison	TX	75001	**800-356-7740***	972-458-6100
	*Cust Svc					
Galvanic Applied Sciences USA Inc	41 Wellman St	Lowell	MA	01851	**866-252-8470**	978-848-2701
GE Infrastructure Sensing	1100 Technology Pk Dr	Billerica	MA	01821	**800-833-9438**	978-437-1000
Gefran ISI Inc	8 Lowell Ave	Winchester	MA	01890	**888-888-4474**	781-729-5249
Gems Sensors Inc	1 Cowles Rd	Plainville	CT	06062	**800-378-1600**	860-747-3000
General Devices Company Inc	1410 S Post Rd	Indianapolis	IN	46239	**800-821-3520**	317-897-7000
Geotech Environmental Equipment Inc	2650 E 40th Ave	Denver	CO	80205	**800-833-7958**	303-320-4764
GfG Instrumentation Inc	1194 Oak Vly Dr Ste 20	Ann Arbor	MI	48108	**800-959-0329**	734-769-0573
Harding Instruments	7741 Wagner Rd NW	Edmonton	AB	T6E5X7	**888-792-1171**	780-462-7100
Hart Scientific Inc	799 E Utah Vly Dr	American Fork	UT	84003	**800-438-4278**	801-763-1600
Healthspace USA Inc	4860 Cox Rd Ste 200	Glen Allen	VA	23060	**866-860-4224**	804-935-8532
HO Trerice Co	12950 W Eight-Mile Rd	Oak Park	MI	48237	**888-873-7423**	248-399-8000
HSQ Technology	26227 Research Rd	Hayward	CA	94545	**800-486-6684**	510-259-1334
Industrial Scientific Corp	7848 Steubenville Pk	Oakdale	PA	15071	**800-338-3287**	412-788-4353
ISCO Inc	4700 Superior St PO Box 82531	Lincoln	NE	68501	**800-228-4250**	402-464-0231
ITT Industries Inc	1133 Westchester Ave	White Plains	NY	10604	**800-254-2823**	914-641-2000
	NYSE: ITT					
Kistler-Morse Corp	150 Venture Blvd	Spartanburg	SC	29306	**800-426-9010**	864-574-2763
Lake Shore Cryotronics	575 McCorkle Blvd	Westerville	OH	43082	**877-969-0010**	614-891-2243
LaMotte Co	802 Washington Ave	Chestertown	MD	21620	**800-344-3100**	410-778-3100
Linear Laboratories	42025 Osgood Rd	Fremont	CA	94539	**800-536-0262**	510-226-0488
Magnetrol International Inc	5300 Belmont Rd	Downers Grove	IL	60515	**800-624-8765**	630-969-4000
Mahr Federal Inc	1144 Eddy St	Providence	RI	02905	**800-343-2050***	401-784-3100
	*Orders					
Malema Engineering Corp	1060 S Rogers Cir	Boca Raton	FL	33487	**800-637-6418**	561-995-0595
MAMAC Systems Inc	8189 Century Blvd	Minneapolis	MN	55317	**800-843-5116**	952-556-4900
Marsh Bellofram Corp	8019 Ohio River Blvd	Newell	WV	26050	**800-727-5646**	304-387-1200
McCrometer Inc	3255 W Stetson Ave	Hemet	CA	92545	**800-220-2279**	951-652-6811
Micro Motion Inc	7070 Winchester Cir	Boulder	CO	80301	**800-522-6277**	303-530-8400
MicroMod Automation Inc	75 Town Centre Dr	Rochester	NY	14623	**800-480-1975**	585-321-9200
MKS Instruments Inc	2 Tech Dr Ste 201	Andover	MA	01810	**800-428-9401**	978-645-5500
Moore Industries International Inc	16650 Schoenborn St	North Hills	CA	91343	**800-999-2900**	818-894-7111
Nearfield Systems Inc	19730 Magellan Dr	Torrance	CA	90502	**800-334-7384**	310-525-7000
NRD LLC	2937 Alt Blvd PO Box 310	Grand Island	NY	14072	**800-525-8076**	716-773-7634
Omega Engineering Inc	1 Omega Dr PO Box 4047	Stamford	CT	06907	**800-826-6342**	203-359-1660
Onset Computer Corp	PO Box 3450	Pocasset	MA	02559	**800-564-4377**	508-759-9500
OPW Fuel Management Systems	6900 Santa Fe Dr	Hodgkins	IL	60525	**800-547-9393**	708-485-4200
Orange Research Inc	140 Cascade Blvd	Milford	CT	06460	**800-989-5657**	203-877-5657
Orion Instruments LLC	2105 Oak Villa Blvd	Baton Rouge	LA	70815	**866-556-7466**	225-906-2343
PakSense Inc	6223 N Discovery Pl	Boise	ID	83713	**877-832-0720**	208-489-9010

	City	State	ZIP	Toll-Free	Phone
Paper Machine Components 11 Old Sugar Hollow Rd	Danbury	CT	06810	**800-869-5747**	203-792-8686
Parker Hannifin Corp Veriflo Div 250 Canal Blvd	Richmond	CA	94804	**800-272-7537**	510-235-9590
PdMA Corp 5909-C Hampton Oaks Pkwy	Tampa	FL	33610	**800-476-6463**	813-621-6463
Pearpoint Inc 72055 Corporate Way	Thousand Palms	CA	92276	**800-688-8094**	760-343-7350
Pentair 7433 Harwin Dr	Houston	TX	77036	**800-545-6258**	
Portage Electric Products Inc 7700 Freedom Ave NW	North Canton	OH	44720	**888-464-7374**	330-499-2727
Porter Instrument Company Inc 245 Township Line Rd PO Box 907	Hatfield	PA	19440	**888-723-4001**	215-723-4000
Potter Electric Signal Company Inc 5757 Phantom Dr Ste 125	Hazelwood	MO	63042	**800-325-3936**	314-878-4321
Pressure Profile Systems Inc 5757 Century Blvd Ste 600	Los Angeles	CA	90045	**888-249-2464**	310-641-8100
RAE Systems 3775 N First St	San Jose	CA	95134	**877-723-2878**	408-952-8200
Raven Industries Inc 205 E Sixth St *NASDAQ: RAVN*	Sioux Falls	SD	57104	**800-243-5435**	605-336-2750
Robertshaw Industrial Products 1602 Mustang Dr	Maryville	TN	37801	**800-228-7429**	865-981-3100
Rochester Gauges Inc of Texas 11616 Harry Hines Blvd	Dallas	TX	75229	**800-821-1829**	972-241-2161
Ronan Engineering Co 21200 Oxnard St	Woodland Hills	CA	91367	**800-327-6626**	
Rosemount Analytical Inc Process Analytical Div 6565 P Davis Industrial Pkwy	Solon	OH	44139	**800-433-6076**	440-914-1261
Sable Systems International Inc 6000 S Ea Ste 1	Las Vegas	NV	89119	**800-330-0465**	702-269-4445
Scully Signal Co 70 Industrial Way	Wilmington	MA	01887	**800-272-8559**	617-692-8600
See Water Inc 121 N Dillon St	San Jacinto	CA	92583	**888-733-9283**	951-487-8073
Sensidyne Inc 16333 Bay Vista Dr	Clearwater	FL	33760	**800-451-9444**	727-530-3602
Sensus USA Inc 8601 Six Forks Rd Stes 300 & 700	Raleigh	NC	27615	**800-638-3748**	919-845-4000
Sierra Instruments Inc 5 Harris Ct Bldg L	Monterey	CA	93940	**800-866-0200**	831-373-0200
SJE-Rhombus 22650 County Hwy 6 PO Box 1708	Detroit Lakes	MN	56502	**800-746-6287**	218-847-1317
SOR Inc 14685 W 105th St	Lenexa	KS	66215	**800-676-6794**	913-888-2630
Spectronics Corp 956 Brush Hollow Rd	Westbury	NY	11590	**800-274-8888**	
Spirax Sarco Inc 1150 Northpoint Blvd	Blythewood	SC	29016	**800-883-4411**	803-714-2000
Sterling Inc 2900 S 160th St *Cust Svc	New Berlin	WI	53151	**800-783-7835***	262-641-8600
Taylor Precision Products LLC 2220 Entrada del Sol Ste A	Las Cruces	NM	88001	**866-843-3905**	
Teledyne Advanced Pollution Instrumentation 9480 Carroll Pk Dr	San Diego	CA	92121	**800-324-5190**	858-657-9800
Teledyne Monitor Labs Inc (TML) 35 Inverness Dr E	Englewood	CO	80112	**800-422-1499**	303-792-3300
Tevet LLC 85 Spring St S	Mosheim	TN	37818	**866-886-8527**	678-905-1300
Thermo Fisher Scientific Inc 81 Wyman St *NYSE: TMO*	Waltham	MA	02454	**800-678-5599**	781-622-1000
Titan Logix Corp 4130 - 93 St	Edmonton	AB	T6E5P5	**877-462-4085**	780-462-4085
Transcat Inc 35 Vantage Pt Dr *NASDAQ: TRNS*	Rochester	NY	14624	**800-800-5001**	585-352-9460
Troxler Electronic Laboratories Inc 3008 E Cornwallis Rd PO Box 12057	Research Triangle Park	NC	27709	**877-876-9537**	919-549-8661
TSI Inc 500 CaRdigan Rd	Shoreview	MN	55126	**800-874-2811**	651-483-0900
Veeder-Root 125 Powder Forest Dr	Simsbury	CT	06070	**888-262-7539**	860-651-2700
Wika Instrument Corp 1000 Wiegand Blvd	Lawrenceville	GA	30043	**888-945-2872**	770-513-8200
Wilmington Instrument Company Inc 332 N Fries Ave	Wilmington	CA	90744	**800-544-2843**	310-834-1133
Winland Electronics Inc 1950 Excel Dr *NYSE: WEX*	Mankato	MN	56001	**800-635-4269**	507-625-7231
World Energy Alternatives LLC 2 Constitution Ctr	Boston	MA	02129	**800-829-3676**	617-889-7300
Yokogawa Corp of America 12530 W Airport Blvd	Sugar Land	TX	77478	**800-888-6400**	281-340-3800
YSI Inc 1700-1725 Brannum Ln *Cust Svc	Yellow Springs	OH	45387	**800-765-4974***	937-767-7241
ZK Celltest Inc 256 Gibraltar Dr Ste 109	Sunnyvale	CA	94089	**800-837-8235**	408-752-0449

204 CONTROLS - TEMPERATURE - RESIDENTIAL & COMMERCIAL

	City	State	ZIP	Toll-Free	Phone
Azonix Corp 900 Middlesex Tpke Bldg 6	Billerica	MA	01821	**800-967-5558**	978-670-6300
CAPP/USA 201 Marple Ave	Clifton Heights	PA	19018	**800-356-8000**	610-394-1100
Cooper Atkins Corp 33 Reeds Gap Rd *Sales	Middlefield	CT	06455	**800-835-5011***	860-349-3473
DeltaTRAK Inc PO Box 398	Pleasanton	CA	94566	**800-962-6776**	925-249-2250
Emerson Climate Technologies - Retail Solutions 1065 Big Shanty Rd NW Ste 100	Kennesaw	GA	30144	**800-829-2724**	770-425-2724
Hansen Technologies Corp 6827 High Grove Blvd	Burr Ridge	IL	60527	**800-426-7368**	630-325-1565
HSQ Technology 26227 Research Rd	Hayward	CA	94545	**800-486-6684**	510-259-1334
Johnson Controls Systems 9410 Bunsen Pkwy Ste 100-B	Louisville	KY	40220	**800-765-7773**	502-671-7300
Kidde-Fenwal Inc 400 Main St *Hum Res	Ashland	MA	01721	**800-872-6527***	508-881-2000
KMC Controls Inc 19476 Industrial Dr	New Paris	IN	46553	**877-444-5622**	574-831-5250
Novar Controls Corp 6060 Rockside Woods Blvd Ste 400	Cleveland	OH	44131	**800-348-1235**	
Portage Electric Products Inc 7700 Freedom Ave NW	North Canton	OH	44720	**888-464-7374**	330-499-2727
Prentke Romich Co 1022 Heyl Rd	Wooster	OH	44691	**800-848-8008**	330-262-1984
Residential Control Systems 11481 Sunrise Gold Cir Ste 1	Rancho Cordova	CA	95742	**888-727-4822**	916-635-6784
Siemens Bldg Technologies Inc 1000 Deerfield Pkwy *General	Buffalo Grove	IL	60089	**800-877-7545***	847-215-1000
Taylor Precision Products LLC 2220 Entrada del Sol Ste A	Las Cruces	NM	88001	**866-843-3905**	
Watlow Winona 1241 Bundy Blvd	Winona	MN	55987	**800-928-5692**	507-454-5300

205 CONTROLS & RELAYS - ELECTRICAL

	City	State	ZIP	Toll-Free	Phone
ABB SSAC 8242 Loop Rd *Tech Supp	Baldwinsville	NY	13027	**800-377-7722***	315-638-1300
Allied Controls Inc 150 E Aurora St	Waterbury	CT	06708	**800-788-0955**	203-757-4200
AMETEK National Controls Corp 1725 Western Dr	West Chicago	IL	60185	**800-323-2593**	630-231-5900
AMX Corp 3000 Research Dr	Richardson	TX	75082	**855-269-8585**	469-624-8585
Anaheim Automation 910 E Orangefair Ln *Sales	Anaheim	CA	92801	**800-345-9401***	714-992-6990
Bright Image Corp 2830 S18th Ave	Broadview	IL	60155	**888-449-5656**	
Bus-tech Inc 26 Crosby Dr	Bedford	MA	01710	**800-284-3172**	
Cleveland Motion Controls Inc 7550 Hub Pkwy	Cleveland	OH	44125	**800-321-8072**	216-524-8800
Contrex Inc 8900 Zachary Ln N	Maple Grove	MN	55369	**800-342-4411**	763-424-7800
DST Controls 651 Stone Rd	Benicia	CA	94510	**800-251-0773**	707-745-5117
Ducommun Inc 23301 Wilmington Ave *NYSE: DCO*	Carson	CA	90745	**800-522-6645**	310-513-7280
Duct-O-Wire Co 345 Adams Cir	Corona	CA	92882	**800-752-6001**	951-735-8220
Easter Owens Electric Co 6692 Fig St	Arvada	CO	80004	**866-204-3707**	303-431-0111
Electric Regulator Corp 6189 El Camino Real	Carlsbad	CA	92009	**800-458-6566**	760-438-7873
Electronic Theatre Controls Inc 3031 Pleasantview Rd	Middleton	WI	53562	**800-688-4116**	608-831-4116
Enercon Engineering Inc 201 Altorfer Ln	East Peoria	IL	61611	**800-218-8831**	309-694-1418
FSI Technologies Inc 668 E Western Ave	Lombard	IL	60148	**800-468-6009**	630-932-9380
Gentec Inc 2625 Dalton	Quebec	QC	G1P3S9	**800-463-4480**	418-651-8000
GET Engineering Corp 9350 Bond Ave	El Cajon	CA	92021	**877-494-1820**	619-443-8295
Glendinning Marine Products 740 Century Cir	Conway	SC	29526	**800-500-2380**	843-399-6146
Globe Electronic Hardware Inc 34-24 56th St	Woodside	NY	11377	**800-221-1505**	718-457-0303
Guardian Electric Mfg Company Inc 1425 Lake Ave	Woodstock	IL	60098	**800-762-0369**	815-334-3600
Honeywell Sensing & Control 11 W Spring St *Cust Svc	Freeport	IL	61032	**800-537-6945***	815-235-5500
Hydrolevel Co 83 Water St	New Haven	CT	06511	**800-654-0768**	203-776-0473
Icm Controls Corp 7313 William Barry Blvd	North Syracuse	NY	13212	**800-365-5525**	315-233-5266
IDEC Corp 1175 Elko Dr	Sunnyvale	CA	94089	**800-262-4332**	408-747-0550
Imperial Irrigation District (IID) PO Box 937	Imperial	CA	92251	**800-303-7756**	760-482-9600
Inertia Dynamics Inc 31 Industrial Pk Rd	New Hartford	CT	06057	**800-800-6445**	860-482-4444
KB Electronics Inc 12095 NW 39th St	Coral Springs	FL	33065	**800-221-6570**	954-346-4900
Leach International Corp 6900 Orangethorpe Ave	Buena Park	CA	90622	**800-232-7700**	714-736-7598
Lutron Electronics Company Inc 7200 Suter Rd *Tech Supp	Coopersburg	PA	18036	**800-523-9466***	610-282-6280
MagneTek Inc N49 W13650 Campbell Dr *NASDAQ: MAG*	Menomonee Falls	WI	53051	**800-288-8178**	
Maxcess International, Inc. 222 W Memorial Rd PO Box 26508	Oklahoma City	OK	73114	**800-333-3433**	405-755-1600
Moog Inc Jamison Rd *NYSE: MOG/A*	East Aurora	NY	14052	**800-336-2112**	716-652-2000
OMRON Corp 1 Commerce Dr	Schaumburg	IL	60173	**800-556-6766**	847-843-7900
OMRON Scientific Technologies Inc 6550 Dumbarton Cir	Fremont	CA	94555	**888-510-4357**	510-608-3400
Ormec Systems Corp 19 Linden Pk	Rochester	NY	14625	**800-656-7632**	585-385-3520
Panasonic Electric Works Corp of America 629 Central Ave	New Providence	NJ	07974	**800-276-6289**	908-464-3550
Parker Hannifin Corp Electromechanical Automation Div 5500 Business Pk Dr	Rohnert Park	CA	94928	**800-358-9068**	707-584-7558
Parker McCrory Manufacturing Co 2000 Forest Ave	Kansas City	MO	64108	**800-662-1038**	816-221-2000
Payne Engineering Co Rt 29 PO Box 70 *Orders	Scott Depot	WV	25560	**800-331-1345***	304-757-7353

Classified Section

Name / Address	City	State	Zip	Toll-Free	Phone
Polytron Corp 4400 Wyland Dr	Elkhart	IN	46516	**888-228-0246**	574-522-0246
PVA Tepla America Inc 251 Corporate Terr	Corona	CA	92879	**800-527-5667***	951-371-2500
*Sales					
RCI Custom Products 801 NE St Ste 2A	Frederick	MD	21701	**800-546-4724**	301-620-9130
Relay Specialties Inc 17 Raritan Rd	Oakland	NJ	07436	**800-526-5376**	201-337-1000
Rockford Systems Inc 4620 Hydraulic Rd	Rockford	IL	61109	**800-922-7533***	815-874-7891
*Cust Svc					
Sendec Corp 72 Perinton Pkwy	Fairport	NY	14450	**800-295-8000**	585-425-3390
Sequence Controls Inc 150 Rosamond St	Carleton	ON	K7C1V2	**800-663-1833**	613-257-7356
SOR Inc 14685 W 105th St	Lenexa	KS	66215	**800-676-6794**	913-888-2630
Sparton 27 Hale Spring Rd	Plaistow	NH	03865	**800-443-4132**	603-382-3840
Sprecher + Schuh 15910 International Plaza Dr	Houston	TX	77032	**877-721-5913**	281-442-9000
Sturdy Corp 1822 Carolina Beach Rd	Wilmington	NC	28401	**800-721-3282**	910-763-2500
Systems East Inc 30 Basil Sawyer Dr	Hampton	VA	23666	**800-230-8734**	757-766-8400
Time Mark Corp 11440 E Pine St	Tulsa	OK	74116	**800-862-2875**	918-438-1220
Time-O-Matic Inc 1015 Maple St	Danville	IL	61832	**800-637-2645**	217-442-0611
Tornatech Inc 7075, Place Robert-Joncas Ste 132	Saint-laurent	QC	H4M2Z2	**800-363-8448**	514-334-0523
Triumph Controls Inc 205 Church Rd	North Wales	PA	19454	**800-322-2885**	215-699-4861
Wago Corp N120 W19129 Freistadt Rd	Germantown	WI	53022	**800-346-7245**	
X-COM Systems LLC 12345-B Sunrise Vly Dr	Reston	VA	20191	**800-342-8408**	703-390-1087
Yaskawa America Inc 2121 Norman Dr S	Waukegan	IL	60085	**800-927-5292**	847-887-7000

206 CONVENIENCE STORES

SEE ALSO Gas Stations ; Grocery Stores

Name / Address	City	State	Zip	Toll-Free	Phone
7-Eleven Inc 1722 Routh Ste 100	Dallas	TX	75221	**800-255-0711**	703-255-1800
Cafepress.com Inc 1850 Gateway Dr Ste 300	Foster City	CA	94404	**877-809-1659**	650-655-3120
Cracker Barrel Convenience Stores Inc 12221 Industriplex Blvd	Baton Rouge	LA	70809	**800-547-4151**	225-753-3200
Fkg Oil Co 721 W Main	Belleville	IL	62220	**800-873-3546**	618-233-6754
Holiday Stationstores 4567 American Blvd W	Bloomington	MN	55437	**800-745-7411**	952-830-8700
Love's Travel Stops & Country Stores Inc 10601 N Pennsylvania Ave	Oklahoma City	OK	73120	**800-388-0983**	
Mac's Convenience Stores Inc 305 Milner Ave Ste 400 4th Fl	Toronto	ON	M1B3V4	**800-268-5574**	
Maverik Inc 880 W Center St	North Salt Lake	UT	84054	**800-789-4455***	801-936-5557
*Cust Svc					
Open Pantry Food Marts 10505 Corporate Dr Ste 101	Pleasant Prairie	WI	53158	**800-242-3358**	262-857-1156
Plaid Pantries Inc 10025 SW Allen Blvd	Beaverton	OR	97005	**800-677-5243**	503-646-4246
QuikTrip Corp 4705 S 129th E Ave	Tulsa	OK	74134	**800-441-0253**	918-615-7700
Sheetz Inc 5700 Sixth Ave	Altoona	PA	16602	**800-487-5444**	814-941-5106
Speedway LLC 500 Speedway Dr	Enon	OH	45323	**800-643-1948***	937-864-3001
*Cust Svc					
Stripes Convenience Stores 4525 Ayers St	Corpus Christi	TX	78415	**800-569-3585**	361-884-2464
NYSE: SUSS					
Wawa Inc 260 W Baltimore Pike	Media	PA	19063	**800-444-9292**	610-358-8000
Xtramart 221 Quinebaug Rd	North Grosvenordale	CT	06255	**800-243-6366**	

207 CONVENTION CENTERS

SEE ALSO Stadiums & Arenas ; Performing Arts Facilities
Listings are alphabetized by city names within state groupings.

Name / Address	City	State	Zip	Toll-Free	Phone
America's Ctr Convention Ctr 701 Convention Plz Ste 300	Saint Louis	MO	63101	**800-325-7962**	314-342-5036
AmericasMart 240 Peachtree St NW Ste 2200	Atlanta	GA	30303	**800-285-6278**	404-220-3000
Asheville Civic Ctr 87 Haywood St	Asheville	NC	28801	**888-464-4218**	828-259-5743
Beaumont Civic Ctr Complex 701 Main St	Beaumont	TX	77701	**800-782-3081**	409-838-3435
Bell Harbor International Conference Ctr 2211 Alaskan Way Pier 66	Seattle	WA	98121	**888-772-4422**	206-441-6666
Buffalo Niagara Convention Ctr 153 Franklin St Convention Ctr Plz	Buffalo	NY	14202	**800-995-7570**	716-855-5555
California Market Ctr 110 E Ninth St	Los Angeles	CA	90079	**800-225-6278**	213-630-3600
Casper Events Ctr 1 Events Dr	Casper	WY	82601	**800-442-2256**	307-235-8441
Centennial Hall Convention Ctr 101 Egan Dr	Juneau	AK	99801	**800-478-4176**	907-586-5283
Chattanooga Convention Ctr 1150 Carter St PO Box 6008	Chattanooga	TN	37402	**800-962-5213**	423-756-0001
City of Pendleton 500 SW Dorion Ave	Pendleton	OR	97801	**800-238-5355**	541-966-0201
Colorado Springs City Auditorium 221 E Kiowa St	Colorado Springs	CO	80903	**800-888-4748**	719-385-5969
Cross Insurance Center 515 Main St	Bangor	ME	04401	**800-745-3000**	207-561-8300
Dallas Convention Ctr 650 S Griffin St	Dallas	TX	75202	**877-850-2100**	214-939-2750
Dallas Market Ctr 2100 Stemmons Fwy Ste 113	Dallas	TX	75207	**800-325-6587**	214-655-6100
Duluth Entertainment Convention Ctr 350 Harbor Dr	Duluth	MN	55802	**800-628-8385**	218-722-5573
El Paso Convention & Performing Arts Ctr 1 Civic Ctr Plz	El Paso	TX	79901	**800-351-6024**	915-534-0600
Elko Convention & Visitors Authority 700 Moren Way	Elko	NV	89801	**800-248-3556**	775-738-4091
Expo Square 4145 E 21st St	Tulsa	OK	74114	**877-781-2660**	918-744-1113
Festival Plaza 101 Crockett St	Shreveport	LA	71101	**888-458-4748**	318-673-5100
Florence Events Ctr 715 Quince St	Florence	OR	97439	**888-968-4086**	541-997-1994
Fort Worth Convention Ctr 1201 Houston St	Fort Worth	TX	76102	**866-630-2588**	817-392-6338
Frontier Airlines Ctr 400 W Wisconsin Ave	Milwaukee	WI	53203	**800-745-3000**	414-908-6000
Gateway Ctr 1 Gateway Dr	Collinsville	IL	62234	**800-289-2388**	618-345-8998
George R Brown Convention Ctr 1001 Avenida de Las Americas	Houston	TX	77010	**800-427-4697**	713-853-8000
Georgia International Convention Ctr 2000 Convention Ctr Concourse	College Park	GA	30337	**888-331-4422**	770-997-3566
Grapevine Convention Ctr, The 1209 S Main St	Grapevine	TX	76051	**866-782-7897**	817-410-3459
Greater Columbus Convention Ctr 400 N High St	Columbus	OH	43215	**800-626-0241**	614-827-2500
Greater Tacoma Convention & Trade Ctr 1500 Broadway	Tacoma	WA	98402	**800-745-3000**	253-830-6601
Hampton Inn Philadelphia Ctr City-Convention Ctr 1301 Race St	Philadelphia	PA	19107	**800-426-7866**	215-665-9100
Hawaii Convention Ctr 1801 Kalakaua Ave	Honolulu	HI	96815	**800-295-6603**	808-943-3500
Henderson Convention Ctr 200 S Water St	Henderson	NV	89015	**877-775-5252**	702-267-2171
Henry B Gonzalez Convention Ctr 200 E Market St	San Antonio	TX	78205	**877-504-8895**	210-207-8500
Horizon Convention Ctr 401 S High St	Muncie	IN	47305	**888-288-8860**	765-288-8860
Hot Springs Convention Ctr (HSCVB) 134 Convention Blvd PO Box 6000	Hot Springs	AR	71902	**800-625-7576**	501-321-2277
International Exposition Ctr 1-X Ctr Dr	Cleveland	OH	44135	**855-436-8683**	216-676-6000
John B Hynes Veterans Memorial Convention Ctr 900 Boylston St	Boston	MA	02115	**800-392-6089**	617-954-2000
John S Knight Ctr 77 E Mill St	Akron	OH	44308	**800-245-4254**	330-374-8900
Kansas City Convention & Entertainment Centers 301 W 13th St	Kansas City	MO	64105	**800-767-7700**	816-513-5000
Kansas Expocentre 1 Expocentre Dr	Topeka	KS	66612	**800-745-3000**	785-235-1986
Kentucky International Convention Ctr 221 S Fourth St	Louisville	KY	40202	**800-701-5831**	502-595-4381
Manatee Convention Ctr 1 Haben Blvd	Palmetto	FL	34221	**800-822-2017**	941-722-3244
Mayo Civic Ctr 30 Civic Ctr Dr SE	Rochester	MN	55904	**800-422-2199**	507-328-2220
Merchandise Mart 222 Merchandise Mart Plz Ste 470	Chicago	IL	60654	**800-677-6278**	312-527-4141
MetraPark 308 6th Ave N	Billings	MT	59101	**800-366-8538**	406-256-2400
Mississippi Coast Coliseum & Convention Ctr 2350 Beach Blvd	Biloxi	MS	39531	**800-726-2781**	228-594-3700
Monterey Conference Ctr 1 Portola Plz	Monterey	CA	93940	**800-742-8091***	831-646-3770
*Sales					
Moody Gardens Convention Ctr 7 Hope Blvd	Galveston	TX	77554	**888-388-8484**	409-741-8484
Myrtle Beach Convention Ctr 2101 N Oak St	Myrtle Beach	SC	29577	**800-537-1690**	843-918-5000
Natchez Convention Ctr 211 Main St	Natchez	MS	39120	**888-475-9144**	601-442-5880
Navy Pier 600 E Grand Ave	Chicago	IL	60611	**800-595-7437**	312-595-7437
New Jersey Convention & Exposition Ctr 97 Sunfield Ave	Edison	NJ	08837	**800-367-0070**	732-417-1400
Oakland Convention Ctr 1001 Broadway	Oakland	CA	94607	**800-228-9290**	510-451-4000
Oakley-Lindsay Ctr 300 Civic Ctr Plaza Ste 237	Quincy	IL	62301	**800-978-4748**	217-223-1000
Ocean Ctr 101 N Atlantic Ave	Daytona Beach	FL	32118	**800-858-6444**	386-254-4500
Ocean Shores Convention Ctr 120 W Chance a La Mer Ave	Ocean Shores	WA	98569	**800-874-6737**	360-289-4411
Office of General Services Corning Tower 41st Fl Empire State Plz	Albany	NY	12242	**877-426-6006**	518-474-3899
Ogden Eccles Conference Ctr 2415 Washington Blvd	Ogden	UT	84401	**866-472-4627**	801-689-8600
Oncenter Complex 800 S State St	Syracuse	NY	13202	**800-776-7548**	315-435-8000
Ontario Convention Ctr 2000 E Convention Ctr Way	Ontario	CA	91764	**800-455-5755**	909-937-3000
Orange County Convention Ctr (OCCC) 9800 International Dr	Orlando	FL	32819	**800-345-9845**	407-685-9800
Oregon Convention Ctr 777 NE Martin Luther King Jr Blvd	Portland	OR	97232	**800-791-2250**	503-235-7575
Palm Springs Convention Ctr 277 N Avenida Caballeros	Palm Springs	CA	92262	**800-898-7256**	760-325-6611
Pennsylvania Convention Ctr 1101 Arch St	Philadelphia	PA	19107	**800-428-9000**	215-418-4700
Phoenix Convention Ctr 100 N Third St	Phoenix	AZ	85004	**800-282-4842**	602-262-6225
Plano Centre 2000 E Springcreek Pkwy	Plano	TX	75074	**800-613-3222**	972-422-0296
Pontchartrain Ctr 4545 Williams Blvd	Kenner	LA	70065	**800-745-3000**	504-465-9985

Name / Address	City	State	Zip	Toll-Free	Phone
Reno-Sparks Convention Ctr 4590 S Virginia St	Reno	NV	89502	**800-367-7366**	775-827-7600
Rushmore Plaza Civic Ctr 444 Mt Rushmore Rd N	Rapid City	SD	57701	**800-468-6463**	605-394-4115
Saint Louis Executive Conference Ctr 701 Convention Plz	Saint Louis	MO	63101	**800-325-7962**	314-342-5050
Salem Conference Ctr 200 Commercial St SE *Sales	Salem	OR	97301	**877-589-1700***	503-589-1700
San Diego Convention Ctr 111 W Harbor Dr	San Diego	CA	92101	**800-525-7322**	619-525-5000
San Jose Convention Center (SJC) 150 W San Carlos St	San Jose	CA	95110	**800-726-5673**	408-792-4194
Santa Monica Civic Auditorium 1855 Main St	Santa Monica	CA	90401	**866-728-3229**	310-458-8551
Savannah International Trade & Convention Ctr 1 International Dr	Savannah	GA	31421	**888-644-6822**	912-447-4000
Seaside Civic & Convention Ctr 415 First Ave	Seaside	OR	97138	**800-394-3303**	503-738-8585
Sharonville Convention Ctr 11355 Chester Rd	Sharonville	OH	45246	**800-294-3179**	513-771-7744
Sioux City Convention Ctr 801 Fourth St	Sioux City	IA	51101	**800-593-2228**	712-279-4800
South Padre Island Convention Centre 7355 Padre Blvd	South Padre Island	TX	78597	**800-657-2373**	956-761-3000
Statehouse Convention Ctr 426 W Markham PO Box 3232	Little Rock	AR	72203	**800-844-4781**	501-376-4781
Tampa Convention Ctr 333 S Franklin St	Tampa	FL	33602	**866-790-4111**	813-274-8511
Tyson Events Ctr 401 Gordon Dr	Sioux City	IA	51101	**800-593-2228**	712-279-4850
US Cellular Ctr 370 First Ave E	Cedar Rapids	IA	52401	**800-745-3000**	319-398-5211
Vancouver Convention & Exposition Centre (VCEC) 1055 Canada Pl	Vancouver	BC	V6C0C3	**866-785-8232**	604-689-8232
Visalia Convention Ctr 303 E Acequia Ave	Visalia	CA	93291	**800-640-4888**	559-713-4000
Washington Convention Ctr Authority 801 Mt Vernon Pl NW	Washington	DC	20001	**800-368-9000**	202-249-3000
Wildwoods Convention Ctr 4501 Boardwalk	Wildwood	NJ	08260	**800-992-9732**	609-729-9000
Yakima Convention Ctr 10 N Eigth St	Yakima	WA	98901	**800-221-0751**	509-575-6062
Yuma Civic Ctr 1440 W Desert Hills Dr	Yuma	AZ	85365	**866-966-0220**	928-373-5040

208 CONVENTION & VISITORS BUREAUS

SEE ALSO Travel & Tourism Information - Canadian ; Travel & Tourism Information - Foreign Travel

Listings are alphabetized by city names.

Name / Address	City	State	Zip	Toll-Free	Phone
Aberdeen Convention & Visitors Bureau 10 Railroad Ave SW PO Box 78	Aberdeen	SD	57401	**800-645-3851**	605-225-2414
Abilene Convention & Visitors Bureau 201 NW Second St	Abilene	KS	67410	**800-569-5915**	785-263-2231
Abingdon Convention & Visitors Bureau 335 Cummings St	Abingdon	VA	24210	**800-435-3440**	276-676-2282
Akron/Summit County Convention & Visitors Bureau 77 E Mill St	Akron	OH	44308	**800-245-4254**	330-374-8900
Albany County Convention & Visitors Bureau 25 Quackenbush Sq	Albany	NY	12207	**800-258-3582**	518-434-1217
Albany Visitors Assn 300 Second Ave SW	Albany	OR	97321	**800-526-2256**	541-928-0911
Albuquerque Convention & Visitors Bureau 20 First Plz Ste 601	Albuquerque	NM	87102	**800-733-9918**	505-842-9918
Alexandria Convention & Visitors Assn 221 King St	Alexandria	VA	22314	**800-388-9119**	703-746-3301
Alexandria/Pineville Area Convention & Visitors Bureau (APACVB) 707 Main St PO Box 1070	Alexandria	LA	71301	**800-551-9546**	318-442-9546
Allegan County Tourist & Recreational Council 3255 122nd Ave Ste 103	Allegan	MI	49010	**888-425-5342**	269-686-9088
Lehigh Valley Visitor Ctr 840 Hamilton St Ste 200	Allentown	PA	18101	**800-747-0561**	610-882-9200
Alpena Area Convention & Visitors Bureau 235 W Chisholm St	Alpena	MI	49707	**800-425-7362**	989-354-4181
Alton Regional Convention & Visitors Bureau (ARCVB) 200 Piasa St	Alton	IL	62002	**800-258-6645**	618-465-6676
Amana Colonies Convention & Visitors Bureau 622 46th Ave	Amana	IA	52203	**800-579-2294**	319-622-7622
Amarillo Convention & Visitor Council 1000 S Polk St	Amarillo	TX	79101	**800-692-1338**	806-374-1497
Lorain County Visitors Bureau 8025 Leavitt Rd	Amherst	OH	44001	**800-334-1673**	440-984-5282
Anaheim/Orange County Visitor & Convention Bureau 800 W Katella Ave	Anaheim	CA	92802	**855-405-5020**	714-765-8888
Anchorage Convention & Visitors Bureau 524 W Fourth Ave	Anchorage	AK	99501	**800-478-6657**	907-276-4118
Anderson/Madison County Visitors & Convention Bureau 6335 S Scatterfield Rd	Anderson	IN	46013	**800-533-6569**	765-643-5633
Steuben County Tourism Bureau 430 N Wayne St Ste 1B	Angola	IN	46703	**888-665-5668**	260-665-5386
Ann Arbor Area Convention & Visitors Bureau 120 W Huron St	Ann Arbor	MI	48104	**800-888-9487**	734-995-7281
Southernmost Illinois Tourism Bureau PO Box 378	Anna	IL	62906	**800-248-4373**	618-833-9928
Annapolis & Anne Arundel County Conference & Visitors Bureau (AAACCVB) 26 W St	Annapolis	MD	21401	**888-302-2852**	410-280-0445
Fox Cities Convention & Visitors Bureau 3433 W College Ave	Appleton	WI	54914	**800-236-6673**	920-734-3358
Arlington Convention & Visitors Bureau 1905 E Randol Mill Rd	Arlington	TX	76011	**800-433-5374**	817-265-7721
Aspen Chamber Resort Assn 425 Rio Grande Pl	Aspen	CO	81611	**800-670-0792**	970-925-1940
Athens Convention & Visitors Bureau 300 N Thomas St	Athens	GA	30601	**800-653-0603**	706-357-4430
Athens County Convention & Visitors Bureau 667 E State St	Athens	OH	45701	**800-878-9767**	740-592-1819
Cobb Travel & Tourism 1 Galleria Pkwy	Atlanta	GA	30339	**800-451-3480**	678-303-2622
Atlantic City Convention & Visitors Authority 2314 Pacific Ave	Atlantic City	NJ	08401	**888-228-4748**	609-348-7100
Auburn-Opelika Tourism Bureau 714 E Glenn Ave	Auburn	AL	36830	**866-880-8747**	334-887-8747
Augusta Metropolitan Convention & Visitors Bureau 1450 Greene St Ste 560	Augusta	GA	30901	**800-726-0243**	706-823-6600
Aurora Area Convention & Visitors Bureau 43 W Galena Blvd	Aurora	IL	60506	**800-477-4369**	630-897-5581
Austin Convention & Visitors Bureau 301 Congress Ave Ste 200	Austin	TX	78701	**800-926-2282**	512-474-5171
Catalina Island Visitors Bureau 1 Green Pier PO Box 217	Avalon	CA	90704	**877-854-1125**	310-510-1520
Baker County Visitors & Convention Bureau 490 Campbell St	Baker City	OR	97814	**800-523-1235**	541-523-3356
Greater Bakersfield Convention & Visitors Bureau 515 Truxtun Ave	Bakersfield	CA	93301	**866-425-7353**	661-852-7282
Baltimore Area Convention & Visitors Assn (BACVA) 100 Light St 12th Fl	Baltimore	MD	21202	**877-225-8466**	410-659-7300
Bandera County Convention & Visitors Bureau 126 State Hwy 16 S PO Box 171	Bandera	TX	78003	**800-364-3833**	830-796-3045
Greater Bangor Convention & Visitors Bureau 40 Harlow St	Bangor	ME	04401	**800-916-6673**	207-947-5205
Clermont County Convention & Visitors Bureau (CCCVB) 410 E Main St PO Box 100	Batavia	OH	45103	**800-796-4282**	513-732-3600
Baton Rouge Convention & Visitors Bureau 359 Third St	Baton Rouge	LA	70801	**800-527-6843**	225-383-1825
Battle Creek/Calhoun County Convention & Visitors Bureau 77 E Michigan Ave Ste 100	Battle Creek	MI	49017	**800-397-2240**	269-962-2240
Beaumont Convention & Visitors Bureau 505 Willow St	Beaumont	TX	77701	**800-392-4401**	409-880-3749
Greene County Convention & Visitors Bureau 1221 Meadowbridge Dr	Beavercreek	OH	45434	**800-733-9109**	937-429-9100
Washington County Visitors Assn 12725 SW Millikan Way Ste 210	Beaverton	OR	97005	**800-537-3149**	503-644-5555
Southern West Virginia Convention & Visitors Bureau 1406 Harper Rd	Beckley	WV	25801	**800-847-4898**	304-252-2244
Bedford County Visitors Bureau 131 S Juliana St	Bedford	PA	15522	**800-765-3331**	814-623-1771
Gaston County Travel & Tourism 620 N Main St	Belmont	NC	28012	**800-849-9994**	704-825-4044
Beloit Convention & Visitors Bureau 500 Public Ave	Beloit	WI	53511	**800-423-5648**	608-365-4838
Bucks County Conference & Visitors Bureau (BCCVB) 3207 St Rd	Bensalem	PA	19020	**800-836-2825**	215-639-0300
Big Spring Convention & Visitor Bureau 215 W Third St PO Box 3359	Big Spring	TX	79720	**866-222-7100**	432-264-6032
Billings Convention & Visitors Bureau 815 S 27th St PO Box 31177	Billings	MT	59107	**800-735-2635**	406-245-4111
Mississippi Gulf Coast Convention & Visitors Bureau 2350 Beach Blvd Ste A	Biloxi	MS	39531	**888-467-4853**	228-896-6699
Greater Birmingham Convention & Visitors Bureau 2200 Ninth Ave N	Birmingham	AL	35203	**800-458-8085**	205-458-8000
Bismarck-Mandan Convention & Visitors Bureau 1600 Burnt Boat Dr	Bismarck	ND	58503	**800-767-3555**	701-222-4308
Bloomington Convention & Visitors Bureau (BCVB) 7900 International Dr Ste 990	Bloomington	MN	55425	**800-346-4289**	952-858-8500
Bloomington-Normal Area Convention & Visitors Bureau 3201 CIRA Dr Ste 201	Bloomington	IL	61704	**800-433-8226**	309-665-0033
Bloomington/Monroe County Convention & Visitors Bureau 2855 N Walnut St	Bloomington	IN	47404	**800-800-0037**	812-334-8900
Columbia-Montour Visitors Bureau 121 Papermill Rd	Bloomsburg	PA	17815	**800-847-4810**	570-784-8279
Mercer County Convention & Visitors Bureau 621 Commerce St	Bluefield	WV	24701	**800-221-3206**	304-325-8438
Boise Convention & Visitors Bureau 250 S Fifth St Ste 300	Boise	ID	83702	**800-635-5240**	208-344-7777
North Carolina High Country Host 1700 Blowing Rock Rd	Boone	NC	28607	**800-438-7500**	828-264-1299
Greater Boston Convention & Visitors Bureau (GBCVB) 2 Copley Pl Ste 105	Boston	MA	02116	**888-733-2678**	617-536-4100
Boulder Convention & Visitors Bureau 2440 Pearl St	Boulder	CO	80302	**800-444-0447**	303-442-2911
Brenham/Washington County Convention & Visitor Bureau 314 S Austin St	Brenham	TX	77833	**888-273-6426**	979-836-3695
Greater Bridgeport Conference & Vistors Ctr 164 W Main St	Bridgeport	WV	26330	**800-368-4324**	304-842-7272
Minneapolis Northwest 6200 Shingle Creek Pkwy Ste 130	Brooklyn Center	MN	55430	**800-541-4364**	763-852-7500
Northwest Pennsylvania's Great Outdoors Visitors Bureau 2801 Maplevale Rd	Brookville	PA	15825	**800-348-9393**	814-849-5197
Brownsville Convention & Visitors Bureau 650 Ruben M Torres Sr Blvd	Brownsville	TX	78521	**800-626-2639**	956-546-3721
Brunswick & The Golden Isles of Georgia Visitors Bureau 4 Glynn Ave	Brunswick	GA	31520	**800-933-2627**	912-265-0620
Buena Park Convention & Visitors Office 6601 Beach Blvd	Buena Park	CA	90621	**800-541-3953**	
Buffalo Niagara Convention & Visitors Bureau 403 Main St Ste 630	Buffalo	NY	14203	**800-283-3256**	716-852-2356
San Mateo County Convention & Visitors Bureau 111 Anza Blvd Ste 410	Burlingame	CA	94010	**800-288-4748**	650-348-7600
Burlington/Alamance County Convention & Visitors Bureau 200 S Main St PO Box 519	Burlington	NC	27216	**800-637-3804**	336-570-1444
Vermont Convention Bureau 60 Main St Ste 100	Burlington	VT	05401	**877-264-3503**	802-860-0606
Cadillac Area Visitors Bureau 201 N Mitchell St	Cadillac	MI	49601	**800-225-2537**	231-775-0657
Tourism Calgary 200 238 11th Ave SE	Calgary	AB	T2G0X8	**800-661-1678**	403-263-8510
Finger Lakes Visitors Connection 25 Gorham St	Canandaigua	NY	14424	**877-386-4669**	585-394-3915
Canton/Stark County Convention & Visitors Bureau 222 Market Ave N	Canton	OH	44702	**800-552-6051**	330-454-1439

Name / Address	City	State	ZIP	Toll-Free	Phone
Cape Girardeau Convention & Visitors Bureau 400 Broadway Ste 100	Cape Girardeau	MO	63701	**800-777-0068**	573-335-1631
Carlsbad Convention & Visitors Bureau 400 Carlsbad Village Dr	Carlsbad	CA	92008	**800-227-5722**	760-434-6093
Hamilton County Convention & Visitors Bureau Inc 37 E Main St	Carmel	IN	46032	**800-776-8687**	317-848-3181
Carrington Convention & Visitors Bureau City Hall 103 10th Ave N PO Box 501	Carrington	ND	58421	**800-641-9668**	701-652-2524
Casper Area Convention & Visitors Bureau 992 N Poplar St	Casper	WY	82601	**800-852-1889**	307-234-5362
Cedar City-Brian Head Tourism & Convention Bureau 581 N Main St	Cedar City	UT	84721	**800-354-4849**	435-586-5124
Cedar Rapids Area Convention & Visitors Bureau 87 16th Ave Ste 200	Cedar Rapids	IA	52404	**800-735-5557**	319-398-5009
Champaign County Convention & Visitors Bureau 108 S Neil St	Champaign	IL	61820	**800-369-6151**	217-351-4133
Chapel Hill/Orange County Visitors Bureau 501 W Franklin St	Chapel Hill	NC	27516	**888-968-2060**	
Charleston Area Convention & Visitors Bureau 423 King St	Charleston	SC	29403	**800-868-8118**	843-853-8000
Charlotte Convention & Visitors Bureau 500 S College St Ste 300	Charlotte	NC	28202	**800-722-1994**	704-334-2282
Chattanooga Area Convention & Visitors Bureau 215 Broad St	Chattanooga	TN	37402	**800-322-3344**	423-756-8687
Chautauqua County Visitors Bureau Chautauqua Main Gate Rt 394 PO Box 1441	Chautauqua	NY	14722	**800-242-4569**	716-357-4569
Cherokee Tribal Travel & Promotions 498 Tsali Blvd	Cherokee	NC	28719	**877-440-9990**	828-359-6492
Chesapeake Conventions & Tourism Bureau (CCT) 860 Greenbrier Cir Ste 101	Chesapeake	VA	23320	**888-889-5551**	757-502-4898
Cheyenne Area Convention & Visitors Bureau 121 W 15th St Ste 202	Cheyenne	WY	82001	**800-426-5009**	307-778-3133
Chicago Office of Tourism & Culture 78 E Washington St 4th Fl	Chicago	IL	60602	**888-871-5311**	312-744-2400
Greater Cincinnati Convention & Visitors Bureau 525 Vine St Ste 1500	Cincinnati	OH	45202	**800-543-2613**	513-621-2142
Pickaway County Visitors Bureau 325 W Main St	Circleville	OH	43113	**800-283-4678**	740-474-3636
Clarksville/Montgomery County Tourist Commission 25 Jefferson St Ste 300	Clarksville	TN	37040	**800-530-2487**	931-647-2331
Clear Lake Convention & Visitors Bureau 205 Main Ave PO Box 188	Clear Lake	IA	50428	**800-285-5338**	641-357-2159
Visit St Petersburg Clearwater 13805 58th St N Ste 2-200	Clearwater	FL	33760	**877-352-3224**	727-464-7200
Brevard County Tourism Development 430 Brevard Ave Ste 150	Cocoa Village	FL	32922	**877-572-3224**	321-433-4470
Park County Travel Council (PCTC) 836 Sheridan Ave PO Box 2454	Cody	WY	82414	**800-393-2639**	307-587-2297
Colby Convention & Visitors Bureau 350 S Range Ste 10	Colby	KS	67701	**800-611-8835**	785-460-7643
Bryan/College Station Convention & Visitors Bureau (BCSCVB) 715 University Dr E	College Station	TX	77840	**800-777-8292**	979-260-9898
Colorado Springs Convention & Visitors Bureau 515 S Cascade Ave	Colorado Springs	CO	80903	**800-888-4748**	719-635-7506
Columbia Convention & Visitors Bureau 300 S Providence Rd	Columbia	MO	65203	**800-652-0987**	573-875-1231
Columbia Metropolitan Convention & Visitors Bureau 1101 Lincoln St PO Box 15	Columbia	SC	29202	**800-264-4884**	803-545-0000
Columbus Area Visitors Ctr 506 Fifth St	Columbus	IN	47201	**800-468-6564**	812-378-2622
Columbus Convention & Visitors Bureau PO Box 789	Columbus	MS	39703	**800-327-2686**	662-329-1191
Greater Columbus Convention & Visitors Bureau 277 W Nationwide Blvd Ste 125	Columbus	OH	43215	**866-397-2657**	614-221-6623
Polk County Travel & Tourism 20 E Mills St PO Box 308	Columbus	NC	28722	**800-440-7848**	828-894-2324
New Hampshire Div of Travel & Tourism Development 172 Pembroke Rd PO Box 1856	Concord	NH	03302	**800-262-6660**	603-271-2665
Coos Bay-North Bend Visitor & Convention Bureau 50 Central Ave	Coos Bay	OR	97420	**800-824-8486**	541-269-0215
Iowa City/Coralville Area Convention & Visitors Bureau 900 First Ave Hayden Fry Way	Coralville	IA	52241	**800-283-6592**	319-337-6592
Corinth Area Convention & Visitors Bureau 215 N Fillmore St	Corinth	MS	38834	**800-748-9048**	662-287-8300
Corpus Christi Convention & Visitors Bureau 101 N Shoreline Blvd Ste 430	Corpus Christi	TX	78401	**800-678-6232**	361-881-1888
Corvallis Tourism 420 NW Second St	Corvallis	OR	97330	**800-334-8118**	541-757-1544
Northern Kentucky Convention & Visitors Bureau (NKYCVB) 50 E RiverCenter Blvd Ste 200	Covington	KY	41011	**877-659-8474**	859-261-4677
Montgomery County Visitors & Convention Bureau 218 E Pike St	Crawfordsville	IN	47933	**800-866-3973**	765-362-5200
Crescent City-Del Norte County Chamber of Commerce (CCDNCVB) 1001 Front St	Crescent City	CA	95531	**800-343-8300**	707-464-3174
Dallas Convention & Visitors Bureau 325 N St Paul St Ste 700	Dallas	TX	75201	**800-232-5527**	214-571-1000
Central Florida Visitors & Convention Bureau 101 Adventure Ct	Davenport	FL	33837	**800-828-7655**	863-420-2586
Tucker County Convention & Visitors Bureau 410 William Ave	Davis	WV	26260	**800-782-2775**	304-259-5315
Dayton/Montgomery County Convention & Visitors Bureau 1 Chamber Plz Ste A	Dayton	OH	45402	**800-221-8235**	937-226-8211
Decatur Area Convention & Visitors Bureau 202 E N St	Decatur	IL	62523	**800-331-4479**	217-423-7000
Decatur/Morgan County Convention & Visitors Bureau (DMCCVB) 719 Sixth Ave SE PO Box 2349	Decatur	AL	35602	**800-232-5449**	256-350-2028
Wicomico County Convention & Visitors Bureau 8480 Ocean Hwy	Delmar	MD	21875	**800-332-8687**	410-548-4914
Denver Metro Convention & Visitors Bureau 1555 California St Ste 300	Denver	CO	80202	**800-480-2010**	303-892-1112
Greater Des Moines Convention & Visitors Bureau 400 Locust St Ste 265	Des Moines	IA	50309	**800-451-2625**	515-286-4960
Detroit Metropolitan Convention & Visitors Bureau 211 W Fort St Ste 1000	Detroit	MI	48226	**877-424-5554**	313-202-1800
Dickinson Convention & Visitors Bureau 72 E Museum Dr	Dickinson	ND	58601	**800-279-7391**	701-483-4988
Dothan Area Convention & Visitors Bureau 3311 Ross Clark Cir	Dothan	AL	36301	**888-449-0212**	334-794-6622
Kent County & Greater Dover Delaware Convention & Visitors Bureau 435 N DuPont Hwy	Dover	DE	19901	**800-233-5368**	302-734-1736
DuQuoin Tourism Commission 20 N Chestnut St PO Box 1037	Du Quoin	IL	62832	**800-455-9570**	618-542-8338
Dublin Convention & Visitors Bureau 9 S High St	Dublin	OH	43017	**800-245-8387**	614-792-7666
Duluth Convention & Visitors Bureau 21 W Superior St Ste 100	Duluth	MN	55802	**800-438-5884**	218-722-4011
Durango Area Tourism Office 111 S Camino del Rio	Durango	CO	81301	**800-525-8855**	970-247-3500
Durham Convention & Visitors Bureau 101 E Morgan St	Durham	NC	27701	**800-446-8604**	919-687-0288
Eagan Convention & Visitors Bureau 1501 Central Pkwy	Eagan	MN	55121	**866-324-2620**	651-675-5546
Visit Eau Claire 4319 Jeffers Rd	Eau Claire	WI	54703	**888-523-3866**	715-831-2345
Effingham Convention & Visitors Bureau 201 E Jefferson Ave	Effingham	IL	62401	**800-772-0750**	217-342-5305
Elgin Area Convention & Visitors Bureau 60 S Grove Ave	Elgin	IL	60120	**800-217-5362**	847-695-7540
Elkhart County Convention & Visitors Bureau 219 Caravan Dr	Elkhart	IN	46514	**800-262-8161**	574-262-8161
Howard County Tourism Council 8267 Main St Side Entrance	Ellicott City	MD	21043	**866-313-6300**	410-313-1900
Grays Harbor Tourism PO Box 1229	Elma	WA	98541	**800-621-9625**	360-482-2651
VisitErie 208 E Bayfront Pkwy Ste 103	Erie	PA	16507	**800-524-3743**	814-454-1000
Eugene Cascades Coast 754 Olive St	Eugene	OR	97440	**800-547-5445**	541-484-5307
Humboldt County Convention & Visitors Bureau 1034 Second St	Eureka	CA	95501	**800-346-3482**	707-443-5097
Evansville Convention & Visitors Bureau 401 SE Riverside Dr	Evansville	IN	47713	**800-433-3025**	812-421-2200
Fairbanks Convention & Visitors Bureau 101 Dunkel St Ste 111	Fairbanks	AK	99701	**800-327-5774**	907-456-5774
Fairfax County Convention & Visitors Bureau (FXVA) 3702 Pender Dr Ste 420	Fairfax	VA	22030	**800-732-4732**	703-790-0643
Convention & Visitors Bureau of Marion County 1000 Cole St Ste A	Fairmont	WV	26554	**800-834-7365**	304-368-1123
Fairmont Convention & Visitors Bureau 323 E Blue Earth Ave	Fairmont	MN	56031	**800-657-3280**	507-235-8585
Fargo-Moorhead Convention & Visitors Bureau 2001 44th St S	Fargo	ND	58103	**800-235-7654**	701-282-3653
Farmington Convention & Visitors Bureau 3041 E Main St	Farmington	NM	87402	**800-448-1240**	505-326-7602
Fayetteville Area Convention & Visitors Bureau (FACVB) 245 Person St	Fayetteville	NC	28301	**800-255-8217**	910-483-5311
Flagstaff Convention & Visitors Bureau 323 W Aspen Ave	Flagstaff	AZ	86001	**800-217-2367**	928-779-7611
Florence Convention & Visitors Bureau 3290 W Radio Dr *General	Florence	SC	29501	**800-325-9005***	843-664-0330
Fond du Lac Convention & Visitors Bureau 171 S Pioneer Rd	Fond du Lac	WI	54935	**800-937-9123**	920-923-3010
Fort Collins Convention & Visitors Bureau 19 Old Town Sq Ste 137	Fort Collins	CO	80524	**800-274-3678**	970-232-3840
Greater Fort Lauderdale Convention & Visitors Bureau 100 E Broward Blvd Ste 200	Fort Lauderdale	FL	33301	**877-272-5465**	954-765-4466
Fort Madison 614 Ninth St	Fort Madison	IA	52627	**800-210-8687**	319-372-5471
Lee County Visitors & Convention Bureau 2201 Second St Ste 600	Fort Myers	FL	33901	**800-237-6444**	239-338-3500
Fort Smith Convention & Visitors Bureau 2 N 'B'	Fort Smith	AR	72901	**800-637-1477**	479-783-8888
Fort Wayne/Allen County Convention & Visitors Bureau 927 S Harrison St	Fort Wayne	IN	46802	**800-767-7752**	260-424-3700
Fort Worth Convention & Visitors Bureau 111 W Fourth St Ste 200	Fort Worth	TX	76102	**800-433-5747**	817-336-8791
Frankenmuth Convention & Visitors Bureau 635 S Main St	Frankenmuth	MI	48734	**800-386-8696**	989-652-6106
Frankfort/Franklin County Tourist & Convention Commission 100 Capitol Ave	Frankfort	KY	40601	**800-960-7200**	502-875-8687
Tourism Council of Frederick County Inc 151 S East St	Frederick	MD	21701	**800-999-3613**	301-600-2888
Fredericksburg Chamber of Commerce 302 E Austin St	Fredericksburg	TX	78624	**888-997-3600**	830-997-6523
Fremont/Sandusky County Convention & Visitors Bureau 712 N St Ste 102	Fremont	OH	43420	**800-255-8070**	419-332-4470
Fresno & Clovis Convention & Visitors Bureau 1550 E Shaw Ave Ste 101	Fresno	CA	93710	**800-788-0836**	559-981-5500
Alachua County Visitors & Convention Bureau 30 E University Ave	Gainesville	FL	32601	**866-778-5002**	352-374-5260
Galena/Jo Daviess County Convention & Visitors Bureau (GJDCCVB) 101 Bouthillier St *General	Galena	IL	61036	**800-747-9377***	815-777-3557
Galesburg Area Convention & Visitors Bureau 2163 E Main St	Galesburg	IL	61401	**800-916-3330**	309-343-2485
Finney County Convention & Visitors Bureau 1511 E Fulton Terr	Garden City	KS	67846	**866-267-4638**	620-275-1900
Georgetown Convention & Visitors Bureau 1101 N College St	Georgetown	TX	78626	**800-436-8696**	512-930-3545
Gettysburg Convention & Visitors Bureau 571 W Middle St	Gettysburg	PA	17325	**800-337-5015**	717-334-6274
Greater Grand Forks Convention & Visitors Bureau 4251 Gateway Dr	Grand Forks	ND	58203	**800-866-4566**	701-746-0444
Grand Junction Visitors & Convention Bureau 740 Horizon Dr	Grand Junction	CO	81506	**800-962-2547**	970-244-1480
Grand Rapids/Kent County Convention & Visitors Bureau 171 Monroe Ave NW Ste 700	Grand Rapids	MI	49503	**800-678-9859**	616-459-8287
Grants Pass Visitors & Convention Bureau 1995 NW Vine St	Grants Pass	OR	97526	**800-547-5927**	541-476-7574
Houma Area Convention & Visitors Bureau 114 Tourist Dr	Gray	LA	70359	**800-688-2732**	985-868-2732
Greeley Convention & Visitors Bureau 902 Seventh Ave	Greeley	CO	80631	**800-449-3866**	970-352-3567

Organization	Address	City	State	ZIP	Toll-Free	Phone
Packer Country Visitor & Convention Bureau	1901 S Oneida St	Green Bay	WI	54304	**888-867-3342**	920-494-9507
Greensboro Area Convention & Visitors Bureau	2200 Pinecroft Rd Ste 200	Greensboro	NC	27407	**800-344-2282**	336-274-2282
Greater Greenville Convention & Visitors Bureau	148 River St Ste 222	Greenville	SC	29601	**800-351-7180**	864-421-0000
Greenville-Pitt County Convention & Visitors Bureau (GPCCVB)	417 Cotanche St Ste 100	Greenville	NC	27858	**800-537-5564**	252-329-4200
Greenwood Convention & Visitors Bureau	111 E Market St	Greenwood	MS	38930	**800-748-9064**	662-453-9197
Alabama Gulf Coast Convention & Visitors Bureau	3150 Gulf Shores Pkwy PO Box 457	Gulf Shores	AL	36547	**800-745-7263**	251-968-7511
Lake County Convention & Visitors Bureau	5465 W Grand Ave Ste 100	Gurnee	IL	60031	**800-525-3669**	847-662-2700
Hagerstown/Washington County Convention & Visitors Bureau	16 Public Sq	Hagerstown	MD	21740	**888-257-2600**	301-791-3246
Hampton Conventions & Visitors Bureau	1919 Commerce Dr Ste 290	Hampton	VA	23666	**800-487-8778**	757-722-1222
Hannibal Convention & Visitors Bureau	505 N Third St	Hannibal	MO	63401	**866-263-4825**	573-221-2477
Jefferson County Convention & Visitors Bureau	37 Washington Ct	Harpers Ferry	WV	25425	**866-435-5698**	304-535-2627
Hershey Harrisburg Region Visitors Bureau	3211 N Front St Ste 301-A	Harrisburg	PA	17110	**877-727-8573**	717-231-7788
Positively Cleveland Visitors Ctr	2207 Forest Hills Rd Ste 100	Harrisburg	PA	17112	**800-321-1001**	216-875-6680
Long Island Convention & Visitors Bureau & Sports Commission	330 Motor Pkwy Ste 203	Hauppauge	NY	11788	**877-386-6654**	
Hays Convention & Visitors Bureau	2700 Vine St PO Box 490	Hays	KS	67601	**800-569-4505**	785-628-8202
Alpine Helen/White County Convention & Visitors Bureau	726 Bruckenstrasse PO Box 730	Helen	GA	30545	**800-858-8027**	706-878-2181
Henderson County Tourist Commission	101 N Water St Ste B	Henderson	KY	42420	**800-648-3128**	270-826-3128
Henderson County Travel & Tourism	201 S Main St	Hendersonville	NC	28792	**800-828-4244**	828-693-9708
Huntingdon County Visitors Bureau	6993 Seven Pt Rd Ste 2	Hesston	PA	16647	**888-729-7869**	814-658-0060
Hickory Metro Convention & Visitors Bureau	1960 13th Ave Dr SE	Hickory	NC	28602	**800-509-2444**	828-322-1335
High Point Convention & Visitors Bureau	300 S Main St	High Point	NC	27260	**800-720-5255**	336-884-5255
Hilton Head Island Visitors & Convention Bureau	1 Chamber Dr PO Box 5647	Hilton Head Island	SC	29938	**800-523-3373**	843-785-3673
Holland Area Convention & Visitors Bureau	76 E Eigth St	Holland	MI	49423	**800-506-1299**	616-394-0000
Hawaii Visitors & Convention Bureau	2270 Kalakaua Ave Ste 801	Honolulu	HI	96815	**800-464-2924**	
Hot Springs Convention & Visitors Bureau	134 Convention Blvd	Hot Springs	AR	71901	**800-543-2284**	501-321-2277
Greater Houston Convention & Visitors Bureau	901 Bagby St Ste 100	Houston	TX	77002	**800-446-8786**	713-437-5200
Cabell-Huntington Convention & Visitors Bureau	PO Box 347	Huntington	WV	25708	**800-635-6329**	304-525-7333
Huntington County Visitors & Convention Bureau	407 N Jefferson St	Huntington	IN	46750	**800-848-4282**	260-359-8687
Huntington Beach Marketing & Visitors Bureau	301 Main St Ste 208	Huntington Beach	CA	92648	**800-729-6232**	714-969-3492
Huntsville/Madison County Convention & Visitor's Bureau	500 Church St Ste 1	Huntsville	AL	35801	**800-843-0468**	256-551-2230
Huron Chamber & Visitors Bureau	1725 Dakota Ave S	Huron	SD	57350	**800-487-6673**	605-352-0000
Greater Hutchinson Convention & Visitors Bureau	117 N Walnut St PO Box 519	Hutchinson	KS	67504	**800-691-4262**	620-662-3391
Incline Village/Crystal Bay Visitors Bureau	969 Tahoe Blvd	Incline Village	NV	89451	**800-468-2463**	775-832-1606
Indiana County Tourist Bureau	2334 Oakland Ave Ste 68	Indiana	PA	15701	**877-746-3426**	724-463-7505
Indianapolis Convention & Visitors Assn	200 S Capitol Ave Ste 300	Indianapolis	IN	46225	**800-862-6912**	317-262-3000
Western Upper Peninsula Convention & Visitor Bureau	405 N Lake St PO Box 706	Ironwood	MI	49938	**800-522-5657**	906-932-4850
Irving Convention & Visitors Bureau	500 W Las Colinas Blvd	Irving	TX	75039	**800-247-8464**	972-252-7476
Ithaca/Tompkins County Convention & Visitors Bureau	904 E Shore Dr	Ithaca	NY	14850	**800-284-8422**	607-272-1313
Jackson County Convention & Visitors Bureau	141 S Jackson St	Jackson	MI	49201	**800-245-5282**	517-764-4440
Metro Jackson Convention & Visitors Bureau	111 E Capitol St Ste 102	Jackson	MS	39202	**800-354-7695**	601-960-1891
Jacksonville Convention & Visitors Bureau	310 E State St	Jacksonville	IL	62650	**800-593-5678**	217-243-5678
Onslow County Tourism	1099 Gum Branch Rd	Jacksonville	NC	28540	**800-932-2144**	
Visit Jacksonville	208 N Laura St Ste 1	Jacksonville	FL	32202	**800-733-2668**	904-798-9111
Jamestown Promotions & Tourism Ctr	404 Louis L'Amour Ln	Jamestown	ND	58401	**800-222-4766**	701-251-9145
Jefferson City Convention & Visitors Bureau	700 E Capitol Ave	Jefferson City	MO	65101	**800-769-4183**	573-632-2820
Clark-Floyd Counties Convention & Tourism Bureau	315 Southern Indiana Ave	Jeffersonville	IN	47130	**800-552-3842**	812-282-6654
Greater Johnstown/Cambria County Convention & Visitors Bureau	111 Roosevelt Blvd Ste A	Johnstown	PA	15906	**800-237-8590**	814-536-7993
Heritage Corridor Convention & Visitors Bureau	339 W Jefferson St	Joliet	IL	60435	**800-926-2262**	815-727-2323
Juneau Convention & Visitors Bureau	101 Egan Dr	Juneau	AK	99801	**888-581-2201**	907-586-1737
Kalamazoo County Convention & Visitors Bureau	141 E Michigan Ave Ste 100	Kalamazoo	MI	49007	**800-888-0509**	269-488-9000
Flathead Convention & Visitors Bureau	15 Depot Pk	Kalispell	MT	59901	**800-543-3105**	406-756-9091
Cabarrus County Convention & Visitors Bureau	3003 Dale Earnhardt Blvd	Kannapolis	NC	28083	**800-848-3740**	704-782-4340
Kansas City Convention & Visitors Assn	1100 Main St Ste 2200	Kansas City	MO	64105	**800-767-7700**	816-221-5242
Kansas City Kansas Convention & Visitors Bureau Inc	901 N Eigth St PO Box 171517	Kansas City	KS	66117	**800-264-1563**	913-321-5800
Tri-Cities Visitor & Convention Bureau	7130 W Grandridge Blvd Ste B	Kennewick	WA	99336	**800-254-5824**	509-735-8486
Kenosha Area Convention & Visitors Bureau	812 56th St	Kenosha	WI	53140	**800-654-7309**	262-654-7307
Kerrville Convention & Visitors Bureau	2108 Sidney Baker St	Kerrville	TX	78028	**800-221-7958**	830-792-3535
Ketchikan Visitors Bureau	131 Front St	Ketchikan	AK	99901	**800-770-3300**	907-225-6166
Key West Visitors Ctr	510 Greene St 1st Fl *General	Key West	FL	33040	**800-533-5397***	305-294-2587
Monroe County Tourist Development Council	1201 White St Ste 102	Key West	FL	33040	**800-242-5229**	305-296-1552
Valley Forge Convention & Visitors Bureau	1000 First Ave Ste 101 *General	King of Prussia	PA	19406	**888-847-4883***	610-834-1550
Kingsport Convention & Visitors Bureau (KCVB)	400 Clinchfield St Ste 100	Kingsport	TN	37660	**800-743-5282**	423-392-8820
Armstrong County Tourist Bureau	125 Market St Ste 2	Kittanning	PA	16201	**888-265-9954**	724-543-4003
Discover Klamath	205 Riverside Dr Ste B	Klamath Falls	OR	97601	**800-445-6728**	541-882-1501
Knoxville Tourism & Sports Corp	301 S Gay St	Knoxville	TN	37902	**800-727-8045**	865-523-7263
Lake Barkley Tourist Commission	82 Days Inn Dr	Kuttawa	KY	42055	**800-355-3885**	270-388-5300
La Crosse Area Convention & Visitors Bureau	410 Veterans Memorial Dr	La Crosse	WI	54601	**800-658-9424**	608-782-2366
Lafayette Convention & Visitors Commission	1400 NW Evangeline Thwy	Lafayette	LA	70501	**800-346-1958**	337-232-3737
Lafayette-West Lafayette Convention & Visitors Bureau	301 Frontage Rd	Lafayette	IN	47905	**800-872-6648**	765-447-9999
Laguna Beach Visitors & Conference Bureau	381 Forest Ave	Laguna Beach	CA	92651	**800-877-1115**	949-497-9229
Southwest Louisiana Convention & Visitors Bureau	1205 N Lakeshore Dr	Lake Charles	LA	70601	**800-456-7952**	337-436-9588
Seminole County Convention & Visitors Bureau	1515 International Pkwy Ste 1013	Lake Mary	FL	32746	**800-800-7832**	407-665-2900
Lake Placid Convention & Visitors Bureau	2608 Main St	Lake Placid	NY	12946	**800-447-5224**	518-523-2445
Chicago Southland Convention & Visitors Bureau	2304 173rd St	Lansing	IL	60438	**888-895-8233**	708-895-8200
Greater Lansing Convention & Visitors Bureau	500 E Michigan Ave Ste 180	Lansing	MI	48912	**888-252-6746**	517-487-0077
Las Cruces Convention & Visitors Bureau	211 N Water St	Las Cruces	NM	88001	**800-429-9488**	575-541-2444
Las Vegas Convention & Visitors Authority	3150 Paradise Rd	Las Vegas	NV	89109	**877-847-4858**	702-892-0711
Greenbrier County Convention & Visitors Bureau	200 W Washington St	Lewisburg	WV	24901	**800-833-2068**	304-645-1000
Lexington Convention & Visitors Bureau	301 E Vine St	Lexington	KY	40507	**800-845-3959**	859-233-7299
Laurel Highlands Visitors Bureau	120 E Main St	Ligonier	PA	15658	**800-333-5661**	724-238-5661
Lima/Allen County Convention & Visitors Bureau	144 S Main St Ste 101	Lima	OH	45801	**888-222-6075**	419-222-6075
Lincoln Convention & Visitors Bureau	1135 M St Ste 300	Lincoln	NE	68508	**800-423-8212**	402-434-5335
Lincoln City Visitor & Convention Bureau	801 SW Hwy 101 Ste 401	Lincoln City	OR	97367	**800-452-2151**	541-996-1274
Lisle Convention & Visitors Bureau	925 Burlington Ave	Lisle	IL	60532	**800-733-9811**	630-769-1000
Little Rock Convention & Visitors Bureau	426 W Markham St PO Box 3232	Little Rock	AR	72203	**800-844-4781**	501-376-4781
Lodi Conference & Visitors Bureau	115 S School St	Lodi	CA	95240	**800-798-1810**	209-365-1195
London/Laurel County Tourist Commission	140 Faith Assembly Church Rd	London	KY	40741	**800-348-0095**	606-878-6900
Long Beach Convention & Visitors Bureau	301 E Ocean Blvd	Long Beach	CA	90802	**800-452-7829**	562-436-3645
Louisville & Jefferson County Convention & Visitors Bureau	401 W Main St Ste 2300	Louisville	KY	40202	**800-626-5646**	502-584-2121
Greater Merrimack Valley Convention & Visitors Bureau	40 French St 2nd Fl	Lowell	MA	01852	**800-443-3332**	978-459-6150
Lubbock Convention & Visitors Bureau	1500 Broadway St 6th Fl	Lubbock	TX	79401	**800-692-4035**	806-747-5232
Lumberton Area Visitors Bureau	3431 Lackey St	Lumberton	NC	28360	**800-359-6971**	910-739-9999
Mackinaw Area Visitors Bureau	10800 US 23	Mackinaw City	MI	49701	**800-666-0160**	231-436-5664
Macon-Bibb County Convention/Visitors Bureau	450 Martin Luther King Jr Blvd	Macon	GA	31201	**800-768-3401**	478-743-1074
Greater Madison Convention & Visitors Bureau	615 E Washington Ave	Madison	WI	53703	**800-373-6376**	608-255-2537
Saint Tammany Parish Tourist & Convention Commission	68099 Hwy 59	Mandeville	LA	70471	**800-634-9443**	985-892-0520
Manhattan Convention & Visitors Bureau	501 Poyntz Ave	Manhattan	KS	66502	**800-759-0134**	785-776-8829
Manitowoc Area Visitor & Convention Bureau	4221 Calumet Ave	Manitowoc	WI	54221	**800-627-4896**	
Greater Mankato Growth	1961 Premier Dr	Mankato	MN	56001	**800-697-0652**	507-385-6640
Mansfield/Richland County Convention & Visitors Bureau	124 N Main St	Mansfield	OH	44902	**800-642-8282**	419-525-1300
Outer Banks Visitors Bureau	1 Visitor Ctr Cir	Manteo	NC	27954	**877-629-4386**	252-473-2138
Marion-Grant County Convention & Visitors Bureau	428 S Washington St Ste 261	Marion	IN	46953	**800-662-9474**	765-668-5435
Williamson County Tourism Bureau	1602 Sioux Dr *General	Marion	IL	62959	**800-433-7399***	618-997-3690
Marquette Country Convention & Visitors Bureau	337 W Washington St	Marquette	MI	49855	**800-544-4321**	906-228-7749
Marshfield Convention & Visitors Bureau	700 S Central Ave PO Box 868	Marshfield	WI	54449	**800-422-4541**	715-384-3454
Mason City Convention & Visitors Bureau	2021 Fourth St SW Hwy 122 W	Mason City	IA	50401	**800-423-5724**	641-422-1663

Name	Address	City	State	ZIP	Toll-Free	Phone
Memphis Convention & Visitors Bureau	47 Union Ave	Memphis	TN	38103	**888-633-9099**	901-543-5300
Merced Conference & Visitors Bureau (MCVB)	710 W 16th St	Merced	CA	95340	**800-446-5353**	209-384-2791
Meridian/Lauderdale County Tourism Bureau	212 Constitution Ave	Meridian	MS	39301	**888-868-7720**	601-482-8001
Greater Miami Convention & Visitors Bureau	701 Brickell Ave Ste 2700	Miami	FL	33131	**800-933-8448**	305-539-3000
LaPorte County Convention & Visitors Bureau	4073 S Franklin St	Michigan City	IN	46360	**800-634-2650**	219-872-5055
Midland County Convention & Visitors Bureau	300 Rodd St Ste 101	Midland	MI	48640	**800-444-9979**	989-839-0340
Visit Milledgeville	200 W Hancock St	Milledgeville	GA	31061	**800-653-1804**	478-452-4687
Greater Milwaukee Convention & Visitors Bureau	648 N Plankinton Ave Ste 425	Milwaukee	WI	53203	**800-554-1448**	414-273-7222
Meet Minneapolis	250 Marquette Ave Ste 1300	Minneapolis	MN	55401	**800-445-7412**	612-767-8000
Minot Convention & Visitors Bureau	1020 S Broadway	Minot	ND	58701	**800-264-2626**	701-857-8206
Modesto Convention & Visitors Bureau	1150 Ninth St Ste C	Modesto	CA	95354	**888-640-8467**	209-526-5588
Quad Cities Convention & Visitors Bureau	1601 River Dr Ste 110	Moline	IL	61265	**800-747-7800**	309-277-0937
Monterey County Convention & Visitors Bureau	PO Box 1770	Monterey	CA	93942	**888-221-1010**	831-657-6400
Montgomery Area Chamber of Commerce Convention & Visitor Bureau	300 Water St	Montgomery	AL	36104	**800-240-9452**	334-261-1100
Montrose Visitor & Convention Bureau	107 S Cascade Ave	Montrose	CO	81401	**888-212-8294**	970-249-5000
Greater Morgantown Convention & Visitors Bureau	68 Donley St	Morgantown	WV	26501	**800-458-7373**	304-292-5081
Knox County Convention & Visitors Bureau	107 S Main St	Mount Vernon	OH	43050	**800-837-5282**	740-392-6102
Mount Vernon Convention & Visitors Bureau	1100 Main St	Mount Vernon	IL	62864	**800-252-5464**	618-242-3151
Muncie Visitors Bureau	3700 S Madison St	Muncie	IN	47302	**800-568-6862**	765-284-2700
Muskegon County Convention & Visitors Bureau	610 W Western Ave	Muskegon	MI	49440	**800-250-9283**	231-724-3100
Nacogdoches Convention & Visitors Bureau	200 E Main St	Nacogdoches	TX	75961	**888-653-3788**	936-564-7351
Napa Valley Conference & Visitors Bureau	600 Main St	Napa	CA	94559	**855-847-6272**	707-251-5895
Greater Naples Marco Island Everglades Convention & Visitors Bureau	2800 Horseshoe Dr	Naples	FL	34104	**800-688-3600**	239-252-2384
Brown County Convention & Visitors Bureau	10 N Van Buren St PO Box 840	Nashville	IN	47448	**800-753-3255**	812-988-7303
Nashville Convention & Visitors Bureau (NCVB)	150 Fourth Ave N Ste G250	Nashville	TN	37219	**800-657-6910**	615-259-4730
Natchez Convention & Visitors Bureau	640 S Canal St	Natchez	MS	39120	**800-647-6724**	601-446-6345
Craven County Convention & Visitors Bureau	203 S Front St	New Bern	NC	28560	**800-437-5767**	252-637-9400
Greater New Braunfels Chamber of Commerce Inc, The	390 S Seguin Ave PO Box 311417	New Braunfels	TX	78130	**800-572-2626**	830-625-2385
Lawrence County Tourist Promotion Agency	229 S Jefferson St	New Castle	PA	16101	**888-284-7599**	724-654-8408
New Orleans Metropolitan Convention & Visitors Bureau	2020 St Charles Ave	New Orleans	LA	70130	**800-672-6124**	504-566-5011
Newberry Area Tourism Assn, The	PO Box 308	Newberry	MI	49868	**800-831-7292**	906-293-5562
Newport Beach Conference & Visitors Bureau	1200 Newport Ctr Dr Ste 120	Newport Beach	CA	92660	**800-216-1598**	949-719-6100
Newport News Tourism Development Office	700 Town Ctr Dr Ste 320	Newport News	VA	23606	**888-493-7386**	757-926-1400
Newton Convention & Visitor Bureau	300 E 17th St S Ste 400	Newton	IA	50208	**800-798-0299**	641-792-0299
Niagara Tourism & Convention Corp	10 Rainbow Blvd	Niagara Falls	NY	14303	**877-325-5787**	716-282-8992
Norfolk Convention & Visitors Bureau	232 E Main St	Norfolk	VA	23510	**800-368-3097**	757-664-6620
Norman Convention & Visitors Bureau	309 E Main St	Norman	OK	73069	**800-767-7260**	405-366-8095
DuPage Convention & Visitors Bureau	915 Harger Rd Ste 240	Oak Brook	IL	60523	**800-232-0502**	630-575-8070
Oak Park Area Convention & Visitors Bureau	1118 Westgate	Oak Park	IL	60301	**888-625-7275**	708-524-7800
Ocean City Convention & Visitors Bureau	4001 Coastal Hwy	Ocean City	MD	21842	**800-626-2326**	410-289-8181
Oconomowoc Convention & Visitors Bureau	174 E Wisconsin Ave	Oconomowoc	WI	53066	**888-936-7463**	262-569-2186
Odessa Convention & Visitors Bureau	700 N Grant Ave Ste 200	Odessa	TX	79761	**800-780-4678**	432-333-7871
Ogden/Weber Convention & Visitors Bureau	2438 Washington Blvd	Ogden	UT	84401	**800-255-8824**	801-778-6250
Oklahoma City Convention & Visitors Bureau	123 Pk Ave	Oklahoma City	OK	73102	**800-225-5652**	405-297-8912
McDowell County Tourism Development Authority	91 S Catawba Ave	Old Fort	NC	28762	**888-233-6111**	828-668-4282
Olympia Lacey Tumwater Visitor & Convention Bureau	103 Sid Snyder Ave SW	Olympia	WA	98501	**877-704-7500**	360-704-7544
Greater Omaha Convention & Visitors Bureau	1001 Farnam St Ste 200	Omaha	NE	68102	**866-937-6624**	402-444-4660
Ontario Area Chamber of Commerce	251 SW 9th St	Ontario	OR	97914	**866-989-8012**	541-889-8012
Ontario Convention & Visitors Bureau	2000 E Convention Ctr Way	Ontario	CA	91764	**800-455-5755**	909-937-3000
Orlando/Orange County Convention & Visitors Bureau Inc	6700 Forum Dr Ste 100	Orlando	FL	32821	**800-972-3304**	407-363-5872
Lake of the Ozarks Convention & Visitors Bureau	5815 Hwy 54 PO Box 1498	Osage Beach	MO	65065	**800-386-5253**	573-348-1599
Ottawa Tourism & Convention Authority	150 Elgin St Ste 1405	Ottawa	ON	K2P1L4	**800-363-4465**	613-237-5150
Ottawa Visitors Ctr	106 W Lafayette St	Ottawa	IL	61350	**888-688-2924**	815-434-2737
Overland Park Convention & Visitors Bureau	9001 W 110th St Ste 100	Overland Park	KS	66210	**800-262-7275**	913-491-0123
Owensboro-Davies County Tourist Commission	215 E Second St	Owensboro	KY	42303	**800-489-1131**	270-926-1100
Oxford Convention & Visitors Bureau	102 Ed Perry Blvd	Oxford	MS	38655	**800-758-9177**	662-232-2367
Oxnard Convention & Visitors Bureau	1000 Town Ctr Dr Ste 130	Oxnard	CA	93036	**800-269-6273**	805-385-7545
Panama City Beach Convention & Visitors Bureau	17001 Panama City Beach Pkwy	Panama City Beach	FL	32413	**800-722-3224**	850-233-5070
Park City Chamber of Commerce/Convention & Visitors Bureau	1850 Sidewinder Dr Ste 320	Park City	UT	84060	**800-453-1360**	435-649-6100
Greater Parkersburg Convention & Visitors Bureau	350 Seventh St	Parkersburg	WV	26101	**800-752-4982**	304-428-1130
Pasadena Convention & Visitors Bureau	300 E Green St	Pasadena	CA	91101	**800-307-7977**	626-795-9311
Pensacola Convention & Visitors Bureau	1401 E Gregory St	Pensacola	FL	32502	**800-874-1234**	850-434-1234
Peoria Area Convention & Visitors Bureau	456 Fulton St Ste 300	Peoria	IL	61602	**800-747-0302**	309-676-0303
Petoskey Area Visitors Bureau	401 E Mitchell St	Petoskey	MI	49770	**800-845-2828**	231-348-2755
Greater Phoenix Convention & Visitors Bureau	400 E Van Buren St Ste 600	Phoenix	AZ	85004	**877-225-5749**	602-254-6500
Pigeon Forge Dept of Tourism	PO Box 1390	Pigeon Forge	TN	37868	**800-251-9100**	865-453-8574
Pine Bluff Convention & Visitors Bureau (PBCVB)	1 Convention Ctr Plz	Pine Bluff	AR	71601	**800-536-7660**	870-536-7600
Greater Pittsburgh Convention & Visitors Bureau	120 Fifth Ave 5th Ave Pl, 1st Level	Pittsburgh	PA	15222	**800-359-0758**	412-281-7711
Plano Convention & Visitors Bureau	2000 E Spring Creek Pkwy	Plano	TX	75074	**800-817-5266**	972-941-5840
Ponca City Tourism	420 E Grand Ave PO Box 1109	Ponca City	OK	74602	**866-763-8092**	580-765-4400
North Olympic Peninsula Visitor & Convention Bureau	338 W First St Ste 104 PO Box 670	Port Angeles	WA	98362	**800-942-4042**	360-452-8552
Port Arthur Convention & Visitors Bureau	3401 Cultural Ctr Dr	Port Arthur	TX	77642	**800-235-7822**	409-985-7822
Lake Erie Shores & Islands Welcome Ctr	770 SE Catawba Rd	Port Clinton	OH	43452	**800-441-1271**	419-734-4386
Indiana Dunes the Casual Coast	1215 N State Rd 49	Porter	IN	46304	**800-283-8687**	219-926-2255
Travel Portland	Pioneer Courthouse Square 701 S.W. Sixth Ave.	Portland	OR	97205	**877-678-5263**	503-275-9750
Providence Warwick Convention & Visitors Bureau	10 Memorial Blvd	Providence	RI	02903	**800-233-1636**	401-456-0200
Utah Valley Convention & Visitors Bureau	111 S University Ave	Provo	UT	84601	**800-222-8824**	801-851-2100
Plumas County Visitors Bureau	550 Crescent St	Quincy	CA	95971	**800-326-2247**	530-283-6345
Quincy Area Convention & Visitors Bureau (QACVB)	532 Gardner Expy	Quincy	IL	62301	**800-978-4748**	217-214-3700
Greater Raleigh Convention & Visitors Bureau	421 Fayetteville St Mall Ste 1505	Raleigh	NC	27602	**800-849-8499**	919-834-5900
Palm Springs Desert Resorts Convention & Visitors Authority	70-100 Hwy 111	Rancho Mirage	CA	92270	**800-967-3767**	760-770-9000
Rapid City Convention & Visitors Bureau	444 Mt Rushmore Rd N	Rapid City	SD	57701	**800-487-3223**	605-718-8484
Reading & Berks County Visitors Bureau	2525 N 12th St Ste 101	Reading	PA	19605	**800-443-6610**	610-375-4085
Rehoboth Beach Convention Ctr	229 Rehoboth Ave	Rehoboth Beach	DE	19971	**888-743-3628**	302-227-4641
Reno-Sparks Convention & Visitors Authority	PO Box 837	Reno	NV	89504	**800-443-1482**	775-827-7600
Richardson Convention & Visitors Bureau	411 W Arapaho Rd Ste 105	Richardson	TX	75080	**888-690-7287**	972-744-4034
Richmond Metropolitan Convention & Visitors Bureau	401 N Third St	Richmond	VA	23219	**800-370-9004**	804-782-2777
Richmond/Wayne County Convention & Tourism Bureau	5701 National Rd E	Richmond	IN	47374	**800-828-8414**	765-935-8687
Ridgecrest Area Convention & Visitors Bureau (RACVB)	643 N China Lake Blvd Ste C	Ridgecrest	CA	93555	**800-847-4830**	760-375-8202
Riverside Convention & Visitors Bureau	3750 University Ave Ste 175	Riverside	CA	92501	**888-748-7733**	951-222-4700
Roanoke Valley Convention & Visitors Bureau	101 Shenandoah Ave NE	Roanoke	VA	24016	**800-635-5535**	540-342-6025
Tunica MS	13625 Hwy 61 N	Robinsonville	MS	38664	**888-488-6422**	
Rochester Convention & Visitors Bureau	30 Civic Ctr Dr SE Ste 200	Rochester	MN	55904	**800-634-8277**	507-288-4331
Visit Rochester	45 E Ave Ste 400	Rochester	NY	14604	**800-677-7282**	585-279-8300
Rockhill-York County Convention & Visitors Bureau	452 S Anderson Rd	Rock Hill	SC	29730	**888-702-1320**	803-329-5200
Rockford Area Convention & Visitors Bureau	102 N Main St	Rockford	IL	61101	**800-521-0849**	815-963-8111
Conference & Visitors Bureau of Montgomery County MD Inc	111 Rockville Pk Ste 800	Rockville	MD	20850	**877-789-6904**	240-777-2060
Greater Rome Convention & Visitors Bureau	402 Civics Ctr Dr	Rome	GA	30161	**800-444-1834**	706-295-5576
Sacramento Convention & Visitors Bureau	1608 'I' St	Sacramento	CA	95814	**800-292-2334**	916-808-7777
Greater Saint Charles Convention & Visitors Bureau	230 S Main St	Saint Charles	MO	63301	**800-366-2427**	636-946-7776
Saint Cloud Area Convention & Visitors Bureau	525 Hwy 10 S Ste 1	Saint Cloud	MN	56304	**800-264-2940**	320-251-4170
Saint Joseph Convention & Visitors Bureau	109 S Fourth St	Saint Joseph	MO	64501	**800-785-0360**	816-233-6688
Auglaize & Mercer Counties Convention & Visitors Bureau	900 Edgewater Dr	Saint Marys	OH	45885	**800-860-4726**	419-394-1294
Salem Convention & Visitors Assn	181 High St NE	Salem	OR	97301	**800-874-7012**	503-581-4325
Rowan County Convention & Visitors Bureau	204 E Innes St Ste 120	Salisbury	NC	28144	**800-332-2343**	704-638-3100
Visit Salt Lake	90 SW Temple	Salt Lake City	UT	84101	**800-541-4955**	801-534-4900

	City	State	ZIP	Toll-Free	Phone
San Angelo Chamber of Commerce 418 W Ave B	San Angelo	TX	76903	**800-252-1381**	325-655-4136
San Antonio Convention & Visitors Bureau 203 S St Marys St Ste 200	San Antonio	TX	78205	**800-447-3372**	210-207-6700
San Francisco Convention & Visitors Bureau 201 Third St Ste 900	San Francisco	CA	94103	**855-847-6272**	415-974-6900
San Jose Convention & Visitors Bureau 408 Almaden Blvd	San Jose	CA	95110	**800-726-5673**	408-295-9600
Puerto Rico Convention Bureau 100 Convention Blvd	San Juan	PR	00907	**800-875-4765**	787-725-2110
Marin Convention & Visitors Bureau 1 Mitchell Blvd Ste B	San Rafael	CA	94903	**866-925-2060**	415-925-2060
Santa Barbara Visitors Bureau & Film Commission 1601 Anacapa St	Santa Barbara	CA	93101	**800-676-1266**	805-966-9222
Santa Clara Convention/Visitors Bureau 1850 Warburton Ave	Santa Clara	CA	95050	**800-272-6822**	408-244-9660
Santa Cruz County Conference & Visitors Council 303 Water St Ste 100	Santa Cruz	CA	95060	**800-833-3494**	831-425-1234
Santa Fe Convention Ctr 201 W Marcy St	Santa Fe	NM	87501	**800-777-2489**	505-955-6200
Santa Monica Convention & Visitors Bureau 1920 Main St Ste B	Santa Monica	CA	90405	**800-544-5319**	310-319-6263
Visit Sarasota County 1777 Main St Ste 302	Sarasota	FL	34236	**800-522-9799**	941-955-0991
Saratoga Convention & Tourism Bureau 60 Railroad Pl Ste 301	Saratoga Springs	NY	12866	**855-424-6073**	518-584-1531
Sault Sainte Marie Convention & Visitors Bureau 225 E Portage Ave	Sault Sainte Marie	MI	49783	**800-647-2858**	906-632-3366
Greater Woodfield Convention & Visitors Bureau 1375 E Woodfield Rd Ste 120	Schaumburg	IL	60173	**800-847-4849**	847-490-1010
Scottsdale Convention & Visitors Bureau 4343 N Scottsdale Rd Ste 170	Scottsdale	AZ	85251	**800-782-1117**	480-421-1004
Lackawanna County Convention & Visitors Bureau 99 Glenmaura National Blvd	Scranton	PA	18507	**800-229-3526**	570-496-1701
Seattle's Convention & Visitors Bureau 701 Pike St Ste 800	Seattle	WA	98101	**866-732-2695**	206-461-5800
Visit MercerCounty PA 50 N Water Ave	Sharon	PA	16146	**800-637-2370**	724-346-3771
Shelby County Office of Tourism 315 E Main St	Shelbyville	IL	62565	**800-874-3529**	217-774-2244
Shepherdsville-Bullitt County Tourist & Convention Commission 395 Paroquet Springs Dr	Shepherdsville	KY	40165	**800-526-2068**	502-543-8687
Shipshewana/LaGrange County Convention & Visitors Bureau 350 S Van Buren St Ste H	Shipshewana	IN	46565	**800-254-8090**	260-768-4008
Shreveport-Bossier Convention & Tourist Bureau 629 Spring St	Shreveport	LA	71101	**800-551-8682**	318-222-9391
Sioux City Tourism Bureau 801 Fourth St	Sioux City	IA	51101	**800-593-2228**	712-279-4800
Sioux Falls Convention & Visitors Bureau 200 N Phillips Ave Ste 102	Sioux Falls	SD	57104	**800-333-2072**	605-336-1620
Sitka Convention & Visitors Bureau 303 Lincoln St Ste 4	Sitka	AK	99835	**800-557-4852**	907-747-5940
Skagway Visitor Information 245 Broadway PO Box 1029	Skagway	AK	99840	**888-762-1898**	907-983-2855
Johnston County Convention & Visitors Bureau 235 E Market St	Smithfield	NC	27577	**800-441-7829**	919-989-8687
South Bend/Mishawaka Convention & Visitors Bureau 401 E Colfax Ave Ste 310	South Bend	IN	46617	**800-519-0577**	
Lake Tahoe Visitors Authority 3066 Lk Tahoe Blvd	South Lake Tahoe	CA	96150	**800-288-2463**	530-544-5050
South Padre Island Convention & Visitors Bureau 7355 Padre Blvd	South Padre Island	TX	78597	**800-767-2373**	956-761-6433
South Sioux City Convention & Visitors Bureau 4401 Dakota Ave	South Sioux City	NE	68776	**866-494-1307**	402-494-1307
Convention & Visitors Bureau-Village of Pinehurst Southern Pines Aberdeen Area 10677 Hwy 15-501	Southern Pines	NC	28387	**800-346-5362**	910-692-3330
Spokane Convention & Visitors Bureau 801 W Riverside Ste 301	Spokane	WA	99201	**800-662-0084**	509-624-1341
Greater Springfield Convention & Visitors Bureau 1441 Main St	Springfield	MA	01103	**800-723-1548**	413-787-1548
Springfield Convention & Visitors Bureau 109 N Seventh St	Springfield	IL	62701	**800-545-7300**	217-789-2360
Springfield Missouri Convention & Visitors Bureau 815 E St Louis St Ste 100	Springfield	MO	65806	**800-678-8767**	417-881-5300
Centre County Convention & Visitors Bureau 800 E Pk Ave	State College	PA	16803	**800-358-5466**	814-231-1400
Pocono Mountains Vacation Bureau 1004 Main St	Stroudsburg	PA	18360	**800-722-9199**	570-421-5791
Racine County Convention & Visitors Bureau 14015 Washington Ave	Sturtevant	WI	53177	**800-272-2463**	262-884-6400
Central Oregon Visitors Association 57100 Beaver Dr Bldg 6 Ste 130	Sunriver	OR	97707	**800-800-8334**	
Superior/Douglas County Convention & Visitors Bureau 305 Harborview Pkwy	Superior	WI	54880	**800-942-5313**	715-392-7151
Tourism Bureau Southwestern Illinois 4387 N. Illinois St Ste 200	Swansea	IL	62226	**800-442-1488**	618-257-1488
Tacoma Regional Convention & Visitor Bureau 1516 Commerce St	Tacoma	WA	98402	**800-272-2662**	253-627-2836
North Lake Tahoe Resort Assn 100 N Lake Blvd	Tahoe City	CA	96145	**800-468-2463**	530-581-6900
North Lake Tahoe Visitors & Convention Bureau PO Box 1757	Tahoe City	CA	96145	**800-462-5196**	530-581-6900
Chambers of Commerce / Tourism 106 E Jefferson St	Tallahassee	FL	32301	**800-628-2866**	850-606-2305
Tampa Bay & Co 401 E Jackson St Ste 2100	Tampa	FL	33602	**877-230-0078**	813-223-1111
Tempe Tourism Office 222 South Mill Ave Ste 120	Tempe	AZ	85281	**866-914-1052**	480-894-8158
Terre Haute Convention & Visitors Bureau 5353 E Margaret Dr	Terre Haute	IN	47803	**800-366-3043**	
Thief River Falls Convention & Visitors Bureau (TRFCVB) 102 Main Ave N	Thief River	MN	56701	**800-657-3700**	218-686-9785
City of Thomasville Tourism Authority 144 E Jackson St	Thomasville	GA	31792	**800-533-4587**	229-226-3424
Three Lakes Information Bureau 1704 Superior St PO Box 268	Three Lakes	WI	54562	**800-972-6103**	715-546-3344
River Country Tourism Bureau PO Box 214	Three Rivers	MI	49093	**800-447-2821**	
Greater Toledo Convention & Visitors Bureau 401 Jefferson Ave	Toledo	OH	43604	**800-243-4667**	419-321-6404
Tomah Convention & Visitors Bureau 901 Kilbourn Ave PO Box 625	Tomah	WI	54660	**800-948-6624**	608-372-2166
Visit Topeka Inc 618 S Kansas Ave	Topeka	KS	66603	**800-235-1030**	785-234-1030
Toronto Convention & Visitors Assn 207 Queen's Quay W Ste 405 PO Box 126	Toronto	ON	M5J1A7	**800-499-2514**	416-203-2600
Smoky Mountain Visitors Bureau 7906 E Lamar Alexander Pkwy	Townsend	TN	37882	**800-525-6834**	865-448-6134
Traverse City Convention & Visitors Bureau 101 W Grandview Pkwy	Traverse City	MI	49684	**800-940-1120**	231-947-1120
Atlanta's DeKalb Convention & Visitors Bureau 1957 Lakeside Pkwy Ste 510	Tucker	GA	30084	**800-999-6055**	770-492-5000
Metropolitan Tucson Convention & Visitors Bureau 100 S Church Ave	Tucson	AZ	85701	**800-638-8350**	520-624-1817
Tulsa Convention & Visitors Bureau 1 W Third St Ste 100	Tulsa	OK	74103	**800-558-3311**	
Colbert County Tourism & Convention Bureau 719 Hwy 72 W PO Box 740425	Tuscumbia	AL	35674	**800-344-0783**	256-383-0783
Tyler Convention & Visitors Bureau (TCVB) 315 N Broadway	Tyler	TX	75702	**800-235-5712**	903-592-1661
Oneida County Convention & Visitors Bureau PO Box 551	Utica	NY	13503	**800-426-3132**	315-724-7221
Vallejo Convention & Visitors Bureau 289 Mare Island Way *General	Vallejo	CA	94590	**866-921-9277***	707-642-3653
Southwest Washington Convention & Visitors Bureau 1220 Main S Ste 220	Vancouver	WA	98660	**877-600-0800**	360-750-1553
Ventura Visitors & Convention Bureau 101 S California St	Ventura	CA	93001	**800-333-2989**	805-648-2075
Iron Range Tourism Bureau 403 N First St	Virginia	MN	55792	**800-777-8497**	218-749-8161
Virginia Beach Convention & Visitor Bureau (VBCVB) 2101 Parks Ave Ste 500	Virginia Beach	VA	23451	**800-700-7702**	757-385-4700
Visalia Convention & Visitors Bureau PO Box 2734	Visalia	CA	93279	**800-524-0303**	559-334-0141
Waco Convention & Visitors Bureau 100 Washington Ave	Waco	TX	76701	**800-321-9226**	254-750-5810
Kallman Worldwide Inc 4 N St Ste 800	Waldwick	NJ	07463	**877-492-7028**	201-251-2600
Warren County Visitors Bureau 22045 Rt 6	Warren	PA	16365	**800-624-7802**	814-726-1222
Kosciusko County Convention & Visitors Bureau (KOSCVB) 111 Capital Dr	Warsaw	IN	46582	**800-800-6090**	574-269-6090
Washington DC Convention & Tourism Corp 901 Seventh St NW 4th Fl	Washington	DC	20001	**800-422-8644**	202-789-7000
Waterloo Convention & Visitor Bureau 500 Jefferson St	Waterloo	IA	50701	**800-728-8431**	319-233-8350
Wausau Central Wisconsin Convention & Visitors Bureau (CWCVB) 219 Jefferson St Ste B	Wausau	WI	54403	**888-948-4748**	715-355-8788
Tioga County Visitors Bureau 2053 Rt 660	Wellsboro	PA	16901	**888-846-4228**	570-724-0635
West Branch Area Chamber of Commerce 422 W Houghton Ave	West Branch	MI	48661	**800-755-9091**	989-345-2821
West Hollywood Convention & Visitors Bureau 8687 Melrose Ave Ste M38	West Hollywood	CA	90069	**800-368-6020**	310-289-2525
Monroe-West Monroe Convention & Visitors Bureau 601 Constitution Dr PO Box 1436	West Monroe	LA	71292	**800-843-1872**	318-387-5691
Palm Beach County Convention & Visitors Bureau 1555 Palm Beach Lakes Blvd Ste 800	West Palm Beach	FL	33401	**800-554-7256**	561-233-3000
Wheeling Convention & Visitors Bureau 1401 Main St	Wheeling	WV	26003	**800-828-3097**	304-233-7709
Wichita Convention & Visitors Bureau 515 Main St Ste 115	Wichita	KS	67202	**800-288-9424**	316-265-2800
Williamsburg Destination Marketing Committee 421 N Boundary St PO Box 3495	Williamsburg	VA	23187	**800-368-6511**	757-229-6511
Martin County Travel & Tourism Authority 100 E Church St PO Box 382	Williamston	NC	27892	**800-776-8566**	252-792-6605
Cape Fear Coast Convention & Visitors Bureau 505 Nutt St Unit A	Wilmington	NC	28401	**877-406-2356**	910-341-4030
Greater Wilmington Convention & Visitors Bureau 100 W Tenth St Ste 20	Wilmington	DE	19801	**800-489-6664**	
Wilson Visitors Bureau 209 Broad St	Wilson	NC	27893	**800-497-7398**	252-243-8440
Winnemucca Convention & Visitors Authority 50 W Winnemucca Blvd	Winnemucca	NV	89445	**800-962-2638**	775-623-5071
Winona Convention & Visitors Bureau 160 Johnson St	Winona	MN	55987	**800-657-4972**	507-452-0735
Winston-Salem Convention & Visitors Bureau 200 Brookstown Ave	Winston-Salem	NC	27101	**866-728-4200**	336-728-4200
Wisconsin Dells Visitors & Convention Bureau 701 Superior St PO Box 390	Wisconsin Dells	WI	53965	**800-223-3557**	608-254-8088
Wayne County Convention & Visitors Bureau 428 W Liberty St	Wooster	OH	44691	**800-362-6474**	330-264-1800
Worcester County Convention & Visitors Bureau 91 Prescott St	Worcester	MA	01605	**866-755-7439**	508-755-7400
Mahoning County Convention & Visitors Bureau 21 W Boardman St	Youngstown	OH	44503	**800-447-8201**	330-740-2130
Yuma Convention & Visitors Bureau 201 N Fourth Ave	Yuma	AZ	85364	**800-293-0071**	928-783-0071

209 CONVEYORS & CONVEYING EQUIPMENT

SEE ALSO Material Handling Equipment

	City	State	ZIP	Toll-Free	Phone
Airfloat LLC 2230 Brush College Rd	Decatur	IL	62526	**800-888-0018**	217-423-6001
Allor Manufacturing Inc 12534 Emerson Dr	Brighton	MI	48116	**888-382-6300**	248-486-4500
AMF Bakery Systems 2115 W Laburnum Ave	Richmond	VA	23227	**800-225-3771**	804-355-7961
Automatic Systems Inc 9230 E 47th St	Kansas City	MO	64133	**800-366-3488**	816-356-0660
Beltservice Corp 4143 Rider Trl N	Earth City	MO	63045	**800-727-2358**	314-344-8500

	City	State	Zip	Toll-Free	Phone
Bilt-Rite Conveyors 735 Industrial Loop Rd	New London	WI	54961	**800-558-3616**	920-982-6600
BW Container Systems 1305 Lakeview Dr	Romeoville	IL	60446	**800-527-0494**	630-759-6800
C & M Conveyor 4598 SR 37	Mitchell	IN	47446	**800-551-3195**	812-849-5647
Cambelt International Corp 2820 West 1100 South	Salt Lake City	UT	84104	**855-226-2358**	801-972-5511
Cambridge International 105 Goodwill Rd	Cambridge	MD	21613	**800-638-9560**	410-901-4979
Carrier Vibrating Equipment Inc 3400 Fern Vly Rd	Louisville	KY	40213	**800-547-7278**	502-969-3171
Christianson Systems Inc 20421 15th St SE PO Box 138	Blomkest	MN	56216	**800-328-8896**	320-995-6141
Conveyor Components Co 130 Seltzer Rd *Cust Svc	Croswell	MI	48422	**800-233-3233***	810-679-4211
Cyclonaire Corp 2922 N Division Ave	York	NE	68467	**800-445-0730**	402-362-2000
Dematic 507 Plymouth Ave NE *Cust Svc	Grand Rapids	MI	49505	**877-725-7500***	
Engineered Products Inc 500 Furman Hall Rd	Greenville	SC	29609	**888-301-1421**	864-234-4888
Evana Automation 5825 Old Boonville Hwy	Evansville	IN	47715	**800-468-6774**	812-479-8246
Feeco International Inc 3913 Algoma Rd	Green Bay	WI	54311	**800-373-9347**	920-468-1000
Flexible Steel Lacing Co 2525 Wisconsin Ave	Downers Grove	IL	60515	**800-323-3444**	630-971-0150
Garvey Corp 208 S Rt 73	Blue Anchor	NJ	08037	**800-257-8581**	609-561-2450
Hansen Manufacturing Corp 5100 W 12th St	Sioux Falls	SD	57107	**800-328-1785**	605-332-3200
Hapman 6002 E N Ave	Kalamazoo	MI	49048	**800-427-6260**	269-343-1675
Intelligrated Products 475 E High St PO Box 899	London	OH	43140	**866-936-7300**	513-701-7300
Jorgensen Conveyors Inc 10303 N Baehr Rd	Mequon	WI	53092	**800-325-7705**	262-242-3089
Kice Industries Inc 5500 N Mill Heights Dr	Wichita	KS	67219	**877-289-5423**	316-744-7151
KWS Mfg Company Ltd 3041 Conveyor Dr	Burleson	TX	76028	**800-543-6558**	817-295-2247
Laitram LLC 200 Laitram Ln	Harahan	LA	70123	**800-535-7631**	504-733-6000
Martin Engineering 1 Martin Pl	Neponset	IL	61345	**800-544-2947**	309-594-2384
Metzgar Conveyor Co Inc 901 Metzgar Dr NW	Comstock Park	MI	49321	**888-266-8390**	616-784-0930
Prab Inc 5944 E Kilgore Rd	Kalamazoo	MI	49048	**800-968-7722**	269-382-8200
Rapat Corp 919 Odonnel St	Hawley	MN	56549	**800-325-6377**	218-483-3344
Rapid Industries 4003 Oaklawn Dr	Louisville	KY	40219	**800-727-4381**	502-968-3645
Renold Jeffrey 2307 Maden Dr	Morristown	TN	37813	**800-251-9012**	423-586-1951
Richards-Wilcox Inc 600 S Lake St	Aurora	IL	60506	**800-253-5668**	
Roll-A-Way Conveyor Inc 2335 N Delaney Rd	Gurnee	IL	60031	**800-747-9024**	847-336-5033
Schroeder Industries LLC 580 W Pk Rd	Leetsdale	PA	15056	**800-722-4810**	724-318-1100
Shick Tube Veyor Corp 4346 Clary Blvd	Kansas City	MO	64130	**877-744-2587**	816-861-7224
Shuttleworth Inc 10 Commercial Rd	Huntington	IN	46750	**800-444-7412**	260-356-8500
Stewart Systems 808 Stewart Ave	Plano	TX	75074	**800-966-5808**	972-422-5808
Sweet Mfg Company Inc 2000 E Leffel Ln *Cust Svc	Springfield	OH	45505	**800-334-7254***	937-325-1511
Swisslog 10825 E 47th Ave	Denver	CO	80239	**800-525-1841**	303-371-7770
Thomas Conveyor Co 555 N Burleson Blvd	Burleson	TX	76028	**800-433-2217**	817-295-7151
Transco Industries Inc 5534 NE 122nd Ave	Portland	OR	97230	**800-545-9991**	503-256-1955
Universal Industries Inc 5800 Nordic Dr	Cedar Falls	IA	50613	**800-553-4446**	319-277-7501
VAC-U-MAX 69 William St	Belleville	NJ	07109	**800-822-8629**	973-759-4600
W & H Systems Inc 120 Asia Pl	Carlstadt	NJ	07072	**800-966-6993**	201-933-7840
Westfalia Technologies Inc 3655 Sandhurst Dr	York	PA	17406	**800-673-2522**	717-764-1115
Whirl Air Flow Corp 20055 177th St	Big Lake	MN	55309	**800-373-3461**	763-262-1200
Wire Belt Company of America 154 Harvey Rd *Cust Svc	Londonderry	NH	03053	**800-922-2637***	603-644-2500
Young Industries Inc 16 Painter St	Muncy	PA	17756	**800-546-3165**	570-546-3165

210 CORD & TWINE

	City	State	Zip	Toll-Free	Phone
Ashaway Line & Twine Manufacturing Co 24 Laurel St	Ashaway	RI	02804	**800-556-7260**	401-377-2221
Atkins & Pearce Inc 1 Braid Way	Covington	KY	41017	**800-837-7477**	859-356-2001
Bridon Cordage LLC 909 E 16th St	Albert Lea	MN	56007	**800-533-6002**	507-377-1601
Carron Net Company Inc 1623 17th St PO Box 177	Two Rivers	WI	54241	**800-558-7768**	920-793-2217
I & I Sling Inc PO Box 2423	Aston	PA	19014	**800-874-3539**	610-485-8500
New England Ropes Inc 848 Airport Rd	Fall River	MA	02720	**800-333-6679**	508-678-8200
Pacific Fibre & Rope Company Inc 903 Flint St	Wilmington	CA	90744	**800-825-7673**	310-834-4567
Pelican Rope Works Inc 4001 W Carriage Dr	Santa Ana	CA	92704	**800-464-7673**	714-545-0116
PlymKraft Inc 479 Export Cir	Newport News	VA	23601	**800-992-0854**	757-595-0364
Puget Sound Rope Corp 1012 Second St	Anacortes	WA	98221	**888-525-8488**	360-293-8488
Rocky Mount Cord Co 381 N Grace St *Orders	Rocky Mount	NC	27804	**800-342-9130***	252-977-9130
Samson Rope Technologies Inc 2090 Thornton Rd *Cust Svc	Ferndale	WA	98248	**800-227-7673***	360-384-4669

211 CORK & CORK PRODUCTS

SEE ALSO Office & School Supplies

	City	State	Zip	Toll-Free	Phone
Expanko Inc 180 Gordon Dr Ste 113	Exton	PA	19341	**800-345-6202**	
Manton Industrial Cork Products Inc 415 Oser Ave Unit U	Hauppauge	NY	11788	**800-663-1921**	631-273-0700
Maryland Cork Co Inc 505 Blue Ball Rd PO Box 126	Elkton	MD	21922	**800-662-2675**	410-398-2955

212 CORPORATE HOUSING

	City	State	Zip	Toll-Free	Phone
Churchill Corporate Services 56 Utter Ave	Hawthorne	NJ	07506	**800-941-7458**	973-636-9400
Coast to Coast Corporate Housing 10773 Los Alamitos Blvd	Los Alamitos	CA	90720	**800-451-9466**	562-795-0250
ExecSuite Third Ave SW Ste 702	Calgary	AB	T2P3B4	**800-667-4980**	403-294-5800
Klein & Company Corporate Housing Services Inc 914 Washington Ave	Golden	CO	80401	**800-208-9826**	303-796-2100
ExecuStay Corp 2222 Corinth Ave	Los Angeles	CA	90064	**800-990-9292**	
Oakwood Crystal City 400 15th St S	Arlington	VA	22202	**877-902-0832**	703-920-9550
Oakwood Worldwide 2222 Corinth Ave	Los Angeles	CA	90064	**800-888-0808**	310-478-1021
SuiteAmerica 4970 Windplay Dr Ste C-1	El Dorado Hills	CA	95762	**800-410-4305**	916-941-7970

213 CORRECTIONAL & DETENTION MANAGEMENT (PRIVATIZED)

SEE ALSO Correctional Facilities - State ; Juvenile Detention Facilities

	City	State	Zip	Toll-Free	Phone
Colorado Correctional Industries 4999 Oakland St *Cust Svc	Denver	CO	80239	**800-685-7891***	719-226-4206
Corrections Corp of America 10 Burton Hills Blvd *NYSE: CXW*	Nashville	TN	37215	**800-624-2931**	615-263-3000

214 CORRECTIONAL FACILITIES

	City	State	Zip	Toll-Free	Phone
Administrative-Maximum US Penitentiary *Florence* PO Box 8500	Florence	CO	81226	**877-623-8426**	719-784-9464
Federal Correctional Complex *Coleman* 846 NE 54th Terr	Coleman	FL	33521	**877-623-8426**	352-689-5000
Federal Correctional Institution					
Butner Old NC Hwy 75 PO Box 1000	Butner	NC	27509	**877-623-8426**	919-575-4541
Englewood 9595 W Quincy Ave	Littleton	CO	80123	**877-623-8426**	303-985-1566
Fairton 655 Fairton-Millville Rd PO Box 280	Fairton	NJ	08320	**877-623-8426**	856-453-1177
Forrest City 1400 Dale Bumpers Rd	Forrest City	AR	72335	**877-623-8426**	870-630-6000
Loretto 772 St Joseph St	Loretto	PA	15940	**877-623-8426**	814-472-4140
Manchester 805 Fox Hollow Rd PO Box 4000	Manchester	KY	40962	**877-623-8426**	606-598-1900
McKean 6975 Rt 59 PO Box 8000	Lewis Run	PA	16738	**877-623-8426**	814-362-8900
Yazoo City 2225 Haley Barbour Pkwy PO Box 5050	Yazoo City	MS	39194	**877-623-8426**	662-751-4800
SeaTac PO Box 13901	Seattle	WA	98198	**877-623-8426**	206-870-5700
Federal Prison Camp					
Duluth 6902 Airport Rd PO Box 1400	Duluth	MN	55814	**877-623-8426**	218-722-8634
Montgomery Maxwell AFB	Montgomery	AL	36112	**877-623-8426**	334-293-2100
Medical Ctr for Federal Prisoners Springfield 1900 W Sunshine St	Springfield	MO	65807	**877-623-8426**	417-862-7041
Metropolitan Correctional Ctr *Chicago* 71 W Van Buren St	Chicago	IL	60605	**877-623-8426**	312-322-0567
US Penitentiary					
Atwater 1 Federal Way PO Box 019001	Atwater	CA	95301	**877-623-8426**	209-386-0257

215 CORRECTIONAL FACILITIES - STATE

SEE ALSO Correctional & Detention Management (Privatized) ; Juvenile Detention Facilities

	City	State	Zip	Toll-Free	Phone
Algoa Correctional Ctr 8501 No More Victims Rd	Jefferson City	MO	65102	**800-392-1111**	573-751-3911
Arizona State Prison Complex-Eyman 4374 E Butte Ave PO Box 3500	Florence	AZ	85132	**866-333-2039**	520-868-0201

Name / Address	City	State	Zip	Toll-Free	Phone
Arkansas Dept of Corrections Maximum Security Unit 2501 State Farm Rd	Tucker	AR	72168	**866-801-3435**	501-842-3800
Arkansas Dept of Corrections Tucker Unit 2400 State Farm Rd PO Box 240	Tucker	AR	72168	**800-682-7377**	501-842-2519
Boonville Correctional Ctr 1216 E Morgan St	Boonville	MO	65233	**800-392-8486**	660-882-6521
Charles E Egeler Correctional Facility 3855 Cooper St	Jackson	MI	49201	**855-444-3911**	517-780-5600
Chillicothe Correctional Ctr 3151 Litton Rd	Chillicothe	MO	64601	**800-392-8486**	660-646-4032
Deerfield Correctional Ctr 21360 Deerfield Dr	Capron	VA	23829	**800-560-4292**	434-658-4368
Fairbanks Correctional Ctr 1931 Eagan Ave	Fairbanks	AK	99701	**877-741-0741**	907-458-6700
G Robert Cotton Correctional Facility 3500 N Elm Rd	Jackson	MI	49201	**855-444-3911**	517-780-5000
Goodman Correctional Institution 4556 Broad River Rd	Columbia	SC	29210	**866-230-7761**	803-896-8565
Huron Valley Correctional Facility 3201 Bemis Rd	Ypsilanti	MI	48197	**855-444-3911**	734-572-9900
Iowa State Penitentiary Ave E & 1st St PO Box 409	Fort Madison	IA	52627	**800-382-0019**	319-372-1908
Kentucky Correctional Institution for Women 3000 Ash Ave	Pewee Valley	KY	40056	**877-687-6818**	502-241-8454
Lee Correctional Institution 990 Wisacky Hwy	Bishopville	SC	29010	**877-846-3472**	803-428-2800
Lorain Correctional Institution 2075 Avon Belden Rd	Grafton	OH	44044	**888-988-4768**	440-748-1049
Luther Luckett Correctional Complex Dawkins Rd PO Box 6	LaGrange	KY	40031	**800-511-1670**	502-222-0363
Mike Durfee State Prison 1412 Wood St	Springfield	SD	57062	**800-537-0025**	605-369-2201
Minnesota Correctional Facility-Fairbault 1101 Linden Ln	Faribault	MN	55021	**800-657-3830**	507-334-0700
Mississippi State Penitentiary Hwy 49 W PO Box 1057	Parchman	MS	38738	**800-844-0898**	662-745-6611
Montana State Prison 400 Conley Lk Rd	Deer Lodge	MT	59722	**888-739-9122**	406-846-1320
Mule Creek State Prison 4001 Hwy 104	Ione	CA	95640	**877-256-6877**	209-274-4911
Nebraska Correctional Ctr for Women 1107 Recharge Rd	York	NE	68467	**877-634-8463**	402-362-3317
Nebraska State Penitentiary 4201 S 14th St	Lincoln	NE	68502	**877-634-8463**	402-471-3161
New Hampshire State Prison for Women 317 Mast Rd	Goffstown	NH	03045	**800-639-1122**	603-668-6137
Northern Regional Correctional Facility 112 Northern Regional Correctional Dr	Moundsville	WV	26041	**866-984-8463**	304-843-4067
Okeechobee Correctional Institution 3420 NE 168th St	Okeechobee	FL	34972	**800-574-5729**	863-462-5400
Palmer Correctional Ctr PO Box 919	Palmer	AK	99645	**877-741-0741**	907-745-5054
Pelican Bay State Prison (PBSP) 5905 Lake Earl Dr PO Box 7000	Crescent City	CA	95531	**877-256-6877**	707-465-1000
Pleasant Valley State Prison 24863 W Jayne Ave PO Box 8500	Coalinga	CA	93210	**877-256-6877**	559-935-4900
Riverbend Maximum Security Institution 7475 Cockrill Bend Blvd	Nashville	TN	37243	**800-770-8277**	615-350-3100
RJ Donovan Correctional Facility at Rock Mountain 480 Alta Rd	San Diego	CA	92179	**877-256-6877**	619-661-6500
SCI-Coal Township 1 Kelley Dr	Coal Township	PA	17866	**800-322-4472**	570-644-7890
South Bay Correctional Facility 600 US Hwy 27 S	South Bay	FL	33493	**800-574-5729**	561-992-9505
Thumb Correctional Facility 3225 John Conley Dr	Lapeer	MI	48446	**855-444-3911**	810-667-2045
Topeka Correctional Facility 815 SE Rice Rd	Topeka	KS	66603	**888-317-8204**	785-296-3317
Wake Correctional Ctr 1000 Rock Quarry Rd	Raleigh	NC	27610	**866-719-0108**	919-733-7988
Warren Correctional Institution 379 Collins Rd	Manson	NC	27553	**866-719-0108**	252-456-3400
Wayne County Boot Camp PO Box 182	Clifton	TN	38425	**855-876-7283**	931-676-3345

216 CREDIT & FINANCING - CONSUMER

SEE ALSO Credit & Financing - Commercial ; Credit Unions ; Banks - Commercial & Savings

Name / Address	City	State	Zip	Toll-Free	Phone
Atlantic Bay Mortgage Group 596 Lynnhaven Pkwy Ste 102	Virginia Beach	VA	23452	**866-877-3143**	757-213-1660
Budget Finance Co 1849 Sawtelle Blvd	Los Angeles	CA	90025	**800-225-6267**	310-696-4050
Credit Acceptance Corp 25505 W 12 Mile Rd	Southfield	MI	48034	**800-634-1506**	248-353-2700
DHI Mortgage Co Ltd 10700 Pecan Park Blvd Ste 450	Austin	TX	78750	**800-315-8434**	512-502-0545
Dollar Loan Ctr LLC 6122 W Sahara Ave	Las Vegas	NV	89146	**866-550-4352**	702-693-5626
Enerbank USA Inc 1245 E Brickyard Rd Ste 600	Salt Lake City	UT	84106	**888-390-1220**	
Farm Credit of The Virginias Aca 106 Sangers Ln	Staunton	VA	24401	**800-559-1016**	540-886-3435
Finance Factors Ltd 1164 Bishop St	Honolulu	HI	96813	**800-648-7136**	808-548-4940
First Insurance Funding Corp 450 Skokie Blvd Ste 1000	Northbrook	IL	60062	**800-837-3707**	
Ford Motor Credit Co 1 American Rd	Dearborn	MI	48121	**800-727-7000**	313-322-3000
Franklin Credit Management Corp 101 Hudson St	Jersey City	NJ	07302	**800-255-5897**	201-604-1800
Gateway Mortgage Group LLC 6910 E 14th St	Tulsa	OK	74112	**877-406-8109**	918-712-9000
General Motors Acceptance Corp (GMAC) 200 Renaissance Ctr	Detroit	MI	48265	**800-200-4622**	877-320-2559
Guaranteed Rate Inc 3940 N Ravenswood	Chicago	IL	60613	**866-934-7283**	773-290-0505
Harley-Davidson Financial Services Inc PO Box 21489	Carson City	NV	89721	**888-691-4337**	
iMortgage Services Inc 2570 Boyce Plz Rd Boyce Plz Iii	Pittsburgh	PA	15241	**888-575-8555**	412-220-7330
MCAP Financial Corp 1140 W Pender St Ste 1400	Vancouver	BC	V6E4G1	**800-977-5877**	604-681-8805
Mercedes-Benz Financial Services USA LLC PO Box 685	Roanoke	TX	76262	**800-654-6222**	
Nelnet Inc 121 S 13th St Ste 204 *NYSE: NNI*	Lincoln	NE	68508	**888-486-4722**	402-458-2370
Nicholas Financial Inc 2454 McMullen Booth Rd Bldg C *NASDAQ: NICK*	Clearwater	FL	33759	**800-237-2721**	727-726-0763
Ontario Centres of Excellence Inc 156 Front St W Ste 200	Toronto	ON	M5J2L6	**866-759-6014**	416-861-1092
PreCash Inc 5120 Woodway Dr Ste 6001	Houston	TX	77056	**800-773-2274**	713-600-2267
Prestige Financial Services Inc 1420 S 500 W	Salt Lake City	UT	84115	**888-822-7422**	801-844-2100
Prime Rate Premium Finance Corp 2141 Enterprise Dr PO Box 100507 *Cust Svc	Florence	SC	29501	**800-777-7458***	843-669-0937
Redwood Credit Union PO Box 6104	Santa Rosa	CA	95406	**800-479-7928**	707-545-4000
Regional Acceptance Corp 1424 E Fire Tower Rd	Greenville	NC	27858	**877-722-7299**	252-321-7700
Sallie Mae 12061 Bluemont Way *Cust Svc	Reston	VA	20190	**888-272-5543***	703-810-3000
Security Finance Corp 181 Security Plc *All	Spartanburg	SC	29307	**800-395-8195***	864-582-8193
Select Portfolio Servicing Inc 3815 SW Temple	Salt Lake City	UT	84115	**800-258-8602**	
SLM Corp 12061 Bluemont Way *NASDAQ: SLM* ■ *Cust Svc	Reston	VA	20190	**888-272-5543***	703-810-3000
Toyota Financial Services 19001 S Western Ave *Cust Svc	Torrance	CA	90501	**800-874-8822***	212-715-7386
Triad Financial Services Inc 4336 Pablo Oaks Ct	Jacksonville	FL	32224	**800-522-2013**	
Wallick & Volk Mortgage 222 E 18th St	Cheyenne	WY	82001	**800-280-8655**	307-634-5941
WebBank Corp 215 S State St Ste 1000	Salt Lake City	UT	84111	**888-881-3789**	801-456-8350
Wells Fargo Education Financial Services PO Box 5185	Sioux Falls	SD	57117	**800-658-3567**	
Wells Fargo Financial Inc 800 Walnut St	Des Moines	IA	50309	**800-735-3008**	515-280-7741
Western Funding Inc PO Box 94858	Las Vegas	NV	89193	**888-434-3122**	702-434-1990

217 COSMETICS, SKIN CARE, AND OTHER PERSONAL CARE PRODUCTS

SEE ALSO Perfumes

Name / Address	City	State	Zip	Toll-Free	Phone
AHAVA North America 330 7th Avenue	New York	NY	10001	**800-366-7254**	
Aire-Master of America Inc 1821 N State Hwy Cc	Nixa	MO	65714	**800-525-0957**	417-725-2691
Apothecary Products 11750 12th Ave S Burnsville	Burnsville	MN	55337	**800-328-2742**	
At Last Naturals Inc 401 Columbus Ave	Valhalla	NY	10595	**800-527-8123**	
Aveda Corp 4000 Pheasant Ridge Dr	Blaine	MN	55449	**800-644-4831**	763-951-4000
Avon Products Inc 1345 Ave of the Americas *NYSE: AVP* ■ *Cust Svc	New York	NY	10017	**800-367-2866***	212-282-7000
Bath & Body Works 7 Limited Pkwy E	Reynoldsburg	OH	43068	**800-395-1001**	
BeautiControl Inc 2121 Midway Rd PO Box 815189	Carrollton	TX	75006	**800-232-8841**	
Belcam Inc Delagar Div 27 Montgomery St	Rouses Point	NY	12979	**800-328-3006**	518-297-3366
BeneFit Cosmetics 225 Bush St *Cust Svc	San Francisco	CA	94104	**800-781-2336***	415-781-8153
Bronner Bros Inc 2141 Powers Ferry Rd	Marietta	GA	30067	**800-241-6151**	770-988-0015
CBI Laboratories 4201 Diplomacy Rd	Fort Worth	TX	76155	**800-822-7546**	972-241-7546
CCA Industries Inc 200 Murray Hill Pkwy *NYSE: CAW* ■ *Cust Svc	East Rutherford	NJ	07073	**800-524-2720***	201-935-3232
Clinique Laboratories Inc 767 Fifth Ave 37th Fl	New York	NY	10153	**800-419-4041**	212-572-3983
Combe Inc 1101 Westchester Ave	White Plains	NY	10604	**800-431-2610**	914-694-5454
Crabtree & Evelyn Ltd 102 Peake Brook Rd	Woodstock	CT	06281	**800-272-2873**	860-928-2761
DEB Inc 2815 Coliseum Centre Dr Ste 600	Charlotte	NC	28217	**800-248-7190**	704-263-4240
Farouk Systems Inc 250 Pennbright Dr	Houston	TX	77090	**800-237-9175**	281-876-2000
Forever Living Products International Inc 7501 E McCormick Pkwy	Scottsdale	AZ	85258	**888-440-2563**	480-998-8888
GOJO Industries Inc 1 GOJO Plz Ste 500	Akron	OH	44311	**800-321-9647**	330-255-6000

	City	State	Zip	Toll-Free	Phone
Guest Supply Inc 4301 US Hwy 1 PO Box 902 *Cust Svc	Monmouth Junction	NJ	08852	**800-446-7819***	609-514-9696
Gurwitch Products LLC 8 Greenway Plz Ste 7	Houston	TX	77046	**888-637-2437**	281-275-7000
H2O Plus Inc 845 W Madison St *Cust Svc	Chicago	IL	60607	**800-242-2284***	312-850-9283
Hillshire Brands 2200 W Don Tyson Pkwy	Springdale	AR	72762	**800-323-7117**	479-290-6397
Jafra Cosmetics International 2451 Townsgate Rd	Westlake Village	CA	91361	**800-551-2345**	805-449-3000
Jan Marini Skin Research Inc 6951 Via Del Oro	San Jose	CA	95119	**800-347-2223**	408-362-0130
John Amico Haircare Products 4731 W 136th St	Crestwood	IL	60445	**800-676-5264**	708-824-4000
John Paul Mitchell Systems 1888 Century Park E ste 1600 *Cust Svc	Los Angeles	CA	90067	**800-793-8790***	
Johnson & Johnson Consumer Products Co 199 Grandview Rd	Skillman	NJ	08558	**866-565-2229**	908-874-1000
Johnson & Johnson Inc 7101 Notre-Dame E	Montreal	QC	H1N2G4	**800-361-8990**	514-251-5100
Key West Aloe 13095 N Telecom Pkwy	Tampa	FL	33637	**800-445-2563**	
L'Oreal USA 575 Fifth Ave	New York	NY	10017	**800-322-2036**	212-818-1500
Luster Products Inc 1104 W 43rd St	Chicago	IL	60609	**800-621-4255**	773-579-1800
Mary Kay Inc PO Box 799045 *Cust Svc	Dallas	TX	75379	**800-627-9529***	972-687-6300
Maybelline New York 575 Fifth Ave PO Box 1010	New York	NY	10017	**800-944-0730**	
Merle Norman Cosmetics Inc 9130 Bellanca Ave	Los Angeles	CA	90045	**800-421-6648**	310-641-3000
Neutrogena Corp 5760 W 96th St	Los Angeles	CA	90045	**800-582-4048**	310-642-1150
Nutramax Laboratories Inc 2208 Lakeside Blvd	Edgewood	MD	21040	**800-925-5187**	410-776-4000
Obagi Medical Products Inc 3760 Kilroy Airport Way Ste 500	Long Beach	CA	90806	**800-636-7546**	562-628-1007
Origins Natural Resources Inc 767 Fifth Ave *Cust Svc	New York	NY	10153	**800-674-4467***	
Paramount Cosmetics Inc 93 Entin Rd Ste 4	Clifton	NJ	07014	**800-522-9880**	973-472-2323
Person & Covey Inc 616 Allen Ave	Glendale	CA	91201	**800-423-2341**	
Pfizer Inc 235 E 42nd St *NYSE: PFE*	New York	NY	10017	**800-879-3477**	212-733-2323
Philosophy Inc 3809 E Watkins	Phoenix	AZ	85034	**800-568-3151**	
Prescriptives Inc 767 Fifth Ave	New York	NY	10153	**866-290-6471**	
Revlon Consumer Products Corp 1501 Williamsboro St	Oxford	NC	27565	**800-473-8566**	212-527-4000
Rozelle Cosmetics 4260 Loop Rd	Westfield	VT	05874	**800-451-4216**	802-744-2270
sephora.com Inc 525 Market St 1st Market Twr 32nd Fl *Cust Svc	San Francisco	CA	94105	**877-737-4672***	415-284-3300
Sothys USA Inc 1500 NW 94th Ave	Miami	FL	33172	**800-325-0503**	305-594-4222
Star Nail Products Inc 29120 Ave Paine	Valencia	CA	91355	**800-762-6245**	661-257-7827
Tom's of Maine Inc 302 Lafayette Ctr	Kennebunk	ME	04043	**800-367-8667**	800-985-3874
ULTA Beauty 1000 Remington Blvd Ste 120	Bolingbrook	IL	60440	**866-983-8582**	630-410-4800
Urban Decay 833 W 16th St	Newport Beach	CA	92663	**800-784-8722**	949-631-4504
Wahl Clipper Corp 2900 Locust St	Sterling	IL	61081	**800-767-9245**	
Wella Corp 6109 DeSoto Ave	Woodland Hills	CA	91367	**800-829-4422**	818-999-5112
Zotos International Inc 100 Tokeneke Rd	Darien	CT	06820	**888-242-4247**	203-655-8911

218 CREDIT & FINANCING - COMMERCIAL

SEE ALSO Credit & Financing - Consumer ; Banks - Commercial & Savings

	City	State	Zip	Toll-Free	Phone
AFCO Credit Corp 14 Wall St	New York	NY	10005	**800-288-6901**	212-401-4400
American AgCredit (ACA) PO Box 1120	Santa Rosa	CA	95402	**800-800-4865**	707-545-1200
Arkansas Capital Corp Group 200 S Commerce St Ste 400	Little Rock	AR	72201	**800-216-7237**	501-374-9247
ATEL Capital Group 600 California St 6th Fl	San Francisco	CA	94108	**800-543-2835**	415-989-8800
Automotive Finance Corp (AFC) 13085 Hamilton Crossing Blvd	Carmel	IN	46032	**888-335-6675**	865-384-8250
AutoStar 114 Ave of the Americas Ste 39	New York	NY	10036	**800-288-6782**	212-930-9400
BMO Financial Corp 1 First Canadian Place 11th Fl	Toronto	ON	M5X1A1	**800-553-0332**	416-359-4440
Bombardier Capital Group 261 Mountain View Dr 4th Fl	Colchester	VT	05446	**800-949-5568**	802-764-5232
Cascade Federal Credit Union 18020 80th Ave S	Kent	WA	98032	**800-562-2853**	425-251-8888
CDC Small Business Finance Corp 2448 Historic Decatur Rd Ste 200	San Diego	CA	92106	**800-611-5170**	619-291-3594
Co-op Finance Assn Inc, The 10100 N Ambassador Dr Ste 315 PO Box 901532	Kansas City	MO	64153	**877-835-5232**	816-214-4200
Colonial Farm Credit Aca 7104 Mechanicsville Tpke PO Box 727	Mechanicsville	VA	23111	**800-777-8908**	804-746-4581
Equity Funding 12505 Bel-Red Rd Ste 200	Bellevue	WA	98005	**866-332-3863**	425-283-1040
Farm Credit Leasing (FCL) 600 Hwy 169 S Ste 300	Minneapolis	MN	55426	**800-444-2929**	952-417-7800
Farm Credit Of Central Florida Aca 115 S Missouri Ave Ste 400	Lakeland	FL	33815	**800-533-2773**	863-682-4117
Farm Credit Of Northwest Florida Aca 5052 Hwy 90	Marianna	FL	32446	**800-527-0647**	850-526-4910
Financial Pacific Co 3455 S 344th Way Ste 300	Federal Way	WA	98001	**800-447-7107**	
First Carolina Corporate Credit Union 7900 Triad Ctr Dr Ste 410	Greensboro	NC	27409	**800-585-4317**	
First Community Financial Corp (FCFC) 4000 N Central Ave Ste 100 *OTC: FMFP*	Phoenix	AZ	85012	**877-777-4778**	602-265-7715
Ford Motor Credit Co 1 American Rd	Dearborn	MI	48121	**800-727-7000**	313-322-3000
GE Vendor Financial Services 1719 Rt 10 E Ste 306	Parsippany	NJ	07054	**800-626-2000**	203-373-2039
Greenstone Farm Credit Services Aca 3515 West Rd	East Lansing	MI	48823	**800-444-3276**	800-968-0061
Imh Financial Corp 7001 N Scottsdale Rd Ste 2050	Scottsdale	AZ	85253	**800-510-6445**	480-840-8400
Imperial PFS (UPAC) 8245 Nieman Rd	Lenexa	KS	66214	**800-877-7848**	913-894-6150
iStar Financial Inc 1114 Ave of the Americas 39th Fl *NYSE: STAR*	New York	NY	10036	**888-603-5847**	212-930-9400
Jackson Purchase Ag Credit Assn PO Box 309	Mayfield	KY	42066	**877-422-4203**	270-247-5613
John Deere Credit Co 6400 NW 86th St	Johnston	IA	50131	**800-275-5322**	515-267-3000
Key Equipment Finance 1000 S McCaslin Blvd	Superior	CO	80027	**888-301-6238**	
Medallion Financial Corp 437 Madison Ave 38th Fl *NASDAQ: TAXI*	New York	NY	10022	**877-633-2554**	212-328-2100
MicroFinancial Inc 16 New England Executive Pk Ste 200 *NASDAQ: MFI*	Burlington	MA	01803	**877-868-3800**	781-994-4800
New York Business Development Corp (NYBDC) 50 Beaver St Ste 500	Albany	NY	12207	**800-923-2504**	518-463-2268
Park Community Federal Credit Union PO Box 18630	Louisville	KY	40261	**800-626-2870**	502-968-3681
PDS Gaming Corp 6280 Annie Oakley Dr	Las Vegas	NV	89120	**800-479-3612**	702-736-0700
Phoenix American Inc 2401 Kerner Blvd	San Rafael	CA	94901	**866-895-5050**	
Phoenix Growth Capital Corp 2401 Kerner Blvd	San Rafael	CA	94901	**866-895-5050**	
Phoenix Leasing Inc 2401 Kerner Blvd	San Rafael	CA	94901	**866-895-5050**	
Pinnacle Business Finance Inc 615 Commerce St Ste 101	Tacoma	WA	98402	**800-566-1993**	253-284-5600
PMC Commercial Trust 17950 Preston Rd Ste 600 *NASDAQ: CMCT*	Dallas	TX	75252	**800-486-3223**	972-349-3200
Priority Capital Inc 174 Green St	Melrose	MA	02176	**800-761-2118**	781-321-8778
Puerto Rico Farm Credit Aca PO Box 363649	San Juan	PR	00936	**800-981-3323**	787-753-0579
Republic Financial Corp 5251 DTC Pkwy Ste 300	Greenwood Village	CO	80111	**800-596-3608**	303-751-3501
Schroder Investment Management North America Inc (SIMNA) 875 Third Ave 22nd Fl	New York	NY	10022	**800-730-2932**	
Siemens Financial Services Inc 170 Wood Ave S	Iselin	NJ	08830	**800-327-4443**	732-590-6500
Snap-on Credit LLC 950 Technology Way Ste 301	Libertyville	IL	60048	**877-777-8455**	
Southgroup & Financial Services Inc 795 Woodlands Pkwy Ste 101	Ridgeland	MS	39157	**855-744-6777**	601-914-3220
Sta International 1400 Old Country Rd Ste 411	Westbury	NY	11590	**866-970-9882**	516-997-2400
Taycor LLC 6065 Bristol Pkwy	Culver City	CA	90230	**800-322-9738**	310-895-7704
Tyndall Federal Credit Union Inc PO Box 59760	Panama City	FL	32412	**888-896-3255**	850-769-9999
Verizon Credit Inc 201 N Tampa St	Tampa	FL	33602	**800-483-7988**	813-229-6000
Wells Fargo 420 Montgomery St *NYSE: WFC*	San Francisco	CA	94104	**800-877-4833**	
Wells Fargo Equipment Finance Inc 733 Marquette Ave Ste 700	Minneapolis	MN	55402	**877-322-8228**	612-667-9876
Western Agcredit PO Box 95850	South Jordan	UT	84095	**800-824-9198**	801-571-9200
Xerox Financial Services Inc 800 Long Ridge Rd	Stamford	CT	06904	**800-275-9376**	203-968-3000

219 CREDIT CARD PROVIDERS & RELATED SERVICES

Companies listed here include those that issue credit cards as well as companies that provide services to these companies (i.e., rewards programs, theft prevention, etc.).

	City	State	Zip	Toll-Free	Phone
American Express Company Inc World Financial Ctr 200 Vesey St *NYSE: AXP*	New York	NY	10285	**800-528-4800**	212-640-2000
Applied Card Systems 50 Applied Card Way	Glen Mills	PA	19342	**866-227-5627**	
Bank of America Card Services 1 Commercial Pl 2nd Fl	Norfolk	VA	23510	**800-732-9194**	757-441-4770

Company	Address	City	State	ZIP	Toll-Free	Phone
Capital One Financial Corp	1680 Capital One Dr *NYSE: COF*	McLean	VA	22102	**800-655-2265**	800-926-1000
Chevron Texaco Credit Card Ctr	PO Box P	Concord	CA	94524	**800-243-8766**	
Diners Club International	111 W Monroe	Chicago	IL	60603	**800-234-6377**	
Intersections Inc	3901 Stonecroft Blvd *NASDAQ: INTX*	Chantilly	VA	20151	**800-695-7536**	703-488-6100
Loan Science	9600 Great Hills Trail E Ste 200	Austin	TX	78759	**866-311-9450**	
MasterCard Inc	2000 Purchase St *NYSE: MA*	Purchase	NY	10577	**800-100-1087**	914-249-2000
Rewards Network	2 N Riverside Plaza Ste 200	Chicago	IL	60606	**866-844-3753**	866-559-3463
Transaction Network Services Inc.	10740 Parkridge Blvd Ste 100	Reston	VA	20191	**866-523-0661**	703-453-8300
Visa Inc	PO Box 8999 *NYSE: V*	San Francisco	CA	94128	**866-765-9644**	415-932-2100
Wright Express Corp	97 Darling Ave *NYSE: WEX*	South Portland	ME	04106	**800-761-7181**	207-773-8171

220 CREDIT REPORTING SERVICES

Company	Address	City	State	ZIP	Toll-Free	Phone
Advantage Credit Inc	32065 Castle Ct Ste 300	Evergreen	CO	80439	**800-670-7993**	303-670-7993
Coface Services North America Inc	50 Millstone Rd	East Windsor	NJ	08520	**877-626-3223**	609-469-0400
Constellation Technology Corp	7887 Bryan Dairy Rd Ste 100	Largo	FL	33777	**800-335-7355**	727-547-0600
Creditors Bureau Associates	420 College St	Macon	GA	31201	**866-949-4213**	478-750-1111
Equifax Credit Marketing Services	1550 Peachtree St NW *NYSE: EFX* ■ *Sales	Atlanta	GA	30309	**800-660-5125***	404-885-8000
Equifax Inc	1550 Peachtree St NW *NYSE: EFX* ■ *Sales	Atlanta	GA	30309	**888-202-4025***	404-885-8000
Experian Information Solutions Inc	475 Anton Blvd *Cust Svc	Costa Mesa	CA	92626	**888-397-3742***	714-830-7000
Fitch Ratings Inc	1 State St Plz	New York	NY	10004	**800-753-4824**	212-908-0500
Kroll Factual Data Inc	5200 Hahns Peak Dr	Loveland	CO	80538	**800-929-3400**	970-663-5700
Merchants Credit Bureau	955 Green St	Augusta	GA	30901	**800-426-5265**	706-823-6246
NACM South Texas Inc	10887 S Wilcrest Dr	Houston	TX	77099	**866-252-6226**	281-228-6100
Screeningone Inc	2233 W 190th St	Torrance	CA	90504	**888-327-6511**	
Tele-Track	5550 Peach Tree Pkwy Ste 600	Norcross	GA	30092	**800-729-6981**	770-449-8809
TransUnion LLC	555 W Adams St	Chicago	IL	60661	**866-922-2100**	
Trudiligence LLC	3190 S Wadsworth Blvd Ste 260	Lakewood	CO	80227	**800-580-0474**	303-692-8445

221 CREDIT UNIONS

Company	Address	City	State	ZIP	Toll-Free	Phone
66 Federal Credit Union	PO Box 1358	Bartlesville	OK	74005	**800-897-6991**	918-336-7662
Affinity Federal Credit Union	73 Mountain View Blvd PO Box 621	Basking Ridge	NJ	07920	**800-325-0808**	
Air Force Federal Credit Union	1560 Cable Ranch Rd Ste 200	San Antonio	TX	78245	**800-227-5328**	210-673-5610
Alaska USA Federal Credit Union	4000 Credit Union Dr PO Box 196613	Anchorage	AK	99503	**800-525-9094**	907-563-4567
Allegacy Federal Credit Union	1691 Westbrook Plaza Dr	Winston-Salem	NC	27103	**800-782-4670**	336-774-3400
America First Credit Union	1344 West 4675 South	Ogden	UT	84405	**800-999-3961**	801-627-0900
American Airlines Employees Federal Credit Union	4151 Amon Carter Blvd PO Box 155489	Fort Worth	TX	76155	**800-533-0035**	817-952-4500
American Eagle Federal Credit Union	417 Main St	East Hartford	CT	06118	**800-842-0145**	860-568-2020
Amoco Federal Credit Union	PO Box 889	Texas City	TX	77592	**800-231-6053**	409-948-8541
Andrews Federal Credit Union (AFCU)	5711 Allentown Rd	Suitland	MD	20746	**800-487-5500**	301-702-5500
ANG Federal Credit Union	PO Box 170204	Birmingham	AL	35217	**800-237-6211**	205-841-4525
APCO Employees Credit Union	750 17th St N	Birmingham	AL	35203	**800-249-2726**	205-257-3601
Arizona Federal Credit Union	PO Box 60070	Phoenix	AZ	85082	**800-523-4603**	602-683-1000
Ascend Federal Credit Union	520 Airpark Dr PO Box 1210	Tullahoma	TN	37388	**800-342-3086**	931-455-5441
Ascentra Credit Union	1710 Grant St	Bettendorf	IA	52722	**800-426-5241**	563-355-0152
Atlanta Postal Credit Union	501 Pulliam St SW Ste 350	Atlanta	GA	30312	**800-849-8431**	404-768-4126
Autotruck Federal Credit Union	3611 Newburg Rd	Louisville	KY	40218	**800-459-2328**	502-459-8981
Bank-Fund Staff Federal Credit Union	PO Box 27755	Washington	DC	20038	**800-923-7328**	202-458-4300
BayPort Credit Union Inc	3711 Huntington Ave	Newport News	VA	23607	**800-928-8801**	757-928-8850
Beacon Credit Union	PO Box 627	Wabash	IN	46992	**800-762-3136**	260-563-7443
Bellco First Federal Credit Union	7600 E OrchaRd Rd Ste 400N	Greenwood Village	CO	80111	**800-235-5261**	303-689-7800
Bethpage Federal Credit Union	899 S Oyster Bay Rd	Bethpage	NY	11714	**800-628-7070**	
BlueCross BlueShield of Tennessee Inc	1 Cameron Hill Cir	Chattanooga	TN	37402	**800-848-0298**	423-755-5600
Campus Federal Credit Union	PO Box 98036	Baton Rouge	LA	70898	**888-769-8841**	225-769-8841
Campus USA Credit Union	PO Box 147029	Gainesville	FL	32614	**800-367-6440**	352-335-9090
CFCU Community Credit Union	1030 Craft Rd	Ithaca	NY	14850	**800-428-8340**	607-257-8500
Chartway Federal Credit Union	160 Newtown Rd	Virginia Beach	VA	23462	**800-678-8765**	757-552-1000
Citadel Federal Credit Union	520 Eagleview Blvd	Exton	PA	19341	**800-666-0191**	610-380-6000
Citizens Equity First Credit Union	5401 W Dirksen Pkwy *Cust Svc	Peoria	IL	61607	**800-633-7077***	309-633-7000
Class Act Federal Credit Union	3620 Fern Vly Rd	Louisville	KY	40219	**800-292-2960**	502-964-7575
Coast Central Credit Union Inc	2650 Harrison Ave	Eureka	CA	95501	**800-974-9727**	707-445-8801
Coastal Federal Credit Union	1000 St Albans Dr	Raleigh	NC	27609	**800-868-4262**	919-420-8000
Commonwealth Credit Union	PO Box 978	Frankfort	KY	40602	**800-228-6420**	502-564-4775
Community America Credit Union (CACU)	9777 Ridge Dr	Lenexa	KS	66219	**800-892-7957**	913-905-7000
Community Resource Federal Credit Union	20 Wade Rd	Latham	NY	12110	**888-783-2211**	518-783-2211
Coors Credit Union	816 Washington Ave	Golden	CO	80401	**800-770-6414**	303-279-6414
Coosa Pines Federal Credit Union	17591 Plant Rd	Childersburg	AL	35044	**800-237-9789**	256-378-5559
Credit Union Acceptance Company LLC	9601 Jones Rd Ste 108	Houston	TX	77065	**866-970-2822**	281-970-2822
Credit Union of Southern California	PO Box 200	Whittier	CA	90608	**866-287-6225**	562-698-8326
Credit Union of Texas	PO Box 517028	Dallas	TX	75251	**800-314-3828**	972-263-9497
Dearborn Federal Credit Union	400 Town Ctr Dr	Dearborn	MI	48126	**888-336-2700**	313-336-2700
Deer Valley Federal Credit Union	16215 N 28th Ave	Phoenix	AZ	85053	**800-579-5051**	602-375-7300
Delta Employees Credit Union	1025 Virginia Ave	Atlanta	GA	30354	**800-544-3328**	404-715-4725
Denver Fire Dept Federal Credit Union (DFDFCU)	2201 Federal Blvd	Denver	CO	80211	**866-880-7770**	303-228-5300
Desert Schools Federal Credit Union	148 N 48th St	Phoenix	AZ	85034	**800-456-9171**	602-433-7000
Digital Employees' Federal Credit Union	220 Donald Lynch Blvd	Marlborough	MA	01752	**800-328-8797**	508-263-6700
Duca Financial Services Credit Union Ltd	5290 Yonge St	Toronto	ON	M2N5P9	**866-900-3822**	416-223-8502
Dupaco Community Credit Union	3999 Pennsylvania Ave	Dubuque	IA	52002	**800-373-7600**	563-557-7600
Educational Employees Credit Union	PO Box 5242	Fresno	CA	93755	**800-538-3328**	559-437-7700
Educators Credit Union (ECU)	1400 N Newman Rd PO Box 081040	Racine	WI	53406	**800-236-5898**	262-886-5900
Eglin Federal Credit Union	838 Eglin Pkwy NE	Fort Walton Beach	FL	32547	**800-367-6159**	850-862-0111
Ent Federal Credit Union	7250 Campus Dr	Colorado Springs	CO	80920	**800-525-9623**	719-574-1100
Evansville Teachers Federal Credit Union	PO Box 5129	Evansville	IN	47716	**800-800-9271**	812-477-9271
FAA Credit Union	PO Box 26406	Oklahoma City	OK	73126	**800-448-1990**	405-682-1990
Faa Federal Credit Union	3920 Whitebrook Dr	Memphis	TN	38118	**800-346-0069**	901-366-0066
Fairwinds Federal Credit Union	3087 N Alafaya Trl	Orlando	FL	32826	**800-443-6887**	407-277-5045
Finance Ctr Federal Credit Union	PO Box 26501	Indianapolis	IN	46226	**800-473-2328**	317-916-7700
Financial Partners Credit Union	PO Box 7005	Downey	CA	90241	**800-950-7328**	562-923-0311
Firefighters Community Credit Union Inc	2300 St Clair Ave NE	Cleveland	OH	44114	**800-621-4644**	216-621-4644
First Community Credit Union (FCCU)	PO Box 1030	Chesterfield	MO	63006	**800-767-8880**	636-728-3333
Fort Knox Federal Credit Union	PO Box 900	Radcliff	KY	40159	**800-756-3678**	502-942-0254
Fort Worth City Credit Union	PO Box 100099	Fort Worth	TX	76185	**888-732-3085**	817-732-2803
Fort Worth Community Credit Union	1905 Forest Ridge Dr PO Box 210848	Bedford	TX	76021	**800-817-8234**	817-835-5000
Forum Credit Union	PO Box 50738	Indianapolis	IN	46250	**800-382-5414**	317-558-6000
Founders Federal Credit Union	607 N Main St *Tech Supp	Lancaster	SC	29720	**888-918-7403***	803-289-5927
Georgia Cu Affiliates	6705 Sugarloaf Pkwy Ste 200	Duluth	GA	30097	**800-768-4282**	770-476-9625
Georgia's Own Credit Union	1155 Peachtree St NE Ste 400	Atlanta	GA	30309	**800-533-2062**	404-874-1166
Gesa Credit Union	51 Gage Blvd PO Box 500	Richland	WA	99352	**888-946-4372**	509-946-1611
Greylock Federal Credit Union	150 W St	Pittsfield	MA	01201	**800-207-5555**	413-236-4000
GTE Federal Credit Union	PO Box 172599	Tampa	FL	33672	**888-871-2690**	813-871-2690
Guadalupe Credit Union	3601 Mimbres Ln	Santa Fe	NM	87507	**800-540-5382**	505-982-8942
Hamilton City Employees Federal Credit Union	309 Ct St	Hamilton	OH	45011	**800-264-5578**	513-868-5881

Name / Address	City	State	ZIP	Toll-Free	Phone
Harbor Credit Union					
800 Weise St	Green Bay	WI	54302	**800-827-4645**	920-431-6688
HarborOne Credit Union					
770 Oak St PO Box 720	Brockton	MA	02301	**800-244-7592**	508-895-1000
Horizon Credit Union					
13224 E Mansfield Ste 300	Spokane Valley	WA	99216	**800-808-6402**	
Hudson Valley Federal Credit Union					
159 Barnegat Rd	Poughkeepsie	NY	12601	**800-468-3011**	845-463-3011
Hughes Federal Credit Union Inc					
PO Box 11900	Tucson	AZ	85734	**866-760-3156**	520-794-8341
I B M Southeast Employees Federal Credit Union					
PO Box 5090	Boca Raton	FL	33431	**888-567-8688**	561-982-4700
Indiana Credit Union League					
5975 Castle Creek Parkway N Ste 300	Indianapolis	IN	46250	**800-285-5300**	317-594-5300
Indiana Members Credit Union (IMCU)					
7110 W Tenth St	Indianapolis	IN	46214	**800-556-9268**	317-248-8556
Island Federal Credit Union					
120 Motor Pkwy	Hauppauge	NY	11788	**800-475-5263**	631-851-1100
Keesler Federal Credit Union					
PO Box 7001	Biloxi	MS	39534	**888-533-7537**	228-385-5500
Kern Schools Federal Credit Union					
PO Box 9506	Bakersfield	CA	93389	**800-221-3311**	661-833-7900
KeyPoint Credit Union					
2805 Bowers Ave	Santa Clara	CA	95051	**888-255-3637**	408-731-4100
Kinecta Federal Credit Union					
1440 Rosecrans Ave PO Box 10003	Manhattan Beach	CA	90266	**800-854-9846**	310-643-5400
L & N Federal Credit Union					
9265 Smyrna Pkwy	Louisville	KY	40229	**800-443-2479**	502-368-5858
La Capitol Federal Credit Union					
PO Box 3398	Baton Rouge	LA	70821	**800-522-2748**	225-342-5055
Lafayette Federal Credit Union (Inc)					
3535 University Blvd W	Kensington	MD	20895	**800-888-6560**	301-929-7990
Landmark Credit Union					
5445 S Westridge Dr PO Box 510910	New Berlin	WI	53151	**800-801-1449**	262-796-4500
Langley Federal Credit Union					
1055 W Mercury Blvd	Hampton	VA	23666	**800-826-7490**	757-827-7200
Leominster Credit Union					
20 Adams St	Leominster	MA	01453	**800-649-4646**	978-537-8021
Local Government Federal Credit Union					
323 W Jones St Ste 600	Raleigh	NC	27603	**888-732-8562**	919-857-2150
Lockheed Federal Credit Union (LFCU)					
2340 Hollywood Way	Burbank	CA	91505	**800-328-5328**	818-565-2020
Los Angeles Federal Credit Union					
PO Box 53032	Los Angeles	CA	90053	**877-695-2328**	818-242-8640
Los Angeles Police Federal Credit Union					
PO Box 10188	Van Nuys	CA	91410	**877-695-2732**	818-787-6520
Members Group Inc, The					
1500 NW 118th St	Des Moines	IA	50325	**800-268-1884**	
Meriwest Credit Union					
PO Box 530953	San Jose	CA	95153	**877-637-4937**	
Midwest America Federal Credit Union					
1104 Medical Pk Dr	Fort Wayne	IN	46825	**800-348-4738**	260-482-3334
Miramar Federal Credit Union					
9494 Miramar Rd	San Diego	CA	92196	**800-640-1228**	858-695-9494
Mission Federal Credit Union					
PO Box 919023	San Diego	CA	92121	**800-500-6328**	858-524-2850
Mountain America Credit Union					
PO Box 9001	West Jordan	UT	84084	**800-748-4302**	801-325-6228
Municipal Credit Union					
PO Box 3205	New York	NY	10007	**866-512-6109**	212-693-4900
Nassau Financial Federal Credit Union					
1325 Franklin Ave Ste 500	Garden City	NY	11530	**800-216-2328**	516-742-4900
Neighbors Federal Credit Union					
PO Box 2831	Baton Rouge	LA	70821	**866-819-2178**	225-819-2178
New England Federal Credit Union					
PO Box 527	Williston	VT	05495	**800-400-8790**	802-879-8790
New Orleans Firemens Federal Credit Union					
PO Box 689	Metairie	LA	70004	**800-647-1689**	504-889-9090
North Country Federal Credit Union Inc					
69 Swift St Ste 100	South Burlington	VT	05403	**800-660-3258**	802-657-6847
North Island Credit Union					
5898 Copley Dr	San Diego	CA	92111	**800-848-5654***	619-656-6525
*Cust Svc					
NuUnion Credit Union					
501 S Capitol Ave	Lansing	MI	48933	**888-267-7200**	517-267-7200
Oklahoma Federal Credit Union					
517 NE 36th St	Oklahoma City	OK	73105	**800-522-8510**	405-524-6467
Orange County's Credit Union					
PO Box 11777	Santa Ana	CA	92711	**888-354-6228**	714-755-5900
Owensboro Federal Credit Union					
717 Harvard Dr PO Box 1189	Owensboro	KY	42302	**800-264-1054**	270-683-1054
Pacific Marine Credit Union					
M C X Complex	Camp Pendleton	CA	92055	**800-736-4500**	760-430-7511
Pacific NW Federal Credit Union (PNWFCU)					
12106 NE Marx St	Portland	OR	97220	**866-692-8669**	503-256-5858
Pacific Service Federal Credit Union					
PO Box 8191	Walnut Creek	CA	94596	**888-858-6878**	925-296-6200
Pearl Harbor Federal Credit Union (PHFCU)					
94-449 Ukee St	Waipahu	HI	96797	**800-987-5583**	
Pennsylvania State Employees Credit Union					
1 Credit Union Pl	Harrisburg	PA	17110	**800-237-7328**	717-234-8484
Pentagon Federal Credit Union					
2930 Eisenhower Ave	Alexandria	VA	22314	**800-247-5626**	
Pine Bluff Cotton Belt Federal Credit Union					
1703 River Pines Blvd	Pine Bluff	AR	71601	**888-249-1904**	870-535-6365
Police & Fire Federal Credit Union					
901 Arch St	Philadelphia	PA	19107	**800-228-8801**	215-931-0300
Portland Teachers Credit Union					
PO Box 3750	Portland	OR	97208	**800-527-3932**	503-228-7077
Premier America Credit Union					
19867 Prairie St PO Box 2178	Chatsworth	CA	91313	**800-772-4000**	818-772-4000
Premier Members Federal Credit Union					
5495 Arapahoe Ave	Boulder	CO	80303	**800-468-0634**	303-657-7000
Provident Central Credit Union					
303 Twin Dolphin Dr	Redwood City	CA	94065	**800-632-4600**	650-508-0300

Name / Address	City	State	ZIP	Toll-Free	Phone
Randolph-Brooks Federal Credit Union					
PO Box 2097	Universal City	TX	78148	**800-580-3300**	210-945-3300
Redstone Federal Credit Union					
220 Wynn Dr NW	Huntsville	AL	35893	**800-234-1234**	256-837-6110
Rhode Island State Employees Credit Union					
160 Francis St	Providence	RI	02903	**855-322-7428**	401-751-7440
Rockland Federal Credit Union					
241 Union St	Rockland	MA	02370	**800-562-7328**	781-878-0232
RTN Federal Credit Union					
600 Main St	Waltham	MA	02452	**800-338-0221**	781-736-9900
SAC Federal Credit Union (SAFCU)					
11515 S 39th St	Bellevue	NE	68123	**800-228-0392**	402-292-8000
Safe 1 Credit Union					
PO Box 2203	Bakersfield	CA	93303	**800-322-4529**	661-327-3818
SAFE Credit Union					
3720 Madison Ave	North Highlands	CA	95660	**800-733-7233**	916-979-7233
Safeamerica Credit Union					
6001 Gibraltar Dr	Pleasanton	CA	94588	**800-972-0999**	925-734-4111
San Antonio Federal Credit Union					
PO Box 1356	San Antonio	TX	78295	**800-234-7228**	210-258-1234
San Diego County Credit Union					
6545 Sequence Dr	San Diego	CA	92121	**877-732-2848**	
San Francisco Federal Credit Union					
770 Golden Gate Ave	San Francisco	CA	94102	**800-852-7598**	415-775-5377
Sb1 Federal Credit Union					
PO Box 7480	Philadelphia	PA	19101	**800-806-9465**	215-569-3700
Schools Financial Credit Union					
1485 Response Rd Ste 126	Sacramento	CA	95815	**800-962-0990**	916-569-5400
Secure First Credit Union					
3000 Winewood Rd	Birmingham	AL	35215	**877-520-2115**	205-520-2115
Security Service Federal Credit Union					
16211 La Cantera Pkwy	San Antonio	TX	78256	**800-527-7328**	210-476-4000
Selco Community Credit Union					
299 E 11th Ave	Eugene	OR	97401	**800-445-4483**	541-686-8000
South Carolina Federal Credit Union					
PO Box 190012	North Charleston	SC	29419	**800-845-0432**	843-797-8300
Space Coast Credit Union					
8045 N Wickham Rd PO Box 419001	Melbourne	FL	32941	**800-447-7228**	321-752-2222
Stanford Federal Credit Union					
1860 Embarcadero Rd	Palo Alto	CA	94303	**888-723-7328**	650-723-2509
Star One Federal Credit Union					
PO Box 3643	Sunnyvale	CA	94088	**866-543-5202**	408-543-5202
State Employees Credit Union of Maryland Inc					
971 Corporate Blvd	Linthicum	MD	21090	**800-879-7328**	410-487-7328
State Employees Federal Credit Union					
700 Patroon Creek Blvd Patroon Creek Corporate Ctr	Albany	NY	12206	**800-727-3328**	518-452-8234
State Employees' Credit Union (SECU)					
PO Box 29606	Raleigh	NC	27626	**888-732-8562**	919-857-2150
Sunstate Federal Credit Union (Inc)					
PO Box 1162	Gainesville	FL	32627	**877-786-7828**	352-381-5200
Teachers Credit Union (TCU)					
PO Box 1395	South Bend	IN	46624	**800-552-4745**	574-284-6247
Teachers Federal Credit Union (TFCU)					
2410 N Ocean Ave	Farmingville	NY	11738	**800-341-4333**	631-698-7000
Tech Credit Union					
10951 Broadway	Crown Point	IN	46307	**800-276-8324**	219-663-5120
Telcoe Federal Credit Union					
820 Lousiana St	Little Rock	AR	72201	**800-482-9009**	501-375-5321
Texans Credit Union					
777 E Campbell Rd	Richardson	TX	75081	**800-843-5295**	972-348-2000
Texas Dow Employees Credit Union (TDECU)					
1001 FM 2004	Lake Jackson	TX	77566	**800-839-1154**	979-297-1154
Tower Federal Credit Union					
7901 Sandy Spring Rd	Laurel	MD	20707	**800-787-8328**	301-497-7000
Travis Federal Credit Union					
1 Travis Way	Vacaville	CA	95687	**800-877-8328**	707-449-4000
Truliant Federal Credit Union					
3200 Truliant Way	Winston-Salem	NC	27103	**800-822-0382**	336-659-1955
Tyco Electronics Federal Credit Union					
PO Box 3449	Redwood City	CA	94064	**888-673-3288**	
U S Employees O C Federal Credit Union					
PO Box 44000	Oklahoma City	OK	73144	**800-227-6366**	405-685-6200
Ukrainian National Federal Credit Union					
215 Second Ave PO Box 160	New York	NY	10003	**866-859-5848**	212-533-2980
United Nations Federal Credit Union (UNFCU)					
24-01 44th Rd Ct Sq Pl	Long Island	NY	11101	**800-891-2471**	347-686-6000
Unitus Community Credit Union					
PO Box 1937	Portland	OR	97207	**800-452-0900**	503-227-5571
University & State Employees Credit Union					
10120 Pacific Heights Blvd Ste 100	San Diego	CA	92121	**866-873-2448**	858-795-6100
University of Hawaii Federal Credit Union					
PO Box 22070	Honolulu	HI	96823	**800-927-3397**	808-983-5500
University of Hawaii Foundation, The					
2444 Dole St Bachman Hall 105	Honolulu	HI	96822	**866-846-4262**	808-956-8849
US Alliance Federal Credit Union					
600 Midland Ave	Rye	NY	10580	**800-431-2754**	
US New Mexico Federal Credit Union (USNMFCU)					
3939 Osuna Rd NE PO Box 129	Albuquerque	NM	87109	**888-342-8766**	505-342-8888
Valley First Credit Union					
PO Box 1411	Modesto	CA	95353	**877-549-4567**	209-549-8500
Vantage Credit Union (VCU)					
PO Box 4433	Bridgeton	MO	63044	**800-522-6009**	314-298-0055
Verity Credit Union					
PO Box 75974	Seattle	WA	98175	**800-444-4589**	206-440-9000
Virginia Credit Union					
7500 Boulders View Dr	Richmond	VA	23225	**800-285-5051**	804-323-6000
Visions Federal Credit Union (VFUC)					
24 McKinley Ave	Endicott	NY	13760	**800-242-2120**	607-754-7900
Vystar Credit Union					
1802 Kernan Blvd S	Jacksonville	FL	32246	**800-445-6289**	904-777-6000
Washington State Employees Credit Union					
330 Union Ave SE	Olympia	WA	98501	**800-562-0999**	360-943-7911
Wescom Credit Union					
123 S Marengo Ave PO Box 7058	Pasadena	CA	91101	**888-493-7266**	626-535-1000
Wings Financial Credit Union					
14985 Glazier Ave Ste 100	Apple Valley	MN	55124	**800-692-2274**	952-997-8000

Name / Address	City	State	ZIP	Toll-Free	Phone
Workers' Credit Union 815 Main St PO Box 900	Fitchburg	MA	01420	**800-221-4020**	978-345-1021
Wright-Patt Credit Union Inc 2455 Executive Pk Blvd PO Box 286	Fairborn	OH	45324	**800-762-0047**	937-912-7000
Y-12 Federal Credit Union 501 Lafayette Dr	Oak Ridge	TN	37830	**800-482-1043**	865-482-1043
Yolo Federal Credit Union 266 W Main St	Woodland	CA	95695	**877-965-6328**	530-668-2700

222 CRUISE LINES

SEE ALSO Travel Agencies ; Casinos ; Cruises - Riverboat ; Ports & Port Authorities

Name / Address	City	State	ZIP	Toll-Free	Phone
Baja Expeditions Inc 3096 Palm St	San Diego	CA	92104	**800-843-6967**	858-581-3311
Blount Small Ship Adventures 461 Water St	Warren	RI	02885	**800-556-7450**	401-247-0955
Bluewater Adventures Ltd 252 E First St Ste 3	North Vancouver	BC	V7L1B3	**888-877-1770**	604-980-3800
Carnival Cruise Lines 3655 NW 87th Ave	Miami	FL	33178	**800-764-7419**	305-599-2600
China Ocean Shipping Co Americas Inc (COSCO) 100 Lighting Way	Secaucus	NJ	07094	**800-242-7354**	201-422-0500
Costa Cruise Lines 200 S Pk Rd Ste 200	Hollywood	FL	33021	**800-462-6782**	954-266-5600
Cruise West 3826 18th Ave W	Seattle	WA	98119	**888-862-8881**	206-283-9322
Cunard Line Ltd 24303 Town Ctr Dr Ste 200	Valencia	CA	91355	**800-728-6273**	661-753-1000
Discovery Cruises Inc 1775 NW 70th Ave	Miami	FL	33126	**800-866-8687**	305-477-2867
Great Lakes Cruise Co 3270 Washtenaw Ave	Ann Arbor	MI	48104	**888-891-0203**	
Holland America Line 300 Elliott Ave W	Seattle	WA	98119	**800-426-0327**	206-281-3535
Hurtigruten 405 Pk Ave	New York	NY	10022	**866-552-0371**	212-319-1300
Lindblad Expeditions 96 Morton St 9th Fl	New York	NY	10014	**800-397-3348**	212-765-7740
Maine Windjammer Cruises PO Box 617	Camden	ME	04843	**800-736-7981**	207-236-2938
Oceania Cruises Inc 8300 NW 33rd St Ste 308	Miami	FL	33122	**800-531-5619**	305-514-2300
Princess Cruises 24844 Rockefeller Ave	Santa Clarita	CA	91355	**800-774-6237**	661-753-0000
Rockport Schooner Cruises PO Box 272	Belfast	ME	04915	**866-732-2473**	207-338-3088
Royal Caribbean International 1050 Caribbean Way	Miami	FL	33132	**800-327-6700**	305-539-6000
Sea Cloud Cruises Inc 282 Grand Ave Ste 3	Englewood	NJ	07631	**888-732-2568**	201-227-9404
SeaDream Yacht Club 601 Brickell Key Dr Ste 1050	Miami	FL	33131	**800-707-4911**	305-631-6110
Star Clippers Inc 760 NW 107th Ave *Resv	Miami	FL	33172	**800-442-0556***	305-442-0550
Travel Dynamics International 132 E 70th St	New York	NY	10021	**800-257-5767**	212-517-7555
Windstar Cruises 2101 Fourth Ave Ste 210 *Resv	Seattle	WA	98121	**800-258-7245***	206-292-9606

223 CRUISES - RIVERBOAT

SEE ALSO Casinos ; Cruise Lines

Name / Address	City	State	ZIP	Toll-Free	Phone
American Cruise Lines 741 Boston Post Rd Ste 200	Guilford	CT	06437	**800-814-6880**	203-453-6800
Englund Marine & Industrial Supply Company Inc 95 Hamburg Ave PO Box 296	Astoria	OR	97103	**800-228-7051**	503-325-4341
French Country Waterways Ltd 24 Bay Rd	Duxbury	MA	02332	**800-222-1236**	781-934-2454
Uniworld 17323 Ventura Blvd	Encino	CA	91316	**800-733-7820**	818-382-7820
Victoria Cruises Inc 57-08 39th Ave *Cust Svc	Woodside	NY	11377	**800-348-8084***	212-818-1680
Viking River Cruises 5700 Canoga Ave Ste 200 *Cust Svc	Woodland Hills	CA	91367	**877-668-4546***	818-227-1234

224 CUTLERY

SEE ALSO Silverware

Name / Address	City	State	ZIP	Toll-Free	Phone
Atlanta Cutlery Corp 2147 Gees Mill Rd	Conyers	GA	30013	**800-883-0300**	770-922-3700
Buck Knives Inc 660 S Lochsa St	Post Falls	ID	83854	**800-326-2825**	208-262-0500
Crescent Manufacturing Co 1310 Majestic Dr	Fremont	OH	43420	**800-537-1330**	419-332-6484
Cutco Corp 1116 E State St	Olean	NY	14760	**800-828-0448**	716-372-3111
Dexter-Russell Inc 44 River St	Southbridge	MA	01550	**800-343-6042**	508-765-0201
Douglas/Quikut Co 118 E Douglas Rd	Walnut Ridge	AR	72476	**800-982-5233**	
Fiskars Brands Inc 2537 Daniels St	Madison	WI	53718	**866-348-5661**	
KA-BAR Knives Inc 200 Homer St	Olean	NY	14760	**800-282-0130**	716-372-5952
Lamson & Goodnow Mfg Co 45 Conway St	Shelburne Falls	MA	01370	**800-872-6564**	413-625-0201
Master Cutlery Inc 700 Penhorn Ave	Secaucus	NJ	07094	**888-271-7229**	201-271-7600
Midwest Tool & Cutlery Co Inc 1210 Progress St PO Box 160	Sturgis	MI	49091	**800-782-4659**	269-651-7964
Ontario Knife Co 26 Empire St	Franklinville	NY	14737	**800-222-5233**	716-676-5527
Pacific Handy Cutter Inc 17819 Gillette Ave *Cust Svc	Irvine	CA	92614	**800-229-2233***	714-662-1033
Professional Cutlery Direct LLC 242 Branford Rd	North Branford	CT	06471	**800-792-6650**	
Queen Cutlery Co 507 Chestnut St *Sales	Titusville	PA	16354	**800-222-5233***	814-827-3673
Rada Manufacturing Co PO Box 838	Waverly	IA	50677	**800-311-9691**	319-352-5454
Swiss Army Brands Inc 7 Victoria Dr PO Box 1212 *Cust Svc	Monroe	CT	06468	**800-442-2706***	203-929-6391
Wenger North America Inc 15 Corporate Dr *Cust Svc	Orangeburg	NY	10962	**800-431-2996***	845-365-3500
WR Case & Sons Cutlery Co 50 Owens Way PO Box 4000	Bradford	PA	16701	**800-523-6350**	

225 CYLINDERS & ACTUATORS - FLUID POWER

SEE ALSO Automotive Parts & Supplies - Mfr

Name / Address	City	State	ZIP	Toll-Free	Phone
Bosch Rexroth Corp 5150 Prairie Stone Pkwy	Hoffman Estates	IL	60192	**800-860-1055**	847-645-3600
Clippard Instrument Lab 7390 Colerain Ave	Cincinnati	OH	45239	**877-245-6247**	513-521-4261
Control Line Equipment Inc 14750 Industrial Pkwy	Cleveland	OH	44135	**888-895-1440**	216-433-7766
Cunningham Manufacturing Co 318 S Webster St	Seattle	WA	98108	**800-767-0038**	206-767-3713
Eckel Mfg Company Inc 8035 N County Rd W	Odessa	TX	79764	**800-654-4779**	432-362-4336
Hader/Seitz Inc 15600 W Lincoln Ave	New Berlin	WI	53151	**877-388-2101**	
Hannon Hydraulics LLC 625 N Loop 12	Irving	TX	75061	**800-333-4266**	972-438-2870
Helac Corp 225 Battersby Ave	Enumclaw	WA	98022	**800-327-2589**	360-825-1601
Hol-Mac Corp 2730-A Hwy 15 PO Box 349	Bay Springs	MS	39422	**800-844-3019**	601-764-4121
Humphrey Products Co 5070 E N Ave PO Box 2008	Kalamazoo	MI	49048	**800-477-8707**	269-381-5500
ITT Industries Inc Engineered Valves Div 33 Centerville Rd	Lancaster	PA	17603	**800-366-1111**	717-509-2200
Luxfer Gas Cylinders 3016 Kansas Ave	Riverside	CA	92507	**800-764-0366**	951-684-5110
Micromatic LLC 525 Berne St	Berne	IN	46711	**800-333-5752**	260-589-2136
Norris Cylinder Co 4818 W Loop 281	Longview	TX	75603	**800-527-8418**	903-757-7633
Parker Hannifin Corp Automation Actuator Div 135 Quadral Dr	Wadsworth	OH	44281	**800-272-7537**	330-336-3511
Parker Hannifin Corp Cylinder Div 500 S Wolf Rd	Des Plaines	IL	60016	**800-272-7537**	847-298-2400
Parker Instrumentation Group 6035 Parkland Blvd	Cleveland	OH	44124	**800-272-7537**	216-896-3000
PHD Inc 9009 Clubridge Dr	Fort Wayne	IN	46809	**800-624-8511**	260-747-6151
Quincy Ortman Cylinders 3501 Wismann Ln PO Box C-2	Quincy	IL	62305	**844-759-4922**	217-277-0321
Sargent Controls & Aerospace 5675 W Burlingame Rd	Tucson	AZ	85743	**800-230-0359**	520-744-1000
Standex International Corp Custom Hoists Div 771 County Rd 30A W PO Box 98	Hayesville	OH	44838	**800-837-4668**	419-368-4721
Tol-O-Matic Inc 3800 County Rd 116	Hamel	MN	55340	**800-328-2174**	763-478-8000
Wabash Technologies 1375 Swan St PO Box 829	Huntington	IN	46750	**800-487-6865**	260-355-4100

226 DATA COMMUNICATIONS SERVICES FOR WIRELESS DEVICES

Companies listed here deliver data such as customized news or stock information, other personalized content, and/or multimedia, audio, and video from the Internet to wireless devices (cellular phones, Personal Digital Assistants, pagers, laptop computers).

Name / Address	City	State	ZIP	Toll-Free	Phone
Accel Networks LLC 4905 34th StS #227	St. Petersburg	FL	33711	**877-406-8585**	
AOL Canada Inc 99 Spadina Ave Ste 200	Toronto	ON	M5V3P8	**888-265-6306**	416-263-8100
Auto Data Direct Inc 1379 Cross Creek Cir	Tallahassee	FL	32301	**866-923-3123**	850-877-8804
BlackBerry 2200 University Ave E Ste 200	Waterloo	ON	N2L3X2	**877-255-2377**	519-888-7465
Broadcast Microwave Services Inc (BMS) 12367 Crosthwaite Cir	Poway	CA	92064	**800-669-9667**	858-391-3050
Buyatab Online Inc 204 - 576 Seymour St	Vancouver	BC	V6B3K1	**888-267-0447**	
Calpop Com Inc 600 W Seventh St	Los Angeles	CA	90017	**866-467-8846**	
Carousel Industries of North America Inc 659 S County Trl	Exeter	RI	02822	**800-401-0760**	
Chatr Wireless 333 Bloor St E 8th Fl	Toronto	ON	M4W1G9	**800-485-9745**	
Cirrus9 Inc 15 Market Sq	Saint John	NB	E2L1E8	**855-643-6691**	
Clevest Solutions Inc 13911 Wireless Way Ste 100	Richmond	BC	V6V3B9	**866-915-0088**	604-214-9700
Cognify PO Box 69337	Oro Valley	AZ	85737	**888-444-7992**	888-264-6439
Com-Net Services Inc 7786 S Commerce Ave	Baton Rouge	LA	70815	**800-676-2137**	225-928-1231
Condo Control Central 10 St Mary Sty Ste 200	Toronto	ON	M5X1C7	**888-762-6636**	

Company	City	State	ZIP	Toll-Free	Phone
Dial800 LLC 9911 Pico Blvd Ste 1200	Los Angeles	CA	90035	**800-700-1987**	800-342-5800
Discover Communications Inc 30 Victoria Crescent	Brampton	ON	L6T1E4	**888-456-8989**	905-455-5600
Doublehorn Communications 1802 W Sixth St	Austin	TX	78703	**855-618-6423**	214-283-1400
DriverDO LLC 734 Massachusetts St	Lawrence	KS	66044	**844-366-6837**	
Dtreds LLC 1329 Shepard Dr Ste 2	Sterling	VA	20164	**877-694-7766**	
DXStorm.com Inc 824 Winston Churchill Blvd	Oakville	ON	L6J7X2	**877-397-8676**	905-842-8262
EDge Interactive Inc 67 Mowat Ave Ste 533	Toronto	ON	M6K3E3	**800-211-5577**	416-494-3343
Execulink Telecom Inc 619 Main St N	Burgessville	ON	N0J1C0	**866-706-1994**	
Fibernetics Corp 605 Boxwood Dr	Cambridge	ON	N3E1A5	**866-973-4237**	519-489-6700
Fibre Noire Internet Inc 550 Ave Beaumont Ste 320	Montreal	QC	H3N1V1	**877-907-3002**	
FreshGrade Inc 301-1447 Ellis St	Kelowna	BC	V1Y2A3	**877-957-7757**	
FundThrough Inc 260 Spadina Ave Ste 400	Toronto	ON	M5T2E4	**800-766-0460**	
Global Relay Communications Inc 220 cambie St	Vancouver	BC	V6B2M9	**866-484-6630**	604-484-6630
GreenSky Trade Credit LLC 1797 Northeast Expy Ste 100	Atlanta	GA	30329	**866-936-0602**	
Hotwire Communications LLC 1 Belmont Ave Ste 1100	Bala Cynwyd	PA	19004	**800-355-5668**	800-409-4733
Huxley Communications Cooperative 102 n main ave	Huxley	IA	50124	**800-231-4922**	515-597-2212
iLeads.com LLC 567 San Nicolas Dr Ste 180	Newport Beach	CA	92660	**877-245-3237**	
Immediatek Inc(NDA) 3301 Airport Fwy Ste 200	Bedford	TX	76021	**888-661-6565**	
Intermec Technologies Corp 6001 36th Ave W *Sales	Everett	WA	98203	**800-934-3163***	425-348-2600
iTalkBB Canada Inc 109 - 235 Yorkland Blvd	North York	ON	M2J4Y8	**877-482-5522**	
Itx Corp 1169 Pittsford Victor Rd Ste 100	Pittsford	NY	14534	**800-600-7785**	585-899-4888
JM Eventsonline ca Inc 155 Colonnade Rd Ste 17	Ottawa	ON	K2E7K1	**866-638-3687**	
Kin Communications Inc 736 Granville St Ste 100	Vancouver	BC	V6Z1G3	**866-684-6730**	604-684-6730
LemonStand eCommerce Inc 912-525 Seymour St	Vancouver	BC	V6B3H7	**855-332-0555**	604-558-0555
Masergy Communications Inc 2740 N Dallas Pkwy Ste 260	Plano	TX	75093	**866-588-5885**	214-442-5700
MediaCore Inc 26 Bastion Sq Ste 205	Victoria	BC	V8W1H9	**877-682-6655**	250-590-9394
Metalink Technologies Inc 417 Wayne Ave PO Box 1124	Defiance	OH	43512	**888-999-8002**	419-782-3472
Mobilicity 101 Exchange Ave	Vaughan	ON	L4K5R6	**877-866-2458**	
Mojio Inc 1080 Howe St 9th Fl	Vancouver	BC	V6Z2T1	**855-556-6546**	
Network Earth Inc 14 Cambridge Ct	Wappingers Falls	NY	12590	**888-201-5160**	
Nitel Inc 1101 W Lk St 6th Fl	Chicago	IL	60607	**888-450-2100**	
NKTelco Inc 301 W S St PO Box 219	New Knoxville	OH	45871	**888-658-3526**	419-753-2457
Oil-Law Records Corp 8 N W 65th St	Oklahoma City	OK	73116	**888-464-5529**	405-840-1631
Outreach Communications 2801 Glenda St	Haltom City	TX	76117	**800-982-3760**	817-288-7200
Pa-Go Mobile Inc 150 NE 95th St Ste 307	Seattle	WA	98115	**877-425-2196**	
Powered By Search Inc 505 Consumers Rd Ste 507	Toronto	ON	M2J4V8	**866-611-5535**	416-840-9044
Redline Communications Inc 302 Town Centre Blvd 3rd Fl	Markham	ON	L3R0E8	**866-633-6669**	905-479-8344
Roam Mobility Inc 400 - 311 Water St	Vancouver	BC	V6B1B8	**888-762-6487**	
Satellite Management Services Inc 4529 E Bwy Rd	Phoenix	AZ	85040	**800-788-8388**	602-386-4444
Smart Cabling Solutions Inc 1250 N Winchester St	Olathe	KS	66061	**877-390-9501**	913-390-9501
SPROUT Wellness Solutions Inc 366 Adelaide St W Ste 301	Toronto	ON	M5V1R9	**866-535-5027**	
Superheat Fgh Services Inc 313 Garnet Dr	New Lenox	IL	60451	**888-508-3226**	
Synchronoss Technologies Inc 200 Crossing Blvd *NASDAQ: SNCR*	Bridgewater	NJ	08807	**866-620-3940**	
TeleCommunication Systems Inc 275 W St Ste 400 *NASDAQ: TSYS*	Annapolis	MD	21401	**800-810-0827**	410-263-7616
TELUS Quebec 6 Rue Jules-A-Brillant	Rimouski	QC	G5L7E4	**866-558-2273**	
TeraGo Networks Inc 55 Commerce Vly Dr W Ste 800	Thornhill	ON	L3T7V9	**866-837-2461**	
Threshold Communications Inc 16541 Redmond Way Ste 245C	Redmond	WA	98052	**844-844-1382**	206-812-6200
Trade Service Company LLC 15092 Ave of Science	San Diego	CA	92128	**800-854-1527**	
Trojan Professional Services Inc 14410 Cerritos Ave	Los Alamitos	CA	90720	**800-451-9723**	
Trulioo Inc 300 - 420 W Hastings St	Vancouver	BC	V6B1L1	**888-773-0179**	
UniteU Technologies Inc 12 Pine Cone Dr	Pittsford	NY	14534	**866-386-4838**	
Weblink Solutions 23950 Craftsman Rd	Calabasas	CA	91302	**866-296-1977**	
WIND Mobile 207 Queens Quay W Ste 710 PO Box 114	Toronto	ON	M5J1A7	**877-946-3184**	
Wireless Analytics LLC 230 N St Ste 4	Danvers	MA	01923	**888-588-5550**	
Zingle Inc 5235 Avenida Encinas Ste A	Carlsbad	CA	92008	**877-946-4536**	
Zyme Solutions Inc 240 Twin Dolphin Dr Ste D	Redwood Shores	CA	94065	**888-200-6629**	650-294-4700

227 DATA PROCESSING & RELATED SERVICES

SEE ALSO Electronic Transaction Processing ; Payroll Services

Company	City	State	ZIP	Toll-Free	Phone
Adxstudio Inc 200 - 1445 Park St	Regina	SK	S4N4C5	**800-508-7811**	306-569-6500
Affinigent Inc 4 Kent Rd Ste 200	York	PA	17402	**800-932-3380**	717-600-0033
Assessment Technology Inc 6700 E Speedway Blvd	Tucson	AZ	85710	**800-367-4762**	520-323-9033
Atlantech Online Inc 1010 Wayne Ave Ste 630	Silver Spring	MD	20910	**800-256-1612**	301-589-3060
Automatic Data Processing Inc (ADP) 1 ADP Blvd *NASDAQ: ADP*	Roseland	NJ	07068	**800-225-5237**	
AutoVision Wireless Inc 360 Deerhide Crescent	Toronto	ON	M9M2Y6	**866-514-8030**	416-747-4444
Beanstalk Data 656 michael wylie dr	Charlotte	NC	28217	**800-892-3997**	
Beanstream Internet Commerce Inc 1803 Douglas St Ste 200	Victoria	BC	V8T5C3	**888-472-0811**	250-472-2326
Blizzard Internet Marketing Inc 50629 Hwy 6	Glenwood Springs	CO	81601	**888-840-5893**	970-928-7875
Blue Rock Technologies 800 Kirts Blvd	Troy	MI	48084	**866-390-8200**	248-786-6100
BlueTie Inc 2480 Browncroft Blvd Ste 2b	Rochester	NY	14625	**800-258-3843**	585-586-2000
BNSF Logistics LLC 4700 S Thompson Ste A202	Springdale	AR	72764	**888-285-4514**	
Capax Global LLC 590 Headquarters Plaza	Morristown	NJ	07960	**888-682-8900**	973-401-0660
Carahsoft Technology Corp 12369 Sunrise Vly Dr Ste D2	Reston	VA	20191	**888-662-2724**	703-871-8500
CCC Information Services Inc 222 Merchandise Mart Plz	Chicago	IL	60654	**800-621-8070**	
Central Service Assn 93 S Coley Rd	Tupelo	MS	38801	**877-842-5962**	662-842-5962
CitiusTech Inc 2 Research Way	Princeton	NJ	08540	**877-248-4871**	
Claimsnet.com Inc 14860 Montfort Dr Ste 250	Dallas	TX	75254	**800-356-1511**	972-458-1701
CNC Software Inc 671 Old Post Rd	Tolland	CT	06084	**800-228-2877**	860-875-5006
Collective Technologies LLC 9433 Bee Caves Rd	Austin	TX	78733	**800-994-1640**	512-263-5500
Colosseum Online Inc 800 Petrolia Rd	Toronto	ON	M3J3K4	**877-739-7873**	416-739-7873
Communication Data Services 1901 Bell Ave	Des Moines	IA	50315	**866-897-7987**	515-246-6837
Computer Services Inc 3901 Technology Dr *OTC: CSVI*	Paducah	KY	42001	**800-545-4274**	270-442-7361
Continental Graphics Corp 4060 N Lakewood Blvd Bldg 801 5th Fl	Long Beach	CA	90808	**800-862-5691**	714-503-4200
Cornwell Data Services Inc 352 Evelyn St	Paramus	NJ	07652	**866-981-1050**	201-261-1050
Crosscom National LLC 900 Deerfield Pkwy	Buffalo Grove	IL	60089	**888-471-6050**	847-520-9200
Cst Data 10725 John Price Rd	Charlotte	NC	28273	**866-383-3282**	704-927-3282
CU*Answers 6000 28th St SE Ste 100	Grand Rapids	MI	49546	**800-327-3478**	616-285-5711
Customer Paradigm Inc 5353 Manhattan Cir Ste 103	Boulder	CO	80303	**888-772-0777**	303-499-9318
D K Global 420 Missouri Ct	Redlands	CA	92373	**866-375-2214**	909-747-0201
D Net Internet Service 208 E Palmer St	Franklin	NC	28734	**877-601-3638**	828-349-3638
Dantom Systems Inc 29241 Beck Rd	Wixom	MI	48393	**866-536-2376**	248-567-7300
Data Dash Inc 3928 Delor St	Saint Louis	MO	63116	**800-211-5988**	314-832-5788
Data Services Inc 31516 Winterplace Pkwy	Salisbury	MD	21804	**800-432-4066**	410-546-2206
Datamark Inc 123 W Mills Ave Ste 400	El Paso	TX	79901	**800-477-1944**	
Desert Dog Marketing LLC 4641 N 12th St Ste 200	Phoenix	AZ	85014	**800-506-0398**	
Destiny Solutions Inc 40 Holly St	Toronto	ON	M4S3C3	**866-403-0500**	416-480-0500
Direct Online Marketing 4727 Jacob St	Wheeling	WV	26003	**800-979-3177**	304-214-4850
Directory One Inc 9135 Katy Fwy Ste 204	Houston	TX	77024	**800-477-1324**	713-465-0051
DirectWest Corp 2550 Sandra Schmirler Way Ste 200	Regina	SK	S4W1A1	**800-667-8201**	306-777-0333
Discovery Research Group 6975 Union Pk Ctr Ste 150	Midvale	UT	84047	**800-678-3748**	
Doc 2 E-file Inc 4500 S Wayside Dr Ste 102	Houston	TX	77087	**888-649-2006**	713-649-2006
Docufree Corp 1175 Northmeadow Pkwy Ste 140	Roswell	GA	30076	**877-220-4350**	770-643-2900
DoxTek Inc 264 W Center St	Orem	UT	84057	**877-705-7226**	
DPF Data Services Group Inc 1990 Swarthmore Ave	Lakewood	NJ	08701	**800-431-4416**	732-370-8840
Dundee Internet Service Inc 168 Riley St	Dundee	MI	48131	**888-222-8485**	734-529-5331
DuVoice Corp 608 State St S Ste 100	Kirkland	WA	98033	**800-888-1057**	425-889-9790

				Toll-Free	Phone
Effective Data Inc 1515 E Wdfield Rd	Schaumburg	IL	60173	**877-825-5233**	847-969-9300
Enhanced Software Products Inc 1811 N Hutchinson Rd	Spokane	WA	99212	**800-456-5750**	509-534-1514
Equifax Inc 1550 Peachtree St NW *NYSE: EFX* ■ *Sales	Atlanta	GA	30309	**888-202-4025***	404-885-8000
Fair Isaac Corp 2665 Long Lake Rd Bldg C *NYSE: FICO* ■ *Cust Svc	Roseville	MN	55113	**888-342-6336***	612-758-5200
Forte Data Systems Inc 3330 Paddock Pkwy	Suwanee	GA	30024	**800-571-8702**	678-208-0206
Genetec Inc 2280 Alfred-Nobel Blvd Ste 400	Montreal	QC	H4S2A4	**866-684-8006**	514-332-4000
GEOSPAN Corp 10900 73rd Ave N Ste 136	Minneapolis	MN	55369	**800-436-7726**	763-493-9320
Glance Networks Inc 1167 Massachusetts Ave	Arlington	MA	02476	**877-452-6236**	781-646-8505
Global Health Care Exchange LLC (GHX) 1315 W Century Dr	Louisville	CO	80027	**800-968-7449**	720-887-7000
Goold Health Systems Inc PO Box 1090	Augusta	ME	04332	**800-832-9672**	207-622-7153
GreenGeeks LLC 5739 Kanan Rd Ste 300	Agoura Hills	CA	91301	**877-326-7483**	310-496-8946
Habanero Consulting Group Inc 510-1111 Melville St	Vancouver	BC	V6E3V6	**866-841-6201**	604-709-6201
Health Management Systems Inc 401 Pk Ave S	New York	NY	10016	**877-357-3268**	212-857-5000
Hivelocity Ventures Corp 8010 Woodland Ctr Blvd Ste 700	Tampa	FL	33614	**888-869-4678**	813-471-0355
Impatica Inc 2430 Don Reid Dr Ste 200	Ottawa	ON	K1H1E1	**800-548-3475**	613-736-9982
Incontrol Technology Inc 1651 e main st	El Cajon	CA	92021	**888-508-1288**	619-270-1260
InfoMine Inc 580 Hornby St Ste 900	Vancouver	BC	V6C3B6	**888-683-2037**	604-683-2037
Innotap 200 North Warner Rd Ste 210	King of Prussia	PA	19406	**855-438-4666**	
Inspired eLearning Inc 613 NW Loop 410 Ste 530	San Antonio	TX	78216	**800-631-2078**	210-579-0224
Internet Nebraska Inc 1719 N Cotner Blvd Ste B	Lincoln	NE	68505	**800-438-4638**	402-434-8680
Kelser Corp 111 Roberts St Ste D	East Hartford	CT	06108	**800-647-5316**	860-528-9819
Kirtley Technology Corp 9s531 Wilmette Ave	Darien	IL	60561	**888-757-0778**	630-512-0213
La Touraine Inc 625 Broadway Ste 700	San Diego	CA	92101	**800-893-8871**	
Learning Enhancement Corp 200 S Wacker Dr Ste 3100	Chicago	IL	60606	**877-272-4610**	312-455-1758
Leatherup Com 955 Venice Blvd	Los Angeles	CA	90015	**800-846-6010**	213-763-6185
LoganBritton Inc 1700 Park St Ste 111	Naperville	IL	60563	**800-362-4352**	
Lowe-Martin Company Inc 400 Hunt Club Rd	Ottawa	ON	K1V1C1	**866-521-9871**	613-741-0962
Lumension Security Inc 8660 E Hartford Dr Ste 300	Scottsdale	AZ	85255	**888-725-7828**	
Mid America Computer Corp PO Box 700	Blair	NE	68008	**800-622-2502**	402-426-6222
Mile High Shooting Accessories LLC 3731 Monarch St	Erie	CO	80516	**877-871-9990**	303-255-9999
Modern Earth 449 Provencher Blvd	Winnipeg	MB	R2J0B8	**866-766-7640**	204-885-2469
Mudiam Inc 7100 regency Sq blvd	Houston	TX	77036	**888-306-2062**	713-484-7266
N-Dimension Solutions Inc 9030 Leslie St Unit 300	Richmond Hill	ON	L4B1G2	**866-837-8884**	905-707-8884
Nakina Systems Inc 80 Hines Rd Ste 200	Ottawa	ON	K2K2T8	**877-625-4627**	613-254-7351
Nexcess.net LLC 21700 Melrose Ave	Southfield	MI	48075	**866-639-2377**	
One Technologies LP 8144 Walnut Hill Ln Ste 600	Dallas	TX	75231	**888-550-8471**	
Openface Inc 3445 Park Ave	Montreal	QC	H2X2H6	**800-865-8585**	514-281-8585
Opinion Access Corp 47-10 32nd Pl	Long Island	NY	11101	**888-489-3282**	718-729-2622
Optimetra Inc 1710 Chapel Hills Dr	Colorado Springs	CO	80920	**800-758-9710**	
Orchid Suites Inc 1309 Emerson St NW	Washington	DC	20011	**877-255-4300**	
P K W Associates Inc 705 E Ordnance Rd Ste 108	Baltimore	MD	21226	**888-358-3900**	443-773-1000
PenTeleData 540 Delaware Ave PO Box 197	Palmerton	PA	18071	**800-281-3564**	
Pinnacle Business Systems Inc 3824 S Blvd St Ste 200	Edmond	OK	73013	**800-311-0757**	
Pinpoint Data 339 Somerset St	North Plainfield	NJ	07060	**866-974-6764**	908-756-9400
Printco Graphics Inc 14112 Industrial Rd	Omaha	NE	68144	**888-593-1080**	402-593-1080
Printmail Systems Inc 23 Friends Ln	Newtown	PA	18940	**800-910-4844**	215-860-4250
PRISMHR 50 Resnik Rd Ste 200	Plymouth	MA	02360	**877-837-4311**	508-747-7261
Protogate Inc 12225 World Trade Dr	San Diego	CA	92128	**877-473-0190**	858-451-0865
Pyramid Consulting Inc 11100 Atlantis Pl	Alpharetta	GA	30022	**877-248-0024**	678-514-3500
Ramco Systems Corp 3150 Brunswick Pk Ste 130	Lawrenceville	NJ	08648	**800-472-6261**	609-620-4800
Rangam Consultants Inc 370 Campus Dr Ste 103	Somerset	NJ	08873	**877-583-7054**	908-704-8843
Red Clay Interactive 22 Buford Village Way Ste 221	Buford	GA	30518	**866-251-2800**	770-297-2430
RedTail Solutions Inc 69 Milk St Ste 100	Westborough	MA	01581	**866-764-7601**	508-983-1900
Renew Data Corp 9500 Arboretum Blvd	Austin	TX	78759	**888-811-3789**	512-276-5500
Right Systems Inc 2600 Willamette Dr NE Ste C	Lacey	WA	98516	**800-571-1717**	360-956-0414
Rugged Systems Inc 13000 Danielson St Q	Poway	CA	92064	**888-584-2673**	858-391-1006
Saepio Technologies Inc 4601 Madison Ave 4th Fl	Kansas City	MO	64112	**877-468-7613**	816-777-2100
Scicom Data Services Ltd 10101 Bren Rd E	Minnetonka	MN	55343	**800-488-9087**	952-933-4200
Shop Floor Automations Inc 5360 Jackson Dr	La Mesa	CA	91942	**877-611-5825**	619-461-4000
Sigma Solutions Inc 422 E Ramsey Rd	San Antonio	TX	78216	**800-567-5964**	210-348-9876
Simplifile LC 4844 North 300 West Ste 202	Provo	UT	84604	**800-460-5657**	801-373-0151
Skybank Financial Services Corp 1444 Biscayne Blvd Ste 309	Miami	FL	33132	**800-617-9980**	
Sof Tec Solutions Inc 384 Inverness Pkwy # 211	Englewood	CO	80112	**888-376-3832**	303-662-1010
Softlayer Technologies Inc 4849 Alpha Rd *Sales	Dallas	TX	75244	**866-398-7638***	214-442-0600
SourceMedical Solutions Inc 100 Grandview Pl Ste 400	Birmingham	AL	35243	**866-245-8093**	
Southern Data Systems Inc 1245 Land O Lakes Dr	Roswell	GA	30075	**888-425-6151**	770-993-7103
Spectrum Data Inc 131 N Third St	Oregon	IL	61061	**800-733-6567**	815-732-6567
SportsDirect Inc 211 Horseshoe Lk Dr	Halifax	NS	B3S1E1	**866-756-9771**	902-835-3320
Storm Internet Services Inc 1760 Courtwood Crescent	Ottawa	ON	K2C2B5	**866-257-8676**	613-567-6585
SunGard Data Systems Inc 680 E Swedesford Rd	Wayne	PA	19087	**866-264-4829**	416-646-5932
Systems House, The 1033 Rte 46 East Ste A202	Clifton	NJ	07013	**800-637-5556**	973-777-8050
Taskstream LLC 71 W 23rd St	New York	NY	10010	**800-311-5656**	212-868-2700
Tax Management Associates Inc 2225 Coronation Blvd	Charlotte	NC	28227	**800-951-5350**	704-847-1234
Techware Distribution Inc 7720 W 78th St	Minneapolis	MN	55439	**800-295-0083**	952-944-0083
Tecnicard Inc 3191 Coral Way Ste 800	Miami	FL	33145	**800-317-6020**	305-442-0018
Teradata Corp 10000 Innovation Dr *NYSE: TDC*	Dayton	OH	45342	**866-548-8348**	
TigerLead Solutions LLC 30700 Russell Ranch Rd Ste 102	Westlake Village	CA	91362	**888-844-3744**	
Townsend Security 724 columbia st nw	Olympia	WA	98501	**800-357-1019**	360-359-4400
Trend 660 American Ave Ste 203	King Of Prussia	PA	19406	**877-330-9900**	610-783-4650
Triton-Tek Inc 445 W Erie St Ste 208	Chicago	IL	60654	**866-387-4866**	312-467-9201
Urban Web Design 102-19 Dallas Rd	Victoria	BC	V8V5A6	**877-889-2573**	250-380-1296
V-fluence Interactive Public Realtions Inc 7770 Regents Rd	San Diego	CA	92122	**877-835-8362**	
Vam USA LLC 19210 Hardy Rd	Houston	TX	77041	**888-863-5204**	713-479-3200
Versasuite 13401 Pond Springs Rd	Austin	TX	78729	**800-903-8774**	512-249-8774
Versatile Systems Inc 4900 Ritter Rd Ste 100 *NYSE: CVE*	Mechanicsburg	PA	17055	**800-262-1622**	
Web Age Solutions Inc 439 University Ave Ste 820	Toronto	ON	M5G1Y8	**866-206-4644**	
Williams Records Management 1925 E Vernon Ave *Cust Svc	Los Angeles	CA	90058	**888-478-3453***	323-234-3453
Wrightsoft Corp 131 Hartwell Ave	Lexington	MA	02421	**800-225-8697**	
XE.com Inc 1145 Nicholson Rd Ste 200	Newmarket	ON	L3Y9C3	**877-932-6640**	416-214-5606
Xiologix 8215 SW Tualatin Sherwood	Tualatin	OR	97062	**888-492-6843**	503-691-4364
Z57 Internet Solutions 10045 Mesa Rim Rd	San Diego	CA	92121	**800-899-8148**	

228 DATING SERVICES

				Toll-Free	Phone
Art Craft Display Inc 500 Business Centre Dr	Lansing	MI	48917	**800-878-0710**	517-485-2221
Ashley Madison Agency, The 2300 Yonge St	Toronto	ON	M4P1E4	**866-742-2218**	
Balnea Spa 319 chemin du Lac Gale	Bromont	QC	J2L2S5	**866-734-2110**	450-534-0604
Caledon Laboratories Ltd 40 Armstrong Ave	Georgetown	ON	L7G4R9	**877-225-3366**	905-877-0101
Cmrg Business Solutions 2401 Trinity Ln	Mckinney	TX	75070	**888-828-8097**	
Digiscribe International LLC 150 Clearbrook Rd Ste 125	Elmsford	NY	10523	**800-686-7577**	
Forest Preserve Dist of Dupage County 1717 31st St	Oak Brook	IL	60523	**800-526-0857**	630-616-8424
Friendfinder Network Inc 6800 Broken Sound Pkwy Ste 200 *TSE: FFN*	Boca Raton	FL	33487	**888-575-8383**	561-912-7000
Herlache Enterprises 6417 W 87th St Ste 3	Oak Lawn	IL	60453	**888-446-8854**	
iGov Technologies Inc 9211 Palm River Rd Ste 110	Tampa	FL	33619	**800-777-9375**	813-612-9470
Omni Cubed Inc 1390 Broadway Ste B155	Placerville	CA	95667	**877-311-1976**	

				Toll-Free	Phone
SVM LP 200 E Howard Ave Ste 220	Des Plaines	IL	60018	**877-300-1786**	
Tarrytown House Estate & Conference Center 49 E Sunnyside Ln	Tarrytown	NY	10591	**800-553-8118**	914-591-8200
Wedding Experience 2307 Douglas Rd Ste 400	Coral Gables	FL	33145	**866-223-9672**	305-421-1260

229 DENTAL ASSOCIATIONS - STATE

SEE ALSO Health & Medical Professionals Associations

				Toll-Free	Phone
Arizona Dental Assn 3193 N Drinkwater Blvd	Scottsdale	AZ	85251	**800-866-2732**	480-344-5777
Arkansas State Dental Assn 7480 Hwy 107	Sherwood	AR	72120	**800-501-2732**	501-834-7650
California Dental Assn 1201 K St	Sacramento	CA	95853	**800-736-7071**	916-443-0505
Colorado Dental Assn 8301 E Prentice Ave Ste 400	Greenwood Village	CO	80111	**866-777-4771**	303-740-6900
Florida Dental Assn 1111 E Tennessee St	Tallahassee	FL	32308	**800-877-9922**	850-681-3629
Georgia Dental Assn 7000 Peachtree Dnwdy Rd NE Ste 200 Bldg 17	Atlanta	GA	30328	**800-432-4357**	404-636-7553
Hawaii Dental Assn 1345 S Beretania St Ste 301	Honolulu	HI	96814	**800-359-6725**	808-593-7956
Illinois State Dental Society 1010 S Second St	Springfield	IL	62704	**888-286-2447**	217-525-1406
Indiana Dental Assn 401 W Michigan St	Indianapolis	IN	46202	**800-562-5646**	317-634-2610
Iowa Dental Assn 8797 NW 54th Ave Ste 100	Johnston	IA	50131	**800-828-2181**	515-331-2298
Louisiana Dental Assn 7833 Office Pk Blvd	Baton Rouge	LA	70809	**800-388-6642**	225-926-1986
Massachusetts Dental Society 2 Willow St Ste 200	Southborough	MA	01745	**800-342-8747**	508-480-9797
Michigan Dental Assn 3657 Okemos Rd Ste 200	Okemos	MI	48864	**800-589-2632**	517-372-9070
Minnesota Dental Assn 1335 Industrial Blvd Ste 200	Minneapolis	MN	55413	**800-950-3368**	612-767-8400
Mississippi Dental Assn 439 B katherine Dr Ste C	Flowood	MS	39232	**866-982-0442**	601-664-9691
Missouri Dental Assn 3340 American Ave	Jefferson City	MO	65109	**800-688-1907**	573-634-3436
Montana Dental Assn 17 1/2 S Last Chance Gulch PO Box 1154	Helena	MT	59624	**800-257-4988**	406-443-2061
Nebraska Dental Assn 7160 S 29th St Ste 1	Lincoln	NE	68516	**888-789-2614**	402-476-1704
Nevada Dental Assn 8863 W Flamingo Rd Ste 102	Las Vegas	NV	89147	**800-962-6710**	702-255-4211
New Mexico Dental Assn 9201 Montgomery Blvd NE Ste 601	Albuquerque	NM	87111	**888-787-1722**	505-294-1368
New York State Dental Assn 20 Corporate Woods Blvd #602	Albany	NY	12211	**800-255-2100**	518-465-0044
North Carolina Dental Society 1600 Evans Rd	Cary	NC	27513	**800-662-8754**	919-677-1396
North Dakota Dental Assn PO Box 1332	Bismarck	ND	58501	**800-444-1330**	701-223-8870
Ohio Dental Assn 1370 Dublin Rd	Columbus	OH	43215	**800-497-6076**	614-486-2700
Oklahoma Dental Assn 317 NE 13th St	Oklahoma City	OK	73104	**800-876-8890**	405-848-8873
Oregon Dental Assn PO Box 3710	Wilsonville	OR	97070	**800-452-5628**	503-218-2010
South Carolina Dental Assn 120 Stonemark Ln	Columbia	SC	29210	**800-327-2598**	803-750-2277
South Dakota Dental Assn 804 N Euclid Ave Ste 103	Pierre	SD	57501	**866-551-8023**	605-224-9133
Texas Dental Assn 1946 S IH-35 Ste 400	Austin	TX	78704	**800-832-1145**	512-443-3675
Virginia Dental Assn (VDA) 3460 Mayland Ct Ste 110	Richmond	VA	23233	**877-726-0850**	804-288-5750
Wisconsin Dental Assn 6737 W Washington St Ste 2360	West Allis	WI	53214	**800-364-7646**	414-276-4520

230 DENTAL EQUIPMENT & SUPPLIES - MFR

				Toll-Free	Phone
3M ESPE Dental Products Div 3M Ctr Bldg 0275-02-SE-03	Saint Paul	MN	55144	**800-634-2249**	651-575-5144
3M Unitek 2724 Peck Rd	Monrovia	CA	91016	**800-634-5300**	
A-dec Inc 2601 Crestview Dr *Cust Svc	Newberg	OR	97132	**800-547-1883***	503-538-7478
Accutron Inc 1733 Parkside Ln	Phoenix	AZ	85027	**800-531-2221**	623-780-2020
Air Techniques Inc 1295 Walt Whitman Rd	Melville	NY	11747	**888-247-8481**	516-433-7676
Alpha Pro Tech Ltd 60 Centurian Dr	Markham	ON	L3R9R2	**800-749-1363**	905-479-0654
Am-Touch Dental 28703 Industry Dr	Valencia	CA	91355	**800-350-4568**	661-294-1213
American Orthodontics Corp 1714 Cambridge Ave	Sheboygan	WI	53081	**800-558-7687**	920-457-5051
Aribex Inc 744 South 400 East	Orem	UT	84097	**866-340-5522**	801-226-5522
Barnhardt Mfg Co 1100 Hawthorne Ln	Charlotte	NC	28205	**800-277-0377**	
Bicon LLC 501 Arborway	Boston	MA	02130	**800-882-4266**	617-524-4443
Brasseler USA 1 Brasseler Blvd	Savannah	GA	31419	**800-841-4522**	
Buffalo Dental Manufacturing Company Inc 159 Lafayette Dr	Syosset	NY	11791	**800-828-0203**	516-496-7200
Centrix Inc 770 River Rd	Shelton	CT	06484	**800-235-5862**	203-929-5582
Coltene/Whaledent Inc 235 Ascot Pkwy	Cuyahoga Falls	OH	44223	**800-221-3046**	330-916-8800
Den-Mat Corp 2727 Skyway Dr	Santa Maria	CA	93455	**800-433-6628**	805-922-8491
DEN-TAL-EZ Group Inc 2 W Liberty Blvd Ste 160	Malvern	PA	19355	**866-383-4636**	610-725-8004
DEN-TAL-EZ Inc Equipment Div 2500 Hwy 31 S	Bay Minette	AL	36507	**800-383-4636**	251-937-6781
Dentsply Caulk 38 W Clarke Ave	Milford	DE	19963	**800-532-2855**	302-422-4511
DENTSPLY International 221 W Philadelphia St PO Box 872	York	PA	17405	**800-800-2888**	717-845-7511
Dentsply International Inc 221 W Philadelphia St PO Box 872 *NASDAQ: XRAY*	York	PA	17405	**800-877-0020**	717-845-7511
Dentsply International Inc Tulsa Dental Div 5100 E Skelly Dr Ste 300	Tulsa	OK	74135	**800-662-1202**	918-493-6598
G & H Wire Company Inc 2165 Earlywood Dr	Franklin	IN	46131	**800-526-1026**	317-346-6655
GC America Inc 3737 W 127th St *Cust Svc	Alsip	IL	60803	**800-323-7063***	708-597-0900
Great Lakes Orthodontic Laboratories Div 200 Cooper Ave	Tonawanda	NY	14150	**800-828-7626**	
Heraeus 300 Heraeus Way *General	South Bend	IN	46614	**800-431-1785***	
Hu-Friedy Mfg Company Inc 3232 N Rockwell St	Chicago	IL	60618	**800-483-7433**	773-975-6100
Hygenic Corp 1245 Home Ave	Akron	OH	44310	**800-321-2135**	330-633-8460
Isolite Systems 111 Castilian Dr	Santa Barbara	CA	93117	**800-560-6066**	805-560-9888
Keystone Dental Inc 144 Middlesex Tpke	Burlington	MA	01803	**866-902-9272**	781-328-3490
Kinetic Instrument Inc 17 Berkshire Blvd	Bethel	CT	06801	**800-233-2346**	203-743-0080
Lancer Orthodontics Inc 1493 Poinsettia Bldg 143 *NYSE: LANZ* ■ *Cust Svc	Vista	CA	92081	**800-854-2896***	760-744-5585
Lang Dental Manufacturing Co 175 Messner Dr	Wheeling	IL	60090	**800-222-5264**	847-215-6622
LifeCore Biomedical LLC 3515 Lyman Blvd *Cust Svc	Chaska	MN	55318	**800-348-4368***	952-368-4300
M & M Innovations 7424 Blythe Island Hwy	Brunswick	GA	31523	**800-688-3384**	912-265-7110
Midwest Dental Equipment Services & Supplies 2700 Commerce St	Wichita Falls	TX	76301	**800-766-2025**	
Myotronics-noromed Inc 5870 S 194th St	Kent	WA	98032	**800-426-0316**	206-243-4214
Net32 Inc 250 Towne Village Dr	Cary	NC	27513	**800-517-1997**	919-468-1177
Nobel Biocare USA Inc 22715 Savi Ranch Pkwy	Yorba Linda	CA	92887	**800-993-8100**	714-282-4800
ORMCO Corp 1717 W Collins Ave *Cust Svc	Orange	CA	92867	**800-854-1741***	714-516-7400
Pentron Clinical Technologies LLC 53 N Plains Industrial Rd	Wallingford	CT	06492	**800-243-3969**	
Practicon Inc 1112 Sugg Pkwy	Greenville	NC	27834	**800-959-9505**	252-752-5183
Premier Dental Products Co 1710 Romano Dr PO Box 4500	Plymouth Meeting	PA	19462	**888-773-6872**	610-239-6000
Quantum Dental Technologies Inc 748 Briar Hill Ave	Toronto	ON	M6B1L3	**866-993-9910**	
Rocky Mountain Orthodontics Inc (RMO Inc) 650 W Colfax Ave	Denver	CO	80204	**800-525-6375**	303-592-8200
Sirona Dental Systems LLC 4835 Sirona Dr Ste 100	Charlotte	NC	28273	**800-659-5977**	704-587-0453
Southern Implants Inc 5 Holland Bldg 209	Irvine	CA	92618	**866-700-2100**	949-273-8505
Stern Empire Dental Lab 1805 W 34th St	Houston	TX	77018	**800-229-0214**	713-688-1301
Sunstar Americas Inc 4635 W Foster Ave	Chicago	IL	60630	**888-777-3101**	
TP Orthodontics Inc 100 Ctr Plz	La Porte	IN	46350	**800-348-8856**	219-785-2591
Water Pik Inc 1730 E Prospect Rd	Fort Collins	CO	80553	**800-525-2774**	

231 DEPARTMENT STORES

				Toll-Free	Phone
Ann & Hope Inc 1 Ann & Hope Way	Cumberland	RI	02864	**877-228-7824**	
Bloomingdale's 1000 Third Ave	New York	NY	10022	**800-950-0047**	212-705-2000
Bob's Sporting Goods 1111 Hudson St	Longview	WA	98632	**800-292-5551**	360-425-3870
Bon-Ton Stores Inc 2801 E Market St *NASDAQ: BONT*	York	PA	17402	**800-945-4438**	717-757-7660
Cookies The Kids Department Store 510 Fulton St	Brooklyn	NY	11201	**877-942-6654**	718-797-3300
Fred's Inc 4300 New Getwell Rd *NASDAQ: FRED*	Memphis	TN	38118	**800-374-7417**	901-365-8880
Gordman 12100 W Ctr Rd	Omaha	NE	68144	**855-290-6454**	402-691-4000
Kohl's Corp N 56 W 17000 Ridgewood Dr *NYSE: KSS*	Menomonee Falls	WI	53051	**855-564-5705**	262-703-7000
Langstons Co 2034 NW Seventh St	Oklahoma City	OK	73106	**800-658-2831**	405-235-9536
Lord & Taylor 424 Fifth Ave	New York	NY	10018	**800-223-7440**	212-391-3344
Macy's 400 Fifth Ave	Pittsburgh	PA	15219	**877-884-3751**	513-573-7912
Macy's Inc 7 W 7th St *NYSE: M*	Cincinnati	OH	45202	**800-261-5385**	513-579-7000
Masters Inc 5741 NW Cornelius Pass Rd	Hillsboro	OR	97124	**877-652-5656**	503-531-3308
Peebles Inc 1 Peebles St	South Hill	VA	23970	**800-723-4548**	800-743-8730

Company / Address	City	State	ZIP	Toll-Free	Phone
Proffitt & Goodson Inc Old Kingston Pl 4800 Old Kingston Pk Ste 200	Knoxville	TN	37919	866-776-3355	865-584-1850
Sears Canada Inc 290 Yonge St Ste 700 *TSE: SCC*	Toronto	ON	M5B2C3	877-987-3277	416-362-1711
SmartBargains Inc 101 S State Rd 7 Ste 201	Hollywood	FL	33023	877-222-6660	
Target Corp 1000 Nicollet Mall *NYSE: TGT* ■ *Cust Svc	Minneapolis	MN	55403	800-440-0680*	612-304-6073
Tongass Trading Co 201 Dock St	Ketchikan	AK	99901	800-235-5102	907-225-5101
Wal-Mart Stores Inc 702 SW Eigth St *NYSE: WMT* ■ *Cust Svc	Bentonville	AR	72716	800-925-6278*	479-273-4000
Walmart.com 1919 Davis St	San Leandro	CA	94577	800-925-6278	

232 DEVELOPMENTAL CENTERS

Residential facilities for the developmentally disabled.

Company / Address	City	State	ZIP	Toll-Free	Phone
Productive Alternatives Inc 1205 N Tower Rd	Fergus Falls	MN	56537	800-627-3529	218-998-5630
Sonoma Developmental Ctr 15000 Arnold Dr	Eldridge	CA	95431	800-862-0007	707-938-6000
Woodward Resource Ctr 1251 334th St	Woodward	IA	50276	888-229-9223	515-438-2600

233 DIAGNOSTIC PRODUCTS

SEE ALSO Medicinal Chemicals & Botanical Products ; Pharmaceutical Companies ; Pharmaceutical Companies - Generic Drugs ; Biotechnology Companies

Company / Address	City	State	ZIP	Toll-Free	Phone
Abaxis Inc 3240 Whipple Rd *NASDAQ: ABAX*	Union City	CA	94587	800-822-2947	510-675-6500
Abbott Laboratories Abbott Diagnostics Div 100 Abbott Pk Rd	Abbott Park	IL	60064	800-387-8378	847-937-6100
Accurate Chemical & Scientific Corp 300 Shames Dr	Westbury	NY	11590	800-645-6264	516-333-2221
Advanced Biotechnologies Inc (ABI) 9108 Guilford Rd	Columbia	MD	21046	800-426-0764	410-792-9779
Akorn Inc 1925 W Field Ct *NASDAQ: AKRX*	Lake Forest	IL	60045	800-932-5676	847-279-6100
ALerCHEK Inc 15 Oak St Ste 302	Springvale	ME	04083	877-282-9542	207-490-2266
Alere Inc 51 Sawyer Rd Ste 200	Waltham	MA	02453	877-441-7440	781-647-3900
Alere San Diego Inc 9975 Summers Ridge Rd	San Diego	CA	92121	866-284-3684	781-647-3900
Alk - Abello Pharmaceuticals Inc 35-151 Brunel Rd	Mississauga	ON	L4Z2H6	800-663-0972	905-290-9952
Allermed Laboratories Inc 7203 Convoy Ct	San Diego	CA	92111	800-221-2748	
Aloha Medicinals Inc 2300 Arrowhead Dr	Carson City	NV	89706	877-835-6091	775-886-6300
Amresco Inc 6681 Cochran Rd	Solon	OH	44139	800-448-4442	440-349-1313
AnaSpec Inc 34801 Campus Dr	Fremont	CA	94555	800-452-5530	510-791-9560
AntiCancer Inc 7917 Ostrow St	San Diego	CA	92111	800-511-2555	858-654-2555
Ascend Therapeutics Inc 607 Herndon Pkwy Ste 110	Herndon	VA	20170	888-412-5751	703-471-4744
Athena Diagnostics Inc 377 Plantation St 2nd Fl	Worcester	MA	01605	800-394-4493	508-756-2886
Bachem-Peninsula Laboratories Inc 305 Old County Rd	San Carlos	CA	94070	800-922-1516	650-801-6090
Baxter Corp 7125 Mississauga Rd	Mississauga	ON	L5N0C2	866-234-2345	905-369-6000
BD Diagnostics 7 Loveton Cir	Sparks	MD	21152	800-666-6433	410-316-4000
Becton Dickinson & Co 1 Becton Dr *NYSE: BDX* ■ *Cust Svc	Franklin Lakes	NJ	07417	888-237-2762*	201-847-6800
Bio-Rad Laboratories 1000 Alfred Nobel Dr *NYSE: BIO*	Hercules	CA	94547	800-424-6723	510-724-7000
Biocell Laboratories Inc 2001 University Dr	Rancho Dominguez	CA	90220	800-222-8382	310-537-3300
BioGenex Laboratories Inc 4600 Norris Canyon Rd	San Ramon	CA	94583	800-421-4149	925-275-0550
Biohelix Corp 500 Cummings Ste 5550	Beverly	MA	01915	866-800-5458	978-927-5056
Biomerica Inc 1533 Monrovia Ave *OTC: BMRA* ■ *Cust Svc	Newport Beach	CA	92663	800-854-3002*	949-645-2111
BioMerieux Inc 595 Anglum Rd	Hazelwood	MO	63042	800-634-7656	314-731-8500
Bionostics Inc 7 Jackson Rd *General	Devens	MA	01434	800-776-3856*	978-772-7070
BiosPacific Inc 5980 Horton St Ste 225	Emeryville	CA	94608	800-344-6686	510-652-6155
Boreal Genomics Inc 5150 El Camino Real	Los Altos	CA	94022	800-681-5644	604-822-8268
Burlington Drug Co Inc 91 Catamount Dr	Milton	VT	05468	800-338-8703	802-893-5105
Calmoseptine Inc 16602 Burke Ln	Huntington Beach	CA	92647	800-800-3405	714-840-3405
Cancap Pharmaceutical Ltd 13111 Vanier Pl Ste 180	Richmond	BC	V6V2J1	877-998-2378	604-278-2188
Cancer Genetics Inc Meadows Office Complex 201 Rt 17 N 2nd Fl	Rutherford	NJ	07070	888-334-4988	201-528-9200
Cangene bioPharma Inc 1111 S Paca St	Baltimore	MD	21230	800-441-4225	410-843-5000
Cedarlane Laboratories Inc 4410 Paletta Ct	Burlington	ON	L7L5R2	800-268-5058	905-878-8891
Chematics Inc PO Box 293	North Webster	IN	46555	800-348-5174	574-834-2406
Cholestech Corp 9975 Summers Ridge Rd	San Diego	CA	92121	866-284-3684	510-732-7200
Chromaprobe Inc 378 Fee Fee Rd	Maryland Heights	MO	63043	888-964-1400	314-738-0001
Cobalt Pharmaceuticals Inc 6500 Kitimat Rd	Mississauga	ON	L5N2B8	866-254-6111	905-814-1820
DakoCytomation 6392 Via Real *Cust Svc	Carpinteria	CA	93013	800-400-3256*	805-566-6655
Diamond Drugs Inc 645 Kolter Dr	Indiana	PA	15701	800-882-6337	724-349-1111
DiaSorin Inc 1951 NW Ave	Stillwater	MN	55082	855-677-0600	651-439-9710
Digestive Care Inc 1120 Win Dr	Bethlehem	PA	18017	877-882-5950	610-882-0349
DMS Pharmaceutical Group Inc 810 Busse Hwy	Park Ridge	IL	60068	877-788-1100	847-518-1100
DuPont Qualicon Henry Clay Rd Bldg 400 Rt 141 PO Box 80400	Wilmington	DE	19880	800-863-6842	302-695-5300
Edgemont Pharmaceuticals LLC 1250 Capital of Texas Hwy S Bldg 3 Ste 400	Austin	TX	78746	888-594-4332	512-550-8555
Edimer Pharmaceuticals Inc 55 Cambridge Pkwy Ste 102W	Cambridge	MA	02142	866-334-4240	617-758-4300
Enzo Biochem Inc 527 Madison Ave *NYSE: ENZ*	New York	NY	10022	800-522-5052	212-583-0100
Enzo Life Sciences Inc 10 Executive Blvd	Farmingdale	NY	11735	800-942-0430	631-694-7070
Euro-Pharm International Canada Inc 9400 Boul Langelier	Montreal	QC	H1P3H8	888-929-0835	514-323-8757
Exalpha Biologicals Inc 2 Shaker Rd Unit B101	Shirley	MA	01464	800-395-1137	
Face Stockholm Ltd 324 Joslen Blvd	Hudson	NY	12534	888-334-3223	518-828-6600
Gen-Probe Inc 10210 Genetic Ctr Dr	San Diego	CA	92121	800-523-5001	858-410-8000
GenBio 15222 Ave of Science Ste A *Tech Supp	San Diego	CA	92128	800-288-4368*	858-592-9300
Gibson Laboratories Inc 1040 Manchester St	Lexington	KY	40508	800-477-4763	859-254-9500
Golden State Medical Supply Inc 5187 Camino Ruiz	Camarillo	CA	93012	800-284-8633	805-477-9866
Guerbet LLC 120 W Seventh St Ste 108	Bloomington	IN	47404	877-729-6679	812-333-0059
Helena Laboratories Inc 1530 Lindbergh Dr	Beaumont	TX	77704	800-231-5663	409-842-3714
Hemagen Diagnostics Inc 9033 Red Branch Rd *OTC: HMGN*	Columbia	MD	21045	800-436-2436	443-367-5500
hermo Fisher Scientific Inc 8365 Valley Pike PO Box 307	Middletown	VA	22645	800-528-0494	800-556-2323
Hitachi Chemical Diagnostics 630 Clyde Ct	Mountain View	CA	94043	800-233-6278	650-961-5501
Honeys Place Inc 640 Glenoaks Blvd	San Fernando	CA	91340	800-910-3246	818-256-1101
Hycor Biomedical Inc 7272 Chapman Ave *Cust Svc	Garden Grove	CA	92841	800-382-2527*	
IDEXX Laboratories Inc 1 IDEXX Dr *NASDAQ: IDXX*	Westbrook	ME	04092	800-548-6733	207-556-0300
ImmucorGamma Inc 3130 Gateway Dr PO Box 5625 *NASDAQ: BLUD* ■ *Cust Svc	Norcross	GA	30091	800-829-2553*	770-441-2051
Immuno-Mycologics Inc (IMMY) 2700 Technology Pl	Norman	OK	73071	800-654-3639	405-360-4669
ImmunoDiagnostics Inc 1 Presidential Way Ste 104	Woburn	MA	01801	800-573-1700	781-938-6300
Immunovision Inc 1820 Ford Ave	Springdale	AR	72764	800-541-0960	479-751-7005
Inova Diagnostics Inc 9900 Old Grove Rd	San Diego	CA	92131	800-545-9495	858-586-9900
Interleukin Genetics Inc 135 Beaver St *OTC: ILIU* ■ *Cust Svc	Waltham	MA	02452	866-990-4363*	781-398-0700
International Immunology Corp 25549 Adams Ave	Murrieta	CA	92562	800-843-2853	951-677-5629
International Isotopes Inc 4137 Commerce Cir *OTC: INIS*	Idaho Falls	ID	83401	800-699-3108	208-524-5300
InVitro International 330 E Orangethorpe Ave Ste D	Placentia	CA	92870	800-246-8487	949-851-8356
Invivoscribe Technologies Inc 6330 Nancy Ridge Dr Ste 106	San Diego	CA	92121	866-623-8105	858-224-6600
Iso-Tex Diagnostics Inc PO Box 909	Friendswood	TX	77549	800-477-4839	
Jackson ImmunoResearch Laboratories Inc 872 W Baltimore Pk PO Box 9	West Grove	PA	19390	800-367-5296	610-869-4024
Kern Health Systems 9700 Stockdale Hwy	Bakersfield	CA	93311	888-466-2219	661-664-5000
Kibow Biotech Inc 4781 W Chester Pike Newtown Business Ctr	Newtown Square	PA	19073	888-271-2560	610-353-5130
Kirkegaard & Perry Laboratories Inc 910 Clopper Rd	Gaithersburg	MD	20878	800-638-3167	301-948-7755
KMI Diagnostics Inc 8201 Central Ave NE Ste P	Minneapolis	MN	55432	888-564-3424	763-231-3313
Kohl & Frisch Ltd 7622 Keele St	Concord	ON	L4K2R5	800-265-2520	
Lawton's Drug Stores Ltd 236 Brownlow Ave Ste 270	Dartmouth	NS	B3B1V5	866-990-1599	902-468-1000

	City	State	Zip	Toll-Free	Phone
LifeScan Inc 1000 Gibraltar Dr	Milpitas	CA	95035	**800-227-8862**	408-263-9789
Maine Biotechnology Services Inc 1037 R Forest Ave	Portland	ME	04103	**800-925-9476**	207-797-5454
Mallinckrodt Inc 675 McDonnell Blvd	Hazelwood	MO	63042	**800-778-7898**	314-654-2000
Marianna Industries Inc 11222 "I" St	Omaha	NE	68137	**800-228-9060**	402-593-0211
Medical Analysis Systems Inc 46360 Fremont Blvd	Fremont	CA	94538	**800-232-3342**	510-979-5000
MEDTOX Diagnostics Inc 1238 Anthony Rd	Burlington	NC	27215	**800-334-1116**	336-226-6311
Meridian Bioscience Inc 3471 River Hills Dr *NASDAQ: VIVO* ■ *Cust Svc	Cincinnati	OH	45244	**800-543-1980***	513-271-3700
Moss Inc PO Box 189	Pasadena	MD	21123	**800-932-6677**	410-768-3442
National Diagnostics Inc 305 Patton Dr	Atlanta	GA	30336	**800-526-3867**	404-699-2121
Neci 334 Hecla St	Lake Linden	MI	49945	**888-648-7283**	906-296-1000
Neogen Corp 620 Lesher Pl *NASDAQ: NEOG*	Lansing	MI	48912	**800-234-5333**	517-372-9200
New Horizons Diagnostics Corp 9110 Red Branch Rd	Columbia	MD	21045	**800-888-5015**	410-992-9357
Odan Laboratories Ltd 325 Stillview Ave	Pointe-Claire	QC	H9R2Y6	**800-387-9342**	514-428-1628
Ondine Biomedical Inc 1100 Melville St	Vancouver	BC	V6E4A6	**800-564-6253**	604-669-0555
OraSure Technologies Inc 220 E First St *NASDAQ: OSUR*	Bethlehem	PA	18015	**800-869-3538**	610-882-1820
Ortho-Clinical Diagnostics Inc 1001 US Rt 202 N PO Box 350	Raritan	NJ	08869	**800-828-6316**	
Oxford Biomedical Research Inc 2165 Avon Industrial Dr	Rochester Hills	MI	48309	**800-692-4633**	248-852-8815
Pacific Biometrics Inc 645 Elliott Ave W Ste 300	Seattle	WA	98119	**800-767-9151**	206-298-0068
Parchem Trading Ltd 415 Huguenot St	New Rochelle	NY	10801	**800-282-3982**	914-654-6800
PBA Health 6300 Enterprise Rd	Kansas City	MO	64120	**800-333-8097**	816-245-5700
Peptides International Inc 11621 Electron Dr	Louisville	KY	40299	**800-777-4779**	502-266-8787
Phadia US Inc 4169 Commercial Ave	Portage	MI	49002	**800-346-4364**	269-492-1940
Pharmaceutical Assoc Inc 1700 Perimeter Rd	Greenville	SC	29605	**888-233-2334**	864-277-7282
Pharmalucence Inc 29 Dunham Rd	Billerica	MA	01821	**800-221-7554**	781-275-7120
Pharmasave Drugs (National) Ltd 8411 - 200th St Ste 201	Langley	BC	V2Y0E7	**800-661-6106**	604-455-2400
Pharmascience Inc 6111 Royalmount Ave Ste 100	Montreal	QC	H4P2T4	**866-853-1178**	514-340-9800
Pharmetics Inc 3695 AutoRt Des Laurentides	Laval	QC	H7L3H7	**877-472-4433**	450-682-8580
Phoenix Pharmaceuticals Inc 330 Beach Rd	Burlingame	CA	94010	**800-988-1205**	650-558-8898
Pointe Scientific Inc 5449 Research Dr PO Box 87188	Canton	MI	48188	**800-445-9853**	734-487-8300
Polymedco Inc 510 Furnace Dock Rd	Cortlandt Manor	NY	10567	**800-431-2123**	914-739-5400
PolyPeptide Laboratories Inc 365 Maple Ave	Torrance	CA	90503	**800-338-4965**	310-782-3569
Polysciences Inc 400 Valley Rd *Cust Svc	Warrington	PA	18976	**800-523-2575***	215-343-6484
Prasco LLC 6125 Commerce Ct	Mason	OH	45040	**866-469-1414**	513-618-3333
Promega Corp 2800 Woods Hollow Rd	Madison	WI	53711	**800-356-9526**	608-274-4330
Prozyme Inc 3832 Bay Ctr Pl	Hayward	CA	94545	**800-457-9444**	510-638-6900
Purdue Pharma 575 Granite Ct	Pickering	ON	L1W3W8	**800-387-5349**	905-420-6400
Qst Consultations Ltd 11275 Edgewater Dr	Allendale	MI	49401	**866-757-4751**	616-895-5461
Quantimetrix Corp 2005 Manhattan Beach Blvd	Redondo Beach	CA	90278	**800-624-8380**	310-536-0006
Quidel Corp 10165 McKellar Ct *NASDAQ: QDEL*	San Diego	CA	92121	**800-874-1517**	858-552-1100
R & D Systems Inc 614 McKinley Pl NE	Minneapolis	MN	55413	**800-343-7475**	612-379-2956
Research & Diagnostic Antibodies 2645 W Cheyenne Ave	North Las Vegas	NV	89032	**800-858-7322**	702-638-7800
Roche Diagnostics Corp (RDC) 9115 Hague Rd PO Box 50457 *Cust Svc	Indianapolis	IN	46250	**800-428-5076***	317-521-2000
Rockland Immunochemicals Inc PO Box 326	Gilbertsville	PA	19525	**800-656-7625**	610-369-1008
Saskatchewan Health Research Foundation 253-111 Research Dr	Saskatoon	SK	S7N3R2	**800-975-1699**	306-975-1680
SCIMEDX Corp 100 Ford Rd	Denville	NJ	07834	**800-221-5598**	973-625-8822
Sigma-Aldrich Corp 3050 Spruce St *NASDAQ: SIAL*	Saint Louis	MO	63103	**800-325-3010**	314-771-5765
Southern Biotechnology Assoc Inc 160A Oxmoor Blvd	Birmingham	AL	35209	**800-722-2255**	205-945-1774
St Renatus LLC 1000 Centre Ave	Fort Collins	CO	80526	**888-686-2314**	970-282-0156
Stanbio Laboratory LP 1261 N Main St	Boerne	TX	78006	**800-531-5535**	830-249-0772
Straight Arrow Products Inc 2020 Highland Ave	Bethlehem	PA	18020	**800-827-9815**	610-882-9606
Strategic Diagnostics Inc 111 Pencader Dr *NASDAQ: SDIX*	Newark	DE	19702	**800-544-8881**	302-456-6789
Streck Inc 7002 S 109th St	Omaha	NE	68128	**800-228-6090**	402-333-1982
Sunovion Pharmaceuticals Inc 84 Waterford Dr	Marlborough	MA	01752	**888-394-7377**	508-481-6700
SurModics Inc 9924 W 74th St *NASDAQ: SRDX*	Eden Prairie	MN	55344	**866-787-6639**	952-829-2700
Tec Laboratories Inc 7100 Tec Labs Way SW	Albany	OR	97321	**800-482-4464**	541-926-4577
Techne Corp 614 McKinley Pl NE *NASDAQ: TECH*	Minneapolis	MN	55413	**800-343-7475**	612-379-8854
Teco Diagnostics 1268 N Lakeview Ave	Anaheim	CA	92807	**800-222-9880**	714-463-1111
Thermo Scientific 12076 Santa Fe Dr PO Box 14428	Lenexa	KS	66215	**800-255-6730**	913-888-0939
Triad Isotopes Inc 4205 Vineland Rd Ste L1	Orlando	FL	32811	**866-310-0086**	407-455-6700
Trinity Biotech PLC 5919 Farnsworth Ct *NASDAQ: TRIB*	Carlsbad	CA	92008	**800-331-2291**	760-929-0500
Tyger Scientific Inc 324 Stokes Ave	Ewing	NJ	08638	**888-329-8990**	609-434-0143
Uman Pharma Inc 100 De L'Industrie Blvd	Candiac	QC	J5R1J1	**877-444-9989**	450-444-9989
Utak Laboratories Inc 25020 Ave Tibbitts	Valencia	CA	91355	**800-235-3442**	661-294-3935
Valeo Pharma Inc 16667 Hymus Blvd Kirkland	Kirkland	QC	H9H4R9	**888-694-0865**	514-694-0150
Wako Chemicals USA Inc 1600 Bellwood Rd	Richmond	VA	23237	**800-992-9256**	804-271-7677
World Wide Packaging LLC 15 Vreeland Rd Ste 4	Florham Park	NJ	07932	**800-950-0390**	973-805-6500
Worthington Biochemical Corp 730 Vassar Ave	Lakewood	NJ	08701	**800-445-9603**	732-942-1660
Xeris Pharmaceuticals Inc 3208 Red River St Ste 300	Austin	TX	78705	**888-570-4781**	
Xttrium Laboratories Inc 1200 E Business Ctr Dr	Mt. Prospect	IL	60056	**800-587-3721**	773-268-5800
Zepto Metrix Corp 872 Main St *Cust Svc	Buffalo	NY	14202	**800-274-5487***	716-882-0920

234 DISPLAYS - EXHIBIT & TRADE SHOW

	City	State	Zip	Toll-Free	Phone
3D Exhibits Inc 2900 Lively Blvd	Elk Grove Village	IL	60007	**800-471-9617**	847-250-9000
Downing Displays Inc 550 Techne Ctr Dr	Milford	OH	45150	**800-883-1800**	513-248-9800
Expon Exhibits 909 Fee Dr	Sacramento	CA	95815	**800-783-9766**	916-924-1600
Gilbert Displays Inc 110 Spagnoli Rd	Melville	NY	11747	**855-577-1100**	631-577-1100
Human Movement LLC 1111 S St	Louisville	CO	80027	**855-464-6601**	
massAV 80 Cambridge St	Burlington	MA	01803	**800-423-7830**	
Siegel Display Products 300 Sixth Ave N	Minneapolis	MN	55401	**800-626-0322**	612-340-1493

235 DISPLAYS - POINT-OF-PURCHASE

SEE ALSO Signs

	City	State	Zip	Toll-Free	Phone
Acrylic Design Assoc 6050 Nathan Ln N	Plymouth	MN	55442	**800-445-2167**	763-559-8395
AMD Industries Inc 4620 W 19th St	Cicero	IL	60804	**800-367-9999**	708-863-8900
Archbold Container Corp 800 W Barre Rd PO Box 10	Archbold	OH	43502	**800-446-2520**	419-445-8865
Array Marketing 45 Progress Ave	Toronto	ON	M1P2Y6	**800-295-4120**	416-299-4865
Art-Phyl Creations 16250 NW 48th Ave	Hialeah	FL	33014	**800-327-8318**	305-624-2333
Chicago Display Marketing Corp 2021 W St	River Grove	IL	60171	**800-681-4340**	708-842-0001
Colony Inc 2500 Galvin Dr	Elgin	IL	60123	**800-735-1300**	847-426-5300
Display Smart LLC 801 W 27th Terr	Lawrence	KS	66046	**888-843-1870**	785-843-1869
Display Technologies LLC 1111 Marcus Ave Ste M68	Lake Success	NY	11042	**800-424-4220**	
Felbro Inc 3666 E Olympic Blvd	Los Angeles	CA	90023	**800-733-5276**	323-263-8686
Frank Mayer & Assoc Inc 1975 Wisconsin Ave	Grafton	WI	53024	**855-294-2875**	
Hunter Display 14 Hewlett Ave	East Patchogue	NY	11772	**800-767-2110**	631-475-5900
Lingo Manufacturing Co 7400 Industrial Rd *Cust Svc	Florence	KY	41042	**800-354-9771***	859-371-2662
MDI Worldwide 38271 W 12-Mile Rd *Sales	Farmington Hills	MI	48331	**800-228-8925***	248-553-1900
Nashville Display 306 Hartmann Dr	Lebanon	TN	37087	**800-251-1150**	615-743-2900
New Dimensions Research Corp 260 Spagnoli Rd	Melville	NY	11747	**800-637-8870**	631-694-1356
Ovation Instore 57-13 49th Pl	Maspeth	NY	11378	**800-553-2202**	718-628-2600
Rapid Displays 4300 W 47th St	Chicago	IL	60632	**800-356-5775**	773-927-1091
Thorco Industries Inc 1300 E 12th St	Lamar	MO	64759	**800-445-3375**	417-682-3375
United Displaycraft 333 E Touhy Ave *General	Des Plaines	IL	60018	**877-632-8767***	847-375-3800
Universal Display & Fixtures Co 726 E Hwy 121	Lewisville	TX	75057	**800-235-0701**	972-221-5022

Classified Section

Company	Address	City	State	ZIP	Toll-Free	Phone
Visual Marketing Inc	154 W Erie St	Chicago	IL	60654	**800-662-8640**	312-664-9177
Vulcan Industries Inc	300 Display Dr	Moody	AL	35004	**888-444-4417**	205-640-2400

DOOR & WINDOW GLASS

SEE Glass - Flat, Plate, Tempered

236 DOORS & WINDOWS - METAL

SEE ALSO Shutters - Window (All Types)

Company	Address	City	State	ZIP	Toll-Free	Phone
AK Draft Seal Ltd	7470 Buller Ave	Burnaby	BC	V5J4S5	**888-520-9009**	604-451-1080
Allan Window Technologies Ltd	131 Caldari Rd	Concord	ON	L4K3Z9	**800-760-5665**	905-738-8600
Amsco Windows Inc	1880 S 1045 W	Salt Lake City	UT	84104	**800-748-4661**	801-978-5000
Anemostat	1220 Watsoncenter Rd PO Box 4938	Carson	CA	90745	**877-423-7426**	310-835-7500
Asi Technologies Inc	5848 N 95th Ct	Milwaukee	WI	53225	**800-558-7068**	414-464-6200
ASSA ABLOY	110 Sargent Dr	New Haven	CT	06511	**800-377-3948**	
Babcock-Davis	9300 73rd Ave N	Brooklyn Park	MN	55428	**888-412-3726**	763-488-9247
Clopay Bldg Products Inc	8585 Duke Blvd	Mason	OH	45040	**800-225-6729**	
Columbia Mfg Corp	14400 S San Pedro St	Gardena	CA	90248	**800-729-3667**	310-327-9300
Cookson Co	2417 S 50th Ave	Phoenix	AZ	85043	**800-294-4358**	602-272-4244
Cornell Iron Works Inc	24 Elmwood Rd	Mountain Top	PA	18707	**800-233-8366**	570-474-6773
Deansteel Manufacturing Co	111 Merchant	San Antonio	TX	78204	**800-825-8271**	210-226-8271
Dominion Bldg Products	6949 Fairbanks N Houston Rd	Houston	TX	77040	**800-826-2617**	
Door Components Inc	7980 Redwood Ave	Fontana	CA	92336	**866-989-3667**	909-770-5700
Dunbarton Corp	PO Box 8577	Dothan	AL	36304	**800-633-7553**	
EFCO Corp	1000 County Rd	Monett	MO	65708	**800-221-4169**	417-235-3193
Electric Power Door	522 W 27th St	Hibbing	MN	55746	**800-346-5760**	218-263-8366
Elixir Industries Inc	24800 Chrisanta Dr Ste 210	Mission Viejo	CA	92691	**800-421-1942**	949-860-5000
Fleming Door Products Ltd	101 Ashbridge Cir	Woodbridge	ON	L4L3R5	**800-263-7515**	
GlassCraft Door Co	2002 Brittmoore Rd	Houston	TX	77043	**800-766-2196**	713-690-8282
Graham Architectural Products Corp	1551 Mt Rose Ave	York	PA	17403	**800-755-6274**	717-849-8100
Hufcor Inc	2101 Kennedy Rd	Janesville	WI	53545	**800-356-6968**	608-756-1241
Hygrade Metal Moulding Manufacturing Corp	1990 Highland Ave	Bethlehem	PA	18020	**800-645-9475**	610-866-2441
International Revolving Door Co	2138 N Sixth Ave	Evansville	IN	47710	**800-745-4726**	812-425-3311
International Window Corp	5625 E Firestone Blvd	South Gate	CA	90280	**800-477-4032**	562-928-6411
Jamison Door Co	55 JV Jamison Dr	Hagerstown	MD	21740	**800-532-3667**	301-733-3100
Jantek Industries	230 Rt 70	Medford	NJ	08055	**888-782-7937**	609-654-1030
Joyce Windows	1125 Berea Industrial Pkwy	Berea	OH	44017	**800-824-7988**	440-239-9100
Kane Manufacturing Corp	515 N Fraley St	Kane	PA	16735	**800-952-6399**	814-837-6464
Krieger Specialty Products Co	4880 Gregg Rd	Pico Rivera	CA	90660	**866-203-5060**	562-695-0645
LaForce Inc	1060 W Mason St	Green Bay	WI	54303	**800-236-8858**	920-497-7100
Lockheed Window Corp	Rt 100 PO Box 166	Pascoag	RI	02859	**800-537-3061**	401-568-3061
Loxcreen Co Inc, The	1630 Old Dunbar Rd PO Box 4004	West Columbia	SC	29172	**800-330-5699**	803-822-8200
M-D Bldg Products Inc	4041 N Santa Fe Ave	Oklahoma City	OK	73118	**800-654-8454*** *Cust Svc	405-528-4411
McKeon Door Co	44 Sawgrass Dr	Bellport	NY	11713	**800-266-9392**	631-803-3000
MM Systems Corp	50 MM Way	Pendergrass	GA	30567	**800-241-3460**	706-824-7500
Moss Supply Company Inc	5001 N Graham St	Charlotte	NC	28269	**800-438-0770**	704-596-8717
National Guard Products Inc	4985 E Raines Rd	Memphis	TN	38118	**800-647-7874**	
Nystrom Inc	9300 73rd Ave N	Minneapolis	MN	55428	**800-547-2635**	763-488-9200
O'Keeffe's Inc	325 Newhall St	San Francisco	CA	94124	**888-653-3333**	415-822-4222
Overhead Door Corp	2501 S State Hwy 121 Bus Ste 200	Lewisville	TX	75067	**800-275-3290**	469-549-7100
Overly Manufacturing Co	574 W Otterman St	Greensburg	PA	15601	**800-979-7300**	724-834-7300
Peelle Co	373 Nesconset Hwy Ste 311	Hauppauge	NY	11788	**800-787-5020**	905-846-4545
Peerless Products Inc	2403 S Main St	Fort Scott	KS	66701	**800-279-9999**	620-223-4610
PGT Industries	1070 Technology Dr	Nokomis	FL	34275	**800-282-6019**	941-480-1600
Quaker Window Products Inc	504 S Hwy 63 PO Box 128	Freeburg	MO	65035	**800-347-0438**	
Raynor Garage Doors	1101 E River Rd	Dixon	IL	61021	**800-472-9667**	815-288-1431
Rebco Inc	1171-1225 Madison Ave	Paterson	NJ	07509	**800-777-0787**	973-684-0200
Reese Enterprises Inc	16350 Asher Ave	Rosemount	MN	55068	**800-328-0953**	651-423-1126
Richards-Wilcox Inc	600 S Lake St	Aurora	IL	60506	**800-253-5668**	
Southeastern Aluminum Products Inc	6701 Suemac Pl	Jacksonville	FL	32254	**800-243-8200*** *Sales	904-781-8200
Southeastern Metals Mfg Company Inc	11801 Industry Dr	Jacksonville	FL	32218	**800-874-0335**	904-757-4200
Special-Lite Inc	PO Box 6	Decatur	MI	49045	**800-821-6531**	269-423-7068
Stanley Access Technologies	65 Scott Swamp Rd	Farmington	CT	06032	**800-722-2377**	860-677-2861
Steelcraft Mfg Co	9017 Blue Ash Rd	Cincinnati	OH	45242	**877-613-8766*** *Cust Svc	513-745-6400
Super Sky Products Inc	10301 N Enterprise Dr	Mequon	WI	53092	**800-558-0467**	262-242-2000
Taylor Bldg Products	631 N First St	West Branch	MI	48661	**800-248-3600**	989-345-5110
Therma-Tru Corp	1750 Indian Wood Cir	Maumee	OH	43537	**800-537-8827**	419-891-7400
Thermo-Twin Industries Inc	1155 Allegheny Ave	Oakmont	PA	15139	**800-641-2211**	412-826-1000
TRACO	71 Progress Ave	Cranberry Township	PA	16066	**800-992-4444**	724-776-7000
Traditional Door Design & Millwork Ltd	261 Regina Rd	Woodbridge	ON	L4L8M3	**877-226-9930**	416-747-1992
Tubelite Inc	4878 Mackinaw Trl	Reed City	MI	49677	**800-866-2227**	
Wayne-Dalton Corp	1 Door Dr PO Box 67	Mount Hope	OH	44660	**800-827-3667**	330-674-7015
West Window Corp	226 Industrial Pk Dr	Martinsville	VA	24112	**800-446-4167**	276-638-2394
Won-Door Corp	1865 South 3480 West	Salt Lake City	UT	84104	**800-453-8494**	801-973-7500

237 DOORS & WINDOWS - VINYL

Company	Address	City	State	ZIP	Toll-Free	Phone
American Exteriors LLC	1169 W Littleton Blvd	Littleton	CO	80120	**800-794-6369**	303-794-6369
Associated Materials Inc Alside Div	PO Box 2010	Akron	OH	44309	**800-922-6009*** *Cust Svc	
CertainTeed Corp	750 E Swedesford Rd	Valley Forge	PA	19482	**800-782-8777*** *Prod Info	610-341-7000
Champion Window Mfg Inc	12121 Champion Way	Cincinnati	OH	45241	**877-424-2674**	513-346-4600
Chelsea Bldg Products	565 Cedar Way	Oakmont	PA	15139	**800-424-3573**	
Harry G Barr Co	6500 S Zero St	Fort Smith	AR	72903	**800-829-2277**	479-646-7891
Larson Manufacturing Co	2333 Eastbrook Dr	Brookings	SD	57006	**888-483-3768*** *Cust Svc	605-692-6115
Moss Supply Company Inc	5001 N Graham St	Charlotte	NC	28269	**800-438-0770**	704-596-8717
PGT Industries	1070 Technology Dr	Nokomis	FL	34275	**800-282-6019**	941-480-1600
Provia Door Inc	2150 SR- 39	Sugarcreek	OH	44681	**800-669-4711*** *General	330-852-4711
Quanex Building Products Corp	1900 W Loop S Ste 1500	Houston	TX	77027	**888-475-0633*** *Cust Svc	713-961-4600
Rehau Inc	1501 EdwaRds Ferry Rd NE	Leesburg	VA	20176	**800-247-9445**	703-777-5255
Royal Group, The	71 Royal Group Crescent	Woodbridge	ON	L4H1X9	**800-263-2353**	905-264-0701
RubbAir Door Div Eckel Industries Inc	100 Groton Shirley Rd	Ayer	MA	01432	**800-966-7822**	978-772-0480
Soft-Lite LLC	10250 Philipp Pkwy	Streetsboro	OH	44241	**800-551-1953**	330-528-3400
Statewide Remodeling Inc	2450 Esters Blvd Ste 200	DFW Airport	TX	75261	**800-317-8283**	214-677-9000
Superseal Mfg Co Inc	PO Box 795	South Plainfield	NJ	07080	**800-433-4873**	908-561-5910
Thermal Industries Inc	3700 Haney C	Murrysville	PA	15668	**800-245-1540**	724-733-3880
Veka Inc	100 Veka Dr	Fombell	PA	16123	**800-654-5589**	724-452-1000
Weather Shield Manufacturing Inc	1 Weather Shield Plz PO Box 309	Medford	WI	54451	**800-222-2995**	715-748-2100
West Window Corp	226 Industrial Pk Dr	Martinsville	VA	24112	**800-446-4167**	276-638-2394
Windsor Windows & Doors	900 S 19th St	West Des Moines	IA	50265	**800-218-6186**	515-223-6660

238 DOORS & WINDOWS - WOOD

SEE ALSO Shutters - Window (All Types) ; Millwork

Company	Address	City	State	ZIP	Toll-Free	Phone
Algoma Hardwoods Inc	1001 Perry St	Algoma	WI	54201	**800-678-8910**	920-487-5221
Allmar Inc	287 Riverton Ave	Winnipeg	MB	R2L0N2	**800-230-5516**	204-668-1000
Andersen Corp	100 Fourth Ave N	Bayport	MN	55003	**888-888-7020**	651-264-5150
Construction Metals LLC	13169 B Slover Ave	Fontana	CA	92337	**800-576-9810**	909-390-9880
Endura Products Inc	8817 W Market St	Colfax	NC	27235	**800-334-2006**	336-668-2472
Great Day Improvements LLC	700 E Highland Rd	Macedonia	OH	44056	**800-230-8301**	330-468-0700

				Toll-Free	Phone
Haley Bros Inc 6291 Orangethorpe Ave	Buena Park	CA	90620	**800-854-5951**	714-670-2112
Industrial Door Company Inc 360 Coon Rapids Blvd	Minneapolis	MN	55433	**888-798-0199**	763-786-4730
Jenkins Mfg Company Inc 1608 Frank Akers Rd	Anniston	AL	36207	**800-633-2323**	256-831-7000
Larson Manufacturing Co 2333 Eastbrook Dr *Cust Svc	Brookings	SD	57006	**888-483-3768***	605-692-6115
Lincoln Wood Products Inc 1400 W Taylor St PO Box 375	Merrill	WI	54452	**800-967-2461**	
Marvin Windows & Doors PO Box 100	Warroad	MN	56763	**888-537-7828**	218-386-1430
Masonite International Corp 201 N Franklin St Ste 300	Tampa	FL	33602	**800-895-2723**	813-877-2726
Mathews Bros Co 22 Perkins Rd	Belfast	ME	04915	**800-615-2004**	207-338-6490
National Vinyl LLC 7 Coburn St	Chicopee	MA	01013	**800-424-5300**	413-420-0548
Pella Corp 102 Main St *Cust Svc	Pella	IA	50219	**877-473-5527***	641-621-1000
Quaker Window Products Inc 504 S Hwy 63 PO Box 128	Freeburg	MO	65035	**800-347-0438**	
Semling-Menke Company Inc PO Box 378	Merrill	WI	54452	**800-333-2206**	715-536-9411
SNE Enterprises Inc 880 Southview Dr	Mosinee	WI	54455	**800-826-5509**	715-693-7000
Trustile Doors LLC 1780 E 66th Ave	Denver	CO	80229	**866-442-5302**	303-286-3931
Vancouver Door Company Inc 203 Fifth St NW	Puyallup	WA	98371	**800-999-3667**	253-845-9581
Weather Shield Manufacturing Inc 1 Weather Shield Plz PO Box 309	Medford	WI	54451	**800-222-2995**	715-748-2100
Windsor Windows & Doors 900 S 19th St	West Des Moines	IA	50265	**800-218-6186**	515-223-6660

DRUGS - MFR

SEE Vitamins & Nutritional Supplements ; Diagnostic Products ; Medicinal Chemicals & Botanical Products ; Pharmaceutical Companies ; Pharmaceutical Companies - Generic Drugs ; Biotechnology Companies

239 DRUG STORES

SEE ALSO Health Food Stores

				Toll-Free	Phone
Allergychoices Inc 2800 National Dr Ste 100	Onalaska	WI	54650	**866-793-1680**	608-793-1580
Arbor Centers for Eyecare 2640 W 183rd St	Homewood	IL	60430	**866-798-6633**	708-798-6633
BCP Veterinary Pharmacy 1614 Webster St	Houston	TX	77003	**800-481-1729**	713-771-1144
Carepoint Inc 215 E Bay St Ste 304	Charleston	SC	29401	**800-296-1825**	843-853-6999
Community Pharmacies LP 16 Commerce Dr Ste 1	Augusta	ME	04332	**800-730-4840**	
CVS Corp 1 CVS Dr *Cust Svc	Woonsocket	RI	02895	**888-607-4287***	401-765-1500
Discount Drug Mart Inc 211 Commerce Dr	Medina	OH	44256	**800-833-6278**	330-725-2340
Drugstore.com Inc 411 108th Ave NE Ste 1400	Bellevue	WA	98004	**800-378-4786**	
Eye Care for Animals 372 S Milwaukee Ave	Wheeling	IL	60090	**877-617-3937**	847-215-3933
Eye Center Surgeons & Associates Ll 401 Meridian St N Ste 200	Huntsville	AL	35801	**800-233-9083**	256-705-3937
Fruth Pharmacy Inc 4016 Ohio River Rd	Point Pleasant	WV	25550	**800-438-5390**	304-675-1612
Gemmel Pharmacy Group Inc 143 N Euclid Ave	Ontario	CA	91762	**888-302-0229**	909-988-0591
General Hearing Corp 175 Brookhollow Esplanade	Harahan	LA	70123	**800-824-3021**	504-733-3767
Harmon Stores Inc 650 Liberty Ave	Union	NJ	07083	**866-427-6661**	
Jean Coutu Group (PJC) Inc 530 Rue Beriault *TSE: PJC.A*	Longueuil	QC	J4G1S8	**877-695-6175**	450-646-9760
Katz Group 10104 103rd Ave Ste 1702 Bell Tower	Edmonton	AB	T5J0H8	**866-323-9695**	780-990-0505
Lee Silsby Compounding Pharmacy 3216 Silsby Rd	Cleveland Heights	OH	44118	**800-918-8831**	216-321-4300
Liberty Drug & Surgical Inc 195 Main St	Chatham	NJ	07928	**877-816-0111**	973-635-6200
Medical Center Pharmacy 2401 N Ocoee St	Cleveland	TN	37311	**877-753-9555**	423-476-5548
Medicap Pharmacies Inc 1 Rider Trail Plaza Dr	Earth City	MO	63045	**800-407-8055**	314-993-6000
Mission Pharmacy Services LLC 201 N Jefferson St Ste 300	Kittanning	PA	16201	**877-758-2039**	
Navarro Discount Pharmacies 9400	Miami	FL	33178	**866-628-2776**	
Nucara Pharmacy 209 E San Marnan Dr	Waterloo	IA	50702	**800-359-2357**	319-236-8891
Oncology Plus Inc 1070 E Brandon Blvd	Brandon	FL	33511	**877-410-0779**	
Pet Health Pharmacy 12012 N 111th Ave	Youngtown	AZ	85363	**800-742-0516**	623-214-2791
Pro-tech Security Sales 1313 W Bagley Rd	Berea	OH	44017	**800-888-4002**	440-239-0100
Revolution Eyewear Inc 997 Flower Glen St	Simi Valley	CA	93065	**800-986-0010**	
Rite Aid Corp 30 Hunter Ln *NYSE: RAD*	Camp Hill	PA	17011	**800-748-3243**	717-761-2633
Rxusa Inc 81 Seaview Blvd	Port Washington	NY	11050	**800-764-3648**	516-467-2500
Skyemed Pharmacy 1332 N Federal Hwy	Pompano Beach	FL	33062	**866-778-8255**	
Symons Capital Management Inc 650 Washington Rd Ste 800	Pittsburgh	PA	15228	**888-344-7740**	412-344-7690
Thrifty White Stores 6055 Nathan Lane N Ste 200	Plymouth	MN	55442	**800-642-3275**	763-513-4300
Transcript Pharmacy Inc 2506 Lakeland Dr Ste 201	Jackson	MS	39232	**866-420-4041**	
Vitacost.com Inc 5400 Broken Sound Blvd NW Ste 500	Boca Raton	FL	33487	**800-381-0759**	
Vitamin Shoppe Inc 2101 91st St *NYSE: VSI*	North Bergen	NJ	07047	**800-223-1216**	201-868-5959
Walgreen Co 200 Wilmot Rd *Cust Svc	Deerfield	IL	60015	**800-925-4733***	847-940-2500

240 DRUGS & PERSONAL CARE PRODUCTS - WHOL

Companies listed here distribute pharmaceuticals, over-the-counter (OTC) drugs, and/or personal care products typically found in drug stores.

				Toll-Free	Phone
Ambient Healthcare Inc 15851 SW 41st St Ste 600	Davie	FL	33331	**877-342-9352**	954-796-3338
AmerisourceBergen Corp 1300 Morris Dr Ste 100 PO Box 959 *NYSE: ABC*	Chesterbrook	PA	19087	**800-829-3132**	610-727-7000
Auspex Pharmaceuticals Inc 3333 N Torrey Pines Court Ste 400	La Jolla	CA	92037	**800-487-7671**	858-558-2400
Bedford Road Pharmacy Inc 11306 Bedford Rd Ne	Cumberland	MD	21502	**800-788-6693**	301-777-1771
BioMotiv LLC 3605 Warrensville Ctr Rd	Cleveland	OH	44122	**800-477-6307**	216-455-3200
Buffalo Supply Inc 1650A Coal Creek Dr	Lafayette	CO	80026	**800-366-1812**	
Cadeau Express Inc 3494 E Sunset Rd	Las Vegas	NV	89120	**800-240-0301**	702-433-1333
Cardinal Health Nuclear Pharmacy Services 7000 Cardinal Pl	Dublin	OH	43017	**800-326-6457**	614-757-5000
Complete Pharmacy Care Inc 4206 Dalrock Rd	Rowlett	TX	75088	**866-804-6937**	972-675-3300
Dakota Drug Inc 28 Main St N	Minot	ND	58703	**800-437-2018**	701-852-2141
DRAXIMAGE Inc 16751 Transcanada Hwy	Kirkland	QC	H9H4J4	**888-633-5343**	514-630-7080
Familiprix Inc 6000 Rue Armand-Viau	Quebec	QC	G2C2C5	**800-463-5160**	418-847-3311
Familymeds Inc 312 Farmington Ave	Farmington	CT	06032	**888-787-2800**	
Ferring Pharmaceuticals Inc 100 Interpace Pkwy	Parsippany	NJ	07054	**888-337-7464**	973-796-1600
Forever Spring 2629 E Craig Rd Ste E	Las Vegas	NV	89030	**800-523-4334**	702-633-4283
Health Coalition Inc 8320 NW 30th Terr	Doral	FL	33122	**800-456-7283**	305-662-2988
Iredale Mineral Cosmetics Ltd 28 Church St	Great Barrington	MA	01230	**877-869-9420**	413-528-1078
J&B Medical Supply Co Inc 50496 W Pontiac Trail	Wixom	MI	48393	**800-980-0047**	248-896-6210
Kinray Inc 152-35 Tenth Ave	Whitestone	NY	11357	**800-854-6729**	718-767-1234
Lil' Drug Store Products Inc 1201 Continental Pl Ne	Cedar Rapids	IA	52402	**800-553-5022**	
London Drugs Ltd 12251 Horseshoe Way	Richmond	BC	V7A4X5	**888-991-2299**	604-272-7400
Mechanical Servants Inc 2755 Thomas St	Melrose Park	IL	60160	**800-351-2000**	708-615-9439
Methapharm Inc 11772 W Sample Rd	Coral Springs	FL	33065	**800-287-7686**	954-341-0795
Morris & Dickson Co Ltd 410 Kay Ln	Shreveport	LA	71115	**800-388-3833**	318-797-7900
Neil Medical Group Inc 2545 Jetport Rd	Kinston	NC	28504	**800-735-9111**	
North Carolina Mutual Wholesale Drug Co 816 Ellis Rd	Durham	NC	27703	**800-800-8551**	919-596-2151
Omegachem Inc 480 rue Perreault	St-romuald	QC	G6W7V6	**800-661-6342**	418-837-4444
Pamlab LLC 4099 Hwy 190 E Service Rd	Covington	LA	70433	**844-639-9725**	985-893-4097
Parmed Pharmaceuticals Inc 4220 Hyde Pk Blvd	Niagara Falls	NY	14305	**800-727-6331**	716-284-5666
Pharmacommunications Group Inc 100 Renfrew Dr	Markham	ON	L3R9R6	**800-267-5409**	905-477-3100
Putney Inc 1 Monument Sq Ste 400	Portland	ME	04101	**866-683-0660**	207-828-0880
Reese Pharmaceutical Co 10617 Frank Ave	Cleveland	OH	44106	**800-321-7178**	
RG Shakour Inc 254 Tpke Rd	Westborough	MA	01581	**800-661-2030**	
Rx Scan 2478 Lackey Old State Rd	Delaware	OH	43015	**800-572-2648**	740-548-1725
Sothys USA Inc 1500 NW 94th Ave	Miami	FL	33172	**800-325-0503**	305-594-4222
Sprout Pharmaceuticals Inc 4208 Six Forks Rd	Raleigh	NC	27609	**844-746-5745**	
Syreon Corp 260 - 1401 W Eighth Ave	Vancouver	BC	V6H1C9	**866-979-7366**	604-676-5900
US WorldMeds LLC 4010 Dupont Cir Ste L-07	Louisville	KY	40207	**888-900-8796**	502-815-8000
Value Drug Mart Assoc Ltd 16504 - 121A Ave	Edmonton	AB	T5V1J9	**888-554-8258**	780-453-1701

241 DUDE RANCHES

SEE ALSO Resorts & Resort Companies

				Toll-Free	Phone
320 Guest Ranch Inc 205 Buffalo Horn Creek Rd	Gallatin Gateway	MT	59730	**800-243-0320**	406-995-4283

Classified Section

Name / Address	City	State	Zip	Toll-Free	Phone
63 Ranch PO Box 979	Livingston	MT	59047	**888-395-5151**	
7 D Ranch 7D Ranch PO Box 100	Cody	WY	82414	**888-587-9885**	307-587-9885
Bar Lazy J Guest Ranch 447 County Rd 3 PO Box N	Parshall	CO	80468	**800-396-6279**	970-725-3437
Black Mountain Ranch 4000 Conger Mesa Rd	McCoy	CO	80463	**800-967-2401**	970-653-4226
Bonanza Creek Country Guest Ranch 523 Bonanza Creek Rd	Martinsdale	MT	59053	**800-476-6045**	406-572-3366
Brooks Lake Lodge & Guest Ranch 458 Brooks Lk Rd	Dubois	WY	82513	**866-213-4022**	
Camp Lebanon 1205 Acorn Rd	Burtrum	MN	56318	**800-816-1502**	320-573-2125
Cherokee Park Ranch 436 Cherokee Hills Dr	Livermore	CO	80536	**800-628-0949**	970-493-6522
Circle Z Ranch PO Box 194	Patagonia	AZ	85624	**888-854-2525**	
CM Ranch 167 Fish Hatchery Rd PO Box 217	Dubois	WY	82513	**800-455-0721**	307-455-2331
Colorado Trails Ranch 12161 County Rd 240	Durango	CO	81301	**800-323-3833**	970-247-5055
Concordia Language Villages 8659 Thorsonveien Rd	Bemidji	MN	56601	**800-450-2214**	218-586-8600
Coulter Lake Guest Ranch 80 County Rd 273	Rifle	CO	81650	**800-858-3046**	970-625-1473
Deer Valley Ranch 16825 County Rd 162	Nathrop	CO	81236	**877-897-1297**	719-395-2353
Drowsy Water Ranch PO Box 147	Granby	CO	80446	**800-845-2292**	970-725-3456
Eatons' Ranch 270 Eatons' Ranch Rd	Wolf	WY	82844	**800-210-1049**	307-655-9285
Elk Mountain Ranch PO Box 910	Buena Vista	CO	81211	**800-432-8812**	
Flying E Ranch 2801 W Wickenburg Way	Wickenburg	AZ	85390	**888-684-2650**	928-684-2690
Fresh Air Fund 633 Third Ave 14th Fl	New York	NY	10017	**800-367-0003**	
Greenhorn Creek Guest Ranch 2116 Greenhorn Ranch Rd	Quincy	CA	95971	**800-334-6939**	530-283-0930
Hawley Mountain Guest Ranch 4188 Main Boulder Rd	McLeod	MT	59052	**877-496-7848**	406-932-5791
Heart Six Ranch 16985 Buffalo Vly Rd PO Box 70	Moran	WY	83013	**888-543-2477**	
Hideout at Flitner Ranch Resort PO Box 206	Shell	WY	82441	**800-354-8637**	307-765-2080
Home Ranch PO Box 822	Clark	CO	80428	**800-688-2982**	970-879-1780
Horse Prairie Ranch 3300 Bachelor Mountain Rd	Dillon	MT	59725	**888-726-2454**	406-681-3166
Kay El Bar Guest Ranch PO Box 2480	Wickenburg	AZ	85358	**800-684-7583**	928-684-7593
Laramie River Dude Ranch 25777 County Rd 103	Jelm	WY	82063	**800-551-5731**	970-435-5716
Latigo Ranch PO Box 237	Kremmling	CO	80459	**800-227-9655**	970-724-9008
Lazy L & B Ranch 1072 E Fork Rd *Cust Svc	Dubois	WY	82513	**800-453-9488***	307-455-2839
Lone Mountain Ranch 750 Lone Mtn Ranch Rd PO Box 160069	Big Sky	MT	59716	**800-514-4644**	406-995-4644
Long Hollow Ranch 71105 Holmes Rd	Sisters	OR	97759	**877-923-1901**	541-923-1901
Lozier's Box R Ranch 552 Willow Creek Rd PO Box 100	Cora	WY	82925	**800-822-8466**	307-367-4868
North Fork Ranch (NFR) 55395 Hwy 285 PO Box B	Shawnee	CO	80475	**800-843-7895**	303-838-9873
Peaceful Valley Ranch 475 Peaceful Vly Rd	Lyons	CO	80540	**800-955-6343**	303-747-2881
Pine Butte Guest Ranch 351 S Fork Rd	Choteau	MT	59422	**877-812-3698**	406-466-2158
Price Canyon Ranch PO Box 39	Rodeo	NM	88056	**800-727-0065**	520-558-2383
Rainbow Trout Ranch (RTR) 1484 FDR 250 PO Box 458	Antonito	CO	81120	**800-633-3397**	719-376-5659
Rancho de la Osa Guest Ranch PO Box 1	Sasabe	AZ	85633	**800-872-6240**	520-240-3797
Rawah Ranch 11447 N County Rd 103	Glendevey	CO	82063	**800-820-3152**	
Rich Ranch 939 Cottonwood Lakes Rd	Seeley Lake	MT	59868	**800-532-4350**	406-677-2317
Smith Fork Ranch 45362 Needle Rock Rd	Crawford	CO	81415	**855-539-1492**	970-921-3454
Sundance Trail Guest Ranch 17931 Red Feather Lakes Rd	Red Feather Lakes	CO	80545	**800-357-4930**	970-224-1222
T Cross Ranch LLC 82 Parque Creek Rd PO Box 638	Dubois	WY	82513	**877-827-6770**	307-455-2206
Tanque Verde Ranch 14301 E Speedway	Tucson	AZ	85748	**800-234-3833**	520-296-6275
Tarryall River Ranch 270015 County Rd 77	Lake George	CO	80827	**800-408-8407**	719-748-1214
Thousand Pines Christian Camp & Conference Center 359 Thousnd Pines Rd	Crestline	CA	92325	**888-423-2267**	909-338-2705
Three Bars Cattle & Guest Ranch 9500 Wycliffe Perry Creek Rd	Cranbrook	BC	V1C7C7	**877-426-5230**	250-426-5230
Triangle C Dude Ranch 3737 Hwy 26	Dubois	WY	82513	**800-661-4928**	307-455-2225
Triple J Wilderness Ranch 91 Mortimer Rd PO Box 310	Augusta	MT	59410	**800-826-1300**	406-562-3653
Tumbling River Ranch 3715 Pk County Rd 62 PO Box 30	Grant	CO	80448	**800-654-8770**	303-838-5981
Vee Bar Guest Ranch 38 Vee Bar Ranch Rd	Laramie	WY	82070	**800-483-3227**	307-745-7036
Vista Verde Guest & Ski Ranch PO Box 770465	Steamboat Springs	CO	80477	**800-526-7433**	970-879-3858
White Stallion Ranch 9251 W Twin Peaks Rd	Tucson	AZ	85743	**888-977-2624**	520-297-0252
Wilderness Trails Ranch 1766 County Rd 302	Durango	CO	81303	**800-527-2624**	970-247-0722
Wind River Ranch PO Box 3410	Estes Park	CO	80517	**800-523-4212**	970-586-4212

242 DUPLICATION & REPLICATION SERVICES

Name / Address	City	State	Zip	Toll-Free	Phone
Corporate Disk Co 4610 Crime Pkwy	McHenry	IL	60050	**800-634-3475**	
Illinois Blueprint Corp 800 SW Jefferson Ave	Peoria	IL	61605	**800-747-7070**	309-676-1300
Online Copy Corp 48815 Kato Rd	Fremont	CA	94539	**800-833-4460**	
Standard Digital Imaging 4426 S 108th St	Omaha	NE	68137	**800-642-8062**	402-592-1292
Thomas Reprographics 600 N Central Expy	Richardson	TX	75080	**800-877-3776**	972-231-7227

243 DUTY-FREE SHOPS

SEE ALSO Gift Shops

Name / Address	City	State	Zip	Toll-Free	Phone
Niagara Duty Free Shop 5726 Falls Ave	Niagara Falls	ON	L2G7T5	**877-642-4337**	905-374-3700
Peace Bridge Duty Free Inc 1 Peace Bridge Plz	Buffalo	NY	14213	**800-361-1302**	
Starboard Cruise Services Inc 8400 NW 36th St	Miami	FL	33166	**800-540-4785**	786-845-7300
Tunnel Duty Free Shop Inc 465 Goyeau St	Windsor	ON	N9A1H1	**800-669-2105**	519-252-2713

EDUCATIONAL INSTITUTIONS

SEE Children's Learning Centers ; Colleges - Tribal ; Colleges & Universities - Historically Black ; Colleges & Universities - Jesuit ; Preparatory Schools - Boarding

244 EDUCATIONAL INSTITUTION OPERATORS & MANAGERS

Name / Address	City	State	Zip	Toll-Free	Phone
Apollo Group Inc 4025 E Elwood St *NASDAQ: APOL*	Phoenix	AZ	85040	**800-990-2765**	
Aqua Data Inc 95 Fifth Ave	Pincourt	QC	J7V5K8	**800-567-9003**	514-425-1010
Axonify Inc 460 Phillip St Ste 300	Waterloo	ON	N2L5J2	**866-317-1992**	519-585-1200
Bridgepoint Education Inc 13500 Evening Creek Dr N Ste 600 *NYSE: BPI*	San Diego	CA	92128	**866-475-0317**	858-486-1710
Capella Education Co 225 S Sixth St 9th Fl *NASDAQ: CPLA* ■ *Cust Svc	Minneapolis	MN	55402	**888-227-3552***	612-339-8650
Career Education Corp (CEC) 2895 Greenspoint Pkwy Ste 600 *NASDAQ: CECO*	Hoffman Estates	IL	60196	**877-559-9222**	847-781-3600
Carney, Sandoe & Associates, Limited Partnersh 44 Bromfield St	Boston	MA	02108	**800-225-7986**	617-542-0260
Center of Vocational Alternative For Men 3770 N High St	Columbus	OH	43214	**877-521-2682**	614-294-7117
Corinthian Colleges Inc 6 Hutton Centre Dr Ste 400 *NASDAQ: COCO*	Santa Ana	CA	92707	**888-370-7589**	916-431-6959
eCornell 950 Danby Rd Ste 150	Ithaca	NY	14850	**866-326-7635**	607-330-3200
Education Management Corp (EDMC) 210 Sixth Ave 33rd Fl *NASDAQ: EDMC*	Pittsburgh	PA	15222	**800-275-2440**	412-562-0900
Elenco Electronics Inc 150 W Carpenter Ave	Wheeling	IL	60090	**800-533-2441**	847-541-3800
ITT Educational Services Inc 13000 N Meridian St *NYSE: ESI*	Carmel	IN	46032	**800-388-3368**	317-706-9200
Laureate Education Inc 650 S Exeter St	Baltimore	MD	21202	**866-452-8732**	410-843-6100
Leona Group LLC 2125 University Pk Dr	Okemos	MI	48864	**800-656-6763**	517-333-9030
LifeLearn Inc 367 Woodlawn Rd W Unit 9	Guelph	ON	N1H7K9	**888-770-2218**	519-767-5043
Lingo Media Corp 151 Bloor St W Ste 703	Toronto	ON	M5S1S4	**866-927-7011**	416-927-7000
N R S I 179 Lafayette Dr	Syosset	NY	11791	**800-331-3117**	516-921-5500
National Heritage Academies 3850 Broadmoor Ave SE Ste 201 *General	Grand Rapids	MI	49512	**877-223-6402***	
Pacific Resources for Education & Learning 900 Ft St Mall Ste 1300	Honolulu	HI	96813	**800-377-4773**	808-441-1300
Safe & Civil Schools 2451 Willamette St	Eugene	OR	97405	**800-323-8819**	541-345-1442
Schoolwires Inc 330 Innovation Blvd Ste 301	State College	PA	16803	**877-427-9413**	
Sylvan Learning Centers 1001 Fleet St	Baltimore	MD	21202	**888-338-2283**	
Vertical Alliance Group Inc 1730 Galleria Oaks	Texarkana	TX	75503	**877-792-3866**	903-792-3866

245 EDUCATIONAL MATERIALS & SUPPLIES

SEE ALSO Educational & Reference Software ; Office & School Supplies

Name / Address	City	State	Zip	Toll-Free	Phone
American Educational Products Inc 401 Hickory St PO Box 2121	Fort Collins	CO	80522	**800-289-9299**	970-484-7445
Carolina Biological Supply Co 2700 York Rd	Burlington	NC	27215	**800-334-5551**	336-584-0381
Carson-Dellosa Publishing Company Inc 7027 Albert Pick Rd	Greensboro	NC	27409	**800-321-0943**	336-632-0084

	City	St	ZIP	Toll-Free	Phone
Center Enterprises Inc 30 Shield St *Orders	West Hartford	CT	06110	**800-542-2214***	860-953-4423
Claridge Products & Equipment Inc 601 Hwy 62 65	Harrison	AR	72601	**800-434-4610**	870-743-2200
Creative Teaching Press Inc 6262 Katella Ave	Cypress	CA	92649	**800-444-4287**	714-895-5047
Delta Education LLC 80 NW Blvd	Nashua	NH	03063	**800-258-1302**	603-889-8899
Didax Inc 395 Main St	Rowley	MA	01969	**800-458-0024**	978-948-2340
Education Ctr Inc 3515 W Market St Ste 200	Greensboro	NC	27403	**800-714-7991**	336-854-0309
Educational Insights Inc 380 N Fairway Dr	Vernon Hills	IL	60061	**800-995-4436**	
Educators Resource Inc 2575 Schillingers Rd *Cust Svc	Semmes	AL	36575	**800-868-2368***	
Evan-Moor Educational Publishers Inc 18 Lower Ragsdale Dr	Monterey	CA	93940	**800-777-4362**	831-649-5901
Excelligence Learning Corp 2 Lower Ragsdale Dr Ste 125	Monterey	CA	93940	**800-627-2829**	831-333-5572
Fisher Science Education 4500 Turnberry Dr	Hanover Park	IL	60133	**800-955-1177**	800-766-7000
Frog Street Press Inc 800 Industrial Blvd Ste 100	Grapevine	TX	76051	**800-884-3764**	
Ghent Manufacturing Inc 2999 Henkle Dr	Lebanon	OH	45036	**800-543-0550**	513-932-3445
Great Source Education Group 181 Ballardvale St	Wilmington	MA	01887	**800-289-4490**	
Guidecraft USA 55508 Hwy 19 W	Winthrop	MN	55396	**800-524-3555**	507-647-5030
Hayes School Publishing Co Inc 321 Pennwood Ave	Pittsburgh	PA	15221	**800-926-0704**	412-371-2373
Incentive Publications Inc 2400 Crestmoor Dr *Mktg	Nashville	TN	37215	**800-967-5325***	615-385-2934
Kaplan Early Learning Co 1310 Lewisville-Clemmons Rd	Lewisville	NC	27023	**800-334-2014**	336-766-7374
Learning Resources 380 N Fairway Dr	Vernon Hills	IL	60061	**800-222-3909**	847-573-8400
Learning Wrap-Ups Inc 1660 W Gordon Ave Ste 4	Layton	UT	84041	**800-992-4966**	801-497-0050
McDonald Publishing 567 Hanley Industrial Ct	Saint Louis	MO	63144	**800-722-8080**	314-781-7400
McGraw-Hill Education 8787 Orion Pl	Columbus	OH	43240	**800-334-7344**	
National School Products 1523 Old Niles Ferry Rd	Maryville	TN	37803	**800-627-9393**	865-984-3960
Questar Assessment Inc 5550 Upper 147th St W *OTC: QUSA* ■ *Cust Svc	Apple Valley	MN	55124	**800-800-2598***	952-997-2700
Rock 'N Learn Inc 105 Commercial Cir	Conroe	TX	77304	**800-348-8445**	936-539-2731
Roylco Inc 3251 Abbeville Hwy PO Box 13409	Anderson	SC	29624	**800-362-8656**	864-296-0043
School Specialty Inc PO Box 1579 *NASDAQ: SCHS*	Appleton	WI	54912	**888-388-3224**	920-734-5712
Teacher Created Resources 6421 Industry Way	Westminster	CA	92683	**888-343-4335**	
Teaching & Learning Co 1204 Buchanan St	Carthage	IL	62321	**800-444-1144**	937-228-6118
TREND Enterprises Inc 300 Ninth Ave SW *Cust Svc	New Brighton	MN	55112	**800-860-6762***	651-631-2850
World*Class Learning Materials PO Box 639	Candler	NC	28715	**800-638-6470**	

246 EDUCATIONAL TESTING SERVICES - ASSESSMENT &

	City	St	ZIP	Toll-Free	Phone
Alpine Testing Inc 51 W Ctr St	Orem	UT	84057	**844-625-7463**	
Barron's Educational Series Inc 250 Wireless Blvd	Hauppauge	NY	11788	**800-645-3476**	631-434-3311
Castle Worldwide Inc 900 Perimeter Pk Rd Ste G	Morrisville	NC	27560	**800-655-4845**	919-572-6880
College Board 45 Columbus Ave	New York	NY	10023	**800-927-4302**	212-713-8000
Fresh Air Educators Inc 203-1568 Carling Ave	Ottawa	ON	K1Z7M4	**866-495-4868**	
General Educational Development Testing Service *American Council on Education* 1 Dupont Cir NW	Washington	DC	20036	**866-205-6267**	202-939-9300
H & H Publishing Company Inc 1231 Kapp Dr	Clearwater	FL	33765	**800-366-4079**	727-442-7760
Kaplan Inc 6301 Kaplan University Ave *Cust Svc	Fort Lauderdale	FL	33309	**800-258-2432***	954-515-3993
McGraw-Hill Cos Inc CTB/McGraw-Hill Div 20 Ryan Ranch Rd	Monterey	CA	93940	**800-538-9547**	831-393-0700
Praxis Series Online Educational Testing Service Teaching & Learning Div (ETS) PO Box 6051	Princeton	NJ	08541	**800-772-9476**	609-771-7395
Prometric 1501 S Clinton St	Baltimore	MD	21224	**866-776-6387**	443-455-8000

247 ELECTRIC COMPANIES - COOPERATIVES (RURAL)

SEE ALSO Utility Companies

Companies listed here are members of the National Rural Electric Cooperative Association; most are consumer-owned, but some are public power districts. In addition, the companies listed are electricity distribution cooperatives. Companies that generate and/or transmit electricity, but do not distribute it, are not included.

Alabama

	City	St	ZIP	Toll-Free	Phone
Baldwin County Electric Membership Corp 19600 Hwy 59	Summerdale	AL	36580	**800-837-3374**	251-989-6247
Central Alabama Electric Co-op 1802 Hwy 31 N	Prattville	AL	36067	**800-545-5735**	334-365-6762
Cherokee Electric Co-op 1550 Clarence Chestnut Bypass PO Box O	Centre	AL	35960	**800-952-2667**	256-927-5524
Covington Electric Co-op Inc 18836 US Hwy 84	Andalusia	AL	36421	**800-239-4121**	334-222-4121
Cullman Electric Co-op 1749 Eva Rd NE PO Box 1168	Cullman	AL	35055	**800-242-1806**	256-737-3201
Dixie Electric Co-op 9100 Atlanta Hwy	Montgomery	AL	36117	**888-349-4332**	334-288-1163
Franklin Electric Co-op Inc 225 Franklin St NW	Russellville	AL	35653	**800-410-2732**	256-332-2730
Joe Wheeler Electric Membership Corp PO Box 460	Trinity	AL	35673	**800-239-6518**	256-552-2300
North Alabama Electric Co-op 41103 US Hwy 72	Stevenson	AL	35772	**800-572-2900**	256-437-2281
Pea River Electric Co-op 1311 W Roy Parker Rd PO Box 969	Ozark	AL	36361	**800-264-7732**	334-774-2545
Pioneer Electric Co-op 300 Herbert St	Greenville	AL	36037	**800-239-3092**	334-382-6636
Sand Mountain Electric Co-op 402 Main St W	Rainsville	AL	35986	**877-843-2512**	256-638-2153
South Alabama Electric Co-op (SAEC) PO Box 449	Troy	AL	36081	**800-556-2060**	334-566-2060
Tallapoosa River Electric Co-op 15163 US Hwy 431 S PO Box 675	Lafayette	AL	36862	**800-332-8732**	334-864-9331
Tombigbee Electric Co-op Inc 7686 US Hwy PO Box 610	Guin	AL	35563	**800-621-8069**	205-468-3325

Alaska

	City	St	ZIP	Toll-Free	Phone
Chugach Electric Assn Inc 5601 Electron Dr	Anchorage	AK	99518	**800-478-7494**	907-563-7494
Copper Valley Electric Assn Inc (CVEA) Mile 187 Glenn Hwy PO Box 45	Glennallen	AK	99588	**866-835-2832**	907-822-3211
Golden Valley Electrical Assn Inc 758 Illinois St	Fairbanks	AK	99701	**800-770-4832**	907-452-1151
Homer Electric Assn Inc 3977 Lake St	Homer	AK	99603	**800-478-8551**	907-235-8551
Nushagak Electric & Telephone Co-op Inc 557 Kenny Wren Rd	Dillingham	AK	99576	**800-478-5296**	907-842-5251

Arizona

	City	St	ZIP	Toll-Free	Phone
Duncan Valley Electric Co-op Inc PO Box 440	Duncan	AZ	85534	**800-669-2503**	928-359-2503
Graham County Electric Inc 9 W Center St	Pima	AZ	85543	**800-577-9266**	928-485-2451
Navopache Electric Co-op Inc 1878 W White Mtn Blvd	Lakeside	AZ	85929	**800-543-6324**	928-368-5118
Sulphur Springs Valley Electric Co-op Inc 350 N Haskell Ave	Willcox	AZ	85643	**877-877-6861**	520-384-2221

Arkansas

	City	St	ZIP	Toll-Free	Phone
Arkansas Valley Electric Co-op Corp 1811 W Commercial St PO Box 47	Ozark	AR	72949	**800-468-2176**	479-667-2176
Ashley-Chicot Electric Co-op Inc 307 E Jefferson St	Hamburg	AR	71646	**800-281-5212**	870-853-5212
Carroll Electric Co-op Corp 920 Hwy 62 Spur	Berryville	AR	72616	**800-432-9720**	870-423-2161
Clay County Electric Co-op Corp 300 N Missouri Ave	Corning	AR	72422	**800-521-2450**	870-857-3521
Craighead Electric Co-op Corp 4314 Stadium Blvd PO Box 7503	Jonesboro	AR	72403	**800-794-5012**	870-932-8301
First Electric Co-op Corp 1000 S JP Wright Loop Rd	Jacksonville	AR	72076	**800-489-7405**	501-982-4545
Mississippi County Electric Co-op 510 N Broadway St	Blytheville	AR	72315	**800-439-4563**	870-763-4563
Ouachita Electric Co-op Corp 700 Bradley Ferry Rd PO Box 877	Camden	AR	71711	**877-252-4538**	870-836-5791
Ozarks Electric Co-op Corp 3641 W Wedington Dr	Fayetteville	AR	72704	**800-521-6144**	479-521-2900
Petit Jean Electric Co-op 270 Quality Dr PO Box 37	Clinton	AR	72031	**800-786-7618**	501-745-2493
Rich Mountain Electric Co-op Inc 515 Janssen PO Box 897	Mena	AR	71953	**877-828-4074**	479-394-4140
South Central Arkansas Electric Co-op 4818 Highway 8 W PO Box 476	Arkadelphia	AR	71923	**800-814-2931**	870-246-6701
Woodruff Electric Co-op PO Box 1619	Forrest City	AR	72336	**888-559-6400**	870-633-2262

California

	City	St	ZIP	Toll-Free	Phone
Anza ElectricCo-op Inc 58470 Hwy 371 PO Box 391909	Anza	CA	92539	**844-311-7201**	951-763-4333
Plumas-Sierra Rural Electric Co-op 73233 SR 70	Portola	CA	96122	**800-555-2207**	530-832-4261
Surprise Valley Electric Co-op 22595 US 395	Alturas	CA	96101	**866-843-2667**	530-233-3511

Colorado

	City	St	ZIP	Toll-Free	Phone
Empire Electric Assn Inc 801 N Broadway	Cortez	CO	81321	**800-709-3726**	970-565-4444

Name / Address	City	State	ZIP	Toll-Free	Phone
Grand Valley Rural Power Lines Inc 845 22 Rd PO Box 190	Grand Junction	CO	81505	**877-760-7435**	970-242-0040
Gunnison County Electric Assn Inc 37250 W Hwy 50 PO Box 180	Gunnison	CO	81230	**800-726-3523**	970-641-3520
Highline Electric Assn 1300 S Interocean Ave	Holyoke	CO	80734	**800-816-2236**	970-854-2236
Holy Cross Energy PO Box 2150	Glenwood Springs	CO	81602	**877-833-2555**	970-945-5491
Intermountain Rural Electric Assn 5496 Hwy 85	Sedalia	CO	80135	**800-332-9540**	303-688-3100
KC Electric Assn 422 Third Ave	Hugo	CO	80821	**800-700-3123**	719-743-2431
La Plata Electric Assn Inc 45 Stewart St	Durango	CO	81303	**888-839-5732**	970-247-5786
Morgan County Rural Electric Assn 20169 US Hwy 34	Fort Morgan	CO	80701	**877-495-6487**	970-867-5688
Mountain Parks Electric Inc 321 W Agate Ave	Granby	CO	80446	**877-887-3378**	970-887-3378
Mountain View Electric Assn Inc 1655 Fifth St	Limon	CO	80828	**800-388-9881**	719-775-2861
Poudre Valley Rural Electric Assn Inc 7649 Rea Pkwy	Fort Collins	CO	80528	**800-432-1012**	970-226-1234
San Isabel Electric 893 E Enterprise Dr	Pueblo West	CO	81007	**800-279-7432**	719-547-2160
San Luis Valley Rural Electric Co-op 3625 US Hwy 160 W	Monte Vista	CO	81144	**800-332-7634**	719-852-3538
San Miguel Power Assn Inc 170 W Tenth Ave	Nucla	CO	81424	**800-864-7256**	970-864-7311
Sangre de Cristo Electric Assn 29780 US Hwy 24	Buena Vista	CO	81211	**800-933-3823**	719-395-2412
Southeast Colorado Power Assn (SECPA) 901 W 3rd	La Junta	CO	81050	**800-332-8634**	719-384-2551
United Power Inc 500 Co-op Way	Brighton	CO	80603	**800-468-8809**	303-659-0551
White River Electric Assn (WREA) PO Box 958	Meeker	CO	81641	**800-922-1987**	970-878-5041
Y-W Electric Assn Inc 250 Main Ave PO Box Y	Akron	CO	80720	**800-660-2291**	970-345-2291
Yampa Valley Electric Assn Inc 435 Mack Ln Ste 203	Craig	CO	81626	**888-873-9832**	970-879-1160

Delaware

Name / Address	City	State	ZIP	Toll-Free	Phone
Delaware Electric Co-op Inc PO Box 600	Greenwood	DE	19950	**800-282-8595**	302-349-3147

Florida

Name / Address	City	State	ZIP	Toll-Free	Phone
Central Florida Electric Co-op Inc 1124 N Young Blvd	Chiefland	FL	32644	**800-227-1302**	352-493-2511
Choctawhatchee Electric Co-op Inc 1350 W Baldwin Ave	DeFuniak Springs	FL	32435	**800-342-0990**	850-892-2111
Clay Electric Co-op Inc 7450 State Rd 100	Keystone Heights	FL	32656	**800-224-4917**	352-473-8000
Escambia River Electric Co-op Inc 3425 Florida 4	Jay	FL	32565	**800-235-3848**	850-675-4521
Florida Keys Electric Co-op Assn 91630 Overseas Hwy	Tavernier	FL	33070	**800-858-8845**	305-852-2431
Gulf Coast Electric Co-op Inc 722 W Hwy 22 PO Box 220	Wewahitchka	FL	32465	**800-333-9392**	850-639-2216
Lee County Electric Co-op Inc 4980 Bayline Dr PO Box 3455	North Fort Myers	FL	33917	**800-282-1643**	239-995-2121
Peace River Electric Co-op Inc 210 Metheny Rd PO Box 1310	Wauchula	FL	33873	**800-282-3824**	
Sumter Electric Co-op Inc PO Box 301	Sumterville	FL	33585	**800-732-6141**	352-793-3801
Suwannee Valley Electric Co-op PO Box 160	Live Oak	FL	32064	**800-752-0025**	386-362-2226
Talquin Electric Co-op Inc 1640 W Jefferson St	Quincy	FL	32351	**888-271-8778**	850-627-7651
West Florida Electric Co-op 5282 Peanut Rd	Graceville	FL	32440	**800-342-7400**	850-263-3231

Georgia

Name / Address	City	State	ZIP	Toll-Free	Phone
Altamaha Electric Membership Corp 611 W Liberty Ave PO Box 346	Lyons	GA	30436	**800-822-4563**	912-526-8181
Amicalola Electric Membership Corp 544 Hwy 515 S	Jasper	GA	30143	**800-282-7411**	706-253-5200
Canoochee Electric Membership Corp 342 E Brazell St	Reidsville	GA	30453	**800-342-0134**	
Central Georgia Electric Membership Corp 923 S Mulberry St	Jackson	GA	30233	**800-222-4877**	770-775-7857
Coastal Electric Co-op 1265 S Coastal Hwy PO Box 109	Midway	GA	31320	**800-421-2343**	912-884-3311
Coweta-Fayette Electric Membership Corp 807 Collinsworth Rd	Palmetto	GA	30268	**877-746-4362**	770-502-0226
Diverse Power Inc 1400 S Davis Rd	LaGrange	GA	30241	**800-845-8362**	706-845-2000
Flint Energies 3 S Macon St	Reynolds	GA	31076	**800-342-3616**	478-847-3415
Grady Electric Membership Corp (EMC) 1499 US Hwy 84 W	Cairo	GA	39828	**877-757-6060**	229-377-4182
Habersham Electric Membership Corp 6135 Georgia 115	Clarkesville	GA	30523	**800-640-6812**	706-754-2114
Hart Electric Membership Corp 1071 Elberton Hwy	Hartwell	GA	30643	**800-241-4109**	706-376-4714
Irwin Electric Membership Corp 915 W Fourth St	Ocilla	GA	31774	**800-237-3745**	229-468-7415
Jackson Electric Membership Corp 850 Commerce Rd	Jefferson	GA	30549	**800-462-3691**	706-367-5281
Jefferson Energy Co-op 3077 Hwy 17 PO Box 457	North Wrens	GA	30833	**877-533-3377**	706-547-2167
Little Ocmulgee Electric Membership Corp 26 W Railroad Ave	Alamo	GA	30411	**800-342-1290**	912-568-7171
Middle Georgia Electric Membership Corp 600 Tippettville Rd	Vienna	GA	31092	**800-342-0144**	229-268-2671
Mitchell Electric Membership Corp 475 Cairo Rd	Camilla	GA	31730	**800-479-6034**	229-336-5221
Ocmulgee Electric Membership Corp 5722 Eastman St	Eastman	GA	31023	**800-342-5509**	478-374-7001
Oconee Electric Membership Corp 3445 US Hwy 80 W	Dudley	GA	31022	**800-522-2930**	478-676-3191
Okefenoke Rural Electric Membership Corp (REMC) 14384 Cleveland St PO Box 602	Nahunta	GA	31553	**800-262-5131**	912-462-5131
Planters Electric Membership Corp 1740 Hwy 25 N PO Box 979	Millen	GA	30442	**888-397-3742**	478-982-4722
Snapping Shoals Electric Membership Corp 14750 Brown Bridge Rd	Covington	GA	30016	**888-999-1416**	770-786-3484
Sumter Electric Membership Corp 1120 Felder St	Americus	GA	31709	**800-342-6978**	229-924-8041
Three Notch Electric Membership Corp PO Box 295	Donalsonville	GA	39845	**800-239-5377**	229-524-5377
Tri-State Electric Membership Corp (TSEMC) 2310 Blue Ridge Dr	Blue Ridge	GA	30513	**800-351-1111**	706-492-3251
Washington Electric Membership Corp 258 N Harris St	Sandersville	GA	31082	**800-552-2577**	478-552-2577

Idaho

Name / Address	City	State	ZIP	Toll-Free	Phone
Clearwater Power Co 4230 Hatwai Rd PO Box 997	Lewiston	ID	83501	**888-743-1501**	208-743-1501
Fall River Rural Electric Co-op Inc 1150 N 3400 E	Ashton	ID	83420	**800-632-5726**	208-652-7431
Idaho County Light & Power Co-op 1065 Hwy 13	Grangeville	ID	83530	**877-212-0424**	208-983-1610
Kootenai Electric Co-op Inc 2451 W Dakota Ave	Hayden	ID	83835	**800-240-0459**	208-765-1200
Raft River Rural Electric Co-op Inc 155 N Main St PO Box 617	Malta	ID	83342	**800-342-7732**	208-645-2211
Salmon River Electric Co-op Inc 1130 Main St PO Box 384	Challis	ID	83226	**877-806-2283**	208-879-2283

Illinois

Name / Address	City	State	ZIP	Toll-Free	Phone
Adams Electric Co-op 700 Eastwood St PO Box 247	Camp Point	IL	62320	**800-232-4797**	217-593-7701
Clinton County Electric Co-op Inc 475 N Main St PO Box 40	Breese	IL	62230	**800-526-7282**	618-526-7282
Corn Belt Energy Corp 1 Energy Way	Bloomington	IL	61705	**800-879-0339**	309-662-5330
Eastern Illini Electric Co-op 330 W Ottawa PO Box 96	Paxton	IL	60957	**800-824-5102**	217-379-2131
Egyptian Electric Co-op Assn PO Box 38	Steeleville	IL	62288	**800-606-1505**	
Illinois Rural Electric Co-op 2 S Main St	Winchester	IL	62694	**800-468-4732**	217-742-3128
Jo-Carroll Energy 793 US Hwy 20 W	Elizabeth	IL	61028	**800-858-5522**	815-858-2207
Menard Electric Co-op 14300 State Hwy 97 PO Box 200	Petersburg	IL	62675	**800-872-1203**	217-632-7746
MJM Electric Co-op Inc (MJMEC) 264 NE St PO Box 80	Carlinville	IL	62626	**800-648-4729**	217-854-3137
Rural Electric Convenience Co-op Co 3973 W SR 104 PO Box 19	Auburn	IL	62615	**800-245-7322**	217-438-6197
Shelby Electric Co-op (SEC) 1355 IL-128 state PO Box 560	Shelbyville	IL	62565	**800-677-2612**	217-774-3986
SouthEastern Illinois Electric Co-op 585 Hwy 142 S PO Box 251	Eldorado	IL	62930	**800-833-2611**	618-273-2611
Southern Illinois Electric Co-op 7420 US Hwy 51 S	Dongola	IL	62926	**800-762-1400**	618-827-3555
Southwestern Electric Co-op Inc 525 US Rt 40 PO Box 549	Greenville	IL	62246	**800-637-8667**	
Spoon River Electric Co-op Inc (SREC) 930 S Fifth Ave PO Box 340	Canton	IL	61520	**877-404-2572**	309-647-2700
Wayne-White Counties Electric Co-op 1501 W Main St	Fairfield	IL	62837	**888-871-7695**	618-842-2196
Western Illinois Electrical Co-op 524 N Madison St PO Box 338	Carthage	IL	62321	**800-576-3125**	217-357-3125

Indiana

Name / Address	City	State	ZIP	Toll-Free	Phone
Bartholomew County Rural Electric Membership Corp 1697 W. Deaver Rd	Columbus	IN	47201	**800-927-5672**	812-372-2546
Boone County Rural Electric Membership Corp 1207 Indianapolis Ave	Lebanon	IN	46052	**800-897-7362**	765-482-2390
Clark County REMC 7810 State Rd 60 PO Box 411	Sellersburg	IN	47172	**800-462-6988**	812-246-3316
Daviess-Martin County REMC 12628 E 75 N PO Box 430	Loogootee	IN	47553	**800-762-7362**	812-295-4200
Decatur County Rural Electric Membership Corp 1430 W Main St PO Box 46	Greensburg	IN	47240	**800-844-7362**	812-663-3391
Hendricks Power Co-op 86 N County Rd 500 E	Avon	IN	46123	**800-876-5473**	317-745-5473
Jackson County Rural Electric Membership Corp 274 E Base Rd	Brownstown	IN	47220	**800-288-4458**	812-358-4458
Jasper County Rural Electric Membership Corp 280 E 400 S	Rensselaer	IN	47978	**888-866-7362**	219-866-4601
Jay County Rural Electric Membership Corp 484 S 200 W PO Box 904	Portland	IN	47371	**800-835-7362**	260-726-7121
Johnson County Rural Electric Membership Corp 750 International Dr	Franklin	IN	46131	**800-382-5544**	317-736-6174
LaGrange County Rural Electric Membership Corp 1995 E US Hwy 20	LaGrange	IN	46761	**877-463-7165**	260-463-7165
Miami-Cass County Rural Electric Membership Corp 3086 W 100 N PO Box 168	Peru	IN	46970	**800-844-6668***	765-473-6668
*General					
Noble REMC 300 Weber Rd PO Box 137	Albion	IN	46701	**800-933-7362**	260-636-2113

				Toll-Free	Phone
Orange County Rural Electric Membership Corp 7133 N State Rd 337 PO Box 208	Orleans	IN	47452	**888-337-5900**	812-865-2229
Parke County Rural Electric Membership Corp 119 W High St	Rockville	IN	47872	**800-537-3913**	765-569-3133
Rush Shelby Energy Inc 2777 S 840 W PO Box 55 *General	Manilla	IN	46150	**800-706-7362***	765-544-2600
South Central Indiana Rural Electric Membership Corp 300 Morton Ave	Martinsville	IN	46151	**800-264-7362**	765-342-3344
Southeastern Indiana Rural Electric Membership Corp 712 S Buckeye St	Osgood	IN	47037	**800-737-4111**	812-689-4111
Southern Indiana Rural Electric Co-op Inc 1776 Tenth St PO Box 219	Tell City	IN	47586	**800-323-2316**	812-547-2316
Steuben County Rural Electric Membership Corp 1212 S Wayne St	Angola	IN	46703	**888-233-9088**	260-665-3563
Tipmont Rural Electric Membership Corp 403 S Main St	Linden	IN	47955	**800-726-3953**	
Wabash County Rural Electric Membership Corp 350 Wedcor Ave	Wabash	IN	46992	**800-563-2146**	260-563-2146
Warren County Rural Electric Membership Corp 15 Midway St PO Box 37	Williamsport	IN	47993	**800-872-7319**	765-762-6114
White County Rural Electric Membership Corp 302 N Sixth St	Monticello	IN	47960	**800-844-7161**	574-583-7161
Whitewater Valley Rural Electric Membership Corp 101 Brownsville Ave	Liberty	IN	47353	**800-529-5557**	765-458-5171
WIN Energy Rural Electric Membership Corp 3981 S US Hwy 41	Vincennes	IN	47591	**800-882-5140**	812-882-5140

Iowa

				Toll-Free	Phone
Access Energy Co-op 1800 W Washington St	Mount Pleasant	IA	52641	**866-242-4232**	319-385-1577
Allamakee-Clayton Electric Co-op (ACEC) 229 Hwy 51 PO Box 715	Postville	IA	52162	**888-788-1551**	563-864-7611
Butler County Rural Electric Co-op 521 N Main PO Box 98	Allison	IA	50602	**888-267-2726**	319-267-2726
Calhoun County Electric Co-op Assn 1015 Tonawanda St PO Box 312	Rockwell City	IA	50579	**800-821-4879**	712-297-7112
Chariton Valley Electric Co-op 2090 Hwy 5 PO Box 486	Albia	IA	52531	**800-475-1702**	641-932-7126
Consumers Energy 2074 242nd St	Marshalltown	IA	50158	**800-696-6552**	641-752-1593
East-Central Iowa Rural Electric Co-op 2400 Bing Miller Ln	Urbana	IA	52345	**877-850-4343**	319-443-4343
Eastern Iowa Light & Power Co-op 600 E Fifth St PO Box 3003	Wilton	IA	52778	**800-728-1242**	563-732-2211
Franklin Rural Electric Co-op 1560 Hwy 65 PO Box 437	Hampton	IA	50441	**800-750-3557**	641-456-2557
Grundy County Rural Electric Co-op 102 E 'G' Ave	Grundy Center	IA	50638	**800-390-7605**	319-824-5251
Hawkeye REC 24049 Iowa 9	Cresco	IA	52136	**800-658-2243**	563-547-3801
Heartland Power Co-op 216 Jackson St PO Box 65	Thompson	IA	50478	**888-584-9732**	641-584-2251
Humboldt County Rural Electric Co-op (HCREC) 1210 13th St N	Humboldt	IA	50548	**800-452-1111**	515-332-1616
Iowa Lakes Electric Co-op 702 S First St	Estherville	IA	51334	**800-225-4532**	712-362-7870
Lyon Rural Electric Co-op 116 S Marshall St	Rock Rapids	IA	51246	**800-658-3976**	712-472-2506
Maquoketa Valley Rural Electric Co-op 109 N Huber St	Anamosa	IA	52205	**800-927-6068**	319-462-3542
Midland Power Co-op 1005 E Lincolnway PO Box 420	Jefferson	IA	50129	**800-833-8876**	515-386-4111
Nishnabotna Valley Rural Electric Co-op 1317 Chatburn Ave	Harlan	IA	51537	**800-234-5122**	712-755-2166
North West REC 1505 Albany Pl SE PO Box 435	Orange City	IA	51041	**800-383-0476**	712-707-4935
Osceola Electric Co-op Inc 1102 Egret Dr PO Box 127	Sibley	IA	51249	**888-754-2519**	712-754-2519
Pella Co-op Electric Assn 2615 Washington St	Pella	IA	50219	**800-619-1040**	641-628-1040
Raccoon Valley Electric Co-op 28725 Hwy 30 PO Box 486	Glidden	IA	51443	**800-253-6211**	712-659-3649
Southern Iowa Electric Co-op Inc 22458 Hwy 2 PO Box 70	Bloomfield	IA	52537	**800-607-2027**	641-664-2277
Southwest Iowa Rural Electric Co-op 1801 Grove Ave	Corning	IA	50841	**888-591-1261**	641-322-3165
TIP Rural Electric Co-op 612 W Des Moines St PO Box 534	Brooklyn	IA	52211	**800-934-7976**	641-522-9221
Western Iowa Power Co-op 809 Iowa 39	Denison	IA	51442	**800-253-5189**	712-263-2943
Woodbury County Rural Electric Co-op Assn 1495 Humboldt Ave	Moville	IA	51039	**800-469-3125**	712-873-3125

Kansas

				Toll-Free	Phone
Ark Valley Electric Co-op Assn 10 E Tenth St	South Hutchinson	KS	67504	**888-297-9212**	620-662-6661
Bluestem Electric Co-op Inc 614 E Hwy 24 PO Box 5	Wamego	KS	66547	**800-558-1580**	785-456-2212
Butler Rural Electric Co-op Assn Inc 216 S Vine St PO Box 1242	El Dorado	KS	67042	**800-464-0060**	316-321-9600
Caney Valley Electric Co-op Assn Inc, The 401 Lawrence St PO Box 308	Cedar Vale	KS	67024	**800-310-8911**	620-758-2262
CMS Electric Co-op Inc 509 E Carthage St	Meade	KS	67864	**800-794-2353**	620-873-2184
DS&O Electric Cooperative Inc 129 W Main St PO Box 286	Solomon	KS	67480	**800-376-3533**	785-655-2011
Heartland Rural Electric Co-op 110 Enterprise St	Girard	KS	66743	**888-835-9585**	620-724-8251
Kaw Valley Electric Co-op Inc 1100 SW Auburn Rd	Topeka	KS	66615	**800-794-2011**	785-478-3444
Lane-Scott Electric Co-op Inc 410 S High	Dighton	KS	67839	**800-407-2217**	620-397-5327
Leavenworth-Jefferson Electric Co-op Inc 507 N Union St	McLouth	KS	66054	**888-796-6111**	
Lyon-Coffey Electric Co-op Inc 1013 N 4th PO Box 229	Burlington	KS	66839	**800-748-7395**	620-364-2116
Midwest Energy Inc 1330 Canterbury Dr	Hays	KS	67601	**800-222-3121**	785-625-3437
Pioneer Electric Co-op Inc 1850 W Oklahoma St PO Box 368	Ulysses	KS	67880	**800-794-9302**	620-356-1211
Prairie Land Electric Co-op Inc 14935 US Hwy 36	Norton	KS	67654	**800-577-3323**	785-877-3323
Radiant Electric Co-op Inc PO Box 390	Fredonia	KS	66736	**800-821-0956**	620-378-2161
Rolling Hills Electric Co-op Inc 122 W Main St PO Box 307	Mankato	KS	66956	**877-906-5903**	785-378-3151
Sumner-Cowley Electric Co-op Inc 2223 N A St PO Box 220	Wellington	KS	67152	**888-326-3356**	620-326-3356
Twin Valley Electric Co-op Inc 501 S Huston Ave	Altamont	KS	67330	**866-784-5500**	620-784-5500
Victory Electric Co-op Assn Inc 3230 N 14th Ave	Dodge City	KS	67801	**800-279-7915**	620-227-2139
Western Co-op Electric Assn Inc 635 S 13th St	WaKeeney	KS	67672	**800-456-6720**	785-743-5561
Wheatland Electric Co-op Inc 101 S Main St	Scott City	KS	67871	**800-762-0436**	620-872-5885

Kentucky

				Toll-Free	Phone
Big Sandy Rural Electric Co-op Corp 504 11th St	Paintsville	KY	41240	**888-789-7322**	606-789-4095
Blue Grass Energy Co-op Corp 1201 Lexington Rd	Nicholasville	KY	40356	**888-546-4243**	859-885-4191
Clark Energy Co-op Inc 2640 Ironworks Rd	Winchester	KY	40391	**800-992-3269**	859-744-4251
Cumberland Valley Electric Inc 6219 N US Hwy 25 E	Gray	KY	40734	**800-513-2677**	
Farmers Rural Electric Co-op Corp 504 S Broadway St	Glasgow	KY	42141	**800-253-2191**	270-651-2191
Grayson Rural Electric Co-op Corp 109 Bagby Pk	Grayson	KY	41143	**800-562-3532**	606-474-5136
Hickman-Fulton Counties Rural Electric Co-op Corp 1702 Moscow Ave	Hickman	KY	42050	**800-633-1391**	270-236-2521
Inter-County Energy Co-op 1009 Hustonville Rd	Danville	KY	40422	**888-266-7322**	859-236-4561
Jackson Energy Co-op 115 Jackson Energy Ln	McKee	KY	40447	**800-262-7480**	606-364-1000
Jackson Purchase Energy Corp 2900 Irvin Cobb Dr	Paducah	KY	42002	**800-633-4044**	270-442-7321
Kenergy Corp 6402 Old Corydon Rd	Henderson	KY	42419	**800-844-4832**	270-826-3991
Licking Valley Rural Electric Co-op Corp 271 Main St	West Liberty	KY	41472	**800-596-6530**	606-743-3179
Nolin Rural Electric Co-op Corp 411 Ring Rd	Elizabethtown	KY	42701	**888-637-4247**	270-765-6153
Owen Electric Co-op Inc 8205 Hwy 127 N PO Box 400	Owenton	KY	40359	**800-372-7612**	502-484-3471
Pennyrile Rural Electric Co-op Corp 2000 Harrison St PO Box 2900 *Cust Svc	Hopkinsville	KY	42241	**800-297-4710***	270-886-2555
Salt River Electric Co-op Corp 111 W Brashear Ave	Bardstown	KY	40004	**800-221-7465**	502-348-3931
Shelby Energy Co-op Inc 620 Old Finchville Rd	Shelbyville	KY	40065	**800-292-6585**	502-633-4420
South Kentucky Rural Electrical Co-op 925 N Main St PO Box 910	Somerset	KY	42502	**800-264-5112**	606-678-4121
Taylor County RECC 625 W Main St PO Box 100	Campbellsville	KY	42719	**800-931-4551**	270-465-4101
Warren Rural Electric Co-op Corp 951 Fairview Ave	Bowling Green	KY	42101	**866-319-3234**	270-842-6541
West Kentucky Rural Electric Co-op Corp PO Box 589	Mayfield	KY	42066	**877-495-7322**	270-247-1321

Louisiana

				Toll-Free	Phone
Beauregard Electric Co-op Inc 1010 E First St	DeRidder	LA	70634	**800-367-0275**	337-463-6221
Concordia Electric Co-op Inc 1865 Hwy 84 W PO Box 98	Jonesville	LA	71343	**800-617-6282**	318-339-7969
Dixie Electric Membership Corp (DEMCO) PO Box 15659	Baton Rouge	LA	70895	**800-262-0221**	225-261-1221
Jefferson Davis Electric Co-op 906 N Lk Arthur Ave PO Box 1229	Jennings	LA	70546	**800-256-5332**	337-824-4330
Pointe Coupee Electric Membership Corp 2506 False River Dr PO Box 160	New Roads	LA	70760	**800-738-7232**	225-638-3751
Southwest Louisiana Electric Membership Corp 3420 NE Evangeline Thruway	Lafayette	LA	70509	**888-275-3626**	337-896-5384
Washington-Saint Tammany Electric Co-op 950 Pearl St PO Box N	Franklinton	LA	70438	**866-672-9773**	985-839-3562

Maine

				Toll-Free	Phone
Eastern Maine Electric Co-op Inc 21 Union St	Calais	ME	04619	**800-696-7444**	207-454-7555

Maryland

				Toll-Free	Phone
Choptank Electric Co-op Inc 24820 Meeting House Rd PO Box 430	Denton	MD	21629	**877-892-0001**	

Michigan

				Toll-Free	Phone
Cherryland Electric Co-op 5930 US 31 S PO Box 298	Grawn	MI	49637	**800-442-8616**	231-486-9200
Great Lakes Energy Co-op 1323 Boyne Ave	Boyne City	MI	49712	**888-485-2537**	

Name / Address	City	State	Zip	Toll-Free	Phone
Midwest Energy Co-op 901 E State St	Cassopolis	MI	49031	**800-492-5989**	
Presque Isle Electric & Gas Co-op PO Box 308	Onaway	MI	49765	**800-423-6634**	989-733-8515

Minnesota

Name / Address	City	State	Zip	Toll-Free	Phone
Agralite Electric Co-op 320 Hwy 12 SE	Benson	MN	56215	**800-950-8375**	320-843-4150
Arrowhead Electric Co-op Inc 5401 W Hwy 61 PO Box 39	Lutsen	MN	55612	**800-864-3744**	218-663-7239
Beltrami Electric Co-op Inc 4111 Technology Dr NW	Bemidji	MN	56601	**800-955-6083**	218-444-2540
Benco Electric Co-op 20946 549 Ave PO Box 8	Mankato	MN	56002	**888-792-3626**	507-387-7963
Brown County Rural Electric Assn 24386 State Hwy 4 PO Box 529	Sleepy Eye	MN	56085	**800-658-2368**	507-794-3331
Clearwater-Polk Electric Co-op 315 Main Ave N	Bagley	MN	56621	**888-694-3833**	218-694-6241
Connexus Energy Co-op 14601 Ramsey Blvd	Ramsey	MN	55303	**877-382-4357**	763-323-2650
Crow Wing Co-op Power & Light Co Hwy 371 N PO Box 507	Brainerd	MN	56401	**800-648-9401**	218-829-2827
Dakota Electric Assn 4300 220th St W	Farmington	MN	55024	**800-874-3409**	651-463-6144
East Central Energy PO Box 39	Braham	MN	55006	**800-254-7944**	
Federated Rural Electric Assn 77100 US Hwy 71 PO Box 69	Jackson	MN	56143	**800-321-3520**	507-847-3520
Freeborn-Mower Co-op Services 2501 E Main St	Albert Lea	MN	56007	**800-734-6421**	507-373-6421
Goodhue County Co-op Electric Assn 1410 Northstar Dr	Zumbrota	MN	55992	**800-927-6864**	507-732-5117
Great River Energy 12300 Elm Creek Blvd	Maple Grove	MN	55369	**888-521-0130**	763-445-5000
Itasca-Mantrap Co-op Electrical Assn 16930 County Rd 6	Park Rapids	MN	56470	**888-713-3377**	218-732-3377
Lake Country Power 2810 Elida Dr	Grand Rapids	MN	55744	**800-421-9959**	
Lake Region Co-op Electrical Assn 1401 S Broadway PO Box 643	Pelican Rapids	MN	56572	**800-552-7658**	218-863-1171
Lyon-Lincoln Electric Co-op Inc (LLEC) 205 W Hwy 14 PO Box 639	Tyler	MN	56178	**800-927-6276**	507-247-5505
McLeod Co-op Power Assn 1231 Ford Ave N	Glencoe	MN	55336	**800-494-6272**	320-864-3148
Meeker Co-op Light & Power Assn 1725 E US Hwy 12 PO Box 68	Litchfield	MN	55355	**800-232-6257**	320-693-3231
Mille Lacs Electric Co-op PO Box 230	Aitkin	MN	56431	**800-450-2191**	218-927-2191
Minnesota Valley Co-op Light & Power Assn 501 S First St	Montevideo	MN	56265	**800-247-5051**	320-269-2163
Minnesota Valley Electric Co-op 125 Minnesota Vly Electric Dr PO Box 77024	Jordan	MN	55352	**800-282-6832**	952-492-2313
Nobles Co-op Electric 22636 US Hwy 59 PO Box 788	Worthington	MN	56187	**800-776-0517**	507-372-7331
North Itasca Electric Co-op Inc 301 Main Ave PO Box 227	Bigfork	MN	56628	**800-762-4048**	218-743-3131
North Star Electric Co-op 441 State Hwy 172 NW PO Box 719	Baudette	MN	56623	**888-634-2202**	218-634-2202
People's Energy Co-op 1775 Lk Shady Ave S	Oronoco	MN	55960	**800-214-2694**	507-367-7000
PKM Electric Co-op Inc 406 N Minnesota St	Warren	MN	56762	**800-552-7366**	218-745-4711
Red Lake Electric Co-op Inc 412 International Dr PO Box 430	Red Lake Falls	MN	56750	**800-245-6068**	218-253-2168
Red River Valley Co-op Power Assn 109 Second Ave E	Halstad	MN	56548	**800-788-7784**	218-456-2139
Renville-Sibley Co-op Power Assn 103 Oak St PO Box 68	Danube	MN	56230	**800-826-2593**	320-826-2593
Roseau Electric Co-op Inc 1107 Third St NE	Roseau	MN	56751	**888-847-8840**	218-463-1543
South Central Electric Assn 71176 Tiell Dr PO Box 150	Saint James	MN	56081	**888-805-7232**	507-375-3164
Stearns ElectricAssn 900 E Kraft Dr	Melrose	MN	56352	**800-962-0655**	320-256-4241
Steele-Waseca Co-op Electric (SWCE) 2411 W Bridge St PO Box 485	Owatonna	MN	55060	**800-526-3514**	507-451-7340
Todd-Wadena Electric Co-op 550 Ash Ave NE PO Box 431	Wadena	MN	56482	**800-321-8932**	218-631-3120
Traverse Electric Co-op Inc 1618 Broadway PO Box 66	Wheaton	MN	56296	**800-927-5443**	320-563-8616
Tri-County Electric Co-op 31110 Co-op Way PO Box 626	Rushford	MN	55971	**800-432-2285**	507-864-7783
Wild Rice Electric Co-op Inc 502 N Main PO Box 438	Mahnomen	MN	56557	**800-244-5709**	218-935-2517
Wright-Hennepin Co-op Electric Assn 6800 Electric Dr PO Box 330	Rockford	MN	55373	**800-943-2667**	763-477-3000

Mississippi

Name / Address	City	State	Zip	Toll-Free	Phone
Alcorn County Electric Power Assn 1909 S Tate St	Corinth	MS	38834	**866-448-3046**	662-287-4402
Central Electric Power Assn 104 E Main St	Carthage	MS	39051	**866-846-5671**	601-267-5671
Coast Electric Power Assn 18020 Hwy Ste 603 *Cust Svc	Kiln	MS	39556	**800-624-3348***	228-363-7000
Dixie Electric Power Assn PO Box 88	Laurel	MS	39441	**888-465-9209**	601-425-2535
Monroe County Electric Power Assn 601 N Main St	Amory	MS	38821	**866-656-2962**	662-256-2962
North East MS EPA 10 PR 2050 PO Box 1037	Oxford	MS	38655	**877-234-6331**	662-234-6331
Pearl River Valley Electric Power Assn 1422 Hwy 13 N PO Box 1217	Columbia	MS	39429	**855-277-8372**	601-736-2666
Southern Pine Electric Power Assn 110 Risher St PO Box 60	Taylorsville	MS	39168	**800-231-5240**	601-785-6511
Southwest Mississippi Electric Power Assn 18671 Hwy 61 PO Box 5	Lorman	MS	39096	**800-287-8564**	
Yazoo Valley Electric Power Assn 2255 Gordon Ave	Yazoo City	MS	39194	**800-281-5098**	662-746-4251

Missouri

Name / Address	City	State	Zip	Toll-Free	Phone
Atchison-Holt Electric Co-op 18585 Industrial Rd PO Box 160	Rock Port	MO	64482	**888-744-5366**	660-744-5344
Barry Electric Co-op 4015 Main St PO Box 307	Cassville	MO	65625	**866-847-2333**	
Barton County Electric Co-op 91 US-160	Lamar	MO	64759	**800-286-5636**	417-682-5636
Black River Electric Co-op 2600 Hwy 67 PO Box 31	Fredericktown	MO	63645	**800-392-4711**	573-783-3381
Boone Electric Co-op 1413 Rangeline St	Columbia	MO	65201	**800-225-8143**	573-449-4181
Callaway Electric Co-op 1313 Co-op Dr PO Box 250	Fulton	MO	65251	**888-642-4840**	573-642-3326
Central Missouri ElectricCo-op Inc 22702 Hwy 65 PO Box 939	Sedalia	MO	65302	**855-875-7165**	660-826-2900
Co-Mo Electric Co-op Inc 29868 Hwy 5 PO Box 220	Tipton	MO	65081	**800-781-0157**	660-433-5521
Consolidated Electric Co-op 3940 E Liberty St	Mexico	MO	65265	**800-621-0091**	573-581-3630
Crawford Electric Co-op Inc 10301 N Service Rd PO Box 10	Bourbon	MO	65441	**800-677-2667**	573-732-4415
Cuivre River Electric Co-op 1112 E Cherry St	Troy	MO	63379	**800-392-3709**	636-528-8261
Farmers' Electric Co-op 201 W Business 36 PO Box 680	Chillicothe	MO	64601	**800-279-0496**	660-646-4281
Gascosage Electric Co-op 803 S Hwy 28 PO Box G	Dixon	MO	65459	**866-568-8243**	573-759-7146
Grundy Electric Co-op Inc 4100 Oklahoma Ave	Trenton	MO	64683	**800-279-2249**	660-359-3941
Howard Electric Co-op 205 Hwy 5 & 240 N PO Box 391	Fayette	MO	65248	**877-352-0122**	660-248-3311
Howell-Oregon Electric Co-op Inc 6327 N US Hwy 63 PO Box 649	West Plains	MO	65775	**855-385-9903**	417-256-2131
Laclede Electric Co-op 1400 E Rt 66	Lebanon	MO	65536	**800-299-3164**	417-532-3164
Lewis County Rural Electric Co-op 18256 Hwy 16 PO Box 68	Lewistown	MO	63452	**888-454-4485**	573-215-4000
Macon Electric Co-op 31571 Bus Hwy 36 E PO Box 157	Macon	MO	63552	**800-553-6901**	660-385-3157
Osage Valley Electric Co-op Assn 1321 N Orange St	Butler	MO	64730	**800-889-6832**	660-679-3131
Ozark Border Electric Co-op 3281 S Westwood	Poplar Bluff	MO	63901	**800-392-0567**	573-785-4631
Pemiscot-Dunklin Electric Co-op Hwy 412 W PO Box 509	Hayti	MO	63851	**800-558-6641**	573-757-6641
Platte-Clay Electric Co-op Inc 1000 W Hwy 92 PO Box 100	Kearney	MO	64060	**800-431-2131**	816-628-3121
Ralls County Electric Co-op 17594 Hwy 19 PO Box 157	New London	MO	63459	**877-985-8711**	573-985-8711
Sac Osage Electric Co-op Inc 4815 E Hwy 54 PO Box 111	El Dorado Springs	MO	64744	**800-876-2701**	417-876-2721
Three Rivers Electric Co-op 1324 E Main St PO Box 918	Linn	MO	65051	**800-892-2251**	573-644-9000
Webster Electric Co-op 1240 Spur Dr	Marshfield	MO	65706	**800-643-4305**	417-859-2216
White River Valley Electric Co-op Inc 2449 State Hwy 76 E	Branson	MO	65616	**800-879-4056**	417-335-9335

Montana

Name / Address	City	State	Zip	Toll-Free	Phone
Beartooth Electric Co-op Inc 1306 N Broadway St PO Box 1110	Red Lodge	MT	59068	**800-472-9821**	406-446-2310
Big Flat Electric Co-op Inc 333 S Seventh St	Malta	MT	59538	**800-242-2040**	406-654-2040
Flathead Electric Co-op Inc 2510 Hwy 2 E	Kalispell	MT	59901	**800-735-8489**	406-751-4483
Glacier Electric Co-op Inc 410 E Main St	Cut Bank	MT	59427	**800-347-6795**	406-873-5566
Hill County Electric Co-op Inc PO Box 2330	Havre	MT	59501	**877-394-7804**	
Lincoln Electric Co-op Inc (LEC) 500 Osloski Rd PO Box 628	Eureka	MT	59917	**800-442-2994**	406-889-3301
Lower Yellowstone Rural Electric Assn Inc 3200 W Holly St PO Box 1047	Sidney	MT	59270	**844-441-5627**	406-488-1602
McCone Electric Co-op Inc 110 Main St	Circle	MT	59215	**800-684-3605**	406-485-3430
Missoula Electric Co-op Inc 1700 W Broadway	Missoula	MT	59808	**800-352-5200**	406-541-4433
Park Electric Co-op Inc 5706 US Hwy 89 S PO Box 1119	Livingston	MT	59047	**888-298-0657**	406-222-3100
Sheridan Electric Co-op Inc PO Box 227	Medicine Lake	MT	59247	**888-472-1533**	406-789-2231
Southeast Electric Co-op Inc (SECO) 110 S Main St	Ekalaka	MT	59324	**888-485-8762**	406-775-8762
Sun River Electric Co-op Inc 310 First Ave S PO Box 309	Fairfield	MT	59436	**800-452-7516**	406-467-2527
Yellowstone Valley Electric Co-op 150 Co-op Way	Huntley	MT	59037	**800-736-5323**	406-348-3411

Nebraska

Name / Address	City	State	Zip	Toll-Free	Phone
Burt County Public Power District 613 N 13th St	Tekamah	NE	68061	**888-835-1620**	402-374-2631
Butler County Rural Public Power District 1331 N Fourth St	David City	NE	68632	**800-230-0569**	402-367-3081

Name	Address	City	State	ZIP	Toll-Free	Phone
Chimney Rock Public Power District	805 W Eigth St PO Box 608	Bayard	NE	69334	**877-773-6300**	308-586-1824
Cornhusker Public Power District	23169 235th Ave PO Box 9	Columbus	NE	68602	**800-955-2773**	402-564-2821
Cuming County Public Power District	500 S Main St	West Point	NE	68788	**877-572-2463**	402-372-2463
Custer Public Power District	625 E SE St PO Box 10	Broken Bow	NE	68822	**888-749-2453**	308-872-2451
Dawson Public Power District	75191 Rd 433	Lexington	NE	68850	**800-752-8305**	308-324-2386
Elkhorn Rural Public Power District	206 N Fourth St	Battle Creek	NE	68715	**800-675-2185**	402-675-2185
Howard Greeley Rural Power	422 Howard Ave PO Box 105	Saint Paul	NE	68873	**800-280-4962**	308-754-4457
KBR Rural Public Power District	374 N Pine St PO Box 187	Ainsworth	NE	69210	**800-672-0009**	402-387-1120
Loup Public Power District (LPPD)	2404 15th St PO Box 988	Columbus	NE	68602	**866-869-2087**	402-564-3171
McCook Public Power District	1510 N Hwy 83	McCook	NE	69001	**800-658-4285**	308-345-2500
Midwest Electric Co-op Corp	104 Washington Ave	Grant	NE	69140	**800-451-3691**	308-352-4356
Nebraska Public Power District	1414 15th St PO Box 499	Columbus	NE	68602	**877-275-6773**	402-564-8561
Norris Public Power District	606 Irving St PO Box 399	Beatrice	NE	68310	**800-858-4707**	402-223-4038
North Central Public Power District	1409 Main St PO Box 90	Creighton	NE	68729	**800-578-1060**	402-358-5112
Northeast Nebraska Public Power District	1410 W Seventh St PO Box 350	Wayne	NE	68787	**800-750-9277**	402-375-1360
Northwest Rural Public Power District	5613 State Hwy 87 PO Box 249	Hay Springs	NE	69347	**800-847-0492**	308-638-4445
Perennial Public Power District	2122 S Lincoln Ave	York	NE	68467	**800-289-0288**	402-362-3355
Polk County Rural Public Power District	115 W 3rd St PO Box 465	Stromsburg	NE	68666	**888-242-5265**	402-764-4381
South Central Public Power District (SCPPD)	275 S Main St PO Box 406	Nelson	NE	68961	**800-557-5254**	402-225-2351
Southern Public Power District (SPPD)	4550 W Husker Hwy PO Box 1687	Grand Island	NE	68803	**800-652-2013**	308-384-2350
Southwest Public Power District	221 S Main St PO Box 289	Palisade	NE	69040	**800-379-7977**	308-285-3295
Stanton County Public Power District	807 Douglas St	Stanton	NE	68779	**877-439-2300**	402-439-2228
Twin Valleys Public Power District	1145 Nasby St	Cambridge	NE	69022	**800-658-4266**	308-697-3315
Wheat Belt Public Power District	2104 Illinois St	Sidney	NE	69162	**800-261-7114**	308-254-5871

Nevada

Name	Address	City	State	ZIP	Toll-Free	Phone
Valley Electric Assn Inc	800 E Hwy 372 PO Box 237	Pahrump	NV	89048	**800-742-3330**	775-727-5312

New Hampshire

Name	Address	City	State	ZIP	Toll-Free	Phone
New Hampshire Electric Co-op	579 Tenney Mtn Hwy	Plymouth	NH	03264	**800-698-2007**	603-536-1800

New Jersey

Name	Address	City	State	ZIP	Toll-Free	Phone
Sussex Rural Electric Co-op	64 County Rt 639 PO Box 346	Sussex	NJ	07461	**877-504-6463**	973-875-5101

New Mexico

Name	Address	City	State	ZIP	Toll-Free	Phone
Columbus Electric Co-op Inc	900 N Gold St PO Box 631	Deming	NM	88031	**800-950-2667**	505-546-8838
Jemez Mountains Electric Co-op	PO Box 128	Espanola	NM	87532	**888-755-2105**	505-753-2105
Mora-San Miguel Electric Co-op	PO Box 240	Mora	NM	87732	**800-421-6773**	575-387-2205
Otero County Electric Co-op Inc	202 Burro Ave PO Box 227	Cloudcroft	NM	88317	**800-548-4660**	575-682-2521
Socorro Electric Co-op Inc	215 Manzanares Ave PO Box H	Socorro	NM	87801	**800-351-7575**	575-835-0560
Springer Electric Co-op Inc	408 Maxwell Ave PO Box 698	Springer	NM	87747	**800-288-1353**	575-483-2421

New York

Name	Address	City	State	ZIP	Toll-Free	Phone
Delaware County Electric Co-op (DCEC)	39 Elm St PO Box 471	Delhi	NY	13753	**866-436-1223**	607-746-2341
Steuben Rural Electric Co-op Inc	9 Wilson Ave	Bath	NY	14810	**800-843-3414**	607-776-4161

North Carolina

Name	Address	City	State	ZIP	Toll-Free	Phone
Albemarle Electric Membership Corp	PO Box 69	Hertford	NC	27944	**800-215-9915**	252-426-5735
Blue Ridge Electric Membership Corp	1216 Blowing Rock Blvd	Lenoir	NC	28645	**800-451-5474**	828-758-2383
Brunswick Electric Membership Corp	795 Ocean Hwy PO Box 826	Shallotte	NC	28459	**800-842-5871**	910-754-4391
Cape Hatteras Electric Co-op	47109 Light Plant Rd PO Box 9	Buxton	NC	27920	**800-454-5616**	252-995-5616
Carteret-Craven Electric Co-op (CCEC)	1300 Hwy 24 W PO Box 1490	Newport	NC	28570	**800-682-2217**	252-247-3107
Central Electric Membership Corp	128 Wilson Rd	Sanford	NC	27331	**800-446-7752**	919-774-4900
Edgecombe-Martin County Electric Membership Corp	NC Hwy 33 E	Tarboro	NC	27886	**800-445-6486**	252-823-2171
EnergyUnited Electric Membership Corp	PO Box 1831	Statesville	NC	28687	**800-522-3793**	704-873-5241
Four County Electric Membership Corp	1822 NC Hwy 53 W PO Box 667	Burgaw	NC	28425	**888-368-7289**	910-259-2171
Halifax Electric Membership Corp	208 Whitfield St	Enfield	NC	27823	**800-690-0522**	252-445-5111
Haywood Electric Membership Corp	376 Grindstone Rd	Waynesville	NC	28785	**800-951-6088**	828-452-2281
Jones-Onslow Electric Membership Corp	259 Western Blvd	Jacksonville	NC	28546	**800-682-1515**	910-353-1940
Lumbee River Electric Membership Corp	PO Box 830	Red Springs	NC	28377	**800-683-5571**	910-843-4131
Pee Dee Electric Membership Corp (PDEMC)	575 US Hwy 52 S	Wadesboro	NC	28170	**800-992-1626**	704-694-2114
Randolph Electric Membership Corp	879 McDowell Rd PO Box 40	Asheboro	NC	27204	**800-672-8212**	336-625-5177
Roanoke Electric Co-op	518 NC 561 W	Aulander	NC	27805	**800-433-2236**	252-539-4600
Rutherford Electric Membership Corp	186 Hudlow Rd PO Box 1569	Forest City	NC	28043	**800-521-0920**	828-245-1621
South River Electric Membership Corp	17494 US 421 S PO Box 931	Dunn	NC	28335	**800-338-5530**	910-892-8071
Surry-Yadkin Electric Membership Corp	510 S Main St	Dobson	NC	27017	**800-682-5903**	336-356-8241
Tideland Electric Membership Corp	25831 Hwy 264 E	Pantego	Nc	27860	**800-637-1079**	252-943-3046
Union Power Co-op	1525 N Rocky River Rd	Monroe	NC	28110	**800-922-6840**	704-289-3145
Wake Electric	100 S Franklin St PO Box 1229	Wake Forest	NC	27588	**800-474-6300**	919-863-6300

North Dakota

Name	Address	City	State	ZIP	Toll-Free	Phone
Burke-Divide Electric Co-op Inc (BDEC)	9549 Hwy 5 W	Columbus	ND	58727	**800-472-2983**	701-939-6671
Capital Electric Co-op Inc	4111 State St	Bismarck	ND	58503	**888-223-1513**	701-223-1513
Cass County Electric Co-op Inc	4100 32nd Ave SW	Fargo	ND	58104	**800-248-3292**	701-356-4400
Dakota Valley Electric Co-op	7296 Hwy 281	Edgeley	ND	58433	**800-342-4671**	701-493-2281
KEM Electric Co-op Inc	107 S Broadway	Linton	ND	58552	**800-472-2673**	701-254-4666
McLean Electric Co-op Inc	4031 Hwy 37 Bypass NW	Garrison	ND	58540	**800-263-4922**	701-463-2291
Mor-Gran-Sou Electric Co-op Inc	202 Sixth Ave W	Flasher	ND	58535	**800-750-8212**	701-597-3301
Mountrail-Williams Electric Co-op	218 58th St W PO Box 1346	Williston	ND	58802	**800-279-2667**	701-577-3765
Nodak Electric Co-op Inc	4000 32nd Ave S	Grand Forks	ND	58201	**800-732-4373**	701-746-4461
Northern Plains Electric Co-op	1515 W Main St	Carrington	ND	58421	**800-882-2500**	701-652-3156
Slope Electric Co-op Inc	116 E 12th St PO Box 338	New England	ND	58647	**800-559-4191**	701-579-4191
Verendrye Electric Co-op Inc	615 Hwy 52	Velva	ND	58790	**800-472-2141**	701-338-2855

Ohio

Name	Address	City	State	ZIP	Toll-Free	Phone
Adams Rural Electric Co-op Inc	4800 SR 125	West Union	OH	45693	**800-283-1846**	937-544-2305
Buckeye Rural Electric Co-op	PO Box 200	Rio Grande	OH	45674	**800-231-2732**	740-379-2025
Butler Rural Electric Co-op Inc (BREC)	3888 Still-Beckett Rd	Oxford	OH	45056	**800-255-2732**	513-867-4400
Carroll Electric Co-op Inc	350 Canton Rd NW	Carrollton	OH	44615	**800-232-7697**	330-627-2116
Darke Rural Electric Co-op Inc	1120 Fort Jefferson Rd	Greenville	OH	45331	**866-692-6330**	937-548-4114
Denier Electric Co Inc	10891 SR- 128	Harrison	OH	45030	**800-676-3282**	513-738-2641
Firelands Electric Co-op Inc	1 Energy Pl PO Box 32	New London	OH	44851	**800-533-8658**	419-929-1571
Frontier Power Co	770 S 2nd St PO Box 280	Coshocton	OH	43812	**800-624-8050**	740-622-6755
Guernsey-Muskingum Electric Co-op	17 S Liberty St	New Concord	OH	43762	**800-521-9879**	740-826-7661
Hancock-Wood Electric Co-op Inc (HWEC)	1399 Business Pk Dr S PO Box 190	North Baltimore	OH	45872	**800-445-4840**	419-257-3241
Holmes-Wayne Electric Co-op Inc	6060 Ohio 83	Millersburg	OH	44654	**866-674-1055**	330-674-1055
Lorain-Medina Rural Electric Co-op Inc	22898 W Rd	Wellington	OH	44090	**800-222-5673**	440-647-2133
Mid Ohio Energy Co-op Inc	555 W Franklin St	Kenton	OH	43326	**888-382-6732**	419-673-7289
North Central Electric Co-op Inc	13978 E County Rd 56	Attica	OH	44807	**800-426-3072**	419-426-3072
North Western Electric Co-op Inc	04125 State Rt 576 PO Box 391	Bryan	OH	43506	**800-647-6932**	419-636-5051
Paulding-Putnam Electric Co-op	910 N Williams St	Paulding	OH	45879	**800-686-2357**	419-399-5015
South Central Power Company Inc	2780 Coon Path Rd	Lancaster	OH	43130	**800-282-5064**	740-653-4422
Union Rural Electric Co-op Inc	15461 US 36E	Marysville	OH	43040	**800-642-1826**	937-642-1826
Washington Electric Co-op Inc	406 Colegate Dr	Marietta	OH	45750	**877-594-9324**	740-373-2141

Oklahoma

Name	Address	City	State	ZIP	Toll-Free	Phone
Alfalfa Electric Co-op Inc	121 E Main St	Cherokee	OK	73728	**888-736-3837**	580-596-3333

Company	Address	City	State	ZIP	Toll-Free	Phone
Canadian Valley Electric Co-op	11277 S 356 PO Box 751	Seminole	OK	74868	**877-382-3680**	405-382-3680
Central Rural Electric Co-op	3304 S Boomer Rd PO Box 1809	Stillwater	OK	74076	**800-375-2884**	405-372-2884
Choctaw Electric Co-op Inc	1033 N 4250 Rd	Hugo	OK	74743	**800-780-6486**	580-326-6486
Cimarron Electric Co-op	PO Box 299	Kingfisher	OK	73750	**800-375-4121**	405-375-4121
Cookson Hills Electric Co-op Inc	1002 E Main St	Stigler	OK	74462	**800-328-2368**	918-967-4614
Cotton Electric Co-op Inc	226 N Broadway	Walters	OK	73572	**800-522-3520**	580-875-3351
Harmon Electric Assn Inc (HEA)	114 N First St PO Box 393	Hollis	OK	73550	**800-643-7769**	580-688-3342
Indian Electric Co-op Inc	2506 E Hwy 64	Cleveland	OK	74020	**800-482-2750**	918-358-2514
Kay Electric Co-op (KEC)	300 W Doolin Ave	Blackwell	OK	74631	**800-535-1079**	580-363-1260
Kiamichi Electric Co-op Inc (KEC)	966 SW Hwy 2 PO Box 340	Wilburton	OK	74578	**800-888-2731**	918-465-2338
Kiwash Electric Co-op Inc	120 W First St	Cordell	OK	73632	**888-832-3362**	580-832-3361
Lake Region Electric Co-op Inc	516 S Lake Region Rd	Hulbert	OK	74441	**800-364-5732**	918-772-2526
Northeast Oklahoma Electric Co-op Inc	443857 E Hwy 60 PO Box 948	Vinita	OK	74301	**800-256-6405**	918-256-6405
Northwestern Electric Co-op Inc	2925 William Ave	Woodward	OK	73802	**800-375-7423**	580-256-7425
Rural Electric Co-op Inc (REC)	801 N Industrial Heights PO Box 609	Lindsay	OK	73052	**800-259-3504**	405-756-3104
Southeastern Electric Co-op Inc	1514 E Hwy 70 PO Box 1370	Durant	OK	74702	**866-924-1315**	580-924-2170
Southwest Rural Electric Assn	700 N Broadway PO Box 310	Tipton	OK	73570	**800-256-7973**	580-667-5281
Tri-County Electric	302 E Glaydas St PO Box 880	Hooker	OK	73945	**800-522-3315**	580-652-2418
Verdigris Valley Electric Co-op	8901 E 146th St N	Collinsville	OK	74021	**800-870-5948**	918-371-2584

Oregon

Company	Address	City	State	ZIP	Toll-Free	Phone
Blachly-Lane Inc	PO Box 70	Junction City	OR	97448	**800-446-8418**	541-688-8711
Consumers Power Inc (CPI)	6990 W Hills Rd PO Box 1180	Philomath	OR	97370	**800-872-9036**	541-929-3124
Midstate Electric Co-op Inc	16755 Finley Butte Rd	La Pine	OR	97739	**800-722-7219**	541-536-2126
Tillamook People's Utility District	1115 Pacific Ave	Tillamook	OR	97141	**800-422-2535**	503-842-2535
Wasco Electric Co-op Inc	105 E Fourth St	The Dalles	OR	97058	**800-341-8580**	541-296-2740
West Oregon Electric Co-op Inc	652 Rose Ave PO Box 69	Vernonia	OR	97064	**800-777-1276**	503-429-3021

Pennsylvania

Company	Address	City	State	ZIP	Toll-Free	Phone
Adams Electric Co-op Inc	1338 Biglerville Rd PO Box 1055	Gettysburg	PA	17325	**888-232-6732**	717-334-2171
Bedford Rural Electric Co-op Inc	8846 Lincoln Hwy	Bedford	PA	15522	**800-808-2732**	814-623-5101
Citizens' Electric Co	1775 Industrial Blvd PO Box 551	Lewisburg	PA	17837	**877-487-9384**	570-524-2231
Claverack Rural Electric Co-op Inc	32750 W US 6	Wysox	PA	18854	**800-326-9799**	570-265-2167
New Enterprise Rural Electric Co-op Inc	3596 Brumbaugh Rd	New Enterprise	PA	16664	**800-270-3177**	814-766-3221
Northwestern Rural Electric Co-op Assn Inc	22534 State Rte Ste 86	Cambridge Springs	PA	16403	**800-352-0014**	800-472-7910
REA Energy Co-op Inc	75 Airport Rd	Indiana	PA	15701	**800-211-5667**	724-349-4800
Somerset Rural Electric Co-op	223 Industrial Pk Rd	Somerset	PA	15501	**800-443-4255**	814-445-4106
Sullivan County Rural Electric Co-op Inc (SCREC)	5675 Rt 87 PO Box 65	Forksville	PA	18616	**800-570-5081**	570-924-3381
Tri-County Rural Electric Co-op Inc	22 N Main St PO Box 526	Mansfield	PA	16933	**800-343-2559**	570-662-2175
United Electric Co-op Inc	29 United Rd	Du Bois	PA	15801	**888-581-8969**	814-371-8570
Valley Rural Electric Co-op Inc	10700 Fairgrounds Rd PO Box 477	Huntingdon	PA	16652	**800-432-0680**	814-643-2650
Warren Electric Co-op Inc (WEC)	320 E Main St PO Box 208	Youngsville	PA	16371	**800-364-8640**	814-563-7548

South Carolina

Company	Address	City	State	ZIP	Toll-Free	Phone
Aiken Electric Co-op Inc	2790 Wagener Rd *Tech Supp	Aiken	SC	29802	**877-264-5368***	803-649-6245
Broad River Electric Co-op Inc	811 Hamrick St	Gaffney	SC	29342	**866-687-2667**	864-489-5737
Coastal Electric Co-op Inc	2269 Jefferies Hwy	Walterboro	SC	29488	**855-880-2743**	843-538-5700
Edisto Electric Co-op Inc	896 Calhoun St	Bamberg	SC	29003	**800-433-3292**	803-245-5141
Laurens Electric Co-op Inc	2254 S Carolina 14	Laurens	SC	29360	**800-942-3141**	
Little River Electric Co-op Inc (LRECI)	PO Box 220	Abbeville	SC	29620	**800-459-2141**	864-366-2141
Lynches River Electric Co-op Inc	1104 W McGregor St	Pageland	SC	29728	**800-922-3486**	843-672-6111
Mid-Carolina Electric Co-op Inc	PO Box 669 *Cust Svc	Lexington	SC	29071	**888-813-8000***	803-749-6555
Newberry Electric Co-op Inc	882 Wilson Rd	Newberry	SC	29108	**800-479-8838**	803-276-1121
Pee Dee Electric Co-op Inc	PO Box 491	Darlington	SC	29540	**866-747-0060**	843-665-4070
Santee Electric Co-op Inc	424 Sumter Hwy	Kingstree	SC	29556	**800-922-1604**	843-355-6187
York Electric Co-op Inc	PO Box 150	York	SC	29745	**800-582-8810**	803-684-4247

South Dakota

Company	Address	City	State	ZIP	Toll-Free	Phone
Black Hills Electric Co-op	25191 Co-op Way PO Box 792	Custer	SD	57730	**800-742-0085**	605-673-4461
Bon Homme Yankton Electric Assn	134 S Lidice St	Tabor	SD	57063	**800-925-2929**	605-463-2507
Butte Electric Co-op	109 Dartmouth Ave	Newell	SD	57760	**800-928-8839**	605-456-2494
Cam-Wal Electric Co-op Inc	404 W Scranton St PO Box 135	Selby	SD	57472	**800-269-7676**	
Charles Mix Electric Assn Inc	440 Lake St	Lake Andes	SD	57356	**800-208-8587**	605-487-7321
Cherry-Todd Electric Co-op Inc	625 W Second St	Mission	SD	57555	**800-856-4417**	605-856-4416
Clay-Union Electric Corp	1410 E Cherry St PO Box 317	Vermillion	SD	57069	**800-696-2832**	605-624-2673
Codington-Clark Electric Co-op	3520 Ninth Ave SW PO Box 880	Watertown	SD	57201	**800-463-8938**	605-886-5848
Dakota Energy Co-op Inc	PO Box 830	Huron	SD	57350	**800-353-8591**	605-352-8591
FEM Electric Assn Inc	PO Box 468	Ipswich	SD	57451	**800-587-5880**	605-426-6891
Grand Electric Co-op Inc	801 Coleman Ave PO Box 39	Bison	SD	57620	**800-592-1803**	605-244-5211
H-D Electric Co-op Inc	423 Third Ave S	Clear Lake	SD	57226	**800-781-7474**	605-874-2171
Lake Region Electric Assn Inc	1212 Main St	Webster	SD	57274	**800-657-5869**	605-345-3379
Moreau-Grand Electric Co-op Inc	405 Ninth St	Timber Lake	SD	57656	**800-952-3158**	605-865-3511
Northern Electric Co-op Inc	39456 133nd St	Bath	SD	57427	**800-529-0310**	605-225-0310
Oahe Electric Co-op Inc	102 S Cranford St PO Box 216	Blunt	SD	57522	**800-640-6243**	605-962-6243
Rosebud Electric Co-op Inc	512 Rosebud Ave PO Box 439	Gregory	SD	57533	**888-464-9304**	605-835-9624
Sioux Valley-Southwestern Electric Co-op Inc	47092 SD Hwy 34 PO Box 216	Colman	SD	57017	**800-234-1960**	605-534-3535
Union County Electric Co-op Inc	122 W Main St	Elk Point	SD	57025	**888-356-3395**	605-356-3395
West Central Electric Co-op Inc	204 Main St PO Box 17	Murdo	SD	57559	**800-242-9232**	605-669-2472
West River Electric Assn Inc	1200 W Fourth Ave PO Box 412	Wall	SD	57790	**888-279-2135**	
Whetstone Valley Electric Co-op	1101 E Fourth Ave	Milbank	SD	57252	**800-568-6631**	605-432-5331

Tennessee

Company	Address	City	State	ZIP	Toll-Free	Phone
Caney Fork Electric Co-op Inc	920 Smithville Hwy PO Box 272	McMinnville	TN	37110	**888-505-3030**	931-473-3116
Chickasaw Electric Co-op	17970 US Hwy 64 E PO Box 459	Somerville	TN	38068	**866-465-3591**	901-465-3591
Fayetteville Public Utilities	408 W College St	Fayetteville	TN	37334	**800-379-2534**	931-433-1522
Forked Deer Electric Co-op	PO Box 67	Halls	TN	38040	**844-333-2729**	731-836-7508
Greeneville Light & Power System	PO Box 1690	Greeneville	TN	37744	**866-466-1438**	423-636-6200
La Follette Utilities Board	302 N Tennessee Ave PO Box 1411	La Follette	TN	37766	**800-352-1340**	423-562-3316
Mountain Electric Co-op Inc	PO Box 180 *Cust Svc	Mountain City	TN	37683	**800-638-3788***	423-727-1800
Newport Utilities	PO Box 519	Newport	TN	37822	**877-779-8581**	423-625-2800
Pickwick Electric Co-op	530 Mulberry Ave	Selmer	TN	38375	**800-372-8258**	731-645-3411
Sequachee Valley Electric Co-op	512 Cedar Ave PO Box 31	South Pittsburg	TN	37380	**800-923-2203**	423-837-8605
Southwest Tennessee Electric Membership Corp	1009 E Main St	Brownsville	TN	38012	**800-772-0472**	731-772-1322
Tennessee Valley Electric Co-op	590 Florence Rd	Savannah	TN	38372	**866-925-4916**	731-925-4916
Tri-County Electric Membership Corp	405 College St	Lafayette	TN	37083	**800-369-2111**	615-666-2111
Upper Cumberland Electric Membership Corp	138 Gordonsville Hwy	South Carthage	TN	37030	**800-261-2940**	615-735-2940

Texas

Company	Address	City	State	ZIP	Toll-Free	Phone
Bandera Electric Co-op Inc	3172 State Hwy 16 N	Bandera	TX	78003	**866-226-3372**	
Big Country Electric Co-op	1010 W S First St PO Box 518	Roby	TX	79543	**888-662-2232**	325-776-2244
Bowie-Cass Electric Co-op Inc	117 N St	Douglassville	TX	75560	**800-794-2919**	903-846-2311
Central Texas Electric Co-op Inc (CTEC)	386 Friendship Ln PO Box 553 *General	Fredericksburg	TX	78624	**800-900-2832***	830-997-2126
Coleman County Electric Co-op Inc	3300 N Hwy 84 PO Box 860	Coleman	TX	76834	**800-560-2128**	325-625-2128
Comanche Electric Co-op Assn	201 W Wrights Ave	Comanche	TX	76442	**800-915-2533**	325-356-2533
Cooke County Electric Co-op	11799 W US Hwy 82 PO Box 530	Muenster	TX	76252	**800-962-0296**	940-759-2211

Company	Address	City	State	ZIP	Toll-Free	Phone
CoServ Electric	7701 S Stemmons Fwy	Corinth	TX	76210	**800-274-4014**	940-321-7800
Deaf Smith Electric Co-op Inc	1501 E First St	Hereford	TX	79045	**800-687-8189**	806-364-1166
Deep East Texas Electric Co-op Inc	880 Texas Hwy 21 E PO Box 736	San Augustine	TX	75972	**800-392-5986**	936-275-2314
Farmers Electric Co-op Inc	2000 E I-30	Greenville	TX	75402	**800-541-2662**	903-455-1715
Fayette Electric Co-op Inc	357 N Washington St	La Grange	TX	78945	**800-874-8290**	979-968-3181
Grayson-Collin Electric Co-op (GCEC)	PO Box 548	Van Alstyne	TX	75495	**800-967-5235**	903-482-7100
Greenbelt Electric Co-op Inc	PO Box 948	Wellington	TX	79095	**800-527-3082**	806-447-2536
Guadalupe Valley Electric Co-op Inc	825 E Sarah Dewitt Dr	Gonzales	TX	78629	**800-223-4832**	830-857-1200
Hamilton County Electric Co-op Assn	420 N Rice St PO Box 753	Hamilton	TX	76531	**800-595-3401**	254-386-3123
Hilco Electric Co-op Inc	115 E Main PO Box 127	Itasca	TX	76055	**800-338-6425**	254-687-2331
Karnes Electric Co-op Inc	1007 N Hwy 123	Karnes City	TX	78118	**888-807-3952**	830-780-3952
Lamar County Electric Co-op Assn	1485 N Main St	Paris	TX	75460	**800-252-8080**	903-784-4303
Lamb County Electric Co-op Inc	2415 S Phelps Ave	Littlefield	TX	79339	**800-365-9000**	806-385-5191
Lyntegar Electric Co-op Inc	PO Box 970	Tahoka	TX	79373	**877-218-2308**	806-561-4588
McLennan County Electric Co-op	1111 Johnson Dr PO Box 357	McGregor	TX	76657	**800-840-2957**	254-840-2871
Medina Electric Co-op Inc	PO Box 370	Hondo	TX	78861	**866-632-3532**	
Navarro County Electric Co-op Inc	3800 Texas 22 PO Box 616	Corsicana	TX	75110	**800-771-9095**	903-874-7411
Navasota Valley Electric Co-op Inc	2281 E US Hwy 79 PO Box 848	Franklin	TX	77856	**800-443-9462**	979-828-3232
North Plains Electric Co-op Inc	14585 Hwy 83 N PO Box 1008	Perryton	TX	79070	**800-272-5482**	806-435-5482
Nueces Electric Co-op (NEC)	709 E Main St PO Box 260970	Robstown	TX	78380	**800-632-9288**	361-387-2581
Panola-Harrison Electric Co-op	410 E Houston St	Marshall	TX	75670	**800-972-1093**	903-935-7936
Pedernales Electric Co-op Inc	PO Box 1	Johnson City	TX	78636	**888-554-4732**	830-868-7155
Rio Grande Electric Co-op Inc	Hwy 90 & State Hwy 131 PO Box 1509	Brackettville	TX	78832	**800-749-1509**	830-563-2444
Sam Houston Electric Co-op Inc	1157 E Church St	Livingston	TX	77351	**800-458-0381**	936-327-5711
San Bernard Electric Co-op Inc	309 W Main St	Bellville	TX	77418	**800-364-3171**	979-865-3171
San Patricio Electric Co-op Inc	402 E Sinton St	Sinton	TX	78387	**888-740-2220**	361-364-2220
South Plains Electric Co-op Inc	PO Box 1830	Lubbock	TX	79408	**800-658-2655**	806-775-7766
Southwest Texas Electric Co-op Inc	101 E Gillis St PO Box 677	Eldorado	TX	76936	**800-643-3980**	325-853-2544
Swisher Electric Co-op Inc	401 SW Second St PO Box 67	Tulia	TX	79088	**800-530-4344**	806-995-3567
Texas Electric Co-ops Inc	1122 Colorado St 24th Fl	Austin	TX	78701	**800-301-2860**	512-454-0311
Tri-County Electric Co-op Inc	600 NW Pkwy	Azle	TX	76020	**800-367-8232**	817-444-3201
Trinity Valley Electric Co-op Inc (TVEC)	1800 Hwy 243 E PO Box 888	Kaufman	TX	75142	**800-766-9576**	972-932-2214
Wharton County Electric Co-op Inc (WCEC)	1815 E Jackson St	El Campo	TX	77437	**800-460-6271**	979-543-6271
Wise Electric Co-op Inc	1900 N Trinity St	Decatur	TX	76234	**888-627-9326**	940-627-2167
Wood County Electric Co-op Inc	501 S Main St	Quitman	TX	75783	**800-762-2203**	903-763-2203

Utah

Company	Address	City	State	ZIP	Toll-Free	Phone
Dixie-Escalante Rural Electric Assn	71 E Hwy 56	Beryl	UT	84714	**800-874-0904**	435-439-5311
Garkane Energy Co-op Inc	120 West 300 South PO Box 465	Loa	UT	84747	**800-747-5403**	435-836-2795

Vermont

Company	Address	City	State	ZIP	Toll-Free	Phone
Vermont Electric Co-op Inc	42 Wescom Rd	Johnson	VT	05656	**800-832-2667**	802-635-2331
Washington Electric Co-op	40 Church St	East Montpelier	VT	05602	**800-932-5245**	802-223-5245

Virginia

Company	Address	City	State	ZIP	Toll-Free	Phone
BARC Electric Co-op	84 High St PO Box 264	Millboro	VA	24460	**800-846-2272**	
Central Virginia Electric Co-op	800 Co-op Way PO Box 247	Lovingston	VA	22949	**800-367-2832**	434-263-8336
Community Electric Co-op	52 W Windsor Blvd	Windsor	VA	23487	**855-700-2667**	757-242-6181
Mecklenburg Electric Co-op	11633 Hwy Ninety Two	Chase City	VA	23924	**800-989-4161**	434-372-6100
Northern Neck Electric Co-op Inc	85 St Johns St PO Box 288	Warsaw	VA	22572	**800-243-2860**	804-333-3621
Northern Virginia Electric Co-op	PO Box 2710	Manassas	VA	20108	**888-335-0500**	703-335-0500
Southside Electric Co-op Inc	2000 W Virgina Ave	Crewe	VA	23930	**800-552-2118**	434-645-7721

Washington

Company	Address	City	State	ZIP	Toll-Free	Phone
Benton Rural Electric Assn (BREA)	402 Seventh St PO Box 1150	Prosser	WA	99350	**800-221-6987**	509-786-2913
Big Bend Electric Co-op	1373 N Hwy 261 PO Box 348	Ritzville	WA	99169	**866-844-2363**	509-659-1700
Columbia Rural Electric Assn Inc	115 E Main St	Dayton	WA	99328	**800-642-1231**	509-382-2578
Elmhurst Mutual Power & Light Co	120 132nd St S	Tacoma	WA	98444	**855-841-2178**	253-531-4646
Energy Northwest	76 N Power Plant Loop	Richland	WA	99354	**800-468-6883**	509-372-5000
Inland Power & Light Company Inc	10110 W Hallett Rd	Spokane	WA	99224	**800-747-7151**	509-747-7151
Nespelem Valley Electric Co-op Inc	1009 F St	Nespelem	WA	99155	**866-377-8642**	509-634-4571
Peninsula Light Co	13315 Goodnough Dr NW	Gig Harbor	WA	98332	**888-809-8021**	253-857-5950
Tanner Electric Co	45710 SE North Bend Way	North Bend	WA	98045	**800-472-0208**	425-888-0623

Wisconsin

Company	Address	City	State	ZIP	Toll-Free	Phone
Adams-Columbia Electric Co-op	401 E Lake St	Friendship	WI	53934	**800-831-8629**	608-339-3346
Barron Electric Co-op	1434 State Hwy 25 N	Barron	WI	54812	**800-322-1008**	715-537-3171
Bayfield Electric Co-op Inc	68460 District St	Iron River	WI	54847	**800-278-0166**	715-372-4287
Chippewa Valley Electric Co-op	317 S Eigth St	Cornell	WI	54732	**800-300-6800**	715-239-6800
Clark Electric Co-op	124 N Main St PO Box 190	Greenwood	WI	54437	**800-272-6188**	715-267-6188
Dunn Energy Co-op	PO Box 220	Menomonie	WI	54751	**800-924-0630**	715-232-6240
Jackson Electric Co-op	N6868 County Rd F PO Box 546	Black River Falls	WI	54615	**800-370-4607**	715-284-5385
Jump River Electric Co-op	PO Box 99	Ladysmith	WI	54848	**866-273-5111**	715-532-5524
Oakdale Electric Co-op	PO Box 128	Oakdale	WI	54649	**800-241-2468**	608-372-4131
Oconto Electric Co-op	PO Box 168 PO Box 168	Oconto Falls	WI	54154	**800-472-8410**	920-846-2816
Pierce Pepin Co-op Services	W7725 US Hwy 10 PO Box 420	Ellsworth	WI	54011	**800-924-2133**	715-273-4355
Polk-Burnett Electric Co-op (PBEC)	1001 State Rd 35	Centuria	WI	54824	**800-421-0283**	715-646-2191
Price Electric Co-op	508 N Lake Ave PO Box 110	Phillips	WI	54555	**800-884-0881**	715-339-2155
Richland Electric Co-op	1027 N Jefferson St	Richland Center	WI	53581	**800-242-8511**	608-647-3173
Riverland Energy Co-op	N28988 State Rd 93 PO Box 277	Arcadia	WI	54612	**800-411-9115**	608-323-3381
Saint Croix Electric Co-op	1925 Ridgeway St	Hammond	WI	54015	**800-924-3407**	715-796-7000
Scenic Rivers Energy Co-op	231 N Sheridan St	Lancaster	WI	53813	**800-236-2141**	608-723-2121
Taylor Electric Co-op	N1831 State Hwy 13	Medford	WI	54451	**800-862-2407**	715-678-2411
Vernon Electric Co-op	110 Saugstad Rd	Westby	WI	54667	**800-447-5051**	608-634-3121

Wyoming

Company	Address	City	State	ZIP	Toll-Free	Phone
Big Horn Rural Electric Co-op	208 S Fifth St PO Box 270	Basin	WY	82410	**800-564-2419**	307-568-2419
Bridger Valley Extreme Access	40014 Business Loop 1-80 PO Box 399	Mountain View	WY	82939	**800-276-3481**	307-786-2800
Carbon Power & Light Inc	100 E Willow Ave PO Box 579	Saratoga	WY	82331	**800-359-0249**	307-326-5206
High Plains Power Inc	1775 E Monroe PO Box 713	Riverton	WY	82501	**800-445-0613**	307-856-9426
High West Energy Inc (HWE)	6270 County Rd 212	Pine Bluffs	WY	82082	**888-834-1657**	307-245-3261
Lower Valley Energy	236 N Washington PO Box 188	Afton	WY	83110	**800-882-5875**	307-885-3175
Powder River Energy Corp (PRE)	221 Main St PO Box 930	Sundance	WY	82729	**800-442-3630**	
Wheatland Rural Electric Assn	2154 S St PO Box 1209	Wheatland	WY	82201	**800-344-3351**	307-322-2125
Wyrulec Co	3978 US Hwy 26/85	Torrington	WY	82240	**800-628-5266**	307-837-2225

248 ELECTRICAL & ELECTRONIC EQUIPMENT & PARTS - WHOL

Company	Address	City	State	ZIP	Toll-Free	Phone
ACF Components & Fasteners Inc	31012 Huntwood Ave	Hayward	CA	94544	**800-227-2901***	510-487-2100
	*Cust Svc					
Actify LLC	7635 Interactive Way Ste 200	Indianapolis	IN	46278	**800-467-0830**	
Adi American Distributors Inc	2 Emery Ave	Randolph	NJ	07869	**800-877-0510**	973-328-1181
Advanced MP Technology	1010 Calle Sombra	San Clemente	CA	92673	**800-492-3113**	949-492-3113
AE Petsche Company Inc	2112 W Div St	Arlington	TX	76012	**844-237-7600**	817-461-9473
Aesco Electronics Inc	2230 Picton Pkwy	Akron	OH	44312	**877-442-6987**	330-245-2630

Company / Address	City	State	ZIP	Toll-Free	Phone
Algo Communication Products Ltd 4500 Beedie St	Burnaby	BC	V5J5L2	**800-226-7722**	604-438-3333
Allied Electronics Inc 7151 Jack Newell Blvd S	Fort Worth	TX	76118	**866-433-5722**	817-595-3500
Allstar Magnetics LLC 6205 NE 63rd St	Vancouver	WA	98661	**800-356-5977**	360-693-0213
America II Electronics Inc 2600 118th Ave N	Saint Petersburg	FL	33716	**800-767-2637**	727-573-0900
Anixter International Inc 2301 Patriot Blvd *NYSE: AXE*	Glenview	IL	60025	**800-492-1212**	224-521-8000
Area 51 Esg Inc 51 Post	Irvine	CA	92618	**877-476-8751**	949-387-0051
Argo International Corp 160 Chubb Ave	Lyndhurst	NJ	07071	**877-274-6468**	201-561-7010
Astrex Inc 205 Express St	Plainview	NY	11803	**800-633-6360**	516-433-1700
Audio-technica Us Inc 1221 Commerce Dr	Stow	OH	44224	**800-667-3745**	330-686-2600
Avnet Inc 2211 S 47th St *NYSE: AVT*	Phoenix	AZ	85034	**888-822-8638**	480-643-2000
B&D Industries Inc 9720 Bell Ave Se	Albuquerque	NM	87123	**866-315-8349**	505-299-4464
Barnett Inc 801 W Bay St	Jacksonville	FL	32204	**888-803-4467**	904-384-6530
Bearcom Inc 4009 Distribution Dr Ste 200 *Sales	Garland	TX	75041	**800-527-1670***	
Becker Electric Supply Inc 1341 E Fourth St	Dayton	OH	45402	**800-762-9515**	937-226-1341
Beyond Components 5 Carl Thompson Rd	Westford	MA	01886	**800-971-4242**	
Billows Electric Supply Co 9100 State Rd	Philadelphia	PA	19136	**877-519-7302**	215-332-9700
Bisco Industries Inc 1500 N Lakeview Ave	Anaheim	CA	92807	**800-323-1232**	
Border States Electric Supply 105 25th St N	Fargo	ND	58102	**800-800-0199**	701-293-5834
Broadfield Distributing Inc 67A Glen Cove Ave	Glen Cove	NY	11542	**800-634-5178**	516-676-2378
Buckles-Smith 801 Savaker Ave	San Jose	CA	95126	**800-833-7362**	408-280-7777
Butler Supply Inc 965 Horan Dr	Fenton	MO	63026	**800-850-9949**	636-349-9000
Byram Laboratories Inc 1 Columbia Rd	Branchburg	NJ	08876	**800-766-1212**	
Cadex Electronics Inc 22000 Fraserwood Way	Richmond	BC	V6W1J6	**800-565-5228**	604-231-7777
Carlton Bates Co 3600 W 69th St	Little Rock	AR	72209	**866-600-6040**	501-562-9100
Cell-Tel Government Systems Inc 8226-B Phillips Hwy Ste 290	Jacksonville	FL	32256	**800-737-7545**	904-363-1111
Century Fasteners Corp 50-20 Ireland St	Elmhurst	NY	11373	**800-221-0769**	718-446-5000
Cms Communications Inc 722 Goddard Ave	Chesterfield	MO	63005	**800-755-9169**	
Codale Electric Supply Inc 5225 West 2400 South PO Box 702070	Salt Lake City	UT	84120	**800-300-6634**	801-975-7300
Communications Supply Corp (CSC) 200 E Lies Rd	Carol Stream	IL	60188	**800-468-2121**	630-221-6400
Components Distributors Inc 2601 Blake St Ste 200	Denver	CO	80205	**800-777-7334**	
Comtel Corp 39810 Grand River Ave Ste 180	Novi	MI	48375	**800-335-2505**	248-888-4730
Corporate Telephone Services 184 W Second St	Boston	MA	02127	**800-274-1211**	617-625-1200
Cortelco Inc 1703 Sawyer Rd	Corinth	MS	38834	**800-288-3132**	662-287-5281
Cross Automation Inc 2001 Oak Pkwy *General	Belmont	NC	28012	**800-272-7537***	704-523-2222
Crum Electric Supply Co 1165 W English Ave	Casper	WY	82601	**800-726-2239**	307-266-1278
Dakota Supply Group (DSG) 2601 Third Ave N	Fargo	ND	58102	**800-437-4702**	701-237-9440
Dee Electronics Inc 2500 16th Ave SW	Cedar Rapids	IA	52404	**800-747-3331**	319-365-7551
Dependable Component Supply Corp 1003 E Newport Ctr Dr	Deerfield Beach	FL	33442	**800-336-7100**	954-283-5800
Digi-Key Corp 701 Brooks Ave S	Thief River Falls	MN	56701	**800-344-4539**	218-681-6674
Diversified Electronics Co Inc PO Box 566	Forest Park	GA	30298	**800-646-7278**	404-361-4840
Dominion Electric Supply Company Inc 5053 Lee Hwy	Arlington	VA	22207	**800-525-5006**	703-536-4400
Dow Electronics Inc 8603 E Adamo Dr	Tampa	FL	33619	**800-627-2900**	813-626-5195
E Sam Jones Distributor Inc 4898 S Atlanta Rd	Smyrna	GA	30080	**800-624-9849**	404-351-3250
Electric Supply & Equipment Co 1812 E Wendover Ave	Greensboro	NC	27405	**800-632-0268**	336-272-4123
Electric Supply Inc 4407 N Manhattan Ave	Tampa	FL	33614	**800-678-1894**	813-872-1894
Electro Brand Inc 1127 S Mannheim Rd Ste 305	Westchester	IL	60154	**800-982-3954**	708-338-4400
Electro-Matic Products Inc 23409 Industrial Pk Ct	Farmington Hills	MI	48335	**888-879-1088**	248-478-1182
ElectroTech Inc 7101 Madison Ave W	Minneapolis	MN	55427	**800-544-4288**	763-544-4288
Elliott Electric Supply Co 2526 N Stallings Dr PO Box 630610	Nacogdoches	TX	75963	**877-777-0242**	936-569-1184
Englewood Electrical Supply 716 Belvedere Dr	Kokomo	IN	46901	**800-417-7543**	765-452-4087
Eric Electronics 2220 Lundy Ave *General	San Jose	CA	95131	**800-495-3742***	408-432-1111
Evans Enterprises Inc 1536 S Western Ave	Oklahoma City	OK	73109	**800-423-8267**	405-631-1344
Facility Solutions Group (FSG) 4401 Westgate Blvd Ste 310	Austin	TX	78745	**800-854-6465**	512-440-7985
FD Lawrence Electric Company Inc 3450 Beekman St *Cust Svc	Cincinnati	OH	45223	**800-582-4490***	513-542-1100
Fiber Instruments Sales Inc 161 Clear Rd *Sales	Oriskany	NY	13424	**800-500-0347***	315-736-2206
Fiber Optic Center New Trust 23 Centre St	New Bedford	MA	02740	**800-473-4237**	508-992-6464
Flame Enterprises Inc 21500 Gledhill St	Chatsworth	CA	91311	**800-854-2255**	818-700-2905
Floyd Bell Inc 720 Dearborn Park Ln	Columbus	OH	43085	**888-356-9323**	614-294-4000
Foxcom Inc 136 Main St Ste 300b	Princeton	NJ	08540	**866-663-7284**	609-514-1800
Friedman Electric 1321 Wyoming Ave	Exeter	PA	18643	**800-545-5517**	570-654-3371
Fromm Electric Supply Corp 2101 Centre Ave PO Box 15147	Reading	PA	19605	**800-360-4441**	610-374-4441
FSG Lighting 4401 Westgate Blvd Ste 310	Austin	TX	78745	**800-854-6465**	512-440-7985
FTG Inc 725 Marshall Phelps Rd	Windsor	CT	06095	**888-610-6020**	860-610-6000
Future Electronics 237 Hymus Blvd *Cust Svc	Pointe-Claire	QC	H9R5C7	**800-675-1619***	514-694-7710
Futurecom Systems Group Inc 3277 Langstaff Rd	Concord	ON	L4K5P8	**800-701-9180**	905-660-5548
Galco Industrial Electronics Inc 26010 Pinehurst Dr	Madison Heights	MI	48071	**888-783-4611**	248-542-9090
GBH Communications Inc 1309 S Myrtle Ave	Monrovia	CA	91016	**800-222-5424**	
George R Peters Assoc Inc PO Box 850	Troy	MI	48099	**800-929-5972**	248-524-2211
Graybar Electric Co Inc 34 N Meramec Ave	Saint Louis	MO	63105	**800-472-9227**	314-573-9200
Hammond Electronics Inc 1230 W Central Blvd *Sales	Orlando	FL	32805	**800-929-3672***	407-849-6060
Hartford Electric Supply Co (HESCO) 30 Inwood Rd Ste 1	Rocky Hill	CT	06067	**800-969-5444**	860-236-6363
Headsets Direct Inc 1454 W Gurley St Ste A	Prescott	AZ	86305	**800-914-7996**	928-777-9100
Heartland Label Printers Inc 1700 Stephen St *General	Little Chute	WI	54140	**800-236-7914***	
Heilind Electronics Inc 58 Jonspin Rd	Wilmington	MA	01887	**800-400-7041**	978-657-4870
Hite Co 3101 Beale Ave	Altoona	PA	16601	**800-252-3598**	814-944-6121
HITEC Group Ltd 1743 Quincy Ave Unit 155	Naperville	IL	60540	**800-288-8303**	
HL Dalis Inc 35-35 24th St	Long Island	NY	11106	**800-453-2547**	718-361-1100
Houston Wire & Cable Co (HWC) 10201 N Loop E	Houston	TX	77029	**800-468-9473**	713-609-2100
IBS Electronics Inc 3506 W Lk Ctr Dr Ste D	Santa Ana	CA	92704	**800-527-2888**	714-751-6633
IMS Inc 340 Progress Dr *General	Manchester	CT	06040	**800-264-9837***	860-649-4415
Independent Electric Supply Inc 1370 Bayport Ave	San Carlos	CA	94070	**855-437-4968**	650-594-9440
Industrial Electric Wire & Cable Inc (IEWC) 5001 S Towne Dr	New Berlin	WI	53151	**800-344-2323**	262-782-2323
Interstate Connecting Components Inc 120 Mt Holly By Pass	Lumberton	NJ	08048	**888-899-1990**	800-422-3911
Interstate Electrical Supply Inc 2300 Second Ave	Columbus	GA	31901	**800-903-4409**	706-324-1000
Jaco Electronics Inc 415 Oser Ave *OTC: JACO*	Hauppauge	NY	11788	**877-373-5226**	
Janesway Electronic Corp 404 N Terr Ave	Mount Vernon	NY	10552	**800-431-1348**	914-699-6710
Jasco Products Inc 10 E Memorial Rd	Oklahoma City	OK	73114	**800-654-8483**	405-752-0710
JH Larson Co 10200 51st Ave N	Plymouth	MN	55442	**800-292-7970**	763-545-1717
Kehoe Component Sales Inc 34 Foley Dr	Sodus	NY	14551	**800-228-7223**	
Kendall Electric Inc 131 Grand Trunk Ave	Battle Creek	MI	49037	**800-632-5422**	269-963-5585
Kikusui America Inc 1633 Bayshore Hwy Ste 331	Burlingame	CA	94010	**877-876-2807**	650-259-5900
Leff Electric 4700 Spring Rd	Cleveland	OH	44131	**800-686-5333**	216-432-3000
Lester Sales Co Inc 4312 W Minnesota St	Indianapolis	IN	46241	**800-544-6183**	317-244-7811
Lewis Electric Supply Company Inc 1306 Second St PO Box 2237	Muscle Shoals	AL	35662	**800-239-0681**	256-383-0681
Lowe Electric Supply Co 1525 Forsyth St PO Box 4767	Macon	GA	31208	**800-868-8661**	478-743-8661
Loyd's Electric Supply Inc (LES) 838 Stonetree Dr	Branson	MO	65616	**800-492-4030**	417-334-2171
Macnica Americas Inc 380 Stevens Ave Ste 206	Solana Beach	CA	92075	**888-399-4937**	760-707-0120
Maltby Electric Supply Company Inc 336 Seventh St	San Francisco	CA	94103	**800-339-0668**	415-863-5000
Mars Electric Co 38868 Mentor Ave	Willoughby	OH	44094	**877-229-7227**	440-946-2250
Marsh Electronics Inc 1563 S 101st St *Cust Svc	Milwaukee	WI	53214	**800-926-2774***	414-475-6000
Mayer Electric Supply Co 3405 Fourth Ave S PO Box 1328	Birmingham	AL	35222	**866-637-1255**	205-583-3500
McNaughton-McKay Electric Company Inc 1357 E Lincoln Ave	Madison Heights	MI	48071	**888-626-2785**	248-399-7500
Metro Wire & Cable Co 6636 Metropolitan Pkwy	Sterling Heights	MI	48312	**800-633-1432**	586-264-3050
Mid-Island Electrical Supply 59 Mall Dr	Commack	NY	11725	**877-324-2636**	631-864-4242

Company	Address	City	State	ZIP	Toll-Free	Phone	Note
Mouser Electronics Corp	1000 N Main St	Mansfield	TX	76063	**800-346-6873**	817-804-3888	
Murdock Industrial Supply	1111 E 1st	Wichita	KS	67202	**800-362-2422**	316-262-4476	
Music People Inc	154 Woodlawn Rd Ste C	Berlin	CT	06037	**800-289-8889**		
NACB Group Inc	10 Starwood Dr	Hampstead	NH	03841	**800-370-2737**	603-329-4551	
Nedco Electronics	594 American Way	Payson	UT	84651	**800-605-2323**	801-465-1790	
Nelson Electric Supply Co Inc	926 State St	Racine	WI	53404	**800-806-3576**	262-635-5050	
NEP Electronics Inc	805 Mittel Dr	Wood Dale	IL	60191	**800-284-7470**	630-595-8500	
NF Smith & Assoc LP	5306 Hollister Rd	Houston	TX	77040	**800-468-7866**	713-430-3000	
Nora Lighting Inc	6505 Gayhart St	Commerce	CA	90040	**800-686-6672**	323-767-2600	
Northern Video Systems Inc	3625 Cincinnati Ave	Rocklin	CA	95765	**800-366-4472**	916-543-4000	
Nsync Services Inc	850 Greenview Dr	Grand Prairie	TX	75050	**866-706-7962**	972-641-7426	
Nu Horizons Electronics Corp	70 Maxess Rd	Melville	NY	11747	**855-326-4757**	631-396-5000	
Nu-Lite Electrical Wholesalers	850 Edwards Ave	Harahan	LA	70123	**800-256-1603**	504-733-3300	
Omni Cable Corp	2 Hagerty Blvd	West Chester	PA	19382	**888-292-6664**	610-701-0100	
One Link Wireless	7321 Broadway Ext	Oklahoma City	OK	73116	**800-259-2929**	405-840-2345	
Paige Electric Company LP	1160 Springfield Rd	Union	NJ	07083	**800-327-2443**	908-687-7810	
Path Master Inc	1960 Midway Dr	Twinsburg	OH	44087	**855-738-2722**	330-425-4994	
Peerless Electronics Inc	700 Hicksville Rd	Bethpage	NY	11714	**800-285-2121**	516-594-3500	
PEI-Genesis	2180 Hornig Rd	Philadelphia	PA	19116	**800-675-1214**	215-673-0400	
Platt Electric Supply	10605 SW Allen Blvd	Beaverton	OR	97005	**800-257-5288**	503-641-6121	
Powell Electronics Inc	200 Commodore Dr	Swedesboro	NJ	08085	**800-235-7880**	856-241-8000	
Power & Telephone Supply Company Inc	2673 Yale Ave	Memphis	TN	38112	**800-238-7514***	901-866-3300	*Cust Svc
Priority Wire & Cable Inc	PO Box 398	North Little Rock	AR	72115	**800-945-5542***	501-372-5444	*General
Professional Electric Products Co (PEPCO)	33210 Lakeland Blvd	Eastlake	OH	44095	**800-872-7000**	440-946-3790	
Projections Unlimited Inc	15311 Varrenca Pkwy	Irvine	CA	92618	**800-551-4405***	714-544-2700	*Cust Svc
QED Inc	1661 W Third Ave	Denver	CO	80223	**800-700-5011**	303-825-5011	
Radiophone Engineering Inc	534 W Walnut St	Springfield	MO	65806	**800-369-2929**	417-862-6653	
Ralph Pill Electrical Supply Co	50 Von Hillern St	Boston	MA	02125	**800-897-1769**	617-265-8800	
Rawson Inc	2010 McAllister	Houston	TX	77092	**800-779-1414**		
Reagan Wireless Corp	720 S Powerline Rd Ste D	Deerfield Beach	FL	33442	**877-724-3266**	954-596-2355	
Red Peacock International Inc	1945 Gardena Ave	Glendale	CA	91204	**877-774-0037**	818-265-7722	
Regency Lighting Co	9261 Jordan Ave	Chatsworth	CA	91311	**800-284-2024**		
Renco Electronics Inc	595 International Pl	Rockledge	FL	32955	**800-645-5828**	321-637-1000	
Rexel Inc	14951 Dallas Pkwy PO Box 9085	Dallas	TX	75254	**888-739-3577**	972-387-3600	
Rexel Ryall Electrical Supplies	11775 E 45th Ave	Denver	CO	80239	**888-739-3577**	303-629-7721	
Richardson Electronics Ltd	40 W 267 Keslinger Rd PO Box 393	LaFox	IL	60147	**800-348-5580***	630-208-2200	*NASDAQ: RELL* ■ *Sales
RS Electronics Inc	34443 Schoolcraft Rd	Livonia	MI	48150	**866-600-6040**	734-525-1155	
Rumsey Electric Co	15 Colwell Ln	Conshohocken	PA	19428	**800-462-2402**	610-832-9000	
S K C Communication Products Inc	8320 Hedge Ln Terr	Shawnee Mission	KS	66227	**800-882-7779**	913-422-4222	
Sager Electronics Inc	19 Lorena Dr	Middleboro	MA	02346	**800-724-3780**	508-947-8888	
Sandusky Electric Inc	1513 Sycamore Line	Sandusky	OH	44870	**800-356-1243**	419-625-4915	
Schuster Electronics Inc	11320 Grooms Rd	Cincinnati	OH	45242	**800-521-1358**		
Sciemetric Instruments Inc	359 Terry Fox Dr Ste 100	Ottawa	ON	K2K2E7	**877-931-9200**	613-254-7054	
Scott Electric	1000 S Main St PO Box S	Greensburg	PA	15601	**800-442-8045**	724-834-4321	
Sennheiser Electronics Corp	1 Enterprise Dr	Old Lyme	CT	06371	**877-736-6434**	860-434-9190	
Shealy Electrical Wholesalers Inc	422 Fairforest Way	Greenville	SC	29607	**800-868-5980**	864-242-6880	
Shepherd Electric Supply	7401 Pulaski Hwy	Baltimore	MD	21237	**800-253-1777***	410-866-6000	*Sales
Signalink Technologies Inc	Units 13 & 14 2550 Acland Rd	Kelowna	BC	V1X7L4	**888-491-3883**	250-491-3883	
Singing Machine Company Inc, The	6601 Lyons Rd Bldg A-7	Coconut Creek	FL	33073	**866-670-6888**	954-596-1000	*OTC: SMDM*
Skywalker Communications Inc	9390 Veterans Memorial Pkwy	O'Fallon	MO	63366	**800-844-9555**	636-272-8025	
Sommer Electric Corp	818 Third St NE	Canton	OH	44704	**800-766-6373**	330-455-9454	
Southern Controls Inc	3511 Wetumpka Hwy	Montgomery	AL	36110	**800-392-5770**		
Spectra Integrated Systems Inc	8100 Arrowridge Blvd	Charlotte	NC	28273	**800-443-7561**	704-525-7099	
Spectra Merchandising International Inc	4230 N Normandy Ave	Chicago	IL	60634	**800-777-5331**	773-202-8408	
Springfield Electric Supply Co	700 N Ninth St	Springfield	IL	62702	**800-747-2101**	217-788-2100	
Standard Electric Co	2650 Trautner Dr	Saginaw	MI	48603	**800-322-0215**	989-497-2100	
Standard Electric Supply Co	222 N Emmber Ln PO Box 651	Milwaukee	WI	53233	**800-776-8222**	414-272-8100	
Stanion Wholesale Electric Co	812 S Main St PO Box F	Pratt	KS	67124	**866-782-6466**	620-672-5678	
State Electric Supply Company Inc	2010 Second Ave	Huntington	WV	25703	**800-624-3417***	304-523-7491	*Cust Svc
Steiner Electric Co	1250 Touhy Ave	Elk Grove Village	IL	60007	**800-783-4637**	847-228-0400	
Steven Engineering Inc	230 Ryan Way	South San Francisco	CA	94080	**800-258-9200**	650-588-9200	
Stoneway Electric Supply Co	402 N Perry St	Spokane	WA	99202	**800-841-1408**	509-535-2933	
Storage Battery Systems Inc (SBS)	N56 W16665 Ridgewood Dr	Menomonee Falls	WI	53051	**800-554-2243**	262-703-5800	
Summit Electric Supply Co	2900 Stanford NE	Albuquerque	NM	87107	**800-824-4400**	505-346-9000	
Surface Mount Distribution Inc (SMD)	1 Oldfield	Irvine	CA	92618	**800-820-7634**	949-470-7700	
Syn-Tech Inc	3100 Ridgelake Dr Ste 101	Metairie	LA	70002	**800-535-7619**	504-835-7825	
Tacoma Electric Supply Inc	1311 S Tacoma Way	Tacoma	WA	98409	**800-422-0540**	253-475-0540	
Taitron Components Inc	28040 W Harrison Pkwy	Valencia	CA	91355	**800-247-2232**	661-257-6060	*NASDAQ: TAIT*
TeL Systems	7235 Jackson Rd	Ann Arbor	MI	48103	**800-686-7235**	734-761-4506	
Telcobuy com L L C	60 Weldon Pkwy	St. Louis	MO	63043	**877-350-0191**		
Tele-Communications Inc	5125 W 140th St	Brookpark	OH	44142	**877-841-8914**	216-267-0800	
Telesource Services LLC	1450 Highwood E	Pontiac	MI	48340	**800-525-4300**	248-335-3000	
Terry-Durin Co	409 Seventh Ave SE	Cedar Rapids	IA	52401	**800-332-8114**	319-364-4106	
TESSCO Technologies Inc	11126 McCormick Rd	Hunt Valley	MD	21031	**800-472-7373**	410-229-1000	*NASDAQ: TESS*
Tri-Ed Distribution Inc	135 Crossways Pk Dr W	Woodbury	NY	11797	**888-874-3336**	516-941-2800	
Tri-State Armature & Electrical Works Inc	330 GE Patterson PO Box 466	Memphis	TN	38126	**800-238-7654**	901-527-8412	
Tri-State Utility Products Inc	1030 Atlanta Industrial Dr	Marietta	GA	30066	**800-282-7985**	770-427-3119	
TTI Inc	2441 NE Pkwy	Fort Worth	TX	76106	**800-225-5884***	817-740-9000	*Sales
Unique Communications Inc	3650 Coral Ridge Dr	Coral Springs	FL	33065	**800-881-8182**	954-735-4002	
United Electrical Sales Ltd	4496 36th St	Orlando	FL	32811	**800-432-5126**	407-246-1992	
United Utility Supply Co-op Inc	4515 Bishop Ln	Louisville	KY	40218	**800-366-4887**	502-957-2568	
Valley Electric Supply Corp	1361 N State Rd PO Box 724	Vincennes	IN	47591	**800-825-7877**	812-882-7860	
Van Meter Industrial Inc	850 32nd Ave SW	Cedar Rapids	IA	52404	**800-247-1410**	319-366-5301	
Venkel Ltd	5900 Shepherd Mtn Cove	Austin	TX	78730	**800-950-8365**	512-794-0081	
Viking Electric Supply Inc	451 Industrial Blvd W	Minneapolis	MN	55413	**800-435-3345**	612-627-1300	
Virginia West Electric Supply Co (WVES)	250 12-th St W	Huntington	WV	25704	**800-624-3433**	304-525-0361	
Voss Lighting	PO Box 22159	Lincoln	NE	68542	**866-292-0529**	402-328-2281	
Vsa Inc	6929 Seward Ave	Lincoln	NE	68507	**800-888-2140**	402-467-3668	
Wabash Electric Supply Inc	1400 S Wabash St	Wabash	IN	46992	**800-552-7777**	260-563-4146	
Walters Wholesale Electric Co	2825 Temple Ave	Signal Hill	CA	90755	**800-700-5483**	562-988-3100	
Werner Electric Supply Co	2341 Industrial Dr	Neenah	WI	54956	**800-236-5026**	920-729-4500	
Wes-Garde Components Group Inc	190 Elliott St	Hartford	CT	06114	**800-554-8866**	860-525-6907	
West-Lite Supply Company Inc	12951 166th St	Cerritos	CA	90703	**800-660-6678**		
Western Extralite Co	1470 Liberty St	Kansas City	MO	64102	**800-279-8833**	816-421-8404	
White Radio LP	5228 Everest Dr	Mississauga	ON	L4W2R4	**877-386-1956**	905-632-6894	
Whitlock Group	12820 W Creekk Pkwy	Richmond	VA	23238	**800-726-9843**	804-273-9100	
Wieland Electric Inc (WEI)	49 International Rd	Burgaw	NC	28425	**800-943-5263**	910-259-5050	
Williams Supply Inc	210 Seventh St	Roanoke	VA	24016	**800-533-6969**	540-343-9333	
Wiremasters Inc	1788 N Pt Rd	Columbia	TN	38401	**800-635-5342**	615-791-0281	
WW Grainger Inc	100 Grainger Pkwy	Lake Forest	IL	60045	**888-361-8649**	847-535-1000	*NYSE: GWW*
XP Power	990 Benicia Ave	Sunnyvale	CA	94085	**800-253-0490**	408-732-7777	
Zack Electronics Inc	1070 Hamilton Rd	Duarte	CA	91010	**800-466-0449**	626-303-0655	

249 ELECTRICAL EQUIPMENT FOR INTERNAL COMBUSTION ENGINES

SEE ALSO Motors (Electric) & Generators ; Automotive Parts & Supplies - Mfr

Company / Address	City	State	Zip	Toll-Free	Phone
American Electronic Components 1101 Lafayette St	Elkhart	IN	46516	**888-847-6552**	574-295-6330
CE Niehoff & Co 2021 Lee St *Tech Supp	Evanston	IL	60202	**800-643-4633***	847-866-6030
Edge Products 1080 S Depot Dr	Ogden	UT	84404	**888-360-3343**	801-476-3343
ETCO Inc Automotive Products Div 3004 62nd Ave E	Bradenton	FL	34203	**800-689-3826**	941-756-8426
Flight Systems Inc 505 Fishing Creek Rd	Lewisberry	PA	17339	**800-403-3728**	717-932-9900
Goodall Manufacturing Co 7558 Washington Ave S	Eden Prairie	MN	55344	**800-328-7730**	952-941-6666
Ignition Systems & Controls LP 6300 W Hwy 80	Midland	TX	79706	**800-777-5559**	432-697-6472
Kelly Aerospace 1404 E S Blvd	Montgomery	AL	36116	**888-461-6077**	334-286-8551
Motorcar Parts & Accessories 2929 California St	Torrance	CA	90503	**800-890-9988**	310-212-7910
NGK Spark Plugs Inc 46929 Magellan	Wixom	MI	48393	**877-473-6767**	248-926-6900
Precision Parts & Remanufacturing Co 4411 SW 19th St	Oklahoma City	OK	73108	**800-654-3846**	405-681-2592
Prestolite Wire Corp 200 Galleria Officentre Ste 212	Southfield	MI	48034	**800-498-3132**	248-355-4422
Remy International Inc 600 Corp Dr *NYSE: REMY*	Pendleton	IN	46064	**800-372-3555**	765-778-6499
Transpo Electronics Inc 2150 Brengle Ave	Orlando	FL	32808	**800-327-6903**	
Van Bergen & Greener Inc 1818 Madison St	Maywood	IL	60153	**800-621-3889**	708-343-4700

250 ELECTRICAL SIGNALS MEASURING & TESTING INSTRUMENTS

Company / Address	City	State	Zip	Toll-Free	Phone
3M Telecommunications Div 6801 River Pl Blvd	Austin	TX	78726	**800-426-8688**	
Aeroflex 35 South Service Rd PO Box 6022	Plainview	NY	11803	**800-843-1553**	913-764-2452
Allied Motion Technologies Inc 495 Commerce Dr Ste 3 *NASDAQ: AMOT*	Amherst	NY	14228	**888-392-5543**	716-242-8634
Analog Devices Inc 3 Technology Way *NASDAQ: ADI*	Norwood	MA	02062	**800-262-5643**	781-329-4700
Anritsu Co 490 Jarvis Dr	Morgan Hill	CA	95037	**800-267-4878**	408-778-2000
Associated Equipment Corp 5043 Farlan Ave	Saint Louis	MO	63115	**800-949-1472**	314-385-5178
Bird Electronic Corp 30303 Aurora Rd	Solon	OH	44139	**866-695-4569**	440-248-1200
Bird Technologies Group Inc 30303 Aurora Rd	Solon	OH	44139	**866-695-4569**	440-248-1200
Bruel & Kjaer Instruments Inc 2815 Colonnades Ct Ste A	Norcross	GA	30071	**800-332-2040**	770-209-6907
Cascade Microtech Inc 2430 NW 206th Ave *NASDAQ: CSCD*	Beaverton	OR	97006	**800-854-8400**	503-601-1000
Chatsworth Data Corp 9735 Lurline Ave	Chatsworth	CA	91311	**877-380-6855**	818-350-5072
Cohu Inc 12367 Crosthwaite Cir *NASDAQ: COHU*	Poway	CA	92064	**800-685-5050**	858-848-8100
Communications Manufacturing Co (CMC) 2234 Colby Ave *Orders	Los Angeles	CA	90064	**800-462-5532***	310-828-3200
Curtis Instruments Inc 200 Kisco Ave	Mount Kisco	NY	10549	**800-777-3433**	914-666-2971
CyberOptics Corp 5900 Golden Hills Dr *NASDAQ: CYBE* ■ *Cust Svc	Minneapolis	MN	55416	**800-746-6315***	763-542-5000
DIT-MCO International Corp 5612 Brighton Terr	Kansas City	MO	64130	**800-821-3487**	816-444-9700
Doble Engineering Co Inc 85 Walnut St	Watertown	MA	02472	**888-443-6253**	617-926-4900
Dranetz-BMI 1000 New Durham Rd	Edison	NJ	08818	**800-372-6832**	732-287-3680
EADS North American Defense Test & Services Inc 4 Goodyear *Cust Svc	Irvine	CA	92618	**800-722-2528***	949-859-8999
EXFO Inc 400 Godin Ave *NASDAQ: EXFO*	Quebec	QC	G1M2K2	**800-663-3936**	418-683-0211
Fluke Biomedical 6920 Seaway Blvd	Everett	WA	98203	**800-443-5853**	425-446-6945
Fluke Corp 6920 Seaway Blvd	Everett	WA	98203	**877-355-3225**	425-446-6100
Fluke Networks Inc 6920 Seaway Blvd	Everett	WA	98203	**800-283-5853**	425-446-4519
Giga-Tronics Inc 4650 Norris Canyon Rd *NASDAQ: GIGA*	San Ramon	CA	94583	**800-726-4442**	925-328-4650
Gleason M & M Precision Systems Corp 300 Progress Rd	Dayton	OH	45449	**800-727-6333**	937-859-8273
Greenlee Textron 1390 Aspen Way	Vista	CA	92081	**800-642-2155**	760-598-8900
Hickok Inc 10514 Dupont Ave *OTC: HICKA*	Cleveland	OH	44108	**800-342-5080**	216-541-8060
Hughes Corp Weschler Instruments Div 16900 Foltz Pkwy	Cleveland	OH	44149	**800-557-0064**	440-238-2550
ILX Lightwave Corp 31950 E Frontage Rd	Bozeman	MT	59715	**800-459-9459**	406-586-1244
Itron Inc 2111 N Molter Rd *NASDAQ: ITRI*	Liberty Lake	WA	99019	**800-635-5461**	509-924-9900
Ixia 26601 W Agoura Rd *NASDAQ: XXIA*	Calabasas	CA	91302	**877-367-4942**	818-871-1800
KLA-Tencor Corp 1 Technology Dr *NASDAQ: KLAC*	Milpitas	CA	95035	**800-600-2829**	408-875-3000
Knopp Inc 1307 66th St	Emeryville	CA	94608	**800-227-1848**	510-653-1661
Landis Gyr Inc 2800 Duncan Rd	Lafayette	IN	47904	**888-390-5733**	765-742-1001
LeCroy Corp 700 Chestnut Ridge Rd *NASDAQ: LCRY*	Chestnut Ridge	NY	10977	**800-553-2769**	845-425-2000
Megger 4271 Bronze Way	Dallas	TX	75237	**800-723-2861**	214-333-3201
Micro Control Co 7956 Main St NE	Minneapolis	MN	55432	**800-328-9923**	763-786-8750
Monroe Electronics Inc 100 Housel Ave	Lyndonville	NY	14098	**800-821-6001**	585-765-2254
National Instruments Corp 11500 N Mopac Expy *NASDAQ: NATI* ■ *Cust Svc	Austin	TX	78759	**800-433-3488***	512-794-0100
Newport Electronics Inc 2229 S Yale St *Cust Svc	Santa Ana	CA	92704	**800-639-7678***	714-540-4914
Phase Matrix Inc 109 Bonaventura Dr	San Jose	CA	95134	**877-447-2736**	408-428-1000
Radiodetection Corp 154 Portland Rd	Bridgton	ME	04009	**877-247-3797**	207-647-9495
Schweitzer E O Mfg Company Inc 450 Enterprise Pkwy	Lake Zurich	IL	60047	**888-870-7350**	847-362-8304
Snap-on Diagnostics 420 Barclay Blvd	Lincolnshire	IL	60069	**800-424-7226**	847-478-0700
TEGAM Inc 10 Tegam Way	Geneva	OH	44041	**800-666-1010**	440-466-6100
Teradyne Inc Assembly Test Div 600 Riverpark Dr	North Reading	MA	01864	**800-837-2396**	978-370-2700
Teradyne Inc Industrial/Consumer Div 600 Riverpark Dr	North Reading	MA	01864	**800-837-2396**	978-370-2700
Trek Inc 11601 Maple Ridge Rd	Medina	NY	14103	**800-367-8735**	585-798-3140
Trilithic Inc 9710 Pk Davis Dr	Indianapolis	IN	46235	**800-344-2412**	317-895-3600
Yokogawa Corp of America 12530 W Airport Blvd	Sugar Land	TX	77478	**800-888-6400**	281-340-3800
Zetec Inc 8226 Bracken Pl SE Ste 100	Snoqualmie	WA	98065	**800-643-1771**	425-974-2700

251 ELECTRICAL SUPPLIES - PORCELAIN

Company / Address	City	State	Zip	Toll-Free	Phone
CoorsTek Inc 600 Ninth St	Golden	CO	80401	**800-821-6110**	303-278-4000
Fair-Rite Products Corp 1 Commerical Row PO Box J	Wallkill	NY	12589	**888-324-7748**	845-895-2055
International Ceramic Engineering 235 Brooks St	Worcester	MA	01606	**800-779-3321**	508-853-4700
Kyocera Industrial Ceramics Corp 5713 E Fourth Plain Rd	Vancouver	WA	98661	**800-826-0527**	360-696-8950
Medler Eelectric Company Inc 2155 Redman Dr	Alma	MI	48801	**800-229-5740**	
Saint-Gobain Advanced Ceramics Latrobe 4702 Rt 982	Latrobe	PA	15650	**800-438-7237**	724-539-6000
Sunbelt Transfomer Ltd 1922 S Martin Luther King Jr Dr	Temple	TX	76504	**800-433-3128**	254-771-3777

252 ELECTROMEDICAL & ELECTROTHERAPEUTIC EQUIPMENT

SEE ALSO Medical Instruments & Apparatus - Mfr

Company / Address	City	State	Zip	Toll-Free	Phone
ABIOMED Inc 22 Cherry Hill Dr *NASDAQ: ABMD*	Danvers	MA	01923	**800-422-8666**	978-777-5410
Affymetrix Inc 3420 Central Expy *NASDAQ: AFFX*	Santa Clara	CA	95051	**888-362-2447**	408-731-5000
Amedica Corp 1885 West 2100 South	Salt Lake City	UT	84119	**855-839-3500**	
Artel 25 Bradley Dr	Westbrook	ME	04092	**888-406-3463**	207-854-0860
Avancen MOD Corp 1156 Bowman Rd Ste 200	Mount Pleasant	SC	29464	**800-607-1230**	
Axiobionics 6111 Jackson Rd Ste 200	Ann Arbor	MI	48103	**800-552-3539**	734-327-2946
Beacon Medaes 1800 Overview Dr	Rock Hill	SC	29730	**888-463-3427**	803-817-5600
Bio Medical Innovations 814 Airport Way	Sandpoint	ID	83864	**800-201-3958**	
Bovie Medical Corp 734 Walt Whitman Rd Ste 207 *NYSE: BVX*	Melville	NY	11747	**800-888-4999**	631-421-5452
Cardiac Science Corp 3303 Monte Villa Pkwy *Cust Svc	Bothell	WA	98021	**800-426-0337***	425-402-2000
CAS Medical Systems Inc 44 E Industrial Rd *NASDAQ: CASM*	Branford	CT	06405	**800-227-4414**	203-488-6056
CNS Response Inc 85 Enterprise Ste 410	Aliso Viejo	CA	92656	**888-545-2677**	949-420-4400
Conmed Corp 525 French Rd *NASDAQ: CNMD*	Utica	NY	13502	**800-448-6506**	315-797-8375
Cook Medical Inc 1186 Montgomery Ln *General	Vandergrift	PA	15690	**800-457-4500***	724-845-8621
Draeger Medical Inc 3135 Quarry Rd	Telford	PA	18969	**800-437-2437**	
Dynatronics Corp 7030 Pk Centre Dr *NASDAQ: DYNT*	Salt Lake City	UT	84121	**800-874-6251**	801-568-7000

Classified Section

Company	Address	City	State	Zip	Toll-Free	Phone
Eigen Video	13366 Grass Vly Ave Ste A	Grass Valley	CA	95945	**888-924-2020**	530-274-1240
Fisher & Paykel Healthcare Inc	173 Technology Dr Ste 100	Irvine	CA	92618	**800-446-3908**	949-453-4000
Gambro Renal Products	14143 Denver W Pkwy	Lakewood	CO	80401	**800-525-2623**	303-232-6800
GE Healthcare Information Technologies	8200 W Tower Ave	Milwaukee	WI	53223	**800-558-5102**	414-355-5000
GN ReSound North America	8001 E Bloomington Fwy	Bloomington	MN	55420	**888-735-4327**	
HealthTronics Inc	9825 Spectrum Dr Bldg 3	Austin	TX	78717	**888-252-6575**	512-328-2892
Inovio Pharmaceuticals Inc	660 W Germantown Pk Ste 110 *NASDAQ: INOVIO*	Plymouth	PA	19462	**877-446-6846**	267-440-4200
IVY Biomedical Systems Inc	11 Business Pk Dr	Branford	CT	06405	**800-247-4614**	203-481-4183
Kelyniam Global Inc	97 River Rd	Canton	CT	06019	**800-280-8192**	
MAQUET Cardiac Assist	15 Law Dr	Fairfield	NJ	07004	**800-777-4222**	973-244-6100
Masimo Corp	40 Parker	Irvine	CA	92618	**800-326-4890**	949-297-7000
Medical Education Technologies Inc (METI)	6300 Edgelake Dr	Sarasota	FL	34240	**866-462-7920**	941-377-5562
Medical Graphics Corp	350 Oak Grove Pkwy *NASDAQ: ANGN*	Saint Paul	MN	55127	**800-950-5597**	651-484-4874
Medtronic Inc	710 Medtronic Pkwy NE *NYSE: MDT* ■ *Cust Svc	Minneapolis	MN	55432	**800-328-2518***	763-514-4000
Medtronic of Canada Ltd	6733 Kitimat Rd	Mississauga	ON	L5N1W3	**800-268-5346**	905-826-6020
Medtronic Perfusion Systems	7611 Northland Dr	Brooklyn Park	MN	55428	**800-328-3320**	763-391-9000
Meridian Medical Technologies Inc	6350 Stevens Forest Rd Ste 301	Columbia	MD	21046	**800-638-8093**	443-259-7800
Misonix Inc	1938 NEW Hwy	Farmingdale	NY	11735	**800-694-9612**	631-694-9555
Mortara Instrument Inc	7865 N 86th St	Milwaukee	WI	53224	**800-231-7437**	414-354-1600
Natus Medical Inc	1501 Industrial Rd *NASDAQ: BABY*	San Carlos	CA	94070	**800-255-3901**	650-802-0400
NeuroMetrix	62 Fourth Ave *NASDAQ: NURO*	Waltham	MA	02451	**888-786-7287**	781-890-9989
Neuromonics Inc	PO Box 351886	Westminster	CO	80035	**866-606-3876**	
O-two Medical Technologies Inc	7575 Kimbel St	Mississauga	ON	L5S1C8	**800-387-3405**	905-677-9410
Oscor Inc	3816 DeSoto Blvd *Cust Svc	Palm Harbor	FL	34683	**800-726-7267***	727-937-2511
Osprey Medical Inc	7600 Executive Dr	Eden Prairie	MN	55344	**855-860-7584**	952-955-8230
Paradigm Medical Industries Inc	4273 South 590 West *OTC: PDMI*	Salt Lake City	UT	84123	**800-742-0671**	801-977-8970
Physio-Control Inc	11811 Willows Rd NE	Redmond	WA	98052	**800-442-1142**	425-867-4000
Positron Corp	530 Oakmont Ln	Westmont	IL	60559	**866-613-7587**	317-576-0183
PP Systems International Inc	110 Haverhill Rd Ste 301	Amesbury	MA	01913	**866-211-9346**	978-834-0505
Respironics Novametrix LLC	5 Technology Dr	Wallingford	CT	06492	**800-345-6443**	724-387-4000
Richard Wolf Medical Instruments Corp	353 Corporate Woods Pkwy	Vernon Hills	IL	60061	**800-323-9653**	847-913-1113
Rockwell Medical Inc	30142 Wixom Rd *NASDAQ: RMTI*	Wixom	MI	48393	**800-449-3353**	248-960-9009
SensorMedics Corp	22745 Savi Ranch Pkwy	Yorba Linda	CA	92887	**800-231-2466**	714-283-2228
Siemens Medical Solutions Inc	51 Valley Stream Pkwy	Malvern	PA	19355	**800-888-7436**	888-826-9702
Solta Medical Inc	25881 Industrial Blvd	Hayward	CA	94545	**877-782-2286**	
Spacelabs Health Care	35301 SE Center St	Snoqualmie	WA	98065	**800-522-7025**	425-396-3300
Thoratec Corp	6035 Stoneridge Dr *NASDAQ: THOR*	Pleasanton	CA	94588	**800-528-2577**	925-847-8600
Vasomedical Inc	180 Linden Ave *OTC: VASO*	Westbury	NY	11590	**800-455-3327**	516-997-4600
Watermark Medical LLC	1641 Worthington Rd Ste 320	West Palm Beach	FL	33409	**877-710-6999**	
Welch Allyn Medical Products	4341 State St Rd	Skaneateles Falls	NY	13152	**800-289-2500**	315-685-4100
Welch Allyn Monitoring Inc	8500 SW Creekside Pl *Cust Svc	Beaverton	OR	97008	**800-289-2500***	503-530-7500
ZOLL Medical Corp	269 Mill Rd	Chelmsford	MA	01824	**800-348-9011**	978-421-9655

253 ELECTRONIC BILL PRESENTMENT & PAYMENT SERVICES

SEE ALSO Application Service Providers (ASPs)

Company	Address	City	State	Zip	Toll-Free	Phone
Alpha Card Services Inc	475 Veit Rd	Huntingdon Valley	PA	19006	**866-253-2227**	
Capital Merchant Solutions Inc	3005 Gill St Ste 2	Bloomington	IL	61704	**877-495-2419**	
FIX Flyer LLC	225 Broadway Ste 1600	New York	NY	10007	**888-349-3593**	
Freedman Financial Associates Inc	8 Essex Ctr Dr 3rd Fl	Peabody	MA	01960	**800-588-8108**	978-531-8108
Heartland Payment Systems Inc	90 Nassau St 2nd Fl *NYSE: HPY*	Princeton	NJ	08542	**888-798-3131**	609-683-3831
Ifrah Financial Services Inc	17300 Chenal Pkwy Ste 150	Little Rock	AR	72223	**800-954-3724**	501-821-7733
Landmark Financial Group LLC	181 Old Post Rd	Southport	CT	06890	**800-437-4214**	203-254-8422
Lear Capital Inc	1990 S Bundy Dr Ste 600	Los Angeles	CA	90025	**800-576-9355**	
Money Movers Inc	PO Box 241	Sebastopol	CA	95473	**800-861-5029**	707-829-5557
U.S. Bankcard Services Inc	17171 E Gale Ave Ste 110	City Of Industry	CA	91745	**888-888-8872**	
USA Technologies Inc	100 Deerfield Ln Ste 140	Malvern	PA	19355	**800-633-0340**	

254 ELECTRONIC COMMUNICATIONS NETWORKS (ECNS)

SEE ALSO Securities Brokers & Dealers ; Securities & Commodities Exchanges

ECNs are computerized trade-matching systems that unite best bid and offer prices and provide anonymity to investors.

Company	Address	City	State	Zip	Toll-Free	Phone
Comm-Works Holdings LLC	1405 Xenium Ln N Ste 120	Minneapolis	MN	55441	**800-853-8090**	763-258-5800
Layer 3 Communications LLC	1555 Oakbrook Dr Ste 100	Norcross	GA	30093	**866-535-3924**	770-225-5300
Network Telephone Services Inc	21135 Erwin St	Woodland Hills	CA	91367	**800-742-5687**	818-992-4300

255 ELECTRONIC COMPONENTS & ACCESSORIES - MFR

SEE ALSO Semiconductors & Related Devices ; Printed Circuit Boards

Company	Address	City	State	Zip	Toll-Free	Phone
3M Electronic Handling & Protection Div	6801 River Pl Blvd	Austin	TX	78726	**800-328-1368**	
3M Interconnect Solutions Div	6801 River Pl Blvd	Austin	TX	78726	**800-225-5373**	512-984-1800
Aavid Thermalloy LLC	70 Commercial St Ste 200	Concord	NH	03301	**855-322-2843**	603-224-9988
Advanced Bionics LLC	28515 Westinghouse Pl	Valencia	CA	91355	**877-829-0026**	661-362-1400
Aeroflex Inc	35 S Service Rd PO Box 6022 *TSE: ARX*	Plainview	NY	11803	**800-843-1553**	516-694-6700
AESP Inc	16295 NW 13th Ave	Miami	FL	33169	**800-446-2377**	305-944-7710
Aldelo LP	4641 Spyres Way Ste 4	Modesto	CA	95356	**800-801-6036**	209-338-5488
Alpha Group, The	3767 Alpha Way	Bellingham	WA	98226	**800-322-5742**	360-647-2360
American International Inc	1040 Avendia Acaso	Camarillo	CA	93012	**800-336-6500**	805-388-6800
American Power Conversion Corp (APC)	132 Fairgrounds Rd *Cust Svc	West Kingston	RI	02892	**800-788-2208***	401-789-5735
AMETEK Automation & Process Technologies	1080 N Crooks	Clawson	MI	48017	**800-635-0289**	248-435-0700
Ametek HDR Power Systems Inc	3563 Interchange Rd	Columbus	OH	43204	**888-797-2685**	614-308-5500
AMETEK Solidstate Controls	875 Dearborn Dr	Columbus	OH	43085	**800-635-7300**	614-846-7500
Amphenol Aerospace	40-60 Delaware Ave	Sidney	NY	13838	**800-678-0141**	607-563-5011
Amphenol RF	4 Old Newtown Rd	Danbury	CT	06810	**800-627-7100**	203-743-9272
Amphenol Spectra-Strip	720 Sherman Ave	Hamden	CT	06514	**800-846-6400**	203-281-3200
Amphenol-Tuchel Electronics	6900 Haggerty Rd Ste 200	Canton	MI	48187	**800-380-8052**	734-451-6400
AmRad Engineering Inc	32 Hargrove Grade	Palm Coast	FL	32137	**800-445-6033**	386-445-6000
Anaren Microwave Inc	6635 Kirkville Rd *NASDAQ: ANEN*	East Syracuse	NY	13057	**800-544-2414**	315-432-8909
Antec Inc	47900 Fremont Blvd	Fremont	CA	94538	**800-222-6832**	510-770-1200
AudioQuest Inc	2621 White Rd	Irvine	CA	92614	**800-747-2770**	949-585-0111
AVG Automation	4140 Utica St	Bettendorf	IA	52722	**877-774-3279**	
Avionic Instruments Inc	1414 Randolph Ave	Avenel	NJ	07001	**800-468-3571**	732-388-3500
Avnet Electronics Marketing Inc	2211 S 47th St	Phoenix	AZ	85034	**888-822-8638**	480-643-2000
Banner Engineering Corp	9714 Tenth Ave N	Minneapolis	MN	55441	**888-373-6767**	763-544-3164
BEI Technologies Inc Industrial Encoder Div	7230 Hollister Ave *Sales	Goleta	CA	93117	**800-350-2727***	805-968-0782
Bergquist Co	18930 W 78th St	Chanhassen	MN	55317	**800-347-4572**	952-835-2322
C & D Technologies Inc	1400 Union Meeting Rd PO Box 3053	Blue Bell	PA	19422	**800-543-8630**	215-619-2700
C&D Technologies	11 Cabot Blvd	Mansfield	MA	02048	**800-233-2765**	508-339-3000
Califone International Inc	9135 Alabama Ave Ste B	Chatsworth	CA	91311	**800-722-0500**	818-407-2400
Camesa Inc	1615 Spur 529	Rosenberg	TX	77471	**800-866-0001**	281-342-4494
Celestica Inc	844 Don Mills Rd *NYSE: CLS*	Toronto	ON	M3C1V7	**888-899-9998**	416-448-5800
City Electric Supply Inc	315 E Prentiss St	Iowa City	IA	52240	**800-272-6111**	319-338-7561
Clary Corp	150 E Huntington Dr	Monrovia	CA	91016	**800-551-6111**	626-359-4486

Classified Section

Company	City	State	ZIP	Toll-Free	Phone
Clinton Electronics Corp 6701 Clinton Rd	Loves Park	IL	61111	**800-549-6393**	815-633-1444
Coilcraft Inc 1102 Silver Lk Rd	Cary	IL	60013	**800-322-2645**	847-639-2361
Comdel Inc 11 Kondelin Rd	Gloucester	MA	01930	**800-468-3144**	978-282-0620
Communications & Power Industries LLC 607 Hansen Way	Palo Alto	CA	94303	**800-231-4818**	650-846-2900
Cooper Industries 600 Travis St Ste 5400 *NYSE: ETN*	Houston	TX	77002	**866-853-4293**	713-209-8400
Cornucopia Tool & Plastics Inc 448 Sherwood Rd PO Box 1915	Paso Robles	CA	93447	**800-235-4144**	805-369-0030
Crystek Crystals Corp 12730 Commonwealth Dr	Fort Myers	FL	33913	**800-237-3061**	239-561-3311
CTS Corp 905 W Blvd N *NYSE: CTS*	Elkhart	IN	46514	**800-757-6686**	574-293-7511
Cyber Power Systems Inc 4241 12th Ave E Ste 400	Shakopee	MN	55379	**877-297-6937**	952-403-9500
Cyberex 5900 Eastport Blvd	Richmond	VA	23231	**800-238-5000**	804-236-3300
Data Device Corp 105 Wilbur Pl *Cust Svc	Bohemia	NY	11716	**800-332-5757***	631-567-5600
Digital Power Corp 41324 Christy St	Fremont	CA	94538	**866-344-7697**	510-353-4023
Dow-Key Microwave Corp 4822 McGrath St	Ventura	CA	93003	**800-266-3695**	805-650-0260
Eby Co 4300 H St	Philadelphia	PA	19124	**800-329-3430**	215-537-4700
Electrex Inc PO Box 948	Hutchinson	KS	67504	**800-319-3676**	
Electrocube Inc 3366 Pomona Blvd	Pomona	CA	91768	**800-515-1112**	909-595-4037
Emerson Network Power Connectivity Solutions 1050 Dearborn Dr	Columbus	OH	43085	**800-275-3500**	614-888-0246
EMF Corp 505 Pokagon Trl	Angola	IN	46703	**800-847-2818**	260-665-9541
Eoff Electric Company Inc 3241 NW Industrial St	Portland	OR	97210	**800-285-3633**	503-222-9411
EPCOS Inc 485-B Rt 1 S Ste 200	Iselin	NJ	08830	**800-689-3717**	
eSilicon Corp 501 Macara Ave	Sunnyvale	CA	94085	**877-769-2447**	408-616-4600
Forbes Snyder Tristate Cash 54 Northampton St	Easthampton	MA	01027	**800-222-4064**	413-529-2950
Franklin Empire Inc 8421 Darnley Rd	Montreal	QC	H4T2B2	**800-361-5044**	514-341-9720
Greenlee Textron 1390 Aspen Way	Vista	CA	92081	**800-642-2155**	760-598-8900
Heliene Inc 520 Allen'S Side Rd	Sault Sainte Marie	ON	P6A6K4	**855-363-2797**	705-575-6556
Hitachi Canada Ltd 5450 Explore Dr Ste 501	Mississauga	ON	L4W5N1	**877-248-4237**	905-629-9300
Hubbell Power Systems Inc 210 N Allen St	Centralia	MO	65240	**800-346-3062**	573-682-5521
Hutchinson Technology Inc 40 W Highland Pk Dr *NASDAQ: HTCH*	Hutchinson	MN	55350	**800-419-1007**	320-587-3797
Instantel Inc 309 Legget Dr	Ottawa	ON	K2K3A3	**800-267-9111**	613-592-4642
Integrated Magnetics Inc 11248 Playa Ct	Culver City	CA	90230	**800-421-6692**	310-391-7213
Interpoint Corp PO Box 97005	Redmond	WA	98073	**800-822-8782**	425-882-3100
InVue Security Products Inc 10715 Sikes Pl Ste 200	Charlotte	NC	28277	**888-257-4272**	704-206-7849
ipDataTel LLC 13110 SW Fwy	Sugar Land	TX	77478	**866-896-1818**	713-452-2700
ITT Industries Inc 1133 Westchester Ave *NYSE: ITT*	White Plains	NY	10604	**800-254-2823**	914-641-2000
JAE Electronics Inc 142 Technology Dr Ste 100	Irvine	CA	92618	**800-523-7278**	949-753-2600
Jenkins Electric Inc 5933 Brookshire Blvd	Charlotte	NC	28216	**800-438-3003**	
Jewell Instruments LLC 850 Perimeter Rd	Manchester	NH	03103	**800-227-5955**	603-669-6400
Johanson Mfg Corp 301 Rockaway Valley Rd	Boonton	NJ	07005	**800-477-1272**	973-334-2676
Kepco Inc 131-38 Sanford Ave	Flushing	NY	11355	**800-526-2324**	718-461-7000
La Marche Mfg Co 106 Bradrock Dr	Des Plaines	IL	60018	**888-232-9562**	847-299-1188
Larco 210 NE Tenth Ave *Cust Svc	Brainerd	MN	56401	**800-523-6996***	218-829-9797
Lenexpo Inc 1293 Mtn View Alviso Rd Ste A	Sunnyvale	CA	94089	**877-536-3976**	408-962-0515
Lexel Imaging Systems Inc 1501 Newtown Pike	Lexington	KY	40511	**800-397-8121**	859-243-5500
Lumex Inc 290 E Helen Rd	Palatine	IL	60067	**800-278-5666**	847-359-2790
MagneTek Inc N49 W13650 Campbell Dr *NASDAQ: MAG*	Menomonee Falls	WI	53051	**800-288-8178**	
Magtech Industries Corp 5625-A S Arville St	Las Vegas	NV	89119	**888-954-4481**	702-364-9998
Marlow Industries Inc 10451 Vista Pk Rd	Dallas	TX	75238	**877-627-5691**	214-340-4900
Maxwell Technologies Inc 5271 Viewridge Ct Ste 100 *NASDAQ: MXWL*	San Diego	CA	92123	**877-511-4324**	858-503-3300
Methode Electronics Inc 7401 W Wilson Ave *NYSE: MEI*	Chicago	IL	60706	**877-316-7700**	708-867-6777
Micro-coax Inc 206 Jones Blvd	Pottstown	PA	19464	**800-223-2629**	610-495-0110
Microwave Filter Company Inc 6743 Kinne St	East Syracuse	NY	13057	**800-448-1666**	315-438-4700
Molex Inc 2222 Wellington Ct *NASDAQ: MOLX* ■ *Cust Svc	Lisle	IL	60532	**800-786-6539***	630-969-4550
MtronPTI 1703 E Hwy 50	Yankton	SD	57078	**800-762-8800**	605-665-9321
Murata Electronics North America Inc 2200 Lake Pk Dr	Smyrna	GA	30080	**800-704-6079**	770-436-1300

Company	City	State	ZIP	Toll-Free	Phone
NewComLink Inc 3900 N Capital Of Texas Hwy Ste 150	Austin	TX	78746	**888-988-0603**	
Newport Corp 1791 Deere Ave *NASDAQ: NEWP* ■ *Sales	Irvine	CA	92606	**800-222-6440***	949-863-3144
Niles Audio Corp 1969 Kellog Ave	Carlsbad	CA	92008	**800-289-4434**	760-710-0992
Nortech Systems Inc 7550 Meridian Cir N Ste 150 *NASDAQ: NSYS*	Maple Grove	MN	55369	**800-237-9576**	952-345-2244
Nortek Security & Control LLC 1950 Camino Vida Roble Ste 150 *Cust Svc	Carlsbad	CA	92008	**800-421-1587***	760-438-7000
NWL Transformers Inc 312 Rising Sun Rd	Bordentown	NJ	08505	**800-742-5695**	609-298-7300
Ohmite Manufacturing Co 1600 Golf Rd Ste 850	Rolling Meadows	IL	60008	**866-964-6483**	847-258-0300
On-Line Strategies Inc 7920 Belt Line Rd Ste 1150	Dallas	TX	75254	**866-237-4900**	214-466-1000
Onyx EMS LLC 2920 Kelly Ave	Watertown	SD	57201	**800-772-7866**	605-886-2519
Panamax Inc 1690 Corporate Cir	Petaluma	CA	94954	**800-472-5555**	707-283-5900
Para Systems Inc *Minuteman UPS* 1455 LeMay Dr	Carrollton	TX	75007	**800-238-7272**	972-446-7363
PCB Group Inc 3425 Walden Ave	Depew	NY	14043	**800-828-8840**	716-684-0001
PG Life Link Inc 167 Gap Way	Erlanger	KY	41018	**800-287-4123**	859-283-5900
Piller Inc 45 Turner Rd	Middletown	NY	10941	**800-597-6937**	
Plastronics Socket Co Inc 2601 Texas Dr *Cust Svc	Irving	TX	75062	**800-582-5822***	972-258-2580
Plug Power Inc 968 Albany-Shaker Rd *NASDAQ: PLUG*	Latham	NY	12110	**877-474-1993**	518-782-7700
Positronic Industries Inc 423 N Campbell Ave PO Box 8247	Springfield	MO	65801	**800-641-4054**	417-866-2322
Post Glover Resistors Inc 1369 Cox Rd *Cust Svc	Erlanger	KY	41018	**800-537-6144***	859-283-0778
Precision Interconnect Corp 10025 SW Freeman Ct	Wilsonville	OR	97070	**800-522-6752**	503-685-9300
Raritan Computer Inc 400 Cottontail Ln	Somerset	NJ	08873	**800-724-8090**	732-764-8886
Record USA 4324 Phil Hargett Ct PO Box 3099 *Sales	Monroe	NC	28111	**800-438-1937***	704-289-9212
RF Industries 7610 Miramar Rd Bldg 6000 *NASDAQ: RFIL*	San Diego	CA	92126	**800-233-1728**	858-549-6340
Samtec Inc 520 Parkeast Blvd	New Albany	IN	47150	**800-726-8329**	812-944-6733
Schumacher Electric Corp 801 E Business Ctr Dr	Mount Prospect	IL	60056	**800-621-5485**	
Scosche Industries Inc PO Box 2901	Oxnard	CA	93034	**800-363-4490**	805-486-4450
Seiko Instruments USA Inc 21221 S Western Ave Ste 250 *Sales	Torrance	CA	90501	**800-688-0817***	310-517-7700
Sendec Corp 72 Perinton Pkwy	Fairport	NY	14450	**800-295-8000**	585-425-3390
Sigma Electronics Inc 1027 Commercial Ave	East Petersburg	PA	17520	**866-569-2681**	717-569-2926
Signal Transformer Company Inc 500 Bayview Ave	Inwood	NY	11096	**866-239-5777**	516-239-5777
Simplex Inc 5300 Rising Moon Rd	Springfield	IL	62711	**800-637-8603**	217-483-1600
SL Power Electronics Inc 6050 King Dr Bldg A	Ventura	CA	93003	**800-235-5929**	805-486-4565
Smart Power Systems Inc 1760 Stebbins Dr	Houston	TX	77043	**800-882-8285**	713-464-8000
SNC Mfg Company Inc 101 W Waukau Ave	Oshkosh	WI	54902	**800-558-3325**	920-231-7370
Standex Electronics Inc 4538 Camberwell Rd	Cincinnati	OH	45209	**866-782-6339**	513-871-3777
Stevens Water Monitoring Systems 12067 NE Glenn Widing Dr Ste 106	Portland	OR	97220	**800-452-5272**	503-469-8000
Superconductor Technologies Inc (STI) 460 Ward Dr *NASDAQ: SCON*	Santa Barbara	CA	93111	**800-727-3648**	805-690-4500
Sypris Electronics LLC 10901 N McKinley Dr	Tampa	FL	33612	**800-937-9220**	813-972-6000
Sypris Solutions Inc 101 Bullitt Ln Ste 450 *NASDAQ: SYPR*	Louisville	KY	40222	**800-588-9119**	502-329-2000
System Sensor 3825 Ohio Ave *Tech Supp	Saint Charles	IL	60174	**800-736-7672***	630-377-6580
Taiyo Yuden (USA) Inc 1930 N Thoreau Dr Ste 190	Schaumburg	IL	60173	**800-348-2496**	847-925-0888
TDI-Transistor Devices Inc 85 Horsehill Rd	Cedar Knolls	NJ	07927	**800-488-6724**	973-267-1900
Telonic Berkeley Inc 1080 La Mirada Ct *Sales	Vista	CA	92081	**800-311-8805***	760-744-8350
Threshold Financial Technologies Inc 3269 American Dr	Mississauga	ON	L4V1X5	**888-414-3733**	905-678-7373
Times Microwave Systems Inc PO Box 5039	Wallingford	CT	06492	**800-867-2629**	203-949-8400
Toshiba America Inc 1251 Ave of the Americas Ste 4100	New York	NY	10020	**800-457-7777**	212-596-0600
Total Technologies Ltd 9710 Research Dr	Irvine	CA	92618	**800-669-4885**	949-465-0200
TRAK Microwave Corp 4726 Eisenhower Blvd	Tampa	FL	33634	**888-283-8444**	813-901-7200
Triton Systems Inc 21405 B St	Long Beach	MS	39560	**866-787-4866**	228-575-3100
TSI Power Corp 1103 W Pierce Ave	Antigo	WI	54409	**800-874-3160**	715-623-0636

				Toll-Free	Phone
United Chemi-Con Inc 9801 W Higgins Rd	Rosemont	IL	60018	**800-344-4539**	847-696-2000
Viatran Corp 3829 Forest Pkwy Ste 500	Wheatfield	NY	14120	**800-688-0030**	716-629-3800
Vicor Corp 25 Frontage Rd *NASDAQ: VICR*	Andover	MA	01810	**800-869-5300**	978-470-2900
Vishay Intertechnology Inc 63 Lancaster Ave *NYSE: VSH*	Malvern	PA	19355	**800-567-6098**	610-644-1300
Wireless Xcessories Group Inc 1840 County Line Rd Ste 301 *OTC: WIRX*	Huntingdon Valley	PA	19006	**800-233-0013**	215-322-4600
World Electronics Sales & Service Inc 3000 Kutztown Rd	Reading	PA	19605	**800-523-0427**	610-939-9800
Xantrex Technology Inc 3700 Gilmore Way	Burnaby	BC	V5G4M1	**800-670-0707**	604-422-8595
Z Communications Inc 14118 Stowe Dr Ste B	Poway	CA	92064	**877-808-1226**	858-621-2700

256 ELECTRONIC ENCLOSURES

				Toll-Free	Phone
Buckeye ShapeForm 555 Marion Rd	Columbus	OH	43207	**800-728-0776**	614-445-8433
Equipto Electronics Corp 351 Woodlawn Ave	Aurora	IL	60506	**800-204-7225**	630-897-4691
TRI MAP International Inc 111 Val Dervin Pkwy	Stockton	CA	95206	**888-687-4627**	209-234-0100
Zero Manufacturing Inc 500 West 200 North	North Salt Lake	UT	84054	**800-959-5050**	801-298-5900

257 ELECTRONIC TRANSACTION PROCESSING

				Toll-Free	Phone
Avid Payment Solutions 950 S Old Woodward Ste 220	Birmingham	MI	48009	**888-855-8644**	
Chase Paymentech Solutions LLC 14221 Dallas Pkwy *Cust Svc	Dallas	TX	75254	**800-708-3740***	
Covera Solutions Inc 1021 Watervliet-Shaker Rd PO Box 13539	Albany	NY	12205	**866-526-8372**	
Elavon 2 Concourse Pkwy Ste 300	Atlanta	GA	30328	**800-725-1243**	678-731-5000
Global Payments Inc 10 Glenlake Pkwy N Twr *NYSE: GPN*	Atlanta	GA	30328	**800-560-2960**	770-829-8000
National Processing Co 5100 Interchange Way *General	Louisville	KY	40229	**877-300-7757***	800-683-2289

258 ELEVATORS, ESCALATORS, MOVING WALKWAYS

				Toll-Free	Phone
Able Services 868 Folsom St	San Francisco	CA	94107	**800-461-9577**	415-546-6534
Abx Engineering 880 Hinckley Rd	Burlingame	CA	94010	**800-366-4588**	650-552-2322
Aerospec Inc 505 E Alamo Dr	Chandler	AZ	85225	**888-854-2376**	480-892-7195
Alabama Graphics & Engineering Supply Inc 2801 Fifth Ave S	Birmingham	AL	35233	**800-292-3806**	205-252-8505
Allana Buick & Bers Inc 990 Commercial St	Palo Alto	CA	94303	**800-378-3405**	650-543-5600
Allied Corrosion Industries Inc 1550 Cobb Industrial Dr	Marietta	GA	30066	**800-241-0809**	770-425-1355
Ally Plm Solutions Inc 9155 Governors Way	Cincinnati	OH	45249	**800-631-5961**	513-984-0480
American Aerospace Controls Inc 570 Smith St	Farmingdale	NY	11735	**888-873-8559**	631-694-5100
AMT Machine Systems Ltd 868 Fwy Dr N	Columbus	OH	43229	**866-204-0660**	614-635-8050
Apex Geoscience Inc 2120 Brandon Dr	Tyler	TX	75703	**800-755-8461**	903-581-8080
Arnold & Assoc 14275 Midway Rd Ste 170	Addison	TX	75001	**800-535-6329**	972-991-1144
Astrodyne Corp 375 Forbes Blvd	Mansfield	MA	02048	**800-823-8082**	508-964-6300
B M Ross & Assoc Ltd 62 N St	Goderich	ON	N7A2T4	**888-524-2641**	519-524-2641
Benesyst Inc 800 Washington Ave N 8th Fl	Minneapolis	MN	55401	**866-786-3366**	800-422-4661
Boyle Energy Services & Technology Inc 28 Locke Rd	Concord	NH	03301	**800-428-8872**	603-227-5200
BRIC Engineered Systems Ltd 1101 Wentworth St W Ste D1	Oshawa	ON	L1J8P7	**800-937-5135**	905-436-8867
Burns Engineering Inc 10201 Bren Rd E	Minnetonka	MN	55343	**800-328-3871**	952-935-4400
Cam Services Inc 5664 Selmaraine Dr	Culver City	CA	90230	**800-576-3050**	310-390-3552
Chisholm Fleming & Assoc 317 Renfrew Dr Ste 301	Markham	ON	L3R9S8	**888-241-4149**	905-474-1458
City of Clarksville 199 10th St	Clarksville	TN	37040	**800-342-1003**	931-645-7464
Clarity Innovations Inc 1001 SE Water Ave Ste 400	Portland	OR	97214	**877-683-3187**	503-248-4300
Clean Ones Corp PO Box 40008	Portland	OR	97204	**800-367-4587**	503-224-5211
Cme Assoc Inc 32 Crabtree Ln	Woodstock	CT	06281	**888-291-3227**	860-928-7848
Controlled Contamination Services LLC 4182 Sorrento Valley Blvd	San Diego	CA	92121	**888-263-9886**	858-457-7598
Corradino Group 200 s Fifth st	Louisville	KY	40202	**800-880-8241**	502-587-7221
Corrpro Canada Inc 10848 - 214 St	Edmonton	AB	T5S2A7	**800-661-8390**	780-447-4565
DBA Engineering Ltd 401 Hanlan Rd	Vaughan	ON	L4L3T1	**800-819-8833**	905-851-0090
Degree Controls Inc 18 Meadowbrook Dr	Milford	NH	03055	**877-334-7332**	603-672-8900
DJ & A PC 3203 S Russell St	Missoula	MT	59801	**800-398-3522**	406-721-4320
Dungan Engineering pa 1574 Hwy 98 E	Columbia	MS	39429	**800-368-2573**	601-731-2600
Dynamic Design Solutions Inc 3565 Centre Cir	Fort Mill	SC	29715	**866-337-2010**	803-548-3609
E C S 2741 S 21st Ave	Broadview	IL	60155	**800-621-0759**	708-338-9700
Elevator Equipment Corp 4035 Goodwin Ave	Los Angeles	CA	90039	**888-577-3326**	323-245-0147
Ems-tech Inc 699 Dundas St W	Belleville	ON	K8N4Z2	**844-450-8324**	613-966-6611
Engineering Data Design Corp 105 Daventry Ln Ste 100	Louisville	KY	40223	**888-678-0683**	502-412-4000
Environmental Health & Engineering Inc 117 Fourth Ave	Needham	MA	02494	**800-825-5343**	781-247-4300
ESE Inc 3600 DowNWind Dr	Marshfield	WI	54449	**800-236-4778**	715-387-4778
Falcon Crest Aviation Supply Inc 8318 Braniff	Houston	TX	77061	**800-833-8229**	713-644-2290
FUTEK Advanced Sensor Technology Inc 10 Thomas	Irvine	CA	92618	**800-233-8835**	949-465-0900
Geotek Engineering & Testing Services Inc 909 E 50th St N	Sioux Falls	SD	57104	**800-354-5512**	605-335-5512
Giffin Koerth Inc 40 University Ave Ste 800	Toronto	ON	M5J1T1	**800-564-5313**	416-368-1700
Giles Engineering Assoc Inc N8 W22350 Johnson Dr	Waukesha	WI	53186	**800-782-0610**	262-544-0118
Globex Corp 3620 Stutz Dr	Canfield	OH	44406	**800-533-8610**	330-533-0030
GMI Building Services Inc 8001 Vickers St	San Diego	CA	92111	**866-803-4464**	
H&S Constructors Inc 1616 Valero Way	Corpus Christi	TX	78469	**800-727-8602**	361-289-5272
HESS Construction + Engineering Services Inc 804 W Diamond Ave Ste 300	Gaithersburg	MD	20878	**800-544-6056**	301-670-9000
HH Angus & Assoc Ltd 1127 Leslie St	Toronto	ON	M3C2J6	**866-955-8201**	416-443-8200
Hunt Guillot & Assoc LLC 603 Reynolds Dr	Ruston	LA	71270	**866-255-6825**	318-255-6825
InfoTech Enterprises America Inc 330 Roberts St Ste 102	East Hartford	CT	06108	**866-746-2133**	860-528-5430
Interlink Network Systems Inc 495 Cranbury Rd	East Brunswick	NJ	08816	**877-872-6947**	732-846-2226
Jedson Engineering 705 Central Ave	Cincinnati	OH	45202	**866-729-3945**	513-965-5999
JM Turner Engineering Inc 1325 College Ave	Santa Rosa	CA	95404	**800-514-4220**	707-528-4503
Johnson Engineering Inc 2122 Johnson St	Fort Myers	FL	33901	**866-367-4400**	239-334-0046
Kelly's Janitorial Service Inc 228 Hazel Ave	Trenton	NJ	08638	**800-227-0366**	609-771-0365
Kussmaul Electronics Company Inc 170 Cherry Ave	West Sayville	NY	11796	**800-346-0857**	631-567-0314
LARON Inc 4255 Santa Fe Dr	Kingman	AZ	86401	**800-248-3430**	928-757-8424
Lochmueller Group 6200 Vogel Rd	Evansville	IN	47715	**800-423-7411**	812-479-6200
MadgeTech Inc 6 Warner Rd	Warner	NH	03278	**877-671-2885**	603-456-2011
Matot Inc 2501 Van Buren St	Bellwood	IL	60104	**800-369-1070**	708-547-1888
Matrix Energy Services Inc 3221 Ramos Cir	Sacramento	CA	95827	**800-556-2123**	916-363-9283
Matrix LLC 19 Ave D	Johnson City	NY	13790	**800-338-5603**	607-766-0700
McQ Inc 1551 Forbes St	Fredericksburg	VA	22405	**866-373-2374**	540-373-2374
Meda Ltd 1575 Lauzon Rd	Windsor	ON	N8S3N4	**888-518-6332**	519-944-7221
Moffitt Corp Inc 1351 13th Ave S Ste 130	Jacksonville Beach	FL	32250	**800-474-3267**	904-241-9944
Monitor Elevator Products Inc 125 Ricefield Ln	Hauppauge	NY	11788	**800-527-9156**	
Motion Control Engineering Inc 11380 White Rock Rd	Rancho Cordova	CA	95742	**800-444-7442**	916-463-9200
Omicron Architecture Engineering Construction Ltd 595 Burrard St Three Bentall Centre Fifth Fl PO Box 49369	Vancouver	BC	V7X1L4	**877-632-3350**	604-632-3350
Radiant Technologies Inc 2835 Pan American Fwy Ne	Albuquerque	NM	87107	**800-289-7176**	505-842-8007
Ricon Corp 7900 Nelson Rd	Panorama City	CA	91402	**800-322-2884**	818-267-3000
Schindler Elevator Corp 20 Whippany Rd	Morristown	NJ	07960	**800-225-3123**	973-397-6500
Schumacher Elevator Co 1 Schumacher Way PO Box 393	Denver	IA	50622	**800-779-5438**	319-984-5676
Technical Systems Integration Inc 816 Greenbrier Cir Ste 208	Chesapeake	VA	23320	**800-566-8744**	757-424-5793
Tulloch Engineering Inc 200 Main St	Thessalon	ON	P0R1L0	**800-797-2997**	705-842-3372
Vaughn Coltrane Pharr & Associates Inc 2060 E Exchange Pl	Tucker	GA	30084	**877-230-5315**	678-567-4513
Waupaca Elevator Co Inc 1726 N BallaRd Rd	Appleton	WI	54911	**800-238-8739**	920-991-9082
York Building Services Inc 99 Grand St Ste 3	Moonachie	NJ	07074	**855-443-9675**	

259 EMBASSIES & CONSULATES - FOREIGN, IN THE US

SEE ALSO Travel & Tourism Information - Foreign Travel

Foreign embassies in the U.S. generally include consular services among their functions. These embassy-based consulates are listed here only if their address differs from the embassy's.

				Toll-Free	Phone
Afghanistan Embassy 2341 Wyoming Ave NW	Washington	DC	20008	**866-323-8609**	202-483-6410

Classified Section

	City	State	ZIP	Toll-Free	Phone
Antigua & Barbuda					
Embassy 3216 New Mexico Ave NW	Washington	DC	20016	**866-978-7299**	202-362-5122
Australia					
Consulate General 1000 Bishop St PH	Honolulu	HI	96813	**866-343-3086**	808-529-8100
Embassy 2005 Massachusetts Ave NW	Washington	DC	20036	**800-345-6541**	202-558-2216
Austria					
Consulate General 11859 Wilshire Blvd Ste 501	Los Angeles	CA	90025	**800-255-2414**	310-444-9310
Embassy 3524 International Ct NW	Washington	DC	20008	**800-255-2414**	202-895-6700
Bahamas					
Embassy 2220 Massachusetts Ave NW	Washington	DC	20008	**800-883-7421**	202-319-2660
Brazil					
Consulate General 8484 Wilshire Blvd Ste 711	Beverly Hills	CA	90211	**877-782-5477**	323-651-2664
Consulate General 1233 W Loop S Ste 1150	Houston	TX	77027	**800-326-2289**	713-961-3063
Bulgaria					
Embassy 1621 22nd St NW	Washington	DC	20008	**800-961-6836**	202-387-0174
Burkina Faso Embassy					
2005 Massachusetts Ave NW	Washington	DC	20008	**800-345-6541**	202-332-5577
Canada					
885 Second Ave 14th Fl	New York	NY	10017	**800-267-8376**	212-848-1100
Consulate General 500 N Akard St Ste 2900	Dallas	TX	75201	**800-267-8376**	214-922-9806
Consulate General 1251 Ave of the Americas Concourse Level	New York	NY	10020	**800-267-8376**	212-596-1628
Embassy 501 Pennsylvania Ave NW	Washington	DC	20001	**800-567-6868**	202-682-1740
Cape Verde					
Embassy 3415 Massachusetts Ave NW	Washington	DC	20007	**800-343-2347**	202-965-6820
Chile					
Embassy 1732 Massachusetts Ave NW	Washington	DC	20036	**855-310-8471**	202-785-1746
Denmark					
Consulate General 875 N Michigan Ave Ste 3950	Chicago	IL	60611	**800-345-6541**	
Fiji Embassy					
1707 L St NW Ste 200	Washington	DC	20036	**800-932-3454**	202-337-8320
France					
Consulate General 205 N Michigan Ave Ste 3700	Chicago	IL	60601	**866-858-4430**	312-327-5200
Consulate General 1395 Brickell Ave Ste 1050	Miami	FL	33131	**877-624-8737**	305-403-4185
Consulate General 777 Post Oak Blvd Ste 600	Houston	TX	77056	**888-902-5322**	713-572-2799
Consulate General 934 Fifth Ave	New York	NY	10021	**800-772-1213**	212-606-3600
Consulate General 540 Bush St	San Francisco	CA	94108	**800-553-4133**	415-397-4330
Consulate General 3475 Piedmont Rd NE Ste 1840	Atlanta	GA	30305	**888-937-2623**	404-495-1660
Embassy 4101 Reservoir Rd NW	Washington	DC	20007	**800-622-6232**	202-944-6000
Germany					
Consulate General 285 Peachtree Ctr Ave NE Ste 901	Atlanta	GA	30303	**866-687-8561**	404-659-4760
Honduras					
Embassy 3007 Tilden St NW	Washington	DC	20008	**800-375-5283**	202-966-7702
Consulate General 540 Arguello Blvd	San Francisco	CA	94118	**866-978-0055**	415-668-0662
Ireland					
Embassy 2234 Massachusetts Ave NW	Washington	DC	20008	**866-560-1050**	202-462-3939
Italy					
Consulate General 150 S Independence Mall W Public Ledger Bldg Ste 1026	Philadelphia	PA	19106	**800-531-0840**	215-592-7329
Consulate General 1300 Post Oak Blvd Ste 660	Houston	TX	77056	**800-637-9314**	713-850-7520
Consulate General 600 Atlantic Ave 17th Fl	Boston	MA	02210	**888-225-5427**	617-722-9201
Embassy 3000 Whitehaven St NW	Washington	DC	20008	**800-222-1222**	202-612-4400
Korea Republic of					
Consulate General 2033 Sixth Ave Ste 1125	Seattle	WA	98121	**800-375-5283**	206-441-1011
Kuwait Embassy					
2940 Tilden St NW	Washington	DC	20008	**800-688-9889**	202-966-0702
Consulate General 4506 Carolinas St	Houston	TX	77004	**877-639-4835**	713-271-6800
Micronesia					
300 E 42nd St Ste 1600	New York	NY	10017	**800-469-4828**	212-697-8370
Consulate 1725 N St NW Ste 910	Washington	DC	20036	**877-730-9753**	202-223-4383
Netherlands					
Consulate General 666 Third Ave 19th Fl	New York	NY	10017	**877-388-2443**	
Embassy 4200 Linnean Ave NW	Washington	DC	20008	**877-388-2443**	
New Zealand					
Embassy 37 Observatory Cir NW	Washington	DC	20008	**855-844-2835**	202-328-4800
Peru					
Consulate General 180 N Michigan Ave Ste 1830	Chicago	IL	60601	**877-714-7378**	312-782-1599
Consulate General 870 Market St Ste 1067	San Francisco	CA	94102	**877-714-7378**	415-362-7136
Consulate General 100 Hamilton Plaza	Paterson	NJ	07505	**877-714-7378**	973-278-3324
Consulate General 5177 Richmond Ave Ste 695	Houston	TX	77056	**877-714-7378**	713-355-9517
Consulate General 3450 Wilshire Blvd Ste 800	Los Angeles	CA	90010	**877-714-7378**	213-252-5910
Consulate General 444 Brickell Ave Ste M135	Miami	FL	33131	**877-714-7378**	
Philippines					
Consulate General 30 N Michigan Ave Ste 2100	Chicago	IL	60602	**888-259-7838**	312-332-6458
Consulate General 447 Sutter St 6th Fl Philippine Ctr Bldg	San Francisco	CA	94108	**877-700-0669**	415-433-6666
Consulate General 556 Fifth Ave	New York	NY	10036	**866-589-1878**	212-764-1330
Embassy 1600 Massachusetts Ave NW	Washington	DC	20036	**800-527-2820**	202-467-9300
Saint Lucia					
Embassy 3216 New Mexico Ave NW	Washington	DC	20016	**800-456-3984**	202-364-6792
Turkey					
Consulate General 1990 Post Oak Blvd Ste 1300	Houston	TX	77056	**888-566-7656**	713-622-5849
Consulate General 6300 Wilshire Blvd Ste 2010	Los Angeles	CA	90048	**800-874-8875**	323-655-8832
Embassy 2525 Massachusetts Ave NW	Washington	DC	20008	**877-367-8875**	202-612-6700

260 EMBROIDERY & OTHER DECORATIVE STITCHING

	City	State	ZIP	Toll-Free	Phone
Branded Emblem Co Inc 7920 Foster St	Overland Park	KS	66204	**800-448-2267**	913-648-0573
CR Daniels Inc 3451 Ellicott Ctr Dr	Ellicott City	MD	21043	**800-933-2638**	410-461-2100
EmbroidMe Inc 2121 Vista Pkwy	West Palm Beach	FL	33411	**877-877-0234**	561-640-7367
Fabri-Quilt Inc 901 E 14th Ave	North Kansas City	MO	64116	**800-279-0622**	816-421-2000
FlagZone LLC 105A Industrial Dr	Gilbertsville	PA	19525	**800-976-4201**	
Gensco Equipment (1990) Inc 53 Carlaw Ave	Toronto	ON	M4M2R6	**800-268-6797**	416-465-7521
Herrschners Inc 2800 Hoover Rd	Stevens Point	WI	54481	**800-713-1239**	715-341-8686
Lion Bros Company Inc 300 Red Brook Blvd *Cust Svc	Owings Mills	MD	21117	**800-365-6543***	
Luv N' Care Ltd 3030 Aurora Ave	Monroe	LA	71201	**800-588-6227**	
Monarch Textile Rental Services Inc 2810 Foundation Dr	South Bend	IN	46628	**800-589-9434**	574-233-9433
Moritz Embroidery Works Inc Pocono Mtn Business Park 405 Industrial Park Dr PO Box 187	Mount Pocono	PA	18344	**800-533-4183**	570-839-9600
MP Global Products Inc 2500 Old Hadar Rd	Norfolk	NE	68701	**888-379-9695**	402-379-9695
National Emblem Inc 17036 S Avalon Blvd	Carson	CA	90746	**800-877-6185**	310-515-5055
Osgood Textile Company Inc 333 Park St	West Springfield	MA	01089	**888-674-6638**	413-737-6488
Penn Emblem Co 10909 Dutton Rd	Philadelphia	PA	19154	**800-793-7366**	
Saint Louis Embroidery 1759 Scherer Pkwy	Saint Charles	MO	63303	**800-457-6676**	636-724-2200
Schweizer Emblem Co 1022 Busse Hwy *Cust Svc	Park Ridge	IL	60068	**800-942-5215***	847-292-1022
Thread Logic 16775 Greystone Ln	Jordan	MN	55352	**800-347-1612**	

261 EMPLOYMENT OFFICES - GOVERNMENT

	City	State	ZIP	Toll-Free	Phone
Employment & Training Administration 200 Constitution Ave NW	Washington	DC	20210	**866-487-2365**	
Colorado Labor & Employment Dept 633 17th St Ste 201	Denver	CO	80203	**800-390-7936**	303-318-8000
Indiana Workforce Development Dept 10 N Senate Ave	Indianapolis	IN	46204	**800-891-6499**	317-232-7670
Iowa Workforce Development 1000 E Grand Ave	Des Moines	IA	50319	**800-562-4692**	515-281-5387
Louisiana Workforce Commission 1001 N 23rd St	Baton Rouge	LA	70802	**877-529-6757**	225-342-3111
Michigan Career Education & Workforce Programs 201 N Washington Sq Victor Office Center	Lansing	MI	48913	**888-253-6855**	517-335-5858
Mississippi Employment Security Commission 1235 Echelon Pkwy PO Box 1699	Jackson	MS	39215	**888-844-3577**	601-321-6000
New Hampshire Employment Security (NHES) 32 S Main St	Concord	NH	03301	**800-852-3400**	603-224-3311
New York Labor Dept WA Harriman Campus Bldg 12	Albany	NY	12240	**888-469-7365**	518-457-9000
Ohio Workforce Developement Office 4020 E Fifth Ave PO Box 1618	Columbus	OH	43219	**888-296-7541**	
Oregon Employment Dept 875 Union St NE	Salem	OR	97311	**877-345-3484**	503-451-2400

262 EMPLOYMENT SERVICES - ONLINE

	City	State	ZIP	Toll-Free	Phone
Advantage RN LLC 8892 Beckett Rd	West Chester	OH	45069	**866-301-4045**	513-874-8717
agriCAREERS Inc 613 Main St PO Box 140	Massena	IA	50853	**800-633-8387**	
All-Star Recruiting LLC 6119 Lyons Rd	Coconut Creek	FL	33073	**800-928-0229**	

Name	Address	City	ST	ZIP	Toll-Free	Phone
Allegiant International LLC	1710 N Main St	Auburn	IN	46706	**866-841-3671**	
Alpha Rae Personnel Inc	347 W Berry St Ste 700	Fort Wayne	IN	46802	**800-837-8940**	260-426-8227
Avjobs Inc	PO Box 260830	Littleton	CO	80163	**888-624-8691**	303-683-2322
Backtrack Inc	8850 Tyler Blvd	Mentor	OH	44060	**800-991-9694**	440-205-8280
Bayside Solutions Inc	6160 Stoneridge Mall Rd Ste 320	Pleasanton	CA	94588	**800-220-0074**	
Bcg Attorney Search	175 S Lk Ave Unit 200	Pasadena	CA	91101	**800-298-6440**	
Bear Staffing Services Inc	47 S Broad St	Woodbury	NJ	08096	**866-580-2327**	
Bowen Workforce Solutions Inc	602 12 Ave Sw Ste 700	Calgary	AB	T2R1J3	**866-692-6936**	403-262-1156
Carolinas Constructions Solutions Inc	6712 Old Pineville Rd	Charlotte	NC	28217	**866-521-5624**	704-578-1567
Catalyst Awareness Inc	355 Elmira Rd N Ste 127	Guelph	ON	N1K1S5	**866-749-3697**	
Chicago Nannies Inc	101 N Marion St Ste 300	Oak Park	IL	60301	**866-900-9605**	708-524-2101
Children First Home Healthcare Service	4448 Edgewater Dr	Orlando	FL	32804	**800-207-0802**	407-513-3000
Clearbridge Technology Group	6 Fortune Dr	Billerica	MA	01821	**877-808-2284**	781-916-2284
Coastal Administrative Services Inc	103 E Holly Ste 214	Bellingham	WA	98225	**800-870-1831**	
ComputerJobs.com Inc	1995 N Pk Pl SE	Atlanta	GA	30339	**800-850-0045**	770-850-0045
Condustrial Inc	105 East N St	Greenville	SC	29601	**888-794-7798**	864-235-3619
Dice Inc	4101 NW Urbandale Dr	Urbandale	IA	50322	**877-386-3323**	515-280-1144
Emerge Financial Wellness Inc	530 Church St Ste 301	Nashville	TN	37219	**800-791-1725**	
EmpireWorks Inc	1940 Olivera Rd.	Concord	CA	94520	**888-278-8200**	
EmplawyerNet	2331 Westwood Blvd	Los Angeles	CA	90064	**800-270-2688**	
EmploymentGuide.com	150 Granby St	Norfolk	VA	23510	**877-876-4039**	
ExecUNet Inc	295 Westport Ave	Norwalk	CT	06851	**800-637-3126**	203-750-1030
Expert Recruiters	883 Helmcken St	Vancouver	BC	V6Z1B1	**888-407-7799**	604-689-3600
Federal Staffing Resources LLC	2200 Somerville Rd Ste 300	Annapolis	MD	21401	**866-886-2300**	410-990-0795
Filter Talent	1425 4th Ave Ste 1000	Seattle	WA	98101	**800-336-0809**	
Galaxy Software Solutions Inc	5820 N Lilley Rd Ste 8	Canton	MI	48187	**877-269-4774**	734-983-9030
Global HR Research LLC	24201 Walden Ctr Dr Ste 206	Bonita Springs	FL	34134	**800-790-1205**	239-274-0048
Guru.com	5001 Baum Blvd Ste 760	Pittsburgh	PA	15213	**888-678-0136**	412-687-1316
HealthCareSource Inc	100 Sylvan Rd Ste 100	Woburn	MA	01801	**800-869-5200**	
HealthForce Ontario Marketing & Recruitment Agency	163 Queen St E	Toronto	ON	M5A1S1	**800-596-4046**	416-862-2200
HR Works Inc	200 WillowBrook Ofc Park	Fairport	NY	14450	**877-219-9062**	585-381-8340
Incepture Inc	8381 Dix Ellis Trail Ste 105	Jacksonville	FL	32225	**877-347-7151**	
Industry Specific Solutions LLC	24901 Northwestern Hwy Ste 400	Southfield	MI	48075	**877-356-3450**	
Intellect Resources Inc	3824 N Elm St Ste 102	Greensboro	NC	27455	**877-554-8911**	
International Foundation of Employee Benefit Plans (IFEBP)	18700 W Bluemound Rd	Brookfield	WI	53045	**888-334-3327**	262-786-6700
JCSI Corporate Staffing	2 South St	Grafton	MA	01519	**888-527-4462**	774-760-1800
JobHive Inc	701 E Bridger Ave Ste 400	Las Vegas	NV	89101	**855-562-4483**	
JobMonkey Inc	PO Box 3956	Seattle	WA	98124	**800-230-1095**	
K A Hamilton & Assoc	159 Perry Hwy Ste 100	Pittsburgh	PA	15229	**800-746-4726**	412-459-0122
Kendall & Davis Company Inc	3668 S Geyer Rd Ste 100	St. Louis	MO	63127	**866-675-3755**	
Kovasys Inc	500 Pl d'Armes Ste 1800	Montreal	QC	H2X2T7	**888-568-2747**	
KWCG Inc	12255 Pkwy Centre Dr	San Diego	CA	92064	**877-464-5924**	
Ll Roberts Group	7475 Skillman St Ste 102c	Dallas	TX	75231	**877-878-6463**	214-221-6463
Maxsys	173 Dalhousie St	Ottawa	ON	K1N7C7	**800-429-5177**	613-562-9943
MDT Labor LLC	2325 Paxton Church Rd Ste B	Harrisburg	PA	17110	**888-454-9202**	
Mind Your Business Inc (myb)	305 Eighth Ave E	Hendersonville	NC	28792	**888-869-2462**	
MonsterTRAK	11845 W Olympic Blvd Ste 500	Los Angeles	CA	90064	**800-999-8725**	
MyOpenJobs LLC	203 Main St Ste 100	Lake Dallas	TX	75065	**800-396-4822**	
National Diversity Newspaper Job Bank	*c/o Morris Communications* 725 Broad St	Augusta	GA	30901	**800-622-6358**	706-724-0851
NationJob Inc	920 Morgan St Ste T	Des Moines	IA	50309	**800-292-7731**	
Net-Temps Inc	55 Middlesex St Ste 220	North Chelmsford	MA	01863	**800-307-0062**	978-251-7272
Nowhirecom	21220 Kelly Rd	Eastpointe	MI	48021	**800-724-8546**	586-778-8491
NSTAR Global Services Inc	120 Partlo St	Garner	NC	27529	**877-678-2766**	
Olesky Associates Inc	865 Washington St Ste 3	Newtonville	MA	02460	**800-486-4330**	781-235-4330
On Time Staffing LLC	2 Aquarium Dr Ferry Terminal Bldg Ste 150	Camden	NJ	08103	**866-333-3007**	
People Plus Industrial Inc	1095 Nebo Rd	Madisonville	KY	42431	**888-825-1500**	270-825-8939
Peoplecomm Inc	148 Woodbine Ave	Northport	NY	11768	**800-735-1629**	
Peterson's Nelnet LLC	121 S 13th St Ste 201	Lincoln	NE	68508	**877-338-7772**	609-896-8669
Placement Strategies Inc	6965 El Camino Real Ste 105-200	Carlsbad	CA	92009	**866-445-0710**	909-597-0668
Platinum Personnel	1475 Ellis St	Kelowna	BC	V1Y2A3	**800-652-1511**	250-979-7200
PRN Health Services Inc	4321 W College Ave Ste 200	Appleton	WI	54914	**888-830-8811**	
Procel Temporary Services	2447 Pacific Coast Hwy Ste 207	Hermosa Beach	CA	90254	**800-338-9905**	310-372-0560
Randstad US L P	2015 S Park Pl	Atlanta	GA	30339	**800-382-7297**	
Renoir Staffing Services Inc	1301 Marina Vlg Pkwy Ste 350	Alameda	CA	94501	**866-672-3709**	
Run Consultants LLC	925 N Point Pkwy Ste 160	Alpharetta	GA	30005	**866-457-2193**	
Salus Group Benefits Inc	37525 Mound Rd	Sterling Heights	MI	48310	**866-991-9907**	
Sesame Software Inc	File 74625 P.O. Box 60000	San Francisco	CA	94160	**866-474-7575**	
Sharf Woodward & Associates Inc	5900 Sepulveda Blvd	Sherman Oaks	CA	91411	**877-482-6687**	818-989-2200
Skillforce Inc	405 Williams Court Ste 100	Baltimore	MD	21220	**866-581-8989**	
Southern Healthcare Agency Inc	PO Box 320999	Flowood	MS	39232	**800-880-2772**	601-933-0037
Sprocket Staffing Services	35 Colby Ave	Manasquan	NJ	08736	**800-269-1441**	
Staffing Options & Solutions Inc	6249 S E St Ste E	Indianapolis	IN	46227	**800-554-7823**	317-791-2456
Staffing Resource Group Inc, The	3505 E Frntage Rd Ste 320	Tampa	FL	33607	**877-774-7742**	
Staffworks Group	20505 W 12 Mile Rd	Southfield	MI	48076	**877-304-9690**	
TalentLens Inc	19500 Bulverde Rd	San Antonio	TX	78259	**888-298-6227**	
Targeted Job Fairs Inc	4441 Glenway Ave	Cincinnati	OH	45205	**800-695-1939**	
Taylor & Hill Inc	9941 Rowlett Rd	Houston	TX	77075	**800-318-0231**	713-941-2671
Teach Away Inc	147 Liberty St	Toronto	ON	M6K3G3	**855-483-2242**	416-628-1386
Teachers on Reserve LLC	604 Sonora Ave	Glendale	CA	91201	**800-457-1899**	818-502-5800
United Personnel Services Inc	289 Bridge St	Springfield	MA	01103	**800-363-8200**	413-736-0800
VetJobs Inc	PO Box 71445	Marietta	GA	30007	**877-838-5627**	770-993-5117
Waterstone Group Inc, The	1145 W Main Ave Ste 209	De Pere	WI	54115	**800-291-3836**	920-964-0333
Zachary Piper LLC	1410 Spring Hill Rd Ste 300	Mclean	VA	22012	**888-487-8812**	703-649-4001

263 ENGINEERING & DESIGN

SEE ALSO Surveying, Mapping, Related Services

Name	Address	City	ST	ZIP	Toll-Free	Phone
Aim Engineering & Surveying Inc	5300 Lee Blvd	Lehigh Acres	FL	33971	**800-226-4569**	239-332-4569
AKRF Inc	440 Pk Ave S	New York	NY	10016	**800-899-2573**	212-696-0670
Alion Science & Technology	1750 Tysons Blvd Ste 1300	McLean	VA	22102	**877-439-9227**	703-918-4480
Allied Power Group LLC	10131 Mills Rd	Houston	TX	77070	**888-830-3535**	281-444-3535
AM Kinney	150 E Fourth St	Cincinnati	OH	45202	**800-265-3682**	513-421-2265
American Engineering Testing Inc	550 Cleveland Ave N	Saint Paul	MN	55114	**800-972-6364**	651-659-9001
Ams Mechanical Systems Inc	140 E Tower Dr	Burr Ridge	IL	60527	**800-794-5033**	630-887-7700
Amset Technical Consulting	1864 S Elmhurst Rd	Mount Prospect	IL	60056	**888-982-6783**	847-229-1155
Apollo Professional Svc	29 Stiles Rd Ste 302	Salem	NH	03079	**866-277-3343**	
Applied Technology & Management Inc	5550 NW 111th Blvd	Gainesville	FL	32653	**800-275-6488**	
ARGO Systems LLC	1362 Mellon Rd Ste 100	Hanover	MD	21076	**877-994-2746**	410-768-2444
ASG Renaissance	22226 Garrison St	Dearborn	MI	48124	**800-238-0890**	313-565-4700
B Jcc Inspections	1000 Banks Draw	Rexford	MT	59930	**877-248-6006**	406-882-4825
Barr Engineering Co	4700 W 77th St	Minneapolis	MN	55435	**800-632-2277**	952-832-2600
Bartlett & West Engineers Inc	1200 SW Executive Dr	Topeka	KS	66615	**888-200-6464**	785-272-2252
Belcan Corp	10200 Anderson Way	Cincinnati	OH	45242	**800-423-5226**	513-891-0972
Bender Engineering Inc	10037 E River St	Irvine	CA	92618	**800-255-5675**	949-458-7560
Bergmann Assoc Inc	28 E Main St 200 1st Federal Plaza	Rochester	NY	14614	**800-724-1168**	585-232-5135
Biff Duncan Associates Inc	450 Shrewsbury Plz	Shrewsbury	NJ	07702	**866-335-2433**	732-876-0263
Bionetics Corp, The	101 Production Dr Ste 100	Yorktown	VA	23693	**800-868-0330**	757-873-0900
BL Cos	355 Research Pkwy	Meriden	CT	06450	**800-301-3077**	203-630-1406
Boudreau-Espley-Pitre Corp	1040 Lorne St Unit 3	Sudbury	ON	P3C4R9	**877-675-7720**	705-675-7720
Braun Intertec Corp	11001 Hampshire Ave S	Bloomington	MN	55438	**800-279-6100**	952-995-2000

Company / Address	City	State	ZIP	Toll-Free	Phone
Brinjac Engineering Inc 114 N Second St	Harrisburg	PA	17101	**877-274-6526**	717-233-4502
Brock Solutions Inc 86 Ardelt Ave	Kitchener	ON	N2C2C9	**877-702-7625**	519-571-1522
C & S Companies (CSCOS) 499 Col Eileen Collins Blvd	Syracuse	NY	13212	**877-277-6583**	315-455-2000
Carlo Gavazzi Inc 750 Hastings Ln	Buffalo Grove	IL	60089	**800-222-2659**	847-465-6100
Carollo Engineers 2700 Ygnacio Vly Rd Ste 300	Walnut Creek	CA	94598	**800-523-5826**	925-932-1710
CAS Inc PO Box 11190	Huntsville	AL	35814	**800-729-8686**	256-971-6126
CDI Corporation 1717 Arch St 35th Fl	Philadelphia	PA	19103	**866-472-2203**	215-569-2200
Civil & Environmental Consultants Inc 333 Baldwin Rd	Pittsburgh	PA	15205	**800-365-2324**	412-429-2324
Clark Engineering Corp 621 Lilac Dr N	Minneapolis	MN	55422	**877-246-9196**	763-545-9196
Concepts NREC 217 Billings Farm Rd	White River Junction	VT	05001	**888-299-8057**	802-296-2321
Corrpro Cos Inc 1055 W Smith Rd	Medina	OH	44256	**800-443-3516**	330-723-5082
CPH Engineers 500 W Fulton St	Sanford	FL	32771	**866-609-0688**	
Craig Test Boring Company Inc 5435 Harding Hwy PO Box 427	Mays Landing	NJ	08330	**800-584-2277**	
CSS-Dynamac Corp 10301 Democracy Ln Ste 300	Fairfax	VA	22030	**800-888-4612**	703-691-4612
CT Consultants Inc 8150 Sterling Ct	Mentor	OH	44060	**800-925-0988**	440-951-9000
Dataline LLC 6703 Albunda Dr PO Box 50816	Knoxville	TN	37950	**800-666-9858**	865-588-7740
Datasyst Engineering & Testing Services Inc S14W33511 Hwy 18	Delafield	WI	53018	**800-969-4050**	262-968-4003
David Evans & Assoc Inc (DEA) 2100 SW River Pkwy	Portland	OR	97201	**800-721-1916**	503-223-6663
Dayton T Brown Inc 1175 Church St	Bohemia	NY	11716	**800-232-6300**	631-589-6300
Deighton Associates Ltd 223 Brock St N Unit 7	Whitby	ON	L1N4H6	**888-219-6605**	905-665-6605
DLZ Corp 6121 Huntley Rd	Columbus	OH	43229	**800-336-5352**	614-888-0040
Doerfer Engineering Corp PO Box 816	Waverly	IA	50677	**877-483-4700**	
Dyer Riddle Mills & Precourt Inc (DRMP) 941 Lk Baldwin Ln	Orlando	FL	32814	**800-375-3767**	407-896-0594
E.S. Fox Ltd 9127 Montrose Rd	Niagara Falls	ON	L2E7J9	**866-233-8933**	905-354-3700
E2 Consulting Engineers Inc 450 E 17th Ave Ste 200	Denver	CO	80203	**888-835-9400**	303-232-9800
EADS Group 1126 Eigth Ave	Altoona	PA	16602	**800-626-0904**	814-944-5035
EarthRes Group Inc 6912 Old Easton Rd PO Box 468	Pipersville	PA	18947	**800-264-4553**	215-766-1211
EMCOR Services Betlem 704 Clinton Ave South	Rochester	NY	14620	**800-423-8536**	585-271-5500
EMK Consultants of Florida Inc 7815 N Dale Mabry Hwy	Tampa	FL	33614	**800-347-2607**	813-931-8900
Engineering & Environmental Consultants Inc 4625 E Ft Lowell Rd	Tucson	AZ	85712	**800-887-2103**	520-321-4625
ENSCO Inc 3110 Fairview Pk Dr Ste 300	Falls Church	VA	22042	**800-367-2682**	703-321-9000
Eoa Inc 1410 Jackson St	Oakland	CA	94612	**800-794-2482**	510-832-2852
Etegent Technologies Ltd 1775 Mentor Ave	Cincinnati	OH	45212	**800-860-4867**	513-631-0579
Fakouri Electrical Engineering Inc 30001 Comercio	Rancho Santa Margarita	CA	92688	**800-669-8862**	
Fanning/Howey Assoc Inc 1200 Irmscher Blvd	Celina	OH	45822	**800-452-3573**	419-586-2292
Farwest Corrosion Control Co 1480 W Artesia Blvd	Gardena	CA	90248	**888-532-7937**	310-532-9524
Fay Spofford & Thorndike LLC 5 Burlington Woods	Burlington	MA	01803	**800-835-8666**	781-221-1000
Flint Surveying & Engineering Company Inc 5370 Miller Rd	Swartz Creek	MI	48473	**800-624-6089**	810-230-1333
Fuss & O'Neill Consulting Engineers Inc 146 Hartford Rd	Manchester	CT	06040	**800-286-2469**	860-646-2469
Gannett Fleming Inc 207 Senate Ave	Camp Hill	PA	17011	**800-233-1055**	717-763-7211
GEI Consultants Inc 400 Unicorn Pk Dr	Woburn	MA	01801	**888-434-9679**	781-721-4000
GeoEngineers Inc 8410 154th Ave NE	Redmond	WA	98052	**888-624-8373**	425-861-6000
GeoSyntec Consultants Inc 5901 Broken Sound Pkwy NW Ste 300	Boca Raton	FL	33487	**866-676-1101**	561-995-0900
Ghafari Assoc Inc 17101 Michigan Ave	Dearborn	MI	48126	**800-289-7822**	313-441-3000
Gillespie, Prudhon & Associates Inc 16111 Se 106th Ave Ste 100	Clackamas	OR	97015	**800-595-2145**	503-657-0424
Greeley & Hansen 100 S Wacker Dr Ste 1400	Chicago	IL	60606	**800-837-9779**	312-558-9000
Haag Engineering Co 4949 W Royal Ln	Irving	TX	75063	**800-527-0168**	214-614-6500
Hammel Green & Abrahamson Inc 701 Washington Ave N	Minneapolis	MN	55401	**888-442-8255**	612-758-4000
Hazen & Sawyer PC 498 Seventh Ave 11th Fl	New York	NY	10018	**800-858-9876**	212-777-8400
HDR Engineering Inc 8404 Indian Hills Dr	Omaha	NE	68114	**800-366-4411**	402-399-1000
Heery International Inc 999 Peachtree St NE	Atlanta	GA	30309	**866-840-3940**	404-881-9880
Henneman Engineering 1605 S State St	Champaign	IL	61820	**888-616-0216**	217-359-1514
Hi-Tech Systems Engineering Co 2700 Old Centre Rd	Portage	MI	49024	**866-312-1893**	269-488-7788
HL Turner Group Inc, The 27 Locke Rd	Concord	NH	03301	**800-305-2289**	603-228-1122
HMC Archtiect 3546 Councours St	Ontario	CA	91764	**800-350-9979**	909-989-9979
HPD, LLC 23563 W Main St	Plainfield	IL	60544	**866-362-0993**	815-609-2000
HRP Associates Inc 197 Scott Swamp Rd	Farmington	CT	06032	**800-246-9021**	
Huitt-Zollars Inc 1717 McKinney Ave Ste 1400	Dallas	TX	75202	**866-667-6572**	214-871-3311
IDD Process & Packaging 5450 Tech Cir	Moorpark	CA	93021	**800-621-4144**	805-529-9890
IDEO 100 Forest Ave	Palo Alto	CA	94301	**866-369-9888**	650-289-3400
Intertek Group PLC 801 Travis St Ste 1500	Houston	TX	77002	**800-967-5352**	713-407-3500
Intrinsix Corp 100 Campus Dr	Marlborough	MA	01752	**800-783-0330**	508-658-7600
James Machine Works LLC 1521 Adams St	Monroe	LA	71201	**800-259-6104**	318-322-6104
JMP Engineering Inc 4026 Meadowbrook Dr Unit 143	London	ON	N6L1C9	**855-228-8668**	519-652-2741
John M. Campbell & Co 1215 Crossroads Blvd	Norman	OK	73072	**800-821-5933**	405-321-1383
Johnson Mirmiran & Thompson (JMT) 72 Loveton Cir	Sparks	MD	21152	**800-472-2310**	410-329-3100
KBR Inc 601 Jefferson St	Houston	TX	77002	**888-203-1112**	713-753-2000
KCI Technologies Inc 936 Ridgebrook Rd	Sparks	MD	21152	**800-572-7496**	410-316-7800
Keith & Schnars PA 6500 N Andrews Ave	Fort Lauderdale	FL	33309	**800-488-1255**	954-776-1616
Ken Garner Manufacturing - Rho Inc 1201 E 28th St # B	Chattanooga	TN	37404	**888-454-7207**	423-698-6200
Kratos Defense & Security Solutions Inc 4820 Eastgate Mall Ste 200	San Diego	CA	92121	**877-548-7911**	858-332-3700
KSA Engineers Inc 140 E Tyler St Ste 600 Ste 600	Longview	TX	75601	**877-572-3647**	903-236-7700
Kta-Tator Inc 115 Technology Dr	Pittsburgh	PA	15275	**800-582-4243**	412-788-1300
Larson Design Group Inc 1000 Commerce Pk Dr Ste 201 PO Box 487	Williamsport	PA	17701	**877-323-6603**	570-323-6603
Lauren Engineers & Constructors Inc 901 S First St	Abilene	TX	79602	**800-433-7300**	325-670-9660
LBA Group Inc 3400 Tupper Dr	Greenville	NC	27834	**800-522-4464**	252-757-0279
LJB Inc 2500 Newmark Dr	Miamisburg	OH	45342	**866-552-3536**	937-259-5000
Lochsa Engineering Inc 6345 S Jones Blvd Ste 100	Las Vegas	NV	89118	**866-606-9784**	702-365-9312
Lumos & Assoc Inc 800 E College Pkwy	Carson City	NV	89706	**800-621-7155**	775-883-7077
Macaulay-Brown Inc 4021 Executive Dr	Dayton	OH	45430	**800-669-4000**	937-426-3421
Management Consulting Inc 1961 Diamond Springs Rd	Virginia Beach	VA	23455	**888-892-0787**	757-460-0879
Mannik & Smith Group Inc 1800 Indian Wood Cir	Maumee	OH	43537	**888-891-6321**	419-891-2222
Maren Engineering 111 W Taft Dr	South Holland	IL	60473	**800-875-1038**	708-333-6250
Martronic Engineering Inc 80 W Cochran St Ste B	Simi Valley	CA	93065	**800-960-0808**	805-583-0808
MBS Assoc Inc 7800 E Kemper Rd Ste 160	Cincinnati	OH	45249	**888-469-9301**	513-645-1600
McDonough Bolyard Peck Inc (MBP) 3040 Williams Dr Williams Plz 1 Ste 300	Fairfax	VA	22031	**800-898-9088**	703-641-9088
McGill Smith Punshon Inc 3700 Park 42 Dr Ste 190B	Cincinnati	OH	45241	**800-759-8065**	513-759-0004
McLaughlin Research Corp 132 Johnnycake Hill Rd	Middletown	RI	02842	**800-556-7154**	401-849-4010
MDA Information Systems Inc 6011 Executive Blvd	Rockville	MD	20852	**800-642-1687**	240-833-8200
Meier Enterprises Inc 12 W. Kennewick Ave	Kennewick	WA	99336	**800-239-7589**	509-735-1589
Merrick & Co 2450 S Peoria St	Aurora	CO	80014	**800-544-1714**	303-751-0741
Michael Baker Corp 100 Airsite Dr Airsite Business Pk *NYSE: BKR*	Moon Township	PA	15108	**800-553-1153**	412-269-6300
Microlynx Systems Ltd 1925 18 Ave Ne Ste 107	Calgary	AB	T2E7T8	**866-835-4332**	403-275-7346
Mikros Engineering Inc 8755 Wyoming Ave N	Brooklyn Park	MN	55445	**800-394-5499**	763-424-4642
Miller Engineers & Scientists 5308 S 12th St	Sheboygan	WI	53081	**800-969-7013**	920-458-6164
Missman Inc 1011 27th Ave PO Box 6040	Rock Island	IL	61201	**800-969-3029**	309-788-7644
Modjeski & Masters Inc 100 Sterling Pkwy Ste 302	Mechanicsburg	PA	17050	**888-663-5375**	717-790-9565
Moffatt & Nichol Engineers 3780 Kilroy Airport Way # 750	Long Beach	CA	90806	**888-399-6609**	562-590-6500
Morgan-Keller Inc 70 Thomas Johnson Dr Ste 200	Frederick	MD	21702	**800-725-5051**	301-663-0626
Morrison Hershfield Group Inc 125 Commerce Valley Dr W Ste 300	Markham	ON	L3T7W4	**888-649-4730**	416-499-3110
Multax Systems Inc 505 N Sepulveda Blvd Ste 7	Manhattan Beach	CA	90266	**800-888-0199**	310-379-8398
Nalpro Business Solutions LLC Brier Hill Ct Bldg C	East Brunswick	NJ	08816	**888-868-6360**	732-390-1400
Nextgen Networks Inc 200 Katonah Ave Ste A	Katonah	NY	10536	**866-639-8436**	
Ninyo & Moore 5710 Ruffin Rd	San Diego	CA	92123	**800-427-0401**	858-576-1000
Nova Pole International Inc 19433 96th Ave Ste 102	Surrey	BC	V4N4C4	**866-874-8889**	604-881-0090
NV5 2525 Natomas Pk Dr Ste 300	Sacramento	CA	95833	**877-941-2068**	916-641-9100
Olsson Assoc 1111 Lincoln Mall Ste 111	Lincoln	NE	68508	**877-831-6389**	402-474-6311
Omni Associates Inc 1 Systems Dr	Appleton	WI	54914	**800-571-6677**	920-735-6900
Operational Technologies Corp 4100 NW Loop 410 Ste 230	San Antonio	TX	78229	**855-276-6136**	210-731-0000

Company / Address	City	State	Zip	Toll-Free	Phone
Orchard Hiltz & McCliment Inc (OHM) 34000 Plymouth Rd	Livonia	MI	48150	**888-522-6711**	734-522-6711
Parkhill Smith & Cooper Inc 4222 85th St	Lubbock	TX	79423	**800-400-6646**	806-473-2200
Passero Associates 242 W Main St Ste 100	Rochester	NY	14614	**800-836-0365**	585-325-1000
Patrick Engineering Inc 4970 Varsity Dr	Lisle	IL	60532	**800-799-7050**	630-795-7200
PCA Engineering Inc 57 Cannonball Rd PO Box 196	Pompton Lakes	NJ	07442	**800-666-7221**	973-616-4501
Pearson Engineering Associates Inc 8825 N 23rd Ave Ste 11	Phoenix	AZ	85021	**866-747-9754**	602-264-0807
Perteet Inc 2707 Colby Ave Ste 900 Ste900	Everett	WA	98201	**800-615-9900**	425-252-7700
Picco Engineering 350 Caldari Rd	Concord	ON	L4K4J4	**888-772-0773**	905-760-9688
Polyengineering Inc 1935 Headland Ave	Dothan	AL	36303	**888-793-4700**	334-793-4700
Porter Consulting Engineers PC 552 State St	Meadville	PA	16335	**800-541-5941**	814-337-4447
Power Engineering Corp PO Box 766	Wilkes-Barre	PA	18703	**800-626-0903**	570-823-8822
PPM Consultants Inc 2508 Ticheli Rd	Monroe	LA	71202	**800-761-8675**	318-323-7270
Professional Service Industries Inc (PSI) 1901 S Meyers Rd Ste 400	Oakbrook Terrace	IL	60181	**800-548-7901**	630-691-1490
Propak Systems Ltd 440 East Lk Rd NE	Airdrie	AB	T4A2J8	**800-408-4434**	403-912-7000
Quality Solutions Inc 128 N First St	Colwich	KS	67030	**888-328-2454**	316-721-3656
Quest Convergence Systems Inc 43 Metcalf Dr	Belleville	IL	62223	**877-933-8776**	618-398-3311
R-S-H Engineering Inc 909 N 18th St Ste 200	Monroe	LA	71201	**888-340-4884**	318-323-4009
RCM Technologies Inc 2500 McClellan Ave Ste 350 *NASDAQ: RCMT*	Pennsauken	NJ	08109	**800-322-2885**	856-356-4500
Ready Technologies Inc 101 Capitol Way N Ste 301	Olympia	WA	98501	**877-892-9104**	360-413-9800
Reliability Center 501 Westover Ave	Hopewell	VA	23860	**800-457-0645**	804-458-0645
Rettew Assoc Inc 3020 Columbia Ave	Lancaster	PA	17603	**800-738-8395**	717-394-3721
Reynolds Smith & Hills Inc 10748 Deerwood Pk Blvd	Jacksonville	FL	32256	**800-741-2014**	904-256-2500
RMF Engineering Inc 5520 Research Pk Dr Ste 300	Baltimore	MD	21228	**800-938-5760**	410-576-0505
Sabre Industries Inc 8653 E Hwy 67	Alvarado	TX	76009	**866-254-3707**	817-852-1700
Schneider Corp 8901 Otis Ave	Indianapolis	IN	46216	**866-973-7100**	317-826-7100
Schofield Brothers of New England Inc 1071 Worcester Rd	Framingham	MA	01701	**800-696-2874**	508-879-0030
SCS Engineers 3900 Kilroy Airport Way Ste 100	Long Beach	CA	90806	**800-326-9544**	562-426-9544
Sebesta Blomberg & Assoc Inc 1450 Energy Park Dr Ste 300	St Paul	MN	55108	**877-706-6858**	651-634-0775
Senga Engineering 1525 E Warner Ave	Santa Ana	CA	92705	**877-878-8159**	714-549-8011
Shive-Hattery Inc (SH) 316 Second St SE Ste 500 PO Box 1599	Cedar Rapids	IA	52406	**800-798-0227**	319-362-0313
Short-Elliott-Hendrickson Inc 3535 Vadnais Ctr Dr	Saint Paul	MN	55110	**800-325-2055**	651-490-2000
Simmons Engineering Corp 400 Regency Dr	Glendale Heights	IL	60139	**800-252-3381**	630-912-2880
Simon & Assoc Inc 3200 Commerce St	Blacksburg	VA	24060	**800-763-4234**	540-951-4234
Simpson Gumpertz & Heger Inc 41 Seyon St Bldg 1 Ste 500	Waltham	MA	02453	**800-729-7429**	781-907-9000
Skelton, Brumwell & Associates Inc 93 Bell Farm Rd Ste 107	Barrie	ON	L4M5G1	**877-726-1141**	705-726-1141
Snowline Engineering 4261 Business Dr	Cameron Park	CA	95682	**800-361-6083**	530-677-2675
Snyder & Assoc Inc PO Box 1159 *General	Ankeny	IA	50023	**888-964-2020***	515-964-2020
Sonalysts Inc 215 Waterford Pkwy N	Waterford	CT	06385	**800-526-8091**	860-442-4355
Spec Ops Inc 319 Business Ln	Ashland	VA	23005	**800-774-3854**	804-752-4790
SPI/Mobile Pulley Works Inc 905 S Ann St	Mobile	AL	36605	**866-334-6325**	251-653-0606
Sponseller Group Inc 1600 Timber Wolf Dr	Holland	OH	43528	**800-776-1625**	419-861-3000
Sproule Associates Ltd 900 N Tower Sun Life Plz 140 Fourth Ave SW	Calgary	AB	T2P3N3	**877-777-6135**	403-294-5500
Stanley Consultants Inc 225 Iowa Ave	Muscatine	IA	52761	**800-553-9694**	563-264-6600
Stantec Inc 400 E Vine St Ste 300 *NYSE: STN*	Lexington	KY	40507	**866-782-6832**	859-233-2100
Steven Schaefer Associates Inc 10411 Medallion Dr	Cincinnati	OH	45241	**800-542-3302**	513-542-3300
Stratasys Inc 7665 Commerce Way *NASDAQ: SSYS*	Eden Prairie	MN	55344	**800-937-3010**	952-937-3000
Sun Engineering Services Inc 5405 Garden Grove Blvd	Westminster	CA	92683	**888-604-5888**	714-379-2300
Sunland Group Inc 1033 La Posada Dr Ste 370	Austin	TX	78752	**866-732-8500**	512-494-0208
Syska & Hennessy Group 11 W 42nd St	New York	NY	10036	**800-328-1600**	212-921-2300
Taber Consultants 3911 W Capitol Ave	West Sacramento	CA	95691	**888-423-0573**	916-371-1690
Taylor & Syfan Consulting Engineers Inc 684 Clarion Ct	San Luis Obispo	CA	93401	**800-579-3881**	805-547-2000
Tectonic Engineering & Surveying Consultants PC 70 Pleasant Hill Rd	Mountainville	NY	10953	**800-829-6531**	845-534-5959
Teledyne Brown Engineering Inc 300 Sparkman Dr	Huntsville	AL	35807	**800-933-2091**	256-726-1000
Terracon 18001 W 106th St	Olathe	KS	66061	**800-593-7777**	913-599-6886
TransCore Holdings Inc 8158 Adams Dr	Hummelstown	PA	17036	**800-923-4824**	717-561-2400
Trayer Engineering Corp 898 Pennsylvania Ave	San Francisco	CA	94107	**800-377-1774**	415-285-7770
TriLeaf Inc 10845 Olive Blvd Ste 310	Saint Louis	MO	63141	**800-652-5552**	314-997-6111
Truevance Management Inc 7666 Blanding Blvd	Jacksonville	FL	32244	**800-285-2028**	904-777-9052
Ulteig Engineers Inc 3350 38th Ave S	Fargo	ND	58104	**888-858-3441**	701-280-8500
Unified Industries Inc 6551 Loisdale Ct Ste 400	Springfield	VA	22150	**800-666-1642**	703-922-9800
United States Steel Corp 600 Grant St *NYSE: X*	Pittsburgh	PA	15219	**866-433-4801**	412-433-1121
UniversalPegasus International Inc 4848 Loop Central Dr *General	Houston	TX	77081	**800-966-1811***	713-977-7770
Valcom Consulting Group Inc 85 Albert St	Ottawa	ON	K1P6A4	**866-561-5580**	613-594-5200
Vanadium Group Corp 134 Three Degree Rd	Pittsburgh	PA	15237	**800-685-0354**	412-367-6060
Vanteon Corp 250 Cross Keys Office Pk Bldg 250	Fairport	NY	14450	**888-506-5677**	585-419-9555
Vectech Pharmaceutical Consultants Inc 12501 E Grand River Ave	Brighton	MI	48116	**800-966-8832**	248-478-5820
Veenstra & Kimm Inc 3000 Westown Pkwy	West Des Moines	IA	50266	**800-241-8000**	515-225-8000
Versar Inc 6850 Versar Ctr *NYSE: VSR* ■ *Cust Svc	Springfield	VA	22151	**800-283-7727***	703-750-3000
VSE Corp 2550 Huntington Ave *NASDAQ: VSEC*	Alexandria	VA	22303	**800-455-4873**	703-960-4600
Wade-Trim Group Inc 500 Griswold Ave Ste 2500	Detroit	MI	48226	**800-482-2864**	313-961-3650
Wallace Roberts & Todd LLC 1700 Market St 28th Fl	Philadelphia	PA	19103	**800-978-4450**	215-732-5215
Walter P Moore 1301 Mckinney St Ste 1100	Houston	TX	77010	**800-364-7300**	713-630-7300
Weston & Sampson Inc 5 Centennial Dr	Peabody	MA	01960	**800-726-7766**	978-532-1900
Willbros Downstream LLC 4400 Post Oak Pkwy Ste 1000	Houston	TX	77027	**888-310-7712**	918-556-3600
Willdan 2401 E Katella Ave Ste 300	Anaheim	CA	92806	**800-424-9144**	714-940-6300
Woodard & Curran 41 Hutchins Dr	Portland	ME	04102	**800-426-4262**	207-774-2112
Zephyr Environmental Corp 2600 Via Fortuna Ste 450	Austin	TX	78746	**800-452-5558**	512-329-5544
Zeton Inc 740 Oval Ct	Burlington	ON	L7L6A9	**877-299-3866**	905-632-3123

264 ENGINES & TURBINES

SEE ALSO Motors (Electric) & Generators ; Aircraft Engines & Engine Parts ; Automotive Parts & Supplies - Mfr

Company / Address	City	State	Zip	Toll-Free	Phone
Arrow Engine Co 2301 E Independence St	Tulsa	OK	74110	**800-331-3662**	918-583-5711
Briggs & Stratton Corp 12301 W Wirth St *NYSE: BGG*	Milwaukee	WI	53222	**800-444-7774**	414-259-5333
Brunswick Corp Mercury Marine Div W 6250 Pioneer Rd	Fond du Lac	WI	54935	**866-408-6372**	920-929-5040
Capstone Turbine Corp 21211 Nordhoff St *NASDAQ: CPST*	Chatsworth	CA	91311	**866-422-7786**	818-734-5300
Chromium Corp 14911 Quorum Dr Ste 600	Dallas	TX	75254	**888-346-4747**	216-271-4910
Clayton Industries 17477 Hurley St	City of Industry	CA	91744	**800-423-4585**	626-435-1200
Cummins Inc 500 Jackson St PO Box 3005 *NYSE: CMI*	Columbus	IN	47201	**800-343-7357**	812-377-5000
Delaware Mfg Industries Corp 3776 Commerce Ct	Wheatfield	NY	14120	**800-248-3642**	716-743-4360
Electro Steam Generator Corp 50 Indel Ave PO Box 438	Rancocas	NJ	08073	**866-617-0764**	609-288-9071
EnPro Industries Inc Fairbanks Morse Engine 701 White Ave	Beloit	WI	53511	**800-356-6955**	
Hatch & Kirk Inc 5111 Leary Ave NW	Seattle	WA	98107	**800-426-2818**	206-783-2766
Hercules Engine Components Co 2770 S Erie St	Massillon	OH	44646	**800-345-0662**	330-830-2498
JASPER Engines & Transmissions 815 Wernsing Rd PO Box 650	Jasper	IN	47547	**800-827-7455**	812-482-1041
John Deere Power Systems 3801 W Ridgeway Ave PO Box 5100	Waterloo	IA	50704	**800-533-6446**	
KMS Ventures Inc 1301 W 25th St Ste 300	Austin	TX	78705	**844-282-7433**	512-474-6312
Kohler Engines 444 Highland Dr	Kohler	WI	53044	**800-544-2444**	920-457-4441
Northern Lights Inc 4420 14th Ave NW	Seattle	WA	98107	**800-762-0165**	206-789-3880
NREC Power Systems 5222 Hwy 311	Houma	LA	70360	**800-851-6732**	985-872-5480
Pratt & Whitney Canada Inc 1000 Marie-Victorin Blvd	Longueuil	QC	J4G1A1	**800-268-8000**	450-677-9411
Springfield ReManufacturing Corp 650 N Broadview Pl	Springfield	MO	65802	**800-772-7733**	417-862-3501
Volvo Penta of the Americas Inc 1300 Volvo Penta Dr	Chesapeake	VA	23320	**800-522-1959**	757-436-2800

Company	Address	City	State	ZIP	Toll-Free	Phone
Wartsila North America Inc	16330 Air Ctr Blvd	Houston	TX	77032	**877-927-8745**	281-233-6200
Westerbeke Corp	150 John Hancock Rd Miles Standish Industrial Pk	Taunton	MA	02780	**800-582-7846**	508-823-7677
Western Diesel Services Inc	1100 Research Blvd	Saint Louis	MO	63132	**855-257-6937**	314-868-8620

265 ENVELOPES

Company	Address	City	State	ZIP	Toll-Free	Phone
ADM Corp	100 Lincoln Blvd	Middlesex	NJ	08846	**800-327-0718**	732-469-0900
Alvah Bushnell Co	519 E Chelten Ave	Philadelphia	PA	19144	**800-255-7434**	215-842-9520
AmericanChurch Inc	525 McClurg Rd PO Box 3120	Youngstown	OH	44513	**800-446-3035**	330-758-4545
B & W Press Inc	401 E Main St	Georgetown	MA	01833	**877-246-3467**	978-352-6100
Bowers Envelope Co	5331 N Tacoma Ave	Indianapolis	IN	46220	**800-333-4321**	317-253-4321
Curtis 1000 Inc	1725 Breckinridge Pkwy Ste 500	Duluth	GA	30096	**877-287-8715**	678-380-9095
Heinrich Envelope Corp	925 Zane Ave N	Minneapolis	MN	55422	**800-346-7957**	763-544-3571
Love Envelopes Inc	10733 E Ute St	Tulsa	OK	74116	**800-532-9747**	918-836-3535
Mackay Envelope Corp	2100 Elm St SE	Minneapolis	MN	55414	**800-622-5299**	
National Church Supply Co, The	PO Box 269	Chester	WV	26034	**800-627-9900**	304-387-5200
Papercone Corp	3200 Fern Vly Rd	Louisville	KY	40213	**800-626-5308**	502-961-9493
Poly-Pak Industries Inc	125 Spagnoli Rd	Melville	NY	11747	**800-969-1993**	
Response Envelope Inc	1340 S Baker Ave	Ontario	CA	91761	**800-750-0046**	909-923-5855
Tension Envelope Corp	819 E 19th St	Kansas City	MO	64108	**800-388-5122**	
Top Flight Inc	1300 Central Ave	Chattanooga	TN	37408	**800-777-3740**	423-266-8171
Western States Envelope & Label Co	4480 N 132nd St	Butler	WI	53007	**800-558-0514**	262-781-5540
Worcester Envelope Co	22 Millbury St	Auburn	MA	01501	**800-343-1398**	508-832-5394

266 EQUIPMENT RENTAL & LEASING

SEE ALSO Credit & Financing - Consumer ; Credit & Financing - Commercial ; Fleet Leasing & Management

266-1 Computer Equipment Leasing

Company	Address	City	State	ZIP	Toll-Free	Phone
Data Sales Company Inc	3450 W Burnsville Pkwy	Burnsville	MN	55337	**800-328-2730**	952-890-8838
Electro Rent Corp	6060 Sepulveda Blvd *NASDAQ: ELRC* ■ *Sales	Van Nuys	CA	91411	**800-688-1111***	818-787-2100
First Equipment Co	PO Box 2129	Addison	TX	75001	**888-780-8631**	972-380-2300
Newport Leasing Inc	4750 Von Karman Ave *Cust Svc	Newport Beach	CA	92660	**800-274-0042***	949-476-8476
Rent-A-PC Inc	265 Oser Ave	Hauppauge	NY	11788	**800-800-8686**	631-273-8888
Summit Funding Group Inc	4680 Parkway Dr Ste 300	Mason	OH	45040	**866-489-1222**	513-489-1222

266-2 Home & Office Equipment Rental (General)

Company	Address	City	State	ZIP	Toll-Free	Phone
Bestway Inc	12400 Coit Rd Ste 950	Dallas	TX	75251	**800-316-4567**	214-630-6655
Brook Furniture Rental Inc	100 N Field Dr Ste 220	Lake Forest	IL	60045	**877-285-7368**	847-810-4000
Buddy's Home Furnishings	6608 E Adamo Dr	Tampa	FL	33619	**866-779-5085**	
Classic Party Rentals	901 W. Hillcrest Blvd	Inglewood	CA	90301	**800-678-3854**	310-535-3660
GFC Leasing Co	2675 Research Pk Dr	Madison	WI	53711	**800-333-5905**	800-677-7877
Independent Rental Inc	2020 S Cushman St	Fairbanks	AK	99701	**888-456-6595**	
LMG Inc	PO Box 770429	Orlando	FL	32877	**888-226-3100**	407-850-0505
Marlin Business Services Inc	300 Fellowship Rd *NASDAQ: MRLN*	Mount Laurel	NJ	08054	**888-479-9111**	
Projection Presentation Technology	5803 Rolling Rd	Springfield	VA	22152	**800-377-7650**	703-912-1334
Rent-A-Center Inc	5501 Headquarters Dr *NASDAQ: RCII*	Plano	TX	75024	**800-422-8186**	
Rug Doctor LP	4701 Old Shepard Pl	Plano	TX	75093	**800-784-3628**	972-673-1400
Somerset Capital Group Ltd	612 Wheelers Farms Rd	Milford	CT	06461	**877-282-9922**	203-701-5100

266-3 Industrial & Heavy Equipment Rental

Company	Address	City	State	ZIP	Toll-Free	Phone
AH Harris & Son Inc	367 Alumni Rd	Newington	CT	06111	**800-382-6555**	860-665-9494
Ahern Rentals Inc	4241 Arville St	Las Vegas	NV	89103	**800-589-6797**	702-362-0623
Allied Steel Construction Co Inc	2211 NW First Terr	Oklahoma City	OK	73107	**800-522-4658**	405-232-7531
Buck & Knobby Equipment Co	6220 Sterns Rd	Ottawa Lake	MI	49267	**855-213-2825**	734-856-2811
Cloverdale Equipment Co	13133 Cloverdale St	Oak Park	MI	48237	**888-388-9182**	248-399-6600
Equipment Technology LLC	341 NW 122nd St	Oklahoma City	OK	73114	**888-748-3841**	
Ervin Leasing Co	3893 Research Pk Dr	Ann Arbor	MI	48108	**800-748-0015**	
Essex Crane Rental Corp	1110 Lake Cook Rd Ste 220	Buffalo Grove	IL	60089	**888-991-4100**	847-215-6500
H & E Equipment Services Inc	11100 Mead Rd *NASDAQ: HEES*	Baton Rouge	LA	70809	**866-467-3682**	225-298-5200
Hawthorne Machinery Co	16945 Camino San Bernardo	San Diego	CA	92127	**800-437-4228**	858-674-7000
HB Rentals LC	5813 Hwy 90 E	Broussard	LA	70518	**800-262-6790**	337-839-1641
Hertz Equipment Rental Corp	225 Brae Blvd	Park Ridge	NJ	07656	**800-654-3131**	201-307-2000
Independent Rental Inc	2020 S Cushman St	Fairbanks	AK	99701	**888-456-6595**	
Klochko Equipment Rental Company Inc	2782 Corbin Ave	Melvindale	MI	48122	**800-783-7368**	313-386-7220
Leppo Inc	PO Box 154	Tallmadge	OH	44278	**800-453-7762**	330-633-3999
Marco Crane & Rigging Co	221 S 35th Ave	Phoenix	AZ	85009	**800-668-2671**	602-272-2671
Maxim Crane Works	1225 Washington Pk	Bridgeville	PA	15017	**877-629-5438**	412-504-0200
Medico Industries Inc	1500 Hwy 315	Wilkes-Barre	PA	18711	**800-633-0027**	570-825-7711
National Construction Rentals Inc	15319 Chatsworth St	Mission Hills	CA	91345	**800-352-5675**	818-221-6000
Norcal Rental Group LLC	318 Stealth Ct	Livermore	CA	94551	**800-649-6629**	925-961-0130
Quantum Analytics	3400 East Third Ave	Foster City	CA	94404	**800-992-4199**	650-312-0900
Raymond Handling Concepts Corp	41400 Boyce Rd	Fremont	CA	94538	**800-675-2500**	510-745-7500
Rush Enterprises Inc	555 IH 35 S Ste 500 *NASDAQ: RUSHA*	New Braunfels	TX	78130	**800-973-7874**	830-626-5200
Safway Services Inc	N 19 W 24200 Riverwood Dr	Waukesha	WI	53188	**800-558-4772**	262-523-6500
Skyworks LLC	100 Thielman Dr	Buffalo	NY	14206	**877-601-5438**	716-822-5438
Star Rentals Inc	1919 Fourth Ave S	Seattle	WA	98134	**800-825-7880**	206-622-7880
Stephenson Equipment Inc (SEI)	7201 Paxton St	Harrisburg	PA	17111	**800-325-6455**	717-564-3434
Sunbelt Rentals Inc	2341 Deerfield Dr *General	Fort Mill	SC	29715	**800-667-9328***	704-348-2676
Tetra Corporate Services LLC	6995 Union Park Ctr Ste 360	Salt Lake City	UT	84047	**800-417-0548**	801-566-2600
Traffic Control Service Inc	2435 Lemon Ave	Signal Hill	CA	90755	**800-763-3999**	
United Rentals	3266 E Washington St	Phoenix	AZ	85233	**844-873-4948**	602-267-3898
United Rentals Inc	224 Selleck St *NYSE: URI*	Stamford	CT	06902	**800-877-3687**	203-622-3131
Western Oilfields Supply Co	3404 State Rd	Bakersfield	CA	93308	**800-742-7246**	661-399-9124

266-4 Medical Equipment Rental

Company	Address	City	State	ZIP	Toll-Free	Phone
American Shared Hospital Services	4 Embarcadero Ctr Ste 3700 *NYSE: AMS*	San Francisco	CA	94111	**800-735-0641**	415-788-5300
Dynasplint Systems Inc	770 Ritchie Hwy Ste W21	Severna Park	MD	21146	**800-638-6771**	410-544-9530
First Lease Inc	1 Walnut Grove Dr Ste 300	Horsham	PA	19044	**866-493-4778**	
Freedom Medical Inc	219 Welsh Pool Rd	Exton	PA	19341	**800-784-8849**	610-903-0200
Universal Hospital Services Inc	7700 France Ave S Ste 275	Minneapolis	MN	55435	**800-847-7368**	952-893-3200

266-5 Transport Equipment Rental

Company	Address	City	State	ZIP	Toll-Free	Phone
Flexi-Van Leasing Inc	251 Monroe Ave	Kenilworth	NJ	07033	**866-965-9288**	908-276-8000
GE Rail Car Services	161 N Clark St 7th Fl	Chicago	IL	60601	**800-626-2000**	312-853-5000
Greenbrier Co	1 Centerpointe Dr Ste 200 *NYSE: GBX*	Lake Oswego	OR	97035	**800-343-7188**	503-684-7000
Procor Ltd	2001 Speers Rd	Oakville	ON	L6L2X9	**888-977-6267**	905-827-4111
Railserve Inc	1691 Phoenix Blvd Ste 110	Atlanta	GA	30349	**800-345-7245**	770-996-6838
TTX Co	101 N Wacker Dr	Chicago	IL	60606	**800-889-4357**	312-853-3223

267 ETHICS COMMISSIONS

Company	Address	City	State	ZIP	Toll-Free	Phone
Federal Election Commission	999 E St NW	Washington	DC	20463	**800-424-9530**	202-694-1100

				Toll-Free	Phone
Arakansas Ethics Commission PO Box 1917	Little Rock	AR	72203	**800-422-7773**	501-324-9600
California Fair Political Practices Commission 428 J St Ste 620	Sacramento	CA	95814	**866-275-3772**	916-322-5660
Georgia Transparency & Campaign Finance Commission 200 Piedmont Ave SE Ste 1402	Atlanta	GA	30334	**866-589-7327**	404-463-1980
Louisiana Ethics Board 617 N Third St LaSalle Bldg Ste 10-36	Baton Rouge	LA	70802	**800-842-6630**	225-219-5600
Maryland Ethics Commission 45 Calvert St 3rd Fl	Annapolis	MD	21401	**877-669-6085**	410-260-7770
Minnesota Campaign Finance & Public Disclosure Board 658 Cedar St Ste 190	Saint Paul	MN	55155	**800-657-3889**	651-296-5148
New Mexico Ethics Administration 325 Don Gaspar St Ste 300	Santa Fe	NM	87501	**800-477-3632**	505-827-3600
Pennsylvania State Ethics Commission 309 Finance Bldg PO Box 11470	Harrisburg	PA	17108	**800-932-0936**	717-783-1610
West Virginia Ethics Commission 210 Brooks St Ste 300	Charleston	WV	25301	**866-558-0664**	304-558-0664

268 EXECUTIVE RECRUITING FIRMS

				Toll-Free	Phone
Boyden World Corp 50 Broadway	Hawthorne	NY	10532	**877-226-9336**	914-747-0093
Christian & Timbers 25825 Science Pk Dr	Cleveland	OH	44122	**800-299-9630**	216-464-8710
Daniel & Yeager (D&Y) 6767 Old Madison Pk Ste 690	Huntsville	AL	35806	**800-955-1919**	
Diversified Search Cos 2005 Market St 33rd Fl	Philadelphia	PA	19103	**800-423-3932**	215-732-6666
Korn/Ferry International 1900 Ave of the Stars Ste 2600 *NYSE: KFY*	Los Angeles	CA	90067	**877-345-3610**	310-552-1834
Management Recruiters International Worldwide Inc 1717 Arch St 36th Fl	Philadelphia	PA	19103	**800-875-4000**	
Russell Reynolds Assoc Inc 200 Pk Ave 23rd Fl	New York	NY	10166	**800-259-0470**	212-351-2000
Spencer Reed Group Inc 6900 College Blvd Ste 1	Overland Park	KS	66211	**800-477-5035**	913-663-4400
Tyler & Co 400 Northridge Rd Ste 1250	Atlanta	GA	30350	**800-989-6789**	770-396-3939
Witt/Kieffer Ford Hadelman & Lloyd 2015 Spring Rd Ste 510	Oak Brook	IL	60523	**888-281-1370**	630-990-1370

269 EXERCISE & FITNESS EQUIPMENT

SEE ALSO Sporting Goods

				Toll-Free	Phone
Body-Solid Inc 1900 Des Plaines Ave	Forest Park	IL	60130	**800-833-1227**	708-427-3500
Cybex International Inc 10 Trotter Dr *NASDAQ: CYBI*	Medway	MA	02053	**888-462-9239**	508-533-4300
Heartline Fitness Products Inc 8041 Cessna Ave Ste 200	Gaithersburg	MD	20879	**800-262-3348**	301-921-0661
Hoggan Health Industries Inc 8020 South 1300 West	West Jordan	UT	84088	**800-678-7888**	801-572-6500
Hoist Fitness Systems Inc 9990 Empire St Ste 130	San Diego	CA	92126	**800-548-5438**	858-578-7676
HYDRO-FIT Inc 160 Madison St *Cust Svc	Eugene	OR	97402	**800-346-7295***	541-484-4361
ICON Health & Fitness Inc 1500 South 1000 West	Logan	UT	84321	**800-999-3756**	435-750-5000
IronMaster LLC 14562 167th Ave SE	Monroe	WA	98272	**800-533-3339**	360-217-7780
Nautilus Inc 16400 SE Nautilus Dr *NYSE: NLS*	Vancouver	WA	98684	**800-628-8458**	360-694-7722
New York Barbells 160 Home St	Elmira	NY	14904	**800-446-1833**	607-733-8038
Precor Inc 20031 142nd Ave NE	Woodinville	WA	98072	**800-786-8404**	425-486-9292
Pro Star Sports Inc 1133 Winchester Ave	Kansas City	MO	64126	**800-821-8482**	816-241-9737
Soloflex Inc 22590 NW Badertscher Rd	Hillsboro	OR	97124	**800-547-8802**	
Spirit Manufacturing Inc 3000 Nestle Rd	Jonesboro	AR	72401	**800-258-4555**	870-935-1107
Star Trac by Unisen Inc 14410 Myford Rd	Irvine	CA	92606	**800-228-6635**	714-669-1660
True Fitness Technology Inc 865 Hoff Rd	O'Fallon	MO	63366	**800-426-6570**	636-272-7100
Vectra Fitness Inc 7901 S 190th St	Kent	WA	98032	**800-283-2872**	425-291-9550
Woodway USA W229 N591 Foster Ct	Waukesha	WI	53186	**800-966-3929**	262-548-6235
York Barbell Co Inc 3300 BoaRd Rd *Cust Svc	York	PA	17406	**800-358-9675***	717-767-6481

270 EXPLOSIVES

				Toll-Free	Phone
Alliant Powder 2299 Snake River Ave	Lewiston	ID	83501	**800-276-9337**	800-379-1732
Austin Powder Co 25800 Science Pk Dr Ste 300	Cleveland	OH	44122	**800-321-0752**	216-464-2400
Buckley Powder Co 42 Inverness Dr E	Englewood	CO	80112	**800-333-2266**	303-790-7007
Dyno Nobel Inc 2795 E Cottonwood Pkwy Ste 500	Salt Lake City	UT	84121	**800-473-2675**	801-364-4800

271 EYE BANKS

SEE ALSO Transplant Centers - Blood Stem Cell ; Organ & Tissue Banks

Eye banks listed here are members of the Eye Bank Association of America (EBAA), an accrediting body for eye banks. The EBAA medical standards for member eye banks are endorsed by the American Academy of Ophthalmology.

				Toll-Free	Phone
Alabama Eye Bank 500 Robert Jemison Rd	Birmingham	AL	35209	**800-423-7811**	
Alcon Laboratories Inc 6201 S Fwy	Fort Worth	TX	76134	**800-862-5266**	817-293-0450
Center for Organ Recovery & Education (CORE) 204 Sigma Dr RIDC Pk	Pittsburgh	PA	15238	**800-366-6777**	412-963-3550
Dakota Lions Sight & Health 4501 W 61st St Ste 201	Sioux Falls	SD	57107	**800-372-3751**	701-250-9390
Donor Network of Arizona 201 W Coolidge St	Phoenix	AZ	85013	**800-447-9477**	602-222-2200
Donor Network West 12667 Alcosta Blvd Ste 600	Oakland	CA	94607	**888-570-9400**	925-480-3101
Eye Bank Assn of America (EBAA) 1015 18th St NW Ste 1010	Washington	DC	20036	**888-491-8833**	202-775-4999
Eye Bank for Sight Restoration Inc 120 Wall St 3rd Fl	New York	NY	10005	**866-287-3937**	212-742-9000
Eye Bank of British Columbia 2550 Willow St Eye Care Ctr 3rd Fl	Vancouver	BC	V5Z3N9	**800-667-2060**	604-875-4567
Heartland Lions Eye Bank 10100 N Ambassador Dr Ste 200	Kansas City	MO	64153	**800-756-4824**	816-454-5454
Idaho Lions Eye Bank 1090 N Cole Rd	Boise	ID	83704	**800-546-6889**	208-338-5466
International Cornea Project 9246 Lightwave Ave Ste 120	San Diego	CA	92123	**800-393-2265**	858-694-0400
International Sight Restoration Inc 3808 Gunn Hwy Ste B	Tampa	FL	33618	**877-477-3210**	813-264-6003
LABS Inc 6933 S Revere Pkwy	Centennial	CO	80112	**866-393-2244**	720-528-4750
LifePoint Inc 3950 Faber Pl Dr	Charleston	SC	29405	**800-462-0755**	843-763-7755
LifeShare of the Carolinas 1200 Ridgefield Blvd Ste 150	Asheville	NC	28806	**800-932-4483**	828-665-0107
Lions Eye Bank of Manitoba & Northwest Ontario Inc 691 Wolseley Ave	Winnipeg	MB	R3G1C3	**800-552-6820**	204-788-8507
Lions Eye Bank of Nebraska Inc *University of Nebraska Medical Ctr* 985541 Nebraska Medical Ctr	Omaha	NE	68198	**800-225-7244**	402-559-4039
Lions Eye Bank of Wisconsin 2401 American Ln	Madison	WI	53704	**877-233-2354**	608-233-2354
Lions Medical Eye Bank & Research Ctr of Eastern Virginia Inc 600 Gresham Dr	Norfolk	VA	23507	**800-453-6059**	
Lone Star Lions Eye Bank 102 E Wheeler St PO Box 347	Manor	TX	78653	**800-977-3937**	512-457-0638
Medical Eye Bank of Maryland 815 Pk Ave	Baltimore	MD	21201	**800-756-4824**	410-752-2020
Midwest Eye Banks 4889 Venture Dr	Ann Arbor	MI	48108	**800-247-7250**	734-780-2100
Minnesota Lions Eye Bank 1000 Westgate Dr Ste 260 *Cust Svc	Saint paul	MN	55114	**866-887-4448***	612-625-5159
National Disease Research Interchange (NDRI) 1628 John F Kennedy Blvd 8 Penn Ctr 8th Fl	Philadelphia	PA	19103	**800-222-6374**	215-557-7361
New Mexico Lions Eye Bank 2501 Yale Blvd SE Ste 100	Albuquerque	NM	87106	**888-616-3937**	505-266-3937
North Carolina Eye Bank Inc 3900 Westpoint Blvd Ste F	Winston-Salem	NC	27103	**800-552-9956**	336-765-0932
Northeast Pennsylvania Lions Eye Bank Inc *Lehigh Valley Hospital* 2346 Jacksonville Rd	Bethlehem	PA	18017	**800-637-2393**	610-625-3800
Old Dominion Eye Bank (ODEF) 9200 Arboretum Pkwy Ste 104	Richmond	VA	23236	**800-832-0728**	804-560-7540
Oregon Lions Sight & Hearing Foundation 1010 NW 22nd Ave Ste 144	Portland	OR	97210	**800-635-4667**	503-413-7399
Regional Tissue Bank QEII Health Sciences Centre 5788 University Ave Rm 431 MacKenzie Bldg	Halifax	NS	B3H1V7	**800-314-6515**	902-473-4171
Rochester Eye & Tissue Bank 524 White Spruce Blvd	Rochester	NY	14623	**800-568-4321**	585-272-7890
Rocky Mountain Lions Eye Bank (RMLEB) 1675 Aurora Crt Ste El2049 PO Box 6026	Aurora	CO	80045	**800-444-7479**	720-848-3937
San Diego Eye Bank (SDEB) 9246 Lightwave Ave Ste 120	San Diego	CA	92123	**800-393-2265**	858-694-0400
SightLife 221 Yale Ave N Ste 450	Seattle	WA	98109	**800-847-5786**	206-682-8500
South Dakota Lions Eye Bank 4501 W 61st St N	Sioux Falls	SD	57107	**800-245-7846**	605-373-1008
Upstate New York Transplant Services Inc 110 Broadway	Buffalo	NY	14203	**800-227-4771**	716-853-6667
Western Texas Lions Eye Bank Alliance 2030 Pullman St Ste 4	San Angelo	TX	76902	**866-226-7632**	325-653-8666

272 FABRIC STORES

SEE ALSO Patterns - Sewing

				Toll-Free	Phone
Everfast Inc 203 Gale Ln *Cust Svc	Kennett Square	PA	19348	**800-213-6366***	610-444-9700
Jo-Ann Fabrics & Crafts 5555 Darrow Rd	Hudson	OH	44236	**888-739-4120**	330-656-2600
Jo-Ann Stores Inc (JAS) 5555 Darrow Rd	Hudson	OH	44236	**888-739-4120**	330-656-2600
Mary Maxim Inc 2001 Holland Ave PO Box 5019	Port Huron	MI	48061	**800-962-9504**	810-987-2000

273 FACILITIES MANAGEMENT SERVICES

SEE ALSO Correctional & Detention Management (Privatized)

Company	City	State	Zip	Toll-Free	Phone
Agracel Inc 2201 Willenborg Ave	Effingham	IL	62401	**800-600-8085**	217-342-4443
ARAMARK Uniform & Career Apparel LLC 2860 Rudder Rd	Memphis	TN	38118	**800-272-6275**	
Financial & Realty Services LLC 1110 Bonifant St Ste 301	Silver Spring	MD	20910	**800-650-9714**	301-650-9112
IAP Worldwide Services Inc 7315 N Atlantic Ave	Cape Canaveral	FL	32920	**877-296-8010**	321-784-7100
New York State Bridge Authority PO Box 1010	Highland	NY	12528	**800-333-8655**	845-691-7245
OMNIPLEX World Services Corp 14151 Pk Meadow Dr Ste 300	Chantilly	VA	20151	**800-356-3406**	703-652-3100
Philotechnics Ltd 201 Renovare Blvd	Oak Ridge	TN	37830	**888-723-9278**	865-483-1551
Phoenix Park 'n Swap 3801 E Washington St	Phoenix	AZ	85034	**800-772-0852**	602-273-1250
United Space Alliance (USA) 600 Gemini Ave	Houston	TX	77058	**800-367-5690**	281-212-6200
Viox Services Inc 15 W Voorhees St	Cincinnati	OH	45215	**888-846-9462**	513-948-8469
Xanterra Parks & Resorts 6312 S Fiddlers Green Cir Ste 600-N	Greenwood Village	CO	80111	**800-236-7916**	303-600-3400

274 FACTORS

Factors are companies that buy accounts receivable (invoices) from other businesses at a discount.

Company	City	State	Zip	Toll-Free	Phone
Action Capital Corp 230 Peachtree St Ste 910	Atlanta	GA	30343	**800-525-7767**	404-524-3181
Advantage Funding Corp 1000 Parkwood Cir SE	Atlanta	GA	30339	**800-241-2274**	770-955-2274
AmeriFactors 215 Celebration Pl Ste 340	Celebration	FL	34747	**800-884-3863**	407-566-1150
Asta Funding Inc 210 Sylvan Ave *NASDAQ: ASFI*	Englewood Cliffs	NJ	07632	**866-389-7627**	201-567-5648
Bibby Financial Services 600 TownPark Ln Ste 450	Kennesaw	GA	30144	**877-882-4229**	
Crestmark Bank 5480 Corporate Dr Ste 350	Troy	MI	48098	**888-999-8050**	
Diversified Funding Services Inc 125 Habersham Dr Ste C	Fayetteville	GA	30214	**888-603-0055**	770-603-0055
Goodman Factors 3010 LBJ Fwy Ste 140	Dallas	TX	75234	**877-446-6362**	972-241-3297
Hamilton Group 100 Elwood Davis Rd	North Syracuse	NY	13212	**800-351-3066**	315-413-0086
LSQ Funding Group LC 2600 Lucien Way Ste 100	Maitland	FL	32751	**800-474-7606**	
Magnolia Financial Inc 187 W Broad St	Spartanburg	SC	29306	**866-573-0611**	864-573-9900
Mazon Assoc Inc 800 W Airport Fwy Ste 900	Irving	TX	75062	**800-442-2740**	972-554-6967
Porter Capital Corp 2112 First Ave N	Birmingham	AL	35203	**800-737-7344**	205-322-5442
Quantum Corporate Funding Ltd 1140 Ave of the Americas 16th Fl	New York	NY	10036	**800-352-2535**	212-768-1200
Riviera Finance 220 Ave I	Redondo Beach	CA	90277	**800-872-7484**	
RTS Financial Service 9300 Metcalf Ste 301	Overland Park	KS	66212	**877-242-4390**	
Seven Oaks Capital Assoc LLC 7854 Anselmo Ln PO Box 82360	Baton Rouge	LA	70810	**800-511-4588**	225-757-1919
TCE Capital Corp 505 Consumers Rd Ste 707	Toronto	ON	M2J4V8	**800-465-0400**	416-497-7400

275 FARM MACHINERY & EQUIPMENT - MFR

SEE ALSO Lawn & Garden Equipment

Company	City	State	Zip	Toll-Free	Phone
ADM Alliance Nutrition Inc 1000 N 30th St	Quincy	IL	62301	**800-292-3333**	217-222-7100
AGCO Corp (AGCO) 4205 River Green Pkwy *NYSE: AGCO*	Duluth	GA	30096	**877-525-4384**	770-813-9200
Alamo Group Inc 1627 E Walnut *NYSE: ALG* ■ *Cust Svc	Seguin	TX	78155	**800-788-6066***	830-379-1480
All-American Co-op PO Box 125	Stewartville	MN	55976	**888-354-4058**	507-533-4222
Allied Systems Co 21433 SW Oregon St	Sherwood	OR	97140	**800-285-7000**	503-625-2560
Amarillo Wind Machine Co 20513 Ave 256	Exeter	CA	93221	**800-311-4498**	559-592-4256
Arts-Way Mfg Co Inc 5556 Hwy 9 PO Box 288 *NASDAQ: ARTW*	Armstrong	IA	50514	**800-535-4517**	712-864-3131
Atom-Jet Industries Ltd 2110 Park Ave	Brandon	MB	R7B0R9	**800-573-5048**	204-728-8590
B & H Manufacturing Inc 141 County Rd 34 E	Jackson	MN	56143	**800-240-3288**	507-847-2802
Berg Equipment Co 2700 W Veterans Pkwy	Marshfield	WI	54449	**800-494-1738**	715-384-2151
Bowie Industries Inc 1004 E Wise St	Bowie	TX	76230	**800-433-0934**	940-872-1106
Brillion Iron Works Inc 200 Pk Ave	Brillion	WI	54110	**855-320-0373**	920-756-2121
Brown Mfg Corp 6001 E Hwy 27	Ozark	AL	36360	**800-633-8909**	
Broyhill Co 1 N Market Sq	Dakota City	NE	68731	**800-228-1003**	402-987-3412
Bucklin Tractor & Implement Co 115 W Railroad PO Box 127	Bucklin	KS	67834	**800-334-4823**	620-826-3271
Buhler Versatile Inc 1260 Clarence Ave	Winnipeg	MB	R3T1T2	**888-524-1003**	204-661-8711
Cal-Coast Dairy Systems Inc 424 S Tegner Rd *Cust Svc	Turlock	CA	95380	**800-732-6826***	209-634-9026
Chick Master Incubator Co 945 Lafayette Rd PO Box 704	Medina	OH	44258	**800-727-8726**	330-722-5591
Conrad-American Inc PO Box 2000 *General	Houghton	IA	52631	**800-553-1791***	
CTB Inc 611 N Higbee St PO Box 2000	Milford	IN	46542	**800-261-8651**	574-658-4191
Custom Products of Litchfield Inc 1715 S Sibley Ave	Litchfield	MN	55355	**800-222-5463**	320-693-3221
Dig Corp 1210 Activity Dr	Vista	CA	92081	**800-322-9146**	760-727-0914
DuraTech Industries International Inc PO Box 1940	Jamestown	ND	58401	**800-243-4601**	701-252-4601
EVH Mfg Company LLC 4895 Red Bluff Rd	Loris	SC	29569	**888-990-2555**	843-756-2555
EZ Trail Inc 1050 E Columbia St PO Box 168	Arthur	IL	61911	**800-677-2802**	217-543-3471
Fabrication JR Tardif Inc 62 Blvd Cartier	Rivi Re-Du-Loup	QC	G5R6B2	**877-962-7273**	418-862-7273
Finn Corp 9281 Le St Dr	Fairfield	OH	45014	**800-543-7166**	513-874-2818
Forsbergs Inc 1210 Pennington Ave PO Box 510 *Cust Svc	Thief River Falls	MN	56701	**800-654-1927***	218-681-1927
Gandy Co 528 Gandrud Rd	Owatonna	MN	55060	**800-443-2476**	507-451-5430
GMP Metal Products Inc 3883 Delor St	Saint Louis	MO	63116	**800-325-9808**	314-481-0300
Hagie Manufacturing Co PO Box 273	Clarion	IA	50525	**800-247-4885**	515-532-2861
Hardi Inc 1500 W 76th St	Davenport	IA	52806	**866-770-7063**	563-386-1730
Hastings Equity Grain Bin Mfg Co 1900 Summit Ave	Hastings	NE	68901	**888-883-2189**	402-462-2189
HCC Inc 1501 First Ave	Mendota	IL	61342	**800-548-6633**	815-539-9371
HD Hudson Manufacturing Co 500 N Michigan Ave	Chicago	IL	60611	**800-977-7293**	312-644-2830
Heartland Equipment Inc 2100 N Falls Blvd	Wynne	AR	72396	**800-530-7617**	
Henderson Manufacturing Inc 1085 S Third St	Manchester	IA	52057	**800-359-4970**	563-927-2828
Herschel-Adams Inc 1301 N 14th St	Indianola	IA	50125	**800-247-2167**	
Hiniker Co 58766 240th St	Mankato	MN	56002	**800-433-5620**	507-625-6621
Hutchinson/Mayrath/TerraTrack Industries 514 W Crawford PO Box 629	Clay Center	KS	67432	**800-523-6993**	785-632-2161
Jamesway Incubator Co Inc 30 High Ridge Ct	Cambridge	ON	N1R7L3	**800-438-8077**	519-624-4646
KBH Corp, The 395 Anderson Blvd	Clarksdale	MS	38614	**800-843-5241**	662-624-5471
Kelley Manufacturing Co 80 Vernon Dr PO Box 1467	Tifton	GA	31793	**800-444-5449**	229-382-9393
Kelly Ryan Equipment Co 900 Kelly Ryan Dr	Blair	NE	68008	**800-640-6967**	402-426-2151
KMW Ltd PO Box 327	Sterling	KS	67579	**800-445-7388**	620-278-3641
Kubota Tractor Corp 3401 Del Amo Blvd	Torrance	CA	90503	**888-458-2682**	310-370-3370
Lindsay Corp 2222 N 111th St *NYSE: LNN*	Omaha	NE	68164	**866-404-5049**	402-829-6800
Loftness Specialized Farm Equipment Inc 650 S Main St PO Box 337	Hector	MN	55342	**800-828-7624**	320-848-6266
Mathews Co 500 Industrial Ave	Crystal Lake	IL	60012	**800-323-7045**	815-459-2210
Mertz Mfg LLC 1701 N Waverly St	Ponca City	OK	74601	**800-654-6433**	580-762-5646
Miller Saint Nazianz Inc 511 E Main St	Saint Nazianz	WI	54232	**800-247-5557**	920-773-2121
Orthman Manufacturing Inc 75765 Rd 435 PO Box B	Lexington	NE	68850	**800-658-3270**	308-324-4654
Osborne Industries Inc 120 N Industrial Ave	Osborne	KS	67473	**800-255-0316**	785-346-2192
Precision Tank & Equipment Company Inc 3503 Conover Rd	Virginia	IL	62691	**800-258-4197**	217-452-7228
Reinke Mfg Co Inc 5325 Reinke Rd	Deshler	NE	68340	**866-365-7381**	402-365-7251
Root-Lowell Manufacturing Co 1000 Foreman Rd PO Box 289	Lowell	MI	49331	**800-748-0098**	616-897-9211
Scranton Mfg Company Inc 101 State St PO Box 336	Scranton	IA	51462	**800-831-1858**	712-652-3396
Shivvers Inc 614 W English St	Corydon	IA	50060	**800-245-9093**	641-872-1005
Simonsen Industries Inc 500 Iowa 31	Quimby	IA	51049	**800-831-4860**	712-445-2211
Sioux Steel Co 196 1/2 E Sixth St	Sioux Falls	SD	57104	**800-557-4689**	605-336-1750
Stock Equipment Co 16490 Chillicothe Rd	Chagrin Falls	OH	44023	**888-742-1249**	440-543-6000
Sudenga Industries Inc 2002 Kingbird Ave	George	IA	51237	**888-783-3642**	712-475-3301
Sun Circle Inc 286 S G St	Arcata	CA	95521	**800-458-6543**	707-822-5777
T-l Irrigation Co 151 E Hwy 6 AB Rd PO Box 1047	Hastings	NE	68902	**800-330-4264**	402-462-4128
Top Air Sprayers 601 S Broad St	Kalida	OH	45853	**800-322-6301**	419-532-3121
Toro Co Irrigation Div 5825 Jasmine St	Riverside	CA	92504	**800-654-1882**	
Unverferth Mfg Company Inc 601 S Broad St	Kalida	OH	45853	**800-322-6301**	419-532-3121
Valmont Industries Inc 1 Valmont Plz *NYSE: VMI*	Omaha	NE	68154	**800-825-6668**	402-963-1000

	City	State	Zip	Toll-Free	Phone
Vermeer Corp 1210 Vermeer Rd E PO Box 200	Pella	IA	50219	**800-829-0051**	641-628-3141
Westfield Industries Ltd 74 Hwy 205 E	Rosenort	MB	R0G1W0	**866-467-7207**	204-746-2396
Wiese Industries Inc 1501 Fifth St PO Box 39	Perry	IA	50220	**800-568-4391**	515-465-9854
Woods Equipment Co 2606 S Illinois Rt 2 PO Box 1000	Oregon	IL	61061	**800-319-6637**	815-732-2141
Wylie Spray Center 702 E 40th St	Lubbock	TX	79404	**888-249-5162**	806-763-1335
Yetter Manufacturing Inc 109 S McDonough St PO Box 358	Colchester	IL	62326	**800-447-5777**	309-776-4111

276 FARM MACHINERY & EQUIPMENT - WHOL

	City	State	Zip	Toll-Free	Phone
Abilene Machine Inc PO Box 129	Abilene	KS	67410	**800-255-0337**	785-655-9455
Ag West Supply Inc 9055 Rickreall Rd	Rickreall	OR	97371	**800-842-2224**	503-363-2332
Agri-Service 300 Agri-Service Way	Kimberly	ID	83341	**800-388-3599**	208-734-7772
Arends & Sons Inc 715 S Sangamon Ave	Gibson City	IL	60936	**800-637-6052**	217-784-4241
Arends Bros Inc 1190 E 1200N Rd	Melvin	IL	60952	**800-356-6811**	217-388-7717
BE Implement Co 1645 FM 403 PO Box 752	Brownfield	TX	79316	**800-725-5435**	806-637-3594
Belarus Tractor International Inc 7842 N Faulkner Rd	Milwaukee	WI	53224	**800-356-2336**	
Bell Equipment Inc 511 Fourth St	Nezperce	ID	83543	**800-343-2355**	208-937-2402
Berchtold Equipment Co Inc 330 E 19th St	Bakersfield	CA	93305	**800-691-7817**	661-323-7817
Blanchard Compact Equipment 1410 Ashville Hwy	Spartanburg	SC	29303	**888-799-3606**	864-582-1245
Burks Tractor Co Inc 3140 Kimberly Rd	Twin Falls	ID	83301	**800-247-7419**	208-733-5543
Carco International Inc 2721 Midland Blvd	Fort Smith	AR	72904	**800-824-3215**	479-441-3270
Carrico Implement Company Inc 3160 US 24 Hwy	Beloit	KS	67420	**877-542-4099**	785-738-5744
Ernie Williams Ltd 2613 Hwy 18 E	Algona	IA	50511	**888-535-4096**	515-295-3561
Farm Implement & Supply Company Inc 1200 S Washington Hwy 183	Plainville	KS	67663	**888-589-6029**	785-434-4824
Farmer Boy Ag Systems Inc PO Box 435	Myerstown	PA	17067	**800-845-3374**	
Farmers Supply Sales Inc 1409 E Ave	Kalona	IA	52247	**800-493-4917**	319-656-2291
Gardner Inc 3641 Interchange Rd	Columbus	OH	43204	**800-848-8946**	614-456-4000
Garton Tractor Inc 2400 N Golden State Blvd	Turlock	CA	95382	**877-872-2767**	209-632-3931
Giles & Ransome Inc Ransome Engine Power Div 2975 Galloway Rd	Bensalem	PA	19020	**877-726-7663**	215-639-4300
Glade & Grove Supply Inc 305 CR 17 W PO Box 760	Avon Park	FL	33826	**800-433-4451**	561-996-3095
Golden Spike Equipment Co 1352 W Main St PO Box 70	Tremonton	UT	84337	**800-821-4474**	435-257-5346
Greenline Equipment 14750 S Pony Express Rd	Bluffdale	UT	84065	**888-201-5500**	801-966-4231
Grossenburg Implement Inc 31341 US Hwy 18	Winner	SD	57580	**800-658-3440**	605-842-2040
Harcourt Equipment 313 Hwy 169 & 175 E	Harcourt	IA	50544	**800-445-5646**	515-354-5332
Hillsboro Equipment Inc E18898 Hwy 33	Hillsboro	WI	54634	**800-521-5133**	608-489-2275
HOLT Texas Ltd 3302 S WW White Rd	San Antonio	TX	78222	**800-275-4658**	210-648-1111
Hoober Inc 3452 Old Philadelphia Pk PO Box 518	Intercourse	PA	17534	**800-732-0017**	717-768-8231
Hultgren Implements Inc 5698 State Hwy 175	Ida Grove	IA	51445	**800-827-1650**	712-364-3105
Hurst Farm Supply Inc 105 Ave D	Abernathy	TX	79311	**800-535-8903**	806-298-2541
Implement Sales Company LLC 1574 Stone Ridge Dr	Stone Mountain	GA	30083	**800-955-9592**	770-908-9439
JD Equipment Inc 1660 US 42 NE	London	OH	43140	**800-659-5646**	614-879-6620
Jerry Pate Turf & Irrigation Inc 301 Schubert Dr	Pensacola	FL	32504	**800-700-7004**	850-479-4653
John Day Co 6263 Abbott Dr	Omaha	NE	68110	**800-767-2273**	402-455-8000
Larchmont Engineering & Irrigation Co 11 Larchmont Ln PO Box 66	Lexington	MA	02420	**877-862-2550**	781-862-2550
Liechty Farm Equipment Inc 1701 S Defiance St	Archbold	OH	43502	**800-272-5898**	419-445-1565
Littau Harvester Inc 855 Rogue Ave	Stayton	OR	97383	**866-262-2495**	503-769-5953
MDMA Equipment Dealers Inc N6291 State Hwy 25	Durand	WI	54736	**888-672-8864**	715-672-8915
Mid-State Equipment Inc W 1115 Bristol Rd	Columbus	WI	53925	**877-677-4020**	920-623-4020
Monroe Tractor & Implement Company Inc 1001 Lehigh Stn Rd	Henrietta	NY	14467	**866-683-5338**	585-334-3867
Peterson Tractor Co 955 Marina Blvd	San Leandro	CA	94577	**800-590-5945**	510-357-6200
Premier Equipment LLC 2025 US Hwy 14 W	Huron	SD	57350	**800-627-5469**	605-352-7100
Revels Tractor Company Inc 2217 N Main St	Fuquay Varina	NC	27526	**800-849-5469**	919-552-5697
Roeder Implement Inc 2550 Rockdale Rd	Dubuque	IA	52003	**800-557-1184**	563-557-1184
Schmidt Machine Co 7013 Ohio 199	Upper Sandusky	OH	43351	**866-368-3814**	419-294-3814
SEMA Equipment Inc 11555 Hwy 60 Blvd	Wanamingo	MN	55983	**800-569-1377**	507-824-2256
Simpson Norton Corp 4144 S Bullard Ave	Goodyear	AZ	85338	**877-859-8676**	623-932-5116
Sioux Automation Ctr Inc 877 First Ave NW	Sioux Center	IA	51250	**866-722-1488**	712-722-1488
Sloan Implement Co 120 N Business 51	Assumption	IL	62510	**800-745-4020**	217-226-4411
Spartan Distributors Inc 487 W Div St	Sparta	MI	49345	**800-822-2216**	616-887-7301
Straub International Inc 214 SW 40th Ave	Great Bend	KS	67530	**800-658-1706**	620-792-5256
Teeter Irrigation Inc 2729 W Oklahoma	Ulysses	KS	67880	**800-524-5497**	620-353-1111
Titan Machinery Inc 7955 179th Ave SE *NASDAQ: TITN*	Wahpeton	ND	58075	**800-654-4313**	701-642-8424
Tom Hassenfritz Equipment Co 1300 W Washington St	Mount Pleasant	IA	52641	**800-634-4885**	319-385-3114
Tractor Supply Co 5401 Virginia Way *NASDAQ: TSCO*	Brentwood	TN	37027	**877-718-6750**	
Washington County Tractor Inc PO Box 1619	Brenham	TX	77834	**800-256-5655**	979-836-4591
Western Implement Co Inc 2919 N Ave	Grand Junction	CO	81504	**800-338-6639**	970-242-7960
White's Inc 4614 Navigation Blvd PO Box 2344	Houston	TX	77011	**800-231-9559**	713-928-2632
Witmer's Inc 39821 SR 14	Salem	OH	44460	**888-427-6025**	330-427-2147
Wyatt-Quarles Seed Co 730 US Hwy 70 W	Garner	NC	27529	**800-662-7591**	919-772-4243

277 FARM PRODUCT RAW MATERIALS

	City	State	Zip	Toll-Free	Phone
ADM Corn Processing 4666 Faries Pkwy	Decatur	IL	62526	**866-574-9690**	217-424-5200
Alliance Grain Co 1306 W Eigth St	Gibson City	IL	60936	**800-222-2451**	217-784-4284
Aurora Co-op Elevator Co 605 12th St PO Box 209	Aurora	NE	68818	**800-642-6795**	402-694-2106
Cargill Inc 15407 McGinty Rd W	Wayzata	MN	55391	**800-227-4455**	952-742-7575
Cargill Ltd 300-240 Graham Ave PO Box 5900	Winnipeg	MB	R3C4C5	**888-855-8558**	204-947-0141
Central Connecticut Co-op Farmers Assn 10 Apel Pl PO Box 8500	Manchester	CT	06042	**800-640-4523**	860-649-4523
Central Iowa Co-op 2829 Westown Pkwy Ste 350	West Des Moines	IA	50266	**800-513-3938**	515-225-1334
Ceres Solutions LLP 2112 Indianapolis Rd PO Box 432	Crawfordsville	IN	47933	**800-878-0952*** *General	765-362-6700
Co-Alliance LLP 5250 E US Hwy 36 Bldg 1000	Avon	IN	46123	**800-525-0272**	317-745-4491
Co-op Elevator Co 7211 E Michigan Ave	Pigeon	MI	48755	**800-968-0601**	989-453-4500
Effingham Equity Inc 201 W Roadway Ave	Effingham	IL	62401	**800-223-1337**	217-342-4101
Farmers Co-op 208 W Depot	Dorchester	NE	68343	**800-642-6439**	402-946-2211
Frontier Co-op 211 S Lincoln PO Box 37	Brainard	NE	68626	**800-869-0379**	402-545-2811
Heartland Co-op 2829 Westown Pkwy Ste 350	West Des Moines	IA	50266	**800-513-3938**	515-225-1334
Italgrani USA Inc 7900 Van Buren St	Saint Louis	MO	63111	**800-274-1274**	314-638-1447
Joy Dog Food PO Box 305	Pinckneyville	IL	62274	**800-245-4125**	
MaxYield Co-op 313 Third Ave NE PO Box 49	West Bend	IA	50597	**800-383-0003**	515-887-7211
NEW Co-op Inc 2626 First Ave S	Fort Dodge	IA	50501	**800-362-2233**	515-955-2040
Northwest Grain Growers Inc 850 N Fourth Ave	Walla Walla	WA	99362	**800-994-4290**	509-525-6510
Parrish & Heimbecker Ltd (P&H) 201 Portage Ave Ste 1400	Winnipeg	MB	R3B3K6	**800-665-8937**	204-956-2030
Pendleton Grain Growers Inc 1000 SW Dorian St PO Box 1248	Pendleton	OR	97801	**800-422-7611**	541-278-5035
Plains Cotton Co-op Assn 3301 E 50th St PO Box 2827	Lubbock	TX	79408	**800-333-8011**	806-763-8011
Scoular Co 2027 Dodge St	Omaha	NE	68102	**800-488-3500**	402-342-3500
South Dakota Wheat Growers Assn 908 Lamont St SE	Aberdeen	SD	57401	**888-429-4902**	605-225-5500
Staplcotn Co-op Assn Inc 214 W Market St	Greenwood	MS	38930	**800-293-6231**	662-453-6231
Stratton Equity Co-op Co Inc 98 Colorado Ave PO Box 25	Stratton	CO	80836	**800-438-7070**	719-348-5326
Western Iowa Co-op 3330 Moville St PO Box 106	Hornick	IA	51026	**800-488-3201**	712-874-3211

278 FARM SUPPLIES

	City	State	Zip	Toll-Free	Phone
Agfinity 260 Factory Rd	Eaton	CO	80615	**800-433-4688**	970-454-4000
AgVantage FS Inc 1600 Eigth St SW	Waverly	IA	50677	**800-346-0058**	319-483-4900
Alforex Seeds 38001 County Rd 27	Woodland	CA	95695	**877-560-5181**	530-666-3331
BFG Supply Co LLC PO Box 479	Burton	OH	44021	**800-883-0234**	440-834-1883
Bleyhl Farm Service Inc 940 E Wine Country Rd	Grandview	WA	98930	**800-862-6806*** *Cust Svc	509-882-2248

Classified Section

Company / Address	City	State	ZIP	Toll-Free	Phone
Bradley Caldwell Inc 200 Kiwanis Blvd *Cust Svc	Hazleton	PA	18202	**800-257-9100***	570-455-7511
Central Valley Co-op 900 30th Pl NW	Owatonna	MN	55060	**800-270-2339**	507-451-1230
CHS Inc 5500 Cenex Dr *NASDAQ: CHSCP*	Inver Grove Heights	MN	55077	**800-232-3639**	651-355-6000
Co-op Feed Dealers Inc 380 Broome Corporate Pkwy PO Box 670 *Cust Svc	Conklin	NY	13748	**800-333-0895***	607-651-9078
Countryside Co-op 514 E Main St	Durand	WI	54736	**800-236-7585**	715-672-8947
CropKing Inc 134 W Dr	Lodi	OH	44254	**800-321-5656**	330-302-4203
Crystal Valley Coop 721 W Humphrey PO Box 210	Lake Crystal	MN	56055	**800-622-2910**	507-726-6455
Dragon Claw USA Inc 16033 Arrow Hwy	Irwindale	CA	91706	**800-238-5296**	626-480-0068
Edon Farmers Co-op Assn Inc 205 S Michigan PO Box 308	Edon	OH	43518	**800-878-4093**	419-272-2121
Evergreen FS Inc 402 N Hershey Rd	Bloomington	IL	61704	**877-963-2392**	309-663-2392
Farm Service Co-op 2308 Pine St	Harlan	IA	51537	**800-452-4372**	712-755-3185
Farmers Co-op Assn 105 Jackson St	Jackson	MN	56143	**800-864-3847**	507-847-4160
Federation Co-op 108 N Water St	Black River Falls	WI	54615	**800-944-1784**	715-284-5354
Fifield Land Co 4307 Fifield Rd	Brawley	CA	92227	**800-536-6395**	760-344-6391
Frenchman Valley Farmers Co-op Exchange 202 Broadway	Imperial	NE	69033	**800-538-2667**	308-882-3200
Gold Star FS Inc 101 NE St	Cambridge	IL	61238	**800-443-8497**	309-937-3369
Gowan Company LLC PO Box 5569	Yuma	AZ	85366	**800-883-1844**	928-783-8844
Grangetto's Farm & Garden Supply Co 1105 W Mission Ave	Escondido	CA	92025	**800-536-4671**	760-745-4671
Growth Products Ltd 80 Lafayette Ave	White Plains	NY	10603	**800-648-7626**	914-428-1316
Hummert International Inc 4500 Earth City Expy	Earth City	MO	63045	**800-325-3055**	314-506-4500
Hutchinson Co-Op PO Box 158	Hutchinson	MN	55350	**800-795-1299**	320-587-4647
Kreamer Feed Inc PO Box 38	Kreamer	PA	17833	**800-767-4537**	570-374-8148
Kugler Co 209 W Third St PO Box 1748	McCook	NE	69001	**800-445-9116**	308-345-2280
Legend Seeds Inc PO Box 241	De Smet	SD	57231	**800-678-3346**	605-854-3346
Martrex Inc 1107 Hazeltine Blvd Ste 535	Minnetonka	MN	55345	**800-328-3627**	952-933-5000
McFarlane Mfg Company Inc 1259 Water St PO Box 100	Sauk City	WI	53583	**800-627-8569**	608-643-3321
Meherrin Agricultural & Chemical Co Inc 413 Main St	Severn	NC	27877	**800-775-0333**	252-585-1744
NEW Co-op Inc 2626 First Ave S	Fort Dodge	IA	50501	**800-362-2233**	515-955-2040
Northwest Wholesale Inc 1567 N Wenatchee Ave	Wenatchee	WA	98801	**800-874-6607**	509-662-2141
Nu Way Co-op Inc PO Box Q	Trimont	MN	56176	**800-445-4118**	507-639-2311
Orangeburg Pecan Company Inc 761 Russell St	Orangeburg	SC	29115	**800-845-6970**	803-534-4277
Orscheln Farm & Home LLC 1800 Overcenter Dr PO Box 698	Moberly	MO	65270	**800-498-5090**	660-263-4377
Panhandle Co-op Assn 401 S Beltline Hwy W *Cust Svc	Scottsbluff	NE	69361	**800-732-4546***	308-632-5301
Paris Farmers' Union PO Box D	South Paris	ME	04281	**800-639-3603**	207-743-8976
Quality Liquid Feeds Inc PO Box 240	Dodgeville	WI	53533	**800-236-2345**	608-935-2345
Red River Specialties Inc 1324 N Hearne Ave Ste 120	Shreveport	LA	71107	**800-256-3344**	318-425-5944
Reedsville Co-op Assn Inc PO Box 460	Reedsville	WI	54230	**800-236-4047**	920-754-4321
S R C Corp PO Box 30676	Salt Lake City	UT	84130	**800-888-4545**	801-268-4500
Siegers Seed Co 13031 Reflections Dr	Holland	MI	49424	**800-962-4999**	616-786-4999
Silver Edge Co-op 39999 Hilton Rd	Edgewood	IA	52042	**800-632-5953**	563-928-6419
Southern FS Inc 2002 E Main St PO Box 728	Marion	IL	62959	**800-492-7684**	618-993-2833
Southern States Co-op Inc 6606 W Broad St	Richmond	VA	23230	**866-372-8272**	804-281-1000
Southern States Frederick Co-op Inc 500 E South St	Frederick	MD	21701	**866-633-5747**	301-663-6164
Stanislaus Farm Supply Co 624 E Service Rd	Modesto	CA	95358	**800-323-0725**	209-538-7070
Tennessee Farmers Co-op 180 Old Nashville Hwy	La Vergne	TN	37086	**800-366-2667**	615-793-8011
United Suppliers Inc 30473 260th St PO Box 538	Eldora	IA	50627	**800-782-5123**	641-858-2341
Van Horn Inc PO Box 380	Cerro Gordo	IL	61818	**800-252-1615**	217-677-2131
Wabash Valley Service Company Inc 909 N Ct St	Grayville	IL	62844	**888-869-8127**	618-375-2311
Western Consolidated Co-op 520 Co Rd 9 PO Box 78	Holloway	MN	56249	**800-368-3310**	320-394-2171
Western Reserve Farm Co-op Inc 14961 S State Ave PO Box 339	Middlefield	OH	44062	**888-427-6672**	440-632-1192
Wilco Farmers 200 Industrial Way	Mount Angel	OR	97362	**800-382-5339**	503-845-6122
Yankton Ag Service 114 Mulberry St	Yankton	SD	57078	**800-456-5528**	605-665-3691

279 FASHION DESIGN HOUSES

SEE ALSO Clothing & Accessories - Mfr

Company / Address	City	State	ZIP	Toll-Free	Phone
Armani Exchange 568 Broadway	New York	NY	10012	**800-717-2929**	212-431-6000
Christian Dior 712 Fifth Ave 37th Fl	New York	NY	10019	**800-929-3467**	212-582-0500
Diane Von Furstenberg 440 W 14th St	New York	NY	10014	**888-472-2383**	212-741-6607
Donna Karan International Inc 550 Seventh Ave *General	New York	NY	10018	**877-316-0975***	212-789-1500
Kay Green Design Inc 859 Outer Rd	Orlando	FL	32814	**800-226-5186**	407-246-7155
Marc Jacobs International 72 Spring St	New York	NY	10012	**877-707-6272**	

280 FASTENERS & FASTENING SYSTEMS

SEE ALSO Hardware - Mfr ; Precision Machined Products

Company / Address	City	State	ZIP	Toll-Free	Phone
Atlas Bolt & Screw Co 1628 Troy Rd	Ashland	OH	44805	**800-321-6977**	419-289-6171
B & G Mfg Company Inc 3067 Unionville Pk	Hatfield	PA	19440	**800-366-3067**	215-822-1925
Captive Fastener Corp 19 Thornton Rd	Oakland	NJ	07436	**800-526-4430**	201-337-6800
ELF Fastening Systems Inc 29019 Solon Rd	Solon	OH	44139	**800-248-2376**	440-248-8655
Ford Fasteners Inc 110 S Newman St	Hackensack	NJ	07601	**800-272-3673**	201-487-3151
Hohmann & Barnard Inc 30 Rasons Ct	Hauppauge	NY	11788	**800-645-0616**	631-234-0600
ITW Brands 955 National Pkwy Ste 95500	Schaumburg	IL	60173	**877-489-2726**	847-944-2260
ITW Buildex 1349 W Bryn Mawr	Itasca	IL	60143	**800-284-5339**	630-595-3500
Mid-States Bolt & Screw Co 4126 Somers Dr	Burton	MI	48529	**800-482-0867**	810-744-0123
Mid-States Screw Corp 1817 18th Ave	Rockford	IL	61104	**888-354-6772**	815-397-2440
Ms Aerospace Inc 13928 Balboa Blvd	Sylmar	CA	91342	**866-487-2365**	818-833-9095
National Rivet & Manufacturing Co 21 E Jefferson St	Waupun	WI	53963	**888-324-5511**	920-324-5511
Ohio Nut & Bolt Co 5250 W 164th St	Brook Park	OH	44142	**800-362-0291**	216-267-2240
Pan American Screw Inc 630 Reese Dr SW *Cust Svc	Conover	NC	28613	**800-951-2222***	828-466-0060
PennEngineering & Manufacturing Corp 5190 Old Easton Rd	Danboro	PA	18916	**800-237-4736**	215-766-8853
Robertson Inc 97 Bronte St N	Milton	ON	L9T2N8	**800-268-5090**	905-878-2861
Scovill Fasteners Inc 1802 Scovill Dr *Cust Svc	Clarkesville	GA	30523	**888-726-8455***	706-754-1000
Stafast Products Inc 505 Lk Shore Blvd	Painesville	OH	44077	**800-782-3278**	440-357-5546

281 FENCES - MFR

SEE ALSO Recycled Plastics Products

Company / Address	City	State	ZIP	Toll-Free	Phone
Acorn Wire & Iron Works Inc 2035 S Racine Ave	Chicago	IL	60608	**800-552-2676**	773-585-0600
Cherry Tree Design 320 Pronghorn Trl	Bozeman	MT	59718	**800-634-3268**	406-582-8800
Conifex Timber Inc 980 700 W Georgia St PO Box 10070	Vancouver	BC	V7Y1B6	**866-301-2949**	604-216-2949
Dare Products Inc 860 Betterly Rd PO Box 157	Battle Creek	MI	49015	**800-922-3273**	269-965-2307
Holland Bowl Mill 120 James St	Holland	MI	49424	**800-774-1230**	616-396-6513
Master Halco Inc 1321 Greenway Dr	Irving	TX	75038	**800-883-8384**	972-714-7300
Merchants Metals Inc 900 Ashwood Pkwy Ste 600	Atlanta	GA	30338	**800-272-6171**	770-960-2880
Riverdale Mills Corp 130 Riverdale St	Northbridge	MA	01534	**800-762-6374**	508-234-8715
Taiga Building Products Ltd 4710 Kingsway Ste 800	Burnaby	BC	V5H4M2	**800-663-1470**	604-438-1471
Tru-Link Fence Co 5440 Touhy Ave	Skokie	IL	60077	**800-568-9300**	847-568-9300
Walnut Hollow Farm Inc 1409 State Rd 23	Dodgeville	WI	53533	**800-395-5995**	608-935-2341

282 FERTILIZERS & PESTICIDES

SEE ALSO Farm Supplies

Company / Address	City	State	ZIP	Toll-Free	Phone
Abell Corp 2500 Sterlington Rd	Monroe	LA	71203	**800-325-7204**	
Agrium Inc 13131 Lk Fraser Dr SE *NYSE: AGU*	Calgary	AB	T2J7E8	**877-247-4861**	403-225-7000
Airgas Specialty Products 2530 Sever Rd Ste 300	Lawrenceville	GA	30043	**800-295-2225**	
Alabama Farmers Co-op Inc PO Box 2227	Decatur	AL	35601	**888-255-2667**	256-353-6843
Amvac Chemical Corp 4100 E Washington Blvd	Los Angeles	CA	90023	**800-424-9300**	323-264-3910

	City	State	Zip	Toll-Free	Phone
California Ammonia Co (CALAMCO) 1776 W March Ln Ste 420	Stockton	CA	95207	**800-624-4200**	209-982-1000
Certis USA LLC 9145 Guilford Rd Ste 175	Columbia	MD	21046	**800-250-5024**	
CFC Farm & Home Ctr 15172 Brandy Rd PO Box 2002	Culpeper	VA	22701	**800-284-2667**	540-825-2200
Coastal Agrobusiness Inc 3702 Evans St PO Box 856	Greenville	NC	27835	**800-758-1828**	252-756-1126
Degesch America Inc PO Box 116	Weyers Cave	VA	24486	**800-330-2525**	540-234-9281
Dow AgroSciences LLC 9330 Zionsville Rd	Indianapolis	IN	46268	**800-331-6451**	317-337-3000
DuPont Crop Protection PO Box 80705	Wilmington	DE	19880	**888-638-7668**	302-774-1000
Enforcer Products Inc PO Box 1060	Cartersville	GA	30120	**888-805-4357**	
FMC Corp 2929 Walnut St *NYSE: FMC*	Philadelphia	PA	19104	**888-548-4486**	215-299-6000
Frit Industries Inc 1792 Jodie Parker Rd	Ozark	AL	36360	**800-633-7685**	334-774-2515
Hillshire Brands 2200 W Don Tyson Pkwy	Springdale	AR	72762	**800-323-7117**	479-290-6397
Intrepid Potash Inc 700 17th St Ste 1700 *NYSE: IPI*	Denver	CO	80202	**800-451-2888**	303-296-3006
JR Simplot Co 999 W Main St Ste 1300	Boise	ID	83702	**800-832-8893**	208-336-2110
Kellogg Garden Products 350 W Sepulveda Blvd	Carson	CA	90745	**800-232-2322**	
Kirby Agri Inc 500 Running Pump Rd PO Box 6277	Lancaster	PA	17607	**800-745-7524**	717-299-2541
Kronos Micronutrients 213 W Moxee Ave PO Box 1167	Moxee	WA	98936	**800-541-4086**	509-248-4911
Landec Ag LLC 201 N Michigan St	Oxford	IN	47971	**800-241-7252**	765-385-1000
Lebanon Seaboard Corp 1600 E Cumberland St	Lebanon	PA	17042	**800-233-0628**	717-273-1685
Miller Chemical & Fertilizer Corp 120 Radio Rd PO Box 333	Hanover	PA	17331	**800-233-2040**	717-632-8921
Na-Churs/Alpine Solutions 421 Leader St	Marion	OH	43302	**800-622-4877**	740-382-5701
PBI/Gordon Corp 1217 W 12th St PO Box 014090	Kansas City	MO	64101	**800-821-7925**	816-421-4070
Potash Corp 1101 Skokie Blvd	Northbrook	IL	60062	**800-667-0403**	847-849-4200
Potash Corp of Saskatchewan Inc 122 First Ave S Ste 500 *NYSE: POT*	Saskatoon	SK	S7K7G3	**800-667-3930**	306-933-8500
Safeguard Chemical Corp 411 Wales Ave	Bronx	NY	10454	**800-536-3170**	718-585-3170
Scotts Miracle Gro Products Inc 14111 Scottslawn Rd	Marysville	OH	43041	**888-270-3714**	937-644-0011
Scotts Miracle-Gro Co 14111 Scottslawn Rd *NYSE: SMG* ■ *Cust Svc	Marysville	OH	43041	**800-543-8873***	937-644-0011
Share Corp 7821 N Faulkner Rd	Milwaukee	WI	53224	**800-776-7192**	414-355-4000
Southern States Chemical Co 1600 E President St	Savannah	GA	31404	**888-337-8922**	912-232-1101
Spectrum Brands 3001 Deming Way	Middleton	WI	53711	**800-566-7899**	608-275-3340
Stoller USA 4001 W Sam Houston Pkwy N Ste 100	Houston	TX	77043	**800-539-5283**	713-461-1493
Summit Chemical Co 235 S Kresson St	Baltimore	MD	21224	**800-227-8664**	410-522-0661
Syngenta Corp 3411 Silverside Rd Ste 100	Wilmington	DE	19810	**800-555-2470**	302-425-2000
Syngenta Crop Protection Inc 410 Swing Rd PO Box 18300	Greensboro	NC	27409	**800-797-5040**	336-632-6000
Tender Corp 106 Burndy Rd	Littleton	NH	03561	**800-258-4696**	603-444-5464
Van Diest Supply Co 1434 220th St PO Box 610	Webster City	IA	50595	**800-779-2424**	515-832-2366
Woodstream Corp 69 N Locust St *All	Lititz	PA	17543	**800-800-1819***	717-626-2125
Y-Tex Corp 1825 Big Horn Ave PO Box 1450	Cody	WY	82414	**800-443-6401**	307-587-5515

283 FESTIVALS - BOOK

	City	State	Zip	Toll-Free	Phone
Boston Globe Book Festival PO Box 55819 PO Box 2378	Boston	MA	02205	**888-694-5623**	
Great Salt Lake Book Festival Utah Humanities Council 202 W 300 N	Salt Lake City	UT	84103	**877-786-7598**	801-359-9670
Los Angeles Times Festival of Books Los Angeles Times 202 W First St	Los Angeles	CA	90012	**800-528-4637**	213-237-2335
National Book Festival Library of Congress 101 Independence Ave SE	Washington	DC	20540	**888-714-4696**	202-707-2777
Texas Book Festival 610 Brazos St Ste 200	Austin	TX	78701	**800-222-8733**	512-477-4055
Virginia Festival of the Book Virginia Foundation for the Humanities 145 Ednam Dr	Charlottesville	VA	22903	**877-451-5098**	434-924-3296

284 FESTIVALS - FILM

	City	State	Zip	Toll-Free	Phone
AFI Fest 2021 N Western Ave	Los Angeles	CA	90027	**866-234-3378**	323-856-7600
Anchorage Film Festival 1231 W Northern Lights Blvd Ste 844	Anchorage	AK	99503	**800-544-0786**	907-338-3761
Austin Film Festival 1801 Salina St Ste 210	Austin	TX	78702	**800-310-3378**	512-478-4795
Chicago International Film Festival Cinema Chicago 30 E Adams St Ste 800	Chicago	IL	60603	**800-982-2787**	312-683-0121
Denver International Film Festival 1510 York 3rd Fl	Denver	CO	80206	**866-293-1566**	303-595-3456
Sarasota Film Festival 332 Cocoanut Ave	Sarasota	FL	34236	**800-435-7352**	941-364-9514
Toronto International Film Festival Inc Reitman Sq 350 King St W	Toronto	ON	M5V3X5	**888-599-8433**	
Worldfest Houston International Film Festival PO Box 56566	Houston	TX	77240	**866-965-9955**	713-629-3700

285 FIRE PROTECTION SYSTEMS

SEE ALSO Safety Equipment - Mfr ; Security Products & Services ; Personal Protective Equipment & Clothing

	City	State	Zip	Toll-Free	Phone
BRK Brands Inc 3901 Liberty St Rd	Aurora	IL	60504	**800-323-9005**	630-851-7330
Fike Corp 704 SW Tenth St	Blue Springs	MO	64015	**877-342-3453**	816-229-3405
Fire & Life Safety America 3017 Vernon Rd	Richmond	VA	23228	**800-252-5069**	804-222-1381
Firecom Inc 39-27 59th St	Woodside	NY	11377	**888-347-3269**	718-899-6100
First Alert Inc 3901 Liberty St Rd	Aurora	IL	60504	**800-323-9005**	630-851-7330
Gamewell FCI 12 Clintonville Rd	Northford	CT	06472	**800-606-1983**	203-484-7161
Honeywell Fire Solutions 1 Fire-Lite Pl	Northford	CT	06472	**800-627-3473**	203-484-7161
Potter Electric Signal Company Inc 5757 Phantom Dr Ste 125	Hazelwood	MO	63042	**800-325-3936**	314-878-4321
Siemens Bldg Technologies Inc Fire Safety Div 8 Fernwood Rd	Florham Park	NJ	07932	**888-303-3353**	973-593-2600
Silent Knight 7550 Meridian Cir Ste 100	Maple Grove	MN	55369	**800-328-0103**	763-493-6400
Task Force Tips Inc 3701 Innovation Way	Valparaiso	IN	46383	**800-348-2686**	219-462-6161
Tyco SimplexGrinnell 50 Technology Dr	Westminster	MA	01441	**800-746-7539**	978-731-2500
Viking Corp 210 N Industrial Pk Dr	Hastings	MI	49058	**800-968-9501**	269-945-9501

286 FIREARMS & AMMUNITION (NON-MILITARY)

SEE ALSO Sporting Goods ; Weapons & Ordnance (Military)

	City	State	Zip	Toll-Free	Phone
Beretta USA Corp 17601 Beretta Dr	Accokeek	MD	20607	**800-237-3882**	301-283-2191
Connecticut Valley Arms (CVA) 1685 Boggs Rd Ste 300	Duluth	GA	30096	**800-320-8767**	770-449-4687
Crosman Corp 7629 Rt 5 & 20	Bloomfield	NY	14469	**800-724-7486**	585-657-6161
Defense Technology/Federal Laboratories 1855 S Loop PO Box 248	Casper	WY	82601	**877-248-3835**	307-235-2136
Federal Cartridge Co 900 Ehlen Dr	Anoka	MN	55303	**800-379-1732**	
Gun Parts Corp 226 Williams Ln	Kingston	NY	12401	**866-686-7424**	845-679-4867
H & R 1871 60 Industrial Rowe	Gardner	MA	01440	**866-776-9292**	
Hornady Manufacturing Co 3625 W Old Potash Hwy	Grand Island	NE	68803	**800-338-3220**	308-382-1390
Knight Rifles 213 Dennis st Athens	Athens	TN	37303	**866-518-4181**	
Lyman Products Corp 475 Smith St	Middletown	CT	06457	**800-225-9626**	860-632-2020
Marlin Firearms Co PO Box 1871 *Cust Svc	Madison	NC	27025	**800-544-8892***	
OF Mossberg & Sons Inc 7 Grasso Ave	North Haven	CT	06473	**800-363-3555**	203-230-5300
Olin Corp Winchester Div 427 N Shamrock St	East Alton	IL	62024	**800-356-2666**	618-258-2000
Remington Arms Company Inc 870 Remington Dr PO Box 700	Madison	NC	27025	**800-243-9700**	336-548-8700
Savage Arms Inc 100 Springdale Rd	Westfield	MA	01085	**800-243-3220**	413-568-7001
SIG SAUER Inc 18 Industrial Dr	Exeter	NH	03833	**866-345-6744**	603-772-2302
Smith & Wesson Corp 2100 Roosevelt Ave *Cust Svc	Springfield	MA	01104	**800-331-0852***	413-781-8300
Smith & Wesson Holding Corp 2100 Roosevelt Ave *NASDAQ: SWHC*	Springfield	MA	01104	**800-372-6454**	413-781-8300
Springfield Armory 420 W Main St	Geneseo	IL	61254	**800-680-6866**	309-944-5631
Taurus International Mfg Inc 16175 NW 49th Ave	Miami	FL	33014	**800-327-3776**	305-624-1115
Weatherby Inc 1605 Commerce Way	Paso Robles	CA	93446	**800-227-2016**	805-227-2600
Williams Gun Sight Co 7389 Lapeer Rd	Davison	MI	48423	**800-530-9028**	810-653-2131

287 FISHING - COMMERCIAL

	City	State	Zip	Toll-Free	Phone
Arctic Storm Management Group LLC 2727 Alaskan Way Pier 69	Seattle	WA	98121	**800-929-0908**	206-547-6557
Nova Fisheries 2532 Yale Ave E	Seattle	WA	98102	**888-458-6682**	206-781-2000

Company	Address	City	State	Zip	Toll-Free	Phone
Ocean Beauty Seafoods Inc	1100 W Ewing St	Seattle	WA	98119	**800-365-8950**	206-285-6800

288 FIXTURES - OFFICE & STORE

SEE ALSO Commercial & Industrial Furniture

Company	Address	City	State	Zip	Toll-Free	Phone
Able Steel Equipment Co Inc	50-02 23rd St	Long Island	NY	11101	**800-428-8722**	718-361-9240
Angola Wire Products Inc	803 Wohlert St	Angola	IN	46703	**800-800-7225**	260-665-9447
Architectural Bronze Aluminum Corp	655 Deerfield Rd Ste 100	Deerfield	IL	60015	**800-339-6581**	
Benner-Nawman Inc	3450 Sabin Brown Rd	Wickenburg	AZ	85390	**800-992-3833**	928-684-2813
Best-Rite Mfg	2885 Lorraine Ave	Temple	TX	76501	**800-749-2258**	
Borroughs Corp	3002 N Burdick St	Kalamazoo	MI	49004	**800-748-0227**	269-342-0161
Boston Group	400 Riverside Ave	Medford	MA	02155	**800-225-1633**	
Churchill Cabinet Co	4616 W 19th St *Sales	Cicero	IL	60804	**800-379-9776***	708-780-0070
Consolidated Storage Cos	225 Main St *Cust Svc	Tatamy	PA	18085	**800-323-0801***	610-253-2775
Cres-Cor	5925 Heisley Rd	Mentor	OH	44060	**877-273-7267**	440-350-1100
Datum Filing Systems Inc	89 Church Rd	Emigsville	PA	17318	**800-828-8018**	717-764-6350
DeBourgh Manufacturing Co	27505 Otero Ave PO Box 981	La Junta	CO	81050	**800-328-8829**	
Dixie Store Fixtures & Sales Company Inc	2425 First Ave N	Birmingham	AL	35203	**800-323-4943**	205-322-2442
Durham Manufacturing Co	201 Main St	Durham	CT	06422	**800-243-3774**	860-349-3427
Econoco Corp	300 Karin Ln	Hicksville	NY	11801	**800-645-7032**	516-935-7700
EQUIPTO	225 Main St	Tatamy	PA	18085	**800-323-0801**	610-253-2775
Ex-Cell Metal Products Inc	11240 Melrose St	Franklin Park	IL	60131	**800-392-3557**	847-451-0451
Frazier Industrial Co	91 Fairview Ave	Long Valley	NJ	07853	**800-859-1342**	908-876-3001
Hamilton Sorter Co Inc	3158 Production Dr	Fairfield	OH	45014	**800-503-9966**	513-870-4400
Handy Store Fixtures Inc	337 Sherman Ave	Newark	NJ	07114	**800-631-4280**	973-242-1600
Hoosier Co	5421 W 86th St PO Box 681064	Indianapolis	IN	46268	**800-521-4184**	317-872-8125
Hufcor Inc	2101 Kennedy Rd	Janesville	WI	53545	**800-356-6968**	608-756-1241
InterMetro Industries Corp	651 N Washington St *Cust Svc	Wilkes-Barre	PA	18705	**800-992-1776***	570-825-2741
International Visual Corp (IVC)	11500 Blvd Armand Bombardier	Montreal	QC	H1E2W9	**866-643-0570**	514-643-0570
Jaken Company Inc	14420 My ford rf	Irvine	CA	90623	**800-401-7225**	714-522-1700
Jesco-Wipco Industries Inc	950 Anderson Rd PO Box 388	Litchfield	MI	49252	**800-455-0019**	517-542-2903
JL Industries Inc	4450 W 78th St Cir	Bloomington	MN	55435	**800-554-6077**	952-835-6850
John Boos & Co	3601 S Banker St PO Box 609	Effingham	IL	62401	**888-431-2667**	217-347-7701
Kardex Systems Inc	114 Westview Ave	Marietta	OH	45750	**800-639-5805**	740-374-9300
Karges Furniture Company Inc	1501 W Maryland St	Evansville	IN	47710	**800-252-7437**	812-425-2291
Killion Industries Inc	1380 Poinsettia Ave	Vista	CA	92081	**800-421-5352**	760-727-5102
Kwik-Wall Co	1010 E Edwards St	Springfield	IL	62703	**800-280-5945**	217-522-5553
LA Darling Co	1401 Hwy 49B	Paragould	AR	72450	**800-643-3499**	870-239-9564
Lista International Corp	106 Lowland St *Cust Svc	Holliston	MA	01746	**800-722-3020***	508-429-1350
Lozier Corp	6336 John J Pershing Dr	Omaha	NE	68110	**800-228-9882**	402-457-8000
Lyon Work Space Products	420 N Main St	Montgomery	IL	60538	**800-433-8488**	630-892-8941
M.E.G. LLC	502 S Green St PO Box 240 *Cust Svc	Cambridge City	IN	47327	**800-645-3315***	
Modernfold Inc	215 W New Rd	Greenfield	IN	46140	**800-869-9685**	
National Partitions	10300 Goldenfern Ln	Knoxville	TN	37931	**888-818-5749**	865-670-2100
NNM Peterson Manufacturing Co	24133 W 143rd St	Plainfield	IL	60544	**800-826-9086**	815-436-9201
Pacific Fixture Company Inc	12860 San Fernando Rd Unit B	Sylmar	CA	91342	**800-272-2349**	818-362-2130
Packard Industries Inc	1515 US 31 N	Niles	MI	49120	**800-253-0866**	269-684-2550
Pan-Osten Co	6944 Louisville Rd	Bowling Green	KY	42101	**800-472-6678**	270-783-3900
Panelfold Inc	10700 NW 36th Ave	Miami	FL	33167	**800-433-3222**	305-688-3501
Pentwater Wire Products Inc (PWP)	474 Carroll St PO Box 947	Pentwater	MI	49449	**877-869-6911**	231-869-6911
Plasticrest Products Inc	4519 W Harrison St	Chicago	IL	60624	**800-828-2163**	773-826-2163
Racks Inc	PO Box 530840	San Diego	CA	92153	**877-920-7225**	619-661-0987
RC Smith Co	14200 Southcross Dr W	Burnsville	MN	55306	**800-747-7648**	952-854-0711
Reeve Store Equipment Co	9131 Bermudez St PO Box 276	Pico Rivera	CA	90660	**800-927-3383**	562-949-2535
Republic Storage Systems LLC	1038 Belden Ave NE *Sales	Canton	OH	44705	**800-477-1255***	330-438-5800
Ridg-U-Rak Inc	120 S Lake St	North East	PA	16428	**866-479-7225**	814-725-8751
Russ Bassett Co	8189 Byron Rd	Whittier	CA	90606	**800-350-2445**	562-945-2445
Salsbury Industries Inc	1010 E 62nd St	Los Angeles	CA	90001	**800-624-5299**	323-846-6700
Sandusky Cabinets Inc	16125 Widmere Rd PO Box 517 *Cust Svc	Arvin	CA	93203	**800-886-8688***	661-854-5551
Semasys Inc	702 Ashland St *Cust Svc	Houston	TX	77007	**800-231-1425***	713-869-8331
Southern Imperial Inc	1400 Eddy Ave *Cust Svc	Rockford	IL	61103	**800-747-4665***	815-877-7041
SpaceGuard Products Inc	711 S Commerce Dr	Seymour	IN	47274	**800-841-0680**	812-523-3044
Spacesaver Corp	1450 Janesville Ave	Fort Atkinson	WI	53538	**800-492-3434**	800-255-8170
Sparks Marketing Group Inc	2828 Charter Rd	Philadelphia	PA	19154	**800-925-7727**	215-676-1100
Spectrum Industries Inc	925 First Ave	Chippewa Falls	WI	54729	**800-235-1262**	715-723-6750
SPG International	11230 Harland Dr	Covington	GA	30014	**877-503-4774**	
Stanley Vidmar Storage Technologies	11 Grammes Rd	Allentown	PA	18103	**800-523-9462**	
Streater Inc	411 S First Ave	Albert Lea	MN	56007	**800-527-4197**	
Structural Concepts Corp	888 Porter Rd	Muskegon	MI	49441	**800-433-9489**	231-798-8888
Stylmark Inc	PO Box 32008	Minneapolis	MN	55432	**800-328-2495**	763-574-7474
Tesko Welding & Manufacturing Co	7350 W Montrose Ave	Norridge	IL	60706	**800-621-4514**	708-452-0045
Timely Inc	10241 Norris Ave	Pacoima	CA	91331	**800-247-6242**	818-492-3500
TJ Hale Co	W 139 N 9499 Hwy 145	Menomonee Falls	WI	53051	**800-236-4253**	262-255-5555
Trendway Corp	13467 Quincy St PO Box 9016	Holland	MI	49422	**800-968-5344**	616-399-3900
Trion Industries Inc	297 Laird St	Wilkes-Barre	PA	18702	**800-444-4665**	570-824-1000
Unarco Material Handling Inc	701 16th Ave E	Springfield	TN	37172	**800-862-7261**	
Viking Metal Cabinet Co	24047 W Lockport St Ste 209	Plainfield	IL	60544	**800-776-7767**	
W/M Display Group	1040 W 40th St	Chicago	IL	60609	**800-443-2000**	773-254-3700
Western Pacific Storage Systems Inc	300 E Arrow Hwy	San Dimas	CA	91773	**800-732-9777**	

289 FLAGS, BANNERS, PENNANTS

Company	Address	City	State	Zip	Toll-Free	Phone
Aaa Flag & Banner Manufacturing Co	8955 National Blvd	Los Angeles	CA	90034	**800-266-4222**	
Annin & Co	105 Eisenhower Pkwy	Roseland	NJ	07068	**888-252-4569**	973-228-9400
Eder Flag Mfg Company Inc	1000 W Rawson Ave	Oak Creek	WI	53154	**800-558-6044**	414-764-3522
National Banner Co	11938 Harry Hines Blvd	Dallas	TX	75234	**800-527-0860**	972-241-2131
Olympus Flag & Banner	9000 W Heather Ave	Milwaukee	WI	53224	**800-558-9620**	414-355-2010

290 FLASH MEMORY DEVICES

Company	Address	City	State	Zip	Toll-Free	Phone
Advanced Micro Devices Inc (AMD)	1 AMD Pl PO Box 3453 *NYSE: AMD*	Sunnyvale	CA	94088	**800-538-8450**	408-749-4000
Kingston Technology Co	17600 Newhope St	Fountain Valley	CA	92708	**800-835-6575**	714-435-2600
Lexar Media Inc	47300 Bayside Pkwy	Fremont	CA	94538	**877-747-4031**	510-413-1200
Micron Technology Inc	8000 S Federal Way *NASDAQ: MU*	Boise	ID	83707	**888-363-2589**	208-368-4000
PNY Technologies Inc	299 Webro Rd	Parsippany	NJ	07054	**800-769-7079**	973-515-9700
SanDisk Corp	601 McCarthy Blvd *NASDAQ: SNDK*	Milpitas	CA	95035	**866-726-3475**	408-801-1000
Sony Electronics Inc	1 Sony Dr *Cust Svc	Park Ridge	NJ	07656	**800-222-7669***	201-930-1000
Spansion Inc	915 DeGuigne Dr *NYSE: CODE*	Sunnyvale	CA	94085	**866-772-6746**	408-962-2500

291 FLEET LEASING & MANAGEMENT

Company	Address	City	State	Zip	Toll-Free	Phone
Allstate Leasing Inc	1 Olympic Pl	Towson	MD	21204	**800-223-4885**	
Donlen Corp	2315 Sanders Rd	Northbrook	IL	60062	**800-323-1483**	847-714-1400
Emkay Inc	805 W Thorndale Ave	Itasca	IL	60143	**800-621-2001**	630-250-7400
Executive Car Leasing Inc	7807 Santa Monica Blvd	Los Angeles	CA	90046	**800-994-2277**	323-654-5000

	City	State	Zip	Toll-Free	Phone
Lease Plan USA 1165 Sanctuary Pkwy	Alpharetta	GA	30004	**800-457-8721**	770-933-9090
Leasing Assoc Inc 12600 N Featherwood Dr Ste 400	Houston	TX	77034	**800-449-4807**	832-300-1300
Motorlease Corp 1506 New Britain Ave	Farmington	CT	06032	**800-243-0182**	860-677-9711
RUAN Transportation Management Systems 666 Grand Ave 3200 Ruan Ctr	Des Moines	IA	50309	**866-782-6669**	515-245-2500

FLOOR COVERINGS - MFR

SEE Tile - Ceramic (Wall & Floor) ; Carpets & Rugs ; Flooring - Resilient

292 FLOOR COVERINGS STORES

	City	State	Zip	Toll-Free	Phone
Boa-Franc Inc 1255-98th St	Saint-georges	QC	G5Y8J5	**800-463-1303**	418-227-1181
Century Tile Supply Co 747 E Roosevelt Rd	Lombard	IL	60148	**888-845-3968**	630-495-2300
Clark-Dunbar Flooring Superstore 3232 Empire Dr	Alexandria	LA	71301	**800-256-1467**	318-445-0262
Dolphin Carpet & Tile 3550 NW 77th Ct	Miami	FL	33122	**800-639-3566**	305-591-4141
Eckards Home Improvement 2402 N Belt Hwy	Saint Joseph	MO	64506	**800-264-2794**	816-279-4522
EG Penner Building Centres 200 Park Rd W	Steinbach	MB	R5G1A1	**800-353-8733**	204-326-1325
Elte 80 Ronald Ave	Toronto	ON	M6E5A2	**888-276-3583**	416-785-7885
Feizy Import & Export Co Ltd 1949 Stemmons Fwy	Dallas	TX	75207	**800-779-0877**	214-747-6000
Floor Coverings International 5250 Triangle Pwy Ste 100 *Sales	Norcross	GA	30092	**800-955-4324***	770-874-7600
Flooring Sales Group 1251 First Ave S	Seattle	WA	98134	**877-478-3577**	206-624-7800
Furniture Outlets USA Inc 140 E Hinks Ln	Sioux Falls	SD	57104	**877-395-8998**	605-336-5000
Hi Tech Data Floors Inc 1885 Swarthmore Ave	Lakewood	NJ	08701	**800-544-8321**	732-905-1799
Lumber Liquidators Inc 1455 VFW Pkwy	West Roxbury	MA	02132	**800-227-0332**	617-327-1222
Quality Craft Ltd 17750-65A Ave Ste 301	Surrey	BC	V3S5N4	**800-663-2252**	604-575-5550
Roysons Corp 40 Vanderhoof Ave	Rockaway	NJ	07866	**888-769-7667**	973-625-7923
Starline Associates Inc 3901 Sw 47th Ave Ste 410	Davie	FL	33314	**866-752-6548**	954-792-1965
Teragren Fine Bamboo Flooring Panels & Veneer 12715 Miller Rd Ne Ste 301	Bainbridge Island	WA	98110	**800-929-6333**	206-842-9477
Tom Duffy Co 5200 Watt Ct Ste B	Fairfield	CA	94534	**800-479-5671**	

293 FLOORING - RESILIENT

SEE ALSO Recycled Plastics Products

	City	State	Zip	Toll-Free	Phone
American Floor Products Company Inc 7977 Cessna Ave	Gaithersburg	MD	20879	**800-342-0424**	
Armstrong World Industries Inc 2500 Columbia Ave *NYSE: AWI* ■ *Cust Svc	Lancaster	PA	17603	**800-233-3823***	717-397-0611
Congoleum Corp 3500 Quakerridge Rd PO Box 3127	Mercerville	NJ	08619	**800-274-3266**	609-584-3000
Expanko Inc 180 Gordon Dr Ste 113	Exton	PA	19341	**800-345-6202**	
Forbo Flooring Systems 8 Maplewood Dr Humboldt Industrial Pk *Cust Svc	Hazleton	PA	18202	**800-842-7839***	
Formica Corp 10155 Reading Rd	Cincinnati	OH	45241	**800-367-6422**	513-786-3400
Fryer-Knowles Inc 205 S Dawson St	Seattle	WA	98108	**800-544-6052**	206-767-7710
Mannington Mills Inc 75 Mannington Mills Rd *Cust Svc	Salem	NJ	08079	**800-356-6787***	856-935-3000
Pergo Inc 3128 Highwoods Blvd Ste 100	Raleigh	NC	27604	**800-337-3746**	
RCA Rubber Co 1833 E Market St	Akron	OH	44305	**800-321-2340**	330-784-1291
Regupol America 33 Keystone Dr	Lebanon	PA	17042	**800-537-8737**	
Roppe Corp 1602 N Union St	Fostoria	OH	44830	**800-537-9527**	419-435-8546
Stonhard Inc 1000 E Pk Ave *Cust Svc	Maple Shade	NJ	08052	**800-854-0310***	856-779-7500
Superior Mfg Group 5655 W 73rd St	Chicago	IL	60638	**800-621-2802**	708-458-4600
Surface Shields Inc 10457 163rd Pl	Orland Park	IL	60467	**800-754-9685**	708-226-9810
Tarkett Inc 1001 Yamaska St E	Farnham	QC	J2N1J7	**800-363-9276**	450-293-3173

294 FLORISTS

SEE ALSO Garden Centers

	City	State	Zip	Toll-Free	Phone
1-800-Flowers.com Inc 1 Old Country Rd Ste 500 *NASDAQ: FLWS*	Carle Place	NY	11514	**800-356-9377**	516-237-6000
Arrow Florist & Park Avenue Greenhouses Inc 757 Pk Ave	Cranston	RI	02910	**800-556-7097**	401-785-1900
Astoria-Pacific Inc 15130 SE 82nd Dr	Clackamas	OR	97015	**800-536-3111**	503-657-3010
Bachman's Inc 6010 Lyndale Ave S	Minneapolis	MN	55419	**888-222-4626**	612-861-7311
Baisch & Skinner Inc 2721 Lasalle St	Saint Louis	MO	63104	**800-523-0013**	314-664-1212
Barry-owen Co Inc 5625 Smithway St	Los Angeles	CA	90040	**800-682-6682**	323-724-4800
Birthday Direct 120 Commerce St	Muscle Shoals	AL	35661	**888-491-9185**	256-381-0310
BloomNation LLC 8889 W Olympic Blvd	Beverly Hills	CA	90211	**877-702-5666**	
Boesen the Florist 3422 Beaver Ave	Des Moines	IA	50310	**800-274-4761**	515-274-4761
Boite a Fleur De Laval Inc La 3266 Boul Sainte-Rose	Laval	QC	H7P4K8	**800-784-3495**	450-622-0341
Burchell Nursery Inc, The 12000 Hwy 120	Oakdale	CA	95361	**800-828-8733**	209-845-8733
Cactus Flower Florists 10822 N Scottsdale Rd	Scottsdale	AZ	85254	**800-922-2887**	480-483-9200
Canada Flowers 4073 Longhurst Ave	Niagara Falls	ON	L2E6G5	**888-705-9999**	905-354-2713
Connell's Map Lee Flowers & Gifts 2408 E Main St	Bexley	OH	43209	**800-790-8980**	614-237-8653
Country Lane Flower Shop 729 S Michigan Ave	Howell	MI	48843	**800-764-7673**	517-546-1111
Danson Decor Inc 3425 Douglas B Floreani	St Laurent	QC	H4S1Y6	**800-363-1865**	514-335-2435
Dr Delphinium Designs & Events 5806 W Lovers Ln & Tollway	Dallas	TX	75225	**800-783-8790**	214-522-9911
Eastern Floral & Gift Shop 818 Butterworth St SW	Grand Rapids	MI	49504	**800-494-2202**	616-949-2200
Felly's Flowers Inc PO Box 6620	Madison	WI	53716	**800-993-7673**	
Flower Patch Inc 4370 S 300 W *General	Murray	UT	84107	**888-865-6858***	801-747-2824
Flower Pot Florists 2314 N Broadway St	Knoxville	TN	37917	**800-824-7792**	865-523-5121
Flowers by Sleeman for All Seasons & Reasons Ltd 1201 Memorial Rd	Houghton	MI	49931	**800-400-4023**	906-482-4023
Formaggio Kitchen on Line LLC 244 Huron Ave	Cambridge	MA	02138	**888-212-3224**	617-354-4750
Foster City Flowers & Gifts 1160 Chess Dr Ste 1	Foster City	CA	94404	**800-970-7673**	650-573-6607
Freeman's Flowers & Event Consultants 2934 Duniven Cir	Amarillo	TX	79109	**800-846-3104**	806-355-4451
Fruit Co, The 2900 Van Horn Dr	Hood River	OR	97031	**800-387-3100**	541-387-3100
FTD Inc 3113 Woodcreek Dr *Cust Svc	Downers Grove	IL	60515	**800-736-3383***	
Gift of Life Foundation 3861 Research Park Dr	Ann Arbor	MI	48108	**866-500-5801**	734-973-1577
Gifts for You LLC 2425 Curtiss St	Downers Grove	IL	60515	**866-443-8748**	630-771-0095
Greeters of Hawaii Ltd 300 Rodgers Blvd Ste 266	Honolulu	HI	96819	**800-366-8559**	808-836-0161
Grower Direct Fresh Cut Flowers 6303 Wagner Rd	Edmonton	AB	T6E4N4	**877-277-4787**	780-436-7774
Hardin's Florist Supply 329 W Bowman Ave	Liberty	NC	27298	**800-672-8226**	336-622-3035
Higdon Florist 201 E 32nd St	Joplin	MO	64804	**800-641-4726**	417-624-7171
Hillcrest Garden 95 W Century Rd	Paramus	NJ	07652	**800-437-7000**	201-599-3030
Howard Bros Florists 8700 S Pennsylvania Ave	Oklahoma City	OK	73159	**800-648-0524**	405-632-4747
John Wolf Florist 6228 Waters Ave	Savannah	GA	31406	**800-944-6435**	912-352-9843
Johnston the Florist Inc 14179 Lincoln Way	North Huntingdon	PA	15642	**800-356-9371**	412-751-2821
Jon's Nursery Inc 24546 Nursery Way	Eustis	FL	32736	**800-322-4289**	352-357-4289
Joyce Florist 2729 S Hampton Rd	Dallas	TX	75224	**800-527-1520**	214-942-1776
Ken's Flower Shop 140 W S Boundary St	Perrysburg	OH	43551	**800-253-0100**	419-874-1333
Kuhn Flowers Inc 3802 Beach Blvd	Jacksonville	FL	32207	**800-458-5846**	904-398-8601
Lester's Florist Inc 2100 Bull St	Savannah	GA	31401	**800-841-1103**	912-233-6066
Lloyd's Florist 9216 Preston Hwy	Louisville	KY	40229	**800-264-1825**	502-968-5428
Martina's Flowers & Gifts 3830 Washington Rd	Augusta	GA	30907	**800-927-1204**	706-863-7172
Mayesh Wholesale Florist Inc 5401 W 104th St	Los Angeles	CA	90045	**888-462-9374**	310-348-4921
Mellano & Co 766 Wall St	Los Angeles	CA	90014	**888-635-5266**	213-622-0796
Metropolitan Plant & Flower Exchange 2125 Fletcher Ave	Fort Lee	NJ	07024	**800-638-7613**	201-944-1050
Midwest Trading Horticultural Supplies Inc 48w805 Il Rt 64	Maple Park	IL	60151	**800-546-9522**	630-365-1990
Nakase Bros Wholesale Nursery 9441 Krepp Dr	Huntington Beach	CA	92646	**800-747-4388**	714-962-6604
Nanz & Kraft Florists Inc 141 Breckenridge Ln	Louisville	KY	40207	**800-897-6551**	502-897-6551
National Floral Supply Inc 3825 LeonaRdtown Rd Ste 4	Waldorf	MD	20601	**800-932-2772**	301-932-7600
Niagara Helicopters Ltd 3731 Victoria Ave	Niagara Falls	ON	L2E6V5	**800-281-8034**	905-357-5672
Norton's Flowers & Gifts 2900 Washtenaw Ave	Ypsilanti	MI	48197	**800-682-8667**	734-434-2700
Nottawaseppi Huron Band of Potawatomi's FireKeepers Development Authority 11177 E Michigan Ave	Battle Creek	MI	49014	**877-353-8777**	
Office Playground Inc 715 Southpoint Blvd Ste 100	Petaluma	CA	94954	**800-458-1948**	415-483-1196

Classified Section

Company / Address	City	State	ZIP	Toll-Free	Phone
Phillip's Flower Shops Inc 524 N Cass Ave	Westmont	IL	60559	**800-356-7257**	630-719-5200
Phoenix Flower Shops 5733 E Thomas Rd Ste 4	Scottsdale	AZ	85251	**888-311-0404**	480-289-4000
Primitives by Kathy Inc 1817 William Penn Way	Lancaster	PA	17601	**866-295-2849**	
Proflowers.com 4840 Eastgate Mall	San Diego	CA	92121	**800-580-2913**	
Provide Commerce Inc 4840 Eastgate Mall *Cust Svc	San Diego	CA	92121	**800-776-3569***	858-729-2800
Sawyer Nursery Inc 5401 Port Sheldon St	Hudsonville	MI	49426	**888-378-7800**	616-669-9094
Schroeder's Flowerland Inc 1530 S Webster Ave	Green Bay	WI	54301	**800-236-4769**	920-436-6363
Smith Southwestern Inc 1850 N Rosemont	Mesa	AZ	85205	**800-783-3909**	480-854-9545
Strange's Florist Inc 3313 Mechanicsville Pk	Richmond	VA	23223	**800-421-4070**	804-321-2200
Sunwest Silver Company Inc 324 Lomas Blvd NW	Albuquerque	NM	87102	**800-771-3781**	505-243-3781
Thirstystone Resources Inc 1304 Corporate Dr	Gainesville	TX	76240	**800-829-6888**	940-668-6793
Tipton & Hurst Inc 1801 N Grant St	Little Rock	AR	72207	**800-666-3333**	501-666-3333
Veldkamp's Flowers 9501 W Colfax Ave	Lakewood	CO	80215	**800-247-3730**	303-232-2673
Villere's Florist 750 Martin Behrman Ave	Metairie	LA	70005	**800-845-5373**	504-833-3716
Viviano Flower Shop 32050 Harper Ave	Saint Clair Shores	MI	48082	**800-848-4266**	586-293-0227
Washington Floral Service Inc 2701 S 35th St	Tacoma	WA	98409	**800-351-5515**	253-472-8343
Watanabe Floral Inc 1607 Hart St	Honolulu	HI	96817	**888-832-9360**	808-832-9360
Winston Bros Inc 131 Newbury St	Boston	MA	02116	**800-457-4901**	617-541-1100
Winward International Inc 3089 Whipple Rd	Union City	CA	94587	**800-888-8898**	510-487-8686
Worrell Corp 305 S Post Rd	Indianapolis	IN	46219	**800-297-9599**	317-895-9708

295 FLOWERS & NURSERY STOCK - WHOL

SEE ALSO Horticultural Products Growers

Company / Address	City	State	ZIP	Toll-Free	Phone
Allstate Floral & Craft Inc 14038 Park Pl	Cerritos	CA	90703	**800-433-4056**	562-926-2302
Ball Horticultural Co 622 Town Rd	West Chicago	IL	60185	**800-879-2255**	630-231-3600
Claymore C Sieck Wholesale Florist 311 E Chase St	Baltimore	MD	21202	**800-624-7134**	410-685-4660
Cleveland Plant & Flower Co 12920 Corporate Dr	Cleveland	OH	44130	**888-231-7569**	216-898-3500
Delaware Valley Wholesale Florist Inc (DVWF) 520 Mantua Blvd N	Sewell	NJ	08080	**800-676-1212**	856-468-7000
Denver Wholesale Florists Co 4800 Dahlia St	Denver	CO	80216	**800-829-8280**	303-399-0970
Distinctive Designs International Inc 120 Sibley Dr	Russellville	AL	35654	**800-243-4787**	256-332-7390
Esprit Miami 3043 NW 107th Ave	Miami	FL	33172	**800-327-2320**	305-591-2244
Florist Distributing Inc 2403 Bell Ave	Des Moines	IA	50321	**800-373-3741**	515-243-5228
Holmberg Farms Inc 13430 Hobson Simmons Rd	Lithia	FL	33547	**800-282-3562**	
Karthauser & Sons Inc W 147 N 11100 Fond du Lac Ave	Germantown	WI	53022	**800-338-8620**	262-255-7815
Kennicott Bros 452 N Ashland Ave	Chicago	IL	60622	**866-346-2826**	312-492-8200
L & L Nursery Supply Co Inc 2552 Shenandoah Way	San Bernardino	CA	92407	**800-624-2517**	909-591-0461
Pittsburgh Cut Flower Co 1901 Liberty Ave	Pittsburgh	PA	15222	**800-837-2837**	412-355-7000
Tapscott's 1403 E 18th St	Owensboro	KY	42303	**800-626-1922**	270-684-2308
Teters Floral Products Inc 1425 S Lillian Ave	Bolivar	MO	65613	**800-999-5996**	417-326-7654
Van Well Nursery 2821 Grant Rd	East Wenatchee	WA	98802	**800-572-1553**	509-886-8189
Van Zyverden Inc 8079 Van Zyverden Rd	Meridian	MS	39305	**800-332-2852**	601-679-8274
Zieger & Sons Inc 6215 Ardleigh St	Philadelphia	PA	19138	**800-752-2003**	215-438-7060

296 FOIL & LEAF - METAL

Company / Address	City	State	ZIP	Toll-Free	Phone
Air Cycle Corp 2200 Ogden Ave Ste 100	Lisle	IL	60532	**800-909-9709**	
Alamo Industrial Inc 1502 East Walnut St	Seguin	TX	78155	**800-356-6286**	
Automotive Resources Inc 12775 Randolph Ridge Ln	Manassas	VA	20109	**800-562-3250**	703-359-6265
B&G Equipment Company Inc 135 Region S Dr	Jackson	GA	30233	**800-544-8811**	678-688-5601
Buff & Shine Manufacturing Inc 2139 E Del Amo Blvd	Compton	CA	90220	**800-659-2833**	310-886-5111
Chem-pak Inc 242 Corning Way	Martinsburg	WV	25405	**800-336-9828**	304-262-1880
Chemetal 39 O'Neil St	EastHampton	MA	01027	**800-807-7341**	413-529-0718
Crown Roll Leaf Inc 91 Illinois Ave	Paterson	NJ	07503	**800-631-3831**	973-742-4000
Diamond Z Manufacturing 11299 Bass Ln	Caldwell	ID	83605	**800-949-2383**	208-585-2929
Hodge Products Inc PO Box 1326	El Cajon	CA	92020	**800-778-2217**	
Ideal Shield LLC 2525 Clark St	Detroit	MI	48209	**866-825-8659**	313-842-7290
Oak-Mitsui Inc 80 First St	Hoosick Falls	NY	12090	**800-424-8802**	518-686-4961
October Company Inc 51 Ferry St	EastHampton	MA	01027	**800-628-9346**	413-527-9380
Precision Hose 2200 Centre Park Ct	Stone Mountain	GA	30087	**877-850-2662**	770-413-5680
Prentex Alloy Fabricators Inc 3108 Sylvan Ave	Dallas	TX	75212	**877-773-6839**	214-748-7837
Shade Systems Inc 4150 Sw 19th St	Ocala	FL	34474	**800-609-6066**	352-237-0135
Vooner Flogard Corp 4729 Stockholm Ct	Charlotte	NC	28273	**800-345-7879**	704-552-9314
Warren Co, The 2201 Loveland Ave	Erie	PA	16506	**800-562-0357**	

297 FOOD PRODUCTS - MFR

SEE ALSO Salt ; Ice - Manufactured ; Livestock & Poultry Feeds - Prepared ; Meat Packing Plants ; Pet Products ; Poultry Processing ; Agricultural Products ; Bakeries ; Beverages - Mfr

Company / Address	City	State	ZIP	Toll-Free	Phone
AlturnaMATS Inc 701 E Spring St Mailbox #9	Titusville	PA	16354	**800-438-9336**	814-827-8884
Contemar Silo Systems Inc 30 Pennsylvania Ave Unit 8	Concord	ON	L4K4A5	**800-567-2741**	905-669-3604
Flatout Inc 1422 Woodland Dr	Saline	MI	48176	**866-944-5445**	734-944-4262
Koss Industrial Inc 1943 Commercial Way	Green Bay	WI	54311	**800-844-6261**	920-469-5300
Remco Products Corp 4735 W 106th St	Zionsville	IN	46077	**800-585-8619**	317-876-9856
Revent Inc 100 Ethel Rd W	Piscataway	NJ	08854	**800-822-9642**	732-777-9433
Thomsen Group LLC 1303 43rd St	Kenosha	WI	53140	**800-558-4018**	
Wixon Inc 1390 E Bolivar Ave	Saint Francis	WI	53235	**800-841-5304**	414-769-3000

297-1 Bakery Products - Fresh

Company / Address	City	State	ZIP	Toll-Free	Phone
Alfred Nickles Bakery Inc 26 N Main St	Navarre	OH	44662	**800-597-9096**	330-879-5635
Bays Corp PO Box 1455	Chicago	IL	60690	**800-367-2297**	
Bimbo Bakeries USA PO Box 976	Horsham	PA	19044	**800-984-0989**	
Calise & Sons Bakery Inc 2 Quality Dr	Lincoln	RI	02865	**800-225-4737**	401-334-3444
De Wafelbakkers LLC 10000 Crystal Hill Rd.	North Little Rock	AR	72113	**800-924-3391**	501-791-3320
Delight Grecian Foods Inc 1201 Tonne Rd	Elk Grove Village	IL	60007	**800-621-4387**	847-364-1010
Dinkel's Bakery 3329 N Lincoln Ave *Orders	Chicago	IL	60657	**800-822-8817***	773-281-7300
Fantini Baking Company Inc 375 Washington St	Haverhill	MA	01832	**800-223-9037**	978-373-1273
Greyston Bakery Inc 104 Alexander St	Yonkers	NY	10701	**800-289-2253**	914-375-1510
H & S Bakery Inc 601 S Caroline St	Baltimore	MD	21231	**800-959-7655**	410-276-7254
Heiners Bakery Inc 1300 Adams Ave	Huntington	WV	25704	**800-776-8411**	304-523-8411
Klosterman Baking Company Inc 4760 Paddock Rd	Cincinnati	OH	45229	**877-301-1004**	513-242-1004
Lawler Foods Ltd Inc PO Box 2558	Humble	TX	77347	**800-541-8285**	281-446-0059
Leidenheimer Baking Co 1501 Simon Bolivar Ave	New Orleans	LA	70113	**800-259-9099**	504-525-1575
Martin's Famous Pastry Shoppe Inc 1000 Potato Roll Ln *Cust Svc	Chambersburg	PA	17201	**800-548-1200***	717-263-9580
McKee Foods Corp PO Box 750 *Cust Svc	Collegedale	TN	37315	**800-522-4499***	423-238-7111
Morabito Baking Company Inc 757 Kohn St	Norristown	PA	19401	**800-525-7747**	610-275-5419
Orlando Baking Company Inc 7777 Grand Ave	Cleveland	OH	44104	**800-362-5504**	216-361-1872
Pan-O-Gold Baking Co 444 E St Germain	Saint Cloud	MN	56304	**800-444-7005**	320-251-9361
Pepperidge Farm Inc 595 Westport Ave *PR	Norwalk	CT	06851	**888-737-7374***	203-846-7000
Piantedosi Baking Company Inc 240 Commercial St	Malden	MA	02148	**800-339-0080**	781-321-3400
Rothbury Farms PO Box 202	Grand Rapids	MI	49501	**877-684-2879**	
Schwebel Baking Co PO Box 6018	Youngstown	OH	44501	**800-860-2867**	330-783-2860
Signature Breads Inc 100 Justin Dr	Chelsea	MA	02150	**888-602-6533**	
Sokol & Co 5315 Dansher Rd *Cust Svc	Countryside	IL	60525	**800-328-7656***	708-482-8250
Tasty Baking Co 4300 S 26th St	Philadelphia	PA	19112	**800-248-2789**	215-221-8500
Wenner Bread Products Inc 33 Rajon Rd	Bayport	NY	11705	**800-869-6262**	631-563-6262
Wolferman's 2500 S Pacific Hwy PO Box 9100	Medford	OR	97501	**800-999-0169**	

297-2 Bakery Products - Frozen

Company / Address	City	State	Zip	Toll-Free	Phone
Athens Pastries & Frozen Foods Inc 13600 Snow Rd	Brookpark	OH	44142	**800-837-5683**	216-676-8500
Bridgford Foods Corp 1308 N Patt St *NASDAQ: BRID*	Anaheim	CA	92801	**800-854-3255**	714-526-5533
Dessert Innovations Inc 25-B Enterprise Blvd	Atlanta	GA	30336	**800-359-7351**	404-691-5000
Eli's Cheesecake Co 6701 W Forest Preserve Dr	Chicago	IL	60634	**800-999-8300**	773-736-3417
Guttenplans Frozen Dough 100 Hwy 36 *General	Middletown	NJ	07748	**888-422-4357***	732-495-9480
James Skinner Baking Co 4657 G St	Omaha	NE	68117	**800-358-7428**	402-734-1672
Main Street Gourmet Inc 170 Muffin Ln	Cuyahoga Falls	OH	44223	**800-678-6246**	330-929-0000
Maplehurst Inc 50 Maplehurst Dr	Brownsburg	IN	46112	**800-344-4235**	317-858-9000
Rhino Foods Inc 79 Industrial Pkwy	Burlington	VT	05401	**800-639-3350**	802-862-0252
Vie de France Yamazaki Inc 2070 Chain Bridge Rd Ste 500 *General	Vienna	VA	22182	**800-446-4404***	703-442-9205

297-3 Butter (Creamery)

Company / Address	City	State	Zip	Toll-Free	Phone
AMPI 315 N Broadway	New Ulm	MN	56073	**800-533-3580**	507-354-8295
Cabot Creamery 193 Home Farm Way	Waitsfield	VT	05673	**888-792-2268**	802-229-9361
Grassland Dairy Products Company Inc N 8790 Fairgrounds Ave PO Box 160	Greenwood	WI	54437	**800-428-8837**	715-267-6182
O-AT-KA Milk Products Co-op Inc 700 Ellicott St	Batavia	NY	14020	**800-828-8152**	585-343-0536
Plainview Milk Products Co-Op 130 Second St SW	Plainview	MN	55964	**800-356-5606**	507-534-3872

297-4 Cereals (Breakfast)

Company / Address	City	State	Zip	Toll-Free	Phone
Big G Cereals PO Box 9452 PO Box 9452	Minneapolis	MN	55440	**800-248-7310**	
Bob's Red Mill Natural Foods Inc 13521 SE Pheasant Ct	Milwaukie	OR	97222	**800-553-2258**	503-654-3215
Homestead Mills 221 N River St PO Box 1115	Cook	MN	55723	**800-652-5233**	218-666-5233
Honeyville Grain Inc 11600 Dayton Dr	Rancho Cucamonga	CA	91730	**888-810-3212**	909-980-9500
Kellogg Co 1 Kellogg Sq PO Box 3599 *NYSE: K* ■ *Cust Svc	Battle Creek	MI	49016	**800-962-1413***	269-961-2000
New England Natural Bakers 74 Fairview St E	Greenfield	MA	01301	**800-910-2884**	413-772-2239
Organic Milling Co 505 W Allen Ave	San Dimas	CA	91773	**800-638-8686**	909-599-0961
Quaker Oats Co 555 W Monroe St	Chicago	IL	60661	**800-367-6287**	312-821-1000
Weetabix Co Inc 300 Nickerson Rd	Marlborough	MA	01752	**800-343-0590**	978-368-0991

297-5 Cheeses - Natural, Processed, Imitation

Company / Address	City	State	Zip	Toll-Free	Phone
AMPI 315 N Broadway	New Ulm	MN	56073	**800-533-3580**	507-354-8295
Berner Foods Inc 2034 E Factory Rd	Dakota	IL	61018	**800-819-8199**	815-563-4222
Burnett Dairy Co-op 11631 SR- 70	Grantsburg	WI	54840	**800-854-2716**	715-689-2468
Cabot Creamery 193 Home Farm Way	Waitsfield	VT	05673	**888-792-2268**	802-229-9361
Cacique Inc 14923 Procter Ave	La Puente	CA	91746	**800-521-6987**	626-961-3399
ConAgra Foods Retail Products Co Deli Foods Group 215 W Field Rd	Naperville	IL	60563	**877-266-2472**	630-857-1000
Dairiconcepts LP 3253 E Chestnut Expy	Springfield	MO	65802	**877-596-4374**	417-829-3400
Dairy Farmers of America Inc 10220 N Ambassador Dr	Kansas City	MO	64153	**888-332-6455**	816-801-6455
Farmdale Creamery Inc 1049 W Baseline St	San Bernardino	CA	92411	**800-346-7306**	909-889-3002
Galaxy Nutritional Foods Inc 66 Whitecap Dr	North Kingstown	RI	02852	**800-441-9419**	401-667-5000
Gossner Foods Inc 1051 N 1000 W	Logan	UT	84321	**800-944-0454**	435-713-6100
Grande Cheese Co 301 E Main St	Lomira	WI	53048	**800-772-3210**	
Hilmar Cheese Company Inc PO Box 910	Hilmar	CA	95324	**888-300-4465**	209-667-6076
Jerome Cheese Co 547 W Nez Perce	Jerome	ID	83338	**800-757-7611**	208-324-8806
Le Sueur Cheese Company Inc 719 N Main St	Le Sueur	MN	56058	**800-247-0871**	507-665-3353
Sargento Foods Inc 1 Persnickety Pl	Plymouth	WI	53073	**800-243-3737**	920-893-8484
Sartori Food Corp 107 Pleasant View Rd *Cust Svc	Plymouth	WI	53073	**800-558-5888***	920-893-6061
Swiss Valley Farms 247 Research Pkwy PO Box 4493	Davenport	IA	52808	**800-747-6113**	563-468-6600
Tropical Cheese Industries Inc 450 Fayette St PO Box 1357	Perth Amboy	NJ	08861	**888-874-4928**	732-442-4898

297-6 Chewing Gum

Company / Address	City	State	Zip	Toll-Free	Phone
Concord Confections Ltd 345 Courtland Ave	Concord	ON	L4K5A6	**800-267-0037**	905-660-8989
Topps Company Inc 1 Whitehall St	New York	NY	10004	**800-489-9149**	212-376-0300
Wrigley Co, The 410 N Michigan Ave	Chicago	IL	60611	**888-985-2064**	312-644-2121

297-7 Coffee - Roasted (Ground, Instant, Freeze-Dried)

Company / Address	City	State	Zip	Toll-Free	Phone
Allegro Coffee Co 12799 Claude Ct	Thornton	CO	80241	**800-530-3995**	303-444-4844
ARCO Coffee Company 2206 Winter St	Superior	WI	54880	**800-283-2726**	715-392-4771
Autocrat Coffee Inc 10 Blackstone Vly Pl	Lincoln	RI	02865	**800-288-6272**	401-333-3300
Boyd Coffee Co 19730 NE Sandy Blvd *Cust Svc	Portland	OR	97230	**800-545-4077***	503-666-4545
Cadillac Coffee Co 194 E Maple Rd	Troy	MI	48083	**800-438-6900**	248-545-2266
Coffee Holding Company Inc 3475 Victory Blvd *NASDAQ: JVA*	Staten Island	NY	10314	**800-458-2233**	718-832-0800
Community Coffee Co PO Box 2311	Baton Rouge	LA	70821	**800-688-0990**	800-884-5282
DeCoty Coffee Company Inc 1920 Austin St	San Angelo	TX	76903	**800-588-8001**	
Farmer Bros Co 20333 S Normandie Ave *NASDAQ: FARM*	Torrance	CA	90502	**800-735-2878**	310-787-5200
Frontier Natural Products Co-op 3021 78th St PO Box 299	Norway	IA	52318	**800-669-3275**	319-227-7996
Hawaiian Isles Kona Coffee Co 2839 Mokumoa St *Orders	Honolulu	HI	96819	**800-657-7716***	808-839-3255
McCullagh Coffee 245 Swan St	Buffalo	NY	14204	**800-753-3473**	
Melitta Canada Inc 50 Ronson Dr Unit 150	Toronto	ON	M9W1B3	**800-565-4882**	
New England Coffee Co 100 Charles St	Malden	MA	02148	**800-225-3537**	
Old Mansion Foods 3811 Corporate Rd PO Box 1838	Petersburg	VA	23805	**800-476-1877**	804-862-9889
Paul deLima Co Inc 7546 Morgan Rd	Liverpool	NY	13090	**800-962-8864**	315-457-3725
Red Diamond Inc 400 Park Ave	Moody	AL	35004	**800-292-4651**	205-577-4000
Reily Foods Co 640 Magazine St	New Orleans	LA	70130	**800-535-1961**	504-524-6131
Royal Cup Coffee 160 Cleage Dr *Cust Svc	Birmingham	AL	35217	**800-366-5836***	
S & D Coffee Inc 300 Concord Pkwy PO Box 1628 *Cust Svc	Concord	NC	28026	**800-933-2210***	704-782-3121
Texas Coffee Co Inc 3297 S M L King Jr Pkwy	Beaumont	TX	77705	**800-259-3400**	409-835-3434
Torke Coffee Roasting Company Inc 3455 Paine Ave	Sheboygan	WI	53081	**800-242-7671**	920-458-4114
Van Roy Coffee Co, The 4569 Spring Rd	Cleveland	OH	44131	**877-826-7669**	216-749-7069
White Coffee Corp 18-35 Steinway Pl	Astoria	NY	11105	**800-221-0140**	718-204-7900

297-8 Confectionery Products

Company / Address	City	State	Zip	Toll-Free	Phone
ADM Cocoa Div 77 W Wacker Dr	Chicago	IL	60601	**800-637-5843**	217-424-5200
Anthony-Thomas Candy Co 1777 Arlingate Ln	Columbus	OH	43228	**877-226-3921**	614-274-8405
Asher's Chocolates 80 Wambold Rd	Souderton	PA	18964	**800-223-4420**	215-721-3000
Atkinson Candy Co 1608 W Frank Ave	Lufkin	TX	75904	**800-231-1203**	936-639-2333
Barry Callebaut USA LLC 400 Industrial Pk Rd	Saint Albans	VT	05478	**866-443-0460**	802-524-9711
Best Sweet Inc 288 Mazeppa Rd	Mooresville	NC	28115	**888-211-5530**	704-664-4300
Blommer Chocolate Co 600 W Kinzie St	Chicago	IL	60610	**800-621-1606**	312-226-7700
Brown & Haley PO Box 1596	Tacoma	WA	98401	**800-426-8400**	
Charms Co 7401 S Cicero Ave	Chicago	IL	60629	**800-267-0037**	773-838-3400
Cherrydale Farms Fundraising 707 N Vly Forge Rd	Lansdale	PA	19446	**877-619-4822**	
Chocolates a la Carte Inc 28455 Livingston Ave *Cust Svc	Valencia	CA	91355	**800-818-2462***	
Eaton Farm Confectioners Inc 30 Burbank Rd	Sutton	MA	01590	**800-343-9300**	508-865-5235
Esther Price Candies Inc 1709 Wayne Ave	Dayton	OH	45410	**800-782-0326**	937-253-2121
Fowler's Chocolate Co 100 River Rock Dr Ste 102	Buffalo	NY	14207	**800-824-2263**	716-877-9983
Gertrude Hawk Chocolates Inc 9 Keystone Pk	Dunmore	PA	18512	**866-932-4295**	800-822-2032
Ghirardelli Chocolate Co 1111 139th Ave	San Leandro	CA	94578	**800-877-9338**	

Classified Section

Company / Address	City	State	Zip	Toll-Free	Phone
Goetze's Candy Company Inc 3900 E Monument St *Orders	Baltimore	MD	21205	**800-295-8058***	410-342-2010
Guittard Chocolate Co 10 GuittaRd Rd	Burlingame	CA	94010	**800-468-2462**	650-697-4427
Harry London Candies Inc 5353 Lauby Rd *Cust Svc	North Canton	OH	44720	**800-333-3629***	330-494-0833
Hershey Co 100 Crystal A Dr *NYSE: HSY* ■ *Cust Svc	Hershey	PA	17033	**800-468-1714***	
Hillside Candy Co 35 Hillside Ave	Hillside	NJ	07205	**800-524-1304**	973-926-2300
James Candy Co 1519 Boardwalk *Orders	Atlantic City	NJ	08401	**800-441-1404***	609-344-1519
Jelly Belly Candy Co 1 Jelly Belly Ln	Fairfield	CA	94533	**800-323-9380**	707-428-2800
Just Born Inc 1300 Stefko Blvd	Bethlehem	PA	18017	**800-445-5787**	610-867-7568
Katharine Beecher Candies 1250 Slate Hill Rd	Camp Hill	PA	17011	**800-233-7082**	717-761-5440
Koeze Co PO Box 9470	Grand Rapids	MI	49509	**800-555-9688**	
Lammes Candies Since 1885 Inc PO Box 1885	Austin	TX	78767	**800-252-1885**	512-310-2223
Lindt & Sprungli USA 1 Fine Chocolate Pl	Stratham	NH	03885	**877-695-4638**	603-778-8100
Lucks Co, The 3003 S Pine St	Tacoma	WA	98409	**800-426-9778**	253-383-4815
Madelaine Chocolate Novelties Inc 9603 Beach Ch Dr	Rockaway Beach	NY	11693	**800-322-1505**	718-945-1500
Malleys Chocolates 13400 Brookpark Rd	Cleveland	OH	44135	**800-835-5684**	216-362-8700
Moonstruck Chocolate Co 6600 N Baltimore Ave	Portland	OR	97203	**800-557-6666**	503-247-3448
Morley Candy Makers Inc 23770 Hall Rd	Clinton Township	MI	48036	**800-651-7263**	586-468-4300
Munson's Candy Kitchen Inc 174 Hop River Rd	Bolton	CT	06043	**888-686-7667**	860-649-4332
Paradise Inc 1200 W MLK Jr Blvd *OTC: PARF*	Plant City	FL	33563	**800-330-8952**	
Pearson's Candy Co 2140 W Seventh St *Cust Svc	Saint Paul	MN	55116	**800-328-6507***	651-698-0356
Pennsylvania Dutch Candies 1250 Slate Hill Rd	Camp Hill	PA	17011	**800-233-7082**	717-761-5440
Russell Stover Candies Inc 4900 Oak St	Kansas City	MO	64112	**800-477-8683**	816-842-9240
See's Candies Inc 210 El Camino Real *Cust Svc	South San Francisco	CA	94080	**800-877-7337***	650-761-2490
Sorbee International Ltd 9990 Global Rd	Philadelphia	PA	19115	**800-654-3997**	215-645-1111
Spangler Candy Co 400 N Portland St PO Box 71 *Sales	Bryan	OH	43506	**888-636-4221***	419-636-4221
Storck USA LP 325 N LaSalle St Ste 400	Chicago	IL	60654	**800-852-5542**	312-467-5700
Sweet Candy Co Inc 3780 W Directors Row	Salt Lake City	UT	84104	**800-669-8669**	801-886-1444
T R Toppers Inc 320 Fairchild	Pueblo	CO	81001	**800-748-4635**	719-948-4902
Tootsie Roll Industries Inc 7401 S Cicero Ave *NYSE: TR*	Chicago	IL	60629	**866-972-6879**	773-838-3400
Vitasoy USA Inc 1 New England Way	Ayer	MA	01432	**800-848-2769**	978-772-6880
Waymouth Farms Inc 5300 Boone Ave	New Hope	MN	55428	**800-527-0094**	763-533-5300
Wolfgang Candy Co 50 E Fourth Ave	York	PA	17404	**800-248-4273**	717-843-5536
World's Finest Chocolate Inc 4801 S Lawndale	Chicago	IL	60632	**888-821-8452**	
Zachary Confections Inc 2130 IN-28 *Cust Svc	Frankfort	IN	46041	**800-445-4222***	

297-9 Cookies & Crackers

Company / Address	City	State	Zip	Toll-Free	Phone
Benzel's Pretzel Bakery Inc 5200 Sixth Ave	Altoona	PA	16602	**800-344-4438**	814-942-5062
Bremner Biscuit Co 4600 Joliet St	Denver	CO	80239	**866-972-6879**	303-371-8180
Christie Cookie Co 1205 Third Ave N	Nashville	TN	37208	**800-458-2447**	615-242-3817
Delyse Inc 505 Reactor Way	Reno	NV	89502	**800-441-6887**	775-857-1811
J & J Snack Foods Corp 6000 Central Hwy *NASDAQ: JJSF*	Pennsauken	NJ	08109	**800-486-9533**	856-665-9533
Joy Cone Co 3435 Lamor Rd	Hermitage	PA	16148	**800-242-2663**	724-962-5747
Keystone Pretzels 124 W Airport Rd	Lititz	PA	17543	**888-572-4500**	
Norse Dairy Systems 1740 Joyce Ave	Columbus	OH	43219	**800-637-2663**	614-294-4931
Pretzels Inc 123 Harvest Rd PO Box 503	Bluffton	IN	46714	**800-456-4838**	260-824-4838
Rudolph Foods Company Inc 6575 Bellefontaine Rd	Lima	OH	45804	**800-241-7675**	419-648-3611
Silver Lake Cookie Company Inc 141 Freeman Ave	Islip	NY	11751	**800-645-9048**	631-581-4000
Snyder's of Hanover 1250 York St PO Box 6917	Hanover	PA	17331	**800-233-7125**	717-632-4477
T. Marzetti Company. PO Box 29163	Columbus	OH	43229	**800-999-1835**	
Tom Sturgis Pretzels Inc 2267 Lancaster Pk	Reading	PA	19607	**800-817-3834**	610-775-0335
Wege Pretzel Co PO Box 334	Hanover	PA	17331	**800-888-4646**	

297-10 Dairy Products - Dry, Condensed, Evaporated

Company / Address	City	State	Zip	Toll-Free	Phone
Abbott Laboratories Ross Products Div 625 Cleveland Ave *PR	Columbus	OH	43215	**800-227-5767***	614-624-7485
AMPI 315 N Broadway	New Ulm	MN	56073	**800-533-3580**	507-354-8295
Dairy Farmers of America Inc 10220 N Ambassador Dr	Kansas City	MO	64153	**888-332-6455**	816-801-6455
Davisco International Inc 719 N Main St	Le Sueur	MN	56058	**800-757-7611**	507-665-8811
Erie Foods International Inc 401 Seventh Ave PO Box 648	Erie	IL	61250	**800-447-1887**	309-659-2233
Foremost Farms USA E10889A Penny Ln	Baraboo	WI	53913	**800-362-9196**	608-355-8700
Gehl's Guernsey Farms Inc N116 W15970 Main St	Germantown	WI	53022	**800-521-2873**	262-251-8572
Instantwhip Foods Inc 2200 Cardigan Ave *Cust Svc	Columbus	OH	43215	**800-544-9447***	614-488-2536
John Volpi & Company Inc 5263 Northrup Ave	St Louis	MO	63110	**800-288-3439**	314-772-8550
Maple Island Inc 2497 Seventh Ave E Ste 105	St Paul	MN	55109	**800-369-1022**	651-773-1000
Milk Products LLC PO Box 150	Chilton	WI	53014	**800-657-0793**	920-849-2348
O-AT-KA Milk Products Co-op Inc 700 Ellicott St	Batavia	NY	14020	**800-828-8152**	585-343-0536
Sinton Dairy Foods Co LLC 3801 Sinton Rd	Colorado Springs	CO	80907	**800-388-4970**	719-633-3821

297-11 Diet & Health Foods

Company / Address	City	State	Zip	Toll-Free	Phone
AMS Health Sciences Inc 4000 N Lindsay	Oklahoma City	OK	73105	**800-426-4267**	405-842-0131
Eden Foods Inc 701 Tecumseh Rd *Cust Svc	Clinton	MI	49236	**800-248-0320***	517-456-7424
Isagenix International LLC 2225 S Price Rd	Chandler	AZ	85286	**877-877-8111**	480-889-5747
Medifast Inc 11445 Cronhill Dr *NYSE: MED*	Owings Mills	MD	21117	**800-209-0878**	
RC Fine Foods PO Box 236	Belle Mead	NJ	08502	**800-526-3953**	908-359-5500
Tahitian Noni International 333 W Riverpark Dr *Cust Svc	Provo	UT	84604	**800-445-2969***	801-234-1000
Vitaminerals Inc 1815 Flower St	Glendale	CA	91201	**800-432-1856**	

297-12 Fats & Oils - Animal or Marine

Company / Address	City	State	Zip	Toll-Free	Phone
Darling International Inc 251 O'Connor Ridge Blvd Ste 300 *NYSE: DAR*	Irving	TX	75038	**855-327-7761**	972-717-0300
GA Wintzer & Son Co 204 W Auglaize St	Wapakoneta	OH	45895	**800-331-1801**	419-739-4900
Jacob Stern & Sons Inc 1464 E Valley Rd *Cust Svc	Santa Barbara	CA	93108	**800-223-7054***	805-565-1411
Werner G Smith Inc 1730 Train Ave *General	Cleveland	OH	44113	**800-535-8343***	216-861-3676

297-13 Fish & Seafood - Canned

Company / Address	City	State	Zip	Toll-Free	Phone
Beaver Street Fisheries Inc 1741 W Beaver St	Jacksonville	FL	32209	**800-874-6426**	904-354-8533
Bumble Bee Seafoods Inc PO Box 85362	San Diego	CA	92186	**800-800-8572**	858-715-4000
Los Angeles Smoking & Curing Co (LASCCO) 1100 W Ewing St	Seattle	WA	98119	**800-365-8950**	206-285-6800
Nelson Crab Inc 3088 Kindred Ave	Tokeland	WA	98590	**800-262-0069**	
Noon Hour Food Products Inc 215 N Des Plaines *Cust Svc	Chicago	IL	60661	**888-463-6332***	312-382-1177
Overwaitea Food Group 19855 92A Ave	Langley	BC	V1M3B6	**800-242-9229**	604-888-1213
Peter Pan Seafoods Inc 2200 Sixth Ave Ste 1000	Seattle	WA	98121	**800-331-3522**	206-728-6000
Petersburg Fisheries PO Box 1147	Petersburg	AK	99833	**877-772-4294**	907-772-4294
Vita Food Products Inc 2222 W Lake St	Chicago	IL	60612	**800-989-8482**	312-738-4500

297-14 Fish & Seafood - Fresh or Frozen

Company / Address	City	State	Zip	Toll-Free	Phone
Blount Seafood Corp 630 Currant Rd *Hotline	Fall River	MA	02720	**800-274-2526***	774-888-1300
Consolidated Catfish Cos LLC 299 S St PO Box 271	Isola	MS	38754	**800-228-3474**	662-962-3101
Crocker & Winsor Seafoods Inc PO Box 51905	Boston	MA	02205	**800-225-1597**	617-269-3100
Freshwater Farm Products LLC 4554 State Hwy 12 E PO Box 850	Belzoni	MS	39038	**800-748-9338**	662-247-4205

Company	City	State	ZIP	Toll-Free	Phone
Gorton's Inc 128 Rogers St	Gloucester	MA	01930	**800-222-6846**	978-283-3000
King & Prince Seafood Corp 1 King & Prince Blvd	Brunswick	GA	31520	**800-841-0205**	912-265-5155
Morey's Seafood International LLC 1218 Hwy 10 S	Motley	MN	56466	**800-808-3474**	218-352-6345
Ocean Beauty Seafoods Inc 1100 W Ewing St	Seattle	WA	98119	**800-365-8950**	206-285-6800
Overwaitea Food Group 19855 92A Ave	Langley	BC	V1M3B6	**800-242-9229**	604-888-1213
Pinnacle Foods Corp 399 Jefferson Rd	Parsippany	NJ	07054	**866-266-7596**	973-541-6620
Riverside Foods Inc 2520 Wilson St	Two Rivers	WI	54241	**800-678-4511**	920-793-4511
Sea Harvest Packing Co PO Box 818	Brunswick	GA	31521	**800-627-4300**	912-264-3212
Stoller Fisheries 1301 18th St PO Box B	Spirit Lake	IA	51360	**800-831-5174**	712-336-1750
Tampa Bay Fisheries Inc 3060 Gallagher Rd	Dover	FL	33527	**800-732-3663**	813-752-8883
UniSea Inc 15400 NE 90th St PO Box 97019	Redmond	WA	98073	**800-535-8509**	425-881-8181

297-15 Flavoring Extracts & Syrups

Company	City	State	ZIP	Toll-Free	Phone
David Michael & Co Inc 10801 Decatur Rd	Philadelphia	PA	19154	**800-363-5286**	215-632-3100
DD Williamson & Company Inc 100 S Spring St	Louisville	KY	40206	**800-227-2635**	502-895-2438
Emerald Kalama Chemical LLC 1296 Third St NW	Kalama	WA	98625	**877-300-9545**	360-673-2550
Frutarom Corp 9500 Railroad Ave	North Bergen	NJ	07047	**866-229-7198**	201-861-9500
I Rice & Company Inc 11500 Roosevelt Blvd Bldg D	Philadelphia	PA	19116	**800-232-6022**	215-673-7423
Jel Sert Co Rt 59 & Conde St	West Chicago	IL	60185	**800-323-2592**	630-876-4838
Kalsec Inc 3713 W Main St	Kalamazoo	MI	49006	**800-323-9320**	269-349-9711
Limpert Bros Inc 202 NW Blvd PO Box 1480	Vineland	NJ	08362	**800-691-1353**	856-691-1353
Lyons Magnus Inc 3158 E Hamilton Ave	Fresno	CA	93702	**800-344-7130**	
Mother Murphy's Labs Inc 2826 S Elm St PO Box 16846	Greensboro	NC	27416	**800-849-1277**	336-273-1737
Nielsen-Massey Vanillas Inc 1550 S Shields Dr	Waukegan	IL	60085	**800-525-7873**	847-578-1550
Phillips Syrup Corp 28025 Ranney Pkwy	Westlake	OH	44145	**800-350-8443**	440-835-8001
Sea Breeze Inc 441 Rt 202	Towaco	NJ	07082	**800-732-2733**	973-334-7777
Sensient Technologies Corp 777 E Wisconsin Ave *NYSE: SXT*	Milwaukee	WI	53202	**800-558-9892**	414-271-6755
Sethness Products Co 3422 W Touhy Ave	Lincolnwood	IL	60712	**888-772-1880**	847-329-2080
Western Syrup Co 13766 Milroy Pl	Santa Fe Springs	CA	90670	**800-521-3888**	562-921-4485
Wild Flavors Inc 1261 Pacific Ave	Erlanger	KY	41018	**800-263-5286**	859-342-3600

297-16 Flour Mixes & Doughs

Company	City	State	ZIP	Toll-Free	Phone
Abitec Corp Inc PO Box 569 *Sales	Columbus	OH	43215	**800-555-1255***	614-429-6464
Bake'n Joy Foods Inc 351 Willow St	North Andover	MA	01845	**800-666-4937**	978-683-1414
Dawn Food Products Inc 3333 Sargent Rd *Cust Svc	Jackson	MI	49201	**800-292-1362***	517-789-4400
Langlois Co 10810 San Sevaine Way	Mira Loma	CA	91752	**800-962-5993**	951-360-3900
Pinnacle Foods Corp 399 Jefferson Rd	Parsippany	NJ	07054	**866-266-7596**	973-541-6620
Rhodes International Inc PO Box 25487 *Cust Svc	Salt Lake City	UT	84125	**800-876-7333***	801-972-0122
Subco Foods Inc 4350 S Taylor Dr	Sheboygan	WI	53081	**800-473-0757**	920-457-7761
Watson Foods Company Inc 301 Heffernan Dr	West Haven	CT	06516	**800-388-3481**	203-932-3000

297-17 Food Emulsifiers

Company	City	State	ZIP	Toll-Free	Phone
ADM Specialty Food Ingredients Div 4666 E Faries Pkwy	Decatur	IL	62526	**800-637-5843**	217-424-5200
American Lecithin Company Inc 115 Hurley Rd Unit 2B	Oxford	CT	06478	**800-364-4416**	203-262-7100
Crest Foods Company Inc 905 Main St	Ashton	IL	61006	**877-273-7893**	815-453-7411
Frutarom Corp 9500 Railroad Ave	North Bergen	NJ	07047	**866-229-7198**	201-861-9500

297-18 Fruits & Vegetables - Dried or Dehydrated

Company	City	State	ZIP	Toll-Free	Phone
Bernard Food Industries Inc 1125 Hartrey Ave	Evanston	IL	60204	**800-323-3663**	847-869-5222
Del Monte Foods Co 1 Maritime Plaza *Cust Svc	San Francisco	CA	94111	**800-543-3090***	415-247-3000
Freskeeto Frozen Foods Inc 8019 Rt 209	Ellenville	NY	12428	**800-356-3663**	845-647-5111
Garry Packing Inc 11272 E Central Ave	Del Rey	CA	93616	**800-248-2126**	559-888-2126
Graceland Fruit Inc 1123 Main St	Frankfort	MI	49635	**800-352-7181**	231-352-7181
Idaho-Pacific Corp 4723 E 100 N PO Box 478 *Sales	Ririe	ID	83443	**800-238-5503***	208-538-6971
Larsen Farms 2650 N 2375 E *Sales	Hamer	ID	83425	**800-767-6104***	208-662-5501
Oregon Potato Co PO Box 3110	Pasco	WA	99302	**800-336-6311**	509-545-4545
Small Planet Foods Inc 106 Woodworth St	Sedro Woolley	WA	98284	**800-624-4123**	360-855-0100
Stapleton-Spence Packing Co 1530 The Alameda Ste 320	San Jose	CA	95126	**800-297-8815**	408-297-8815
Sunsweet Growers Inc 901 N Walton Ave	Yuba City	CA	95993	**800-417-2253**	530-674-5010

297-19 Fruits & Vegetables - Pickled

Company	City	State	ZIP	Toll-Free	Phone
Beaverton Foods Inc 7100 NW Century Blvd	Hillsboro	OR	97124	**800-223-8076**	503-646-8138
Best Maid Products Inc PO Box 1809	Fort Worth	TX	76101	**800-447-3581**	817-335-5494
Cain's Foods Inc 114 E Main St	Ayer	MA	01432	**800-225-0601**	978-772-0300
Clorox Co 1221 Broadway *NYSE: CLX* ■ *Cust Svc	Oakland	CA	94612	**800-424-9300***	510-271-7000
Conway Import Co Inc 11051 W Addison St	Franklin Park	IL	60131	**800-323-8801**	847-455-5600
Eastern Foods Inc 1000 Naturally Fresh Blvd	Atlanta	GA	30349	**800-765-1950**	
GLK Foods LLC 11 Clark St	Shortsville	NY	14548	**855-572-8800**	
Kaplan & Zubrin Inc 146 Kaighns Ave	Camden	NJ	08103	**800-248-1736**	856-964-1083
Langlois Co 10810 San Sevaine Way	Mira Loma	CA	91752	**800-962-5993**	951-360-3900
Lee Kum Kee Inc 14841 Don Julian Rd *Orders	City of Industry	CA	91746	**800-654-5082***	626-709-1888
Litehouse Inc 1109 N Ella Ave	Sandpoint	ID	83864	**800-669-3169**	208-265-3700
MA Gedney Co 2100 Stoughton Ave	Chaska	MN	55318	**888-244-0653**	952-448-2612
Maurice's Gourmet Barbeque PO Box 6847	West Columbia	SC	29171	**800-628-7423**	803-791-5887
McIlhenny Co Hwy 329 *Orders	Avery Island	LA	70513	**800-634-9599***	337-365-8173
Moody Dunbar Inc 2000 Waters Edge Dr Ste 21	Johnson City	TN	37604	**800-251-8202**	423-952-0100
NewStar Fresh Foods LLC 900 Work St	Salinas	CA	93901	**888-782-7220**	831-758-7800
Olds Products Co 10700 88th Ave	Pleasant Prairie	WI	53158	**800-233-8064**	262-947-3500
Spring Glen Fresh Foods Inc 314 Spring Glen Dr PO Box 518	Ephrata	PA	17522	**800-641-2853**	717-733-2201
T Marzetti Co 1105 Schrock Rd	Columbus	OH	43229	**800-999-1835**	614-846-2232
Walden Farms 1209 W St Georges Ave	Linden	NJ	07036	**800-229-1706**	

297-20 Fruits, Vegetables, Juices - Canned or Preserved

Company	City	State	ZIP	Toll-Free	Phone
American Spoon Foods Inc 1668 Clarion Ave	Petoskey	MI	49770	**800-222-5886**	231-347-9030
Apple & Eve Inc 2 Seaview Blvd	Port Washington	NY	11050	**866-487-2365**	516-621-1122
Braswell Food Co 226 N Zetterower Ave	Statesboro	GA	30458	**800-673-9388**	912-764-6191
Bruce Foods Corp PO Box 1030	New Iberia	LA	70561	**800-299-9082**	337-365-8101
Campbell Soup Co 1 Campbell Pl *NYSE: CPB*	Camden	NJ	08103	**800-257-8443**	856-342-4800
Carriage House Cos Inc, The 196 Newton St	Fredonia	NY	14063	**800-828-8915**	716-673-1000
Cincinnati Preserving Company Inc 3015 E Kemper Rd *Cust Svc	Cincinnati	OH	45241	**800-222-9966***	513-771-2000
Cornelius Seed Corn Co 14760 317th Ave	Bellevue	IA	52031	**800-218-1862**	563-672-3463
Del Monte Foods Co 1 Maritime Plaza *Cust Svc	San Francisco	CA	94111	**800-543-3090***	415-247-3000
Del Monte Fresh Produce Co 241 Sevilla Ave *Cust Svc	Coral Gables	FL	33134	**800-950-3683***	305-520-8400
Don Pepino Sales Co 123 Railroad Ave	Williamstown	NJ	08094	**888-281-6400**	856-629-7429
Escalon Premier Brands 1905 McHenry Ave	Escalon	CA	95320	**800-255-5750**	209-838-7341
Furmano Foods Inc 770 Cannery Rd PO Box 500	Northumberland	PA	17857	**877-877-6032**	570-473-3516
Giorgio Foods Inc PO Box 96	Temple	PA	19560	**800-220-2139**	610-926-2139
Hanover Foods Corp 1550 York St PO Box 334 *OTC: HNFSA*	Hanover	PA	17331	**800-888-4646**	717-632-6000
Hirzel Canning Company & Farms 411 Lemoyne Rd	Northwood	OH	43619	**800-837-1631**	419-693-0531
HJ Heinz Co 1 PPG Pl Ste 3100	Pittsburgh	PA	15230	**800-255-5750**	412-456-5700
House Foods America Corp 7351 Orangewood Ave	Garden Grove	CA	92841	**877-333-7077**	714-901-4350

Classified Section

Company	Address	City	State	ZIP	Toll-Free	Phone
Jasper Wyman & Son	PO Box 100 *Sales	Milbridge	ME	04658	**800-341-1758***	
JM Smucker Co	1 Strawberry Ln *NYSE: SJM*	Orrville	OH	44667	**888-550-9555**	330-682-3000
Johanna Foods Inc	20 Johanna Farm Rd PO Box 272	Flemington	NJ	08822	**800-727-6700**	908-788-2200
Lakeside Foods Inc	808 Hamilton St	Manitowoc	WI	54220	**800-466-3834**	920-684-3356
Lassonde Pappas	1 Colons Dr Ste 200	Carneys Point	NJ	08069	**800-257-7019**	856-455-1000
Leelanau Fruit Co	2900 SW Bay Shore Dr	Suttons Bay	MI	49682	**800-431-0718**	231-271-3514
Lyons Magnus Inc	3158 E Hamilton Ave	Fresno	CA	93702	**800-344-7130**	
Moody Dunbar Inc	2000 Waters Edge Dr Ste 21	Johnson City	TN	37604	**800-251-8202**	423-952-0100
Morgan Foods Inc	90 W Morgan St	Austin	IN	47102	**888-430-1780**	812-794-1170
Mott's LLP	PO Box 869077 *Consumer Info	Plano	TX	75086	**800-426-4891***	
Mrs Clark's Foods	740 SE Dalbey Dr	Ankeny	IA	50021	**800-736-5674**	515-299-6400
Muir Glen Organic Tomato Products	PO Box 9452	Minneapolis	MN	55440	**800-624-4123**	800-248-7310
National Fruit Product Co Inc	701 Fairmont Ave	Winchester	VA	22601	**800-655-4022**	540-723-9614
Ocean Spray Cranberries Inc	1 Ocean Spray Dr	Lakeville-Middleboro	MA	02349	**800-662-3263**	508-946-1000
Odwalla Inc	1625 North Market Blvd	Sacramento	CA	95834	**800-952-5210**	
Pacific Coast Producers	631 N Cluff Ave	Lodi	CA	95240	**877-618-4776**	209-367-8800
Pastorelli Food Products Inc	162 N Sangamon St	Chicago	IL	60607	**800-767-2829**	312-666-2041
Simply Orange Juice Co	2659 Orange Ave	Apopka	FL	32703	**800-871-2653**	
Stanislaus Food Products Co	1202 D St	Modesto	CA	95354	**800-327-7201**	
Stapleton-Spence Packing Co	1530 The Alameda Ste 320	San Jose	CA	95126	**800-297-8815**	408-297-8815
Sun Orchard Inc	1198 W Fairmont Dr	Tempe	AZ	85282	**800-505-8423**	
Talk O'Texas Brands Inc	1610 Roosevelt St	San Angelo	TX	76905	**800-749-6572**	325-655-6077
Tip Top Canning Co	505 S Second St PO Box 126	Tipp City	OH	45371	**800-352-2635**	937-667-3713
Truitt Bros Inc	1105 Front St NE	Salem	OR	97301	**800-547-8712**	503-362-3674
Vegetable Juices Inc	7400 S Narragansett Ave *General	Chicago	IL	60638	**888-776-9752***	708-924-9500
Zeigler Beverage Co	1513 N Broad St *Sales	Lansdale	PA	19446	**800-854-6123***	215-855-5161

297-21 Fruits, Vegetables, Juices - Frozen

Company	Address	City	State	ZIP	Toll-Free	Phone
Apio Inc	PO Box 727 *Sales	Guadalupe	CA	93434	**800-454-1355***	805-343-2835
Bernatello's	PO Box 729	Maple Lake	MN	55358	**800-622-6935**	952-831-6622
Capitol City Produce	16550 Commercial Ave	Baton Rouge	LA	70816	**800-349-1583**	225-272-8153
Coloma Frozen Foods Inc	4145 Coloma Rd	Coloma	MI	49038	**800-642-2723**	269-849-0500
Dole Food Company Inc	1 Dole Dr *NYSE: DOLE*	Westlake Village	CA	91362	**800-232-8888**	818-879-6600
Giorgio Foods Inc	PO Box 96	Temple	PA	19560	**800-220-2139**	610-926-2139
Graceland Fruit Inc	1123 Main St	Frankfort	MI	49635	**800-352-7181**	231-352-7181
HJ Heinz Co	1 PPG Pl Ste 3100	Pittsburgh	PA	15230	**800-255-5750**	412-456-5700
HPC Foods Ltd	288 Libby St	Honolulu	HI	96819	**877-370-0919**	808-848-2431
JR Simplot Co	999 W Main St Ste 1300	Boise	ID	83702	**800-832-8893**	208-336-2110
Lakeside Foods Inc	808 Hamilton St	Manitowoc	WI	54220	**800-466-3834**	920-684-3356
Leelanau Fruit Co	2900 SW Bay Shore Dr	Suttons Bay	MI	49682	**800-431-0718**	231-271-3514
McCain Foods Ltd	181 Bay St Ste 3600	Toronto	ON	M5J2T3	**800-938-7799**	416-955-1700
McCain Foods USA Inc	2275 Cabot Dr	Lisle	IL	60532	**800-938-7799**	
Mrs Clark's Foods	740 SE Dalbey Dr	Ankeny	IA	50021	**800-736-5674**	515-299-6400
NORPAC Foods Inc	930 W Washington St	Stayton	OR	97383	**800-733-9311**	503-769-2101
Penobscot McCrum LLC	28 Pierce St	Belfast	ME	04915	**800-435-4456**	207-338-4360

297-22 Gelatin

Company	Address	City	State	ZIP	Toll-Free	Phone
Gelita USA Inc	PO Box 927	Sioux City	IA	51102	**800-223-9244**	712-943-5516
Langlois Co	10810 San Sevaine Way	Mira Loma	CA	91752	**800-962-5993**	951-360-3900
Nitta Gelatin Inc	598 Airport Blvd Ste 900	Morrisville	NC	27560	**888-648-8287**	919-238-3300
Subco Foods Inc	4350 S Taylor Dr	Sheboygan	WI	53081	**800-473-0757**	920-457-7761

297-23 Grain Mill Products

Company	Address	City	State	ZIP	Toll-Free	Phone
ACH Food Cos Inc	7171 Goodlet Farms Pkwy	Cordova	TN	38016	**800-691-1106**	901-381-3000
ADM Corn Processing Div	4666 E Faries Pkwy	Decatur	IL	62526	**800-637-5843**	217-424-5200
ADM Milling Co (ADM)	8000 W 110th St	Overland Park	KS	66210	**800-422-1688**	913-491-9400
Ag Processing Inc	12700 W Dodge Rd PO Box 2047	Omaha	NE	68103	**800-247-1345**	402-496-7809
Bay State Milling Co	100 Congress St	Quincy	MA	02169	**800-553-5687**	
Blendex Company Inc	11208 Electron Dr	Louisville	KY	40299	**800-626-6325**	502-267-1003
Chelsea Milling Co	201 W N St PO Box 460	Chelsea	MI	48118	**800-727-2460**	734-475-1361
Farmers Rice Co-op	PO Box 15223	Sacramento	CA	95851	**800-326-2799**	916-923-5100
Gold Medal	PO Box 9452	Minneapolis	MN	55440	**800-248-7310**	
Hodgson Mill Inc	1100 Stevens Ave	Effingham	IL	62401	**800-347-0105**	217-347-0105
House-Autry Mills Inc	7000 US Hwy 301 S	Four Oaks	NC	27524	**800-849-0802**	
Indian Harvest Specialtifoods Inc	1012 Paul Bunyan Dr SE *Orders	Bemidji	MN	56601	**800-346-7032***	
Knappen Milling Co	110 S Water St	Augusta	MI	49012	**800-562-7736**	269-731-4141
Mallet & Company Inc	51 Arch St Ext	Carnegie	PA	15106	**800-245-2757**	412-276-9000
Manildra Group USA	4210 Shawnee Mission Pkwy Ste 312A	Shawnee Mission	KS	66205	**800-323-8435**	913-362-0777
Mennel Milling Co	128 W Crocker St	Fostoria	OH	44830	**800-688-8151**	419-435-8151
MGP Ingredients Inc	100 Commercial St PO Box 130 *NASDAQ: MGPI*	Atchison	KS	66002	**800-255-0302**	913-367-1480
Morrison Milling Co	319 E Prairie St	Denton	TX	76201	**800-531-7912**	940-387-6111
North Dakota Mill & Elevator	1823 Mill Rd	Grand Forks	ND	58203	**800-538-7721**	701-795-7000
Pacific Grain Products International Inc	351 Hanson Way PO Box 2060 *Cust Svc	Woodland	CA	95776	**800-333-0110***	530-662-5056
Pacific International Rice Mills Inc	845 Kentucky Ave	Woodland	CA	95695	**800-747-4764**	530-661-6028
Producers Rice Mill Inc	PO Box 1248	Stuttgart	AR	72160	**800-369-7675**	870-673-4444
RiceTec Inc	1925 FM 2917 PO Box 1305	Alvin	TX	77511	**877-580-7423**	281-393-3532
Rock River Lumber & Grain Co	5502 Lyndon Rd PO Box 68	Prophetstown	IL	61277	**800-605-4333**	815-537-5131
Shawnee Milling Company Inc	201 S Broadway PO Box 1567	Shawnee	OK	74802	**800-654-2600**	405-273-7000
Siemer Milling Co	111 W Main St PO Box 670	Teutopolis	IL	62467	**800-826-1065**	217-857-3131
Wilkins-Rogers Inc	27 Frederick Rd *Cust Svc	Ellicott City	MD	21043	**877-438-4338***	410-465-5800

297-24 Honey

Company	Address	City	State	ZIP	Toll-Free	Phone
Barkman Honey	120 Santa Fe St	Hillsboro	KS	67063	**800-364-6623**	
Dutch Gold Honey Inc	2220 Dutch Gold Dr	Lancaster	PA	17601	**800-846-2753**	717-393-1716
Glorybee Foods Inc	120 N Seneca Rd	Eugene	OR	97402	**800-456-7923**	541-689-0913
Honey Acres	1557 Hwy 67 N	Ashippun	WI	53003	**800-558-7745**	
Honeytree Inc	8570 M 50	Onsted	MI	49265	**800-968-1889**	517-467-2482
Silverbow Honey Company Inc	1120 E Wheeler Rd	Moses Lake	WA	98837	**866-444-6639**	509-765-6616

297-25 Ice Cream & Frozen Desserts

Company	Address	City	State	ZIP	Toll-Free	Phone
Anderson Erickson Dairy Co	2420 E University Ave	Des Moines	IA	50317	**800-234-7257**	515-265-2521
Baldwin Richardson Foods Company Inc	20201 S La Grange Rd Ste 200 *Cust Svc	Frankfort	IL	60423	**866-644-2732***	815-464-9994
Broughton Foods Co	1701 Green St	Marietta	OH	45750	**800-283-2479**	740-373-4121
Cedar Crest Specialties Inc	7269 Hwy 60 PO Box 260 *Hotline	Cedarburg	WI	53012	**800-877-8341***	262-377-7252
Coleman Dairy Inc	6901 I-30	Little Rock	AR	72209	**800-365-1551**	501-748-1700
Creamland Dairies Inc	PO Box 961447	Albuquerque	NM	87105	**800-395-7004**	505-247-0721
Farrs Better Foods	2575 South 300 West	South Salt lake City	UT	84115	**877-553-2777**	801-484-8724
Galliker Dairy Company Inc	143 Donald Ln	Johnstown	PA	15907	**800-477-6455**	814-266-8702
Gandy's Dairies Inc	201 University Blvd	Lubbock	TX	79415	**877-382-4357**	806-762-8844
Graeter's Inc	2145 Reading Rd	Cincinnati	OH	45202	**800-721-3323**	513-721-3323
Green Foods Corp	2220 Camino Del Sol	Oxnard	CA	93030	**800-777-4430**	805-983-7470

	City	State	ZIP	Toll-Free	Phone
Hershey Creamery Co 301 S Cameron St	Harrisburg	PA	17101	**888-240-1905**	717-238-8134
Hiland Dairy Co PO Box 2270	Springfield	MO	65801	**800-641-4022**	417-862-9311
J & J Snack Foods Corp 6000 Central Hwy *NASDAQ: JJSF*	Pennsauken	NJ	08109	**800-486-9533**	856-665-9533
Perry's Ice Cream Company Inc 1 Ice Cream Plz	Akron	NY	14001	**800-873-7797**	716-542-5492
Schwan Food Co 115 W College Dr	Marshall	MN	56258	**800-533-5290**	507-532-3274
Sugar Creek Foods International 301 N El Paso St	Russellville	AR	72801	**800-445-2715**	
Turkey Hill Dairy Inc 2601 River Rd	Conestoga	PA	17516	**800-693-2479**	717-872-5461
Turner Dairy Farms Inc 1049 Jefferson Rd	Pittsburgh	PA	15235	**800-892-1039**	412-372-2211
Umpqua Dairy Products Co 1686 Se N St PO Box 1306	Grants Pass	OR	97526	**800-222-6455**	541-672-2638
Wells Enterprises Inc 1 Blue Bunny Dr *All	Le Mars	IA	51031	**888-309-1742***	712-546-4000
YoCream International Inc 5858 NE 87th Ave	Portland	OR	97220	**800-962-7326**	503-256-3754

297-26 Meat Products - Prepared

	City	State	ZIP	Toll-Free	Phone
Aidells Sausage Co 1625 Alvarado St	San Leandro	CA	94577	**877-243-3557**	510-614-5450
Albertville Quality Foods Inc 130 Quality Dr	Albertville	AL	35950	**800-353-2806**	256-840-9923
Alderfer Inc 382 Main St PO Box 2 *Sales	Harleysville	PA	19438	**800-222-2319***	
Aliments Asta Inc 511 Ave De La Gare	St Alexandre-De-Kamouraska	QC	G0L2G0	**800-463-1355**	418-495-2728
American Foods Group Inc 544 Acme St	Green Bay	WI	54302	**800-345-0293**	920-437-6330
Ballard's Farm Sausage Inc 7275 Right Fork Wilson Creek *General	Wayne	WV	25570	**800-346-7675***	304-272-5147
Bar-S Foods Co PO Box 29049	Phoenix	AZ	85038	**800-699-4115**	
Berks Packing Company Inc 307-323 Bingaman St PO Box 5919	Reading	PA	19610	**800-882-3757**	
Best Provision Company Inc 144 Avon Ave	Newark	NJ	07108	**800-631-4466**	973-242-5000
Bridgford Foods Corp 1308 N Patt St *NASDAQ: BRID*	Anaheim	CA	92801	**800-854-3255**	714-526-5533
Burger's Ozark Country Cured Hams Inc 32819 hwy 87	California	MO	65018	**800-203-4424**	573-796-3134
Caribbean Products Ltd 3624 Falls Rd	Baltimore	MD	21211	**888-689-5068**	
Carl Buddig & Co 950 175th St	Homewood	IL	60430	**888-633-5684**	708-798-0900
Carlton Foods Corp 880 Texas 46	New Braunfels	TX	78130	**800-628-9849**	830-625-7583
Cattaneo Bros Inc 769 Caudill St	San Luis Obispo	CA	93401	**800-243-8537**	805-543-7188
Cher-Make Sausage Co 2915 Calumet Ave	Manitowoc	WI	54220	**800-242-7679**	920-683-5980
Chicago Meat Authority Inc (CMA) 1120 W 47th Pl	Chicago	IL	60609	**800-383-3811**	773-254-3811
Chicopee Provision Co Inc 19 Sitarz St	Chicopee	MA	01013	**800-924-6328**	413-594-4765
Citterio USA Corp 2008 SR 940	Freeland	PA	18224	**800-435-8888**	570-636-3171
Cloverdale Foods Co 3015 34th St NW	Mandan	ND	58554	**800-669-9511**	
Cook's Ham Inc 200 S Second St	Lincoln	NE	68508	**800-332-8400**	402-475-6700
Daniele Inc PO Box 106	Pascoag	RI	02859	**800-451-2535**	401-568-6228
Dewied International Inc 5010 IH- 10 E	San Antonio	TX	78219	**800-992-5600**	210-661-6161
Dietz & Watson Inc 5701 Tacony St	Philadelphia	PA	19135	**800-333-1974**	215-831-9000
Family Brands International LLC 1001 Elm Hill Rd PO Box 429	Lenoir City	TN	37771	**800-356-4455**	
Fred Usinger Inc 1030 N Old World Third St	Milwaukee	WI	53203	**800-558-9998**	414-276-9100
Gallo Salame 2411 Baumann Ave	San Lorenzo	CA	94580	**800-988-6464**	
Gaytan Foods 15430 Proctor Ave	City Of Industry	CA	91745	**800-242-9826**	626-330-4553
Habbersett Scrapple Inc 103 S Railroad Ave	Bridgeville	DE	19933	**800-338-4727**	
Hatfield Quality Meats Inc 2700 Clemens Rd	Hatfield	PA	19440	**800-743-1191**	215-368-2500
Hazle Park Packing Co 260 Washington Ave Hazle Pk	Hazletownship	PA	18202	**800-238-4331**	570-455-7571
Hormel Foods Corp 1 Hormel Pl *NYSE: HRL*	Austin	MN	55912	**800-523-4635**	507-437-5611
John Morrell & Co 805 E Kemper Rd	Cincinnati	OH	45246	**800-722-1127**	513-346-3540
Johnsonville Sausage LLC PO Box 906	Sheboygan Falls	WI	53085	**888-556-2728**	
Jones Dairy Farm 800 Jones Ave	Fort Atkinson	WI	53538	**800-635-6637**	920-563-2431
Kayem Foods Inc 75 Arlington St	Chelsea	MA	02150	**800-426-6100**	617-889-1600
Kent Quality Foods Inc 703 Leonard St NW	Grand Rapids	MI	49504	**800-748-0141**	
Kessler's Inc 1201 Hummel Ave	Lemoyne	PA	17043	**800-382-1328**	717-763-7162
Kiolbassa Provision Co 1325 S Brazos St	San Antonio	TX	78207	**800-456-5465**	713-747-7383
Kronos Products Inc 1 Kronos Dr	Glendale Heights	IL	60139	**800-621-0099**	
Maid-Rite Steak Company Inc 105 Keystone Industrial Pk	Dunmore	PA	18512	**800-233-4259**	570-343-4748
Marathon Enterprises Inc 9 Smith St	Englewood	NJ	07631	**800-722-7388**	201-935-3330
Miller Packing Co 1122 Industrial Way PO Box 1390	Lodi	CA	95241	**800-624-2328**	209-339-2310
Natural Casing Co 410 E Railroad St PO Box A	Peshtigo	WI	54157	**877-515-0270**	
Neto Sausage Co Inc 288 Brokaw Rd	Santa Clara	CA	95050	**888-482-6386**	408-296-0818
Oberto Sausage Co 7060 S 238th St	Kent	WA	98032	**877-453-7591**	253-854-7056
Odom's Tennessee Pride Sausage Inc 1201 Neelys Bend Rd	Madison	TN	37115	**866-484-8641**	615-868-1360
Old Wisconsin Sausage Co 5030 PlaybiRd Rd	Sheboygan	WI	53083	**877-451-7988**	
Palmyra Bologna Company Inc 230 N College St	Palmyra	PA	17078	**800-282-6336**	717-838-6336
Park 100 Foods Inc 326 E Adams St	Tipton	IN	46072	**800-854-6504**	765-675-3480
Peer Foods Group Inc 1200 W 35th St 3rd Fl	Chicago	IL	60609	**800-365-5644**	773-927-1440
Plumrose USA Inc 1901 Butterfield Rd Ste 305	Downers Grove	IL	60515	**800-526-4909**	732-624-4040
Pocino Foods Co 14250 Lomitas Ave	City of Industry	CA	91746	**800-345-0150**	626-968-8000
Randolph Packing Co 275 Roma Jean Pkwy	Streamwood	IL	60107	**800-451-1607**	630-830-3100
Reser's Fine Foods Inc 15570 SW Jenkins Rd	Beaverton	OR	97006	**800-333-6431**	503-643-6431
Sadler's Smokehouse Ltd PO Box 1088	Henderson	TX	75653	**800-777-5581**	903-655-7265
Sahlen Packing Company Inc 318 Howard St	Buffalo	NY	14206	**800-466-8165**	716-852-8677
Schaller & Weber Inc 22-35 46th St *Orders	Astoria	NY	11105	**800-847-4115***	718-721-5480
Silver Star Meats Inc 1720 Middletown Rd PO Box 393	McKees Rocks	PA	15136	**800-548-1321**	412-771-5539
Stampede Meat Inc 7351 S 78th Ave	Bridgeview	IL	60455	**800-353-0933**	
Standard Meat Company LP 5105 Investment Dr	Dallas	TX	75236	**866-859-6313**	214-561-0561
Stock Yards Packing Co Inc 2457 W North Ave	Melrose Park	IL	60160	**877-785-9273**	
Sugar Creek Packing Co 2101 Kenskill Ave	Washington Court House	OH	43160	**800-848-8205**	740-335-7440
Sysco Kansas City Inc 1915 E Kansas City Rd	Olathe	KS	66061	**800-735-3341**	913-829-5555
TF Kinnealey & Company Inc 1100 Pearl St	Brockton	MA	02301	**800-225-4950**	508-638-7700
Tyson Prepared Foods Inc 5701 McNutt Rd	Santa Teresa	NM	88008	**888-301-7304**	575-589-0100
US Premium Beef LLC (USPB) 12200 N Ambassador Dr PO Box 20103	Kansas City	MO	64163	**866-877-2525**	816-713-8800
Vienna Sausage Manufacturing Co 2501 N Damen Ave	Chicago	IL	60647	**800-366-3647**	773-278-7800
Vollwerth & Co 200 Hancock St PO Box 239	Hancock	MI	49930	**800-562-7620**	906-482-1550
Wimmer's Meat Products Inc 126 W Grant St *Cust Svc	West Point	NE	68788	**800-762-9865***	402-372-2437

297-27 Milk & Cream Products

	City	State	ZIP	Toll-Free	Phone
Alta Dena Dairy 17851 E Railrd *Orders	City of Industry	CA	91748	**800-535-1369***	
AMPI 315 N Broadway	New Ulm	MN	56073	**800-533-3580**	507-354-8295
Anderson Erickson Dairy Co 2420 E University Ave	Des Moines	IA	50317	**800-234-7257**	515-265-2521
Broughton Foods Co 1701 Green St	Marietta	OH	45750	**800-283-2479**	740-373-4121
Clover Farms Dairy PO Box 14627	Reading	PA	19612	**800-323-0123**	610-921-9111
Cloverland Green Spring Dairy Inc 2701 Loch Raven Rd *Orders	Baltimore	MD	21218	**800-492-0094***	410-235-4477
Coleman Dairy Inc 6901 I-30	Little Rock	AR	72209	**800-365-1551**	501-748-1700
Dean Foods Co 2711 N Haskell Ave Ste 3400 *NYSE: DF*	Dallas	TX	75204	**800-395-7004**	214-303-3400
Eagle Family Foods Inc 1 Strawberry Ln	Orrville	OH	44667	**888-656-3245**	
Galliker Dairy Company Inc 143 Donald Ln	Johnstown	PA	15907	**800-477-6455**	814-266-8702
Guida-Seibert Dairy Co 433 Pk St	New Britain	CT	06051	**800-832-8929**	860-224-2404
Harrisburg Dairies Inc 2001 Herr St	Harrisburg	PA	17105	**800-692-7429**	717-233-8701
Heritage Foods LLC 4002 Westminster Ave *Orders	Santa Ana	CA	92703	**800-321-5960***	714-775-5000
Hiland Dairy Co PO Box 2270	Springfield	MO	65801	**800-641-4022**	417-862-9311
Kemps LLC 1270 Energy Ln	Saint Paul	MN	55108	**800-322-9566**	651-379-6500
Land O'Lakes Inc Dairyman's Div 400 S 'M' St	Tulare	CA	93274	**800-328-4155**	559-687-8287

Company / Address	City	State	ZIP	Toll-Free	Phone
Lifeway Foods Inc 6431 W Oakton St *NASDAQ: LWAY*	Morton Grove	IL	60053	**877-281-3874**	847-967-1010
Marcus Dairy Inc 4 Eagle Rd	Danbury	CT	06810	**800-243-2511**	203-748-5611
Milkco Inc 220 Deaverview Rd	Asheville	NC	28806	**800-842-8021**	828-254-9560
Oakhurst Dairy 364 Forest Ave	Portland	ME	04101	**800-482-0718**	207-772-7468
Parmalat Canada Ltd 405 the W Mall 10th Fl	Toronto	ON	M9C5J1	**800-563-1515**	
Prairie Farms Dairy Inc 1100 N Broadway St	Carlinville	IL	62626	**800-654-2547**	217-854-2547
Producers Dairy Foods Inc 250 E Belmont Ave	Fresno	CA	93701	**800-660-1171**	559-264-6583
Royal Crest Dairy Inc 350 S Pearl St	Denver	CO	80209	**888-226-6455**	303-777-2227
Shamrock Foods 3900 E Camelback Rd Ste 300	Phoenix	AZ	85018	**800-289-3663**	602-477-2500
Smith Dairy 1381 Dairy Ln	Orrville	OH	44667	**800-776-7076**	330-683-8710
Southeast Milk Inc 1950 SE Hwy 484 PO Box 3790	Belleview	FL	34420	**800-598-7866**	
Superior Dairy Inc 4719 Navarre Rd SW	Canton	OH	44706	**800-597-5460**	330-477-4515
Umpqua Dairy Products Co 1686 Se N St PO Box 1306	Grants Pass	OR	97526	**800-222-6455**	541-672-2638
United Dairy Farmers 3955 Montgomery Rd *General	Cincinnati	OH	45212	**866-837-4833***	513-396-8700
United Dairy Inc 300 N Fifth St	Martins Ferry	OH	43935	**800-252-1542**	740-633-1451
WhiteWave Foods Co 12002 Airport Way	Broomfield	CO	80021	**888-820-9283**	303-635-4000

297-28 Nuts - Edible

Company / Address	City	State	ZIP	Toll-Free	Phone
Azar Nut Co 1800 NW Dr	El Paso	TX	79912	**800-351-8178**	915-877-4079
Hines Nut Co Inc 990 S St Paul St	Dallas	TX	75201	**800-561-6374**	214-939-0253
John B Sanfilippo & Son Inc 1703 N Randall Rd *NASDAQ: JBSS*	Elgin	IL	60123	**800-874-8734**	847-289-1800
Kar's Nuts 1200 E 14 Mile Rd	Madison Heights	MI	48071	**800-527-6887**	248-588-1903
King Nut Co 31900 Solon Rd	Solon	OH	44139	**800-860-5464**	440-248-8484
Priester Pecan Company Inc PO Box 381	Fort Deposit	AL	36032	**800-277-3226**	334-227-4301
South Georgia Pecan Co 309 S Lee St	Valdosta	GA	31601	**800-627-6630**	229-244-1321
Trophy Nut Company Inc 320 N Second St	Tipp City	OH	45371	**800-729-6887**	937-667-8478
Young Pecan Co 1831 W Evans St Ste 200 *All	Florence	SC	29501	**800-829-6864***	843-662-8591

297-29 Oil Mills - Cottonseed, Soybean, Other Vegetable Oils

Company / Address	City	State	ZIP	Toll-Free	Phone
Abitec Corp Inc PO Box 569 *Sales	Columbus	OH	43215	**800-555-1255***	614-429-6464
Ag Processing Inc 12700 W Dodge Rd PO Box 2047	Omaha	NE	68103	**800-247-1345**	402-496-7809
American Lecithin Company Inc 115 Hurley Rd Unit 2B	Oxford	CT	06478	**800-364-4416**	203-262-7100
Cargill Inc 15407 McGinty Rd W	Wayzata	MN	55391	**800-227-4455**	952-742-7575
Owensboro Grain Co 822 E Second St	Owensboro	KY	42303	**800-874-0305**	270-926-2032
Planters Cotton Oil Mill Inc 2901 Planters Dr	Pine Bluff	AR	71601	**800-264-7070**	870-534-3631

297-30 Oils - Edible (Margarine, Shortening, Table Oils, etc)

Company / Address	City	State	ZIP	Toll-Free	Phone
ACH Food Cos Inc 7171 Goodlet Farms Pkwy	Cordova	TN	38016	**800-691-1106**	901-381-3000
Golden Foods/Golden Brands LLC 2520 Seventh St Rd	Louisville	KY	40208	**800-622-3055**	502-636-3712
Par-Way Tryson Co 107 Bolte Ln	Saint Clair	MO	63077	**800-844-4554**	636-629-4545
Ventura Foods LLC 40 Pt Dr	Brea	CA	92821	**800-421-6257**	714-257-3700

297-31 Pasta

Company / Address	City	State	ZIP	Toll-Free	Phone
Dakota Growers Pasta Company Inc 1 Pasta Ave	Carrington	ND	58421	**866-569-4411**	701-652-2855
Monterey Pasta Co 2315 Moore Ave	Fullerton	CA	92833	**800-588-7782**	
New World Pasta Co 85 Shannon Rd *Sales	Harrisburg	PA	17112	**800-730-5957***	717-526-2200
OB Macaroni Co PO Box 53 *Orders	Fort Worth	TX	76101	**800-553-4336***	817-335-4629
Peking Noodle Co Inc 1514 N San Fernando Rd	Los Angeles	CA	90065	**877-735-4648**	323-223-2023

297-32 Peanut Butter

Company / Address	City	State	ZIP	Toll-Free	Phone
Carriage House Cos Inc, The 196 Newton St	Fredonia	NY	14063	**800-828-8915**	716-673-1000
Jimbo's Jumbos Inc 185 Peanut Dr PO Box 465 *General	Edenton	NC	27932	**800-334-4771***	
JM Smucker Co 1 Strawberry Ln *NYSE: SJM*	Orrville	OH	44667	**888-550-9555**	330-682-3000
John B Sanfilippo & Son Inc 1703 N Randall Rd *NASDAQ: JBSS*	Elgin	IL	60123	**800-874-8734**	847-289-1800
Producers Peanut Company Inc PO Box 250	Suffolk	VA	23434	**800-847-5491**	757-539-7496

297-33 Salads - Prepared

Company / Address	City	State	ZIP	Toll-Free	Phone
D'Arrigo Bros Company of California Inc PO Box 850 *Cust Svc	Salinas	CA	93902	**800-995-5939***	831-455-4500
Earth Island 9201 Owensmouth Ave	Chatsworth	CA	91311	**888-394-3949**	818-725-2820
Herold's Salads Inc 17512 Miles Ave	Cleveland	OH	44128	**800-427-2523**	216-991-7500
Kayem Foods Inc 75 Arlington St	Chelsea	MA	02150	**800-426-6100**	617-889-1600
Ready Pac Produce Inc 4401 Foxdale Ave	Irwindale	CA	91706	**800-800-7822**	
Reser's Fine Foods Inc 15570 SW Jenkins Rd	Beaverton	OR	97006	**800-333-6431**	503-643-6431
Sandridge Food Corp (SFC) 133 Commerce Dr	Medina	OH	44256	**800-672-2523**	330-725-2348
Suter Company Inc 258 May St	Sycamore	IL	60178	**800-435-6942**	815-895-9186

297-34 Sandwiches - Prepared

Company / Address	City	State	ZIP	Toll-Free	Phone
Bridgford Foods Corp 1308 N Patt St *NASDAQ: BRID*	Anaheim	CA	92801	**800-854-3255**	714-526-5533
Cloverdale Foods Co 3015 34th St NW	Mandan	ND	58554	**800-669-9511**	
Hormel Foods Corp 1 Hormel Pl *NYSE: HRL*	Austin	MN	55912	**800-523-4635**	507-437-5611
Konop Cos 1725 Industrial Dr	Green Bay	WI	54302	**800-770-0477**	920-468-8517
Landshire Inc 12 Tucker Dr	Caseyville	IL	62232	**800-969-2747**	618-293-6525

297-35 Snack Foods

Company / Address	City	State	ZIP	Toll-Free	Phone
Better Made Snack Foods Inc 10148 Gratiot Ave	Detroit	MI	48213	**800-332-2394**	313-925-4774
Bickel's Snack Foods 1120 Zinns Quarry Rd	York	PA	17404	**800-233-1933**	717-843-0738
Cape Cod Potato Chip Co 100 Breed's Hill Rd	Hyannis	MA	02601	**888-881-2447**	508-775-3358
Evans Food Group Ltd 4118 S Halsted St	Chicago	IL	60609	**888-643-8267**	773-254-7400
Frito-Lay North America 7701 Legacy Dr	Plano	TX	75024	**800-352-4477**	972-334-7000
Golden Flake Snack Foods Inc 1 Golden Flake Dr	Birmingham	AL	35205	**800-239-2447**	205-323-6161
Herr Foods Inc 20 Herr Dr PO Box 300	Nottingham	PA	19362	**800-344-3777**	610-932-9330
Mike-Sell's Potato Chip Co 333 Leo St PO Box 115	Dayton	OH	45404	**800-257-4742**	937-228-9400
Mission Foods 1159 Cottonwood Ln Ste 200	Irving	TX	75038	**800-443-7994**	972-232-5000
Smith Bros Co 3501 W 48th Pl	Chicago	IL	60632	**800-621-0225**	773-927-3737
Snacks Unlimited 1 General Mills Blvd	Minneapolis	MN	55426	**800-248-7310**	763-764-7600
Snyder of Berlin 1313 Stadium Dr	Berlin	PA	15530	**800-374-7949**	814-267-4641
Uncle Ray's LLC 14245 Birwood St	Detroit	MI	48238	**800-800-3286**	313-834-0800
UTZ Quality Foods Co 900 High St	Hanover	PA	17331	**800-367-7629**	717-637-6644
Wise Foods Inc 228 Rasely St Ste 75	Berwick	PA	18603	**888-759-4401**	770-426-5821
Wyandot Inc 135 Wyandot Ave	Marion	OH	43302	**800-992-6368**	740-383-4031

297-36 Specialty Foods

Company / Address	City	State	ZIP	Toll-Free	Phone
Armanino Foods of Distinction Inc 30588 San Antonio St *OTC: AMNF*	Hayward	CA	94544	**800-255-5855**	510-441-9300
Avanti Foods 109 Depot St	Walnut	IL	61376	**800-243-3739**	815-379-2155
Beech-Nut Nutrition Corp 1 Nutritious Pl	Amsterdam	NY	12010	**800-233-2468**	
Border Foods Inc 4065 J St SE	Deming	NM	88030	**800-323-4358**	
Bruce Foods Corp PO Box 1030	New Iberia	LA	70561	**800-299-9082**	337-365-8101
Camino Real Foods Inc 2638 E Vernon Ave	Vernon	CA	90058	**800-421-6201**	323-585-6599
Campbell Soup Co 1 Campbell Pl *NYSE: CPB*	Camden	NJ	08103	**800-257-8443**	856-342-4800
Cromers Inc 1700 Huger St	Columbia	SC	29201	**800-322-7688**	

Company / Address	City	State	Zip	Toll-Free	Phone
Cuisine Solutions Inc 1501 Moran Rd Unit 100 *OTC: CUSI*	Sterling	VA	20166	**888-285-4679**	703-270-2900
D & D Foods Inc 9425 N 48th St	Omaha	NE	68152	**800-208-0364**	402-571-4113
Del Monte Foods Co 1 Maritime Plaza *Cust Svc	San Francisco	CA	94111	**800-543-3090***	415-247-3000
Deli Express 16101 W 78th St	Eden Prairie	MN	55344	**800-328-8184**	
Durrset Amigos Ltd 4669 Hwy 90 W	San Antonio	TX	78237	**800-580-3477**	210-798-5360
Eden Foods Inc 701 Tecumseh Rd *Cust Svc	Clinton	MI	49236	**800-248-0320***	517-456-7424
El Encanto Inc 2001 Fourth St SW PO Box 293	Albuquerque	NM	87103	**800-888-7336**	505-243-2722
Ener-G Foods Inc 5960 First Ave S PO Box 84487	Seattle	WA	98124	**800-331-5222**	206-767-3928
Gerber Products Co 445 State St	Fremont	MI	49412	**800-284-9488**	
Hain Celestial Group Inc 4600 Sleepytime Dr *NASDAQ: HAIN*	Boulder	CO	80301	**800-434-4246**	
Hanover Foods Corp 1550 York St PO Box 334 *OTC: HNFSA*	Hanover	PA	17331	**800-888-4646**	717-632-6000
HJ Heinz Co 1 PPG Pl Ste 3100	Pittsburgh	PA	15230	**800-255-5750**	412-456-5700
Home Market Foods Inc 140 Morgan Dr	Norwood	MA	02062	**800-367-8325**	781-948-1500
Hormel Foods Corp 1 Hormel Pl *NYSE: HRL*	Austin	MN	55912	**800-523-4635**	507-437-5611
JM Smucker Co 1 Strawberry Ln *NYSE: SJM*	Orrville	OH	44667	**888-550-9555**	330-682-3000
Juanita's Foods Inc PO Box 847 PO Box 847	Wilmington	CA	90748	**800-303-2965**	
Kahiki Foods Inc 1100 Morrison Rd	Columbus	OH	43230	**855-524-4540**	614-322-3180
La Reina Inc 316 N Ford Blvd	Los Angeles	CA	90022	**800-367-7522**	323-268-2791
Mancini Foods PO Box 157	Zolfo Springs	FL	33890	**800-741-1778**	
McCain Foods Ltd 181 Bay St Ste 3600	Toronto	ON	M5J2T3	**800-938-7799**	416-955-1700
McCain Foods USA Inc 2275 Cabot Dr	Lisle	IL	60532	**800-938-7799**	
Michael Angelo's Gourmet Foods Inc 200 Michael Angelo Way	Austin	TX	78728	**877-482-5426**	512-218-3500
Morgan Foods Inc 90 W Morgan St	Austin	IN	47102	**888-430-1780**	812-794-1170
Mott's LLP PO Box 869077 *Consumer Info	Plano	TX	75086	**800-426-4891***	
Nardone Bros Baking Company Inc 420 New Commerce Blvd	Wilkes-Barre	PA	18706	**800-822-5320**	570-823-0141
Overhill Farms Inc 2727 E Vernon Ave *NYSE: OFI*	Vernon	CA	90058	**800-859-6406**	323-582-9977
Papa John's International Inc PO Box 99900 *NASDAQ: PZZA*	Louisville	KY	40269	**877-547-7272**	
Pastorelli Food Products Inc 162 N Sangamon St	Chicago	IL	60607	**800-767-2829**	312-666-2041
Pinnacle Foods Corp 399 Jefferson Rd	Parsippany	NJ	07054	**866-266-7596**	973-541-6620
Preferred Meal Systems Inc 5240 St Charles Rd *Cust Svc	Berkeley	IL	60163	**800-886-6325***	708-318-2500
Quaker Oats Co 555 W Monroe St	Chicago	IL	60661	**800-367-6287**	312-821-1000
Ruiz Foods Inc PO Box 37	Dinuba	CA	93618	**800-477-6474**	559-591-5510
Schwan Food Co 115 W College Dr	Marshall	MN	56258	**800-533-5290**	507-532-3274
Small Planet Foods Inc 106 Woodworth St	Sedro Woolley	WA	98284	**800-624-4123**	360-855-0100
Suter Company Inc 258 May St	Sycamore	IL	60178	**800-435-6942**	815-895-9186
Windsor Foods 3355 W Alabama St Ste 730	Houston	TX	77098	**800-458-4054**	713-843-5200
Winter Gardens Quality Foods Inc 304 Commerce St PO Box 339	New Oxford	PA	17350	**800-242-7637**	717-624-4911

297-37 Spices, Seasonings, Herbs

Company / Address	City	State	Zip	Toll-Free	Phone
Abco Laboratories Inc 2450 S Watney Way	Fairfield	CA	94533	**800-678-2226**	707-432-2200
American Outdoor Products Inc 6350 Gunpark Dr	Boulder	CO	80301	**800-641-0500**	303-581-0518
Benson's Gourmet Seasonings PO Box 638	Azusa	CA	91702	**800-325-5619**	626-969-4443
Blendex Company Inc 11208 Electron Dr	Louisville	KY	40299	**800-626-6325**	502-267-1003
Frontier Natural Products Co-op 3021 78th St PO Box 299	Norway	IA	52318	**800-669-3275**	319-227-7996
Fuchs North America 9740 Reisterstown Rd	Owings Mills	MD	21117	**800-365-3229**	410-363-1700
Johnny's Fine Foods Inc 319 E 25th St *General	Tacoma	WA	98421	**800-962-1462***	253-383-4597
McCormick & Company Inc McCormick Flavor Div 226 Schilling Cir	Hunt Valley	MD	21031	**800-322-7742**	410-771-7500
McCormick Ingredients 18 Loveton Cir	Sparks	MD	21152	**800-632-5847**	410-771-7301
Newly Weds Foods Inc 4140 W Fullerton Ave	Chicago	IL	60639	**800-621-7521**	773-489-7000
Pepsi Bottling Ventures LLC 4141 Parklake Ave Ste 600	Raleigh	NC	27612	**800-662-8792**	919-865-2300
Precision Foods Inc 11457 Olde Cabin Rd Ste 100	Saint Louis	MO	63141	**800-442-5242**	314-567-7400
Sabra Dipping Co LLC 2420 49th St	Astoria	NY	11103	**888-957-2272**	
SensoryEffects Flavor Co 231 Rock Industrial Park Dr	Bridgeton	MO	63044	**800-422-5444**	314-291-5444
Spice Hunter Inc 184 Suburban Rd PO Box 8110	San Luis Obispo	CA	93403	**800-444-3061**	
Spice World Inc 8101 Presidents Dr	Orlando	FL	32809	**800-433-4979**	
World Spice Inc 223 E Highland Pkwy	Roselle	NJ	07203	**800-234-1060**	908-245-0600

297-38 Sugar & Sweeteners

Company / Address	City	State	Zip	Toll-Free	Phone
C & H Sugar Co Inc 2300 Contra Costa Blvd Ste 600	Pleasant Hill	CA	94523	**800-773-1803**	
Western Sugar Co-op 7555 E Hampden Ave Ste 600	Denver	CO	80231	**800-523-7497**	303-830-3939

297-39 Syrup - Maple

Company / Address	City	State	Zip	Toll-Free	Phone
Carriage House Cos Inc, The 196 Newton St	Fredonia	NY	14063	**800-828-8915**	716-673-1000
Maple Grove Farms of Vermont 1052 Portland St	Saint Johnsbury	VT	05819	**800-525-2540**	802-748-5141
Pinnacle Foods Corp 399 Jefferson Rd	Parsippany	NJ	07054	**866-266-7596**	973-541-6620
Richards Maple Products Inc 545 Water St	Chardon	OH	44024	**800-352-4052**	
Sea Breeze Inc 441 Rt 202	Towaco	NJ	07082	**800-732-2733**	973-334-7777

297-40 Tea

Company / Address	City	State	Zip	Toll-Free	Phone
Bigelow Tea 201 Black Rock Tpke	Fairfield	CT	06825	**888-244-3569**	
Celestial Seasonings Inc 4600 Sleepytime Dr	Boulder	CO	80301	**800-351-8175**	303-530-5300
Redco Foods Inc 1 Hansen Island	Little Falls	NY	13365	**800-556-6674**	315-823-1300
S & D Coffee Inc 300 Concord Pkwy PO Box 1628 *Cust Svc	Concord	NC	28026	**800-933-2210***	704-782-3121

297-41 Vinegar & Cider

Company / Address	City	State	Zip	Toll-Free	Phone
Boyajian Inc 144 Will Dr *General	Canton	MA	02021	**800-965-0665***	781-828-9966
Heintz & Weber Co Inc 150 Reading Ave	Buffalo	NY	14220	**800-438-6878**	716-852-7171
MA Gedney Co 2100 Stoughton Ave	Chaska	MN	55318	**888-244-0653**	952-448-2612
Mizkan Americas Inc 1661 Feehanville Dr Ste 300	Mount Prospect	IL	60056	**800-323-4358**	847-590-0059
National Fruit Product Co Inc 701 Fairmont Ave	Winchester	VA	22601	**800-655-4022**	540-723-9614
Pastorelli Food Products Inc 162 N Sangamon St	Chicago	IL	60607	**800-767-2829**	312-666-2041

297-42 Yeast

Company / Address	City	State	Zip	Toll-Free	Phone
Brolite Products Inc 1900 S Pk Ave	Streamwood	IL	60107	**888-276-5483**	630-830-0340
DSM Food Specialties Inc 45 Waterview Blvd	Parsippany	NJ	07054	**800-526-0189**	973-257-1063
Lesaffre Yeast Corp 7475 W Main St *Cust Svc	Milwaukee	WI	53214	**877-677-7000***	
Minn-Dak Yeast Company Inc 18175 Red River Rd W	Wahpeton	ND	58075	**800-348-0991**	701-642-3300
Ohly Americas 3388 Bacon St	Rhinelander	WI	54501	**800-321-2689**	320-587-2481

298 FOOD PRODUCTS - WHOL

SEE ALSO Beverages - Whol

Company / Address	City	State	Zip	Toll-Free	Phone
Quantum Inc PO Box 2791	Eugene	OR	97402	**800-448-1448**	541-345-5556

298-1 Baked Goods - Whol

Company / Address	City	State	Zip	Toll-Free	Phone
Wheat Montana Farms Inc 10778 US Hwy 287	Three Forks	MT	59752	**800-535-2798**	406-285-3614

298-2 Coffee & Tea - Whol

Company / Address	City	State	Zip	Toll-Free	Phone
Barrie House Coffee Company Inc 4 Warehouse ln	Elmsford	NY	10523	**800-876-2233**	

				Toll-Free	Phone
Becharas Bros Coffee Co Inc 14501 Hamilton Ave	Highland Park	MI	48203	800-944-9675	313-869-4700
Capricorn Coffees Inc 353 Tenth St	San Francisco	CA	94103	800-541-0758	415-621-8500
Coffee Bean International 9120 NE Alderwood Rd	Portland	OR	97220	800-877-0474	503-227-4490
Coffee Masters Inc 7606 Industrial Ct	Spring Grove	IL	60081	800-334-6485	815-675-0088
Red Diamond Inc 400 Park Ave	Moody	AL	35004	800-292-4651	205-577-4000
Royal Cup Coffee 160 Cleage Dr *Cust Svc	Birmingham	AL	35217	800-366-5836*	

298-3 Confectionery & Snack Foods - Whol

				Toll-Free	Phone
AMCON Distributing Co 7405 Irvington Rd *NYSE: DIT*	Omaha	NE	68122	888-201-5997	402-331-3727
Brown & Haley PO Box 1596	Tacoma	WA	98401	800-426-8400	
Burklund Distributors Inc 2500 N Main St Ste 3	East Peoria	IL	61611	800-322-2876	309-694-1900
Continental Concession Supplies Inc 575 Jericho Turnpike Ste 300	Jericho	NY	11753	800-516-0090	516-739-8777
Eby-Brown Co 280 W Shuman Blvd Ste 280	Naperville	IL	60563	800-553-8249	630-778-2800
Foreign Candy Company Inc 1 Foreign Candy Dr	Hull	IA	51239	800-831-8541	712-439-1496
Frito-Lay North America 7701 Legacy Dr	Plano	TX	75024	800-352-4477	972-334-7000
Harold Levinson Assoc (HLA) 21 Banfi Plz	Farmingdale	NY	11735	800-325-2512	631-962-2400
Hines Nut Co Inc 990 S St Paul St	Dallas	TX	75201	800-561-6374	214-939-0253
Keilson-Dayton Co 107 Commerce Pk Dr	Dayton	OH	45404	800-759-3174	937-236-1070
Kennedy Wholesale Inc 16014 Adelante St	Irwindale	CA	91706	877-292-2639	818-241-9977
McDonald Wholesale Co 2350 W Broadway St	Eugene	OR	97402	877-722-5503	541-345-8421
Sultana Distribution Services Inc 600 Food Ctr Dr	Bronx	NY	10474	877-617-5500	718-617-5500
Trophy Nut Company Inc 320 N Second St	Tipp City	OH	45371	800-729-6887	937-667-8478

298-4 Dairy Products - Whol

				Toll-Free	Phone
Ambriola Company Inc 7 Patton Dr	West Caldwell	NJ	07006	800-962-8224	
AMPI 315 N Broadway	New Ulm	MN	56073	800-533-3580	507-354-8295
Broughton Foods Co 1701 Green St	Marietta	OH	45750	800-283-2479	740-373-4121
Clofine Dairy Products Inc 1407 New Rd	Linwood	NJ	08221	800-441-1001	609-653-1000
Clover-Stornetta Farms Inc PO Box 750369	Petaluma	CA	94975	800-237-3315	707-769-3235
Cream-O-Land Dairy Inc 529 Cedar Ln	Florence	NJ	08518	800-220-6455	609-499-3601
Erie Foods International Inc 401 Seventh Ave PO Box 648	Erie	IL	61250	800-447-1887	309-659-2233
Hillcrest Foods 2695 E 40th St	Cleveland	OH	44115	800-952-4344	216-361-4625
Luberski Inc 310 N Harbor Blvd Ste 205	Fullerton	CA	92832	800-326-3220	714-680-3447
Maryland & Virginia Milk Producers Co-op Assn Inc 1985 Isaac Newton Sq W	Reston	VA	20190	800-552-1976	703-742-6800
Masters Gallery Foods Inc 328 County Hwy PP PO Box 170 *General	Plymouth	WI	53073	800-236-8431*	920-893-8431
Plains Dairy Products 300 N Taylor St	Amarillo	TX	79107	800-365-5608	806-374-0385
Prairie Farms Dairy Inc 1100 N Broadway St	Carlinville	IL	62626	800-654-2547	217-854-2547
Roberts Dairy Co 2901 Cuming St	Omaha	NE	68131	800-779-4321	402-344-4321
Rockview Dairies Inc 7011 Stewart & Gray Rd	Downey	CA	90241	800-423-2479	562-927-5511
Sure Winner Foods Inc 2 Lehner Rd	Saco	ME	04072	800-640-6447	207-282-1258
Umpqua Dairy Products Co 1686 Se N St PO Box 1306	Grants Pass	OR	97526	800-222-6455	541-672-2638

298-5 Fish & Seafood - Whol

				Toll-Free	Phone
Beaver Street Fisheries Inc 1741 W Beaver St	Jacksonville	FL	32209	800-874-6426	904-354-8533
Blount Seafood Corp 630 Currant Rd *Hotline	Fall River	MA	02720	800-274-2526*	774-888-1300
ConAgra Foods Foodservice Co 5 ConAgra Dr	Omaha	NE	68102	800-357-6543	
Golden-Tech International Inc 2461 152nd Ave NE	Redmond	WA	98052	800-311-8090	425-869-1461
Inland Seafood Corp 1651 Montreal Cir	Tucker	GA	30084	800-883-3474	404-350-5850
Ipswich Shellfish Co Inc 8 Hayward St	Ipswich	MA	01938	800-477-9424	978-356-4371
Maine Lobster Direct 48 Union Wharf	Portland	ME	04101	800-556-2783	
Metropolitan Poultry & Seafood Co 1920 Stanford Ct	Landover	MD	20785	800-522-0060	301-772-0060
Morey's Seafood International LLC 1218 Hwy 10 S	Motley	MN	56466	800-808-3474	218-352-6345
Quirch Foods Co 7600 NW 82nd Pl	Miami	FL	33166	800-458-5252	305-691-3535
Sager's Seafood Plus Inc 4802 Bridal Wreath Dr	Richmond	TX	77406	800-929-3474	281-342-8833
Slade Gorton Company Inc 225 Southampton St	Boston	MA	02118	800-225-1573	617-442-5800
Stavis Seafoods Inc 212 Northern Ave Ste 305	Boston	MA	02210	800-390-5103	617-482-6349
Troyer Foods Inc 17141 State Rd 4	Goshen	IN	46528	800-876-9377	574-533-0302

298-6 Frozen Foods (Packaged) - Whol

				Toll-Free	Phone
Cedar Farms 2100 Hornig Rd	Philadelphia	PA	19116	800-220-2217	215-934-7100
ConAgra Foods Foodservice Co 5 ConAgra Dr	Omaha	NE	68102	800-357-6543	
Dot Foods Inc 1 Dot Way PO Box 192	Mount Sterling	IL	62353	800-366-3687	217-773-4411

298-7 Fruits & Vegetables - Fresh - Whol

				Toll-Free	Phone
Albert's Organics Inc 3268 E Vernon Ave	Vernon	CA	90058	800-899-5944	
Alpine Fresh Inc 9300 NW 58th St Ste 201	Miami	FL	33178	800-292-8777	305-594-9117
Banacol Marketing Corp 355 Alhambra Cir Ste 1510	Coral Gables	FL	33134	877-324-7619	305-441-9036
Belair Produce Company Inc 7226 Pkwy Dr	Hanover	MD	21076	888-782-8008	410-782-8000
Bix Produce Co 1415 L'Orient St	Saint Paul	MN	55117	800-642-9514	651-487-8000
Calavo Growers Inc 1141-A Cummings Rd *NASDAQ: CVGW*	Santa Paula	CA	93060	800-654-8758	805-525-1245
Caro Foods Inc 2324 Bayou Blue Rd	Houma	LA	70364	800-395-2276	985-872-1483
Costa Fruit & Produce 18 Bunker Hill Industrial Pk PO Box 290754	Boston	MA	02129	800-322-1374	617-241-8007
Crosset Company Inc 10295 Toebben Dr	Independence	KY	41051	800-347-4902	859-283-5830
Del Monte Fresh Produce Co 241 Sevilla Ave *Cust Svc	Coral Gables	FL	33134	800-950-3683*	305-520-8400
Dole Food Company Hawaii 802 Mapunapuna St	Honolulu	HI	96819	800-697-9100	808-861-8015
Egan Bernard & Co 1900 Old Dixie Hwy	Fort Pierce	FL	34946	800-327-6676	
Frieda's Inc 4465 Corporate Ctr Dr	Los Alamitos	CA	90720	800-241-1771	714-826-6100
General Produce Co 1330 N 'B' St	Sacramento	CA	95814	800-366-4991	916-441-6431
H Smith Packing Corp 99 Ft Fairfield Rd	Presque Isle	ME	04769	800-393-9898	207-764-4540
Hearn Kirkwood 7251 Standard Dr *General	Hanover	MD	21076	800-777-9489*	410-712-6000
Hollar & Greene Produce Co Inc 230 Cabbage Rd PO Box 3500	Boone	NC	28607	800-222-1077	828-264-2177
Indianapolis Fruit Company Inc 4501 Massachusetts Ave	Indianapolis	IN	46218	800-377-2425	317-546-2425
Kegel's Produce Inc 2851 Old Tree Dr	Lancaster	PA	17603	800-535-3435	717-392-6612
Melissa's/World Variety Produce Inc 5325 S Soto St	Vernon	CA	90058	800-588-0151	
Moore Food Distributors Co 9910 Page Ave	Saint Louis	MO	63132	800-467-7878	314-426-1300
Muir Enterprises Inc 3575 West 900 South PO Box 26775	Salt Lake City	UT	84104	877-268-2002	801-363-7695
North Bay Produce Inc PO Box 988	Traverse City	MI	49685	800-678-1941	
Organic Valley Family of Farms 1 Organic Way	LaFarge	WI	54639	888-444-6455	
Pacific Coast Fruit Co 201 NE Second Ave Ste 100	Portland	OR	97232	800-423-4945	503-234-6411
Produce Source Partners 13167 Telcourt Rd	Ashland	VA	23005	800-344-4728	804-262-8300
Progressive Produce Co 5790 Peachtree St	Los Angeles	CA	90040	800-900-0757	323-890-8100
ProPacificfresh 70 Pepsi Way PO Box 1069	Durham	CA	95938	888-232-0908	530-893-0596
Sambazon Inc 1160 Calle Cordillera	San Clemente	CA	92673	877-726-2296	949-498-8618
Sandridge Food Corp (SFC) 133 Commerce Dr	Medina	OH	44256	800-672-2523	330-725-2348
Taylor Farms Inc PO Box 1649	Salinas	CA	93902	866-675-6120	831-676-9765
W. R. Vernon Produce Co PO Box 4054	Winston-Salem	NC	27101	800-222-6406	336-725-9741

298-8 Groceries - General Line

				Toll-Free	Phone
Acme Food Sales Inc 5940 1st Ave S	Seattle	WA	98108	800-777-2263	206-762-5150
Active Organics Inc 1097 Yates St	Lewisville	TX	75057	800-541-1478	972-221-7500

Company / Address	City	State	Zip	Toll-Free	Phone
Affiliated Foods Inc 1401 W Farmers Ave	Amarillo	TX	79118	**800-234-3661**	806-372-3851
Albert Guarnieri Co 1133 E Market St	Warren	OH	44483	**800-686-2639**	330-394-5636
AMCON Distributing Co 7405 Irvington Rd *NYSE: DIT*	Omaha	NE	68122	**888-201-5997**	402-331-3727
Amster-Kirtz Co 2830 Cleveland Ave NW	Canton	OH	44709	**800-257-9338**	330-535-6021
Animal Supply Company LLC 32001 32nd Ave S Ste 420	Federal Way	WA	98001	**800-323-2963**	253-237-0400
Apetito Canada Ltd 12 Indell Ln	Brampton	ON	L6T3Y3	**800-268-8199**	905-799-1022
Associated Food Stores Inc 1850 West 2100 South *Cust Svc	Salt Lake City	UT	84119	**888-574-7100***	801-973-4400
Associated Grocers Inc 8600 Anselmo Ln	Baton Rouge	LA	70810	**800-637-2021**	225-444-1000
Associated Grocers of New England Inc 11 Co-op Way	Pembroke	NH	03275	**800-242-2248**	603-223-6710
Associated Grocers of the South 3600 Vanderbilt Rd	Birmingham	AL	35217	**800-695-6051**	205-841-6781
Associated Wholesalers Inc PO Box 67	Robesonia	PA	19551	**800-927-7771**	610-693-3161
Brenham Wholesale Grocery Co 602 W First St	Brenham	TX	77833	**800-392-4869**	979-836-7925
Camp Olympia 723 Olympia Dr	Trinity	TX	75862	**800-735-6190**	936-594-2541
Cash-Wa Distributing Co 401 W Fourth St	Kearney	NE	68845	**800-652-0010**	308-237-3151
Coastal Pacific Food Distributors Inc (CPFD) 1015 Performance Dr	Stockton	CA	95206	**800-500-2611**	209-983-2454
Deb-El Food Products LLC 2 Papetti Plaza	Elizabeth	NJ	07206	**800-421-0330**	908-351-0330
Devault Foods 1 Devault Ln	Devault	PA	19432	**800-426-2874**	610-644-2536
DiCarlo Distributors Inc 1630 N Ocean Ave	Holtsville	NY	11742	**800-342-2756**	631-758-6000
Dutch Valley Bulk Food Distributors Inc 7615 Lancaster Ave	Myerstown	PA	17067	**800-733-4191**	717-933-4191
F Mcconnell & Sons Inc 11102 Lincoln Hwy E	New Haven	IN	46774	**800-552-0835**	260-493-6607
Farner-Bocken Co 1751 US Hwy 30 E PO Box 368	Carroll	IA	51401	**800-274-8692**	712-792-3503
Feesers Inc 5561 Grayson Rd	Harrisburg	PA	17111	**800-326-2828**	717-564-4636
Field Trip Factory 2211 N Elston Ave Ste 304	Chicago	IL	60614	**800-987-6409**	
Flavor Dynamics Inc 640 Montrose Ave	South Plainfield	NJ	07080	**888-271-8424**	908-822-8855
Food Services of America Inc 16100 N 71st St Ste 400	Scottsdale	AZ	85254	**800-528-9346**	480-927-4000
Fuji Health Science Inc 3 Terri Ln Ste 12	Burlington	NJ	08016	**877-385-4777**	609-386-3030
G r Manufacturing Inc 4800 Commerce Dr	Trussville	AL	35173	**800-841-8001**	205-655-8001
George E DeLallo Co Inc 6390 Rt 30	Jeannette	PA	15644	**877-335-2556**	724-523-6577
Gold Coast Ingredients Inc 2429 Yates Ave	Commerce	CA	90040	**800-352-8673**	323-724-8935
Granite Falls Energy LLC 15045 Hwy 23 SE	Granite Falls	MN	56241	**877-485-8595**	320-564-3100
Grocery People Ltd, The 14505 Yellowhead Trl	Edmonton	AB	T5L3C4	**800-461-9401**	780-447-5700
Grocery Supply Co 130 Hillcrest Dr	Sulphur Springs	TX	75482	**800-231-1938**	903-885-7621
Hannaford Bros Co 145 Pleasant Hill Rd	Scarborough	ME	04074	**800-213-9040**	
Hansen Beverage Co 2661 Green River Rd	Corona	CA	92879	**877-265-3632**	800-426-7367
Harris Soup Co, The 17711 NE Riverside Pkwy	Portland	OR	97230	**800-307-7687**	503-257-7687
Honor Foods 1801 N Fifth St	Philadelphia	PA	19122	**800-462-2890**	215-236-1700
Imperial Trading Co Inc 701 Edwards Ave *Cust Svc	Elmwood	LA	70123	**800-775-4504***	504-733-1400
Jace Holdings Ltd 6649 Butler Crescent	Saanichton	BC	V8M1Z7	**800-667-8280**	250-483-1715
JM Swank Co 395 Herky St	North Liberty	IA	52317	**800-593-6333**	319-626-3683
Johnson Bros Bakery Supply 10731 N Interstate 35	San Antonio	TX	78233	**877-446-2767**	800-590-2575
Jonathan Lord Corp 87 Carlough Rd	Bohemia	NY	11716	**800-814-7517**	631-563-4445
Jordano's Inc 550 S Patterson Ave	Santa Barbara	CA	93111	**800-325-2278**	805-964-0611
Kings Super Markets Inc 700 Lanidex Plaza	Parsippany	NJ	07054	**800-325-4647**	
La Petite Bretonne Inc 1210 Boul Mich Le-Bohec	Blainville	QC	J7C5S4	**800-361-3381**	450-435-3381
Larue Coffee 2631 S 156th Cir	Omaha	NE	68130	**800-658-4498**	402-333-9099
Laurel Grocery Co Inc 129 Barbourville Rd	London	KY	40744	**800-467-6601**	
Magnetic Springs Water Co 1917 Joyce Ave	Columbus	OH	43219	**800-572-2990**	614-421-1780
Maines Paper & Food Service Co 101 Broome Corporate Pkwy	Conklin	NY	13748	**800-366-3669**	607-779-1200
McLane Company Inc 4747 McLane Pkwy	Temple	TX	76504	**800-299-1401**	254-771-7500
McLane Foodservice Inc 2085 Midway Rd	Carrollton	TX	75006	**800-299-1401**	972-364-2000
Merchants Co 1100 Edwards St	Hattiesburg	MS	39401	**800-451-8346**	601-583-4351
Mineral Resources International 1990 W 3300 S	Ogden	UT	84401	**800-731-7866**	801-731-7040
Nuherbs co 3820 Penniman Ave	Oakland	CA	94619	**800-233-4307**	510-534-4372
Olean Wholesale Grocery Co-op Inc 1587 Haskell Rd PO Box 1070	Olean	NY	14760	**888-835-3026**	716-372-2020
Oppenheimer Cos Inc 877 W Main Ste 700	Boise	ID	83702	**800-727-9939**	208-343-4883
P J Noyes Company Inc 89 Bridge St	Lancaster	NH	03584	**800-522-2469**	603-788-4952
Paris Gourmet of New York Inc 145 Grand St	Carlstadt	NJ	07072	**800-727-8791**	
Performance Foodservice 12500 W Creek Pkwy	Richmond	VA	23238	**800-535-5053**	804-484-7700
Peter Gillhams Natural Vitality 4879 Fountain Ave	Los Angeles	CA	90029	**888-324-9904**	
Piggly Wiggly Carolina Company Inc PO Box 118047	Charleston	SC	29423	**800-243-9880**	843-554-9880
Purity Wholesale Grocers Inc 5400 Broken Sound Blvd NW	Boca Raton	FL	33487	**800-323-6838**	561-994-9360
Rishi Tea LLC 185 S 33rd Ct	Milwaukee	WI	53208	**866-747-4483**	414-747-4001
Rutan Poly Industries Inc 39 Siding Pl	Mahwah	NJ	07430	**800-872-1474**	201-529-1474
S Abraham & Sons Inc PO Box 1768 *General	Grand Rapids	MI	49501	**866-248-3163***	616-453-6358
Shamrock Foods 3900 E Camelback Rd Ste 300	Phoenix	AZ	85018	**800-289-3663**	602-477-2500
Shanks Extracts Inc 350 Richardson Dr	Lancaster	PA	17603	**800-346-3135**	717-393-4441
Southco Distributing Co 2201 S John St	Goldsboro	NC	27530	**800-969-3172**	919-735-8012
Specialty Brands Of America Inc 1400 Old Country Rd	Westbury	NY	11590	**877-795-3599**	516-997-6969
Super Store Industries 16888 McKinley Ave PO Box 549	Lathrop	CA	95330	**888-292-8004**	209-858-2010
SUPERVALU Inc 7075 Flying Cloud Dr *NYSE: SVU* ■ *Cust Svc	Eden Prairie	MN	55344	**877-322-8228***	952-828-4000
SYGMA Network Inc 5550 Blazer Pkwy Ste 300	Dublin	OH	43017	**877-441-1144**	
Sysco Central Ohio Inc 2400 Harrison Rd	Columbus	OH	43204	**800-735-3341**	614-272-0655
Sysco Denver Inc 5000 Beeler St	Denver	CO	80238	**800-366-6696**	303-585-2000
Sysco Food Services of Idaho Inc 5710 Pan Am Ave	Boise	ID	83716	**800-747-9726**	208-345-9500
Sysco Grand Rapids 3700 Sysco Ct SE	Grand Rapids	MI	49512	**800-669-6967**	616-949-3700
Sysco Hampton Roads Inc 7000 Harbour View Blvd	Suffolk	VA	23435	**800-234-2451**	757-673-4000
Thoms Proestler Co 8001 TPC Rd	Rock Island	IL	61204	**800-747-1234**	309-787-1234
Topco Assoc LLC 7711 Gross Pt Rd	Skokie	IL	60077	**888-423-0139**	847-676-3030
Unified Grocers Inc 5200 Sheila St	Commerce	CA	90040	**800-724-7762**	323-264-5200
Vistar/VSA Corp 12650 E Arapahoe Rd	Centennial	CO	80112	**800-880-9900**	303-662-7100
W L Halsey Grocery Company Inc PO Box 6485	Huntsville	AL	35824	**800-621-0240**	256-772-9691
Wakefern Food Corp 600 York St	Elizabeth	NJ	07207	**800-746-7748**	908-527-3300
Winkler Inc 535 E Medcalf St	Dale	IN	47523	**800-621-3843**	812-937-4421
Wood-Fruitticher Grocery Company Inc 2900 Alton Rd	Birmingham	AL	35210	**800-328-0026**	205-836-9663

298-9 Meats & Meat Products - Whol

Company / Address	City	State	Zip	Toll-Free	Phone
Bruss Co 3548 N Kostner Ave	Chicago	IL	60641	**800-621-3882**	773-282-2900
Calumet Diversified Meats Inc 10000 80th Ave	Pleasant Prairie	WI	53158	**800-752-7427**	262-947-7200
Cambridge Packing Co Inc 41-43 Foodmart Rd	Boston	MA	02118	**800-722-6726**	617-269-6700
Cardinal Meat Specialists Ltd 155 Hedgedale Rd	Brampton	ON	L6T5P3	**800-363-1439**	905-459-4436
Cell Response Formulation LLC 4115 S Pub Pl	Jackson	WY	83002	**888-364-7839**	307-734-7839
ConAgra Foods Foodservice Co 5 ConAgra Dr	Omaha	NE	68102	**800-357-6543**	
Cusack Wholesale Meat Inc 301 SW 12th St	Oklahoma City	OK	73109	**800-241-6328**	405-232-2114
Deen Meats PO Box 4155 PO Box 4155	Fort Worth	TX	76164	**800-333-3953**	817-335-2257
Heartland Meat Company Inc 3461 Main St	Chula Vista	CA	91911	**888-407-3668**	619-407-3668
Manda Fine Meats 2445 Sorrel Ave	Baton Rouge	LA	70802	**800-343-2642**	225-344-7636
Michael's Finer Meats & Seafoods 3775 Zane Trace Dr	Columbus	OH	43228	**800-282-0518**	614-527-4900
Midamar Corp PO Box 218	Cedar Rapids	IA	52406	**800-362-3711**	319-362-3711
Paper Pak Industries (PPI) 1941 N White Ave	La Verne	CA	91750	**888-293-6529**	909-392-1750
Porky Products Corp 400 Port Carteret Dr *General	Carteret	NJ	07008	**800-952-0265***	732-541-0200
Quality Meats & Seafoods 700 Ctr St	West Fargo	ND	58078	**800-342-4250**	701-282-0202
Quirch Foods Co 7600 NW 82nd Pl	Miami	FL	33166	**800-458-5252**	305-691-3535
Sampco Inc 651 W Washington Blvd Ste 300	Chicago	IL	60661	**800-767-0689**	312-346-1506
Trim-Rite Food Corp 801 Commerce Pkwy	Carpentersville	IL	60110	**800-626-9442**	847-649-3400
Troyer Foods Inc 17141 State Rd 4	Goshen	IN	46528	**800-876-9377**	574-533-0302
U W Provision Company Inc PO Box 620038	Middleton	WI	53562	**800-832-0517**	608-836-7421
Williams Sausage Company Inc 5132 Old Troy Hickman Rd	Union City	TN	38261	**866-626-4282**	731-885-5841

298-10 Poultry, Eggs, Poultry Products - Whol

Company / Address	City	State	Zip	Toll-Free	Phone
Butts Foods Inc 2596 Bransford Ave	Nashville	TN	37204	**800-962-8570**	731-423-3456
Chino Valley Ranchers 5611 Peck Rd	Arcadia	CA	91006	**800-354-4503**	
Dutt & Wagner of Virginia Inc 1142 W Main St	Abingdon	VA	24210	**800-688-2116**	276-628-2116
House of Raeford Farms Inc 520 E Central Ave	Raeford	NC	28376	**800-888-7539**	910-875-5161
Metropolitan Poultry & Seafood Co 1920 Stanford Ct	Landover	MD	20785	**800-522-0060**	301-772-0060
Norbest Inc PO Box 890	Moroni	UT	84646	**800-453-5327**	
Quirch Foods Co 7600 NW 82nd Pl	Miami	FL	33166	**800-458-5252**	305-691-3535
Troyer Foods Inc 17141 State Rd 4	Goshen	IN	46528	**800-876-9377**	574-533-0302
Zacky Farms 13200 Crossroads Pkwy N Ste 250	City of Industry	CA	91746	**800-888-0235**	562-641-2020

298-11 Specialty Foods - Whol

Company / Address	City	State	Zip	Toll-Free	Phone
Charles C. Parks Co 500 Belvedere Dr	Gallatin	TN	37066	**800-873-2406**	615-452-2406
ConAgra Foods Foodservice Co 5 ConAgra Dr	Omaha	NE	68102	**800-357-6543**	
Conway Import Co Inc 11051 W Addison St	Franklin Park	IL	60131	**800-323-8801**	847-455-5600
CRS Onesource 2803 Tamarack Rd PO Box 1984	Owensboro	KY	42302	**800-264-0710**	270-684-1469
Ellis Coffee Co 2835 Bridge St	Philadelphia	PA	19137	**800-822-3984**	215-537-9500
Essex Grain Products 9 Lee Blvd	Frazer	PA	19355	**800-441-1017**	610-647-3800
Hain Celestial Group Inc 4600 Sleepytime Dr *NASDAQ: HAIN*	Boulder	CO	80301	**800-434-4246**	
Industrial Commodities Inc PO Box 4380	Glen Allen	VA	23060	**800-523-7902**	
J Sosnick & Sons Inc 258 Littlefield Ave	South San Francisco	CA	94080	**800-223-2194**	650-952-2226
Joffrey's Coffee & Tea Co 3803 Corporex Pk Dr	Tampa	FL	33619	**800-458-5282**	813-250-0404
John E Koerner & Company Inc 4820 Jefferson Hwy	New Orleans	LA	70121	**800-333-1913**	
Love & Quiches Desserts 178 Hanse Ave	Freeport	NY	11520	**800-525-5251**	516-623-8800
O S F Flavors Inc 40 Baker Hollow Rd	Windsor	CT	06095	**800-466-6015**	860-298-8350
Otto Brehm Inc PO Box 249	Yonkers	NY	10710	**800-272-6886**	914-968-6100
Producers Rice Mill Inc PO Box 1248	Stuttgart	AR	72160	**800-369-7675**	870-673-4444
Rain Creek Baking Co, The 2401 W Almond Ave	Madera	CA	93637	**800-530-0505**	559-674-4445
ReNew Life Formulas Inc 2076 Sunnydale Blvd	Clearwater	FL	33765	**800-830-1800**	727-450-1061
Schreiber Foods International Inc 600 E Crescent Ave Ste 103	Upper Saddle River	NJ	07458	**800-631-7070**	201-327-3535
Silver Springs Bottled Water Company Inc PO Box 926	Silver Springs	FL	34489	**800-556-0334**	
Sturm Foods Inc PO Box 287	Manawa	WI	54949	**800-347-8876**	920-596-2511
Sugar Foods Corp 950 Third Ave 21st Fl	New York	NY	10022	**800-732-8963**	212-753-6900
Sunsweet Growers Inc 901 N Walton Ave	Yuba City	CA	95993	**800-417-2253**	530-674-5010
Sysco Indianapolis LLC 4000 W 62nd St	Indianapolis	IN	46268	**800-347-3920**	317-291-2020
United Sugars Corp 7803 Glenroy Rd Ste 300	Bloomington	MN	55439	**800-984-3585**	952-896-0131

299 FOOD PRODUCTS MACHINERY

SEE ALSO Food Service Equipment & Supplies

Company / Address	City	State	Zip	Toll-Free	Phone
Alto-Shaam Inc W 164 N 9221 Water St PO Box 450	Menomonee Falls	WI	53052	**800-329-8744**	262-251-3800
American Permanent Ware Inc 729 Third Ave	Dallas	TX	75226	**800-527-2100**	214-421-7366
Anderson International Corp 6200 Harvard Ave	Cleveland	OH	44105	**800-336-4730**	216-641-1112
Atlas Metal Industries 1135 NW 159th Dr *Cust Svc	Miami	FL	33169	**800-762-7565***	305-625-2451
Atlas Pacific Engineering Co 1 Atlas Ave	Pueblo	CO	81001	**800-588-5438**	719-948-3040
Belshaw Bros Inc 1750 22nd Ave S	Seattle	WA	98144	**800-578-2547**	206-322-5474
Bettcher Industries Inc PO Box 336	Vermilion	OH	44089	**800-321-8763**	440-965-4422
Brewmatic Co 20333 S Normandie Ave PO Box 2959	Torrance	CA	90509	**800-421-6860**	310-787-5444
C Cretors & Co 3243 N California Ave	Chicago	IL	60618	**800-228-1885**	773-588-1690
Carlisle Cos Inc 13925 Ballantyne Corporate Pl Ste 400 *NYSE: CSL*	Charlotte	NC	28277	**800-248-5995**	704-501-1100
Casa Herrerra Inc 2655 N Pine St	Pomona	CA	91767	**800-624-3916**	909-392-3930
CE Rogers Co 1895 Frontage Rd	Mora	MN	55051	**800-279-8081**	320-679-2172
Chester-Jensen Company Inc PO Box 908	Chester	PA	19016	**800-685-3750**	610-876-6276
Cleveland Range Co 1333 E 179th St	Cleveland	OH	44110	**800-338-2204**	216-481-4900
CPM Wolverine Proctor LLC 251 Gibraltar Rd	Horsham	PA	19044	**800-428-0846**	215-443-5200
Delfield Co 980 S Isabella Rd	Mount Pleasant	MI	48858	**800-733-8821**	989-773-7981
Duke Manufacturing Co 2305 N Broadway	Saint Louis	MO	63102	**800-735-3853**	314-231-1130
Dunkley International Inc 1910 Lake St	Kalamazoo	MI	49001	**800-666-1264**	269-343-5583
Edlund Company Inc 159 Industrial Pkwy	Burlington	VT	05401	**800-772-2126**	802-862-9661
Feldmeier Equipment Inc 6800 Townline Rd	Syracuse	NY	13211	**800-258-0118**	315-454-8608
Fish Oven & Equipment Corp 120 W Kent Ave	Wauconda	IL	60084	**877-526-8720**	847-526-8686
Food Warming Equipment Company Inc 7900 S Rt 31 *Sales	Crystal Lake	IL	60014	**800-222-4393***	815-459-7500
Frymaster LLC 8700 Line Ave *Cust Svc	Shreveport	LA	71106	**800-221-4583***	318-865-1711
Garland Commercial Industries 185 S St	Freeland	PA	18224	**800-424-2411**	570-636-1000
Globe Food Equipment Co 2153 Dryden Rd	Dayton	OH	45439	**800-347-5423**	937-299-5493
Great Western Mfg Co Inc 2017 S Fourth St PO Box 149	Leavenworth	KS	66048	**800-682-3121**	913-682-2291
Grindmaster Crathco Systems Inc 4003 Collins Ln	Louisville	KY	40245	**800-695-4500**	502-425-4776
GS Blodgett Corp 44 Lakeside Ave	Burlington	VT	05401	**800-331-5842**	802-658-6600
Hayes & Stolz Industrial Manufacturing Co 3521 Hemphill St PO Box 11217	Fort Worth	TX	76110	**800-725-7272**	817-926-3391
Heat & Control Inc 21121 Cabot Blvd	Hayward	CA	94545	**800-227-5980**	510-259-0500
Henny Penny Corp 1219 US 35 W PO Box 60	Eaton	OH	45320	**800-417-8417**	937-456-8400
Hobart Corp 701 S Ridge Ave *Cust Svc	Troy	OH	45374	**800-333-7447***	937-332-3000
Key Technology Inc 150 Avery St *NASDAQ: KTEC*	Walla Walla	WA	99362	**877-341-5668**	509-529-2161
Kwik Lok Corp 2712 S 16th Ave PO Box 9548	Yakima	WA	98909	**800-688-5945**	509-248-4770
Lawrence Equipment Inc 2034 Peck Rd	El Monte	CA	91733	**800-423-4500**	626-442-2894
Lewis M Carter Mfg Co PO Box 428	Donalsonville	GA	39845	**800-332-8232**	229-524-2197
LK Industries 1357 W Beaver St	Jacksonville	FL	32209	**800-531-4975**	904-354-8882
Lucks Co, The 3003 S Pine St	Tacoma	WA	98409	**800-426-9778**	253-383-4815
Manitowoc Beverage Equipment 2100 Future Dr	Sellersburg	IN	47172	**800-367-4233**	812-246-7000
Market Forge Industries Inc 35 Garvey St	Everett	MA	02149	**866-698-3188**	617-387-4100
Marlen International Inc 4780 NW 41st St Ste 100	Riverside	MO	64150	**800-862-7536**	
Merco-Savory Inc 1111 N Hadley Rd *Cust Svc	Fort Wayne	IN	46804	**800-547-2513***	260-459-8200
Microfluidics International Corp 90 Glacier Dr Ste 1000	Westwood	MA	02090	**800-370-5452**	617-969-5452
Middleby Corp 1400 Toastmaster Dr *NASDAQ: MIDD*	Elgin	IL	60120	**800-331-5842**	847-741-3300
Nitta Casings Inc 141 Southside Ave *Cust Svc	Bridgewater	NJ	08807	**800-526-3970***	908-218-4400
Oliver Products Co 445 Sixth St NW	Grand Rapids	MI	49504	**800-253-3893**	616-456-7711
Peerless Food Equipment 500 S Vandemark Rd	Sidney	OH	45365	**800-999-3327**	937-492-4158
Peerless Machinery Corp 500 S Vandenmark Rd PO Box 769	Sidney	OH	45365	**877-795-7377**	937-492-4158
Piper Products Inc 300 S 84th Ave	Wausau	WI	54401	**800-544-3057**	715-842-2724
Pitco Frialator Inc PO Box 501	Concord	NH	03302	**800-258-3708**	603-225-6684
Prince Castle Inc 355 E Kehoe Blvd	Carol Stream	IL	60188	**800-722-7853**	630-462-8800
Ross Industries Inc 5321 Midland Rd	Midland	VA	22728	**800-336-6010**	540-439-3271
S Howes Company Inc 25 Howard St	Silver Creek	NY	14136	**888-255-2611**	716-934-2611
SaniServ Inc 451 E County Line Rd	Mooresville	IN	46158	**800-733-8073**	317-831-7030
Schlueter Co 310 N Main St	Janesville	WI	53545	**800-359-1700**	608-755-5444
Server Products Inc 3601 Pleasant Hill Rd PO Box 98	Richfield	WI	53076	**800-558-8722**	262-628-5600
Sonic Corp 1 Research Dr	Stratford	CT	06615	**866-493-1378**	203-375-0063
Southbend Inc 1100 Old Honeycutt Rd	Fuquay Varina	NC	27526	**800-755-4777**	919-762-1000
Stoelting LLC 502 Hwy 67	Kiel	WI	53042	**800-558-5807**	920-894-2293
Taylor 750 N Blackhawk Blvd	Rockton	IL	61072	**800-255-0626**	815-624-8333
Town Food Service Equipment Co 72 Beadel St	Brooklyn	NY	11222	**800-221-5032**	718-388-5650
Union Standard Equipment Co 801 E 141st St	Bronx	NY	10454	**877-282-7333**	718-585-0200
United Bakery Equipment Co Inc 15815 W 110th St	Lenexa	KS	66219	**888-823-2253**	913-541-8700
Univex Corp 3 Old Rockingham Rd	Salem	NH	03079	**800-258-6358**	603-893-6191

Company	Address	City	State	ZIP	Toll-Free	Phone
Urschel Laboratories Inc	2503 Calumet Ave PO Box 2200	Valparaiso	IN	46384	**844-877-2435**	219-464-4811
Van Doren Sales Inc	10 NE Cascade Ave	East Wenatchee	WA	98802	**866-886-1837**	509-886-1837
Viking Range Corp	111 Front St	Greenwood	MS	38930	**888-845-4641**	662-455-1200
Wells Bloomfield Industries	10 Sunnen Dr	Saint Louis	MO	63143	**888-356-5362**	
Wilbur Curtis Company Inc	6913 Acco St	Montebello	CA	90640	**800-421-6150**	323-837-2300
Winston Industries LLC	2345 Carton Dr	Louisville	KY	40299	**800-234-5286**	502-495-5400

300 FOOD SERVICE

SEE ALSO Restaurant Companies

Company	Address	City	State	ZIP	Toll-Free	Phone
A'viands LLC	1751 County Rd B W Ste 300	Roseville	MN	55113	**888-872-3788**	651-631-0940
Advance Food Company Inc	9987 Carver Rd Ste 500	Cincinnati	OH	45242	**800-969-2747**	
American Food & Vending Corp	124 Metropolitan Pk Dr	Syracuse	NY	13088	**800-466-9261**	315-457-9950
Bran-Zan Holdings Inc	1548 Barclay Blvd	Buffalo Grove	IL	60089	**866-266-9670**	
Canteen Service Co	712 Industrial Dr	Owensboro	KY	42301	**800-467-2471**	270-683-2471
Canteen Vending Services *Compass Group*	2400 Yorkmont Rd	Charlotte	NC	28217	**800-357-0012**	704-328-4000
Cara Operations Ltd	199 Four Valley Dr	Vaughan	ON	L4K0B8	**800-860-4082**	905-760-2244
Centerplate	2187 Atlantic St	Stamford	CT	06902	**800-698-6992**	203-975-5900
Compass Group North American Div (CGNAD)	2400 Yorkmont Rd	Charlotte	NC	28217	**800-357-0012**	704-328-4000
Five Star Food Service Inc	6005 Century Oaks Dr Ste 100	Chattanooga	TN	37416	**800-327-0043**	423-643-2600
Food Bank For New York City	39 Broadway 10th Fl	New York	NY	10006	**866-692-3663**	212-566-7855
General Mills Inc	1 General Mills Blvd *NYSE: GIS*	Minneapolis	MN	55426	**800-248-7310**	
Guest Services Inc	3055 Prosperity Ave	Fairfax	VA	22031	**800-345-7534**	703-849-9300
Institutional Wholesale Co	535 Dry Vly Rd	Cookeville	TN	38506	**800-239-9588**	931-537-4000
Island Oasis	141 Norfolk St PO Box 769	Walpole	MA	02081	**800-777-4752**	508-660-1176
Love & Quiches Desserts	178 Hanse Ave	Freeport	NY	11520	**800-525-5251**	516-623-8800
Morrison Management Specialists Inc	5801 Peachtree Dunwoody Rd *General	Atlanta	GA	30342	**800-225-4368***	
Open Kitchen Inc	1161 W 21st St	Chicago	IL	60608	**800-339-5334**	312-666-5335
Signature Services Corp	2705 Hawes Ave	Dallas	TX	75235	**800-929-5519**	214-353-2661
Sodexo Inc	9801 Washingtonian Blvd	Gaithersburg	MD	20878	**800-763-3946**	
Sportservice Corp	40 Fountain Plz	Buffalo	NY	14202	**800-828-7240**	716-858-5000
Summit Food Service Distributors Inc	580 Industrial Rd	London	ON	N5V1V1	**800-265-9267**	519-453-3410
Universal Sodexho	9801 Washingtonian Blvd	Gaithersburg	MD	20878	**888-763-3967**	301-987-4000

301 FOOD SERVICE EQUIPMENT & SUPPLIES

SEE ALSO Food Products Machinery

Company	Address	City	State	ZIP	Toll-Free	Phone
Adams-Burch Inc	1901 Stanford Ct *Cust Svc	Landover	MD	20785	**800-347-8093***	301-276-2000
Advance Tabco	200 Heartland Blvd	Edgewood	NY	11717	**800-645-3166**	631-242-4800
Atlanta Fixture & Sales Co	3185 NE Expy	Atlanta	GA	30341	**800-282-1977**	770-455-8844
Bargreen Ellingson Inc	2925 70th Ave E	Fife	WA	98424	**866-722-2665**	253-722-2600
Boelter Cos Inc	N22W23685 Ridgeview Pkwy W	West Waukesha	WI	53188	**800-263-5837**	262-523-6200
Bolton & Hay Inc	2701 Delaware Ave	Des Moines	IA	50317	**800-362-1861**	515-265-2554
Browne & Co	100 Esna Pk Dr	Markham	ON	L3R1E3	**866-306-3672**	905-475-6104
Browne-Halco Inc	788 Morris Turnpike Ste 202	Short Hills	NJ	07078	**888-289-1005**	973-232-1065
Cambro Manufacturing Co	5801 Skylab Rd	Huntington Beach	CA	92647	**800-833-3003**	714-848-1555
Carlisle FoodService Products Inc	4711 E Hefner Rd	Oklahoma City	OK	73131	**800-654-8210**	405-475-5600
Curtis Restaurant Supply & Equipment Co	6577 E 40th St	Tulsa	OK	74145	**800-766-2878**	918-622-7390
Eagle Group Inc	100 Industrial Blvd	Clayton	DE	19938	**800-441-8440**	302-653-3000
Edward Don & Co	2500 S Harlem Ave *Cust Svc	North Riverside	IL	60546	**800-777-4366***	
Genpak Carthage	505 E Cotton St	Carthage	TX	75633	**800-626-6695**	903-693-7151
Hotel & Restaurant Supply Inc	5020 Arundel Rd PO Box 6	Meridian	MS	39302	**800-782-6651**	601-482-7127
Intedge Mfg	1875 Chumley Rd	Woodruff	SC	29388	**866-969-9605**	864-969-9601
InterMetro Industries Corp	651 N Washington St *Cust Svc	Wilkes-Barre	PA	18705	**800-992-1776***	570-825-2741
Kittredge Equipment Co Inc	100 Bowles Rd	Agawam	MA	01001	**800-423-7082**	413-304-4100
Lakeside Manufacturing Inc	4900 W Electric Ave	West Milwaukee	WI	53219	**800-558-8565**	414-902-6400
Lancaster Colony Commercial Products Inc	3902 Indianola Ave	Columbus	OH	43214	**800-292-7260**	614-263-2850
Maines Paper & Food Service Co	101 Broome Corporate Pkwy	Conklin	NY	13748	**800-366-3669**	607-779-1200
McLane Foodservice Inc	2085 Midway Rd	Carrollton	TX	75006	**800-299-1401**	972-364-2000
N Wasserstrom & Sons Inc	2300 Lockbourne Rd	Columbus	OH	43207	**800-444-4697**	614-228-5550
PBI Market Equipment Inc	2667 Gundry Ave	Signal Hill	CA	90755	**800-421-3753**	562-595-4785
Perkins Equipment Div	630 John Hancock Rd	Taunton	MA	02780	**800-733-5708**	508-824-2800
RAPIDS Wholesale Equipment Co	6201 S Gateway Dr	Marion	IA	52302	**800-472-7431**	319-447-1670
Restaurant Technologies Inc	2250 Pilot Knob Rd Ste 100	Mendota Heights	MN	55120	**888-796-4997**	651-796-1600
Service Ideas Inc	2354 Ventura Dr	Woodbury	MN	55125	**800-328-4493**	651-730-8800
Smith & Greene Co	19015 66th Ave S	Kent	WA	98032	**800-232-8050**	425-656-8000
Standex International Corp Food Service Equipment Group	11 Keewaydin Dr *NYSE: SXI*	Salem	NH	03079	**800-647-1284**	603-893-9701
TriMark USA Inc	505 Collins St	South Attleboro	MA	02703	**800-755-5580**	508-399-2400
US Foods Culinary Equipment & Supplies	2621 Fairview Ave N Ste 2	Roseville	MN	55113	**866-636-2338**	651-638-8993
Vollrath Co LLC, The	1236 N 18th St	Sheboygan	WI	53081	**800-624-2051**	920-457-4851
Wasserstrom Co	477 S Front St	Columbus	OH	43215	**866-634-8927**	614-228-6525

302 FOOTWEAR

Company	Address	City	State	ZIP	Toll-Free	Phone
Acor Orthopaedic Inc	18530 S Miles Pkwy	Cleveland	OH	44128	**800-237-2267**	216-662-4500
Acushnet Co	333 Bridge St	Fairhaven	MA	02719	**800-225-8500**	508-979-2000
Aerosoles Inc	201 Meadow Rd	Edison	NJ	08817	**800-798-9478**	732-985-6900
Aldo Shoes	2300 Emile Belanger	Montreal	QC	H4R3J4	**888-818-2536**	514-747-2536
Allen-Edmonds Shoe Corp	201 E Seven Hills Rd *Cust Svc	Port Washington	WI	53074	**800-235-2348***	262-235-6512
Asics America Corp	29 Parker Ste 100	Irvine	CA	92618	**800-333-8404**	949-453-8888
Badorf Shoe Co Inc	1958 Auction Rd	Manheim	PA	17545	**800-325-1545**	717-653-0155
Barbour Welting Company Div Barbour Corp	1001 N Montello St	Brockton	MA	02301	**800-955-9649**	508-583-8200
Brooks Sports Inc	19910 N Creek Pkwy Ste 200	Bothell	WA	98011	**800-227-6657**	
Capezio/Ballet Makers Inc	1 Campus Rd *Acctg	Totowa	NJ	07512	**800-533-1887***	973-595-9000
Chinese Laundry Shoes	3485 S La Cienega Blvd	Los Angeles	CA	90016	**888-935-8825**	310-838-2103
Clark Cos NA	156 Oak St *Cust Svc	Newton Upper Falls	MA	02464	**800-211-5461***	617-964-1222
Cole-Haan	8701 Keystone Crossing	Indianapolis	IN	46240	**800-695-8945**	317-810-0160
Consolidated Shoe Company Inc	22290 Timberlake Rd	Lynchburg	VA	24502	**800-368-7463**	434-239-0391
Cowtown Boots	11401 Gateway Blvd W	El Paso	TX	79936	**800-580-2698**	915-593-2929
Crocs Inc	6328 Monarch Pk Pl *NASDAQ: CROX*	Niwot	CO	80503	**866-306-3179**	303-848-7000
Danner Shoe Manufacturing Co	17634 NE Airport *Cust Svc	Portland	OR	97230	**800-345-0430***	503-251-1100
Deckers Outdoor Corp	495-A S Fairview Ave *NYSE: DECK*	Goleta	CA	93117	**877-337-8333**	805-967-7611
Drew Shoe Corp	252 Quarry Rd	Lancaster	OH	43130	**800-837-3739**	740-653-4271
East Lion Corp	318 Brea Canyon Rd	City of Industry	CA	91789	**877-939-1818**	626-912-1818
Eastland Shoe Mfg Corp	4 Meeting House Rd	Freeport	ME	04032	**888-988-1998**	207-865-6314
ES Originals Inc	440 9th Ave 7th Fl *General	New York	NY	10001	**800-677-6577***	212-736-8124
Famous Footwear	247 Junction Rd *Cust Svc	Madison	WI	53717	**800-888-7198***	608-833-3340
Finish Line Inc, The	3308 N Mitthoeffer Rd *NASDAQ: FINL*	Indianapolis	IN	46235	**888-777-3949**	317-899-1022
Florsheim Inc	333 W Estabrook Blvd	Glendale	WI	53212	**866-454-0449**	
Foot Locker Inc	112 W 34th St *NYSE: FL*	New York	NY	10120	**800-952-5210**	212-720-3700
Footstar Inc	933 MacArthur Blvd	Mahwah	NJ	07430	**800-322-2885**	201-934-2000
Gateway Shoe Co	910 Kehro Mill Rd Ste 112	Ballwin	MO	63011	**800-539-6063**	636-256-7050
Georgia Boot Inc	39 E Canal St	Nelsonville	OH	45764	**877-795-2410**	740-753-1951

Company / Address	City	State	Zip	Toll-Free	Phone
HH Brown Shoe Company Inc 124 W Putnam Ave	Greenwich	CT	06830	**888-444-2769**	203-661-2424
Hush Puppies Co 9341 Courtland Dr NE	Rockford	MI	49351	**866-699-7365**	616-866-5500
Impo International Inc PO Box 639	Santa Maria	CA	93456	**800-367-4676**	
Inter-Pacific Corp 2257 Colby Ave	Los Angeles	CA	90064	**877-605-8414**	310-473-7591
John Reyer Shoe Store 40 S Water Ave *Cust Svc	Sharon	PA	16146	**800-245-1550***	
Johnston & Murphy Inc 1415 Murfreesboro Rd	Nashville	TN	37217	**800-424-2854**	615-367-7168
Justin Boot Co Inc 610 W Daggett St *Cust Svc	Fort Worth	TX	76104	**800-548-1021***	817-332-7797
K-Swiss Inc 31248 Oak Crest Dr *NASDAQ: KSWS*	Westlake Village	CA	91361	**800-938-8000**	818-706-5100
Kaepa USA Inc 9050 Autobahn Dr Ste 500	Dallas	TX	75237	**800-880-9200**	
Keds Corp 1400 Industries Rd	Richmond	IN	47374	**800-680-0966**	
Kenneth Cole Productions Inc 603 W 50th St *NYSE: KCP*	New York	NY	10019	**800-536-2653**	212-265-1500
LaCrosse Footwear Inc 17634 NE Airport *Cust Svc	Portland	OR	97230	**800-323-2668***	
Lady Foot Locker (LFL) 112 W 34th St	New York	NY	10120	**800-991-6686**	212-720-3700
Lake Catherine Footwear 3770 Malvern Rd PO Box 6048	Hot Springs	AR	71901	**800-819-1901**	
Lamey-Wellehan Inc 940 Turner St	Auburn	ME	04210	**800-370-6900**	207-784-6595
Lucchese Boot Co 20 ZANE GREY	El Paso	TX	79906	**800-637-6888**	888-582-1883
Marty's Shoe Outlet Inc 121 Carver Ave *General	Westwood	NJ	07675	**888-662-7897***	201-497-6637
Merrell Footwear 9341 Courtland Dr NE *Cust Svc	Rockford	MI	49351	**800-288-3124***	616-866-5500
Mizuno USA 4925 Avalon Ridge Pkwy	Norcross	GA	30071	**800-966-1211**	770-441-5553
Munro & Co Inc 3770 Malvern Rd 71901 PO Box 6048	Hot Springs	AR	71902	**800-819-1901**	501-262-6000
New Balance Athletic Shoe Inc 20 Guest St Brighton Landing	Brighton	MA	02135	**800-595-9138**	617-783-4000
Nike Inc 1 Bowerman Dr *NYSE: NKE* ■ *Cust Svc	Beaverton	OR	97005	**800-344-6453***	503-671-6453
Novus Inc 655 Calle Cubitas	Guaynabo	PR	00969	**888-530-4546**	787-272-4546
ONGUARD Industries 1850 Clark Rd	Havre de Grace	MD	21078	**800-365-2282**	410-272-2000
Otomix Inc 747 Glasgow Ave	Inglewood	CA	90301	**800-701-7867**	310-215-6100
Payless ShoeSource Inc 3231 SE Sixth Ave	Topeka	KS	66607	**877-452-7500**	785-233-5171
Phoenix Footwear Group Inc 5937 Darwin Ct Ste 109 *OTC: PXFG*	Carlsbad	CA	92008	**888-218-7275**	760-602-9688
Propet USA Inc 2415 W Valley Hwy N	Auburn	WA	98001	**800-877-6738**	253-854-7600
Puma North America Inc 10 Lyberty Way *General	Westford	MA	01886	**888-565-7862***	978-698-1000
PW Minor & Son Inc 3 Tread Easy Ave	Batavia	NY	14020	**800-333-4067**	585-343-1500
Red Wing Shoe Company Inc 314 Main St *Cust Svc	Red Wing	MN	55066	**800-733-9464***	651-388-8211
Reebok International Ltd 1895 JW Foster Blvd	Canton	MA	02021	**866-870-1743**	781-401-5000
RG Barry Corp 13405 Yarmouth Dr NW *NASDAQ: DFZ*	Pickerington	OH	43147	**800-848-7560**	614-864-6400
Rockport Company Inc 1895 JW Foster Blvd	Canton	MA	02021	**800-828-0545**	781-401-5000
Rocky Shoes & Boots Inc 39 E Canal St *NASDAQ: RCKY*	Nelsonville	OH	45764	**877-795-2410**	740-753-3130
Romika USA LLC 3405 Del Webb Ave NE	Salem	OR	97301	**888-777-4174**	503-588-8117
SAS Shoemakers 1717 SAS Dr	San Antonio	TX	78224	**877-782-7463**	
Saucony Inc 191 Spring St	Lexington	MA	02420	**800-282-6575**	
Saxon Shoes Inc 11800 W Broad St Ste 2750 *General	Richmond	VA	23233	**800-686-5616***	804-285-3473
Sebago Inc 9341 Courtland Dr	Rockford	MI	49351	**866-699-7367**	616-866-5500
Shoe Carnival Inc 7500 E Columbia St *NASDAQ: SCVL* ■ *Cust Svc	Evansville	IN	47715	**800-430-7463***	812-867-6471
Shoe Show of Rocky Mountain Inc 2201 Trinity Church Rd *Cust Svc	Concord	NC	28027	**888-557-4637***	704-782-4143
Skechers USA Inc 228 Manhattan Beach Blvd *NYSE: SKX* ■ *Cust Svc	Manhattan Beach	CA	90266	**800-746-3411***	310-318-3100
Spalding PO Box 90015	Bowling Green	KY	42103	**855-253-4533**	
Stride Rite Corp 191 Spring St *Cust Svc	Lexington	MA	02420	**800-299-6575***	617-824-6000
Super Shoe Stores Inc 601 Dual Hwy	Hagerstown	MD	21740	**866-842-7510**	
Teva Sport Sandals 123 N Leroux St *General	Flagstaff	AZ	86001	**800-367-8382***	928-779-5938
Timberland Co, The 200 Domain Dr *NYSE: VFC*	Stratham	NH	03885	**800-258-0855**	603-772-9500
Trimfoot Co LLC 115 Trimfoot Terr	Farmington	MO	63640	**800-325-6116**	
Vans Inc 15700 Shoemaker Ave	Santa Fe Springs	CA	90670	**855-909-8267**	
Weinbrenner Shoe Co Inc 108 S Polk St *General	Merrill	WI	54452	**800-569-6817***	715-536-5521
West Coast Shoe Co 52828 NW Shoe Factory Ln PO Box 607	Scappoose	OR	97056	**800-326-2711**	503-543-7114
Weyco Group Inc 333 W Estabrook Blvd *NASDAQ: WEYS*	Glendale	WI	53212	**866-454-0449**	414-908-1880

303 FORESTRY SERVICES

SEE ALSO Timber Tracts

Company / Address	City	State	Zip	Toll-Free	Phone
Resource Management Service LLC 31 Inverness Ctr Pkwy Ste 360	Birmingham	AL	35242	**800-995-9516**	
Vestra Resources Inc 5300 Aviation Dr	Redding	CA	96002	**877-983-7872**	530-223-2585

304 FOUNDATIONS - COMMUNITY

SEE ALSO Charitable & Humanitarian Organizations

Company / Address	City	State	Zip	Toll-Free	Phone
Arizona Community Foundation 2201 E Camelback Rd Ste 405B	Phoenix	AZ	85016	**800-222-8221**	602-381-1400
Cleveland Foundation 1422 Euclid Ave Ste 1300	Cleveland	OH	44115	**877-554-5054**	216-861-3810
Colorado Trust 1600 Sherman St	Denver	CO	80203	**888-847-9140**	303-837-1200
Community Foundation for Greater New Haven 70 Audubon St	New Haven	CT	06510	**877-829-5500**	203-777-2386
Dayton Foundation 40 N Main St Ste 500	Dayton	OH	45423	**877-222-0410**	937-222-0410
Foundation for the Carolinas 217 S Tryon St	Charlotte	NC	28202	**800-973-7244**	704-973-4500
Hawaii Community Foundation 65-1279 Kawaihae Rd	Kamuela	HI	96743	**888-731-3863**	808-537-6333
Minneapolis Foundation 80 S Eigth St 800 IDS Ctr	Minneapolis	MN	55402	**866-305-0543**	612-672-3878
New York Community Trust 909 Third Ave 22nd Fl	New York	NY	10022	**877-829-5500**	212-686-0010
Omaha Community Foundation (OCF) 302 S 36th St Ste 100	Omaha	NE	68131	**800-794-3458**	402-342-3458
Saint Paul Foundation, The 101 Fifth St E Ste 2400	Saint Paul	MN	55101	**800-875-6167**	651-224-5463

305 FOUNDATIONS - CORPORATE

SEE ALSO Charitable & Humanitarian Organizations

Company / Address	City	State	Zip	Toll-Free	Phone
Cargill Foundation 15407 McGinty Rd W Ste 46	Wayzata	MN	55391	**800-227-4455**	877-765-8867
CIGNA Foundation 900 Cottage Grove Rd *NYSE: CI*	Bloomfield	CT	06002	**866-438-2446**	
Coca-Cola Foundation Inc PO Box 1734	Atlanta	GA	30301	**800-438-2653**	
Dow Chemical Company Foundation 2030 Dow Ctr	Midland	MI	48674	**800-331-6451**	989-636-1000
General Mills Foundation PO Box 9452	Minneapolis	MN	55440	**800-248-7310**	
General Motors Foundation Inc PO Box 33170	Detroit	MI	48232	**800-222-1020**	
Hallmark Corp Foundation 2501 McGee St	Kansas City	MO	64108	**800-425-5627**	
Humana Foundation Inc 500 W Main St Ste 208	Louisville	KY	40202	**888-431-4748**	502-580-4140
Lutheran Community Foundation 625 Fourth Ave S Ste 200	Minneapolis	MN	55415	**800-365-4172**	612-340-4110
Principal Financial Group Foundation Inc 711 High St	Des Moines	IA	50392	**800-986-3343**	502-855-3673
Revlon Foundation Inc 237 Pk Ave *Cust Svc	New York	NY	10017	**800-473-8566***	
SBC Foundation 130 E Travis St Ste 350	San Antonio	TX	78205	**800-591-9663**	
Scripps Howard Foundation 312 Walnut St PO Box 5380	Cincinnati	OH	45201	**800-888-3000**	513-977-3035
Wal-Mart Foundation 702 SW Eigth St *NYSE: WMT*	Bentonville	AR	72716	**800-438-6278**	479-273-4000
Whirlpool Foundation 2000 N M-63	Benton Harbor	MI	49022	**800-952-9245**	269-923-5000
Xerox Foundation 45 Glover Ave	Norwalk	CT	06856	**800-275-9376**	

306 FOUNDATIONS - PRIVATE

SEE ALSO Charitable & Humanitarian Organizations

Company / Address	City	State	Zip	Toll-Free	Phone
AIDS Foundation of Chicago 200 W Jackson Blvd Ste 2200	Chicago	IL	60606	**866-895-2437**	312-922-2322
Amity Foundation of California 2260 Watson Way	Vista	CA	92083	**888-508-9269**	

Name / Address	City	State	Zip	Toll-Free	Phone
Annie E Casey Foundation 701 St Paul St	Baltimore	MD	21202	**800-222-1099**	410-547-6600
Art Gallery of Ontario 317 Dundas St W	Toronto	ON	M5T1G4	**877-225-4246**	416-979-6660
Arthur Vining Davis Foundations 225 Water St	Jacksonville	FL	32202	**888-427-4313**	904-359-0670
Bill & Melinda Gates Foundation PO Box 23350	Seattle	WA	98102	**800-728-3843**	206-709-3100
Careers The Next Generation Foundation 10470 176 St Nw	Edmonton	AB	T5S1L3	**888-757-7172**	780-426-3414
Carnegie Corp of New York 437 Madison Ave	New York	NY	10022	**800-336-7323**	212-371-3200
Centre for Addiction & Mental Health Foundation 901 King St W Ste 502	Toronto	ON	M5V3H5	**800-414-0471**	416-979-6909
Colonial Williamsburg Foundation PO Box 1776	Williamsburg	VA	23187	**800-447-8679**	757-229-1000
Corporation for Public Broadcasting (CPB) 401 Ninth St NW	Washington	DC	20004	**800-272-2190**	202-879-9600
Dave Thomas Foundation for Adoption 716 Mt Airyshire Blvd Ste 100	Columbus	OH	43235	**800-275-3832**	
David Suzuki Foundation 2211 Fourth Ave W	Vancouver	BC	V6K4S2	**800-453-1533**	604-732-4228
Ewing Marion Kauffman Foundation (EMKF) 4801 Rockhill Rd	Kansas City	MO	64110	**800-385-1607**	816-932-1000
FJC 520 Eighth Ave 20th Fl	New York	NY	10018	**888-448-3352**	212-714-0001
Florida School Choice Fund Inc PO Box 1670	Jacksonville	FL	33601	**877-735-7837**	
Free Methodist Foundation, The 8050 Spring Arbor Rd	Spring Arbor	MI	49283	**800-325-8975**	517-750-2727
Gates Family Foundation 1390 Lawrence St	Denver	CO	80204	**866-590-4377**	303-722-1881
Georgia Northwestern Technical College Foundation Inc 1 Maurice Culberson Dr Sw	Rome	GA	30161	**866-983-4682**	706-295-6842
Granite State Independent Living Foundation 21 Chenell Dr	Concord	NH	03301	**800-826-3700**	603-228-9680
Hearst Foundation, The 300 W 57th St 26th Fl.	New York	NY	10019	**800-841-7048**	212-649-3750
Idaho Community Foundation Inc 210 W State St	Boise	ID	83702	**800-657-5357**	208-342-3535
Kansas Health Foundation 309 E Douglas	Wichita	KS	67202	**800-373-7681**	316-262-7676
Kate B Reynolds Charitable Trust 128 Reynolda Village	Winston-Salem	NC	27106	**800-485-9080**	336-397-5500
Kidango Inc 44000 Old Warm Springs Blvd	Fremont	CA	94538	**800-262-4252**	408-258-3710
Kiwanis International Foundation 3636 Woodview Trace	Indianapolis	IN	46268	**800-549-2647**	317-875-8755
Liberty Fund Inc 8335 Allison Pt Trial Ste 300	Indianapolis	IN	46250	**800-955-8335**	317-842-0880
Lumina Foundation for Education 30 S Meridian St Ste 700	Indianapolis	IN	46204	**800-834-5756**	317-951-5300
Meadows Foundation Inc 3003 Swiss Ave	Dallas	TX	75204	**800-826-9431**	214-826-9431
Michael J Fox Foundation for Parkinson's Research Grand Central Stn PO Box 4777	New York	NY	10163	**800-708-7644**	
National Foundation for Cancer Research (NFCR) 4600 E W Hwy Ste 525	Bethesda	MD	20814	**800-321-2873**	301-654-1250
National PTA 1250 N Pitt St	Alexandria	VA	22314	**800-307-4782**	703-518-1200
Nellie Mae Education Foundation 1250 Hancock St Ste 205N	Quincy	MA	02169	**877-635-5436**	781-348-4200
Ottawa Regional Cancer Foundation The 1500 Alta Vista Dr	Ottawa	ON	K1G3Y9	**855-247-3527**	613-247-3527
Patient Advocate Foundation Inc 700 Thimble Shoals Blvd Ste 200	Newport News	VA	23606	**800-532-5274**	
Pew Charitable Trusts 2005 Market St 1 Commerce Sq Ste 1700	Philadelphia	PA	19103	**800-351-6801**	215-575-9050
Phi Kappa Phi Foundation 7576 Goodwood Blvd	Baton Rouge	LA	70806	**800-804-9880**	225-388-4917
Public Welfare Foundation 1200 U St NW	Washington	DC	20009	**800-275-7934**	202-965-1800
Richard King Mellon Foundation 500 Grant St Ste 4106	Pittsburgh	PA	15219	**800-424-9836**	412-392-2800
Robert R McCormick Tribune Foundation 205 N Michigan Ave Ste 4300	Chicago	IL	60611	**800-435-7352**	312-445-5000
Robert Wood Johnson Foundation PO Box 2316	Princeton	NJ	08543	**877-843-7953**	
Salesforce.Com Foundation The Landmark @ One Market Ste 300	San Francisco	CA	94105	**800-667-6389**	
Seva Foundation 1786 Fifth St	Berkeley	CA	94710	**877-764-7382**	510-845-7382
Student Veterans of America PO Box 77673	Washington	DC	20013	**866-320-3826**	202-223-4710
Texas Methodist Foundation 11709 Boulder Ln Ste 100	Austin	TX	78726	**800-933-5502**	512-331-9971
Tides Canada Foundation 400-163 W Hastings St	Vancouver	BC	V6B1H5	**866-843-3722**	604-647-6611
Universitas Foundation of Canada 3005 Ave Maricourt	Quebec	QC	G1W4T8	**877-710-7377**	418-651-8975
Women's Independence Scholarship Program Inc (WISP) 4900 Randall Pkwy Ste H	Wilmington	NC	28403	**866-255-7742**	910-397-7742
XanGo Goodness 2889 Ashton Blvd	Lehi	UT	84043	**877-469-2646**	801-816-8000

307 FOUNDRIES - INVESTMENT

Name / Address	City	State	Zip	Toll-Free	Phone
Consolidated Casting Corp 1501 S I-45	Hutchins	TX	75141	**800-649-5289**	972-225-7305
Remet Corp 210 Commons Rd	Utica	NY	13502	**877-939-0171**	315-797-8700
Waltek Inc 14310 Sunfish Lk Blvd	Ramsey	MN	55303	**800-937-9496**	763-427-3181

308 FOUNDRIES - IRON & STEEL

SEE ALSO Foundries - Nonferrous (Castings)

Name / Address	City	State	Zip	Toll-Free	Phone
Allegheny Technologies Inc 1000 Six PPG Pl *NYSE: ATI* ■ *Sales	Pittsburgh	PA	15222	**800-258-3586***	412-394-2800
Alloy Engineering & Casting Co 1700 W Washington St	Champaign	IL	61821	**800-348-2880**	217-398-3200
American Cast Iron Pipe Co (ACIPCO) 1501 31st Ave N	Birmingham	AL	35207	**800-442-2347**	205-325-7701
Bremen Castings Inc 500 N Baltimore St	Bremen	IN	46506	**800-837-2411**	
Castalloy Inc 1701 Industrial Ln PO Box 827	Waukesha	WI	53189	**800-211-0900**	262-547-0070
Columbia Steel Casting Co Inc 10425 N Bloss Ave	Portland	OR	97203	**800-547-9471**	503-286-0685
Complex Steel & Wire Corp 36254 Annapolis St	Wayne	MI	48184	**800-521-0666**	734-326-1600
Delta Centrifugal Corp PO Box 1043 *Sales	Temple	TX	76503	**888-433-3100***	254-773-9055
EJ Group Inc 301 Spring St	East Jordan	MI	49727	**800-874-4100**	231-536-2261
Farrar Corp 142 W Burns St	Norwich	KS	67118	**800-536-2215**	620-478-2212
Frog Switch & Mfg Co 600 E High St	Carlisle	PA	17013	**800-233-7194**	717-243-2454
Harrison Steel Castings Co Inc 900 S Mound St	Attica	IN	47918	**800-659-4722**	765-762-2481
Hensley Industries Inc 2108 Joe Field Rd PO Box 29779	Dallas	TX	75229	**888-406-6262**	972-241-2321
Hitachi Metals America Ltd 2 Manhattanville Rd Ste 301	Purchase	NY	10577	**800-777-5757**	914-694-9200
Howco Metals Management 9611 Telge Rd	Houston	TX	77095	**800-392-7720**	281-649-8800
Jencast PO Box 1509	Coffeyville	KS	67337	**800-331-2662**	620-251-5700
Neenah Foundry Co 2121 Brooks Ave	Neenah	WI	54956	**800-558-5075**	920-725-7000
Rodney Hunt Co 46 Mill St	Orange	MA	01364	**800-448-8860**	978-544-2511
Sentinel Bldg Systems Inc 237 S Fourth St PO Box 348	Albion	NE	68620	**800-327-0790**	402-395-5076
Sharon Coating LLC 277 Sharpsville Ave	Sharon	PA	16146	**800-456-1794**	724-983-6464
Sioux City Foundry Co 801 Div St	Sioux City	IA	51102	**800-831-0874**	712-252-4181
Standard Alloys & Mfg PO Box 969	Port Arthur	TX	77640	**800-231-8240**	409-983-3201
Steel Service Corp 2260 Flowood Dr PO Box 321425	Jackson	MS	39232	**800-844-9222**	601-939-9222
Talladega Castings & Machine Co Inc 228 N Ct St	Talladega	AL	35160	**800-766-6708**	256-362-5550
Talladega Machinery & Supply Co Inc 301 N Johnson Ave PO Box 736 *Cust Svc	Talladega	AL	35161	**800-289-8672***	256-362-4124
Tyler Pipe Co 11910 CR 492	Tyler	TX	75706	**800-527-8478**	903-882-5511
US Pipe & Foundry Co 2 Chase Corporate Drive Ste 200	Birmingham	AL	35244	**866-347-7473**	
Waukesha Foundry Company Inc 1300 Lincoln Ave	Waukesha	WI	53186	**800-727-0741**	262-542-0741
Waupaca Foundry 1955 Brunner Dr PO Box 249	Waupaca	WI	54981	**800-669-6820**	715-258-6611

309 FOUNDRIES - NONFERROUS (CASTINGS)

SEE ALSO Foundries - Iron & Steel

Name / Address	City	State	Zip	Toll-Free	Phone
Bunting Bearings Corp 1001 Holland Pk Blvd	Holland	OH	43528	**888-286-8464**	419-866-7000
Consolidated Metco Inc 13940 N Rivergate Blvd *Sales	Portland	OR	97203	**800-547-9473***	
Deco Products Co 506 Sanford St	Decorah	IA	52101	**800-327-9751**	563-382-4264
Del Mar Die Casting Co 12901 S Western Ave	Gardena	CA	90249	**800-624-7468**	323-321-0600
Electric Materials Co 50 S Washington St	North East	PA	16428	**800-356-2211**	814-725-9621
General Die Casters Inc 2150 Highland Rd	Twinsburg	OH	44087	**800-332-2278**	330-657-2300
Halex Co 23901 Aurora Rd	Bedford Heights	OH	44146	**800-749-3261**	
Lee Brass Co 1800 Golden Springs Rd *General	Anniston	AL	36207	**800-876-1811***	
Littlestown Foundry Inc 150 Charles St PO Box 69	Littlestown	PA	17340	**800-471-0844**	717-359-4141
Madison-Kipp Corp 201 Waubesa St	Madison	WI	53704	**800-356-6148**	
Magnolia Metal Corp 10675 Bedford Ave Ste 200	Omaha	NE	68134	**800-228-4043**	402-455-8760
NGK Metals Corp 917 Hwy 11 S	Sweetwater	TN	37874	**800-523-8268**	423-337-5500
Piad Precision Casting Corp 112 Industrial Pk Rd	Greensburg	PA	15601	**800-441-9858**	724-838-5500
Premier Die Casting Co 1177 Rahway Ave	Avenel	NJ	07001	**800-394-3006**	732-634-3000
Premier Tool & Die Cast Corp 9886 N Tudor Rd	Berrien Springs	MI	49103	**800-417-8717**	269-471-7715
Reliable Castings Corp 3530 Spring Grove Ave	Cincinnati	OH	45223	**866-722-2278**	513-541-2627
Stahl Specialty Co 111 E Pacific PO Box 6	Kingsville	MO	64061	**800-821-7852**	816-597-3322
Talladega Castings & Machine Co Inc 228 N Ct St	Talladega	AL	35160	**800-766-6708**	256-362-5550

Company	Address	City	State	ZIP	Toll-Free	Phone
Techni-Cast Corp	11220 Garfield Ave	South Gate	CA	90280	**800-923-4585**	562-923-4585
United Titanium Inc	3450 Old Airport Rd	Wooster	OH	44691	**800-321-4938**	330-264-2111

310 FRAMES & MOULDINGS

Company	Address	City	State	ZIP	Toll-Free	Phone
Alexandria Moulding	20352 Powerdam Rd	Alexandria	ON	K0C1A0	**866-377-2539**	613-525-2784
Groovfold Inc	1050 W State St	Newcomerstown	OH	43832	**800-367-1133**	740-498-8363
Larson-Juhl	3900 Steve Reynolds Blvd	Norcross	GA	30093	**800-221-4123**	
North American Enclosures Inc	65 Jetson Ln	Central Islip	NY	11722	**800-645-9209**	631-234-9500
Quanex Building Products	2270 Woodale Dr	Mounds View	MN	55112	**800-233-4383**	763-231-4000
Royal Mouldings Ltd	135 Bearcreek Rd PO Box 610	Marion	VA	24354	**800-368-3117**	276-783-8161
Woodgrain Distribution	80 Shelby St	Montevallo	AL	35115	**800-756-0199**	205-665-2546

FRAMES & MOULDINGS - METAL

SEE Doors & Windows - Metal

311 FRANCHISES

SEE ALSO Real Estate Agents & Brokers ; Restaurant Companies ; Staffing Services ; Travel Agency Networks ; Weight Loss Centers & Services ; Remodeling, Refinishing, Resurfacing Contractors ; Business Service Centers ; Candles ; Car Rental Agencies ; Children's Learning Centers ; Cleaning Services ; Convenience Stores ; Health Food Stores ; Home Inspection Services ; Hotels & Hotel Companies ; Ice Cream & Dairy Stores ; Laundry & Drycleaning Services ; Optical Goods Stores ; Pest Control Services ; Printing Companies - Commercial Printers ; Auto Supply Stores ; Automotive Services ; Bakeries ; Beauty Salons

Please see the category on Hotel & Resort Operation & Management for listings of hotel franchises.

Company	Address	City	State	ZIP	Toll-Free	Phone
1-800-Got-Junk	887 Great Northern Way	Vancouver	BC	V5T4T5	**800-468-5865**	
1-800-Water Damage	1167 Mercer St	Seattle	WA	98109	**800-928-3732**	206-381-3041
ABC Seamless	3001 Fiechtner Dr	Fargo	ND	58103	**800-732-6577**	701-293-5952
ActionCOACH	5781 S Ft Apache Rd	Las Vegas	NV	89148	**888-483-2828**	702-795-3188
Aire Serv Heating & Air Conditioning Inc	1020 N University Parks Dr Ste 101	Waco	TX	76707	**855-259-2280**	254-523-3600
Aire-Master of America Inc	1821 N State Hwy Cc	Nixa	MO	65714	**800-525-0957**	417-725-2691
All Tune & Lube Brakes & More Inc	8334 Veteran's Hwy	Millersville	MD	21108	**877-978-1758**	410-987-1011
AmeriSpec Inc	3839 Forest Hill Irene Rd	Memphis	TN	38125	**877-769-5217**	901-820-8500
Archadeck	2924 Emerywood Pkwy Ste 101	Richmond	VA	23294	**800-722-4668**	804-353-6999
Baskin-Robbins Inc	130 Royall St	Canton	MA	02021	**800-859-5339**	781-737-3000
Beef O'Bradys Inc	5660 W Cypress St Ste A	Tampa	FL	33607	**800-728-8878**	813-226-2333
Benjamin Franklin Plumbing	50 Central Ave Ste 920	Sarasota	FL	34236	**800-471-0809**	941-366-9692
Big Apple Bagels	500 Lk Cook Rd Ste 475	Deerfield	IL	60015	**800-251-6101**	847-948-7520
Bojangles' Restaurants Inc	9432 Southern Pine Blvd	Charlotte	NC	28273	**800-366-9921**	704-335-1804
Boston Pizza Restaurants LP	1501 LBJ Fwy Ste 450	Dallas	TX	75234	**866-277-8721**	972-484-9022
BrickKicker Inc	849 N Ellsworth St	Naperville	IL	60563	**800-821-1820**	
Candy Bouquet International Inc	510 Mclean St	Little Rock	AR	72202	**877-226-3901**	501-375-9990
Captain D's LLC	624 Grassmere Park Dr Ste 30	Nashville	TN	37211	**800-314-4819**	615-391-5461
CardSmart Retail Corp	11 Executive Ave	Edison	NJ	08817	**888-782-7050**	
Carlson Wagonlit Travel Inc	701 Carlson Pkwy	Minnetonka	MN	55305	**800-213-7295**	
Carvel Express	200 Glenridge Pt Pkwy Ste 200	Atlanta	GA	30342	**800-322-4848**	
CertaPro Painters Ltd	150 Green Tree Rd Ste 1003	Oaks	PA	19456	**800-689-7271**	
Certified Restoration DryCleaning Network LLC	2060 Coolidge Hwy	Berkley	MI	48072	**800-963-2736**	
Charley's Grilled Subs	2500 Farmers Dr Ste 140	Columbus	OH	43235	**800-437-8325**	614-923-4700
Checkers Drive-In Restaurants Inc	4300 W Cypress St Ste 600	Tampa	FL	33607	**800-800-8072**	813-283-7000
Chester's International LLC	3500 Colonnade Pkwy Ste 325	Birmingham	AL	35243	**800-554-4537**	205-949-4690
Cleaning Authority	7230 Lee DeForest Dr	Columbia	MD	21046	**888-658-0659**	410-740-1900
Closet Factory	12800 S Broadway	Los Angeles	CA	90061	**800-838-7995**	310-516-7000
Coffee Beanery Ltd, The	3429 Pierson Pl	Flushing	MI	48433	**800-441-2255**	
Cold Stone Creamery Inc	9311 E Via De Ventura *Cust Svc	Scottsdale	AZ	85258	**866-452-4252***	480-362-4800
Color-Glo International	7111 Ohms Ln	Minneapolis	MN	55439	**800-333-8523**	952-835-1338
ComForcare Senior Services Inc	2520 Telegraph Rd Ste 100	Bloomfield Hills	MI	48302	**800-886-4044**	248-745-9700
Computer Explorers	12715 Telge Rd	Cypress	TX	77429	**800-531-5053**	
Computer Troubleshooters USA	755 Commerce Dr Ste 605	Decatur	GA	30030	**877-704-1702**	800-877-0020
Contours Express Inc	156 Imperial Way	Nicholasville	KY	40356	**855-589-9662**	
Cookies By Design Inc	1865 Summit Ave Ste 605	Plano	TX	75074	**800-945-2665**	972-398-9536
Coverall Cleaning Concepts	5201 Congress Ave Ste 275	Boca Raton	FL	33487	**800-537-3371**	866-296-8944
Craters & Freighters	331 Corporate Cir Ste J	Golden	CO	80401	**800-736-3335**	
Creative Colors International Inc	19015 S Jodi Rd Ste E	Mokena	IL	60448	**800-933-2656**	708-478-1437
Critter Control Inc	9435 E Cherry Bend Rd	Traverse City	MI	49684	**800-451-6544**	231-947-2400
CruiseOne Inc	1201 W Cypress Creek Rd Ste 100	Fort Lauderdale	FL	33309	**800-278-4731**	
D'Angelo Sandwich Shops	600 Providence Hwy	Dedham	MA	02026	**800-727-2446**	781-461-1200
Dairy Queen	7505 Metro Blvd	Minneapolis	MN	55439	**800-883-4279**	952-830-0200
Decor & You Inc	900 Main St S	Southbury	CT	06488	**800-477-3326**	203-264-3500
Decorating Den Systems Inc	8659 Commerce Dr	Easton	MD	21601	**800-332-3367**	410-822-9001
DirectBuy Inc	8450 Broadway	Merrillville	IN	46410	**800-320-3462**	219-736-1100
Domino's Pizza Inc	30 Frank Lloyd Wright Dr *NYSE: DPZ*	Ann Arbor	MI	48106	**800-253-8182**	734-930-3030
Dr Vinyl & Assoc Ltd	1350 SE Hamblen Rd *General	Lees Summit	MO	64081	**800-531-6600***	816-525-6060
DreamMaker Bath & Kitchen by Worldwide	510 N Valley Mills Dr Ste 304	Waco	TX	76710	**800-583-2133**	
Dunkin' Donuts	130 Royall St *Cust Svc	Canton	MA	02021	**800-859-5339***	781-737-3000
Duraclean International Inc	220 W Campus Dr	Arlington Heights	IL	60004	**800-862-5326**	847-704-7100
Edible Arrangements LLC	95 Barnes Rd *Cust Svc	Wallingford	CT	06492	**877-363-7848***	304-894-8901
EmbroidMe Inc	2121 Vista Pkwy	West Palm Beach	FL	33411	**877-877-0234**	561-640-7367
Express Employment Professionals	8516 NW Expy	Oklahoma City	OK	73162	**800-222-4057**	405-840-5000
Express Oil Change	1880 S Pk Dr	Hoover	AL	35244	**888-945-1771**	205-945-1771
Extreme Pita	2187 Dunwin Dr	Mississauga	ON	L5L1X2	**800-563-6688**	905-820-7887
Famous Dave's of America Inc	12701 Whitewater Dr Ste 200 *NASDAQ: DAVE*	Minnetonka	MN	55343	**800-929-4040**	952-294-1300
Fast-Fix Jewelry & Watch Repairs	451 Altamonte Ave	Altamonte Springs	FL	32701	**800-359-0407**	407-261-1595
FasTracKids International Ltd	6900 E Belleview Ave Ste 100	Greenwood Village	CO	80111	**888-576-6888**	303-224-0200
Figaro's Italian Pizza Inc	1500 Liberty St SE Ste 160	Salem	OR	97302	**888-344-2767**	503-371-9318
Fish Window Cleaning Services Inc	200 Enchanted Pkwy	Manchester	MO	63021	**877-707-3474**	636-779-1500
Floor Coverings International	5250 Triangle Pwy Ste 100 *Sales	Norcross	GA	30092	**800-955-4324***	770-874-7600
Fox's Pizza Den Inc	4425 Willaim Penn Hwy	Murrysville	PA	15668	**800-899-3697**	724-733-7888
Furniture Medic	3839 S Forest Hill Irene Rd	Memphis	TN	38125	**800-877-9933**	
GNC Inc	300 Sixth Ave 14th Fl *NYSE: GNC*	Pittsburgh	PA	15222	**877-462-4700**	
Goddard Systems Inc	1016 W Ninth Ave	King of Prussia	PA	19406	**800-463-3273**	610-265-8510
Grease Monkey International	7450 E Progress Pl	Greenwood Village	CO	80111	**800-822-7706**	303-308-1660
Great American Cookie Company Inc	3300 Chambers Rd Ste 170	Horseheads	NY	14845	**877-639-2361**	
Great Clips Inc	7700 France Ave S Ste 425	Minneapolis	MN	55435	**800-999-5959**	952-893-9088
Great Harvest Bread Co	28 S Montana St	Dillon	MT	59725	**800-442-0424**	406-683-6842
Great Steak & Potato Co	9311 E Via de Ventura	Scottsdale	AZ	85258	**866-452-4252**	480-362-4800
Griswold Special Care Inc	717 Bethlehem Pike Ste 300	Erdenheim	PA	19038	**855-303-9470**	215-402-0200
Growth Coach, The	10700 Montgomery Rd Ste 300	Cincinnati	OH	45242	**888-292-7992**	
Gymboree Corp	500 Howard St *NASDAQ: GYMB*	San Francisco	CA	94105	**877-449-6932**	415-278-7000
Handyman Matters Inc	12567 W Cedar Dr	Lakewood	CO	80228	**866-349-6946**	303-984-0177
Hayes Handpiece Franchises Inc	5375 Avenida Encinas Ste C	Carlsbad	CA	92008	**800-228-0521**	760-602-0521
Homes & Land Magazine Affiliates LLC	1830 E Pk Ave	Tallahassee	FL	32301	**800-277-7800**	850-575-0189
HomeTeam Inspection Service Inc	575 Chamber Dr	Milford	OH	45150	**800-598-5297**	
HomeVestors of America Inc	6500 Greenville Ave Ste 400	Dallas	TX	75206	**866-200-6475**	972-761-0046
HouseMaster	92 E Main St Ste 301	Somerville	NJ	08876	**800-526-3939**	732-469-6565

Company	Address	City	State	ZIP	Toll-Free	Phone
Ident-A-Kid Services of America	1780 102nd Ave N Ste 100	Saint Petersburg	FL	33716	**800-890-1000**	727-577-4646
IHOP Corp	450 N Brand Blvd	Glendale	CA	91203	**866-444-5144**	818-240-6055
Instant Imprints	5897 Oberlin Dr Ste 200	San Diego	CA	92121	**800-542-3437**	858-642-4848
Interim HealthCare Inc	1601 Sawgrass Corporate Pkwy	Sunrise	FL	33323	**800-338-7786**	954-858-6000
Jackson Hewitt Inc	3 Sylvan Way Ste 301 *OTC: JHTXQ*	Parsippany	NJ	07054	**800-234-1040**	
Jazzercise Inc	2460 Impala Dr *Cust Svc	Carlsbad	CA	92010	**800-348-4748***	760-476-1750
Jenny Craig International Inc	5770 Fleet St	Carlsbad	CA	92008	**800-443-2331**	760-696-4000
Juice It Up! Franchise Corp	17915 Sky Pk Cir Ste J	Irvine	CA	92614	**888-705-8423**	949-475-0146
KFC Corp	1441 Gardiner Ln	Louisville	KY	40213	**800-225-5532**	920-923-2321
Kinderdance International Inc	5238 Valleypointe Pkwy	Roanoke	VA	24019	**800-554-2334**	321-984-4448
Kitchen Tune-Up Inc	813 Cir Dr	Aberdeen	SD	57401	**800-333-6385**	605-225-4049
Lawn Doctor Inc	142 SR 34	Holmdel	NJ	07733	**800-845-0580**	800-631-5660
Learning Express Inc	29 Buena Vista St	Devens	MA	01434	**888-725-8697**	978-889-1000
Liberty Tax Service Inc	1716 Corporate Landing Pkwy *Cust Svc	Virginia Beach	VA	23454	**800-790-3863***	757-493-8855
Little Caesars Inc	2211 Woodward Ave	Detroit	MI	48201	**800-722-3727**	313-983-6409
Little Gym International Inc	7001 N Scottsdale Rd *General	Paradise Valley	AZ	85253	**888-228-2878***	
Living Assistance Services Inc	937 Haverford Rd Ste 200	Bryn Mawr	PA	19010	**800-365-4189**	
Mad Science Group	8360 Bougainville St Ste 201	Montreal	QC	H4P2G1	**800-586-5231**	514-344-4181
Magnetsigns Adv Inc	4225 38th St	Camrose	AB	T4V3Z3	**800-219-8977**	780-672-8720
Maid Brigade USA/Minimaid Canada	4 Concourse Pkwy Ste 200	Atlanta	GA	30328	**866-800-7470**	770-551-9630
MaidPro Corp	180 Canal St	Boston	MA	02114	**888-624-3776**	617-742-8787
Manhattan Bagel Co Inc	555 Zang St Ste 300	Lakewood	CO	80228	**800-224-3563**	303-568-8000
Martinizing Dry Cleaning	8944 Columbia Rd Ste J	Loveland	OH	45140	**800-827-0207**	
Mathnasium LLC	5120 W Goldleaf Cir Ste 300	Los Angeles	CA	90056	**877-601-6284**	323-421-8000
McDonald's Corp	1 McDonald's Plz *NYSE: MCD*	Oak Brook	IL	60523	**800-244-6227**	630-623-3000
Medicap Pharmacies Inc	1 Rider Trail Plaza Dr	Earth City	MO	63045	**800-407-8055**	314-993-6000
Merle Norman Cosmetics Inc	9130 Bellanca Ave	Los Angeles	CA	90045	**800-421-6648**	310-641-3000
Merlin Corp	3815 E Main St	Saint Charles	IL	60174	**800-652-9910**	630-513-8200
Midas International Corp	1300 Arlington Heights Rd	Itasca	IL	60143	**800-621-8545**	630-438-3000
Minuteman Press International Inc	61 Executive Blvd	Farmingdale	NY	11735	**800-645-3006**	631-249-1370
Money Mailer LLC	12131 Western Ave	Garden Grove	CA	92841	**800-468-5865**	714-889-3800
Mr Appliance Corp	304 E Church Ave	Killeen	TX	76541	**888-998-2011**	
Mr Handyman International LLC	3948 Ranchero Dr Ste 1C *Cust Svc	Ann Arbor	MI	48108	**855-632-2126***	800-289-4600
Mr Hero Restaurants	7010 Engle Rd Ste 100	Middleburg Heights	OH	44130	**888-860-5082**	440-625-3080
My Favorite Muffin	500 Lk Cook Rd Ste 475	Deerfield	IL	60015	**800-251-6101**	847-948-7520
National Property Inspections Inc (NPI)	9375 Burt St Ste 201	Omaha	NE	68114	**800-333-9807**	402-333-9807
Navis Pack & Ship Centers	6551 S Revere Pkwy Ste 250	Centennial	CO	80111	**800-344-3528**	
OpenWorks	4742 N 24th St Ste 450	Phoenix	AZ	85016	**800-777-6736**	602-224-0440
Orange Julius of America	7505 Metro Blvd	Minneapolis	MN	55439	**866-793-7582**	952-830-0200
Padgett Business Services	160 Hawthorne Pk	Athens	GA	30606	**800-723-4388**	
Pak Mail Centers of America Inc	7173 S Havana St Ste 600 *Cust Svc	Centennial	CO	80112	**800-778-6665***	303-957-1000
Party City Corp	25 Green Pond Rd Ste 1	Rockaway	NJ	07866	**800-727-8924**	973-453-8600
Perkins Restaurant & Bakery	6075 Poplar Ave Ste 800	Memphis	TN	38119	**800-877-7375**	901-766-6400
Perma-Glaze Inc	1638 Research Loop Rd Ste 160	Tucson	AZ	85710	**800-332-7397**	520-722-9718
Petland Inc	250 Riverside St	Chillicothe	OH	45601	**800-221-5935**	740-775-2464
Physicians Weight Loss Centers of America Inc	395 Springside Dr	Akron	OH	44333	**800-205-7887**	330-666-7952
Pizza Inn Inc	3551 Plano Pkwy *NASDAQ: RAVE*	The Colony	TX	75056	**877-574-9924**	
Pizza Ranch Inc	204 19th St SE	Orange City	IA	51041	**800-321-3401**	
Plato's Closet	23021 Outer Dr	Allen Park	MI	48101	**800-592-8049**	313-278-2300
Postal Connections of America	6136 Frisco Sq Blvd Ste 400	Frisco	TX	75034	**800-767-8257**	
PostalAnnex+ Inc	7580 Metropolitan Dr Ste 200	San Diego	CA	92108	**800-456-1525**	619-563-4800
PostNet International Franchise Corp	1819 Wazee St	Denver	CO	80202	**800-841-7171**	303-771-7100
Precision Auto Care Inc	748 Miller Dr SE *OTC: PACI*	Leesburg	VA	20175	**866-944-8863**	
PremierGarage Systems LLC	21405 N 15th Ln	Phoenix	AZ	85027	**866-590-9411**	480-483-3030
Pressed4Time Inc	8 Clock Tower Pl Ste 110	Maynard	MA	01754	**800-423-8711**	
Primrose School Franchising Co	3660 Cedarcrest Rd	Acworth	GA	30101	**800-745-0677**	770-529-4100
Priority Management Systems Inc	11160 Silversmith Pl	Richmond	BC	V7A5E4	**800-437-1032**	604-214-7772
ProForma	8800 E Pleasant Vly Rd	Independence	OH	44131	**800-825-1525**	216-520-8400
Property Damage Appraisers Inc (PDA)	6100 SW Blvd Ste 200	Fort Worth	TX	76109	**800-749-7324**	
RadioShack Corp	300 RadioShack Cir *NYSE: RSH*	Fort Worth	TX	76102	**800-843-7422**	817-882-9380
Rainbow International	1010 N University Pk Dr	Waco	TX	76707	**855-724-6269**	254-756-5463
Re-Bath LLC	16879 N 75th Ave Ste 101	Peoria	AZ	85382	**800-426-4573**	
RE/MAX International Inc	5075 S Syracuse St *Cust Svc	Denver	CO	80237	**800-525-7452***	303-770-5531
Realty Executives International Inc	7600 N 16th St Ste 100	Phoenix	AZ	85020	**800-252-3366**	602-957-0747
Rescuecom Corp	2560 Burnet Ave	Syracuse	NY	13206	**800-737-2837**	
Results Travel	701 Carlson Pkwy	Minnetonka	MN	55305	**800-456-4000**	763-212-5000
Right at Home Inc	6464 Crt St Ste 150	Omaha	NE	68106	**877-697-7537**	402-697-7537
RSVP Publications	6730 W Linebaugh Ave Ste 201	Tampa	FL	33625	**800-360-7787**	813-960-7787
Sea Tow Services International Inc	1560 Youngs Ave PO Box 1178	Southold	NY	11971	**800-473-2869**	631-765-3660
Second Cup Ltd	6303 Airport Rd	Mississauga	ON	L4V1R8	**877-212-1818**	
Signs by Tomorrow USA Inc	8681 Robert Fulton Dr	Columbia	MD	21046	**800-765-7446**	410-312-3600
Sir Speedy Inc	26722 Plaza Dr	Mission Viejo	CA	92691	**800-854-8297**	949-348-5000
Snap-on Inc	2801 80th St *NYSE: SNA*	Kenosha	WI	53143	**877-762-7664**	262-656-5200
Sport Clips Inc	110 Briarwood Dr	Georgetown	TX	78628	**800-872-4247**	512-869-1201
Spring-Green Lawn Care Corp	11909 Spaulding School Dr	Plainfield	IL	60585	**800-435-4051**	815-436-8777
Stork News of America Inc	1305 Hope Mills Rd Ste A	Fayetteville	NC	28304	**800-633-6395**	910-429-2229
Stretch-N-Grow International Inc	PO Box 7599	Seminole	FL	33775	**800-348-0166**	
Successories Inc	1040 Holland Dr	Boca Raton	FL	33487	**800-535-2773**	
SuperCoups	350 Revolutionary Dr	East Taunton	MA	02718	**800-626-2620**	508-977-2000
Supercuts	7201 Metro Blvd	Minneapolis	MN	55439	**877-857-2070**	
Terminix International Company LP	860 Ridge Lk Blvd	Memphis	TN	38120	**855-212-6399**	866-399-0453
Treats International Franchise Corp	238 Queen St S 2nd Fl	Mississauga	ON	L5M1L5	**800-461-4003**	613-563-4073
Truly Nolen of America Inc	3636 E Speedway Blvd	Tucson	AZ	85716	**800-468-7859**	800-528-3442
Tuffy Assoc Corp	7150 Granite Cir	Toledo	OH	43617	**800-228-8339**	419-865-6900
UPS Store, The	6060 Cornerstone Ct W	San Diego	CA	92121	**800-789-4623**	858-455-8800
Valpak Direct Marketing Systems Inc	8605 Largo Lakes Dr	Largo	FL	33773	**800-237-6266**	
Wild Birds Unlimited Inc	11711 N College Ave Ste 146	Carmel	IN	46032	**800-326-4928**	317-571-7100
WineStyles Inc	5515 Mills Civic Pkwy Ste 110	West Des Moines	IA	50266	**866-424-9463**	
Wing Zone Franchise Corp	900 Cir 75 Pkwy Ste 930	Atlanta	GA	30339	**877-946-4966**	404-875-5045
Wireless Toyz Ltd	29155 NW Hwy	Southfield	MI	48034	**866-237-2624**	248-426-8200
Wireless Zone	34 Industrial Pk Pl	Middletown	CT	06457	**888-881-2622**	860-632-9494
Woodcraft Supply LLC	1177 Rosemar Rd	Parkersburg	WV	26105	**800-535-4482**	
World Inspection Network International Inc	12345 Lk City Way NE Ste 365	Seattle	WA	98125	**800-309-6753**	
Worldwide Express	2602 McKinney Ave Ste 400	Dallas	TX	75204	**800-758-7447**	214-720-2400
WSI Internet	5580 Explorer Dr Ste 600	Mississauga	ON	L4W4Y1	**888-678-7588**	905-678-7588
Ziebart International Corp	1290 E Maple Rd	Troy	MI	48083	**800-877-1312**	248-588-4100

312 FREIGHT FORWARDERS

SEE ALSO Logistics Services (Transportation & Warehousing)

Company	Address	City	State	ZIP	Toll-Free	Phone
A & S Services Group LLC	310 N Zarfoss Dr	York	PA	17404	**800-227-6782**	717-759-3017
Advance Transportation Systems Inc	1125 Glendale Milford Rd	Cincinnati	OH	45215	**800-878-4849**	513-771-4848
Airways Freight Corp	3849 W Wedington Dr	Fayetteville	AR	72704	**800-643-3525**	479-442-6301
Allen Lund Company Inc	4529 Angeles Crest Hwy Ste 300	La Canada	CA	91011	**800-777-6142**	

Company / Address	City	State	Zip	Toll-Free	Phone
Arrow Freight Management Inc 1001 Berryville st	El Paso	TX	79928	**888-598-9891**	
Autobahn Freight Lines Ltd 27 Automatic Rd	Brampton	ON	L6S5N8	**877-989-9994**	416-741-5454
Axsun Inc 4900 Armand Frappier	Saint-Hubert	QC	J3Z1G5	**888-992-9786**	450-445-3003
Barthco International Inc 5101 S Broad St *General	Philadelphia	PA	19112	**877-401-6400***	215-238-8600
Blue-Grace Logistics LLC 2846 S Falkenburg Rd	Riverview	FL	33578	**800-697-4477**	813-641-0357
BNX Shipping Inc 910 E 236th St	Carson	CA	90745	**844-221-3091**	310-764-0999
CDS Logistics Management Inc 1225 Bengies Rd Ste A	Baltimore	MD	21220	**866-649-9559**	410-314-8000
Cold Star Freight Systems Inc 1015 Henry Eng Pl	Victoria	BC	V9B6B2	**800-201-1277**	250-381-3399
Combined Express Inc 3685 Marshall Ln	Bensalem	PA	19020	**800-777-0458**	215-633-1535
ContainerWorld Forwarding Services Inc 16133 Blundell Rd	Richmond	BC	V6W0A3	**877-838-8880**	604-276-1300
Continental Traffic Service Inc (CTSI) 5100 Poplar Ave 15th Fl	Memphis	TN	38137	**888-836-5135**	901-766-1500
Evans Delivery Company Inc PO Box 268	Pottsville	PA	17901	**800-666-7885**	570-385-9048
FESCO Agencies NA Inc 1000 Second Ave Ste 1310	Seattle	WA	98104	**800-275-3372**	206-583-0860
Fetch Logistics Inc 25 Northpointe Pkwy Ste 200	Amherst	NY	14228	**800-964-4940**	716-689-4556
Freight Logistics Inc PO Box 1712	Medford	OR	97501	**800-866-7882**	541-734-5617
Frontier Logistics LP 1806 S 16th St	La Porte	TX	77571	**800-610-6808**	
Gold Coast Freightways Inc 12250 NW 28th Ave	Miami	FL	33167	**877-465-3585**	305-687-3560
HA Logistics Inc 5175 Johnson Dr	Pleasanton	CA	94588	**800-449-5778**	925-251-9300
Interdom LLC 11800 S 75th Ave Ste 2N	Palos Heights	IL	60463	**800-935-0851**	
J & A Freight Systems Inc 4704 Irving Park Rd Ste 8	Chicago	IL	60641	**877-668-3378**	
Knitney Lines Inc PO Box 350 *General	Scranton	PA	18505	**866-564-8639***	570-457-5060
L E Coppersmith Inc 525 S Douglas St	El Segundo	CA	90245	**888-827-4388**	310-607-8000
LeanLogistics Inc 1351 S Waverly Rd	Holland	MI	49423	**866-584-7280**	616-738-6400
Logistics Plus Inc 1406 Peach St	Erie	PA	16501	**866-564-7587**	814-461-7600
Longhorn Imports Inc 2202 E Union Bower	Irving	TX	75061	**800-641-8348**	972-721-9102
Lynden Inc 18000 International Blvd Ste 800	Seattle	WA	98188	**888-596-3361**	206-241-8778
Metro Express Transportation Services Inc 875 Fee Fee Rd	St. Louis	MO	63043	**800-805-0073**	314-993-1511
MSM Transportation Inc 124 Commercial Rd	Bolton	ON	L7E1K4	**800-667-4175**	905-951-6800
Oceane Marine Shipping Inc 407 E Maple St	Cumming	GA	30040	**888-262-3263**	770-888-5941
Phoenix International Freight Services Ltd 14701 Charlson Rd	Eden Prairie	MN	55347	**855-229-6128**	952-937-6761
Pioneer Transfer LLC 2034 S St Aubin St PO Box 2567	Sioux City	IA	51106	**800-325-4650**	
Primary Freight Services Inc 6545 Caballero Blvd	Buena Park	CA	90620	**800-635-0013**	310-635-3000
Quality Customs Broker Inc 4464 S Whitnall Ave	Saint Francis	WI	53235	**888-813-4647**	414-482-9447
Quality Transportation 36-40 37th St Ste 201	Long Island	NY	11101	**800-677-2838**	212-308-6333
R & D Transportation Services Inc 4036 Adolfo Rd	Camarillo	CA	93012	**800-966-7114**	805-529-7511
Recon Logistics LLC 10205 Queens Way Ste 5	Chagrin Falls	OH	44023	**866-424-7153**	440-708-2306
Rmx Global Logistics 35715 US Hwy 40 Bldg B	Evergreen	CO	80439	**888-824-7365**	
Rock-It Cargo USA Inc 5432 W 104th St	Los Angeles	CA	90045	**800-973-1727**	310-410-0935
Rogers & Brown Custom Brokers Inc 2 Cumberland St	Charleston	SC	29401	**866-738-8197**	843-577-3630
Romar Transportation Systems Inc 3500 S Kedzie Ave	Chicago	IL	60632	**800-621-5416**	773-376-8800
Satellite Logistics Group Inc 12621 Featherwood Ste 390	Houston	TX	77034	**877-795-7540**	281-902-5500
Schenker of Canada Ltd 5935 Airport Rd 10th Fl	Mississauga	ON	L4V1W5	**800-461-3686**	905-676-0676
Scott Logistics Corp PO Box 391	Rome	GA	30162	**800-893-6689**	706-234-1184
Senvoy LLC 115 SE Yamhill St	Portland	OR	97214	**866-373-6869**	503-234-7722
Sho-Air International 5401 Argosy Ave	Huntington Beach	CA	92649	**800-227-9111**	949-476-9111
Smith Systems Transportation Inc 417 Ninth Ave	Scottsbluff	NE	69361	**800-897-5571**	
Sotech Nitram Inc 1695 Boul Laval	Laval	QC	H7S2M2	**877-664-8726**	450-975-2100
Sunset Transportation Inc 11325 Concord Village Ave	St Louis	MO	63123	**800-849-6540**	
Terminal Corp, The 2001 E McComas St Ste A	Baltimore	MD	21224	**800-560-7207**	
Thompson, Ahern & Company Ltd 6299 Airport Rd Ste 506	Mississauga	ON	L4V1N3	**877-262-8226**	905-677-3471
Time Definite Services Inc 1360 Madeline Ln Ste 300	Elgin	IL	60124	**800-466-8040**	
Total Quality Logistics Inc (TQL) 4289 Ivy Pointe Blvd	Cincinnati	OH	45245	**800-580-3101**	513-831-2600
Towne Air Freight 24805 US 20 W	South Bend	IN	46628	**800-726-6654**	423-636-3380
Trademark Transportation Inc 739 Vandalia St	Saint Paul	MN	55114	**800-646-2550**	651-646-2500
Trans-Border Global Freight Systems Inc 2103 Route 9	Round Lake	NY	12151	**800-493-9444**	518-785-6000
TransCore Link Logistics Corp 6660 Kennedy Rd Ste 205	Mississauga	ON	L5T2M9	**800-263-6149**	
TRANSInternational System Inc 130 E Wilson Bridge Rd Ste 150 Ste 150	Worthington	OH	43085	**800-340-7540**	614-891-4942
Transit Systems Inc 999 Old Eagle School Rd Ste 114	Wayne	PA	19087	**800-626-1257**	
Transportation Management Assoc Inc 344 Oak Grove Church Rd	Mocksville	NC	27028	**800-745-8292**	
TransX Group of Cos 2595 Inkster Blvd	Winnipeg	MB	R3C2E6	**877-558-9444**	204-632-6694
Travelers Transportation Services Inc 195 Heart Lk Rd South	Brampton	ON	L6W3N6	**800-265-8789**	905-457-8789
Triple B Forwarders Inc 1511 Glen Curtis St	Carson	CA	90746	**800-228-8465**	310-604-5840
Tucker Company Worldwide Inc 900 Dudley Ave	Cherry Hill	NJ	08002	**800-229-7780**	856-317-9600
Worldtrans Services Inc 7130 Miramar Rd Ste 100a	San Diego	CA	92121	**800-736-3769**	858-536-7900

313 FREIGHT TRANSPORT - DEEP SEA (DOMESTIC PORTS)

Company / Address	City	State	Zip	Toll-Free	Phone
Alaska Marine Lines Inc 5615 W Marginal Way SW *Cust Svc	Seattle	WA	98106	**800-326-8346***	206-763-4244
Berman Moving & Storage Inc 23800 Corbin Dr	Cleveland	OH	44128	**800-333-0582**	216-663-8816
Coastal Transportation Inc 4025 13th Ave W	Seattle	WA	98119	**800-544-2580**	206-282-9979
Crowley Maritime Corp 9487 Regency Square Blvd	Jacksonville	FL	32225	**800-276-9539**	904-727-2200
Freightquote.com Inc 16025 W 113th St	Lenexa	KS	66219	**800-323-5441**	
Hapag-Lloyd America Inc 401 E Jackson St	Tampa	FL	33602	**800-282-8977**	813-276-4600
International Shipholding Corp 11 N Water Ste 18290 *NYSE: ISH*	Mobile	AL	36602	**800-826-3513**	251-243-9100
Matson Navigation Co 555 12th St *Cust Svc	Oakland	CA	94607	**800-462-8766***	510-628-4000
Northland Services Inc 6700 W Marginal Way SW	Seattle	WA	98106	**800-426-3113**	206-763-3000
Overseas Shipholding Group Inc 666 Third Ave	New York	NY	10017	**800-851-9677**	212-953-4100
Seaboard Marine 8001 NW 79th Ave	Miami	FL	33166	**866-676-8886**	305-863-4444
Totem Ocean Trailer Express Inc 32001 32nd Ave S Ste 200	Federal Way	WA	98001	**800-426-0074**	253-449-8100
Trailer Bridge Inc 10405 New Berlin Rd E *OTC: TRBRQ*	Jacksonville	FL	32226	**800-554-1589**	904-751-7100
US Shipping Corp 399 Thornall St 8th Fl	Edison	NJ	08837	**866-942-6592**	732-635-1500
Western Pioneer Inc 4601 Shilshole Ave NW	Seattle	WA	98107	**800-426-6783**	206-789-1930
Young Bros Ltd PO Box 3288	Honolulu	HI	96801	**800-572-2743**	808-543-9311

314 FREIGHT TRANSPORT - DEEP SEA (FOREIGN PORTS)

Company / Address	City	State	Zip	Toll-Free	Phone
Antillean Marine Shipping Corp 3038 NW N River Dr	Miami	FL	33142	**888-633-6361**	305-633-6361
Atlantic Container Line (ACL) 50 Cardinal Dr	Westfield	NJ	07090	**800-225-1235**	908-518-5300
Fednav Ltd 1000 Rue de la GauchetiFre O Bureau 3500 *General	Montreal	QC	H3B4W5	**800-678-4842***	514-878-6500
Hamburg Sud North America Inc 465 S St	Morristown	NJ	07960	**888-228-8241**	973-775-5300
Hapag-Lloyd America Inc 401 E Jackson St	Tampa	FL	33602	**800-282-8977**	813-276-4600
Interlog USA Inc 2818A Anthony Ln S	Minneapolis	MN	55418	**800-603-6030**	612-789-3456
International Shipholding Corp 11 N Water Ste 18290 *NYSE: ISH*	Mobile	AL	36602	**800-826-3513**	251-243-9100
K Line America Inc 8730 Stony Pt Pkwy Ste 400	Richmond	VA	23235	**800-609-3221**	804-560-3600
Mckeil Marine Ltd 208 Hillyard St	Hamilton	ON	L8L6B6	**800-454-4780**	905-528-4780
Northern Transportation Co Ltd 42003 Mackenzie Hwy	Hay River	NT	X0E0R9	**866-935-6825**	867-587-2442
Overseas Shipholding Group Inc 666 Third Ave	New York	NY	10017	**800-851-9677**	212-953-4100
Seaboard Marine 8001 NW 79th Ave	Miami	FL	33166	**866-676-8886**	305-863-4444
Tidewater Inc 601 Poydras St Ste 1900 *NYSE: TDW*	New Orleans	LA	70130	**800-678-8433**	504-568-1010
Tropical Shipping 5 E 11th St	Riviera Beach	FL	33404	**800-367-6200**	561-881-3900

315 FREIGHT TRANSPORT - INLAND WATERWAYS

Company / Address	City	State	Zip	Toll-Free	Phone
A & B Freight Line Inc 4805 Sandy Hollow Rd	Rockford	IL	61125	**800-231-2235**	815-874-4700

Company	Address	City	State	Zip	Toll-Free	Phone
American Commercial Barge Lines Inc	1701 E Market St	Jeffersonville	IN	47130	**800-457-6377**	
AMJ Campbell International	1445 Courtneypark Dr E	Mississauga	ON	L5T2E3	**800-363-6683**	905-670-6683
Andrie Inc	561 E Western Ave	Muskegon	MI	49442	**800-722-2421**	231-728-2226
Best Way Logistics	14004 Century Ln	Grandview	MO	64030	**877-923-7892**	816-767-8008
Crowley Maritime Corp	9487 Regency Square Blvd	Jacksonville	FL	32225	**800-276-9539**	904-727-2200
Custom Global Logistics LLC	317 W Lk St	Northlake	IL	60164	**800-446-8336**	
Delmar International Inc	10636 Cote de Liesse	Montreal	QC	H8T1A5	**888-433-5627**	514-636-8800
Falcon Express Transportation Inc	6804 Virginia Manor Rd	Beltsville	MD	20705	**800-296-9696**	240-264-1215
Fednav Ltd	1000 Rue de la GauchetiFre O Bureau 3500	Montreal	QC	H3B4W5	**800-678-4842***	514-878-6500
	*General					
Focus Logistics Inc	1311 Howard Dr	West Chicago	IL	60185	**877-924-3600**	630-231-8200
Hackbarth Delivery Service Inc	3504 Brookdale Dr N	Mobile	AL	36618	**800-277-3322**	251-478-1401
J S Logistics	4550 Gustine Ave	Saint Louis	MO	63116	**800-814-2634**	314-832-6008
Keltic Transportation Inc	90 MacNaughton Ave Caledonia Industrial Park	Moncton	NB	E1H3L9	**888-854-1233**	506-854-1233
Kreative Carriers Transportation & Logistic Services Inc	61 Bluewater Rd	Bedford	NS	B4B1G8	**888-274-2444**	
LTI Trucking Services Inc	411 N 10th St Ste 500	St. Louis	MO	63101	**800-642-7222**	
Mackie Group	933 Bloor St W	Oshawa	ON	L1J5Y7	**800-565-4646**	905-728-2400
Milgram & Company Ltd	400 - 645 Wellington	Montreal	QC	H3C0L1	**800-879-6144**	514-288-2161
Roy Miller Freight Lines LLC	3165 E Coronado St	Anaheim	CA	92806	**800-336-5673**	714-632-5511
SCI Logistics Ltd	180 Attwell Dr Ste 600	Toronto	ON	M9W6A9	**866-773-7735**	416-401-3011
Stone Belt Freight Lines Inc	101 W Dillman Rd	Bloomington	IN	47403	**800-264-2340**	812-824-6741
Summit Travel Group	830 Menlo Ave Ste 110	Menlo Park	CA	94025	**877-232-4465**	650-373-4400
Tidewater Barge Lines Inc	6305 NW Old Lower River Rd	Vancouver	WA	98660	**800-562-1607**	360-693-1491
Tri-line Carriers L.p	235185 Ryan Rd	Rocky View	AB	T1X0K1	**800-661-9191**	
Van-Kam Freightways Ltd	10155 Grace Rd	Surrey	BC	V3V3V7	**800-663-2161**	604-582-7451
Vedder Transportation Group, The	400 Riverside Rd	Abbotsford	BC	V2S4P4	**866-857-1375**	
Versacold International Corp	2115 Commissioner St	Vancouver	BC	V5L1A6	**800-563-2653**	604-255-4656

316 FRUIT GROWERS

SEE ALSO Crop Preparation Services ; Wines - Mfr

316-1 Berry Growers

Company	Address	City	State	Zip	Toll-Free	Phone
Driscoll Strawberry Assoc Inc	345 Westridge Dr	Watsonville	CA	95077	**800-871-3333**	
Jasper Wyman & Son	PO Box 100	Milbridge	ME	04658	**800-341-1758***	
	*Sales					

316-2 Citrus Growers

Company	Address	City	State	Zip	Toll-Free	Phone
Egan Bernard & Co	1900 Old Dixie Hwy	Fort Pierce	FL	34946	**800-327-6676**	
Limoneira Co	1141 Cummings Rd	Santa Paula	CA	93060	**866-321-8953**	805-525-5541
	NASDAQ: LMNR					

316-3 Deciduous Tree Fruit Growers

Company	Address	City	State	Zip	Toll-Free	Phone
Capital Agricultural Property Services Inc	801 Warrenville Rd Ste 150	Lisle	IL	60532	**800-243-2060**	630-434-9150
Hudson River Fruit Distributors	65 Old Indian Rd	Milton	NY	12547	**800-640-2774**	
National Fruit Product Co Inc	701 Fairmont Ave	Winchester	VA	22601	**800-655-4022**	540-723-9614
Oregon Cherry Growers Inc	1520 Woodrow NE	Salem	OR	97301	**800-367-2536**	503-364-8421
Rice Fruit Co	2760 Carlisle Rd	Gardners	PA	17324	**800-627-3359**	717-677-8131

316-4 Fruit Growers (Misc)

Company	Address	City	State	Zip	Toll-Free	Phone
Brooks Tropicals Inc	18400 SW 256th St PO Box 900160	Homestead	FL	33090	**800-327-4833**	305-247-3544
Calavo Growers Inc	1141-A Cummings Rd	Santa Paula	CA	93060	**800-654-8758**	805-525-1245
	NASDAQ: CVGW					
Del Monte Fresh Produce Co	241 Sevilla Ave	Coral Gables	FL	33134	**800-950-3683***	305-520-8400
	*Cust Svc					
Dole Food Company Inc	1 Dole Dr	Westlake Village	CA	91362	**800-232-8888**	818-879-6600
	NYSE: DOLE					

316-5 Grape Vineyards

Company	Address	City	State	Zip	Toll-Free	Phone
Spring Mountain Vineyards	2805 Spring Mtn Rd	Saint Helena	CA	94574	**877-769-4637**	707-967-4188
Windsor Vineyards	205 Concourse Blvd	Santa Rosa	CA	95403	**800-289-9463**	

317 FUEL DEALERS

Company	Address	City	State	Zip	Toll-Free	Phone
AC & T Company Inc	11535 Hopewell Rd	Hagerstown	MD	21740	**800-458-3835**	301-582-2700
Aero ALL-GAS Company Inc, The	3150 Main St	Hartford	CT	06120	**800-255-4277**	860-278-2376
Alvin Hollis & Co	1 Hollis St	South Weymouth	MA	02190	**800-649-5090**	781-335-2100
AmeriGas Partners LP	460 N Gulph Rd	King of Prussia	PA	19406	**800-427-4968**	610-337-7000
	NYSE: APU					
Apollo Oil LLC	1175 Early Dr	Winchester	KY	40391	**800-473-5823**	859-744-5444
Automotive Service Inc	910 Mtn Home Rd PO Box 2157	Sinking Spring	PA	19608	**800-383-3421**	610-678-3421
Blossman Gas Inc	809 Washington Ave	Ocean Springs	MS	39564	**800-256-7762**	888-256-7762
Bowden Oil Company Inc	PO Box 145	Sylacauga	AL	35150	**800-280-0393**	256-245-5611
Burns & McBride Inc	240 S DuPont Hwy	New Castle	DE	19720	**800-756-5110**	302-656-5110
D F Richard Inc	124 Broadway	Dover	NH	03821	**800-649-6457**	603-742-2020
Ed Staub & Sons Petroleum Inc	1301 Esplanade Ave	Klamath Falls	OR	97601	**800-435-3835**	
Farm & Home Oil Co	3115 State Rd	Telford	PA	18969	**800-776-7263**	
FC Haab Company Inc	2314 Market St	Philadelphia	PA	19103	**800-486-5663**	215-563-0800
Ferrellgas Partners LP	1 Liberty Plaza	Liberty	MO	64068	**888-337-7355**	816-792-1600
	NYSE: FGP					
First Corporate Sedans Inc	60 E 42nd St Ste 2424	New York	NY	10165	**800-473-8876**	212-972-2282
Fred M Schildwachter & Sons Inc	1400 Ferris Pl	Bronx	NY	10461	**800-642-3646**	718-828-2500
Glassmere Fuel Service Inc	1967 Saxonburg Blvd	Tarentum	PA	15084	**800-235-9054**	724-265-4646
Kingston Oil Supply Corp	2926 Rt 32 N	Saugerties	NY	12477	**800-755-6726**	845-247-2200
Kolkhorst Petroleum Co	1685 E Washington	Navasota	TX	77868	**800-548-6671**	936-825-6868
Lazzari Fuel Company LLC	11 Industrial Way	Brisbane	CA	94005	**800-242-7265**	415-467-2970
Lincoln Land Oil Co	PO Box 4307	Springfield	IL	62708	**800-238-4912**	217-523-5050
Martin Resource Management Corp (MRMC)	PO Box 191	Kilgore	TX	75663	**888-334-7473**	903-983-6200
Metro Energy Group	1011 Hudson Ave	Ridgefield	NJ	07657	**800-951-2941**	201-941-3470
Mirabito Fuel Group Inc	49 Ct St PO Box 5306	Binghamton	NY	13902	**800-934-9480**	607-352-2800
Mitchell Supreme Fuel Co	532 Freeman St	Orange	NJ	07050	**800-832-7090**	973-678-1800
Mutual Liquid Gas & Equipment Co Inc	17117 S Broadway St	Gardena	CA	90248	**800-633-3574**	323-321-3771
Phelps Sungas Inc	224 Cross Rd	Geneva	NY	14456	**800-458-1085**	315-789-3285
Sharp Energy Inc	648 Ocean Hwy	Pocomoke City	MD	21851	**888-742-7740**	
Shipley Energy	415 Norway St	York	PA	17403	**800-839-1849**	717-848-4100
Star Gas Partners LP	2187 Atlantic St	Stamford	CT	06902	**800-960-7546**	203-328-7310
	NYSE: SGU					
Stripes Convenience Stores	4525 Ayers St	Corpus Christi	TX	78415	**800-569-3585**	361-884-2464
	NYSE: SUSS					
Suburban Propane LP	1 Suburban Plz 240 Rt 10 W PO Box 206	Whippany	NJ	07981	**800-776-7263**	973-887-5300
Super Save Group	19395 Langley By-pass	Surrey	BC	V3S6K1	**800-665-2800**	604-533-4423
Wilson of Wallingford Inc	221 Rogers Ln PO Box 185	Wallingford	PA	19086	**888-607-2621**	610-566-7600
Wo Stinson & Son Ltd	4726 Bank St	Ottawa	ON	K1T3W7	**800-267-9714**	613-822-7400
Woodruff Energy	73 Water St PO Box 777	Bridgeton	NJ	08302	**800-557-1121**	856-455-1111
Worley & Obetz Inc	85 White Oak Rd PO Box 429	Manheim	PA	17545	**800-697-6891**	717-665-6891

318 FUND-RAISING SERVICES

Company	Address	City	State	Zip	Toll-Free	Phone
A All Languages Ltd	421 Bloor St E Ste 306	Toronto	ON	M4W3T1	**800-567-8100**	416-975-5000
AccuConference	6300 Ridglea Pl Ste 318	Ft Worth	TX	76116	**800-977-4607**	
Air Compressor Solutions	3001 Kermit Hwy	Odessa	TX	79764	**800-527-4137**	432-335-5900
Amerilist Inc	978 Route 45 Ste L2	Pomona	NY	10970	**800-457-2899**	845-362-6737

Company / Address	City	State	Zip	Toll-Free	Phone
APC Integrated Services Inc 770 SPIRIT OF SAINT LOUIS Blvd	CHESTERFIELD	MO	63005	**888-294-7886**	
Avantpage Translations 1138 Villaverde Ln	Davis	CA	95618	**877-269-5264**	530-750-2040
Barchart.com Inc 330 S Wells Ste 618	Chicago	IL	60606	**800-238-5814**	312-554-8122
Barnet Associates LLC 2 Round Lake Rd	Ridgefield	CT	06877	**888-827-7070**	
Barton Cotton Inc 3030 Waterview Ave	Baltimore	MD	21230	**800-638-4652**	800-348-1102
BeenVerified Inc 307 Fifth Ave 16th Fl	New York	NY	10016	**888-579-5910**	
Bentz Whaley Flessner 7251 Ohms Ln	Minneapolis	MN	55439	**800-921-0111**	952-921-0111
Brakeley Briscoe Inc 322 W Bellevue Ave Ste 204	San Mateo	CA	94402	**800-416-3086**	650-344-8883
Cargill Assoc Inc 4701 Altamesa Blvd	Fort Worth	TX	76133	**800-433-2233**	817-292-9374
Central Ontario Healthcare Procurement Alliance 95 Mural St	Richmond Hill	ON	L4B3G2	**866-897-8812**	905-886-5319
Concord Servicing Corp 4150 N Drinkwater Blvd	Scottsdale	AZ	85251	**866-493-6393**	
Cox North America Inc 8181 Coleman Rd	Haslett	MI	48840	**800-822-8114**	517-339-3330
Creative Sign Designs 12801 Commodity Pl Ste 200	Tampa	FL	33626	**800-804-4809**	813-818-7100
Crosbie & Company Inc 150 King St W Sun Life Financial Tower 15th Fl	Toronto	ON	M5H1J9	**866-873-7002**	416-362-7726
CSA Group 178 Rexdale Blvd	Toronto	ON	M9W1R3	**800-463-6727**	416-747-4000
eLawMarketing 25 Robert Pitt Dr Ste 209G	Monsey	NY	10952	**866-833-6245**	
Extended Presence 3570 E 12th Ave Ste 200	Denver	CO	80206	**800-398-8957**	303-325-8600
Fam Funds 384 N Grand St PO Box 310	Cobleskill	NY	12043	**800-721-5391**	518-234-4393
Field Nation LLC 310 Fourth Ave S Ste 8100	Minneapolis	MN	55415	**877-573-4353**	
FilterBoxx Water & Environmental Corp 5716 Burbank Rd SE	Calgary	AB	T2H1Z4	**877-868-4747**	403-203-4747
Gale Force Petroleum Inc 100 King St W Ste 5700	Toronto	ON	M5X1C7	**888-440-3411**	
Galveston Central Appraisal District 9850 Emmett F Lowry Expy Ste A	Texas City	TX	77591	**866-277-4725**	409-935-1980
Gilligan & Ferneman LLC 1754 Business Ctr Ln	Kissimmee	FL	34758	**800-720-4152**	
Global Pacific Financial Services Ltd 10430 144 St	Surrey	BC	V3T4V5	**800-561-1177**	
Greater Giving Inc 1920 N W Amberglen Pkwy Ste 140	Beaverton	OR	97006	**800-276-5992**	
GroveWare Technologies Ltd 90 Eglinton Ave E Ste 411	Toronto	ON	M4P2Y3	**877-701-9378**	
IFS Financial Services Inc 250 Brownlow Ave Ste 1	Dartmouth	NS	B3B1W9	**800-565-1153**	902-481-6106
Info Cubic LLC 9250 E Costilla Ave Ste 525	Greenwood Village	CO	80112	**877-360-4636**	303-220-0170
Intronix Technologies Inc 26 McEwan Dr West Unit 15	Bolton	ON	L7E1E6	**800-819-9996**	905-951-3361
Issuer Direct Corp 500 Perimeter Park Dr Ste D	Morrisville	NC	27560	**877-481-4014**	
LW Robbins Assoc 201 Summer St	Holliston	MA	01746	**800-229-5972**	
Mail Dispatch LLC 9710 Distribution Ave	San Diego	CA	92121	**800-275-0450**	
MyUSACorporation.com Inc 1 Radisson Plz Ste 800	New Rochelle	NY	10801	**877-330-2677**	
Nomadic Display Capitol Inc 5617 Industrial Dr	Springfield	VA	22151	**800-336-5019**	703-912-4700
NorAm Capital Holdings Inc 15303 N Dallas Pkwy Ste 1030	Addison	TX	75001	**888-886-6726**	
Nova Express Millennium Inc 105 - 14271 Knox Way	Richmond	BC	V6V2Z4	**877-566-6839**	604-278-8044
oberoSPM 7560 Airport Rd Unit 12	Mississauga	ON	L4T4H4	**888-815-2996**	
OnCorp Direct Inc 1033 Bay St Ste 313	Toronto	ON	M5S3A5	**800-461-7772**	416-964-2677
Parenty Reitmeier Inc 605 Des Meurons St	Winnipeg	MB	R2H2R1	**877-445-3737**	204-237-3737
Payment Services Corp Inc 360 Albert St Ste 1220	Ottawa	ON	K1R7X7	**866-972-0616**	
Phone Ware Inc 8902 Activity Rd	San Diego	CA	92126	**800-243-8329**	858-459-3000
Practice Concepts 2706 Harbor Blvd	Costa Mesa	CA	92626	**877-778-2020**	714-545-5110
QCSS Inc 21925 Field Pkwy Ste 210	Deer Park	IL	60010	**888-229-7046**	847-229-7046
Reed Brennan Media Associates Inc 628 Virginia Dr	Orlando	FL	32803	**800-708-7311**	407-894-7300
Round Sky Inc 848 N Rainbow Blvd Ste 326	Las Vegas	NV	89107	**855-450-3618**	
Ruotolo Assoc Inc (RA) 29 Broadway Ste 210	Cresskill	NJ	07626	**800-786-8656**	201-568-3898
Sureshred Security 3166 Diablo Ave	Hayward	CA	94545	**888-606-0008**	510-784-1150
Synergent 2 Ledgeview Dr	Westbrook	ME	04092	**800-341-0180**	207-773-5671
TeamBonding 298 Tosca Dr	Stoughton	MA	02072	**888-398-8326**	
Thermosoft International Corp 701 corporate Woods Pkwy	Vernon Hills	IL	60061	**800-308-8057**	847-279-3800
Thetubestore Inc 120 Lancing Dr	Hamilton	ON	L8W3A1	**877-570-0979**	905-570-0979
Townsend Oil Company Inc 27 Cherry St PO Box 90	Danvers	MA	01923	**800-888-2888**	
Trademark Co, The 344 Maple Ave W Ste 151	Vienna	VA	22180	**800-906-8626**	
Vantage Sourcing LLC 328 Ross Clark Cir	Dothan	AL	36303	**866-580-4562**	

319 FURNACES & OVENS - INDUSTRIAL PROCESS

Company / Address	City	State	Zip	Toll-Free	Phone
Ajax Tocco Magnethermic Corp 1745 Overland Ave NE	Warren	OH	44483	**800-547-1527**	330-372-8511
Alabama Specialty Products Inc 152 Metal Samples Rd PO Box 8	Munford	AL	36268	**888-388-1006**	256-358-5200
Alpha 1 Induction Service Ctr Inc 1525 Old Alum Creek Dr	Columbus	OH	43209	**800-991-2599**	614-253-8900
Armor Group Inc, The 4600 N Mason-Montgomery Rd	Mason	OH	45040	**800-255-0393**	
AVS Inc 60 Fitchburg Rd	Ayer	MA	01432	**800-772-0710**	978-772-0710
BriskHeat Corp 1055 Gibbard Ave	Columbus	OH	43201	**800-848-7673**	614-294-3376
Cambridge Engineering Inc PO Box 1010	Chesterfield	MO	63006	**800-899-1989**	636-532-2233
CCI Thermal Technologies Inc 5918 Roper Rd *Cust Svc	Edmonton	AB	T6B3E1	**800-661-8529***	780-466-3178
CMI EFCO Inc 435 W Wilson St	Salem	OH	44460	**877-225-2674**	330-332-4661
Despatch Industries Inc 8860 207th St W	Lakeville	MN	55044	**800-726-0110**	952-469-5424
Detroit Radiant Product Co 21400 Hoover Rd	Warren	MI	48089	**800-222-1100**	586-756-0950
Detroit Stoker Co 1510 E First St	Monroe	MI	48161	**800-786-5374**	734-241-9500
Eclipse Inc 1665 Elmwood Rd	Rockford	IL	61103	**888-826-3473**	815-877-3031
Fast Heat Inc 776 Oaklawn Ave	Elmhurst	IL	60126	**877-747-8575**	630-833-5400
Gas-Fired Products Inc 305 Doggett St	Charlotte	NC	28203	**800-830-3983**	704-372-3485
Glenro Inc 39 McBride Ave	Paterson	NJ	07501	**888-453-6761**	973-279-5900
Glo-Quartz Electric Heater Company Inc 7084 Maple St *Sales	Mentor	OH	44060	**800-321-3574***	440-255-9701
Heatrex Inc PO Box 515	Meadville	PA	16335	**800-394-6589**	814-724-1800
Inductoheat Inc 32251 N Avis Dr	Madison Heights	MI	48071	**800-624-6297**	248-585-9393
Inductotherm Group 10 Indel Ave PO Box 157	Rancocas	NJ	08073	**800-257-9527**	609-267-9000
Industronics Service Co 489 Sullivan Ave	South Windsor	CT	06074	**800-878-1551**	860-289-1551
Ipsen Inc PO Box 6266	Rockford	IL	61125	**800-727-7625**	815-332-4941
John Zink Company LLC 11920 E Apache St	Tulsa	OK	74116	**800-421-9242**	918-234-1800
Johnson Gas Appliance Co 520 E Ave NW	Cedar Rapids	IA	52405	**800-553-5422**	319-365-5267
Novatec Inc 222 Thomas Ave	Baltimore	MD	21225	**800-237-8379**	410-789-4811
Paragon Industries Inc 2011 S Town E Blvd	Mesquite	TX	75149	**800-876-4328**	972-288-7557
Pillar Induction Co 21905 Gateway Rd	Brookfield	WI	53045	**800-558-7733**	262-317-5300
Pyronics Inc 17700 Miles Rd	Cleveland	OH	44128	**800-883-9218**	216-662-8800
Radyne Corp 211 W Boden St	Milwaukee	WI	53207	**800-236-8360**	414-481-8360
Rapid Engineering Inc 1100 7-Mile Rd NW	Comstock Park	MI	49321	**800-536-3461**	616-784-0500
Red-Ray Mfg Co Inc 10-22 County Line Rd	Branchburg	NJ	08876	**800-883-9218**	908-722-0040
Selas Heat Technology Company LLC 130 Keystone Dr	Montgomeryville	PA	18936	**800-523-6500**	215-646-6600
ST Johnson Co 925 Stanford Ave	Oakland	CA	94608	**800-225-1348**	510-652-6000
Steelman Industries Inc 2800 Hwy 135 N	Kilgore	TX	75662	**800-287-6633**	903-984-3061
StrikoDynarad 501 E Roosevelt Ave	Zeeland	MI	49464	**855-787-4561**	616-772-3705
Surface Combustion Inc 1700 Indian Wood Cir	Maumee	OH	43537	**800-537-8980**	419-891-7150
Tempco Electric Heater Corp 607 N Central Ave	Wood Dale	IL	60191	**888-268-6396**	630-350-2252
Thermal Circuits Inc 1 Technology Way	Salem	MA	01970	**800-808-4328**	978-745-1162
Thermal Engineering Corp 2741 The Blvd	Columbia	SC	29209	**800-331-0097**	803-783-0750
Trent Inc 201 Leverington Ave	Philadelphia	PA	19127	**800-544-8736**	215-482-5000
Truheat Inc 700 Grand St	Allegan	MI	49010	**800-879-6199**	269-673-2145

320 FURNITURE - MFR

SEE ALSO Recycled Plastics Products ; Cabinets - Wood ; Fixtures - Office & Store ; Mattresses & Adjustable Beds ; Baby Products

320-1 Commercial & Industrial Furniture

Company / Address	City	State	Zip	Toll-Free	Phone
Abco Office Furniture 4121 Rushton St	Florence	AL	35630	**800-336-0070**	256-767-4100
Adelphia Steel Equipment Co 7372 State Rd	Philadelphia	PA	19136	**800-865-8211**	215-333-6300
Allied Plastics Company Inc 2001 Walnut St *Cust Svc	Jacksonville	FL	32206	**800-999-0386***	904-359-0386
Allsteel Inc 2210 Second Ave *Cust Svc	Muscatine	IA	52761	**888-255-7833***	563-272-4800
Anthro Corp 10450 SW Manhasset Dr	Tualatin	OR	97062	**800-325-3841**	503-691-2556
Bestar Inc 4220 Villeneuve St	Lac-Megantic	QC	G6B2C3	**888-823-7827**	819-583-1017

Company	Address	City	State	Zip	Toll-Free	Phone
Bevco Precision Manufacturing Co	21320 Doral Rd	Waukesha	WI	53186	**800-864-2991**	262-798-9200
BGD Cos Inc	5323 Lakeland Ave N	Minneapolis	MN	55429	**800-699-3537**	612-338-6804
Biofit Engineered Products	15500 Biofit Way	Bowling Green	OH	43402	**800-597-0246**	419-823-1089
Borroughs Corp	3002 N Burdick St	Kalamazoo	MI	49004	**800-748-0227**	269-342-0161
Bright Chair Co	51 Railroad Ave	Middletown	NY	10940	**888-524-5997**	845-343-2196
Carolina Business Furniture LLC	535 Archdale Blvd	Archdale	NC	27263	**800-763-0212**	336-431-9400
Cramer Inc	1222 Quebec St	North Kansas City	MO	64116	**800-366-6700**	
Danver	1 Grand St	Wallingford	CT	06492	**888-441-0537**	203-269-2300
Dar-Ran Furniture Industries	2402 Shore St	High Point	NC	27263	**800-334-7891**	336-861-2400
Dauphin North America	300 Myrtle Ave *Cust Svc	Boonton	NJ	07005	**800-631-1186***	973-263-1100
Emeco	805 W Elm Ave	Hanover	PA	17331	**800-366-5951**	717-637-5951
Ergotron Inc	1181 Trapp Rd *Sales	Saint Paul	MN	55121	**800-888-8458***	651-681-7600
Fillip Metal Cabinet Co	4500 W 47th St	Chicago	IL	60632	**800-535-0733**	773-733-7527
First Office	1204 E Sixth St	Huntingburg	IN	47542	**800-983-4415**	
Flex-Y-Plan Industries Inc	6960 W Ridge Rd *Cust Svc	Fairview	PA	16415	**800-458-0552***	814-474-1565
Flexible-Montisa	323 Acorn St *Cust Svc	Plainwell	MI	49080	**800-875-6836***	269-924-0730
Geiger International Inc	6095 Fulton Industrial Blvd SW	Atlanta	GA	30336	**800-456-6452**	404-344-1100
Global Industries Inc	17 W Stow Rd	Marlton	NJ	08053	**800-220-1900**	856-596-3390
Groupe Lacasse LLC	99 St-Pierre St	Sainte-Pie	QC	J0H1W0	**888-522-2773**	450-772-2495
Gunlocke Company LLC	1 Gunlocke Dr *Cust Svc	Wayland	NY	14572	**800-828-6300***	585-728-5111
H Wilson Co	2245 Delany Rd	Waukegan	IL	60087	**800-245-7224**	
Hausmann Industries Inc	130 Union St	Northvale	NJ	07647	**888-428-7626**	201-767-0255
Haworth Inc	1 Haworth Ctr	Holland	MI	49423	**800-344-2600**	616-393-3000
Herman Miller Inc	855 E Main Ave *NASDAQ: MLHR*	Zeeland	MI	49464	**888-443-4357**	616-654-3000
High Point Furniture Industries Inc	1104 Bedford St PO Box 2063	High Point	NC	27261	**800-447-3462**	336-431-7101
Hirsh Industries Inc	3636 Westown Pkwy Ste 100	West Des Moines	IA	50266	**800-383-7414**	515-299-3200
HON Co	200 Oak St	Muscatine	IA	52761	**800-553-8230**	563-272-7100
Huot Manufacturing Co	550 Wheeler St N	Saint Paul	MN	55104	**800-832-3838**	651-646-1869
IAC Industries	895 Beacon St	Brea	CA	92821	**800-989-1422**	714-990-8997
Indiana Furniture	1224 Mill St	Jasper	IN	47546	**800-422-5727**	812-482-5727
Invincible Office Furniture Co	842 S 26th St PO Box 1117	Manitowoc	WI	54220	**877-682-4601**	920-682-4601
Izzydesign	17237 Van Wagoner Rd	Spring Lake	MI	49456	**800-543-5449**	616-916-9369
Jasper Desk Co	415 E Sixth St *Cust Svc	Jasper	IN	47546	**800-365-7994***	812-482-4132
Jasper Seating Company Inc	*Jasper Group* 225 Clay St	Jasper	IN	47546	**800-622-5661**	812-482-3204
Khoury Inc	1129 Webster Ave PO Box 1746	Waco	TX	76703	**800-725-6765**	254-754-5481
KI	1330 Bellevue St	Green Bay	WI	54302	**800-424-2432**	920-468-8100
Kimball Hospitality	1180 E 16th St	Jasper	IN	47549	**800-634-9510**	276-666-8933
Kimball Office Furniture Co	1600 Royal St	Jasper	IN	47549	**800-482-1818**	
Knoll Inc	1235 Water St *NYSE: KNL* ■ *Cust Svc	East Greenville	PA	18041	**800-343-5665***	215-679-7991
Lakeside Manufacturing Inc	4900 W Electric Ave	West Milwaukee	WI	53219	**800-558-8565**	414-902-6400
LB Furniture Industries LLC	99 S Third St	Hudson	NY	12534	**800-221-8752**	518-828-1501
Luxor Div EBSCO Industries Inc	2245 Delany Rd	Waukegan	IL	60087	**800-323-4656**	847-244-1800
Magna Design Inc	26246 Twelve Trees Ln NW	Poulsbo	WA	98370	**800-426-1202**	360-394-1300
Martin Furniture	2345 Britannia Blvd *Cust Svc	San Diego	CA	92154	**800-268-5669***	
Marvel Group Inc	3843 W 43rd St *Cust Svc	Chicago	IL	60632	**800-621-8846***	
Maxon Furniture Inc	660 SW 39th St Ste 150 *Cust Svc	Renton	WA	98057	**800-876-4274***	
Mayline Group	619 N Commerce St PO Box 728	Sheboygan	WI	53082	**800-822-8037**	920-457-5537
MLP Seating Corp	950 Pratt Blvd	Elk Grove Village	IL	60007	**800-723-3030**	847-956-1700
National Office Furniture	1205 Kimball Blvd	Jasper	IN	47549	**800-482-1717**	
NER Data Products Inc	307 S Delsea Dr	Glassboro	NJ	08028	**888-637-3282**	
Neutral Posture Inc	3904 N Texas Ave	Bryan	TX	77803	**800-446-3746**	979-778-0502
Nomanco Inc	501 Nmc Dr	Zebulon	NC	27597	**800-345-7279**	919-269-6500
Nova Solutions Inc	421 Industrial Ave	Effingham	IL	62401	**800-730-6682**	217-342-7070
Office Chairs Inc	14815 Radburn Ave	Santa Fe Springs	CA	90670	**866-624-4968**	562-802-0464
Open Plan Systems Inc	4700 Deepwater Terminal Rd	Richmond	VA	23234	**844-677-6771**	804-275-2468
Paoli Inc	201 E Martin St	Orleans	IN	47452	**800-472-8669**	
Penco Products Inc	1820 Stonehenge Dr	Oaks	PA	19456	**800-562-1000**	
Plymold	615 Centennial Dr	Kenyon	MN	55946	**800-759-6653**	
Reconditioned Systems Inc (RSI)	2636 S Wilson St Ste 105	Tempe	AZ	85282	**800-280-5000**	480-968-1772
Robertson Furniture Company Inc	890 Elberton St	Toccoa	GA	30577	**800-241-0713**	706-886-1494
Rush Industries Inc	118 N Wrenn St	High Point	NC	27260	**800-524-0258**	336-886-7700
Safco Products Co	9300 W Research Ctr Rd *Cust Svc	New Hope	MN	55428	**800-328-3020***	763-536-6700
Shure Manufacturing Corp	1901 W Main St	Washington	MO	63090	**800-227-4873**	636-390-7100
Spectrum Industries Inc	925 First Ave	Chippewa Falls	WI	54729	**800-235-1262**	715-723-6750
Steelcase Inc	801 44th St SE PO Box 1967 *NYSE: SCS*	Grand Rapids	MI	49501	**888-783-3522**	616-247-2710
Stylex	PO Box 5038	Delanco	NJ	08075	**800-257-5742**	
TAB Products Co	605 Fourth St	Mayville	WI	53050	**888-466-8228**	
Techline USA LLC	500 S Div St	Waunakee	WI	53597	**800-356-8400**	608-849-4181
Tennsco Corp	201 Tennsco Dr PO Box 1888 *Cust Svc	Dickson	TN	37056	**866-446-8686***	615-446-8000
Trendway Corp	13467 Quincy St PO Box 9016	Holland	MI	49422	**800-968-5344**	616-399-3900
Tuohy Furniture Corp	42 St Albans Pl *Cust Svc	Chatfield	MN	55923	**800-533-1696***	507-867-4280
Viking Acoustical Corp	21480 Heath Ave	Lakeville	MN	55044	**800-328-8385**	952-469-3405
Vitro Seating Products Inc	201 Madison St *Cust Svc	Saint Louis	MO	63102	**800-325-7093***	314-241-2265
Watson Furniture Group Inc	26246 Twelve Trees Ln NW	Poulsbo	WA	98370	**800-426-1202**	360-394-1300
West Coast Industries Inc	10 Jackson St	San Francisco	CA	94111	**800-243-3150**	415-621-6656
Workplace Systems Inc	562 Mammoth Rd	Londonderry	NH	03053	**800-258-9700**	603-622-3727
Wright Line LLC	160 Gold Star Blvd	Worcester	MA	01606	**800-225-7348**	508-852-4300

320-2 Household Furniture

Company	Address	City	State	Zip	Toll-Free	Phone
Albany Industries Inc	504 N Glenfield Rd	New Albany	MS	38652	**877-534-9804**	662-534-9800
Ameriwood Industries Inc	410 E S First St *General	Wright City	MO	63390	**800-489-3351***	636-745-3351
Ashley Furniture Industries Inc	1 Ashley Way	Arcadia	WI	54612	**800-477-2222**	608-323-6225
Baby's Dream Furniture Inc	411 Industrial Blvd	Buena Vista	GA	31803	**800-835-2742**	229-649-4404
Bassett Furniture Industries Inc	3525 Fairystone Pk Hwy PO Box 626 *NASDAQ: BSET*	Bassett	VA	24055	**877-525-7070**	714-222-1010
Broyhill Furniture Industries Inc	3483 Hickory Blvd *Cust Svc	Hudson	NC	28638	**800-225-0265***	
Brueton Industries Inc	146 Hanse Ave *Cust Svc	Freeport	NY	11520	**800-221-6783***	516-379-3400
Bush Industries Inc	1 Mason Dr	Jamestown	NY	14701	**800-950-4782**	716-665-2000
Carrom	218 E Dowland St	Ludington	MI	49431	**800-223-6047**	231-845-1263
Century Furniture LLC	401 11th St NW	Hickory	NC	28601	**800-852-5552**	828-328-1851
DeFehr Furniture Ltd	125 Furniture Pk	Winnipeg	MB	R2G1B9	**877-333-3471**	204-988-5630
Dutailier Group Inc	299 Rue Chaput	Sainte-Pie	QC	J0H1W0	**800-363-9817**	450-772-2403
El Ran Furniture Ltd	2751 Transcanada Hwy	Pointe-Claire	QC	H9R1B4	**800-361-6546**	514-630-5656
Ethan Allen Interiors Inc	Ethan Allen Dr *NYSE: ETH*	Danbury	CT	06811	**888-324-3571**	
Evenflo Company Inc	1801 Commerce Dr	Piqua	OH	45356	**800-233-5921**	
Finnleo Sauna	575 Cokato St E	Cokato	MN	55321	**800-346-6536**	
Hooker Furniture Corp	440 E Commonwealth Blvd *NASDAQ: HOFT* ■ *Cust Svc	Martinsville	VA	24112	**800-422-1511***	276-632-0459
Human Touch	3030 Walnut Ave	Long Beach	CA	90807	**800-742-5493**	562-426-8700
La-Z-Boy Inc	1284 N Telegraph Rd *NYSE: LZB*	Monroe	MI	48162	**800-375-6890**	734-242-1444
Lamont Ltd	1530 Bluff Rd	Burlington	IA	52601	**800-553-5621**	319-753-5131
Leathercraft	PO Box 639	Conover	NC	28613	**800-627-1561**	
Little Tikes Co, The	2180 Barlow Rd *Cust Svc	Hudson	OH	44236	**800-321-0183***	

Classified Section

Company	City	State	ZIP	Toll-Free	Phone
Mantua Mfg Co 7900 Northfield Rd *Orders	Walton Hills	OH	44146	**800-333-8333***	
McGuire Furniture Co 1201 Bryant St	San Francisco	CA	94103	**800-662-4847**	415-626-1414
Mitchell Gold & Bob Williams Co (MGBW) 135 One Comfortable Pl	Taylorsville	NC	28681	**800-789-5401**	828-632-9200
Pearson Co 1420 Progress Ave	High Point	NC	27260	**800-225-0265**	336-882-8135
Robern Inc 701 N Wilson Ave	Bristol	PA	19007	**800-877-2376**	215-826-9800
Room & Board Inc 4600 Olson Memorial Hwy	Golden Valley	MN	55422	**800-301-9720**	763-521-4431
Rumble Tuff Inc 865 North 1430 West	Orem	UT	84057	**855-228-8388**	801-609-8168
Rush Industries Inc 118 N Wrenn St	High Point	NC	27260	**800-524-0258**	336-886-7700
Sauder Woodworking Co 502 Middle St PO Box 156 *Cust Svc	Archbold	OH	43502	**800-523-3987***	419-446-2711
Schnadig International Corp 4200 Tudor Ln	Greensboro	NC	27410	**800-468-8730**	
Sico North America Inc 7525 Cahill Rd	Minneapolis	MN	55439	**800-328-6138**	952-941-1700
Standard Furniture Mfg Company Inc 801 Hwy 31 S *General	Bay Minette	AL	36507	**877-788-1899***	251-937-6741
Stanley Furniture Co Inc 200 North Hamilton St *NASDAQ: STLY*	High Point	NC	27260	**877-772-4858**	
Storkcraft Baby 7433 Nelson Rd	Richmond	BC	V6W1G3	**877-274-0277**	604-274-5121
Suncast Corp 701 N Kirk Rd	Batavia	IL	60510	**800-444-3310**	630-879-2050
Techline USA LLC 500 S Div St	Waunakee	WI	53597	**800-356-8400**	608-849-4181
Walter E Smithe Furniture Inc 1251 W Thorndale Ave	Itasca	IL	60143	**800-948-4263**	630-285-8000
Whittier Wood Products 3787 W First Ave PO Box 2827	Eugene	OR	97402	**800-653-3336**	541-687-0213
Zenith Products Corp 400 Lukens Dr	New Castle	DE	19720	**800-892-3986**	

320-3 Institutional & Other Public Buildings Furniture

Company	City	State	ZIP	Toll-Free	Phone
Achieva Inc 197 Funder Dr PO Box 729	Mocksville	NC	27028	**800-788-7213**	336-751-7104
Adden Furniture Inc 710 Chelmsford St	Lowell	MA	01851	**800-625-3876**	978-454-7848
American Desk 1302 Industrial Blvd	Temple	TX	76504	**800-433-3142**	
American Seating Co 401 American Seating Ctr NW *Cust Svc	Grand Rapids	MI	49504	**800-748-0268***	616-732-6600
Artco-Bell Corp 1302 Industrial Blvd	Temple	TX	76504	**877-778-1811**	254-778-1811
Bretford Manufacturing Inc 11000 Seymour Ave	Franklin Park	IL	60131	**800-521-9614**	847-678-2545
Brodart Co 500 Arch St	Williamsport	PA	17701	**800-233-8467**	570-326-2461
ENOCHS Examining Room Furniture PO Box 50559 *Cust Svc	Indianapolis	IN	46250	**800-428-2305***	
ErgoGenesis LLC 1 BodyBilt Pl	Navasota	TX	77868	**800-364-5299**	936-825-1700
Fleetwood Group Inc 11832 James St	Holland	MI	49424	**800-257-6390**	616-396-1142
Fordham Equipment Co 1204 Village Market Place Ste 262	Morrisville	NC	27560	**866-467-0708**	919-467-0708
Gaylord Bros 7282 William Barry Blvd	Syracuse	NY	13212	**800-345-5330**	315-457-5070
Gunlocke Company LLC 1 Gunlocke Dr *Cust Svc	Wayland	NY	14572	**800-828-6300***	585-728-5111
Hard Mfg Company Inc 230 Grider St	Buffalo	NY	14215	**800-873-4273**	
Herman Miller for Health Care 855 E Main Ave PO Box 302	Zeeland	MI	49464	**888-443-4357**	616-654-3000
Hill-Rom Services Inc 1069 SR 46 E	Batesville	IN	47006	**800-267-2337**	812-934-7777
Hussey Seating Co 38 Dyer St Ext	North Berwick	ME	03906	**800-341-0401**	207-676-2271
Imperial Woodworks Inc PO Box 7835 PO Box 7835	Waco	TX	76714	**800-234-6624**	
Irwin Seating Company Inc 3251 Fruit Ridge NW	Grand Rapids	MI	49544	**866-464-7946**	616-574-7400
Joerns Healthcare 5001 Joerns Dr	Stevens Point	WI	54481	**800-826-0270**	715-341-3600
Kimball Hospitality 1180 E 16th St	Jasper	IN	47549	**800-634-9510**	276-666-8933
KLN Steel Products Co 2 Winnco Dr	San Antonio	TX	78218	**800-624-9101**	210-227-4747
LB Furniture Industries LLC 99 S Third St	Hudson	NY	12534	**800-221-8752**	518-828-1501
List Industries Inc 401 Jim Moran Blvd	Deerfield Beach	FL	33442	**800-776-1342**	954-429-9155
Luxor Div EBSCO Industries Inc 2245 Delany Rd	Waukegan	IL	60087	**800-323-4656**	847-244-1800
Meco Corp 1500 Industrial Rd	Greeneville	TN	37745	**800-251-7558**	
Midwest Folding Products Inc 1414 S Western Ave	Chicago	IL	60608	**800-621-4716**	312-666-3366
Mitchell Furniture Systems Inc 1700 W St Paul Ave	Milwaukee	WI	53233	**800-290-5960**	414-342-3111
Mity-Lite Inc 1301 West 400 North	Orem	UT	84057	**800-909-8034**	801-224-0589
MLP Seating Corp 950 Pratt Blvd	Elk Grove Village	IL	60007	**800-723-3030**	847-956-1700
Nemschoff Healthcare Furniture and Clinic Furniture 909 N Eigth St *Cust Svc	Sheboygan	WI	53081	**800-203-8916***	
New Holland Church Furniture 313 Prospect St PO Box 217	New Holland	PA	17557	**800-648-9663**	
Shelby Williams Industries Inc 810 W Hwy 25/70 *General	Newport	TN	37821	**800-873-3252***	423-623-0031
Sico North America Inc 7525 Cahill Rd	Minneapolis	MN	55439	**800-328-6138**	952-941-1700
Spectrum Industries Inc 925 First Ave	Chippewa Falls	WI	54729	**800-235-1262**	715-723-6750
Sturdisteel Co PO Box 2655	Waco	TX	76702	**800-433-3116**	
Tesco Industries LP 1035 E Hacienda	Bellville	TX	77418	**800-699-5824**	
TMI Systems Design Corp 50 S Third Ave W	Dickinson	ND	58601	**800-456-6716**	701-456-6716
UMF Medical 1316 Eisenhower Blvd	Johnstown	PA	15904	**800-638-5322**	814-266-8726
Virco Manufacturing Corp 2027 Harpers Way *NASDAQ: VIRC* ■ *Cust Svc	Torrance	CA	90501	**800-448-4726***	310-533-0474
Wieland 13737 Main St PO Box 1000	Grabill	IN	46741	**888-943-5263**	260-627-3686
Winco Inc 5516 SW First Ln	Ocala	FL	34474	**800-237-3377**	352-854-2929
Worden Company Inc 199 E 17th St	Holland	MI	49423	**800-748-0561**	616-392-1848

320-4 Outdoor Furniture

Company	City	State	ZIP	Toll-Free	Phone
Belson Outdoors Inc 111 N River Rd	North Aurora	IL	60542	**800-323-5664**	630-897-8489
Bemis Manufacturing Co 300 Mill St	Sheboygan Falls	WI	53085	**800-558-7651**	920-467-4621
Brown Jordan Co 9860 Gidley St	El Monte	CA	91731	**800-743-4252**	
Cox Industries Inc 860 Cannon Bridge Rd PO Box 1124	Orangeburg	SC	29116	**800-476-4401**	803-534-7467
DuMor Inc PO Box 142	Mifflintown	PA	17059	**800-598-4018**	717-436-2106
Gardenside Ltd 808 Anthony St Ste 140	Berkeley	CA	94710	**888-999-8325**	415-455-4500
Hatteras Hammocks Inc 305 Industrial Blvd	Greenville	NC	27834	**800-643-3522**	252-758-0641
J Robert Scott Inc 500 N Oak St	Inglewood	CA	90302	**877-207-5130**	310-680-4300
Kay Park Recreation Corp 1301 Pine St *Cust Svc	Janesville	IA	50647	**800-553-2476***	
Mallin Casual Furniture 1 Minson Way	Montebello	CA	90640	**800-251-6537**	
Minson Corp 1 Minson Way	Montebello	CA	90640	**800-251-6537**	323-513-1041
OW Lee Company Inc 1822 E Francis St	Ontario	CA	91761	**800-776-9533**	909-947-3771
RJ Thomas Mfg Company Inc PO Box 946	Cherokee	IA	51012	**800-762-5002**	712-225-5115
Twin Oaks Hammocks 138 Twin Oaks Rd	Louisa	VA	23093	**800-688-8946**	540-894-5125
Wabash Valley Manufacturing Inc 505 E Main St	Silver Lake	IN	46982	**800-253-8619**	260-352-2102
Walpole Woodworkers Inc 767 E St Rt 7 *Cust Svc	Walpole	MA	02081	**800-343-6948***	508-668-2800

321 FURNITURE - WHOL

Company	City	State	ZIP	Toll-Free	Phone
Adirondack Direct 3040 48th Ave	Long Island	NY	11101	**800-221-2444**	718-204-4500
ATD-American Co 135 Greenwood Ave	Wyncote	PA	19095	**866-283-9327**	215-576-1380
Brown & Saenger 711 W Russell St PO Box 84040	Sioux Falls	SD	57118	**800-952-3509**	605-336-1960
Business Furniture Corp 6102 Victory Way	Indianapolis	IN	46278	**800-774-5544**	317-216-1600
California Office Furniture 1724 Tenth St	Sacramento	CA	95811	**877-442-6959**	916-442-6959
Carithers Wallace Courtenay Co 4343 NE Expy	Atlanta	GA	30340	**800-292-8220**	770-493-8200
Carroll Seating Company Inc 10 Lincoln St	Kansas City	KS	66103	**800-972-3779**	816-471-2929
Champion Industries Inc PO Box 2968 PO Box 2968 *OTC: CHMP*	Huntington	WV	25728	**800-624-3431**	304-528-2791
COECO Office Systems Co 2521 N Church St	Rocky Mount	NC	27804	**800-682-6844**	252-977-1121
Egan Visual Inc 300 Hanlan Rd	Woodbridge	ON	L4L3P6	**888-609-8886**	905-851-2826
Evergreen Enterprises Inc 5915 Midlothian Trnpk	Richmond	VA	23225	**800-774-3837**	804-231-1800
EVS Ltd 3702 W Sample St	South Bend	IN	46619	**800-364-3218**	574-233-5707
Glover Sales Group LLC 221 Cockeysville Rd	Cockeysville	MD	21030	**800-966-9016**	410-771-8000
Heritage Office Furnishings 1588 Rand Ave	Vancouver	BC	V6P3G2	**888-775-4555**	604-688-2381
J L Business Interiors Inc 515 Schoenhaar Dr PO Box 303	West Bend	WI	53090	**866-338-5524**	262-338-2221
Kentwood Office Furniture Inc 3063 Breton Rd SE	Grand Rapids	MI	49512	**877-698-6250**	616-957-2320
Najarian Furniture Company Inc 17560 Rowland St	City of Industry	CA	91748	**888-781-3088**	626-839-8700
National Business Furniture Inc 735 N Water St Ste 440 *Sales	Milwaukee	WI	53202	**800-558-1010***	414-276-8511

Company / Address	City	State	ZIP	Toll-Free	Phone
Nevers Industries Inc 14125 21st Ave N	Minneapolis	MN	55447	**800-258-5591**	763-210-4206
North Country Business Products Inc 1112 S Railroad St SE	Bemidji	MN	56601	**800-937-4140**	218-751-4140
Office Environments Inc 11407 Granite St	Charlotte	NC	28273	**888-861-2525**	704-714-7200
Office Star Products 1901 S Archibald PO Box 3520	Ontario	CA	91761	**800-950-7262**	909-930-2000
Paragon Furniture Management Inc 2224 E Randol Mill Rd	Arlington	TX	76011	**800-451-8546**	817-633-3242
R & M Office Furniture 9615 Oates Dr	Sacramento	CA	95827	**800-660-1756**	916-362-1756
Superior Medical Supply Inc 11005 Dover St Unit 1100	Broomfield	CO	80021	**877-460-1411**	303-460-1411
Trade Products Corp 12124 Popes Head Rd	Fairfax	VA	22030	**888-352-3580**	703-502-9000
Trinity Hardwood Distributors Inc 110 East Oregon	Dallas	TX	75203	**800-492-9856**	214-948-3001
Wasserstrom Co 477 S Front St	Columbus	OH	43215	**866-634-8927**	614-228-6525

322 FURNITURE STORES

SEE ALSO Department Stores

Company / Address	City	State	ZIP	Toll-Free	Phone
Activeforevercom 10799 N 90th St	Scottsdale	AZ	85260	**800-377-8033**	480-459-3202
Addison House Interiors Inc 5201 Nw 77th Ave Ste 400	Doral	FL	33166	**800-426-2988**	305-640-2400
Afinety Inc 1956 Cotner Ave	Los Angeles	CA	90025	**877-423-4638**	310-996-2700
Agati Inc 1219 W Lake St	Chicago	IL	60607	**866-418-8710**	312-829-1977
All Makes Office Equipment Co 2558 Farnam St	Omaha	NE	68131	**800-341-2413**	402-341-2413
American Furniture Warehouse Co 8501 Grant St	Thornton	CO	80229	**888-615-9415**	303-289-3300
American Home Furnishings 3535 Menaul Blvd NE	Albuquerque	NM	87107	**800-854-6755**	505-883-2211
American Surplus Inc 1 Noyes Ave Bldg B	Rumford	RI	02916	**800-876-3736**	401-434-4355
Andreas Furniture Company Inc 114 Dover Rd Ne	Sugarcreek	OH	44681	**800-846-7448**	330-852-2494
Arizona Leather Company Inc 4235 Schaefer Ave	Chino	CA	91710	**888-669-5328**	909-993-5101
August Inc 354 Congress Park Dr	Centerville	OH	45459	**800-318-5242**	937-434-2520
Bar Productscom Inc 1990 Lake Ave SE	Largo	FL	33771	**800-256-6396**	727-584-2093
Barn Furniture Mart Inc 6206 N Sepulveda Blvd	Van Nuys	CA	91411	**888-302-2276**	818-780-4070
Beaufurn LLC 5269 US Hwy 158	Advance	NC	27006	**888-766-7706**	
Best Material Handling Inc 4754 N Chestnut St	Colorado Springs	CO	80907	**800-933-5270**	719-599-9191
Blackledge Furniture 233 Sw Second St	Corvallis	OR	97333	**800-782-4851**	541-753-4851
Boss Chair Inc 5353 Jillson St	Commerce	CA	90040	**800-593-1888**	323-262-1919
Cardi's Furniture 1 Furniture Way	Swansea	MA	02777	**866-419-4096**	508-379-7510
Casual Designs Furniture Inc 36523 Lighthouse Rd	Selbyville	DE	19975	**888-629-1717**	302-436-8224
Charlotte Appliances Inc 3200 Lake Ave	Rochester	NY	14612	**800-244-0405**	585-663-5050
City Furniture Inc 6701 N Hiatus Rd	Tamarac	FL	33321	**888-882-5436**	954-597-2200
Cumberland Furniture 321 Terminal St Sw	Grand Rapids	MI	49548	**800-401-7877**	
Dates Weiser Furniture Corp 1700 Broadway St	Buffalo	NY	14212	**800-466-7037**	716-891-1700
El Dorado Furniture Corp 4200 NW 167th St	Miami	FL	33054	**888-451-7800**	305-624-2400
Epoch Design 17617 Ne 65th St Ste 2	Redmond	WA	98052	**800-589-7990**	425-284-0880
Ethan Allen Interiors Inc Ethan Allen Dr *NYSE: ETH*	Danbury	CT	06811	**888-324-3571**	
Gibraltar Steel Furniture Inc 9976 Westwanda Dr	Beverly Hills	CA	90210	**800-416-3635**	310-276-8889
Gracious Living Corp 7200 Martin Grove Rd	Woodbridge	ON	L4L9J3	**800-465-5660**	905-264-5660
Gressco Ltd 328 Moravian Vly Rd	Waunakee	WI	53597	**800-345-3480**	608-849-6300
Haverty Furniture Cos Inc 780 Johnson Ferry Rd NE Ste 800 *NYSE: HVT*	Atlanta	GA	30342	**888-428-3789**	404-443-2900
Heliodyne Corp 4910 Seaport Ave	Richmond	CA	94804	**888-878-8750**	510-237-9614
Hurwitz-Mintz Furniture Co 1751 Airline Dr	Metairie	LA	70001	**888-957-9555**	504-378-1000
IcwUSACom Inc 1487 Kingsley Dr	Medford	OR	97504	**800-558-4435**	541-608-2824
IKEA 420 Alan Wood Rd	Conshohocken	PA	19428	**800-434-4532**	610-834-0180
Interior Design Services Inc 209 Powell Pl	Brentwood	TN	37027	**800-433-7446**	615-376-1200
International Contract Furnishings Inc (ICF) 19 Ohio Ave	Norwich	CT	06360	**800-237-1625**	860-886-1700
Inviting Home.com 4700 SW 51st St Unit 219	Davie	FL	33314	**866-751-6606**	781-444-8001
Jayson Home & Garden 1885 N Clybourn Ave	Chicago	IL	60614	**800-472-1885**	773-248-8180
Jerome's Furniture Warehouse 16960 Mesamint St	San Diego	CA	92127	**866-633-4094**	
Lack's Valley Stores Ltd 1300 San Patricia St	Pharr	TX	78577	**800-870-6999**	956-702-3361
Living Spaces Furniture LLC 14501 Artesia Blvd	La Mirada	CA	90638	**877-266-7300**	
MacKenzie-Childs LLC 3260 SR- 90	Aurora	NY	13152	**888-665-1999**	315-364-7123
Massoud Furniture Manufacturing Inc 8351 Moberly Ln	Dallas	TX	75227	**800-762-2797**	214-388-8655
Mathis Bros Furniture Inc 6611 S 101 St E Ave *Cust Svc	Tulsa	OK	74133	**800-329-3434***	918-461-7785
Maynard Furniture Company Inc 725 Anderson St	Belton	SC	29627	**866-420-5249**	864-338-7751
Miskelly Furniture 101 Airport Rd	Jackson	MS	39208	**888-939-6288**	601-939-6288
Morris Furniture Co Inc 2377 Commerce Ctr Dr	Fairborn	OH	45324	**800-243-0000**	937-874-7100
Moser Corp 601 N 13th St	Rogers	AR	72756	**800-632-4564**	479-636-3481
N o a Medical Industries Inc 801 Terry Ln	Washington	MO	63090	**800-633-6068**	636-239-7600
N Tepperman Ltd 2595 Ouellette Ave	Windsor	ON	N8X4V8	**800-265-5062**	519-969-9700
Nashville Office Interiors 1621 Church St	Nashville	TN	37203	**877-342-0294**	615-329-1811
Nebraska Furniture Mart Inc 700 S 72nd St	Omaha	NE	68114	**800-336-9136**	402-397-6100
Nickerson Business Supplies 876A Lebanon St	Monroe	OH	45050	**888-385-9922**	513-539-6600
Nucraft Furniture Co 5151 W River Dr	Comstock Park	MI	49321	**877-682-7238**	616-784-6016
Olum's of Binghamton Inc 3701 Vestal Pkwy E *Cust Svc	Vestal	NY	13850	**855-264-8674***	607-729-5775
Otterbine Barebo Inc 3840 Main Rd E	Emmaus	PA	18049	**800-237-8837**	610-965-6018
Parker Furniture 10375 SW Beaverton-Hillsdale Hwy	Beaverton	OR	97005	**866-515-9673**	503-644-0155
Patioshoppers Inc 41188 Sandalwood Cir	Murrieta	CA	92562	**800-940-6123**	951-696-1700
Pier 1 Kids 100 Pier 1 Pl	Fort Worth	TX	76102	**800-433-4035**	817-252-8000
Porters of Racine 301 Sixth St	Racine	WI	53403	**800-558-3245**	262-633-6363
Preservation Technologies LP 111 Thomson Park Dr	Cranberry Township	PA	16066	**800-416-2665**	724-779-2111
Reborn Cabinets 2981 E La Palma Ave	Anaheim	CA	92806	**888-273-2676**	714-630-2220
Regency Seating Inc 2375 Romig Rd	Akron	OH	44320	**866-816-9822**	330-848-3700
Rocky Top Furniture Inc 8957 Lexington Rd	Lancaster	KY	40444	**800-332-1143**	859-548-2828
Rosewood Industries Inc 1203 E Central Ter	Stigler	OK	74462	**800-228-3306**	
Rotmans Furniture & Carpet 725 Southbridge St	Worcester	MA	01610	**800-768-6267**	508-755-5276
Sam Clar Office Furniture Inc 1221 Diamond Way	Concord	CA	94520	**800-726-2527**	925-602-3900
Schmidt-Goodman Office Products 1920 N Broadway	Rochester	MN	55906	**800-247-0663**	507-282-3870
Sedlak Interiors Inc 34300 Solon Rd	Solon	OH	44139	**800-260-2949**	440-248-2424
Selden's Home Furnishings 1802 62nd Ave E	Tacoma	WA	98424	**800-870-7880**	253-922-5700
Sheely's Furniture & Appliance Company Inc 11450 S Ave	North Lima	OH	44452	**877-549-9144**	330-549-3901
Shops at Carolina Furniture of Williamsburg 5425 Richmond Rd	Williamsburg	VA	23188	**800-582-8916**	757-565-3000
Sit 'n Sleep 14300 S Main St	Gardena	CA	90248	**877-262-4006**	310-604-8903
Slumberland Inc 3060 Centerville Rd	Little Canada	MN	55117	**888-957-7586**	651-482-7500
Smart Furniture Inc 430 Market St	Chattanooga	TN	37402	**888-467-6278**	423-267-7007
Smith Village Home Furnishings 34 N Main St	Jacobus	PA	17407	**800-242-1921**	717-428-1921
Stageright Corp 495 Pioneer Pkwy	Clare	MI	48617	**800-438-4499**	989-386-7393
Standard Office Supply 35 Sheridan St Nw	Washington	DC	20011	**888-829-4820**	202-829-4820
Star Furniture Company Inc 16666 Barker Springs Rd	Houston	TX	77084	**800-364-6661**	281-492-6661
Steinhafels W 231 N 1013 County Hwy F *Cust Svc	Waukesha	WI	53186	**866-351-4600***	262-436-4600
Sunnyland Outdoor & Casual Furniture 7879 Spring Vly Rd Ste 125	Dallas	TX	75254	**877-239-3716**	972-239-3716
Tri-boro Shelving & Partition Corp 300 Dominion Dr	Farmville	VA	23901	**800-633-3070**	434-315-5600
Trinity Business Furniture 6089 Kennedy Rd	Trinity	NC	27370	**855-311-6660**	336-472-6660
Urban Barn Ltd 4085 Marine Way Ste 1	Burnaby	BC	V5J5E2	**844-456-2200**	604-456-2200
USA Baby 793 Springer Dr	Lombard	IL	60148	**800-767-9464**	630-652-0600
Value City Furniture 4300 E Fifth Ave	Columbus	OH	43219	**888-751-8552**	888-672-2411
Victory Furniture 9040 W Pico Blvd	Los Angeles	CA	90035	**800-953-2000**	
Walker's Furniture Inc 3808 N Sullivan Rd Bldg 22-C	Spokane Valley	WA	99216	**866-667-6655**	509-535-1995
Warehouse Home Furnishings Distributors Inc 1851 Telfair St PO Box 1140	Dublin	GA	31021	**800-456-0424**	
Wayside Furniture Inc 1367 Canton Rd	Akron	OH	44312	**877-499-3968**	330-733-6221
Weekends Only Inc 349 Marshall Ave 3rd Fl	Saint Louis	MO	63119	**855-803-5888**	314-447-1500
Wells Home Furnishings 101 Bowers Rd	Charleston	WV	25314	**800-249-7753**	304-343-3600
WG&R Furniture Co 900 Challenger Dr	Green Bay	WI	54311	**888-947-7782**	920-469-4880
Wieser & Cawley Furniture 1301 Colegate Dr	Marietta	OH	45750	**800-339-0094**	740-373-1676

Company	Address	City	State	ZIP	Toll-Free	Phone
Workplace Resource LLC	4400 NE Loop 410 Ste 130	San Antonio	TX	78218	**800-580-3000**	512-472-7300
WS Badcock Corp (WSBC)	PO Box 497	Mulberry	FL	33860	**800-223-2625**	

323 GAMES & GAMING

SEE ALSO Toys, Games, Hobbies ; Casino Companies ; Casinos ; Lotteries, Games, Sweepstakes

Company	Address	City	State	ZIP	Toll-Free	Phone
Ac Coin & Slot	201 W Decatur Ave	Pleasantville	NJ	08232	**800-284-7568**	609-641-7811
American Gaming & Electronics	9500 W 55th St Ste A	Countryside	IL	60525	**800-336-6630**	708-290-2100
Amtote International Inc	11200 Pepper Rd	Hunt Valley	MD	21031	**800-345-1566**	410-771-8700
Arachnid Inc	6212 Material Ave	Loves Park	IL	61111	**800-435-8319**	815-654-0212
Aristocrat Technologies	7230 Amigo St	Las Vegas	NV	89119	**800-748-4156**	702-270-1000
Douglas Press Inc	2810 Madison St	Bellwood	IL	60104	**800-323-0705**	708-547-8400
Gaming Partners International Corp	1700 Industrial Rd *NASDAQ: GPIC*	Las Vegas	NV	89102	**800-728-5766**	702-384-2425
International Game Technology (IGT)	9295 Prototype Dr *NYSE: IGT*	Reno	NV	89521	**800-522-4700**	775-448-7777
Konami Gaming Inc	585 Trade Ctr Dr	Las Vegas	NV	89119	**866-544-7568**	702-616-1400
Scientific Games Corp	750 Lexington Ave 25th Fl *NASDAQ: SGMS*	New York	NY	10022	**800-827-2946**	212-754-2233
Smart Industries Corp	1626 Delaware Ave	Des Moines	IA	50317	**800-553-2442**	515-265-9900
Valley-Dynamo	7224 Burns Rd	Richland Hills	TX	76118	**800-826-7856**	972-595-5365
Video King Gaming Systems (VKGS LLC)	2717 N 118 Cir Ste 210	Omaha	NE	68164	**800-635-9912**	402-951-2970
WMS Gaming Inc	800 S Northpoint Blvd	Waukegan	IL	60085	**800-522-4700**	847-785-3000

324 GARDEN CENTERS

SEE ALSO Seed Companies ; Horticultural Products Growers

Company	Address	City	State	ZIP	Toll-Free	Phone
Earl May Seed & Nursery	208 N Elm St	Shenandoah	IA	51603	**877-800-5556**	712-246-1020
Gardener's Supply Co	128 Intervale Rd	Burlington	VT	05401	**800-863-1700**	802-660-3500
Greenbrier Farms Inc	225 Sign Pine Rd	Chesapeake	VA	23322	**800-829-2141**	757-421-2141
Home & Garden Showplace	8600 W Bryn Mawr	Chicago	IL	60631	**877-502-4641**	773-695-5000
Home Depot Inc	2455 Paces Ferry Rd NW *NYSE: HD* ■ *Cust Svc	Atlanta	GA	30339	**800-553-3199***	770-433-8211
Johnson's Garden Centers	2707 W 13th St	Wichita	KS	67203	**888-542-8463**	316-942-1443
JW Jung Seed Co	335 S High St	Randolph	WI	53956	**800-297-3123**	
Lowe's Cos Inc	1000 Lowe's Blvd *NYSE: LOW*	Mooresville	NC	28117	**800-445-6937**	704-758-1000
McKay Nursery Company Inc	750 S Monroe St PO Box 185	Waterloo	WI	53594	**800-236-4242**	920-478-2121
Milaeger's Inc	4838 Douglas Ave	Racine	WI	53402	**800-669-1229**	262-639-2040
Panhandle Co-op Assn	401 S Beltline Hwy W *Cust Svc	Scottsbluff	NE	69361	**800-732-4546***	308-632-5301
Plants of the Southwest	3095 Agua Fria Rd	Santa Fe	NM	87507	**800-788-7333**	505-438-8888
Pleasant View Gardens Inc	7316 Pleasant St	Loudon	NH	03307	**866-862-2974**	603-435-8361
Ritchie Tractor	1746 W Lmar Alxander Pkwy	Maryville	TN	37801	**888-319-0282**	865-981-3199
Round Butte Seed Growers Inc	505 C St	Culver	OR	97734	**866-385-7001**	541-546-5222
Village Nurseries	1589 N Main St	Orange	CA	92867	**800-542-0209**	
Wal-Mart Stores Inc	702 SW Eigth St *NYSE: WMT* ■ *Cust Svc	Bentonville	AR	72716	**800-925-6278***	479-273-4000
Weingartz Supply Co	46061 Van Dyke Ave	Utica	MI	48317	**855-669-7278**	586-731-7240
White Flower Farm Inc	30 Irene St *Cust Svc	Torrington	CT	06790	**800-411-6159***	860-496-9624

325 GAS STATIONS

SEE ALSO Convenience Stores

Company	Address	City	State	ZIP	Toll-Free	Phone
Alpena Oil Co Inc	235 Water St	Alpena	MI	49707	**800-968-1098**	989-356-1098
AMBEST Inc	5115 Maryland Way	Brentwood	TN	37027	**800-910-7220**	615-371-5187
B&t Service Station Contractors	630 S Frontage Rd	Nipomo	CA	93444	**888-862-2552**	805-929-8944
BP PLC	28100 Torch Pkwy *NYSE: BP*	Warrenville	IL	60555	**800-333-3991**	
Busler Enterprises Inc	2601 N St Joseph Ave	Evansville	IN	47720	**800-457-3232**	812-424-7511
Chevron Corp	6001 Bollinger Canyon Rd *NYSE: CVX* ■ *Cust Svc	San Ramon	CA	94583	**800-368-8357***	925-842-1000
Dakota Plains Co-op	151 Ninth Ave NW	Valley City	ND	58072	**800-288-7922**	701-845-0812
Dunlap Oil Company Inc	759 S Haskell Ave	Willcox	AZ	85643	**800-854-1646**	520-384-2248
Englefield Oil Co	447 James Pkwy *Cust Svc	Heath	OH	43056	**800-837-4458***	740-928-8215
Exxon Mobil Corp	5959 Las Colinas Blvd *NYSE: XOM*	Irving	TX	75039	**800-252-1800**	972-444-1000
Forward Corp	219 N Front St	Standish	MI	48658	**800-664-4501**	989-846-4501
GasAmerica Services Inc	2700 W Main St	Greenfield	IN	46140	**800-643-1948**	317-468-2515
Gate Petroleum Co	9540 San Jose Blvd PO Box 23627	Jacksonville	FL	32241	**866-571-1982**	904-737-7220
Houston Food Bank, The	535 Portwall St	Houston	TX	77029	**866-384-4277**	713-223-3700
Hunt & Sons Inc	5750 S Watt Ave	Sacramento	CA	95829	**800-734-2999**	916-383-4868
Imperial Oil Resources Ltd	237 Fourth Ave SW PO Box 2480 Stn M	Calgary	AB	T2P3M9	**800-567-3776**	
Jubitz Corp	33 NE Middlefield Rd	Portland	OR	97211	**800-523-0600**	503-283-1111
Monroe Oil Co	519 E Franklin St *General	Monroe	NC	28112	**800-452-2717***	704-289-5438
NELLA Oil Co	2360 Lindbergh St	Auburn	CA	95602	**800-995-0401**	530-885-0401
Ney Oil Company Inc	145 S Water St	Ney	OH	43549	**800-962-9839**	419-658-2324
O'Connell Oil Assoc Inc	545 Merrill Rd	Pittsfield	MA	01201	**800-464-4894**	413-499-4800
Pilot Travel Centers LLC	5508 Lonas Dr	Knoxville	TN	37939	**800-562-6210**	865-938-1439
RaceTrac Petroleum Inc	3225 Cumberland Blvd Ste 100	Atlanta	GA	30339	**888-636-5589**	770-431-7600
Rip Griffin Truck Travel Ctr Inc	4710 Fourth St	Lubbock	TX	79416	**800-333-9330**	806-795-8785
Sampson-Bladen Oil Co Inc	510 Commerce St PO Box 469	Clinton	NC	28329	**800-849-4177**	910-592-4177
Scott-Gross Company Inc	664 Magnolia Ave	Lexington	KY	40505	**800-967-6874**	
Shirtcliff Oil Co	PO Box 6003	Myrtle Creek	OR	97457	**800-422-0536**	541-863-5268
Speedway LLC	500 Speedway Dr *Cust Svc	Enon	OH	45323	**800-643-1948***	937-864-3001
Spencer Cos Inc	120 Woodson St	Huntsville	AL	35801	**800-633-2910**	256-533-1150
Thornton Oil Corp	10101 Linn Stn Rd Ste 200	Louisville	KY	40223	**800-928-8022**	502-425-8022
Town Pump Inc	600 S Main St	Butte	MT	59701	**800-823-4931**	406-497-6700
TravelCenters of America	24601 Ctr Ridge Rd Ste 200	Westlake	OH	44145	**800-632-9240**	440-808-9100
True North Energy LLC	5565 Airport Hwy	Toledo	OH	43615	**888-245-9336**	419-868-6800
UPI Energy LP	105 Silvercreek Pkwy N Ste 200	Guelph	ON	N1H8M1	**800-396-2667**	519-821-2667
Vermont Gas Systems Inc	85 Swift St	South Burlington	VT	05403	**800-639-8081**	802-863-4511
W & H Co-op Oil Co	407 13th St N	Humboldt	IA	50548	**800-392-3816**	515-332-2782
Wallis Oil Co	106 E Washington St	Cuba	MO	65453	**800-467-6652**	573-885-2277
Wesco Inc	1460 Whitehall Rd	Muskegon	MI	49445	**800-968-0200**	

326 GAS TRANSMISSION - NATURAL GAS

Companies that transmit or store natural gas but do not distribute it.

Company	Address	City	State	ZIP	Toll-Free	Phone
ANR Pipeline Co	717 Texas St	Houston	TX	77002	**800-827-5267**	832-320-5230
Boardwalk Pipeline Partners LP	3800 Frederica St *NYSE: BWP*	Owensboro	KY	42301	**866-913-2122**	270-686-3620
Cheniere Energy Inc	700 Milam St Ste 800 *NYSE: LNG*	Houston	TX	77002	**877-375-5002**	713-375-5000
Duke Energy Corp	550 S Tryon St Mail Drop WP 890	Charlotte	NC	28202	**800-521-2232**	713-627-5400
Gas Transmission-Northwest	1400 SW Fifth Ave Ste 900	Portland	OR	97201	**888-750-6275**	
Iroquois Gas Transmission System LP	1 Corporate Dr Ste 600	Shelton	CT	06484	**800-888-3982**	203-925-7200
Kern River Gas Transmission Co	2755 E Cottonwood Pkwy Ste 300	Salt Lake City	UT	84121	**800-420-7500**	801-937-6000
Kinder Morgan	1001 Louisiana St Ste 1000 *NYSE: KMI*	Houston	TX	77002	**800-247-4122**	713-369-9000
Kinder Morgan Energy Partners LP	500 Dallas St Ste 1000 *NYSE: KMI*	Houston	TX	77002	**866-208-3372**	713-369-9000
Kinder Morgan Management LLC	500 Dallas St 1 Allen Ctr Ste 1000 *NYSE: KMI*	Houston	TX	77002	**800-781-4152**	713-369-9000
Northern Natural Gas Co	1111 S 103rd St	Omaha	NE	68124	**877-654-0646**	402-398-7000
Questar Gas Management Co	PO Box 45360	Salt Lake City	UT	84145	**800-323-5517**	801-324-5111
Spark Energy Gas LP	2105 Citywest Blvd	Houston	TX	77042	**877-547-7275**	
TransCanada Pipelines Ltd	450 First St SW	Calgary	AB	T2P5H1	**800-661-3805**	403-920-2000

				Toll-Free	Phone
Tri-Gas & Oil Company Inc 3941 Federalsburg Hwy PO Box 465	Federalsburg	MD	21632	**800-638-7802**	410-754-8184
WBI Energy 1250 W Century Ave	Bismarck	ND	58503	**877-924-4677**	701-530-1064
WBI Holdings Inc 1250 W Century Ave *General	Bismarck	ND	58503	**877-924-4677***	
Williams Gas Pipeline Gulfstream 1905 Intermodal Cir Ste 310	Palmetto	FL	34221	**800-440-8475**	
Williams Partners LP 1 Williams Ctr *NYSE: WPZ*	Tulsa	OK	74172	**800-600-3782**	918-573-2000

327 GASKETS, PACKING, SEALING DEVICES

SEE ALSO Automotive Parts & Supplies - Mfr

				Toll-Free	Phone
Akron Gasket & Packing Enterprises Inc 445 NE Ave	Tallmadge	OH	44278	**800-888-2088**	330-633-3742
American Casting & Manufacturing Corp 51 Commercial St	Plainview	NY	11803	**800-342-0333**	516-349-7010
American Packing & Gasket Co (APG) 6039 Armour Dr PO Box 213	Houston	TX	77020	**800-888-5223**	713-675-5271
APM Hexseal Corp 44 Honeck St	Englewood	NJ	07631	**800-498-9034**	201-569-5700
Apple Rubber Products Inc 310 Erie St *Cust Svc	Lancaster	NY	14086	**800-828-7745***	716-684-6560
AR Thomson Group 7930 130th St	Surrey	BC	V3W0H7	**800-410-9116**	604-507-6050
Atlantic Gasket Corp 3908 Frankford Ave	Philadelphia	PA	19124	**800-229-8881**	215-533-6400
Auburn Manufacturing Co 29 Stack St	Middletown	CT	06457	**800-427-5387**	860-346-6677
AW Chesterton Co 500 Unicorn Pk Dr	Woburn	MA	01801	**888-400-4872**	781-438-7000
Bal Seal Engineering Company Inc 19650 Pauling	Foothill Ranch	CA	92610	**800-366-1006**	949-460-2100
Bentley Mfg Company Inc 520 Pk Industrial Dr	La Habra	CA	90631	**800-424-2425**	562-501-2955
California Gasket & Rubber Corp 533 W Collins Ave	Orange	CA	92867	**800-635-7084**	310-323-4250
Calpico Inc 1387 San Mateo Ave	South San Francisco	CA	94080	**800-998-9115**	650-588-2241
CE Conover & Company Inc 4106 Blanche Rd	Bensalem	PA	19020	**800-266-6837**	215-639-6666
CGR Products Inc 4655 US Hwy 29 N	Greensboro	NC	27405	**877-313-6785**	336-621-4568
Chicago Gasket Co 1285 W N Ave	Chicago	IL	60622	**800-833-5666**	773-486-3060
Chicago-Wilcox Mfg Co 16928 State St PO Box 126	South Holland	IL	60473	**800-323-5282**	
Cometic Gasket Inc 8090 Auburn Rd	Concord	OH	44077	**800-752-9850**	440-354-0777
Corpus Christi Gasket & Fastener Inc PO Box 4074	Corpus Christi	TX	78469	**800-460-6366**	361-884-6366
Ct Gasket & Polymer Company Inc 12308 Cutten Rd	Houston	TX	77066	**800-299-1685**	
Eagle Burgmann Industries LP 10035 Brookriver Dr *General	Houston	TX	77040	**800-303-7735***	
Flow Dry Technology Inc 379 Albert Rd PO Box 190	Brookville	OH	45309	**800-533-0077**	937-833-2161
Flowserve Corp 5215 N O'Connor Blvd Ste 2300 *NYSE: FLS*	Irving	TX	75039	**800-350-1082**	972-443-6500
Gasket Manufacturing Co 18001 Main St	Gardena	CA	90248	**800-442-7538**	310-217-5600
Gaskets Inc 301 W Hwy 16	Rio	WI	53960	**800-558-1833**	920-992-3137
Houston Mfg Specialty Company Inc 9909 Wallisville Rd	Houston	TX	77013	**800-231-6030**	713-675-7400
IG Inc 720 S Sara Rd	Mustang	OK	73064	**800-654-8433**	405-376-9393
Ilene Industries Inc 301 Stanley Blvd	Shelbyville	TN	37160	**800-251-1602**	931-684-8731
Industrial Custom Products Inc 2801 37th Ave NE	Minneapolis	MN	55421	**800-654-0886**	612-781-2255
Industrial Gasket & Shim Company Inc (IGS) 200 Country Club Rd	Meadow Lands	PA	15347	**800-229-1447**	724-222-5800
Intek Plastic Inc 1000 Spiral Blvd	Hastings	MN	55033	**888-468-3531**	
Interface Solutions Inc 216 Wohlsen Way	Lancaster	PA	17603	**800-942-7538**	
Jade Engineered Plastic Inc 121 Broadcommon Rd	Bristol	RI	02809	**800-557-9155**	401-253-4440
Kimber Manufacturing Inc 555 Taxter Rd Ste 235	Elmsford	NY	10523	**888-243-4522**	406-758-2222
Lamons Gasket Co 7300 Airport Blvd	Houston	TX	77061	**800-231-6906**	713-222-0284
Marco Rubber 35 Woodworkers Way	Seabrook	NH	03874	**800-775-6525**	603-468-3600
Netherland Rubber Co 2931 Exon Ave	Cincinnati	OH	45241	**800-582-1877**	513-733-0883
Novagard Solutions Inc 5109 Hamilton Ave	Cleveland	OH	44114	**800-380-0138**	216-881-8111
Ohio Gasket & Shim Company Inc 976 Evans Ave	Akron	OH	44305	**800-321-2438**	330-630-2030
Omega Shielding Products Inc 1384 Pompton Ave	Cedar Grove	NJ	07009	**800-828-5784**	973-890-7455
Pacific States Felt & Mfg Company Inc 23850 Clawiter Rd	Hayward	CA	94545	**800-566-8866**	510-783-0277
Pemko Mfg Company Inc 4226 Transport St	Ventura	CA	93003	**800-283-9988**	805-642-2600
PPC Mechanical Seals 2769 Mission Dr	Baton Rouge	LA	70805	**800-731-7325**	225-356-4333
Press-Seal Gasket Corp 2424 W State Blvd	Fort Wayne	IN	46808	**800-348-7325**	260-436-0521
Presscut Industries Inc 1730 Briercroft Ct	Carrollton	TX	75006	**800-442-4924**	972-389-0615
Rotor Clip Company Inc 187 Davidson Ave *Cust Svc	Somerset	NJ	08873	**800-557-6867***	732-469-7333
Schlegel Systems Inc 1555 Jefferson Rd	Rochester	NY	14623	**888-924-7694**	585-427-7200
Seal Methods Inc 11915 Shoemaker Ave	Santa Fe Springs	CA	90670	**800-423-4777**	562-944-0291
Sealing Devices Inc 4400 Walden Ave *Cust Svc	Lancaster	NY	14086	**800-727-3257***	716-684-7600
Sealing Equipment Products Co Inc 123 Airpark Industrial Rd *Cust Svc	Alabaster	AL	35007	**800-633-4770***	
Sorbothane Inc 2144 State Rt 59	Kent	OH	44240	**800-838-3906**	330-678-9444
Specification Rubber Products Inc 1568 First St N	Alabaster	AL	35007	**800-633-3415**	205-663-2521
Sur-Seal Gasket & Packing Inc 6156 Wesselman Rd	Cincinnati	OH	45248	**800-345-8966**	
T & E Industries Inc 215 Watchung Ave *Sales	Orange	NJ	07050	**800-245-7080***	973-672-5454
Triseal Corp 11920 Price Rd	Hebron	IL	60034	**800-910-7325**	815-648-2473
UTEX Industries Inc 10810 Katy Fwy Ste 100	Houston	TX	77043	**800-359-9230**	713-467-1000
Vellumoid Inc 54 Rockdale St	Worcester	MA	01606	**800-609-5558**	508-853-2500
William H Harvey 4334 S 67th St	Omaha	NE	68117	**800-321-9532**	402-331-1175
Zero International Inc 415 Concord Ave	Bronx	NY	10455	**800-635-5335**	718-585-3230

328 GIFT SHOPS

SEE ALSO Card Shops ; Duty-Free Shops ; Home Furnishings Stores

				Toll-Free	Phone
Atlantic Center For The Arts Inc 1414 Art Ctr Ave	New Smyrna Beach	FL	32168	**800-393-6975**	386-427-6975
Brookstone Inc 1 Innovation Way *Cust Svc	Merrimack	NH	03054	**800-846-3000***	603-880-9500
CM Paula Co 6049 Hi-Tek Ct	Mason	OH	45040	**800-543-4464**	
Disney Consumer Products 500 S Buena Vista St *PR	Burbank	CA	91521	**855-553-4763***	818-560-1000
GiftCertificates.com 11510 Blondo St	Omaha	NE	68164	**800-773-7368**	
Historical Research Ctr Inc 2107 Corporate Dr	Boynton Beach	FL	33426	**800-985-9956**	
Mole Hollow Candles Ltd 208 Charlton Rd Rt 20 PO Box 223 *Cust Svc	Sturbridge	MA	01566	**800-445-6653***	
Olympia Promotions & Distribution 226 E Jericho Tpke	Mineola	NY	11501	**800-846-7874**	516-775-4500
Oregon Connection 1125 S First St	Coos Bay	OR	97420	**800-255-5318**	541-267-7804
San Francisco Music Box Co 5370 W 95th St	Prairie Village	KS	66207	**800-227-2190**	
Sanrio Inc 570 Eccles Ave	South San Francisco	CA	94080	**800-759-6454**	650-952-2880
Silver Towne LP 120 E Union City Pike PO Box 424	Winchester	IN	47394	**800-788-7481**	765-584-7481
Tuesday Morning Corp 6250 LBJ Fwy *NASDAQ: TUES*	Dallas	TX	75240	**800-457-0099**	972-387-3562
Wendell August Forge Inc 2074 Leesburg-Grove City Rd	Mercer	PA	16137	**866-354-5192**	724-748-9501
Yankee Candle Company Inc PO Box 110	South Deerfield	MA	01373	**877-803-6890**	413-665-8306

329 GIFTS & NOVELTIES - WHOL

				Toll-Free	Phone
Accoutrements 10915 47th Ave W	Mukilteo	WA	98275	**800-886-2221**	425-349-3838
Blair Cedar & Novelty Works Inc 680 W US Hwy 54	Camdenton	MO	65020	**800-325-3943**	573-346-2235
Drysdales Inc 3220 S Memorial Dr	Tulsa	OK	74145	**800-444-6481**	918-664-6481
Fridgedoor.com 65 School St	Quincy	MA	02169	**800-955-3741**	617-770-7913
Hayes Specialties Corp 1761 E Genesee	Saginaw	MI	48601	**800-248-3603**	989-755-6541
Hornung's Golf Products Inc 815 Morris St	Fond du Lac	WI	54935	**800-323-3569**	920-922-2640
Sanrio Inc 570 Eccles Ave	South San Francisco	CA	94080	**800-759-6454**	650-952-2880
Star Sales Company Inc 1803 N Central St	Knoxville	TN	37917	**800-347-9494**	781-933-2145
Trends International LLC 5188 W 74th St	Indianapolis	IN	46268	**866-406-7771**	317-388-1212
Unique Industries Inc 4750 League Island Blvd	Philadelphia	PA	19112	**800-888-0559**	215-336-4300
US Balloon Mfg Company Inc 140 58th St	Brooklyn	NY	11220	**800-285-4000**	718-492-9700
Variety Distributors Inc 609 Seventh St	Harlan	IA	51537	**800-274-1095**	712-755-2184
WinCraft Inc 1124 W Fifth St	Winona	MN	55987	**800-533-8006**	507-454-5510

330 GLASS - FLAT, PLATE, TEMPERED

				Toll-Free	Phone
AGC Flat Galss North America Inc 11175 Cicero Dr Ste 400	Alpharetta	GA	30022	**800-251-0441**	404-446-4200

				Toll-Free	Phone
Anthony International 12391 Montera Ave	Sylmar	CA	91342	**800-772-0900**	818-365-9451
Apogee Enterprises Inc 4400 W 78th St Ste 520 *NASDAQ: APOG*	Minneapolis	MN	55435	**877-752-3432**	952-835-1874
Basco Shower Enclosures 7201 Snider Rd	Mason	OH	45040	**800-543-1938**	513-573-1900
Binswanger Glass 965 Ridge Lk Blvd Ste 305	Memphis	TN	38120	**800-365-9922**	
Bullseye Glass Co 3722 SE 21st Ave	Portland	OR	97202	**888-220-3002**	503-232-8887
D & W Inc 941 Oak St	Elkhart	IN	46514	**800-255-0829**	574-264-9674
Glaz-Tech Industries Inc 2207 E Elvira Rd	Tucson	AZ	85756	**800-755-8062**	520-629-0268
Gray Glass Co 217-44 98th Ave	Queens Village	NY	11429	**800-523-3320**	718-217-2943
Guardian Industries Corp 2300 Harmon Rd	Auburn Hills	MI	48326	**800-822-5599**	248-340-1800
Hartung Agalite Glass Co 17830 W Valley Hwy	Seattle	WA	98188	**800-552-2227**	425-656-2626
Hartung Glass Industries 10450 SW Ridder Rd	Wilsonville	OR	97070	**800-552-2227**	503-682-3846
Kokomo Opalescent Glass Co 1310 S Market St	Kokomo	IN	46902	**877-475-6329**	765-457-8136
Northwestern Industries Inc 2500 W Jameson St	Seattle	WA	98199	**800-426-2771**	206-285-3140
ODL Inc 215 E Roosevelt Ave	Zeeland	MI	49464	**800-253-3900**	616-772-9111
Oldcastle BuildingEnvelope 5005 Lyndon B Johnson Fwy Ste 1050	Dallas	TX	75244	**866-653-2278**	
Prelco Inc 94 Blvd Cartier	Rivi Re-Du-Loup	QC	G5R2M9	**800-463-1325**	418-862-2274
Rainbow Art Glass Inc 1761 Rt 34 S	Farmingdale	NJ	07727	**800-526-2356**	732-681-6003
Spectrum Glass Co PO Box 646	Woodinville	WA	98072	**800-426-3120**	425-483-6699
Tru Vue Inc 9400 W 55th St	McCook	IL	60525	**800-621-8339**	708-485-5080
Viracon Inc 800 Pk Dr	Owatonna	MN	55060	**800-533-2080**	507-451-9555
Virginia Mirror Co Inc 300 Moss St S	Martinsville	VA	24112	**800-368-3011**	276-632-9816
Wasco Products Inc 85 Spencer Dr Unit A	Wells	ME	04073	**800-388-0293**	207-324-8060

331 GLASS FIBERS

				Toll-Free	Phone
Capitol Aluminum & Glass Corp 1276 W Main St	Bellevue	OH	44811	**800-331-8268**	419-483-7050
Fiberoptics Technology Inc 1 Quassett Rd *Cust Svc	Pomfret	CT	06258	**800-433-5248***	860-928-0443
Novatech Group Inc 160 Murano St	Sainte-julie	QC	J3E0C6	**844-986-8001**	
Sentinel Process 3265 Sunset Ln	Hatboro	PA	19040	**800-345-3569**	919-462-7108

331-4 Military Hospitals

				Toll-Free	Phone
Brooke Army Medical Ctr (BAMC) 3551 Roger Brooke Dr	Fort Sam Houston	TX	78234	**800-443-2262**	210-916-4141
Darnall Army Medical Ctr 36000 Darnall Loop	Fort Hood	TX	76544	**800-305-6421**	254-288-8000
David Grant US Air Force Medical Ctr 101 Bodin Cir	Travis AFB	CA	94535	**800-264-3462**	707-423-3735
Keller Army Community Hospital 900 Washington Rd	West Point	NY	10996	**800-552-2907**	845-938-7992
Naval Hospital Bremerton 1 Bo1 Rd	Bremerton	WA	98312	**800-422-1383**	360-475-4000
Tripler Army Medical Ctr 1 Jarrett White Rd Tripler AMC	Honolulu	HI	96859	**877-880-2184**	808-433-6661
US Air Force 375th Medical Group 310 W Losey St	Scott AFB	IL	62225	**866-683-2778**	

332 GLASS PRODUCTS - INDUSTRIAL (CUSTOM)

				Toll-Free	Phone
Abrisa Technologies 200 S Hallock Dr	Santa Paula	CA	93060	**877-622-7472**	
Flex-O-Lite Inc 50 Crestwood Executive Ctr Ste 522	Saint Louis	MO	63126	**800-325-9525**	
Henderson Glass Inc 715 S Blvd E	Rochester Hills	MI	48307	**800-694-0672**	
King Precision Glass Inc 177 S Indian Hill Blvd	Claremont	CA	91711	**866-554-2773**	909-626-3526
Lang-Mekra North America LLC 101 Tillessen Blvd	Ridgeway	SC	29130	**888-635-7248**	803-337-5264
Lenoir Mirror Company Inc 401 Kincaid St	Lenoir	NC	28645	**800-438-8204**	828-728-3271
North American Specialty Glass 2175 Kumry Rd PO Box 70	Trumbauersville	PA	18970	**888-785-5962**	215-536-0333
Precision Electronic Glass Inc 1013 Hendee Rd	Vineland	NJ	08360	**800-982-4734**	856-691-2234
Richland Glass Company Inc 1640 SW Blvd	Vineland	NJ	08360	**800-959-0312**	856-691-1697
Swift Glass Company Inc 131 W 22nd St	Elmira Heights	NY	14903	**800-537-9438**	607-733-7166

333 GLASSWARE - LABORATORY & SCIENTIFIC

				Toll-Free	Phone
Ace Glass Inc 1430 NW Blvd PO Box 688	Vineland	NJ	08360	**800-223-4524**	856-692-3333
Bellco Glass Inc 340 Edrudo Rd	Vineland	NJ	08360	**800-257-7043**	856-691-1075
Quadrex Corp PO Box 3881 *Sales	Woodbridge	CT	06525	**800-275-7033***	203-393-3112
Wale Apparatus Co Inc 400 Front St	Hellertown	PA	18055	**800-334-9253**	610-838-7047
WB Bottle Supply Company Inc 3400 S Clement Ave	Milwaukee	WI	53207	**800-738-3931**	414-482-4300

334 GLASSWARE & POTTERY - HOUSEHOLD

SEE ALSO Table & Kitchen Supplies - China & Earthenware

				Toll-Free	Phone
Anchor Hocking Co 519 Pierce Ave	Lancaster	OH	43130	**800-562-7511**	740-681-6478
Berney-Karp Inc 3350 E 26th St	Los Angeles	CA	90058	**800-237-6395**	323-260-7122
Blenko Glass Co PO Box 67	Milton	WV	25541	**877-425-3656**	304-743-9081
Ceramo Company Inc 681 Kasten Dr	Jackson	MO	63755	**800-325-8303**	573-243-3138
Enesco LLC 225 Windsor Dr	Itasca	IL	60143	**800-436-3726**	630-875-5300
Fenton Art Glass Co 700 Elizabeth St *Cust Svc	Williamstown	WV	26187	**800-933-6766***	304-375-6122
Friedman Bros Decorative Arts 9015 NW 105th Way	Medley	FL	33178	**800-327-1065**	305-887-3170
Gardner Glass Products Inc 301 Elkin Hwy PO Box 1570	North Wilkesboro	NC	28659	**800-334-7267**	
Haeger Industries Inc 7 Maiden Ln *Cust Svc	Dundee	IL	60118	**800-288-2529***	847-426-3441
Haggerty Enterprises Inc 370 Kimberly Dr	Carol Stream	IL	60188	**800-336-5282**	630-315-3300
Libbey Inc 300 Madison Ave PO Box 10060 *NYSE: LBY*	Toledo	OH	43699	**888-794-8469**	419-325-2100
Marshall Pottery 4901 Elysian Fields Rd	Marshall	TX	75672	**888-768-8721**	903-927-5400
Pfaltzgraff Co PO Box 21769	York	PA	17402	**800-999-2811**	
Swarovski North America Ltd 1 Kenney Dr	Cranston	RI	02920	**800-289-4900**	401-463-6400

335 GLOBAL DISTRIBUTION SYSTEMS (GDSS)

A global distribution system (GDS) is a computer reservations system that includes reservations databases of air travel suppliers in many countries. GDSs typically are owned jointly by airlines operating in different countries.

				Toll-Free	Phone
Amadeus North America Inc 3470 NW 82nd Ave Ste 1000	Miami	FL	33122	**888-262-3387**	305-499-6000
Pegasus Solutions Inc 5430 LBJ Fwy Ste 1100	Dallas	TX	75240	**800-843-4343**	214-234-4000

336 GOURMET SPECIALTY SHOPS

				Toll-Free	Phone
Graber Olive House Inc 315 E Fourth St	Ontario	CA	91764	**800-996-5483**	
Harry & David Holdings Inc 2500 S Pacific Hwy *Cust Svc	Medford	OR	97501	**877-322-1200***	
Hickory Farms Inc 811 Madison Ave	Toledo	OH	43604	**800-753-8558**	
Logan Farms Honey Glazed Hams 10560 Westheimer Rd	Houston	TX	77042	**800-833-4267**	713-781-4335

337 GOVERNMENT - CITY

				Toll-Free	Phone
Bridgeport City Hall 999 Broad St	Bridgeport	CT	06604	**800-978-2828**	203-576-7201
Cheyenne City Hall 2101 O'Neil Ave	Cheyenne	WY	82001	**855-491-1859**	307-637-6200
Greenville City Hall 206 S Main St	Greenville	SC	29601	**800-829-4477**	864-232-2273
Ocean City City Hall 301 Baltimore Ave	Ocean City	MD	21842	**800-626-2326**	410-289-8931
Ottawa City Hall 110 Laurier Ave W	Ottawa	ON	K1P1J1	**866-261-9799**	613-580-2400
San Diego City Hall 202 C St	San Diego	CA	92101	**866-470-1308**	619-533-4000

338 GOVERNMENT - COUNTY

				Toll-Free	Phone
Aiken County 828 Richland Ave W	Aiken	SC	29801	**866-876-7074**	803-642-2012
Aleutians East Borough 3380 C St Ste 205	Anchorage	AK	99503	**888-383-2699**	907-274-7555
Allen County 1 N Washington St	Iola	KS	66749	**866-444-1407**	620-365-1407
Allen Parish PO Box 1280	Oberlin	LA	70655	**888-639-4868**	337-639-4868
Ashe County Chamber of Commerce 1 N Jefferson Ave Ste C PO Box 31	West Jefferson	NC	28694	**888-343-2743**	336-846-9550
Assumption Parish 4813 Hwy 1 PO Box 520	Napoleonville	LA	70390	**800-315-9513**	985-369-7435
Atchison County 405 S Main St PO Box 243	Rock Port	MO	64482	**800-989-4115**	660-744-6562
Auglaize County 209 S Blackhoof St Ste 201	Wapakoneta	OH	45895	**877-836-3206**	419-739-6710

	City	State	ZIP	Toll-Free	Phone
Bath County PO Box 309	Warm Springs	VA	24484	**888-823-1710**	540-839-7221
Bay County 515 Ctr Ave Ste 101	Bay City	MI	48708	**877-229-9960**	989-895-4280
Bell County 101 E Central Ave PO Box 480	Belton	TX	76513	**800-460-2355**	254-933-5160
Bennington County 100 Veterans Memorial Dr	Bennington	VT	05201	**800-229-0252**	802-447-3311
Benzie County 448 Ct Pl	Beulah	MI	49617	**800-315-3593**	231-882-9671
Blaine County 420 Ohio St	Chinook	MT	59523	**800-666-6124**	406-442-9830
Boone County 601 N Main St	Belvidere	IL	61008	**877-225-7077**	815-547-4770
Box Elder County 01 S Main St	Brigham City	UT	84302	**877-390-2326**	435-734-3300
Bucks County 55 E Ct St	Doylestown	PA	18901	**888-942-8257**	215-348-6000
Burleigh County 514 E Thayer Ave PO Box 1055	Bismarck	ND	58502	**877-222-6682**	701-222-6690
Butler County 205 W Central Ave	El Dorado	KS	67042	**800-822-6104**	316-322-4300
Camden County 520 Market St Rm 102	Camden	NJ	08102	**866-226-3362**	856-225-5300
Carbon County PO Box 1017	Rawlins	WY	82301	**800-228-3547**	
Caribou County 159 S Main	Soda Springs	ID	83276	**800-972-7660**	208-547-4324
Carroll County 8215 Black Oak Rd	Mount Carroll	IL	61053	**800-485-0145**	815-244-2035
Carter County 101 1St Ave SW	Ardmore	OK	73401	**800-231-8668**	580-223-8162
Charlevoix County 203 Antrim St	Charlevoix	MI	49720	**800-548-9157**	231-547-7200
Cherokee County 165 E Sixth St Ste 203 Ste 203	Rusk	TX	75785	**800-541-2524**	903-683-6540
Chester County 313 W Market St Ste 6202 PO Box 2748	West Chester	PA	19380	**800-692-1100**	610-344-6100
Chisago County 313 N Main St	Center City	MN	55012	**888-234-1246**	651-257-1300
Clarke County 100 Church St PO Box 689	Quitman	MS	39355	**877-462-3222**	601-776-5701
Clinton County 137 Margaret St Ste 208	Plattsburgh	NY	12901	**877-873-7283**	518-565-4600
Coconino County 219 E Cherry Ave	Flagstaff	AZ	86001	**800-559-9289**	928-774-5011
Collin County 200 S McDonald St Ste 120	McKinney	TX	75069	**800-336-5996**	972-548-4100
Comal County 199 Main Plaza	New Braunfels	TX	78130	**877-724-9475**	830-221-1100
County of Greene 93 E High St	Waynesburg	PA	15370	**888-852-5399**	724-852-5210
Crawford County 225 N Beaumont Rd	Prairie du Chien	WI	53821	**877-794-2372**	608-326-0200
Crow Wing County 326 Laurel St	Brainerd	MN	56401	**888-829-6680**	218-824-1067
Dauphin County 2 S Second St 3rd Fl	Harrisburg	PA	17101	**800-328-0058**	717-780-6636
Dorchester County 501 Ct Ln	Cambridge	MD	21613	**800-272-9829**	410-228-1700
Elk County PO Box 606	Howard	KS	67349	**877-504-2490**	620-374-2490
Emmet County 200 Div St Ste 130	Petoskey	MI	49770	**866-731-1204**	231-348-1702
Esmeralda County PO Box 547	Goldfield	NV	89013	**800-884-4072**	775-485-6309
Franklin County 355 W Main St	Malone	NY	12953	**800-397-8686**	518-483-6770
Fremont County 450 N Second St	Lander	WY	82520	**800-967-2297**	307-332-2405
Gates County 200 Ct St	Gatesville	NC	27938	**800-272-9829**	252-357-2411
Gila County 1400 E Ash St	Globe	AZ	85501	**800-304-4452**	928-425-3231
Graham County 34 Wall St Ste 407	Asheville	NC	28801	**866-962-6246**	828-255-0182
Grant County 35 C St NW PO Box 37	Ephrata	WA	98823	**800-572-0119**	509-754-2011
Greeley County 510 Broadway PO Box 656	Tribune	KS	67879	**888-204-1781**	620-376-2548
Green County 1016 16th Ave	Monroe	WI	53566	**800-947-3529**	608-328-9430
Greenbrier County 200 W Washington St	Lewisburg	WV	24901	**800-833-2068**	304-647-6602
Hancock County 12630 Broad St	Sparta	GA	31087	**800-255-0135**	706-444-5746
Hardin County 495 Main St	Savannah	TN	38372	**800-552-3866**	731-925-3921
Hardy County 204 Washington St Rm 111	Moorefield	WV	26836	**800-222-1222**	304-530-0250
Harlan County 311 Main St	Alma	NE	68920	**800-762-5498**	
Harper County 201 N Jennings Ave	Anthony	KS	67003	**877-537-2110**	620-842-5555
Harris County 112 S College St PO Box 426	Hamilton	GA	31811	**888-478-0010**	706-628-0010
Hidalgo County 100 N Closner	Edinburg	TX	78539	**888-318-2811**	956-318-2100
Hinsdale County 311 N Henson St	Lake City	CO	81235	**877-944-7575**	970-944-2225
Hudspeth County 109 Brown St	Sierra Blanca	TX	79851	**888-368-4689**	915-369-2331
Indiana County 350 N Fourth St	Indiana	PA	15701	**888-559-6355**	724-465-3805
Jackson County 3405 S Main St PO Box 155	Newport	AR	72043	**800-234-1040**	870-523-6011
Jefferson County PO Box 890	Dandridge	TN	37725	**877-237-3847**	865-397-9642
Johnson County 111 S Cherry St Ste 1200	Olathe	KS	66061	**800-766-3777**	913-715-0775
Kane County 78 S 100 E	Kanab	UT	84741	**800-733-5263**	435-644-5033
King County 401 5th Ave Ste 800	Seattle	WA	98104	**800-325-6165**	206-296-1586
Klamath County 305 Main St	Klamath Falls	OR	97601	**800-377-6094**	541-883-5134
La Porte County 813 Lincolnway	La Porte	IN	46350	**800-654-3441**	219-326-6808
Lafourche Parish 402 Green St PO Box 5548	Thibodaux	LA	70302	**800-834-8832**	985-446-8427
Lake County 895 Michigan Ave PO Box 130	Baldwin	MI	49304	**800-245-3240**	231-745-4331
LaSalle County 707 E Etna Rd	Ottawa	IL	61350	**800-247-5243**	815-433-3366
Lawrence County County Courthouse 430 Court St	New Castle	PA	16101	**855-564-6116**	724-658-2541
Leavenworth County 300 Walnut St	Leavenworth	KS	66048	**855-893-9533**	913-684-0421
Leelanau County 8527 E Government Ctr Dr	Suttons Bay	MI	49682	**866-256-9711**	231-256-9824
Lewis County 499 US Hwy 33 E Ste 102	Weston	WV	26452	**800-296-7329**	304-269-7328
Lincoln County PO Box 978	Brookhaven	MS	39602	**800-613-4667**	601-833-1411
Madison County 248 SW Range Ave PO Box 237	Madison	FL	32340	**877-272-3642**	850-973-2788
Marion County 100 S Main St	Palmyra	MO	63461	**888-870-5943**	573-769-2549
McCreary County Tourist Commission PO Box 699	Whitley City	KY	42653	**877-209-1012**	606-376-3008
McKean County 500 W Main St	Smethport	PA	16749	**800-482-1280**	814-887-5571
McKenzie County PO Box 699	Watford City	ND	58854	**800-701-2804**	701-444-2804
Mercer County 621 Commerce St PO Box 4088	Bluefield	WV	24701	**800-221-3206**	304-325-8438
Morgan County 1226 Knoxville Hwy	Wartburg	TN	37887	**888-205-5017**	
Morrison County 213 SE First Ave	Little Falls	MN	56345	**866-401-1111**	320-632-2941
Napa County 1195 Third St Ste 310	Napa	CA	94559	**877-279-2976**	707-253-4421
Nassau County PO Box 870	Fernandina Beach	FL	32035	**888-615-4398**	904-491-7300
Nelson County 210 B Ave W Ste 203	Lakota	ND	58344	**800-472-2286**	701-247-2462
Newton County 201 N 3rd St	Kentland	IN	47951	**888-663-9866**	219-474-6081
Northumberland County 201 Market St 2nd Fl	Sunbury	PA	17801	**800-692-4332**	570-988-4167
Northwest Arctic Borough PO Box 1110	Kotzebue	AK	99752	**800-478-1110**	907-442-2500
Noxubee County 503 S Washington St PO Box 308	Macon	MS	39341	**800-487-0165**	
Orange County 200 Dailey Dr	Orange	VA	22960	**866-803-8641**	540-661-4550
Park County 1002 Sheridan Ave	Cody	WY	82414	**800-786-2844**	307-527-8510
Perry County 333 7th St	Tell City	IN	47586	**888-343-6262**	812-547-7933
Pickett County 1 Courthouse Sq Ste 200	Byrdstown	TN	38549	**888-406-4704**	931-864-3798
Pike County 506 Broad St	Milford	PA	18337	**866-681-4947**	570-296-7613
Pine County 635 Northridge Dr NW	Pine City	MN	55063	**800-450-7463**	320-591-1400
Pocahontas County PO Box 275	Marlinton	WV	24954	**800-336-7009**	
Portage County 449 S Meridian St 7th Fl	Ravenna	OH	44266	**800-772-3799**	330-297-3600
Pulaski County 100 N Main St Ste 202	Somerset	KY	42501	**877-655-7154**	606-678-4853
Putnam County 130 Orie Griffin Blvd PO Box 1578	Palatka	FL	32177	**800-426-9975**	386-329-0800
Raleigh County 215 Main St	Beckley	WV	25801	**800-509-6568**	304-255-9178
Ramsey County 15 W Kellogg Blvd	Saint Paul	MN	55102	**866-520-7225**	651-266-8000
Randolph County 110 S Main St	Huntsville	MO	65259	**844-277-6555**	660-277-5822
Roane County 1209 N Kentucky St	Kingston	TN	37763	**888-483-1377**	865-376-5556
Rutland Region Chamber of Commerce 50 Merchants Row	Rutland	VT	05701	**800-756-8880**	802-773-2747
Salem County 94 Market St	Salem	NJ	08079	**877-222-3737**	856-935-7510
San Bernardino County 385 N Arrowhead Ave	San Bernardino	CA	92415	**888-818-8988**	909-387-8306
Santa Fe County 102 Grant Ave	Santa Fe	NM	87504	**877-607-0741**	505-986-6200
Sargent County 355 Main St	Forman	ND	58032	**866-634-8387**	701-724-6241
Sawyer County 10610 Main St Ste 10	Hayward	WI	54843	**877-699-4110**	715-634-4866
Shelby County 612 Ct St	Harlan	IA	51537	**800-735-3942**	712-755-3831
Susquehanna County 75 Public Ave	Montrose	PA	18801	**800-932-0313**	570-278-4600
Towns County 1411 Jack Dayton Cir	Young Harris	GA	30582	**800-984-1543**	706-896-4966
Trego County 18001 283 Hwy	WaKeeney	KS	67672	**877-962-7248**	785-743-6385
Trempealeau County 36245 Main St	Whitehall	WI	54773	**877-538-2311**	715-538-2311
Turner County PO Box 191	Ashburn	GA	31714	**800-436-7442**	229-567-2334
Uintah County 147 E Main St	Vernal	UT	84078	**800-966-4680**	435-781-0770
Union County 1103 S First St	Clayton	NM	88415	**800-390-7858**	575-374-9253
Vermillion County 255 S Main St	Newport	IN	47966	**800-340-8155**	765-492-5345
Waller County 836 Austin St	Hempstead	TX	77445	**800-901-4412**	979-826-3357
Wilcox County 103 N Broad St	Abbeville	GA	31001	**866-694-5824**	229-467-2737
Winneshiek County 201 W Main St	Decorah	IA	52101	**866-227-9874**	563-382-9219
Wood County 1 Courthouse Sq	Bowling Green	OH	43402	**866-860-4140**	419-354-9000
Yates County 417 Liberty St	Penn Yan	NY	14527	**866-212-5160**	315-536-5120
Yazoo County PO Box 186	Yazoo City	MS	39194	**800-381-0662**	662-746-1815

339 GOVERNMENT - STATE

SEE ALSO Sports Commissions & Regulatory Agencies - State ; Student Assistance Programs ; Veterans Nursing Homes - State ; Correctional Facilities - State ; Employment Offices - Government ; Ethics Commissions ; Governors - State ; Legislation Hotlines ; Lotteries, Games, Sweepstakes ; Parks - State

339-1 Alabama

				Toll-Free	*Phone*
Administrative Office of Alabama Courts 300 Dexter Ave	Montgomery	AL	36104	**866-954-9411**	334-954-5000
Conservation & Natural Resources Dept 64 N Union St PO Box 301450	Montgomery	AL	36130	**800-262-3151**	334-242-3486
Crime Victims Compensation Commission 5845 Carmichael Rd	Montgomery	AL	36117	**800-541-9388**	334-290-4420
Emergency Management Agency 5898 County Rd 41 PO Box 2160	Clanton	AL	35046	**800-843-0699**	205-280-2200
Mental Health & Mental Retardation Dept 100 N Union St PO Box 301410	Montgomery	AL	36130	**800-367-0955**	334-242-3454
Public Health Dept 201 Monroe St	Montgomery	AL	36104	**800-252-1818**	334-206-5300
Public Service Commission 100 N Union St RSA Union PO Box 304260	Montgomery	AL	36130	**800-392-8050**	334-242-5218
Rehabilitation Services Dept 602 S Lawrence St	Montgomery	AL	36104	**800-441-7607**	334-293-7500
Securities Commission 770 Washington Ave Ste 570	Montgomery	AL	36130	**800-222-1253**	334-242-2984
State Parks Div 64 N Union St	Montgomery	AL	36130	**800-252-7275**	
Tourism Department 401 Adams Ave PO Box 4927	Montgomery	AL	36104	**800-252-2262**	334-242-4169

339-2 Alaska

				Toll-Free	*Phone*
Banking Securities & Corporations Div 333 Willoughby Ave Fl 9 PO Box 110807	Juneau	AK	99801	**888-925-2521**	907-465-2521
Enterprise Technology Services Div PO Box 110206	Juneau	AK	99811	**888-565-8680**	
Housing Finance Corp 4300 Boniface Pkwy 99504 PO Box 101020	Anchorage	AK	99504	**800-478-2432**	907-338-6100
Military & Veterans Affairs Dept (DMVA) PO Box 5800	Fort Richardson	AK	99505	**888-248-3682**	907-428-6896
Postsecondary Education Commission 3030 Vintage Blvd PO Box 110510	Juneau	AK	99801	**800-441-2962**	907-465-2962
Vocational Rehabilitation Div 801 W Tenth St Ste 200	Juneau	AK	99801	**800-478-2815**	907-465-2814

339-3 Arizona

				Toll-Free	*Phone*
Attorney General 1275 W Washington St	Phoenix	AZ	85007	**888-377-6108**	602-542-5025
Children Youth & Families Div 1789 W Jefferson St	Phoenix	AZ	85007	**866-229-5553**	602-542-0419
Historic Preservation Office 1300 W Washington St	Phoenix	AZ	85007	**800-285-3703**	602-542-4174
Legislature Capitol Complex 1700 W Washington St	Phoenix	AZ	85007	**800-352-8404**	602-926-3559
Motor Vehicle Div PO Box 2100	Phoenix	AZ	85001	**800-251-5866**	602-255-0072
Rehabilitation Services Admin 1789 W Jefferson St 2nd Fl NW	Phoenix	AZ	85007	**800-563-1221**	602-542-3332
Tourism Office 1110 W Washington St Ste 155	Phoenix	AZ	85007	**888-520-3434**	602-364-3700
Treasurer 1700 W Washington St 1st Fl	Phoenix	AZ	85007	**877-365-8310**	602-542-7800
Weights & Measures Dept 4425 W Olive Ave Ste 134	Glendale	AZ	85302	**800-277-6675**	602-771-4920

339-4 Arkansas

				Toll-Free	*Phone*
Attorney General 323 Ctr St Ste 200 *Consumer Info	Little Rock	AR	72201	**800-482-8982***	501-682-2007
Child Support Enforcement Office 1509 W Seventh St	Little Rock	AR	72201	**800-264-2445**	501-682-8398
Crime Victims Reparations Board 323 Ctr St Ste 200	Little Rock	AR	72201	**800-448-3014**	501-682-1020
Game & Fish Commission 2 Natural Resource Dr	Little Rock	AR	72205	**800-364-4263**	501-223-6300
Highway & Transportation Dept 10324 I- 30	Little Rock	AR	72209	**800-245-1672**	501-569-2000
Insurance Dept 1200 W Third St	Little Rock	AR	72201	**800-282-9134**	501-371-2600
Parks & Tourism Dept 1 Capitol Mall	Little Rock	AR	72201	**800-628-8725**	501-682-7777
Rehabilitation Services 525 W Capitol Ave	Little Rock	AR	72201	**800-330-0632**	501-296-1600
Securities Dept 201 E Markham St Rm 300	Little Rock	AR	72201	**800-981-4429**	501-324-9260
Vital Records Div 4815 W Markham St Slot 44	Little Rock	AR	72205	**800-637-9314**	501-661-2336
Worker's Compensation Commission 324 S Spring St	Little Rock	AR	72203	**800-622-4472**	501-682-3930

339-5 California

				Toll-Free	*Phone*
Arts Council 1300 'I' St Ste 930	Sacramento	CA	95814	**800-201-6201**	916-322-6555
Child Support Services Dept PO Box 419064	Sacramento	CA	95741	**866-901-3212**	916-464-5000
Corporations Dept 1515 K St Ste 200	Sacramento	CA	95814	**866-275-2677**	916-445-7205
Corrections Dept PO Box 942883	Sacramento	CA	94283	**877-256-6877**	
Fish & Game Dept 1416 Ninth St 12th Fl	Sacramento	CA	95814	**888-334-2258**	916-445-0411
Health Care Services Dept PO Box 997413 MS 8502	Sacramento	CA	95899	**800-735-2929**	
Housing Finance Agency 500 Capitol Mall Ste 1400	Sacramento	CA	95814	**877-922-5432**	916-322-3991
Parks & Recreation Dept PO Box 942896	Sacramento	CA	94296	**800-777-0369**	916-653-6995
Public Utilities Commission 505 Van Ness Ave	San Francisco	CA	94102	**800-848-5580**	415-703-2782
Teacher Credentialing Commission 1900 Capitol Ave	Sacramento	CA	95814	**888-921-2682**	916-445-7254
Veterans Affairs Dept 1227 'O' St	Sacramento	CA	95814	**800-221-8998**	916-653-2158
Victim Compensation Program PO Box 3036	Sacramento	CA	95812	**800-777-9229**	

339-6 Colorado

				Toll-Free	*Phone*
Aging & Adult Services Div 1575 Sherman St Ground Fl	Denver	CO	80203	**800-773-1366**	303-866-2636
Housing & Finance Authority 1981 Blake St	Denver	CO	80202	**800-877-2432**	303-297-2432
Natural Resources Dept 1313 Sherman St Rm 718	Denver	CO	80203	**800-536-5308**	303-866-3311
Parks & Outdoor Recreation Div 1313 Sherman St Rm 618 *Campground Resv	Denver	CO	80203	**800-678-2267***	303-866-3437
Public Health & Environment Dept (CDPHE) 4300 Cherry Creek Dr S	Denver	CO	80246	**800-886-7689**	303-692-2000
Public Utilities Commission 1560 Broadway Ste 250	Denver	CO	80203	**800-888-0170**	303-894-2000
Regulatory Agencies Dept 1560 Broadway Ste 1550	Denver	CO	80202	**800-886-7675**	303-894-7855
State Court Administrator 1301 Pennsylvania St Ste 300	Denver	CO	80203	**800-888-0001**	303-837-3668
Supreme Court 1560 Broadway Ste 1800	Denver	CO	80202	**877-888-1370**	303-866-6400
Victims Programs Office 700 Kipling St Ste 1000	Lakewood	CO	80215	**888-282-1080**	303-239-5719
Vocational Rehabilitation Div 1575 Sherman St 4th Fl	Denver	CO	80203	**866-870-4595**	303-866-4150
Workers Compensation Div 633 17th St Ste 400	Denver	CO	80202	**888-390-7936**	303-318-8700

339-7 Connecticut

				Toll-Free	*Phone*
Banking Dept 260 Constitution Plaza	Hartford	CT	06103	**800-831-7225**	860-240-8299
Chief Medical Examiner 11 Shuttle Rd	Farmington	CT	06032	**800-842-1508**	860-679-3980
Consumer Protection Dept 165 Capitol Ave	Hartford	CT	06106	**800-842-2649**	860-713-6100
Emergency Management and Homeland Security Div 25 Sigourney St 6th Fl	Hartford	CT	06106	**800-397-8876**	860-256-0800
Higher Education Dept 61 Woodland St	Hartford	CT	06105	**800-842-0229**	860-947-1800
Public Utility Control Dept 10 Franklin Sq	New Britain	CT	06051	**800-382-4586**	860-827-2935
Rehabilitation Services Bureau 25 Sigourney St 11th Fl	Hartford	CT	06106	**800-537-2549**	860-424-4844
State Parks Div 79 Elm St	Hartford	CT	06106	**866-287-2757**	860-424-3000
Veterans Affairs Dept 287 W St	Rocky Hill	CT	06067	**800-447-0961**	860-721-5891
Victim Services Office 225 Spring St 4th Fl	Wethersfield	CT	06109	**800-822-8428**	
Workers' Compensation Commission 21 Oak St 4th Fl	Hartford	CT	06106	**800-223-9675**	860-493-1500
Dept of Consumer Protection 165 Capitol Ave	Hartford	CT	06106	**800-842-2649**	860-713-6100
Dept of Consumer Protection 165 Capitol Ave	Hartford	CT	06106	**800-842-2649**	860-713-6100

339-8 Delaware

				Toll-Free	*Phone*
Agriculture Dept 2320 S DuPont Hwy	Dover	DE	19901	**800-282-8685**	302-739-4811
Child Support Enforcement Div (DCSE) 84A Christiana Rd	New Castle	DE	19720	**800-464-4357**	302-577-7171
Emergency Management Agency 165 Brick Store Landing Rd	Smyrna	DE	19977	**877-729-3362**	302-659-3362
Parks & Recreation Div 89 Kings Hwy *Campground Resv	Dover	DE	19901	**877-987-2757***	302-739-9200
Tourism Office 99 Kings Hwy	Dover	DE	19901	**866-284-7483**	302-739-4271
Weights & Measures Office 2320 S DuPont Hwy	Dover	DE	19901	**800-282-8685**	302-739-4811

339-9 District of Columbia

	City	State	Zip	Toll-Free	Phone
Convention & Tourism Corp 901 7th St NW 4th Fl	Washington	DC	20001	**800-422-8644**	202-789-7000

339-10 Florida

	City	State	Zip	Toll-Free	Phone
Attorney General State Capitol PL-01	Tallahassee	FL	32399	**866-966-7226**	850-487-1963
Business & Professional Regulation Dept 1940 N Monroe St	Tallahassee	FL	32399	**866-532-1440**	850-487-1395
Consumer Services Div 2005 Apalachee Pkwy	Tallahassee	FL	32399	**800-435-7352**	
Education Dept 325 W Gaines St Ste 1514	Tallahassee	FL	32399	**800-445-6739**	850-245-0505
Financial Services Dept 200 E Gaines St	Tallahassee	FL	32399	**800-342-2762**	850-413-3100
Insurance Regulation Office 200 E Gaines St	Tallahassee	FL	32301	**800-342-2762**	850-413-3140
Recreation & Parks Div 3900 Commonwealth Blvd MS 500 *Campground Resv	Tallahassee	FL	32399	**800-326-3521***	850-245-2157
Secretary of State RA Gray Bldg 500 S Bronough St	Tallahassee	FL	32399	**800-955-8771**	850-245-6500
Vocational Rehabilitation Services Div 2002 Old St Augustine Rd Bldg A	Tallahassee	FL	32301	**800-451-4327**	850-245-3399

339-11 Georgia

	City	State	Zip	Toll-Free	Phone
State Government Information 7 Martin Luther King JrDr Ste 643	Atlanta	GA	30303	**800-436-7442**	678-436-7442
Arts Council 260 14th St NW Ste 401	Atlanta	GA	30318	**800-222-6006**	404-685-2400
Corrections Dept 300 Patrol Rd Forsyth	Atlanta	GA	31029	**888-343-5627**	404-656-4661
Emergency Management Agency (GEMA) 935 E Confederate Ave SE PO Box 18055	Atlanta	GA	30316	**800-879-4362**	404-635-7000
Environmental Protection Div 2 Martin Luther King Jr Dr Ste 1152 E Tower	Atlanta	GA	30334	**888-373-5947**	404-657-5947
Governor's Office of Consumer Protection 2 ML King Jr Dr Ste 356	Atlanta	GA	30334	**800-869-1123**	
Securities & Business Regulation Div 2 Martin Luther King Jr Dr W Tower Ste 802	Atlanta	GA	30334	**844-753-7825**	478-207-2440
Tourism Div 75 Fifth St NW Ste 1200 *Resv	Atlanta	GA	30308	**800-255-0056***	404-962-4000

339-12 Hawaii

	City	State	Zip	Toll-Free	Phone
Child Support Enforcement Agency 601 Kamokila Blvd Ste 251	Kapolei	HI	96707	**888-317-9081**	
Taxation Dept 830 Punchbowl St Rm 221	Honolulu	HI	96813	**800-222-3229**	808-587-4242
Vocational Rehabilitation Div 1901 Bachelot St	Honolulu	HI	96817	**800-316-8005**	808-586-9744

339-13 Idaho

	City	State	Zip	Toll-Free	Phone
Aging Commission (ICOA) 341 W Washington Fl 3 PO Box 83720	Boise	ID	83702	**800-926-2588**	208-334-3833
Arts Commission 2410 Old Penitentiary Rd	Boise	ID	83712	**800-278-3863**	208-334-2119
Board of Medicine 1755 N Westgate Dr Ste 140 PO Box 83720	Boise	ID	83704	**800-333-0073**	208-327-7000
Crime Victims Compensation Program PO Box 83720	Boise	ID	83720	**800-950-2110**	208-334-6000
Department of Commerce 700 W State St PO Box 83720	Boise	ID	83720	**800-842-5858**	208-334-2470
Homeland Security Bureau 4040 W Guard St Bldg 600	Boise	ID	83705	**800-344-0984**	208-422-3040
Housing & Finance Assn 565 W Myrtle Ave	Boise	ID	83702	**800-526-7145**	208-331-4882
Parks & Recreation Dept 5657 Warm Springs Ave	Boise	ID	83716	**855-514-2429**	
Public Utilities Commission PO Box 83720	Boise	ID	83720	**800-432-0369**	208-334-0300
Real Estate Commission 575 E Parkcenter Blvd Ste 180	Boise	ID	83706	**866-447-5411**	208-334-3285
Tax Commission 800 E Pk Blvd	Boise	ID	83712	**800-972-7660**	208-334-7660
Tourism Development Div 700 W State St PO Box 83720 *General	Boise	ID	83720	**800-847-4843***	208-334-2470

339-14 Illinois

	City	State	Zip	Toll-Free	Phone
Child Support Enforcement Div 509 S Sixth St	Springfield	IL	62701	**800-447-4278**	
Crime Victims Services Div 100 W Randolf Rd 13th Fl	Chicago	IL	60601	**800-228-3368**	312-814-2581
Human Services Dept 100 S Grand Ave E 3rd Fl	Springfield	IL	62762	**800-843-6154**	217-557-1601
Mental Health Div 100 W Randolf St Ste 3-400	Chicago	IL	60601	**800-252-2923**	312-814-2811
Revenue Dept 101 W Jefferson St	Springfield	IL	62702	**800-732-8866**	217-782-3336
Secretary of State 213 State Capitol	Springfield	IL	62756	**800-252-8980**	217-782-2201
Tourism Bureau 100 W Randolph St Ste 3-400	Chicago	IL	60601	**800-226-6632**	312-814-4732
Veterans Affairs Dept James R. Thompson Ctr 100 W Randolph Ste 5-570	Chicago	IL	60601	**800-437-9824**	312-814-5391
Workers' Compensation Commission 100 W Randolph St 8th Fl	Chicago	IL	60601	**866-352-3033**	312-814-6611

339-15 Indiana

	City	State	Zip	Toll-Free	Phone
State Government Information 402 W Washington St Rm W160A	Indianapolis	IN	46204	**800-457-8283**	317-233-0800
Child Support Bureau 402 W Washington St	Indianapolis	IN	46204	**800-840-8757**	317-232-2350
Consumer Protection Div 402 W Washington St 5th Fl	Indianapolis	IN	46204	**800-382-5516**	317-232-6330
Disability Aging & Rehabilitative Services Div 402 W Washington St Rm W451	Indianapolis	IN	46204	**800-545-7763**	317-232-1147
Environmental Management Dept 100 N Senate Ave Rm 1301	Indianapolis	IN	46204	**800-451-6027**	317-232-8611
Family & Social Services Admin 402 W Washington St Rm W461 PO Box 7083	Indianapolis	IN	46207	**800-545-7763**	
General Assembly State House 200 W Washington St	Indianapolis	IN	46204	**800-382-9842**	317-232-9600
Insurance Dept 311 W Washington St Ste 300 *Cust Svc	Indianapolis	IN	46204	**800-622-4461***	317-232-2385
State Parks & Reservoirs Div 402 W Washington St Rm W298	Indianapolis	IN	46204	**800-622-4931**	317-232-4124
Tourism Development Office 1 N Capitol Ave Ste 100	Indianapolis	IN	46204	**800-457-8283**	317-232-8860
Victims Services Div 101 W Washington St Ste 1170 East Tower	Indianapolis	IN	46204	**800-353-1484**	317-232-1233

339-16 Iowa

	City	State	Zip	Toll-Free	Phone
Adult Children & Family Services Div 1305 E Walnut St	Des Moines	IA	50319	**800-735-2942**	515-281-8746
Child Support Recovery Unit PO Box 9125	Des Moines	IA	50306	**888-229-9223**	
Consumer Protection Div 1305 E Walnut St 2nd Fl	Des Moines	IA	50319	**888-777-4590**	515-281-5926
Elder Affairs Dept 510 E 12th St Ste 2	Des Moines	IA	50309	**800-532-3213**	515-242-3333
Motor Vehicle Div 100 Euclid Ave PO Box 9204	Des Moines	IA	50306	**800-532-1121**	515-244-9124
Revenue & Finance Dept 1305 E Walnut	Des Moines	IA	50319	**800-367-3388**	515-281-3204
Utilities Board 1375 E Ct Ave Rm 69	Des Moines	IA	50319	**877-565-4450**	515-725-7300

339-17 Kansas

	City	State	Zip	Toll-Free	Phone
Consumer Protection Div 534 S Kansas Ave Ste 1210	Topeka	KS	66603	**800-452-6727**	785-296-5059
Healing Arts Board 800 SW Jackson Lower Level Ste A	Topeka	KS	66612	**888-886-7205**	785-296-7413
Insurance Dept 420 SW Ninth St	Topeka	KS	66612	**800-432-2484**	785-296-3071
Travel & Tourism Development Div 1020 S Kansas Ave Ste 200	Topeka	KS	66612	**800-252-6727**	785-296-2009
Treasurer 900 SW Jackson St Ste 201	Topeka	KS	66612	**800-432-0386**	785-296-3171
Workers' Compensation Div 401 SW Topeka Blvd Ste 2	Topeka	KS	66603	**800-332-0353**	785-296-4000

339-18 Kentucky

	City	State	Zip	Toll-Free	Phone
State Government Information 229 W Main St Ste 400	Frankfort	KY	40601	**877-855-3573**	502-875-3733
Arts Council 500 Mero St 21st Fl Capital Plaza Tower	Frankfort	KY	40601	**888-833-2787**	502-564-3757
Child Support Div 730 Schenkel Ln	Frankfort	KY	40601	**800-248-1163**	502-564-2285
Consumer Protection Div 1024 Capital Ctr Dr Ste 200	Frankfort	KY	40601	**888-432-9257**	502-696-5389
Crime Victims Compensation Board 130 Brighton Pk Blvd	Frankfort	KY	40601	**800-469-2120**	502-573-2290
Education Professional Standards Board 100 Airport Dr 3rd Fl	Frankfort	KY	40601	**888-598-7667**	502-564-4606
Financial Institutions Dept 1025 Capital Ctr Dr Ste 200	Frankfort	KY	40601	**800-223-2579**	502-573-3390
Fish & Wildlife Resources Dept 1 Game Farm Rd	Frankfort	KY	40601	**800-858-1549**	502-564-3400
General Assembly 700 Capitol Ave State Capitol Bldg	Frankfort	KY	40601	**800-372-7181**	502-564-8100
Historical Society 100 W Broadway	Frankfort	KY	40601	**877-444-7867**	502-564-1792
Housing Corp 1231 Louisville Rd	Frankfort	KY	40601	**800-633-8896**	502-564-7630

Name / Address	City	State	ZIP	Toll-Free	Phone
Insurance Dept 215 W Main St	Frankfort	KY	40602	**800-595-6053**	502-564-3630
Public Service Commission PO Box 615	Frankfort	KY	40602	**800-772-4636**	502-564-3940
Real Estate Commission (KREC) 10200 Linn Stn Rd Ste 201 *General	Louisville	KY	40223	**888-373-3300***	502-429-7250
Travel and Tourism Dept 500 Mero St Ste 2200	Frankfort	KY	40601	**800-225-8747**	502-564-4930
Veterans Affairs Dept (KDVA) 1111B Louisville Rd	Frankfort	KY	40601	**800-572-6245**	502-564-9203
Vocational Rehabilitation Dept 275 E Main St MS 2E-K	Frankfort	KY	40601	**800-372-7172**	502-564-4440
Workers Claims Dept (DWC) 657 Chamberlin Ave	Frankfort	KY	40601	**800-554-8601**	502-564-5550

339-19 Louisiana

Name / Address	City	State	ZIP	Toll-Free	Phone
Community Services Office 627 N 4th St	Baton Rouge	LA	70802	**888-524-3578**	
Consumer Protection Office PO Box 94095	Baton Rouge	LA	70804	**800-351-4889**	
Education Dept PO Box 94064	Baton Rouge	LA	70804	**877-453-2721**	
Environmental Quality Dept 602 N Fifth St	Baton Rouge	LA	70802	**866-896-5337**	225-219-5337
Housing Finance Agency 2415 Quail Dr	Baton Rouge	LA	70808	**888-454-2001**	225-763-8700
Insurance Dept PO Box 94214	Baton Rouge	LA	70804	**800-259-5300**	225-342-5900
Legislature PO Box 94062	Baton Rouge	LA	70804	**800-256-3793**	225-342-2456
Office of the Governor PO Box 94004	Baton Rouge	LA	70804	**866-366-1121**	225-342-7015
Public Service Commission PO Box 91154	Baton Rouge	LA	70821	**800-256-2397**	225-342-4404
Real Estate Commission PO Box 14785	Baton Rouge	LA	70898	**800-821-4529**	225-765-0191
Revenue Dept 617 N Third St PO Box 201	Baton Rouge	LA	70801	**855-307-3893**	
State Parks Office PO Box 44426	Baton Rouge	LA	70804	**888-677-1400**	225-342-8111
Veterans Affairs Dept PO Box 94095	Baton Rouge	LA	70804	**877-432-8982**	225-219-5000
Wildlife & Fisheries Dept PO Box 98000	Baton Rouge	LA	70898	**800-442-2511**	225-765-2800

339-20 Maine

Name / Address	City	State	ZIP	Toll-Free	Phone
State Government Information 26 Edison Dr	Augusta	ME	04330	**888-577-6690**	207-624-9494
Consumer Protection Unit 6 State House Stn	Augusta	ME	04333	**800-436-2131**	207-626-8849
Economic & Community Development Dept 59 State House Stn	Augusta	ME	04333	**800-541-5872**	207-624-9800
Elder Services Office 11 Statehouse Stn	Augusta	ME	04333	**800-624-8404**	
Environmental Protection Dept 17 State House Stn	Augusta	ME	04333	**800-452-1942**	207-287-7688
Financial Institutions Bureau 35 Anthony Ave 11 State House Stn	Augusta	ME	04333	**800-452-1926**	207-624-8090
Governor 1 State House Stn	Augusta	ME	04333	**888-577-6690**	207-287-3531
Insurance Bureau 34 State House Stn	Augusta	ME	04333	**800-300-5000**	207-624-8475
Rehabilitation Services Bureau 150 State House Stn	Augusta	ME	04333	**800-698-4440**	
Tourism Office 59 State House Stn	Augusta	ME	04333	**888-624-6345**	

339-21 Maryland

Name / Address	City	State	ZIP	Toll-Free	Phone
State Government Information State House	Annapolis	MD	21401	**800-811-8336**	410-974-3901
Assessments & Taxation Dept 301 W Preston St 8th Fl	Baltimore	MD	21201	**888-246-5941**	410-767-1184
Court of Appeals 361 Rowe Blvd 4th Fl	Annapolis	MD	21401	**800-926-2583**	410-260-1500
Criminal Injuries Compensation Board 6776 Reisterstown Rd Ste 206	Baltimore	MD	21215	**888-679-9347**	410-585-3010
Department of Budget & Management 45 Calvert St	Annapolis	MD	21401	**800-705-3493**	
Education Dept 200 W Baltimore St	Baltimore	MD	21201	**888-246-0016**	410-767-0100
Emergency Management Agency 5401 Rue St Lo Dr	Reisterstown	MD	21136	**877-636-2872**	410-517-3600
Environment Dept 1800 Washington Blvd	Baltimore	MD	21230	**800-633-6101**	410-537-3000
Higher Education Commision 839 Bestgate Rd Ste 400	Annapolis	MD	21401	**800-974-0203**	410-260-4500
Housing & Community Development Dept 100 Community Pl	Crownsville	MD	21032	**800-756-0119**	
Insurance Administration 525 St Paul Pl	Baltimore	MD	21202	**800-492-6116**	410-468-2000
Natural Resources Dept 580 Taylor Ave	Annapolis	MD	21401	**877-620-8367**	410-260-8021
Parole & Probation Div 6776 Reisterstown Rd	Baltimore	MD	21215	**877-227-8031**	410-585-3500
Physician Quality Assurance Board 4201 Patterson Ave	Baltimore	MD	21215	**800-492-6836**	410-764-4777
Public Service Commission 6 St Paul St 16th Fl	Baltimore	MD	21202	**800-492-0474**	410-767-8000
State Forest & Park Service 580 Taylor Ave Rm E-3 *Campground Resv	Annapolis	MD	21401	**877-620-8367***	410-260-8186
State Police 1201 Reisterstown Rd	Pikesville	MD	21208	**800-525-5555**	410-653-4200
Teacher Certification & Accreditation Div 200 W Baltimore St	Baltimore	MD	21201	**866-772-8922**	410-767-0412
Tourism Development Office 217 E Redwood St 9th Fl	Baltimore	MD	21202	**800-543-1036**	410-767-3400
Treasurer 80 Calvert St Rm 109	Annapolis	MD	21401	**800-974-0468**	410-260-7533
Veterans Affairs Dept 31 Hopkins Plaza Rm 1231	Baltimore	MD	21201	**800-446-4926**	410-230-4444
Vital Records Div 6550 Reisterstown Rd	Baltimore	MD	21215	**800-832-3277**	410-764-3038

339-22 Massachusetts

Name / Address	City	State	ZIP	Toll-Free	Phone
Banks Div 1000 Washington St Ste 710	Boston	MA	02118	**800-495-2265**	617-956-1501
Child Support Enforcement Div 51 Sleeper St 4th Fl	Boston	MA	02205	**800-332-2733**	617-660-1234
Executive Office of Transportation 10 Pk Plaza Ste 3170	Boston	MA	02116	**800-219-9936**	617-973-7000
Insurance Div 1000 Washington St Ste 810	Boston	MA	02118	**877-563-4467**	617-521-7794
Parole Board 12 Mercer Rd	Natick	MA	01760	**888-298-6272**	508-650-4500
Revenue Dept PO Box 7010	Boston	MA	02204	**800-392-6089**	617-626-2201
Travel & Tourism Office 10 Pk Plaza Ste 4510	Boston	MA	02116	**800-227-6277**	617-973-8500

339-23 Michigan

Name / Address	City	State	ZIP	Toll-Free	Phone
Attorney General 525 W Ottawa St	Lansing	MI	48933	**877-765-8388**	517-373-1110
Child Support Office 235 S Grand Ave PO Box 30037	Lansing	MI	48933	**866-661-0005**	
Civil Service Dept Capitol Commons Ctr 400 S Pine St	Lansing	MI	48913	**800-788-1766**	517-373-3030
Community Health Dept Capitol View Bldg 201 Townsend St	Lansing	MI	48913	**800-649-3777**	517-373-3740
Crime Victims Services Commission 320 S Walnut St Garden Level Lewis Cass Bldg	Lansing	MI	48913	**877-251-7373**	
Economic Development Corp (MEDC) 300 N Washington Sq	Lansing	MI	48913	**888-522-0103**	517-373-9808
eLibrary Information 702 W Kalamazoo St PO Box 30007	Lansing	MI	48909	**877-479-0021**	517-373-4331
Financial & Insurance Regulation PO Box 30220	Lansing	MI	48909	**877-999-6442**	517-373-0220
Parks & Recreation Div PO Box 30257 *Campground Resv	Lansing	MI	48909	**800-447-2757***	517-373-9900
Travel Michigan 300 N Washington Sq	Lansing	MI	48913	**888-784-7328**	517-373-0670

339-24 Minnesota

Name / Address	City	State	ZIP	Toll-Free	Phone
Aging Board 540 Cedar St	Saint Paul	MN	55155	**800-882-6262**	651-431-2500
Arts Board 400 Sibley St Ste 200	Saint Paul	MN	55101	**800-866-2787**	651-215-1600
Attorney General 1400 Bremer Tower 445 Minnesota St	Saint Paul	MN	55101	**800-657-3787**	651-296-3353
Attorney General's Office 445 Minnesota St Ste 1400	Saint Paul	MN	55101	**800-657-3787**	651-296-3353
Employment & Economic Development Dept (DEED) 1st National Bank Bldg 332 Minnesota St Ste E200	Saint Paul	MN	55101	**800-657-3858**	651-259-7114
Finance Dept 658 Cedar St Ste 400	Saint Paul	MN	55155	**800-627-3529**	651-201-8000
Governor 130 State Capitol 75 Rev Dr Martin Luther King Jr Blvd	Saint Paul	MN	55155	**800-657-3717**	651-201-3400
Health Dept PO Box 64975	Saint Paul	MN	55164	**888-345-0823**	651-201-5000
Historical Society 345 Kellogg Blvd W	Saint Paul	MN	55102	**800-657-3773**	651-259-3000
Housing Finance Authority 400 Sibley St Ste 300	Saint Paul	MN	55101	**800-657-3769**	651-296-7608
Labor & Industry Dept 443 Lafayette Rd N	Saint Paul	MN	55155	**800-342-5354**	651-284-5005
Legislature 75 Constitution Ave State Capitol	Saint Paul	MN	55155	**800-657-3550**	651-296-2146
Medical Practice Board 2829 University Ave SE Ste 500	Minneapolis	MN	55414	**800-657-3709**	612-617-2130
Natural Resources Dept 500 Lafayette Rd	Saint Paul	MN	55155	**888-646-6367**	651-296-6157
Parks & Recreation Div 500 Lafayette Rd	Saint Paul	MN	55155	**888-646-6367**	651-296-6157
Public Utilities Commission 121 Seventh Pl E Ste 350	Saint Paul	MN	55101	**800-657-3782**	651-296-7124
Revenue Dept 600 N Roberts St	Saint Paul	MN	55101	**800-652-9094**	651-296-3403
Transportation Dept 395 John Ireland Blvd	Saint Paul	MN	55155	**800-657-3774**	651-296-3000
Workers'' Compensation Div 443 Lafayette Rd	Saint Paul	MN	55155	**800-342-5354**	651-284-5005

339-25 Mississippi

Name / Address	City	State	ZIP	Toll-Free	Phone
State Government Information 200 S Lamar Ste 800	Jackson	MS	39201	**877-290-9487**	601-351-5023

				Toll-Free	Phone
Banking & Consumer Finance Dept PO Box 23729	Jackson	MS	39225	**800-844-2499**	601-359-1031
Child Support Enforcement Div 750 N State St	Jackson	MS	39202	**800-345-6347**	601-359-4929
Consumer Protection Div PO Box 22947	Jackson	MS	39225	**800-281-4418**	601-359-4230
Contractors Board 215 Woodline Dr Ste B	Jackson	MS	39232	**800-880-6161**	601-354-6161
Emergency Management Agency PO Box 5644	Pearl	MS	39288	**800-222-6362**	601-933-6362
Family & Children Services Div 750 N State St	Jackson	MS	39202	**800-345-6347**	601-359-4570
Higher Learning Institutions Board of Trustees 3825 Ridgewood Rd Ste 915	Jackson	MS	39211	**800-327-2980**	601-432-6198
Insurance Dept 1001 Woolfolk State Office Bldg 501 NW St PO Box 79	Jackson	MS	39201	**800-562-2957**	601-359-3569
Rehabilitation Services Dept 1281 Highway 51 PO Box 1698	Madison	MS	39110	**800-443-1000**	

339-26 Missouri

				Toll-Free	Phone
Child Support Enforcement Div PO Box 109002	Jefferson City	MO	65102	**800-859-7999**	
Consumer Protection Div 207 W High St PO Box 899	Jefferson City	MO	65102	**800-392-8222**	573-751-3321
Elementary & Secondary Education Dept 205 Jefferson St PO Box 480	Jefferson City	MO	65101	**800-735-2966**	573-751-4212
Finance Div PO Box 716	Jefferson City	MO	65102	**888-246-7225**	573-751-3242
Higher Education Dept 3515 Amazonas Dr	Jefferson City	MO	65109	**800-473-6757**	573-751-2361
Natural Resources Dept PO Box 176 *Cust Svc	Jefferson City	MO	65102	**800-361-4827***	573-751-3443
Professional Registration Div 3605 Missouri Blvd PO Box 1335	Jefferson City	MO	65102	**800-735-2966**	573-751-0293
Public Service Commission 200 Madison St PO Box 360	Jefferson City	MO	65102	**800-819-3180**	573-751-3234
Securities Div 600 W Main St PO Box 1276	Jefferson City	MO	65102	**800-721-7996**	573-751-4704
State Courts Administrator PO Box 104480	Jefferson City	MO	65110	**888-541-4894**	
State Parks Div PO Box 176	Jefferson City	MO	65102	**800-334-6946**	573-751-2479
Supreme Court 207 W High St	Jefferson City	MO	65101	**888-541-4894**	573-751-4144
Tourism Div PO Box 1055	Jefferson City	MO	65102	**800-519-2100**	573-751-4133
Transportation Dept 105 W Capitol Ave	Jefferson City	MO	65102	**888-275-6636**	573-751-2551
Vocational & Adult Education Div 3024 Dupont Cir PO Box 480	Jefferson City	MO	65109	**877-222-8963**	573-751-3251
Workers Compensation Div PO Box 58	Jefferson City	MO	65102	**800-775-2667**	573-751-4231

339-27 Montana

				Toll-Free	Phone
Arts Council PO Box 202201	Helena	MT	59620	**800-282-3092**	406-444-6430
Banking & Financial Institutions Div Rm 155 Mitchell Bldg 125 N Roberts St PO Box 200101	Helena	MT	59620	**800-914-8423**	406-841-2920
Child & Family Services Div PO Box 8005	Helena	MT	59604	**866-820-5437**	406-841-2400
Consumer Protection Office PO Box 200151	Helena	MT	59620	**800-481-6896**	406-444-4500
Information Technology Services Div 125 N Roberts St	Helena	MT	59601	**800-628-4917**	406-444-2700
Revenue Dept PO Box 5805	Helena	MT	59604	**866-859-2254**	406-444-6900
Securities Dept 840 Helena Ave	Helena	MT	59601	**800-332-6148**	406-444-2040
Victim Services Office 2225 11th Ave PO Box 201410	Helena	MT	59620	**800-498-6455**	406-444-1907
Vital Records Bureau 111 N Sanders St	Helena	MT	59604	**888-877-1946**	406-444-4228

339-28 Nebraska

				Toll-Free	Phone
Arts Council 1004 Farnam St	Omaha	NE	68131	**800-341-4067**	402-595-2122
Child Support Enforcement Div PO Box 95026	Lincoln	NE	68509	**877-631-9973**	402-471-3121
Economic Development Dept 301 Centennial Mall S PO Box 94666	Lincoln	NE	68509	**800-426-6505**	402-471-3747
Emergency Management Agency 1300 Military Rd	Lincoln	NE	68508	**877-297-2368**	402-471-7421
Environmental Quality Dept 1200 N St Ste 400	Lincoln	NE	68508	**877-253-2603**	402-471-2186
Health & Human Services Dept 301 Centennial Mall S	Lincoln	NE	68508	**800-430-3244**	402-471-3121
Historical Society 1500 R St	Lincoln	NE	68501	**800-833-6747**	402-471-3270
Insurance Dept 941 O St Ste 400	Lincoln	NE	68508	**877-564-7323**	402-471-2201
Investment Finance Authority 1230 'O' St Ste 200	Lincoln	NE	68508	**800-204-6432**	402-434-3900
Public Service Commission 1200 N St Ste 300	Lincoln	NE	68508	**800-526-0017**	402-471-3101
Travel & Tourism Div PO Box 98907	Lincoln	NE	68509	**877-632-7275**	402-471-3796
Vocational Rehabilitation Services Div 3901 N 27th St Ste 6	Lincoln	NE	68521	**800-472-3382**	402-471-3231
Workers' Compensation Court 1010 Lincoln Mall Ste 100	Lincoln	NE	68508	**800-599-5155**	402-471-6468

339-29 Nevada

				Toll-Free	Phone
Child Support Enforcement Office 1470 College Pkwy	Carson City	NV	89706	**800-992-0900**	775-684-0500
Economic Development Commission 808 W Nye Ln	Carson City	NV	89703	**800-336-1600**	775-687-9900
Motor Vehicles Dept 555 Wright Way	Carson City	NV	89711	**877-368-7828**	775-684-4368
Secretary of State 101 N Carson St Ste 3	Carson City	NV	89701	**800-450-8594**	775-684-5708
Tourism Commission 401 N Carson St	Carson City	NV	89701	**800-237-0774**	775-687-4322
Welfare Div 1470 College Pkwy	Carson City	NV	89706	**800-992-0900**	775-684-0500

339-30 New Hampshire

				Toll-Free	Phone
Banking Dept 53 Regional Dr Ste 200	Concord	NH	03301	**800-437-5991**	603-271-3561
Child Support Services 129 Pleasant St	Concord	NH	03301	**800-852-3345**	603-271-4427
Division of Vital Records Administration 71 S Fruit St	Concord	NH	03301	**800-735-2964**	603-271-4650
Environmental Services Dept 29 Hazen Dr PO Box 95	Concord	NH	03301	**800-735-2964**	603-271-3503
Housing Finance Authority PO Box 5087	Manchester	NH	03108	**800-439-7247**	603-472-8623
Public Utilities Commission 21 S Fruit St Ste 10 *Consumer Assistance	Concord	NH	03301	**800-852-3793***	603-271-2431
Travel & Tourism Development Office PO Box 1856	Concord	NH	03302	**800-262-6660**	603-271-2665
Victims' Assistance Commission 33 Capitol St	Concord	NH	03301	**800-300-4500**	603-271-1284
Vocational Rehabilitation Office 21 S Fruit St Ste 20	Concord	NH	03301	**800-299-1647**	603-271-3471

339-31 New Jersey

				Toll-Free	Phone
Banking & Insurance Dept 20 W State St PO Box 325	Trenton	NJ	08625	**800-446-7467**	609-292-7272
Child Support Office 175 S Broad St PO Box 8068	Trenton	NJ	08650	**877-655-4371**	
Mental Health Services Div PO Box 272	Trenton	NJ	08625	**800-382-6717**	609-777-0700
Military & Veterans' Affairs Dept 101 Eggert Crossing Rd	Lawrenceville	NJ	08648	**800-624-0508**	609-530-4600
Motor Vehicle Commission 225 E State St PO Box 160	Trenton	NJ	08666	**888-486-3339**	609-292-6500
Securities Bureau 153 Halsey St Sixth Fl PO Box 47029	Newark	NJ	07101	**866-446-8378**	973-504-3600
Travel & Tourism Div 225 W State St PO Box 460	Trenton	NJ	08625	**800-847-4865**	609-599-6540
Victims of Crime Compensation Board 50 Pk Pl	Newark	NJ	07102	**877-658-2221**	973-648-2107

339-32 New Mexico

				Toll-Free	Phone
Children Youth & Families Dept PO Box 5160	Santa Fe	NM	87502	**800-610-7610**	800-432-2075
Crime Victims Reparation Commission 8100 Mountain Rd NE Ste 106	Albuquerque	NM	87110	**800-306-6262**	505-841-9432
Department of Veterans Services 490 Old SF Trail	Santa Fe	NM	87504	**866-433-8387**	505-827-6300
Economic Development Dept PO Box 20003	Santa Fe	NM	87504	**800-374-3061**	505-827-0300
Environment Dept 1190 St Francis Dr Ste 4050	Santa Fe	NM	87502	**800-219-6157**	505-827-2855
Highway & Transportation Dept (NMDOT) 1120 Cerrillos Rd PO Box 1149 *General	Santa Fe	NM	87504	**800-432-4269***	505-827-5100
Lieutenant Governor 490 Old Santa Fe Trail Rm 417	Santa Fe	NM	87501	**800-432-4406**	505-476-2250
Mortgage Finance Authority 344 Fourth St SW	Albuquerque	NM	87102	**800-444-6880**	505-843-6880
Secretary of State 325 Don Gaspar Ave Ste 300	Santa Fe	NM	87503	**800-477-3632**	505-827-3600
Tourism Dept 491 Old Santa Fe Trail	Santa Fe	NM	87503	**800-545-2070**	
Vital Records & Health Statistics Bureau 1105 S St Francis Dr	Santa Fe	NM	87502	**866-534-0051**	505-827-0121
Vocational Rehabilitation Div 435 St Michaels Dr Bldg D	Santa Fe	NM	87505	**800-224-7005**	505-954-8500
Workers' Compensation Admin 2410 Ctr Ave SE PO Box 27198	Albuquerque	NM	87125	**800-255-7965**	505-841-6000

339-33 New York

				Toll-Free	Phone
Aging Office 2 Empire State Plaza	Albany	NY	12223	**800-342-9871**	
Banking Dept 1 State St	New York	NY	10004	**877-226-5697**	800-342-3736
Division of Consumer Protection 5 Empire State Plaza Ste 2101	Albany	NY	12223	**800-697-1220**	518-474-3514

Name / Address	City	State	Zip	Toll-Free	Phone
Empire State Development 30 S Pearl St	Albany	NY	12245	**800-782-8369**	518-292-5100
Health Dept Empire State Plaza Corning II Tower	Albany	NY	12237	**866-881-2809**	
Historic Preservation Div PO Box 189	Waterford	NY	12188	**800-456-2267**	518-237-8643
Mental Health Office 44 Holland Ave	Albany	NY	12229	**800-597-8481**	518-474-4403
Motor Vehicles Dept 6 Empire State Plaza	Albany	NY	12228	**800-368-1186**	518-473-5595
Office of Court Admin 25 Beaver St Rm 852	New York	NY	10004	**800-268-7869**	212-428-2100
Parks Recreation & Historic Preservation Office 1 Empire State Plaza *Campground Resv	Albany	NY	12238	**800-456-2267***	518-474-0456
Taxation & Finance Dept WA Harriman Campus Bldg 9	Albany	NY	12227	**800-225-5829**	518-457-5149
Temporary & Disability Assistance Office 40 N Pearl St 16th Fl	Albany	NY	12243	**800-342-3009**	518-473-1090
Tourism Div PO Box 2603	Albany	NY	12223	**800-225-5697**	518-473-1064
Veterans' Affairs Div 333 E Washington St Ste 430	Albany	NY	12223	**888-838-7697**	315-428-4046
Vital Records Office PO Box 2602	Albany	NY	12220	**877-854-4481**	518-474-3077
Workers' Compensation Board 328 State St	Schenectady	NY	12305	**877-632-4996**	518-462-8880

339-34 North Carolina

Name / Address	City	State	Zip	Toll-Free	Phone
Marine Fisheries Div PO Box 769	Morehead City	NC	28557	**800-682-2632**	252-726-7021
Parks & Recreation Div 217 W Jones St 1615 MSC	Raleigh	NC	27604	**877-722-6762**	919-707-9300
Tourism Div 301 N Wilmington St	Raleigh	NC	27601	**800-847-4862**	919-733-4171
Transportation Dept 1 S Wilmington St	Raleigh	NC	27611	**877-368-4968**	
Utilities Commission 4325 Mail Service Ctr	Raleigh	NC	27699	**866-380-9816**	919-733-7328
Victims Compensation Services Div 4232 Mail Service Ctr	Raleigh	NC	27699	**800-826-6200**	919-733-7974

339-35 North Dakota

Name / Address	City	State	Zip	Toll-Free	Phone
Accountancy Board 2701 S Columbia Rd	Grand Forks	ND	58201	**800-532-5904**	701-775-7100
Agriculture Dept 600 E Blvd Ave Dept 602	Bismarck	ND	58505	**800-242-7535**	701-328-2231
Attorney General 600 E Blvd Ave Dept 125	Bismarck	ND	58505	**800-366-6888**	701-328-2210
Child Support Enforcement Div 1600 E Century Ave Ste 7	Bismarck	ND	58501	**800-231-4255**	701-328-3582
Consumer Protection Div 1050 E Interstate Ave Ste 200	Bismarck	ND	58503	**800-472-2600**	701-328-3404
Crime Victims Compensation Program PO Box 5521	Bismarck	ND	58506	**800-445-2322**	701-328-6195
Economic Development & Finance Div 1600 E Century Ave Ste 200-B	Bismarck	ND	58503	**866-432-5682**	701-328-5300
Financial Institutions Dept 2000 Schafer St Ste G	Bismarck	ND	58501	**800-366-6888**	701-328-9933
Housing Finance Agency PO Box 1535	Bismarck	ND	58502	**800-292-8621**	701-328-8080
Insurance Dept 600 E Blvd Ave Dept 401	Bismarck	ND	58505	**800-247-0560**	701-328-2440
Parks & Recreation Dept 1600 E Century Ave Ste 3	Bismarck	ND	58503	**800-807-4723**	701-328-5357
Secretary of State 600 E Blvd Ave Dept 108	Bismarck	ND	58505	**800-352-0867**	701-328-2900
Tourism Div 1600 Eentury Ave Ste 200S	Bismarck	ND	58502	**800-435-5663**	701-328-2525
Veterans Affairs Dept 4201 38th St S Ste 104	Fargo	ND	58104	**866-634-8387**	701-239-7165
Vocational Rehabilitation Div 1237 W Divide Ave Ste 2	Bismarck	ND	58501	**800-755-2745**	701-328-8800
Workers Compensation 1600 E Century Ave Ste 1000	Bismarck	ND	58503	**800-777-5033**	701-328-3800

339-36 Ohio

Name / Address	City	State	Zip	Toll-Free	Phone
Agriculture Dept 8995 E Main St	Reynoldsburg	OH	43068	**800-282-1955**	614-728-6201
Consumer Protection Section 30 E Broad St 14th Fl	Columbus	OH	43215	**800-282-0515**	614-466-8831
Education Dept 25 S Front St	Columbus	OH	43215	**877-644-6338**	614-995-1545
Financial Institutions Div 77 S High St 21st Fl	Columbus	OH	43266	**866-278-0003**	614-728-8400
Highway Patrol (OSHP) 1970 W Broad St PO Box 182074	Columbus	OH	43223	**877-772-8765**	614-466-2660
Insurance Dept 50 W Town St Third Fl Ste 300	Columbus	OH	43215	**800-686-1526**	614-644-2658
Mental Health Dept 30 E Broad St 8th Fl	Columbus	OH	43215	**888-636-4889**	614-466-2596
Parks & Recreation Div 2045 Morse Rd Bldg C-3	Columbus	OH	43229	**800-282-7275**	614-265-6561
Taxation Dept 30 E Broad St 22nd Fl PO Box 530	Columbus	OH	43215	**888-405-4089**	614-466-2166
Travel & Tourism Div PO Box 1001	Columbus	OH	43216	**800-282-5393**	614-466-8844
Wildlife Div 2045 Morse Rd Bldg G	Columbus	OH	43229	**800-945-3543**	614-265-6300
Workers' Compensation Bureau 30 W Spring St	Columbus	OH	43215	**800-644-6292**	614-644-6292

339-37 Oklahoma

Name / Address	City	State	Zip	Toll-Free	Phone
Child Support Enforcement Div PO Box 248822	Oklahoma City	OK	73124	**800-522-2922**	405-522-2273
Commerce Dept 900 N Stiles Ave	Oklahoma City	OK	73104	**800-879-6552**	405-815-6552
Environmental Quality Dept 707 N Robinson Ave PO Box 1677	Oklahoma City	OK	73101	**800-869-1400**	405-702-1000
Housing Finance Agency 100 NW 63rd St Ste 200	Oklahoma City	OK	73116	**800-256-1489**	405-848-1144
Insurance Dept (OID) 3625 NW 56th Ste 100	Oklahoma City	OK	73152	**800-522-0071**	405-521-2828
Parks Div PO Box 52002	Oklahoma City	OK	73152	**800-654-8240**	405-230-8300
Rehabilitative Services Dept 5501 N Portland Ave	Oklahoma City	OK	73112	**800-845-8476**	405-951-3400
Wildlife Conservation Dept (ODWC) PO Box 53465	Oklahoma City	OK	73152	**800-522-8039**	405-521-4660

339-38 Oregon

Name / Address	City	State	Zip	Toll-Free	Phone
Crime Victims Service Div 1162 Ct St NE	Salem	OR	97301	**877-877-9392**	503-378-4400
Dept of Transportation 355 Capitol St NE Ste 135 Rm 222	Salem	OR	97301	**888-275-6368**	503-986-4000
Financial Fraud/Consumer Protection Section 1162 Ct St NE	Salem	OR	97301	**877-877-9392**	503-378-4400
Fish & Wildlife Dept (ODFW) 3406 Cherry Ave NE	Salem	OR	97303	**800-720-6339**	503-947-6000
Legislative Assembly 900 Ct St NE	Salem	OR	97301	**800-332-2313**	
Oregon Business Development Dept (OBDD) 775 Summer St NE Ste 200 *General	Salem	OR	97301	**800-735-2900***	503-986-0123
Parks & Recreation Dept (OPRD) 725 Summer St NE Ste C	Salem	OR	97301	**800-551-6949**	503-986-0707
Vocational Rehabilitation Services Office (OVRS) 700 Summer St NE E-87	Salem	OR	97301	**877-277-0513**	800-692-9666

339-39 Pennsylvania

Name / Address	City	State	Zip	Toll-Free	Phone
Banking Dept 17 N Second St Market Square Plz	Harrisburg	PA	17101	**800-722-2657**	717-783-4721
Insurance Dept 1326 Strawberry Sq	Harrisburg	PA	17120	**877-881-6388**	
Public Utility Commission 400 N St Keystone Bldg PO Box 3265	Harrisburg	PA	17120	**800-692-7380**	717-783-1740
State Parks Bureau PO Box 8551	Harrisburg	PA	17105	**888-727-2757**	717-787-6640
Transportation Dept 400 N St	Harrisburg	PA	17120	**800-932-4600**	717-787-2838
Vocational Rehabilitation Office (OVR) 1521 N Sixth St	Harrisburg	PA	17102	**800-442-6351**	717-787-5244
Workers Compensation Bureau 1171 S Cameron St Rm 324	Harrisburg	PA	17104	**800-482-2383**	717-783-5421

339-40 Rhode Island

Name / Address	City	State	Zip	Toll-Free	Phone
Higher Education Assistance Authority (RIHEAA) 560 Jefferson Blvd	Warwick	RI	02886	**800-922-9855**	401-736-1100
Tourism Div 315 Iron Horse Way Ste 101	Providence	RI	02908	**800-556-2484**	

339-41 South Carolina

Name / Address	City	State	Zip	Toll-Free	Phone
State Government Information 1301 Gervais St Ste 710	Columbia	SC	29201	**866-340-7105**	803-771-0131
Child Support Enforcement Office 3150 Harden St Ext	Columbia	SC	29203	**800-768-5858**	803-898-9210
Commerce Dept 1201 Main St Ste 1600	Columbia	SC	29201	**800-868-7232**	803-737-0400
Veterans Affairs Div 1205 Pendleton St Ste 463	Columbia	SC	29201	**800-827-1000**	803-734-0200
Vocational Rehabilitation Dept 1410 Boston Ave PO Box 15	West Columbia	SC	29171	**800-832-7526**	803-896-6500

339-42 South Dakota

Name / Address	City	State	Zip	Toll-Free	Phone
Child Support Div 700 Governors Dr	Pierre	SD	57501	**800-286-9145**	605-773-3641
Crime Victims' Compensation Program 700 Governors Dr	Pierre	SD	57501	**800-696-9476**	605-773-6317
DEPARTMENT OF HEALTH 600 E Capitol Ave	Pierre	SD	57501	**800-738-2301**	605-773-4961
Economic Development Office 711 E Wells Ave	Pierre	SD	57501	**800-872-6190**	605-773-3301
Parks & Recreation Div 523 E Capitol Ave *Campground Resv	Pierre	SD	57501	**800-710-2267***	605-773-3391
Rehabilitation Services Div 500 E Capitol Ave	Pierre	SD	57501	**800-265-9684**	605-773-3195

	City	State	Zip	Toll-Free	Phone
Tourism Office 711 E Wells Ave	Pierre	SD	57501	**800-952-3625**	605-773-3301

339-43 Tennessee

	City	State	Zip	Toll-Free	Phone
Child Support Services Div 400 Deaderick St 12th Fl	Nashville	TN	37248	**800-838-6911**	615-313-4880
Economic & Community Development Dept (ECD) 312 Eigth Ave N 11th Fl	Nashville	TN	37243	**877-768-6374**	615-741-1888
Mental Health & Developmental Disabilities Dept 425 Fifth Ave N 3rd Fl	Nashville	TN	37243	**800-669-1851**	615-532-6500
Real Estate Commission 500 James Robertson Pkwy Ste 180	Nashville	TN	37243	**800-342-4031**	615-741-2273
Securities Div 500 James Robertson Pkwy Ste 680	Nashville	TN	37243	**800-863-9117**	615-741-2947
State Parks Div 401 Church St 7th Fl	Nashville	TN	37243	**888-867-2757**	615-532-0001
Supreme Court 511 Union St Nashville City Ctr Ste 600	Nashville	TN	37219	**800-448-7970**	615-741-2687

339-44 Texas

	City	State	Zip	Toll-Free	Phone
State Government Information 1501 N Congress Ste 4224	Austin	TX	78711	**877-452-9060**	512-936-9500
Aging & Disability Services 701 W 51st St Ste W253	Austin	TX	78751	**888-388-6332**	512-438-3011
Agriculture Dept PO Box 12847 *Cust Svc	Austin	TX	78711	**800-835-5832***	512-463-7476
Arts Commission 920 Colorado Ste 501 PO Box 13406	Austin	TX	78701	**800-252-9415**	512-463-5535
Banking Dept 2601 N Lamar Blvd	Austin	TX	78705	**877-276-5554**	512-475-1300
Child Support Div 300 W 15th St	Austin	TX	78701	**800-252-8014**	512-460-6000
Comptroller of Public Accounts 111 E 17th St	Austin	TX	78774	**800-531-5441**	512-463-4600
Consumer Protection Div PO Box 12548 *General	Austin	TX	78711	**800-621-0508***	
Crime Victims Services Div PO Box 12198	Austin	TX	78711	**800-983-9933**	512-936-1200
Environmental Quality Commission (TCEQ) 12100 Pk 35 Cir PO Box 13087	Austin	TX	78711	**800-735-2989**	512-239-1000
General Land Office 1700 N Congress Ave Ste 935	Austin	TX	78701	**800-998-4456**	512-463-5001
Governor PO Box 12428	Austin	TX	78711	**800-843-5789**	512-463-2000
Insurance Dept 333 Guadalupe St PO Box 149104	Austin	TX	78714	**800-252-3439**	512-463-6169
Medical Board PO Box 2018 *Cust Svc	Austin	TX	78768	**800-248-4062***	512-305-7010
Motor Vehicle Div 4000 Jackson Ave PO Box 2293	Austin	TX	78731	**888-368-4689**	
Parks & Wildlife Dept 4200 Smith School Rd	Austin	TX	78744	**800-792-1112**	512-389-4800
Public Utility Commission PO Box 13326	Austin	TX	78711	**888-782-8477**	512-936-7000
Railroad Commission PO Box 12967	Austin	TX	78711	**877-228-5740**	512-463-7131
Veterans Commission PO Box 12277	Austin	TX	78711	**800-252-8387**	512-463-5538
Vital Statistics Bureau 1100 W 49th St PO Box 12040	Austin	TX	78756	**888-963-7111**	
Workers Compensation Commission 7551 Metro Ctr Dr *Cust Svc	Austin	TX	78744	**800-252-7031***	512-804-4000

339-45 Utah

	City	State	Zip	Toll-Free	Phone
Aging & Adult Services Div 195 N 1950 W Rm 325	Salt Lake City	UT	84116	**877-424-4640**	801-538-3910
Child & Family Services Div 195 N 1950 W Rm 225	Salt Lake City	UT	84116	**855-323-3237**	801-538-4100
Community & Economic Development Dept 60 E S Temple 3rd Fl	Salt Lake City	UT	84111	**855-204-9046**	801-538-8680
Environmental Quality Dept 195 N 1950 W	Salt Lake City	UT	84116	**800-458-0145**	801-536-4400
Governor 350 N State St Ste 200 PO Box 142220	Salt Lake City	UT	84114	**800-705-2464**	801-538-1000
Labor Commission PO Box 146600	Salt Lake City	UT	84114	**800-530-5090**	801-530-6800
Lieutenant Governor PO Box 142325	Salt Lake City	UT	84114	**800-705-2464**	
Motor Vehicle Div PO Box 30412	Salt Lake City	UT	84130	**800-368-8824**	801-297-7780
Occupational & Professional Licensing Div PO Box 146741	Salt Lake City	UT	84111	**866-275-3675**	801-530-6628
Office of Tourism 300 N State St	Salt Lake City	UT	84114	**800-200-1160**	801-538-1900
Parks & Recreation Div 1594 W N Temple Ste 116	Salt Lake City	UT	84116	**800-322-3770**	801-538-7220
Rehabilitation Office 250 E 500 S	Salt Lake City	UT	84111	**800-473-7530**	801-538-7530
Workers' Compensation Fund 100 W Towne Ridge Pkwy	Sandy	UT	84070	**800-446-2667**	385-351-8000

339-46 Virginia

	City	State	Zip	Toll-Free	Phone
Aging & Rehabilitative Services Dept 8004 Franklin Farms Dr	Richmond	VA	23229	**800-552-5019**	804-662-7000
Child Support Enforcement Div 730 E Broad St	Richmond	VA	23219	**800-468-8894**	
Criminal Injuries Compensation Fund (CICF) PO Box 26927	Richmond	VA	23261	**800-552-4007**	
Governor 1111 E Broad St PO Box 1475	Richmond	VA	23219	**800-828-1120**	804-786-2211
Health Professions Dept 9960 Mayland Dr Ste 300	Henrico	VA	23233	**800-533-1560**	804-367-4400
Housing Development Authority 601 S Belvidere St	Richmond	VA	23220	**800-968-7837**	804-782-1986
Information Technologies Agency (VITA) 11751 Meadowville Ln	Chester	VA	23836	**866-637-8482**	
State Parks Div 203 Governor St Ste 306 *Resv	Richmond	VA	23219	**800-933-7275***	
Vital Records Div 2001 Maywill St PO Box 1000	Richmond	VA	23230	**877-572-6333**	804-662-6200

339-47 Washington

	City	State	Zip	Toll-Free	Phone
Child Support Div PO Box 11520	Olympia	WA	98411	**800-442-5437**	
Financial Institutions Dept PO Box 41200	Olympia	WA	98504	**877-746-4334**	360-902-8703
Health Dept PO Box 47890	Olympia	WA	98504	**800-525-0127**	360-236-4501
Historical Society 1911 Pacific Ave	Tacoma	WA	98402	**888-238-4373**	253-272-3500
Housing Finance Commission 1000 Second Ave Ste 2700	Seattle	WA	98104	**800-767-4663**	206-464-7139
Natural Resources Dept 1111 Washington St SE PO Box 47000	Olympia	WA	98504	**800-258-5990**	360-902-1000
Revenue Dept PO Box 47478	Olympia	WA	98504	**800-647-7706**	360-705-6714
Social & Health Services Dept PO Box 45130	Olympia	WA	98504	**800-737-0617**	360-902-8400
State Parks & Recreation Commission 1111 Israel Rd SW *Campground Resv	Olympia	WA	98504	**888-226-7688***	360-902-8500
Utilities & Transportation Commission 1300 S Evergreen Pk Dr SW PO Box 47250	Olympia	WA	98504	**888-333-9882**	360-664-1160
Veterans Affairs Dept PO Box 41150	Olympia	WA	98504	**800-562-2308**	360-753-5586
Vocational Rehabilitation Div PO Box 45340	Olympia	WA	98504	**800-637-5627**	360-438-8000

339-48 West Virginia

	City	State	Zip	Toll-Free	Phone
Child Support Enforcement Bureau 231 Capitol St Ste 111	Charleston	WV	25301	**800-571-4864**	304-347-8688
Children & Families Bureau 350 Capitol St Rm R-730	Charleston	WV	25301	**800-642-8589**	304-558-0628
Community Development Div 1900 Kanawha Blvd E	Charleston	WV	25311	**800-982-3386**	304-558-2234
Consumer Protection Div 812 Quarrier St 1st Fl	Charleston	WV	25301	**800-368-8808**	304-558-8986
Crime Victims Compensation Fund 1900 Kanawha Blvd E Rm W-334	Charleston	WV	25305	**877-562-6878**	304-347-4850
Development Office 1900 Kanawah Blvd E Bldg 6 Rm 525B	Charleston	WV	25305	**800-982-3386**	304-558-2234
Housing Development Fund 814 Virginia St E	Charleston	WV	25301	**800-933-9843**	304-345-6475
Insurance Commission PO Box 50540	Charleston	WV	25305	**888-879-9842**	304-558-3354
Motor Vehicles Div 5707 Maccorkle Ave SE Ste 400	Charleston	WV	25304	**800-642-9066**	304-558-3900
Public Service Commission 208 Brooke St PO Box 812	Charleston	WV	25301	**800-344-5113**	304-340-0300
Rehabilitation Services Div 107 Capitol St	Charleston	WV	25301	**800-642-8207**	
Secretary of State 1900 Kanawha Blvd E Bldg 1 Ste 157K	Charleston	WV	25305	**866-767-8683**	304-558-6000
Securities Div 1900 Kanawha Blvd E Bldg 1 Rm W-100	Charleston	WV	25305	**877-982-9148**	304-558-2257
State Parks and Forests 324 4th Ave	Charleston	WV	25305	**800-225-5982**	304-558-2764
Tourism Div 90 MacCorkle Ave SW	Charleston	WV	25303	**800-225-5982**	
Treasurer 1900 Kanawha Blvd E Bldg 1 Ste E-145	Charleston	WV	25305	**800-422-7498**	304-558-5000
Veterans Affairs Div 1321 Plaza E Ste 101	Charleston	WV	25301	**888-838-2332**	304-558-3661

339-49 Wisconsin

	City	State	Zip	Toll-Free	Phone
Crime Victims Services Office PO Box 7951	Madison	WI	53707	**800-446-6564**	608-264-9497
Housing & Economic Development Authority 201 W Washington Ave Ste 700	Madison	WI	53703	**800-334-6873**	608-266-7884
Insurance Commission PO Box 7873	Madison	WI	53707	**800-236-8517**	608-266-3585
Legislature State Capitol	Madison	WI	53702	**800-362-9472**	608-266-9960

	City	State	Zip	Toll-Free	Phone
Parks & Recreation Bureau 101 S Webster St PO Box 7921	Madison	WI	53707	**888-936-7463**	608-266-2621
Public Instruction Dept 125 S Webster St PO Box 7841	Madison	WI	53707	**800-441-4563**	608-266-3390
Teacher Education & Licensing Bureau 125 S Webster St	Madison	WI	53703	**800-441-4563**	608-266-3390
Treasurer PO Box 2114	Madison	WI	53707	**855-375-2274**	
Veterans Affairs Dept 201 W Washington Ave PO Box 7843	Madison	WI	53703	**800-947-8387**	608-266-1311
Vocational Rehabilitation Div 201 East Washington Avenue PO Box 7852	Madison	WI	53707	**800-442-3477**	608-261-0050

339-50 Wyoming

	City	State	Zip	Toll-Free	Phone
Aging Div 6101 Yellowstone Rd N Rm 259B	Cheyenne	WY	82002	**800-442-2766**	307-777-7986
Highway Patrol (WHP) 5300 Bishop Blvd	Cheyenne	WY	82009	**800-442-9090**	307-777-4301
State Parks & Historical Sites Div 2301 Central Ave	Cheyenne	WY	82002	**877-996-7275**	307-777-6323
Tourism Div 1520 Etchepare Cir	Cheyenne	WY	82007	**800-225-5996**	307-777-7777

340 GOVERNMENT - US - EXECUTIVE BRANCH

SEE ALSO Cemeteries - National ; Coast Guard Installations ; Military Bases ; Parks - National - US

	City	State	Zip	Toll-Free	Phone
USA Freedom Corps 1201 New York Ave NW	Washington	DC	20005	**800-833-3722**	202-606-5000

340-1 US Department of Agriculture

	City	State	Zip	Toll-Free	Phone
Department of Agriculture (USDA) 1400 Independence Ave SW	Washington	DC	20250	**844-433-2774**	202-720-3631
Center for Nutrition Policy & Promotion (CNPP) 3101 Pk Ctr Dr 10th Fl	Alexandria	VA	22302	**888-779-7264**	703-305-7600
Food & Nutrition Service *Food Stamp Program* 3101 Pk Ctr Dr	Alexandria	VA	22302	**800-221-5689**	703-305-2022
Forest Service (USFS) 1400 Independence Ave SW	Washington	DC	20050	**800-832-1355**	202-205-8333
Forest Service Regional Offices *Region 8 (Southern Region)* 1720 Peachtree St Ste 760S	Atlanta	GA	30309	**877-372-7248**	404-347-4177
National Agricultural Statistics Service (NASS) 1400 Independence Ave SW	Washington	DC	20250	**800-727-9540**	202-720-2707

340-2 US Department of Commerce

	City	State	Zip	Toll-Free	Phone
Economic Development Administration 1401 Constitution Ave NW	Washington	DC	20230	**888-469-3146**	202-482-2900
Minority Business Development Agency Regional Offices *Chicago Region* 105 W Adams St Ste 2300	Chicago	IL	60603	**888-324-1551**	312-353-0182
National Environmental Satellite Data & Information Service *National Coastal Data Development Ctr* Bldg 1100 Ste 101	Stennis Space Center	MS	39529	**866-732-2382**	228-688-2936
National Institute of Standards & Technology (NIST) 100 Bureau Dr Sp 1070	Gaithersburg	MD	20899	**800-877-8339**	301-975-6478
National Marine Fisheries Service Regional Offices *Pacific Islands Region* 1601 Kapiolani Blvd Rm 1110	Honolulu	HI	96814	**888-674-7411**	808-944-2200
National Technical Information Service (NTIS) 5285 Port Royal Rd *Orders	Springfield	VA	22161	**800-553-6847***	703-605-6000
North American Industry Classification System (NAICS) US Census Bureau 4600 Silver Hill Rd	Washington	DC	20233	**800-923-8282**	301-763-4636
US Census Bureau Regional Offices *Atlanta* 101 Marietta St NW Ste 3200	Atlanta	GA	30303	**800-424-6974**	404-730-3832
Boston 4 Copley Pl Ste 301	Boston	MA	02117	**800-562-5721**	617-424-4501
Chicago 1111 W 22nd St Ste 400	Oak Brook	IL	60523	**800-865-6384**	630-288-9200
Denver 6900 W Jefferson Ave Ste 100	Denver	CO	80235	**800-852-6159**	303-264-0202
Los Angeles 15350 Sherman Way Ste 300	Van Nuys	CA	91406	**800-992-3530**	818-267-1700
New York 32 Old Slip 9th Fl	New York	NY	10005	**800-991-2520**	212-584-3400
Philadelphia 833 Chestnut St Ste 504	Philadelphia	PA	19107	**800-262-4236**	215-717-1800
US Patent & Trademark Office PO Box 1450	Alexandria	VA	22313	**800-786-9199**	571-272-1000

340-3 US Department of Defense

	City	State	Zip	Toll-Free	Phone
Defense Commissary Agency 1300 E Ave	Fort Lee	VA	23801	**877-332-2471**	804-734-8000
Defense Contract Audit Agency 8725 John J Kingman Rd Ste 2135	Fort Belvoir	VA	22060	**855-414-5892**	703-767-3265
Defense Contract Management Agency 6350 Walker Ln Ste 300	Alexandria	VA	22310	**888-576-3262**	
Defense Information Systems Agency PO Box 4502	Arlington	VA	22204	**844-247-3457**	
Defense Technical Information Ctr (DTIC) 8725 John J Kingman Rd Ste 0944	Fort Belvoir	VA	22060	**800-225-3842**	703-767-9100
Defense Threat Reduction Agency 8725 John T Kingman Rd MS 6201	Fort Belvoir	VA	22060	**800-701-5096**	703-767-5870

340-4 US Department of Defense - Department of the Army

	City	State	Zip	Toll-Free	Phone
US Army War College 122 Forbes Ave	Carlisle	PA	17013	**800-453-0992**	717-245-3131

340-5 US Department of Defense - Department of the Navy

	City	State	Zip	Toll-Free	Phone
Military Sealift Command 914 Charles Morris Ct SE Washington Navy Yard	Washington	DC	20398	**800-793-5784**	
Navy Personnel Command (NPC) 5720 Integrity Dr	Millington	TN	38055	**866-827-5672**	901-874-3165

340-6 US Department of Education

	City	State	Zip	Toll-Free	Phone
Department of Education *Inspector General's Fraud & Abuse Hotline* 400 Maryland Ave SW	Washington	DC	20202	**800-647-8733**	
Office of Vocational & Adult Education 400 Maryland Ave SW Room 4W116	Washington	DC	20202	**800-872-5327**	
US Dept of Education *Region 6* 1999 Bryan St Ste 1620	Dallas	TX	75201	**877-521-2172**	214-661-9600
National Institute for Literacy (NIFL) 1775 'I' St NW Ste 730	Washington	DC	20006	**800-228-8813**	202-233-2025
Secretary of Education 400 Maryland Ave SW	Washington	DC	20202	**800-872-5327**	202-401-3000

340-7 US Department of Energy

	City	State	Zip	Toll-Free	Phone
Department of Energy (DOE) 1000 Independence Ave SW	Washington	DC	20585	**800-342-5363**	202-586-5450
Federal Energy Regulatory Commission 888 First St NE	Washington	DC	20426	**866-208-3372**	202-502-8004
Federal Energy Regulatory Commission Regional Offices *Portland* 888 First St NE Fox Tower Ste 550	Washington	DC	20426	**866-208-3372**	202-502-6088
Power Marketing Administrations *Bonneville Power Administration* 905 NE 11th Ave	Portland	OR	97232	**800-282-3713**	503-230-3000

340-8 US Department of Health & Human Services

	City	State	Zip	Toll-Free	Phone
Department of Health & Human Services (HHS) 330 Independence Ave SW	Washington	DC	20201	**877-696-6775**	202-619-0150
US Health & Human Services Department *Region 9* 90 7th St Ste 4-100	San Francisco	CA	94103	**800-368-1019**	
Agency for Healthcare Research & Quality 540 Gaither Rd	Rockville	MD	20850	**800-358-9295**	301-427-1200
Agency for Toxic Substances & Disease Registry 4770 Buford Hwy NE	Atlanta	GA	30341	**800-232-4636**	
AIDSinfo PO Box 6303	Rockville	MD	20849	**800-448-0440**	301-519-0459
Centers for Disease Control & Prevention *National Center for Chronic Disease Prevention & Health Promotion (NCCDPHP)* 4770 Buford Hwy NE	Atlanta	GA	30341	**800-232-4636**	
National Center for Emerging & Zoonotic Infectious Diseases 1600 Clifton Rd	Atlanta	GA	30333	**800-232-4636**	404-639-3311
National Center for Environmental Health 4770 Buford Hwy Bldg 101	Atlanta	GA	30341	**800-232-4636**	404-639-3311
National Center for Health Marketing 1600 Clifton Rd NE	Atlanta	GA	30333	**800-311-3435**	404-639-3311
National Center for HIV/AIDS Viral Hepatitis STD & TB Prevention 1600 Clifton Rd	Atlanta	GA	30333	**800-232-4636**	
National Center for Immunization & Respiratory Diseases 1600 Clifton Rd NE MS E-05	Atlanta	GA	30333	**800-232-4636**	
National Center for Injury Prevention & Control (NCIPC) 4770 Buford Hwy NE	Atlanta	GA	30341	**800-232-4636**	
National Center for Public Health Informatics 1600 Clifton Rd NE	Atlanta	GA	30333	**800-232-4636**	
National Center on Birth Defects & Developmental Disabilities 1600 Clifton Rd	Atlanta	GA	30329	**800-232-4636**	404-639-3311
National Institute for Occupational Safety & Health 200 Independence Ave SW	Washington	DC	20201	**800-356-4674**	404-639-3286
National Office of Public Health Genomics 4770 Buford Hwy MS K-89	Atlanta	GA	30341	**877-442-9719**	770-488-8510
Travelers Health 1600 Clifton Rd NE	Atlanta	GA	30333	**800-232-4636**	
Centers for Medicare & Medicaid Services *Medicare Hotline* 7500 Security Blvd	Baltimore	MD	21244	**800-633-4227**	
Child Welfare Information Gateway 1250 Maryland Ave SW 8th Fl	Washington	DC	20024	**800-394-3366**	703-385-7565
Food & Drug Administration *Center for Devices & Radiological Health (CDRH)* 10903 New Hampshire Ave WO66-5429	Silver Spring	MD	20993	**800-638-2041**	301-796-7100
Center for Food Safety & Applied Nutrition 5100 Paint Branch Pkwy	College Park	MD	20740	**888-723-3366**	
National Center for Toxicological Research 3900 N Ctr Rd	Jefferson	AR	72079	**800-638-3321**	870-543-7000

				Toll-Free	Phone
Pacific Region					
1301 Clay St Ste 1180N	Oakland	CA	94612	**877-696-6775**	
Health Resources & Services Administration (HRSA)					
5600 Fishers Ln	Rockville	MD	20857	**888-275-4772**	301-443-2216
National Child Care Information & Technical Assistance Ctr (NCCIC)					
9300 Lee Hwy	Fairfax	VA	22031	**877-296-2250**	
National Clearinghouse for Alcohol & Drug Information					
11426 Rockville Pk PO Box 2345	Rockville	MD	20847	**800-729-6686**	
National Hansen's Disease Program (NHDP)					
1770 Physicians Pk Dr	Baton Rouge	LA	70816	**800-221-9393**	
National Institutes of Health					
National Cancer Institute					
Public Inquiries Office 6116 Executive Blvd Rm 3036A	Bethesda	MD	20892	**800-422-6237**	301-435-3848
National Center for Complementary & Alternative Medicine					
National Institutes of Health 31 Ctr Dr Bldg 31	Bethesda	MD	20892	**888-644-6226**	301-594-7103
National Institute of Mental Health					
6001 Executive Blvd Rm 8184 MSC 9663	Bethesda	MD	20892	**866-615-6464**	301-443-4513
National Institute of Neurological Disorders & Stroke					
PO Box 5801	Bethesda	MD	20824	**800-352-9424**	301-496-5751
National Institute on Deafness & Other Communication Disorders					
31 Ctr Dr Bldg 31 Rm 3C35	Bethesda	MD	20892	**800-241-1044**	301-496-7243
National Library of Medicine					
National Institutes of Health 8600 Rockville Pike Bldg 38	Bethesda	MD	20894	**888-346-3656**	301-594-5983
National Mental Health Information Ctr					
PO Box 42557	Washington	DC	20015	**800-487-4889**	
National Women's Health Information Ctr					
200 Independence Ave S.W	Washington	DC	20201	**800-994-9662**	
NIH Osteoporosis & Related Bone Diseases-National Resource Ctr					
2 AMS Cir	Bethesda	MD	20892	**800-624-2663**	202-223-0344
Office of Public Health & Science					
200 Independence Ave SW Rm 716G	Washington	DC	20201	**877-696-6775**	202-690-7694
Substance Abuse & Mental Health Services Administration (SAMHSA)					
1 Choke Cherry Rd	Rockville	MD	20857	**877-726-4727**	240-276-2000
Center for Mental Health Services					
1 Choke Cherry Ln	Rockville	MD	20857	**877-726-4727**	
Center for Substance Abuse Prevention					
1 Choke Cherry Rd	Rockville	MD	20857	**877-726-4727**	240-276-2420
Center for Substance Abuse Treatment					
1 Choke Cherry Rd PO Box 2345	Rockville	MD	20857	**877-726-4727**	240-276-2130

340-9 US Department of Homeland Security

				Toll-Free	Phone
Ready Campaign					
500 C St SW Ste 714	Washington	DC	20472	**800-621-3362**	
Federal Emergency Management Agency (FEMA)					
500 C St SW	Washington	DC	20472	**800-621-3362**	
FEMA for Kids					
500 C St SW Ste 714	Washington	DC	20472	**800-621-3362**	
National Flood Insurance Program					
500 C St SW	Washington	DC	20472	**888-379-9531**	
Federal Emergency Management Agency Regional Offices (FEMA)					
Region 1 99 High St	Boston	MA	02110	**877-336-2734**	617-956-7551
Region 3					
1 Independence Mall 615 Chestnut St 6th Fl	Philadelphia	PA	19106	**800-621-3362**	215-931-5500
Region 5					
536 S Clark St 6th Fl	Chicago	IL	60605	**877-336-2627**	312-408-5500
Region 6 800 N Loop 288	Denton	TX	76209	**800-426-5460**	940-898-5399
Region 9					
1111 Broadway Ste 1200	Oakland	CA	94607	**877-336-2627**	510-627-7100
Transportation Security Administration (TSA)					
601 S 12th St	Arlington	VA	22202	**866-289-9673**	
Federal Air Marshal Service					
601 S 12th St	Arlington	VA	22202	**866-289-9673**	
US Citizenship & Immigration Services Regional Offices					
Eastern Region					
70 Kimball Ave	South Burlington	VT	05403	**800-767-1833**	
US Coast Guard					
National Maritime Ctr					
100 Forbes Dr	Martinsburg	WV	25404	**888-427-5662**	304-433-3400
US Coast Guard Academy					
15 Mohegan Ave	New London	CT	06320	**800-883-8724**	860-444-8500
US Customs & Border Protection					
1300 Pennsylvania Ave NW	Washington	DC	20229	**877-227-5511**	703-526-4200
US Immigration & Customs Enforcement (ICE)					
425 'I' St NW	Washington	DC	20536	**866-347-2423**	202-514-1900

340-10 US Department of Housing & Urban Development

				Toll-Free	Phone
Department of Housing & Urban Development (HUD)					
451 Seventh St SW	Washington	DC	20410	**800-569-4287**	202-708-0685
Public Affairs Office					
451 Seventh St SW	Washington	DC	20410	**800-333-4636**	202-708-0980
Department of Housing & Urban Development Regional Offices					
Boston 10 Cswy St 3rd Fl	Boston	MA	02222	**800-225-5342**	617-994-8200
Mid-Atlantic Region					
100 Penn Sq E	Philadelphia	PA	19107	**800-225-5342**	215-656-0500
New York City Regional Office					
26 Federal Plaza Ste 3541	New York	NY	10278	**800-496-4294**	212-264-8000
Pacific/Hawaii Region					
600 Harrison St 3rd Fl	San Francisco	CA	94107	**800-347-3739**	415-489-6572
Rocky Mountain Region					
1670 Bdwy 25th Fl	Denver	CO	80202	**800-955-2232**	303-672-5440
HUD Office of Fair Housing & Equal Opportunity					
451 Seventh St SW	Washington	DC	20410	**800-669-9777**	202-708-1112
Housing Discrimination Hotline					
451 Seventh St SW	Washington	DC	20410	**800-333-4636**	202-708-1112
HUD Office of Public & Indian Housing					
451 Seventh St SW Rm 4100	Washington	DC	20410	**800-955-2232**	202-708-0950
Real Estate Assessment Ctr					
550 12th St SW Ste 100	Washington	DC	20410	**888-245-4860**	202-708-1112

340-11 US Department of the Interior

				Toll-Free	Phone
Bureau of Indian Affairs Regional Offices (BIA)					
Alaska Region					
3601 C St Ste 1100	Anchorage	AK	99503	**800-645-8397**	907-271-1536
National Wild Horse & Burro Program					
1849 C St NW Rm. 5665	Washington	DC	20240	**866-468-7826**	202-208-3801
Bureau of Land Management Regional Offices					
Eastern States Office					
7450 Boston Blvd	Springfield	VA	22153	**800-370-3936**	703-440-1600
National Interagency Fire Ctr					
3833 S Development Ave	Boise	ID	83705	**877-471-2262**	208-387-5512
US Fish & Wildlife Service (USFWS)					
1849 C St NW	Washington	DC	20240	**800-344-9453**	202-208-4717
US Fish & Wildlife Service Regional Offices					
Great Lakes/Big Rivers Region					
5600 American Blvd W Ste 900	Bloomington	MN	55437	**800-877-8339**	612-713-5360
US Geological Survey (USGS)					
12201 Sunrise Valley Dr	Reston	VA	20192	**888-275-8747**	703-648-6723
Ask USGS					
12201 Sunrise Valley Dr	Reston	VA	20192	**888-275-8747**	703-648-5953

340-12 US Department of Justice

				Toll-Free	Phone
Community Oriented Policing Services (COPS)					
1100 Vermont Ave NW 10th Fl	Washington	DC	20530	**800-421-6770**	202-514-5328
Federal Bureau of Prisons					
National Institute of Corrections					
320 First St NW	Washington	DC	20534	**800-995-6423**	202-307-3106
National Institute of Corrections Information Cent					
11900 E Cornell Ave Unit C	Aurora	CO	80014	**800-877-1461**	
National Criminal Justice Reference Service					
PO Box 6000	Rockville	MD	20849	**800-851-3420**	301-240-7760
Office of Justice Programs					
Bureau of Justice Assistance					
810 Seventh St NW	Washington	DC	20531	**888-744-6513**	202-616-6500
Office for Victims of Crime					
810 Seventh St NW 8th Fl	Washington	DC	20531	**800-363-0441**	202-307-5983
Office of Special Counsel for Immigration-Related Unfair Employment Practices					
950 Pennsylvania Ave NW	Washington	DC	20038	**800-255-7688**	202-616-5594
US Marshals Service					
401 Courthouse Square	Alexandria	VA	22314	**800-336-0102***	202-307-9100
*General					
US Parole Commission					
5550 Friendship Blvd Rm 420	Chevy Chase	MD	20815	**888-585-9103**	301-492-5990

340-13 US Department of Labor

				Toll-Free	Phone
Department of Labor (DOL)					
200 Constitution Ave NW	Washington	DC	20210	**866-487-2365**	202-693-4650
Department of Labor					
Job Corps					
200 Constitution Ave NW Ste N4463	Washington	DC	20210	**800-733-5627**	202-693-3000
Office of Administrative Law Judges					
200 Constitution Ave NW Ste 400 N.	Washington	DC	20210	**877-889-5627**	202-693-7300
Public Affairs Office					
200 Constitution Ave NW	Washington	DC	20210	**866-487-2365**	202-693-4650
Employment & Training Administration					
200 Constitution Ave NW	Washington	DC	20210	**866-487-2365**	
Bureau of Labor Statistics					
Consumer Price Index					
2 Massachusetts Ave NE	Washington	DC	20212	**800-877-8339**	202-691-5200
Mountain-Plains Information Office					
2300 Main St Ste 1190	Kansas City	MO	64108	**800-487-9004**	816-285-7000
New York-New Jersey Information Office					
201 Varick St Rm 808	New York	NY	10014	**800-877-8339**	646-264-3600
Southeast Information Office					
61 Forsyth St	Atlanta	GA	30303	**800-347-3764**	404-893-4222
Employment & Training Administration Regional Offices					
Region 3- Atlanta					
Federal Ctr 61 Forsyth St SW Rm 6M12	Atlanta	GA	20210	**877-872-5627**	
Employment Standards Administration					
200 Constitution Ave NW Rm S2321	Washington	DC	20210	**866-487-2365**	202-693-0200
Office of Labor-Management Standards (OLMS)					
200 Constitution Ave NW Rm N-1519	Washington	DC	20210	**866-487-2365**	
Mine Safety & Health Administration (MSHA)					
1100 Wilson Blvd	Arlington	VA	22209	**800-746-1553**	202-693-9400
Occupational Safety & Health Administration (OSHA)					
200 Constitution Ave NW	Washington	DC	20210	**800-321-6742**	202-693-1999
Occupational Safety & Health Administration Regional Offices					
Region 1					
JFK Federal Bldg Rm E-340	Boston	MA	02203	**800-321-6742**	617-565-9860
Region 10					
300 Fifth Ave Ste 1280	Seattle	WA	98104	**800-321-6742***	206-757-6700
*Help Line					
Region 2					
201 Varick St Ste 670	New York	NY	10014	**800-321-6742**	212-337-2378
Region 3					
Curtis Ctr 170 S Independence Mall W Ste 740W	Philadelphia	PA	19106	**800-321-6742**	215-861-4900
Office of Disability Employment Policy					
200 Constitution Ave NW Ste S1303	Washington	DC	20210	**866-633-7365**	202-693-7880
Secretary of Labor					
200 Constitution Ave NW Rm S2018	Washington	DC	20210	**866-487-2365**	202-693-6000
Women's Bureau					
200 Constitution Ave NW Rm S3002	Washington	DC	20210	**800-827-5335**	202-693-6710
Region 10					
1111 Third Ave Ste 620	Seattle	WA	98101	**800-827-5335**	206-553-1534
Women's Bureau Regional Offices					
Region 2					
201 Varick St Rm 602	New York	NY	10014	**800-827-5335**	212-337-2389

	City	State	Zip	Toll-Free	Phone
Region 3 200 Constitution Ave NW Ste 631E	Washington	DC	20210	**800-827-5335**	866-487-2365
Region 4 Sam Nunn Federal Ctr 61 Forsyth St SW Ste 6B75	Atlanta	GA	30303	**800-827-5335**	404-562-2336
Region 5 Federal Bldg 230 S Dearborn St Rm 1022	Chicago	IL	60604	**800-827-5335**	312-353-6985
Region 6 Federal Bldg 525 Griffin St Ste 735	Dallas	TX	75202	**800-827-5335**	972-850-4700
Region 7 2300 Main St Ste 1050	Kansas City	MO	64108	**800-827-5335**	816-285-7233
Region 8 1999 Broadway Ste 1620 PO Box 46550	Denver	CO	80201	**800-827-5335**	303-844-1286
Region 9 90 Seventh St Ste 2650	San Francisco	CA	94103	**800-827-5335**	415-625-2638

340-14 US Department of State

	City	State	Zip	Toll-Free	Phone
Bureau of Consular Affairs 2201 C St NW SA-29	Washington	DC	20520	**888-407-4747**	202-501-4444
Office of Children's Issues SA-17 9th Fl	Washington	DC	20522	**888-407-4747**	202-501-4444
Passport Services 1111 19th St NW Ste 500	Washington	DC	20524	**888-874-7793**	877-487-2778
Colorado Passport Agency *Colorado Agency* 3151 S Vaughn Way Ste 600	Aurora	CO	80014	**888-874-7793**	877-487-2778
International Boundary & Water Commission - US & Mexico 4171 N Mesa Ste C-100	El Paso	TX	79902	**800-262-8857**	915-832-4101
Passport Services Regional Offices *Boston Agency* 10 Cswy St Rm 247 Tip O'Neill Federal Bldg	Boston	MA	02222	**877-487-2778**	
Chicago Agency Kluczynski Federal Bldg 230 S Dearborn St 18th Fl	Chicago	IL	60604	**877-487-2778**	
Connecticut Agency 850 Canal St	Stamford	CT	06902	**877-487-2778**	
Honolulu Agency 300 Ala Moana Bldg Ste 1-330	Honolulu	HI	96850	**877-487-2778**	
Los Angeles Agency 11000 Wilshire Blvd Ste 1000	Los Angeles	CA	90024	**877-487-2778**	
New Orleans Agency 365 Canal St Ste 1300	New Orleans	LA	70130	**877-487-2778**	
New York Agency 376 Hudson St 10th Fl	New York	NY	10014	**877-487-2778**	
Philadelphia Agency US Custom House 200 Chesnut St Rm 103	Philadelphia	PA	19106	**877-487-2778**	
San Francisco Agency 95 Hawthorne St 5th Fl	San Francisco	CA	94105	**877-487-2778**	
Washington (DC) Agency 600 19th St NW 1st Floor Sidewalk Level	Washington	DC	20006	**877-487-2778**	

340-15 US Department of Transportation

	City	State	Zip	Toll-Free	Phone
Safety Hotline 800 Independence Ave SW	Washington	DC	20591	**800-255-1111**	
Federal Aviation Administration Northwest Mountain Region 1601 Lind Ave SW	Renton	WA	98057	**800-220-5715**	425-227-2001
Federal Highway Administration *National Highway Institute* 4600 Fairfax Dr Ste 800	Arlington	VA	22203	**877-558-6873**	703-235-0500
Federal Motor Carrier Safety Administration (FMCSA) 1200 New Jersey Ave SE	Washington	DC	20590	**800-832-5660**	
Federal Railroad Administration Regional Offices (FRA) *Region 1* 55 Broadway Room 1077	Cambridge	MA	02142	**800-724-5991**	617-494-2302
Region 2 Baldwin Tower Ste 660 1510 Chester Pike	Crum Lynne	PA	19022	**800-724-5992**	610-521-8200
Region 3 61 Forsyth St SW Ste 16T20	Atlanta	GA	30303	**800-724-5993**	404-562-3800
Region 4 200 W Adams St	Chicago	IL	60606	**800-724-5040**	312-353-6203
Region 6 901 Locust St Ste 464	Kansas City	MO	64106	**800-724-5996**	816-329-3840
Region 8 703 Broadway St Ste 650	Vancouver	WA	98660	**800-724-5998**	360-696-7536
Maritime Administration (MARAD) 1200 New Jersey Ave SE *Hotline	Washington	DC	20590	**800-996-2723***	202-366-5807
Maritime Administration *US Merchant Marine Academy* 300 Steamboat Rd	Kings Point	NY	11024	**866-546-4778**	516-773-5387
National Highway Traffic Safety Administration (NHTSA) 1200 New Jersey Ave SE	Washington	DC	20590	**888-327-4236**	202-366-9550
National Center for Statistics & Analysis 1200 New Jersey Ave SE	Washington	DC	20590	**800-934-8517**	202-366-1503
Vehicle Research & Test Ctr 10820 SR 347 PO Box B37	East Liberty	OH	43319	**800-262-8309**	937-666-4511
National Highway Traffic Safety Administration Regional Offices *NHTSA Region 3* 1200 New Jersey Ave Ste 6700	Washington	DC	20590	**888-327-4236**	
Pipeline & Hazardous Materials Safety Administration *Office of Hazardous Materials Safety* 1200 New Jersey Ave SE	Washington	DC	20590	**800-467-4922**	202-366-4433
Research & Innovative Technology Administration (RITA) 1200 New Jersey Ave SE	Washington	DC	20590	**800-853-1351**	202-366-7582
Bureau of Transportation Statistics 1200 New Jersey Ave SE	Washington	DC	20590	**800-853-1351**	202-366-1270
Office of Research Development & Technology 1200 New Jersey Ave SE	Washington	DC	20590	**800-853-1351**	
Saint Lawrence Seaway Development Corp 1200 New Jersey Ave SE	Washington	DC	20590	**800-785-2779**	202-366-0091
Secretary of Transportation 1200 New Jersey Ave SE	Washington	DC	20590	**855-368-4200**	

340-16 US Department of the Treasury

	City	State	Zip	Toll-Free	Phone
Department of the Treasury 1500 Pennsylvania Ave NW	Washington	DC	20220	**800-359-3898**	202-622-2000
Alcohol & Tobacco Tax & Trade Bureau 1310 G St NW Ste 300	Washington	DC	20220	**877-882-3277**	202-453-2000
Bureau of Engraving & Printing 14th & C Sts SW	Washington	DC	20228	**877-874-4114**	
Bureau of the Public Debt PO Box 7015	Parkersburg	WV	26106	**800-722-2678**	
TreasuryDirect PO Box 7015	Parkersburg	WV	26106	**800-722-2678**	304-480-7711
Comptroller of the Currency 250 E St SW *Cust Svc	Washington	DC	20219	**800-613-6743***	202-874-5000
Internal Revenue Service (IRS) 1111 Constitution Ave NW	Washington	DC	20224	**800-829-1040**	202-622-9511
Taxpayer Advocate Service 77 K St NE Ste 1500	Washington	DC	20002	**877-777-4778**	202-803-9000
US Mint 801 Ninth St NW *Cust Svc	Washington	DC	20220	**800-872-6468***	202-354-7462
San Francisco 155 Hermann St	San Francisco	CA	94102	**800-872-6468**	415-575-8000
West Point (NY) PO Box 37	West Point	NY	10996	**800-872-6468**	

340-17 US Department of Veterans Affairs

	City	State	Zip	Toll-Free	Phone
Department of Veterans Affairs (VA) 810 Vermont Ave NW *Cust Svc	Washington	DC	20420	**800-827-1000***	202-461-7600
Public & Intergovernmental Affairs Office 810 Vermont Ave NW	Washington	DC	20420	**800-273-8255**	
Secretary of Veterans Affairs *Board of Veterans' Appeals* 810 Vermont Ave NW	Washington	DC	20420	**800-923-8387**	
Center for Women Veterans 810 Vermont Ave NW	Washington	DC	20420	**800-827-1000**	
Veterans Benefits Administration 810 Vermont Ave NW	Washington	DC	20420	**800-827-1000**	
Veterans Health Administration 810 Vermont Ave NW	Washington	DC	20420	**800-827-1000**	202-273-5400
Gulf War Veterans Information 50 Irving St NW	Washington	DC	20422	**800-313-2232**	
Office of Research & Development 810 Vermont Ave NW MC 12	Washington	DC	20420	**800-827-1000**	

340-18 US Independent Agencies Government Corporations & Quasi-Official Agencies

Included also among these listings are selected Federal Boards, Committees, and Commissions.

	City	State	Zip	Toll-Free	Phone
Federal Election Commission 999 E St NW	Washington	DC	20463	**800-424-9530**	202-694-1100
Architectural & Transportation Barriers Compliance Board 1331 F St NW Ste 1000	Washington	DC	20004	**800-872-2253**	202-272-0080
Commodity Futures Trading Commission 1155 21 St NW 1155 21 St NW	Washington	DC	20581	**866-366-2382**	202-418-5000
Consumer Product Safety Commission (CPSC) 4340 E W Hwy Ste 502	Bethesda	MD	20814	**800-638-2772**	301-504-7923
Corp for National & Community Service *AmeriCorps USA* 1201 New York Ave NW	Washington	DC	20525	**800-833-3722**	202-606-5000
Learn & Serve America 1201 New York Ave NW	Washington	DC	20525	**800-833-3722**	202-606-5000
Senior Corps 1201 New York Ave NW	Washington	DC	20525	**800-833-3722**	202-606-5000
Defense Nuclear Facilities Safety Board 625 Indiana Ave NW Ste 700	Washington	DC	20004	**800-788-4016**	202-694-7000
Denali Commission 510 L St Ste 410	Anchorage	AK	99501	**888-480-4321**	907-271-1414
US National Response Team 1200 Pennsylvania Ave NW	Washington	DC	20593	**800-424-9346**	202-267-2675
Environmental Protection Agency Regional Offices *Region 1* 1 Congress St Ste 1100	Boston	MA	02114	**888-372-7341**	617-918-1111
Region 10 1200 Sixth Ave Ste 900	Seattle	WA	98101	**800-424-4372**	206-553-1200
Region 3 1650 Arch St	Philadelphia	PA	19103	**800-438-2474**	215-814-5000
Region 4 Federal Ctr 61 Forsyth St SW	Atlanta	GA	30303	**800-241-1754**	404-562-9900
Region 6 1445 Ross Ave Ste 1200	Dallas	TX	75202	**800-887-6063**	214-665-2200
Region 8 1595 Wynkoop St	Denver	CO	80202	**800-227-8917**	303-312-6312
Region 9 75 Hawthorne St	San Francisco	CA	94105	**866-372-9378**	415-947-8000
Equal Employment Opportunity Commission (EEOC) 1801 L St NW	Washington	DC	20507	**800-669-4000**	202-663-4191
Equal Employment Opportunity Commission Regional Offices *Atlanta District* 100 Alabama St SW Ste 4R30	Atlanta	GA	30303	**800-669-6820**	
Birmingham District 1130 22nd St S Ste 2000	Birmingham	AL	35205	**800-669-4000**	205-212-2100
Charlotte District 129 W Trade St Ste 400	Charlotte	NC	28202	**800-669-4000**	704-344-6682

	City	State	Zip	Toll-Free	Phone
Chicago District 500 W Madison St Ste 2800	Chicago	IL	60661	**800-669-4000**	312-353-2713
Dallas District 207 S Houston St 3rd Fl	Dallas	TX	75202	**800-669-4000**	214-253-2700
Houston District 1201 Louisiana St 6th Fl	Houston	TX	77002	**800-669-4000**	
Los Angeles District 255 E Temple St 4th Fl	Los Angeles	CA	90012	**800-669-4000**	
New York District 33 Whitehall St 5th Fl	New York	NY	10004	**866-408-8075**	212-336-3620
Philadelphia District 801 Market St Ste 1300	Philadelphia	PA	19107	**800-669-4000**	
Saint Louis District 1222 Spruce St Rm 8.100	Saint Louis	MO	63103	**800-669-4000**	314-539-7800
San Francisco District 450 Golden Gate Ave 5 W PO Box 36025	San Francisco	CA	94102	**800-669-4000**	
Export-Import Bank of the US 811 Vermont Ave NW	Washington	DC	20571	**800-565-3946**	202-565-3946
Federal Communications Commission (FCC) 445 12th St SW	Washington	DC	20554	**888-225-5322**	
Federal Deposit Insurance Corp 550 17th St NW	Washington	DC	20429	**877-275-3342**	202-898-7192
Federal Deposit Insurance Corp Regional Offices					
Atlanta Area Office 10 Tenth St NW Ste 800	Atlanta	GA	30309	**800-765-3342**	678-916-2200
Boston Area Office 15 Braintree Hill Office Pk Ste 300	Braintree	MA	02184	**866-728-9953**	781-794-5500
Chicago Area Office 300 S Riverside Plaza Ste 1700	Chicago	IL	60606	**800-944-5343**	312-382-6000
Dallas Area Office 1601 Bryan St	Dallas	TX	75201	**800-568-9161**	214-754-0098
Kansas City Area Office 2345 Grand Blvd Ste 1200	Kansas City	MO	64108	**800-209-7459**	816-234-8000
Memphis Area Office 5100 Poplar Ave Ste 1900	Memphis	TN	38137	**800-210-6354**	901-685-1603
New York Area Office 350 5th Ave Ste 1200	New York	NY	11215	**800-334-9593**	917-320-2500
San Francisco Area Office 25 Jessie St at Ecker Sq Ste 2300	San Francisco	CA	94105	**800-756-3558**	415-546-0160
National Do Not Call Registry 600 Pennsylvania Ave NW	Washington	DC	20580	**888-382-1222**	
Federal Trade Commission Regional Offices					
East Central Region 1111 Superior Ave Ste 200	Cleveland	OH	44114	**877-382-4357**	216-263-3455
Midwest Region 55 W Monroe St Ste 1825	Chicago	IL	20580	**877-382-4357**	
NortheastRegion 1 Bowling Green Ste 318	New York	NY	10004	**877-382-4357**	212-607-2829
Northwest Region 915 Second Ave Rm 2896	Seattle	WA	98174	**877-382-4357**	
Southeast Region 60 Forsyth St SW	Atlanta	GA	30303	**877-282-4357**	404-656-1390
Southwest Region 1999 Bryan St Ste 2150	Dallas	TX	75201	**877-382-4357**	
Western Region 901 Market St Ste 570	San Francisco	CA	94103	**877-382-4357**	
Federal Citizen Information Center PO Box 100	Pueblo	CO	81009	**888-878-3256**	
General Services Administration Regional Offices					
Region 1 - New England 10 Cswy St Rm 1010 Thomas P O'Neill Federal Bldg	Boston	MA	02222	**866-734-1727**	617-565-5860
Region 3 - Mid-Atlantic Strawbridge Bldg 20 N 8th St	Philadelphia	PA	19107	**800-333-4636**	215-446-5100
Region 4 - Southeast Sunbelt 1800 F St NW Ste 600	Washington	DC	20405	**800-333-4636**	
Region 8 - Rocky Mountain Denver Federal Ctr Bldg 41	Denver	CO	80225	**888-999-4777**	303-236-7329
Indian Arts & Crafts Board Dept of the Interior 1849 C St NW MS 2528-MIB	Washington	DC	20240	**888-278-3253**	202-208-3773
Merit Systems Protection Board (MSPB) 1615 M St NW	Washington	DC	20419	**800-209-8960**	202-653-7200
Merit Systems Protection Board Regional Offices (MSPB)					
Atlanta Region 401 W Peachtree St NW 10th Fl	Atlanta	GA	30308	**800-209-8960**	404-730-2755
Denver Field Office 165 S Union Blvd Ste 318	Lakewood	CO	80228	**800-209-8960**	303-969-5101
National Archives & Records Administration					
Archival Research Catalog 8601 Adelphi Rd	College Park	MD	20740	**866-272-6272**	
Office of the Federal Register 800 N Capitol St NW Ste 700-K	Washington	DC	20002	**877-684-6448**	202-741-6000
Northeast Region 380 Trapelo Rd	Waltham	MA	02452	**866-406-2379**	781-663-0130
Pacific Alaska Region 6125 Sand Pt Way NE	Seattle	WA	98115	**866-325-7208**	206-336-5115
National Credit Union Administration 1775 Duke St *Fraud Hotline	Alexandria	VA	22314	**800-827-9650***	703-518-6300
National Endowment for the Humanities (NEH) 400 7th St SW	Washington	DC	20506	**800-634-1121**	202-606-8400
National Labor Relations Board (NLRB) 1099 14th St NW	Washington	DC	20570	**866-667-6572**	202-273-1991
National Labor Relations Board Regional Offices					
Region 1 10 Cswy St 6th Fl	Boston	MA	02222	**866-667-6572**	617-565-6700
Region 11 4035 University Pkwy Ste 200	Winston-Salem	NC	27106	**866-667-6572**	336-631-5201
Region 14 1222 Spruce St Rm 8.302	Saint Louis	MO	63103	**866-667-6572**	314-539-7770
Region 16 Federal Bldg 819 Taylor St Rm 8A24	Fort Worth	TX	76102	**866-667-6572**	817-978-2921
Region 18 330 Second Ave S Ste 790	Minneapolis	MN	55401	**866-667-6572**	612-348-1757
Region 20 901 Market St Ste 400	San Francisco	CA	94103	**866-667-6572**	415-356-5130
Region 25 575 N Pennsylvania St Ste 238	Indianapolis	IN	46204	**866-667-6572**	317-226-7381
Region 3 Niagara Ctr Bldg 130 S Elmwood Ave Ste 630	Buffalo	NY	14202	**866-667-6572**	716-551-4931
Region 31 11150 W Olympic Blvd Ste 700	Los Angeles	CA	90064	**866-667-6572**	310-235-7352
Region 8 1240 E Ninth St Rm 1695	Cleveland	OH	44199	**866-667-6572**	216-522-3715
Region 9 550 Main St Rm 3003	Cincinnati	OH	45202	**866-667-6572**	513-684-3686
National Railroad Passenger Corp 60 Massachusetts Ave NE	Washington	DC	20002	**800-872-7245**	202-906-3741
National Science Foundation (NSF) 4201 Wilson Blvd	Arlington	VA	22230	**800-877-8339**	703-292-5111
Nuclear Regulatory Commission Regional Offices					
Region 1 2100 Renaissance Blvd	King of Prussia	PA	19406	**800-432-1156**	610-337-5000
Region 2 61 Forsyth St SW Ste 23T85	Atlanta	GA	30303	**800-577-8510**	404-562-4400
Region 3 2443 Warrenville Rd Ste 210	Lisle	IL	60532	**800-522-3025**	630-829-9500
Region 4 1600 E Lamar Blvd	Arlington	TX	76011	**800-952-9677**	817-860-8100
Occupational Safety & Health Review Commission Regional Offices					
Atlanta Region 100 Alabama St SW Rm 2R90	Atlanta	GA	30303	**800-321-6742**	404-562-1640
Office of Special Counsel 1730 M St NW Ste 218	Washington	DC	20036	**800-872-9855**	202-254-3600
Office of Special Counsel Regional Offices					
Dallas Field Office 525 Griffin St Rm 824 PO Box 103	Dallas	TX	75202	**800-872-9855**	214-747-1519
San Francisco Bay Area Field Office Federal Bldg 1301 Clay St Ste 1220-N	Oakland	CA	94612	**800-872-9855**	510-637-3460
Peace Corps 1111 20th St NW	Washington	DC	20526	**800-424-8580**	202-692-1040
Peace Corps Regional Offices					
Atlanta Regional Office 1111 20th St NW	Washington	DC	20526	**855-855-1961**	404-562-3456
Chicago Regional Office 55 W Monroe St Ste 450	Chicago	IL	60603	**800-424-8580**	312-353-4990
Dallas Regional Office 1100 Commerce St Ste 427	Dallas	TX	75242	**855-855-1961**	
Denver Regional Office 1999 Broadway Ste 2205	Denver	CO	80202	**855-855-1961**	
Los Angeles Regional Office 2361 Rosecrans Ave Ste 155	El Segundo	CA	90245	**800-424-8580**	310-356-1100
Mid-Atlantic Regional Office 1525 Wilson Blvd Ste 100	Arlington	VA	22209	**800-424-8580**	202-692-1040
New York Regional Office 201 Varick St Ste 1025	New York	NY	10014	**800-424-8580**	212-352-5440
Northwest Regional Office 1601 Fifth Ave Ste 605	Seattle	WA	98101	**800-424-8580**	206-553-5490
San Francisco Regional Office 1301 Clay St Ste 620-N	Oakland	CA	94612	**800-424-8580**	510-452-8444
Pension Benefit Guaranty Corp 1200 K St NW *Cust Svc	Washington	DC	20005	**800-400-7242***	202-326-4000
Railroad Retirement Board 844 N Rush St	Chicago	IL	60611	**877-772-5772**	312-751-4300
Selective Service System 1515 Wilson Blvd	Arlington	VA	22209	**888-655-1825**	847-688-6888
Selective Service System Regional Offices					
Region 1 PO Box 94638	Palatine	IL	60094	**888-655-1825**	847-688-6888
Region 2 PO Box 94638	Palatine	IL	60094	**888-655-1825**	847-688-6888
Small Business Administration (SBA) 409 Third St SW	Washington	DC	20416	**800-827-5722**	202-205-6600
Region 10 701 Fifth Ave Ste 2900	Seattle	WA	98104	**800-772-1213**	206-615-2236
Small Business Administration Regional Offices					
Region 6 1301 Young St	Dallas	TX	75202	**800-772-1213**	214-767-9401
Social Security Administration (SSA) 6401 Security Blvd	Baltimore	MD	21235	**800-772-1213**	410-965-8904
Social Security Administration Regional Offices					
Region 2 26 Federal Plaza Rm 40-102	New York	NY	10278	**800-772-1213**	212-264-4036
Region 4 61 Forsyth St SW Ste 23T30	Atlanta	GA	30303	**800-772-1213**	
Region 5 600 W Madison St PO Box 8280	Chicago	IL	60680	**800-772-1213**	312-575-4050
US Commission on Civil Rights Regional Offices					
Midwestern Regional Office 55 W Monroe St Ste 410	Chicago	IL	60603	**800-552-6843**	312-353-8311
US Election Assistance Commission 1201 New York Ave NW Ste 300	Washington	DC	20005	**866-747-1471**	202-566-3100
US General Services Administration 1800 F St NW	Washington	DC	20405	**800-488-3111**	
US Postal Service (USPS) 475 L'Enfant Plaza W SW *Cust Svc	Washington	DC	20260	**800-275-8777***	202-268-2000

341 GOVERNMENT - US - JUDICIAL BRANCH

341-1 US Bankruptcy Courts

	City	State	Zip	Toll-Free	Phone
US Bankruptcy Court					
Alaska 605 W Fourth Ave Ste 138	Anchorage	AK	99501	**800-859-8059**	907-271-2655
Eastern District of Washington 904 W Riverside Ave Ste 304	Spokane	WA	99201	**800-519-2549**	509-353-2404
Minnesota 300 S Fourth St 7W US Courthouse	Minneapolis	MN	55415	**866-260-7337**	612-664-5260
Missouri Eastern 111 S Tenth St 4th Fl	Saint Louis	MO	63102	**866-803-9517**	314-244-4500

Name / Address	City	State	Zip	Toll-Free	Phone
Pennsylvania Middle 197 S Main St	Wilkes-Barre	PA	18701	**877-298-2053**	570-831-2500
Texas Northern 1100 Commerce St Rm 1254	Dallas	TX	75242	**800-442-6850**	214-753-2000
Wisconsin Eastern US Courthouse 517 E Wisconsin Ave Rm 126	Milwaukee	WI	53202	**877-781-7277**	414-297-3291

341-2 US District Courts

Name / Address	City	State	Zip	Toll-Free	Phone
US District Court Colorado 901 19th St	Denver	CO	80294	**800-359-8699**	303-844-3433
US District Court for the District of Alaska 222 W Seventh Ave Ste 4	Anchorage	AK	99513	**866-243-3814**	907-677-6100
US District Court Mississippi Southern PO Box 23552	Jackson	MS	39201	**866-517-7682**	601-965-4439
US District Court Nebraska 111 S 18th Plaza Ste 1152	Omaha	NE	68102	**866-220-4381**	402-661-7350
US District Court North Carolina Western 401 W Trade St	Charlotte	NC	28202	**866-851-1605**	704-350-7400
US District Court Oklahoma Northern 333 W Fourth St	Tulsa	OK	74103	**866-213-1957**	918-699-4700
US District Court Vermont 11 Elmwood Ave Rm 506 PO Box 945	Burlington	VT	05402	**800-837-8718**	802-951-6301

341-3 US Supreme Court

Name / Address	City	State	Zip	Toll-Free	Phone
Roberts John G Jr US Supreme Ct Bldg 1 1st St NE	Washington	DC	20543	**800-772-1213**	202-479-3000
Kennedy Anthony M US Supreme Ct Bldg 1 1st St NE	Washington	DC	20543	**800-772-1213**	202-479-3000
Scalia Antonin US Supreme Ct Bldg 1 1st St NE	Washington	DC	20543	**800-772-1213**	202-479-3000
Stevens John Paul US Supreme Ct Bldg 1 1st St NE	Washington	DC	20543	**800-772-1213**	202-479-3000

342 GOVERNMENT - US - LEGISLATIVE BRANCH

SEE ALSO Legislation Hotlines

Name / Address	City	State	Zip	Toll-Free	Phone
Library of Congress *National Library Service for the Blind & Physically Handicapped* 1291 Taylor St NW	Washington	DC	20011	**888-657-7323**	202-707-5100
US Copyright Office 101 Independence Ave SE	Washington	DC	20559	**877-476-0778**	202-707-3000
Tourism Abbotsford Society 34561 Delair Rd	Abbotsford	BC	V2S2E1	**888-332-2229**	604-859-1721
US Government Printing Office Bookstore (GPO) 732 N Capitol St NW	Washington	DC	20401	**866-512-1800**	202-512-1800

342-1 US Senators, Representatives, Delegates

The circled letter S denotes that a listing is for a senator.

Name / Address	City	State	Zip	Toll-Free	Phone
Hahn Janice (Rep D - CA) 404 Cannon Bldg	Washington	DC	20515	**855-328-7332**	202-225-8220
Frankel Lois (Rep D - FL) 1037 Longworth Bldg	Washington	DC	20515	**866-264-0957**	202-225-9890
Sablan Gregorio (Rep D - MP) 423 Cannon Bldg	Washington	DC	20515	**877-446-3465**	202-225-2646
ⓈScott Tim (Sen R - SC) 520 Hart Senate Office Bldg	Washington	DC	20510	**855-425-6324**	202-224-6121
Lummis Cynthia M (Rep R - WY) 2433 Rayburn HOB	Washington	DC	20515	**888-879-3599**	202-225-2311

343 GOVERNORS - STATE

Listings for governors are organized by state names.

Name / Address	City	State	Zip	Toll-Free	Phone
Malloy Dan (D) 210 Capitol Avey	Hartford	CT	06106	**800-406-1527**	

344 GRAPHIC DESIGN

SEE ALSO Typesetting & Related Services

Name / Address	City	State	Zip	Toll-Free	Phone
Adrenalin Inc 54 W 11th Ave	Denver	CO	80204	**888-757-5646**	303-454-8888
Armada Group Inc, The 325 Soquel Ave Ste A	Santa Cruz	CA	95062	**800-408-2120**	
B&B Image Group 1712 Marshall St NE	Minneapolis	MN	55413	**888-788-9461**	612-788-9461
BrandEquity International 7 Great Meadow Rd	Newton	MA	02462	**800-969-3150**	
Cottonimages.Com Inc 10481 Nw 28th St	Miami	FL	33172	**888-642-7999**	305-251-2560
David Berman Developments 340 Selby Ave	Ottawa	ON	K2A3X6	**800-665-1809**	613-728-6777
Firstbase Services Ltd 34609 Delair Rd	Abbotsford	BC	V2S2E1	**800-758-2922**	604-850-5334
Goldmark Group Inc, The 1155 Bloomfield Ave	Clifton	NJ	07012	**800-632-9632**	973-777-5720
Graphic Reproduction 1381 Franquette Ave Bldg B1	Concord	CA	94520	**800-498-9939**	925-674-0900
H & H Graphics Inc 854 N Prince St	Lancaster	PA	17603	**866-338-7569**	717-393-3941
Hudson Printing & Graphic Design 611 S Mobberly Ave	Longview	TX	75602	**800-530-4888**	903-758-1773
Imprimis Group Inc 4835 Lyndon B Johnson Fwy	Dallas	TX	75244	**888-772-9682**	972-419-1700
Kane Graphical Corp 2255 W Logan Blvd	Chicago	IL	60647	**800-992-2921**	
Lansmont Corp Ryan Ranch Research Pk 17 Mandeville Ct	Monterey	CA	93940	**800-526-7666**	831-655-6600
Lucas Color Card 4900 N Santa Fe Ave	Oklahoma City	OK	73118	**888-845-8227**	405-524-1811
Metro Creative Graphics Inc 519 Eigth Ave	New York	NY	10018	**800-223-1600**	212-947-5100
Mike Davis & Associates Inc 15505 Long Vista Dr # 200	Austin	TX	78728	**888-836-8442**	512-836-8442
Newhall Klein Inc 6109 W Kl Ave	Kalamazoo	MI	49009	**866-639-4255**	269-544-0844
Offwhite 521 Ft St	Marietta	OH	45750	**800-606-1610**	740-373-9010
Printing House Ltd, The 1403 Bathurst St	Toronto	ON	M5R3H8	**800-874-0870**	416-536-6113
QuadSystems LLC N61 W23044 Harry's Way	Sussex	WI	53089	**866-246-7693**	
Screen Works Inc 3970 Image Dr	Dayton	OH	45414	**800-536-9111**	937-264-9111
Signature Graphics Inc 1000 Signature Dr	Porter	IN	46304	**800-356-3235**	219-926-4994
Spire Inc 65 Bay St	Boston	MA	02125	**877-350-8837**	617-350-8837
Subia Corp 6612 Gulton Ct NE	Albuquerque	NM	87109	**800-275-2636**	505-345-2636
Theprinters.com 3500 E College Ave	State College	PA	16801	**800-359-2097**	814-237-7600
Vango Graphics Inc 1371 S Inca St	Denver	CO	80223	**877-722-6168**	303-722-6109
West Canadian Digital Imaging Inc 200 - 1601 Ninth Ave SE	Calgary	AB	T2G0H4	**800-267-2555**	403-245-2555
William Fox Munroe Inc 3 E Lancaster Ave	Shillington	PA	19607	**800-344-2402**	610-775-4521

345 GROCERY STORES

SEE ALSO Wholesale Clubs ; Convenience Stores ; Gourmet Specialty Shops ; Health Food Stores ; Ice Cream & Dairy Stores ; Bakeries

Name / Address	City	State	Zip	Toll-Free	Phone
A.G. Ferrari Foods 2000 N Loop Rd	Alameda	CA	94502	**877-878-2783**	510-346-2100
Acme Markets Inc 75 Valley Stream Pkwy	Malvern	PA	19355	**877-932-7948**	610-889-4000
Advanced Orthomolecular Research Inc 3900 - 12 St Ne	Calgary	AB	T2E8H9	**800-387-0177**	403-250-9997
Alaska Commercial Co 550 W 64th Ave Ste 200	Anchorage	AK	99518	**800-563-0002**	907-273-4600
ALDI Inc 1200 N Kirk Rd	Batavia	IL	60510	**800-366-2324**	630-879-8100
Amax Nutrasource Inc 14291 E Don Julian Rd	City Of Industry	CA	91746	**800-893-5306**	626-961-6600
Ascenta Health Ltd 4-15 Garland Ave	Dartmouth	NS	B3B0A6	**866-224-1775**	902-435-7329
Autry Greer & Sons Inc 2850 W Main St	Mobile	AL	36612	**800-999-7750**	251-457-8655
Bashas Inc 22402 S Bashas Rd	Chandler	AZ	85248	**800-755-7292**	480-895-9350
BI-LO LLC PO Box B	Jacksonville	SC	32203	**800-967-9105**	800-768-4438
Big Y Foods Inc 2145 Roosevelt Ave *Cust Svc	Springfield	MA	01102	**800-828-2688***	413-784-0600
Brookshire Bros Ltd 1201 Ellen Trout Dr	Lufkin	TX	75904	**855-467-7837**	936-634-8155
Byrd Cookie Company Inc 6700 Waters Ave	Savannah	GA	31406	**800-291-2973**	912-355-1716
Capitol Distributing Inc 3500 E Commercial Ct	Meridian	ID	83642	**800-769-5659**	208-888-5112
Econo Foods 1600 Stephenson	Iron Mountain	MI	49801	**877-295-4558**	906-774-1911
El Matador Foods Inc 7201 Bayway Dr	Baytown	TX	77520	**800-470-2447**	281-424-4555
EuroPharma Inc 955 Challenger Dr	Green Bay	WI	54311	**866-598-5487**	920-406-6500
Federated Group Inc 3025 W Salt Creek Ln	Arlington Heights	IL	60005	**800-234-0011**	847-577-1200
Food City 1005 N Arizona Ave	Chandler	AZ	85224	**800-755-7292**	480-857-2198
FreshDirect Inc 23-30 Borden Ave	Long Island	NY	11101	**866-511-1240**	718-928-1000
Frontera Foods Inc 449 N Clark St Ste 205	Chicago	IL	60654	**800-509-4441**	312-595-1624
Fry's Food Stores of Arizona Inc 500 S 99th Ave	Tolleson	AZ	85353	**866-221-4141**	
G & J Land & Marine Food Distributors 506 Front St	Morgan City	LA	70380	**800-256-9187**	985-385-2620
GermanDeli.com 601 Westport Pkwy, Ste 100	Grapevine	TX	76051	**877-437-6269**	817-410-9955
Giant Eagle Inc 101 Kappa Dr *Cust Svc	Pittsburgh	PA	15238	**800-553-2324***	412-963-6200
Giant Food Inc 8301 Professional Pl Ste 115	Landover	MD	20785	**888-469-4426**	
Giant Food Stores Inc 1149 Harrisburg Pike	Carlisle	PA	17013	**888-814-4268**	717-249-4000
Golub Corp 461 Nott St	Schenectady	NY	12308	**800-666-7667**	
Gs Foods Inc 5925 S Alcoa Ave	Vernon	CA	90058	**800-273-6637**	323-581-6161
Hancock County Co-op Oil Assn 245 State St	Garner	IA	50438	**800-924-2667**	641-923-2635

				Toll-Free	Phone
Heinen's Inc 4540 Richmond Rd	Cleveland	OH	44128	**855-475-2300**	
Holly Poultry Inc 2221 Berlin St	Baltimore	MD	21230	**800-342-9464**	410-727-6210
IGA Inc 8725 W Higgins Rd Ste 350	Chicago	IL	60631	**800-321-5442**	773-693-4520
Ingles Markets Inc 2913 US Hwy 70 W *NASDAQ: IMKTA*	Black Mountain	NC	28711	**800-635-5066**	828-669-2941
International Gourmet Foods Inc 7520 Fullerton Rd	Springfield	VA	22153	**800-522-0377**	703-569-4520
International Plastics Inc 185 Commerce Ctr	Greenville	SC	29615	**800-820-4722**	864-297-8000
InVite Health Inc 1 Garden State Plz	Paramus	NJ	07652	**800-349-0929**	201-587-2222
K-VA-T Food Stores Inc PO Box 1158	Abingdon	VA	24212	**800-826-8451**	276-623-5100
Klass Ingredients Inc 3885 N Buffalo St	Orchard Park	NY	14127	**800-662-6577**	716-662-6665
Kroger Co 1014 Vine St *NYSE: KR*	Cincinnati	OH	45202	**800-576-4377**	513-762-4000
Kuukpik Corp PO Box 89187	Nuiqsut	AK	99789	**866-480-6220**	907-480-6220
Lake Erie Frozen Foods Co 1830 Orange Rd	Ashland	OH	44805	**800-766-8501**	419-289-9204
Life Force International Corp 495 Raleigh Ave	El Cajon	CA	92064	**800-531-4877**	858-218-3200
Loblaw Cos Ltd 1 President's Choice Cir	Brampton	ON	L6Y5S5	**888-495-5111**	905-459-2500
Lorann Oils 4518 Aurelius Rd	Lansing	MI	48910	**800-862-8620**	517-882-0215
Lowes Food Stores Inc 1381 Old Mill Cir Ste 200	Winston-Salem	NC	27103	**800-669-5693**	336-659-0180
Martin & Bayley Inc 1311 A W Main	Carmi	IL	62821	**800-876-2511**	618-382-2334
McClancy Seasoning Co 1 Spice Rd	Fort Mill	SC	29707	**800-843-1968**	803-548-2366
Meijer Inc 2929 Walker Ave NW	Grand Rapids	MI	49544	**800-543-3704**	616-453-6711
Meijer Stores Inc 2929 Walker Ave NW	Grand Rapids	MI	49544	**800-543-3704**	616-453-6711
Merchants Grocery Co 800 Maddox Dr PO Box 1268	Culpeper	VA	22701	**877-897-9893**	540-825-0786
Mother's Market & Kitchen 1890 Newport Blvd	Costa Mesa	CA	92627	**800-595-6667**	949-631-4741
Natural Healthy Concepts 310 N Westhill Blvd	Appleton	WI	54914	**866-505-7501**	920-968-2350
Nature's Best 6 Pt Dr Ste 300	Brea	CA	92821	**800-800-7799**	714-255-4600
Overwaitea Food Group 19855 92A Ave	Langley	BC	V1M3B6	**800-242-9229**	604-888-1213
Peapod LLC 9933 Woods Dr	Skokie	IL	60077	**800-573-2763**	847-583-9400
Piggly Wiggly Carolina Company Inc PO Box 118047	Charleston	SC	29423	**800-243-9880**	843-554-9880
Publix Super Markets Inc 3300 Publix Corporate Pkwy *PR	Lakeland	FL	33811	**800-242-1227***	863-688-1188
Rainbow Grocery Co-op Inc 1745 Folsom St	San Francisco	CA	94103	**877-720-2667**	415-863-0620
Raley's 500 W Capitol Ave PO Box 15618	Sacramento	CA	95852	**800-925-9989**	916-373-3333
Ralphs Grocery Co 1014 Vine St *Cust Svc	Cincinnati	OH	45202	**800-576-4377***	
Resource Plus 9636 Heckscher Dr	Jacksonville	FL	32226	**888-678-8966**	
Roasterie Inc, The 1204 W 27th St	Kansas City	MO	64108	**800-376-0245**	816-931-4000
Schnuck Markets Inc 11420 Lackland Rd	Saint Louis	MO	63146	**800-264-4400**	314-994-4400
Shop 'n Save 10461 Manchester Rd	Kirkwood	MO	63122	**800-428-6974**	314-984-0900
Shoppers Food & Pharmacy 10501 Martin Luther King Jr Hwy	Bowie	MD	20720	**800-866-0514**	240-544-0180
ShopRite PO Box 7812	Edison	NJ	08818	**800-746-7748**	
ShopRite Supermarkets Inc 600 York St	Elizabeth	NJ	07207	**800-746-7748**	908-527-3300
Smart & Final Inc 600 Citadel Dr	Commerce	CA	90040	**800-894-0511**	323-869-7500
Starco Impex Inc 2710 S 11th St	Beaumont	TX	77701	**866-740-9601**	
Stop & Shop Supermarket Co 1385 Hancock St	Quincy	MA	02169	**800-767-7772**	781-397-0006
Super H Mart Inc 2550 Pleasant Hill Rd	Duluth	GA	30096	**877-427-7386**	678-543-4000
Supermercado Mi Tierra LLC 9520 International Blvd	Oakland	CA	94603	**800-225-9902**	510-567-8617
SUPERVALU Inc 7075 Flying Cloud Dr *NYSE: SVU* ■ *Cust Svc	Eden Prairie	MN	55344	**877-322-8228***	952-828-4000
Supreme Mfg Company Inc 5 Connerty Ct	East Brunswick	NJ	08816	**800-772-7632**	732-254-0087
Village Super Market Inc 733 Mountain Ave *NASDAQ: VLGEA*	Springfield	NJ	07081	**800-746-7748**	973-467-2200
VitaDigest.com 20687-2 Amar Rd Ste 258	Walnut	CA	91789	**877-848-2168**	
Waldbaums 2 Paragon Dr	Montvale	NJ	07645	**866-443-7374**	
Wedge Community Co-Op Inc 2105 Lyndale Ave S	Minneapolis	MN	55405	**800-535-4555**	612-871-3993
Wegmans Food Markets Inc 1500 Brooks Ave PO Box 30844	Rochester	NY	14603	**800-934-6267**	585-328-2550
Weis Markets 1000 S Second St PO Box 471 *NYSE: WMK*	Sunbury	PA	17801	**866-999-9347**	
Western Bagel Baking Corp 7814 Sepulveda Blvd	Van Nuys	CA	91405	**800-555-0882**	818-786-5847
WinCo Foods Inc PO Box 5756	Boise	ID	83705	**888-674-6854**	208-377-0110
Wing Hing Foods Inc 2539 E Philadelphia St	Ontario	CA	91761	**855-734-2742**	
ZeaVision LLC 716-I Crown Industrial Ct	Chesterfield	MO	63005	**866-833-2800**	314-628-1000

346 GYM & PLAYGROUND EQUIPMENT

				Toll-Free	Phone
American Athletic Inc (AAI) 200 American Ave	Jefferson	IA	50129	**800-247-3978**	515-386-3125
American Playground Corp 2328 Jefferson St	Anderson	IN	46016	**800-541-1602**	765-642-0288
BCI Burke Company Inc 660 Van Dyne Rd	Fond du Lac	WI	54937	**800-356-2070**	920-921-9220
Columbia Cascade Co 1300 SW Sixth Ave Ste 310	Portland	OR	97201	**800-547-1940**	503-223-1157
Grounds For Play Inc 1401 E Dallas St	Mansfield	TX	76063	**800-552-7529**	
Jaypro Sports Inc 976 Hartford Tpke *Cust Svc	Waterford	CT	06385	**800-243-0533***	860-447-3001
Landscape Structures Inc 601 Seventh St S	Delano	MN	55328	**800-328-0035**	763-972-3391
Miracle Recreation Equipment Co 878 Hwy 60	Monett	MO	65708	**800-523-4202**	417-235-6917
PlayCore Inc 401 Chestnut St Ste 410	Chattanooga	TN	37402	**877-762-7563**	
Playworld Systems Inc 1000 Buffalo Rd	Lewisburg	PA	17837	**800-233-8404**	570-522-9800
School-Tech Inc 745 State Cir	Ann Arbor	MI	48108	**800-521-2832**	
SportsPlay Equipment Inc 5642 Natural Bridge Ave	Saint Louis	MO	63120	**800-727-8180**	314-389-4140

347 GYPSUM PRODUCTS

				Toll-Free	Phone
American Gypsum Co 3811 Turtle Creek Blvd Ste 1200	Dallas	TX	75219	**866-439-5800**	214-530-5500
Canadian Gypsum Company Inc 350 Burnhamthorpe Rd W 5th Fl	Mississauga	ON	L5B3J1	**800-565-6607**	905-803-5600
CertainTeed Gypsum 2424 Lakeshore Rd W	Mississauga	ON	L5J1K4	**800-233-8990**	905-823-9881
National Gypsum Co 2001 Rexford Rd	Charlotte	NC	28211	**800-628-4662**	704-365-7300
PABCO Gypsum 37851 Cherry St	Newark	CA	94560	**877-449-7786**	510-792-9555
USG Corp 550 W Adams St *NYSE: USG*	Chicago	IL	60661	**800-874-4968**	312-436-4000

348 HAIRPIECES, WIGS, TOUPEES

				Toll-Free	Phone
Aderans Hair Goods Inc *Simplicity Hair Extensions* 9135 Independence Ave *Sales	Chatsworth	CA	91311	**877-413-5225***	
Alkinco PO Box 278	New York	NY	10116	**800-424-7118**	212-719-3070
Headstart Hair For Men Inc 3395 Cypress Gardens Rd	Winter Haven	FL	33884	**800-645-6525**	863-324-5559
HPH Corp 1529 SE 47th Terr	Cape Coral	FL	33904	**800-654-9884**	239-540-0085
Jacquelyn Wigs 15 W 37th St 4th Fl	New York	NY	10018	**800-272-2424**	212-302-2266
Jean Paree Weegs Inc 4041 South 700 East Ste 2 *Orders	Salt Lake City	UT	84107	**800-422-9447***	
Jon Renau Collection 2510 Island View Way	Vista	CA	92081	**800-462-9447**	760-598-0067
Louis Ferre Inc 302 Fifth Ave Ste 10	New York	NY	10001	**800-695-1061**	212-239-1600
National Fiber Technology LLC 300 Canal St *Cust Svc	Lawrence	MA	01840	**800-842-2751***	978-686-2964
Peggy Knight Solutions Inc 1750 Bridgeway	Sausalito	CA	94965	**800-997-7753**	415-289-1777
Rene Of Paris 9135 Independence Ave 9th Fl *Sales	Chatsworth	CA	90212	**800-353-7363***	
Wig America Co 27317 Industrial Blvd	Hayward	CA	94545	**800-338-7600**	510-887-9579
World of Wigs 2305 E 17th St	Santa Ana	CA	92705	**800-794-5572**	714-547-4461
YK International Co 3246 W Montrose Ave	Chicago	IL	60618	**800-266-5254**	773-583-5270

349 HANDBAGS, TOTES, BACKPACKS

SEE ALSO Sporting Goods ; Tarps, Tents, Covers ; Leather Goods - Personal ; Luggage, Bags, Cases

				Toll-Free	Phone
Dow Cover Co Inc 373 Lexington Ave	New Haven	CT	06513	**800-735-8877**	203-469-5394
Kate Spade 135 5th Ave	New York	NY	10010	**866-999-5283**	212-358-0420
Vera Bradley Designs 2208 Production Rd	Fort Wayne	IN	46808	**800-975-8372**	260-482-4673

350 HARDWARE - MFR

				Toll-Free	Phone
Aceco 4419 Federal Way	Boise	ID	83716	**800-359-7012**	208-343-7712
Acorn Manufacturing Company Inc 457 School St	Mansfield	MA	02048	**800-835-0121**	

Company / Address	City	State	ZIP	Toll-Free	Phone
Acryline USA Inc 2015 Becancour	Lyster	QC	G0S1V0	**800-567-0920**	
Adams Rite Manufacturing Co 10027 S 51st St Ste 102	Phoenix	AZ	85044	**800-872-3267**	909-632-2300
AGM Container Controls Inc 3526 E Ft Lowell Rd	Tucson	AZ	85716	**800-995-5590**	520-881-2130
Albion Industries Inc 800 N Clark St	Albion	MI	49224	**800-835-8911**	517-629-9441
Allied Fastener & Tool Inc 1130 Ng St	Lake Worth	FL	33460	**877-353-3731**	561-585-2113
American Bolt & Screw Manufacturing Corp 601 Kettering Dr	Ontario	CA	91761	**800-325-0844**	909-390-0522
Arrow Lock Co 100 Arrow Dr	New Haven	CT	06511	**800-839-3157**	
Assa Abloy of Canada Ltd 160 Four Vly Dr	Vaughan	ON	L4K4T9	**800-461-3007**	905-738-2466
ASSA Inc 110 Sargent Dr	New Haven	CT	06511	**800-235-7482**	203-624-5225
Attwood Corp 1016 N Monroe St	Lowell	MI	49331	**844-808-5704**	616-897-9241
Automotive Racing Products Inc 1863 Eastman Ave	Ventura	CA	93003	**800-826-3045**	805-339-2200
Bad Dog Tools 24 Broadcommon Rd	Bristol	RI	02809	**800-252-1330**	401-253-1330
Baier Marine Company Inc 2920 Airway Ave	Costa Mesa	CA	92626	**800-455-3917**	
Baldwin Hardware Corp 841 E Wyomissing Blvd	Reading	PA	19611	**800-566-1986**	610-777-7811
Band-It-IDEX Inc 4799 Dahlia St	Denver	CO	80216	**800-525-0758**	303-320-4555
Barnhill Bolt Company Inc 2500 Princeton Dr Ne	Albuquerque	NM	87107	**800-472-3900**	505-884-1808
Baron Mfg Company LLC 1200 Capitol Dr	Addison	IL	60101	**800-368-8585**	630-628-9110
Belwith International Ltd 3100 Broadway Ave	Grandville	MI	49418	**800-235-9484**	
Berenson Corp 2495 Main St	Buffalo	NY	14214	**800-333-0578**	716-833-2402
Best Access Systems 6161 E 75th St	Indianapolis	IN	46250	**855-365-2407**	317-849-2250
Bete Fog Nozzle Inc 50 Greenfield St	Greenfield	MA	01301	**800-235-0049**	413-772-0846
Blum Inc 7733 Old Plank Rd	Stanley	NC	28164	**800-438-6788**	704-827-1345
Bommer Industries Inc PO Box 187	Landrum	SC	29356	**800-334-1654**	864-457-3301
Brainerd Mfg Company Inc 140 Business Pk Dr	Winston-Salem	NC	27107	**800-652-7277**	336-769-4077
Bronze Craft Corp 37 Will St	Nashua	NH	03060	**800-488-7747**	603-883-7747
Cal-Royal Products Inc 6605 Flotilla St	City Of Commerce	CA	90040	**800-876-9258**	323-888-6601
Charles Leonard Inc 145 Kennedy Dr	Hauppauge	NY	11788	**800-999-7202**	631-273-6700
Chicago Nut & Bolt Inc 150 Covington Dr	Bloomingdale	IL	60108	**888-529-8600**	630-529-8600
Circle Bolt & Nut Company Inc 158 Pringle St	Kingston	PA	18704	**800-548-2658**	570-718-6001
Classic Brass Inc 2051 Stoneman Cir	Lakewood	NY	14750	**800-869-3173**	716-763-1400
Cloud-rider Designs Ltd 1260 Eighth Ave	Regina	SK	S4R1C9	**800-632-1255**	306-761-2119
Coast Tool Co 2099 edison ave	San leandro	CA	94577	**888-675-3737**	510-569-1945
Colonial Bronze Co 511 Winsted Rd *All	Torrington	CT	06790	**800-355-7903***	860-489-9233
Component Hardware Group Inc 1890 Swarthmore Ave	Lakewood	NJ	08701	**800-526-3694**	732-363-4700
Corbin Russwin Inc 225 Episcopal Rd	Berlin	CT	06037	**800-438-1951**	860-225-7411
Craft Inc 1929 County St PO Box 3049	South Attleboro	MA	02703	**800-827-2388**	508-761-7917
Daemar Inc 861 Cranberry Ct	Oakville	ON	L6L6J7	**800-387-7115**	905-847-6500
Dahl Bros Canada Ltd 2600 S Sheridan Way	Mississauga	ON	L5J2M4	**800-268-5355**	905-822-2330
Dayton Superior Corp 1125 Byers Rd	Miamisburg	OH	45342	**800-745-3700**	937-866-0711
DE-STA-CO 1025 Doris Rd	Auburn Hills	MI	48326	**888-337-8226**	248-836-6700
Dixie Industries 3510 N Orchard Knob Ave	Chattanooga	TN	37406	**800-933-4943**	423-698-3323
Door Engineering & Mfg LLC 400 Cherry St	Kasota	MN	56050	**800-959-1352**	507-931-6910
DORMA Group North America Dorma Dr	Reamstown	PA	17567	**800-523-8483**	717-336-3881
Doug Mockett & Company Inc 1915 Abalone Ave	Torrance	CA	90501	**800-523-1269**	310-318-2491
Drivekore Inc 101 Wesley Dr	Mechanicsburg	PA	17055	**800-382-1311**	717-697-7440
Duo Fast Northeast 22 Tolland St	East Hartford	CT	06108	**888-399-5712**	860-289-6861
Dynamation Research Inc 2301 Pontius Ave	Los Angeles	CA	90064	**800-726-7997**	310-477-1224
East Teak Trading Group Inc 1106 Drake Rd	Donalds	SC	29638	**800-338-5636**	864-379-2111
Eberhard Hardware Manufacturing Ltd 1523 Bellmill Rd	Tillsonburg	ON	N4G0C9	**800-567-3344**	519-688-3443
Eberhard Mfg Co PO Box 368012	Cleveland	OH	44149	**800-334-6706**	440-238-9720
Emtek Products Inc 15250 Stafford St	City of Industry	CA	91744	**800-356-2741**	626-961-0413
Engineered Products Co (EPCO) 601 Kelso St PO Box 108	Flint	MI	48506	**888-414-3726**	810-767-2050
ER Wagner Mfg Company Inc 4611 N 32nd St	Milwaukee	WI	53209	**800-558-5596**	414-871-5080
ESPE Mfg Company Inc 9220 Ivanhoe St *Cust Svc	Schiller Park	IL	60176	**800-367-3773***	847-678-8950
Fastbolt Corp 200 Louis St	South Hackensack	NJ	07606	**800-631-1980**	201-440-9100
Faultless Caster 3438 Briley Pk Blvd N *Cust Svc	Nashville	TN	37207	**800-322-7359***	
Folger Adam Security Inc 4634 S Presa St	San Antonio	TX	78223	**888-745-0530**	210-533-1231
Freud America Inc 218 Feld Ave	High Point	NC	27263	**800-334-4107**	336-434-3171
Fulton Corp 303 Eigth Ave	Fulton	IL	61252	**800-252-0002**	
G G Schmitt & Sons Inc 2821 Old Tree Dr	Lancaster	PA	17603	**866-724-6488**	717-394-3701
Genie Co 1 Door Dr PO Box 67	Mount Hope	OH	44660	**800-354-3643**	
Granite Security Products Inc 4801 Esco Dr	Fort Worth	TX	76140	**877-948-6723**	469-735-4901
Grass America Inc 1202 Hwy 66 S	Kernersville	NC	27284	**800-334-3512**	
H & C Tool Supply Corp 235 Mount Read Blvd	Rochester	NY	14611	**800-323-4624**	585-235-5700
HA Guden Company Inc 99 Raynor Ave	Ronkonkoma	NY	11779	**800-344-6437**	631-737-2900
Hager Co 139 Victor St	Saint Louis	MO	63104	**800-325-9995**	314-772-4400
Halex Corp 750 S Reservoir St	Pomona	CA	91766	**800-576-1636**	909-622-3537
Hampton Products International Corp 50 Icon	Foothill Ranch	CA	92610	**800-562-5625**	949-472-4256
Helton Industries Ltd 30840 Peardonville Rd	Abbotsford	BC	V2T6K2	**877-300-7412**	604-854-3660
Hi Tech Seals Inc 9211-41 Ave	Edmonton	AB	T6E6R5	**800-661-6055**	780-438-6055
Hindley Mfg Company Inc 9 Havens St	Cumberland	RI	02864	**800-323-9031**	401-722-2550
Hudson Lock Inc 81 Apsley St	Hudson	MA	01749	**800-434-8960**	
Inpower LLC 3555 Africa Rd	Galena	OH	43021	**866-548-0965**	740-548-0965
Inventory Sales Co 9777 Reavis Rd	St Louis	MO	63123	**866-417-3801**	314-776-6200
Jacknob Corp 290 Oser Ave PO Box 18032	Hauppauge	NY	11788	**800-424-7495**	631-546-6560
Jacob Holtz Co 10 Industrial Hwy MS-6 Airport Business Complex B	Lester	PA	19029	**800-445-4337**	215-423-2800
Jarvis Caster Co 881 Lower Brownsville Rd	Jackson	TN	38301	**800-995-9876**	
Kaba Ilco Corp 400 Jeffreys Rd	Rocky Mount	NC	27804	**800-334-1381**	252-446-3321
Kanebridge Corp 153 Bauer Dr	Oakland	NJ	07436	**888-222-9221**	201-337-2300
Kason Industries Inc 57 Amlajack Blvd	Newnan	GA	30265	**800-935-3550**	770-304-3000
Keystone Electronics Corp 31-07 20th Rd	Astoria	NY	11105	**800-221-5510**	718-956-8900
Knape & Vogt Manufacturing Co 2700 Oak Industrial Dr NE	Grand Rapids	MI	49505	**800-253-1561**	616-459-3311
LE Johnson Products Inc 2100 Sterling Ave	Elkhart	IN	46516	**800-837-5664**	574-293-5664
Le Smith Co 1030 E Wilson St PO Box 766	Bryan	OH	43506	**888-537-6484**	419-636-4555
Liberty Hardware Mfg Corp 140 Business Pk Dr	Winston-Salem	NC	27107	**800-542-3789**	
Lockmasters Security Institute 2101 John C Watts Dr	Nicholasville	KY	40356	**800-654-0637**	859-885-6041
Master Lock Company LLC 137 W Forest Hill Ave PO Box 927	Oak Creek	WI	53154	**800-464-2088**	
Medeco Security Locks Inc 3625 Alleghany Dr	Salem	VA	24153	**800-839-3157**	540-380-5000
Mountz Inc 1080 N 11th St	San Jose	CA	95112	**888-925-2763**	408-292-2214
Nagel Chase Inc 2323 Delaney Rd	Gurnee	IL	60031	**800-323-4552**	
Nik-O-Lok Co 3130 N Mitthoeffer Rd	Indianapolis	IN	46235	**800-428-4348**	317-899-6955
Norshield Corp 3232 Mobile Hwy	Montgomery	AL	36108	**855-859-3716**	334-551-0650
P M Industrial Supply Co 9613 Canoga Ave	Chatsworth	CA	91311	**800-382-3684**	818-341-9180
Paneloc Corp PO Box 547	Farmington	CT	06034	**800-394-6711**	860-677-6711
Payson Casters Inc 2323 N Delaney Rd	Gurnee	IL	60031	**800-323-4552**	847-336-6200
PDQ Manufacturing 2754 Creek Hill Rd	Leola	PA	17540	**800-441-9692**	717-656-4281
PL Porter Co 3000 Winona Ave	Burbank	CA	91504	**888-236-5165**	818-526-2600
Purdy Corp 101 Prospect Ave	Cleveland	OH	44115	**800-547-0780**	
Qual-Craft Industries PO Box 559	Stoughton	MA	02072	**800-231-5647**	781-344-1000
Renovator's Supply Inc Renovators Old ML	Millers Falls	MA	01349	**800-659-2211**	413-423-3300
Rockford Process Control Inc 2020 Seventh St	Rockford	IL	61104	**800-228-3779**	815-966-2000
Rocky Mountain Hardware Inc 1020 Airport Way PO Box 4108	Hailey	ID	83333	**888-788-2013**	208-788-2013
Rousseau Metal Inc 105 Ave De Gasp Ouest	St Jean-Port-Joli	QC	G0R3G0	**866-463-4270**	418-598-3381
Rutherford Controls Int'l Corp 210 Shearson Crescent	Cambridge	ON	N1T1J6	**800-265-6630**	519-621-7651
RWM Casters Co PO Box 668	Gastonia	NC	28053	**800-634-7704**	
S Parker Hardware Manufacturing Corp PO Box 9882	Englewood	NJ	07631	**800-772-7537**	201-569-1600
Salice America Inc 2123 Crown Centre Dr	Charlotte	NC	28227	**800-222-9652**	704-841-7810
Sargent & Greenleaf Inc 1 Security Dr	Nicholasville	KY	40356	**800-826-7652**	859-885-9411
Sargent Manufacturing Co 100 Sargent Dr	New Haven	CT	06511	**800-727-5477**	
Saturn Fasteners Inc 425 S Varney St	Burbank	CA	91502	**800-947-9414**	818-846-7145
Savant Manufacturing Inc 2930 Hwy 383 PO Box 520	Kinder	LA	70648	**800-326-6880**	337-738-5896

Classified Section

Company	Address	City	State	ZIP	Toll-Free	Phone
Seastrom Mfg Company Inc	456 Seastrom St	Twin Falls	ID	83301	**800-634-2356**	208-737-4300
Sebewaing Tool & Engineering Co	415 Union St	Sebewaing	MI	48759	**800-453-2207**	989-883-2000
Securitron Magnalock Corp	10027 S 51st St Ste 102 *Sales	Phoenix	AZ	85044	**800-624-5625***	623-582-4626
Shepherd Caster Corp	203 Kerth St	Saint Joseph	MI	49085	**800-253-0868**	269-983-7351
Sherwood Windows Ltd	37 Iron St	Toronto	ON	M9W5E3	**800-770-5256**	416-675-3262
Signature Hardware	2700 Crescent Springs Pike	Erlanger	KY	41017	**866-855-2284**	859-647-7564
Simpson Strong-Tie Company Inc	5956 W Las Positas Blvd	Pleasanton	CA	94588	**800-925-5099**	925-560-9000
Spalding Hardware Ltd	1616 10 Ave SW	Calgary	AB	T3C0J5	**800-837-0850**	
Spokane Hardware Supply Inc	2001 E Trent Ave	Spokane	WA	99202	**800-888-1663**	509-535-1663
Suncor Stainless Inc	70 Armstrong Rd	Plymouth	MA	02360	**800-218-7702**	508-732-9191
Sunex International Inc	100 Roe Rd	Travelers Rest	SC	29690	**800-833-7869**	864-834-8759
Tides Marine Inc	3251 SW 13th Dr	Deerfield Beach	FL	33442	**800-420-0949**	954-420-0949
Tiffin Metal Products Co	450 Wall St	Tiffin	OH	44883	**800-537-0983**	
Trimark Corp	PO Box 350	New Hampton	IA	50659	**800-447-0343**	641-394-3188
Trimco/Builders Brass Works	3528 Emery St	Los Angeles	CA	90023	**800-637-8746**	323-262-4191
Truth Hardware Inc	700 W Bridge St *Cust Svc	Owatonna	MN	55060	**800-866-7884***	507-451-5620
TS Distributors Inc	4404 Windfern Rd	Houston	TX	77041	**800-392-3655**	832-467-5400
Unicorp	291 Cleveland St	Orange	NJ	07050	**800-526-1389**	973-674-1700
Weber-Knapp Co	441 Chandler St	Jamestown	NY	14701	**800-828-9254**	716-484-9135
Weiser Lock A Masco Co	19701 Da Vinci	Lake Forest	CA	92610	**800-677-5625**	
Woodbury Box Company Inc	301 McIntosh Pkwy	Thomaston	GA	30286	**800-722-2061**	
Wright Tool Company Inc	1 Wright Dr	Barberton	OH	44203	**800-321-2902**	330-848-0600
Yale Residential Security Products Inc	100 Yale Ave *Cust Svc	Lenoir City	TN	37771	**800-438-1951***	
Yale Security Inc.ÿ	1902 Airport Rd	Monroe	NC	28110	**800-438-1951**	
Yardley Products Corp	10 W College Ave	Yardley	PA	19067	**800-457-0154**	215-493-2723

351 HARDWARE - WHOL

Company	Address	City	State	ZIP	Toll-Free	Phone
Aarch Caster & Equipment	314 Axminister Dr	Fenton	MO	63026	**888-349-0220**	636-349-0220
Action Bolt & Tool Co (WURTH)	2051 E Blue Heron Blvd	Riviera Beach	FL	33404	**800-423-0700**	561-845-8800
Aero-Space Southwest Inc	21450 N Third Ave	Phoenix	AZ	85027	**800-289-2779**	623-582-2779
All-Pro Fasteners Inc	1916 Peyco Dr N	Arlington	TX	76001	**800-361-6627**	817-467-5700
Allied International	13207 Bradley Ave *General	Sylmar	CA	91342	**800-533-8333***	818-364-2333
Associated Steel Corp	18200 Miles Rd	Cleveland	OH	44128	**800-321-9300**	
Baer Supply Co	909 Forest Edge Dr	Vernon Hills	IL	60061	**800-944-2237**	847-913-2237
Bargain Supply Co	844 E Jefferson St	Louisville	KY	40206	**800-322-5226**	502-562-5000
Barnett Inc	801 W Bay St	Jacksonville	FL	32204	**888-803-4467**	904-384-6530
Blish-Mize Co	223 S Fifth St	Atchison	KS	66002	**800-995-0525**	913-367-1250
Bostwick-Braun Co	PO Box 912	Toledo	OH	43697	**800-777-9640**	419-259-3600
Builders Hardware & Supply Company Inc	1516 15th Ave W	Seattle	WA	98119	**800-828-1437**	206-281-3700
Cascade Wholesale Hardware Inc	5650 NW *General	Hillsboro	OR	97124	**800-877-9987***	503-614-2600
Caster Technology Corp	11552 Markon Dr	Garden Grove	CA	92841	**866-547-8090**	714-893-6886
Compatico Inc	4710 44th St SE	Grand Rapids	MI	49512	**800-336-1772**	616-940-1772
Conveyer & Caster Corp	3501 Detroit Ave	Cleveland	OH	44113	**800-777-0600**	216-631-4448
Denver Wire Rope & Supply Inc	4100 Dahlia St	Denver	CO	80216	**800-873-3697**	303-377-5166
Desoto Sales Inc	20945 Osborne St	Canoga Park	CA	91304	**800-826-9779**	818-998-0853
Dixie Construction Products Inc	970 Huff Rd NW	Atlanta	GA	30318	**800-992-1180**	404-351-1100
Earnest Machine Products Co	12502 Plz Dr	Cleveland	OH	44130	**800-327-6378**	216-362-1100
EB Bradley Co	5080 S Alameda St	Los Angeles	CA	90058	**800-533-3030**	323-585-9201
Fastec Industrial	2219 Eddie Williams Rd	Johnson City	TN	37601	**800-837-2505**	
Fastenal Co	2001 Theurer Blvd *NASDAQ: FAST*	Winona	MN	55987	**877-507-7555**	507-454-5374
General Fasteners Co	37584 Amrhein Rd Ste 150	Livonia	MI	48150	**800-945-2658**	734-452-2400
Handy Hardware Wholesale Inc	8300 Tewantin Dr	Houston	TX	77061	**800-364-3835**	713-644-1495
Hans Johnsen Co	8901 Chancellor Row *Sales	Dallas	TX	75247	**800-879-1515***	214-879-1550
Harbor Freight Tools	3491 Mission Oaks Blvd	Camarillo	CA	93011	**800-444-3353**	805-445-4791
Hardware Distribution Warehouses Inc (HDW)	6900 Woolworth Rd *Cust Svc	Shreveport	LA	71129	**800-256-8527***	318-686-8527
Hardware Suppliers of America Inc (HSI)	1400 E Fire Tower Rd	Greenville	NC	27858	**800-334-5625**	
Hawaii Nut & Bolt Inc	905 Ahua St	Honolulu	HI	96819	**800-764-6887**	808-834-1919
Hillman Group Inc	10590 Hamilton Ave	Cincinnati	OH	45231	**800-800-4900**	513-851-4900
Hodell-natco Industries Inc	7825 Hub Pkwy	Cleveland	OH	44125	**800-321-4862**	216-447-0165
Home Depot Supply	3100 Cumberland Blvd Ste 1480	Atlanta	GA	30339	**855-615-8372**	770-852-9000
House-Hasson Hardware Inc	3125 Water Plant Rd	Knoxville	TN	37914	**800-333-0520**	865-525-0471
Industrial Hardware & Specialties Inc	17B Kentucky Ave	Paterson	NJ	07503	**800-684-4010**	973-684-4010
J & E Supply & Fastner Company Inc	1903 SE 59th St	Oklahoma City	OK	73129	**800-677-7922**	405-670-1234
Jay Cee Sales & Rivet Inc	32861 Chesley Dr	Farmington	MI	48336	**800-521-6777**	248-478-2150
Jensen Distribution Services	PO Box 3708 *General	Spokane	WA	99220	**800-234-1321***	
JSJ Corp Dake Div	724 Robbins Rd	Grand Haven	MI	49417	**800-846-3253**	616-842-7110
Karl W Richter Inc	350 Middlefield Rd	Toronto	ON	M1S5B1	**877-597-8665**	416-757-8951
Kentec Inc	3250 Centerville Hwy	Snellville	GA	30039	**800-241-0148**	770-985-1907
Max Tool Inc	119b Citation Ct	Birmingham	AL	35209	**800-783-6298**	205-942-2466
Monroe Hardware Co	101 N Sutherland Ave	Monroe	NC	28110	**800-222-1974**	704-289-3121
Oasis Stage Werks Inc	249 S Rio Grande St	Salt Lake City	UT	84101	**800-952-6865**	801-363-0364
Omaha Wholesale Hardware Co	PO Box 3628	Omaha	NE	68102	**800-238-4566**	402-444-1673
Onity Inc	2232 Northmont Pkwy Ste 100	Duluth	GA	30096	**800-424-1433**	
Orgill Inc	3742 Tyndale Dr	Memphis	TN	38125	**800-347-2860**	901-754-8850
Parts Assoc Inc	12420 Plz Dr	Parma	OH	44130	**800-321-1128**	216-433-7700
Regitar USA Inc	2575 Container Dr	Montgomery	AL	36109	**877-734-4827**	334-244-1885
Repairclinic.com Inc	48600 Michigan Ave	Canton	MI	48188	**800-269-2609**	734-495-3079
Ryobi Technologies Inc	1428 Pearman Dairy Rd	Anderson	SC	29625	**800-525-2579**	
Serv-a-lite Products Inc	3451 Morton Dr	East Moline	IL	61244	**800-800-4900**	
Signal Industrial Products Corp	1601 Cowart St	Chattanooga	TN	37408	**800-728-1326**	423-756-4980
Silicone Specialties Inc	430 S Rockford Ave	Tulsa	OK	74120	**888-243-0672**	918-587-5567
Specialty Bolt & Screw Inc	235 Bowles Rd	Agawam	MA	01001	**800-322-7878**	413-789-6700
Standard Supply & Distributing Co	1431 Regal Row	Dallas	TX	75247	**800-460-7801**	214-630-7800
Supply Technologies LLC	6065 Parkland Blvd	Cleveland	OH	44124	**800-695-8650**	440-947-2100
Techni-Tool Inc	1547 N Trooper Rd PO Box 1117 *Cust Svc	Worcester	PA	19490	**800-832-4866***	610-941-2400
Triangle Fastener Corp	1925 Preble Ave *General	Pittsburgh	PA	15233	**800-486-1832***	412-321-5000
Wallace Hardware Company Inc	5050 S Davy Crockett Pkwy PO Box 6004	Morristown	TN	37815	**800-776-0976**	423-586-5650
Wurth Revcar Fasteners Inc	3845 Thirlane Rd	Roanoke	VA	24019	**877-999-8784**	
WW Grainger Inc	100 Grainger Pkwy *NYSE: GWW*	Lake Forest	IL	60045	**888-361-8649**	847-535-1000

352 HEALTH CARE PROVIDERS - ANCILLARY

SEE ALSO Vision Correction Centers ; Home Health Services ; Hospices

Company	Address	City	State	ZIP	Toll-Free	Phone
Amedisys Inc	5959 S Sherwood Forest Blvd Ste 300 *NASDAQ: AMED*	Baton Rouge	LA	70816	**800-464-0020**	225-292-2031
American Family Care	3700 Cahaba Beach Rd	Birmingham	AL	35242	**800-258-7535**	205-403-8902
American Red Cross In Greater New York (Inc)	520 W 49th St	New York	NY	10019	**877-733-2767**	
AmeriHealth Mercy Health Plan	8040 Carlson Rd Ste 500	Harrisburg	PA	17112	**888-991-7200**	717-651-3540
AmSurg Corp	1A Burton Hills Blvd *NASDAQ: AMSG*	Nashville	TN	37215	**800-945-2301**	615-665-1283
CareSource	230 N Main St	Dayton	OH	45402	**800-488-0134**	937-224-3300
Children's Bureau of Southern California	1910 Magnolia Ave	Los Angeles	CA	90004	**800-730-3933**	213-342-0100
DaVita Inc	1551 Wewatta St *NYSE: DVA*	Denver	CO	80202	**800-310-4872**	303-405-2100
Fresenius Medical Care North America	920 Winter St	Waltham	MA	02451	**800-662-1237**	781-699-9000
Hanger Orthopedic Group Inc	10910 Domain Dr Ste 300	Austin	TX	78758	**877-442-6437**	512-777-3800

Name / Address	City	State	Zip	Toll-Free	Phone
HealthDrive Corp 888 Worcester St	Wellesley	MA	02482	**888-964-6681**	
HealthSouth Corp 3660 Grandview Pkwy Ste 200 *NYSE: HLS*	Birmingham	AL	35243	**800-765-4772**	205-967-7116
Healthways Inc 701 Cool Springs Blvd *NASDAQ: HWAY*	Franklin	TN	37067	**800-327-3822**	
MedCath Inc 10720 Sikes Pl Ste 300 *NASDAQ: MDTH*	Charlotte	NC	28277	**800-461-9330**	704-708-6600
Miracle-Ear Inc 5000 Cheshire Pkwy N	Minneapolis	MN	55446	**800-464-8002**	
Radiation Therapy Services Inc 2270 Colonial Blvd	Fort Myers	FL	33907	**800-437-1619**	239-931-7275
SCAN Health Plan 3800 Kilroy Airport Way Ste 100	Long Beach	CA	90806	**800-247-5091**	562-989-5100
US Physical Therapy 1300 W Sam Houston Pkwy S Ste 300 *NYSE: USPH*	Houston	TX	77042	**800-580-6285**	713-297-7000

353 HEALTH CARE SYSTEMS

SEE ALSO General Hospitals - US

Health Care Systems are one or more hospitals owned, leased, sponsored, or managed by a central organization. Single-hospital systems are not included here; however, some large hospital networks or alliances may be listed.

Name / Address	City	State	Zip	Toll-Free	Phone
Addus HealthCare Inc 2401 S Plum Grove Rd *NASDAQ: ADUS*	Palatine	IL	60067	**888-233-8746**	847-303-5300
Adventist Health 2100 Douglas Blvd	Roseville	CA	95661	**877-336-3566**	916-781-2000
Albert Einstein Healthcare Network 5501 Old York Rd	Philadelphia	PA	19141	**800-346-7834**	215-456-7890
American Caresource Holdings Inc 222 W. LAS COLINAS BLVD Ste 500N *NASDAQ: ANCI*	IRVING	TX	75039	**800-370-5994**	
American Kidney Stone Management Ltd (AKSM) 797 Thomas Ln	Columbus	OH	43214	**800-637-5188**	614-447-0281
American Renal Assoc Inc 66 Cherry Hill Dr	Beverly	MA	01915	**877-997-3625**	978-922-3080
Amery Regional Medical Ctr 265 Griffin St E	Amery	WI	54001	**800-424-5273**	715-268-8000
Appalachian Regional Healthcare Service (ARH) 80 Hospital Dr PO Box 8086	Barbourville	KY	40906	**888-654-0015**	859-226-2440
Banner Health 1441 N 12th St	Phoenix	AZ	85006	**866-451-3399**	602-495-4000
Baptist Health South Florida Inc 6000 University Dr	Coral Gables	FL	33146	**800-622-2838**	786-662-7000
Baptist Memorial Health Care Corp 350 N Humphreys Blvd	Memphis	TN	38120	**800-422-7847**	901-227-5920
Benedictine Health System 503 E Third St Ste 400	Duluth	MN	55805	**800-833-7208**	218-786-2370
Catholic Healthcare Partners 615 Elsinore Pl	Cincinnati	OH	45202	**877-700-4647**	513-639-2800
Centra Health Inc 1920 Atherholt Rd	Lynchburg	VA	24501	**800-947-5442**	434-947-3000
Christiana Care Health System 501 W 14th St	Wilmington	DE	19801	**855-250-9594**	302-366-1929
CHRISTUS Schumpert Health System 1 St Mary Pl	Shreveport	LA	71101	**844-444-8440**	318-681-4500
CHRISTUS Spohn Health System 1702 Santa Fe St	Corpus Christi	TX	78404	**800-247-6574**	361-881-3000
Community Health Systems Inc 4000 Meridian Blvd *NYSE: CYH*	Franklin	TN	37067	**888-373-9600**	615-465-7000
Community Services Group (CSG) 320 Highland Dr PO Box 597	Mountville	PA	17554	**877-907-7970**	717-285-7121
Crozer-Keystone Health System (CKHS) 190 W Sproul Rd	Springfield	PA	19064	**800-254-3258**	610-328-8700
Eastern Maine Healthcare Systems (EMHS) 43 Whiting Hill Rd	Brewer	ME	04412	**844-364-4473**	207-973-7050
Fairview Health Services 2450 Riverside Ave	Minneapolis	MN	55454	**800-824-1953**	612-672-6000
Great Plains Health Alliance Inc 625 Third St	Phillipsburg	KS	67661	**800-432-2779**	785-543-2111
Greenville Hospital System (GHS) 701 Grove Rd	Greenville	SC	29605	**877-447-4636**	864-455-8976
Guthrie Healthcare System 1 Guthrie Sq	Sayre	PA	18840	**888-448-8474**	570-887-4401
HCA Midwest Health System 903 E 104th St Ste 500	Kansas City	MO	64131	**800-386-9355**	816-508-4000
Health Net Of Arizona Inc 1230 W Washington St	Tempe	AZ	85281	**800-291-6911**	602-794-1400
Henry Ford Health System 1 Ford Pl	Detroit	MI	48202	**800-436-7936**	
IASIS Healthcare Corp 117 Seaboard Ln Bldg E	Franklin	TN	37067	**877-898-6080**	615-844-2747
ICG Link Inc 7003 Chadwick Dr Ste 111	Brentwood	TN	37027	**877-397-7605**	615-370-1530
Inova Health System 8110 Gatehouse Rd	Falls Church	VA	22042	**855-694-6682**	
INTEGRIS Health Inc 3300 NW Expy	Oklahoma City	OK	73112	**888-951-2277**	405-951-2277
Intermountain HealthCare 36 S State St *Hum Res	Salt Lake City	UT	84111	**800-843-7820***	801-442-2000
Kindred Healthcare Inc 680 S Fourth Ave *NYSE: KND*	Louisville	KY	40202	**800-545-0749**	502-596-7300
LifePoint Health 330 Seven Springs Way *NASDAQ: LPNT*	Brentwood	TN	37027	**888-982-9144**	615-920-7000
Lifespring Inc 460 Spring St	Jeffersonville	IN	47130	**800-456-2117**	812-280-2080
MedCath Inc 10720 Sikes Pl Ste 300 *NASDAQ: MDTH*	Charlotte	NC	28277	**800-461-9330**	704-708-6600
MedStar Health 5565 Sterrett Pl 5th Fl.	Columbia	MD	21044	**877-772-6505**	410-772-6500
Methodist Health Care System 6565 Fannin St	Houston	TX	77030	**877-726-9362**	713-790-3311
Methodist Healthcare Ministries of South Texas Inc 4507 Medical Dr	San Antonio	TX	78229	**800-959-6673**	210-692-0234
Methodist Hospitals of Dallas 1441 N Beckley Ave	Dallas	TX	75203	**800-725-9664**	214-947-8181
Northwestern Counseling & Support Services Inc 107 Fisher Pond Rd	Saint Albans	VT	05478	**800-834-7793**	802-524-6554
Palomar Pomerado Health 15615 Pomerado Rd	Poway	CA	92064	**800-628-2880**	858-613-4000
Premier Inc 12255 El Camino Real	San Diego	CA	92130	**877-777-1552**	858-481-2727
Riverside-San Bernardino County Indian Health Inc (RSBCIH) 11555 1/2 Potrero Rd	Banning	CA	92220	**800-732-8805**	951-849-4761
Schumacher Group 200 Corporate Blvd Ste 201	Lafayette	LA	70508	**800-893-9698**	
Scripps Health 4275 Campus Pt Ct	San Diego	CA	92121	**800-727-4777**	
Sea Mar Community Health Ctr 1040 S Henderson St	Seattle	WA	98108	**855-289-4503**	206-763-5277
Senior Whole Health LLC (SWH) 58 Charles St	Cambridge	MA	02141	**888-794-7268**	617-494-5353
Shriners Hospitals for Children 2900 N Rocky Pt Dr	Tampa	FL	33607	**800-237-5055**	813-281-0300
Southern Illinois Healthcare 1239 E Main St	Carbondale	IL	62902	**866-744-2468**	618-457-5200
SSM Healthy 1000 N Lee Ave	Oklahoma City	OK	73102	**866-203-5846**	618-242-4600
Sutter Health 2200 River Plaza	Sacramento	CA	95833	**888-888-6044**	916-733-8800
Texas Health Resources 612 E. Lamar Blvd Ste 900	Arlington	TX	76011	**877-847-9355**	
TheraCare 116 W 32nd St 8th Fl	New York	NY	10001	**800-505-7000**	212-564-2350
Universal Health Services Inc 367 S Gulph Rd *NYSE: UHS*	King of Prussia	PA	19406	**800-347-7750**	610-768-3300
University of Maryland Medical System 22 S Greene St	Baltimore	MD	21201	**800-492-5538**	410-328-8667
University of Pittsburgh Medical Ctr Health System 200 Lothrop St	Pittsburgh	PA	15213	**800-533-8762**	412-647-2345
Vantage Health Plan Inc 130 Desiard St Ste 300	Monroe	LA	71201	**888-823-1910**	318-361-0900
Veterans Health Administration 810 Vermont Ave NW	Washington	DC	20420	**800-827-1000**	202-273-5400
Washington County Mental Health Services Inc (WCMHS) PO Box 647	Montpelier	VT	05601	**800-649-2642**	802-229-0591
West Penn Allegheny Health System 4800 Friendship Ave	Pittsburgh	PA	15224	**800-994-6610**	
Wheaton Franciscan Healthcare 3801 Spring St	Racine	WI	53405	**877-304-6332**	262-687-4011

354 HEALTH & FITNESS CENTERS

SEE ALSO Spas - Health & Fitness ; Weight Loss Centers & Services

Name / Address	City	State	Zip	Toll-Free	Phone
Algoma University College 1520 Queen St E	Sault Sainte Marie	ON	P6A2G4	**888-254-6628**	705-949-2301
Auberge et spa Le Nordik Inc 16 ch Nordik	Old Chelsea	QC	J9B2P7	**866-575-3700**	819-827-1111
Big Fitness 5 Progress St	Seekonk	MA	02771	**800-383-2008**	401-885-5200
Brick Bodies Fitness Services Inc 201 Old Padonia Rd	Cockeysville	MD	21030	**866-952-7425**	410-252-8058
Contours Express Inc 156 Imperial Way	Nicholasville	KY	40356	**855-589-9662**	
Corporate Fitness Works Inc 1200 16th St N	St Petersburg	FL	33705	**855-417-9697**	301-417-9697
Crunch Fitness International 220 W 19th St	New York	NY	10011	**888-227-8624**	212-370-0998
Dumbell Man Fitness Equipment, The 655 Hawaii Ave	Torrance	CA	90503	**800-432-6266**	310-381-2900
Equinox Fitness Holdings Inc 895 Broadway	New York	NY	10003	**866-332-6549**	212-677-0180
Fitness Depot 1808 Lower Roswell Rd	Marietta	GA	30068	**800-974-6828**	770-971-6828
Flex Hr 10700 Medlock Bridge Rd Ste 206	Johns Creek	GA	30097	**877-735-3947**	770-814-4225
G & G Fitness Equipment Inc 7350 Transit Rd	Williamsville	NY	14221	**800-537-0516**	716-633-2527
Healthtrax Fitness & Wellness 2345 Main St	Glastonbury	CT	06033	**800-998-0880**	860-652-7066
Iron Tribe Franchise LLC 300 27th St S	Birmingham	AL	35233	**855-226-8699**	205-226-8669
Jonas Fitness Inc 16969 n texas ave	Webster	TX	77598	**800-324-9800**	
Kinderdance International Inc 5238 Valleypointe Pkwy	Roanoke	VA	24019	**800-554-2334**	321-984-4448
Little Gym International Inc 7001 N Scottsdale Rd *General	Paradise Valley	AZ	85253	**888-228-2878***	
Mdr Fitness Corp 14101 Nw Fourth St	Sunrise	FL	33325	**866-521-7337**	954-845-9500
Peoplefit Health & Fitness Center 237 Lexington St Ste 110	Woburn	MA	01801	**855-784-4663**	781-932-9332
Premier & Curzons Fitness Clubs 5100 Dixie Rd	Mississauga	ON	L4W1C9	**866-371-7307**	905-602-9912
Scotch Malt Whiskey Society 10210 Nw 50th St	Sunrise	FL	33351	**800-990-1991**	954-749-2440
Shockoe Commerce Group LLC 11 S 12th St 4th Fl	Richmond	VA	23219	**866-570-0498**	804-343-3441
TuffStuff Fitness Equipment Inc 13971 Norton Ave	Chino	CA	91710	**888-884-8275**	909-629-1600

Name / Address	City	State	ZIP	Toll-Free	Phone
Work Out World 762 SR- 18	Brunswick	NJ	08816	**888-564-6969**	732-390-7390
World Health 7222 Edgemont Blvd NW	Calgary	AB	T3A2X7	**866-278-4131**	403-239-4048

355 HEALTH FOOD STORES

Name / Address	City	State	ZIP	Toll-Free	Phone
Christopher Enterprises 155 West 2050 North	Spanish Fork	UT	84660	**800-453-1406**	
Ginsberg's Foods Inc 29 Ginsberg Ln PO Box 17	Hudson	NY	12534	**800-999-6006**	518-828-4004
GNC Inc 300 Sixth Ave 14th Fl *NYSE: GNC*	Pittsburgh	PA	15222	**877-462-4700**	
Juice It Up! Franchise Corp 17915 Sky Pk Cir Ste J	Irvine	CA	92614	**888-705-8423**	949-475-0146
Netrition Inc 25 Corporate Cir Ste 118	Albany	NY	12203	**888-817-2411**	518-464-0765
Whole Foods Market Inc 550 Bowie St *NASDAQ: WFM*	Austin	TX	78703	**888-992-6227**	512-477-4455

HEATING EQUIPMENT - ELECTRIC

SEE Air Conditioning & Heating Equipment - Residential

356 HEALTH & MEDICAL INFORMATION - ONLINE

Name / Address	City	State	ZIP	Toll-Free	Phone
At Health Inc 7829 Center Blvd SE	Snoqualmie	WA	98065	**888-284-3258**	425-292-0329
BabyCenter LLC 163 Freelon St	San Francisco	CA	94107	**866-241-2229**	415-537-0900
eMedicine.com Inc 8420 W Dodge Rd Ste 402	Omaha	NE	68114	**866-241-9601**	402-341-3222
MedlinePlus National Library of Medicine 8600 Rockville Pk	Bethesda	MD	20894	**888-346-3656**	301-594-5983
Pain.com *Dannemiller Memorial Educational Foundation* 5711 NW Pkwy	San Antonio	TX	78246	**800-328-2308**	210-572-2512
PubMed US National Library of Medicine 8600 Rockville Pike	Bethesda	MD	20894	**888-346-3656**	

357 HEATING EQUIPMENT - GAS, OIL, COAL

SEE ALSO Furnaces & Ovens - Industrial Process ; Air Conditioning & Heating Equipment - Commercial/Industrial ; Air Conditioning & Heating Equipment - Residential ; Boiler Shops

Name / Address	City	State	ZIP	Toll-Free	Phone
Aerco International Inc 159 Paris Ave	Northvale	NJ	07647	**800-526-0288**	201-768-2400
Aquatherm Industries Inc 1940 Rutgers University Blvd	Lakewood	NJ	08701	**800-535-6307**	
Bosch Thermotechnology 340 Mad River Pk	Waitsfield	VT	05673	**800-283-3787**	
Electro-Flex Heat Inc 5 Northwood Rd	Bloomfield	CT	06002	**800-585-4213**	860-242-6287
Empire Comfort Systems Inc 918 Freeburg Ave	Belleville	IL	62222	**800-851-3153**	618-233-7420
Freeman Gas Inc 1186 Asheville Hwy	Spartanburg	SC	29303	**800-277-5730**	864-582-5475
Hearth & Home Technologies Inc 7571 215th St W	Lakeville	MN	55044	**888-427-3973**	952-985-6000
John Zink Company LLC 11920 E Apache St	Tulsa	OK	74116	**800-421-9242**	918-234-1800
LB White Company Inc W 6636 LB White Rd	Onalaska	WI	54650	**800-345-7200**	608-783-5691
Meeder Equipment Co 12323 Sixth St	Rancho Cucamonga	CA	91739	**800-423-3711**	909-463-0600
Powrmatic Inc 2906 Baltimore Blvd PO Box 439	Finksburg	MD	21048	**800-966-9100**	410-833-9100
Rasmussen Iron Works Inc 12028 E Philadelphia St	Whittier	CA	90601	**888-301-0440**	562-696-8718
Raypak Inc 2151 Eastman Ave	Oxnard	CA	93030	**800-438-4328**	805-278-5300
Reimers Electra Steam Inc 4407 Martinsburg Pk PO Box 37	Clear Brook	VA	22624	**800-872-7562**	540-662-3811
Roberts-Gordon Inc 1250 William St PO Box 44	Buffalo	NY	14240	**800-828-7450**	716-852-4400
RW Beckett Corp PO Box 1289	Elyria	OH	44036	**800-645-2876**	440-327-1060
Schwank Inc 2 Schwank Way at Hwy 56N	Waynesboro	GA	30830	**877-446-3727**	
Spectrolab Inc 12500 Gladstone Ave	Sylmar	CA	91342	**800-936-4888**	818-365-4611
Taco Inc 1160 Cranston St	Cranston	RI	02920	**888-778-2733**	401-942-8000
Thermal Solutions LLC PO Box 3244	Lancaster	PA	17604	**800-860-5726**	717-239-7642
Utica Boilers Inc PO Box 4729	Utica	NY	13504	**800-325-5479**	866-847-6656
Water Furnace International Inc 9000 Conservation Way	Fort Wayne	IN	46809	**800-222-5667**	260-478-5667
Wayne Combustion Systems 801 Glasgow Ave	Fort Wayne	IN	46803	**855-929-6327**	260-425-9200
Williams Comfort Products 250 W Laurel St	Colton	CA	92324	**866-677-8444**	909-825-0993

358 HEAVY EQUIPMENT DISTRIBUTORS

SEE ALSO Farm Machinery & Equipment - Whol ; Industrial Equipment & Supplies (Misc) - Whol

Name / Address	City	State	ZIP	Toll-Free	Phone
4Rivers Equipment 3763 Monarch St	Frederick	CO	80516	**800-490-6162**	303-833-5900
Adams Air & Hydraulics Inc 7209 E Adamo Dr	Tampa	FL	33619	**800-282-4165**	813-626-4128
Adept Corp 4601 N Susquehanna Trl	York	PA	17406	**800-451-2254**	717-266-3606
Admar Supply Co Inc 1950 Brighton Henriett	Rochester	NY	14623	**800-836-2367**	585-272-9390
Air Center Inc 2175 Stephenson Hwy	Troy	MI	48083	**800-247-2959**	248-619-7800
Akhurst Machinery Ltd 1669 Foster's Way (Annacis Island)	Delta	BC	V3M6S7	**888-265-4336**	604-540-1430
Alban Tractor Co 8531 Pulaski Hwy	Baltimore	MD	21237	**800-492-6994**	410-686-7777
Alta Equipment Co 28775 Beck Rd	Wixom	MI	48393	**800-261-9642**	248-449-6700
Anderson Equipment Co 1000 Washington Pk	Bridgeville	PA	15017	**800-414-4554**	412-343-2300
Andrews & Hamilton Company Inc 3829 S Miami Blvd	Durham	NC	27703	**800-443-6866**	919-787-4100
Apex Packing & Rubbr Co 1855 New Hwy Ste D	Farmingdale	NY	11735	**800-645-9110**	631-420-8150
Arnold Machinery Co 2975 West 2100 South *Cust Svc	Salt Lake City	UT	84119	**800-821-0548***	801-972-4000
Bacon-Universal Company Inc 918 Ahua St	Honolulu	HI	96819	**800-352-3508**	808-839-7202
Balzer Pacific Equipment Co 2136 SE Eigth Ave	Portland	OR	97214	**800-442-0966**	503-232-5141
Bane Machinery Inc PO Box 541355	Dallas	TX	75354	**800-594-2263**	214-352-2468
Baron Oilfield Supply Ltd 9515-108 St	Grande Prairie	AB	T8V5R7	**888-532-5661**	780-532-5661
Belt Tech Industrial Inc 2574 E 700 S	Washington	IN	47501	**877-554-2358**	812-644-7623
Bevco Sales International Inc 9354 194 St	Surrey	BC	V4N4E9	**800-663-0090**	604-888-1455
Blue Giant Equipment Corp 85 Heart Lk Rd South	Brampton	ON	L6W3K2	**800-668-7078**	905-457-3900
Burns Controls Co 13735 Beta Rd	Dallas	TX	75244	**800-442-2010**	972-233-6712
C M S North America 4095 Korona Ct Se	Caledonia	MI	49316	**800-931-6083**	616-698-9970
Cameron Instruments Inc 173 Woolwich St	Guelph	ON	N1H3V4	**888-863-8010**	519-824-7111
Canimex Inc 285 Saint-Georges St	Drummondville	QC	J2C4H3	**855-777-1335**	819-477-1335
Cherry's Industrial Equipment 600 Morse Ave	Elk Grove Village	IL	60007	**800-350-0011**	
Cleveland Bros Equipment Company Inc 5300 Paxton St	Harrisburg	PA	17111	**866-551-4602**	717-564-2121
Colby Equipment Company Inc 3048 Ridgeview Dr	Indianapolis	IN	46226	**800-443-2981**	317-545-4221
Coleman Instrument Co 11575 Goldcoast Dr	Cincinnati	OH	45249	**800-899-5745**	513-489-5745
Colorid LLC 20480 Chartwls Ctr Dr	Cornelius	NC	28031	**888-682-6567**	704-987-2238
Delta t Systems Inc 2171 State Rd 175	Richfield	WI	53076	**800-733-4204**	262-628-0331
Diamond Equipment Inc 1060 E Diamond Ave	Evansville	IN	47711	**800-258-4428**	812-425-4428
Ecoa Industrial Products 5051 NW 37th Ave	Miami	FL	33142	**800-433-3833**	
Elliott & Frantz Inc 450 E Church Rd	King Of Prussia	PA	19406	**800-220-3025**	610-279-5200
Empire Southwest Co 1725 S Country Club Dr	Mesa	AZ	85210	**800-367-4731**	480-633-4000
Erb Equipment Co Inc 200 Erb Industrial Dr	Fenton	MO	63026	**800-634-9661**	636-349-0200
Exact Metrology Inc 11575 Goldcoast Dr	Cincinnati	OH	45246	**866-722-2600**	513-831-6620
Falcon Executive Aviation Inc 4766 E Falcon Dr	Mesa	AZ	85215	**800-237-2359**	480-832-0704
Florida Handling Systems Inc 2651 State Rd 60 W	Bartow	FL	33830	**800-664-3380**	863-534-1212
Fordia Inc 2745 de Miniac Ville Saint Laurent	Saint Laurent	QC	H4S1E5	**800-768-7274**	514-336-9211
Formers by Ernie Inc 7905 Almeda Genoa Rd Ste B	Houston	TX	77075	**866-991-3455**	713-991-3455
Foxx Equipment Co 421 Southwest Blvd	Kansas City	MO	64108	**800-821-2254**	816-421-3600
Franks Supply Company Inc 3311 Stanford Dr NE	Albuquerque	NM	87107	**800-432-5254**	505-884-0000
Garden State Engine & Equipment Co 3509 US Hwy 22	Somerville	NJ	08876	**800-479-3857**	908-534-5444
General Equipment & Supplies Inc 4300 Main Ave	Fargo	ND	58103	**800-437-2924**	701-282-2662
Glauber Equipment Corp 1600 Commerce Pkwy	Lancaster	NY	14086	**888-452-8237**	716-681-1234
Global Equipment Marketing Inc PO Box 810483	Boca Raton	FL	33481	**866-750-8662**	561-750-8662
Green Line Hose & Fittings (B.C.) Ltd 1477 Derwent Way	Delta	BC	V3M6N3	**800-665-5444**	604-525-6700
Grimstad S84w18887 Enterprise Dr	Muskego	WI	53150	**877-474-6782**	414-422-2300
H Gr Industrial Surplus 20001 Euclid Ave	Euclid	OH	44117	**866-447-7117**	216-486-4567
Hammond Drives & Equipment Inc 8527 Midland Rd	Freeland	MI	48623	**888-695-2239**	989-695-2239
Handi-Ramp 510 N Ave	Libertyville	IL	60048	**800-876-7267**	847-680-7700
Heavy Machines Inc 3926 E Rains Rd	Memphis	TN	38118	**888-366-9028**	901-260-2200
Henderson Sewing Machine Company Inc Waits Dr Industrial Park	Andalusia	AL	36420	**800-824-5113**	334-222-2451
Hooper Handling Inc 5590 Camp Rd	Hamburg	NY	14075	**800-649-5590**	716-649-5590
Hydra-Fab Fluid Power Inc 3585 Laird Rd Unit 5	Mississauga	ON	L5L5Z8	**866-466-9866**	905-569-1819

Company / Address	City	State	Zip	Toll-Free	Phone
Identity Automation LP 8833 N Sam Houston Pkwy W	Houston	TX	77064	**877-221-8401**	
ILMO Products Company Inc 7 Eastgate Dr	Jacksonville	IL	62650	**888-243-9353**	217-245-2183
Improved Construction Methods 1040 N Redmond Rd	Jacksonville	AR	72076	**877-494-5793**	
Innovent Air Handling Equipment 60 28th Ave N	Minneapolis	MN	55411	**877-218-4129**	612-877-4800
Janell Inc 6130 Cornell Rd	Cincinnati	OH	45242	**888-489-9111**	513-489-9111
John Fabick Tractor Co 1 Fabick Dr *Cust Svc	Fenton	MO	63026	**800-845-9188***	636-343-5900
Kibble Equipment 1150 S Victory Dr	Mankato	MN	56001	**800-624-8983**	507-387-8201
Leavitt Machinery & Rentals Inc 24389 Fraser Hwy	Langley	BC	V2Z2L3	**877-850-6499**	604-607-4450
M R L Equipment Company Inc PO Box 31154	Billings	MT	59107	**877-788-2907**	406-869-9900
M&M Pump & Supply Inc 1125 Olivette Executive Pkwy Ste 110	St. Louis	MO	63132	**800-369-1450**	314-395-8122
M.G. Newell Corp 301 Citation Ct	Greensboro	NC	27409	**800-334-0231**	336-393-0100
M.H. Equipment Co 2001 E Hartman Rd	Chillicothe	IL	61523	**888-564-2191**	309-579-8020
Machinery & Equipment Company Inc 3401 Bayshore Blvd	Brisbane	CA	94005	**800-227-4544**	415-467-3400
Magnus Equipment 4500 Beidler Rd	Willoughby	OH	44094	**800-394-8964**	440-942-8488
Maltz Sales Company Inc 67 Green St	Foxboro	MA	02035	**800-370-0439**	508-203-2400
Markem-Imaje Inc 5448 Timberlea Blvd	Mississauga	ON	L4W2T7	**800-267-5108**	
Mckinney Petroleum Equipment Inc 3926 Halls Mill Rd	Mobile	AL	36693	**800-476-7867**	251-661-8800
Methods Machine Tools Inc 65 Union Ave	Sudbury	MA	01776	**877-668-4262**	978-443-5388
Mississippi Valley Equipment Company Inc 1198 Pershall Rd	Saint Louis	MO	63137	**800-325-8001**	314-869-8600
Mister Safety Shoes Inc 6-2300 Finch Ave W	Toronto	ON	M9M2Y3	**800-707-0051**	416-746-3000
Mobile Parts Inc 2472 Evans Rd PO Box 327	Val Caron	ON	P3N1P5	**800-461-4055**	705-897-4955
Modern Automation Inc 134 Tennsco Dr	Dickson	TN	37055	**800-921-9705**	615-446-1990
Monroe Tractor & Implement Company Inc 1001 Lehigh Stn Rd	Henrietta	NY	14467	**866-683-5338**	585-334-3867
Moodie Implement Co 80335 US Hwy 87 W	Lewistown	MT	59457	**877-278-5531**	406-538-5433
Mustang Tractor & Equipment Co 12800 NW Fwy	Houston	TX	77040	**800-256-1001**	713-460-2000
O'keefe Elevator Company Inc 1402 Jones St	Omaha	NE	68102	**800-369-6317**	402-345-4056
Ohio Machinery Co 3993 E Royalton Rd	Broadview Heights	OH	44147	**800-837-6200**	440-526-6200
Optimal Engineering Systems 6901 Woodley Ave	Van Nuys	CA	91406	**888-777-1826**	818-222-9200
Oxford Alloys Inc 2632 Tee Dr	Baton Rouge	LA	70814	**800-562-3355**	225-273-4800
Patten Industries Inc 635 W Lake St	Elmhurst	IL	60126	**877-688-6812**	630-279-4400
Petersen Inc 1527 North 2000 West	Ogden	UT	84404	**800-410-6789**	801-732-2000
Pneumatic & Hydraulic Systems Company Inc 1338 Petroleum Pkwy	Broussard	LA	70518	**877-836-1999**	337-839-1999
Power Motive Corp 5000 Vasquez Blvd	Denver	CO	80216	**800-627-0087**	303-355-5900
Profile Food Ingredients LLC 1151 Timber Dr	Elgin	IL	60123	**877-632-1700**	847-622-1700
Quest Engineering Inc 2300 Edgewood Ave South	Minneapolis	MN	55426	**800-328-4853**	952-546-4441
R R Floody Co 5065 27th Ave	Rockford	IL	61109	**800-678-6639**	815-399-1931
R&M Materials Handling Inc 4501 Gateway Blvd	Springfield	OH	45502	**800-955-9967**	937-328-5100
Rasmussen Equipment Co 3333 West 2100 South	Salt Lake City	UT	84119	**800-453-8032**	801-972-5588
RBI Corp 10201 Cedar Ridge Dr	Ashland	VA	23005	**800-444-7370**	
Rencor Controls Inc 21 Sullivan Pkwy	Fort Edward	NY	12828	**866-472-7030**	518-747-4171
RJM Sales Inc 454 Park Ave	Scotch Plains	NJ	07076	**800-752-9055**	908-322-7880
Rk Controls 5901 Corvette St	Commerce	CA	90040	**877-305-8451**	323-887-7066
Roland Machinery Co 816 N Dirksen Pkwy	Springfield	IL	62702	**800-252-2926**	217-789-7711
Rudd Equipment Co 4344 Poplar Level Rd	Louisville	KY	40213	**800-527-2282**	502-456-4050
S & s Industrial Equipment & Supply Company Inc 7 Chelten Way	Trenton	NJ	08638	**800-282-3506**	609-695-3800
SDT North America Inc PO Box 682	Cobourg	ON	K9A4R5	**800-667-5325**	905-377-1313
Sidel Systems Usa Inc 12500 El Camino Real	Atascadero	CA	93422	**800-668-5003**	805-462-1250
Simark Controls Ltd 10509-46 St S E Ste 10509	Calgary	AB	T2C5C2	**800-565-7431**	403-236-0580
Southeastern Equipment Company Inc 10874 E Pike Rd	Cambridge	OH	43725	**800-798-5438**	740-432-6303
Southwest Materials Handling Company Inc 4719 Almond St	Dallas	TX	75247	**866-674-6067**	214-630-1375
Stan Houston Equipment Co 501 S Marion Rd	Sioux Falls	SD	57106	**800-952-3033**	605-336-3727
Stoffel Equipment Company Inc 7764 N 81st St	Milwaukee	WI	53223	**800-354-7502**	414-354-7500
Tipco Punch Inc 1 Coventry Rd	Brampton	ON	L6T4B1	**800-544-8444**	905-791-9811
Titan Machinery 644 East Beaton Dr	West Fargo	ND	58078	**800-548-7747**	701-356-0130
Toll Gas & Welding Supply 3005 Niagara Ln N	Plymouth	MN	55447	**877-865-5427**	763-551-5300
Tool Technology Distributors Inc 3110 Osgood Ct	Fremont	CA	94539	**800-335-8437**	510-656-8220
Triflo International Inc 1000 FM 830	Willis	TX	77318	**800-332-0993**	936-856-8551
Tyler Equipment Corp 251 Shaker Rd	East Longmeadow	MA	01028	**800-292-6351**	413-525-6351
US Equipment Company Inc 8311 Sorensen Ave	Santa Fe Springs	CA	90670	**800-255-4731**	
Valin Corp 555 E California Ave	Sunnyvale	CA	94086	**800-774-5630**	408-730-9850
Valley Litho Supply Inc 1047 Haugen Ave	Rice Lake	WI	54868	**800-826-6781**	
Victor L Phillips Co 4100 Gardner Ave	Kansas City	MO	64120	**800-878-9290**	816-241-9290
Wajax Industrial Components LP 2200 52 Nd Ave	Lachine	QC	H8T2Y3	**866-546-3267**	514-636-3333
Wallace b e Products Corp 71 N Bacton Hill Rd	Frazer	PA	19355	**800-553-5438**	610-647-1400
Westbrook Engineering 23501 Mound Rd	Warren	MI	48091	**800-899-8182**	586-759-3100
White's Farm Supply Inc 4154 State Rt 31	Canastota	NY	13032	**800-633-4443**	315-697-2214
Winchester Equipment Co 121 Indian Hollow Rd	Winchester	VA	22603	**800-323-3581**	
Wojanis Inc 1001 Montour W Ind Park	Coraopolis	PA	15108	**800-345-9024**	724-695-1415
Wyoming Machinery Co 5300 Old W Yellowstone Hwy	Casper	WY	82604	**800-244-0527**	307-472-1000

359 HELICOPTER TRANSPORT SERVICES

SEE ALSO Air Charter Services ; Ambulance Services

Company / Address	City	State	Zip	Toll-Free	Phone
Accel Aviation Accessories LLC 11900 Lacy Ln	Fort Myers	FL	33966	**877-999-2391**	
Air Logistics Inc 4605 Industrial Dr	New Iberia	LA	70560	**800-365-6771**	337-365-6771
Bristow Alaska Inc 1915 Donald Ave	Fairbanks	AK	99701	**800-686-4080**	907-452-1197
Carson Helicopters 952 Blooming Glen Rd	Perkasie	PA	18944	**800-523-2335**	215-249-3535
Coastal Helicopters Inc 8995 Yandukin Dr	Juneau	AK	99801	**800-789-5610**	907-789-5600
Corporate Helicopters of San Diego 3753 John J Montgomery Dr Ste 2	San Diego	CA	92123	**800-345-6737**	858-505-5650
Eagle Copters Ltd 823 Mctavish Rd NE	Calgary	AB	T2E7G9	**800-564-6469**	403-250-7370
Island Express Helicopter Service 1175 Queens Hwy S *Cust Svc	Long Beach	CA	90802	**800-228-2566***	310-510-2525
Midwest Helicopter Airways Inc 525 Executive Dr	Willowbrook	IL	60527	**800-323-7609**	630-325-7860
PHI Inc 2001 SE Evangeline Thwy PO Box 90808 *NASDAQ: PHII*	Lafayette	LA	70508	**866-815-7101**	337-235-2452
Victoria International Airport 1962 Canso Rd	North Saanich	BC	V8L5V5	**866-844-4354**	250-656-3987
VIH Logging Ltd 1962 Canso Rd	North Saanich	BC	V8L5V5	**866-844-4354**	250-656-3987
Yellowhead Helicopters Ltd 3010 Selwyn Rd	Valemount	BC	V0E2Z0	**888-566-4401**	250-566-4401

360 HOLDING COMPANIES

SEE ALSO Conglomerates

A holding company is a company that owns enough voting stock in another firm to control management and operations by influencing or electing its board of directors.

360-1 Airlines Holding Companies

Company / Address	City	State	Zip	Toll-Free	Phone
Frontier Airlines Inc 7001 Tower Rd	Denver	CO	80249	**800-265-5505**	720-374-4200
JetBlue Airways Corp 118-29 Queens Blvd *NASDAQ: JBLU*	Forest Hills	NY	11375	**800-538-2583**	718-286-7900

360-2 Bank Holding Companies

Company / Address	City	State	Zip	Toll-Free	Phone
Access National Corp 1800 Robert Fulton Dr Ste 310 *NASDAQ: ANCX*	Reston	VA	20191	**800-931-0370**	703-871-2100
Accuristix 2844 Bristol Cir	Oakville	ON	L6H6G4	**866-356-6830**	905-829-9927
Allegheny Valley Bank 5137 Butler St *OTC: AVLY*	Pittsburgh	PA	15201	**888-397-3742**	412-781-1464
Alpine Bank of Colorado 2200 Grand Ave	Glenwood Springs	CO	81601	**888-425-7463**	970-945-2424
AMB Financial Corp 8230 Hohman Ave *OTC: AMFC*	Munster	IN	46321	**800-436-5113**	219-836-5870
Amboy Bancorp 3590 US Hwy 9 S	Old Bridge	NJ	08857	**800-942-6269**	732-591-8700
Ameriana Bancorp 2118 Bundy Ave *NASDAQ: ASBI*	New Castle	IN	47362	**866-844-7584**	765-529-2230

				Toll-Free	Phone
American National Bank 628 Main St *NASDAQ: AMNB*	Danville	VA	24541	**800-240-8190**	434-792-5111
American River Bankshares 3100 Zinfandel Dr Ste 450 *NASDAQ: AMRB*	Rancho Cordova	CA	95670	**800-544-0545**	
American State Bank 1401 Ave Q	Lubbock	TX	79401	**800-531-1401**	806-767-7000
Anchor BanCorp Wisconsin Inc 25 W Main St *NYSE: ABCW*	Madison	WI	53707	**800-252-6246**	608-252-8700
Andrus Transportation Services LLC 3185 East Deseret Dr North	Saint George	UT	84790	**800-888-5838**	435-673-1566
Annapolis Bancorp Inc 1000 Bestgate Rd *NASDAQ: ANNB*	Annapolis	MD	21401	**800-555-5455**	410-224-4455
Arrow Financial Corp 250 Glen St *NASDAQ: AROW*	Glens Falls	NY	12801	**800-937-5449**	518-415-4307
Associated Banc-Corp 1200 Hansen Rd *NYSE: ASB* ■ *PR	Green Bay	WI	54304	**800-236-2722***	920-491-7000
Atlantic Coast Bank (ACFC) 505 Haines Ave *NASDAQ: ACFC*	Waycross	GA	31501	**800-342-2824**	912-283-4711
BancorpSouth Inc 2910 W Jackson St *NYSE: BXS*	Tupelo	MS	38801	**888-797-7711**	662-680-2000
Bank Independent 710 S Montgomery Ave	Sheffield	AL	35660	**877-865-5050**	256-386-5000
Bank Mutual Corp 4949 W Brown Deer Rd *NASDAQ: BKMU*	Milwaukee	WI	53223	**844-256-8684**	414-354-1500
Bank of Commerce Holdings 1901 Churn Creek Rd *NASDAQ: BOCH*	Redding	CA	96002	**800-421-2575**	530-224-3333
Bank of Hawaii Corp 130 Merchant St 20th Fl *NYSE: BOH*	Honolulu	HI	96813	**888-643-3888**	
Bank of South Carolina Corp 256 Meeting St *NASDAQ: BKSC*	Charleston	SC	29401	**800-523-4175**	843-724-1500
Bank of the Ozarks Inc 12615 Chenal Pkwy PO Box 8811 *NASDAQ: OZRK*	Little Rock	AR	72211	**800-628-3552**	501-978-2265
Banner Bank PO Box 907 *NASDAQ: BANR*	Walla Walla	WA	99362	**800-272-9933**	509-527-3636
Bar Harbor Bankshares 82 Main St PO Box 400 *NYSE: BHB*	Bar Harbor	ME	04609	**888-853-7100**	207-288-3314
Barnes Transportation Services Inc 2309 Whitley Rd	Wilson	NC	27895	**800-898-5897**	
Bay Bank 2328 W Joppa Rd *NASDAQ: BYBK*	Lutherville	MD	21093	**800-222-6566**	410-494-2580
BB & T Corp 200 W Second St *NYSE: BBT*	Winston-Salem	NC	27101	**800-226-5228**	336-733-1470
BBCN Bank 3731 Wilshire Blvd Ste 1000 *NASDAQ: NARA*	Los Angeles	CA	90010	**888-811-6272**	213-639-1700
Benny Whitehead Inc 3265 S Eufaula Ave	Eufaula	AL	36027	**800-633-7617**	334-687-8055
Berkshire Hills Bancorp Inc 24 N St *NYSE: BHLB*	Pittsfield	MA	01201	**800-773-5601**	413-443-5601
Bmo Bankcorp Inc 111 W Monroe St	Chicago	IL	60603	**888-340-2265**	
Boston Private Financial Holdings Inc 10 Post Office Sq *NASDAQ: BPFH*	Boston	MA	02109	**855-738-8916**	617-912-1900
Brannen Banks Of Florida Inc PO Box 1929	Inverness	FL	34451	**866-546-8273**	352-726-1221
Bridge Capital Holdings 55 Almaden Blvd Ste 200 *NASDAQ: BBNK* ■ *General	San Jose	CA	95113	**866-273-4265***	408-423-8500
Broadway Financial Corp 4800 Wilshire Blvd *NASDAQ: BYFC*	Los Angeles	CA	90010	**888-988-2265**	323-634-1700
Brookline Bank PO Box 470469 *NASDAQ: BRKL* ■ *Cust Svc	Brookline	MA	02445	**877-668-2265***	617-730-3520
Bryn Mawr Bank Corp 801 Lancaster Ave *NASDAQ: BMTC*	Bryn Mawr	PA	19010	**855-381-2631**	610-525-1700
C & F Financial Corp 802 Main St PO Box 391 *NASDAQ: CFFI*	West Point	VA	23181	**800-583-3863**	804-843-4584
Camden National Corp 2 Elm St *NYSE: CAC*	Camden	ME	04843	**800-860-8821**	207-236-8821
Capital City Bank Group Inc PO Box 900 *NASDAQ: CCBG*	Tallahassee	FL	32302	**888-671-0400**	850-402-7500
Capitol City Bancshares Inc 562 Lee St SW	Atlanta	GA	30311	**866-758-6395**	404-752-6067
Capitol Federal Financial 700 Kansas Ave *NASDAQ: CFFN*	Topeka	KS	66603	**888-822-7333**	785-235-1341
Cardinal Financial Corp 8270 Greensboro Dr Ste 500 *NASDAQ: CFNL*	McLean	VA	22102	**800-473-3247**	703-584-3400
Carolina Bank Holdings Inc 101 N Spring St *NASDAQ: CLBH*	Greensboro	NC	27401	**800-472-3272**	336-288-1898
Cascade Bancorp 1100 NW Wall St *NASDAQ: CACB* ■ *Cust Svc	Bend	OR	97701	**877-617-3400***	541-385-6205
Cathay General Bancorp Inc 777 N Broadway *NASDAQ: CATY*	Los Angeles	CA	90012	**800-922-8429**	213-625-4700
Central Federal Corp 601 Main St *NASDAQ: CFBK*	Wellsville	OH	14895	**866-668-4606**	330-666-7979
Central Pacific Financial Corp PO Box 3590 *NYSE: CPF*	Honolulu	HI	96811	**800-342-8422**	808-544-0500
Central Valley Community Bancorp 7100 N Financial Dr Ste 101 *NASDAQ: CVCY*	Fresno	CA	93720	**866-294-9588**	559-298-1775
Century Bancorp Inc 400 Mystic Ave *NASDAQ: CNBKA*	Medford	MA	02155	**866-823-6887**	781-393-4160
CFS Bancorp Inc 707 Ridge Rd *NASDAQ: CITZ*	Munster	IN	46321	**866-622-1370**	219-513-5123
Chemical Financial Corp 333 E Main St *NASDAQ: CHFC*	Midland	MI	48640	**800-867-9757**	989-839-5350
Citizens Financial Group Inc 1 Citizens Dr	Riverside	RI	02915	**800-922-9999**	401-456-7000
Clifton Savings Bancorp Inc 1433 Van Houten Ave *NASDAQ: CSBK*	Clifton	NJ	07013	**888-562-6727**	973-473-2200
CNB Financial Corp 1 S Second St PO Box 42 *NASDAQ: CCNE*	Clearfield	PA	16830	**800-492-3221**	814-765-9621
Colorado Business Bank 821 17th St	Denver	CO	80202	**800-574-4714**	303-293-2265
Columbia Bank 1301 A St Ste 800 *NASDAQ: COLB*	Tacoma	WA	98402	**800-305-1905**	253-305-1900
Commercial National Financial Corp 900 Ligonier St *OTC: CNAF*	Latrobe	PA	15650	**800-803-2265**	724-539-3501
Community Bank Shares of Indiana Inc 101 W Spring St *NASDAQ: YCB*	New Albany	IN	47150	**866-944-2004**	812-944-2224
Community Bank System Inc 5790 Widewaters Pkwy *NYSE: CBU*	Syracuse	NY	13214	**800-847-2911**	315-445-2282
Community Investors Bancorp Inc 119 S Sandusky Ave *OTC: CIBN*	Bucyrus	OH	44820	**800-222-4955**	419-562-7055
Community Shores Bank Corp 1030 W Norton Ave *OTC: CSHB*	Muskegon	MI	49441	**888-853-6633**	231-780-1800
Compass Bancshares Inc 15 S 20th St	Birmingham	AL	35233	**800-266-7277**	205-297-3584
Crazy Woman Creek Bancorp Inc PO Box 1020	Buffalo	WY	82834	**877-684-2766**	307-684-5591
Cullen/Frost Bankers Inc 100 W Houston St *NYSE: CFR*	San Antonio	TX	78205	**800-562-6732**	210-220-4011
CVB Financial Corp 701 N Haven Ave PO Box 51000 *NASDAQ: CVBF*	Ontario	CA	91764	**888-222-5432**	909-980-4030
Dime Community Bancshares Inc 209 Havemeyer St *NASDAQ: DCOM*	Brooklyn	NY	11211	**800-321-3463**	718-782-6200
Doral Financial Corp 1441 F D Roosevelt Ave *NYSE: DRL*	San Juan	PR	00920	**866-296-3743**	787-749-4949
Eagle Bancorp Inc 7815 Woodmont Ave *NASDAQ: EGBN*	Bethesda	MD	20814	**800-364-8313**	240-497-2044
East West Bancorp Inc 1881 W Main St *NASDAQ: EWBC*	Alhambra	CA	91801	**888-895-5650**	626-308-2012
Eastern Bank Corp 265 Franklin St *Cust Svc	Boston	MA	02110	**800-327-8376***	617-897-1008
Eastern Virginia Bankshares Inc 330 Hospital Rd *NASDAQ: EVBS* ■ *General	Tappahannock	VA	22560	**866-296-3743***	804-443-8400
Enterprise Financial Services Corp 150 N Meramec Ave *NASDAQ: EFSG*	Clayton	MO	63105	**800-396-8141**	314-725-5500
Evans Bancorp Inc 1 Grimsby Dr *NYSE: EVBN*	Hamburg	NY	14075	**866-310-0763**	716-926-2000
Farmer State Bank of Sublette 303 S Pennsylvania Ave PO Box 20	Sublette	IL	61367	**866-269-1722**	815-849-5242
Farmers Capital Bank Corp PO Box 309 *NASDAQ: FFKT*	Frankfort	KY	40602	**800-776-9437**	502-227-1668
Fauquier Bankshares Inc 10 Courthouse Sq *NASDAQ: FBSS*	Warrenton	VA	20186	**800-638-3798**	540-347-2700
FFD Financial Corp 321 N Wooster Ave *OTC: FFDF*	Dover	OH	44622	**800-558-3424**	330-364-7777
FFW Corp 1205 N Cass St *OTC: FFWC*	Wabash	IN	46992	**800-377-4984**	260-563-3185
Fidelity Federal Bancorp 18 NW Fourth St *OTC: FDLB*	Evansville	IN	47708	**800-280-8280**	812-424-0921
Financial Institutions Inc 220 Liberty St *NASDAQ: FISI*	Warsaw	NY	14569	**866-296-3743**	585-786-1100
First American Bank Corp 1650 Louis Ave	Elk Grove Village	IL	60009	**866-449-1150**	847-952-3700
First Bancorp 341 N Main St *NASDAQ: FBNC*	Troy	NC	27371	**800-548-9377**	910-576-6171
First Banctrust Corp 101 S Central Ave *OTC: FIRT*	Paris	IL	61944	**800-228-6381**	217-465-6381

Classified Section

Company	City	State	ZIP	Toll-Free	Phone
First Banks Inc 135 N Meramec Ave	Clayton	MO	63105	**800-760-2265**	314-854-4600
First Busey Corp 100 W University Ave *NASDAQ: BUSE*	Champaign	IL	61820	**800-672-8739**	217-365-4516
First Citizens Bancorp Inc PO Box 29 *OTC: FCBN*	Columbia	SC	29202	**888-612-4444**	919-716-4588
First Citizens Bank 350 S Beverly D Ste 150	Beverly Hills	CA	90212	**888-323-4732**	
First Citizens National Bank Charitable Foundation PO Box 1708	Mason City	IA	50402	**800-423-1602**	641-423-1600
First Commonwealth Financial Corp 601 Philadelphia St *NYSE: FCF*	Indiana	PA	15701	**800-711-2265**	724-349-7220
First Community Corp (FCC) 5455 Sunset Blvd *NASDAQ: FCCO*	Lexington	SC	29072	**800-829-6372**	803-951-0555
First Defiance Financial Corp 601 Clinton St *NASDAQ: FDEF*	Defiance	OH	43512	**800-472-6292**	419-782-5015
First Financial Bancorp (FFB) 255 E Fifth St Ste 700 *NASDAQ: FFBC*	Cincinnati	OH	45202	**877-322-9530**	
First Financial Bankshares Inc PO Box 701 *NASDAQ: FFIN*	Abilene	TX	79604	**888-588-2623**	325-627-7155
First Financial Corp 1 First Financial Plz *NASDAQ: THFF*	Terre Haute	IN	47807	**800-511-0045**	812-238-6000
First FSB of Frankfort 216 W Main St PO Box 535	Frankfort	KY	40602	**888-818-3372**	502-223-1638
First Horizon National Corp 165 Madison *NYSE: FHN*	Memphis	TN	38103	**800-489-4040**	901-523-4444
First Interstate Bancsystem Inc 401 N 31st St *NASDAQ: FIBK*	Billings	MT	59101	**888-752-3341**	406-255-5000
First Merchants Corp 200 E Jackson St *NASDAQ: FRME*	Muncie	IN	47305	**800-205-3464**	765-747-1500
First Midwest Bancorp Inc 1 Pierce Pl Ste 1500 *NASDAQ: FMBI*	Itasca	IL	60143	**800-322-3623**	630-875-7200
First National Lincoln Corp 223 Main St PO Box 940	Damariscotta	ME	04543	**800-564-3195**	207-563-3195
First National of Nebraska Inc PO BOX 2490	Omaha	NE	68197	**800-688-7070**	402-341-0500
First of Long Island Corp 10 Glen Head Ave *NASDAQ: FLIC*	Glen Head	NY	11545	**800-554-8969**	516-671-4900
First South Bancorp Inc 1311 Carolina Ave *NASDAQ: FSBK*	Washington	NC	27889	**800-946-4178**	252-946-4178
First Southern Bank 301 S Ct St *General	Florence	AL	35630	**800-625-7131***	256-718-4200
First United Corp 19 S Second St *NASDAQ: FUNC*	Oakland	MD	21550	**888-692-2654**	
FirstFed Bancorp Inc 1630 Fourth Ave N PO Box 340	Bessemer	AL	35020	**800-436-5112**	205-428-8472
Flushing Financial Corp 1979 Marcus Ave *NASDAQ: FFIC*	New Hyde Park	NY	11042	**800-581-2889**	718-961-5400
German American Bancorp 711 Main St *NASDAQ: GABC*	Jasper	IN	47546	**800-482-1314**	812-482-1314
Glacier Bancorp Inc PO Box 27 *NASDAQ: GBCI*	Kalispell	MT	59903	**800-735-4371**	406-756-4200
Great American Bancorp Inc 1311 S Neil St *OTC: GTPS*	Champaign	IL	61820	**800-962-4284**	217-356-2265
Greene County Bancorp Inc 302 Main St *NASDAQ: GCBC*	Catskill	NY	12414	**888-439-4272**	518-943-2600
Greenwood Racing Inc 3001 St Rd	Bensalem	PA	19020	**888-238-2946**	215-639-9000
Guaranty Bancshares Inc 100 W Arkansas St PO Box 1158	Mount Pleasant	TX	75455	**888-572-9881**	903-572-9881
Hancock Holding Co 2510 14th St	Gulfport	MS	39501	**800-522-6542**	228-868-4727
Hanmi Bank 3660 Wilshire Blvd Ste PH-A	Los Angeles	CA	90010	**877-808-4266**	213-382-2200
Harleysville Savings Financial Corp 271 Main St *NASDAQ: HARL*	Harleysville	PA	19438	**888-256-8828**	215-256-8828
Heartland Financial USA Inc 1398 Central Ave *NASDAQ: HTLF*	Dubuque	IA	52001	**888-739-2100**	563-589-2100
Heritage Bank 101 N Main St	Jonesboro	GA	30236	**866-971-0106**	770-478-8881
Heritage Commerce Corp 150 Almaden Blvd *NASDAQ: HTBK*	San Jose	CA	95113	**800-468-9716**	408-947-6900
Heritage Financial Corp 201 Fifth Ave SW *NASDAQ: HFWA*	Olympia	WA	98501	**800-962-4284**	360-943-1500
HF Financial Corp 225 S Main Ave *NASDAQ: HFFC*	Sioux Falls	SD	57104	**800-244-2149**	605-333-7556
High Country Bancorp Inc 7360 W Hwy 50 PO Box 309 *OTC: HCBC*	Salida	CO	81201	**800-201-0557**	719-539-2516
HMN Financial Inc 1016 Civic Ctr Dr NW *NASDAQ: HMNF*	Rochester	MN	55901	**888-257-2000**	507-535-1309
Home City Financial Corp 2454 N Limestone St *OTC: HCFL*	Springfield	OH	45503	**866-421-2331**	937-390-0470
HSBC North America Holdings Inc 2700 Sanders Rd	Prospect Heights	IL	60070	**800-975-4722**	847-564-5000
Huntington Bancshares Inc 7 Easton Oval *NASDAQ: HBAN*	Columbus	OH	43219	**800-480-2265**	
IBERIABANK Corp 200 W Congress St *NASDAQ: IBKC*	Lafayette	LA	70501	**800-968-0801**	
Independent Bank Corp 230 W Main St *NASDAQ: IBCP*	Ionia	MI	48846	**888-300-3193**	616-527-2400
Keweenaw Financial Corp 235 Quincy St	Hancock	MI	49930	**866-482-0404**	906-482-0404
KeyCorp 127 Public Sq *NYSE: KEY*	Cleveland	OH	44114	**800-539-9055**	216-689-8481
Lake Sunapee Bank 9 Main St PO Box 29	Newport	NH	03773	**800-281-5772**	603-863-5772
Lakeland Bancorp Inc 250 Oak Ridge Rd *NASDAQ: LBAI*	Oak Ridge	NJ	07438	**866-224-1379**	973-697-2000
Lakeland Financial Corp 202 E Ctr St *NASDAQ: LKFN*	Warsaw	IN	46580	**800-827-4522**	574-267-6144
LNB Bancorp Inc 457 Broadway *NASDAQ: LNBB*	Lorain	OH	44052	**800-860-1007**	440-989-3348
Logansport Financial Corp 723 E Broadway *OTC: LOGN*	Logansport	IN	46947	**800-541-9154**	574-722-3855
Macatawa Bank Corp 10753 Macatawa Dr PO Box 3119 *NASDAQ: MCBC*	Holland	MI	49424	**877-820-2265**	616-820-1444
Malaga Financial Corp 2514 Via Tejon *OTC: MLGF*	Palos Verdes Estates	CA	90274	**866-275-2677**	310-375-9000
MB Financial Inc 6111 N River Rd *NASDAQ: MBFI*	Rosemont	IL	60018	**888-422-6562**	
MBT Financial Corp 102 E Front St *NASDAQ: MBTF*	Monroe	MI	48161	**800-321-0032**	734-241-3431
Mercantile Bank 200 N 33rd St PO Box 3455 *NYSE: MBCR*	Quincy	IL	62305	**800-405-6372**	217-223-7300
Mercantile Bank Corp 310 Leonard St NW *NASDAQ: MBWM*	Grand Rapids	MI	49504	**888-345-6296**	616-406-3000
Merchants Bancshares Inc PO Box 1009 *NASDAQ: MBVT*	Burlington	VT	05402	**800-322-5222**	802-658-3400
Mesa Systems Inc 681 Railroad Blvd	Grand Junction	CO	81505	**800-654-3225**	970-241-6450
Mid Penn Bancorp Inc 349 Union St *NASDAQ: MPB*	Millersburg	PA	17061	**866-642-7736**	717-692-2133
MidSouth Bancorp Inc 102 Versailles Blvd *NYSE: MSL*	Lafayette	LA	70501	**800-213-2265**	337-237-8343
MidWestOne Financial Group Inc 102 S Clinton St PO Box 1700 *NASDAQ: MOFG* ■ *Cust Svc	Iowa City	IA	52240	**800-247-4418***	319-356-5800
MutualFirst Financial Inc 110 E Charles St *NASDAQ: MFSF*	Muncie	IN	47305	**800-382-8031**	765-747-2800
NASB Financial Inc 12520 S 71 Hwy *NASDAQ: NASB*	Grandview	MO	64030	**800-677-6272**	816-765-2200
National Bankshares Inc 101 Hubbard St *NASDAQ: NKSH*	Blacksburg	VA	24060	**800-552-4123**	540-951-6300
National Penn Bancshares Inc PO Box 547 *NASDAQ: NPBC*	Boyertown	PA	19512	**800-822-3321**	
NBT Bancorp Inc 52 S Broad St *NASDAQ: NBTB*	Norwich	NY	13815	**800-628-2265**	607-337-2265
North State Bank Inc 6204 Falls of Neuse Rd	Raleigh	NC	27609	**877-357-2265**	919-787-9696
Northbridge Financial Corp 105 Adelaide St W Ste 700	Toronto	ON	M5H1P9	**855-620-6262**	416-350-4400
Northeast Bancorp 500 Canal St *NASDAQ: NBN*	Lewiston	ME	04240	**800-284-5989**	207-786-3245
Northeast Indiana Bancorp Inc 648 N Jefferson St *OTC: NIDB*	Huntington	IN	46750	**800-550-3372**	260-356-3311
Northern States Financial Corp 1601 N Lewis Ave *OTC: NSFC*	Waukegan	IL	60085	**800-339-4432**	847-244-6000
Northwest Bancorp Inc PO Box 128	Warren	PA	16365	**800-859-1000**	814-728-7263
Ocwen Financial Corp 1661 Worthington Rd Ste 100 PO Box 24737 *NYSE: OCN*	West Palm Beach	FL	33409	**800-746-2936**	561-681-8000
Ohio Valley Banc Corp 420 Third Ave *NASDAQ: OVBC*	Gallipolis	OH	45631	**800-468-6682**	740-446-2631
Old Point Financial Corp 1 W Mellen St PO Box 3392 *NASDAQ: OPOF*	Hampton	VA	23663	**800-952-0051**	757-728-1200
Old Second Bancorp Inc 37 S River St *NASDAQ: OSBC*	Aurora	IL	60506	**877-866-0202**	630-892-0202
Opus Bank 19900 MacArthur Blvd 12th Fl	Irvine	CA	92612	**855-678-7226**	949-250-9800
Owen Community Bank 279 E Morgan St	Spencer	IN	47460	**800-690-2095**	812-829-2095

Company / Address	City	State	ZIP	Toll-Free	Phone
Pacific Mercantile Bancorp 949 S Coast Dr Ste 105 *NASDAQ: PMBC* ■ *General	Costa Mesa	CA	92626	**877-450-2265***	714-438-2600
Pacific Premier Bancorp Inc 1600 Sunflower Ave *NASDAQ: PPBI*	Costa Mesa	CA	92626	**888-388-5433**	714-431-4000
Park Bancorp Inc 5400 S Pulaski Rd *OTC: PFED*	Chicago	IL	60632	**888-727-5333**	773-582-8616
Park National Bank 50 N Third St PO Box 3500 *NYSE: PRK*	Newark	OH	43058	**888-791-8633**	740-349-8451
Pathfinder Bancorp Inc 214 W First St *NASDAQ: PBHC*	Oswego	NY	13126	**800-811-5620**	315-343-0057
Patriot National Bancorp Inc 900 Bedford St *NASDAQ: PNBK*	Stamford	CT	06901	**888-728-7468**	203-251-7200
Peapack-Gladstone Bank 500 Hills Dr Ste 300 PO Box 700 *NASDAQ: PGC*	Bedminster	NJ	07921	**800-742-7595**	908-234-0700
Peoples Bancorp Inc 138 Putnam St *NASDAQ: PEBO*	Marietta	OH	45750	**800-374-6123**	740-373-3155
Peoples Bancorp of North Carolina Inc 518 W 'C' St *NASDAQ: PEBK*	Newton	NC	28658	**800-948-7195**	828-464-5620
PlainsCapital Corp 2323 Victory Ave Ste 1400	Dallas	TX	75219	**866-762-8392**	214-252-4100
PNC Financial Services Group Inc 249 Fifth Ave 1 PNC Plz *NYSE: PNC*	Pittsburgh	PA	15222	**877-762-2000**	412-762-2000
Princeton National Bancorp Inc 606 S Main St *OTC: PNBC*	Princeton	IL	61356	**888-897-2276**	309-662-4444
PrivateBancorp Inc 120 S LaSalle St *NASDAQ: PVTB*	Chicago	IL	60603	**800-662-7748**	
Prosperity Bancshares Inc 1301 N Mechanic *NYSE: PB*	El Campo	TX	77437	**800-862-9098**	979-543-1426
Provident Bank 3756 Central Ave *NASDAQ: PROV*	Riverside	CA	92506	**800-442-5201**	951-686-6060
Pulaski Financial Corp 12300 Olive Blvd *NASDAQ: PULB*	Saint Louis	MO	63141	**888-649-3320**	314-878-2210
Quad City Bank & Trust 3551 Seventh St *NASDAQ: QCRH*	Moline	IL	61265	**866-676-0551**	309-736-3580
RBC Centura Banks Inc PO Box 1220	Rocky Mount	NC	27802	**800-769-2553**	
Regions Financial Corp 1900 Fifth Ave N *NYSE: RF*	Birmingham	AL	35203	**866-688-0658**	
Renasant Corp 209 Troy St PO Box 709 *NASDAQ: RNST* ■ *Cust Svc	Tupelo	MS	38802	**800-680-1601***	662-680-1001
Republic Bancorp Inc 601 W Market St *NASDAQ: RBCAA*	Louisville	KY	40202	**888-540-5363**	502-584-3600
Republic First Bancorp Inc 50 S 16th St Ste 2400 *NASDAQ: FRBK*	Philadelphia	PA	19102	**888-875-2265**	215-735-4422
Richline Group Inc 6701 Nob Hill Rd	Tamarac	FL	33321	**800-327-1808**	
S&T Bancorp Inc 800 Philadelphia St *NASDAQ: STBA*	Indiana	PA	15701	**800-325-2265**	724-349-1800
Salisbury Bancorp Inc 5 Bissell St PO Box 1868 *NASDAQ: SAL*	Lakeville	CT	06039	**800-222-9801**	860-435-9801
Sandy Spring Bancorp Inc 17801 Georgia Ave *NASDAQ: SASR*	Olney	MD	20832	**800-399-5919**	301-774-6400
SCBT Financial Corp 950 John C Calhoun Dr *NASDAQ: SCBT*	Orangeburg	SC	29115	**800-277-2175**	803-534-2175
Seacoast Banking Corp of Florida PO Box 9012 PO Box 9012 *NASDAQ: SBCF* ■ *All	Stuart	FL	34995	**800-706-9991***	772-287-4000
Sierra Bancorp 86 N Main St PO Box 1930 *NASDAQ: BSRR*	Porterville	CA	93257	**888-454-2265**	559-782-4900
Simmons First National Corp 501 Main St *NASDAQ: SFNC*	Pine Bluff	AR	71601	**866-246-2400**	870-541-1000
Southern Missouri Bancorp Inc 531 Vine St *NASDAQ: SMBC*	Poplar Bluff	MO	63901	**855-452-7272**	573-778-1800
SouthFirst Bancshares Inc 126 N Norton Ave PO Box 167 *OTC: SZBI*	Sylacauga	AL	35150	**800-239-1492**	256-245-4365
Southside Bancshares Inc 1201 S Beckham Ave *NASDAQ: SBSI*	Tyler	TX	75701	**877-639-3511**	903-531-7111
Southwest Bancorp Inc 608 S Main St PO Box 1988 *NASDAQ: OKSB*	Stillwater	OK	74076	**888-762-4762**	
Southwest Georgia Financial Corp 201 First St SE *NYSE: SGB*	Moultrie	GA	31768	**888-683-2265**	229-985-1120
Sun Bancorp Inc (SNBC) 226 Landis Ave *NASDAQ: SNBC*	Vineland	NJ	08360	**800-786-9066**	
Sunshine Financial Inc 1400 E Park Ave	Tallahassee	FL	32301	**800-468-3993**	850-219-7200
SunTrust Banks Inc 303 Peachtree St NE *NYSE: STI*	Atlanta	GA	30308	**800-786-8787**	404-588-7711
Sussex Bank 200 Munsonhurst Rd *NASDAQ: SBBX*	Franklin	NJ	07416	**800-511-9900**	973-827-2914
SVB Financial Group 3005 Tasman Dr *NASDAQ: SIVB*	Santa Clara	CA	95054	**800-760-9644**	408-654-7400
SY Bancorp Inc 1040 E Main St *NASDAQ: SYBT*	Louisville	KY	40206	**800-625-9066**	502-582-2571
Synovus Financial Corp 1111 Bay Ave Ste 500 PO Box 120 *NYSE: SNV*	Columbus	GA	31902	**888-796-6887**	706-649-2311
Timberland Bancorp Inc 624 Simpson Ave *NASDAQ: TSBK*	Hoquiam	WA	98550	**800-562-8761**	360-533-4747
Titonka Bancshares Inc PO Box 309	Titonka	IA	50480	**866-985-3247**	515-928-2142
Tower Financial Corp 116 E Berry St *NASDAQ: TOFC*	Fort Wayne	IN	46802	**800-731-2265**	
TriCo Bancshares 63 Constitution Dr *NASDAQ: TCBK*	Chico	CA	95973	**800-922-8742**	530-898-0300
Trustco Bank Corp NY PO Box 1082 *NASDAQ: TRST*	Schenectady	NY	12301	**800-670-3110**	518-377-3311
Trustmark National Bank 248 E Capitol St PO Box 291 *NASDAQ: TRMK* ■ *Cust Svc	Jackson	MS	39201	**800-243-2524***	601-208-5111
UMB Financial Corp 1010 Grand Blvd *NASDAQ: UMBF*	Kansas City	MO	64106	**800-821-2171**	816-860-7000
Umpqua Holdings Corp 1 SW Columbia St Ste 1200 *NASDAQ: UMPQ*	Portland	OR	97258	**866-486-7782**	503-727-4100
Union Bankshares Inc 20 Lower Main St *NASDAQ: UNB*	Morrisville	VT	05661	**866-862-1891**	802-888-6600
United Bancorp Inc 201 S Fourth St *NASDAQ: UBCP*	Martins Ferry	OH	43935	**888-275-5566**	740-633-0445
United Bancshares Inc 100 S High St PO Box 67 *NASDAQ: UBOH*	Columbus Grove	OH	45830	**800-837-8111**	419-659-2141
United Community Banks Inc PO Box 398 *NASDAQ: UCBI*	Blairsville	GA	30514	**866-270-7100**	706-781-2265
United Community Financial Corp PO Box 1111 *NASDAQ: UCFC*	Youngstown	OH	44501	**877-272-7661**	330-742-0500
United Security Bancshares Inc PO Box 249 *NASDAQ: USBI*	Thomasville	AL	36784	**866-546-8273**	334-636-5424
Unity Bancorp Inc 64 Old Hwy 22 *NASDAQ: UNTY*	Clinton	NJ	08809	**800-618-2265**	908-730-7630
Universal Enterprises Inc 8030 SW Nimbus	Beaverton	OR	97008	**800-547-5740**	503-644-8723
Univest Corp of Pennsylvania 14 N Main St PO Box 64197 *NASDAQ: UVSP*	Souderton	PA	18964	**877-723-5571**	
US Bancorp 800 Nicollet Mall *NYSE: USB* ■ *Cust Svc	Minneapolis	MN	55402	**800-872-2657***	651-466-3000
Valley National Bancorp 1455 Valley Rd *NYSE: VLY*	Wayne	NJ	07470	**800-522-4100**	973-305-8800
Veteran's Truck Line Inc 800 Black Hawk Dr	Burlington	WI	53105	**800-456-9476**	262-539-3400
VIST Financial Corp PO Box 6219 PO Box 6219 *NASDAQ: VIST*	Wyomissing	PA	19610	**888-238-3330**	610-926-7632
Washington Federal Inc 425 Pike St *NASDAQ: WAFD*	Seattle	WA	98101	**800-324-9375**	206-624-7930
Washington Trust Bancorp Inc 23 Broad St *NASDAQ: WASH*	Westerly	RI	02891	**800-475-2265**	401-348-1200
Wayne Bank 717 Main St	Honesdale	PA	18431	**800-598-5002**	570-253-1455
Wayne Savings Bancshares Inc 151 N Market St *NASDAQ: WAYN*	Wooster	OH	44691	**800-414-1103**	330-264-5767
Webster City Federal Bancorp 820 Des Moines St *NYSE: WCFB*	Webster City	IA	50595	**866-519-4004**	515-832-3071
Webster Financial Corp PO Box 10305 *NYSE: WBS*	Waterbury	CT	06726	**800-325-2424**	
West Bancorp Inc PO Box 65020 *NASDAQ: WTBA*	West Des Moines	IA	50265	**800-810-2301**	515-222-2300
West Side Unlimited Corp 4201 16th Ave SW	Cedar Rapids	IA	52404	**800-373-2957**	319-390-4466
Westfield Financial Inc 141 Elm St *NASDAQ: WFD*	Westfield	MA	01085	**800-995-5734**	413-568-1911
Westwood Holdings Group Inc 200 Crescent Ct Ste 1200 *NYSE: WHG*	Dallas	TX	75201	**800-687-0372**	214-756-6900
Winona National Bankÿÿÿ PO Box 499	Winona	MN	55987	**800-546-4392**	507-454-4320
WSFS Financial Corp 500 Delaware Ave *NASDAQ: WSFS*	Wilmington	DE	19801	**888-973-7226**	302-792-6000
WTB Financial Corp PO Box 2127	Spokane	WA	99210	**800-788-4578**	

360-3 Holding Companies (General)

Company	City	State	Zip	Toll-Free	Phone
Alutiiq LLC 3909 Arctic Blvd Ste 400	Anchorage	AK	99503	**800-829-8547**	907-222-9500
American Standard Cos Inc 1 Centennial Ave	Piscataway	NJ	08855	**800-442-1902**	
AMETEK Inc 1100 Cassatt Rd PO Box 1764 *NYSE: AME*	Berwyn	PA	19312	**800-473-1286**	610-647-2121
Atlas Copco North America LLC 7 Campus Dr Ste 200	Parsippany	NJ	07054	**800-732-6762**	973-397-3432
Atlas World Group Inc 1212 St George Rd	Evansville	IN	47711	**800-252-8885**	812-424-2222
Boca Resorts 501 E Camino Real	Boca Raton	FL	33432	**888-543-1277**	561-447-3000
BT Conferencing Inc 150 Newport Ave. Ext, Ste 301	North Quincy	MA	02171	**866-770-8777**	
CBRL Group Inc PO Box 787	Lebanon	TN	37088	**800-333-9566**	
CenturyTel Inc 100 Centurylink Dr PO Box 4065 *NYSE: CTL*	Monroe	LA	71211	**877-290-5458**	318-388-9000
Clayton Holdings LLC 100 BeaRd Sawmill Rd Ste 200	Shelton	CT	06484	**877-291-5301**	203-926-5600
Comcast Corp 1701 JFK Blvd *NASDAQ: CMCSA*	Philadelphia	PA	19103	**800-266-2278**	215-665-1700
ConAgra Foods Inc 1 ConAgra Dr *NYSE: CAG*	Omaha	NE	68102	**877-266-2472**	402-240-4000
CONSOL Energy Inc 1000 Consol Energy Dr *NYSE: CNX*	Canonsburg	PA	15317	**800-544-8024**	724-485-4000
CUI Global Inc 20050 SW 112th Ave *NASDAQ: CUI*	Tualatin	OR	97062	**800-275-4899**	503-612-2300
Dectron International Inc 4300 Poirier Blvd	Montreal	QC	H4R2C5	**888-332-8766**	514-334-9609
Deluxe Corp 3680 N Victoria St *NYSE: DLX*	Shoreview	MN	55126	**800-328-7205**	651-483-7111
Dicke Safety Products 1201 Warren Ave	Downers Grove	IL	60515	**877-891-0050**	630-969-0050
Elvis Presley Enterprises Inc 3734 Elvis Presley Blvd	Memphis	TN	38116	**800-238-2000**	901-332-3322
ESCO Technologies Inc 9900A Clayton Rd *NYSE: ESE*	Saint Louis	MO	63124	**800-368-5948**	314-213-7200
Esmark Steel Group 2500 Euclid Ave	Chicago Heights	IL	60411	**800-323-0340**	708-756-0400
Eyak Corp, The 360 W Benson Blvd Ste 210	Anchorage	AK	99503	**800-478-7161**	907-334-6971
FedEx Corp 3610 Hacks Cross Rd *NYSE: FDX*	Memphis	TN	38125	**800-463-3339**	901-369-3600
Fresh Del Monte Produce Co 241 Sevilla Ave PO Box 149222 *NYSE: FDP* ■ *Cust Svc	Coral Gables	FL	33134	**800-950-3683***	305-520-8400
George Weston Ltd 22 St Clair Ave E *TSE: WN*	Toronto	ON	M4T2S7	**800-564-6253**	416-922-2500
Hitch Enterprises Inc 309 Northridge Cir PO Box 1308	Guymon	OK	73942	**800-951-2533**	580-338-8575
Home Capital Group Inc 145 King St W Ste 2300 *TSE: HCG*	Toronto	ON	M5H1J8	**800-990-7881**	416-360-4663
Hunt Consolidated Inc 1900 N Akard St	Dallas	TX	75201	**800-424-9300**	214-978-8000
Icahn Enterprises LP 767 Fifth Ave 47th Fl *NASDAQ: IEP*	New York	NY	10153	**800-255-2737**	212-702-4300
IsoRay Medical Inc 350 Hills St Ste 106	Richland	WA	99354	**877-447-6729**	509-375-1202
Kyocera International Inc 8611 Balboa Ave	San Diego	CA	92123	**877-248-4237**	858-576-2600
Liberty Diversified International Inc 5600 Hwy 169 N	New Hope	MN	55428	**800-421-1270**	763-536-6600
Marsh & McLennan Cos Inc 1166 Ave of the Americas *NYSE: MMC*	New York	NY	10036	**866-374-2662**	212-345-5000
McKesson Corp 1 Post St *NYSE: MCK*	San Francisco	CA	94104	**800-482-3784**	415-983-8300
MDC Holdings Inc 4350 S Monaco St Ste 500 *NYSE: MDC*	Denver	CO	80237	**888-500-7060**	303-773-1100
NewMarket Corp 330 S Fourth St *NYSE: NEU*	Richmond	VA	23219	**800-625-5191**	804-788-5000
NextWave Wireless Inc 10350 Science Ctr Dr Ste 210 *OTC: WAVE*	San Diego	CA	92121	**800-461-9330**	858-731-5300
North American Stainless Inc 6870 Hwy 42 East	Ghent	KY	41045	**800-499-7833**	502-347-6000
Nustar GP Holdings LLC PO Box 781609 *NYSE: NSH*	San Antonio	TX	78248	**800-866-9060**	210-918-2000
OKI Developments Inc 1416 112th Ave NE	Bellevue	WA	98004	**877-465-3654**	425-454-2800
Omega International Inc 1937 NE Loop 410 Ste 200	San Antonio	TX	78217	**888-558-0701**	210-805-8808
Otc Global Holdings 5151 San Felipe Ste 2200	Houston	TX	77056	**877-737-8511**	713-358-5450
Otter Tail Corp 4334 18th Ave SW PO Box 9156 *NASDAQ: OTTR*	Fargo	ND	58106	**866-410-8780**	218-739-8479
Pro-Dex Inc 2361 McGaw Ave *NASDAQ: PDEX*	Irvine	CA	92614	**800-562-6204**	
Revlon Inc 237 Pk Ave *NYSE: REV*	New York	NY	10017	**800-473-8566**	212-527-4000
Sandvik Inc 1702 Nevins Rd	Fair Lawn	NJ	07410	**800-726-3845**	201-794-5000
SGS North America Inc 201 State Rt 17 N	Rutherford	NJ	07070	**800-645-5227**	201-508-3000
Shenandoah Telecommunications Co 500 Shentel Way *NASDAQ: SHEN*	Edinburg	VA	22824	**800-743-6835**	540-984-5224
Siebert Financial Corp 885 Third Ave *NASDAQ: SIEB*	New York	NY	10022	**877-327-8379**	212-644-2400
Sumitomo Corp of America 600 Third Ave 42nd Fl	New York	NY	10016	**877-980-3283**	212-207-0700
Telephone & Data Systems Inc 30 N La Salle St Ste 4000 *NYSE: TDS*	Chicago	IL	60602	**877-337-1575**	312-630-1900
ThyssenKrupp Elevator 9280 Crestwyn Hills Dr	Memphis	TN	38125	**877-230-0303**	901-261-1800
Toyota Motor North America Inc 601 Lexington Ave 49th Fl	New York	NY	10022	**800-331-4331**	
Tredegar Corp 1100 Boulders Pkwy *NYSE: TG*	North Chesterfield	VA	23225	**800-411-7441**	804-330-1000
Union Pacific Corp 1400 Douglas St *NYSE: UNP*	Omaha	NE	68179	**888-870-8777**	402-544-5000
VENSURE Employer Services Inc 4140 E Baseline Rd Ste 201	Mesa	AZ	85206	**800-409-8958**	
Warren Equities Inc 27 Warren Way	Providence	RI	02905	**866-867-4075**	401-781-9900
WEDGE Group Inc 1415 Louisiana St Ste 3000	Houston	TX	77002	**888-563-5383**	713-739-6500
Williams Cos Inc 1 Williams Ctr *NYSE: WMB*	Tulsa	OK	74103	**800-945-5426**	918-573-2000
Worthington Direct Holdings LLC 6301 Gaston Ave Ste 670	Dallas	TX	75214	**800-599-6636**	
YRC Worldwide Inc 10990 Roe Ave *NASDAQ: YRCW*	Overland Park	KS	66211	**800-846-4300**	913-696-6100

360-4 Insurance Holding Companies

Company	City	State	Zip	Toll-Free	Phone
AFLAC Inc 1932 Wynnton Rd *NYSE: AFL*	Columbus	GA	31999	**800-992-3522**	706-323-3431
AIG SunAmerica Inc 21650 Oxnard St	Woodland Hills	CA	91367	**800-445-7862**	
Allstate Corp 2775 Sanders Rd *NYSE: ALL*	Northbrook	IL	60062	**800-255-7828**	847-402-5000
AMBAC Financial Group Inc 1 State St Plz 15th Fl *OTC: ABKFQ*	New York	NY	10004	**800-221-1854**	212-668-0340
American Fidelity Assurance Co 2000 N Classen Blvd	Oklahoma City	OK	73106	**800-654-8489**	405-523-2000
Americo Life Inc 300 W 11th St *General	Kansas City	MO	64105	**800-231-0801***	816-391-2000
Anthem Insurance Cos Inc 120 Monument Cir Ste 200	Indianapolis	IN	46204	**800-331-1476**	317-488-6000
Aon Corp 200 E Randolph St	Chicago	IL	60601	**877-384-4276**	312-381-1000
Assurant Group 11222 Quail Roost Dr	Miami	FL	33157	**800-852-2244**	305-253-2244
Bexil Corp 11 Hanover Sq *OTC: BXLC*	New York	NY	10005	**800-937-5449**	212-785-0400
Capitol Transamerica Corp 1600 Aspen Commons	Middleton	WI	53562	**800-475-4450**	608-829-4200
Chubb Corp 15 Mountain View Rd *NYSE: CB*	Warren	NJ	07059	**800-252-4670**	908-903-2000
Citizens Financial Corp 12910 Shelbyville Rd Ste 300 *OTC: CFIN*	Louisville	KY	40243	**800-843-7752**	502-244-2420
CNA Financial Corp 333 S Wabash Ave *NYSE: CNA*	Chicago	IL	60604	**800-262-4357**	312-822-5000
Conseco Inc 11825 N Pennsylvania St *NYSE: CNO*	Carmel	IN	46032	**866-595-2255**	
CUNA Mutual Group 5910 Mineral Pt Dr	Madison	WI	53705	**800-937-2644**	608-238-5851
Donegal Group Inc 1195 River Rd *NASDAQ: DGICA*	Marietta	PA	17547	**800-877-0600**	717-426-1931
EMC Insurance Group Inc 717 Mulberry St *NASDAQ: EMCI*	Des Moines	IA	50309	**800-447-2295**	515-280-2511
Everest Re Group Ltd 477 Martinsville Rd PO Box 830	Liberty Corner	NJ	07938	**800-269-6660**	908-604-3000
Federated Insurance Cos 121 E Pk Sq PO Box 328	Owatonna	MN	55060	**800-533-0472**	507-455-5200
GMAC Insurance Holdings Inc PO Box 3199	Winston-Salem	NC	27102	**888-293-5108**	
Harleysville Group Inc 355 Maple Ave *NASDAQ: HGIC*	Harleysville	PA	19438	**800-523-6344**	215-256-5000
Hartford Financial Services Group Inc 690 Asylum Ave *NYSE: HIG*	Hartford	CT	06115	**866-553-5663**	860-547-5000
Horace Mann Educators Corp 1 Horace Mann Plz *NYSE: HMN*	Springfield	IL	62715	**800-999-1030**	217-789-2500

Company / Address	City	State	Zip	Toll-Free	Phone
Investors Title Co 121 N Columbia St *NASDAQ: ITIC*	Chapel Hill	NC	27514	**800-326-4842**	919-968-2200
Kansas City Life Insurance Co 3520 Broadway *NASDAQ: KCLI*	Kansas City	MO	64111	**800-821-6164**	816-753-7000
Kingsway America Inc (KAI) 150 NW Pt Blvd	Elk Grove Village	IL	60007	**800-232-0631**	847-700-9100
Legal & General America Inc 1701 Research Blvd	Rockville	MD	20850	**800-638-8428**	301-279-4800
Lincoln National Corp (LNC) 150 N Radnor-Chester Rd *NYSE: LNC*	Radnor	PA	19087	**877-275-5462**	484-583-1400
Manulife Financial Corp 200 Bloor St E *NYSE: MFC*	Toronto	ON	M4W1E5	**800-795-9767**	416-926-3000
Markel Corp 4521 Highwoods Pkwy *NYSE: MKL*	Glen Allen	VA	23060	**877-566-6323**	800-431-1270
Meadowbrook Insurance Group Inc 26255 American Dr *NYSE: MIG*	Southfield	MI	48034	**800-482-2726**	248-358-1100
Midland Co 7000 Midland Blvd	Amelia	OH	45102	**800-759-9008**	800-543-2644
Mutual of Omaha Co 3300 Mutual of Omaha Plz	Omaha	NE	68175	**800-775-6000**	402-342-7600
Navigators Group Inc 1 Penn Plz 32nd Fl *NASDAQ: NAVG*	New York	NY	10119	**866-408-1922**	212-244-2333
Pacific Mutual Holding Co 700 Newport Ctr Dr	Newport Beach	CA	92660	**800-347-7787**	949-219-3011
Phoenix Cos Inc, The 1 American Row PO Box 5056 *NYSE: PNX*	Hartford	CT	06102	**800-628-1936**	860-403-5000
PICO Holdings Inc 7979 Ivanhoe Ave Ste 301 *NASDAQ: PICO*	La Jolla	CA	92037	**888-389-3222**	858-456-6022
PMI Group Inc 3003 Oak Rd *OTC: PMI*	Walnut Creek	CA	94597	**800-288-1970**	
ProAssurance Corp 100 Brookwood Pl Ste 300 *NYSE: PRA*	Birmingham	AL	35209	**800-282-6242**	205-877-4400
Protective Life Corp 2801 Hwy 280 S *NYSE: PL*	Birmingham	AL	35223	**800-333-3418**	205-268-1000
Reinsurance Group of America Inc 1370 Timberlake Manor Pkwy *NYSE: RGA*	Chesterfield	MO	63017	**800-985-4326**	636-736-7000
RLI Corp 9025 N Lindbergh Dr *NYSE: RLI* ■ *Cust Svc	Peoria	IL	61615	**800-331-4929***	309-692-1000
Security Benefit Group of Cos 1 Security Benefit Pl	Topeka	KS	66636	**800-888-2461**	785-438-3000
Selective Insurance Group Inc 40 Wantage Ave *NASDAQ: SIGI*	Branchville	NJ	07890	**800-777-9656**	973-948-3000
StanCorp Financial Group Inc 1100 SW Sixth Ave *NYSE: SFG*	Portland	OR	97204	**800-368-1135**	
Summit Holding Southeast Inc PO Box 600	Gainesville	GA	30503	**800-971-2667**	678-450-5825
Sun Life Financial Inc 150 King St W *TSE: SLF*	Toronto	ON	M5H1J9	**877-786-5433**	416-979-9966
Torchmark Corp 3700 S Stonebridge Dr *NYSE: TMK*	McKinney	TX	75070	**877-577-3899**	972-569-4000
Travelers Cos Inc 385 Washington St *NYSE: TRV*	Saint Paul	MN	55102	**800-328-2189**	651-310-7911
ULLICO Inc 1625 Eye St NW	Washington	DC	20006	**800-431-5425**	
United Fire Group 118 Second Ave SE PO Box 73909	Cedar Rapids	IA	52407	**800-332-7977**	319-399-5700
United Trust Group Inc (UTGI) 5250 S Sixth St *OTC: UTGN*	Springfield	IL	62705	**800-323-0050**	217-241-6410
Universal American Corp (UAFC) 44 S Broadway Ste 1200 *NYSE: UAM*	White Plains	NY	10601	**866-249-8668**	914-934-5200
UnumProvident Corp 1 Fountain Sq	Chattanooga	TN	37402	**800-262-0018**	423-294-1011
Western & Southern Financial Group 400 Broadway	Cincinnati	OH	45202	**800-333-5222**	513-629-1800
White Mountains Insurance Group Ltd 80 S Main St *NYSE: WTM*	Hanover	NH	03755	**866-295-3762**	603-640-2200

360-5 Utilities Holding Companies

Company / Address	City	State	Zip	Toll-Free	Phone
AGL Resources Inc 10 Peachtree Pl PO Box 4569 *NYSE: GAS* ■ *Cust Svc	Atlanta	GA	30309	**866-977-4278***	404-584-4000
ALLETE Inc 30 W Superior St *NYSE: ALE*	Duluth	MN	55802	**800-228-4966**	218-279-5000
Ameren Corp 1901 Chouteau Ave *NYSE: AEE*	Saint Louis	MO	63103	**800-552-7583**	314-621-3222
American Electric Power Company Inc 1 Riverside Plz *NYSE: AEP* ■ *Cust Svc	Columbus	OH	43215	**800-277-2177***	614-716-1000
American States Water Co 630 E Foothill Blvd *NYSE: AWR*	San Dimas	CA	91773	**800-999-4033**	909-394-3600
American Water Works Co Inc 1025 Laurel Oak Rd *NYSE: AWK*	Voorhees	NJ	08043	**888-282-6816**	856-346-8200
Artesian Resources Corp 664 Churchmans Rd *NASDAQ: ARTNA*	Newark	DE	19702	**800-332-5114**	302-453-6900
Atmos Energy Corp 5430 LBJ Fwy Ste 1800 *NYSE: ATO*	Dallas	TX	75240	**888-286-6700**	972-934-9227
Black Hills Corp 625 Ninth St *NYSE: BKH*	Rapid City	SD	57701	**866-264-8003**	605-721-1700
CenterPoint Energy Inc 1111 Louisiana St *NYSE: CNP* ■ *Cust Svc	Houston	TX	77002	**800-495-9880***	713-207-1111
CH Energy Group Inc 284 S Ave *NYSE: CHG*	Poughkeepsie	NY	12601	**800-527-2714**	845-452-2000
CMS Energy Corp 1 Energy Plz *NYSE: CMS*	Jackson	MI	49201	**800-477-5050**	517-788-0550
Connecticut Water Service Inc 93 W Main St *NASDAQ: CTWS*	Clinton	CT	06413	**800-286-5700**	860-669-8636
Consolidated Edison Inc 4 Irving Pl *NYSE: ED*	New York	NY	10003	**800-752-6633**	212-460-4600
Dominion Resources Inc 120 Tredegar St *NYSE: D*	Richmond	VA	23219	**800-552-4034**	804-819-2000
DPL Inc 1065 Woodman Dr *NYSE: DPL*	Dayton	OH	45432	**800-433-8500**	800-736-3001
DTE Energy Co 1 Energy Plz *NYSE: DTE*	Detroit	MI	48226	**800-477-4747**	313-235-4000
Duquesne Light Holdings Inc 411 Seventh Ave	Pittsburgh	PA	15219	**888-393-7000**	412-393-7000
Dynegy Inc 601 Travis St Ste 1400 *NYSE: DYN*	Houston	TX	77002	**800-633-4704**	713-507-6400
Edison International 2244 Walnut Grove Ave *NYSE: EIX* ■ *Cust Svc	Rosemead	CA	91770	**800-655-4555***	626-302-1212
Energen Corp 605 Richard Arrington Blvd N *NYSE: EGN*	Birmingham	AL	35203	**800-654-3206**	205-326-2700
Entergy Corp 639 Loyola Ave *NYSE: ETR*	New Orleans	LA	70113	**800-368-3749**	504-576-4000
FirstEnergy Corp 76 S Main St *NYSE: FE*	Akron	OH	44308	**800-633-4766**	
FPL Group Inc *NextEra Energy Inc* 700 Universe Blvd *NYSE: NEE*	Juno Beach	FL	33408	**888-218-4392**	561-694-4000
Holly Energy Partners LP 100 Crescent Ct Ste 1600	Dallas	TX	75201	**800-642-1687**	214-871-3555
MidAmerican Energy Holdings Co 666 Grand Ave PO Box 657	Des Moines	IA	50303	**800-329-6261**	
National Fuel Gas Co 6363 Main St *NYSE: NFG* ■ *Cust Svc	Williamsville	NY	14221	**800-365-3234***	716-857-7000
National Grid USA Service Company Inc 25 Research Dr	Westborough	MA	01582	**800-548-8000**	508-389-2000
New Jersey Resources Corp 1415 Wyckoff Rd *NYSE: NJR*	Wall	NJ	07719	**800-221-0051**	732-938-1000
NSTAR 800 Boylston St *NYSE: NST*	Boston	MA	02199	**800-592-2000**	617-424-2000
OGE Energy Corp 321 N Harvey St *NYSE: OGE*	Oklahoma City	OK	73102	**800-272-9741**	405-553-3000
PG & E Corp 77 Beale St 24th Fl *NYSE: PCG*	San Francisco	CA	94105	**800-743-5000**	415-267-7000
Pinnacle West Capital Corp 400 N Fifth St *NYSE: PNW*	Phoenix	AZ	85004	**800-457-2983**	602-250-1000
PNM Resources Inc Alvarado Sq *NYSE: PNM*	Albuquerque	NM	87158	**888-342-5766**	505-241-2700
PPL Corp 2 N Ninth St *NYSE: PPL*	Allentown	PA	18101	**800-342-5775**	610-774-5151
Progress Energy Inc 410 S Wilmington St *NYSE: PGN*	Raleigh	NC	27601	**800-452-2777**	919-546-6111
Public Service Enterprise Group Inc 80 Pk Plz *NYSE: PEG* ■ *Cust Svc	Newark	NJ	07102	**800-436-7734***	973-430-7000
Questar Corp 333 S State St PO Box 45433 *NYSE: STR*	Salt Lake City	UT	84145	**800-323-5517**	801-324-5000
SCANA Corp 220 Operation Way *NYSE: SCG*	Cayce	SC	29033	**800-251-7234**	803-217-9000
Sempra Energy Corp 101 Ash St *NYSE: SRE*	San Diego	CA	92101	**800-411-7343**	619-696-2000
Unitil Corp 6 Liberty Ln W *NYSE: UTL*	Hampton	NH	03842	**800-852-3339**	603-772-0775
Vectren Corp 211 NW Riverside Dr PO Box 209 *NYSE: VVC*	Evansville	IN	47702	**800-227-1376**	812-491-4000
Westar Energy Inc 818 S Kansas Ave *NYSE: WR*	Topeka	KS	66612	**800-383-1183**	785-575-6300
WGL Holdings Inc 101 Constitution Ave NW *NYSE: WGL*	Washington	DC	20080	**800-645-3751**	703-750-2000
Wisconsin Energy Corp 231 W Michigan St *NYSE: WEC* ■ *General	Milwaukee	WI	53203	**800-242-9137***	414-221-2345

361 HOME FURNISHINGS - WHOL

Company	Address	City	State	Zip	Toll-Free	Phone
AA Importing Co Inc	7700 Hall St	Saint Louis	MO	63147	**800-325-0602***	314-383-8800
*Cust Svc						
Adleta Co	1645 Diplomat Dr Ste 200	Carrollton	TX	75006	**800-423-5382**	972-620-5600
Architex International	3333 Commercial Ave	Northbrook	IL	60062	**800-621-0827**	847-205-1333
B & F System Inc	3920 S Walton Walker	Dallas	TX	75236	**877-586-2926**	214-333-2111
Bettendorf-Stanford	1370 W Main St	Salem	IL	62881	**800-548-2253**	618-548-3555
Bishop Distributing Co	5200 36th St SE	Grand Rapids	MI	49512	**800-748-0363***	
*Cust Svc						
Bisque Imports	1 Belmont Ave	Belmont	NC	28012	**888-568-5991**	704-829-9290
Boston Warehouse Trading Corp	59 Davis Ave	Norwood	MA	02062	**800-811-2672**	781-769-8550
BR Funsten & Co	5200 Watt Ct Ste B	Fairfield	CA	94534	**888-261-2871**	209-825-5375
C & F Enterprises Inc	819 Bluecrab Rd	Newport News	VA	23606	**888-889-9868**	757-310-6100
Caber Sure Fit Inc	25A E Pearce St Unit 1	Richmond Hill	ON	L4B2M9	**800-520-3152**	905-886-5849
Cambridge Silversmith Ltd	116 Lehigh Dr	Fairfield	NJ	07004	**800-890-3366**	973-227-4400
Carlton Group Inc	120 Landmark Dr	Greensboro	NC	27409	**800-722-7824**	336-668-7677
Carnations Home Fashions Inc	53 Jeanne Dr	Newburgh	NY	12550	**800-866-8949**	212-679-6017
CCA Global Partners	4301 Earth City Expy	Earth City	MO	63045	**800-466-6984**	314-506-0000
CDC Distributors	10511 Medallion Dr	Cincinnati	OH	45241	**800-678-2321**	513-771-3100
Cookshack	2304 N Ash St	Ponca City	OK	74601	**800-423-0698**	580-765-3669
Cool Gear International LLC	10 Cordage Park Cir	Plymouth	MA	02360	**855-393-2665**	
Decorative Crafts Inc	50 Chestnut St	Greenwich	CT	06830	**800-431-4455**	203-531-1500
Derr Flooring Company Inc	525 Davisville Rd PO Box 912	Willow Grove	PA	19090	**800-523-3457**	215-657-6300
Down Under Linen & Bedding Ctr	5170 Dixie Rd	Mississauga	ON	L4W1E3	**888-624-6484**	905-624-5854
Fabricut Inc	9303 E 46th St	Tulsa	OK	74145	**800-999-8200**	918-622-7700
Farrey's Wholesale Hardware Company Inc	1850 NE 146th St	North Miami	FL	33181	**888-854-5483**	305-947-5451
Georgian Plantation Shutter Co	455 Wilbanks Dr	Ball Ground	GA	30107	**888-684-0382**	678-454-1100
Home Design Outlet Center	400 County Ave	Secaucus	NJ	07094	**800-701-0388**	
Home Essentials & Beyond Inc	200 Theodore Conrad Dr	Jersey City	NJ	07305	**800-417-6218**	732-590-3600
Horizons Window Fashions Inc	1705 Waukegan Rd	Waukegan	IL	60085	**800-858-2352**	
Innovative Hearth Products	2701 S Harbor Blvd	Santa Ana	CA	92704	**866-328-4537**	
Jackson George N Ltd	1139 Mcdermot Ave	Winnipeg	MB	R3E0V2	**800-665-8978**	204-786-3821
JJ Haines & Company Inc	6950 Aviation Blvd	Glen Burnie	MD	21061	**800-922-9248**	
Kanawha Scales & Systems Inc	Rock Branch Industrial Pk 303 Jacobson Dr	Poca	WV	25159	**800-955-8321**	304-755-8321
Kiefer Specialty Flooring Inc	2910 Falling Waters Blvd	Lindenhurst	IL	60046	**800-322-5448**	847-245-8450
L Bornstein & Co Inc	321 Washington St	Somerville	MA	02143	**800-842-1111**	617-776-3555
Lanz Cabinet Shop Inc	3025 W Seventh Pl	Eugene	OR	97402	**800-788-6332**	541-485-4050
Legendary Whitetails	820 Enterprise Dr	Slinger	WI	53086	**800-875-9453**	
Legends of England	3520 Roberts Cut Off Rd	Fort Worth	TX	76114	**800-578-1065**	817-236-3141
Longust Distributing Inc	2432 W Birchwood Ave	Mesa	AZ	85202	**800-352-0521**	480-820-6244
Lonseal Inc	928 E 238th St	Carson	CA	90745	**800-832-7111**	310-830-7111
M Block & Sons Inc	5020 W 73rd St	Bedford Park	IL	60638	**800-621-8845**	708-728-8400
Maxtex Inc	3620 Francis Cir	Alpharetta	GA	30004	**800-241-1836**	770-772-6757
MDS	N30 W22377 Green Rd Ste C	Waukesha	WI	53186	**888-523-2611**	
More Space Place Inc	5040 140th Ave N	Clearwater	FL	33760	**888-731-3051**	
National Glass Ltd	5744 198th St	Langley	BC	V3A7J2	**800-663-8168**	604-530-2311
Omega Moulding Company Ltd	1 Saw Grass Dr	Bellport	NY	11713	**800-289-6634**	
OneCoast Network LLC	230 Spring St Ste 1800	Atlanta	GA	30303	**866-592-5514**	
Pompanoosuc Mills Corp	Route 5 PO Box 238	East Thetford	VT	05043	**800-757-4061**	
Regent Products Corp	8999 Palmer St	River Grove	IL	60171	**800-583-1002**	708-583-1000
Santec Inc	3501 Challenger St	Torrance	CA	90503	**800-284-4050**	310-542-0063
Selective Enterprises Inc	10701 Texland Blvd	Charlotte	NC	28273	**800-334-1207**	704-588-3310
Sewing Source Inc, The	PO Box 639	Spring Hope	NC	27882	**800-849-6945**	252-478-3900
Shelving Inc	32 S Squirrel Rd	Auburn Hills	MI	48326	**800-637-9508**	248-852-8600
Sobel Westex Inc	2670 Western Ave	Las Vegas	NV	89109	**888-887-6235**	
SOG Specialty Knives & Tools LLC	6521 212th St SW	Lynnwood	WA	98036	**888-405-6433**	425-771-6230
Southern Tile Distributors Inc	4590 Village Ave	Norfolk	VA	23502	**800-333-8970**	757-855-8041
Springs Window Fashions LP	7549 Graber Rd	Middleton	WI	53562	**877-792-0002**	608-836-1011
Stephen Miller Gallery	800 Santa Cruz Ave	Menlo Park	CA	94025	**888-566-8833**	650-327-5040
Sterling Cut Glass Company Inc	5020 Olympic Blvd	Erlanger	KY	41018	**800-543-1317**	859-283-2333
T & A Supply Company Inc	6821 S 216th St Bldg A PO Box 927	Kent	WA	98032	**800-562-2857**	253-872-3682
Tailored Living LLC	1927 N Glassell St	Orange	CA	92865	**866-675-8819**	
Thompson Olde Inc	3250 Camino Del Sol	Oxnard	CA	93030	**800-827-1565**	805-983-0388
Three Hands Corp	13259 Ralston Ave	Sylmar	CA	91342	**800-443-5443**	818-833-1200
Virginia Tile Co	28320 Plymouth Rd	Livonia	MI	48150	**877-356-7461**	734-762-2400
Wanke Cascade Co	6330 N Cutter Cir	Portland	OR	97217	**800-365-5053**	503-289-8609
Weightech	1649 Country Elite Dr	Waldron	AR	72958	**800-457-3720**	479-637-4182
WMF Americas Inc	3512 Faith Church Rd	Indian Trail	NC	28079	**800-966-3009**	704-882-3898

362 HOME FURNISHINGS STORES

SEE ALSO Department Stores ; Furniture Stores

Company	Address	City	State	Zip	Toll-Free	Phone
Altmeyer Home Stores Inc	6515 Rt 22	Delmont	PA	15626	**800-394-6628**	724-468-3434
Amcon Block & Precast Inc	2211 Hwy 10 S	Saint Cloud	MN	56304	**888-251-6030**	320-251-6030
Anna's Linens Inc	3550 Hyland Ave	Costa Mesa	CA	92626	**866-266-2728**	714-850-0504
Art Material Services Inc	625 Joyce Kilmer Ave	New Brunswick	NJ	08901	**888-522-5526**	732-545-8888
Bauerware LLC	3886 17th St	San Francisco	CA	94114	**877-864-5662**	415-864-3886
Beacon Products LLC	2041 58th Ave Cir E	Bradenton	FL	34203	**800-345-4928**	
Bed Bath & Beyond Inc	650 Liberty Ave	Union	NJ	07083	**800-462-3966**	908-688-0888
NASDAQ: BBBY						
Besco Electric Supply Co	711 S 14th St	Leesburg	FL	34748	**800-541-6618**	
Bitterman Scales LLC	413 Radcliff Rd	Willow Street	PA	17584	**877-464-3009**	717-464-3009
Blanco America Inc	110 Mount Holly By-Pass	Lumberton	NJ	08048	**800-451-5782**	
Bristol Aluminum	5514 Bristol Emilie Rd	Levittown	PA	19057	**800-338-5532**	215-946-3160
Burlington Coat Factory	1830 Rt 130 N	Burlington	NJ	08016	**855-355-2875**	609-387-7800
Container Store, The	500 Freeport Pkwy	Coppell	TX	75019	**800-733-3532**	972-538-6000
Cost Plus Inc	200 Fourth St	Oakland	CA	94607	**877-967-5362**	510-893-7300
NASDAQ: CPWM						
Cutlery & More LLC	135 Prairie Lk Rd	East Dundee	IL	60118	**800-650-9866**	
Design Within Reach Inc	711 Canal St 3rd fl 3rd Fl	Stamford	CT	06902	**800-944-2233**	203-614-0600
OTC: DWRI						
DirectBuy Inc	8450 Broadway	Merrillville	IN	46410	**800-320-3462**	219-736-1100
Force Flow Inc	2430 Stanwell Dr	Concord	CA	94520	**800-893-6723**	
GEARYS Beverly Hills	351 N Beverly Dr	Beverly Hills	CA	90210	**800-793-6670**	310-273-4741
Gracious Home	1220 Third Ave	New York	NY	10021	**800-338-7809**	212-517-6300
Grand Rapids Scale Company Inc	4215 Stafford Ave Sw	Grand Rapids	MI	49548	**800-348-5701**	616-538-7080
Granite City Electric Supply Co	19 Quincy Ave	Quincy	MA	02169	**800-850-9400**	617-472-6500
Gump's	135 Post St	San Francisco	CA	94108	**800-766-7628**	415-982-1616
Habitat Housewares	3801 Old Seward Hwy Ste 7	Anchorage	AK	99503	**800-770-1856**	907-561-1856
Hammacher Schlemmer & Co	9307 N Milwaukee Ave	Niles	IL	60714	**800-321-1484**	
Hussong Manufacturing Company Inc	204 Industrial Park Rd	Lakefield	MN	56150	**800-253-4904**	507-662-6641
Kirkland's Inc	5310 Maryland Way	Brentwood	TN	37027	**877-541-4855**	
NASDAQ: KIRK						
Kitchen Collection Inc	71 E Water St	Chillicothe	OH	45601	**888-548-2651***	740-773-9150
*General						
Kwik-Covers LLC	811 Ridge Rd	Webster	NY	14580	**866-586-9620**	585-787-9620
Lindamar Industries Inc	1603 Commerce Way	Paso Robles	CA	93446	**800-235-1811**	805-237-1910
Litelab Corp	251 Elm St	Buffalo	NY	14203	**800-238-4120**	716-856-4491
Lynx Grills Inc	5895 Rickenbacker Rd	Commerce	CA	90040	**888-289-5969**	323-838-1770
Mason Structural Steel Inc	7500 Northfield Rd	Walton Hills	OH	44146	**800-686-1223**	440-439-1040
Mattress Firm Inc	5815 Gulf Fwy	Houston	TX	77023	**800-821-6621**	713-923-1090
Michael C Fina Inc	545 Fifth Ave	New York	NY	10022	**800-289-3462**	212-557-2500

	City	State	Zip	Toll-Free	Phone
Pier 1 Imports Inc					
100 Pier 1 Pl	Fort Worth	TX	76102	**800-245-4595**	817-252-8000
NYSE: PIR					
Restoration Hardware Inc					
2900 N MacArthur Dr Ste 100	Tracy	CA	95376	**800-910-9836**	
Seattle Lighting Fixture Co					
222 Second Ave Ext S	Seattle	WA	98104	**800-689-1000***	206-622-4736
*Cust Svc					
Sentran LLC					
4355 E Lowell St Ste F	Ontario	CA	91761	**888-545-8988**	909-605-1544
Southern Wholesale Flooring Company Inc					
955B Cobb Pl Blvd	Kennesaw	GA	30144	**800-282-7590**	770-514-7110
Sur La Table					
5701 Sixth Ave S Ste 486	Seattle	WA	98108	**800-243-0852**	
Timberlane Inc					
150 Domorah Dr	Montgomeryville	PA	18936	**800-250-2221**	215-616-0600
TJX Cos Inc					
770 Cochituate Rd	Framingham	MA	01701	**800-926-6299**	508-390-1000
NYSE: TJX					
Topaz Lighting Corp					
925 Waverly Ave	Holtsville	NY	11742	**800-666-2852**	631-758-5507
Totalcomp Scales & Components					
13-01 Pollitt Dr Ste 2	Fair Lawn	NJ	07410	**800-631-0347**	201-797-2718
Villeroy & Boch Tableware Ltd					
3535 Us Hwy 1	Princeton	NJ	08540	**800-536-2284**	
Williams-Sonoma Inc					
3250 Van Ness Ave	San Francisco	CA	94109	**800-838-2589**	415-421-7900
NYSE: WSM					
World Class Lighting					
14350 60th St N	Clearwater	FL	33760	**877-499-6753**	727-524-7661
Z Gallerie Inc					
1855 W 139th St	Gardena	CA	90249	**800-358-8288**	310-630-1200

363 HOME HEALTH SERVICES

SEE ALSO Hospices

	City	State	Zip	Toll-Free	Phone
Abbi Home Care Inc					
6453 SW Blvd	Benbrook	TX	76132	**877-383-2224**	817-377-0889
Advantage Home Health Care Inc					
4008 N Wheeling Ave	Muncie	IN	47304	**800-884-5088**	765-284-1211
Alacare Home Health & Hospice					
2400 John Hawkins Pkwy	Birmingham	AL	35244	**800-852-4724**	205-981-8000
Allcare Medical Inc					
125 Newtown Rd Ste 300	Plainview	NY	11803	**800-244-4660**	
Almost Family Inc					
9510 Ormsby Stn Rd Ste 300	Louisville	KY	40223	**800-828-9769**	502-891-1000
NASDAQ: AFAM					
Altamed Health Services Corp					
500 Citadel Dr Ste 490	Los Angeles	CA	90040	**877-462-2582**	323-725-8751
Amedisys Inc					
5959 S Sherwood Forest Blvd Ste 300	Baton Rouge	LA	70816	**800-464-0020**	225-292-2031
NASDAQ: AMED					
American HomePatient Inc					
5200 Maryland Way Ste 400	Brentwood	TN	37027	**800-890-7271**	615-221-8884
Androscoggin Home Health Services Inc					
PO Box 819	Lewiston	ME	04243	**800-482-7412**	207-777-7740
Anthelio Healthcare Solutions Inc					
5400 LBJ Fwy Ste 200	Dallas	TX	75240	**855-268-4354**	214-257-7000
Apria Healthcare Group Inc					
26220 Enterprise Ct	Lake Forest	CA	92630	**800-277-4288**	949-639-2000
ARK Diagnostics Inc					
48089 Fremont Blvd	Fremont	CA	94538	**877-869-2320**	510-270-6270
Aroostook Home Health Services					
658 Main St Ste 2	Caribou	ME	04736	**877-688-9977**	207-492-8290
Bayada Nurses Home Care Specialists					
290 Chester Ave	Moorestown	NJ	08057	**877-591-1527**	856-231-1000
Calea Ltd					
2785 Skymark Ave Unit 2	Mississauga	ON	L4W4Y3	**888-909-3299**	905-238-1234
CanCare Health Services Inc					
45 Sheppard Ave E Ste 204	Toronto	ON	M2N5W9	**877-226-6995**	416-226-6995
Care Partners					
68 Sweeten Creek Rd	Asheville	NC	28803	**800-627-1533**	828-252-2255
Caresource Health Plan					
740 SE Seventh St	Grants Pass	OR	97526	**888-460-0185**	541-471-4106
Carestar Inc					
5566 Cheviot Rd	Cincinnati	OH	45247	**866-834-4712**	513-618-8300
Carter Healthcare					
3105 S Meridian Ave	Oklahoma City	OK	73119	**888-951-1112**	405-947-7700
Casepro Inc					
21738 Hardy Oak Blvd	San Antonio	TX	78258	**888-999-2594**	210-496-8050
Central Vermont Home Health & Hospice					
600 Granger Rd	Barre	VT	05641	**800-286-1219**	802-223-1878
Christian Homes Inc					
200 N Postville Dr	Lincoln	IL	62656	**800-535-8717**	217-732-9651
ComForcare Senior Services Inc					
2520 Telegraph Rd Ste 100	Bloomfield Hills	MI	48302	**800-886-4044**	248-745-9700
Commonwealth Health Corporation Inc					
800 Park St	Bowling Green	KY	42101	**800-786-1581**	270-745-1500
Confident Care Corp					
3 University Plz Dr Ste 340	Hackensack	NJ	07601	**866-839-2273**	201-498-9400
Continucare Corp					
7200 Corporate Ctr Dr Ste 600	Miami	FL	33126	**866-312-7154**	305-500-2000
Coram Healthcare Corp					
555 17th St Ste 1500	Denver	CO	80202	**800-267-2642**	
Delaware Hospice Inc					
3515 Silverside Rd	Wilmington	DE	19810	**800-838-9800**	302-478-5707
Dermatran Health Solutions					
1504 market st	Redding	CA	96001	**855-675-5210**	
Fletcher'S Medical Supplies Inc					
6851 S Distribution Ave	Jacksonville	FL	32256	**855-541-7809**	904-387-4481
General Healthcare Resources Inc					
2250 Hickory Rd Ste 240	Plymouth Meeting	PA	19462	**800-879-4471**	610-834-1122
Genesis Home Care Inc					
116 E Heritage Dr	Tyler	TX	75703	**800-947-0273**	903-509-3374
Griswold Special Care Inc					
717 Bethlehem Pike Ste 300	Erdenheim	PA	19038	**855-303-9470**	215-402-0200
Hamacher Resource Group LLC					
8801 W Heather Ave	Milwaukee	WI	53224	**800-888-0889**	
Help At Home Inc					
1 N State St Ste 800	Chicago	IL	60602	**800-404-3191**	312-762-0900
Home Bound Healthcare Inc					
1615 Vollmer Rd	Flossmoor	IL	60422	**800-444-7028**	708-798-0800
Home Instead Inc					
13323 California St	Omaha	NE	68154	**888-484-5759**	402-498-4466
Home IV Care & Nutritional Service					
30 Ebco Cir Ste 102	Waynesboro	VA	22980	**800-552-6576**	
Home Staff Inc					
5517 N Cumberland Ave Ste 915	Chicago	IL	60656	**800-806-6924**	773-467-6002
Homewatch International Inc					
7100 E Belleview Ave Ste 303	Greenwood Village	CO	80111	**800-777-9770**	303-758-5111
Hospice Atlanta-Visiting Nurse Health System					
1244 Pk Vista Dr	Atlanta	GA	30319	**866-374-4776**	404-869-3000
IntegraCare Holdings Inc					
2559 SW Grapevine Pkwy Ste 300	Grapevine	TX	76051	**800-735-2988**	817-310-4999
Interim HealthCare Inc					
1601 Sawgrass Corporate Pkwy	Sunrise	FL	33323	**800-338-7786**	954-858-6000
Kelly Home Care Services Inc					
999 W Big Beaver Rd	Troy	MI	48084	**800-755-8636**	248-362-4444
Lakewood Health System					
49725 County 83	Staples	MN	56479	**800-525-1033**	218-894-1515
LHC Group LLC					
901 Hugh Wallis Rd S	Lafayette	LA	70508	**866-542-4768**	337-289-8188
NASDAQ: LHCG					
Lifelink Foundation Inc					
409 Bayshore Blvd	Tampa	FL	33606	**800-262-5775**	813-253-2640
Living Assistance Services Inc					
937 Haverford Rd Ste 200	Bryn Mawr	PA	19010	**800-365-4189**	
Mackenzie Eason & Associates					
3023 S University Dr Ste 230	Fort Worth	TX	76109	**866-392-3139**	817-922-9152
Mains'l Services Inc					
7000 78th Ave N	Brooklyn Park	MN	55445	**800-441-6525**	
Med Team Home Health Care					
131 S Beckham Ave	Tyler	TX	75702	**800-825-2873**	903-592-9747
Medical Ctr at Princeton Home Care					
905 Herrontown Rd	Princeton	NJ	08540	**877-932-8395**	609-497-4900
Medical Services of America Inc (MSA)					
171 Monroe Ln	Lexington	SC	29072	**800-845-5850**	803-957-0500
Mena Hospital Commission					
311 Morrow St N	Mena	AR	71953	**800-394-6185**	479-394-2534
Meridian Health System Inc					
1967 Hwy 34, Bldg C, Ste 104	Wall	NJ	07719	**800-560-9990**	
Metro Pavia Health System Inc					
MaraMar Plz Bldg Avenida San Patricio Ste 950-960	Guaynabo	PR	00968	**888-882-0882**	
National Home Health Care Corp					
700 White Plains Rd Ste 275	Scarsdale	NY	10583	**800-422-4661**	914-722-9000
New Choices Inc					
2501 18th St Ste 201	Bettendorf	IA	52722	**888-355-5502**	563-355-5502
New York Health Care Inc					
33 W Hawthorne Ave 3rd Fl	Valley Stream	NY	11580	**888-978-6942**	718-375-6700
OTC: BBAL					
North Los Angel County Regional Ctr					
15400 Sherman Way Ste 170	Van Nuys	CA	91406	**800-430-4263**	818-778-1900
Ohel Children's Home & Family Services Inc					
4510 16th Ave	Brooklyn	NY	11204	**800-603-6435**	718-851-6300
Ontario Medical Supply Ltd					
1100 Algoma Rd	Ottawa	ON	K1B0A3	**800-804-1112**	613-244-8620
Passport Program-western					
925 Euclid Ave Ste 600	Cleveland	OH	44115	**800-626-7277**	216-621-0303
Pediatric Services of America Inc					
310 Technology Pkwy	Norcross	GA	30092	**800-408-4442**	770-441-1580
Personal-Touch Home Care Inc					
186-18 Hillside Ave	Jamaica	NY	11432	**888-275-4147**	718-468-2500
PreCheck Inc					
2500 E T C Jester Blvd Ste	Houston	TX	77008	**800-999-9861**	
Promera Health					
61 accord park dr	Norwell	MA	02061	**888-878-9058**	
Right at Home Inc					
6464 Crt St Ste 150	Omaha	NE	68106	**877-697-7537**	402-697-7537
Selfhelp Community Services Inc					
520 Eigth Ave 5th Fl	New York	NY	10018	**866-735-1234**	
Society'S Assets Inc					
5200 Washington Ave Ste 225	Racine	WI	53406	**800-378-9128**	262-637-9128
Solano Coalition for Bett					
1 Harbor Ctr Ste 270	Suisun City	CA	94585	**800-978-7547**	707-863-4440
Sta-Home Hospice					
406 Briarwood Dr Bldg 200	Jackson	MS	39206	**800-782-4663**	601-956-5100
Star Multi Care Services Inc					
115 Broad Hollow Rd Ste 275	Melville	NY	11747	**877-920-0600**	631-424-7827
SunCrest Healthcare Inc					
9510 Ormsby Station Rd Ste 300	Louisville	KY	40223	**800-845-6987**	615-627-9267
Sunrise Home Health Services					
3200 Broadway Blvd Ste 260	Garland	TX	75043	**800-296-7823**	972-278-1414
Verecom Technologies Inc					
61 Broadway	New York	NY	10006	**888-562-2468**	
Visiting Nurse Assn of Morris County (Inc)					
175 South St	Morristown	NJ	07960	**800-938-4748**	973-539-1216
Vna of Rhode Island					
475 Kilvert St	Warwick	RI	02886	**800-638-6274**	401-574-4900
WorldMed Assist					
1230 Mtn Side Ct	Concord	CA	94521	**866-999-3848**	

364 HOME IMPROVEMENT CENTERS

SEE ALSO Construction Materials

	City	State	Zip	Toll-Free	Phone
Above Security Inc					
955 Michele-Bohec Blvd Ste 244	Blainville	QC	J7C5J6	**866-430-8166**	450-430-8166
Alaska Industrial Hardware Inc					
2192 Viking Dr	Anchorage	AK	99501	**800-478-7201**	907-276-7201

				Toll-Free	Phone
Arlington Coal & Lumber Company Inc 41 Pk Ave	Arlington	MA	02476	**800-649-8101**	781-643-8100
Atlanta Hardwood Corp 5596 Riverview Rd SE	Mableton	GA	30126	**800-476-5393**	404-792-2290
Busy Beaver Bldg Centers 2940 Library Rd	Pittsburgh	PA	15234	**800-732-0999**	412-882-6633
Hacienda Home Centers Inc 1255 Bosque Farms Blvd	Bosque Farms	NM	87068	**800-944-0704**	505-869-2637
Home Depot Inc 2455 Paces Ferry Rd NW *NYSE: HD* ■ *Cust Svc	Atlanta	GA	30339	**800-553-3199***	770-433-8211
Len-Co Lumber Corp 1445 Seneca St	Buffalo	NY	14210	**800-258-4585**	716-822-0243
Linen Chest Inc 4455 AutoRt Des Laurentides	Laval	QC	H7L5X8	**800-363-3832**	514-341-7077
Lowe's Cos Inc 1000 Lowe's Blvd *NYSE: LOW*	Mooresville	NC	28117	**800-445-6937**	704-758-1000
Lowe's Home Centers Inc PO Box 1111	North Wilkesboro	NC	28656	**800-445-6937**	
Manta Group Ltd, The 1300-350 Bay St	Toronto	ON	M5H2S6	**866-626-8247**	416-483-5166
Martin Door Manufacturing Inc 2828 South 900 West	Salt Lake City	UT	84119	**800-388-9310**	801-973-9310
National Lumber 71 Maple St	Mansfield	MA	02048	**800-370-9663**	508-339-8020
Northern Tool & Equipment Co 2800 Southcross Dr W *Cust Svc	Burnsville	MN	55306	**800-222-5381***	952-894-9510
Pandel Inc 21 River Dr	Cartersville	GA	30120	**800-537-3868**	770-382-1034
Paramount Builders Inc 501 Central Dr	Virginia Beach	VA	23454	**888-340-9002**	757-340-9000
Preverco Inc 285 Rue De Rotterdam	Saint-augustin-de-desmaures	QC	G3A2E5	**877-667-2725**	418-878-8930
Reisterstown Lumber Co, The PO Box 337	Reisterstown	MD	21136	**800-289-8739**	410-833-1300
RONA Inc 220 Ch du Tremblay *TSE: RON*	Boucherville	QC	J4B8H7	**877-599-5900**	514-599-5100
Simonson Properties Co 535 1st St NE	Saint Cloud	MN	56304	**888-843-8789**	320-252-9385
Solutioninc Technologies Ltd 5692 Bloomfield St	Halifax	NS	B3K1T2	**888-496-2221**	902-420-0077
Stanton Carpet Corp 211 Robbins Ln	Syosset	NY	11791	**888-809-2989**	516-822-5878
WE Aubuchon Company Inc 95 Aubuchon Dr	Westminster	MA	01473	**800-431-2712**	978-874-0521

365 HOME INSPECTION SERVICES

				Toll-Free	Phone
AmeriSpec Inc 3839 Forest Hill Irene Rd	Memphis	TN	38125	**877-769-5217**	901-820-8500
BrickKicker Inc 849 N Ellsworth St	Naperville	IL	60563	**800-821-1820**	
HomeTeam Inspection Service Inc 575 Chamber Dr	Milford	OH	45150	**800-598-5297**	
HouseMaster 92 E Main St Ste 301	Somerville	NJ	08876	**800-526-3939**	732-469-6565
Insparisk LLC 71-19 80th St Ste 8205	Glendale	NY	11385	**888-464-6772**	
iv3 Solutions Corp 50 Minthorn Blvd Ste 301	Markham	ON	L3T7X8	**877-995-2651**	
National Property Inspections Inc (NPI) 9375 Burt St Ste 201	Omaha	NE	68114	**800-333-9807**	402-333-9807
Remote Access Technology Inc 61 Atlantic St	Dartmouth	NS	B2Y4P4	**877-356-2728**	902-434-4405
World Inspection Network International Inc 12345 Lk City Way NE Ste 365	Seattle	WA	98125	**800-309-6753**	

366 HOME SALES & OTHER DIRECT SELLING

				Toll-Free	Phone
4Life Research 9850 South 300 West *Sales	Sandy	UT	84070	**888-454-3374***	801-256-3102
Advocare International Lp 2801 Summit Ave	Plano	TX	75074	**800-542-4800**	972-665-5800
Amway Corp 7575 Fulton St E	Ada	MI	49355	**800-253-6500**	616-787-4000
Avon Products Inc 1345 Ave of the Americas *NYSE: AVP* ■ *Cust Svc	New York	NY	10017	**800-367-2866***	212-282-7000
Color Me Beautiful 7000 Infantry Ridge Rd Ste 200	Manassas	VA	20109	**800-265-6763**	
Colorado Prime Foods 500 Bi-County Blvd Ste 400	Farmingdale	NY	11735	**800-365-2404**	631-694-1111
Conklin Company Inc 551 Valley Pk Dr	Shakopee	MN	55379	**800-888-8838**	952-445-6010
Corbin Turf & Ornamental Supply 1105 Old Buncombe Rd	Greenville	SC	29617	**800-476-4504**	864-233-2113
Dew-El Corp 10841 Paw Paw Dr	Holland	MI	49424	**800-443-3935**	616-396-6554
Email Co, The 15 Kainona Ave	Toronto	ON	M3H3H4	**877-933-6245**	
Getconnect 14114 Dallas Pkwy Ste 430	Dallas	TX	75254	**888-200-1831**	
Golden Neo-Life Diamite International 3500 Gateway Blvd	Fremont	CA	94538	**800-432-5842**	
Image Iv Systems Inc 512 S Varney St	Burbank	CA	91502	**800-473-5424**	818-841-0756
JR Watkins Inc 150 Liberty St PO Box 5570	Winona	MN	55987	**800-243-9423**	507-457-3300
Kaeser & Blair Inc 4236 Grissom Dr	Batavia	OH	45103	**800-642-0790**	
KMA One 6815 Meadowridge Ct	Alpharetta	GA	30005	**888-500-2536**	770-886-4000
Kwik Kafe Company Inc 204 Furnace St	Bluefield	VA	24605	**800-533-4066**	276-322-4691
Magnets.com 51 Pacific Ave Ste 4	Jersey City	NJ	07304	**866-229-8237**	
Mail Shark 4125 New Holland Rd	Mohnton	PA	19540	**888-457-4275**	
Mary Kay Inc PO Box 799045 *Cust Svc	Dallas	TX	75379	**800-627-9529***	972-687-6300
Melaleuca Inc 3910 S Yellowstone Hwy *Sales	Idaho Falls	ID	83402	**800-282-3000***	208-522-0700
Mt Shasta Spring Water Company Inc 1878 Twin View Blvd	Redding	CA	96003	**800-922-6227**	530-246-8800
Noevir USA Inc 1095 Main St	Irvine	CA	92614	**800-872-8817**	949-660-1111
Pampered Chef Ltd 1 Pampered Chef Ln	Addison	IL	60101	**888-687-2433**	
Partylite Gifts Inc 59 Armstrong Rd	Plymouth	MA	02360	**888-999-5706**	508-830-3100
Poly Expert Inc 850 ave Munck	Laval	QC	H7S1B1	**877-384-5060**	514-384-5060
PostcardMania 2145 Sunnydale Blvd Bldg 101	Clearwater	FL	33765	**800-628-1804**	
Princess House Inc 470 Miles Standish Blvd *Sales	Taunton	MA	02780	**800-622-0039***	508-823-0711
Qivana 5255 Edgewood Dr	Provo	UT	84604	**888-874-8262**	
Reliv International Inc 136 Chesterfield Industrial Blvd *NASDAQ: RELV*	Chesterfield	MO	63005	**800-735-4887**	636-537-9715
Saladmaster Inc 230 Westway Pl Ste 101	Arlington	TX	76018	**800-765-5795**	817-633-3555
Shaklee Corp 4747 Willow Rd	Pleasanton	CA	94588	**800-742-5533**	925-924-2000
SK Food Group Inc 4600 37th Ave SW	Seattle	WA	98126	**800-722-6290**	206-935-8100
Smartpak Equine LLC 40 Grissom Rd Ste 500	Plymouth	MA	02360	**888-752-5171**	774-773-1000
Specialty Merchandise Corp 996 Flower Glen St *Orders	Simi Valley	CA	93065	**800-345-4762***	805-578-5500
Success Motivation International Inc 4567 Lakeshore Dr *Sales	Waco	TX	76710	**888-391-0050***	254-776-9966
Sunrider International 1625 Abalone Ave *Orders	Torrance	CA	90501	**888-278-6743***	310-781-3808
TouchPoint Technologies LLC 2319 Oak Myrtle Ln Ste 104	Wesley Chapel	FL	33544	**877-898-6824**	
Vector Marketing Co 322 Houghton Ave	Olean	NY	14760	**800-828-0448**	
Verndale Corp, The 28 Damrell St Ste 300	Boston	MA	02127	**866-942-8376**	
WEBCARGO Inc 800 Pl Victoria Ste 2603 Tour de la bourse CP 329	Montreal	QC	H4Z1G8	**866-905-0123**	
WebEyeCare Inc 10 Canal St Ste 302	Bristol	PA	19007	**888-536-7480**	

367 HOME WARRANTY SERVICES

				Toll-Free	Phone
American Home Shield 889 Ridge Lake Blvd PO Box 851	Memphis	TN	38120	**800-776-4663**	901-537-8000
Asset Marketing Systems Insurance Services LLC 15050 Ave of Science	San Diego	CA	92128	**888-303-8755**	
Blue Ribbon Home Warranty Inc 95 S Wadsworth Blvd	Lakewood	CO	80226	**800-571-0475**	303-986-3900
Cross Country Home Services 1625 NW 136th Ave Ste 200 *Cust Svc	Sunrise	FL	33323	**800-778-8000***	954-845-2468
Cypress Care Inc 2736 Meadow Church Rd Ste 300	Duluth	GA	30097	**800-419-7191**	
First American Home Buyers Protection Corp 7833 Haskell Ave PO Box 10180	Van Nuys	CA	91410	**800-444-9030**	818-781-5050
Home Security of America Inc 310 N Midvale Blvd	Madison	WI	53705	**800-367-1448**	
Warrantech Corp Inc 2200 Hwy 121	Bedford	TX	76021	**800-833-8801**	817-785-6601

368 HORSE BREEDERS

SEE ALSO Livestock Improvement Services

				Toll-Free	Phone
Darby Dan Farm 3225 Old Frankfort Pk	Lexington	KY	40510	**888-321-0424**	859-254-0424
Glencrest Farm 1576 Moores Mill Rd PO Box 4468	Midway	KY	40347	**800-903-0136**	859-233-7032
Mill Ridge Farm 2800 Bowman Mill Rd	Lexington	KY	40513	**800-950-6397**	859-231-0606

369 HORTICULTURAL PRODUCTS GROWERS

SEE ALSO Seed Companies ; Garden Centers

				Toll-Free	Phone
Altman Specialty Plants Inc 3742 Blue BiRd Canyon Rd	Vista	CA	92084	**800-773-7667**	760-744-8191
Aris Horticulture Inc 115 Third St SE	Barberton	OH	44203	**800-232-9557**	
Battlefield Farms Inc 23190 Clarks Mtn Rd	Rapidan	VA	22733	**800-722-0744**	

Company	Address	City	State	ZIP	Toll-Free	Phone
Bay City Flower Company Inc	2265 Cabrillo Hwy S	Half Moon Bay	CA	94019	**800-399-5858***	650-726-5535
	*Sales					
Bettinger Farms Inc	11602 Frankfort Rd	Swanton	OH	43558	**855-629-7661**	419-829-2771
Burgett Floral Inc	868 Fuller NE	Grand Rapids	MI	49503	**800-404-2999**	616-456-1999
CD Ford & Sons Inc	PO Box 300	Geneseo	IL	61254	**800-383-4661**	309-944-4661
Color Spot Nurseries Inc	2575 Olive Hill Rd	Fallbrook	CA	92028	**800-554-4065**	760-695-1480
Costa Nursery Farms Inc	21800 SW 162nd Ave	Miami	FL	33170	**800-327-7074**	
Cuthbert Greenhouses Inc	4900 Hendron Rd	Groveport	OH	43125	**800-321-1939**	614-836-3866
Dallas Johnson Greenhouse Inc	2802 Twin City Dr	Council Bluffs	IA	51501	**800-445-4794**	712-366-0407
Dan Schantz Farm & Greenhouses LLC	8025 Spinnerstown Rd	Zionsville	PA	18092	**800-451-3064**	610-967-2181
DeLeon's Bromeliads Co	13745 SW 216th St	Miami	FL	33170	**800-448-8649**	305-238-6028
Dramm & Echter Inc	1150 Quail Gardens Dr	Encinitas	CA	92024	**800-854-7021**	760-436-0188
Ever-Bloom Inc	4701 Foothill Rd	Carpinteria	CA	93013	**800-388-8112**	805-684-5566
Farmers West	5300 Foothill Rd	Carpinteria	CA	93013	**800-549-0085**	805-684-5531
Garden State Growers	99 Locust Grove Rd	Pittstown	NJ	08867	**800-288-8484**	908-730-8888
Green Valley Floral Co	24999 Potter Rd	Salinas	CA	93908	**800-228-1255**	831-424-7691
Greenleaf Nursery Co	28406 Hwy 82	Park Hill	OK	74451	**800-331-2982**	918-457-5172
Harts Nursery of Jefferson Inc	4049 Jefferson-Scio Rd	Jefferson	OR	97352	**800-356-9335**	541-327-3366
Johannes Flowers Inc	4990 Foothill Rd	Carpinteria	CA	93013	**800-365-9476**	805-684-5686
Kerry's Nursery Inc	21840 SW 258th St	Homestead	FL	33031	**800-331-9127**	
Knox Nursery Inc	940 Avalon Rd	Winter Garden	FL	34787	**800-441-5669**	
Kurt Weiss Greenhouses Inc	95 Main St	Center Moriches	NY	11934	**800-344-7805**	631-878-2500
Matsui Nursery Inc	1645 Old Stage Rd	Salinas	CA	93908	**800-793-6433**	831-422-6433
McLellan Botanicals	2352 San Juan Rd	Aromas	CA	95004	**800-467-2443**	
Metrolina Greenhouses Inc	16400 Huntersville-Concord Rd	Huntersville	NC	28078	**800-543-3915**	704-875-1371
Nurserymen's Exchange	2651 N Cabrillo Hwy	Half Moon Bay	CA	94019	**800-227-5229***	650-712-4195
	*General					
Ocean Breeze International (OBI)	3910 Via Real	Carpinteria	CA	93013	**888-715-8888**	805-684-1747
Panzer Nursery Inc	17980 W Baseline Rd	Beaverton	OR	97006	**888-212-5327**	503-645-1185
Parks Bros Farm Inc	6733 Parks Rd	Van Buren	AR	72956	**800-334-5770**	479-474-1125
Post Gardens Inc	21189 Huron River Dr	Rockwood	MI	48173	**800-834-4630**	734-379-9688
Rockwell Farms Inc	332 Rockwell Farms Rd	Rockwell	NC	28138	**800-635-6576**	
Smith Gardens Inc	4164 Meridian St Ste 400	Bellingham	WA	98226	**800-755-6256**	360-733-4671
Speedling Inc	4447 Old 41 Hwy S	Ruskin	FL	33570	**800-881-4769***	
	*Cust Svc					
Sun Valley Floral Farms Inc	3160 Upper Bay Rd	Arcata	CA	95521	**800-747-0396**	
Woodburn Nursery & Azaleas	13009 McKee School Rd NE	Woodburn	OR	97071	**888-634-2232***	503-634-2231
	*Sales					
Young's Plant Farm	PO Box 3410	Auburn	AL	36830	**800-304-8609**	

370 HOSE & BELTING - RUBBER OR PLASTICS

SEE ALSO Automotive Parts & Supplies - Mfr

Company	Address	City	State	ZIP	Toll-Free	Phone
ABC Industrie	PO Box 77	Warsaw	IN	46581	**800-426-0921**	574-267-5166
Aero Rubber Company Inc	8100 W 185th St	Tinley Park	IL	60487	**800-662-1009**	708-430-4900
American Hose & Rubber Co	3645 E 44th St	Tucson	AZ	85713	**800-272-7537**	520-514-1666
Ammeraal Beltech USA	7501 N St Louis Ave	Skokie	IL	60076	**800-323-4170***	847-673-6720
	*Cust Svc					
Apache Hose & Belting Co Inc	4805 Bowling St SW	Cedar Rapids	IA	52404	**800-553-5455***	319-365-0471
	*Sales					
Atco Rubber Products Inc	7101 Atco Dr	Fort Worth	TX	76118	**800-877-3828**	817-595-2894
Belterra Corp	1638 Fosters Way	Delta	BC	V3M6S6	**888-860-5600**	604-540-1950
Belting Industries Company Inc	20 Boright Ave	Kenilworth	NJ	07033	**800-843-2358**	908-272-8591
Carlstar Group LLC, The	725 Cool Springs Blvd Ste 500	Franklin	TN	37067	**866-773-2926**	615-503-0220
Chemprene Inc	483 Fishkill Ave	Beacon	NY	12508	**800-431-9981**	845-831-2800
Cobon Plastics Corporation	90 S St	Newark	NJ	07114	**800-360-1324**	973-344-6330
Coilhose Pneumatics Inc	19 Kimberly Rd	East Brunswick	NJ	08816	**800-424-9300**	732-390-8480
Cooper Tire & Rubber Co	701 Lima Ave	Findlay	OH	45840	**800-854-6288**	419-423-1321
	NYSE: CTB					
Dormont Manufacturing Co	6015 Enterprise Dr	Export	PA	15632	**800-367-6668**	
Fenner Drives	311 W Stiegel St	Manheim	PA	17545	**800-243-3374***	717-665-2421
	*Sales					
Flexaust Co	1510 Armstrong Rd	Warsaw	IN	46580	**800-343-0428**	574-267-7909
Freelin-Wade Co	1730 NE Miller St	McMinnville	OR	97128	**888-373-9233**	503-434-5561
Gates Corp	1551 Wewatta St	Denver	CO	80202	**800-709-6001**	303-744-1911
Habasit ABT Inc	150 Industrial Pk Rd	Middletown	CT	06457	**800-522-2358**	860-632-2211
Habasit Belting Inc	1400 Clinton St	Buffalo	NY	14206	**800-325-1585**	716-824-8484
HBD/Thermoid Inc	1301 W Sandusky Ave	Bellefontaine	OH	43311	**800-543-8070**	937-593-5010
Industrial Rubber Works	1700 Nicholas Blvd	Elk Grove Village	IL	60007	**800-852-1855**	847-952-1800
Key Fire Hose Corp (KFH)	PO Box 7107	Dothan	AL	36302	**800-447-5666**	334-671-5532
Legg Company Inc	325 E Tenth St	Halstead	KS	67056	**800-835-1003***	
	*Sales					
Lockwood Products Inc	5615 Willow Ln	Lake Oswego	OR	97035	**800-423-1625**	503-635-8113
Mattracks Systems	202 Cleveland Ave E	Karlstad	MN	56732	**877-436-7800**	218-436-7000
Mulhern Belting Inc	148 Bauer Dr	Oakland	NJ	07436	**800-253-6300**	201-337-5700
NewAge Industries Inc	145 James Way	SouthHampton	PA	18966	**800-506-3924**	215-526-2300
Parker Fluid Connectors Group	6035 Parkland Blvd	Cleveland	OH	44124	**800-272-7537***	216-896-3000
	*General					
Ro-Lab American Rubber Co Inc	8830 W Linne Rd	Tracy	CA	95304	**800-678-0726**	209-836-0965
Salem-Republic Rubber Co	475 W California Ave	Sebring	OH	44672	**800-686-4199**	330-938-9801
Sparks Belting Co	3800 Stahl Dr SE	Grand Rapids	MI	49546	**800-451-4537**	616-949-2750
Swan Hose	1201 Delaware Ave	Marion	OH	43302	**800-848-8707**	
Titeflex Corp	603 Hendee St	Springfield	MA	01139	**800-765-2525**	413-739-5631
Unaflex LLC	1350 S Dixie Hwy E	Pompano Beach	FL	33064	**800-327-1286**	954-943-5002

371 HOSPICES

SEE ALSO Specialty Hospitals

Company	Address	City	State	ZIP	Toll-Free	Phone
HomeCare of East Alabama Medical Ctr	665 Opelika Rd	Auburn	AL	36830	**866-542-4768**	334-826-3131
Hospice of Marshall County	408 Martling Rd	Albertville	AL	35951	**888-334-9336**	256-891-7724
Hospice of the Valley	240 Johnston St SE	Decatur	AL	35601	**877-260-3657**	256-350-5585
Hospice of West Alabama	3851 Loop Rd	Tuscaloosa	AL	35404	**877-362-7522**	205-523-0101
Hospice of Arizona	19820 N Seventh Ave Ste 130	Phoenix	AZ	85027	**888-330-8560**	602-678-1313
Arkansas Hospice	14 Parkstone Cir	North Little Rock	AR	72116	**877-257-3400**	501-748-3333
Hospice Home Care	2200 S Bowman	Little Rock	AR	72211	**800-479-1219**	501-296-9043
Community Hospice Inc	4368 Spyres Way	Modesto	CA	95356	**866-645-4567**	209-578-6300
Elizabeth Hospice	150 W Crest St	Escondido	CA	92025	**800-797-2050**	760-737-2050
Hinds Hospice	1616 W Shaw Ste C-1	Fresno	CA	93711	**800-400-4677**	559-248-8591
Hoffmann Hospice of the Valley	8501 Brimhall Rd Bldg 100	Bakersfield	CA	93312	**888-833-3900**	661-410-1010
Hospice of Redlands Community Hospital	350 Terracina Blvd	Redlands	CA	92373	**888-397-4999**	909-335-5643
Livingston Memorial Visiting Nurse Assn Hospice	1996 Eastman Ave Ste 101	Ventura	CA	93003	**800-830-8881**	805-642-1608
Seasons Hospice & Palliative Care of California-Orange	750 The City Dr	Orange	CA	92868	**877-508-0644**	714-980-0900
VITAS Healthcare Corp of California	990 W 190th St Ste 120	Torrance	CA	90502	**800-582-9533**	305-374-4143
VITAS Healthcare Corp of San Gabriel Cities	1343 N Grand Ave	Covina	CA	91724	**866-418-4827**	
VNA & Hospice of Northern California	1900 Powell St Ste 300	Emeryville	CA	94608	**800-698-1273**	510-450-8596
VNA & Hospice of Southern California	150 W First St Ste 270	Claremont	CA	91711	**888-357-3574**	909-624-3574
Hospice & Palliative Care of Northern Colorado	2726 W 11th St Rd	Greeley	CO	80634	**800-564-5563**	970-352-8487
Hospice & Palliative Care of Western Colorado	2754 Compass Dr Ste 377	Grand Junction	CO	81506	**866-310-8900**	970-241-2212
Hospice of Boulder County	2594 Trilridge Dr E	Lafayette	CO	80026	**877-986-4766**	303-449-7740
Hospice of Southeastern Connecticut Inc	227 Dunham St	Norwich	CT	06360	**877-654-4035**	860-848-5699
Compassionate Care Hospice of Delaware	702 Wilmington Ave	Wilmington	DE	19805	**800-219-0092***	302-993-9090
	*General					
Bigbend Hospice	1723 Mahan Ctr Blvd	Tallahassee	FL	32308	**800-772-5862**	850-878-5310
Chapters Health System	12973 Telecom Pkwy Ste 100	Temple Terrace	FL	33637	**866-204-8611**	813-871-8111
Community Hospice of Northeast Florida	4266 Sunbeam Rd	Jacksonville	FL	32257	**866-274-6614**	904-268-5200
Covenant Hospice	5041 N 12th Ave	Pensacola	FL	32504	**800-541-3072**	850-433-2155
Gulfside Hospice Inc	6224 Lafayette St	New Port Richey	FL	34652	**800-561-4883**	727-845-5707

Name / Address	City	State	ZIP	Toll-Free	Phone
Hope Hospice 9470 HealthPark Cir	Fort Myers	FL	33908	**800-835-1673**	239-482-4673
Hospice by the Sea 1531 W Palmetto Pk Rd	Boca Raton	FL	33486	**800-633-2577**	561-395-5031
Hospice of Lake & Sumter Inc 2445 Ln Pk Rd	Tavares	FL	32778	**888-728-6234**	352-343-1341
Hospice of Marion County 3231 SW 34th Ave	Ocala	FL	34474	**888-482-5018**	352-873-7400
Hospice of Northeast Florida 4266 Sunbeam Rd	Jacksonville	FL	32257	**866-253-6681**	904-268-5200
Hospice of Palm Beach County 5300 E Ave	West Palm Beach	FL	33407	**800-287-4722**	561-848-5200
Hospice of Saint Francis Inc 1250 Grumman Pl Ste B	Titusville	FL	32780	**866-269-4240**	321-269-4240
Hospice of the Comforter 480 W Central Pkwy	Altamonte Springs	FL	32714	**877-696-6775**	407-682-0808
Hospice of the Treasure Coast 5090 Dunn Rd	Fort Pierce	FL	34981	**800-299-4677**	772-462-8900
Lifepath Hospice 3010 W Azeele St	Tampa	FL	33609	**800-209-2200**	813-877-2200
Tidewell Hospice 5955 Rand Blvd	Sarasota	FL	34238	**800-959-4291**	941-552-7500
Treasure Coast Hospice 1201 SE Indian St	Stuart	FL	34997	**800-299-4677**	772-403-4500
Visiting Nurse Assn of the Treasure Coast 1110 35th Ln	Vero Beach	FL	32960	**800-749-5760**	772-567-5551
VITAS Hospice Care 201 S Biscayne Blvd Ste 400 *General	Miami	FL	33131	**800-582-9533***	305-374-4143
Heyman HospiceCare 420 E Second Ave	Rome	GA	30161	**800-324-1078**	706-509-3200
Hospice Atlanta-Visiting Nurse Health System 1244 Pk Vista Dr	Atlanta	GA	30319	**866-374-4776**	404-869-3000
Hospice of NE Georgia Medical Ctr 2150 Limestone Pkwy Ste 222	Gainesville	GA	30501	**888-572-3900**	770-533-8888
Hospice of Southwest Georgia 114 A Mimosa Dr	Thomasville	GA	31792	**800-290-6567**	229-584-5500
Hospice Savannah Inc PO Box 13190	Savannah	GA	31416	**888-355-4911**	912-355-2289
Pine Pointe Hospice & Palliative Care 6261 Peak Rd	Macon	GA	31210	**800-211-1084**	478-633-5660
Trinity Hospital of Augusta 2803 Wrightsboro Rd Ste 38	Augusta	GA	30909	**800-999-6673**	706-729-6000
United Hospice of Atlanta 1626 Jeurgens Ct	Norcross	GA	30093	**800-222-0321**	770-279-6200
Carle Hospice 611 W Park St	Urbana	IL	61801	**800-239-3620**	217-383-3311
Harbor Light Hospice 800 Roosevelt Rd Bldg C Ste 206	Glen Ellyn	IL	60137	**800-419-0542**	630-300-3716
Hospice of Kankakee Valley Inc 482 Main St Nw	Bourbonnais	IL	60914	**855-871-4695**	815-939-4141
Hospice of Lincolnland 1000 Health Ctr Dr	Mattoon	IL	61938	**800-454-4055**	
Hospice of Southern Illinois 305 S Illinois St	Belleville	IL	62220	**800-233-1708**	618-235-1703
Joliet Area Community Hospice 250 Water Stone Cir	Joliet	IL	60431	**800-360-1817**	815-740-4104
OSF Hospice 2265 W Altorfer Dr	Peoria	IL	61615	**800-673-5288**	
Center for Hospice Care Inc 111 Sunnybrook Ct	South Bend	IN	46637	**800-413-9083**	574-243-3100
Hosparus Inc 502 Hausfeldt Ln	New Albany	IN	47150	**800-895-5633**	812-945-4596
Hospice of the Calumet Area 600 Superior Ave	Munster	IN	46321	**888-303-0180**	219-922-2732
Cedar Valley Hospice 2101 Kimball Ave Ste 401	Waterloo	IA	50702	**800-617-1972**	319-272-2002
Hospice of Siouxland 4300 Hamilton Blvd	Sioux City	IA	51104	**800-383-4545**	712-233-4100
Mercy Medical Center North Iowa 1000 4th St SW	Mason City	IA	50401	**800-297-4719**	641-428-6208
Harry Hynes Memorial Hospice 313 S Market St	Wichita	KS	67202	**800-767-4965**	316-265-9441
Hospice of Reno County 1600 N Lorraine	Hutchinson	KS	67502	**800-267-6891**	620-665-2473
Midland Hospice Care 200 SW Frazier Cir	Topeka	KS	66606	**800-491-3691**	785-232-2044
Community Hospice 1480 Carter Ave	Ashland	KY	41101	**800-926-6184**	606-329-1890
Heritage Hospice 120 Enterprise Dr PO Box 1213	Danville	KY	40423	**800-203-6633**	859-236-2425
Hospice of Lake Cumberland 100 Pkwy Dr	Somerset	KY	42503	**800-937-9596**	606-679-4389
Hospice of Southern Kentucky 5872 Scottsville Rd	Bowling Green	KY	42104	**800-344-9479**	270-782-3402
Hospice of the Bluegrass 2312 Alexandria Dr	Lexington	KY	40504	**800-876-6005**	859-276-5344
Lourdes Homecare & Hospice 2855 Jackson St	Paducah	KY	42003	**800-870-7460**	270-444-2262
Saint Anthony's Hospice 2410 S Green St	Henderson	KY	42420	**866-380-2326**	270-826-2326
CommCare Corp 601 Poydras St 2755 Pan American Life Center	New Orleans	LA	70130	**877-792-5434**	504-324-8950
Hospice of Acadiana 2600 Johnston St Ste 200	Lafayette	LA	70503	**800-738-2226**	337-232-1234
Hospice of Baton Rouge 9063 Siegen Ln	Baton Rouge	LA	70810	**888-447-0433**	225-767-4673
Coastal Hospice & Palliative Care 2604 Old Ocean City Rd PO Box 1733	Salisbury	MD	21804	**800-780-7886**	410-742-8732
Gilchrist Hospice Care 11311 McCormick Rd	Hunt Valley	MD	21031	**800-735-2258**	443-849-8200
Hospice of the Chesapeake 445 Defense Hwy *General	Annapolis	MD	21401	**877-462-1101***	410-987-2003
Montgomery Hospice 1355 Piccard Dr Ste 100	Rockville	MD	20850	**800-994-6610**	301-921-4400
Baystate Visiting Nurse Assn & Hospice 50 Maple St	Springfield	MA	01103	**800-249-8298**	413-794-6411
Community VNA 10 Emory St	Attleboro	MA	02703	**800-220-0110**	508-222-0118
Hospice & Palliative Care of Cape Cod Inc 765 Attucks Ln	Hyannis	MA	02601	**800-642-2423**	508-957-0200
Hospice Care 100 Sylvan Rd	Woburn	MA	01801	**866-279-7103**	781-569-2888
Hospice of the North Shore 75 Sylvan St Ste B102	Danvers	MA	01923	**888-283-1722**	978-774-7566
Merrimack Valley Hospice 360 Merrimack St Bldg 9	Lawrence	MA	01843	**800-933-5593**	
Old Colony Hospice 1 Credit Union Way	Randolph	MA	02368	**800-370-1322**	781-341-4145
Angela Hospice Home Care 14100 Newburgh Rd *General	Livonia	MI	48154	**866-464-7810***	734-464-7810
Arbor Hospice & Home Care 2366 Oak Vly Dr	Ann Arbor	MI	48103	**888-992-2273**	734-662-5999
Hospice at Home 4025 Health Pk Ln	Saint Joseph	MI	49085	**800-717-3811**	269-429-7100
Hospice of Henry Ford Health System 2799 W Grand Blvd	Detroit	MI	48202	**800-436-7936**	248-585-5270
Hospice of Holland Inc 270 Hoover Blvd	Holland	MI	49423	**800-255-3522**	616-396-2972
Hospice of Lansing 4052 Legacy Pkwy Ste 200	Lansing	MI	48911	**877-882-4500**	517-882-4500
Hospice of Michigan 400 Mack Ave	Detroit	MI	48201	**888-247-5701**	313-578-5000
MidMichigan Home Care 3007 N Saginaw Rd	Midland	MI	48640	**800-852-9350**	989-633-1400
Munson Healthcare 1105 Sixth St	Traverse City	MI	49684	**800-468-6766**	231-935-5000
Pediatric Special Care Inc 17040 W 12 Mile Rd Ste 200	Southfield	MI	48076	**800-282-7337**	248-557-4800
Fairview Hospice 2450 26th Ave S	Minneapolis	MN	55406	**800-285-5647**	612-728-2455
Health Partners 8170 33rd Ave S	Minneapolis	MN	55425	**800-247-7015**	952-883-6877
Hospice Ministries 450 Towne Ctr Blvd	Ridgeland	MS	39157	**800-273-7724**	601-898-1053
Fair View Nursing Home 1714 W 16th St	Sedalia	MO	65301	**877-222-4114**	660-827-1594
Heartland Hands-Hope Hospice 137 N Belt Hwy	Saint Joseph	MO	64506	**800-443-1143**	816-271-7190
Odyssey Healthcare of Kansas City 4911 S Arrowhead Dr	Independence	MO	64055	**800-944-4357**	816-795-1333
Saint Luke's Home Care & Hospice 3100 Broadway St Ste 1000	Kansas City	MO	64111	**888-303-7576**	816-756-1160
SSM Hospice 2 Harbor Bend Ct	Lake Saint Louis	MO	63367	**800-835-1212**	314-989-2700
VNA Hospice Care (VNA) 11440 Olive Blvd Ste 200	Creve Coeur	MO	63141	**800-392-4740**	314-918-7171
VNA of Greater St Louis *Hospice Care* 11440 Olive Blvd Ste 200	Creve Coeur	MO	63141	**800-392-4740**	314-918-7171
Visiting Nurse Assn 12565 W Ctr Rd Ste 100	Omaha	NE	68144	**800-456-8869**	402-342-5566
Family Home Hospice 1701 W Charleston Blvd	Las Vegas	NV	89102	**800-748-6773**	702-242-7000
Concord Regional Visiting Nurse Assoc Hospice Program 30 Pillsbury St	Concord	NH	03301	**800-924-8620**	603-224-4093
Home Health & Hospice Care 7 Executive Park Dr	Merrimack	NH	03054	**800-887-5973**	603-882-2941
Hospice of New Jersey 400 Broadacres Dr 1St Fl	Bloomfield	NJ	07003	**800-501-0451**	973-893-0818
Karen Ann Quinlan Hospice 99 Sparta Ave	Newton	NJ	07860	**800-882-1117**	973-383-0115
Lighthouse Hospice 1040 Kings Hwy N Ste 100 *General	Cherry Hill	NJ	08034	**888-467-7423***	856-414-1155
Samaritan Hospice 5 Eves Dr Ste 300	Marlton	NJ	08053	**800-229-8183**	856-596-1600
South Jersey Healthcare HospiceCare 2848 S Delsea Dr Bldg 1	Vineland	NJ	08360	**800-770-7547**	
VNA of Central Jersey (VNACJ) 176 Riverside Ave	Red Bank	NJ	07701	**800-862-3330**	
Catskill Area Hospice & Palliative Care Inc 1 Birchwood Dr	Oneonta	NY	13820	**800-306-3870**	607-432-6773
East End Hospice 481 Westhampton-Riverhead Rd PO Box 1048	WestHampton Beach	NY	11978	**877-513-0099**	631-288-8400
HomeCare & Hospice 1225 W State St	Olean	NY	14760	**800-339-7011**	716-372-5735
Hospice Care Inc 4277 Middle Settlement Rd	New Hartford	NY	13413	**800-317-5661**	315-735-6484
Hospice Care Network 99 Sunnyside Blvd	Woodbury	NY	11797	**800-405-6731**	516-832-7100
Hospice Family Care 550 E Main St	Batavia	NY	14020	**800-719-7129**	585-343-7596
Hospice of Orange & Sullivan Counties 800 Stony Brook Ct	Newburgh	NY	12550	**800-924-0157**	845-561-6111
Hospice of Saint Lawrence Valley 6805 State Hwy 11	Potsdam	NY	13676	**888-827-1000**	315-265-3105
Niagara Hospice 4675 Sunset Dr	Lockport	NY	14094	**800-662-1220**	716-439-4417
CarePartners Mountain Area Hospice PO Box 5779	Asheville	NC	28813	**800-627-1533**	828-255-0231
Covenant Care Home 600 Mount Moriah Church Rd	Lumberton	NC	28360	**877-708-7689**	910-738-7777
Four Seasons Hospice & Palliative Care 571 S Allen Rd	Flat Rock	NC	28731	**866-466-9734**	828-692-6178
Hospice & Palliative CareCenter 101 Hospice Ln	Winston-Salem	NC	27103	**888-876-3663**	336-768-3972
Hospice of Alamance Caswell 914 Chapel Hill Rd	Burlington	NC	27215	**800-588-8879**	336-532-0100
Hospice of Rutherford County 374 Hudlow Rd PO Box 336	Forest City	NC	28043	**800-218-2273**	828-245-0095
Hospice of Stanly County 960 N First St	Albemarle	NC	28001	**800-230-4236**	704-983-4216
Hospice of Wake County Inc 250 Hospice Cir	Raleigh	NC	27607	**888-900-3959**	919-828-0890

Name	Address	City	State	ZIP	Toll-Free	Phone
Kitty Askins Hospice Ctr	107 Handley Pk Ct	Goldsboro	NC	27534	**800-692-4442**	919-735-5887
Lower Cape Fear Hospice & Life Care	1414 Physicians Dr	Wilmington	NC	28401	**800-733-1476**	910-796-7900
Richmond County Hospice	1119 N US Hwy 1	Rockingham	NC	28379	**800-322-2997**	910-997-4464
Hospice of the Red River Valley	1701 38th St S Ste 101	Fargo	ND	58103	**800-237-4629**	701-356-1500
Bridge Home Health & Hospice	15100 Birchaven Ln	Findlay	OH	45840	**800-982-3306**	419-423-5351
FairHope Hospice & Palliative Care Inc	282 Sells Rd	Lancaster	OH	43130	**800-994-7077**	740-654-7077
Heartland Hospice Services	333 N Summit St	Toledo	OH	43604	**800-366-1232**	419-252-5500
Homereach Hospice	800 McConnell Dr	Columbus	OH	43214	**800-837-2455**	614-566-5377
Hospice of Central Ohio	2269 Cherry Vly Rd	Newark	OH	43055	**800-804-2505**	740-344-0311
Hospice of Cincinnati	4360 Cooper Rd	Cincinnati	OH	45242	**800-691-7255**	513-891-7700
Hospice of Dayton	324 Wilmington Ave	Dayton	OH	45420	**800-653-4490**	937-256-4490
Hospice of Medina County	5075 Windfall Rd	Medina	OH	44256	**800-700-4771**	330-722-4771
Hospice of Miami County	550 Summit Ave Ste 101	Troy	OH	45373	**800-372-0009**	937-335-5191
Hospice of North Central Ohio	1050 Dauch Dr	Ashland	OH	44805	**800-952-2207**	419-281-7107
Hospice of Northwest Ohio	30000 E River Rd	Perrysburg	OH	43551	**866-661-4001**	419-661-4001
Hospice of the Cleveland Clinic	6801 Brecksville Rd Ste 10	Independence	OH	44131	**800-263-0403**	216-444-9819
Hospice of the Western Reserve	300 E 185th St	Cleveland	OH	44119	**800-707-8922**	216-383-2222
Hospice of Visiting Nurse Service	3358 Ridgewood Rd	Akron	OH	44333	**800-335-1455**	330-665-1455
Quaker Heights Nursing Home Inc	514 High St	Waynesville	OH	45068	**800-319-1317**	513-897-6050
State of the Heart Home Health & Hospice	1350 N Broadway	Greenville	OH	45331	**800-417-7535**	937-548-2999
Stein Hospice Service	1912 Hayes Ave Ste 3	Sandusky	OH	44870	**800-625-5269**	419-625-5269
Valley Hospice Inc	380 Summit Ave	Steubenville	OH	43952	**877-467-7423**	740-284-4440
Visiting Nurse Assn of Ohio	2500 E 22nd St	Cleveland	OH	44115	**877-698-6264**	216-931-1400
Grace Hospice	6400 S Lewis Ave Ste 1000	Tulsa	OK	74136	**800-659-0307**	918-744-7223
Lovejoy Hospice	939 SE Eigth St	Grants Pass	OR	97526	**888-758-8569**	541-474-1193
Willamette Valley Hospice	1015 Third St NW	Salem	OR	97304	**800-555-2431**	503-588-3600
Berks VNA	1170 Berkshire Blvd	Wyomissing	PA	19610	**855-843-8627**	
Celtic Healthcare	150 Scharberry Ln	Mars	PA	16046	**800-355-8894**	
Chandler Hall Hospice	99 Barclay St	Newtown	PA	18940	**888-603-1973**	215-860-4000
Compassionate Care Hospice	3331 St Rd Ste 410	Bensalem	PA	19020	**800-584-8165**	215-245-3525
Family Hospice & Palliative Care	50 Moffett St	Pittsburgh	PA	15243	**800-513-2148**	412-572-8800
Forbes Hospice	4800 Friendship Ave	Pittsburgh	PA	15224	**800-381-8080**	412-578-5000
Holy Redeemer Home Care & Hospice	12265 Townsend Rd Ste 400	Philadelphia	PA	19154	**888-678-8678**	
Hospice of Central Pennsylvania	1320 Linglestown Rd	Harrisburg	PA	17110	**866-779-7374**	717-732-1000
Hospice of Lancaster County	685 Good Dr PO Box 4125	Lancaster	PA	17604	**888-236-9563**	717-295-3900
Lehigh Valley Hospice	2166 S 12th St Ste 401	Allentown	PA	18103	**888-584-2273**	610-969-0300
SUN Home Health Services Inc	61 Duke St PO Box 232	Northumberland	PA	17857	**888-478-6227**	570-473-8320
VITAS Healthcare Corp of Pennsylvania	1787 Sentry Pk W Bldg 16 Ste 400	Blue Bell	PA	19422	**800-582-9533**	305-374-4143
VNA	154 Hindman Rd	Butler	PA	16001	**877-862-6659**	724-282-6806
VNA Hospice & Home Health of Lackawanna County	301 Delaware Ave	Olyphant	PA	18447	**800-936-7671**	570-383-5180
Home Hospice Care of Rhode Island	1085 N Main St	Providence	RI	02904	**800-338-6555**	401-415-4200
Hospice Community Care	PO Box 993	Rock Hill	SC	29731	**800-895-2273**	803-329-1500
Hospice of the Upstate	1835 Rogers Rd	Anderson	SC	29621	**800-261-8636**	864-224-3358
McLeod Hospice	1203 E Cheves St	Florence	SC	29506	**800-768-4556**	843-777-2564
Open Arms Hospice	1836 W Georgia Rd	Simpsonville	SC	29680	**866-473-6276**	864-688-1700
Palmetto Health Home Care & Hospice	1400 Pickens St	Columbia	SC	29202	**800-238-1884**	803-296-3100
Alive Hospice Inc	1718 Patterson St	Nashville	TN	37203	**800-327-1085**	615-327-1085
Amedisys Hospice	209 10th Ave S Ste 512	Nashville	TN	37203	**800-659-2633**	423-587-9484
Baptist Trinity Home Care & Hospice	6019 Walnut Grove Rd	Memphis	TN	38120	**800-422-7847**	901-226-5000
Hospice of Chattanooga	4411 Oakwood Dr	Chattanooga	TN	37416	**800-267-6828**	423-892-4289
Methodist Alliance Hospice	6400 Shelby View Dr Ste 101	Memphis	TN	38134	**800-541-8277**	901-516-1999
AseraCare Hospice of Austin	14205 Burnet Rd	Austin	TX	78728	**800-332-3982**	512-218-9890
AseraCare Hospice of Milwaukee	7160 Dallas Pkwy Ste 400	Plano	TX	75024	**800-598-5132**	262-785-1356
CHRISTUS Spohn Hospice	6200 Saratoga Blvd Bldg B Ste 104	Corpus Christi	TX	78414	**844-444-8440**	361-994-3400
Community Hospice of Texas	6100 Western Pl Ste 150	Fort Worth	TX	76107	**800-226-0373**	817-870-2795
Hendrick Hospice Care	1682 Hickory St	Abilene	TX	79601	**800-622-8516**	325-677-8516
Home Hospice of Grayson County	505 W Ctr St	Sherman	TX	75090	**888-233-7455**	903-868-9315
Hospice at the Texas Medical Ctr	1905 Holcombe Blvd	Houston	TX	77030	**800-630-7894**	713-467-7423
Hospice Austin	4107 Spicewood Springs Rd Ste 100	Austin	TX	78759	**800-445-3261**	512-342-4700
Hospice Brazos Valley	502 W 26th St	Bryan	TX	77803	**800-824-2326**	979-821-2266
Hospice House Foundation Inc	903 n sam houston ave	Odessa	TX	79761	**877-428-3581**	432-580-0067
Hospice of East Texas	4111 University Blvd	Tyler	TX	75701	**800-777-9860**	903-266-3400
Hospice of Midland	911 W Texas Ave	Midland	TX	79701	**800-339-1180**	432-682-2855
Hospice of San Angelo	36 E Twohig St PO Box 471	San Angelo	TX	76903	**800-499-6524**	325-658-6524
Hospice of South Texas	605 E Locust Ave	Victoria	TX	77901	**800-874-6908**	361-572-4300
Hospice of Wichita Falls	4909 Johnson Rd	Wichita Falls	TX	76310	**800-378-2822**	940-691-0982
Lubbock Regional Mental Health Mental Retardation Center	1602 10th St	Lubbock	TX	79401	**800-687-7581**	806-766-0310
Capital Hospice Inc	2900 Telestar Ct	Falls Church	VA	22042	**855-571-5700**	703-538-2065
Good Samaritan Hospice	2408 Electric Rd	Roanoke	VA	24018	**888-466-7809**	540-776-0198
Hospice of the Piedmont	675 Peter Jefferson Pkwy Ste 300	Charlottesville	VA	22911	**800-975-5501**	434-817-6900
Mary Washington Hospice	5012 Southpoint Pkwy	Fredericksburg	VA	22407	**800-257-1667**	540-741-1667
Evergreen Hospice Services	12822 124th Ln NE	Kirkland	WA	98034	**877-980-7500**	425-899-1070
Harbors Home Health & Hospice	201 Seventh St	Hoquiam	WA	98550	**800-772-1319**	360-532-5454
Hospice of Spokane	121 S Arthur St	Spokane	WA	99202	**800-467-7423**	509-456-0438
Providence Hospice of Seattle	425 Pontius Ave N Ste 300	Seattle	WA	98109	**888-782-4445**	206-320-4000
Providence Sound Home Care & Hospice	3432 S Bay Rd NE	Olympia	WA	98506	**800-869-7062**	360-459-8311
Hospice of Huntington	1101 Sixth Ave	Huntington	WV	25701	**800-788-5480**	304-529-4217
Hospice of the Panhandle	330 Hospice Ln	Kearneysville	WV	25430	**800-345-6538**	304-264-0406
Kanawha Hospice Care	1606 Kanawha Blvd W	Charleston	WV	25387	**800-560-8523**	304-768-8523
Aurora VNA Zilber Family Hospice	1155 N Honey Creek Pkwy	Wauwatosa	WI	53213	**888-206-6955**	414-615-5900
Beloit Regional Hospice	655 Third St Ste 200	Beloit	WI	53511	**877-363-7421**	608-363-7421
Gundersen Lutheran at Home HomeCare & Hospice	914 Green Bay St *General	La Crosse	WI	54601	**800-362-9567***	608-775-8400
Hospice Alliance	10220 Prairie Ridge Blvd	Pleasant Prairie	WI	53158	**800-830-8344**	262-652-4400
HospiceCare	5395 E Cheryl Pkwy	Madison	WI	53711	**800-553-4289**	608-276-4660
Theda Care at Home	3000 E College Ave	Appleton	WI	54915	**800-984-5554**	920-969-0919
Unity Hospice	2366 Oak Ridge Cir	De Pere	WI	54115	**800-990-9249**	920-338-1111
VITAS Healthcare Corp	2675 N Mayfair Rd Ste 500	Wauwatosa	WI	53226	**866-418-4827**	414-257-2600

372 HOSPITAL HOSPITALITY HOUSES

Name	Address	City	State	ZIP	Toll-Free	Phone
American Cancer Society Hope Lodge of Baltimore	636 W Lexington St	Baltimore	MD	21201	**888-227-6333**	410-547-2522
American Cancer Society Hope Lodge of Charleston	269 Calhoun St	Charleston	SC	29401	**800-227-2345**	843-958-0930
American Cancer Society Hope Lodge Worcester	7 Oak St	Worcester	MA	01609	**800-227-2345**	508-792-2985
American Cancer Society Joe Lee Griffin Hope Lodge	1104 Ireland Way	Birmingham	AL	35205	**800-227-2345**	205-558-7860
American Cancer Society Winn-Dixie Hope Lodge	250 Williams St NW	Atlanta	GA	30303	**800-227-2345**	404-327-9200
Atlanta Hospital Hospitality House	1815 S Ponce De Leon Ave NE	Atlanta	GA	30307	**855-286-9658**	404-377-6333
Bannister Family House	406 Dickinson St	San Diego	CA	92103	**800-926-8273**	619-543-7977
Barnes Lodge	4520 Clayton Ave	Saint Louis	MO	63110	**800-551-3492**	314-652-4319
Baylor Plaza Hotel	3600 Gaston Ave	Dallas	TX	75246	**800-422-9567**	
Beacon House	1301 N Third St	Marquette	MI	49855	**800-562-9753**	906-225-7100
Carolyn Scott Rainbow House	7815 Harney St	Omaha	NE	68114	**800-642-8822**	402-955-7815
Casa Esperanza	1005 Yale NE	Albuquerque	NM	87106	**866-654-1338**	505-246-2700
Children's Hope House	7922 W Jefferson Blvd	Fort Wayne	IN	46804	**800-706-9941**	260-459-8550
Children's House at Johns Hopkins	1915 McElderry St	Baltimore	MD	21205	**800-933-5470**	410-614-2560
Conine Clubhouse	1005 Joe DiMaggio Dr	Hollywood	FL	33021	**866-532-4362**	954-265-5324
Cynthia C. & William E. Perry Pavilion	9400 Turkey Lake Rd	Orlando	FL	32819	**800-447-1435**	321-842-8844
Gift of Life Transplant House	705 Second St SW	Rochester	MN	55902	**800-479-7824**	507-288-7470

Classified Section

	City	State	Zip	Toll-Free	Phone
Hubbard House, The 29 W Miller St	Orlando	FL	32806	**800-648-3818**	407-649-6886
Inn at Virginia Mason 1006 Spring St	Seattle	WA	98104	**800-283-6453**	206-583-6453
Kohl's House at Children's Memorial Hospital 225 E Chicago Ave	Chicago	IL	60611	**800-543-7362**	312-227-4000
Mario Pastega Guest House 3505 NW Samaritan Dr	Corvallis	OR	97330	**800-863-5241**	541-768-4650
Nebraska House 983285 Nebraska Medical Ctr	Omaha	NE	68198	**800-401-4444**	402-559-5000
Rosenbaum Family House 30 Family House Dr PO Box 8228	Morgantown	WV	26506	**855-988-2273**	304-598-6094
Steven's Hope for Children Inc 1014 W Foothill Blvd Ste B	Upland	CA	91786	**866-378-3836**	909-373-0678
Travis & Beverly Cross Guest Housing Ctr 9320 SW Barnes Rd	Portland	OR	97225	**888-550-1575**	503-216-1575
Zachary & Elizabeth Fisher House 111 Rockville Pk Ste 420	Rockville	MD	20850	**888-294-8560**	

373 HOSPITAL HOSPITALITY HOUSES - RONALD MCDONALD HOUSE

	City	State	Zip	Toll-Free	Phone
Ronald McDonald House Charities (RMHC) 1 Kroc Dr	Oak Brook	IL	60523	**855-670-4787**	630-623-7048
Akron 245 Locust St	Akron	OH	44302	**800-262-0333**	330-253-5400
Albany 139 S Lake Ave	Albany	NY	12208	**866-244-8464**	518-438-2655
Albuquerque 1011 Yale Ave NE	Albuquerque	NM	87106	**877-842-8960**	505-842-8960
Ann Arbor 1600 Washington Heights	Ann Arbor	MI	48104	**800-544-8684**	734-994-4442
Chattanooga 200 Central Ave	Chattanooga	TN	37403	**855-670-4787**	423-778-4300
Cleveland 10415 Euclid Ave	Cleveland	OH	44106	**800-223-2273**	216-229-5758
Durham 506 Alexander Ave	Durham	NC	27705	**866-244-8464**	919-286-9305
Falls Church 3312 Gallows Rd	Falls Church	VA	22042	**855-227-7435**	703-698-7080
Fort Myers 16100 Roserush Ct	Fort Myers	FL	33908	**800-435-7352**	239-437-0202
Galveston 301 14th St	Galveston	TX	77550	**800-275-2946**	409-762-8770
Hershey 745 W Governor Rd	Hershey	PA	17033	**800-732-0999**	717-533-4001
Huntington 1500 17th St	Huntington	WV	25701	**855-227-7435**	304-529-1122
Kansas City 2502 Cherry St	Kansas City	MO	64108	**888-353-4537**	816-842-8321
Las Vegas 2323 Potosi St	Las Vegas	NV	89146	**888-248-1561**	702-252-4663
Philadelphia 3925 Chestnut St	Philadelphia	PA	19104	**800-723-0999**	215-387-8406
Phoenix 501 E Roanoke Ave	Phoenix	AZ	85004	**877-333-2978**	602-264-2654
Providence 45 Gay St	Providence	RI	02905	**888-353-4537**	401-274-4447
Seattle 5130 40th Ave NE	Seattle	WA	98105	**866-987-9330**	206-838-0600
Wilmington 1901 Rockland Rd	Wilmington	DE	19803	**888-656-4847**	302-656-4847
Winston-Salem 419 S Hawthorne Rd	Winston-Salem	NC	27103	**855-227-7435**	336-723-0228
Gainesville 1600 SW 14th St	Gainesville	FL	32608	**800-435-7352**	352-374-4404

374 HOSPITALS

SEE ALSO Veterans Nursing Homes - State ; Health Care Providers - Ancillary ; Health Care Systems ; Hospices

HOSPITALS - DEVELOPMENTAL DISABILITIES

374-1 Children's Hospitals

	City	State	Zip	Toll-Free	Phone
Arnold Palmer Hospital for Children & Women 92 W Miller St	Orlando	FL	32806	**800-648-3818**	407-649-9111
Children's Healthcare of Atlanta at Egleston 1405 Clifton Rd NE	Atlanta	GA	30322	**888-785-7778**	404-785-6000
Children's Healthcare of Atlanta at Scottish Rite 1001 Johnson Ferry Rd NE	Atlanta	GA	30342	**888-785-7778**	404-785-5252
Children's Hospital 200 Henry Clay Ave	New Orleans	LA	70118	**800-299-9511**	504-899-9511
Children's Hospital Medical Ctr of Akron 1 Perkins Sq	Akron	OH	44308	**800-262-0333**	330-543-1000
Children's Hospitals & Clinics Minneapolis 2525 Chicago Ave	Minneapolis	MN	55404	**866-225-3251**	612-813-6000
Children's Institute of Pittsburgh 1405 Shady Ave	Pittsburgh	PA	15217	**877-433-1109**	412-420-2400
Children's Medical Ctr 1 Children's Plaza	Dayton	OH	45404	**800-228-4055**	937-641-3000
Children's Mercy Hospital & Clinics 2401 Gillham Rd	Kansas City	MO	64108	**866-512-2168**	816-234-3000
Children's National Medical Ctr (CNMC) 111 Michigan Ave NW	Washington	DC	20010	**800-884-5433**	202-476-5000
Children's Specialized Hospital 150 New Providence Rd	Mountainside	NJ	07092	**888-244-5373**	908-233-3720
Cincinnati Children's Hospital Medical Ctr 3333 Burnet Ave	Cincinnati	OH	45229	**800-344-2462**	513-636-4200
Copper Hills Youth Ctr 5899 Rivendell Dr	West Jordan	UT	84081	**800-776-7116**	
CS Mott Children's Hospital 1500 E Medical Ctr Dr	Ann Arbor	MI	48109	**800-211-8181**	734-936-4000
Devereux 1291 Stanley Rd NW PO Box 1688	Kennesaw	GA	30156	**800-342-3357**	678-303-5233
Devereux Cleo Wallace 8405 Church Ranch Blvd	Westminster	CO	80021	**800-456-2536**	303-466-7391
Devereux Hospital & Children's Ctr of Florida 8000 Devereux Dr	Melbourne	FL	32940	**800-338-3738**	321-242-9100
Driscoll Children's Hospital 3533 S Alameda St	Corpus Christi	TX	78411	**800-324-5683**	361-694-5000
Gillette Children's Specialty Healthcare 200 E University Ave	Saint Paul	MN	55101	**800-719-4040**	651-291-2848
Gulf Coast Treatment Ctr 1015 Mar-Walt Dr	Fort Walton Beach	FL	32547	**800-537-5433**	850-863-4160
Hawthorn Ctr 18471 Haggerty Rd	Northville	MI	48167	**855-444-3911**	248-349-3000
Helen DeVos Children's Hospital 100 Michigan St NE	Grand Rapids	MI	49503	**800-222-1222**	616-391-9000
HSC Pediatric Ctr 1731 Bunker Hill Rd NE	Washington	DC	20017	**800-226-4444**	202-832-4400
JD McCarty Ctr for Children with Developmental Disabilities 2002 E Robinson St	Norman	OK	73071	**800-777-1272**	405-307-2800
Kennedy Krieger Institute 707 N Broadway	Baltimore	MD	21205	**800-873-3377**	443-923-9200
KidsPeace Orchard Hills Campus 5300 Kids Peace Dr	Orefield	PA	18069	**800-257-3223**	
Lucile Packard Children's Hospital (LPCH) 725 Welch Rd	Palo Alto	CA	94304	**800-995-5724**	650-497-8000
Mary Bridge Children's Hospital & Health Ctr 317 Martin Luther King Jr Way	Tacoma	WA	98405	**800-552-1419**	253-403-1400
Miami Children's Hospital 3100 SW 62nd Ave	Miami	FL	33155	**800-432-6837**	305-666-6511
New York City Children's Ctr-Queens Campus (NYCCC) 74-03 Commonwealth Blvd	Bellerose	NY	11426	**800-597-8481**	718-264-4500
Phoenix Children's Hospital 1919 E Thomas Rd	Phoenix	AZ	85016	**888-908-5437**	602-546-1000
Rady Children's Hospital (RCH) 3020 Children's Way MC 5101	San Diego	CA	92123	**800-788-9029**	858-576-1700
Saint Louis Children's Hospital 1 Children's Pl	Saint Louis	MO	63110	**800-427-4626**	314-454-6000
Seattle Children's Hospital 4800 Sand Pt Way NE	Seattle	WA	98105	**866-987-2000**	206-987-2000
Shriners Hospitals for Children Boston 51 Blossom St	Boston	MA	02114	**800-255-1916**	617-722-3000
Shriners Hospitals for Children Canada 1529 Cedar Ave	Montreal	QC	H3G1A6	**800-361-7256**	514-842-4464
Shriners Hospitals for Children Cincinnati 3229 Burnet Ave	Cincinnati	OH	45229	**800-875-8580**	513-872-6000
Shriners Hospitals for Children Erie 1645 W Eigth St	Erie	PA	16505	**800-873-5437**	814-875-8700
Shriners Hospitals for Children Galveston 2900 Rocky Pt Dr	Tampa	Fl	33607	**844-739-0849**	813-281-0300
Shriners Hospitals for Children Greenville 950 W Faris Rd	Greenville	SC	29605	**800-361-7256**	864-271-3444
Shriners Hospitals for Children Lexington 1900 Richmond Rd	Lexington	KY	40502	**800-668-4634**	859-266-2101
Shriners Hospitals for Children Los Angeles 3160 Geneva St	Los Angeles	CA	90020	**888-486-5437**	213-388-3151
Shriners Hospitals for Children Philadelphia 3551 N Broad St	Philadelphia	PA	19140	**800-281-4050**	215-430-4000
Shriners Hospitals for Children Salt Lake City Fairfax Rd & Virginia St	Salt Lake City	UT	84103	**800-313-3745**	801-536-3500
Shriners Hospitals for Children Tampa 12502 N Pine Dr	Tampa	FL	33612	**800-237-5055**	813-972-2250
Streamwood Behavioral Health Ctr 1400 E Irving Pk Rd	Streamwood	IL	60107	**800-272-7790**	630-837-9000
Texas Children's Hospital 6621 Fannin St	Houston	TX	77030	**800-364-5437**	832-824-1000
Texas Scottish Rite Hospital for Children 2222 Welborn St	Dallas	TX	75219	**800-421-1121**	214-559-5000
Women's & Children's Hospital of Buffalo 219 Bryant St	Buffalo	NY	14222	**800-462-7653**	716-878-7000
Youth Villages Inner Harbour 4685 Dorsett Shoals Rd	Douglasville	GA	30135	**800-255-8657**	770-852-6333

374-2 General Hospitals - Canada

	City	Prov	Postal Code	Toll-Free	Phone
Belleville General Hospital 265 Dundas St E	Belleville	ON	K8N5A9	**800-483-2811**	613-969-7400
British Columbia's Women's Hospital & Health Centre 4500 Oak St	Vancouver	BC	V6H3N1	**888-300-3088**	604-875-2424
Brockville General Hospital 75 Charles St	Brockville	ON	K6V1S8	**800-567-7415**	613-345-5645
Centre Hospitalier Le Gardeur 911 Montee des Pionniers	Terrebonne	QC	J6V2H2	**888-654-7525**	450-654-7525
Centre Hospitalier Pierre Boucher 1333 Boul Jacques-Cartier E	Longueuil	QC	J4M2A5	**866-277-3553**	450-468-8111
Children's Hospital of Eastern Ontario 401 Smyth Rd	Ottawa	ON	K1H8L1	**866-797-0007**	613-737-7600
CHU Sainte-Justine 3175 Ch de la Cote-Sainte-Catherine	Montreal	QC	H3T1C5	**888-235-3667**	514-345-4931
Colchester Regional Hospital 207 Willow St	Truro	NS	B2N5A1	**800-460-2110**	902-893-4321
Concordia Hospital 1095 Concordia Ave	Winnipeg	MB	R2K3S8	**888-315-9257**	204-667-1560
Cornwall Community Hospital 840 McConnell Ave	Cornwall	ON	K6H5S5	**866-263-1560**	613-938-4240
Credit Valley Hospital 2200 Eglinton Ave W	Mississauga	ON	L5M2N1	**877-292-4284**	905-813-2200
Hotel Dieu Hospital 166 Brock St	Kingston	ON	K7L5G2	**855-544-3400**	613-544-3310
Jeffrey Hale - St Brigid's Hospital 1250 ch Sainte-Foy	Quebec	QC	G1S2M6	**888-984-5333**	418-684-5333
Joseph Brant Memorial Hospital (JBMH) 1230 N Shore Blvd	Burlington	ON	L7S1W7	**800-810-0000**	905-632-3730
Kelowna General Hospital (KGH) 2268 Pandosy St	Kelowna	BC	V1Y1T2	**888-877-4442**	250-862-4000
Lakeridge Health Oshawa 1 Hospital Ct	Oshawa	ON	L1G2B9	**866-338-1778**	905-576-8711
Lions Gate Hospital 231 E 15th St	North Vancouver	BC	V7L2L7	**800-984-1131**	604-988-3131
Montfort Hospital 713 Montreal Rd	Ottawa	ON	K1K0T2	**866-670-4621**	613-746-4621
Montreal Heart Institute 5000 Belanger St E	Montreal	QC	H1T1C8	**855-922-6387**	514-376-3330

Hospital	Address	City	State/Prov	Postal Code	Toll-Free	Phone
Pembroke Regional Hospital	705 MacKay St	Pembroke	ON	K8A1G8	**866-996-0991**	613-732-2811
Ross Memorial Hospital (RMH)	10 Angeline St N	Lindsay	ON	K9V4M8	**800-510-7365**	705-324-6111
Rouge Valley Ajax & Pickering	580 Harwood Ave S	Ajax	ON	L1S2J4	**866-752-6989**	905-683-2320
Saint Joseph's Lifecare Centre	99 Wayne Gretzky Pkwy	Brantford	ON	N3S6T6	**888-699-7817**	519-751-7096
Saint Michael's Hospital	30 Bond St	Toronto	ON	M5B1W8	**866-797-0000**	416-360-4000
Saskatoon City Hospital	701 Queen St	Saskatoon	SK	S7K0M7	**855-655-7612**	306-655-8000
Stratford General Hospital	46 General Hospital Dr	Stratford	ON	N5A2Y6	**888-275-1102**	519-272-8210
Timmins & District Hospital	700 Ross Ave E	Timmins	ON	P4N8P2	**888-340-3003**	705-267-2131

374-3 General Hospitals - US

Hospital	Address	City	State	Zip	Toll-Free	Phone
Abbott Northwestern Hospital	800 E 28th St	Minneapolis	MN	55407	**800-582-5175**	612-863-4000
Advocate Sherman Hospital	1425 N Randall Rd	Elgin	IL	60123	**800-397-9000**	847-742-9800
Affiliated Community Medical Centers (ACMC)	101 Willmar Ave SW	Willmar	MN	56201	**888-225-6580**	320-231-5000
Affinity Medical Ctr	875 Eigth St NE	Massillon	OH	44646	**800-999-6673**	330-832-8761
Aiken Regional Medical Centers	302 University Pkwy	Aiken	SC	29801	**800-245-3679**	803-641-5000
Akron General Medical Ctr	400 Wabash Ave	Akron	OH	44307	**800-221-4601**	330-344-6000
Alaska Native Medical Ctr (ANMC)	4315 Diplomacy Dr *Admitting	Anchorage	AK	99508	**800-478-6661***	907-563-2662
Albert Einstein Medical Ctr	5501 Old York Rd	Philadelphia	PA	19141	**800-346-7834**	
Alexian Bros Medical Ctr	800 Biesterfield Rd	Elk Grove Village	IL	60007	**800-432-5005**	847-437-5500
Allegiance Health	205 NE Ave	Jackson	MI	49201	**800-872-6480**	517-788-4800
Allen Memorial Hospital	1825 Logan Ave	Waterloo	IA	50703	**888-343-4165**	319-235-3941
Alpena Regional Medical Ctr	1501 W Chisholm St	Alpena	MI	49707	**800-556-8842**	989-356-7000
Alton Memorial Hospital	1 Memorial Dr	Alton	IL	62002	**800-994-6610**	618-463-7311
Altoona Regional Health System Altoona Hospital	620 Howard Ave	Altoona	PA	16601	**877-855-8152**	814-889-2011
Altru Hospital	1200 S Columbia Rd	Grand Forks	ND	58201	**800-732-4277**	701-780-5000
Alvarado Hospital Medical Ctr	6655 Alvarado Rd	San Diego	CA	92120	**800-258-2723**	619-287-3270
Annie Penn Hospital	618 S Main St	Reidsville	NC	27320	**866-391-2734**	336-951-4000
Appleton Medical Ctr	1818 N Meade St	Appleton	WI	54911	**800-236-4101**	920-731-4101
Arkansas Valley Regional Medical Ctr (AVRMC)	1100 Carson Ave	La Junta	CO	81050	**877-696-6775**	719-384-5412
Arrowhead Regional Medical Ctr	400 N Pepper Ave	Colton	CA	92324	**855-422-8029**	909-580-1000
Ashtabula County Medical Ctr (ACMC)	2420 Lake Ave	Ashtabula	OH	44004	**866-213-2262**	440-997-2262
Aspirus Wausau Hospital	333 Pine Ridge Blvd	Wausau	WI	54401	**800-283-2881**	715-847-2121
Atrium Medical Ctr	1 Medical Ctr Dr	Middletown	OH	45005	**800-338-4057**	513-424-2111
Auburn Regional Medical Ctr	202 N Div St Plaza 1	Auburn	WA	98001	**866-268-7223**	253-833-7711
Augusta Medical Ctr (AMC)	78 Medical Ctr Dr PO Box 1000	Fishersville	VA	22939	**800-932-0262**	540-932-4000
Aurora Sinai Medical Ctr	945 N 12th St	Milwaukee	WI	53201	**888-863-5502**	414-219-2000
Aventura Hospital	20900 Biscayne Blvd	Aventura	FL	33180	**800-523-5772**	305-682-7000
Avera Queen of Peace Hospital	525 N Foster St	Mitchell	SD	57301	**888-531-1685**	605-995-2000
Avera Saint Luke's Hospital	305 S State St	Aberdeen	SD	57401	**800-658-3535**	605-622-5000
Baltimore Washington Medical Ctr	301 Hospital Dr	Glen Burnie	MD	21061	**800-994-6610**	410-787-4000
Banner Del E Webb Memorial Hospital	14502 W Meeker Blvd	Sun City West	AZ	85375	**800-254-4357**	623-214-4000
Baptist Health	1 Trillium Way	Corbin	KY	40701	**800-395-4435**	606-528-1212
Baptist Health Louisville	4000 Kresge Way	Louisville	KY	40207	**800-489-3002**	502-897-8100
Baptist Health Paducah (WBH)	2501 Kentucky Ave	Paducah	KY	42003	**877-271-4176**	270-575-2100
Baptist Hospital of Miami	8900 SW 88th St	Miami	FL	33176	**800-994-6610**	786-596-1960
Baptist Medical Ctr	1225 N State St	Jackson	MS	39202	**800-948-6262**	601-968-1000
Baptist Memorial Hospital Golden Triangle	2520 Fifth St N	Columbus	MS	39703	**800-422-7847**	662-244-1000
Baptist Memorial Hospital Union City	1201 Bishop St	Union City	TN	38261	**800-344-2470**	731-885-2410
Bassett Healthcare Network	1 Atwell Rd	Cooperstown	NY	13326	**800-227-7388**	607-547-3456
Baxter Regional Medical Ctr	624 Hospital Dr	Mountain Home	AR	72653	**800-695-3627**	870-424-1000
Bay Area Medical Ctr (BAMC)	3100 Shore Dr	Marinette	WI	54143	**888-788-2070**	715-735-4200
Bay Medical Ctr	615 N Bonita Ave	Panama City	FL	32401	**800-268-2435**	850-769-1511
Bay Regional Medical Ctr (BRMC)	1900 Columbus Ave	Bay City	MI	48708	**800-656-3950**	989-894-3000
Bayhealth Medical Ctr	21 W Clarke Ave	Milford	DE	19963	**877-453-7107**	302-430-5738
Baylor Regional Medical Ctr at Grapevine	1650 W College St	Grapevine	TX	76051	**800-422-9567**	817-481-1588
Bayshore Medical Ctr	4000 Spencer Hwy	Pasadena	TX	77504	**800-465-4837**	713-359-2000
Beaufort Memorial Hospital	955 Ribaut Rd	Beaufort	SC	29902	**877-532-6472**	843-522-5200
Beloit Health System	1969 W Hart Rd	Beloit	WI	53511	**800-637-2641**	608-363-5724
Benefis HealthSystems *East Campus*	1101 26th St S	Great Falls	MT	59405	**800-648-6632**	406-455-5000
Beth Israel Deaconess Medical Ctr (BIDMC)	330 Brookline Ave	Boston	MA	02215	**800-667-5356**	617-667-7000
Bethesda Hospital	2951 Maple Ave	Zanesville	OH	43701	**800-322-4762**	740-454-4000
Billings Clinic	2800 Tenth Ave N	Billings	MT	59101	**800-332-7156**	406-238-2501
Blessing Hospital	Broadway at 11th St	Quincy	IL	62301	**866-460-3933**	217-223-8400
Blount Memorial Hospital	907 E Lamar Alexander Pkwy	Maryville	TN	37804	**800-448-0219**	865-983-7211
Bluefield Regional Medical Ctr (BRMC)	500 Cherry St	Bluefield	WV	24701	**800-994-6610**	304-327-1100
Bon Secours Community Hospital	160 E Main St	Port Jervis	NY	12771	**866-522-4984**	845-858-7000
Bon Secours Memorial Regional Medical Ctr	8260 Atlee Rd	Mechanicsville	VA	23116	**888-455-3766**	804-764-6000
Bon Secours Saint Mary's Hospital	5801 Bremo Rd	Richmond	VA	23226	**877-342-1500**	804-285-2011
Braddock Hospital	12500 Willowbrook Rd	Cumberland	MD	21502	**888-369-1122**	240-964-7000
Brattleboro Memorial Hospital Inc	17 Belmont Ave Ste 1	Brattleboro	VT	05301	**866-972-5266**	802-257-0341
Broadlawns Medical Ctr	1801 Hickman Rd	Des Moines	IA	50314	**866-904-5755**	515-282-2200
Bronson Methodist Hospital	601 John St	Kalamazoo	MI	49007	**800-276-6766**	269-341-7654
BronxCare Family Wellness Center	1276 Fulton Ave	Bronx	NY	10456	**877-451-9361**	718-590-1800
Brooksville Regional Hospital	17240 Cortez Blvd	Brooksville	FL	34601	**844-455-8708**	352-796-5111
Bryan LGH Medical Ctr East	1600 S 48th St	Lincoln	NE	68506	**800-742-7844**	402-481-7333
Buena Vista Regional Medical Ctr	PO Box 309	Storm Lake	IA	50588	**877-401-8030**	712-732-4030
Buffalo General Hospital	100 High St	Buffalo	NY	14203	**800-506-6480**	716-859-5600
Cambridge Medical Ctr (CMC)	701 S Dellwood St	Cambridge	MN	55008	**800-252-4133**	763-689-7700
Cape Cod Hospital	27 Pk St	Hyannis	MA	02601	**800-545-5014**	508-771-1800
Capital Medical Ctr	3900 Capital Mall Dr SW	Olympia	WA	98502	**888-677-9757**	360-754-5858
Capital Regional Medical Ctr (CRMC)	2626 Capital Medical Blvd	Tallahassee	FL	32308	**800-994-6610**	850-325-5000
Carilion New River Valley Medical Ctr	2900 Lamb Cir	Christiansburg	VA	24073	**800-432-7874**	540-731-2000
Carolinas Medical Center-NorthEast	920 Church St N	Concord	NC	28025	**800-575-1275**	704-403-1275
Carolinas Medical Center-University	8800 N Tryon St	Charlotte	NC	28262	**800-821-1535**	704-863-6000
Carolinas Medical Ctr Mercy	2001 Vail Ave	Charlotte	NC	28207	**800-821-1535**	
Catholic Medical Ctr (CMC)	100 McGregor St	Manchester	NH	03102	**800-437-9666**	603-668-3545
Catskill Regional Medical Ctr	68 Harris-Bushville Rd PO Box 800	Harris	NY	12742	**888-846-5945**	845-794-3300
Cedars-Sinai Medical Ctr (CSMC)	8700 Beverly Blvd	Los Angeles	CA	90048	**800-233-2771**	310-423-3277
Centegra Memorial Medical Ctr	3701 Doty Rd	Woodstock	IL	60098	**877-236-8347**	815-338-2500
Central Carolina Hospital	1135 Carthage St	Sanford	NC	27330	**800-292-2262**	919-774-2100
Central DuPage Hospital	25 N Winfield Rd	Winfield	IL	60190	**800-223-9776**	630-933-1600
Central Texas Medical Ctr (CTMC)	1301 Wonder World Dr	San Marcos	TX	78666	**800-927-9004**	512-353-8979
CGH Medical Ctr (CGHMC)	100 E LeFevre Rd	Sterling	IL	61081	**800-625-4790**	815-625-0400
Chandler Regional Hospital	475 S Dobson Rd	Chandler	AZ	85224	**877-728-5414**	480-728-3000
Chesapeake Regional Medical Ctr	736 Battlefield Blvd N	Chesapeake	VA	23320	**800-456-8121**	757-312-8121
Christ Hospital	2139 Auburn Ave	Cincinnati	OH	45219	**800-527-8919**	513-585-2000
CHRISTUS Hospital - St Elizabeth	2830 Calder St	Beaumont	TX	77702	**866-683-3627**	409-892-7171
CHRISTUS Saint Mary Hospital	3600 Gates Blvd PO Box 3696	Port Arthur	TX	77642	**866-683-3627**	409-985-7431
CHRISTUS Schumpert Highland	1453 E Bert Kouns	Shreveport	LA	71105	**888-681-4138**	318-681-4500
City Hospital	2500 Hospital Dr	Martinsburg	WV	25401	**888-988-1362**	304-264-1000
CJW Medical Ctr	7101 Jahnke Rd	Richmond	VA	23225	**800-468-6620**	804-320-3911
Clarion Hospital (CH)	1 Hospital Dr	Clarion	PA	16214	**800-522-0505**	814-226-9500
Claxton-Hepburn Medical Ctr	214 King St	Ogdensburg	NY	13669	**888-220-0042**	315-393-3600
Clearfield Hospital	809 Tpke Ave PO Box 992	Clearfield	PA	16830	**800-281-8000**	814-765-5341
Cleveland Clinic	9500 Euclid Ave	Cleveland	OH	44195	**800-223-2273**	216-444-2200
Cleveland Clinic Hospital	2950 Cleveland Clinic Blvd	Weston	FL	33331	**866-293-7866**	954-689-5000
Clifton Springs Hospital & Clinic	2 Coulter Rd	Clifton Springs	NY	14432	**888-786-4347**	315-462-9561

Name / Address	City	State	ZIP	Toll-Free	Phone
Clinton Memorial Hospital (CMH) 610 W Main St PO Box 600	Wilmington	OH	45177	**800-803-9648**	937-382-6611
Coffeyville Regional Medical Ctr 1400 W Fourth St	Coffeyville	KS	67337	**800-540-2762**	620-251-1200
Colquitt Regional Medical Ctr (CRMC) 3131 S Main St PO Box 40	Moultrie	GA	31768	**888-262-2762**	229-985-3420
Columbia Memorial Hospital 71 Prospect Ave	Hudson	NY	12534	**866-539-1370**	518-828-7601
Columbia Saint Mary's Hospital Ozaukee 13111 N Port Washington Rd	Mequon	WI	53097	**800-457-6004**	262-243-7300
Columbus Regional Hospital 2400 E 17th St	Columbus	IN	47201	**800-841-4938**	812-379-4441
Community Hospital Anderson (CHA) 1515 N Madison Ave	Anderson	IN	46011	**800-777-7775**	765-298-4242
Community Hospital of Long Beach 1720 Termino Ave	Long Beach	CA	90804	**800-994-6610**	562-498-1000
Community Hospital of the Monterey Peninsula (CHOMP) 23625 Holman Hwy	Monterey	CA	93940	**888-452-4667**	831-624-5311
Community Medical Ctr (CMC) 99 Hwy 37 W	Toms River	NJ	08755	**888-724-7123**	732-557-8000
Conroe Regional Medical Ctr 504 Medical Ctr Blvd	Conroe	TX	77304	**888-633-2687**	936-539-1111
Contra Costa Health Services 2500 Alhambra Ave	Martinez	CA	94553	**877-661-6230**	925-370-5000
Conway Regional Hospital 2302 College Ave	Conway	AR	72032	**800-245-3314**	501-329-3831
Cooper University Hospital 3 Cooper Plz	Camden	NJ	08103	**800-826-6737**	856-342-2000
Copley Hospital Inc 528 Washington Hwy	Morrisville	VT	05661	**888-833-8329**	802-888-8888
Coral Gables Hospital Inc (CGH) 3100 Douglas Rd	Coral Gables	FL	33134	**866-728-3677**	305-445-8461
Corning Hospital 176 Denison Pkwy E	Corning	NY	14830	**877-750-2042**	607-937-7200
Creighton University Medical Ctr 601 N 30th St	Omaha	NE	68131	**800-368-5097**	402-449-4000
Dallas County Hospital 610 10th St	Perry	IA	50220	**800-877-7541**	515-465-3547
Danbury Hospital (DH) 24 Hospital Ave	Danbury	CT	06810	**800-516-3658**	203-739-7000
Danville Regional Medical Ctr 142 S Main St	Danville	VA	24541	**800-688-3762**	434-799-2100
Davis Hospital & Medical Ctr (DHMC) 1600 W Antelope Dr	Layton	UT	84041	**877-898-6080**	801-807-1000
Davis Memorial Hospital 812 Gorman Ave	Elkins	WV	26241	**888-477-6895**	304-636-3300
Deaconess Hospital 600 Mary St	Evansville	IN	47747	**800-677-3422**	812-450-5000
Decatur Memorial Hospital 2300 N Edward St	Decatur	IL	62526	**866-364-3600**	217-876-8121
Delaware County Memorial Hospital 501 N Lansdowne Ave	Drexel Hill	PA	19026	**877-884-1564**	610-284-8100
Delnor-Community Hospital (DCH) 300 Randall Rd	Geneva	IL	60134	**800-223-9776**	630-208-3000
Desert Regional Medical Ctr 1150 N Indian Canyon Dr	Palm Springs	CA	92262	**800-491-4990**	760-323-6511
DesPeres Hospital 2345 Dougherty Ferry Rd	Saint Louis	MO	63122	**888-457-5203**	314-966-9100
Doctors Hospital 5100 W Broad St	Columbus	OH	43228	**800-432-3309**	614-544-1000
Doctors Hospital at White Rock Lake 9440 Poppy Dr	Dallas	TX	75218	**866-893-8446**	214-820-0111
Doctors Hospital of Laredo 10700 McPherson Rd	Laredo	TX	78045	**844-244-4874**	956-523-2000
Dominican Hospital (DH) 1555 Soquel Dr	Santa Cruz	CA	95065	**866-466-1401**	831-462-7700
East Georgia Regional Medical Ctr (EGRMC) 1499 Fair Rd	Statesboro	GA	30458	**844-455-8708**	912-486-1000
East Jefferson General Hospital (EJGH) 4200 Houma Blvd	Metairie	LA	70006	**866-280-7737**	504-454-4000
Eastern New Mexico Medical Ctr 405 W Country Club Rd	Roswell	NM	88201	**800-222-1222**	575-622-8170
Edinburg Regional Medical Ctr (ERMC) 1102 W Trenton Rd	Edinburg	TX	78539	**800-465-5585**	956-388-6000
Elliot Hospital 1 Elliot Way Ste 100	Manchester	NH	03103	**800-922-4999**	603-627-1669
Enloe Medical Ctr 1531 Esplanade	Chico	CA	95926	**800-822-8102**	530-332-7300
Erlanger Medical Ctr 975 E Third St	Chattanooga	TN	37403	**877-849-8338**	423-778-7000
Essentia Health 502 E Second St	Duluth	MN	55805	**855-469-6532**	218-786-8376
Evanston Hospital 2650 Ridge Ave	Evanston	IL	60201	**888-364-6400**	847-570-2000
Fairfield Medical Ctr (FMC) 401 N Ewing St	Lancaster	OH	43130	**800-548-2627**	740-687-8000
Fairview Hospital 18101 Lorain Ave	Cleveland	OH	44111	**800-801-2273**	216-444-0261
Fairview University Medical Ctr Mesabi 750 E 34th St	Hibbing	MN	55746	**888-870-8626**	218-262-4881
FHN Memorial Hospital 1045 W Stephenson St	Freeport	IL	61032	**800-747-4131**	815-599-6000
Finley Hospital 350 N Grandview Ave	Dubuque	IA	52001	**800-582-1891**	563-582-1881
Firelands Regional Medical Ctr 1111 Hayes Ave	Sandusky	OH	44870	**800-342-1177**	419-557-7400
Fisher-Titus Medical Ctr (FTMC) 272 Benedict Ave	Norwalk	OH	44857	**800-589-3862**	419-668-8101
Florida Hospital Heartland Medical Ctr 4200 Sun 'n Lake Blvd PO Box 9400	Sebring	FL	33871	**800-756-4447**	863-314-4466
Flowers Hospital 4370 W Main St	Dothan	AL	36305	**877-456-9617**	334-793-5000
Floyd Medical Ctr 304 Turner McCall Blvd	Rome	GA	30165	**866-874-2772**	706-509-5000
Floyd Memorial Hospital 1850 State St	New Albany	IN	47150	**800-423-1513**	812-944-7701
Forrest General Hospital 6051 US Hwy 49	Hattiesburg	MS	39402	**800-503-5980**	601-288-7000
Fountain Valley Regional Hospital & Medical Ctr 17100 Euclid St	Fountain Valley	CA	92708	**866-904-6871**	714-966-7200
Franciscan St. Elizabeth Health 1501 Hartford St	Lafayette	IN	47904	**800-371-6011**	765-423-6011
Frankfort Regional Medical Ctr 299 King's Daughters Dr	Frankfort	KY	40601	**888-696-4505**	502-875-5240
Franklin Community Health Network 111 Franklin Health Commons	Farmington	ME	04938	**800-398-6031**	207-778-6031
Franklin Square Hospital Ctr 9000 Franklin Sq Dr	Baltimore	MD	21237	**888-404-3549**	443-777-7000
Frick Hospital 508 S Church St	Mount Pleasant	PA	15666	**877-771-1234**	724-547-1500
Gateway Regional Medical Ctr (GRMC) 2100 Madison Ave *General	Granite City	IL	62040	**800-422-6237***	618-798-3000
Genesis Medical Ctr Illini Campus 801 Illini Dr	Silvis	IL	61282	**800-250-6020**	309-792-9363
George Washington University Hospital 900 23rd St NW	Washington	DC	20037	**888-449-3627**	202-715-4000
Glacial Ridge Hospital Foundation Inc 10 Fourth Ave SE	Glenwood	MN	56334	**866-667-4747**	320-634-4521
GlenOaks Hospital 701 Winthrop Ave	Glendale Heights	IL	60139	**866-751-7127**	630-545-8000
Glens Falls Hospital 100 Pk St	Glens Falls	NY	12801	**800-994-6610**	518-926-1000
Golden Valley Memorial Hospital 1600 N Second St	Clinton	MO	64735	**888-225-6903**	660-885-5511
Good Samaritan Hospital 10 E 31st St	Kearney	NE	68847	**800-277-4306**	308-865-7100
Good Samaritan Hospital of Maryland 5601 Loch Raven Blvd	Baltimore	MD	21239	**855-633-5655**	410-532-8000
Good Samaritan Regional Medical Ctr 3600 NW Samaritan Dr	Corvallis	OR	97330	**888-872-0760**	541-768-5111
Grady Memorial Hospital 2220 Iowa Ave	Chickasha	OK	73018	**800-299-9665**	405-224-2300
Grand Strand Regional Medical Ctr 809 82nd Pkwy	Myrtle Beach	SC	29572	**800-342-2383**	843-692-1000
Greenview Regional Hospital 1801 Ashley Cir	Bowling Green	KY	42104	**800-605-1466**	270-793-1000
Greenwich Hospital 5 Perryridge Rd	Greenwich	CT	06830	**800-657-8355**	203-863-3000
Gulf Coast Medical Ctr 13681 Doctors Way	Fort Myers	FL	33912	**800-809-9906**	239-343-1000
Gundersen Lutheran Medical Ctr 1836 S Ave	La Crosse	WI	54601	**800-362-9567**	608-782-7300
Hannibal Regional Hospital 6500 Hospital Dr	Hannibal	MO	63401	**888-426-6425**	573-248-1300
Hanover Hospital 300 Highland Ave	Hanover	PA	17331	**800-673-2426**	717-637-3711
Harbor Hospital Ctr 3001 S Hanover St	Baltimore	MD	21225	**800-280-9006**	410-350-3200
Harlan ARH Hospital 81 Ballpark Rd	Harlan	KY	40831	**800-274-9375**	606-573-8100
Harrington Memorial Hospital (HMH) 100 S St	Southbridge	MA	01550	**800-416-6072**	508-765-9771
Harrisburg Hospital 111 S Front St	Harrisburg	PA	17101	**888-782-5678**	717-782-3131
Harrison Memorial Hospital 2520 Cherry Ave	Bremerton	WA	98310	**866-844-9355**	360-377-3911
Hartford Hospital 80 Seymour St	Hartford	CT	06102	**800-545-7664**	860-545-5000
Hays Medical Ctr (HMC) 2220 Canterbury Dr	Hays	KS	67601	**800-248-0073**	785-650-2759
Heart of Lancaster Regional Medical Ctr 1500 Highland Dr	Lititz	PA	17543	**800-999-6673**	717-625-5000
Henry Ford Hospital 2799 W Grand Blvd	Detroit	MI	48202	**800-999-4340**	313-916-2600
Heritage Valley Health System 1000 Dutch Ridge Rd	Beaver	PA	15009	**877-771-4847**	724-728-7000
High Point Regional Health System (HPRHS) 601 N Elm St PO Box HP-5	High Point	NC	27262	**877-878-7644**	336-878-6000
Hillcrest Baptist Medical Ctr 3000 Herring Ave	Waco	TX	76708	**800-793-6030**	254-202-2000
Hoag Hospital Irvine (HHI) 16200 Sand Canyon Ave	Irvine	CA	92618	**800-309-9729**	949-764-4624
Holmes Regional Medical Ctr 1350 Hickory St	Melbourne	FL	32901	**800-716-7737**	321-434-7000
Holy Cross Hospital 1500 Forest Glen Rd	Silver Spring	MD	20910	**800-358-9001**	301-754-7000
Holy Family Memorial Medical Ctr 2300 Western Ave PO Box 1450	Manitowoc	WI	54220	**800-994-3662**	920-320-2011
Holy Redeemer Hospital & Medical Ctr 1648 Huntingdon Pk	Meadowbrook	PA	19046	**800-818-4747**	215-947-3000
Holy Rosary Healthcare 2600 Wilson St	Miles City	MT	59301	**800-843-3820**	406-233-2600
Hospital of Saint Raphael 1450 Chapel St	New Haven	CT	06511	**888-700-6543**	203-789-3000
Hospital of the University of Pennsylvania 3400 Spruce St	Philadelphia	PA	19104	**800-789-7366**	215-662-4000
Howard County General Hospital 5755 Cedar Ln	Columbia	MD	21044	**866-323-4615**	410-740-7890
Hunt Regional Healthcare 4215 Joe Ramsey Blvd	Greenville	TX	75401	**855-854-2283**	903-408-5000
Hurley Medical Ctr 1 Hurley Plz	Flint	MI	48503	**800-336-8999**	810-262-9000
Hutchinson Regional Healthcare System 1701 E 23rd Ave	Hutchinson	KS	67502	**800-267-6891**	620-665-2000
Indiana University Hospital 550 N University Blvd	Indianapolis	IN	46202	**800-248-1199**	317-274-5000
INTEGRIS Baptist Regional Health Ctr 200 Second Ave SW	Miami	OK	74355	**888-951-2277**	918-542-6611
INTEGRIS Bass Baptist Health Ctr 600 S Monroe	Enid	OK	73701	**888-951-2277**	580-233-2300
INTEGRIS Southwest Medical Ctr 4401 S Western St	Oklahoma City	OK	73109	**888-949-3816**	405-636-7000
Intermountain Healthcare Logan Regional Hospital 500 E 1400 N	Logan	UT	84341	**800-442-4845**	435-716-1000

Name / Address	City	State	ZIP	Toll-Free	Phone
Irvington General Hospital 95 Old Short Hills Rd	West Orange	NJ	07052	**888-724-7123**	
Ivinson Memorial Hospital 255 N 30th St	Laramie	WY	82072	**877-858-0990**	307-742-2141
Jackson County Memorial Hospital 1200 E Pecan St	Altus	OK	73521	**800-595-0455**	580-379-5000
Jackson Purchase Medical Ctr 1099 Medical Ctr Cir	Mayfield	KY	42066	**800-994-6610**	270-251-4100
Jennie Stuart Medical Ctr 320 W 18th St PO Box 2400	Hopkinsville	KY	42241	**800-887-5762**	270-887-0100
Jersey Shore University Medical Ctr 1945 Rt 33	Neptune	NJ	07753	**800-560-9990**	732-775-5500
John D Archbold Memorial Hospital 915 Gordon Ave	Thomasville	GA	31792	**800-341-1009**	229-228-2000
John Muir Medical Ctr (JMMC) 1601 Ygnacio Valley Rd	Walnut Creek	CA	94598	**844-398-5376**	925-939-3000
Jordan Hospital 275 Sandwich St	Plymouth	MA	02360	**800-256-7326**	508-746-2000
Kadlec Regional Medical Ctr 888 Swift Blvd	Richland	WA	99352	**800-780-6067**	509-946-4611
Kaiser Permanente Foundation Hospital 9400 E Rosecrans Ave	Bellflower	CA	90706	**866-279-8954**	562-461-3000
Kaiser Permanente Harbor City Medical Ctr 25825 S Vermont Ave	Harbor City	CA	90710	**800-464-4000**	310-325-5111
Kaiser Permanente Hospital 441 N Lakeview Ave	Anaheim	CA	92807	**800-464-4000**	714-279-4000
Kaiser Permanente Medical Center-South Sacramento 6600 Bruceville Rd	Sacramento	CA	95823	**800-464-4000**	916-688-2000
Kaiser Permanente Medical Ctr 1200 El Camino Real	South San Francisco	CA	94080	**800-464-4000**	650-742-2000
Kaiser Permanente Parma Medical Ctr 12301 Snow Rd	Cleveland	OH	44130	**800-524-7372**	216-362-2000
Kaiser Permanente Riverside Medical Ctr 10800 Magnolia Ave *Cust Svc	Riverside	CA	92505	**800-464-4000***	951-353-2000
Kaiser Permanente Walnut Creek Medical Ctr 1425 S Main St	Walnut Creek	CA	94596	**800-464-4000**	925-295-4000
Kalispell Regional Medical Ctr 310 Sunnyview Ln	Kalispell	MT	59901	**800-228-1574**	406-752-5111
Katherine Shaw Bethea Hospital 403 E First St	Dixon	IL	61021	**800-582-9731**	815-288-5531
Kaweah Delta Hospital 400 W Mineral King Ave	Visalia	CA	93291	**800-717-5670**	559-624-2000
Kennedy Health System-Cherry Hill 2201 Chapel Ave W	Cherry Hill	NJ	08002	**866-224-0264**	856-488-6500
Kenosha Medical Ctr 6308 Eigth Ave	Kenosha	WI	53143	**800-994-6610**	262-656-2011
Kent General Hospital 640 S State St	Dover	DE	19901	**888-761-8300**	302-674-4700
Kent Hospital 455 Toll Gate Rd	Warwick	RI	02886	**800-892-9291**	401-737-7000
King's Daughters Medical Ctr 2201 Lexington Ave	Ashland	KY	41101	**888-377-5362**	606-408-4000
Kingman Regional Medical Ctr (KRMC) 3269 Stockton Hill Rd	Kingman	AZ	86409	**877-757-2101**	928-757-2101
Kishwaukee Community Hospital 1 Kish Hospital Dr	DeKalb	IL	60115	**800-397-1521**	815-756-1521
La Porte Hospital (LPH) 1007 Lincolnway PO Box 250	La Porte	IN	46350	**800-235-6204**	219-326-1234
Lahey Clinic Foundation Inc 41 Mall Rd	Burlington	MA	01805	**800-524-3955**	781-744-8000
Lake Region Hospital 712 S Cascade St	Fergus Falls	MN	56537	**800-439-6424**	218-736-8000
Lakeland Medical Center-Niles 31 N St Joseph Ave	Niles	MI	49120	**800-968-0115**	269-683-5510
Lakewood Hospital 14519 Detroit Ave	Lakewood	OH	44107	**866-588-2264**	216-521-4200
Lancaster Regional Medical Ctr 250 College Ave	Lancaster	PA	17603	**877-456-9617**	717-291-8211
Lankenau Medical Ctr 100 E Lancaster Ave	Wynnewood	PA	19096	**866-225-5654**	484-476-2000
Lapeer Regional Hospital 1375 N Main St	Lapeer	MI	48446	**888-327-0671**	810-667-5500
Laughlin Memorial Hospital 1420 Tuscolum Blvd	Greeneville	TN	37745	**800-852-7157**	423-787-5000
Lawrence Memorial Hospital (LMH) 325 Maine St	Lawrence	KS	66044	**800-749-4144**	785-505-5000
LDS Hospital 8th Ave & C St	Salt Lake City	UT	84143	**888-301-3880**	801-408-1100
Lea Regional Medical Ctr 5419 N Lovington Hwy	Hobbs	NM	88240	**877-492-8001**	575-492-5000
Legacy Emanuel Hospital & Health Ctr 2801 N Gantenbein Ave	Portland	OR	97227	**888-598-4232**	503-413-2200
Legacy Good Samaritan Hospital 1015 NW 22nd Ave	Portland	OR	97210	**800-733-9959**	503-335-3500
Legacy Salmon Creek Hospital 2211 NE 139th St	Vancouver	WA	98686	**877-270-5566**	360-487-1000
Lehigh Valley Health Network 700 E Broad St	Hazleton	PA	18201	**800-528-1234**	570-501-4000
Liberty Hospital 2525 Glenn Hendren Dr	Liberty	MO	64068	**800-344-3829**	816-781-7200
Lifeline Medical Assoc LLC 99 Cherry Hill Rd Ste 220	Parsippany	NJ	07054	**800-845-2785**	973-316-0307
Lima Memorial Hospital 1001 Bellefontaine Ave	Lima	OH	45804	**877-362-5672**	419-228-3335
Lodi Memorial Hospital 975 S Fairmont Ave	Lodi	CA	95240	**800-323-3360**	209-334-3411
Logan Regional Medical Ctr 20 Hospital Dr	Logan	WV	25601	**888-982-9144**	304-831-1101
Loma Linda University Medical Ctr 11234 Anderson St	Loma Linda	CA	92354	**877-558-6248**	909-558-4000
Long Island College Hospital (LICH) 339 Hicks St	Brooklyn	NY	11201	**800-227-8922**	718-780-1000
Lovelace Medical Ctr 5400 Gibson Blvd SE	Albuquerque	NM	87108	**888-281-6531**	505-262-7000
Lower Keys Medical Ctr 5900 College Rd	Key West	FL	33040	**800-355-2470**	305-294-5531
Loyola University Medical Ctr 2160 S First Ave	Maywood	IL	60153	**888-584-7888**	
Lutheran Hospital of Indiana 7950 W Jefferson Blvd	Fort Wayne	IN	46804	**800-444-2001**	260-435-7001
MacNeal Hospital 3249 S Oak Pk Ave	Berwyn	IL	60402	**888-622-6325**	708-783-9100
Maine Medical Ctr (MMC) 22 Bramhall St	Portland	ME	04102	**877-339-3107**	207-662-0111
Manatee Memorial Hospital 206 Second St E	Bradenton	FL	34208	**844-854-9613**	941-746-5111
Margaret Mary Community Hospital Inc 321 Mitchell Ave PO Box 226	Batesville	IN	47006	**800-562-5698**	812-934-6624
Maricopa Medical Ctr 2601 E Roosevelt St	Phoenix	AZ	85008	**866-749-2876**	602-344-5011
Marietta Memorial Hospital 401 Matthew St	Marietta	OH	45750	**800-523-3977**	740-374-1400
Marin General Hospital 250 Bon Air Rd	Greenbrae	CA	94904	**888-996-9644**	415-925-7000
Marina Del Rey Hospital 4650 Lincoln Blvd	Marina del Rey	CA	90292	**888-600-5600**	310-823-8911
Martha Jefferson Hospital (MJH) 500 Martha Jefferson Dr	Charlottesville	VA	22902	**888-652-6663**	434-654-7000
Martin Memorial Health Systems (MMHS) 200 SE Hospital Ave PO Box 9010	Stuart	FL	34994	**800-368-3375**	772-287-5200
Mary Washington Hospital 1001 Sam Perry Blvd	Fredericksburg	VA	22401	**800-395-2455**	540-741-1100
Marymount Hospital 12300 McCracken Rd	Garfield Heights	OH	44125	**800-801-2273**	216-581-0500
Maui Memorial Hospital 221 Mahalani St	Wailuku	HI	96793	**800-427-5940**	808-244-9056
Mayo Clinic Health System Austin 1000 First Dr NW	Austin	MN	55912	**888-609-4065**	507-433-7351
Mayo Clinic Health System Southwest Minnesota 1025 Marsh St	Mankato	MN	56001	**800-327-3721**	507-625-4031
Mayo Clinic Hospital 5777 E Mayo Blvd	Phoenix	AZ	85054	**888-266-0440**	480-342-2000
Meadville Medical Ctr (MMC) 751 Liberty St	Meadville	PA	16335	**800-254-5164**	814-333-5000
Medcenter One Hospital 300 N Seventh St	Bismarck	ND	58501	**800-932-8758**	701-323-6000
Medical Ctr Enterprise (MCE) 400 N Edwards St	Enterprise	AL	36330	**800-994-6610**	334-347-0584
Memorial Health System (MHS) *Central* 1400 E Boulder St	Colorado Springs	CO	80909	**877-422-3648**	719-365-5000
Memorial Healthcare Ctr 826 W King St	Owosso	MI	48867	**800-206-8706**	989-723-5211
Memorial Hermann Memorial City Hospital 921 Gessner Rd	Houston	TX	77024	**800-526-2121**	713-242-3000
Memorial Hospital 325 S Belmont St	York	PA	17405	**800-436-4326**	717-843-8623
Memorial Hospital & Health Care Ctr 800 W Ninth St	Jasper	IN	47546	**800-852-7279**	812-996-2345
Memorial Hospital of Rhode Island (MHRI) 111 Brewster St	Pawtucket	RI	02860	**800-647-4362**	401-729-2000
Memorial Hospital of South Bend 615 N Michigan St	South Bend	IN	46601	**800-850-7913**	574-647-1000
Memorial Hospital of Sweetwater County 1200 College Dr *General	Rock Springs	WY	82901	**866-571-0944***	307-362-3711
Memorial Medical Ctr 1615 Maple Ln	Ashland	WI	54806	**877-611-1988**	715-685-5500
Mercer County Joint Township Community Hospital 800 W Main St	Coldwater	OH	45828	**888-844-2341**	419-678-2341
Mercy 1235 E Cherokee	Springfield	MO	65804	**800-909-8326**	417-820-2000
Mercy General Health Partners *Muskegon Campus* 1500 E Sherman Blvd	Muskegon	MI	49444	**800-368-4125**	231-672-2000
Mercy Hospital 144 State St	Portland	ME	04101	**800-293-6583**	207-879-3000
Mercy Hospital & Trauma Ctr 1000 Mineral Pt Ave	Janesville	WI	53548	**800-756-4147**	608-756-6000
Mercy Iowa City 500 E Market St	Iowa City	IA	52245	**800-637-2942**	319-339-0300
Mercy Medical Ctr (MMC) 345 St Paul Pl	Baltimore	MD	21202	**800-636-3729**	410-332-9000
Mercy Medical Ctr North Iowa 1000 Fourth St SW	Mason City	IA	50401	**800-433-3883**	641-428-7000
Mercy Memorial Health Ctr (MMHC) 1011 14th Ave NW	Ardmore	OK	73401	**888-637-2937**	580-223-5400
Meritus Health 11116 Medical Campus Rd	Hagerstown	MD	21742	**800-735-2258**	301-790-8000
Methodist Hospital 1701 N Senate Blvd PO Box 1367	Indianapolis	IN	46202	**800-899-8448**	317-962-2000
Methodist Hospital of Southern California 300 W Huntington Dr	Arcadia	CA	91007	**888-388-2838**	626-898-8000
Metro Health Hospital 5900 Byron Ctr Ave	Wyoming	MI	49519	**800-968-0051**	616-252-7200
MetroHealth Medical Ctr 2500 MetroHealth Dr	Cleveland	OH	44109	**800-554-5251**	216-778-7800
Metroplex Hospital 2201 S Clear Creek Rd	Killeen	TX	76549	**800-926-7664**	254-526-7523
MetroWest Medical Ctr 115 Lincoln St	Framingham	MA	01702	**800-357-6060**	508-383-1000
Miami Valley Hospital 1 Wyoming St *All	Dayton	OH	45409	**800-544-0630***	937-208-8000
Mid Coast Hospital 123 Medical Ctr Dr	Brunswick	ME	04011	**800-994-6610**	207-729-0181
Middlesex Hospital 28 Crescent St	Middletown	CT	06457	**800-548-2394**	860-358-6000
Midland Memorial Hospital 2200 W Illinois Ave	Midland	TX	79701	**800-833-2916**	432-685-1111
Midlands Community Hospital 11111 S 84th St	Papillion	NE	68046	**855-524-4001**	402-593-3000
Mille Lacs Health System 200 Elm St N	Onamia	MN	56359	**877-535-3154**	320-532-3154

Name / Address	City	State	Zip	*Toll-Free*	*Phone*
Missouri Baptist Hospital of Sullivan 751 Sappington Bridge Rd	Sullivan	MO	63080	**800-939-2273**	573-468-4186
Missouri Baptist Medical Ctr 3015 N Ballas Rd	Saint Louis	MO	63131	**800-392-0936**	314-996-5000
Monmouth Medical Ctr 300 Second Ave	Long Branch	NJ	07740	**888-724-7123**	732-222-5200
Monroe Clinic Hospital 515 22nd Ave	Monroe	WI	53566	**800-338-0568**	608-324-2000
Moore Regional Hospital 155 Memorial Dr PO Box 3000	Pinehurst	NC	28374	**866-415-2778**	910-715-1000
Morris Hospital 150 W High St	Morris	IL	60450	**877-743-3123**	815-942-2932
Morristown Medical Ctr 100 Madison Ave	Morristown	NJ	07960	**877-310-7226**	973-971-5000
Morton Plant Hospital 300 Pinellas St	Clearwater	FL	33756	**800-229-2273**	727-462-7000
Moses H Cone Memorial Hospital 1200 N Elm St	Greensboro	NC	27401	**866-391-2734**	336-832-7000
Mount Carmel West Hospital 793 W State St	Columbus	OH	43222	**800-346-1009**	614-234-5000
Mount Nittany Medical Ctr 1800 E Pk Ave	State College	PA	16803	**866-686-6171**	814-231-7000
Mount Sinai Hospital Medical Ctr of Chicago California Ave 15th St	Chicago	IL	60608	**877-448-7848**	773-542-2000
Mount Sinai Medical Ctr, The 1 Gustave L Levy Pl	New York	NY	10029	**800-637-4627**	212-241-6500
Mount Sinai of Queens 25-10 30th Ave	Astoria	NY	11102	**800-968-7637**	718-932-1000
Mountain View Hospital 1000 East 100 North	Payson	UT	84651	**877-865-9738**	801-465-7000
Nacogdoches Medical Ctr 4920 NE Stallings Dr	Nacogdoches	TX	75965	**866-898-8446**	936-569-9481
Nashville General Hospital 1818 Albion St	Nashville	TN	37208	**800-318-2596**	615-341-4000
Natchitoches Parish Hospital 501 Keyser Ave	Natchitoches	LA	71457	**888-728-8383**	318-214-4200
Nebraska Medical Ctr, The 4350 Dewey Ave	Omaha	NE	68105	**800-922-0000**	402-552-2000
New England Baptist Hospital 125 Parker Hill Ave	Boston	MA	02120	**855-370-6324**	617-754-5000
New Hanover Regional Medical Ctr 2131 S 17th St	Wilmington	NC	28401	**877-228-8135**	910-343-7000
New York Presbyterian Hospital 525 E 68th St	New York	NY	10021	**888-694-5700**	212-746-5454
Newport Hospital (NH) 11 Friendship St	Newport	RI	02840	**866-401-0002**	401-845-1646
North Central Bronx Hospital 3424 Kossuth Ave	Bronx	NY	10467	**877-207-2134**	718-519-5000
North Fulton Hospital 3000 Hospital Blvd	Roswell	GA	30076	**877-228-3638**	770-751-2500
North Shore Medical Ctr 1100 NW 95th St	Miami	FL	33150	**800-984-3434**	305-835-6000
North Shore University Hospital 300 Community Dr	Manhasset	NY	11030	**888-214-4065**	516-562-0100
North Suburban Medical Ctr (NSMC) 9191 Grant St	Thornton	CO	80229	**877-647-7440**	303-451-7800
Northern Westchester Hospital 400 E Main St	Mount Kisco	NY	10549	**877-469-4362**	914-666-1200
Northport Medical Ctr 2700 Hospital Dr	Northport	AL	35476	**866-840-0750**	205-333-4500
Northwest Hospital & Medical Ctr 1550 N 115th St	Seattle	WA	98133	**877-694-4677**	206-364-0500
Northwest Hospital Ctr 5401 Old Ct Rd	Randallstown	MD	21133	**800-876-1175**	410-521-2200
Northwest Texas Hospital 1501 S Coulter	Amarillo	TX	79106	**800-887-1114**	806-354-1000
Norwegian-American Hospital 1044 N Francisco St	Chicago	IL	60622	**877-624-9333**	773-292-8200
Oakhill Hospital 11375 Cortez Blvd	Brooksville	FL	34613	**877-442-2362**	352-596-6632
Oakwood Annapolis Hospital 33155 Annapolis Rd	Wayne	MI	48184	**800-543-9355**	734-467-4000
Oakwood Heritage Hospital 10000 Telegraph Rd	Taylor	MI	48180	**800-543-9355**	313-295-5000
Oakwood Hospital & Medical Ctr 18101 Oakwood Blvd	Dearborn	MI	48124	**800-543-9355**	313-593-7000
Oakwood Southshore Medical Ctr 5450 Fort St	Trenton	MI	48183	**800-543-9355**	734-671-3800
Ocean Medical Ctr (OMC) 425 Jack Martin Blvd	Brick	NJ	08724	**800-560-9990**	732-840-2200
Ochsner Clinic Foundation Hospital 1514 Jefferson Hwy	New Orleans	LA	70121	**800-343-0269**	504-842-3000
Ochsner Medical Ctr West Bank 2500 Belle Chasse Hwy	Gretna	LA	70056	**800-231-5257**	504-391-5454
Oconomowoc Memorial Hospital 791 Summit Ave	Oconomowoc	WI	53066	**800-242-0313**	262-569-9400
Ogden Regional Medical Ctr 5475 Adams Ave Pkwy	Ogden	UT	84405	**877-870-3745**	801-479-2111
Olympic Medical Ctr 939 Caroline St	Port Angeles	WA	98362	**888-362-6260**	360-417-7000
Orange City Area Health System 1000 Lincoln Cir SE	Orange City	IA	51041	**800-808-6264**	712-737-4984
Orange Coast Memorial Medical Ctr (OCMMC) 9920 Talbert Ave	Fountain Valley	CA	92708	**877-597-4777**	714-378-7000
Orange Regional Medical Ctr 60 Prospect Ave	Middletown	NY	10940	**888-321-6762**	845-343-2424
Oregon Health & Science University Hospital 3181 SW Sam Jackson Pk Rd	Portland	OR	97239	**800-292-4466**	503-494-8311
Orlando Regional Medical Ctr (ORMC) 1414 Kuhl Ave	Orlando	FL	32806	**800-424-6998**	321-841-5111
OSF Saint Anthony Medical Ctr 5666 E State St	Rockford	IL	61108	**800-343-3185**	815-226-2000
OSF Saint Francis Medical Ctr 530 NE Glen Oak Ave	Peoria	IL	61637	**888-627-5673**	309-655-2000
OSF Saint Mary Medical Ctr 3333 N Seminary St	Galesburg	IL	61401	**877-795-0416**	309-344-3161
Ottumwa Regional Health Ctr 1001 Pennsylvania Ave	Ottumwa	IA	52501	**800-933-6742**	641-684-2300
Ouachita County Medical Ctr (OCMC) PO Box 797	Camden	AR	71711	**877-836-2472**	870-836-1000
Our Lady of Lourdes Medical Ctr 1600 Haddon Ave	Camden	NJ	08103	**888-568-7337**	856-757-3500
Owensboro Medical Health Systems (OMHS) 811 E Parish Ave PO Box 20007	Owensboro	KY	42303	**877-888-6647**	270-688-2000
Palestine Regional Medical Ctr 2900 S Loop 256	Palestine	TX	75801	**800-222-1222**	903-731-1000
Palms West Hospital (PWH) 13001 Southern Blvd	Loxahatchee	FL	33470	**877-549-9337**	561-798-3300
Parkland Health Ctr 1101 W Liberty St	Farmington	MO	63640	**800-734-3944**	573-756-6451
Parkridge East Hospital 941 Spring Creek Rd	Chattanooga	TN	37412	**800-605-1527**	423-894-7870
Parkview Hospital 2200 Randallia Dr	Fort Wayne	IN	46805	**888-737-9311**	260-373-4000
Parkview Medical Ctr 400 W 16th St	Pueblo	CO	81003	**800-543-4046**	719-584-4000
Peace River Regional Medical Ctr 2500 Harbor Blvd	Port Charlotte	FL	33952	**888-941-2495**	941-766-4122
PeaceHealth St Joseph Medical Ctr 2901 Squalicum Pkwy	Bellingham	WA	98225	**800-541-7209**	360-734-5400
Pender Memorial Hospital 507 E Fremont St	Burgaw	NC	28425	**888-815-5188**	910-259-5451
Peninsula Regional Medical Ctr 100 E Carroll St	Salisbury	MD	21801	**800-543-7780**	410-546-6400
Penn Presbyterian Medical Ctr (PPMC) 39th & Market Sts	Philadelphia	PA	19104	**800-789-7366**	215-662-8000
Penn State Milton S Hershey Medical Ctr 500 University Dr	Hershey	PA	17033	**800-731-3032**	717-531-8521
Pennsylvania Hospital 800 Spruce St	Philadelphia	PA	19107	**800-789-7366**	215-829-3000
Penrose Hospital 2222 N Nevada Ave	Colorado Springs	CO	80907	**800-398-2045**	719-776-5000
Phoebe Putney Memorial Hospital 417 W Third Ave PO Box 3770	Albany	GA	31706	**877-312-1167**	229-312-1000
Piedmont Medical Ctr 222 S Herlong Ave	Rock Hill	SC	29732	**800-222-4218**	803-329-1234
Pinnacle Health Hospital at Community General 4300 Londonderry Rd	Harrisburg	PA	17109	**888-782-5678**	717-652-3000
Placentia-Linda Hospital 1301 N Rose Dr	Placentia	CA	92870	**888-754-9729**	714-993-2000
Plains Regional Medical Ctr 2100 N ML King Blvd	Clovis	NM	88101	**800-923-6980**	505-769-2141
POH Regional Medical Ctr 50 N Perry St	Pontiac	MI	48342	**888-327-0671**	248-338-5000
Poplar Bluff Regional Medical Ctr 2620 N Westwood Blvd	Poplar Bluff	MO	63901	**855-444-7276**	573-785-7721
Poplar Bluff Regional Medical Ctr South Campus 3100 Oak Grove Rd	Poplar Bluff	MO	63901	**855-444-7276**	
Port Huron Hospital (PHH) 1221 Pine Grove Ave	Port Huron	MI	48060	**888-327-0671**	810-987-5000
Portsmouth Regional Hospital 333 Borthwick Ave	Portsmouth	NH	03801	**800-685-8282**	603-436-5110
Poudre Valley Hospital 1024 S Lemay Ave	Fort Collins	CO	80524	**800-994-6610**	970-495-7000
Prairie Lakes Hospital & Care Ctr 401 Ninth Ave NW	Watertown	SD	57201	**877-917-7547**	605-882-7000
Pratt Regional Medical Ctr Corp 200 Commodore St	Pratt	KS	67124	**877-572-2787**	620-672-7451
Presbyterian Hospital 1100 Central Ave SE	Albuquerque	NM	87106	**888-977-2333**	505-841-1234
Presbyterian Kaseman Hospital 8300 Constitution Ave NE	Albuquerque	NM	87110	**800-356-2219**	505-291-2000
ProMedica 2142 N Cove Blvd	Toledo	OH	43606	**866-865-4677**	419-291-5437
Providence Centralia Hospital 914 S Scheuber Rd *Help Line	Centralia	WA	98531	**877-736-2803***	360-736-2803
Providence Hospitals 2435 Forest Dr	Columbia	SC	29204	**877-256-5381**	803-256-5300
Providence Medford Medical Ctr 1111 Crater Lk Ave	Medford	OR	97504	**877-541-0588**	541-732-5000
Providence Medical Ctr 8929 Parallel Pkwy	Kansas City	KS	66112	**800-281-7777**	913-596-4000
Providence Portland Medical Ctr 4805 NE Glisan St	Portland	OR	97213	**800-833-8899**	503-215-1111
Providence Sacred Heart Medical Ctr 101 W Eigth Ave	Spokane	WA	99204	**800-442-8534**	509-474-3170
Providence Saint Peter Hospital (PSPH) 413 Lilly Rd NE	Olympia	WA	98506	**888-492-9480**	360-491-9480
Providence Saint Vincent Medical Ctr 9205 SW Barnes Rd Ste 20	Portland	OR	97225	**800-677-6752**	503-216-2401
Providence St Mary Medical Ctr 401 W Poplar St PO Box 1477	Walla Walla	WA	99362	**877-215-7833**	509-525-3320
Qualis Health PO Box 33400	Seattle	WA	98133	**800-949-7536**	206-364-9700
Quality of Life Health Services Inc 1411 Piedmont Cutoff PO Box 97	Gadsden	AL	35902	**888-490-0131**	256-492-0131
Queens Hospital Ctr 82-68 164th St	Jamaica	NY	11432	**888-692-6116**	718-883-3000
Raulerson Hospital 1796 Hwy 441 N	Okeechobee	FL	34972	**877-549-9337**	863-763-2151
Redlands Community Hospital Foundation PO Box 3391	Redlands	CA	92373	**888-397-4999**	909-335-5500
Regional Medical Ctr, The 3000 St Matthews Rd	Orangeburg	SC	29118	**800-476-3377**	803-395-2200
Reston Hospital Ctr 1850 Town Ctr Pkwy *General	Reston	VA	20190	**888-327-8882***	703-689-9000
Retreat Hospital 2621 Grove Ave	Richmond	VA	23220	**800-888-3627**	804-254-5100
Richland Hospital Inc, The 333 E Second St	Richland Center	WI	53581	**888-467-7485**	608-647-6321
Riddle Memorial Hospital 1068 W Baltimore Pike	Media	PA	19063	**866-225-5654**	484-227-9400
Rideout Memorial Hospital 726 Fourth St	Marysville	CA	95901	**888-923-3800**	530-749-4300
Ridgeview Medical Ctr (RMC) 500 S Maple St	Waconia	MN	55387	**800-967-4620**	952-442-2191

Name / Address	City	State	ZIP	Toll-Free	Phone
River Oaks Hospital 1525 River Oaks Rd W	New Orleans	LA	70123	**800-366-1740**	504-734-1740
River Parishes Hospital 500 Rue De Sante	Laplace	LA	70068	**800-231-5275**	985-652-7000
Riverside Methodist Hospital 3535 Olentangy River Rd	Columbus	OH	43214	**800-837-7555**	614-566-5000
Riverton Memorial Hospital LLC 2100 W Sunset Dr	Riverton	WY	82501	**888-982-9144**	307-856-4161
Riverview Hospital 395 Westfield Rd	Noblesville	IN	46060	**800-523-6001**	317-773-0760
Robert J Dole VA Medical Center 5500 E Kellogg St	Wichita	KS	67218	**888-878-6881**	316-685-2221
Robert Packer Hospital 1 Guthrie Sq	Sayre	PA	18840	**888-448-8474**	570-888-6666
Robert Wood Johnson University Hospital 1 Robert Wood Johnson Pl	New Brunswick	NJ	08901	**888-637-9584**	732-828-3000
Rochester General Health System (RGHS) 1425 Portland Ave	Rochester	NY	14621	**877-922-5465**	585-922-4000
Rose Medical Ctr 4567 E Ninth Ave	Denver	CO	80220	**866-746-4282**	303-320-2121
Rowan Regional Medical Ctr (RRMC) 612 Mocksville Ave	Salisbury	NC	28144	**888-844-0080**	704-210-5000
Rush-Copley Medical Ctr (RCMC) 2000 Ogden Ave	Aurora	IL	60504	**866-426-7539**	630-978-6200
Sacred Heart HealthCare System 421 Chew St	Allentown	PA	18102	**800-994-6610**	610-776-4500
Sacred Heart Hospital 900 W Clairemont Ave	Eau Claire	WI	54701	**888-445-4554**	715-717-4121
Sacred Heart Hospital of Pensacola 5151 N Ninth Ave	Pensacola	FL	32504	**800-874-1026**	850-416-7000
Sacred Heart Medical Ctr 1255 Hilyard St	Eugene	OR	97401	**800-288-7444**	541-686-7300
Saint Agnes HealthCare 900 S Caton Ave	Baltimore	MD	21229	**800-875-8750**	410-368-6000
Saint Alexius Hospital *Broadway Campus* 3933 S Broadway	Saint Louis	MO	63118	**800-245-1431**	314-865-7000
Saint Alphonsus Regional Medical Ctr 1055 N Curtis Rd	Boise	ID	83706	**877-401-3627**	208-367-2121
Saint Anthony Hospital 1000 N Lee St	Oklahoma City	OK	73101	**800-227-6964**	405-272-7000
Saint Anthony's Medical Ctr 10010 Kennerly Rd	Saint Louis	MO	63128	**800-554-9550**	314-525-1000
Saint Barnabas Medical Ctr 94 Old Short Hills Rd	West Orange	NJ	07052	**888-724-7123**	973-322-5000
Saint Charles Mercy Hospital 2600 Navarre Ave	Oregon	OH	43616	**888-987-6372**	419-696-7200
Saint Cloud Hospital 1406 Sixth Ave	Saint Cloud	MN	56303	**800-835-6652**	320-251-2700
Saint Elizabeth Hospital 1506 S Oneida St	Appleton	WI	54915	**800-223-7332**	920-738-2000
Saint Francis Health Ctr 1700 SW Seventh St	Topeka	KS	66606	**855-578-3726**	785-295-8000
Saint Francis Hospital & Medical Ctr 114 Woodland St	Hartford	CT	06105	**800-993-4312**	860-714-4000
Saint Francis Medical Ctr 601 Hamilton Ave	Trenton	NJ	08629	**888-216-3293**	609-599-5000
Saint John's Hospital 800 E Carpenter St	Springfield	IL	62702	**855-228-4438**	217-544-6464
Saint Joseph Hospital 700 Broadway	Fort Wayne	IN	46802	**800-258-0974**	260-425-3000
Saint Joseph Medical Ctr (SJMC) 1717 S J St	Tacoma	WA	98405	**888-825-3227**	
Saint Joseph Mercy Ann Arbor 5301 McAuley Dr	Ypsilanti	MI	48197	**866-522-8268**	734-712-3456
Saint Joseph Mercy Oakland 44405 Woodward Ave	Pontiac	MI	48341	**800-396-1313**	248-858-3000
Saint Joseph's Hospital 2661 County Hwy I	Chippewa Falls	WI	54729	**877-723-1811**	715-723-1811
Saint Joseph's Hospital Health Ctr 301 Prospect Ave	Syracuse	NY	13203	**888-785-6371**	315-448-5111
Saint Luke's Hospital & Regional Trauma Ctr 915 E First St	Duluth	MN	55805	**866-261-5915**	218-249-5555
Saint Luke's Hospital of New Bedford 101 Page St	New Bedford	MA	02740	**800-497-1727**	508-997-1515
Saint Luke's Regional Medical Ctr 2720 Stone Pk Blvd	Sioux City	IA	51104	**800-352-4660**	712-279-3500
Saint Mary Mercy Hospital 36475 Five-Mile Rd	Livonia	MI	48154	**800-464-7492**	734-655-4800
Saint Mary's Health Care System 1230 Baxter St	Athens	GA	30606	**800-233-7864**	706-389-3000
Saint Mary's Hospital 2251 N Shore Dr *Cust Svc	Rhinelander	WI	54501	**800-578-0840***	715-361-2000
Saint Mary's Hospital & Regional Medical Ctr 2635 N Seventh St	Grand Junction	CO	81502	**800-458-3888**	
Saint Mary's Hospital Medical Ctr 1726 Shawano Ave	Green Bay	WI	54303	**800-666-5606**	920-498-4200
Saint Mary-Corwin Medical Ctr 1008 Minnequa Ave	Pueblo	CO	81004	**800-228-4039**	719-557-4000
Saint Rita's Medical Ctr (SRMC) 730 W Market St	Lima	OH	45801	**800-232-7762**	419-227-3361
Saint Thomas Hospital 4220 HaRding Rd	Nashville	TN	37205	**800-400-5800**	615-222-2111
Saint Vincent Charity Hospital (SVCH) 2351 E 22nd St	Cleveland	OH	44115	**800-750-0750**	216-861-6200
Saint Vincent Hospital 835 S Van Buren St	Green Bay	WI	54301	**800-236-3030**	920-433-0111
Saint Vincent Hospital-Worcester Medical Ctr 123 Summer St	Worcester	MA	01608	**877-633-2368**	508-363-5000
Saint Vincent's Medical Ctr 2800 Main St	Bridgeport	CT	06606	**877-255-7847**	203-576-6000
Salem Hospital 665 Winter St SE	Salem	OR	97301	**800-876-1718**	
Salinas Valley Memorial Hospital (SVMH) 450 E Romie Ln	Salinas	CA	93901	**800-813-4673**	831-757-4333
Samaritan Medical Ctr 830 Washington St	Watertown	NY	13601	**877-888-6138**	315-785-4000
San Francisco General Hospital Medical Ctr 1001 Potrero Ave Ste 1E21	San Francisco	CA	94110	**800-723-7140**	415-206-8426
Sarah Bush Lincoln Health Ctr (SBLHC) 1000 Health Ctr Dr PO Box 372	Mattoon	IL	61938	**800-345-3191**	217-258-2525
Sarasota Memorial Hospital 1700 S Tamiami Trl	Sarasota	FL	34239	**800-764-8255**	941-917-9000
Scheurer Hospital Inc 170 N Caseville Rd	Pigeon	MI	48755	**800-690-9972**	989-453-3223
Schneck Medical Ctr 411 W Tipton St	Seymour	IN	47274	**800-234-9222**	812-522-2349
Scott & White Memorial Hospital 2401 S 31st St	Temple	TX	76508	**800-792-3710**	254-724-2111
Scripps Green Hospital 10666 N Torrey Pines Rd	La Jolla	CA	92037	**800-727-4777**	858-455-9100
Scripps Memorial Hospital-La Jolla 9888 Genesee Ave	La Jolla	CA	92037	**800-727-4777**	
Sentara Careplex Hospital 3000 Coliseum Dr	Hampton	VA	23666	**800-736-8272**	757-736-1000
Sentara Obici Hospital 2800 Godwin Blvd	Suffolk	VA	23434	**800-736-8272**	757-934-4000
Sentara Virginia Beach General Hospital 1060 First Colonial Rd	Virginia Beach	VA	23454	**800-736-8272**	757-395-8000
Seton Medical Ctr 1900 Sullivan Ave	Daly City	CA	94015	**800-371-2176**	650-992-4000
Shands Hospital at the University of Florida 1600 SW Archer Rd	Gainesville	FL	32610	**855-483-7546**	352-265-0111
Shannon Medical Ctr (SMC) 120 E Harris Ave	San Angelo	TX	76903	**800-368-1019**	325-653-6741
Sharp Grossmont Hospital (SGH) 5555 Grossmont Ctr Dr	La Mesa	CA	91942	**800-827-4277**	619-740-6000
Shore Memorial Hospital 9507 Hospital Ave PO Box 17	Nassawadox	VA	23413	**800-834-7035**	757-414-8000
Sierra Vista Regional Medical Ctr (SVRMC) 1010 Murray Ave	San Luis Obispo	CA	93405	**866-904-6871**	805-546-7600
Sinai Grace Hospital 6071 W Outer Dr	Detroit	MI	48235	**888-362-2500**	313-966-3300
SJH Regional Medical Ctr (SJHRMC) 1505 W Sherman Ave	Vineland	NJ	08360	**800-770-7547**	856-641-8000
Skaggs Community Health Ctr 545 Branson Landing Blvd PO Box 650	Branson	MO	65615	**800-994-6610**	417-335-7000
Skyline Medical Ctr 3441 Dickerson Pike	Nashville	TN	37207	**800-242-5662**	615-769-2000
Soldiers + Sailors Memorial Hospital 32-36 Central Ave	Wellsboro	PA	16901	**800-808-5287**	570-723-7764
Somerset Medical Ctr (SMC) 110 Rehill Ave	Somerville	NJ	08876	**888-637-9584**	908-685-2200
Sonora Regional Medical Ctr (SRMC) 1000 Greenly Rd *Compliance	Sonora	CA	95370	**877-336-3566***	209-536-5000
South Nassau Communities Hospital 1 Healthy Way	Oceanside	NY	11572	**877-768-8462**	516-632-3000
South Shore Hospital 55 Fogg Rd	South Weymouth	MA	02190	**800-439-2370**	781-340-8000
Southeast Georgia Health System Brunswick Campus 2415 Parkwood Dr	Brunswick	GA	31520	**844-882-7227**	912-466-7000
Southeast Missouri Hospital (SMH) 1701 Lacey St	Cape Girardeau	MO	63701	**800-800-5123**	573-334-4822
Southwest General Hospital (SGH) 7400 Barlite Blvd	San Antonio	TX	78224	**877-898-6080**	210-921-2000
Southwestern Vermont Medical Ctr 100 Hospital Dr	Bennington	VT	05201	**800-422-6237**	802-442-6361
Sparrow Health System 1215 E Michigan Ave	Lansing	MI	48912	**800-772-7769**	517-364-1000
Spartanburg Regional Medical Ctr (SRMC) 101 E Wood St	Spartanburg	SC	29303	**800-318-2596**	864-560-6000
Spectrum Health Blodgett Campus 100 Michigan St NE	Grand Rapids	MI	49503	**866-989-7999**	616-774-7444
SSM Health 620 E Monroe St	Mexico	MO	65265	**844-776-9355**	573-582-5000
St Agnes Hospital 430 E Div St	Fond du Lac	WI	54935	**800-922-3400**	920-929-2300
St Alexius Medical Ctr 900 E Broadway Ave	Bismarck	ND	58501	**877-530-5550**	701-530-7755
St John Detroit Riverview Ctr 7733 E Jefferson Ave	Detroit	MI	48214	**866-501-3627**	
St John Providence Health System 28000 Dequindre	Warren	MI	48092	**866-501-3627**	
St Mary's of Michigan (STMH) 800 S Washington Ave	Saginaw	MI	48601	**877-738-6672**	989-907-8115
St Petersburg General Hospital 6500 38th Ave N	Saint Petersburg	FL	33710	**800-733-0610**	727-384-1414
St. John Providence 28000 Dequindre	Warren	MI	48092	**866-501-3627**	586-573-5000
Stonewall Jackson Memorial Hospital (SJMH) 230 Hospital Plaza	Weston	WV	26452	**866-637-0471**	304-269-8000
Stormont-Vail Regional Health Ctr 1500 SW Tenth Ave	Topeka	KS	66604	**800-432-2951**	785-354-6000
Strong Memorial Hospital *University of Rochester Medical Ctr* 601 Elmwood Ave	Rochester	NY	14642	**800-999-6673**	585-275-2100
Summa Barberton Hospital 155 Fifth St NE	Barberton	OH	44203	**888-905-6071**	330-615-3000
Sutter Auburn Faith Community Hospital (SAFH) 11815 Education St	Auburn	CA	95602	**800-478-8837**	530-888-4500
Sutter Medical Ctr of Santa Rosa 3325 Chanate Rd	Santa Rosa	CA	95404	**800-651-5111**	707-576-4006
SwedishAmerican Hospital 1401 E State St	Rockford	IL	61104	**800-322-4724**	815-968-4400
Tacoma General Hospital 315 MLK Jr Way	Tacoma	WA	98405	**800-552-1419**	253-403-1000
Terre Haute Regional Hospital (THRH) 3901 S Seventh St	Terre Haute	IN	47802	**866-270-2311**	812-232-0021
Terrebonne General Medical Ctr (TGMC) 8166 Main St	Houma	LA	70360	**888-850-6270**	985-873-4141
Texas Healthcare PLLC 2821 Lackland Rd Ste 300	Fort Worth	TX	76116	**877-238-6200**	817-378-3640
Theda Clark Medical Ctr 130 Second St	Neenah	WI	54956	**800-236-3122**	920-729-3100

Classified Section

Name / Address	City	State	Zip	Toll-Free	Phone
Thibodaux Regional Medical Ctr (TRMC)					
602 N Acadia Rd	Thibodaux	LA	70301	**800-822-8442**	985-447-5500
Thomas Hospital					
750 Morphy Ave	Fairhope	AL	36532	**800-422-2027**	251-928-2375
Thomas Jefferson University Hospital					
111 S 11th St	Philadelphia	PA	19107	**800-533-3669**	215-955-6000
Thomasville Medical Ctr					
207 Old Lexington Rd	Thomasville	NC	27360	**888-844-0080**	336-472-2000
Tift Regional Medical Ctr					
1641 Madison Ave	Tifton	GA	31794	**800-648-1935**	229-382-7120
TJ Samson Community Hospital					
1301 N Race St	Glasgow	KY	42141	**800-651-5635**	270-651-4444
Torrance Memorial Medical Ctr					
3330 Lomita Blvd	Torrance	CA	90505	**866-843-2572**	310-325-9110
Town & Country Hospital					
6001 Webb Rd	Tampa	FL	33615	**866-463-7449**	813-888-7060
Triangle Orthopedic Assoc PA					
120 William Penn Plz	Durham	NC	27704	**800-359-3053**	919-220-5255
Trident Medical Ctr					
9330 Medical Plz Dr	Charleston	SC	29406	**866-492-9085**	843-797-7000
Trinity Hospital Saint Joseph's					
1 W Burdick Expy	Minot	ND	58701	**800-247-1316**	701-857-5000
Trinity Medical Ctr					
1 Burdick Expy W PO Box 5020	Minot	ND	58702	**800-862-0005**	701-857-5000
Trinity Medical Ctr West					
4000 Johnson Rd	Steubenville	OH	43952	**877-271-4176**	740-264-8000
Tristar Southern Hills Medical Ctr					
391 Wallace Rd	Nashville	TN	37211	**800-242-5662**	615-781-4000
Tucson Medical Ctr					
5301 E Grant Rd	Tucson	AZ	85712	**800-526-5353**	520-327-5461
Tufts Medical Ctr (TMC)					
800 Washington St	Boston	MA	02111	**866-220-3699**	617-636-5000
Tulane Medical Ctr (TMC)					
1415 Tulane Ave	New Orleans	LA	70112	**800-588-5800**	504-988-5263
Twin County Regional Hospital					
200 Hospital Dr	Galax	VA	24333	**800-295-3342**	276-236-8181
UAB Medical West					
995 Ninth Ave SW	Bessemer	AL	35022	**800-994-6610**	205-481-7000
UAMS Medical Ctr					
4301 W Markham St	Little Rock	AR	72205	**877-467-6560**	501-686-7000
UC Irvine Healthcare					
101 the City Dr S	Orange	CA	92868	**877-824-3627**	714-456-7890
UH Parma Medical Center (PCGH)					
7007 Powers Blvd	Parma	OH	44129	**855-292-4292**	440-743-3000
United Hospital					
333 N Smith Ave	Saint Paul	MN	55102	**800-869-1320**	651-241-8000
United Hospital Ctr					
327 Medical pk Dr	Bridgeport	WV	26330	**800-607-8888**	304-624-2121
University Health Care System					
1350 Walton Way	Augusta	GA	30901	**866-591-2502**	706-722-9011
University Hospital					
4502 Medical Dr	San Antonio	TX	78229	**866-864-5226**	210-358-4000
University Hospital SUNY Upstate Medical University					
750 E Adams St	Syracuse	NY	13210	**877-464-5540**	315-464-5540
University Hospitals of Cleveland					
11100 Euclid Ave	Cleveland	OH	44106	**866-844-2273**	216-844-1000
University Medical Ctr at Princeton (UMCP)					
253 Witherspoon St	Princeton	NJ	08540	**877-932-8935**	609-497-4304
University of Chicago Medical Ctr					
5841 S Maryland Ave	Chicago	IL	60637	**888-824-0200**	773-702-1000
University of Connecticut Health Ctr					
John Dempsey Hospital					
263 Farmington Ave	Farmington	CT	06030	**800-535-6232**	860-679-2000
University of Illinois Medical Ctr					
1740 W Taylor St	Chicago	IL	60612	**866-600-2273**	312-996-3900
University of Louisville Hospital					
530 S Jackson St	Louisville	KY	40202	**800-891-0947**	502-562-3000
University of Minnesota Medical Ctr Fairview - University Campus					
500 Harvard St	Minneapolis	MN	55455	**800-688-5252**	612-273-3000
University of Nebraska Medical Ctr					
42nd and Emile	Omaha	NE	68198	**877-726-4727**	402-559-4000
University of Pittsburgh Medical Ctr (UPMC)					
Horizon 110 N Main St	Greenville	PA	16125	**888-447-1122**	724-588-2100
Passavant					
9100 Babcock Blvd	Pittsburgh	PA	15237	**800-533-8762**	412-367-6700
Shadyside					
5230 Centre Ave	Pittsburgh	PA	15232	**800-533-8762**	412-623-2121
South Side 2000 Mary St	Pittsburgh	PA	15203	**800-533-8762**	412-488-5550
University of Texas Medical Branch Hospitals					
301 University Blvd	Galveston	TX	77555	**800-201-0527**	409-772-1011
University of Toledo Medical Center, The					
3000 Arlington Ave	Toledo	OH	43614	**800-321-8383**	419-383-4000
University of Vermont Medical Center, The (FAHC)					
111 Colchester Ave	Burlington	VT	05401	**800-358-1144**	802-847-0000
University of Virginia Health System					
1215 Lee St	Charlottesville	VA	22908	**800-251-3627**	434-924-0211
University of Wisconsin Hospital & Clinics					
600 Highland Ave	Madison	WI	53792	**800-323-8942**	608-263-6400
UPMC Mercy Hospital					
1400 Locust St	Pittsburgh	PA	15219	**800-446-3797**	412-232-8111
UPMC Presbyterian					
200 Lothrop St	Pittsburgh	PA	15213	**877-986-9862**	412-647-8762
Upper Valley Medical Ctr (UVMC)					
3130 N County Rd 25-A	Troy	OH	45373	**866-608-3463**	937-440-4000
UVA Culpeper Hospital					
501 Sunset Ln	Culpeper	VA	22701	**866-608-4749**	540-829-4100
UW Medicine Eastside Hospital & Specialty					
3100 Northup Way	Bellevue	WA	98004	**877-520-5000**	
Valdese General Hospital (VGH)					
720 Malcolm Blvd Ste 200	Valdese	NC	28690	**800-994-6610**	828-874-2251
Valley Baptist Medical Ctr Brownsville					
1040 W Jefferson St	Brownsville	TX	78520	**855-720-7448**	956-698-5400
Valley Health System					
223 N Van Dien Ave	Ridgewood	NJ	07450	**800-825-5391**	201-447-8000
Valley Medical Ctr					
400 S 43rd St	Renton	WA	98055	**855-923-4633**	425-228-3450
Valley Regional Medical Ctr					
100-A E Alton Gloor Blvd	Brownsville	TX	78526	**877-813-6455**	956-350-7000
Vanderbilt University Medical Ctr					
1215 21st Ave S	Nashville	TN	37232	**877-936-8422**	615-322-5000
Vassar Bros Medical Ctr					
45 Reade Pl	Poughkeepsie	NY	12601	**877-729-2444**	845-454-8500
Vaughan Regional Medical Ctr					
1015 Medical Ctr Pkwy	Selma	AL	36701	**800-994-6610**	334-418-4100
Ventura County Medical Center					
3291 Loma Vista Rd	Ventura	CA	93003	**800-369-7437**	805-652-6000
Virginia Baptist Hospital					
3300 Rivermont Ave	Lynchburg	VA	24503	**866-749-4455**	434-947-4000
Washington Hospital Ctr					
110 Irving St NW	Washington	DC	20010	**855-546-1686**	202-877-7000
Waukesha Memorial Hospital					
725 American Ave	Waukesha	WI	53188	**800-326-2011**	262-928-1000
Weirton Medical Ctr					
601 Colliers Way	Weirton	WV	26062	**800-994-6610**	304-797-6000
Wentworth-Douglass Hospital					
789 Central Ave	Dover	NH	03820	**877-201-7100**	603-742-5252
Wesley Long Community Hospital					
501 N Elam Ave	Greensboro	NC	27403	**866-391-2734**	336-832-1000
Wesley Medical Ctr					
5001 Hardy St	Hattiesburg	MS	39402	**877-456-9617**	601-268-8000
West Suburban Hospital Medical Ctr					
3 Erie Ct	Oak Park	IL	60302	**866-938-7256**	708-383-6200
West Valley Medical Ctr					
1717 Arlington Ave	Caldwell	ID	83605	**866-270-2311**	208-459-4641
Westerly Hospital					
25 Wells St	Westerly	RI	02891	**800-933-5960**	401-596-6000
Wheaton Franciscan Healthcare					
3801 Spring St	Racine	WI	53405	**877-304-6332**	262-687-4011
All Saints 3801 Spring St	Racine	WI	53405	**877-304-6332**	262-687-4011
Whittier Hospital Medical Ctr					
9080 Colima Rd	Whittier	CA	90605	**800-613-4291**	562-945-3561
Wilcox Memorial Hospital (WMH)					
3-3420 Kuhio Hwy	Lihue	HI	96766	**877-709-9355**	808-245-1100
Williamson ARH Hospital					
260 Hospital Dr	South Williamson	KY	41503	**888-654-0015***	606-237-1700
*General					
Woodland Heights Medical Ctr					
505 S John Redditt Dr	Lufkin	TX	75904	**800-222-1222**	936-634-8311
Wuesthoff Medical Ctr Rockledge					
110 Longwood Ave	Rockledge	FL	32955	**877-456-9617**	321-636-2211
Wyoming Medical Ctr					
1233 E Second St	Casper	WY	82601	**800-822-7201**	307-577-7201
Yavapai Regional Medical Ctr					
1003 Willow Creek Rd	Prescott	AZ	86301	**877-843-9762**	928-445-2700

374-5 Psychiatric Hospitals

Listings here include state psychiatric facilities as well as private psychiatric hospitals.

Name / Address	City	State	Zip	Toll-Free	Phone
Adventist Behavioral Health					
14901 Broschart Rd	Rockville	MD	20850	**800-204-8600**	301-251-4500
Arizona State Hospital					
2500 E Van Buren St	Phoenix	AZ	85008	**877-588-5163**	602-244-1331
Atascadero State Hospital					
10333 S Camino Real	Atascadero	CA	93422	**844-210-6207**	805-468-2000
Aurora Las Encinas Hospital					
2900 E Del Mar Blvd	Pasadena	CA	91107	**800-792-2345**	626-795-9901
Austin State Hospital					
4110 Guadalupe St	Austin	TX	78751	**866-407-3773**	512-452-0381
Banner Behavioral Health Hospital					
7575 E Earll Dr	Scottsdale	AZ	85251	**800-254-4357**	480-941-7500
Brentwood A Behavioral Health Co					
1006 Highland Ave	Shreveport	LA	71101	**877-678-7500**	318-678-7500
Bronx Psychiatric Ctr					
1500 Waters Pl	Bronx	NY	10461	**800-597-8481**	718-931-0600
BryLin Hospitals					
1263 Delaware Ave	Buffalo	NY	14209	**800-727-9546**	716-886-8200
Buffalo Psychiatric Ctr					
400 Forest Ave	Buffalo	NY	14213	**800-597-8481**	716-885-2261
Caro Ctr 2000 Chambers Rd	Caro	MI	48723	**888-556-0490**	989-673-3191
Carrier Clinic					
252 County Rd 601	Belle Mead	NJ	08502	**800-933-3579**	908-281-1000
Catawba Hospital					
5525 Catawba Hospital Dr	Catawba	VA	24070	**800-451-5544**	540-375-4200
Cedar Springs Behavioral Health System					
2135 Southgate Rd	Colorado Springs	CO	80906	**800-888-1088**	719-633-4114
Central Louisiana State Hospital					
242 W Shamrock St	Pineville	LA	71360	**866-666-8335**	318-484-6200
Central Washington Hospital					
1201 S Miller St	Wenatchee	WA	98801	**800-365-6428**	509-662-1511
Chester Mental Health Ctr					
1315 Lehman Dr	Chester	IL	62233	**800-843-6154**	618-826-4571
Chicago Lakeshore Hospital					
4840 N Marine Dr	Chicago	IL	60640	**800-888-0560***	773-878-9700
*Cust Svc					
Clifton T Perkins Hospital Ctr					
8450 Dorsey Run Rd	Jessup	MD	20794	**877-463-3464**	410-724-3000
College Hospital					
10802 College Pl	Cerritos	CA	90703	**800-352-3301**	562-924-9581
College Hospital Costa Mesa					
301 Victoria St	Costa Mesa	CA	92627	**800-773-8001**	949-642-2734
Creedmoor Psychiatric Ctr					
79-25 Winchester Blvd	Queens Village	NY	11427	**800-597-8481**	718-464-7500
Del Amo Hospital					
23700 Camino Del Sol	Torrance	CA	90505	**800-533-5266**	310-530-1151
Delaware Psychiatric Ctr					
1901 N Dupont Hwy Main Bldg	New Castle	DE	19720	**800-652-2929**	302-255-9399
Eastern State Hospital (ESH)					
4601 Ironbound Rd	Williamsburg	VA	23188	**800-994-6610**	757-253-5161
Elmira Psychiatric Ctr					
100 Washington St	Elmira	NY	14901	**800-597-8481**	607-737-4711
Fair Oaks Hospital					
5352 Linton Blvd	Delray Beach	FL	33484	**866-904-6871**	561-498-4440
Fairfax Hospital					
10200 NE 132nd St	Kirkland	WA	98034	**800-435-7221**	425-821-2000

Name	Address	City	State	ZIP	Toll-Free	Phone
Fairmount Behavioral Health System	561 Fairthorne Ave	Philadelphia	PA	19128	**800-235-0200**	215-487-4000
Fort Lauderdale Hospital	1601 E Las Olas Blvd	Fort Lauderdale	FL	33301	**800-585-7527**	954-463-4321
Four Winds Hospital	800 Cross River Rd	Katonah	NY	10536	**800-528-6624**	914-763-8151
Friends Hospital	4641 Roosevelt Blvd	Philadelphia	PA	19124	**800-889-0548**	215-831-4600
Georgia Regional Hospital at Savannah	1915 Eisenhower Dr	Savannah	GA	31406	**800-436-7442**	912-356-2011
Green Oaks Hospital	7808 Clodus Fields Dr	Dallas	TX	75251	**800-866-6554**	972-991-9504
Griffin Memorial Hospital	900 E Main St *General	Norman	OK	73071	**800-955-3468***	405-321-4880
Hamilton Ctr Inc	PO Box 4323	Terre Haute	IN	47804	**800-742-0787**	812-231-8323
Havenwyck Hospital	1525 University Dr	Auburn Hills	MI	48326	**800-401-2727**	248-373-9200
Hill Crest Behavioral Health Services	6869 Fifth Ave S	Birmingham	AL	35212	**800-292-8553**	205-833-9000
Holly Hill Hospital	3019 Falstaff Rd	Raleigh	NC	27610	**800-447-1800**	919-250-7000
Horsham Clinic	722 E Butler Pk	Ambler	PA	19002	**800-237-4447**	215-643-7800
Jewish Hospital & St Mary's HealthCare	200 Abraham Flexner Way	Louisville	KY	40202	**800-451-3637**	502-587-4011
Kalamazoo Psychiatric Hospital	1312 Oakland Dr	Kalamazoo	MI	49008	**888-509-7007**	269-337-3000
Kerrville State Hospital	721 Thompson Dr	Kerrville	TX	78028	**888-963-7111**	830-896-2211
Kingsboro Psychiatric Ctr	681 Clarkson Ave	Brooklyn	NY	11203	**800-597-8481**	
Lakeside Behavioral Health System	2911 Brunswick Rd	Memphis	TN	38133	**800-232-5253**	901-377-4700
Langley Porter Psychiatric Institute	401 Parnassus Ave	San Francisco	CA	94143	**800-723-7140**	415-476-7000
McLean Hospital	115 Mill St	Belmont	MA	02478	**800-333-0338**	617-855-2000
Meadows Psychiatric Ctr	132 The Meadows Dr	Centre Hall	PA	16828	**800-641-7529**	814-364-2161
Memorial Hermann Prevention & Recovery Ctr (MHPARC)	3043 Gessner	Houston	TX	77080	**800-464-7272**	713-939-7272
Menninger Clinic	12301 S Main St PO Box 809045	Houston	TX	77035	**800-351-9058**	713-275-5000
Middle Tennessee Mental Health Institute	221 Stewarts Ferry Pike	Nashville	TN	37214	**800-770-8277**	615-902-7400
Mohawk Valley Psychiatric Ctr	1400 Noyes St	Utica	NY	13502	**800-597-8481**	315-738-3800
Napa State Hospital	2100 Napa-Vallejo Hwy	Napa	CA	94558	**866-762-0972**	707-253-5000
New Mexico Behavioral Health Institute	3695 Hot Springs Blvd	Las Vegas	NM	87701	**800-446-5970**	505-454-2100
North Dakota State Hospital	2605 Cir Dr	Jamestown	ND	58401	**888-862-7342**	701-253-3650
Northwest Missouri Psychiatric Rehabilitation Ctr	3505 Frederick Ave	Saint Joseph	MO	64506	**800-273-8255**	816-387-2300
Oregon State Hospital	2600 Ctr St NE	Salem	OR	97301	**800-544-7078**	503-945-2800
Pembroke Hospital	199 Oak St	Pembroke	MA	02359	**800-222-2237**	781-829-7000
Pilgrim Psychiatric Ctr	998 Crooked Hill Rd	West Brentwood	NY	11717	**800-597-8481**	631-761-3500
Pine Rest Christian Mental Health Services	300 68th St SE PO Box 165	Grand Rapids	MI	49501	**800-678-5500**	616-455-5000
Poplar Springs Hospital	350 Poplar Dr	Petersburg	VA	23805	**866-546-2229**	804-733-6874
Psychiatric Institute of Washington	4228 Wisconsin Ave NW	Washington	DC	20016	**800-369-2273**	202-885-5600
Richard H Hutchings Psychiatric Ctr	620 Madison St	Syracuse	NY	13210	**800-690-6639**	
Ridge Behavioral Health System	3050 Rio Dosa Dr	Lexington	KY	40509	**800-753-4673**	859-269-2325
River Park Hospital	1230 Sixth Ave	Huntington	WV	25701	**800-621-2673**	304-526-9111
Riverview Psychiatric Ctr	250 Arsenal St 11 State House Stn	Augusta	ME	04330	**888-261-6684**	207-624-4600
Rogers Memorial Hospital Inc	34700 Valley Rd	Oconomowoc	WI	53066	**800-767-4411**	262-646-4411
Sheppard Pratt Health System (SPHS)	6501 N Charles St	Baltimore	MD	21285	**800-627-0330**	410-938-3000
Spring Harbor Hospital	123 Andover Rd	Westbrook	ME	04092	**888-524-0080**	207-761-2200
Springfield Hospital Ctr	6655 Sykesville Rd	Sykesville	MD	21784	**800-333-7564**	410-970-7000
Thomas B Finan Ctr	10102 Country Club Rd SE PO Box 1722	Cumberland	MD	21502	**888-854-0035**	301-777-2405
Timberlawn Mental Health System	4600 Samuell Blvd	Dallas	TX	75228	**800-426-4944**	214-381-7181
Torrance State Hospital	121 Longview Dr PO Box 111	Torrance	PA	15779	**866-816-9212**	724-459-8000
University Behavioral Ctr	2500 Discovery Dr	Orlando	FL	32826	**800-999-0807**	407-281-7000
Walter P Reuther Psychiatric Hospital	30901 Palmer Rd	Westland	MI	48186	**877-765-8388**	734-367-8400
Western Mental Health Institute	11100 Hwy 64 W	Bolivar	TN	38008	**800-770-8277**	731-228-2000
Western State Hospital	9601 Steilacoom Blvd SW	Tacoma	WA	98498	**877-501-2233**	253-582-8900
Westwood Lodge Hospital	45 Clapboardtree St	Westwood	MA	02090	**800-222-2237**	781-762-7764
William R Sharpe Jr Hospital	936 Sharpe Hospital Rd	Weston	WV	26452	**866-384-5250**	304-269-1210

374-6 Rehabilitation Hospitals

Name	Address	City	State	ZIP	Toll-Free	Phone
Allied Services Rehabilitation Hospital	475 Morgan Hwy	Scranton	PA	18508	**888-734-2272**	570-348-1300
Bryn Mawr Rehab Hospital	414 Paoli Pike	Malvern	PA	19355	**888-876-8764**	484-596-5400
Burke Rehabilitation Hospital	785 Mamaroneck Ave	White Plains	NY	10605	**888-992-8753**	914-597-2500
Charlotte Institute of Rehabilitation	1100 Blythe Blvd	Charlotte	NC	28203	**800-634-2256**	704-355-4300
Craig Hospital	3425 S Clarkson St	Englewood	CO	80113	**800-247-0257**	303-789-8000
Drake Ctr	151 W Galbraith Rd	Cincinnati	OH	45216	**800-948-0003**	513-418-2500
Edwin Shaw Rehab	1621 Flickinger Rd	Akron	OH	44312	**800-221-4601**	330-784-1271
Frazier Rehabilitation Institute	220 Abraham Flexner Way	Louisville	KY	40202	**800-333-2230**	502-582-7400
Gaylord Hospital	Gaylord Farms Rd PO Box 400	Wallingford	CT	06492	**866-429-5673**	203-284-2800
HealthSouth Chattanooga Rehabilitation Hospital	3660 Grandview Pkwy Ste 200	Birmingham	AL	35243	**800-765-4772**	205-967-7116
HealthSouth Harmarville Rehabilitation Hospital	320 Guys Run Rd	Pittsburgh	PA	15238	**800-765-4772**	412-828-1300
HealthSouth Hospital of Pittsburgh	320 Guys Run Rd	Pittsburgh	PA	15238	**800-765-4772**	412-828-1300
HealthSouth MountainView Regional Rehabilitation Hospital	1160 Van Voorhis Rd	Morgantown	WV	26505	**800-388-2451**	304-598-1100
HealthSouth Nittany Valley Rehabilitation Hospital	550 W College Ave	Pleasant Gap	PA	16823	**800-842-6026**	814-359-3421
HealthSouth Rehabilitation Hospital of Altoona	2005 Vly View Blvd	Altoona	PA	16602	**800-873-4220**	814-944-3535
HealthSouth Rehabilitation Hospital of Austin	1215 Red River	Austin	TX	78701	**800-765-4772**	512-474-5700
HealthSouth Rehabilitation Hospital of Erie	143 E Second St	Erie	PA	16507	**800-765-4772**	814-878-1230
HealthSouth Rehabilitation Hospital of Kingsport	113 Cassel Dr	Kingsport	TN	37660	**800-454-7422**	423-246-7240
Madonna Rehabilitation Hospital	5401 S St	Lincoln	NE	68506	**800-676-5448**	402-489-7102
Magee Rehabilitation Hospital	1513 Race St	Philadelphia	PA	19102	**800-966-2433**	215-587-3000
Marianjoy Rehabilitation Hospital	26 W 171 Roosevelt Rd	Wheaton	IL	60187	**800-462-2366**	630-462-4000
Mary Free Bed Rehabilitation Hospital	235 Wealthy St SE	Grand Rapids	MI	49503	**800-528-8989**	616-242-0300
Methodist Rehabilitation Ctr	1350 E Woodrow Wilson Dr	Jackson	MS	39216	**800-223-6672**	601-981-2611
Northeast Rehabilitation Hospital	70 Butler St	Salem	NH	03079	**800-439-2370**	603-893-2900
Rancho Los Amigos National Rehabilitation Ctr	7601 E Imperial Hwy	Downey	CA	90242	**877-726-2461**	562-401-7111
Rehabilitation Hospital of Indiana	4141 Shore Dr	Indianapolis	IN	46254	**866-510-2273**	317-329-2000
Rehabilitation Institute of Chicago	345 E Superior St *Admitting	Chicago	IL	60611	**800-354-7342***	312-238-1000
Shadyside Nursing & Rehabilitation Ctr	5609 Fifth Ave	Pittsburgh	PA	15232	**800-366-1232**	412-362-3500
Southern Indiana Rehabilitation Hospital	3104 Blackiston Blvd	New Albany	IN	47150	**800-737-7090**	812-941-8300
Spalding Rehabilitation Hospital	900 Potomac St	Aurora	CO	80011	**800-367-3309**	303-367-1166
Spaulding Rehabilitation Hospital	125 Nashua St	Boston	MA	02114	**888-774-0055**	617-573-7000
TIRR Memorial Hermann Hospital	1333 Moursund St	Houston	TX	77030	**800-447-3422**	713-799-5000

374-7 Specialty Hospitals

Name	Address	City	State	ZIP	Toll-Free	Phone
Barbara Ann Karmanos Cancer Institute	4100 John R St	Detroit	MI	48201	**800-527-6266**	
Bascom Palmer Eye Institute	900 NW 17th St	Miami	FL	33136	**800-329-7000**	305-326-6000
Brigham & Women's Hospital	75 Francis St	Boston	MA	02115	**800-722-5520**	617-732-5500
Dana-Farber Cancer Institute	44 Binney St	Boston	MA	02115	**866-408-3324**	617-632-3000
Dermatology Assoc of Atlanta	5555 Pchtrdnwyd Ste 190	Atlanta	GA	30324	**800-233-0706**	404-256-4457
Eleanor Slater Hospital	14 Harrington Rd	Cranston	RI	02920	**800-438-8477**	401-462-2339
Fox Chase Cancer Ctr	333 Cottman Ave	Philadelphia	PA	19111	**888-369-2427**	215-728-6900
Georgia Cancer Specialists Pc (GCS)	1872 Montreal Rd	Tucker	GA	30084	**800-491-5991**	770-496-9443
H Lee Moffitt Cancer Ctr & Research Institute	University of S Florida 12902 Magnolia Dr	Tampa	FL	33612	**800-456-3434**	888-663-3488
Hughston Orthopedic Hospital	100 Frist Ct	Columbus	GA	31908	**855-795-3609**	706-494-2100
Kindred Hospital Atlanta	705 Juniper St	Atlanta	GA	30308	**800-255-0135**	404-873-2871
Kindred Hospital Kansas City	8701 Troost Ave	Kansas City	MO	64131	**800-545-0749**	816-995-2000
Leahi Hospital	3675 Kilauea Ave	Honolulu	HI	96816	**800-845-6733**	808-733-8000
MD Anderson Cancer Ctr	1515 Holcombe Blvd	Houston	TX	77030	**800-889-2094**	713-792-2121
Memorial Sloan-Kettering Cancer Ctr	1275 York Ave	New York	NY	10065	**800-525-2225**	212-639-2000

Name / Address	City	State	Zip	Toll-Free	Phone
Midwestern Regional Medical Ctr (MRMC) 2520 Elisha Ave	Zion	IL	60099	**800-615-3055**	847-872-4561
National Jewish Medical & Research Ctr 1400 Jackson St PO Box 17169	Denver	CO	80206	**877-225-5654**	303-388-4461
New York Eye & Ear Infirmary 310 E 14th St	New York	NY	10003	**800-522-4582**	212-979-4000
Odessa Regional Medical Ctr 520 E Sixth St	Odessa	TX	79761	**877-898-6080**	432-582-8000
Roswell Park Cancer Institute Elm and Carlton St	Buffalo	NY	14263	**877-275-7724**	716-845-2300
Saint Vincent Women's Hospital 8111 Township Line Rd	Indianapolis	IN	46260	**800-582-8258**	317-415-8111
Samuel Mahelona Memorial Hospital 4800 Kawaihau Rd	Kapaa	HI	96746	**800-845-6733**	808-822-4961
Siteman Cancer Ctr 4921 Parkview Pl	Saint Louis	MO	63110	**800-600-3606**	314-362-5196
Stanford Cancer Ctr 875 Lake Blake Wilbur Dr	Stanford	CA	94305	**800-422-6237**	650-498-6000
Straith Hospital for Special Surgery 23901 Lahser Rd	Southfield	MI	48034	**800-994-6610**	248-357-3360
Texas Ctr for Infectious Diseases 2303 SE Military Dr	San Antonio	TX	78223	**800-839-5864**	210-534-8857
Texas Orthopedic Hospital 7401 Main St	Houston	TX	77030	**866-783-4549**	713-799-8600
UC Davis Cancer Ctr 4501 X St	Sacramento	CA	95817	**800-362-5566**	916-734-5800
Women's & Children's Hospital (WCH) 4600 Ambassador Caffery Pkwy	Lafayette	LA	70508	**888-569-8331**	337-521-9100

374-8 Veterans Hospitals

Listings for veterans hospitals are organized by states, and then by city names within those groupings.

Name / Address	City	State	Zip	Toll-Free	Phone
Alexandria Veterans Affairs Medical Ctr 2495 Shreveport Hwy 71 N	Pineville	LA	71360	**800-375-8387**	318-473-0010
Altoona VA Medical Ctr 2907 Pleasant Vly Blvd	Altoona	PA	16602	**877-626-2500**	
Alvin C York Medical Ctr 3400 Lebanon Pike	Murfreesboro	TN	37129	**800-228-4973**	615-867-6000
Batavia VA Medical Ctr 222 Richmond Ave	Batavia	NY	14020	**800-273-8255**	585-297-1000
Bath Veterans Affairs Medical Ctr 76 Veterans Ave	Bath	NY	14810	**877-845-3247**	607-664-4000
Carl Vinson Veterans Affairs Medical Ctr 1826 Veterans Blvd	Dublin	GA	31021	**800-595-5229**	478-272-1210
Central Texas Veterans Health Care System 1901 Veterans Memorial Dr	Temple	TX	76504	**800-423-2111**	254-778-4811
Colmery-O'Neil Veterans Affairs Medical Ctr 2200 SW Gage Blvd	Topeka	KS	66622	**800-574-8387**	785-350-3111
Dayton Va Medical Ctr 4100 W Third St	Dayton	OH	45428	**800-368-8262**	937-268-6511
Denver Veterans Affairs Medical Ctr 1055 Clermont St	Denver	CO	80220	**888-336-8262**	303-399-8020
Dwight D Eisenhower V A Medical Ctr 4101 South 4th St	Leavenworth	KS	66048	**800-952-8387**	913-682-2000
East Orange Campus of the VA New Jersey Health Care System (NJHCS) 385 Tremont Ave *General	East Orange	NJ	07018	**844-872-4681***	
Erie VA Medical Ctr 135 E 38th St	Erie	PA	16504	**800-274-8387**	814-868-8661
Harry S Truman Memorial Veterans Hospital 800 Hospital Dr	Columbia	MO	65201	**877-222-8387**	573-814-6000
Huntington Veterans Affairs Medical Ctr 1540 Spring Valley Dr	Huntington	WV	25704	**800-827-8244**	304-429-6741
James H Quillen Veterans Affairs Medical Ctr Corner of Lamont & Veterans Way PO Box 4000	Mountain Home	TN	37684	**877-573-3529**	423-926-1171
Jerry L Pettis Memorial Veterans Affairs Medical Ctr 11201 Benton St	Loma Linda	CA	92357	**800-827-1000**	909-825-7084
John J Pershing Veterans Affairs Medical Ctr 1500 N Westwood Blvd	Poplar Bluff	MO	63901	**888-557-8262**	573-686-4151
Louis A Johnson Veterans Affairs Medical Ctr 1 Medical Ctr Dr	Clarksburg	WV	26301	**800-733-0512**	304-623-3461
Louis Stokes Cleveland Veterans Affairs Medical Ctr 10701 E Blvd	Cleveland	OH	44106	**888-838-6446**	216-791-3800
Malcom Randall VAMC NF/SGVHS 1601 SW Archer Rd	Gainesville	FL	32608	**800-324-8387**	352-376-1611
Northern Arizona VA Health Care System 500 Hwy 89 N	Prescott	AZ	86313	**800-949-1005**	928-445-4860
Overton Brooks Veterans Affairs Medical Ctr 510 E Stoner Ave	Shreveport	LA	71101	**800-863-7441**	318-221-8411
Richard L. Roudebush VA Medical Ctr 1481 W Tenth St	Indianapolis	IN	46202	**888-878-6889**	317-988-4498
Salem Veterans Affairs Medical Ctr 1970 Roanoke Blvd	Salem	VA	24153	**888-982-2463**	540-982-2463
San Francisco VA Medical Ctr 4150 Clement St	San Francisco	CA	94121	**877-487-2838**	415-221-4810
Sierra NV Healthcare Systems (VA Medical Ctr) 975 Kirman Ave	Reno	NV	89502	**888-838-6256**	775-786-7200
Southern Arizona Veterans Healthcare System 3601 S Sixth Ave	Tucson	AZ	85723	**800-470-8262**	520-792-1450
Stratton Veterans Affairs Medical Ctr 113 Holland Ave	Albany	NY	12208	**800-223-4810**	518-626-5000
Thomas E Creek Veterans Affairs Medical Ctr 6010 Amarillo Blvd W	Amarillo	TX	79106	**800-687-8262**	806-355-9703
Tomah Veterans Affairs Medical Ctr 500 E Veterans St	Tomah	WI	54660	**800-872-8662**	608-372-3971
Tuscaloosa VA Medical Ctr 3701 Loop Rd E	Tuscaloosa	AL	35404	**888-269-3045**	205-554-2000
U.S. Department of Veterans Affairs 325 E 'H' St	Iron Mountain	MI	49801	**800-215-8262**	906-774-3300
VA Hudson Valley Health Care System *Castle Point Campus* 41 Castle Pt Rd	Wappingers Falls	NY	12590	**877-222-8387**	845-831-2000
Montrose Campus 2094 Albany Post Rd PO Box 100	Montrose	NY	10548	**800-269-8749**	914-737-4400
VA Medical Ctr 2400 Hospital Rd	Tuskegee	AL	36083	**800-214-8387**	334-727-0550
Veterans Affairs Long Beach Medical Ctr 5901 E Seventh St	Long Beach	CA	90822	**888-769-8387**	562-826-8000
Veterans Affairs Medical Ctr 7180 Highland Dr	Pittsburgh	PA	15206	**866-482-7488**	412-365-4900
Veterans Affairs Outpatient Clinic 1515 W Pleasant St Bldg 1	Knoxville	IA	50138	**800-816-8878**	641-842-3101
Veterans Affairs Puget Sound Medical Ctr 1660 S Columbian Way	Seattle	WA	98108	**800-329-8387**	206-762-1010
WG Bill Hefner Veterans Affairs Medical Ctr 1601 Brenner Ave	Salisbury	NC	28144	**800-469-8262**	704-638-9000
White River Junction Veterans Affairs Medical Ctr 215 N Main St	White River Junction	VT	05009	**866-687-8387**	802-295-9363

375 HOT TUBS, SPAS, WHIRLPOOL BATHS

Name / Address	City	State	Zip	Toll-Free	Phone
Alaglass Swimming Pools 165 Sweet Bay Rd	Saint Matthews	SC	29135	**877-655-7179**	
Atlantic Spas & Billiards 8721 Glenwood Ave	Raleigh	NC	27617	**800-849-8827**	919-783-7447
Bath-Tec Inc PO Box 1118	Ennis	TX	75120	**800-526-3301**	972-646-5279
Best Bath Systems 723 Garber St	Caldwell	ID	83605	**866-333-8657**	208-342-6823
Cal Spas Inc 1462 E Ninth St	Pomona	CA	91766	**800-225-7727**	909-623-8781
Hydro Systems Inc 29132 Ave Paine	Valencia	CA	91355	**800-747-9990**	661-775-0686
Jason International Inc 8328 MacArthur Dr	North Little Rock	AR	72118	**800-255-5766**	501-771-4477
Kallista Inc 1227 N Eigth St Ste 2 *Cust Svc	Sheboygan	WI	53081	**888-452-5547***	920-457-4441
Koral Industries Inc 1504 S Kaufman St	Ennis	TX	75119	**800-627-2441**	972-875-6555
Marquis Spas Corp 596 Hoffman Rd	Independence	OR	97351	**800-275-0888**	503-838-0888
Master Spas Inc 6927 Lincoln Pkwy	Fort Wayne	IN	46804	**800-860-7727**	260-436-9100
Plastic Development Co Inc 75 Palmer Industrial Rd PO Box 4007	Williamsport	PA	17701	**800-451-1420**	
Royal Baths Manufacturing Co 14635 Chrisman Rd	Houston	TX	77039	**800-826-0074**	281-442-3400
Spa Manufacturers 6060 Ulmerton Rd	Clearwater	FL	33760	**877-530-9493**	727-530-9493
Spurlin Industries Inc 625 Main St	Palmetto	GA	30268	**800-749-4475**	770-463-1644
Thermo Spas Inc 155 E St	Wallingford	CT	06492	**800-876-0158**	
Watertech Whirlpool Bath & Spa 2507 Plymouth Rd	Johnson City	TN	37601	**800-289-8827**	
Watkins Mfg Corp 1280 Pk Ctr Dr	Vista	CA	92081	**800-999-4688**	

376 HOTEL RESERVATIONS SERVICES

Name / Address	City	State	Zip	Toll-Free	Phone
AC Central Reservations Inc 201 Tilton Rd London Sq Mall Ste 17B	Northfield	NJ	08225	**888-227-6667**	609-383-8880
Advance Reservations Inn Arizona PO Box 950	Tempe	AZ	85280	**800-456-0682**	480-990-0682
Alexandria & Arlington Bed & Breakfast Networks (AABBN) 4938 Hampden Ln Ste 164	Bethesda	MD	20814	**888-549-3415**	703-549-3415
Alliance Reservations Network 21640 N 19th Ave Ste C102 *Cust Svc	Phoenix	AZ	85027	**800-419-1545***	602-444-9993
Anchorage Alaska Bed & Breakfast Assn (AABBA) PO Box 242623	Anchorage	AK	99524	**888-584-5147**	907-272-5909
B & B Agency of Boston 47 Commercial Wharf Ste 3	Boston	MA	02110	**800-248-9262**	
Bed & Breakfast Atlanta 790 N Ave Ste 202	Atlanta	GA	30306	**800-967-3224**	404-875-0525
Bed & Breakfast Cape Cod PO Box 2250	Mashpee	MA	02649	**800-556-3815**	508-255-3824
Branson's Best Reservations 2875 Green Mtn Dr	Branson	MO	65616	**800-335-2555**	417-339-2204
Capitol Reservations 1730 Rhode Island Ave NW	Washington	DC	20036	**800-619-4337**	202-452-1270
Colonial Williamsburg Reservation Ctr PO Box 1776	Williamsburg	VA	23187	**800-447-8679**	757-229-1000
Greater New Orleans Hotel & Lodging Assn 2020 St Charles Ave 5th Fl	New Orleans	LA	70130	**866-366-1121**	504-525-2264
Hawaii's Best Bed & Breakfasts 571 Pauku St	Kailua	HI	96734	**800-262-9912**	808-263-3100
Holiday Inn Express & Suites 5001 Brougham Dr	Drayton Valley	AB	T7A0A1	**877-444-3110**	780-515-9888
Hot Rooms 875 N. Michigan Ave Ste 3100	Chicago	IL	60611	**800-468-3500**	773-468-7666
Jackson Hole Central Reservations (JHCR) 140 E Broadway Ste 24 PO Box 2618	Jackson	WY	83001	**888-838-6606**	307-733-4005
Key West Key 726 Passover Ln	Key West	FL	33040	**800-881-7321**	
Know Before You Go Reservations 8000 International Dr	Orlando	FL	32819	**800-749-1993**	407-352-9813
Lasvegastickets.com 5030 Paradise Rd Ste B108	Las Vegas	NV	89119	**800-597-7469**	702-597-1588
Leading Hotels of the World 485 Lexington Ave Ste 401	New York	NY	10017	**800-745-8883**	212-515-5600
Luxe Worldwide Hotels 11461 W Sunset Blvd	Los Angeles	CA	90049	**888-336-3745**	310-440-3090
Nantucket Accommodations 2 Windy Way	Nantucket	MA	02554	**866-743-3330**	508-228-9559

Name / Address	City	State	Zip	Toll-Free	Phone
National Corporate Housing 365 Herndon Pkwy Ste 111	Herndon	VA	20170	**866-229-4720**	
New Otani North America Reservation Ctr 120 S Los Angeles St *Cust Svc	Los Angeles	CA	90012	**800-421-8795***	213-629-1200
Ocean City Hotel-Motel-Restaurant Assn PO Box 340	Ocean City	MD	21843	**800-626-2326**	410-289-6733
Quikbook 381 Pk Ave S 3rd Fl	New York	NY	10016	**800-789-9887**	212-779-7666
Resort 2 Me 975 Cass St	Monterey	CA	93940	**800-757-5646**	831-642-6622
San Diego Concierge 4379 30th St Ste 4	San Diego	CA	92104	**800-979-9091**	619-280-4121
Stay Aspen Snowmass 425 Rio Grande Pl	Aspen	CO	81611	**888-649-5982**	970-925-9000
Vacation Co 42 New Orleans Rd Ste 102	Hilton Head Island	SC	29928	**800-845-7018**	843-686-6100
Washington DC Accommodations 2201 Wisconsin Ave NW Ste C-120	Washington	DC	20007	**800-503-3330**	202-289-2220
Winter Park Resort 85 Parsenn Rd *Resv	Winter Park	CO	80482	**800-903-7275***	970-726-5514

377 HOTELS - CONFERENCE CENTER

Name / Address	City	State	Zip	Toll-Free	Phone
Airlie Conference Ctr 6809 Airlie Rd	Warrenton	VA	20187	**800-288-9573**	540-347-1300
BALSAMS Grand Resort Hotel, The 1000 Cold Spring Rd	Dixville Notch	NH	03576	**800-255-0800**	
Banff Centre, The 107 Tunnel Mtn Dr PO Box 1020	Banff	AB	T1L1H5	**800-884-7574**	403-762-6100
Chaminade 1 Chaminade Ln	Santa Cruz	CA	95065	**800-283-6569**	831-475-5600
Chateau Elan Resort & Conference Ctr 100 Rue Charlemagne	Braselton	GA	30517	**800-233-9463**	678-425-0900
Chattanoogan, The 1201 Broad St	Chattanooga	TN	37402	**877-756-1684**	423-756-3400
Cheyenne Mountain Conference Resort 3225 Broadmoor Vly Rd	Colorado Springs	CO	80906	**800-428-8886**	719-538-4000
Conference Ctr at NorthPointe 100 Green Meadows Dr S	Lewis Center	OH	43035	**866-233-9393**	614-880-4300
Cook Hotel & Conference Ctr 3848 W Lakeshore Dr	Baton Rouge	LA	70808	**866-610-2665**	225-383-2665
Country Springs Hotel & Conference Ctr 2810 Golf Rd	Pewaukee	WI	53072	**800-247-6640**	262-547-0201
Crystal Mountain Resort 12500 Crystal Mtn Dr	Thompsonville	MI	49683	**800-968-7686**	231-378-2000
Delta Sherbrooke Hotel & Conference Centre 2685 Rue King O	Sherbrooke	QC	J1L1C1	**800-268-1133**	819-822-1989
Dolce Atlanta-Peachtree 201 Aberdeen Pkwy	Peachtree City	GA	30269	**800-983-6523**	770-487-2666
Dolce Hayes Mansion 200 Edenvale Ave	San Jose	CA	95136	**866-981-3300**	408-226-3200
Doral Arrowwood Conference Resort 975 Anderson Hill Rd	Rye Brook	NY	10573	**844-211-0512**	844-214-5500
Emory Conference Ctr Hotel 1615 Clifton Rd	Atlanta	GA	30329	**800-933-6679**	404-712-6000
Evergreen Marriott Conference Resort 4021 Lakeview Dr	Stone Mountain	GA	30083	**800-228-9290**	770-879-9900
Founders Inn 5641 Indian River Rd	Virginia Beach	VA	23464	**800-926-4466**	757-424-5511
Georgetown University Hotel & Conference Ctr 3800 Reservoir Rd NW	Washington	DC	20057	**888-902-1606**	202-687-3200
Glen Cove Mansion Hotel & Conference Ctr 200 Dosoris Ln	Glen Cove	NY	11542	**877-782-9426**	516-671-6400
Grandover Resort & Conference Ctr 1000 Club Rd	Greensboro	NC	27407	**800-472-6301**	336-294-1800
Hamilton Park Hotel & Conference Ctr 175 Pk Ave	Florham Park	NJ	07932	**877-999-3223**	973-377-2424
Hickory Ridge Marriott Conference Hotel 10400 Fernwood Rd	Bethesda	IL	20817	**800-334-0344**	301-380-3000
Hidden Valley Resort & Conference Ctr 1 Craighead Dr PO Box 4420	Hidden Valley	PA	15502	**800-452-2223**	814-443-8000
Hilton Scranton & Conference Ctr 100 Adams Ave	Scranton	PA	18503	**800-445-8667**	570-343-3000
Hotel at Auburn University & Dixon Conference Ctr, The 241 S College St	Auburn	AL	36830	**800-228-2876**	334-821-8200
Hotels Etc Inc 7712 Hampton Pl Bldg 11C	Loganville	GA	30052	**877-967-7283**	
Hyatt Place New York Midtown South 52-54 W 36th	New York	NY	10015	**888-492-8847**	
Inn at Aspen 38750 Hwy 82	Aspen	CO	81611	**800-222-7736**	
Inn at Virginia Tech & Skelton Conference Ctr 901 Prices Fork Rd	Blacksburg	VA	24061	**877-200-3360**	540-231-8000
Ivey Spencer Leadership Centre 551 Windermere Rd	London	ON	N5X2T1	**888-678-6926**	519-679-4546
James L Allen Ctr 2169 Campus Dr	Evanston	IL	60208	**877-755-2227**	847-467-7000
Kingbridge Centre, The 12750 Jane St	King City	ON	L7B1A3	**800-827-7221**	905-833-3086
Kingsgate Marriott Conference Ctr at the University of Cincinnati 151 Goodman St	Cincinnati	OH	45219	**800-228-9290**	513-487-3800
Kingsmill Resort & Spa 1010 Kingsmill Rd	Williamsburg	VA	23185	**800-832-5665**	757-253-1703
Lakeview Golf Resort & Spa 1 Lakeview Dr	Morgantown	WV	26508	**800-624-8300**	304-594-1111
Lansdowne Resort 44050 Woodridge Pkwy	Leesburg	VA	20176	**877-513-8400**	703-729-8400
Lodge At Breckenridge, The 112 Overlook Dr	Breckenridge	CO	80424	**800-736-1607**	970-453-9300
Marietta Conference Ctr & Resort 500 Powder Springs St	Marietta	GA	30064	**888-685-2500**	770-427-2500
Marriott Montgomery Prattville at Capitol Hill 2500 Legends Cir *Resv	Prattville	AL	36066	**800-593-6429***	334-290-1235
Millennium Broadway Hotel New York 145 W 44th St	New York	NY	10036	**800-622-5569**	212-768-4400
National Ctr for Employee Development (NCED) 2701 E Imhoff Rd	Norman	OK	73071	**866-438-6233**	405-366-4420
NAV Canada Training & Conference Ctr 1950 Montreal Rd	Cornwall	ON	K6H6L2	**877-832-6416**	613-936-5800
Oak Brook Hills Marriott Resort 3500 Midwest Rd	Oak Brook	IL	60523	**800-228-9290**	630-850-5555
Oak Ridge Hotel & Conference Ctr 1 Oak Ridge Dr *Sales	Chaska	MN	55318	**800-737-9588***	952-368-3100
Penn Stater Conference Ctr Hotel 215 Innovation Blvd	State College	PA	16803	**800-233-7505**	814-863-5000
PNK (River City) LLC 777 River City Casino Blvd	Saint Louis	MO	63125	**888-578-7289**	
Renaissance Portsmouth Hotel & Waterfront Conference Ctr 425 Water St	Portsmouth	VA	23704	**888-839-1775**	757-673-3000
Resort at Squaw Creek 400 Squaw Creek Rd PO Box 3333	Olympic Valley	CA	96146	**800-327-3353**	530-583-6300
Saratoga Hilton 534 Broadway	Saratoga Springs	NY	12866	**800-445-8667**	518-584-4000
Skamania Lodge 1131 SW Skamania Lodge Way PO Box 189	Stevenson	WA	98648	**800-221-7117**	509-427-7700
Snowbird Ski & Summer Resort Hwy 210 PO Box 929000	Snowbird	UT	84092	**800-453-3000**	801-742-2222
Stoweflake Mountain Resort & Spa 1746 Mountain Rd PO Box 369	Stowe	VT	05672	**800-253-2232**	802-253-7355
University of Maryland University College Marriott Conference Ctr Hotel 3501 University Blvd E	Adelphi	MD	20783	**800-721-7033**	301-985-7300
Vdara Condo Hotel LLC 3950 Las Vegas Blvd	Las Vegas	NV	89119	**866-718-2489**	
White Oaks Conference Resort & Spa 253 Taylor Rd SS4 *Resv	Niagara-on-the-Lake	ON	L0S1J0	**800-263-5766***	905-688-2550
Woodlands Resort & Conference Ctr, The 2301 N Millbend Dr *Resv	The Woodlands	TX	77380	**800-433-2624***	281-367-1100
Wyndham Peachtree Conference Ctr 2443 Hwy 54 W	Peachtree City	GA	30269	**800-996-3426**	770-487-2000

378 HOTELS - FREQUENT STAY PROGRAMS

Name / Address	City	State	Zip	Toll-Free	Phone
Aava Whistler Hotel Ltd 4005 Whistler Way	Whistler	BC	V0N1B4	**800-663-5644**	604-932-2522
Apple Farm Bakery 2015 Monterey St	San Luis Obispo	CA	93401	**800-255-2040**	805-544-6100
Beach Terrace Motor Inn 3400 Atlantic Ave	Wildwood	NJ	08260	**800-841-8416**	609-522-8100
Bear Creek Mountain Resort 101 Doe Mtn Ln	Macungie	PA	18062	**866-754-2822**	610-641-7101
Broadway Plaza Hotel 1155 Broadway	New York	NY	10001	**877-504-6835**	212-679-7665
Buena Vista Motor Inn 1599 Lombard St	San Francisco	CA	94123	**800-835-4980**	415-923-9600
Chestnut Mountain Resort 8700 Chestnut Dr	Galena	IL	61036	**800-397-1320**	
Christie Lodge PO Box 1196	Avon	CO	81620	**888-325-6343**	970-845-4504
Chukchansi Gold Resort & Casino 711 Lucky Ln	Coarsegold	CA	93614	**866-794-6946**	
Country Hearth Inn Inc 50 Glenlake Pkwy NE Ste 350	Atlanta	GA	30328	**888-443-2784**	770-393-2662
Crowne Plaza Niagara Falls - Fallsview 5685 Falls Ave	Niagara Falls	ON	L2E6W7	**800-263-7135**	905-374-4447
Danfords Hotel & Marina 25 E Broadway	Port Jefferson	NY	11777	**800-332-6367**	
Days Inn Hinton-Jasper Hotel 358 Smith St	Hinton	AB	T7V2A1	**800-259-4827**	780-817-1960
FairBridge Inns LLC 421 W Riverside Ave Ste 407	Spokane	WA	99201	**877-866-8090**	
Fairmont San Francisco Hotel, The 950 Mason St	San Francisco	CA	94108	**800-257-7544**	415-772-5000
Gainey Suites Hotel 7300 E Gainey	Scottsdale	AZ	85258	**800-970-4666**	480-922-6969
GrandLife Hotels Inc 310 W Broadway	New York	NY	10013	**800-965-3000**	212-965-3000
Harbor Hotel Provincetown 698 Commercial St Cape Cod	Provincetown	MA	02657	**855-447-8696**	
Harbour Towers Hotel & Suites 345 Quebec St	Victoria	BC	V8V1W4	**800-663-5896**	250-385-2405
Hinton Lakeview Inns & Suites 500 Smith St	Hinton	AB	T7V2A1	**877-355-3500**	780-865-2575
Holiday Inn Baltimore Inner Harbor Hotel 301 W Lombard St	Baltimore	MD	21201	**877-834-3613**	410-685-3500
Horseshoe Valley Resort Ltd 1101 Horseshoe Vly Rd - Comp 10 RR 1	Barrie	ON	L4M4Y8	**800-461-5627**	705-835-2790
Hotel Blue 717 Central Ave Nw	Albuquerque	NM	87102	**877-878-4868**	505-924-2400
Hotel Shangri La 1301 Ocean Ave	Santa Monica	CA	90401	**877-999-1301**	310-394-2791
Hyatt Gold Passport Program 9805 Q St PO Box 27089	Omaha	NE	68127	**800-233-1234**	
Inn at Mamas Fish House 799 Poho Pl	Paia	HI	96779	**800-860-4852**	808-579-8488
Intercontinental San Francisco 888 Howard St	San Francisco	CA	94103	**888-811-4273**	
Kontiki Beach Resort 2290 N Fulton Beach Rd	Rockport	TX	78382	**800-388-0649**	361-729-2318
Lahaina Shores Beach Resort 475 Front St	Lahaina	HI	96761	**866-934-9176**	
LeisureLink Inc 90 S 400 W Ste 300	Salt Lake City	UT	84101	**855-840-2249**	
London West Hollywood Hotel 1020 N San Vicente Blvd	West Hollywood	CA	90069	**866-282-4560**	
Meadowmere Resort 74 Main St	Ogunquit	ME	03907	**800-633-8718**	207-646-9661
Menominee Hotel PO Box 760	Keshena	WI	54135	**800-343-7778**	715-799-3600

Name / Address	City	State	Zip	Toll-Free	Phone
Oak Plantation Resort & Suites Condominium Association Inc					
4090 Enchanted Oaks Cir	Kissimmee	FL	34741	**888-411-4141**	
Omni Hotels Select Guest Loyalty Program					
11819 Miami St 3rd Fl	Omaha	NE	68164	**800-843-6664***	
*Cust Svc					
Perry Group International					
1 Market Plz Ste 3600	San Francisco	CA	94105	**800-580-3950**	415-434-0135
Plaza Hotel, The					
5th Ave at Central Park S	New York	NY	10019	**888-850-0909**	212-759-3000
Prince Preferred Guest Program					
100 Holomoana St	Honolulu	HI	96815	**800-774-6234**	
Pueblo Bonito Hotels & Resorts					
4350 La Jolla Village Dr	San Diego	CA	92122	**800-990-8250**	858-642-2050
Raintree Resorts Management Company LLC					
PO Box 350	Teton Village	WY	83025	**866-352-9777**	307-734-9777
Ramada Plaza Beach Resort					
1500 Miracle Strip Pkwy Se	Fort Walton Beach	FL	32548	**800-874-8962**	850-243-9161
Red Lion Hotel 621 21St St	Lewiston	ID	83501	**800-232-6730**	208-799-1000
Resorts of the Canadian Rockies Inc					
1505 17th Ave SW	Calgary	AB	T2T0E2	**800-258-7669**	403-254-7669
Sky Lodge, The					
201 Heber Ave Main St	Park City	UT	84068	**888-876-2525**	435-658-2500
Starwood Hotels Preferred Guest Program					
111 Westchester Ave	White Plains	NY	10604	**888-625-4988**	512-834-2426
Sunstream Hotels & Resorts					
6231 Estero Blvd	Fort Myers Beach	FL	33931	**844-652-3696**	239-765-4111
Tahoe Biltmore Lodge & Casino					
PO Box 115	Crystal Bay	NV	89402	**800-245-8667**	775-831-0660
Terranea Resort & Spa					
100 Terranea Way	Rancho Palos Verdes	CA	90275	**866-547-3066**	310-265-2800
TRYP Hotels Worldwide Inc					
395 Rue De La Couronne	Quebec	QC	G1K7X4	**800-267-2002**	
Twin Pine Casino					
22223 Hwy 29 PO Box 789	Middletown	CA	95461	**800-564-4872**	707-987-0197
Vacationer RV Resort					
1581 East Main St	El Cajon	CA	92021	**877-626-4409**	
W New York- Union Square					
201 Park Ave S	New York	NY	10003	**877-822-0000**	212-253-9119
Washington Jefferson LLC					
318 W 51st St	New York	NY	10019	**888-567-7550**	212-246-7550
Wedmore Place LLC					
5810 Wessex Hundred	Williamsburg	VA	23185	**866-933-6673**	
Wyndham ByRequest Program					
PO Box 4090	Aberdeen	SD	57401	**800-996-3426**	

379 HOTELS & HOTEL COMPANIES

SEE ALSO Resorts & Resort Companies ; Casino Companies ; Corporate Housing ; Hotel Reservations Services ; Hotels - Conference Center ; Hotels - Frequent Stay Programs

Name / Address	City	State	Zip	Toll-Free	Phone
1886 Crescent Hotel & Spa					
75 Prospect Ave	Eureka Springs	AR	72632	**877-342-9766**	479-253-9766
70 Park Avenue Hotel					
70 Pk Ave at 38th St	New York	NY	10016	**877-707-2752**	212-973-2400
Academy Hotel Colorado Springs, The					
8110 N Academy Blvd	Colorado Springs	CO	80920	**800-766-8524**	719-598-5770
Acadia Inn 98 Eden St	Bar Harbor	ME	04609	**800-638-3636**	207-288-3500
Acapulco Hotel & Resort					
2505 S Atlantic Ave	Daytona Beach Shores	FL	32118	**855-922-3224**	386-761-2210
Accent Inns Vancouver Airport					
10551 St Edwards Dr	Richmond	BC	V6X3L8	**800-663-0298**	604-273-3311
Accent Inns Vancouver-Burnaby					
3777 Henning Dr	Burnaby	BC	V5C6N5	**800-663-0298**	604-473-5000
Acqua Hotel					
555 Redwood Hwy	Mill Valley	CA	94941	**888-662-9555**	415-380-0400
Acqualina					
17875 Collins Ave	Sunny Isles Beach	FL	33160	**877-312-9742**	305-918-8000
Adams Oceanfront Resort					
4 Read St	Dewey Beach	DE	19971	**800-448-8080**	302-227-3030
Admiral Fell Inn					
888 S Broadway Historic Fell's Pt	Baltimore	MD	21231	**866-583-4162**	410-522-7377
Admiral on Baltimore					
2 Baltimore Ave	Rehoboth Beach	DE	19971	**888-882-4188**	302-227-1300
Adolphus, The					
1321 Commerce St	Dallas	TX	75202	**800-221-9083**	214-742-8200
Adventureland Inn					
305 34th Ave NW	Altoona	IA	50009	**800-910-5382**	515-265-7321
Affina Dumont					
150 E 34th St	New York	NY	10016	**866-233-4642**	212-481-7600
Affinia 50 155 E 50th St	New York	NY	10022	**866-246-2203**	212-751-5710
Affinia Chicago					
155 E 50th St	New York	NY	10022	**866-246-2203**	212-751-5710
Affinia Gardens					
215 E 64th St	New York	NY	10065	**866-233-4642**	212-355-1230
Affinia Manhattan					
371 Seventh Ave	New York	NY	10001	**866-246-2203**	212-563-1800
Airport Settle Inn					
2620 S Packerland Dr	Green Bay	WI	54313	**800-688-9052**	920-499-1900
Airtel Plaza Hotel					
7277 Valjean Ave	Van Nuys	CA	91406	**877-939-9268**	818-997-7676
Ala Moana Hotel					
410 Atkinson Dr	Honolulu	HI	96814	**800-367-6025**	808-955-4811
Albert at Bay Suite Hotel					
435 Albert St	Ottawa	ON	K1R7X4	**800-267-6644**	613-238-8858
Albion Hotel					
1650 James Ave	Miami Beach	FL	33139	**877-782-3557***	305-913-1000
*General					
Alexis Hotel 1007 First Ave	Seattle	WA	98104	**866-356-8894**	206-624-4844
Alpenhof Lodge					
3255 W Village Dr	Teton Village	WY	83025	**800-732-3244**	307-733-3242
Ambassador Hotel					
2308 W Wisconsin Ave	Milwaukee	WI	53233	**888-322-3326**	414-345-5000
Ambrosia House Tropical Lodging					
622 Fleming St	Key West	FL	33040	**800-535-9838**	305-296-9838
America's Best Franchising Inc					
America's Best Inns & Suites					
50 Glen Lake Pkwy NE Ste 350	Atlanta	GA	30328	**800-237-8466**	770-393-2662
AmericInn International LLC					
250 Lake Dr E	Chanhassen	MN	55317	**800-634-3444***	952-294-5000
*Resv					
Ameristar Casino & Hotel					
3200 N Ameristar Dr	Kansas City	MO	64161	**888-777-8700**	816-414-7000
Ameristar Casino Hotel Council Bluffs					
2200 River Rd	Council Bluffs	IA	51501	**866-667-3386**	712-328-8888
Ameritel Inn Boise Towne Square					
7965 W Emerald St	Boise	ID	83704	**800-600-6001**	208-378-7000
Ameritel Inn Pocatello					
1440 Pocatello Bench Rd	Pocatello	ID	83201	**800-600-6001**	208-234-7500
Amway Grand Plaza Hotel					
187 Monroe Ave NW	Grand Rapids	MI	49503	**800-253-3590**	616-774-2000
Anaheim Plaza Hotel & Suites					
1700 S Harbor Blvd	Anaheim	CA	92802	**800-631-4144**	714-772-5900
Andaz San Diego 600 F St	San Diego	CA	92101	**877-489-4489**	619-849-1234
Andrews Hotel					
624 Post St	San Francisco	CA	94109	**800-926-3739**	415-563-6877
Angler's Inn 265 N Millward	Jackson	WY	83001	**800-867-4667**	307-733-3682
Antler Inn					
43 W Pearl St PO Box 575	Jackson	WY	83001	**800-483-8667**	307-733-2535
Apple Tree Inn					
9508 N Div St	Spokane	WA	99218	**800-323-5796**	509-466-3020
Applewood Manor Inn					
62 Cumberland Cir	Asheville	NC	28801	**800-442-2197**	828-254-2244
Aqua Bamboo 2425 Kuhio Ave	Honolulu	HI	96815	**855-747-0754**	808-922-7777
Aqua Hospitality Corp					
445 Seaside Ave	Honolulu	HI	96815	**855-747-0755**	808-923-2345
Aqua Waikiki Wave					
2299 Kuhio Ave	Honolulu	HI	96815	**855-747-0754**	808-922-1262
ARC the Hotel Ottawa					
140 Slater St	Ottawa	ON	K1P5H6	**800-699-2516**	613-238-2888
Argonaut Hotel					
495 Jefferson St	San Francisco	CA	94109	**866-415-0704**	415-563-0800
Arizona Charlie's Boulder Casino & Hotel					
4575 Boulder Hwy	Las Vegas	NV	89121	**888-236-9066**	702-951-5800
Arizona Charlie's Decatur Casino & Hotel					
740 S Decatur Blvd	Las Vegas	NV	89107	**888-236-8645**	702-258-5200
Arizona Inn 2200 E Elm St	Tucson	AZ	85719	**800-933-1093**	
Ashland Springs Hotel					
212 E Main St	Ashland	OR	97520	**888-795-4545**	541-488-1700
Asticou Inn					
15 Peabody Dr	Northeast Harbor	ME	04662	**800-258-3373**	207-276-3344
Aston Hotels & Resorts					
2155 Kalakaua Ave Ste 500	Honolulu	HI	96815	**800-775-4228**	808-931-1400
Astor Crowne Plaza					
739 Canal St	New Orleans	LA	70130	**877-408-9661**	504-962-0500
Astor Hotel, The					
924 E Juneau Ave	Milwaukee	WI	53202	**800-558-0200**	414-271-4220
Atheneum Suite Hotel & Conference Ctr					
1000 Brush Ave	Detroit	MI	48226	**800-772-2323**	313-962-2323
Atlantic Eyrie Lodge					
6 Norman Rd	Bar Harbor	ME	04609	**800-422-2883**	
Atlantic Sands Hotel					
101 N Boardwalk	Rehoboth Beach	DE	19971	**800-422-0600**	302-227-2511
Atrium Hotel					
18700 MacArthur Blvd	Irvine	CA	92612	**800-854-3012**	949-833-2770
Auberge du Soleil					
180 Rutherford Hill Rd	Rutherford	CA	94573	**800-348-5406**	707-963-1211
Auberge du Vieux-Port					
97 Rue de la Commune E	Montreal	QC	H2Y1J1	**888-660-7678**	514-876-0081
Auberge Saint-Antoine					
8 rue Saint-Antoine	Quebec	QC	G1K4C9	**888-692-2211**	418-692-2211
Austin Hotel & Spa					
305 Malvern Ave	Hot Springs	AR	71901	**877-623-6697**	501-623-6600
Avalon Corporate Furnished Apartments					
1553 Empire Blvd	Webster	NY	14580	**800-934-9763**	585-671-4421
Avalon Hotel 16 W Tenth St	Erie	PA	16501	**888-295-4949**	814-459-2220
Avenue Inn & Spa					
33 Wilmington Ave	Rehoboth Beach	DE	19971	**800-433-5870**	
Avenue Plaza Resort					
2111 St Charles Ave	New Orleans	LA	70130	**800-614-8685**	504-566-1212
Ayres Hotel Anaheim					
2550 E Katella Ave	Anaheim	CA	92806	**800-595-5692**	714-634-2106
Bahama House					
2001 S Atlantic Ave	Daytona Beach Shores	FL	32118	**888-687-1894**	
Balance Rock Inn					
21 Albert Meadow	Bar Harbor	ME	04609	**800-753-0494**	207-288-2610
Balboa Park Inn					
3402 Pk Blvd	San Diego	CA	92103	**800-938-8181**	619-298-0823
Bally's Casino Tunica					
1450 Bally's Blvd	Robinsonville	MS	38664	**866-422-5597**	
Balmoral Inn					
120 Balmoral Ave	Biloxi	MS	39531	**800-393-9131**	228-388-6776
Bar Harbor Hotel-Bluenose Inn					
90 Eden St	Bar Harbor	ME	04609	**800-445-4077**	207-288-3348
Barnstead Inn					
349 Bonnet St	Manchester Center	VT	05255	**800-331-1619**	802-362-1619
Baronne Plaza Hotel					
201 Baronne St	New Orleans	LA	70112	**888-756-0083**	504-522-0083
Barrington Hotel & Suites					
263 Shepherd of the Hills Expy	Branson	MO	65616	**800-760-8866**	417-334-8866
Bay Club Hotel & Marina					
2131 Shelter Island Dr	San Diego	CA	92106	**800-672-0800**	619-224-8888
Bay Park Hotel					
1425 Munras Ave	Monterey	CA	93940	**800-338-3564***	831-649-1020
*Resv					
Baymont Inn					
4025 McDonald Dr	Dubuque	IA	52003	**800-337-0550**	563-582-3752
Beacher's Lodge					
6970 A1A S	Saint Augustine	FL	32080	**800-527-8849**	904-471-8849
Beacon Hotel					
720 Ocean Dr	Miami Beach	FL	33139	**877-674-8200**	305-674-8200
Beacon Hotel & Corporate Quarters					
1615 Rhode Island Ave NW	Washington	DC	20036	**800-823-1700**	202-296-2100

Name / Address	City	State	Zip	Toll-Free	Phone
Beaver Creek Lodge 26 Avon Dale Ln	Beaver Creek	CO	81620	**800-525-7280**	970-845-9800
Beecher Hill LLC 9991 Beecher Hill Rd	Peshastin	WA	98847	**866-414-0559**	509-548-0559
Beechwood Hotel 363 Plantation St	Worcester	MA	01605	**800-344-2589**	508-754-5789
Bell Tower Hotel 300 S Thayer St	Ann Arbor	MI	48104	**800-562-3559**	734-769-3010
Bell Tower Inn 1235 Second St SW	Rochester	MN	55902	**800-448-7583**	507-289-2233
Bellasera Hotel 221 Ninth St S	Naples	FL	34102	**855-990-0301**	239-649-7333
Bellevue Club Hotel 11200 SE Sixth St	Bellevue	WA	98004	**800-579-1110**	425-454-4424
Bellmoor, The 6 Christian St	Rehoboth Beach	DE	19971	**800-425-2355**	302-227-5800
Belvedere Hotel 319 W 48th St	New York	NY	10036	**800-492-8122**	212-245-7000
Ben Lomond Suites LLC 2510 Washington Blvd	Ogden	UT	84401	**877-627-1900**	801-627-1900
Benjamin, The 125 E 50th St	New York	NY	10022	**866-222-2365**	212-715-2500
Benson, The 309 SW Broadway	Portland	OR	97205	**800-663-1144**	503-228-2000
Berkeley Hotel, The 1200 E Cary St	Richmond	VA	23219	**888-780-4422**	804-780-1300
Bernards Inn 27 Mine Brook Rd	Bernardsville	NJ	07924	**888-766-0002**	908-766-0002
Bernardus Lodge 415 Carmel Valley Rd	Carmel Valley	CA	93924	**800-223-2533**	831-658-3400
Best Western Chincoteague Island 7105 Maddox Blvd	Chincoteague Island	VA	23336	**800-553-6117**	757-336-6557
Best Western International Inc 6201 N 24th Pkwy	Phoenix	AZ	85016	**800-528-1234**	602-957-4200
Best Western Laguna Brisas Spa Hotel 1600 S Coast Hwy	Laguna Beach	CA	92651	**888-296-6834**	949-497-7272
Best Western Victorian Inn 487 Foam St	Monterey	CA	93940	**800-232-4141**	831-373-8000
Betsy Hotel 1440 Ocean Dr	Miami Beach	FL	33139	**866-792-3879**	305-531-6100
Beverly Hills Hotel 9641 Sunset Blvd	Beverly Hills	CA	90210	**800-650-1842**	310-276-2251
Beverly Hilton 9876 Wilshire Blvd	Beverly Hills	CA	90210	**800-605-8896**	310-274-7777
Beverly Wilshire - A Four Seasons Hotel 9500 Wilshire Blvd	Beverly Hills	CA	90212	**800-545-4000**	310-275-5200
Bienville House Hotel 320 Decatur St	New Orleans	LA	70130	**800-535-7836**	504-529-2345
Billings C'mon Inn Hotel 2020 Overland Ave	Billings	MT	59102	**800-655-1170**	406-655-1100
Billings Hotel & Convention Ctr 1223 Mullowney Ln	Billings	MT	59101	**800-537-7286**	406-248-7151
Biltmore Greensboro Hotel 111 W Washington St *General	Greensboro	NC	27401	**800-332-0303***	336-272-3474
Biltmore Hotel & Suites 2151 Laurelwood Rd	Santa Clara	CA	95054	**800-255-9925**	408-988-8411
Biltmore Hotel Oklahoma 401 S Meridian Ave	Oklahoma City	OK	73108	**800-522-6620**	405-947-7681
Biltmore Suites 205 W Madison St	Baltimore	MD	21201	**800-868-5064**	410-728-6550
Bismarck Expressway Suites 180 E Bismarck Expy	Bismarck	ND	58504	**888-774-5566**	701-222-3311
Blackfoot Inn 5940 Blackfoot Trl SE	Calgary	AB	T2H2B5	**800-661-1151**	403-252-2253
Blackwell, The 2110 Tuttle Pk Pl	Columbus	OH	43210	**866-247-4003**	614-247-4000
Blakely New York 136 W 55th St	New York	NY	10019	**800-735-0710**	212-245-1800
Blantyre 16 Blantyre Rd PO Box 995	Lenox	MA	01240	**844-881-0104**	413-637-3556
Blue Horizon Hotel 1225 Robson St	Vancouver	BC	V6E1C3	**800-663-1333**	604-688-1411
Blue Moon Hotel 944 Collins Ave	Miami Beach	FL	33139	**800-553-7739**	305-673-2262
Blue Parrot Inn 409 Angela St	Key West	FL	33040	**800-549-4430**	305-296-0033
Bluenose Inn & Suites 636 Bedford Hwy	Halifax	NS	B3M2L8	**800-553-5339**	800-565-2301
Boardwalk Plaza Hotel 2 Olive Ave	Rehoboth Beach	DE	19971	**800-332-3224**	302-227-7169
Bodega Bay Lodge 103 Coast Hwy 1 *Resv	Bodega Bay	CA	94923	**888-875-2250***	707-875-3525
Bohemian Hotel Celebration 700 Bloom St	Celebration	FL	34747	**888-249-4007**	407-566-6000
Bond Place Hotel 65 Dundas St E	Toronto	ON	M5B2G8	**800-268-9390**	416-362-6061
Boone Tavern Hotel of Berea College 100 S Main St	Berea	KY	40403	**800-366-9358**	859-985-3700
Borgata Hotel Casino & Spa 1 Borgata Way	Atlantic City	NJ	08401	**877-786-9900**	609-317-1000
Boston Harbor Hotel 70 Rowes Wharf	Boston	MA	02110	**800-752-7077**	617-439-7000
Boston Park Plaza Hotel & Towers 50 Pk Plz	Boston	MA	02116	**800-225-2008**	617-426-2000
Boulder Adventure Lodge (A-Lodge) 91 Four Mile Canyon Rd	Boulder	CO	80302	**800-556-3446**	435-335-7460
Boulder Station Hotel & Casino 4111 Boulder Hwy	Las Vegas	NV	89121	**800-683-7777**	702-432-7777
Bourbon Orleans - A Wyndham Historic Hotel 717 Orleans St	New Orleans	LA	70116	**866-513-9744**	504-523-2222
Bradley Inn 3063 Bristol Rd	New Harbor	ME	04554	**800-942-5560**	207-677-2105
Brazilian Court, The 301 Australian Ave	Palm Beach	FL	33480	**800-552-0335**	561-655-7740
Breakers at Waikiki, The 250 Beach Walk	Honolulu	HI	96815	**800-426-0494**	808-923-3181
Breakers Hotel & Suites 105 Second St	Rehoboth Beach	DE	19971	**800-441-8009**	302-227-6688
Breakwater Inn 1711 Glacier Ave	Juneau	AK	99801	**888-586-6303**	
Brent House Hotel 1512 Jefferson Hwy	New Orleans	LA	70121	**800-535-3986**	504-842-4140
Bridgewater Hotel 723 First Ave	Fairbanks	AK	99701	**800-528-4916**	
Bristol Hotel 1055 First Ave	San Diego	CA	92101	**800-662-4477**	619-232-6141
Brookshire Suites 120 E Lombard St	Baltimore	MD	21202	**855-345-5033**	410-625-1300
Brookstown Inn 200 Brookstown Ave	Winston-Salem	NC	27101	**800-845-4262**	336-725-1120
Brookstreet Hotel 525 Legget Dr	Ottawa	ON	K2K2W2	**888-826-2220**	613-271-1800
Brown County Inn 51 State Rd 46	Nashville	IN	47448	**800-772-5249**	812-988-2291
Brown Hotel, The 335 W Broadway St	Louisville	KY	40202	**888-888-5252**	502-583-1234
Brown Palace Hotel 321 17th St	Denver	CO	80202	**800-321-2599**	303-297-3111
Brown's Wharf Inn 121 Atlantic Ave	Boothbay Harbor	ME	04538	**800-334-8110**	207-633-5440
Bryant Park Hotel 40 W 40th St	New York	NY	10018	**877-640-9300**	212-869-0100
Budget Host International 2307 Roosevelt Dr	Arlington	TX	76016	**800-283-4678**	817-861-6088
Budget Suites of America 2770 N Hwy 360	Grand Prairie	TX	75050	**866-877-2000**	972-647-2500
Buena Vista Suites 8203 World Ctr Dr *Resv	Orlando	FL	32821	**800-537-7737***	407-239-8588
Business Inn 180 MacLaren St	Ottawa	ON	K2P0L3	**800-363-1777**	613-232-1121
C'mon Inn Grand Forks 3051 32nd Ave S	Grand Forks	ND	58201	**800-255-2323**	701-775-3320
California Hotel & Casino 12 E Ogden Ave	Las Vegas	NV	89101	**800-634-6505**	702-385-1222
Cambridge Suites Hotel Halifax 1583 Brunswick St	Halifax	NS	B3J3P5	**800-565-1263**	902-420-0555
Cambridge Suites Hotel Toronto 15 Richmond St E	Toronto	ON	M5C1N2	**800-463-1990**	416-368-1990
Canad Inns - Club Regent Casino Hotel 1415 Regent Ave W	Winnipeg	MB	R2C3B2	**888-332-2623**	204-667-5560
Canad Inns Fort Garry 1824 Pembina Hwy	Winnipeg	MB	R3T2G2	**888-332-2623**	204-261-7450
Canad Inns Garden City 2100 McPhillips St	Winnipeg	MB	R2V3T9	**888-332-2623**	204-633-0024
Canad Inns Polo Park 1405 St Matthews Ave	Winnipeg	MB	R3G0K5	**888-332-2623**	204-775-8791
Canal Park Lodge 250 Canal Pk Dr	Duluth	MN	55802	**800-777-8560**	218-279-6000
Canandaigua Inn on the Lake 770 S Main St	Canandaigua	NY	14424	**800-228-2801**	585-394-7800
Canary Hotel 31 W Carrillo	Santa Barbara	CA	93101	**866-999-5401**	805-884-0300
Cannery Casino & Hotel, The *Cannery Casino Resorts LLC* 2121 E Craig Rd	North Las Vegas	NV	89030	**866-999-4899**	702-507-5700
Capital Hill Hotel & Suites 88 Albert St	Ottawa	ON	K1P5E9	**800-463-7705**	613-235-1413
Capital Hotel 111 W Markham St	Little Rock	AR	72201	**877-637-0037**	501-374-7474
Capitol Plaza Hotel & Conference Ctr 100 State St	Montpelier	VT	05602	**800-274-5252**	802-223-5252
Capitol Plaza Hotel Jefferson City 415 W McCarty St	Jefferson City	MO	65101	**800-338-8088**	573-635-1234
Capt Hirams Resort 1606 Indian River Dr	Sebastian	FL	32958	**888-447-2671**	772-589-4345
Caribe Royale Orlando All-Suites Hotel & Convention Ctr 8101 World Ctr Dr *Resv	Orlando	FL	32821	**800-823-8300***	407-238-8000
Carlson *Radisson Hotels & Resorts* 701 Carlson Pkwy	Minnetonka	MN	55305	**800-333-3333**	763-212-5000
Carlson Hotels Worldwide *Country Inns & Suites by Carlson* 11340 Blondo St Ste 100	Omaha	NE	68164	**800-600-7275**	
Carlton on Madison Ave 88 Madison Ave *Resv	New York	NY	10016	**800-601-8500***	212-532-4100
Carlyle Hotel, The 1731 New Hampshire Ave NW	Washington	DC	20009	**877-301-0019**	202-234-3200
Carmel River Inn 26600 Oliver Rd	Carmel	CA	93923	**800-882-8142**	831-624-1575
Carnegie Hotel 1216 W State of Franklin Rd	Johnson City	TN	37604	**866-757-8277**	423-979-6400
Carolina Inn 211 Pittsboro St	Chapel Hill	NC	27516	**800-962-8519**	919-933-2001
Carousel Beachfront Hotel & Suites 11700 Coastal Hwy	Ocean City	MD	21842	**800-641-0011**	410-524-1000
Carousel Inn & Suites 1530 S Harbor Blvd	Anaheim	CA	92802	**800-854-6767**	714-758-0444
Cartier Place Suite Hotel 180 Cooper St	Ottawa	ON	K2P2L5	**800-236-8399**	613-236-5000
Casa Madrona Hotel 801 Bridgeway *General	Sausalito	CA	94965	**800-288-0502***	415-332-0502
Casa Monica Hotel 95 Cordova St *Help Line	Saint Augustine	FL	32084	**800-648-1888***	904-827-1888
Casa Munras Hotel 700 Munras Ave	Monterey	CA	93940	**800-222-2446**	831-375-2411
Casablanca Hotel 147 W 43rd St	New York	NY	10036	**888-922-7225**	212-869-1212
Cascades Inn 3226 Shepherd of the Hills Expy	Branson	MO	65616	**800-588-8424**	417-335-8424
Casino Royale Hotel 3411 Las Vegas Blvd S	Las Vegas	NV	89109	**800-854-7666**	702-737-3500

Name / Address	City	State	Zip	Toll-Free	Phone
Castle in the Sand Hotel 3701 Atlantic Ave	Ocean City	MD	21842	**800-552-7263**	410-289-6846
Castle Inn & Suites 1734 S Harbor Blvd	Anaheim	CA	92802	**800-227-8530**	714-774-8111
Castle on the Hudson 400 Benedict Ave	Tarrytown	NY	10591	**800-616-4487**	914-631-1980
Center Court Historic Inn & Cottages 1075 Duval St C-19	Key West	FL	33040	**800-797-8787**	305-296-9292
Century Hotel South Beach 140 Ocean Dr	Miami Beach	FL	33139	**877-659-8855**	305-674-8855
Century Plaza Hotel & Spa 1015 Burrard St	Vancouver	BC	V6Z1Y5	**800-663-1818**	604-687-0575
Century Suites Hotel 300 SR-446	Bloomington	IN	47401	**800-766-5446**	812-336-7777
Chamberlain West Hollywood 1000 Westmount Dr	West Hollywood	CA	90069	**877-686-2082**	310-657-7400
Chancellor Hotel on Union Square 433 Powell St	San Francisco	CA	94102	**800-428-4748**	415-362-2004
Chandler Inn 26 Chandler St	Boston	MA	02116	**800-842-3450**	617-482-3450
Charles Hotel Harvard Square 1 Bennett St	Cambridge	MA	02138	**800-882-1818**	617-864-1200
Charleston Place 205 Meeting St	Charleston	SC	29401	**888-635-2350**	843-722-4900
Charter at Beaver Creek 120 Offerson Rd PO Box 5310	Avon	CO	81620	**800-525-6660**	970-949-6660
Chase Hotel at Palm Springs 200 W Arenas Rd	Palm Springs	CA	92262	**877-532-4273**	760-320-8866
Chase Park Plaza 212 N KingsHwy Blvd *Resv	Saint Louis	MO	63108	**877-587-2427***	314-633-3000
Chateau Louis Hotel & Conference Centre 11727 Kingsway	Edmonton	AB	T5G3A1	**800-661-9843**	780-452-7770
Chateau on the Lake 415 N State Hwy 265	Branson	MO	65616	**888-333-5253**	417-334-1161
Chateau Vaudreuil Suites Hotel 21700 Rt Transcanada Hwy	Vaudreuil-Dorion	QC	J7V8P3	**800-363-7896**	450-455-0955
Chateau Versailles 1659 Sherbrooke St W	Montreal	QC	H3H1E3	**888-933-8111**	514-933-3611
Chelsea Savoy Hotel 204 W 23rd St	New York	NY	10011	**866-929-9353**	212-929-9353
Chesterfield Hotel 363 Cocoanut Row	Palm Beach	FL	33480	**800-243-7871**	561-659-5800
Chestnut Hill Hotel 8229 Germantown Ave	Philadelphia	PA	19118	**800-628-9744**	215-242-5905
Chiltern Inn 11 Cromwell Harbor Rd	Bar Harbor	ME	04609	**800-709-0114**	207-288-3371
Chimo Hotel 1199 Joseph Cyr St	Ottawa	ON	K1J7T4	**800-387-9779**	613-744-1060
Choice Hotels International Inc 10750 Columbia Pk *NYSE: CHH*	Silver Spring	MD	20901	**800-424-6423**	301-592-5000
Choice Hotels International, Inc. 997 New Loudon Rd	Latham	NY	12110	**800-424-6423**	518-785-0931
Choice Hotelsÿ 3050 University Pkwy	Winston-Salem	NC	27105	**877-424-6423**	
Chrysalis Inn & Spa 804 Tenth St	Bellingham	WA	98225	**888-808-0005**	360-756-1005
Churchill Hotel 1914 Connecticut Ave NW	Washington	DC	20009	**800-424-2464**	202-797-2000
Cincinnatian Hotel 601 Vine St	Cincinnati	OH	45202	**800-942-9000**	513-381-3000
Circus Circus Hotel & Casino Reno 500 N Sierra St	Reno	NV	89503	**800-648-5010**	775-329-0711
Circus Circus Hotel Casino & Theme Park Las Vegas 2880 Las Vegas Blvd S *Resv	Las Vegas	NV	89109	**800-634-3450***	702-734-0410
Cleftstone Manor 92 Eden St	Bar Harbor	ME	04609	**888-288-4951**	207-288-8086
Cliff House at Pikes Peak 306 Canyon Ave	Manitou Springs	CO	80829	**888-212-7000**	
Clinton Inn Hotel 145 Dean Dr	Tenafly	NJ	07670	**800-275-4411**	201-871-3200
ClubHouse Hotel & Suites Sioux Falls 2320 S Louise Ave	Sioux Falls	SD	57106	**866-534-8700**	605-361-8700
Coast Edmonton House Suite Hotel 1090 W Georgia S Ste 900	Vancouver	BC	V6E3V7	**800-716-6199**	604-682-7982
Coast Plaza Hotel 1316 33 St Ne	Calgary	AB	T2A6B6	**800-661-1464**	403-248-8888
Coastal Inn Concorde 379 Windmill Rd	Dartmouth	NS	B3A1J6	**800-565-1565**	902-465-7777
Coastal Inns Inc 111 Warwick St Box 280	Digby	NS	B0V1A0	**800-665-7829**	800-401-1155
Coastal Palms Hotel 120th St Coastal Hwy	Ocean City	MD	21842	**800-641-0011**	
Cocca's Inn & Suites Corner of Wolf Rd & Central Ave	Albany	NY	12205	**888-426-2227**	518-459-2240
Coffee Exchange 207 Wickenden St	Providence	RI	02903	**877-263-3334**	401-273-1198
Colby Hill Inn 33 The Oaks PO Box 779	Henniker	NH	03242	**800-531-0330**	603-428-3281
Colonnade Hotel 120 Huntington Ave	Boston	MA	02116	**800-962-3030**	617-424-7000
Colorado Belle Hotel & Casino 2100 S Casino Dr *Resv	Laughlin	NV	89029	**877-460-0777***	702-298-4000
Columbia Gorge Hotel 4000 Westcliff Dr	Hood River	OR	97031	**800-345-1921**	541-386-5566
Columns, The 3811 St Charles Ave	New Orleans	LA	70115	**800-445-9308**	504-899-9308
Comfort Inn & Suites Milwaukee 916 E State St	Milwaukee	WI	53202	**800-424-6423**	414-276-8800
Commander Hotel 1401 Atlantic Ave	Ocean City	MD	21842	**888-289-6166**	
Commonwealth Park Suites Hotel 901 Bank St	Richmond	VA	23219	**888-343-7301**	804-343-7300
Conch House Heritage Inn 625 Truman Ave	Key West	FL	33040	**800-207-5806**	305-293-0020
Conch House Marina Resort 57 Comares Ave	Saint Augustine	FL	32080	**800-940-6256**	904-829-8646
Contactpointe of Pittsburgh 2593 Wexford Bayne Rd Ste 200	Sewickley	PA	15143	**877-255-4916**	412-788-0680
Cooper Hotel & Conference Ctr 12230 Preston Rd	Dallas	TX	75230	**800-444-5187**	972-386-0306
Copley Square Hotel 47 Huntington Ave	Boston	MA	02116	**800-225-7062**	617-536-9000
Cornhusker Hotel, The 333 S 13th St	Lincoln	NE	68508	**866-706-7706**	402-474-7474
Cosmopolitan Hotel Toronto 8 Colborne St	Toronto	ON	M5E1E1	**800-958-3488**	416-350-2000
Country Inn at the Mall 936 Stillwater Ave *Resv	Bangor	ME	04401	**800-244-3961***	207-941-0200
Country Inn Lake Resort 1332 Airport Rd	Hot Springs	AR	71913	**800-822-7402**	501-767-3535
Courtyard Fort Lauderdale Beach 440 Seabreeze Blvd	Fort Lauderdale	FL	33316	**888-236-2427**	954-524-8733
Cove Inn 900 Broad Ave S	Naples	FL	34102	**800-255-4365**	239-262-7161
Cowboy Village Resort 120 S Flat Creek Dr PO Box 38	Jackson	WY	83001	**800-962-4988**	307-733-3121
Creekside Inn 3400 El Camino Real	Palo Alto	CA	94306	**800-492-7335**	650-493-2411
Crest Hotel & Suites 1670 James Ave	Miami Beach	FL	33139	**800-531-3880**	305-531-0321
Cross Creek Resort 3815 Pennsylvania 8	Titusville	PA	16354	**800-461-3173**	814-827-9611
Crown American Hotels Co Pasquerilla Plz	Johnstown	PA	15907	**800-245-9295**	814-533-4600
Crown Reef Resort 2913 S Ocean Blvd	Myrtle Beach	SC	29577	**877-435-9125**	843-626-8077
Crowne Plaza Chateau Lacombe 10111 Bellamy Hill	Edmonton	AB	T5J1N7	**800-661-8801**	780-428-6611
Crowne Plaza Syracuse 701 E Genesee St	Syracuse	NY	13210	**888-227-6963**	315-479-7000
Crystal Beach Suites & Health Club 6985 Collins Ave	Miami Beach	FL	33141	**888-643-4630**	305-865-9555
Crystal Inn 185 S State St Ste 1300 *General	Salt Lake City	UT	84111	**800-662-2525***	801-320-7200
Crystal Inn Salt Lake City Downtown 230 W 500 S	Salt Lake City	UT	84101	**800-662-2525**	801-328-4466
Curtis, The 1405 Curtis St	Denver	CO	80202	**800-525-6651**	303-571-0300
Custom Hotel 8639 Lincoln Blvd	Los Angeles	CA	90045	**877-287-8601**	310-645-0400
Dan'l Webster Inn 149 Main St	Sandwich	MA	02563	**800-444-3566**	508-888-3622
Dauphine Orleans Hotel 415 Dauphine St	New Orleans	LA	70112	**800-521-7111**	504-586-1800
Davenport Hotel, The 10 S Post St	Spokane	WA	99201	**800-899-1482**	509-455-8888
Days Inns Worldwide Inc 215 W 94th St Broadway	New York	NY	10025	**800-225-3297**	212-866-6400
Daytona Beach Resort & Conference Ctr 2700 N Atlantic Ave	Daytona Beach	FL	32118	**800-654-6216**	386-672-3770
Daytona Inn Beach Resort 219 S Atlantic Ave *General	Daytona Beach	FL	32118	**800-874-1822***	386-252-3626
Dearborn Inn the - A Marriott Hotel 20301 Oakwood Blvd	Dearborn	MI	48124	**800-228-9290**	313-271-2700
Deerfoot Inn & Casino 1000 11500 35th St SE	Calgary	AB	T2Z3W4	**877-236-5225**	403-236-7529
Del Monte Lodge Renaissance Rochester Hotel & Spa, The 41 N Main St	Pittsford	NY	14534	**866-237-5979**	585-381-9900
DELAMAR Greenwich Harbor 500 Steamboat Rd	Greenwich	CT	06830	**866-335-2627**	203-661-9800
Delta King Riverboat Hotel 1000 Front St	Sacramento	CA	95814	**800-825-5464**	916-444-5464
Desert Riviera Hotel 610 E Palm Canyon Dr	Palm Springs	CA	92264	**866-270-8322**	760-327-5314
Destination Hotels & Resorts Inc 10333 E Dry Creek Rd Ste 450	Englewood	CO	80112	**855-893-1011**	303-799-3830
Diamond Head Inn 605 Diamond St	San Diego	CA	92109	**888-478-7829**	858-273-1900
Dinah's Garden Hotel 4261 El Camino Real	Palo Alto	CA	94306	**800-227-8220**	650-493-2844
Dolphin Beach Resort 4900 Gulf Blvd	Saint Pete Beach	FL	33706	**800-237-8916**	727-360-7011
Dolphin Inn 1705 Atlantic Ave	Virginia Beach	VA	23451	**800-365-3467**	757-491-1420
Donatello, The 501 Post St	San Francisco	CA	94102	**800-258-2366**	415-441-7100
Doubletree Claremont 555 W Foothill Blvd	Claremont	CA	91711	**800-222-8733**	909-626-2411
Doubletree Hotel Downtown Wilmington Legal District 700 N King St	Wilmington	DE	19801	**800-222-8733**	302-655-0400
Doubletree North Shore Hotel 9599 Skokie Blvd	Skokie	IL	60077	**800-445-8667**	847-679-7000
Downtown Erie Hotel 18 W 18th St	Erie	PA	16501	**800-832-9101**	814-456-2961
Drake Hotel, The 140 E Walton Pl	Chicago	IL	60611	**800-553-7253**	312-787-2200
Driftwood Hotel 435 Willoughby Ave	Juneau	AK	99801	**800-544-2239**	907-586-2280
Driftwood Shores Resort 88416 First Ave	Florence	OR	97439	**800-422-5091**	541-997-8263
Driskill Hotel 604 Brazos St	Austin	TX	78701	**800-252-9367**	512-474-5911
Drury Hotels Company LLC 721 Emerson Rd Ste 400	Saint Louis	MO	63141	**800-378-7946**	314-429-2255
Duke Towers- All Condominium Hotel 807 W Trinity Ave	Durham	NC	27701	**866-385-3869**	919-687-4444
Duke's 8th Avenue Hotel 630 W Eigth Ave	Anchorage	AK	99501	**800-478-4837**	907-274-6213
Dunes Manor Hotel 2800 Baltimore Ave	Ocean City	MD	21842	**800-523-2888**	410-289-1100
Dunhill Hotel 237 N Tryon St	Charlotte	NC	28202	**800-354-4141**	704-332-4141

	City	State	Zip	Toll-Free	Phone
Dynasty Suites 1235 W Colton Ave *General	Redlands	CA	92374	**800-874-8958***	909-793-6648
Eagle Mountain House 179 Carter Notch Rd PO Box 804	Jackson	NH	03846	**800-966-5779**	603-383-9111
East Canyon Hotel & Spa 288 E Camino Monte Vista	Palm Springs	CA	92262	**877-324-6835**	760-320-1928
Eden House 1015 Fleming St	Key West	FL	33040	**800-533-5397**	
Edgewater Beach Hotel 1901 Gulf Shore Blvd N	Naples	FL	34102	**866-624-1695**	888-564-1308
Edgewater Hotel 2411 Alaskan Way Pier 67	Seattle	WA	98121	**800-624-0670**	206-728-7000
Edgewater Resort 200 Edgewater Cir	Hot Springs	AR	71913	**800-234-3687**	501-767-3311
Edgewater Resort & Waterpark 2400 London Rd	Duluth	MN	55812	**800-777-7925**	218-728-3601
Edmonds Harbor Inn & Suites 130 W Dayton	Edmonds	WA	98020	**800-441-8033**	425-771-5021
El Cortez Hotel & Casino 600 E Fremont St	Las Vegas	NV	89101	**800-634-6703**	702-385-5200
El Rey Inn 1862 Cerillos Rd	Santa Fe	NM	87505	**800-521-1349**	505-982-1931
El Tovar Hotel 1 Main St	Grand Canyon	AZ	86023	**888-297-2757**	928-638-2631
Elan Hotel 8435 Beverly Blvd	Los Angeles	CA	90048	**866-203-2212**	323-658-6663
Eldorado Hotel 309 W San Francisco St	Santa Fe	NM	87501	**800-955-4455**	505-988-4455
Eldorado Hotel Casino 345 N Virginia St *Resv	Reno	NV	89501	**800-879-8879***	775-786-5700
Eldridge Hotel 701 Massachusetts St	Lawrence	KS	66044	**800-527-0909**	785-749-5011
Eliot Hotel, The 370 Commonwealth Ave	Boston	MA	02215	**800-443-5468**	617-267-1607
Elk Country Inn 480 W Pearl St PO Box 1255	Jackson	WY	83001	**800-483-8667**	307-733-2364
Elvis Presley's Heartbreak Hotel 3677 Elvis Presley Blvd	Memphis	TN	38116	**877-777-0606**	901-332-1000
Embassy Hotel & Suites 25 Cartier St	Ottawa	ON	K2P1J2	**800-661-5495**	613-237-2111
Emerald Queen Hotel & Casino 5700 Pacific Hwy E	Fife	WA	98424	**888-820-3555**	253-922-2000
Emerson Resort & Spa 5340 Rt 28	Mount Tremper	NY	12457	**877-688-2828**	845-688-2828
Emily Morgan Hotel 705 E Houston St	San Antonio	TX	78205	**800-824-6674**	210-225-5100
Empire Landmark Hotel & Conference Centre 1400 Robson St	Vancouver	BC	V6G1B9	**800-830-6144**	604-687-0511
Enclave Suites of Orlando 6165 Carrier Dr	Orlando	FL	32819	**800-457-0077**	407-351-1155
Epoque Hotels 2500 NE 135th St Ste 502	North Miami	FL	33181	**866-376-7831**	305-538-9697
Ethan Allen Hotel 21 Lake Ave Ext	Danbury	CT	06811	**800-742-1776**	203-744-1776
Euro-Suites Hotel University Centre 501 Chestnut Ridge Rd	Morgantown	WV	26505	**800-678-4837**	
Evergreen Lodge 250 S Frontage Rd W	Vail	CO	81657	**800-284-8245**	970-476-7810
Excalibur Hotel & Casino 3850 Las Vegas Blvd S	Las Vegas	NV	89109	**877-750-5464**	702-597-7777
Executive Hotel Vintage Court 650 Bush St	San Francisco	CA	94108	**888-388-3932**	415-392-4666
Executive Inn 978 Phillips Ln	Louisville	KY	40209	**888-205-8144**	502-367-6161
Executive Inn Group Corp *Executive Hotels & Resorts* 1080 Howe St 8th Fl	Vancouver	BC	V6Z2T1	**866-642-6888**	604-642-5250
Executive Pacific Plaza Hotel 400 Spring St	Seattle	WA	98104	**888-388-3932**	206-623-3900
Executive Suite Hotel 4360 SpenaRd Rd	Anchorage	AK	99517	**888-315-2378**	907-243-6366
Expressway Hotels 4303 17th Ave S	Fargo	ND	58103	**877-239-4303**	701-239-4303
Extended Stay America 11525 N Community House Rd Ste 100	Charlotte	NC	28277	**800-804-3724**	980-345-1600
Extended Stay Hotels *Crossland Economy Studios* 11525 N Community House Rd Ste 100	Charlotte	NC	28277	**800-804-3724**	980-345-1600
Extended StayAmerica 11525 N Community House Rd Ste 100	Charlotte	NC	28277	**800-804-3724**	980-345-1600
StudioPLUS Deluxe Studios 530 Woods Lake Rd	Greenville	SC	29607	**800-804-3724**	864-288-4300
Fairbanks Princess Riverside Lodge 4477 Pikes Landing Rd	Fairbanks	AK	99709	**800-426-0500**	907-455-4477
Fairmont Hotels & Resorts Inc 100 Wellington St W TD Ctr Ste 1600 *General	Toronto	ON	M5K1B7	**800-441-3313***	416-874-2600
Fairmount Hotel, The 401 S Alamo St	San Antonio	TX	78205	**877-229-8808**	210-224-8800
Fargo C'mon Inn Hotel 4338 20th Ave SW	Fargo	ND	58103	**800-334-1570**	701-277-9944
Fearrington House 2000 Fearrington Village Ctr	Pittsboro	NC	27312	**800-277-0130**	919-542-2121
Fenwick Inn 13801 Coastal Hwy	Ocean City	MD	21842	**800-492-1873**	410-250-1100
Fiesta Henderson 777 W Lk Mead Pkwy	Henderson	NV	89015	**888-899-7770**	702-558-7000
Findlay Inn & Conference Ctr 200 E Main Cross St *Cust Svc	Findlay	OH	45840	**800-825-1455***	419-422-5682
Fireside Inn & Suites 25 Airport Rd	West Lebanon	NH	03784	**877-258-5900**	603-298-5900
First Gold Hotel 270 Main St	Deadwood	SD	57732	**800-274-1876**	605-578-9777
Fisherman's Wharf Inn 22 Commercial St	Boothbay Harbor	ME	04538	**800-628-6872**	207-633-5090

	City	State	Zip	Toll-Free	Phone
Fitger's Inn 600 E Superior St	Duluth	MN	55802	**888-348-4377**	218-722-8826
Fitzpatrick Manhattan Hotel 687 Lexington Ave	New York	NY	10022	**800-367-7701**	212-355-0100
Flagship All Suites Resort 60 N Maine Ave	Atlantic City	NJ	08401	**800-647-7890**	609-343-7447
Foley House Inn 14 W Hull St Chippewa Sq	Savannah	GA	31401	**800-647-3708**	912-232-6622
Foot of the Mountain Motel 200 W Arapahoe Ave	Boulder	CO	80302	**866-773-5489**	303-442-5688
Foothills Inn 1625 N La Crosse St	Rapid City	SD	57701	**877-428-5666**	605-348-5640
Fort Garry, The 222 Broadway	Winnipeg	MB	R3C0R3	**800-665-8088**	204-942-8251
Fort Marcy Hotel Suites 321 Kearney Ave	Santa Fe	NM	87501	**888-667-2775**	505-988-2800
Four Points by Sheraton Charlotte 315 E Woodlawn Rd	Charlotte	NC	28217	**800-368-7764**	704-522-0852
Four Points by Sheraton French Quarter 541 Bourbon St	New Orleans	LA	70130	**866-716-8133**	504-524-7611
Four Queens Hotel & Casino 202 Fremont St	Las Vegas	NV	89101	**800-634-6045**	702-385-4011
Four Sails Resort Hotel 3301 Atlantic Ave	Virginia Beach	VA	23451	**800-227-4213**	757-491-8100
Four Seasons Hotels Inc 1165 Leslie St	Toronto	ON	M3C2K8	**800-332-3442**	416-449-1750
Francis Marion Hotel, The 387 King St	Charleston	SC	29403	**877-756-2121**	843-722-0600
Franklin, The 164 E 87th St	New York	NY	10128	**800-607-4009**	212-369-1000
Fremont Hotel & Casino 200 Fremont St	Las Vegas	NV	89101	**800-634-6460**	702-385-3232
French Quarter Suites Hotel 1119 N Rampart St	New Orleans	LA	70116	**800-457-2253**	504-524-7725
G6 Hospitality LLC *Motel 6* 4001 International Pkwy	Carrollton	TX	75007	**800-466-8356**	972-360-9000
Galt House Hotel 140 N Fourth St	Louisville	KY	40202	**800-843-4258**	502-589-5200
Garden City Hotel 45 Seventh St	Garden City	NY	11530	**877-549-0400**	516-747-3000
Garden Court Hotel 520 Cowper St	Palo Alto	CA	94301	**800-824-9028**	650-322-9000
Garden Place Hotel 6461 Transit Rd	Depew	NY	14043	**877-456-4097**	716-683-7990
Gardens Hotel 526 Angela St	Key West	FL	33040	**800-526-2664**	305-294-2661
Garland, The 4222 Vineland Ave	North Hollywood	CA	91602	**800-238-3759**	818-980-8000
Garrett's Desert Inn 311 Old Santa Fe Trl	Santa Fe	NM	87501	**800-888-2145**	505-982-1851
Gaslamp Plaza Suites 520 E St	San Diego	CA	92101	**800-874-8770**	619-232-9500
Gastonian, The 220 E Gaston St	Savannah	GA	31401	**800-322-6603**	912-232-2869
Gateways Inn 51 Walker St	Lenox	MA	01240	**888-492-9466**	413-637-2532
Gaylord Opryland Hotel & Convention Ctr 2800 Opryland Dr	Nashville	TN	37214	**888-236-2427**	615-889-1000
Geneva on the Lake 1001 Lochland Rd	Geneva	NY	14456	**800-343-6382**	315-789-7190
George Washington University Inn 824 New Hampshire Ave NW	Washington	DC	20037	**800-424-9671**	202-337-6620
Georgetown Inn 1310 Wisconsin Ave	Washington	DC	20007	**866-971-6618**	202-333-8900
Georgian Court Hotel 773 Beatty St	Vancouver	BC	V6B2M4	**800-663-1155**	604-682-5555
Georgian Hotel 1415 Ocean Ave	Santa Monica	CA	90401	**800-538-8147**	310-395-9945
Georgian Resort 384 Canada St	Lake George	NY	12845	**800-525-3436**	518-668-5401
Georgian Terrace Hotel 659 Peachtree St NE	Atlanta	GA	30308	**800-651-2316**	404-897-1991
Gideon Putnam Resort & Spa 24 Gideon Putnam Rd	Saratoga Springs	NY	12866	**800-452-7275**	518-584-3000
Glass House Inn 3202 W 26th St	Erie	PA	16506	**800-956-7222**	814-833-7751
Glen Grove Suites 2837 Yonge St	Toronto	ON	M4N2J6	**800-565-3024**	416-489-8441
Glendorn 1000 Glendorn Dr	Bradford	PA	16701	**800-843-8568**	814-362-6511
Glenerin Inn, The 1695 The Collegeway	Mississauga	ON	L5L3S7	**877-991-9971**	905-828-6103
Glenmore Inn 2720 Glenmore Trl SE	Calgary	AB	T2C2E6	**800-661-3163**	403-279-8611
Glidden House 1901 Ford Dr	Cleveland	OH	44106	**866-812-4537**	216-231-8900
Glorietta Bay Inn 1630 Glorietta Blvd	Coronado	CA	92118	**800-283-9383**	619-435-3101
Gold Coast Hotel & Casino 4000 W Flamingo Rd	Las Vegas	NV	89103	**800-331-5334**	702-367-7111
Goldbelt Hotel Juneau 51 Egan Dr	Juneau	AK	99801	**888-478-6909**	907-586-6900
Golden Eagle Resort 511 Mountain Rd PO Box 1090	Stowe	VT	05672	**800-626-1010**	802-253-4811
Golden Hotel, The 800 11th St	Golden	CO	80401	**800-233-7214**	303-279-0100
Goldener Hirsch Inn 7570 Royal St E *Cust Svc	Park City	UT	84060	**800-252-3373***	435-649-7770
Good Hotel *Good Hotel* 112 Seventh St	San Francisco	CA	94103	**800-444-5819**	415-621-7001
Good-Nite Inn Fremont 4135 Cushing Pkwy	Fremont	CA	94538	**800-648-3466**	510-656-9307
Gouverneur Hotel Montreal (Place-Dupuis) 1000 Sherbrooke St W Ste 2300	Montreal	QC	H3A3R3	**888-910-1111**	
Governor Calvert House 58 State Cir	Annapolis	MD	21401	**800-847-8882**	410-263-2641
Governor's Inn 210 Richards Blvd	Sacramento	CA	95811	**800-999-6689**	916-448-7224

Name / Address	City	State	Zip	Toll-Free	Phone
Grafton on Sunset 8462 W Sunset Blvd	West Hollywood	CA	90069	**800-821-3660**	323-654-4600
Graham, The 1075 Thomas Jefferson St NW	Washington	DC	20007	**855-341-1292**	202-337-0900
Gramercy Park Hotel 2 Lexington Ave	New York	NY	10010	**866-784-1300**	212-920-3300
Grand America Hotel 555 S Main St	Salt Lake City	UT	84111	**800-621-4505**	801-258-6000
Grand Country Inn Grand Country Sq 1945 W Hwy 76	Branson	MO	65616	**888-505-4096**	417-335-3535
Grand Del Mar 5300 Grand Del Mar Ct	San Diego	CA	92130	**855-314-2030**	858-314-2000
Grand Gateway Hotel 1721 N LaCrosse St	Rapid City	SD	57701	**866-742-1300**	605-342-8853
Grand Hotel Minneapolis, The 615 Second Ave S	Minneapolis	MN	55402	**866-843-4726**	612-288-8888
Grand Hotel of Cape May Beach Ave	Cape May	NJ	08204	**800-257-8550**	609-884-5611
Grand Oaks Hotel 2315 Green Mountain Dr	Branson	MO	65616	**800-553-6423**	
Grand Summit Hotel 570 Springfield Ave	Summit	NJ	07901	**800-346-0773**	908-273-3000
Grande Colonial 910 Prospect St	La Jolla	CA	92037	**888-828-5498**	
Grant Plaza Hotel 465 Grant Ave	San Francisco	CA	94108	**800-472-6899**	415-434-3883
Granville Island Hotel 1253 Johnston St *Resv	Vancouver	BC	V6H3R9	**800-663-1840***	604-683-7373
Great Divide Lodge 550 Village Rd PO Box 8059	Breckenridge	CO	80424	**888-400-9590**	970-547-5550
Green Mountain Inn 18 Main St PO Box 60	Stowe	VT	05672	**800-253-7302**	802-253-7301
Green Valley Ranch Resort Casino & Spa 2300 Paseo Verde Pkwy *Resv	Henderson	NV	89052	**866-782-9487***	702-617-7777
Grey Bonnet Inn 831 Rt 100 N	Killington	VT	05751	**800-342-2086**	
Greyfield Inn 4 N Second St Ste 300	Fernandina Beach	FL	32034	**866-401-8581**	904-261-6408
Habana Inn 2200 NW 40th St	Oklahoma City	OK	73112	**800-988-2221**	405-525-0730
Habitat Suites 500 E Highland Mall Blvd	Austin	TX	78752	**800-535-4663**	512-467-6000
Hacienda The at Hotel Santa Fe 1501 Paseo del Peralta	Santa Fe	NM	87501	**855-825-9876**	505-955-7805
Halekulani Hotel 2199 Kalia Rd	Honolulu	HI	96815	**800-367-2343**	808-923-2311
Half Moon Bay Lodge & Conference Ctr 2400 S Cabrillo Hwy	Half Moon Bay	CA	94019	**800-710-0778**	650-726-9000
Halifax Marriott Harborfront Hotel 1919 Upper Water St	Halifax	NS	B3J3J5	**800-450-4442**	902-421-1700
Halliburton House Inn 5184 Morris St	Halifax	NS	B3J1B3	**888-512-3344**	902-420-0658
Hallmark Inns & Resorts 15455 Hallmark Dr Ste 200	Lake Oswego	OR	97035	**888-448-4449**	503-635-4555
Handlery Union Square Hotel 351 Geary St	San Francisco	CA	94102	**800-995-4874**	415-781-7800
Hanover Inn 2 E Wheelock St	Hanover	NH	03755	**800-443-7024**	603-643-4300
Harbor Court Hotel 165 Steuart St	San Francisco	CA	94105	**866-792-6283**	415-882-1300
Harbor View Hotel 131 N Water St Martha's Vineyard PO Box 7	Edgartown	MA	02539	**800-225-6005**	508-627-7000
Harborside Hotel & Marina 55 W St	Bar Harbor	ME	04609	**800-328-5033**	207-288-5033
Harborside Inn 1 Christie's Landing	Newport	RI	02840	**800-427-9444**	401-846-6600
Hard Rock Hotel & Casino Biloxi 777 Beach Blvd	Biloxi	MS	39530	**877-877-6256**	228-374-7625
Hard Rock Hotel San Diego 207 Fifth Ave	San Diego	CA	92101	**866-751-7625**	619-702-3000
Harrah's Council Bluffs 1 Harrahs Blvd	Council Bluffs	IA	51501	**800-342-7724**	712-329-6000
Harrah's Joliet 151 N Joliet St	Joliet	IL	60432	**800-522-4700**	815-740-7800
Harraseeket Inn 162 Main St	Freeport	ME	04032	**800-342-6423**	207-865-9377
Hartness House Inn 30 Orchard St	Springfield	VT	05156	**800-732-4789**	802-885-2115
Harvard Square Hotel 110 Mt Auburn St Harvard Sq	Cambridge	MA	02138	**800-458-5886**	617-864-5200
Harvest Inn 1 Main St	Saint Helena	CA	94574	**800-950-8466**	707-963-9463
Hassayampa Inn 122 E Gurley St *Cust Svc	Prescott	AZ	86301	**800-322-1927***	
Hastings House Country House Hotel 160 Upper Ganges Rd	Salt Spring Island	BC	V8K2S2	**800-661-9255**	250-537-2362
Hawaiian Inn 2301 S Atlantic Ave	Daytona Beach Shores	FL	32118	**800-922-3023**	386-255-5411
Hawthorne Hotel 18 Washington Sq W	Salem	MA	01970	**800-729-7829**	978-744-4080
Hawthorne Inn & Conference Ctr 420 High St	Winston-Salem	NC	27101	**877-777-3099**	336-777-3000
Heartland Inns 87-2nd St *Resv	Coralville	IA	52241	**800-334-3277***	319-351-8132
Henley Park Hotel 926 Massachusetts Ave NW	Washington	DC	20001	**800-222-8474**	202-638-5200
Henlopen Hotel 511 N Boardwalk	Rehoboth Beach	DE	19971	**800-441-8450**	302-227-2551
Heritage Inn, The 34521 Postal Ln	Lewes	DE	19958	**800-669-9399**	
Hermitage Hotel 231 Sixth Ave N	Nashville	TN	37219	**888-888-9414**	615-244-3121
Hermosa Inn 5532 N Palo Cristi Rd	Paradise Valley	AZ	85253	**800-241-1210**	602-955-8614
Hershey Lodge 325 University Dr	Hershey	PA	17033	**844-330-1802**	717-533-3311
Hilgard House Hotel & Suites 927 Hilgard Ave	Los Angeles	CA	90024	**800-826-3934**	310-208-3945
Hilltop Inn of Vermont 3472 Airport Rd	Montpelier	VT	05602	**877-609-0003**	802-229-5766
Hilton Worldwide 7930 Jones Branch Dr	McLean	VA	22102	**800-445-8667**	703-883-1000
Historic Bullock Hotel 633 Main St	Deadwood	SD	57732	**800-336-1876**	
Historic French Market Inn 509 Decatur St	New Orleans	LA	70130	**800-366-2743**	504-561-5621
Historic Inns of Annapolis 58 State Cir	Annapolis	MD	21401	**800-847-8882**	410-263-2641
HLC Hotels Inc 7080 Abercorn St PO Box 13069	Savannah	GA	31416	**800-344-4378**	912-352-4493
Holiday Inn 301 Government St	Mobile	AL	36602	**888-465-4329**	251-694-0100
Holiday Inn Express DFW North 4550 W John Carpenter Fwy	Irving	TX	75063	**800-465-4329**	
Holiday Inn Resort Daytona Beach Oceanfront 1615 S Atlantic Ave	Daytona Beach	FL	32118	**800-874-0975**	386-255-0921
Horton Grand Hotel 311 Island Ave	San Diego	CA	92101	**800-542-1886**	619-544-1886
Hospitality International Inc 1726 Montreal Cir	Tucker	GA	30084	**800-251-1962**	
Master Hosts Inns & Resorts 1726 Montreal Cir	Tucker	GA	30084	**800-247-4677**	
Passport Inn 1726 Montreal Cir	Tucker	GA	30084	**800-251-1962**	
Red Carpet Inn 1726 Montreal Cir	Tucker	GA	30084	**800-247-4677**	
Scottish Inns 1726 Montreal Cir	Tucker	GA	30084	**800-251-1962**	
Hospitality Suites Resort 409 N Scottsdale Rd	Scottsdale	AZ	85257	**800-445-5115**	480-949-5115
Hotel & Suites Normandin 4700 Pierre-Bertrand Blvd	Quebec	QC	G2J1A4	**800-463-6721**	418-622-1611
Hotel 1000 1000 First Ave	Seattle	WA	98104	**877-315-1088**	206-957-1000
Hotel 140 140 Clarendon St	Boston	MA	02116	**800-714-0140**	617-585-5600
Hotel 43 981 Grove St	Boise	ID	83702	**800-243-4622**	208-342-4622
Hotel 71 71 St Pierre St	Quebec	QC	G1K4A4	**888-692-1171**	418-692-1171
Hotel Abri 127 Ellis St	San Francisco	CA	94102	**866-778-6169**	415-392-8800
Hotel Adagio 550 Geary St	San Francisco	CA	94102	**855-687-7262**	415-775-5000
Hotel Allegro Chicago 171 W Randolph St	Chicago	IL	60601	**800-643-1500**	312-236-0123
Hotel Ambassadeur 3401 Blvd Ste-Anne	Quebec	QC	G1E3L4	**800-363-4619**	418-666-2828
Hotel Ambassador 1324 S Main St *General	Tulsa	OK	74119	**888-408-8282***	918-587-8200
Hotel Andra 2000 Fourth Ave	Seattle	WA	98121	**877-448-8600**	206-448-8600
Hotel at Old Town Wichita 830 E First St	Wichita	KS	67202	**877-265-3869**	316-267-4800
Hotel Avante 860 E El Camino Real	Mountain View	CA	94040	**800-538-1600**	650-940-1000
Hotel Beacon 2130 Broadway	New York	NY	10023	**800-572-4969**	212-787-1100
Hotel Bedford 118 E 40th St	New York	NY	10016	**800-221-6881**	212-697-4800
Hotel Bel-Air 701 Stone Canyon Rd	Los Angeles	CA	90077	**800-648-4097**	310-472-1211
Hotel Bijou 111 Mason St	San Francisco	CA	94102	**877-568-2733**	415-771-1200
Hotel Boulderado 2115 13th St	Boulder	CO	80302	**800-433-4344**	303-442-4344
Hotel Burnham 1 W Washington St	Chicago	IL	60602	**866-690-1986**	312-782-1111
Hotel Captain Cook 939 W Fifth Ave	Anchorage	AK	99501	**800-843-1950**	907-276-6000
Hotel Chateau Bellevue 16 Rue de la Porte	Quebec	QC	G1R4M9	**877-849-1877**	418-692-2573
Hotel Chateau Laurier 1220 Pl George-V Ouest	Quebec	QC	G1R5B8	**877-522-8108**	418-522-8108
Hotel Classique 2815 Laurier Blvd	Quebec	QC	G1V4H3	**800-463-1885**	418-658-2793
Hotel Colorado 526 Pine St	Glenwood Springs	CO	81601	**800-544-3998**	970-945-6511
Hotel Commonwealth 500 Commonwealth Ave	Boston	MA	02215	**866-784-4000**	617-933-5000
Hotel Congress 311 E Congress St	Tucson	AZ	85701	**800-722-8848**	520-622-8848
Hotel Contessa 306 W Market St	San Antonio	TX	78205	**866-435-0900**	210-229-9222
Hotel de Anza 233 W Santa Clara St	San Jose	CA	95113	**800-843-3700**	408-286-1000
Hotel Deca 4507 Brooklyn Ave NE	Seattle	WA	98105	**800-899-0251**	206-634-2000
Hotel Del Sol 3100 Webster St	San Francisco	CA	94123	**877-433-5765**	415-921-5520
Hotel Deluxe 729 SW 15th Ave	Portland	OR	97205	**866-895-2094**	503-219-2094
Hotel Derek 2525 W Loop S	Houston	TX	77027	**866-292-4100**	713-961-3000
Hotel Drisco 2901 Pacific Ave	San Francisco	CA	94115	**800-738-7477**	415-346-2880
Hotel du Pont 11th & Market Sts	Wilmington	DE	19801	**800-441-9019**	302-594-3100
Hotel Durant 2600 Durant Ave	Berkeley	CA	94704	**800-738-7477**	510-845-8981
Hotel Edison 228 W 47th St	New York	NY	10036	**800-637-7070**	212-840-5000
Hotel Encanto de Las Cruces 705 S Telshor Blvd	Las Cruces	NM	88011	**866-383-0443**	575-522-4300
Hotel Galvez - A Wyndham Historic Hotel 2024 Seawall Blvd	Galveston	TX	77550	**800-996-3426**	409-765-7721
Hotel George 15 E St NW *General	Washington	DC	20001	**800-546-7866***	202-347-4200
Hotel Grand Pacific 463 Belleville St	Victoria	BC	V8V1X3	**800-663-7550**	250-386-0450

Name	Address	City	State	ZIP	Toll-Free	Phone
Hotel Grand Victorian	2325 W Hwy 76	Branson	MO	65616	**800-324-8751**	417-336-2935
Hotel Granduca	1080 Uptown Pk Blvd	Houston	TX	77056	**888-472-6382**	713-418-1000
Hotel Griffon	155 Steuart St	San Francisco	CA	94105	**800-321-2201**	415-495-2100
Hotel Jerome	330 E Main St	Aspen	CO	81611	**855-331-7213**	
Hotel La Rose	308 Wilson St	Santa Rosa	CA	95401	**800-527-6738**	707-579-3200
Hotel Le Bleu	370 Fourth Ave	Brooklyn	NY	11215	**866-427-6073**	718-625-1500
Hotel Le Cantlie Suites	1110 Sherbrooke St W	Montreal	QC	H3A1G9	**800-567-1110**	514-842-2000
Hotel Le Capitole	972 St Jean St	Quebec	QC	G1R1R5	**800-261-9903**	418-694-4444
Hotel Le Clos Saint-Louis	69 St Louis St	Quebec	QC	G1R3Z2	**800-461-1311**	418-694-1311
Hotel Le Germain Toronto	30 Mercer St	Toronto	ON	M5V1H3	**866-345-9501**	416-345-9500
Hotel Le Marais	717 Conti St	New Orleans	LA	70130	**800-935-8740**	504-525-2300
Hotel le Priori	15 du Sault-au-Matelot St	Quebec	QC	G1K3Y7	**800-351-3992**	418-692-3992
Hotel Le Soleil	567 Hornby St	Vancouver	BC	V6C2E8	**877-632-3030**	604-632-3000
Hotel Le St-James	355 St Jacques St	Montreal	QC	H2Y1N9	**866-841-3111**	514-841-3111
Hotel Lombardy	2019 Pennsylvania Ave NW	Washington	DC	20006	**800-424-5486**	202-828-2600
Hotel Lord-Berri	1199 Berri St	Montreal	QC	H2L4C6	**888-363-0363**	514-845-9236
Hotel Lucia	400 SW Broadway	Portland	OR	97205	**877-225-1717**	503-225-1717
Hotel Lumen	6101 Hillcrest Ave	Dallas	TX	75205	**800-908-1140**	214-219-2400
Hotel Lusso	808 West Sprague Avenue *General	Spokane	WA	99201	**800-899-1482***	509-747-9750
Hotel Madera	1310 New Hampshire Ave NW	Washington	DC	20036	**800-546-7866**	202-296-7600
Hotel Manoir Victoria	44 Cote du Palais	Quebec	QC	G1R4H8	**800-463-6283**	418-692-1030
Hotel Mark Twain	345 Taylor St	San Francisco	CA	94102	**877-854-4106**	415-673-2332
Hotel Marlowe Cambridge	25 Edwind H Land Blvd	Cambridge	MA	02141	**800-825-7140**	617-868-8000
Hotel Max	620 Stewart St	Seattle	WA	98101	**866-833-6299**	206-728-6299
Hotel Mead	451 E Grand Ave	Wisconsin Rapids	WI	54494	**800-843-6323**	715-423-1500
Hotel Mela	120 W 44th St	New York	NY	10036	**877-452-6352**	212-710-7000
Hotel Metro	411 E Mason St	Milwaukee	WI	53202	**877-638-7620**	414-272-1937
Hotel Monaco Chicago	225 N Wabash Ave	Chicago	IL	60601	**866-610-0081**	312-960-8500
Hotel Monaco Denver	1717 Champa St	Denver	CO	80202	**800-990-1303**	303-296-1717
Hotel Monaco Portland	506 SW Washington at Fifth Ave	Portland	OR	97204	**866-861-9514**	503-222-0001
Hotel Monaco Salt Lake City	15 West 200 South *Resv	Salt Lake City	UT	84101	**800-805-1801***	801-595-0000
Hotel Monaco Seattle	1101 Fourth Ave	Seattle	WA	98101	**800-715-6513**	206-621-1770
Hotel Monte Vista	100 N San Francisco St	Flagstaff	AZ	86001	**800-545-3068**	928-779-6971
Hotel Monteleone	214 Royal St	New Orleans	LA	70130	**866-338-4684**	504-523-3341
Hotel Murano	1320 Broadway Plz	Tacoma	WA	98402	**888-862-3255**	253-238-8000
Hotel Nikko San Francisco	222 Mason St	San Francisco	CA	94102	**866-636-4556**	415-394-1111
Hotel Northampton	36 King St	NorthHampton	MA	01060	**800-547-3529**	413-584-3100
Hotel Oceana *Santa Barbara*	202 W Cabrillo Blvd	Santa Barbara	CA	93101	**800-965-9776**	805-965-4577
Hotel Omni Mont-Royal	1050 Sherbrooke St W	Montreal	QC	H3A2R6	**800-843-6664**	514-284-1110
Hotel Orrington	1710 Orrington Ave	Evanston	IL	60201	**888-677-4648**	847-866-8700
Hotel Pacific	300 Pacific St	Monterey	CA	93940	**800-554-5542**	831-373-5700
Hotel Phillips	106 W 12th St	Kansas City	MO	64105	**877-704-5341**	816-221-7000
Hotel Plaza Athenee	37 E 64th St	New York	NY	10065	**800-447-8800**	212-734-9100
Hotel Plaza Quebec	3031 Laurier Blvd	Sainte-Foy	QC	G1V2M2	**800-567-5276**	418-658-2727
Hotel Plaza Real	125 Washington Ave	Santa Fe	NM	87501	**855-752-9273**	505-988-4900
Hotel Preston	733 Briley Pkwy	Nashville	TN	37217	**800-407-4324**	615-361-5900
Hotel Provincial	1024 Rue Chartres	New Orleans	LA	70116	**800-535-7922**	504-581-4995
Hotel Rex	562 Sutter St *Resv	San Francisco	CA	94102	**800-433-4434***	415-433-4434
Hotel Rodney	142 Second St	Lewes	DE	19958	**800-824-8754**	302-645-6466
Hotel Roger Williams	131 Madison Ave *Resv	New York	NY	10016	**888-448-7788***	212-448-7000
Hotel Rouge	1315 16th St NW	Washington	DC	20036	**800-738-1202**	202-232-8000
Hotel Royal Plaza	1905 Hotel Plaza Blvd	Lake Buena Vista	FL	32830	**888-662-4683**	407-828-2828
Hotel Ruby Foo's	7655 Decarie Blvd	Montreal	QC	H4P2H2	**800-361-5419**	514-731-7701

Name	Address	City	State	ZIP	Toll-Free	Phone
Hotel Saint Francis	210 Don Gaspar Ave	Santa Fe	NM	87501	**800-529-5700**	505-983-5700
Hotel Saint Marie	827 Toulouse St	New Orleans	LA	70112	**800-366-2743**	504-561-8951
Hotel San Carlos	202 N Central Ave	Phoenix	AZ	85004	**866-253-4121**	602-253-4121
Hotel Santa Barbara	533 State St	Santa Barbara	CA	93101	**888-259-7700**	805-957-9300
Hotel Santa Fe	1501 Paseo de Peralta	Santa Fe	NM	87501	**855-825-9876**	505-982-1200
Hotel Sax Chicago	333 N Dearborn St	Chicago	IL	60610	**855-880-1240**	312-245-0333
Hotel Sepia	3135 Ch St-Louis	Sainte-Foy	QC	G1W1R9	**888-301-6837**	418-653-4941
Hotel Shelley	844 Collins Ave	Miami Beach	FL	33139	**877-762-3477**	305-531-3341
Hotel Solamar	435 Sixth Ave	San Diego	CA	92101	**877-230-0300**	619-819-9500
Hotel Strasburg, The	213 S Holliday St	Strasburg	VA	22657	**800-348-8327**	540-465-9191
Hotel Teatro	1100 14th St	Denver	CO	80202	**888-727-1200**	303-228-1100
Hotel The Queen Mary	1126 Queens Hwy	Long Beach	CA	90802	**877-342-0738**	562-435-3511
Hotel Triton	342 Grant Ave	San Francisco	CA	94108	**800-800-1299**	415-394-0500
Hotel Universel	2300 Ch St-Foy	Quebec	QC	G1V1S5	**800-463-4495**	418-653-5250
Hotel Utica	102 Lafayette St	Utica	NY	13502	**877-906-1912**	315-724-7829
Hotel Valencia Santana Row	355 Santana Row	San Jose	CA	95128	**866-842-0100**	408-551-0010
Hotel Valley Ho	6850 E Main St	Scottsdale	AZ	85251	**866-882-4484**	480-376-4600
Hotel Viking	1 Bellevue Ave	Newport	RI	02840	**800-556-7126**	401-847-3300
Hotel Vintage Park	1100 Fifth Ave	Seattle	WA	98101	**800-853-3914**	206-624-8000
Hotel Wales	1295 Madison Ave	New York	NY	10128	**866-925-3746**	212-876-6000
Hotel XIXe Siecle *Lhotel*	262 St Jacques St W	Vieux-Quebec	QC	H2Y1N1	**877-553-0019**	514-985-0019
Hotel ZaZa Dallas	2332 Leonard St	Dallas	TX	75201	**800-597-8399**	214-468-8399
Hotel ZaZa Houston	5701 Main St *Resv	Houston	TX	77005	**888-880-3244***	713-526-1991
HP Hotels Inc	1 Chase Corporate Dr Ste 210	Birmingham	AL	35244	**800-576-3467**	205-879-7004
Humphrey's Half Moon Inn & Suites	2303 Shelter Island Dr	San Diego	CA	92106	**800-542-7400**	619-224-3411
Hyannis Holiday Motel	131 Ocean St	Hyannis	MA	02601	**800-423-1551**	508-775-1639
Hyannis Travel Inn	18 N St	Hyannis	MA	02601	**800-352-7190**	508-775-8200
Hyatt Carmel Highlands	120 Highlands Dr	Carmel	CA	93923	**800-633-7313**	831-620-1234
Hyatt Hotels Corp	71 S Wacker Dr *NYSE: H*	Chicago	IL	60606	**888-591-1234**	312-750-1234
Grand Hyatt Hotels	71 S Wacker Dr *Resv	Chicago	IL	60606	**800-233-1234***	312-750-1234
Hyatt Place Hotels	71 S Wacker Dr	Chicago	IL	60606	**888-492-8847**	312-750-1234
Hyatt Regency Hotels	71 S Wacker Dr *Resv	Chicago	IL	60606	**800-233-1234***	312-750-1234
Park Hyatt Hotels	71 S Wacker Dr *Resv	Chicago	IL	60606	**800-233-1234***	312-750-1234
Ilikai Hotel & Suites	1777 Ala Moana Blvd	Honolulu	HI	96815	**866-536-7973**	808-949-3811
Imperial of Waikiki	205 Lewers St	Honolulu	HI	96815	**800-347-2582**	808-923-1827
Indigo Inn	1 Maiden Ln	Charleston	SC	29401	**800-845-7639**	843-577-5900
Ingleside Inn	200 W Ramon Rd	Palm Springs	CA	92264	**800-772-6655**	760-325-0046
Inlet Tower Suites	1200 L St	Anchorage	AK	99501	**800-544-0786**	907-276-0110
Inn & Spa at Loretto	211 Old Santa Fe Trl	Santa Fe	NM	87501	**800-727-5531**	505-988-5531
Inn Above Tide, The	30 El Portal	Sausalito	CA	94965	**800-893-8433**	415-332-9535
Inn at Camachee Harbor	201 Yacht Club Dr	Saint Augustine	FL	32084	**800-688-5379**	904-825-0003
Inn at Gig Harbor	3211 56th St NW	Gig Harbor	WA	98335	**800-795-9980**	253-858-1111
Inn at Harbour Town	7 Lighthouse Ln *Resv	Hilton Head Island	SC	29928	**800-732-7463***	843-363-8100
Inn at Langley	400 First St PO Box 835	Langley	WA	98260	**800-843-3779**	360-221-3033
Inn at Montchanin Village	528 Montchanin Rd	Montchanin	DE	19710	**800-269-2473**	302-888-2133
Inn at Morro Bay	60 State Pk Rd	Morro Bay	CA	93442	**800-321-9566**	805-772-5651
Inn at Otter Crest	301 Otter Crest Loop	Otter Rock	OR	97369	**800-452-2101**	541-765-2111
Inn at Pelican Bay	800 Vanderbilt Beach Rd	Naples	FL	34108	**800-597-8770**	239-597-8777
Inn at Perry Cabin	308 Watkins Ln	Saint Michaels	MD	21663	**800-722-2949**	410-745-2200
Inn at Reading, The	1040 N Pk Rd	Wyomissing	PA	19610	**800-383-9713**	610-372-7811
Inn at Saint John	939 Congress St	Portland	ME	04102	**800-636-9127**	207-773-6481
Inn at Spanish Head	4009 SW Hwy 101	Lincoln City	OR	97367	**800-452-8127**	541-996-2161
Inn at the Market	86 Pine St	Seattle	WA	98101	**800-446-4484**	206-443-3600

Name / Address	City	State	Zip	Toll-Free	Phone
Inn At The Quay 900 Quayside Dr	New Westminster	BC	V3M6G1	**800-663-2001**	604-520-1776
Inn at Union Square 440 Post St	San Francisco	CA	94102	**800-288-4346**	415-397-3510
Inn at, The Tides, The 800 Coast Hwy 1	Bodega Bay	CA	94923	**800-541-7788**	707-875-2751
Inn by the Lake 3300 Lk Tahoe Blvd	South Lake Tahoe	CA	96150	**800-877-1466**	530-542-0330
Inn of Long Beach 185 Atlantic Ave	Long Beach	CA	90802	**800-230-7500**	562-435-3791
Inn of the Anasazi 113 Washington Ave	Santa Fe	NM	87501	**888-767-3966**	505-988-3030
Inn of the Governors 101 W Alameda St	Santa Fe	NM	87501	**800-234-4534**	505-982-4333
Inn on Biltmore Estate 1 Antler Hill Rd	Asheville	NC	28803	**800-411-3812**	828-225-1600
Inn on Fifth 699 Fifth Ave S	Naples	FL	34102	**888-403-8778**	239-403-8777
Inn on Gitche Gumee 8517 Congdon Blvd	Duluth	MN	55804	**800-317-4979**	218-525-4979
Inn on Lake Superior 350 Canal Pk Dr	Duluth	MN	55802	**888-668-4352**	218-726-1111
Inn on the Alameda 303 E Alameda St	Santa Fe	NM	87501	**888-984-2121**	505-984-2121
Inn on the Paseo 630 Paseo de Peralta	Santa Fe	NM	87501	**855-984-8200**	505-984-8200
Inns at Mill Falls 312 Daniel Webster Hwy	Meredith	NH	03253	**800-622-6455**	
InnSuites Hospitality Trust InnSuites Hotels & Suites 475 N Granada Ave	Tucson	AZ	85701	**800-842-4242**	520-622-0923
InnSuites Hotel Tempe/Phoenix Airport 1651 W Baseline Rd	Tempe	AZ	85283	**800-841-4242**	480-897-7900
InterContinental Hotels Group (IHG) 3 Ravinia Dr Ste 100	Atlanta	GA	30346	**800-621-0555**	770-604-2000
Holiday Inn Hotels & Resorts 3 Ravinia Dr Ste 100	Atlanta	GA	30346	**800-725-8232**	770-604-2000
Hotel Indigo 3 Ravinia Dr Ste 100	Atlanta	GA	30346	**800-334-5194**	770-604-2000
Staybridge Suites 3 Ravinia Dr Ste 100	Atlanta	GA	30346	**800-465-4329**	770-604-2000
International Hotel 20 Second Ave SW	Rochester	MN	55902	**800-940-6811**	
International House Hotel 221 Camp St	New Orleans	LA	70130	**800-633-5770**	504-553-9550
Iroquois New York 49 W 44th St	New York City	NY	10036	**800-332-7220**	212-840-3080
Island Hotel, The 690 Newport Ctr Dr	Newport Beach	CA	92660	**866-554-4620**	949-759-0808
Jack London Inn 444 Embarcadero W	Oakland	CA	94607	**800-549-8780**	510-444-2032
Jackson Hole Lodge 420 W Broadway PO Box 1805	Jackson	WY	83001	**800-604-9404**	307-733-2992
James Chicago, The 55 E Ontario	Chicago	IL	60611	**888-526-3778**	312-337-1000
James Gettys Hotel 27 Chambersburg St	Gettysburg	PA	17325	**888-900-5275**	717-337-1334
Jameson Inns *Jameson Inns* 115 Ann Denard Dr	Washington	GA	30673	**800-526-3766**	706-678-7925
Jared Coffin House 29 Broad St *Cust Svc	Nantucket	MA	02554	**800-248-2405***	508-228-2400
Jefferson Hotel 101 W Franklin St	Richmond	VA	23220	**800-424-8014**	804-788-8000
Jolly Hotel Madison Towers 22 E 38th St *Resv	New York	NY	10016	**888-726-0528***	212-802-0600
Jolly Roger Inn 640 W Katella Ave	Anaheim	CA	92802	**888-296-5986**	714-782-7500
Kahala Mandarin Oriental Hotel Hawaii Resort 5000 Kahala Ave	Honolulu	HI	96816	**800-367-2525**	808-739-8888
Kawada Hotel 200 S Hill St	Los Angeles	CA	90012	**800-752-9232**	213-621-4455
Kellogg Hotel & Conference Ctr 219 S Harrison Rd Michigan State University Campus	East Lansing	MI	48824	**800-875-5090**	517-432-4000
Kensington Court Ann Arbor 610 Hilton Blvd *Orders	Ann Arbor	MI	48108	**800-344-7829***	734-761-7800
Kensington Park Hotel 450 Post St	San Francisco	CA	94102	**800-553-1900**	415-788-6400
Kensington Riverside Inn 1126 Memorial Dr NW	Calgary	AB	T2N3E3	**877-313-3733**	403-228-4442
Keswick Hall 701 Club Dr	Keswick	VA	22947	**888-778-2565**	434-979-3440
Key Lime Inn 725 Truman Ave	Key West	FL	33040	**800-549-4430**	305-294-5229
Killington Grand Resort Hotel & Conference Ctr 4763 Killington Rd	Killington	VT	05751	**800-621-6867**	802-422-5001
Kimball Terrace Inn 10 Huntington Rd	Northeast Harbor	ME	04662	**800-454-6225**	207-276-3383
Kimberly Hotel 145 E 50th St	New York	NY	10022	**800-683-0400**	212-755-0400
Kimpton Hotel & Restaurant Group 422 SW Broadway	Portland	OR	97205	**800-263-2305**	503-228-1212
Kimpton Hotel & Restaurant Group LLC 222 Kearny St Ste 200	San Francisco	CA	94108	**800-546-7866**	415-397-5572
Kimpton Hotel & Restaurant Group, LLC 10050 S DeAnza Blvd	Cupertino	CA	95014	**800-499-1408**	415-397-5572
King Kamehameha's Kona Beach Hotel 75-5660 Palani Rd	Kailua-Kona	HI	96740	**800-367-2111**	808-329-2911
King Pacific Lodge 255 W First St	North Vancouver	BC	V7M3G8	**855-825-9378**	604-987-5452
Kinzie Hotel 20 W Kinzie St	Chicago	IL	60654	**877-262-5341**	312-395-9000
Kitano New York 66 Pk Ave E 38th St	New York	NY	10016	**800-548-2666**	212-885-7000
Knob Hill Inn 960 N Main St PO Box 1327	Ketchum	ID	83340	**800-526-8010**	208-726-8010
Kona Kai Resort 1551 Shelter Island Dr	San Diego	CA	92106	**800-566-2524**	619-221-8000
L' Appartement Hotel 455 Sherbrooke W	Montreal	QC	H3A1B7	**800-363-3010**	514-284-3634
L'Ermitage Beverly Hills Hotel 9291 Burton Way	Beverly Hills	CA	90210	**877-235-7582**	310-278-3344
L'Hotel du Vieux-Quebec 1190 St Jean St	Quebec	QC	G1R1S6	**800-361-7787**	418-692-1850
L'Hotel Quebec 3115 des Hotels Ave	Sainte-Foy	QC	G1W3Z6	**800-567-5276**	418-658-5120
La Fonda 100 E San Francisco St	Santa Fe	NM	87501	**800-523-5002**	505-982-5511
La Pensione Hotel 606 W Date St	San Diego	CA	92101	**800-232-4683**	619-236-8000
La Posada Hotel & Suites 1000 Zaragoza St *Resv	Laredo	TX	78040	**800-444-2099***	956-722-1701
La Quinta Inn & Suites Secaucus Meadowlands 350 Lighting Way *General	Secaucus	NJ	07094	**800-753-3757***	201-863-8700
Lafayette Hotel 600 St Charles Ave	New Orleans	LA	70130	**800-366-2743**	504-524-4441
Lafayette Hotel & Suites San Diego 2223 El Cajon Blvd	San Diego	CA	92104	**800-468-3531**	619-296-2101
Lafayette Park Hotel 3287 Mt Diablo Blvd	Lafayette	CA	94549	**855-382-8632**	925-283-3700
Lake Louise Inn 210 Village Rd PO Box 209	Lake Louise	AB	T0L1E0	**800-661-9237**	403-522-3791
Lake Lure Inn & Spa, The 2771 Memorial Hwy	Lake Lure	NC	28746	**888-434-4970**	828-625-2526
Lake Placid Lodge 144 Lodge Way	Lake Placid	NY	12946	**877-523-2700**	518-523-2700
Lakeside Inn 100 N Alexander St	Mount Dora	FL	32757	**800-556-5016**	352-383-4101
Lakeview on the Lake 8696 E Lake Rd	Erie	PA	16511	**888-558-8439**	814-899-6948
Lamothe House Hotel 621 Esplanade Ave	New Orleans	LA	70116	**800-535-7815**	
Lancaster Hotel 701 Texas St	Houston	TX	77002	**800-231-0336**	713-228-9500
Landmark Inn 230 N Front St *General	Marquette	MI	49855	**888-752-6362***	906-228-2580
Langdon Hall Country House Hotel & Spa 1 Langdon Dr	Cambridge	ON	N3H4R8	**800-268-1898**	519-740-2100
Langham Boston, The 250 Franklin St	Boston	MA	02110	**800-791-7781**	617-451-1900
Lantern Lodge Motor Inn 411 N College St	Myerstown	PA	17067	**800-262-5564**	717-866-6536
LaPlaya Resort & Suites 2500 N Atlantic Ave	Daytona Beach	FL	32118	**800-224-5052**	386-672-0990
Latham Hotel, The 135 S 17th St	Philadelphia	PA	19103	**877-528-4261**	215-563-7474
Laurel Inn 444 Presidio Ave	San Francisco	CA	94115	**800-552-8735**	415-346-7431
Le Chamois 4557 Blackcomb Way	Whistler	BC	V0N1B4	**866-944-7853**	604-932-8700
Le Meridian 20 Sidney St	Cambridge	MA	02139	**800-543-4300**	617-577-0200
Le Meridien Chambers Minneapolis 901 Hennepin Ave *General	Minneapolis	MN	55403	**877-782-0116***	612-767-6900
Le M,ridien Dallas, The Stoneleigh 2927 Maple Ave	Dallas	TX	75201	**888-625-4988**	214-871-7111
Le Merigot - A JW Marriott Beach Hotel & Spa 1740 Ocean Ave	Santa Monica	CA	90401	**888-539-7899**	310-395-9700
Le Montrose Suite Hotel 900 Hammond St	West Hollywood	CA	90069	**800-776-0666**	310-855-1115
Le Nouvel Montreal Hotel & Spa 1740 Rene-Levesque Blvd W	Montreal	QC	H3H1R3	**800-363-6063**	514-931-8841
Le Parc Suite Hotel 733 NW Knoll Dr *Resv	West Hollywood	CA	90069	**800-578-4837***	877-591-9556
Le Port-Royal Hotel & Suites 144 St Pierre St	Quebec	QC	G1K8N8	**866-417-2777**	418-692-2777
Le Richelieu Hotel 1234 Chartres St	New Orleans	LA	70116	**800-535-9653**	504-529-2492
Le Saint Sulpice 414 Rue St Sulpice *General	Montreal	QC	H2Y2V5	**877-785-7423***	514-288-1000
Leisure Sports Inc 7077 Koll Ctr Pkwy Ste 110	Pleasanton	CA	94566	**888-239-0930**	925-600-1966
Lenox Hotel 61 Exeter St	Boston	MA	02116	**800-225-7676**	617-536-5300
Leola Village Inn & Suites 38 Deborah Dr	Leola	PA	17540	**877-669-5094**	717-656-7002
Les Suites Hotel Ottawa 130 Besserer St	Ottawa	ON	K1N9M9	**866-682-0879**	613-232-2000
Library Hotel 299 Madison Ave	New York	NY	10017	**877-793-7323**	212-983-4500
Lighthouse Club Hotel 201 60th St	Ocean City	MD	21842	**888-371-5400**	410-524-5400
Lighthouse Lodge & Suites 1150 Lighthouse Ave	Pacific Grove	CA	93950	**800-858-1249**	
Linden Row Inn 100 E Franklin St	Richmond	VA	23219	**800-348-7424**	804-783-7000
Listel Hotel, The 1300 Robson St	Vancouver	BC	V6E1C5	**800-663-5491**	604-684-8461
Little America Hotel & Resort Cheyenne 2800 W Lincolnway	Cheyenne	WY	82009	**800-445-6945**	307-775-8400
Little America Hotel & Towers Salt Lake City 555 S Main St	Salt Lake City	UT	84101	**800-453-9450**	801-258-6568
Little America Hotel Flagstaff 2515 E Butler Ave	Flagstaff	AZ	86004	**800-352-4386**	928-779-7900
Little America Hotels & Resorts 500 S Main St	Salt Lake City	UT	84101	**800-281-7899**	801-596-5700
Little Nell, The 675 E Durant Ave	Aspen	CO	81611	**888-843-6355**	970-920-4600
Lodge & Spa at Cordillera 2205 Cordillera Way	Edwards	CO	81632	**800-877-3529**	970-926-2200
Lodge At Breckenridge, The 112 Overlook Dr	Breckenridge	CO	80424	**800-736-1607**	970-453-9300

Name / Address	City	State	ZIP	Toll-Free	Phone
Lodge at the Mountain Village 1415 Lowell Ave	Park City	UT	84060	**800-453-1360**	435-649-0800
Lodge on the Desert 306 N Alvernon Way	Tucson	AZ	85711	**877-498-6776**	520-320-2000
Lofts Hotel & Suites 55 E Nationwide Blvd *General	Columbus	OH	43215	**877-902-9022***	614-461-2663
Lone Oak Lodge 2221 N Fremont St *General	Monterey	CA	93940	**800-283-5663***	831-372-4924
Long House Alaskan Hotel 4335 Wisconsin St	Anchorage	AK	99517	**888-243-2133**	907-243-2133
Lonsdale Quay Hotel 123 Carrie Cates Ct	North Vancouver	BC	V7M3K7	**800-836-6111**	604-986-6111
Lookout Inn 6901 Lookout Rd	Boulder	CO	80301	**800-530-1513**	877-234-4779
Lord Elgin Hotel 100 Elgin St	Ottawa	ON	K1P5K8	**800-267-4298**	613-235-3333
Lord Nelson Hotel & Suites 1515 S Pk St	Halifax	NS	B3J2L2	**800-565-2020**	902-423-6331
Lord Stanley Suites on the Park 1889 Alberni St	Vancouver	BC	V6G3G7	**888-767-7829**	604-688-9299
Los Angeles Athletic Club 431 W Seventh St	Los Angeles	CA	90014	**800-421-8777**	213-625-2211
LQ Management LLC 909 Hidden Ridge Ste 600	Irving	TX	75038	**800-753-3757**	214-492-6600
La Quinta Inn & Suites 909 Hidden Ridge Ste 600	Irving	TX	75038	**800-753-3757**	214-492-6600
Luxe Hotel Rodeo Drive 360 N Rodeo Dr	Beverly Hills	CA	90210	**800-468-3541**	310-273-0300
Luxe Hotel Sunset Blvd 11461 Sunset Blvd	Los Angeles	CA	90049	**800-468-3541**	310-476-6571
Luxe Worldwide Hotels 11461 W Sunset Blvd	Los Angeles	CA	90049	**888-336-3745**	310-440-3090
Luxor Hotel & Casino 3900 Las Vegas Blvd S *Resv	Las Vegas	NV	89119	**800-288-1000***	702-262-4000
MacArthur Place 29 E MacArthur St	Sonoma	CA	95476	**800-722-1866**	707-938-2929
Madison Concourse Hotel & Governors Club 1 W Dayton St	Madison	WI	53703	**800-356-8293**	608-257-6000
Madison Hotel, The 1 Convent Rd	Morristown	NJ	07960	**800-526-0729**	973-285-1800
Madison the - A Loews Hotel 667 Madison Ave	New York	NY	10065	**800-235-6397**	212-521-2000
Magnolia Hotel & Spa, The 623 Courtney St	Victoria	BC	V8W1B8	**877-624-6654**	250-381-0999
Magnolia Hotel Dallas 1401 Commerce St	Dallas	TX	75201	**888-915-1110**	214-915-6500
Magnolia Hotel Denver 818 17th St	Denver	CO	80202	**888-915-1110**	303-607-9000
Magnolia Hotel Houston 1100 Texas Ave	Houston	TX	77002	**888-915-1110**	713-221-0011
Main Street Station Hotel & Casino 200 N Main St	Las Vegas	NV	89101	**800-713-8933**	702-387-1896
Maison Dupuy Hotel 1001 Toulouse St	New Orleans	LA	70112	**800-535-9177**	504-586-8000
Malaga Inn 359 Church St	Mobile	AL	36602	**800-235-1586**	251-438-4701
Mandarin Oriental Hotel Group (USA) 345 California St Ste 1250	San Francisco	CA	94104	**800-526-6566**	415-772-8800
Mandarin Oriental Miami 500 Brickell Key Dr	Miami	FL	33131	**800-526-6566**	305-913-8288
Mandarin Oriental New York 80 Columbus Cir	New York	NY	10023	**866-801-8880**	212-805-8800
Mandarin Oriental San Francisco 222 Sansome St	San Francisco	CA	94104	**800-526-6566**	415-276-9888
Mandarin Oriental Washington DC 1330 Maryland Ave SW	Washington	DC	20024	**888-888-1778**	202-554-8588
Manor House Inn 106 W St	Bar Harbor	ME	04609	**800-437-0088**	207-288-3759
Mansfield, The 12 W 44th St	New York	NY	10036	**800-255-5167**	212-277-8700
Mansion on Forsyth Park 700 Drayton St	Savannah	GA	31401	**888-213-3671**	912-238-5158
Mansion View Inn & Suites 529 S Fourth St	Springfield	IL	62701	**800-252-1083**	217-544-7411
Maple Hill Farm Bed & Breakfast Inn 11 Inn Rd	Hallowell	ME	04347	**800-622-2708**	207-622-2708
Marina Inn at Grande Dunes 8121 Amalfi Pl *Resv	Myrtle Beach	SC	29572	**877-913-1333***	843-913-1333
Mark Spencer Hotel 409 SW 11th Ave	Portland	OR	97205	**800-548-3934**	503-224-3293
Mark Twain Hotel 225 NE Adams St	Peoria	IL	61602	**866-325-6351**	309-676-3600
Market Pavilion Hotel 225 E Bay St	Charleston	SC	29401	**877-440-2250**	843-723-0500
Marquesa Hotel 600 Fleming St	Key West	FL	33040	**800-869-4631**	305-292-1919
Marquette Hotel, The 710 Marquette Ave	Minneapolis	MN	55402	**800-328-4782**	612-333-4545
Marriott Charleston Hotel 170 Lockwood Blvd	Charleston	SC	29403	**888-236-2427**	843-723-3000
Marriott Columbus 800 Front Ave	Columbus	GA	31901	**800-455-9261**	706-324-1800
Ritz-Carlton Hotel Co LLC 4445 Willard Ave Ste 800	Chevy Chase	MD	20815	**800-241-3333**	301-547-4700
Martha Washington Hotel & Spa, The 150 W Main St	Abingdon	VA	24210	**888-999-8078**	276-628-3161
Maryland Inn 16 Church Cir	Annapolis	MD	21401	**800-847-8882**	410-263-2641
Matrix Hotel 10640-100 Ave	Edmonton	AB	T5J3N8	**866-465-8150**	780-429-2861
Maumee Bay Lodge & Conference Ctr 1750 Pk Rd Ste 2	Oregon	OH	43616	**800-282-7275**	419-836-1466
Mayfair Hotel & Spa 3000 Florida Ave	Coconut Grove	FL	33133	**800-433-4555**	305-441-0000
Mayflower Inn 118 Woodbury Rd	Washington	CT	06793	**800-585-7198**	860-868-9466
Mayflower Park Hotel 405 Olive Way	Seattle	WA	98101	**800-426-5100**	206-623-8700
Mayo Clinic 4500 San Pablo Rd	Jacksonville	FL	32224	**888-255-4458**	904-992-9992
McKinley Grand Hotel 320 Market Ave S	Canton	OH	44702	**844-378-9476**	330-454-5000
MCM Elegante Suites 4250 Ridgemont Dr	Abilene	TX	79606	**888-897-9644**	325-698-1234
Meeting Street Inn 173 Meeting St	Charleston	SC	29401	**800-842-8022**	843-723-1882
Menger Hotel 204 Alamo Plz	San Antonio	TX	78205	**800-345-9285**	210-223-4361
Mercer Hotel 147 Mercer St	New York	NY	10012	**888-918-6060**	212-966-6060
Meridian Plaza Resort 2310 N Ocean Blvd	Myrtle Beach	SC	29577	**800-323-3011**	843-626-4734
Metropolitan Hotel Vancouver 645 Howe St	Vancouver	BC	V6C2Y9	**800-667-2300**	604-687-1122
Metterra Hotel on Whyte 10454 82nd Ave	Edmonton	AB	T6E4Z7	**866-465-8150**	780-465-8150
Meyer Jabara Hotels 1601 Belvedere Rd Ste 407 S	West Palm Beach	FL	33406	**877-696-8671**	561-689-6602
Miami International Airport Hotel NW 20th St & Le Jeune Rd	Miami	FL	33122	**800-327-1276**	305-871-4100
Midtown Hotel 220 Huntington Ave	Boston	MA	02115	**800-343-1177**	617-262-1000
Mill Street Inn 75 Mill St	Newport	RI	02840	**800-392-1316**	401-849-9500
Mill Valley Inn 165 Throckmorton Ave	Mill Valley	CA	94941	**855-334-7946**	415-389-6608
Mills House Hotel 115 Meeting St	Charleston	SC	29401	**800-874-9600**	843-577-2400
Milner Hotel Boston 78 Charles St S	Boston	MA	02116	**877-645-6377**	617-426-6220
Milner Hotels Inc 1538 Centre St	Detroit	MI	48226	**877-645-6377**	313-963-3950
Minto Place Suite Hotel 185 Lyons St N	Ottawa	ON	K1R7Y4	**800-267-3377**	613-232-2200
Mira Monte Inn & Suites 69 Mt Desert St	Bar Harbor	ME	04609	**800-553-5109**	
Mirabeau Park Hotel 1100 N Sullivan Rd	Spokane Valley	WA	99037	**866-584-4674**	509-924-9000
Mirbeau Inn & Spa 851 W Genesee St	Skaneateles	NY	13152	**877-647-2328**	315-685-5006
Mission Inn 3649 Mission Inn Ave	Riverside	CA	92501	**800-843-7755**	951-784-0300
Misty Harbor & Barefoot Beach Resort 118 Weirs Rd	Gilford	NH	03249	**800-336-4789**	603-293-4500
Miyako Hotel Los Angeles 328 E First St	Los Angeles	CA	90012	**800-228-6596**	213-617-2000
MODA Hotel 900 Seymour St	Vancouver	BC	V6B3L9	**877-683-5522**	604-683-4251
Mojave A Desert Resort 73721 Shadow Mtn Dr *Resv	Palm Desert	CA	92260	**800-391-1104***	760-346-6121
Molly Pitcher Inn 88 Riverside Ave	Red Bank	NJ	07701	**800-221-1372**	732-747-2500
Monarch Hotel & Conference Ctr 12566 SE 93rd Ave	Clackamas	OR	97015	**800-492-8700**	503-652-1515
Mondrian Hotel 8440 Sunset Blvd	West Hollywood	CA	90069	**800-525-8029**	323-650-8999
Monmouth Plantation 36 Melrose Ave	Natchez	MS	39120	**800-828-4531**	601-442-5852
Monte Carlo Inn-Airport Suites 7035 Edwards Blvd	Mississauga	ON	L5T2H8	**800-363-6400**	905-564-8500
Monterey Bay Inn 242 Cannery Row	Monterey	CA	93940	**800-424-6242**	831-373-6242
Monterey Hotel 406 Alvarado St	Monterey	CA	93940	**800-966-6490**	831-375-3184
Monterey Inn Resort & Conference Centre 2259 Prince of Wales Dr	Ottawa	ON	K2E6Z8	**800-565-1311**	613-288-3500
Monterey Plaza Hotel & Spa 400 Cannery Row	Monterey	CA	93940	**800-334-3999**	831-646-1700
Morgans Hotel 237 Madison Ave	New York	NY	10016	**800-606-6090**	212-686-0300
Morgans Hotel Group Co 475 Tenth Ave *NASDAQ: MHGC*	New York	NY	10018	**800-606-6090**	212-277-4100
Morrison-Clark Historic Inn & Restaurant 1015 L St NW	Washington	DC	20001	**800-332-7898**	202-898-1200
Mosaic Hotel 125 S Spalding Dr	Beverly Hills	CA	90212	**800-463-4466**	310-278-0303
Mosser Hotel 54 Fourth St	San Francisco	CA	94103	**800-227-3804**	415-986-4400
Motel 6 Wichita 465 S Webb Rd	Wichita	KS	67207	**800-466-8356**	316-684-6363
Mount View Hotel & Spa 1457 Lincoln Ave	Calistoga	CA	94515	**800-816-6877**	707-942-6877
Mountain Haus 292 E Meadow Dr	Vail	CO	81657	**800-237-0922**	970-476-2434
Mountain Lake Hotel 115 Hotel Cir	Pembroke	VA	24136	**800-346-3334**	540-626-7121
Mountain Villas 9525 W Skyline Pkwy	Duluth	MN	55810	**866-688-4552**	218-624-5784
Muse, The 130 W 46th St	New York	NY	10036	**877-692-6873**	212-485-2400
Mutiny Hotel 2951 S Bayshore Dr	Miami	FL	33133	**888-868-8469**	305-441-2100
Napa River Inn 500 Main St	Napa	CA	94559	**877-251-8500**	707-251-8500
National Hotel 1677 Collins Ave	Miami Beach	FL	33139	**800-327-8370**	305-532-2311
Nativo Lodge Hotel 6000 Pan American Fwy NE	Albuquerque	NM	87109	**888-628-4861**	505-798-4300
New Castle Hotels & Resorts 2 Corporate Dr	Shelton	CT	06484	**800-321-2211**	203-925-8370
New Haven Hotel 229 George St	New Haven	CT	06510	**800-644-6835**	203-498-3100
New Otani Kaimana Beach Hotel 2863 Kalakaua Ave	Honolulu	HI	96815	**800-356-8264**	808-923-1555
New York Palace Hotel 455 Madison Ave	New York	NY	10022	**800-697-2522**	212-888-7000
New York's Hotel Pennsylvania 401 Seventh Ave	New York	NY	10001	**800-223-8585**	212-736-5000
Newport Beach Hotel & Suites 1 Wave Ave	Middletown	RI	02842	**800-655-1778**	401-846-0310

				Toll-Free	*Phone*
Newport Beachside Hotel & Resort					
16701 Collins Ave	Miami Beach	FL	33160	**800-327-5476**	305-949-1300
Newport Harbor Hotel & Marina					
49 America's Cup Ave	Newport	RI	02840	**800-955-2558**	401-847-9000
Nine Zero Hotel					
90 Tremont St	Boston	MA	02108	**866-906-9090**	617-772-5800
Nittany Lion Inn					
200 W Pk Ave	State College	PA	16803	**800-233-7505**	814-865-8500
Norwood Hotel					
112 Marion St	Winnipeg	MB	R2H0T1	**888-888-1878**	204-233-4475
O Henry Hotel					
624 Green Vly Rd	Greensboro	NC	27408	**800-965-8259**	336-854-2000
Ocean Forest Plaza					
5523 N Ocean Blvd	Myrtle Beach	SC	29577	**800-845-6701***	843-497-0044
*General					
Ocean Key Resort					
424 Atlantic Ave	Virginia Beach	VA	23451	**800-955-9700**	757-425-2200
Ocean Pointe Suites at Key Largo					
500 Burton Dr	Tavernier	FL	33070	**800-882-9464**	305-853-3000
Ocean Reef Club					
35 Ocean Reef Dr Ste 200	Key Largo	FL	33037	**888-422-9944**	305-367-2611
Ocean Resort Hotel Waikiki					
175 Paoakalani Ave	Honolulu	HI	96815	**877-367-1912**	808-922-3861
Ocean Sky Hotel & Resort					
4060 Galt Ocean Dr	Fort Lauderdale	FL	33308	**800-678-9022**	954-565-6611
Ocean Walk Resort					
300 N Atlantic	Daytona Beach	FL	32118	**888-743-2561**	386-323-4800
OHANA Waikiki Beachcomber Hotel					
2300 Kalakaua Ave	Honolulu	HI	96815	**866-956-4262**	808-922-4646
Old Mill Toronto					
21 Old Mill Rd	Toronto	ON	M8X1G5	**866-653-6455**	416-236-2641
Omni Hotels 4001 Maple Ave	Dallas	TX	75219	**800-843-6664**	402-952-6664
Omni La Mansion del Rio					
112 College St	San Antonio	TX	78205	**800-292-7300**	210-518-1000
One Washington Cir Hotel					
1 Washington Cir NW	Washington	DC	20037	**800-424-9671**	202-872-1680
Onyx Hotel 155 Portland St	Boston	MA	02114	**866-660-6699**	617-557-9955
Opus Hotel 322 Davie St	Vancouver	BC	V6B5Z6	**866-642-6787**	
Orchard Garden Hotel					
466 Bush St	San Francisco	CA	94108	**888-717-2881**	415-399-9807
Orchard Hotel					
665 Bush St	San Francisco	CA	94108	**888-717-2881**	415-362-8878
Orchards Inn of Sedona					
254 Hwy N 89 A	Sedona	AZ	86336	**855-474-7719**	
Orient Express Hotels Inc					
1155 Ave of the Americas	New York	NY	10036	**800-237-1236**	212-302-5055
NYSE: OEH					
Orlando, The					
8384 W Third St	Los Angeles	CA	90048	**800-624-6835**	323-658-6600
Orleans Las Vegas Hotel & Casino					
4500 W Tropicana Ave	Las Vegas	NV	89103	**800-675-3267**	702-365-7111
Outrigger Enterprises Group					
2375 Kuhio Ave	Honolulu	HI	96815	**800-462-6262**	808-921-6941
Outrigger Hotels & Resorts					
2375 Kuhio Ave	Honolulu	HI	96815	**800-688-7444**	808-921-6941
Outrigger Waikiki on the Beach					
2335 Kalakaua Ave	Honolulu	HI	96815	**800-688-7444**	808-923-0711
Oxford Hotel 1600 17th St	Denver	CO	80202	**800-228-5838**	303-628-5400
Oxford Suites Boise					
1426 S Entertainment Ave	Boise	ID	83709	**888-322-8001***	208-322-8000
*General					
Oxford Suites Spokane Valley					
15015 E Indiana Ave	Spokane Valley	WA	99216	**866-668-7848**	509-847-1000
Oxford Suites Spokane-Downtown					
115 W N River Dr	Spokane	WA	99201	**800-774-1877**	509-353-9000
Oyster Point Hotel, The					
146 Bodman Pl	Red Bank	NJ	07701	**800-345-3484**	732-530-8200
Pacific Beach Hotel					
2490 Kalakaua Ave	Honolulu	HI	96815	**800-367-6060**	808-922-1233
Pacific Inn					
600 Marina Dr	Seal Beach	CA	90740	**866-466-0300**	562-493-7501
Pacific Inn Resort & Conference Centre					
1160 King George Hwy	Surrey	BC	V4A4Z2	**800-667-2248**	604-535-1432
Pacific Shores Inn					
4802 Mission Blvd	San Diego	CA	92109	**888-478-7829**	858-483-6300
Pacific Terrace Hotel					
610 Diamond St	San Diego	CA	92109	**800-344-3370**	858-581-3500
Painted Buffalo Inn					
400 W Broadway PO Box 2547	Jackson	WY	83001	**800-288-3866**	307-733-4340
Palace Casino 158 Howard Ave	Biloxi	MS	39530	**800-725-2239**	228-432-8888
Palace Hotel					
2 New Montgomery St	San Francisco	CA	94105	**866-716-8136**	415-512-1111
Palace Station Hotel & Casino					
2411 W Sahara Ave	Las Vegas	NV	89102	**800-634-3101***	702-367-2411
*Resv					
Palmer House Hilton					
17 E Monroe St	Chicago	IL	60603	**800-445-8667**	312-726-7500
Pan Pacific Hotel Vancouver					
999 Canada Pl Ste 300	Vancouver	BC	V6C3B5	**800-937-1515**	604-662-8111
Pan Pacific Seattle					
2125 Terry Ave	Seattle	WA	98121	**877-324-4856**	206-264-8111
Pantages Hotel					
200 Victoria St	Toronto	ON	M5B1V8	**866-852-1777**	416-362-1777
Par-A-Dice Hotel					
21 Blackjack Blvd	East Peoria	IL	61611	**800-727-2342**	309-699-7711
Paramount Hotel 724 Pine St	Seattle	WA	98101	**877-821-2011**	206-292-9500
Paris Las Vegas					
3655 Las Vegas Blvd S	Las Vegas	NV	89109	**800-342-7724**	800-522-4700
Park Shore Waikiki Hotel					
2586 Kalakaua Ave	Honolulu	HI	96815	**866-536-7975**	808-954-7426
Park South Hotel					
124 E 28th St	New York	NY	10016	**800-315-4642**	212-448-0888
Park Vista Resort Hotel					
705 Cherokee OrchaRd Rd PO Box 30	Gatlinburg	TN	37738	**800-227-5622***	865-436-9211
*Sales					
Parkway Inn					
125 N Jackson St PO Box 494	Jackson	WY	83001	**800-247-8390**	

				Toll-Free	*Phone*
Paso Robles Inn					
1103 Spring St	Paso Robles	CA	93446	**800-676-1713**	805-238-2660
Peabody Memphis					
149 Union Ave	Memphis	TN	38103	**800-732-2639**	901-529-4000
Peacock Suites					
1745 S Anaheim Blvd	Anaheim	CA	92805	**800-522-6401**	714-535-8255
Peery Hotel					
110 West 300 South	Salt Lake City	UT	84101	**800-331-0073**	801-521-4300
Pegasus International Hotel					
501 Southard St	Key West	FL	33040	**800-397-8148**	305-294-9323
Pelham Hotel					
444 Common St	New Orleans	LA	70130	**888-856-4486**	504-522-4444
Pelican Grand Beach Resort Condominium Associati					
2000 N Ocean Blvd	Fort Lauderdale	FL	33305	**800-525-6232**	954-568-9431
Penguin Hotel					
1418 Ocean Dr	Miami Beach	FL	33139	**800-499-7964**	305-534-9334
Peninsula Beverly Hills					
9882 S Santa Monica Blvd	Beverly Hills	CA	90212	**800-462-7899**	310-551-2888
Peninsula Chicago					
108 E Superior St	Chicago	IL	60611	**866-288-8889**	312-337-2888
Peninsula New York					
700 Fifth Ave	New York	NY	10019	**800-262-9467**	212-956-2888
Penn's View Hotel					
14 N Front St	Philadelphia	PA	19106	**800-331-7634**	215-922-7600
Peppermill Hotel & Casino					
2707 S Virginia St	Reno	NV	89502	**800-648-6992**	775-826-2121
Pfister Hotel					
424 E Wisconsin Ave	Milwaukee	WI	53202	**800-558-8222**	414-273-8222
Phillips Beach Plaza Hotel					
1301 Atlantic Ave	Ocean City	MD	21842	**800-492-5834**	410-289-9121
Phoenix Grand Hotel Salem					
201 Liberty St SE	Salem	OR	97301	**877-540-7800**	503-540-7800
Phoenix Hotel					
601 Eddy St	San Francisco	CA	94109	**800-248-9466**	415-776-1380
Phoenix Park Hotel					
520 N Capitol St	Washington	DC	20001	**800-824-5419**	202-638-6900
Pier 5 Hotel					
711 Eastern Ave	Baltimore	MD	21202	**866-583-4162**	410-539-2000
Pillars Hotel at New River Sound					
111 N Birch Rd	Fort Lauderdale	FL	33304	**800-241-3333**	954-467-9639
Pine Crest Inn					
85 Pine Crest Ln	Tryon	NC	28782	**800-633-3001**	828-859-9135
Pines Lodge					
141 Scott Hill Rd	Beaver Creek	CO	81620	**800-859-8242***	970-429-5043
*Resv					
Place D'Armes Hotel					
625 St Ann St	New Orleans	LA	70116	**800-366-2743**	504-524-4531
Place Louis Riel All-Suite Hotel					
190 Smith St	Winnipeg	MB	R3C1J8	**800-665-0569**	204-947-6961
Planters Inn					
112 N Market St	Charleston	SC	29401	**800-845-7082**	843-722-2345
Platinum Hotel					
211 E Flamingo Rd	Las Vegas	NV	89169	**877-211-9211***	702-365-5000
*General					
Plaza Hotel & Casino					
1 Main St PO Box 760	Las Vegas	NV	89101	**800-634-6575**	702-386-2110
Plaza on the River Resort Club Hotel					
121 W St	Reno	NV	89501	**800-628-5974**	775-786-2200
Plaza Suite Hotel Resort					
620 S Peters St	New Orleans	LA	70130	**800-770-6721**	
Plaza Suites Silicon Valley					
3100 Lakeside Dr	Santa Clara	CA	95054	**800-345-1554**	408-748-9800
Plump Jack's Squaw Valley Inn					
1920 Squaw Vly Rd PO Box 2407	Olympic Valley	CA	96146	**800-323-7666**	530-583-1576
Point Plaza Suites & Conference Hotel					
950 J Clyde Morris Blvd	Newport News	VA	23601	**800-841-1112**	757-599-4460
Pontchartrain Hotel					
2031 St Charles Ave	New Orleans	LA	70130	**800-708-6652**	504-524-0581
Port-O-Call Hotel					
1510 Boardwalk	Ocean City	NJ	08226	**800-334-4546**	609-399-8812
Portland Harbor Hotel					
468 Fore St	Portland	ME	04101	**888-798-9090**	207-775-9090
Portland Regency Hotel					
20 Milk St	Portland	ME	04101	**800-727-3436**	207-774-4200
Portofino Hotel & Yacht Club					
260 Portofino Way	Redondo Beach	CA	90277	**800-468-4292**	310-379-8481
Portofino Inn & Suites Anaheim					
1831 S Harbor Blvd	Anaheim	CA	92802	**800-398-3963***	714-782-7600
*Resv					
Portola Plaza Hotel					
2 Portola Plaza	Monterey	CA	93940	**888-222-5851**	831-649-4511
Post Hotel, The					
200 Pipestone Rd PO Box 69	Lake Louise	AB	T0L1E0	**800-661-1586**	403-522-3989
Prairie Band Casino & Resort					
12305 150th Rd	Mayetta	KS	66509	**888-727-4946**	785-966-7777
Preferred Hotel Group					
Preferred Hotels & Resorts Worldwide Inc					
311 S Wacker Dr Ste 1900	Chicago	IL	60606	**800-650-1281**	312-913-0400
Summit Hotels & Resorts					
311 S Wacker Dr Ste 1900	Chicago	IL	60606	**800-650-1281**	312-913-0400
President Abraham Lincoln Hotel & Conference Ctr (PALHACC)					
701 E Adams St	Springfield	IL	62701	**855-610-8733**	217-544-8800
Prestige Harbourfront Resort & Convention Centre					
251 Harbourfront Dr Ne	Salmon Arm	BC	V1E2W7	**877-737-8443**	250-833-5800
Prince Conti Hotel					
830 Conti St	New Orleans	LA	70112	**800-366-2743**	504-529-4172
Prince George Hotel, The					
1725 Market St	Halifax	NS	B3J3N9	**800-565-1567**	902-425-1986
Princess Bayside Beach Hotel & Golf Ctr					
4801 Coastal Hwy	Ocean City	MD	21842	**888-622-9743***	410-723-2900
*General					
Princess Royale Oceanfront Hotel & Conference Ctr					
9100 Coastal Hwy	Ocean City	MD	21842	**800-476-9253**	410-524-7777
Providence Biltmore Hotel					
11 Dorrance St	Providence	RI	02903	**800-294-7709**	
Publick House Historic Resort					
277 Main St Rt 131	Sturbridge	MA	01566	**800-782-5425***	508-347-3313
*Cust Svc					

	City	State	Zip	Toll-Free	Phone
Puffin Inn 4400 SpenaRd Rd	Anchorage	AK	99517	**800-478-3346**	907-243-4044
Quality Hotel-airport 7228 Wminster Hwy	Richmond	BC	V6X1A1	**877-244-3051**	604-244-3051
Quality Inn Halifax Airport Hotel 60 Sky Blvd Halifax International Airport	Goffs	NS	B2T1K3	**800-667-3333**	902-873-3000
Quebec Inn 7175 Blvd Hamel Ouest	Quebec	QC	G2G1B6	**800-567-5276**	418-872-9831
Queen Anne Hotel 1590 Sutter St	San Francisco	CA	94109	**800-227-3970**	415-441-2828
Quimby House Inn 109 Cottage St	Bar Harbor	ME	04609	**800-344-5811**	207-288-5811
Rabbit Hill Inn 48 Lower Waterford Rd PO Box 55	Lower Waterford	VT	05848	**800-626-3215**	802-748-5168
Radisson Butler Blvd 4700 Salisbury Rd	Jacksonville	FL	32256	**888-201-1718**	904-281-9700
Radisson Chicago-O'Hare Hotel 1450 E Touhy Ave	Des Plaines	IL	60018	**888-201-1718**	847-296-8866
Radisson Hotel Bloomington Mall of America 1700 American Blvd E *Resv	Bloomington	MN	55425	**800-967-9033***	952-854-8700
Radisson Milwaukee North Shore 7065 N Port Washington Rd	Milwaukee	WI	53217	**800-395-7046**	414-351-6960
Raffaello Hotel 201 E Delaware Pl	Chicago	IL	60611	**800-916-4339**	312-943-5000
Railroad Pass Hotel & Casino 2800 S Boulder Hwy	Henderson	NV	89002	**800-654-0877**	702-294-5000
Ramada Middletown 425 E Main Rd	Middletown	RI	02842	**800-854-9517**	401-846-3555
Ramada Plaza & Conference Ctr 4900 Sinclair Rd	Columbus	OH	43229	**800-272-6232**	614-846-0300
Ranch at Steamboat 1800 Ranch Rd	Steamboat Springs	CO	80487	**888-686-8075**	970-879-3000
Ranch Inn 45 E Pearl St	Jackson	WY	83001	**800-348-5599**	307-733-6363
Raphael Kansas City 325 Ward Pkwy	Kansas City	MO	64112	**800-821-5343**	816-756-3800
Red Jacket Beach Resort 39 Todd Rd	South Yarmouth	MA	02664	**800-227-3263**	508-398-6941
Red Lion Hotels Corp 201 W N River Dr Ste 100 *NYSE: RLH* ■ *Resv	Spokane	WA	99201	**800-733-5466***	
Red Rock Resort Spa & Casino 11011 W Charleston Blvd	Las Vegas	NV	89135	**866-767-7773**	702-797-7777
Regency Fairbanks Hotel 95 Tenth Ave	Fairbanks	AK	99701	**800-478-1320**	907-459-2700
Regency Suites Calgary 610 Fourth Ave SW	Calgary	AB	T2P0K1	**800-468-4044**	403-231-1000
Regency Suites Hotel Midtown Atlanta 975 W Peachtree St	Atlanta	GA	30309	**800-642-3629**	404-876-5003
Remington Suite Hotel 220 Travis St	Shreveport	LA	71101	**800-444-6750**	318-425-5000
Residence & Conference Centre - Toronto 1760 Finch Ave E	Toronto	ON	M2J5G3	**877-225-8664**	416-491-8811
Rhett House Inn 1009 Craven St	Beaufort	SC	29902	**888-480-9530**	843-524-9030
Richmond, The 1757 Collins Ave	Miami Beach	FL	33139	**855-627-3767**	305-538-2331
Rittenhouse Hotel 210 W Rittenhouse Sq	Philadelphia	PA	19103	**800-635-1042**	215-546-9000
Ritz-Carlton Dallas 2121 McKinney Ave *Resv	Dallas	TX	75201	**800-960-7082***	214-922-0200
Riu Hotel Florida Beach 3101 Collins Ave	Miami	FL	33140	**888-666-8816**	305-673-5333
River's Edge Resort Cottages 4200 Boat St	Fairbanks	AK	99709	**800-770-3343**	907-474-0286
Riveredge Resort Hotel 17 Holland St	Alexandria Bay	NY	13607	**800-365-6987**	315-482-9917
Riverside Hotel 620 E Las Olas Blvd	Fort Lauderdale	FL	33301	**800-325-3280**	954-467-0671
Riverstone Billings Inn 880 N 29th St	Billings	MT	59101	**800-231-7782**	406-252-6800
Riviera Hotel 1431 Robson St	Vancouver	BC	V6G1C1	**888-699-5222**	604-685-1301
Road King Inn Columbia Mall 3300 30th Ave S	Grand Forks	ND	58201	**800-707-1391**	
Robert Treat Hotel 50 Pk Pl	Newark	NJ	07102	**800-569-2300**	973-622-1000
Rock View Resort 1049 Parkview Dr	Hollister	MO	65672	**800-375-9530**	417-334-4678
Rocklin Park Hotel 5450 China Garden Rd	Rocklin	CA	95677	**888-630-9400**	916-630-9400
Roger Smith Hotel 501 Lexington Ave	New York	NY	10017	**800-445-0277**	212-755-1400
Roosevelt Hotel 45 E 45th St	New York	NY	10017	**888-833-3969**	212-661-9600
Rose Hotel 807 Main St	Pleasanton	CA	94566	**800-843-9540**	925-846-8802
Rosedale on Robson Suite Hotel 838 Hamilton St	Vancouver	BC	V6B6A2	**800-661-8870**	604-689-8033
Rosellen Suites at Stanley Park 2030 Barclay St	Vancouver	BC	V6G1L5	**888-317-6648**	604-689-4807
Rosen Centre Hotel 9840 International Dr	Orlando	FL	32819	**800-204-7234**	407-996-9840
Rosen Hotels & Resorts Inc 9840 International Dr	Orlando	FL	32819	**800-204-7234**	407-996-9840
Rosen Plaza Hotel 9700 International Dr	Orlando	FL	32819	**800-366-9700**	407-996-9700
Rosen Shingle Creek 9939 Universal Blvd	Orlando	FL	32819	**866-996-9939**	407-996-9939
Rosewood Hotels & Resorts 500 Crescent Ct Ste 300	Dallas	TX	75201	**888-767-3966**	214-880-4200
Roslyn Claremont Hotel 1221 Old Northern Blvd	Roslyn	NY	11576	**800-626-9005**	516-625-2700
Rough Creek Lodge 5165 County Rd 2013	Glen Rose	TX	76043	**877-907-0754**	254-965-3700
Royal Garden at Waikiki Hotel 440 Olohana St	Honolulu	HI	96815	**800-989-0971**	808-943-0202
Royal Holiday Beach Resort 1988 Beach Blvd *Resv	Biloxi	MS	39531	**800-874-0402***	228-388-7553
Royal Park Hotel-brookshire & The Commons 600 E University Dr	Rochester	MI	48307	**800-339-2761**	248-652-2600
Royal Regency Hotel 165 Tuckahoe Rd	Yonkers	NY	10710	**800-215-3858**	914-476-6200
Royal Sonesta Hotel Boston 40 Edwin H Land Blvd	Cambridge	MA	02142	**800-766-3782**	617-806-4200
Royal Sonesta Hotel New Orleans 300 Bourbon St	New Orleans	LA	70130	**800-766-3782**	504-586-0300
Royal Sun Inn 1700 S Palm Canyon Dr	Palm Springs	CA	92264	**800-619-4786**	760-327-1564
Royalton Hotel 44 W 44th St	New York	NY	10036	**800-606-6090**	212-869-4400
Saint Anthony the - A Wyndham Historic Hotel 300 E Travis St	San Antonio	TX	78205	**800-996-3426**	210-227-4392
Saint Michaels Harbour Inn & Marina 101 N Harbor Rd	Saint Michaels	MD	21663	**800-955-9001**	410-745-9001
Saint Paul Hotel 350 Market St	Saint Paul	MN	55102	**800-292-9292**	651-292-9292
Saint Regis Hotel 602 Dunsmuir St	Vancouver	BC	V6B1Y6	**800-770-7929**	604-681-1135
Saint Regis Hotel Winnipeg 285 Smith St	Winnipeg	MB	R3C1K9	**800-663-7344**	204-942-0171
Salisbury Hotel 123 W 57th St	New York	NY	10019	**888-692-5757**	212-246-1300
Sam's Town Hotel & Casino Shreveport 315 Clyde Fant Pkwy	Shreveport	LA	71101	**877-770-7867**	
Sam's Town Hotel & Gambling Hall 5111 Boulder Hwy	Las Vegas	NV	89122	**800-897-8696**	702-456-7777
San Carlos Hotel 150 E 50th St	New York	NY	10022	**800-722-2012**	212-755-1800
Sands Casino Resort Bethlehem 77 Sands Blvd	Bethlehem	PA	18015	**877-726-3777**	
Sands Ocean Club Resort 9550 Shore Dr *General	Myrtle Beach	SC	29572	**888-999-8485***	
Sands Regency Casino Hotel 345 N Arlington Ave *Resv	Reno	NV	89501	**800-233-4939***	775-348-2200
Sandwich Lodge & Resort 54 Rt 6A - Old King's Hwy	Sandwich	MA	02563	**800-282-5353**	508-888-2275
Sanibel Inn 937 E Gulf Dr	Sanibel	FL	33957	**866-565-5480**	239-472-3181
Santa Barbara Inn 901 E Cabrillo Blvd	Santa Barbara	CA	93103	**800-231-0431**	805-966-2285
Santa Maria Inn 801 S Broadway	Santa Maria	CA	93454	**800-462-4276**	805-928-7777
Saratoga Hilton 534 Broadway	Saratoga Springs	NY	12866	**800-445-8667**	518-584-4000
Satellite Hotel 411 Lakewood Cir	Colorado Springs	CO	80910	**800-423-8409**	719-596-6800
Savoy Suites Georgetown 2505 Wisconsin Ave NW	Washington	DC	20007	**877-301-0002**	202-337-9700
Scotsman Inn West 5922 W Kellogg St	Wichita	KS	67209	**800-950-7268**	316-943-3800
Sea Ranch Lodge 60 Sea Walk Dr PO Box 44	The Sea Ranch	CA	95497	**800-732-7262**	707-785-2371
Sea View Hotel 9909 Collins Ave	Bal Harbour	FL	33154	**800-447-1010**	305-866-4441
Seaport Hotel & World Trade Ctr 1 Seaport Ln	Boston	MA	02210	**877-732-7678**	617-385-4000
Seaside Inn 541 E Gulf Dr	Sanibel Island	FL	33957	**866-565-5092**	239-472-1400
Seattle Convention Ctr Pike Street 1011 Pike St	Seattle	WA	98101	**800-225-5466**	206-682-8282
Sedona Rouge Hotel & Spa 2250 W SR- 89A	Sedona	AZ	86336	**866-312-4111**	928-203-4111
Seelbach Hilton Louisville 500 S Fourth St	Louisville	KY	40202	**800-333-3399**	502-585-3200
Senate Luxury Suites 900 SW Tyler St	Topeka	KS	66612	**800-488-3188**	785-233-5050
Sentinel Hotel 614 SW 11th Ave	Portland	OR	97205	**888-246-5631**	503-224-3400
Serrano Hotel 405 Taylor St	San Francisco	CA	94102	**866-575-9941**	415-885-2500
Setai, The 2001 Collins Ave	Miami Beach	FL	33139	**888-625-7500**	305-520-6000
Shades of Green on Walt Disney World Resort 1950 W Magnolia Palm Dr	Lake Buena Vista	FL	32830	**888-593-2242**	407-824-3400
Shelburne Murray Hill 303 Lexington Ave	New York	NY	10016	**866-233-4642**	212-689-5200
Shephard's Beach Resort 619 S Gulfview Blvd	Clearwater Beach	FL	33767	**800-237-8477**	727-441-6875
Sheraton Delfina Santa Monica 530 W Pico Blvd	Santa Monica	CA	90405	**888-625-4988**	310-399-9344
Sheraton Gateway Hotel Los Angeles 6101 W Century Blvd	Los Angeles	CA	90045	**888-627-7104**	310-642-1111
Sheraton Suites Calgary Eau Claire 255 Barclay Parade SW	Calgary	AB	T2P5C2	**866-716-8134**	403-266-7200
Sherry-Netherland Hotel 781 Fifth Ave	New York	NY	10022	**877-743-7710**	212-355-2800
Shilo Inn Hotel Salt Lake City 206 SW Temple	Salt Lake City	UT	84101	**800-222-2244**	
Shilo Inn Suites Hotel Portland Airport 117707 NE Airport Way	Portland	OR	97220	**800-222-2244**	503-252-7500
Shilo Inn Suites Salem 3304 Market St	Salem	OR	97301	**800-222-2244**	503-581-4001
Shilo Inns Suites Hotels 11600 SW Shilo Ln	Portland	OR	97225	**800-222-2244**	503-641-6565
Siena Hotel 1505 E Franklin St	Chapel Hill	NC	27514	**800-223-7379**	919-929-4000
Silver Cloud Hotel Seattle Broadway 1100 Broadway	Seattle	WA	98122	**800-590-1801**	206-325-1400
Silver Cloud Inn Seattle-Lake Union 1150 Fairview Ave N *General	Seattle	WA	98109	**800-330-5812***	206-447-9500

Name / Address	City	State	ZIP	Toll-Free	Phone
Silver Cloud Inn University District 5036 25th Ave NE	Seattle	WA	98105	**800-205-6940**	206-526-5200
Silver King Hotel 1485 Empire Ave	Park City	UT	84060	**888-667-2775**	435-649-5500
Silver Smith Hotel & Suites 10 S Wabash Ave	Chicago	IL	60603	**800-979-0084**	312-372-7696
SilverBirch Hotels & Resorts 1600 - 1030 W Georgia St	Vancouver	BC	V6E2Y3	**800-661-1232**	604-646-2447
Silverdale Beach Hotel 3073 NW Bucklin Hill Rd	Silverdale	WA	98383	**800-544-9799**	360-698-1000
Simonton Court Historic Inn & Cottages 320 Simonton St	Key West	FL	33040	**800-944-2687**	
Sir Francis Drake Hotel 450 Powell St	San Francisco	CA	94102	**800-795-7129**	415-392-7755
Ski Bromont 150 Champlain	Bromont	QC	J2L1A2	**866-276-6668**	450-534-2200
Sky Hotel 709 E Durant Ave	Aspen	CO	81611	**800-882-2582**	970-925-6760
Snell House 21 Atlantic Ave	Bar Harbor	ME	04609	**866-763-5524**	207-288-8004
Snowbird Mountain Lodge 4633 Santeetlah Rd	Robbinsville	NC	28771	**800-941-9290**	828-479-3433
Snowy Owl Inn 41 Village Rd	Waterville Valley	NH	03215	**800-766-9969**	603-236-8383
Sofia Hotel 150 W Broadway	San Diego	CA	92101	**800-826-0009**	619-234-9200
SoHo Grand Hotel 310 W Broadway	New York	NY	10013	**800-965-3000**	212-965-3000
SoHo Metropolitan Hotel 318 Wellington St W	Toronto	ON	M5V3T4	**866-764-6638**	416-599-8800
Somerset Inn 2601 W Big Beaver Rd	Troy	MI	48084	**800-228-8769**	248-643-7800
Sonesta Hotel & Suites Coconut Grove 2889 McFarlane Rd	Miami	FL	33133	**800-766-3782**	305-529-2828
Soniat House 1133 Chartres St	New Orleans	LA	70116	**800-544-8808**	504-522-0570
Sophie Station Suites 1717 University Ave	Fairbanks	AK	99709	**800-528-4916**	
South Beach Marina Inn & Vacation Rentals 232 S Sea Pines Dr	Hilton Head Island	SC	29928	**800-367-3909**	843-671-6498
South Pier Inn on the Canal 701 Lake Ave S	Duluth	MN	55802	**800-430-7437**	218-786-9007
South Point Hotel & Casino 9777 Las Vegas Blvd S	Las Vegas	NV	89183	**866-796-7111**	702-796-7111
Southampton Inn 91 Hill St	SouthHampton	NY	11968	**800-832-6500**	631-283-6500
Southernmost On the Beach 508 S St	Key West	FL	33040	**800-354-4455**	305-296-6577
Southfork Hotel 1600 N Central Expy	Plano	TX	75074	**877-386-4383**	972-578-8555
Southway Inn 2431 Bank St	Ottawa	ON	K1V8R9	**877-688-4929**	613-737-0811
Spindrift Inn 652 Cannery Row	Monterey	CA	93940	**800-841-1879**	831-646-8900
Spring Creek Ranch 1800 Spirit Dance Rd	Jackson	WY	83001	**800-443-6139**	307-733-8833
St James Hotel 406 Main St	Red Wing	MN	55066	**800-252-1875**	651-388-2846
St Julien Hotel & Spa 900 Walnut St	Boulder	CO	80302	**877-303-0900**	720-406-9696
Stamford Suites 720 Bedford St	Stamford	CT	06901	**866-394-4365**	203-359-7300
Stanley Hotel 333 Wonderview Ave	Estes Park	CO	80517	**800-976-1377**	970-586-3371
Star Island Resort 5000 Ave of the Stars	Kissimmee	FL	34746	**800-513-2820**	407-997-8000
Starwood Hotels & Resorts Worldwide Inc 1111 Westchester Ave *NYSE: HOT* ■ *Cust Svc	White Plains	NY	10604	**888-625-5144***	914-640-8100
Saint Regis Hotels & Resorts 1111 Westchester Ave	White Plains	NY	10604	**888-625-4988**	914-640-8100
Westin Hotels & Resorts 1111 Westchester Ave	White Plains	NY	10604	**888-625-5144**	914-640-8100
State Plaza Hotel 2117 E St NW	Washington	DC	20037	**800-424-2859**	202-861-8200
Stockyards Hotel 109 E Exchange Ave	Fort Worth	TX	76164	**800-423-8471**	817-625-6427
Stone Castle Hotel & Conference Ctr, The 3050 Green Mtn Dr	Branson	MO	65616	**800-677-6906**	417-335-4700
Stonebridge Inn 300 Carriage Way PO Box 5008	Snowmass Village	CO	81615	**800-922-7242**	970-923-2420
Stonewall Jackson Hotel & Conference Ctr 24 S Market St	Staunton	VA	24401	**866-880-0024**	540-885-4848
Stoney Creek Inn 101 Mariner's Way	East Peoria	IL	61611	**800-659-2220**	309-694-1300
Strater Hotel 699 Main Ave	Durango	CO	81301	**800-247-4431**	970-247-4431
Stratford Hotel 242 Powell St	San Francisco	CA	94102	**888-688-0038**	415-397-7080
Strathcona Hotel 60 York St	Toronto	ON	M5J1S8	**800-268-8304**	416-363-3321
Strathcona Hotel, The 919 Douglas St	Victoria	BC	V8W2C2	**800-663-7476**	250-383-7137
Stratosphere Tower Hotel & Casino 2000 S Las Vegas Blvd	Las Vegas	NV	89104	**800-998-6937**	702-380-7777
Sturbridge Host Hotel & Conference Ctr 366 Main St	Sturbridge	MA	01566	**800-582-3232**	508-347-7393
Suites at Fisherman's Wharf 2655 Hyde St	San Francisco	CA	94109	**800-227-3608**	415-771-0200
Suites Hotel in Canal Park, The 325 Lake Ave S	Duluth	MN	55802	**800-794-1716**	218-727-4663
Summit Lodge & Spa 4359 Main St	Whistler	BC	V0N1B4	**888-913-8811**	604-932-2778
Sun Viking Lodge 2411 S Atlantic Ave	Daytona Beach Shores	FL	32118	**800-874-4469**	386-252-6252
Suncoast Hotel & Casino 9090 Alta Dr	Las Vegas	NV	89145	**877-677-7111**	702-636-7111
Sundial Boutique Hotel 4340 Sundial Crescent	Whistler	BC	V0N1B4	**800-661-2321**	604-932-2321
Sunset Inn Travel Apartments 1111 Burnaby St	Vancouver	BC	V6E1P4	**800-786-1997**	604-688-2474
Sunset Marquis Hotel & Villas 1200 N Alta Loma Rd	West Hollywood	CA	90069	**800-858-9758**	310-657-1333
Sunset Station Hotel & Casino 1301 W Sunset Rd	Henderson	NV	89014	**888-786-7389**	702-547-7777
Surf & Sand Resort 1555 S Coast Hwy	Laguna Beach	CA	92651	**877-741-5908**	949-497-4477
Surfsand Resort 148 W Gower Rd	Cannon Beach	OR	97110	**800-547-6100**	503-436-2274
Surfside Inn 1211 Atlantic Ave	Virginia Beach	VA	23451	**800-437-2497**	757-428-1183
Surrey Hotel 20 E 76th St	New York	NY	10021	**866-233-4642**	212-288-3700
Swag, The 2300 Swag Rd	Waynesville	NC	28785	**800-789-7672**	828-926-0430
Taj Boston 15 Arlington St	Boston	MA	02116	**866-969-1825**	617-536-5700
Taj Campton Place 340 Stockton St	San Francisco	CA	94108	**866-969-1825**	415-781-5555
Teton Mountain Lodge & Spa 3385 Cody Ln	Teton Village	WY	83025	**800-631-6271**	307-201-6066
Thayer Hotel 674 Thayer Rd	West Point	NY	10996	**800-247-5047**	845-446-4731
Tickle Pink Inn at Carmel Highlands 155 Highland Dr	Carmel	CA	93923	**800-635-4774**	831-624-1244
Tidewater Inn & Conference Ctr 101 E Dover St	Easton	MD	21601	**800-237-8775**	410-822-1300
Time, The 224 W 49th St	New York	NY	10019	**877-846-3692**	212-246-5252
Times Hotel & Suites 6515 Wilfrid-Hamel Blvd	L'Ancienne-Lorette	QC	G2E5W3	**888-902-4444**	418-877-7788
Tivoli Lodge 386 Hanson Ranch Rd	Vail	CO	81657	**800-451-4756**	970-476-5615
Topaz Hotel 1733 N St NW	Washington	DC	20036	**800-775-1202**	202-393-3000
Town & Country Inn 20 State RT 2 *General	Shelburne	NH	03581	**800-325-4386***	603-466-3315
Town & Country Inn & Conference Ctr 2008 Savannah Hwy	Charleston	SC	29407	**800-334-6660**	843-571-1000
Town Inn Suites 620 Church St	Toronto	ON	M4Y2G2	**800-387-2755**	416-964-3311
Townsend Hotel 100 Townsend St	Birmingham	MI	48009	**800-548-4172**	248-642-7900
Trans World Corp (TWC) 545 Fifth Ave Ste 940 *OTC: TWOC*	New York	NY	10017	**877-407-9037**	212-983-3355
Travelodge Virginia Beach 1909 Atlantic Ave	Virginia Beach	VA	23451	**800-578-7878**	757-425-0650
Tremont Chicago 100 E Chestnut St	Chicago	IL	60611	**866-716-8147**	312-751-1900
Trianon Old Naples 955 Seventh Ave S	Naples	FL	34102	**877-482-5228**	239-435-9600
Tropical Winds Oceanfront Hotel 1398 N Atlantic Ave	Daytona Beach	FL	32118	**800-245-6099**	386-258-1016
Tropicana Inn & Suites 1540 S Harbor Blvd	Anaheim	CA	92802	**800-828-4898**	714-635-4082
Trump International Hotel & Tower 725 Fifth Ave	New York	NY	10022	**888-448-7867**	312-588-8000
Tugboat Inn 80 Commercial St PO Box 267	Boothbay Harbor	ME	04538	**800-248-2628**	207-633-4434
Tuscany Suites & Casino 255 E Flamingo Rd *Resv	Las Vegas	NV	89169	**877-887-2261***	702-893-8933
Twin Farms 452 Royalton Tpke PO Box 115	Barnard	VT	05031	**800-894-6327**	802-234-9999
UMass Hotel at the Campus Ctr 1 Campus Ctr Way	Amherst	MA	01003	**877-822-2110**	413-549-6000
Umstead Hotel & Spa 100 Woodland Pond	Cary	NC	27513	**866-877-4141**	919-447-4000
Union Station A Wyndham Historic Hotel PO Box 4090	Aberdeen	SD	57401	**800-996-3426**	
University Inn Seattle 4140 Roosevelt Way NE	Seattle	WA	98105	**800-733-3855**	206-632-5055
University Place 310 SW Lincoln St	Portland	OR	97201	**866-845-4647**	503-221-0140
US Grant, The 326 Broadway	San Diego	CA	92101	**866-716-8136**	619-232-3121
US Suites 4970 Windplay Dr C1 *Cust Svc	El Dorado Hills	CA	95762	**800-877-8483***	916-941-7970
Valley River Inn 1000 Vly River Way	Eugene	OR	97401	**800-543-8266**	541-743-1000
Vanderbilt Grace 41 Mary St	Newport	RI	02840	**888-826-4255**	401-846-6200
Varscona Hotel 8208 106th St	Edmonton	AB	T6E6R9	**866-465-8150**	780-434-6111
Velvet Cloak Inn, The 1505 Hillsborough St	Raleigh	NC	27605	**888-828-0335**	919-828-0333
Viceroy Palm Springs 415 S BelaRdo Rd	Palm Springs	CA	92262	**866-781-9923**	760-320-4117
Viceroy Santa Monica 1819 Ocean Ave	Santa Monica	CA	90401	**888-622-4567**	310-260-7500
Victoria Inn Winnipeg 1808 Wellington Ave	Winnipeg	MB	R3H0G3	**877-842-4667**	204-786-4801
Victoria Regent Hotel, The 1234 Wharf St	Victoria	BC	V8W3H9	**800-663-7472**	250-386-2211
Victorian Condo-Hotel & Conference Ctr 6300 Seawall Blvd	Galveston	TX	77551	**800-231-6363**	409-740-3555
Villa Florence 225 Powell St	San Francisco	CA	94102	**800-553-4411**	415-397-7700
Villa Royale Inn 1620 Indian Trl	Palm Springs	CA	92264	**800-245-2314**	760-327-2314
Village Latch Inn 101 Hill St PO Box 3000	SouthHampton	NY	11968	**800-545-2824**	631-283-2160
Villagio Inn & Spa 6481 Washington St	Yountville	CA	94599	**800-351-1133**	707-944-8877
Vintage Inn Napa Valley 6541 Washington St *Cust Svc	Yountville	CA	94599	**800-351-1133***	
Vintners Inn 4350 Barnes Rd	Santa Rosa	CA	95403	**800-421-2584**	707-575-7350
Virginian Lodge 750 W Broadway PO Box 1052	Jackson Hole	WY	83001	**800-262-4999**	307-733-2792
Virginian Suites 1500 Arlington Blvd	Arlington	VA	22209	**866-371-1446**	703-522-9600

Name / Address	City	State	Zip	Toll-Free	Phone
Viscount Gort Hotel 1670 Portage Ave	Winnipeg	MB	R3J0C9	**800-665-1122**	204-775-0451
Viscount Suite Hotel 4855 E Broadway Blvd *Resv	Tucson	AZ	85711	**800-527-9666***	520-745-6500
Vista Host Inc 10370 Richmond Ave Ste 150	Houston	TX	77042	**800-257-3000**	713-267-5800
Voyageur Lakewalk Inn 333 E Superior St	Duluth	MN	55802	**800-258-3911**	218-722-3911
Waikiki Parc Hotel 2233 Helumoa Rd	Honolulu	HI	96815	**800-422-0450**	808-921-7272
Waikiki Resort Hotel 2460 Koa Ave	Honolulu	HI	96815	**800-367-5116**	808-922-4911
Waldorf Towers, The 100 E 50th St	New York	NY	10022	**800-925-3673**	212-355-3100
Warwick Denver Hotel 1776 Grant St	Denver	CO	80203	**800-203-3232**	303-861-2000
Warwick Melrose Hotel 3015 Oak Lawn Ave	Dallas	TX	75219	**800-521-7172**	214-521-5151
Warwick New York Hotel 65 W 54th St	New York	NY	10019	**800-223-4099**	212-247-2700
Warwick Seattle Hotel 401 Lenora St	Seattle	WA	98121	**800-426-9280**	206-443-4300
Washington Court Hotel 525 New Jersey Ave NW	Washington	DC	20001	**800-321-3010**	202-628-2100
Washington Duke Inn & Golf Club 3001 Cameron Blvd	Durham	NC	27705	**800-443-3853**	919-490-0999
Washington Plaza Hotel 10 Thomas Cir NW Massachusetts Ave at 14th St	Washington	DC	20005	**800-424-1140**	202-842-1300
Washington Square Hotel 103 Waverly Pl	New York	NY	10011	**800-222-0418**	212-777-9515
Waterfront Hotel 10 Washington St	Oakland	CA	94607	**888-842-5333**	510-836-3800
Waters Edge Hotel 25 Main St	Tiburon	CA	94920	**888-662-9555**	415-789-5999
Wauwinet, The 120 Wauwinet Rd PO Box 2580	Nantucket	MA	02584	**800-426-8718**	508-228-0145
Weber's Inn 3050 Jackson Rd *Resv	Ann Arbor	MI	48103	**800-443-3050***	734-769-2500
Wedgewood Hotel 845 Hornby St	Vancouver	BC	V6Z1V1	**800-663-0666**	604-689-7777
Wedgewood Resort Hotel 212 Wedgewood Dr	Fairbanks	AK	99701	**800-528-4916**	
Wellington Hotel 871 Seventh Ave	New York	NY	10019	**800-652-1212**	212-247-3900
Wellington Resort 551 Thames St	Newport	RI	02840	**800-228-2968**	401-849-1770
Wentworth Mansion 149 Wentworth St	Charleston	SC	29401	**888-466-1886**	843-853-1886
Westgate Branson Woods 2201 Roark Vly Rd	Branson	MO	65616	**877-253-8572**	417-334-2324
Westgate Painted Mountain Country Club 6302 E McKellips Rd	Mesa	AZ	85215	**888-433-3707**	480-654-3611
Westin Houston Downtown, The 1520 Texas Ave	Houston	TX	77002	**800-427-4697**	713-228-1520
Westmark Hotels Inc 300 Elliott Ave W	Seattle	WA	98119	**800-544-0970**	
White Elephant Inn & Cottages 50 Easton St	Nantucket	MA	02554	**800-475-2637**	508-228-2500
White Swan Inn 845 Bush St	San Francisco	CA	94108	**800-999-9570**	415-775-1755
Whitney the - A Wyndham Historic Hotel 610 Poydras St	New Orleans	LA	70130	**800-996-3426**	504-581-4222
Wickaninnish Inn 500 Osprey Ln PO Box 250	Tofino	BC	V0R2Z0	**800-333-4604**	250-725-3100
Williamsburg Lodge 310 S England St *Cust Svc	Williamsburg	VA	23185	**800-447-8679***	757-229-1000
Willows Historic Palm Springs Inn 412 W Tahquitz Canyon Way	Palm Springs	CA	92262	**800-966-9597**	760-320-0771
Willows Hotel 555 W Surf St	Chicago	IL	60657	**877-207-2111**	773-528-8400
Willows Lodge 14580 NE 145th St	Woodinville	WA	98072	**877-424-3930**	425-424-3900
Windsor Arms Hotel 18 St Thomas St	Toronto	ON	M5S3E7	**877-999-2767**	416-971-9666
Windsor Court Hotel 300 Gravier St	New Orleans	LA	70130	**888-596-0955**	504-523-6000
Wonder View Inn & Suites 50 Eden St PO Box 25	Bar Harbor	ME	04609	**888-439-8439**	207-288-3358
Woodloch Pines Inc 731 Welcome Lk Rd	Hawley	PA	18428	**800-966-3562**	570-685-8000
Woodmark Hotel on Lake Washington 1200 Carillon Pt	Kirkland	WA	98033	**800-822-3700**	425-822-3700
Wort Hotel 50 N Glenwood *Cust Svc	Jackson	WY	83001	**800-322-2727***	307-733-2190
Wyndham Hotel Group					
Baymont Inn & Suites 1023 Eighth Ave NW	Aberdeen	SD	57401	**800-337-0550**	
Ramada 949 Route 46 *Resv	Parsippany	NJ	07054	**877-212-2733***	
Travelodge PO Box 4090 *Resv	Aberdeen	SD	57041	**800-525-4055***	312-427-8000
Wyndham Vacation Resorts 6277 Sea Harbor Dr	Orlando	FL	32821	**800-251-8736**	
Wyndham Lake Buena Vista 1850 Hotel Plaza Blvd	Lake Buena Vista	FL	32830	**800-624-4109**	407-828-4444
Wynfrey Hotel 1000 Riverchase Galleria	Birmingham	AL	35244	**800-633-7313**	205-705-1234
Wynn Las Vegas 3131 Las Vegas Blvd S	Las Vegas	NV	89109	**877-321-9966**	702-770-7000
Yarmouth Resort 343 Main St Rt 28	West Yarmouth	MA	02673	**877-838-3524**	508-775-5155
Yogo Inn 211 E Main St	Lewistown	MT	59457	**800-860-9646**	406-535-8721
Yorktowne Hotel 48 E Market St	York	PA	17401	**800-233-9324**	717-848-1111

380 ICE - MANUFACTURED

Name / Address	City	State	Zip	Toll-Free	Phone
Hanover Foods Corp 1550 York St PO Box 334 *OTC: HNFSA*	Hanover	PA	17331	**800-888-4646**	717-632-6000
House of Flavors Inc 110 N William St	Ludington	MI	49431	**800-930-7740**	231-845-7369
Icemakers Inc 3711 Fifth Ct N *General	Birmingham	AL	35222	**800-467-2181***	205-591-2791
Reddy Ice Holdings Inc 8750 N Central Expy Ste 1800 *OTC: RDDYQ*	Dallas	TX	75231	**800-683-4423**	214-526-6740

381 ICE CREAM & DAIRY STORES

Name / Address	City	State	Zip	Toll-Free	Phone
Baskin-Robbins Inc 130 Royall St	Canton	MA	02021	**800-859-5339**	781-737-3000
Carvel Express 200 Glenridge Pt Pkwy Ste 200	Atlanta	GA	30342	**800-322-4848**	
Cloverland Green Spring Dairy Inc 2701 Loch Raven Rd *Orders	Baltimore	MD	21218	**800-492-0094***	410-235-4477
Cold Stone Creamery Inc 9311 E Via De Ventura *Cust Svc	Scottsdale	AZ	85258	**866-452-4252***	480-362-4800
Dairy Queen 7505 Metro Blvd	Minneapolis	MN	55439	**800-883-4279**	952-830-0200
Kilwins Quality Confections Inc (KQC) 1050 Bay View Rd	Petoskey	MI	49770	**888-454-5946**	
Royal Crest Dairy Inc 350 S Pearl St	Denver	CO	80209	**888-226-6455**	303-777-2227

382 IMAGING EQUIPMENT & SYSTEMS - MEDICAL

SEE ALSO Medical Instruments & Apparatus - Mfr

Name / Address	City	State	Zip	Toll-Free	Phone
Agfa Corp 611 River Dr	Elmwood Park	NJ	07407	**888-274-8626**	201-440-2500
Alpine Solutions Inc 3222 Corte Malpaso Ste 204	Camarillo	CA	93012	**855-388-1883**	805-388-1699
BrainLAB Inc 3 Westbrook Corp Ctr	Westchester	IL	60154	**800-784-7700**	708-409-1343
Dentsply International Inc 221 W Philadelphia St PO Box 872 *NASDAQ: XRAY*	York	PA	17405	**800-877-0020**	717-845-7511
Digirad Corp 13950 Stowe Dr *NASDAQ: DRAD*	Poway	CA	92064	**800-947-6134**	858-726-1600
Dornier MedTech America Inc 1155 Roberts Blvd	Kennesaw	GA	30144	**800-367-6437**	770-426-1315
Hitachi Medical Systems America Inc 1959 Summit Commerce Pk	Twinsburg	OH	44087	**800-800-3106**	330-425-1313
Hologic Inc 35 Crosby Dr *NASDAQ: HOLX*	Bedford	MA	01730	**800-523-5001**	781-999-7300
iCAD Inc 98 Spit Brook Rd Ste 100 *NASDAQ: ICAD*	Nashua	NH	03062	**866-280-2239**	603-882-5200
ImageWorks 250 Clearbrook Rd	Elmsford	NY	10523	**800-592-6666**	914-592-6100
ITT Night Vision & Imaging 7635 Plantation Rd	Roanoke	VA	24019	**800-448-8678**	540-563-0371
Merge Helathcare 350 N Orleans St 1st Fl	Chicago	IL	60654	**877-446-3743**	312-565-6868
One Call Medical Inc (OCM) 20 Waterview Blvd PO Box 614	Parsippany	NJ	07054	**800-872-2875**	973-257-1000
Philips 5000 Marina Blvd Ste 100 *Cust Svc	Brisbane	CA	94005	**877-328-2808***	650-228-5555
Philips Medical Systems 3000 Minuteman Rd	Andover	MA	01810	**800-934-7372**	978-659-3000
Precision Optics Corp Inc 22 E Broadway *OTC: PEYE*	Gardner	MA	01440	**800-447-2812**	978-630-1800
S & S Technology 10625 Telge Rd	Houston	TX	77095	**800-231-1747**	281-815-1300
Shimadzu Medical Systems 20101 S Vermont Ave *General	Torrance	CA	90502	**800-477-1227***	310-217-8855
Siemens Medical Solutions Inc 51 Valley Stream Pkwy	Malvern	PA	19355	**800-888-7436**	888-826-9702
SonoSite Inc 21919 30th Dr SE *NASDAQ: SONO*	Bothell	WA	98021	**888-482-9449**	425-951-1200
Stereotaxis Inc 4320 Forest Pk Ave *NASDAQ: STXS*	Saint Louis	MO	63108	**866-646-2346**	314-678-6100
Topcon Medical Systems Inc 111 Bauer Dr	Oakland	NJ	07436	**800-223-1130**	201-599-5100
Toshiba America Inc 1251 Ave of the Americas Ste 4100	New York	NY	10020	**800-457-7777**	212-596-0600
Toshiba America Medical Systems Inc 2441 Michelle Dr *Cust Svc	Tustin	CA	92780	**800-521-1968***	714-730-5000
Varian Medical Systems Inc 3100 Hansen Way *NYSE: VAR*	Palo Alto	CA	94304	**800-544-4636**	650-493-4000
Vision-Sciences Inc 40 Ramland Rd S *NASDAQ: VSCI*	Orangeburg	NY	10962	**800-874-9975**	845-365-0600
Wolf X-Ray Corp 100 W Industry Ct *Cust Svc	Deer Park	NY	11729	**800-356-9729***	631-242-9729

383 IMAGING SERVICES - DIAGNOSTIC

Company	Address	City	State	ZIP	Toll-Free	Phone
Alliance Imaging Inc	100 Bayview Cir Ste 400	Newport Beach	CA	92660	**800-544-3215**	949-242-5300
Center for Diagnostic Imaging	5775 Wayzata Blvd Ste 190	Saint Louis Park	MN	55416	**800-537-0005**	952-541-1840
Johns Dental Laboratory Inc	423 S 13th St	Terre Haute	IN	47807	**800-457-0504**	812-232-6026
Medical Resources Inc	1455 Broad St	Bloomfield	NJ	07003	**800-537-7272**	973-707-1100

384 INCENTIVE PROGRAM MANAGEMENT SERVICES

SEE ALSO Conference & Events Coordinators

Many of the companies listed here provide travel as a reward for employees or corporate customers in order to boost sales or employee performance. Most of these companies are members of the Society of Incentive & Travel Executives. Some of the companies listed offer merchandise or other types of incentives as well.

Company	Address	City	State	ZIP	Toll-Free	Phone
Beatty Group International	9800 Beaverton Hillsdale Ste 105	Beaverton	OR	97005	**800-285-6215**	503-644-3340
ITAGroup	4600 Westown Pkwy	West Des Moines	IA	50266	**800-257-1985**	
Marketing Innovators International Inc	9701 W Higgins Rd	Rosemont	IL	60018	**800-543-7373**	
Motivation Through Incentives Inc	10400 W 103 St Ste 10	Overland Park	KS	66214	**800-826-3464**	
Provident Travel	11309 Montgomery Rd	Cincinnati	OH	45249	**800-354-8108**	513-247-1100
Student Advantage LLC	280 Summer St	Boston	MA	02210	**800-333-2920**	
USMotivation	7840 Roswell Rd Bldg 100 3rd Fl	Atlanta	GA	30350	**866-885-4702**	
Viktor Incentives & Meetings	4020 Copper View Ste 130	Traverse City	MI	49684	**800-748-0478**	231-947-0882

385 INDUSTRIAL EQUIPMENT & SUPPLIES (MISC) - WHOL

Company	Address	City	State	ZIP	Toll-Free	Phone
AaronEquipment Company Inc	735 E Green St PO Box 80	Bensenville	IL	60106	**800-492-2766**	630-350-2200
Abatix Corp	2400 Skyline Dr Ste 400	Mesquite	TX	75149	**800-426-3983**	214-381-0322
Accurate Air Engineering Inc	16207 Carmennita Rd	Cerritos	CA	90703	**800-438-5577**	562-484-6370
Adco Manufacturing Inc	2170 Academy Ave	Sanger	CA	93657	**888-608-5946**	559-875-5563
AIM Supply Co	7337 Bryan Dairy Rd	Largo	FL	33777	**800-999-0125**	727-544-6211
Aimco	10000 SE Pine St	Portland	OR	97216	**800-852-1368**	
Airgas Inc	259 N Radnor-Chester Rd Ste 100 *NYSE: ARG*	Radnor	PA	19087	**800-255-2165**	610-687-5253
Alamo Iron Works Inc	943 AT&T Ctr Pkwy	San Antonio	TX	78219	**800-292-7817**	210-223-6161
Atlantic Lift Truck Inc	2945 Whittington Ave	Baltimore	MD	21230	**800-638-4566**	410-644-7777
Austin Pump & Supply Co	PO Box 17037	Austin	TX	78760	**800-252-9692**	512-442-2348
Barnes Distribution	1301 E Ninth St Ste 700	Cleveland	OH	44114	**800-726-9626**	216-416-7200
Bearing Distributors Inc	8000 Hub Pkwy	Cleveland	OH	44125	**888-423-4872**	216-642-9100
Berendsen Fluid Power	401 S Boston Ave Ste 1200	Tulsa	OK	74103	**800-360-2327**	918-592-3781
Bolttech Mannings	501 Mosside Blvd	North Versailles	PA	15137	**888-846-8827**	724-872-4873
Brake Supply Company Inc	5501 Foundation Blvd	Evansville	IN	47725	**800-457-5788**	812-467-1000
Brauer Material Handling Systems Inc	226 Molly Walton Dr	Hendersonville	TN	37075	**800-645-6083**	
Briggs Equipment	10540 N Stemmons Fwy	Dallas	TX	75220	**800-606-1833**	214-630-0808
Briggs Industrial Equipment	10550 N Stemmons Fwy	Dallas	TX	75220	**800-516-9206**	214-630-0808
C & H Distributors LLC	770 S 70th St *Sales	Milwaukee	WI	53214	**800-558-9966***	414-443-1700
Canadian Bearings Ltd	1600 Drew Rd	Mississauga	ON	L5S1S5	**800-229-2327**	905-670-6700
Carolina Material Handling Services Inc	PO Box 6	Columbia	SC	29202	**800-922-6709**	803-695-0149
Cascade Machinery & Electric Inc	4600 E Marginal Way S	Seattle	WA	98134	**800-289-0500**	206-762-0500
Cisco-Eagle	2120 Valley View Ln	Dallas	TX	75234	**888-877-3861**	972-406-9330
CMC Construction Services	9103 E Almeda Rd	Houston	TX	77054	**877-297-9111**	713-799-1150
Conveyco Technologies Inc	PO Box 1000	Bristol	CT	06011	**800-229-8215**	860-589-8215
Cross Co	4400 Piedmont Pkwy	Greensboro	NC	27410	**800-858-1737**	336-856-6000
Cummins Southern Plains Inc	PO Box 90027	Arlington	TX	76004	**800-516-4354**	817-640-6801
Deacon Industrial Supply Co Inc	165 Boro Line Rd	King of Prussia	PA	19406	**800-726-9800**	610-265-5322
Detroit Pump & Mfg Co	450 Fair St Bldg D	Ferndale	MI	48220	**800-686-1662**	248-544-4242
Drago Supply Co	740 Houston Ave	Port Arthur	TX	77640	**877-609-7975**	409-983-4911
Dueco	N4 W22610 Bluemound Rd	Waukesha	WI	53186	**800-558-4004**	262-547-8500
Duncan Industrial Solutions	3450 S MacArthur Blvd	Oklahoma City	OK	73179	**800-375-9470**	405-688-2300
DXP Enterprises Inc	7272 Pinemont Dr *NASDAQ: DXPE*	Houston	TX	77040	**800-830-3973**	713-996-4700
Eastern Lift Truck Company Inc	549 E Linwood Ave	Maple Shade	NJ	08052	**866-980-7175**	856-779-8880
Edgen Corp	18444 Highland Rd	Baton Rouge	LA	70809	**866-334-3648**	225-756-9868
Endries International Inc	714 W Ryan St PO Box 69	Brillion	WI	54110	**800-852-5821**	920-756-5381
Engman-Taylor Company Inc (ETCO)	W142 N9351 Fountain Blvd	Menomonee Falls	WI	53051	**800-236-1975**	262-255-9300
Enpro Inc	121 S LombaRd Rd	Addison	IL	60101	**800-323-2416**	630-629-3504
FCx Performance	3000 E 14th Ave	Columbus	OH	43219	**800-253-6223**	614-324-6050
Florida Detroit Diesel-Allison Inc	5040 University Blvd W	Jacksonville	FL	32216	**888-812-4440**	904-737-7330
Forklifts of Minnesota Inc	2201 W 94th St	Bloomington	MN	55431	**800-752-4300**	952-887-5400
FUJIFILM Graphic System USA Inc	45 Crosby Dr	Bedford	MA	01730	**800-755-3854**	781-271-4400
FW Webb Co	160 Middlesex Tpke	Bedford	MA	01730	**800-343-7555**	781-272-6600
Ganesh Machinery	20869 Plummer St	Chatsworth	CA	91311	**888-542-6374**	818-349-9166
Gas Equipment Company Inc	11616 Harry Hines Blvd	Dallas	TX	75229	**800-821-1829**	972-241-2333
General Tool & Supply Co Inc	2705 NW Nicolai St	Portland	OR	97210	**800-526-9328**	503-226-3411
Geneva Scientific Inc	11 N Batavia Ave	Batavia	IL	60510	**800-338-2697**	
Gosiger Inc	108 McDonough St	Dayton	OH	45402	**877-288-1538**	937-228-5174
H G Makelim Co	219 Shaw Rd	South San Francisco	CA	94080	**800-471-0590**	650-873-4757
Hagemeyer North America Inc	1460 Tobias Gadson Blvd	Charleston	SC	29407	**877-462-7070**	843-745-2400
Haggard & Stocking Assoc	5318 Victory Dr	Indianapolis	IN	46203	**800-622-4824**	317-788-4661
Hahn Systems Co Inc	6312 SE Ave	Indianapolis	IN	46203	**800-201-4246**	317-243-3796
Harrington Industrial Plastics LLC	14480 Yorba Ave	Chino	CA	91710	**800-213-4528**	909-597-8641
HD Supply Waterworks Ltd	PO Box 1419	Thomasville	GA	31799	**800-492-6909**	800-950-7659
Herc-U-Lift Inc	5655 Hwy 12 W PO Box 69	Maple Plain	MN	55359	**800-362-3500**	763-479-2501
Hull Lift Truck Inc	28747 Old US 33 W	Elkhart	IN	46516	**888-284-0364**	574-293-8651
IBT Inc	9400 W 55th St	Merriam	KS	66203	**800-332-2114**	913-677-3151
Illinois Auto Electric Co	700 Enterprise St	Aurora	IL	60504	**800-683-8484**	630-862-3300
Indeck Power Equipment Co	1111 Willis Ave	Wheeling	IL	60090	**800-446-3325**	847-541-8300
Indoff Inc	11816 Lackland Rd	Saint Louis	MO	63146	**800-486-7867**	314-997-1122
Industrial Controls Distributors Inc (ICD)	1776 Bloomsbury Ave *Sales	Ocean	NJ	07712	**800-281-4788***	732-918-9000
Industrial Diesel Inc	8705 Harmon Rd	Fort Worth	TX	76177	**800-323-3659**	817-232-1071
J. H. Bennett & Company Inc	PO Box 8028 *General	Novi	MI	48376	**800-837-5426***	248-596-5100
Jabo Supply Corp	5164 County Rd 64/66	Huntington	WV	25705	**800-334-5226**	304-736-8333
Jefferds Corp	2070 Winfield Rd	Saint Albans	WV	25177	**888-848-6216**	304-755-8111
Kimball Midwest	4800 Robert Rd	Columbus	OH	43228	**800-233-1294**	614-219-6100
Lewis Goetz & Company Inc	1571 Grandview Ave	Paulsboro	NJ	08066	**800-257-6239**	856-579-1421
Lewis-Goetz & Co Inc	650 Washington Rd Ste 210	Pittsburgh	PA	15228	**800-989-0447**	412-341-7100
Lipten Company LLC	28054 Ctr Oaks Ct	Wixom	MI	48393	**800-860-0790**	248-374-8910
Logan Corp	555 Seventh Ave	Huntington	WV	25701	**888-853-4751**	304-526-4700
M & L Industries Inc	1210 St Charles St *General	Houma	LA	70360	**800-969-0068***	985-876-2280
Mac-Gray Corp	404 Wyman St Ste 400 *NYSE: TUC*	Waltham	MA	02451	**888-622-4729**	781-487-7600
Machinery Sales Co	17253 Chestnut St	City of Industry	CA	91748	**800-588-8111**	626-581-9211
Machinery Systems Inc	614 E State Pkwy	Schaumburg	IL	60173	**866-428-1502**	847-882-8085
Mahar Tool Supply Co Inc	112 Williams St	Saginaw	MI	48605	**800-456-2427**	989-799-5530
Martin Supply Co	200 Appleton Ave	Sheffield	AL	35660	**800-828-8116**	256-383-3131
McCall Handling Co	8801 Wise Ave	Dundalk	MD	21222	**888-870-0685**	410-388-2600
McGill Hose & Coupling Inc	41 Benton Dr PO Box 408	East Longmeadow	MA	01028	**800-669-1467**	413-525-3977
McKinley Equipment Corp	17611 Armstrong Ave	Irvine	CA	92614	**800-770-6094**	949-261-9222
Medart Inc	124 Manufacturers Dr *Cust Svc	Arnold	MO	63010	**800-888-7181***	636-282-2300
Minnesota Supply Company Inc	6470 Flying Cloud Dr	Eden Prairie	MN	55344	**800-869-1028**	952-828-7300
Modern Group Ltd	2501 Durham Rd	Bristol	PA	19007	**800-223-3827**	215-943-9100

Company / Address	City	State	Zip	Toll-Free	Phone
Motion Industries Inc 1605 Alton Rd	Birmingham	AL	35210	**800-526-9328**	205-956-1122
MSC Industrial Direct Co 75 Maxess Rd *NYSE: MSM*	Melville	NY	11747	**800-645-7270**	516-812-2000
Multiquip Inc 18910 Wilmington Ave	Carson	CA	90746	**800-421-1244**	310-537-3700
NC Machinery Co 17025 W Valley Hwy	Tukwila	WA	98188	**800-562-4735**	425-251-9800
Nebraska Machinery Co Inc 3501 S Jeffers St	North Platte	NE	69101	**800-494-9560**	308-532-3100
Nelson-Jameson Inc 2400 E Fifth St PO Box 647	Marshfield	WI	54449	**800-826-8302**	715-387-1151
Newman's Inc 3003 Texas 225	Pasadena	TX	77503	**800-231-3505**	713-675-8631
Nu-Life Environmental Inc PO Box 1527	Easley	SC	29641	**800-654-1752**	864-855-5155
O Berk Co 3 Milltown Ct	Union	NJ	07083	**800-631-7392**	908-851-9500
Pacific Power Group 600 S 56th Pl	Ridgefield	WA	98642	**800-882-3860**	360-887-7400
Piping & Equipment Inc 9100 Canniff St	Houston	TX	77017	**888-889-9683**	713-947-9393
Production Tool Supply 8655 E Eight Mile Rd	Warren	MI	48089	**800-366-3600**	586-755-7770
R & M Energy Systems 301 Premier Rd *Sales	Borger	TX	79007	**888-262-8645***	806-274-5293
R B M Co 2700 Texas Ave	Knoxville	TN	37921	**800-521-5656**	865-524-8621
Red Ball Oxygen Co Inc 609 N Market	Shreveport	LA	71107	**800-551-8150**	318-425-3211
Rem Sales Inc 910 Gay Hill Rd	Windsor	CT	06095	**877-689-1860**	860-687-3400
Remstar International Inc 41 Eisenhower Dr	Westbrook	ME	04092	**800-639-5805**	
Rex Supply Co 3715 Harrisburg Blvd	Houston	TX	77003	**800-369-0669**	713-222-2251
Riekes Equipment Co PO Box 3392	Omaha	NE	68103	**800-856-0931**	402-593-1181
Robert Dietrick Co Inc PO Box 605	Fishers	IN	46038	**866-767-1888**	317-842-1991
RS Hughes Company Inc 1162 Sonora Ct	Sunnyvale	CA	94086	**877-774-8443**	818-686-9111
Ryan Herco Products Corp 3010 N San Fernando Blvd	Burbank	CA	91504	**800-848-1141**	818-841-1141
S.l.c. Meter Service Inc 10375 Dixie Hwy	Davisburg	MI	48350	**800-433-4332**	248-625-0667
Shively Bros Inc 2919 S Grand Travers St PO Box 1520	Flint	MI	48501	**800-530-9352**	810-232-7401
Smith Power Products Inc 3065 W California Ave	Salt Lake City	UT	84104	**800-658-5352**	801-415-5000
Sooner Pipe LLC 1331 Lamar St Ste 970 4 Houston Ctr	Houston	TX	77010	**800-888-9161**	713-759-1200
Southern Pump & Tank Co 4800 N Graham St *Cust Svc	Charlotte	NC	28269	**800-477-2826***	704-596-4373
Strategic Distribution Inc 1414 Radcliffe St Ste 300	Bristol	PA	19007	**800-322-2644**	215-633-1900
Teeco Products Inc 16881 Armstrong Ave	Irvine	CA	92606	**800-854-3463**	949-261-6295
Texas Process Equipment Co 5215 Ted St	Houston	TX	77040	**800-828-4114**	713-460-5555
Travers Tool Company Inc 128-15 26th Ave *Cust Svc	Flushing	NY	11354	**800-221-0270***	718-886-7200
Valtra Inc 7141 Paramount Blvd	Pico Rivera	CA	90660	**800-989-5244**	562-949-8625
Vellano Bros Inc 7 Hemlock St	Latham	NY	12110	**800-342-9855**	518-785-5537
Voto Manufacturers Sales Co 500 N Third St PO Box 1299	Steubenville	OH	43952	**800-848-4010**	740-282-3621
Werres Corp 807 E S St	Frederick	MD	21701	**800-638-6563**	301-620-4000
Wilson Supply Co 1302 Conti St	Houston	TX	77002	**800-874-5930**	713-237-3700
Windsor Factory Supply Ltd 730 N Service Rd	Windsor	ON	N8X3J3	**800-387-2659**	519-966-2202
Yamazen Inc 735 E Remington Rd	Schaumburg	IL	60173	**800-882-8558**	847-490-8130

386 INDUSTRIAL MACHINERY, EQUIPMENT, & SUPPLIES

SEE ALSO Rolling Mill Machinery ; Textile Machinery ; Woodworking Machinery ; Conveyors & Conveying Equipment ; Food Products Machinery ; Furnaces & Ovens - Industrial Process ; Machine Shops ; Material Handling Equipment ; Packaging Machinery & Equipment ; Paper Industries Machinery ; Printing & Publishing Equipment & Systems

Company / Address	City	State	Zip	Toll-Free	Phone
ABB Inc 501 Merritt 7 *Prod Info	Norwalk	CT	06851	**800-626-4999***	203-750-2200
Accu Therm Inc PO Box 249	Monroe City	MO	63456	**888-925-4332**	573-735-1060
Acme Electric N85 W12545 Westbrook Crossing	Menomonee Falls	WI	53051	**800-334-5214**	910-738-1121
Acorn Gencon Plastics Inc 15125 Proctor Ave	City of Industry	CA	91746	**800-782-7706**	626-968-6681
Adept Technology Inc 5960 Inglewood Dr *NASDAQ: ADEP*	Pleasanton	CA	94588	**800-292-3378**	925-245-3400
Aeroglide Corp 100 Aeroglide Dr	Cary	NC	27511	**800-722-7483**	919-851-2000
Alemite LLC 1057-521 Corporate Ctr Dr Ste 100	Fort Mill	SC	29715	**800-267-8022**	803-802-0001
Allentown Equipment 1733 90th St	Sturtevant	WI	53177	**800-553-3414**	
American Baler Co 800 E Centre St	Bellevue	OH	44811	**800-843-7512**	419-483-5790
AO Smith Water Products Co 500 Tennessee Waltz Pkwy	Ashland City	TN	37015	**800-527-1953**	
Apache Stainless Equipment Corp 200 W Industrial Dr PO Box 538	Beaver Dam	WI	53916	**800-444-0398**	920-356-9900
Ats Systems Oregon Inc 2121 NE Jack London St	Corvallis	OR	97330	**800-564-6253**	541-758-3329
Azon USA Inc 643 W Crosstown Pkwy	Kalamazoo	MI	49008	**800-788-5942**	269-385-5942
Bauer-Pileco Inc 100 N FM 3083 E	Conroe	TX	77303	**800-474-5326**	713-691-3000
Besser Co 801 Johnson St	Alpena	MI	49707	**800-530-9980**	989-354-4111
Blower Application Company Inc N 114 W 19125 Clinton Dr	Germantown	WI	53022	**800-959-0880**	262-255-5580
Charles Ross & Son Co 710 Old Willets Path	Hauppauge	NY	11788	**800-243-7677**	631-234-0500
Chemineer Inc 5870 Poe Ave	Dayton	OH	45414	**800-643-0641**	937-454-3200
Chief Automotive Systems Inc 1924 E Fourth St	Grand Island	NE	68802	**800-445-9262**	308-384-9747
Clean Diesel Technologies Inc 4567 Telephone Rd Ste 206 *NASDAQ: CDTI*	Ventura	CA	93003	**800-661-9963**	805-639-9458
CMA Dishmachines 12700 Knott St	Garden Grove	CA	92841	**800-854-6417**	714-898-8781
Corotec Corp 145 Hyde Rd	Farmington	CT	06032	**800-423-0348**	860-678-0038
CUNO Inc 400 Research Pkwy	Meriden	CT	06450	**800-243-6894**	203-237-5541
Davis-Ulmer Sprinkler Company Inc 1 Commerce Dr	Amherst	NY	14228	**877-691-3200**	716-691-3200
Despatch Industries Inc 8860 207th St W	Lakeville	MN	55044	**800-726-0110**	952-469-5424
Diamond Power International Inc 2600 E Main St	Lancaster	OH	43130	**800-848-5086**	740-687-6500
Dings Co 4740 W Electric Ave	Milwaukee	WI	53219	**800-494-1918**	414-672-7830
Ecodyne Ltd 4475 Corporate Dr	Burlington	ON	L7L5T9	**888-326-3963**	905-332-1404
Enerflex Systems Ltd 1331 Macleod Trail SE Ste 904 *TSE: EFX*	Calgary	AB	T2G0K3	**800-242-3178**	403-387-6377
Engis Corp 105 W Hintz Rd	Wheeling	IL	60090	**800-993-6447**	847-808-9400
Equipment Manufacturing Corp (EMC) 14930 Marquardt Ave	Santa Fe Springs	CA	90670	**888-833-9000**	562-623-9394
FANUC America Corp 3900 W Hamlin Rd	Rochester Hills	MI	48309	**800-477-6268**	248-377-7000
Farrel Corp 25 Main St	Ansonia	CT	06401	**800-800-7290**	203-736-5500
Fluid Management Inc 1023 S Wheeling Rd	Wheeling	IL	60090	**800-462-2466**	847-537-0880
Forward Technology Inc 260 Jenks Ave *Cust Svc	Cokato	MN	55321	**800-307-6040***	320-286-2578
Fusion Inc 4658 E 355th St	Willoughby	OH	44094	**800-626-9501**	440-946-3300
Gamajet Cleaning Systems Inc 604 Jeffers Cir *Sales	Exton	PA	19341	**877-426-2538***	610-408-9940
General Equipment Co 620 Alexander Dr SW PO Box 334 *Cust Svc	Owatonna	MN	55060	**800-533-0524***	507-451-5510
George Koch Sons LLC 10 S 11th Ave	Evansville	IN	47712	**888-873-5624**	812-465-9600
Glastender Inc 5400 N Michigan Rd	Saginaw	MI	48604	**800-748-0423**	989-752-4275
Gougler Industries Inc 711 Lake St	Kent	OH	44240	**800-527-2282**	330-673-5826
Graham Corp 20 Florence Ave *NYSE: GHM* ■ *Orders	Batavia	NY	14020	**800-828-8150***	585-343-2216
Gregory Poole Equipment Co 4807 Beryl Rd PO Box 469	Raleigh	NC	27606	**800-451-7278**	919-828-0641
Hamon Research-Cottrell Inc 58 E Main St	Somerville	NJ	08876	**800-445-6578**	908-685-4000
Harrington Hoists Inc 401 W End Ave	Manheim	PA	17545	**800-233-3010**	717-665-2000
Hfw Industries Inc 196 Philadelphia St PO Box 8	Buffalo	NY	14207	**800-937-9311**	716-875-3380
Hosokawa Polymer Systems 63 Fuller Way	Berlin	CT	06037	**800-233-6112**	860-828-0541
Husky Injection Molding Systems Ltd 500 Queen St S	Bolton	ON	L7E5S5	**800-465-4875**	905-951-5000
Hydro-Thermal Corp 400 Pilot Ct	Waukesha	WI	53188	**800-952-0121**	262-548-8900
Jesco-Wipco Industries Inc 950 Anderson Rd PO Box 388	Litchfield	MI	49252	**800-455-0019**	517-542-2903
Kobelco Stewart Bolling Inc (KSBI) 1600 Terex Rd	Hudson	OH	44236	**800-464-0064**	330-655-3111
Koch Membrane Systems Inc 850 Main St	Wilmington	MA	01887	**888-677-5624**	978-694-7000
Kois Bros Equipment Company Inc 5200 Colorado Blvd	Commerce	CO	80022	**800-672-6010**	303-298-7370
Komline-Sanderson Engineering Corp 12 Holland Ave	Peapack	NJ	07977	**800-225-5457**	908-234-1000
Lawton Industries Inc 4353 Pacific St	Rocklin	CA	95677	**800-692-2600**	916-624-7895
Lesman Instrument Co 135 Bernice Dr	Bensenville	IL	60106	**800-953-7626**	630-595-8400
Lightnin 135 Mt Read Blvd	Rochester	NY	14611	**877-247-3797**	585-436-5550
Littleford Day Inc 7451 Empire Dr	Florence	KY	41042	**800-365-8555**	859-525-7600
Lmt USA Inc 1081 S Northpoint Blvd	Waukegan	IL	60085	**800-225-0852**	
Marathon Equipment Co PO Box 1798	Vernon	AL	35592	**800-633-8974**	205-695-9105
Maruka USA Inc 400 Commons Way	Rockaway	NJ	07866	**800-631-0426**	973-983-1000
Materials Transportation Co (MTC) 1408 S Commerce PO Box 1358	Temple	TX	76503	**800-433-3110**	254-298-2900
McNeil & NRM Inc 96 E Crosier St	Akron	OH	44311	**800-669-2525**	330-253-2525

Company	Address	City	State	Zip	Toll-Free	Phone
MEGTEC Systems Inc	830 Prosper Rd *Cust Svc	De Pere	WI	54115	**800-558-5535***	920-336-5715
Michigan Fluid Power Inc	4556 Spartan Industrial Dr SW	Grandville	MI	49418	**800-635-0289**	616-538-5700
Michigan Wheel Corp	1501 Buchanan Ave SW	Grand Rapids	MI	49507	**800-369-4335**	616-452-6941
Mico Inc	1911 Lee Blvd	North Mankato	MN	56003	**800-477-6426**	507-625-6426
Micro-Poise Measurment Systems LLC	1624 Englewood Ave	Akron	OH	44305	**800-428-3812**	330-784-1251
Minuteman International Inc	111 S Rohlwing Rd	Addison	IL	60101	**800-323-9420**	630-627-6900
Mississippi Welders Supply Co	5150 W Sixth St	Winona	MN	55987	**800-657-4422**	507-454-5231
Monroe Environmental Corp	810 W Front St	Monroe	MI	48161	**800-992-7707**	734-242-7654
Moody-Price LLC	18320 Petroleum Dr	Baton Rouge	LA	70809	**800-272-9832**	
Mueller Steam Specialty	1491 NC Hwy 20 W	Saint Pauls	NC	28384	**800-334-6259**	910-865-8241
National Super Service Company Inc	3115 Frenchman Rd *Cust Svc	Toledo	OH	43607	**800-677-1663***	419-531-2121
Neumayer Equipment Company Inc	5060 Arsenal St	Saint Louis	MO	63139	**800-843-4563**	314-772-4501
Nexen Group Inc	560 Oak Grove Pkwy	Vadnais Heights	MN	55127	**800-843-7445**	651-484-5900
Nilfisk-Advance Inc	14600 21st Ave N *Cust Svc	Plymouth	MN	55447	**800-989-2235***	
Nordson Corp	28601 Clemens Rd *NASDAQ: NDSN*	Westlake	OH	44145	**800-321-2881**	440-892-1580
Oil & Gas Equipment Corp	8 Rd 350	Flora Vista	NM	87415	**800-868-9624**	505-333-2300
Oscar Wilson Engines & Parts Inc	826 Lone Star Dr	O Fallon	MO	63366	**800-233-3723**	636-978-1313
Pall Corp	2200 Northern Blvd *NYSE: PLL*	East Hills	NY	11548	**800-645-6532**	516-484-5400
Parkson Corp	1401 W Cyperess Creek Rd	Fort Lauderdale	FL	33309	**888-727-5766**	
Paul Mueller Co	1600 W Phelps St *OTC: MUEL*	Springfield	MO	65802	**800-683-5537**	417-831-3000
PDQ Manufacturing Inc	1698 Scheuring Rd	De Pere	WI	54115	**800-227-3373**	920-983-8333
Peach State Integrated Technologies Inc	3005 Business Pk Dr	Norcross	GA	30071	**800-998-6517**	678-327-2000
Peerless Manufacturing Co	14651 N Dallas Pkwy Ste 500 *NASDAQ: PMFG*	Dallas	TX	75254	**877-879-7634**	214-357-6181
Permadur Industries Inc	186 Rt 206 S	Hillsborough	NJ	08844	**800-392-0146**	908-359-9767
Peterson Machine Tool Inc	1100 N Union St	Council Grove	KS	66846	**800-835-3528**	
Phillips Machine Service Inc	367 George St	Beckley	WV	25801	**800-733-1521**	304-255-0537
Pioneer/Eclipse Corp	1 Eclipse Rd *Cust Svc	Sparta	NC	28675	**800-367-3550***	336-372-8080
Pipe & Tube Supply Inc	1407 N Cypress	North Little Rock	AR	72114	**800-770-8823**	501-372-6556
Premier Safety & Service Inc	2 Industrial Pk Dr	Oakdale	PA	15071	**800-828-1080**	724-693-8699
PSB Industries Inc	PO Box 1318	Erie	PA	16512	**800-829-1119**	814-453-3651
PTI Technologies Inc	501 Del Norte Blvd	Oxnard	CA	93030	**800-331-2701**	805-604-3700
R&R Products Inc	3334 E Milber St	Tucson	AZ	85714	**800-528-3446**	520-889-3593
Rockford Industrial Welding Supply Inc	4646 Linden Rd	Rockford	IL	61109	**800-226-1904**	815-226-1900
Rotary Lift	2700 Lanier Dr	Madison	IN	47250	**800-445-5438**	812-273-1622
Salem Tools Inc	1602 Midland Rd	Salem	VA	24153	**800-390-4348**	540-389-0233
Shop-Vac Corp	2323 Reach Rd	Williamsport	PA	17701	**800-347-5096**	570-326-0502
SJF Material Handling Equipment	211 Baker Ave	Winsted	MN	55395	**800-598-5532**	320-485-2824
STI Electronics Inc	261 Palmer Rd	Madison	AL	35758	**888-650-3006**	256-461-9191
Super Products LLC	17000 W Cleveland Ave	New Berlin	WI	53151	**800-837-9711**	262-784-7100
Swiss Precision Instruments Inc	11450 Markon Dr	Garden Grove	CA	92841	**888-774-8200**	714-799-1555
Synventive Molding Solutions Inc	10 Centennial Dr	Peabody	MA	01960	**800-367-5662**	978-750-8065
Tennant Co	701 N Lilac Dr *NYSE: TNC* ■ *Cust Svc	Minneapolis	MN	55422	**800-553-8033***	763-540-1200
Thermotron Industries Co	291 Kollen Pk Dr	Holland	MI	49423	**800-409-3449**	616-393-4580
Thomas Engineering Inc	575 W Central Rd	Hoffman Estates	IL	60192	**800-634-9910**	847-358-5800
Timesavers Inc	11123 89th Ave N	Maple Grove	MN	55369	**800-537-3611**	763-488-6600
Tool Smith Company Inc	1300 Fourth Ave S PO Box 2384	Birmingham	AL	35233	**800-317-8665**	205-323-2576
Unified Brands	1055 Mendell Davis Dr	Jackson	MS	39272	**888-994-7636**	
USM Corp	32 Stevens St	Haverhill	MA	01830	**800-361-2056**	978-374-0303
Vacudyne Inc	375 E Joe Orr Rd	Chicago Heights	IL	60411	**800-459-9591**	708-757-5200
Van Air Systems Inc	2950 Mechanic St	Lake City	PA	16423	**800-840-9906**	814-774-2631
Vermeer Midsouth Inc	1200 Vermeer Cv	Cordova	TN	38018	**800-264-4123**	901-758-1928
Videojet Technologies Inc	1500 Mittel Blvd *Cust Svc	Wood Dale	IL	60191	**800-843-3610***	630-860-7300
W M Sprinkman Corp	4234 Courtney Rd	Franksville	WI	53126	**800-816-1610**	262-835-2390
Western Hydro Corp	3449 Enterprise Ave	Hayward	CA	94545	**800-972-5945**	510-783-9166
WH Bagshaw Company Inc	1 Pine St Ext PO Box 766	Nashua	NH	03060	**800-343-7467**	603-883-7758
Windsor K„rcher Group	1351 W Stanford Ave	Englewood	CO	80110	**800-444-7654**	303-762-1800
Yale Carolinas Inc (YCI)	9839 S Tryon St	Charlotte	NC	28273	**800-844-1454**	704-588-6930

387 INFORMATION RETRIEVAL SERVICES (GENERAL)

SEE ALSO Investigative Services

Company	Address	City	State	Zip	Toll-Free	Phone
33Across Inc	229 W 28th St 12th Fl	New York	NY	10001	**888-297-4094**	
411 Local Search Corp Inc	1200 Eglinton Ave E Ste 300 N York	Toronto	ON	M3C1H9	**866-411-4411**	416-849-1432
Acquizition.biz Inc	1100 Rene-Levesque Blvd W 24th Fl	Montreal	QC	H3B4X9	**866-499-0334**	514-499-0334
AdMobilize LLC	1680 Michigan Ave Ste 736	Miami	FL	33139	**855-236-6245**	
Advantix Solutions Group	1202 Richardson Dr Ste 200	Richardson	TX	75080	**866-238-2684**	
Airespring Inc	6060 Sepulveda Blvd Ste 220	Van Nuys	CA	91411	**888-389-2899**	818-786-8990
AirPair Inc	875 Howard St	San Francisco	CA	94103	**800-487-0668**	
Amigos Library Services	14400 Midway Rd	Dallas	TX	75244	**800-843-8482**	972-851-8000
AnswerDash Inc	4000 Mason Rd New Ventures Facility Fluke Hall	Seattle	WA	98195	**800-311-5786**	
AOAExcel Inc	243 N Lindbergh Blvd Fl 1	St. Louis	MO	63141	**800-365-2219**	
Apmetrix Inc	5414 Oberlin Dr Ste 200	San Diego	CA	92121	**800-490-3184**	
AppsHosting Inc	13772 Goldenwest St Ste 321	Westminster	CA	92683	**877-625-6610**	
Arkadin Inc	5 Concourse Pkwy Ste 1600	Atlanta	GA	30328	**866-551-1432**	
AroundWire.Com LLC	18107 Sherman Way Ste 206	Reseda	CA	91335	**888-382-3793**	
Audio Authority Corp	2048 Mercer Rd	Lexington	KY	40511	**800-322-8346**	859-233-4599
Beepi	240 Third St Ste 200	Los Altos	CA	94022	**888-542-3374**	
Best Telecom Inc	262 E End Ave	Beaver	PA	15009	**888-365-2273**	
Bliss Direct Media	641 15Th Ave Ne	Saint Joseph	MN	56374	**800-578-7947**	320-271-1600
BloomNet Inc	1 Old Country Rd Ste 500	Carle Place	NY	11514	**866-256-6663**	
Blue Box Group Inc	119 Pine St Ste 200	Seattle	WA	98101	**800-613-4305**	
Bocada Inc	5555 Lakeview Dr	Kirkland	WA	98033	**866-262-2321**	425-818-4400
BoeFly LLC	50 W 72nd St Ste C6	New York	NY	10023	**800-277-3158**	
Branding Brand	2313 East Carson St	Pittsburgh	PA	15203	**888-979-5018**	
Broadband Dynamics LLC	8757 E Via De Commercio	Scottsdale	AZ	85258	**888-801-1034**	
BurrellesLuce	30 B Vreeland Rd PO Box 674	Florham Park	NJ	07932	**800-631-1160**	973-992-6600
C Spire	1018 Highland Colony Pkwy Ste 300	Ridgeland	MS	39157	**855-277-4735**	
CallDirek	2200 S Dixie Hwy Ste 401	Miami	FL	33133	**866-673-4735**	
Camperoo Inc	2900 Weslayan St Ste 545	Houston	TX	77027	**888-538-8809**	
Care Zone Inc	1463 East Republican St Ste 198	Seattle	WA	98112	**888-407-7785**	
CatholicMatch LLC	211 E Grandview Ave	Zelienople	PA	16063	**888-605-3977**	
CharityUSA.com LLC	600 University St Ste 1000 One Union Square	Seattle	WA	98101	**888-811-5271**	206-268-5400
Chemical Abstracts Service (CAS)	2540 Olentangy River Rd	Columbus	OH	43202	**800-848-6538**	614-447-3600
Citation Communications Inc	1855 Indian Rd Ste 207	West Palm Beach	FL	33409	**800-286-5109**	561-688-0330
CloudSway LLC	711 Pacific Ave	Tacoma	WA	98402	**855-212-5683**	
CompleteCampaigns.com Inc	3635 Ruffin Rd 3rd Fl	San Diego	CA	92123	**888-217-9600**	
ComTech21	1 Barnes Park S	Wallingford	CT	06492	**877-312-5564**	
Comwave Networks Inc	61 Wildcat Rd	Toronto	ON	M3J2P5	**877-474-6638**	416-663-9700
ConceptShare Inc	130 Slater St	Ottawa	ON	K1P6E2	**844-227-7848**	613-903-4431
Conjur Inc	460 Totten Pond Rd	Waltham	MA	02451	**855-648-5919**	
ConvergeOne LLC	3344 Hwy 149	Eagan	MN	55121	**888-321-6227**	
Crosslake Communications	35910 County Rd 66 PO Box 70	Crosslake	MN	56442	**800-992-8220**	218-692-2777
CU Conferences	8711 Watson Rd Ste 200	St. Louis	MO	63119	**888-465-6010**	
Curatel LLC	1605 W Olympic Blvd Ste 800	Los Angeles	CA	90015	**866-287-2366**	
Custom Toll Free	10940 Wilshire Blvd 17th Fl	Los Angeles	CA	90024	**800-287-8664**	800-933-3030

Classified Section

Company / Address	City	State	ZIP	Toll-Free	Phone
CypherWorX Inc 3349 Monroe Ave	Rochester	NY	14618	**888-685-4440**	
Data Transmission Network Corp 9110 W Dodge Rd Ste 200	Omaha	NE	68114	**800-485-4000**	402-390-2328
Dataium LLC 2525 Perimeter Pl Dr Ste 105	Nashville	TN	37214	**877-896-3282**	
Deal Interactive LLC 3 Park Ave 39th Fl	New York	NY	10016	**888-415-4888**	
DebtFolio Inc 35 Braintree Hill Office Park Ste 107	Braintree	MA	06084	**866-876-3654**	
Declara Inc 977 Commercial St	Palo Alto	CA	94303	**877-216-0604**	
DFT Communications 40 Temple St	Fredonia	NY	14063	**877-653-3100**	716-673-3000
Dialog 2250 Perimeter Pk Dr Ste 300	Morrisville	NC	27560	**800-334-2564**	919-804-6400
DocAuto Inc 3500 Pkwy Ln Ste 270	Norcross	GA	30092	**800-362-2886**	770-242-6747
DPL Group, The 53 Clark Rd	Rothesay	NB	E2E2K9	**800-561-8880**	506-847-2347
DrivingSales LLC 8871 S Sandy Pkwy Ste 250	Sandy	UT	84070	**866-943-8371**	
Druva Software Inc 150 Mathilda Place, STE 450	Sunnyvale	CA	94086	**888-248-4976**	
DSG Tag Systems Inc 5455 152nd St Ste 214	Surrey	BC	V3S5A5	**877-589-8806**	
EatStreet Inc 131 W Wilson St Ste 400	Madison	WI	53715	**866-654-8777**	
EBSCO Information Services PO Box 1943	Birmingham	AL	35201	**800-758-5995**	205-991-6600
Edufii Inc 2078 Parker St Ste 200	San Luis Obispo	CA	93401	**800-439-8505**	
Ekahau Inc 1851 Alexander Bell Dr Ste 300	Reston	VA	20191	**866-435-2428**	
ELM Resources 12950 Race Track Rd Ste 201	Tampa	FL	33626	**866-524-8198**	
EMC Corporation of Canada 120 Adelaide St W 14th Fl Ste 1400	Toronto	ON	M5H1T1	**800-858-1410**	416-628-5973
Environmental Data Resources Inc 440 Wheelers Farms Rd	Milford	CT	06460	**800-352-0050**	203-783-0300
eScreen Inc 7500 W 110th St Ste 500	Overland Park	KS	66210	**800-881-0722**	913-327-5915
Everlaw 2020 Milvia St Ste 220	Berkeley	CA	94704	**844-383-7529**	
EverTrue LLC 330 Congress St 2nd Fl	Boston	MA	02210	**855-387-8783**	
Everwise Corp 1178 Broadway 4th Fl	New York	NY	10001	**888-734-0011**	
ezCater Inc 101 Arch St Ste 1510	Boston	MA	02110	**800-488-1803**	
FamilySearch 35 N W Temple St	Salt Lake City	UT	84150	**866-406-1830**	
FishHound LLC 15720 Ventura Blvd Ste 220	Encino	CA	91436	**800-469-0224**	
Fluidware 12 York St 2nd Fl	Ottawa	ON	K1N5S6	**866-218-5127**	
FOI Services Inc 704 Quince OrchaRd Rd Ste 275	Gaithersburg	MD	20878	**800-654-1147**	301-975-9400
FOIA Group Inc (FGI) 1250 Connecticut Ave NW Ste 200	Washington	DC	20036	**888-461-7951**	
Forex Newscom 55 Water St 50th Fl	New York	NY	10041	**888-503-6739**	
Franchise Information Services Inc 4075 Wilson Boulevard Ste 410	Arlington	VA	22203	**800-485-9570**	703-740-4700
Frontier Networks Inc 530 Kipling Ave	Toronto	ON	M8Z5E3	**866-833-2323**	416-847-5240
FTJ FundChoice LLC 2300 Litton Ln Ste 102	Hebron	KY	41048	**800-379-2513**	
Geotab Inc 1081 S Service Rd W	Oakville	ON	L6L6K3	**877-436-8221**	416-434-4309
GigMasters.com Inc 33 S Main St	Norwalk	CT	06854	**866-342-9794**	
Healthcare Management Systems Inc (HMS) 3102 W End Ave Ste 400	Nashville	TN	37203	**800-383-3317**	615-383-7300
Helixstorm Inc 41619 Margarita Rd Ste 202	Temecula	CA	92591	**888-434-3549**	
Helpjuice Inc 211 E Seventh St Ste 620	Austin	TX	78701	**888-256-0808**	888-230-3420
Homes.com Inc 150 Granby St	Norfolk	VA	23510	**866-675-1058**	
Host Department LLC 45277 Fremont Blvd Ste 11	Fremont	CA	94538	**866-887-4678**	
I Am Athlete LLC PO Box 667	Santa Monica	CA	90406	**877-462-7979**	
IBISWorld Inc 11755 Wilshire blvd 11th fl	Los Angeles	CA	90025	**800-330-3772**	
IdeaTek Communications LLC 10400 E 69th St PO Box 258	Buhler	KS	67522	**855-433-2835**	
IMVU Inc PO Box 390012	Mountain View	CA	94039	**866-761-0975**	650-321-8334
InComm Conferencing Inc 208 Harristown Rd Ste 101	Glen Rock	NJ	07452	**877-804-2062**	
infoUSA Inc 5711 S 86th Cir	Omaha	NE	68127	**800-321-0869**	800-835-5856
Infrastructure Networks Inc 1718 Fry Rd Ste 116	Houston	TX	77084	**855-333-4638**	281-740-3226
Innovative Telecom Solutions Inc 9 Vela Way	Edgewater	NJ	07020	**800-510-3000**	
Intelletrace Inc 448 Ignacio Blvd	Novato	CA	94945	**800-618-5877**	
ISLC Inc 14 Savannah Hwy	Beaufort	SC	29906	**888-828-4752**	843-770-1000
Kahuna Inc 555 Bryant St Ste 322	Palo Alto	CA	94301	**844-465-2486**	
Kaleo Software Inc 2041 Rosecrans Ave Ste 245	El Segundo	CA	90245	**888-937-8945**	
LaughStub LLC 2038 Armacost Ave	Los Angeles	CA	90025	**800-927-0939**	
LexisNexis Martindale-Hubbell 121 Chanlon Rd	New Providence	NJ	07974	**800-526-4902**	
Lingo Inc 7901 Jones Branch Dr 9th Fl	Mclean	VA	22102	**888-546-4699**	
LINQ Services 1200 Steuart St Unit C3	Baltimore	MD	21230	**800-421-5467**	
Merrill DataSite 225 Varick St	New York	NY	10014	**866-399-3770**	
MERX Networks Inc 6 Antares Dr Phase II Unit 103	Ottawa	ON	K2E8A9	**800-964-6379**	613-727-4900
MessageBank LLC 250 W 57Th St Ste 1001	New York	NY	10107	**800-989-8001**	212-333-9300
MobileIQ Inc 4800 Baseline Rd Ste E104-247	Boulder	CO	80303	**866-261-8600**	
MOGL Loyalty Services Inc 9645 Scranton Rd Ste 110	San Diego	CA	92121	**888-664-5669**	
Mountain Telephone Co 405 Main St	West Liberty	KY	41472	**800-939-3121**	606-743-3121
National Technical Information Service (NTIS) 5285 Port Royal Rd *Orders	Springfield	VA	22161	**800-553-6847***	703-605-6000
New Pros Data Inc 155 Hidden Ravines Dr	Powell	OH	43065	**800-837-5478**	740-201-0410
NewCloud Networks 160 Inverness Dr W	Englewood	CO	80112	**855-255-5001**	
Newsbank Inc 5801 Pelican Bay Blvd Ste 600	Naples	FL	34108	**800-243-7694**	239-263-6004
Next Net Media LLC 316 California Ave Ste 804	Reno	NV	89509	**800-737-5820**	
Nexxtworks Inc 30798 Us Hwy 19 N	Palm Harbor	FL	34684	**888-533-8353**	
Niche Directories LLC 909 N Sepulveda Blvd 11th Fl	El Segundo	CA	90026	**877-242-9330**	
Oceus Networks Inc 1895 Preston White Dr Ste 300	Reston	VA	20191	**877-816-2599**	703-234-9200
Oklahoma Telephone & Telegraph Inc 26 N Otis Ave	Dustin	OK	74839	**800-869-1989**	
OneClass 65 Bloor St E Unit 1902	Toronto	ON	M4W3L4	**855-392-6946**	
OneMorePallet.com 9891 Montgomery Rd Ste 122	Cincinnati	OH	45242	**855-438-1667**	
OurParents Inc 8521 Leesburg Pk Ste 310	Vienna	VA	22182	**866-629-1634**	
Ovid Technologies Inc 333 Seventh Ave 20th Fl	New York	NY	10001	**800-950-2035**	646-674-6300
PackLate.com Inc 100 Four Falls Corporate Ctr Ste 104	West Conshohocken	PA	19428	**877-472-2552**	
Pinnacle Communications Corp 19821 Executive Park Cir	Germantown	MD	20874	**800-644-9101**	301-601-0777
PK4 Media Inc 1600 E Franklin Ave Ste C	El Segundo	CA	90245	**888-320-6281**	
PriceWaiter LLC 426 Market St	Chattanooga	TN	37421	**855-671-9889**	
Pure Auto LLC 164 Market St Ste 250	Charleston	SC	29401	**877-860-7873**	
Purple Communications Inc 595 Menlo Dr	Rocklin	CA	95765	**800-900-9478**	
Questia Media America Inc 1 N State St Ste 900	Chicago	IL	60602	**800-759-4726**	800-889-0097
Rallyorg 995 Market St 2nd Fl	San Francisco	CA	94105	**888-648-2220**	
RealtyShares Inc 637 Natoma St Ste 5	San Francisco	CA	94103	**855-880-6050**	415-450-6234
Reaslo Inc 5214F Diamond Heights Blvd Ste 217	San Francisco	CA	94131	**888-870-7889**	
RefWorks LLC 7200 Wisconsin Ave Ste 601	Bethesda	MD	20814	**800-843-7751**	301-961-6700
Rentals Inc 3585 Engineering Dr	Norcross	GA	30092	**888-501-7368**	
Reputation Rhino LLC 711 Third Ave 12th Fl	New York	NY	10017	**888-975-3331**	
Riviera Cellular & Telecommunicat PO Box 997	Riviera	TX	78379	**877-296-3232**	361-296-3232
SchoolDocs LLC 5944 Luther Ln Ste 600	Dallas	TX	75225	**866-311-2293**	
Scoot & Doodle Inc 2625 Middlefield Rd Ste 223	Palo Alto	CA	94306	**888-563-9224**	
Scott Enterprises Inc 2225 Downs Dr 6th Fl Exce Stes.	Erie	PA	16509	**877-866-3445**	814-868-9500
Scripted Inc 135 Stillman St	San Francisco	CA	94107	**800-797-4470**	
Seize The Deal LLC 1851 N Greenville Ave Ste 100	Richardson	TX	75081	**866-210-0881**	
Sell My Timeshare Now LLC 383 Central Ave Ste 260	Dover	NH	03820	**877-815-4227**	603-516-0200
Senior-Living.com Inc 8521 Leesburg Pk Ste 310	Vienna	VA	22182	**866-342-4297**	
ShopVisible LLC 945 East Paces Ferry Rd Ste 1475	Atlanta	GA	30326	**866-493-7037**	
SkyBlox LLC 244 Peters St Ste 7	Atlanta	GA	30313	**866-632-9685**	
Smarty Ants Inc 1400 Rollins Rd	Burlingame	CA	94010	**877-905-2687**	
Social Annex Inc 5301 Beethoven St Ste 260	Los Angeles	CA	90066	**866-802-8806**	
Social Strategy1 5000 Sawgrass Village Cir Ste 30	Ponte Vedra Beach	FL	32082	**877-771-3366**	
Sogetel Inc 111, rue du 12-Novembre	Nicolet	QC	J3T1S3	**866-764-3835**	
Southwest Communications Inc 4100 N Mulberry Dr Ste 160	Kansas City	MO	64116	**800-383-5533**	816-298-4100
SPACECONNECTION Inc, The 10530 Victory Blvd	North Hollywood	CA	91606	**800-537-7223**	818-754-1100
SpinGo Solutions Inc 14193 S Minuteman Dr Ste 100	Draper	UT	84020	**877-377-4646**	
SpotOn Inc 2350 Kerner Blvd Ste 380	San Rafael	CA	94901	**877-814-4102**	
Stickk.com LLC 39 E 30th St Ste 4	New York	NY	10016	**866-578-4255**	

Company	Address	City	State	ZIP	Toll-Free	Phone
TelcoIQ	4300 Forbes Blvd Ste 110	Lanham	MD	20706	**877-835-2647**	202-595-1500
TelSpan Inc	101 W Washington St E Tower Ste 1200	Indianapolis	IN	46204	**800-800-1729**	
Thomson Financial	22 Thomson Pl	Boston	MA	02210	**888-216-1929**	617-856-2000
TodoCast Inc	31831 Camino Capistrano Ste 301	San Juan Capistrano	CA	92675	**866-510-7889**	
TouchLogic Corp	30 Kinnear Ct Ste 602	Richmond Hill	ON	L4B1K8	**877-707-0207**	
Touchstorm LLC	355 Lexington Ave 12th Fl	New York	NY	10017	**877-794-6101**	
Trada Inc	1023 Walnut St	Boulder	CO	80302	**877-871-1835**	
Trapit Inc	2390 El Camino Real Ste 220	Palo Alto	CA	94306	**844-987-2748**	
TruSignal LLC	25 6th Ave N	St. Cloud	MN	56303	**855-569-0426**	
US News University Connection LLC	9417 Princess Palm Ave	Tampa	FL	33619	**866-442-6587**	
USA Communications Inc	920 E 56th St Ste B	Kearney	NE	68847	**877-234-0102**	
uShip Inc	205 Brazos St	Austin	TX	78701	**800-698-7447**	
Vanilla Forums Inc	414 McGill St, Ste 800	Montreal	QC	H2Y1S1	**866-845-0815**	
Vectus Inc	18685 Main St 101 PMB 360	Huntington Beach	CA	92648	**866-483-2887**	
Vessel Metrics LLC	3 Church Cir Ste 325	Annapolis	MD	21401	**888-214-1710**	
Vetstreet	780 Township Line Rd	Yardley	PA	19067	**888-799-8387**	215-493-0621
Vinely	1 Kendall Sq Bldg 400 B4202	Cambridge	MA	02139	**888-294-1128**	
VoIP Innovations Inc	8 Penn Ctr W Ste 101	Pittsburgh	PA	15276	**877-478-6471**	
West Group	610 Opperman Dr *Cust Svc	Eagan	MN	55123	**800-328-4880***	651-687-7000
WhoKnows Inc	425 BRdway St	Redwood City	CA	94063	**877-338-2763**	
Wholeshare Inc	2431 Mission St	San Francisco	CA	94110	**800-625-4605**	
XTRAC LLC	245 Summer St	Boston	MA	02210	**855-975-3569**	
Yesware Inc	75 Kneeland St Fl 15	Boston	MA	02111	**855-937-9273**	
YouVisit LLC	20533 Biscayne Blvd Ste 1322	Aventura	FL	33180	**866-585-7158**	

388 INK

Company	Address	City	State	ZIP	Toll-Free	Phone
Braden Sutphin Ink Co	3650 E 93rd St	Cleveland	OH	44105	**800-289-6872**	216-271-2300
Central Ink Corp	1100 Harvester Rd	West Chicago	IL	60185	**800-345-2541**	630-231-6500
Color Resolutions International	575 Quality Blvd	Fairfield	OH	45014	**800-346-8570**	513-552-7200
Deco Chem Inc	3502 N Home St	Mishawaka	IN	46545	**888-332-6465**	574-259-3787
Gans Ink & Supply Company Inc	1441 Boyd St	Los Angeles	CA	90033	**800-421-6167**	323-264-2200
Independent Ink Inc	13700 Gramercy Pl	Gardena	CA	90249	**800-446-5538**	310-523-4657
International Coatings Co	13929 166th St	Cerritos	CA	90703	**800-423-4103**	562-926-1010
Matsui International Company Inc	1501 W 178th St	Gardena	CA	90248	**800-359-5679**	310-767-7812
Nazdar	8501 Hedge Ln Terr	Shawnee	KS	66227	**800-767-9942**	913-422-1888
Nor-Cote International Inc	506 Lafayette Ave	Crawfordsville	IN	47933	**800-488-9180**	765-362-9180
Reaxis Inc	941 Robinson Hwy	Mcdonald	PA	15057	**800-426-7273**	
Sensient Technologies Corp	777 E Wisconsin Ave *NYSE: SXT*	Milwaukee	WI	53202	**800-558-9892**	414-271-6755
Sericol Inc	1101 W Cambridge Dr	Kansas City	KS	66103	**800-737-4265**	913-342-4060
Siegwerk USA Co	3535 SW 56th St	Des Moines	IA	50321	**800-728-8200**	515-471-2100
Sun Chemical Corp	35 Waterview Blvd	Parsippany	NJ	07054	**800-543-2323**	973-404-6000
Toyo Ink America LLC	1225 N Michael Dr *General	Wood Dale	IL	60191	**866-969-8696***	
U-mark Inc	102 Iowa Ave	Belleville	IL	62220	**866-383-6275**	618-235-7500
US Ink Corp	651 Garden St	Carlstadt	NJ	07072	**800-423-8838**	201-935-8666

389 INSULATION & ACOUSTICAL PRODUCTS

Company	Address	City	State	ZIP	Toll-Free	Phone
Anco Products Inc (API)	2500 S 17th St	Elkhart	IN	46517	**800-837-2626**	574-293-5574
Applegate Insulation Manufacturing Inc	1000 Highview Dr	Webberville	MI	48892	**800-627-7536**	517-521-3545
CertainTeed Corp	750 E Swedesford Rd *Prod Info	Valley Forge	PA	19482	**800-782-8777***	610-341-7000
Claremont Sales Corp	35 Winsome Dr PO Box 430	Durham	CT	06422	**800-222-4448**	860-349-4499
Dryvit Systems Inc	1 Energy Way	West Warwick	RI	02893	**800-556-7752**	401-822-4100
Industrial Insulation Group LLC (IIG)	2100 Line St	Brunswick	GA	31520	**800-334-7997**	303-978-2000
Isolatek International Inc	41 Furnace St	Stanhope	NJ	07874	**800-631-9600**	973-347-1200
ITW Insulation Systems	1370 E 40th St Ste 1 Bldg 7	Houston	TX	77022	**800-231-1024**	
Johns Manville Corp	717 17th St PO Box 5108 *Prod Info	Denver	CO	80217	**800-654-3103***	303-978-2000
Knauf Insulation	1 Knauf Dr	Shelbyville	IN	46176	**800-825-4434**	317-398-4434
MIT International	77 Massachusetts Ave *General	Cambridge	TX	02139	**800-228-9290***	617-253-1000
Nu-Wool Company Inc	2472 Port Sheldon Rd	Jenison	MI	49428	**800-748-0128**	616-669-0100
Rock Wool Manufacturing Co	1400 Seventh Ct PO Box 506 *Sales	Leeds	AL	35094	**800-874-7625***	205-699-6121
Scott Industries Inc	1573 Hwy 136 W PO Box 7	Henderson	KY	42419	**800-951-9276**	270-831-2037
Soundcoat Co	1 Burt Dr	Deer Park	NY	11729	**800-394-8913**	631-242-2200
Thermafiber Inc	3711 W Mill St	Wabash	IN	46992	**888-834-2371**	260-563-2111
Thermwell Products Co	420 Rt 17 S	Mahwah	NJ	07430	**800-526-5265**	201-684-4400

390 INSURANCE AGENTS, BROKERS, SERVICES

Company	Address	City	State	ZIP	Toll-Free	Phone
A Plus Benefits Inc	395 West 600 North	Lindon	UT	84042	**800-748-5102**	801-443-1090
Actuarial Systems Corp	15840 Monte St Ste 108	Sylmar	CA	91342	**800-950-2082**	
Affinion Group Inc	6 High Ridge Pk	Stamford	CT	06905	**800-251-2148**	203-956-1000
Agency Software Inc	215 W Commerce Dr	Hayden Lake	ID	83835	**800-342-7327**	208-762-7188
Alliance Worldwide Investigative Group Inc	4 Executive Park Dr	Clifton Park	NY	12065	**800-579-2911**	518-514-2944
Amfed Cos LLC	576 Highland Colony Pkwy	Ridgeland	MS	39157	**800-264-8085**	601-853-4949
ANCO Insurance	1111 Briarcrest Dr PO Box 3889	Bryan	TX	77802	**800-749-1733**	979-776-2626
Andreini & Co	220 W 20th Ave	San Mateo	CA	94403	**800-969-2522**	650-573-1111
Andrew G Gordon Inc	306 Washington St	Norwell	MA	02061	**866-243-2259**	781-659-2262
Aon Risk Services Inc	200 E Randolph St	Chicago	IL	60601	**877-384-4276**	312-381-1000
Argenia LLC	11524 Fairview Rd	Little Rock	AR	72212	**800-482-5968**	501-227-9670
Arthur J Gallagher & Co	2 Pierce Pl *NYSE: AJG*	Itasca	IL	60143	**888-285-5106**	630-773-3800
Arthur J. Glatfelter Agency Inc	PO Box 2726	York	PA	17405	**800-233-1957**	717-741-0911
Assurity Life Insurance Co	PO Box 82533	Lincoln	NE	68501	**800-869-0355**	402-476-6500
Badger Mutual Insurance Co	1635 W National Ave	Milwaukee	WI	53204	**800-837-7833**	414-383-1234
Beckerman & Co	430 Lake Ave	Colonia	NJ	07067	**800-339-1836**	732-499-9200
Benefit & Risk Management Services Inc	10860 Gold Ctr Dr Ste 300	Rancho Cordova	CA	95670	**888-326-2555**	916-858-2950
Berkley Risk Administrators Company LLC	222 S Ninth St Ste 1300	Minneapolis	MN	55402	**800-449-7707**	612-766-3000
Bilbrey Insurance Services Inc	5701 Greendale Rd	Johnston	IA	50131	**800-383-0116**	
Bischoff Insurance Agency Inc	1300 Oakridge Dr Ste 100	Fort Collins	CO	80525	**888-229-5558**	970-223-9400
Burnham & Flower Group Inc	315 S Kalamazoo Mall	Kalamazoo	MI	49007	**888-748-7966**	269-381-1173
C P H & Associates	711 S Dearborn St Unit 205	Chicago	IL	60605	**800-875-1911**	312-987-9823
Cailor Fleming & Assoc Inc	4610 Market St	Youngstown	OH	44512	**800-796-8495**	330-782-8068
Callbright Corp	6700 Hollister	Houston	TX	77040	**877-462-2552**	
CalSurance	681 S Parker St Ste 300	Orange	CA	92868	**800-762-7800**	714-939-0800
Capital Analysts Inc	218 Glenside Ave	Wyncote	PA	19095	**800-242-1421**	
Carl Nelson Insurance Agency I	1519 N 11th Ave	Hanford	CA	93230	**800-582-4264**	559-584-4495
Casswood Insurance Agency Ltd	5 Executive Pk Dr	Clifton Park	NY	12065	**800-972-2242**	518-373-8700
CBIZ Benefits & Insurance Services of Maryland Inc	44 Baltimore St *Cust Svc	Cumberland	MD	21502	**800-615-8418***	301-777-1500
Clark Insurance	PO Box 3543	Portland	ME	04104	**800-773-4300**	207-774-6257
Clifford & Rano Insurance Agency Inc	57 Cedar St	Worcester	MA	01609	**800-660-8284**	508-752-8284
Cross Financial Corp	74 Gilman Rd PO Box 1388	Bangor	ME	04401	**800-999-7345**	207-947-7345
Cumbre Inc	3333 Concours Ste 5100	Ontario	CA	91764	**800-998-7986**	909-484-2456
DailyAccess Corp	307 University Blvd N Bldg 3 Ste 1500	Mobile	AL	36688	**877-859-5735**	251-665-1800
Dale Barton Agency Inc	1100 East 6600 South	Salt Lake City	UT	84121	**866-288-1666**	801-288-1600
Daniel & Henry Co	1001 Highlands Plaza Dr W Ste 500	Saint Louis	MO	63110	**800-256-3462**	314-421-1525
Distinguished Programs Group LLC, The	1180 Ave Of The Americas 16th Fl	New York	NY	10036	**888-355-4626**	212-297-3100
Dyatech LLC	805 S Wheatley St Ste 600	Ridgeland	MS	39157	**866-651-4222**	601-914-1004
Eagan Insurance Agency Inc	2629 N Cswy Blvd	Metairie	LA	70002	**888-882-9600**	504-836-9600
Elant Inc	46 Harriman Dr	Goshen	NY	10924	**800-501-3936**	

Company / Address	City	State	ZIP	Toll-Free	Phone
Emery & Webb Inc 989 Main St	Fishkill	NY	12524	800-942-5818	845-896-6727
Employers Insurance Company of Nevada 9790 Gateway Dr Ste 100	Reno	NV	89521	888-682-6671	
Encon Group Inc 500-1400 Blair Pl	Ottawa	ON	K1J9B8	800-267-6684	613-786-2000
Endurance Specialty Holdings Ltd 767 Third Ave 5th Fl *NYSE: ENH*	New York	NY	10017	855-838-7792	212-209-6500
FairMarket Life Settlements Corp 435 Ford Rd Ste 120	St Louis Park	MN	55426	866-326-3757	
Faribo Insurance Agency Inc 1404 Seventh St NW	Faribault	MN	55021	888-923-0430	507-334-3929
Farmers Fire Insurance Co 2875 Eastern Blvd	York	PA	17402	800-537-0928	717-751-4435
Farris Evans Insurance Agency Inc 1568 Union Ave	Memphis	TN	38104	800-395-8207	901-274-5424
FDI Group Inc 39500 High Pointe Blvd Ste 400	Novi	MI	48375	800-828-0759	
Fortun Insurance Agency Inc 365 Palermo Ave	Coral Gables	FL	33134	877-643-2055	305-445-3535
Fred C Churchinc 41 Wellman St	Lowell	MA	01851	800-225-1865	978-458-1865
Fred Loya Insurance 1800 Lee Trevino Ste 201	El Paso	TX	79936	800-554-0595	915-590-5692
Fringe Benefits Management Co 3101 Sessions Rd	Tallahassee	FL	32303	800-872-0345	850-425-6200
Frontier Adjusters of America Inc 4745 N Seventh St Ste 320	Phoenix	AZ	85014	800-426-7228	
GCube Insurance Services Inc 3101 Wcoast Hwy Ste 100	Newport Beach	CA	92663	877-903-4777	949-515-9981
Gebco Insurance Assoc 8600 LaSalle Rd Ste 338	Towson	MD	21286	800-464-3226	410-668-3100
Gerrity Baker Williams Inc 3 Goldmine Rd	Flanders	NJ	07836	800-548-2329	973-426-1500
Graham Co, The 1 Penn Sq W 25th Fl	Philadelphia	PA	19102	888-472-4262	215-567-6300
Haas & Wilkerson Inc 4300 Shawnee Mission Pkwy	Fairway	KS	66205	800-821-7703	913-432-4400
HealthSCOPE Benefits Inc 27 Corporate Hill Dr	Little Rock	AR	72205	877-240-0135	501-225-1551
Healy Group Inc, The 53800 Generations Dr	South Bend	IN	46635	800-667-4613	574-271-6000
Herbert H. Landy Insurance Agency Inc 75 Second Ave Ste 410	Needham	MA	02494	800-336-5422	
Hibbs Hallmark & Co 501 Shelley Dr	Tyler	TX	75701	800-765-6767	
Hinkle Insurance Agency Inc 600 Olde Hickory Rd Ste 200	Lancaster	PA	17601	877-408-1418	717-560-9733
Holmes Murphy & Assoc Inc 3001 Westown Pkwy	West Des Moines	IA	50266	800-247-7756	515-223-6800
Horton Group, The 10320 Orland Pkwy	Orland Park	IL	60467	800-383-8283	708-845-3000
Housing Authority Risk Retention Group Inc PO Box 189	Cheshire	CT	06410	800-873-0242	203-272-8220
Hub International Ltd 1065 Ave of the Americas	New York	NY	10018	800-456-5293	212-338-2000
Human Arc Corp 1457 East 40th St	Cleveland	OH	44103	800-828-6453	216-431-5200
Hunt Insurance Agency Inc 12000 S Harlem Ave	Palos Heights	IL	60463	800-772-6484	708-361-5300
Hylant Group 811 Madison Ave	Toledo	OH	43624	800-249-5268	419-255-1020
Independant Insurance Services In 3956 N Pine St	Davenport	IA	52806	800-373-1562	563-383-5555
Insurance Services Office Inc (ISO) 545 Washington Blvd	Jersey City	NJ	07310	800-888-4476	201-469-2000
InterWest Insurance Services Inc 3636 American River Dr 2nd Fl	Sacramento	CA	95864	800-444-4134	916-679-2960
J Smith Lanier & Co 300 W Tenth St	West Point	GA	31833	800-226-4522	706-645-2211
Jack Ogren & Company Inc 6929 Hohman Ave	Hammond	IN	46324	888-489-4235	219-933-0076
Jake A Parrott Insurance Agency Inc 2508 N Herritage St	Kinston	NC	28501	800-727-7688	252-523-1041
James Greene & Assoc Inc 275 W Kiehl Ave	Sherwood	AR	72120	800-422-3384	501-834-4001
Jas. D. Collier & Co 606 S Mendenhall Rd Ste 200 *General	Memphis	TN	38117	800-511-1548*	
Jmd Group LLC 720 Walnut St	Chattanooga	TN	37402	866-251-0361	423-265-8111
Johns Eastern Co Inc PO Box 110259 Lakewood Branch *General	Sarasota	FL	34211	877-326-5326*	941-907-3100
KAFL Inc 85 Allen St Ste 300	Rochester	NY	14608	800-272-6488	585-271-6400
Keenan & Assoc 2355 Crenshaw Blvd Ste 200 PO Box 4328	Torrance	CA	90501	800-654-8102	310-212-3344
Kelsey National Corp 3030 S Bundy Dr	Los Angeles	CA	90066	800-366-5656	310-390-1000
Kraus-Anderson Insurance 420 Gateway Blvd	Burnsville	MN	55337	800-207-9261	952-707-8200
Lawley Service Insurance 361 Delaware Ave *Cust Svc	Buffalo	NY	14202	800-860-5741*	716-849-8618
Le Mars Insurance Co PO Box 1608	Le Mars	IA	51031	800-545-6480	
Leap/Carpenter/Kemps Insurance Agency 3187 Collins Dr	Merced	CA	95348	800-221-0864	209-384-0727
leavitt group Enterprises 216 S 200 W	Cedar City	UT	84720	800-264-8085	435-586-6553
Lewer Agency Inc 4534 Wornall Rd	Kansas City	MO	64111	800-821-7715	
Lincoln General Insurance Co 3501 Concord Rd	York	PA	17402	800-876-3350	717-757-0000
LISI Inc 1600 W Hillsdale Blvd	San Mateo	CA	94402	866-570-5474	650-348-4131
Loesel Schaaf Insurance Agency Inc 3537 W 12th St	Erie	PA	16505	877-718-9935	814-833-5433
Loomis Co 850 N Pk Rd	Wyomissing	PA	19610	800-782-0392	610-374-4040
Lovitt & Touche Inc 7202 E Rosewood St Ste 200 PO Box 32702	Tucson	AZ	85710	800-426-2756	520-722-3000
Maga Ltd 2610 Lk Cook Rd	Riverwoods	IL	60015	800-533-6242	847-940-8866
Managed Care of America Inc 1910 Cochran Rd Ste 605	Pittsburgh	PA	15220	800-922-4966	412-922-2803
Managed HealthCare Northwest Inc 422 East Burnside St Suite 215 PO Box 4629	Portland	OR	97208	800-648-6356	503-413-5800
Marsh & Mclennan Agency 250 Pehle Ave	Saddle Brook	NJ	07663	800-669-6330	201-845-6600
Marshall & Sterling Inc 110 Main St	Poughkeepsie	NY	12601	800-333-3766	845-454-0800
McGriff Seibels & Williams Inc 2211 Seventh Ave S	Birmingham	AL	35233	800-476-2211	205-252-9871
Mesirow Financial Insurance Services Div 353 N Clark St	Chicago	IL	60654	800-453-0600	312-595-6200
MGM Industries Inc 287 Freehill Rd	Hendersonville	TN	37075	800-476-5584	615-824-6572
MIC Services Insurance Inc 170 Kinnelon Rd - Ste 11	Kinnelon	NJ	07405	800-355-2662	973-492-2828
Michigan Insurance Co 1700 E Beltline Ne PO Box 152120, Ste 100	Grand Rapids	MI	49515	888-606-6426	616-447-3600
Mike Moss Agency Inc 803 S Dogwood	Siloam Springs	AR	72761	800-447-0163	479-524-5111
Miller-Lewis Benefit Consultants 121 E Sixth Ave	Lancaster	OH	43130	800-734-3198	740-654-4055
Minnesota Lawyers Mutual Insurance Co 333 S Seventh St Ste 2200	Minneapolis	MN	55402	800-422-1370	
MSI Benefits Group Inc 245 Townpark Dr Ste 100	Kennesaw	GA	30144	800-580-1629	770-425-1231
Multiplan inc 115 Fifth Ave	New York	NY	10003	800-922-4362	212-780-2000
National Electronic Attachment Inc 3577 Pkwy Ln Ste 250	Norcross	GA	30092	800-782-5150	770-441-3203
National Farm Life Insurance Co 6001 Bridge St	Fort Worth	TX	76112	800-772-7557	817-451-9550
NCCI Holdings Inc 901 Peninsula Corporate Cir *Cust Svc	Boca Raton	FL	33487	800-622-4123*	561-893-1000
Newbury Corp 222 Ames St	Dedham	MA	02026	800-688-1825	
Northwest Administrators Inc 2323 Eastlake Ave E	Seattle	WA	98102	877-304-6702	206-329-4900
Oswald Cos 1100 Superior Ave Ste 1500	Cleveland	OH	44114	855-467-9253	216-367-8787
Otis-Magie Insurance Agency Inc 332 W Superior St Ste 700	Duluth	MN	55802	800-241-2425	218-722-7753
Pacesetter Claims Service Inc 2871 N Hwy 167	Catoosa	Ok	74015	888-218-4880	918-665-8887
Paradigm Equity Strategies LLC 1611 - A Akron Peninsula Rd	Akron	OH	44313	888-249-5727	330-475-1690
Parker Smith & Feek Inc 2233 112th Ave NE *Cust Svc	Bellevue	WA	98004	800-457-0220*	425-709-3600
Parkville Insurances Services Inc 15242 E Whittier Blvd PO Box 1275	Whittier	CA	90603	800-350-2702	562-945-2702
Piedmont Community Health Plan Inc 2512 Langhorne Rd	Lynchburg	VA	24501	800-400-7247	434-947-4463
Policemen's Annuity & Benefit Fund of Chicago 221 N LaSalle St Ste 1626	Chicago	IL	60601	800-656-6606	312-744-3891
POMCO 2425 James St	Syracuse	NY	13206	800-934-2459	315-432-9171
Purves & Assoc Insurance 500 Fourth St	Davis	CA	95616	800-681-2025	530-756-5561
Rampart Brokerage Corp 1983 Marcus Ave Ste C130	New Hyde Park	NY	11042	800-772-6727	516-538-7000
Reid Jones McRorie & Williams Inc 2200 Executive St PO Box 669248	Charlotte	NC	28208	800-785-2604	704-537-0012
Renaissance Group 981 Worcester St	Wellesley	MA	02482	800-514-2667	
RSI Insurance Brokers Inc 2801 Bristol St Ste 200	Costa Mesa	CA	92626	800-828-5273	714-546-6616
Sahouri Insurance & Associates Inc 8200 Grnsburg Dr Ste 1550	Mclean	VA	22102	855-242-6660	703-883-0500
Scott Danahy Naylon Company Inc (SDN) 300 Spindrift Dr	Williamsville	NY	14221	800-728-6362	716-633-3400
Security Escrow & Title Insurance Agency 337 South Main Ste 110	Cedar City	UT	84720	855-319-9820	435-867-0402
Selectpath Benefits & Financial Inc 310-700 Richmond St	London	ON	N6A5C7	888-327-5777	519-675-1177
Selectquote Insurance Services 595 Market St 10th Fl	San Francisco	CA	94105	800-670-3213	415-543-7338
Senior Market Sales Inc (SMS) 8420 W Dodge Rd 5th Fl	Omaha	NE	68114	800-786-5566	402-397-3311
SilverStone Group 11516 Miracle Hills Dr Ste 100	Omaha	NE	68154	800-288-5501	402-964-5400
Stallings Crop Insurance Corp PO Box 6100	Lakeland	FL	33807	800-721-7099	863-647-2747
Stanley Mcdonald Agency of Illinois 2018 State Rd	La Crosse	WI	54601	800-344-3948	608-788-6160
Star Casualty Insurance Company Inc PO Box 451037	Miami	FL	33134	877-782-7210	
Starkweather & Shepley Inc 60 Catamore Blvd	East Providence	RI	02914	800-854-4625	401-435-3600
Sullivan Curtis Monroe 1920 Main St	Irvine	CA	92614	800-427-3253	949-250-7172
Swan & Sons-Morss Company Inc 309 E Water St	Elmira	NY	14902	877-407-1657	607-734-6283
Tabb Brockenbrough & Ragland LLC 4905 Dickens Rd	Richmond	VA	23230	800-296-0531	804-355-7984
Teachers Protective Mutual Life Insurance Co 116-118 N Prince St	Lancaster	PA	17603	800-555-3122	717-394-7156
Tetrault Insurance Agency Inc 4317 Acushnet Ave	New Bedford	MA	02745	800-696-9991	508-995-8365

Name / Address	City	State	ZIP	Toll-Free	Phone
U S Risk Insurance Group Inc 10210 N Central Expy	Dallas	TX	75231	**800-926-9155**	214-265-7090
Union Central Life Insurance Co, The 1876 Waycross Rd PO Box 40888	Cincinnati	OH	45240	**877-546-3863**	
United Underwriters Inc PO Box 971000	Orem	UT	84097	**866-686-4833**	801-226-2662
Usasia Insurance Services 319 Union Ave	Pomona	CA	91768	**800-372-4822**	909-618-0288
Van Dyk Group Inc, The 12800 Long Beach Blvd	Beach Haven	NJ	08008	**800-222-0131**	609-492-1511
Van Zandt Emrich & Cary Inc 12401 Plantside Dr	Louisville	KY	40299	**800-928-7355**	502-456-2001
VIVA Health Inc 1222 14th Ave S	Birmingham	AL	35205	**800-633-1542**	205-939-1718
Wallace Welch Willingham 300 First Ave S 5th Fl	Saint Petersburg	FL	33701	**800-783-5085**	727-522-7777
Weber Insurance Corp 505 Corporate Dr W	Langhorne	PA	19047	**888-860-0400**	215-860-0400
West Point Underwriters LLC 7785 66th St	Pinellas Park	FL	33781	**800-688-6213**	727-507-7565
Wharton Group 101 S Livingston Ave	Livingston	NJ	07039	**800-521-2725**	973-992-5775
William Penn Assn 709 Brighton Rd	Pittsburgh	PA	15233	**800-848-7366**	412-231-2979
Willis Group Holdings Ltd 200 Liberty St 1 World Financial Ctr *NYSE: WSH*	New York	NY	10281	**800-234-8596**	212-915-8888
Wolverine Mutual Insurance Co 1 Wolverine Way	Dowagiac	MI	49047	**800-733-3320**	269-782-3451

391 INSURANCE COMPANIES

SEE ALSO Viatical Settlement Companies ; Home Warranty Services

391-1 Animal Insurance

Name / Address	City	State	ZIP	Toll-Free	Phone
Canadian Livestock Insurance 480 University Ave Ste 412	Toronto	ON	M5G1V2	**800-727-1502**	416-510-8191
Equisport Agency Inc 2306 Eastways Rd PO Box 269	Bloomfield Hills	MI	48304	**800-432-1215**	248-644-1215
Henry Equestrian Insurance Brokers 28 Victoria St	Aurora	ON	L4G1P9	**800-565-4321**	905-727-1144
Pet's Health Plan 3840 Greentree Ave SW	Canton	OH	44706	**800-807-6724**	
Veterinary Pet Insurance Inc PO Box 2344	Brea	CA	92822	**800-872-7387**	

391-2 Life & Accident Insurance

Name / Address	City	State	ZIP	Toll-Free	Phone
Acacia Life Insurance Co 7315 Wisconsin Ave	Bethesda	MD	20814	**800-444-1889**	301-280-1000
Advance Insurance Company of Kansas 1133 SW Topeka Blvd	Topeka	KS	66629	**800-530-5989**	785-273-9804
Aetna Inc 151 Farmington Ave *NYSE: AET*	Hartford	CT	06156	**800-872-3862**	860-273-0123
Allianz Life Insurance Company of North America PO Box 1344	Minneapolis	MN	55416	**800-950-5872**	
Allstate Life Insurance Co 3100 Sanders Rd Allstate W Plz *Cust Svc	Northbrook	IL	60062	**800-366-1411***	847-402-5000
American Amicable Life Insurance Co PO Box 2549	Waco	TX	76702	**800-736-7311**	254-297-2777
American Equity Investment Life Insurance Co 6000 Westown Pkwy	West Des Moines	IA	50266	**888-221-1234**	515-221-0002
American Family Life Assurance Company of Columbus (AFLAC) 1932 Wynnton Rd *Cust Svc	Columbus	GA	31999	**800-992-3522***	706-323-3431
American Family Life Insurance Co 6000 American Pkwy	Madison	WI	53783	**800-692-6326**	608-249-2111
American Family Mutual Insurance Co 6000 American Pkwy *Cust Svc	Madison	WI	53783	**800-374-0008***	608-249-2111
American Income Life Insurance Co (AIL) 1200 Wooded Acres	Waco	TX	76710	**800-433-3405**	254-761-6400
American Republic Insurance Co 601 Sixth Ave *Cust Svc	Des Moines	IA	50309	**800-247-2190***	
American Standard Insurance Company of Wisconsin 6000 American Pkwy	Madison	WI	53783	**800-692-6326**	608-249-2111
American United Life Insurance Co 1 American Sq 510A PO Box 368	Indianapolis	IN	46206	**800-537-6442**	317-285-1877
Americo Financial Life & Annuity Insurance Co PO Box 410288	Kansas City	MO	64141	**800-231-0801**	
Ameritas Direct 5900 'O' St	Lincoln	NE	68510	**800-555-4655**	
Ameritas Life Insurance Corp 5900 'O' St	Lincoln	NE	68510	**800-745-1112**	402-467-1122
Anthem Life Insurance Co 6740 N High St Ste 200	Worthington	OH	43085	**800-551-7265**	614-436-0688
Arch Insurance Group Inc 1 Liberty Plz 53rd Fl	New York	NY	10006	**866-993-9978**	212-651-6500
Assurant Employee Benefits 2323 Grand Blvd	Kansas City	MO	64108	**800-733-7879**	816-474-2345
Aurora National Life Assurance Co PO Box 4490	Hartford	CT	06147	**800-265-2652**	
Baltimore Life Cos 10075 Red Run Blvd	Owings Mills	MD	21117	**800-628-5433**	410-581-6600
Bankers Fidelity Life Insurance Co 4370 Peachtree Rd *NASDAQ: AAME*	Atlanta	GA	30319	**866-458-7504**	404-266-5500
Bankers Life & Casualty Co 111 E Wacker Dr Ste 2100	Chicago	IL	60601	**800-231-9150**	312-396-6000
Banner Life Insurance Co 1701 Research Blvd	Rockville	MD	20850	**800-638-8428**	301-279-4800
Beneficial Financial Group 55 N 300 W	Salt Lake City	UT	84145	**800-233-7979**	801-933-1100
Best Life & Health Insurance Co 2505 McCabe Way	Irvine	CA	92614	**800-433-0088**	949-253-4080
Catholic Order of Foresters 355 Shuman Blvd	Naperville	IL	60563	**800-617-4176**	630-983-4900
Central States Health & Life Company of Omaha 1212 N 96th St	Omaha	NE	68114	**800-826-6587**	402-397-1111
CIGNA 900 Cottage Grove Rd	Hartford	CT	06002	**800-244-6224**	860-226-6000
Citizens Insurance Company of America 400 E Anderson Ln	Austin	TX	78752	**800-880-5044**	512-837-7100
Citizens Security Life Insurance Co 12910 Shelbyville Rd Ste 300	Louisville	KY	40243	**800-843-7752**	502-244-2420
Colonial Life & Accident Insurance Co 1200 Colonial Life Blvd	Columbia	SC	29210	**800-325-4368**	
Colonial Penn Life Insurance Co 399 Market St	Philadelphia	PA	19181	**800-523-9100**	215-928-8000
Columbus Life Insurance Co 400 E Fourth St PO Box 5737	Cincinnati	OH	45201	**800-677-9595**	800-677-9696
Companion Life Insurance Co 7909 Parklane Rd Ste 200	Columbia	SC	29223	**800-753-0404**	803-735-1251
Concord Group Insurance Cos 4 Bouton St	Concord	NH	03301	**800-852-3380**	
Conseco Annuity Assurance Co 11825 N Pennsylvania St	Carmel	IN	46032	**866-595-2255**	
Conseco Senior Health Insurance Co 11825 N Pennsylvania St	Carmel	IN	46032	**866-595-2255**	
Continental Assurance Co 333 S Wabash Ave	Chicago	IL	60604	**800-251-2148**	312-822-5000
COUNTRY Insurance & Financial Services 1705 Towanda Ave	Bloomington	IL	61701	**888-211-2555**	866-268-6879
Creative Mktg International Corp 11460 Tomahawk Creek Pkwy	Leawood	KS	66211	**800-992-2642**	913-814-0510
Crump Insurance Services Inc 105 Eisenhower Pkwy	Roseland	NJ	07068	**800-222-0087**	973-461-2100
ELCO Mutual Life & Annuity 916 Sherwood Dr	Lake Bluff	IL	60044	**888-872-7954**	847-295-6000
Epic Life Insurance Co 1765 W Broadway *Sales	Madison	WI	53713	**800-236-8809***	608-223-2100
Equitable Life & Casualty Insurance Co 3 Triad Ctr *Cust Svc	Salt Lake City	UT	84180	**877-358-4060***	
Erie Family Life Insurance Co 100 Erie Insurance Pl	Erie	PA	16530	**800-458-0811**	814-870-2000
Farm Bureau Life Insurance Co 5400 University Ave	West Des Moines	IA	50266	**800-247-4170**	515-225-5400
Farm Family Life Insurance Co PO Box 656	Albany	NY	12201	**800-948-3276**	518-431-5000
Federal Life Insurance Co Mutual 3750 W Deerfield Rd	Riverwoods	IL	60015	**800-233-3750**	847-520-1900
Federated Life Insurance Co 121 E Pk Sq PO Box 328	Owatonna	MN	55060	**800-533-0472**	507-455-5200
Federated Mutual Insurance Co 121 E Pk Sq PO Box 328	Owatonna	MN	55060	**800-533-0472**	507-455-5200
First UNUM Life Insurance Co 2211 Congress St	Portland	ME	04122	**800-633-7491**	207-575-2211
FirstCare 1901 W Loop 289 Ste #9	Lubbock	TX	79407	**800-884-4901**	806-784-4300
Gerber Life Insurance Co 1311 Mamaroneck Ave	White Plains	NY	10605	**800-704-2180**	914-272-4000
Go Medico 1515 S 75th St	Omaha	NE	68124	**800-228-6080**	402-391-6900
Grange Insurance 671 S High St	Columbus	OH	43206	**800-422-0550**	
Great-West Life & Annuity Insurance Co 8515 E OrchaRd Rd	Greenwood Village	CO	80111	**800-537-2033**	303-737-3000
Great-West Life Assurance Co 100 Osborne St	Winnipeg	MB	R3C3A5	**800-990-6654**	204-946-1190
Greek Catholic Union of the USA 5400 Tuscarawas Rd	Beaver	PA	15009	**800-722-4428**	724-495-3400
Guarantee Trust Life Insurance Co 1275 Milwaukee Ave	Glenview	IL	60025	**800-338-7452**	847-699-0600
Guardian Life Insurance Company of America 7 Hanover Sq	New York	NY	10004	**888-600-4667**	212-598-8000
GuideOne Mutual Insurance Co 1111 Ashworth Rd	West Des Moines	IA	50265	**877-448-4331**	515-267-5000
Harleysville Mutual Insurance Co 355 Maple Ave	Harleysville	PA	19438	**800-523-6344**	215-256-5000
Hartford Life & Accident Insurance Co 1 Hartford Plz	Hartford	CT	06155	**877-896-9320**	860-547-5000
Harvey Watt & Co 475 N Central Ave	Atlanta	GA	30354	**800-241-6103**	404-767-7501
HCC Life Insurance Co 225 Townpark Dr Ste 145	Kennesaw	GA	30144	**800-447-0460**	770-973-9851
Horace Mann Life Insurance Co 1 Horace Mann Plaza	Springfield	IL	62715	**800-999-1030**	217-789-2500
Humana Inc 500 W Main St *NYSE: HUM*	Louisville	KY	40202	**800-486-2620**	502-580-1000
Illinois Mutual Life Insurance Co 300 SW Adams St	Peoria	IL	61634	**800-380-6688**	309-674-8255
Indiana Farm Bureau Insurance Co 225 SE St PO Box 1250	Indianapolis	IN	46206	**800-723-3276**	317-692-7200
Industrial Alliance Insurance & Financial Services 1080 Grande Allee W PO Box 1907 Stn Therminus	Quebec	QC	G1K7M3	**800-463-6236**	418-684-5000
Insurance Marketing Agencies Inc 306 Main St	Worcester	MA	01608	**800-891-1226**	508-753-7233
Investors Heritage Life Insurance Co (IHLIC) 200 Capital Ave PO Box 717	Frankfort	KY	40602	**800-422-2011**	502-223-2361
Jackson National Life Insurance Co 1 Corporate Way	Lansing	MI	48951	**800-644-4565**	517-381-5500
John Hancock New York 100 Summit Lake Dr	Valhalla	NY	10595	**800-732-5543**	877-391-3748
Lafayette Life Insurance Co 400 Broadway	Cincinnati	OH	45202	**800-443-8793**	
Life Insurance Co of Alabama 302 Broad St	Gadsden	AL	35901	**800-226-2371**	256-543-2022

Company / Address	City	State	ZIP	Toll-Free	Phone
Lincoln Heritage Life Insurance Co 4343 E Camelback Rd Ste 400 Ste 400	Phoenix	AZ	85018	**800-438-7180**	602-957-1650
Lincoln National Life Insurance Co 1300 S Clinton St	Fort Wayne	IN	46802	**800-454-6265**	
London Life Insurance Co 255 Dufferin Ave	London	ON	N6A4K1	**800-990-6654**	519-432-5281
Loyal American Life Insurance Co *Great American Financial Resources Inc* PO Box 26580	Austin	TX	78755	**800-315-5522**	800-545-4269
Madison National Life Insurance Company Inc PO Box 5008	Madison	WI	53705	**800-356-9601**	608-830-2000
Medico Group 1515 S 75th St	Omaha	NE	68124	**800-228-6080**	402-391-6900
MetLife Inc 200 Pk Ave *NYSE: MET*	New York	NY	10166	**800-638-5433**	212-578-2211
MetLife Investors Insurance Co 5 Pk Plz Ste 1900	Irvine	CA	92614	**800-848-3854**	
Midland National Life Insurance Co 1 Sammons Plz	Sioux Falls	SD	57193	**800-923-3223**	605-335-5700
Modern Woodmen of America 1701 First Ave	Rock Island	IL	61201	**800-447-9811**	309-786-6481
Mutual Insurance Company of Arizona PO Box 33180	Phoenix	AZ	85067	**800-352-0402**	602-956-5276
Mutual of America Life Insurance Co 320 Pk Ave	New York	NY	10022	**800-468-3785**	212-224-1600
Mutual of Omaha Insurance Co Mutual of Omaha Plaza	Omaha	NE	68175	**800-775-6000**	402-342-7600
Mutual Trust Life Insurance Co 1200 Jorie Blvd	Oak Brook	IL	60522	**800-323-7320**	630-990-1000
National Guardian Life Insurance Co (NGL) 2 E Gilman St	Madison	WI	53703	**800-548-2962**	608-257-5611
National Mutual Benefit 6522 Grand Teton Plaza	Madison	WI	53719	**800-779-1936**	608-833-1936
National Western Life Insurance Co 850 E Anderson Ln *NASDAQ: NWLI*	Austin	TX	78752	**800-531-5442**	512-836-1010
Nationwide Life & Annuity Insurance Co 1 Nationwide Pl	Columbus	OH	43215	**800-882-2822**	614-249-7111
Nationwide Mutual Insurance Co 5100 Rings Rd	Dublin	OH	43017	**800-543-3747**	877-669-6877
New York Life Insurance & Annuity Corp 51 Madison Ave	New York	NY	10010	**800-598-2019**	212-576-7000
North Carolina Mutual Life Insurance Co 411 W Chapel Hill St	Durham	NC	27701	**800-626-1899**	919-682-9201
Ohio State Life Insurance Co PO Box 410288	Kansas City	MO	64141	**800-752-1387**	
Old American Insurance Co 3520 Broadway	Kansas City	MO	64111	**800-733-6242**	816-753-7000
OneAmerica Financial Partners Inc (PML) PO Box 368	Indianapolis	IN	46206	**800-249-6269**	317-285-1877
Oxford Life Insurance Co 2721 N Central Ave *Cust Svc	Phoenix	AZ	85004	**800-308-2318***	602-263-6666
Pacific Guardian Life Insurance Company Ltd 1440 Kapiolani Blvd Ste 1700	Honolulu	HI	96814	**800-367-5354**	808-955-2236
Pacific Life Insurance Co 700 Newport Ctr Dr	Newport Beach	CA	92660	**800-800-7646**	949-219-3011
Pan-American Life Insurance Co 601 Poydras St *Life Ins	New Orleans	LA	70130	**877-939-4550***	
Partner Reinsurance Co of the US 1 Greenwich Plaza	Greenwich	CT	06830	**800-831-9146**	203-485-4200
Pekin Life Insurance Co 2505 Ct St *OTC: PKIN*	Pekin	IL	61558	**800-322-0160**	309-346-1161
Penn Insurance & Annuity Co 600 Dresher Rd *Cust Svc	Horsham	PA	19044	**800-523-0650***	215-956-8000
Penn Mutual Life Insurance Co 600 Dresher Rd *Cust Svc	Horsham	PA	19044	**800-523-0650***	215-956-8000
Penn Treaty Network America Insurance Co 3440 Lehigh St	Allentown	PA	18103	**800-362-0700**	
Physicians Life Insurance Co 2600 Dodge St	Omaha	NE	68131	**800-228-9100**	402-633-1000
Physicians Mutual Insurance Co 2600 Dodge St	Omaha	NE	68131	**800-228-9100**	402-633-1000
Pro Assurance Corp 1250 23rd St NW Ste 250	Washington	DC	20037	**800-613-3615**	202-969-1866
Property-Owners Insurance Co PO Box 30660	Lansing	MI	48909	**800-288-8740**	517-323-1200
Prudential Financial Inc 751 Broad St *NYSE: PRU*	Newark	NJ	07102	**800-843-7625**	973-802-6000
RBC Liberty Insurance PO Box 789	Greenville	SC	29602	**800-551-8354**	864-609-8111
Reliable Life Insurance Co 100 King St W PO Box 557	Hamilton	ON	L8N3K9	**800-465-0661**	905-523-5587
Reliance Standard Life Insurance 2001 Market St Ste 1500	Philadelphia	PA	19103	**800-351-7500**	267-256-3500
Sabre Healthdirect Inc 590 Alden Rd	Markham	ON	L3R8N2	**800-314-3346**	905-305-9900
Security Life Insurance Co of America 10901 Red Cir Dr	Minnetonka	MN	55343	**800-328-4667**	952-544-2121
Security Mutual Life Insurance Co of New York 100 Court St PO Box 1625	Binghamton	NY	13901	**800-927-8846**	607-723-3551
Security National Financial Corp (SNFC) 5300 South 360 West Ste 250 PO Box 57250 *NASDAQ: SNFCA*	Salt Lake City	UT	84123	**800-574-7117**	801-264-1060
Sentry Life Insurance Co 1800 N Pt Dr	Stevens Point	WI	54481	**800-373-6879**	715-346-6000
Settlers Life Insurance Co 1969 Lee Hwy	Bristol	VA	24201	**800-523-2650**	276-645-4300
Shenandoah Life Insurance Co 2301 Brambleton Ave	Roanoke	VA	24015	**800-848-5433**	540-985-4400
Slovene National Benefit Society 247 W Allegheny Rd	Imperial	PA	15126	**800-843-7675**	724-695-1100
Standard Life Insurance Company of Indiana 10689 N Pennsylvania St	Indianapolis	IN	46280	**800-222-3216**	317-574-6201
State Life Insurance Co 1 American Sq PO Box 368 *Cust Svc	Indianapolis	IN	46206	**800-537-6442***	317-285-2300
Sun Life Assurance Company of Canada 1 Sun Life Executive Pk PO Box 9133	Wellesley Hills	MA	02481	**800-786-5433**	781-237-6030
Symetra Life Insurance Co 777 108th Ave Ne Ste 1200	Bellevue	WA	98004	**800-574-0233**	425-256-8000
Texas Life Insurance Co 900 Washington PO Box 830	Waco	TX	76703	**800-283-9233**	254-752-6521
Thrivent Financial for Lutherans 4321 N BallaRd Rd	Appleton	WI	54919	**800-847-4836**	920-684-3225
TIAA-CREF 730 Third Ave	New York	NY	10017	**866-842-2442**	212-490-9000
Transamerica Occidental Life Insurance Co 1150 S Olive St *Cust Svc	Los Angeles	CA	90015	**800-852-4678***	213-742-2111
Trustmark Insurance Co 400 Field Dr	Lake Forest	IL	60045	**888-246-9949**	847-615-1500
United Heritage Life Insurance Co PO Box 7777	Meridian	ID	83680	**800-657-6351**	208-493-6100
United Insurance Holdings Corp 360 Central Ave Ste 900 *NASDAQ: UIHC*	Saint Petersburg	FL	33701	**800-861-4370**	800-295-8016
United Investors Life Insurance Co 2801 Hwy 280 S	Birmingham	AL	35223	**800-866-9933**	205-268-1000
United Life Insurance Co PO Box 73909	Cedar Rapids	IA	52407	**800-332-7977**	319-399-5700
United of Omaha Life Insurance Co Mutual of Omaha Plaza	Omaha	NE	68175	**800-775-6000**	402-342-7600
United World Life Insurance Co 3300 Mutual of Omaha Plz	Omaha	NE	68175	**800-775-6000**	402-342-7600
USAA Life Insurance Co (USAA) 9800 Fredericksburg Rd	San Antonio	TX	78288	**800-531-8000**	210-531-8722
Utica National Insurance Group 180 Genesee St	New Hartford	NY	13413	**800-274-1914**	315-734-2000
Variable Annuity Life Insurance Co (VALIC) 2929 Allen Pkwy	Houston	TX	77019	**800-448-2542**	
Washington National Insurance Co 11825 N Pennsylvania St	Carmel	IN	46032	**866-595-2255**	
Western & Southern Life Insurance Co 400 Broadway	Cincinnati	OH	45202	**800-926-1993**	
Western Fraternal Life Assn (WFLA) 1900 First Ave NE	Cedar Rapids	IA	52402	**877-935-2467**	319-363-2653
Western United Life Assurance Co 929 W Sprague Ave PO Box 2290 *General	Spokane	WA	99210	**800-247-2045***	509-835-2500
Western-Southern Life Assurance Co 400 Broadway	Cincinnati	OH	45202	**866-832-7719**	
William Penn Life Insurance Co of New York 100 Quentin Roosevelt Blvd	Garden City	NY	11530	**800-346-4773**	516-794-3700
Woman's Life Insurance Society 1338 Military St PO Box 5020	Port Huron	MI	48061	**800-521-9292**	810-985-5191

391-3 Medical & Hospitalization Insurance

Companies listed here provide managed care and/or traditional hospital and medical service plans to individuals and/or groups. Managed care companies typically offer plans as Health Maintenance Organizations (HMOs), Preferred Provider Organizations (PPOs), Exclusive Provider Organizations (EPOs), and/or Point of Service (POS) plans. Other types of hospital and medical service plans offered by companies listed here include indemnity plans and medical savings accounts.

Company / Address	City	State	ZIP	Toll-Free	Phone
AARP Health Care Options PO Box 1017	Montgomeryville	PA	18936	**800-523-5800**	
Aetna Inc 151 Farmington Ave *NYSE: AET*	Hartford	CT	06156	**800-872-3862**	860-273-0123
Aetna US Healthcare Inc 980 Jolly Rd	Blue Bell	PA	19422	**800-872-3862**	215-775-4800
Alberta Blue Cross 10009 108th St NW	Edmonton	AB	T5J3C5	**800-661-6995**	780-498-8100
American Specialty Health Plans 10221 Wateridge Cir	San Diego	CA	92121	**800-848-3555**	
AMERIGROUP Corp 4425 Corporation Ln *NYSE: AGP*	Virginia Beach	VA	23462	**800-600-4441**	757-490-6900
Anthem Blue Cross & Blue Shield 2015 Staples Mill Rd	Richmond	VA	23230	**800-451-1527**	804-354-7000
Anthem Blue Cross & Blue Shield Maine 2 Gannett Dr *Cust Svc	South Portland	ME	04106	**800-482-0966***	207-822-7000
Anthem Blue Cross & Blue Shield of Connecticut 370 Bassett Rd	North Haven	CT	06473	**800-922-1742**	800-922-4670
Anthem Blue Cross & Blue Shield of Nevada 9133 W Russell Rd	Las Vegas	NV	89148	**800-332-3842**	702-228-2583
Anthem Blue Cross Blue Shield Colorado 700 Broadway	Denver	CO	80273	**800-654-9338**	303-831-2131
Arkansas Blue Cross Blue Shield PO Box 2181	Little Rock	AR	72203	**800-238-8379**	501-712-1114
AvMed 4300 NW 89th Blvd	Gainesville	FL	32606	**800-346-0231**	352-372-8400
Benecaid Health Benefit Solutions Inc 185 The W Mall Ste 800	Toronto	ON	M9C5L5	**877-797-7448**	416-626-8786
Blue Care Network of Michigan 20500 Civic Ctr Dr	Southfield	MI	48076	**800-662-6667**	248-799-6400
Blue Cross & Blue Shield of Alabama 450 Riverchase Pkwy E	Birmingham	AL	35244	**800-292-8868**	205-988-2200
Blue Cross & Blue Shield of Kansas City 2301 Main St	Kansas City	MO	64108	**800-892-6048**	816-395-2222
Blue Cross & Blue Shield of Michigan 600 Lafayette Blvd E	Detroit	MI	48226	**855-237-3501**	313-225-9000
Blue Cross & Blue Shield of Mississippi PO Box 1043	Jackson	MS	39215	**800-222-8046**	601-932-3704
Blue Cross & Blue Shield of Montana 560 N Pk Ave PO Box 4309	Helena	MT	59604	**800-447-7828**	406-437-5000
Blue Cross & Blue Shield of Nebraska 1919 Aksarben Dr PO Box 3248	Omaha	NE	68180	**800-422-2763**	402-982-7000

Company / Address	City	State	ZIP	Toll-Free	Phone
Blue Cross & Blue Shield of New Mexico PO Box 27630	Albuquerque	NM	87125	**800-835-8699**	505-291-3500
Blue Cross & Blue Shield of North Carolina 1965 Ivory Creek Blvd *Cust Svc	Durham	NC	27702	**800-446-8053***	919-489-7431
Blue Cross & Blue Shield of Oklahoma 1215 S Boulder Ave *Cust Svc	Tulsa	OK	74119	**800-942-5837***	918-560-3500
Blue Cross & Blue Shield of Rhode Island 500 Exchange St	Providence	RI	02903	**800-637-3718**	401-459-1000
Blue Cross & Blue Shield of Texas Inc 1001 E Lookout Dr	Richardson	TX	75082	**800-521-2227**	972-766-6900
Blue Cross & Blue Shield of Vermont 445 Industrial Ln *Cust Svc	Montpelier	VT	05602	**800-247-2583***	802-223-6131
Blue Cross Blue Shield of Arizona 2444 W Las Palmaritas Dr	Phoenix	AZ	85021	**800-232-2345**	602-864-4400
Blue Cross Blue Shield of Delaware PO Box 1991	Wilmington	DE	19899	**800-572-4400**	800-876-7639
Blue Cross Blue Shield of Georgia 3350 Peachtree Rd NE *Cust Svc	Atlanta	GA	30326	**800-441-2273***	404-842-8000
Blue Cross Blue Shield of Kansas 1133 SW Topeka Blvd	Topeka	KS	66629	**800-432-0216**	785-291-7000
Blue Cross Blue Shield of Louisiana 5525 Reitz Ave	Baton Rouge	LA	70898	**800-599-2583**	225-295-3307
Blue Cross Blue Shield of Massachusetts 401 Pk Dr	Boston	MA	02215	**800-262-2583**	617-246-5000
Blue Cross Blue Shield of North Dakota 4510 13th Ave S	Fargo	ND	58121	**800-342-4718**	701-282-1100
Blue Cross Blue Shield of Wyoming 4000 House Ave	Cheyenne	WY	82001	**800-851-9145**	307-634-1393
Blue Cross of California 2 Gannett Dr	South Portland	ME	04106	**800-999-3643**	800-482-0966
Blue Cross of Idaho 3000 E Pine Ave	Meridian	ID	83642	**800-274-4018**	208-345-4550
Blue Cross of Northeastern Pennsylvania 19 N Main St *Cust Svc	Wilkes-Barre	PA	18711	**800-577-3742***	
BlueCross BlueShield of Western New York 257 W Genesee St	Buffalo	NY	14240	**800-888-0757**	716-887-6900
Capital District Physicians' Health Plan 500 Patroon Creek Blvd	Albany	NY	12206	**888-258-0477**	518-641-3000
Capital Health Plan PO Box 15349	Tallahassee	FL	32317	**800-390-1434**	850-383-3333
Carelink Health Plans 500 Virginia St E Ste 400	Charleston	WV	25301	**800-348-2922**	304-348-2900
Cdspi 155 Lesmill Rd	Toronto	ON	M3B2T8	**800-561-9401**	416-296-9401
Centene Corp 7700 Forsyth Blvd *NYSE: CNC* ■ *General	Saint Louis	MO	63105	**800-293-0056***	314-725-4477
Chiropractic Health Plan of California PO Box 190	Clayton	CA	94517	**800-995-2442**	310-210-5400
CIGNA Healthcare 900 Cottage Grove Rd	Hartford	CT	06152	**800-433-5768**	860-226-6000
CIGNA Healthcare of North Carolina Inc 701 Corporate Ctr Dr	Raleigh	NC	27607	**800-942-1654**	919-854-7000
Community Care 218 W Sixth St	Tulsa	OK	74119	**800-278-7563**	918-594-5200
CompBenefits Corp 100 Mansell Ct E Ste 400	Roswell	GA	30076	**800-633-1262**	770-552-7101
Comprehensive Health Services Inc (CHSI) 10701 Parkridge Blvd Ste 200	Reston	VA	20191	**800-638-8083**	703-760-0700
ConnectiCare Inc 175 Scott Swamp Rd *Cust Svc	Farmington	CT	06032	**800-251-7722***	860-674-5700
Coventry Health Care Inc 6705 Rockledge Dr Ste 900 *NYSE: CVH*	Bethesda	MD	20817	**866-667-3062**	301-581-0600
Coventry Health Care of Delaware Inc 750 Prides Crossing Ste 200	Newark	DE	19713	**800-833-7423**	
Coventry Health Care of Georgia Inc 1100 Cir 75 Pkwy Ste 1400	Atlanta	GA	30339	**800-470-2004**	678-202-2100
Coventry Health Care of Iowa Inc 4320 114th St	Urbandale	IA	50322	**800-470-6352**	515-225-1234
Coventry Health Care of Kansas Inc 8320 Ward Pkwy	Kansas City	MO	64114	**800-969-3343**	
Coventry Health Care of Louisiana Inc 1720 S Sykes Dr *Sales	Bismarck	ND	58504	**800-341-6613***	
Coventry Health Care of Nebraska Inc 15950 W Dodge Rd Ste 100	Omaha	NE	68164	**855-449-2889**	402-498-9030
Dakotacare 2600 W 49th St PO Box 7406	Sioux Falls	SD	57117	**800-325-5598**	605-334-4000
Davis Vision Inc 711 Troy-Schenectady Rd	Latham	NY	12110	**800-999-5431**	
Dean Health Insurance Inc 1277 Deming Way	Madison	WI	53717	**800-279-1301**	608-836-1400
Delta Dental Insurance Company of Alaska PO Box 1809	Alpharetta	GA	30023	**800-521-2651**	
Delta Dental of Arizona PO Box 43026	Phoenix	AZ	85080	**800-352-6132**	
Delta Dental of Arkansas 1513 Country Club Rd PO Box 15965	Sherwood	AR	72120	**800-462-5410**	501-835-3400
Delta Dental of Colorado 4582 S Ulster St Ste 800	Denver	CO	80237	**800-233-0860**	303-741-9300
Delta Dental of Idaho 555 E Parkcenter Blvd PO Box 2870	Boise	ID	83706	**800-356-7586**	208-489-3580
Delta Dental of Indiana PO Box 30416	Lansing	MI	48909	**800-524-0149**	
Delta Dental of Iowa 9000 Northpark Dr Ste 13 *Cust Svc	Johnston	IA	50131	**800-544-0718***	515-261-5500
Delta Dental of Kansas 1619 N Waterfront Pkwy PO Box 789769	Wichita	KS	67201	**800-234-3375**	316-264-4511
Delta Dental of Kentucky 10100 Linn Stn Rd PO Box 242810 *Cust Svc	Louisville	KY	40223	**800-955-2030***	
Delta Dental of Louisiana PO Box 1803	Alpharetta	GA	30023	**800-422-4234**	
Delta Dental of Maryland 1 Delta Dr	Mechanicsburg	PA	17055	**800-932-0783**	717-766-8500
Delta Dental of Massachusetts 465 Medford St *Cust Svc	Boston	MA	02129	**800-872-0500***	617-886-1000
Delta Dental of Michigan PO Box 30416	Lansing	MI	48909	**800-524-0149**	
Delta Dental of Minnesota PO Box 330	Minneapolis	MN	55440	**800-553-9536**	651-406-5900
Delta Dental of Missouri 12399 Gravois Rd Ste 2	Saint Louis	MO	63127	**800-392-1167**	314-656-3000
Delta Dental of Montana PO Box 1803	Alpharetta	GA	30023	**800-422-4234**	
Delta Dental of New Jersey 1639 State Rt 10	Parsippany	NJ	07054	**800-624-2633**	973-285-4000
Delta Dental of New Jersey Inc PO Box 222	Parsippany	NJ	07054	**800-452-9310**	
Delta Dental of New Mexico 2500 Louisiana Blvd NE Ste 600	Albuquerque	NM	87110	**800-999-0963**	505-883-4777
Delta Dental of New York 1 Delta Dr	Mechanicsburg	PA	17055	**800-932-0783**	717-766-8500
Delta Dental of Ohio PO Box 30416	Lansing	MI	48909	**800-524-0149**	
Delta Dental of Oklahoma 16 NW 63rd St Ste 201	Oklahoma City	OK	73116	**800-522-0188**	405-607-2100
Delta Dental of Pennsylvania 1 Delta Dr	Mechanicsburg	PA	17055	**800-932-0783**	
Delta Dental of Rhode Island 10 Charles St	Providence	RI	02904	**800-598-6684**	401-752-6000
Delta Dental of South Dakota 720 N Euclid Ave PO Box 1157	Pierre	SD	57501	**800-627-3961**	605-224-7345
Delta Dental of Tennessee 240 Venture Cir *Cust Svc	Nashville	TN	37228	**800-223-3104***	615-255-3175
Delta Dental of Virginia 4818 Starkey Rd	Roanoke	VA	24014	**800-367-3531**	540-989-8000
Delta Dental of West Virginia 1 Delta Dr	Mechanicsburg	PA	17055	**800-932-0783**	717-766-8500
Delta Dental of Wisconsin 2801 Hoover Rd PO Box 828	Stevens Point	WI	54481	**800-236-3713**	715-344-6087
Delta Dental of Wyoming 6234 Yellowstone Rd PO Box 29	Cheyenne	WY	82009	**800-735-3379**	307-632-3313
Delta Dental Plan of North Carolina 343 E Six Forks Rd Ste 180	Raleigh	NC	27609	**800-662-8856**	919-832-6015
EmblemHealth Co 55 Water St	New York	NY	10041	**800-447-8255**	646-447-5000
Excellus BlueCross BlueShield PO Box 22999	Rochester	NY	14692	**800-278-1247**	585-454-1700
Excellus BlueCross BlueShield of Central New York 333 Butternut Dr	Syracuse	NY	13214	**800-633-6066**	315-671-6400
EyeMed Vision Care 4000 Luxottica Pl	Mason	OH	45040	**800-521-3605**	513-765-4321
Fallon Community Health Plan Inc 10 Chestnut St Ste 7	Worcester	MA	01608	**800-333-2535**	508-799-2100
First Choice Health Plan 600 University St Ste 1400	Seattle	WA	98101	**800-467-5281**	
First Priority Health 19 N Main St	Wilkes-Barre	PA	18711	**800-822-8753**	
Foster Thomas Inc 1788 Forest Dr	Annapolis	MD	21401	**800-372-3626**	
Geisinger Health Plan 100 N Academy Ave	Danville	PA	17822	**800-447-4000**	570-271-8760
Great American Supplemental Benefits PO Box 26580	Austin	TX	78755	**866-459-4272**	
Group Health Co-op 320 Westlake Ave N Ste 100	Seattle	WA	98109	**888-901-4636**	206-448-5600
Hanover Insurance Co 440 Lincoln St	Worcester	MA	01653	**800-853-0456**	508-855-1000
Harvard Pilgrim Health Care Inc 93 Worcester St	Wellesley	MA	02481	**888-888-4742**	617-509-1000
Hawaii Dental Service 700 Bishop St Ste 700	Honolulu	HI	96813	**800-232-2533**	808-521-1431
Hawaii Medical Service Assn 818 Keeaumoku St	Honolulu	HI	96822	**800-776-4672**	808-948-6111
Health Alliance Plan 2850 W Grand Blvd	Detroit	MI	48202	**800-422-4641**	313-872-8100
Health Net Inc 21650 Oxnard St *NYSE: HNT*	Woodland Hills	CA	91367	**800-848-4747**	818-676-6000
Health Tradition Health Plan 1808 E Main St	Onalaska	WI	54650	**800-545-8499**	608-781-9692
HealthAmerica Pennsylvania Inc 3721 Tecport Dr PO Box 67103	Harrisburg	PA	17111	**800-788-6445**	
HealthCare USA 10 S Broadway Ste 1200	Saint Louis	MO	63102	**800-213-7792**	314-241-5300
HealthPartners Inc PO Box 1309	Minneapolis	MN	55440	**800-883-2177**	952-883-5000
Healthplex Inc 333 Earl Ovington Blvd *Cust Svc	Uniondale	NY	11553	**800-468-0608***	516-542-2200
HealthPlus of Michigan 2050 S Linden Rd	Flint	MI	48532	**800-332-9161**	810-230-2000
Heritage Summit HealthCare of Florida Inc PO Box 2928	Lakeland	FL	33806	**800-282-7644**	863-665-6629
Highmark Inc 120 Fifth Ave Pl	Pittsburgh	PA	15222	**800-992-0246**	412-544-7000
Humana Inc 500 W Main St *NYSE: HUM*	Louisville	KY	40202	**800-486-2620**	502-580-1000
Humana Military Healthcare Services 500 W Main St *General	Louisville	KY	40201	**800-444-5445***	
Independence Blue Cross 1901 Market St	Philadelphia	PA	19103	**800-275-2583**	
Independent Health 511 Farber Lakes Dr	Buffalo	NY	14221	**800-247-1466**	716-631-3001
IOA Re Inc 190 W Germantown Pk Ste 200	East Norriton	PA	19401	**800-462-2300**	610-940-9000

Company / Address	City	State	ZIP	Toll-Free	Phone
Kaiser Foundation Health Plan Inc 1 Kaiser Plz	Oakland	CA	94612	**800-464-4000**	408-972-3000
Kaiser Permanente 3495 Piedmont Rd NE Piedmont Ctr Bldg 9	Atlanta	GA	30305	**800-611-1811**	404-364-7000
Kaiser Permanente Hawaii 711 Kapiolani Blvd	Honolulu	HI	96813	**800-966-5955**	808-432-0000
Kaiser Permanente Northwest 500 NE Multnomah St Ste 100	Portland	OR	97232	**800-813-2000**	503-813-2000
LA Care Health Plan 555 W Fifth St 29th Fl	Los Angeles	CA	90013	**888-839-9909**	213-694-1250
Lexington Veteran Affairs Medical Center 1101 Veterans Dr	Lexington	KY	40502	**877-222-8387**	859-233-4511
MEDICA 401 Carlson Pkwy *Cust Svc	Minnetonka	MN	55305	**800-952-3455***	952-992-2900
Medical Benefits Mutual Life Insurance Co 1975 Tamarack Rd	Newark	OH	43058	**800-423-3151**	740-522-8425
Medical Mutual of Ohio 2060 E Ninth St	Cleveland	OH	44115	**800-700-2583**	216-687-7000
Memorial Health Partners 4700 Waters Ave	Savannah	GA	31404	**800-537-0690**	912-350-8000
MetLife Inc 200 Pk Ave *NYSE: MET*	New York	NY	10166	**800-638-5433**	212-578-2211
Molina Healthcare Inc 200 Oceangate Ste 100 *NYSE: MOH*	Long Beach	CA	90802	**888-562-5442**	562-435-3666
MVP Health Care 625 State St	Schenectady	NY	12305	**800-777-4793**	518-370-4793
ODS Cos 601 SW Second Ave	Portland	OR	97204	**888-221-0802**	503-228-6554
Oxford Health Plans LLC 48 Monroe Tpke	Trumbull	CT	06611	**800-444-6222**	203-459-9100
Oxford Health Plans (NJ) Inc 111 Wood Ave S Ste 2	Iselin	NJ	08830	**800-201-6920**	732-623-1000
Pacificare of Texas 6200 NW Pkwy	San Antonio	TX	78249	**800-624-7272**	210-474-5000
Paramount Health Care 1901 Indian Wood Cir	Maumee	OH	43537	**800-462-3589**	419-887-2525
Physicians Plus Insurance Corp 2650 Novation Pkwy Ste 200	Madison	WI	53713	**800-545-5015**	608-282-8900
Preferred CommunityChoice PPO 218 W Sixth St	Tulsa	OK	74119	**800-884-4776**	918-594-5200
Preferred Health Systems Inc 8535 E 21st St N	Wichita	KS	67206	**800-990-0345**	316-609-2345
Premera Blue Cross 7001 220th St SW *Cust Svc	Mountlake Terrace	WA	98043	**800-722-1471***	425-918-4000
Premera Blue Cross Blue Shield of Alaska 2550 Denali St Ste 1404 *Cust Svc	Anchorage	AK	99503	**800-508-4722***	907-258-5065
Priority Health 1231 E Beltline NE	Grand Rapids	MI	49525	**800-942-0954**	616-942-0954
Regence Blue Cross Blue Shield of Oregon PO Box 1071	Portland	OR	97207	**888-734-3623**	888-675-6570
Regence BlueCross BlueShield of Utah 2890 E Cottonwood Pkwy *Cust Svc	Salt Lake City	UT	84121	**800-624-6519***	801-333-2100
Rocky Mountain Health Plans 2775 Crossroads Blvd PO Box 10600	Grand Junction	CO	81502	**800-843-0719**	970-244-7760
SafeGuard Health Enterprises Inc 95 Enterprise Ste 100	Aliso Viejo	CA	92656	**800-880-1800**	949-425-4300
Sagamore Health Network 11555 N Meridian St Ste 400	Carmel	IN	46032	**800-364-3469**	317-573-2886
Scott & White Health Plan 2401 S 31st St	Temple	TX	76508	**800-321-7947**	254-298-3000
Sharp Health Plan 4305 University Ave Ste 200	San Diego	CA	92105	**800-359-2002**	619-228-2300
Spectera Inc 6220 Old Dobbin Ln Liberty 6, Ste 200	Columbia	MD	21045	**800-638-3120**	410-265-6033
Trillium Community Health Plan Inc 1800 Millrace Dr	Eugene	OR	97403	**800-910-3906**	541-431-1950
Tufts Associated Health Plans 705 Mt Auburn St	Watertown	MA	02472	**800-462-0224**	617-972-9400
Union Pacific Railroad Employees' Health Systems 1040 North 2200 West	Salt Lake City	UT	84116	**800-547-0421**	801-595-4300
UnitedHealth Group Inc 9900 Bren Rd E *NYSE: UNH*	Minnetonka	MN	55343	**800-328-5979**	952-936-1300
Unity Health Insurance 840 Carolina St	Sauk City	WI	53583	**800-362-3308**	608-643-2491
Univera Healthcare 205 Pk Club Ln	Buffalo	NY	14221	**877-883-9577**	716-847-1480
Voya Services Co 230 Park Ave	New York	NY	10169	**855-663-8692**	860-580-4646
Washington Dental Service 9706 Fourth Ave NE	Seattle	WA	98115	**800-367-4104**	206-522-1300
WellCare Group Inc 8735 Henderson Rd	Tampa	FL	33634	**866-765-4385**	813-290-6200
WellCare Health Plans Inc PO Box 31372	Tampa	FL	33631	**866-530-9491**	

391-4 Property & Casualty Insurance

Company / Address	City	State	ZIP	Toll-Free	Phone
Accident Fund Co 232 S Capitol Ave PO Box 40790 *Mktg	Lansing	MI	48901	**888-276-0327***	517-342-4200
ACE USA 436 Walnut St PO Box 1000	Philadelphia	PA	19106	**866-357-3797**	215-640-1000
Addison Insurance Co 118 Second Ave SE PO Box 73909	Cedar Rapids	IA	52401	**800-332-7977**	319-399-5700
Aegis Security Inc PO Box 3153	Harrisburg	PA	17105	**800-233-2160**	717-657-9671
Agricultural Workers Mutual Auto Insurance Co PO Box 88	Fort Worth	TX	76101	**800-772-7424**	817-831-9900
ALLIED Group Inc 1100 Locust St	Des Moines	IA	50391	**800-532-1436**	515-508-4211
Allied Insurance 1100 Locust St	Des Moines	CA	50391	**800-532-1436**	
American Commerce Insurance Co 3590 Twin Creeks Dr	Columbus	OH	43204	**800-848-2945**	614-308-3366
American Family Mutual Insurance Co 6000 American Pkwy *Cust Svc	Madison	WI	53783	**800-374-0008***	608-249-2111
American Modern Home Insurance Co PO Box 5323	Cincinnati	OH	45201	**800-543-2644**	513-943-7200
American National Property & Casualty Co 1949 E Sunshine St	Springfield	MO	65899	**800-333-2860**	417-887-0220
American Southern Insurance Co 3715 Northside Pkwy NW Bldg 400 Ste 800	Atlanta	GA	30327	**800-241-1172**	404-266-9599
AMERISAFE Inc 2301 Hwy 190 W *NASDAQ: AMSF*	DeRidder	LA	70634	**800-256-9052**	337-463-9052
Amerisure Insurance Co 26777 Halsted Rd Ste 200	Farmington Hills	MI	48331	**800-257-1900**	248-615-9000
Amica Mutual Insurance Co 100 Amica Way	Lincoln	RI	02865	**800-652-6422**	
Arbella Mutual Insurance Co 1100 Crown Colony Dr	Quincy	MA	02169	**800-972-5348**	617-328-2800
Armed Forces Insurance Exchange (AFI) PO Box G	Fort Leavenworth	KS	66027	**800-255-0187**	800-255-6792
Arrowpoint Capital Whitehall Corporate Ctr Ste 3 3600 Arco Corporate Dr	Charlotte	NC	28273	**866-236-7750**	704-522-2000
Associated Industries Of Massachusetts Mutual Insurance Com PO Box 4070	Burlington	MA	01803	**866-270-3354**	781-221-1600
AssuranceAmerica Corp 5500 I- N Pkwy Ste 600	Atlanta	GA	30328	**800-450-7857**	770-952-0200
Auto-Owners Insurance Co 6101 Anacapri Blvd	Lansing	MI	48917	**800-346-0346**	517-323-1200
Avemco Insurance Co 411 Aviation Way	Frederick	MD	21701	**800-874-9125**	301-694-5700
Baldwin & Lyons Inc 111 Congressional Blvd Ste 500 *NASDAQ: BWINB*	Carmel	IN	46032	**800-644-5501**	317-636-9800
Berkshire Hathaway Group (BHG) 3024 Harney St	Omaha	NE	68131	**800-223-2064**	402-536-3100
Berkshire Hathaway Homestates Cos (BHHC) PO Box 2048	Omaha	NE	68103	**888-495-8949**	
Bituminous Insurance Cos 320 18th St	Rock Island	IL	61201	**800-475-4477**	
Brotherhood Mutual Insurance Co (BMI) 6400 Brotherhood Way PO Box 2589 *Cust Svc	Fort Wayne	IN	46825	**800-333-3735***	
Brown & Brown Insurance PO Box 1718	Tacoma	WA	98401	**800-562-8171**	253-396-5500
California Casualty Insurance Group 1900 Alameda De Las Pulgas	San Mateo	CA	94403	**866-680-5143**	650-574-4000
Canada Life Assurance Co, The 330 University Ave	Toronto	ON	M5G1R8	**888-252-1847**	416-597-1456
Canal Insurance Co 400 E Stone Ave PO Box 7	Greenville	SC	29601	**800-452-6911**	
Capitol Indemnity Corp 1600 Aspen Commons	Middleton	WI	53562	**800-475-4450**	608-829-4200
Capitol Insurance Cos 1600 Aspen Commons PO Box 5900	Middleton	WI	53562	**800-475-4450**	608-829-4200
Carolina Casualty Insurance Co 5011 Gate Pkwy Ste 200	Jacksonville	FL	32256	**800-874-8053**	904-363-0900
Central Insurance Cos 800 S Washington St	Van Wert	OH	45891	**800-736-7000**	419-238-1010
Century-National Insurance Co 12200 Sylvan St PO Box 3999 *Cust Svc	North Hollywood	CA	91606	**800-894-8384***	818-760-0880
Chubb & Son 15 Mountain View Rd	Warren	NJ	07059	**800-252-4670**	908-903-2000
Church Mutual Insurance Co 3000 Schuster Ln	Merrill	WI	54452	**800-554-2642**	715-536-5577
Civil Service Employees Insurance Co 2121 N California Blvd Ste 989	Walnut Creek	CA	94596	**800-282-6848**	
Colorado Farm Bureau Mutual Insurance Co PO Box 5647	Denver	CO	80217	**800-315-5998**	303-749-7500
Commerce Insurance Co 211 Main St	Webster	MA	01570	**800-221-1605**	508-943-9000
Concord Group Insurance Cos 4 Bouton St	Concord	NH	03301	**800-852-3380**	
Continental Casualty Co 333 S Wabash Ave	Chicago	IL	60685	**800-262-2000**	312-822-5000
Continental Western Group 11201 Douglas Ave	Urbandale	IA	50322	**800-235-2942**	515-473-3000
Cornhusker Casualty Co PO Box 2048	Omaha	NE	68103	**888-495-8949**	
Country Mutual Insurance Co 1701 Towanda Ave *Cust Svc	Bloomington	IL	61701	**888-211-2555***	309-821-3000
Crum & Forster Insurance Inc 305 Madison Ave PO Box 1973	Morristown	NJ	07962	**800-690-5520**	973-490-6600
Cumberland Insurance Group 633 Shiloh Pike	Bridgeton	NJ	08302	**800-232-6992**	
Cumberland Mutual Fire Insurance Co 633 Shiloh Pk	Bridgeton	NJ	08302	**800-232-6992**	
Dairyland Insurance Co 1800 N Pt Dr *Sales	Stevens Point	WI	54481	**866-445-5364***	715-346-6000
Donegal Mutual Insurance Co 1195 River Rd PO Box 302	Marietta	PA	17547	**800-877-0600**	717-426-1931
Economical Insurance Group, The 111 Westmount Rd S PO Box 2000	Waterloo	ON	N2J4S4	**800-265-2180**	519-570-8200
Endurance Reinsurance Corp of America 750 Third Ave Fl 18 & 19	New York	NY	10017	**888-221-3894**	212-471-2800
Erie Indemnity Co *Erie Insurance Group* 100 Erie Insurance Pl *NASDAQ: ERIE*	Erie	PA	16530	**800-458-0811**	814-870-2000

Company / Address	City	State	ZIP	Toll-Free	Phone
Erie Insurance Exchange 100 Erie Insurance Pl	Erie	PA	16530	**800-458-0811**	814-870-2000
Erie Insurance Property & Casualty Co 100 Erie Insurance Pl	Erie	PA	16530	**800-458-0811**	814-870-2000
Everest Reinsurance Co 477 Martinsville Rd	Liberty Corner	NJ	07938	**800-269-6660**	908-604-3000
Farm Family Casualty Insurance Co PO Box 656	Albany	NY	12201	**800-843-3276**	518-431-5000
Farmers Alliance Mutual Insurance Co 1122 N Main PO Box 1401	McPherson	KS	67460	**800-362-1075**	620-241-2200
Farmers Insurance Exchange 4680 Wilshire Blvd	Los Angeles	CA	90010	**855-808-6599**	323-932-3200
Farmers Mutual Hail Insurance Company of Iowa 6785 Westown Pkwy	West Des Moines	IA	50266	**800-247-5248**	515-282-9104
Farmers Mutual Insurance Company of Nebraska 1220 Lincoln Mall	Lincoln	NE	68508	**800-742-7433**	402-434-8300
FCCI Insurance Group 6300 University Pkwy	Sarasota	FL	34232	**800-226-3224**	941-907-3224
Federated Mutual Insurance Co 121 E Pk Sq PO Box 328	Owatonna	MN	55060	**800-533-0472**	507-455-5200
Fhm Insurance Co 4601 Touchton Rd E Bldg 300 Ste 3150	Jacksonville	FL	32246	**800-393-0001**	904-724-9890
Fireman's Fund Insurance Co 1465 N McDowell Blvd	Petaluma	CA	94954	**866-386-3932**	
First Insurance Company of Hawaii Ltd 1100 Ward Ave PO Box 2866	Honolulu	HI	96803	**800-272-5202**	808-527-7777
Florida Family Insurance Services LLC 27599 Riverview Ctr Blvd Ste 100 PO Box 136001	Bonita Springs	FL	34136	**888-850-4663**	239-495-4700
Florida Farm Bureau Insurance Cos 5700 SW 34th St	Gainesville	FL	32608	**866-275-7322**	352-378-1321
FM Global 270 Central Ave PO Box 7500	Johnston	RI	02919	**800-343-7722**	401-275-3000
Foremost Insurance Co 5600 Beech Tree Ln	Caledonia	MI	49316	**800-532-4221**	
Frankenmuth Insurance 1 Mutual Ave	Frankenmuth	MI	48787	**800-234-4433**	989-652-6121
Franklin Mutual Insurance Co 5 Broad St	Branchville	NJ	07826	**800-842-0551**	973-948-3120
General Star National Insurance Co 695 E Main St Financial Ctr	Stamford	CT	06901	**800-624-5237**	203-328-5000
Germania Farm Mutual Insurance Assn 507 Hwy 290 E	Brenham	TX	77833	**800-392-2202**	979-836-5224
Golden Eagle Insurance Corp 525 B St	San Diego	CA	92101	**888-398-8924**	610-832-8240
Grain Dealers Mutual Insurance Co 6201 Corporate Dr	Indianapolis	IN	46278	**800-428-7081**	317-388-4500
Grange Mutual Casualty Co 671 S High St	Columbus	OH	43206	**800-422-0550**	
Great Northern Insurance Co 15 Mtn View Rd *Cust Svc	Warren	NJ	07059	**800-252-4670***	908-903-2000
Great West Casualty Co 1100 W 29th St PO Box 277	South Sioux City	NE	68776	**800-228-8602**	402-494-2411
Grinnell Mutual Reinsurance Co 4215 Hwy 146 PO Box 790	Grinnell	IA	50112	**800-362-2041**	641-269-8000
GuideOne Mutual Insurance Co 1111 Ashworth Rd	West Des Moines	IA	50265	**877-448-4331**	515-267-5000
Hagerty Insurance Agency LLC 141 River's Edge Dr Ste 200 PO Box 1303	Traverse City	MI	49684	**877-922-9701**	231-947-6868
Hanover Insurance Co 440 Lincoln St	Worcester	MA	01653	**800-853-0456**	508-855-1000
Harco National Insurance Co PO Box 68309	Schaumburg	IL	60168	**800-448-4642**	
Harleysville Insurance Co of New Jersey 112 W Park Dr	Mount Laurel	NJ	08054	**800-322-5521**	856-642-9779
Harleysville Worcester Insurance Co 120 Front St Ste 400	Worcester	MA	01608	**800-225-7387**	508-754-6666
Hartford's Omni Auto Plan PO Box 105440	Atlanta	GA	30348	**800-243-5860**	770-952-4500
Hingham Mutual Fire Insurance Co 230 Beal St	Hingham	MA	02043	**800-341-8200**	781-749-0841
Hortica Insurance 1 Horticultural Ln PO Box 428	Edwardsville	IL	62025	**800-851-7740**	618-656-4240
HSB Group Inc 1 State St	Hartford	CT	06103	**800-472-1866**	860-722-1866
ICW Group 11455 El Camino Real	San Diego	CA	92130	**800-877-1111**	858-350-2400
IMT Group, The PO Box 1336	Des Moines	IA	50266	**800-274-3531**	
Indiana Farmers Mutual Insurance Co 10 W 106th St	Indianapolis	IN	46290	**800-666-6460**	317-846-4211
Injured Workers Insurance Fund 8722 Loch Raven Blvd	Towson	MD	21286	**800-264-4943**	410-494-2000
Insurance Company of the West 11455 El Camino Real	San Diego	CA	92130	**800-877-1111**	858-350-2400
Intact Insurance 700 University Ave Mn 3 Ste 1500	Toronto	ON	M5G0A1	**877-341-1464**	844-489-3768
James A Scott & Son Inc PO Box 10489	Lynchburg	VA	24506	**800-365-0101**	434-832-2100
Lititz Mutual Insurance Co 2 N Broad St PO Box 900	Lititz	PA	17543	**800-626-4751**	717-626-4751
Lumbermen's Underwriting Alliance (LUA) 1905 NW Corporate Blvd PO Box 3061	Boca Raton	FL	33431	**800-327-0630**	561-994-1900
Main Street America Group 55 W St	Keene	NH	03431	**800-258-5310**	603-352-4000
MAPFRE USA Corp 211 Main St	Webster	MA	01570	**800-922-8276**	
Markel Specialty Commercial 4600 Cox Rd	Glen Allen	VA	23060	**800-416-4364**	
Mercer Insurance Group Inc 10 N Hwy 31 PO Box 278	Pennington	NJ	08534	**800-223-0534**	609-737-0426
Merchants Insurance Group 250 Main St	Buffalo	NY	14202	**800-462-1077**	716-849-3333
Mercury Insurance Group 4484 Wilshire Blvd *NYSE: MCY*	Los Angeles	CA	90010	**800-956-3728**	323-937-1060
Michigan Millers Mutual Insurance Co 2425 E Grand River Ave PO Box 30060	Lansing	MI	48912	**800-888-1914**	
Mid-Continent Group 1437 S Boulder Ave W PO Box 1409	Tulsa	OK	74119	**800-722-4994**	918-587-7221
Middlesex Mutual Assurance Co 213 Ct St PO Box 891	Middletown	CT	06457	**800-622-3780**	
Midwest Employers Casualty Co 14755 N Outer 40 Dr Ste 300	Chesterfield	MO	63017	**877-975-2667**	636-449-7000
Millers First Insurance Co 111 E Fourth St	Alton	IL	62002	**800-558-0500**	618-463-3636
Montgomery Mutual Insurance Co 13830 Ballantyne Corporate Pl Ste 300	Charlotte	NC	28277	**800-561-0178**	704-759-7661
Mutual of Enumclaw Insurance Co 1460 Wells St	Enumclaw	WA	98022	**800-366-5551**	360-825-2591
National Farmers Union Property & Casualty Co 5619 DTC Pkwy Ste 300	Greenwood Village	CO	80111	**800-347-1961**	303-337-5500
National Fire & Marine Insurance Co 3024 Harney St	Omaha	NE	68131	**866-720-7861**	402-536-3000
National Grange Mutual Insurance Co 55 W St	Keene	NH	03431	**800-258-5310**	603-352-4000
National Interstate Corp 3250 I- Dr *NASDAQ: NATL*	Richfield	OH	44286	**800-929-1500**	330-659-8900
Nationwide Mutual Fire Insurance Co 1 Nationwide Plaza	Columbus	OH	43215	**877-669-6877**	614-249-7111
Nationwide Mutual Insurance Co 1 Nationwide Plaza	Columbus	OH	43215	**877-669-6877**	614-249-7111
Nautilus Insurance Group LLC 7233 E Butherus Dr	Scottsdale	AZ	85260	**800-842-8972**	480-951-0905
New Era Life Insurance Co PO Box 4884	Houston	TX	77210	**800-552-7879**	
New Jersey Manufacturers Insurance Co 301 Sullivan Way	West Trenton	NJ	08628	**800-232-6600**	609-883-1300
New Mexico Mutual Casualty Co PO Box 27825	Albuquerque	NM	87125	**800-788-8851**	505-345-7260
New York Central Mutual Fire Insurance Co (NYCM) 1899 Central Plz E	Edmeston	NY	13335	**800-234-6926**	
North American Specialty Insurance Co 650 Elm St Ste 600	Manchester	NH	03101	**800-542-9200**	603-644-6600
Northern Security Insurance Co PO Box 188	Montpelier	VT	05601	**800-451-5000**	802-223-2341
Northland Insurance Co 385 Washington St	Saint Paul	MN	55102	**800-237-9334**	
Northwestern Pacific Indemnity Co 15 Mtn View Rd *Claims	Warren	NJ	07059	**800-252-4670***	908-903-2000
Odyssey Re Holdings Corp 300 First Stamford Pl	Stamford	CT	06902	**866-745-4440**	203-977-8000
Ohio Casualty Insurance Co 9450 SewaRd Rd	Fairfield	OH	45014	**800-843-6446**	513-603-2400
Ohio Indemnity Co 250 E Broad St 7th Fl	Columbus	OH	43215	**800-628-8581**	614-228-2800
Old Dominion Insurance Co 4601 Touchton Rd E Ste 330 Ste 3400	Jacksonville	FL	32246	**800-226-0875**	904-642-3000
OneBeacon Insurance Group N 605 US-169 Ste 800	Plymouth	MN	55441	**800-662-0156**	781-332-7000
Oregon Mutual Insurance Co PO Box 808	McMinnville	OR	97128	**800-888-2141**	503-472-2141
Pacific Specialty Insurance Co 3601 Haven Ave	Menlo Park	CA	94025	**800-962-1172**	
Peerless Insurance Co 62 Maple Ave	Keene	NH	03431	**800-542-5385**	603-352-3221
Pekin Insurance (FAIA) 2505 Ct St	Pekin	IL	61558	**800-322-0160**	309-346-1161
Penn National Insurance Co 2 N Second St PO Box 2361	Harrisburg	PA	17101	**800-388-4764**	717-234-4941
Pennsylvania Manufacturers Assn Co 380 Sentry Pkwy	Blue Bell	PA	19422	**800-222-2749**	
Pharmacists Mutual Insurance Co 808 Hwy 18 W PO Box 370 *General	Algona	IA	50511	**800-247-5930***	
Philadelphia Consolidated Holding Corp 231 Saint Asaph's Rd Ste 100	Bala Cynwyd	PA	19004	**888-647-8639**	610-617-7900
Philadelphia Contributionship Insurance Co 212 S Fourth St *Cust Svc	Philadelphia	PA	19106	**888-627-1752***	215-627-1752
Pinnacol Assurance 7501 E Lowry Blvd	Denver	CO	80230	**800-873-7242**	303-361-4000
Preferred Employers Insurance Co PO Box 85478 *Cust Svc	San Diego	CA	92186	**888-472-9001***	866-472-9602
Preferred Mutual Insurance Co 1 Preferred Way	New Berlin	NY	13411	**800-333-7642**	607-847-6161
Princeton Excess & Surplus Lines Insurance Co 555 College Rd E	Princeton	NJ	08543	**800-544-2378**	609-243-4200
Princeton Insurance Co 746 Alexander Rd PO Box 5322	Princeton	NJ	08540	**800-334-0588**	609-452-9404
Progressive Casualty Insurance Co 6300 Wilson Mills Rd Campus E	Mayfield Village	OH	44143	**800-776-4737**	440-461-5000
Providence Mutual Fire Insurance Co 340 E Ave	Warwick	RI	02886	**877-763-1800**	401-827-1800
Prudential Financial Inc 751 Broad St *NYSE: PRU*	Newark	NJ	07102	**800-843-7625**	973-802-6000
QBE Holdings Inc Wall St Plz 88 Pine St	New York	NY	10005	**800-362-5448**	212-422-1212
Quincy Mutual Fire Insurance Co 57 Washington St	Quincy	MA	02169	**800-899-1116**	
Republic Western Insurance Co 2721 N Central Ave *Claims	Phoenix	AZ	85004	**800-528-7134***	
RLI Insurance Co 9025 N Lindbergh Dr	Peoria	IL	61615	**800-331-4929**	309-692-1000
Royal & SunAlliance Insurance Co of Canada (RSA) 18 York St Ste 800	Toronto	ON	M5J2T8	**800-268-8406**	416-366-7511

Company / Address	City	State	ZIP	Toll-Free	Phone
RTW Inc 8500 Normandale Lk Blvd Ste 1400 PO Box 390327 *Sales	Bloomington	MN	55437	800-789-2242*	952-893-0403
Rural Mutual Insurance Company Inc 1241 John Q Hammons Dr PO Box 5555	Madison	WI	53705	800-362-7881	608-836-5525
Safe Auto Insurance Co 4 Easton Oval PO Box 182109	Columbus	OH	43219	800-723-3288	614-231-0200
Safeway Insurance Group 790 Pasquinelli Dr	Westmont	IL	60559	800-273-0300	630-887-8300
Sagamore Insurance Co 111 Congressional Blvd Ste 500	Carmel	IN	46032	800-317-9402	
Savers Property & Casualty Insurance Co 11880 College Blvd Ste 500	Overland Park	KS	66210	800-482-2726	800-351-1411
Scottsdale Insurance Co 8877 N Gainey Ctr Dr	Scottsdale	AZ	85258	800-423-7675	480-365-4000
Secura Insurance Cos PO Box 819	Appleton	WI	54912	800-558-3405	920-739-3161
Sentry Insurance Co 2 Technology Park Dr	Westford	MA	01886	800-373-6879	
Sompo Japan Insurance Co of America 777 Third Ave 28th Fl	New York	NY	10017	800-208-3614	212-416-1200
SS Nesbitt & Co Inc 3500 Blue Lake Dr	Birmingham	AL	35243	800-422-3223	205-262-2700
Star Insurance Co 26255 American Dr	Southfield	MI	48034	800-482-2726	248-358-4020
State Auto Property & Casualty Insurance Co 518 E Broad St	Columbus	OH	43215	800-444-9950	614-464-5000
State Compensation Insurance Fund PO Box 8192	Pleasanton	CA	94588	866-721-3498	415-565-1234
State Farm Insurance 333 First Commerce Dr	Aurora	ON	L4G8A4	877-659-1570	
STOPS Inc 8855 Grissom Pkwy	Titusville	FL	32780	866-632-2161	321-383-4111
Texas Mutual Insurance Co 6210 E Hwy 290	Austin	TX	78723	888-532-5246	512-224-3800
Tokio Marine Life 230 Pk Ave	New York	NY	10169	800-628-2796	212-297-6600
Topa Insurance Corp 24025 Park Sorrento Ste 300	Calabasas	CA	91302	877-353-8672	310-201-0451
Tower Group Inc 120 Broadway 14th Fl *NASDAQ: TWGP*	New York	NY	10271	877-883-6599	212-655-2000
Transcontinental Insurance Co 333 S Wabash Ave CNA Ctr	Chicago	IL	60604	800-262-2000	312-822-5000
Transportation Insurance Co 333 S Wabash Ave	Chicago	IL	60604	800-437-8854	312-822-5000
ULLICO Casualty Co 1625 I St NW	Washington	DC	20006	800-431-5425	
Unico American Corp 23251 Mulholland Dr	Woodland Hills	CA	91364	800-669-9800	818-591-9800
Union Standard Insurance Co 122 W Carpenter Fwy Ste 350	Irving	TX	75039	800-444-0049	972-719-2400
United Fire & Casualty Co 118 Second Ave SE *NASDAQ: UFCS*	Cedar Rapids	IA	52407	800-332-7977	319-399-5700
United Heartland Inc PO Box 3026	Milwaukee	WI	53201	866-206-5851	
United National Group 3 Bala Plz E Ste 300	Bala Cynwyd	PA	19004	800-333-0352	610-664-1500
United National Insurance Co 3 Bala Plz E Ste 300	Bala Cynwyd	PA	19004	800-333-0352	610-664-1500
Universal Insurance Holding Inc (UIH) 1110 W Commerical Blvd Ste 100 *NYSE: UVE*	Fort Lauderdale	FL	33309	800-509-5586	
USA Workers' Injury Network 1250 S Capital of Texas Hwy Bldg 3 Ste 500 *Cust Svc	Austin	TX	78746	800-872-0020*	
USAA Property & Casualty Insurance Group 9800 Fredericksburg Rd	San Antonio	TX	78288	800-531-8722	210-531-8722
Utica First Insurance Co 5981 Airport Rd	Oriskany	NY	13424	800-456-4556	315-736-8211
Utica National Insurance Group 180 Genesee St	New Hartford	NY	13413	800-274-1914	315-734-2000
Vermont Mutual Insurance Co 89 State St PO Box 188	Montpelier	VT	05601	800-451-5000	802-223-2341
Victoria Insurance 22901 Millcreek Blvd	Cleveland	OH	44122	800-888-8424	216-896-6990
Vigilant Insurance Co 15 Mtn View Rd *Claims	Warren	NJ	07059	800-252-4670*	908-903-2000
West Bend Mutual Insurance Co 1900 S 18th Ave	West Bend	WI	53095	800-236-5010	262-334-5571
Western National Mutual Insurance Co 5350 W 78th St	Edina	MN	55439	800-862-6070	952-835-5350
Western Reserve Group, The 1685 Cleveland Rd	Wooster	OH	44691	800-362-0426	330-262-9060
Wisconsin Reinsurance Corp 2810 City View Dr	Madison	WI	53707	800-939-9473	608-242-4500
Zenith Insurance Co PO Box 9055	Van Nuys	CA	91409	800-440-5020	818-713-1000

391-5 Surety Insurance

Company / Address	City	State	ZIP	Toll-Free	Phone
AMBAC Assurance Corp 1 State St Plaza 15th Fl	New York	NY	10004	800-221-1854	212-658-7470
American Public Life Insurance Co 2305 Lakeland Dr PO Box 925	Jackson	MS	39205	800-256-8606	601-936-6600
Bond Pro LLC 1501 E Second Ave	Tampa	FL	33605	888-789-4985	
Catholic Mutual Group 10843 Old Mill Rd	Omaha	NE	68154	800-228-6108	402-551-8765
Central Insurance Cos 800 S Washington St	Van Wert	OH	45891	800-736-7000	419-238-1010
Century Insurance Group 465 Cleveland Ave	Westerville	OH	43082	877-855-8462	614-895-2000
Chubb Specialty Insurance 82 Hopmeadow St	Simsbury	CT	06070	800-252-4670	860-408-2000
CNA Surety Corp 333 S Wabash Ave *NYSE: L*	Chicago	IL	60604	877-672-6115	312-822-5000
Copic Insurance Co 7351 Lowry Blvd	Denver	CO	80230	800-421-1834	720-858-6000
Dentists Insurance Co 1201 K St 17th Fl	Sacramento	CA	95814	800-733-0634	800-733-0633
Doctors' Co, The 185 Greenwood Rd	Napa	CA	94558	800-421-2368	
Euler Hermes ACI 800 Red Brook Blvd 4th Fl	Owings Mills	MD	21117	877-883-3224	410-753-0753
Everest Reinsurance Co 477 Martinsville Rd	Liberty Corner	NJ	07938	800-269-6660	908-604-3000
Federated Mutual Insurance Co 121 E Pk Sq PO Box 328	Owatonna	MN	55060	800-533-0472	507-455-5200
Financial Guaranty Insurance Co 125 Pk Ave 6th Fl	New York	NY	10017	800-352-0001	212-312-3000
Fireman's Fund Insurance Co 1465 N McDowell Blvd	Petaluma	CA	94954	866-386-3932	
First Insurance Company of Hawaii Ltd 1100 Ward Ave PO Box 2866	Honolulu	HI	96803	800-272-5202	808-527-7777
Illinois State Medical Inter-Insurance Exchange (ISMIE) 20 N Michigan Ave Ste 700	Chicago	IL	60602	800-782-4767	312-782-2749
Insurance Company of the West 11455 El Camino Real	San Diego	CA	92130	800-877-1111	858-350-2400
International Fidelity Insurance Co (IFIC) 1 Newark Ctr 20th Fl	Newark	NJ	07102	800-333-4167	973-624-7200
JP Everhart & Co PO Box 2683	Waco	TX	76702	888-622-8575	
Kansas Medical Mutual Insurance Co (KaMMCO) 623 SW Tenth Ave Ste 200	Topeka	KS	66612	800-232-2259	785-232-2224
Life of the South Insurance Co 10151 Deerwood Pk Blvd Bldg 100	Jacksonville	FL	32256	800-888-2738	904-350-9660
Louisiana Medical Mutual Insurance Co 1 Galleria Blvd Ste 700	Metairie	LA	70001	800-452-2120	
Media/Professional Insurance Inc 1201 Walnut Ste 1800	Kansas City	MO	64106	866-282-0565	816-471-6118
Medical Assurance Inc 100 Brookwood Pl Ste 300 *Cust Svc	Birmingham	AL	35209	800-282-6242*	205-877-4400
Medical Mutual Group 700 Spring Forest Rd	Raleigh	NC	27609	800-662-7917	919-872-7117
Medical Mutual Insurance Company of Maine 1 City Ctr Ste 9	Portland	ME	04112	800-942-2791	207-775-2791
Medical Mutual Liability Insurance Society of Maryland 225 International Cir PO Box 8016	Hunt Valley	MD	21030	800-492-0193	410-785-0050
Medical Protective Co 5814 Reed Rd	Fort Wayne	IN	46835	800-463-3776	260-485-9622
Mortgage Guaranty Insurance Corp 270 E Kilbourn Ave	Milwaukee	WI	53202	800-558-9900	414-347-6480
NCMIC Insurance Co 14001 University Ave	Clive	IA	50325	800-769-2000	515-313-4500
Norcal Mutual Insurance Company Inc 560 Davis St	San Francisco	CA	94111	800-652-1051	415-397-9700
Old Republic Insured Automotive Services Inc 8282 S Memorial Dr	Tulsa	OK	74133	800-331-3780	918-307-1000
Old Republic Surety 445 S Moorlands Rd Ste 200	Brookfield	WI	53005	800-217-1792	262-797-2640
Pekin Life Insurance Co 2505 Ct St *OTC: PKIN*	Pekin	IL	61558	800-322-0160	309-346-1161
Penn National Insurance Co 2 N Second St PO Box 2361	Harrisburg	PA	17101	800-388-4764	717-234-4941
Pennsylvania Medical Society Liability Insurance Co (PMSLIC) 1700 Bent Creek Blvd PO Box 2080	Mechanicsburg	PA	17050	800-445-1212	844-466-7225
Podiatry Insurance Company of America 3000 Meridian Blvd Ste 400	Franklin	TN	37067	800-251-5727	615-984-2005
Pre-Paid Legal Services Inc 1 Pre-Paid Way	Ada	OK	74820	800-654-7757	580-436-1234
Princeton Insurance Co 746 Alexander Rd PO Box 5322	Princeton	NJ	08540	800-334-0588	609-452-9404
ProAssurance 20 Allen Ave Ste 430	Saint Louis	MO	63119	800-282-6242	314-961-7700
ProMutual Group 13th Fl 4th Fl	Boston	MA	02111	800-225-6168	
Protective Insurance Co 111 Congressional Blvd Ste 500	Carmel	IN	46032	800-644-5501	
Radian Asset Assurance Inc *Radian Group Inc, The* 335 Madison Ave 25th Fl	New York	NY	10017	877-723-4261	212-983-3100
Radian Group Inc 1601 Market St *NYSE: RDN*	Philadelphia	PA	19103	800-523-1988	215-564-6600
Reciprocal of America 4200 Innslake Dr Ste 102	Glen Allen	VA	23060	800-284-8847	804-747-8600
Republic Mortgage Insurance Co 101 N Cherry St Ste 101	Winston-Salem	NC	27101	800-999-7642	
RLI Insurance Co 9025 N Lindbergh Dr	Peoria	IL	61615	800-331-4929	309-692-1000
Rose & Kiernan Inc 99 Troy Rd	East Greenbush	NY	12061	866-488-6582	518-244-4245
State Volunteer Mutual Insurance Co 101 W Pk Dr Ste 300	Brentwood	TN	37027	800-342-2239	615-377-1999
Surety Group Inc 3715 Northside Pkwy NW Ste 1-315	Atlanta	GA	30327	800-486-8211	404-352-8211
Texas Hospital Insurance Exchange 8310 N Capital of Texas Hwy Ste 250	Austin	TX	78731	800-792-0060	512-451-5775
Texas Lawyers Insurance Exchange (TLIE) 1801 S MoPac Ste 300	Austin	TX	78746	800-252-9332	512-480-9074
Transamerica 4333 Edgewood Rd NE	Cedar Rapids	IA	52499	800-852-4678	319-355-8511
Triad Guaranty Insurance Corp 101 S Stratford Rd *Cust Svc	Winston-Salem	NC	27104	888-691-8074*	336-723-1282

Company	Address	City	State	ZIP	Toll-Free	Phone
ULLICO Casualty Co	1625 I St NW	Washington	DC	20006	**800-431-5425**	
United Guaranty Corp (UGC)	230 N Elm St	Greensboro	NC	27401	**800-334-8966**	
United National Group	3 Bala Plz E Ste 300	Bala Cynwyd	PA	19004	**800-333-0352**	610-664-1500
Utica National Insurance Group	180 Genesee St	New Hartford	NY	13413	**800-274-1914**	315-734-2000
Vision Financial Corp	PO Box 506	Keene	NH	03431	**800-793-0223**	
Warranty Group Inc, The	175 W Jackson 11th Fl	Chicago	IL	60604	**800-621-2130**	312-356-3000
Western World Insurance Co	400 Parson's Pond Dr	Franklin Lakes	NJ	07417	**888-847-8600**	201-847-8600
XL Specialty Insurance Co	70 Seaview Ave	Stamford	CT	06902	**877-263-7995**	203-964-5200
Zurich North America	1400 American Ln	Schaumburg	IL	60196	**800-382-2150**	847-605-6000

391-6 Title Insurance

Most title insurance companies also provide other real estate services such as escrow, flood certification, appraisals, etc.

Company	Address	City	State	ZIP	Toll-Free	Phone
Attorney's Title Insurance Fund Inc	6545 Corporate Ctr Blvd	Orlando	FL	32822	**800-336-3863**	407-240-3863
Chicago Title & Trust Co	171 N Clark St	Chicago	IL	60601	**800-621-1919**	312-223-2000
Commonwealth Land Title Insurance Co	601 Riverside Ave	Jacksonville	FL	32204	**888-866-3684**	
Community Title & Escrow Ltd	2600 State St Bldg D	Alton	IL	62002	**800-854-4049**	618-466-7755
Entitle Direct Group Inc	281 Tresser Blvd 6th Fl	Stamford	CT	06901	**877-936-8485**	203-724-1150
Fidelity National Title Group Inc	601 Riverside Ave	Jacksonville	FL	32204	**888-866-3684**	904-854-8100
Fidelity National Title Insurance Co	7025 N Scottsdale Rd	Scottsdale	AZ	85258	**888-934-3354**	480-344-6400
Fidelity National Title Insurance Company of Oregon	900 SW Fifth Ave Mezzanine Level	Portland	OR	97204	**888-934-3354**	503-223-8338
First American Corp	1 First American Way *NYSE: FAF*	Santa Ana	CA	92707	**800-854-3643**	714-250-3000
Hanover Insurance Co	440 Lincoln St	Worcester	MA	01653	**800-853-0456**	508-855-1000
Meridian Title Corp	202 S Michigan St	South Bend	IN	46601	**800-777-1574**	574-232-5845
Mississippi Valley Title Insurance Co	315 Tom Bigbee St	Jackson	MS	39201	**800-647-2124**	601-969-0222
Monroe Title Insurance Corp	47 W Main St	Rochester	NY	14614	**800-966-6763**	585-232-4950
North American Title Co	1855 Gateway Blvd Ste 600	Concord	CA	94520	**800-566-0370**	925-935-5599
Northpoint Escrow & Title LLC	10800 NE Eighth St Ste 200	Bellevue	WA	98004	**877-678-1678**	425-453-8880
Old Republic National Title Insurance Co (ORTIG)	400 Second Ave S	Minneapolis	MN	55401	**800-328-4441**	612-371-1111
Stewart Information Services Corp	1980 Post Oak Blvd Ste 800 *NYSE: STC*	Houston	TX	77056	**800-729-1900**	713-625-8100
Stewart REI Data Inc	1980 Post Oak Blvd Ste 800	Houston	TX	77056	**800-729-1900**	212-922-0050
Stewart Title Guaranty Co	1980 Post Oak Blvd Ste 800	Houston	TX	77056	**800-729-1900**	713-625-8100
Title Guaranty of Hawaii Inc	235 Queen St	Honolulu	HI	96813	**800-222-3229**	808-533-6261
Title Resources Guaranty Co (TRGC)	8111 LBJ Fwy Ste 1200	Dallas	TX	75251	**800-526-8018**	972-644-6500
US Recordings Inc	2925 Country Dr	Little Canada	MN	55117	**877-272-5250**	651-765-6400
USHEALTH Group Inc	300 Burnett St Ste 200	Fort Worth	TX	76102	**800-387-9027**	

391-7 Travel Insurance

Most of the companies listed here are insurance agencies and brokerages that specialize in selling travel insurance policies, rather than the insurers who underwrite the policies.

Company	Address	City	State	ZIP	Toll-Free	Phone
Access America	2805 N Parham Rd	Richmond	VA	23294	**800-284-8300**	
All Aboard Benefits	6162 E Mockingird Ln Ste 104	Dallas	TX	75214	**800-462-2322**	214-821-6677
Continental Assurance Co	333 S Wabash Ave	Chicago	IL	60604	**800-251-2148**	312-822-5000
Highway To Health Inc	1 Radnor Corporate Ctr Ste 100	Radnor	PA	19087	**888-243-2358**	
Ingle International	460 Richmond St W Ste 100	Toronto	ON	M5V1Y1	**800-360-3234**	416-730-8488
Insurance Consultants International	19760 Knights Crossing Ste 1C	Monument	CO	80132	**800-576-2674**	719-573-9080
International SOS Assistance Inc	3600 Horizon Blvd Ste 300	Trevose	PA	19053	**800-441-2668**	215-244-1500
Pan-American Life Insurance Co	601 Poydras St *Life Ins	New Orleans	LA	70130	**877-939-4550***	
Travel Insured International	855 Winding Brook Dr PO Box 280568	Glastonbury	CT	06033	**800-243-3174**	
Wallach & Company Inc	107 W Federal St	Middleburg	VA	20118	**800-237-6615**	540-687-3166

392 INTERCOM EQUIPMENT & SYSTEMS

Company	Address	City	State	ZIP	Toll-Free	Phone
Anacom General Corp	1240 S Claudina St	Anaheim	CA	92805	**800-955-9540**	714-774-8484
Clever Devices Ltd	300 Crossways Pk Dr	Woodbury	NY	11797	**800-872-6129**	516-433-6100
Crest Healthcare Supply	195 Third St	Dassel	MN	55325	**800-328-8908**	320-275-3382
David Clark Company Inc	360 Franklin St *Cust Svc	Worcester	MA	01615	**800-298-6235***	508-751-5800
Lee Dan Communications Inc	155 Adams Ave	Hauppauge	NY	11788	**800-231-1414**	631-231-1414

393 INTERIOR DESIGN

Company	Address	City	State	ZIP	Toll-Free	Phone
24 Asset Management Corp	2020 Camino del Rio N Ste 900	San Diego	CA	92108	**855-414-2424**	
Accent	7171 Mercy Rd Ste 200	Omaha	NE	68106	**800-397-7243**	402-397-9920
Accord Creditor Services LLC	PO Box 10005	Newnan	GA	30271	**800-373-0760**	
AdHub LLC, The	146 Alexander St	Rochester	NY	14607	**866-712-2986**	585-442-2585
Ark TeleServices	2 E Merrick Rd	Valley Stream	NY	11580	**800-898-5367**	
ARS National Services Inc	201 W Grand Ave	Escondido	CA	92025	**800-456-5053**	
Arvato Digital Services LLC	29011 Commerce Ctr Dr	Valencia	CA	91355	**800-223-1478**	
ATG Technologies Inc	2639 N Monroe St Cedars Bldg B Ste 200	Tallahassee	FL	32303	**800-775-7790**	
BizQuest LLC	2100 E Rt 66 Ste 200	Glendora	CA	91740	**888-280-3815**	
Building Service Inc (BSI)	W222 N630 Cheaney Rd	Waukesha	WI	53186	**866-353-3600**	262-955-6400
C m Buck & Associates Inc	6850 Guion Rd	Indianapolis	IN	46268	**800-382-3961**	317-293-5704
Canada Media Fund	50 Wellington St E Ste 202	Toronto	ON	M5E1C8	**877-975-0766**	416-214-4400
CardTrak LLC	4055 Tamiami Trail	Port Charlotte	FL	33952	**800-344-7714**	
Carenet Healthcare Services	11845 Interstate 10 W Ste 400	San Antonio	TX	78230	**800-809-7000**	
Cascade Receivables Management LLC	101 Second St Ste 100	Petaluma	CA	94952	**888-417-1531**	
CBE Companies Inc	1309 Technology Pkwy	Cedar Falls	IA	50613	**800-925-6686**	
Ci Radar LLC	4046 Wetherburn Way Ste 1	Norcross	GA	30092	**888-421-0617**	678-680-2103
CLASSIC HOSTESS INC	2 Skillman St Ste 313	Brooklyn	NY	11205	**888-280-6539**	
Cleanwise Inc	1100 E Woodfield Rd Ste 200	Schaumburg	IL	60173	**877-255-5230**	
CMS Mid-Atlantic Inc	295 Totowa Rd	Totowa	NJ	07512	**800-267-1981**	
CO-OP Financial Services Inc	9692 Haven Ave	Rancho Cucamonga	CA	91730	**800-782-9042**	
CoinLab Inc	811 1st Ave Ste 480	Seattle	WA	98104	**855-522-2646**	
Corrective Education Company LLC	2825 Cottonwood Pkwy Ste 500	Salt Lake City	UT	84121	**877-318-0983**	
D P Brown of Saginaw Inc	2845 Universal Dr	Saginaw	MI	48603	**877-799-9400**	989-799-9400
Decorating Den Systems Inc	8659 Commerce Dr	Easton	MD	21601	**800-332-3367**	410-822-9001
Digital Dialogue LLC	3252 University Dr Ste 165	Auburn Hills	MI	48326	**800-205-4268**	
DirectEmployers.com	9002 N Purdue Rd Quad III Ste 100	Indianapolis	IN	46268	**866-268-6206**	317-874-9000
eCollect LLC	5000 Euclid Ave Ste 4403	Cleveland	OH	44103	**888-569-6001**	
Etheridge Printing Co	4434 Mcewen Rd	Dallas	TX	75244	**800-834-2709**	214-827-8151
First Reliance Holdings LLC	275 N Pointe Pkwy Ste 60	Amherst	NY	14228	**877-495-8938**	
Fisher Group Inc	3571 South 300 West	Salt Lake City	UT	84115	**800-365-8920**	
Fortitude Business Solutions LLC	PO Box 2095	Daphne	AL	36526	**877-577-2644**	
GCS Service Inc	370 Wabasha St N	St. Paul	MN	55102	**800-822-2303**	
Global R&D Consulting Group	3200 Autoroute Laval Ouest	Laval	GA	30022	**866-770-5577**	
Goldec Hamm's Manufacturing Ltd	6760 65 Ave	Red Deer	AB	T4P1A5	**800-661-1665**	403-343-6607
Good Leads	224 Main St Unit 2B	Salem	NH	03079	**866-894-5323**	603-870-8150
Grant & Weber Inc	26610 Agoura Rd Ste 209	Calabasas	CA	91302	**800-333-1656**	818-871-7700
Imagine Advertising & Publishing Inc	6141 Crooked Creek Rd	Norcross	GA	30092	**866-832-3214**	770-734-0966
Influence Technologies Inc	1342 La Colina Dr	Tustin	CA	92780	**877-420-2766**	
Innovadex LLC	7930 Santa Fe 3rd Fl	Overland Park	KS	66204	**877-292-7279**	913-307-9010
InstaGift LLC	117 West Glenwood Dr	Birmingham	AL	35209	**877-870-3463**	
Intland GmbH	968 Inverness Way	Sunnyvale	CA	94087	**866-468-5210**	
Invisible Hand Networks Inc	670 Broadway Ste 302	New York	NY	10012	**866-637-5286**	212-400-7416

Classified Section

Company / Address	City	State	Zip	Toll-Free	Phone
JobDiva 116 John St. Ste 1406	New York	NY	10038	**866-562-3482**	
Jomax LLC 14100 N 83rd Ave Ste 235	Peoria	AZ	85381	**888-866-0721**	
Kay Green Design Inc 859 Outer Rd	Orlando	FL	32814	**800-226-5186**	407-246-7155
Kear IT Inc 1510-H Caton Ctr Dr	Baltimore	MD	21227	**877-532-7481**	
Lehman Hardware & Appliances Inc 4779 Kidron Rd	Dalton	OH	44618	**888-438-5346**	
Lewellen & Best Displays Inc 101 Knell St	Montgomery	IL	60538	**800-250-7565**	630-896-2500
Loanio Inc 25 Smith St Ste 301	Nanuet	NY	10954	**800-624-8830**	
Logic PD Inc 6201 Bury Dr	Eden Prairie	MN	55346	**855-461-3802**	952-941-8071
Matrix Companies, The 7162 Reading Rd Ste 250	Cincinnati	OH	45237	**877-550-7973**	513-351-1222
MGM Mirage Design Group Inc 3260 Industrial Rd	Las Vegas	NV	89109	**800-929-1111**	866-761-7111
Mo-Tires Ltd 2830 5 Ave N	Lethbridge	AB	T1H0P1	**800-774-3888**	403-329-4533
MTI America PO Box 667140	Pompano Beach	FL	33066	**800-553-2155**	
myFreightWorld LLC 7133 W 95th St	Overland Park	KS	66212	**877-549-9438**	
Networld Media Group LLC 13100 Eastpoint Park Blvd Ste 100	Louisville	KY	40223	**877-441-7545**	
Nitelines USA Inc 3065 Peachtree Industrial Blvd Ste 210	Duluth	GA	30097	**877-337-2563**	
Noritsu Technical Services 6900 Noritsu Ave	Buena Park	CA	90620	**888-435-7448**	
Pioneer Magnetics 1745 Berkeley St	Santa Monica	CA	90404	**800-269-6426**	310-829-6751
Polygon Network PO Box 4806	Dillon	CO	80435	**800-221-4435**	
Primeritus Financial Services Inc 440 Metroplex Dr	Nashville	TN	37211	**888-833-4238**	
QualiTest Ltd 1139 Post Rd	Fairfield	CT	06824	**877-882-9540**	
Quippi Corp 444 S Cedros Ave Ste 410	La Jolla	CA	92037	**888-978-4774**	
RealtyBid International Inc 3225 Rainbow Dr Ste 248	Rainbow City	AL	35906	**877-518-5600**	
Recruiting Toolbox PO Box 2573	Redmond	WA	98073	**888-823-2030**	425-557-2100
Regatta Travel Solutions Inc 325 Winding River Ln Ste 201B	Charlottesville	VA	22911	**800-605-5093**	
Renbor Sales Solutions Inc 256 Thornway Ave	Thornhill	ON	L4J7X8	**855-257-2537**	416-671-3555
Rev.com Inc 251 Kearny St 8th Fl	San Francisco	CA	94108	**888-369-0701**	
Sacor Financial Inc 1911 Douglas Blvd 85-126	Roseville	CA	95661	**866-556-0231**	
Sales Gauge 1186 Old Marlborough Rd	Concord	MA	01742	**877-406-0493**	781-910-0077
Sea Pearl Seafood Company Inc 14120 Shell Belt Rd	Bayou La Batre	AL	36509	**800-872-8804**	251-824-2129
Setina Manufacturing Company Inc 2926 Yelm Hwy Se	Olympia	WA	98501	**800-426-2627**	
Smart LLC Smart TuitionOne Woodbridge Ctr Ste 800	Woodbridge	NJ	07095	**866-395-2986**	
Springboard Nonprofit Consumer Credit Management Inc 4351 Latham St	Riverside	CA	92501	**888-425-3453**	
Star Exhibits & Environments Inc 6920 93rd Ave N	Minneapolis	MN	55445	**800-419-7827**	763-561-4655
StreamSend 78 York St	Sacramento	CA	95814	**877-439-4078**	916-326-5407
TaskUs Inc 3233 Donald Douglas Loop S Ste 3	Santa Monica	CA	90405	**888-400-8275**	
TernPro Inc 1431 Washington Blvd Apt 1703	Detroit	MI	48226	**888-483-8779**	
Tetra Tech Architects & Engineers Cornell Business & Technology Park 10 Brown Rd	Ithaca	NY	14850	**877-882-7241**	607-277-7100
TMP Direct 600 International Dr	Mount Olive	NJ	07828	**800-328-2439**	
Trading Post of Kittery 301 US Rte 1 PO Box 904	Kittery	ME	03904	**800-872-4867**	
Training Industry Inc 401 Harrison Oaks Blvd Ste 300	Cary	NC	27513	**866-298-4203**	
TrueAccord Corp 148 Townsend St Ste 26	San Francisco	CA	94107	**866-611-2731**	
Uhl Company Inc 9065 zachary ln n	Maple grove	MN	55369	**800-815-3820**	763-425-7226
UsTrendy INC 1842 Beacon St Ste 404	Brookline	MA	02445	**888-535-1187**	
Venuelabs 505 Fifth Ave S Ste 300	Seattle	WA	98104	**866-333-7328**	425-633-1510
Villa Lighting Supply Inc 2929 Chouteau Ave	Saint Louis	MO	63103	**800-325-0963**	
Walls 360 Inc 5054 Bond St	Las Vegas	NV	89118	**888-244-9969**	
Warranty Life Services Inc 4152 Meridian St Ste 105-29	Bellingham	WA	98226	**888-927-7269**	
Worldwide Court Reporters 3000 Weslayan St Ste 235	Houston	TX	77027	**800-745-1101**	713-572-2000
Wyse Meter Solutions Inc RPO Newmarket Court PO Box 95530	Newmarket	ON	L3Y8J8	**866-681-9465**	
Yale Club of New York City, The 50 Vanderbilt Ave	New York	NY	10017	**800-335-9253**	212-716-2100

394 INTERNET BACKBONE PROVIDERS

Companies that are, in effect, Internet service providers for Internet Service Providers (ISPs).

Company / Address	City	State	Zip	Toll-Free	Phone
BT Americas Inc 2160 E Grand Ave	El Segundo	CA	90245	**888-767-2988**	408-330-2700
Cogent Communications Group Inc 1015 31st St NW *NASDAQ: CCOI*	Washington	DC	20007	**877-875-4432**	202-295-4200
iPass Inc 3800 Bridge Pkwy *NASDAQ: IPAS*	Redwood Shores	CA	94065	**877-236-3807**	650-232-4100
Level 3 Communications Inc 1025 Eldorado Blvd *NYSE: LVLT*	Broomfield	CO	80021	**877-453-8353**	720-888-1000
nFrame Inc 701 Congressional Blvd Ste 100	Carmel	IN	46032	**877-570-7827**	317-805-3759
SunGard Availability Services 680 E Swedesford Rd	Wayne	PA	19087	**800-468-7483**	484-582-2000
Verio Inc 8300 E Maplewood Ave Ste 400 *Sales	Greenwood Village	CO	80111	**800-438-8374***	561-912-2555
Verizon Business 1 Verizon Way *Cust Svc	Basking Ridge	NJ	07920	**877-297-7816***	908-559-2000
XO Communications Inc 13865 Sunrise Vly Dr	Herndon	VA	20171	**866-349-0134**	703-547-2000

395 INTERNET BROADCASTING

Company / Address	City	State	Zip	Toll-Free	Phone
Audible Inc 1 Washington Pk	Newark	NJ	07102	**888-283-5051**	973-820-0400
BankCard Services 3055 Wilshire Blvd 3rd Fl	Los Angeles	CA	90010	**888-339-0100**	213-365-1122
Compugen Inc 100 Via Renzo Dr	Richmond Hill	ON	L4S0B8	**800-387-5045**	905-707-2000
Eventure Interactive Inc 3420 Bristol St Fl 6	Costa Mesa	CA	92626	**855-986-5669**	
Media Temple Inc 8520 National Blvd Bldg A	Culver City	CA	90232	**877-578-4000**	
OMT Inc 1-1717 Dublin Ave	Winnipeg	MB	R3H0H2	**888-665-0501**	204-786-3994
Yodle Inc 330 W 34th St 18th Fl	New York	NY	10001	**877-276-5104**	

396 INTERNET DOMAIN NAME REGISTRARS

Company / Address	City	State	Zip	Toll-Free	Phone
Acumenex Com 2201 Brant St	Burlington	ON	L7P3N8	**877-788-5028**	
AITDomains.com 421 Maiden Ln	Fayetteville	NC	28301	**877-549-2881**	
Allied Infosecurity Inc 1009 W 9th Ave Ste B	King Of Prussia	PA	19406	**866-240-0094**	
Best Registration Services Inc 1418 S Third St	Louisville	KY	40208	**800-977-3475**	502-637-4528
Domain-It! 9891 Montgomery Rd *General	Cincinnati	OH	45242	**866-269-2355***	513-351-4222
DomainPeople Inc 550 Burrard St Ste 200 Bentall Twr 5	Vancouver	BC	V6C2B5	**877-734-3667**	604-639-1680
Dotster 8100 NE Pkwy Dr Ste 300 PO Box 821066	Vancouver	WA	98682	**800-401-5250**	360-449-5800
Dotster Inc PO Box 821066	Vancouver	WA	98682	**800-401-5250**	360-253-2210
Dynadot LLC PO Box 345 *Cust Svc	San Mateo	CA	94401	**866-652-2039***	650-585-1961
easyDNS 219 Dufferin St Ste 304A	Toronto	ON	M6K3J1	**888-677-4741**	416-535-8672
Etera Solutions Llc 354 TurnPk St Ste 203	Canton	MA	02021	**888-536-6515**	
Jsa Technologies 201 Main St Ste 1320	Fort Worth	TX	76102	**877-572-8324**	
Livecareer Inc 1432 Washington St	San Francisco	CA	94109	**800-652-8430**	
Mindbody Online 4051 Broad St Ste 220	Sn Luis Obisp	CA	93401	**877-755-4279**	
Moniker Online Services LLC 20 SW 27th Ave Ste 201	Pompano Beach	FL	33069	**800-688-6311**	
Name.com LLC 2500 E Second Ave 2nd Fl	Denver	CO	80206	**800-365-0006**	720-249-2374
Network Solutions LLC 13861 Sunrise Valley Dr Ste 300	Herndon	VA	20171	**800-361-5712**	703-668-4600
Omedix Inc 15849 N 71st St Ste 100	Scottsdale	AZ	85254	**877-866-3349**	
Piraeus Consulting LLC 1408 4th Ave, Ste 400	Seattle	WA	98101	**866-747-2387**	
PrimeConnections Contact Solutions LLC 301 Brazos St Ste 615	Austin	TX	78701	**866-976-2747**	
Register.com Inc 575 Eigth Ave 8th Fl	New York	NY	10018	**888-734-4783**	
SI Holdings 3267 Bee Caves Rd Ste 107	Austin	TX	78746	**866-551-4646**	
Terraine Inc 5912-A Toole Dr	Nashville	TN	37230	**800-531-1242**	
Threadpoint LLC 24881 Alicia Pkwy Ste E #310	Laguna Hills	CA	92653	**866-631-1595**	

397 INTERNET SEARCH ENGINES, PORTALS, DIRECTORIES

Name / Address	City	State	Zip	Toll-Free	Phone
Ancestry 360 W 4800 N	Provo	UT	84604	**800-262-3787**	801-705-7000
Ancestry.com 360 W 4800 N *Cust Svc	Provo	UT	84604	**800-262-3787***	801-705-7000
BioSpace Inc 90 New Montgomery St Ste 414	San Francisco	CA	94105	**888-246-7722**	877-277-7585
Genealogy.com 360 West 4800 North	Provo	UT	84604	**800-262-3787**	801-705-7000
HomeAdvisor 14023 Denver W Pkwy Ste 200	Golden	CO	80401	**800-474-1596**	303-963-7200
Hotelrooms.com Inc 108-18 Queens Blvd	Forest Hills	NY	11375	**800-486-7000**	718-730-6000
Law Engine 7660-H Fay Avenue Ste 342	La Jolla	CA	92037	**800-894-2889**	858-456-1234
NewsHub 100 Lombard St Ste 203	Toronto	ON	M5C1M3	**800-889-9487**	416-536-4827
Nursing Ctr 323 Norristown Rd Ste 200	Ambler	PA	19002	**800-346-7844**	800-787-8985
RootsWeb.com 360 W 4800 N	Provo	UT	84604	**800-262-3787**	801-705-7000
Tucows Inc 96 Mowat Ave *TSE: TC*	Toronto	ON	M6K3M1	**800-371-6992**	416-535-0123
Wired News Wired 520 Third St Ste 305	San Francisco	CA	94107	**800-769-4733**	
YELLOWPAGES.com LLC 208 S Akard	Dallas	TX	75202	**866-329-7118**	

398 INTERNET SERVICE PROVIDERS (ISPS)

Name / Address	City	State	Zip	Toll-Free	Phone
ABT Internet Inc 175 E Shore Rd	Great Neck	NY	11023	**800-367-3414**	516-829-5484
Access US 712 N Second St Ste 300	Saint Louis	MO	63102	**800-638-6373**	314-655-7700
Aplus.net Internet Services 3680 Victoria St N	Shoreview	MN	55126	**877-275-8763**	858-410-6929
AT & T Inc 175 E Houston St PO Box 2933 *NYSE: AT&T*	San Antonio	TX	78299	**800-351-7221**	210-821-4105
Cable One Inc 210 E Earll Drive	Phoenix	AZ	85012	**877-692-2253**	602-364-6000
Cincinnati Bell Inc 221 E Fourth St *NYSE: CBB*	Cincinnati	OH	45202	**800-387-3638**	513-397-9900
ClearSail Communications LLC 3950 Braxton	Houston	TX	77063	**888-905-0888**	713-230-2800
Direct Internet Access 141 Desiard St PO Box 7263	Monroe	LA	71201	**800-296-2249**	
DSLextreme.com 21540 Plummer St Ste A	Chatsworth	CA	91311	**866-243-8638**	
EarthLink Inc 1375 Peachtree St NE *NASDAQ: ELNK*	Atlanta	GA	30309	**866-383-3080**	404-815-0770
Expedient Communications 810 Parish St	Pittsburgh	PA	15220	**877-570-7827**	412-316-7800
Frontline Communications PO Box 98	Orangeburg	NY	10962	**888-376-6854**	
HughesNet 11717 Exploration Ln	Germantown	MD	20876	**866-347-3292**	301-428-5500
iSelect Internet Inc 1420 W Kettleman Ln Ste E	Lodi	CA	95242	**877-837-1427**	209-334-0496
Net Access Corp 2300 15th St Ste 300	Denver	CO	80202	**800-638-6336**	973-590-5000
NetZero Inc 21301 Burbank Blvd	Woodland Hills	CA	91367	**800-638-9376**	818-287-3000
New Edge Networks 3000 Columbia House Blvd Ste 106	Vancouver	WA	98661	**877-725-3343**	360-693-9009
ProtoSource Network 2511 W Shaw Ave Ste 102	Fresno	CA	93711	**866-490-8600**	
Road Runner Group 60 Columbus Cir 60 Columbus Cir	New York	NY	10023	**866-689-3678**	703-345-3422
TOAST.net 4841 Monroe St Ste 307	Toledo	OH	43623	**888-862-7863**	419-292-2200
Verio Inc 8300 E Maplewood Ave Ste 400 *Sales	Greenwood Village	CO	80111	**800-438-8374***	561-912-2555
Verizon Business 1 Verizon Way *Cust Svc	Basking Ridge	NJ	07920	**877-297-7816***	908-559-2000

399 INVENTORY SERVICES

Name / Address	City	State	Zip	Toll-Free	Phone
Douglas-Guardian Services Corp 14800 St Mary's Ln	Houston	TX	77079	**800-255-0552**	281-531-0500
MSI Inventory Service Corp PO Box 320129	Flowood	MS	39232	**800-820-1460**	601-939-0130
WIS International 9265 Sky Park Ct Ste 100	San Diego	CA	92123	**800-268-6848**	858-565-8111

400 INVESTIGATIVE SERVICES

SEE ALSO Security & Protective Services ; Information Retrieval Services (General) ; Public Records Search Services

Name / Address	City	State	Zip	Toll-Free	Phone
ASK Services Inc 42180 Ford Rd Ste 101	Canton	MI	48187	**888-416-1313**	734-983-9040
Aurico Reports Inc 116 W Eastman St	Arlington Heights	IL	60004	**866-255-1852**	
Bombet Cashio & Assoc 11220 N Harrells Ferry Rd	Baton Rouge	LA	70816	**800-256-5333**	225-275-0796
Camping Investigations 4427 N 27th Ave	Phoenix	AZ	85017	**800-862-8458**	602-864-7860
Capitol Detective Agency 2922 N 18th Pl	Phoenix	AZ	85016	**800-346-0347**	602-265-3462
Claims Verification Inc 6700 N Andrews Ave Ste 200	Ft. Lauderdale	FL	33309	**888-284-2000**	
Donan Engineering Co Inc 11321 Plantside Dr	Louisville	KY	40299	**800-482-5611**	
Douglas Baldwin & Assoc PO Box 1249	La Canada	CA	91012	**800-392-3950**	818-952-4433
Eastern Security Inc 303 Wyman St Ste 300	Waltham	MA	02451	**888-491-8181**	
Gregg Investigations Inc 500 E Milwaukee St	Janesville	WI	53545	**800-866-1976**	
Inquiries Inc 129 N W St	Easton	MD	21601	**866-987-3767**	410-819-3711
International Investigators Inc 3216 N Pennsylvania St	Indianapolis	IN	46205	**800-403-8111**	317-925-1496
Kessler International 45 Rockefeller Plz Ste 2000	New York	NY	10111	**800-932-2221**	212-286-9100
Michael Ramey & Assoc Inc PO Box 744	Danville	CA	94526	**800-321-0505**	
North Winds Investigations Inc 119 S Second St PO Box 1654	Rogers	AR	72756	**800-530-4514**	479-925-1612
Owens & Assoc Investigations 8765 Aero Dr Ste 306	San Diego	CA	92123	**800-297-1343**	
Palmer Investigative Services 624 W Gurley St Ste A	Prescott	AZ	86304	**800-280-2951**	928-778-2951
Research Assoc Inc 27999 Clemens Rd	Cleveland	OH	44145	**800-255-9693**	440-892-9439
Rick Johnson & Assoc of Colorado 1649 Downing St	Denver	CO	80218	**800-530-2300**	303-296-2200
Southern Research Company Inc 2850 Centenary Blvd	Shreveport	LA	71104	**888-772-6952**	318-227-9700
Starside Security & Investigation Inc 1930 S Brea Canyon Rd Ste 220	Diamond Bar	CA	91765	**888-478-2774**	909-396-9999
Stewart & Assoc Inc 50 W Douglas St Ste 1200	Freeport	IL	61032	**888-310-2840**	815-235-3807
Vericon Resources Inc 3550 Engineering Dr Ste 225	Norcross	GA	30092	**800-795-3784**	770-457-9922
VTS Investigations LLC PO Box 971	Elgin	IL	60121	**800-538-4464**	
Wood & Tait Inc 64-5249 Kauakea Rd	Kamuela	HI	96743	**800-774-8585**	808-885-5090

401 INVESTMENT ADVICE & MANAGEMENT

SEE ALSO Securities Brokers & Dealers ; Commodity Contracts Brokers & Dealers ; Investment Guides - Online ; Mutual Funds

Name / Address	City	State	Zip	Toll-Free	Phone
Acumen Capital Finance Partners Ltd 404 Sixth Ave S W Ste 700	Calgary	AB	T2P0R9	**888-422-8636**	403-571-0300
Advent Capital Management LLC 1065 Ave of the Americas 31st Fl	New York	NY	10018	**888-523-8368**	212-482-1600
AGF Management Ltd 66 Wellington St W 31st Fl	Toronto	ON	M5K1E9	**800-268-8583**	905-214-8203
Aldebaran Capital LLC 10293 N Meridian St Ste 100	Indianapolis	IN	46290	**888-742-7827**	317-818-7827
AllianceBernstein Holding LP (AB) 1345 Ave of the Americas *NYSE: AB* ■ *Cust Svc	New York	NY	10105	**800-221-5672***	212-486-5800
American Capital Partners LLC 205 Oser Ave	Hauppauge	NY	11788	**800-393-0493**	631-851-0918
American Century Investments Inc 4500 Main St PO Box 419200	Kansas City	MO	64111	**800-345-2021**	816-531-5575
Ameriprise Financial Inc 834 Ameriprise Financial Ctr *NYSE: AMP*	Minneapolis	MN	55474	**866-673-3673**	612-671-3131
Ameriprise Financial Services Inc 70100 Ameriprise Financial Ctr	Minneapolis	MN	55474	**866-483-8434**	
Amivest Capital Management 703 Market St 18th Fl	San Francisco	CA	94103	**800-541-7774**	
AmSouth Investment Services Inc (AIS) 250 Riverchase Pkwy E 4th Fl	Birmingham	AL	35244	**866-512-3479**	
Analytic Investors LLC 555 W Fifth St 50th Fl	Los Angeles	CA	90013	**800-618-1872**	213-688-3015
Appleton Group Wealth Management LLC 100 W Lawrence St 3/F Apple	Wisconsin	WI	54911	**866-993-7727**	920-993-7727
Appleton Partners Inc 1 Post Office Sq 6th Fl	Boston	MA	02109	**800-338-0745**	617-338-0700
ARGI Investment Services LLC 1914 Stanley Gault Pkwy	Louisville	KY	40223	**866-568-9719**	502-753-0609
Aristotle Capital Management LLC 11100 Santa Monica Blvd Ste 1700	Los Angeles	CA	90025	**877-478-4722**	310-478-4005
Asset Strategy Consultants LLC 6 N Park Dr Ste 208	Hunt Valley	MD	21030	**866-344-8282**	410-528-8282
AssetMark Inc 1655 Grant St 10th Fl	Concord	CA	94520	**800-664-5345**	
Atlantic Trust 100 E Pratt St 23rd Fl	Baltimore	MD	21202	**866-644-4144**	410-539-4660
Attain Capital Management LLC 1 E Wacher Dr 30th Fl	Chicago	IL	60601	**800-311-1145**	312-604-0926
Badgley Phelps & Bell Inc 1420 Fifth Ave Ste 3200	Seattle	WA	98101	**800-869-7173**	206-623-6172
Bahl & Gaynor Inc 212 E Third St Ste 200	Cincinnati	OH	45202	**800-341-1810**	513-287-6100
Bailard Biehl & Kaiser Group 950 Tower Ln Ste 1900	Foster City	CA	94404	**800-224-5273**	650-571-5800
Bartlett & Co 600 Vine St Ste 2100	Cincinnati	OH	45202	**800-800-4612**	513-621-4612
Beacon Trust Co 163 Madison Ave Ste 600	Morristown	NJ	07960	**866-377-8090**	973-377-8090
Becker Capital Management Inc 1211 S W Fifth Ave Ste 2185	Portland	OR	97204	**800-551-3998**	503-223-1720

Classified Section

Company / Address	City	State	Zip	Toll-Free	Phone
Bell Investment Advisors 1111 Broadway Ste 1630	Oakland	CA	94607	800-700-0089	510-433-1066
Berkshire Advisors Inc 2240 Ridgewood Rd	Wyomissing	PA	19610	800-566-4325	610-376-6970
Bessemer Trust Co 630 Fifth Ave	New York	NY	10111	866-271-7403	212-708-9100
Boenning & Scattergood Inc 200 Barr Harbor Dr Four Tower Bridge Ste 300	West Conshohocken	PA	19428	800-883-1212	610-832-1212
Bogdahn Group, The 4901 Vineland Rd Ste 600	Orlando	FL	32811	866-240-7932	
Boston Advisors Inc 1 Liberty Sq 10th Fl	Boston	MA	02109	800-523-5903	617-348-3100
Boston Family Office LLC, The 88 Broad St 2nd Fl	Boston	MA	02110	800-900-4401	617-624-0800
Boston Financial Data Services 2000 Crown Colony Dr	Quincy	MA	02169	888-772-2337	617-483-5000
Bouchey Financial Group Ltd 1819 Fifth Ave	Troy	NY	12180	800-783-0339	518-720-3333
Brandes Investment Partners LP 11988 El Camino Real Ste 500	San Diego	CA	92130	800-237-7119	858-755-0239
Brandywine Capital Associates 113 East Evans St	West Chester	PA	19380	888-344-2920	610-344-2910
Brandywine Global Investment Management LLC 2929 Arch St 8th Fl	Philadelphia	PA	19104	800-348-2499	215-609-3500
Brown &Tedstrom Inc 1700 Broadway Ste 500	Denver	CO	80290	800-883-9361	303-863-7231
Brown Investment Advisory & Trust Co 901 S Bond St Ste 400	Baltimore	MD	21231	800-645-3923	410-537-5400
BTS Asset Management Inc 420 Bedford St Ste 340	Lexington	MA	02420	800-343-3040	
Calamos Asset Management Inc 2020 Calamos Ct *NASDAQ: CLMS*	Naperville	IL	60563	800-582-6959	630-245-7200
Caldwell Trust Co 1400 Ctr Rd Ste Two	Venice	FL	34292	800-338-9476	941-493-3600
Callan Assoc Inc 101 California St Ste 3500	San Francisco	CA	94111	800-227-3288	415-974-5060
Cambiar Investors Inc 2401 E Second Ave Ste 500	Denver	CO	80206	888-673-9950	
Cambria Capital LLC 488 E Winchester St Ste 200	Salt Lake City	UT	84107	877-226-0477	
Cameron Thomson Group Ltd 390 Bay St Ste 1706	Toronto	ON	M5H2Y2	800-395-9943	416-350-5009
CapFinancial Partners LLC 4208 Six Forks Rd Ste 1700	Raleigh	NC	27609	800-216-0645	919-870-6822
Capital Group Cos Inc 333 S Hope St	Los Angeles	CA	90071	800-421-8511	213-615-0514
Capital Growth Management LP 1 International Pl	Boston	MA	02110	800-345-4048	617-737-3225
Capital Research & Management Co (CRMC) 333 S Hope St	Los Angeles	CA	90071	800-421-4225	213-486-9200
Carolinas Investment Consulting LLC 5605 Carnegie Blvd Ste 400	Charlotte	NC	28209	800-255-2904	704-643-2455
Casey Research LLC 55 NE Fifth Ave	Delray Beach	FL	33483	888-512-2739	602-445-2736
Casgrain & Company Ltd 1200 Mcgill College Ave 21st Fl	Montreal	QC	H3B4G7	800-361-8738	514-871-8080
Century Wealth Management LLC 1770 Kirby Pkwy Ste 117	Memphis	TN	38138	855-850-5532	901-850-5532
Churchill Corporate Services 56 Utter Ave	Hawthorne	NJ	07506	800-941-7458	973-636-9400
Clark Capital Management Group Inc (CCMG) 1650 Market St 1 Liberty Pl 53rd Fl	Philadelphia	PA	19103	800-766-2264	215-569-2224
Cohen & Steers Inc 280 Pk Ave 10th Fl *NYSE: CNS*	New York	NY	10017	800-330-7348	212-832-3232
Columbia Threadneedle Investments 1 Financial Ctr	Boston	MA	02111	800-426-3750	
Commonwealth Financial Network 29 Sawyer Rd	Waltham	MA	02453	800-237-0081	781-736-0700
Compak Asset Management 1801 Dove St	Newport Beach	CA	92660	800-388-9700	
Conestoga Capital Advisors LLC 259 N Radnor Chester Rd Radnor Ct Ste 120	Radnor	PA	19087	800-320-7790	484-654-1380
Connors Investor Services Inc 1210 Broadcasting Rd Ste 200	Wyomissing	PA	19610	877-376-7418	610-376-7418
Cornerstone Advisors Asset Management Inc 74 W Broad St Ste 340	Bethlehem	PA	18018	800-923-0900	610-694-0900
Creative Financial Group (CFG) 16 Campus Blvd	Newtown Square	PA	19073	800-893-4824	610-325-6100
Crestwood Advisors LLC 50 Federal St Ste 810	Boston	MA	02110	877-273-7896	617-523-8880
Crown Financial Ministries 601 Broad St SE	Gainesville	GA	30501	800-722-1976	770-534-1000
Cullinan Associates Inc 295 N Hubbards Ln 2nd Fl	Louisville	KY	40207	800-611-4841	502-893-0300
Cumberland Private Wealth Management Inc 99 Yorkville Ave Ste 300	Toronto	ON	M5R3K5	800-929-8296	416-929-1090
Curran Investment Management 30 S Pearl St Omni Plz 9th Fl	Albany	NY	12207	866-432-1246	518-391-4246
DailyFX 55 Water St 50th Fl	New York	NY	10041	888-503-6739	212-897-7660
Design ProfessionalXL Group 2959 Salinas Hwy	Monterey	CA	93940	800-227-4284	831-649-5522
Driehaus Capital Management Inc 25 E Erie St	Chicago	IL	60611	800-688-8819	312-587-3800
Duff & Phelps Investment Management Co 200 S Wacker Dr Ste 500	Chicago	IL	60606	800-338-8214	312-263-2610
Eagle Asset Management 880 Carillon Pkwy	Saint Petersburg	FL	33716	800-237-3101	
Earnest Partners LLC 1180 Peachtree St Ste 2300	Atlanta	GA	30309	800-322-0068	404-815-8772
Edgar Lomax Co 6564 Loisdale Ct Ste 310	Springfield	VA	22150	866-205-0524	703-719-0026
Elan Financial Services 225 W Sta Sq Dr Ste 620	Pittsburgh	PA	15219	877-935-2637	
Eliot Rose Asset Management LLC 1000 Chapel View Blvd Ste 240	Cranston	RI	02920	866-585-5100	401-588-5100
Estrada Hinojosa & Company Inc 1717 Main St LB47	Dallas	TX	75201	800-676-5352	214-658-1670
Federated Investors 1001 Liberty Ave Federated Investors Twr *NYSE: FII*	Pittsburgh	PA	15222	800-245-0242	412-288-1900
Fidelity Investments Institutional Services Company Inc 82 Devonshire St	Boston	MA	02109	800-343-3548	617-563-9840
Fiduciary Management Inc of Milwaukee 100 E Wisconsin Ave Ste 2200	Milwaukee	WI	53202	800-264-7684	414-226-4545
First Pacific Advisors Inc 11400 W Olympic Blvd Ste 1200	Los Angeles	CA	90064	800-982-4372	310-473-0225
Fischer Francis Trees & Watts Inc 200 Pk Ave 11th Fl	New York	NY	10166	866-392-4090	212-681-3000
Fisher Investments 13100 Skyline Blvd	Woodside	CA	94062	800-550-1071	
Flexible Plan Investments Ltd 3883 Telegraph Rd Ste 100	Bloomfield Hills	MI	48302	800-347-3539	248-642-6640
FMR Corp 82 Devonshire St	Boston	MA	02109	800-343-3548	
Foothills Asset Management Ltd 8767 E Via de Ventura Ste 175	Scottsdale	AZ	85258	800-663-9870	480-777-9870
Ford Equity Research Inc 11722 Sorrento Vly Rd Ste I	San Diego	CA	92121	800-842-0207	858-755-1327
Formula Growth Ltd 1010 Sherbrooke St W Ste 2300	Montreal	QC	H3A2R7	877-343-6654	514-288-5136
Fort Washington Investment Advisors Inc 303 Broadway Ste 1200	Cincinnati	OH	45202	888-244-8167	513-361-7600
Franklin Resources Inc 1 Franklin Pkwy Bdge 970 1st Fl *NYSE: BEN*	San Mateo	CA	94403	800-632-2301	650-312-2000
Front Street Capital 33 Yonge St Ste 600	Toronto	ON	M5E1G4	800-513-2832	416-364-1990
Frontier Investment Management Co 8401 N Central Expy Ste 300	Dallas	TX	75225	800-553-8034	972-934-2590
Gannett Welsh & Kotler LLC 222 Berkeley St 15th Fl	Boston	MA	02116	800-225-4236	617-236-8900
Global Cash Card 7 Corporate Park Ste 130	Irvine	CA	92606	888-220-4477	949-751-0360
Goldman Sachs Asset Management (GSAM) 200 W St	New York	NY	10282	800-526-7384	212-902-1000
Greystone Managed Investments Inc 300 Park Centre 1230 Blackfoot Dr	Regina	SK	S4S7G4	800-213-4286	306-779-6400
Hamilton Capital Management 5025 Arlington Centre Blvd	Columbus	OH	43220	888-833-5951	614-273-1000
Harris Assoc LP 111 South Wacker Dr Ste 4600	Chicago	IL	60606	800-731-0700	312-646-3600
Haywood Securities Inc Waterfront Centre 200 Burrard St Ste 700	Vancouver	BC	V6C3L6	800-663-9499	604-697-7100
HD Vest Financial Services 6333 N State Hwy 161 4th Fl	Irving	TX	75038	866-218-8206	972-870-6000
Hengehold Capital Management LLC 6116 Harrison Ave	Cincinnati	OH	45247	877-598-5120	513-598-5120
Herndon Plant Oakley Ltd 800 N Shoreline Blvd Ste 2200 South	Corpus Christi	TX	78401	800-888-4894	361-888-7611
Holland Capital Management LP 303 W Madison St Ste 700	Chicago	IL	60606	800-295-9779	312-553-4830
Hyperion Capital Management Inc 200 Vessey St 3 World Financial Ctr	New York	NY	10281	800-497-3746	212-549-8400
ICM Asset Management Inc 601 W Main Ave	Spokane	WA	99201	800-488-4075	509-455-3588
ICON Advisers Inc 5299 DTC Blvd Ste 1200	Greenwood Village	CO	80111	800-828-4881	303-790-1600
IGM Financial Inc 447 Portage Ave 1 Canada Ctr *NYSE: IGM*	Winnipeg	MB	R3B3H5	888-746-6344	
Integra Capital Ltd 2020 Winston Park Dr Ste 200	Oakville	ON	L6H6X7	800-363-2480	905-829-1131
Investment Scorecard Inc 601 Grassmere Park Dr Ste 1	Nashville	TN	37211	800-555-6035	615-301-1975
Jatheon Technologies Inc British Colonial Bldg 8 Wellington St E Mezzanine Level	Toronto	ON	M5E1C5	888-528-4366	416-840-0418
Jeffrey Matthews Financial Group LLC, The 30B Vreeland Rd Ste 210	Florham Park	NJ	07932	888-467-3636	973-805-6222
Johnson Investment Counsel Inc 3777 W Fork Rd	Cincinnati	OH	45247	800-541-0170	513-661-3100
JPMorgan Fleming Asset Management PO Box 8528	Boston	MA	02266	800-480-4111	
Jra Financial Advisors 7373 Kirkwood Ct Ste 300	Maple Grove	MN	55369	800-278-5988	763-315-8000
Kayne Anderson Capital Advisors LP 1800 Ave of the Stars 3rd Fl	Los Angeles	CA	90067	800-638-1496	
KCM Investment Advisors LLC 750 Lindaro St Ste 250	San Rafael	CA	94901	888-287-5555	415-461-7788
Killen Group Inc 1189 Lancaster Ave	Berwyn	PA	19312	877-454-5536	610-296-7222
Kirr Marbach & Co Investment Management 621 Washington St	Columbus	IN	47201	800-808-9444	812-376-9444
Laird Norton Tyee 801 Second Ave Ste 1600	Seattle	WA	98104	800-426-5105	206-464-5100
Landaas & Co 411 E Wisconsin Ave 20th Fl	Milwaukee	WI	53202	800-236-1096	414-223-1099
Laurentian Bank Securities Inc 1981 McGill College Ave Ste 100	Montreal	QC	H3A3K3	888-350-8577	514-350-2800
Leconte Wealth Management LLC 703 William Blount Dr	Maryville	TN	37801	888-236-6630	865-379-8200
Leerink Swann & Co 1 Federal St 37th Fl	Boston	MA	02110	800-808-7525	
Lexington Wealth Management 12 Waltham St	Lexington	MA	02421	800-626-1566	781-860-7745
Linscomb & Williams Inc 1400 Post Oak Blvd Ste 1000	Houston	TX	77056	800-960-1200	713-840-1000
Logan Capital Management Inc 6 Coulter Ave Ste 2000	Ardmore	PA	19003	800-215-1100	

Company / Address	City	State	ZIP	Toll-Free	Phone
Loomis Sayles & Company Inc LP PO Box 219594	Kansas City	MO	64121	**800-343-2029**	800-633-3330
Lord Abbett & Co 90 Hudson St	Jersey City	NJ	07302	**888-522-2388**	201-827-2000
Mackenzie Financial Corp 180 Queen St W	Toronto	ON	M5V3K1	**888-653-7070**	416-922-5322
Madison Investment Advisors Inc 550 Science Dr	Madison	WI	53711	**800-767-0300**	608-274-0300
Manarin Investment Counsel Ltd 505 N 210th St	Omaha	NE	68022	**800-397-1167**	402-330-1166
Manchester Financial Inc 2815 Townsgate Rd Ste 100	Westlake Village	CA	91361	**800-492-1107**	805-495-4405
Marketocracy Inc 1208 W Magnolia Ste 236	Fort Worth	TX	76104	**877-462-4180**	
Marquette Asset Management 60 S Sixth St Ste 3900	Minneapolis	MN	55402	**866-661-3770**	612-661-3770
Marshall & Sullivan Inc 1109 First Ave Ste 200	Seattle	WA	98101	**800-735-7290**	206-621-9014
Mercer Global Advisors Inc 1801 E Cabrillo Blvd	Santa Barbara	CA	93108	**800-258-1559**	800-898-4642
MFS Investment Management 500 Boylston St	Boston	MA	02116	**877-960-6077**	617-954-5000
Mission Wealth Management LLC 1123 Chapala St 3rd Fl	Santa Barbara	CA	93101	**888-642-7221**	805-882-2360
Morley Financial Services Inc 1300 SW Fifth Ave Ste 3300	Portland	OR	97201	**800-548-4806**	503-484-9300
Morningstar Inc 22 W Washington St *NASDAQ: MORN* ■ *Orders	Chicago	IL	60606	**800-735-0700***	312-696-6000
Morrow & Co LLC 470 W Ave	Stamford	CT	06902	**800-662-5200**	203-658-9400
Navellier Securities Corp 1 E Liberty St Ste 504	Reno	NV	89501	**800-887-8671**	775-785-2300
Neiman Funds Management LLC 6631 Main St	Williamsville	NY	14221	**877-385-2720**	
Neuberger Berman LLC 605 Third Ave	New York	NY	10158	**800-223-6448**	
NorthCoast Asset Management LLC 1 Greenwich Office Park	Greenwich	CT	06831	**800-274-5448**	203-532-7000
Northern Trust Company of Connecticut 300 Atlantic St Ste 400	Stamford	CT	06901	**866-876-9944**	312-630-0779
Northwestern Mutual Investment Services LLC 611 E Wisconsin Ave Ste 300	Milwaukee	WI	53202	**866-664-7737**	
Odlum Brown Ltd 250 Howe St Ste 1100	Vancouver	BC	V6C3S9	**866-636-8222**	604-669-1600
Osborne Partners Capital Management LLC 580 California St Ste 1900	San Francisco	CA	94104	**800-362-7734**	415-362-5637
Pacific Investment Management Company LLC 840 Newport Ctr Dr	Newport Beach	CA	92660	**800-387-4626**	949-720-6000
Parady Financial Group Inc 340 Heald Way Ste 226	The Villages	FL	32163	**855-701-4351**	352-751-3016
Parsons Capital Management Inc 10 Weybosset St Ste 1000	Providence	RI	02903	**888-521-2440**	401-521-2440
Payden & Rygel 333 S Grand Ave	Los Angeles	CA	90071	**800-572-9336**	213-625-1900
Peak Financial Management Inc 281 Winter St Ste 160	Waltham	MA	02451	**877-567-9500**	781-487-9500
Peninsula Asset Management Inc 1111 Third Ave W Ste 340	Bradenton	FL	34205	**800-269-6417**	
Personal Capital Corp 726 Main St	Redwood City	CA	94063	**855-855-8005**	
Pittenger & Anderson Inc 5533 S 27th St Ste 201	Lincoln	NE	68512	**800-897-1588**	402-328-8800
Primary Global Research LLC 1975 W El Camino Real Ste 300	Mountain View	CA	94040	**888-893-1688**	
Primerica Financial Services 3120 Breckinridge Blvd	Duluth	GA	30099	**800-257-4725**	770-381-1000
Producers Financial 5350 Tomah Dr Ste 3800	Colorado Springs	CO	80918	**800-985-5549**	719-535-0739
Prudential Financial Inc 751 Broad St *NYSE: PRU*	Newark	NJ	07102	**800-843-7625**	973-802-6000
Putnam Investments 30 Dan Rd PO Box 8383	Canton	MA	02021	**888-478-8626**	617-292-1000
PVG Asset Management Corp 24918 Genesee Trl Rd	Golden	CO	80401	**800-777-0818**	303-526-0548
QCI Asset Management 40A Grove St	Pittsford	NY	14534	**800-836-3960**	585-218-2060
R N Croft Financial Group Inc 218 Steeles Ave E	Thornhill	ON	L3T1A6	**877-249-2884**	905-695-7777
Radnor Financial Advisors Inc 485 Devon Park Dr Ste 119	Wayne	PA	19087	**888-271-9922**	610-975-0280
Raymond James Ltd 2200-925 W Georgia St Cathedral Pl	Vancouver	BC	V6C3L2	**888-545-6624**	604-659-8000
Retirement System Group Inc 108 Corporate Park Dr	White Plains	NY	10604	**855-549-6689**	212-503-0100
Riverfront Investment Group LLC 1214 E Cary St	Richmond	VA	23219	**866-583-0744**	804-549-4800
RNC Genter Capital Management 11601 Wilshire Blvd 25th Fl	Los Angeles	CA	90025	**800-877-7624**	310-477-6543
Roffman Miller Assoc Inc 1835 Market St Ste 500	Philadelphia	PA	19103	**800-995-1030**	215-981-1030
Ronald Blue & Company LLC 300 Colonial Ctr Pkwy Ste 300	Roswell	GA	30076	**800-841-0362**	770-280-6000
Rothschild North America Inc 1251 Ave of the Americas 51st Fl	New York	NY	10020	**844-726-3863**	212-403-3500
Royce & Assoc LLC 745 Fifth Ave	New York	NY	10151	**800-221-4268**	
Ruane Cunniff & Goldfarb Inc 9 W 57th St Ste 5000	New York	NY	10019	**800-686-6884**	212-832-5280
Russell Investment Group 1301 Second Ave Ste 18	Seattle	WA	98101	**800-787-7354**	
Russell Investments 1301 Second Ave 18th Fl	Seattle	WA	98101	**800-426-7969**	206-505-7877
Saturna Capital Corp 1300 N State St	Bellingham	WA	98225	**888-732-6262**	360-734-9900
Schultz Collins Lawson Chambers Inc 455 Market St Ste 1250	San Francisco	CA	94105	**877-291-2205**	415-291-3000
Segall Bryant & Hamill 540 W Madison St Ste 1900	Chicago	IL	60606	**800-836-4265**	312-474-1222
Select Portfolio Management Inc 120 Vantis	Aliso Viejo	CA	92656	**800-445-9822**	949-975-7900
Sheaff Brock Investment Advisors LLC 10401 N Meridian St Ste 100	Indianapolis	IN	46290	**866-575-5700**	317-705-5700
Signalert Corp 150 Great Neck Rd Ste 301	Great Neck	NY	11021	**800-829-6229**	516-829-6444
Signator Investors Inc 197 Clarendon St C-8	Boston	MA	02116	**800-543-6611**	
Smith Graham & Co 600 Travis St Ste 6900	Houston	TX	77002	**800-739-4470**	713-227-1100
Sound Shore Management Inc 8 Sound Shore Dr Ste 180	Greenwich	CT	06830	**800-551-1980**	203-629-1980
South Texas Money Management Ltd 700 N Saint Mary's Ste 100	San Antonio	TX	78205	**800-805-1385**	210-824-8916
Sovereign Society, The 98 S E Sixth Ave Ste 2	Delray Beach	FL	33483	**866-584-4096**	888-358-8125
Spero-Smith Investment Advisers Inc 3601 Green Rd Ste 102	Cleveland	OH	44122	**800-794-7545**	216-464-6266
Spire Investment Partners LLC 7918 Jones Branch Dr Ste 750	Mclean	VA	22102	**888-737-8907**	703-748-5800
Stansberry & Assoc Investment Research LLC 1217 Saint Paul St	Baltimore	MD	21202	**888-261-2693**	
State Universities Retirement System of Illinois 1901 Fox Dr	Champaign	IL	61820	**800-275-7877**	217-378-8800
Stoever Glass & Company Inc 30 Wall St	New York	NY	10005	**800-223-3881**	
Systematic Financial Management LP 300 Frank W Burr Blvd Seventh Fl Glenpoint Ctr E 7th Fl	Teaneck	NJ	07666	**800-258-0497**	201-928-1982
T Rowe Price Assoc Inc 100 E Pratt St	Baltimore	MD	21202	**800-638-7890**	410-345-2000
Tamarac Inc 701 Fifth Ave 14th Fl	Seattle	WA	98104	**866-525-8811**	
TAMRO Capital Partners LLC 1701 Duke St Ste 250	Alexandria	VA	22314	**888-816-2925**	703-740-1000
TCI Wealth Advisors Inc 4011 E Sunrise Dr	Tucson	AZ	85718	**877-733-1859**	520-733-1477
Technomart RGA Inc 401 Washington Ave Ste 1101	Baltimore	MD	21204	**800-877-6555**	410-828-6555
Thompson Siegel & Walmsley Inc 6806 Paragon Pl Ste 300	Richmond	VA	23230	**800-697-1056**	804-353-4500
Tom Johnson Investment Management Inc 201 Robert S Kerr Ave	Oklahoma City	OK	73102	**888-404-8546**	405-236-2111
Treflie Capital Management 35 Ezekills Holw	Sag Harbor	NY	11963	**866-236-3363**	631-725-2500
TYGH Capital Management Inc 1211 S W Fifth Ave Ste 2100	Portland	OR	97204	**800-972-0150**	503-972-0150
US Global Investors Inc 7900 Callaghan Rd *NASDAQ: GROW*	San Antonio	TX	78229	**800-873-8637**	210-308-1234
USAA Investment Management 9800 Fredericksburg Rd PO Box 659453	San Antonio	TX	78288	**800-531-8722**	
Value Line Asset Management 220 E 42nd St	New York	NY	10017	**800-634-3583**	212-907-1500
Vanguard Group 455 Devon Pk Dr	Wayne	PA	19087	**800-662-7447**	610-669-1000
VCI Emergency Vehicle 43 jefferson ave	Berlin	NJ	08009	**800-394-2162**	856-768-2162
Vontobel Asset Management Inc 1540 Broad Way Ave 38th Fl *General	New York	NY	10036	**800-445-8872***	212-415-7000
Waddell & Reed Financial Inc 6300 Lamar Ave *NYSE: WDR*	Overland Park	KS	66201	**888-923-3355**	913-236-2000
WE Donoghue & Company Inc 629 Washington St	Norwood	MA	02062	**800-642-4276**	
Wealth Conservancy Inc, The 1525 Spruce St Ste 300	Boulder	CO	80302	**888-440-1919**	303-444-1919
Webb Financial Group 7900 Xerxes Ave S Ste 1920	Minneapolis	MN	55431	**800-927-9322**	952-837-3200
Weiss Research Inc 15430 Endeavour Dr	Jupiter	FL	33478	**800-291-8545**	
Wentworth Hauser & Violich (WHV) 301 Battery St	San Francisco	CA	94111	**800-204-2650**	415-981-6911
Wilbanks, Smith & Thomas Asset Management LLC 150 W Main St Ste 1700	Norfolk	VA	23510	**800-229-3677**	757-623-3676
Wilshire Assoc Inc 1299 Ocean Ave Ste 700	Santa Monica	CA	90401	**855-626-8281**	310-451-3051
Woodmont Investment Counsel LLC 401 Commerce St Ste 5400	Nashville	TN	37219	**800-278-8003**	615-297-6144
Workplace Answers LLC 3701 Executive Ctr Dr Ste 201	Austin	TX	78731	**866-861-4410**	
Wright Investors' Service 440 Wheelers Farms Rd	Milford	CT	06461	**800-232-0013**	203-783-4400
Yacktman Asset Management Co 6300 Bridgepoint Pkwy Bldg 1 Ste 320	Austin	TX	78730	**800-835-3879**	512-767-6700

402 INVESTMENT COMPANIES - SMALL BUSINESS

The companies listed here conform to the Small Business Administration's standards for investing.

Company / Address	City	State	ZIP	Toll-Free	Phone
Galliard Capital Management Inc 800 La Salle Ave Ste 1100	Minneapolis	MN	55402	**800-717-1617**	612-667-3220
GamePlan Financial Marketing LLC 300 ParkBrooke Pl Ste 200 *Cust Svc	Woodstock	GA	30189	**800-886-4757***	678-238-0601
Hornor Townsend & Kent Inc (HTK) 600 Dresher Rd Ste C1C	Horsham	PA	19044	**800-289-9999**	
Impact Seven Inc 147 Lk Almena Dr	Almena	WI	54805	**800-685-9353**	715-357-3334
UMB Capital Corp 1010 Grand Blvd	Kansas City	MO	64106	**800-821-2171**	816-860-7000

Classified Section

403 INVESTMENT COMPANIES - SPECIALIZED SMALL BUSINESS

Companies listed here conform to the Small Business Administration's requirements for investment in minority companies.

Company	Address	City	State	Zip	Toll-Free	Phone
Al Copeland Investments Inc	1001 Harimaw Ct S	Metairie	LA	70001	**800-401-0401**	504-830-1000
ALCO Inc	6925 - 104 St	Edmonton	AB	T6H2L5	**800-563-1498**	780-435-3502
Security Credit Services LLC	2653 W Oxford Loop Ste 108	Oxford	MS	38655	**866-699-7889**	662-281-7220
Smith Affiliated Capital (SAC)	800 Third Ave 12th Fl	New York	NY	10022	**888-387-3298**	212-644-9440

404 INVESTMENT GUIDES - ONLINE

SEE ALSO Buyer's Guides - Online

Company	Address	City	State	Zip	Toll-Free	Phone
Briefing.com Inc	401 N Michigan Ste 2910	Chicago	IL	60611	**800-752-3013***	312-670-4463
	*General					
EDGAR Online Inc	11200 Rockville Pk Ste 310	Rockville	MD	20852	**800-732-0330**	301-287-0300
	NASDAQ: EDGR					
eSignal	3955 Pt Eden Way	Hayward	CA	94545	**800-815-8256**	510-266-6000
FactSet Research Systems Inc	601 Merritt 7 3rd Fl	Norwalk	CT	06851	**877-322-8738**	203-810-1000
	NYSE: FDS					
Harris myCFO Inc	2200 Geng Rd Ste 100	Palo Alto	CA	94303	**866-966-1130**	650-210-5000
Hoover's Inc	5800 Airport Blvd	Austin	TX	78752	**800-486-8666**	512-374-4500
InvestorPlace.com	2420A Gehman Ln 2420A Gehman Ln	Lancaster	PA	17602	**800-219-8592**	
Stockwatch	700 W Georgia St PO Box 10371	Vancouver	BC	V7Y1J6	**800-268-6397**	604-687-1500
TheStreet.com Inc	14 Wall St 15th Fl	New York	NY	10005	**800-562-9571**	212-321-5000
	NASDAQ: TST					

405 INVESTMENT (MISC)

SEE ALSO Real Estate Investment Trusts (REITs) ; Royalty Trusts ; Securities Brokers & Dealers ; Venture Capital Firms ; Commodity Contracts Brokers & Dealers ; Franchises ; Investment Guides - Online ; Mortgage Lenders & Loan Brokers ; Mutual Funds ; Investment Newsletters ; Banks - Commercial & Savings

Company	Address	City	State	Zip	Toll-Free	Phone
ABRY Partners LLC	111 Huntington Ave 29th Fl	Boston	MA	02199	**800-777-3674**	617-859-2959
Adams Express Co	500 E Pratt St Ste 1300	Baltimore	MD	21202	**800-638-2479**	410-752-5900
	NYSE: ADX					
Central Securities Corp	630 Fifth Ave Ste 820	New York	NY	10111	**866-593-2507**	212-698-2020
	NYSE: CET					
Counsel Corp	1211 Ave of the Americas Ste 2902	New York	NY	10036	**866-296-3743**	212-696-0100
	NYSE: CXS					
DPEC Capital Inc	135 Fifth Ave	New York	NY	10010	**844-574-3577**	301-590-6500
Enerplus Resources Fund	3000 Dome Tower 333 7th Ave SW Ste 3000	Calgary	AB	T2P2Z1	**800-319-6462**	403-298-2200
Fidelity Investments Charitable Gift Fund	PO Box 770001	Cincinnati	OH	45277	**800-262-6039**	
Haverford Trust Co	3 Radnor Corp Ctr Ste 450	Radnor	PA	19087	**888-995-1979**	610-995-8700
HomeVestors of America Inc	6500 Greenville Ave Ste 400	Dallas	TX	75206	**866-200-6475**	972-761-0046
Main Street Capital Corp	1300 Post Oak Blvd	Houston	TX	77056	**800-966-1559**	713-350-6000
	NYSE: MAIN					
Moors & Cabot Inc	111 Devonshire St	Boston	MA	02109	**800-426-0501**	617-426-0500
Pembina Pipeline Corp	585 Eighth Ave SW	Calgary	AB	T2P1G1	**888-428-3222**	403-231-7500
	TSE: PPL					
Superior Plus Income Fund	840-7 Ave SW Ste 1400	Calgary	AB	T2P3G2	**866-490-7587**	403-218-2970
Thomas H Lee Partners	100 Federal St	Boston	MA	02110	**877-456-3427**	617-227-1050

406 JANITORIAL & CLEANING SUPPLIES - WHOL

Company	Address	City	State	Zip	Toll-Free	Phone
Brady Industries Inc	7055 Lindell Rd	Las Vegas	NV	89118	**800-293-4698**	702-876-3990
C&T Design & Equipment Company Inc	2750 Tobey Dr	Indianapolis	IN	46219	**800-966-3374**	317-898-9602
Culinary Depot Inc	2 Melnick Dr	Monsey	NY	10952	**888-845-8200**	
Fitch Co	2201 Russell St	Baltimore	MD	21230	**800-933-4824**	410-539-1953
Industrial Soap Co	722 S Vandeventer Ave	Saint Louis	MO	63110	**800-405-7627**	314-241-6363
J. Ennis Fabrics Ltd	12122 - 68 St	Edmonton	AB	T5B1R1	**800-663-6647**	
Kellermeyer Co	475 W Woodland Cir	Bowling Green	OH	43402	**800-445-7415**	419-255-3022
Rose Products & Services Inc	545 Stimmel Rd	Columbus	OH	43223	**800-264-1568**	614-443-7647

Company	Address	City	State	Zip	Toll-Free	Phone
Taylor Freezers of California	221 Harris Ct	South San Francisco	CA	94080	**877-978-4800**	

407 JEWELERS' FINDINGS & MATERIALS

Company	Address	City	State	Zip	Toll-Free	Phone
Cranesmart Systems Inc	4908 97 St NW	Edmonton	AB	T6E5S1	**888-562-3222**	780-437-2986
Cyber-Rain Inc	6345 Balboa Blvd Ste 230	Encino	CA	91316	**877-888-1452**	
David H Fell & Company Inc	6009 Bandini Blvd	Commerce	CA	90040	**800-822-1996**	323-722-9992
Delta M Corp	1003 Larsen Dr	Oak Ridge	TN	37830	**800-922-0083**	
Emme E2MS LLC	PO Box 2251	Bristol	CT	06011	**800-396-0523**	
Findings Inc	160 Water St	Keene	NH	03431	**800-225-2706**	603-352-3717
FoodChek Systems Inc	1414 8 St. S.W. Ste 450	Calgary	AB	T2R1J6	**877-298-0208**	403-269-9424
Fugro-Roadware Inc	2505 Meadowvale Blvd	Mississauga	ON	L5N5S2	**800-828-2726**	905-567-2870
George Kelk Corp	48 Lesmill Rd	Toronto	ON	M3B2T5	**888-275-5355**	416-445-5850
Humboldt Manufacturing Co	875 Tollgate Rd	Elgin	IL	60123	**800-544-7220**	708-456-6300
Krohn Industries Inc	PO Box 98	Carlstadt	NJ	07072	**800-526-6299**	201-933-9696
Lee's Morvillo Group	160 Niantic Ave	Providence	RI	02907	**800-821-1700**	401-353-1740
Modern Machine & Tool Company Inc	11844 Jefferson Ave	Newport News	VA	23606	**800-482-1835**	757-873-1212
Northern Digital Inc	103 Randall Dr	Waterloo	ON	N2V1C5	**877-634-6340**	519-884-5142
Paul H Gesswein & Co	255 Hancock Ave	Bridgeport	CT	06605	**800-544-2043**	203-366-5400
Precision Specialties Co	1201 East Pecan St	Sherman	TX	75090	**800-527-3295**	
Rainwise Inc	25 Federal St	Bar Harbor	ME	04609	**800-762-5723**	207-288-5169
Romanoff International Supply Corp	9 Deforest St	Amityville	NY	11701	**800-221-7448***	631-842-2400
	*Cust Svc					
Romet Ltd	1080 Matheson Blvd East	Mississauga	ON	L4W2V2	**800-387-3201**	905-624-1591
SIE Computing Solutions Inc	10 Mupac Dr	Brockton	MA	02301	**800-926-8722**	508-588-6110
Signalisation Ver-Mac Inc	1781 Bresse	Quebec	QC	G2G2V2	**888-488-7446**	418-654-1303
Space Optics Research Labs LLC	7 Stuart Rd	Chelmsford	MA	01824	**800-552-7675**	978-250-8640
Stuller Settings Inc	PO Box 87777	Lafayette	LA	70598	**800-877-7777**	
SymCom Inc	222 Disk Dr	Rapid City	SD	57701	**800-843-8848**	605-348-5580
Viconics Technologies Inc	9245 Langelier Blvd	Saint-Leonard	QC	H1P3K9	**800-563-5660**	514-321-5660
Victor Settings Inc	25 Brook Ave	Maywood	NJ	07607	**800-322-9008**	201-845-4433

408 JEWELRY - COSTUME

Company	Address	City	State	Zip	Toll-Free	Phone
1928 Jewelry Co	3000 W Empire Ave	Burbank	CA	91504	**800-227-1928**	818-841-1928
A & Z Hayward Co	655 Waterman Ave	East Providence	RI	02914	**800-556-7462**	401-438-0550
C & J Jewelry Company Inc	100 Dupont Dr	Providence	RI	02907	**888-527-4268**	401-944-2200

409 JEWELRY - PRECIOUS METAL

Company	Address	City	State	Zip	Toll-Free	Phone
American Achievement Corp	7211 Cir S Rd	Austin	TX	78745	**800-531-5055**	512-444-0571
Balfour	7211 Cir S Rd	Austin	TX	78745	**800-225-3687**	
Byard F Brogan Inc	PO Box 0369	Glenside	PA	19038	**800-232-7642**	215-885-3550
Diablo Mfg Company Inc	900 Golden Gate Terr PO Box 1108	Grass Valley	CA	95945	**800-551-2233***	530-272-2241
	*Cust Svc					
Hammerman Bros Inc	50 W 57th St 12th Fl	New York	NY	10019	**800-223-6436**	212-956-2800
Harry Klitzner Co, The	530 Wellington Ave Ste 11	Cranston	RI	02910	**800-621-0161**	
Harry Winston Inc	718 Fifth Ave	New York	NY	10019	**800-988-4110**	212-399-1000
Ira Green Inc	177 Georgia Ave	Providence	RI	02905	**800-663-7487***	401-467-4770
	*General					
Jacmel Jewelry Inc	3030 47th Ave	Long Island	NY	11101	**800-945-4300**	
James Avery Craftsman Inc	145 Avery Rd N	Kerrville	TX	78029	**800-283-1770**	830-895-1122
Jostens Inc	3601 Minnesota Ave Ste 400	Minneapolis	MN	55435	**800-235-4774**	952-830-3300
Kinsley & Sons Inc	24 S Church St Ste A	Union	MO	63084	**800-468-4428***	
	*General					
Maui Divers of Hawaii	1520 Liona St	Honolulu	HI	96814	**800-462-4454**	808-946-7979
Mtm Recognition Corp	3201 SE 29th St	Oklahoma City	OK	73115	**877-686-7464**	405-670-4545
Novell Design Studio	2100 Felver Ct	Rahway	NJ	07065	**888-668-3551**	
OC Tanner Co	1930 S State St	Salt Lake City	UT	84115	**800-453-7490**	

Company / Address	City	State	Zip	Toll-Free	Phone
Ostbye & Anderson Inc 10055 51st Ave N	Minneapolis	MN	55442	**866-553-1515**	763-553-1515
Relios Inc 6815 Academy Pkwy W NE	Albuquerque	NM	87109	**800-827-6543**	505-345-5304
Robert S Fisher & Company Inc 280 Sheffield St	Mountainside	NJ	07092	**800-526-8052**	908-928-0002
Stanley Creations Inc 1414 Willow Ave	Melrose Park	PA	19027	**800-220-1414**	215-635-6200
Sunshine Minting Inc 7600 Mineral Dr Ste 700	Coeur d'Alene	ID	83815	**800-274-5837**	208-772-9592
Terryberry Co 2033 Oak Industrial Dr NE	Grand Rapids	MI	49505	**800-253-0882**	616-458-1391
Tiffany & Co 727 Fifth Ave *NYSE: TIF* ■ *Orders	New York	NY	10022	**800-526-0649***	212-755-8000
Wheeler Mfg Co Inc 107 Main Ave PO Box 629	Lemmon	SD	57638	**800-843-1937**	605-374-3848
Wright & Lato 2100 Felver Ct	Rahway	NJ	07065	**800-724-1855**	973-674-8700

410 JEWELRY STORES

Company / Address	City	State	Zip	Toll-Free	Phone
Aucoin-Hart 1525 Metairie Rd	Metairie	LA	70005	**800-992-8743**	504-834-9999
Ben Bridge Jeweler Inc PO Box 1908 *Cust Svc	Seattle	WA	98111	**888-917-9171***	206-239-6811
Ben Moss Jewellers 300-201 Portage Ave	Winnipeg	MB	R3B3K6	**888-236-6677**	204-947-6682
Birks & Mayors Inc 1240 du Sq-Phillips St	Montreal	QC	H3B3H4	**800-758-2511**	
Blue Nile Inc 705 Fifth Ave S Ste 900 *NASDAQ: NILE*	Seattle	WA	98104	**800-242-2728**	206-336-6700
Borsheim's Inc 120 Regency Pkwy	Omaha	NE	68114	**800-642-4438**	402-391-0400
Coleman E Adler & Sons Inc 722 Canal St	New Orleans	LA	70130	**800-925-7912**	504-523-5292
DGSE Cos Inc 11311 Reeder Rd *NYSE: DGSE*	Dallas	TX	75229	**800-527-5307**	972-484-3662
Dunkin's Diamonds Inc 897 Hebron Rd	Heath	OH	43056	**877-343-4883**	
Fantasy Diamond Corp 1550 W Carrol Ave	Chicago	IL	60607	**800-621-4445**	312-583-3200
Finks Jewelry Inc 3545 Electric Rd	Roanoke	VA	24018	**800-699-7464**	540-342-2991
Freeman Jewelers Inc 76 Merchants Row	Rutland	VT	05701	**800-451-4167**	802-773-2792
Garfield Refining Co 810 East Cayuga St	Philadelphia	PA	19124	**800-523-0968**	
GN Diamond LLC 800 Chestnut St	Philadelphia	PA	19107	**800-724-8810**	215-925-0217
H Stern Jewelers Inc 645 Fifth Ave	New York	NY	10022	**800-747-8376**	212-688-0300
H. E. Murdock Co Inc 88 Main St	Waterville	ME	04901	**888-974-1805**	207-873-7036
Harry Ritchie's Jewelers Inc 956 Willamette St *Cust Svc	Eugene	OR	97401	**800-935-2850***	541-686-1787
Harry Winston Inc 718 Fifth Ave	New York	NY	10019	**800-988-4110**	212-399-1000
Helzberg Diamonds 1825 Swift Ave	North Kansas City	MO	64116	**800-435-9237**	816-842-7780
Jay Roberts Jewelers 515 Rt 73 S	Marlton	NJ	08053	**888-828-8463**	856-596-8600
JewelryWeb.com Inc 98 Cuttermill Rd Ste 464	Great Neck	NY	11021	**800-955-9245**	516-482-3982
Kay Jewelers 375 Ghent Rd	Akron	OH	44333	**800-681-8796**	330-668-5000
King's Jewelry & Loan 800 S Vermont Ave	Los Angeles	CA	90005	**800-378-1111**	213-383-5555
Lori Bonn Jewelery 114 Linden St	Oakland	CA	94607	**877-507-4206**	
Lux Bond & Green Inc 46 Lasalle Rd	West Hartford	CT	06107	**800-524-7336**	
Morgan & Co 1131 Glendon Ave	Los Angeles	CA	90024	**800-458-4367**	310-208-3377
Osterman Jewelers 375 Ghent Rd	Akron	OH	44333	**800-844-7130**	330-668-5000
Reeds Jewelers Inc PO Box 2229 *Orders	Wilmington	NC	28402	**877-406-3266***	910-350-3100
Rogers Jewelry Co PO Box 3151	Modesto	CA	95353	**800-877-4221**	
Ross Simons Jewelers Inc 9 Ross Simons Dr	Cranston	RI	02920	**800-835-0919**	
Samuels Jewelers 9607 Research Blvd Ste 100 Bldg F	Austin	TX	78759	**877-202-2870**	512-369-1400
Shane Co 9790 E Arapahoe Rd	Greenwood Village	CO	80112	**866-467-4263**	
Shreve Crump & Low Inc 39 Newbury St	Boston	MA	02116	**800-328-4326**	617-267-9100
Sol Jewelry Designs Inc 550 S Hill St Ste 1020	Los Angeles	CA	90013	**888-323-7772**	213-622-7772
Tiffany & Co 727 Fifth Ave *NYSE: TIF* ■ *Orders	New York	NY	10022	**800-526-0649***	212-755-8000
Trabert & Hoeffer 111 E Oak St	Chicago	IL	60611	**800-539-3573**	312-787-1654
Van Cleef & Arpels Inc 744 Fifth Ave	New York	NY	10019	**877-826-2533**	212-896-9284
Wixon Jewelers Inc 9955 Lyndale Ave S	Minneapolis	MN	55420	**800-853-7667**	952-881-8862
Zale Corp 6201 15th Ave *NYSE: ZLC* ■ *Cust Svc	Brooklyn	NY	11219	**866-249-2593***	718-921-8137
Zales Jewelers Div 901 W Walnut Hill Ln *Cust Svc	Irving	TX	75038	**800-311-5393***	972-580-4000

411 JEWELRY, WATCHES, GEMS - WHOL

Company / Address	City	State	Zip	Toll-Free	Phone
Alishaev Bros Inc 20 W 47th St Ste 203	New York	NY	10036	**877-859-6020**	
Broco Products Inc 18624 Syracuse Ave	Cleveland	OH	44110	**800-321-0837**	216-531-0880
Charles & Colvard Ltd 170 Southport Dr *NASDAQ: CTHR*	Morrisville	NC	27560	**877-202-5467**	
Circa Inc 415 Madison Ave 19th Fl	New York	NY	10017	**877-876-5493**	212-486-6013
Continental Coin Corp 5627 Sepulveda Blvd	Van Nuys	CA	91411	**800-552-6467**	818-781-4232
EH Ashley & Company Inc 1 White Squadron Rd	Riverside	RI	02915	**800-735-7424**	401-431-0950
Empire Diamond Corp 350 Fifth Ave Ste 4000	New York	NY	10118	**800-728-3425**	212-564-4777
Frederick Goldman Inc 154 W 14th St	New York	NY	10011	**800-221-3232**	
Gemex Systems Inc 6040 W Executive Dr Ste A	Mequon	WI	53092	**866-694-3639**	262-242-1111
Gerson Co 1450 S Lone Elm Rd	Olathe	KS	66061	**800-444-8172**	913-262-7400
Identification Plates Inc 1555 High Point Dr	Mesquite	TX	75149	**800-395-2570**	972-216-1616
Jewel-Craft Inc 4122 Olympic Blvd	Erlanger	KY	41018	**800-525-5482**	859-282-2400
Joseph Blank Inc 62 W 47th St Ste 808	New York	NY	10036	**800-223-7666**	212-575-9050
Kendra Scott Design Inc 1400 S Congress Ave Ste A-170	Austin	TX	78704	**866-677-7023**	512-499-8400
Lashbrook Designs 131 E 13065 S	Draper	UT	84020	**888-252-7388**	
Leo Wolleman Inc 45 W 45th St 10th Fl	New York	NY	10036	**800-223-5667**	212-840-1881
Metal Marketplace International (MMI) 718 Sansom St	Philadelphia	PA	19106	**800-523-9191**	215-592-8777
Mikimoto (America) Company Ltd 680 Fifth Ave 4th Fl	New York	NY	10019	**844-341-0579**	212-457-4500
Seno Jewelry LLC 259 W 30th St 10th Fl	New York	NY	10001	**888-468-0888**	
World Minerals Inc 130 Castilian Dr	Goleta	CA	93117	**800-893-4445**	805-562-0200

412 JUVENILE DETENTION FACILITIES

SEE ALSO Correctional & Detention Management (Privatized) ; Correctional Facilities - State
Listings are organized alphabetically by states.

Company / Address	City	State	Zip	Toll-Free	Phone
Arkansas Juvenile Access & Treatment Ctr 425 W Capitol Ste 1620	Little Rock	AR	72201	**877-727-3468**	501-324-8900
Cuyahoga Hills Juvenile Correctional Facility 4321 Green Rd	Highland Hills	OH	44128	**800-872-3132**	216-464-8200
Fairbanks Youth Facility 1502 Wilbur St	Fairbanks	AK	99701	**800-478-2686**	907-451-2150
Ferris School 959 Centre Rd	Wilmington	DE	19805	**800-292-9582**	302-993-3800
Johnson Youth Ctr 3252 Hospital Dr	Juneau	AK	99801	**800-780-9972**	907-586-9433
Logansport Juvenile Correctional Facility 1118 S St Rd 25	Logansport	IN	46947	**800-800-5556**	574-753-7571
McLaughlin Youth Ctr 2600 Providence Dr	Anchorage	AK	99508	**800-478-2221**	907-261-4399
New Castle County Detention Ctr 963 Centre Rd	Wilmington	DE	19805	**800-969-4357**	302-633-3100
State Training School 3211 Edgington Ave	Eldora	IA	50627	**800-362-2178**	641-858-5402
Ventura Youth Correctional Facility 3100 Wright Rd	Camarillo	CA	93010	**866-232-5627**	805-485-7951
Woodland Hills Youth Development Ctr 3965 Stewarts Ln	Nashville	TN	37218	**855-418-1622**	615-532-2000

LABELS - FABRIC

SEE Narrow Fabric Mills

413 LABELS - OTHER THAN FABRIC

Company / Address	City	State	Zip	Toll-Free	Phone
Accurate Dial & Nameplate Inc 329 Mira Loma Ave	Glendale	CA	91204	**800-400-4455**	323-245-9181
Acro Labels Inc 2530 Wyandotte Rd	Willow Grove	PA	19090	**800-355-2235**	215-657-5366
Alcop Adhesive Label Co 826 Perkins Ln	Beverly	NJ	08010	**888-313-3017**	609-871-4400
AME Label Corp 25155 W Ave Stanford	Valencia	CA	91355	**866-278-9268**	661-257-2200
Arch Crown Tags Inc 460 Hillside Ave	Hillside	NJ	07205	**800-526-8353**	973-731-6300
Avery Dennison Corp 207 Goode Ave *NYSE: AVY* ■ *Cust Svc	Glendale	CA	91203	**888-567-4387***	626-304-2000
Best Label Co 2900 Faber St	Union City	CA	94587	**800-637-5333**	510-489-5400
Blue Ribbon Tag & Label Corp 4035 N 29th Ave	Hollywood	FL	33020	**800-433-4974**	954-922-9292
Brady Corp 6555 W Good Hope Rd *NYSE: BRC* ■ *Cust Svc	Milwaukee	WI	53223	**800-541-1686***	414-358-6600

Name / Address	City	State	Zip	Toll-Free	Phone
Brady Identification Solutions 6555 W Good Hope Rd *Cust Svc	Milwaukee	WI	53223	**800-537-8791***	414-358-6600
CCL Label Inc 161 Worcester Rd Ste 502	Framingham	MA	01701	**877-240-9772**	508-872-4511
Cellotape Inc 47623 Fremont Blvd	Fremont	CA	94538	**800-231-0608**	510-651-5551
Clamp Swing Pricing Company Inc 8386 Capwell Dr	Oakland	CA	94621	**800-227-7615**	510-567-1600
Data Label Inc 1000 Spruce St	Terre Haute	IN	47807	**800-457-0676**	812-232-0408
DeskTop Labels 7277 Boone Ave N	Minneapolis	MN	55428	**800-241-9730**	
Discount Labels Inc 4115 Profit Ct	New Albany	IN	47150	**800-995-9500**	
East West Label Co 1000 E Hector St	Conshohocken	PA	19428	**800-441-7333**	610-825-0410
Ennis Inc PO Box D	Wolfe City	TX	75496	**800-527-1008**	972-775-9801
General Data Co Inc 4354 Ferguson Dr	Cincinnati	OH	45245	**800-733-5252**	513-752-7978
Gilbreth Packaging Systems 3001 State Rd	Croydon	PA	19021	**800-630-2413**	
Grand Rapids Label Co 2351 Oak Industrial Dr NE	Grand Rapids	MI	49505	**800-552-5215**	616-459-8134
Green Bay Packaging Inc 1700 Webster Ct	Green Bay	WI	54302	**800-236-8400**	920-433-5111
Harris Industries Inc 5181 Argosy Ave	Huntington Beach	CA	92649	**800-222-6866**	714-898-8048
Impact Label Corp 3434 S Burdick St	Kalamazoo	MI	49001	**800-820-0362**	269-381-4280
International Label & Printing Company Inc 2550 United Ln	Elk Grove Village	IL	60007	**800-244-1442**	
Labelmaster Co 5724 N Pulaski Rd	Chicago	IL	60646	**800-621-5808**	773-478-0900
Labeltape Inc 5100 Beltway Dr SE	Caledonia	MI	49316	**800-928-4537**	616-698-1830
Lancer Label 301 S 74th St *Cust Svc	Omaha	NE	68114	**800-228-7074***	
McCourt Label Co 20 Egbert Ln	Lewis Run	PA	16738	**800-458-2390**	814-362-3851
MPI Label Systems Inc 450 Courtney Rd	Sebring	OH	44672	**800-423-0442**	330-938-2134
National Printing Converters Inc 18 S Murphy Ave	Brazil	IN	47834	**800-877-6724**	
Phifer Inc 4400 Kauloosa Ave PO Box 1700	Tuscaloosa	AL	35401	**800-633-5955**	205-345-2120
Print-O-Tape Inc 755 Tower Rd	Mundelein	IL	60060	**800-346-6311**	847-362-1476
Printed Systems 1265 Gillingham Rd *Sales	Neenah	WI	54956	**800-352-2332***	
Quikstik Labels 220 Broadway	Everett	MA	02149	**800-225-3496**	617-389-7570
Reidler Decal Corp 264 Industrial Pk Rd PO Box 8	Saint Clair	PA	17970	**800-628-7770**	
Shamrock Scientific Specialty Systems Inc 34 Davis Dr	Bellwood	IL	60104	**800-323-0249**	708-547-9005
Smyth Cos Inc 1085 Snelling Ave N	Saint Paul	MN	55108	**800-473-3464**	651-646-4544
Spectrum Label Corp 30803 San Clemente St	Hayward	CA	94544	**800-545-2235**	510-477-0707
Spinnaker Coating Inc 518 E Water St	Troy	OH	45373	**800-543-9452**	937-332-6500
Tape & Label Converters Inc 8231 Allport Ave	Santa Fe Springs	CA	90670	**888-285-2462**	562-945-3486
Tapecon Inc 10 Latta Rd	Rochester	NY	14612	**800-333-2407**	585-621-8400
TAPEMARK Co 1685 Marthaler Ln	St Paul	MN	55118	**800-535-1998**	651-455-1611
Weber Marking Systems Inc 711 W Algonquin Rd *Sales	Arlington Heights	IL	60005	**800-843-4242***	847-364-8500
Whitlam Label Company Inc 24800 Sherwood Ave	Center Line	MI	48015	**800-755-2235**	586-757-5100
Wright Global Graphics 5115 Prospect St	Thomasville	NC	27360	**800-678-9019**	336-472-4200
WS Packaging Group Inc 2571 S. Hemlock Rd	Green Bay	WI	54229	**800-236-3424**	800-818-5481

414 LABOR UNIONS

Name / Address	City	State	Zip	Toll-Free	Phone
AFT Healthcare 555 New Jersey Ave NW	Washington	DC	20001	**800-238-1133**	202-879-4491
Air Line Pilots Assn 535 Herndon Pkwy	Herndon	VA	20170	**877-331-1223**	703-689-2270
Amalgamated Transit Union (ATU) 10000 New Hampshire Ave	Silver Spring	MD	20903	**888-240-1196**	202-537-1645
American Federation of Government Employees 80 F St NW	Washington	DC	20001	**888-844-2343**	202-737-8700
American Federation of Labor & Congress of Industrial Organizations (AFL-CIO) 815 16th St NW	Washington	DC	20006	**877-850-4959**	202-637-5000
American Federation of Musicians of the US & Canada (AFM) 1501 Broadway Ste 600	New York	NY	10036	**800-762-3444**	212-869-1330
American Federation of Teachers (AFT) 555 New Jersey Ave NW	Washington	DC	20001	**800-238-1133**	202-879-4400
Association of Professional Flight Attendants 1004 W Euless Blvd	Euless	TX	76040	**800-395-2732**	817-540-0108
B.C. Government & Service Employees' Union 4911 Canada Way	Burnaby	BC	V5G3W3	**800-663-1674**	604-291-9611
Brotherhood of Locomotive Engineers & Trainmen (BLET) 1370 Ontario St Mezzanine Level	Cleveland	OH	44113	**877-772-5772**	216-241-2630
Directors Guild of America 7920 W Sunset Blvd	Los Angeles	CA	90046	**800-421-4173**	310-289-2000
Glass Molders Pottery Plastics & Allied Workers International Union 608 E Baltimore Pike	Media	PA	19063	**855-670-4787**	610-565-5051
Inlandboatmen's Union of the Pacific (IBU) 1711 W Nickerson St Ste D	Seattle	WA	98119	**800-562-6000**	206-284-6001
International Alliance of Theatrical Stage Employees Moving Picture Technicians (IATSE) 1430 Broadway 20th Fl	New York	NY	10018	**800-456-3863**	212-730-1770
International Assn of Bridge Structural Ornamental & Reinforcing Iron Workers 1750 New York Ave NW Ste 400	Washington	DC	20006	**800-368-0105**	202-383-4800
International Longshore & Warehouse Union 1188 Franklin St 4th Fl	San Francisco	CA	94109	**866-266-0013**	415-775-0533
International Organization of Masters Mates & Pilots 700 Maritime Blvd	Linthicum Heights	MD	21090	**877-667-5522**	410-850-8700
International Union of Bricklayers & Allied Craftworkers (BAC) 1776 eye St NW	Washington	DC	20006	**888-880-8222**	202-783-3788
International Union of Painters & Allied Trades (IUPAT) 7234 Pkwy Dr	Hanover	MD	21076	**800-554-2479**	410-564-5900
International Union of Police Assn 1549 Ringling Blvd Ste 600	Sarasota	FL	34236	**800-247-4872**	941-487-2560
International Union Security Police & Fire Professionals of America (SPFPA) 25510 Kelly Rd	Roseville	MI	48066	**800-228-7492**	586-772-7250
National Air Traffic Controllers Assn (NATCA) 1325 Massachusetts Ave NW	Washington	DC	20005	**800-266-0895**	202-628-5451
Ocsea-Afscme Local 390 Worthington Rd Ste A	Westerville	OH	43082	**800-969-4702**	614-865-4700
Ontario Nurses Association 85 Grenville St Ste 400	Toronto	ON	M5S3A2	**800-387-5580**	416-964-8833
Power Worker's Union, The 244 Eglinton Ave E	Toronto	ON	M4P1K2	**800-958-8798**	416-481-4491
Screen Actors Guild (SAG) 5757 Wilshire Blvd	Los Angeles	CA	90036	**800-724-0767**	323-954-1600
Seafarers International Union 5201 Auth Way	Camp Springs	MD	20746	**800-252-4674**	301-899-0675
Service Employees International Union 1800 Massachusetts Ave NW	Washington	DC	20036	**800-424-8592**	202-730-7000
Sheet Metal Workers International Assn (SMWIA) 1750 New York Ave NW 6th Fl	Washington	DC	20006	**800-251-7045**	202-783-5880
Shopper Local 2222 Sedwick Rd # 102	Durham	NC	27713	**877-251-4592**	
Transportation Communications International Union 3 Research Pl	Rockville	MD	20850	**877-772-5772**	301-948-4910
Unifor 301 Laurier Ave W	Ottawa	ON	K1P6M6	**877-230-5201**	613-230-5200
Union of American Physicians & Dentists 180 Grand Ave Ste 1380	Oakland	CA	94612	**800-622-0909**	510-839-0193
United Brotherhood of Carpenters & Joiners of America 101 Constitution Ave NW	Washington	DC	20001	**800-530-5090**	202-546-6206
United Food & Commercial Workers International Union (UFCW) 1775 K St NW	Washington	DC	20006	**800-551-4010**	202-223-3111
United Food & Commercial Workers Union Local 555 7095 SW Sandburg St	Tigard	OR	97281	**800-452-8329**	503-684-2822
United Scenic Artists 29 W 38th St 15th Fl	New York	NY	10018	**800-456-3863**	212-581-0300
United Transportation Union 14600 Detroit Ave	Cleveland	OH	44107	**800-558-8842**	216-228-9400
Writers Guild of America West (WGAw) 7000 W Third St	Los Angeles	CA	90048	**800-421-4182**	323-951-4000

415 LABORATORIES - DENTAL

SEE ALSO Laboratories - Medical

Name / Address	City	State	Zip	Toll-Free	Phone
1 Biotechnology PO Box 758	Oneco	FL	34264	**800-951-4246**	941-355-8451
Alcopro Inc 2547 Sutherland Ave	Knoxville	TN	37919	**800-227-9890**	865-525-4900
American Health Associates 671 Ohio Pk Ste K	Cincinnati	IN	45245	**800-522-7556**	
Applied Diagnostics Inc 1140 Business Center Dr Ste 370	Houston	TX	77043	**855-239-8378**	713-271-4133
Boos Dental Laboratory 1000 Boone Ave N Ste 660	Golden Valley	MN	55427	**800-333-2667**	763-544-1446
BRLI No 2 Acquisition Corp 207 Perry Pkwy	Gaithersburg	MD	20877	**888-729-1206**	301-519-2100
C B D 11603 Crosswinds Way Ste 100	San Antonio	TX	78233	**888-858-8663**	210-590-3033
Calgary Laboratory Services 3535 Research Rd NW	Calgary	AB	T2L2K8	**800-661-3450**	403-770-3500
Carolina Medical Lab 1815 Back Creek Dr	Charlotte	NC	28213	**800-963-3522**	704-598-8818
Cleveland HeartLab Inc 6701 Carnegie Ave Ste 500	Cleveland	OH	44103	**866-358-9828**	
Coast2Coast Diagnostics Inc 600 N Tustin Ave Ste 110	Santa Ana	CA	92705	**800-730-9263**	
Cytolab Pathology Services 6825 216th St Sw	Lynnwood	WA	98036	**800-845-6167**	425-712-8020
Dental Technologies Inc (DTI) 5601 Arnold Rd	Dublin	CA	94568	**800-229-0936**	925-829-3611
Distinctive Dental Studio Ltd. Inc 1504 Wall St	Naperville	IL	60563	**800-552-7890**	630-369-4600
DynaLifeDX Diagnostic Laboratory Services 10150 - 102 St Ste 200	Edmonton	AB	T5J5E2	**800-661-9876**	780-451-3702
Elisa Act Biotechnologies 109 Carpenter Dr	Sterling	VA	20165	**800-553-5472**	
First Dental Health 5771 Copley Dr Ste 101	San Diego	CA	92111	**800-334-7244**	
Foundation Laboratory 1716 W Holt Ave	Pomona	CA	91768	**800-843-7190**	909-623-9301
Gamma Dynacare Medical Laboratories Inc 115 Midair Ct	Brampton	ON	L6T5M3	**800-668-2714**	
Genetics Associates Inc 1916 Patterson St Ste 400	Nashville	TN	37203	**800-331-4363**	615-327-4532
Highlands Pathology Consultants Pc 2175 Hwy 75 Ste 4	Blountville	TN	37617	**877-696-6775**	423-323-5290
Imaging Healthcare Specialists Medical Group Inc 6256 Greenwich Dr Ste 150	San Diego	CA	92122	**866-558-4320**	
Integrated Regional Laboratories Inc 5361 NW 33rd Ave	Ft. Lauderdale	FL	33309	**800-522-0232**	
Interactive Medical Connections Inc 700 Gemini St Ste 110	Houston	TX	77058	**800-480-8040**	281-486-4434
Kaylor Dental Laboratory Inc 619 N Florence St	Wichita	KS	67212	**800-657-2549**	316-943-3226
Kimball Genetics Inc 8490 Upland Dr Ste 100	Englewood	CO	80112	**800-444-9111**	

Name / Address	City	State	Zip	Toll-Free	Phone
LifeScan Laboratory Inc 5255 W Golf	Skokie	IL	60077	**800-270-0037**	
Modern Dental Laboratory USA LLC 13228 SE 30th St Ste C-6	Bellevue	WA	98005	**877-711-8778**	
Molecular Imaging Services Inc 10 Whitaker Ct	Bear	DE	19701	**866-937-8855**	
MRI Group 2100 Harrisburg Pk	Lancaster	PA	17601	**888-674-1377**	717-291-1016
O'Brien Dental Lab Inc 4311 SW Research Way	Corvallis	OR	97333	**800-445-5941**	541-754-1238
Pathology & Cytology Laboratories Inc 290 Big Run Rd	Lexington	KY	40503	**800-264-0514**	859-278-9513
PersonalizeDx 2980 Scott St	Vista	CA	92081	**877-429-6643**	
Phenopath Laboratories PLLC 551 N 34th St Ste 100	Seattle	WA	98103	**888-927-4366**	206-374-9000
Posca Bros Dental Laboratory Inc 641 W Willow St	Long Beach	CA	90806	**800-537-6722**	562-427-1811
Quality Bioresources Inc 1015 N Austin St	Seguin	TX	78155	**888-674-7224**	830-372-4797
Roe Dental Laboratory Inc 9565 Midwest Ave	Garfield Heights	OH	44125	**800-228-6663**	216-663-2233
Roman Research Inc 800 Franklin St	Hanson	MA	02341	**800-225-8652**	
Rose Radiology Boot Ranch 4133 Woodlands Pkwy	Palm Harbor	FL	34685	**877-674-7673**	727-781-3888
Vista Imaging Services Inc 3941 Park Dr Ste 20-463	El Dorado Hills	CA	95762	**855-972-9729**	415-272-3925
Warde Medical Laboratory 300 W Textile Rd	Ann Arbor	MI	48108	**800-876-6522**	734-214-0300

416 LABORATORIES - DRUG-TESTING

SEE ALSO Laboratories - Medical

Name / Address	City	State	Zip	Toll-Free	Phone
ArcticDx Inc MaRS Centre S Tower 101 College St Ste 200	Toronto	ON	M5G1L7	**866-964-5182**	
Bio-Reference Laboratories Inc 481 Edward H Ross Dr *NASDAQ: BRLI*	Elmwood Park	NJ	07407	**800-229-5227**	
DrugScan Inc 200 Precision Rd Ste 200 PO Box 347	Horsham	PA	19044	**800-235-4890**	
LabOne Inc 10101 Renner Blvd	Lenexa	KS	66219	**800-646-7788**	913-888-1770
MEDTOX Scientific Inc 402 W County Rd D *NASDAQ: MTOX*	Saint Paul	MN	55112	**800-832-3244**	651-636-7466
US Drug Testing Laboratories Inc 1700 S Mt Prospect Rd	Des Plaines	IL	60018	**800-235-2367**	847-375-0770

417 LABORATORIES - GENETIC TESTING

SEE ALSO Laboratories - Medical

Name / Address	City	State	Zip	Toll-Free	Phone
Blood Systems Laboratories 2424 W Erie Dr	Tempe	AZ	85282	**800-288-2199**	602-343-7000
BRT Laboratories Inc 400 W Franklin St	Baltimore	MD	21201	**800-765-5170**	410-225-9595
Center for Genetic Testing at Saint Francis 6465 S Yale Ave	Tulsa	OK	74136	**877-789-6001**	918-502-1720
Commonwealth Biotechnologies Inc 601 Biotech Dr	Richmond	VA	23235	**800-735-9224**	804-648-3820
DNA Diagnostics Ctr 1 DDC Way	Fairfield	OH	45014	**800-362-2368**	513-881-7800
DNA Paternity Lab of Utah 2749 E Parleys Way Ste 100	Salt Lake City	UT	84109	**800-362-5559**	801-466-3872
Genetic Profiles Corp 10675 Treena St Ste 103	San Diego	CA	92131	**800-551-7763**	
Genetica DNA Laboratories Inc 8740 Montgomery Rd	Cincinnati	OH	45236	**800-433-6848**	513-985-9777
GenQuest DNA Analysis Laboratory 133 Coney Island Dr	Sparks	NV	89431	**877-362-5227**	775-358-0652
Genzyme Genetics 3400 Computer Dr	Westborough	MA	01581	**800-255-7357**	508-898-9001
Identity Genetics Inc 47927 213th St	Aurora	SD	57002	**800-861-1054**	
Laboratory Corp of America Holdings 358 S Main St *NYSE: LH*	Burlington	NC	27215	**800-334-5161**	336-584-5171
LABS Inc 6933 S Revere Pkwy	Centennial	CO	80112	**866-393-2244**	720-528-4750
Maxxam Analytics Inc 335 LaiRd Rd Ste 2	Guelph	ON	N1G4P7	**877-706-7678**	
Medical Genetics Consultants 819 DeSoto St	Ocean Springs	MS	39564	**800-362-4363**	
Memorial Blood Centers (MBC) 737 Pelham Blvd *Cust Svc	Saint Paul	MN	55114	**888-448-3253***	651-332-7000
Molecular Pathology Laboratory Network Inc 250 E Broadway	Maryville	TN	37804	**800-932-2943**	865-380-9746
NMS Labs 3701 Welsh Rd	Willow Grove	PA	19090	**800-522-6671**	215-657-4900
Paternity Testing Corp (PTC) 300 Portland St	Columbia	MO	65201	**888-837-8323**	573-442-9948
Rhode Island Blood Ctr 405 Promenade St	Providence	RI	02908	**800-283-8385**	401-453-8360
South Texas Blood & Tissue Ctr 6211 IH-10 W	San Antonio	TX	78201	**800-292-5534**	210-731-5555
State University of New York Upstate Medical University Tissue Typing Laboratory 750 E Adams St	Syracuse	NY	13210	**877-464-5540**	315-464-4775
University of North Texas Health Science Ctr 3500 Camp Bowie Blvd	Fort Worth	TX	76107	**800-687-7580**	817-735-2000

Classified Section

418 LABORATORIES - MEDICAL

SEE ALSO Laboratories - Dental ; Laboratories - Drug-Testing ; Laboratories - Genetic Testing ; Organ & Tissue Banks ; Blood Centers

Name / Address	City	State	Zip	Toll-Free	Phone
ABC American Bio-clinical 2730 N Main St Ste 101	Los Angeles	CA	90031	**800-262-1688**	
Accugenix Inc 223 Lake Dr	Newark	DE	19702	**877-274-8371**	302-292-8888
Ariosa Diagnostics Inc 5945 Optical Ct	San Jose	CA	95138	**855-927-4672**	
Arkansas Anatomic Pathology Services pa 411 E Matthews Ave	Jonesboro	AR	72401	**800-764-0447**	870-930-3518
Atherotech Inc 201 London Pkwy	Birmingham	AL	35211	**800-719-9807**	
Aurum Ceramic Dental Laboratories Ltd 115 17 Ave SW	Calgary	AB	T2S0A1	**800-665-8815**	403-228-5120
Bio-Reference Laboratories Inc 481 Edward H Ross Dr *NASDAQ: BRLI*	Elmwood Park	NJ	07407	**800-229-5227**	
Boval Company LP 505 W Industrial Blvd	Cleburne	TX	76031	**800-635-1706**	817-645-1706
Calvert Labs 1225 Crescent Green Ste 115	Cary	NC	27518	**800-300-8114**	919-459-8653
Canadian Medical Laboratories Ltd 6560 Kennedy Rd	Mississauga	ON	L5T2X4	**800-263-0801**	
Cell Signaling Technology Inc 3 Trask Ln	Danvers	MA	01923	**877-678-8324**	978-867-2300
Cmi 6704 Guada Coma Dr	Schertz	TX	78154	**800-840-1070**	210-967-6169
Cml Healthcare Inc Unit 1 60 Courtneypark Dr W	Mississauga	ON	L5W0B3	**800-263-0801**	905-565-0043
DIANON Systems Inc 1 Forest Pkwy	Shelton	CT	06484	**800-328-2666**	203-926-7100
Equipoise Dental Laboratory Inc 85 Portland Ave	Bergenfield	NJ	07621	**800-999-4950**	201-385-4750
Genetrack Biolabs Inc 401-1508 Broadway W	Vancouver	BC	V6J1W8	**888-828-1899**	604-325-7282
Genova Diagnostics 63 Zillicoa St	Asheville	NC	28801	**800-522-4762**	828-253-0621
Global Neuro-Diagnostics LP 2670 Firewheel Dr Ste B	Flower Mound	TX	75028	**866-848-2522**	
Great Plains Laboratory Inc 11813 W 77th St	Overland Park	KS	66214	**800-288-0383**	913-341-8949
Harmony Dental Lab 758 W Duval St	Jacksonville	FL	32202	**888-354-3594**	904-354-4467
Health Network Laboratory 2024 Lehigh St	Allentown	PA	18103	**877-402-4221**	610-402-8170
Identigene LLC 2495 South West Temple	Salt Lake City	UT	84115	**888-404-4363**	801-462-1401
Igenex 795 San Antonio Rd	Palo Alto	CA	94303	**800-832-3200**	650-424-1191
Keller Laboratories Inc 160 Larkin Williams Industrial Ct	Fenton	MO	63026	**800-325-3056**	636-600-4200
LabOne Inc 10101 Renner Blvd	Lenexa	KS	66219	**800-646-7788**	913-888-1770
Laboratory Corp of America Holdings 358 S Main St *NYSE: LH*	Burlington	NC	27215	**800-334-5161**	336-584-5171
Medical Diagnostic Laboratories LLC 2439 Kuser Rd	Hamilton	NJ	08690	**877-269-0090**	609-570-1000
National Genetics Institute 2440 S Blvd Ste 235	Los Angeles	CA	90064	**800-352-7788**	310-996-0036
Nebraska Lablinc LLC 5440 S St Ste 100	Lincoln	NE	68506	**866-886-5462**	402-484-5462
NeuroScience Inc 373 280th St	Osceola	WI	54020	**888-342-7272**	715-294-2144
NMS Labs 3701 Welsh Rd	Willow Grove	PA	19090	**800-522-6671**	215-657-4900
Norgen Biotek Corp 3430 Schmon Pkwy	Thorold	ON	L2V4Y6	**866-667-4362**	905-227-8848
North Coast Clinical Laboratory Inc 2215 Cleveland Rd	Sandusky	OH	44870	**800-325-5737**	419-626-6012
Opmedic Group Inc 1361 Beaumont Ave Ste 301	Mount-royal	QC	H3P2W3	**888-776-2732**	514-345-8535
Parkway Clinical Laboratories Inc 3494 Progress Dr	Bensalem	PA	19020	**800-327-2764**	215-245-5112
Path Logic Inc 950 Riverside Pkwy Ste 90	West Sacramento	CA	95605	**855-291-4528**	
Physician's Automated Laboratory Inc (PALLAB) 9830 Brimhall Rd	Bakersfield	CA	93312	**800-675-2271**	661-829-2260
Quest Diagnostics at Nichols Institute 33608 Ortega Hwy	San Juan Capistrano	CA	92675	**800-642-4657**	949-728-4000
Quest Diagnostics Inc 3 Giralda Farms *NYSE: DGX*	Madison	NJ	07940	**800-222-0446**	201-393-5000
South Bend Medical Foundation 530 N Lafayette Blvd	South Bend	IN	46601	**800-544-0925**	574-234-4176
Specialty Laboratories Inc 27027 Tourney Rd *Sales	Valencia	CA	91355	**800-421-7110***	661-799-6543
Sunrise Medical Laboratories Inc 250 Miller Pl *Cust Svc	Hicksville	NY	11801	**800-782-0282***	631-435-1515
Visalia Medical Lab 5400 West Hillsdale Ave	Visalia	CA	93291	**800-486-2362**	559-562-1222

419 LABORATORY ANALYTICAL INSTRUMENTS

SEE ALSO Glassware - Laboratory & Scientific ; Laboratory Apparatus & Furniture

Name / Address	City	State	Zip	Toll-Free	Phone
Abaxis Inc 3240 Whipple Rd *NASDAQ: ABAX*	Union City	CA	94587	**800-822-2947**	510-675-6500
American Biologics 1180 Walnut Ave	Chula Vista	CA	91911	**800-227-4473**	619-429-8200
BD Biosciences 2350 Qume Dr	San Jose	CA	95131	**800-223-8226**	408-432-9475

				Toll-Free	Phone
Bio/Data Corp PO Box 347	Horsham	PA	19044	**800-257-3282**	215-441-4000
Bioanalytical Systems Inc 2701 Kent Ave *NASDAQ: BASI*	West Lafayette	IN	47906	**800-845-4246**	765-463-4527
BioTek Instruments Inc 100 Tigan St PO Box 998	Winooski	VT	05404	**888-451-5171**	802-655-4740
Buehler Ltd 41 Waukegan Rd *Sales	Lake Bluff	IL	60044	**800-283-4537***	847-295-6500
California Analytical Instruments Inc 1312 W Grove Ave	Orange	CA	92865	**800-959-0949**	714-974-5560
Caliper Life Sciences Inc 68 Elm St	Hopkinton	MA	01748	**800-762-4000**	508-435-9500
CAO Group Inc 4628 Skyhawk Dr	West Jordan	UT	84084	**877-877-9778**	801-256-9282
CDS Analytical Inc 465 Limestone Rd PO Box 277	Oxford	PA	19363	**800-541-6593**	610-932-3636
CEM Corp 3100 Smith Farm Rd	Matthews	NC	28104	**800-726-3331**	704-821-7015
Cepheid 904 E Caribbean Dr *NASDAQ: CPHD*	Sunnyvale	CA	94089	**888-838-3222**	408-541-4191
Cetac Technologies Inc 14306 Industrial Rd	Omaha	NE	68144	**800-369-2822**	402-733-2829
Chrom Tech Inc 5995 149th St W Ste 102	Apple Valley	MN	55124	**800-822-5242**	952-431-6000
CMI Inc 316 E Ninth St	Owensboro	KY	42303	**866-835-0690**	270-685-6545
CompuMed Inc 5777 W Century Blvd Ste 360	Los Angeles	CA	90045	**800-421-3395**	310-258-5000
Corning Inc Life Sciences Div 836 N St Bldg 300 Ste 3401	Tewksbury	MA	01876	**800-492-1110**	978-442-2200
Datacolor 5 Princess Rd *General	Lawrenceville	NJ	08648	**800-340-1007***	609-924-2189
Eberbach Corp 505 S Maple Rd	Ann Arbor	MI	48103	**800-422-2558**	734-665-8877
FEI Co 5350 NE Dawson Creek Dr *NASDAQ: FEIC* ■ *Cust Svc	Hillsboro	OR	97124	**866-693-3426***	503-726-7500
Fisher Scientific Company Inc 112 Colonnade Rd	Ottawa	ON	K2E7L6	**800-234-7437**	613-226-8874
Gambro BCT 10811 W Collins Ave	Lakewood	CO	80215	**877-339-4228**	303-231-4357
Gatan Inc 5794 W Las Positas Blvd	Pleasanton	CA	94588	**888-887-3377**	925-463-0200
GrayWolf Sensing Solutions LLC 6 Research Dr	Shelton	CT	06484	**800-218-7997**	203-402-0477
Hach Co PO Box 389	Loveland	CO	80539	**800-227-4224**	970-669-3050
Hamilton Co 4970 Energy Way	Reno	NV	89502	**800-648-5950**	775-858-3000
Harvard Bioscience Inc 84 October Hill Rd *NASDAQ: HBIO*	Holliston	MA	01746	**800-272-2775**	508-893-8999
Helena Laboratories Inc 1530 Lindbergh Dr	Beaumont	TX	77704	**800-231-5663**	409-842-3714
Horiba Instruments Inc 17671 Armstrong Ave	Irvine	CA	92614	**800-446-7422**	949-250-4811
hygiena LLC 941 Avenida Acaso	Camarillo	CA	93012	**877-494-4364**	805-388-8007
Illumina Inc 9885 Towne Centre Dr *NASDAQ: ILMN*	San Diego	CA	92121	**800-809-4566**	858-202-4500
Instrumentation Laboratory Inc 180 Hartwell Rd *Sales	Bedford	MA	01730	**800-955-9525***	781-861-0710
ISCO Inc 4700 Superior St PO Box 82531	Lincoln	NE	68501	**800-228-4250**	402-464-0231
Labcon North America Inc 3700 Lkeville Hwy	Petaluma	CA	94954	**800-227-1466**	707-766-2100
LaMotte Co 802 Washington Ave	Chestertown	MD	21620	**800-344-3100**	410-778-3100
Leco Corp 3000 Lakeview Ave	Saint Joseph	MI	49085	**800-292-6141**	269-985-5496
Li Cor Inc PO Box 4425	Lincoln	NE	68504	**800-447-3576**	402-467-3576
Luminex Corp 12212 Technology Blvd *NASDAQ: LMNX*	Austin	TX	78727	**888-219-8020**	512-219-8020
Mandel Scientific Company Inc 2 Admiral Pl	Guelph	ON	N1G4N4	**888-883-3636**	519-763-9292
Med-Plus Medical Supplies 17 Vanderbilt Ave	Brooklyn	NY	11205	**888-433-2300**	718-222-4416
Micromeritics Instrument Corp 1 Micromeritics Dr	Norcross	GA	30093	**800-229-5052**	770-662-3620
Modal Shop Inc, The 1776 Mentor Ave	Cincinnati	OH	45212	**800-860-4867**	513-351-9919
Molecular Devices Inc (MDI) 1311 Orleans Dr	Sunnyvale	CA	94089	**800-635-5577**	408-747-1700
Monogram Biosciences Inc 345 Oyster Pt Blvd	South San Francisco	CA	94080	**800-777-0177**	650-635-1100
MPD Inc 316 E Ninth St	Owensboro	KY	42303	**866-225-5673**	270-685-6200
New Objective Inc 2 Constitution Way	Woburn	MA	01801	**888-220-2998**	781-933-9560
Nova Biomedical Corp 200 Prospect St *Sales	Waltham	MA	02454	**800-458-5813***	781-894-0800
OI Corp 151 Graham Rd PO Box 9010	College Station	TX	77842	**800-653-1711**	979-690-1711
Olis Inc 130 Conway Dr Ste A B & C	Bogart	GA	30622	**800-852-3504**	706-353-6547
Pall Life Sciences 600 S Wagner Rd	Ann Arbor	MI	48103	**800-521-1520**	734-665-0651
Particle Measuring Systems Inc 5475 Airport Blvd *Cust Svc	Boulder	CO	80301	**800-238-1801***	303-443-7100
Photo Research Inc 9731 Topanga Canyon Pl	Chatsworth	CA	91311	**877-424-6423**	818-341-5151
Response Biomedical Corp 1781 75th Ave W *TSE: RBM*	Vancouver	BC	V6P6P2	**888-591-5577**	604-456-6010
Sakura Finetek USA Inc 1750 W 214th St	Torrance	CA	90501	**800-725-8723**	310-972-7800
Schroer Manufacturing Co 511 Osage Ave	Kansas City	KS	66105	**800-444-1579**	913-281-1500
Scientific Industries Inc 70 Orville Dr	Bohemia	NY	11716	**888-850-6208**	631-567-4700
SEER Technology Inc 2681 Parleys Way Ste 201	Salt Lake City	UT	84109	**877-505-7337**	801-746-7888
Sheldon Laboratory Systems Inc 102 Kirk St PO Box 836	Crystal Springs	MS	39059	**800-531-7604**	601-892-2731
Shimadzu Scientific Instruments Inc 7102 Riverwood Dr	Columbia	MD	21046	**800-477-1227**	410-381-1227
Siskiyou Corp 110 Sw Booth St	Grants Pass	OR	97526	**877-313-6418**	541-479-8697
Smart Imaging Technologies Inc 1770 Saint James Pl Ste 414	Houston	TX	77056	**877-280-1100**	713-589-3500
Soilmoisture Equipment Corp 801 S Kellogg Ave	Goleta	CA	93117	**888-964-0040**	805-964-3525
Sparton Corp 425 N Martingale Rd Ste 2050	Schaumburg	IL	60173	**800-772-7866**	847-762-5800
Spectra Services Inc 6359 Dean Pkwy	Ontario	NY	14519	**800-955-7732**	585-265-4320
Spectrum Laboratories Inc 18617 Broadwick St	Rancho Dominguez	CA	90220	**800-634-3300**	310-885-4600
Spectrum Systems Inc 3410 W Nine-Mile Rd	Pensacola	FL	32526	**800-432-6119**	850-944-3392
STARR Life Sciences Corp 333 Allegheny Ave Ste 300	Oakmont	PA	15139	**866-978-2779**	
Supelco Inc 595 N Harrison Rd	Bellefonte	PA	16823	**800-247-6628**	814-359-3441
Tekran Instruments Corp 230 Tech Ctr Dr	Knoxville	TN	37912	**888-383-5726**	865-688-0688
Temptronic Corp 41 Hampden Rd *Tech Support	Mansfield	MA	02048	**800-558-5080***	781-688-2300
Thermo Fisher Scientific Inc 81 Wyman St *NYSE: TMO*	Waltham	MA	02454	**800-678-5599**	781-622-1000
Toptica Photonics Inc 1286 Blossom Dr Ste 1	Victor	NY	14564	**877-277-9897**	585-657-6663
Transgenomic Inc 12325 Emmet St *OTC: TBIO*	Omaha	NE	68164	**888-233-9283**	402-452-5400
Upchurch Scientific Inc 619 Oak St	Oak Harbor	WA	98277	**800-426-0191**	360-679-2528
Waters Corp 34 Maple St *NYSE: WAT*	Milford	MA	01757	**800-252-4752**	508-478-2000
ZTR Control Systems Inc 8050 County Rd 101 East	Minneapolis	MN	55379	**855-724-5987**	

420 LABORATORY APPARATUS & FURNITURE

SEE ALSO Scales & Balances ; Glassware - Laboratory & Scientific ; Laboratory Analytical Instruments

				Toll-Free	Phone
Baker Company Inc 161 Gatehouse Rd PO Box E	Sanford	ME	04073	**800-992-2537**	207-324-8773
Bel-Art Products Inc 661 Rte 23 S	Wayne	NJ	07440	**800-423-5278**	973-694-0500
Boekel Scientific 855 Pennsylvania Blvd	Feasterville	PA	19053	**800-336-6929**	215-396-8200
Caliper Life Sciences Inc 68 Elm St	Hopkinton	MA	01748	**800-762-4000**	508-435-9500
Cole-Parmer Instrument Co 625 E Bunker Ct	Vernon Hills	IL	60061	**800-323-4340**	847-549-7600
Corning Inc Life Sciences Div 836 N St Bldg 300 Ste 3401	Tewksbury	MA	01876	**800-492-1110**	978-442-2200
Edstrom Industries Inc 819 Bakke Ave	Waterford	WI	53185	**800-558-5913**	262-534-5181
Ika-Works Inc 2635 Northchase Pkwy SE	Wilmington	NC	28405	**800-733-3037**	910-452-7059
Kalamazoo Technical Furniture 6450 Vly Industrial Dr	Kalamazoo	MI	49009	**800-832-5227**	
Kewaunee Scientific Corp 2700 W Front St PO Box 1842 *NASDAQ: KEQU*	Statesville	NC	28687	**800-824-6626**	704-873-7202
Knf Neuberger Inc 2 Black Forest Rd	Trenton	NJ	08691	**800-323-4340**	609-890-8600
Labconco Corp 8811 Prospect Ave *Cust Svc	Kansas City	MO	64132	**800-821-5525***	816-333-8811
Nalge Nunc International 75 Panorama Creek Dr	Rochester	NY	14625	**800-625-4327**	585-586-8800
Omnicell Inc 1201 Charleston Rd *NASDAQ: OMCL*	Mountain View	CA	94043	**800-850-6664**	650-251-6100
Pacific Combustion Engineering Co 2107 Border Ave	Torrance	CA	90501	**800-342-4442**	310-212-6300
Parr Instrument Co 211 53rd St	Moline	IL	61265	**800-872-7720**	309-762-7716
Parter Medical Products Inc 17015 Kingsview Ave	Carson	CA	90746	**800-666-8282**	310-327-4417
Percival Scientific Inc 505 Research Dr	Perry	IA	50220	**800-695-2743**	515-465-9363
Preston Industries Inc 6600 W Touhy Ave	Niles	IL	60714	**800-229-7569**	847-647-0611
Thermal Product Solutions 2821 Old Rt 15 PO Box 150	New Columbia	PA	17856	**800-586-2473**	570-538-7200
Thermo Fisher Scientific Inc 81 Wyman St *NYSE: TMO*	Waltham	MA	02454	**800-678-5599**	781-622-1000
ThermoGenesis Corp 2711 Citrus Rd *NASDAQ: KOOL*	Rancho Cordova	CA	95742	**800-783-8357**	916-858-5100
Thomas Scientific 1654 High Hill Rd PO Box 99	Swedesboro	NJ	08085	**800-345-2100**	856-467-2000

421 LADDERS

Company / Address	City	State	Zip	Toll-Free	Phone
ALACO Ladder Co 5167 G St	Chino	CA	91710	**888-310-7040**	909-591-7561
Ballymore Co 501 Gunnard Carlson Dr	Coatesville	PA	19365	**800-762-8327**	610-593-5062
Cotterman Co 130 Seltzer Rd	Croswell	MI	48422	**800-552-3337**	810-679-4400
Duo-Safety Ladder Corp 513 W Ninth Ave	Oshkosh	WI	54902	**877-386-5377**	920-231-2740
Lynn Ladder & Scaffolding Company Inc 20 Boston St	Lynn	MA	01904	**800-225-2510**	781-598-6010
Werner Co 93 Werner Rd	Greenville	PA	16125	**888-523-3371**	
Wing Enterprises Inc 1198 N Spring Creek	Springville	UT	84663	**866-872-5901**	801-489-3684

422 LANDSCAPE DESIGN & RELATED SERVICES

Company / Address	City	State	Zip	Toll-Free	Phone
Cagwin & Dorward Inc 1565 S Novato Blvd Ste B	Novato	CA	94947	**800-891-7710**	415-892-7710
Creative Environments 8920 S Hardy Dr	Tempe	AZ	85284	**855-777-9305**	480-458-4100
Environmental Earthscapes Inc 5075 S Swan Rd	Tucson	AZ	85706	**800-571-1575**	520-571-1575
Landscape Concepts Management 31745 Alleghany Rd	Grayslake	IL	60030	**866-655-3800**	847-223-3800
Lipinski Landscape & Irrigation Contractors Inc 100 Sharp Rd	Marlton	NJ	08053	**800-644-6035**	
Mission Landscape Services Inc 536 E Dyer Rd	Santa Ana	CA	92707	**800-545-9963**	
US Lawns 4700 Millenia Blvd Ste 240	Orlando	FL	32839	**800-875-2967**	

423 LANGUAGE SCHOOLS

SEE ALSO Translation Services

Company / Address	City	State	Zip	Toll-Free	Phone
Agape English Language Institute (AELI) 610 Pickens St PO Box 12504	Columbia	SC	29201	**877-476-2354**	803-799-3452
AmeriSpan Unlimited 1334 Walnut St 6 Fl	Philadelphia	PA	19107	**800-879-6640**	215-751-1100
Boston Academy of English 38 Chauncy St 8th Fl	Boston	MA	02111	**800-704-9313**	
Boston Academy of English inc 38 Chauncy St 8th Fl	Boston	MA	02111	**800-704-9313**	
Colorado School of English 331 14th St	Denver	CO	80202	**877-234-0654**	720-932-8900
Cultural Ctr for Language Studies 3191 Coral Way Ste 114	Miami	FL	33145	**800-704-8181**	305-529-2257
ESL Instruction & Consulting Inc 42 Broad St NW	Atlanta	GA	30303	**877-579-2366**	404-577-2366
Lingua School Inc 225 E Las Olas Blvd 6th Fl	Fort Lauderdale	FL	33301	**888-654-6482**	954-577-9955
POLY Languages Institute Inc (POLY) 5757 Wilshire Blvd Ste 510	Los Angeles	CA	90036	**877-738-5787**	323-933-9399
Tamwood International College 300-909 Burrard St	Vancouver	BC	V6Z2N2	**866-533-0123**	604-899-4480

424 LASER EQUIPMENT & SYSTEMS - MEDICAL

SEE ALSO Medical Instruments & Apparatus - Mfr

Company / Address	City	State	Zip	Toll-Free	Phone
BioLase Technology Inc 4 Cromwell	Irvine	CA	92618	**800-699-9462**	888-424-6527
Candela Corp 530 Boston Post Rd *NASDAQ: CLZR*	Wayland	MA	01778	**800-733-8550**	508-358-7400
Cynosure Inc 5 Carlisle Rd *NASDAQ: CYNO*	Westford	MA	01886	**800-886-2966**	978-256-4200
Iridex Corp 1212 Terra Bella Ave *NASDAQ: IRIX* ■ *Cust Svc	Mountain View	CA	94043	**800-388-4747***	650-940-4700
Laserscope 3070 Orchard Dr	San Jose	CA	95134	**800-878-3399**	408-943-0636
Lumenis Ltd 2033 Gateway Pl Ste 200	San Jose	CA	95110	**877-586-3647**	408-764-3000
PhotoMedex Inc 40 Ramland Rd S, 2nd Fl Ste 200 *NASDAQ: PHMD*	Orangeburg	NY	10962	**888-966-1010**	215-619-3600
Spectranetics Corp 9965 Federal Dr *NASDAQ: SPNC*	Colorado Springs	CO	80921	**800-231-0978**	719-447-2000
Trimedyne Inc 15091 Bake Pkwy *OTC: TMED*	Irvine	CA	92618	**800-733-5273**	949-559-5300

425 LASERS - INDUSTRIAL

Company / Address	City	State	Zip	Toll-Free	Phone
AGL Corp 2202 N Redmond Rd PO Box 189	Jacksonville	AR	72076	**800-643-9696**	501-982-4433
Baublys Control Laser Corp 7101 Tpc Dr Ste 100	Orlando	FL	32822	**866-612-8619**	407-926-3500
Coherent Inc 5100 Patrick Henry Dr *NASDAQ: COHR* ■ *Sales	Santa Clara	CA	95054	**800-527-3786***	408-764-4000
Continuum 3150 Central Expy	Santa Clara	CA	95051	**888-532-1064**	408-727-3240
Electro Scientific Industries Inc 13900 NW Science Pk Dr *NASDAQ: ESIO* ■ *Cust Svc	Portland	OR	97229	**800-331-4708***	503-641-4141
GSI Group Inc 125 Middlesex Tpke *NASDAQ: GSIG*	Bedford	MA	01730	**800-342-3757**	781-266-5700
IPG Photonics Corp 50 Old Webster Rd *NASDAQ: IPGP*	Oxford	MA	01540	**877-980-1550**	508-373-1100
Laser Excel N6323 Berlin Rd PO Box 279	Green Lake	WI	54941	**800-285-6544**	920-294-6544
Leica Geosystems Inc 3498 Kraft Ave SE *Sales	Grand Rapids	MI	49512	**800-367-9453***	616-977-4189
Synrad Inc 4600 Campus Pl	Mukilteo	WA	98275	**800-796-7231**	425-349-3500

426 LAUNDRY & DRYCLEANING SERVICES

SEE ALSO Linen & Uniform Supply

Company / Address	City	State	Zip	Toll-Free	Phone
Admiral Inc 10 Taylor Ave	Annapolis	MD	21401	**800-864-4429**	410-267-8381
Coinmach Service Corp 303 Sunnyside Blvd Ste 70	Plainview	NY	11803	**877-264-6622**	516-349-8555
Crown Management Services Inc 1501 N Guillemard St	Pensacola	FL	32501	**800-844-5280**	850-438-7578
Dove Cleaners Inc 1560 Yonge St	Toronto	ON	M4T2S9	**866-999-3683**	416-413-7900
Martinizing Dry Cleaning 8944 Columbia Rd Ste J	Loveland	OH	45140	**800-827-0207**	
Nu-Yale Cleaners 6300 Hwy 62	Jeffersonville	IN	47130	**888-644-7400**	812-285-7400
Pressed4Time Inc 8 Clock Tower Pl Ste 110	Maynard	MA	01754	**800-423-8711**	

LAUNDRY EQUIPMENT - HOUSEHOLD

SEE Appliances - Major - Mfr ; Appliances - Whol

427 LAUNDRY EQUIPMENT & SUPPLIES - COMMERCIAL & INDUSTRIAL

Company / Address	City	State	Zip	Toll-Free	Phone
Coinmach Service Corp 303 Sunnyside Blvd Ste 70	Plainview	NY	11803	**877-264-6622**	516-349-8555
Colmac Industries Inc PO Box 72	Colville	WA	99114	**800-926-5622**	509-684-4505
Edro Corp 37 Commerce St *Sales	East Berlin	CT	06023	**800-628-6434***	860-828-0311
Ellis Corp 1400 W Bryn Mawr Ave	Itasca	IL	60143	**800-611-6806**	630-250-9222
GA Braun Inc 461 E Brighton Ave	Syracuse	NY	13212	**800-432-7286**	315-475-3123
Kemco Systems Inc 11500 47th St N	Clearwater	FL	33762	**800-633-7055**	727-573-2323
Minnesota Chemical Co 2285 Hampden Ave	Saint Paul	MN	55114	**800-328-5689**	651-646-7521
Thermal Engineering of Arizona Inc 2250 W Wetmore Rd	Tucson	AZ	85705	**866-832-7278**	520-888-4000

428 LAW FIRMS

SEE ALSO Legal Professionals Associations ; Litigation Support Services ; Arbitration Services - Legal ; Bar Associations - State

Company / Address	City	State	Zip	Toll-Free	Phone
Advocacy Center for Persons With Disabilities 2728 Centerview Dr Ste 102	Tallahassee	FL	32301	**800-342-0823**	850-488-9071
Ahmad, Zavitsanos, Anaipakos, Alavi & Mensing PC 1 Houston Ctr 1221 McKinney St Ste 3460	Houston	TX	77010	**800-856-8153**	713-655-1101
Alan b Harris Attorney at Law 409 N Texas Ave	Odessa	TX	79761	**800-887-1676**	432-580-3118
Armentor Glenn Law Corp 300 Stewart St	Lafayette	LA	70501	**800-960-5551**	337-233-1471
Arnold & Itkin LLP 6009 Memorial Dr	Houston	TX	77007	**888-493-1629**	713-222-3800
Arns Law Firm, The 515 Folsom St Fl 3	San Francisco	CA	94105	**800-495-7800**	415-495-7800
Atkinson Conway & Gagnon Inc 420 L St Ste 500	Anchorage	AK	99501	**800-478-1900**	907-276-1700
Attorney Aid Divorce & Bankruptcy Center Inc 3605 Long Beach Blvd Ste 300	Long Beach	CA	90807	**877-905-5297**	562-988-0885
Barker Martin PS 719 Second Ave Ste 1200	Seattle	WA	98104	**888-381-9806**	360-756-9806
Barnes & Thornburg 11 S Meridian St	Indianapolis	IN	46204	**800-236-1352**	317-236-1313
Barris, Sott, Denn & Driker PLLC 333 W Fort St Ste 1200	Detroit	MI	48226	**877-529-8750**	313-965-9725
BCF LLP 25th Fl 1100 Rene-Levesque Blvd W	Montreal	QC	H3B5C9	**866-511-8501**	514-397-8500
Berding & Weil LLP 2175 N California Blvd Ste 500	Walnut Creek	CA	94596	**800-838-2090**	925-838-2090
Berger & Montague PC 1622 Locust St	Philadelphia	PA	19103	**800-424-6690**	215-875-3000
Black Mann & Graham LLP 2905 Corporate Cir	Flower Mound	TX	75028	**888-293-0505**	972-353-4174
Blasingame, Burch, Garrard & Ashley PC 440 College Ave	Athens	GA	30603	**866-354-3544**	706-354-4000
Blitt & Gaines Pc 661 Glenn Ave	Wheeling	IL	60090	**888-920-0620**	847-403-4900
Blue Williams LLP 3421 N Causeway Blvd Ste 900	Metairie	LA	70002	**800-326-4991**	504-831-4091

Classified Section

Name / Address	City	State	ZIP	Toll-Free	Phone
Boies Schiller & Flexner LLP 5301 Wisconsin Ave NW	Washington	DC	20015	**877-224-0464**	202-237-2727
Boren, Oliver & Coffey LLP 59 N Jefferson St	Martinsville	IN	46151	**800-403-9971**	765-342-0147
Brewer & Pritchard 3 Riverway Ste 1800	Houston	TX	77024	**800-445-8710**	713-209-2950
Broyles Kight & Ricafort PC 8250 Haverstick Rd Ste 100	Indianapolis	IN	46240	**888-834-2692**	317-571-3600
Buchanan Ingersoll & Rooney PC 301 Grant St 1 Oxford Ctr 20th Fl	Pittsburgh	PA	15219	**800-444-6738**	412-562-8800
Bull, Housser & Tupper LLP 900 Howe St Ste 900	Vancouver	BC	V6Z2M4	**866-687-6575**	604-687-6575
Burns Burns Walsh & Walsh pa 704 Topeka Ave	Lyndon	KS	66451	**888-528-3186**	785-828-4418
Cameron, Hodges, Coleman, LaPointe & Wright PA 111 N Magnolia Ave Ste 1350	Orlando	FL	32801	**888-841-5030**	407-841-5030
Cavanagh Law Firm, The 1850 N Central Ave	Phoenix	AZ	85004	**888-824-3476**	602-322-4000
Cellino & Barnes PC 2500 Main Pl Tower 350 Main St	Buffalo	NY	14202	**800-888-8888**	716-854-2020
Charles d Hankey Law Office PC 434 E New York St	Indianapolis	IN	46202	**800-520-3633**	317-634-8565
Clark, Gagliardi & Miller PC 99 Court St	White Plains	NY	10601	**800-734-5694**	
Cocciardi & Associates Inc 4 Kacey Ct	Mechanicsburg	PA	17055	**800-377-3024**	717-766-4500
Cochran Firm LLC 111 E Main St	Dothan	AL	36301	**800-843-3476**	334-793-1555
Cohen Highley LLP 255 Queens Ave	London	ON	N6A5R8	**800-563-1020**	519-672-9330
Collins & Lacy PC 1330 Lady St 6th Fl	Columbia	SC	29201	**888-648-0526**	803-256-2660
Cooley Godward Kronish LLP 3000 El Camino Real	Palo Alto	CA	94306	**888-654-2411**	650-843-5000
Coon Brent & Associates Law Firm Pc 215 Orleans St	Beaumont	TX	77701	**866-335-2666**	409-835-2666
Cooper Legal Services Dwayne e Cooper Atty at Law 8411 Tuskin Way	Indianapolis	IN	46278	**800-959-1825**	317-873-3600
Copple, Rockey, Mckeever & Schlecht PC LLO 2425 Taylor Ave	Norfolk	NE	68701	**888-860-2425**	402-371-4300
Cozen O'Connor 1900 Market St	Philadelphia	PA	19103	**800-523-2900**	215-665-2000
Cullen, Weston, Pines & Bach LLP 122 W Washington Ave Ste 900	Madison	WI	53703	**866-443-8661**	608-807-0752
Dale L Buchanan & Associates PC 6576 E Brainerd Rd	Chattanooga	TN	37421	**800-813-8783**	423-894-2552
Daniel & Stark Law Offices 100 W William Joel Bryan Pkwy	Bryan	TX	77803	**800-474-1233**	254-776-6200
Davies Pearson PC 920 Fawcett Ave	Tacoma	WA	98401	**800-439-1112**	253-620-1500
Davis Law Firm 10500 Heitage Blvd Ste 102	San Antonio	TX	78201	**800-770-0127**	210-444-4444
Day Pitney LLP 242 Trumbull St	Hartford	CT	06103	**866-667-6572**	860-275-0100
Dechert LLP 2929 Arch St Cira Ctr	Philadelphia	PA	19104	**800-328-4880**	215-994-4000
Dennis, Corry, Porter & Smith LLP 14 Piedmont Ctr 3535 Piedmont Rd NE Ste 900	Atlanta	GA	30305	**800-735-0838**	404-365-0102
Dickstein Shapiro LLP 1825 Eye St NW	Washington	DC	20006	**800-203-3447**	202-420-2200
Docken & Co 900-800 6 Ave Sw	Calgary	AB	T2P3G3	**877-269-3612**	403-269-3612
Domengeaux Wright Roy & Edwards LLC 556 Jefferson St Ste 500	Lafayette	LA	70501	**800-375-6186**	337-233-3033
Donati Law Firm LLP 1545 Union Ave	Memphis	TN	38104	**800-521-0578**	901-278-1004
Dorsey & Whitney LLP 50 S Sixth St Ste 1500	Minneapolis	MN	55402	**800-759-4929**	612-340-2600
Elliott, Ostrander & Preston PC Union Bank Tower 707 SW Washington St Ste 1500	Portland	OR	97205	**866-716-3410**	503-224-7112
Ellis Ged & Bodden pa 7171 N Federal Hwy	Boca Raton	FL	33487	**888-342-3476**	561-995-1966
Emerson Thomson & Bennett LLC 1914 Akron Peninsula Rd	Akron	OH	44313	**800-822-8113**	330-434-9999
Evan K Thalenberg Law Offices 216 E Lexington St	Baltimore	MD	21202	**800-778-1181**	410-625-9100
Faegre & Benson LLP 90 S Seventh St 2200 Wells Fargo Bldg	Minneapolis	MN	55402	**800-328-4393**	612-766-7000
Farr, Farr, Emerich, Hackett & Carr PA Earl D Farr Bldg 99 Nesbit St	Punta Gorda	FL	33950	**855-327-7529**	941-639-1158
Farris, Riley & Pitt LLP 2025 Third Ave N Ste 400	Birmingham	AL	35203	**888-580-5176**	205-324-1212
Field Law 10235 101 St Nw Ste 2000	Edmonton	AB	T5J3G1	**800-222-6479**	780-423-3003
Fish & Richardson PC 1 Marina Park Dr	Boston	MA	02110	**800-818-5070**	617-542-5070
Foley & Lardner LLP 777 E Wisconsin Ave	Milwaukee	WI	53202	**855-225-5341**	414-271-2400
Foster Pepper Pllc 1111 Third Ave Ste 3400	Seattle	WA	98101	**800-995-5902**	206-447-4400
Fraser Stryker PC LLO 500 Energy Plz 409 S 17th St	Omaha	NE	68102	**800-544-6041**	402-341-6000
Frost Brown Todd LLC 201 E Fifth St 2200 PNC Ctr	Cincinnati	OH	45202	**866-559-6446**	513-651-6800
Fulbright & Jaworski LLP 1301 McKinney St Ste 5100	Houston	TX	77010	**866-385-2744**	713-651-5151
Gallagher, Gams, Pryor, Tallan & Littrell LLP 471 E Broad St 19th Fl	Columbus	OH	43215	**866-378-1624**	614-228-5151
Garan Lucow Miller PC 1000 Woodbridge St	Detroit	MI	48207	**800-875-1530**	313-446-1530
Garden City Group LLC 105 Maxess Rd	Melville	NY	11747	**888-404-8013**	631-470-5000
Gibson Dunn & Crutcher LLP 333 S Grand Ave Ste 4600	Los Angeles	CA	90071	**888-203-1112**	213-229-7000
Gislason & Hunter LLP 2700 S Broadway	New Ulm	MN	56073	**800-469-0234**	507-354-3111
Glancy Prongay & Murray LLP 1801 Ave Of The Stars	Los Angeles	CA	90067	**888-773-9224**	310-201-9150
Goldberg Weisman Cairo 1 E Wacker Dr Ste 3800	Chicago	IL	60601	**800-464-4772**	312-464-1234
Goodell Devries Leech & Dann LLP 1 S St 20th Fl	Baltimore	MD	21202	**888-229-4354**	410-783-4000
Gunster Yoakley & Stewart Pa 777 S Flagler Dr Ste 500 E	West Palm Beach	FL	33401	**800-749-1980**	561-655-1980
Gurstel Chargo LLP 6681 Country Club Dr	Golden Valley	MN	55427	**877-750-6335**	763-267-6700
Harman, Claytor, Corrigan & Wellman A Professional Corp PO Box 70280	Richmond	VA	23255	**877-747-4229**	804-747-5200
Harrang Long Gary Rudnick PC 360 E 10th Ave Ste 300	Eugene	OR	97401	**800-315-4172**	541-485-0220
Harris Wyatt & Amala Attorneys at Law 5778 Commercial St Se	Salem	OR	97306	**800-853-2144**	503-378-7744
Hartnett Law Firm, The 2920 N Pearl St	Dallas	TX	75201	**800-900-9702**	214-742-4655
Herman Herman Katz & Cotlar LLP 820 Okeefe Ave	New Orleans	LA	70113	**844-943-7626**	504-581-4892
Hertz Schram & Saretsky Pc 1760 S Telegraph Rd Ste 300	Bloomfield Hills	MI	48302	**866-775-5987**	248-335-5000
Hopkins & Carley A Law Corp PO Box 1469	San Jose	CA	95109	**800-829-3676**	408-286-9800
Horowitt, Darryl J. - Coleman & Horowitt LLP 499 W Shaw Ave Ste 116	Fresno	CA	93704	**800-891-8362**	559-248-4820
Iowa Legal Aid 1111 Ninth St Ste 230	Des Moines	IA	50314	**800-992-8161**	515-243-2151
Jacko Law Group PC 5920 Friars Rd Ste 208	San Diego	CA	92108	**866-497-2298**	619-298-2880
Jeansonne & Remondet LLC 365 Canal St Ste 1600	New Orleans	LA	70130	**800-446-2745**	337-237-4370
Jenkins Fenstermaker PLLC 325 Eighth St	Huntington	WV	25701	**866-617-4736**	304-523-2100
John C. Heath, Attorney at Law PLLC 360 N Cutler Dr	Salt Lake City	UT	84054	**800-756-9681**	
Joseph, Greenwald & Laake PA 6404 Ivy Ln Ste 400	Rockville	MD	20770	**877-412-7429**	301-220-2200
Katz Law Office Ltd 2408 W Cermak Rd	Chicago	IL	60608	**866-352-3033**	773-847-8982
Kelley & Ferraro LLP 2200 Key Tower 127 Pub Sq	Cleveland	OH	44114	**800-398-1795**	216-202-3450
Kelly Mike Law Group LLC 500 Taylor St Ste 400	Columbia	SC	29201	**866-692-0123**	803-726-0123
King & Schickli PLLC 247 N Broadway	Lexington	KY	40507	**888-364-5712**	859-252-0889
Kirkland & Ellis LLP 200 E Randolph Dr	Chicago	IL	60601	**800-647-7600**	312-861-2000
Kirkpatrick & Lockhart Preston Gates Ellis LLP 210 Sixth Ave	Pittsburgh	PA	15222	**800-452-8260**	412-355-6500
Kline & Specter A Professional Corp 1525 Locust St 19th Fl	Philadelphia	PA	19102	**800-243-1100**	215-772-1000
Larson King LLP 30 E Seventh St Ste 2800	Saint Paul	MN	55101	**877-373-5501**	651-312-6500
Lawton & Cates SC 10 E Doty St Ste 400	Madison	WI	53703	**800-900-4539**	608-282-6200
Legal Aid 126 W Adams St Fl 7	Jacksonville	FL	32202	**866-356-8371**	904-356-8371
Legal Aid Society of Palm Beach County Inc 423 Fern St Ste 200	West Palm Beach	FL	33401	**800-403-9353**	561-655-8944
Lesperance & Martineau 1440 Rue Sainte-catherine O	Montreal	QC	H3G1R8	**888-273-8387**	514-861-4831
Lewis Wagner 501 Indiana Ave #200	Indianapolis	IN	46202	**800-237-0505**	317-237-0500
Littler Mendelson PC 650 California St 20th Fl	San Francisco	CA	94108	**888-548-8537**	415-433-1940
Lloyd & McDaniel PLC 11405 Park Rd Ste 200	Louisville	KY	40223	**866-548-2486**	502-585-1880
Lloyd Gray Whitehead & Monroe PC 2501 20th Pl S Ste 300	Birmingham	AL	35223	**800-967-7299**	205-967-8822
Lopez Mchugh LLP 1123 Admiral Peary Way	Philadelphia	PA	19112	**877-703-7070**	215-952-6910
Lorber Greenfield & Polito LLP 13985 Stowe Dr	Poway	CA	92064	**800-659-8821**	858-513-1020
Lorge & Lorge Law Firm 501 W Willow St	Bear Creek	WI	54922	**800-529-2946**	715-752-3304
Lynch, Traub, Keefe & Errante A Professional Corp 52 Trumbull St	New Haven	CT	06506	**888-692-7403**	203-787-0275
Mallilo & Grossman 16309 Northern Blvd	Flushing	NY	11358	**866-593-6274**	718-461-6633
May, Adam, Gerdes & Thompson LLP 503 S Pierre St	Pierre	SD	57501	**800-636-8803**	605-224-8803
McAfee & Taft A Professional Corp 2 Leadership Sq 211 N Robinson Ste 1000	Oklahoma City	OK	73102	**800-235-9621**	405-235-9621
Mccallum, Hoaglund, Cook & Irby LLP 905 Montgomery Hwy Ste 201	Vestavia	AL	35216	**866-974-8145**	205-824-7767
McGuireWoods LLP 901 E Cary St 1 James Ctr	Richmond	VA	23219	**877-712-8778**	804-775-1000
McLennan Ross LLP 600 W Chambers 12220 Stony Plain Rd	Edmonton	AB	T5N3Y4	**800-567-9200**	780-482-9200
Meisner & Associates Pc 30200 Telegraph Rd Ste 467	Bingham Farms	MI	48025	**800-470-4433**	248-644-4433
Milbank Tweed Hadley & McCloy LLP 1 Chase Manhattan Plaza	New York	NY	10005	**800-229-0543**	212-530-5000
Miller & Chevalier Chartered 655 15th St NW Ste 900	Washington	DC	20005	**866-628-4282**	202-626-5800
Miller Johnson Snell & Cummiskey PLC 250 Monroe Ave NW Ste 800 PO Box 306	Grand Rapids	MI	49503	**800-772-1213**	616-831-1700
Morgan & Weisbrod 6800 W Loop S Ste 450	Bellaire	TX	77401	**877-898-1581**	713-838-0003
Morgan Lewis & Bockius LLP 1701 Market St	Philadelphia	PA	19103	**866-963-7137**	215-963-5000
Morrison Scott Alan Law Offices of pa 141 W Patrick St Ste 300	Frederick	MD	21701	**866-220-5185**	301-694-6262

Name / Address	City	State	ZIP	Toll-Free	Phone
Munsch Hardt Kopf Harr Pc 500 N Akard St	Dallas	TX	75201	**800-321-6742**	214-855-7500
Nahon, Saharovich & Trotz PLC 488 S Menhenhall Rd	Memphis	TN	38117	**800-529-4004**	901-683-7000
Nelson & Kennard 2180 Harvard St Ste 160 PO Box 13807	Sacramento	CA	95815	**866-920-2295**	
Nelson Mullins Riley & Scarborough LLP 1320 Main St 17th Fl	Columbia	SC	29201	**800-237-2000**	803-799-2000
New Haven Legal Assistance Association Inc 426 State St	New Haven	CT	06510	**877-829-5500**	203-946-4811
Niedner, Bodeux, Carmichael, Huff, Lenox & Pashos LLP 131 Jefferson St	Saint Charles	MO	63301	**888-572-2192**	636-949-9300
Nysarc Inc 393 Delaware Ave	Delmar	NY	12054	**800-735-8924**	518-439-8311
O'Reilly Rancilio PC Sterling Town Ctr 12900 Hall Rd Ste 350	Sterling Heights	MI	48313	**800-708-3528**	586-726-1000
Ohio Legal Assistance Foundation 10 W Broad St Ste 950	Columbus	OH	43215	**800-877-9772**	614-715-8560
Orrick Herrington & Sutcliffe LLP 666 Fifth Ave	New York	NY	10103	**866-342-5259**	212-506-5000
Pallett Valo LLP 77 City Ctr Dr Ste 300	Mississauga	ON	L5B1M5	**800-323-3781**	905-273-3300
Parker Poe Adams & Bernstein LLP 3 Wachovia Ctr 401 S Tryon St Ste 3000	Charlotte	NC	28202	**866-602-5893**	704-372-9000
Parr Richey Obremsky & Morton 201 N Illinois St Ste 300	Indianapolis	IN	46204	**888-337-7766**	317-269-2500
Pellettieri Rabstein & Altman 100 Nassau Pk Blvd	Princeton	NJ	08540	**800-432-5297**	609-520-0900
Perkins Coie LLP 1201 Third Ave Ste 4800	Seattle	WA	98101	**888-720-8382**	206-359-8000
Polsinelli Shalton Flanigan Suelthaus PC 700 W 47th St Ste 1000	Kansas City	MO	64112	**800-422-0893**	816-753-1000
Portnoff Law Associates Ltd 1000 Sandy Hill Rd Ste 1	Norristown	PA	19401	**866-211-9466**	484-690-9300
Proskauer Rose LLP 1585 Broadway	New York	NY	10036	**866-444-3272**	212-969-3000
Quarles & Brady LLP 411 E Wisconsin Ave Ste 2400	Milwaukee	WI	53202	**800-654-2200**	414-277-5000
Rad Law Firm 2001 Beach St Ste 600	Fort Worth	TX	76103	**800-598-1090**	817-465-8733
Rainwater, Holt & Sexton PA 6315 Ranch Dr	Little Rock	AR	72223	**800-434-4800**	
Relin, Goldstein & Crane LLP 28 E Main St Ste 1800	Rochester	NY	14614	**888-984-2351**	585-325-6202
Reminger & Reminger Company LPa 101 W Prospect Ave	Cleveland	OH	44115	**800-486-1311**	216-687-1311
Rendigs, Fry, Kiely & Dennis LLP 600 Vine St Ste 2650	Cincinnati	OH	45202	**800-274-2330**	513-381-9200
Reynolds, Mirth, Richards & Farmer LLP Manulife Pl 10180-101 St Ste 3200	Edmonton	AB	T5J3W8	**800-661-7673**	780-425-9510
Rodey Dickason Sloan Akin & Robb P A 201 Third St NW Ste 2200	Albuquerque	NM	87102	**800-226-2935**	505-765-5900
Ross & Matthews PC 3650 Lovell Ave	Fort Worth	TX	76107	**800-458-6982**	817-255-2000
Ross, Banks, May, Cron & Cavin PC 7700 San Felipe Ste 550	Houston	TX	77063	**866-896-1492**	713-626-1200
Rowley Chapman & Barney Ltd 63 E Main St Ste 501	Mesa	AZ	85201	**888-476-8411**	480-833-1113
Sachs Waldman Pc 1000 Farmer St	Detroit	MI	48226	**800-638-6722**	313-965-3464
Sackett & Associates 1055 Lincoln Ave	San Jose	CA	95125	**800-913-3000**	408-295-7755
Schlichter, Bogard & Denton 100 S Fourth St Ste 900	St. Louis	MO	63102	**800-873-5297**	314-621-6115
Schneiderman & Sherman 23938 Research Dr Ste 300	Farmington Hills	MI	48335	**866-867-7688**	248-539-7400
Schroeder Group, The 20800 Swenson Dr Ste 475	Waukesha	WI	53186	**800-372-3020**	262-798-8220
Searcy Denney Scarola Barnhart Po Box 3626	West Palm Beach	FL	33402	**800-780-8607**	561-686-6300
Settle & Pou PC 3333 Lee Pkwy 8th Fl	Dallas	TX	75219	**800-538-4661**	214-520-3300
Shean Law Offices 1114 N College Ave	Bloomington	IN	47404	**877-743-2652**	812-332-3643
Shook Hardy & Bacon LLP 2555 Grand Blvd	Kansas City	MO	64108	**855-380-7584**	816-474-6550
Sidley Austin LLP 787 Seventh Ave	New York	NY	10019	**800-306-5230**	312-853-7000
Sieben Polk PA 1640 S Frontage Rd Ste 200	Hastings	MN	55033	**800-620-1829**	651-437-3148
Silver & Archibald LLP 997 S Milledge Ave	Athens	GA	30605	**877-526-6281**	706-548-8122
Sindel, Sindel & Noble PC 8008 Carondelet Ave Ste 301	Saint Louis	MO	63105	**866-489-5504**	314-721-6040
Siskinds LLP 680 Waterloo St PO Box 2520	London	ON	N6A3V8	**877-672-2121**	519-672-2121
Slack & Davis LLP 2705 Bee Caves Rd Ste 220	Austin	TX	78746	**800-455-8686**	512-795-8686
Smith Hartvigsen PLLC The Walker Ctr 175 South Main St Ste 300	Salt Lake City	UT	84111	**877-825-2064**	801-413-1600
Smith, Sovik, Kendrick & Sugnet PC 250 S Clinton St Ste 600	Syracuse	NY	13202	**800-675-0011**	315-474-2911
Snell & Wilmer LLP 1 Arizona Ctr 400 E Van Buren St Ste 1900	Phoenix	AZ	85004	**800-322-0430**	602-382-6000
Spence Law Firm LLC 15 S Jackson St	Jackson	WY	83001	**800-967-2117**	307-733-7290
Spilman Thomas & Battle PLLC Spilman Cntr 300 Knwh Blv Spilman Ctr Spilman Center Ste 100	Charleston	WV	25301	**800-967-8251**	304-340-3838
Stark & Stark 993 Lenox Dr Bldg 2	Lawrenceville	NJ	08648	**800-535-3425**	609-896-9060
Stearns Weaver Miller Weissler Alhadeff & Sitterson P.A. 150 W Flagler St Ste 2200	Miami	FL	33130	**866-293-7866**	305-789-3200
Steele Law Firm p C The 949 County Rt 53	Oswego	NY	13126	**877-496-2687**	315-216-4721
Stueve Siegel Hanson LLP 460 Nichols Rd Ste 200	Kansas City	MO	64112	**800-714-0360**	816-714-7100
Sutherland Asbill & Brennan LLP 999 Peachtree St NE	Atlanta	GA	30309	**855-857-9769**	404-853-8000
Sweeney Law Firm 8109 Lima Rd	Fort Wayne	IN	46818	**866-793-6339**	260-420-3137
Taylor Law Offices Pc 122 E Washington Ave	Effingham	IL	62401	**800-879-2250**	
Taylor Wellons Politz & Duhe Aplc 8550 United Plz Blvd Ste 101	Baton Rouge	LA	70809	**877-850-1047**	225-387-9888
Texas Legal Services Center Inc 815 Brazos St Ste 1100	Austin	TX	78701	**888-343-4414**	512-477-6000
Thompson Hine LLP 127 Public Sq 3900 Key Ctr	Cleveland	OH	44114	**877-257-3382**	216-566-5500
Thorp Reed & Armstrong LLP 301 Grant St 14th Fl	Pittsburgh	PA	15219	**800-949-3120**	412-394-7711
Townsend James r 150 Dufferin Ave	London	ON	N6A5N6	**888-354-0448**	519-672-5272
Vinson & Elkins LLP 1001 Fannin St 1st City Tower Ste 2500	Houston	TX	77002	**877-610-2009**	713-758-2222
White Buffalo Club 160 West Gill Ave Ste 200	Jackson	WY	83001	**888-256-8182**	307-734-4900
Williams, Turner & Holmes PC 200 N Sixth St Ste 103	Grand Junction	CO	81501	**800-548-6528**	970-242-6262
Woodcock Washburn LLP 2929 Arch St Fl 12	Philadelphia	PA	19104	**877-843-4821**	215-568-3100

429 LAWN & GARDEN EQUIPMENT

SEE ALSO Farm Machinery & Equipment - Mfr

Name / Address	City	State	ZIP	Toll-Free	Phone
Ames True Temper Inc 465 Railroad Ave	Camp Hill	PA	17011	**800-393-1846**	
Armatron International Inc 15 Highland Ave	Malden	MA	02148	**800-343-3280**	781-321-2300
Artcraft Company Inc, The 200 John L Dietsch Blvd	North Attleboro	MA	02763	**800-659-4042**	508-695-4042
Binkley & Hurst LP 133 Rothsville Stn Rd	Lititz	PA	17543	**800-414-4705**	717-626-4705
Brinly-Hardy Co 3230 Industrial Pkwy	Jeffersonville	IN	47130	**800-626-5329**	812-218-7200
California Flexrake Corp 9620 Gidley St	Temple City	CA	91780	**800-266-4200**	626-443-4026
Carswell Distributing Co 3750 N Liberty St	Winston-Salem	NC	27105	**800-929-1948**	336-767-7700
CMD Products 1410 Flightline Dr Ste D	Lincoln	CA	95648	**800-210-9949**	916-434-0228
Commerce Corp 7603 Energy Pkwy	Baltimore	MD	21226	**800-883-0234**	410-255-3500
Corona Clipper Inc 22440 Tomasco Canyon Rd	Corona	CA	92883	**800-234-2547**	951-737-6515
Dultmeier Sales LLC 13808 Industrial Rd	Omaha	NE	68137	**888-677-5054**	402-333-1444
EarthWay Products Inc 1009 Maple St	Bristol	IN	46507	**800-294-0671**	574-848-7491
Echo Inc 400 Oakwood Rd	Lake Zurich	IL	60047	**800-673-1558**	847-540-8400
Encore Manufacturing Company Inc 2415 Ashland Ave	Beatrice	NE	68310	**800-267-4255**	
Gilmour Mfg Group 2537 Daniels St Somerset *Cust Svc	Madison	WI	53718	**866-348-5661***	
Grassland Equipment & Irrigation Corp 892-898 Troy Schenectady Rd	Latham	NY	12110	**800-564-5587**	518-785-5841
Green Depot Inc 1 Ivy Hill Rd	Brooklyn	NY	11211	**800-238-5008**	718-782-2991
Harnack Co 6016 Nordic Dr *Cust Svc	Cedar Falls	IA	50613	**800-772-2022***	319-277-0660
Hutson 306 Andrus Dr	Murray	KY	42071	**866-488-7662**	270-886-3994
Kanequip Inc 1451 S Second Ave	Dodge City	KS	67801	**800-359-1108**	620-225-0016
Lawn Equipment Parts Co 1475 River Rd	Marietta	PA	17547	**800-365-3726**	717-426-5200
Lodi Irrigation 1301 E Armstrong Rd	Lodi	CA	95242	**800-634-7272**	
MacKissic Inc PO Box 111	Parker Ford	PA	19457	**800-348-1117**	610-495-7181
Master Mark Plastics 210 Ampe Dr *Cust Svc	Paynesville	MN	56362	**800-535-4838***	320-243-7318
Melnor Inc 109 Tyson Dr	Winchester	VA	22603	**877-283-0697**	540-722-5600
Midwest Bio-systems Inc 28933 35 E St	Tampico	IL	61283	**877-649-2114**	815-438-7200
MTD Products Inc 5965 Grafton Rd	Valley City	OH	44280	**800-800-7310**	330-225-2600
Oliver M Dean Inc 125 Brooks St	Worcester	MA	01606	**800-648-3326**	508-856-9100
Precision Products Inc 316 Limit St *Cust Svc	Lincoln	IL	62656	**800-225-5891***	217-735-1590
Rugg Mfg Company Inc 105 Newton St	Greenfield	MA	01302	**800-633-8772**	413-773-5471
Simplicity Manufacturing Inc PO Box 702	Milwaukee	WI	53201	**800-837-6836**	
Smithco Inc 34 W Ave	Wayne	PA	19087	**877-833-7648**	610-688-4009
Stens Corp 2424 Cathy Ln	Jasper	IN	47546	**800-457-7444**	812-482-2526
Stihl Inc 536 Viking Dr *Cust Svc	Virginia Beach	VA	23452	**800-467-8445***	757-486-9100
Storr Tractor Co 3191 Rt 22	Branchburg	NJ	08876	**800-526-3802**	908-722-9830
Swisher Mower & Machine Company Inc 1602 Corporate Dr	Warrensburg	MO	64093	**800-222-8183**	660-747-8183

Classified Section

	City	State	Zip	Toll-Free	Phone
Toro Co 8111 Lyndale Ave	Bloomington	MN	55420	**888-384-9939**	
NYSE: TTC					
Toro Company Commercial Products Div 8111 Lyndale Ave	Bloomington	MN	55420	**800-348-2424***	952-888-8801
*Cust Svc					
Tuff Torq Corp 5943 Commerce Blvd	Morristown	TN	37814	**866-572-3441**	423-585-2000
Weathermatic 3301 W Kingsley Rd	Garland	TX	75041	**888-484-3776**	972-278-6131
Wesspur Tree Equipment 2121 Iron St	Bellingham	WA	98225	**800-268-2141**	360-734-5242

430 LEATHER GOODS - PERSONAL

SEE ALSO Clothing & Accessories - Mfr ; Footwear ; Handbags, Totes, Backpacks ; Leather Goods (Misc) ; Luggage, Bags, Cases

	City	State	Zip	Toll-Free	Phone
Buxton Co 245 Cadwell Dr	Springfield	MA	01104	**800-426-3638**	413-734-5900
Coach Inc 516 W 34th St	New York	NY	10001	**800-444-3611**	212-594-1850
NYSE: COH					
Dooney & Bourke Inc 1 Regent St	East Norwalk	CT	06855	**800-347-5000***	203-853-7515
*Cust Svc					

431 LEATHER GOODS (MISC)

	City	State	Zip	Toll-Free	Phone
Action Co 1425 N Tennessee St	McKinney	TX	75069	**800-937-3700***	972-542-8700
*Sales					
Auburn Leather Co 125 N Caldwell St	Auburn	KY	42206	**800-635-0617**	270-542-4116
Gould & Goodrich Leather Inc 709 E McNeil St	Lillington	NC	27546	**800-277-0732**	910-893-2071
Hunter Company Inc 3300 W 71st Ave	Westminster	CO	80030	**800-676-4868**	303-427-4626

432 LEATHER TANNING & FINISHING

	City	State	Zip	Toll-Free	Phone
Hermann Oak Leather Co 4050 N First St	Saint Louis	MO	63147	**800-325-7950**	314-421-1173
Leatherock International Inc 5285 Lovelock St	San Diego	CA	92110	**800-466-6667**	619-299-7625
Showa Best Glove Inc 579 Edison St	Menlo	GA	30731	**800-241-0323**	

433 LEGISLATION HOTLINES

	City	State	Zip	Toll-Free	Phone
Alabama State Legislature State House 11 S Union St	Montgomery	AL	36130	**800-499-3051**	334-242-7600
Florida Bill Status 111 W Madison St Rm 704	Tallahassee	FL	32399	**800-342-1827**	850-488-4371
Maryland Dept of Legislative Services 90 State Cir	Annapolis	MD	21401	**800-492-7122**	410-946-5400
Massachusetts Bill Status 1 Ashburton Pl Rm 1611	Boston	MA	02108	**800-392-6090**	617-727-7030
Nevada Bill Status 401 S Carson St	Carson City	NV	89701	**800-978-2878**	775-684-3360
New Jersey Bill Status State House Annex PO Box 068	Trenton	NJ	08625	**800-792-8630**	609-292-4840
New York Bill Status 202 Legislative Office Bldg	Albany	NY	12248	**800-342-9860**	518-455-4218
North Dakota Legislative Council Services State Capitol Bldg 600 E Blvd Ave	Bismarck	ND	58505	**800-366-6888**	701-328-2916
Washington Bill Status PO Box 40600	Olympia	WA	98504	**800-562-6000**	360-786-7573
West Virginia Bill Status State Capitol Complex Rm MB27 Bldg 1	Charleston	WV	25305	**877-565-3447**	304-347-4836
Wisconsin Bill Status 1 E Main St	Madison	WI	53708	**800-362-9472**	608-266-9960
Wyoming Legislative Service Office 3001 E Pershing Blvd	Cheyenne	WY	82002	**800-342-9570**	307-777-7881

434 LIBRARIES

SEE ALSO Library Systems - Regional - Canadian

434-1 Medical Libraries

	City	State	Zip	Toll-Free	Phone
Leon S McGoogan Library of Medicine University of Nebraska Medical Ctr 986705 Nebraska Medical Ctr.	Omaha	NE	68198	**866-800-5209**	402-559-6221
Moody Medical Library 914 Market st	Galveston	TX	77555	**866-235-5223**	409-772-2372
National Library of Medicine National Institutes of Health 8600 Rockville Pike Bldg 38	Bethesda	MD	20894	**888-346-3656**	301-594-5983
Oregon Health & Science University *Bone Marrow Transplant Program (OHSU)* 3181 SW Sam Jackson Pk Rd	Portland	OR	97239	**800-222-1222**	503-494-1617
Raymon H Mulford Library *Medical College of Ohio Toledo* 3000 Arlington Ave	Toledo	OH	43614	**800-321-8383**	419-383-4225
Ruth Lilly Medical Library 975 W Walnut St IB 100	Indianapolis	IN	46202	**877-952-1988**	317-274-7182
Saint Louis University 221 N Grand Blvd	Saint Louis	MO	63103	**800-758-3678**	314-977-7288
State University of New York at Buffalo *Health Sciences Library (HSL)* 3435 Main St Abbott Hall Rm 102	Buffalo	NY	14214	**866-432-5849**	716-829-3900
Texas A & M University Rudder Tower Ste 205	College Station	TX	77843	**888-890-5667**	979-845-8901
University of California Irvine *Library* PO Box 19557	Irvine	CA	92623	**800-848-4722**	949-824-6836
University of Nebraska Medical Ctr McGoogan Library of Medicine 986705 Nebraska Medical Ctr	Omaha	NE	68198	**866-800-5209**	402-559-4006
University of Pennsylvania 3451 Walnut St	Philadelphia	PA	19104	**800-537-5487**	215-898-5000
University of Tennessee Health Science Ctr *Health Sciences Library & Biocommunications Ctr* 877 Madison Ave	Memphis	TN	38103	**877-747-0004**	901-448-5634
University of Texas Southwestern Medical Ctr at Dallas Library, The 5323 Harry Hines Blvd	Dallas	TX	75390	**866-645-6455**	214-648-2001
West Virginia University PO Box 6009	Morgantown	WV	26506	**800-344-9881**	304-293-2121

434-2 Presidential Libraries

	City	State	Zip	Toll-Free	Phone
Abraham Lincoln Presidential Library & Museum 112 N Sixth St	Springfield	IL	62701	**800-610-2094**	217-557-6250
Dwight D Eisenhower Presidential Library & Museum 200 SE Fourth St	Abilene	KS	67410	**877-746-4453**	785-263-6700
Franklin D Roosevelt Presidential Library & Museum 4079 Albany Post Rd	Hyde Park	NY	12538	**800-337-8474**	845-486-7770
Harry S Truman Presidential Library & Museum 500 W Hwy 24	Independence	MO	64050	**800-833-1225**	816-268-8200
John F Kennedy Presidential Library & Museum Columbia Pt	Boston	MA	02125	**866-535-1960**	617-514-1600
LBJ Library & Museum 2313 Red River St	Austin	TX	78705	**800-874-6451**	512-721-0216
Ronald Reagan Presidential Library & Museum 40 Presidential Dr	Simi Valley	CA	93065	**800-410-8354**	805-522-2977
Rutherford B Hayes Presidential Ctr Spiegel Grove	Fremont	OH	43420	**800-998-7737**	419-332-2081
Woodrow Wilson Presidential Library 20 N Coalter St PO Box 24	Staunton	VA	24401	**888-496-6376**	540-885-0897

434-3 Public Libraries

Listings for public libraries are alphabetized by city name within each state grouping.

	City	State	Zip	Toll-Free	Phone
Alachua County Library District 401 E University Ave	Gainesville	FL	32601	**866-341-2730**	352-334-3900
Alameda County Library 2450 Stevenson Blvd	Fremont	CA	94538	**888-663-0660**	510-745-1500
Allen County Public Library 900 Library Plaza	Fort Wayne	IN	46802	**800-448-6160**	260-421-1200
Alpena County George N Fletcher Public Library 211 N First Ave	Alpena	MI	49707	**877-737-4106**	989-356-6188
Arlington Public Library 101 E Abram St	Arlington	TX	76010	**888-227-7669**	817-459-6900
Arrowhead Library System 210 Dodge St	Janesville	WI	53548	**855-352-9003**	608-758-6690
Atlantic City Free Public Library 1 N Tennessee Ave	Atlantic City	NJ	08401	**800-621-3362**	609-345-2269
Baltimore County Public Library 320 York Rd	Towson	MD	21204	**800-705-3493**	410-887-6100
Bangor Public Library 145 Harlow St	Bangor	ME	04401	**800-442-4293**	207-947-8336
Beauregard Parish Library 205 S Washington Ave	DeRidder	LA	70634	**800-524-6239**	337-463-6217
Bethlehem Area Public Library 11 W Church St	Bethlehem	PA	18018	**800-732-0999**	610-867-3761
Bloomfield Township Public Library 1099 Lone Pine Rd	Bloomfield Hills	MI	48302	**800-318-2596**	248-642-5800
Blue Grass Regional Library 104 E Sixth St	Columbia	TN	38401	**888-345-5575**	931-388-9282
Bolivar County Library 104 S Leflore Ave	Cleveland	MS	38732	**888-268-8076**	662-843-2774
Bristol Public Library 5 High St	Bristol	CT	06010	**877-603-7323**	860-584-7787
Bronx Library Ctr 310 E Kings Bridge Rd	Bronx	NY	10458	**800-342-3688**	718-579-4244
Brookfield Public Library 1900 N Calhoun Rd	Brookfield	WI	53005	**866-868-3947**	262-782-4140
Brunswick-Glynn County Regional Library 208 Gloucester St	Brunswick	GA	31520	**800-222-6748**	912-279-3740
Cambridge Public Library 244 S Birch St	Cambridge	MN	55008	**877-721-4862**	763-689-7390
Camden County Library 203 Laurel Rd	Voorhees	NJ	08043	**877-222-3737**	856-772-1636
Canton Public Library 1200 S Canton Ctr Rd	Canton	MI	48188	**888-988-6300**	734-397-0999
Carmel Clay Public Library 55 Fourth Ave SE	Carmel	IN	46032	**800-908-4490**	317-844-3361
Carnegie Regional Library 49 W Seventh St	Grafton	ND	58237	**800-568-5964**	701-352-2754
Carol Stream Public Library 616 Hiawatha Dr	Carol Stream	IL	60188	**800-829-1040**	630-653-0755
Caroline County Public Library 100 Market St	Denton	MD	21629	**800-832-3277**	410-479-1343
Carrollton Public Library 4220 N Josey Ln	Carrollton	TX	75010	**888-727-2978**	972-466-4800
Cerritos Civic Ctr 18025 Bloomfield Ave	Cerritos	CA	90703	**866-402-7433**	562-916-1350
City of Carlsbad Library 1250 Carlsbad Village Dr	Carlsbad	CA	92008	**866-230-2273**	760-434-2870
City of Palm Springs 300 S Sunrise Way	Palm Springs	CA	92262	**800-611-1911**	760-322-7323

Classified Section

Library	Address	City	State	Zip	Toll-Free	Phone
Clarksville Montgomery County Public Library	350 Pageant Ln	Clarksville	TN	37040	**877-239-6635**	931-648-8826
Clearwater Public Library	100 N Osceola Ave	Clearwater	FL	33755	**800-342-8060**	727-562-4970
Columbus Public Library	3000 Macon Rd	Columbus	GA	31906	**800-652-0782**	706-243-2669
Contra Costa County Library	75 Santa Barbara Rd	Pleasant Hill	CA	94523	**800-984-4636**	925-646-6423
Corsicana Public Library	100 N 12th St	Corsicana	TX	75110	**877-648-2836**	903-654-4810
Cumberland County Public Library	300 Maiden Ln	Fayetteville	NC	28301	**866-488-7386**	910-483-1580
Cuyahoga County Public Library	2111 Snow Rd	Parma	OH	44134	**800-749-5560**	216-398-1800
Daly City Public Library	40 Wembley Dr	Daly City	CA	94015	**888-227-7669**	650-991-8025
Daniel Boone Regional Library	100 W Broadway	Columbia	MO	65203	**800-324-4806**	573-443-3161
Danville Public Library	319 N Vermilion St	Danville	IL	61832	**866-235-6096**	217-477-5220
DeKalb County Public Library	215 Sycamore St	Decatur	GA	30030	**800-677-1116**	404-370-3070
DeKalb Public Library	309 Oak St	DeKalb	IL	60115	**888-268-2824**	815-756-9568
Delaware County District Library	84 E Winter St	Delaware	OH	43015	**866-862-7286**	740-362-3861
Des Plaines Public Library	1501 Ellinwood Ave	Des Plaines	IL	60016	**800-829-1040**	847-827-5551
Deschutes Public Library	507 NW Wall St	Bend	OR	97701	**855-268-3767**	541-312-1020
DeSoto Public Library	211 E Pleasant Run Rd Ste C	DeSoto	TX	75115	**800-886-9008**	972-230-9656
Downey City Library (DCL)	11121 Brookshire Ave	Downey	CA	90241	**877-846-3452**	562-904-7360
East Brunswick Public Library	2 Jean Walling Civic Ctr	East Brunswick	NJ	08816	**800-829-1040**	732-390-6950
EG Fisher Public Library	1289 Ingleside Ave	Athens	TN	37303	**800-552-6843**	423-745-7782
El Centro Public Library	539 State St	El Centro	CA	92243	**877-482-5656**	760-337-4565
Elk Grove Village Public Library	1001 Wellington Ave	Elk Grove Village	IL	60007	**800-252-8980**	847-439-0447
Englewood Public Library	1000 Englewood Pkwy, Englewood Civic Ctr 1st Fl	Englewood	CO	80110	**866-922-9006**	303-762-2560
Escanaba Public Library	400 Ludington St	Escanaba	MI	49829	**800-992-9012**	906-786-4463
Evanston Public Library	1703 Orrington Ave	Evanston	IL	60201	**888-253-7003**	847-448-8600
Fall River Public Library	104 N Main St	Fall River	MA	02720	**800-331-3764**	508-324-2700
Farr Regional Library	1939 61st Ave	Greeley	CO	80634	**888-861-7323**	970-506-8550
Fayette County Library	216 W Market St	Somerville	TN	38068	**866-465-3591**	901-465-5248
Fayette County Public Library	531 Summit St	Oak Hill	WV	25901	**855-275-5737**	304-465-0121
Finger Lakes Library System	119 E Green St	Ithaca	NY	14850	**800-909-3557**	607-273-4074
First Regional Library	370 W Commerce St	Hernando	MS	38632	**800-446-0892**	662-429-4439
Flagler County Public Library (FCPL)	2500 Palm Coast Pkwy NW	Palm Coast	FL	32137	**877-863-5244**	386-446-6763
Forsyth County Public Library	201 N Chestnut St FL 5	Winston-Salem	NC	27101	**866-345-1884**	336-703-2665
Fort Smith Public Library	3201 Rogers Ave	Fort Smith	AR	72903	**866-660-0885**	479-783-0229
Free Library of Philadelphia	1901 Vine St	Philadelphia	PA	19103	**800-732-0999**	215-686-5322
Fremont Main Library	2400 Stevenson Blvd	Fremont	CA	94538	**800-434-0222**	510-745-1400
Friendswood Public Library	416 S Friendswood Dr	Friendswood	TX	77546	**800-696-3493**	281-482-7135
Gaston County Public Library	1555 E Garrison Blvd	Gastonia	NC	28054	**888-241-3115**	704-868-2164
Genesee District Library	G-4195 W Pasadena Ave	Flint	MI	48504	**866-732-1120**	810-732-0110
Glendora Public Library & Cultural Ctr	140 S Glendora Ave	Glendora	CA	91741	**866-275-3772**	626-852-4891
Grande Prairie Public Library	3479 W 183rd St	Hazel Crest	IL	60429	**800-321-9511**	708-798-5563
Greenville County Library	25 Heritage Green Pl	Greenville	SC	29601	**866-275-7273**	864-242-5000
Harford County Public Library	1221-A Brass Mill Rd	Belcamp	MD	21017	**800-944-7403**	410-575-6761
Helen B Hoffman Plantation Library	501 N Fig Tree Ln	Plantation	FL	33317	**800-774-5866**	954-797-2140
Henderson County Public Library	301 N Washington St	Hendersonville	NC	28739	**866-866-2362**	828-697-4725
Henry County Public Library System	1001 Florence McGarity Blvd	McDonough	GA	30252	**877-527-3712**	770-954-2806
High Point Public Library (HPPL)	901 N Main St	High Point	NC	27262	**877-772-8346**	336-883-3660
Hillsboro Public Library	2850 NE Brookwood Pkwy	Hillsboro	OR	97124	**855-870-0049**	503-615-6500
Hilton Head Library	11 Beach City Rd	Hilton Head Island	SC	29926	**800-860-1444**	843-255-6500
Hockessin Library	1023 Valley Rd	Hockessin	DE	19707	**888-352-7722**	302-239-5160
Hood County Public Library	222 N Travis St	Granbury	TX	76048	**800-452-9292**	817-573-3569
Horseshoe Bend Regional Library	207 NW St	Dadeville	AL	36853	**855-336-0333**	256-825-9232
Houston Public Library	500 McKinney St	Houston	TX	77002	**800-318-2596**	832-393-1313
Huntington Beach Public Library (HBPL)	7111 Talbert Ave	Huntington Beach	CA	92648	**800-565-0148**	714-842-4481
Hurst Public Library	901 Precinct Line Rd	Hurst	TX	76053	**800-344-8377**	817-788-7300
Indianhead Federated Library System	1538 Truax Blvd	Eau Claire	WI	54703	**800-321-5427**	715-839-5082
Iowa City Public Library	123 S Linn St	Iowa City	IA	52240	**866-862-6877**	319-356-5200
Jackson County Public Library (JCPL)	303 W Second St	Seymour	IN	47274	**877-275-7673**	812-522-3412
Jefferson-Madison Regional Library	201 E Market St	Charlottesville	VA	22902	**866-979-1555**	434-979-7151
Jersey City Free Public Library	472 Jersey Ave	Jersey City	NJ	07302	**800-443-0315**	201-547-4501
John F Kennedy Library (JFKL)	190 W 49th St	Hialeah	FL	33012	**877-738-5622**	305-821-2700
Johnson County Library	PO Box 2933	Shawnee Mission	KS	66201	**800-386-8501**	913-826-4600
Juneau Public Libraries	292 Marine Way	Juneau	AK	99801	**800-478-4176**	907-586-5324
Kent District Library	814 W River Ctr Dr NE	Comstock Park	MI	49321	**877-243-2466**	616-784-2007
Kirkwood Library	6000 Kirkwood Hwy	Wilmington	DE	19808	**888-352-7722**	302-995-7663
Kitsap Regional Library	1301 Sylvan Way	Bremerton	WA	98310	**877-883-9900**	360-405-9100
Lake Agassiz Regional Library (LARL)	118 Fifth St S PO Box 900	Moorhead	MN	56560	**800-247-0449**	218-233-3757
Lawrence Public Library	707 Vermont St	Lawrence	KS	66044	**888-657-7323**	785-843-3833
Lawton Public Library	110 SW Fourth St	Lawton	OK	73501	**855-895-8064**	580-581-3450
Lewis & Clark Library	120 S Last Chance Gulch	Helena	MT	59601	**800-733-2767**	406-447-1690
Linda Hall Library	5109 Cherry St	Kansas City	MO	64110	**800-662-1545**	816-363-4600
Lorain Public Library System	351 W Sixth St	Lorain	OH	44052	**800-322-7323**	440-244-1192
Los Angeles County Public Library	7400 E Imperial Hwy	Downey	CA	90242	**888-794-9466**	562-940-8462
Lucy Robbins Welles Library	95 Cedar St	Newington	CT	06111	**800-842-1423**	860-665-8700
Manhattan Public Library	629 Poyntz Ave	Manhattan	KS	66502	**800-432-2796**	785-776-4741
Mansfield-Richland County Public Library	43 W Third St	Mansfield	OH	44902	**877-795-2111**	419-521-3100
McCracken County Public Library	555 Washington St	Paducah	KY	42003	**866-829-7532**	270-442-2510
Merced County Library	2100 O St	Merced	CA	95340	**866-249-0773**	209-385-7643
Meriden Public Library	105 Miller St	Meriden	CT	06450	**800-567-0902**	203-238-2344
Meridian-Lauderdale County Public Library	2517 Seventh St	Meridian	MS	39301	**800-318-2596**	601-693-6771
Mid Wisconsin Federated Library System	112 Clinton St	Horicon	WI	53032	**800-660-6899**	920-485-0833
Mid-Continent Public Library	15616 E 24 Hwy	Independence	MO	64050	**800-318-2596**	816-836-5200
Milwaukee Public Library	814 W Wisconsin Ave	Milwaukee	WI	53233	**866-947-7363**	414-286-3000
Missouri River Regional Library	214 Adams St	Jefferson City	MO	65101	**800-949-7323**	573-634-2464
Mobile Public Library	701 Government St	Mobile	AL	36602	**877-322-8228**	251-208-7073
Mohave Educational Services Cooperative Inc	625 E Beale St	Kingman	AZ	86401	**800-742-2437**	928-753-6945
Monroe County Library System	3700 S Custer Rd	Monroe	MI	48161	**800-462-2050**	734-241-5277
Monroe County Public Library System	700 Fleming St	Key West	FL	33040	**877-772-8346**	305-292-3595
Monrovia Public Library	321 S Myrtle Ave	Monrovia	CA	91016	**888-620-1749**	626-256-8274
Monterey Public Library	625 Pacific St	Monterey	CA	93940	**800-338-0505**	831-646-3932
Mount Laurel Library	100 Walt Whitman Ave	Mount Laurel	NJ	08054	**888-576-5529**	856-234-7319
Muskegon Area District Library	4845 Airline Rd	Muskegon	MI	49444	**877-569-4801**	231-737-6248
Nacogdoches Public Library	1112 N St	Nacogdoches	TX	75961	**800-252-5400**	936-559-2970
Napa City-County Library	580 Coombs St	Napa	CA	94559	**877-848-7030**	707-253-4241
Nassau Library System	900 Jerusalem Ave	Uniondale	NY	11553	**800-662-1220**	516-292-8920
New Bedford Free Public Library (NBFPL)	613 Pleasant St	New Bedford	MA	02740	**877-336-2627**	508-991-6275
New Braunfels Public Library	700 E Common St	New Braunfels	TX	78130	**800-434-8013**	830-221-4300
New Canaan Library	151 Main St	New Canaan	CT	06840	**800-545-2433**	203-594-5000
New Castle County Library	750 Library Ave	Newark	DE	19711	**877-225-7351**	302-731-7550
New Castle Public Library	424 Delaware St	New Castle	DE	19720	**877-225-7351**	302-328-1995
New Fairfield Free Public Library	2 Brush Hill Rd	New Fairfield	CT	06812	**877-227-7487**	203-312-5679
Northern New York Library Network	6721 Us Hwy 11	Potsdam	NY	13676	**877-833-1674**	315-265-1119
Northern Waters Library Service	3200 E Lakeshore Dr	Ashland	WI	54806	**800-228-5684**	715-682-2365
Norwalk Public Library	1 Belden Ave	Norwalk	CT	06850	**800-382-9463**	203-899-2780
Old Bridge Public Library	1 Old Bridge Plz	Old Bridge	NJ	08857	**800-829-1040**	732-721-5600
Onslow County Public Library	58 Doris Ave E	Jacksonville	NC	28540	**800-351-1697**	910-455-7350
Orion Township Public Library	825 Joslyn Rd	Lake Orion	MI	48362	**877-924-7467**	248-693-3000
Owatonna Public Library	105 N Elm St	Owatonna	MN	55060	**800-657-3864**	507-444-2460

				Toll-Free	Phone
Parkersburg & Wood County Public Library 3100 Emerson Ave	Parkersburg	WV	26104	**800-642-8674**	304-420-4587
Paul Sawyier Public Library 319 Wapping St	Frankfort	KY	40601	**800-829-3676**	502-352-2665
Pawtucket Public Library 13 Summer St	Pawtucket	RI	02860	**800-359-3090**	401-725-3714
Peter White Public Library 217 N Front St	Marquette	MI	49855	**800-992-9012**	906-228-9510
Pierce County Library System 3005 112th St E	Tacoma	WA	98446	**800-346-0995**	253-536-6500
Pima County Public Library 101 N Stone Ave	Tucson	AZ	85701	**877-705-5437**	520-594-5600
Placer County Library 350 Nevada St	Auburn	CA	95603	**800-488-4308**	530-886-4500
Ponca City Library 515 E Grand Ave	Ponca City	OK	74601	**800-522-8165**	580-767-0345
Portage County District Library 10482 S St	Garrettsville	OH	44231	**800-500-5179**	330-527-4378
Provo City Library 550 N University Ave	Provo	UT	84601	**800-914-8931**	801-852-6650
Puyallup Public Library 324 S Meridian	Puyallup	WA	98371	**866-862-4232**	253-841-5454
Racine Public Library 75 Seventh St	Racine	WI	53403	**888-529-0061**	262-636-9241
Ramapo Catskill Library System 619 Rt 17-M	Middletown	NY	10940	**800-327-7343**	845-343-1131
Ramsey County Public Library 4570 N Victoria St	Shoreview	MN	55126	**888-335-9632**	651-486-2200
Rancho Cucamonga Public Library 7368 Archibald Ave	Rancho Cucamonga	CA	91730	**800-655-4555**	909-477-2720
Rangeview Library District 5877 E 120th Ave	Thornton	CO	80602	**800-222-3937**	303-288-2001
Richardson Public Library 900 Civic Ctr Dr	Richardson	TX	75080	**800-735-2989**	972-744-4350
Richmond Public Library 325 Civic Ctr Plaza	Richmond	CA	94804	**800-833-2900**	510-620-6555
Riverside City Public Library 3581 Mission Inn Ave	Riverside	CA	92501	**888-225-7377**	951-826-5201
S Central Library Syst 4610 S Biltmore Ln	Madison	WI	53718	**855-516-7257**	608-246-7970
Saint Clair County Library System 210 McMorran Blvd	Port Huron	MI	48060	**877-987-7323**	810-987-7323
Saint George Library Ctr 5 Central Ave	Staten Island	NY	10301	**800-342-3688**	718-442-8560
Saint Paul Public Library 90 W Fourth St	Saint Paul	MN	55102	**888-335-9632**	651-266-7000
Saline County Public Library 1800 Smithers	Benton	AR	72015	**800-476-4466**	501-778-4766
San Benito Public Library 101 W Rose St	San Benito	TX	78586	**800-444-1187**	956-361-3860
San Diego Public Library 820 E St	San Diego	CA	92101	**866-470-1308**	619-236-5800
Santa Clara County Library 14600 Winchester Blvd	Los Gatos	CA	95032	**800-286-1991**	408-293-2326
Scott County Library System 13090 Alabama Ave S	Savage	MN	55378	**877-772-8346**	952-707-1770
Shelbyville-Shelby County Public Library 57 W Broadway	Shelbyville	IN	46176	**866-466-4438**	317-398-7121
Shreve Memorial Library 424 Texas St	Shreveport	LA	71101	**866-783-5462**	318-226-5897
Somerset County Library 1 Vogt Dr	Bridgewater	NJ	08807	**888-313-3532**	908-526-4016
Southeastern Library System of Oklahoma (SEPLSO) 401 N Second St	McAlester	OK	74501	**800-215-6494**	918-426-0456
Southwest Wisconsin Library System 1775 Fourth St	Fennimore	WI	53809	**866-866-3393**	608-822-3393
Stockton-San Joaquin County Public Library (SSJCPL) 605 N El Dorado St	Stockton	CA	95202	**866-805-7323**	209-937-8416
Superior Public Library 1530 Tower Ave	Superior	WI	54880	**866-894-4899**	715-394-8860
Sutter County Library 750 Forbes Ave	Yuba City	CA	95991	**800-533-2873**	530-822-7137
Teaneck Public Library 840 Teaneck Rd	Teaneck	NJ	07666	**800-245-1377**	201-837-4171
Teton County Public Library 125 Virginian Ln	Jackson	WY	83001	**800-878-2167**	307-733-2164
Timberland Regional Library 415 Tumwater Blvd SW	Tumwater	WA	98501	**877-284-6237**	360-943-5001
Tippecanoe County Public Library 627 S St	Lafayette	IN	47901	**800-542-7818**	765-429-0100
Tompkins County Public Library 101 E Green St	Ithaca	NY	14850	**800-772-7267**	607-272-4557
Troy-Miami County Public Library 419 W Main St	Troy	OH	45373	**866-657-8556**	937-339-0502
Tufts Library 46 Broad St	Weymouth	MA	02188	**888-283-3757**	781-337-1402
Vernon Parish Library 1401 Nolan Trace	Leesville	LA	71446	**800-737-2231**	337-239-2027
Veterans Memorial Library 301 S University Ave	Mount Pleasant	MI	48858	**888-520-8103**	989-773-3242
Waco-McLennan County Library 1717 Austin Ave	Waco	TX	76701	**800-433-7300**	254-750-5941
Walton-De Funiak Library 3 Cir Dr	DeFuniak Springs	FL	32435	**800-342-0141**	850-892-3624
Warren County-Vicksburg Public Library 700 Veto St	Vicksburg	MS	39180	**800-721-7222**	601-636-6411
Washington County Library 8595 Central Pk Pl	Woodbury	MN	55125	**800-657-3750**	651-275-8500
Waterford Township Public Library 5168 Civic Ctr Dr	Waterford	MI	48329	**800-318-2596**	248-674-4831
Watertown Free Public Library 123 Main St	Watertown	MA	02472	**800-829-3676**	617-972-6431
Watertown Public Library 100 S Water St	Watertown	WI	53094	**800-829-3676**	920-262-4090
Weatherford Public Library 1014 Charles St	Weatherford	TX	76086	**800-489-0190**	817-598-4150
Weber County Library 2464 Jefferson Ave	Ogden	UT	84401	**866-678-5342**	801-337-2632
Welles-Turner Memorial Library 2407 Main St	Glastonbury	CT	06033	**800-411-9671**	860-652-7719
Wells County Public Library 200 W Washington St	Bluffton	IN	46714	**800-824-6111**	260-824-1612
West Allis Public Library 7421 W National Ave	West Allis	WI	53214	**800-877-8339**	414-302-8500
West Florida Regional Library 200 W Gregory St	Pensacola	FL	32501	**800-435-7352**	850-436-5060
West Islip Public Library 3 Higbie Ln	West Islip	NY	11795	**866-833-1122**	631-661-7080
West Orange Public Library 46 Mt Pleasant Ave	West Orange	NJ	07052	**800-345-7587**	973-736-0198
West Palm Beach Public Library 411 Clematis St	West Palm Beach	FL	33401	**866-472-7275**	561-868-7700
Westerville Public Library 126 S State St	Westerville	OH	43081	**800-816-0662**	614-882-7277
Wharton County Library 1920 N Fulton St	Wharton	TX	77488	**800-244-5492**	979-532-8080
Willingboro Public Library 220 Willingboro Pkwy	Willingboro	NJ	08046	**866-321-9571**	609-877-6668
Wilson County Public Library 249 W Nash St	Wilson	NC	27893	**877-321-2652**	252-237-5355
Woburn Public Library 45 Pleasant St	Woburn	MA	01801	**800-392-6089**	781-933-0148
Woodland Public Library 250 First St	Woodland	CA	95695	**800-321-2752**	530-661-5980
Woodridge Public Library 3 Plaza Dr	Woodridge	IL	60517	**800-279-0400**	630-964-7899
Woonsocket Harris Public Library 303 Clinton St	Woonsocket	RI	02895	**800-359-3090**	401-769-9044

434-4 Special Collections Libraries

				Toll-Free	Phone
AIDS Library 1233 Locust St 2nd Fl	Philadelphia	PA	19107	**877-613-4533**	215-985-4851
Bentley Historical Library 1150 Beal Ave	Ann Arbor	MI	48109	**866-233-6661**	734-764-3482

434-5 State Libraries

				Toll-Free	Phone
Arkansas State Library 900 W Capitol Ste 100	Little Rock	AR	72201	**866-801-3435**	501-682-2053
California State Library 900 N St	Sacramento	CA	95814	**800-952-5666**	916-654-0261
Connecticut State Library 231 Capitol Ave	Hartford	CT	06106	**866-886-4478**	860-757-6510
Delaware Div of Libraries 497 S Red Haven Ln	Dover	DE	19901	**800-829-4059**	302-739-4748
Idaho Commission for Libraries (ICFL) 325 W State St	Boise	ID	83702	**800-458-3271**	208-334-2150
Illinois State Library 300 S Second St	Springfield	IL	62701	**800-665-5576**	217-782-2994
Kentucky Dept for Libraries & Archives 300 Coffee Tree Rd	Frankfort	KY	40602	**800-372-2968**	502-564-8300
Library of Michigan, The 702 W Kalamazoo St PO Box 30007	Lansing	MI	48909	**800-726-7323**	517-373-1580
Massachusetts Board of Library Commissioners 98 N Washington St	Boston	MA	02114	**800-952-7403**	617-725-1860
Nebraska Library Commission 1200 N St Ste 120	Lincoln	NE	68508	**800-307-2665**	402-471-2045
Nevada State Library & Archives (NSLA) 100 N Stewart St	Carson City	NV	89701	**800-922-2880**	775-684-3360
North Dakota State Library (NDSL) 604 E Blvd Ave Dept 250	Bismarck	ND	58505	**800-472-2104**	701-328-4622
Oklahoma Dept of Libraries 200 NE 18th St	Oklahoma City	OK	73105	**800-522-8116**	405-521-2502
South Dakota State Library 800 Governors Dr	Pierre	SD	57501	**800-423-6665**	605-773-3131
State Library of Ohio 274 E First Ave Ste 100	Columbus	OH	43201	**800-686-1532**	614-644-7061
Tennessee State Library & Archives 403 Seventh Ave N	Nashville	TN	37243	**877-850-4959**	615-741-2764
Utah State Library 250 N 1950 W Ste A	Salt Lake City	UT	84116	**800-662-9150**	801-715-6777
Vermont Dept of Libraries 109 State St	Montpelier	VT	05609	**888-350-0950**	802-828-3261
West Virginia Library Commission 1900 Kanawha Blvd E	Charleston	WV	25305	**800-642-9021**	304-558-2041
Wisconsin Department of Public Instruction 125 S Webster St PO Box 7841	Madison	WI	53707	**800-441-4563**	608-266-3390

434-6 University Libraries

Listings for university libraries are arranged by states.

				Toll-Free	Phone
Abilene Christian University Brown Library (ACU) 760 Library Ct	Abilene	TX	79699	**800-460-6228**	325-674-2000
Andrews University James White Library 4190 Admin Dr	Berrien Springs	MI	49104	**800-253-2874**	269-471-3264
Angelo State University Henderson Library 2025 S Johnson St	San Angelo	TX	76909	**800-946-8627**	325-942-2051
Appalachian State University *Belk Library* 218 College St PO Box 32026	Boone	NC	28608	**877-423-0086**	828-262-2300
Ashland University Library 509 College Ave	Ashland	OH	44805	**866-434-5222**	419-289-5400
Auburn University 202 Mary Martin Hall *Admissions	Auburn University	AL	36849	**866-389-6770***	334-844-6425
Barry University 11300 NE Second Ave	Miami Shores	FL	33161	**800-756-6000**	305-899-3000

Name / Address	City	State	ZIP	Toll-Free	Phone
Barry Memorial Library					
11300 NE Second Ave	Miami Shores	FL	33161	**800-756-6000**	305-899-3000
Bowling Green State University Jerome Library (BGSU)					
1001 E Wooster St	Bowling Green	OH	43403	**866-246-6732**	419-372-2051
Brown University Rockefeller Library					
10 Prospect St	Providence	RI	02912	**877-668-4493**	401-863-2162
California Lutheran University Pearson Library					
60 W Olsen Rd	Thousand Oaks	CA	91360	**877-258-3678**	805-493-3250
College of the Holy Cross Dinand Library					
1 College St	Worcester	MA	01610	**877-433-1843**	508-793-2642
College of William & Mary Swem Library					
PO Box 8794	Williamsburg	VA	23187	**800-462-3683**	757-221-3072
Cunningham Memorial Library					
510 N 6 1/2 St	Terre Haute	IN	47809	**800-851-4279**	812-237-2580
Denison University Doane Library					
400 W Loop	Granville	OH	43023	**800-336-4766**	740-587-6235
DePauw University West Library					
11 E Larabee St	Greencastle	IN	46135	**800-447-2495**	765-658-4420
Drexel University Hagerty Library					
33rd St & Market St	Philadelphia	PA	19104	**888-278-8825**	215-895-2767
East Stroudsburg University Kemp Library					
200 Prospect St	East Stroudsburg	PA	18301	**877-422-1378**	570-422-3465
Eastern Connecticut State University Smith Library					
83 Windham St	Willimantic	CT	06226	**800-578-1449**	860-465-4506
Eastern Michigan University Halle Library					
955 W Cir Dr	Ypsilanti	MI	48197	**888-888-3465**	734-487-0020
Edinboro University of Pennsylvania Baron-Forness Library (EUB)					
200 Tartan Rd	Edinboro	PA	16444	**888-845-2890**	814-732-2273
Ferris State University					
1201 S State St	Big Rapids	MI	49307	**800-433-7747**	231-591-2000
FLITE Library					
1010 Campus Dr	Big Rapids	MI	49307	**800-433-7747**	231-591-3602
Florida A & M University					
1700 Lee Hall Dr Rm G-7					
Foote-Hilyer Administration Ctr	Tallahassee	FL	32307	**866-642-1198**	850-599-3000
Coleman Memorial Library					
1500 S Martin Luther King Blvd	Tallahassee	FL	32307	**800-540-6754**	850-599-3370
Florida Atlantic University (FAU)					
777 Glades Rd	Boca Raton	FL	33431	**800-299-4328***	561-297-3000
*Admissions					
Fordham University					
441 E Fordham Rd	Bronx	NY	10458	**800-367-3426**	718-817-3240
Francis Marion University Rogers Library					
PO Box 100547	Florence	SC	29502	**800-368-7551**	
Franklin & Marshall College Shadek-Fackenthal Library					
450 College Ave	Lancaster	PA	17604	**866-366-7655**	717-291-4223
Gallaudet University Library					
800 Florida Ave NE	Washington	DC	20002	**800-995-0550**	202-651-5217
George Mason University					
4400 University Dr	Fairfax	VA	22030	**888-627-6612**	703-993-1000
George Washington University					
2121 'I' St NW	Washington	DC	20052	**866-498-3382**	202-994-1000
Georgia Institute of Technology Library					
225 N Ave NW	Atlanta	GA	30332	**888-225-7804**	404-894-4500
Gonzaga University Foley Library					
502 E Boone Ave	Spokane	WA	99258	**800-498-5941**	509-323-5931
Grand Valley State University Zumberge Library					
1 Campus Dr	Allendale	MI	49401	**800-879-0581**	616-331-3252
Grinnell College Burling Library					
6th Ave High St	Grinnell	IA	50112	**800-247-0113**	641-269-3371
Hawaii Pacific University					
1164 Bishop St Ste 200	Honolulu	HI	96813	**866-225-5478**	808-544-0200
Meader Library					
1060 Bishop St	Honolulu	HI	96813	**866-225-5478**	808-544-0210
Hope College Van Wylen Library					
53 Graves Pl	Holland	MI	49423	**800-968-7850**	616-395-7790
Illinois Institute of Technology					
10 W 33rd St	Chicago	IL	60616	**800-448-2329**	312-567-3025
Indiana University of Pennsylvania Stapleton Library					
1011 S Dr	Indiana	PA	15705	**888-342-2383**	724-357-2340
Indiana University-Purdue University Indianapolis					
Library					
755 W Michigan St	Indianapolis	IN	46202	**888-422-0499**	317-274-0462
Kent State University					
800 E. Summit St PO Box 5190	Kent	OH	44242	**800-988-5368**	330-672-2121
Lawrence University Mudd Library					
711 E Boldt Way	Appleton	WI	54911	**800-432-5427**	920-832-6750
Louisiana Tech University Prescott Memorial Library					
PO Box 10408	Ruston	LA	71272	**877-557-2575**	318-257-3555
Marquette University Raynor Memorial Library					
1355 W Wisconsin Ave	Milwaukee	WI	53233	**800-876-1715**	414-288-7556
Mercer University					
1400 Coleman Ave	Macon	GA	31207	**800-637-2378**	478-301-2650
Michigan State University Library					
100 Library	East Lansing	MI	48824	**800-500-1554**	517-353-8700
Middlebury College Library					
110 Storrs Ave	Middlebury	VT	05753	**800-829-1040**	802-443-5494
Minnesota State University Mankato					
Memorial Library					
PO Box 8419	Mankato	MN	56002	**800-722-0544**	507-389-5952
Montana State University					
Billings					
1500 University Dr	Billings	MT	59101	**800-565-6782**	406-657-2011
New Mexico State University (NMSU)					
MSC-3A PO Box 30001	Las Cruces	NM	88003	**800-662-6678***	575-646-3121
*Admissions					
North Carolina State University Libraries					
CB 7111	Raleigh	NC	27695	**877-601-0590**	919-515-2843
Northeastern Illinois University Williams Library					
5500 N St Louis Ave	Chicago	IL	60625	**800-393-0865**	773-442-4470
Northwestern State University Watson Memorial Library					
913 University Pkwy	Natchitoches	LA	71497	**888-540-9657**	318-357-4477
Ohio Northern University Heterick Memorial Library					
525 S Main St	Ada	OH	45810	**866-943-5787**	419-772-2181
Ohio State University					
154 W 12th Ave	Columbus	OH	43210	**800-426-5046**	614-292-3980
Libraries					
1858 Neil Ave Mall	Columbus	OH	43210	**800-555-1212**	614-292-6175

Name / Address	City	State	ZIP	Toll-Free	Phone
Ohio University					
120 Chubb Hall	Athens	OH	45710	**800-858-6843**	740-593-1000
Oklahoma State University					
219 Student Union Bldg	Stillwater	OK	74078	**800-852-1255**	405-744-5000
Oral Roberts University Library					
7777 S Lewis Ave	Tulsa	OK	74171	**800-678-8876**	918-495-6723
Pace University 1 Pace Plz	New York	NY	10038	**866-722-3338**	212-346-1200
Pacific University Library					
2043 College Way	Forest Grove	OR	97116	**800-677-6712**	503-352-1400
Peru State College Library					
600 Hoyt St PO Box 10	Peru	NE	68421	**800-742-4412**	402-872-3815
Regent University					
Library					
1000 Regent University Dr	Virginia Beach	VA	23464	**888-249-1822**	757-352-4916
Rhodes College Barret Library					
2000 N Pkwy	Memphis	TN	38112	**800-844-5969**	901-843-3000
Saginaw Valley State University Zahnow Library					
7400 Bay Rd	University Center	MI	48710	**800-968-9500**	989-964-4240
Saint John's University Alcuin Library					
2835 Abbey Plaza	Collegeville	MN	56321	**800-544-1489**	320-363-2122
Salisbury University Blackwell Library					
1101 Camden Ave	Salisbury	MD	21801	**888-543-0148**	410-543-6130
Seattle University Lemieux Library					
901 12th Ave	Seattle	WA	98122	**800-426-7123**	206-296-6210
Simmons College Beatley Library					
300 The Fenway	Boston	MA	02115	**800-831-4284**	617-521-2780
Sixth Floor Museum					
411 Elm St Ste 120 Dealey Plz	Dallas	TX	75202	**888-485-4854**	214-747-6660
South Dakota State University Briggs Library					
N Campus Dr PO Box 2115	Brookings	SD	57007	**800-786-2038**	605-688-5106
Southern Illinois University Edwardsville					
Lovejoy Library					
30 Hairpin Dr PO Box 1063	Edwardsville	IL	62026	**888-328-5168**	618-650-4636
Stanford University Green Library					
557 Escondido Mall	Stanford	CA	94305	**800-521-0600**	650-723-2300
Stetson University DuPont-Ball Library					
421 N Woodland Blvd	DeLand	FL	32723	**800-688-0101**	386-822-7183
Syracuse University Bird Library					
222 Waverly Ave	Syracuse	NY	13244	**866-722-7858**	315-443-2093
Texas A & M University					
Rudder Tower Ste 205	College Station	TX	77843	**888-890-5667**	979-845-8901
Texas Christian University Mary Couts Burnett Library					
2800 S University Dr	Fort Worth	TX	76129	**866-321-7428**	817-257-7000
Texas Tech University Libraries					
18th & Boston Ave PO Box 40002	Lubbock	TX	79409	**888-270-3369**	806-742-2265
Tuskegee University Ford Motor Co Library/Learning Resource Ctr					
Hollis Burke Frissell Library Bldg	Tuskegee	AL	36088	**800-622-6531**	334-727-8894
University at Albany University Libraries					
1400 Washington Ave	Albany	NY	12222	**800-342-4146**	518-442-3600
University of Alabama					
PO Box 870132	Tuscaloosa	AL	35487	**800-933-2262***	205-348-6010
*Admissions					
Gorgas Library					
Information Ctr First Fl	Tuscaloosa	AL	35487	**888-764-5603**	205-348-6047
University of Alaska Fairbanks					
PO Box 757480	Fairbanks	AK	99775	**800-478-1823**	907-474-7500
University of Arkansas					
232 Silas Hunt Hall	Fayetteville	AR	72701	**800-377-8632***	479-575-5346
*Admissions					
University of California Irvine					
Library PO Box 19557	Irvine	CA	92623	**800-848-4722**	949-824-6836
University of Cincinnati Langsam Library					
PO Box 210033	Cincinnati	OH	45221	**866-397-3382**	513-556-1515
University of Colorado at Colorado Springs					
Kraemer Family Library					
1420 Austin Bluffs Pkwy					
PO Box 7150	Colorado Springs	CO	80918	**800-990-8227**	719-255-3295
Babbidge Library					
369 Fairfield Rd Unit 2005	Storrs	CT	06269	**888-603-9635**	860-486-2219
University of Florida Libraries					
PO Box 117001	Gainesville	FL	32611	**877-351-2377**	352-392-0342
University of Georgia Library					
320 S Jackson St	Athens	GA	30602	**877-314-5560**	706-542-0621
University of Idaho					
875 Perimeter Dr	Moscow	ID	83844	**888-884-3246**	208-885-6111
University of Maine					
5713 Chadbourne Hall	Orono	ME	04469	**877-486-2364***	207-581-1110
*Admissions					
University of Maryland					
7569 Baltimore Ave	College Park	MD	20742	**800-422-5867***	301-405-1000
*Admissions					
University of Memphis McWherter Library					
126 Ned R McWherter Library	Memphis	TN	38152	**866-670-6147**	901-678-2201
University of Miami Richter Library					
PO Box 248214	Coral Gables	FL	33124	**800-708-6754**	305-284-3551
University of Michigan Dearborn					
Mardigian Library					
4901 Evergreen Rd	Dearborn	MI	48128	**877-619-6650**	313-593-5445
University of Minnesota Crookston					
UMC Library					
2900 University Ave	Crookston	MN	56716	**800-862-6466**	218-281-8399
University of Minnesota Duluth					
Kathryn A. Martin Library					
416 Library Dr	Duluth	MN	55812	**866-999-6995**	218-726-8102
Williams Library					
1 Library Loop	University	MS	38677	**800-891-4596**	662-915-7091
University of Missouri Kansas City					
Nichols Library					
800 E 51st St	Kansas City	MO	64110	**800-775-8652**	816-235-1534
University of Montana Missoula					
Mansfield Library					
32 Campus Dr	Missoula	MT	59812	**800-240-4939**	406-243-2053
University of North Texas Libraries					
1155 Union Cir PO Box 305190	Denton	TX	76203	**877-872-0264**	940-565-2413
University of Pennsylvania Van Pelt Library					
3420 Walnut St	Philadelphia	PA	19104	**877-784-8379**	215-898-7091
Hillman Library					
3960 Forbes Ave	Pittsburgh	PA	15260	**888-465-4329**	412-648-7710

	City	State	Zip	Toll-Free	Phone
University of Richmond 28 Westhampton Way	Richmond	VA	23173	**800-700-1662**	804-289-8000
University of Saint Thomas O'Shaughnessy-Frey Library 2115 Summit Ave	Saint Paul	MN	55105	**800-328-6819**	651-962-5494
University of South Carolina 1600 Hampton St	Columbia	SC	29208	**800-868-5872**	803-777-7000
University of South Florida Polytechnic *Lakeland* 3433 Winter Lake Rd	Lakeland	FL	33803	**800-873-5636**	863-667-7000
University of Southern California *Doheny Memorial Library* 3550 Trousdale Pkwy University Pk Campus	Los Angeles	CA	90089	**800-775-7330**	213-740-4039
University of Tennessee Knoxville *Hodges Library* 1015 Volunteer Blvd	Knoxville	TN	37996	**800-426-9119**	865-974-4351
University of Toledo Carlson Library 2801 W Bancroft St MS 509	Toledo	OH	43606	**800-586-5336**	419-530-2324
University of Utah Marriott Library Marriott Library 295 S 1500 E	Salt Lake City	UT	84112	**800-458-0145**	801-581-8558
University of Wisconsin Eau Claire *McIntyre Library* 105 Garfield Ave	Eau Claire	WI	54702	**877-267-1384**	715-836-3715
University of Wisconsin Stout *Library* 315 Tenth Ave E	Menomonie	WI	54751	**866-716-6685**	715-232-1215
University of Wisconsin Superior *Jim Dan Hill Library* PO Box 2000	Superior	WI	54880	**877-232-1727**	715-394-8343
University of Wyoming Libraries PO Box 3334	Laramie	WY	82071	**800-442-6757**	307-766-3190
Virginia Commonwealth University Cabell Library 901 Pk Ave PO Box 842033	Richmond	VA	23284	**844-352-7399**	804-828-1105
Washington State University PO Box 641040	Pullman	WA	99164	**888-468-6978**	509-335-3564
Weber State University 3848 Harrison Blvd	Ogden	UT	84408	**800-848-7770**	801-626-6000
Stewart Library 2901 University Cir	Ogden	UT	84408	**877-306-3140**	801-626-6403
Wesleyan University Olin Library 252 Church St	Middletown	CT	06459	**800-421-1561**	860-685-2660
West Virginia University PO Box 6009	Morgantown	WV	26506	**800-344-9881**	304-293-2121
Western Illinois University 1 University Cir *Admissions	Macomb	IL	61455	**877-742-5948***	309-298-1414
Malpass Library 1 University Cir	Macomb	IL	61455	**800-413-6544**	309-298-2762
Western Michigan University Waldo Library 1903 W Michigan Ave	Kalamazoo	MI	49008	**866-533-3438**	269-387-5202
Western Oregon University Hamersly Library 345 N Monmouth Ave	Monmouth	OR	97361	**877-877-1593**	503-838-8418
Xavier University Library 3800 Victory Pkwy	Cincinnati	OH	45207	**888-468-4509**	513-745-3881

435 LIBRARY ASSOCIATIONS - STATE & PROVINCE

	City	State	Zip	Toll-Free	Phone
Illinois Library Assn (ILA) 33 W Grand Ave Ste 301	Chicago	IL	60610	**877-565-1896**	312-644-1896
New York Library Assn (NYLA) 6021 State Farm Rd *General	Guilderland	NY	12084	**800-252-6952***	518-432-6952
Solano County Library 1150 Kentucky St	Fairfield	CA	94533	**866-572-7587**	
State Education Resource Center 25 Industrial Park Rd	Middletown	CT	06457	**800-842-8678**	860-632-1485

436 LIBRARY SYSTEMS - REGIONAL - CANADIAN

	City	State	Zip	Toll-Free	Phone
North Ontario Library Service 334 Regent St	Sudbury	ON	P3C4E2	**800-461-6348**	705-675-6467

437 LIGHT BULBS & TUBES

	City	State	Zip	Toll-Free	Phone
Advanced Lighting Technologies Inc 7905 Cochran Rd Ste 300	Glenwillow	OH	44139	**888-440-2358**	440-519-0500
AETEK UV Systems 1229 Lakeview Ct	Romeoville	IL	60446	**800-333-2304**	630-226-4200
Bayco Products Inc 640 Sanden Blvd	Wylie	TX	75098	**800-233-2155**	469-326-9400
Eye Lighting International NA 9150 Hendricks Rd *Cust Svc	Mentor	OH	44060	**888-665-2677***	440-350-7000
Interlectric Corp 1401 Lexington Ave	Warren	PA	16365	**800-722-2184**	814-723-6061
LCD Lighting Inc 37 Robinson Blvd	Orange	CT	06477	**800-826-9465**	203-795-1520
Ledtronics Inc 23105 Kashiwa Ct	Torrance	CA	90505	**800-579-4875**	310-534-1505
Light Sources Inc 37 Robinson Blvd	Orange	CT	06477	**800-826-9465**	203-799-7877
Litetronics International Inc 4101 W 123rd St	Alsip	IL	60803	**800-860-3392**	708-389-8000
OSRAM Sylvania Glass Technologies 131 Portsmouth Ave	Exeter	NH	03833	**800-258-8290**	603-772-4331
Philips Lighting Co 200 Franklin Sq Dr	Somerset	NJ	08873	**800-555-0050**	
Sun Ergoline Inc 1 Walter Kratz Dr	Jonesboro	AR	72401	**888-771-0996**	
Technical Consumer Products Inc 325 Campus Dr	Aurora	OH	44202	**800-324-1496**	
Trojan Inc 198 Trojan St	Mount Sterling	KY	40353	**800-264-0526**	859-498-0526
Ushio America Inc 5440 Cerritos Ave	Cypress	CA	90630	**800-326-1960**	714-236-8600
UVP Inc 2066 W 11th St *Cust Svc	Upland	CA	91786	**800-452-6788***	909-946-3197
Venture Lighting International Inc 32000 Aurora Rd	Solon	OH	44139	**800-451-2606**	440-248-3510

438 LIGHTING EQUIPMENT - VEHICULAR

	City	State	Zip	Toll-Free	Phone
Able 2 Products Company Inc PO Box 543	Cassville	MO	65625	**800-641-4098**	417-847-4791
Avtec Inc 6 Industrial Pk	Cahokia	IL	62206	**800-552-8832**	618-337-7800
Federal Signal Corp Emergency Products Div 2645 Federal Signal Dr	University Park	IL	60466	**800-264-3578**	708-534-3400
JW Speaker Corp N 120 W 19434 Freistadt Rd PO Box 1011	Germantown	WI	53022	**800-558-7288**	262-251-6660
Luminator 900 Klein Rd	Plano	TX	75074	**800-388-8205**	972-424-6511
Peterson Manufacturing Co 4200 E 135th St	Grandview	MO	64030	**800-821-3490**	816-765-2000
Teledyne Lighting & Display Products 12964 Panama St	Los Angeles	CA	90066	**800-563-4020**	310-823-5491
Truck-Lite Company Inc 310 E Elmwood Ave *Cust Svc	Falconer	NY	14733	**800-562-5012***	716-665-6214
Vehicle Safety Mfg LLC 408 Central Ave *General	Newark	NJ	07107	**800-832-7233***	973-643-3000

439 LIGHTING FIXTURES & EQUIPMENT

	City	State	Zip	Toll-Free	Phone
Altman Lighting Inc 57 Alexander St	Yonkers	NY	10701	**800-425-8626**	914-476-7987
American Fluorescent Corp 2345 Ernie Krueger Cir	Waukegan	IL	60087	**800-873-2326**	847-249-5970
American Louver Co 7700 N Austin Ave	Skokie	IL	60077	**800-772-0355**	847-470-3300
Brinkmann Corp 4215 McEwen Rd	Dallas	TX	75244	**800-527-0717**	972-387-4939
Commercial Lighting Industries 81161 Indio Blvd	Indio	CA	92201	**800-755-0155**	760-343-2704
Con-Tech Lighting 2783 Shermer Rd	Northbrook	IL	60062	**800-728-0312**	847-559-5500
Cooper Industries 600 Travis St Ste 5400 *NYSE: ETN*	Houston	TX	77002	**866-853-4293**	713-209-8400
Corbett Lighting Inc 14508 Nelson Ave	City of Industry	CA	91744	**800-533-8769**	626-336-4511
Dazor Lighting Solutions 2079 Congressional	Saint Louis	MO	63146	**800-345-9103**	314-652-2400
Dual-Lite Inc 701 Millennium Blvd	Greenville	SC	29607	**866-898-0131**	864-678-1000
ELK Lighting Creativity 12 Willow Ln	Nesquehoning	PA	18240	**800-613-3261**	
Elk Lighting Inc 12 Willow Lane	Nesquehoning	PA	18240	**866-283-1953**	
Energy Focus Inc 32000 Aurora Rd *OTC: EFOI*	Solon	OH	44139	**800-327-7877**	440-715-1300
Fulton Industries Inc 135 E Linfoot St PO Box 377	Wauseon	OH	43567	**800-537-5012**	419-335-3015
Gardco Lighting 1611 Clovis Barker Rd	San Marcos	TX	78666	**800-227-0758**	512-753-1000
GE Lighting Systems Inc 3010 Spartanburg Hwy	East Flat Rock	NC	28726	**888-694-3533**	828-693-2000
HE Williams Inc 831 W Fairview Ave	Carthage	MO	64836	**866-358-4065**	417-358-4065
High End Systems Inc 2105 Gracy Farms Ln	Austin	TX	78758	**800-890-8989**	512-836-2242
Hinkley Lighting 12600 Berea Rd	Cleveland	OH	44111	**800-446-5539**	216-671-3300
Holophane 214 Oakwood Ave PO Box 3004	Newark	OH	43058	**866-465-6742**	740-345-9631
Hydrel 12881 Bradley Ave	Sylmar	CA	91342	**866-533-9901**	
Kenall Mfg 1020 Lakeside Dr	Gurnee	IL	60031	**800-453-6255**	847-360-8200
Kichler Lighting 7711 E Pleasant Vly Rd PO Box 318010	Cleveland	OH	44131	**866-558-5706**	
Koehler-Bright Star Inc 380 Stewart Rd *Cust Svc	Hanover Township	PA	18706	**800-788-1696***	570-825-1900
Kurtzon Lighting Inc 1420 S Talman Ave	Chicago	IL	60608	**800-837-8937**	773-277-2121
Lamplight Farms Inc W140 N4900 Lilly Rd *Cust Svc	Menomonee Falls	WI	53051	**888-473-1088***	262-781-9590
Ledalite Architectural Products 19750-92A Ave	Langley	BC	V1M3B2	**800-665-5332**	604-888-6811
Legion Lighting Company Inc 221 Glenmore Ave	Brooklyn	NY	11207	**800-453-4466**	718-498-1770
Lighting Quotient, The 114 Boston Post Rd	West Haven	CT	06516	**800-222-0193**	203-931-4455
Lithonia Lighting 1 Lithonia Way	Conyers	GA	30012	**800-858-7763**	770-922-9000
Luxo Corp 5 Westchester Plz	Elmsford	NY	10523	**800-222-5896**	914-345-0067
Mag Instrument Inc 2001 S Hillman Ave	Ontario	CA	91761	**800-289-6241**	909-947-1006
Mercury Lighting Products Company Inc 20 Audrey Pl	Fairfield	NJ	07004	**800-637-2584**	973-244-9444

Name / Address	City	State	ZIP	Toll-Free	Phone
Minka Group 1151 W Bradford Ct	Corona	CA	92882	**800-221-7977**	951-735-9220
Mule Lighting Inc 46 Baker St	Providence	RI	02905	**800-556-7690**	401-941-4446
Musco Sports Lighting LLC 100 First Ave W PO Box 808	Oskaloosa	IA	52577	**800-825-6020**	641-673-0411
North Star Lighting Inc 2150 Parkes Dr	Broadview	IL	60155	**800-229-4330**	708-681-4330
Norwell Manufacturing Inc 82 Stevens St	East Taunton	MA	02718	**800-822-2831**	508-823-1751
Pacific Coast Lighting 20238 Plummer St	Chatsworth	CA	91311	**800-709-9004**	818-886-9751
Paramount Industries Inc 304 N Howard St	Croswell	MI	48422	**800-521-5405**	810-679-2551
Paul C Buff Inc 2725 Bransford Ave	Nashville	TN	37204	**800-443-5542**	615-383-3982
Philips Canlyte, Inc 3015 Louis Amos *All	Lachine	QC	H8T1C4	**800-668-2770***	514-636-0670
Philips Holding USA Inc 1251 Ave of the Americas	New York	NY	10020	**800-453-6860**	212-536-0500
Philips Luminaire 776 S Green St	Tupelo	MS	38804	**800-234-1890**	
Prescolite Inc 701 Millennium Blvd	Greenville	SC	29607	**888-777-4832**	864-678-1000
RAB Lighting 170 Ludlow Ave	Northvale	NJ	07647	**888-722-1000**	201-784-8600
Rejuvenation Inc 2550 NW Nicolai St	Portland	OR	97210	**888-401-1900**	503-231-1900
Renova Lighting Systems Inc 20 Middlesex Rd	Mansfield	MA	02048	**800-635-6682**	401-682-1850
Schonbek Worldwide Lighting Inc 61 Industrial Blvd	Plattsburgh	NY	12901	**800-836-1892**	518-563-7500
Sea Gull Lighting Products LLC A Generations Brands Co 301 W Washington St	Riverside	NJ	08075	**800-347-5483**	856-764-0500
SIMKAR Corp 700 Ramona Ave	Philadelphia	PA	19120	**800-523-3602**	215-831-7700
Spectrolab Inc 12500 Gladstone Ave	Sylmar	CA	91342	**800-936-4888**	818-365-4611
Strand Lighting 10911 Petal St	Dallas	TX	75238	**800-733-0564**	214-647-7880
Streamlight Inc 30 Eagleville Rd	Eagleville	PA	19403	**800-523-7488**	610-631-0600
Super Sky Products Inc 10301 N Enterprise Dr	Mequon	WI	53092	**800-558-0467**	262-242-2000
Tech Lighting LLC 7400 Linda Ave	Skokie	IL	60077	**800-522-5315**	847-410-4400
Tri-Lite Inc 1642 N Besly Ct	Chicago	IL	60642	**800-322-5250**	773-384-7765
Troy-CSL Lighting Inc 14508 Nelson Ave	City of Industry	CA	91744	**800-533-8769**	626-336-4511
Western Reflections 261 Commerce Way *Cust Svc	Gallatin	TN	37066	**800-507-8302***	615-451-9700

440 LIME

Name / Address	City	State	ZIP	Toll-Free	Phone
Carmeuse North America 11 Stanwix St 11th Fl	Pittsburgh	PA	15222	**866-243-0965**	412-995-5500
Cheney Lime & Cement 478 Graystone Rd PO Box 160	Allgood	AL	35013	**800-752-8282**	205-625-3031
Graymont Inc 10991 Shellbridge Way Ste 200	Richmond	BC	V6X3C6	**866-207-4292**	604-276-9331
Texas Lime Co 15865 Farm Rd 1434 PO Box 851	Cleburne	TX	76033	**800-772-8000**	817-641-4433

441 LIMOUSINE SERVICES

Name / Address	City	State	ZIP	Toll-Free	Phone
Alliance Limousine Inc 14553 Delano St Ste 210	Van Nuys	CA	91411	**800-954-5466**	
American Coach Limousine 1100 Jorie Blvd Ste 314	Oak Brook	IL	60523	**888-709-5466**	630-629-0001
American Limousines Inc 4401 E Fairmount Ave	Baltimore	MD	21224	**800-787-1690**	410-522-0400
Arizona Limousines Inc 8900 N Central Ave Ste 101	Phoenix	AZ	85020	**800-678-0033**	602-267-7097
Bayview Limousine Service 15701 Nelson Pl S	Seattle	WA	98188	**800-606-7880**	206-824-6200
Carey Executive Limousine 245 University Ave	Atlanta	GA	30315	**800-241-3943**	404-223-2000
Carey International Inc 4530 Wisconsin Ave NW	Washington	DC	20016	**800-336-4646**	202-895-1200
Classic Transportation Group 1600 Locust Ave	Bohemia	NY	11716	**800-291-8090**	631-567-5100
Elite Limousine Service Inc 1059 12th Ave Ste E	Honolulu	HI	96816	**800-776-2098**	808-735-2431
Gateway Limousines 1550 Gilbreth Rd	Burlingame	CA	94010	**800-486-7077**	650-697-5548
International Chauffeured Service Worldwide 53 E 34th St	New York	NY	10016	**800-266-5254**	212-213-0302
Mears Transportation Group 324 W Gore St	Orlando	FL	32806	**800-759-5219**	407-422-4561
Park Cities Limousine 7129 Harry Hines Blvd	Dallas	TX	75235	**888-559-0708**	214-824-0011
Pontarelli Limousine Service 2225 W Hubbard St	Chicago	IL	60612	**800-322-5466**	312-226-5466
R & R Limousine 4403 Kiln Ct	Louisville	KY	40218	**800-582-5576**	502-458-1862
Regency Limousine International 83-03 24th Ave	East Elmhurst	NY	11370	**866-302-2201**	718-507-4000
Royal Coachman Worldwide 88 Ford Rd Ste 26	Denville	NJ	07834	**800-472-7433**	973-400-3200
Starlite Limousines LLC PO Box 13542	Scottsdale	AZ	85267	**800-875-4104**	480-422-3619
Teddy's Transportation System Inc 25 Van Zant St	Norwalk	CT	06855	**800-888-3339**	203-866-2231
US Coachways Inc 100 St Mary's Ave Ste 2B	Staten Island	NY	10305	**800-359-5991**	718-477-4242
XYZ Two Way Radio Inc 275 20th St	Brooklyn	NY	11215	**800-535-3377**	718-499-2007

442 LINEN & UNIFORM SUPPLY

Name / Address	City	State	ZIP	Toll-Free	Phone
Ace ImageWear 4120 Truman Rd	Kansas City	MO	64127	**800-366-0564**	816-231-5737
Ace-Tex Enterprises 7601 Central St	Detroit	MI	48210	**800-444-3800**	313-834-4000
AmeriPride Services Inc 10801 Wayzata Blvd *Cust Svc	Minnetonka	MN	55305	**800-750-4628***	952-738-4200
Apparelmaster 123 Harrison Ave	Harrison	OH	45030	**877-543-1678**	513-202-1600
Arrow Uniform Rental Inc 6400 Monroe Blvd	Taylor	MI	48180	**888-332-7769**	313-299-5000
Cintas Corp PO Box 625737 *NASDAQ: CTAS*	Cincinnati	OH	45262	**800-786-4367**	513-459-1200
Continental Linen Services 4200 Manchester Rd	Kalamazoo	MI	49001	**800-878-4357**	
Domestic Linen Supply & Laundry Co Inc 30555 NW Hwy	Farmington Hills	MI	48334	**800-344-3555**	248-737-2000
G & K Services Inc 5995 Opus Pkwy Ste 500	Minnetonka	MN	55343	**800-452-2737**	952-912-5500
Healthcare Services Group Inc (HCSG) 3220 Tillman Dr Ste 300	Bensalem	PA	19020	**800-486-3289**	215-639-4274
Industrial Towel & Uniform Inc 2700 S 160th St	New Berlin	WI	53151	**800-767-2487**	262-782-1950
Iron City Uniform Rental 6640 Frankstown Ave	Pittsburgh	PA	15206	**800-532-2010**	412-661-2001
Model Coverall Service Inc 100 28th St SE	Grand Rapids	MI	49548	**800-968-6491**	616-241-6491
Morgan Services Inc 323 N Michigan Ave	Chicago	IL	60601	**888-966-7426**	312-346-3181
Prudential Overall Supply PO Box 11210	Santa Ana	CA	92711	**800-767-5536**	949-250-4855
Roscoe Co 3535 W Harrison St *Cust Svc	Chicago	IL	60624	**888-476-7263***	773-722-5000
Sitex Corp 1300 Commonwealth Dr	Henderson	KY	42420	**800-278-3537**	270-827-3537
Summit Golf Brands Inc 8 W 40th St 2nd Fl	New York	NY	10018	**800-926-8010**	212-302-7255
Textile Care Services Inc 225 Wood Lk Dr SE	Rochester	MN	55904	**800-422-0945**	
Unitech Services Group 295 Parker St	Springfield	MA	01151	**800-344-3824**	413-543-6911
US Linen & Uniform Inc 1106 Harding St	Richland	WA	99352	**888-875-4636**	509-946-6125
Valiant Products Corp 2727 Fifth Ave W *Cust Svc	Denver	CO	80204	**800-347-2727***	303-892-1234

443 LIQUOR STORES

Name / Address	City	State	ZIP	Toll-Free	Phone
Ferry Plaza Wine Merchant Administration Offices 101 The Embarcadero	San Francisco	CA	94105	**866-991-9400**	415-288-0470
Fox Run Vineyards 670 State Rt 14	Penn Yan	NY	14527	**800-636-9786**	315-536-4616
Gold Standard Enterprises Inc 5100 W Dempster St	Skokie	IL	60077	**888-942-9463**	847-674-4200
Patz & Hall Wine Co 851 Napa Vly Corporate Way Ste A	Napa	CA	94558	**877-265-6700**	707-265-7700
Pearlstine Distributors Inc (PDI) 1600 Chrlston Rgonal Pkwy	Charleston	SC	29492	**800-922-1048**	843-388-6800
Saratoga Liquor Company Inc 3215 James Day Ave	Superior	WI	54880	**800-472-6923**	715-394-4487
Spec's Wines Spirits & Finer Foods 2410 Smith St	Houston	TX	77006	**888-526-8787**	713-526-8787
Touring & Tasting 125 S Quarantina St	Santa Barbara	CA	93103	**800-850-4370**	805-965-2813
Wiederkehr Wine Cellars Inc 3324 Swiss Family Dr	Altus	AR	72821	**800-622-9463**	479-468-3551
Wine Club, The 1431 S Village Way	Santa Ana	CA	92705	**800-966-5432**	714-835-6485
Wine.com Inc 114 Sansome St 3rd Fl	San Francisco	CA	94104	**800-592-5870**	415-291-9500
WineShop At Home 525 Airpark Rd	Napa	CA	94558	**800-946-3746**	707-253-0200
Zachys Wine & Liquor Inc 16 E Pkwy	Scarsdale	NY	10583	**800-723-0241**	914-723-0241

444 LITIGATION SUPPORT SERVICES

Name / Address	City	State	ZIP	Toll-Free	Phone
Al Betz & Assoc Inc 125 Airport Dr Ste 30	Westminster	MD	21157	**877-402-3376**	410-875-3376
Alderson Reporting Co 1155 Connecticut Ave NW Ste 200	Washington	DC	20036	**800-367-3376**	202-289-2260
Allied Court Reporters Inc 115 Phenix Ave	Cranston	RI	02920	**888-443-3767**	401-946-5500
Atkinson-Baker Inc (ABI) 500 N Brand Blvd 3rd Fl	Glendale	CA	91203	**800-288-3376**	818-551-7300
Boccardo Law Firm Inc, The 111 W Saint John St Ste 400	San Jose	CA	95113	**800-662-9807**	

Name / Address	City	State	Zip	Toll-Free	Phone
Brian Loncar & Associates P c 1104 Travis St	Wichita Falls	TX	76301	800-239-4878	
Compex Legal Services Inc 325 S Maple Ave *Cust Svc	Torrance	CA	90503	800-426-6739*	
Courtroom Sciences Inc 4950 N O'Connor Rd	Irving	TX	75062	800-514-5879	972-717-1773
DecisionQuest 21535 Hawthorne Blvd Ste 310	Torrance	CA	90503	877-833-2474	310-618-9600
Depobook Reporting Services 1600 G St Ste 101	Modesto	CA	95354	800-830-8885	209-544-6466
DOAR Litigation Consulting 170 Earle Ave	Lynbrook	NY	11563	800-875-8705	516-823-4000
Douglas & London P C 59 Maiden Ln Fl 6	New York	NY	10038	888-596-9790	
Eric Buchanan & Associates Pllc 414 Mccallie Ave	Chattanooga	TN	37402	877-634-2506	
FTI Consulting 909 Commerce Rd Ste 1400 *NYSE: FCN*	Annapolis	MD	21401	800-334-5701	410-224-8770
Hahn & Bowersock Corp 151 Kalmus Dr Ste L1	Costa Mesa	CA	92626	800-660-3187	
Jane Rose Reporting 80 Fifth Ave	New York	NY	10011	800-825-3341	212-727-7773
Jury Research Institute 2617 Danville Blvd PO Box 100	Alamo	CA	94507	800-233-5879	925-932-5663
Novus Law LLC 8770 W Bryn Mawr Ave	Chicago	IL	60631	877-668-8752	
Professional Shorthand Reporters Inc (PSR) 601 Poydras St Ste 1615	New Orleans	LA	70130	800-536-5255	504-529-5255
Ralph Rosenberg Court Reporters Inc 1001 Bishop St Ste 2460	Honolulu	HI	96813	888-524-5888	
Stahancyk Kent & Hook P C Duniway Plz 2400 SW 4th Ave	Portland	OR	97201	877-673-7632	
US Legal Support Inc 363 N Sam Houston Pkwy E Ste 900	Houston	TX	77060	800-567-8757	713-653-7100
Veritext LLC 290 W Mt Pleasant Ave Ste 3200	Livingston	NJ	07039	800-567-8658	
Wilkes & McHugh P A 1 N Dale Mabry Hwy Ste 800	Tampa	FL	33609	800-255-5070	

445 LIVESTOCK - WHOL

SEE ALSO Cattle Ranches, Farms, Feedlots (Beef Cattle) ; Hog Farms

Name / Address	City	State	Zip	Toll-Free	Phone
All West Select Sires 450 N Hill Blvd	Burlington	WA	98233	800-426-2697	
Blue Grass Stockyard 375 Lisle Industrial Ave PO Box 1023	Lexington	KY	40588	800-621-3972	859-255-7701
Empire Livestock Marketing LLC 5001 Brittonfield Pkwy	East Syracuse	NY	13057	800-462-8802	315-433-9129
Equity Co-op Livestock Sales Assn 401 Commerce Ave	Baraboo	WI	53913	800-362-3989	608-356-8311
High Plains Livestock Exchange LLC 28601 US Hwy 34	Brush	CO	80723	866-842-5115	970-842-5115
Lewiston Sales Inc 21241 Dutchmans Crossing Rd	Lewiston	MN	55952	800-732-6334	507-523-2112
Lynch Livestock Co 331 Third St NW	Waucoma	IA	52171	800-468-3178	563-776-3311
Prairie Livestock LLC 2139 Barton Ferry Rd PO Box 636	West Point	MS	39773	800-647-6350	662-494-5651
Producers Livestock Marketing Assn 4809 S 114th St	Omaha	NE	68137	800-257-4046	402-597-9189
Roswell Livestock Auction Sales Inc 900 N Garden PO Box 2041	Roswell	NM	88202	800-748-1541	575-622-5580
Turner County Stockyard 1315 US Hwy 41 S	Ashburn	GA	31714	800-344-9808	229-567-3371
United Producers Inc 8351 N High St Ste 250	Columbus	OH	43235	800-456-3276	
Winner Livestock Auction Co 31690 Livestock Barn Rd	Winner	SD	57580	800-201-0451	605-842-0451

446 LIVESTOCK & POULTRY FEEDS - PREPARED

Name / Address	City	State	Zip	Toll-Free	Phone
AC Nutrition 158 N Main St	Winters	TX	79567	800-588-3333	325-754-4546
ADM Alliance Nutrition Inc 1000 N 30th St	Quincy	IL	62301	800-292-3333	217-222-7100
AG Partners Inc 512 S Eigth St PO Box 467	Lake City	MN	55041	800-772-2990	651-345-3328
Ag Processing Inc 12700 W Dodge Rd PO Box 2047	Omaha	NE	68103	800-247-1345	402-496-7809
Agri-King Inc 18246 Waller Rd	Fulton	IL	61252	800-435-9560	815-589-2525
Ahrberg Milling Co 200 S Depot St PO Box 968	Cushing	OK	74023	800-324-0267	918-225-0267
Alabama Farmers Co-op Inc PO Box 2227	Decatur	AL	35601	888-255-2667	256-353-6843
Albion Laboratories Inc 101 N Main St	Clearfield	UT	84015	800-453-2406	801-773-4631
Bagdad Roller Mills Inc 5740 Elmburg Rd	Bagdad	KY	40003	800-928-3333	502-747-8968
Belstra Milling Company Inc 424 15th St	Demotte	IN	46310	800-276-2789	
BioZyme Inc 6010 Stockyards Expy	Saint Joseph	MO	64504	800-821-3070	816-238-3326
Blue Seal Feeds Inc 2905 US Hwy 61 N *Cust Svc	Muscatine	IA	52761	866-647-1212*	
Buckeye Nutrition 330 E Schultz Ave	Dalton	OH	44618	800-417-6460	
Cumberland Valley Co-op Assn 908 Mt Rock Rd	Shippensburg	PA	17257	800-488-2197	717-532-2197
D & D Commodities Ltd PO Box 359	Stephen	MN	56757	800-543-3308	
Darling International Inc 251 O'Connor Ridge Blvd Ste 300 *NYSE: DAR*	Irving	TX	75038	855-327-7761	972-717-0300
Diamond V Mills Inc PO Box 74570	Cedar Rapids	IA	52407	800-373-7234	319-366-0745
Eagle Roller Mill Co 1101 Airport Rd	Shelby	NC	28150	800-223-9108	704-487-5061
Effingham Equity Inc 201 W Roadway Ave	Effingham	IL	62401	800-223-1337	217-342-4101
Elenbaas Co 411 W Front St	Sumas	WA	98295	800-808-6954	360-988-5811
First Co-op Assn (FCA) 960 Riverview Dr PO Box 60	Cherokee	IA	51012	877-753-5400	712-225-5400
FL Emmert Co Inc 2007 Dunlap St	Cincinnati	OH	45214	800-441-3343	513-721-5808
Flint River Mills Inc 1100 Dothan Rd *Cust Svc	Bainbridge	GA	39817	800-841-8502*	229-246-2232
FM Brown's Sons Inc 205 Woodrow Ave PO Box 2116	Sinking Spring	PA	19608	800-334-8816	610-678-4567
Form-A-Feed Inc (FAF) 740 Bowman St	Stewart	MN	55385	800-422-3649	320-562-2413
Friona Industries LP 500 S Taylor St Ste 601	Amarillo	TX	79101	800-658-6014	806-374-1811
Furst-McNess Co 120 E Clark St	Freeport	IL	61032	800-435-5100	815-235-6151
Harvest Land Co-op 711 Front St PO Box 278	Morgan	MN	56266	800-245-5819	507-249-3196
Hog Slat 315 S Sycamore St	Flora	IN	46929	800-949-4647	574-967-3776
Hubbard Feeds Inc 111 W Cherry St Ste 500	Mankato	MN	56001	800-869-7219	507-388-9400
JBS United Inc 4310 State Rd 38 W	Sheridan	IN	46069	800-382-9909	317-758-4495
JD Heiskell & Co 116 W Cedar St	Tulare	CA	93274	800-366-1886	559-685-6100
John A Van Den Bosch Co 4511 Holland Ave	Holland	MI	49424	800-968-6477	
Kay Dee Feed Company Inc 1919 Grand Ave *Cust Svc	Sioux City	IA	51106	800-831-4815*	712-277-2011
Kemin Industries Inc 2100 Maury St	Des Moines	IA	50317	800-777-8307	515-559-5100
Land O'Lakes Inc Western Feed Div 4001 Lexington Ave N	Arden Hills	MN	55126	800-328-9680	
Manna Pro Corp 707 Spirit 40 Pk Dr Ste 150	Chesterfield	MO	63005	800-690-9908	
Mark Hershey Farms Inc 479 Horseshoe Pk	Lebanon	PA	17042	888-801-3301	717-867-4624
Merrick's Inc 2415 Parview Rd PO Box 620307	Middleton	WI	53562	800-637-7425	608-831-3440
Milk Specialties Co 7500 Flying Cloud Dr Ste 500	Eden Prairie	MN	55344	800-323-4274	952-942-7310
Mountaire Corp PO Box 1320	Millsboro	DE	19966	877-887-1490	302-934-1100
Moyer & Son Inc 113 E Reliance Rd	Souderton	PA	18964	866-669-3747	215-799-2000
NRV Inc N8155 American St	Ixonia	WI	53036	800-558-0002	920-261-7000
Oberbeck Grain Co 700 Walnut St	Highland	IL	62249	800-632-2012	618-654-2387
OMCO Inc 214 E Mill St	Odon	IN	47562	800-525-0272	812-636-7362
Producers Co-op Assoc 300 E Buffalo St	Girard	KS	66743	800-442-2809	620-724-8241
Provimi North America Inc 10 Collective Way	Brookville	OH	45309	888-522-2420	937-770-2400
Quali Tech Inc 318 Lake Hazeltine Dr	Chaska	MN	55318	800-328-5870	952-448-5151
Ralco Nutrition Inc 1600 Hahn Rd	Marshall	MN	56258	800-533-5306	
Rangen Inc 115 13th Ave S *Cust Svc	Buhl	ID	83316	800-657-6446*	208-543-6421
Seminole Feed 335 NE Watula Ave PO Box 940	Ocala	FL	34470	800-683-1881	352-732-4143
Star Milling Co 24067 Water St	Perris	CA	92570	800-733-6455	951-657-3143
Triple Crown Nutrition Inc 319 Barry Ave S Ste 303	Wayzata	MN	55391	800-451-9916	
Trouw Nutrition 115 Executive Dr	Highland	IL	62249	800-365-1357	618-654-2070
Vita Plus Corp 2514 Fish Hatchery Rd	Madison	WI	53713	800-362-8334	608-256-1988
Zeigler Bros Inc 400 GaRdner Stn Rd	Gardners	PA	17324	800-841-6800	717-677-6181

447 LOGGING

Name / Address	City	State	Zip	Toll-Free	Phone
Canal Wood LLC 2430 Main St	Conway	SC	29526	866-587-1460	843-488-9663
Cousineau Inc 3 Valley Rd PO Box 58	North Anson	ME	04958	877-268-7463	207-635-4445
Greif Inc 425 Winter Rd *NYSE: GEF*	Delaware	OH	43015	877-781-9797	740-549-6000
Midwest Walnut Co 1914 Postevin St	Council Bluffs	IA	51503	800-592-5688	712-325-9191
Roseburg Forest Products Co PO Box 1088	Roseburg	OR	97470	800-245-1115	541-679-3311

448 LOGISTICS SERVICES (TRANSPORTATION & WAREHOUSING)

SEE ALSO Trucking Companies ; Freight Forwarders ; Marine Services ; Rail Transport Services ; Commercial Warehousing

Name / Address	City	State	Zip	Toll-Free	Phone
A Duie Pyle Inc 650 Westtown Rd	West Chester	PA	19381	800-523-5020	610-696-5800

Classified Section

Name / Address	City	State	Zip	Toll-Free	Phone
Access Business Group 7575 Fulton St E	Ada	MI	49355	**800-253-6500***	616-787-6000
*Cust Svc					
Acme Wire Products Co 7 Broadway Ave	Mystic	CT	06355	**800-723-7015**	860-572-0511
ADS Tactical Inc Lynnwood Plz 621 Lynnhaven Pkwy Ste 400	Virginia Beach	VA	23452	**800-948-9433**	757-481-7758
AN Deringer Inc 64 N Main St	Saint Albans	VT	05478	**800-448-8108**	802-524-8110
APL Logistics Inc 16220 N Scottsdale Rd Ste 300	Scottsdale	AZ	85254	**866-896-2005**	
Associated Global Systems Inc 3333 New Hyde Pk Rd	New Hyde Park	NY	11042	**800-645-8300***	516-627-8910
*Cust Svc					
Atlantic Bulk Carrier Corp PO Box 112	Providence Forge	VA	23140	**800-966-0030**	804-966-5459
B-H Transfer Co 750 Sparta Rd PO Box 151	Sandersville	GA	31082	**800-342-6462**	478-552-5119
Bender Group 345 Parr Cir	Reno	NV	89512	**800-621-9402**	775-788-8800
Bulldog Hiway Express 3390 Buffalo Ave	Charleston	SC	29418	**800-331-9515**	843-744-1651
Cdo Technologies Inc 5200 Sprngfeld St Ste 320	Dayton	OH	45431	**866-307-6616**	937-258-0022
Central Transportation Systems Inc 4105 Rio Bravo Ste 100	El Paso	TX	79902	**800-283-3106**	
CH Robinson Worldwide Inc 14701 Charlson Rd	Eden Prairie	MN	55347	**855-229-6128***	952-683-3950
NASDAQ: CHRW ■ *Cust Svc					
Clean Air Technology Inc 41105 Capital Dr	Canton	MI	48187	**800-459-6320**	
Clipper Exxpress Inc 9014 Heritage Pkwy Ste 300	Woodridge	IL	60517	**800-678-2547**	630-739-0700
Coyote Logistics LLC 191 E Deerpath Rd	Lake Forest	IL	60045	**877-626-9683**	847-295-2424
Crane Worldwide Logistics LLC 1500 Rankin Rd	Houston	TX	77073	**888-870-2726**	281-443-2777
Daniel F Young Inc 1235 Westlakes Dr Ste 255	Berwyn	PA	19312	**866-407-0083**	610-725-4000
Daniel Group Ltd, The 400 Clarice Ave Ste 200	Charlotte	NC	28204	**877-967-4242**	
Danny Herman Trucking Inc PO Box 55	Mountain City	TN	37683	**800-251-7500**	423-727-9061
Dennis K Burke Inc 284 Eastern Ave PO Box 6069	Chelsea	MA	02150	**800-289-2875**	617-884-7800
Dependable Highway Express Inc 2440 S 48th Ave	Phoenix	AZ	85043	**800-472-2037**	602-278-4401
Distribution & Marking Services Inc (DMSI) 10709 Granite St Ste Q	Charlotte	NC	28273	**844-325-3741**	704-749-7300
Dohrn Transfer Co 625 Third Ave	Rock Island	IL	61201	**888-364-7621**	309-794-0723
DSC Logistics 1750 S Wolf Rd	Des Plaines	IL	60018	**800-372-1960**	
Expeditors International of Washington Inc 1015 Third Ave 12th Fl	Seattle	WA	98104	**800-284-7474**	206-674-3400
NASDAQ: EXPD					
FedEx Supply Chain Services Inc 5455 Darrow Rd	Hudson	OH	44236	**800-463-3339**	901-369-3600
Fremont Contract Carriers Inc (FCC) 865 S Bud Blvd	Fremont	NE	68025	**800-228-9842**	
Griffin Transport Services 5360 Capital Ct	Reno	NV	89502	**800-361-5028**	775-331-8010
Gypsum Express Ltd 8280 Sixty Rd PO Box 268	Baldwinsville	NY	13027	**800-621-7901**	315-638-2201
H E Whitlock Inc 4808 Dillon Dr PO Box 8030	Pueblo	CO	81008	**866-933-0709**	
Hanson Logistics 2900 S State St	Saint Joseph	MI	49085	**888-772-1197**	269-982-1390
Higher Ed Growth LLC 5400 S Lakeshore Dr Ste 101	Tempe	AZ	85283	**866-433-8532**	
Horizon Air Freight Inc 152-15 Rockaway Blvd	Jamaica	NY	11434	**800-221-6028**	718-528-3800
Hub Group Inc 2000 Clearwater Dr	Oak Brook	IL	60523	**800-377-5833**	630-271-3600
NASDAQ: HUBG					
JB Hunt Transport Services Inc 615 JB Hunt Corporate Dr	Lowell	AR	72745	**800-643-3622**	479-820-0000
NASDAQ: JBHT					
Kenco Group Inc 2001 Riverside Dr	Chattanooga	TN	37406	**800-758-3289**	
Kintetsu World Express USA Inc 1 Jericho Plz Ste 100	Jericho	NY	11753	**800-275-4045**	516-933-7100
Kuehne & Nagel Inc 10 Exchange Pl	Jersey City	NJ	07302	**866-914-0444**	201-413-5500
L&B Transport LLC 708 US190 PO Box 74870	Port Allen	LA	70767	**800-545-9401**	225-387-0894
Landstar Logistics Inc 13410 Sutton Pk Dr S	Jacksonville	FL	32224	**800-872-9400**	904-398-9400
LeSaint Logistics 868 W Crossroads Pkwy	Romeoville	IL	60446	**877-566-9375**	630-243-5950
M & J Transportation 3536 Nicholson Ave	Kansas City	MO	64120	**866-298-3858**	816-231-6733
Matson Logistics Inc 555 12th St	Oakland	CA	94607	**800-762-8766**	510-628-4000
McElroy Truck Lines Inc 111 80 Spur PO Box 104	Cuba	AL	36907	**800-992-7863**	205-392-5579
Meridian IQ 11501 Outlook St Ste 500	Overland Park	KS	66211	**877-246-4909**	
Metropolitan Trucking Inc (MRTK) 299 Market St	Saddle Brook	NJ	07663	**800-967-3278**	
Midwest Specialized Transportation Inc PO Box 6418	Rochester	MN	55903	**800-927-8007**	507-424-4838
Mitsui & Co (USA) Inc 200 Pk Ave	New York	NY	10166	**877-248-4237**	212-878-4000
MySupplyChainGroup LLC 1500 First Ave N Ste A111	Birmingham	AL	35203	**888-444-7786**	205-706-4300
National Distributors Inc 1517 Avco Blvd	Sellersburg	IN	47172	**800-334-9677**	812-246-6306
National Freight Inc (NFI) 1515 Burnt Mill Rd	Cherry Hill	NJ	08003	**877-634-3777***	
*General					
Navis Logistics Network 6551 S Revere Pkwy Ste 250	Centennial	CO	80111	**800-344-3528**	
Oakley Transport Inc 101 ABC Rd	Lake Wales	FL	33859	**800-969-8265**	863-638-1435
ODW Logistics Inc 1580 Williams Rd	Columbus	OH	43207	**800-743-7062**	614-497-1660
Pegasus Logistics Group Inc 306 Airline Dr Ste 100	Coppell	TX	75019	**800-997-7226**	469-671-0300
Pierce Distribution Services Co PO Box 15600	Loves Park	IL	61132	**800-466-7397**	
Ponvia Technology Inc 49-T Sherwood Ter	Lake Bluff	IL	60045	**877-217-0875**	
Radiant Logistics Inc Third Fl 405 114Th Ave Se	Bellevue	WA	98004	**800-843-4784**	425-943-4599
Red Rock Distributing Co 1 NW 50th St	Oklahoma City	OK	73118	**800-323-7109**	405-677-3373
Red Star Oil 802 Purser Dr	Raleigh	NC	27603	**800-774-6033**	919-772-1944
Renodis Inc 476 Robert St N	Saint Paul	MN	55101	**866-200-8986**	651-556-1200
RIM Logistics Ltd 200 N Gary Ave	Roselle	IL	60172	**888-275-0937**	630-595-0610
Rinchem Company Inc 6133 Edith Blvd NE	Albuquerque	NM	87107	**888-375-2436**	505-345-3655
Rural Health Resource Center 525 S Lake Ave Ste 320	Duluth	MN	55802	**800-997-6685**	218-727-9390
Ryder System Inc 11690 NW 105th St	Miami	FL	33178	**800-297-9337**	305-500-3726
NYSE: R					
S & H Express Inc 400 Mulberry St	York	PA	17403	**800-637-9782**	717-848-5015
Schneider National Inc 3101 S Packerland Dr PO Box 2545	Green Bay	WI	54306	**800-558-6767**	920-592-2000
Seko Worldwide Inc 1100 Arlington Heights Rd Ste 600	Itasca	IL	60143	**800-323-1235**	630-919-4800
Shaker Group Inc, The 862 Albany Shaker Rd	Latham	NY	12110	**800-267-0314**	518-786-9286
Slay Industries Inc 1441 Hampton Ave	Saint Louis	MO	63139	**800-852-7529**	314-647-7529
Store Opening Solutions (SOS) 800 Middle Tennessee Blvd	Murfreesboro	TN	37129	**877-388-9262**	
Survival Systems Training Ltd 40 Mount Hope Ave	Dartmouth	NS	B2Y4K9	**800-788-3888**	902-465-3888
Taylor Protocols Inc 16040 Christensen Rd Ste 315	Tukwila	WA	98188	**877-355-8229**	206-283-8144
Technical Transportation Inc 1701 W Northwest Hwy Ste 100	Grapevine	TX	76051	**800-852-8726**	
Thoroughbred Direct Intermodal Services 5165 Campus Dr Ste 400	Plymouth Meeting	PA	19462	**877-250-2902**	610-567-3360
TRANSFLO Terminal Services Inc 500 Water St Ste J975	Jacksonville	FL	32202	**866-872-6735**	
Transplace 3010 Gaylord Pkwy Ste 200	Frisco	TX	75034	**866-413-9266**	
TSS Inc 110 E Old Settlers Blvd	Round Rock	TX	78664	**844-681-8158**	512-310-1000
UPS Supply Chain Solutions 12380 Morris Rd	Alpharetta	GA	30005	**800-742-5727**	913-693-6151
Vimich Traffic Logistics 12201 Tecumseh Rd E	Tecumseh	ON	N8N1M3	**800-284-1045**	
Weber Logistics 13530 Rosecrans Ave	Santa Fe Springs	CA	90670	**855-469-3237**	
Wilheit Packaging LLC 1527 May Dr	Gainesville	GA	30507	**800-727-4421**	770-532-4421
Willson International Ltd 2345 Argentia Rd Ste 201	Mississauga	ON	L5N8K4	**800-754-1918**	905-363-1133
Wise Consulting Associates Inc 54 Scott Adam Rd Ste 206	Hunt Valley	MD	21030	**800-654-4550**	410-628-0100
XPO Logistics Inc 6805 Perimeter Dr	Dublin	OH	43016	**800-837-7584**	614-923-1400

449 LONG-TERM CARE FACILITIES

SEE ALSO Retirement Communities ; Veterans Nursing Homes - State ; Long-Term Care Facilities Operators

Free-standing facilities accredited by the Joint Commission on Accreditation of Health-care Organizations. Listings in this category are organized alphabetically by states.

Name / Address	City	State	Zip	Toll-Free	Phone
Area Agency On Aging 9549 Koger Blvd Gadsden Bldg Ste 100	St Petersburg	FL	33702	**800-963-5337**	727-570-9696
Area Agency On Aging 10b Inc 1550 Corporate Woods Pkwy	Uniontown	OH	44685	**800-421-7277**	330-896-9172
Armed Forces Retirement Home - Washington 3700 N Capitol St NW	Washington	DC	20011	**800-422-9988***	
*Admissions					
Casa Colina Ctr for Rehabilitation 255 E Bonita Ave	Pomona	CA	91769	**800-926-5462**	909-596-7733
Central Boston Elder Services Inc 2315 Washington St	Boston	MA	02119	**800-922-2275**	617-277-7416
Comprehensive Care Management Corp (CCM) 1250 Waters Pl Tower 1 Ste 602	Bronx	NY	10461	**877-226-8500**	
Extended Care Hospital Westminster 206 Hospital Cir	Westminster	CA	92683	**800-236-9747**	714-891-2769
Front Porch Communities & Services 303 N Glenoaks Blvd	Burbank	CA	91502	**800-233-3709**	
Hennis Care Centre 1720 Cross St	Dover	OH	44622	**800-241-1044**	330-364-8849
Heritage Ctr 1201 W Buena Vista Rd	Evansville	IN	47710	**800-704-0700**	812-429-0700
Hope Network 3075 Orchard Vista Dr SE	Grand Rapids	MI	49546	**800-695-7273**	616-301-8000
Jewish Home Lifecare 120 W 106th St	New York	NY	10025	**800-544-0304**	212-870-5000

Classified Section

				Toll-Free	Phone
Kindred Hospital Greensboro 2401 Southside Blvd	Greensboro	NC	27406	**877-836-2671**	336-271-2800
La Jolla Nursing & Rehabilitation Ctr 2552 Torrey Pines Rd	La Jolla	CA	92037	**800-861-0086**	858-453-5810
ManorCare Health Services - Mountainside 1180 Rt 22 W	Mountainside	NJ	07092	**800-366-1232**	908-654-0020
North Adams Common Nursing Home 175 Franklin St	North Adams	MA	01247	**800-445-4560**	413-664-4041
Oklahoma Veterans Ctr Norman 1776 E Robinson St	Norman	OK	73071	**800-782-5218**	405-360-5600
Presbyterian SeniorCare-Westminster Place 1215 Hulton Rd	Oakmont	PA	15139	**877-772-6500**	412-828-5600
Redstone Highlands Health Care Ctr 6 Garden Ctr Dr	Greensburg	PA	15601	**800-732-0999**	724-832-8400
St.Vincent Health 2001 W 86th St	Indianapolis	IN	46260	**866-338-2345**	317-338-2345
Williamstown Commons Nursing & Rehabilitation Ctr 25 Adams Rd	Williamstown	MA	01267	**800-445-4560**	413-458-2111

450 LONG-TERM CARE FACILITIES OPERATORS

				Toll-Free	Phone
Active Day/Senior Care Inc 400 Redland Ct Ste 114	Owings Mills	MD	21117	**877-435-3372**	866-724-9599
ElderWood Senior Care 7 Limestone Dr	Williamsville	NY	14221	**888-826-9663**	716-633-3900
Five Star Quality Care Inc 400 Centre St *NYSE: FVE*	Newton	MA	02458	**866-230-1286**	617-796-8387
Genesis HealthCare Corp 101 E State St	Kennett Square	PA	19348	**800-944-7776**	610-444-6350
Odyssey HealthCare Inc 717 N Harwood St	Dallas	TX	75201	**855-865-5894**	214-922-9711
Sun Healthcare Group Inc 18831 Von Karman Ste 400 *NASDAQ: SUNH*	Irvine	CA	92612	**800-729-6600**	949-255-7100

451 LOTTERIES, GAMES, SWEEPSTAKES

SEE ALSO Games & Gaming

				Toll-Free	Phone
British Columbia Lottery Corp (BCLC) 74 W Seymour St	Kamloops	BC	V2C1E2	**866-815-0222**	250-828-5500
Catfish Bend Casinos II LLC 3001 Winegard Dr	Burlington	IA	52601	**866-792-9948**	319-753-2946
Choctaw Casino Resorts 3735 Choctaw Rd	Durant	OK	74701	**888-652-4628**	580-920-0160
Cliff Castle Casino 555 W Middle Verde Rd	Camp Verde	AZ	86322	**800-381-7568**	928-567-7999
Colorado Lottery 212 W Third St Ste 210	Pueblo	CO	81003	**800-999-2959**	719-546-2400
Cypress Bayou Casino 832 Martin Luther King Rd	Charenton	LA	70523	**800-284-4386**	
Fortune Bay Resort & Casino 1430 Bois Forte Rd	Tower	MN	55790	**800-992-7529**	218-753-6400
Georgia Lottery Corp 250 Williams St NW Ste 3000	Atlanta	GA	30303	**800-425-8259**	404-215-5000
Idaho Lottery 1199 Shoreline Ln Ste 100	Boise	ID	83702	**800-432-5688**	208-334-2600
Kansas Lottery 128 N Kansas Ave	Topeka	KS	66603	**800-544-9467**	785-296-5700
Kentucky Lottery Corp 1011 W Main St	Louisville	KY	40202	**800-937-8946**	502-560-1500
Montana Lottery 2525 N Montana Ave	Helena	MT	59601	**800-425-1435**	406-444-5825
Nebraska Lottery 1800 "O" St PO Box 98901	Lincoln	NE	68509	**800-587-5200**	402-471-6100
New Hampshire Lottery Commission 14 Integra Dr	Concord	NH	03301	**800-852-3324**	603-271-3391
Ohio Lottery Commission 615 W Superior Ave	Cleveland	OH	44113	**800-686-4208**	216-787-3200
River Rock Entertainment Authority 3250 Hwy 128 E	Geyserville	CA	95441	**877-883-7777**	707-857-2777
San Felipe's Casino Hollywood 25 Hagon Rd	Algodones	NM	87001	**877-529-2946**	505-867-6700
Soboba Casino 23333 Soboba Rd	San Jacinto	CA	92583	**866-476-2622**	951-665-1000
Washington State Lottery PO Box 43000	Olympia	WA	98504	**800-732-5101**	360-664-4720
Wyandotte Nation Casino 100 Jackpot Pl	Wyandotte	OK	74370	**866-447-4946**	918-678-4946

452 LUGGAGE, BAGS, CASES

SEE ALSO Handbags, Totes, Backpacks ; Leather Goods - Personal

				Toll-Free	Phone
Anvil Cases 15730 Salt Lake Ave	City of Industry	CA	91745	**800-359-2684**	626-968-4100
Calzone Case Co 225 Black Rock Ave *Cust Svc	Bridgeport	CT	06605	**800-243-5152***	203-367-5766
CH Ellis Co Inc 2432 SE Ave *Sales	Indianapolis	IN	46201	**800-466-3351***	317-636-3351
Coach Inc 516 W 34th St *NYSE: COH*	New York	NY	10001	**800-444-3611**	212-594-1850
Delsey Luggage 6735 Business Pkwy Ste A	Elkridge	MD	21075	**800-558-3344**	410-796-5655
Mercury Luggage Manufacturing Co 4843 Victor St	Jacksonville	FL	32207	**800-874-1885**	904-334-8801
Platt Luggage Inc 4051 W 51st St	Chicago	IL	60632	**800-222-1555**	773-838-2000
SKB Corp 434 W Levers Pl *Sales	Orange	CA	92867	**800-410-2024***	714-637-1252

				Toll-Free	Phone
Targus Inc 1211 N Miller St	Anaheim	CA	92806	**877-482-7487**	714-765-5555
Travelpro USA 700 Banyan Trl	Boca Raton	FL	33431	**800-741-7471**	561-998-2824
Zero Manufacturing Inc 500 West 200 North	North Salt Lake	UT	84054	**800-959-5050**	801-298-5900

453 MACHINE SHOPS

SEE ALSO Precision Machined Products

				Toll-Free	Phone
Acme Cryogenics Inc 2801 Mitchell Ave	Allentown	PA	18103	**800-422-2790**	610-966-4488
American Grinding & Machine Co 2000 N Mango Ave	Chicago	IL	60639	**877-988-4343**	773-889-4343
Brandywine Machine Company Inc 300 Creek Rd	Downingtown	PA	19335	**800-523-7128**	
Burger & Brown Engineering Inc 4500 E 142nd St	Grandview	MO	64030	**800-764-3518**	816-878-6675
Chalmers & Kubeck Inc 150 Commerce Dr	Aston	PA	19014	**800-242-5637**	610-494-4300
Chant Engineering 59 Industrial Dr	New Britain	PA	18901	**888-567-0983**	215-230-4260
Consolidated Bottle Corp 77 Union St	Toronto	ON	M6N3N2	**800-561-1354**	416-656-7777
Custom Brackets 32 Alpha Park	Cleveland	OH	44143	**800-530-2289**	440-446-0819
Digital Machining Systems LLC 929 Ridge Rd	Duson	LA	70529	**800-530-8945**	337-984-6013
Egge Machine Company Inc 11707 Slauson Ave	Santa Fe Springs	CA	90670	**800-866-3443**	562-945-3419
Femco Machine Co 754 S Main St Ext	Punxsutawney	PA	15767	**800-458-3445**	814-938-9763
Furmanite America 101 Old Underwood Rd	La Porte	TX	77571	**800-444-5572**	281-842-5100
Granite State Manufacturing Co 124 Joliette St	Manchester	NH	03102	**800-464-7646**	
Haas Automation Inc 2800 Sturgis Rd	Oxnard	CA	93030	**800-331-6746**	805-278-1800
Highway Machine Company Inc (HMC) 3010 S Old US Hwy 41	Princeton	IN	47670	**866-990-9462**	812-385-3639
Industrial Tool Inc 9210 52nd Ave N *Sales	New Hope	MN	55428	**800-776-4455***	763-533-7244
J C Steele & Sons Inc 710 S Mulberry St	Statesville	NC	28677	**800-278-3353**	704-872-3681
Kurt Manufacturing Co 5280 Main St NE	Minneapolis	MN	55421	**800-458-7855**	763-572-1500
Laser Excel N6323 Berlin Rd PO Box 279	Green Lake	WI	54941	**800-285-6544**	920-294-6544
LaVezzi Precision Inc 999 Regency Dr	Glendale Heights	IL	60139	**800-323-1772**	630-582-1230
Lemco Tool Corp 1850 Metzger Ave	Cogan Station	PA	17728	**800-233-8713**	570-494-0620
Lith-O-Roll Corp 9521 Telstar Ave	El Monte	CA	91731	**800-423-4176**	626-579-0340
Litton Engineering Laboratories 200 Litton Dr Ste 200	Grass Valley	CA	95945	**800-821-8866**	530-273-6176
Marshall Screw Products Co 3820 Chandler Dr Ne	Minneapolis	MN	55421	**800-321-6727**	
Micro Instrument Corp (MIC) 1199 Emerson St PO Box 60619	Rochester	NY	14606	**800-200-3150**	585-458-3150
Peeco 7050 W Ridge Rd	Fairview	PA	16415	**800-235-9382**	814-474-5561
Poly Cycle Inc 5501 Campbells Run Rd	Pittsburgh	PA	15205	**800-394-4333**	412-747-1101
Quality Mfg Company Inc (QMI) PO Box 616	Winchester	KY	40392	**866-460-6459**	859-744-0420
Santinelli International Inc 325 Oser Ave	Hauppauge	NY	11788	**800-644-3343**	631-435-3343
Scheirer Machine Company Inc 3200 Industrial Blvd	Bethel Park	PA	15102	**800-448-4590**	412-833-6500
Schmiede Corp 1865 Riley Creek Rd PO Box 1630	Tullahoma	TN	37388	**800-535-1851**	931-455-4801
Standard Locknut Inc 1045 E 169th St	Westfield	IN	46074	**800-783-6887**	317-867-0100
Tier One LLC 31 Pecks Ln	Newtown	CT	06470	**877-251-2228**	203-426-3030
Twin City EDM 7940 Rancher Rd NE	Fridley	MN	55432	**800-397-0338**	763-783-7808
Unisource Manufacturing Inc 8040 NE 33rd Dr	Portland	OR	97211	**800-234-2566**	503-281-4673
Vescio Threading Co 14002 Anson Ave	Santa Fe Springs	CA	90670	**800-361-4218**	562-802-1868
Wahlco Inc 2722 S Fairview St	Santa Ana	CA	92704	**800-423-5432**	714-979-7300
Weldmac Manufacturing Co 1451 N Johnson Ave	El Cajon	CA	92020	**800-252-1533**	619-440-2300
Windham Manufacturing Company Inc 8520 Forney Rd	Dallas	TX	75227	**888-965-0093**	214-388-0511
Windings Inc PO Box 566	New Ulm	MN	56073	**800-795-8533**	507-359-2034
Xtek Inc 11451 Reading Rd	Cincinnati	OH	45241	**888-332-9835**	513-733-7800

454 MACHINE TOOLS - METAL CUTTING TYPES

SEE ALSO Machine Tools - Metal Forming Types ; Metalworking Devices & Accessories

				Toll-Free	Phone
Abbco Inc 2401 American Ln	Elkgrove Vlg	IL	60007	**866-986-6546**	630-595-7115
Allied Tool Products 9334 N 107th St	Milwaukee	WI	53224	**800-558-5147**	414-355-8280
Barnes International Inc 814 Chestnut St PO Box 1203	Rockford	IL	61105	**800-435-4877**	815-964-8661
Crafts Technology 91 Joey Dr	Elk Grove Village	IL	60007	**800-323-6802**	847-758-3100

Classified Section

Company	City	State	Zip	Toll-Free	Phone
Darex 210 E Hersey St PO Box 730	Ashland	OR	97520	**800-597-6170**	541-488-2224
Davenport Machine Inc 167 Ames St	Rochester	NY	14611	**800-344-5748**	585-235-4545
EH Wachs Co 600 Knightsbridge Pkwy	Lincolnshire	IL	60069	**800-323-8185**	847-537-8800
Extrude Hone Corp 235 Industry Blvd	Irwin	PA	15642	**800-835-3668**	724-863-5900
Flow International Corp 23500 64th Ave S *NASDAQ: FLOW*	Kent	WA	98032	**800-446-3569**	253-850-3500
GF Machining Solutions 560 Bond St	Lincolnshire	IL	60069	**800-282-1336**	847-913-5300
Gleason Corp 1000 University Ave	Rochester	NY	14607	**800-727-6333**	585-473-1000
Grob Inc 1731 Tenth Ave	Grafton	WI	53024	**800-225-6481**	262-377-1400
Hanchett Manufacturing Inc 906 N State St	Big Rapids	MI	49307	**800-454-7463**	231-796-7678
Hardinge Inc 1 Hardinge Dr *NASDAQ: HDNG*	Elmira	NY	14902	**800-843-8801**	607-734-2281
Hause Machines 809 S Pleasant St	Montpelier	OH	43543	**800-932-8665**	419-485-3158
Huffman Corp 1050 Huffman Way	Clover	SC	29710	**888-483-3626**	803-222-4561
Hurco Cos Inc 1 Technology Way *NASDAQ: HURC* ■ *Sales	Indianapolis	IN	46268	**800-634-2416***	317-293-5309
Hypertherm Inc 21 Great Hollow Rd PO Box 5010	Hanover	NH	03755	**800-643-0030**	603-643-3441
Hypneumat Inc 5900 W Franklin Dr	Franklin	WI	53132	**800-228-9949**	414-423-7400
Kaufman Mfg Co 547 S 29th St PO Box 1056	Manitowoc	WI	54221	**800-420-6641**	920-684-6641
Klingelhofer Corp 165 Mill Ln	Mountainside	NJ	07092	**800-879-5546**	908-232-7200
Koike Aronson Inc 635 W Main St PO Box 307	Arcade	NY	14009	**800-252-5232**	585-492-2400
Kyocera Tycom Corp 3565 Cadillac	Costa Mesa	CA	92626	**800-823-7284**	714-428-3600
Makino 7680 Innovation Way	Mason	OH	45040	**888-625-4661**	513-573-7200
McLean Inc 3409 E Miraloma Ave *Cust Svc	Anaheim	CA	92806	**800-451-2424***	714-996-5451
NNT Corp 1320 Norwood Ave	Itasca	IL	60143	**800-556-9999**	630-875-9600
North American Products Corp 1180 Wernsing Rd *Cust Svc	Jasper	IN	47546	**800-457-7468***	812-482-2000
Oliver of Adrian Inc 1111 E Beecher St PO Box 189	Adrian	MI	49221	**877-668-0885**	517-263-2132
Parker Majestic Inc 300 N Pike Rd	Sarver	PA	16055	**866-572-7537**	724-352-1551
Peddinghaus Corp 300 N Washington Ave	Bradley	IL	60915	**800-786-2448**	815-937-3800
Pioneer Broach Co 6434 Telegraph Rd	Los Angeles	CA	90040	**800-621-1945**	323-728-1263
Rothenberger USA 4455 Boeing Dr	Rockford	IL	61109	**800-545-7698**	815-397-7617
Rottler Mfg 8029 S 200th St	Kent	WA	98032	**800-452-0534**	253-872-7050
S & M Machine Service Inc 109 E Highland Dr	Oconto Falls	WI	54154	**800-323-1579**	920-846-8130
Servo Products Co 34940 Lakeland Blvd	Eastlake	OH	44095	**800-521-7359**	440-942-9999
Setco Sales Co 5880 Hillside Ave	Cincinnati	OH	45233	**800-543-0470**	513-941-5110
SNK America Inc 1150 Feehanville Dr	Mount Prospect	IL	60056	**888-765-6224**	847-364-0801
Southwestern Industries Inc 2615 Homestead Pl	Rancho Dominguez	CA	90220	**800-421-6875**	310-608-4422
Sunnen Products Co 7910 Manchester Ave	Saint Louis	MO	63143	**800-325-3670**	314-781-2100
Technidrill Systems Inc 429 Portage Blvd	Kent	OH	44240	**844-313-7012**	330-678-9980
Thermal Dynamics Corp 82 Benning St	West Lebanon	NH	03784	**800-752-7621**	603-298-5711
Tool-Flo Mfg Inc 7803 Hansen Rd	Houston	TX	77061	**800-345-2815**	713-941-1080
Toyoda Machinery USA Inc 316 W University Dr	Arlington Heights	IL	60004	**800-257-2985**	847-253-0340
TRU TECH Systems Inc 24550 N River Rd PO Box 46965	Mount Clemens	MI	48043	**877-878-8324**	586-469-2700
US Tool Grinding Inc 701 S Desloge Dr	Desloge	MO	63601	**800-222-1771**	573-431-3856
Vernon Tool Company Ltd 503 Jones Rd	Oceanside	CA	92054	**800-452-1542**	760-433-5860
WF Meyers Co 1008 13th St	Bedford	IN	47421	**800-457-4055**	812-275-4485
Whitney Tool Company Inc 906 R St PO Box 545	Bedford	IN	47421	**800-536-1971**	812-275-4491
Wisconsin Machine Tool Corp 3225 Gateway Rd Ste 100	Brookfield	WI	53045	**800-243-3078**	262-317-3048

455 MACHINE TOOLS - METAL FORMING TYPES

SEE ALSO Rolling Mill Machinery ; Tool & Die Shops ; Machine Tools - Metal Cutting Types ; Metalworking Devices & Accessories

Company	City	State	Zip	Toll-Free	Phone
Advanced Hydraulics Inc 13568 Vintage Pl	Chino	CA	91710	**888-581-8079**	909-590-7644
Amada America Inc 7025 Firestone Blvd	Buena Park	CA	90621	**800-626-6612**	714-739-2111
Badge A Minit Ltd 345 N Lewis Ave	Oglesby	IL	61348	**800-223-4103**	815-883-8822
Bliss Clearing Niagara (BCN) 1004 E State St	Hastings	MI	49058	**800-642-5477**	269-948-3300
Bradbury Company Inc 1200 E Cole	Moundridge	KS	67107	**800-397-6394**	620-345-6394
Cyril Bath Co 1610 Airport Rd	Monroe	NC	28110	**800-801-1418**	704-289-8531
DR Sperry & Co 623 Rathbone Ave	Aurora	IL	60506	**888-997-9297**	630-892-4361
Edwards Manufacturing Co 1107 Sykes St	Albert Lea	MN	56007	**800-373-8206**	507-373-8206
Emery Corp PO Box 1104	Morganton	NC	28680	**800-255-0537**	828-433-1536
Erie Press Systems 1253 W 12th St PO Box 4061	Erie	PA	16512	**800-222-3608**	814-455-3941
Grant Assembly Technologies 90 Silliman Ave	Bridgeport	CT	06605	**800-227-2150**	203-366-4557
Greenerd Press & Machine Company Inc 41 Crown St PO Box 886	Nashua	NH	03061	**800-877-9110**	603-889-4101
Heim LP 6360 W 73rd St	Chicago	IL	60638	**800-927-9393**	708-496-7450
Mate Precision Tooling Inc 1295 Lund Blvd	Anoka	MN	55303	**800-328-4492**	763-421-0230
Mega Manufacturing Inc PO Box 457	Hutchinson	KS	67504	**800-338-5471**	620-663-1127
Murata Machinery USA Inc 2120 Queen City Dr	Charlotte	NC	28208	**800-428-8469**	
Pacific Press Technologies 714 Walnut St	Mount Carmel	IL	62863	**800-851-3586**	618-262-8666
Presses Inc 6360 W 73rd St	Chicago	IL	60638	**800-927-9393**	708-496-7400
Reed 28 Sword St	Auburn	MA	01501	**800-343-6068**	508-753-6530
Schleuniger Inc 87 Colin Dr *Tech Supp	Manchester	NH	03103	**877-902-1470***	603-668-8117
Strippit Inc/LVD 12975 Clarence Ctr Rd	Akron	NY	14001	**800-828-1527**	716-542-4511
Tetrahedron Assoc Inc PO Box 710157	San Diego	CA	92171	**800-958-3872**	619-661-0552
Tools for Bending Inc 194 W Dakota Ave *Cust Svc	Denver	CO	80223	**800-873-3305***	303-777-7170
Williams White & Co 600 River Dr	Moline	IL	61265	**877-797-7650**	
Wysong Inc 4820 US 29 N	Greensboro	NC	27405	**800-299-7664**	336-621-3960

456 MAGAZINES & JOURNALS

SEE ALSO Periodicals Publishers

456-1 Agriculture & Farming Magazines

Company	City	State	Zip	Toll-Free	Phone
Alfa Corp 2108 E S Blvd	Montgomery	AL	36116	**800-964-2532**	334-288-0375
American Agriculturist 5227-B Baltimore Pike	Littlestown	PA	17340	**800-441-1410**	717-359-0150
Beef Magazine 7900 International Dr Ste 300 *Cust Svc	Minneapolis	MN	55425	**800-722-5334***	952-851-9329
Dairy Herd Management 10901 W 84th Terr	Lenexa	KS	66214	**800-255-5113**	913-438-8700
Farm Industry News 7900 International Dr Ste 300 *Cust Svc	Minneapolis	MN	55425	**800-722-5334***	952-851-9329
Farm Journal 30 S 15th Ste 900	Philadelphia	PA	19102	**800-331-9310**	215-557-8900
Farm Show Magazine 20088 Kenwood Trial	Lakeville	MN	55044	**800-834-9665**	
Georgia Farm Bureau News 1620 Bass Rd	Macon	GA	31210	**800-342-1192**	478-474-8411
Hoard's Dairyman Magazine 28 Milwaukee Ave W PO Box 801	Fort Atkinson	WI	53538	**800-245-8222**	920-563-5551
Iowa Farm Bureau Spokesman Magazine 5400 University Ave	West Des Moines	IA	50266	**866-598-3693**	515-225-5413
Kansas Living Magazine 2627 KFB Plz	Manhattan	KS	66503	**800-406-3053**	785-587-6000
Pork Report 1776 NW 114th St PO Box 9114	Des Moines	IA	50325	**800-456-7675**	515-223-2600
Soybean Digest 7900 International Dr Ste 300 *Cust Svc	Minneapolis	MN	55425	**800-722-5334***	952-851-4667
Tennessee Farm Bureau News 147 Bear Creek Pike	Columbia	TN	38401	**877-876-2222**	931-388-7872
Texas Farm Bureau 7420 Fish Pond Rd PO Box 2689	Waco	TX	76710	**800-488-7872**	254-772-3030
Top Producer Magazine 1818 Market St 31st Fl	Philadelphia	PA	19103	**800-320-7992**	

456-2 Art & Architecture Magazines

Company	City	State	Zip	Toll-Free	Phone
AmericanStyle Magazine 3000 Chestnut Ave Ste 304	Baltimore	MD	21211	**800-642-4314**	410-889-3093
Architectural Digest 4 Times Sq 18th Fl	New York	NY	10036	**800-365-8032**	
Architectural Record Magazine 2 Penn Plaza 9th Fl	New York	NY	10121	**800-393-6343**	646-849-7100
Art in America Magazine 575 Broadway *Cust Svc	New York	NY	10012	**800-925-8059***	212-941-2800
Artforum International Magazine 350 Seventh Ave 19th Fl	New York	NY	10001	**800-966-2783**	212-475-4000
Artist's Magazine, The 4700 E Galbraith Rd	Cincinnati	OH	45236	**800-422-2550**	513-531-2222
ARTnews Magazine 48 W 38th St 9th Fl	New York	NY	10018	**800-284-4625**	212-398-1690
Design/Build Business Magazine 3030 Salt Creek Ln Ste 200	Arlington Heights	IL	60005	**800-547-7377**	847-454-2714
HOW Design Magazine 4700 E Galbraith Rd *Cust Svc	Cincinnati	OH	45236	**800-333-1115***	513-531-2690
Metropolis Magazine 205 Lexington Ave 17th Fl	New York	NY	10016	**800-344-3046**	212-627-9977

Name / Address	City	State	ZIP	Toll-Free	Phone
Pastel Journal 4700 E Galbraith Rd	Cincinnati	OH	45236	800-422-2550	513-531-2222
Southwest Art Magazine 10901 W 120th Ave Ste 350	Broomfield	CO	80021	877-212-1938	303-442-0427
Sunshine Artist Magazine 4075 LB McLeod Rd Ste E	Orlando	FL	32811	800-597-2573	407-648-7479

456-3 Automotive Magazines

Name / Address	City	State	ZIP	Toll-Free	Phone
American Iron Magazine 1010 Summer St *Cust Svc	Stamford	CT	06905	877-693-3572*	203-425-8777
AutoWeek Magazine 1155 Gratiot Ave *Circ	Detroit	MI	48207	888-288-6954*	313-446-6000
Cycle World Magazine 1499 Monrovia Ave	Newport Beach	CA	92663	800-456-3084	949-720-5300
Easyriders Magazine 28210 Dorothy Dr	Agoura Hills	CA	91301	800-323-3484	818-889-8740
Grassroots Motorsports Magazine 915 Ridgewood Ave	Holly Hill	FL	32117	800-520-8292	386-239-0523
Hemmings Motor News 222 Main St	Bennington	VT	05201	800-227-4373	802-442-3101
Hot Rod Magazine 6420 Wilshire Blvd *Orders	Los Angeles	CA	90048	800-800-4681*	323-782-2000
Hot Rod Network 774 S Placentia Ave	Placentia	CA	92870	800-926-8207	
Motor Trend Magazine 6420 Wilshire Blvd 7th Fl	Los Angeles	CA	90048	800-800-6848	323-782-2000
Motorcycle Consumer News Magazine 3 Burroughs	Irvine	CA	92618	888-333-0354	949-855-8822
National Speed Sport News Magazine 142 F S Cardigan Way	Mooresville	NC	28117	866-455-2531	704-489-5231
Off-Road Magazine 2400 E Katella Ave 7th fl	Anaheim	CA	92806	877-462-6752	714-848-8880
Road & Track Magazine 1499 Monrovia Ave	Newport Beach	CA	92663	800-835-6422	949-720-5300
Stock Car Racing Magazine PO Box 420235	Palm Coast	FL	32142	800-333-2633	

456-4 Boating Magazines

Name / Address	City	State	ZIP	Toll-Free	Phone
Blue Water Sailing Magazine 747 Aquidneck Ave Ste 201 Ste 201	Middletown	RI	02842	888-800-7245	401-847-7612
Power & Motoryacht Magazine 260 Madison Ave 4th Fl	New York	NY	10016	800-284-8036	860-767-3200
SAIL Magazine 98 N Washington St Ste 107	Boston	MA	02114	877-388-7761	617-720-8600
Sailing World Magazine 55 Hammarlund Way *Cust Svc	Middletown	RI	02842	866-436-2460*	401-845-5100
Sea Magazine 17782 Cowan St Ste C	Irvine	CA	92614	800-873-7327	949-660-6150
Yachting Magazine 55 Hammarlund Way	Middletown	RI	02842	800-999-0869	

456-5 Business & Finance Magazines

Name / Address	City	State	ZIP	Toll-Free	Phone
Advisor Today 2901 Telestar Ct	Falls Church	VA	22042	800-247-4074	
Alaska Business Monthly 501 W Northern Lights Blvd Ste 100	Anchorage	AK	99503	800-770-4373	907-276-4373
American Banker Magazine 1 State St Plaza 27th Fl	New York	NY	10004	800-221-1809	212-803-8200
Appraisal Journal 200 W Madison Ste 1500	Chicago	IL	60606	888-756-4624	
Area Development Magazine 400 Post Ave Ste 304	Westbury	NY	11590	800-735-2732	516-338-0900
Arkansas Business LP 122 E Second St	Little Rock	AR	72201	888-322-6397	501-372-1443
Association Management Magazine 1575 'I' St NW	Washington	DC	20005	888-950-2723	202-371-0940
Banking Strategies Magazine 115 S LaSalle St Ste 3300	Chicago	IL	60603	888-224-0037	312-553-4600
Black Enterprise Magazine 130 Fifth Ave *Cust Svc	New York	NY	10011	800-727-7777*	212-242-8000
British Standards Institution, The 12110 Sunset Hills Rd Ste 200	Reston	VA	20190	800-862-4977	703-437-9000
Business Facilities Magazine 44 Apple St Ste 3	Tinton Falls	NJ	07724	800-524-0337	732-842-7433
Business Insurance Magazine 711 Third Ave	New York	NY	10017	877-812-1587	212-210-0100
Business Journal, The 25 E Boardman St	Youngstown	OH	44501	800-837-6397	330-744-5023
California Real Estate Magazine 525 S Virgil Ave	Los Angeles	CA	90020	888-811-5281	213-739-8200
Central New York Business Journal, The 269 W Jefferson St	Syracuse	NY	13202	800-836-3539	315-579-3919
CFO Magazine 253 Summer St	Boston	MA	02210	800-772-1119	617-345-9700
Columbus Business First 303 W Nationwide Blvd	Columbus	OH	43215	800-486-3289	614-461-4040
Communications News PO Box 866	Osprey	FL	34229	800-827-9715	941-539-7579
Contract Design Magazine 770 Broadway	New York	NY	10004	800-697-8859	
Crain's Chicago Business Magazine 150 N Michigan Ave 16th Fl	Chicago	IL	60601	877-812-1590	312-649-5200
Crain's Cleveland Business Magazine 700 W St Clair Ave Ste 310	Cleveland	OH	44113	888-909-9111	216-522-1383
Crain's Detroit Business Magazine 1155 Gratiot Ave	Detroit	MI	48207	888-909-9111	313-446-6000
Crain's New York Business Magazine 685 Third Ave 3rd Fl	New York	NY	10017	877-824-9379	212-210-0100
Drug Topics Magazine 24950 Country Club Blvd Ste 200 *Cust Svc	North Olmsted	OH	44070	877-922-2022*	440-891-2792
E-Commerce Times (ECT) 16133 Ventura Blvd Ste 700	Encino	CA	91436	877-328-5500	818-461-9700
Editor & Publisher Magazine 17782 Cowan Ste C	Irvine	CA	92614	855-896-7433	949-660-6150
Expansion Management Magazine 1300 E Ninth St	Cleveland	OH	44114	866-505-7173	216-696-7000
Fast Company Magazine 7 World Trade Ctr	New York	NY	10007	800-542-6029	212-389-5300
Finance & Commerce 730 Second Ave S US Trust Bldg Ste 100	Minneapolis	MN	55402	800-451-9998	612-333-4244
Forbes Magazine 60 Fifth Ave	New York	NY	10011	800-295-0893	212-366-8900
Franchising World Magazine 1501 K St NW Ste 350	Washington	DC	20005	800-543-1038	202-628-8000
Harvard Business Review 60 Harvard Way	Boston	MA	02163	800-274-3214	617-783-7500
Health Facilities Management Magazine 155 N Wacker Dr Ste 400	Chicago	IL	60606	800-621-6902	312-893-6800
Hospitals & Health Networks Magazine 155 N Wacker Ste 400	Chicago	IL	60606	800-621-6902	312-893-6800
HRMagazine 1800 Duke St	Alexandria	VA	22314	800-283-7476	703-548-3440
Inc Magazine 7 World Trade Ctr	New York	NY	10007	800-234-0999	212-389-5377
Independent Agent Magazine 127 S Peyton St	Alexandria	VA	22314	800-221-7917	
Indianapolis Business Journal 41 E Washington St Ste 200	Indianapolis	IN	46204	800-428-7081	317-634-6200
Journal of Accountancy 220 Leigh Farm Rd	Durham	NC	27707	888-777-7077	
Journal of Financial Planning Assn 7535 E Hampden Ave Ste 600	Denver	CO	80231	800-322-4237	303-759-4900
Journal of Property Management 430 N Michigan Ave	Chicago	IL	60611	800-837-0706	
Law Enforcement Technology Magazine 1233 Janesville Ave	Fort Atkinson	WI	53538	800-547-7377	
Leadership Journal 465 Gundersen Dr	Carol Stream	IL	60188	800-777-3136	630-260-6200
Lodging Magazine 385 Oxford Vly Rd Ste 420	Yardley	PA	19067	800-394-5157	215-321-9662
Marketing News 311 S Wacker Dr Ste 5800	Chicago	IL	60606	800-262-1150	312-542-9000
Mergers & Acquisitions Magazine 1 State St Plz *Cust Svc	New York	NY	10004	888-807-8667*	212-803-6051
Mississippi Business Journal 200 N Congress St	Jackson	MS	39201	800-283-4625	601-364-1000
National Assn of Credit Management 8840 Columbia 100 Pkwy	Columbia	MD	21045	800-955-8815	410-740-5560
National Association of Housing and Redevelopment Officials 630 'I' St NW	Washington	DC	20001	877-866-2476	202-289-3500
New Accountant Magazine 3525 W Peterson Ave	Chicago	IL	60659	888-641-3169	773-866-9900
Palm Beach Daily Business Review 324 Datura St Ste 140	West Palm Beach	FL	33401	800-777-7300	561-820-2060
PCBE Inc PO Box 1575	Tacoma	WA	98401	800-540-8322	253-404-0891
Pensions & Investments Magazine 711 Third Ave *Cust Svc	New York	NY	10017	888-446-1422*	212-210-0100
Print Magazine 10151 Carver Rd Ste 200	Blue Ash	OH	45242	877-860-9145	513-531-2690
Purchasing Magazine 225 Wyman St	Waltham	MA	02451	888-393-5000	
Realtor Magazine 430 N Michigan Ave 9th Fl	Chicago	IL	60611	800-874-6500	312-329-8458
Rough Notes Company Inc, The 11690 Technology Dr	Carmel	IN	46032	800-428-4384	317-582-1600
Self-Employed America Magazine PO Box 241	Annapolis Junction	MD	20701	800-649-6273	
Selling Power Magazine 1140 International Pkwy	Fredericksburg	VA	22406	800-752-7355	540-752-7000
Signal Magazine 4400 Fair Lakes Ct	Fairfax	VA	22033	800-336-4583	703-631-6100
Sloan Management Review 77 Massachusetts Ave E60-100	Cambridge	MA	02139	800-876-5764	617-253-7170
Strategic Finance Magazine 10 Paragon Dr Ste 1	Montvale	NJ	07645	800-638-4427	201-573-9000
Training Magazine 27020 Noble Rd	Excelsior	MN	55331	877-865-9361	847-559-7596
Triangle Business Journal 3600 Glenwood Ave Ste 100	Raleigh	NC	27612	800-275-9356	919-878-0010
Utah Business Magazine 90 S 400 W Ste 650	Salt Lake City	UT	84101	866-294-1660	801-568-0114
Your Church Magazine 465 Gundersen Dr	Carol Stream	IL	60188	877-247-4787	630-260-6200

456-6 Children's & Youth Magazines

Name / Address	City	State	ZIP	Toll-Free	Phone
Creative Kids Magazine PO Box 8813	Waco	TX	76714	800-998-2208	254-756-3337
Cricket Media Inc 30 Grove St Ste C	Peterborough	NH	03458	800-821-0115	
Girls' Life Acqusition Co 4529 Hartford Rd	Baltimore	MD	21214	800-931-2237	410-426-9600
New Moon Magazine PO Box 161287	Duluth	MN	55816	800-381-4743	218-878-9673
Odyssey Magazine 30 Grove St Ste C	Peterborough	NH	03458	800-821-0115	603-924-7209

Name / Address	City	State	ZIP	Toll-Free	Phone
Owl Magazine 10 Lower Spadina Ave Ste 400	Toronto	ON	M5V2Z2	**800-551-6957**	416-340-2700
Turtle Magazine 1100 Waterway Blvd	Indianapolis	IN	46202	**800-558-2376**	317-634-1100
Wild Animal Baby Magazine 11100 Wildlife Ctr Dr	Reston	VA	20190	**800-822-9919**	
Your Big Backyard Magazine 11100 Wildlife Ctr Dr	Reston	VA	20190	**800-822-9919**	

456-7 Computer & Internet Magazines

Name / Address	City	State	ZIP	Toll-Free	Phone
Computer Magazine 10662 Los Vaqueros Cir *Orders	Los Alamitos	CA	90720	**800-272-6657***	714-821-8380
Computers in Libraries Magazine 143 Old Marlton Pk	Medford	NJ	08055	**800-300-9868**	609-654-6266
Computerworld Magazine 1 Speen St	Framingham	MA	01701	**800-343-6474**	508-879-0700
eContent Magazine 143 Old Marlton Pike Ste 3	Medford	NJ	08055	**800-300-9868**	609-654-6266
Federal Computer Week Magazine 3141 Fairview Pk Dr Ste 777	Falls Church	VA	22042	**877-534-2208**	703-876-5100
IEEE Computer Graphics & Applications Magazine 10662 Los Vaqueros Cir PO Box 3014	Los Alamitos	CA	90720	**800-272-6657**	714-821-8380
IEEE Micro Magazine 10662 Los Vaqueros Cir PO Box 3014	Los Alamitos	CA	90720	**800-272-6657**	714-821-8380
Information Today Magazine 143 Old Marlton Pk	Medford	NJ	08055	**800-300-9868**	609-654-6266
InformationWeek Magazine 600 Community Dr	Manhasset	NY	11030	**855-569-5945**	516-562-5000
InfoWorld Inc 501 Second St Fl 6	San Francisco	CA	94107	**800-227-8365**	415-243-4344
Law Technology News 120 Broadway 5th Fl *Cust Svc	New York	NY	10271	**800-888-8300***	212-457-7905
Macworld Magazine 501 Second St Ste 600 *Cust Svc	San Francisco	CA	94107	**800-288-6848***	415-243-0505
MultiMedia Schools Magazine 143 Old Marlton Pk	Medford	NJ	08055	**800-300-9868**	609-654-6266
Network World Magazine 492 Old Connecticut Path Ste 200 PO Box 9208	Framingham	MA	01701	**800-622-1108**	
Oracle Magazine 500 Oracle Pkwy	Redwood Shores	CA	94065	**800-392-2999**	650-506-7000
Searcher: The Magazine for Database Professionals 143 Old Marlton Pk	Medford	NJ	08055	**800-300-9868**	609-654-6266
Ziff Davis, LLC 28 E 28th St	New York	NY	10016	**800-289-0429**	212-503-3500

456-8 Education Magazines & Journals

Name / Address	City	State	ZIP	Toll-Free	Phone
Academe Magazine 1133 19th St NW Ste 200	Washington	DC	20036	**800-424-2973**	202-737-5900
AEA Advocate Magazine 345 E Palm Ln	Phoenix	AZ	85004	**800-352-5411**	602-264-1774
Alabama School Journal 422 Dexter Ave	Montgomery	AL	36104	**800-392-5839**	334-834-9790
American Educator Magazine 555 New Jersey Ave NW	Washington	DC	20001	**800-238-1133**	202-879-4400
American Teacher Magazine 555 New Jersey Ave NW	Washington	DC	20001	**800-238-1133**	202-879-4400
Arkansas Educator Magazine 1500 W Fourth St	Little Rock	AR	72201	**800-632-0624**	501-375-4611
Chronicle of Higher Education, The 1255 23rd St NW Ste 700	Washington	DC	20037	**800-728-2803**	202-466-1000
Colorado School Journal 101 W. Colfax Ave Ste 800	Denver	CO	80202	**800-336-7678**	303-837-1500
Education Ctr Inc 3515 W Market St Ste 200	Greensboro	NC	27403	**800-714-7991**	336-854-0309
Education Week Magazine 6935 Arlington Rd	Bethesda	MD	20814	**800-346-1834**	301-280-3100
Educational Leadership Magazine 1703 N Beauregard St	Alexandria	VA	22311	**800-933-2723**	703-578-9600
Harvard Educational Review 8 Story St 1st Fl	Cambridge	MA	02138	**877-930-4473**	617-495-3432
ISTA Advocate Magazine 150 W Market St Ste 900	Indianapolis	IN	46204	**800-382-4037**	317-263-3400
Journal of Physical Education Recreation & Dance (JOPERD) 1900 Assn Dr	Reston	VA	20191	**800-213-7193**	703-476-3400
KEA News 401 Capital Ave	Frankfort	KY	40601	**800-231-4532**	502-875-2889
Library Journal 160 Varick St 11th Fl	New York	NY	10013	**800-588-1030**	646-380-0700
Louisiana Association of Educators 8322 One Kalais Ave	Baton Rouge	LA	70809	**800-256-4523**	225-343-9243
MAA FOCUS 1529 18th St NW	Washington	DC	20036	**800-741-9415**	202-387-5200
Maine Educator Magazine 35 Community Dr	Augusta	ME	04330	**800-332-8529**	207-622-5866
MEA Voice Magazine 1216 Kendale Blvd PO Box 2573	East Lansing	MI	48826	**800-292-1934**	517-332-6551
Minnesota Educator Magazine 41 Sherburne Ave	Saint Paul	MN	55103	**800-652-9073**	651-227-9541
Missouri State Teachers Assn 407 S Sixth St *General	Columbia	MO	65201	**800-392-0532***	573-442-3127
MTA Today Magazine 20 Ashburton Pl	Boston	MA	02108	**800-392-6175**	617-878-8000
NCAE News Bulletin PO Box 27347	Raleigh	NC	27611	**800-662-7924**	919-832-3000
NCTM News Bulletin 1906 Assn Dr	Reston	VA	20191	**800-235-7566**	703-620-9840
New Hampshire Educator Magazine 9 S Spring St	Concord	NH	03301	**866-556-3264**	603-224-7751
New York Teacher Magazine 800 Troy-Schenectady Rd	Latham	NY	12110	**800-342-9810**	518-213-6000
NSEA Voice Magazine 605 S 14th St Ste 200	Lincoln	NE	68508	**800-742-0047**	402-475-7611
Ohio Education Assn (OEA) 225 E Broad St PO Box 2550	Columbus	OH	43216	**800-282-1500**	614-228-4526
Oklahoma Education Association 323 E Madison PO Box 18485	Oklahoma City	OK	73154	**800-522-8091**	405-528-7785
Oregon Education Magazine (OEA) 6900 SW Atlanta St Bldg 1	Portland	OR	97223	**800-858-5505**	503-684-3300
Scholastic Coach & Athletic Director Magazine 557 Broadway *General	New York	NY	10012	**800-724-6527***	212-343-6100
Teacher Magazine 6935 Arlington Rd Ste 100	Bethesda	MD	20814	**800-346-1834**	301-280-3100
TSTA Advocate Magazine 316 W 12th St	Austin	TX	78701	**877-275-8782**	512-476-5355
Vermont NEA Today Magazine 10 Wheelock St	Montpelier	VT	05602	**800-649-6375**	802-223-6375
Virginia Journal of Education 116 S Third St	Richmond	VA	23219	**800-552-9554**	804-648-5801
West Virginia School Journal 1558 Quarrier St	Charleston	WV	25311	**800-642-8261**	304-346-5315
Young Children Magazine 1313 L St NW Ste 500 PO Box 97156	Washington	DC	20005	**800-424-2460**	202-232-8777

456-9 Entertainment & Music Magazines

Name / Address	City	State	ZIP	Toll-Free	Phone
American Cinematographer Magazine 1782 N Orange Dr	Los Angeles	CA	90028	**800-448-0145**	323-969-4333
Bass Player Magazine 28 E 28th St 12th Fl *Cust Svc	New York	NY	10016	**866-246-3595***	212-378-0400
Canadian Musician Magazine 4056 Dorchester Rd	Niagara Falls	ON	L2E6M9	**800-363-6336**	905-374-8878
Dance Magazine 333 Seventh Ave 11th Fl	New York	NY	10001	**800-331-1750**	212-979-4800
Down Beat Magazine 102 N Haven Rd	Elmhurst	IL	60126	**800-554-7470**	651-251-9682
Entertainment Weekly Magazine 1675 Broadway	New York	NY	10019	**800-828-6882**	212-522-5600
Film Comment Magazine 165 W 65th St	New York	NY	10023	**888-313-6085**	212-875-5610
Grammy Magazine 3030 Olympic Blvd	Santa Monica	CA	90404	**800-423-2017**	310-392-3777
Guitar Player Magazine 28 E 28th St 12th Fl *Cust Svc	New York	NY	10016	**800-289-9839***	212-378-0400
Hollywood Reporter 5055 Wilshire Blvd Ste 600	Los Angeles	CA	90036	**866-525-2150**	323-525-2000
Jazziz Magazine 2650 N Military Trail Ste 140	Boca Raton	FL	33431	**888-852-9987**	561-893-6868
JazzTimes Magazine 85 Quincy Ave Ste 2	Quincy	MA	02169	**800-437-5828**	617-706-9110
Keyboard Magazine 28 E 28th St 12th Fl *Cust Svc	New York	NY	10016	**800-483-2433***	212-378-0400
Live Design 249 W 17th St *Sales	New York	NY	10011	**866-505-7173***	212-204-4272
Multichannel News 28 E 28th St 12th Fl *Cust Svc	New York	NY	10016	**888-343-5563***	917-281-4700
Playbill Magazine 525 Seventh Ave Ste 1801	New York	NY	10018	**800-533-4330**	212-557-5757
Pollstar 4697 W Jacquelyn Ave	Fresno	CA	93722	**800-344-7383**	559-271-7900
Rolling Stone Magazine 1290 Ave of the Americas 2nd Fl	New York	NY	10104	**800-639-3865**	800-283-1549
TV Guide Magazine LLC 11 West 42nd St 16th Fl	New York	NY	10036	**800-866-1400**	212-852-7500
Videomaker Magazine 1350 E Ninth St PO Box 4591	Chico	CA	95927	**800-284-3226**	530-891-8410

456-10 Fraternal & Special Interest Magazines

Name / Address	City	State	ZIP	Toll-Free	Phone
AARP the Magazine 601 E St NW	Washington	DC	20049	**888-687-2277**	202-434-3525
AAUW Outlook Magazine 1111 16th St NW	Washington	DC	20036	**800-326-2289**	202-785-7700
Adoptive Families Magazine 108 West 39th St Ste 805	New York	NY	10018	**800-372-3300**	646-366-0830
Columbia Magazine 1 Columbus Plaza	New Haven	CT	06510	**800-380-9995**	203-752-4000
Commentary Magazine 561 7th Ave 16th Fl	New York	NY	10018	**800-829-6270**	212-891-1400
Eagle Magazine 1623 Gateway Cir S	Grove City	OH	43123	**800-648-5080**	614-883-2200
Elks Magazine 2750 N Lakeview Ave	Chicago	IL	60614	**800-892-8384**	773-755-4700
Lion Magazine 300 W 22nd St *Circ	Oak Brook	IL	60523	**800-710-7822***	630-571-5466
Royal Neighbor Magazine 230 16th St	Rock Island	IL	61201	**800-627-4762**	309-788-4561
United Commercial Travellers 1801 Watermark Dr Ste 100	Columbus	OH	43215	**800-848-0123**	614-228-3276
WOODMEN Magazine 1700 Farnam St	Omaha	NE	68102	**800-225-3108**	402-342-1890

456-11 General Interest Magazines

	City	State	Zip	Toll-Free	Phone
Alfred Hitchcock Mystery Magazine 44 Wall St Ste 904	New York	NY	10005	**800-220-7443**	
Atlantic Monthly Magazine 600 New Hampshire Ave NW *Cust Svc	Washington	DC	20037	**800-234-2411***	202-266-6000
Black Enterprise Magazine 130 Fifth Ave *Cust Svc	New York	NY	10011	**800-727-7777***	212-242-8000
Booklist Magazine 50 E Huron St	Chicago	IL	60611	**800-545-2433**	
Bridal Guide Magazine 330 Seventh Ave 10th Fl	New York	NY	10001	**800-472-7744**	212-838-7733
Canadian Living Magazine 25 Sheppard Ave W Ste 100	Toronto	ON	M2N6S7	**800-387-6332**	416-733-7600
Christianity Today 465 Gundersen Dr *Cust Svc	Carol Stream	IL	60188	**800-222-1840***	630-260-6200
College Outlook & Career Opportunities Magazine 20 E Gregory Blvd	Kansas City	MO	64114	**800-274-8867**	816-361-0616
Consumer Reports Magazine 101 Truman Ave *Orders	Yonkers	NY	10703	**800-333-0663***	914-378-2000
Cook's Illustrated Magazine PO Box 470739 *Circ	Brookline	MA	02447	**800-526-8442***	617-232-1000
Cosmopolitan Magazine 300 W 57th St	New York	NY	10019	**866-879-6636**	212-649-2000
Country Magazine 1610 North 2nd St Ste 102	Milwaukee	WI	53212	**888-861-1265**	414-423-0100
Cuisine Magazine 2200 Grand Ave	Des Moines	IA	50312	**800-311-3995**	
Elle Magazine 1633 Broadway 44th Fl	New York	NY	10019	**800-876-8775**	212-903-5000
Ellery Queen Mystery Magazine (EQMM) 267 Broadway 4th Fl	New York	NY	10007	**800-220-7443**	
Essence Magazine 135 W 50th St 4th Fl	New York	NY	10020	**800-274-9398**	
Family Cir Magazine 375 Lexington Ave 9th Fl	New York	NY	10017	**800-627-4444**	
Food & Wine Magazine 1120 Ave of the Americas Ste 9	New York	NY	10036	**800-333-6569**	813-979-6625
Franchise Handbook 5555 N Port Washington Rd Ste 305	Milwaukee	WI	53217	**800-272-0246**	414-882-2878
Futurist Magazine 7910 Woodmont Ave Ste 450	Bethesda	MD	20814	**800-989-8274**	301-656-8274
Harper's Magazine 666 Broadway 11th Fl	New York	NY	10012	**800-444-4653**	212-420-5720
Interview Magazine 575 Broadway 5th Fl	New York	NY	10012	**800-925-9574**	212-941-2900
Latina Media Ventures LLC 625 Madison Ave 3rd Fl	New York	NY	10022	**888-489-7753**	212-642-0200
Lucky Inc 4 Times Sq	New York	NY	10036	**888-959-5203**	614-277-0827
Marie Claire Magazine 300 W 57th St 34th Fl	New York	NY	10019	**800-777-3287**	515-282-1607
Martha Stewart Living Magazine 601 W 26th St 25th Fl	New York	NY	10001	**800-999-6518**	
Men's Journal LLC 1290 Ave of the Americas 2nd Fl	New York	NY	10104	**800-677-6367**	
Ms Magazine 1600 Wilson Blvd Ste 801	Arlington	VA	22209	**866-672-6363**	703-522-4201
New York Review of Books 435 Hudson St 3rd Fl	New York	NY	10014	**800-354-0050**	212-757-8070
People Magazine Rockefeller Ctr Time & Life Bldg	New York	NY	10020	**800-541-9000**	212-522-3347
Psychology Today Magazine 115 E 23 St 9th Fl	New York	NY	10010	**800-931-2237**	212-260-7210
Reminisce Magazine 1610 N 2nd St Ste 102	Milwaukee	NY	53212	**888-859-7838**	414-423-0100
Saturday Evening Post, The 1100 Waterway Blvd	Indianapolis	IN	46202	**800-829-5576**	317-634-1100
Self Magazine 4 Times Sq	New York	NY	10036	**800-274-6111**	212-286-2860
Simple & Delicious 5400 S 60th St	Greendale	WI	53129	**800-344-6913**	414-423-0100
Smithsonian Magazine 600 Maryland Ave Ste 6001	Washington	DC	20024	**800-766-2149**	202-633-6090
Sun Magazine 8815 Conroy Windermere Rd Ste 130	Orlando	FL	32835	**888-218-9968**	407-477-2815
Taste of Home Magazine 5400 S 60th St	Greendale	WI	53129	**800-344-6913**	414-423-0100
Utne Reader Magazine 12 N 12th St Ste 400 *Cust Svc	Minneapolis	MN	55403	**800-736-8863***	612-338-5040
Vanity Fair Magazine 4 Times Sq	New York	NY	10036	**800-365-0635**	
Western Living Magazine 2608 Granville St Ste 560	Vancouver	BC	V6H3V3	**800-363-3272**	604-877-7732
Wilson Quarterly Magazine 1300 Pennsylvania Ave NW 1 Woodrow Wilson Plaza *Orders	Washington	DC	20004	**888-947-9018***	202-691-4000
Women's Wear Daily Magazine 750 Third Ave 5th Fl	New York	NY	10017	**800-289-0273**	212-630-4600

456-12 Government & Military Magazines

	City	State	Zip	Toll-Free	Phone
Air Force Magazine 1501 Lee Hwy	Arlington	VA	22209	**800-727-3337**	703-247-5800
Air Force Times Magazine 6883 Commercial Dr	Springfield	VA	22159	**800-368-5718**	703-750-7400
ARMY Magazine 2425 Wilson Blvd	Arlington	VA	22201	**800-336-4570**	703-841-4300
FRA Today 125 NW St	Alexandria	VA	22314	**800-372-1924**	703-683-1400
Governing Magazine 1100 Connecticut Ave NW Ste 1300	Washington	DC	20036	**800-940-6039**	202-862-8802
Navy Times Magazine 6883 Commercial Dr *Cust Svc	Springfield	VA	22159	**800-368-5718***	703-750-7400
Public Employee Magazine 1625 L St NW	Washington	DC	20036	**800-792-0045**	202-429-1130
Soldier of Fortune Magazine 2135 11th St	Boulder	CO	80302	**800-377-2789**	303-449-3750

456-13 Health & Fitness Magazines

	City	State	Zip	Toll-Free	Phone
American Fitness Magazine 15250 Ventura Blvd Ste 200	Sherman Oaks	CA	91403	**800-446-2322**	818-905-0040
Cooking Light Magazine 2100 Lakeshore Dr	Birmingham	AL	35209	**800-366-4712**	205-445-6000
Diabetes Forecast Magazine 1701 N Beauregard St	Alexandria	VA	22311	**800-676-4065**	703-549-1500
Fitness Rx for Men Magazine 21 Bennetts Rd	Setauket	NY	11733	**800-653-1151**	631-751-9696
Flex Magazine 21100 Erwin St	Woodland Hills	CA	91367	**877-527-8342**	412-235-0203
Heart & Soul Magazine 15480 Annapolis Rd Ste 202-225	Bowie	MD	20715	**800-834-8813**	
Ironman Magazine 1701 Ives Ave	Oxnard	CA	93033	**800-447-0008**	805-385-3500
Men's Health Magazine 400 S Tenth St	Emmaus	PA	18098	**800-666-2303**	610-967-5171
Muscle & Fitness Hers Magazine 21100 Erwin St	Woodland Hills	CA	91367	**800-340-8954**	
Prevention Magazine 733 Third Ave	Emmaus	PA	10017	**800-813-8070**	
Vegetarian Times 300 N Continental Blvd Ste 650	El Segundo	CA	90245	**800-573-1900**	310-356-4100

456-14 Hobby & Personal Interests Magazines

	City	State	Zip	Toll-Free	Phone
American Photo Magazine 1633 Broadway 43rd Fl	New York	NY	10019	**800-274-4514**	212-767-6000
Antique Trader 700 E State St	Iola	WI	54990	**800-258-0929**	715-445-2214
AOPA Pilot Magazine 421 Aviation Way	Frederick	MD	21701	**800-872-2672**	301-695-2000
Arabian Horse World Magazine 1316 Tamson Dr Ste 101	Cambria	CA	93428	**800-955-9423**	805-771-2300
Bead & Button Magazine 21027 Crossroads Cir *Cust Svc	Waukesha	WI	53186	**800-533-6644***	262-796-8776
BeadStyle Magazine 21027 Crossroads Cir *Cust Svc	Waukesha	WI	53186	**800-533-6644***	262-796-8776
Better Homes & Gardens WOOD Magazine 1716 Locust St	Des Moines	IA	50309	**800-374-9663**	
Bicycling Magazine 400 S Tenth St	Emmaus	PA	18098	**800-666-2806**	
Bird Talk Magazine 3 Burroughs *Resv	Irvine	CA	92618	**800-695-6088***	949-855-8822
Birds & Blooms Magazine 5400 S 60th St	Greendale	WI	53129	**888-860-8040**	
BirdWatching Magazine 25 Braintree Hill Office Pk Ste 404	Braintree	MA	02184	**877-252-8141**	
Blood-Horse Magazine PO Box 911088	Lexington	KY	40591	**800-866-2361**	859-278-2361
Cat Fancy Magazine 3 Burroughs *Cust Svc	Irvine	CA	92618	**800-546-7730***	949-855-8822
Ceramics Monthly 600 N Cleveland Ave Ste 210	Westerville	OH	43082	**800-342-3594**	614-794-5867
Chess Life Magazine PO Box 3967 *Sales	Crossville	TN	38557	**800-903-8723***	931-787-1234
Classic Trains Magazine 21027 Crossroads Cir PO Box 1612	Waukesha	WI	53186	**800-533-6644**	262-796-8776
Coin World Magazine 911 S Vandemark Rd	Sidney	OH	45365	**866-519-7298**	937-498-0800
Crafts 'n Things Magazine PO Box 926	Sidney	OH	45365	**866-222-3621**	
Creating Keepsakes Magazine 14850 Pony Express Rd	Bluffdale	UT	84065	**888-247-5282**	801-816-8300
Daily Racing Form 100 Broadway 7th Fl *Cust Svc	New York	NY	10005	**800-306-3676***	212-366-7600
Digital Photographer Magazine 12121 Wilshire Blvd 12th Fl	Los Angeles	CA	90025	**800-537-4619**	310-820-1500
Dog Fancy Magazine 3 Burroughs *Cust Svc	Irvine	CA	92618	**800-546-7730***	949-855-8822
Equus Magazine 656 Quince OrchaRd Rd Ste 600 *Cust Svc	Gaithersburg	MD	20878	**800-829-5910***	301-977-3900
Family Handyman Magazine 2915 Commers Dr Ste 700	Eagan	MN	55121	**800-285-4961**	
Fine Woodworking Magazine 63 S Main St PO Box 5506	Newtown	CT	06470	**800-283-7252**	203-426-8171
Flying Magazine 460 N. Orlando Ave. Ste 200 *Cust Svc	Winter Park	FL	32789	**800-678-0797***	407-628-4802
Horse Illustrated Magazine 3 Burroughs	Irvine	CA	92618	**888-588-4677**	949-855-8822
McCall Patterns Magazine 120 Broadway	New York	NY	10271	**800-782-0323**	
McCall's Quilting Magazine 741 Corporate Cir Ste A	Golden	CO	80401	**800-944-0736**	303-215-5600

Name / Address	City	State	Zip	Toll-Free	Phone
Model Airplane News 20 Westport Rd	Wilton	CT	06897	**800-988-6488**	203-431-9000
Nuts & Volts Magazine 430 Princeland Ct	Corona	CA	92879	**800-783-4624*** *Orders	951-371-8497
Outdoor Photographer Magazine 12121 Wilshire Blvd 12th Fl	Los Angeles	CA	90025	**800-283-4410*** *Cust Svc	310-820-1500
Outside Magazine 400 Market St	Santa Fe	NM	87501	**888-909-2382*** *General	505-989-7100
Paper Crafts Magazine 14512 S Ctr Point Way Ste 600	Bluffdale	UT	84065	**800-727-2387**	801-816-8300
PC Gamer Magazine 4000 Shoreline Ct Ste 400	South San Francisco	CA	94080	**877-404-1337**	650-238-2505
Popular Woodworking Magazine 4700 E Galbraith Rd	Cincinnati	OH	45236	**877-860-9140*** *Cust Svc	513-531-2690
QST Magazine 225 Main St	Newington	CT	06111	**888-277-5289**	860-594-0200
Quilter's Newsletter Magazine 741 Corporate Cir Ste A	Golden	CO	80401	**800-477-6089**	303-215-5600
Quiltmaker Magazine 741 Corporate Cir Ste A	Golden	CO	80401	**800-388-7023**	800-881-6634
Radio Control Boat Modeler 88 Danbury Rd	Wilton	CT	06897	**888-235-2021**	203-431-9000
Rock & Gem Magazine 290 Maple Ct Ste 232	Ventura	CA	93003	**866-377-4666**	805-644-3824
Rug Hooking Magazine 5067 Ritter Rd	Mechanicsburg	PA	17055	**866-375-8626**	717-796-0411
Scale Auto Magazine 21027 Crossroads Cir	Waukesha	WI	53186	**800-533-6644*** *Cust Svc	262-796-8776
Shutterbug Magazine 1419 Chaffee Dr Ste 1	Titusville	FL	32780	**800-829-3340**	321-269-3212
Smoke Magazine 26 Broadway	New York	NY	10004	**800-766-2633**	212-391-2060
Threads Magazine 63 S Main St PO Box 5506	Newtown	CT	06470	**866-505-4687*** *General	203-426-8171
Wine Spectator Magazine 387 Pk Ave S 8th Fl	New York	NY	10016	**800-752-7799*** *Orders	212-684-4224
Woodshop News 10 Bokum Rd	Essex	CT	06426	**800-444-7686**	860-767-8227
Woodsmith Magazine 2200 Grand Ave	Des Moines	IA	50312	**800-333-5075*** *Cust Svc	

456-15 Law Magazines & Journals

Name / Address	City	State	Zip	Toll-Free	Phone
Alabama Lawyer Magazine 415 Dexter Ave	Montgomery	AL	36104	**800-354-6154**	334-269-1515
Arizona Attorney Magazine 4201 N 24th St Ste 200	Phoenix	AZ	85016	**866-482-9227**	602-252-4804
Arkansas Lawyer Magazine 2224 Cottondale Ln	Little Rock	AR	72202	**800-609-5668**	501-375-4606
Bench & Bar of Minnesota Magazine 600 Nicollet Mall Ste 380	Minneapolis	MN	55402	**800-366-4812**	612-333-1183
Colorado Lawyer Magazine 1900 Grant St 9th Fl	Denver	CO	80203	**800-332-6736**	303-860-1115
Florida Bar Journal 651 E Jefferson St	Tallahassee	FL	32399	**800-342-8060**	850-561-5600
Georgia Bar Journal 104 Marietta St NW Ste 100	Atlanta	GA	30303	**866-773-2782**	404-527-8700
Hawaii Bar Journal 1100 Alakea St Ste 1000	Honolulu	HI	96813	**888-586-1056**	808-537-1868
Journal of the Kansas Bar Assn 1200 SW Harrison St	Topeka	KS	66612	**800-928-3111**	785-234-5696
Legal Management: Journal of the Assn of Legal Administrators (ALA) 75 Tri State International Ste 222	Lincolnshire	IL	60069	**877-675-5571**	847-267-1252
Maine Bar Journal 124 State St PO Box 788	Augusta	ME	04332	**800-475-7523**	207-622-7523
Maryland Bar Journal 520 W Fayette St	Baltimore	MD	21201	**800-492-1964**	410-685-7878
Michigan Bar Journal 306 Townsend St	Lansing	MI	48933	**888-726-3678**	517-346-6300
Montana Lawyer Magazine 7 W Sixth Ave Ste 2B	Helena	MT	59601	**888-385-9119**	406-442-7660
New York Law Journal 120 Broadway 5th Fl	New York	NY	10271	**877-256-2472**	
New York State Bar News 1 Elk St	Albany	NY	12207	**800-442-3863**	518-463-3200
Oregon State Bar Bulletin, The 16037 SW Upper Boones Ferry Rd PO Box 231935	Tigard	OR	97281	**800-452-8260**	503-620-0222
Texas Bar Journal 1414 Colorado St Ste 902	Austin	TX	78701	**800-204-2222**	512-463-1463
Washington Lawyer Magazine 1101 K St NW Ste 200	Washington	DC	20005	**877-333-2227**	202-737-4700
Washington State Bar News 1325 Fourth Ave Ste 600	Seattle	WA	98101	**800-945-9722**	

456-16 Medical Magazines & Journals

Name / Address	City	State	Zip	Toll-Free	Phone
Access Magazine 444 N Michigan Ave Ste 3400	Chicago	IL	60611	**800-243-2342**	312-440-8900
American Journal of Psychiatry 1000 Wilson Blvd Ste 1825	Arlington	VA	22209	**800-368-5777**	703-907-7300
Annals of Internal Medicine Magazine 190 N Independence Mall W	Philadelphia	PA	19106	**800-523-1546**	215-351-2400
Connecticut Medicine Magazine 160 St Ronan St	New Haven	CT	06511	**800-842-8440**	203-865-0587
Dental Economics Magazine 1421 S Sheridan Rd	Tulsa	OK	74112	**800-331-4463**	
Diabetes Advisor Magazine 1701 N Beauregard St	Alexandria	VA	22311	**800-342-2383**	800-806-7801
Family Practice Management 11400 Tomahawk Creek Pkwy	Leawood	KS	66211	**800-274-2237**	913-906-6000
Internal Medicine News 5635 Fishers Ln Ste 6000	Rockville	MD	20852	**877-524-9336**	240-221-2400
Journal of Practical Nursing (JPN) 1940 Duke St Ste 200	Alexandria	VA	22314	**800-655-4845**	703-933-1003
Journal of the American Dietetic Assn 1600 John F Kennedy Blvd	Philadelphia	PA	19103	**800-654-2452**	
Journal of the American Medical Assn (JAMA) PO Box 10946	Chicago	IL	60654	**800-262-2350**	312-670-7827
Journal of the American Pharmacists Assn 2215 Constitution Ave NW	Washington	DC	20037	**800-237-2742**	202-628-4410
Journal of the Louisiana State Medical Society 6767 Perkins Rd Ste 100	Baton Rouge	LA	70808	**800-375-9508**	225-763-8500
Journal of the Medical Assn of Georgia 1849 The Exchange Ste 200	Atlanta	GA	30339	**800-282-0224**	678-303-9290
Journal of the Mississippi State Medical Assn PO Box 2548	Ridgeland	MS	39158	**800-898-0251**	601-853-6733
Mayo Clinic Proceedings Magazine 200 First St SW Siebens Bldg 7-70	Rochester	MN	55905	**800-654-2452*** *Cust Svc	507-284-2094
Missouri Medicine Magazine PO Box 1028	Jefferson City	MO	65102	**800-869-6762**	573-636-5151
NASW News 750 First St NE Ste 700	Washington	DC	20002	**800-227-3590**	202-408-8600
New England Journal of Medicine 10 Shattuck St	Boston	MA	02115	**800-843-6356**	617-734-9800
Nursing Spectrum Greater New York/New Jersey Metro Magazine 1721 Moon Lk Blvd Ste 540	Hoffman Estates	IL	60169	**800-770-0866**	
Ohio Medicine Magazine 3401 Mill Run Dr	Hilliard	OH	43026	**800-766-6762**	614-527-6762
Pharmacy Today Magazine 2215 Constitution Ave NW	Washington	DC	20037	**800-237-2742**	202-628-4410
Psychotherapy Networker 5135 MacArthur Blvd NW	Washington	DC	20016	**888-851-9498**	202-537-8950
Social Work Magazine 750 First St NE Ste 700	Washington	DC	20002	**800-227-3590**	202-408-8600
US Pharmacist Magazine 100 Ave of the Americas	New York	NY	10013	**800-825-4696**	
Virginia Medical News 2924 Emerywood Pkwy Ste 300	Richmond	VA	23294	**800-746-6768**	
West Virginia Medical Journal PO Box 4106	Charleston	WV	25364	**800-257-4747**	304-925-0342

456-17 Political & Current Events Magazines

Name / Address	City	State	Zip	Toll-Free	Phone
American Spectator Magazine 933 N. Kenmore St Ste 405	Arlington	VA	22201	**800-524-3469**	703-807-2011
Foreign Affairs 58 E 68th St	New York	NY	10065	**800-829-5539*** *Cust Svc	212-434-9527
Freeman, The 30 S Broadway	Irvington-on-Hudson	NY	10533	**800-960-4333*** *Sales	914-591-7230
Maclean's Magazine 1 Mt Pleasant Rd 11th Fl	Toronto	ON	M4Y2Y5	**800-268-9119**	416-764-1300
Mother Jones Magazine 222 Sutter St Ste 600	San Francisco	CA	94108	**800-438-6656**	415-321-1700
Nation Magazine 33 Irving Pl 8th Fl	New York	NY	10003	**800-333-8536*** *Cust Svc	212-209-5400
National Journal 600 New Hampshire Ave NW	Washington	DC	20037	**800-613-6701**	202-739-8400
New Republic, The 1620 L St NW Ste 300C	Washington	DC	20036	**800-827-1289**	202-508-4444
Newsweek Magazine 7 Hanover Sq	New York	NY	10004	**800-631-1040*** *Cust Svc	
Reason Magazine 3415 S Sepulveda Blvd Ste 400	Los Angeles	CA	90034	**888-732-7668*** *Cust Svc	310-391-2245
US News & World Report 1050 Thomas Jefferson St NW	Washington	DC	20007	**800-836-6397**	202-955-2000

456-18 Religious & Spiritual Magazines

Name / Address	City	State	Zip	Toll-Free	Phone
B'Nai B'Rith Magazine 2020 K St NW 7th Fl	Washington	DC	20006	**888-388-4224**	202-857-6600
Biblical Archaeology Review 4710 41st St NW	Washington	DC	20016	**800-221-4644**	202-364-3300
Body & Soul 42 Pleasant St	Watertown	MA	02472	**800-999-6518**	617-449-5506
Catholic Digest PO Box 6015	New London	CT	06320	**800-678-2836**	860-437-3012
Charisma Magazine 600 Rinehart Rd	Lake Mary	FL	32746	**800-749-6500**	407-333-0600
Christianity Today Magazine 465 Gundersen Dr	Carol Stream	IL	60188	**800-999-1704**	630-260-6200
Episcopal Life Magazine 815 Second Ave Episcopal Church Ctr	New York	NY	10017	**800-334-7626**	212-716-6000
Lutheran Magazine 8765 W Higgins Rd	Chicago	IL	60631	**800-638-3522**	
Moment Magazine 4115 Wisconsin Ave NW Ste 10	Washington	DC	20016	**800-777-1005**	202-363-6422
Presbyterians Today Magazine 100 Witherspoon St	Louisville	KY	40202	**800-728-7228**	800-872-3283
Today's Christian Woman Magazine 465 Gundersen Dr	Carol Stream	IL	60188	**877-247-4787*** *Orders	630-260-6200
US Catholic Magazine 205 W Monroe	Chicago	IL	60606	**800-328-6515*** *Cust Svc	312-236-7782

456-19 Science & Nature Magazines

	City	State	Zip	Toll-Free	Phone
American Scientist Magazine 3106 E NC Hwy 54 PO Box 13975	Research Triangle Park	NC	27709	**800-243-6534**	919-549-4691
Archaeology Magazine 36-36 33rd St	Long Island	NY	11106	**877-275-9782**	718-472-3050
Audubon Magazine 225 Varick St 7th Fl *Cust Svc	New York	NY	10014	**800-274-4201***	212-979-3000
Aviation Week & Space Technology Magazine 1200 G St NW	Washington	DC	20005	**800-525-5003**	
BioScience 1444 'I' St NW Ste 200	Washington	DC	20005	**800-992-2427**	202-628-1500
BioTechniques 52 Vanderbilt Ave 7th Fl	New York	NY	10017	**800-606-6246**	212-520-2777
E/The Environmental Magazine 28 Knight St PO Box 5098	Norwalk	CT	06851	**800-321-6742**	203-854-5559
Friends of the Earth Magazine 1100 15th St NW	Washington	DC	20005	**877-843-8687**	202-783-7400
National Parks Magazine 777 Sixth St NW Ste 700 *General	Washington	DC	20001	**800-628-7275***	202-223-6722
National Wildlife Magazine 11100 Wildlife Ctr Dr *Cust Svc	Reston	VA	20190	**800-822-9919***	703-438-6000
Nature National Press Bldg 529 14th St NW Ste 968	Washington	DC	20045	**800-524-0384**	202-737-2355
Orion Magazine 187 Main St	Great Barrington	MA	01230	**888-909-6568**	413-528-4422
Physics Today Magazine 1 Physics Ellipse	College Park	MD	20740	**800-344-6902**	301-209-3040
Science Magazine 1200 New York Ave NW	Washington	DC	20005	**866-434-2227**	202-326-6500
Science News 1719 N St NW *Cust Svc	Washington	DC	20036	**800-552-4412***	202-785-2255
Sierra Magazine 85 Second St 2nd Fl	San Francisco	CA	94105	**866-338-1015**	415-977-5500
Sky & Telescope Magazine 90 Sherman St	Cambridge	MA	02140	**800-253-0245**	617-864-7360
Smithsonian Air & Space Magazine PO Box 37012 *Cust Svc	Washington	DC	20013	**800-766-2149***	202-633-6070
Tech Briefs Media Group 261 Fifth Ave Ste 1901	New York	NY	10016	**888-456-3398**	212-490-3999

456-20 Sports Magazines

	City	State	Zip	Toll-Free	Phone
American Rifleman Magazine 11250 Waples Mill Rd	Fairfax	VA	22030	**800-672-3888**	
Bassmaster Magazine 3500 Blue Lake Dr Ste 330	Birmingham	FL	35243	**877-227-7872**	
Climbing Magazine 5720 Flatiron Pkwy	Boulder	CO	80301	**800-829-5895**	
Competitor Magazine 9477 Waples St Ste 150	San Diego	CA	92121	**800-311-1255**	
Ducks Unlimited Magazine 1 Waterfowl Way	Memphis	TN	38120	**800-453-8257**	901-758-3825
Hockey News Magazine 25 Sheppard Ave Ste 100	Toronto	ON	M2N6S7	**888-361-9768**	514-848-7000
Journal of the Philosophy of Sport 1607 N Market St	Champaign	IL	61820	**800-747-4457**	217-351-5076
Salt Water Sportsman Magazine 460 N Orlando Ave Ste 200	Winter Park	FL	32789	**800-759-2127**	407-628-4802
Ski Magazine 5720 Flatiron Pkwy	Boulder	CO	80301	**888-444-8151**	303-253-6300
Snow Goer Magazine 10405 6th Ave N Ste 210	Plymouth	MN	55441	**800-710-5249**	
Sport Fishing Magazine 460 N Orlando Ave Ste 200	Orlando	FL	32789	**800-879-0496**	
Sports Afield Magazine 15621 Chemical Ln	Huntington Beach	CA	92649	**800-451-4788**	714-373-4910
Sports Business Daily 120 W Morehead St Ste 310	Charlotte	NC	28202	**800-829-9839**	704-973-1410
Sports Spectrum Magazine 105 Corporate Blvd Ste 2	Indian Trail	NC	28079	**866-821-2971**	704-821-2971
Travel + Leisure Magazine 225 Liberty St	New York	NY	10281	**800-452-9292**	212-382-5600

456-21 Trade & Industry Magazines

	City	State	Zip	Toll-Free	Phone
AAPG Explorer Magazine 1444 S Boulder Ave	Tulsa	OK	74119	**800-364-2274**	918-584-2555
Aerospace America Magazine 1801 Alexander Bell Dr Ste 500	Reston	VA	20191	**800-639-2422**	703-264-7500
Air Conditioning Heating & Refrigeration News 2401 W Big Beaver Rd Ste 700	Troy	MI	48084	**800-837-8337**	248-362-3700
American Salon Magazine 757 Third Ave 5th Fl	New York	NY	10017	**866-871-0656**	323-966-4662
American Society of Civil Engineers (ASCE) 1801 Alexander Bell Dr	Reston	VA	20191	**800-548-2723**	703-295-6300
Automotive News Magazine 1155 Gratiot Ave	Detroit	MI	48207	**877-812-1584**	313-446-0450
Bartender Magazine PO Box 158 *Sales	Liberty Corner	NJ	07938	**800-829-4222***	908-766-6006
Builder Magazine 1 Thomas Cir NW Ste 600	Washington	DC	20005	**800-325-6180**	202-452-0800
Building Design & Construction Magazine 3030 W Salt Creek Ln Ste 201	Arlington Heights	IL	60005	**888-811-3288**	847-391-1000
Chemical Processing Magazine 1501 E. Woodfield Rd Ste 400N	Schaumburg	IL	60173	**800-343-4048**	630-467-1300
Chemical Week Magazine 140 E 45th St 2 Grand Central Tower,40th Fl *Cust Svc	New York	NY	10017	**866-501-7540***	212-884-9528
Civil Engineering Magazine 1801 Alexander Bell Dr	Reston	VA	20191	**800-548-2723**	703-295-6300
DaySpa Magazine 7628 Densmore Ave	Van Nuys	CA	91406	**800-442-5667**	818-782-7328
Design News 225 Wyman St	Waltham	MA	02451	**800-869-6882**	763-746-2792
Designfax Magazine 2506 Tamiami Trail North	Nokomis	FL	34275	**877-245-6247**	941-966-9521
EDN Magazine 303 Second St *Orders	San Francisco	CA	94107	**800-446-6551***	415-947-6000
Electronic Component News 100 Enterprise Dr Ste 600	Rockaway	NJ	07866	**877-650-5160**	973-920-7000
Engineering News-Record (ENR) 350 fifth Ave Ste 6000	New York	NY	10118	**877-876-8208**	646-849-7100
EPRI Journal 3420 Hillview Ave	Palo Alto	CA	94304	**800-313-3774**	650-855-2121
Fine Homebuilding Magazine 63 S Main St PO Box 5506	Newtown	CT	06470	**800-283-7252**	203-426-8171
Food Processing Magazine 555 W Pierce Rd Ste 301	Itasca	IL	60143	**800-755-5505**	630-467-1300
Giftware News 704 N Wells St	Chicago	IL	60654	**800-229-1967**	312-849-2220
Home Media Retailing 4590 MacArthur Ste 500	Newport Beach	CA	92660	**800-371-6897**	714-759-4661
Institute of Scrap Recycling Industries Magazine 1615 L St NW Ste 6000	Washington	DC	20036	**800-767-7236**	202-662-8500
Journal of Petroleum Technology 222 Palisades Creek Dr	Richardson	TX	75080	**800-456-6863**	972-952-9393
Journal of Protective Coatings & Linings 2100 Wharton St Ste 310	Pittsburgh	PA	15203	**800-837-8303**	412-431-8300
Land Line Magazine 1 NW Oodia Dr PO Box 1000	Grain Valley	MO	64029	**800-444-5791**	816-229-5791
Modern Machine Shop Magazine 6915 Valley Ave	Cincinnati	OH	45244	**800-950-8020**	513-527-8800
Nailpro Magazine 7628 Densmore Ave	Van Nuys	CA	91406	**800-442-5667**	818-782-7328
Nails Magazine 3520 Challenger St	Torrance	CA	90503	**888-624-5744**	310-533-2400
National Fisherman Magazine 121 Free St	Portland	ME	04101	**800-959-5073**	207-842-5600
National Fitness Trade Journal PO Box 2490	White City	OR	97503	**877-867-7835**	541-830-0400
Oil & Gas Journal PO Box 2002	Tulsa	OK	74101	**800-633-1656**	918-831-9423
Plant Services Magazine 555 W Pierce Rd Ste 301	Itasca	IL	60143	**800-872-9141**	630-467-1300
Pro Lights & Staging News Magazine 6000 S Eastern Ste 14-J *General	Las Vegas	NV	89119	**888-667-7438***	702-932-5585
Proceedings of the IEEE Magazine 445 Hoes Ln	Piscataway	NJ	08855	**800-678-4333**	732-562-5478
Qualified Remodeler Magazine 1233 Janesville Ave	Fort Atkinson	WI	53538	**800-547-7377**	732-372-7668
Quality Progress Magazine 600 N Plankinton Ave PO Box 3005 *Cust Svc	Milwaukee	WI	53201	**800-248-1946***	414-272-8575
Women's Wear Daily Magazine 750 Third Ave 5th Fl	New York	NY	10017	**800-289-0273**	212-630-4600
Writer's Digest 4700 E Galbraith Rd *Cust Svc	Cincinnati	OH	45236	**800-283-0963***	513-531-2690

456-22 Travel & Regional Interest Magazines

	City	State	Zip	Toll-Free	Phone
Alaska Magazine 301 Arctic Slope Ave Ste 300	Anchorage	AK	99518	**800-288-5892**	386-246-0444
Arizona Highways Magazine 2039 W Lewis Ave	Phoenix	AZ	85009	**800-543-5432**	
Baltimore Magazine 1000 Lancaster St Ste 400 *Cust Svc	Baltimore	MD	21202	**800-935-0838***	410-752-4200
Buffalo Spree Magazine 100 Corporate Pkwy Ste 220	Buffalo	NY	14226	**855-697-7733**	716-783-9119
Cape Cod Life Magazine 13 Steeple St Ste 204 PO Box 1439	Mashpee	MA	02649	**800-698-1717**	508-419-7381
Caribbean Travel & Life Magazine 460 N Orlando Ave Ste 200 *Sales	Winter Park	FL	32789	**800-289-9399***	407-628-4802
Chesapeake Bay Magazine 1819 Bay Ridge Ave Ste 180	Annapolis	MD	21403	**800-283-2883**	410-263-2662
Chicago Magazine 435 N Michigan Ave Ste 1100	Chicago	IL	60611	**800-999-0879**	312-222-8999
Cleveland Magazine 1422 Euclid Ave Ste 730	Cleveland	OH	44115	**800-210-7293**	216-771-2833
Connecticut Magazine 35 Nutmeg Dr	Trumbull	CT	06611	**800-645-4328**	203-380-6600
Departures Magazine 1120 Ave of the Americas	New York	NY	10036	**888-424-0106**	212-642-1999
Down East 680 Commercial St	Rockport	ME	04856	**800-766-1670**	207-594-9544
Family Motor Coaching Magazine 8291 Clough Pk	Cincinnati	OH	45244	**800-543-3622**	513-474-3622
Guest Informant Magazine 725 Broad St	Augusta	GA	30901	**800-622-6358**	706-724-0851
Hamptons Magazine 67 Hampton Rd Ste 201	SouthHampton	NY	11968	**866-891-3144**	631-283-7125
Hana Hou Magazine (Hawaiian Airlines) 1144 Tenth Ave Ste 401	Honolulu	HI	96816	**888-733-3336**	808-733-3333

				Toll-Free	Phone
Honolulu Magazine 1000 Bishop St Ste 405	Honolulu	HI	96813	**800-788-4230**	808-534-7546
Houston LifeStyle Magazine 10707 Corporate Dr Ste 170	Stafford	TX	77477	**866-505-4456**	281-240-2445
Indianapolis Monthly Magazine 40 Monument Cir Ste 100 *Circ	Indianapolis	IN	46204	**888-403-9005***	317-237-9288
InsideFlyer Magazine 1930 Frequent Flyer Pt	Colorado Springs	CO	80915	**888-407-4747**	719-597-8889
Islands Magazine 460 N Orlando Ave Ste 200	Winter Park	FL	32789	**800-250-1523**	515-237-3697
Jacksonville Magazine 1261 King St	Jacksonville	FL	32204	**800-962-0214**	904-389-3622
Key Magazine PO Box 111266	Memphis	TN	38111	**866-636-7447**	901-458-3912
Key: This Week in Chicago Magazine 222 W Ontario St Ste 420	Chicago	IL	60654	**877-866-0966**	312-943-0838
Los Angeles Confidential Magazine 717 N Highland Ave Unit 10	Los Angeles	CA	90038	**866-891-3144**	310-289-7300
Los Angeles Magazine 5900 Wilshire Blvd 10th Fl *Cust Svc	Los Angeles	CA	90036	**800-876-5222***	323-801-0100
Louisville Magazine 137 W Muhammad Ali Blvd Ste 102	Louisville	KY	40202	**866-832-0011**	502-625-0100
Memphis Magazine 460 Tennessee St Ste 200	Memphis	TN	38103	**800-288-9999**	901-521-9000
Michigan Out-of-Doors Magazine (MOOD) 2101 Wood St PO Box 30235	Lansing	MI	48912	**800-777-6720**	517-371-1041
Midwest Living Magazine 1716 Locust St	Des Moines	IA	50309	**800-678-8093**	515-247-2982
Milwaukee Magazine 126 N Jefferson St	Milwaukee	WI	53202	**800-662-4818**	414-273-1101
Minneapolis-Saint Paul Magazine 220 S Sixth St Ste 500	Minneapolis	MN	55402	**800-999-5589**	612-339-7571
MotorHome Magazine 2750 Park View Ct Ste 240 *Cust Svc	Oxnard	CA	93036	**800-678-1201***	805-667-4100
National Geographic Traveler Magazine 1145 17th St NW	Washington	DC	20036	**800-647-5463**	202-857-7000
Nevada Magazine 401 N Carson St	Carson City	NV	89701	**855-729-7117**	775-687-5416
New Jersey Monthly Magazine 55 Pk Pl PO Box 920	Morristown	NJ	07963	**888-419-0419**	973-539-8230
New Mexico Magazine PO Box 12002	Santa Fe	NM	87504	**800-898-6639**	
New Orleans Magazine 110 Veterans Blvd Ste 123 *Edit	Metairie	LA	70005	**877-221-3512***	504-828-1380
New York Magazine 75 Varick St	New York	NY	10013	**800-678-0900**	212-508-0700
Ohio Magazine 1422 Euclid Ave Ste 730	Cleveland	OH	44115	**800-210-7293**	216-771-2833
Orange Coast Magazine 3701 Birch St Ste 100	Newport Beach	CA	92660	**800-397-8179**	949-862-1133
Oregon Coast Magazine 88906 Highway 101 N Ste 2B	Florence	OR	97439	**800-348-8401**	541-997-8401
Orlando Magazine 801 N Magnolia Ave Ste 201	Orlando	FL	32803	**866-356-3075**	407-423-0618
Palm Beach Illustrated Magazine 1000 N Dixie Hwy Ste C	West Palm Beach	FL	33401	**800-308-7346**	561-659-6160
Phoenix Magazine 15169 N Scottsdale Ste 310	Scottsdale	AZ	85254	**866-481-6970**	480-664-3960
San Francisco Magazine 243 Vallejo St	San Francisco	CA	94111	**866-736-2499**	415-398-2800
Southern Accents Magazine 2100 Lakeshore Dr	Birmingham	AL	35209	**877-262-5866**	205-445-6000
Southern Living Magazine 2100 Lakeshore Dr	Birmingham	AL	35209	**800-366-4712**	205-445-6000
Travel Agent Magazine 757 Third Ave 5th Fl	New York	NY	10017	**855-424-6247**	212-895-8200
Travelhost Magazine 10701 N Stemmons Fwy	Dallas	TX	75220	**800-527-1782**	972-556-0541
Western Outdoors Magazine 185 Avenida La Pata	San Clemente	CA	92673	**800-290-2929**	949-366-0030
Yankee Magazine 1121 Main St PO Box 520	Dublin	NH	03444	**800-288-4284**	603-563-8111

457 MAGNETS - PERMANENT

				Toll-Free	Phone
Electron Energy Corp 924 Links Ave	Landisville	PA	17538	**800-824-2735**	717-898-2294
Eneflux Armtek Magnetics Inc 700 Hicksville Rd Ste 110	Bethpage	NY	11714	**877-363-3589**	516-576-3434
Flexmag Industries Inc 107 Industry Rd	Marietta	OH	45750	**800-543-4426**	740-374-8024
Magnetic Component Engineering Inc 2830 Lomita Blvd	Torrance	CA	90505	**800-989-5656**	
Magnum Magnetics Corp 801 Masonic Pk Rd	Marietta	OH	45750	**800-258-0991**	740-373-7770
Mohr Corp PO Box 1600	Brighton	MI	48114	**800-223-6647**	810-225-9494

458 MAIL ORDER HOUSES

SEE ALSO Seed Companies ; Checks - Personal & Business ; Computer Stores ; Art Supply Stores ; Book, Music, Video Clubs

				Toll-Free	Phone
2 Checkoutcom Inc 1785 O'Brien Rd	Columbus	OH	43228	**877-294-0273**	614-921-2450
Advanced Image Direct 1415 S Acacia Ave	Fullerton	CA	92831	**800-540-3848**	714-502-3900
Aeromedixcom LLC Po Box 14730	Jackson	WY	83002	**888-362-7123**	307-732-2642
Backcountry.com 2607 South 3200 West Ste A *Orders	West Valley City	UT	84119	**800-409-4502***	
Brokers Worldwide 701C Ashland Ave	Folcroft	PA	19032	**800-624-5287**	610-461-3661
Chadwick's of Boston 500 Bic Dr Bldg 4	Milford	CT	06461	**877-330-3393**	
Childcraft Education Corp 1156 Four Star Dr	Mount Joy	PA	17552	**800-631-5652**	
Cinmar LLC 5566 W Chester Rd	West Chester	OH	45069	**888-263-9850**	
Crutchfield Corp 1 Crutchfield Pk *Sales	Charlottesville	VA	22911	**888-955-6000***	434-817-1000
Current USA Inc 1005 E Woodmen Rd *Cust Svc	Colorado Springs	CO	80920	**800-848-2848***	
Daniel Smith Artist Materials PO Box 84268	Seattle	WA	98124	**800-426-6740**	206-223-9599
Design Toscano Inc 1400 Morse Ave	Elk Grove Village	IL	60007	**800-525-5141**	847-952-0100
Digi-Key Corp 701 Brooks Ave S	Thief River Falls	MN	56701	**800-344-4539**	218-681-6674
EVINE Live Inc 6740 Shady Oak Rd	Eden Prairie	MN	55344	**800-676-5523**	
Fingerhut 6509 Flying Cloud Dr	Eden Prairie	MN	55344	**800-208-2500**	
Forestry Suppliers Inc 205 W Rankin St *Cust Svc	Jackson	MS	39201	**800-752-8460***	601-354-3565
Gaiam Inc 833 W S Boulder Rd Ste C *NASDAQ: GAIA*	Louisville	CO	80027	**877-989-6321**	303-222-3600
Gardens Alive Inc 5100 Schenley Pl	Lawrenceburg	IN	47025	**800-222-1222**	513-354-1482
Hammacher Schlemmer & Co 9307 N Milwaukee Ave	Niles	IL	60714	**800-321-1484**	
Hanna Andersson Corp 1010 NW Flanders St *Cust Svc	Portland	OR	97209	**800-222-0544***	
Harry & David Holdings Inc 2500 S Pacific Hwy *Cust Svc	Medford	OR	97501	**877-322-1200***	
Hello Direct Inc 77 NE Blvd	Nashua	NH	03062	**800-435-5634**	
J Crew Group Inc 770 Broadway	New York	NY	10003	**800-562-0258**	212-209-2500
Jackson & Perkins 2 Floral Ave *Cust Svc	Hodges	SC	29653	**800-292-4769***	
JC Whitney 761 Progress Pkwy	La Salle	IL	61301	**866-529-5530**	
JDR Microdevices Inc 229 Polaris Ave Ste 17	Mountain View	CA	94043	**800-538-5000**	650-625-1400
Lands' End Inc 1 Lands' End Ln *Orders	Dodgeville	WI	53595	**800-963-4816***	
Levenger 420 S Congress Ave *Cust Svc	Delray Beach	FL	33445	**800-544-0880***	561-276-2436
LL Bean Inc 15 Casco St	Freeport	ME	04033	**800-341-4341**	207-552-3080
Mary Maxim Inc 2001 Holland Ave PO Box 5019	Port Huron	MI	48061	**800-962-9504**	810-987-2000
Miles Kimball Co 250 City Ctr Bldg *Cust Svc	Oshkosh	WI	54906	**855-202-7394***	920-231-3800
Movies Unlimited Inc 3015 Darnell Rd	Philadelphia	PA	19154	**800-668-4344**	215-637-4444
Mystic Stamp Co 9700 Mill St	Camden	NY	13316	**866-660-7147**	315-245-2690
NASCO International Inc 901 Janesville Ave *Orders	Fort Atkinson	WI	53538	**800-558-9595***	920-563-2446
National Wholesale Company Inc 400 National Blvd	Lexington	NC	27292	**800-480-4673**	
Norm Thompson Outfitters Inc 3188 NW Aloclek Dr	Hillsboro	OR	97124	**800-547-1160**	877-718-7899
Now Courier Inc PO Box 6066	Indianapolis	IN	46206	**800-543-6066**	
NRC Sports Inc 603 Pleasant St	Paxton	MA	01612	**800-243-5033**	
Oriental Trading Company Inc 5455 S 90th St	Omaha	NE	68127	**800-875-8480**	402-596-1200
Patagonia Inc 259 W Santa Clara St PO Box 150 *Cust Svc	Ventura	CA	93001	**800-638-6464***	805-643-8616
Roaman's 2300 SE Ave	Indianapolis	IN	46283	**800-677-0229**	
S & S Worldwide Inc 75 Mill St *Orders	Colchester	CT	06415	**800-243-9232***	860-537-3451
SkyMall Inc 1520 E Pima St	Phoenix	AZ	85034	**800-759-6255**	
Specialty Catalog Corp 400 Manley St	West Bridgewater	MA	02379	**800-364-9060**	508-638-7000
StubHub Inc 199 Fremont St Fl 4	San Francisco	CA	94105	**866-788-2482**	415-222-8400
Sunnyland Farms Inc PO Box 8200	Albany	GA	31706	**800-999-2488**	
Tech4Learning Inc 10981 San Diego Mission Rd Ste 120	San Diego	CA	92108	**877-834-5453**	619-563-5348
Tog Shop Inc 30 Tozer Rd	Beverly	MA	01915	**800-767-6666**	978-922-2040
TravelSmith Outfitters 773 San Marin Dr Ste 2300	Novato	CA	94945	**800-770-3387**	
Unicover Corp 1 Unicover Ctr *Cust Svc	Cheyenne	WY	82008	**800-443-4225***	307-771-3000
Unistar-Sparco Computers Inc 7089 Ryburn Dr	Millington	TN	38053	**800-840-8400**	901-872-2272
Van Dyke Supply Co 39771 Sd Hwy 34	Woonsocket	SD	57385	**800-279-7985**	704-279-7985
Victorian Trading Co 15600 W 99th St *Cust Svc	Lenexa	KS	66219	**800-700-2035***	913-438-3995
Wild Wings LLC 2101 S Hwy 61	Lake City	MN	55041	**800-445-4833**	651-345-5355

	City	State	ZIP	Toll-Free	Phone
Williams-Sonoma Inc 3250 Van Ness Ave *NYSE: WSM*	San Francisco	CA	94109	**800-838-2589**	415-421-7900
Wintersilks Inc PO Box 196	Jessup	PA	18434	**800-648-7455**	800-718-3687
Women's International Pharmacy Inc PO Box 6468	Madison	WI	53716	**800-279-5708**	608-221-7800
Woodcraft Supply LLC 1177 Rosemar Rd	Parkersburg	WV	26105	**800-535-4482**	
Zappos.com 400 E Stewart Ave	Las Vegas	NV	89101	**800-927-7671**	

459 MALLS - SHOPPING

	City	State	ZIP	Toll-Free	Phone
Antique Mall 1251 S Virginia St	Reno	NV	89502	**888-316-6255**	775-324-4141
Arizona Mills 5000 Arizona Mills Cir	Tempe	AZ	85282	**877-746-6642**	480-491-7300
Aspen Grove Lifestyle Ctr 7301 S Santa Fe Dr	Littleton	CO	80120	**877-225-5337**	
Bayshore Town Center 5800 N Bayshore Dr Ste A256	Glendale	WI	53217	**800-235-4636**	414-963-8780
Boulder Arts & Crafts 1421 Pearl St Mall	Boulder	CO	80302	**866-656-2667**	303-443-3683
Boynton Beach Mall 801 N Congress Ave	Boynton Beach	FL	33426	**877-746-6642**	561-736-7902
Bronx Council on the Arts 1738 Hone Ave	Bronx	NY	10461	**866-564-5226**	718-931-9500
Burlington Mall 75 Middlesex Tpke	Burlington	MA	01803	**877-746-6642**	781-272-8667
Copley Place 100 Huntington Ave Ste 100	Boston	MA	02116	**877-746-6642**	617-262-6600
Del Amo Fashion Ctr 3525 Carson St	Torrance	CA	90503	**877-746-6642**	310-542-8525
Design Ctr of the Americas (DCOTA) 1855 Griffin Rd	Dania Beach	FL	33004	**877-992-9204**	954-920-7997
Ellenton Premium Outlets 5461 Factory Shops Blvd	Ellenton	FL	34222	**888-267-2121**	941-723-1150
Fairlane Town Ctr 18900 Michigan Ave	Dearborn	MI	48126	**800-992-9500**	
Fallbrook Ctr 6633 Fallbrook Ave	West Hills	CA	91307	**866-718-1649**	818-885-9700
Fashion Island Shopping Ctr 401 Newport Ctr Dr	Newport Beach	CA	92660	**855-658-8527**	949-721-2000
Festival Flea Market Mall 2900 W Sample Rd	Pompano Beach	FL	33073	**800-353-2627**	954-979-4555
Franklin Mills 1455 Franklin Mills Cir *General	Philadelphia	PA	19154	**877-746-6642***	215-632-1500
Gardner Village 1100 West 7800 South	West Jordan	UT	84088	**800-662-4335**	801-566-8903
Genesee Valley Ctr 3341 S Linden Rd	Flint	MI	48507	**866-236-1128**	810-732-4000
Great Lakes Mall 7850 Mentor Ave	Mentor	OH	44060	**877-746-6642**	440-255-6900
Green Hills Antique Mall 4108 Hillsboro Pk	Nashville	TN	37215	**888-316-6255**	615-383-9851
Greenwood Park Mall 1251 US Hwy 31 N	Greenwood	IN	46142	**877-746-6642**	317-881-6758
Grove, The 189 The Grove Dr	Los Angeles	CA	90036	**888-315-8883**	323-900-8080
Historic Old Town Fort Collins 19 Old Town Sq Ste 230	Fort Collins	CO	80524	**866-203-5939**	970-484-6500
Ingram Park Mall 6301 NW Loop 410	San Antonio	TX	78238	**877-746-6642**	210-684-9570
Irving Mall 3880 Irving Mall	Irving	TX	75062	**877-746-6642**	972-255-0571
King of Prussia Mall 160 N Gulph Rd	King of Prussia	PA	19406	**877-746-6642**	610-265-5727
Liberty Tree Mall 100 Independence Way	Danvers	MA	01923	**877-746-6642**	978-777-0794
Meyerland Plaza 420 Meyerland Plaza	Houston	TX	77096	**888-675-2275**	713-349-0245
Mill Creek Mall 654 Millcreek Mall	Erie	PA	16565	**800-615-3535**	814-868-9000
Mills at Jersey Gardens, The 651 Kapkowski Rd	Elizabeth	NJ	07201	**877-789-2327**	908-354-5900
North East Mall 1101 Melbourne St Ste 1000	Hurst	TX	76053	**877-746-6642**	817-284-3427
Orland Square 288 Orland Sq	Orland Park	IL	60462	**877-746-6642**	708-349-1646
Outlets at Anthem 4250 W Anthem Way	Phoenix	AZ	85086	**888-482-5834**	623-465-9500
Potomac Mills 2700 Potomac Mills Cir	Woodbridge	VA	22192	**877-746-6642**	703-496-9301
Prime Outlets San Marcos 3939 S IH-35	San Marcos	TX	78666	**800-331-5479**	512-396-2200
River Oaks Ctr 96 River Oaks Ctr Dr	Calumet City	IL	60409	**877-746-6642**	708-868-0600
Rolling Oaks Mall 6909 N Loop 1604 E	San Antonio	TX	78247	**877-746-6642**	210-651-5513
Roosevelt Field Mall 630 Old Country Rd	Garden City	NY	11530	**877-746-6642**	516-742-8001
Seminole Towne Ctr 200 Towne Ctr Cir	Sanford	FL	32771	**877-746-6642**	407-323-2262
Shops at Woodlake 725 Woodlake Rd	Kohler	WI	53044	**855-444-2838**	920-459-1713
Solomon Pond Mall 601 Donald Lynch Blvd	Marlborough	MA	01752	**877-746-6642**	508-303-6255
South Coast Plaza 3333 Bristol St	Costa Mesa	CA	92626	**800-782-8888**	
South Shore Plaza 250 Granite St	Braintree	MA	02184	**877-746-6642**	781-843-8200
Southdale Ctr 10 Southdale Ctr	Edina	MN	55435	**877-746-6642**	952-925-7874
Southern Park Mall 7401 Market St	Youngstown	OH	44512	**877-746-6642**	330-758-4511
SouthPark Mall 4400 Sharon Rd	Charlotte	NC	28211	**888-726-5930**	704-364-4411
SouthPointe Pavilions 2910 Pine Lake Rd Ste Q	Lincoln	NE	68516	**800-733-2767**	402-421-2114
Square One Mall 1201 Broadway	Saugus	MA	01906	**877-746-6642**	781-233-8787
Stoneridge Shopping Ctr 1 Stoneridge Mall	Pleasanton	CA	94588	**877-746-6642**	925-463-2778
Stonestown Galleria 3251 20th Ave	San Francisco	CA	94132	**800-326-3264**	415-564-8848
Tacoma Mall 4502 S Steele St Ste 1177	Tacoma	WA	98409	**877-746-6642**	253-475-4565
Tanger Outlet Ctr San Marcos 4015 S IH-35 Ste 319	San Marcos	TX	78666	**800-408-8424**	512-396-7446
Tri-County Mall 11700 Princeton Pike	Cincinnati	OH	45246	**866-905-4675**	513-671-0120
Tysons Corner Ctr 1961 Chain Bridge Rd Ste 305	McLean	VA	22102	**877-247-5223**	703-847-7300
University Park Mall 6501 N Grape Rd	Mishawaka	IN	46545	**877-746-6642**	574-277-2223
Viejas Outlet Ctr 5005 Willows	Alpine	CA	91901	**877-303-2695**	619-659-2070
West Point Market 1711 W Market St	Akron	OH	44313	**800-838-2156**	330-864-2151
Westchester, The 125 Westchester Ave	White Plains	NY	10601	**877-746-6642**	914-421-1333
Westmoreland Mall 5256 Rt 30 E	Greensburg	PA	15601	**800-333-7310**	724-836-5025

460 MALTING PRODUCTS

SEE ALSO Breweries

	City	State	ZIP	Toll-Free	Phone
Premier Malt Products Inc 25760 Groesbeck Hwy Ste 103 *Cust Svc	Warren	MI	48089	**800-521-1057***	586-443-3355

461 MANAGED CARE - BEHAVIORAL HEALTH

	City	State	ZIP	Toll-Free	Phone
American Behavioral Benefits Managers 2204 Lakeshore Dr Ste 135	Birmingham	AL	35209	**800-925-5327**	205-871-7814
Anthem Inc 120 Monument Cir	Indianapolis	IN	46204	**800-999-7222**	317-488-6000
APS Healthcare Inc 44 S Broadway Ste 1200	White Plains	NY	10601	**800-305-3720**	
Associated Behavioral Health Care Inc 4700 42nd Ave SW Ste 470	Seattle	WA	98116	**800-858-6702**	206-935-1282
Bensinger DuPont & Assoc (BDA) 134 N LaSalle St Ste 2200	Chicago	IL	60602	**800-227-8620**	312-726-8620
CIGNA Behavioral Health Inc 11095 Viking Dr Ste 350	Eden Prairie	MN	55344	**800-753-0540**	703-907-7730
Comprehensive EAP 4 Mt Royal Ave	Marlborough	MA	01752	**800-344-1011**	
ComPsych Corp 455 N City Front Plaza Dr NBC Tower 13th Fl	Chicago	IL	60611	**800-851-1714**	312-595-4000
COPE Inc 1120 G St NW Ste 550	Washington	DC	20005	**800-247-3054**	202-628-5100
CorpCare Assoc Inc 7000 Peachtree Dunwoody Rd Bldg 4 Ste 300	Atlanta	GA	30328	**800-728-9444**	
EAP Consultants Inc 3901 Roswell Rd Ste 340	Marietta	GA	30062	**800-869-0276**	770-951-9970
EAP Systems 500 W Cummings Pk	Woburn	MA	01801	**800-535-4841**	781-935-8850
FEI Behavioral Health 11700 W Lk Pk Dr	Milwaukee	WI	53224	**800-782-1948**	414-359-1055
Gilsbar Inc PO Box 998	Covington	LA	70434	**800-445-7227**	985-892-3520
Holman Group 9451 Corbin Ave	Northridge	CA	91324	**800-321-2843**	818-704-1444
Hurst Place 209 Limeridge Rd E	Hamilton	ON	L9A2S6	**888-521-8300**	289-426-5302
Interface EAP Inc (IEAP) 10370 Richmond Ave Ste 1100 PO Box 421879	Houston	TX	77042	**800-324-4327**	713-781-3364
Magellan Health Services Inc 55 Nod Rd *NASDAQ: MGLN*	Avon	CT	06001	**800-424-4399**	860-507-1900
Managed Health Network Inc 1600 Los Gamos Dr Ste 300	San Rafael	CA	94903	**800-327-2133**	
MENTOR Network, The 313 Congress St 5th Fl	Boston	MA	02210	**800-388-5150**	617-790-4800
MHNet Behavioral Health 9606 N MoPac Exwy Ste 600	Austin	TX	78759	**888-646-6889**	
National Employee Assistance Services Inc N 17 W 24100 Riverwood Dr Ste 300	Waukesha	WI	53188	**800-634-6433**	262-574-2500
New Directions Behavioral Health LLC PO Box 6729	Leawood	KS	66206	**800-624-5544**	
Perspectives Ltd 20 N Clark St Ste 2650	Chicago	IL	60602	**800-866-7556**	312-558-5318
Providence Service Corp 64 E Broadway *NASDAQ: PRSC*	Tucson	AZ	85701	**800-747-6950**	520-748-7108
Stuecker & Assoc Inc 1930 Bishop Ln Watterson Towers Ste 1001	Louisville	KY	40218	**800-799-9327**	502-452-9227
United Behavioral Health Inc 425 Market St 27th Fl	San Francisco	CA	94105	**800-888-2998**	415-547-5000
ValueOptions Inc 12369 Sunrise Vly Dr Ste C	Reston	VA	20191	**877-334-0077**	703-390-6800

Classified Section

462 MANAGEMENT SERVICES

SEE ALSO Educational Institution Operators & Managers ; Facilities Management Services ; Hotels & Hotel Companies ; Incentive Program Management Services ; Investment Advice & Management ; Pharmacy Benefits Management Services ; Association Management Companies

Company / Address	City	State	ZIP	Toll-Free	Phone
2 Places At 1 Time Inc 270 Peachtree St 20th Fl	Atlanta	GA	30303	877-275-2237	
360 Technologies Inc 15401 Debba Dr	Austin	TX	78734	888-883-0360	512-266-7360
ABELSoft Inc 3310 S Service Rd	Burlington	ON	L7N3M6	800-267-2235	
Acc Technical Services Inc 106 Dwight Park Cir	Syracuse	NY	13209	855-484-4500	315-484-4500
Accompass 1052 Yonge St	Toronto	ON	M4W2L1	866-969-8588	416-969-8588
Ace Products Management G 12801 W Silver Spring Rd	Butler	WI	53007	800-294-9007	262-754-1289
Act2 Retirement Consulting LLC 5120 Watchwood Path	Columbia	MD	21044	866-992-9256	
Alcazar Networks Inc 419 State Ave Ste 3	Emmaus	PA	18049	800-349-6192	484-664-2800
AllMed Healthcare Management Inc 621 SW Alder St Ste 740	Portland	OR	97205	888-289-6015	503-274-9916
Altus Consulting Corp 38699 Old Wheatland Rd	Waterford	VA	20197	800-300-4505	703-929-4000
Amarillo Economic Development Corp 801 S Fillmore Ste 205	Amarillo	TX	79101	800-333-7892	806-379-6411
AmerAssist Inc 8415 Pulsar Pl	Columbus	OH	43240	877-294-9707	
American Dental Partners Inc 401 Edgewater Pl Ste 430 *NASDAQ: ADPI*	Wakefield	MA	01880	800-838-6563	781-213-6500
American Utility Management Inc 2211 S York Rd Ste 320	Oak Brook	IL	60523	866-520-1245	
AMFM Inc 240 Capitol St Ste 500	Charleston	WV	25301	800-348-1623	304-344-1623
Archway Marketing Services Inc 19850 S Diamond Lake Rd	Rogers	MN	55374	866-779-9855	763-428-3300
Arcweb Technologies LLC 234 Market St 5th Fl	Philadelphia	PA	19106	800-846-7980	
Auto Profit Masters 250 E Dry Creek Rd	Littleton	CO	80122	866-826-7911	303-795-5838
Avatar Management Services Inc 8157 Bavaria Dr E	Macedonia	OH	44056	800-728-2827	330-963-3900
Baker Krizner Financial Planning 2230 N Limestone St	Springfield	OH	45503	888-390-8753	937-390-8750
Bankruptcy Management Solutions Inc 5 Peters Canyon Rd Ste 200	Irvine	CA	92606	800-634-7734	
Banyan Water Inc 11002-B Metric Blvd	Austin	TX	78758	800-276-1507	
Bcn Transportation Services 3650 W Liberty Rd	Ann Arbor	MI	48103	800-891-9911	734-994-4100
Benefact Consulting Group 6285 Northam Dr Ste 200	Mississauga	ON	L4V1X5	855-829-2225	
Benefit Advantage Inc 3431 Commodity Ln	Green Bay	WI	54304	800-686-6829	920-339-0351
Benetrends Inc 1180 Welsh Rd	North Wales	PA	19454	866-423-6387	267-498-0059
Beyond the Arc Inc 2600 Tenth St Ste 616	Berkeley	CA	94710	877-676-3743	
Birner Dental Management Services Inc 1777 S Harrison St Ste 1400	Denver	CO	80210	877-898-1083	303-691-0680
Brenton Productions Inc 179 Gasoline Alley Ste 102A	Mooresville	NC	02777	800-572-7798	
Brillio 100 Town Sq Pl Ste 308	Jersey City	NJ	07310	800-317-0575	
BSC America Inc 803 Bel Air Rd	Bel Air	MD	21014	800-764-7400	
Capital Realty Advisors Inc 600 Sandtree Dr Ste 109	Palm Beach Gardens	FL	33403	800-940-1088	561-624-5888
Carolina Advanced Digital Inc 133 Triangle Trade Dr	Cary	NC	27513	800-435-2212	919-663-2211
Carpedia International Ltd 75 Navy St	Oakville	ON	L6J2Z1	877-445-8288	
Catchpole Corp, The 10 High St Ste 502	Boston	MA	02110	866-431-2666	781-431-2666
CE Resource Inc 1482 Stone Point Dr Ste 100	Roseville	CA	95661	800-707-5644	
Chally Group Worldwide Inc 3123 Research Blvd	Dayton	OH	45420	800-254-5995	937-259-1200
Chartis Group LLC 220 W Kinzie St 5th Fl	Chicago	IL	60654	877-667-4700	
Cirro Energy Services Inc 2745 Dallas Pkwy Ste 200	Plano	TX	75093	866-791-1911	
Clayton L Scroggins Associates Inc 200 Northland Blvd	Cincinnati	OH	45246	800-359-3970	513-771-7070
Cleantech Open, The 336 Portage Rd	Palo Alto	CA	94306	888-989-6736	
Clover Global Group 2431 W Irving Park Rd	Chicago	IL	60618	888-256-8370	773-267-6767
Coast Dental Services Inc 4010 W Boy Scout Blvd Ste 1100	Tampa	FL	33607	800-327-6453	813-288-1999
Coker Consulting 2400 Lakeview Pkwy Ste 400	Alpharetta	GA	30009	800-345-5829	
Communibiz Inc Po Box 30062	Billings	MT	59107	877-266-0979	406-259-1252
Compmanagement Inc PO Box 884	Dublin	OH	43017	800-825-6755	614-376-5300
Concentra Inc 5080 Spectrum Dr Ste 1200 W	Addison	TX	75001	866-944-6046	
Corizon 105 Westpark Dr Ste 200	Brentwood	TN	37027	800-729-0069	
Cortex Consultants Inc 1218 Langley St	Victoria	BC	V8W1W2	866-931-1192	250-360-1492
CorVel Corp 2010 Main St Ste 600 *NASDAQ: CRVL*	Irvine	CA	92614	888-726-7835	949-851-1473
Corvirtus LLC 1011 N Weber St	Colorado Springs	CO	80903	800-322-5329	
CRAssoc Inc 8580 Cinderbed Rd Ste 2400	Newington	VA	22122	877-272-8960	703-550-8145
DealNet Capital Corp 325 Milner Ave Ste 300	Toronto	ON	M1B5N1	855-912-3444	
Deep East Texas Council of Governments 274 e lamar st	Jasper	TX	75951	800-256-6848	409-384-5704
DevFacto Technologies Inc 2250 Scotia Place Tower 1 10060 Jasper Ave	Edmonton	AB	T5J3R8	877-323-3832	587-520-9118
Digital Street Inc 69550 Highway 111 Ste 201	Rancho Mirage	CA	92270	866-464-5100	
Dresser & Associates Inc 243 US Route 1	Scarborough	ME	04074	866-885-7212	207-885-0809
Eagle's Flight, Creative Training Excellence Inc 489 Clair Rd W	Guelph	ON	N1L0H7	800-567-8079	519-767-1747
EBUSINESS STRATEGIS LLC 18318 Fern Trl Ctr	Houston	TX	77084	888-647-3249	281-647-6183
Edgemark Partners 4510 cox rd	Glen Allen	VA	23060	800-488-0289	804-967-2000
Eisenbach Consulting LLC 921 Shiloh Rd B-300	Tyler	TX	75703	800-977-4020	
Elitexpo Cargo Systems 845 Commerce Dr	South Elgin	IL	60177	800-543-5484	
Ensave Energy Performance Inc 65 Millet St Ste 105	Richmond	VT	05477	800-732-1399	
Enterey Inc 9900 Irvine Ctr Dr Ste 100	Irvine	CA	92618	800-691-2349	
Ephor Group LLC 24 E Greenway Plz Ste 440	Houston	TX	77046	800-379-9330	
FCC Services 7951 E Maplewood Ave Ste 225	Greenwood Village	CO	80111	888-275-3227	
File Keepers LLC 6277 E Slauson Ave	Los Angeles	CA	90040	800-332-3453	323-728-3133
Firm Consulting Group 2107 W Cass St Ste B	Tampa	FL	33606	877-636-9525	
First Health Group Corp *Coventry* 3200 Highland Ave	Downers Grove	IL	60515	800-247-2898	630-737-7900
Flippen Group, The 1199 Haywood Dr	College Station	TX	77845	800-316-4311	979-693-7660
Foster Lake & Pond Management Inc 9020 White Oak Rd PO Box 1294	Garner	NC	27529	888-525-6348	919-772-8548
Franchise Brands LLC 325 Bic Dr	Milford	CT	06461	800-797-2308	
Franchise Co, The (TFC) 5399 Eglinton Ave W Ste 110	Etobicoke	ON	M9C5K9	800-294-5591	416-620-3960
Geo-instruments Inc 24 Celestial Dr	Narragansett	RI	02882	800-477-2506	
Gottlieb Martin & Associates Inc 4932 Sunbeam Rd	Jacksonville	FL	32257	800-833-9986	904-346-3088
Group Management Services Inc 3296 Columbia Rd Ste 101	Richfield	OH	44286	888-823-2084	330-659-0100
Grove Consultants International, The 1000 Oreilly Ave	San Francisco	CA	94129	800-494-7683	415-561-2500
Harkcon 1390 Chain Bridge Rd 570	Mclean	VA	22101	800-499-6456	
HealthAxis Inc 7301 N State Hwy 161	Irving	TX	75039	888-974-2947	972-443-5000
Hg Solutions 3701 S Lawrence St	Tacoma	WA	98409	866-988-2626	253-588-2626
Hill Physicians Medical Group Inc 2409 Camino Ramon PO Box 5080	San Ramon	CA	94583	800-445-5747	925-820-8300
Howard Simon & Associates Inc 304 Saunders Rd	Riverwoods	IL	60015	800-424-7526	847-945-0340
HowGood Inc 33 Flatbush Ave 5th Fl	Brooklyn	NY	11217	888-601-3015	
Hru Inc. Technical Resources 3451 Dunckel Rd	Lansing	MI	48911	888-205-3446	517-272-5888
Hygieneering Inc 7575 Plz Ct	Willowbrook	IL	60527	800-444-7154	630-654-2550
ICM Inc 310 N First St	Colwich	KS	67030	877-456-8588	316-796-0900
IHL Consulting Group 1064 Cedarview Ln	Franklin	TN	37067	888-445-6777	615-591-2955
In Touch Business Consultants 11370 66th St 132	Largo	FL	33773	877-676-5492	
INFOCUS Marketing Inc 4245 Sigler Rd	Warrenton	VA	20187	800-708-5478	
Insperity Inc 19001 Crescent Springs Dr	Kingwood	TX	77339	800-237-3170	866-715-3552
IQ Systems Inc 5595 Equity Ave Ste 300	Reno	NV	89502	866-842-4748	775-352-2301
Jolt Consulting Group 112 Spring St Ste 301	Saratoga Springs	NY	12866	877-249-6262	
Keating Technologies Inc 25 Royal Crest Court Ste 120	Markham	ON	L3R9X4	877-532-8464	905-479-0230
Keiro Services 325 S Boyle Ave	Los Angeles	CA	90033	800-366-2624	323-980-7555
Klemmer & Associates Leaders 1340 commerce st	Petaluma	CA	94954	800-577-5447	707-559-7722
Kotter International 5 Bennett St	Cambridge	MA	02138	855-400-4712	617-600-6787
Latitude Consulting Group Inc 100 E Michigan Ave Ste 200	Saline	MI	48176	888-577-2797	
Learning Unlimited 5810 E Skelly Dr Ste 500	Tulsa	OK	74135	888-622-4203	918-622-3292
Legal Club of America Corp 7771 W Oakland Park Blvd Ste 217	Sunrise	FL	33351	800-316-5387	954-377-0222
Lifewings Partners LLC 9198 Crestwyn Hills Dr	Memphis	TN	38125	800-290-9314	
Lost Recovery Network Lrni 406 dixon st	Vidalia	GA	30474	877-693-1456	912-537-3901

Company / Address	City	State	Zip	Toll-Free	Phone
M2 Logistics Inc 2413 Hazelwood Ln	Green Bay	WI	54304	**800-391-5121**	920-569-8800
Macadamian Technologies Inc 165 Rue Wellington	Gatineau	QC	J8X2J3	**877-779-6336**	819-772-0300
Material & Contract Services LLC 5820 Stoneridge Mall Rd	Pleasanton	CA	94588	**866-772-9250**	925-460-0397
Mattersight Corp 200 S Wacker Ste 3100	Chicago	IL	60606	**877-235-6925**	
MavenWire LLC 630 Freedom Business Ctr 3rd Fl	King Of Prussia	PA	19406	**866-343-4870**	
Medcor Inc 4805 W Prime Pkwy	McHenry	IL	60050	**877-696-6775**	815-363-9500
Medexcel USA Inc 484 Temple Hill Rd	New Windsor	NY	12553	**800-563-6384**	845-565-3700
Metropolitan Health Networks Inc 777 Yamato Rd Ste 510 *NYSE: MDF*	Boca Raton	FL	33431	**800-221-5487**	561-805-8500
MHM Services Inc 1593 Spring Hill Rd Ste 600	Vienna	VA	22182	**800-416-3649**	703-749-4600
Mid Ohio Regional Planning Commission 111 Liberty St Ste 100	Columbus	OH	43215	**800-750-0750**	614-228-2663
Mikan Associates Consulting 141 W Jackson Blvd Ste 1520	Chicago	IL	60604	**888-902-1970**	847-613-6010
Mitchell Selling Dynamics 1360 Puritan Ave	Birmingham	MI	48009	**800-328-9696**	248-644-8092
Modis Inc 10201 Centurion Pkwy N Ste 400	Jacksonville	FL	32256	**800-372-2788**	904-360-2300
Mutual Fund Store LLC, The 11095 Metcalf Ave Ste 220	Overland Park	KS	66210	**800-375-3000**	
MyLLC.com Inc 5716 Corsa Ave Ste 110	Westlake Village	CA	91362	**888-886-9552**	
Napa Networks Inc 245 Stafford Rd West Ste 202	Ottawa	ON	K2H9E8	**888-641-1113**	613-248-3417
Navigate Power LLC 2211 N Elston Ave Ste 309	Chicago	IL	60614	**888-601-1789**	
Navtech Seminars & Gps Supply 5501 Backlick Rd Ste 230	Springfield	VA	22151	**800-628-0885**	703-256-8900
Netcracker Technology Corp 95 Sawyer Rd University Ofc Pk III	Waltham	MA	02453	**800-477-5785**	781-419-3300
New Ventures West PO Box 591525	San Francisco	CA	94159	**800-332-4618**	
Ohm Systems Inc 10250 Chester Rd	Cincinnati	OH	45215	**800-878-0646**	513-771-0008
Olympique Expert Building Care 26232 Enterprise Ct	Lake Forest	CA	92630	**866-659-6747**	949-455-0796
Organo Gold International Inc 5505 hovander rd	Ferndale	WA	98248	**877-674-2661**	
Orion Registrar Inc 7850 vance dr	Arvada	CO	80003	**800-446-0674**	303-456-6010
Path-2 Ventures LLC 223 E Blvd	Charlotte	NC	28203	**888-692-1057**	
Patricia Seybold Group 210 Commercial St	Boston	MA	02109	**855-310-0101**	617-742-5200
Pediatrix Medical Group Inc 1301 Concord Terr	Sunrise	FL	33323	**800-243-3839**	954-384-0175
PeopleWorks Inc 6158 10th Ave	Aurelia	IA	51005	**888-404-3646**	
Peridrome Corp 284 Park Pl	Brooklyn	NY	11238	**877-363-7770**	
PFSweb Inc 505 Millennium Dr Ste 500 *NASDAQ: PFSW*	Allen	TX	75013	**888-330-5504**	972-881-2900
Pinpoint Technologies 17802 Irvine Blvd Ste 215	Tustin	CA	92780	**866-603-7770**	714-505-7600
Pinyon Environmental Engineering Resources 9100 W Jewell Ave Ste 200	Denver	CO	80232	**888-641-7337**	303-980-5200
Pitney Bowes Management Services 90 Pk Ave	New York	NY	10016	**800-322-8000**	212-808-3800
Playback Now Inc 3139 Campus Dr Ste 700	Norcross	GA	30071	**800-241-7785**	770-447-0616
Pmalliance Inc 2075 Spencers Way Ste 201	Stone Mountain	GA	30087	**866-808-3735**	770-938-4947
Porter Medical Ctr Inc 115 Porter Dr	Middlebury	VT	05753	**800-994-6610**	802-388-4701
Portico Healthnet 2610 University Ave W	Saint Paul	MN	55114	**866-489-4899**	651-603-5100
Power Wellness 2055 W Army Trl Rd Ste 124	Addison	IL	60101	**877-888-2988**	630-570-2600
PreviMed Inc 1164 Malibu Dr	San Jose	CA	95157	**800-565-3901**	
PrimeGenesis LLC 200 W Hill Rd	Stamford	CT	06902	**866-805-7777**	203-323-8501
Progesys Inc 4020 Blvd le Corbusier Ste 201	Laval	QC	H7L5R2	**877-274-8815**	450-667-7646
Prospect Medical Holdings Inc 10780 Santa Monica Blvd Ste 400	Los Angeles	CA	90025	**800-708-3230**	310-943-4500
Protocol Driven Healthcare Inc 40 Morristown Rd Ste 2D	Bernardsville	NJ	07924	**888-816-4006**	515-277-1376
Provell Inc 855 Village Center Drive Ste 116	North Oaks	MN	55127	**800-624-2946**	952-258-2000
PVA Consulting Group Inc 20865 Ch de la Cote Nord Ste 200	Boisbriand	QC	J7E4H5	**877-970-1970**	450-970-1970
Quality Media Resources Inc 10929 Se 23rd St	Bellevue	WA	98004	**800-800-5129**	425-455-0558
RBN Energy LLC 2323 S Shepherd Dr Ste 1010	Houston	TX	77019	**888-400-9838**	
Realstreet Staffing 2500 Wallington Way Ste 208	Marriottsville	MD	21104	**877-480-8002**	410-480-8002
Recordflow 1751 e garry ave	Santa Ana	CA	92705	**877-896-7350**	
Red Spot Interactive 1001 jupiter park dr	Jupiter	FL	33458	**800-401-7931**	
Redmonk LLC 93 S Jackson St	Seattle	WA	98104	**866-733-6665**	
Retirement Advantage Inc, The 47 Park Pl Ste 850	Appleton	WI	54914	**888-872-2364**	
RGFCC Corp 627 Cady Dr	Fort Washington	MD	20744	**888-389-1230**	
RHA Health Services Inc 17 Church St	Asheville	NC	28801	**866-742-2428**	828-232-6844
Rideau Inc 473 Deslauriers	Montreal	QC	H4N1W2	**800-363-6464**	
River West Meeting Associates Inc 3616 N Lincoln Ave	Chicago	IL	60613	**888-534-5292**	773-755-3000
Robert Ferrilli LLC 41 S Haddon Ave Ste 7	Haddonfield	NJ	08033	**888-864-3282**	
Roco Rescue 7077 Exchequer Dr	Baton Rouge	LA	70809	**800-647-7626**	225-755-7626
Ruggie Wealth Management 2100 Lk Eustis Dr	Tavares	FL	32778	**888-343-2711**	352-343-2700
School Innovations & Advocacy Inc 11130 Sun Ctr Dr Ste 100	Rancho Cordova	CA	95670	**877-954-4357**	
Scott Sheldon LLC 3985 Medina Rd Ste 220	Medina	OH	44256	**877-467-7552**	330-952-1671
SEA Ltd 7349 Worthington-Galena Rd	Columbus	OH	43085	**800-782-6851**	
Select Medical Corp 4714 Gettysburg Rd	Mechanicsburg	PA	17055	**888-735-6332**	717-972-1100
Service Intelligence Inc 1061 Red Venture Dr Ste 175	Fort Mill	SC	29707	**800-263-2980**	
Seton Hotel 144 E 40th St	New York	NY	10016	**866-697-3866**	212-889-5301
Shaker Consulting Group Inc 3201 Entp Pkwy Ste 360	Cleveland	OH	44122	**888-485-7633**	
Sheridan Healthcare Inc 1613 NW 136th Ave Ste 200	Sunrise	FL	33323	**800-437-2672**	
Solutions 21 152 Wabash St	Pittsburgh	PA	15220	**866-765-2121**	
Solutions AE Inc 236 Auburn Ave	Atlanta	GA	30303	**888-562-4441**	
Southern Solutions Group Inc 4305 Poplar Creek Ln	High Point	NC	27265	**866-581-6055**	
SpawGlass Construction Corp 13800 W Rd	Houston	TX	77041	**800-771-0422**	281-970-5300
Spectrum Healthcare Resources Inc 12647 Olive Blvd Ste 600	Saint Louis	MO	63141	**800-325-3982**	
SSA Consultants Inc 9331 Bluebonnet Blvd	Baton Rouge	LA	70810	**800-634-2758**	225-769-2676
Staples Construction Company Inc 1501 Eastman Ave	Ventura	CA	93003	**800-881-4650**	805-658-8786
Stock & Option Solutions Inc 6399 San Ignacio Ave Ste 100	San Jose	CA	95119	**888-767-0199**	408-979-8700
Stop Hunger Now 615 Hillsborough St Ste 200	Raleigh	NC	27603	**888-501-8440**	919-839-0689
Summit Energy Services Inc 10350 Ormsby Pk Pl Ste 400	Louisville	KY	40223	**866-907-8664**	502-429-3800
Surge Resources 920 Candia Rd	Manchester	NH	03109	**800-787-4387**	603-623-0007
Talent Curve 14 Bridle Path	Pittsboro	NC	27312	**866-494-0248**	
Team Quality Services Inc 4483 County Rd 19 Ste B	Auburn	IN	46706	**866-568-8326**	260-572-0060
Telcom Corp 1499 W Palmetto Park Rd Ste 214	Boca Raton	FL	33486	**800-394-5448**	561-394-5448
TeleProviders Inc 23461 Southpointe Dr Ste 185	Laguna Hills	CA	92653	**888-999-4244**	
Three Rivers Planning & Development District Inc 75 S Main St PO Box 690	Pontotoc	MS	38863	**877-489-6911**	662-489-2415
Traffic Group Inc, The 9900 Franklin Sq Dr	Baltimore	MD	21236	**800-583-8411**	410-931-6600
Trisoft Technologies Inc 14429 Independence Dr	Plainfield	IL	60544	**866-364-7031**	
TTG Consultants 4727 Wilshire Blvd	Los Angeles	CA	90010	**800-736-8840**	323-936-6600
Turpin Sales & Marketing Inc 330 Cold Spring Ave	West Springfield	MA	01089	**877-377-7573**	
Unisource NTC 1560 Holly Court Ste 200	Thousand Oaks	CA	91360	**800-736-8470**	
Vanir Construction Management Inc 4540 Duckhorn Dr Ste 300	Sacramento	CA	95834	**888-912-1201**	916-575-8887
Vendors Exchange International Inc 8700 Brookpark Rd	Cleveland	OH	44129	**800-321-2311**	216-432-1800
Verisk Analytics 545 Washington Blvd *NASDAQ: VRSK*	Jersey City	NJ	07310	**800-888-4476**	201-469-3000
Vertigraph Inc 12959 Jupiter Rd Ste 252	Dallas	TX	75238	**800-989-4243**	214-340-9436
VetStrategy 30 Whitmore Rd	Woodbridge	ON	L4L7Z4	**866-901-6471**	
Vetter Health Services Inc 20220 Harney St	Elkhorn	NE	68022	**800-388-4264**	402-895-3932
Volt VIEWtech Inc 4761 E Hunter Ave	Anaheim	CA	92807	**888-396-9927**	714-695-3377
Wicklander Zulawski & Associates Inc 4932 Main St	Downers Grove	IL	60515	**800-222-7789**	630-852-6800
Winfree Marketing & Sales Institute 1905 Arnold Palmer Blvd	Louisville	KY	40245	**800-616-9260**	502-253-0700
Zimmet Healthcare Consulting LLC 4006 Us Hwy 9	Morganville	NJ	07751	**877-763-2001**	732-970-0733

463 MANNEQUINS & DISPLAY FORMS

Company / Address	City	State	Zip	Toll-Free	Phone
Siegel & Stockman USA 126 W 25th St	New York	NY	10001	**888-515-8949**	212-633-0138
Silvestri Studio Inc 8125 Beach St	Los Angeles	CA	90001	**800-647-8874**	323-277-4420

464 MARINE SERVICES

SEE ALSO Freight Transport - Deep Sea (Domestic Ports) ; Freight Transport - Deep Sea (Foreign Ports) ; Freight Transport - Inland Waterways ; Logistics Services (Transportation & Warehousing)

Company / Address	City	State	Zip	Toll-Free	Phone
AEP River Operations 16150 Main Cir Dr Ste 400	Chesterfield	MO	63017	**800-621-3362**	636-530-2100

Classified Section

	City	State	ZIP	Toll-Free	Phone
Andrie Inc 561 E Western Ave	Muskegon	MI	49442	**800-722-2421**	231-728-2226
Bay Houston Towing Co 2243 Milford St	Houston	TX	77253	**800-324-3755**	713-529-3755
Crowley Maritime Corp 9487 Regency Square Blvd	Jacksonville	FL	32225	**800-276-9539**	904-727-2200
Edison Chouest Offshore 16201 E Main St	Galliano	LA	70354	**866-925-5161**	985-601-4444
Foss Maritime Co 1151 Fairview Ave N	Seattle	WA	98119	**800-562-2711**	
General Steamship Agencies Inc 575 Redwood Hwy Ste 200	Mill Valley	CA	94941	**855-859-3123**	415-389-5200
Great Lakes Towing Co 4500 Div Ave	Cleveland	OH	44102	**800-321-3663**	216-621-4854
Hawaiian Tug & Barge 1331 N Nimitz Hwy PO Box 3288	Honolulu	HI	96817	**800-572-2743**	808-543-9311
Hopkins-Carter Company Inc 3300 NW 21st St	Miami	FL	33142	**800-595-9656**	305-635-7377
Hornbeck Offshore Services Inc 103 Northpark Blvd Ste 300 *NYSE: HOS*	Covington	LA	70433	**800-642-9816**	985-727-2000
Kinder Morgan Bulk Terminals Inc 7116 Hwy 22	Sorrento	LA	70778	**800-232-1627**	225-675-5387
Marquette Transportation Company LLC 5525 Mounes St	New Orleans	LA	70123	**800-735-5845**	504-733-5845
McAllister Towing & Transportation Co Inc 17 Battery Pl Ste 1200	New York	NY	10004	**888-774-0400**	212-269-3200
New York State Canal Corp 200 Southern Blvd PO Box 189	Albany	NY	12201	**800-422-6254**	518-436-2700
Odyssey Marine Exploration Inc 5215 W Laurel St *NASDAQ: OMEX*	Tampa	FL	33607	**800-458-4646**	813-876-1776
Sause Bros 3710 NW Front Ave	Portland	OR	97210	**800-488-4167**	503-222-1811
Sea Tow Services International Inc 1560 Youngs Ave PO Box 1178	Southold	NY	11971	**800-473-2869**	631-765-3660
SSA Marine 1131 SW Klickitat Way	Seattle	WA	98134	**800-422-3505**	206-623-0304
Tidewater Inc 601 Poydras St Ste 1900 *NYSE: TDW*	New Orleans	LA	70130	**800-678-8433**	504-568-1010
Virginia International Terminals Inc 7737 Hampton Blvd *General	Norfolk	VA	23505	**800-541-2431***	757-440-7000

465 MARKET RESEARCH FIRMS

SEE ALSO

	City	State	ZIP	Toll-Free	Phone
1stWEST Financial Corp 1536 Cole Blvd Ste 333	Lakewood	CO	80401	**866-670-3443**	
Aberdeen Group Inc 451 D St Ste 710	Boston	MA	02210	**800-577-7891**	617-854-5200
Ameresco Canada Inc 90 Sheppard Ave E	North York	ON	M2N3A1	**888-483-7267**	416-512-7700
AML Partners LLC 4 Grand Cove Way	Edgewater	NJ	07020	**866-790-5095**	201-484-8835
Amphenol Optimize Manufacturing Co 528 N Mariposa Rd Bldg. A	Nogales	AZ	85621	**800-288-4746**	520-397-7015
AQA International LLC 501 Commerce Dr, NE	Columbia	SC	29223	**800-281-4384**	
Arbitron Inc 9705 Patuxent Woods Dr *NYSE: ARB*	Columbia	MD	21046	**800-543-7300**	410-312-8000
Bensussen Deutsch & Assoc Inc (BDA) 15525 Woodinville-Redmond Rd NE	Woodinville	WA	98072	**800-451-4764**	425-492-6111
Bridge Metrics LLC 830 S Greenville Ave	Allen	TX	75002	**877-801-7158**	
C & R Research Services Inc 500 N Michigan Ave Ste 1200	Chicago	IL	60611	**800-543-9393**	312-828-9200
CattleLog 10305 102nd Terrace	Sebastian	FL	32958	**866-239-2665**	
comScore Inc 11950 Democracy Dr # 600	Reston	VA	20190	**866-276-6972**	703-438-2000
Connected Nation Inc 444 N Capitol St, NW	Washington	DC	20001	**877-846-7710**	
Contact 101 Inc 777 N Rainbow Blvd Ste 250	Las Vegas	NV	89107	**888-731-2397**	
Cross Commerce Media Inc 130 Madison Ave	New York	NY	10016	**888-890-0020**	
Datassential 1762 Westwood Blvd Ste 250	Los Angeles	CA	90024	**877-886-3687**	
Demand Metric 562 Wellington St	London	ON	N6A3R5	**866-947-7744**	519-495-9619
eXelate 7 W 22nd St 9th Fl	New York	NY	10010	**877-896-3282**	646-380-4400
Gallup Inc 1001 Gallup Dr	Omaha	NE	68102	**888-500-8282**	402-951-2003
Gallup Organization 901 F St NW	Washington	DC	20004	**877-242-5587**	202-715-3030
Gartner Inc 56 Top Gallant Rd *NYSE: IT*	Stamford	CT	06902	**866-471-2526**	203-964-0096
GRFI Ltd 400 E Randolph St Ste 700	Chicago	IL	60601	**888-856-5161**	
Gulf of Maine Research Institute, The 350 Commercial St	Portland	ME	04101	**866-447-2111**	207-772-2321
InBios International Inc 562 First Ave S Ste 600	Seattle	WA	98104	**866-462-4671**	206-344-5821
Information Resources Inc 150 N Clinton St	Chicago	IL	60661	**866-262-5973**	312-726-1221
Innovairre Communications LLC 825 Hylton Rd	Pennsauken	NJ	08110	**856-663-2500**	
Institute for Corporate Productivity Inc 411 First Ave S Ste 403	Seattle	WA	98104	**866-375-4427**	206-624-6565
International Data Corp (IDC) 5 Speen St	Framingham	MA	01701	**800-343-4952**	508-872-8200
Investorideas com 145 Tyee Dr Number 1573	Point Roberts	WA	98281	**800-665-0411**	
Invoke Solutions Inc 375 Totten Pond Rd	Waltham	MA	02451	**866-687-4367**	781-810-2700
JD Power & Assoc 2625 Townsgate Rd Ste 100	Westlake Village	CA	91361	**800-274-5372**	805-418-8000
Kazan, McClain, Abrams, Fernandez, Lyons & Farrise PLC Jack London Market 55 Harrison St Ste 400	Oakland	CA	94607	**877-995-6372**	
Knowledge Works Inc 5750 Old Orchard Rd Ste 250	Skokie	IL	60077	**866-825-3400**	847-853-6117
M/A/R/C Research 1660 Westridge Cir	Irving	TX	75038	**800-884-6272**	972-983-0400
Maritz Research Inc 1355 N Hwy Dr	Fenton	MO	63099	**877-462-7489**	385-695-2940
Market Decisions LLC 75 Washington Ave Ste 206	Portland	ME	04101	**800-293-1538**	207-767-6440
MarketVision Research Inc 10300 Alliance Rd Ste 200	Cincinnati	OH	45242	**800-232-4250**	513-791-3100
Micro-Tech Consultants Inc 1686 Jessica Pl	Santa Rosa	CA	95403	**800-752-8878**	707-575-4820
MORPACE International Inc 31700 Middlebelt Rd Ste 200 *General	Farmington Hills	MI	48334	**800-881-1723***	248-737-5300
National Research Corp 1245 Q St *NASDAQ: NRCI*	Lincoln	NE	68508	**800-388-4264**	402-475-2525
NPD Group Inc 900 W Shore Rd	Port Washington	NY	11050	**866-444-1411**	516-625-0700
OnCard Marketing Inc 276 Fifth Ave Ste 608	New York	NY	10001	**866-996-8729**	
Open Minds 163 York St	Gettysburg	PA	17325	**877-350-6463**	717-334-1329
Opinion Research Corp (ORC) 902 Carnegie Ctr Ste 220	Princeton	NJ	08540	**800-444-4672**	
RateHub.ca 411 Richmond St E Ste 208	Toronto	ON	M5A3S5	**800-679-9622**	
RDA Group 450 Enterprise Ct	Bloomfield Hills	MI	48302	**800-669-7324**	248-332-5000
Reis Inc 530 Fifth Ave 5th Fl *NASDAQ: REIS*	New York	NY	10036	**800-366-7347**	212-921-1122
Relevancy Group LLC, The 1010 Shenandoah Dr	Spring Lake	NJ	07762	**877-972-6886**	
Ruf Strategic Solutions 1533 E Spruce St	Olathe	KS	66061	**800-829-8544**	
Seneca Consulting Group Inc 111 Smithtown Byp Ste 112	Hauppauge	NY	11788	**866-442-2472**	631-577-4092
Sharetracker LLC 1480 E Hwy MM	Ashland	MO	65010	**866-977-7171**	
Standards Council of Canada 270 Albert St Ste 200	Ottawa	ON	K1P6N7	**800-844-6790**	613-238-3222
Strategy Institute 401 Richmond St W Ste 401	Toronto	ON	M5V3A8	**866-298-9343**	
TRC Holdings Inc 1300 Virginia Dr Ste 200	Fort Washington	PA	19034	**800-275-2827**	215-641-2200
Unmetric Inc 2001 Victoria Rd	Chicago	IL	60060	**855-558-5588**	
Walker Information Inc 301 Pennsylvania Pkwy	Indianapolis	IN	46280	**800-334-3939**	317-843-3939
Westat Inc 1600 Research Blvd	Rockville	MD	20850	**800-669-6820**	301-251-1500
XtremeEDA Corp 200-25 Holland Ave	Ottawa	ON	K1Y4R9	**800-586-0280**	613-728-5912
Zolato Inc 2801 First Ave Ste 306	Seattle	WA	98121	**866-557-6716**	

466 MARKING DEVICES

	City	State	ZIP	Toll-Free	Phone
American Marking Systems Inc 1015 Paulison Ave PO Box 1677	Clifton	NJ	07011	**800-782-6766**	973-478-5600
Cable Markers Company Inc 13805-C Alton Pkwy	Irvine	CA	92618	**800-746-7655**	
CH Hanson Co 2000 N Aurora Rd	Naperville	IL	60563	**800-827-3398**	630-848-2000
Cosco Industries Inc 7220 W Wilson Ave	Harwood Heights	IL	60706	**800-296-8970**	708-867-5800
Excelsior Marking Products 888 W Waterloo Rd	Akron	OH	44314	**800-433-3615**	330-745-2300
Hitt Marking Devices Inc 3231 W MacArthur Blvd	Santa Ana	CA	92704	**800-969-6699**	714-979-1405
Huntington Park Rubber Stamp 2761 E Slauson Ave PO Box 519	Huntington Park	CA	90255	**800-882-0029**	323-582-6461
Infosight Corp PO Box 5000	Chillicothe	OH	45601	**800-401-0716**	740-642-3600
Jackson Marking Products Co 9105 N Rainbow Ln	Mount Vernon	IL	62864	**800-782-6722**	618-242-1334
La-Co/Markal Co 1201 Pratt Blvd	Elk Grove Village	IL	60007	**800-621-4025**	847-956-7600
Matthews International Corp Marking Products Div 6515 Penn Ave	Pittsburgh	PA	15206	**800-775-7775**	412-665-2500
Menke Marking Devices 13253 Alondra Blvd	Santa Fe Springs	CA	90670	**800-231-6023**	562-921-1380
New Method Steel Stamps Inc 31313 Kendall Ave	Fraser	MI	48026	**800-582-0199**	586-293-0200
Norwood Marking Systems 2538 Wisconsin Ave	Downers Grove	IL	60515	**800-626-3464**	630-968-0646
Schwaab Inc 11415 W Burleigh St	Milwaukee	WI	53222	**800-935-9877**	414-771-4150
Schwerdtle Stamp Co 166 Elm St	Bridgeport	CT	06604	**800-535-0004**	203-330-2750
Signet Marking Devices 3121 Red Hill Ave	Costa Mesa	CA	92626	**800-421-5150**	714-549-0341
Stamp-Rite Inc 154 S Larch St	Lansing	MI	48912	**800-328-1988**	517-487-5071
Tacoma Rubber Stamp & Sign 919 Market St	Tacoma	WA	98402	**800-544-7281**	253-383-5433

Company / Address	City	State	Zip	Toll-Free	Phone
Volk Corp 23936 Industrial Pk Dr	Farmington Hills	MI	48335	**800-521-6799***	248-477-6700
*Cust Svc					
Wendell's Inc 6601 Bunker Lk Blvd NW PO Box 458	Ramsey	MN	55303	**800-936-3355**	763-576-8200

467 MASS TRANSPORTATION (LOCAL & SUBURBAN)

SEE ALSO Bus Services - Intercity & Rural

Company / Address	City	State	Zip	Toll-Free	Phone
Alameda-Contra Costa Transit District 1600 Franklin St 10th Fl	Oakland	CA	94612	**877-878-8883**	510-891-4777
Alaska Marine Highway System 6858 Glacier Hwy PO Box 112505	Juneau	AK	99801	**800-642-0066**	907-465-3941
Altamont Commuter Express (ACE) 949 E Ch St	Stockton	CA	95202	**800-411-7245**	
Caledonia Haulers LLC 420 W Lincoln St PO Box 31	Caledonia	MN	55921	**800-325-4728**	507-725-9000
Cape Cod Regional Transit Authority (CCRTA) 215 Iyannough Rd PO Box 1988	Hyannis	MA	02601	**800-352-7155**	508-775-8504
Catalina Express Berth 95	San Pedro	CA	90731	**800-481-3470**	310-519-7971
Central Puget Sound Regional Transit Authority 401 S Jackson St	Seattle	WA	98104	**800-201-4900**	206-398-5000
Cliff Viessman Inc 215 First Ave PO Box 175	Gary	SD	57237	**800-328-2408**	605-272-5241
Delaware Transit Corp 119 Lower Beach St Ste 100	Wilmington	DE	19805	**800-652-3278**	302-576-6000
GO Transit 20 Bay St Ste 600	Toronto	ON	M5J2W3	**888-438-6646**	416-869-3200
Horizon Freight System Inc 6600 Bessemer Ave	Cleveland	OH	44127	**800-480-6829**	216-341-7410
Karl's Transport Inc PO Box 333	Antigo	WI	54409	**800-922-8707**	715-623-2033
Los Angeles County Metropolitan Transportation Authority 1 Gateway Plz	Los Angeles	CA	90012	**800-621-7828**	213-922-6000
Mission Petroleum Carriers Inc 8450 Mosley	Houston	TX	77075	**800-737-9911**	713-943-8250
New Jersey Transit Corp 1 Penn Plz E	Newark	NJ	07105	**800-772-3606***	973-491-7000
*Cust Svc					
Niagara Frontier Transit Metro System Inc 181 Ellicott St Ste 1	Buffalo	NY	14203	**877-294-9434**	716-855-7300
Northern Indiana Commuter Transportation District 33 E US Hwy 12	Chesterton	IN	46304	**800-743-3333**	219-926-5744
Office Movers Inc 6500 Kane Way	Elkridge	MD	21075	**800-331-4025**	410-799-7704
Packard Transport Inc 24021 S Municipal Dr PO Box 380	Channahon	IL	60410	**800-467-9260**	815-467-9260
Pierce Transit 3701 96th St SW PO Box 99070	Lakewood	WA	98499	**800-562-8109**	253-581-8000
Regional Transportation Commission of Southern Nevada (RTC) 600 S Grand Central Pkwy Ste 350	Las Vegas	NV	89106	**800-228-3911**	702-676-1500
Regional Transportation District (RTD) 1600 Blake St	Denver	CO	80202	**800-366-7433**	303-628-9000
Reliable Carriers Inc 41555 Koppernick Rd	Canton	MI	48187	**800-521-6393**	734-453-6677
Riverside Transit Agency (RTA) 1825 Third St PO Box 59968	Riverside	CA	92517	**800-800-7821**	951-565-5000
San Mateo County Transit District 1250 San Carlos Ave PO Box 3006	San Carlos	CA	94070	**800-660-4287**	650-508-6200
Santa Clara Valley Transportation Authority (VTA) 3331 N First St	San Jose	CA	95134	**800-894-9908**	408-321-5555
Sonoma County Transit 355 W Robles Ave	Santa Rosa	CA	95407	**800-345-7433**	707-585-7516
Southern California Regional Rail Authority 700 S Flower St Ste 2600	Los Angeles	CA	90017	**800-371-5465**	213-452-0200
Suburban Mobility Authority for Regional Transportation (SMART) 535 Griswold St Ste 600 Buhl Bldg	Detroit	MI	48226	**866-962-5515**	313-223-2100
Utah Transit Authority 3600 S 700 W PO Box 30810	Salt Lake City	UT	84130	**888-743-3882**	801-262-5626
VIA Metropolitan Transit 800 W Myrtle St	San Antonio	TX	78212	**866-362-4200**	210-362-2000
Virginia Railway Express (VRE) 1500 King St Ste 202	Alexandria	VA	22314	**800-743-3873**	703-684-1001
VPSI Inc 1220 Rankin Dr	Troy	MI	48083	**800-826-7433**	248-597-3500
York County Transportation Authority 1230 Roosevelt Ave	York	PA	17404	**800-632-9063**	717-846-5562

468 MATCHES & MATCHBOOKS

Company / Address	City	State	Zip	Toll-Free	Phone
DD Bean & Sons Co 207 Peterborough St	Jaffrey	NH	03452	**800-366-2824**	603-532-8311
Maryland Match Corp 605 Alluvion St	Baltimore	MD	21230	**800-423-0013**	410-752-8164

469 MATERIAL HANDLING EQUIPMENT

SEE ALSO Conveyors & Conveying Equipment

Company / Address	City	State	Zip	Toll-Free	Phone
Abell-Howe Crane Inc 2143 Internationale Pkwy Ste 400	Woodridge	IL	60517	**800-366-0068**	
Advance Lifts Inc 701 Kirk Rd	Saint Charles	IL	60174	**800-843-3625**	630-584-9881
Air Technical Industries 7501 Clover Ave	Mentor	OH	44060	**800-321-9680**	440-951-5191
American Crane & Equipment Corp 531 Old Swede Rd	Douglassville	PA	19518	**877-877-6778**	610-385-6061
American Power Pull Corp 550 W Linfoot St PO Box 109	Wauseon	OH	43567	**800-808-5922**	419-335-7050
ATAP Inc 130 Industry way	Eastaboga	AL	36260	**800-362-2827**	256-362-2221
Autoquip Corp 1058 W Industrial Rd	Guthrie	OK	73044	**888-811-9876**	405-282-5200
Bayhead Products Corp 173 Crosby Rd	Dover	NH	03820	**800-229-4323**	603-742-3000
Berns Co 1250 W 17th St	Long Beach	CA	90813	**800-421-3773**	562-437-0471
BGK Finishing Systems 4131 Pheasant Ridge Dr NE	Minneapolis	MN	55449	**800-663-5498**	763-784-0466
Busse/SJI Corp 124 N Columbus St	Randolph	WI	53956	**800-882-4995**	
Cascade Corp 2201 NE 201st Ave	Fairview	OR	97024	**800-227-2233**	503-669-6300
NYSE: CASC					
Clark Material Handling Co 700 Enterprise Dr	Lexington	KY	40510	**866-252-5275**	859-422-6400
Columbus McKinnon Corp 140 John James Audubon Pkwy	Amherst	NY	14228	**800-888-0985**	716-689-5400
NASDAQ: CMCO					
Craneveyor Corp 1524 Potrero Ave	South El Monte	CA	91733	**888-501-0050**	
Crosby Group, The 2801 Dawson Rd	Tulsa	OK	74110	**800-772-1500**	918-834-4611
Crysteel Mfg Inc 52182 Ember Rd	Lake Crystal	MN	56055	**800-533-0494***	507-726-2728
*Orders					
Dematic 507 Plymouth Ave NE	Grand Rapids	MI	49505	**877-725-7500***	
*Cust Svc					
Detroit Hoist Co 6650 Sterling Dr N	Sterling Heights	MI	48312	**800-521-9126**	586-268-2600
Downs Crane & Hoist Company Inc 8827 Juniper St	Los Angeles	CA	90002	**800-748-5994**	323-589-6061
Drake-Scruggs Equipment Inc 2000 S Dirksen Pkwy	Springfield	IL	62703	**877-799-0398**	217-753-3871
Escalera Inc 708 S Industrial Dr PO Box 1359	Yuba City	CA	95993	**800-622-1359**	530-673-6318
Excellon Automation Inc 20001 S Rancho Way	Rancho Dominguez	CA	90220	**800-392-3556**	310-668-7700
FL Smidth Inc 2040 Ave C	Bethlehem	PA	18017	**800-523-9482**	610-264-6011
Genie Industries Inc 18340 NE 76th St	Redmond	WA	98052	**800-536-1800**	425-881-1800
Gunnebo-Johnson Corp 1240 N Harvard Ave	Tulsa	OK	74115	**800-331-5460***	918-832-8933
*Sales					
Harlan Materials Handling Corp 27 Stanley Rd	Kansas City	KS	66115	**800-255-4262**	913-342-5650
Harlo Corp PO Box 129	Grandville	MI	49468	**800-391-4151**	616-538-0550
Harper Trucks Inc PO Box 12330	Wichita	KS	67277	**800-835-4099**	316-942-1381
Hilman Inc 12 Timber Ln	Marlboro	NJ	07746	**888-276-5548***	732-462-6277
*Cust Svc					
Indusco Group 1200 W Hamburg St	Baltimore	MD	21230	**800-727-0665**	410-727-0665
Iowa Mold Tooling Co Inc (IMT) 500 W US Hwy 18	Garner	IA	50438	**800-247-5958**	641-923-3711
Kelly Systems Inc 422 N Western Ave	Chicago	IL	60612	**800-258-8237**	312-733-3224
Konecranes America 7300 Chippewa Blvd	Houston	TX	77086	**800-231-0241**	281-445-2225
Kornylak Corp 400 Heaton St	Hamilton	OH	45011	**800-837-5676**	513-863-1277
Landoll Corp 1900 N St	Marysville	KS	66508	**800-446-5175***	785-562-5381
*Cust Svc					
Leebaw Mfg Company Inc PO Box 553	Canfield	OH	44406	**800-841-8083**	
Lift-All Company Inc 1909 McFarland Dr	Landisville	PA	17538	**800-909-1964**	717-898-6615
Liftone 440 E Westinghouse Blvd	Charlotte	NC	28273	**855-543-8663**	
Lovegreen Industrial Services Inc 2280 Sibley Ct	Eagan	MN	55122	**800-262-8284**	651-890-1166
Magline Inc 1205 W Cedar St	Standish	MI	48658	**800-624-5463**	
Manitex Inc 3000 S Austin Ave	Georgetown	TX	78626	**877-314-3390**	512-942-3000
Matot Inc 2501 Van Buren St	Bellwood	IL	60104	**800-369-1070**	708-547-1888
Maxon Industries Inc 11921 Slauson Ave	Santa Fe Springs	CA	90670	**800-227-4116**	562-464-0099
Mazzella Lifting Technologies 21000 Aerospace Pkwy	Cleveland	OH	44142	**800-362-4601**	440-239-7000
McGuire W194 N11481 McCormick Dr PO Box 309	Germantown	WI	53022	**800-624-8473**	518-828-7652
Mertz Mfg LLC 1701 N Waverly St	Ponca City	OK	74601	**800-654-6433**	580-762-5646
Morris Material Handling Inc 315 W Forest Hill Ave	Oak Creek	WI	53154	**800-933-3001**	414-764-6200
NMC-Wollard Inc 2021 Truax Blvd	Eau Claire	WI	54703	**800-656-6867**	715-835-3151
North American Industries Inc 80 Holton St	Woburn	MA	01801	**800-847-8470**	781-897-4100
Nutting 450 Pheasant Ridge Dr	Watertown	SD	57201	**800-533-0337**	605-882-3000
Ohio Magnetics Inc 5400 Dunham Rd	Maple Heights	OH	44137	**800-486-6446**	216-662-8484
Pettibone Michigan 1100 Superior Ave	Baraga	MI	49908	**800-467-3884**	906-353-4800
Positech Corp 191 N Rush Lk Rd	Laurens	IA	50554	**800-831-6026**	712-841-4548
Process Equipment Inc 2770 Welborn St PO Box 1607	Pelham	AL	35124	**888-663-2028**	205-663-5330
Production Equipment Co 401 Liberty St	Meriden	CT	06450	**800-758-5697**	203-235-5795
Proserv Anchor Crane Group 455 Aldine Bender PO Box 670965	Houston	TX	77060	**800-835-2223**	281-405-9048
PTR Baler & Compactor Co 2207 E Ontario St	Philadelphia	PA	19134	**800-523-3654**	215-533-5100
Pucel Enterprises Inc 1440 E 36th St	Cleveland	OH	44114	**800-336-4986**	216-881-4604
Raymond Corp 22 S Canal St	Greene	NY	13778	**800-235-7200***	607-656-2311
*General					
RKI Inc 2301 Central Pkwy	Houston	TX	77092	**800-346-8988**	713-688-4414

Classified Section

	City	State	ZIP	Toll-Free	Phone
Royal Tractor Co Inc 109 Overland Pk Pl	New Century	KS	66031	**888-782-7278**	913-782-2598
Scott Industrial Systems Inc 4433 Interpoint Blvd PO Box 1387	Dayton	OH	45401	**800-416-6023**	937-233-8146
Shepard Niles 220 N Genesee St	Montour Falls	NY	14865	**800-481-2260**	607-535-7111
Sherman & Reilly Inc 400 W 33rd St *Sales	Chattanooga	TN	37401	**800-251-7780***	423-756-5300
Solazyme Inc 225 Gateway Blvd *NASDAQ: SZYM*	South San Francisco	CA	94080	**877-917-9075**	650-780-4777
Southeast Industrial Equipment Inc 12200 Steele Creek Rd	Charlotte	NC	28273	**866-696-9125**	704-399-9700
Southworth Products Corp PO Box 1380	Portland	ME	04104	**800-743-1000**	207-878-0700
Steel King Industries Inc 2700 Chamber St	Stevens Point	WI	54481	**800-826-0203**	715-341-3120
Streator Dependable Manufacturing Co 1705 N Shabbona St	Streator	IL	61364	**800-795-0551**	815-672-0551
Taylor-Dunn Manufacturing Co 2114 W Ball Rd	Anaheim	CA	92804	**800-688-8680**	714-956-4040
Terex Corp Crane Div 202 Raleigh St	Wilmington	NC	28412	**877-794-5284**	910-395-8500
Terex-Telelect Inc 500 Oakwood Rd PO Box 1150	Watertown	SD	57201	**800-982-8975**	605-882-4000
Thern Inc 5712 Industrial Pk Rd PO Box 347	Winona	MN	55987	**800-843-7648**	507-454-2996
Triple/S Dynamics Inc 1031 S Haskell Ave PO Box 151027	Dallas	TX	75315	**800-527-2116**	214-828-8600
Valley Craft 2001 S Hwy 61	Lake City	MN	55041	**800-328-1480**	651-345-3386
WA Charnstrom Co 5391 12th Ave E *Cust Svc	Shakopee	MN	55379	**800-328-2962***	
Waldon Mfg LLC 201 W Oklahoma Ave	Fairview	OK	73737	**866-283-2759**	580-227-3711
Western Hoist Inc 1839 Cleveland Ave	National City	CA	91950	**888-994-6478**	619-474-3361
Whiting Corp 26000 Whiting Way	Monee	IL	60449	**800-861-5744**	
Wiggins Lift Company Inc 2571 Cortez St	Oxnard	CA	93031	**800-350-7821**	805-485-7821
WinHolt Equipment Group 141 Eileen Way	Syosset	NY	11791	**800-444-3595**	516-222-0335

470 MATTRESSES & ADJUSTABLE BEDS

SEE ALSO Household Furniture

	City	State	ZIP	Toll-Free	Phone
Bechik Products Inc 1020 Discovery Rd Ste 150	Eagan	MN	55121	**800-328-6569**	651-698-0364
Bergad Inc 747 Eljer Way	Ford City	PA	16226	**888-476-8664**	724-763-2883
Bowles Mattress Co Inc 1220 Watt St	Jeffersonville	IN	47130	**800-223-7509**	812-288-8614
Classic Sleep Products Inc 8214 Wellmoor Ct	Jessup	MD	20794	**877-707-7533**	410-904-0006
Comfortex Inc 1680 Wilkie Dr	Winona	MN	55987	**800-445-4007**	507-454-6579
Corsicana Bedding Inc PO Box 1050	Corsicana	TX	75151	**800-323-4349**	903-872-2591
Cotton Belt Inc 401 E Sater St	Pinetops	NC	27864	**800-849-4192**	252-827-4192
Englander Northeast 12 Esquire Rd	North Billerica	MA	01862	**800-370-8700**	
Imperial Bedding Co 720 11th St PO Box 5347	Huntington	WV	25703	**800-529-3321**	304-529-3321
Jackson Mattress Company Inc 3154 Camden Rd	Fayetteville	NC	28306	**800-763-7378**	910-425-0131
Jamison Bedding Inc PO Box 681948 *Cust Svc	Franklin	TN	37068	**800-255-1883***	615-794-1883
King Koil Licensing Company Inc 7501 S Quincy St Ste 130	Willowbrook	IL	60527	**800-525-8331**	
Kingsdown Inc 126 W Holt St *Cust Svc	Mebane	NC	27302	**800-354-5464***	919-563-3531
Kolcraft Enterprises Inc 10832 NC Hwy 211 E *Cust Svc	Aberdeen	NC	28315	**800-453-7673***	910-944-9345
Leggett & Platt Inc Number 1 Leggett Rd PO Box 757 *NYSE: LEG*	Carthage	MO	64836	**800-888-4569**	417-358-8131
Northwest Bedding 6102 S Hayford Rd	Spokane	WA	99224	**800-456-7686**	509-244-3000
Omaha Bedding Co 4011 S 60th St	Omaha	NE	68117	**800-279-9018**	402-733-8600
Palliser Furniture Upholstery Ltd 70 Lexington Park	Winnipeg	MB	R2G4H2	**866-444-0777**	204-988-5600
Restonic Mattress 201 James E Casey Dr	Buffalo	NY	14206	**800-898-6075**	716-895-1414
Restonic Mattress Corp 737 Main St	Buffalo	NY	14203	**800-898-6075**	
Riverside Mattress Co 225 Dunn Rd	Fayetteville	NC	28312	**888-288-5195**	910-483-0461
Serta Mattress/AW Inc 8415 ARdmore Rd	Landover	MD	20785	**888-557-3782**	301-322-1000
Sleep Train Inc 2205 Plz Dr	Rocklin	CA	95765	**800-919-2337**	
Southerland Inc 1973 Southerland Dr *Cust Svc	Nashville	TN	37207	**800-443-1183***	615-226-9650
Tempur-Pedic International Inc 1713 Jaggie Fox Way *NYSE: TPX*	Lexington	KY	40511	**800-821-6621**	
Therapedic International 1375 Jersey Ave	North Brunswick	NJ	08902	**800-233-7467**	

471 MEASURING, TESTING, CONTROLLING INSTRUMENTS

SEE ALSO Electrical Signals Measuring & Testing Instruments

	City	State	ZIP	Toll-Free	Phone
ABB Inc 501 Merritt 7 *Prod Info	Norwalk	CT	06851	**800-626-4999***	203-750-2200
All Weather Inc 1165 National Dr	Sacramento	CA	95834	**800-824-5873**	916-928-1000
AMETEK Inc Test & Calibration Instruments Div 8600 Somerset Dr	Largo	FL	33773	**800-733-5427**	727-538-6132
AMETEK US Gauge 820 Pennsylvania Blvd	Feasterville	PA	19053	**888-631-5454**	215-355-6900
Beta LaserMike Inc 8001 Technology Blvd	Dayton	OH	45424	**800-886-9935**	937-233-9935
Bruel & Kjaer Instruments Inc 2815 Colonnades Ct Ste A	Norcross	GA	30071	**800-332-2040**	770-209-6907
Cambridge Technology Inc 25 Hartwell Ave	Lexington	MA	02421	**800-342-3757**	781-541-1600
Canberra Industries Inc 800 Research Pkwy *Sales	Meriden	CT	06450	**800-243-3955***	203-238-2351
Clayton Industries 17477 Hurley St	City of Industry	CA	91744	**800-423-4585**	626-435-1200
Crane Nuclear Inc 2825 Cobb International Blvd	Kennesaw	GA	30152	**800-795-8013**	770-424-6343
Cubic Transportation Systems Inc 5650 Kearny Mesa Rd	San Diego	CA	92111	**800-937-5449**	858-268-3100
Danaher Corp 2200 Pennsylvania Ave NW Ste 800 *NYSE: DHR*	Washington	DC	20037	**800-833-9200**	202-828-0850
Davis Instrument Corp 3465 Diablo Ave	Hayward	CA	94545	**800-678-3669**	510-732-9229
Delta Cooling Towers Inc PO Box 315	Rockaway	NJ	07866	**800-289-3358**	973-586-2201
Dynisco LLC 38 Forge Pkwy *General	Franklin	MA	02038	**800-396-4726***	508-541-9400
Emerson Process Management CSI 835 Innovation Dr	Knoxville	TN	37932	**800-675-4726**	865-675-2110
Endevco Corp 30700 Rancho Viejo Rd	San Juan Capistrano	CA	92675	**800-982-6732**	949-493-8181
Enidine Inc 7 Centre Dr	Orchard Park	NY	14127	**800-852-8508**	716-662-1900
Fairfield Industries Inc 1111 Gillingham Ln	Sugar Land	TX	77478	**800-231-9809**	281-275-7500
Fiber Instruments Sales Inc 161 Clear Rd *Sales	Oriskany	NY	13424	**800-500-0347***	315-736-2206
Fisher Research Laboratory Inc 1465H Henry Brennan Ste H	El Paso	TX	79936	**800-685-5050**	915-225-0333
Garrett Metal Detectors 1881 W State St	Garland	TX	75042	**800-234-6151**	972-494-6151
George Risk Industries Inc 802 S Elm St *OTC: RSKIA* ■ *Sales	Kimball	NE	69145	**800-523-1227***	308-235-4645
GFI Genfare 751 Pratt Blvd	Elk Grove Village	IL	60007	**877-247-3797**	847-593-8855
Gleason M & M Precision Systems Corp 300 Progress Rd	Dayton	OH	45449	**800-727-6333**	937-859-8273
Goodrich Corp 2730 W Tyvola Rd 4 Coliseum Ctr *NYSE: GR*	Charlotte	NC	28217	**800-735-7899**	704-423-7000
Herman H Sticht Company Inc 45 Main St Ste 701	Brooklyn	NY	11201	**800-221-3203**	718-852-7602
Hexagon Metrology Inc 250 Circuit Dr	North Kingstown	RI	02852	**800-343-7933**	401-886-2000
Interface Inc 7401 E Butherus Dr	Scottsdale	AZ	85260	**800-947-5598**	480-948-5555
L-3 Avionics Systems 5353 52nd St SE	Grand Rapids	MI	49512	**800-253-9525**	616-949-6600
Leica Geosystems Inc 3498 Kraft Ave SE *Sales	Grand Rapids	MI	49512	**800-367-9453***	616-977-4189
Ludlum Measurements Inc 501 Oak St	Sweetwater	TX	79556	**800-622-0828**	325-235-5494
Magnetic Analysis Corp 103 Fairview Park Dr	Elmsford	NY	10523	**800-463-8622**	914-699-9450
Marposs Corp 3300 Cross Creek Pkwy	Auburn Hills	MI	48326	**888-627-7677**	248-370-0404
Metrix Instrument Co 8824 Fallbrook Dr	Houston	TX	77064	**800-638-7494**	713-461-2131
Metrosonics 1060 Corporate Ctr Dr	Oconomowoc	WI	53066	**800-245-0779**	262-567-9157
Metrotech Corp 3251 Olcott St	Santa Clara	CA	95054	**800-446-3392**	408-734-1400
MTS Systems Corp 14000 Technology Dr *NASDAQ: MTSC* ■ *Cust Svc	Eden Prairie	MN	55344	**800-328-2255***	952-937-4000
Mustang Dynamometer 2300 Pinnacle Pkwy	Twinsburg	OH	44087	**888-468-7826**	330-963-5400
Ohmart/VEGA Corp 4241 Allendorf Dr	Cincinnati	OH	45209	**800-367-5383**	513-272-0131
Oxford Instruments Measurement Systems 300 Bake Ave Ste 150	Concord	MA	01742	**800-447-4717**	
Preco Electronics Inc 10335 W Emerald St	Boise	ID	83704	**866-977-7326**	208-323-1000
Rochester Gauges Inc of Texas 11616 Harry Hines Blvd	Dallas	TX	75229	**800-821-1829**	972-241-2161
Rudolph Technologies Inc 1 Rudolph Rd PO Box 1000 *NASDAQ: RTEC*	Flanders	NJ	07836	**877-467-8365**	973-691-1300
Setra Systems Inc 159 Swanson Rd	Boxborough	MA	01719	**800-257-3872**	978-263-1400
Sierra Monitor Corp 1991 Tarob Ct *OTC: SRMC*	Milpitas	CA	95035	**888-509-1970**	408-262-6611

Company / Address	City	State	Zip	Toll-Free	Phone
Smiths Detection 2202 Lakeside Blvd	Edgewood	MD	21040	**800-297-0955**	410-510-9100
Sorrento Electronics Inc 4949 Greencraig Ln	San Diego	CA	92123	**800-252-1180**	858-522-8300
SuperFlow Technologies Group 4747 Centennial Blvd	Colorado Springs	CO	80919	**800-471-7701**	719-471-1746
Taber Industries 455 Bryant St	North Tonawanda	NY	14120	**800-333-5300**	716-694-4000
Testing Machines Inc 40 McCullough Dr *General	New Castle	DE	19720	**800-678-3221***	302-613-5600
Thermo Fisher Scientific Inc 81 Wyman St *NYSE: TMO*	Waltham	MA	02454	**800-678-5599**	781-622-1000
Unilux Inc 59 N Fifth St	Saddle Brook	NJ	07663	**800-522-0801**	201-712-1266
Vaisala Inc 10-D Gill St	Woburn	MA	01801	**888-824-7252**	781-933-4500
White's Electronics Inc 1011 Pleasant Valley Rd *Sales	Sweet Home	OR	97386	**800-999-9147***	800-547-6911

472 MEAT PACKING PLANTS

SEE ALSO Poultry Processing

Company / Address	City	State	Zip	Toll-Free	Phone
Abbyland Foods Inc 502 E Linden St PO Box 69	Abbotsford	WI	54405	**800-732-5483**	715-223-6386
Allen Bros Inc 3737 S Halsted St	Chicago	IL	60609	**800-548-7777**	773-890-5100
Alpine Meats 9850 Lowr Sacramento Rd	Stockton	CA	95210	**800-399-6328**	209-477-2691
American Foods Group Inc 544 Acme St	Green Bay	WI	54302	**800-345-0293**	920-437-6330
Carolina Packers Inc 2999 S Bright Leaf Blvd	Smithfield	NC	27577	**800-682-7675**	919-934-2181
Central Nebraska Packing Inc 2800 E Eigth St *Cust Svc	North Platte	NE	69103	**800-445-2881***	308-532-1250
Chisesi Bros Meat Packing Co 5221 Jefferson Hwy	New Orleans	LA	70123	**800-966-3550**	504-822-3550
Clougherty Packing Co 3049 E Vernon Ave *Sales	Los Angeles	CA	90058	**800-846-7635***	
Comer Packing 1000 Poplar St PO Box 33	Aberdeen	MS	39730	**800-748-8916**	662-369-9325
ConAgra Foods Retail Products Co Deli Foods Group 215 W Field Rd	Naperville	IL	60563	**877-266-2472**	630-857-1000
Cudahy Patrick Inc 1 Sweet Apple-Wood Ln	Cudahy	WI	53110	**800-486-6900**	414-744-2000
Curtis Packing Co 2416 Randolph Ave	Greensboro	NC	27406	**800-852-7890**	336-275-7684
Eddy Packing Company Inc 404 Airport Dr	Yoakum	TX	77995	**800-292-2361**	361-293-2361
Farm Boy Meats 2761 N Kentucky Ave	Evansville	IN	47711	**800-852-3976**	812-425-5231
Food Consulting Co, The 13724 Recuerdo Dr	Del Mar	CA	92014	**800-793-2844**	858-793-4658
Greater Omaha Packing Company Inc 3001 L St	Omaha	NE	68107	**800-747-5400**	402-731-1700
Harris Ranch Beef Co 16277 S McCall Ave PO Box 220	Selma	CA	93662	**800-742-1955**	
Hatfield Quality Meats Inc 2700 Clemens Rd	Hatfield	PA	19440	**800-743-1191**	215-368-2500
J Freirich Foods Inc 815 W Kerr St PO Box 1529	Salisbury	NC	28144	**800-554-4788**	704-636-2621
JH Routh Packing Company Inc 4413 W Bogart Rd	Sandusky	OH	44870	**800-446-6759**	419-626-2251
John Morrell & Co 805 E Kemper Rd	Cincinnati	OH	45246	**800-722-1127**	513-346-3540
Long Prairie Packing Co 10 Riverside Dr	Long Prairie	MN	56347	**800-996-6440**	320-732-2171
Morrilton Packing Company Inc 51 Blue Diamond Dr	Morrilton	AR	72110	**800-264-2475**	501-354-2474
National Beef Packing Co LLC 12200 Ambassador Dr Ste 500 PO Box 20046	Kansas City	MO	64163	**800-449-2333**	
Olymel LP 2200 Pratte Ave Pratte	Saint-Hyacinthe	QC	J2S4B6	**800-361-7990**	450-771-0400
Pearl Meat Packing Company Inc 27 York Ave	Randolph	MA	02368	**800-462-3022**	781-228-5100
Plumrose USA Inc 1901 Butterfield Rd Ste 305	Downers Grove	IL	60515	**800-526-4909**	732-624-4040
Quality Meats & Seafoods 700 Ctr St	West Fargo	ND	58078	**800-342-4250**	701-282-0202
Quincy Street Inc 13350 Quincy St	Holland	MI	49424	**800-784-6290**	616-399-3330
Rose Packing Company Inc 65 S Barrington Rd	South Barrington	IL	60010	**800-323-7363**	847-381-5700
Sam Hausman Meat Packer Inc 4261 Beacon	Corpus Christi	TX	78403	**800-364-5521**	361-883-5521
Sioux-Preme Packing Co 4241 US 75th Ave *General	Sioux Center	IA	51250	**800-735-7675***	
Superior Farms 1480 Drew Ave Ste 100	Davis	CA	95618	**800-228-5262**	530-758-3091
Thompson Packers Inc 550 Carnation St	Slidell	LA	70460	**800-989-6328**	985-641-6640
Travis Meats Inc 7210 Clinton Hwy PO Box 670	Powell	TN	37849	**800-247-7606**	865-938-9051
Tyson Fresh Meats Inc 800 Stevens Port Dr	Dakota Dunes	SD	57049	**800-416-2269**	605-235-2061

473 MEDICAL ASSOCIATIONS - STATE

SEE ALSO Health & Medical Professionals Associations

Association / Address	City	State	Zip	Toll-Free	Phone
Alabama Medical Assn 19 S Jackson St	Montgomery	AL	36104	**800-239-6272**	
Alaska State Medical Assn 4107 Laurel St	Anchorage	AK	99508	**800-951-8712**	907-562-0304
Arizona Medical Assn, The (ArMA) 810 W Bethany Home Rd	Phoenix	AZ	85013	**800-482-3480**	602-246-8901
Colorado Medical Society 7351 Lowry Blvd	Denver	CO	80230	**800-654-5653**	720-859-1001
Connecticut State Medical Society 160 St Ronan St	New Haven	CT	06511	**800-406-1527**	203-865-0587
Delmarva Foundation For Medical Care Inc (DFMC) 28464 Marlboro Ave	Easton	MD	21601	**800-999-3362**	410-822-0697
Hawaii Medical Assn 1360 S Beretania St	Honolulu	HI	96816	**888-536-2792**	808-536-7702
Illinois State Medical Society 20 N Michigan Ave Ste 700	Chicago	IL	60602	**800-782-4767**	312-782-1654
Indiana State Medical Assn 322 Canal Walk	Indianapolis	IN	46202	**800-257-4762**	317-261-2060
Iowa Medical Society 1001 Grand Ave	West Des Moines	IA	50265	**800-747-3070**	515-223-1401
Kansas Medical Society 623 SW Tenth Ave	Topeka	KS	66612	**800-332-0156**	785-235-2383
Louisiana State Medical Society 6767 Perkins Rd Ste 100	Baton Rouge	LA	70808	**800-375-9508**	225-763-8500
Maine Medical Assn 30 Assn Dr	Manchester	ME	04351	**800-772-0815**	207-622-3374
Maryland State Medical Society 1211 Cathedral St	Baltimore	MD	21201	**800-492-1056**	410-539-0872
Massachusetts Medical Society (MMS) 860 Winter St	Waltham	MA	02451	**800-322-2303**	781-893-4610
Medical Assn of Georgia (MAG) 1849 The Exchange Ste 200	Atlanta	GA	30339	**800-282-0224**	678-303-9290
Missouri State Medical Assn 113 Madison St	Jefferson City	MO	65101	**800-869-6762**	573-636-5151
Montana Medical Assn 2021 11th Ave Ste 1	Helena	MT	59601	**877-443-4000**	406-443-4000
New Hampshire Medical Society 7 N State St	Concord	NH	03301	**800-564-1909**	603-224-1909
New Jersey Medical Society 2 Princess Rd	Lawrenceville	NJ	08648	**800-706-7893**	609-896-1766
New Mexico Medical Society (NMMS) 316 Osuna Rd NE Ste 501	Albuquerque	NM	87107	**800-748-1596**	505-828-0237
New York State Medical Society 865 Merrick Ave PO Box 5404	Westbury	NY	11590	**800-523-4405**	516-488-6100
North Carolina Medical Society 222 N Person St	Raleigh	NC	27601	**800-722-1350**	919-833-3836
Ohio State Medical Assn 3401 Mill Run Dr	Hilliard	OH	43026	**800-766-6762**	614-527-6762
Oregon Medical Assn (OMA) 11740 SW 68th Pkwy Ste 100	Portland	OR	97223	**877-605-3229**	503-619-8000
Pennsylvania Medical Society 777 E Pk Dr	Harrisburg	PA	17111	**800-228-7823**	717-558-7750
Rhode Island Medical Society 235 Promenade St Ste 500	Providence	RI	02908	**800-343-7776**	401-331-3207
South Carolina Medical Assn 132 W Pk Blvd	Columbia	SC	29210	**800-327-1021**	803-798-6207
Texas Medical Assn 401 W 15th St	Austin	TX	78701	**800-880-1300**	512-370-1300
Vermont Medical Society 134 Main St	Montpelier	VT	05601	**800-640-8767**	802-223-7898
Virginia Medical Society 4205 Dover Rd	Richmond	VA	23221	**800-746-6768**	804-353-2721
Washington State Medical Assn 2033 Sixth Ave Ste 1100	Seattle	WA	98121	**800-552-0612**	206-441-9762
West Virginia State Medical Assn 4307 MacCorkle Ave SE PO Box 4106	Charleston	WV	25364	**800-257-4747**	304-925-0342
Wisconsin State Medical Society 330 E Lakeside St	Madison	WI	53701	**866-442-3800**	
Wyoming Medical Society 122 E 17th St	Cheyenne	WY	82001	**888-879-3599**	307-635-2424

474 MEDICAL & DENTAL EQUIPMENT & SUPPLIES - WHOL

Company / Address	City	State	Zip	Toll-Free	Phone
A Plus International Inc 5138 Eucalyptus Ave	Chino	CA	91710	**800-762-1123**	909-591-5168
ABC Home Medical Supply Inc 15 E Uwchlan Ave Ste 430	Exton	PA	19341	**866-897-8588**	
Ace Medical Inc 94-910 Moloalo St	Waipahu	HI	96797	**866-678-3601**	808-678-3600
Aeroflow Inc 3165 Sweeten Creek Rd	Asheville	NC	28803	**888-345-1780**	
Aktina Medical Physics Corp 360 N Route 9W	Congers	NY	10920	**888-433-3380**	845-268-0101
Alpha Imaging Inc 4455 Glenbrook Rd	Willoughby	OH	44094	**800-331-7327**	440-953-3800
Amber Diagnostics Inc 2180 Premier Row	Orlando	FL	32809	**866-919-2959**	407-438-7847
Amendia Inc 1755 W Oak Pkwy	Marietta	GA	30062	**877-755-3329**	678-445-3784
American Medical ID 949 Wakefield Ste 100	Houston	TX	77018	**800-363-5985**	
Ampronix Inc 15 Whatney	Irvine	CA	92618	**800-400-7972**	949-273-8000
Andrew Technologies LLC 1421 Edinger Ave Ste D	Tustin	CA	92780	**888-959-7674**	
Anesthesia Service Inc 1821 N Classen Blvd	Oklahoma City	OK	73106	**800-336-3356**	405-525-3588
Ansar Group Inc, The 240 S Eigth St	Philadelphia	PA	19107	**888-883-7804**	215-922-6088

Classified Section

Company / Address	City	State	ZIP	Toll-Free	Phone
Aqueduct Medical Inc 665 Third St Ste 20	San Francisco	CA	94107	**877-365-4325**	
Avalign Technologies Inc 272 E Deerpath Rd Ste 208	Lake Forest	IL	60045	**855-282-5446**	
Banyan International Corp 11629 49th Pl W	Mukilteo	WA	98275	**888-782-8548**	325-677-1372
Benco Dental Co 295 CenterPoint Blvd	Pittston	PA	18640	**800-462-3626**	
Bisco Dental Products (Canada) Inc 2571 Smith St	Richmond	BC	V6X2J1	**800-667-8811**	604-276-8662
Blue Ridge X-Ray Company Inc 120 Vista Blvd	Arden	NC	28704	**800-727-7290**	
Burkhart Dental Supply Co 2502 S 78th St *Cust Svc	Tacoma	WA	98409	**800-562-8176***	253-474-7761
Butler Animal Health Supply LLC 400 Metro Pl N *PR	Dublin	OH	43017	**888-691-2724***	614-761-9095
Byram Healthcare Centers Inc 120 Bloomingdale Rd	White Plains	NY	10605	**800-354-4054**	914-286-2000
CAN-med Healthcare 200 Bluewater Rd	Bedford	NS	B4B1G9	**800-565-7553**	902-455-4649
Canadian Hospital Specialties ULC 2810 Coventry Rd	Oakville	ON	L6H6R1	**800-461-1423**	905-825-9300
CardioMed Supplies Inc 199 Saint David St	Lindsay	ON	K9V5K7	**800-387-9757**	705-328-2518
CCS Medical Inc 1505 LBJ Fwy Ste 600	Farmers Branch	TX	75234	**800-726-9811**	800-260-8193
Connect America LLC 2193 W Chester Pk	Broomall	PA	19008	**800-654-6100**	
Core Medical Imaging Inc 6161 Ne 175th St Ste 201	Kenmore	WA	98028	**800-809-9729**	425-485-4330
Dectro International Inc 1000 Blvd du Parc-Technologique	Quebec	QC	G1P4S3	**800-463-5566**	418-650-0303
Dedicated Distribution Inc 640 Miami Ave	Kansas City	KS	66105	**800-325-8367**	913-371-2200
Derma Sciences Inc 214 Carnegie Ctr Ste 100	Princeton	NJ	08540	**800-825-4325**	609-514-4744
Dr Fresh Inc 6645 Caballero Blvd	Buena Park	CA	90620	**866-373-7371**	714-690-1573
Enthermics Inc W164 N9221 Water St	Menomonee Falls	WI	53051	**800-862-9276**	262-251-8356
Evans-Sherratt Co 13050 Northend Ave	Oak Park	MI	48237	**800-248-3826**	248-584-5500
Expeditor Systems Inc 4090 Nine McFarland Dr	Alpharetta	GA	30004	**800-226-8158**	
Global Medical Imaging LLC 222 Rampart St	Charlotte	NC	28203	**800-958-9986**	
Global Medical LLC 8332 Bristol Ct Ste 108	Jessup	MD	20794	**800-528-1001**	
Goetze Dental 3939 NE 33 Terrace	Kansas City	MO	64117	**800-692-0804**	816-413-1200
Griswold Machine & Engineering Inc 8530 M 60	Union City	MI	49094	**800-248-2054**	517-741-4300
Grogans Health Care Supply Inc 1016 S Broadway St	Lexington	KY	40504	**800-365-1020**	859-254-6661
Hanson Medical Systems Inc 1954 Howell Branch Rd Ste 203	Winter Park	FL	32792	**877-671-3883**	407-671-3883
Healthcom 1600 W Jackson St	Sullivan	IL	61951	**800-525-6237**	
Henry Schein Inc 135 Duryea Rd *NASDAQ: HSIC*	Melville	NY	11747	**800-582-2702**	631-843-5500
Hospi Tel Manufacturing Corp 545 N Arlington Ave Ste 7	East Orange	NJ	07017	**800-631-0462**	973-678-7100
International Manufacturing Group Inc 879 F St Ste 120	West Sacramento	CA	95605	**800-775-6412**	
Jorgensen Laboratories Inc 1450 Van Buren Ave	Loveland	CO	80538	**800-525-5614**	970-669-2500
Karl Storz Endoscopy-america Inc 600 Corporate Pt	Culver City	CA	90230	**800-321-1304**	310-338-8100
KCI Medical Canada Inc 75 Courtneypark Dr W Unit No 2	Mississauga	ON	L5W0E3	**800-668-5403**	905-565-7187
Kentec Medical Inc 17871 Fitch	Irvine	CA	92614	**800-825-5996**	949-863-0810
Keystone Industries 480 S Democrat Rd	Gibbstown	NJ	08027	**800-333-3131**	856-663-4700
Leeches USA Ltd 300 Shames Dr	Westbury	NY	11590	**800-645-3569**	516-333-2570
LENSAR Inc 2800 Discovery Dr	Orlando	FL	32826	**888-536-7271**	
Les Wilkins & Assoc Inc 6850 35th Ave NE	Seattle	WA	98115	**800-426-6634**	206-522-0908
Life-Assist Inc 11277 Sunrise Park Dr	Rancho Cordova	CA	95742	**800-824-6016**	
Mabis Healthcare Inc 1931 Norman Dr	Waukegan	IL	60085	**800-526-4753**	
Mada Medical Products Inc 625 Washington Ave	Carlstadt	NJ	07072	**800-526-6370**	201-460-0454
Maquet-Dynamed Inc 235 Shields Ct	Markham	ON	L3R8V2	**800-227-7215**	905-752-3300
Marketlab Inc 6850 Southbelt Dr	Caledonia	MI	49316	**866-237-3722**	
MC Healthcare Products Inc 4658 Ontario St	Beamsville	ON	L0R1B4	**800-268-8671**	
McKesson Medical Group Extended Care 8121 Tenth Ave N	Golden Valley	MN	55427	**800-328-8111**	
McKesson Medical-Surgical 8741 Landmark Rd	Richmond	VA	23228	**800-446-3008**	415-983-8300
Mesa Laboratories Inc 12100 W Sixth Ave *NASDAQ: MLAB* *Sales	Lakewood	CO	80228	**800-992-6372***	303-987-8000
Mio 2930 Arbutus St	Vancouver	BC	V6J3Y9	**877-770-1116**	604-224-9184
Moore Medical Corp 389 John Downey Dr *Sales	New Britain	CT	06050	**800-234-1464***	860-826-3600
Neuro-Tec Inc 975 Cobb Pl Blvd Ste 301	Kennesaw	GA	30144	**800-554-3407**	

Company / Address	City	State	ZIP	Toll-Free	Phone
Nihon Kohden America Inc 90 Icon	Foothill Ranch	CA	92610	**800-325-0283**	949-580-1555
novoGI Inc PO Box 12363	Atlanta	GA	30355	**866-295-7125**	
Oakworks Inc 923 E Wellspring Rd	New Freedom	PA	17349	**800-558-8850**	717-235-6807
Omega Medical Health Systems Inc 1200 E High St Ste 106	Pottstown	PA	19464	**866-716-6342**	
Omron Healthcare Inc 1925 W Field Ct	Lake Forest	IL	60045	**877-216-1333**	847-680-6200
Optonol Inc P.O. Box 2367	Kansas City	KS	66110	**877-707-3937**	
Oral-B Laboratories 600 Clipper Dr Ste 200	Belmont	CA	94002	**800-566-7252**	
Orthopedic Designs North America Inc 5912 Breckenridge Pkwy Ste F	Tampa	FL	33610	**888-635-8535**	
Otto Bock Healthcare North America Inc 2 Carlson Pkwy N Ste 100	Minneapolis	MN	55447	**800-328-4058**	763-553-9464
Patterson Cos Inc 1031 Mendota Heights Rd *NASDAQ: PDCO*	Saint Paul	MN	55120	**800-328-5536**	651-686-1600
Pearson Dental Supplies Inc 13161 Telfair Ave	Sylmar	CA	91342	**800-535-4535**	818-362-2600
Permobil Inc 6961 Eastgate Blvd	Lebanon	TN	37090	**800-736-0925**	615-443-2839
PerSys Medical Co 5310 Elm St	Houston	TX	77081	**888-737-7978**	
Platinum Medical Imaging LLC 1027 SW 30th Ave	Deerfield Beach	FL	33442	**888-673-5151**	
Precision BioLogic Inc 140 Eileen Stubbs Ave	Dartmouth	NS	B3B0A9	**800-267-2796**	902-468-6422
Prestige Medical Corporation International 8600 Wilbur Ave	Northridge	CA	91324	**800-762-3333**	818-993-3030
Prima Tech USA 277 Faison McGowan Rd Ste 2	Kenansville	NC	28349	**800-458-7454**	910-296-6116
Radiancy Inc 40 Ramland Rd S Ste 200	Orangeburg	NY	10962	**888-661-2220**	845-398-1647
RedRick Technologies Inc 21624 Adelaide Rd	Mount Brydges	ON	N0L1W0	**800-340-9511**	519-264-2400
Reshape Medical 100 Calle Iglesia	San Clemente	CA	92672	**844-937-7374**	
Rgh Enterprises Inc 1810 Summit Commerce Pk	Twinsburg	OH	44087	**800-307-5930**	330-963-6998
Roka Bioscience Inc 20 Independence Blvd 4th Fl	Warren	NJ	07059	**855-765-2246**	908-605-4700
Saebo Inc 2725 Water Ridge Pkwy Ste 320 Six LakePointe Plaza	Charlotte	NC	28217	**888-284-5433**	
SameDay Security Inc 133 S Church St	Las Cruces	NM	88001	**866-572-3274**	
Savoy Technical Services Inc 4301 Hwy 27 South	Sulphur	LA	70665	**877-703-3235**	337-558-6071
Sebacia Inc 2905 Premiere Pkwy Ste 150	Duluth	GA	30097	**888-935-4411**	
SinuSys Corp 4030 Fabian Way	Palo Alto	CA	94303	**855-474-6879**	650-213-9988
SmartScrubs LLC 3400 E Mcdowell Rd	Phoenix	AZ	85008	**800-800-5788**	
Somagen Diagnostics Inc 9220 25th Ave	Edmonton	AB	T6N1E1	**800-661-9993**	780-702-9500
Specialty Surgical Products Inc 1131 Us Hwy 93 N	Victor	MT	59875	**888-878-0811**	406-961-0102
Surgical Principals Inc 1625 S Tacoma Way	Tacoma	WA	98409	**888-801-9251**	
Sysmex America Inc 1 Nelson C White Pkwy	Mundelein	IL	60060	**800-379-7639**	847-996-4500
Tech West Vacuum Inc 2625 N Argyle Ave	Fresno	CA	93727	**800-428-7139**	559-291-1650
Technical Instrument San Francisco 1826 Rollins Rd	Burlingame	CA	94010	**866-800-9797**	650-651-3000
Tetra Medical Supply Corp 6364 W Gross Pt Rd *Cust Svc	Niles	IL	60714	**800-621-4041***	847-647-0590
Thermedx LLC 31200 Solon Rd Unit 1	Solon	OH	44139	**888-542-9276**	440-542-0883
TPC Advance Technology Inc 18525 Gale Ave	City Of Industry	CA	91748	**800-560-8222**	626-810-4337
Trans Med USA Inc 31 Progress Ave	Tyngsboro	MA	01879	**800-442-1142**	978-649-1970
Tri State Distribution Inc 600 Vista Dr	Sparta	TN	38583	**800-392-9824**	
Triangle X-ray Co 4900 Thornton Rd Ste 117	Raleigh	NC	27616	**866-763-9729**	919-876-6156
Trudell Medical Group Ltd 758 Third St	London	ON	N5V5J7	**800-757-4881**	519-685-8800
Valeritas Inc 750 Rt 202 S Ste 600	Bridgewater	NJ	08807	**855-384-8848**	908-927-9920
VWR International 100 Matsonford Rd Bldg 1 Ste 200	Radnorpa	PA	19087	**800-932-5000**	610-431-1700
William V MacGill & Co 1000 N LombaRd Rd	Lombard	IL	60148	**800-323-2841**	630-889-0500
Zee Medical Inc 22 Corporate Pk	Irvine	CA	92606	**800-435-7763**	

MEDICAL FACILITIES

SEE Substance Abuse Treatment Centers ; Developmental Centers ; Health Care Providers - Ancillary ; Hospices ; Hospitals ; Imaging Services - Diagnostic

475 MEDICAL INSTRUMENTS & APPARATUS - MFR

SEE ALSO Imaging Equipment & Systems - Medical ; Medical Supplies - Mfr

Company / Address	City	State	ZIP	Toll-Free	Phone
Accurate Surgical & Scientific Instruments Corp 300 Shames Dr	Westbury	NY	11590	**800-645-3569**	516-333-2570

Company / Address	City	State	ZIP	Toll-Free	Phone
Accuray Inc 1310 Chesapeake Terr *NASDAQ: ARAY*	Sunnyvale	CA	94089	**888-522-3740**	408-716-4600
ACIST Medical Systems Inc 7905 Fuller Rd	Eden Prairie	MN	55344	**888-667-6648**	952-941-3507
Acme United Corp 60 Round Hill Rd *NYSE: ACU*	Fairfield	CT	06824	**800-835-2263**	203-254-6060
Ad-tech Medical Instrument Inc 1901 William St	Racine	WI	53404	**800-776-1555**	262-634-1555
AESCULAP Inc 3773 Corporate Pkwy	Center Valley	PA	18034	**800-282-9000**	
Allied Healthcare Products Inc 1720 Sublette Ave *NASDAQ: AHPI*	Saint Louis	MO	63110	**800-444-3954**	314-771-2400
Altimate Medical Inc 262 W First St	Morton	MN	56270	**800-342-8968**	507-697-6393
Andover Healthcare Inc 9 Fanaras Dr	Salisbury	MA	01952	**800-432-6686**	978-465-0044
Artisan Laboratories Inc 2532 Se Hawthorne Blvd	Portland	OR	97214	**800-222-6721**	503-238-6006
Aspen Medical Products 6481 Oak Cyn	Irvine	CA	92618	**800-295-2776**	949-681-0200
Atrium Medical Corp 5 Wentworth Dr	Hudson	NH	03051	**800-528-7486**	603-880-1433
B Braun Medical Inc 824 12th Ave	Bethlehem	PA	18018	**800-523-9676**	610-691-5400
Bard Access Systems Inc 605 North 5600 West	Salt Lake City	UT	84116	**800-443-5505**	801-522-5000
Bard Inc Peripheral Vascular 1625 W Third St	Tempe	AZ	85281	**800-321-4254**	480-894-9515
Baxter International Inc 1 Baxter Pkwy *NYSE: BAX*	Deerfield	IL	60015	**800-422-9837**	847-948-2000
BD Medical 9450 S State St	Sandy	UT	84070	**888-237-2762**	801-565-2300
Becton Dickinson & Co 1 Becton Dr *NYSE: BDX* ■ *Cust Svc	Franklin Lakes	NJ	07417	**888-237-2762***	201-847-6800
Beekley Corp 1 Prestige Ln	Bristol	CT	06010	**800-233-5539**	860-583-4700
Best Theratronics Ltd 413 March Rd	Ottawa	ON	K2K0E4	**866-792-8598**	613-591-2100
Best Vascular 4350 International Blvd Ste A	Norcross	GA	30093	**800-668-6783**	770-717-0904
Bio Compression Systems Inc 120 W Commercial Ave	Moonachie	NJ	07074	**800-888-0908**	201-939-0716
BioCardia Inc 125 Shoreway Rd Ste B	San Carlos	CA	94070	**800-624-1179**	650-226-0120
Biodex Medical Systems Inc 20 Ramsay Rd	Shirley	NY	11967	**800-224-6339**	631-924-9000
Bioflex Low Intensity Laser System 411 Horner Ave	Etobicoke	ON	M8W4W3	**888-557-4004**	416-251-1055
BioMerieux Inc 595 Anglum Rd	Hazelwood	MO	63042	**800-634-7656**	314-731-8500
Biomet Microfixation Inc 1520 Tradeport Dr	Jacksonville	FL	32218	**800-874-7711**	904-741-4400
Bioseal 167 W Orangethorpe Ave	Placentia	CA	92870	**800-441-7325**	714-528-4695
Biosense Webster Inc 3333 S Diamond Canyon Rd	Diamond Bar	CA	91765	**800-729-9010**	909-839-8500
Blackburn's Physicians Pharmacy Inc 301 Corbet St	Tarentum	PA	15084	**800-472-2440**	724-224-9100
Boston Scientific Corp 1 Boston Scientific Pl *NYSE: BSX*	Natick	MA	01760	**888-272-1001**	508-650-8000
Braemar Inc 1285 Corporate Ctr Dr	Eagan	MN	55121	**800-328-2719**	651-286-8620
Bunnell Inc 436 Lawndale Dr	Salt Lake City	UT	84115	**800-800-4358**	801-467-0800
Cadwell Laboratories Inc 909 N Kellogg St	Kennewick	WA	99336	**800-245-3001**	509-735-6481
Cambridge Heart Inc 46 Jonspin Rd	Wilmington	MA	01887	**888-226-9283**	978-654-7600
CardiacAssist Inc 240 Alpha Dr	Pittsburgh	PA	15238	**800-373-1607**	412-963-7770
Cardica Inc 900 Saginaw Dr *NASDAQ: CRDC*	Redwood City	CA	94063	**888-544-7194**	650-364-9975
Cardiovascular Systems Inc 1225 Old H 8 NW	St Paul	MN	55112	**877-274-0360**	651-259-1600
CareFusion Corp 3750 Torrey View Ct *NYSE: CFN*	San Diego	CA	92130	**888-876-4287**	858-617-2000
CAS Medical Systems Inc 44 E Industrial Rd *NASDAQ: CASM*	Branford	CT	06405	**800-227-4414**	203-488-6056
Celsion Corp 10220-L Old Columbia Rd *NASDAQ: CLSN*	Columbia	MD	21046	**888-504-7965**	410-290-5390
Chad Therapeutics Inc 2975 Horseshoe Dr S Ste 600 *OTC: CHADQ*	Naples	FL	34104	**800-423-8870**	239-687-1285
Conmed Corp 525 French Rd *NASDAQ: CNMD*	Utica	NY	13502	**800-448-6506**	315-797-8375
ConMed Endoscopic Technologie 525 French Rd	Utica	NY	13502	**800-225-1332**	315-797-8375
CONMED Linvatec 11311 Concept Blvd *Cust Svc	Largo	FL	33773	**800-448-6506***	727-392-6464
Cook Inc PO Box 4195	Bloomington	IN	47402	**800-457-4500**	812-339-2235
Cook Medical Inc 1186 Montgomery Ln *General	Vandergrift	PA	15690	**800-457-4500***	724-845-8621
Cook Urological Inc PO Box 4195	Bloomington	IN	47402	**800-457-4500**	812-339-2235
Cooper Cos Inc 6140 Stoneridge Mall Rd Ste 590 *NYSE: COO*	Pleasanton	CA	94588	**888-822-2660**	925-460-3600
CooperSurgical Inc 95 Corporate Dr	Trumbull	CT	06611	**800-645-3760**	203-929-6321
Cordis Corp 14201 NW 60th Ave	Miami Lakes	FL	33014	**800-327-7714**	800-447-7585
Corpak Medsystems Inc 1001 Asbury Dr	Buffalo Grove	IL	60089	**800-323-6305**	847-403-3400
CP Medical Inc 803 NE 25th Ave	Portland	OR	97232	**800-950-2763**	503-232-1555
CR Bard Inc Urological Div 8195 Industrial Blvd	Covington	GA	30014	**800-526-4455**	770-784-6100
Cutera Inc 3240 Bayshore Blvd *NASDAQ: CUTR*	Brisbane	CA	94005	**888-428-8372**	415-657-5500
Cutting Edge Products LLC 1000 Turk Hill Rd	Fairport	NY	14450	**800-497-0539**	252-830-5577
Dale Medical Products Inc PO Box 1556	Plainville	MA	02762	**800-343-3980**	
Davol Inc 100 Crossings Blvd *Cust Svc	Warwick	RI	02886	**800-556-6756***	
Defibtech LLC 741 Boston Post Rd Ste 201	Guilford	CT	06437	**866-333-4248**	203-453-4507
Encision Inc 6797 Winchester Cir *OTC: ECIA*	Boulder	CO	80301	**800-998-0986**	303-444-2600
Endologix Inc 11 Studebaker *NASDAQ: ELGX*	Irvine	CA	92618	**800-983-2284**	949-457-9546
Eternity Healthcare Inc Ste 1 8755 Ash St	Vancouver	BC	V6P6T3	**855-324-1110**	
ev3 Inc 3033 Campus Dr	Plymouth	MN	55441	**800-716-6700**	763-398-7000
First Quality Products Inc 121 N Rd	Mcelhattan	PA	17748	**800-227-3551**	570-769-6900
Gaymar Industries Inc 10 Centre Dr	Orchard Park	NY	14127	**800-828-7341**	716-662-2551
GEM Edwards Inc 5640 Hudson Industrial Pkwy PO Box 429	Hudson	OH	44236	**800-733-7976**	
GF Health Products Inc 2935 NE Pkwy	Atlanta	GA	30360	**800-347-5678**	770-447-1609
Great Basin Scientific Inc 420 E S Temple Ste A	Salt Lake City	UT	84111	**888-360-4022**	801-990-1055
Haemonetics Corp 400 Wood Rd *NYSE: HAE*	Braintree	MA	02184	**800-225-5242**	781-848-7100
Hartwell Medical Corp 6354 Corte Del Abeto Ste F	Carlsbad	CA	92011	**800-633-5900**	760-438-5500
Henry Troemner LLC 201 Wolf Dr	Thorofare	NJ	08086	**800-352-7705**	856-686-1600
Hill-Rom Services Inc 1069 SR 46 E	Batesville	IN	47006	**800-267-2337**	812-934-7777
Hoggan Health Industries Inc 8020 South 1300 West	West Jordan	UT	84088	**800-678-7888**	801-572-6500
Hospira Inc 275 N Field Dr *NYSE: HSP*	Lake Forest	IL	60045	**877-946-7747**	224-212-2000
Hospital Marketing Services Company Inc 162 Great Hill Rd	Naugatuck	CT	06770	**800-786-5094**	203-723-1466
Hypertension Diagnostics Inc 730 Bldg Ste 295	Minneapolis	MN	55402	**888-785-7392**	651-687-9999
Implant Sciences Corp 500 Research Dr *OTC: IMSC*	Wilmington	MA	01887	**877-732-7333**	978-752-1700
Inovise Medical Inc 8770 SW Nimbus Ave Ste D	Beaverton	OR	97008	**877-466-8473**	503-431-3800
Insulet Corp 9 Oak Park Dr	Bedford	MA	01730	**800-591-3455**	781-457-5000
Integra LifeSciences Holdings Corp 311 Enterprise Dr *NASDAQ: IART*	Plainsboro	NJ	08536	**800-654-2873**	609-275-0500
Intuitive Surgical Inc 1266 Kifer Rd Bldg 101 *NASDAQ: ISRG*	Sunnyvale	CA	94086	**888-868-4647**	408-523-2100
Joerns Healthcare 5001 Joerns Dr	Stevens Point	WI	54481	**800-826-0270**	715-341-3600
Johnson Matthey Medical Products 1401 King Rd	West Chester	PA	19380	**800-442-1405**	610-648-8000
Kensey Nash Corp 735 Pennsylvania Dr *NASDAQ: KNSY* ■ *General	Exton	PA	19341	**800-322-2885***	484-713-2100
Kinamed Inc 820 Flynn Rd	Camarillo	CA	93012	**800-827-5775**	805-384-2748
Kirwan Surgical Products Inc 180 Enterprise Dr	Marshfield	MA	02050	**888-547-9267**	781-834-9500
Knit Rite Inc 120 Osage Ave	Kansas City	KS	66105	**800-821-3094**	913-281-4600
Lake Region Mfg Company Inc 340 Lk Hazeltine Dr	Chaska	MN	55318	**866-899-1392**	
Landice Inc 111 Canfield Ave	Randolph	NJ	07869	**800-526-3423**	973-927-9010
MAQUET Cardiac Assist 15 Law Dr	Fairfield	NJ	07004	**800-777-4222**	973-244-6100
Medi-Nuclear Corp Inc 4610 Littlejohn St	Baldwin Park	CA	91706	**800-321-5981**	626-960-9822
Medica Corp 5 Oak Park Dr	Bedford	MA	01730	**800-777-5983**	781-275-4892
Medone Surgical Inc 670 Tallevast Rd	Sarasota	FL	34243	**866-633-6631**	941-359-3129
Medovations Inc 102 E Keefe Ave	Milwaukee	WI	53212	**800-558-6408**	414-265-7620
MedRx Inc 1200 Starkey Rd Ste 105	Largo	FL	33771	**888-392-1234**	727-584-9600
Medtronic Inc 710 Medtronic Pkwy NE *NYSE: MDT* ■ *Cust Svc	Minneapolis	MN	55432	**800-328-2518***	763-514-4000
Medtronic Neurosurgery 125 Cremona Dr *Cust Svc	Goleta	CA	93117	**800-468-9710***	800-633-8766
Medtronic Perfusion Systems 7611 Northland Dr	Brooklyn Park	MN	55428	**800-328-3320**	763-391-9000
Megadyne Medical Products Inc 11506 S State St	Draper	UT	84020	**800-747-6110**	801-576-9669
Mercury Medical 11300 49th St N	Clearwater	FL	33762	**800-237-6418**	727-573-0088
Meridian Medical Technologies Inc 6350 Stevens Forest Rd Ste 301	Columbia	MD	21046	**800-638-8093**	443-259-7800

Classified Section

Company / Address	City	State	Zip	Toll-Free	Phone
Merit Medical Systems Inc 1600 W Merit Pkwy *NASDAQ: MMSI*	South Jordan	UT	84095	**800-356-3748**	801-253-1600
MicroAire Surgical Instruments Inc 3590 Grand Forks Blvd	Charlottesville	VA	22911	**800-722-0822**	
Microlife USA Inc 1617 Gulf to Bay Blvd Second Fl Ste B	Clearwater	FL	33755	**888-314-2599**	727-451-0484
Midmark Corp 60 Vista Dr	Versailles	OH	45380	**800-643-6275**	937-526-3662
MiMedx Group Inc 1775 W Oak Commons Ct Ne	Marietta	GA	30062	**888-543-1917**	
Minntech Corp 14605 28th Ave N	Minneapolis	MN	55447	**800-328-3345**	763-553-3300
Mott Corp 84 Spring Ln	Farmington	CT	06032	**800-289-6688**	860-747-6333
MPM Medical Inc 2301 Crown Ct	Irving	TX	75038	**800-232-5512**	972-893-4090
Mui Scientific 145 Traders Blvd E	Mississauga	ON	L4Z3L3	**800-303-6611**	905-890-5525
Nasiff Associates 841 County Rt 37	Central Square	NY	13036	**866-627-4332**	315-676-2346
Novosci 2021 Airport Rd	Conroe	TX	77301	**800-854-0567**	281-363-4949
Nspire Health Inc 1830 Lefthand Cir	Longmont	CO	80501	**800-574-7374**	303-666-5555
Nubenco Medical 1 Kalisa Way Ste 207	Paramus	NJ	07652	**800-633-1322**	201-967-9000
NuVasive Inc 7475 Lusk Blvd *NASDAQ: NUVA*	San Diego	CA	92121	**800-475-9131**	858-909-1800
NxStage Medical Inc 439 S Union St 5th Fl *NASDAQ: NXTM*	Lawrence	MA	01843	**866-697-8243**	978-687-4700
Occk Inc 1710 W Schilling Rd	Salina	KS	67401	**800-526-9731**	785-827-9383
Ortho Technology Inc 17401 Commerce Park Blvd	Tampa	FL	33647	**800-999-3161**	813-991-5896
Ortho-Clinical Diagnostics Inc 1001 US Rt 202 N PO Box 350	Raritan	NJ	08869	**800-828-6316**	
ORTHOCON Inc 1 Bridge St Ste 121	Irvington	NY	10533	**888-445-6784**	914-357-2600
Osteomed Corp 3885 Arapaho Rd *Cust Svc	Addison	TX	75001	**800-456-7779***	972-677-4600
Oxus America Inc 1685 Northfield Dr	Rochester Hills	MI	48309	**888-475-1568**	
Pepose Vision Institute PC 1815 Clarkson Rd	Chesterfield	MO	63017	**877-862-2020**	636-728-0111
Peregrine Surgical Ltd 51 Britain Dr	New Britain	PA	18901	**877-348-0456**	215-348-0456
Pilling Surgical 2917 Weck Dr *Cust Svc	Research Triangle Park	NC	27709	**866-246-6990***	919-544-8000
Prism Medical Ltd Unit 2 485 Millway Ave	Concord	ON	L4K3V4	**877-304-5438**	416-260-2145
Prodigy Diabetes Care LLC 2701-A Hutchison McDonald Rd PO Box 481928	Charlotte	NC	28269	**800-366-5901**	
Promedica Inc 114 Douglas Rd E	Oldsmar	FL	34677	**800-899-5278**	813-854-1905
Pronk Technologies Inc 8933 Lankershim Blvd	Sun Valley	CA	91352	**800-609-9802**	818-768-5600
Propper Mfg Company Inc 36-04 Skillman Ave *Cust Svc	Long Island	NY	11101	**800-832-4300***	718-392-6650
Pryor Products 1819 Peacock Blvd	Oceanside	CA	92056	**800-854-2280**	760-724-8244
ResMed Inc 9001 Spectrum Ctr Blvd *NYSE: RMD*	San Diego	CA	92123	**800-424-0737**	858-836-5000
Saint Jude Medical St Jude Medical Inc *NYSE: STJ*	St Paul	MN	55117	**800-328-9634**	651-756-2000
Salter Labs 100 Sycamore Rd	Arvin	CA	93203	**800-421-0024**	661-854-3166
Sechrist Industries Inc 4225 E La Palma Ave	Anaheim	CA	92807	**800-732-4747**	714-579-8400
Shofu Dental Corp 1225 Stone Dr	San Marcos	CA	92078	**800-827-4638**	760-736-3277
Siemens Medical Solutions Inc 51 Valley Stream Pkwy	Malvern	PA	19355	**800-888-7436**	888-826-9702
Smith & Nephew Inc Endoscopy Div 150 Minuteman Rd	Andover	MA	01810	**800-343-5717**	978-749-1000
Smiths Medical MD Inc 1265 Grey Fox Rd	Saint Paul	MN	55112	**800-258-5361**	651-633-2556
Sorin Group USA Inc 14401 W 65th Way	Arvada	CO	80004	**800-289-5759**	303-424-0129
Specialty Silicone Fabricators 3077 Rollie Gates Dr	Paso Robles	CA	93446	**800-394-4284**	805-239-4284
Starplex Scientific Inc 50 A Steinway Blvd	Etobicoke	ON	M9W6Y3	**800-665-0954**	416-674-7474
STERIS Corp 5960 Heisley Rd *NYSE: STE*	Mentor	OH	44060	**800-548-4873**	440-354-2600
Stryker Canada LP 45 Innovation Dr	Hamilton	ON	L9H7L8	**800-668-8324**	
Stryker Corp 2825 Airview Blvd *NYSE: SYK*	Kalamazoo	MI	49002	**800-616-1406**	269-385-2600
Synergetics USA Inc 3845 Corporate Ctr Dr *NASDAQ: SURG*	O'Fallon	MO	63368	**800-600-0565**	636-939-5100
Techno-Aide Inc 7117 Centennial Blvd	Nashville	TN	37209	**800-251-2629**	615-350-7030
TERATECH Corp 77-79 Terr Hall Ave	Burlington	MA	01803	**866-837-2766**	781-270-4143
Terumo Cardiovascular Systems Corp 6200 Jackson Rd	Ann Arbor	MI	48103	**800-262-3304**	734-663-4145
Terumo Medical Corp 2101 Cottontail Ln	Somerset	NJ	08873	**800-283-7866**	732-302-4900
TFX Medical Inc 50 Plantation Dr	Jaffrey	NH	03452	**800-548-6600**	603-532-7706
Topcon Medical Systems Inc 111 Bauer Dr	Oakland	NJ	07436	**800-223-1130**	201-599-5100
United States Endoscopy Group Inc 5976 Heisley Rd	Mentor	OH	44060	**800-769-8226**	440-639-4494
Urologix Inc 14405 21st Ave N	Minneapolis	MN	55447	**800-475-1403**	763-475-1400
Utah Medical Products Inc 7043 S 300 W *NASDAQ: UTMD*	Midvale	UT	84047	**866-754-9789**	801-566-1200
Vasamed Inc 7615 Golden Triangle Dr Ste A	Eden Prairie	MN	55344	**800-695-2737**	
Vascular Solutions Inc 6464 Sycamore Ct *NASDAQ: VASC*	Minneapolis	MN	55369	**877-979-4300**	763-656-4300
Ventana Medical Systems Inc 1910 Innovation Pk Dr	Tucson	AZ	85755	**800-227-2155**	520-887-2155
Veridex LLC 700 US Hwy Rt 202 S	Raritan	NJ	08869	**877-837-4339**	
Vital Signs Inc 20 Campus Rd	Totowa	NJ	07512	**800-932-0760**	973-790-1330
VitalAire Canada Inc 6990 Creditview Rd Unit 6	Mississauga	ON	L5N8R9	**888-629-0202**	
Vivosonic Inc 120-5525 Eglinton Ave W	Toronto	ON	M9C5K5	**877-255-7685**	416-231-9997
W A Baum Company Inc 620 Oak St	Copiague	NY	11726	**888-281-6061**	631-226-3940
WalkMed Infusion LLC 6555 S Kenton St Ste 304	Centennial	CO	80111	**800-578-0555**	303-420-9569
Wells Johnson Co 8000 S Kolb Rd	Tucson	AZ	85756	**800-528-1597**	520-298-6069
Wexler Surgical Supplies 11333 Chimney Rock Rd	Houston	TX	77035	**800-414-1076**	713-723-6900

476 MEDICAL SUPPLIES - MFR

SEE ALSO Personal Protective Equipment & Clothing

Company / Address	City	State	Zip	Toll-Free	Phone
Adhesives Research Inc 400 Seaks Run Rd PO Box 100	Glen Rock	PA	17327	**800-445-6240**	717-235-7979
Adroit Medical Systems Inc 1146 CaRding Machine Rd	Loudon	TN	37774	**800-267-6077**	
Advanced Sterilization Products (ASP) 33 Technology Dr	Irvine	CA	92618	**888-783-7723**	
AESCULAP Inc 3773 Corporate Pkwy	Center Valley	PA	18034	**800-282-9000**	
Allergan 2525 Dupont Dr PO Box 19534	Irvine	CA	92612	**800-347-4500**	714-246-4500
Allied Healthcare Products Inc 1720 Sublette Ave *NASDAQ: AHPI*	Saint Louis	MO	63110	**800-444-3954**	314-771-2400
AMG Medical Inc 8505 Dalton	Montreal	QC	H4T1V5	**800-363-2381**	514-737-5251
Animas Corp 200 Lawrence Dr	West Chester	PA	19380	**877-937-7867**	610-644-8990
Armstrong Medical Industries Inc 575 Knightsbridge Pkwy *Cust Svc	Lincolnshire	IL	60069	**800-323-4220***	847-913-0101
Arthrex Inc 1370 Creekside Blvd	Naples	FL	34108	**800-934-4404**	239-643-5553
Aspen Surgical 6945 Southbelt Dr SE	Caledonia	MI	49316	**888-364-7004**	616-698-7100
Avery Dennison Corp 207 Goode Ave *NYSE: AVY* ■ *Cust Svc	Glendale	CA	91203	**888-567-4387***	626-304-2000
Baxter International Inc 1 Baxter Pkwy *NYSE: BAX*	Deerfield	IL	60015	**800-422-9837**	847-948-2000
Baylis Medical Company Inc 5959 Trans-Canada Hwy	Montreal	QC	H4T1A1	**800-850-9801**	514-488-9801
Becton Dickinson & Co 1 Becton Dr *NYSE: BDX* ■ *Cust Svc	Franklin Lakes	NJ	07417	**888-237-2762***	201-847-6800
Beltone Electronics Corp 2601 Patriot Blvd	Glenview	IL	60026	**800-235-8663**	847-832-3300
BioHorizons Inc 2300 Riverchase Ctr	Birmingham	AL	35244	**888-246-8338**	205-967-7880
Biomet Inc 56 E Bell Dr PO Box 587	Warsaw	IN	46582	**800-348-9500**	574-267-6639
Bristol-Myers Squibb Co 345 Pk Ave *NYSE: BMY*	New York	NY	10154	**800-332-2056**	212-546-4000
BSN Medical Inc 5825 Carnegie Blvd	Charlotte	NC	28209	**800-552-1157**	704-554-9933
Burke Inc 1800 Merriam Ln *Sales	Kansas City	KS	66106	**800-255-4147***	
Capstone Therapeutics Corp 1275 W Washington St Ste 101 *OTC: CAPS*	Tempe	AZ	85281	**800-937-5520**	602-286-5520
Centurion Medical Products 100 Centurion Way	Williamston	MI	48895	**800-248-4058**	517-546-5400
Chattanooga Group 4717 Adams Rd	Hixson	TN	37343	**800-592-7329**	423-870-2281
Community Surgical Supply Inc 1390 Rt 37 W	Toms River	NJ	08755	**800-349-2990**	732-349-2990
Consensus Orthopedics Inc 1115 Windfield Way Ste 100	El Dorado Hills	CA	95762	**800-638-2041**	916-355-7100
Conventus Orthopaedics Inc 10200 73rd Ave N Ste 122	Maple Grove	MN	55369	**855-418-6466**	763-515-5000
Cramer Products Inc 153 W Warren St	Gardner	KS	66030	**800-345-2231**	913-856-7511
Cyberonics Inc 100 Cyberonics Blvd The Cyberonics Bldg *NASDAQ: CYBX*	Houston	TX	77058	**800-332-1375**	281-228-7262
DeRoyal Industries Inc 200 DeBusk Ln	Powell	TN	37849	**800-251-9864**	865-938-7828
DJ Orthopedics Inc 1430 Decision St	Vista	CA	92081	**800-321-9549**	760-727-1280

Company / Address	City	State	Zip	Toll-Free	Phone
Dynarex Corporation 10 Glenshaw St	Orangeburg	NY	10962	**888-335-7500**	845-365-8200
Ehob Inc 250 N Belmont Ave	Indianapolis	IN	46222	**800-899-5553**	317-972-4600
Ergodyne Corp 1021 Bandana Blvd E Ste 220	Saint Paul	MN	55108	**800-225-8238**	651-642-9889
Exactech Inc 2320 NW 66th Ct *NASDAQ: EXAC*	Gainesville	FL	32653	**800-392-2832**	352-377-1140
Female Health Co 515 N State St Ste 2225	Chicago	IL	60654	**800-882-6655**	312-595-9123
Ferno-Washington Inc 70 Weil Way	Wilmington	OH	45177	**800-733-3766**	937-382-1451
Fillauer Inc PO Box 5189	Chattanooga	TN	37406	**800-251-6398**	423-624-0946
Freeman Manufacturing Co 900 W Chicago Rd	Sturgis	MI	49091	**800-253-2091**	269-651-2371
GF Health Products Inc 2935 NE Pkwy	Atlanta	GA	30360	**800-347-5678**	770-447-1609
Halyard Health 20202 Windrow Dr	Lake Forest	CA	92630	**800-448-3569**	949-206-2700
Hanger Orthopedic Group Inc 10910 Domain Dr Ste 300	Austin	TX	78758	**877-442-6437**	512-777-3800
Hanger Prosthetics & Orthopedics Inc 10910 Domain Dr Ste 300	Austin	TX	78758	**877-442-6437**	
Helvoet Pharma Inc 9012 Pennsauken Hwy	Pennsauken	NJ	08110	**800-874-3586**	856-663-2202
Hermell Products Inc 9 Britton Dr	Bloomfield	CT	06002	**800-233-2342**	860-242-6550
Hollister Inc 2000 Hollister Dr	Libertyville	IL	60048	**800-323-4060**	847-680-1000
Hospira Inc 275 N Field Dr *NYSE: HSP*	Lake Forest	IL	60045	**877-946-7747**	224-212-2000
Hoveround Corp 2151 Whitfield Industrial Way	Sarasota	FL	34243	**800-542-7236**	941-739-6200
Howard Leight Industries 7828 Waterville Rd	San Diego	CA	92154	**800-430-5490**	
Hy-Tape International Inc PO Box 540	Patterson	NY	12563	**800-248-0101**	
ICU Medical Inc 951 Calle Amanecer *NASDAQ: ICUI*	San Clemente	CA	92673	**800-824-7890**	949-366-2183
Ideal Tape Co 1400 Middlesex St	Lowell	MA	01851	**800-284-3325**	
Invacare Corp 1 Invacare Way *NYSE: IVC*	Elyria	OH	44036	**800-333-6900**	440-329-6000
Johnson & Johnson Consumer Products Co 199 Grandview Rd	Skillman	NJ	08558	**866-565-2229**	908-874-1000
Johnson & Johnson Inc 7101 Notre-Dame E	Montreal	QC	H1N2G4	**800-361-8990**	514-251-5100
K-Tube Technologies 13400 Kirkham Way	Poway	CA	92064	**800-394-0058**	858-513-9229
Kinetic Concepts Inc (KCI) PO Box 659508 *Cust Svc	San Antonio	TX	78265	**800-275-4524***	
Langer Inc 2905 Veterans' Memorial Hwy	Ronkonkoma	NY	11779	**800-645-5520**	
LPS Industries Inc 10 Caesar Pl *Sales	Moonachie	NJ	07074	**800-275-6577***	201-438-3515
M & C Specialties Co 90 James Way *Cust Svc	SouthHampton	PA	18966	**800-441-6996***	215-322-1600
Medical Action Industries Inc (MAI) 500 Expy Dr S *NASDAQ: MDCI*	Brentwood	NY	11717	**800-645-7042**	631-231-4600
Medtronic Inc 710 Medtronic Pkwy NE *NYSE: MDT* ■ *Cust Svc	Minneapolis	MN	55432	**800-328-2518***	763-514-4000
Medtronic MiniMed Inc 18000 Devonshire St	Northridge	CA	91325	**800-646-4633**	
Medtronic Powered Surgical Solutions 4620 N Beach St	Fort Worth	TX	76137	**800-643-2773**	817-788-6400
Medtronic Surgical Technologies 6743 Southpoint Dr N	Jacksonville	FL	32216	**800-874-5797**	904-296-9600
Mentor Corp 201 Mentor Dr *NASDAQ: MENT*	Santa Barbara	CA	93111	**800-525-0245**	805-879-6000
Mettler Electronics Corp 1333 S Claudina St	Anaheim	CA	92805	**800-854-9305**	714-533-2221
Microtek Medical Holdings Inc 13000 Deerfield Pkwy Ste 300	Alpharetta	GA	30004	**800-777-7977**	678-896-4400
Microtek Medical Inc 512 N Lehmberg Rd	Columbus	MS	39702	**800-824-3027**	662-327-1863
MicroVention Inc 1311 Valencia Ave	Tustin	CA	92780	**800-990-8368**	714-247-8000
Milestone Scientific Inc 220 S Orange Ave *OTC: MLSS*	Livingston	NJ	07039	**800-862-1125**	973-535-2717
Miracle-Ear Inc 5000 Cheshire Pkwy N	Minneapolis	MN	55446	**800-464-8002**	
Monaghan Medical Corp 5 Latour Ave Ste 1600	Plattsburgh	NY	12901	**800-833-9653**	518-561-7330
MP Biomedicals LLC 3 Hutton Ctr Dr Ste 100	Santa Ana	CA	92707	**800-633-1352**	949-833-2500
Nearly Me Technologies Po Box 21475	Waco	TX	76702	**800-887-3370**	254-662-1752
NELCO Inc 3 Gill St Unit D	Woburn	MA	01801	**800-635-2613**	781-933-1940
Nice-Pak Products Inc 2 Nice-Pak Pk	Orangeburg	NY	10962	**800-444-6725**	845-365-1700
NorMed 4310 S 131 Pl Ste 160	Seattle	WA	98168	**800-288-8200**	
Nu-Hope Laboratories Inc 12640 Branford St	Pacoima	CA	91331	**800-899-5017**	818-899-7711
Ortho Development Corp 12187 S Business Pk Dr	Draper	UT	84020	**800-429-8339**	801-553-9991
Orthofix Inc 1720 Bray Central Dr	McKinney	TX	75069	**800-527-0404**	469-742-2500
OrthoPro LLC 3939 S Wasatch Blvd Ste 19	Salt Lake City	UT	84124	**866-746-0208**	
Osteomed Corp 3885 Arapaho Rd *Cust Svc	Addison	TX	75001	**800-456-7779***	972-677-4600
Pacific Medical Inc 1700 N Chrisman Rd	Tracy	CA	95304	**800-726-9180**	
Passy-Muir Inc 4521 Campus Dr Pmb 273	Irvine	CA	92612	**800-634-5397**	949-833-8255
Phonic Ear Inc 2080 Lakeville Hwy	Petaluma	CA	94954	**800-227-0735**	707-769-1110
Phygen LLC 2301 Dupont Ave Ste 510	Irvine	CA	92612	**800-939-7008**	
Posey Co 5635 Peck Rd	Arcadia	CA	91006	**800-447-6739**	626-443-3143
Precision Dynamics Corp 13880 Del Sur St	San Fernando	CA	91340	**800-847-0670**	818-897-1111
Pride Mobility Products Corp 182 Susquehanna Ave	Exeter	PA	18643	**800-800-8586**	
Pro Orthopedic Devices Inc 2884 E Ganley Rd	Tucson	AZ	85706	**800-523-5611**	520-294-4401
Prosthetic Design Inc 700 Harco Dr	Clayton	OH	45315	**800-459-0177**	937-836-1464
Retractable Technologies Inc 511 Lobo Ln *NYSE: RVP*	Little Elm	TX	75068	**888-806-2626**	972-294-1010
Rusch Inc 2917 Weck Dr PO Box 12600	Research Triangle Park	NC	27709	**866-246-6990**	919-544-8000
Sas Safety Corp 3031 Gardenia Ave	Long Beach	CA	90807	**800-262-0200**	562-427-2775
Siemens Hearing Instruments Inc 10 Constitution Ave PO Box 1397	Piscataway	NJ	08855	**800-766-4500**	
Smith & Nephew Inc 1450 E Brooks Rd *Cust Svc	Memphis	TN	38116	**800-238-7538***	901-396-2121
Smiths Medical ASD Inc 160 Weymouth St	Rockland	MA	02370	**800-258-5361**	781-878-8011
Smiths Medical MD Inc 1265 Grey Fox Rd	Saint Paul	MN	55112	**800-258-5361**	651-633-2556
Smiths Medical Respiratory Support Products 5200 Upper Metro Pl Ste 200	Dublin	OH	43017	**800-258-5361**	214-618-0218
Sonic Innovations Inc 2501 Cottontail Ln	Somerset	NJ	08873	**888-678-4327**	888-423-7834
Southmedic Inc 50 Alliance Blvd	Barrie	ON	L4M5K3	**800-463-7146**	705-726-9383
Span-America Medical Systems Inc 70 Commerce Ctr *NASDAQ: SPAN*	Greenville	SC	29615	**800-888-6752**	864-288-8877
Spenco Medical Corp PO Box 2501	Waco	TX	76702	**800-877-3626**	
Standard Textile Company Inc 1 Knollcrest Dr	Cincinnati	OH	45237	**800-999-0400**	513-761-9255
Starkey Laboratories Inc 6700 Washington Ave S	Eden Prairie	MN	55344	**800-328-8602**	952-941-6401
STERIS Corp 5960 Heisley Rd *NYSE: STE*	Mentor	OH	44060	**800-548-4873**	440-354-2600
Sunrise Medical Inc 2842 Business Pk Ave	Fresno	CA	93727	**800-333-4000**	
Surgical Appliance Industries Inc 3960 Rosslyn Dr	Cincinnati	OH	45209	**800-888-0867**	
Synovis Life Technologies Inc 2575 University Ave *NASDAQ: SYNO*	Saint Paul	MN	55114	**800-255-4018**	651-796-7300
Synthes USA 1302 Wrights Ln E	West Chester	PA	19380	**800-523-0322**	610-719-5000
Tamarack Habilitation Technologies Inc 1670 94th Ln NE	Blaine	MN	55449	**866-795-0057**	763-795-0057
TIDI Products LLC 570 Enterprise Dr	Neenah	WI	54956	**800-521-1314**	
TSO3 Inc 2505 Dalton Ave	Quebec	QC	G1P3S5	**866-715-0003**	418-651-0003
Utah Medical Products Inc 7043 S 300 W *NASDAQ: UTMD*	Midvale	UT	84047	**866-754-9789**	801-566-1200
Vital Signs Inc 20 Campus Rd	Totowa	NJ	07512	**800-932-0760**	973-790-1330
Volcano Corp 3721 Valley Centre Dr Ste 500	San Diego	CA	92130	**800-228-4728**	
West Pharmaceutical Services Inc 101 Gordon Dr *NYSE: WST*	Lionville	PA	19341	**800-345-9800**	610-594-2900
Wright Medical Group Inc 5677 Airline Rd *NASDAQ: WMGI*	Arlington	TN	38002	**800-238-7188**	901-867-9971
Wright Medical Technology Inc 5677 Airline Rd	Arlington	TN	38002	**800-238-7188**	901-867-9971
Zimmer Inc 1800 W Ctr St PO Box 708	Warsaw	IN	46580	**800-613-6131**	574-267-6131

477 MEDICAL TRANSCRIPTION SERVICES

Companies listed here have a national or regional clientele base.

Company / Address	City	State	Zip	Toll-Free	Phone
Carrier Services of Tennessee Inc 2534 N Mount Juliet Rd	Mount Juliet	TN	37122	**800-825-7508**	615-758-9757
FreightPros 3307 Northland Dr Ste 360	Austin	TX	78731	**888-297-6968**	
MediGrafix Inc 9 Fairway Ln Ste C	Blythewood	SC	29016	**888-744-1301**	803-261-6387
Thomas Transcription Services Inc PO Box 26613	Jacksonville	FL	32226	**888-878-2889**	904-751-5058
Warren Gibson Ltd 206 Church St South PO Box 100	Alliston	ON	L9R1T9	**800-461-4374**	705-435-4342

478 MEDICINAL CHEMICALS & BOTANICAL PRODUCTS

SEE ALSO Vitamins & Nutritional Supplements ; Diagnostic Products ; Pharmaceutical Companies ; Pharmaceutical Companies - Generic Drugs ; Biotechnology Companies

Companies listed here manufacture medicinal chemicals and botanical products in bulk for sale to pharmaceutical, vitamin, and nutritional product companies.

Company	Address	City	State	Zip	Toll-Free	Phone
Acic Fine Chemicals Inc	81 St Claire Blvd	Brantford	ON	N3S7X6	**800-265-6727**	519-751-3668
Array BioPharma Inc (*NASDAQ: ARRY*)	3200 Walnut St	Boulder	CO	80301	**877-633-2436**	303-381-6600
Avanti Polar Lipids Inc	700 Industrial Pk Dr	Alabaster	AL	35007	**800-227-0651**	205-663-2494
Bachem Bioscience Inc	3132 Kashiwa St	Torrance	CA	90505	**888-422-2436**	310-539-4171
Balchem Corp (*NASDAQ: BCPC*)	52 Sunrise Pk Rd PO Box 600	New Hampton	NY	10958	**877-407-8289**	845-326-5613
Bedford Laboratories Inc	300 Northfield Rd	Bedford	OH	44146	**800-562-4797**	440-232-3320
Ben Venue Laboratories Inc	300 Northfield Rd	Bedford	OH	44146	**800-989-3320*** (*General)	440-232-3320
Bio-Botanica Inc	75 Commerce Dr	Hauppauge	NY	11788	**800-645-5720**	631-231-5522
Cambrex Corp (*NYSE: CBM*)	1 Meadowlands Plz	East Rutherford	NJ	07073	**866-286-9133**	201-804-3000
Charm Sciences Inc	659 Andover St	Lawrence	MA	01843	**800-343-2170**	978-687-9200
Cyanotech Corp (*NASDAQ: CYAN*)	73-4460 Queen Kaahumanu Hwy Ste 102	Kailua-Kona	HI	96740	**800-453-1187*** (*Sales)	808-326-1353
Designing Health Inc	28410 Witherspoon Pkwy	Valencia	CA	91355	**800-774-7387**	661-257-1705
Flora Mfg & Distributing Ltd	7400 Fraser Park Dr	Burnaby	BC	V5J5B9	**888-436-6697**	604-436-6000
George Uhe Company Inc	219 River Dr	Garfield	NJ	07026	**800-850-4075**	201-843-4000
Greer Laboratories Inc	639 Nuway Cir NE PO Box 800	Lenoir	NC	28645	**800-378-3906*** (*Cust Svc)	828-754-5327
ICC Industries Inc	460 Pk Ave	New York	NY	10022	**800-422-1720**	212-521-1700
Interchem Corp	120 Rt 17 N	Paramus	NJ	07652	**800-261-7332**	201-261-7333
Johnson Matthey Pharma Services	25 Patton Rd	Devens	MA	01434	**800-444-8544**	978-784-5000
Lannett Company Inc (LCI) (*NYSE: LCI*)	13200 Townsend Rd	Philadelphia	PA	19154	**800-325-9994**	215-333-9000
LycoRed Corp	377 Crane St	Orange	NJ	07051	**877-592-6733**	973-882-0322
NHK Laboratories Inc	12230 E Florience Ave	Santa Fe Springs	CA	90670	**866-645-5227**	562-944-5400
Nutra Pharma Corp	12502 W Atlantic Blvd	Coral Springs	FL	33071	**877-895-5647**	954-509-0911
Nutraceutix Inc	9609 153rd Ave NE	Redmond	WA	98052	**800-548-3222**	425-883-9518
One Lambda Inc	21001 Kittridge St	Canoga Park	CA	91303	**800-822-8824**	818-702-0042
PendoPharm Inc	6111 Royalmount	Montreal	QC	H4P2T4	**866-926-7653*** (*Cust Svc)	514-340-5045
Rainbow Light Nutritional Sys Inc	100 Ave Tea	Santa Cruz	CA	95060	**800-635-1233**	
Scientific Protein Laboratories Inc	700 E Main St PO Box 158	Waunakee	WI	53597	**800-334-4775**	608-849-5944
Siegfried USA LLC	33 Industrial Pk Rd	Pennsville	NJ	08070	**877-763-8630*** (*Cust Svc)	856-678-3601
Sigma-Aldrich Corp (*NASDAQ: SIAL*)	3050 Spruce St	Saint Louis	MO	63103	**800-325-3010**	314-771-5765
Spectrum Laboratory Products Inc	14422 S San Pedro St	Gardena	CA	90248	**800-772-8786*** (*General)	310-516-8000
SPI Pharma	Rockwood Office Park Fl 2	Wilmington	DE	19809	**800-789-9755**	302-576-8567
SST Corp	635 Brighton Rd	Clifton	NJ	07012	**800-222-0921**	973-473-4300
Starwest Botanicals Inc	11253 Trade Ctr Dr	Rancho Cordova	CA	95742	**888-273-4372*** (*General)	916-638-8100
Terry Laboratories Inc	7005 Technology Dr	Melbourne	FL	32904	**800-367-2563**	321-259-1630
Tri-K Industries Inc	2 Stewart Ct PO Box 10	Denville	NJ	07834	**800-526-0372**	973-298-8850
TSI Health Sciences Inc	305 S Fourth St E Ste 101	Missoula	MT	59801	**877-549-9123**	406-549-9123
United-Guardian Inc (UGI) (*NASDAQ: UG*)	230 Marcus Blvd PO Box 18050	Hauppauge	NY	11788	**800-645-5566**	631-273-0900

479 METAL - STRUCTURAL (FABRICATED)

Company	Address	City	State	Zip	Toll-Free	Phone
Aerospace America Inc	900 Harry Truman Pkwy	Bay City	MI	48706	**800-237-6414**	989-684-2121
AmChel Communications Inc	2800 Capital St	Wylie	TX	75098	**866-388-6959**	972-442-1030
American BOA Inc	1420 Redi Rd	Cumming	GA	30040	**800-856-4580**	770-889-9400
Amerimax Home Products Inc	450 Richardson Dr	Lancaster	PA	17603	**800-347-2586**	717-299-3711
Anchor Fabrication Ltd	1200 Lawson Rd	Fort Worth	TX	76131	**800-635-0386**	817-498-2521
Apex Industries Inc	100 Millennium Blvd	Moncton	NB	E1E2G8	**800-268-3331**	506-857-1620
Baron Metal Industries Inc	101 Ashbridge Cir	Woodbridge	ON	L4L3R5	**800-263-7515**	416-749-2111
Braden Mfg LLC	5199 N Mingo Rd	Tulsa	OK	74117	**800-272-3360**	
Central Minnesota Fabricating Inc	2725 W Gorton Ave	Willmar	MN	56201	**800-839-8857**	320-235-4181
CENTRIA	1005 Beaver Grade Rd	Moon Township	PA	15108	**800-759-7474**	412-299-8000
Cessco Fabrication & Engineering Ltd	7310-99 St	Edmonton	AB	T6E3R8	**800-272-9698**	780-433-9531
Chase Industries Inc	10021 Commerce Park Dr	Cincinnati	OH	45246	**800-543-4455**	513-860-5565
CMC Alamo Steel Co	2784 Old Dallas Rd	Waco	TX	76705	**800-500-0333**	254-799-2471
CMC Capitol City Steel	14501 S IH 35	Buda	TX	78610	**888-682-7337**	512-282-8820
CMC Rebar Georgia	251 Hosea Rd	Lawrenceville	GA	30045	**888-682-7337**	770-963-6251
Craig Manufacturing Ltd	96 Mclean Ave	Hartland	NB	E7P2K5	**800-565-5007**	506-375-4493
Discount RampsCom LLC	760 S Indiana Ave	West Bend	WI	53095	**888-651-3431**	262-338-3431
Don Young Co	8181 Ambassador Row	Dallas	TX	75247	**800-367-0390**	214-630-0934
Dropbox Inc	401 S 9th St	Ironton	OH	45638	**888-388-7768**	
Etobicoke Ironworks Ltd	141 Rivalda Rd	Weston	ON	M9M2M6	**866-274-6971**	416-742-7111
Excel Bridge Manufacturing Co	12001 Shoemaker Ave	Santa Fe Springs	CA	90670	**800-548-0054**	562-944-0701
Fabral Inc	3449 Hempland Rd	Lancaster	PA	17601	**800-477-2741**	717-397-2741
Garaga Inc	8500 25th Ave	St Georges	QC	G6A1K5	**800-464-2724**	418-227-2828
GLM Industries LP	1508 - Eighth St	Nisku	AB	T9E7S6	**800-661-9828**	780-955-2233
Grain Belt Supply Company Inc	PO Box 615	Salina	KS	67402	**800-447-0522**	785-827-4491
Herber Aircraft Service Inc	1401 E Franklin Ave	El Segundo	CA	90245	**800-544-0050**	310-322-9575
J. C. Macelroy Company Inc	PO Box 850	Piscataway	NJ	08855	**800-622-3576**	732-572-7100
Jesse Engineering Co	1840 Marine View Dr	Tacoma	WA	98422	**800-468-3595**	253-922-7433
JH Industries Inc	1981 E Aurora Rd	Twinsburg	OH	44087	**800-321-4968**	330-963-4105
Linetec	725 S 75th Ave	Wausau	WI	54401	**888-717-1472**	715-843-4100
Manko Window Systems Inc	800 Hayes Dr	Manhattan	KS	66502	**800-642-1488**	785-776-9643
Mason Corp	123 W Oxmoor Rd	Birmingham	AL	35209	**800-868-4100**	205-942-4100
McElroy Metal Inc	1500 Hamilton Rd	Bossier City	LA	71111	**800-562-3576**	318-747-8097
Merchant & Evans Inc	308 Connecticut Dr	Burlington	NJ	08016	**800-257-6215**	609-387-3033
Midwest Metal Products Co	2100 W Mt Pleasant Rd	Muncie	IN	47302	**888-741-1044**	
Mobility Center Inc	6693 Dixie Hwy	Bridgeport	MI	48722	**866-361-7559**	989-777-0910
Nabco Entrances Inc	S82W18717 Gemini Dr	Muskego	WI	53150	**888-679-3319**	262-679-0045
Nello Capital Inc	211 W Washington St Ste 2000	South Bend	IN	46601	**800-806-3556**	574-288-3632
Nucor Corp (*NYSE: NUE*)	1915 Rexford Rd	Charlotte	NC	28211	**800-294-1322**	704-366-7000
Owen Industries Inc	501 Ave H	Carter Lake	IA	51510	**800-831-9252**	712-347-5500
Paxton & Vierling Steel Co	500 Ave H Carter Lake	Carter Lake	IA	51510	**800-831-9252**	
Price Steel Ltd	13500 156 St	Edmonton	AB	T5V1L3	**800-661-6789**	780-447-9999
Processed Metals Innovators LLC	600 21st Ave	Bloomer	WI	54724	**888-877-7277**	715-568-1700
Qualico Steel Co Inc	PO Box 149	Webb	AL	36376	**866-234-5382**	334-793-1290
Ralston Metal Products Ltd	50 Watson Rd S	Guelph	ON	N1L1E2	**800-265-7611**	
Rodney Hunt Co	46 Mill St	Orange	MA	01364	**800-448-8860**	978-544-2511
RSDC of Michigan LLC	1775 Holloway Dr	Holt	MI	48842	**877-881-7732**	
Schuff Steel Inc	1920 Ledo Rd	Albany	GA	31707	**866-252-4628**	678-821-7061
Sims Cab Depot	200 Moulinette Rd	Long Sault	ON	K0C1P0	**800-225-7290**	613-534-2289
Southland Steel Fabricators Inc	251 Greensburg St	Greensburg	LA	70441	**800-738-7734**	225-222-4141
Steele Solutions Inc	9909 S 57th St	Franklin	WI	53132	**888-542-5099**	414-367-5099
Steffes Corp	3050 Hwy 22 N	Dickinson	ND	58601	**888-783-3337**	701-483-5400
Stupp Bros Inc	3800 Weber Rd	Saint Louis	MO	63125	**800-535-9999**	314-638-5000
T. Bruce Sales Inc	9 Carbaugh St	West Middlesex	PA	16159	**800-944-0738**	724-528-9961
Tie Down Engineering Inc	255 Villanova Dr SW	Atlanta	GA	30336	**800-241-1806**	404-344-0000
United Window & Door Manufacturing Inc	24-36 Fadem Rd	Springfield	NJ	07081	**800-848-4550**	973-912-0600
Val-Fab Inc	218 Jackson St	Neenah	WI	54956	**888-482-5322**	920-722-1009
Wahlcometroflex Inc	29 Lexington St	Lewiston	ME	04240	**800-272-6652**	207-784-2338
WaUSAu Window & Wall Systems	7800 International Dr	Wausau	WI	54401	**877-678-2983**	715-845-2161

Classified Section

Company / Address	City	State	ZIP	Toll-Free	Phone
Wojan Window & Door Corp 217 Stover Rd	Charlevoix	MI	49720	**800-632-9827**	231-547-2931
WSF Industries Inc 7 Hackett Dr	Tonawanda	NY	14150	**800-874-8265**	716-692-4930
Zimmerman Metals Inc 201 E 58th Ave	Denver	CO	80216	**800-247-4202**	303-294-0180

480 METAL COATING, PLATING, ENGRAVING

Company / Address	City	State	ZIP	Toll-Free	Phone
Alumicor Ltd 290 Humberline Dr	Toronto	ON	M9W5S2	**877-258-6426**	416-745-4222
American Nickeloid Co 2900 Main St	Peru	IL	61354	**800-645-5643**	815-223-0373
AST Products Inc 9 Linnell Cir	Billerica	MA	01821	**877-667-4500**	978-667-4500
BL Downey Company LLC 2125 Gardner Rd	Broadview	IL	60155	**800-323-1206**	708-345-8000
Charlotte Anodizing Products Inc 591 E Packard Hwy	Charlotte	MI	48813	**800-818-6945**	517-543-1911
Chem Processing Inc 3910 Linden Oaks Dr	Rockford	IL	61109	**800-262-2119**	815-874-8118
Chemart Co 15 New England Way	Lincoln	RI	02865	**800-521-5001**	401-333-9200
Continental Studwelding Ltd 35 Devon Rd	Brampton	ON	L6T5B6	**800-848-9442**	905-792-3650
CVD Diamond Corp 2061 Piper Ln	London	ON	N5V3S5	**877-457-9903**	519-457-9903
Deposition Sciences Inc 3300 Coffey Ln	Santa Rosa	CA	95403	**866-433-7724**	707-573-6700
East Side Plating Inc 8400 SE 26th Pl	Portland	OR	97202	**800-394-8554**	503-654-3774
Everlube Products 100 Cooper Cir	Peachtree City	GA	30269	**800-428-7802**	770-261-4800
FW Gartner Thermal Spraying Ltd 25 Southbelt Industrial Dr	Houston	TX	77047	**888-439-4872**	713-225-0010
Galvan Industries Inc 7320 Millbrook Rd *General	Harrisburg	NC	28075	**800-277-5678***	704-455-5102
GM Nameplate Inc 2040 15th Ave W	Seattle	WA	98119	**800-366-7668**	206-284-2200
Hadronics Inc 4570 Steel Pl	Cincinnati	OH	45209	**800-829-0826**	513-321-9350
Ingot Metal Company Ltd 111 Fenmar Dr	Weston	ON	M9L1M3	**800-567-7774**	416-749-1372
J & M Plating Inc 4500 Kishwaukee St	Rockford	IL	61109	**877-344-3044**	815-964-4975
LB Foster Co 415 Holiday Dr *NASDAQ: FSTR*	Pittsburgh	PA	15220	**800-255-4500**	
Lorin Industries 1960 S Roberts St	Muskegon	MI	49443	**800-654-1159**	231-722-1631
Magnetic Metals Corp 1900 Hayes Ave	Camden	NJ	08105	**800-257-8174**	856-964-7842
Master Finish Co 2020 Nelson SE PO Box 7505	Grand Rapids	MI	49510	**877-590-5819**	
Max Levy Autograph Inc 2710 Commerce Way	Philadelphia	PA	19154	**800-798-3675**	215-842-3675
Metal Cladding Inc 230 S Niagara St	Lockport	NY	14094	**800-432-5513**	
Meziere Enterprises Inc 220 S Hale Ave	Escondido	CA	92029	**800-208-1755**	760-746-3273
National Coatings Inc 3520 Rennie School Rd	Traverse City	MI	49685	**888-947-2557**	231-943-2557
Nd Industries Inc 1000 N Crooks Rd	Clawson	MI	48017	**800-471-5000**	248-288-0000
Nor-Ell Inc 851 Hubbard Ave	Saint Paul	MN	55104	**877-276-4075**	651-487-1441
O E C Graphics Inc 555 W Waukau Ave PO Box 2443	Oshkosh	WI	54902	**800-388-7770**	920-235-7770
Pioneer Metal Finishing LLC 486 Globe Ave	Green Bay	WI	54304	**877-721-1100**	
Plasma Ruggedized Solutions Inc 2284 Ringwood Ave Ste A	San Jose	CA	95131	**800-994-7527**	408-954-8405
Premier Die Casting Co 1177 Rahway Ave	Avenel	NJ	07001	**800-394-3006**	732-634-3000
Roesch Inc 100 N 24th St	Belleville	IL	62222	**800-423-6243**	
Sapa Inc 7933 NE 21st Ave	Portland	OR	97211	**800-547-0790**	503-802-3000
Towne Technologies Inc 6-10 Bell Ave PO Box 460	Somerville	NJ	08876	**800-837-2515**	908-722-9500
Ultra-tech Enterprises Inc 4701 Taylor Rd	Punta Gorda	FL	33950	**800-293-2001**	941-575-2000
US Chrome Corp 175 Garfield Ave	Stratford	CT	06615	**800-637-9019**	
Willington Cos 11 Middle River Dr	Stafford Springs	CT	06076	**877-967-4743**	860-684-4281

481 METAL FABRICATING - CUSTOM

Company / Address	City	State	ZIP	Toll-Free	Phone
Afco Industries Inc 3400 Roy St	Alexandria	LA	71302	**800-551-6576**	
Brakewell Steel Fabricator Inc 55 Leone Ln	Chester	NY	10918	**888-914-9131**	845-469-9131
Chicago Metal Fabricators Inc 3724 S Rockwell St	Chicago	IL	60632	**877-400-5995**	773-523-5755
Cross Bros Inc 5255 Sheila St	Los Angeles	CA	90040	**866-939-1057**	323-266-2000
CSM Metal Fabricating & Engineering Inc 1800 S San Pedro St	Los Angeles	CA	90015	**800-272-4806**	213-748-7321
Demsey Manufacturing Co 78 New Wood Rd	Watertown	CT	06795	**800-533-6739**	860-274-6209
Fabricated Components Inc PO Box 431	Stroudsburg	PA	18360	**800-233-8163**	570-421-4110
International Extrusions Inc 5800 Venoy Rd	Garden City	MI	48135	**800-242-8876**	734-427-8700
Liquidmetal Technologies Inc (LQMT) 30452 Esperanza *OTC: LQMT*	Rancho Santa Margarita	CA	92688	**888-203-1112**	949-635-2100
Lucasey Manufacturing Corp 2744 E 11th St PO Box 14023	Oakland	CA	94601	**800-582-2739**	510-534-1435
MP Metal Products Inc W1250 Elmwood Ave	Ixonia	WI	53036	**800-824-6744**	920-261-9650
Sommer Metalcraft Corp 315 Poston Dr	Crawfordsville	IN	47933	**888-876-6637**	765-362-6201
Unifab Corp 5260 Lovers Ln *General	Portage	MI	49002	**800-648-9569***	269-382-2803
White River Distributors Inc 720 Ramsey	Batesville	AR	72501	**800-548-7219**	870-793-2374

482 METAL FORGINGS

Company / Address	City	State	ZIP	Toll-Free	Phone
A & A Global Industries Inc 17 Stenersen Ln	Cockeysville	MD	21030	**800-638-6000**	410-252-1020
Alcoa Wheel Products International 1600 Harvard Ave	Cleveland	OH	44105	**800-242-9898**	216-641-3600
Aluminum Precision Products Inc 3333 W Warner St	Santa Ana	CA	92704	**800-411-8983**	714-546-8125
Anchor-Harvey Components LLC 600 W Lamm Rd	Freeport	IL	61032	**888-367-4464**	815-233-3833
Brainerd Industries Inc 680 Precision Ct	Miamisburg	OH	45342	**800-790-0430**	937-228-0488
Ellwood City Forge 800 Commercial Ave	Ellwood City	PA	16117	**800-843-0166**	724-752-0055
Federal Flange 4014 Pinemont St	Houston	TX	77018	**800-231-0150**	713-681-0606
Ferguson Perforating & Wire Co 130 Ernest St	Providence	RI	02905	**800-341-9800**	401-941-8876
Fine Line Production 2221 Regal Pkwy	Euless	TX	76040	**800-887-5625**	817-267-6750
Forged Products Inc (FPI) 6505 N Houston Rosslyn Rd	Houston	TX	77091	**800-876-3416**	713-462-3416
Frontier Metal Stamping Inc 3764 Puritan Way	Erie	CO	80516	**888-316-1266**	303-458-5129
Green Bay Drop Forge 1341 State St	Green Bay	WI	54304	**800-824-4896**	920-432-6401
H & L Tooth Company Inc 10055 E 56 St N	Tulsa	OK	74117	**800-458-6684**	918-272-0951
Jorgensen Forge Corp 8531 E Marginal Way S	Tukwila	WA	98108	**800-231-5382**	206-762-1100
Kerkau Manufacturing Co 1321 S Valley Ctr Dr	Bay City	MI	48706	**800-248-5060**	989-686-0350
Liberty Forge Inc PO Box 1210	Liberty	TX	77575	**800-231-2377**	
Machine Specialty & Manufacturing Inc 215 Rousseau Rd	Youngsville	LA	70592	**800-256-1292**	337-837-0020
Mercer Forge Corp 200 Brown St	Mercer	PA	16137	**800-558-5075**	724-662-2750
MMD Equipment 121 High Hill Rd	Swedesboro	NJ	08085	**800-433-1382**	856-467-3200
Norforge & Machining Inc 195 N Dean St	Bushnell	IL	61422	**800-839-3706**	309-772-3124
Performance Stamping Company Inc 20 Lk Marian Rd	Carpentersville	IL	60110	**800-935-0393**	847-426-2233
Phoenix Forging Company Inc 800 Front St	Catasauqua	PA	18032	**800-444-3674**	610-264-2861
Randall Bearings Inc 1046 Greenlawn Ave PO Box 1258	Lima	OH	45802	**800-626-7071**	419-223-1075
Saint Croix Forge Inc 5195 Scandia Trl	Forest Lake	MN	55025	**866-668-7642**	651-464-8967
Scot Forge Co 8001 Winn Rd PO Box 8	Spring Grove	IL	60081	**800-435-6621**	847-587-1000
Steel Industries Inc (SII) 12600 Beech-Daly Rd	Redford Township	MI	48239	**877-783-3599**	
Talan Products Inc 18800 Cochran Ave	Cleveland	OH	44110	**877-419-2805**	216-458-0170
Thoro'Bred Inc 5020 E La Palma Ave	Anaheim	CA	92807	**877-585-5152**	714-779-2581
Western Forge & Flange Co 687 County Rd 2201	Cleveland	TX	77327	**800-352-6433**	281-727-7060
Wozniak Industries Inc Commercial Forged Products Div 5757 W 65th St	Bedford Park	IL	60638	**800-637-2695**	708-458-1220
Wrought Washer Manufacturing Inc 2100 S Bay St	Milwaukee	WI	53207	**800-558-5217**	414-744-0771
Young Manufacturing Inc 2331 N 42nd St	Grand Forks	ND	58203	**800-451-9884**	701-772-5541

483 METAL HEAT TREATING

Company / Address	City	State	ZIP	Toll-Free	Phone
Akron Steel Treating Co 336 Morgan Ave	Akron	OH	44311	**800-364-2782**	330-773-8211
Bluewater Thermal Solutions 201 Brookfield Pwy Ste 102	Greenville	SC	29607	**877-990-0050**	864-990-0050
Curtiss-Wright Corp 10 Waterview Blvd 2nd Fl *NYSE: CW*	Parsippany	NJ	07054	**855-449-0995**	973-541-3700
Euclid Heat Treating Co 1340 E 222nd St	Euclid	OH	44117	**800-962-2909**	216-481-8444
FPM LLC 1501 S Lively Blvd	Elk Grove Village	IL	60007	**877-437-6432**	847-228-2525
Gibraltar Industries Inc 3556 Lakeshore Rd *NASDAQ: ROCK*	Buffalo	NY	14219	**800-247-8368**	716-826-6500
HI TecMetal Group Inc 1101 E 55th St	Cleveland	OH	44103	**877-484-2867**	216-881-8100
Industrial Steel Treating Inc 613 Carroll St	Jackson	MI	49202	**800-253-9534**	

Company	Address	City	State	ZIP	Toll-Free	Phone
Miller Consolidated Industries Inc	2221 Arbor Blvd	Dayton	OH	45439	**800-589-4133**	937-294-2681
Nitrex Metal Inc	3474 Poirier Blvd	Saint-Laurent	QC	H4R2J5	**877-335-7191**	514-335-7191
Rex Heat Treat	951 W Eigth St PO Box 270	Lansdale	PA	19446	**800-220-4739**	215-855-1131
Stahl Specialty Co	111 E Pacific PO Box 6	Kingsville	MO	64061	**800-821-7852**	816-597-3322
Texas Heat Treating Inc	155 Texas Ave	Round Rock	TX	78664	**800-580-5884**	512-255-5884

484 METAL INDUSTRIES (MISC)

SEE ALSO Steel - Mfr ; Wire & Cable ; Foundries - Investment ; Foundries - Iron & Steel ; Foundries - Nonferrous (Castings) ; Metal Heat Treating ; Metal Tube & Pipe

Company	Address	City	State	ZIP	Toll-Free	Phone
Alcoa Inc	390 Park Ave	New York	NY	10022	**800-523-9596**	412-553-4545
Alcoa Primary Metals	900 S Gay St Riverview Twr Ste 1100	Knoxville	TN	37902	**800-852-0238**	865-594-4700
Allegheny Technologies Inc	1000 Six PPG Pl *NYSE: ATI* ■ *Sales	Pittsburgh	PA	15222	**800-258-3586***	412-394-2800
Allvac Inc	2020 Ashcraft Ave PO Box 5030	Monroe	NC	28110	**800-841-5491**	704-289-4511
Altech LLC	242 America Pl	Jeffersonville	IN	47130	**800-264-8256**	812-282-8256
Ampco Metal Inc	1117 E Algonquin Rd	Arlington Heights	IL	60005	**800-844-6008**	847-437-6000
Anaheim Extrusion Company Inc	1330 N Kraemer Blvd PO Box 6380	Anaheim	CA	92806	**800-660-3318**	714-630-3111
Arvinyl Metal Laminates Corp	233 N Sherman Ave	Corona	CA	92882	**800-278-4695**	
Big River Zinc Corp	2401 Mississippi Ave	Sauget	IL	62201	**800-274-4002**	618-274-5000
Broco Inc	10868 Bell Ct	Rancho Cucamonga	CA	91730	**800-845-7259**	909-483-3222
Bunting Magnetics Co	500 S Spencer Ave	Newton	KS	67114	**800-835-2526**	316-284-2020
Cannon Muskegon Corp	2875 Lincoln St PO Box 506	Muskegon	MI	49441	**800-253-0371**	231-755-1681
Cardinal Aluminum Co	6910 Preston Hwy *Cust Svc	Louisville	KY	40219	**800-398-7833***	502-969-9302
Chase Brass & Copper Co	14212 Selwyn Dr	Montpelier	OH	43543	**800-537-4291**	419-485-3193
Chicago Extruded Metals Co (CXM)	1601 S 54th Ave *Cust Svc	Cicero	IL	60804	**800-323-8102***	
Croft LLC	107 Oliver Emmerich Dr	McComb	MS	39648	**800-437-8421**	601-684-6121
Curtis Steel Company LLC (CSC)	6504 Hurst St PO Box 7469	Houston	TX	77008	**800-749-4621**	713-861-4621
Custom Aluminum Products Inc	414 Div St	South Elgin	IL	60177	**800-745-6333**	847-717-5000
Doe Run Co, The	1801 Pk 270 Dr Ste 300	Saint Louis	MO	63146	**800-356-3786**	314-453-7100
Dynamet Inc	195 Museum Rd	Washington	PA	15301	**800-237-9655**	724-228-1000
Elmet Technologies Inc	1560 Lisbon St	Lewiston	ME	04240	**800-343-8008**	207-333-6100
Glines & Rhodes Inc	189 E St	Attleboro	MA	02703	**800-343-1196**	508-226-2000
H Kramer & Co	1345 W 21st St	Chicago	IL	60608	**800-621-2305**	312-226-6600
Haynes International Inc	1020 W Pk Ave PO Box 9013 *NASDAQ: HAYN*	Kokomo	IN	46904	**800-354-0806**	765-456-6000
Hoover & Strong Inc	10700 Trade Rd *Cust Svc	North Chesterfield	VA	23236	**800-759-9997***	
Hussey Copper Ltd	100 Washington St	Leetsdale	PA	15056	**800-733-8866**	724-251-4200
Industrial Tectonics Inc	7222 Huron River Dr	Dexter	MI	48130	**866-816-8904**	734-426-4681
JW Aluminum	435 Old Mt Holly Rd *Sales	Mount Holly	SC	29445	**877-586-5314***	
Kaiser Aluminum Corp	27422 Portola Pkwy Ste 200 *Sales	Foothill Ranch	CA	92610	**800-873-2011***	949-614-1740
Light Metals Corp	2740 Prairie St SW	Wyoming	MI	49509	**888-363-8257**	616-538-3030
Linemaster Switch Corp	29 Plaine Hill Rd	Woodstock	CT	06281	**800-974-3668**	860-974-1000
Loxcreen Co Inc, The	1630 Old Dunbar Rd PO Box 4004	West Columbia	SC	29172	**800-330-5699**	803-822-8200
Lucas-Milhaupt Inc	5656 S Pennsylvania Ave	Cudahy	WI	53110	**800-558-3856**	414-769-6000
Luvata Appleton LLC	553 Carter Ct	Kimberly	WI	54136	**866-488-0217**	920-749-3820
Luvata Ohio Inc	1376 Pittsburgh Dr	Delaware	OH	43015	**800-749-5510**	740-363-1981
Magnetech Industrial Services Inc	800 Nave Rd SE *General	Massillon	OH	44646	**800-837-1614***	330-830-3500
Memry Corp	3 Berkshire Blvd	Bethel	CT	06801	**866-466-3679**	203-739-1100
Metglas Inc	440 Allied Dr	Conway	SC	29526	**800-581-7654**	843-349-7319
Micro Surface Engr Inc	1550 E Slauson Ave	Los Angeles	CA	90011	**800-322-5832**	323-582-7348
Midland Industries Inc	1424 N Halsted St	Chicago	IL	60642	**800-662-8228**	312-664-7300
Mueller Brass Co	2199 Lapeer Ave	Port Huron	MI	48060	**800-553-3336**	810-987-7770
Mueller Industries Inc	8285 Tournament Dr Ste 150 *NYSE: MLI*	Memphis	TN	38125	**800-348-8464**	901-753-3200
NN Inc	2000 Waters Edge Dr Bldg 3 Ste 12 *NASDAQ: NNBR*	Johnson City	TN	37604	**877-888-0002**	423-743-9151
Noranda Aluminum Inc	801 Crescent Ctr Dr Ste 600	Franklin	TN	37067	**800-325-8112**	615-771-5700
Novelis North America	3560 Lenox Rd Ste 2000	Atlanta	GA	30326	**800-892-1819**	404-760-4000
Patrick Industries Inc Patrick Metals Div	5020 Lincolnway E	Mishawaka	IN	46544	**800-922-9692**	574-255-9692
Revere Copper Products Inc	1 Revere Pk	Rome	NY	13440	**800-448-1776**	315-338-2022
Ross Metals Corp	27 W 47th St	New York	NY	10036	**800-334-7191**	
Southwire Co	1 Southwire Dr	Carrollton	GA	30119	**800-444-1700**	770-832-4242
Special Metals Corp	4317 Middle Settlement Rd	New Hartford	NY	13413	**800-334-8351**	315-798-2900
Taber Extrusions LP	915 S Elmira Ave	Russellville	AR	72802	**800-563-6853**	479-968-1021
Titanium Metals Corp (TIMET)	224 Vly Creek Blvd Ste 200 *NYSE: TIE*	Exton	PA	19341	**800-753-1550**	610-968-1300
Tree Island Industries	3933 Boundary Rd	Richmond	BC	V6V1T8	**800-663-0955**	604-524-3744
Valmont Industries Inc	1 Valmont Plz *NYSE: VMI*	Omaha	NE	68154	**800-825-6668**	402-963-1000
Victory White Metal Co	6100 Roland Ave	Cleveland	OH	44127	**800-635-5050**	216-271-1400
Wah Chang	1600 Old Salem Rd NE	Albany	OR	97321	**888-926-4211**	541-926-4211
Wiley Sanders Truck Lines Inc	PO Box 707 PO Box 707	Troy	AL	36081	**800-392-8017**	
Xyron Inc	8465 N 90th St Ste 6	Scottsdale	AZ	85258	**800-793-3523**	480-443-9419

485 METAL PRODUCTS - HOUSEHOLD

Company	Address	City	State	ZIP	Toll-Free	Phone
All-Clad Metalcrafters LLC	424 Morganza Rd *Cust Svc	Canonsburg	PA	15317	**800-255-2523***	724-745-8300
Calphalon Corp	PO Box 583	Toledo	OH	43697	**800-809-7267**	
Le Creuset of America Inc	114 Bob Gifford Blvd	Early Branch	SC	29916	**877-418-5547**	803-943-4308
Lifetime Brands Inc	1000 Steward Ave *NASDAQ: LCUT*	Garden City	NY	11530	**800-252-3390**	516-683-6000
ME Heuck Co	1600 Beech St *Cust Svc	Terre Haute	IN	47804	**866-634-3825***	812-238-5000
Meyer Corp	1 Meyer Pl *Cust Svc	Vallejo	CA	94590	**800-888-3883***	707-551-2800
Nordic Ware	5005 Hwy 7	Minneapolis	MN	55416	**877-466-7342**	952-920-2888
Saladmaster Inc	230 Westway Pl Ste 101	Arlington	TX	76018	**800-765-5795**	817-633-3555
Whitesell Corp	2703 Avalon Ave *General	Muscle Shoals	AL	35661	**855-227-4515***	256-248-8500
Wilton Armetale Co	PO Box 600	Mount Joy	PA	17552	**800-779-4586**	
Wilton Industries Inc	2240 W 75th St	Woodridge	IL	60517	**800-794-5866**	630-963-7100

486 METAL PRODUCTS (MISC)

Company	Address	City	State	ZIP	Toll-Free	Phone
Aerodyne Alloys LLC	350 Pleasant Vly Rd	South Windsor	CT	06074	**800-243-4344**	860-289-6011
Alexandria Extrusion Co	401 County Rd 22 NW	Alexandria	MN	56308	**800-568-6601**	320-763-6537
Aluchem Inc	1 Landy Ln	Cincinnati	OH	45215	**800-336-8519**	513-733-8519
Aluminum Ladder Co	1430 W Darlington St	Florence	SC	29501	**800-752-2526**	843-662-2595
Bead Industries Inc	11 Cascade Blvd	Milford	CT	06460	**800-297-4851**	203-301-0270
Carolina Carports Inc	187 Cardinal Ridge Trl	Dobson	NC	27017	**800-670-4262**	
Flinchbaugh Engineering Inc	4387 Run Way	York	PA	17406	**866-967-5334**	717-755-1900
General Magnaplate Corp	1331 Us Rt 1	Linden	NJ	07036	**800-441-6173**	908-862-6200
Lechler Inc	445 Kautz Rd *Cust Svc	Saint Charles	IL	60174	**800-777-2926***	630-377-6611
Liberty Safe & Security Products Inc	1199 W Utah Ave	Payson	UT	84651	**800-247-5625**	801-925-1000
Metalworking Group Inc	9070 Pippin Rd	Cincinnati	OH	45251	**800-476-9409**	513-521-4114
Polar Ware Co	502 Hwy 67 *Cust Svc	Kiel	WI	53042	**800-237-3655***	
Precision Valve Corp	800 Westchester Ave	Rye Brook	NY	10573	**866-686-8464**	914-969-6500
Viking Materials Inc	3225 Como Ave SE *General	Minneapolis	MN	55414	**800-682-3942***	612-617-5800
Visual Planning Corp	71 Meadowbank Dr	Ottawa	ON	K2G0P4	**800-361-1192**	613-563-8727

487 METAL STAMPINGS

SEE ALSO Closures - Metal or Plastics ; Electronic Enclosures ; Metal Stampings - Automotive

Company / Address	City	State	ZIP	Toll-Free	Phone
Accurate Perforating Co 3636 S Kedzie Ave	Chicago	IL	60632	**800-621-0273**	773-254-3232
Admiral Craft Equipment Corp 940 S Oyster Bay Rd	Hicksville	NY	11801	**800-223-7750**	516-433-3535
All New Stamping Co 10801 Lower Azusa Rd	El Monte	CA	91731	**800-877-7775**	
American Metalcraft Inc 2074 George St	Melrose Park	IL	60160	**800-333-9133**	708-345-1177
American Products LLC 597 Evergreen Rd	Strafford	MO	65757	**855-736-2135**	417-736-2135
Arrow Tru-Line Inc 2211 S Defiance St	Archbold	OH	43502	**877-285-7253**	419-446-2785
Ataco Steel Products Corp PO Box 270	Cedarburg	WI	53012	**800-536-4822**	262-377-3000
Bazz Houston Co 12700 Western Ave	Garden Grove	CA	92841	**800-385-9608**	714-898-2666
Btd Mfg Inc 1111 13th Ave SE	Detroit Lakes	MN	56501	**866-562-3986**	
Dayton Rogers Manufacturing Co 8401 W 35 W Service Dr	Minneapolis	MN	55449	**800-677-8881**	763-784-7714
Delta Consolidated Industries Inc 4800 Krueger Dr	Jonesboro	AR	72401	**800-643-0084**	870-935-3711
Diamond Manufacturing Co 243 W Eigth St	Wyoming	PA	18644	**800-233-9601**	570-693-0300
Diamond Perforated Metals Inc 7300 W Sunnyview Ave	Visalia	CA	93291	**800-642-4334**	559-651-1889
DORMA Architectural Hardware DORMA Dr Drawer AC	Reamstown	PA	17567	**800-523-8483**	717-336-3881
Fulton Industries Inc 135 E Linfoot St PO Box 377	Wauseon	OH	43567	**800-537-5012**	419-335-3015
GMP Metal Products Inc 3883 Delor St	Saint Louis	MO	63116	**800-325-9808**	314-481-0300
Hannibal Industries Inc 3851 S Santa Fe Ave	Los Angeles	CA	90058	**888-246-7074**	323-588-4261
Hendrick Manufacturing Co 1 Seventh Ave *Cust Svc	Carbondale	PA	18407	**800-225-7373***	
Heyco Products 1800 Industrial Way N	Toms River	NJ	08755	**800-526-4182**	732-286-1800
Hobson & Motzer Inc 30 Air Line Dr	Durham	CT	06422	**800-476-5111**	860-349-1756
HPL Stampings Inc 425 Enterprise Pkwy	Lake Zurich	IL	60047	**800-927-0397**	847-540-1400
HTT Inc. 1828 Oakland Ave	Sheboygan	WI	53081	**866-270-4710**	920-453-5300
Innovative Stamping Corp 2068 E Gladwick St	Compton	CA	90220	**800-400-0047**	310-537-6996
Jagemann Stamping Co 5757 W Custer St	Manitowoc	WI	54220	**888-337-7853**	920-682-4633
Ken-Tron Manufacturing Inc PO Box 21250	Owensboro	KY	42304	**800-872-9336**	270-684-0431
Kennedy Manufacturing Co 1260 Industrial Dr	Van Wert	OH	45891	**800-413-8665**	419-238-2442
Kickhaefer Mfg Co (KMC) 1221 S Pk St PO Box 348	Port Washington	WI	53074	**800-822-6080**	262-377-5030
Knaack Manufacturing Co 420 E Terra Cotta Ave	Crystal Lake	IL	60014	**800-456-7865**	815-459-6020
Midwest Wire Products LLC 649 S Lansing Ave PO Box 770	Sturgeon Bay	WI	54235	**800-445-0225**	920-743-6591
Penn United Technology Inc 799 N Pike Rd	Cabot	PA	16023	**866-572-7537**	724-352-1507
Quality Perforating Inc 166 Dundaff St	Carbondale	PA	18407	**800-872-7373**	570-282-4344
Saunders Manufacturing Co 65 Nickerson Hill Rd	Readfield	ME	04355	**800-341-4674**	207-685-9860
Stack-On Products Co 1360 N Old Rand Rd	Wauconda	IL	60084	**800-323-9601**	847-526-1611
Steel City Corp 190 N Meridian Rd	Youngstown	OH	44501	**800-321-0350**	330-792-7663
Stewart EFI LLC 45 Old Waterbury Rd	Thomaston	CT	06787	**800-393-5387**	860-283-8213
Waterloo Industries Inc 139 W Forest Hill Ave *Cust Svc	Oak Creek	WI	53154	**800-558-5528***	

488 METAL STAMPINGS - AUTOMOTIVE

SEE ALSO Automotive Parts & Supplies - Mfr

Company / Address	City	State	ZIP	Toll-Free	Phone
Advance Engineering Co 7505 Baron Dr	Canton	MI	48187	**800-497-6388**	313-537-3500
American Metal & Plastics Inc 450 32nd St SW	Grand Rapids	MI	49548	**800-382-0067**	616-452-6061
C Cowles & Co Inc 83 Water St	New Haven	CT	06511	**800-624-4483**	203-865-3117
Decoma International Inc *Magna Exteriors & Interiors* 50 Casmir Ct	Concord	ON	L4K4J5	**888-348-2398**	905-669-2888
Lake Air 7709 Winpark Dr	Minneapolis	MN	55427	**888-785-2422**	763-546-0994
Philippi-Hagenbuch Inc 7424 W Plank Rd	Peoria	IL	61604	**800-447-6464**	309-697-9200
Polar ware 502 Hgwy 67 PO Box 366	Kiel	WI	53402	**800-237-3655**	
Radar Industries 27101 Grosbeck Hwy	Warren	MI	48089	**800-779-0301**	248-358-3570
Spartanburg Steel Products Inc 1290 New Cut Rd PO Box 6428	Spartanburg	SC	29304	**888-974-7500**	864-585-5211
Stewart EFI LLC 45 Old Waterbury Rd	Thomaston	CT	06787	**800-393-5387**	860-283-8213

Company / Address	City	State	ZIP	Toll-Free	Phone
Syracuse Stamping Co 1054 S Clinton St	Syracuse	NY	13202	**800-581-5555**	315-476-5306

489 METAL TUBE & PIPE

Company / Address	City	State	ZIP	Toll-Free	Phone
AK Tube LLC 30400 E Broadway	Walbridge	OH	43465	**800-955-8031**	419-661-4150
American Cast Iron Pipe Co (ACIPCO) 1501 31st Ave N	Birmingham	AL	35207	**800-442-2347**	205-325-7701
Atlas Tube 1855 E 122nd St	Chicago	IL	60633	**800-733-5683**	773-646-4500
Bull Moose Tube Co 1819 Clarkson Rd Ste 100	Chesterfield	MO	63017	**800-325-4467**	636-537-2600
California Steel & Tube 16049 Stephens St	City of Industry	CA	91745	**800-338-8823**	626-968-5511
Cerro Flow Products Inc PO Box 66800	Saint Louis	MO	63166	**888-237-7611**	618-337-6000
Charlotte Pipe & Foundry Co 2109 Randolph Rd	Charlotte	NC	28207	**800-438-6091**	704-372-5030
Dixie Pipe Sales Inc 2407 Broiller	Houston	TX	77054	**800-733-3494**	713-796-2021
Earle M Jorgensen Co 10650 S Alameda St *Sales	Lynwood	CA	90262	**800-336-5365***	323-567-1122
Energy Alloys LLC 350 Glenborough Ste 300	Houston	TX	77067	**866-448-9831**	832-601-5800
Felker Bros Corp 22 N Chestnut Ave	Marshfield	WI	54449	**800-826-2304**	715-384-3121
Hanna Steel Corp 3812 Commerce Ave PO Box 558	Fairfield	AL	35064	**800-633-8252**	205-780-1111
Hannibal Industries Inc 3851 S Santa Fe Ave	Los Angeles	CA	90058	**888-246-7074**	323-588-4261
Hydro Aluminum North America 999 Corporate Blvd Ste 100	Linthicum	MD	21090	**888-935-5752**	
International Metal Hose Co 520 Goodrich Rd	Bellevue	OH	44811	**800-458-6855**	419-483-7690
Jackson Tube Service Inc 8210 Industry Pk Dr	Piqua	OH	45356	**800-543-8910**	937-773-8550
Leavitt Tube 1717 W 115th St	Chicago	IL	60643	**800-532-8488**	773-239-7700
LeFiell Manufacturing Co 13700 Firestone Blvd	Santa Fe Springs	CA	90670	**800-451-5971**	562-921-3411
Lock Joint Tube Inc 515 W Ireland Rd	South Bend	IN	46614	**800-257-6859**	574-299-5326
Morris Coupling Co 2240 W 15th St	Erie	PA	16505	**800-426-1579**	814-459-1741
Northwest Pipe Co 12005 N Burgard *NASDAQ: NWPX*	Portland	OR	97203	**800-989-9631**	503-285-1400
Outokumpu Stainless Pipe Inc 1101 N Main St	Wildwood	FL	34785	**800-731-7473**	352-748-1313
Plymouth Tube Co 29 W 150 Warrenville Rd *Mktg	Warrenville	IL	60555	**800-323-9506***	630-393-3550
Quality Edge Inc 2712 Walkent Dr NW	Walker	MI	49544	**888-784-0878**	
Southland Tube Inc 3525 Richard Arrington Blvd N	Birmingham	AL	35234	**800-543-9024**	205-251-1884
Stupp Corp 12555 Ronaldson Rd	Baton Rouge	LA	70807	**800-535-9999**	225-775-8800
Synalloy Corp 775 Spartan Blvd Ste 102 PO Box 5627 *NASDAQ: SYNL* ■ *Orders	Spartanburg	SC	29304	**800-937-5449***	864-585-3605
Tex-Tube Co 1503 N Post Oak Rd	Houston	TX	77055	**800-839-7473**	713-686-4351
Tube Methods Inc PO Box 460	Bridgeport	PA	19405	**800-220-2123**	610-279-7700
Tube Processing Corp 604 E Le Grande Ave	Indianapolis	IN	46203	**800-295-4119**	317-787-1321
Valmont Industries Inc 1 Valmont Plz *NYSE: VMI*	Omaha	NE	68154	**800-825-6668**	402-963-1000
Wheatland Tube Co 700 S Dock St	Sharon	PA	16146	**800-257-8182**	
Yarde Metals Inc 45 Newell St	Southington	CT	06489	**800-444-9494**	860-406-6061

490 METAL WORK - ARCHITECTURAL & ORNAMENTAL

Company / Address	City	State	ZIP	Toll-Free	Phone
Alabama Metal Industries Corp (AMICO) 3245 Fayette Ave	Birmingham	AL	35208	**800-366-2642**	205-787-2611
Alvarado Mfg Company Inc 12660 Colony St	Chino	CA	91710	**800-423-4143**	909-591-8431
American Stair Corp Inc 642 Forestwood Dr	Romeoville	IL	60446	**800-872-7824**	
Ameristar Fence Products Inc 1555 N Mingo Rd	Tulsa	OK	74116	**888-333-3422**	918-835-0898
ATAS International Inc 6612 Snowdrift Rd	Allentown	PA	18106	**800-468-1441**	610-395-8445
Bedford Machine & Tool Inc 2103 John Williams Blvd	Bedford	IN	47421	**800-264-1948**	812-275-1948
Bil-Jax Inc 125 Taylor Pkwy	Archbold	OH	43502	**800-537-0540**	419-445-8915
Brand Energy & Infrastructure Services Inc 1325 Cobb International Dr Ste A-1	Kennesaw	GA	30152	**855-746-4477**	678-285-1400
Construction Specialties Inc 3 Werner Way	Lebanon	NJ	08833	**800-972-7214**	908-236-0800
Duvinage Corp 60 W Oak Ridge Dr	Hagerstown	MD	21740	**800-541-2645**	301-733-8255
Fisher & Ludlow Tru-Weld Grating 2000 Corporate Dr Ste 400	Wexford	PA	15090	**800-334-2047**	724-934-5320

Company	Address	City	State	ZIP	Toll-Free	Phone
Goldline International Inc	1601 Cloverfield Blvd 100 S Tower	Santa Monica	CA	90404	**877-376-2646**	310-587-1423
Hafele America Company Inc	3901 Cheyenne Dr	Archdale	NC	27263	**800-423-3531*** *Cust Svc	336-889-2322
Hapco Inc	26252 Hillman Hwy	Abingdon	VA	24210	**800-368-7171**	276-628-7171
Irvine Access Floors Inc	9425 Washington Blvd	Laurel	MD	20723	**800-969-8870**	301-617-9333
Jerith Mfg Company Inc	14400 McNulty Rd	Philadelphia	PA	19154	**800-344-2242**	215-676-4068
King Architectural Metals Inc	PO Box 271169	Dallas	TX	75227	**800-542-2379**	
Lapmaster International LLC	501 W Algonquin Rd	Mount Prospect	IL	60056	**877-352-8637**	224-659-7101
NSK America Corp	1800 Global Pkwy	Hoffman Estates	IL	60192	**800-585-4675**	847-843-7664
Overly Manufacturing Co	574 W Otterman St	Greensburg	PA	15601	**800-979-7300**	724-834-7300
Quickmill Inc	760 Rye St	Peterborough	ON	K9J6W9	**800-295-0509**	705-745-2961
Spider Staging Corp	365 Upland Dr	Tukwila	WA	98188	**877-774-3370**	206-575-6445
Steel Ceilings Inc	451 E Coshocton St	Johnstown	OH	43031	**800-848-0496**	740-967-1063
Superior Aluminum Products Inc	555 E Main St PO Box 430	Russia	OH	45363	**800-548-8656**	937-526-4065
T Tech Inc	510 Guthridge Ct	Norcross	GA	30092	**800-370-1530**	770-455-0676
Tate Access Floors Inc	7510 Montevideo Rd	Jessup	MD	20794	**800-231-7788**	410-799-4200
VELUX America Inc	450 Old BrickyaRd Rd	Greenwood	SC	29648	**866-358-3589**	864-941-4700
Vicwest Corp	1296 S Service Rd W	Oakville	ON	L6L5T7	**800-265-6583**	905-825-2252
Wolf Robotics LLC	4600 Innovation Dr	Fort Collins	CO	80525	**866-965-3911**	970-225-7600
Wooster Products Inc	1000 Spruce St PO Box 6005	Wooster	OH	44691	**800-321-4936**	330-264-2844

491 METALS SERVICE CENTERS

Company	Address	City	State	ZIP	Toll-Free	Phone
A & B Aluminum & Brass Foundry	11165 Denton Dr	Dallas	TX	75229	**800-743-4995**	972-247-3579
A&B Process Systems Corp	201 S Wisconsin Ave	Stratford	WI	54484	**888-258-2789**	715-687-4332
ABC Metals Inc	500 W Clinton St	Logansport	IN	46947	**800-238-8470**	
Abt Foam LLC	259 Murdock Rd	Troutman	NC	28166	**800-438-6057**	704-528-9806
Accurate Alloys Inc	5455 Irwindale Ave	Irwindale	CA	91706	**800-842-2222**	626-338-4012
Acier Picard Inc	3000 Rue De L' Etchemin	Levis	QC	G6W7X6	**888-834-0646**	418-834-8300
Action Stainless & Alloys Inc	1505 Halsey Way	Carrollton	TX	75007	**800-749-2523**	972-466-1500
Advanced Support Products Inc	24227 Fm 2978 Rd	Tomball	TX	77375	**800-941-5737**	281-357-1277
Aladdin Steel Inc	PO Box 89	Gillespie	IL	62033	**800-637-4455**	217-839-2121
Alaskan Copper & Brass Co	3223 Sixth Ave S	Seattle	WA	98134	**800-552-7661**	206-623-5800
Alfiniti Inc	1152 rue Manic	Chicoutimi	QC	G7K1A2	**800-334-8731**	418-696-2545
All American Grating Inc	3001 Grand Ave	Pittsburgh	PA	15225	**800-962-9692**	412-771-6970
All Foils Inc	16100 Imperial Pkwy	Strongsville	OH	44149	**800-521-0054**	440-572-3645
All Metals Industries Inc	PO Box 807	Belmont	NH	03220	**800-654-6043**	603-267-7023
Alliance Corp	2395 Meadowpine Blvd	Mississauga	ON	L5N7W6	**888-821-4797**	905-821-4797
Allied Sinterings Inc	29 Briar Ridge Rd	Danbury	CT	06810	**877-875-0464**	
Alro Steel Corp	3100 E High St	Jackson	MI	49204	**800-877-2576**	517-787-5500
Aluminum & Stainless Inc	PO Box 3484	Lafayette	LA	70502	**800-252-9074**	337-837-4381
Aluminum Distributing	2930 Sw Second Ave	Fort Lauderdale	FL	33315	**866-825-9271**	954-523-6474
American Aluminum Extrusion Company LLC	1 Saint Lawrence Ave	Beloit	WI	53511	**877-896-2236**	608-361-1800
American Chrome Co	518 W Crossroads Pkwy	Bolingbrook	IL	60440	**800-562-4488**	630-685-2200
American Douglas Metals Inc	783 Thorpe Rd	Orlando	FL	32824	**800-428-0023**	407-855-6590
American Strip Steel Inc	901 Coopertown Rd	Delanco	NJ	08075	**800-526-1216**	
AMI Metals Inc	1738 General George Patton Dr	Brentwood	TN	37027	**800-727-1903**	615-377-0400
Amstek Metal LLC	2408 W Mcdonough	Joliet	IL	60436	**800-551-9473**	815-725-2520
Applied Laser Technologies	8404 Venture Cir	Schofield	WI	54476	**888-359-3002**	715-359-3002
Art Iron Inc	860 Curtis St	Toledo	OH	43609	**800-472-1113**	419-241-1261
ASA Alloys Inc	81 Steinway Blvd	Etobicoke	ON	M9W6H6	**800-387-9166**	416-213-0000
Atlas Steel Products Co	7990 Bavaria Rd	Twinsburg	OH	44087	**800-444-1682**	330-425-1600
Basic Metals Inc	W180 Nn11819 River Ln	Germantown	WI	53022	**800-989-1996**	262-255-9034
BC Wire Rope & Rigging	2720 E Regal Park Dr	Anaheim	CA	92806	**800-669-5919**	714-666-8000
Berlin Metals LLC	3200 Sheffield Ave	Hammond	IN	46327	**800-754-8867**	219-933-0111
BMG Metals Inc	950 Masonic Ln	Richmond	VA	23231	**800-552-1510**	804-226-1024
Bobco Metals Co	2000 S Alameda St	Los Angeles	CA	90058	**877-952-6226**	
Bohler-Uddeholm North America	2505 Millenium Dr	Elgin	IL	60124	**800-638-2520**	630-883-3100
Brown-Strauss Steel	2495 Uravan St	Aurora	CO	80011	**800-677-2778*** *Sales	303-371-2200
Cambridge Street Metal Corp (CSM)	82 Stevens St	East Taunton	MA	02718	**800-254-7580**	508-822-2278
Chatham Steel Corp	501 W Boundary St	Savannah	GA	31401	**800-800-1337**	912-233-5751
Cherokee Steel Supply	196 Leroy Anderson Dr	Monroe	GA	30655	**800-729-0334**	770-207-4621
Chicago Tube & Iron Co	1 Chicago Tube Dr	Romeoville	IL	60446	**800-972-0217*** *Cust Svc	815-834-2500
City Pipe & Supply Corp	PO Box 2112	Odessa	TX	79760	**844-307-4044**	432-332-1541
Clayton Metals Inc	546 Clayton Ct	Wood Dale	IL	60191	**800-323-7628**	
Coastal Corrosion Control Surveys LLC	10172 Mammoth Ave	Baton Rouge	LA	70814	**800-894-2120**	225-275-6131
Columbia Pipe & Supply Co	1120 W Pershing Rd	Chicago	IL	60609	**888-429-4635**	773-927-6600
Consolidated Steel Services Inc	632 Glendale Vly Blvd	Fallentimber	PA	16639	**800-237-8783**	814-944-5890
Consumers Pipe & Supply Co	5832 E 61st St	Los Angeles	CA	90040	**800-338-7473**	323-685-6870
Contractors Steel Co	36555 Amrhein Rd	Livonia	MI	48150	**800-521-3946**	734-464-4000
Damascus Steel Casting Co	Blockhouse Rd Run Extn	New Brighton	PA	15066	**800-920-2210**	724-846-2770
Decker Steel & Supply Inc	4500 Train Ave	Cleveland	OH	44102	**800-321-6100**	216-281-7900
Domtech Inc	40 East Davis St	Trenton	ON	K8V6S4	**888-278-8258**	613-394-4884
Dubose National Energy Services Inc	PO Box 499	Clinton	NC	28329	**800-590-2150**	910-590-2151
East Coast Metals	171 Ruth Rd	Harleysville	PA	19438	**800-355-2060**	215-256-9550
Eaton Steel Corp	10221 Capital Ave	Oak Park	MI	48237	**800-527-3851**	248-398-3434
Ed Fagan Inc	769 Susquehanna Ave	Franklin Lakes	NJ	07417	**800-335-6827**	201-891-4003
Extrudex Aluminum Ltd	411 Chrislea Rd	Woodbridge	ON	L4L8N4	**800-668-7210**	416-745-4444
Field System Machining Inc	720 Schneider Dr	South Elgin	IL	60177	**800-789-2814**	847-468-1313
Fox Valley Spring Company Inc	N915 Craftsmen Dr	Greenville	WI	54942	**800-776-2645**	920-757-7777
GB Tubulars Inc	950 Threadneedle St Ste 130	Houston	TX	77079	**888-245-3848**	713-465-3585
General Steel Inc	PO Box 1503	Macon	GA	31202	**800-476-2794**	478-746-2794
Gibbs Wire & Steel Company Inc	Metals Dr PO Box 520	Southington	CT	06489	**800-800-4422**	860-621-0121
Hanna Steel Corp	3812 Commerce Ave PO Box 558	Fairfield	AL	35064	**800-633-8252**	205-780-1111
Hansen Architectural Systems	5500 Se Alexander St	Hillsboro	OR	97123	**800-599-2965**	503-356-0959
Howard Precision Metals Inc	PO Box 240127	Milwaukee	WI	53224	**800-444-0311**	414-355-9611
Hynes Industries	3760 Oakwood	Youngstown	OH	44515	**800-321-9257**	
Industrial Material Corp	7701 Harborside Dr	Galveston	TX	77554	**800-701-4462**	409-744-4538
International Mold Steel Inc	6796 Powerline Dr	Florence	KY	41042	**800-625-6653**	859-342-6000
Ken-Mac Metals Inc	17901 Englewood Dr	Cleveland	OH	44130	**800-831-9503**	440-234-7500
Key Bellevilles Inc	100 Key Ln	Leechburg	PA	15656	**800-245-3600**	724-295-5111
KGS Steel Inc	3725 Pine Ln	Bessemer	AL	35022	**800-533-3846**	205-425-0800
Kivort Steel	380 Hudson River Rd	Waterford	NY	12188	**800-462-2616**	518-590-7233
Klein Steel Service	105 Vanguarden Pkwy	Rochester	NY	14606	**800-477-6789*** *Cust Svc	585-328-4000
Kreher Steel Company LLC	1550 N 25th Ave	Melrose Park	IL	60160	**800-323-0745**	
Lapham-Hickey Steel Corp	5500 W 73rd St	Chicago	IL	60638	**800-323-8443**	708-496-6111
Latrobe Specialty Steel Co	2626 Ligonier St	Latrobe	PA	15650	**888-245-7856**	724-537-7711
Lindquist Steels Inc	1050 Woodend Rd	Stratford	CT	06615	**800-243-9637**	
Livingston Pipe & Tube Inc	1612 Rt 4 N	Staunton	IL	62088	**800-548-7473**	618-635-8700
LMS Reinforcing Steel Group Inc	6320 148th St	Surrey	BC	V3S3C4	**888-698-2008**	604-598-9930
Loveman Steel Corp	5455 Perkins Rd	Bedford Heights	OH	44146	**800-568-3626**	
Maas-Hansen Steel Corp	2435 E 37th St PO Box 58364	Vernon	CA	90058	**800-647-8335**	323-586-0171
Majestic Steel USA	5300 Majestic Pkwy	Cleveland	OH	44146	**800-321-5590**	440-786-2666
Marmon/Keystone Corp	PO Box 992	Butler	PA	16003	**800-544-1748**	724-283-3000
Matenaer Corp	810 Schoenhaar Dr	West Bend	WI	53090	**800-254-0873**	262-338-0700
Mazel & Company Inc	4300 W Ferdinand St	Chicago	IL	60624	**800-525-4023**	773-533-1600
McNichols Co	9401 Corporate Lake Dr	Tampa	FL	33634	**877-884-4653**	
Merfish Pipe & Supply Co	PO Box 15879	Houston	TX	77220	**800-869-5731**	713-869-5731
Merit USA	620 Clark Ave	Pittsburg	CA	94565	**800-445-6374**	

Classified Section

Company / Address	City	State	Zip	Toll-Free	Phone
Metal Supermarkets IP Inc 520 Abilene Dr 2nd Fl	Mississauga	ON	L5T2H7	**866-867-9344**	905-362-8226
MultAlloy Inc 8511 Monroe St	Houston	TX	77061	**800-568-9551**	
Murphy & Nolan Inc 340 Peat St PO Box 6689	Syracuse	NY	13217	**800-836-6385**	315-474-8203
Napco Steel Inc 1800 Arthur Dr	West Chicago	IL	60185	**800-292-8010**	630-293-1900
National Specialty Alloys LLC 18250 Keith Harrow Blvd *General	Houston	TX	77084	**800-847-5653***	281-345-2115
National Tube Supply Co 925 Central Ave	University Park	IL	60466	**800-229-6872**	708-534-2700
New Process Steel Corp 5800 Westview Dr	Houston	TX	77055	**800-392-4989**	713-686-9631
North American Steel Co 18300 Miles Ave	Cleveland	OH	44128	**800-321-9310**	216-475-7300
Northwest Aluminum Specialties Inc 2929 W Second St	The Dalles	OR	97058	**800-626-2241**	541-296-6161
O'neal Flat Rolled Metals 1229 S Fulton Ave	Brighton	CO	80601	**800-336-3365**	303-654-0300
O'Neal Steel Inc 744 41st St N	Birmingham	AL	35222	**800-861-8272**	205-599-8000
Olympic Steel Inc 5096 Richmond Rd *NASDAQ: ZEUS*	Bedford Heights	OH	44146	**800-321-6290**	216-292-3800
OnlineMetals.com 1138 W Ewing	Seattle	WA	98119	**800-533-6350**	
Owen Industries Inc 501 Ave H	Carter Lake	IA	51510	**800-831-9252**	712-347-5500
Pacesetter Steel Service Inc 1045 Big Shanty Rd	Kennesaw	GA	30144	**800-749-6505**	770-919-8000
Pacific Steel & Recycling 1401 Third St NW	Great Falls	MT	59404	**800-889-6264**	406-771-7222
Paco Steel & Engineering Corp 19818 S Alameda St	Rancho Dominguez	CA	90221	**800-421-1473**	310-537-6375
Palmer Manufacturing 18 N Bechtle Ave	Springfield	OH	45504	**800-457-5456**	937-323-6339
Paragon Steel Enterprises LLC 4211 County Rd 61	Butler	IN	46721	**800-411-5677**	260-868-1100
Parker Steel Co PO Box 2883	Toledo	OH	43606	**800-333-4140**	419-473-2481
Peerless Steel Corp 2450 Austin	Troy	MI	48083	**800-482-3947**	248-528-3200
Pentz Design Pattern & Foundry 14823 Main St Ne	Duvall	WA	98019	**800-411-6555**	425-788-6490
Perforated Tubes Inc 4850 Fulton St E	Ada	MI	49301	**888-869-5736**	616-942-4550
Peterson Steel Corp 61 W Mountain St	Worcester	MA	01606	**800-325-3245**	508-853-3630
Phillips & Johnston Inc 21w179 Hill Ave	Glen Ellyn	IL	60137	**877-411-8823**	630-469-8150
Phoenix Metals Co 4685 Buford Hwy	Norcross	GA	30071	**800-241-2290**	770-447-4211
Pioneer Steel Corp 7447 Intervale St	Detroit	MI	48238	**800-999-9440**	313-933-9400
Posner Industries Inc 8641 Edgeworth Dr	Capitol Heights	MD	20743	**888-767-6377**	301-350-1000
Precision Steel Warehouse Inc 3500 Wolf Rd	Franklin Park	IL	60131	**800-323-0740**	847-455-7000
Rancocas Metals Corp 35 Indel Ave	Rancocas	NJ	08073	**800-762-6382**	609-267-4120
Rangers Die Casting Co 10828 S Alameda St	Lynwood	CA	90262	**877-386-9969**	310-764-1800
Rayco Industries Inc 1502 Valley Rd	Richmond	VA	23222	**800-505-7111**	804-321-7111
Rolled Alloys Inc 125 W Sterns Rd	Temperance	MI	48182	**800-521-0332**	734-847-0561
Rolled Steel Products Corp 2187 Garfield Ave	Los Angeles	CA	90040	**800-400-7833**	323-723-8836
Russel Metals Inc 6600 Financial Dr *TSE: RUS*	Mississauga	ON	L5N7J6	**800-268-0750**	905-819-7777
Saginaw Pipe Company Inc 1980 Hwy 31 S PO Box 8	Saginaw	AL	35137	**800-433-1374**	205-664-3670
Salit Steel Ltd 7771 Stanley Ave	Niagara Falls	ON	L2E6V6	**800-263-7110**	905-354-5691
Service Steel Aerospace Corp 4609 70th St E	Fife	WA	98424	**800-426-9794**	
Shamrock Steel Sales Inc 238 W County Rd S	Odessa	TX	79763	**800-299-2317**	432-337-2317
Sheffield Metals International Inc 5467 Evergreen Pkwy	Sheffield Village	OH	44054	**800-283-5262**	440-934-8500
Siskin Steel & Supply Co Inc 1901 Riverfront Pkwy	Chattanooga	TN	37408	**800-756-3671**	423-756-3671
Skyline Steel LLC 8 Woodhollow Rd Ste 102	Parsippany	NJ	07054	**866-875-9546**	
Soleno Inc 1160 Rt 133 CP 837	Saint-jean-sur-richelieu	QC	J2X4J5	**877-633-7473**	450-347-7855
Solon Manufacturing Co 425 Center St	Chardon	OH	44024	**800-323-9717**	440-286-7149
Southern Copper & Supply Company Inc 875 Yeager Pkwy	Pelham	AL	35124	**800-289-2728**	205-664-9440
Southern Wire Corp 8045 Metro Rd	Olive Branch	MS	38654	**800-238-0333**	662-890-4873
Specialty Pipe & Tube Inc PO Box 516	Mineral Ridge	OH	44440	**800-842-5839**	330-505-8262
Spectra Aluminum Products Inc 95 Reagens Industrial Pkwy	Bradford	ON	L3Z2A4	**866-999-2586**	905-778-8093
State Pipe & Supply Inc 9615 S Norwalk Blvd	Santa Fe Springs	CA	90670	**800-733-6410**	562-695-5555
Staub Metals Corp 7747 E Rosecrans Ave	Paramount	CA	90723	**800-447-8282**	562-602-2200
Steel Supply Co, The 5101 Newport Dr	Rolling Meadows	IL	60008	**800-323-7571**	
Steel Unlimited Inc 456 W Valley Blvd	Rialto	CA	92376	**800-544-6453**	909-873-1222
Steel Warehouse Company Inc 2722 W Tucker Dr	South Bend	IN	46619	**800-348-2529**	574-236-5100
Supra Alloys Inc 351 Cortez Cir	Camarillo	CA	93012	**888-647-8772**	805-388-2138
Sylvania Steel Corp 4169 Holland Sylvania Rd *General	Toledo	OH	43623	**800-435-0986***	419-885-3838
Taco Metals Inc 50 NE 179th St	Miami	FL	33162	**800-653-8568**	305-652-8566
TCI Aluminum/North Inc 2353 Davis Ave	Hayward	CA	94545	**800-824-6197**	510-786-3750
Terra Nova Steel & Iron (Ontario) Inc 3595 Hawkestone Rd	Mississauga	ON	L5C2V1	**877-427-0269**	905-273-3872
Texas Pipe & Supply Co Inc 2330 Holmes Rd	Houston	TX	77051	**800-233-8736**	713-799-9235
ThyssenKrupp Materials NA 22355 W 11 Mile Rd	Southfield	MI	48033	**800-926-2600**	248-233-5600
Tioga Pipe Supply Company Inc 2450 Wheatsheaf Ln	Philadelphia	PA	19137	**800-523-3678**	215-831-0700
Tomson Steel Co (Inc) PO Box 940	Middletown	OH	45042	**800-837-3001**	
Trident Steel Corp 12825 Flushing Meadows Dr Ste 110	St. Louis	MO	63131	**800-777-9687**	314-822-0500
Triple-S Steel Supply LLC 6000 Jensen Dr	Houston	TX	77026	**800-231-1034**	713-697-7105
Tubular Steel Inc 1031 Executive Pkwy Dr	Saint Louis	MO	63141	**800-388-7491**	314-851-9200
Turret Steel Industries Inc 105 Pine St	Imperial	PA	15126	**800-245-4800**	724-218-1014
United Aluminum Corp 100 United Dr	North Haven	CT	06473	**800-243-2515**	203-239-5881
United States Brass & Copper Co Inc 1401 Brook Dr	Downers Grove	IL	60515	**800-821-2854**	630-629-9340
Universal Steel Co 6600 Grant Ave	Cleveland	OH	44105	**800-669-2645**	216-883-4972
Valiant Steel & Equipment Inc 6455 Old Peachtree Rd	Norcross	GA	30071	**800-939-9905**	770-417-1235
Viking Materials Inc 3225 Como Ave SE *General	Minneapolis	MN	55414	**800-682-3942***	612-617-5800
Vista Metals Inc 65 Ballou Blvd	Bristol	RI	02809	**800-431-4113**	401-253-1772
West Central Steel Inc 110 19th St NW PO Box 1178	Willmar	MN	56201	**800-992-8853**	320-235-4070
Westfield Steel Inc 530 State Rd 32 W	Westfield	IN	46074	**800-622-4984**	
White Aluminum Products LLC 2101 US Hwy 441	Leesburg	FL	34748	**888-474-5884**	
Willbanks Metals Inc 1155 NE 28th St	Fort Worth	TX	76106	**800-772-2352**	817-625-6161
Wire Rope Industries Ltd 5501 Trans-Canada Hwy	Pointe-claire	QC	H9R1B7	**800-565-5501**	514-697-9711
Wiscolift Inc W6396 Speciality Dr	Greenville	WI	54942	**800-242-3477**	920-757-8832
Wisconsin Steel & Tube Corp 1555 N Mayfair Rd	Milwaukee	WI	53226	**800-279-8335**	414-453-4441
Wrisco Industries Inc 355 Hiatt Dr Ste B	Palm Beach Gardens	FL	33418	**800-627-2646**	561-626-5700

492 METALWORKING DEVICES & ACCESSORIES

SEE ALSO Tool & Die Shops ; Machine Tools - Metal Cutting Types ; Machine Tools - Metal Forming Types

Company / Address	City	State	Zip	Toll-Free	Phone
Acme Industrial Co 441 Maple Ave	Carpentersville	IL	60110	**800-323-5582**	847-428-3911
Advanced Machine & Engineering Co 2500 Latham St	Rockford	IL	61103	**800-225-4263**	815-962-6076
Allied Machine & Engineering Corp 120 Deeds Dr	Dover	OH	44622	**800-321-5537**	330-343-4283
American Drill Bushings Co (ADB) 5740 Hunt Rd	Valdosta	GA	31606	**800-423-4425**	229-253-8928
ASKO Inc 501 W Seventh Ave	Homestead	PA	15120	**800-321-1310**	412-461-4110
ATI Metal Working Products 1 Teledyne Pl	La Vergne	TN	37086	**888-926-4211**	615-641-4200
Besly Cutting Tools Inc 16200 Woodmint Ln	South Beloit	IL	61080	**800-435-2965**	815-389-2231
Big Kaiser Precision Tooling Inc 641 Fargo Ave	Elk Grove Village	IL	60007	**888-866-5776**	847-228-7660
Buck Chuck Co 2155 Traversefield Dr	Traverse City	MI	49686	**800-228-2825**	
Carbro Corp 15724 Condon Ave PO Box 278	Lawndale	CA	90260	**888-738-4400**	310-643-8400
Carl Zeiss Industrial Metrology 6250 Sycamore Ln N	Maple Grove	MN	55369	**800-327-9735**	763-744-2400
CJT Koolcarb Inc 494 Mission St	Carol Stream	IL	60188	**800-323-2299**	630-690-5933
Cline Tool & Service Co PO Box 866	Newton	IA	50208	**866-561-3022**	641-792-7081
Deltronic Corp 3900 W Segerstrom Ave	Santa Ana	CA	92704	**800-451-6922**	714-545-5800
Detroit Edge Tool Co 6570 E Nevada St	Detroit	MI	48234	**800-404-2038**	313-366-4120
Edmunds Gages 45 Spring Ln	Farmington	CT	06032	**800-878-1622**	860-677-2813
Forkardt 2155 Traverse Field Dr	Traverse City	MI	49686	**800-544-3823**	231-995-8300
Fullerton Tool Company Inc 121 Perry St	Saginaw	MI	48602	**855-722-7243**	989-799-4550
Garr Tool Co 7800 N Alger Rd	Alma	MI	48801	**800-248-9003**	989-463-6171
Gilman USA 1230 Cheyenne Ave PO Box 5	Grafton	WI	53024	**800-445-6267**	262-377-2434
Glastonbury Southern Gage 46 Industrial Pk Rd	Erin	TN	37061	**800-251-4243**	931-289-4243
Guhring Inc 1445 Commerce Ave	Brookfield	WI	53045	**800-776-6170**	262-784-6730

Company / Address	City	State	ZIP	Toll-Free	Phone
Hannibal Carbide Tool Inc 5000 Paris Gravel Rd	Hannibal	MO	63401	**800-451-9436**	573-221-2775
Hardinge Inc 1 Hardinge Dr *NASDAQ: HDNG*	Elmira	NY	14902	**800-843-8801**	607-734-2281
Hayden Twist Drill & Tool Company Inc 22822 Globe St	Warren	MI	48089	**800-521-1780**	586-754-7700
Hougen Manufacturing Inc 3001 Hougen Dr *Orders	Swartz Creek	MI	48473	**800-426-7818***	810-635-7111
Huron Machine Products Inc 228 SW 21st Terr	Fort Lauderdale	FL	33312	**800-327-8186**	
Husqvarna Construction Products 17400 W 119th St	Olathe	KS	66061	**800-288-5040**	
Industrial Tools Inc (ITI) 1111 S Rose Ave	Oxnard	CA	93033	**800-266-5561**	805-483-1111
Jergens Inc 15700 S Waterloo Rd	Cleveland	OH	44110	**800-537-4367**	877-486-1454
KEO Cutters Inc 25040 Easy St	Warren	MI	48089	**888-390-2050**	586-771-2050
Lancaster Knives Inc 165 Ct St	Lancaster	NY	14086	**800-869-9666**	716-683-5050
Lovejoy Tool Company Inc 133 Main St	Springfield	VT	05156	**800-843-8376**	802-885-2194
Melin Tool Co 5565 Venture Dr Unit C	Cleveland	OH	44130	**800-521-1078**	216-362-4230
Micro 100 Tool Corp 1410 E Pine Ave	Meridian	ID	83642	**800-421-8065**	208-888-7310
NED Corp 31 Town Forest Rd	Oxford	MA	01540	**800-343-6086**	
Niagara Cutter Inc 2805 Bellingham Dr	Troy	MI	48083	**800-832-8326**	716-689-8400
North American Tool Corp 215 Elmwood Ave	South Beloit	IL	61080	**800-872-8277**	815-389-2300
Onsrud Cutter LP 800 Liberty Dr	Libertyville	IL	60048	**800-234-1560**	847-362-1560
OSG Tap & Die Inc 676 E Fullerton Ave	Glendale Heights	IL	60139	**800-837-2223**	630-790-1400
Phillips Corp 7390 Coca Cola Dr	Hanover	MD	21076	**800-878-4242**	410-564-2929
Powers Fasteners Inc 2 Powers Ln	Brewster	NY	10509	**800-524-3244**	914-235-6300
Regal-Beloit Corp 200 State St *NYSE: RBC*	Beloit	WI	53511	**800-672-6495**	608-364-8800
Reiff & Nestor Co 50 Reiff St	Lykens	PA	17048	**800-521-3422**	717-453-7113
S-T Industries Inc 301 Armstrong Blvd N PO Box 517	Saint James	MN	56081	**800-326-2039**	507-375-3211
Scotchman Industries Inc 180 E Hwy 14	Philip	SD	57567	**800-843-8844**	605-859-2542
Seco Tools 2805 Bellingham Dr	Troy	MI	48083	**800-832-8326**	248-528-5200
Spiralock Corp 25235 Dequindre Rd	Madison Heights	MI	48071	**800-521-2688**	248-543-7800
Star Cutter Co 23461 Industrial Pk Dr	Farmington	MI	48335	**877-635-3488**	248-474-8200
Starrett Webber Gage Div 24500 Detroit Rd	Cleveland	OH	44145	**800-255-3924**	440-835-0001
Stilson Products 15935 Sturgeon St	Roseville	MI	48066	**888-400-5978**	586-778-1100
Tapmatic Corp 802 S Clearwater Loop *General	Post Falls	ID	83854	**800-854-6019***	208-773-8048
Thread Check Inc 390 Oser Ave	Hauppauge	NY	11788	**800-767-7633**	631-231-1515
TM Smith Tool International Corp 360 Hubbard Ave	Mount Clemens	MI	48043	**800-521-4894**	586-468-1465
United Drill Bushing Corp 12200 Woodruff Ave	Downey	CA	90241	**800-486-3466**	562-803-1521
Viking Drill & Tool Inc 355 State St	Saint Paul	MN	55107	**800-328-4655**	651-227-8911
Walker Magnetics Group Inc 20 Rockdale St	Worcester	MA	01606	**800-962-4638**	508-853-3232
Walter USA Inc N22 W23855 Ridgeview Pkwy W	Waukesha	WI	53188	**800-945-5554**	
Zenith Cutter Co 5200 Zenith Pkwy	Loves Park	IL	61111	**800-223-5202**	815-282-5200

493 METALWORKING MACHINERY

SEE ALSO Rolling Mill Machinery

Company / Address	City	State	ZIP	Toll-Free	Phone
Armstrong Mfg Co 2700 SE Tacoma St	Portland	OR	97202	**800-426-6226**	503-228-8381
Bartell Machinery Systems LLC 6321 Elmer Hill Rd	Rome	NY	13440	**800-537-8473**	315-336-7600
Belvac Production Machinery Inc 237 Graves Mill Rd	Lynchburg	VA	24502	**800-423-5822**	434-239-0358
Eubanks Engineering Co 3022 Inland Empire Blvd	Ontario	CA	91764	**800-729-4208**	909-483-2456
Pannier Corp 207 Sandusky St	Pittsburgh	PA	15212	**877-726-6437**	412-323-4900
Pines Technology 30505 Clemens Rd	Westlake	OH	44145	**800-207-2840**	440-835-5553
Red Bud Industries 200 B & E Industrial Dr *Cust Svc	Red Bud	IL	62278	**800-851-4612***	618-282-3801
Rowe Machinery & Automation Inc 76 Hinckley Rd	Clinton	ME	04927	**800-247-2645**	207-426-2351
Sweed Machinery Inc 653 Second Ave PO Box 228 *Sales	Gold Hill	OR	97525	**800-888-1352***	541-855-1512

494 METERS & OTHER COUNTING DEVICES

Company / Address	City	State	ZIP	Toll-Free	Phone
AMETEK Inc Dixson Div 287 27 Rd	Grand Junction	CO	81503	**888-302-0639**	970-242-8863
AMETEK Sensor Technology Drexelbrook Div 205 Keith Valley Rd *Cust Svc	Horsham	PA	19044	**800-553-9092***	215-674-1234
Auto Meter Products Inc 413 W Elm St	Sycamore	IL	60178	**866-248-6356**	815-895-8141
Badger Meter Inc 4545 W Brown Deer Rd *NYSE: BMI*	Milwaukee	WI	53224	**800-876-3837**	414-355-0400
Clark-Reliance Corp 16633 Foltz Pkwy	Strongsville	OH	44149	**800-238-4027**	440-572-1500
Duncan Solutions Inc 633 W Wisconsin Ave Ste 1600	Milwaukee	WI	53203	**888-993-8622**	
Electro-Sensors Inc 6111 Blue Cir Dr *NASDAQ: ELSE*	Minnetonka	MN	55343	**800-328-6170**	952-930-0100
Elster American Meter Co 2221 Industrial Rd	Nebraska City	NE	68410	**877-595-6254**	402-873-8200
Eugene Ernst Products Company Inc PO Box 925	Farmingdale	NJ	07727	**800-992-2843**	732-938-5641
Greenwald Industries 212 Middlesex Ave	Chester	CT	06412	**800-221-0982**	860-526-0800
Laser Technology Inc 7070 S Tucson Way	Englewood	CO	80112	**800-280-6113**	303-649-1000
Maxima Technologies Stewart Warner 1811 Rohrerstown Rd	Lancaster	PA	17601	**800-676-1837**	717-581-1000
PMP Corp 25 Security Dr *Cust Svc	Avon	CT	06001	**800-243-6628***	860-677-9656
POM Inc 200 S Elmira Ave PO Box 430	Russellville	AR	72802	**800-331-7275**	479-968-2880
Sparling Instruments Company Inc 4097 N Temple City Blvd *Sales	El Monte	CA	91731	**800-800-3569***	626-444-0571
Thomas G Faria Corp 385 Norwich-New London Tpke	Uncasville	CT	06382	**800-473-2742**	860-848-9271

495 MICROGRAPHICS PRODUCTS & SERVICES

Company / Address	City	State	ZIP	Toll-Free	Phone
BMI Imaging Systems 1115 E Arques Ave	Sunnyvale	CA	94085	**800-359-3456**	408-736-7444
Comstor Productivity Ctr Inc 441 W Sharp Ave	Spokane	WA	99201	**800-776-2451**	509-534-5080
DPF Data Services Group Inc 1990 Swarthmore Ave	Lakewood	NJ	08701	**800-431-4416**	732-370-8840
DST Output 5220 Robert J Mathews Pkwy	El Dorado Hills	CA	95762	**800-441-7587**	916-939-4960
Eye Communication Systems Inc 455 E Industrial Dr	Hartland	WI	53029	**800-558-2153**	262-367-1360
HF Group Inc 203 W Artesia Blvd	Compton	CA	90220	**800-421-5000**	310-605-0755
Indus International Inc 340 S Oak St PO Box 890	West Salem	WI	54669	**800-843-9377**	608-786-0300

496 MILITARY BASES

496-1 Air Force Bases

Base / Address	City	State	ZIP	Toll-Free	Phone
Cannon Air Force Base 110 E Sextant Ave Ste 1150	Cannon AFB	NM	88103	**877-283-3858**	575-784-4131
Eielson Air Force Base 354 Broadway St Unit 2B	Eielson AFB	AK	99702	**800-538-6647**	907-377-1110
Kirtland Air Force Base 2000 Wyoming Blvd SE Ste A-1	Kirtland AFB	NM	87117	**877-246-1453**	505-846-5991
Laughlin Air Force Base 561 Liberty Dr Ste 3	Laughlin AFB	TX	78843	**866-966-1020**	830-298-5988
Little Rock Air Force Base 1250 Thomas Ave	Little Rock AFB	AR	72099	**800-557-6815**	501-987-1110
Luke Air Force Base 14185 W Falcon St	Luke AFB	AZ	85309	**800-321-1080**	623-856-5853
Malmstrom Air Force Base 7410 Flightline Dr Bldg 300	Malmstrom AFB	MT	59402	**866-731-4633**	406-731-1110
Maxwell Air Force Base 55 Le May Plaza S	Maxwell AFB	AL	36112	**877-353-6807**	334-953-2014
McConnell Air Force Base 57837 Coffeyville St Ste 271	McConnell AFB	KS	67221	**877-272-7337**	316-759-6100
Mountain Home Air Force Base 366 Gunfighter Ave Ste 314	Mountain Home AFB	ID	83648	**855-366-0140**	208-828-6800
Seymour Johnson Air Force Base 1510 Wright Bros Ave	Seymour Johnson AFB	NC	27531	**800-525-0102**	919-722-0027
Shaw Air Force Base 517 Lance Ave Ste 106	Shaw AFB	SC	29152	**800-235-7776**	803-895-2019
Sheppard Air Force Base 419 G Ave Ste 3	Sheppard AFB	TX	76311	**877-676-1847**	940-676-2511
Tyndall Air Force Base 445 Suwannee Rd 101	Tyndall AFB	FL	32403	**800-356-5273**	850-283-1110
Vance Air Force Base 246 Brown Pkwy	Vance AFB	OK	73705	**866-966-1020**	580-213-7476
Whiteman Air Force Base 1081 Arnold Ave Bldg 59 Ste 104	Whiteman AFB	MO	65305	**866-363-8667**	660-687-6123

496-2 Army Bases

Base / Address	City	State	ZIP	Toll-Free	Phone
Fort Leonard Wood Bldg 744	Fort Leonard Wood	MO	65473	**800-350-7746**	573-596-0131

Name / Address	City	State	Zip	Toll-Free	Phone
Fort Polk 2030 14th St	Fort Polk	LA	71459	**800-752-4658**	337-531-2911
Fort Riley 405 Pershing Ct	Fort Riley	KS	66442	**800-273-8255**	785-239-2022

496-3 Naval Installations

Name / Address	City	State	Zip	Toll-Free	Phone
Naval Air Station Jacksonville 6801 Roosevelt Blvd	Jacksonville	FL	32212	**800-849-6024**	904-542-2338
Naval Air Station Joint Reserve Base New Orleans 301 Russell Ave	New Orleans	LA	70143	**800-729-7327**	504-678-3254
Naval Air Station Patuxent River 22268 Cedar Point Road Bldg 409	Patuxent River	MD	20670	**877-995-5247**	301-342-3000
Naval Air Station Pensacola 190 Radford Blvd	Pensacola	FL	32508	**800-628-9466**	
Naval Base San Diego 3455 Senn Rd	San Diego	CA	92136	**877-995-5247**	619-556-1011
Naval Station Mayport PO Box 280032	Mayport	FL	32228	**800-872-7245**	904-270-5401
U.S. Fleet Forces Command 1562 Mitscher Ave Ste 250	Norfolk	VA	23551	**800-473-3549**	757-836-3630

497 MILITARY SERVICE ACADEMIES

Name / Address	City	State	Zip	Toll-Free	Phone
US Air Force Academy (USAFA) 2304 Cadet Dr Ste 2300	Air Force Academy	CO	80840	**800-443-9266**	719-333-1110
US Naval Academy 121 Blake Rd *Admissions	Annapolis	MD	21402	**888-249-7707***	410-293-1000

498 MILLWORK

SEE ALSO Shutters - Window (All Types) ; Lumber & Building Supplies ; Doors & Windows - Wood ; Home Improvement Centers

Name / Address	City	State	Zip	Toll-Free	Phone
Anlin Industries 1665 Tollhouse Rd	Clovis	CA	93611	**800-287-7996**	559-322-1531
Boiseries Raymond Inc 11880, 56e Ave	Montreal	QC	H1E2L6	**800-361-6577**	514-494-1141
Buffelen Woodworking Co 1901 Taylor Way	Tacoma	WA	98421	**800-423-8810**	253-627-1191
Cain Millwork Inc 1 Cain Pkwy	Rochelle	IL	61068	**800-417-3511**	815-561-9700
Canamould Extrusions Inc 101a Roytec Rd	Woodbridge	ON	L4L8A9	**866-874-6762**	905-264-4436
Carter-Lee ProBuild 1717 W Washington St	Indianapolis	IN	46222	**800-344-9242**	317-639-5431
Cascade Wood Products Inc PO Box 2429	White City	OR	97503	**800-423-3311**	541-826-2911
Central Woodwork Inc 870 Keough Rd	Collierville	TN	38017	**800-788-3775**	901-363-4141
Commercial & Architectural Products Inc PO Box 250	Dover	OH	44622	**800-377-1221**	330-343-6621
Contact Industries Inc 9200 SE Sunnybrook Blvd Ste 200	Clackamas	OR	97015	**800-547-1038**	503-228-7361
Cox Interior Inc 1751 Old Columbia Rd	Campbellsville	KY	42718	**800-733-1751**	
Dashwood Industries Ltd 69323 Richmond St	Centralia	ON	N0M1K0	**800-265-4284**	519-228-6624
Delden Manufacturing Company Inc 3530 N Kimball Dr	Kansas City	MO	64161	**800-821-3708**	816-413-1600
Dorris Lumber & Moulding Co, The 2601 Redding Ave	Sacramento	CA	95820	**800-827-5823**	916-452-7531
Graves Lumber Co 1315 S Cleveland-Massillon Rd	Copley	OH	44321	**877-500-5515**	330-666-1115
HB&G Inc PO Box 589	Troy	AL	36081	**800-264-4424**	334-566-5000
Horner Millwork Corp 1255 Grand Army Hwy	Somerset	MA	02726	**800-543-5403**	508-679-6479
Huttig Bldg Products Inc (HBP) 555 Maryville University Dr Ste 400 *OTC: HBPI*	Saint Louis	MO	63141	**800-325-4466**	314-216-2600
Inline Fibreglass Ltd 30 Constellation Ct	Toronto	ON	M9W1K1	**866-566-5656**	416-679-1171
Jeld-Wen Inc PO Box 1329	Klamath Falls	OR	97601	**800-535-3936**	
Lafayette Wood-Works Inc 3004 Cameron St	Lafayette	LA	70506	**800-960-3311**	337-233-5250
Laflamme Doors & Windows Corp 39 Industrielle	St. Apollinaire	QC	G0S2E0	**800-463-1922**	
Louisiana-Pacific Corp 414 Union St Ste 2000 *NYSE: LPX*	Nashville	TN	37219	**888-820-0325**	615-986-5600
Mann & Parker Lumber Company Inc, The 335 N Constitution Ave	New Freedom	PA	17349	**800-632-9098**	717-235-4834
Menzner Lumber & Supply Co PO Box 217	Marathon	WI	54448	**800-257-1284**	
Michbi Doors Inc 75 Emjay Blvd	Brentwood	NY	11717	**800-854-4541**	631-231-9050
Milliken Millwork Inc 6361 Sterling Dr N	Sterling Heights	MI	48312	**800-686-9218**	586-264-0950
Nana Wall Systems Inc 707 Redwood Hwy	Mill Valley	CA	94941	**800-873-5673**	415-383-3148
New England Garage Door 15 Campanelli Cir	Canton	MA	02021	**800-676-7734**	781-821-2737
Nickell Moulding Company Inc 3015 Mobile Dr	Elkhart	IN	46515	**800-838-2151**	574-264-3129
Paltech Enterprises Inc 2560 Bing Miller Ln	Urbana	IA	52345	**800-949-1006**	319-443-2700
Quanex Building Products 2270 Woodale Dr	Mounds View	MN	55112	**800-233-4383**	763-231-4000
Randall Bros Inc 665 Marietta St NW *Cust Svc	Atlanta	GA	30313	**800-476-4539***	404-892-6666
Raynor Garage Doors 1101 E River Rd	Dixon	IL	61021	**800-472-9667**	815-288-1431
Reeb Millwork Corp 7475 Henry Clay Blvd	Liverpool	NY	13088	**800-862-8622**	315-451-6699
Royal Cup Coffee and Tea 160 Cleage Dr	Birmingham	AL	35217	**800-366-5836**	
Shanahan's LP 8400-124 St	Surrey	BC	V3W6K1	**888-591-5999**	604-591-5111
Shuster's Bldg Components 2920 Clay Pk	Irwin	PA	15642	**800-676-0640**	724-446-7000
Somerset Door & Column Co 174 Sagamore St	Somerset	PA	15501	**800-242-7916**	814-444-9427
Southern Staircase Inc 6025 Shiloh Rd Ste E	Alpharetta	GA	30005	**800-874-8408**	770-888-7333
Sundt Construction 2620 S 55th St	Tempe	AZ	85282	**800-280-3000**	480-293-3000
Sunrise Mfg. Inc 2665 Mercantile Dr	Rancho Cordova	CA	95742	**800-748-6529**	916-635-6262
Tru Tech Corp 20 Vaughan Vly Blvd	Vaughan	ON	L4H0B1	**888-760-0099**	905-856-0096
Werzalit of America Inc 40 Holly Ave	Bradford	PA	16701	**800-999-3730**	814-362-3881
Woodgrain Millworks Inc 300 NW 16th St	Fruitland	ID	83619	**888-783-5485**	208-452-3801
Young Mfg Company Inc 521 S Main St PO Box 167	Beaver Dam	KY	42320	**800-545-6595**	270-274-3306

499 MINERAL PRODUCTS - NONMETALLIC

SEE ALSO Insulation & Acoustical Products

Name / Address	City	State	Zip	Toll-Free	Phone
Buffalo Crushed Stone Co Inc 2544 Clinton St	Buffalo	NY	14224	**800-543-3860**	716-826-7310
Burgess Pigment Company Inc 525 Beck Blvd PO Box 349	Sandersville	GA	31082	**800-841-8999**	478-552-2544
Eagle-Picher Minerals Inc 9785 Gateway Dr Ste 1000 *Cust Svc	Reno	NV	89521	**800-228-3865***	775-824-7600
Graphel Corp 6115 Centre Pk Dr PO Box 369	West Chester	OH	45071	**800-255-1104**	513-779-6166
Graphite Sales Inc 16710 W Pk Cir Dr	Chagrin Falls	OH	44023	**800-321-4147**	440-543-8221
Hill & Griffith Co 1085 Summer St	Cincinnati	OH	45204	**800-543-0425**	513-921-1075
La Habra Products Inc 4125 E La Palma Ave Ste 250	Anaheim	CA	92807	**866-516-0061**	714-778-2266
Miller & Co LLC 9700 W Higgins Rd Ste 1000	Rosemont	IL	60018	**800-727-9847**	847-696-2400
Miller Studio 734 Fair Ave NW	New Philadelphia	OH	44663	**800-332-0050**	330-339-1100
Multicoat Corp 23331 Antonio Pkwy	Rancho Santa Margarita	CA	92688	**877-685-8426**	949-888-7100
Oil-Dri Corp of America 410 N Michigan Ave Ste 400 *NYSE: ODC*	Chicago	IL	60611	**800-645-3747**	312-321-1515
Silbrico Corp 6300 River Rd	Hodgkins	IL	60525	**800-323-4287**	708-354-3350
US Diamond Wheel Co 101 Kendall Pt Dr	Oswego	IL	60543	**800-223-0457**	800-851-1095
USG Corp 550 W Adams St *NYSE: USG*	Chicago	IL	60661	**800-874-4968**	312-436-4000
Von Roll Isola USA 200 Von Roll Dr	Schenectady	NY	12306	**800-654-7652**	518-344-7100

500 MINING - COAL

Name / Address	City	State	Zip	Toll-Free	Phone
Alpha Natural Resources Inc 1 Alpha Pl PO Box 16429 *OTC: ANR*	Bristol	VA	24209	**866-322-5742**	276-619-4410
Cloud Peak Energy Inc (RTEA) 505 S Gillette Ave PO Box 3009	Gillette	WY	82717	**866-470-4300**	307-687-6000
JM Huber Corp 499 Thornall St 8th Fl	Edison	NJ	08837	**877-418-0038**	732-549-8600
Knight Hawk Coal LLC 500 Cutler-Trico Rd	Percy	IL	62272	**855-611-2625**	618-426-3662
Natural Resource Partners LP 601 Jefferson St Ste 3600 *NYSE: NRP*	Houston	TX	77002	**888-334-7102**	713-751-7507
Peabody Energy Corp Peabody Plz 701 Market St	St. Louis	MO	63101	**866-470-4500**	314-342-3400
Westmoreland Coal Co 9540 S Maroon Cir Ste 200 *NASDAQ: WLB*	Englewood	CO	80112	**855-922-6463**	719-442-2600

501 MINING - METALS

Name / Address	City	State	Zip	Toll-Free	Phone
Agnico-Eagle Mines Ltd 145 King St E Ste 500 *NYSE: AEM*	Toronto	ON	M5C2Y7	**888-822-6714**	416-947-1212
B2 Gold Corp 595 Burrard St Ste 3100 PO Box 49143	Vancouver	BC	V7X1J1	**800-316-8855**	604-681-8371
Badger Mining Corp 409 S Church St PO Box 328	Berlin	WI	54923	**800-932-7263**	920-361-2388
Barrick Gold Corp TD Canada Trust Tower 161 Bay St PO Box 212 *NYSE: ABX*	Toronto	ON	M5J2S1	**800-720-7415**	416-861-9911
BCM Resources Corp 1040 W Georgia St	Vancouver	BC	V6E4H1	**888-646-0144**	604-646-0144

Company / Address	City	State	Zip	Toll-Free	Phone
Crystallex International Corp 8 King St E Ste 1201	Toronto	ON	M5C1B5	**800-738-1577**	416-203-2448
Eldorado Gold Corp 550 Burrard St *NYSE: ELD*	Vanouver	BC	V6C2B5	**888-353-8166**	604-687-4018
First Quantum Minerals Ltd 543 Granville St 8th Fl *TSE: FM*	Vancouver	BC	V6C1X8	**888-688-6577**	604-688-6577
Gold Reserve Inc 926 W Sprague Ave Ste 200 *TSE: GRZ*	Spokane	WA	99201	**800-625-9550**	509-623-1500
Goldcorp Inc 666 Burrard St Ste 3400 *NYSE: G*	Vancouver	BC	V6C2X8	**800-567-6223**	604-696-3000
Golden Star Resources Ltd 150 King St W Ste 1200 *NYSE: GSS*	Toronto	ON	M5H1J9	**800-553-8436**	303-830-9000
Hecla Mining Co 800 W Pender St Ste 970 *NYSE: HL*	Vancouver	BC	V6C2V6	**800-432-5291**	604-682-6201
IAMGOLD Corp 401 Bay St Ste 3200 PO Box 153 *TSE: IMG*	Toronto	ON	M5H2Y4	**888-464-9999**	416-360-4710
IBC Advanced Alloys Corp 570 Granville St Ste 1200	Vancouver	BC	V6C3P1	**800-373-3251**	604-685-6263
Kinross Gold Corp 25 York St 17th Fl *NYSE: KGC*	Toronto	ON	M5J2V5	**866-561-3636**	416-365-5123
Materion Corp 6070 Parkland Blvd *NYSE: MTRN*	Mayfield Heights	OH	44124	**800-321-2076**	216-486-4200
North American Palladium Ltd 1 University Ave Ste 402 *TSE: PDL*	Toronto	ON	M5J2J2	**888-360-7590**	416-360-7590
NovaGold Resources Inc 789 W Pender St Ste 720 *NYSE: NG*	Vancouver	BC	V6C1H2	**866-699-6227**	604-669-6227
Pacific Rim Mining Corp 625 Howe St Ste 1050 *OTC: PFRMF*	Vancouver	BC	V6C2T6	**888-775-7097**	604-689-1976
Rubicon Minerals Corp 44 Victoria St Ste 400 *NYSE: RBY*	Toronto	ON	M5C1Y2	**866-365-4706**	604-623-3333
Sherritt International Corp 1133 Yonge St *TSE: S*	Toronto	ON	M4T2Y7	**800-704-6698**	416-924-4551
Silver Standard Resources Inc 999 W Hastings St Ste 1180 *TSE: SSO*	Vancouver	BC	V6C2W2	**888-338-0046**	604-689-3846
Teck Cominco American Inc 501 N Riverpoint Blvd Ste 300	Spokane	WA	99202	**866-225-0198**	509-747-6111
US Energy Corp 877 N Eigth W *NASDAQ: USEG*	Riverton	WY	82501	**800-776-9271**	307-856-9271
Western Copper Corp 1040 W Georgia St FL 15	Vancouver	BC	V6E4H1	**888-966-9995**	604-684-9497
Wharf Resources USA Inc 10928 Wharf Rd	Lead	SD	57754	**800-567-6223**	605-584-1441

502 MINING - MINERALS

502-1 Chemical & Fertilizer Minerals Mining

Company / Address	City	State	Zip	Toll-Free	Phone
American Borate Corp 5700 Cleveland St Ste 350	Virginia Beach	VA	23462	**800-486-1072**	757-490-2242
New Riverside Ochre Co 75 Old River Rd SE *Orders	Cartersville	GA	30121	**800-248-0176***	770-382-4568
Potash Corp 1101 Skokie Blvd	Northbrook	IL	60062	**800-667-0403**	847-849-4200
Searles Valley Minerals 9401 Indian Creek Pkwy Ste 1000	Overland Park	KS	66210	**800-637-2775**	913-344-9500
Solvay Chemicals Inc 3333 Richmond Ave	Houston	TX	77098	**800-765-8292**	713-525-6800
United Salt Corp 4800 San Felipe St	Houston	TX	77056	**800-554-8658**	713-877-2600

502-2 Clay, Ceramic, Refractory Minerals Mining

Company / Address	City	State	Zip	Toll-Free	Phone
AMCOL International Corp 2870 Forbs Ave *NYSE: ACO* ■ *General	Hoffman Estates	IL	60192	**800-962-8586***	847-851-1500
I-Minerals Inc 880 - 580 Hornby St	Vancouver	BC	V6C3B6	**877-303-6573**	604-303-6573
Imerys USA Inc 100 Mansell Ct E Ste 300	Roswell	GA	30076	**800-843-3222**	770-645-3300
Milwhite Inc 5487 S Padre Island Hwy	Brownsville	TX	78521	**800-442-0082**	956-547-1970
Riverside Clay Co Inc 201 Truss Ferry Rd	Pell City	AL	35128	**800-924-0637**	205-338-3366
Riverside Refractories Inc 201 Truss Ferry Rd	Pell City	AL	35128	**800-924-0637**	205-338-3366
RT Vanderbilt Company Inc 30 Winfield St *Cust Svc	Norwalk	CT	06855	**800-243-6064***	203-853-1400
US Silica Co 8490 Progress Dr Ste 300	Frederick	MD	21701	**800-243-7500**	304-258-2500
Wyo-Ben Inc 1345 Discovery Dr *Cust Svc	Billings	MT	59102	**800-548-7055***	406-652-6351

502-3 Minerals Mining (Misc)

Company / Address	City	State	Zip	Toll-Free	Phone
Harborlite 130 Castilian Dr	Santa Barbara	CA	93117	**800-893-4445**	805-562-0200
ILC Resources 3301 106th Cir	Urbandale	IA	50322	**800-247-2133**	515-243-8106
RT Vanderbilt Company Inc 30 Winfield St *Cust Svc	Norwalk	CT	06855	**800-243-6064***	203-853-1400
Stornoway Diamond Corp 980 W First St Ste 118 *TSE: SWY*	North Vancouver	BC	V7P3N4	**877-331-2232**	604-983-7750
Vanderbilt Minerals Corp 30 Winfield St	Norwalk	CT	06855	**800-243-6064**	203-853-1400
WGI Heavy Minerals Inc 810 E Sherman Ave *TSE: WG*	Coeur d'Alene	ID	83814	**888-542-7638**	208-666-6000

502-4 Sand & Gravel Pits

Company / Address	City	State	Zip	Toll-Free	Phone
Edward C Levy Co 9300 Dix Ave	Dearborn	MI	48120	**877-938-0007**	313-843-7200
Fisher Sand & Gravel Co 3948 First ST SW	Underwood	ND	58576	**800-932-8740**	701-442-5600
Hills Materials Co 3975 Sturgis Rd	Rapid City	SD	57702	**800-325-7056**	605-394-3300
Janesville Sand & Gravel Co (JSG) 1110 Harding St	Janesville	WI	53547	**800-955-7702**	608-754-7701
LG Everist Inc 300 S Phillips Ave Ste 200	Sioux Falls	SD	57117	**800-843-7992**	605-334-5000
Mark Sand & Gravel Co 525 Kennedy Pk Rd PO Box 458	Fergus Falls	MN	56537	**800-427-8316**	218-736-7523
Pike Industries Inc 3 Eastgate Pk Rd	Belmont	NH	03220	**800-283-0803**	603-527-5100
Pounding Mill Quarry Corp 171 St Clair S Crossing	Bluefield	VA	24605	**888-661-7625**	276-326-1145
US Silica Co 8490 Progress Dr Ste 300	Frederick	MD	21701	**800-243-7500**	304-258-2500

502-5 Stone Quarries - Crushed & Broken Stone

Company / Address	City	State	Zip	Toll-Free	Phone
Edward C Levy Co 9300 Dix Ave	Dearborn	MI	48120	**877-938-0007**	313-843-7200
Harney Rock & Paving Co 457 S Date Ave	Burns	OR	97720	**888-298-2681**	541-573-7855
HB Mellot Estate Inc 100 Mellott Dr	Warfordsburg	PA	17267	**800-634-5634**	301-678-2050
Hills Materials Co 3975 Sturgis Rd	Rapid City	SD	57702	**800-325-7056**	605-394-3300
Hunt Midwest Enterprises Inc 8300 NE Underground Dr	Kansas City	MO	64161	**800-551-6877**	816-455-2500
Hunt Midwest Mining Inc 8300 NE Underground Dr	Kansas City	MO	64161	**800-551-6877**	816-455-2500
LG Everist Inc 300 S Phillips Ave Ste 200	Sioux Falls	SD	57117	**800-843-7992**	605-334-5000
Pike Industries Inc 3 Eastgate Pk Rd	Belmont	NH	03220	**800-283-0803**	603-527-5100
Pounding Mill Quarry Corp 171 St Clair S Crossing	Bluefield	VA	24605	**888-661-7625**	276-326-1145
Texas Crushed Stone Co 5300 S IH-35 PO Box 1050	Georgetown	TX	78627	**800-772-8272**	512-930-0106
Tilcon NY Inc 162 Old Mill Rd	West Nyack	NY	10994	**800-872-7762**	845-358-4500
Vulcan Materials Co 1200 Urban Ctr Dr PO Box 385014 *NYSE: VMC*	Birmingham	AL	35238	**800-615-4331**	205-298-3000
Vulcan Materials Company Western Div 3200 San Fernando Rd *NYSE: VMC*	Los Angeles	CA	90065	**800-615-4331**	323-258-2777

502-6 Stone Quarries - Dimension Stone

Company / Address	City	State	Zip	Toll-Free	Phone
American Clay Enterprises LLC 2418 Second St SW	Albuquerque	NM	87102	**866-404-1634**	505-243-5300
Eden Stone Company Inc W4520 Lime Rd	Eden	WI	53019	**800-472-2521**	920-477-2521
Pounding Mill Quarry Corp 171 St Clair S Crossing	Bluefield	VA	24605	**888-661-7625**	276-326-1145

503 MISSILES, SPACE VEHICLES, PARTS

SEE ALSO Weapons & Ordnance (Military)

Company / Address	City	State	Zip	Toll-Free	Phone
Esterline Mason 13955 Balboa Blvd	Sylmar	CA	91342	**800-232-7700**	818-361-3366
HITCO Carbon Composites Inc 1600 W 135th St	Gardena	CA	90249	**800-421-5444**	310-527-0700
International Launch Services (ILS) 1875 Explorer St Ste 700	Reston	VA	20190	**800-852-4980**	571-633-7400
Lockheed Martin Corp 6801 Rockledge Dr *NYSE: LMT*	Bethesda	MD	20817	**866-562-2363**	301-897-6000
Lockheed Martin Space Systems Co Michoud Operations 13800 Old Gentilly Rd	New Orleans	LA	70129	**866-562-2363**	504-257-3311

504 MOBILE HOMES & BUILDINGS

Name / Address	City	State	Zip	Toll-Free	Phone
American Homestar Corp 2450 S Shore Blvd Ste 300	League City	TX	77573	**800-313-5570**	281-334-9700
Cavalier Homes Inc 32 Wilson Blvd PO Box 300	Addison	AL	35540	**800-743-2284**	
Cavco Industries Inc 1001 N Central Ave 8th Fl. *NASDAQ: CVCO*	Phoenix	AZ	85004	**800-790-9111**	602-256-6263
Destiny Industries LLC 250 R W Bryant Rd	Moultrie	GA	31788	**866-782-6600**	
Fleetwood Homes of Idaho Inc 2611 E Comstock Ave	Nampa	ID	83687	**800-334-8958**	208-466-2438
Fleetwood Homes of Virginia Inc 90 Weaver St	Rocky Mount	VA	24151	**866-890-6206**	540-483-5171
Franklin Homes Inc 10655 Hwy 43	Russellville	AL	35653	**800-332-4511**	
Hometown America LLC 150 N Wacker Dr Ste 2800	Chicago	IL	60606	**888-735-4310**	312-604-7500
Horton Homes Inc 101 Industrial Blvd	Eatonton	GA	31024	**800-657-4000**	706-485-8506
Jacobsen Homes 600 Packard Ct	Safety Harbor	FL	34695	**800-843-1559**	727-726-1138
Luxury Retreats International Inc 5530 St Patrick St Ste 2210	Montreal	QC	H4E1A8	**877-993-0100**	514-393-8844
Manufactured Housing Enterprises Inc 09302 St Rt 6 Rt 6	Bryan	OH	43506	**800-821-0220**	419-636-4511
McGrath RentCorp 5700 Las Positas Rd *NASDAQ: MGRC*	Livermore	CA	94551	**800-962-4284**	925-606-9200
Nashua Homes of Idaho Inc PO Box 170008	Boise	ID	83717	**855-766-0222**	208-345-0222
Nobility Homes Inc 3741 SW Seventh St *OTC: NOBH*	Ocala	FL	34474	**800-476-6624**	352-732-5157
R-Anell Custom Homes Inc 235 Anthony Grave Rd *Cust Svc	Crouse	NC	28033	**800-951-5511***	704-483-5511
Ritz-Craft Corp of Pennsylvania Inc 15 Industrial Pk Rd	Mifflinburg	PA	17844	**800-326-9836**	570-966-1053
River Birch Homes Inc 400 River Birch Dr	Hackleburg	AL	35564	**888-760-3314**	205-935-1997
Satellite Industries Inc 2530 Xenium Ln N	Minneapolis	MN	55441	**800-328-3332**	
Skyline Corp 2520 By-Pass Rd *NYSE: SKY*	Elkhart	IN	46514	**800-348-7469**	574-294-6521
Wick Buildings 405 Walter Rd	Mazomanie	WI	53560	**855-438-9425**	

505 MODELLING AGENCIES

Name / Address	City	State	Zip	Toll-Free	Phone
Women Management 199 Lafayette St 7th Fl	New York	NY	10012	**800-838-3006**	212-334-7480

506 MODELING SCHOOLS

Name / Address	City	State	Zip	Toll-Free	Phone
Frederick Taylor University 346 Rheem Blvd Ste 203	Moraga	CA	94556	**800-988-4622**	
Mercy College of Ohio 2221 Madison Ave	Toledo	OH	43604	**888-806-3729**	419-251-1313
Pima Medical Institute 3350 E Grant Rd Ste 200	Tucson	AZ	85716	**888-556-7334**	520-326-1600
Regional Occupational Programs 300 Dana St	Fort Bragg	CA	95437	**800-451-9999**	707-964-9000
Rhino Medical Staffing 2000 E Lamar Blvd Ste 250	Arlington	TX	76006	**866-267-4466**	817-795-2295

507 MOPS, SPONGES, WIPING CLOTHS

SEE ALSO Brushes & Brooms ; Cleaning Products

Name / Address	City	State	Zip	Toll-Free	Phone
A&B Wiper Supply Inc 5601 Paschall Ave	Philadelphia	PA	19143	**800-333-7247**	215-482-6100
Abco Cleaning Products 6800 NW 36th Ave	Miami	FL	33147	**888-694-2226**	305-694-2226
Bro-Tex Inc 800 Hampden Ave	Saint Paul	MN	55114	**800-328-2282**	651-645-5721
Butler Home Products LLC 237 Cedar Hill St	Marlborough	MA	01752	**888-318-8521**	508-597-8000
Continental Manufacturing Co 305 Rock Industrial Pk Dr	Bridgeton	MO	63044	**800-325-1051**	314-656-4301
Disco Inc 1895 Brannan Rd	McDonough	GA	30253	**800-325-1051**	770-474-7575
Ettore Products Co 2100 N Loop Rd	Alameda	CA	94502	**800-438-8673**	510-748-4130
Golden Star Inc 4770 N Belleview Ave Ste 209	Kansas City	MO	64116	**800-821-2792**	816-842-0233
United Textile Company Inc 751-143rd Ave *General	San Leandro	CA	94578	**800-233-0077***	510-276-2288
Wipe-Tex International Corp 110 E 153rd St	Bronx	NY	10451	**800-643-9607**	718-665-0787

508 MORTGAGE LENDERS & LOAN BROKERS

SEE ALSO Banks - Commercial & Savings

Name / Address	City	State	Zip	Toll-Free	Phone
21st Mortgage Corp 620 Market St Ste 100	Knoxville	TN	37902	**800-955-0021**	865-292-2120
AAA Financial Corp 4613 N University Dr	Coral Springs	FL	33065	**800-881-2530**	954-344-2530
Ascentium Capital LLC 23970 Hwy 59 N	Kingwood	TX	77339	**866-722-8500**	
BRT Realty Trust 60 Cutter Mill Rd Ste 303 *NYSE: BRT*	Great Neck	NY	11021	**800-450-5816**	516-466-3100
Canada Deposit Insurance Corp 50 O'Connor St 17th Fl	Ottawa	ON	K1P6L2	**800-461-2342**	613-996-2081
CitiMortgage Inc 1000 Technology Dr *Cust Svc	O'Fallon	MO	63368	**800-283-7918***	
Dominion Lending Centres Inc 2215 Coquitlam Ave	Port Coquitlam	BC	V3B1J6	**866-928-6810**	
EverHome Mortgage Co 301 W Bay St *Cust Svc	Jacksonville	FL	32202	**800-669-9721***	888-882-3837
Fannie Mae 3900 Wisconsin Ave NW *OTC: FNMA*	Washington	DC	20016	**800-732-6643**	202-752-7000
First Eastern Mortgage Corp 100 Brickstone Sq	Andover	MA	01810	**800-777-2240**	978-749-3100
First Equity Mortgage Bankers 9300 S Dadeland Blvd Ste 500	Miami	FL	33156	**800-973-3654**	305-666-3333
First Financial Services Inc (FFSI) 6230 Fairview Rd Ste 450	Charlotte	NC	28210	**866-506-9090**	
Freddie Mac 8200 Jones Branch Dr	McLean	VA	22102	**800-424-5401**	703-903-2000
North Central Region 333 W Wacker Dr Ste 2500	Chicago	IL	60606	**800-373-3343**	312-407-7400
Northeast Region 8200 Jones Branch Dr	McLean	VA	22102	**800-373-3343**	703-903-2000
Southeast/Southwest Region 2300 Windy Ridge Pkwy Ste 200N	Atlanta	GA	30339	**800-373-3343**	770-857-8800
George Mason Mortgage Corp 4100 Monu Crnr Dr Ste 100	Fairfax	VA	22030	**800-867-6859**	703-273-2600
Guild Mortgage Co 5898 Copley Dr 4th & 5th Fl	San Diego	CA	92111	**800-365-4441**	
HomeSteps 500 Plano Pkwy	Carrollton	TX	75010	**800-972-7555**	
HSBC Bank USA 2929 Walden Ave	Depew	NY	14043	**800-338-4626**	
Huntington Mortgage Co 7575 Huntington Pk Dr	Columbus	OH	43235	**800-323-4695**	614-480-6505
Inland Mortgage Corp 2901 Butterfield Rd	Oak Brook	IL	60523	**800-826-8228**	630-218-8000
LendingTree Inc 11115 Rushmore Dr	Charlotte	NC	28277	**800-555-8733**	704-541-5351
Lion Inc 200 Martin Ln Ste A	Elk Grove	IL	60007	**800-867-6320**	872-228-5466
loanDepot 26642 Towne Centre Dr	Foothill Ranch	CA	92610	**888-337-6888**	
Merix Financial Inc 390 Bay St 18th Fl Ste 500	Toronto	ON	M5H2Y2	**877-637-4914**	
Midland Mortgage Co PO Box 26648	Oklahoma City	OK	73126	**800-654-4566**	
MMA Capital Management LLC (MuniMae) 621 E Pratt St Ste 600 *OTC: MMAB*	Baltimore	MD	21202	**855-650-6932**	443-263-2900
Mortgage Investors Group 8320 E Walker Springs Ln	Knoxville	TN	37923	**800-489-8910**	865-691-8910
Mortgage Resources Inc (MRI) 425 S Woods Mill Rd Ste 100	Chesterfield	MO	63017	**800-965-9910**	314-576-5577
National Rural Utilities Co-op Finance Corp 2201 Co-op Way	Herndon	VA	20171	**800-424-2954**	703-709-6700
Payscape Advisors 729 Lambert Dr Ne	Atlanta	GA	30324	**888-351-6565**	
PHH Mortgage Corp 3000 Leadenhall Rd	Mount Laurel	NJ	08054	**800-210-8849**	
Plaza Home Mortgage Inc 5090 Shoreham Pl Ste 206	San Diego	CA	92122	**866-260-2529**	858-346-1208
Redwood Trust Inc 1 Belvedere Pl Ste 300 *NYSE: RWT*	Mill Valley	CA	94941	**866-269-4976**	415-389-7373
Regions Mortgage Inc 215 Forrest St	Hattiesburg	MS	39401	**800-986-2462**	
Residential Mortgage LLC 100 Calais Dr	Anchorage	AK	99503	**888-357-2707**	907-222-8800
Safeguard Properties Inc 7887 Safeguard Cir	Valley View	OH	44125	**800-852-8306**	216-739-2900
Softgate Systems Inc 330 Passaic Ave	Fairfield	NJ	07004	**888-477-7297**	973-830-1575
SunTrust Mortgage Inc 1001 Semmes Ave	Richmond	VA	23224	**800-634-7928**	
Truwest Credit Union PO Box 3489	Scottsdale	AZ	85271	**855-878-9378**	480-441-5900
Universal American Mortgage Co 700 NW 107th Ave	Miami	FL	33172	**800-741-8262**	
Universal Lending Corp (ULC) 6775 E Evans Ave	Denver	CO	80224	**800-758-4063**	
Vanderbilt Mortgage & Finance Inc 500 Alcoa Trl	Maryville	TN	37804	**800-970-7250**	
Verico Capital Mortgages Inc 106-18 Deakin St	Ottawa	ON	K2E8B7	**877-459-4414**	613-228-3888
Wells Fargo Home Mortgage 2840 Ingersoll Ave	Des Moines	IA	50312	**800-401-1957**	515-237-5196

509 MORTUARY, CREMATORY, CEMETERY PRODUCTS & SERVICES

Name / Address	City	State	Zip	Toll-Free	Phone
AJ Desmond & Sons Funeral Directors 2600 Crooks Rd	Troy	MI	48084	**800-210-7135**	248-362-2500
Baue Funeral Homes 620 Jefferson St	Saint Charles	MO	63301	**888-724-0073**	636-940-1000
Carriage Services Inc 3040 Post Oak Blvd Ste 300 *NYSE: CSV*	Houston	TX	77056	**866-332-8400**	713-332-8400
Church & Chapel Metal Arts Inc 2616 W Grand Ave	Chicago	IL	60612	**800-992-1234**	
Dignity Memorial 1929 Allen Pkwy	Houston	TX	77019	**800-894-2024**	713-522-5141
Forest Lawn Memorial-Parks & Mortuaries 1712 S Glendale Ave	Glendale	CA	91205	**800-204-3131**	323-254-3131
Mount Sinai Memorial Park 5950 Forest Lawn Dr	Los Angeles	CA	90068	**800-600-0076**	323-469-6000
Neptune Society 4312 Woodman Ave 3rd Fl	Sherman Oaks	CA	91423	**888-637-8863**	
Spring Grove Cemetery 4521 Spring Grove Ave	Cincinnati	OH	45232	**888-853-2230**	513-681-7526
Stewart Enterprises Inc 1333 S Clearview Pkwy *NASDAQ: STEI*	New Orleans	LA	70121	**877-239-3264**	713-522-5141
Woodlawn Cemetery Inc, The Webster Ave & E 233rd St	Bronx	NY	10470	**877-496-6352**	718-920-0500

510 MOTION PICTURE DISTRIBUTION & RELATED SERVICES

Name / Address	City	State	Zip	Toll-Free	Phone
Baker & Taylor Inc 2550 W Tyvola Rd Ste 300	Charlotte	NC	28217	**800-775-1800**	
Crown Media Holdings Inc 12700 Ventura Blvd Ste 200 *NASDAQ: CRWN*	Studio City	CA	91604	**800-479-7328**	818-755-2400
Extreme Reach Inc 75 2nd Ave Ste 720 *NASDAQ: DGIT*	Needham	MA	02494	**877-769-9382**	781-577-2016
Facets Multimedia Inc 1517 W Fullerton Ave *Cust Svc	Chicago	IL	60614	**800-331-6197***	773-281-9075
First Run Features 630 Ninth Ave Ste 1213	New York	NY	10036	**800-229-8575**	212-243-0600
Ingram Entertainment Inc 2 Ingram Blvd	La Vergne	TN	37089	**800-621-1333**	615-287-4000
Insight Media 2162 Broadway	New York	NY	10024	**800-233-9910**	212-721-6316
Kino International Corp 333 W 39th St Rm 503	New York	NY	10018	**800-562-3330**	212-629-6880
Kultur International Films Ltd PO Box 755	Forked River	NJ	08731	**888-329-2580**	
Sony Pictures Entertainment Inc 10202 W Washington Blvd	Culver City	CA	90232	**855-327-7669**	310-244-4000
Twentieth Century Fox Home Entertainment Inc 2121 Ave of the Stars Ste 100	Los Angeles	CA	90067	**877-369-7867**	310-369-3900
Warner Bros Entertainment Inc 4000 Warner Blvd	Burbank	CA	91522	**800-778-7879**	818-954-1853

511 MOTION PICTURE PRE- & POST-PRODUCTION SERVICES

Name / Address	City	State	Zip	Toll-Free	Phone
Crossman Post Production LLC 35 Lone Hollow	Sandy	UT	84092	**888-553-1958**	801-553-1958
Go Edit Inc 5614 Cahuenga Blvd	North Hollywood	CA	91601	**800-833-9200**	818-284-6260
Raleigh Studios Worldwide 5300 Melrose Ave	Hollywood	CA	90038	**888-960-3456**	323-466-3111

512 MOTION PICTURE PRODUCTION - SPECIAL INTEREST

SEE ALSO Motion Picture & Television Production ; Animation Companies

Name / Address	City	State	Zip	Toll-Free	Phone
Active Parenting Publishers 1955 Vaughn Rd Ste 108	Kennesaw	GA	30144	**800-825-0060**	770-429-0565
American Educational Products Inc 401 Hickory St PO Box 2121	Fort Collins	CO	80522	**800-289-9299**	970-484-7445
Coastal Training Technologies Corp 500 Studio Dr	Virginia Beach	VA	23452	**866-333-6888**	757-498-9014
CRM Learning 2218 Faraday Ave Ste 110	Carlsbad	CA	92008	**800-421-0833**	760-431-9800
Hammond Communications Group Inc 173 Trade St	Lexington	KY	40511	**888-424-1878**	859-254-1878
Intaglio LLC 5809 Cross Roads Commerce Pkwy Ste 200	Grand Rapids	MI	49519	**800-632-9153**	616-243-3300
Keystone Learning Systems LLC 6030 Daybreak Cir Ste A150 116	Clarksville	MD	21029	**800-949-5590**	410-800-4000
Kultur International Films Ltd PO Box 755	Forked River	NJ	08731	**888-329-2580**	
Learning Communications LLC 5520 Trabuco Rd	Irvine	CA	92620	**800-622-3610**	
Medcom Trainex 6060 Phyllis Dr *Cust Svc	Cypress	CA	90630	**800-877-1443***	
National Film Board of Canada Stn Centre-Ville PO Box 6100	Montreal	QC	H3C3H5	**800-267-7710**	514-283-9000
Nightingale-Conant Corp 6245 W Howard St *Cust Svc	Niles	IL	60714	**800-557-1660***	
PADI Americas 30151 Tomas St	Rancho Santa Margarita	CA	92688	**800-527-8378**	949-858-7234

513 MOTION PICTURE & TELEVISION PRODUCTION

SEE ALSO Motion Picture Production - Special Interest ; Animation Companies

Name / Address	City	State	Zip	Toll-Free	Phone
Audio General Inc (AGI) 1680 Republic Rd	Huntingdon Valley	PA	19006	**866-866-2600**	267-288-0300
Audio Video Systems Inc 14120 Sullyfield Cir	Chantilly	VA	20151	**877-287-1175**	703-263-1002
Aurora Pictures Inc 5249 Chicago Ave	Minneapolis	MN	55417	**800-346-9487**	612-821-6490
Bioquant Image Analysis Corp 5611 Ohio Ave	Nashville	TN	37209	**800-221-0549**	615-350-7866
Bullfrog Films Inc 372 Dautrich Rd	Reading	PA	19606	**800-543-3764**	610-779-8226
Cev Multimedia Ltd 1020 SE Loop 289	Lubbock	TX	79404	**877-610-5017**	806-745-8820
CGI Communications Inc 130 E Main St	Rochester	NY	14604	**800-398-3029**	585-427-0020
Cintrex Audio Visual 656 Axminister Dr	Fenton	MO	63026	**800-325-9541**	636-343-0178
Columbia TriStar Motion Picture Group 10202 W Washington Blvd	Culver City	CA	90232	**855-327-7669**	310-244-4000
Communca Inc 31 N Erie St	Toledo	OH	43604	**800-800-7890**	
Eastco Multi Media Solutions Inc 3646 California Rd	Orchard Park	NY	14127	**800-365-8273**	716-662-0536
Event Producers Inc 5724 Salmen St	New Orleans	LA	70123	**866-903-6949**	504-466-4066
High Speed Productions Inc 1303 Underwood Ave	San Francisco	CA	94124	**888-520-9099**	415-822-3083
Kantola Productions LLC 55 Sunnyside Ave	Mill Valley	CA	94941	**800-280-1180**	415-381-9363
NBA Entertainment 450 Harmon Meadow Blvd	Secaucus	NJ	07094	**866-648-4668**	201-865-1500
Pacific Title Archives 10717 Vanowen St	North Hollywood	CA	91605	**800-968-9111**	818-760-4223
PayReel Inc 24928 Genesee Trl Rd	Golden	CO	80401	**800-352-7397**	303-526-4900
Rodgers & Hammerstein Organization, The 229 W 28th St 11th Fl	New York	NY	10001	**800-400-8160**	212-541-6600
Samson Technologies Inc 45 Gilpin Ave	Hauppauge	NY	11788	**800-372-6766**	631-784-2200
Smp Communications Corp 7626 E Greenway Rd Ste 100	Scottsdale	AZ	85260	**888-796-3342**	480-905-4100
Sony Pictures Entertainment Inc 10202 W Washington Blvd	Culver City	CA	90232	**855-327-7669**	310-244-4000
Sony Pictures Television 10202 W Washington Blvd	Culver City	CA	90232	**800-327-3325**	310-244-4000
Swank Motion Pictures Inc 10795 Watson Rd	St Louis	MO	63127	**888-248-8757**	314-984-6000
Universal Studios Inc 100 Universal City Plaza	Universal City	CA	91608	**800-864-8377**	
Viacom Entertainment Group 1515 Broadway	New York	NY	10036	**800-516-4399**	212-258-6000
Video Symphony Entertraining Inc 266 E Magnolia Blvd	Burbank	CA	91502	**888-370-7589**	818-557-6500
Vision Global AR Ltee 80, Queen St Ste 301	Montreal	QC	H3C2N5	**800-667-7690**	514-879-0020
Vista Electronics Inc 27525 Newhall Ranch Rd	Valencia	CA	91355	**800-847-8299**	661-294-9820
Warner Bros Entertainment Inc 4000 Warner Blvd	Burbank	CA	91522	**800-778-7879**	818-954-1853
Warner Home Video 4000 Warner Blvd Bldg 168	Burbank	CA	91522	**866-373-4389**	

MOTION PICTURE THEATERS

SEE Theaters - Motion Picture

514 MOTOR SPEEDWAYS

Name / Address	City	State	Zip	Toll-Free	Phone
Atlanta Motor Speedway PO Box 500	Hampton	GA	30228	**877-926-7849**	770-946-4211
Auto Club Speedway 9300 Cherry Ave	Fontana	CA	92335	**800-944-7223**	909-429-5000
Bandimere Speedway 3051 S Rooney Rd	Morrison	CO	80465	**888-737-5253**	303-697-6001
Brainerd International Raceway 5523 Birchdale Rd	Brainerd	MN	56401	**866-444-4455**	218-824-7223
Bristol Motor Speedway 151 Speedway Blvd	Bristol	TN	37620	**866-415-4158**	423-989-6933
Carolina Dragway 302 Dragstrip Rd	Jackson	SC	29803	**877-471-7223**	803-471-2285
Chicagoland Speedway 500 Speedway Blvd	Joliet	IL	60433	**888-629-7223**	815-722-5500
Darlington Raceway 1301 Harry Bird Hwy	Darlington	SC	29532	**866-459-7223**	
Heartland Park Topeka 7530 SW Topeka Blvd	Topeka	KS	66619	**800-437-2237**	785-862-4781
Hickory Motor Speedway 3130 Hwy 70 SE	Newton	NC	28658	**800-843-8725**	828-464-3655
Holland NASCAR Motorsports Complex 11586 Holland Glenwood Rd	Holland	NY	14080	**866-655-0257**	716-537-2272
Kentucky Speedway 1 Speedway Blvd *Resv	Sparta	KY	41086	**888-652-7223***	859-567-3400
Las Vegas Motor Speedway 7000 Las Vegas Blvd N	Las Vegas	NV	89115	**800-644-4444**	702-644-4444
Lime Rock Park 60 White Hollow Rd	Lakeville	CT	06039	**800-722-3577**	860-435-5000
Maple Grove Raceway 30 Stauffer Pk Ln	Mohnton	PA	19540	**877-814-2538**	610-856-7812

Name / Address	City	State	ZIP	Toll-Free	Phone
Martinsville Speedway 340 Speedway Rd	Martinsville	VA	24112	**877-722-3849**	
Michigan International Speedway 12626 US 12	Brooklyn	MI	49230	**800-354-1010**	517-592-6666
Mid-Ohio Sports Car Course 7721 Steam Corners Rd PO Box 3108	Lexington	OH	44904	**800-643-6446**	419-884-4000
Pocono Raceway Long Pond Rd PO Box 500	Long Pond	PA	18334	**800-722-3929**	570-646-2300
Road America N 7390 Hwy 67	Elkhart Lake	WI	53020	**800-365-7223**	920-892-4576
Road Atlanta Raceway 5300 Winder Hwy	Braselton	GA	30517	**800-849-7223**	770-967-6143
Sebring International Raceway 113 Midway Dr	Sebring	FL	33870	**800-626-7223**	863-655-1442
Sonoma Raceway Hwy S 37 & 121	Sonoma	CA	95476	**800-870-7223**	707-938-8448
South Boston Speedway 1188 James D Hagood Hwy PO Box 1066	South Boston	VA	24592	**877-440-1540**	434-572-4947
Summit Motorsports Park 1300 Ohio 18	Norwalk	OH	44857	**800-729-6455**	419-668-5555
Texas Motorplex 7500 W Hwy 287	Ennis	TX	75119	**800-668-6775**	972-878-2641

515 MOTOR VEHICLES - COMMERCIAL & SPECIAL PURPOSE

SEE ALSO Snowmobiles ; Weapons & Ordnance (Military) ; Campers, Travel Trailers, Motor Homes ; Motorcycles & Motorcycle Parts & Accessories ; All-Terrain Vehicles ; Automobiles - Mfr

Name / Address	City	State	ZIP	Toll-Free	Phone
Allied Body Works Inc 625 S 96th St *General	Seattle	WA	98108	**800-733-7450***	206-763-7811
Art Moehn 2200 Seymour Rd	Jackson	MI	49201	**866-495-5942**	
Auto Crane Co PO Box 580697	Tulsa	OK	74158	**888-848-5445**	918-836-0463
Auto Truck Inc 1420 Brewster Creek Blvd	Bartlett	IL	60103	**877-284-4440**	630-860-5600
Bianchi Motors Inc 8430 Peach St	Erie	PA	16509	**866-979-8132**	814-864-5809
Carnegie Body Co 9500 Brookpark Rd	Cleveland	OH	44129	**800-362-1989**	216-749-5000
Champion Bus Inc 331 Graham Rd	Imlay City	MI	48444	**800-776-4943**	810-724-6474
Coach & Equipment Manufacturing Corp 130 Horizon Pk Dr PO Box 36	Penn Yan	NY	14527	**800-724-8464**	
Columbia ParCar Corp 1115 Commercial Ave	Reedsburg	WI	53959	**800-222-4653**	608-524-8888
Curtis Industries LLC 111 Higgins St	Worcester	MA	01606	**800-343-7676**	
Dealers Truck Equipment Co 2460 Midway St	Shreveport	LA	71108	**800-259-7569**	318-635-7567
Diamond Coach Corp 2300 W Fourth St PO Box 489	Oswego	KS	67356	**800-442-4645**	620-795-2191
Dick Gores Rv World 14590 Duval Pl W	Jacksonville	FL	32218	**800-635-7008**	904-741-5100
Douglass Truck Bodies Inc 231 21st St	Bakersfield	CA	93301	**800-635-7641**	661-327-0258
E-Z-GO 1451 Marvin Griffin Rd	Augusta	GA	30906	**800-241-5855**	
Ebus Inc 9250 Washburn Rd	Downey	CA	90242	**888-925-4263**	562-904-3474
Elliott Machine Works Inc 1351 Freese Works Pl	Galion	OH	44833	**800-299-0412**	419-468-4709
Erie Vehicle Co 60 E 51st St	Chicago	IL	60615	**888-550-3743**	773-536-6300
Fleet Engineers Inc 1800 E Keating Ave *Cust Svc	Muskegon	MI	49442	**800-333-7890***	231-777-2537
Fleet Equipment Corp 567 Commerce St	Franklin Lakes	NJ	07417	**800-631-0873**	201-337-3294
Fontaine Modification Co 9827 Mt Holly Rd	Charlotte	NC	28214	**800-366-8246**	704-391-1355
Fontaine Truck Equipment Co 7574 Commerce Cir	Trussville	AL	35173	**800-874-9780**	205-661-4900
Ford of Ocala Inc 2816 NW Pine Ave	Ocala	FL	34475	**888-255-1788**	352-732-4800
General Body Manufacturing Co 7110 Jensen Dr	Houston	TX	77093	**800-395-8585**	713-692-5177
Gillig Corp 25800 Clawiter Rd	Hayward	CA	94545	**800-735-1500**	510-785-1500
Gowans-Knight Co Inc 49 Knight St	Watertown	CT	06795	**800-352-4871**	860-274-8801
Hackney & Sons Inc 911 W 5th St PO Box 880	Washington	NC	27889	**800-763-0700**	252-946-6521
Heil Environmental Ltd 2030 Hamilton Pl Blvd Ste 200	Chattanooga	TN	37421	**866-367-4345**	423-899-9100
Hercules Manufacturing Co 800 Bob Posey St	Henderson	KY	42420	**800-633-3031**	270-826-9501
Johnson Refrigerated Truck Bodies 215 E Allen St *Sales	Rice Lake	WI	54868	**800-922-8360***	715-234-7071
Joyce Koons Buick Gmc 10660 Automotive Dr	Manassas	VA	20109	**866-755-0072**	
Kann Manufacturing Corp PO Box 400	Guttenberg	IA	52052	**800-806-5266**	563-252-2035
Kesler-Schaefer Auto Auction Inc 5333 W 46th St PO Box 53203	Indianapolis	IN	46254	**800-959-5722**	317-297-2300
Kidron Inc 13442 Emerson Rd	Kidron	OH	44636	**800-321-5421**	330-857-3011
Labrie Environmental Group 175 du Pont	Saint-Nicolas	QC	G7A2T3	**800-463-6638**	418-831-8250
Laird Noller Ford Inc 2245 SW Topeka Blvd	Topeka	KS	66611	**800-632-3673**	785-235-9211
Leson Chevrolet Co Inc 1501 Westbank Express	Harvey	LA	70058	**877-496-2420**	504-366-4381
Liberty Toyota Scion 4397 Rt 130 S	Burlington	NJ	08016	**888-809-7798**	609-386-6300
Libertyville Chevrolet Inc 1001 S Milwaukee Ave *Sales	Libertyville	IL	60048	**877-520-1807***	847-281-5330
Lodal Inc 620 N Hooper St PO Box 2315	Kingsford	MI	49802	**800-435-3500**	906-779-1700
Lumberton Honda Mitsubishi Inc 301 Wintergreen Dr	Lumberton	NC	28358	**855-712-9438**	910-739-9871
Luther Brookdale Chevrolet 6701 Brooklyn Blvd	Brooklyn Center	MN	55429	**800-716-1271**	
LZ Truck Equipment Inc 1881 Rice St	Saint Paul	MN	55113	**800-247-1082**	651-488-2571
M. H. Eby Inc PO Box 127	Blue Bell	PA	17506	**800-292-4752**	717-354-4971
Matt Castrucci Auto Mall of Dayton 3013 Mall Pk Dr	Dayton	OH	45459	**855-204-5293**	
Mc-Coy-Mills 700 W Commonwealth *Sales	Fullerton	CA	92832	**888-434-3145***	
McDaniel Motor Co 1111 Mt Vernon Ave	Marion	OH	43302	**877-362-0288**	740-389-2355
McGuire Cadillac Inc 910 Rt 1 N	Woodbridge	NJ	07095	**866-552-4208**	
McNeilus Cos Inc 524 County Rd 34 E PO Box 70	Dodge Center	MN	55927	**800-265-1098**	507-374-6321
Mel Rapton Inc 3630 Fulton Ave	Sacramento	CA	95821	**800-529-3053**	916-482-5400
Mickey Truck Bodies Inc 1305 Trinity Ave PO Box 2044	High Point	NC	27261	**800-334-9061**	336-882-6806
Mike Castrucci Ford Sales Inc 1020 SR- 28	Milford	OH	45150	**855-902-6741**	513-831-7010
Miller Industries Inc 8503 Hilltop Dr *NYSE: MLR*	Ooltewah	TN	37363	**800-292-0330**	423-238-4171
Momentum Bmw Ltd 10002 SW Fwy	Houston	TX	77074	**800-731-8114**	
Monroe Truck Equipment Inc 1051 W Seventh St	Monroe	WI	53566	**800-356-8134**	608-328-8127
Morgan Corp 111 Morgan Way PO Box 588	Morgantown	PA	19543	**800-666-7426**	610-286-5025
Morgan Olson Corp 1801 S Nottawa Rd	Sturgis	MI	49091	**800-233-4823**	269-659-0200
Morse Operations Inc 3790 W Blue Herron Blvd	Riviera Beach	FL	33404	**800-755-2593**	
Motor Coach Industries International Co 1700 E Golf Rd Ste 300	Schaumburg	IL	60173	**800-743-3624**	847-285-2000
Murrays Ford Inc 3007 Blinker Pkwy	Du Bois	PA	15801	**800-371-6601**	814-371-6600
Nacarato GMC Truck Inc 519 New Paul Rd	La Vergne	TN	37086	**888-392-8486**	615-280-2800
Noble Ford Mercury Inc 2406 N Jefferson Way	Indianola	IA	50125	**800-496-9984**	515-961-8151
North Florida Lincoln Mercury 4620 Southside Blvd	Jacksonville	FL	32216	**888-457-1949**	877-941-1435
Obs Inc 1324 WTuscarawas St PO Box 6210	Canton	OH	44706	**800-362-9592**	330-453-3725
Omaha Standard Inc 3501 S 11th St Ste 1	Council Bluffs	IA	51501	**800-279-2201**	712-328-7444
Oshkosh Truck Corp 2307 Oregon St	Oshkosh	WI	54903	**800-392-9921**	920-235-9150
Parkhurst Manufacturing Co 18999 Hwy Y	Sedalia	MO	65301	**800-821-7380**	660-826-8685
Pierce Mfg Inc 2600 American Dr PO Box 2017 *Cust Svc	Appleton	WI	54912	**888-974-3723***	920-832-3000
Porter Truck Sales LP 135 McCarty St	Houston	TX	77029	**800-956-2408**	713-672-2400
Prevost Car Inc 35 boul Gagnon	Sainte-Claire	QC	G0R2V0	**877-773-8678**	418-883-3391
Quad-City Peterbilt Inc 8100 N Fairmount St	Davenport	IA	52806	**866-601-8607**	
R & B Car Company Inc 3811 S Michigan St	South Bend	IN	46614	**800-260-1833**	
R & S/Godwin Truck Body Co LLC 5168 S US Hwy 23 PO Box 420	Ivel	KY	41642	**800-826-7413**	606-874-2151
R&H Motor Cars Ltd 9727 Reisterstown Rd	Owings Mills	MD	21117	**844-233-2593**	
Rapid Chevrolet Company Inc 2323 E Mall Dr	Rapid City	SD	57701	**800-456-2105**	605-343-1282
Rdk Truck Sales Inc 3214 E Adamo Dr	Tampa	FL	33605	**877-735-4636**	813-241-0711
Reading Truck Body Inc 201 Hancock Blvd *All	Reading	PA	19611	**800-458-2226***	
RKI Inc 2301 Central Pkwy	Houston	TX	77092	**800-346-8988**	713-688-4414
Rocket Supply Corp 404 N Rt 115 PO Box 98	Roberts	IL	60962	**800-252-6871**	
Rush Truck Center - Lubbock 4515 Ave A	Lubbock	TX	79404	**888-987-2458**	806-747-2579
Rydell Chevrolet Inc 18600 Devonshire St	Northridge	CA	91324	**866-697-5167**	319-234-4601
Saf-T-Cab Inc PO Box 2587	Fresno	CA	93745	**800-344-7491**	559-268-5541
Sanders Ford Inc 1135 Lejeune Blvd *General	Jacksonville	NC	28540	**888-897-8527***	910-455-1911
Scania USA Inc 121 Interpark Blvd Ste 601	San Antonio	TX	78216	**800-272-2642**	210-403-0007
Scelzi Equipment Inc 1030 W Gladstone St	Azusa	CA	91702	**866-972-3594**	626-334-0573
Schetky Northwest Sales Inc 8430 NE Killingsworth St	Portland	OR	97220	**800-255-8341**	503-287-4141
Segway Inc 14 Technology Dr	Bedford	NH	03110	**866-473-4929**	603-222-6000
Shealy's Truck Ctr Inc 1340 Bluff Rd	Columbia	SC	29201	**800-951-8580**	803-771-0176
Snethkamp Chrysler Dodge Jeep Ram 11600 Telegraph Rd	Redford	MI	48239	**888-455-6146**	313-255-2700
Somerset Welding & Steel Inc 10558 Somerset Pk	Somerset	PA	15501	**800-777-2671**	814-444-3400

Classified Section

Company	Address	City	State	ZIP	Toll-Free	Phone
Spartan Motors Inc	1541 Reynolds Rd *NASDAQ: SPAR*	Charlotte	MI	48813	**800-937-5449**	517-543-6400
STAHL/A Scott Fetzer Co	3201 W Old Lincoln Way	Wooster	OH	44691	**800-277-8245**	330-264-7441
Sterling Truck Corp	12120 Telegraph Rd *Cust Svc	Redford Township	MI	48239	**800-385-4357***	800-785-4357
Steve Hopkins Inc	2499 Auto Mall Pkwy	Fairfield	CA	94533	**877-873-3913**	707-427-1000
Steve Landers Toyota	10825 Colonel Glenn Rd	Little Rock	AR	72204	**888-314-4350**	501-568-5800
Sunbury Motor Co	943 N Fourth St	Sunbury	PA	17801	**800-358-8090**	570-286-7746
Superior Auto Sales Inc	5201 Camp Rd	Hamburg	NY	14075	**866-439-9637**	716-649-6695
Superior Motors Inc	282 John C Calhoun Dr	Orangeburg	SC	29115	**877-375-4759**	
Superior Trailer Sales Co	501 Hwy 80	Sunnyvale	TX	75182	**800-637-0324**	972-226-3893
Sutphen Corp	PO Box 158	Amlin	OH	43002	**800-726-7030**	614-889-1005
Sweeney Buick	7997 Market St	Youngstown	OH	44512	**877-360-4928**	
Ten-8 Fire Equipment Inc	2904 59th Ave Dr E	Bradenton	FL	34203	**877-989-7660**	941-756-7779
Thomson-Macconnell Cadillac Inc	2820 Gilbert Ave	Cincinnati	OH	45206	**877-472-0738**	513-334-4239
Tom Roush Inc	525 W David Brown Dr	Westfield	IN	46074	**800-382-4619**	317-896-5561
Trailercraft Inc	1301 E 64th Ave	Anchorage	AK	99518	**800-478-3238**	907-563-3238
Truck Utilities Inc	2370 English St	Saint Paul	MN	55109	**800-869-1075**	651-484-3305
Tymco Inc	225 E Industrial Blvd PO Box 2368	Waco	TX	76703	**800-258-9626**	254-799-5546
Unicell Body Co	571 Howard St *Cust Svc	Buffalo	NY	14206	**800-628-8914***	716-853-8628
United Ford Parts & Distribtion Ctr Inc	12007 E 61st St	Broken Arrow	OK	74012	**800-800-9001**	918-317-6800
Valley Chevrolet Inc	601 Kidder St	Wilkes-Barre	PA	18702	**877-207-9214**	570-821-2772
Vista-pro Automotive LLC	15 Century Blvd Ste 600	Nashville	TN	37214	**888-250-2676**	615-622-2200
Volvo Honolulu	704 Ala Moana Blvd	Honolulu	HI	96813	**888-892-2456**	
Wendle Motors Inc	9000 N Div	Spokane	WA	99218	**888-685-7177**	
Wheeled Coach Industries Inc	2737 Forsyth Rd	Winter Park	FL	32792	**800-342-0720**	407-677-7777
Wichita Kenworth Inc	5115 N Broadway	Wichita	KS	67219	**800-825-5558**	316-838-0867
York Automotive Group Inc	6019 W Central Ave	Toledo	OH	43615	**866-390-8894**	

516 MOTORCYCLES & MOTORCYCLE PARTS & ACCESSORIES

Company	Address	City	State	ZIP	Toll-Free	Phone
American Honda Motor Company Inc	1919 Torrance Blvd	Torrance	CA	90501	**800-999-1009**	310-783-3170
Corbin	2360 Technology Pkwy	Hollister	CA	95023	**800-538-7035**	831-634-1100
Edelbrock Corp	2700 California St	Torrance	CA	90503	**800-739-3737**	310-781-2222
Fulmer Co	122 Gayoso Ave	Memphis	TN	38103	**844-438-5637**	901-525-5711
Hed Cycling Products	1735 Terrace Dr	Roseville	MN	55113	**888-246-3639**	651-653-0202
Kawasaki Motors Corp USA	PO Box 25252	Santa Ana	CA	92799	**866-802-9381**	949-770-0400
Lehman Trikes Inc	125 Industrial Dr *CVE: LHT*	Spearfish	SD	57783	**888-394-3357**	605-642-2111
National Cycle Inc	2200 Maywood Dr	Maywood	IL	60153	**877-972-7336**	708-343-0400
Persons Majestic Mfg Co	PO Box 370	Huron	OH	44839	**800-772-2453**	419-433-9057
Rivco Products Inc	440 S Pine St	Burlington	WI	53105	**888-801-8222**	262-763-8222
Yamaha Motor Corp USA	6555 Katella Ave *Cust Svc	Cypress	CA	90630	**800-656-7695***	

MOTORS - FLUID POWER

SEE Pumps & Motors - Fluid Power

517 MOTORS (ELECTRIC) & GENERATORS

SEE ALSO Automotive Parts & Supplies - Mfr

Company	Address	City	State	ZIP	Toll-Free	Phone
ADS/Transicoil	9 Iron Bridge Dr	Collegeville	PA	19426	**800-323-7115**	484-902-1100
AO Smith Corp	11270 W Pk Pl Ste 170 PO Box 245008 *NYSE: AOS*	Milwaukee	WI	53224	**800-359-4065**	414-359-4000
AO Smith Electrical Products Co	531 N Fourth St	Tipp City	OH	45371	**800-543-9450**	937-667-2431
Arco Electric Products Corp	2325 E Michigan Rd	Shelbyville	IN	46176	**800-428-4370**	317-398-9713
Aura Systems Inc	1310 E Grand Ave *OTC: AUSI*	El Segundo	CA	90245	**800-909-2872**	310-643-5300
Autotrol Corp	365 E Prairie St PO Box 557	Crystal Lake	IL	60039	**800-228-6207**	815-459-3080
Bluffton Motor Works LLC	410 E Spring St	Bluffton	IN	46714	**800-579-8527**	260-827-2200
Bodine Electric Co	201 Northfield Rd	Northfield	IL	60093	**800-726-3463**	773-478-3515
Bosch Rexroth Corp	5150 Prairie Stone Pkwy	Hoffman Estates	IL	60192	**800-860-1055**	847-645-3600
CALEX Manufacturing Co	2401 Stanwell Dr	Concord	CA	94520	**800-542-3355**	925-687-4411
Continental Electric Motors Inc	23 Sebago St	Clifton	NJ	07013	**800-335-6718**	
Dumore Corp	1030 Veterans St	Mauston	WI	53948	**888-467-8288**	608-847-6420
Elwood Corp High Performance Motors Group	2701 N Green Bay Rd	Racine	WI	53404	**800-558-9489**	262-637-6591
Engine Power Source Inc	348 Bryant Blvd	Rock Hill	SC	29732	**800-374-7522**	704-944-1999
Five Star Electric of Houston Inc	19424 Pk Row Ste 100	Houston	TX	77084	**888-492-7090**	281-492-7090
FLANDERS Inc	8101 Baumgart Rd PO Box 23130	Evansville	IN	47724	**855-875-5888**	812-867-7421
Franklin Electric Co Inc	9255 Coverdale Rd *NASDAQ: FELE*	Fort Wayne	IN	46809	**800-962-3787**	260-824-2900
Generac Power Systems Inc	PO Box 8	Waukesha	WI	53187	**888-436-3722**	262-544-4811
Glentek Inc	208 Standard St	El Segundo	CA	90245	**877-470-6742**	310-322-3026
Himoinsa Power Systems Inc	16002 W 110th St	Lenexa	KS	66219	**866-710-2988**	913-495-5557
Joliet Equipment Corp	1 Doris Ave	Joliet	IL	60433	**800-435-9350**	815-727-6606
Kraft Power Corp	199 Wildwood Ave	Woburn	MA	01801	**800-969-6121**	781-938-9100
Kurz Electric Solutions Inc	1325 McMahon Dr	Neenah	WI	54956	**800-776-3629**	920-886-8200
Marathon Electric Inc	100 E Randolf St PO Box 8003	Wausau	WI	54402	**800-616-7077**	715-675-3311
Martindale Electric Co	1375 Hird Ave	Cleveland	OH	44107	**800-344-9191**	216-521-8567
Molon Motor & Coil Corp	300 N Ridge Ave	Arlington Heights	IL	60005	**800-526-6867**	847-253-6000
Morrill Motors Inc	229 S Main Ave	Erwin	TN	37650	**888-743-7001**	
Motor Appliance Corp	601 International Ave	Washington	DC	63090	**800-622-3406**	636-532-3406
Motor Products Owosso Corp	201 S Delaney Rd	Owosso	MI	48867	**800-248-3841**	
MTU Onsite Energy Corp	100 Power Dr	Mankato	MN	56001	**800-325-5450**	507-625-7973
Nidec Motor Corp	8050 W Florissant Ave	Saint Louis	MO	63136	**888-637-7333**	
PennEngineering & Manufacturing Corp	5190 Old Easton Rd	Danboro	PA	18916	**800-237-4736**	215-766-8853
Petrotech Inc	151 Brookhollow Esplanade	New Orleans	LA	70123	**800-486-8850**	504-620-6600
Piller Inc	45 Turner Rd	Middletown	NY	10941	**800-597-6937**	
Polyspede Electronics Company Inc	6770 Twin Hills Ave	Dallas	TX	75231	**888-476-5944**	214-363-7245
RAE Corp	4615 Prime Pkwy	McHenry	IL	60050	**800-323-7049**	815-385-3500
Sag Harbor Industries Inc	1668 Sag Harbor Tpke	Sag Harbor	NY	11963	**800-724-5952**	631-725-0440
Shinano Kenshi Corp	5737 Mesmer Ave	Culver City	CA	90230	**800-755-0752**	818-889-5028
Specialty Motors Inc	25060 Ave Tibbitts	Valencia	CA	91355	**800-232-2612**	661-257-7388
Sterling Electric Inc	7997 Allison Ave *Cust Svc	Indianapolis	IN	46268	**800-654-6220***	317-872-0471
Stimple & Ward Co	3400 Babcock Blvd	Pittsburgh	PA	15237	**800-792-6457**	412-364-5200
Swiger Coils Systems Inc	4677 Mfg Rd	Cleveland	OH	44135	**800-321-3310**	216-362-7500
Tampa Armature Works Inc	6312 78th St	Riverview	FL	33578	**866-465-8905**	813-621-5661
Toshiba International Corp	13131 W Little York Rd	Houston	TX	77041	**800-231-1412**	713-466-0277
Unitron LP	10925 Miller Rd PO Box 38902	Dallas	TX	75238	**800-527-1279**	214-340-8600
Vicor Corp	25 Frontage Rd *NASDAQ: VICR*	Andover	MA	01810	**800-869-5300**	978-470-2900
Wolverine Power Systems Inc	3229 80th Ave	Zeeland	MI	49464	**800-485-8068**	616-879-0040
Yamaha Motor Corp USA	6555 Katella Ave *Cust Svc	Cypress	CA	90630	**800-656-7695***	
Yaskawa America Inc	2121 Norman Dr S	Waukegan	IL	60085	**800-927-5292**	847-887-7000

518 MOVING COMPANIES

SEE ALSO Trucking Companies

Companies that have the moving of household belongings as their primary business.

Company	Address	City	State	ZIP	Toll-Free	Phone
A Colonial Moving & Storage Co	17 Mercer St	Hackensack	NJ	07601	**877-549-7783**	201-343-5777
Ace World Wide Moving	1900 E College Ave	Cudahy	WI	53110	**800-558-3980**	414-764-1000
Air Van Moving Group	2340 130th Ave NE Ste 201	Bellevue	WA	98005	**800-989-8905**	425-629-4101
Allied International NA Inc	700 Oakmont Ln	Westmont	IL	60559	**800-444-6787**	630-570-3500
American Red Ball International	9750 Third Ave NE Ste 200	Seattle	WA	98115	**800-669-6424**	206-526-1730
American Red Ball Transit Company Inc	PO Box 1127	Indianapolis	IN	46206	**800-733-8139**	

Classified Section

	City	State	Zip	Toll-Free	Phone
Andrews Van Lines Inc 310 S Seventh St *Cust Svc	Norfolk	NE	68701	**800-228-8146***	402-371-5440
Arnoff Moving & Storage Inc 1282 Dutchess Tpke	Poughkeepsie	NY	12603	**800-633-6683**	845-471-1504
Atlantic Relocation Systems Inc 1314 Chattahoochee Ave NW *Cust Svc	Atlanta	GA	30318	**800-241-1140***	404-351-5311
Atlas Van Lines Inc 1212 St George Rd	Evansville	IN	47711	**800-638-9797**	812-424-2222
Bekins Van Lines LLC 8010 Castleton Rd	Indianapolis	IN	46250	**800-456-8092**	
Berger Transfer & Storage Inc 2950 Long Lk Rd	Saint Paul	MN	55113	**877-268-2101**	
Beverly Hills Transfer & Storage Co 15500 S Main St	Gardena	CA	90248	**800-999-7114**	
Bohrens Moving & Storage Inc 3 Applegate Dr	Robbinsville	NJ	08691	**800-326-4736**	609-208-1470
Buehler Moving & Storage 3899 Jackson St	Denver	CO	80205	**800-234-6683**	303-388-4000
Callan & Woodworth Moving & Storage 900 Hwy 212	Michigan City	IN	46360	**800-584-0551**	269-447-1578
Cartwright Cos, The 11901 Cartwright Ave	Grandview	MO	64030	**800-821-2334**	
Castine Moving & Storage 1235 Chestnut St	Athol	MA	01331	**800-225-8068**	978-249-9105
Coast to Coast Moving & Storage Co 136 41st St	Brooklyn	NY	11232	**800-872-6683**	718-443-5800
Cook Moving Systems Inc 1845 Dale Rd	Buffalo	NY	14225	**800-828-7144**	
Corrigan Moving Systems 23923 Research Dr	Farmington Hills	MI	48335	**800-267-7442**	
East Side Moving & Storage 4836 SE Powell Blvd	Portland	OR	97206	**800-547-4600**	503-777-4181
Graebel Van Lines Inc 16346 Airport Cir	Aurora	CO	80011	**800-568-0031**	303-214-6683
Hilford Moving & Storage 1595 Arundell Ave	Ventura	CA	93003	**800-739-6683**	805-642-0221
Hollister Moving & Storage 1650 Lana Way	Hollister	CA	95023	**800-767-8580**	831-637-6250
I-Go Van & Storage 9820 S 142nd St	Omaha	NE	68138	**800-228-9276**	402-891-1222
Johnson Storage & Moving Co 221 Broadway	Denver	CO	80202	**800-289-6683**	303-778-6683
King Relocation Services 13535 Larwin Cir	Santa Fe Springs	CA	90670	**800-854-3679**	
Lido Van & Storage Co Inc 2152 Alton Pkwy Ste N	Irvine	CA	92606	**800-339-5436**	949-863-9000
Mayflower Transit LLC 1 Mayflower Dr	Fenton	MO	63026	**800-325-3924**	636-305-4000
McCollister's Transportation Group Inc 1800 Rt 130 N PO Box 9	Burlington	NJ	08016	**800-257-9595**	609-386-0600
National Van Lines Inc 2800 W Roosevelt Rd	Broadview	IL	60155	**877-590-2810**	708-450-2900
Nationwide Van Lines Inc 1421 NW 65th Ave	Plantation	FL	33313	**800-310-0056**	954-585-3945
Nelson Westerberg Inc 1500 Arthur Ave	Elk Grove Village	IL	60007	**800-245-2080**	847-437-2080
NorthStar Moving Corp 9120 Mason Ave	Chatsworth	CA	91311	**800-275-7767**	818-727-0128
Palmer Moving & Storage 24660 Dequindre Rd	Warren	MI	48091	**800-521-3954**	586-436-3804
Paxton Van Lines Inc 5300 Port Royal Rd	Springfield	VA	22151	**800-336-4536**	703-321-7600
Pickens-Kane Moving Co 410 N Milwaukee Ave	Chicago	IL	60610	**888-871-9998**	312-942-0330
S & M Moving Systems Inc 12128 Burke St	Santa Fe Springs	CA	90670	**800-528-4561**	562-567-2100
Security Storage Co 1701 Florida Ave NW	Washington	DC	20009	**888-903-7695**	202-234-5600
Smith Dray Line 320 Frontage Rd	Greenville	SC	29611	**866-642-6389**	
Starving Students Moving & Storage Co 1850 Sawtelle Blvd Ste 300	Los Angeles	CA	90025	**888-931-6683**	
Stevens Worldwide Van Lines 527 W Morley Dr	Saginaw	MI	48601	**888-860-4566**	800-678-3836
Suddath Cos 815 S Main St	Jacksonville	FL	32207	**800-395-7100**	904-352-2577
Truckin Movers Corp 1031 Harvest St	Durham	NC	27704	**800-334-1651**	919-682-2300
Two Guys Relocation Systems Inc 3571 Pacific Hwy	San Diego	CA	92101	**800-896-4897**	619-296-7995
Two Men & A Truck International Inc 3400 Belle Chase Way	Lansing	MI	48911	**800-345-1070**	517-394-7210
United Van Lines Inc 1 United Dr	St. Louis	MO	63026	**877-740-3040**	636-343-3900
Von Paris Enterprises Inc 8691 Larkin Rd	Savage	MD	20763	**800-866-6355**	410-888-8500
Wald Relocation Services Ltd 8708 W Little York Rd Ste 190	Houston	TX	77040	**800-527-1408**	713-512-4800
Wheaton Van Lines Inc 8010 Castleton Rd	Indianapolis	IN	46250	**800-932-7799**	317-849-7900

519 MUSEUMS

SEE ALSO Museums - Children's ; Museums & Halls of Fame - Sports
Listings for museums are organized alphabetically within state and province groupings.
(Canadian provinces are interfiled among the US states, in alphabetical order.)

	City	State	Zip	Toll-Free	Phone
390th Memorial Museum 6000 E Valencia Rd	Tucson	AZ	85706	**800-639-4992**	520-574-0287
Abraham Lincoln Presidential Library & Museum 112 N Sixth St	Springfield	IL	62701	**800-610-2094**	217-557-6250
Air Zoo, The 6151 Portage Rd	Portage	MI	49002	**866-524-7966**	269-382-6555
Alabama Constitution Village 109 Gates Ave	Huntsville	AL	35801	**800-678-1819**	256-564-8100
Alaska Native Heritage Ctr 8800 Heritage Ctr Dr	Anchorage	AK	99504	**800-315-6608**	907-330-8000
Alaska State Museum 395 Whittier St	Juneau	AK	99801	**800-440-2919**	907-465-2901
Alexandria Archaeology Museum 105 N Union St Ste 327	Alexandria	VA	22314	**800-367-7623**	703-746-4399
Alexandria Black History Museum 902 Wythe St	Alexandria	VA	22314	**800-367-7623**	703-838-4356
Aljira Ctr for Contemporary Arts 591 Broad St	Newark	NJ	07102	**800-852-7699**	973-622-1600
American Airlines CR Smith Museum 4601 Hwy 360 at FAA Rd	Fort Worth	TX	76155	**877-277-6484**	817-967-1560
American Jazz Museum 1616 E 18th St	Kansas City	MO	64108	**800-734-3447**	816-474-8463
American Saddlebred Museum 4083 Iron Works Pkwy	Lexington	KY	40511	**800-829-4438**	859-259-2746
Amon Carter Museum 3501 Camp Bowie Blvd	Fort Worth	TX	76107	**800-573-1933**	817-738-1933
Antique Car Museum/Grovewood Gallery 111 Grovewood Rd	Asheville	NC	28804	**877-622-7238**	828-253-7651
Ardenwood Historic Farm 34600 Ardenwood Blvd	Fremont	CA	94555	**888-327-2757**	510-544-2797
Arizona State Capitol Museum 1700 W Washington St	Phoenix	AZ	85007	**800-228-4710**	602-542-4675
Arizona State University Art Museum 10th St & Mill Ave Nelson Fine Arts Ctr Arizona State University	Tempe	AZ	85287	**855-278-5080**	480-965-2787
Arkansas Arts Ctr 501 E Ninth St	Little Rock	AR	72202	**800-264-2787**	501-372-4000
Arkansas State University Museum PO Box 490	State University	AR	72467	**800-342-2923**	870-972-2074
B & O Railroad Museum 901 W Pratt St	Baltimore	MD	21223	**866-468-7630**	410-752-2490
B Carroll Reece Museum PO Box 70660	Johnson City	TN	37614	**855-590-3878**	423-439-4392
B'nai B'rith Klutznick National Jewish Museum 1120 20th St NW	Washington	DC	20036	**888-388-4224**	202-857-6600
Bailey Matthews Shell Museum 3075 Sanibel-Captiva Rd PO Box 1580	Sanibel	FL	33957	**888-679-6450**	239-395-2233
Baltimore Museum of Art 10 Art Museum Dr	Baltimore	MD	21218	**800-735-2964**	443-573-1700
Banneker-Douglas Museum 84 Franklin St	Annapolis	MD	21401	**877-634-6361**	410-216-6180
Belle Meade Plantation 5025 Harding Pk	Nashville	TN	37205	**800-270-3991**	615-356-0501
Bellevue Arts Museum 510 Bellevue Way NE	Bellevue	WA	98004	**800-367-2648**	425-519-0770
Birmingham Civil Rights Institute 520 16th St N	Birmingham	AL	35203	**866-328-9696**	205-328-9696
Black Cultural Centre for Nova Scotia 10 Cherry Brook Rd	Cherry Brook	NS	B2Z1A8	**800-465-0767**	902-434-6223
Boca Raton Museum of Art 501 Plaza Real Mizner Pk	Boca Raton	FL	33432	**866-481-1689**	561-392-2500
Broward County Historical Commission 151 SW Second St	Fort Lauderdale	FL	33301	**866-682-2258**	954-765-4670
Buffalo Museum of Science 1020 Humboldt Pkwy	Buffalo	NY	14211	**866-291-6660**	716-896-5200
California State Archives 1020 'O' St	Sacramento	CA	95814	**800-633-5155**	916-653-7715
California State Railroad Museum 125 "I" St 111 'I' St	Sacramento	CA	95814	**866-240-4655**	916-323-9280
Calvert Marine Museum 14200 Solomons Island Rd PO Box 97	Solomons	MD	20688	**800-735-2258**	410-326-2042
Canada Agriculture Museum Prince of Wales Dr PO Box 9724 Stn T	Ottawa	ON	K1G5A3	**866-442-4416**	613-991-3044
Canada Science & Technology Museum 1867 St Laurent Blvd PO Box 9724	Ottawa	ON	K1G5A3	**866-442-4416**	613-991-3044
Canadian Museum of Civilization 100 Laurier St	Gatineau	QC	K1A0M8	**800-555-5621**	819-776-7000
Canadian Museum of Contemporary Photography 380 Sussex Dr PO Box 427 Stn A	Ottawa	ON	K1N9N4	**800-319-2787**	613-990-1985
Canadian Museum of Nature 240 McLeod St	Ottawa	ON	K2P2R1	**800-263-4433**	613-566-4700
Center for Creative Photography 1030 N Olive Rd	Tucson	AZ	85721	**888-472-4732**	520-621-7968
Center for Western Studies 2101 S Summit Ave Augustana College	Sioux Falls	SD	57197	**800-727-2844**	605-274-4007
Chabot Space & Science Ctr 10000 Skyline Blvd	Oakland	CA	94619	**800-704-9804**	510-336-7300
Challenger Learning Ctr (CLC) 316 Washington Ave Wheeling Jesuit University	Wheeling	WV	26003	**800-624-6992**	304-243-2279
Charlotte Nature Museum 1658 Sterling Rd	Charlotte	NC	28209	**800-935-0553**	704-372-6261
Cherokee Heritage Ctr & National Museum 21192 S Keeler Dr	Park Hill	OK	74451	**888-999-6007**	918-456-6007
Cheyenne Depot Museum 121 W 15th St Ste 300	Cheyenne	WY	82001	**800-544-2151**	307-632-3905
Children's Museum of Indianapolis 3000 N Meridian St	Indianapolis	IN	46208	**800-820-6214**	317-334-3322
Cincinnati Art Museum 953 Eden Pk Dr	Cincinnati	OH	45202	**877-472-4226**	513-721-2787
Cincinnati History Museum 1301 Western Ave Cincinnati Museum Ctr	Cincinnati	OH	45203	**800-733-2077**	513-287-7000
Circus World Museum 550 Water St	Baraboo	WI	53913	**866-693-1500**	608-356-8341
Cleveland Museum of Art 11150 E Blvd *Sales	Cleveland	OH	44106	**800-469-4449***	216-421-7340
Cleveland Museum of Natural History 1 Wade Oval Dr	Cleveland	OH	44106	**800-317-9155**	216-231-4600
Cloisters Museum Fort Tryon Pk	New York	NY	10040	**800-662-3397**	212-923-3700

Name / Address	City	State	ZIP	Toll-Free	Phone
Colorado Railroad Museum 17155 W 44th Ave	Golden	CO	80403	**800-365-6263**	303-279-4591
Conner Prairie Living History Museum 13400 Allisonville Rd	Fishers	IN	46038	**800-966-1836**	317-776-6000
Corning Museum of Glass 1 Museum Way *Cust Svc	Corning	NY	14830	**800-732-6845***	607-937-5371
COSI Columbus 333 W Broad St	Columbus	OH	43215	**888-819-2674**	614-228-2674
Country Music Hall of Fame & Museum 222 Fifth Ave S	Nashville	TN	37203	**800-852-6437**	615-416-2001
Dayton Art Institute 456 Belmonte Pk N	Dayton	OH	45405	**800-272-8258**	937-223-5277
de Saisset Museum at Santa Clara University 500 El Camino Real	Santa Clara	CA	95053	**866-554-6800**	408-554-4528
DeGrazia Gallery in the Sun 6300 N Swan Rd	Tucson	AZ	85718	**800-545-2185**	520-299-9191
Delaware Art Museum 2301 Kentmere Pkwy	Wilmington	DE	19806	**866-232-3714**	302-571-9590
DeWitt Wallace Decorative Arts Museum 326 Francis St W	Williamsburg	VA	23185	**800-447-8679**	
Dittrick Museum of Medical History 11000 Euclid Ave	Cleveland	OH	44106	**800-368-4723**	216-368-3648
Dwight D Eisenhower Presidential Library & Museum 200 SE Fourth St	Abilene	KS	67410	**877-746-4453**	785-263-6700
EAA AirVenture Museum 3000 Poberezny Rd	Oshkosh	WI	54902	**888-322-3229**	920-426-4800
Edgar Allan Poe Museum 1914 E Main St	Richmond	VA	23223	**888-213-2763**	804-648-5523
Electric City Trolley Station & Museum 300 Cliff St	Scranton	PA	18503	**800-732-0999**	570-963-6590
Elisabet Ney Museum 304 E 44th St	Austin	TX	78751	**800-680-7289**	512-458-2255
EnergyExplorium 13339 Hagers Ferry Rd	Huntersville	NC	28078	**800-777-0003**	980-875-5600
Estes-Winn Memorial Automobile Museum 111 Grovewood Rd	Asheville	NC	28804	**877-622-7238**	828-253-7651
Exploratorium, The 3601 Lyon St	San Francisco	CA	94123	**800-232-9698**	415-561-0360
Fireworks Fine Crafts Gallery 3307 Utah Ave S	Seattle	WA	98134	**800-505-8882**	206-682-8707
Fisheries Museum of the Atlantic 68 Bluenose Dr PO Box 1363	Lunenburg	NS	B0J2C0	**866-579-4909**	902-634-4794
Fitger's Brewery Museum 600 E Superior St	Duluth	MN	55802	**888-348-4377**	218-722-8826
Florida Heritage Museum 167 San Marco Ave	Saint Augustine	FL	32084	**800-268-7252**	904-829-9729
Florida Holocaust Museum 55 Fifth St S	Saint Petersburg	FL	33701	**800-388-4069**	727-820-0100
Flying Leatherneck Aviation Museum Anderson Ave MCAS Miramar	San Diego	CA	92145	**877-359-8762**	858-693-1723
Folk Art Ctr PO Box 9545	Asheville	NC	28815	**888-672-7717**	828-298-7928
Fort Caspar Museum 4001 Fort Caspar Rd	Casper	WY	82604	**800-877-7353**	307-235-8462
Fort Henry National Historic Site PO Box 213 *Cust Svc	Kingston	ON	K7L4V8	**800-437-2233***	613-542-7388
Fort McHenry National Monument & Historic Shrine 2400 E Fort Ave	Baltimore	MD	21230	**866-945-7920**	410-962-4290
Fort Worth Museum of Science & History 1600 Gendy St	Fort Worth	TX	76107	**888-255-9300**	817-255-9300
Franklin D Roosevelt Presidential Library & Museum 4079 Albany Post Rd	Hyde Park	NY	12538	**800-337-8474**	845-486-7770
Franklin Institute Science Museum 222 N 20th St	Philadelphia	PA	19103	**800-732-0999**	215-448-1200
Fraternal Order of Alaska State Troopers Museum 245 W Fifth Ave	Anchorage	AK	99501	**800-770-5050**	907-279-5050
Geological Museum 1000 E University Ave	Laramie	WY	82071	**800-842-2776**	307-766-2646
Gerald R Ford Museum 303 Pearl St NW	Grand Rapids	MI	49504	**800-888-9487**	616-254-0400
Gilcrease Museum 1400 N Gilcrease Museum Rd	Tulsa	OK	74127	**888-655-2278**	918-596-2700
Gillespie Museum of Minerals 421 N Woodland Blvd Unit 8403	DeLand	FL	32723	**800-688-0101**	386-822-7330
Glessner House Museum 1800 S Prairie Ave	Chicago	IL	60616	**800-657-0687**	312-326-1480
Goethe Institut Atlanta/German Cultural Ctr 1197 Peachtree St NE	Atlanta	GA	30361	**888-446-3843**	404-892-2388
Graceland (Elvis Presley Mansion) 3734 Elvis Presley Blvd	Memphis	TN	38116	**800-238-2000**	901-332-3322
Grand Rapids Art Museum 101 Monroe Ctr	Grand Rapids	MI	49503	**800-272-8258**	616-831-1000
Grandmother's Buttons Museum 9814 Royal St	Saint Francisville	LA	70775	**800-580-6941**	225-635-4107
Greenfield Village 20900 Oakwood Blvd	Dearborn	MI	48124	**800-835-5237**	313-271-1620
Guggenheim Hermitage Museum 3355 Las Vegas Blvd S Venetian Resort Hotel & Casino	Las Vegas	NV	89109	**800-329-6109**	212-423-3575
Guinness World Records Museum 4943 Clifton Hill	Niagara Falls	ON	L2G3N5	**866-656-0310**	905-357-4330
Hale Farm & Village 2686 Oakhill Rd PO Box 296	Bath	OH	44210	**800-589-9703**	330-666-3711
Hallie Ford Museum of Art 700 State St	Salem	OR	97301	**844-232-7228**	503-370-6855
Harry S Truman Presidential Library & Museum 500 W Hwy 24	Independence	MO	64050	**800-833-1225**	816-268-8200
Harry S Truman's Little White House Museum 111 Front St	Key West	FL	33040	**800-435-7352**	305-294-9911
Henricus Historical Park Henricus Pk Rd	Chester	VA	23836	**800-514-3849**	804-748-1613
Henry Ford Museum 20900 Oakwood Blvd	Dearborn	MI	48124	**800-835-5237**	313-271-1620
Heritage of the Americas Museum 12110 Cuyamaca College Dr W	El Cajon	CA	92019	**800-234-1597**	619-670-5194
Heritage Square Museum 3800 Homer St	Los Angeles	CA	90031	**800-375-1771**	323-225-2700
High Desert Museum 59800 S Hwy 97	Bend	OR	97702	**866-632-9992**	541-382-4754
Hiller Aviation Museum 601 Skyway Rd	San Carlos	CA	94070	**888-500-1555**	650-654-0200
Historic Jonesborough Visitors Ctr & Museum 117 Boone St	Jonesborough	TN	37659	**866-401-4223**	423-753-1010
Historical Lawmen Museum 845 Motel Blvd	Las Cruces	NM	88007	**800-332-2121**	575-525-1911
Hollywood Wax Museum 6767 Hollywood Blvd	Hollywood	CA	90028	**800-214-3661**	323-462-5991
Holocaust Memorial Ctr 28123 OrchaRd Lake Rd	Farmington Hills	MI	48334	**800-875-5275**	248-553-2400
Honolulu Academy of Arts 900 S Beretania St	Honolulu	HI	96814	**866-385-3849**	808-532-8700
Huntsville Museum of Art 300 Church St SW	Huntsville	AL	35801	**800-786-9095**	256-535-4350
Illinois State Military Museum 1301 N MacArthur Blvd	Springfield	IL	62702	**800-732-8868**	217-761-3910
Indian Pueblo Cultural Ctr 2401 12th St NW	Albuquerque	NM	87104	**866-855-7902**	505-843-7270
Indian River Lifesaving Station Museum 25039 Costal Hwy	Rehoboth Beach	DE	19971	**877-987-2757**	302-227-6991
Indian Temple Mound Museum 107 Miracle Strip Pkwy SW	Fort Walton Beach	FL	32548	**866-847-1301**	850-833-9500
Institute of Texan Cultures 801 E Durango Blvd	San Antonio	TX	78205	**800-447-3372**	210-458-2300
Intel Museum 2200 Mission College Blvd	Santa Clara	CA	95052	**800-628-8686**	408-765-0503
International Civil Rights Ctr & Museum 134 S Elm St	Greensboro	NC	27401	**800-748-7116**	336-274-9199
International Museum of the Horse 4089 Iron Works Pkwy	Lexington	KY	40511	**800-678-8813**	859-259-4232
International Women's Air & Space Museum 1501 N Marginal Rd Burke Lakefront Airport	Cleveland	OH	44114	**877-287-4752**	216-623-1111
Intrepid Sea-Air-Space Museum W 46th St & 12th Ave Pier 86	New York	NY	10036	**877-957-7447**	212-245-0072
Invent Now, Inc 3701 Highland Park NW	North Canton	OH	44720	**800-968-4332**	
Iowa Gold Star Military Museum 7105 NW 70th Ave	Johnston	IA	50131	**800-294-6607**	515-252-4531
Ivan Franko Museum 1040 - 555 Main St 595 Pritchard Ave	Winnipeg	MB	R3B1C3	**866-747-9323**	204-947-1782
Japanese American National Museum 369 E First St	Los Angeles	CA	90012	**800-461-5266**	213-625-0414
Jewish Museum of Maryland 15 Lloyd St *All	Baltimore	MD	21202	**800-235-4045***	410-732-6400
John E Conner Museum 905 W Santa Gertrudis Ave 700 University Blvd.	Kingsville	TX	78363	**800-726-8192**	361-593-2810
John F Kennedy Presidential Library & Museum Columbia Pt	Boston	MA	02125	**866-535-1960**	617-514-1600
Journey Museum 222 New York St	Rapid City	SD	57701	**877-343-8220**	605-394-6923
Kansas Museum of History 6425 SW Sixth St	Topeka	KS	66615	**800-279-3730**	785-272-8681
Kelsey Museum of Archaeology 434 S State St University of Michigan	Ann Arbor	MI	48109	**800-562-3559**	734-763-3559
Kenosha Public Museum 5500 First Ave	Kenosha	WI	53140	**888-258-9966**	262-653-4140
Kent State University Museum PO Box 5190	Kent	OH	44242	**800-988-5368**	330-672-3450
Kentucky Derby Museum 704 Central Ave	Louisville	KY	40208	**800-273-3729**	502-637-1111
Kingsley Plantation 11676 Palmetto Ave	Jacksonville	FL	32226	**877-874-2478**	904-251-3537
Kruger Street Toy & Train Museum 144 Kruger St	Wheeling	WV	26003	**877-242-8133**	304-242-8133
Lacrosse Hall of Fame & Museum 113 W University Pkwy	Baltimore	MD	21210	**866-877-7550**	410-235-6882
Lafayette Museum 1122 Lafayette St	Lafayette	LA	70501	**800-346-1958**	337-234-2208
Lake Shore Railway Museum 31 Wall St Lake Shore Historical Society	North East	PA	16428	**800-945-0340**	814-725-1911
Laura Ingalls Wilder Museum & Home 3068 Hwy A	Mansfield	MO	65704	**877-924-7126**	
LBJ Library & Museum 2313 Red River St	Austin	TX	78705	**800-874-6451**	512-721-0216
Leanin' Tree Museum of Western Art 6055 Longbow Dr	Boulder	CO	80301	**800-525-0656**	303-530-1442
Lone Star Flight Museum 2002 Terminal Dr	Galveston	TX	77554	**888-359-5736**	409-740-7722
Louisiana State Museum 751 Chartres St	New Orleans	LA	70116	**800-568-6968**	504-568-6968
Louisville Science Ctr 727 W Main St	Louisville	KY	40202	**800-591-2203**	502-561-6100
Manitou Cliff Dwellings Museum 10 Cliff Rd	Manitou Springs	CO	80829	**800-354-9971**	719-685-5242
Marbles Kids Museum 201 E Hargett St	Raleigh	NC	27601	**800-745-3000**	919-834-4040
Marian Koshland Science Museum 6th & E Sts NW	Washington	DC	20001	**888-567-4526**	202-334-1201
Mariners' Museum 100 Museum Dr	Newport News	VA	23606	**800-581-7245**	757-596-2222
Marjorie Barrick Museum 4505 S Maryland Pkwy	Las Vegas	NV	89154	**877-895-0334**	702-895-3381
Maryland Historical Society Museum & Library 201 W Monument St	Baltimore	MD	21201	**800-537-5487**	410-685-3750
Meadows Museum of Art at Centenary College 2911 Centenary Blvd	Shreveport	LA	71104	**800-234-4448**	318-869-5169
Meteor Crater & Museum of Astrogeology Exit 233 Off I-40 Meteor Crater Rd	Winslow	AZ	86047	**800-289-5898**	
Metropolitan Museum of Art 1000 Fifth Ave	New York	NY	10028	**800-468-7386**	212-879-5500

Name	Address	City	State	Zip	Toll-Free	Phone
Mid Atlantic Center for The Arts	1048 Washington St	Cape May	NJ	08204	**800-275-4278**	609-884-5404
Mill City Museum	704 S Second St	Minneapolis	MN	55401	**800-657-3773**	612-341-7555
Milwaukee Art Museum	700 N Art Museum Dr	Milwaukee	WI	53202	**888-322-3326**	414-224-3200
Minneapolis Institute of Arts	2400 Third Ave S	Minneapolis	MN	55404	**888-642-2787**	612-870-3000
Minnesota Discovery Ctr	1005 Discovery Dr	Chisholm	MN	55719	**800-372-6437**	218-254-7959
Minnesota Historical Society History Ctr Museum	345 Kellogg Blvd W	Saint Paul	MN	55102	**800-657-3773**	651-259-3001
Minnesota State University Moorhead Regional Science Ctr	1104 Seventh Ave S	Moorhead	MN	56563	**800-593-7246**	218-477-2920
Miramont Castle Museum	9 Capitol Hill Ave	Manitou Springs	CO	80829	**888-685-1011**	719-685-1011
Mississippi Agriculture & Forestry Museum/National Agricultural Aviation Museum	1150 Lakeland Dr	Jackson	MS	39216	**800-844-8687**	601-359-1100
Mississippi Museum of Art	380 S Lamar St	Jackson	MS	39201	**866-843-9278**	601-960-1515
Mississippi Museum of Natural Science	2148 Riverside Dr	Jackson	MS	39202	**800-467-2757**	601-576-6000
Mississippi River Museum	125 N Front St	Memphis	TN	38103	**800-507-6507**	901-576-7241
MIT Museum	265 Massachusetts Ave	Cambridge	MA	02139	**800-228-9000**	617-253-4444
Modern Art Museum of Fort Worth	3200 Darnell St	Fort Worth	TX	76107	**866-824-5566**	817-738-9215
Montana Historical Society Museum	225 N Roberts St	Helena	MT	59620	**800-243-9900**	406-444-2694
Museum of Anthropology	Wake Forest University Wingate Rd PO Box 7267	Winston-Salem	NC	27109	**888-925-3622**	336-758-5282
Museum of Art & Archaeology	1 Pickard Hall	Columbia	MO	65211	**866-447-9821**	573-882-3591
Museum of Arts & Sciences	352 S Nova Rd	Daytona Beach	FL	32114	**866-439-4769**	386-255-0285
Museum of Contemporary Religious Art	221 N Grand Blvd	Saint Louis	MO	63103	**800-442-1142**	314-977-7170
Museum of Early Southern Decorative Arts (MESDA)	924 S Main St	Winston-Salem	NC	27101	**800-441-5303**	336-721-7360
Museum of Geology	501 E St Joseph St S Dakota School of Mines & Technology	Rapid City	SD	57701	**800-544-8162**	605-394-2467
Museum of Glass	1801 Dock St	Tacoma	WA	98402	**866-468-7386*** *General	253-284-4750
Museum of History & Art	1100 Orange Ave	Coronado	CA	92118	**866-599-7242**	619-435-7242
Museum of Making Music	5790 Armada Dr	Carlsbad	CA	92008	**877-551-9976**	760-438-5996
Museum of Missouri Military History	2302 Militia Dr	Jefferson City	MO	65101	**888-526-6664**	573-638-9603
Museum of Natural History & Science	1301 Western Ave Cincinnati Museum Ctr	Cincinnati	OH	45203	**800-733-2077**	513-287-7000
Museum of Nebraska History	15th & P St PO Box 82554	Lincoln	NE	68508	**800-833-6747**	402-471-4754
Museum of Northern Arizona	3101 N Ft Valley Rd	Flagstaff	AZ	86001	**800-423-1069**	928-774-5211
Museum of Science & Industry	5700 S Lk Shore Dr	Chicago	IL	60637	**800-468-6674**	773-684-1414
Museum of the Mountain Man	700 E Hennick St	Pinedale	WY	82941	**877-686-6266**	307-367-4101
Museum of Tolerance	9786 W Pico Blvd	Los Angeles	CA	90035	**800-900-9036**	310-553-8403
Museum of World Treasures	835 E First St	Wichita	KS	67202	**888-700-1311**	316-263-1311
Museums at 18th & Vine	1616 E 18th St	Kansas City	MO	64108	**800-734-3447**	816-474-8463
Museums of Oglebay Institute	1330 National Rd	Wheeling	WV	26003	**800-624-6988**	304-242-7272
Mystic Seaport -- The Museum of America & the Sea	75 Greenmanville Ave PO Box 6000	Mystic	CT	06355	**888-973-2767**	860-572-0711
Naples Museum of Art	5833 Pelican Bay Blvd	Naples	FL	34108	**800-597-1900**	239-597-1111
National Afro-American Museum & Cultural Ctr	1350 Brush Row Rd PO Box 578	Wilberforce	OH	45384	**800-752-2603**	937-376-4944
National Border Patrol Museum	4315 Woodrow Bean TransMtn Rd	El Paso	TX	79924	**877-276-8738**	915-759-6060
National Corvette Museum	350 Corvette Dr	Bowling Green	KY	42101	**800-538-3883**	270-781-7973
National Cowgirl Museum & Hall of Fame	1720 Gendy St	Fort Worth	TX	76107	**800-476-3263**	817-336-4475
National Farm Toy Museum	1110 16th Ave SE	Dyersville	IA	52040	**877-475-2727**	563-875-2727
National Geographic Society Explorers Hall	1145 17th St NW	Washington	DC	20036	**800-647-5463**	
National Inventors Hall of Fame	3701 Highland Park NW	North Canton	OH	44720	**800-968-4332**	
National Mississippi River Museum & Aquarium	350 E Third St	Dubuque	IA	52001	**800-226-3369**	563-557-9545
National Museum of Dentistry	31 S Greene St	Baltimore	MD	21201	**866-787-8637**	410-706-0600
National Museum of Natural History (Smithsonian Institution)	10th St & Constitution Ave NW	Washington	DC	20560	**866-868-7774**	202-633-1000
National Museum of Naval Aviation	1750 Radford Blvd Ste C	Pensacola	FL	32508	**800-247-6289*** *General	850-452-3604
National Museum of the American Indian (Smithsonian Institution)	1 Bowling Green	New York	NY	10004	**800-242-6624**	212-514-3700
National Museum of Wildlife Art	2820 Rungius Rd PO Box 6825	Jackson	WY	83002	**800-313-9553**	307-733-5771
National Museum of Women in the Arts	1250 New York Ave NW	Washington	DC	20005	**866-875-4627**	202-783-5000
National Music Museum	414 E Clark St	Vermillion	SD	57069	**877-225-0027**	605-677-5306
National Ornamental Metal Museum	374 Metal Museum Dr	Memphis	TN	38106	**877-881-2326**	901-774-6380
National Railroad Museum	2285 S Broadway St	Green Bay	WI	54304	**866-468-7630**	920-437-7623
National Scouting Museum	1329 W Walnut Hill Ln	Irving	TX	75038	**800-303-3047**	972-580-2100
National Watch & Clock Museum	514 Poplar St	Columbia	PA	17512	**800-368-6511**	717-684-8261
NAUTICUS the National Maritime Ctr	1 Waterside Dr	Norfolk	VA	23510	**800-664-1080**	757-664-1000
New Brunswick Museum	1 Market Sq	Saint John	NB	E2L4Z6	**888-268-9595**	506-643-2300
New Hampshire Institute of Art	148 Concord St	Manchester	NH	03104	**866-241-4918**	603-623-0313
New Mexico Museum of Art	107 W Palace Ave	Santa Fe	NM	87501	**877-567-7380**	505-476-5072
New Mexico Museum of Space History	Top of Hwy 2001	Alamogordo	NM	88311	**877-333-6589**	575-437-2840
Newark Museum	49 Washington St	Newark	NJ	07102	**888-370-6765**	973-596-6550
Newsome House Museum & Cultural Ctr	2803 Oak Ave	Newport News	VA	23607	**888-493-7386**	757-247-2360
North Carolina Museum of Natural Sciences	11 W Jones St	Raleigh	NC	27601	**877-462-8724**	919-733-7450
North Dakota Game & Fish Dept	100 N Bismarck Expy	Bismarck	ND	58501	**800-406-6409**	701-328-6300
North Museum of Natural History & Science	400 College Ave	Lancaster	PA	17603	**800-732-0999**	717-291-3941
Nottoway Plantation	31025 Louisiana Hwy 1	White Castle	LA	70788	**866-527-6884**	225-545-2730
Oakland Museum of California	1000 Oak St	Oakland	CA	94607	**888-625-6873*** *General	510-238-2200
Ohio Historical Society	1982 Velma Ave	Columbus	OH	43211	**800-686-6124**	614-297-2300
Oklahoma City Museum of Art	415 Couch Dr	Oklahoma City	OK	73102	**800-579-9278**	405-236-3100
Oklahoma City National Memorial & Memorial Ctr Museum	620 N Harvey Ave	Oklahoma City	OK	73102	**888-542-4673**	405-235-3313
Old Florida Museum	259 San Marco Ave	Saint Augustine	FL	32084	**800-813-3208**	904-824-8874
Old Salem	600 S Main St	Winston-Salem	NC	27101	**800-441-5305**	336-721-7300
Ontario Science Centre	770 Don Mills Rd	Toronto	ON	M3C1T3	**888-696-1110**	416-696-1000
Orange County Regional History Ctr	65 E Central Blvd	Orlando	FL	32801	**800-965-2030**	407-836-8500
Oregon Museum of Science & Industry	1945 SE Water Ave	Portland	OR	97214	**800-955-6674**	503-797-4000
Oriental Institute Museum	1155 E 58th St University of Chicago	Chicago	IL	60637	**800-791-9354**	773-702-9514
Orlando Museum of Art	2416 N Mills Ave	Orlando	FL	32803	**800-435-7352**	407-896-4231
Orlando Science Ctr	777 E Princeton St	Orlando	FL	32803	**888-672-4386**	407-514-2000
Pacific Science Ctr	200 Second Ave N	Seattle	WA	98109	**800-664-8775**	206-443-2001
Patriots Point Naval & Maritime Museum	40 Patriots Pt Rd	Mount Pleasant	SC	29464	**800-248-3508**	803-771-0131
Peabody Essex Museum	161 Essex St	Salem	MA	01970	**866-745-1876**	978-745-1876
Pennsylvania Academy of the Fine Arts Museum (PAFA)	118 N Broad St	Philadelphia	PA	19102	**800-799-7233**	215-972-7600
Pennsylvania Anthracite Heritage Museum	Bald Mountain Rd Ste 1	Scranton	PA	18504	**800-732-0999**	570-963-4804
Penobscot Marine Museum	5 Church St PO Box 498	Searsport	ME	04974	**800-268-8030**	207-548-2529
Philadelphia Museum of Art	2600 Benjamin Franklin Pkwy	Philadelphia	PA	19130	**800-732-0999**	215-763-8100
Plaquemine Lock State Historic Site	57730 Main St	Plaquemine	LA	70764	**877-987-7158**	225-687-7158
Polynesian Cultural Ctr	55-370 Kamehameha Hwy	Laie	HI	96762	**800-367-7060**	808-293-3005
Pony Express National Museum	914 Penn St	Saint Joseph	MO	64503	**800-530-5930**	816-279-5059
Port Townsend Marine Science Ctr	532 Battery Way	Port Townsend	WA	98368	**800-566-3932**	360-385-5582
Pueblo Grande Museum & Archaeological Park	4619 E Washington St	Phoenix	AZ	85034	**877-706-4408**	602-495-0901
Queens Museum of Art	New York City Bldg	Queens	NY	11368	**866-867-9665**	718-592-9700
Randall Museum	199 Museum Way	San Francisco	CA	94114	**866-807-7148**	415-554-9600
RCMP Heritage Ctr	5907 Dewdney Ave	Regina	SK	S4T0P4	**866-567-7267**	306-522-7333
Reynolda House Museum of American Art	2250 Reynolda Rd	Winston-Salem	NC	27106	**888-663-1149**	336-758-5150
Reynolds-Alberta Museum	6426 40 Ave PO Box 6360	Wetaskiwin	AB	T9A2G1	**800-661-4726**	780-361-1351
Richmond National Battlefield Park	3215 E Broad St	Richmond	VA	23223	**866-733-7768**	804-226-1981
Ripley's Believe It or Not! Museum	19 San Marco Ave	Saint Augustine	FL	32084	**800-226-6545**	904-824-1606
Roberson Museum & Science Ctr	30 Front St	Binghamton	NY	13905	**888-269-5325**	607-772-0660
Robert Hull Fleming Museum	61 Colchester Ave University of Vermont	Burlington	VT	05405	**888-382-1222**	802-656-0750
Rockford Art Museum	711 N Main St	Rockford	IL	61103	**800-521-0849**	815-968-2787
Rocky Mount Museum	200 Hyder Hill Rd PO Box 160	Piney Flats	TN	37686	**888-538-1791**	423-538-7396
Ronald Reagan Presidential Library & Museum	40 Presidential Dr	Simi Valley	CA	93065	**800-410-8354**	805-522-2977
Roscoe Village	600 N Whitewoman St	Coshocton	OH	43812	**800-877-1830**	740-622-7644
Royal British Columbia Museum (RBCM)	675 Belleville St	Victoria	BC	V8W9W2	**888-447-7977**	250-356-7226
Royal Canadian Military Institute	426 University Ave	Toronto	ON	M5G1S9	**800-585-1072**	416-597-0286

Name / Address	City	State	Zip	Toll-Free	Phone
Royal Saskatchewan Museum 2445 Albert St	Regina	SK	S4P4W7	**866-984-4964**	306-787-2815
Royal Tyrrell Museum of Palaeontology Hwy 838 Midland Provincial Pk	Drumheller	AB	T0J0Y0	**888-440-4240**	403-823-7707
Saint Louis Science Ctr 5050 Oakland Ave	Saint Louis	MO	63110	**800-456-7572**	314-289-4400
Salem Witch Museum 19 1/2 Washington Sq N	Salem	MA	01970	**800-392-6100**	978-744-1692
San Diego Natural History Museum 1788 El Prado PO Box 121390	San Diego	CA	92101	**877-946-7797**	619-232-3821
Sauder Village 22611 SR 2	Archbold	OH	43502	**800-590-9755**	419-446-2541
Sci-Port Discovery Ctr 820 Clyde Fant Pkwy	Shreveport	LA	71101	**877-724-7678**	318-424-3466
Science Central 1950 N Clinton St	Fort Wayne	IN	46805	**888-240-7268**	260-424-2400
Science Museum of Minnesota 120 W Kellogg Blvd	Saint Paul	MN	55102	**800-221-9444**	651-221-9444
Science Museum Oklahoma 2100 NE 52nd St	Oklahoma City	OK	73111	**800-532-7652**	405-602-6664
Shaker Village of Pleasant Hill 3501 Lexington Rd	Harrodsburg	KY	40330	**800-734-5611**	859-734-5411
Sheldon Jackson Museum 104 College Dr	Sitka	AK	99835	**800-587-0430**	907-747-8981
Sixth Floor Museum 411 Elm St Ste 120 Dealey Plz	Dallas	TX	75202	**888-485-4854**	214-747-6660
Smith Robertson Museum & Cultural Ctr 528 Bloom St	Jackson	MS	39202	**800-354-7695**	601-960-1457
Solomon R Guggenheim Museum 1071 Fifth Ave	New York	NY	10128	**800-329-6109**	212-423-3500
Southern University Museum of Art (SUSLA) 3050 Martin Luther King Jr Dr	Shreveport	LA	71107	**800-458-1472**	318-670-6000
Springfield Museums 21 Edwards St	Springfield	MA	01103	**800-625-7738**	413-263-6800
Stan Hywet Hall & Gardens 714 N Portage Path	Akron	OH	44303	**888-836-5533**	330-836-5533
State Historical Society of Missouri, The 1020 Lowry St	Columbia	MO	65201	**800-747-6366**	573-882-1187
Stranahan House Museum Inc 335 SE Sixth Ave	Fort Lauderdale	FL	33301	**800-435-7352**	954-524-4736
Studebaker National Museum 201 Chapin St	South Bend	IN	46601	**888-391-5600**	574-235-9714
Tampa Museum of Art 120 W Gasparilla Plaza	Tampa	FL	33602	**866-790-4111**	813-274-8131
Taylor & Messick Inc 325 Walt Messick Rd	Harrington	DE	19952	**800-237-1272**	302-398-3729
Tech Museum of Innovation 201 S Market St	San Jose	CA	95113	**800-660-4287**	408-294-8324
Tennessee State Museum 505 Deaderick St	Nashville	TN	37243	**800-407-4324**	615-741-2692
Texas Memorial Museum 2400 Trinity St	Austin	TX	78705	**800-687-4132**	512-471-1604
Toledo Museum of Art 2445 Monroe St	Toledo	OH	43620	**800-644-6862**	419-255-8000
Turtle Bay Exploration Park 840 Auditorium Dr	Redding	CA	96001	**800-887-8532**	530-243-8850
Tweed Museum of Art 1201 ordean Ct	Duluth	MN	55812	**866-999-6995**	218-726-8222
University Galleries 400 SW 13th St Fine Arts Bldg B PO Box 115803	Gainesville	FL	32611	**800-745-3000**	352-273-3000
University Museum 3219 Hudson Rd University of Northern Iowa	Cedar Falls	IA	50614	**800-772-2736**	319-273-2188
University of Alaska Museum of the North 907 Yukon Dr	Fairbanks	AK	99775	**866-478-2721**	907-474-7505
University of South Carolina McKissick Museum University of S Carolina 816 Bull St	Columbia	SC	29208	**888-825-9711**	803-777-7251
Upper Room Chapel & Museum 1908 Grand Ave	Nashville	TN	37212	**800-972-0433**	615-340-7200
USS Hornet Museum 707 W Hornet Ave Pier 3	Alameda	CA	94501	**800-555-8355**	510-521-8448
USS Lexington Museum on the Bay 2914 N Shoreline Blvd	Corpus Christi	TX	78402	**800-523-9539**	361-888-4873
Virginia War Museum 9285 Warwick Blvd	Newport News	VA	23607	**888-493-7386**	757-247-8523
Walker Art Ctr 1750 Hennepin Ave	Minneapolis	MN	55403	**888-339-4496**	612-375-7600
Washington Pavilion of Arts & Science 301 S Main PO Box 984	Sioux Falls	SD	57104	**877-927-4728**	605-367-6000
Weatherspoon Art Museum 500 Tate St	Greensboro	NC	27402	**877-862-4123**	336-334-5770
West Baton Rouge Museum 845 N Jefferson Ave	Port Allen	LA	70767	**888-881-6811**	225-336-2422
West Virginia State Museum 1900 Kanawha Blvd E The Cultural Ctr	Charleston	WV	25305	**800-946-9471**	304-558-0220
Western Museum of Mining & Industry 225 N Gate Blvd	Colorado Springs	CO	80921	**800-752-6558**	719-488-0880
Wheelwright Museum of the American Indian 704 Camino Lejo	Santa Fe	NM	87505	**800-607-4636**	505-982-4636
Whitney Museum of American Art 945 Madison Ave	New York	NY	10021	**800-944-8639**	212-570-3600
Will Rogers Memorial Museum 1720 W Will Rogers Blvd	Claremore	OK	74017	**800-324-9455**	918-341-0719
Winterthur Museum & Country Estate 5105 Kennett Pk	Winterthur	DE	19735	**800-448-3883**	302-888-4600
Wisconsin Historical Museum 30 N Carroll St	Madison	WI	53703	**888-748-7479**	608-264-6555
Wisconsin Maritime Museum 75 Maritime Dr	Manitowoc	WI	54220	**866-724-2356**	920-684-0218
Wisconsin State Fair Park 640 S 84th St	West Allis	WI	53214	**800-884-3247**	414-266-7033
Woolaroc Ranch Museum & Wildlife Preserve 1925 Woolaroc Ranch Rd	Bartlesville	OK	74003	**888-966-5276**	918-336-0307
World of Coca-Cola Atlanta 121 Baker St NW	Atlanta	GA	30313	**888-855-5701**	404-676-5151
Yale Ctr for British Art 1080 Chapel St PO Box 208280	New Haven	CT	06510	**877-274-8278**	203-432-2800

520 MUSEUMS - CHILDREN'S

Children's museums are organized alphabetically by states.

Name / Address	City	State	Zip	Toll-Free	Phone
Children's Museum of Oak Ridge 461 W Outer Dr	Oak Ridge	TN	37830	**877-524-1223**	865-482-1074
Children's Museum of Richmond 2626 W Broad St	Richmond	VA	23220	**866-737-5965**	804-474-7000
Cinergy Children's Museum 1301 Western Ave Cincinnati Museum Ctr	Cincinnati	OH	45203	**800-733-2077**	513-287-7000
Discovery Ctr of Springfield 438 E St Louis St	Springfield	MO	65806	**888-636-4395**	417-862-9910
Discovery Place 301 N Tryon St	Charlotte	NC	28202	**800-935-0553**	704-372-6261
EdVenture Children's Museum 211 Gervais St	Columbia	SC	29201	**888-236-2427**	803-779-3100
Exploration Place 300 N McLean Blvd	Wichita	KS	67203	**877-904-1444**	316-660-0600
Kansas Cosmosphere & Space Ctr 1100 N Plum St	Hutchinson	KS	67501	**800-397-0330**	620-662-2305
Please Touch Museum Memorial Hall Fairmount Pk 4231 Ave of the Republic	Philadelphia	PA	19131	**800-732-0999**	215-963-0667
Young at Art Children's Museum 751 SW 121st Ave	Davie	FL	33325	**800-435-7352**	954-424-0085

521 MUSEUMS & HALLS OF FAME - SPORTS

Name / Address	City	State	Zip	Toll-Free	Phone
1932 & 1980 Lake Placid Winter Olympic Museum Olympic Ctr 2634 Main St	Lake Placid	NY	12946	**800-462-6236**	518-523-1655
American Museum of Fly Fishing 4104 Main Rd	Manchester	VT	05254	**800-333-1550**	802-362-3300
Baseball Hall of Fame 910 S 3rd St	Minneapolis	MN	55415	**888-375-9707**	612-375-9707
Canadian Golf Hall of Fame & Museum Glen Abbey Golf Course 1333 Dorval Dr Ste 1	Oakville	ON	L6M4X7	**800-263-0009**	905-849-9700
Cheap Joe's Art Stuff Inc 374 Industrial Park Dr	Boone	NC	28607	**800-227-2788**	828-263-5472
Don Garlits Museums 13700 SW 16th Ave	Ocala	FL	34473	**877-271-3278**	352-245-8661
Greyhound Hall of Fame 407 S Buckeye Ave	Abilene	KS	67410	**800-932-7881**	785-263-3000
Hendrick Motorsports Museum 4400 Papa Joe Hendrick Blvd	Charlotte	NC	28262	**877-467-4890**	
Improv Asylum 216 Hanover St	Boston	MA	02113	**888-396-6887**	617-263-6887
International Bowling Museum & Hall of Fame 621 Six Flags Dr	Arlington	TX	76011	**800-514-2695**	817-385-8215
International Snowmobile Hall of Fame 1521 N Railroad St	Eagle River	WI	54521	**800-746-8963**	715-479-2186
International Tennis Hall of Fame & Museum 194 Bellevue Ave	Newport	RI	02840	**800-745-3000**	401-849-3990
Legends of the Game Baseball Museum 1000 Ballpark Way	Arlington	TX	76011	**866-274-9053**	
Louisville Slugger Museum 800 W Main St	Louisville	KY	40202	**877-775-8443**	502-585-5226
Mississippi Sports Hall of Fame & Museum 1152 Lakeland Dr	Jackson	MS	39216	**800-280-3263**	601-982-8264
Missouri Sports Hall of Fame 3861 E Stan Musial Dr	Springfield	MO	65809	**800-498-5678**	417-889-3100
Motorcycle Hall of Fame Museum 13515 Yarmouth Dr	Pickerington	OH	43147	**800-262-5646**	614-856-2222
Naismith Memorial Basketball Hall of Fame 1000 W Columbus Ave	Springfield	MA	01105	**877-446-6752**	413-781-6500
National Baseball Hall of Fame & Museum 25 Main St	Cooperstown	NY	13326	**888-425-5633**	607-547-7200
National Fresh Water Fishing Hall of Fame 10360 Hall of Fame Dr PO Box 690	Hayward	WI	54843	**866-268-4333**	715-634-4440
National Museum of Racing & Hall of Fame 191 Union Ave	Saratoga Springs	NY	12866	**800-562-5394**	518-584-0400
National Softball Hall of Fame & Museum 2801 NE 50th St	Oklahoma City	OK	73111	**800-654-8337**	405-424-5266
National Sprint Car Hall of Fame & Museum 1 Sprint Capital Pl	Knoxville	IA	50138	**800-874-4488**	641-842-6176
North Carolina Sports Hall of Fame 5 E Edenton St NC Museum of History	Raleigh	NC	27601	**877-627-6724**	919-807-7900
Paul W Bryant Museum 300 Paul W Bryant Dr *General	Tuscaloosa	AL	35487	**866-772-2327***	205-348-4668
Texas Sports Hall of Fame 1108 S University Parks Dr	Waco	TX	76706	**800-567-9561**	254-756-1633
U.S. National Ski Hall of Fame 610 Palms Ave	Ishpeming	MI	49849	**800-648-0720**	906-485-6323
University of Iowa Athletics Hall of Fame 2425 Prairie Meadow Dr	Iowa City	IA	52242	**877-462-6342**	319-384-1031
Us Art Company Inc 66 Pacella Park Dr	Randolph	MA	02368	**800-872-7826**	781-986-6500

522 MUSIC DISTRIBUTORS

Name / Address	City	State	Zip	Toll-Free	Phone
A-r Editions Inc 1600 Aspen Cmns Ste 100	Middleton	WI	53562	**800-736-0070**	608-836-9000
Allegro Corp 20048 NE San Rafael St	Portland	OR	97230	**800-288-2007**	503-491-8480
Baker & Taylor Inc 2550 W Tyvola Rd Ste 300	Charlotte	NC	28217	**800-775-1800**	
Gotham Distributing Corp 60 Portland Rd	Conshohocken	PA	19428	**800-446-8426**	610-649-7650

Company	Address	City	State	ZIP	Toll-Free	Phone
Malaco Music Group Inc	3023 W Northside Dr	Jackson	MS	39213	**800-272-7936***	601-982-4522
	*Cust Svc					
Select-O-Hits Inc	1981 Fletcher Creek Dr	Memphis	TN	38133	**800-346-0723**	901-388-1190

523 MUSIC PROGRAMMING SERVICES

Company	Address	City	State	ZIP	Toll-Free	Phone
Muzak LLC	3318 Lakemont Blvd	Fort Mill	SC	29708	**888-689-2559**	770-246-3941

524 MUSIC STORES

SEE ALSO Book, Music, Video Clubs

Company	Address	City	State	ZIP	Toll-Free	Phone
Amazon.com Inc	1200 12th Ave S Ste 1200	Seattle	WA	98144	**800-201-7575***	206-266-1000
	NASDAQ: AMZN ■ *Cust Svc					
Anonymizer Inc	6755 Mira Mesa Blvd Ste 123-164	San Diego	CA	92121	**888-270-0141**	
Best Buy Company Inc	7601 Penn Ave S	Minneapolis	MN	55423	**888-237-8289**	612-291-1000
	NYSE: BBY					
CD Universe	101 N Plains Industrial Rd	Wallingford	CT	06492	**800-231-7937**	203-294-1648
CD Warehouse	900 N Broadway	Oklahoma City	OK	73102	**800-641-9394**	919-577-6000
DSN Group Inc	152 Lorraine Dr	Lake Zurich	IL	60047	**888-445-2919**	
FirstCom Music	1325 Capital Pkwy Ste 109	Carrollton	TX	75006	**800-858-8880***	972-446-8742
	*Cust Svc					
Global Electronic Music Marketplace	PO Box 4062	Palm Springs	CA	92263	**800-207-4366**	
Hastings Entertainment Inc	3601 Plains Blvd	Amarillo	TX	79102	**877-427-8464***	
	NASDAQ: HAST ■ *Cust Svc					
Med-Tech Resource Inc	29485 Airport Rd	Eugene	OR	97402	**888-627-7779**	
Mississippi Music Inc	222 N Main St	Hattiesburg	MS	39401	**800-844-5821**	601-544-5821
Test com Inc	1501 Euclid Ave Ste 407	Cleveland	OH	44115	**877-502-8600**	
V-Technologies LLC	675 W Johnson Ave	Cheshire	CT	06705	**800-462-4016**	

525 MUSICAL INSTRUMENT STORES

Company	Address	City	State	ZIP	Toll-Free	Phone
Alamo Music Ctr	425 N Main Ave	San Antonio	TX	78205	**800-822-5010**	210-224-1010
American Musical Supply	PO Box 152	Spicer	MN	56288	**800-458-4076**	320-796-2088
Amro Music Stores	2918 Poplar Ave	Memphis	TN	38111	**800-626-2676***	901-323-8888
	*General					
Annex Pro Inc	49 Dunlevy Ave Ste 220	Vancouver	BC	V6A3A3	**800-682-6639**	604-682-6639
Brook Mays Music Co	8605 John Carpenter Fwy	Dallas	TX	75247	**800-637-8966***	214-631-0928
	*Cust Svc					
Buddy Rogers Music Inc	6891 Simpson Ave	Cincinnati	OH	45239	**800-536-2263**	513-729-1950
Cascio Interstate Music	13819 W National Ave	New Berlin	WI	53151	**800-462-2263**	262-789-7600
Cream City Music	12505 W Bluemound Rd	Brookfield	WI	53005	**800-800-0087**	262-860-1800
Elderly Instruments	1100 N Washington Ave	Lansing	MI	48906	**888-473-5810**	517-372-7890
First Act Inc	745 Boylston St	Boston	MA	02116	**888-551-1115**	617-226-7888
Fletcher Music Centers Inc	3966 Airway Cir	Clearwater	FL	33762	**800-258-1088**	727-571-1088
Foxes Music Co	416 S Washington St	Falls Church	VA	22046	**800-446-4414**	703-533-7393
Front End Audio	130 Hunter Village Dr Ste D	Irmo	SC	29063	**888-228-4530**	803-748-0914
Gigasonic	260 E Gish Rd	San Jose	CA	95112	**888-246-4442**	408-573-1400
Graves Piano & Organ Company Inc	5798 Karl Rd	Columbus	OH	43229	**800-686-4322**	614-847-4322
International Violin Co Ltd	1421 Clarkview Rd	Baltimore	MD	21209	**800-542-3538**	410-832-2525
JW Pepper & Son Inc	2480 Industrial Blvd	Paoli	PA	19301	**800-345-6296**	610-648-0500
Lone Star Percussion	10611 Control Pl	Dallas	TX	75238	**866-792-0143**	214-340-0835
Music & Arts Centers Inc	4626 Wedgewood Blvd	Frederick	MD	21703	**888-731-5396**	
Musician's Friend Inc	PO Box 7479	Westlake Village	CA	91359	**800-391-8762**	801-501-8110
Musiciansbuy.com Inc	7830 Byron Dr Ste 1	West Palm Beach	FL	33404	**877-778-7845**	561-842-7451
Quantum Audio Designs Inc	6408 State Hwy 77	Benton	MO	63736	**888-545-4404**	573-545-4404
Stanton's Sheet Music	330 S Fourth St	Columbus	OH	43215	**800-426-8742**	614-224-4257
Strait Music Co	2428 W Ben White Blvd	Austin	TX	78704	**800-725-8877**	512-476-6927
Sweetwater Sound Inc	5501 US Hwy 30 W	Fort Wayne	IN	46818	**800-222-4700**	260-432-8176
Tom Lee Music Ltd	929 Granville St	Vancouver	BC	V6Z1L3	**888-886-6533**	604-685-8471
West Music Inc	1212 Fifth St PO Box 5521	Coralville	IA	52241	**800-373-2000**	319-351-2000
Woodwind & Brasswind	4004 Technology Dr	South Bend	IN	46628	**800-348-5003**	574-251-3500
World Music Supply	2414 W Seventh St	Muncie	IN	47302	**800-867-4611**	765-213-6085

526 MUSICAL INSTRUMENTS

Company	Address	City	State	ZIP	Toll-Free	Phone
Alembic Inc	3005 Wiljan Ct	Santa Rosa	CA	95407	**800-322-5893**	707-523-2611
Avedis Zildjian Co	22 Longwater Dr	Norwell	MA	02061	**800-229-8672**	781-871-2200
Carvin Corp	12340 World Trade Dr	San Diego	CA	92128	**800-854-2235**	858-487-8700
CF Martin & Company Inc	510 Sycamore St PO Box 329	Nazareth	PA	18064	**888-433-9177**	610-759-2837
Chime Master Systems	PO Box 936	Lancaster	OH	43130	**800-344-7464**	
Daisy Rock Guitars	16320 Roscoe Blvd Ste 100	Van Nuys	CA	91410	**877-693-2479**	
Davitt & Hanser Music Co	3015 Kustom Dr	Hebron	KY	41048	**800-999-5558**	859-817-7100
Deering Banjo Co	3733 Kenora Dr	Spring Valley	CA	91977	**800-845-7791**	619-464-8252
Edwards Instrument Co	530 S Hwy H	Elkhorn	WI	53121	**800-562-6838**	262-723-4221
Ernie Ball	151 Suburban Rd	San Luis Obispo	CA	93401	**866-823-2255**	805-544-7726
Fender Musical Instruments Corp	17600 N Perimeter Dr Ste 100	Scottsdale	AZ	85255	**800-488-1818***	480-596-9690
	*Cust Svc					
George Heinl & Co	201 Church St	Toronto	ON	M5B1Y7	**800-387-7858**	416-363-0093
Getzen Company Inc	530 S Cty Hwy H PO Box 440	Elkhorn	WI	53121	**800-366-5584**	262-723-4221
GHS Corp	2813 Wilber Ave	Battle Creek	MI	49037	**800-388-4447**	
Gibson Guitar Corp	309 Plus Pk Blvd	Nashville	TN	37217	**800-444-2766**	615-871-4500
Gibson Piano Ventures Inc	309 Plus Pk Blvd	Nashville	TN	37217	**800-444-2766**	615-871-4500
Hammond Suzuki USA Inc	743 Annoreno Dr	Addison	IL	60101	**888-765-2900**	630-543-0277
Hohner Inc	1000 Technology Pk Dr	Glen Allen	VA	23059	**800-446-6010**	804-515-1900
J D'Addario & Company Inc	595 Smith St	Farmingdale	NY	11735	**800-323-2746**	631-439-3300
JD Calato Mfg Company Inc	4501 Hyde Pk Blvd	Niagara Falls	NY	14305	**800-358-4590***	716-285-3546
	*Cust Svc					
Lindeblad Piano Restoration	101 Us 46	Pine Brook	NJ	07058	**888-587-4266**	
Lowrey Organ Co	989 AEC Dr	Wood Dale	IL	60191	**800-451-5939**	
Lyon & Healy Harps Inc	168 N Ogden Ave	Chicago	IL	60607	**800-621-3881**	312-786-1881
Maas-Rowe Carillons Inc	2255 Meyers Ave	Escondido	CA	92029	**800-854-2023**	
Manhasset Specialty Co	3505 Fruitvale Blvd	Yakima	WA	98902	**800-795-0965**	509-248-3810
Marimba One Inc	901 O St Ste D	Arcata	CA	95521	**888-990-6663**	707-822-9570
Morley Pedals	325 Cary Pt Dr	Cary	IL	60013	**800-284-5172**	847-639-4646
Organ Supply Industries Inc	2320 W 50th St	Erie	PA	16506	**800-458-0289**	814-835-2244
PianoDisc	4111 N Fwy Blvd	Sacramento	CA	95834	**800-566-3472**	916-567-9999
Prestini Musical Instruments Inc	2020 N Aurora Dr	Nogales	AZ	85628	**800-528-6569***	520-287-4931
	*General					
Remo Inc	28101 Industry Dr	Valencia	CA	91355	**800-525-5134**	661-294-5600
Rhythm Tech	29 Beechwood Ave	New Rochelle	NY	10801	**800-726-2279**	914-636-6900
Sabian Ltd	219 Main St.	Meductic	NB	E6H2L5	**800-817-2242**	506-272-2019
Saint Louis Music Inc	1400 Ferguson Ave	Saint Louis	MO	63133	**800-727-4512**	314-727-4512
Schaff Piano Supply Co	451 Oakwood Rd	Lake Zurich	IL	60047	**800-747-4266**	847-438-4556
Schecter Guitar Research Inc	10953 Pendleton St	Sun Valley	CA	91352	**800-660-6621**	
Schulmerich Carillons Inc	Carillon Hill	Sellersville	PA	18960	**800-772-3557**	215-257-2771
Steinway & Sons	1 Steinway Pl	Long Island	NY	11105	**800-783-4692**	718-721-2600
Suzuki Musical Instrument Corp	PO Box 710459	Santee	CA	92072	**800-854-1594***	619-258-1896
	*Cust Svc					
Ultimate Support Systems Inc	5836 Wright Dr	Loveland	CO	80538	**800-525-5628**	
Wenger Corp	555 Pk Dr PO Box 448	Owatonna	MN	55060	**800-493-6437**	507-455-4100
Wicks Pipe Organ Co	1100 Fifth St	Highland	IL	62249	**877-654-2191***	618-654-2191
	*Cust Svc					

527 MUTUAL FUNDS

Company	Address	City	State	ZIP	Toll-Free	Phone
32 Degrees Capital	650 635-8th Ave S W	Calgary	AB	T2P3M3	**866-695-1069**	403-695-1074
ACG Advisory Services Inc	1640 Huguenot Rd	Midlothian	VA	23113	**800-231-6409**	804-323-1886

Classified Section

Name / Address	City	State	ZIP	Toll-Free	Phone
Agilith Capital Inc Victory Bldg 80 Richmond St W Ste 203	Toronto	ON	M5H2A4	866-345-1231	416-915-0284
Alerus Retirement Solutions 2 Pine Tree Dr Ste 400	Arden Hills	MN	55112	800-795-2697	
Alger Family of Funds PO Box 8480	Boston	MA	02266	800-992-3863	
American Century Proprietary Holdings Inc PO Box 419200	Kansas City	MO	64141	800-345-2021	816-531-5575
Aquila Group of Funds 380 Madison Ave Ste 2300	New York	NY	10017	800-437-1020	212-697-6666
Artisan Funds PO Box 8412 *Cust Svc	Boston	MA	02266	800-344-1770*	
Ascendant Advisors LLC 4 Oaks Pl 1330 Post Oak Blvd Ste 1550	Houston	TX	77056	800-552-6010	
Aston Funds PO Box 9765	Providence	RI	02940	800-992-8151	312-268-1400
Baron Funds 767 Fifth Ave 49th Fl	New York	NY	10153	800-992-2766	212-583-2000
Calvert Investments Inc 4550 Montgomery Ave Ste 1000N	Bethesda	MD	20814	800-368-2748	301-951-4800
CGM Funds 38 Newbury St Ste 8	Boston	MA	02116	800-345-4048	617-859-7714
Chandler Asset Management Inc 6225 Lusk Blvd	San Diego	CA	92121	800-317-4747	858-546-3737
CIBC Mellon Global Securities Services Co 320 Bay St PO Box 1	Toronto	ON	M5H4A6	888-439-2457	416-643-5000
Claremont Companies Inc 1 Lakeshore Center	Bridgewater	MA	02324	800-848-9077	508-279-4300
Clipper Fund 2949 E Elvira Rd Ste 101	Tucson	AZ	85756	800-432-2504	
CornerCap Investment Counsel Inc 1355 Peachtree St NE The Peachtree Ste 1700	Atlanta	GA	30309	800-728-0670	404-870-0700
Cozad Asset Management Inc 2501 Galen Dr	Champaign	IL	61821	800-437-1686	217-356-8363
Davis Funds 2949 E Elvira Rd Ste 101	Tucson	AR	85756	800-279-0279	
Dodge & Cox Funds 30 Dan Rd PO Box 8422	Canton	MA	02021	800-621-3979	
Domini Social Investments PO Box 9785	Providence	RI	02940	800-582-6757	
Dreyfus Family of Funds PO Box 55299	Boston	MA	02205	800-843-5466	
Eaton Vance Mutual Funds 2 International Pl	Boston	MA	02110	800-225-6265	617-482-8260
Equity Investment Corp 3007 Piedmont Rd Ste 200	Atlanta	GA	30305	877-342-0111	404-239-0111
Essex Financial Services Inc 176 Westbrook Rd	Essex	CT	06426	800-900-5972	860-767-4300
Ferguson Wellman Capital Management Inc 888 S W Fifth Ave	Portland	OR	97204	800-327-5765	503-226-1444
Fidelity Advisor Funds PO Box 770002	Cincinnati	OH	45277	800-522-7297	
Fidelity Investment Funds PO Box 770001	Cincinnati	OH	45277	800-343-3548	
Fidelity Investments Institutional Operations Company Inc PO Box 770002	Cincinnati	OH	45277	877-208-0098	
Fidelity Partnership 1995 483 Bay St Ste 200	Toronto	ON	M5G2N7	800-263-4077	416-307-5200
First American Funds PO Box 701	Milwaukee	WI	53201	800-677-3863	
Fondaction Bureau 103 2175 Blvd de Maisonneuve Est	Montreal	QC	H2K4S3	800-253-6665	514-525-5505
Fort Pitt Capital Group Inc 680 Andersen Dr Foster Plz Ten	Pittsburgh	PA	15220	800-471-5827	412-921-1822
Galecki Financial Management Inc 7743 W Jefferson Blvd	Fort Wayne	IN	46804	800-838-6441	260-436-8525
GAMCO Investors Inc 1 Corporate Ctr *NYSE: GBL*	Rye	NY	10580	800-422-3554	914-921-5100
Glenmede Funds 1650 Market St Ste 1200	Philadelphia	PA	19103	800-966-3200	215-419-6000
Goldman Sachs 200 W St *NYSE: GS*	New York	NY	10282	800-526-7384	212-902-1000
Greystone Investment Management LLC 3805 Edwards Rd Ste 180	Cincinnati	OH	45209	877-293-0908	513-731-8444
Hartford Mutual Funds 30 Dan Rd Ste 55022	Canton	MA	02021	888-843-7824	
Heartland Funds 789 N Water St Ste 500	Milwaukee	WI	53202	800-432-7856	414-347-7777
ICMARC 777 N Capitol St NE Ste 600 *General	Washington	DC	20002	800-669-7471*	202-962-4600
ING Funds 7337 E Doubletree Ranch Rd	Scottsdale	AZ	85258	800-992-0180	
Invesco 11 Greenway Plaza Ste 100	Houston	TX	77046	800-959-4246	713-626-1919
Invesco Trimark Ltd 5140 Yonge St Ste 800	Toronto	ON	M2N6X7	800-874-6275	416-590-9855
John Hancock Funds 601 Congress St	Boston	MA	02210	800-338-8080	617-375-1500
Lazard Funds 30 Rockefeller Plz 57th Fl	New York	NY	10112	800-823-6300	
Lincluden Investment Management 1275 N Service Rd W Ste 607	Oakville	ON	L6M3G4	800-532-7071	905-825-9000
Loomis Sayles Funds 1 Financial Ctr	Boston	MA	02111	800-633-3330	617-482-2450
Mairs & Power Funds 332 Minnesota St Ste W-1520	Saint Paul	MN	55101	800-304-7404	651-222-8478
Market Traders Institute 400 Colonial Ctr Pkwy Ste 350	Lake Mary	FL	32746	800-866-7431	407-740-0900
MASTER Teacher Inc, The 2600 Leadership Ln	Manhattan	KS	66505	800-669-9633	
MD Physician Services Inc 1870 Alta Vista Dr	Ottawa	ON	K1G6R7	800-267-4022	613-731-4552
Missouri State Employees' Retirement System 907 Wildwood Dr	Jefferson City	MO	65109	800-827-1063	573-632-6100
Monetta Family of Mutual Funds 1776A S Naperville Rd Ste 100	Wheaton	IL	60189	800-241-9772	630-462-9800

Name / Address	City	State	ZIP	Toll-Free	Phone
Morgan Meighen & Associates Ltd 10 Toronto St	Toronto	ON	M5C2B7	866-443-6097	416-366-2931
Mutual Benefit Group 409 Penn St PO Box 577	Huntingdon	PA	16652	800-283-3531	814-643-3000
Neuberger Berman Funds PO Box 8403	Boston	MA	02266	800-877-9700	212-476-8800
New Mexico Educational Retirement Board 701 Camino de Los Marquez PO Box 26129	Santa Fe	NM	87502	866-691-2345	505-827-8030
Nicholas Family of Funds 700 N Water St Ste 1010	Milwaukee	WI	53202	800-227-5987	414-272-6133
Norris, Perne & French LLP 40 Pearl St N W Ste 300	Grand Rapids	MI	49503	800-748-0544	616-459-3421
Northern Funds PO Box 75986	Chicago	IL	60675	800-595-9111	
Northern Institutional Funds 801 S Canal St C5S	Chicago	IL	60607	800-637-1380	
Northstar Investment Advisors LLC 700 17th St Ste 2350	Denver	CO	80202	800-204-6199	303-832-2300
Novare Capital Management 521 E Morehead St The Morehead Bldg Ste 510	Charlotte	NC	28202	877-334-3698	704-334-3698
Oak Assoc Funds PO Box 8233	Denver	CO	80201	888-462-5386	
Oakmark Family of Funds 330 W nineth St	Kansas City	MO	64105	800-625-6275	617-483-8327
Old Dominion Capital Management Inc 815 E Jefferson St	Charlottesville	VA	22902	800-446-2029	434-977-1550
OppenheimerFunds Inc 225 Liberty St	New York	NY	10281	800-525-7048	
Pax World Fund Family 30 Penhallow St Ste 400	Portsmouth	NH	03801	800-767-1729	603-431-8022
Phillips, Hager & North Investment Management Ltd 200 Burrard St 20th Fl	Vancouver	BC	V6C3N5	800-661-6141	604-408-6100
PIMCO Institutional Funds PO Box 219024	Kansas City	MO	64121	800-927-4648	
Pioneer Funds 60 State St	Boston	MA	02109	800-225-6292	617-742-7825
Priviti Capital Corp 850 444 Fifth Ave S W	Calgary	AB	T2P2T8	855-333-9943	403-263-9943
Punch & Associates Inc 3601 W 76th St Ste 225	Edina	MN	55435	800-241-5552	952-224-4350
Putnam Family of Funds PO Box 41203	Providence	RI	02940	800-225-1581	
Rainier Investment Management Mutual Funds 601 Union St Ste 2801	Seattle	WA	98101	800-536-4640	
Redwood Asset Management Inc Richmond Adelaide Centre 120 Adelaide St W Ste 2400	Toronto	ON	M5H1T1	877-313-7011	416-368-8898
RidgeWorth Funds 50 Hurt Plaza Ste 1400	Atlanta	GA	30305	866-595-2470	
Ross Smith Asset Management Inc 407 - 8th Avenue S.W Ste 305	Calgary	AB	T2P1E5	888-494-6893	
Rydex Funds 805 King Farm Blvd Ste 600 *Cust Svc	Rockville	MD	20850	800-820-0888*	301-296-5100
Sandstone Asset Management Inc 115 101 - Sixth St SW	Calgary	AB	T2P5K7	866-318-6140	403-218-6125
School Employees Retirement System of Ohio 300 E Broad St Ste 100	Columbus	OH	43215	800-878-5853	614-222-5853
SEAMARK Asset Management Ltd 1801 Hollis St Ste 810	Halifax	NS	B3J3N4	888-303-5055	902-423-9367
Security Funds 1 Security Benefit Pl	Topeka	KS	66636	800-888-2461	785-438-3000
SEI 1 Freedom Vly Dr *NASDAQ: SEIC*	Oaks	PA	19456	800-342-5734	610-676-1000
Selected Funds PO Box 8243	Boston	MA	02266	800-243-1575	
Sequoia Fund Inc 767 Fifth Ave Ste 4701	New York	NY	10153	800-686-6884	212-832-5280
Sound Shore Fund 3 Canal Plz	Portland	ME	04101	800-754-8758	
SSgA Funds 1 Lincoln St	Boston	MA	02111	800-997-7327	617-786-3000
State Farm Mutual Funds PO Box 219548	Kansas City	MO	64121	800-447-4930	
State Teachers Retirement System of Ohio 275 E Broad St	Columbus	OH	43215	888-227-7877	
Steadyhand Investment Funds Limited Partnership 1747 W Third Ave	Vancouver	BC	V6J1K7	888-888-3147	
Steele Capital Management Inc 788 Main St #200	Dubuque	IA	52001	800-397-2097	563-588-2097
TCW Group Inc 865 S Figueroa St Ste 1800	Los Angeles	CA	90017	800-386-3829	213-244-0000
Terracap Group 100 Sheppard Ave E Ste 502	Toronto	ON	M2N6N5	800-363-3207	416-222-9345
TFS Capital LLC 10 N High St Ste 500	West Chester	PA	19380	888-837-4446	
Thornburg Investment Management Funds 2300 N Ridgetop Rd	Santa Fe	NM	87506	800-533-9337	505-984-0200
Torray Fund 7501 Wisconsin Ave Ste 750 W	Bethesda	MD	20814	800-443-3036	301-493-4600
Trillium Asset Management LLC 2 Financial Ctr 60 S St Ste 1100	Boston	MA	02111	800-548-5684	617-423-6655
Trinity Fiduciary Partners LLC 106 Decker Court Ste 226	Irving	TX	75062	877-334-1283	
Vaughan Nelson Investment Management LP 600 Travis St Ste 6300	Houston	TX	77002	888-888-8676	713-224-2545
Vested Business Brokers Inc 50 Karl Ave # 102	Smithtown	NY	11787	877-735-5224	631-265-7300
Victory Funds 4900 Tiedeman Rd PO Box 182593	Brooklyn	OH	44144	800-539-3863	
Welch Group LLC, The 3940 Montclair Rd 5th Fl	Birmingham	AL	35213	800-709-7100	205-879-5001
Wilshire Mutual Funds Inc PO Box 219512	Kansas City	MO	64121	888-200-6796	

528 NAVIGATION & GUIDANCE INSTRUMENTS & SYSTEMS

Company / Address	City	State	ZIP	Toll-Free	Phone
Adducent Technology Inc 230 Parque Margarita	Rohnert Park	CA	94928	**800-648-0656**	707-478-8136
Alpine Electronics of America 19145 Gramercy Pl	Torrance	CA	90501	**800-257-4631**	310-326-8000
Butler National Corp 19920 W 161st St *OTC: BUKS*	Olathe	KS	66062	**800-690-6903**	913-780-9595
CMI Inc 316 E Ninth St	Owensboro	KY	42303	**866-835-0690**	270-685-6545
Cubic Corp 9333 Balboa Ave PO Box 85587 *NYSE: CUB*	San Diego	CA	92186	**800-937-5449**	858-277-6780
Cubic Defense Systems 9333 Balboa Ave	San Diego	CA	92123	**800-937-5449**	858-277-6780
Del Mar Avionics 1601 Alton Pkwy Ste C	Irvine	CA	92606	**800-854-0481**	949-250-3200
DRS C3 Systems LLC 400 Professional Dr	Gaithersburg	MD	20879	**800-694-5005**	301-921-8100
DRS Technologies Inc 5 Sylvan Way	Parsippany	NJ	07054	**800-694-5005**	973-898-1500
DRS Training & Control Systems 645 Anchors St NW	Fort Walton Beach	FL	32548	**800-694-5005**	850-302-3000
Flash Technology Corp 332 Nichol Mill Ln	Franklin	TN	37067	**888-313-5274**	615-503-2000
FLIR Systems Inc 27700-A SW Pkwy Ave *NASDAQ: FLIR*	Wilsonville	OR	97070	**877-773-3547**	503-498-3547
Frontier Electronic Systems Corp 4500 W Sixth Ave	Stillwater	OK	74074	**800-677-1769**	405-624-1769
Garmin Ltd 1200 E 151st St *NASDAQ: GRMN*	Olathe	KS	66062	**888-442-7646**	913-397-8200
General Dynamics C4 Systems 400 John Quincy Adams Rd Bldg 80	Taunton	MA	02780	**877-449-0600**	
Goodrich Corp 2730 W Tyvola Rd 4 Coliseum Ctr *NYSE: GR*	Charlotte	NC	28217	**800-735-7899**	704-423-7000
Innovative Solutions & Support Inc 720 Pennsylvania Dr *NASDAQ: ISSC*	Exton	PA	19341	**866-359-7876**	610-646-9800
Interstate Electronics Corp 602 E Vermont Ave PO Box 3117	Anaheim	CA	92803	**800-854-6979**	714-758-0500
ITT Industries Inc 1133 Westchester Ave *NYSE: ITT*	White Plains	NY	10604	**800-254-2823**	914-641-2000
Jewell Instruments LLC 850 Perimeter Rd	Manchester	NH	03103	**800-227-5955**	603-669-6400
Kollsman Inc 220 Daniel Webster Hwy	Merrimack	NH	03054	**800-772-9603**	603-889-2500
L-3 Avionics Systems 5353 52nd St SE	Grand Rapids	MI	49512	**800-253-9525**	616-949-6600
L-3 Communications Corp Aviation Recorders Div 6000 Fruitville Rd	Sarasota	FL	34232	**877-726-2228**	941-371-0811
L-3 Communications Corp Communication Systems East Div 1 Federal St	Camden	NJ	08103	**800-339-6197**	856-338-3000
L-3 Communications Corp Randtron Antenna Systems Div 130 Constitution Dr *Sales	Menlo Park	CA	94025	**866-900-7270***	650-326-9500
Laitram LLC 200 Laitram Ln	Harahan	LA	70123	**800-535-7631**	504-733-6000
Lockheed Martin Corp 6801 Rockledge Dr *NYSE: LMT*	Bethesda	MD	20817	**866-562-2363**	301-897-6000
Lowrance Electronics Inc 12000 E Skelly Dr	Tulsa	OK	74128	**800-628-4487**	918-437-6881
Lycoming Engines 652 Oliver St	Williamsport	PA	17701	**800-258-3279**	570-323-6181
Mackay Communications Inc 3691 Trust Dr	Raleigh	NC	27616	**888-798-7979**	281-478-6245
Newcon Optik 105 Sparks Ave	North York	ON	M2H2S5	**877-368-6666**	416-663-6963
Onboard Systems International 13915 NW Third Ct	Vancouver	WA	98685	**800-275-0883**	360-546-3072
Oregon Aero Inc 34020 Skyway Dr	Scappoose	OR	97056	**800-888-6910**	503-543-7399
Raymarine Inc 21 Manchester St	Merrimack	NH	03054	**800-539-5539**	603-881-5200
Rockwell Collins Inc 400 Collins Rd NE *NYSE: COL*	Cedar Rapids	IA	52498	**888-721-3094**	319-295-1000
Rostra Precision Controls Inc 2519 Dana Dr *Cust Svc	Laurinburg	NC	28352	**800-782-3379***	910-276-4853
SELEX Inc 11300 W 89th St	Overland Park	KS	66214	**800-765-0861**	913-495-2600
Shadin LP 6831 Oxford St	St Louis Park	MN	55426	**800-328-0584**	952-927-6500
Superior Air Parts Inc 621 S Royal Ln Ste 100	Coppell	TX	75019	**800-420-4727**	972-829-4600
Systron Donner Inertial 355 Lennon Ln	Walnut Creek	CA	94598	**866-234-4976**	925-979-4400
Trimble Navigation Ltd 935 Stewart Dr *NASDAQ: TRMB*	Sunnyvale	CA	94085	**800-538-7800**	408-481-8000
Trutrak Flight Systems Inc 1500 S Old Missouri Rd	Springdale	AR	72764	**866-878-8725**	479-751-0250
Tyonek Mfg Group Inc 229 Palmer Rd	Madison	AL	35758	**877-258-6200**	256-258-6200
Whistler Group Inc 13016 N Walton Blvd *Cust Svc	Bentonville	AR	72712	**800-531-0004***	479-273-6012
Wipaire Inc 1700 Henry Ave	South St. Paul	MN	55075	**888-947-2473**	651-451-1205
XRS Corporation 12900 Whitewater Dr Ste 300	Hopkins	MN	55343	**800-348-7227**	
Zonar Systems LLC 18200 Cascade Ave S	Seattle	WA	98188	**877-843-3847**	206-878-2459

529 NEWS SYNDICATES, SERVICES, BUREAUS

Company / Address	City	State	ZIP	Toll-Free	Phone
AccountingWEB Inc PO Box 2252	Westerville	OH	43086	**866-688-1678**	
AccuWeather Inc 385 Science Pk Rd *Sales	State College	PA	16803	**800-566-6606***	814-235-8650
American Baptist News Service PO Box 851	Valley Forge	PA	19482	**800-222-3872**	610-768-2000
American Chiropractor, The 8619 NW 68Th St	Miami	FL	33166	**888-369-1396**	
Argus Interactive Agency Inc 217 N Main St Ste 200	Santa Ana	CA	92701	**866-595-9597**	
Disaster News Network (DNN) PO Box 1746	Ellicott City	MD	21041	**888-384-3028**	443-393-3330
FurnitureDealer.net Inc PO Box 22251	Eagan	MN	55122	**866-387-6357**	
Gateway Newstands 240 Chrislea Rd	Woodbridge	ON	L4L8V1	**800-942-5351**	905-851-9652
Inman News 1100 Marina Village Pkwy Ste 102	Alameda	CA	94501	**800-775-4662**	510-658-9252
Kagan 981 Calle Amanecer	San Clemente	CA	92673	**800-933-2667**	949-369-6310
Kansas Press Assn Inc 5423 SW Seventh St	Topeka	KS	66606	**855-572-1863**	785-271-5304
King Features Syndicate Inc 300 W 57th St 15th Fl	New York	NY	10019	**800-708-7311**	212-969-7550
Levy Home Entertainment LLC 1420 Kensington Rd Ste 300	Oak Brook	IL	60523	**800-549-5389**	708-547-4400
Los Angeles Times-Washington Post News Service Inc 1150 15th St NW	Washington	DC	20071	**800-627-1150**	202-334-6000
Market Wire Inc 100 N Sepulveda Blvd Ste 325 *General	El Segundo	CA	90245	**800-774-9473***	310-765-3200
New York Times News Service Div 620 Eigth Ave 9th Fl	New York	NY	10018	**800-698-4637**	212-556-7652
NewRetirement LLC 100 Pine St Ste 590	San Francisco	CA	94111	**866-441-0246**	415-738-2435
PR Photos 4521 Pga Blvd	Palm Beach Gardens	FL	33418	**866-551-7827**	
Religion News Service (RNS) 529 14th St NW Ste 425	Washington	DC	20045	**800-767-6781**	202-463-8777
Softomate LLC 901 N Pitt St Ste 325	Alexandria	VA	22314	**877-243-8735**	
United Methodist News Service 810 12th Ave S	Nashville	TN	37203	**800-251-8140**	615-742-5470
Washington Post Writers Group 1150 15th St NW	Washington	DC	20071	**800-879-9794**	202-334-6375
Website Magazine Inc 999 E Touhy Ave	Des Plaines	IL	60018	**800-817-1518**	773-628-2779

530 NEWSLETTERS

530-1 Banking & Finance Newsletters

Company / Address	City	State	ZIP	Toll-Free	Phone
Banking Daily 1801 S Bell St	Arlington	VA	22202	**800-372-1033**	
Bankruptcy Court Decisions 360 Hiatt Dr	Palm Beach Gardens	FL	33418	**800-621-5463**	561-622-6520
Commercial Lending Litigation News 360 Hiatt Dr	Palm Beach Gardens	FL	33418	**800-621-5463**	561-622-6520
Consumer Bankruptcy News 360 Hiatt Dr	Palm Beach Gardens	FL	33418	**800-621-5463**	561-622-6520
Credit Union Directors Newsletter 5710 Mineral Pt Rd	Madison	WI	53705	**800-356-9655**	608-231-4000
Electronic Commerce & Law Report 1801 S Bell St	Arlington	VA	22202	**800-372-1033**	
International Business & Finance Daily 1801 S Bell St	Arlington	VA	22202	**800-372-1033**	
International Tax Monitor 1801 S Bell St	Arlington	VA	22202	**800-372-1033**	
Louisiana Banker PO Box 2871	Baton Rouge	LA	70821	**888-249-3050**	225-387-3282

530-2 Business & Professional Newsletters

Company / Address	City	State	ZIP	Toll-Free	Phone
Antitrust & Trade Regulation Daily 1801 S Bell St	Arlington	VA	22202	**800-372-1033**	
CD Publications 8204 Fenton St	Silver Spring	MD	20910	**800-666-6380**	301-588-6380
Corporate Writer & Editor 111 E Wacker Dr Ste 500	Chicago	IL	60601	**800-878-5331**	312-960-4140
Customer Communicator, The (TCC) 712 Main St Ste 187B	Boonton	NJ	07005	**800-232-4317**	973-265-2300
Daily Report for Executives 1801 S Bell St	Arlington	VA	22202	**800-372-1033**	
Daily Tax Report 1801 S Bell St	Arlington	VA	22202	**800-372-1033**	
Distribution Ctr Management (DCM) 712 Main St Ste 187B	Boonton	NJ	07005	**800-232-4317**	973-265-2300
Downtown Idea Exchange (DIX) 712 Main St Ste 187B	Boonton	NJ	07005	**800-232-4317**	973-265-2300
Federal EEO Advisor 360 Hiatt Dr	Palm Beach Gardens	FL	33418	**800-341-7874**	561-622-6520
Government Employee Relations Report 1801 S Bell St	Arlington	VA	22202	**800-372-1033**	

Classified Section

					Toll-Free	Phone
Journal of Employee Communication Management	316 N Michigan Ave Ste 400	Chicago	IL	60601	**800-878-5331**	312-960-4100
Law Officer's Bulletin	610 Opperman Dr	Eagan	MN	55123	**800-344-5008**	651-687-7000
Manager's Intelligence Report (MIR)	316 N Michigan Ave Ste 400	Chicago	IL	60601	**800-878-5331**	
Payroll Practitioner's Monthly	3 Bethesda Metro Ctr Ste 250	Bethesda	MD	20814	**800-372-1033**	
Ragan Communications Inc	316 N Michigan Ave Ste 400	Chicago	IL	60601	**800-878-5331**	312-960-4100
Teamwork Newsletter	2222 Sedwick Dr	Durham	NC	27713	**800-223-8720**	
Working Together	360 Hiatt Dr	Palm Beach Gardens	FL	33418	**800-621-5463**	561-622-6520

530-3 Computer & Internet Newsletters

					Toll-Free	Phone
Biotechnology Software	140 Huguenot St 3rd Fl	New Rochelle	NY	10801	**800-654-3237**	914-740-2100
Business Intelligence Advisor	37 Broadway Ste 1	Arlington	MA	02474	**800-964-5118**	781-648-8700
Computer Economics Report, The	2082 Business Ctr Dr Ste 240	Irvine	CA	92612	**800-326-8100**	949-831-8700
Cutter Consortium	37 Broadway Ste 1	Arlington	MA	02474	**800-964-5118**	781-648-8700
Microprocessor Report	355 Chesley Ave	Mountain View	CA	94040	**800-413-2881**	408-270-3772
Washington Internet Daily	2115 Ward Ct NW	Washington	DC	20037	**800-771-9202**	202-872-9200

530-4 Education Newsletters

					Toll-Free	Phone
Early Childhood Report	360 Hiatt Dr	Palm Beach Gardens	FL	33418	**800-621-5463**	561-622-6520
Education Grants Alert	360 Hiatt Dr	Palm Beach Gardens	FL	33418	**800-621-5463**	561-622-6520
Educational Research Newsletter	PO Box 2347	South Portland	ME	04116	**800-321-7471**	207-632-1954
New York Education Law Report	360 Hiatt Dr	Palm Beach	FL	33418	**800-341-7874**	561-622-6520
School Law News	360 Hiatt Dr	Palm Beach Gardens	FL	33418	**800-341-7874**	
Special Education Report	360 Hiatt Dr *Sales	Palm Beach Gardens	FL	33418	**800-621-5463***	561-622-6520

530-5 Energy & Environmental Newsletters

					Toll-Free	Phone
Chemical Regulation Reporter	1801 S Bell St	Arlington	VA	22202	**800-372-1033**	
Clean Air Report	1919 S Eads St Ste 201	Arlington	VA	22202	**800-424-9068**	703-416-8505
Coal Outlook	1200 G St NW Ste 1100	Washington	DC	20005	**800-752-8878**	212-904-3070
Daily Environment Report	1801 S Bell St	Arlington	VA	22202	**800-372-1033**	
Electric Utility Week	2 Penn Plz 25th Fl	New York	NY	10121	**800-752-8878**	212-904-3070
Environment Reporter	1801 S Bell St	Arlington	VA	22202	**800-372-1033**	
Gas Daily	1200 G St NW Ste 1000	Washington	DC	20005	**800-752-8878**	202-383-2000
Global Power Report	2 Penn Plz 25th Fl	New York	NY	10121	**800-752-8878**	
Inside FERC	2 Penn Plz 25th Fl	New York	NY	10121	**800-752-8878**	
Inside NRC	2 Penn Plz 25th Fl	New York	NY	10121	**800-752-8878**	
Megawatt Daily	2 Penn Plz 25th Fl	New York	NY	10121	**800-752-8878**	212-904-3070
Northeast Power Report	2 Penn Plz 25th Fl	New York	NY	10121	**800-752-8878**	
NuclearFuel	1200 G St NW Ste 1000	Washington	DC	20005	**800-228-9290**	202-383-2000
Nucleonics Week	2 Penn Plaza 25th Fl	New York	NY	10121	**800-752-8878**	212-904-3070
Oil Price Information Service	3349 Hwy 138 Bldg D Ste D *Cust Svc	Wall	NJ	07719	**888-301-2645***	732-901-8800
OPIS	9737 Washingtonian Blvd Ste 200	Gaithersburg	MD	20878	**888-301-2645**	301-287-2645
Solid Waste Assn of North America (SWANA)	1100 Wayne Ave Ste 700	Silver Spring	MD	20910	**800-467-9262**	301-585-2898
State Environment Daily	1801 S Bell St	Arlington	VA	22202	**800-372-1033**	
Toxics Law Reporter	1801 S Bell St	Arlington	VA	22202	**800-372-1033**	
Utility Environment Report	2 Penn Plz 25th Fl	New York	NY	10121	**800-752-8878**	
Water Tech Online	19 British American Blvd W	Latham	NY	12110	**888-431-2877**	

530-6 General Interest Newsletters

					Toll-Free	Phone
Bottom Line/Personal	281 Tresser Blvd 8th Fl *Cust Svc	Stamford	CT	06901	**800-678-5835***	800-274-5611
NRTA/AARP Bulletin	601 E St NW	Washington	DC	20049	**888-867-2277**	202-434-2277
Preferred Traveler	4501 Forbes Blvd	Lanham	MD	20706	**866-679-8655**	

530-7 Government & Law Newsletters

					Toll-Free	Phone
Alcoholic Beverage Control	PO Box 27491	Richmond	VA	23261	**800-552-3200**	804-213-4565
American Association for Justice	777 6th St NW Ste 200	Washington	DC	20001	**800-424-2727**	202-965-3500
Bankruptcy Law Letter	610 Opperman Dr	Eagan	MN	55123	**800-937-8529**	651-687-7000
BD Week	9737 Washingtonian Blvd Ste 100	Gaithersburg	MD	20878	**866-777-8567**	646-223-6771
Bioethics Legal Review	1617 JFK Blvd Ste 1750	Philadelphia	PA	19103	**877-256-2472**	215-557-2300
Class Action Litigation Report	1801 S Bell St	Arlington	VA	22202	**800-372-1033**	
Community Development Digest	8204 Fenton St	Silver Spring	MD	20910	**800-666-6380**	301-588-6380
Community Health Funding Week	8204 Fenton St	Silver Spring	MD	20910	**800-666-6380**	301-588-6380
Computer Technology Law Report	1801 S Bell St	Arlington	VA	22202	**800-372-1033**	
Consumer Financial Services Law Report	360 Hiatt Dr	Palm Beach Gardens	FL	33418	**800-621-5463**	561-622-6520
Corporate Compliance & Regulatory	1617 JFK Blvd Ste 1750	Philadelphia	PA	19103	**877-256-2472**	215-557-2300
Criminal Law Reporter	1801 S Bell St	Arlington	VA	22202	**800-372-1033**	
Daily Labor Report	1801 S Bell St	Arlington	VA	22202	**800-372-1033**	
Development Director's Letter	8204 Fenton St	Silver Spring	MD	20910	**800-666-6380**	301-588-6380
Disability Law Compliance Report	610 Opperman Dr *Cust Svc	Eagan	MN	55123	**800-328-4880***	651-687-7000
e-Commerce Law & Strategy	1617 JFK Blvd Ste 1750	Philadelphia	PA	19103	**877-256-2472**	215-557-2300
e-Discovery Law & Strategy	1617 JFK Blvd Ste 1750	Philadelphia	PA	19103	**877-256-2472**	215-557-2300
Employment Discrimination Report	1801 S Bell St	Arlington	VA	22202	**800-372-1033**	
Expert Evidence Report	1801 S Bell St	Arlington	VA	22202	**800-372-1033**	
Family Law Reporter	1801 S Bell St	Arlington	VA	22202	**800-372-1033**	
Federal Assistance Monitor	8204 Fenton St	Silver Spring	MD	20910	**800-666-6380**	301-588-6380
Federal Contracts Report	1801 S Bell St	Arlington	VA	22202	**800-372-1033**	
Franchising Business & Law Alert	1617 JFK Blvd Ste 1750	Philadelphia	PA	19103	**877-256-2472**	215-557-2300
Health Law Reporter	1801 S Bell St	Arlington	VA	22202	**800-372-1033**	
Homeland Security Funding Week	8204 Fenton St	Silver Spring	MD	20910	**800-666-6380**	301-588-6380
Hospital Litigation Reporter	590 Dutch Vly Rd NE	Atlanta	GA	30324	**800-926-7926**	404-881-1141
Hospitality Law	360 Hiatt Dr	Palm Beach Gardens	FL	33418	**800-621-5463**	561-622-6520
Insurance Coverage Law Bulletin, The	1617 JFK Blvd Ste 1750	Philadelphia	PA	19103	**877-256-2472**	215-557-2300
Internet Law & Strategy	1617 JFK Blvd Ste 1750	Philadelphia	PA	19103	**877-256-2472**	215-557-2300
IRS Practice Adviser	1801 S Bell St	Arlington	VA	22202	**800-372-1033**	
Medical Research Law & Policy Report	1801 S Bell St	Arlington	VA	22202	**800-372-1033**	
Medicare Compliance Alert	11300 Rockville Pk Ste 1100	Rockville	MD	20852	**800-929-4824**	301-287-2700
Mergers & Acquisitions Law Report	1801 S Bell St	Arlington	VA	22202	**800-372-1033**	
Money & Politics Report	1801 S Bell St	Arlington	VA	22202	**800-372-1033**	
Municipal Litigation Reporter	590 Dutch Vly Rd NE	Atlanta	GA	30324	**800-926-7926**	404-881-1141
Patent Trademark & Copyright Law Daily	1801 S Bell St	Arlington	VA	22202	**800-372-1033**	
Pharmaceutical Law & Industry Report	1801 S Bell St	Arlington	VA	22202	**800-372-1033**	
Privacy & Data Security Law Resource Center	1801 S Bell St	Arlington	VA	22202	**800-372-1033**	
Real Estate Law Report	610 Opperman Dr *Cust Svc	Eagan	MN	55123	**800-328-4880***	651-687-7000
Roll Call	77 K St NE	Washington	DC	20002	**800-432-2250**	202-650-6500
Securities Law Daily	1801 S Bell St	Arlington	VA	22202	**800-372-1033**	
UCG Holdings	11300 Rockville Pike Ste 1100	Rockville	MD	20852	**800-929-4824**	301-287-2700
Virginia Dept of Taxation	1957 Westmoreland St PO Box 1115	Richmond	VA	23230	**800-828-1120**	804-367-8037
Workplace Law Report	1801 S Bell St	Arlington	VA	22202	**800-372-1033**	
World Securities Law Report	1801 S Bell St	Arlington	VA	22202	**800-372-1033**	

530-8 Health & Social Issues Newsletters

					Toll-Free	Phone
Affordable Housing Update	8204 Fenton St	Silver Spring	MD	20910	**800-666-6380**	301-588-6380
Aging News Alert	8204 Fenton St	Silver Spring	MD	20910	**800-666-6380**	301-588-6385

Name / Address	City	State	ZIP	Toll-Free	Phone
AICR Newsletter 1759 R St NW	Washington	DC	20009	**800-843-8114**	202-328-7744
APCO Bulletin 351 N Williamson Blvd	Daytona Beach	FL	32114	**888-272-6911**	386-322-2500
Cancer Letter PO Box 9905	Washington	DC	20016	**800-513-7042**	202-362-1809
Children & Youth Funding Report 8204 Fenton St	Silver Spring	MD	20910	**800-666-6380**	301-588-6380
Consumer Reports On Health 101 Truman Ave	Yonkers	NY	10703	**800-234-1645**	914-378-2000
Disability Funding Week 8204 Fenton St	Silver Spring	MD	20910	**800-666-6380**	
Dr. Sinatra 95 Old Shoals Rd	Arden	NC	28704	**800-304-1708**	
Environment of Care Leader 9737 Washintonian Blvd Ste 100 *Cust Svc	Gaithersburg	MD	20878	**800-929-4824***	301-287-2700
Harvard Women's Health Watch PO Box 9308	Big Sandy	TX	75755	**877-649-9457**	
Health After 50 750 Third Ave Fl 6	New York	NY	10017	**800-829-0422**	
Health Care Daily Report 1801 S Bell St	Arlington	VA	22202	**800-372-1033**	
Health Law Week 590 Dutch Vly Rd NE	Atlanta	GA	30324	**800-926-7926**	404-881-1141
Healthcare Disparities Report 8204 Fenton St	Silver Spring	MD	20910	**800-666-6380**	301-588-6385
Home Health Line 11300 Rockville Pk Ste 1100	Rockville	MD	20852	**800-929-4824**	301-287-2700
International Medical Device Regulatory Monitor 300 N Washington St Ste 200	Falls Church	VA	22046	**888-838-5578**	703-538-7600
Mayo Clinic Health Letter 200 First St NW	Rochester	MN	55905	**800-291-1128**	
Medicare Compliance Alert 11300 Rockville Pk Ste 1100	Rockville	MD	20852	**800-929-4824**	301-287-2700
OSHA Up-to-Date Newsletter 1121 Spring Lk Dr *Cust Svc	Itasca	IL	60143	**800-621-7615***	630-285-1121

530-9 Investment Newsletters

Name / Address	City	State	ZIP	Toll-Free	Phone
Cabot Market Letter 176 N St PO Box 2049 *Orders	Salem	MA	01970	**800-326-8826***	978-745-5532
Chartist Newsletter PO Box 758	Seal Beach	CA	90740	**800-942-4278**	562-596-2385
Commodity Research Bureau 330 S Wells St Ste 612	Chicago	IL	60606	**800-621-5271**	312-554-8456
Dow Theory Forecasts 7412 Calumet Ave	Hammond	IN	46324	**800-233-5922**	
DRIP Investor 7412 Calumet Ave	Hammond	IN	46324	**800-233-5922**	219-852-3200
Elliott Wave Theorist PO Box 1618	Gainesville	GA	30503	**800-336-1618**	770-536-0309
Fabian's Investment Resources 300 New Jersey Ave NW Ste 500	Washington	DC	20001	**800-950-8765**	267-295-8713
Global Market Perspective PO Box 1618	Gainesville	GA	30503	**800-336-1618**	770-536-0309
Gold Newsletter PO Box 84900	Phoenix	AZ	85071	**800-877-8847**	
Option Advisor 5151 Pfeiffer Rd Ste 250	Cincinnati	OH	45242	**800-448-2080**	513-589-3800
Personal Finance Newsletter 7600A Leesburg Pk W Bldg Ste 300	Falls Church	VA	22043	**800-832-2330**	703-394-4931
Peter Dag Portfolio Strategy & Management, The 65 Lk Front Dr	Akron	OH	44319	**800-833-2782**	330-644-2782
Profitable Investing 9201 Corporate Blvd	Rockville	MD	20850	**800-219-8592**	301-250-2200
Richard Young's Intelligence Report 700 Indian Springs Dr *Cust Svc	Lancaster	PA	17601	**800-219-8592***	
Systems & Forecasts 150 Great Neck Rd Ste 301	Great Neck	NY	11021	**800-982-4372**	516-829-6444
Utility Forecaster 7600A Leesburg Pk W Bldg Ste 300	Falls Church	VA	22043	**800-832-2330**	703-394-4931

530-10 Marketing & Sales Newsletters

Name / Address	City	State	ZIP	Toll-Free	Phone
Book Marketing Update PO Box 2887	Taos	NM	87571	**888-468-7386**	575-751-3398
Marketing Library Services 143 Old Marlton Pk	Medford	NJ	08055	**800-300-9868**	609-654-6266
Sales Leader 2222 Sedwick Dr	Durham	NC	27713	**800-223-8720**	

530-11 Media & Communications Newsletters

Name / Address	City	State	ZIP	Toll-Free	Phone
Communications Daily 2115 Ward Ct NW	Washington	DC	20037	**800-771-9202**	202-872-9200
First Draft 316 N Michigan Ave Ste 400	Chicago	IL	60601	**800-878-5331**	800-493-4867
Jack O'Dwyer's PR Newsletter 271 Madison Ave Ste 600	New York	NY	10016	**866-395-7710**	212-679-2471
Media Industry Newsletter (MIN) 110 William St 11th Fl	New York	NY	10038	**888-707-5814**	212-621-4880
Media Law Reporter 1801 S Bell St	Arlington	VA	22202	**800-372-1033**	
Media Relations Report 316 N Michigan Ave Ste 400	Chicago	IL	60601	**800-878-5331**	312-960-4100
Speechwriter's Newsletter 316 N Michigan Ave Ste 400	Chicago	IL	60601	**800-878-5331**	312-960-4100
State Telephone Regulation Report 2115 Ward Ct NW	Washington	DC	20037	**800-771-9202**	202-872-9200
Telecom AM 2115 Ward Ct NW	Washington	DC	20037	**800-771-9202**	202-872-9200

530-12 Science & Technology Newsletters

Name / Address	City	State	ZIP	Toll-Free	Phone
Flame Retardancy News 49 Walnut Pk Bldg 2	Wellesley	MA	02481	**866-285-7215**	781-489-7301
Food Ingredient News 49 Walnut Pk Bldg 2	Wellesley	MA	02481	**866-285-7215**	781-489-7301
Frost & Sullivan 7550 IH 10 W Ste 400	San Antonio	TX	78229	**877-463-7678**	210-348-1000
Genetic Engineering News 140 Huguenot St 3rd Fl	New Rochelle	NY	10801	**888-211-4235**	914-740-2100
Geophysical Research Letter 2000 Florida Ave NW	Washington	DC	20009	**800-966-2481**	202-462-6900

530-13 Trade & Industry Newsletters

Name / Address	City	State	ZIP	Toll-Free	Phone
AviationWeek 1200 G St NW Ste 900	Washington	DC	20005	**800-525-5003**	
Construction Claims Monthly 2222 Sedwick Rd	Durham	NC	27713	**800-223-8720**	
Construction Labor Report 1801 S Bell St	Arlington	VA	22202	**800-372-1033**	
Cotton's Week 7193 Goodlett Farms Pkwy	Cordova	TN	38016	**888-232-1738**	901-274-9030
DealersEdge PO Box 606	Barnegat Light	NJ	08006	**800-321-5312**	609-879-4456
Funeral Service Insider 3349 Hwy 138 Bldg D Ste D	Wall	NJ	07719	**800-500-4585**	
Kiplinger Agriculture Letter 1729 H St NW	Washington	DC	20006	**800-544-0155**	202-887-6400
Metals Week 2 Penn Plaza	New York	NY	10121	**800-752-8878**	
PhotoSource 5106 Louetta Rd	Spring	TX	77379	**800-786-6277**	281-370-2220
Pro Farmer 6612 Chancellor Dr Ste 300 *Cust Svc	Cedar Falls	IA	50613	**800-772-0023***	319-277-1278
Questex LLC 275 Grove St Ste 2-130	Newton	MA	02466	**888-552-4346**	617-219-8300
Shopping Centers Today 1221 Ave of the Americas	New York	NY	10020	**888-427-2885**	646-728-3800
Uniform Commercial Code Law Letter 610 Opperman Dr *Cust Svc	Eagan	MN	55123	**800-328-4880***	651-687-7000
Union Labor Report 1801 S Bell St	Arlington	VA	22202	**800-372-1033**	

531 NEWSPAPERS

SEE ALSO Newspaper Publishers

531-1 Daily Newspapers - Canada

Name / Address	City	Prov	Postal Code	Toll-Free	Phone
Calgary Herald 215-16th St SE PO Box 2400 Stn M	Calgary	AB	T2E7P5	**800-372-9219**	403-235-7100
Calgary Sun 2615 12th St NE	Calgary	AB	T2E7W9	**877-624-1463**	403-410-1010
Edmonton Journal 10006 - 101 St	Edmonton	AB	T5J2S6	**800-232-9486**	780-429-5100
Edmonton Sun 4990 92nd Ave Ste 250	Edmonton	AB	T6B3A1	**877-468-2401**	780-468-0100
Vancouver Sun 200 Granville St Ste 1	Vancouver	BC	V6C3N3	**866-372-3707**	604-605-2000
Winnipeg Free Press 1355 Mountain Ave	Winnipeg	MB	R2X3B6	**800-542-8900**	204-697-7000
L'Acadie-Nouvelle 476 St-Pierre W	Caraquet	NB	E1W1B7	**800-561-2255**	506-727-4444
Telegraph-Journal 210 Crown St PO Box 2350	Saint John	NB	E2L3V8	**888-295-8665**	
Chronicle Herald, The PO Box 610	Halifax	NS	B3J2T2	**800-563-1187**	902-426-2811
Journal Le Droit 47 Clarence St	Ottawa	ON	K1N9K1	**800-267-6961**	613-562-0555
London Free Press 369 York St PO Box 2280	London	ON	N6A4G1	**866-541-6757**	519-679-1111
National Post 1450 Don Mills Rd Ste 300	Toronto	ON	M3B3R5	**800-267-6568**	416-383-2300
Observer, The 140 S Front St	Sarnia	ON	N7T7M8	**866-541-6757**	519-344-3641
Ottawa Citizen 1101 Baxter Rd PO Box 5020	Ottawa	ON	K2C3M4	**800-267-6100**	613-829-9100
Ottawa Sun PO Box 9729	Ottawa	ON	K1G5H7	**877-624-1463**	613-739-7000
Spectator, The 44 Frid St	Hamilton	ON	L8N3G3	**800-263-6902**	905-526-3333
Toronto Star 1 Yonge St	Toronto	ON	M5E1E6	**800-268-9756**	416-869-4949
Toronto Sun 333 King St E	Toronto	ON	M5A3X5	**888-786-7821**	416-947-2222
Windsor Star, The 167 Ferry St	Windsor	ON	N9A4M5	**800-265-5647**	519-255-5711
Le Devoir 2050 Bleury St 9th Fl	Montreal	QC	H3A3M9	**800-463-7559**	514-985-3333
Regina Leader Post 1964 Pk St	Regina	SK	S4P3G4	**800-667-9999**	306-781-5211

531-2 Daily Newspapers - US

Listings here are organized by city names within state groupings. Most of the fax numbers given connect directly to the newsroom.

Name / Address	City	State	ZIP	Toll-Free	Phone
Anniston Star 4305 McClellan Blvd PO Box 189	Anniston	AL	36202	**866-814-9253**	256-236-1551
Birmingham News 2201 Fourth Ave N	Birmingham	AL	35203	**800-283-4001**	205-325-4444

				Toll-Free	Phone
Decatur Daily 201 First Ave SE	Decatur	AL	35601	**888-353-4612**	256-353-4612
Dothan Eagle PO Box 1968	Dothan	AL	36302	**800-811-1771**	334-792-3141
Gadsden Times 401 Locust St	Gadsden	AL	35901	**800-762-2464**	256-549-2000
Huntsville Times 2317 S Memorial Pkwy	Huntsville	AL	35801	**800-239-5271**	256-532-4000
Montgomery Advertiser 425 Molton St	Montgomery	AL	36104	**877-424-0007**	334-262-1611
Tuscaloosa News 315 28th Ave	Tuscaloosa	AL	35401	**800-888-8639**	205-345-0505
Anchorage Daily News 1001 Northway Dr	Anchorage	AK	99508	**800-478-4200**	907-257-4200
East Valley Tribune 120 W First Ave	Mesa	AZ	85210	**877-728-5414**	480-898-6500
Arizona Republic 200 E Van Buren St	Phoenix	AZ	85004	**800-331-9303**	602-444-8000
Arizona Daily Star 4850 S Pk Ave	Tucson	AZ	85714	**800-695-4492**	520-573-4343
Jonesboro Sun 518 Carson St	Jonesboro	AR	72401	**800-237-5341**	870-935-5525
Arkansas Democrat-Gazette 121 E Capital St *Cust Svc	Little Rock	AR	72203	**800-482-1121***	501-378-3400
Ventura County Star 550 Camarillo Ctr Dr	Camarillo	CA	93010	**800-221-7827**	805-437-0000
Chico Enterprise Record 400 E Pk Ave PO Box 9	Chico	CA	95927	**877-229-8655**	530-891-1234
Times-Standard 930 Sixth St	Eureka	CA	95501	**800-514-0301**	707-498-1817
Fresno Bee 1626 E St	Fresno	CA	93786	**800-877-3400**	559-441-6111
Sentinel, The 300 W Sixth St	Hanford	CA	93230	**800-582-0471**	559-582-0471
Lodi News-Sentinel 125 N Church St	Lodi	CA	95240	**877-333-4507**	209-369-2761
Investor's Business Daily 12655 Beatrice St	Los Angeles	CA	90066	**800-831-2525**	310-448-6000
Los Angeles Times 202 W First St	Los Angeles	CA	90012	**800-528-4637**	213-237-5000
Appeal-Democrat 1530 Ellis Lk Dr PO Box 431	Marysville	CA	95901	**800-831-2345**	530-741-2345
Modesto Bee 1325 H St	Modesto	CA	95354	**800-776-4233**	209-578-2000
Monterey County Herald 2200 Garden Rd	Monterey	CA	93940	**800-688-1808**	831-372-3311
Marin Independent Journal 150 Alameda Del Prado	Novato	CA	94949	**877-229-8655**	415-883-8600
Desert Sun 750 N Gene Autry Trl	Palm Springs	CA	92263	**800-233-3741**	760-322-8889
Antelope Valley Press 37404 Sierra Hwy	Palmdale	CA	93550	**888-874-2527**	661-273-2700
Pasadena Star-News 911 E Colorado Blvd	Pasadena	CA	91106	**800-788-1200**	626-578-6300
Record Searchlight PO Box 492397	Redding	CA	96049	**800-666-1331**	530-243-2424
Press-Enterprise 3450 14th St	Riverside	CA	92501	**877-473-6397**	951-684-1200
Sacramento Bee PO Box 15779 *Cust Svc	Sacramento	CA	95852	**800-284-3233***	916-321-1000
Sun, The 4030 N Georgia Blvd	San Bernardino	CA	92407	**800-922-0922**	909-889-9666
San Diego Daily Transcript 2131 Third Ave	San Diego	CA	92101	**800-697-6397**	619-232-4381
San Diego Union-Tribune 350 Camino De La Reina	San Diego	CA	92108	**800-244-6397**	619-299-3131
San Francisco Chronicle 901 Mission St	San Francisco	CA	94103	**866-732-4766**	415-777-1111
Tribune, The 3825 S Higuera St	San Luis Obispo	CA	93401	**800-477-8799**	805-781-7800
San Mateo County Times 477 Ninth Ave Ste 110	San Mateo	CA	94402	**800-870-6397**	650-348-4321
Orange County Register 625 N Grand Ave	Santa Ana	CA	92701	**877-469-7344**	714-796-7000
Press Democrat 427 Mendocino Ave	Santa Rosa	CA	95401	**800-675-5056**	707-546-2020
Record, The PO Box 900	Stockton	CA	95201	**800-606-9741**	209-943-6397
Daily Breeze 5215 Torrance Blvd	Torrance	CA	90503	**800-253-2687**	310-540-5511
Vallejo Times Herald 440 Curtola Pkwy	Vallejo	CA	94590	**800-600-1141**	707-644-1141
Daily Press 13891 Pk Ave PO Box 1389	Victorville	CA	92393	**844-287-3897**	760-241-7744
Durango Herald 1275 Main Ave	Durango	CO	81301	**800-530-8318**	970-247-3504
Coloradoan, The 1300 Riverside Ave	Fort Collins	CO	80524	**877-424-0063**	970-493-6397
Daily Sentinel PO Box 668	Grand Junction	CO	81502	**800-332-5832**	970-242-5050
Loveland Daily Reporter-Herald 201 E Fifth St	Loveland	CO	80537	**800-244-5613**	970-669-5050
Pueblo Chieftain 825 W Sixth St PO Box 440	Pueblo	CO	81003	**800-279-6397**	719-544-3520
News-Times 333 Main St	Danbury	CT	06810	**877-542-6057**	203-744-5100
Hartford Courant 285 Broad St	Hartford	CT	06115	**800-524-4242**	860-241-6200
Journal Inquirer 306 Progress Dr PO Box 510	Manchester	CT	06045	**800-237-3606**	860-646-0500
Record-Journal 11 Crown St	Meriden	CT	06450	**800-228-6915**	203-235-1661
New Haven Register 40 Sargent Dr	New Haven	CT	06511	**800-925-2509**	203-789-5200
Delaware State News 110 Galaxy Dr PO Box 737	Dover	DE	19903	**800-282-8586**	302-674-3600
Washington Post 1301 K St NW	Washington	DC	20071	**800-627-1150**	202-334-6000
El Nuevo Herald 3511 NW 91st Ave	Doral	FL	33172	**866-949-6722**	305-376-3535
South Florida Sun-Sentinel 200 E Las Olas Blvd *Cust Svc	Fort Lauderdale	FL	33301	**800-548-6397***	954-356-4000
Northwest Florida Daily News PO Box 2949	Fort Walton Beach	FL	32549	**800-755-1185**	850-863-1111
Florida Times-Union 1 Riverside Ave	Jacksonville	FL	32202	**800-472-6397**	904-359-4111
Ledger, The 300 W Lime St	Lakeland	FL	33815	**888-431-7323**	863-802-7000
Daily Commercial 212 E Main St	Leesburg	FL	34748	**877-688-3028**	352-365-8200
Naples Daily News 1100 Immokalee Rd	Naples	FL	34102	**800-404-7343**	239-213-6000
Orlando Sentinel 633 N Orange Ave	Orlando	FL	32801	**800-974-7488**	407-420-5000
Seminole Herald PO Box 1667	Sanford	FL	32772	**800-955-8770**	407-322-2611
Sarasota Herald-Tribune 1741 Main St	Sarasota	FL	34236	**866-284-7102**	941-953-7755
Highlands Today 315 US Hwy 27 N *General	Sebring	FL	33870	**866-607-2187***	863-386-5800
Vero Beach Press-Journal PO Box 1268	Vero Beach	FL	32961	**866-894-9851**	772-562-2315
Palm Beach Post 2751 S Dixie Hwy	West Palm Beach	FL	33405	**800-432-7595**	561-820-4100
Athens Banner-Herald 1 Press Pl	Athens	GA	30601	**800-533-4252**	706-549-0123
Augusta Chronicle 725 Broad St	Augusta	GA	30901	**866-249-8223**	706-724-0851
Columbus Ledger-Enquirer 17 W 12th St	Columbus	GA	31901	**800-282-7859**	706-324-5526
Gainesville Times 345 Green St NW	Gainesville	GA	30501	**800-395-5005**	770-532-1234
Macon Telegraph 120 Broadway	Macon	GA	31201	**800-679-6397**	478-744-4200
Telegraph, The 1675 Montpelier Ave Ste B	Macon	GA	31201	**800-342-5845**	
Valdosta Daily Times PO Box 968	Valdosta	GA	31603	**800-600-4838**	229-244-1880
Honolulu Advertiser 500 Ala Moana Blvd	Honolulu	HI	96813	**800-801-5999**	808-529-4747
Maui News 100 Mahalani St	Wailuku	HI	96793	**888-683-1115**	808-244-3981
Idaho Statesman PO Box 40	Boise	ID	83707	**800-635-8934**	208-377-6400
Post-Register PO Box 1800	Idaho Falls	ID	83403	**800-574-6397**	208-522-1800
Idaho State Journal 305 S Arthur Ave	Pocatello	ID	83204	**800-669-9777**	208-232-4161
Daily Herald 155 E Algonquin Rd	Arlington Heights	IL	60005	**888-903-4070**	847-427-4300
Belleville News-Democrat 120 S Illinois St	Belleville	IL	62220	**800-642-3878**	618-234-1000
Pantagraph PO Box 2907	Bloomington	IL	61702	**800-747-7323**	309-829-9000
Southern Illinoisan 710 N Illinois Ave PO Box 2108	Carbondale	IL	62902	**800-228-0429**	618-529-5454
Chicago Tribune 435 N Michigan Ave	Chicago	IL	60611	**800-874-2863**	312-222-3232
Commercial-News 17 W N St	Danville	IL	61832	**877-732-8258**	217-446-1000
Herald & Review 601 E Williams St	Decatur	IL	62523	**800-437-2533**	217-429-5151
Journal-Standard 27 S State Ave	Freeport	IL	61032	**800-325-6397**	815-232-1171
News-Tribune 426 Second St	La Salle	IL	61301	**800-892-6452**	815-223-3200
Macomb Journal 203 N Randolph St	Macomb	IL	61455	**800-747-5401**	309-833-2114
Reporter 12247 S Harlem Ave	Palos Heights	IL	60463	**800-633-4227**	708-448-6161
Peoria Journal Star 1 News Plz	Peoria	IL	61643	**800-225-5757**	309-686-3000
Quincy Herald-Whig 130 S Fifth St	Quincy	IL	62301	**800-373-9444**	217-223-5100
Rock Island Argus 1724 Fourth Ave	Rock Island	IL	61201	**800-660-2472**	309-786-6441
Shelbyville Daily Union 100 W Main St	Shelbyville	IL	62565	**800-772-1213**	217-774-2161
State Journal-Register PO Box 219	Springfield	IL	62705	**800-397-6397**	217-788-1300
Herald Bulletin 1133 Jackson St	Anderson	IN	46016	**800-750-5049**	765-622-1212
Times-Mail 813 16th St PO Box 849	Bedford	IN	47421	**800-333-2451**	812-275-3355
Republic, The 333 Second St	Columbus	IN	47201	**800-876-7811**	812-372-7811
Truth, The PO Box 487	Elkhart	IN	46515	**800-585-5416**	574-294-1661
Evansville Courier & Press 300 E Walnut St	Evansville	IN	47713	**800-288-3200**	812-424-7711
Journal Gazette 600 W Main St	Fort Wayne	IN	46802	**888-966-4532**	260-461-8773
Goshen News 114 S Main St PO Box 569	Goshen	IN	46527	**800-487-2151**	574-533-2151
Indianapolis Star 307 N Pennsylvania St	Indianapolis	IN	46204	**800-669-7827**	317-444-4000
Kokomo Tribune (KT) 300 N Union St PO Box 9014	Kokomo	IN	46901	**800-382-0696**	765-459-3121
Journal & Courier 217 N Sixth St *News Rm	Lafayette	IN	47901	**800-407-5813***	765-423-5511
Chronicle-Tribune 610 S Adams St	Marion	IN	46953	**800-955-7888**	765-664-5111
Muncie Star-Press 345 S High St	Muncie	IN	47305	**800-783-7827**	765-747-5700
Times, The 601 W 45th Ave	Munster	IN	46321	**800-837-3232**	219-933-3200
South Bend Tribune 225 W Colfax Ave	South Bend	IN	46626	**800-220-7378**	574-235-6464
Tribune-Star PO Box 149	Terre Haute	IN	47808	**800-783-8742**	812-231-4200
Hawk Eye, The 800 S Main St PO Box 10	Burlington	IA	52601	**800-397-1708**	319-754-8461
Gazette, The 501 Second Ave SE	Cedar Rapids	IA	52401	**800-397-8333**	319-398-8333
Daily Nonpareil 535 W Broadway Ste 300	Council Bluffs	IA	51503	**800-283-1882**	712-328-1811
Quad-City Times 500 E Third St	Davenport	IA	52801	**800-437-4641**	563-383-2200

Name / Address	City	State	ZIP	Toll-Free	Phone
Des Moines Register 715 Locust St	Des Moines	IA	50309	**800-247-5346**	515-284-8000
Telegraph Herald 801 Bluff St	Dubuque	IA	52001	**800-553-4801**	563-588-5611
Messenger, The 713 Central Ave	Fort Dodge	IA	50501	**800-622-6613**	515-573-2141
Globe-Gazette 300 N Washington St PO Box 271	Mason City	IA	50402	**800-421-0546**	641-421-0500
Ottumwa Courier 213 E Second St	Ottumwa	IA	52501	**800-532-1504**	641-684-4611
Sioux City Journal 515 Pavonia St	Sioux City	IA	51101	**800-397-3530**	712-293-4300
Pilot Tribune PO Box 1187	Storm Lake	IA	50588	**800-447-1985**	712-732-3130
Waterloo Cedar Falls Courier PO Box 540	Waterloo	IA	50701	**800-798-1730**	319-291-1421
Hutchinson News 300 W Second St	Hutchinson	KS	67504	**800-766-3311**	620-694-5700
Salina Journal PO Box 740	Salina	KS	67402	**800-827-6363**	785-823-6363
Topeka Capital-Journal 616 SE Jefferson St	Topeka	KS	66607	**800-777-7171**	785-295-1111
Wichita Eagle, The 825 E Douglas Ave	Wichita	KS	67202	**800-200-8906**	316-268-6000
Times-Tribune, The 201 N Kentucky Ave	Corbin	KY	40701	**877-629-9722**	606-528-2464
News-Enterprise 408 W Dixie Ave	Elizabethtown	KY	42701	**877-246-2322**	270-769-1200
State Journal, The 1216 Wilkinson Blvd	Frankfort	KY	40601	**800-621-3362**	502-227-4556
Lexington Herald-Leader 100 Midland Ave	Lexington	KY	40508	**800-999-8881**	859-231-3100
Courier-Journal 525 W Broadway PO Box 740031	Louisville	KY	40201	**800-765-4011**	502-582-4011
Alexandria Daily Town Talk PO Box 7558	Alexandria	LA	71306	**800-523-8391**	318-487-6397
Daily Advertiser, The 1100 Bertrand Dr	Lafayette	LA	70506	**800-526-8720**	337-289-6300
American Press 4900 Hwy 90 E *News Rm	Lake Charles	LA	70615	**800-442-2511***	337-494-4080
News-Star 411 N Fourth St	Monroe	LA	71201	**888-677-2524**	318-322-5161
Times-Picayune 3800 Howard Ave	New Orleans	LA	70125	**800-925-0000**	504-826-3279
Times 222 Lake St	Shreveport	LA	71101	**800-551-8892**	318-459-3200
Bangor Daily News 491 Main St PO Box 1329	Bangor	ME	04402	**800-432-7964**	207-990-8000
Sun-Journal PO Box 4400	Lewiston	ME	04243	**800-482-0759**	207-784-5411
Morning Sentinel 31 Front St	Waterville	ME	04901	**800-287-1945**	207-873-3341
Baltimore Sun 501 N Calvert St	Baltimore	MD	21278	**800-829-8000**	410-332-6000
Cumberland Times-News 19 Baltimore St	Cumberland	MD	21502	**800-742-8149**	301-722-4600
Star Democrat 29088 Airpark Dr PO Box 600	Easton	MD	21601	**888-634-4002**	410-822-1500
Frederick News Post 200 E Patrick St	Frederick	MD	21701	**800-486-1177**	301-662-1177
Daily Times 618 Beam St	Salisbury	MD	21801	**877-335-6278**	410-749-7171
Cape Cod Times 319 Main St	Hyannis	MA	02601	**800-451-7887**	508-775-1200
Haverhill Gazette 100 Turnpike St	N Andover	MA	01831	**888-411-3245**	978-946-2000
Berkshire Eagle 75 S Church St PO Box 1171	Pittsfield	MA	01202	**800-234-7404**	413-447-7311
Patriot Ledger 400 Crown Colony Dr PO Box 699159	Quincy	MA	02269	**888-782-2267**	617-786-7000
Daily Telegram 133 N Winter St	Adrian	MI	49221	**800-968-5111**	517-265-5111
Battle Creek Enquirer 155 W Van Buren St	Battle Creek	MI	49017	**800-333-4139**	269-964-7161
Bay City Times 311 Fifth St	Bay City	MI	48708	**800-727-7661**	989-895-8551
Detroit Free Press 615 W Lafayette Blvd	Detroit	MI	48226	**800-395-3300**	313-222-6400
Detroit News 615 W Lafayette Blvd *General	Detroit	MI	48226	**800-395-3300***	313-222-2300
Flint Journal 200 E First St *Circ	Flint	MI	48502	**800-875-6200***	810-766-6100
Holland Sentinel 54 W Eigth St	Holland	MI	49423	**800-633-4227**	616-392-2311
Jackson Citizen Patriot 100 E Michigan Ave Ste 100	Jackson	MI	49201	**877-213-3754**	
Kalamazoo Gazette 401 S Burdick St	Kalamazoo	MI	49007	**800-466-6397**	269-345-3511
Lansing State Journal 120 E Lenawee St	Lansing	MI	48919	**800-234-1719**	517-377-1000
Midland Daily News 124 McDonald St	Midland	MI	48640	**877-411-2762**	989-835-7171
Muskegon Chronicle 981 Third St	Muskegon	MI	49440	**800-783-3161**	231-722-3161
Times Herald 911 Military St	Port Huron	MI	48060	**800-462-4057**	810-985-7171
Saginaw News 203 S Washington Ave	Saginaw	MI	48607	**877-611-6397**	989-752-7171
Herald-Palladium 3450 Hollywood Rd	Saint Joseph	MI	49085	**800-356-4262**	269-429-2400
Duluth News-Tribune 424 W First St *Circ	Duluth	MN	55802	**800-456-8080***	218-723-5281
Free Press 418 S Second St	Mankato	MN	56001	**800-657-4662**	507-625-4451
Star Tribune 425 Portland Ave	Minneapolis	MN	55488	**800-827-8742**	612-673-4000
Saint Cloud Times 3000 Seventh St N PO Box 768	Saint Cloud	MN	56303	**855-336-0360**	320-255-8700
West Central Tribune PO Box 839	Willmar	MN	56201	**800-450-1150**	320-235-1150
Hattiesburg American 825 N Main St	Hattiesburg	MS	39401	**800-844-2637**	601-582-4321

Name / Address	City	State	ZIP	Toll-Free	Phone
Clarion-Ledger, The 201 S Congress St	Jackson	MS	39201	**877-850-5343**	601-961-7000
Meridian Star, The PO Box 1591	Meridian	MS	39302	**800-232-2525**	601-693-1551
Northeast Mississippi Daily Journal 1242 S Green St	Tupelo	MS	38804	**800-264-6397**	662-842-2611
Southeast Missourian 301 Broadway St	Cape Girardeau	MO	63701	**800-879-1210**	573-335-6611
Columbia Daily Tribune 101 N Fourth St	Columbia	MO	65201	**800-333-6799**	573-815-1700
Columbia Missourian 221 S Eigth St	Columbia	MO	65201	**855-270-6572**	573-882-5700
Jefferson City News Tribune 210 Monroe St	Jefferson City	MO	65101	**888-892-6333**	573-636-3131
Joplin Globe 117 E Fourth St	Joplin	MO	64801	**800-444-8514**	417-623-3480
Kansas City Star 1729 Grand Ave	Kansas City	MO	64108	**877-962-7827**	
Daily American Republic 208 Poplar St PO Box 7	Poplar Bluff	MO	63901	**888-276-2242**	573-785-1414
Springfield News Leader 651 N Boonville Ave	Springfield	MO	65806	**800-445-1059**	417-836-1100
Billings Gazette 401 N 28th St	Billings	MT	59101	**800-543-2505**	406-657-1200
Montana Standard 25 W Granite St	Butte	MT	59701	**800-877-1074**	406-496-5500
Great Falls Tribune 205 River Dr S	Great Falls	MT	59405	**800-438-6600**	406-791-1444
Independent Record 317 Cruse Ave	Helena	MT	59601	**800-523-2272**	406-447-4000
Missoulian PO Box 8029	Missoula	MT	59807	**800-366-7102**	406-523-5200
Grand Island Independent 422 W First St	Grand Island	NE	68801	**800-658-3160**	308-382-1000
Lincoln Journal-Star 926 P St	Lincoln	NE	68508	**800-742-7315**	402-475-4200
Norfolk Daily News PO Box 977	Norfolk	NE	68702	**877-371-1020**	402-371-1020
Omaha World-Herald 1314 Douglas St	Omaha	NE	68102	**800-284-6397**	402-444-1000
Nevada Appeal 580 Mallory Way *General	Carson City	NV	89701	**877-689-3249***	775-882-2111
Reno Gazette-Journal 955 Kuenzli St	Reno	NV	89502	**800-970-7366**	775-788-6397
Foster's Daily Democrat 150 Venture Dr	Dover	NH	03820	**800-660-8310**	603-742-4455
Union Leader 100 William Loeb Dr	Manchester	NH	03109	**800-562-8218**	603-668-4321
Valley News 24 Interchange Dr	West Lebanon	NH	03784	**800-874-2226**	603-298-8711
Courier-Post 301 Cuthbert Blvd	Cherry Hill	NJ	08002	**800-677-6289**	856-663-6000
Asbury Park Press 3601 Hwy 66 PO Box 1550	Neptune	NJ	07754	**800-883-7737**	732-922-6000
Star-Ledger, The 1 Star Ledger Plz	Newark	NJ	07102	**800-501-2100**	973-877-4141
New Jersey Herald 2 Spring St	Newton	NJ	07860	**800-423-3725**	973-383-1500
Home News Tribune 92 E Main St Ste 202	Somerville	NJ	08876	**800-627-4663**	732-246-5500
Trentonian 600 Perry St	Trenton	NJ	08618	**855-549-6525**	609-989-7800
Daily Journal 891 E Oak Rd	Vineland	NJ	08360	**800-222-0104**	856-691-5000
Albuquerque Journal 7777 Jefferson St NE	Albuquerque	NM	87109	**800-990-5765**	505-823-7777
Las Cruces Sun-News 256 W Las Cruces Ave	Las Cruces	NM	88005	**877-827-7200**	575-541-5400
Times Union 645 Albany Shaker Rd PO Box 15000	Albany	NY	12212	**877-263-7995**	518-454-5420
Buffalo News 1 News Plz PO Box 100	Buffalo	NY	14240	**800-777-8640**	716-849-4444
Evening Observer 8-10 E Second St PO Box 391	Dunkirk	NY	14048	**800-836-0931**	716-366-3000
Star-Gazette 201 Baldwin St	Elmira	NY	14902	**800-836-8970**	607-734-5151
Post-Star 76 Lawrence St	Glens Falls	NY	12801	**800-724-2543**	518-792-3131
Register-Star 364 Warren St	Hudson	NY	12534	**800-836-4069**	518-828-1616
Post-Journal 15 W Second St	Jamestown	NY	14701	**866-756-9600**	716-487-1111
Newsday Inc 235 Pinelawn Rd	Melville	NY	11747	**888-280-4719**	631-843-2700
Times Herald-Record 40 Mulberry St PO Box 2046	Middletown	NY	10940	**800-295-2181**	845-341-1100
Financial Times 1330 Ave of the Americas	New York	NY	10019	**800-628-8088**	212-641-6500
New York Daily News 450 W 33rd St 3rd Fl	New York	NY	10001	**800-692-6397**	212-210-2100
New York Post 1211 Ave of the Americas	New York	NY	10036	**800-552-7678**	212-930-8000
Olean Times-Herald 639 Norton Dr	Olean	NY	14760	**800-722-8812**	716-372-3121
Daily Star 102 Chestnut St PO Box 250	Oneonta	NY	13820	**800-721-1000**	607-432-1000
Press-Republican 170 Margaret St PO Box 459	Plattsburgh	NY	12901	**800-288-7323**	518-561-2300
Poughkeepsie Journal 85 Civic Ctr Plz	Poughkeepsie	NY	12601	**800-765-1120**	845-437-4800
Democrat & Chronicle 55 Exchange Blvd	Rochester	NY	14614	**800-790-9565**	585-232-7100
Daily Gazette 2345 Maxon Rd Ext PO Box 1090	Schenectady	NY	12301	**800-262-2211**	518-374-4141
Post-Standard PO Box 4915	Syracuse	NY	13221	**866-447-3787**	315-470-0011
Watertown Daily Times 260 Washington St	Watertown	NY	13601	**800-642-6222**	315-782-1000
Courier-Tribune 500 Sunset Ave	Asheboro	NC	27203	**800-488-0444**	336-625-2101
Asheville Citizen Times 14 O'Henry Ave	Asheville	NC	28801	**800-800-4204**	828-252-5622
Charlotte Observer, The 600 S Tryon St	Charlotte	NC	28202	**800-332-0686**	704-358-5000

Name / Address	City	State	ZIP	Toll-Free	Phone
Herald-Sun, The 2828 Pickett Rd	Durham	NC	27705	**866-348-6479**	919-419-6500
Fayetteville Observer 458 Whitfield St	Fayetteville	NC	28306	**800-345-9895**	910-323-4848
Gaston Gazette 1893 Remount Rd	Gastonia	NC	28054	**800-527-5226**	704-869-1700
News & Record 200 E Market St	Greensboro	NC	27401	**800-553-6880**	336-373-7000
Times-News PO Box 490	Hendersonville	NC	28793	**800-849-8050**	828-692-0505
Hickory Daily Record 1100 Pk Pl	Hickory	NC	28602	**800-849-8586**	828-322-4510
Daily News 724 Bell Fork Rd PO Box 196	Jacksonville	NC	28541	**877-878-2120**	910-353-1171
News & Observer 215 S McDowell St	Raleigh	NC	27602	**800-522-4205**	919-829-4500
Winston-Salem Journal 418 N Marshall St	Winston-Salem	NC	27101	**800-642-0925**	336-727-7211
Bismarck Tribune 707 E Front Ave	Bismarck	ND	58504	**866-476-5348**	701-223-2500
Forum, The 101 N Fifth St	Fargo	ND	58102	**800-274-5445**	701-235-7311
Star Beacon PO Box 2100	Ashtabula	OH	44005	**800-554-6768**	440-998-2323
Chillicothe Gazette 50 W Main St	Chillicothe	OH	45601	**877-424-0215**	740-773-2111
Cincinnati Enquirer 312 Elm St	Cincinnati	OH	45202	**800-876-4500**	513-721-2700
Kentucky Post 1720 Gilbert Ave	Cincinnati	OH	45202	**877-667-4265**	513-721-9900
Plain Dealer 1801 Superior Ave	Cleveland	OH	44114	**800-362-0727**	216-999-5000
Columbus Dispatch 34 S Third St	Columbus	OH	43215	**800-942-2745**	614-461-5000
Dayton Daily News 1611 S Main St	Dayton	OH	45409	**888-397-6397**	937-225-2000
Chronicle-Telegram 225 E Ave	Elyria	OH	44035	**800-848-6397**	440-329-7000
Record-Courier 1050 W Main St PO Box 5199	Kent	OH	44240	**800-560-9657**	330-541-9400
Lancaster Eagle-Gazette 138 W Chestnut St	Lancaster	OH	43130	**877-513-7355**	740-654-1321
Lima News 3515 Elida Rd	Lima	OH	45807	**800-686-9924**	419-223-1010
Morning Journal 1657 Broadway Ave	Lorain	OH	44052	**888-757-0727**	440-245-6901
News Journal 70 W Fourth St	Mansfield	OH	44903	**800-472-5547**	419-522-3311
Marion Star, The 163 E Center St	Marion	OH	43302	**877-987-2782**	740-387-0400
Times Leader 200 S Fourth St	Martins Ferry	OH	43935	**800-244-5671**	740-633-1131
Medina Gazette 885 W Liberty St	Medina	OH	44256	**800-633-4623**	330-725-4166
Times Reporter 629 Wabash Ave NW	New Philadelphia	OH	44663	**800-686-5577**	330-364-5577
Advocate, The 22 N First St	Newark	OH	43055	**877-424-0208**	740-345-4053
Portsmouth Daily Times 637 Sixth St	Portsmouth	OH	45662	**800-582-7277**	740-353-3101
Sandusky Register 314 W Market St	Sandusky	OH	44870	**800-466-1243**	419-625-5500
Springfield News-Sun 202 N Limestone St	Springfield	OH	45503	**800-441-6397**	937-328-0300
Blade 541 N Superior St	Toledo	OH	43660	**800-245-3317**	419-724-6000
Tribune Chronicle 240 Franklin St SE	Warren	OH	44482	**888-550-8742**	330-841-1600
News-Herald 7085 Mentor Ave	Willoughby	OH	44094	**800-947-2737**	440-951-0000
Daily Record 212 E Liberty St PO Box 918	Wooster	OH	44691	**800-686-2958**	330-264-1125
Vindicator, The 107 Vindicator Sq PO Box 780	Youngstown	OH	44501	**877-700-4647**	330-747-1471
Times Recorder 34 S Fourth St	Zanesville	OH	43701	**888-217-2614**	740-452-4561
Enid News & Eagle 227 W Broadway PO Box 3451	Enid	OK	73701	**800-299-6397**	580-548-8186
Oklahoman, The 9000 N Broadway	Oklahoma City	OK	73114	**800-375-6397**	405-475-3311
Tulsa World 315 S Boulder Ave	Tulsa	OK	74103	**800-897-3557**	918-583-2161
Albany Democrat-Herald 600 Lyons St SW PO Box 130	Albany	OR	97321	**877-634-2867**	541-926-2211
Bulletin, The 1777 SW Chandler Ave	Bend	OR	97702	**800-503-3933**	541-382-1811
Daily Courier 409 SE Seventh St	Grants Pass	OR	97526	**800-228-0457**	541-474-3700
Medford Mail Tribune PO Box 1108	Medford	OR	97501	**800-452-4011**	541-776-4411
Oregonian 1320 SW Broadway *News Rm	Portland	OR	97201	**800-723-3638***	503-221-8100
News-Review 345 NE Winchester St	Roseburg	OR	97470	**800-863-3321**	541-672-3321
Morning Call PO Box 1260	Allentown	PA	18105	**800-666-5492**	610-820-6500
Altoona Mirror 301 Cayuga Ave	Altoona	PA	16602	**800-222-1962**	814-946-7411
Dispatch, The 116 E Market St	Blairsville	PA	15717	**800-221-9282**	724-459-6100
Butler Eagle 114 W Diamond St	Butler	PA	16001	**800-842-8098**	724-282-8000
Express-Times 30 N Fourth St	Easton	PA	18042	**800-360-3601**	610-258-7171
Erie Times-News 205 W 12th St	Erie	PA	16534	**800-352-0043**	814-870-1600
Evening Sun 135 Baltimore St PO Box 514	Hanover	PA	17331	**800-877-3786**	717-637-3736
Patriot-News 812 Market St	Harrisburg	PA	17101	**800-692-7207**	717-255-8100
Hazleton Standard Speaker 21 N Wyoming St *Cust Svc	Hazleton	PA	18201	**800-843-6680***	570-455-3636
Tribune-Democrat 425 Locust St	Johnstown	PA	15907	**855-255-5975**	814-532-5050
Intelligencer Journal 8 W King St PO Box 1328	Lancaster	PA	17603	**800-809-4666**	717-291-8622
Lancaster New Era 8 W King St PO Box 1328	Lancaster	PA	17603	**800-809-4666**	717-291-8811
Lebanon Daily News 718 Poplar St	Lebanon	PA	17042	**800-457-5929**	717-272-5611
Meadville Tribune 947 Federal Ct	Meadville	PA	16335	**800-879-0006**	814-724-6370
Philadelphia Inquirer 801 Market St Ste 300 PO Box 8263	Philadelphia	PA	19107	**800-341-3413**	215-854-2000
Pittsburgh Tribune-Review 503 Martindale St 3rd Fl	Pittsburgh	PA	15212	**800-909-8742**	412-321-6460
Delaware County Daily Times 500 Mildred Ave	Primos	PA	19018	**888-799-6299**	610-622-8800
Scranton Times-Tribune 149 Penn Ave	Scranton	PA	18503	**800-228-4637**	570-348-9100
Herald, The 52 S Dock St	Sharon	PA	16146	**800-981-1692**	724-981-6100
Centre Daily Times 3400 E College Ave	State College	PA	16801	**800-327-5500**	814-238-5000
Pocono Record 511 Lenox St	Stroudsburg	PA	18360	**800-530-6310**	570-421-3000
Valley News Dispatch 210 Fourth Ave	Tarentum	PA	15084	**877-698-2553**	800-909-8742
Herald-Standard 8 E Church St	Uniontown	PA	15401	**800-342-8254**	724-439-7500
Observer-Reporter 122 S Main St	Washington	PA	15301	**800-222-6397**	724-222-2200
Daily Local News 250 N Bradford Ave	West Chester	PA	19382	**800-568-7355**	610-696-1775
Times Leader, The 15 N Main St	Wilkes-Barre	PA	18711	**800-427-8649**	570-829-7100
Williamsport Sun-Gazette 252 W Fourth St	Williamsport	PA	17701	**800-339-0289**	570-326-1551
Providence Journal 75 Fountain St	Providence	RI	02902	**888-697-7656**	401-277-7303
Anderson Independent-Mail PO Box 2507	Anderson	SC	29622	**800-859-6397**	864-224-4321
Island Packet 10 Buck Island Rd	Bluffton	SC	29910	**877-706-8100**	843-706-8100
State, The 1401 Shop Rd	Columbia	SC	29201	**800-888-5353**	803-771-6161
Greenville News 305 S Main St	Greenville	SC	29601	**800-800-5116**	864-298-4100
Sun News 914 Frontage Rd E	Myrtle Beach	SC	29578	**800-568-1800**	843-626-8555
Spartanburg Herald-Journal 189 W Main St	Spartanburg	SC	29306	**800-922-4158**	864-582-4511
Aberdeen American News 124 S Second St	Aberdeen	SD	57402	**800-925-4100**	605-225-4100
Capital Journal 333 W Dakota Ave	Pierre	SD	57501	**800-537-0025**	605-224-7301
Rapid City Journal 507 Main St	Rapid City	SD	57701	**800-843-2300**	605-394-8300
Argus Leader 200 S Minnesota Ave	Sioux Falls	SD	57104	**800-530-6397**	605-331-2200
Jackson Sun 245 W LaFayette St	Jackson	TN	38301	**800-372-3922**	731-427-3333
Kingsport Times-News 701 Lynn Garden Dr	Kingsport	TN	37660	**800-251-0328**	423-246-8121
Knoxville News-Sentinel 2332 News Sentinel Dr	Knoxville	TN	37921	**800-237-5821**	865-521-8181
Commercial Appeal 495 Union Ave	Memphis	TN	38103	**800-444-6397**	901-529-2345
Citizen Tribune 1609 W First N St PO Box 625	Morristown	TN	37815	**800-624-0281**	423-581-5630
Tennessean 1100 Broadway	Nashville	TN	37203	**800-342-8237**	615-257-0928
Abilene Reporter-News 101 Cypress St	Abilene	TX	79601	**866-604-2020**	325-673-4271
Austin American-Statesman 305 S Congress Ave	Austin	TX	78704	**800-445-9898**	512-445-4040
Brownsville Herald, The 1135 E Van Buren St	Brownsville	TX	78520	**800-488-4301**	956-542-4301
Brazosport Facts 720 S Main St	Clute	TX	77531	**800-864-8340**	979-265-7411
Caller-Times 820 N Lower Broadway	Corpus Christi	TX	78401	**800-827-2011**	361-884-2011
Dallas Morning News 508 Young St	Dallas	TX	75202	**800-431-0010**	214-977-8222
Denton Record-Chronicle 314 E Hickory St	Denton	TX	76201	**800-275-1722**	940-387-3811
Galveston County Daily News 8522 Teichman Rd PO Box 628	Galveston	TX	77553	**800-561-3611**	409-683-5200
Valley Morning Star PO Box 511	Harlingen	TX	78551	**877-786-7612**	956-430-6200
Houston Chronicle 801 Texas Ave	Houston	TX	77002	**800-735-3800**	713-362-7171
Laredo Morning Times 111 Esperanza Dr	Laredo	TX	78041	**800-232-7907**	956-728-2500
Longview News-Journal 320 E Methvin St	Longview	TX	75601	**800-825-9799**	903-757-3311
Lubbock Avalanche-Journal 710 Ave J	Lubbock	TX	79401	**800-692-4021**	806-762-8844
Lufkin Daily News 300 Ellis Ave	Lufkin	TX	75904	**888-664-8792**	936-632-6631
Monitor, The 1400 E Nolana Loop	McAllen	TX	78504	**800-366-4343**	956-683-4000
Midland Reporter-Telegram PO Box 1650	Midland	TX	79702	**800-542-3952**	432-682-5311
Odessa American PO Box 2952	Odessa	TX	79760	**800-592-4433**	432-337-4661
San Angelo Standard-Times 34 W Harris Ave	San Angelo	TX	76903	**800-588-1884**	325-659-8200
San Antonio Express-News Ave E & Third St	San Antonio	TX	78205	**800-555-1551**	210-250-3000
Herald Democrat 603 S Sam Rayburn Fwy	Sherman	TX	75090	**800-827-7183**	903-893-8181
Texarkana Gazette 315 Pine St *General	Texarkana	TX	75501	**888-784-4747***	903-794-3311
Tyler Morning Telegraph PO Box 2030	Tyler	TX	75710	**800-772-1213**	903-597-8111

Name	Address	City	State	Zip	Toll-Free	Phone
Victoria Advocate	PO Box 1518	Victoria	TX	77902	**800-234-8108**	361-575-1451
Waco Tribune-Herald	900 Franklin Ave	Waco	TX	76701	**800-678-8742**	254-757-5757
Times Record News	PO Box 120	Wichita Falls	TX	76307	**800-627-1646**	940-767-8341
Herald Journal	75 W 300 N	Logan	UT	84321	**800-275-0423**	435-752-2121
Standard-Examiner	332 Standard Way	Ogden	UT	84404	**888-221-7070**	801-625-4200
Deseret News	30 E 100 S Suite 400 PO Box 1257	Salt Lake City	UT	84110	**800-999-7511**	801-236-6000
Burlington Free Press	100 Bank St	Burlington	VT	05401	**800-427-3124**	802-863-3441
Rutland Herald	PO Box 668	Rutland	VT	05702	**800-498-4296**	
Bristol Herald-Courier	320 Bob Morrison Blvd	Bristol	VA	24201	**888-228-2098**	276-669-2181
Free Lance Star	616 Amelia St	Fredericksburg	VA	22401	**800-877-0500**	540-374-5000
News & Advance	PO Box 10129	Lynchburg	VA	24506	**800-275-8830**	434-385-5555
Martinsville Bulletin	PO Box 3711	Martinsville	VA	24115	**800-234-6575**	276-638-8801
Virginian-Pilot	150 W Bramelton Ave	Norfolk	VA	23510	**800-446-2004**	757-446-2000
Roanoke Times	201 W Campbell Ave SW	Roanoke	VA	24011	**800-346-1234**	540-981-3340
News Leader	11 N Central Ave	Staunton	VA	24401	**800-793-2459**	540-885-7281
Winchester Star	2 N Kent St	Winchester	VA	22601	**800-296-8639**	540-667-3200
Daily World	315 S Michigan St	Aberdeen	WA	98520	**800-829-7880**	360-532-4000
Kitsap Sun	PO Box 259	Bremerton	WA	98337	**888-377-3711**	360-377-3711
Tri-City Herald	333 W Canal Dr	Kennewick	WA	99336	**800-874-0445**	509-582-1500
Skagit Valley Herald	1000 E College Way PO Box 578	Mount Vernon	WA	98273	**800-683-3300**	360-424-3251
Peninsula Daily News	305 W First St PO Box 1330	Port Angeles	WA	98362	**800-826-7714**	360-452-2345
Seattle Post-Intelligencer	101 Elliott Ave W 2nd Fl	Seattle	WA	98119	**800-542-0820**	206-448-8000
News Tribune	1950 S State St	Tacoma	WA	98405	**800-388-8742**	253-597-8742
Columbian	701 W Eigth St PO Box 180	Vancouver	WA	98660	**800-743-3391**	360-694-3391
Wenatchee World	14 N Mission St	Wenatchee	WA	98801	**800-572-4433**	509-663-5161
Yakima Herald-Republic	PO Box 9668	Yakima	WA	98909	**800-343-2799**	509-248-1251
Register-Herald	801 N Kanawha St	Beckley	WV	25801	**800-950-0250**	304-255-4400
Charleston Gazette	1001 Virginia St E	Charleston	WV	25301	**800-982-6397**	304-348-5140
Clarksburg Exponent Telegram	324 Hewes Ave	Clarksburg	WV	26301	**800-982-6034**	304-626-1400
Exponent Telegram	324 Hewes Ave	Clarksburg	WV	26301	**800-982-6034**	
Herald-Dispatch	946 Fifth Ave	Huntington	WV	25701	**800-444-2446**	304-526-4000
Journal, The	207 W King St	Martinsburg	WV	25402	**800-448-1895**	304-263-8931
Beloit Daily News	149 State St	Beloit	WI	53511	**800-356-3411**	608-365-8811
Leader-Telegram	701 S Farwell St	Eau Claire	WI	54701	**800-236-8808**	715-833-9200
Green Bay Press-Gazette	PO Box 23430	Green Bay	WI	54305	**800-422-7128**	920-431-8400
Janesville Gazette	1 S Parker Dr PO Box 5001	Janesville	WI	53547	**800-362-6712**	608-754-3311
Kenosha News	5800 Seventh Ave	Kenosha	WI	53140	**800-292-2700**	262-657-1000
La Crosse Tribune	401 N Third St	La Crosse	WI	54601	**800-262-0420**	608-782-9710
Capital Times	1901 Fish Hatchery Rd	Madison	WI	53713	**800-362-8333**	608-252-6400
Wisconsin State Journal	1901 Fish Hatchery Rd	Madison	WI	53713	**800-362-8333**	608-252-6200
Herald Times Reporter	902 Franklin St	Manitowoc	WI	54221	**800-783-7323**	920-684-4433
Milwaukee Journal Sentinel	333 W State St	Milwaukee	WI	53201	**800-456-5943**	414-224-2000
Sheboygan Press	632 Center Ave PO Box 358	Sheboygan	WI	53081	**800-686-3900**	920-457-7711
Waukesha County Freeman	801 N Barstow St PO Box 7	Waukesha	WI	53187	**800-762-6219**	262-542-2501
Wausau Daily Herald	800 Scott St	Wausau	WI	54403	**800-477-4838**	715-842-2101
Wyoming Tribune-Eagle	702 W Lincolnway	Cheyenne	WY	82001	**800-561-6268**	307-634-3361

531-3 National Newspapers

Name	Address	City	State	Zip	Toll-Free	Phone
Circle Media Inc	5817 Old Leeds Rd	Irondale	AL	35210	**800-356-9916**	
High Country News	119 Grand Ave	Paonia	CO	81428	**800-311-5852**	970-527-4898
Sentinel Systems Corp	1620 Kipling St	Lakewood	CO	80215	**800-456-9955**	303-242-2000
News-banner Publications Inc	125 N Johnson St	Bluffton	IN	46714	**800-579-7476**	260-824-0224
Ottawa Herald Inc	104 S Cedar St	Ottawa	KS	66067	**800-467-8383**	785-242-4700
Christian Science Monitor	210 Massachusetts Ave	Boston	MA	02115	**800-453-3432**	617-450-2000
Lawyers Weekly Inc	10 Milk St Ste 1000	Boston	MA	02108	**800-444-5297**	617-451-7300
Drummer & Wright Cnty Journal	108 Central Ave	Buffalo	MN	55313	**800-880-5047**	763-682-1221
Lakeview Publishing of Elbow Lake Inc	35 Central Ave N	Elbow Lake	MN	56531	**877-852-2796**	218-685-5326
Lewistown News-argus	521 W Main St	Lewistown	MT	59457	**800-879-5627**	406-535-3401
Wall Street Journal, The	1211 Ave of the Americas *General	New York	NY	10036	**800-568-7625***	212-416-2000
Sentinel Power Services Inc	7517 E Pine St	Tulsa	OK	74115	**800-831-9550**	918-359-0350
Bedford Gazette	424 W Penn St	Bedford	PA	15522	**800-242-4250**	814-623-1151
USA Today	7950 Jones Branch Dr *Cust Svc	McLean	VA	22108	**800-872-0001***	703-854-3400
Charleston Newspapers Ltd	1001 Virginia St E	Charleston	WV	25301	**800-982-6397**	304-348-4848
Winneconne News	908 E Main St	Winneconne	WI	54986	**800-545-5026**	920-582-4541

531-4 Weekly Newspapers

Listings here are organized by city names within state groupings.

Name	Address	City	State	Zip	Toll-Free	Phone
Birmingham Times	115 Third Ave W	Birmingham	AL	35204	**866-456-4995**	205-251-5158
Gardena Valley News	15005 S Vermont Ave	Gardena	CA	90247	**800-329-6351**	310-329-6351
Glendora Highlander Press	1210 N Azusa Canyon Rd	West Covina	CA	91790	**800-788-1200**	626-962-8811
Independent, The	2250 First St	Livermore	CA	94550	**877-952-3588**	925-447-8700
Los Angeles Downtown News	1264 W First St	Los Angeles	CA	90026	**877-338-1010**	213-481-1448
Mammoth Times, The	PO Box 3929	Mammoth Lakes	CA	93546	**800-427-7623**	760-934-3929
Milpitas Post	59 Marylinn Dr	Milpitas	CA	95035	**800-870-6397**	408-262-2454
Aurora Sentinel	14305 E Alameda Ave Ste 200	Aurora	CO	80012	**855-269-4484**	303-750-7555
Bridgeport News	1000 Bridgeport Ave *Advestisement	Shelton	CT	06484	**855-247-8573***	203-926-2080
Milford Mirror	1000 Bridgeport Ave *Advestisement	Shelton	CT	06484	**800-372-2790***	203-402-2315
Reminder, The	PO Box 210	Vernon	CT	06066	**888-456-2211**	860-875-3366
Stratford Star	1000 Bridgeport Ave *Advestisement	Shelton	CT	06484	**800-372-2790***	203-402-2319
Dialog, The	1925 Delaware Ave	Wilmington	DE	19806	**877-225-7870**	302-573-3109
Dover Post	1196 S Little Creek Rd	Dover	DE	19901	**800-942-1616**	302-678-3616
Clay Today	3513 US Hwy 17	Fleming Island	FL	32003	**888-434-9844**	904-264-3200
Miami Today	710 Brickell Ave	Miami	FL	33131	**800-283-2707**	305-358-2663
Osceola News-Gazette	108 Church St	Kissimmee	FL	34741	**866-354-2637**	407-846-7600
Revue & News, The	319 N Main St	Alpharetta	GA	30004	**800-342-9819**	770-442-3278
Galena Gazette	716 S Bench St	Galena	IL	61036	**800-373-6397**	815-777-0019
Times Record	219 S College Ave	Aledo	IL	61231	**800-784-6776**	309-582-5112
Banner-Gazette	490 E State Rd 60 PO Box 38	Pekin	IN	47165	**800-889-3390**	812-967-3176
Hendricks County Flyer	8109 Kingston St Ste 500	Avon	IN	46123	**800-359-3747**	317-272-5800
Papers, The	206 S Main St PO Box 188	Milford	IN	46542	**800-733-4111**	574-658-4111
Avoyelles Journal	105 N Main St	Marksville	LA	71351	**800-565-4321**	318-253-5413
Times of Acadiana	1100 Bertrand Dr	Lafayette	LA	70506	**877-289-2216**	337-289-6300
Coastal Journal	97 Commercial St	Bath	ME	04530	**800-649-6241**	207-443-6241
Baltimore Times	2513 N Charles St	Baltimore	MD	21218	**800-944-7403**	410-366-3900
Ada/Cascade/Forest Hills Advance	PO Box 9	Jenison	MI	49429	**800-439-0960**	616-669-2700
Advisor & Source Newspapers	48075 Van Dyke Ave	Shelby Township	MI	48317	**800-252-7345**	586-731-1000
Camden Publications	331 E Bell St	Camden	MI	49232	**800-222-6336**	517-368-0365
Cedar Springs Post	36 E Maple PO Box 370	Cedar Springs	MI	49319	**888-937-4514**	616-696-3655
Dearborn Times-Herald	13730 Michigan Ave	Dearborn	MI	48126	**866-468-7630**	313-584-4000
Voice, The	51180 Bedford St	New Baltimore	MI	48047	**800-561-2248**	586-716-8100
Morrison County Record	216 SE First St	Little Falls	MN	56345	**888-637-2345**	320-632-2345
Farmington Press	218 N Washington St	Farmington	MO	63640	**800-455-0206**	573-756-8927
Jefferson County Journal	1405 N Truman Blvd	Festus	MO	63028	**800-365-0820**	636-937-9811
Washington Missourian	14 W Main St PO Box 336	Washington	MO	63090	**888-239-7701**	636-239-7701
Bellevue Leader	604 Fort Crook Rd N	Bellevue	NE	68005	**800-284-6397**	402-733-7300
West Nebraska Register	PO Box 608	Grand Island	NE	68802	**800-652-2229**	308-382-4660
Hunterdon County Democrat	8 Minneakoning Rd	Flemington	NJ	08822	**888-782-7533**	908-782-4747

Classified Section

Name / Address	City	State	Zip	Toll-Free	Phone
Twin-Boro News 210 Knickerbocker Rd	Cresskill	NJ	07626	**888-473-2673**	201-894-6715
Queens Courier 38-15 Bell Blvd	Bayside	NY	11361	**800-275-8777**	718-224-5863
Plains Reporter PO Box 1447	Williston	ND	58802	**800-950-2165**	701-572-2165
West Fargo Pioneer 101 5th St N	West Fargo	ND	58078	**888-382-1222**	701-451-5718
Cuyahoga Falls News-Press 1050 W Main St PO Box 5199	Kent	OH	44240	**800-560-9657**	330-541-9421
Dublin Villager 7801 N Central Dr	Lewis Center	OH	43035	**866-790-4502**	740-888-6100
Early Bird, The 5312 Sebring Warner Rd	Greenville	OH	45331	**866-627-4557**	937-548-3330
Forest Hills Journal 394 WaRds Corner Rd Ste 170	Loveland	OH	45140	**888-894-2113**	513-248-8600
Gateway News 1050 West Main St	Kent	OH	44240	**800-560-9657**	330-541-9400
Hilliard This Week 7801 N Central Dr	Lewis Center	OH	43035	**888-837-4342**	740-888-6100
Reynoldsburg This Week 7801 N Central Dr	Lewis Center	OH	43035	**888-837-4342**	740-888-6100
Suburban Press & Metro Press 1550 Woodville Rd	Millbury	OH	43447	**800-300-6158**	419-836-2221
Upper Arlington News 7801 N Central Dr	Lewis Center	OH	43035	**800-860-1267**	740-888-6000
Westerville This Week 7801 N Central Dr	Lewis Center	OH	43035	**888-837-4342**	740-888-6100
Almanac, The 2600 Boyce Plz Rd Ste 142	Pittsburgh	PA	15241	**800-222-6397**	724-941-7725
York Sunday News 1891 Loucks Rd	York	PA	17408	**888-629-4095**	717-767-6397
Bluffton Today 52 Persimmon St	Bluffton	SC	29910	**855-665-8549**	843-815-0800
Chronicle Independent 909 W Dekalb St *General	Camden	SC	29020	**800-922-5431***	803-432-6157
Georgetown Times 615 Front St	Georgetown	SC	29440	**800-772-1213**	843-546-4148
Star, The 404 E Martintown Rd Ste 2	North Augusta	SC	29841	**888-397-3742**	803-279-2793
Valley Town Crier 1811 N 23rd St	McAllen	TX	78501	**800-621-3362**	956-682-2423
World, The 403 US Rt 302-Berlin	Barre	VT	05641	**800-639-9753**	802-479-2582
Fauquier Times-Democrat 39 Culpeper St	Warrenton	VA	20186	**888-351-1660**	540-347-4222
Loudoun Times-Mirror PO Box 359	Leesburg	VA	20178	**888-351-1660**	703-777-1111
Mechanicsville Local 6400 Mechanicsville Tpke	Mechanicsville	VA	23111	**800-468-3382**	804-746-1235
Tribune Newspapers of Snohomish County 127 Ave C Ste B PO Box 499	Snohomish	WA	98291	**877-894-4663**	360-568-4121

531-5 Weekly Newspapers - Alternative

Name / Address	City	State	Zip	Toll-Free	Phone
Chico News & Review 353 E Second St	Chico	CA	95928	**866-703-3873**	530-894-2300
LA Weekly 6715 Sunset Blvd	Los Angeles	CA	90028	**866-789-6188**	
San Luis Obispo New Times 505 Higuera St	San Luis Obispo	CA	93401	**800-546-4219**	805-546-8208
Orlando Weekly 1505 E Colonial Dr St Ste 200	Orlando	FL	32803	**800-474-7576**	407-377-0400
Creative Loafing Atlanta 384 Northyards Blvd Ste 600	Atlanta	GA	30313	**888-242-0208**	404-688-5623
Chicago Reader 11 E Illinois St	Chicago	IL	60611	**888-473-5362**	312-828-0350
Metro Times 733 St Antoine St	Detroit	MI	48226	**866-501-3627**	313-961-4060
Minneapolis/St. Paul City Pages 401 N Third St Ste 550	Minneapolis	MN	55401	**844-387-6962**	612-375-1015
Reno News & Review 708 N Ctr St	Reno	NV	89501	**866-703-3873**	916-498-1234
Long Island Press 575 Underhill Blvd Ste 210	Syosset	NY	11791	**800-545-6683**	516-284-3300
Dayton City Paper 126 N Main St Ste 240	Dayton	OH	45402	**888-228-3630**	937-222-8855
Scene 1468 W Ninth St Ste 805	Cleveland	OH	44113	**877-598-8703**	216-241-7550
Memphis Flyer 460 Tennessee St	Memphis	TN	38103	**877-292-3804**	901-521-9000
Metro Pulse 602 S Gay St Ste Mezzanine	Knoxville	TN	37902	**800-686-4208**	865-522-5399
Austin Chronicle PO Box 49066	Austin	TX	78765	**866-271-4900**	512-454-5766
Houston Press 1621 Milam St Ste 100	Houston	TX	77002	**877-926-8300**	713-280-2400
Pacific Northwest Inlander 9 S Washington St	Spokane	WA	99201	**888-431-9911**	509-325-0634

532 NURSES ASSOCIATIONS - STATE

SEE ALSO Health & Medical Professionals Associations

Name / Address	City	State	Zip	Toll-Free	Phone
Alabama State Nurses Assn (ASNA) 360 N Hull St	Montgomery	AL	36104	**800-270-2762**	334-262-8321
Alaska Municipal League Joint Insurance Association 807 G St Ste 356	Anchorage	AK	99501	**800-337-3682**	907-258-2625
Arizona Osteopathic Medical Association 5150 N 16th St Ste A122	Phoenix	AZ	85016	**888-266-6699**	602-266-6699
Delaware Nurses Assn (DNA) 4765 Ogletown-Stanton Rd Ste L10	Newark	DE	19713	**800-626-4081**	302-733-5880
Federal Hearings & Appeals Services Inc 117 W Main St	Plymouth	PA	18651	**800-664-7177**	570-779-5122
Georgia Municipal Association 201 Pryor St SW	Atlanta	GA	30303	**888-488-4462**	404-688-0472
Georgia Nurses Assn (GNA) 3032 Briarcliff Rd NE	Atlanta	GA	30329	**800-324-0462**	404-325-5536
Hawaii Nurses Assn (HNA) 949 Kapiolani Blvd Ste 107	Honolulu	HI	96814	**800-617-2677**	808-531-1628
Idaho Nurses Assn (INA) 1850 E Southern Ave Ste 1	Tempe	AZ	85224	**888-721-8904**	
Illinois Health Care Association 1029 S Fourth St	Springfield	IL	62703	**800-252-8988**	217-528-6455
Illinois Nurses Assn (INA) 105 W Adams St Ste 2101	Chicago	IL	60603	**800-262-2500**	312-419-2900
Indiana Association of School Principals Inc 11025 E 25th St	Indianapolis	IN	46229	**800-285-2188**	317-891-9900
Iowa Mortgage Association 8800 Nw 62nd Ave	Johnston	IA	50131	**800-800-2353**	515-286-4352
Kentucky Bankers Association 600 W Main St Ste 400	Louisville	KY	40202	**800-392-4045**	502-582-2453
Kentucky Hospital Association 2501 Nelson Miller Pkwy Ste 200	Louisville	KY	40223	**800-945-4542**	502-426-6220
Louisiana State Nurses Assn, The (LSNA) 5713 Superior Dr Ste A-6	Baton Rouge	LA	70816	**800-457-6378**	225-201-0993
Maryland Municipal League Insurance Agency Inc 1212 W St Ste 100	Annapolis	MD	21401	**800-492-7121**	410-268-5514
Massachusetts Nurses Assn (MNA) 340 Tpke St	Canton	MA	02021	**800-882-2056**	781-821-4625
Mha an Association of Montana Health Care Providers 1720 Ninth Ave	Helena	MT	59601	**800-351-3551**	406-442-1911
Michigan Nurses Assn (MNA) 2310 Jolly Oak Rd	Okemos	MI	48864	**888-646-8773**	517-349-5640
Minnesota Nurses Assn (MNA) 345 Randolph Ave Ste 200	Saint Paul	MN	55102	**800-536-4662**	651-646-4807
Nebraska Nurses Assn (NNA) PO Box 3107	Kearney	NE	68848	**800-582-3014**	402-475-3859
New Jersey State Nurses Assn (NJSNA) 1479 Pennington Rd	Trenton	NJ	08618	**800-662-0108**	609-883-5335
New York State Nurses Assn (NYSNA) 11 Cornell Rd	Latham	NY	12110	**800-724-6976**	518-782-9400
North Carolina Nurses Assn (NCNA) 103 Enterprise St PO Box 12025	Raleigh	NC	27605	**800-626-2153**	919-821-4250
Ohio a C e p 3510 Snouffer Rd Ste 100	Columbus	OH	43235	**888-642-2374**	614-792-6506
Ohio Nurses Assn (ONA) 4000 E Main St	Columbus	OH	43213	**800-735-0056**	614-237-5414
Oregon Nurses Assn (ONA) 18765 SW Boones Ferry Rd	Tualatin	OR	97062	**800-634-3552**	503-293-0011
Pennsylvania Assn of Staff Nurses & Allied Professionals (PASNAP) 1 Fayette St Ste 475	Conshohocken	PA	19428	**800-500-7850**	610-567-2907
Red Hat Society Store 431 S Acacia Ave	Fullerton	CA	92831	**866-386-2850**	714-738-0001
South Carolina Education Association, The 421 Zimalcrest Dr	Columbia	SC	29210	**800-422-7232**	803-772-6553
South Dakota Nurses Assn (SDNA) PO Box 1015	Pierre	SD	57501	**888-425-3032**	605-945-4265
Tennessee State Employees Association 627 Woodland St	Nashville	TN	37206	**800-251-8732**	615-256-4533
Utah Nurses Assn (UNA) 4505 S Wastch Blvd Ste 330B	Salt Lake City	UT	84124	**800-338-7657**	801-272-4510
Vermont State Nurses Assn (VSNA) 100 Dorset St Ste 13	South Burlington	VT	05403	**800-540-9390**	802-651-8886
Washington State Nurses Assn (WSNA) 575 Andover Pk W Ste 101	Seattle	WA	98188	**800-231-8482**	206-575-7979
West Virginia Nurses Assn (WVNA) 1007 Bigley Ave Ste 308	Charleston	WV	25302	**800-400-1226**	304-342-1169

533 OFFICE & SCHOOL SUPPLIES

SEE ALSO Office Supply Stores ; Pens, Pencils, Parts ; Printing & Photocopying Supplies ; Writing Paper

Name / Address	City	State	Zip	Toll-Free	Phone
Acroprint Time Recorder Co 5640 Departure Dr	Raleigh	NC	27616	**800-334-7190**	919-872-5800
American Product Distributors Inc (APD) 8350 Arrowridge Blvd	Charlotte	NC	28273	**800-849-5842**	704-522-9411
American Solutions for Business 31 E Minnesota Ave PO Box 218	Glenwood	MN	56334	**800-862-3690**	
Arlington Industries Inc 1616 Lakeside Dr	Waukegan	IL	60085	**800-323-4147**	847-689-2754
Aurora Corp of America 3500 Challenger St	Torrance	CA	90503	**800-327-8508**	310-793-5650
Avery Dennison Corp 207 Goode Ave *NYSE: AVY* ■ *Cust Svc	Glendale	CA	91203	**888-567-4387***	626-304-2000
Avery Dennison Worldwide Office Products Div 207 Goode Ave	Glendale	CA	91203	**800-462-8379**	626-304-2000
Bartizan Corp 217 Riverdale Ave	Yonkers	NY	10705	**800-899-2278**	914-965-7977
Baumgarten's 144 Ottley Dr	Atlanta	GA	30324	**800-247-5547**	404-874-7675
Business Stationery LLC 4944 Commerce Pkwy	Cleveland	OH	44128	**800-234-9954**	216-514-1277
C-Line Products Inc 1100 E Business Ctr Dr	Mount Prospect	IL	60056	**800-323-6084**	847-827-6661
Cardinal Office Products Inc 576 E Main St	Frankfort	KY	40601	**800-589-5886**	502-875-3300
Case Logic Inc 6303 Dry Creek Pkwy	Longmont	CO	80503	**800-925-8111**	303-652-1000
Champion Industries Inc PO Box 2968 PO Box 2968 *OTC: CHMP*	Huntington	WV	25728	**800-624-3431**	304-528-2791
Dahle North America Inc 49 Vose Farm Rd Ste 110	Peterborough	NH	03458	**800-243-8145**	603-924-0003
Deflect-O Corp 7035 E 86th St	Indianapolis	IN	46250	**800-428-4328**	

Company	Address	City	State	ZIP	Toll-Free	Phone
Douglas Stewart Co, The	2402 Advance Rd	Madison	WI	53718	**800-279-2795**	608-221-1155
Eaton Office Supply Company Inc	180 John Glenn Dr	Buffalo	NY	14228	**800-365-3237**	716-691-6100
GBS Corp	7233 Freedom Ave NW	North Canton	OH	44720	**800-552-2427**	330-494-5330
International Imaging Materials Inc	310 Commerce Dr	Amherst	NY	14228	**888-464-4625**	716-691-6333
Lakeshore Learning Materials	2695 E Dominguez St	Carson	CA	90895	**800-778-4456**	
Lee Products Co	800 E 80th St	Bloomington	MN	55420	**800-989-3544**	952-854-3544
Magna Visual Inc	9400 Watson Rd	Sappington	MO	63126	**800-843-3399**	
PBS Supply Company Inc	7013 S 216th St	Kent	WA	98032	**877-727-7515**	253-395-5550
PerfectData Corp	1323 Conshohocken Rd	Plymouth Meeting	PA	19462	**800-973-7332**	
Staples Business Advantage	500 Staples Dr	Framingham	MA	01702	**877-826-7755**	
TAB Products Co	605 Fourth St	Mayville	WI	53050	**888-466-8228**	
United Stationers Inc	1 PkwyN Blvd Ste 100	Deerfield	IL	60015	**855-275-6947**	847-627-7000
Van Ausdall & Farrar Inc	6430 E 75th St	Indianapolis	IN	46250	**800-467-7474**	317-634-2913
Weeks-Lerman Group	58-38 Page Pl	Maspeth	NY	11378	**800-544-5959**	718-803-5000

534 OFFICE SUPPLY STORES

Company	Address	City	State	ZIP	Toll-Free	Phone
Audit & Adjustment Company Inc	20700 44th Ave W Ste 100	Lynnwood	WA	98036	**800-526-1074**	425-776-9797
BenefitHelp Solutions Inc	10505 SE 17th Ave	Milwaukie	OR	97222	**888-398-8057**	503-219-3679
C M School Supply Inc	940 N Central Ave	Upland	CA	91786	**800-464-6681**	909-982-9695
Create-a-card Inc	16 Brasswood Rd	Saint James	NY	11780	**800-753-6867**	631-584-2273
Danby Group LLP, The	3060-A Business Park Dr	Norcross	GA	30071	**800-262-2629**	770-416-9844
DBI Inc	912 E Michigan Ave	Lansing	MI	48912	**800-968-1324**	517-485-3200
Discover Group Inc	2741 W 23rd St	Brooklyn	NY	11224	**866-456-6555**	718-456-4500
Eakes Office Plus	617 W Third St	Grand Island	NE	68801	**800-652-9396**	308-382-8026
Econ-o-copy Inc	4437 Trenton St Ste A	Metairie	LA	70006	**877-256-0310**	504-457-0032
Egyptian Stationers Inc	129 W Main St *Cust Svc	Belleville	IL	62220	**800-642-3949***	618-234-2323
EIS Electro Imaging Systems	6553 Las Positas Rd	Livermore	CA	94551	**800-207-4757**	
Envoy Plan Services Inc	901 Calle Amanecer Ste 200	San Clemente	CA	92673	**800-248-8858**	949-366-5070
FASCore LLC	8515 E Orchard Rd	Greenwood Village	CO	80111	**800-232-0859**	800-537-2033
Friend's Professional Stationery Inc	1535 Lewis Ave	Zion	IL	60099	**800-323-4394**	
Gobin's Inc	615 N Santa Fe Ave	Pueblo	CO	81003	**800-425-2324**	719-544-2324
Hurst Group	257 E Short St	Lexington	KY	40507	**800-926-4423**	859-255-4422
Kennedy Office Supply	4211-A Atlantic Ave	Raleigh	NC	27604	**800-733-9401**	919-878-5400
Lamination Depot Inc	1505 E McFadden Ave	Santa Ana	CA	92705	**800-925-0054**	714-954-0632
Latta's School Supply	1502 Fourth Ave	Huntington	WV	25701	**800-624-3501**	304-523-8400
Matik Inc	33 Brook St	West Hartford	CT	06110	**800-245-1628**	860-232-2323
McCowan Design & Mfg Ltd	1760 Birchmount Rd	Toronto	ON	M1P2H7	**888-782-5189**	416-291-7111
Mg Scientific Inc	8500 107th St	Pleasant Prairie	WI	53158	**800-343-8338**	262-947-7000
Northern Business Products Inc	PO Box 16127	Duluth	MN	55816	**800-647-8775**	218-726-0167
Novacopy Inc	7251 Appling Farms Pkwy	Memphis	TN	38133	**800-264-0637**	901-388-3399
Office Depot Inc	2200 Old Germantown Rd *NASDAQ: ODP*	Delray Beach	FL	33445	**800-937-3600**	561-438-4800
Opus Framing Ltd	3445 Cornett Rd	Vancouver	BC	V5M2H3	**800-663-6953**	604-435-9991
Phillips Group	501 Fulling Mill Rd	Middletown	PA	17057	**800-538-7500**	717-944-0400
Prestige Graphics Inc	9630 Ridgehaven Ct Ste B	San Diego	CA	92123	**800-383-9361**	858-560-8213
Printers & Stationers Inc	113 N Ct St	Florence	AL	35630	**800-624-5334**	256-764-8061
ShurTech Brands	32150 Just Imagine Dr	Avon	OH	44011	**800-321-0253**	440-937-7000
Smith & Butterfield Co Inc	2800 Lynch Rd	Evansville	IN	47711	**800-321-6543**	812-422-3261
Stationers Inc	1945 Fifth Ave	Huntington	WV	25703	**800-862-7200**	304-528-2780
Supply Room Cos Inc	14140 N Washington Hwy	Ashland	VA	23005	**800-849-7239**	804-412-1200
Techneal Inc	2100 S Reservoir St	Pomona	CA	91766	**800-545-6325**	909-465-6325
Total Merchant Concepts Inc	12300 NE Fourth Plain Rd A	Vancouver	WA	98682	**888-249-9919**	360-253-5934
Triplett Office Essentials Corp	3553 109th St	Urbandale	IA	50322	**800-437-5034**	515-270-9150
Variant Microsystems	4128 Business Ctr Dr	Fremont	CA	94538	**800-827-4268**	510-440-2870
Veritas Press	1250 Belle Meade Dr	Lancaster	PA	17601	**800-922-5082**	717-519-1974
WALZ Label & Mailing Systems	624 High Point Ln	East Peoria	IL	61611	**877-971-1500**	309-698-1500
Wist Office Products Co	107 W Julie Dr	Tempe	AZ	85283	**800-999-9478**	480-921-2900

535 OIL & GAS EXTRACTION

Company	Address	City	State	ZIP	Toll-Free	Phone
A H Belo Corp	508 Young St PO Box 224866 *NYSE: AHC*	Dallas	TX	75202	**800-230-1074**	214-977-8200
Allied-Horizontal Wireline Services LLC	15995 N Barker's Landing Ste 140	Houston	TX	77079	**888-494-9580**	713-343-7280
Anadarko Petroleum Corp	1201 Lk Robbins Dr *NYSE: APC*	Spring	TX	77380	**800-800-1101**	832-636-1000
Apache Corp	2000 Post Oak Blvd Ste 100 *NYSE: APA*	Houston	TX	77056	**800-272-2434**	713-296-6000
Aramco Services Co	9009 W Loop S	Houston	TX	77096	**866-287-3592**	713-432-4000
Baytex Energy Corp	2800 520 - Third Ave SW	Calgary	AB	T2P0R3	**800-524-5521**	587-952-3000
BP Canada Energy Co	240 Fourth Ave SW	Calgary	AB	T2P2H8	**877-833-1359**	403-233-1359
BP Canada Energy Resources Co	240- Fourth Ave SW	Calgary	AB	T2P2H8	**800-255-4268**	403-233-1313
BP PLC	28100 Torch Pkwy *NYSE: BP*	Warrenville	IL	60555	**800-333-3991**	
Breitling Energy Corp	Ste 12000 1910 PACIFIC Ave Ste 12000	Dallas	TX	75201	**866-884-0224**	214-716-2600
Cabot Oil & Gas Corp	840 Gessner Rd Ste 1200 *NYSE: COG*	Houston	TX	77024	**800-434-3985**	281-848-2799
Callon Petroleum Co	200 N Canal St *NYSE: CPE*	Natchez	MS	39120	**800-451-1294**	601-442-1601
Canadian Natural Resources Ltd (CNRL)	855 Second St SW Ste 2500 *NYSE: CNQ*	Calgary	AB	T2P4J8	**888-878-3700**	403-517-6700
Chevron Corp	6001 Bollinger Canyon Rd *NYSE: CVX* ■ *Cust Svc	San Ramon	CA	94583	**800-368-8357***	925-842-1000
Cimmaron Field Services Inc	303 W Wall St Bank of America Tower Ste 600	Midland	TX	79701	**877-944-2705**	
ClearStream Energy Services LP	2112 Premier Way	Sherwood Park	AB	T8H2G4	**855-410-9835**	780-410-9835
Comstock Resources Inc	5300 Town & Country Blvd Ste 500 *NYSE: CRK*	Frisco	TX	75034	**800-929-4884**	972-668-8800
Corridor Resources Inc	5475 Spring Garden Rd	Halifax	NS	B3J3T2	**888-429-4511**	902-429-4511
Delta Oil & Gas Inc	700 W Pender St Ste 604	Vancouver	BC	V6C1G8	**866-355-3644**	604-602-1500
Denbury Resources Inc	5320 Legacy Dr *NYSE: DNR* ■ *General	Plano	TX	75024	**800-348-9030***	972-673-2000
Devon Energy Corp	20 N Broadway *NYSE: DVN*	Oklahoma City	OK	73102	**877-860-5820**	405-235-3611
DKRW Advanced Fuels LLC	5444 Westheimer Ste 1560	Houston	TX	77056	**855-876-4595**	
Doyon Ltd	1 Doyon Pl Ste 300	Fairbanks	AK	99701	**888-478-4755**	907-459-2000
Eagle Energy Trust	500 4 Ave SW Ste 2710	Calgary	AB	T2P2V6	**855-531-1575**	403-531-1575
EnCana Corp	500 Ctr St SE Po Box 2850 *NYSE: ECA*	Calgary	AB	T2G1A6	**888-568-6322**	403-645-2000
EQT Corp	625 Liberty Ave Ste 1700 *NYSE: EQT*	Pittsburgh	PA	15222	**800-242-1776**	412-553-5700
Extreme Plastics Plus Inc	148 Roush Cir	Fairmont	WV	26554	**866-408-2837**	
Exxon Mobil Corp	5959 Las Colinas Blvd *NYSE: XOM*	Irving	TX	75039	**800-252-1800**	972-444-1000
Gear Energy Ltd	2600 500 - Fourth Ave SW	Calgary	AB	T2P2V6	**877-494-3430**	403-538-8435
Geoforce Inc	750 Canyon Dr Ste 140	Coppell	TX	75019	**888-574-3878**	972-546-3878
GeoResources Inc	110 Cypress Stn Dr Ste 220 *NASDAQ: GEOI*	Williston	ND	58802	**855-538-0599**	281-537-9920
Husky Energy Inc	707 Eigth Ave SW PO Box 6525 *TSE: HSE*	Calgary	AB	T2P3G7	**877-262-2111**	403-298-6111
JM Huber Corp	499 Thornall St 8th Fl	Edison	NJ	08837	**877-418-0038**	732-549-8600
Loftin Equipment Company Inc	12 N 45th Ave	Phoenix	AZ	85043	**800-437-4376**	602-272-9466
Luca International Group LLC	39650 Liberty St Ste 410	Fremont	CA	94538	**877-988-6688**	510-498-8829
MCW Energy Group Ltd	344 Mira Loma Ave	Glendale	CA	91204	**800-979-1897**	
Newfield Exploration Co	363 N Sam Houston Pkwy E Ste 100 *NYSE: NFX*	Houston	TX	77060	**866-902-0562**	281-847-6000
Noble Energy Inc	100 Glenborough Dr Ste 100 *NYSE: NBL*	Houston	TX	77067	**800-220-5824**	281-872-3100
Nomad Energy Inc	22762 Westheimer Pkwy Ste 515	Houston	TX	77450	**866-387-0287**	
North Atlantic Refining Ltd	29 Pippy Pl PO Box 40	St. John's	NL	A1B3X2	**877-635-3645**	709-463-8811

				Toll-Free	Phone
NW Natural 220 NW Second Ave PO Box 6017	Portland	OR	97209	**800-422-4012**	503-226-4211
Ohio Gas Co PO Box 528	Bryan	OH	43506	**800-331-7396**	419-636-1117
OriginClear Inc 5645 W Adams Blvd	Los Angeles	CA	90016	**877-999-6645**	323-939-6645
Pemex Procurement International Inc 10344 sam houston park dr	Houston	TX	77064	**888-254-1487**	713-430-3100
Penn Virginia Corp 100 Matsonford Rd Ste 200 *NYSE: PVA*	Radnor	PA	19087	**877-316-5288**	610-687-8900
Penn West Petroleum Ltd Ninth Ave SW Ste 200 *TSE: PWT*	Calgary	AB	T2P1K3	**866-693-2707**	403-777-2500
Perf-O-Log Inc 101 Bolton St	Lafayette	LA	70508	**888-892-8276**	
Petroleum Development Corp (PDC) 120 Genesis Blvd PO Box 26 *NASDAQ: PDCE*	Bridgeport	WV	26330	**800-624-3821**	303-860-5800
Pioneer Natural Resources Co 5205 N O'Connor Blvd Ste 200 *NYSE: PXD*	Irving	TX	75039	**888-234-6372**	972-444-9001
Primexx Energy Partners Ltd 4849 Greenville Ave Two Energy Sq Ste 1600	Dallas	TX	75206	**800-754-5908**	214-369-5909
Rife Resources Ltd 400 144 - Fourth Ave SW	Calgary	AB	T2P3N4	**888-257-1873**	403-221-0800
Saguaro Resources Ltd 3000 500 - Fourth Ave SW	Calgary	AB	T2P2V6	**855-835-4434**	403-453-3040
Seneca Resources Corp 1201 Louisiana St Ste 400	Houston	TX	77002	**800-365-3234**	713-654-2600
Shell Canada Ltd 400 Fourth Ave SW	Calgary	AB	T2P0J4	**877-656-3111**	403-691-3111
Shell Oil Co 910 Louisanna St	Houston	TX	77002	**888-467-4355**	713-241-6161
Sinopec Daylight Energy Ltd 112-4th Ave SW Sun Life Plz E Tower Ste 2700	Calgary	AB	T2P0H3	**877-266-6901**	403-266-6900
Southwestern Energy Co 2350 N Sam Houston Pkwy E Ste 300 *NYSE: SWN*	Houston	TX	77032	**866-322-0801**	832-796-1000
Strata Oil & Gas Inc 10010 - 98 St PO Box 7770	Peace River	AB	T8S1T3	**877-237-5443**	403-237-5443
Suncor Energy Inc 150 - 6 Ave SW PO Box 2844 *NYSE: SU*	Calgary	AB	T2P3E3	**800-558-9071**	403-296-8000
Sunoco Inc 1735 Market St Ste LL *NYSE: SUN*	Philadelphia	PA	19103	**800-786-6261**	215-977-3000
Swift Energy Co 16825 Northchase Dr Ste 400 *NYSE: SFY*	Houston	TX	77060	**800-777-2412**	281-874-2700
Teine Energy Ltd 2300 520 - Third Ave SW	Calgary	AB	T2P0R3	**866-900-2711**	403-698-8300
Tengasco Inc 11121 Kingston Pk Ste E *NYSE: TGC*	Knoxville	TN	37934	**888-669-0684**	865-675-1554
Termo Co, The 3275 Cherry Ave	Long Beach	CA	90807	**888-260-4715**	
Titan Oil & Gas Services Inc 6809 King Ave W Bldg E	Billings	MT	59106	**800-406-5209**	406-945-5036
Unit Corp 7130 S Lewis Ave Ste 1000 *NYSE: UNT*	Tulsa	OK	74136	**800-722-3612**	918-493-7700
Value Creation Inc 1100 635 - Eighth Ave SW	Calgary	AB	T2P3M3	**855-908-8800**	403-539-4500
Vangold Resources Ltd 7681 Prince Edward St	Vancouver	BC	V5X3R4	**866-684-1974**	604-684-1974
Wagner Oil Co 500 Commerce St Ste 600	Fort Worth	TX	76102	**800-457-5332**	817-335-2222
Warren Resources Inc 1114 Ave of the Americas 34th Fl *NASDAQ: WRES*	New York	NY	10036	**877-587-9494**	212-697-9660
Whitecap Resources Inc 3800 525 - 8th Ave SW	Calgary	AB	T2P1G1	**866-590-5289**	403-266-0767
Wilshire Enterprises Inc 100 Eagle Rock Ave Ste 100 *OTC: WLSE*	East Hanover	NJ	07936	**888-697-3962**	973-585-7770
XTO Energy Inc 810 Houston St	Fort Worth	TX	76102	**800-299-2800**	817-870-2800
ZaZa Energy Corp 1301 McKinney St Ste 2800 *NASDAQ: ZAZA*	Houston	TX	77010	**866-202-3048**	713-595-1900

536 OIL & GAS FIELD EQUIPMENT

				Toll-Free	Phone
Alberta Oil Tool 9530 60th Ave	Edmonton	AB	T6E0C1	**877-432-3404**	780-434-8566
Baker Hughes Inc (BHI) 2929 Allen Pkwy Ste 1200 *NYSE: BHI*	Houston	TX	77019	**800-229-7447**	713-439-8600
Carbo Ceramics Inc 575 N. Dairy Ashford Rd. Ste 300 *NYSE: CRR*	Houston	TX	77079	**800-551-3247**	281-921-6400
Cuming Corp 225 Bodwell St	Avon	MA	02322	**800-432-6464**	508-580-2660
Dril-Quip Inc 13550 Hempstead Hwy *NYSE: DRQ*	Houston	TX	77040	**877-316-2631**	713-939-7711
Drillers Service Inc 1792 Highland Ave NE	Hickory	NC	28601	**800-334-2308**	828-322-1100
FMC Technologies Inc 1803 Gears Rd *NYSE: FTI*	Houston	TX	77067	**800-356-4898**	281-591-4000
GEFCO Inc (GEFCO) 2215 S Van Buren	Enid	OK	73703	**800-759-7441**	580-234-4141
Harbison-Fischer 901 N Crowley Rd	Crowley	TX	76036	**800-364-7867**	817-297-2211
M & M Supply Co 909 W Peach Ave PO Box 548	Duncan	OK	73534	**800-424-9300**	580-252-7879
Morris Industries Inc 777 Rt 23	Pompton Plains	NJ	07444	**800-835-0777**	973-835-6600
Morrison Bros Co 570 E Seventh St	Dubuque	IA	52001	**800-553-4840**	563-583-5701
Schramm Inc 800 E Virginia Ave	West Chester	PA	19380	**888-737-9438**	610-696-2500
ShawCor Ltd 25 Bethridge Rd *TSE: SCL/A*	Toronto	ON	M9W1M7	**855-744-5789**	416-743-7111
Southern Company Inc 3101 Carrier St	Memphis	TN	38116	**800-264-7626**	901-345-2531
Surface Equipment Corp 337 Cargill Rd	Kilgore	TX	75662	**800-256-7732**	903-984-0400
Tam International Inc 4620 Southerland Rd	Houston	TX	77092	**800-462-7617**	713-462-7617
Titan Specialties Inc 11785 Hwy 152 *Sales	Pampa	TX	79065	**800-692-4486***	806-665-3781
Weatherford International Inc 515 Post Oak Blvd Ste 600 *NYSE: WFT*	Houston	TX	77027	**866-398-0010**	713-693-4000
Winston F2S Corp 1604 Cherokee Trace	White Oak	TX	75693	**800-527-8465**	903-757-7341

537 OIL & GAS FIELD EXPLORATION SERVICES

				Toll-Free	Phone
Allied Oilfield Machine and Pump LLC 202 Hulon Moreland Rd	Levelland	TX	79336	**855-378-4787**	
Arctic Slope Regional Corp 1230 Agvik St PO Box 129	Barrow	AK	99723	**800-770-2772**	907-852-8633
Belvedere Terminals Inc 138 107th Ave Ste 313	Treasure Island	FL	33706	**800-716-8515**	
Bill Barrett Corp 1099 18th St Ste 2300 *NYSE: BBG*	Denver	CO	80202	**800-826-6762**	303-293-9100
Breitburn Energy Partners LP 515 S Flower St Ste 4800 *NASDAQ: BBEP*	Los Angeles	CA	90071	**800-732-0330**	213-225-5900
Chaparral Energy Inc 701 Cedar Lake Blvd	Oklahoma City	OK	73114	**866-478-8770**	405-478-8770
Dawson Geophysical Co 508 W Wall St Ste 800 *NASDAQ: DWSN*	Midland	TX	79701	**800-332-9766**	432-684-3000
Enbase LLC 3303 Louisiana St Ste 210	Houston	TX	77006	**888-400-2719**	
EOG Resources Inc 1111 Bagby Sky Lobby 2 *NYSE: EOG*	Houston	TX	77002	**877-363-3647**	713-651-7000
EXCO Resources Inc 12377 Merit Dr Ste 1700 *NYSE: XCO*	Dallas	TX	75251	**888-788-9449**	214-368-2084
Fidelity Exploration & Production Co 1801 California St Ste 2500	Denver	CO	80202	**800-986-3133**	303-893-3133
Intercept Energy Services Inc 11464 - 149 St	Edmonton	AB	T5M1W7	**877-975-0558**	
Jankovich Co, The Berth 74	San Pedro	CA	90731	**800-836-5355**	
Mustang Fuel Corp 9800 N Oklahoma Ave	Oklahoma City	OK	73114	**800-332-9400**	405-748-9400
New Jersey Natural Gas Co 1415 Wyckoff Rd	Wall	NJ	07719	**800-221-0051**	732-938-1480
Panhandle Royalty Co 5400 N Grand Blvd Grand Ctr Bldg Ste 300	Oklahoma City	OK	73112	**800-884-4225**	405-948-1560
Patterson-UTI Energy Inc 450 Gears Rd Ste 500 *NASDAQ: PTEN*	Houston	TX	77067	**866-387-1933**	281-765-7100
Power Service Products Inc PO Box 1089	Weatherford	TX	76086	**800-643-9089**	817-599-9486
Quicksilver Resources Inc 777 W Rosedale St Ste 300 *OTC: KWKAQ*	Fort Worth	TX	76104	**877-665-8600**	817-665-5000
Radius Professional HDD Tools 1614 N Main St	Weatherford	TX	76086	**800-892-9114**	
Superior Energy Services Inc 601 Poydras St Ste 2400 *NYSE: SPN*	New Orleans	LA	70130	**800-259-7774**	504-587-7374
Surepoint Technologies Group Inc 744 - 4th Ave SW Ste 1000	Calgary	AB	T2P3T4	**855-777-7873**	
TGC Industries Inc 101 E Pk Blvd Ste 955 *NASDAQ: TGE*	Plano	TX	75074	**800-223-7470**	972-881-1099
Veritas DGC Inc 10300 Townpark Dr	Houston	TX	77072	**800-028-1299**	832-351-8300
Walter Oil & Gas Corp 1100 Louisiana St Ste 200	Houston	TX	77002	**888-756-7880**	713-659-1221

538 OIL & GAS FIELD SERVICES

SEE ALSO Oil & Gas Field Exploration Services

				Toll-Free	Phone
Allamon Tool Company Inc 18935 Freeport Dr	Montgomery	TX	77356	**877-449-5433**	
Argus Machine Company Ltd 5820 97th St NW	Edmonton	AB	T6E3J1	**888-434-9451**	780-434-9451
Atlanta Petroleum Equipment Co 4732 N Royal Atlanta Dr	Tucker	GA	30084	**800-562-4060**	770-491-6644
B & R Eckel's Transport Ltd 5514B - 50 Ave	Bonnyville	AB	T9N2K8	**800-661-3290**	780-826-3889
Baker Hughes Inc (BHI) 2929 Allen Pkwy Ste 1200 *NYSE: BHI*	Houston	TX	77019	**800-229-7447**	713-439-8600
Calfrac Well Services Ltd 411 8 Ave SW	Calgary	AB	T2P1E3	**866-770-3722**	403-266-6000

Company / Address	City	State	Zip	Toll-Free	Phone
Camex Equipment Sales & Rental Inc 1806 Second St	Nisku	AB	T9E0W8	**877-955-2770**	780-955-2770
CarbonWrap Solutions LLC 2820 E Ft Lowell Rd	Tucson	AZ	85716	**866-380-1269**	520-292-3109
Central Industries Inc 11438 Cronridge Dr Ste W	Owings Mills	MD	21117	**800-304-8484**	
Colloid Environmental Technologies Co (CETCO) 2870 Forbs Ave	Hoffman Estates	IL	60192	**800-527-9948**	847-851-1899
Cps Building Company Ltd 4327 Red Bank Rd	Cincinnati	OH	45227	**877-295-9876**	513-271-9026
Dalmac Oilfield Services Inc 4934 - 89 St	Edmonton	AB	T6E5K1	**888-632-5622**	780-988-8510
Danos & Curole Marine Contractors Inc 13083 Louisiana 308	Larose	LA	70373	**800-487-5971**	985-693-3313
Diamond Services Corp 503 S DeGravelle Rd	Amelia	LA	70340	**800-879-1162**	985-631-2187
Dwfritz Automation Inc 12100 SW Tualatin Rd	Wilsonville	OR	97070	**800-763-4161**	503-598-9393
Fairweather LLC 9525 King St	Anchorage	AK	99515	**800-319-8802**	907-346-3247
FESCO Ltd 1000 Fesco Ave	Alice	TX	78332	**800-375-3479**	361-661-7000
GOTCO International Inc 11410 Spring Cypress Rd	Tomball	TX	77375	**800-683-7746**	281-376-3784
Gulf Offshore Logistics LLC 120 White Rose Dr	Raceland	LA	70394	**866-532-1060**	
Helix Energy Solutions Inc 400 N Sam Houston Pkwy E Ste 400 *NYSE: HLX*	Houston	TX	77060	**888-345-2347**	281-618-0400
Indel-Davis Inc 4401 S Jackson Ave	Tulsa	OK	74107	**800-331-6300**	918-587-2151
Koch Specialty Plant Services 12221 E Sam Houston Pkwy N	Houston	TX	77044	**800-765-9177**	713-427-7700
LaBarge Coating LLC 211 N Bdwy Ste 3050	Saint Louis	MO	63102	**866-992-4191**	314-646-3400
Leam Drilling Systems Inc 2027a Airport Rd	Conroe	TX	77301	**800-426-5349**	
Mansfield Oil Co 1025 Airport Pkwy SW	Gainesville	GA	30501	**800-695-6626**	
Matrix Service Co 5100 E Skelly Dr 74135 *NASDAQ: MTRX*	Tulsa	OK	74135	**866-367-6879**	
MGS Services LLC 18775 N Frederick Ave Ste E	Gaithersburg	MD	20879	**877-647-4255**	301-330-9793
Milbar Hydro-Test Inc 651 Aero Dr	Shreveport	LA	71107	**800-259-8210**	318-227-8210
NANA Regional Corporation Inc 1001 E Benson Blvd	Kotzebue	AK	99752	**800-478-3301**	907-442-3301
Newpark Mats & Integrated Services LLC 2700 Research Forest Dr Ste 100	The Woodlands	TX	77381	**877-628-7623**	281-362-6800
NOW Inc 7402 N Eldridge Pkwy	Houston	TX	77041	**800-228-2893**	281-823-4700
Oceaneering International Inc 11911 FM 529 *NYSE: OII*	Houston	TX	77041	**877-680-5478**	713-329-4500
Platinum Control Technologies Corp 2822 W Fifth St	Fort Worth	TX	76107	**877-374-1115**	817-529-6485
Pride International Inc 5847 San Felipe St Ste 3300	Houston	TX	77057	**877-736-3772**	713-789-1400
Production Management Industries LLC 9761 Hwy 90 E	Morgan City	LA	70380	**888-229-3837**	985-631-3837
Questor Technology Inc 1121 940 - Sixth Ave SW	Calgary	AB	T2P3T1	**844-477-8669**	403-571-1530
Rig-Chem Inc 132 Thompson Rd	Houma	LA	70363	**800-375-7208**	985-873-7208
Schlumberger Wireline & Testing 210 Schlumberger Dr	Sugar Land	TX	77478	**800-272-7328**	281-285-4551
Shaw Pipeline Services Inc 4250 N Sam Houston Pkwy E Ste 180	Houston	TX	77032	**866-912-5314**	832-601-0850
Sound & Cellular Inc 824 W Yellowstone Hwy	Casper	WY	82601	**800-689-7256**	307-234-7256
Supreme Oil Co 2109 W Monte Vista Rd	Phoenix	AZ	85009	**800-752-7888**	
Team Inc 200 Hermann Dr *NYSE: TISI*	Alvin	TX	77511	**800-662-8326**	281-331-6154
Terroco Industries Ltd Site 14 RR Ste 1 Box 10	Red Deer	AB	T4N5E1	**800-670-1100**	403-346-1171
TK Stanley Inc 6739 Hwy 184	Waynesboro	MS	39367	**800-477-2855**	
Trican Well Service Ltd 645 Seventh Ave SW Ste 2900 *TSE: TCW*	Calgary	AB	T2P4G8	**877-473-2008**	403-266-0202
Valiant Corp 6555 Hawthorne Dr	Windsor	ON	N8T3G6	**888-825-4268**	519-974-5200

539 OIL & GAS WELL DRILLING

Company / Address	City	State	Zip	Toll-Free	Phone
Callon Petroleum Co 200 N Canal St *NYSE: CPE*	Natchez	MS	39120	**800-451-1294**	601-442-1601
Cyclone Drilling Inc PO Box 908	Gillette	WY	82717	**800-318-3724**	307-682-4161
Diamond Offshore Drilling Inc 15415 Katy Fwy *NYSE: DO*	Houston	TX	77094	**800-848-1980**	281-492-5300
Doyon Drilling Inc 11500 C St Ste 200	Anchorage	AK	99515	**800-478-9675**	907-563-5530
GEO Drilling Fluids Inc 1431 Union Ave	Bakersfield	CA	93305	**800-438-7436**	661-325-5919
Helmerich & Payne Inc 1437 S Boulder Ave *NYSE: HP*	Tulsa	OK	74119	**800-205-4913**	918-742-5531
Hercules Offshore Inc 9 Greenway Plaza Ste 2200 *NASDAQ: HERO*	Houston	TX	77046	**888-647-1715**	713-350-5100
Iron Horse Energy Services Inc 1901 Dirkson Dr NE	Redcliff	AB	T0J2P0	**877-526-4666**	403-526-4600
Justiss Oil Company Inc 1120 E Oak St	Jena	LA	71342	**800-256-2501**	318-992-4111
Kicking Horse Energy Inc 1520-700 6 Ave SW	Calgary	AB	T2P0T8	**877-672-2121**	403-234-8663
Maverick Directional Services 25615 Oakhurst Dr	Spring	TX	77386	**866-459-0233**	281-364-1212
McClelland Oilfield Rentals Limited Patnership 8720-110 St	Grande Prairie	AB	T8V8K1	**866-539-3656**	780-539-3656
Nabors Drilling International Ltd 515 W Greens Rd Ste 1000	Houston	TX	77067	**877-344-7529**	281-874-0035
Noble Corp 13135 S Dairy Ashford Rd Ste 800 *NYSE: NE*	Sugar Land	TX	77478	**877-285-4162**	281-276-6100
Parker Drilling Co 1401 Enclave Pkwy Ste 600 *NYSE: PKD*	Houston	TX	77077	**800-468-9716**	281-406-2000
Patterson-UTI Energy Inc 450 Gears Rd Ste 500 *NASDAQ: PTEN*	Houston	TX	77067	**866-387-1933**	281-765-7100
Scientific Drilling Controls Inc 16701 Greenspoint Pk Dr Ste 200	Houston	TX	77060	**800-514-8949**	281-443-3300
Total Energy Services Ltd 2550 300-5th Ave SW Ste 2550 *NYSE: TOT*	Calgary	AB	T2P3C4	**877-818-6825**	403-216-3939
Transocean Inc 4 Greenway Plaza *NYSE: RIG*	Houston	TX	77046	**877-440-0173**	713-232-7500
U.S. Energy Development Corp 2350 N Forest Rd	Getzville	NY	14068	**800-636-7606**	716-636-0401
Unit Corp 7130 S Lewis Ave Ste 1000 *NYSE: UNT*	Tulsa	OK	74136	**800-722-3612**	918-493-7700
Vermilion Energy Trust 3500 520 Third Ave SW *TSE: VET*	Calgary	AB	T2P0R3	**866-895-8101**	403-269-4884
Xtreme Drilling & Coil Services Corp 9805 Katy Freeway Ste 650	Houston	TX	77024	**800-564-6253**	403-262-9500

540 OILS & GREASES - LUBRICATING

SEE ALSO Chemicals - Specialty ; Petroleum Refineries

Company / Address	City	State	Zip	Toll-Free	Phone
American Lubrication Equipment Corp 11212A McCormick Rd PO Box 1350	Hunt Valley	MD	21030	**888-252-9300**	
Amsoil Inc 925 Tower Ave *Sales	Superior	WI	54880	**800-777-7094***	715-392-7101
Anderol Inc 215 Merry Ln	East Hanover	NJ	07936	**888-263-3765**	973-887-7410
Axel Plastics Research Laboratories Inc 5820 Broadway	Woodside	NY	11377	**800-332-2935**	718-672-8300
BG Products Inc 740 S Wichita St	Wichita	KS	67213	**800-961-6228**	316-265-2686
BP Lubricants USA Inc 1500 Valley Rd	Wayne	NJ	07470	**800-333-3991**	973-633-2200
Canada Forgings Inc 130 Hagar St	Welland	ON	L3B5P8	**800-263-0440**	905-735-1220
Castrol Industrial North America Inc 150 W Warrenville Rd	Naperville	IL	60563	**877-641-1600**	
Chem-Trend LP 1445 McPherson Pk Dr	Howell	MI	48843	**800-727-7730**	517-546-4520
CRC Industries Inc 885 Louis Dr *Cust Svc	Warminster	PA	18974	**800-556-5074***	215-674-4300
D-A Lubricant Co 1340 W 29th St	Indianapolis	IN	46208	**800-645-5823**	317-923-5321
Elco Corp 1000 Belt Line St	Cleveland	OH	44109	**800-321-0467**	216-749-2605
Fiske Bros Refining Co 129 Lockwood St	Newark	NJ	07105	**800-733-4755**	973-589-9150
Hangsterfer's Laboratories Inc 175 Ogden Rd	Mantua	NJ	08051	**800-433-5823**	856-468-0216
Hercules Chemical Company Inc 111 S St	Passaic	NJ	07055	**800-221-9330**	973-778-5000
Houghton International Inc 945 Madison Ave PO Box 930	Valley Forge	PA	19482	**888-459-9844**	610-666-4000
Hydrotex Inc 12920 Senlac D Ste 190	Farmers Branch	TX	75234	**800-527-9439**	
ITW Rocol North America 3650 W Lake Ave	Glenview	IL	60026	**800-452-5823**	847-657-5278
Jackson Oil & Solvents Inc 1970 Kentucky Ave	Indianapolis	IN	46221	**800-221-4603**	317-636-4421
Jet-Lube Inc 4849 Homestead Rd Ste 232	Houston	TX	77226	**800-538-5823**	713-670-5700
Kluber Lubrication North America LP 32 Industrial Dr	Londonderry	NH	03053	**800-447-2238**	603-647-4104
Leadership Performance Sustainability Laboratories 4647 Hugh Howell Rd	Tucker	GA	30084	**800-241-8334**	
Lubrication Engineers Inc 300 Bailey Ave	Fort Worth	TX	76107	**800-537-7683**	817-834-6321
Lubrication Technologies Inc 900 Mendelssohn Ave N	Golden Valley	MN	55427	**800-328-5573**	763-545-0707
Lubrizol Corp 29400 Lakeland Blvd *NYSE: LZ*	Wickliffe	OH	44092	**800-380-5397**	440-943-4200
Metalworking Lubricants Co 25 Silverdome Industrial Park	Pontiac	MI	48342	**800-394-5494**	248-332-3500
Northtown Products Inc 5202 Argosy Ave	Huntington Beach	CA	92649	**800-972-7274**	714-897-0700
Oil Ctr Research LLC 106 Montrose Ave	Lafayette	LA	70503	**800-256-8977**	337-993-3559
Orelube Corp, The 20 Sawgrass Dr	Bellport	NY	11713	**800-645-9124**	631-205-9700
Perkins Oil Company Inc 4707 Pflaum Rd	Madison	WI	53718	**800-634-9937**	608-221-4736
Primrose Oil Company Inc 11444 Denton Dr	Dallas	TX	75229	**800-275-2772**	972-241-1100

Company	Address	City	State	Zip	Toll-Free	Phone
Schaeffer Mfg Company Inc	102 Barton St	Saint Louis	MO	63104	**800-325-9962***	314-865-4100
	*Cust Svc					
Schultz Lubricants Inc	164 Shrewsbury St	West Boylston	MA	01583	**800-262-3962**	508-835-4446
Shell Lubricants	1000 Main 12th Fl	Houston	TX	77002	**888-743-5586***	713-241-6161
	*Cust Svc					
Smitty's Supply Inc	63399 Hwy 51 N PO Box 530	Roseland	LA	70456	**800-256-7575**	985-748-9687
Southwestern Petroleum Corp	PO Box 961005	Fort Worth	TX	76161	**800-877-9372**	817-332-2336
Sun Drilling Products Corp	503 Main St	Belle Chasse	LA	70037	**800-962-6490**	504-393-2778
Texas Refinery Corp	840 N Main St	Fort Worth	TX	76164	**800-827-0711**	817-332-1161
Total Lubricants USA	5 N Stiles St	Linden	NJ	07036	**800-323-3198**	908-862-9300
Valvoline Co	3499 Blazer Pkwy PO Box 14000	Lexington	KY	40512	**800-832-6825**	859-357-7777
WD-40 Co	1061 Cudahy Pl	San Diego	CA	92110	**800-448-9340**	619-275-1400
	NASDAQ: WDFC					

541 OPHTHALMIC GOODS

SEE ALSO Personal Protective Equipment & Clothing

Company	Address	City	State	Zip	Toll-Free	Phone
Aearo Co	5457 W 79th St	Indianapolis	IN	46268	**877-327-4332**	317-692-6666
Art-Craft Optical Company Inc	57 Goodway Dr S	Rochester	NY	14623	**800-828-8288**	585-546-6640
Bausch & Lomb Inc	1400 N Goodman St	Rochester	NY	14609	**800-553-5340**	585-338-6000
Beitler-Mckee Optical Co	160 S 22nd St	Pittsburgh	PA	15203	**800-989-4700**	412-481-4700
Bolle Inc	9200 Cody St	Overland Park	KS	66214	**800-423-3537**	913-752-3400
CIBA Vision Corp	11460 Johns Creek Pkwy	Duluth	GA	30097	**800-875-3001**	678-415-3937
Conforma Laboratories Inc	4705 Colley Ave	Norfolk	VA	23508	**800-426-1700**	757-321-0200
Cooper Cos Inc	6140 Stoneridge Mall Rd Ste 590	Pleasanton	CA	94588	**888-822-2660**	925-460-3600
	NYSE: COO					
CooperVision Inc	209 High Point Dr Ste 200	Victor	NY	14564	**800-538-7850**	585-385-6810
Costa Del Mar	2361 Mason Ave Ste 100	Daytona Beach	FL	32117	**800-447-3700**	386-274-4000
DAC Vision	3630 W Miller Ste 350	Garland	TX	75041	**800-800-1550**	972-677-2700
Eye-Kraft Optical Inc	8 McLeland Rd	Saint Cloud	MN	56303	**888-455-2022**	
Gargoyles Inc	500 George Washington Hwy	Smithfield	RI	02917	**866-807-0195**	401-231-3800
Gentex Optics Inc	324 Main St	Simpson	PA	18407	**800-736-0554**	570-282-3550
Homer Optical Company Inc	2401 Linden Ln	Silver Spring	MD	20910	**800-627-2710**	301-585-9060
Icare Industries Inc	4399 35th St N	Saint Petersburg	FL	33714	**877-422-7352**	727-526-0501
IcareLabs	4399 35th St N	Saint Petersburg	FL	33714	**877-422-7352**	
Johnson & Johnson Vision Care Inc	7500 Centurion Pkwy	Jacksonville	FL	32256	**800-843-2020**	800-874-5278
LBI Eyewear	20801 Nordhoff St	Chatsworth	CA	91311	**800-423-5175***	818-407-1890
	*Cust Svc					
Maui Jim Inc	721 Wainee St	Lahaina	HI	96761	**888-352-2001**	808-661-8841
Night Optics USA Inc	15182 Triton Ln Ste 101	Huntington Beach	CA	92649	**800-306-4448**	714-899-4475
Oakley Inc	1 Icon	Foothill Ranch	CA	92610	**800-403-7449***	949-951-0991
	*Cust Svc					
Serengeti Eyewear Inc	9200 Cody St	Overland Park	KS	66214	**800-423-3537***	913-752-3400
	*Cust Svc					
Sigma Corp of America	15 Fleetwood Ct	Ronkonkoma	NY	11779	**800-896-6858**	631-585-1144
Signature Eyewear Inc	498 N Oak St	Inglewood	CA	90302	**800-765-3937**	310-330-2700
	OTC: SEYE					
STAAR Surgical Co	1911 Walker Ave	Monrovia	CA	91016	**800-352-7842**	626-303-7902
	NASDAQ: STAA					
Transitions Optical Inc	9251 Belcher Rd	Pinellas Park	FL	33782	**800-533-2081**	727-545-0400
US Vision Inc	1 Harmon Dr Glen Oaks Industrial Pk	Glendora	NJ	08029	**866-435-7111**	856-228-1000
Vision-Ease Lens Inc	7000 Sunwood Dr NW	Ramsey	MN	55303	**800-328-3449***	320-251-8140
	*Cust Svc					
Walman Optical Company Inc	801 12th Ave N	Minneapolis	MN	55411	**800-873-9256**	612-520-6000
X-Cel Optical Company Inc	806 S Benton Dr	Sauk Rapids	MN	56379	**800-747-9235***	320-251-8404
	*General					
Younger Optics	2925 California St	Torrance	CA	90503	**800-366-5367**	310-783-1533

542 OPTICAL GOODS STORES

Company	Address	City	State	Zip	Toll-Free	Phone
Art Partners LLC	284 S Sharon Amity Rd	Charlotte	NC	28211	**888-472-6866**	
Barnett & Ramel Optical Co	7154 N 16th St	Omaha	NE	68112	**800-228-9732**	
Cliff Weil Inc	8043 Industrial Pk Rd	Mechanicsville	VA	23116	**800-446-9345**	804-746-1321
Empire Vision Centers	2921 Erie Blvd E	Syracuse	NY	13224	**877-959-4160**	315-446-5120
Eye Glass World Inc	2435 Commerce Ave Bldg 2200	Duluth	GA	30096	**800-637-3597**	
Eye-Mart Express Inc	13800 Senlac Dr Ste 200	Farmers Branch	TX	75234	**888-372-2763**	972-488-2002
For Eyes/Insight Optical	285 W 74th Pl	Hialeah	FL	33014	**877-688-9891**	305-557-9004
General Vision Services LLC	520 Eigth Ave 9th Fl	New York	NY	10018	**855-653-0586**	212-729-5300
Henry Ford OptimEyes	655 W 13-Mile Rd	Madison Heights	MI	48071	**800-393-2273**	248-588-9300
JAK Enterprises Inc	8309 N Knoxville Ave	Peoria	IL	61615	**800-752-3295**	309-692-8222
JC Penney Optical Co	821 N Central Expressway	Plano	TX	75075	**866-435-7111**	972-516-1393
LensCrafters Inc	4000 Luxottica Pl	Mason	OH	45040	**877-753-6727**	513-765-4321
Magnifying Ctr	10086 W McNab Rd	Tamarac	FL	33321	**800-364-1612**	954-722-1580
National Vision Inc	296 Grayson Hwy	Lawrenceville	GA	30045	**800-637-3597***	770-822-3600
	*Cust Svc					
Native Eyewear Inc	1444 Wazee St Ste 215	Denver	CO	80202	**888-776-2848**	
Omni Optical Lab	3255 Executive Blvd Ste 100	Beaumont	TX	77705	**800-364-6664**	
Opti Care Eye Health Center	87 Grandview Ave	Waterbury	CT	06708	**800-334-3937**	203-574-2020
Optical Distributor Group LLC	12301 NW 39th St	Coral Springs	FL	33065	**800-852-8089**	914-347-7400
Rite-Style Optical Co	12240 Emmet St	Omaha	NE	68164	**800-373-3200**	612-520-6058
Rx Optical	1700 S Pk St	Kalamazoo	MI	49001	**800-792-2737**	269-342-0003
Sterling Optical	520 Eigth Ave 23rd Fl	New York	NY	10018	**800-393-7789**	516-390-2117
SVS Vision	140 Macomb Pl	Mount Clemens	MI	48043	**800-787-4600**	586-468-7612
Tryiton Eyewear LLC	147 Post Rd E	Westport	CT	06880	**888-896-3885**	203-544-0770
Union Eyecare Centers	4750 Beidler Rd	Willoughby	OH	44094	**800-443-9699**	216-986-9700
US Vision Inc	1 Harmon Dr Glen Oaks Industrial Pk	Glendora	NJ	08029	**866-435-7111**	856-228-1000
Visionworks of America Inc	175 E Houston St	San Antonio	TX	78205	**800-669-1183**	210-340-3531
Vistar Eye Center Inc	707 S Jefferson St	Roanoke	VA	24016	**866-615-5454**	540-855-5100
Vogue Optical Inc	20 Great George St	Charlottetown	PE	C1A4J6	**866-594-3937**	902-566-3326

543 OPTICAL INSTRUMENTS & LENSES

SEE ALSO Laboratory Analytical Instruments

Company	Address	City	State	Zip	Toll-Free	Phone
Allergan Inc	2525 Dupont Dr	Irvine	CA	92612	**800-347-4500**	714-246-4500
	NYSE: AGN					
American Polarizers Inc	141 S Seventh St	Reading	PA	19602	**800-736-9031**	610-373-5177
American Technology Network Corp	1341 San Mateo Ave	South San Francisco	CA	94080	**800-910-2862**	650-875-0130
Applied Fiber Inc	PO Box 1339	Leesburg	GA	31763	**800-226-5394**	229-759-8301
B E Meyers & Co Inc	9461 Willows Rd NE	Redmond	WA	98052	**800-327-5648**	425-881-6648
Burris Company Inc	331 E Eigth St	Greeley	CO	80631	**888-228-7747**	970-356-1670
Bushnell Corp	9200 Cody St	Overland Park	KS	66214	**800-423-3537**	913-752-3400
ChromaGen Vision LLC	326 W Cedar St Ste 1	Kennett Square	PA	19348	**855-473-2323**	
Conoptics International Sales Corp	19 Eagle Rd	Danbury	CT	06810	**800-748-3349**	203-743-3349
CST/Berger Corp	255 W Fleming St	Watseka	IL	60970	**800-435-1859**	815-432-5237
Deltronic Corp	3900 W Segerstrom Ave	Santa Ana	CA	92704	**800-451-6922**	714-545-5800
Edmund Optics Inc	101 E Gloucester Pk	Barrington	NJ	08007	**800-363-1992**	856-547-3488
Epilog Corp	16371 Table Mtn Pkwy	Golden	CO	80403	**888-437-4564**	303-277-1188
Fosta-Tek Optics Inc	320 Hamilton St	Leominster	MA	01453	**866-221-9157**	978-534-6511
G-S Supplies	408 St Paul St	Rochester	NY	14605	**800-295-3050**	585-295-0250
Gould Technology LLC	1121 Benfield Blvd Stes J-P	Millersville	MD	21108	**800-544-6853**	410-987-5600
ITT Night Vision & Imaging	7635 Plantation Rd	Roanoke	VA	24019	**800-448-8678**	540-563-0371
Kollmorgen Corp Electro-Optical Div	50 Prince St	NorthHampton	MA	01060	**877-282-1168**	413-586-2330
LaserMax Corp	3495 Winton Pl	Rochester	NY	14623	**800-527-3703**	585-272-5420
Lyric Optical Company Wholsle	3533 Cardiff Ave	Cincinnati	OH	45209	**800-543-7376**	513-321-2456
Meade Instruments Corp	27 Hubble	Irvine	CA	92618	**800-626-3233**	949-451-1450
	NASDAQ: MEAD					
Mirrotek International LLC	90 Dayton Ave	Passaic	NJ	07055	**888-659-3030**	973-472-1400
Newport Corp	1791 Deere Ave	Irvine	CA	92606	**800-222-6440***	949-863-3144
	NASDAQ: NEWP ■ *Sales					
Optical Gaging Products Inc	850 Hudson Ave	Rochester	NY	14621	**800-647-4243**	585-544-0450

Company / Address	City	State	Zip	Toll-Free	Phone
Parker Hannifin Corp Daedal Div 1140 Sandy Hill Rd	Irwin	PA	15642	**800-245-6903**	724-861-8200
Photon Technology International Inc 300 Birmingham Rd PO Box 272	Birmingham	NJ	08011	**877-784-4349**	609-894-4420
ProPhotonix Inc 32 Hampshire Rd *OTC: STKR*	Salem	NH	03079	**877-941-8631**	603-893-8778
Ross Optical Industries Inc 1410 Gail Borden Pl	El Paso	TX	79935	**800-880-5417**	915-595-5417
Seiler Instrument & Mfg Company Inc 3433 Tree Court Industrial Blvd	Saint Louis	MO	63122	**800-489-2282**	314-968-2282
SheerVision Inc(NDA) 4030 Palos Verdes Dr N Ste 104	Rolling Hills Estates	CA	90274	**877-678-4274**	310-265-8918
Sorenson Media Inc 13961 Minuteman Dr Ste 100	Draper	UT	84020	**888-767-3676**	801-501-8650
Stevens Water Monitoring Systems 12067 NE Glenn Widing Dr Ste 106	Portland	OR	97220	**800-452-5272**	503-469-8000
Veeco Instruments Inc 1 Terminal Dr *NASDAQ: VECO*	Plainview	NY	11803	**888-724-9511**	516-677-0200
Western Ophthalmics Corp 19019 36th Ave W Ste G	Lynnwood	WA	98036	**800-426-9938**	425-672-9332
Zygo Corp Laurel Brook Rd *NASDAQ: ZIGO*	Middlefield	CT	06455	**800-994-6669**	860-347-8506

544 ORGAN & TISSUE BANKS

SEE ALSO Eye Banks

Company / Address	City	State	Zip	Toll-Free	Phone
Alamo Tissue Service Ltd 5844 Rocky Point Dr	San Antonio	TX	78249	**800-226-9091**	210-738-2663
AlloSource 6278 S Troy Cir	Centennial	CO	80111	**888-873-8330**	720-873-0213
Bio-Tissue 7000 SW 97th Ave Ste 211	Miami	FL	33173	**888-296-8858**	305-412-4430
Bone Bank Allografts 4808 Research Dr *Sales	San Antonio	TX	78240	**800-397-0088***	210-696-7616
California Cryobank Inc 11915 La Grange Ave	Los Angeles	CA	90025	**866-927-9622**	310-443-5244
Community Tissue Services 3573 Bristol Pike Ste 201	Bensalem	PA	19020	**800-684-7783**	215-245-4506
Comprehensive Tissue Ctr 11402 University Ave Rm 7415	Edmonton	AB	T6G2J3	**866-407-1970**	780-407-7510
Cryobiology Inc 4830D Knightsbridge Blvd	Columbus	OH	43214	**800-359-4375**	614-451-4375
Cryogenic Laboratories Inc 1944 Lexington Ave N	Roseville	MN	55113	**800-466-2796**	651-489-8000
Donor Alliance Inc 720 S Colorado Blvd Ste 800-N	Denver	CO	80246	**888-868-4747**	303-329-4747
Donor Network West 12667 Alcosta Blvd Ste 600	Oakland	CA	94607	**888-570-9400**	925-480-3101
Gift of Hope Organ & Tissue Donor Network 425 Spring Lake Dr	Itasca	IL	60143	**877-577-3747**	630-758-2600
Gift of Life Donor Program 401 N Third St	Philadelphia	PA	19123	**800-543-6391**	215-557-8090
Indiana Donor Network 3760 Guion Rd	Indianapolis	IN	46222	**888-275-4676**	317-685-0389
Kentucky Organ Donor Affiliates (KODA) 10160 Linn Station Rd	Louisville	KY	40223	**800-525-3456**	502-581-9511
LifeBanc 4775 Richmond Rd	Cleveland	OH	44128	**888-558-5433**	216-752-5433
LifeCell Corp 1 Millennium Way	Branchburg	NJ	08876	**800-226-2714**	
Lifeline of Ohio 770 Kinnear Rd Ste 200	Columbus	OH	43212	**800-525-5667**	614-291-5667
LifeLink Tissue Bank 8510 Sunstate St	Tampa	FL	33634	**800-683-2400**	813-886-8111
LifeNet 1864 Concert Dr	Virginia Beach	VA	23453	**800-847-7831**	757-464-4761
LifeNet Health Northwest 501 SW 39th St	Renton	WA	98057	**800-858-2282**	425-981-8900
LifeShare Transplant Donor Services of Oklahoma 4705 NW Expy	Oklahoma City	OK	73132	**888-580-5680**	405-840-5551
Lifesharing Community Organ & Tissue Donation 3465 Camino del Rio S Ste 410	San Diego	CA	92108	**866-797-2366**	619-521-1983
Louisiana Organ Procurement Agency (LOPA) 3545 N I-10 Service Rd Ste 300	Metairie	LA	70002	**800-521-4483**	
Mid-America Transplant Services (MTS) 1110 Highlands Plz Dr E Ste 100	Saint Louis	MO	63110	**888-376-4854**	314-735-8200
Musculoskeletal Transplant Foundation 125 May St Ste 300	Edison	NJ	08837	**800-946-9008**	732-661-0202
Nevada Donor Network Inc 2061 E Sahara Ave	Las Vegas	NV	89104	**855-683-6667**	702-796-9600
New England Organ Bank 60 First Ave	Waltham	MA	02451	**800-446-6362**	617-244-8000
New York Cryo 900 Northern Blvd Ste 230	Great Neck	NY	11021	**877-769-2796**	516-487-2700
OneLegacy Transplant Donor Network 221 S Figueroa St Ste 500	Los Angeles	CA	90012	**800-786-4077**	213-229-5600
Regional Tissue Bank QEII Health Sciences Centre 5788 University Ave Rm 431 MacKenzie Bldg	Halifax	NS	B3H1V7	**800-314-6515**	902-473-4171
Rocky Mountain Tissue Bank 2993 S Peoria St Ste 390	Aurora	CO	80014	**800-424-5169**	303-337-3330
ScienceCare Inc 21410 N 19th Ave Ste 126	Phoenix	AZ	85027	**800-417-3747**	602-331-3641
Sierra Donor Services 1760 Creekside Oak Dr Ste 220	Sacramento	CA	95833	**877-401-2546**	916-567-1600
South Texas Blood & Tissue Ctr 6211 IH-10 W	San Antonio	TX	78201	**800-292-5534**	210-731-5555
Southeast Tissue Alliance (SETA) 6241 NW 23rd St Ste 400	Gainesville	FL	32653	**866-432-1164**	352-248-2114
Wright Medical Technology Inc 5677 Airline Rd	Arlington	TN	38002	**800-238-7188**	901-867-9971

545 PACKAGE DELIVERY SERVICES

Company / Address	City	State	Zip	Toll-Free	Phone
Crosscountry Courier Inc PO Box 4030	Bismarck	ND	58502	**800-521-0287**	701-222-8498
DHL Global Mail 2700 S Commerce Pkwy Ste 400	Weston	FL	33331	**800-805-9306**	954-903-6300
Dynamex Inc 5429 LBJ Fwy Ste 1000 *Cust Svc	Dallas	TX	75240	**888-478-1660***	214-560-9000
Federal Express Europe Inc 3610 Hacks Cross Rd	Memphis	TN	38125	**800-463-3339**	901-369-3600
FedEx Custom Critical Inc 1475 Boettler Rd *Cust Svc	Uniontown	OH	44685	**800-463-3339***	234-310-4090
Hot Shot Delivery Inc 747 N Shepherd Dr Ste 100 PO Box 701189	Houston	TX	77007	**866-261-3184**	713-869-5525
Network Global Logistics (NGL) 320 Interlocken Pkwy Ste 100	Broomfield	CO	80021	**866-938-1870**	
One Source Industries LLC 185 Technology Dr	Irvine	CA	92618	**800-899-4990**	
Priority Express Courier 5 Chelsea Pkwy	Boothwyn	PA	19061	**800-526-4646**	610-364-3300
Purolator Inc 5995 Avebury Rd	Mississauga	ON	L5R3T8	**888-744-7123**	905-712-8101
Unishippers Assn Inc 746 E Winchester Ste 200	Salt Lake City	UT	84107	**800-999-8721**	
United Parcel Service Inc (UPS) 55 Glenlake Pkwy NE *NYSE: UPS* ■ *Cust Svc	Atlanta	GA	30328	**800-742-5877***	404-828-6000
Washington Express Service LLC 12240 Indian Creek Ct Ste 100	Beltsville	MD	20705	**800-939-5463**	301-210-0899
World Courier Inc 1313 Fourth Ave	New Hyde Park	NY	11040	**800-221-6600**	516-354-2600
Worldwide Express 2602 McKinney Ave Ste 400	Dallas	TX	75204	**800-758-7447**	214-720-2400
WPX Delivery Solutions 3320 W Valley Hwy N Ste 111	Auburn	WA	98001	**800-562-1091**	253-876-2760

546 PACKAGING MACHINERY & EQUIPMENT

Company / Address	City	State	Zip	Toll-Free	Phone
A-B-C Packaging Machine Corp 811 Live Oak St	Tarpon Springs	FL	34689	**800-237-5975**	727-937-5144
AMS Filling Systems 2500 Chestnut Tree Rd	Honey Brook	PA	19344	**800-647-5390**	610-942-4200
ARPAC Group 9511 W River St	Schiller Park	IL	60176	**800-496-7210**	847-678-9034
Automated Packaging Systems Inc 10175 Phillip Pkwy *Sales	Streetsboro	OH	44241	**800-527-0733***	330-528-2000
B & H Manufacturing Co 3461 Roeding Rd	Ceres	CA	95307	**888-643-0444**	209-556-6160
Barry-Wehmiller Cos Inc 8020 Forsyth Blvd	Saint Louis	MO	63105	**800-862-8020**	314-862-8000
Barry-Wehmiller Cos Inc Accraply Div 3580 Holly Ln N	Plymouth	MN	55447	**800-328-3997**	763-557-1313
Belco Packaging Systems Inc 910 S Mountain Ave	Monrovia	CA	91016	**800-833-1833**	626-357-9566
Brenton LLC 4750 County Rd 13 NE	Alexandria	MN	56308	**800-535-2730**	320-852-7705
Campbell Wrapper Corp 1415 Fortune Ave	De Pere	WI	54115	**800-727-4210**	920-983-7100
Data Technology Inc 14225 Dayton Cir Ste 4 *General	Omaha	NE	68137	**888-334-9300***	402-891-0711
Delkor Systems Inc 8700 Rendova St NE	Circle Pines	MN	55014	**800-328-5558**	763-783-0855
Dynaric Inc 5740 Bayside Rd	Virginia Beach	VA	23455	**800-526-0827**	
E-pak Machinery Inc 1535 S State Rd 39	La Porte	IN	46350	**800-328-0466**	219-393-5541
Flexicon Corp 2400 Emrick Blvd	Bethlehem	PA	18020	**888-353-9426**	610-814-2400
Hartness International Inc 1200 Garlington Rd PO Box 26509	Greenville	SC	29616	**800-845-8791**	864-297-1200
Heat Seal LLC 4580 E 71st St	Cleveland	OH	44125	**800-342-6329**	216-341-2022
Kirk Rudy Inc 125 Lorraine Pkwy	Woodstock	GA	30188	**800-897-1910**	770-427-4203
Krones Inc 9600 S 58th St PO Box 321801	Franklin	WI	53132	**800-752-3787**	414-409-4000
Lantech Inc 11000 Bluegrass Pkwy	Louisville	KY	40299	**800-866-0322**	502-815-9109
Loveshaw Corp 2206 Easton Tpke *Cust Svc	South Canaan	PA	18459	**800-747-1586***	570-937-4921
Mooney General Paper Co 1451 Chestnut Ave PO Box 3800	Hillside	NJ	07205	**800-882-8846**	973-926-3800
MTS Medication Technologies Inc 2003 Gandy Blvd N Ste 800 *General	Saint Petersburg	FL	33702	**800-845-0053***	
National Instrument LLC 4119 Fordleigh Rd	Baltimore	MD	21215	**866-258-1914**	410-764-0900
New Jersey Machine Inc 56 Etna Rd *Sales	Lebanon	NH	03766	**800-432-2990***	603-448-0300
New Way Packaging Machinery Inc 210 Blettner Ave	Hanover	PA	17331	**844-801-3711**	717-637-2133
Ossid Corp 4000 College Rd	Battleboro	NC	27809	**800-334-8369**	252-446-6177
Packaging Systems International Inc 4990 Acoma St	Denver	CO	80216	**800-525-6110**	303-296-4445

Company	Address	City	State	ZIP	Toll-Free	Phone
Pearson Packaging Systems	8120 W Sunset Hwy	Spokane	WA	99224	**800-732-7766**	509-838-6226
Quadrel Labeling Systems	7670 Jenther Dr	Mentor	OH	44060	**800-321-8509**	440-602-4700
Rollstock Inc	5720 Brighton Ave	Kansas City	MO	64130	**800-295-2949**	616-570-0430
Shibuya Hoppmann Corp	13129 Airpark Dr Ste 120 *Cust Svc	Elkwood	VA	22718	**800-368-3582***	540-829-2564
Standard Knapp Inc	63 Pickering St *Cust Svc	Portland	CT	06480	**800-628-9565***	860-342-1100
SWF Cos	1949 E Manning Ave	Reedley	CA	93654	**800-344-8951**	559-638-8484
Thiele Technologies	315 27th Ave NE	Minneapolis	MN	55418	**800-932-3647**	612-782-1200
Triangle Package Machinery Co	6655 W Diversey Ave	Chicago	IL	60707	**800-621-4170**	773-889-0200
Universal Labeling Systems Inc	3501 Eigth Ave S	Saint Petersburg	FL	33711	**877-236-0266**	727-327-2123
US Digital Media Inc	1929 W Lone Cactus Dr	Phoenix	AZ	85027	**877-992-3766**	623-587-4900
Wulftec International Inc	209 Wulftec St	Ayer's Cliff	QC	J0B1C0	**877-985-3832**	819-838-4232

547 PACKAGING MATERIALS & PRODUCTS - PAPER OR PLASTICS

SEE ALSO Paper Converters ; Plastics Foam Products ; Coated & Laminated Paper ; Bags - Paper ; Bags - Plastics ; Blister Packaging

Company	Address	City	State	ZIP	Toll-Free	Phone
Acme Paper & Supply Company Inc	8229 Sandy Ct PO Box 422	Savage	MD	20763	**800-462-5812**	410-792-2333
Adhesive Packaging Specialties Inc	PO Box 31	Peabody	MA	01960	**800-222-1117**	978-531-3300
Admiral Packaging Inc	10 Admiral St	Providence	RI	02908	**800-556-6454**	401-274-7000
Advance Bag & Packaging Technologies	5720 Williams Lk Rd	Waterford	MI	48329	**800-475-2247**	248-674-3126
Alliance Rubber Co	210 Carpenter Dam Rd	Hot Springs	AR	71901	**800-626-5940**	
American Packaging Corp	777 Driving Pk Ave	Rochester	NY	14613	**800-551-8801**	585-254-9500
American Packaging Corp Extrusion Div	777 Driving Pk Ave	Rochester	NY	14613	**800-551-8801**	585-254-9500
Apco Extruders Inc	180 National Rd *Orders	Edison	NJ	08817	**800-942-8725***	732-287-3000
Automated Packaging Systems Inc	10175 Phillip Pkwy *Sales	Streetsboro	OH	44241	**800-527-0733***	330-528-2000
BagcraftPapercon	3900 W 43rd St	Chicago	IL	60632	**800-621-8468**	773-254-8000
Bedford Industries Inc	1659 Rowe Ave *Cust Svc	Worthington	MN	56187	**877-233-3673***	507-376-4136
Bemis Co Inc Bemis Clysar Div	2451 Badger Ave	Oshkosh	WI	54903	**888-425-9727**	920-303-7800
Bemis Company Inc Paper Packaging Div	2445 Deer Pk Blvd	Omaha	NE	68105	**800-541-4303**	
BPM Inc	200 W Front St	Peshtigo	WI	54157	**800-826-0494**	715-582-4551
Bryce Corp	4505 Old Lamar Ave	Memphis	TN	38118	**800-238-7277**	901-369-4400
Burrows Paper Corp Packaging Group	2000 Commerce Ctr Dr	Franklin	OH	45005	**800-732-1933**	937-746-1933
Carton Service Inc	First Quality Dr PO Box 702 *General	Shelby	OH	44875	**800-533-7744***	419-342-5010
Charter Films Inc	1901 Winter St PO Box 277	Superior	WI	54880	**877-411-3456**	715-395-8258
Command Plastic Corp	124 W Ave	Tallmadge	OH	44278	**800-321-8001**	330-434-3497
Consolidated Container Co (CCC)	3101 Towercreek Pkwy Ste 300 *Sales	Atlanta	GA	30339	**888-831-2184***	678-742-4600
Crawford Industries LLC	1414 Crawford Dr	Crawfordsville	IN	47933	**800-428-0840**	
Crown Packaging Corp	17854 Chesterfld Airport Rd	Chesterfield	MO	63005	**800-883-9400**	636-681-8000
Cryovac Food Packaging & Food Solutions	100 Rogers Bridge Rd	Duncan	SC	29334	**800-391-5645**	
DuPont Packaging & Industrial Polymers	Barley Mill Plaza 26-2122 PO Box 80026	Wilmington	DE	19880	**800-438-7225**	703-305-7666
Exopack LLC	23810 China Lake Ct PO Box 5687	Katy	TX	77494	**877-447-3539**	864-596-7140
Fisher Container Corp	1111 Busch Pkwy	Buffalo Grove	IL	60089	**800-837-2247**	847-541-0000
Flextron Industries Inc	720 Mt Rd	Aston	PA	19014	**800-633-2181**	610-459-4600
Flower City Tissue Mills Inc	700 Driving Pk Ave	Rochester	NY	14613	**800-595-2030**	585-458-9200
FPC Flexible Packaging Corp	1891 Eglinton Ave E	Toronto	ON	M1L2L7	**888-288-7386**	416-288-3060
General Plastic Extrusions Inc	1238 Kasson Dr	Prescott	WI	54021	**800-532-3888**	715-262-3806
Genpak Corp	68 Warren St	Glens Falls	NY	12801	**800-626-6695**	518-798-9511
Gift Wrap Co	338 Industrial Blvd *General	Midway	GA	31320	**800-443-4429***	
Grayling Industries	1008 Branch Dr	Alpharetta	GA	30004	**800-635-1551**	770-751-9095
Green Bay Packaging Inc	1700 Webster Ct	Green Bay	WI	54302	**800-236-8400**	920-433-5111
Huhtamaki Inc North America	9201 Packaging Dr	DeSoto	KS	66018	**800-255-4243**	913-583-3025
Indiana Ribbon Inc	106 N Second St	Wolcott	IN	47995	**800-531-3100**	219-279-2112
Innovative Enterprises Inc	25 Town & Country Dr	Washington	MO	63090	**800-280-0300**	636-390-0300
International Paper Co	6400 Poplar Ave *NYSE: IP* *Prod Info	Memphis	TN	38197	**800-223-1268***	901-419-9000
LallyPak Inc	1209 Central Ave	Hillside	NJ	07205	**800-523-8484**	908-351-4141
Laminations	3010 E Venture Dr	Appleton	WI	54911	**800-925-2626**	920-831-0596
LPS Industries Inc	10 Caesar Pl *Sales	Moonachie	NJ	07074	**800-275-6577***	201-438-3515
Novacel	21 Third St	Palmer	MA	01069	**877-668-2235**	413-283-3468
Pactiv Corp	1900 W Field Ct	Lake Forest	IL	60045	**888-828-2850**	847-482-2000
Pak West Paper & Packaging	4042 W Garry Ave	Santa Ana	CA	92704	**800-927-7299**	714-557-7420
Pratt Industries USA	1800C Sarasota Pkwy	Conyers	GA	30013	**800-835-2088**	770-918-5678
Printpack Inc	2800 Overlook PkwyNE	Atlanta	GA	30339	**800-669-6820**	404-460-7000
Robinson Industries Inc	3051 W Curtis Rd	Coleman	MI	48618	**877-465-4055**	989-465-6111
Rollprint Packaging Products Inc	320 S Stewart Ave	Addison	IL	60101	**800-276-7629**	630-628-1700
Sabert Corp	2288 Main St Ext	Sayreville	NJ	08872	**800-722-3781**	
Sealed Air Corp Packaging Products Div	301 Mayhill St	Saddle Brook	NJ	07663	**800-648-9093**	201-712-7000
UFP Technologies Inc	172 E Main St *NASDAQ: UFPT*	Georgetown	MA	01833	**800-372-3172**	978-352-2200
Unger Co	12401 Berea Rd	Cleveland	OH	44111	**800-321-1418**	216-252-1400
Viskase Cos Inc	8205 S Cass Ste 115	Darien	IL	60561	**800-323-8562**	630-874-0700
Warp Bros Flex-O-Glass Inc	4647 W Augusta Blvd	Chicago	IL	60651	**800-621-3345**	773-261-5200
Wausau Paper Corp	100 Paper Pl *NYSE: WPP*	Mosinee	WI	54455	**800-723-0008**	715-693-4470
Weyerhaeuser Co	33663 Weyerhaeuser Way S *NYSE: WY*	Federal Way	WA	98003	**800-525-5440**	253-924-2345
Winpak Ltd	100 Salteaux Crescent *TSE: WPK*	Winnipeg	MB	R3J3T3	**800-841-2600**	204-889-1015
WS Packaging Group Inc	2571 S. Hemlock Rd	Green Bay	WI	54229	**800-236-3424**	800-818-5481

548 PACKING & CRATING

Company	Address	City	State	ZIP	Toll-Free	Phone
Allied Container Systems Inc	201 N Civic Dr Ste 180	Walnut Creek	CA	94596	**800-943-6510**	
Craters & Freighters	331 Corporate Cir Ste J	Golden	CO	80401	**800-736-3335**	
Fapco Inc	216 Post Rd	Buchanan	MI	49107	**800-782-0167**	269-695-6889
Navis Logistics Network	6551 S Revere Pkwy Ste 250	Centennial	CO	80111	**800-344-3528**	
Navis Pack & Ship Centers	6551 S Revere Pkwy Ste 250	Centennial	CO	80111	**800-344-3528**	
Packaging Services of Maryland Inc	16461 Elliott Pkwy	Williamsport	MD	21795	**800-223-6255**	301-223-6200
Southern States Packaging Co	PO Box 650	Spartanburg	SC	29304	**800-621-2051**	
Tech Packaging Inc	13241 Bartram Pk Blvd Ste 601	Jacksonville	FL	32258	**866-453-8324**	904-288-6403
Unicep Packaging Inc	1702 Industrial Dr	Sandpoint	ID	83864	**800-354-9396**	208-265-9696

549 PAINTS, VARNISHES, RELATED PRODUCTS

Company	Address	City	State	ZIP	Toll-Free	Phone
Aervoe Industries Inc	PO Box 485	Gardnerville	NV	89410	**800-227-0196**	775-783-3100
Aexcel Corp	7373 Production Dr	Mentor	OH	44060	**800-854-0782**	440-974-3800
Akron Paint & Varnish Inc	1390 Firestone Pkwy	Akron	OH	44301	**800-772-3452**	330-773-8911
American Safety Technologies Inc	565 Eagle Rock Ave	Roseland	NJ	07068	**800-631-7841**	973-403-2600
Behr Process Corp	3400 W Segerstrom Ave	Santa Ana	CA	92704	**800-854-0133**	714-545-7101
Benjamin Moore & Co	101 Paragon Dr	Montvale	NJ	07645	**800-344-0400**	201-573-9600
BryCoat Inc	207 Vollmer Ave	Oldsmar	FL	34677	**800-989-8788**	727-490-1000
California Products Corp	150 Dascomb Rd	Andover	MA	01810	**800-225-1141**	978-623-9980
Carboline Co	350 Hanley Industrial Ct	Saint Louis	MO	63144	**800-848-4645**	314-644-1000
Coating & Adhesive Corp (CAC)	1901 Popular St PO Box 1080	Leland	NC	28451	**800-410-2999**	910-371-3184
Color Wheel Paint Mfg Co Inc	2814 Silver Star Rd	Orlando	FL	32808	**855-862-6639**	407-293-6810
DAP Products Inc	2400 Boston St Ste 200 *Cust Svc	Baltimore	MD	21224	**800-543-3840***	410-675-2100
Davis Paint Company Inc	1311 Iron St PO Box 7589	North Kansas City	MO	64116	**800-821-2029**	816-471-4447
Day-Glo Color Corp	4515 St Clair Ave	Cleveland	OH	44103	**800-424-9300**	216-391-7070
Diamond Vogel Paints	1110 Albany Pl SE PO Box 380	Orange City	IA	51041	**800-728-6435**	712-737-8880
Duckback Products	2644 Hegan Ln PO Box 980	Chico	CA	95927	**800-825-5382**	

Company	Address	City	State	Zip	Toll-Free	Phone
Dunn-Edwards Corp	4885 E 52nd Pl	Los Angeles	CA	90058	**800-537-4098**	323-771-3330
DuPont Automotive	950 Stephenson Hwy PO Box 7013	Troy	MI	48007	**800-533-1313**	248-583-8000
DuPont Performance Coatings	1007 Market St	Wilmington	DE	19898	**800-441-7515**	302-774-1000
Farrell-Calhoun Inc	221 E Carolina Ave	Memphis	TN	38126	**888-832-7735**	901-526-2211
Ferro Corp	6060 Parkland Blvd	Mayfield Heights	IN	44124	**800-321-3314**	216-875-5600
Ferro Corp Plastics Colorants Div	6060 Parkland Blvd Ste 250	Mayfield Heights	OH	44124	**800-521-9094**	419-682-3311
FinishMaster Inc	115 W Washington St 700 S	Indianapolis	IN	46204	**888-311-3678**	317-237-3678
Gemini Coatings Inc	421 SE 27th St	El Reno	OK	73036	**800-262-5710**	405-262-5710
Harrison Paint Co	1329 Harrison Ave SW	Canton	OH	44706	**800-321-0680**	330-455-5125
HB Fuller Co	1200 Willow Lk Blvd PO Box 64683 *NYSE: FUL*	Saint Paul	MN	55164	**888-423-8553**	651-236-5900
Hentzen Coatings Inc	6937 W Mill Rd	Milwaukee	WI	53218	**800-236-6589**	414-353-4200
Hudson Color Concentrates Inc	50 Francis St	Leominster	MA	01453	**888-858-9065**	978-537-3538
Insl-X Products Corp	101 Paragon Dr *Cust Svc	Montvale	NJ	07645	**800-225-5554***	
Kelly-Moore Paint Company Inc	987 Commercial St	San Carlos	CA	94070	**800-874-4436**	650-592-8337
Kenyon Plastering Inc	4001 W Indian School Rd	Phoenix	AZ	85019	**800-949-4319**	602-233-1191
Kop-Coat Inc	436 Seventh Ave 1850 Koppers Bldg	Pittsburgh	PA	15219	**800-221-4466**	412-227-2426
Lancaster Distributing Co	1310 Union St *General	Spartanburg	SC	29302	**800-845-8287***	864-583-3011
Lansco Colors	1 Blue Hill Plaza 11th Fl PO Box 1685	Pearl River	NY	10965	**800-526-2783**	845-507-5942
Mantros-Haeuser & Company Inc	1175 Post Rd E *General	Westport	CT	06880	**800-344-4229***	203-454-1800
Masterchem Industries LLC	3135 Old Hwy M	Imperial	MO	63052	**866-774-6371**	
Minwax Co	10 Mountainview Rd	Upper Saddle River	NJ	07458	**800-523-9299**	
Mobile Paint Manufacturing Co	4775 Hamilton Blvd	Theodore	AL	36582	**800-621-6952**	251-443-6110
Muralo Company Inc	148 E Fifth St	Bayonne	NJ	07002	**800-631-3440**	201-437-0770
Neogard Div Jones-blair Co	2728 Empire Central St	Dallas	TX	75235	**800-492-9400**	214-353-1600
O'Leary Paint	300 E Oakland Ave	Lansing	MI	48906	**800-477-2066**	517-487-2066
Painters Supply & Equipment Co	25195 Brest Rd	Taylor	MI	48180	**800-589-8100**	734-946-8119
Parker Paint Mfg Co Inc	3003 S Tacoma Way	Tacoma	WA	98409	**855-862-6639**	
Penn Color Inc	400 Old Dublin Pk	Doylestown	PA	18901	**866-617-7366**	215-345-6550
Pioneer Mfg	4529 Industrial Pkwy	Cleveland	OH	44135	**800-877-1500**	216-671-5500
PPG Industries Inc	17451 Von Karman Ave	Irvine	CA	92614	**800-544-3338**	949-474-0400
Red Spot Paint & Varnish Co Inc	1107 E Louisiana St	Evansville	IN	47711	**877-777-4778**	812-428-9100
Republic Powdered Metals Inc	2628 Pearl Rd	Medina	OH	44256	**800-382-1218**	
Rodda Paint Co	6107 N Marine Dr	Portland	OR	97203	**800-452-2315**	503-521-4300
RPM International Inc	2628 Pearl Rd *NYSE: RPM*	Medina	OH	44256	**800-776-4488**	330-273-5090
Rust-Oleum Corp	11 E Hawthorn Pkwy	Vernon Hills	IL	60061	**800-323-3584**	847-367-7700
Samuel Cabot Inc	100 Hale St	Newburyport	MA	01950	**800-877-8246**	978-465-1900
Seymour of Sycamore Inc	917 Crosby Ave	Sycamore	IL	60178	**800-435-4482**	815-895-9101
Sheboygan Paint Company Inc	1439 N 25th St PO Box 417	Sheboygan	WI	53082	**800-773-7801**	920-458-2157
Sherwin-Williams Automotive Finishes	4440 Warrensville Ctr Rd	Warrensville Heights	OH	44128	**800-798-5872**	216-332-8330
Sterling-Clark-Lurton Corp	PO Box 130	Norwood	MA	02062	**800-225-9872**	781-762-5400
Textured Coatings Of America	2422 E 15th St	Panama City	FL	32405	**800-454-0340**	850-769-0347
Tnemec Company Inc	6800 Corporate Dr	Kansas City	MO	64120	**800-863-6321**	816-483-3400
Troy Corp	8 Vreeland Rd PO Box 955	Florham Park	NJ	07932	**800-448-2843**	973-443-4200
Valspar Refinish Inc	210 Crosby St *Cust Svc	Picayune	MS	39466	**800-844-3691***	800-845-2500
Whitmore Manufacturing Co	PO Box 9300	Rockwall	TX	75087	**800-699-6318**	972-771-1000
Willamette Valley Co	1075 Arrowsmith St	Eugene	OR	97402	**800-333-9826**	541-484-9621
WM Barr & Company Inc	2105 Ch Ave	Memphis	TN	38109	**800-238-2672**	901-775-0100
Wolf Gordon Inc	33-00 47th Ave	Long Island	NY	11101	**800-347-0550**	
Yenkin-Majestic Paint Corp	1920 Leonard Ave	Columbus	OH	43219	**800-848-1898**	614-253-8511

550 PALLETS & SKIDS

Company	Address	City	State	Zip	Toll-Free	Phone
Anderson Forest Products Inc	1267 Old Edmonton Rd	Tompkinsville	KY	42167	**800-489-6778**	270-487-6778
Clinch-Tite Corp	5264 Lake St PO Box 456 *General	Sandy Lake	PA	16145	**800-241-0900***	724-376-7315
Hill Wood Products Inc	9483 Ashawa Rd	Cook	MN	55723	**800-788-9689**	218-666-5933
Hunter Woodworks Inc	21038 S Wilmington Ave PO Box 4937	Carson	CA	90749	**800-966-4751**	323-775-2544
Pallet Consultants Corp	PO Box 1692	Pompano Beach	FL	33061	**888-782-2909**	954-946-2212
Pallet Masters Inc	655 E Florence Ave	Los Angeles	CA	90001	**800-675-2579**	323-758-6559
PalletOne Inc	1470 US Hwy 17 S	Bartow	FL	33830	**800-771-1148**	863-533-1147
Potomac Supply Corp	1398 Kinsale Rd *Sales	Kinsale	VA	22488	**800-365-3900***	804-472-2527
Tasler Inc	1804 Tasler Dr	Webster City	IA	50595	**800-482-7537**	515-832-5200

551 PAPER - MFR

SEE ALSO Packaging Materials & Products - Paper or Plastics

551-1 Coated & Laminated Paper

Company	Address	City	State	Zip	Toll-Free	Phone
Appleton Papers Inc	825 E Wisconsin Ave PO Box 359	Appleton	WI	54912	**888-593-9546**	920-734-9841
Avery Dennison Worldwide Graphics Div	207 Goode Ave Bldg 8	Glendale	CA	44077	**800-443-9380**	440-358-3700
BPM Inc	200 W Front St	Peshtigo	WI	54157	**800-826-0494**	715-582-4551
Diversified Labeling Solutions	1285 Hamilton Pkwy	Itasca	IL	60143	**800-397-3013**	630-625-1225
Fortifiber Building Systems Group	300 Industrial Dr	Fernley	NV	89408	**800-773-4777**	775-333-6400
Horizon Paper Co Inc	1010 Washington Blvd	Stamford	CT	06901	**866-358-0855**	203-358-0855
Lofton Label Inc	6290 Claude Way	Inver Grove Heights	MN	55076	**877-447-8118**	651-552-6257
Nashua Corp	11 Trafalgar Sq 2nd Fl	Nashua	NH	03063	**800-430-7488**	603-880-2323
National/AZON	1148 Rochester Rd	Troy	MI	48083	**800-325-5939**	
Technicote Westfield Inc	222 Mound Ave	Miamisburg	OH	45342	**800-358-4448**	937-859-4448
TST/Impreso Inc	652 Southwestern Blvd	Coppell	TX	75019	**800-527-2878**	972-462-0100
Wausau Paper Corp	100 Paper Pl *NYSE: WPP*	Mosinee	WI	54455	**800-723-0008**	715-693-4470
Wausau Paper Corp Specialty Paper Div	100 Paper Pl	Mosinee	WI	54455	**800-723-0008**	715-693-4470
Wcp Solutions	6703 S 234th St Ste 120	Kent	WA	98032	**877-398-3030**	

551-2 Writing Paper

Company	Address	City	State	Zip	Toll-Free	Phone
Anna Griffin Inc	99 Armour Dr	Atlanta	GA	30324	**888-817-8170**	404-817-8170
Crane & Co Inc	30 S St *Cust Svc	Dalton	MA	01226	**800-268-2281***	
Geographics	108 Main St 3rd Fl	Norwalk	CT	06851	**800-436-4919**	
Gordon Paper Company Inc	PO Box 1806	Norfolk	VA	23501	**800-457-7366**	757-464-3581
Louisiana Assn For, The Blind, The	1750 Claiborne Ave	Shreveport	LA	71103	**877-913-6471**	318-635-6471
Mohawk Fine Papers Inc	465 Saratoga St	Cohoes	NY	12047	**800-843-6455**	518-237-1740
Performance Office Papers	21565 Hamburg Ave	Lakeville	MN	55044	**800-458-7189**	
Schurman Fine Papers	500 Chadbourne Rd *Sales	Fairfield	CA	94533	**800-789-1649***	
Southworth Co	265 Main St	Agawam	MA	01001	**800-225-1839**	413-789-1200
Specialty Loose Leaf Inc	1 Cabot St	Holyoke	MA	01040	**800-227-3623**	413-532-0106
Top Flight Inc	1300 Central Ave	Chattanooga	TN	37408	**800-777-3740**	423-266-8171
Wausau Paper Corp	100 Paper Pl *NYSE: WPP*	Mosinee	WI	54455	**800-723-0008**	715-693-4470
Wausau Paper Corp Printing & Writing Paper Div	1 Clark's Island	Wausau	WI	54403	**800-723-0008**	715-693-4470

552 PAPER - WHOL

Company	Address	City	State	Zip	Toll-Free	Phone
Anchor Paper Company Inc	480 Broadway St	Saint Paul	MN	55101	**800-652-9755**	651-298-1311
AT Clayton & Co Inc	300 Atlantic St	Stamford	CT	06901	**800-282-5298**	203-658-1200
Atlantic Packaging Co	806 N 23rd St	Wilmington	NC	28405	**800-722-5841**	910-343-0624

Company / Address	City	State	Zip	Toll-Free	Phone
Cole Papers Inc 1300 N 38th St	Fargo	ND	58102	**800-800-8090**	701-282-5311
Dennis Paper Co 910 Acorn Dr	Nashville	TN	37210	**800-441-5684**	615-883-9010
Field Paper Co 3950 D St	Omaha	NE	68107	**800-969-3435**	402-733-3600
Gpa Specialty Printable Sbstrt 8740 W 50th St	McCook	IL	60525	**800-395-9000**	773-650-2020
GreenLine Paper Company Inc 631 S Pine St	York	PA	17403	**800-641-1117**	717-845-8697
Hearn Paper Co 556 N Meridian Rd	Youngstown	OH	44509	**800-225-2989**	330-792-6533
Kelly Paper Co 288 Brea Canyon Rd	Walnut	CA	91789	**800-675-3559**	
Lindenmeyr Book Publishing Papers 521 Fifth Ave	New York	NY	10175	**800-842-8480**	
Lindenmeyr Munroe 14 Research Pkwy	Wallingford	CT	06492	**800-842-8480**	
Lindenmeyr Munroe Central Central National-Gottesman Inc 3 Manhattanville Rd	Purchase	NY	10577	**800-221-3042**	
Lindenmeyr Munroe Paper Corp 115 Moonachie Ave	Moonachie	NJ	07074	**800-221-3042**	201-440-6491
Mac Papers 3300 Phillips Hwy PO Box 5369	Jacksonville	FL	32207	**800-622-2968**	904-348-3300
Midland Paper 101 E Palatine Rd	Wheeling	IL	60090	**800-323-8522**	847-777-2700
Millcraft Paper Co 6800 Grant Ave	Cleveland	OH	44105	**800-860-2482**	216-441-5500
Morrisette Paper Company Inc 5925 Summit Ave PO Box 20768	Browns Summit	NC	27214	**800-822-8882**	336-375-1515
Murnane Paper Corp 345 W Fischer Farm Rd	Elmhurst	IL	60126	**855-632-8191**	630-530-8222
Newell Paper Co 1212 Grand Ave	Meridian	MS	39301	**800-844-8894**	
PaperDirect Inc 1005 E Woodmen Rd	Colorado Springs	CO	80920	**800-272-7377**	
Redd Paper Co 3851 Ctr Loop	Orlando	FL	32808	**800-961-6656**	407-299-6656
Rohn Industries Inc 862 Hersey St	St. Paul	MN	55114	**800-289-8580**	651-647-1300
Roosevelt Paper Co 1 Roosevelt Dr	Mount Laurel	NJ	08054	**800-523-3470**	856-303-4100
Spicers Paper Inc 12310 Slauson Ave	Santa Fe Springs	CA	90670	**800-774-2377**	562-698-1199
Unisource Worldwide Inc 6600 Governors Lake Pkwy	Norcross	GA	30071	**800-864-7687**	770-447-9000
White Paper Co 9990 River Way	Delta	BC	V4G1M9	**888-840-7300**	604-951-3900

553 PAPER CONVERTERS

Company / Address	City	State	Zip	Toll-Free	Phone
Ameri-Fax Corp 6520 W 20th Ave Unit 2	Hialeah	FL	33016	**800-262-8214**	
BagcraftPapercon 3900 W 43rd St	Chicago	IL	60632	**800-621-8468**	773-254-8000
C-P Flexible Packaging 15 Grumbacher Rd	York	PA	17406	**800-815-0667**	717-764-1193
Caraustar Industries Inc 5000 Austell-Powder Springs Rd Ste 300	Austell	GA	30106	**800-858-1438**	770-948-3100
Case Paper Company Inc 500 Mamaroneck Ave	Harrison	NY	10528	**800-222-2922**	914-899-3500
Cindus Corp 515 Stn Ave	Cincinnati	OH	45215	**800-543-4691**	
Crusader Paper Company Inc 350 Holt Rd	North Andover	MA	01845	**800-421-0007**	
International Converter Inc 17153 Industrial Hwy	Caldwell	OH	43724	**800-848-6623**	740-732-5665
Kanzaki Specialty Papers 1 Monarch Pl Ste 800	Springfield	MA	01144	**888-526-9254**	
Lauterbach Group Inc W222 N5710 Miller Way *Sales	Sussex	WI	53089	**800-841-7301***	262-820-8130
Max International Converters Inc 2360 Dairy Rd	Lancaster	PA	17601	**800-233-0222**	
Pacon Corp 2525 N Casaloma Dr	Appleton	WI	54912	**800-333-2545**	
Paper Systems Inc 185 S Pioneer Blvd	Springboro	OH	45066	**888-564-6774**	937-746-6841
PM Co 9220 Glades Dr	Fairfield	OH	45011	**800-327-4359**	513-825-7626
Protect-All Inc 109 Badger Pkwy	Darien	WI	53114	**888-432-8526**	
Spectra-Kote Corp 301 E Water St	Gettysburg	PA	17325	**800-241-4626**	717-334-3177
Spinnaker Coating Inc 518 E Water St	Troy	OH	45373	**800-543-9452**	937-332-6500
TimeMed Labeling Systems Inc 144 Tower Dr *Cust Svc	Burr Ridge	IL	60527	**800-323-4840***	630-986-1800
Tufco Technologies Inc PO Box 23500 *NASDAQ: TFCO*	Green Bay	WI	54305	**800-558-8145**	920-336-0054

554 PAPER FINISHERS (EMBOSSING, COATING, GILDING, STAMPING)

Company / Address	City	State	Zip	Toll-Free	Phone
Colad Group 801 Exchange St	Buffalo	NY	14210	**800-950-1755**	716-961-1776
Complemar Partners 500 Lee Rd Ste 200	Rochester	NY	14606	**800-388-7254**	585-647-5800
Loroco Industries Inc 5000 Creek Rd	Cincinnati	OH	45242	**800-215-9474**	513-891-9544
Madison Cutting Die Inc 2547 Progress Rd	Madison	WI	53716	**800-395-9405**	608-221-3422
Walton Press (WP) 402 Mayfield Dr	Monroe	GA	30655	**800-354-0235**	770-267-2596

555 PAPER INDUSTRIES MACHINERY

Company / Address	City	State	Zip	Toll-Free	Phone
Baumfolder Corp 1660 Campbell Rd	Sidney	OH	45365	**800-543-6107**	937-492-1281
Cranston Machinery Company Inc 2251 SE Oak Grove Blvd	Oak Grove	OR	97267	**800-547-1012**	503-654-7751
Entwistle Co Dietzco Div 6 Bigelow St	Hudson	MA	01749	**800-445-8909**	508-481-4000
Pemco Inc 3333 Crocker Ave	Sheboygan	WI	53082	**888-310-1898**	920-458-2500

556 PAPER MILLS

SEE ALSO Paperboard Mills ; Pulp Mills

Company / Address	City	State	Zip	Toll-Free	Phone
Advanced Poly Packaging Inc 1331 Emmitt Rd	Akron	OH	44306	**800-754-4403**	330-785-4000
Arjobex America Mill 10901 Westlake Dr	Charlotte	NC	28273	**800-765-9278**	
Armor Protective Packaging 951 Jones St	Howell	MI	48843	**800-365-1117**	517-546-1117
BPM Inc 200 W Front St	Peshtigo	WI	54157	**800-826-0494**	715-582-4551
Burrows Paper Corp 501 W Main St	Little Falls	NY	13365	**800-272-7122**	315-823-2300
Cad Store Inc, The 15353 N 91st Ave	Peoria	AZ	85381	**800-576-6789**	623-931-7936
Cauthorne Paper Co 12124 S Washington Hwy	Ashland	VA	23005	**800-552-3011**	804-798-6999
Climax Manufacturing Co 7840 SR 26	Lowville	NY	13367	**800-225-4629**	315-376-8000
Conder Flag Co 4705 Dwight Evans Rd	Charlotte	NC	28217	**800-868-3524**	
FiberMark North America, Inc. 161 Wellington Rd *Cust Svc	Brattleboro	VT	05302	**800-784-8558***	802-257-0365
Finch Paper LLC 1 Glen St	Glens Falls	NY	12801	**800-833-9983**	518-793-2541
Frankston Packaging 699 N Frankston Hwy	Frankston	TX	75763	**800-881-1495**	903-876-2550
Green Field Paper Co 7196 Clairemont Mesa Blvd	San Diego	CA	92111	**888-402-9979**	858-565-2585
Inland Empire Paper Co 3320 N Argonne	Millwood	WA	99212	**866-437-7711**	509-924-1911
International Paper Co 6400 Poplar Ave *NYSE: IP* ■ *Prod Info	Memphis	TN	38197	**800-223-1268***	901-419-9000
K D M Enterprise LLC 820 Commerce Pkwy	Carpentersville	IL	60110	**877-591-9768**	847-783-0333
Kimberly-Clark Corp 351 Phelps Dr *NYSE: KMB*	Irving	TX	75038	**888-525-8388**	972-281-1200
M&A Advisor LLC, The 108-18 Queens Blvd 2nd Fl	Forest Hills	NY	11375	**877-996-3743**	718-997-7900
Marq Packaging Systems Inc 3801 W Washington Ave	Yakima	WA	98903	**800-998-4301**	509-966-4300
Merchants Paper Co 4625 SE 24th Ave	Portland	OR	97202	**800-605-6301**	503-235-2171
Monadnock Paper Mills Inc 117 Antrim Rd *Orders	Bennington	NH	03442	**800-221-2159***	603-588-3311
Nelson Jit Packaging Supplies Inc 4022 W Turney Ave Ste 3	Phoenix	AZ	85019	**800-939-3647**	623-939-3365
Pratt Industries USA 1800C Sarasota Pkwy	Conyers	GA	30013	**800-835-2088**	770-918-5678
Schweitzer-Mauduit International Inc 100 N Pt Ctr E Ste 600 *NYSE: SWM*	Alpharetta	GA	30022	**800-514-0186**	770-569-4271
Verso Corp 6775 Lenox Ctr Ct Ste 400 *NYSE: VRS*	Memphis	TN	38115	**877-837-7606**	
West Linn Paper Co 4800 Mill St	West Linn	OR	97068	**800-989-3608**	503-557-6500
Xamax Industries Inc 63 Silvermine Rd	Seymour	CT	06483	**888-926-2988**	203-888-7200

557 PAPER PRODUCTS - SANITARY

Company / Address	City	State	Zip	Toll-Free	Phone
Associated Hygienic Products LLC 3400 River Green Ct Ste 600 *General	Duluth	GA	30096	**800-757-0927***	770-497-9800
Atlas Paper Mills LLC 3301 NW 107th St	Miami	FL	33167	**800-562-2860**	305-636-5740
Hoffmaster 2920 N Main St	Oshkosh	WI	54901	**800-327-9774**	920-235-9330
Kimberly-Clark Corp 351 Phelps Dr *NYSE: KMB*	Irving	TX	75038	**888-525-8388**	972-281-1200
Nice-Pak Products Inc 2 Nice-Pak Pk	Orangeburg	NY	10962	**800-444-6725**	845-365-1700
Principle Business Enterprises Inc PO Box 129	Dunbridge	OH	43414	**800-467-3224**	419-352-1551
SCA Americas 2929 Arch St Ste 2600 *Cust Svc	Philadelphia	PA	19104	**800-328-9043***	610-499-3700
Wausau Paper Corp 100 Paper Pl *NYSE: WPP*	Mosinee	WI	54455	**800-723-0008**	715-693-4470

558 PAPER PRODUCTS - WHOL

Company	Address	City	State	Zip	Toll-Free	Phone
American Hotel Register Co	100 S Milwaukee Ave	Vernon Hills	IL	60061	**800-323-5686**	847-743-3000
American Paper & Twine Co	7400 Cockrill Bend Blvd	Nashville	TN	37209	**800-251-2437**	615-350-9000
Atlantic Paper & Twine Co Inc	85 York Ave	Pawtucket	RI	02904	**800-613-0950**	401-725-0950
BGR Inc	6392 Gano Rd	West Chester	OH	45069	**800-628-9195**	513-755-7100
Brame Specialty Company Inc	PO Box 27	Durham	NC	27702	**800-533-2041**	919-683-1331
Butler-Dearden Paper Service Inc	PO Box 1069	Boylston	MA	01505	**800-634-7070**	508-869-9000
Central Paper Products Co Inc	350 Gay St Brown Ave Industrial Pk	Manchester	NH	03103	**800-339-4065**	603-624-4065
Dacotah Paper Co	3940 15th Ave NW	Fargo	ND	58102	**800-270-6352**	701-281-1734
Ernest Paper Products	5777 Smithway St	Commerce	CA	90040	**800-233-7788**	
Fleetwood-Signode	3624 W Lake Ave	Glenview	IL	60026	**800-862-7997**	630-268-9999
Garland C Norris Co	1101 Terry Rd	Apex	NC	27502	**800-331-8920**	919-387-1059
Gem State Paper & Supply Co	1801 Highland Ave E	Twin Falls	ID	83303	**800-727-2737**	208-733-6081
H. T. Berry Co Inc	PO Box B	Canton	MA	02021	**800-736-2206**	781-828-6000
Heartland Paper Co	808 W Cherokee St *Cust Svc	Sioux Falls	SD	57104	**800-843-7922***	605-336-1190
Johnston Paper Co	2 Eagle Dr	Auburn	NY	13021	**800-800-7123**	315-253-8435
Landsberg Orora	1640 S Greenwood Ave *Cust Svc	Montebello	CA	90640	**888-526-3723***	323-832-2000
Leonard Paper Co	725 N Haven St *Cust Svc	Baltimore	MD	21205	**800-327-5547***	
M Conley Co	1312 Fourth St SE	Canton	OH	44707	**800-362-6001**	330-456-8243
Mayfield Paper Co	1115 S Hill St	San Angelo	TX	76903	**800-725-1441**	325-653-1444
National Paper & Sanitary Supply	2511 S 156th Cir	Omaha	NE	68130	**800-647-2737**	402-330-5507
Nichols Paper & Supply Company Inc	PO Box 291	Muskegon	MI	49443	**800-442-0213**	231-799-2120
Pacific Packaging Products Inc	24 Industrial Way	Wilmington	MA	01887	**800-777-0300**	978-657-9100
Packaging Distribution Services Inc (PDS)	2308 Sunset Rd	Des Moines	IA	50321	**800-747-2699**	515-243-3156
Paterson Pacific Parchment Co	625 Greg St	Sparks	NV	89431	**800-678-8104**	775-353-3000
Phillips Distribution Inc	3000 E Houston St	San Antonio	TX	78220	**800-580-2397**	210-227-2397
Pollock Paper & Packaging	1 Pollock Pl *Cust Svc	Grand Prairie	TX	75050	**800-843-7320***	972-263-2126
S. Freedman & Sons Inc	3322 Pennsy Dr	Landover	MD	20785	**800-545-7277**	301-322-5000
Saint Louis Paper & Box Co	3843 Garfield Ave	Saint Louis	MO	63113	**800-779-7901**	314-531-7900
Schwarz	8338 Austin Ave	Morton Grove	IL	60053	**800-323-4903**	
Shorr Packaging Inc	800 N Commerce St	Aurora	IL	60504	**888-885-0055**	630-978-1000
Snyder Paper Corp	250 26th St Dr SE PO Box 758	Hickory	NC	28603	**800-222-8562**	828-328-2501
TSN Inc	4001 Salazar Way PO Box 679 *General	Frederick	CO	80530	**888-997-5959***	303-530-0600
Unisource Worldwide Inc	6600 Governors Lake Pkwy	Norcross	GA	30071	**800-864-7687**	770-447-9000

559 PAPERBOARD & CARDBOARD - DIE-CUT

Company	Address	City	State	Zip	Toll-Free	Phone
Alvah Bushnell Co	519 E Chelten Ave	Philadelphia	PA	19144	**800-255-7434**	215-842-9520
Blanks/USA Inc	7700 68th Ave N #7	Minneapolis	MN	55428	**800-328-7311**	
Crescent Cardboard Company LLC	100 W Willow Rd	Wheeling	IL	60090	**888-293-3956**	847-537-3400
Demco Inc	4810 Forest Run Rd *Orders	Madison	WI	53704	**800-356-1200***	608-241-1201
GBS Filing Solutions	224 Morges Rd	Malvern	OH	44644	**800-873-4427**	330-494-5330
Tap Packaging Solutions	2160 Superior Ave	Cleveland	OH	44114	**800-827-5679**	216-781-6000
Topps Company Inc	1 Whitehall St	New York	NY	10004	**800-489-9149**	212-376-0300
University Products Inc	517 Main St	Holyoke	MA	01040	**800-628-1912**	413-532-3372

560 PAPERBOARD MILLS

SEE ALSO Paper Mills ; Pulp Mills

Company	Address	City	State	Zip	Toll-Free	Phone
Cascades Inc	404 Marie-Victorin Blvd *TSE: CAS*	Kingsey Falls	QC	J0A1B0	**800-361-4070**	819-363-5100
Combined Technologies Inc	13970 W Polo Trl Dr	Lake Forest	IL	60045	**877-968-4855**	847-968-4855
FiberMark North America, Inc.	161 Wellington Rd *Cust Svc	Brattleboro	VT	05302	**800-784-8558***	802-257-0365
International Paper Co	6400 Poplar Ave *NYSE: IP* ■ *Prod Info	Memphis	TN	38197	**800-223-1268***	901-419-9000
Newman & Company Inc	6101 Tacony St	Philadelphia	PA	19135	**800-523-3256**	215-333-8700
Packaging Corp of America	1955 W Field Ct *NYSE: PKG*	Lake Forest	IL	60045	**800-456-4725**	
Pactiv Corp	1900 W Field Ct	Lake Forest	IL	60045	**888-828-2850**	847-482-2000
Superior Packaging Solutions	26858 Almond Ave	Redlands	CA	92374	**844-792-2626**	800-680-2393
WinterBell Co	2018 Brevard Rd	High Point	NC	27263	**800-685-2957**	336-887-2651

561 PARKING SERVICE

Company	Address	City	State	Zip	Toll-Free	Phone
Ace Parking Management Inc	645 Ash St *General	San Diego	CA	92101	**855-223-7275***	619-233-6624
Baltimore County Revenue Authority	115 Towsontown Blvd E	Baltimore	MD	21286	**888-246-5384**	410-887-3127
Colonial Parking Inc	1050 Thomas Jefferson St NW Ste 100	Washington	DC	20007	**877-777-4778**	202-295-8100
Edison Properties LLC	100 Washington St	Newark	NJ	07102	**888-727-5327**	973-643-0895
Park 'N Fly	2060 Mt Paran Rd Ste 207 *Cust Svc	Atlanta	GA	30327	**800-325-4863***	
Park To Fly Inc	7800 Narcoossee Rd	Orlando	FL	32822	**888-851-8875**	407-851-8875
Parking Panda Corp	3422 Fait Ave	Baltimore	MD	21224	**800-232-6415**	
Standard Parking Corp	900 N Michigan Ave Ste 1600	Chicago	IL	60611	**888-700-7275**	312-274-2000
Valet Parking Service	1335 S Flower St	Los Angeles	CA	90015	**800-794-7275**	213-342-3388

PARKS - AMUSEMENT

SEE Amusement Park Companies ; Amusement Parks

562 PARKS - NATIONAL - CANADA

Company	Address	City	State	Zip	Toll-Free	Phone
Parks Canada	25-7-N Eddy St	Gatineau	QC	K1A0M5	**888-773-8888**	613-860-1251
Banff National Park	PO Box 900	Banff	AB	T1L1K2	**877-737-3783**	403-762-1550
Glacier National Park	PO Box 350	Revelstoke	BC	V0E2S0	**866-787-6221**	250-837-7500
Kluane National Park & Reserve of Canada	PO Box 5495	Haines Junction	YT	Y0B1L0	**877-852-3100**	867-634-7250
Mingan Archipelago National Park Reserve of Canada	1340 de la Digue St	Havre-Saint-Pierre	QC	G0G1P0	**877-737-3783**	418-538-3331
Mount Revelstoke National Park of Canada	PO Box 350	Revelstoke	BC	V0E2S0	**866-787-6221**	250-837-7500
Point Pelee National Park of Canada	407 Monarch Ln RR 1	Leamington	ON	N8H3V4	**888-773-8888**	519-322-2365
Prince Albert National Park of Canada	Northern Prairies Field Unit PO Box 100 *Campground Resv	Waskesiu Lake	SK	S0J2Y0	**877-737-3783***	306-663-4522
Prince Edward Island National Park of Canada	2 Palmers Ln *Campground Resv	Charlottetown	PE	C1A5V8	**800-663-7192***	902-672-6350
Riel House National Historic Site of Canada	330 River Rd	Winnipeg	MB	R2M3Z8	**877-852-3100**	204-257-1783
Wapusk National Park of Canada	PO Box 127	Churchill	MB	R0B0E0	**888-773-8888**	204-675-8863

563 PARKS - NATIONAL - US

SEE ALSO Nature Centers, Parks, Other Natural Areas ; Cemeteries - National ; Parks - State

Company	Address	City	State	Zip	Toll-Free	Phone
Boston Harbor Islands National Recreation Area	408 Atlantic Ave Ste 228	Boston	MA	02110	**877-874-2478**	617-223-8666
Brice's Crossroads National Battlefield Site	2680 Natchez Trace Pkwy	Tupelo	MS	38804	**800-305-7417**	662-680-4025
Cabrillo National Monument	1800 Cabrillo Memorial Dr	San Diego	CA	92106	**800-236-7916**	619-557-5450
Carl Sandburg Home National Historic Site	81 Carl Sadburg Ln	Flat Rock	NC	28731	**877-642-4743**	828-693-4178
Casa Grande Ruins National Monument	1100 W Ruins Dr	Coolidge	AZ	85128	**877-642-4743**	520-723-3172
Cedar Breaks National Monument	2390 W Hwy 56 Ste 11	Cedar City	UT	84720	**877-642-4743**	435-586-9451
Chaco Culture National Historical Park	PO Box 220	Nageezi	NM	87037	**877-642-4743**	505-786-7014
Chamizal National Memorial	800 S San Marcial St	El Paso	TX	79905	**877-642-4743**	915-532-7273
Chattahoochee River National Recreation Area	1978 Island Ford Pkwy	Atlanta	GA	30350	**877-874-2478**	678-538-1200
Chiricahua National Monument	12856 E Rhyolite Creek Rd	Willcox	AZ	85643	**877-444-6777**	520-824-3560
Colonial National Historical Park	PO Box 210	Yorktown	VA	23690	**866-945-7920**	757-898-3400

Name / Address	City	State	Zip	Toll-Free	Phone
Colorado National Monument 1750 Rim Rock Dr	Fruita	CO	81521	**866-945-7920**	970-858-3617
Cumberland Gap National Historical Park 91 Bartlett Pk Rd PO Box 1848	Middlesboro	KY	40965	**888-831-7526**	606-248-2817
Cumberland Island National Seashore 101 Wheeler St	Saint Marys	GA	31558	**877-860-6787**	912-882-4336
Curecanti National Recreation Area 102 Elk Creek	Gunnison	CO	81230	**866-713-9688**	970-641-2337
Cuyahoga Valley National Park 15610 Vaughn Rd	Brecksville	OH	44141	**800-445-9667**	216-524-1497
De Soto National Memorial 8300 Desoto Memorial Hwy	Bradenton	FL	34209	**888-831-7526**	941-792-0458
Death Valley National Park PO Box 579	Death Valley	CA	92328	**866-713-9688**	760-786-3200
Eleanor Roosevelt National Historic Site 4097 Albany Post Rd	Hyde Park	NY	12538	**800-337-8474**	845-229-9115
Eugene O'Neill National Historic Site 1000 Kuss Rd	Danville	CA	94526	**866-945-7920**	925-838-0249
Fort McHenry National Monument & Historic Shrine 2400 E Fort Ave	Baltimore	MD	21230	**866-945-7920**	410-962-4290
Fort Pulaski National Monument US Hwy 80 E	Savannah	GA	31410	**800-228-5150**	912-786-5787
Fort Vancouver National Historic Site 612 E Reserve St	Vancouver	WA	98661	**800-832-3599**	360-816-6230
Gates of the Arctic National Park & Preserve 4175 Geist Rd	Fairbanks	AK	99709	**866-869-6887**	907-457-5752
Harry S Truman National Historic Site 223 N Main St	Independence	MO	64050	**877-642-4743**	816-254-2720
Hohokam Pima National Monument c/o Casa Grande Ruins National Monument 1100 W Ruins Dr	Coolidge	AZ	85228	**866-705-5711**	520-723-3172
Hopewell Furnace National Historic Site 2 Mark Bird Ln	Elverson	PA	19520	**866-705-5711**	610-582-8773
Jefferson National Expansion Memorial 11 N Fourth St	Saint Louis	MO	63102	**855-733-4522**	314-655-1700
Knife River Indian Villages National Historic Site 564 County Rd 37 PO Box 9	Stanton	ND	58571	**866-705-5711**	701-745-3300
Lava Beds National Monument 1 Indian Well Headquarters	Tulelake	CA	96134	**866-705-5711**	530-260-0537
Natchez Trace National Scenic Trail 2680 Natchez Trace Pkwy	Tupelo	MS	38804	**800-305-7417**	662-680-4025
New Orleans Jazz National Historical Park 419 Decatur St	New Orleans	LA	70130	**877-520-0677**	504-589-4806
Oregon Caves National Monument 19000 Caves Hwy	Cave Junction	OR	97523	**877-245-9022**	541-592-2100
Ozark National Scenic Riverways 404 Watercress Dr PO Box 490	Van Buren	MO	63965	**877-444-6777**	573-323-4236
Pinnacles National Monument 5000 Hwy 146	Paicines	CA	95043	**877-444-6777**	831-389-4485
Piscataway Park c/o Ft Washington Pk 13551 Ft Washington Rd	Fort Washington	MD	20744	**866-705-5711**	301-763-4600
Point Reyes National Seashore 1 Bear Valley Rd	Point Reyes Station	CA	94956	**877-874-2478**	415-464-5100
Poverty Point National Monument c/o Poverty Pt State Historic Site PO Box 276	Epps	LA	71237	**888-926-5492**	318-926-5492
Red Hill Patrick Henry National Memorial 1250 Red Hill Rd	Brookneal	VA	24528	**800-514-7463**	434-376-2044
Richmond National Battlefield Park 3215 E Broad St	Richmond	VA	23223	**866-733-7768**	804-226-1981
Ross Lake National Recreation Area 810 State Rt 20	Sedro Woolley	WA	98284	**866-705-5711**	360-854-7200
Russell Cave National Monument 3729 County Rd 98	Bridgeport	AL	35740	**866-705-5711**	256-495-2672
Saint Paul's Church National Historic Site 897 S Columbus Ave	Mount Vernon	NY	10550	**866-705-5711**	914-667-4116
Salt River Bay National Historical Park & Ecological Preserve c/o Christiansted National Historic Site 2100 Church St Ste 100	Christiansted	VI	00820	**866-705-5711**	340-773-1460
San Antonio Missions National Historical Park 2202 Roosevelt Ave	San Antonio	TX	78210	**866-945-7920**	210-534-8833
Santa Monica Mountains National Recreation Area 401 W Hillcrest Dr	Thousand Oaks	CA	91360	**888-275-8747**	805-370-2300
Shenandoah National Park 3655 US Hwy 211E	Luray	VA	22835	**800-732-0911**	540-999-3500
Steamtown National Historic Site 150 S Washington Ave	Scranton	PA	18503	**888-693-9391**	570-340-5200
Thomas Jefferson Memorial c/o National Capital Parks - Central 900 Ohio Dr SW	Washington	DC	20024	**866-705-5711**	202-426-6841
Tupelo National Battlefield 2680 Natchez Trace Pkwy	Tupelo	MS	38804	**800-305-7417**	662-680-4025
Voyageurs National Park 360 Hwy 11 E	International Falls	MN	56649	**888-381-2873**	218-283-6600
Wrangell-Saint Elias National Park & Preserve Mile 1068 Richardson Hwy PO Box 439	Copper Center	AK	99573	**866-705-5711**	907-822-5234

564 PARKS - STATE

SEE ALSO Nature Centers, Parks, Other Natural Areas ; Parks - National - Canada ; Parks - National - US

Name / Address	City	State	Zip	Toll-Free	Phone
Afton State Park 6959 Peller Ave S	Hastings	MN	55033	**800-366-8917**	651-436-5391
Aiken State Natural Area 1145 State Pk Rd	Windsor	SC	29856	**866-345-7275**	803-649-2857
Albert E. Sleeper State Park 6573 State Pk Rd	Caseville	MI	48725	**800-447-2757**	989-856-4411
Alfred A. Loeb State Park 725 Summer St NE Ste C	Salem	OR	97301	**800-551-6949**	503-986-0707
Alsea Bay Historic Interpretive Ctr 725 Summer St NE Ste C	Salem	OR	97301	**800-551-6949**	
Arkansas Museum of Natural Resources 3853 Smackover Hwy	Smackover	AR	71762	**888-287-2757**	870-725-2877
Assateague State Park 7307 Stephen Decatur Hwy	Berlin	MD	21811	**888-432-2267**	410-641-2120
Babcock State Park 486 Babcock Rd	Clifftop	WV	25831	**800-225-5982**	304-438-3004
Bannack State Park 4200 Bannack Rd	Dillon	MT	59725	**855-922-6768**	406-834-3413
Battle Ground Lake State Park 18002 NE 249th St	Battle Ground	WA	98604	**888-226-7688**	360-687-4621
Bayou Segnette State Park 7777 Westbank Expy	Westwego	LA	70094	**888-677-2296**	504-736-7140
Beacon Rock State Park 34841 State Rd 14	Skamania	WA	98648	**888-226-7688**	509-427-8265
Bear Creek Lake State Park 22 Bear Creek Lk Rd	Cumberland	VA	23040	**800-933-7275**	804-492-4410
Beartown State Park HC 64 PO Box 189 *General	Hillsboro	WV	24946	**800-225-5982***	304-653-4254
Beaver Creek Nature Area 20641 SD Hwy 1806 25495 485th Ave	Fort Pierre	SD	57532	**800-710-2267**	605-223-7660
Beaver Dunes State Park Hwy 270 N	Beaver	OK	73932	**800-654-8240**	580-625-3373
Beavers Bend Resort Park PO Box 10	Broken Bow	OK	74728	**800-435-5514**	580-494-6300
Bentsen-Rio Grande Valley State Park 2800 S Bensen Palm Dr	Mission	TX	78572	**800-792-1112**	956-585-1107
Bethpage State Park Bethpage Pkwy	Farmingdale	NY	11735	**800-456-2267**	516-249-0701
Beverly Beach State Park 198 NE 123rd St	Newport	OR	97365	**800-452-5687**	
Big Foot Beach State Park 1452 Wells St	Lake Geneva	WI	53147	**888-936-7463**	262-248-2528
Big Ridge State Park 1015 Big Ridge Rd	Maynardville	TN	37807	**800-471-5305**	865-992-5523
Big Shoals State Park PO Box G	White Springs	FL	32096	**877-635-3655**	386-397-4331
Big Stone Lake State Park 35889 Meadowbrook State Pk Rd	Ortonville	MN	56278	**888-646-6367**	320-839-3663
Black River State Forest 101 S Webster St PO Box 7921	Madison	WI	53707	**888-936-7463**	608-266-2621
Bladon Springs State Park 3921 Bladon Rd	Bladon Springs	AL	36919	**800-252-7275**	251-754-9207
Blue Licks Battlefield State Resort Park Hwy 68	Mount Olivet	KY	41064	**800-443-7008**	
Blue Mounds State Park 1410 161st St	Luverne	MN	56156	**888-646-6367**	507-283-1307
Bob Straub State Park US 101	Pacific City	OR	97112	**800-551-6949**	
Bonnie Lure State Recreation Area 11321 SW Terwilliger Blvd	Portland	OR	97219	**800-551-6949**	
Bridal Veil Falls State Scenic Viewpoint E Bridal Veil Rd PO Box 100	Bridal Veil	OR	97010	**800-551-6949**	
Buck's Pocket State Park 393 County Rd 174	Grove Oak	AL	35975	**800-760-4089**	256-659-2000
Buckhorn Lake State Resort Park 4441 Kentucky Hwy 1833	Buckhorn	KY	41721	**800-325-0058**	
Bullards Beach State Park PO Box 569	Bandon	OR	97411	**800-551-6949**	541-347-2209
Caesars Head State Park 8155 Geer Hwy	Cleveland	SC	29635	**866-345-7275**	864-836-6115
Caledon State Park 11617 Caledon Rd	King George	VA	22485	**800-933-7275**	540-663-3861
Calhoun Falls State Recreation Area 46 Maintenance Shop Rd	Calhoun Falls	SC	29628	**866-345-7275**	864-447-8267
California State Railroad Museum 125 'I' St 111 'I' St	Sacramento	CA	95814	**866-240-4655**	916-323-9280
Cane Creek State Park 50 State Pk Rd	Star City	AR	71667	**888-287-2757**	870-628-4714
Cape Arago State Park Cape Arago Hwy	Coos Bay	OR	97420	**800-551-6949**	541-888-3778
Carley State Park 19041 Hwy 74	Altura	MN	55910	**888-646-6367**	507-932-3007
Carlsbad State Beach c/o San Diego Coast District Office 4477 Pacific Hwy	San Diego	CA	92110	**800-777-0369**	760-438-3143
Casselman River Bridge State Park 580 Taylor Ave Tawes State Ofc Bldg	Annapolis	MD	21401	**877-620-8367**	
Cathedral Caverns State Park 637 Cave Rd	Woodville	AL	35776	**800-252-7275**	256-728-8193
Cathedral State Park Rt 1 12 Cathedral Way	Aurora	WV	26705	**800-225-5982**	304-735-3771
Cedars of Lebanon State Park 328 Cedar Forest Rd	Lebanon	TN	37090	**800-250-8615**	615-443-2769
Centenary State Historic Site 3522 College St	Jackson	LA	70748	**888-677-2364**	225-634-7925
Charles A. Lindbergh State Park 1615 Lindbergh Dr S PO Box 364	Little Falls	MN	56345	**888-646-6367**	320-616-2525
Charles Towne Landing State Historic Site 1500 Old Towne Rd	Charleston	SC	29407	**866-345-7275**	843-852-4200
Cheaha Resort State Park 19644 Hwy 281	Delta	AL	36258	**800-610-5801**	256-488-5111
Chemin-A-Haut State Park 14656 State Pk Rd	Bastrop	LA	71220	**888-677-2436**	318-283-0812
Cheraw State Park 100 State Pk Rd	Cheraw	SC	29520	**800-868-9630**	843-537-9656
Cherokee State Park N 4475 Rd	Langley	OK	74350	**866-602-4653**	918-435-8066
Cherry Creek State Park 4201 S Parker Rd	Aurora	CO	80014	**866-265-6447**	303-699-3860
Chester State Park 759 State Pk Dr	Chester	SC	29706	**866-345-7275**	803-385-2680
Chewacla State Park 124 Shell Toomer Pkwy	Auburn	AL	36830	**800-252-7275**	334-887-5621
Chickasaw State Park 26955 US Hwy 43	Gallion	AL	36742	**800-760-4089**	334-295-8230
Chicot State Park 3469 Chicot Pk Rd	Ville Platte	LA	70586	**888-677-2442**	337-363-2403
Chugach State Park 18620 Seward Highway	Anchorage	AK	99516	**800-478-6196**	907-345-5014

Listing	City	State	ZIP	Toll-Free	Phone
Clermont State Historic Site					
1 Clermont Ave	Germantown	NY	12526	**800-456-2267**	518-537-4240
Cline Falls State Scenic Viewpoint					
62976 OB Riley Rd	Redmond	OR	97756	**800-551-6949**	
Connecticut Valley Railroad State Park					
1 Railroad Ave PO Box 452	Essex	CT	06426	**866-526-2014**	860-767-0103
Conway Cemetery State Park					
140 Boat Dock Cove Rd 1 Capitol Mall	Bull Shoals	AR	72169	**888-287-2757**	
Coopers Rock State Forest					
61 County Line Dr	Bruceton Mills	WV	26525	**800-225-5982**	304-594-1561
Coquille Myrtle Grove State Natural Site					
PO Box 569	Myrtle Point	OR	97458	**800-551-6949**	
Cossatot River State Park-Natural Area					
1980 Hwy 278 W	Wickes	AR	71973	**877-665-6343**	870-385-2201
Cove Lake State Park					
110 Cove Lake Ln	Caryville	TN	37714	**800-250-8615**	423-566-9701
Crissey Field State Recreation Site					
1655 Hwy 101 N	Brookings	OR	97415	**800-551-6949**	541-469-2021
Crow Wing State Park					
3124 State Pk Rd	Brainerd	MN	56401	**888-646-6367**	218-825-3075
Crown Point State Historic Site					
21 Grandview Dr	Crown Point	NY	12928	**800-456-2267**	518-597-4666
Crystal Lake State Park					
96 Bellwater Ave	Barton	VT	05822	**888-409-7579**	802-525-6205
Crystal River Preserve State Park					
3266 N Sailboat Ave	Crystal River	FL	34428	**800-326-3521**	352-563-0450
Cumberland Falls State Resort Park					
7351 Hwy 90	Corbin	KY	40701	**800-325-0063**	
Cuyamaca Rancho State Park					
13652 Hwy 79	Julian	CA	92036	**800-444-7275**	760-765-0755
Cypremort Point State Park					
306 Beach Ln	Cypremort Point	LA	70538	**888-867-4510**	337-867-4510
D River State Recreation Site					
725 Summer St NE Ste C	Salem	OR	97301	**800-551-6949**	541-994-7341
Dabney State Recreation Area					
725 Summer St NE Ste C	Salem	OR	97301	**800-551-6949**	503-695-2261
Darlingtonia State Natural Site					
84505 Hwy 101 S	Florence	OR	97439	**800-551-6949**	541-997-3851
Dash Point State Park					
5700 SW Dash Pt Rd	Federal Way	WA	98023	**888-226-7688**	253-661-4955
Davy Crockett Birthplace State Park					
1245 Davy Crockett Pk Rd	Limestone	TN	37681	**800-250-8615**	423-257-2167
DeGray Lake Resort State Park					
2027 State Pk Entrance Rd	Bismarck	AR	71929	**800-737-8355**	501-865-2801
Del Rey Beach State Recreation Site					
100 Peter Iredale Rd	Hammond	OR	97121	**800-551-6949**	
Delaware State Park					
5202 US Rt 23 N	Delaware	OH	43015	**866-644-6727**	740-548-4631
Denali State Park					
7278 E Bogard Rd	Wasilla	AK	99654	**800-478-6196**	907-745-3975
Depoe Bay Whale Center					
Oregon Parks and Recreation Department 58 US-101 198 NE 123rd St	Depoe Bay	OR	97341	**800-551-6949**	541-765-3304
Devil's Den State Park					
11333 W Arkansas Hwy 74	West Fork	AR	72774	**888-742-8701**	479-761-3325
Devil's Lake State Recreation Area					
198 NE 123rd St	Lincoln City	OR	97367	**800-551-6949**	
Devils Fork State Park					
161 Holcombe Cir	Salem	SC	29676	**866-345-7275**	864-944-2639
Disney/Little Blue State Park					
Hwy 28 E	Disney	OK	74340	**800-622-6317**	918-435-8066
Douthat State Park					
14239 Douthat State Pk Rd *General	Millboro	VA	24460	**800-933-7275***	540-862-8100
Dreher Island State Recreation Area					
3677 State Pk Rd	Prosperity	SC	29127	**866-345-7275**	803-364-4152
Driftwood Beach State Recreation Site					
5580 S Coast Hwy	Newport	OR	97366	**800-551-6949**	
Dripping Springs State Park					
16830 Dripping Springs Rd	Okmulgee	OK	74447	**800-622-6317**	918-756-5971
Edgar Evins State Park					
1630 Edgar Evins State Pk Rd	Silver Point	TN	38582	**800-250-8619**	931-858-2446
Edisto Beach State Park					
8377 State Cabin Rd	Edisto Island	SC	29438	**800-315-3087**	843-869-2756
Eldorado Canyon State Park					
9 Kneale Rd PO Box B	Eldorado Springs	CO	80025	**866-265-6447**	303-494-3943
Ellmaker State Wayside					
198 NE 123rd St	Newport	OR	97365	**800-551-6949**	
Fair Haven Beach State Park					
14985 State Park Rd *General	Sterling	NY	13156	**800-456-2267***	315-947-5205
Fairview-Riverside State Park					
119 Fairview Dr	Madisonville	LA	70447	**888-677-3247**	985-845-3318
False Cape State Park					
4001 Sandpiper Rd *General	Virginia Beach	VA	23456	**800-933-7275***	757-426-7128
Father Hennepin State Park					
41294 Father Hennepin Pk Rd PO Box 397	Isle	MN	56342	**888-646-6367**	320-676-8763
FD Roosevelt State Park					
2970 GA Hwy 190	Pine Mountain	GA	31822	**800-864-7275**	706-663-4858
Fillmore Glen State Park					
1686 St Rt 38	Moravia	NY	13118	**800-456-2267**	315-497-0130
Fogarty Creek State Recreation Area					
725 Summer St NE Ste C	Salem	OR	97341	**800-551-6949**	
Fontainebleau State Park					
67825 US Hwy 190	Mandeville	LA	70448	**888-677-3668**	985-624-4443
Forestville/Mystery Cave State Park					
21071 County 118	Preston	MN	55965	**888-646-6367**	507-352-5111
Former Governors' Mansion State Historic Site					
612 E Blvd Ave	Bismarck	ND	58505	**866-243-5352**	701-328-2666
Fort Cobb Lake State Park					
27022 Copperhead Rd	Fort Cobb	OK	73038	**800-622-6317**	405-643-2249
Fort Jesup State Historic Site					
32 Geoghagan Rd	Many	LA	71449	**888-677-5378**	318-256-4117
Fort McAllister State Historic Park					
3894 Ft McAllister Rd	Richmond Hill	GA	31324	**800-864-7275**	912-727-2339
Fort Pillow State Historic Park					
3122 Pk Rd	Henning	TN	38041	**800-250-8615**	731-738-5581
Fort Ridgely State Park					
72158 County Rd 30	Fairfax	MN	55332	**888-646-6367**	507-426-7840
Fort Rock State Natural Area					
725 Summer St NE Ste C	Salem	OR	97739	**800-551-6949**	
Fort Saint Jean Baptiste State Historic Site					
155 Jefferson St	Natchitoches	LA	71457	**888-677-7853**	318-357-3101
Fort Snelling State Park					
101 Snelling Lake Rd	Saint Paul	MN	55111	**888-646-6367**	612-725-2389
Foss State Park 10252 Hwy 44	Foss	OK	73647	**800-622-6317**	580-592-4433
Frank Jackson State Park					
100 Jerry Adams Dr	Opp	AL	36467	**800-760-4089**	334-493-6988
Frontenac State Park					
29223 County 28 Blvd	Frontenac	MN	55026	**888-646-6367**	651-345-3401
Frozen Head State Natural Area					
964 Flat Fork Rd	Wartburg	TN	37887	**800-250-8615**	423-346-3318
Gambrill State Park					
8602 Gambrill Pk Rd	Frederick	MD	21702	**800-830-3974**	301-271-7574
George H. Crosby Manitou State Park					
c/o Tettegouche State Pk 5702 Hwy 61	Silver Bay	MN	55614	**888-646-6367**	218-226-6365
George T. Bagby State Park & Lodge					
330 Bagby Pkwy	Fort Gaines	GA	39851	**877-591-5575**	229-768-2571
Giant Springs State Park					
4600 Giant Springs Rd	Great Falls	MT	59405	**855-922-6768**	406-454-5840
Glacial Lakes State Park					
25022 County Rd 41	Starbuck	MN	56381	**888-646-6367**	320-239-2860
Gleneden Beach State Recreation Site					
198 NE 123rd St	Newport	OR	97365	**800-551-6949**	
Golden Gate Canyon State Park					
92 Crawford Gulch Rd	Golden	CO	80403	**866-265-6447**	303-582-3707
Goose Creek State Park					
2190 Camp Leach Rd	Washington	NC	27889	**877-722-6762**	252-923-2191
Gooseberry Falls State Park					
3206 Hwy 61	Two Harbors	MN	55616	**888-646-6367**	218-834-3855
Government Island State Recreation Area					
725 Summer St NE Ste C	Salem	OR	97301	**800-551-6949**	
Governor Daniel Dunklin's Grave State Historic Site					
104 Dunklin Dr 2901 Hwy 61	Herculaneum	MO	65102	**800-334-6946**	
Governor Patterson Memorial State Recreation Site					
5580 S Coast Hwy 5580 S Coast Hwy	Waldport	OR	97394	**800-551-6949**	
Grand Isle State Park					
Admiral Craik Dr	Grand Isle	LA	70358	**888-787-2559**	985-787-2559
Grand Portage State Park					
9393 E Hwy 61	Grand Portage	MN	55605	**888-646-6367**	218-475-2360
Great Plains State Park					
22487 E 1566 Rd	Mountain Park	OK	73559	**800-622-6317**	580-569-2032
Great River Bluffs State Park					
43605 Kipp Dr	Winona	MN	55987	**888-646-6367**	507-643-6849
H. B. Van Duzer Forest State Scenic Corridor					
198 NE 123rd St	Otis	OR	97368	**800-551-6949**	
Hacklebarney State Park					
119 Hacklebarney Rd 119 Hacklebarney Rd	Long Valley	NJ	07853	**800-659-4044**	908-638-6969
Half Moon Bay State Beach					
c/o San Mateo Coast Sector Office 95 Kelly Ave	Half Moon Bay	CA	94019	**800-444-7275**	650-726-8819
Hamlin Beach State Park					
1 Hamlin Beach Blvd W	Hamlin	NY	14464	**800-456-2267**	585-964-2462
Hampson Archeological Museum State Park					
PO Box 156	Wilson	AR	72395	**888-742-8701**	870-655-8622
Hampton Plantation State Historic Site					
1950 Rutledge Rd	McClellanville	SC	29458	**800-315-3087**	843-546-9361
Harmonie State Park					
3451 Harmonie State Pk Rd	New Harmony	IN	47631	**866-622-6746**	812-682-4821
Harriman State Park					
3489 Green Canyon Rd	Island Park	ID	83429	**866-634-3246**	208-558-7368
Havenwoods State Forest					
6141 N Hopkins St	Milwaukee	WI	53209	**888-936-7463**	414-527-0232
Hawaii Information Consortium (HIC)					
201 Merchant St Ste 1805	Honolulu	HI	96813	**800-295-0089**	808-695-4620
Hearst San Simeon State Historical Monument					
750 Hearst Castle Rd	San Simeon	CA	93452	**800-444-4445**	805-927-2020
Heceta Head Lighthouse State Scenic Viewpoint					
93111 Hwy 101 N	Florence	OR	97439	**800-551-6949**	
Heritage Hill State Historical Park					
2640 S Webster Ave	Green Bay	WI	54301	**800-721-5150**	920-448-5150
Herman Davis State Park					
Corner of Ark 18 Baltimore St	Manila	AR	72201	**888-287-2757**	
Heyburn State Park					
57 Chatcolet Rd	Plummer	ID	83851	**866-634-3246**	208-686-1308
Hickory Knob State Resort Park					
1591 Resort Dr	McCormick	SC	29835	**800-491-1764**	864-391-2450
Hoffman Memorial State Wayside					
PO Box 569	Mytrle Point	OR	97458	**800-551-6949**	
Holliday Lake State Park					
2759 State Pk Rd	Appomattox	VA	24522	**800-933-7275**	434-248-6308
Honey Creek State Park					
901 State Pk Rd	Grove	OK	74344	**800-622-6317**	918-786-9447
Hudson River Islands State Park					
Schodack Island State Pk	Schodack Landing	NY	12156	**800-456-2267**	518-732-0187
Hueco Tanks State Historic Site					
6900 Hueco Tanks Rd Ste 1	El Paso	TX	79938	**800-792-1112**	915-857-1135
Hunting Island State Park					
2555 Sea Island Pkwy	Hunting Island	SC	29920	**800-315-3087**	843-838-2011
Huntington Beach State Park					
16148 Ocean Hwy	Murrells Inlet	SC	29576	**800-491-1764**	843-237-4440
Huntington State Park					
PO Box 1343	Huntington	UT	84528	**800-322-3770**	435-687-2491
Jacksonport State Park					
1 Capitol Mall	Newport	AR	72112	**888-287-2757**	870-523-2143
Janes Island State Park					
26280 Alfred Lawson Dr	Crisfield	MD	21817	**877-620-8367**	410-968-1565
Jenny Wiley State Resort Park					
75 Theatre Ct	Prestonsburg	KY	41653	**800-325-0142**	
Jimmie Davis State Park					
1209 State Pk Rd	Chatham	LA	71226	**888-677-2263**	318-249-2595

Name / Address	City	State	Zip	Toll-Free	Phone
John Boyd Thacher State Park 1 Hailes Cave Rd	Voorheesville	NY	12186	**800-456-2267**	518-872-1237
John Jay Homestead State Historic Site PO Box 832	Katonah	NY	10536	**800-456-2267**	914-232-5651
John Paul Jones State Historic Site c/o Bureau of Parks & Lands	Bangor	ME	04401	**800-452-1942**	207-941-4014
Jordan Lake State Recreation Area 280 State Pk Rd	Apex	NC	27523	**877-722-6762**	919-362-0586
Joseph H. Stewart State Recreation Area 35251 Hwy 62	Prospect	OR	97536	**800-452-5687**	541-560-3334
Justin P. Wilson Cumberland Trail State Park 220 Pk Rd	Caryville	TN	38555	**800-342-3145**	423-566-2229
Kam Wah Chung State Heritage Site (KWC) 725 Summer St NE Ste C	Salem	OR	97301	**800-551-6949**	503-986-0707
Kenlake State Resort Park 542 Kenlake Rd	Hardin	KY	42048	**800-325-0143**	270-474-2211
Keystone State Park 1926 S Hwy 151	Sand Springs	OK	74063	**800-654-8240**	918-865-4991
Koberg Beach State Recreation Site 725 Summer St NE Ste C	Salem	OR	97301	**800-551-6949**	503-986-0707
Lake Barkley State Resort Park 3500 State Pk Rd	Cadiz	KY	42211	**800-325-1708**	
Lake Bistineau State Park 103 State Pk Rd	Doyline	LA	71023	**888-677-2478**	318-745-3503
Lake Bruin State Park 201 State Pk Rd	Saint Joseph	LA	71366	**888-677-2784**	318-766-3530
Lake Carmi State Park 460 Marsh Farm Rd *Resv	Enosburg Falls	VT	05450	**888-409-7579***	802-933-8383
Lake Cascade State Park 970 Dam Rd	Cascade	ID	83611	**866-634-3246**	208-382-6544
Lake Chicot State Park 2542 Hwy 257	Lake Village	AR	71653	**800-264-2430**	870-265-5480
Lake Claiborne State Park 225 State Pk Rd	Homer	LA	71040	**888-677-2524**	318-927-2976
Lake D'Arbonne State Park 3628 Evergreen Rd	Farmerville	LA	71241	**888-677-5200**	318-368-2086
Lake Greenwood State Recreation Area 302 State Pk Rd	Ninety Six	SC	29666	**866-345-7275**	864-543-3535
Lake Kegonsa State Park 2405 Door Creek Rd *General	Stoughton	WI	53589	**888-947-2757***	608-873-9695
Lake Lurleen State Park 13226 Lake Lurleen Rd	Coker	AL	35452	**800-760-4089**	205-339-1558
Lake Murray State Park 120 N Robinson Ave 6th Fl	Oklahoma City	OK	73152	**800-652-6552**	
Lake Owyhee State Park 725 Summer St NE Ste C	Salem	OR	97301	**800-551-6949**	503-986-0707
Lake Wapello State Park 15248 Campground Rd	Drakesville	IA	52552	**866-495-4868**	641-722-3371
Lake Wissota State Park 18127 County Hwy O	Chippewa Falls	WI	54729	**800-847-9367**	715-382-4574
Lake Wister State Park 25567 US Hwy 270	Wister	OK	74966	**800-622-6317**	918-655-7212
Lakepoint Resort State Park 104 Lakepoint Dr	Eufaula	AL	36027	**800-544-5253**	334-687-8011
LaPine State Park 15800 State Recreation Rd	La Pine	OR	97739	**800-551-6949**	
LeFleur's Bluff State Park 2140 Riverside Dr	Jackson	MS	39202	**800-237-6278**	601-987-3923
Lewis & Clark State Recreation Site 725 Summer St NE Ste C	Salem	OR	97301	**800-551-6949**	503-986-0707
Lincoln State Park Hwy 162 PO Box 216	Lincoln City	IN	47552	**877-478-3657**	812-937-4710
Little Pee Dee State Park 1298 State Pk Rd	Dillon	SC	29536	**800-491-1764**	843-774-8872
Little Talbot Island State Park 12157 Heckscher Dr	Jacksonville	FL	32226	**800-326-3521**	904-251-2320
Little White House State Historic Site 401 Little White House Rd	Warm Springs	GA	31830	**800-864-7275**	706-655-5870
Longfellow-Evangeline State Historic Site 1200 N Main St	Saint Martinville	LA	70582	**888-677-2900**	337-394-3754
Los Adaes State Historic Site 6354 Hwy 485	Robeline	LA	71469	**888-677-5378**	318-472-9449
Louisiana State Arboretum 4213 Chicot Pk Rd	Ville Platte	LA	70586	**888-677-6100**	337-363-6289
Lovers Key State Park 8700 Estero Blvd	Fort Myers Beach	FL	33931	**800-326-3521**	239-463-4588
Lower Wekiva River Preserve State Park 1800 Wekiwa Cir	Apopka	FL	32712	**800-326-3521**	407-884-2008
Manhattan Beach State Recreation Site 725 Summer St NE Ste C	Salem	OR	97301	**800-551-6949**	503-986-0707
Mansfield State Historic Site 15149 Hwy 175	Mansfield	LA	71052	**888-677-6267**	318-872-1474
Marksville State Historic Site 837 ML King Dr	Marksville	LA	71351	**888-253-8954**	318-253-8954
Mary Jane Thurston State Park 1466 State Rt 65	McClure	OH	43534	**866-644-6727**	419-832-7662
Mastodon State Historic Site 1050 Charles J Becker Dr	Imperial	MO	63052	**800-334-6946**	636-464-2976
Meaher State Park 5200 Battleship Pkwy	Spanish Fort	AL	36577	**800-252-7275**	251-626-5529
Merkle Wildlife Sanctuary 580 Taylor Ave	Annapolis	MD	21401	**877-620-8367**	
Middle Bass Island State Park 1719 Fox Rd	Middle Bass Island	OH	43446	**866-644-6727**	419-285-0311
Millsite State Park Ferron Canyon Rd PO Box 1343	Huntington	UT	84528	**800-322-3770**	435-384-2552
Missouri State Parks PO Box 176	Jefferson City	MO	65102	**800-334-6946**	
Monte Sano State Park 5105 Nolen Ave	Huntsville	AL	35801	**800-252-7275**	256-534-3757
Montgomery Bell State Resort Park 1020 Jackson Hill Rd	Burns	TN	37029	**800-250-8613**	615-797-9052
Moore State Park Mill St	Paxton	MA	01612	**800-437-5922**	508-792-3969
Morgan Run Natural Environment Area Benros Ln	Eldersburg	MD	21784	**800-830-3974**	410-461-5005
Moro Bay State Park 6071 US Hwy 600	Jersey	AR	71651	**888-742-8701**	870-463-8555
Morro Bay State Park 60 State Pk Rd Morro Bay State Pk Rd	Morro Bay	CA	93442	**800-777-0369**	
Myakka River State Park 13208 SR 72	Sarasota	FL	34241	**800-326-3521**	941-361-6511
Myre-Big Island State Park 19499 780th Ave	Albert Lea	MN	56007	**888-646-6367**	507-379-3403
Natural Bridge Battlefield Historic State Park 7502 Natural Bridge Rd	Tallahassee	FL	32305	**800-326-3521**	850-922-6007
Natural Bridge State Resort Park 2135 Natural Bridge Rd	Slade	KY	40376	**800-325-1710**	
Nelson Dewey State Park PO Box 658	Cassville	WI	53806	**888-936-7463**	608-725-5374
Neskowin Beach State Recreation Site 198 NE 123rd St	Neskowin	OR	97149	**800-551-6949**	
New Germany State Park 349 Headquarters Ln	Grantsville	MD	21536	**800-830-3974**	301-895-5453
Newport State Park 475 County Rd NP	Ellison Bay	WI	54210	**800-847-9367**	920-854-2500
North Santiam State Recreation Area PO Box 549	Detroit	OR	97342	**800-551-6949**	
North Toledo Bend State Park 2907 N Toledo Pk Rd	Zwolle	LA	71486	**888-677-6400**	318-645-4715
Northern Highland - American Legion State Forest 4125 County Hwy M	Boulder Junction	WI	54512	**800-847-9367**	715-385-2727
Oak Mountain State Park 200 Terr Dr PO Box 278	Pelham	AL	35124	**800-252-7275**	205-620-2520
OC&E Woods Line State Trail 46000 Hwy 97 N 46000 Hwy 97 N	Chiloquin	OR	97624	**800-551-6949**	541-883-5558
Occoneechee State Park 1192 Occoneechee Pk Rd	Clarksville	VA	23927	**800-933-7275**	434-374-2210
Oceanside Beach State Recreation Site 13000 Whiskey Creek Rd W	Tillamook	OR	97141	**800-551-6949**	
Oconee State Park 624 State Pk Rd	Mountain Rest	SC	29664	**888-803-0844**	864-638-5353
Old Town San Diego State Historic Park 4002 Wallace St	San Diego	CA	92110	**800-777-0369**	619-220-5422
Oleta River State Park 3400 NE 163rd St	North Miami Beach	FL	33160	**800-326-3521**	305-919-1846
Oliver Inlet State Marine Park 400 Willoughby Ave PO Box 111071	Juneau	AK	99801	**855-277-4491**	907-465-4563
Ona Beach State Park 5580 S Coast Hwy	Newport	OR	97366	**800-551-6949**	
Onondaga Cave State Park 7556 Hwy H	Leasburg	MO	65535	**877-422-6766**	573-245-6576
Ontario State Recreation Site 23751 Old Hwy 30	Huntington	OR	97907	**800-551-6949**	
Osage Hills State Park 2131 Osage Hills State Pk Rd	Pawhuska	OK	74056	**800-622-6317**	918-336-4141
Oscar Scherer State Park 1843 S Tamiami Trail	Osprey	FL	34229	**800-326-3521**	941-483-5956
Otter Point State Recreation Site PO Box 1345	Gold Beach	OR	97444	**800-551-6949**	
Ozark Folk Ctr State Park 1032 Pk Ave	Mountain View	AR	72560	**800-264-3655**	870-269-3851
Paint Creek State Park 280 Taylor Rd	Bainbridge	OH	45612	**866-644-6727**	937-981-7061
Palmetto Island State Park 19501 Pleasant Rd	Abbeville	LA	70510	**888-677-3668**	337-893-3930
Panther State Forest HC 63 PO Box Box 923	Panther	WV	24872	**800-225-5982**	304-938-2252
Paradise Point State Recreation Site PO Box 1345	Port Orford	OR	97465	**800-551-6949**	
Paris Mountain State Park 2401 State Pk Rd	Greenville	SC	29609	**866-345-7275**	864-244-5565
Paul M. Grist State Park 1546 Grist Rd	Selma	AL	36701	**800-252-7275**	334-872-5846
Paynes Creek Historic State Park 888 Lake Branch Rd	Bowling Green	FL	33834	**800-326-3521**	863-375-4717
Pennyrile Forest State Resort Park 20781 Pennyrile Lodge Rd	Dawson Springs	KY	42408	**800-325-1711**	
Picacho State Recreation Area 1416 Ninth St PO Box 942896	Sacramento	CA	95814	**800-777-0369**	916-653-6995
Pickett State Park 4605 Pickett Pk Hwy	Jamestown	TN	38556	**877-260-0010**	931-879-5821
Pine Grove Furnace State Park 1100 Pine Grove Rd	Gardners	PA	17324	**888-727-2757**	717-486-7174
Pine Mountain State Resort Park 1050 State Pk Rd	Pineville	KY	40977	**800-325-1712**	
Pipestem Resort State Park PO Box 150	Pipestem	WV	25979	**800-225-5982**	304-466-1800
Pocahontas State Park 10301 State Pk Rd	Chesterfield	VA	23832	**800-933-7275**	804-796-4255
Pocomoke River State Park 3461 Worcester Hwy	Snow Hill	MD	21863	**877-620-8367**	410-632-2566
Pocomoke State Forest 580 Taylor Ave	Annapolis	MD	21401	**877-620-8367**	
Port Hudson State Historic Site 236 Hwy 61	Jackson	LA	70748	**888-677-3400**	225-654-3775
Potawatomi State Park 3740 County Rd PD	Sturgeon Bay	WI	54235	**800-847-9367**	920-746-2890
Poverty Point Reservoir State Park 1500 Poverty Pt Pkwy	Delhi	LA	71232	**800-474-0392**	318-878-7536
Poverty Point State Historic Site 6859 Hwy 577	Pioneer	LA	71266	**888-926-5492**	318-926-5492
Presque Isle State Park 301 Peninsula Dr Ste 1	Erie	PA	16505	**888-727-2757**	814-833-7424
Priest Lake State Park 314 Indian Creek Pk Rd *Resv	Coolin	ID	83821	**888-922-6743***	208-443-2200
Prompton State Park c/o Lackawanna	North Abington Township	PA	18414	**888-727-2757**	570-945-3239
Providence Mountains State Recreation Area 1416 Ninth St	Sacramento	CA	95814	**800-777-0369**	
Queen Wilhelmina State Park 3877 Arkansas 88	Mena	AR	71953	**888-287-2757**	479-394-2863

Name / Address	City	State	Zip	Toll-Free	Phone
Ravine Gardens State Park 1600 Twigg St	Palatka	FL	32177	**800-326-3521**	386-329-3721
Raymond Gary State Park Hwy 70	Fort Towson	OK	74735	**800-622-6317**	580-873-2307
Raymond R Andy Guest Jr Shenandoah River State Park 350 Daughter of Stars Dr	Bentonville	VA	22610	**800-933-7275**	540-622-6840
Rebel State Historic Site 1260 Hwy 1221	Marthaville	LA	71450	**888-677-3600**	318-472-6255
Red Fleet State Park 8750 North Hwy 191	Vernal	UT	84078	**800-322-3770**	435-789-4432
Rickwood Caverns State Park 370 Rickwood Pk Rd	Warrior	AL	35180	**800-252-7275**	205-647-9692
Robbers Cave State Park Hwy 2 N	Wilburton	OK	74578	**800-654-8240**	918-465-2565
Rock Bridge Memorial State Park 5901 S Hwy 163	Columbia	MO	65203	**800-334-6946**	573-449-7402
Rock Island State Park 82 Beach Rd	Rock Island	TN	38581	**800-250-8614**	931-686-2471
Rock Springs Run State Reserve 30601 CR 433	Sorrento	FL	32776	**800-326-3521**	407-884-2008
Roland Cooper State Park 285 Deer Run Dr	Camden	AL	36726	**800-252-7275**	334-682-4838
Rough River Dam State Resort Park 450 Lodge Rd	Falls of Rough	KY	40119	**800-325-1713**	
Saint Bernard State Park 501 St Bernard Pkwy	Braithwaite	LA	70040	**888-677-7823**	504-682-2101
Saint Croix State Park 30065 St Croix Pk Rd	Hinckley	MN	55037	**888-646-6367**	320-384-6591
Saint Mary's River State Park c/o Pt Lookout State Pk 11175 Pt Lookout Rd	Scotland	MD	20687	**800-830-3974**	301-872-5688
Sakatah Lake State Park 50499 Sakatah Lake State Pk Rd	Waterville	MN	56096	**888-646-6367**	507-362-4438
Salt Springs State Park c/o Lackawanna	North Abington Township	PA	18414	**888-727-2757**	570-945-3239
Sam Houston Jones State Park 107 Sutherland Rd	Lake Charles	LA	70611	**888-677-7264**	337-855-2665
Sandy Point State Park 1100 E College Pkwy	Annapolis	MD	21409	**877-620-8836**	410-974-2149
Savanna Portage State Park 55626 Lake Pl	McGregor	MN	55760	**888-646-6367**	218-426-3271
Schoharie Crossing State Historic Site 129 Schoharie St PO Box 140	Fort Hunter	NY	12069	**800-456-2267**	518-829-7516
Schuyler Mansion State Historic Site 32 Catherine St	Albany	NY	12202	**800-456-2267**	518-434-0834
Scioto Trail State Park 144 Lake Rd	Chillicothe	OH	45601	**866-644-6727**	
Senate House State Historic Site 296 Fair St	Kingston	NY	12401	**800-456-2267**	845-338-2786
Seneca Fouts Memorial State Natural Area Wygant Trail	Hood River	OR	97014	**800-551-6949**	
Sequoyah Bay State Park 6237 E 100th St N	Wagoner	OK	74467	**800-622-6317**	918-683-0878
Sesquicentennial State Park 9564 Two Notch Rd	Columbia	SC	29223	**888-245-9300**	803-788-2706
Seyon Lodge State Park 1 National Life Dr	Vermont	VT	05620	**888-409-7579**	802-584-3829
Shackford Head State Park 106 Hogan Ave	Bangor	ME	04401	**800-400-6856**	207-941-4014
Sibley State Park 800 Sibley Pk Rd	New London	MN	56273	**888-646-6367**	320-354-2055
Smithgall Woods Conservation Area & Lodge 61 Tsalaki Trl	Helen	GA	30545	**800-864-7275**	706-878-3087
Snowdale State Park 501 S 439	Salina	OK	74361	**800-622-6317**	918-434-2651
Soldiers Delight Natural Environment Area 5100 Deer Park Rd	Owings Mills	MD	21117	**800-830-3974**	410-461-5005
Somers Cove Marina 715 Broadway PO Box 67	Crisfield	MD	21817	**800-967-3474**	410-968-0925
Soudan Underground Mine State Park 1302 McKinley Park Rd	Soudan	MN	55782	**888-646-6367**	218-753-2245
South Arkansas Arboretum PO Box 7010	El Dorado	AR	71731	**888-287-2757**	
South Beach State Park 5580 S Coast Hwy	Newport	OR	97366	**800-452-5687**	541-867-4715
South Toledo Bend State Park 120 Bald Eaglel Rd	Anacoco	LA	71403	**888-398-4770**	337-286-9075
Spavinaw State Park 555 S Main	Spavinaw	OK	74366	**800-622-6317**	918-589-2651
Split Rock Creek State Park 50th Ave	Jasper	MN	56144	**888-646-6367**	507-348-7908
Split Rock Lighthouse State Park 3755 Split Rock Lighthouse Rd	Two Harbors	MN	55616	**800-366-8917**	218-595-7625
State Forest State Park 56750 Hwy 14	Walden	CO	80480	**866-265-6447**	970-723-8366
Steinaker State Park 4335 N Hwy 191	Vernal	UT	84078	**800-322-3770**	435-789-4432
Stone Mountain State Park 3042 Frank Pkwy	Roaring Gap	NC	28668	**877-722-6762**	336-957-8185
Stonefield Beach State Recreation Site 725 Summer St NE 84505 Hwy 101 S	Salem	OR	97301	**800-551-6949**	
Strouds Run State Park 2045 Morse Rd	Columbus	OH	43229	**800-945-3543**	740-592-2302
Succor Creek State Natural Area 1298 Lk Owyhee Dam Rd	Adrian	OR	97901	**800-551-6949**	
Tettegouche State Park 5702 Hwy 61	Silver Bay	MN	55614	**800-366-8917**	218-226-6365
Three Island Crossing State Park 1083 S Three Island Pk Dr	Glenns Ferry	ID	83623	**888-922-6743**	208-366-2394
Tickfaw State Park 27225 Patterson Rd	Springfield	LA	70462	**888-981-2020**	225-294-5020
Tims Ford State Park 570 Tims Ford Dr	Winchester	TN	37398	**800-471-5295**	931-962-1183
Tokatee Klootchman State Natural Site 93111 Hwy 101 N	Florence	OR	97439	**800-551-6949**	
Tombigbee State Park 264 Cabin Dr	Tupelo	MS	38804	**800-467-2757**	662-842-7669
Torrey Pines State Reserve c/o San Diego Coast District 4477 Pacific Hwy	San Diego	CA	92110	**866-240-4655**	858-755-2063
Touvelle State Recreation Site Table Rock Rd 3792 N River Rd	Central Point	OR	97502	**800-551-6949**	541-983-2277
Tub Springs State Wayside 12845 Green Springs Hwy 3792 N River Rd	Ashland	OR	97520	**800-551-6949**	
Twin Bridges State Park 14801 Hwy 137 S	Fairland	OK	74343	**800-622-6317**	918-540-2545
Twin Lakes State Park 788 Twin Lakes Rd	Green Bay	VA	23942	**800-933-7275**	434-392-3435
Umpqua Lighthouse State Park 84505 Hwy 101 S	Florence	OR	97439	**800-551-6949**	
Unicoi State Park & Lodge 1788 Hwy 356 Rd	Helen	GA	30545	**800-573-9659**	
Unity Lake State Recreation Site 725 Summer St NE Ste C	Salem	OR	97301	**800-551-6949**	541-932-4453
Upper Sioux Agency State Park 5908 Hwy 67	Granite Falls	MN	56241	**800-366-8917**	320-564-4777
Van Buren State Park 12259 Township Rd 218	Van Buren	OH	45889	**866-644-6727**	419-832-7662
W.B. Nelson State Recreation Site 5580 S Coast Hwy	Newport	OR	97366	**800-551-6949**	
Wah-Sha-She State Park HC 75 Hwy 60	Copan	OK	74022	**800-622-6317**	918-532-4334
Walt Whitman House State Historic Site 330 Mickle Blvd	Camden	NJ	08103	**800-843-6420**	
Watts Towers of Simon Rodia State Historic Park 1765 E 107th St 1925 Las Virgenes	Calabasas	CA	91302	**866-240-4655**	213-847-4646
White River State Park 801 W Washington St	Indianapolis	IN	46204	**800-665-9056**	317-233-2434
Whitewater State Park 19041 Hwy 74	Altura	MN	55910	**800-366-8917**	507-932-3007
Willamette Stone State Heritage Site 11321 SW Terwilliger Blvd	Portland	OR	97219	**800-551-6949**	
Willard Bay State Park 900 West 650 North Ste A	Willard	UT	84340	**800-322-3770**	435-734-9494
William M. Tugman State Park 72549 Hwy 101	Lakeside	OR	97449	**800-551-6949**	
Willow River State Park 1034 County Hwy A	Hudson	WI	54016	**800-847-9367**	715-386-5931
Winchuck State Recreation Site 1655 Hwy 101 N	Brookings	OR	97415	**800-551-6949**	
Wind Creek State Park 4325 Al Hwy 128	Alexander City	AL	35010	**800-252-7275**	256-329-0845
Winter Quarters State Historic Site 4929 Hwy 608	Newellton	LA	71357	**888-677-9468**	888-677-2784
Yachats Ocean Road State Natural Site 5580 S Coast Hwy	Newport	OR	97366	**800-551-6949**	
Youghiogheny River Natural Resources Management Area c/o Deep Creek Lake State Pk 898 State Pk Rd	Swanton	MD	21561	**877-620-8367**	301-387-5563

565 PARTY GOODS

Name / Address	City	State	Zip	Toll-Free	Phone
Amscan Inc 80 Grasslands Rd	Elmsford	NY	10523	**800-444-8887**	914-345-2020
Balloons Everywhere Inc 16474 Greeno Rd	Fairhope	AL	36532	**800-239-2000**	
Paper Store Inc 20 Main St	Acton	MA	01720	**844-480-7100**	
Party City Corp 25 Green Pond Rd Ste 1	Rockaway	NJ	07866	**800-727-8924**	973-453-8600

566 PATTERNS - INDUSTRIAL

Name / Address	City	State	Zip	Toll-Free	Phone
Freeman Mfg & Supply Co 1101 Moore Rd	Avon	OH	44011	**800-321-8511**	440-934-1902
Hub Pattern Corp 2113 Salem Ave	Roanoke	VA	24016	**800-482-3505**	540-342-3505

567 PATTERNS - SEWING

Name / Address	City	State	Zip	Toll-Free	Phone
Bonfit America Inc 5741 Buckingham Pkwy Unit A	Culver City	CA	90232	**800-526-6348**	310-204-7880
McCall Pattern Co 615 McCall Rd	Manhattan	KS	66502	**800-255-2762**	

568 PAWN SHOPS

Name / Address	City	State	Zip	Toll-Free	Phone
EZCORP Inc 1901 Capital Pkwy *NASDAQ: EZPW*	Austin	TX	78746	**800-873-7296**	512-314-3400
First Cash Financial Services Inc 690 E Lamar Blvd Ste 400 *NASDAQ: FCFS*	Arlington	TX	76011	**800-290-4598**	817-460-3947
Maxium Financial Services Inc 30 Vogell Rd Ste 1	Richmond Hill	ON	L4B3K6	**800-379-5888**	905-780-6150
Resurgent Capital Services L P 15 S Main St Ste 600	Greenville	SC	29601	**888-665-0374**	

569 PAYROLL SERVICES

SEE ALSO Data Processing & Related Services

Name / Address	City	State	Zip	Toll-Free	Phone
Advantage Payroll Services Inc 126 Merrow Rd PO Box 1330 *Cust Svc	Auburn	ME	04211	**800-876-0178***	207-784-0178

Name / Address	City	State	Zip	Toll-Free	Phone
Automatic Data Processing Inc (ADP) 1 ADP Blvd *NASDAQ: ADP*	Roseland	NJ	07068	**800-225-5237**	
CheckPoint HR 2035 Lincoln Hwy Ste 1080	Edison	NJ	08817	**800-385-0331**	732-287-8270
Corporate Business Solutions LLC 600 S Tower 225 Peachtree St NE	Atlanta	GA	30303	**800-239-8182**	404-521-6030
Employers Resource Management Co 1301 S Vista Ave Ste 200	Boise	ID	83705	**800-574-4668**	208-376-3000
Hiregenics 47742 Van Dyke Ave	Shelby Township	MI	48317	**866-315-5489**	
Media Services 500 S Sepulveda Blvd 4th Fl	Los Angeles	CA	90049	**800-738-0409**	310-440-9600
Patriot Staffing & Services Llc 47 Eggert Ave	Metuchen	NJ	08840	**888-412-6999**	
Paychex Inc 911 Panorama Trl S *NASDAQ: PAYX*	Rochester	NY	14625	**800-828-4411**	585-385-6666
Paychex Major Market Services 12647 Alcosta Blvd Ste 200	San Ramon	CA	94583	**888-243-9329**	925-242-0700
SurePayroll 2350 Ravine Way Ste 100	Glenview	IL	60025	**877-954-7873**	847-676-8420

570 PENS, PENCILS, PARTS

SEE ALSO Office & School Supplies ; Art Materials & Supplies - Mfr

Name / Address	City	State	Zip	Toll-Free	Phone
Alvin & Company Inc 1335 Blue Hills Ave	Bloomfield	CT	06002	**800-444-2584**	860-243-8991
Avery Dennison Corp 207 Goode Ave *NYSE: AVY* ■ *Cust Svc	Glendale	CA	91203	**888-567-4387***	626-304-2000
Dixon Ticonderoga Co 195 International Pkwy	Heathrow	FL	32746	**800-824-9430**	407-829-9000
Dri Mark Products Inc 999 S Oyster Bay Rd Ste 312	Bethpage	NY	11714	**800-645-9118**	516-484-6200
Harcourt Pencil Co 7765 S 175 W	Milroy	IN	46156	**800-428-6584**	
Listo Pencil Corp 1925 Union St	Alameda	CA	94501	**800-547-8648**	510-522-2910
Musgrave Pencil Company Inc 701 W Ln St	Shelbyville	TN	37160	**800-736-2450**	931-684-3611
National Pen Corp (NPC) 12121 Scripps Summit Dr Ste 200	San Diego	CA	92131	**800-854-1000**	858-675-3000

571 PERFORMING ARTS FACILITIES

SEE ALSO Stadiums & Arenas ; Theaters - Broadway ; Theaters - Resident ; Convention Centers
Most of the fax numbers provided for these facilities are for the box office.

Name / Address	City	State	Zip	Toll-Free	Phone
A Contemporary Theatre (ACT) 700 Union St Kreielsheimer Pl	Seattle	WA	98101	**888-584-4849**	206-292-7660
Adrienne Arsht Ctr for the Performing Arts of Miami-Dade County Inc 1300 Biscayne Blvd	Miami	FL	33132	**877-949-6722**	786-468-2000
Alabama Theatre 4750 Hwy 17 S	North Myrtle Beach	SC	29582	**800-342-2262**	843-272-1111
Alberta Bair Theater for the Performing Arts 2722 Third Ave N Ste 200 PO Box 1556	Billings	MT	59103	**877-321-2074**	406-256-8915
American Stage 163 Third St N	Saint Petersburg	FL	33731	**800-435-7352**	727-823-1600
Andy Williams Moon River Theatre 2500 Hwy 76	Branson	MO	65616	**800-666-6094**	417-334-1800
Artpark 450 S Fourth St	Lewiston	NY	14092	**877-325-5787**	716-754-9000
Arts Ctr of Coastal Carolina 14 Shelter Cove Ln	Hilton Head Island	SC	29928	**888-860-2787**	843-686-3945
Auditorium Theatre 50 E Congress Pkwy	Chicago	IL	60605	**800-982-2787**	312-341-2310
Barbara B Mann Performing Arts Hall 13350 FSW Pkwy	Fort Myers	FL	33919	**800-440-7469**	239-489-3033
Bass Performance Hall 4th & Calhoun Sts	Fort Worth	TX	76102	**877-212-4280**	817-212-4300
Berklee Performance Ctr 136 Massachusetts Ave	Boston	MA	02115	**877-237-5533**	617-747-2261
Blossom Music Ctr Tickets 1145 W Steels Corners Rd	Cuyahoga Falls	OH	44223	**800-745-3000**	330-920-8040
Boisfeuillet Jones Atlanta Civic Ctr 395 Piedmont Ave	Atlanta	GA	30308	**877-430-7596**	404-523-6275
Boston Symphony Hall 301 Massachusetts Ave	Boston	MA	02115	**888-266-1200**	617-266-1492
Broadway Ctr for the Performing Arts 901 Broadway	Tacoma	WA	98402	**800-291-7593**	253-591-5890
Broward Ctr for the Performing Arts 201 SW Fifth Ave	Fort Lauderdale	FL	33312	**877-311-7469**	954-462-0222
Bushnell Ctr for the Performing Arts 166 Capitol Ave	Hartford	CT	06106	**888-824-2874**	860-987-6000
California Ctr for the Arts 340 N Escondido Blvd	Escondido	CA	92025	**800-988-4253**	760-839-4138
California Theatre of Performing Arts 562 W Fourth St	San Bernardino	CA	92401	**800-745-3000**	909-885-5152
Carnegie Hall 881 Seventh Ave	New York	NY	10019	**800-728-3843**	212-247-7800
Carolina Opry 8901 Hwy 17 N	Myrtle Beach	SC	29572	**800-843-6779**	
Center for the Arts 103 Ctr for the Arts	Buffalo	NY	14260	**800-745-3000**	716-645-2787
Centre in the Square 101 Queen St N	Kitchener	ON	N2H6P7	**800-265-8977**	519-578-1570
Cerritos Ctr for the Performing Arts 12700 Ctr Ct Dr	Cerritos	CA	90703	**800-300-4345**	562-916-8501
Chester Fritz Auditorium 3475 University Ave	Grand Forks	ND	58202	**800-375-4068**	701-777-3076
Cheyenne Civic Ctr 510 W 20th St	Cheyenne	WY	82001	**877-691-2787**	307-637-6364
Christel DeHaan Fine Arts Ctr 1400 E Hanna Ave University of Indianapolis	Indianapolis	IN	46227	**800-232-8634**	317-788-3566
Cincinnati Playhouse in the Park 962 Mt Adams Cir	Cincinnati	OH	45202	**800-582-3208**	513-345-2242
Circuit Playhouse, The 51 S Cooper St	Memphis	TN	38104	**888-648-8154**	901-725-0776
Citi Performing Arts Ctr Wang Theatre 270 Tremont St	Boston	MA	02116	**800-982-2787**	
Contemporary Arts Ctr 900 Camp St	New Orleans	LA	70130	**800-568-6968**	504-528-3805
Curtis M Phillips Ctr for the Performing Arts 315 Hull Rd PO Box 112750	Gainesville	FL	32611	**800-905-2787**	352-392-1900
Cutler Majestic Theatre at Emerson College 219 Tremont St	Boston	MA	02116	**888-627-7115**	617-824-8000
David A. Straz Jr Ctr for, The Performing Arts, The 1010 N WC MacInnes Pl	Tampa	FL	33602	**800-955-1045**	813-222-1000
Denver Ctr for the Performing Arts 1101 13th St	Denver	CO	80204	**800-641-1222**	303-893-4000
Denver Performing Arts Complex 1400 Curtis St 1St Fl	Denver	CO	80204	**800-745-3000**	720-865-4220
Diana Wortham Theatre at Pack Place 2 S Pack Sq	Asheville	NC	28801	**800-999-2160**	828-257-4530
DuPont Theatre 1007 N Market St	Wilmington	DE	19801	**800-338-0881**	302-656-4401
EJ Thomas Performing Arts Hall 198 Hill St University of Akron	Akron	OH	44325	**800-745-3000**	330-972-7570
El Paso Convention & Performing Arts Ctr 1 Civic Ctr Plz	El Paso	TX	79901	**800-351-6024**	915-534-0600
Fairfield University Fairfield University 1073 N Benson Rd	Fairfield	CT	06824	**877-278-7396**	203-254-4010
Festival Concert Hall *North Dakota State University* PO Box 5691	Fargo	ND	58105	**800-726-1724**	701-231-7932
Flat Rock Playhouse 2661 Greenville Hwy	Flat Rock	NC	28731	**866-732-8008**	828-693-0731
Florence Events Ctr 715 Quince St	Florence	OR	97439	**888-968-4086**	541-997-1994
Fox Theatre 660 Peachtree St NE	Atlanta	GA	30308	**855-285-8499**	404-881-2100
Fulton Opera House Foundation 12 N Prince St PO Box 1865	Lancaster	PA	17603	**888-480-1265**	717-397-7425
Gary Soren Smith Ctr for the Fine & Performing Arts *Ohlone College* 43600 Mission Blvd	Fremont	CA	94539	**800-309-2131**	510-659-6031
Grand 1894 Opera House 2020 Postoffice St	Galveston	TX	77550	**800-821-1894**	409-765-1894
Grand Ole Opry 2804 Opryland Dr	Nashville	TN	37214	**800-733-6779**	615-871-6779
Grand Rapids Civic Theatre 30 N Div Ave	Grand Rapids	MI	49503	**888-823-6837**	616-222-6650
Grand, The 818 N Market St	Wilmington	DE	19801	**800-374-7263**	302-658-7897
Greer Garson Theatre Ctr 1600 St Michael's Dr College of Santa Fe	Santa Fe	NM	87505	**800-456-2673**	505-473-6011
Guthrie Theater 818 S Second St *Resv	Minneapolis	MN	55415	**877-447-8243***	612-377-2224
Hale Centre Theater 3333 S Decker Lake Dr	West Valley City	UT	84119	**877-829-5500**	801-984-9000
Heinz Hall for the Performing Arts 600 Penn Ave	Pittsburgh	PA	15222	**800-743-8560**	412-392-4900
Heymann Performing Arts Ctr 1373 S College Rd	Lafayette	LA	70503	**800-745-3000**	337-291-5540
Hollywood Bowl 2301 N Highland Ave	Hollywood	CA	90068	**800-745-3000**	323-850-2000
Hopkins Ctr for the Arts 6041 Wilson Hall	Hanover	NH	03755	**800-451-4067**	603-646-2422
Jefferson Ctr 541 Luck Ave Ste 221	Roanoke	VA	24016	**866-345-2550**	540-343-2624
John Anson Ford Theatres 2580 Cahuenga Blvd E	Hollywood	CA	90068	**800-352-0050**	323-461-3673
John F Kennedy Ctr for the Performing Arts 2700 F St NW	Washington	DC	20566	**800-444-1324**	202-416-8000
Joseph Meyerhoff Symphony Hall 1212 Cathedral St	Baltimore	MD	21201	**877-276-1444**	410-783-8100
Juanita K Hammons Hall for the Performing Arts 901 S National Ave	Springfield	MO	65897	**888-476-7849**	417-836-6776
Knoxville Civic Auditorium/Coliseum 500 Howard Baker Jr Ave	Knoxville	TN	37915	**877-995-9961**	865-215-8900
Krannert Ctr for the Performing Arts 500 S Goodwin Ave	Urbana	IL	61801	**800-527-2849**	217-333-6700
Lake Charles Civic Ctr 900 Lakeshore Dr	Lake Charles	LA	70601	**888-620-1749**	337-491-1256
Legends Theater 1600 W Hwy 76	Branson	MO	65616	**800-374-7469**	417-339-3003
Liacouras Ctr 1776 N Broad St	Philadelphia	PA	19121	**800-298-4200**	215-204-2400
Lied Ctr for Performing Arts 301 N 12th St	Lincoln	NE	68588	**800-432-3231**	402-472-4700
Lila Cockrell Theatre 200 E Market St *General	San Antonio	TX	78205	**877-504-8895***	210-207-8500
Long Wharf Theatre 222 Sargent Dr	New Haven	CT	06511	**800-782-8497**	203-787-4282
Lyric Opera House 110 W Mt Royal Ave	Baltimore	MD	21201	**800-872-7245**	410-685-5086
Macon City Auditorium 415 First St	Macon	GA	31201	**877-532-6144**	478-751-9152
Mahaffey Theater for the Performing Arts 400 First St S	Saint Petersburg	FL	33701	**800-435-7352**	727-892-5798
Marcus Ctr for the Performing Arts 929 N Water St	Milwaukee	WI	53202	**888-612-3500**	414-273-7206
Maryland Hall for the Creative Arts 801 Chase St	Annapolis	MD	21401	**866-438-3808**	410-263-5544
McCallum Theatre 73000 Fred Waring Dr	Palm Desert	CA	92260	**866-889-2787**	760-340-2787

Name / Address	City	State	Zip	Toll-Free	Phone
Merriweather Post Pavilion (MPP) 10475 Little Patuxent Pkwy	Columbia	MD	21044	**877-435-9849**	410-715-5550
Michigan Theater 603 E Liberty St	Ann Arbor	MI	48104	**800-745-3000**	734-668-8397
Morris Performing Arts Ctr 211 N Michigan St	South Bend	IN	46601	**800-537-6415**	574-235-9190
Music Box Dinner Playhouse 196 Hughes St	Swoyersville	PA	18704	**800-698-7529**	570-283-2195
New Jersey Performing Arts Ctr 1 Ctr St	Newark	NJ	07102	**888-466-5722**	973-642-8989
Norwalk Concert Hall 125 E Ave	Norwalk	CT	06851	**800-357-9577**	203-854-7900
Ocean Ctr 101 N Atlantic Ave	Daytona Beach	FL	32118	**800-858-6444**	386-254-4500
Omaha Community Playhouse 6915 Cass St	Omaha	NE	68132	**888-782-4338**	402-553-0800
One World Theatre 7701 Bee Caves Rd	Austin	TX	78746	**888-616-0522**	512-330-9500
Orchestra Hall 1111 Nicollet Mall	Minneapolis	MN	55403	**800-292-4141**	612-371-5600
Orpheum Theatre 409 S 16th St	Omaha	NE	68102	**866-434-8587**	402-345-0202
Pabst Theater 144 E Wells St	Milwaukee	WI	53202	**866-948-6483**	414-286-3205
Palace, Theatre, The 1420 Celebrity Cir Broadway at the Beach	Myrtle Beach	SC	29577	**888-841-2787**	843-448-9224
Pantages Theater 901 Broadway	Tacoma	WA	98402	**800-291-7593**	253-591-5890
Pantages Theatre 6233 Hollywood Blvd	Los Angeles	CA	90028	**800-430-8903**	
Paramount Theatre 123 Third Ave SE	Cedar Rapids	IA	52401	**800-369-8863**	319-398-5226
Parkland College Theatre 2400 W Bradley Ave	Champaign	IL	61821	**800-346-8089**	217-351-2528
Patriots Theater Memorial Dr	Trenton	NJ	08608	**866-847-7682**	609-984-8484
Philharmonic Ctr for the Arts 5833 Pelican Bay Blvd	Naples	FL	34108	**800-597-1900**	239-597-1111
Pikes Peak Ctr 190 S Cascade Ave	Colorado Springs	CO	80903	**866-464-2626**	719-477-2100
Playhouse Square 1501 Euclid Ave Ste 200	Cleveland	OH	44115	**866-546-1353**	216-771-4444
Plaza Live, The 425 N Bumby Ave	Orlando	FL	32803	**877-435-9849**	407-228-1220
Raymond F Kravis Ctr for the Performing Arts 701 Okeechobee Blvd	West Palm Beach	FL	33401	**800-572-8471**	561-832-7469
Rialto Theater 310 S Ninth St	Tacoma	WA	98402	**800-291-7593**	253-591-5890
Robinson Ctr 101 S. Spring St PO Box 3232	Little Rock	AR	72201	**800-844-4781**	501-376-4781
Ruth Eckerd Hall 1111 McMullen Booth Rd	Clearwater	FL	33759	**800-875-8682**	727-791-7060
Ryman Auditorium 116 Fifth Ave N	Nashville	TN	37219	**800-733-6779**	615-458-8700
San Antonio Municipal Auditorium 200 E Market St PO Box 1809	San Antonio	TX	78205	**877-504-8895**	210-207-8500
San Jose Convention Center (SJC) 150 W San Carlos St	San Jose	CA	95110	**800-726-5673**	408-792-4194
San Jose Ctr for the Performing Arts 255 Almaden Blvd	San Jose	CA	95113	**800-726-5673**	408-792-4111
Savannah Civic Ctr 301 W Oglethorp Ave	Savannah	GA	31401	**800-337-1101**	912-651-6550
Scottsdale Ctr for the Performing Arts 7380 E Second St	Scottsdale	AZ	85251	**800-309-8532**	480-994-2787
Severance Hall 11001 Euclid Ave	Cleveland	OH	44106	**800-686-1141**	216-231-7300
Shea's Performing Arts Ctr 646 Main St	Buffalo	NY	14202	**866-341-5945**	716-847-1410
Shepherd of the Hills Homestead & Outdoor Theatre 5586 W Hwy 76	Branson	MO	65616	**800-653-6288**	417-334-4191
Spokane Civic Theatre 1020 N Howard St	Spokane	WA	99201	**800-325-7328**	509-325-1413
Stambaugh Auditorium 1000 Fifth Ave	Youngstown	OH	44504	**866-516-2269**	330-747-5175
Starlight Theatre 4600 Starlight Rd Swope Pk	Kansas City	MO	64132	**800-776-1730**	816-363-7827
Stranahan Theater 4645 Heatherdowns Blvd	Toledo	OH	43614	**866-381-7469**	419-381-8851
Strand Theatre 619 Louisiana Ave	Shreveport	LA	71101	**800-313-6373**	318-226-1481
Symphony Ctr 220 S Michigan Ave *Cust Svc	Chicago	IL	60604	**800-223-7114***	312-294-3000
Tarrytown Music Hall 13 Main St PO Box 686	Tarrytown	NY	10591	**877-840-0457**	914-631-3390
Tennessee Performing Arts Ctr 505 Deaderick St	Nashville	TN	37219	**866-455-2823**	615-782-4000
University of Texas at Austin Performing Arts Ctr E 23rd St & E Robert Dedman Dr	Austin	TX	78713	**800-687-6010**	512-471-1444
University of West Florida Ctr for Fine & Performing Arts 11000 University Pkwy Bldg 82	Pensacola	FL	32514	**800-263-1074**	850-474-2000
Van Wezel Performing Arts Ctr 777 N Tamiami Trl	Sarasota	FL	34236	**800-826-9303**	941-953-3368
Victoria Theatre 138 N Main St	Dayton	OH	45402	**888-228-3630**	937-228-3630
Victoria Vaudeville Theater 1228 Market St	Wheeling	WV	26003	**800-505-7464**	304-233-7464
Wang Theatre 270 Tremont St	Boston	MA	02116	**800-982-2787**	
Weidner Ctr for the Performing Arts 2420 Nicolet Dr University of Wisconsin at Green Bay	Green Bay	WI	54311	**800-895-0071**	920-465-2726
Westport Country Playhouse 25 Powers Ct	Westport	CT	06880	**888-927-7529**	203-227-4177
Wharton Ctr for the Performing Arts Michigan State University	East Lansing	MI	48824	**800-942-7866**	517-432-2000
Wheeler Opera House 320 E Hyman St	Aspen	CO	81611	**866-449-0464**	970-920-5770
Wichita Falls CVB 1000 Fifth St	Wichita Falls	TX	76301	**800-799-6732**	
Williams Performing Arts Ctr *Abilene Christian University* 1600 Campus Ct	Abilene	TX	79601	**800-460-6228**	325-674-2199
Wilma Theater 265 S Broad St	Philadelphia	PA	19107	**800-732-0999**	215-893-9456
Wiltern Theatre 3790 Wilshire Blvd	Los Angeles	CA	90010	**800-348-8499**	213-388-1400
Wolf Trap Foundation for the Performing Arts 1645 Trap Rd	Vienna	VA	22182	**877-965-3872**	703-255-1900

572 PERFORMING ARTS ORGANIZATIONS

SEE ALSO Arts & Artists Organizations

572-1 Dance Companies

Name / Address	City	State	Zip	Toll-Free	Phone
Aspen Santa Fe Ballet 0245 Sage Way	Aspen	CO	81611	**866-449-0464**	970-925-7175
Axis Dance Co 1428 Alice St Ste 200	Oakland	CA	94612	**800-838-3006**	510-625-0110
Ballet Magnificat 5406 I-55 N	Jackson	MS	39211	**866-617-3257**	601-977-1001
Buglisi Dance Theatre 229 W 42nd St Ste 502	New York	NY	10036	**800-754-0797**	212-719-3301
Collage Dance Theatre 2934 1/2 Beverly Glen Cir	Los Angeles	CA	90077	**866-300-4287**	818-784-8669
Dance Theatre of Harlem Inc 466 W 152nd St	New York	NY	10031	**800-538-2538**	212-690-2800
Dayton Ballet 140 N Main St	Dayton	OH	45402	**800-745-3000**	937-449-5060
Dayton Contemporary Dance Co 840 Germantown St	Dayton	OH	45402	**888-228-3630**	937-228-3232
Doug Varone & Dancers 37 W 32nd St	New York	NY	10001	**800-366-2100**	212-279-3344
Houston Ballet 601 Preston St	Houston	TX	77002	**800-828-2787**	713-523-6300
Mark Morris Dance Group 3 Lafayette Ave	Brooklyn	NY	11217	**800-957-1046**	718-624-8400
Miami City Ballet 2200 Liberty Ave	Miami Beach	FL	33139	**877-929-7010**	305-929-7000
Milwaukee Ballet 504 W National Ave	Milwaukee	WI	53204	**888-612-3500**	414-643-7677
Minnesota Ballet 301 W First St Ste 800	Duluth	MN	55802	**800-627-3529**	218-529-3742
Oakland Ballet Co 2201 Broadway Ste 206	Oakland	CA	94612	**866-711-6037**	510-893-3132
Pennsylvania Ballet 1819 John F Kennedy Blvd	Philadelphia	PA	19103	**800-732-0999**	215-551-7000
Pittsburgh Ballet Theatre 2900 Liberty Ave	Pittsburgh	PA	15201	**800-441-1414**	412-281-0360
Sacramento Ballet 1631 K St	Sacramento	CA	95814	**800-925-9989**	916-552-5800
San Francisco Ballet 455 Franklin St	San Francisco	CA	94102	**888-622-2108**	415-865-2000

572-2 Opera Companies

Name / Address	City	State	Zip	Toll-Free	Phone
Dallas Opera 8350 N Central Expy Ste 210	Dallas	TX	75206	**888-353-4537**	214-443-1000
Florentine Opera Co 700 N Water St Ste 950	Milwaukee	WI	53202	**800-326-7372**	414-291-5700
Florida Grand Opera 8390 NW 25th St	Miami	FL	33122	**800-741-1010**	305-854-1643
Fort Worth Opera 1300 Gendy St	Fort Worth	TX	76107	**877-396-7372**	817-731-0833
Glimmerglass Festival 7300 State Hwy 80 PO Box 191	Cooperstown	NY	13326	**866-568-2388**	607-547-0700
Houston Grand Opera 510 Preston St	Houston	TX	77002	**800-626-7372**	713-546-0200
Kentucky Opera Assn 323 W Broadway Ste 601	Louisville	KY	40202	**800-690-9236**	502-584-4500
Minnesota Opera 620 N First St	Minneapolis	MN	55401	**800-676-6737**	612-333-2700
Opera Omaha 1625 Farnam St Ste 100	Omaha	NE	68102	**877-346-7372**	402-346-4398
Opera San Jose 2149 Paragon Dr	San Jose	CA	95131	**800-745-3000**	408-437-4450
Palm Beach Opera 415 S Olive Ave	West Palm Beach	FL	33401	**800-435-7352**	561-833-7888
Portland Opera 211 SE Caruthers St	Portland	OR	97214	**866-739-6737**	503-241-1407
Santa Fe Opera, The 301 Opera Dr	Santa Fe	NM	87506	**800-280-4654**	505-986-5900
Sarasota Opera 61 N Pineapple Ave	Sarasota	FL	34236	**866-951-0111**	941-366-8450
Seattle Opera PO Box 9248 *Sales	Seattle	WA	98109	**800-426-1619***	206-389-7600
Toledo Opera 425 Jefferson Ave Ste 601	Toledo	OH	43604	**866-860-9048**	419-255-7464
Tulsa Opera 1610 S Boulder Ave	Tulsa	OK	74119	**866-298-2530**	918-582-4035
Wichita Grand Opera 225 W Douglas Ave Century II Performing Arts Ctr.	Wichita	KS	67202	**855-755-7328**	316-683-3444

572-3 Orchestras

Name / Address	City	State	Zip	Toll-Free	Phone
Acadiana Symphony Orchestra 412 Travis St	Lafayette	LA	70503	**800-826-4919**	337-232-4277

Organization / Address	City	State	Zip	Toll-Free	Phone
Austin Symphony Orchestra 1101 Red River St	Austin	TX	78701	**888-462-3787**	512-476-6064
Baltimore Symphony Orchestra 1212 Cathedral St	Baltimore	MD	21201	**877-276-1444**	410-783-8100
Bangor Symphony Orchestra PO Box 1441 *General	Bangor	ME	04402	**800-639-3221***	207-942-5555
Boston Pops 301 Massachusetts Ave Symphony Hall	Boston	MA	02115	**888-266-1200**	617-266-1492
Boston Symphony Orchestra 301 Massachusetts Ave Symphony Hall	Boston	MA	02115	**888-266-1200**	617-266-1492
Chamber Orchestra of Philadelphia 1520 Locust St Ste 500	Philadelphia	PA	19102	**800-732-0999**	215-545-5451
Chicago Symphony Orchestra 220 S Michigan Ave	Chicago	IL	60604	**800-223-7114**	312-294-3000
Cleveland Orchestra, The 11001 Euclid Ave Severance Hall	Cleveland	OH	44106	**800-686-1141**	216-231-1111
Colorado Symphony Orchestra 1000 14th St Unit 15	Denver	CO	80202	**877-292-7979**	303-623-7876
Columbus Symphony Orchestra 55 E State St	Columbus	OH	43215	**800-745-3000**	614-228-9600
Corpus Christi Symphony Orchestra 555 N Carancahua St Tower II Ste 410 Ste 410	Corpus Christi	TX	78401	**877-286-6683**	361-883-6683
Dayton Philharmonic Orchestra 126 N Main St Ste 210	Dayton	OH	45402	**888-228-3630**	937-224-3521
Detroit Symphony Orchestra 3711 Woodward Ave	Detroit	MI	48201	**800-434-6340**	313-576-5111
Dubuque Symphony Orchestra 2728 Asbury Rd Ste 900	Dubuque	IA	52001	**866-803-9280**	563-557-1677
Edmonton Symphony Orchestra 9720 102nd Ave	Edmonton	AB	T5J4B2	**800-563-5081**	780-428-1108
Flagstaff Symphony Orchestra 113 E Aspen Ave # A	Flagstaff	AZ	86001	**888-520-7214**	928-774-5107
Illinois Symphony Orchestera 524 E Capitol Ave	Springfield	IL	62701	**800-401-7222**	217-522-2838
Indianapolis Symphony Orchestra 45 Monument Cir	Indianapolis	IN	46204	**800-366-8457**	317-262-1100
Kansas City Symphony 1703 Wyandotte Ste 200	Kansas City	MO	64108	**877-829-5590**	816-471-1100
Kennedy Ctr Opera House Orchestra John F Kennedy Ctr for the Performing Arts 2700 F St NW	Washington	DC	20566	**800-444-1324**	
Lexington Philharmonic 161 N Mill St	Lexington	KY	40507	**888-494-4226**	859-233-4226
Milwaukee Symphony Orchestra 1101 N Market St STE 100	Milwaukee	WI	53202	**888-367-8101**	414-273-7121
Minnesota Orchestra 1111 Nicollet Mall Orchestra Hall	Minneapolis	MN	55403	**800-292-4141**	612-371-5600
Modesto Symphony Orchestra 911 13th St	Modesto	CA	95354	**877-488-3380**	209-523-4156
National Symphony Orchestra 2700 F St NW	Washington	DC	20566	**800-444-1324**	202-416-8000
New World Symphony 500 17th St	Miami Beach	FL	33139	**800-597-3331**	305-673-3330
Orchestra New England PO Box 200123	New Haven	CT	06520	**800-595-4849**	203-777-4690
Orchestre Symphonique de Montreal 260 de Maisonneuve Blvd W 2nd Fl	Montreal	QC	H2X1Y9	**888-842-9951**	514-842-9951
Oregon Symphony Orchestra 921 SW Washington St Ste 200	Portland	OR	97205	**800-228-7343**	503-228-4294
Phoenix Symphony 1 N First St Ste 200	Phoenix	AZ	85004	**800-776-9080**	602-495-1117
Pittsburgh Symphony Orchestra 600 Penn Ave Heinz Hall for the Performing Arts	Pittsburgh	PA	15222	**800-743-8560**	412-566-7366
River City Brass Band Inc 500 Grant St Ste 2720	Pittsburgh	PA	15219	**800-292-7222**	412-434-7222
Saint Louis Symphony Orchestra 718 N Grand Blvd	Saint Louis	MO	63103	**800-232-1880**	314-533-2500
Santa Fe Symphony Orchestra & Chorus Inc 551 W Cordova Rd Ste D Ste D	Santa Fe	NM	87505	**800-480-1319**	505-983-3530
Sarasota Orchestra 709 N Tamiami Trl	Sarasota	FL	34236	**866-508-0611**	941-953-4252
Seattle Symphony 200 University St	Seattle	WA	98101	**866-833-4747**	206-215-4700
South Bend Symphony Orchestra (SBSO) 127 N Michigan St	South Bend	IN	46601	**800-537-6415**	574-232-6343
Spokane Symphony PO Box 365	Spokane	WA	99210	**800-899-1482**	509-624-1200
Symphony Nova Scotia 6101 University Ave Dalhousie Arts Ctr	Halifax	NS	B3H4R2	**800-874-1669**	902-494-3820
Tacoma Symphony 901 Broadway Ste 600	Tacoma	WA	98402	**800-291-7593**	253-272-7264
Toledo Symphony 1838 Parkwood Ave	Toledo	OH	43604	**800-348-1253**	419-246-8000
Vermont Symphony Orchestra 2 Church St Ste 3B	Burlington	VT	05401	**800-876-9293**	802-864-5741
Virginia Symphony Orchestra 861 Glenrock Rd Ste 200	Norfolk	VA	23502	**855-876-7677**	757-466-3060
Westchester Philharmonic 123 Main St Lobby Level	White Plains	NY	10601	**800-553-0031**	914-682-3707
Windsor Symphony Orchestra 487 Oullette Ave	Windsor	ON	N9A4J2	**888-327-8327**	519-973-1238

572-4 Theater Companies

Organization / Address	City	State	Zip	Toll-Free	Phone
A Contemporary Theatre (ACT) 700 Union St Kreielsheimer Pl	Seattle	WA	98101	**888-584-4849**	206-292-7660
Actors Theatre of Louisville 316 W Main St	Louisville	KY	40202	**800-428-5849**	502-584-1205
Alabama Shakespeare Festival 1 Festival Dr	Montgomery	AL	36117	**800-841-4273**	334-271-5300
American Stage 163 Third St N	Saint Petersburg	FL	33731	**800-435-7352**	727-823-1600
Arkansas Repertory Theatre 601 Main St PO Box 110	Little Rock	AR	72201	**866-684-3737**	501-378-0445
Corn Stock Theatre 1700 Pk Rd	Peoria	IL	61604	**800-220-1185**	309-676-2196
Guthrie Theater 818 S Second St *Resv	Minneapolis	MN	55415	**877-447-8243***	612-377-2224
Lincoln Ctr Theater 150 W 65th St	New York	NY	10023	**800-432-7250**	
Maltz Jupiter Theatre 1001 E Indiantown Rd	Jupiter	FL	33477	**800-445-1666**	561-743-2666
Nebraska Repertory Theatre PO Box 880201	Lincoln	NE	68588	**800-432-3231**	402-472-2072
Omaha Community Playhouse 6915 Cass St	Omaha	NE	68132	**888-782-4338**	402-553-0800
Pacific Repertory Theater PO Box 222035	Carmel	CA	93922	**866-622-0709**	831-622-0700
Pasadena Playhouse, The 39 S El Molino Ave	Pasadena	CA	91101	**800-733-2767**	626-356-7529
People's Light & Theatre Co 39 Conestoga Rd	Malvern	PA	19355	**800-732-0999**	610-647-1900
Perseverance Theatre 914 Third St	Douglas	AK	99824	**855-462-8497**	907-364-2421
Pittsburgh Public Theater 621 Penn Ave	Pittsburgh	PA	15222	**800-732-0999**	412-316-8200
Seattle Repertory Theatre (SRT) 155 Mercer St PO Box 900923	Seattle	WA	98109	**877-900-9285**	206-443-2210
Shakespeare Theatre 516 Eigth St SE	Washington	DC	20003	**877-487-8849**	202-547-3230
Theatre For A New Audience 154 Christopher St Ste 3D	New York	NY	10014	**866-811-4111**	212-229-2819
Tihati Productions Ltd 3615 Harding Ave Ste 507	Honolulu	HI	96816	**877-846-5554**	808-735-0292
Wilma Theater 265 S Broad St	Philadelphia	PA	19107	**800-732-0999**	215-893-9456
Yale Repertory Theatre 1120 Chapel St PO Box 1257	New Haven	CT	06505	**800-973-2837**	203-432-1234

573 PERFUMES

SEE ALSO Cosmetics, Skin Care, and Other Personal Care Products

Company / Address	City	State	Zip	Toll-Free	Phone
Avon Products Inc 1345 Ave of the Americas *NYSE: AVP* ■ *Cust Svc	New York	NY	10017	**800-367-2866***	212-282-7000
Chanel Inc 15 E 57th St	New York	NY	10022	**800-550-0005**	212-355-5050
Crabtree & Evelyn Ltd 102 Peake Brook Rd	Woodstock	CT	06281	**800-272-2873**	860-928-2761
Eagle Marketing Inc Perfume Originals Products Div 2412 Sequoia Pk	Yukon	OK	73099	**800-233-7424**	
Elizabeth Arden Inc 2400 NE 145th Ave 2nd Fl *NASDAQ: RDEN*	Miramar	FL	33027	**800-326-7337**	954-364-6900
Key West Aloe 13095 N Telecom Pkwy	Tampa	FL	33637	**800-445-2563**	
ULTA Beauty 1000 Remington Blvd Ste 120	Bolingbrook	IL	60440	**866-983-8582**	630-410-4800

574 PERSONAL EMERGENCY RESPONSE SYSTEMS

Company / Address	City	State	Zip	Toll-Free	Phone
AlertOne Services Inc 1000 Commerce Park Dr Ste 300 *Cust Svc	Williamsport	PA	17701	**866-581-4540***	
Life Alert 16027 Ventura Blvd	Encino	CA	91436	**800-920-3410**	818-700-7000
LifeFone 16 Yellowstone Ave	White Plains	NY	10607	**888-687-0451**	

575 PERSONAL PROTECTIVE EQUIPMENT & CLOTHING

SEE ALSO Safety Equipment - Mfr ; Safety Equipment - Whol ; Sporting Goods ; Medical Supplies - Mfr

Company / Address	City	State	Zip	Toll-Free	Phone
Aearo Co 5457 W 79th St	Indianapolis	IN	46268	**877-327-4332**	317-692-6666
Allen-Vanguard Corp 2400 St Laurent Blvd	Ottawa	ON	K1G5B4	**800-644-9078**	613-739-9646
Ansell Healthcare Inc 111 S Wood Ave Ste 210	Iselin	NJ	08830	**800-365-2282**	732-345-5400
Bell Sports Corp 6225 N St Hwy 161 Ste 300	Irving	TX	75038	**866-525-2357**	469-417-6600
Biomarine Inc 456 Creamery Way	Exton	PA	19341	**800-378-2287**	610-524-8800
Bullard Co 1898 Safety Way	Cynthiana	KY	41031	**800-227-0423**	859-234-6611
David Clark Company Inc 360 Franklin St *Cust Svc	Worcester	MA	01615	**800-298-6235***	508-751-5800
Encon Safety Products Co 6825 W Sam Houston Pkwy N PO Box 3826	Houston	TX	77041	**800-283-6266**	713-466-1449
Fibre-Metal 2000 Plainfield Pk	Cranston	RI	02921	**800-430-4110**	
Fire-End & Croker Corp 7 Westchester Plz	Elmsford	NY	10523	**800-759-3473**	914-592-3640
Galls Inc 2680 Palumbo Dr	Lexington	KY	40509	**800-477-7766**	859-266-7227
General Econopak Inc 1725 N Sixth St	Philadelphia	PA	19122	**888-871-8568**	215-763-8200
Globe Mfg Co 37 Loudon Rd	Pittsfield	NH	03263	**800-232-8323**	603-435-8323
Graham Medical Products 2273 Larsen Rd *Cust Svc	Green Bay	WI	54303	**800-558-6765***	920-494-8701

Company / Address	City	State	Zip	Toll-Free	Phone
Handgards Inc 901 Hawkins Blvd	El Paso	TX	79915	**800-351-8161**	
HeatMax Inc 505 Hill Rd PO Box 1191	Dalton	GA	30721	**800-432-8629**	706-226-1800
Honeywell Safety Products 2000 Plainfield Pike *Cust Svc	Cranston	RI	02921	**800-430-4110***	401-943-4400
ILC Dover Inc 1 Moonwalker Rd	Frederica	DE	19946	**800-631-9567**	302-335-3911
Kappler Inc 115 Grimes Dr PO Box 490	Guntersville	AL	35976	**800-600-4019**	256-505-4005
Lakeland Industries Inc 701-7 Koehler Ave *NASDAQ: LAKE*	Ronkonkoma	NY	11779	**800-645-9291**	631-981-9700
Landauer Inc 2 Science Rd *NYSE: LDR*	Glenwood	IL	60425	**800-323-8830**	708-755-7000
Louis M Gerson Company Inc 16 Commerce Blvd	Middleboro	MA	02346	**800-225-8623**	508-947-4000
MCR Safety 5321 E Shelby Dr	Memphis	TN	38118	**800-955-6887**	901-795-5810
Medline Industries Inc 1 Medline Pl *Cust Svc	Mundelein	IL	60060	**800-351-1512***	847-949-5500
Miller Products Company Inc 2511 S Tricenter Blvd	Durham	NC	27713	**800-782-7437**	919-313-2100
Moldex Metric Inc 10111 W Jefferson Blvd	Culver City	CA	90232	**800-421-0668**	310-837-6500
MTS Safety Products Inc (MTS) PO Box 204 *General	Golden	MS	38847	**800-647-8168***	
National Safety Apparel Inc (NSA) 15825 Industrial Pkwy	Cleveland	OH	44135	**800-553-0672**	
Newtex Industries Inc 8050 Victor Mendon Rd	Victor	NY	14564	**800-836-1001**	585-924-9135
Plastic Safety Systems Inc 2444 Baldwin Rd	Cleveland	OH	44104	**800-662-6338**	
PolyConversions Inc 505 Condit Dr	Rantoul	IL	61866	**888-893-3330**	217-893-3330
Precept Medical Products Inc 370 Airport Rd PO Box 2400	Arden	NC	28704	**800-851-4431**	828-681-0209
Saf-T-Gard International Inc 205 Huehl Rd	Northbrook	IL	60062	**800-548-4273**	847-291-1600
Safariland LLC 13386 International Pkwy	Jacksonville	FL	32218	**800-347-1200**	904-741-5400
Safe-T-Gard Corp 12105 W Cedar Dr *Cust Svc	Lakewood	CO	80228	**800-356-9026***	303-763-8900
Scott Health & Safety 4320 Goldmine Rd PO Box 569	Monroe	NC	28110	**800-247-7257**	704-291-8300
Seattle Manufacturing Corp 6930 Salashan Pkwy	Ferndale	WA	98248	**800-426-6251**	360-366-5534
Sellstrom Manufacturing Co 2050 Hammond Dr	Schaumburg	IL	60173	**800-323-7402**	847-358-2000
Standard Textile Company Inc 1 Knollcrest Dr	Cincinnati	OH	45237	**800-999-0400**	513-761-9255
Steel Grip Inc 1501 E Voorhees St	Danville	IL	61832	**800-223-1595**	217-442-6240
Steiner Industries 5801 N Tripp Ave	Chicago	IL	60646	**800-621-4515**	773-588-3444
Strong Enterprises Inc 11236 Satellite Blvd	Orlando	FL	32837	**800-344-6319**	407-859-9317
Tingley Rubber Corp 1551 S Washington Ave Ste 403 Ste 403 *Cust Svc	Piscataway	NJ	08854	**800-631-5498***	
United Pioneer Co 2777 Summer St Ste 206	Stamford	CT	06905	**800-466-9823**	
Uvex Safety Inc 900 Douglas Pk *General	Smithfield	RI	02917	**800-682-0839***	
White Knight Engineered Products 9525 Monroe Rd Ste 100	Charlotte	NC	28270	**888-743-4700**	704-542-6876
Wolf X-Ray Corp 100 W Industry Ct *Cust Svc	Deer Park	NY	11729	**800-356-9729***	631-242-9729

576 PEST CONTROL SERVICES

Company / Address	City	State	Zip	Toll-Free	Phone
A 1 Termite & Pest Control Inc 2686 Morganton Blvd Sw	Lenoir	NC	28645	**800-532-7378**	828-758-4312
Al Hoffer's Pest Protection Inc 12329 NW 35 St	Coral Springs	FL	33065	**866-549-7987**	
Bain Pest Control Service Inc 1320 Middlesex St	Lowell	MA	01851	**800-272-3661**	978-452-9621
Bird Solutions International 1338 N Melrose Dr Ste H	Vista	CA	92083	**800-210-9514**	760-758-9747
Burns Pest Elimination Inc 2620 W Grovers Ave	Phoenix	AZ	85053	**877-971-4782**	602-971-4782
Copesan Services Inc W175 N5711 Technology Dr	Menomonee Falls	WI	53051	**800-267-3726**	
Dewey Services Inc 939 E Union St	Pasadena	CA	91106	**877-339-3973**	626-568-9248
Fischer Environmental Service Inc 1980 Surgi Dr	Mandeville	LA	70448	**800-391-2565**	
Gilbert Industries Inc 5611 Krueger Dr	Jonesboro	AR	72401	**800-643-0400**	870-932-6070
Green Lawn Fertilizing Inc 1004 Saunders Ln	West Chester	PA	19380	**888-581-5296**	
Home Paramount Pest Control Cos Inc PO Box 850	Forest Hill	MD	21050	**888-888-4663**	410-510-0700
Horizon Termite & Pest Control Corp 45 Cross Ave	Midland Park	NJ	07432	**888-612-2847**	201-447-2530
Jp Mchale Pest Management Inc 241 Bleakley Ave	Buchanan	NY	10511	**800-479-2284**	
Knockout Pest Control Inc 1009 Front St	Uniondale	NY	11553	**800-244-7378**	516-489-7817
Lawn Doctor Inc 142 SR 34	Holmdel	NJ	07733	**800-845-0580**	800-631-5660
Massey Services Inc 315 Groveland St E	Orlando	FL	32804	**888-262-7739**	407-645-2500
McCall Service Inc 2861 College St	Jacksonville	FL	32205	**800-342-6948**	904-389-5561
NaturaLawn of America Inc 1 E Church St	Frederick	MD	21701	**800-989-5444**	301-694-5440
Orkin Exterminating Co Inc 2170 Piedmont Rd NE	Atlanta	GA	30324	**844-499-3453**	877-250-1652
Pest Shield Pest Control Inc 15329 Tradesman	San Antonio	TX	78249	**888-728-8237**	210-525-8823
Plunkett's Pest Control 40 NE 52nd Way	Fridley	MN	55421	**866-906-1780**	218-723-8464
Presto-X Co 1221 S Saddle Creek Rd Ste 101	Omaha	NE	68106	**800-759-1942**	
Schendel Pest Services 1035 SE Quincy St	Topeka	KS	66612	**800-591-7378**	785-232-9357
Smithereen Exterminators Inc 7400 N Melvina Ave	Niles	IL	60714	**800-336-3500**	847-647-0010
Spring-Green Lawn Care Corp 11909 Spaulding School Dr	Plainfield	IL	60585	**800-435-4051**	815-436-8777
Terminix International Company LP 860 Ridge Lk Blvd	Memphis	TN	38120	**855-212-6399**	866-399-0453
TruGreen ChemLawn 860 Ridge Lk Blvd	Memphis	TN	38120	**866-369-9539**	
Truly Nolen of America Inc 3636 E Speedway Blvd	Tucson	AZ	85716	**800-468-7859**	800-528-3442
TruTech LLC PO Box 6849	Marietta	GA	30065	**800-842-7296**	770-977-2034
Waltham Services Inc 817 Moody St	Waltham	MA	02453	**866-974-7378**	781-893-1810
Western Exterminator Co 305 N Crescent Way	Anaheim	CA	92801	**800-698-2440**	714-517-9000

PESTICIDES

577 PET PRODUCTS

SEE ALSO Leather Goods - Personal ; Livestock & Poultry Feeds - Prepared

Company / Address	City	State	Zip	Toll-Free	Phone
Arctic Glacier Holdings Inc 625 Henry Ave	Winnipeg	MB	R3A0V1	**888-573-9237**	204-772-2473
Bailey Farms LLC 549 Karem Dr	Marshall	WI	53559	**800-655-1705**	
BioZyme Inc 6010 Stockyards Expy	Saint Joseph	MO	64504	**800-821-3070**	816-238-3326
Clorox Co 1221 Broadway *NYSE: CLX* ■ *Cust Svc	Oakland	CA	94612	**800-424-9300***	510-271-7000
Companion Pets Inc (CPI) 2001 N Black Canyon Hwy	Phoenix	AZ	85009	**800-646-3611**	602-255-0166
Doctors Foster & Smith Inc 2253 Air Pk Rd PO Box 100	Rhinelander	WI	54501	**800-826-7206**	715-369-3305
Doskocil Mfg Company Inc PO Box 1246	Arlington	TX	76004	**877-738-6283**	
Eagle Pack Pet Foods Inc 200 Ames Pond Dr	Tewksbury	MA	01876	**800-255-5959**	574-259-7834
Efficas Inc 7007 Winchester Cir Ste 120	Boulder	CO	80301	**866-446-0388**	303-381-2070
FL Emmert Co Inc 2007 Dunlap St	Cincinnati	OH	45214	**800-441-3343**	513-721-5808
Hartz Mountain Corp, The 400 Plz Dr	Secaucus	NJ	07094	**800-275-1414**	
Healthy Pet 6960 Salashan Pkwy	Ferndale	WA	98248	**800-242-2287**	360-734-7415
IAMS Co 3700 Ohio 65 *Cust Svc	Leipsic	OH	45856	**800-675-3849***	419-943-4267
Jeffers Inc 310 W Saunders Rd PO Box 100	Dothan	AL	36301	**800-533-3377**	334-793-6257
John A Van Den Bosch Co 4511 Holland Ave	Holland	MI	49424	**800-968-6477**	
Joy Dog Food PO Box 305	Pinckneyville	IL	62274	**800-245-4125**	
Kaytee Products Inc 521 Clay St	Chilton	WI	53014	**800-669-9580**	920-849-2321
Manna Pro Corp 707 Spirit 40 Pk Dr Ste 150	Chesterfield	MO	63005	**800-690-9908**	
Mark Hershey Farms Inc 479 Horseshoe Pk	Lebanon	PA	17042	**888-801-3301**	717-867-4624
MIDWEST Homes for Pets 3142 S Cowan Rd PO Box 1031	Muncie	IN	47302	**800-428-8560**	765-289-3355
Moyer & Son Inc 113 E Reliance Rd	Souderton	PA	18964	**866-669-3747**	215-799-2000
Multipet International Inc 265 W Commercial Ave	Moonachie	NJ	07074	**800-900-6738**	201-438-6600
Natural Life Pet Products Inc 205 E 29th St	Pittsburg	KS	66762	**800-367-2391**	620-230-0888
Nestle Purina PetCare Co 801 Chouteau Ave	Saint Louis	MO	63102	**800-778-7462**	314-982-1000
North States Industries Inc 1507 92nd Ln NE	Blaine	MN	55449	**800-848-8421**	763-486-1756
Orrco Inc 515 Collins Blvd PO Box 147	Orrville	OH	44667	**800-321-3085**	330-683-5015
Pet Safe International 10427 Electric Ave *Cust Svc	Knoxville	TN	37932	**800-732-2677***	865-777-5404
Pet Supermarket Inc 1100 International Pkwy	Sunrise	FL	33323	**866-434-1990**	954-351-0834
Pet Valu Canada Inc 225 Royal Crest Crt	Markham	ON	L3R9X6	**800-845-4759**	905-946-1200
PETCO Animal Supplies Inc 9125 Rehco Rd	San Diego	CA	92121	**877-738-6742**	858-453-7845
PetFoodDirect.com 189 Main St *Cust Svc	Harleysville	PA	19438	**877-738-3663***	215-513-1999
Petland Inc 250 Riverside St	Chillicothe	OH	45601	**800-221-5935**	740-775-2464

Company	Address	City	State	ZIP	Toll-Free	Phone
PetMed Express Inc	1441 SW 29th Ave *NASDAQ: PETS*	Pompano Beach	FL	33069	**800-738-6337**	954-979-5995
PETsMART Inc	19601 N 27th Ave *NASDAQ: PETM* ■ *Cust Svc	Phoenix	AZ	85027	**800-738-1385***	623-580-6100
Prevue Pet Products Inc	224 N Maplewood Ave	Chicago	IL	60612	**800-243-3624**	312-243-3624
Prince Corp	8351 County Rd H	Marshfield	WI	54449	**800-777-2486**	715-384-3105
Ralco Nutrition Inc	1600 Hahn Rd	Marshall	MN	56258	**800-533-5306**	
Rolf C. Hagen Corp	305 Forbes Blvd *Cust Svc	Mansfield	MA	02048	**800-724-2436***	508-339-9531
Star Milling Co	24067 Water St	Perris	CA	92570	**800-733-6455**	951-657-3143
Sunshine Mills Inc	500 Sixth St SW	Red Bay	AL	35582	**800-633-3349**	256-356-9541
Texas Farm Products Co	915 S Fredonia St	Nacogdoches	TX	75964	**800-392-3110**	936-564-3711
Triumph Pet Industries Inc	500 Sixth St SW	Red Bay	AL	35582	**800-633-3349**	256-356-9541
United Pacific Pet	12060 Cabernet Dr	Fontana	CA	92337	**800-979-3333**	951-360-8550
United Pharmacal Company of Missouri Inc	3705 Pear St	Saint Joseph	MO	64503	**800-254-8726**	816-233-8800
Wild Birds Unlimited Inc	11711 N College Ave Ste 146	Carmel	IN	46032	**800-326-4928**	317-571-7100

578 PETROLEUM & PETROLEUM PRODUCTS - WHOL

Company	Address	City	State	ZIP	Toll-Free	Phone
A.R. Sandri Inc	400 Chapman St	Greenfield	MA	01301	**800-628-1900**	413-772-2121
Allied Oil & Supply Inc	2209 S 24th St	Omaha	NE	68108	**800-333-3717**	402-344-4343
Aos Thermal Compounds LLC	22 Meridian Rd Ste 6	Eatontown	NJ	07724	**888-662-7337**	732-389-5514
Atlas Oil Co	24501 Ecorse Rd	Taylor	MI	48180	**800-878-2000**	313-292-5500
Axeon Specialty Products LLC	750 Washington Blvd Ste 600	Stamford	CT	06901	**855-378-4958**	
Boyett Petroleum	601 McHenry Ave	Modesto	CA	95350	**800-545-9212**	209-577-6000
BP Lubricants USA Inc	1500 Valley Rd	Wayne	NJ	07470	**800-333-3991**	973-633-2200
Bretthauer Oil Co	453 SW Washington St	Hillsboro	OR	97123	**800-359-3113**	503-648-2531
Campbell Oil Company Inc	611 Erie St S	Massillon	OH	44646	**800-589-8555**	330-833-8555
Cargill Energy	PO Box 9300	Minneapolis	MN	55440	**800-227-4455**	952-742-7575
Carson	3125 NW 35th Ave	Portland	OR	97210	**800-998-7767**	503-224-8500
Condon Oil Co	126 E Jackson St	Ripon	WI	54971	**800-452-1212**	920-748-3186
Consolidated Energy Co	910 Main St	Jesup	IA	50648	**800-338-3021**	319-827-1211
Dickey Transport	401 E Fourth St	Packwood	IA	52580	**800-247-1081**	319-695-3601
Dominion Aviation Services Inc	7511 Airfield Dr	Richmond	VA	23237	**800-366-7793**	804-271-7793
Doss Aviation Inc	3670 Rebecca Ln	Colorado Springs	CO	80917	**888-803-4415**	719-570-9804
Drake Petroleum Co Inc	221 Quinebaug Rd	North Grosvenordale	CT	06255	**800-243-6366**	
Earhart Petroleum Inc	1494 Lytle Rd	Troy	OH	45373	**800-686-2928**	937-335-2928
Englefield Oil Co	447 James Pkwy *Cust Svc	Heath	OH	43056	**800-837-4458***	740-928-8215
Farm & Home Oil Co	3115 State Rd	Telford	PA	18969	**800-776-7263**	
Federated Co-ops Inc	502 S Second St	Princeton	MN	55371	**800-638-8228**	763-389-2582
Gassco	7515 Lindsay Rd	Bakersfield	CA	93313	**800-390-7837**	661-832-7406
Gate Petroleum Co	9540 San Jose Blvd PO Box 23627	Jacksonville	FL	32241	**866-571-1982**	904-737-7220
Glacial Lakes Energy LLC	301 20th Ave SE PO Box 933	Watertown	SD	57201	**866-934-2676**	605-882-8480
Global Partners LP	800 S St Ste 200 *NYSE: GLP*	Waltham	MA	02454	**800-685-7222**	781-894-8800
Hasco Oil Company Inc	2800 Temple Ave	Long Beach	CA	90806	**800-456-8491**	562-595-8491
Heartland Petroleum LLC	4001 E Fifth Ave	Columbus	OH	43219	**800-889-7831**	614-441-4001
Johnson Oil Co (JOC)	1113 E Sara DeWitt Dr	Gonzales	TX	78629	**800-284-2432**	
Lanman Oil Co Inc	PO Box 108	Charleston	IL	61920	**800-677-2819**	
Lard Oil Company Inc	914 Florida Blvd SW	Denham Springs	LA	70726	**800-738-7738**	225-664-3311
Leffler Energy Inc	15 Mt Joy St	Mount Joy	PA	17552	**800-984-1411**	
Licking Valley Oil Inc	PO Box 246	Butler	KY	41006	**800-899-9449**	859-472-7111
Main-Care Energy	PO Box 11029	Albany	NY	12211	**800-542-5552**	
Maritime Energy Inc	234 Pk St PO Box 485	Rockland	ME	04841	**800-333-4489**	207-594-4487
Martin Eagle Oil Company Inc	2700 James St	Denton	TX	76205	**800-316-6148**	940-383-2351
Martin Midstream Partners LP	4200 Stone Rd *NASDAQ: MMLP*	Kilgore	TX	75662	**800-256-6644**	903-983-6200
McCall Oil & Chemical Corp	5480 NW Front Ave	Portland	OR	97210	**800-622-2558**	503-221-6400
McNeece Brothers Oil Company Inc	691 E Heil Ave	El Centro	CA	92243	**877-782-6543**	760-352-4721
National Oil & Gas Inc	409 N Main St	Bluffton	IN	46714	**800-322-8454**	260-824-2220
NOCO Energy Corp	2440 Sheridan Dr	Tonawanda	NY	14150	**800-500-6626**	716-833-6626
Offen Petroleum Inc	5100 E 78th Ave	Commerce	CO	80022	**866-657-3835**	303-297-3835
Orange Line Oil Company Inc	404 E Commercial St	Pomona	CA	91767	**800-492-6864**	909-623-0533
PetroLiance LLC	739 N State St	Elgin	IL	60123	**800-628-7231**	877-738-7699
Pro Petroleum Inc	4965 N Sloan Ln	Las Vegas	NV	89115	**877-791-4900**	
R K Allen Oil Inc	36002 AL Hwy 21	Talladega	AL	35161	**800-445-5823**	256-362-4261
R Kidd Fuels Corp	1172 Twinney Dr	Newmarket	ON	L3Y9E2	**866-274-2315**	
Ramos Oil Company Inc	1515 S River Rd *Cust Svc	West Sacramento	CA	95691	**800-477-7266***	916-371-2570
Reeder Distributors Inc	5450 Wilbarger St	Fort Worth	TX	76119	**800-722-3103**	817-429-5957
Retif Oil & Fuel Inc	527 Destrehan Ave	Harvey	LA	70058	**800-349-9000**	504-349-9000
Rex Oil Co Inc	814 & 1000 Lexington Ave	Thomasville	NC	27360	**800-843-0572**	336-472-3368
Rhinehart Oil Company Inc	585 E State Rd	American Fork	UT	84003	**801-756-5233**	801-756-9681
Senergy Petroleum LLC	622 S 56th Ave	Phoenix	AZ	85043	**800-964-0076**	602-272-6795
Sierra Energy	1020 Winding Creek Rd Ste 100	Roseville	CA	95678	**800-576-2264**	916-218-1600
Southern Maryland Oil Co Inc (SMO)	109 N Maple Ave	La Plata	MD	20646	**888-222-3720**	
Spencer Cos Inc	120 Woodson St	Huntsville	AL	35801	**800-633-2910**	256-533-1150
Sprague Energy	185 International Dr Ste 200	Portsmouth	NH	03801	**800-225-1560**	603-431-1000
Stern Oil Company Inc	PO Box 218	Freeman	SD	57029	**800-477-2744**	605-925-7999
Sun Coast Resources Inc	6405 Cavalcade St Bldg 1	Houston	TX	77028	**800-677-3835**	713-844-9600
Taylor Enterprises Inc (TEI)	2586 Southport Rd	Spartanburg	SC	29302	**800-922-3149**	864-573-9518
Technical Gas Products Inc	66 Leonardo Dr	North Haven	CT	06473	**800-847-0745**	
Tesoro Corp	1225 17th St	Denver	CO	80202	**800-299-0570**	
Texas Enterprises Inc	5005 E Seventh St	Austin	TX	78702	**800-545-4412**	512-385-2167
Titan Laboratories	1380 Zuni St PO Box 40567	Denver	CO	80204	**800-848-4826**	
Tropic Oil Company Inc	10002 NW 89th Ave	Miami	FL	33178	**866-645-3835**	305-888-4611
Tulco Oils Inc	5240 E Pine	Tulsa	OK	74115	**800-375-2347**	918-838-3354
Turner Gas Company Inc	PO Box 26554	Salt Lake City	UT	84126	**800-932-4277**	801-973-6886
Ullman Oil Inc	PO Box 23399	Chagrin Falls	OH	44023	**800-543-5195**	440-543-5195
Valor Oil	1200 Alsop Ln	Owensboro	KY	42303	**800-544-5823**	844-468-2567
Varouh Oil Inc	970 Griswold Rd	Elyria	OH	44035	**866-482-7684**	440-324-5025
Vesco Oil Corp	16055 W 12-Mile Rd	Southfield	MI	48076	**800-527-5358**	
Walthall Oil Company Inc	2510 Allen Rd	Macon	GA	31216	**800-633-5685**	478-781-1234
Warex Terminals Corp	1 S Water St PO Box 488	Newburgh	NY	12550	**800-724-0818**	845-561-4000
Warren Oil Company Inc	PO Box 1507	Dunn	NC	28335	**800-779-6456**	910-892-6456
Western Petroleum Co	9531 W 78th St	Eden Prairie	MN	55344	**800-972-3835**	952-941-9090
Western States Petroleum Inc	450 S 15th Ave	Phoenix	AZ	85007	**800-220-1353**	602-252-4011
World Fuel Services Corp	9800 NW 41st St Ste 400 *NYSE: INT*	Miami	FL	33178	**800-345-3818**	305-428-8000
Yorkston Oil Company Inc	2801 Roeder Ave	Bellingham	WA	98225	**800-401-2201**	360-734-2201

579 PETROLEUM REFINERIES

Company	Address	City	State	ZIP	Toll-Free	Phone
A H Belo Corp	508 Young St PO Box 224866 *NYSE: AHC*	Dallas	TX	75202	**800-230-1074**	214-977-8200
Allegheny Petroleum Products Co	999 Airbrake Ave	Wilmerding	PA	15148	**800-600-2900**	412-829-1990
BP PLC	28100 Torch Pkwy *NYSE: BP*	Warrenville	IL	60555	**800-333-3991**	
Calumet Specialty Products Partners LP	2780 Waterfront Pkwy E Dr Ste 200 *NASDAQ: CLMT*	Indianapolis	IN	46214	**800-437-3188**	317-328-5660
Chevron Canada Ltd	1200 - 1050 W Pender St	Vancouver	BC	V6E3T4	**800-663-1650**	604-668-5300
Chevron Corp	6001 Bollinger Canyon Rd *NYSE: CVX* ■ *Cust Svc	San Ramon	CA	94583	**800-368-8357***	925-842-1000
CITGO Petroleum Corp	1293 Eldridge Pkwy	Houston	TX	77077	**800-424-9300**	832-486-4700
Cross Oil Refining & Marketing Inc	484 E Sixth St	Smackover	AR	71762	**800-725-3066**	870-881-8700
Exxon Mobil Corp	5959 Las Colinas Blvd *NYSE: XOM*	Irving	TX	75039	**800-252-1800**	972-444-1000

Classified Section

Company / Address	City	State	Zip	Toll-Free	Phone
Hart Petroleum 323 Skidmores Rd	Deer Park	NY	11729	**800-796-3342**	631-667-3200
Imperial Oil Resources Ltd 237 Fourth Ave SW PO Box 2480 Stn M	Calgary	AB	T2P3M9	**800-567-3776**	
International Group Inc 85 Old Eagle School Rd	Wayne	PA	19087	**800-852-6537**	610-687-9030
Motiva Enterprises LLC 700 Milam St	Houston	TX	77002	**877-668-4825**	713-277-8000
Murphy Oil Corp 200 Peach St	El Dorado	AR	71730	**888-289-9314**	870-862-6411
SEMCO ENERGY Gas Co 1411 Third St Ste A	Port Huron	MI	48060	**800-624-2019**	
Star-Seal 6596 New Peachtree Rd	Atlanta	GA	30340	**800-779-6066**	770-455-6551
Sunoco Inc 1735 Market St Ste LL *NYSE: SUN*	Philadelphia	PA	19103	**800-786-6261**	215-977-3000

580 PETROLEUM STORAGE TERMINALS

Company / Address	City	State	Zip	Toll-Free	Phone
Buckley Oil Company Inc 1809 Rock Island St	Dallas	TX	75207	**800-721-4147**	214-421-4147
Cary Oil Company Inc 110 Mackenan Dr	Cary	NC	27511	**800-227-9645**	919-462-1100
Central Crude Inc 4187 Hwy 3059 PO Box 1863	Lake Charles	LA	70602	**800-245-8408**	337-436-1000
Gresham Petroleum Co 415 Pershing Ave P O Box 690	Indianola	MS	38751	**800-748-8934**	662-884-5000
Jack Becker Distributors Inc 6800 Suemac Pl	Jacksonville	FL	32254	**800-488-8411**	
Link Energy LLC 39 Rivalda Rd 2nd Fl	Toronto	ON	M9M2M4	**855-444-5465**	
Magellan Midstream Partners LP 1 Williams Ctr *NYSE: MMP*	Tulsa	OK	74172	**800-574-6671**	918-574-7000
MFA Oil Co 1 Ray Young Dr	Columbia	MO	65205	**800-366-0200**	573-442-0171
Molo Oil Company Inc 123 Southern Ave	Dubuque	IA	52003	**877-983-3761**	563-557-7540
Sweetwater Valley Oil Company Inc 1236 New Hwy 68	Sweetwater	TN	37874	**800-362-4519**	423-337-6671
W.H. Breshears Inc 720 B St	Modesto	CA	95354	**800-637-4427**	209-522-7291

581 PHARMACEUTICAL & DIAGNOSTIC PRODUCTS - VETERINARY

Company / Address	City	State	Zip	Toll-Free	Phone
Abbott Laboratories Animal Health Div 1401 Sheridan Rd	North Chicago	IL	60064	**888-299-7416**	847-937-6100
Addison Biological Laboratory Inc 507 N Cleveland Ave	Fayette	MO	65248	**800-331-2530**	660-248-2215
Alltech Inc 3031 Catnip Hill Pike	Nicholasville	KY	40356	**800-289-8324**	859-885-9613
Bimeda-MTC Animal Health Inc 420 Beaverdale Rd	Cambridge	ON	N3C2W4	**888-524-6332**	519-654-8000
Bio-Serv 3 Foster Lane Ste 201	Flemington	NJ	08822	**800-996-9908**	908-284-2155
Bioniche Life Sciences Inc. 231 Dundas St E *TSE: BNC*	Belleville	ON	K8N1E2	**800-265-5464**	613-966-8058
Biovet Inc 4375 Ave Beaudry	Saint-Hyacinthe	QC	J2S8W2	**888-824-6838**	450-771-7291
Biovet USA Inc 9025 Penn Ave S	Bloomington	MN	55431	**877-824-6838**	952-884-3113
Boehringer Ingelheim Vetmedica Inc 2621 N Belt Hwy	Saint Joseph	MO	64506	**800-821-7467**	816-233-2571
Cut-Heal Animal Care Products Inc 923 S Cedar Hill Rd	Cedar Hill	TX	75104	**800-288-4325**	972-293-9700
Delmont Laboratories Inc 715 Harvard Ave PO Box 269	Swarthmore	PA	19081	**800-562-5541**	610-543-2747
DMS Laboratories Inc 2 Darts Mill Rd	Flemington	NJ	08822	**800-567-4367**	908-782-3353
Dominion Veterinary Laboratories Inc 1199 Sanford St	Winnipeg	MB	R3E3A1	**800-465-7122**	204-589-7361
Elanco Animal Health 2500 Innovation Way	Greenfield	IN	46140	**877-352-6261**	317-276-2000
Heska Corp 3760 Rocky Mtn Ave *NASDAQ: HSKA*	Loveland	CO	80538	**800-464-3752**	970-493-7272
IMMVAC Inc 6080 Bass Ln	Columbia	MO	65201	**800-944-7563**	573-443-5363
King Bio Pharmaceuticals Inc 3 Westside Dr	Asheville	NC	28806	**800-543-3245**	828-255-0201
Lake Immunogenics Inc 348 Berg Rd	Ontario	NY	14519	**800-648-9990**	
Lloyd Inc 604 W Thomas Ave PO Box 130	Shenandoah	IA	51601	**800-831-0004**	712-246-4000
Luitpold Pharmaceuticals Inc 1 Luitpold Dr PO Box 9001	Shirley	NY	11967	**800-645-1706**	631-924-4000
Merial Ltd 3239 Satellite Blvd Bldg 500	Duluth	GA	30096	**888-637-4251**	678-638-3000
MVP Laboratories Inc 4805 G St	Omaha	NE	68117	**800-856-4648**	402-331-5106
Nutra-Blend Inc 3200 Second St	Neosho	MO	64850	**800-657-5657**	
Pfizer Inc Animal Health Group 235 E 42nd St	New York	NY	10017	**800-879-3477**	212-733-2323
Renco Corp 116 Third Ave N	Minneapolis	MN	55401	**800-359-8181**	612-338-6124
Texas Vet Lab Inc 1702 N Bell St	San Angelo	TX	76903	**800-284-8403**	
Veterinary Pharmacies of America Inc 2854 Antoine Dr	Houston	TX	77092	**877-838-7979**	
Vetoquinol Canada Inc 2000 Ch Georges	Lavaltrie	QC	J5T3S5	**800-363-1700**	450-586-2252

582 PHARMACEUTICAL COMPANIES

SEE ALSO Vitamins & Nutritional Supplements ; Diagnostic Products ; Medicinal Chemicals & Botanical Products ; Pharmaceutical & Diagnostic Products - Veterinary ; Pharmaceutical Companies - Generic Drugs ; Biotechnology Companies

Company / Address	City	State	Zip	Toll-Free	Phone
Abbott Laboratories Pharmaceutical Products Div 100 Research Dr Bioresearch Ctr	Worcester	MA	01605	**866-427-8477**	224-667-6100
Accucaps Industries Ltd 2125 Ambassador Dr	Windsor	ON	N9C3R5	**800-665-7210**	519-969-5404
Allergan Inc 2525 Dupont Dr *NYSE: AGN*	Irvine	CA	92612	**800-347-4500**	714-246-4500
Alva-Amco Pharmacal Cos Inc 7711 Merrimac Ave	Niles	IL	60714	**800-792-2582**	847-663-0700
Amneal Pharmaceuticals LLC 75 Adams Ave *NYSE: IPAH*	Hauppauge	NY	11788	**866-525-7270**	631-952-0214
Amphastar Pharmaceuticals Inc 11570 Sixth St	Rancho Cucamonga	CA	91730	**800-423-4136**	909-980-9484
Apotex Inc 150 Signet Dr	Toronto	ON	M9L1T9	**800-268-4623**	416-749-9300
AstraZeneca Canada Inc 1004 Middlegate Rd	Mississauga	ON	L4Y1M4	**800-565-5877**	905-277-7111
AstraZeneca Pharmaceuticals LP 1800 Concord Pk PO Box 15437	Wilmington	DE	19850	**800-236-9933**	
Bausch & Lomb Inc 1400 N Goodman St	Rochester	NY	14609	**800-553-5340**	585-338-6000
Bausch & Lomb Pharmaceuticals Inc 8500 Hidden River Pkwy *Cust Svc	Tampa	FL	33637	**800-323-0000***	800-553-5340
Baxter International Inc 1 Baxter Pkwy *NYSE: BAX*	Deerfield	IL	60015	**800-422-9837**	847-948-2000
Bayer Inc 77 Belfield Rd	Toronto	ON	M9W1G6	**800-622-2937**	416-248-0771
Blistex Inc 1800 Swift Dr *Cust Svc	Oak Brook	IL	60523	**800-837-1800***	
Boehringer Ingelheim Pharmaceuticals Inc 900 Ridgebury Rd	Ridgefield	CT	06877	**800-243-0127**	203-798-9988
Botanical Laboratories Inc 1441 W Smith Rd	Ferndale	WA	98248	**800-232-4005**	360-384-5656
Bristol-Myers Squibb Canada Inc 2344 Alfred-Nobel Blvd Ste 300 *Cust Svc	Montreal	QC	H4S0A4	**800-267-0005***	514-333-3200
Bristol-Myers Squibb Co 345 Pk Ave *NYSE: BMY*	New York	NY	10154	**800-332-2056**	212-546-4000
Care-Tech Laboratories Inc 3224 S KingsHwy Blvd	Saint Louis	MO	63139	**800-325-9681**	314-772-4610
CB Fleet Co Inc 4615 Murray Pl	Lynchburg	VA	24502	**866-255-6960**	434-528-4000
Chembio Diagnostics Inc 3661 Horseblock Rd *NASDAQ: CEMI*	Medford	NY	11763	**844-243-6246**	631-924-1135
Combe Inc 1101 Westchester Ave	White Plains	NY	10604	**800-431-2610**	914-694-5454
Covalon Technologies Ltd 405 Britannia Rd E Ste 106	Mississauga	ON	L4Z3E6	**877-711-6055**	905-568-8400
DPT Laboratories Ltd 318 McCullough	San Antonio	TX	78215	**866-225-5378**	210-476-8150
Dynavax Technologies Corp 2929 Seventh St Ste 100 *NASDAQ: DVAX*	Berkeley	CA	94710	**877-848-5100**	510-848-5100
Edwards Lifesciences Corp 1 Edwards Way *NYSE: EW*	Irvine	CA	92614	**800-424-3278**	949-250-2500
Eisai Inc 100 Tice Blvd	Woodcliff Lake	NJ	07677	**866-613-4724**	201-692-1100
Eli Lilly & Co Lilly Corporate Ctr *NYSE: LLY* ■ *Prod Info	Indianapolis	IN	46285	**800-545-5979***	317-276-2000
Eli Lilly Canada Inc 3650 Danforth Ave	Toronto	ON	M1N2E8	**888-545-5972**	416-694-3221
Endo Pharmaceuticals Holdings Inc 100 Endo Blvd *Cust Svc	Chadds Ford	PA	19317	**800-462-3636***	610-558-9800
First Priority Inc 1590 Todd Farm Dr	Elgin	IL	60123	**800-650-4899**	847-289-1600
Forest Pharmaceutical Inc 13600 Shoreline Dr	Earth City	MO	63045	**800-678-1605**	314-493-7000
G & W Laboratories Inc 111 Coolidge St	South Plainfield	NJ	07080	**800-922-1038**	908-753-2000
Galderma Laboratories Inc 14501 N Fwy	Fort Worth	TX	76177	**866-735-4137**	817-961-5000
Germiphene Corp 1379 Colborne St E PO Box 1748	Brantford	ON	N3T5M1	**800-265-9931**	519-759-7100
GlaxoSmithKline Inc 7333 Mississauga Rd N	Mississauga	ON	L5N6L4	**800-387-7374**	905-819-3000
Halocarbon Products Corp PO Box 661	River Edge	NJ	07661	**800-338-5803**	201-262-8899
Hoffmann-LaRoche Inc 340 Kingsland St	Nutley	NJ	07110	**800-526-6367**	973-235-5000
Hope Pharmaceuticals Inc 16416 N 92nd St Ste 125	Scottsdale	AZ	85260	**800-755-9595**	
Hospira Inc 275 N Field Dr *NYSE: HSP*	Lake Forest	IL	60045	**877-946-7747**	224-212-2000
Humco Holding Group Inc 7400 Alumax Dr	Texarkana	TX	75501	**800-662-3435**	903-334-6200
Immtech Pharmaceuticals 1 N End Ave	New York	NY	10282	**877-898-8038**	212-791-2911
Jaapharm Canada Inc 510 Rowntree Dairy Rd Bldg B	Woodbridge	ON	L4L8H2	**800-465-9587**	905-851-7885
Janssen Pharmaceutica Inc 1125 Trenton-Harbourton Rd	Titusville	NJ	08560	**800-526-7736**	609-730-2000

Company	Address	City	State	ZIP	Toll-Free	Phone
Jazz Pharmaceuticals Inc	3180 Porter Dr	Palo Alto	CA	94304	**866-997-3688**	650-496-3777
Juniper Pharmaceuticals Inc	33 Arch St *NASDAQ: CBRX*	Boston	MA	02110	**866-566-5636**	973-994-3999
Keryx Biopharmaceuticals Inc	750 Lexington Ave 20th Fl *NASDAQ: KERX*	New York	NY	10022	**800-903-0247**	212-531-5965
King Bio Pharmaceuticals Inc	3 Westside Dr	Asheville	NC	28806	**800-543-3245**	828-255-0201
Konsyl Pharmaceuticals Inc	8050 Industrial Pk Rd	Easton	MD	21601	**800-356-6795**	410-822-5192
Kramer Laboratories Inc	8778 SW Eigth St	Miami	FL	33174	**800-824-4894**	305-223-1287
Major Pharmaceutical Co	31778 Enterprise Dr	Livonia	MI	48150	**800-875-0123**	734-743-6161
Medical Products Laboratories Inc	9990 Global Rd	Philadelphia	PA	19115	**800-523-0191**	215-677-2700
Medicis Pharmaceutical Corp	7720 N Dobson Rd *Cust Svc	Scottsdale	AZ	85256	**866-246-8245***	800-321-4576
Melaleuca Inc	3910 S Yellowstone Hwy *Sales	Idaho Falls	ID	83402	**800-282-3000***	208-522-0700
Mentholatum Company Inc	707 Sterling Dr	Orchard Park	NY	14127	**800-688-7660**	716-677-2500
Merck & Company Inc	1 Merck Dr PO Box 100 *NYSE: MRK* ■ *Cust Svc	Whitehouse Station	NJ	08889	**800-672-6372***	908-423-1000
Mikart Inc	1750 Chattahoochee Ave NW	Atlanta	GA	30318	**888-464-5278**	404-351-4510
Mission Pharmacal	PO Box 786099	San Antonio	TX	78278	**800-531-3333**	210-696-8400
Mylan	1000 Mylan Blvd	Canonsburg	PA	15317	**800-527-4278**	724-514-1800
Mylan Pharmaceuticals Inc	781 Chestnut Ridge Rd	Morgantown	WV	26505	**800-796-9526**	
Neos Therapeutics	2940 N Hwy 360 Ste 100	Grand Prairie	TX	75050	**844-375-8324**	972-408-1300
Novartis Pharmaceuticals Canada Inc	385 boul Bouchard	Dorval	QC	H9S1A9	**800-465-2244**	514-631-6775
Novartis Pharmaceuticals Co	10401 Cornhusker Hwy	Waverly	NE	68462	**888-669-6682**	862-778-2100
Novo Nordisk of North America Inc	100 College Rd W	Princeton	NJ	08540	**800-727-6500**	609-987-5800
Novo Nordisk Pharmaceuticals Inc	800 Scudders Mill Rd *Cust Svc	Princeton	NJ	08536	**800-727-6500***	609-987-5800
Numark Laboratories Inc	164 Northfield Ave	Edison	NJ	08837	**800-338-8079**	
Odor Management Inc	18-6 E Dundee Rd Ste 101	Barrington	IL	60010	**800-662-6367**	847-304-9111
Particle Dynamics International LLC	2629 S Hanley Rd	Saint Louis	MO	63144	**800-452-4682**	314-968-2376
Pfizer Animal Health	5 Giralda Farms	Madison	NJ	07940	**888-963-8471**	
Pfizer Canada Inc	17300 TransCanada Hwy	Kirkland	QC	H9J2M5	**800-463-6001**	514-695-0500
Pfizer Inc	235 E 42nd St *NYSE: PFE*	New York	NY	10017	**800-879-3477**	212-733-2323
Procter & Gamble Pharmaceuticals Canada Inc	PO Box 355 Stn A	Toronto	ON	M5W1C5	**800-668-0150**	416-730-4711
Prometheus Laboratories Inc	9410 Carroll Pk Dr	San Diego	CA	92121	**888-892-8391**	
ProPhase Labs Inc	621 Shady Retreat Rd *NASDAQ: PRPH*	Doylestown	PA	18901	**800-505-2653**	215-345-0919
Protide Pharmaceuticals Inc	505 Oakwood Rd Ste 200	Lake Zurich	IL	60047	**800-552-3569**	847-726-3100
QLT USA Inc	887 Great Northern Way Ste 250	Vancouver	CO	80525	**877-764-3131**	970-482-5868
Qualicaps Inc	6505 Franz Warner Pkwy	Whitsett	NC	27377	**800-227-7853**	336-449-3900
Qualitest Pharmaceuticals	130 Vintage Dr	Huntsville	AL	35811	**800-444-4011**	
Quintiles Canada Inc	18 Rue Elderidge *General	Dollard-des-Ormeaux	QC	H9A2P4	**866-267-4479***	514-855-0888
Quintiles Transnational Corp	4820 Emperor Blvd	Durham	NC	27703	**866-267-4479**	919-998-2000
Regis Technologies Inc	8210 Austin Ave	Morton Grove	IL	60053	**800-323-8144**	847-967-6000
Rules-based Medicine Inc	3300 Duval Rd	Austin	TX	78759	**866-726-6277**	512-835-8026
Salix Pharmaceuticals Inc	8510 Colonnade Ctr Dr *NASDAQ: SLXP*	Raleigh	NC	27615	**800-508-0024**	919-862-1000
SciClone Pharmaceuticals Inc	950 Tower Ln Ste 900 *NASDAQ: SCLN*	Foster City	CA	94404	**800-724-2566**	650-358-3456
Sigma-Tau Pharmaceutical Inc	9841 Washingtonian Blvd Ste 500	Gaithersburg	MD	20878	**800-447-0169**	301-948-1041
Silipos Inc	7049 Williams Rd	Niagara Falls	NY	14304	**800-229-4404**	716-283-0700
SISU Inc	7635 N Fraser Way Ste 102	Burnaby	BC	V5J0B8	**800-663-4163**	604-420-6610
Solvay America Inc	3333 Richmond Ave *General	Houston	TX	77098	**800-365-6565***	713-525-6000
Sovereign Pharmaceuticals Ltd	7590 Sand St	Fort Worth	TX	76118	**877-248-0228**	817-284-0429
SSS Co	71 University Ave	Atlanta	GA	30315	**800-237-3843**	404-521-0857
Sucampo Pharmaceuticals Inc	805 King Farm Blvd Ste 550 *NASDAQ: SCMP*	Rockville	MD	20850	**877-825-3327**	301-961-3400
Taro Pharmaceuticals Inc	130 E Dr	Brampton	ON	L6T1C1	**800-268-1975**	905-791-8276
UCB Pharma Inc	1950 Lake Pk Dr	Smyrna	GA	30080	**800-477-7877**	770-970-7500
United Therapeutics Corp	1040 Spring St *NASDAQ: UTHR*	Silver Spring	MD	20910	**877-864-8437**	301-608-9292
Upsher-Smith Laboratories Inc	6701 Evenstad Dr	Maple Grove	MN	55369	**800-654-2299**	763-315-2000
Vivus Inc	1172 Castro St *NASDAQ: VVUS*	Mountain View	CA	94040	**800-607-0088**	650-934-5200
WF Young Inc	302 Benton Dr	East Longmeadow	MA	01028	**800-628-9653**	413-526-9999
Wright Group, The	6428 Airport Rd	Crowley	LA	70526	**800-201-3096**	337-783-3096
ZLB Behring LLC	1020 First Ave PO Box 61501	King of Prussia	PA	19406	**800-683-1288**	610-878-4000
Zogenix Inc	12400 High Bluff Dr Ste 650	San Diego	CA	92130	**866-964-3649**	858-259-1165

583 PHARMACEUTICAL COMPANIES - GENERIC DRUGS

SEE ALSO Vitamins & Nutritional Supplements ; Diagnostic Products ; Medicinal Chemicals & Botanical Products ; Pharmaceutical & Diagnostic Products - Veterinary ; Pharmaceutical Companies ; Biotechnology Companies

Company	Address	City	State	ZIP	Toll-Free	Phone
Apotex Corp	2400 N Commerce Pkwy Ste 400	Weston	FL	33326	**877-427-6839**	
Biotools Inc	17546 Bee Line Hwy	Jupiter	FL	33458	**866-286-6571**	561-625-0133
E Fougera & Co	60 Baylis Rd	Melville	NY	11747	**800-645-9833**	631-454-6996
Glenwood LLC	111 Cedar Ln	Englewood	NJ	07631	**800-542-0772**	201-569-0050
Healthpoint	3909 Hulen St *Cust Svc	Fort Worth	TX	76107	**800-441-8227***	817-900-4000
Impax Laboratories Inc	30831 Hun2od Ave *NASDAQ: IPXL*	Hayward	CA	94544	**877-994-6729**	510-240-6450
Mericon Industries Inc	8819 N Pioneer Rd	Peoria	IL	61615	**800-242-6464**	309-693-2150
Morton Grove Pharmaceuticals Inc	6451 Main St	Morton Grove	IL	60053	**800-346-6854**	847-967-5600
Mylan Pharmaceuticals ULC	85 Advance Rd	Etobicoke	ON	M8Z2S6	**800-575-1379**	416-236-2631
Nephron Pharmaceuticals Corp	4121 SW 34th St	Orlando	FL	32811	**800-443-4313**	407-999-2225
NuCare Pharmaceuticals Inc	622 W Katella Ave	Orange	CA	92867	**888-482-9545**	
Par Pharmaceutical Cos Inc	6 Ram Ridge Rd *NYSE: PRX*	Chestnut Ridge	NY	10977	**800-828-9393**	201-802-4000
Par Pharmaceutical Inc	1 Ram Ridge Rd	Spring Valley	NY	10977	**800-828-9393**	201-802-4000
Payless Drug Stores Inc	16100 SW 72nd Ave PO Box 230969	Portland	OR	97224	**800-330-3665**	503-626-9436
Perrigo Co	515 Eastern Ave *NYSE: PRGO*	Allegan	MI	49010	**800-719-9260**	269-673-8451
Pharmaceutical Calibrations & Instrumentation LLC	8100 Brownleigh Dr Ste 100-A	Raleigh	NC	27617	**877-724-2257**	
Skilled Care Pharmacy Inc	6175 Hi Tek Ct	Mason	OH	45040	**800-334-1624**	513-459-7455
Taro Pharmaceuticals USA Inc	3 Skyline Dr	Hawthorne	NY	10532	**800-544-1449**	914-345-9001
Teva Pharmaceutical USA	1090 Horsham Rd *NYSE: TEVA*	North Wales	PA	19454	**800-545-8800**	215-591-3000
TruTouch Technologies Inc	73 Carriage Way	Sudbury	MA	01776	**866-721-6221**	
UDL Laboratories Inc	1718 Northrock Ct	Rockford	IL	61103	**800-435-5272**	800-848-0462
USL Pharma	301 S Cherokee St	Denver	CO	80223	**800-654-2299**	303-607-4500
West-Ward Pharmaceutical Corp	401 Industrial Way W *Cust Svc	Eatontown	NJ	07724	**800-631-2174***	732-542-1191
X-Gen Pharmaceuticals Inc	300 Daniels Zenker Dr	Horseheads	NY	14845	**866-390-4411**	

584 PHARMACY ASSOCIATIONS - STATE

SEE ALSO Health & Medical Professionals Associations

Association	Address	City	State	ZIP	Toll-Free	Phone
Alabama Pharmacy Assn	1211 Carmichael Way *General	Montgomery	AL	36106	**877-877-3962***	334-271-4222
Alaska Pharmacist's Assn	203 W 15th Ave Ste 100	Anchorage	AK	99501	**800-228-9290**	907-563-8880
California Pharmacists Assn (CPhA)	4030 Lennane Dr	Sacramento	CA	95834	**866-365-7472**	916-779-1400
Georgia Pharmacy Assn (GPhA)	50 Lenox Pointe NE	Atlanta	GA	30324	**888-871-5590**	404-231-5074
Indiana Pharmacists Alliance	729 N Pennsylvania St	Indianapolis	IN	46204	**800-516-0313**	317-634-4968
Iowa Pharmacy Assn	8515 Douglas Ave Ste 16	Des Moines	IA	50322	**866-512-1800**	515-270-0713
Kansas Pharmacists Assn	1020 SW Fairlawn Rd	Topeka	KS	66604	**888-792-6273**	785-228-2327
Kentucky Pharmacists Assn	1228 US 127 S	Frankfort	KY	40601	**800-922-1557**	502-227-2303
Louisiana Pharmacists Assn	450 Laurel St Ste 1400	Baton Rouge	LA	70801	**877-252-5100**	225-346-6883
Maryland Pharmacists Assn	9115 Guilford Rd Ste 200	Columbia	MD	21046	**877-463-3464**	410-727-0746
Massachusetts Pharmacists Assn	500 W Cummings Pk Ste 3475	Woburn	MA	01801	**888-772-7227**	781-933-1107
Michigan Pharmacists Assn	408 Kalamazoo Plz	Lansing	MI	48933	**800-227-2345**	517-484-1466

Name / Address	City	State	Zip	Toll-Free	Phone
Minnesota Pharmacists Assn (MPhA) 1935 W County Rd B2	Roseville	MN	55113	**800-451-8349**	651-697-1771
Mississippi Pharmacists Assn 341 Edgewood Terr Dr	Jackson	MS	39206	**800-421-2408**	601-981-0416
Missouri Pharmacy Assn 211 E Capitol Ave	Jefferson City	MO	65101	**800-468-4672**	573-636-7522
Nebraska Pharmacists Assn 6221 S 58th St Ste A	Lincoln	NE	68516	**866-365-7472**	402-420-1500
Pharmacists Society of the State of New York 210 Washington Ave Ext	Albany	NY	12203	**800-632-8822**	518-869-6595
Texas Pharmacy Assn 12007 Research Blvd Ste 201	Austin	TX	78759	**800-505-5463**	512-836-8350
Washington State Pharmacy Assn 411 Williams Ave S	Renton	WA	98057	**800-562-6000**	425-228-7171

585 PHARMACY BENEFITS MANAGEMENT SERVICES

A pharmacy benefits management service (PBM) is a company that manages various pharmacy-related aspects of a health insurance plan, such as the assignment of pharmacy cards, claims filing and processing, formulary management, etc. For the most part, PBM clients are insurance companies, HMOs, or PPOs rather than individuals or pharmacies.

Name / Address	City	State	Zip	Toll-Free	Phone
BioScrip 1600 Bdwy Ste 950 *NASDAQ: BIOS*	Denver	CO	80202	**877-409-2301**	720-697-5200
Caremark Rx Inc PO Box 832407	Richardson	TX	75083	**877-460-7766**	
CoreSource Inc 400 Field Dr	Lake Forest	IL	60045	**800-832-3332**	847-604-9200
Health Smart Rx 1301 E Ninth St	Cleveland	OH	44114	**800-681-6912**	
Maxor National Pharmacy Services Corp 320 S Polk St Ste 100	Amarillo	TX	79101	**800-658-6146**	806-324-5400
MedImpact Healthcare Systems Inc 10680 Treena St Ste 500	San Diego	CA	92131	**800-788-2949**	858-566-2727
Prescription Solutions 3515 Harbor Blvd	Costa Mesa	CA	92626	**800-788-4863**	
Prime Therapeutics Inc 1305 Corporate Ctr Dr	Eagan	MN	55121	**800-858-0723**	612-777-4000
ScripNet 10050 Banburry Cross Dr Ste 290	Las Vegas	NV	89144	**888-880-8562**	702-248-2692
Script Care Inc 6380 Folsom Dr	Beaumont	TX	77706	**800-880-9988**	
ScriptSave 4911 E Broadway Blvd Ste 200	Tucson	AZ	85711	**800-347-5985**	
Serve You Custom Prescription Management 10201 Innovation Dr Ste 600	Milwaukee	WI	53226	**888-243-6890**	414-410-8100
Walgreens Health Services 1411 Lake Cook Rd	Deerfield	IL	60015	**800-207-2568**	

586 PHARMACY MANAGEMENT SERVICES

Companies that provide long-term care pharmacy services to individuals with special needs (e.g., chronic disease or advanced age); and those that provide pharmacy management services to hospitals or other institutions.

Name / Address	City	State	Zip	Toll-Free	Phone
Accredo Health Group Inc 1640 Century Ctr Pkwy	Memphis	TN	38134	**877-222-7336**	901-385-3600
McKesson Pharmaceutical 1 Post St	San Francisco	CA	94104	**800-571-2889**	415-983-8300
Omnicare Inc 201 E 4th St *NYSE: OCR*	Cincinnati	OH	45202	**800-342-5627**	800-990-6664

587 PHOTO PROCESSING & STORAGE

Name / Address	City	State	Zip	Toll-Free	Phone
Advanced Photographic Solutions 1525 Hardeman Ln	Cleveland	TN	37312	**800-241-9234**	423-479-5481
Burrell Imaging 1311 Merrillville Rd	Crown Point	IN	46307	**800-348-8732**	219-663-3210
Candid Color Systems Inc 1300 Metropolitan Ave	Oklahoma City	OK	73108	**800-336-4550**	405-947-8747
Dale Laboratories 2960 Simms St	Hollywood	FL	33020	**800-327-1776**	954-925-0103
H & H Color Lab Inc 8906 E 67th St	Raytown	MO	64133	**800-821-1305**	816-358-6677
iMemories 9181 E Bell Rd	Scottsdale	AZ	85260	**800-845-7986**	
McKenna Pro Imaging 2800 Falls Ave *General	Waterloo	IA	50701	**800-238-3456***	319-235-6265
Meisel Visual Imaging 2019 McKenzie Dr	Carrollton	TX	75006	**800-527-5186**	214-688-4950
Photo USA 2140 Colonial Ave	Roanoke	VA	24015	**888-234-6320**	540-344-0961
Yahoo! Photos 701 First Ave	Sunnyvale	CA	94089	**888-267-7574**	408-349-3300

588 PHOTOCOPYING EQUIPMENT & SUPPLIES

SEE ALSO Business Machines - Whol

Name / Address	City	State	Zip	Toll-Free	Phone
Coast to Coast Business Equipment Inc 8 Vanderbilt	Irvine	CA	92619	**877-382-4357**	949-457-7300
Imaging Supplies Company Inc 804 Woodland Ave	Sanford	NC	27330	**800-518-1152**	919-776-1152
Masterfile Corp 3 Concorde Gate 4th Fl	Toronto	ON	M3C3N7	**800-387-9010**	416-929-3000
Northwest Print Strategies Inc 8175 Sw Nimbus Ave	Beaverton	OR	97008	**800-648-5156**	503-641-5156
Oce-USA Inc 5450 N Cumberland Ave	Chicago	IL	60656	**800-877-6232**	773-714-8500
R & D Computers 6767 Peachtree Industrial Blvd Ste B	Atlanta	GA	30092	**800-350-3071**	770-416-0103
Sharp Electronics Corp 1 Sharp Plz	Mahwah	NJ	07430	**800-237-4277**	201-529-8200
Toshiba America Inc 1251 Ave of the Americas Ste 4100	New York	NY	10020	**800-457-7777**	212-596-0600
Xerox Canada Ltd 5650 Yonge St	North York	ON	M2M4G7	**800-939-3769**	
Xerox Corp 45 Glover Ave PO Box 4505 *NYSE: XRX*	Norwalk	CT	06856	**800-327-9753**	203-968-3000

589 PHOTOGRAPH STUDIOS - PORTRAIT

Name / Address	City	State	Zip	Toll-Free	Phone
Cherry Hill Photo Enterprises Inc 4 East Stow Rd	Marlton	NJ	08053	**800-969-2440**	
Freestyle Photo Biz 5124 Sunset Blvd	Hollywood	CA	90027	**800-292-6137**	
George STREET Photo & Video LLC 230 W Huron St Ste 3W	Chicago	IL	60654	**866-831-4103**	
Jostens Inc 3601 Minnesota Ave Ste 400	Minneapolis	MN	55435	**800-235-4774**	952-830-3300
MarathonFoto 3490 Martin Hurst Rd	Tallahassee	FL	32312	**800-424-3686**	972-330-7656
Portrait Express 441 N Water St	Silverton	OR	97381	**800-228-3759**	503-873-6365
Portraits International 10835 Rockley Rd	Houston	TX	77099	**888-838-1495**	281-879-8444
Ripcho Studio 7630 Lorain Ave	Cleveland	OH	44102	**800-686-7427**	216-631-0664

590 PHOTOGRAPHIC EQUIPMENT & SUPPLIES

SEE ALSO Cameras & Related Supplies - Retail

Name / Address	City	State	Zip	Toll-Free	Phone
Agfa Corp 611 River Dr	Elmwood Park	NJ	07407	**888-274-8626**	201-440-2500
Anton/Bauer Inc 14 Progress Dr	Shelton	CT	06484	**800-422-3473**	203-929-1100
Ballantyne Strong Inc 13710 FNB Pkwy *NYSE: BTN* ■ *General	Omaha	NE	68154	**800-424-1215***	
Beta Screen Corp 707 Commercial Ave	Carlstadt	NJ	07072	**800-272-7336**	201-939-2400
Carr Corp 1547 11th St	Santa Monica	CA	90401	**800-952-2398**	310-587-1113
Casio Inc 570 Mt Pleasant Ave *Cust Svc	Dover	NJ	07801	**800-634-1895***	973-361-5400
Ceiva Logic Inc 214 E Magnolia Blvd *Tech Supp	Burbank	CA	91502	**877-693-7263***	818-562-1495
Champion Photochemistry 7895 Tranmere Dr	Mississauga	ON	L5S1V9	**800-387-3430**	905-670-7900
Da-Lite Screen Company Inc 3100 N Detroit St	Warsaw	IN	46581	**800-622-3737**	574-267-8101
Douthitt Corp 245 Adair St	Detroit	MI	48207	**800-368-8448**	313-259-1565
Draper Shade & Screen Co 411 S Pearl St	Spiceland	IN	47385	**800-238-7999**	765-987-7999
Identatronics Inc 165 N Lively Blvd *Cust Svc	Elk Grove Village	IL	60007	**800-323-5403***	847-437-2654
InFocus Corp 13190 SW 68th Pkwy Ste 200	Portland	OR	97223	**877-388-8385**	503-207-4700
Matthews Studio Equipment Group 2405 W Empire Ave	Burbank	CA	91504	**800-237-8263**	818-843-6715
MVM Products LLC 940 Calle Amanecer Ste K	San Clemente	CA	92673	**888-246-5832**	949-366-1470
Navitar Inc 200 Commerce Dr *Cust Svc	Rochester	NY	14623	**800-828-6778***	585-359-4000
Nikon Inc 1300 Walt Whitman Rd *Cust Svc	Melville	NY	11747	**800-645-6687***	631-547-4200
Panavision Inc 6219 DeSoto Ave	Woodland Hills	CA	91367	**800-260-1846**	818-316-1000
Peter Pepper Products Inc 17929 S Susana Rd	Compton	CA	90221	**800-496-0204**	310-639-0390
Phase One Inc 200 Broadhollow Rd Ste 312	Melville	NY	11747	**888-742-7366**	631-757-0400
Research Technology International Inc 4700 W Chase Ave *Sales	Lincolnwood	IL	60712	**800-323-7520***	847-677-3000
Schneider Optics Century Div 7701 Haskell Ave	Van Nuys	CA	91406	**800-228-1254**	818-766-3715
Sharp Electronics Corp 1 Sharp Plz	Mahwah	NJ	07430	**800-237-4277**	201-529-8200
Sony Corp of America 550 Madison Ave	New York	NY	10022	**800-282-2848**	212-833-6800
Stewart Filmscreen Corp 1161 W Sepulveda Blvd	Torrance	CA	90502	**800-762-4999**	310-784-5300
Tiffen Company LLC 90 Oser Ave	Hauppauge	NY	11788	**800-645-2522**	631-273-2500
Toshiba America Inc 1251 Ave of the Americas Ste 4100	New York	NY	10020	**800-457-7777**	212-596-0600
Visual Departures Ltd 48 Sheffield Business Park Ste 195	Ashley Falls	MA	01222	**800-628-2003**	
Vivitar Corp 195 Carter Dr	Edison	NJ	08817	**800-592-9541**	732-248-1306
Vutec Corp 11711 W Sample Rd	Coral Springs	FL	33065	**800-770-4700**	954-545-9000

591 PHOTOGRAPHY - COMMERCIAL

Company	Address	City	State	Zip	Toll-Free	Phone
Universal Image	PO Box 77090	Winter Garden	FL	34787	**800-553-5499**	407-352-5302

592 PHOTOGRAPHY - STOCK

Company	Address	City	State	Zip	Toll-Free	Phone
Alaska Stock Images	2505 Fairbanks St	Anchorage	AK	99503	**800-487-4285**	907-276-1343
Corbis Corp	710 Second Ave Ste 200	Seattle	WA	98104	**800-260-0444**	646-613-4000
Custom Medical Stock Photo Inc	3660 W Irving Pk Rd	Chicago	IL	60618	**800-373-2677**	773-267-3100
Image Works	PO Box 443	Woodstock	NY	12498	**800-475-8801**	845-679-8500
Photo Researchers Inc	307 Fifth Ave 3rd Fl	New York	NY	10016	**800-833-9033**	212-758-3420

593 PIECE GOODS & NOTIONS

SEE ALSO Fabric Stores

Company	Address	City	State	Zip	Toll-Free	Phone
Advanced Probing Systems Inc	2300 Central Ave	Boulder	CO	80301	**800-631-0005**	303-939-9384
Associated Fabrics Corp	15-01 Pollitt Dr Unit 7	Fair Lawn	NJ	07410	**800-232-4077**	
B Berger Co	1380 Highland Rd	Macedonia	OH	44056	**800-288-8400*** *Cust Svc	330-425-3838
Baum Textile Mills Inc	812 Jersey Ave	Jersey City	NJ	07310	**866-842-7631**	201-659-0444
Blank Quilting Corp	*Blank Quilting* 49 West 37th St 14th fl.	New York	NY	10018	**800-294-9495**	
Blumenthal Lansing Co	30 Two Bridges Rd Ste 110	Fairfield	NJ	07004	**800-448-9749**	201-935-6220
Bob Barker Company Inc	PO Box 429	Fuquay Varina	NC	27526	**800-334-9880**	
Brookwood Cos Inc	25 W 45th St 11th Fl	New York	NY	10036	**800-426-5468**	212-551-0100
Burch Fabrics Group	4200 Brockton Dr SE	Grand Rapids	MI	49512	**800-841-8111**	616-698-2800
Criterion Thread Company Inc	21744 98th Ave	Queens Village	NY	11429	**800-695-0080*** *General	718-464-4200
Dunlap Industries Inc	297 Industrial Park Rd	Dunlap	TN	37327	**800-251-7214**	
Duralee Fabrics Ltd Inc	1775 Fifth Ave	Bay Shore	NY	11706	**800-275-3872*** *Cust Svc	631-273-8800
EE Schenck Co	6000 N Cutter Cir	Portland	OR	97217	**800-433-0722**	503-284-4124
Hanes Cos Inc	500 N McLin Creek Rd	Conover	NC	28613	**877-252-3052**	828-464-4673
Hoffman California Fabrics Inc	25792 Obrero Dr	Mission Viejo	CA	92691	**800-547-0100**	
Janlynn Corp	2070 Westover Rd	Chicopee	MA	01022	**800-445-5565**	413-206-0002
Keyston Bros	2801 Academy Way Ste A	Sacramento	CA	95815	**800-453-1112**	916-927-5851
Lew Jan Textile Corp	366 Veterans Memorial Hwy	Commack	NY	11725	**800-899-0531**	
Marcus Bros Textiles Inc	980 Ave of the Americas	New York	NY	10018	**800-548-8295**	212-354-8700
McKee Surfaces	PO Box 230	Muscatine	IA	52761	**800-553-9662*** *Cust Svc	563-263-2421
Meow Inc	307 W 36th St 16th Fl	New York	NY	10018	**888-485-6738**	
Miami Corp, The	720 Anderson Ferry Rd	Cincinnati	OH	45238	**800-543-0448**	513-451-6700
Pine Cone Hill Inc	125 Pecks Rd	Pittsfield	MA	01201	**877-586-4771**	
Prym-Dritz Corp	950 Brisack Rd	Spartanburg	SC	29303	**800-255-7796*** *Cust Svc	864-576-5050
Robert Allen Fabrics Inc	225 Foxboro Blvd	Foxboro	MA	02035	**800-333-3777**	
Robert Kaufman Company Inc	PO Box 59266	Los Angeles	CA	90059	**800-877-2066**	310-538-3482
Schott International Inc	2850 Gilchrist Rd	Akron	OH	44305	**877-661-2121**	330-794-2121
Scovill Fasteners Inc	1802 Scovill Dr	Clarkesville	GA	30523	**888-726-8455*** *Cust Svc	706-754-1000
Spradling International Inc	200 Cahaba Vly Pkwy PO Box 1668	Pelham	AL	35124	**800-333-0955**	205-985-4206
Tiger Button Company Inc	307 W 38th St	New York	NY	10018	**800-223-2754**	212-594-0570
United Notions Inc	13800 Hutton St	Dallas	TX	75234	**800-527-9447**	972-484-8901
US Button Corp	328 Kennedy Dr	Putnam	CT	06260	**800-243-1842**	860-928-2707
Velcro USA Inc	406 Brown Ave	Manchester	NH	03103	**800-225-0180**	603-669-4880
Waterbury Button Co	1855 Peck Ln	Cheshire	CT	06410	**800-928-1812**	
Young Fashions Inc	10300 Perkins Rd	Baton Rouge	LA	70810	**800-824-4154**	225-766-1010

594 PIPE & PIPE FITTINGS - METAL (FABRICATED)

SEE ALSO Metal Tube & Pipe

Company	Address	City	State	Zip	Toll-Free	Phone
Alloy Stainless Products Co	611 Union Blvd	Totowa	NJ	07512	**800-631-8372**	973-256-1616
AY McDonald Manufacturing Co	4800 Chavenelle Rd PO Box 508	Dubuque	IA	52002	**800-292-2737*** *Cust Svc	563-583-7311
BendTec Inc	366 Garfield Ave	Duluth	MN	55802	**800-236-3832**	218-722-0205
Campbell Manufacturing Inc	127 E Spring St	Bechtelsville	PA	19505	**800-523-0224**	610-367-2107
Carpenter Powder Products	600 Mayer St	Bridgeville	PA	15017	**866-790-9092**	412-257-5102
Central Pipe Supply Inc	101 Ware Rd PO Box 5470	Pearl	MS	39288	**800-844-7700**	601-939-3322
Champion Mfg Industries Inc	6021 N Galena Rd	Peoria	IL	61614	**800-452-7473**	309-685-1031
Classic Tube	80 Rotech Dr	Lancaster	NY	14086	**800-882-3711**	716-759-1800
Colonial Engineering Inc	6400 Corporate Ave	Portage	MI	49002	**800-374-0234**	269-323-2495
Controls Southeast Inc	PO Box 7500	Charlotte	NC	28241	**877-788-3030**	704-588-3030
Douglas Bros	423 Riverside Industrial Pkwy	Portland	ME	04103	**800-341-0926**	207-797-6771
Elkhart Products Corp	1255 Oak St	Elkhart	IN	46514	**800-284-4851**	574-264-3181
Empire Industries Inc	180 Olcott St	Manchester	CT	06040	**800-243-4844**	860-647-1431
Fuller Industrial	65 Nelson Rd	Lively	ON	P3Y1P4	**888-524-3777**	705-682-2777
General Plug & Mfg Co Inc	455 Main St	Grafton	OH	44044	**800-289-7584**	440-926-2411
H-P Products Inc	512 W Gorgas St	Louisville	OH	44641	**800-822-8356**	330-875-5556
Kelly Pipe Company LLC	11680 Bloomfield Ave	Santa Fe Springs	CA	90670	**800-305-3559**	562-868-0456
MicroGroup Inc	7 Industrial Pk Rd	Medway	MA	02053	**800-255-8823**	508-533-4925
Mills Iron Works Inc	14834 Maple Ave	Gardena	CA	90248	**800-421-2281**	323-321-6520
Milwaukee Valve Company Inc	16550 W Stratton Dr	New Berlin	WI	53151	**800-348-6544**	262-432-2800
National Excelsior Co	1999 N Ruby St	Melrose Park	IL	60160	**855-373-9235**	708-343-4225
NIBCO Inc	1516 Middlebury St	Elkhart	IN	46515	**800-234-0227**	574-295-3000
Nor-Cal Products Inc	1967 S Oregon St	Yreka	CA	96097	**800-824-4166**	530-842-4457
Parker Hannifin Corp Brass Products Div	100 Parker Dr	Otsego	MI	49078	**800-272-7537**	269-694-9411
Penn Machine Co	106 Stn St	Johnstown	PA	15905	**800-736-6872**	814-288-1547
Pevco Sys Intl Inc	1401 Tangier Dr	Baltimore	MD	21220	**800-296-7382**	410-931-8800
Piping Technology & Products Inc	3701 Holmes Rd PO Box 34506	Houston	TX	77051	**866-746-9172**	713-422-2271
R & B Wagner Inc	PO Box 423	Butler	WI	53007	**888-243-6914**	414-214-0444
Richards Industries Inc	3170 Wasson Rd	Cincinnati	OH	45209	**800-543-7311*** *Cust Svc	513-533-5600
Romac Industries Inc	21919 20th Ave SE	Bothell	WA	98021	**800-426-9341**	425-951-6200
Star Pipe LLC	4018 Westhollow Pkwy	Houston	TX	77082	**800-999-3009**	281-558-3000
Synalloy Corp	775 Spartan Blvd Ste 102 PO Box 5627 *NASDAQ: SYNL* ■	Spartanburg	SC	29304	**800-937-5449*** *Orders	864-585-3605
Tate Andale Inc	1941 Lansdowne Rd	Baltimore	MD	21227	**800-296-8283**	410-247-8700
Tru-Flex Metal Hose Corp	2391 S State Rd 263 PO Box 247	West Lebanon	IN	47991	**800-255-6291**	765-893-4403
Tube Processing Corp	604 E Le Grande Ave	Indianapolis	IN	46203	**800-295-4119**	317-787-1321
Tylok International Inc	1061 E 260th St	Euclid	OH	44132	**800-321-0466**	216-261-7310
Universal Tube Inc	2607 Bond St	Rochester Hills	MI	48309	**800-394-8823**	248-853-5100
US Pipe & Foundry Co	2 Chase Corporate Drive Ste 200	Birmingham	AL	35244	**866-347-7473**	
Victaulic Co	4901 Kesslersville Rd	Easton	PA	18040	**800-742-5842*** *Sales	610-559-3300
World Wide Fittings Inc	7501 N Natchez Ave	Niles	IL	60714	**800-393-9894**	847-588-2200

595 PIPE & PIPE FITTINGS - PLASTICS

Company	Address	City	State	Zip	Toll-Free	Phone
Advanced Drainage Systems Inc	4640 Trueman Blvd	Hilliard	OH	43026	**800-821-6710**	
CertainTeed Corp	750 E Swedesford Rd	Valley Forge	PA	19482	**800-782-8777*** *Prod Info	610-341-7000
Chemtrol Div NIBCO Inc	1516 Middlebury St	Elkhart	IN	46516	**800-234-0227**	574-295-3000
Chevron Phillips Chemical Company Performance Pipe Div	5085 W Pk Blvd Ste 500	Plano	TX	75093	**800-527-0662**	972-599-6600
Diamond Plastics Corp	1212 Johnstown Rd PO Box 1608	Grand Island	NE	68802	**800-782-7473**	308-384-4400
Endot Industries Inc	60 Green Pond Rd	Rockaway	NJ	07866	**800-443-6368**	973-625-8500

				Toll-Free	Phone
Excalibur Extrusions Inc 110 E Crowther Ave	Placentia	CA	92870	**800-648-6804**	714-528-8834
Fernco Inc 300 S Dayton St	Davison	MI	48423	**800-521-1283**	810-653-9626
Hancor Inc PO Box 1047	Findlay	OH	45839	**888-892-2694**	419-422-6521
Hobas Pipe USA LP 1413 E Richey Rd	Houston	TX	77073	**800-856-7473**	281-821-2200
Isco Industries 926 Baxter Ave PO Box 4545	Louisville	KY	40204	**800-345-4726**	502-583-6591
JM Manufacturing Company Inc 5200 West Century Blvd	Los Angeles	CA	90045	**800-621-4404**	
Lasco Fittings Inc 414 Morgan St PO Box 116	Brownsville	TN	38012	**800-776-2756**	731-772-3180
Maloney Technical Products 1300 E Berry St	Fort Worth	TX	76119	**800-231-7236**	817-923-3344
Mueller Plastics Corp 3070 E Cedar	Ontario	CA	91761	**800-348-8464**	909-930-2060
National Pipe & Plastics Inc 3421 Old Vestal Rd	Vestal	NY	13850	**800-836-4350**	
Nebraska Plastics Inc PO Box 45	Cozad	NE	69130	**800-445-2887**	308-784-2500
North American Pipe Corp 2801 Post Oak Blvd Ste 600	Houston	TX	77056	**855-624-7473**	713-840-7473
Oil Creek Plastics Inc 45619 State Hwy 27 PO Box 385	Titusville	PA	16354	**800-537-3661**	814-827-3661
Texas United Pipe Inc 11627 N Houston Rosslyn Rd *Sales	Houston	TX	77086	**800-966-8741***	281-448-3276
Vinylplex Inc 1800 Atkinson Ave	Pittsburg	KS	66762	**877-779-7473**	620-231-8290
Vinyltech Corp 201 S 61st Ave	Phoenix	AZ	85043	**800-255-3924**	602-233-0071

596 PIPELINES (EXCEPT NATURAL GAS)

				Toll-Free	Phone
BP PLC 28100 Torch Pkwy *NYSE: BP*	Warrenville	IL	60555	**800-333-3991**	
Chevron Pipe Line Co 4800 Fournace Pl	Bellaire	TX	77401	**877-596-2800**	713-432-6000
Colonial Pipeline Co 1185 Sanctuary Pkwy Ste 100	Alpharetta	GA	30009	**800-275-3004**	678-762-2200
Country Mark Co-op 1200 Refinery Rd	Mount Vernon	IN	47620	**800-832-5490**	
Enbridge Energy Partners LP 1100 Louisiana Ste 3300 *NYSE: EEP*	Houston	TX	77002	**800-481-2804**	713-821-2000
Genesis Energy LP 919 Milam Ste 2100 *NYSE: GEL*	Houston	TX	77002	**800-284-3365**	713-860-2500
Imperial Oil Resources Ltd 237 Fourth Ave SW PO Box 2480 Stn M	Calgary	AB	T2P3M9	**800-567-3776**	
Kinder Morgan Energy Partners LP 500 Dallas St Ste 1000 *NYSE: KMI*	Houston	TX	77002	**866-208-3372**	713-369-9000
Kinder Morgan Management LLC 500 Dallas St 1 Allen Ctr Ste 1000 *NYSE: KMI*	Houston	TX	77002	**800-781-4152**	713-369-9000
Magellan Midstream Partners LP 1 Williams Ctr *NYSE: MMP*	Tulsa	OK	74172	**800-574-6671**	918-574-7000
MarkWest Energy Partners LP 1515 Arapahoe St Tower 1 Ste 1600 *NYSE: MWE*	Denver	CO	80202	**800-730-8388**	303-925-9200
Plains All American Pipeline LP 333 Clay St Ste 1600 *NYSE: PAA* ■ *Mktg	Houston	TX	77002	**866-753-3619***	713-646-4100
Sunoco Inc 1735 Market St Ste LL *NYSE: SUN*	Philadelphia	PA	19103	**800-786-6261**	215-977-3000
Valero LP PO Box 696000	San Antonio	TX	78269	**800-333-3377**	210-345-2233

597 PLANETARIUMS

				Toll-Free	Phone
Cernan Earth & Space Ctr 2000 N Fifth Ave Triton College	River Grove	IL	60171	**800-972-7000**	708-456-0300
Community College of Southern Nevada Planetarium & Observatory 3200 E Cheyenne Ave	North Las Vegas	NV	89030	**800-630-7563**	702-651-4759
Dreyfuss Planetarium 49 Washington St	Newark	NJ	07102	**888-370-6765**	973-596-6529
Gheens Science Hall & Rauch Planetarium Rauch Planetarium University of Louisville	Louisville	KY	40292	**800-996-7566**	502-852-6664
John Deere Planetarium 820 38th St Augustana College	Rock Island	IL	61201	**800-798-8100**	309-794-7327
Kitt Peak National Observatory 950 N Cherry Ave	Tucson	AZ	85719	**888-809-4012**	520-318-8600
Space Transit Planetarium 3280 S Miami Ave	Miami	FL	33129	**866-268-0250**	305-646-4200

598 PLASTICS - LAMINATED - PLATE, SHEET, PROFILE SHAPES

				Toll-Free	Phone
Connecticut Laminating Company Inc 162 James St	New Haven	CT	06513	**800-753-9119**	203-787-2184
Current Inc 30 Tyler St PO Box 120183	East Haven	CT	06512	**877-436-6542**	203-469-1337
DuPont Surfaces 4417 Lancaster Pk CRP 728/3105	Wilmington	DE	19805	**800-448-9835**	302-774-1000
Formica Corp 10155 Reading Rd	Cincinnati	OH	45241	**800-367-6422**	513-786-3400
Franklin Fibre-Lamitex Corp 903 E 13th St	Wilmington	DE	19802	**800-233-9739**	302-652-3621
Hartson-kennedy Cabinet Top Company Inc 522 W 22nd St PO Box 3095	Marion	IN	46953	**800-388-8144**	765-668-8144
Insulfab Plastics Inc 834 Hayne St	Spartanburg	SC	29301	**800-845-7599**	864-582-7506
Insultab Inc 45 Industrial Pkwy *Cust Svc	Woburn	MA	01801	**800-468-4822***	781-935-0800
Iten Industries 4602 Benefit Ave *Orders	Ashtabula	OH	44004	**800-227-4836***	440-997-6134
Lakeland Plastics Inc (LP) 1550 McCormick Blvd	Mundelein	IL	60060	**800-454-4006**	847-680-1550
Madico Inc 64 Industrial Pkwy	Woburn	MA	01801	**800-456-4331**	781-935-7850
Olon Industries Inc 42 Armstrong Ave	Georgetown	ON	L7G4R9	**800-387-2319**	905-877-7300
Petro Plastics Company Inc 450 S Ave	Garwood	NJ	07027	**800-486-4738**	908-789-1200
Reef Industries Inc 9209 Almeda Genoa Rd	Houston	TX	77075	**800-231-6074**	713-507-4200
Rowmark Inc 2040 Industrial Dr	Findlay	OH	45840	**800-243-3339**	419-425-2407
Sabin Corp 3800 Constitution Ave PO Box 788	Bloomington	IN	47403	**800-457-4500**	812-339-2235
Spaulding Composites Co 55 Nadeau Dr	Rochester	NH	03867	**800-801-0560**	603-332-0555
Techniform Industries Inc 2107 Hayes Ave	Fremont	OH	43420	**800-691-2816**	419-332-8484
V-T Industries Inc 1000 Industrial Pk	Holstein	IA	51025	**800-827-1615**	712-368-4381
Wilmington Fibre Specialty Co 700 Washington St	New Castle	DE	19720	**800-220-5132**	302-328-7525
Wilsonart International Inc 2400 Wilson Pl *Cust Svc	Temple	TX	76504	**800-433-3222***	254-207-7000

599 PLASTICS - UNSUPPORTED - FILM, SHEET, PROFILE SHAPES

SEE ALSO Blister Packaging

				Toll-Free	Phone
Advance Bag & Packaging Technologies 5720 Williams Lk Rd	Waterford	MI	48329	**800-475-2247**	248-674-3126
AEP Industries Inc 125 Phillips Ave *NASDAQ: AEPI*	South Hackensack	NJ	07606	**800-999-2374**	201-641-6600
Anaheim Custom Extruders 4640 E La Palma Ave *Cust Svc	Anaheim	CA	92807	**800-229-2760***	714-693-8508
Arlon Graphics 2811 S Harbor Blvd	Santa Ana	CA	92704	**800-232-7161**	714-540-2811
Atlas Roofing Falcon Foam Div 8240 Byron Ctr Rd SW	Byron Center	MI	49315	**800-917-9138**	
Avery Dennison Worldwide Graphics Div 207 Goode Ave Bldg 8	Glendale	CA	44077	**800-443-9380**	440-358-3700
Brandywine Investment Group Homalite Div 11 Brookside Dr	Wilmington	DE	19804	**800-346-7802**	302-652-3686
Catalina Graphic Films Inc 27001 Agoura Rd Ste 100	Calabasas Hills	CA	91301	**800-333-3136**	818-880-8060
Clopay Plastic Products Co 8585 Duke Blvd	Mason	OH	45040	**800-282-2260**	513-770-4800
Coburn Co, The 834 E Milwaukee St	Whitewater	WI	53190	**800-776-7042**	262-473-2822
Crown Plastics Co 116 May Dr	Harrison	OH	45030	**800-368-0238**	513-367-0238
CUE Inc 11 Leonberg Rd	Cranberry Township	PA	16066	**800-283-4621**	724-772-5225
Dielectrics Industries Inc 300 Burnett Rd	Chicopee	MA	01020	**800-472-7286**	413-594-8111
Dunmore Corp 145 Wharton Rd	Bristol	PA	19007	**800-444-0242**	215-781-8895
E S Robbins Corp 2802 Avalon Ave	Muscle Shoals	AL	35661	**866-934-6018**	256-248-2400
Enflo Corp 315 Lake Ave	Bristol	CT	06010	**888-887-4093**	860-589-0014
Gary Plastic Packaging Corp 1340 Viele Ave	Bronx	NY	10474	**800-221-8150**	718-893-2200
General Formulations Inc 309 S Union St	Sparta	MI	49345	**800-253-3664**	616-887-7387
GSE Lining Technology Inc 19103 Gundle Rd	Houston	TX	77073	**800-435-2008**	281-443-8564
Kayline Processing Inc 31 Coates St *Sales	Trenton	NJ	08611	**800-367-5546***	609-695-1449
Kendall Packaging Corp 10200 N Port Washington Rd	Mequon	WI	53092	**800-237-0951**	262-404-1200
Kimoto Tech Inc PO Box 1783	Cedartown	GA	30125	**888-546-6861**	770-748-2643
Lavanture Products Co 22825 Gallatin Way	Elkhart	IN	46514	**800-348-7625**	574-264-0658
Mitsubishi Polyester Film LLC 2001 Hood Rd	Greer	SC	29650	**800-334-1934**	864-879-5000
MPI Technologies 37 E St	Winchester	MA	01890	**888-674-8088**	781-729-8300
Natvar 8720 US Hwy 70 W	Clayton	NC	27520	**800-395-6288**	909-594-3660
New Hampshire Plastics Inc 1 Bouchard St	Manchester	NH	03103	**800-258-3036**	603-669-8523
Northland Plastics Inc 1420 S 16th St PO Box 290	Sheboygan	WI	53081	**800-776-7163**	
Orcon Corp 1570 Atlantic St *General	Union City	CA	94587	**800-227-0505***	510-489-8100
Penn Fibre Plastics 2434 Bristol Rd *Cust Svc	Bensalem	PA	19020	**800-662-7366***	
Plaskolite Inc 1770 Joyce Ave	Columbus	OH	43219	**800-848-9124**	614-294-3281
Polyfil 74 Green Pond Rd	Rockaway	NJ	07866	**866-765-9345**	973-627-4070
Polyvinyl Films Inc PO Box 753	Sutton	MA	01590	**800-343-6134**	508-865-3558

Company / Address	City	State	Zip	Toll-Free	Phone
Primex Plastics Corp 1235 N 'F' St	Richmond	IN	47374	800-222-5116	765-966-7774
Prinsco Inc 108 W Hwy 7 PO Box 265	Prinsburg	MN	56281	800-992-1725	320-222-6800
Raven Industries Inc 205 E Sixth St *NASDAQ: RAVN*	Sioux Falls	SD	57104	800-243-5435	605-336-2750
Shepherd CE Company Inc 2221 Canada Dry St	Houston	TX	77023	800-324-6733	713-924-4300
Shield Pack LLC 411 Downing Pines Rd	West Monroe	LA	71292	800-551-5185	318-387-4743
SLM Manufacturing Corp 215 Davidson Ave	Somerset	NJ	08873	800-526-3708	732-469-7500
Soliant LLC 1872 Hwy 9 Bypass	Lancaster	SC	29720	800-288-9401	803-285-9401
Southern Film Extruders Inc 2319 English Rd	High Point	NC	27262	800-334-6101	336-885-8091
Summit Plastics Inc 107 S Laurel St	Summit	MS	39666	800-790-7117	601-276-7500
Thermoplastic Processes Inc 1268 Valley Rd	Stirling	NJ	07980	888-554-6400	908-561-3000
VCF Films Inc 1100 Sutton Ave	Howell	MI	48843	888-905-7680	
VPI Corp 3123 S Ninth St *Orders	Sheboygan	WI	53081	800-874-4240*	920-458-4664
Watersaver Company Inc 5870 E 56th Ave	Commerce	CO	80022	800-525-2424	303-289-1818
Zippertubing Co 7150 W Erie St	Chandler	AZ	85226	855-289-1874	480-285-3990

600 PLASTICS FOAM PRODUCTS

Company / Address	City	State	Zip	Toll-Free	Phone
A-Z Sponge & Foam Products Ltd 811 Cundy Ave Annacis Island	Delta	BC	V3M5P6	800-665-3990	604-525-1665
ACH Foam Technologies LLC 5250 Sherman St	Denver	CO	80216	800-525-8697	303-297-3844
Aero Plastics Inc 91 Citation Dr	Concord	ON	L4K2Y8	877-660-2376	905-738-9010
Allied Aerofoam Products LLC 216 Kelsey Ln	Tampa	FL	33619	800-338-9140	813-626-0090
American Excelsior Co 850 Ave H E	Arlington	TX	76011	800-777-7645	
Balcan Plastics Ltd 9340 Meaux St	Saint Leonard	QC	H1R3H2	877-422-5226	514-326-0200
Barger Packaging Inc 2901 Oakland Ave	Elkhart	IN	46517	888-525-2845	
Belle-Pak Packaging Inc 7465 Birchmount Rd	Markham	ON	L3R5X9	800-565-2137	905-475-5151
Bulldog Bag Ltd 13631 Vulcan Way	Richmond	BC	V6V1K4	800-665-1944	604-273-8021
Carpenter Co 5016 Monument Ave	Richmond	VA	23230	800-288-3830	804-359-0800
Cellofoam North America Inc 1917 Rockdale Industrial Blvd	Conyers	GA	30012	800-241-3634	770-929-3688
Clark Foam Products Corp 655 Remington Blvd	Bolingbrook	IL	60440	888-284-2290	630-226-5900
Clayton Corp 866 Horan Dr *Cust Svc	Fenton	MO	63026	800-729-8220*	636-349-5333
Conglom Inc 2600 Marie-Curie Ave	Saint-Laurent	QC	H4S2C3	877-333-0098	514-333-6666
Creative Foam Corp 300 N Alloy Dr	Fenton	MI	48430	800-529-4149	810-629-4149
Custom Pack Inc 662 Exton Cmns	Exton	PA	19341	800-722-7005	610-321-2525
Dart Container Corp 500 Hogsback Rd	Mason	MI	48854	800-248-5960	
Dow Chemical Company, The 1881 W Oak Pkwy	Marietta	GA	30062	800-331-6451	770-428-2684
Elliott Company of Indianapolis Inc 9200 Zionsville Rd *Orders	Indianapolis	IN	46268	800-545-1213*	317-291-1213
Enduro Composites Inc 16602 Central Green Blvd	Houston	TX	77032	800-231-7271	713-358-4000
Federal Foam Technologies Inc 600 Wisconsin Dr	New Richmond	WI	54017	800-898-9559	715-246-9500
FLEXSTAR Packaging Inc 13320 River Rd	Richmond	BC	V6V1W7	800-663-1177	604-273-9277
Flextron Industries Inc 720 Mt Rd	Aston	PA	19014	800-633-2181	610-459-4600
Foam Molders & Specialty Corp 20004 State Rd	Cerritos	CA	90703	800-378-8987	
Fomo Products Inc 2775 Barber Rd	Norton	OH	44203	800-321-5585	330-753-4585
Free Flow Packaging International Inc 1090 Mills Way	Redwood City	CA	94063	800-866-9946	650-261-5300
Future Foam Inc 1610 Ave N Council Bluffs	Council Bluffs	IA	51501	800-733-8061	712-323-9122
FXI 1400 N Providence Rd	Media	PA	19063	800-355-3626	610-744-2300
G & T Industries Inc 1001 76th St SW	Byron Center	MI	49315	800-968-6035	
Gaco Western Inc 200 W Mercer St Ste 202	Seattle	WA	98119	800-456-4226	206-575-0450
General Plastics Mfg Co 4910 S Burlington Way	Tacoma	WA	98409	800-806-6051	253-473-5000
Guardian Packaging Inc 3615 Security St	Garland	TX	75042	800-259-1502	214-349-1500
Gunther Mele Ltd 30 Craig St	Brantford	ON	N3R7J1	888-486-8437	519-756-4330
Hibco Plastics Inc 1820 Us 601 Hwy	Yadkinville	NC	27055	800-849-8683	336-463-2391
Intertrade Industries Ltd 14600 Commerce Ln	Huntington Beach	CA	92649	800-944-9277	714-894-5566
NAP Windows & Doors Ltd 2150 Enterprise Way	Kelowna	BC	V1Y6H7	888-762-5311	250-762-5343
North Carolina Foam Industries Inc 1515 Carter St	Mount Airy	NC	27030	800-346-8229	336-789-9161
Pacific Packaging Products Inc 24 Industrial Way	Wilmington	MA	01887	800-777-0300	978-657-9100
Perfect Turf Inc 622 Sandpebble Dr	Schaumburg	IL	60193	888-796-8873	
Pinova Holdings Inc 2801 Cook St	Brunswick	GA	31520	888-807-2958	
Plastic & Steel Supply Company Inc 50 Tannery Rd Readington Industrial Ctr Bldg 3	Branchburg	NJ	08876	800-407-3726	908-534-6111
Plastipak Industries Inc 150 Industriel Blvd	Boucherville	QC	J4B2X3	800-387-7452	450-650-2200
Poly Molding LLC 96 Fourth Ave	Haskell	NJ	07420	800-229-7161	973-835-7161
Polymer Industries LLC 10526 Alabama Hwy 40 PO Box 32	Henagar	AL	35978	877-489-0039	256-657-5197
Prolamina Corp 840 S Waukegan Rd Ste 208	Lake Forest	IL	60045	877-536-2628	
RL Adams Plastics Inc 5955 Crossroads Commerce	Wyoming	MI	49519	800-968-2241	616-261-4400
Robbie Manufacturing Inc 10810 Mid America Ave	Lenexa	KS	66219	800-255-6328	913-492-3400
Sekisui Voltek LLC 100 Shepard St	Lawrence	MA	01843	800-225-0668	978-685-2557
Sonoco 1 N Second St *NYSE: SON*	Hartsville	SC	29550	800-377-2692	
Storopack Inc 12007 S Woodruff Ave	Downey	CA	90241	800-829-1491	562-803-5582
ThermoSafe Brands 3930 N Ventura Dr Ste 450	Arlington Heights	IL	60004	800-323-7442	847-398-0110
ThermoServ 3901 Pipestone Rd	Dallas	TX	75212	800-635-5559	214-631-0307
Topp Industries Inc 420 N State Rd 25 PO Box 420	Rochester	IN	46975	800-354-4534	574-223-3681
UFP Technologies Inc 172 E Main St *NASDAQ: UFPT*	Georgetown	MA	01833	800-372-3172	978-352-2200
WinCup 4640 Lewis Rd	Stone Mountain	GA	30083	800-292-2877	770-938-5281

601 PLASTICS MACHINING & FORMING

SEE ALSO Plastics Molding - Custom

Company / Address	City	State	Zip	Toll-Free	Phone
Bardes Plastics Inc 5225 W Clinton Ave *Cust Svc	Milwaukee	WI	53223	800-558-5161*	
East Jordan Plastics Inc PO Box 575	East Jordan	MI	49727	800-353-1190	
Empire West Inc 9270 Graton Rd PO Box 511	Graton	CA	95444	800-521-4261	707-823-1190
Engineered Plastics Inc 211 Chase St	Gibsonville	NC	27249	800-711-1740	336-449-4121
Fabri-Form Co 200 S Friendship Dr	New Concord	OH	43762	800-837-2574	740-826-5000
Fabri-Kal Corp 600 Plastics Pl	Kalamazoo	MI	49001	800-888-5054	269-385-5050
FNW Industrial Plastics Inc 12500 Jefferson Ave PO Box 2778	Newport News	VA	23602	800-721-2590	757-874-7795
Formall Inc 3908 Fountain Vly Dr	Knoxville	TN	37918	800-643-3676	865-922-7514
Inline Plastics Corp 42 Canal St	Shelton	CT	06484	800-826-5567	203-924-2015
Innovize Inc 500 Oak Grove Pkwy	Saint Paul	MN	55127	877-605-6580	
McNeal Enterprises Inc 2031 Ringwood Ave	San Jose	CA	95131	800-562-6325	408-922-7290
Meyer Plastics Inc 5167 E 65th St	Indianapolis	IN	46220	800-968-4131	317-259-4131
Perkasie Industries Corp PO Box 179 *Sales	Perkasie	PA	18944	800-523-6747*	215-257-6581
Placon Corp 6096 McKee Rd	Madison	WI	53719	800-541-1535	608-271-5634
Polygon Co 103 Industrial Pk Dr PO Box 176	Walkerton	IN	46574	800-918-9261	574-586-3145
Quadrant Engineering Plastic Products USA 2120 Fairmont Ave PO Box 14235	Reading	PA	19612	800-366-0300	610-320-6600
Ray Products Company Inc 1700 Chablis Ave	Ontario	CA	91761	800-423-7859	909-390-9906
Thermo-Fab Corp 76 Walker Rd	Shirley	MA	01464	888-494-9777	978-425-2311
Total Plastics Inc 3316 Pagosa Ct	Indianapolis	IN	46226	800-382-4635	317-543-3540

602 PLASTICS MATERIALS - WHOL

Company / Address	City	State	Zip	Toll-Free	Phone
A Daigger & Company Inc 620 Lakeview Pkwy	Vernon Hills	IL	60061	800-621-7193	847-816-5060
Aetna Plastics Corp 1702 St Clair Ave	Cleveland	OH	44114	800-634-3074	216-781-4421
AIN Plastics Inc 1750 E Heights Dr *Cust Svc	Madison Heights	MI	48071	877-246-7700*	248-356-4000
Aztec Supply 954 N Batavia St	Orange	CA	92867	800-836-3210	714-771-6580
Bamberger Polymers Inc 2 Jericho Plz Ste 109	Jericho	NY	11753	800-888-8959	516-622-3600
Buckley Industries Inc 1850 E 53rd St N	Wichita	KS	67219	800-835-2779	316-744-7587
Calsak Corp 1411 West 190th St Ste 400	Gardena	CA	90248	888-663-6005	310-719-9500
Cope Plastics Inc 4441 Industrial Dr	Godfrey	IL	62002	800-851-5510	618-466-0221
Delta Polymers Midwest Inc 6685 Sterling Dr N	Sterling Heights	MI	48312	800-860-6848	586-795-2900
E Hofmann Plastics 51 Centennial Rd	Orangeville	ON	L9W3R1	855-452-4014	

				Toll-Free	Phone
El Mar Plastics Inc 109 W 134th St	Los Angeles	CA	90061	**800-255-5210**	310-436-6444
H Muehlstein & Company Inc 10 Westport Rd	Wilton	CT	06897	**800-257-3746**	203-855-6000
Laird Plastics Inc 6800 Broken Sound Pkwy Ste 150	Boca Raton	FL	33487	**800-243-9696**	561-443-9100
M Holland Co 400 Skokie Blvd Ste 600	Northbrook	IL	60062	**877-578-4000**	847-272-7370
Momentum Technologies Inc (MTI) 1507 Boettler Rd	Uniontown	OH	44685	**800-720-0261**	330-896-5900
Nytef Plastics Ltd Inc 6643 42nd Terr N	West Palm Beach	FL	33407	**800-646-9833**	561-840-9499
Orange County Industrial Plastics Inc 4811 E La Palma Ave	Anaheim	CA	92807	**800-974-6247**	714-632-9450
Plastic Film Corporation of America Inc 1287 Naperville Dr	Romeoville	IL	60446	**800-654-6589**	630-887-0800
Plastics International Inc 7600 Anagram Dr	Eden Prairie	MN	55344	**800-776-7769**	952-934-2303
Port Plastics Inc 15325 Fairfield Ranch Rd Ste 150	Chino Hills	CA	91709	**800-800-0039**	480-813-6118
Regal Plastic Supply Co 111 E Tenth Ave	North Kansas City	MO	64116	**800-627-2102**	816-421-6290
Ryan Herco Products Corp 3010 N San Fernando Blvd	Burbank	CA	91504	**800-848-1141**	818-841-1141
San Diego Plastics Inc 2220 Mckinley Ave	National City	CA	91950	**800-925-4855**	619-477-4855
Seelye Plastics Inc 9700 Newton Ave S	Bloomington	MN	55431	**800-328-2728**	
Sekisui America Corp 333 Meadowlands Pkwy *General	Secaucus	NJ	07094	**866-260-5851***	201-423-7960
Superior Oil Co Inc 1402 N Capitol Ave Ste 100	Indianapolis	IN	46202	**800-553-5480**	317-781-4400
Tekra Corp 16700 W Lincoln Ave	New Berlin	WI	53151	**800-448-3572**	262-784-5533

603 PLASTICS MOLDING - CUSTOM

				Toll-Free	Phone
Akron Porcelain & Plastics Co 2739 Cory Ave PO Box 15157	Akron	OH	44314	**800-737-9664**	330-745-2159
Alladin Plastics Inc 140 Industrial Dr	Surgoinsville	TN	37873	**877-536-4693**	423-345-2351
American Metal & Plastics Inc 450 32nd St SW	Grand Rapids	MI	49548	**800-382-0067**	616-452-6061
Berry Plastics Corp 101 Oakley St	Evansville	IN	47710	**877-662-3779**	812-424-2904
Confer Plastics Inc (CPI) 97 Witmer Rd	North Tonawanda	NY	14120	**800-635-3213**	716-693-2056
Cuyahoga Molded Plastics Corp 1265 Babbitt Rd	Cleveland	OH	44132	**800-805-9549**	216-261-2744
D-M-E Co 29111 Stephenson Hwy	Madison Heights	MI	48071	**800-626-6653**	248-398-6000
Double H Plastics Inc 50 W St Rd	Warminster	PA	18974	**800-523-3932**	215-674-4100
EFP Corp 223 Middleton Run Rd	Elkhart	IN	46516	**800-205-8537**	574-295-4690
Elgin Molded Plastics 909 Grace St	Elgin	IL	60120	**800-548-5483**	847-931-2455
Ensinger Putnam Precision Molding 11 Danco Rd	Putnam	CT	06260	**800-752-7865**	860-928-7911
Evco Plastics 100 W N St PO Box 497	DeForest	WI	53532	**800-507-6000**	
Filtertek Inc 11411 Price Rd	Hebron	IL	60034	**800-248-2461**	815-648-1001
Flambeau Inc 15981 Valplast Rd	Middlefield	OH	44062	**800-457-5252**	440-632-1631
Gruber Systems Inc 25636 Ave Stanford	Valencia	CA	91355	**800-257-4070**	661-257-4060
Lehigh Valley Plastics Inc 187 N Commerce Way	Bethlehem	PA	18017	**800-354-5344**	484-893-5500
Molded Fiber Glass Cos 2925 MFG Pl PO Box 675	Ashtabula	OH	44005	**800-860-0196**	440-997-5851
Molding Corp of America 10349 Norris Ave	Pacoima	CA	91331	**800-423-2747**	818-890-7877
MXL Industries Inc 1764 Rohrerstown Rd	Lancaster	PA	17601	**800-233-0159**	717-569-8711
Plaspros Inc 1143 Ridgeview Dr	McHenry	IL	60050	**800-752-7776**	815-430-2300
Plastic Components Inc N 116 W 18271 Morse Dr	Germantown	WI	53022	**877-253-1496**	
Sabin Corp 3800 Constitution Ave PO Box 788	Bloomington	IN	47403	**800-457-4500**	812-339-2235
Seitz LLC 212 Industrial Ln	Torrington	CT	06790	**800-261-2011**	860-489-0476
Steere Enterprises Inc 285 Commerce St	Tallmadge	OH	44278	**800-875-4926**	330-633-4926
Tuthill Corp Plastics Group 2050 Sunnydale Blvd	Clearwater	FL	33765	**800-634-2695**	727-446-8593
Universal Plastic Mold Inc 13245 Los Angeles St	Baldwin Park	CA	91706	**888-893-1587**	
Westlake Plastics Co PO Box 127	Lenni	PA	19052	**800-999-1700**	610-459-1000

604 PLASTICS & OTHER SYNTHETIC MATERIALS

604-1 Synthetic Fibers & Filaments

				Toll-Free	Phone
Consolidated Fibers 8100 S Blvd	Charlotte	NC	28273	**800-243-8621**	
Deltech Corp 11911 Scenic Hwy	Baton Rouge	LA	70807	**800-424-9300**	225-775-0150
DuPont Advanced Fibers Systems 5401 Jefferson Davis Hwy	Richmond	VA	23234	**800-441-7515**	804-383-3845
Fairfield Processing Corp 88 Rose Hill Ave	Danbury	CT	06810	**800-980-8000**	203-744-2090
Hexcel Corp 281 Tresser Blvd 16th Fl *NYSE: HXL*	Stamford	CT	06901	**800-444-3923**	800-688-7734
Honeywell Specialty Materials 101 Columbia Rd	Morristown	NJ	07962	**800-222-0094**	973-455-2145
International Fiber Corp 50 Bridge St	North Tonawanda	NY	14120	**888-698-1936**	716-693-4040
INVISTA 4123 E 37th St N	Wichita	KS	67220	**877-446-8478**	316-828-1000
Nylon Corp of America 333 Sundial Ave	Manchester	NH	03103	**800-851-2001**	603-627-5150
TenCate Grass North America 1131 Broadway St	Dayton	TN	37321	**800-251-1033**	423-775-0792
United Plastic Fabricating Inc 165 Flagship Dr	North Andover	MA	01845	**800-638-8265**	

604-2 Synthetic Resins & Plastics Materials

				Toll-Free	Phone
A Schulman Inc 3550 W Market St *NASDAQ: SHLM*	Akron	OH	44333	**800-547-3746**	330-666-3751
Akcros Chemicals America 500 Jersey Ave *Cust Svc	New Brunswick	NJ	08901	**800-500-7890***	732-220-6882
Asahi Kasei Plastics North America Inc 900 E Van Riper Rd *Cust Svc	Fowlerville	MI	48836	**800-993-5382***	517-223-2000
Bayer Inc 77 Belfield Rd	Toronto	ON	M9W1G6	**800-622-2937**	416-248-0771
Bayer MaterialScience LLC 100 Bayer Rd	Pittsburgh	PA	15205	**800-662-2927**	412-777-2000
Canplas Industries Ltd 500 Veterans Dr	Barrie	ON	L4M4V3	**800-461-1771**	705-726-3361
Cartec International Inc 106 Powder Mill Rd	Canton	CT	06019	**800-821-4434**	860-693-9395
Daikin America Inc 20 Olympic Dr *Cust Svc	Orangeburg	NY	10962	**800-365-9570***	845-365-9500
Dow Chemical Co 2030 Dow Ctr *NYSE: DOW* ■ *Cust Svc	Midland	MI	48674	**800-422-8193***	989-636-1463
DSM Engineering Plastics Inc 2267 W Mill Rd	Evansville	IN	47720	**800-333-4237**	812-435-7500
DuPont Engineering Polymers Lancaster Pike Rt 141 Barley Mill Plz Bldg 22	Wilmington	DE	19805	**800-441-7515**	302-999-4592
Eastman Chemical Co 200 S Wilcox Dr *NYSE: EMN* ■ *Cust Svc	Kingsport	TN	37660	**800-327-8626***	423-229-2000
Engineered Polymer Solutions Inc 1400 N State St	Marengo	IL	60152	**800-654-4242**	
Essco Inc 1933 Highland Rd	Twinsburg	OH	44087	**800-321-2664**	216-524-4141
Gallagher Corp 3908 Morrison Dr	Gurnee	IL	60031	**800-524-8597**	847-249-3440
Goldsmith & Eggleton Inc 300 First St	Wadsworth	OH	44281	**800-321-0954**	330-336-6616
Heritage Plastics Inc 1002 Hunt St	Picayune	MS	39466	**800-245-4623**	601-798-8663
Huntsman Corp 500 Huntsman Way *NYSE: HUN*	Salt Lake City	UT	84108	**888-490-8484**	801-584-5700
Indelco Plastics Corp 6530 Cambridge St	Minneapolis	MN	55426	**800-486-6456**	952-925-5075
Interplastic Corp 1225 Wolters Blvd	Saint Paul	MN	55110	**800-736-5497**	651-481-6860
Kraton Performance Polymers Inc 15710 John F Kennedy Blvd Ste 300 *NYSE: KRA*	Houston	TX	77032	**800-457-2866**	281-504-4950
Lewcott Corp 86 Providence Rd *Sales	Millbury	MA	01527	**800-225-7725***	508-865-1791
Lord Corp 111 Lord Dr	Cary	NC	27511	**877-275-5673**	919-468-5979
Minova USA Inc 150 Carley Ct	Georgetown	KY	40324	**800-626-2948**	502-863-6800
Mitsui Chemicals America Inc 800 Westchester Ave	Rye Brook	NY	10573	**800-972-7252**	914-253-0777
Neville Chemical Co 2800 Neville Rd *Cust Svc	Pittsburgh	PA	15225	**877-704-4200***	412-331-4200
NOVA Chemicals Corp 1000 Seventh Ave SW PO Box 2518	Calgary	AB	T2P5C6	**866-289-6682**	403-750-3600
Osterman & Company Inc 726 S Main St	Cheshire	CT	06410	**800-914-4437**	203-272-2233
Perstorp Polyols Inc 600 Matzinger Rd *Cust Svc	Toledo	OH	43612	**800-537-0280***	419-729-5448
Plastics Color & Compounding Inc 14201 Paxton Ave	Calumet City	IL	60409	**800-922-9936**	
PolyOne Corp 33587 Walker Rd *NYSE: POL*	Avon Lake	OH	44012	**866-765-9663**	440-930-1000
Reichhold Inc 2400 Ellis Rd	Durham	NC	27703	**800-448-3482**	919-990-7500
Resinall Corp PO Box 195	Severn	NC	27877	**800-421-0561**	
RheTech Inc 1500 E N Territorial Rd	Whitmore Lake	MI	48189	**800-869-1230**	734-769-0585
Rogers Corp 1 Technology Dr	Rogers	CT	06263	**800-237-2267**	860-774-9605
RTP Co 580 E Front St	Winona	MN	55987	**800-433-4787**	507-454-6900
Rutland Plastic Technologies 10021 Rodney St	Pineville	NC	28134	**800-438-5134**	704-553-0046
Sartomer Co 502 Thomas Jones Way	Exton	PA	19341	**800-345-8247**	610-363-4100
Sterling Fibers Inc 5005 Sterling Way *Cust Svc	Pace	FL	32571	**800-342-3779***	850-994-5311
Ticona LLC 8040 Dixie Hwy	Florence	KY	41042	**800-833-4882**	859-372-3244

Company	Address	City	State	Zip	Toll-Free	Phone
Tube-Mac Industries Ltd	853 Arvin Ave	Stoney Creek	ON	L8E5N8	**877-643-8823**	905-643-8823
Vi-Chem Corp	55 Cottage Grove St SW	Grand Rapids	MI	49507	**800-477-8501**	616-247-8501
Westlake Chemical Corp	2801 Post Oak Blvd Ste 600	Houston	TX	77056	**888-953-3623**	713-960-9111
NYSE: WLK						

604-3 Synthetic Rubber

Company	Address	City	State	Zip	Toll-Free	Phone
AirBoss of America Corp Rubber Compounding	101 Glasgow St	Kitchener	ON	N2G4X8	**800-294-5723**	519-576-5565
Akrochem Corp	255 Fountain St	Akron	OH	44304	**800-321-2260**	330-535-2100
Goodyear Tire & Rubber Co	200 Innovation Way	Akron	OH	44316	**800-321-2136***	330-796-2121
NASDAQ: GT ■ *Cust Svc						
Lanxess Corp	111 RIDC Pk W Dr	Pittsburgh	PA	15275	**800-526-9377**	412-809-1000
Midwest Elastomers Inc	700 Industrial Dr PO Box 412	Wapakoneta	OH	45895	**800-786-3539**	419-738-8844
Teknor Apex Co	505 Central Ave	Pawtucket	RI	02861	**800-556-3864**	401-725-8000
Textile Rubber & Chemical Company Inc	1300 Tiarco Dr SW	Dalton	GA	30721	**800-727-8453**	706-277-1300

605 PLASTICS PRODUCTS - FIBERGLASS REINFORCED

Company	Address	City	State	Zip	Toll-Free	Phone
Crane Composites Inc	23525 W Eames St	Channahon	IL	60410	**800-435-0080**	815-467-8600
Fibergrate Composite Structures Inc	5151 Beltline Rd Ste 700	Dallas	TX	75254	**800-527-4043**	972-250-1633
Glastic Corp	4321 Glenridge Rd	Cleveland	OH	44121	**800-360-1319**	216-486-0100
GMI Composites Inc	1355 W Sherman Blvd	Muskegon	MI	49441	**800-330-4045**	231-755-1611
McClarin Plastics Inc	15 Industrial Dr	Hanover	PA	17331	**800-233-3189**	717-637-2241
Red Ewald Inc	2669 US 181	Karnes City	TX	78118	**800-242-3524**	830-780-3304

606 PLASTICS PRODUCTS - HOUSEHOLD

Company	Address	City	State	Zip	Toll-Free	Phone
Bow Plastics Ltd	5700 Cote de Liesse	Montreal	QC	H4T1B1	**800-852-8527**	514-735-5671
Eagle Affiliates Inc	1000 S Second St	Plainfield	NJ	07063	**800-237-9255**	908-757-4464
GT Water Products Inc	5239 N Commerce Ave	Moorpark	CA	93021	**800-862-5647**	805-529-2900
Home Products International Inc	4501 W 47th St	Chicago	IL	60632	**800-327-3534**	773-890-1010
Igloo Products Corp	777 Igloo Rd	Katy	TX	77494	**866-509-3503**	713-584-6800
Iris USA Inc	11111 80th Ave	Pleasant Prairie	WI	53158	**800-320-4747**	262-612-1000
Kraftware Corp	270 Cox St	Roselle	NJ	07203	**800-221-1728***	
*Cust Svc						
Maryland Plastics Inc	251 E Central Ave	Federalsburg	MD	21632	**800-544-5582***	410-754-5566
*Cust Svc						
Prolon Inc	305 Industrial Ave	Port Gibson	MS	39150	**800-628-7749**	601-437-4211
Sterilite Corp	PO Box 524	Townsend	MA	01469	**800-225-1046**	
TAP Plastics Inc	6475 Sierra Ln	Dublin	CA	94568	**800-894-0827**	925-829-4889
Thermos Co	475 N Martingale Rd Ste 1100	Schaumburg	IL	60173	**800-243-0745**	847-439-7821
Tupperware Corp	14901 S Orange Blossom Trail	Orlando	FL	32837	**800-468-9716***	407-826-5050
NYSE: TUP ■ *Cust Svc						

607 PLASTICS PRODUCTS (MISC)

Company	Address	City	State	Zip	Toll-Free	Phone
7-sigma Inc	2843 26th Ave S	Minneapolis	MN	55406	**888-722-8396**	612-722-5358
Acrylic Plastic Products Company Inc	4815 Hwy 80 W	Jackson	MS	39209	**800-331-8819**	601-922-2651
Aigner Index Inc	23 Mac Arthur Ave	New Windsor	NY	12553	**800-242-3919**	845-562-4510
All States Inc	602 N 12th St	Saint Charles	IL	60174	**800-621-5837***	773-728-0525
*Cust Svc						
American Window & Glass Inc	2715 Lynch Rd	Evansville	IN	47711	**877-671-6943**	812-464-9400
Amerimade Technology Inc	449 Mtn Vista Pkwy	Livermore	CA	94551	**800-938-3824**	925-243-9090
Avery Dennison Fastener Div	224 Industrial Rd	Fitchburg	MA	01420	**800-225-5913**	
AXYS Technologies Inc	2045 Mills Rd	Sidney	BC	V8L5X2	**877-792-7878**	250-655-5850
Bemis Manufacturing Co	300 Mill St	Sheboygan Falls	WI	53085	**800-558-7651**	920-467-4621
Blackmore Company Inc	10800 Blackmore Ave	Belleville	MI	48111	**800-874-8660**	734-483-8661
Bowman Mfg Company Inc	17301 51st Ave Ne	Arlington	WA	98223	**800-962-4660**	360-435-5005
Burco Molding Inc	15015 Herriman Blvd	Noblesville	IN	46060	**888-883-6656**	317-773-5699
C. L. Smith Co	1311 S 39th St	Saint Louis	MO	63110	**800-264-1202**	314-771-1202
CMI Plastics Inc	222 Pepsi Way	Ayden	NC	28513	**877-395-1920**	252-746-2171
Cool Polymers Inc	51 Circuit Dr	North Kingstown	RI	02852	**888-811-3787**	401-739-7602
Coverbind Corp	3200 Corporate Dr	Wilmington	NC	28405	**800-366-6060**	910-799-4116
Crystal-Like Plastics	21701 Plummer St	Chatsworth	CA	91311	**800-554-6091**	323-849-1735
Custom Accents	1940 Lunt Ave	Elk Grove Village	IL	60007	**888-553-6789**	847-640-4725
DelStar Technologies Inc	220 E St Elmo Rd	Austin	TX	78745	**800-521-6713**	512-447-7000
Den Hartog Industries Inc	4010 Hospers Dr S PO Box 425	Hospers	IA	51238	**800-342-3408**	712-752-8432
Easyturf	2750 La Mirada Dr	Vista	CA	92081	**866-353-3518**	760-789-7772
Engineered Polymers Corp (EPC)	1020 Maple Ave E	Mora	MN	55051	**800-388-2155**	320-679-3232
Enor Corp	245 Livingston St	Northvale	NJ	07647	**800-977-6427**	201-750-1680
Fiberglass Specialties Inc	PO Box 1340	Henderson	TX	75653	**800-527-1459**	903-657-6522
Fusion Optix Inc	19 Wheeling Ave	Woburn	MA	01801	**866-506-8300**	781-995-0805
Garner Industries Inc	7201 N 98th St PO Box 29709	Lincoln	NE	68507	**800-228-0275**	402-434-9100
Genova Products Inc	7034 E Court St	Davison	MI	48423	**800-521-7488**	810-744-4500
GenPore	1136 Morgantown Rd PO Box 380	Reading	PA	19607	**800-654-4391**	610-374-5171
Gessner Products Company Inc	241 N Main St	Ambler	PA	19002	**800-874-7808**	215-646-7667
Glasteel-stabilit America Inc	285 Industrial Dr	Moscow	TN	38057	**800-238-5546**	901-877-3010
GPK Products Inc	1601 43rd St NW	Fargo	ND	58102	**800-437-4670**	701-277-3225
GWI Inc	8 Pomerleau St	Biddeford	ME	04005	**866-494-2020**	207-286-8686
Habasit America	805 Satellite Blvd	Suwanee	GA	30024	**800-458-6431**	
Hanscom Inc	331 Market St	Warren	RI	02885	**877-725-6788**	401-247-1999
Harbec Plastics Inc	369 SR- 104	Ontario	NY	14519	**888-521-4416**	585-265-0010
Hygolet Inc	349 SE Second Ave	Deerfield Beach	FL	33441	**800-494-6538**	954-481-8601
Ideal Pet Products Inc	24735 Ave Rockefeller	Valencia	CA	91355	**800-378-4385**	661-294-2266
Kalwall Corp	1111 Candia Rd PO Box 237	Manchester	NH	03105	**800-258-9777**	603-627-3861
King Plastic Corp	1100 N Toledo Blade Blvd	North Port	FL	34288	**800-780-5502**	941-493-5502
Lamvin Inc	4675 N Ave	Oceanside	CA	92056	**800-446-6329**	760-806-6400
Landmark Plastic Corp	1331 Kelly Ave	Akron	OH	44306	**800-242-1183**	330-785-2200
Leaktite Corp	40 Francis St	Leominster	MA	01453	**800-392-0039**	978-537-8000
LHR Services & Equipment Inc lc-disc	4200 Fm 1128 Rd	Pearland	TX	77584	**800-943-2324**	713-943-2324
Little Kids Inc	225 Chapman St Ste 202	Providence	RI	02905	**800-545-5437**	401-454-7600
LSP Products Group Inc	3689 Arrowhead Dr	Carson City	NV	89706	**800-854-3215**	
Magic Plastics Inc	25215 Ave Stanford	Valencia	CA	91355	**800-369-0303**	661-257-4485
MedGyn Products Inc	100 W Industrial Rd	Addison	IL	60101	**800-451-9667**	630-627-4105
Micro Plastics Inc	11 Industry Ln Hwy 178 N PO Box 149	Flippin	AR	72634	**800-466-1467**	870-453-2261
MOCAP Inc	409 Parkway Dr	Park Hills	MO	63601	**800-633-6775**	314-543-4000
Mold-Rite Plastics LLC	1 Plant St	Plattsburgh	NY	12901	**800-432-5277**	518-561-1812
Mylan Technologies Inc	1000 Mylan Blvd	Canonsburg	PA	15317	**800-294-1322**	724-514-1800
Neil Enterprises Inc	450 E Bunker Ct	Vernon Hills	IL	60061	**800-621-5584**	847-549-7627
Nordson MEDICAL	3325 S Timberline Rd	Fort Collins	CO	80525	**888-404-5837**	970-267-5200
Pac Tec	12365 Haynes St	Clinton	LA	70722	**877-554-2544**	
Plastikon Industries Inc	688 Sandoval Way	Hayward	CA	94544	**800-370-0858**	510-400-1010
Plastpro Inc	5200 W Century Blvd 9F	Los Angeles	CA	90045	**800-779-0561**	310-693-8600
Pleiger Plastics Co	PO Box 1271	Washington	PA	15301	**800-753-4437**	724-228-2244
Plitek LLC	69 Rawls Rd	Des Plaines	IL	60018	**800-966-1250**	
Porex Technologies Corp	500 Bohannon Rd	Fairburn	GA	30213	**800-241-0195***	770-964-1421
*Cust Svc						
Precision Thermoplastic Components Inc	PO Box 1296	Lima	OH	45802	**800-860-4505**	419-227-4500
Prism Plastics Inc	1544 Hwy 65	New Richmond	WI	54017	**877-246-7535**	715-246-7535
Randall Mfg LLC	722 Church Rd	Elmhurst	IL	60126	**800-323-7424**	630-782-0001
Rayner Covering Systems Inc	665 Schneider Dr	South Elgin	IL	60177	**800-648-0757**	847-695-2264
Rogan Corp	3455 Woodhead Dr	Northbrook	IL	60062	**800-584-5662**	847-498-2300
Rohrer Corp	717 Seville Rd PO Box 1009	Wadsworth	OH	44282	**800-243-6640**	330-335-1541
Rubbermaid Commercial Products (RCP)	3124 Valley Ave	Winchester	VA	22601	**800-347-9800**	540-667-8700
Safety Technology International Inc	2306 Airport Rd	Waterford	MI	48327	**800-888-4784**	248-673-9898
Shakespeare Monofilaments & Specialty Polymers	6111 Shakespeare Rd	Columbia	SC	29223	**800-845-2110**	803-754-7011
Smith McDonald Corp	1270 Niagara St	Buffalo	NY	14213	**800-753-8548**	

					Toll-Free	Phone
Spears Manufacturing Co	PO Box 9203	Sylmar	CA	91392	**800-862-1499**	818-364-1611
Spilltech Environmental Inc	1627 Odonoghue St	Mobile	AL	36615	**800-228-3877**	
Stant Corp	1620 Columbia Ave	Connersville	IN	47331	**800-822-3121**	765-825-3121
Steinwall Inc	1759 116th Ave NW	Coon Rapids	MN	55448	**800-229-9199**	763-767-7060
Syndicate Sales Inc	PO Box 756	Kokomo	IN	46903	**800-428-0515**	765-457-7277
Technetics Group	3125 Damon Way	Burbank	CA	91505	**800-618-4701**	818-841-9667
Thombert Inc	316 E Seventh St N	Newton	IA	50208	**800-433-3572**	
TMI LLC	5350 Campbells Run Rd	Pittsburgh	PA	15205	**800-888-9750**	412-787-9750
Triad Products Co	1801 W 'B' St *General	Hastings	NE	68901	**888-253-4227***	402-462-2181
Trippnt Inc	8830 NE 108th St	Kansas City	MO	64157	**800-874-7768**	816-792-2604
TSE Industries Inc	4370 112th Terr N	Clearwater	FL	33762	**800-237-7634**	727-573-7676
Ultra-Poly Corp	102 Demi Rd PO Box 330	Portland	PA	18351	**800-932-0619**	570-897-7500
Univenture Inc	13311 Industrial Pkwy	Marysville	OH	43040	**800-992-8262**	
Viziflex Seels Inc	406 N Midland Ave	Saddle Brook	NJ	07663	**800-627-7752**	
World Class Plastics Inc	7695 SR- 708	Russells Point	OH	43348	**800-954-3140**	937-843-4927
Wren Assoc Ltd	124 Wren Pkwy	Jefferson City	MO	65109	**800-881-2249**	573-893-2249
Yeti Coolers	3411 Hidalgo St	Austin	TX	78702	**888-872-0227**	512-394-9384
Zadro Products Inc	5422 Argosy Ave	Huntington Beach	CA	92649	**800-468-4348**	714-892-9200
ZAGG Inc	3855 South 500 West Ste J	Salt Lake City	UT	84115	**800-700-9244**	801-263-0699

608 PLUMBING FIXTURES & FITTINGS - METAL

					Toll-Free	Phone
Acorn Engineering Co	15125 Proctor Ave PO Box 3527	City of Industry	CA	91744	**800-488-8999**	626-336-4561
American Brass Manufacturing Co	5000 Superior Ave	Cleveland	OH	44103	**800-431-6440**	216-431-6565
Anderson Copper & Brass Co	7231 W Laraway Rd	Frankfort	IL	60423	**800-323-5284**	708-535-9030
Barclay Products Ltd	4000 Porett Dr Ste B	Gurnee	IL	60031	**800-446-9700**	847-244-1234
Bradley Corp	W 142 N 9101 Fountain Blvd	Menomonee Falls	WI	53051	**800-272-3539**	262-251-6000
Central Brass Mfg Company Inc	2950 E 55th St	Cleveland	OH	44127	**800-321-8630**	216-883-0220
Champion-Arrowhead LLC	5147 Alhambra Ave	Los Angeles	CA	90032	**800-332-4267**	323-221-9137
Chicago Faucets A Geberit Co	2100 S Clearwater Dr	Des Plaines	IL	60018	**800-323-5060**	847-803-5000
Eljer Inc	1 Centennial Ave	Piscataway	NJ	08855	**800-442-1902**	
Fisher Manufacturing Co	PO Box 60	Tulare	CA	93275	**800-421-6162**	
Fluidmaster Inc	30800 Rancho Viejo Rd	San Juan Capistrano	CA	92675	**800-631-2011**	949-728-2000
Gerber Plumbing Fixtures LLC	2500 International Pkwy	Woodridge	IL	60517	**888-648-8466**	
Grohe America Inc	241 Covington Dr	Bloomingdale	IL	60108	**800-444-7643**	630-582-7711
Hansgrohe Inc	1490 Bluegrass Lakes Pkwy	Alpharetta	GA	30004	**800-334-0455**	770-360-9880
In-Sink-Erator	4700 21st St	Racine	WI	53406	**800-558-5712**	262-554-5432
Josam Co	525 W US Hwy 20	Michigan City	IN	46360	**800-365-6726**	219-872-5531
Keeney Manufacturing Co	1170 Main St *Cust Svc	Newington	CT	06111	**800-243-0526***	860-666-3342
Kohler Plumbing North America	444 Highland Dr	Kohler	WI	53044	**800-456-4537**	920-457-4441
LDR Industries Inc	600 N Kilbourn Ave	Chicago	IL	60624	**800-545-5230**	773-265-3000
Masco Corp	21001 Van Born Rd *NYSE: MAS*	Taylor	MI	48180	**888-627-6397**	313-274-7400
Microphor Inc	452 E Hill Rd *Orders	Willits	CA	95490	**800-358-8280***	707-459-5563
Moen Inc	25300 Al Moen Dr *Cust Svc	North Olmsted	OH	44070	**800-289-6636***	440-962-2000
Moen Inc CSI Bath Accessories Div	25300 Al Moen Dr	North Olmsted	OH	44070	**800-289-6636**	440-962-2000
Oatey Co	4700 W 160th St *Cust Svc	Cleveland	OH	44135	**800-321-9532***	216-267-7100
Price Pfister Inc	19701 Da Vinci St	Lake Forest	CA	92610	**800-732-8238**	949-672-4000
Sloan Valve Co	10500 Seymour Ave	Franklin Park	IL	60131	**800-982-5839**	847-671-4300
Speakman Co	400 Anchor Mill Rd	New Castle	DE	19720	**800-537-2107**	
Sterling Plumbing	444 Highland Dr *Cust Svc	Kohler	WI	53044	**888-783-7546***	920-457-4441
Symmons Industries Inc	31 Brooks Dr	Braintree	MA	02184	**800-796-6667**	781-848-2250
T & S Brass & Bronze Works Inc	PO Box 1088 *Cust Svc	Travelers Rest	SC	29690	**800-476-4103***	864-834-4102
Water Pik Inc	1730 E Prospect Rd	Fort Collins	CO	80553	**800-525-2774**	
Water Saver Faucet Co	701 W Erie St *Parts	Chicago	IL	60654	**800-973-7278***	312-666-5500
Waterworks Operating Company LLC	60 Backus Ave	Danbury	CT	06810	**800-899-6757**	203-546-6000
Woodford Manufacturing Co	2121 Waynoka Rd *Sales	Colorado Springs	CO	80915	**800-621-6032***	

609 PLUMBING FIXTURES & FITTINGS - PLASTICS

					Toll-Free	Phone
1st Mechanical	1295 Bluegrass Lakes Pkwy	Alpharetta	GA	30004	**888-346-0792**	770-346-0792
Absocold Corp	PO Box 1545	Richmond	IN	47375	**800-843-3714**	765-935-7501
All-Temp Refrigeration Services Inc	271 Hwy 1085	Madisonville	LA	70447	**888-626-1277**	
Alpha Energy Solutions Inc	7200 Distribution Dr	Louisville	KY	40258	**888-212-6324**	502-968-0121
American Moistening Company Inc	10402 Rodney St	Pineville	NC	28134	**800-948-5540**	704-889-7281
Apex Piping Systems Inc	302 Falco Dr	Wilmington	DE	19804	**888-995-2739**	302-995-6136
Applied Mechanical Systems Inc	5598 Wolf Creek Pk	Dayton	OH	45426	**888-854-3073**	937-854-3073
Aqua Bath Company Inc	921 Cherokee Ave	Nashville	TN	37207	**800-232-2284**	615-227-0017
Arneg Canada Inc	18 Rue Richelieu	Lacolle	QC	J0J1J0	**800-363-3439**	450-246-3837
Arneg LLC	750 Old Hargrave Rd	Lexington	NC	27295	**800-276-3487**	336-956-5300
Aurora Contractors Inc	100 Raynor Ave	Ronkonkoma	NY	11779	**866-423-2197**	631-981-3785
Automatic Fire Sprinkler Inc	7272 Mars Dr	Huntington Beach	CA	92647	**800-436-2066**	714-841-2066
B & B Trade Distribution Centre	1950 Oxford St E	London	ON	N5V2Z8	**800-265-0382**	519-679-1770
Belding Tank Technologies Inc	200 N Gooding St PO Box 160	Belding	MI	48809	**800-253-4252**	616-794-1130
Blauch Bros Inc	911 Chicago Ave	Harrisonburg	VA	22802	**888-881-3939**	540-434-2589
Blue Mountain Air Inc	707 Aldridge Rd	Vacaville	CA	95688	**800-889-2085**	
Blue Sky Energy Inc	2598 Fortune Way Ste K	Vista	CA	92081	**800-493-7877**	760-597-1642
Boland	30 W Watkins Mill Rd	Gaithersburg	MD	20878	**800-552-6526**	240-306-3000
Broadway Mechanical	873 81st Ave	Oakland	CA	94621	**800-862-4930**	510-746-4000
Brower Mechanical Inc	4060 Alvis Ct	Rocklin	CA	95677	**877-816-6649**	916-624-0808
C H Garmong & Son Inc	3050 Poplar St	Terre Haute	IN	47803	**800-894-2962**	812-234-3714
Cambridgeport Air Systems	8 Fanaras Dr	Salisbury	MA	01952	**877-648-2872**	978-465-8481
Can-am Plumbing Inc	151 Wyoming St	Pleasanton	CA	94566	**800-786-9797**	925-846-1833
Casto Technical Services Inc	540 Leon Sullivan Way	Charleston	WV	25301	**800-232-2221**	304-346-0549
Claybar Constracting Inc	424 Macnab St	Dundas	ON	L9H2L3	**866-801-9305**	905-627-8000
Cole Industrial Inc	5924 203rd St SW	Lynnwood	WA	98036	**800-627-2653**	425-774-6602
Colite International Ltd	5 Technology Cir	Columbia	SC	29203	**800-760-7926**	803-926-7926
Concepts Av Integration	3712 S 132nd St	Omaha	NE	68144	**877-422-3933**	402-298-5011
Continental Fire Sprinkler Co	4518 S 133rd St	Omaha	NE	68137	**800-543-5170**	402-330-5170
D'vontz	7208 E 38th St	Tulsa	OK	74145	**877-322-3600**	918-622-3600
Danamark Watercare Ltd	2-90 Walker Dr	Brampton	ON	L6T4H6	**888-326-2627**	
Dispensing Dynamics International	1020 Bixby Dr	City of Industry	CA	91745	**800-888-3698**	626-961-3691
Dornbracht Americas Inc	1700 Executive Dr S Ste 600	Duluth	GA	30096	**800-774-1181**	
Effective Solar Products LLC	601 Crescent Ave	Lockport	LA	70374	**888-824-0090**	985-532-0800
Ferrandino & Son Inc	71 Carolyn Blvd	Farmingdale	NY	11735	**866-571-4609**	516-735-0097
Finken Plumbing Heating & Cooling	628 19th Ave NE	Saint Joseph	MN	56374	**877-346-5367**	320-258-2005
Fire Fighter Sales & Service Co	791 Commonwealth Dr	Warrendale	PA	15086	**888-412-3473**	724-720-6000
Florestone Products Company Inc	2851 Falcon Dr	Madera	CA	93637	**800-446-8827**	559-661-4171
Fujitsu General America Inc	353 Rt 46 W	Fairfield	NJ	07004	**888-888-3424**	973-575-0380
Housh-the Home Energy Experts	18 South Main St	Monroe	OH	45050	**866-611-5752**	513-793-6374
Hussung Mechanical Contractors	6913 Enterprise Dr	Louisville	KY	40214	**800-446-2738**	502-375-3500
Imperial Manufacturing Group Inc	40 Industrial Park St	Richibucto	NB	E4W4A4	**800-561-3100**	506-523-9117
Ingenuity Ieq	3600 Centennial Dr	Midland	MI	48642	**800-669-9726**	989-496-2233
Iron City Pipe & Supply	330 E Broadway St	Jackson	OH	45640	**877-286-7447**	740-286-8080
James Lane Air Conditioning Company Inc	5024 Old Jacksboro Hwy	Wichita Falls	TX	76302	**800-460-2204**	940-766-0244
Jet Industries Inc	1935 Silverton Rd NE PO Box 7362	Salem	OR	97303	**800-659-0620**	503-363-2334
Kinetics Mechanical Service Inc	6691 Brisa St	Livermore	CA	94550	**866-567-7378**	925-245-6200

Company / Address	City	State	Zip	Toll-Free	Phone
KITCO Fiber Optics Inc 5269 Cleveland St	Virginia Beach	VA	23462	**866-643-5220**	757-518-8100
Kohler Canada Company Hytec Plumbing Products Div 4150 Spallumcheen Dr	Armstrong	BC	V0E1B6	**800-871-8311**	250-546-3067
L B Plastics Inc PO Box 907	Mooresville	NC	28115	**800-752-7739**	704-663-1543
M Davis & Sons Inc 19 Germay Dr	Wilmington	DE	19804	**800-913-2847**	302-998-3385
Maax Corp 160 St Joseph Blvd	Lachine	QC	H8S2L3	**888-957-7816**	877-438-6229
Maintenx 2202 N Howard Ave	Tampa	FL	33607	**855-751-0075**	
Matco-Norca Inc Rt 22	Brewster	NY	10509	**800-431-2082**	845-278-7570
Mechanical Design Systems Inc 6302 Aaron Ln	Clinton	MD	20735	**877-960-0301**	301-877-9600
Mechanical Systems of Dayton 4401 Springfield St	Dayton	OH	45431	**800-254-9455**	937-254-3235
Meckley Services Inc 5701 General Washington Dr Ste O	Alexandria	VA	22312	**877-632-5539**	703-333-2040
Meier Supply Company Inc 530 Bloomingburg Rd	Middletown	NY	10940	**800-418-3216**	845-733-5666
Mohr Power Solar Inc 1452 Pomona Rd	Corona	CA	92882	**800-637-6527**	951-736-2000
National Meter & Automation 7220 S Fraser St	Centennial	CO	80112	**877-212-8340**	303-339-9100
Noveo Technologies Inc 9655 A Ignace St	Brossard	QC	J4Y2P3	**877-314-2044**	450-444-2044
Nupla Corp 11912 Sheldon St	Sun Valley	CA	91352	**800-872-7661**	818-768-6800
Pedal Valves Inc 13625 River Rd	Luling	LA	70070	**800-431-3668**	985-785-9997
Phybridge Inc 3495 Laird Rd Ste 12	Mississauga	ON	L5L5S5	**888-901-3633**	905-901-3633
Prier Products Inc 4515 E 139th St	Grandview	MO	64030	**800-362-1463**	816-763-4100
S R C Refrigeration 6615 19 Mile Rd	Sterling Heights	MI	48314	**800-521-0398**	586-254-0610
Solar Store LLC, The 2833 N Country Club Rd	Tucson	AZ	85716	**877-264-6374**	520-322-5180
Star Services 4663 Halls Mill Rd	Mobile	AL	36693	**800-661-9050**	251-661-4050
State Supply Co 597 Seventh St E	Saint Paul	MN	55130	**877-775-7705**	651-774-5985
Thetford Corp 7101 Jackson Ave PO Box 1285	Ann Arbor	MI	48106	**800-521-3032**	734-769-6000
Thetford Corp Recreational Vehicle Group 2901 E Bristol St Ste B	Elkhart	IN	46514	**800-831-1076**	574-266-7980
Thompson Industrial Services LLC 104 N Main	Sumter	SC	29150	**800-849-8040**	803-773-8005
Tri-state Fabricators Inc 1146 Ferris Rd	Amelia	OH	45102	**888-523-1488**	513-752-5005
Tudi Mechanical Systems of Tampa Inc 343 Munson Ave	Mc Kees Rocks	PA	15136	**877-367-8834**	412-771-4100
Verigent LLC 149 Plantation Ridge Dr Ste 100	Mooresville	NC	28117	**877-637-6422**	704-658-3271
Wisco Supply Inc 815 S Saint Vrain St	El Paso	TX	79901	**800-947-2689**	915-544-8294
Worly Plumbing Supply Inc 54 E Harrison St	Delaware	OH	43015	**800-365-1175**	740-363-1151
Zampell Cos 9 Stanley Tucker Dr	Newburyport	MA	01950	**877-926-7355**	978-465-0055
Zehnder America Inc 6 Merrill Industrial Dr Ste 7	Hampton	NH	03842	**888-778-6701**	603-601-8544

610 PLUMBING FIXTURES & FITTINGS - VITREOUS CHINA & EARTHENWARE

Company / Address	City	State	Zip	Toll-Free	Phone
American Standard Cos Inc Bath & Kitchen Products Div 1 Centennial Ave PO Box 6820	Piscataway	NJ	08855	**800-442-1902**	
Briggs Plumbing Products 300 Eagle Rd	Goose Creek	SC	29445	**800-888-4458**	
Eljer Inc 1 Centennial Ave	Piscataway	NJ	08855	**800-442-1902**	
Gerber Plumbing Fixtures LLC 2500 International Pkwy	Woodridge	IL	60517	**888-648-6466**	
Kohler Plumbing North America 444 Highland Dr	Kohler	WI	53044	**800-456-4537**	920-457-4441
Mansfield Plumbing Products Inc 150 E First St	Perrysville	OH	44864	**877-850-3060**	419-938-5211
Microphor Inc 452 E Hill Rd	Willits	CA	95490	**800-358-8280***	707-459-5563
*Orders					
Peerless Pottery Inc 319 S Fifth St	Rockport	IN	47635	**866-457-5785**	800-457-5785
Sterling Plumbing 444 Highland Dr	Kohler	WI	53044	**888-783-7546***	920-457-4441
*Cust Svc					
Sunrise Specialty Co 930 98th Ave	Oakland	CA	94603	**800-444-4280**	510-729-7277
Toto USA Inc 1155 Southern Rd	Morrow	GA	30260	**888-295-8134**	770-282-8686

611 PLUMBING, HEATING, AIR CONDITIONING EQUIPMENT & SUPPLIES - WHOL

SEE ALSO Refrigeration Equipment - Whol

Company / Address	City	State	Zip	Toll-Free	Phone
Aaron & Company Inc PO Box 8310	Piscataway	NJ	08855	**800-734-4822**	732-752-8200
AB Young Cos Inc 15305 Stony Creek Way	Noblesville	IN	46060	**800-886-7001**	317-565-5000
Air Monitor Corp 1050 Hopper Ave	Santa Rosa	CA	95403	**800-247-3569**	707-544-2706
Altmas Products 1201 Francisco St	Torrance	CA	90502	**800-678-6463**	310-559-4093
American Backflow Specialties 3940 Home Ave	San Diego	CA	92105	**800-662-5356**	619-527-2525
American Faucet & Coating Corp 3280 Corporate Vw	Vista	CA	92081	**800-621-8383**	760-598-5895
American Granby Inc 7652 Morgan Rd	Liverpool	NY	13090	**800-776-2266**	315-451-1100
Anderson Tube Company Inc 1400 Fairgrounds Rd	Hatfield	PA	19440	**800-523-2258**	215-855-0118
Applied Membranes Inc 2325 Cousteau Ct	Vista	CA	92081	**800-321-9321**	760-727-3711
Applied Thermal Systems 8401 73rd Ave N Ste 74	Brooklyn Park	MN	55428	**800-479-4783**	763-535-5545
Arizona Partsmaster Inc 7125 W Sherman St PO Box 23169	Phoenix	AZ	85043	**888-924-7278**	602-233-3580
Arizona Wholesale Supply Co 2020 E University Dr	Phoenix	AZ	85034	**866-977-6849**	602-258-7901
BA Robinson Company Ltd 619 Berry St	Winnipeg	MB	R3H0S2	**866-903-6275**	204-784-0150
Baker Distributing Co 14610 Breakers Dr Ste 100	Jacksonville	FL	32258	**844-289-0033**	800-217-4698
Barnett Inc 801 W Bay St	Jacksonville	FL	32204	**888-803-4467**	904-384-6530
Bartle & Gibson Company Ltd 13475 Ft Rd NW	Edmonton	AB	T5A1C6	**800-661-5615**	780-472-2850
Bascom-Turner Instrument 111 Downey St	Norwood	MA	02062	**800-225-3298**	781-769-9660
Be-Cool Inc 310 Woodside Ave	Essexville	MI	48732	**800-691-2667**	989-895-9699
Best Plumbing Specialties 3039 Ventrie Ct	Myersville	MD	21773	**800-448-6710**	
Broedell Plumbing Supply Inc 1601 Commerce Ln	Jupiter	FL	33458	**888-328-2383**	561-743-6663
Butcher Distributors Inc 101 Boyce Rd	Broussard	LA	70518	**800-960-0008**	337-837-2088
Caroplast Inc PO Box 668405	Charlotte	NC	28266	**800-327-5797**	704-394-4191
Central Arizona Supply 208 S Country Club Dr	Mesa	AZ	85210	**800-416-6490**	480-834-5817
City Plumbing & Electric Supply Co 730 EE Butler Pkwy	Gainesville	GA	30501	**800-260-2024**	770-532-4123
City Supply Corp 2326 Bell Ave	Des Moines	IA	50321	**800-400-2377**	515-288-3211
Cleveland Plumbing Supply Company Inc 143 E Washington St	Chagrin Falls	OH	44022	**800-331-1078**	440-247-2555
Coburn Supply Company Inc 390 Pk St Ste 100	Beaumont	TX	77701	**800-832-8492**	409-838-6363
Consolidated Supply Co 7337 SW Kable Ln	Tigard	OR	97224	**800-929-5810**	503-620-7050
D-S Pipe & Supply Company Inc 1301 Wicomico St Ste 3	Baltimore	MD	21230	**800-368-8880**	410-539-8000
Delta T Inc 8323 Loch Lomond Dr	Pico Rivera	CA	90660	**800-928-5828**	
Desco Plumbing & Heating Supply Inc 65 Worcester Rd	Etobicoke	ON	M9W5N7	**800-564-5146**	416-213-1555
Duncan Supply Company Inc 910 N Illinois St	Indianapolis	IN	46204	**800-382-5528**	317-634-1335
Duravit USA Inc 2205 Northmont Pkwy Ste 200	Duluth	GA	30096	**888-387-2848**	770-931-3575
East Coast Metal Distributors, Inc 1313 South Briggs Ave	Durham	NC	27703	**844-227-9531**	
Eastern Pennsylvania Supply Co 700 Scott St	Wilkes-Barre	PA	18705	**800-432-8075**	570-823-1181
Emerson-Swan Inc 300 Pond St	Randolph	MA	02368	**800-346-9219**	781-986-2000
Everett J Prescott Inc 32 Prescott St	Gardiner	ME	04345	**800-357-2447**	207-582-1851
Ferguson Enterprises Inc 12500 Jefferson Ave	Newport News	VA	23602	**800-721-2590**	757-874-7795
First Supply LLC 6800 Gisholt Dr	Madison	WI	53713	**800-236-9795**	608-222-7799
Four Seasons Inc 1801 Waters Ridge Dr	Lewisville	TX	75057	**888-505-4567**	972-316-8100
Fresno Distributing Company Inc 2055 E McKinley Ave	Fresno	CA	93703	**800-655-2542**	559-442-8800
Gateway Supply Company Inc 1312 Hamrick St	Columbia	SC	29202	**800-922-5312**	803-771-7160
Gensco Inc 4402 20th St E	Tacoma	WA	98424	**877-620-8203**	253-620-8203
Goodin Co 2700 N Second St	Minneapolis	MN	55411	**800-328-8433**	612-588-7811
Granite Group Wholesalers LLC 6 Storrs St	Concord	NH	03301	**800-258-3690**	603-224-1901
Greenscape Pump Services Inc 1425 Whitlock Ln Ste 108	Carrollton	TX	75006	**877-401-4774**	972-446-0037
Hajoca Corp 127 Coulter Ave	Ardmore	PA	19003	**888-328-2383**	610-649-1430
Harri Plumbing & Heating Inc 809 W 12th St	Juneau	AK	99801	**800-478-3190**	907-586-3190
Harry Cooper Supply Company Inc 605 N Sherman Pkwy	Springfield	MO	65802	**800-426-6737**	417-865-8392
Henry Quentzel Plumbing Supply Co 379 Throop Ave	Brooklyn	NY	11221	**800-889-2294**	718-455-6600
Hercules Industries Inc 1310 W Evans Ave	Denver	CO	80223	**800-356-5350**	303-937-1000
Hydro-flo Products Inc 3655 N 124th St	Brookfield	WI	53005	**800-843-3569**	262-781-2810
I D Booth Inc PO Box 579	Elmira	NY	14902	**888-432-6684**	607-733-9121
JE Sawyer & Company Inc 64 Glen St	Glens Falls	NY	12801	**800-724-3983**	
JH Larson Co 10200 51st Ave N	Plymouth	MN	55442	**800-292-7970**	763-545-1717
John M Frey Co Inc 2735 62nd St Ct	Bettendorf	IA	52722	**800-397-3739**	563-332-9200
Johnson Supply Inc 10151 Stella Link Rd	Houston	TX	77025	**800-833-5455**	713-830-2499
Keller Supply Company Inc 3209 17th Ave W	Seattle	WA	98119	**800-285-3302**	206-285-3300
Kelly's Pipe & Supply Co Inc 2124 Industrial Rd	Las Vegas	NV	89102	**888-382-4957**	

	City	State	Zip	Toll-Free	Phone
Lee Supply Corp 6610 Guion Rd	Indianapolis	IN	46268	**800-873-1103**	317-290-2500
Masters' Supply Inc 4505 Bishop Ln	Louisville	KY	40218	**800-388-6353**	
May Supply Company Inc 1775 Erickson Ave	Harrisonburg	VA	22801	**800-296-9997**	540-433-2611
McGuire Manufacturing 60 Grandview Ct	Cheshire	CT	06410	**800-676-1832**	203-699-1801
Mid-Lakes Distributing Inc 1029 W Adams St	Chicago	IL	60607	**888-733-2700**	312-733-1033
Mid-States Supply Co 1716 Guinotte Ave	Kansas City	MO	64120	**800-825-1410**	816-842-4290
Minvalco Inc 3340 Gorham Ave	Minneapolis	MN	55426	**800-642-9090**	952-920-0131
Morley-Murphy Co 200 S Washington St Ste 305	Green Bay	WI	54301	**877-499-3171**	920-499-3171
Morrison Supply Company Inc 311 E Vickery Blvd	Fort Worth	TX	76104	**800-451-9343**	817-870-2227
Morrow Control & Supply Co 810 Marion Motley Ave Ne	Canton	OH	44705	**800-362-9830**	330-452-9791
Mountain States Pipe & Supply Co 111 W Las Vegas St	Colorado Springs	CO	80903	**800-777-7173**	719-634-5555
Mountain Supply Co 2101 Mullan Rd	Missoula	MT	59808	**800-821-1646**	406-543-8255
New York Replacement Parts Corp 19 School St	Yonkers	NY	10701	**800-228-4718**	914-965-0122
Newton Distributing Company Inc 966 Watertown St	Newton	MA	02465	**877-837-7745**	617-969-4002
Niagara Conservation Corp 45 Horsehill Rd	Cedar Knolls	NJ	07927	**800-831-8383**	973-829-0800
Northwest Pipe Fittings Inc 33 S Eigth St W	Billings	MT	59101	**800-937-4737**	406-252-0142
Peabody Supply Co Inc PO Box 669	Peabody	MA	01960	**800-445-5816**	978-532-2200
Pepco Sales of Dallas Inc 11310 Gemini Ln	Dallas	TX	75229	**877-737-2699**	972-823-8700
Plumb Supply Co 1622 NE 51st Ave	Des Moines	IA	50313	**800-483-9511**	515-262-9511
Plumbers Supply Co 1000 E Main St	Louisville	KY	40206	**800-626-5133**	502-582-2261
Plumbing Distributors Inc 1025 Old Norcross Rd	Lawrenceville	GA	30046	**800-262-9231**	770-963-9231
Prima Supply Inc 4603 Poplar Level Rd Ste 1	Louisville	KY	40213	**888-810-5043**	502-966-4578
Rampart Supply Inc 1801 N Union Blvd	Colorado Springs	CO	80909	**800-748-1837**	719-482-7333
Reeves-Wiedeman Co Inc 14861 W 100th St	Lenexa	KS	66215	**800-365-0024**	913-492-7100
Refrigeration Sales Corp 9450 Allen Dr Ste A	Valley View	OH	44125	**866-894-8200**	216-881-7800
Republic Plumbing Supply Company Inc 890 Providence Hwy	Norwood	MA	02062	**800-696-3900**	
Roberts-Hamilton 6601 Pkwy Cir Ste A	Brooklyn Center	MN	55430	**800-888-2222**	763-315-0100
Robertson Heating Supply Co 2155 W Main St	Alliance	OH	44601	**800-433-9532**	330-821-9180
Rundle-Spence Manufacturing Co PO Box 510008	New Berlin	WI	53151	**800-783-6060**	262-782-3000
Schumacher & Seiler Inc 10 W Aylesbury Rd	Timonium	MD	21093	**800-992-9356**	410-465-7000
Security Supply Corp 196 Maple Ave	Selkirk	NY	12158	**800-333-2226**	518-767-2226
Standard Air & Lite Corp 2406 Woodmere Dr	Pittsburgh	PA	15205	**800-472-2458**	412-920-6505
Sunbelt Marketing Investment Corp 3255 S Sweetwater Rd	Lithia Springs	GA	30122	**800-257-5566**	770-739-3740
Swan Corp, The 515 Olive St Ste 900	St. Louis	MO	63101	**800-325-7008**	314-231-8148
TBA LLC 6700 Enterprise Dr	Louisville	KY	40214	**800-626-3525**	502-367-0222
Temperature Systems Inc 5001 Voges Rd	Madison	WI	53718	**800-366-0930**	608-271-7500
Therm Air Sales Corp 1413 41st Stn	Fargo	ND	58102	**800-726-7520**	701-282-9500
Thermal Corp 1264 Slaughter Rd	Madison	AL	35758	**800-633-2962**	256-837-1122
Upturn Solutions Inc 1396 Riverside Rd	Bigfork	MT	59911	**866-891-4363**	
US Airconditioning Distributors 16900 Chestnut St	City of Industry	CA	91748	**800-937-7222**	626-854-4500
Vamac Inc 4201 Jacque St	Richmond	VA	23230	**800-768-2622**	804-353-7811
WA Roosevelt Co 2727 Commerce St	La Crosse	WI	54603	**800-279-2726**	608-781-2000
Ward Manufacturing LLC 117 Gulick St	Blossburg	PA	16912	**800-248-1027**	570-638-2131
Waxman Industries Inc 24460 Aurora Rd *OTC: WXMN*	Bedford Heights	OH	44146	**800-201-7298**	440-439-1830
Wayne Pipe & Supply Inc 6040 Innovation Blvd	Fort Wayne	IN	46818	**800-552-3697**	260-423-9577
Western Nevada Supply Co 950 S Rock Blvd	Sparks	NV	89431	**800-648-1230**	775-359-5800
Woodhill Supply Inc 4665 Beidler Rd	Willoughby	OH	44094	**800-362-6111**	440-269-1100

612 PLYWOOD & VENEERS

SEE ALSO Lumber & Building Supplies ; Home Improvement Centers

	City	State	Zip	Toll-Free	Phone
Bacon Veneer Co 6951 High Grove Blvd	Burr Ridge	IL	60527	**800-443-7995**	630-323-1414
California Panel & Veneer Co 14055 Artesia Blvd	Cerritos	CA	90703	**800-451-1745**	562-926-5834
Capitol Plywood Inc 160 Commerce Cir	Sacramento	CA	95815	**800-326-1505**	916-922-8861
Columbia Forest Products Inc Columbia Plywood Div 7900 Triad Ctr Dr Ste 200	Greensboro	NC	27409	**800-637-1609**	
Constantine's Wood Ctr 1040 E Oakland Pk Blvd	Fort Lauderdale	FL	33334	**800-443-9667**	954-561-1716
Darlington Veneer Company Inc 225 Fourth St	Darlington	SC	29532	**800-845-2388**	843-393-3861
Fiber-Tech Industries Inc 2000 Kenskill Ave	Washington Court House	OH	43160	**800-879-4377**	740-335-9400
Flexible Materials Inc 1202 Port Rd	Jeffersonville	IN	47130	**800-244-6492**	812-280-7000
G-L Veneer Co Inc 2224 E Slauson Ave	Huntington Park	CA	90255	**800-588-5003**	323-582-5203
Harbor Sales 1000 Harbor Ct	Sudlersville	MD	21668	**800-345-1712**	
Inland Plywood Co 375 N Cass Ave	Pontiac	MI	48342	**800-521-4355**	248-334-4706
Louisiana-Pacific Corp 414 Union St Ste 2000 *NYSE: LPX*	Nashville	TN	37219	**888-820-0325**	615-986-5600
Murphy Hardwood Plywood 2350 Prairie Rd	Eugene	OR	97402	**888-461-4545**	541-461-4545
Murphy Plywood Co 2350 Prairie Rd	Eugene	OR	97402	**888-461-4545**	541-461-4545
Norbord Inc 1 Toronto St Ste 600 *TSE: NBD*	Toronto	ON	M5C2W4	**888-667-2673**	416-365-0705
North American Plywood Corp 12343 Hawkins St *Sales	Santa Fe Springs	CA	90670	**800-421-1372***	562-941-7575
Phillips Plywood Company Inc 13599 Desmond St *Cust Svc	Pacoima	CA	91331	**800-649-6410***	818-897-7736
Plywood Supply Inc 7036 NE 175th St	Kenmore	WA	98028	**888-774-9663**	425-485-8585
Roseburg Forest Products Co PO Box 1088	Roseburg	OR	97470	**800-245-1115**	541-679-3311
States Industries Inc 29495 W Enid Rd	Eugene	OR	97402	**800-626-1981**	541-688-7871
Stimson Lumber Co 520 SW Yamhill St Ste 700	Portland	OR	97204	**800-445-9758**	503-222-1676
United Plywood & Lumber Inc 1640 Mims Ave SW	Birmingham	AL	35211	**800-272-6486**	205-925-7601

613 POINT-OF-SALE (POS) & POINT-OF-INFORMATION (POI) SYSTEMS

	City	State	Zip	Toll-Free	Phone
3M Digital Signage 600 Ericksen Ave NE Ste 200	Bainbridge Island	WA	98110	**888-464-7239**	206-855-2000
Checkpoint Systems Inc 101 Wolf Dr *NYSE: CKP*	Thorofare	NJ	08086	**800-257-5540**	856-848-1800
Datalogic Scanning 959 Terry St	Eugene	OR	97402	**800-695-5700**	541-683-5700
Kiosk Information Systems Inc (KIS) 346 S Arthur Ave *General	Louisville	CO	80027	**800-509-5471***	303-466-5471
Micros Systems Inc 7031 Columbia Gateway Dr *NASDAQ: MCRS*	Columbia	MD	21046	**800-937-2211**	443-285-6000
MTI Inc 1050 NW 229th Ave	Hillsboro	OR	97124	**800-426-6844**	503-648-6500
NextG Networks Inc 890 Tasman Dr	Milpitas	CA	95035	**877-486-9377**	
PAR Technology Corp 8383 Seneca Tpke *NYSE: PAR*	New Hartford	NY	13413	**800-448-6505**	315-738-0600
SeePoint Technology LLC 2619 Manhattan Beach Blvd	Redondo Beach	CA	90278	**888-587-1777**	310-725-9660
TouchSystems Corp 220 Tradesmen Dr	Hutto	TX	78634	**800-320-5944**	512-846-2424
UTC RETAIL Inc 100 Rawson Rd	Victor	NY	14564	**800-349-0546**	
VeriFone Inc 2099 Gateway Pl Ste 600 *NYSE: PAY*	San Jose	CA	95110	**800-837-4366**	408-232-7800
VeriFone Systems Inc 88 W Plumeria Dr Ste 600 *NYSE: PAY*	San Jose	CA	95134	**800-837-4366**	408-232-7800

614 POLITICAL ACTION COMMITTEES

SEE ALSO Civic & Political Organizations

	City	State	Zip	Toll-Free	Phone
AFL-CIO Committee on Political Education 815 16th St NW	Washington	DC	20006	**855-712-8441**	
American Academy of Ophthalmology PAC Governmental Affairs Div 20 F St NW Ste 400	Washington	DC	20001	**866-561-8558**	202-737-6662
American Apparel & Footwear Assn PAC 1601 N Kent St Ste 1200	Arlington	VA	22209	**800-520-2262**	703-524-1864
American Assn of Nurse Anesthetists PAC (AANAPAC) 222 S Prospect Ave	Park Ridge	IL	60068	**855-526-2262**	847-692-7050
American Assn of Orthodontists PAC 401 N Lindbergh Blvd	Saint Louis	MO	63141	**800-424-2841**	314-993-1700
American Bankers Assn PAC (ABAPAC) 1120 Connecticut Ave NW	Washington	DC	20036	**800-226-5377**	
American Chiropractic Assn PAC (ACA-PAC) 1701 Clarendon Blvd	Arlington	VA	22209	**800-986-4636**	703-276-8800
American Dental Assn 1111 14th St NW Ste 1100	Washington	DC	20005	**800-353-2237**	202-898-2424
American Family Life Assurance Co PAC (AFLAC PAC) 1932 Wynnton Rd Ste 300 *NYSE: AFL* ■ *Cust Svc	Columbus	GA	31999	**800-992-3522***	706-323-3431
American Hospital Assn PAC (AHAPAC) 325 Seventh St NW	Washington	DC	20004	**800-424-4301**	202-638-1100
American Moving & Storage Assn PAC 1611 Duke St	Alexandria	VA	22314	**888-849-2672**	703-683-7410
American Nurses Assn PAC (ANA PAC) 8515 Georgia Ave Ste 400	Silver Spring	MD	20910	**800-274-4262**	301-628-5000

Classified Section

Name / Address	City	State	ZIP	Toll-Free	Phone
American Pharmacists Assn PAC 2215 Constitution Ave NW	Washington	DC	20037	**800-237-2742**	202-628-4410
American Society of Travel Agents PAC 1101 King St Ste 490	Alexandria	VA	22314	**800-275-2782**	703-739-2782
American Veterinary Medical Assn PAC (AVMA) 1910 Sunderland Pl NW	Washington	DC	20036	**800-321-1473**	202-789-0007
Associated General Contractors PAC 2300 Wilson Blvd Ste 400	Arlington	VA	22201	**800-242-1767**	703-548-3118
Burlington Northern Santa Fe Corp (BNSF) 500 New Jersey Ave NW Ste 550	Washington	DC	20001	**800-964-9386**	202-347-8662
BUSPAC 700 13th St NW Ste 575	Washington	DC	20005	**800-283-2877**	202-842-1645
Coca-Cola Nonpartisan Committee for Good Government PO Box 1734	Atlanta	GA	30301	**800-438-2653**	
College of American Pathologists PAC 1350 I St NW Ste 590	Washington	DC	20005	**800-392-9994**	202-354-7100
DGA-PAC 7920 W Sunset Blvd	Los Angeles	CA	90046	**800-421-4173**	310-289-2000
ESOP Assn PAC 1726 M St NW Ste 501	Washington	DC	20036	**866-366-3832**	202-293-2971
FRAN-PAC 1501 K St Ste 350	Washington	DC	20005	**800-543-1038**	202-628-8000
Friends Committee on National Legislation (FCNL) 245 Second St NE	Washington	DC	20002	**800-630-1330**	202-547-6000
IATSE PAC 1430 Broadway 20th Fl	New York	NY	10018	**844-422-9273**	212-730-1770
Ironworkers Political Action League 1750 New York Ave NW Ste 400	Washington	DC	20006	**800-368-0105**	202-383-4800
Liberal Party of Canada 81 Metcalfe St	Ottawa	ON	K1P6M8	**888-542-3725**	
Manufactured Housing Institute PAC (MHI PAC) 1655 N Ft Myer Dr Ste 104	Arlington	VA	22209	**800-505-5500**	703-558-0400
MassMutual PAC 1295 State St	Springfield	MA	01111	**800-272-2216**	413-788-8411
Motorola PAC 600 N US Hwy 45	Libertyville	IL	60048	**800-102-2344**	
NA of Home Builders PAC 1201 15th St NW	Washington	DC	20005	**800-368-5242**	202-266-8200
NA of Retired Federal Employees 606 N Washington St	Alexandria	VA	22314	**800-627-3394**	703-838-7760
NAADAC PAC 44 Canal Center Plz Ste 301	Alexandria	VA	22314	**800-377-1136**	703-741-7686
NASBIC PAC 1100 H St NW Ste 610	Washington	DC	20005	**800-471-6153**	202-628-5055
National Confectioners Assn PAC (NCA) 8320 Old Courthouse Rd Ste 300	Vienna	VA	22182	**800-433-1200**	202-534-1440
National Multi Housing Council PAC 1850 M St NW Ste 540	Washington	DC	20036	**866-987-7367**	202-974-2300
National Pork Producers Council PAC 122 C St NW Ste 875	Washington	DC	20001	**866-844-9416**	202-347-3600
National Sunflower Assn PAC 2401 46th Ave SE Ste 206	Mandan	ND	58554	**888-718-7033**	701-328-5100
NRA Institute for Legislative Action 11250 Waples Mill Rd	Fairfax	VA	22030	**800-392-8683**	
Ontario Pc Party 19 Duncan St	Toronto	ON	M5H3H1	**800-903-6453**	416-861-9593
Outdoor Adv Assn of America Inc (OAAA) 1850 M St NW Ste 1040	Washington	DC	20036	**800-325-3694**	202-833-5566
Outdoor Amusement Business Assn PAC (OABA-PAC) 1035 S Semoran Blvd Ste 1045A	Winter Park	FL	32792	**800-517-6222**	407-681-9444
Petroleum Marketers Assn of America's Small Business Community 1901 N Fort Myer Dr Ste 500	Arlington	VA	22209	**888-372-7341**	703-351-8000
Planned Parenthood Action Fund Inc 1110 Vermont Ave NW	Washington	DC	20005	**800-430-4907**	202-973-4800
REITPAC 1875 'I' St NW Ste 600	Washington	DC	20006	**800-362-7348**	202-739-9400
Title Industry PAC (TIPAC) 1828 L St NW Ste 705	Washington	DC	20036	**800-787-2582**	202-296-3671

615 POLITICAL PARTIES (MAJOR)

SEE ALSO Civic & Political Organizations

Name / Address	City	State	ZIP	Toll-Free	Phone
Libertarian Party 2600 Virginia Ave NW Ste 200	Washington	DC	20037	**800-353-2887**	202-333-0008
Republican National Committee (RNC) 310 First St SE	Washington	DC	20003	**800-445-5768**	202-863-8500

615-1 Democratic State Committees

Name / Address	City	State	ZIP	Toll-Free	Phone
Florida Democratic Party 214 S Bronough St	Tallahassee	FL	32301	**855-352-7233**	850-222-3411
Hawaii Democratic Party 1050 Ala Moana Blvd Ste D-26	Honolulu	HI	96814	**844-596-2980**	808-596-2980
Idaho Democratic Party 943 W Overland Rd	Meridian	ID	83642	**800-626-0471**	208-336-1815
Indiana Democratic Party 115 W Washington St Ste 1165	Indianapolis	IN	46204	**800-223-3387**	317-231-7100
New Mexico Democratic Party (DPNM) 8214 Second St NW ste A	Albuquerque	NM	87114	**800-624-2457**	505-830-3650
Oklahoma Democratic Party 4100 N Lincoln Blvd	Oklahoma City	OK	73105	**800-547-5600**	405-427-3366
South Carolina Democratic Party 915 Lady St Ste 111	Columbia	SC	29250	**800-841-1817**	803-799-7798
Virginia Democratic Party 1710 E Franklin St 2nd Fl	Richmond	VA	23223	**800-322-1144**	804-644-1966

615-2 Republican State Committees

Name / Address	City	State	ZIP	Toll-Free	Phone
Alabama Republican Party 3505 Lorna Rd Ste 219	Birmingham	AL	35216	**800-274-8683**	205-212-5900
Texas Republican Party 1108 Lavaca Ste 500	Austin	TX	78701	**800-525-5555**	512-477-9821

616 PORTALS - VOICE

Voice portals permit users to access web-based messaging as well as various types of Internet information (e.g., weather, stock quotes, driving directions, etc.) via the telephone (wired or wireless).

Name / Address	City	State	ZIP	Toll-Free	Phone
GoSolo Technologies Inc 5410 Mariner St Ste 175	Tampa	FL	33609	**866-246-7656**	

617 PORTS & PORT AUTHORITIES

SEE ALSO Cruise Lines ; Airports

Name / Address	City	State	ZIP	Toll-Free	Phone
Georgia Ports Authority PO Box 2406	Savannah	GA	31402	**800-342-8012**	912-964-3811
Hamilton Port Authority 605 James St N 6th Fl	Hamilton	ON	L8L1K1	**800-263-2131**	905-525-4330
Illinois International Port District 3600 E 95th St	Chicago	IL	60617	**800-843-7678**	773-646-4400
Indiana Port Commission 150 W Market St Ste 100	Indianapolis	IN	46204	**800-232-7678**	317-232-9200
International Port of Dutch Harbor PO Box 610	Unalaska	AK	99685	**800-526-6731**	907-581-1251
Kodiak Port & Harbor 403 Marine Way	Kodiak	AK	99615	**800-563-4254**	907-486-8080
Mississippi State Port Authority at Gulfport 2510 14th St Ste 1450	Gulfport	MS	39501	**877-881-4367**	228-865-4300
North Carolina State Ports Authority 2202 Burnett Blvd PO Box 9002	Wilmington	NC	28402	**800-334-0682**	910-763-1621
Oregon International Port of Coos Bay 125 Central Ave Ste 300 PO Box 1215	Coos Bay	OR	97420	**800-463-3339**	541-267-7678
Port Canaveral 445 Challenger Rd	Cape Canaveral	FL	32920	**888-767-8226**	321-783-7831
Port Everglades 1850 Eller Dr	Fort Lauderdale	FL	33316	**800-421-0188**	954-523-3404
Port Freeport 1001 N Gulf Blvd	Freeport	TX	77541	**800-362-5743**	979-233-2667
Port Metro Vancouver 999 Canada Pl	Vancouver	BC	V6C3T4	**888-767-8826**	604-665-9000
Port of Anchorage 2000 Anchorage Port Rd	Anchorage	AK	99501	**877-650-8400**	907-343-6200
Port of Astoria 422 Gateway Ave	Astoria	OR	97103	**800-860-4093**	503-325-4521
Port of Baltimore *Maryland Port Administration* 401 E Pratt St	Baltimore	MD	21202	**800-638-7519***	
*General					
Port of Brownsville 1000 Foust Rd	Brownsville	TX	78521	**800-378-5395**	956-831-4592
Port of Corpus Christi 222 Power St	Corpus Christi	TX	78401	**800-580-7110**	361-882-5633
Port of Duluth *Duluth Seaway Port Authority* 1200 Port Terminal Dr	Duluth	MN	55802	**800-232-0703**	218-727-8525
Port of Everett 2911 Bond St Ste 202	Everett	WA	98201	**800-729-7678**	425-259-3164
Port of Milwaukee 2323 S Lincoln Memorial Dr	Milwaukee	WI	53207	**800-367-5690**	414-286-3511
Port of New Orleans 1350 Port of New Orleans Pl	New Orleans	LA	70130	**800-776-6652**	504-522-2551
Port of Orange *Orange County Navigation Port District* 1201 Childers Rd	Orange	TX	77630	**800-368-3749**	409-883-4363
Port of Palm Beach 1 E 11th St Ste 600	Riviera Beach	FL	33404	**877-377-1737**	561-842-4201
Port of Pensacola 700 S Barracks St	Pensacola	FL	32502	**800-711-1712**	850-436-5070
Port of Port Lavaca-Point Comfort *Calhoun Port Authority* PO Box 397	Point Comfort	TX	77978	**800-933-3643**	361-987-2813
Port of Portland 7200 NE Airport Way	Portland	OR	97218	**800-547-8411**	503-415-6000
Port of Richmond Commission 900 E Broad St	Richmond	VA	23219	**800-467-4943**	804-646-6335
Port of San Diego 3165 Pacific Hwy	San Diego	CA	92101	**800-854-2757**	619-686-6200
Port of San Francisco Pier 1 The Embarcadero	San Francisco	CA	94111	**800-479-5314**	415-274-0400
Port of Seattle PO Box 1209	Seattle	WA	98111	**800-426-7817**	206-728-3000
Port of Seward PO Box 167	Seward	AK	99664	**855-445-7131**	907-224-3138
Port of South Louisiana 171 Belle Terre Blvd PO Box 909	LaPlace	LA	70068	**866-536-8300**	985-652-9278
Port of Stockton 2201 W Washington St	Stockton	CA	95203	**800-344-3213**	209-946-0246
Port of Vancouver 3103 NW Lower River Rd	Vancouver	WA	98660	**800-475-8012**	360-693-3611
Sitka Harbor 617 Katlian St	Sitka	AK	99835	**866-948-8683**	907-747-3439
South Carolina State Ports Authority 176 Concord St	Charleston	SC	29401	**800-845-7106**	843-723-8651
Tampa Port Authority 1101 Channelside Dr	Tampa	FL	33602	**800-741-2297**	813-905-7678
Toledo-Lucas County Port Authority 1 Maritime Plaza	Toledo	OH	43604	**800-969-4700**	419-243-8251
Wrangell Harbor PO Box 531	Wrangell	AK	99929	**800-347-4462**	907-874-3736

618 POULTRY PROCESSING

SEE ALSO Meat Packing Plants

Name / Address	City	State	ZIP	Toll-Free	Phone
American Dehydrated Foods Inc 3801 E Sunshine	Springfield	MO	65809	**800-456-3447**	417-881-7755

Company / Address	City	State	Zip	Toll-Free	Phone
Amick Farms Inc 2079 Batesburg Hwy	Batesburg	SC	29006	**800-926-4257**	803-532-1400
Brakebush Bros Inc N4993 Sixth Dr	Westfield	WI	53964	**800-933-2121**	608-296-2121
Claxton Poultry Farms 8816 Hway 301 PO Box 428	Claxton	GA	30417	**888-739-3181**	912-739-3181
Culver Duck Farms Inc PO Box 910	Middlebury	IN	46540	**800-825-9225**	574-825-9537
Echo Lake Farm Produce Co PO Box 279	Burlington	WI	53105	**800-888-3447**	
Fieldale Farms Corp 555 Broiler Blvd	Baldwin	GA	30511	**800-241-5400**	706-778-5100
Foster Farms Inc PO Box 306 PO Box 457	Livingston	CA	95334	**800-255-7227**	
House of Raeford Farms Inc 520 E Central Ave	Raeford	NC	28376	**800-888-7539**	910-875-5161
Jennie-O Turkey Store 2505 Willmar Ave SW	Willmar	MN	56201	**800-621-3505**	320-235-2622
Koch Foods Inc 1300 Higgins Rd Ste 100	Park Ridge	IL	60068	**800-837-2778**	847-384-5940
Marshall Durbin Co 2830 Commerce Blvd *Sales	Birmingham	AL	35210	**800-245-8204***	205-380-3251
Michael Foods Inc 301 Carlson Pkwy Ste 400	Minnetonka	MN	55305	**800-328-5474**	952-258-4000
Mountaire Farms 17269 NC Hwy 71 N	Lumber Bridge	NC	28357	**877-887-1490**	910-843-5942
OK Foods Inc PO Box 1787	Fort Smith	AR	72902	**800-635-9441**	
Olymel LP 2200 Pratte Ave Pratte	Saint-Hyacinthe	QC	J2S4B6	**800-361-7990**	450-771-0400
Perdue Farms Inc 31149 Old Ocean City Rd	Salisbury	MD	21804	**800-473-7383**	410-543-3000
Pilgrim's Corp 1770 Promontory Cir *NASDAQ: PPC*	Greeley	CO	80634	**800-321-1470**	
Sonstegard Foods Co 5005 S Bur Oak Pl Ste 102	Sioux Falls	SD	57108	**800-533-3184**	
Tip Top Poultry Inc 327 Wallace Rd	Marietta	GA	30062	**800-241-5230**	770-973-8070
Tyson Foods Inc 2210 W Oaklawn Dr PO Box 2020 *NYSE: TSN*	Springdale	AR	72762	**800-643-3410**	479-290-4000
Valley Fresh Inc 3600 E Linwood Ave	Turlock	CA	95380	**800-523-4635**	209-669-5600
West Liberty Foods LLC 228 W Second St	West Liberty	IA	52776	**888-511-4500**	319-627-6000

619 POWER TRANSMISSION EQUIPMENT - MECHANICAL

SEE ALSO Bearings - Ball & Roller

Company / Address	City	State	Zip	Toll-Free	Phone
Allied-Locke Industries 1088 Corregidor Rd	Dixon	IL	61021	**800-435-7752**	815-288-1471
American Metal Bearing Co 7191 Acacia Ave	Garden Grove	CA	92841	**800-888-3048**	714-892-5527
Ameridrives Couplings 1802 Pittsburgh Ave PO Box 4000	Erie	PA	16502	**800-352-0141**	814-480-5000
AmeriDrives International 1802 Pittsburgh Ave	Erie	PA	16502	**800-352-0141**	814-480-5000
Barden Corp 200 Pk Ave	Danbury	CT	06810	**800-243-1060**	203-744-2211
Beemer Precision Inc 230 New York Dr PO Box 3080	Fort Washington	PA	19034	**800-836-2340**	215-646-8440
Bird Precision 1 Spruce St PO Box 540569 *Cust Svc	Waltham	MA	02454	**800-454-7369***	781-894-0160
Bishop-Wisecarver Corp 2104 Martin Way	Pittsburg	CA	94565	**888-580-8272**	925-439-8272
Buckeye Power Sales Company Inc 6850 Commerce Ct Dr PO Box 489	Blacklick	OH	43004	**800-523-3587**	614-861-6000
Cangro Industries Long Island Transmission Co 495 Smith St	Farmingdale	NY	11735	**800-422-9210**	631-454-9000
Carlyle Johnson Machine Co (CJM) 291 Boston Tpke	Bolton	CT	06043	**888-629-4867**	860-643-1531
Certified Power Inc 970 Campus Dr	Mundelein	IL	60060	**888-905-7411**	847-573-3800
Diamond Chain Co 402 Kentucky Ave *Cust Svc	Indianapolis	IN	46225	**800-872-4246***	317-638-6431
Force Control Industries Inc 3660 Dixie Hwy	Fairfield	OH	45014	**800-829-3244**	513-868-0900
General Bearing Corp 44 High St *Sales	West Nyack	NY	10994	**800-431-1766***	845-358-6000
GGB North America 700 Mid Atlantic Pkwy PO Box 189	Thorofare	NJ	08086	**888-840-2349**	856-848-3200
Hebeler Corp 2000 Military Rd	Tonawanda	NY	14150	**800-486-4709**	716-873-9300
Helical Products Co Inc 901 W McCoy Ln	Santa Maria	CA	93455	**877-353-9873**	805-928-3851
Horton Inc 2565 Walnut St	Saint Paul	MN	55113	**800-621-1320**	651-361-6400
John Deere Coffeyville Works Inc 2624 N US Hwy	Coffeyville	KS	67337	**800-844-1337**	
Kamatics Corp 1330 Blue Hills Ave	Bloomfield	CT	06002	**866-540-5760**	860-243-9704
Kingsbury Inc 10385 Drummond Rd *Sales	Philadelphia	PA	19154	**866-581-5464***	215-824-4000
Linn Gear Co 100 N Eigth St PO Box 397	Lebanon	OR	97355	**800-547-2471**	541-259-1211
Magtrol Inc 70 Gardenville Pkwy W	Buffalo	NY	14224	**800-828-7844**	716-668-5555
Marland Clutch 2032 VALLEYDALE Rd	Birmingham	AL	35244	**800-216-3515**	
Maurey Manufacturing Corp 410 Industrial Pk Rd	Holly Springs	MS	38635	**800-284-2161**	
Nook Industries 4950 E 49th St	Cleveland	OH	44125	**800-321-7800**	216-271-7900
NSK Corp 4200 Goss Rd	Ann Arbor	MI	48105	**888-446-5675**	800-675-9930
NTN Bearing Corp of America 1600 E Bishop Ct	Mount Prospect	IL	60056	**800-323-2358**	847-298-7500
OPW Engineered Systems 2726 Henkle Dr *Cust Svc	Lebanon	OH	45036	**800-547-9393***	513-932-9114
Peer Bearing Co 2200 Norman Dr S	Waukegan	IL	60085	**800-433-7337**	847-578-1000
Pic Design Corp 86 Benson Rd PO Box 1004	Middlebury	CT	06762	**800-243-6125**	203-758-8272
RBC Bearings Inc 3131 W Segerstrom Ave PO Box 1953	Santa Ana	CA	92704	**866-722-2376**	714-546-3131
Real Goods Solar 833 W S Boulder Rd *NASDAQ: RSGE*	Louisville	CO	80027	**888-567-6527**	
Regal-Beloit Corp 200 State St *NYSE: RBC*	Beloit	WI	53511	**800-672-6495**	608-364-8800
Renold Ajax Inc 100 Bourne St	Westfield	NY	14787	**800-251-9012**	716-326-3121
Schaeffler Group USA Inc 308 Springhill Farm Rd	Fort Mill	SC	29715	**800-361-5841**	803-548-8500
Solomon Corp 103 W Main	Solomon	KS	67480	**800-234-2867**	785-655-2191
Stock Drive Products/Sterling Instrument 2101 Jericho Tpke	New Hyde Park	NY	11040	**800-737-7436**	516-328-3300
TB Wood's Inc 440 N Fifth Ave	Chambersburg	PA	17201	**888-829-6637**	717-264-7161
US Tsubaki Inc 301 E Marquardt Dr	Wheeling	IL	60090	**800-323-7790**	847-459-9500
Warner Electric 449 Gardner St	South Beloit	IL	61080	**800-825-6544**	815-389-3771
Waukesha Bearings Corp W 231 N 2811 Roundy Cir E Ste 200	Pewaukee	WI	53072	**888-832-3517**	262-506-3000
Zero-Max Inc 13200 Sixth Ave N	Plymouth	MN	55441	**800-533-1731**	763-546-4300

620 PRECISION MACHINED PRODUCTS

SEE ALSO Machine Shops ; Aircraft Parts & Auxiliary Equipment

Company / Address	City	State	Zip	Toll-Free	Phone
Abbott Interfast Corp 190 Abbott Dr	Wheeling	IL	60090	**800-877-0789**	847-459-6200
Alger Mfg Company Inc 724 S Bon View Ave	Ontario	CA	91761	**800-854-9833**	909-986-4591
Bay Swiss Mfg Company Inc 5 Airpark Vista Blvd	Dayton	NV	89403	**800-247-3207**	775-246-7100
Biddle Precision Components Inc 701 S Main St	Sheridan	IN	46069	**800-428-4387**	317-758-4451
Boker's Inc 3104 Snelling Ave	Minneapolis	MN	55406	**800-927-4377**	612-729-9365
Cox Manufacturing Co 5500 N Loop 1604 E	San Antonio	TX	78247	**800-900-7981**	210-657-7731
Davies Molding LLC 350 Kehoe Blvd	Carol Stream	IL	60188	**800-554-9208**	630-510-8188
Elyria Mfg Corp 145 Northrup St PO Box 479	Elyria	OH	44035	**866-365-4171**	440-365-4171
Enoch Manufacturing Co 14242 SE 82nd Dr	Clackamas	OR	97015	**888-659-2660**	503-659-2660
Fairchild Auto-mated Parts Inc 10 White St	Winsted	CT	06098	**800-927-2545**	860-379-2725
Farrar Corp 142 W Burns St	Norwich	KS	67118	**800-536-2215**	620-478-2212
FCI Inc 4661 Giles Rd	Cleveland	OH	44135	**800-321-1032**	216-251-5200
Gates Albert Inc 3434 Union St	North Chili	NY	14514	**800-937-9311**	585-594-9401
Greystone of Lincoln Inc 7 Wellington Rd	Lincoln	RI	02865	**800-446-1761**	401-333-0444
H & H Swiss Screw Machine Products Company Inc 1478 Chestnut Ave	Hillside	NJ	07205	**800-826-9985**	
Horspool & Romine Manufacturing Inc 5850 Marshall St	Oakland	CA	94608	**800-446-2263**	
Kenlee Precision Corp 1701 Inverness Ave	Baltimore	MD	21230	**800-969-5278**	410-525-3800
Kerr Lakeside Inc 26841 Tungsten Rd	Euclid	OH	44132	**800-487-5377**	216-261-2100
Komet Of America Inc 2050 Mitchell Blvd	Schaumburg	IL	60193	**800-865-6638**	847-923-8400
Liberty Brass Turning Company Inc 38-01 Queens Blvd	Long Island	NY	11101	**800-345-5939**	718-784-2911
Metric Machining Co 1425 S Vineyard Ave	Ontario	CA	91761	**800-937-9311**	909-947-9222
Mold-Masters Injectioneering LLC 103 Peyerk Ct Ste E	Romeo	MI	48065	**800-387-2483**	586-752-6551
MSK Precision Products Inc 10101 NW 67th St	Tamarac	FL	33321	**800-992-5018**	954-776-0770
Multimatic Products Inc 390 Oser Ave	Hauppauge	NY	11788	**800-767-7633**	631-231-1515
New Castle Industries Inc 1399 Countyline Rd	New Castle	PA	16101	**800-897-2830**	724-656-5620
Omni-Lite Industries Canada Inc 17210 Edwards Rd	Cerritos	CA	90703	**800-577-6664**	562-404-8510
Pacific Aerospace & Electronics Inc 434 Olds Stn Rd	Wenatchee	WA	98801	**855-285-5200**	509-667-9600
Precisionform Inc 148 W Airport Rd	Lititz	PA	17543	**800-233-3821**	717-560-7610
Production Products Co 6176 E Molloy Rd	East Syracuse	NY	13057	**800-800-6652**	315-431-7200
RB Royal Industries Inc 1350 S Hickory St PO Box 1168	Fond du Lac	WI	54936	**800-892-1550**	920-921-1550
Roberts Automatic Products Inc 880 Lake Dr	Chanhassen	MN	55317	**800-879-9837**	952-949-1000
RW Screw Products Inc 999 Oberlin Rd SW	Massillon	OH	44647	**866-797-2739**	330-837-9211
SFS intec Inc Spring St & Van Reed Rd	Wyomissing	PA	19610	**800-234-4533**	610-376-5751

Company / Address	City	State	Zip	Toll-Free	Phone
Smith & Richardson Manufacturing Co PO Box 589	Geneva	IL	60134	**800-426-0876**	630-232-2581
Sperry Automatics Company Inc 1372 New Haven Rd PO Box 717	Naugatuck	CT	06770	**800-923-3709**	203-729-4589
Superior Products Inc 3786 Ridge Rd	Cleveland	OH	44144	**800-651-9490**	216-651-9400
Talladega Machinery & Supply Co Inc 301 N Johnson Ave PO Box 736	Talladega	AL	35161	**800-289-8672*** *Cust Svc	256-362-4124
Torco Inc 1330 Old 41 Hwy NW	Marietta	GA	30060	**800-876-5228**	770-427-3704
Trace-A-Matic Inc (T-A-M) 1570 Commerce Ave	Brookfield	WI	53045	**877-375-0217**	262-797-7300
Tri Tool Inc 3041 Sunrise Blvd	Rancho Cordova	CA	95742	**800-345-5015**	916-288-6100
Xaloy Inc 1399 Countyline Rd	New Castle	PA	16101	**800-897-2830**	

621 PREPARATORY SCHOOLS - BOARDING

SEE ALSO

Schools listed here are independent, college-preparatory schools that provide housing facilities for students and teachers. All are members of The Association of Boarding Schools (TABS), and many are considered to be among the top prep schools in the United States.

School / Address	City	State	Zip	Toll-Free	Phone
Albert College 160 Dundas St W	Belleville	ON	K8P1A6	**800-952-5237**	613-968-5726
American Boychoir School 19 Lambert Dr	Princeton	NJ	08540	**800-627-7468**	609-924-5858
Army & Navy Academy 2605 Carlsbad Blvd PO Box 3000	Carlsbad	CA	92018	**888-762-2338**	760-729-2385
Avon Old Farms School 500 Old Farms Rd	Avon	CT	06001	**800-464-2866**	860-404-4100
Bement School 94 Main St PO Box 8	Deerfield	MA	01342	**877-405-3949**	413-774-7061
Ben Lippen School 7401 Monticello Rd	Columbia	SC	29203	**800-777-2227**	803-786-7200
Berkshire School 245 N Undermountain Rd	Sheffield	MA	01257	**866-738-5500**	413-229-8511
Brewster Academy 80 Academy Dr	Wolfeboro	NH	03894	**800-842-9961**	603-569-7200
CFS the School at Church Farm PO Box 2000	Paoli	PA	19301	**800-439-4745**	610-363-7500
Chaminade College Preparatory School 425 S Lindbergh Blvd	Saint Louis	MO	63131	**877-378-6847**	314-993-4400
Chatham Hall 800 Chatham Hall Cir	Chatham	VA	24531	**877-644-2941**	434-432-2941
Christ School 500 Christ School Rd	Arden	NC	28704	**800-422-3212**	828-684-6232
Christchurch School 49 Seahorse Ln	Christchurch	VA	23031	**800-296-2306**	804-758-2306
Concord Academy 166 Main St	Concord	MA	01742	**800-768-2983**	978-402-2200
Culver Academies 1300 Academy Rd	Culver	IN	46511	**800-528-5837**	574-842-7000
Darlington School 1014 Cave Spring Rd	Rome	GA	30161	**800-368-4437**	706-235-6051
Darrow School 110 Darrow Rd	New Lebanon	NY	12125	**877-432-7769**	518-794-6000
Dunn School 2555 Hwy 154 PO Box 98	Los Olivos	CA	93441	**800-287-9197**	805-688-6471
Episcopal High School 1200 N Quaker Ln	Alexandria	VA	22302	**877-933-4347**	703-933-4062
Fay School 48 Main St	Southborough	MA	01772	**800-933-2925**	508-485-0100
Foxcroft School 22407 Foxhound Ln	Middleburg	VA	20117	**800-858-2364**	540-687-5555
George School 1690 Newtown-Langhorne Rd	Newtown	PA	18940	**888-804-1300**	215-579-6547
Gilmour Academy 34001 Cedar Rd	Gates Mills	OH	44040	**800-533-5140**	440-442-1104
Greenwood School 14 Greenwood Ln	Putney	VT	05346	**800-380-9218**	802-387-4545
Hargrave Military Academy (HMA) 200 Military Dr	Chatham	VA	24531	**800-432-2480**	434-432-2481
Hawaii Preparatory Academy 65-1692 Kohala Mountain Rd	Kamuela	HI	96743	**800-644-4481**	808-885-7321
Hebron Academy 339 Rd PO Box 309	Hebron	ME	04238	**888-432-7664**	207-966-2100
Hill School 717 E High St	Pottstown	PA	19464	**877-651-2800**	610-326-1000
Hillside School 404 Robin Hill Rd	Marlborough	MA	01752	**800-344-8328**	508-485-2824
Holderness School Chapel Ln PO Box 1879	Plymouth	NH	03264	**877-262-1492**	603-536-1747
Howe Military School PO Box 240	Howe	IN	46746	**888-462-4693**	260-562-2131
Indian Springs School 190 Woodward Dr	Pelham	AL	35124	**888-843-9477*** *General	205-988-3350
Kent School PO Box 2006	Kent	CT	06757	**800-538-5368**	860-927-6111
Kiski School 1888 Brett Ln	Saltsburg	PA	15681	**877-547-5448**	724-639-3586
Landmark School 429 Hale St PO Box 227	Prides Crossing	MA	01965	**866-333-0859**	978-236-3010
Lawrence Academy Powderhouse Rd PO Box 992	Groton	MA	01450	**800-977-4698**	978-448-6535
Lawrenceville School 2500 Main St PO Box 6008	Lawrenceville	NJ	08648	**800-735-2030**	609-896-0400
Linden Hall School for Girls 212 E Main St	Lititz	PA	17543	**800-258-5778**	717-626-8512
Linsly School 60 Knox Ln	Wheeling	WV	26003	**866-648-1893**	304-233-3260
Massanutten Military Academy 614 S Main St	Woodstock	VA	22664	**877-466-6222**	540-459-2167
McCallie School 500 Dodds Ave	Chattanooga	TN	37404	**800-234-2163**	423-624-8300
Mercersburg Academy 300 E Seminary St	Mercersburg	PA	17236	**800-588-2550**	717-328-6173
Milton Hershey School PO Box 830	Hershey	PA	17033	**800-322-3248**	717-520-2100
New York Military Academy 78 Academy Ave	Cornwall On Hudson	NY	12520	**888-275-6962**	845-534-3710
Northfield Mount Hermon School 1 Lamplighter Way	Gill	MA	01354	**866-664-4483**	413-498-3227
Olney Friends School 61830 Sandy Ridge Rd	Barnesville	OH	43713	**800-303-4291**	740-425-3655
Perkiomen School 200 Seminary St PO Box 130	Pennsburg	PA	18073	**866-966-9998**	215-679-9511
Phelps School 583 Sugartown Rd	Malvern	PA	19355	**800-344-8328**	610-644-1754
Phillips Academy 180 Main St	Andover	MA	01810	**877-445-5477**	978-749-4000
Phillips Exeter Academy 20 Main St	Exeter	NH	03833	**800-245-2525**	603-772-4311
Proctor Academy 204 Main St PO Box 500	Andover	NH	03216	**800-626-4907**	603-735-6000
Purnell School 51 Pottersville Rd PO Box 500	Pottersville	NJ	07979	**800-228-9290**	908-439-2154
Putney School 418 Houghton Brook Rd	Putney	VT	05346	**800-999-9080**	802-387-5566
Rabun Gap-Nacoochee School 339 Nacoochee Dr	Rabun Gap	GA	30568	**800-543-7467**	706-746-7467
Randolph-Macon Academy 200 Academy Dr	Front Royal	VA	22630	**800-272-1172**	540-636-5200
Riverside Military Academy 2001 Riverside Dr	Gainesville	GA	30501	**800-462-2338**	770-532-6251
Saint Andrew's College 15800 Yonge St	Aurora	ON	L4G3H7	**877-378-1899**	905-727-3178
Saint Andrew's School 3900 Jog Rd	Boca Raton	FL	33434	**888-357-7332**	561-210-2000
Saint Bernard Preparatory School 1600 St Bernard Dr SE	Cullman	AL	35055	**800-722-0999**	256-739-6682
Saint Catherine's School 6001 Grove Ave	Richmond	VA	23226	**800-648-4982**	804-288-2804
Saint John's Northwestern Military Academy 1101 N Genesee St	Delafield	WI	53018	**800-752-2338**	262-646-7115
Saint John's Preparatory School 1857 Watertower Rd PO Box 4000	Collegeville	MN	56321	**800-525-7737**	320-363-3321
Saint John's-Ravenscourt School 400 S Dr	Winnipeg	MB	R3T3K5	**800-437-0040**	204-477-2400
Saint Mary's School 900 Hillsborough St	Raleigh	NC	27603	**800-948-2557**	919-424-4000
Saint Michael's University School 3400 Richmond Rd	Victoria	BC	V8P4P5	**800-661-5199**	250-592-2411
San Marcos Academy 2801 Ranch to Market 12	San Marcos	TX	78666	**800-428-5120*** *Admissions	512-353-2400
Scattergood Friends School 1951 Delta Ave	West Branch	IA	52358	**888-737-4636**	319-643-7628
Shattuck-Saint Mary's School 1000 Shumway Ave PO Box 218	Faribault	MN	55021	**800-421-2724**	507-333-1616
Solebury School 6832 Phillips Mill Rd	New Hope	PA	18938	**800-675-6900**	215-862-5261
Storm King School 314 Mountain Rd	Cornwall On Hudson	NY	12520	**800-225-9144**	845-534-7892
Stuart Hall School 235 W Frederick St PO Box 210	Staunton	VA	24402	**888-306-8926**	540-885-0356
Valley Forge Military Academy & College 1001 Eagle Rd	Wayne	PA	19087	**800-234-8362**	610-989-1300
Vermont Academy PO Box 500	Saxtons River	VT	05154	**800-698-8867**	802-869-6229
Virginia Episcopal School 400 VES Rd	Lynchburg	VA	24503	**800-937-3582**	434-385-3607
Wasatch Academy 120 South 100 West	Mount Pleasant	UT	84647	**800-634-4690**	435-462-1400
Wayland Academy 101 N University Ave	Beaver Dam	WI	53916	**800-860-7725**	920-885-3373
Webb School PO Box 488	Bell Buckle	TN	37020	**888-733-9322**	931-389-9322
West Nottingham Academy 1079 Firetower Rd	Colora	MD	21917	**866-381-3684**	410-658-5556
Western Reserve Academy 115 College St	Hudson	OH	44236	**877-486-2048**	330-650-9717
Wilbraham & Monson Academy 423 Main St	Wilbraham	MA	01095	**800-616-3659**	413-596-6811
Woodlands Academy of the Sacred Heart 760 E Westleigh Rd	Lake Forest	IL	60045	**888-234-3080**	847-234-4300
Worcester Academy 81 Providence St	Worcester	MA	01604	**800-235-6426**	508-754-5302
Wyoming Seminary 201 N Sprague Ave	Kingston	PA	18704	**877-996-7361**	570-270-2160

622 PREPARATORY SCHOOLS - NON-BOARDING

School / Address	City	State	Zip	Toll-Free	Phone
Glen Mills Schools PO Box 5001	Concordville	PA	19331	**800-441-2064**	610-459-8100
Iolani School 563 Kamoku St	Honolulu	HI	96826	**888-879-8970**	808-949-5355
RenWeb School Management Software 101 E Renfro St Ste A	Burleson	TX	76028	**866-800-6593**	

623 PRESS CLIPPING SERVICES

Company / Address	City	State	Zip	Toll-Free	Phone
Appian Analytics Inc 2000 Crow Canyon Pl Ste 300	San Ramon	CA	94583	**877-757-7646**	
Art Resource Inc 536 Broadway 5th Fl	New York	NY	10012	**888-505-8666**	212-505-8700
Attendee Management Inc 15572 Ranch Rd 12 Ste 1	Wimberley	TX	78676	**877-947-5174**	512-847-5174
BurrellesLuce 30 B Vreeland Rd PO Box 674	Florham Park	NJ	07932	**800-631-1160**	973-992-6600

Company	Address	City	State	ZIP	Toll-Free	Phone
Datatech Labs	8000 e quincy ave	Denver	CO	80237	**888-288-3282**	303-770-3282
Florida Newsclips LLC	PO Box 2190	Palm Harbor	FL	34682	**800-442-0332**	
FlyData Inc	1043 N Shoreline Blvd Ste 200	Mountain View	CA	94043	**855-427-9787**	
InfySource Ltd	8345 NW 66th St	Miami	FL	33166	**800-275-7503**	
Insight Investments Corp	611 Anton Blvd Ste 700	Costa Mesa	CA	92626	**888-442-1441**	714-939-2300
Kentucky Press Assn	101 Consumer Ln *Cust Svc	Frankfort	KY	40601	**800-264-5721***	502-223-8821
LCS Technologies Inc	11230 Gold Express Dr Ste 310-140	Gold River	CA	95670	**855-277-5527**	
Oklahoma Press Service Inc	3601 N Lincoln Blvd	Oklahoma City	OK	73105	**888-815-2672**	405-524-4421
South Carolina Press Services Inc	106 Outlet Pointe Blvd PO Box 11429	Columbia	SC	29210	**888-727-7377**	803-750-9561
South Dakota Newspaper Services	1125 32nd Ave	Brookings	SD	57006	**800-658-3697**	605-692-4300
Thrive Networks Inc	836 North St Bldg 300 Ste 3201	Tewksbury	MA	01876	**866-205-2810**	978-461-3999
Virginia Press Services Inc	11529 Nuckols Rd	Glen Allen	VA	23059	**800-849-8717**	804-521-7570
West Virginia Press Association	3422 Pennsylvania Ave	Charleston	WV	25302	**800-235-6881**	304-342-6908

624 PRINTED CIRCUIT BOARDS

SEE ALSO Semiconductors & Related Devices ; Electronic Components & Accessories - Mfr

Company	Address	City	State	ZIP	Toll-Free	Phone
3Dlabs Inc Ltd	1901 McCarthy Blvd	Milpitas	CA	95035	**800-464-3348**	408-530-4700
Acromag Inc	30765 S Wixom Rd	Wixom	MI	48393	**877-295-7092**	248-624-1541
Advanced Circuits Inc	21101 E 32nd Pkwy	Aurora	CO	80011	**800-979-4722**	303-576-6610
Bourns Inc	1200 Columbia Ave	Riverside	CA	92507	**877-426-8767**	951-781-5690
Centon Electronics Inc	27412 Aliso Viejo Pkwy	Aliso Viejo	CA	92656	**800-234-9292**	949-855-9111
Circuit Express Inc	229 S Clark Dr	Tempe	AZ	85281	**800-979-4722**	
Creative Labs Inc	1901 McCarthy Blvd *Cust Svc	Milpitas	CA	95035	**800-998-1000***	408-428-6600
Crucial Technology	3475 E Commercial Ct	Meridian	ID	83642	**800-336-8915**	208-363-5790
Data Translation Inc	100 Locke Dr *OTC: DATX*	Marlborough	MA	01752	**800-525-8528**	508-481-3700
Dataram Corp	777 Alexander Rd Ste 100 *NASDAQ: DRAM*	Princeton	NJ	08540	**800-328-2726**	609-799-0071
Dynatem Inc	23263 Madero Ste C	Mission Viejo	CA	92691	**800-543-3830**	949-855-3235
GE Fanuc Embedded Systems Inc	7401 Snaproll NE	Albuquerque	NM	87109	**888-790-1820**	505-875-0600
GoldenRAM Computer Products	13 Whatney	Irvine	CA	92618	**800-222-8861**	949-460-9000
Hauppauge Computer Works Inc	91 Cabot Ct	Hauppauge	NY	11788	**800-443-6284**	631-434-1600
Hauppauge Digital Inc	91 Cabot Ct *OTC: HAUP*	Hauppauge	NY	11788	**800-443-6284**	631-434-1600
Holaday Circuits Inc	11126 Bren Rd W	Minnetonka	MN	55343	**800-362-3303**	952-933-3303
Intel Corp	2200 Mission College Blvd *NASDAQ: INTC* ■ *Cust Svc	Santa Clara	CA	95052	**800-628-8686***	408-765-8080
Jabil Circuit Inc	10560 ML King St N *NYSE: JBL*	Saint Petersburg	FL	33716	**877-217-6328**	727-577-9749
Kimball Electronics	13700 Reptron Blvd	Tampa	FL	33626	**800-903-8328**	813-814-5000
Kimball Electronics Group	1038 E 15th St	Jasper	IN	47549	**800-482-1616**	812-634-4200
Libra Industries Inc	7770 Div Dr	Mentor	OH	44060	**800-825-1674**	440-974-7770
Lone Star Circuits	901 Hensley Ln	Wylie	TX	75098	**800-303-9266**	214-291-1427
Micron Technology Inc	8000 S Federal Way *NASDAQ: MU*	Boise	ID	83707	**888-363-2589**	208-368-4000
Natel Engineering Co Inc	9340 Owensmouth Ave	Chatsworth	CA	91311	**800-590-5774**	818-734-6500
Parallax Inc	599 Menlo Dr Ste 100	Rocklin	CA	95765	**888-512-1024**	916-624-8333
Plexus Corp	1 Plexus Way PO Box 156 *NASDAQ: PLXS*	Neenah	WI	54957	**877-733-7260**	920-722-3451
Progress Instruments Inc	807 NW Commerce Dr	Lees Summit	MO	64086	**800-580-9881**	816-524-4442
Promise Technology Inc	580 Cottonwood Dr *Sales	Milpitas	CA	95035	**800-888-0245***	408-228-1400
Quatech Inc	5675 Hudson Industrial Pkwy	Hudson	OH	44236	**800-553-1170**	330-655-9000
RadiSys Corp	5445 NE Dawson Creek Dr *NASDAQ: RSYS*	Hillsboro	OR	97124	**800-950-0044**	503-615-1100
SAE Circuits Colorado Inc	4820 N 63rd St	Boulder	CO	80301	**800-234-9001**	303-530-1900
SigmaTron International Inc	2201 Landmeier Rd *NASDAQ: SGMA*	Elk Grove Village	IL	60007	**800-700-9095**	847-956-8000
Sopark Corp	3300 S Pk Ave	Buffalo	NY	14218	**866-576-7275**	716-822-0434
Spectrum Signal Processing by Vecima	2700 Production Way Ste 300	Burnaby	BC	V5A4X1	**800-663-8986**	604-676-6700
Unicircuit Inc	8192 Southpark Ln	Littleton	CO	80120	**800-648-6449**	303-730-0505
Unigen Corp	45388 Warm Springs Blvd	Fremont	CA	94539	**800-826-0808**	510-668-2088
Westak Inc	1225 Elko Dr	Sunnyvale	CA	94089	**800-387-3766**	408-734-8686
Wintec Industries Inc	675 Sycamore Dr	Milpitas	CA	95035	**866-989-4683**	408-856-0500
ZTEST Electronics Inc	523 Mcnicoll Ave	North York	ON	M2H2C9	**866-393-4891**	416-297-5155

625 PRINTING COMPANIES - BOOK PRINTERS

Company	Address	City	State	ZIP	Toll-Free	Phone
Adair Printing Technologies	7850 Second St	Dexter	MI	48130	**800-637-5025**	734-426-2822
Bang Printing Inc	3323 Oak St	Brainerd	MN	56401	**800-328-0450**	218-829-2877
CJK	3962 Virginia Ave	Cincinnati	OH	45227	**800-598-7808**	513-271-6035
Claitor's Law Books & Publishing	PO Box 261333	Baton Rouge	LA	70826	**800-274-1403**	225-344-0476
Cookbook Publishers Inc	9825 Widmer Rd	Lenexa	KS	66215	**800-227-7282**	913-492-5900
Cushing-Malloy Inc	1350 N Main St	Ann Arbor	MI	48104	**888-295-7244**	734-663-8554
E & M Bindery Inc	11 Peekay Dr	Clifton	NJ	07014	**800-736-2463**	973-777-9300
Garlich Printing Co	525 Rudder Rd	Fenton	MO	63026	**800-276-2622**	636-349-8000
Gospel Publishing House	1445 N Boonville Ave *Orders	Springfield	MO	65802	**800-641-4310***	417-862-2781
Houchen Bindery Ltd	340 First St	Utica	NE	68456	**800-869-0420**	402-534-2261
John Henry Co	5800 W Grand River Ave	Lansing	MI	48906	**800-748-0517**	517-323-9000
Jostens Inc	3601 Minnesota Ave Ste 400	Minneapolis	MN	55435	**800-235-4774**	952-830-3300
Library Reproduction Service	14214 S Figueroa St	Los Angeles	CA	90061	**800-255-5002**	
Moran Printing Inc	5425 Florida Blvd	Baton Rouge	LA	70806	**800-211-8335**	225-923-2550
Mossberg & Company Inc	301 E Sample St	South Bend	IN	46601	**800-428-3340**	574-289-9253
Publishers Press Inc	100 Frank E Simon Ave	Shepherdsville	KY	40165	**800-627-5801**	502-955-6526
Rose Printing Company Inc	2503 Jackson Bluff Rd	Tallahassee	FL	32304	**800-227-3725**	850-576-4151
RR Donnelley	111 S Wacker Dr	Chicago	IL	60606	**800-742-4455**	
Sheridan Group	11311 McCormick Rd Ste 260	Hunt Valley	MD	21031	**800-352-2210**	410-785-7277
Smith-Edwards-Dunlap Co	2867 E Allegheny Ave	Philadelphia	PA	19134	**800-829-0020**	215-425-8800
United Record Pressing LLC	453 Chestnut St	Nashville	TN	37203	**866-407-3165**	615-259-9396
Versa Press Inc	1465 Springbay Rd	East Peoria	IL	61611	**800-447-7829**	
Whitehall Printing Co	4244 Corporate Sq	Naples	FL	34104	**800-321-9290**	
Wright Color Graphics	9051 Sunland Blvd	Sun Valley	CA	91352	**877-246-8877**	818-246-8877

626 PRINTING COMPANIES - COMMERCIAL PRINTERS

Company	Address	City	State	ZIP	Toll-Free	Phone
1-800 Postcards Inc	121 Varick St	New York	NY	10013	**800-767-8227**	
4over Inc	5900 San Fernando Rd	Glendale	CA	91202	**877-782-2737**	
A&h Lithoprint Inc	2540 S 27th Ave	Broadview	IL	60155	**855-305-7628**	708-345-1196
Accu-Label Inc	2021 Research Dr	Fort Wayne	IN	46808	**888-482-5223**	260-482-5223
Acculink	1055 Greenville Blvd Sw	Greenville	NC	27834	**800-948-4110**	252-321-5805
AdMail Express Inc	31640 Hayman St	Hayward	CA	94544	**800-273-6245**	
Adp Media Group LLC	7700 Camp Bowie W Blvd Ste B	Fort Worth	TX	76116	**800-925-5700**	817-244-2740
Aka Printing & Mailing Inc	44 Joseph Mills Dr	Fredericksburg	VA	22408	**800-232-1515**	540-373-1111
Allied Photocopy Inc	1821 University Dr NW	Huntsville	AL	35801	**877-539-2973**	256-539-2973
Allied Printing Services Inc	1 Allied Way	Manchester	CT	06045	**800-225-8777**	860-643-1101
AlphaGraphics Inc	215 S State St Ste 320	Salt Lake City	UT	84111	**800-955-6246**	801-595-7270
Amidon Graphics	1966 Benson Ave	Saint Paul	MN	55116	**800-328-6502**	651-690-2401
Ampco Manufacturers Inc	9 Burbidge St Ste 101	Coquitlam	BC	V3K7B2	**800-663-5482**	604-472-3800
Angstrom Graphics	2025 McKinley St	Hollywood	FL	33020	**800-634-1262**	954-920-7300
Angstrom Graphics Inc	4437 E 49th St	Cleveland	OH	44125	**800-634-1262**	216-271-5300
Annan & Bird Lithographers Ltd	1060 Tristar Dr	Mississauga	ON	L5T1H9	**800-565-5618**	905-670-0604
Arandell Inc	N 82 W 13118 Leon Rd	Menomonee Falls	WI	53051	**800-558-8724**	262-255-4400
Arkansas Graphics Inc	800 S Gaines St	Little Rock	AR	72201	**877-918-4847**	501-376-8436

Classified Section

Company / Address	City	State	Zip	Toll-Free	Phone
Aus-Tex Printing & Mailing 2431 Forbes Dr	Austin	TX	78754	**800-472-7581**	512-476-7581
B & D Litho of Arizona 3820 N 38th Ave	Phoenix	AZ	85019	**800-735-0375**	602-269-2526
B H G Inc PO Box 309	Garrison	ND	58540	**800-658-3485**	701-463-2201
Bassett Printing Corp 3321 Fairystone Park Hwy	Bassett	VA	24055	**800-336-5102**	
BCW Diversified 514 E 31st St	Anderson	IN	46016	**800-433-4229**	765-644-2033
Beckmanxmo 376 Morrison Rd	Columbus	OH	43213	**800-864-2232**	614-864-2232
Bel Aire Displays 506 W Ohio Ave	Richmond	CA	94804	**877-439-4320**	510-439-4300
Bertek Systems Inc 133 Bryce Blvd	Fairfax	VT	05454	**800-367-0210**	802-752-3170
Better Label & Products Inc 3333 Empire Blvd SW	Atlanta	GA	30354	**800-448-1813**	404-763-8440
BFC Forms Service Inc 1051 N Kirk Rd	Batavia	IL	60510	**800-774-6840**	630-879-9240
Bibbero Systems Inc 1300 N McDowell Blvd	Petaluma	CA	94954	**800-242-2376**	707-778-3131
Bolger LLC 3301 Como Ave SE	Minneapolis	MN	55414	**866-264-3287**	651-645-6311
Bonanza Press Inc 19860 141st Pl NE	Woodinville	WA	98072	**800-233-0008**	425-486-3399
Bradley Graphic Solutions Inc 941 Mill Rd	Bensalem	PA	19020	**800-638-8223**	215-638-8771
Brady Palmer Label Corp 1791 Rt 6 Carmel PO Box 490	New York	NY	10512	**800-783-3097**	
Brenner Printing Inc 1234 Triplett St	San Antonio	TX	78216	**877-349-4024**	210-349-4024
Brimar Industries Inc 64 Outwater Ln	Garfield	NJ	07026	**800-274-6271**	
Burns Printing Inc 6131 Industrial Heights Dr	Knoxville	TN	37909	**866-288-5618**	865-584-2265
Burton & Mayer Inc W140 N9000 Lilly Rd	Menomonee Falls	WI	53051	**800-236-1770**	262-781-0770
Campbell Printing Co 2017 Cleveland Hwy	Dalton	GA	30721	**866-828-5240**	706-259-3344
Canfield & Tack Inc 925 Exchange St *General	Rochester	NY	14608	**800-836-0861***	585-235-7710
Carlson Craft Inc 1750 Tower Blvd	North Mankato	MN	56003	**800-774-6848**	
Cathedral Corp 632 Ellsworth Rd Griffis Technology Park	Rome	NY	13441	**800-698-0299**	315-338-0021
Century Marketing Solutions LLC 3000 Cameron St	Monroe	LA	71201	**800-256-6000**	
Challenge Printing Co, The 2 Bridewell Pl	Clifton	NJ	07014	**800-654-1234**	973-471-4700
Champion Industries Inc PO Box 2968 PO Box 2968 *OTC: CHMP*	Huntington	WV	25728	**800-624-3431**	304-528-2791
Click2mail 3103 10th St N Ste 201	Arlington	VA	22201	**866-665-2787**	703-521-9029
Cober Evolving Solutions 1351 Strasburg Rd	Kitchener	ON	N2R1H2	**800-263-7136**	519-745-7136
Color Ad Inc 19627 S Santa Fe Ave	Rancho Dominguez	CA	90221	**888-264-6991**	
Concord Litho Group 92 Old Tpke Rd	Concord	NH	03301	**800-258-3662**	603-225-3328
Content Management Corp 37900 Central Ct	Newark	CA	94560	**877-495-3720**	510-505-1100
Copy Cat Printing 365 N Broadwell Ave	Grand Island	NE	68803	**800-400-8520**	308-384-8520
Coral Color Process Ltd 50 Mall Dr	Commack	NY	11725	**800-564-7303**	631-543-5200
Cosmos Communications Inc 11-05 44th Dr	Long Island	NY	11101	**800-223-5751**	718-482-1800
Courier Graphics Corp 2621 S 37th St	Phoenix	AZ	85034	**800-454-6381**	602-437-9700
Courier Printing 1 Courier Pl	Smyrna	TN	37167	**800-467-0444**	615-355-4000
Coyle Reproductions Inc 14949 Firestone Blvd	La Mirada	CA	90638	**866-269-5373**	714-690-8200
Craftsman Printing Inc 120 Citation Ct	Birmingham	AL	35209	**800-543-1051**	205-942-3939
Crossmark Graphics Inc 16100 W Overland Dr	New Berlin	WI	53151	**800-236-1994**	262-821-1343
Datamark Graphics Inc 603 W Bailey St	Asheboro	NC	27203	**888-629-6300**	
David A Smith Printing Inc 742 S 22nd St	Harrisburg	PA	17104	**800-564-3117**	717-564-3719
Davis Direct Inc 1241 Newell Pkwy	Montgomery	AL	36110	**877-277-0878**	334-277-0878
Di Graphics Inc 4850 Ward Rd	Wheat Ridge	CO	80033	**800-433-2257**	303-425-0510
Digital Room Inc 8000 Haskell Ave	Van Nuys	CA	91406	**866-266-5047**	
Direct Connection Printing & Mailing 1968 Yeager Ave	La Verne	CA	91750	**800-420-9937**	909-392-2334
Document Security Systems Inc 200 Canal View Blvd Ste 300 *NYSE: DSS*	Rochester	NY	14623	**877-407-8031**	585-325-3610
Dolphin Shirt Co 757 Buckley Rd	San Luis Obispo	CA	93401	**800-377-3256**	805-541-2566
Dome Printing 340 Commerce Cir	Sacramento	CA	95815	**800-343-3139**	
Dowling Graphics Inc 12920 Automobile Blvd	Clearwater	FL	33762	**800-749-6933**	727-573-5997
Downeast Graphics & Printing Inc 477 Washington Jct Rd	Ellsworth	ME	04605	**800-427-5582**	207-667-5582
Drug Package Inc 901 Drug Package Ln	O'Fallon	MO	63366	**800-325-6137**	
Dupli Graphics Corp 6761 Thompson Rd N	Syracuse	NY	13211	**800-724-2477**	
DuraColor 1840 Oakdale Ave	Racine	WI	53406	**877-899-7900**	
Emerald City Graphics 23328 66th Ave S *General	Kent	WA	98032	**877-631-5178***	253-520-2600
FCL Graphics Inc 4600 N Olcott Ave	Harwood Heights	IL	60706	**800-274-3380**	708-867-5500
Fineline Printing Group 8081 Zionsville Rd	Indianapolis	IN	46268	**877-334-7687**	317-872-4490
Flagship Press Inc 150 Flagship Dr	North Andover	MA	01845	**800-733-1520**	978-975-3100
Flexo Impressions 8647 Eagle Creek Pkwy	Savage	MN	55378	**800-752-2357**	952-884-9442
Fort Orange Press Inc 11 Sand Creek Rd	Albany	NY	12205	**800-777-3233**	518-489-3233
Fotoprint 975 Pandora Ave	Victoria	BC	V8V3P4	**888-382-8211**	250-382-8218
Franklin Imaging LLC 500 Schrock Rd	Columbus	OH	43229	**877-885-6894**	614-885-6894
Fruitridge Printing & Lithograph Inc 3258 Stockton Blvd	Sacramento	CA	95820	**800-835-4846**	916-452-9213
Fundcraft Publishing Inc 410 Hwy 72 W	Collierville	TN	38027	**800-964-5715**	901-853-7070
Garrity Print Solutions 109 Research Dr	Harahan	LA	70123	**877-568-1555**	504-733-9654
Gazette Publishing Inc 1114 Broadway	Wheaton	MN	56296	**800-567-8303**	320-563-8146
Genie Repros Inc 2211 Hamilton Ave	Cleveland	OH	44114	**877-496-6611**	216-696-6677
Georgia Printco 90 S Oak St	Lakeland	GA	31635	**866-572-0146**	
Globe Ticket & Label Co 11 Eisenhower Ln S	Lombard	IL	60148	**800-523-5968**	
Goetz Printing Co, The 7939 Angus Ct	Springfield	VA	22153	**866-245-0977**	703-569-8232
Gooding Company Inc 5568 Davison Rd	Lockport	NY	14094	**800-769-7768**	716-434-5501
Graphics Type & Color Enterprises Inc 2300 NW Seventh Ave	Miami	FL	33127	**800-433-9298**	305-591-7600
Grit Commercial Printing Inc 80 Choate Cir	Montoursville	PA	17754	**800-872-0409**	570-368-8021
Grove Printing Corp 4225 Howard Ave	Kensington	MD	20895	**877-290-5793**	301-571-1024
Harper Engraving & Printing Co 2626 Fisher Rd	Columbus	OH	43204	**800-848-5196**	614-276-0700
Hart Industries Inc 11412 Cronridge Dr	Owings Mills	MD	21117	**800-638-2700**	410-581-1900
Harty Press Inc, The PO Box 324	New Haven	CT	06513	**800-654-0562**	203-562-5112
Heyman Printing LLC 2083 Holmgren Way	Green Bay	WI	54304	**800-236-4815**	920-499-4815
Hickory Printing Group Inc 725 Reese Dr SW	Conover	NC	28613	**800-442-5679**	828-465-3431
Ideal Jacobs Corp 515 Valley St	Maplewood	NJ	07040	**877-873-4332**	973-275-5100
imageMEDIA Inc 425 E Spruce	St Tarpon Springs	FL	34689	**866-885-4468**	727-772-8889
Immedia Inc 3311 Broadway St NE	Minneapolis	MN	55413	**866-832-2734**	612-524-3400
Inland Arts & Graphics Inc 14440 Edison Dr	New Lenox	IL	60451	**800-437-6003**	
IntegraColor 3210 Innovative Way	Mesquite	TX	75149	**800-933-9511**	972-289-0705
Intelligencer Printing Co 330 Eden Rd	Lancaster	PA	17601	**800-233-0107**	
Interprint Inc 12350 US Hwy 19 N	Clearwater	FL	33764	**800-749-5152**	727-531-8957
Interprint LLC 7111 Hayvenhurst Ave	Van Nuys	CA	91406	**800-926-9873**	818-989-3600
J & A Printing Inc PO Box 457	Hiawatha	IA	52233	**800-793-1781**	319-393-1781
Jena Communications 125 Stokes Ave	Stroudsburg	PA	18360	**800-367-5362**	570-476-6900
John Roberts Co 9687 E River Rd	Coon Rapids	MN	55433	**800-551-1534**	763-755-5500
Kay Toledo Tag Inc PO Box 5038	Toledo	OH	43612	**800-822-8247**	419-729-5479
Kelly Press Inc 1701 Cabin Branch Dr	Cheverly	MD	20785	**888-535-5940**	301-386-2800
Kennickell Printing Co 1700 E President St	Savannah	GA	31404	**800-673-6455**	
Knox Services 2250 Fourth Ave	San Diego	CA	92101	**800-995-6694**	619-233-9700
Koza Inc 2910 S Main St	Pearland	TX	77581	**800-594-5555**	281-485-1462
La Crosse Graphics Inc 3025 East Ave S	La Crosse	WI	54601	**800-832-2503**	608-788-2500
Label Systems Inc 4111 Lindbergh Dr	Addison	TX	75001	**800-220-9552**	972-387-4512
Label Works 2025 Lookout Dr	North Mankato	MN	56003	**800-522-3558**	
Lake Erie Graphics Inc 5372 W 130th St	Brook Park	OH	44142	**888-293-7397**	216-265-7575
Lane Press Inc 87 Meadowland Dr PO Box 130	Burlington	VT	05402	**800-733-3740**	802-863-5555
Laser Image Inc 2451 N Stemmons Fwy	Dallas	TX	75207	**866-812-3491**	
Lasting Impressions Inc 7406 43rd Ave NE	Marysville	WA	98270	**866-859-7625**	360-659-1255
Lew A. Cummings Company Inc 4 Peters Brook Dr	Hooksett	NH	03106	**800-647-0035**	
Litho-Krome Co 5700 Old Brim Dr	Midland	GA	31820	**800-572-8028**	706-562-7900
LogoNation Inc PO Box 3847 Ste 102	Mooresville	NC	28117	**800-955-7375**	704-799-0612
Lowen Corp PO Box 1528	Hutchinson	KS	67504	**800-835-2365**	620-663-2161
Lti Printing Inc 518 N Centerville Rd	Sturgis	MI	49091	**800-592-6990**	269-651-7574
M & R Sales & Service Inc 1n 372 Main St	Glen Ellyn	IL	60137	**800-736-6431**	630-858-6101
M&D Printing 515 University Ave	Henry	IL	61537	**888-242-7552**	309-364-3957

Company / Address	City	State	Zip	Toll-Free	Phone
M. Lee Smith Publishers LLC PO Box 5094	Brentwood	TN	37024	**800-274-6774**	615-373-7517
Magna IV 2401 Commercial Ln	Little Rock	AR	72206	**800-946-2462**	501-376-2397
Marina Graphic Center 12901 Cerise Ave	Hawthorne	CA	90250	**800-974-5777**	310-970-1777
Mercersburg Printing 9964 Buchanan Trl W	Mercersburg	PA	17236	**800-955-3902**	717-328-3902
Mercury Press Inc 1910 S Nicklas St	Oklahoma City	OK	73128	**800-423-5984**	405-682-3468
Merrill Corp 1 Merrill Cir	Saint Paul	MN	55108	**800-688-4400**	651-646-4501
Midland Information Resources Co 5440 Corporate Pk Dr	Davenport	IA	52807	**800-232-3696**	563-359-3696
Mines Press Inc, The 231 Croton Ave	Cortlandt Manor	NY	10567	**800-447-6788**	914-788-1698
Minuteman Press International Inc 61 Executive Blvd	Farmingdale	NY	11735	**800-645-3006**	631-249-1370
Modern Way Printing & Fulfillment 8817 Production Ln	Ooltewah	TN	37363	**800-603-5135**	423-238-4500
Morris Printing Group 3212 Hwy 30 E	Kearney	NE	68847	**800-445-6621**	308-236-7888
MR Label Inc 5018 Gray Rd	Cincinnati	OH	45232	**888-522-3526**	513-681-2088
Nameplate & Panel Technology 387 Gundersen Dr	Carol Stream	IL	60188	**800-833-8397**	630-690-9360
ND Graphic Product Ltd 55 Interchange Way Unit 1	Concord	ON	L4K5W3	**800-811-0194**	416-663-6416
Northern Ohio Printing Inc 4721 Hinckley Indus Pkwy	Cleveland	OH	44109	**800-407-7284**	216-398-0000
Nta Graphics South Inc 501 Republic Cir	Birmingham	AL	35214	**888-798-2123**	205-798-2123
Pacific Color Graphics 440 Boulder Ct 100d	Pleasanton	CA	94566	**888-551-1482**	925-600-3006
Page International Communications 2748 Bingle Rd	Houston	TX	77055	**888-464-8484**	713-464-8484
Paradigm Imaging Group 1590 Metro Dr Ste 116	Costa Mesa	CA	92626	**888-221-7226**	714-432-7226
Pazazz Printing Inc 5584 Cote-de-Liesse	Montreal	QC	H4P1A9	**866-449-4417**	514-856-3330
PBM Graphics Inc 3700 S Miami Blvd	Durham	NC	27703	**800-849-8100**	919-544-6222
Peake DeLancey Printers LLC 2500 Schuster Dr	Cheverly	MD	20781	**800-521-7325**	301-341-4600
Perkinson Reprographics Inc 735 E Brill St	Phoenix	AZ	85006	**888-330-8782**	602-393-3131
Platon Digital Graphics 136 Oregon St	El Segundo	CA	90245	**800-499-0292**	
Pollock Printing Company Inc 928 Sixth Ave South	Nashville	TN	37203	**800-349-1205**	615-255-0526
Premier Graphics LLC 1248 W Fourth St	Mansfield	OH	44906	**800-511-4881**	203-378-6200
Print Direction Inc 1600 Indian Brook Way	Norcross	GA	30093	**877-435-1672**	770-446-6446
Print Papa 1920 Lafayette St Ste L	Santa Clara	CA	95050	**800-657-7181**	408-567-9553
Print Works 3850 98 St Nw	Edmonton	AB	T6E3L2	**888-452-8921**	780-452-8921
Printing Images Inc 12266 Wilkins Ave A	Rockville	MD	20852	**866-685-4356**	301-984-1140
PrintingForLess.com Inc 100 PFL Way	Livingston	MT	59047	**800-930-6040**	
PrintPlace.com 1130 Ave H E	Arlington	TX	76011	**877-405-3949**	817-701-3555
Prisma Graphic Corp 2937 E Broadway Rd	Phoenix	AZ	85040	**800-379-5777**	602-243-5777
Production Press Inc 307 E Morgan St	Jacksonville	IL	62650	**800-231-3880**	217-243-3353
ProForma 8800 E Pleasant Vly Rd	Independence	OH	44131	**800-825-1525**	216-520-8400
Progress Printing Co 2677 Waterlick Rd	Lynchburg	VA	24502	**800-572-7804**	
Prosource Fitness Equipment 6503 Hilburn Dr	Raleigh	NC	27613	**877-781-8077**	919-781-8077
Publication Printers Corp 2001 S Platte River Dr	Denver	CO	80223	**888-824-0303**	303-936-0303
Quick Color Solutions Inc 829 Knox Rd	Mc Leansville	NC	27301	**877-698-0951**	336-698-0951
Quick Tab Ii Inc 241 Heritage Dr	Tiffin	OH	44883	**800-332-5081**	419-448-6622
Rand Graphics Inc 500 S Florence St	Wichita	KS	67209	**800-435-7263**	316-942-1218
Regal Press Inc, The 129 Guild St	Norwood	MA	02062	**800-447-3425**	781-769-3900
Reindl Printing Inc 1300 Johnson St	Merrill	WI	54452	**800-236-9637**	715-536-9537
Reni Publishing Inc 150 Third St SW	Winter Haven	FL	33880	**800-274-2812**	
Rinaldi Printing Co 4514 E Adamo Dr	Tampa	FL	33605	**800-766-3224**	813-247-3921
RMF Printing Technologies Inc 50 Pearl St	Lancaster	NY	14086	**800-828-7999**	716-683-7500
Robyn Inc 7717 W Britton Rd	Oklahoma City	OK	73132	**877-211-9711**	
Rogers Printing Inc PO Box 215	Ravenna	MI	49451	**800-622-5591**	231-853-2244
Rotary Multiforms Inc 1340 E 11 Mile Rd	Madison Heights	MI	48071	**800-762-5644**	586-558-7960
Senton Printing & Packaging Inc 1669 Oxford St E	London	ON	N5V2Z5	**800-445-9808**	519-455-5500
Sharprint Silkscreen & Graphics Inc 4200 W Wrightwood Ave	Chicago	IL	60639	**888-800-5646**	773-862-9300
Sheridan Group 11311 McCormick Rd Ste 260	Hunt Valley	MD	21031	**800-352-2210**	410-785-7277
Sign-ups & Banners Corp 2764 W T C Jester Blvd	Houston	TX	77018	**877-682-7979**	713-682-7979
Sir Speedy Inc 26722 Plaza Dr	Mission Viejo	CA	92691	**800-854-8297**	949-348-5000
SMS Productions Inc 10555 Guilford Rd Ste 114	Jessup	MD	20794	**800-289-7671**	301-953-0011
Solisco Inc 120 10e Rue	Scott	QC	G0S3G0	**800-463-4188**	418-387-8908
Solo Printing Inc 7860 NW 66th St	Miami	FL	33166	**800-325-0118**	305-594-8699
Southland Printing Company Inc 213 Airport Dr	Shreveport	LA	71107	**800-241-8662**	318-221-8662
Sp Mount 1306 E 55th St	Cleveland	OH	44103	**800-503-5022**	216-881-3316
Spartan Graphics Inc 200 Applewood Dr	Sparta	MI	49345	**800-747-4477**	616-887-8243
Square 1 Art LLC 5470 Oakbrook Pkwy Ste E	Norcross	GA	30093	**888-332-3294**	678-906-2291
Stafford Printing Co 2707 Jefferson Davis Hwy	Stafford	VA	22554	**800-774-6831**	540-659-4554
Streeter Printing Inc 9880 Via Pasar	San Diego	CA	92126	**866-787-3383**	858-566-0866
Super Color Digital LLC 16761 Hale Ave	Irvine	CA	92606	**800-979-4446**	949-622-0010
Swift Print Communication 1248 Research Blvd	Saint Louis	MO	63132	**800-545-1141**	314-991-4300
Tenenz Inc 9655 Penn S Ave	Minneapolis	MN	55431	**800-888-5803**	
Times Printing Company Inc 100 Industrial Dr	Random Lake	WI	53075	**800-236-4396**	920-994-4396
Total Printing Systems 201 S Gregory St	Newton	IL	62448	**800-465-5200**	
Transfer Express Inc 7650 Tyler Blvd	Mentor	OH	44060	**800-622-2280**	440-918-1900
Travers Printing Inc 32 Mission St	Gardner	MA	01440	**800-696-0530**	978-632-0530
Tuttle Law Print Inc 414 Quality Ln	Rutland	VT	05701	**800-776-7682**	
Valassis Communications Inc 19975 Victor Pkwy *NYSE: VCI*	Livonia	MI	48152	**800-437-0479**	734-591-3000
Valley Offset Printing Inc 160 S Sheridan Ave	Valley Center	KS	67147	**888-895-7913**	316-755-0061
Victorystore.Com Inc 5200 SW 30Th St	Davenport	IA	52802	**866-241-2295**	
Walter Snyder Printer Inc 691 River St	Troy	NY	12180	**888-272-9774**	518-272-8881
Warren Printing & Mailing Inc 5000 Eagle Rock Blvd	Los Angeles	CA	90041	**888-468-6976**	323-258-2621
Watson Label Products 10616 Trenton Ave	Saint Louis	MO	63132	**800-678-6715**	314-493-9300
Watt Printing Co 4544 Hinckley Industrial Pkwy	Cleveland	OH	44109	**800-273-2170**	216-398-2000
Weatherall Printing Co 1349 Cliff Gookin Blvd	Tupelo	MS	38801	**800-273-6043**	662-842-5284
Weldon Williams & Lick Inc 711 N A St	Fort Smith	AR	72901	**800-242-4995**	479-783-4113
Wells Printing Company Inc 6030 Perimeter Pkwy	Montgomery	AL	36116	**800-264-4958**	334-281-3449
Wendling Printing Co 111 Beech St	Newport	KY	41071	**800-998-9553**	859-261-8300
Wentworth Printing Corp 101 N 12th St	West Columbia	SC	29169	**800-326-0784**	803-796-9990
West Press Printing & Copying 1663 W Grant Rd	Tucson	AZ	85745	**888-637-0337**	520-624-4939
Xlibris Corp 1663 Liberty Dr Ste 200	Bloomington	IN	47403	**888-795-4274**	
Zookbinders Inc 151-K S Pfingsten Rd Ste	Deerfield	IL	60015	**800-810-5745**	

627 PRINTING & PHOTOCOPYING SUPPLIES

Company / Address	City	State	Zip	Toll-Free	Phone
Abco Distribution Inc 6282 Proprietors Rd	Worthington	OH	43085	**800-821-9435**	
Buckeye Business Products Inc 3830 Kelley Ave	Cleveland	OH	44114	**800-837-4323**	
Chromaline Corp 4832 Grand Ave	Duluth	MN	55807	**800-328-4261**	218-628-2217
Color Imaging Inc 4350 Peachtree Industrial Blvd Ste 100	Norcross	GA	30071	**800-783-1090**	770-840-1090
DuraLine Imaging Inc 110 Commercial Blvd	Flat Rock	NC	28731	**800-982-3872**	828-692-1301
Graphic Controls LLC 400 Exchange St	Buffalo	NY	14204	**800-669-1535**	
Hurst Chemical Co 2360 Eastman Ave Ste 108 *Cust Svc	Oxnard	CA	93030	**800-723-2004***	
Image One Corp 13201 Capital Ave	Oak Park	MI	48237	**800-799-5377**	248-414-9955
Ink Technology Corp 18320 Lanken Ave	Cleveland	OH	44119	**800-633-2826**	216-486-6720
LexJet Corp 1680 Fruitville Rd 3rd Fl	Sarasota	FL	34236	**800-453-9538**	941-330-1210
Light Impressions 100 Carlson Rd	Rochester	NY	14610	**800-975-6429**	
Micro Solutions Enterprises (MSE) 8201 Woodley Ave	Van Nuys	CA	91406	**800-673-4968**	818-407-7500
NER Data Products Inc 307 S Delsea Dr	Glassboro	NJ	08028	**888-637-3282**	
Pad Print Machinery of Vermont Inc 201 Tennis Way	East Dorset	VT	05253	**800-272-7764**	802-362-0844
Rayven Inc 431 Griggs St N *Cust Svc	Saint Paul	MN	55104	**800-878-3776***	651-642-1112
WNC Supply LLC 37841 N 16th St	Phoenix	AZ	85086	**800-538-5108**	623-594-4602

628 PRINTING & PUBLISHING EQUIPMENT & SYSTEMS

SEE ALSO Printers

Company / Address	City	State	Zip	Toll-Free	Phone
Brackett Inc 75115 SE Forbes Ave Bldg 451 J	Topeka	KS	66619	**800-255-3506**	785-862-2205
Brandtjen & Kluge Inc 539 Blanding Woods Rd	Saint Croix Falls	WI	54024	**800-826-7320**	715-483-3265
Burgess Industries Inc (BII) 7500 Boone Ave N Ste 111	Brooklyn Park	MN	55428	**800-233-2589**	763-553-7800
Gravograph-New Hermes Inc 2200 Northmont Pkwy	Duluth	GA	30096	**800-843-7637**	770-623-0331
Heidelberg USA Inc 1000 Gutenberg Dr *Cust Svc	Kennesaw	GA	30144	**888-472-9655***	770-419-6500
LasscoWizer Inc 485 Hague St	Rochester	NY	14606	**800-854-6595**	585-436-1934
Mark Andy Inc 18081 Chesterfield Airport Rd	Chesterfield	MO	63005	**800-700-6275**	636-532-4433
Pamarco Global Graphics 235 E 11th Ave	Roselle	NJ	07203	**800-365-6510**	908-241-1200
Presstek Inc 55 Executive Dr *NASDAQ: PRST*	Hudson	NH	03051	**800-422-3616**	603-595-7000
Rosback Co 125 Hawthorne Ave	Saint Joseph	MI	49085	**800-542-2420**	269-983-2582
Xerox Corp 45 Glover Ave PO Box 4505 *NYSE: XRX*	Norwalk	CT	06856	**800-327-9753**	203-968-3000

629 PUBLIC BROADCASTING ORGANIZATIONS

SEE ALSO Television Networks - Broadcast ; Radio Networks

Prison industries are programs established by federal and state governments that provide work for inmates while they are incarcerated as well as on-the-job training to help them become employable on release. At the same time, prison industries provide quality goods and services at competitive prices.

Company / Address	City	State	Zip	Toll-Free	Phone
Alabama Correctional Industries 1400 Lloyd St	Montgomery	AL	36107	**800-224-7007**	334-261-3600
Alabama Educational Television Commission 2112 11th Ave S Ste 400	Birmingham	AL	35205	**800-239-5233**	205-328-8756
Alabama Public Television (APT) 2112 11th Ave S Ste 400	Birmingham	AL	35205	**800-239-5233**	205-328-8756
Annenberg Media 1301 Pennsylvania Ave NW ste302	Washington	DC	20004	**800-532-7637**	
Arkansas Correctional Industries (ACI) 6841 W. 13th St	Pine Bluff	AR	71602	**877-635-7213**	870-730-0385
Arkansas Educational Television Network (AETN) 350 S Donaghey Ave	Conway	AR	72034	**800-662-2386**	501-682-2386
Badger State Industries (BSI) 3099 E Washington Ave PO Box 8990	Madison	WI	53708	**800-862-1086**	608-240-5200
Blue Ridge Public Television 1215 McNeil Dr	Roanoke	VA	24015	**888-332-7788**	540-344-0991
California Public Radio 4100 Vachell Ln	San Luis Obispo	CA	93401	**800-549-8855**	805-549-8855
Capitol Steps Productions Inc 210 N Washington St	Alexandria	VA	22314	**800-733-7837**	703-683-8330
Commonwealth Club of California 595 Market St 2nd Fl	San Francisco	CA	94105	**800-933-7548**	415-597-6700
Connecticut Public Broadcasting Inc (CPBI) 1049 Asylum Ave	Hartford	CT	06105	**800-683-2112**	860-278-5310
Cornhusker State Industries 800 Pioneers Blvd	Lincoln	NE	68502	**800-348-7537**	402-471-4597
Corporation for Public Broadcasting (CPB) 401 Ninth St NW	Washington	DC	20004	**800-272-2190**	202-879-9600
Correctional Enterprises of Connecticut 24 Wolcott Hill Rd	Wethersfield	CT	06109	**800-842-1146**	860-263-6839
East Tennessee Public Communications Corp 1611 E Magnolia Ave	Knoxville	TN	37917	**844-686-2378**	865-595-0220
Federal Prison Industries Inc 320 First St NW	Washington	DC	20534	**800-827-3168**	
Georgia Correctional Industries 2984 Clifton Springs Rd	Decatur	GA	30034	**800-282-7130**	404-244-5100
Georgia Public Broadcasting (GPB) 260 14th St NW	Atlanta	GA	30318	**800-222-6006**	
GPB Education 260 14th St NW	Atlanta	GA	30318	**888-501-8960**	404-685-2550
Hawaii Public Television 2350 Dole St	Honolulu	HI	96822	**800-238-4847**	808-973-1000
Idaho Public Television (IPTV) 1455 N Orchard St	Boise	ID	83706	**800-543-6868**	208-373-7220
Independent Television Service (ITVS) 651 Brannan St Ste 410	San Francisco	CA	94107	**800-621-6196**	415-356-8383
Iowa Prison Industries (IPI) 1445 E Grand Ave	Des Moines	IA	50316	**800-670-4537**	515-242-5770
Kentucky Correctional Industries 1041 Leestown Rd	Frankfort	KY	40601	**800-828-9524**	502-573-1040
Kentucky Educational Television (KET) 600 Cooper Dr	Lexington	KY	40502	**800-432-0951**	859-258-7000
KUAC FM/TV PO Box 755620	Fairbanks	AK	99775	**800-727-6543**	907-474-7491
Louisiana Public Broadcasting 7733 Perkins Rd	Baton Rouge	LA	70810	**800-973-7246**	225-767-5660
Maine Public Broadcasting Network (MPBN) 65 Texas Ave	Bangor	ME	04401	**800-884-1717**	207-941-1010
Maryland Public Television (MPT) 11767 Owings Mills Blvd	Owings Mills	MD	21117	**800-223-3678**	410-581-4201
Massachusetts Correctional Industries 1 Industries Dr Bldg A PO Box 188	Norfolk	MA	02056	**800-222-2211**	508-850-1070
Minnesota Public Radio (MPR) 480 Cedar St	Saint Paul	MN	55101	**800-228-7123**	651-290-1212
Mississippi Authority for Educational Television 3825 Ridgewood Rd	Jackson	MS	39211	**800-850-4406**	601-432-6565
Missouri Vocational Enterprises 1717 Industrial Dr PO Box 1898 *Sales	Jefferson City	MO	65102	**800-392-8486***	573-751-6663
Montana Public Radio 32 Campus Dr University of Montana	Missoula	MT	59812	**800-325-1565**	406-243-4931
Montana Public Television 183 Visual Communications Bldg	Bozeman	MT	59717	**800-426-8243**	866-832-0829
National Captioning Institute (NCI) 3725 Concorde Pkwy Ste 100	Chantilly	VA	20151	**800-825-6758**	703-917-7600
National Educational Telecommunications Assn (NETA) 939 S Stadium Rd	Columbia	SC	29201	**866-270-5141**	803-799-5517
Nebraska Educational Telecommunications (NET) 1800 N 33rd St	Lincoln	NE	68503	**800-868-1868**	
New Hampshire Public Television (NHPTV) 268 Mast Rd	Durham	NH	03824	**800-639-8408**	603-868-1100
New Jersey Bureau of State Use Industries 163 N Olden Ave PO Box 867	Trenton	NJ	08625	**800-321-6524**	
New York Correctional Industries 550 Broadway	Albany	NY	12204	**800-436-6321**	518-436-6321
Ohio Penal Industries (OPI) 1221 McKinley Ave	Columbus	OH	43222	**800-237-3454**	614-752-0287
Oklahoma Correctional Industries 3402 N Martin Luther King Ave	Oklahoma City	OK	73111	**800-522-3565**	405-425-7500
PEN Products 2010 E New York St	Indianapolis	IN	46201	**800-736-2550**	317-955-6800
Pennsylvania Correctional Industries PO Box 47 *General	Camp Hill	PA	17001	**877-673-3724***	717-425-7292
Prairie Public Broadcasting Inc 207 N Fifth St	Fargo	ND	58102	**800-359-6900**	701-241-6900
Public Broadcasting Council of Central New York 506 Old Liverpool Rd PO Box 2400	Syracuse	NY	13220	**800-451-9269**	315-453-2424
Public Broadcasting Northwest Pennsylvania 8425 Peach St	Erie	PA	16509	**800-727-8854**	814-864-3001
Public Broadcasting Service (PBS) 2100 Crystal Dr	Arlington	VA	22202	**866-864-0828**	703-739-5000
Rocky Mountain Public Broadcasting Network (RMPB) 1089 Bannock St	Denver	CO	80204	**800-274-6666**	303-892-6666
Rough Rider Industries 3303 E Main Ave	Bismarck	ND	58506	**800-732-0557**	701-328-6161
Small Station Assn KRWG-TV PO Box 30001	Las Cruces	NM	88003	**877-308-2408**	575-646-2222
Smoky Hills Public Television (SHPTV) 604 Elm St	Bunker Hill	KS	67626	**800-337-4788**	785-483-6990
South Dakota Public Broadcasting (SDPB) 555 N Dakota St PO Box 5000	Vermillion	SD	57069	**800-456-0766**	605-677-5861
Tennessee Rehabilitative Initiative in Correction (TRICOR) 240 Great Cir Rd Ste 310	Nashville	TN	37228	**800-958-7426**	615-741-5705
Texas Public Radio (TPR) 8401 Datapoint Dr Ste 800	San Antonio	TX	78229	**800-622-8977**	210-614-8977
ThinkTV 110 S Jefferson St	Dayton	OH	45402	**800-247-1614**	937-220-1600
TRAC Media Services 2030 E Speedway Blvd Ste 210	Tucson	AZ	85719	**888-299-1866**	520-299-1866
Twin Cities Public Television Inc 172 E Fourth St	Saint Paul	MN	55101	**866-229-1300**	651-222-1717
University of North Carolina Ctr for Public Television (UNC-TV) 10 TW Alexander Dr PO Box 14900	Research Triangle Park	NC	27709	**800-906-5050**	919-549-7000
Vermont Public Television (VPT) 204 Ethan Allen Ave	Colchester	VT	05446	**800-639-7811**	802-655-4800
WAMC/Northeast Public Radio 318 Central Ave	Albany	NY	12206	**800-323-9262**	518-465-5233
West Central Illinois Educational Telecommunications Corp PO Box 6248	Springfield	IL	62708	**800-232-3605**	217-483-7887
West Virginia Correctional Industries 617 Leon Sullivan Way	Charleston	WV	25301	**800-525-5381**	304-558-6054
Wisconsin Educational Communications Board 3319 W Beltline Hwy	Madison	WI	53713	**800-422-9707**	608-264-9600
Wisconsin Public Radio (WPR) 821 University Ave	Madison	WI	53706	**800-747-7444**	
Wisconsin Public Television (WPT) 821 University Ave	Madison	WI	53706	**800-422-9707**	608-263-2121
Wyoming Public Television 2660 Peck Ave	Riverton	WY	82501	**800-495-9788**	307-856-6944

630 PUBLIC INTEREST RESEARCH GROUPS (PIRGS) - STATE

SEE ALSO Consumer Interest Organizations

Companies listed here contractually assume human resources responsibilities for client companies in exchange for a fee, thus allowing the client company to focus on its true company business. The PEO establishes and maintains an employer relationship with the workers assigned to its client companies, with the PEO and the client company each having specific rights and responsibilities toward the employees.

Company / Address	City	State	Zip	Toll-Free	Phone
Adams Keegan Inc 6055 Primacy Pkwy Ste 300	Memphis	TN	38119	**800-621-1308**	901-683-5353
ADP TotalSource Co 10200 Sunset Dr	Miami	FL	33173	**800-447-3237**	305-630-1000
Advice Media LLC PO Box 982064	Park City	UT	84098	**800-260-9497**	
Alcott Group 71 Executive Blvd	Farmingdale	NY	11735	**888-425-2688**	631-420-0100
Allevity HR & Payroll 870 Manzanita Ct Ste A	Chico	CA	95926	**800-447-8233**	530-345-2486
Allied Employer Group 4400 Buffalo Gap Rd Ste 4500	Abilene	TX	79606	**800-495-3836**	325-695-5822
AlphaStaff Inc 800 Corporate Dr Ste 600	Fort Lauderdale	FL	33334	**888-335-9545**	954-267-1760
ALTRES Inc 967 Kapiolani Blvd	Honolulu	HI	96814	**888-425-8737**	808-591-4940
Assent Consulting Inc 2 Grand Central Twr 140 E 45th St	New York	NY	10017	**866-627-4473**	
Axcet HR Solutions *Axel* 8325 Lenexa Dr Ste 410	Lenexa	KS	66214	**800-801-7557**	913-383-2999

	City	State	ZIP	Toll-Free	Phone
Barrett Business Services Inc 8100 NE Pkwy Dr Ste 200 *NASDAQ: BBSI*	Vancouver	WA	98662	800-494-5669	360-828-0700
Brandmovers Inc 590 Means St Ste 250	Atlanta	GA	30318	888-463-4933	
Chipton-ross Inc 343 Main St	El Segundo	CA	90245	800-927-9318	310-414-7800
Co-Advantage Resources 3350 Buschwood Park Dr Ste 200	Tampa	FL	33618	800-868-1016	813-935-2000
CrowdSource Solutions Inc 33 Bronze Pointe	Swansea	IL	62226	855-276-9376	
Diversified Hum Res Inc 3020 E Camelback Rd Ste 213	Phoenix	AZ	85016	888-870-5588	480-941-5588
Doherty Employment Group 7625 Parklawn Ave *Sales	Edina	MN	55435	888-297-0495*	952-832-8383
Employee Management Services 435 Elm St	Cincinnati	OH	45202	888-651-1536	513-651-3244
FrontPage Local 1660 Hotel Cir N Ste 600	San Diego	CA	92108	800-521-7338	
Human Capital 2055 Crooks Rd Lowr Level	Rochester Hills	MI	48309	888-736-9071	
Iconma LLC 850 Stephenson Hwy Ste 612	Troy	MI	48083	888-451-2519	
Identity Theft Resource Center 3625 Ruffin Rd Ste 204	San Diego	CA	92123	888-400-5530	858-693-7935
Innovate E-Commerce Inc 160 N Craig St	Pittsburgh	PA	15213	888-771-9606	
Inspirage Inc 600 108th Ave NE Ste 540	Bellevue	WA	98004	855-517-4250	
Manpower Inc. 8170 W Sahara Ave Ste 207	Las Vegas	NV	89101	888-333-1597	702-363-2626
Marvel Consultants Inc 28601 Chagrin Blvd Ste 210	Cleveland	OH	44122	800-338-1257	216-292-2855
Mountain Ltd 19 Yarmouth Dr Ste 301	New Gloucester	ME	04260	800-322-8627	207-688-6200
New York Public Interest Research Group (NYPIRG) 9 Murray St	New York	NY	10007	800-342-3377	212-349-6460
Oasis Outsourcing 4511 Woodland Corporate Blvd	Tampa	FL	33614	866-709-9401	813-864-8429
Oasis Outsourcing Inc 2054 Vista Pkwy Ste 300 *General	West Palm Beach	FL	33411	888-627-4735*	
OSF Global Services Inc 6655 Blvd Pierre Bertrand, 204-14	Quebec City	QC	G2K1M1	888-548-4344	
Pay Plus Benefits Inc 1110 N Ctr Pkwy Ste B	Kennewick	WA	99336	888-531-5781	509-735-1143
People Lease Inc 689 Town Ctr Blvd Ste B	Ridgeland	MS	39157	800-723-3025	601-987-3025
Personnel Management Inc PO Box 6657	Shreveport	LA	71136	800-259-4126	318-869-4555
Professional Staff Management Inc 6801 Lake Plaza Dr Ste D-405	Indianapolis	IN	46220	800-967-5515	317-816-7007
Progressive Employer Services 6407 Parkland Dr	Sarasota	FL	34243	888-925-2990	941-925-2990
Recon Management Services Inc 3649 S Beglis Pkwy	Sulphur	LA	70665	888-301-4662	337-583-4662
Red Foundry Inc 1608 S Ashland Ave	Chicago	IL	60608	888-406-1099	
Reserves Network, The 22021 Brookpark Rd	Cleveland	OH	44126	866-876-2020	440-779-6681
Resource Management Inc 281 Main St Ste 5 *Cust Svc	Fitchburg	MA	01420	800-508-0048*	
RMPersonnel Inc 4707 Montana Ave	El Paso	TX	79903	866-333-7176	915-565-7674
Staff One Inc 8111 LBJ Fwy	Dallas	TX	75251	800-771-7823	
Strom Aviation Inc 109 S Elm St	Waconia	MN	55387	800-356-6440	952-544-3611
Summit Technical Services Inc 355 Centerville Rd	Warwick	RI	02886	800-643-7372	401-736-8323
Sycara Inc 6263 N Scottsdale Rd Ste 180	Scottsdale	AZ	85250	855-479-2272	
Synygy Pte. Ltd 2501 Seaport Dr	Chester	PA	19013	877-883-5395	610-494-3300
T & t Staff Management Inc 511 Executive Ctr Blvd	El Paso	TX	79902	800-598-1647	915-771-0393
Tilson HR Inc 1530 American Way Ste 200	Greenwood	IN	46143	800-276-3976	317-885-3838
Training Assoc Corp, The 289 Tpke Rd	Westborough	MA	01581	800-241-8868	508-890-8500
TriNet Group Inc 1100 San Leandro Blvd Ste 300	San Leandro	CA	94577	888-874-6388	510-352-5000
VJV IT 96 Linwood Plz	Fort Lee	NJ	07024	800-614-7561	
VS Management of NY Inc 3281 Veterans Memorial Hwy	Ronkonkoma	NY	11779	877-778-7648	

631 PUBLIC POLICY RESEARCH CENTERS

	City	State	ZIP	Toll-Free	Phone
AARP Public Policy Institute 601 E St NW	Washington	DC	20049	888-687-2277	202-434-2277
Acton Institute for the Study of Religion & Liberty 161 Ottawa Ave NW Ste 301	Grand Rapids	MI	49503	800-345-2286	616-454-3080
Allegheny Institute for Public Policy 305 Mt Lebanon Blvd Ste 208	Pittsburgh	PA	15234	800-242-2184	412-440-0079
American Enterprise Institute for Public Policy Research (AEI) 1150 17th St NW	Washington	DC	20036	800-862-5801	202-862-5800
Ashbrook Ctr 401 College Ave Ashland University	Ashland	OH	44805	877-289-5411	419-289-5411
Atlantic Council of the United States 1101 15th St NW 11th Fl	Washington	DC	20005	800-311-9410	202-463-7226
Brookings Institution 1775 Massachusetts Ave NW	Washington	DC	20036	800-275-1447	202-797-6000
Capital Research Ctr 1513 16th St NW	Washington	DC	20036	800-459-3950	202-483-6900
Carnegie Endowment for International Peace 1779 Massachusetts Ave NW	Washington	DC	20036	877-866-3070	202-483-7600
Carter Ctr 1 Copenhill Ave 453 Freedom Pkwy	Atlanta	GA	30307	800-550-3560	404-420-5100
Center for Animals & Public Policy Tufts Univ School of Veterinary Medicine 200 Westboro Rd	North Grafton	MA	01536	888-748-8387	508-839-7920
Center for Cognitive Liberty & Ethics PO Box 73481	Davis	CA	95617	888-950-6463	530-750-7912
Center for Law & Social Policy (CLASP) 1015 15th St NW Ste 400	Washington	DC	20005	800-821-4367	202-906-8000
Center for Policy Research Syracuse University 426 Eggers Hall	Syracuse	NY	13244	800-325-3535	315-443-3114
Committee for Economic Development (CED) 2000 L St NW Ste 700	Washington	DC	20036	800-676-7353	202-296-5860
Foundation for Economic Education (FEE) 30 S Broadway	Irvington-on-Hudson	NY	10533	800-960-4333	404-554-9980
Heritage Foundation 214 Massachusetts Ave NE	Washington	DC	20002	800-546-2843	202-546-4400
Hudson Institute 1015 15th St NW Ste 600	Washington	DC	20005	888-554-1325	202-974-2400
Independent Institute 100 Swan Way	Oakland	CA	94621	800-927-8733	510-632-1366
Institute for Humane Studies 3434 Washington Blvd Ste 440	Arlington	VA	22201	800-697-8799	703-993-4880
Institute for Justice 901 N Glebe Rd Ste 900	Arlington	VA	22203	888-322-6397	703-682-9320
Institute for Policy Studies (IPS) 1112 16th St NW Ste 600	Washington	DC	20036	877-564-6833	202-234-9382
Institute of Government & Public Affairs Univ of Illinois 1007 W Nevada St	Urbana	IL	61801	866-794-3340	217-333-3340
Institute of World Politics 1521 16th St NW	Washington	DC	20036	888-566-9497	202-462-2101
Malcolm Wiener Ctr for Social Policy John F Kennedy School of Government Harvard University 79 John F Kennedy St	Cambridge	MA	02138	866-845-6596	617-496-4082
Manpower Demonstration Research Corp 16 E 34th St 19th Fl	New York	NY	10016	800-221-3165	212-532-3200
Margaret Chase Smith Policy Ctr University of Maine York Complex Ste 4	Orono	ME	04469	877-486-2364	207-581-1648
Princeton Institute for International & Regional Studies (PIIRS) Princeton University Bendheim Hall	Princeton	NJ	08544	888-486-3339	609-258-4852
Public Agenda 6 E 39th St	New York	NY	10016	800-659-4044	212-686-6610
RAND Corp 1776 Main St	Santa Monica	CA	90401	877-584-8642	310-393-0411
Reason Public Policy Institute 3415 S Sepulveda Blvd Ste 400	Los Angeles	CA	90034	888-732-7668	310-391-2245
Rockford Institute 928 N Main St	Rockford	IL	61103	800-383-0680	815-964-5053
Urban Institute 2100 M St NW	Washington	DC	20037	866-518-3874	202-833-7200
World Policy Institute (WPI) 220 Fifth Ave 9th Fl	New York	NY	10001	800-207-8354	212-481-5005
Worldwatch Institute 1776 Massachusetts Ave NW	Washington	DC	20036	877-539-9946	202-452-1999

632 PUBLIC RECORDS SEARCH SERVICES

SEE ALSO Investigative Services

	City	State	ZIP	Toll-Free	Phone
Accufax PO Box 35563	Tulsa	OK	74153	800-256-8898	
All-Search & Inspection Inc 1108 E S Union Ave	Midvale	UT	84047	800-227-3152	801-984-8160
American Driving Records Inc 2860 Gold Tailings Ct PO Box 1970	Rancho Cordova	CA	95670	800-766-6877	916-456-3200
AmRent 250 E BRd St 21st Fl	Columbus	OH	43215	800-324-4595	713-266-1870
Applicant Insight Ltd 5396 School Rd PO Box 458	New Port Richey	FL	34652	800-771-7703	
Apscreen Inc PO Box 80639	Rancho Santa Margarita	CA	92688	800-277-2733	949-646-4003
Background Bureau Inc 2019 Alexandria Pike	Highland Heights	KY	41076	800-854-3990	859-781-3400
Background Information Services Inc 1800 30th St Ste 204	Boulder	CO	80301	800-433-6010	303-442-3960
Capitol Lien Records & Research Inc 1010 N Dale St	Saint Paul	MN	55117	800-845-4077	651-488-0100
Capitol Services Inc 206 E 9th St Ste 1300	Austin	TX	78701	800-345-4647	
CARCO Group Inc 5000 Corporate Ct	Holtsville	NY	11742	800-645-4556	631-862-9300
CCH Washington Service Bureau Inc 1015 15th St NW 10th Fl	Washington	DC	20005	800-955-5219	202-312-6600
CDI Credit Inc 6160 Peachtree Dunwoody Rd NE Ste B-210	Atlanta	GA	30328	800-633-3961	770-350-5070
Charles Jones LLC PO Box 8488	Trenton	NJ	08650	800-792-8888	
Colby Attorneys Service Company Inc 111 Washington Ave Ste 703	Albany	NY	12210	800-832-1220	
CoreLogic SafeRent 7300 Westmore Rd Ste 3	Rockville	MD	20850	866-873-3651	
CT Lien Solutions 2727 Allen Pkwy Ste 1000	Houston	TX	77019	800-833-5778	
D+H CollateralGuard RC (CSRS) 4126 Norland Ave Ste 200	Burnaby	BC	V5G3S8	866-873-9780	604-637-4000
Doc-U-Search Inc 63 Pleasant St PO Box 777	Concord	NH	03301	800-332-3034	
Driving Records Facilities PO Box 1086	Glen Burnie	MD	21061	800-772-5510	
Edge Information Management Inc 1682 W Hibiscus Blvd	Melbourne	FL	32901	800-725-3343	321-722-3343
Employment Screening Services Inc 627 E Sprague St Ste 100	Spokane	WA	99202	800-473-7778	509-624-3851
Explore Information Services LLC 2900 Lone Oak Pkwy Ste 140 PO Box 21636	St. Paul	MN	55121	800-531-9125	

Name / Address	City	State	Zip	Toll-Free	Phone
Fidelifacts 42 Broadway Ste 1548	New York	NY	10004	**800-678-0007**	212-425-1520
Government Liaison Services Inc (GLS) 200 N Glebe Rd Ste 321	Arlington	VA	22203	**800-642-6564**	703-524-8200
HireRight Inc 5151 California Ave	Irvine	CA	92617	**800-400-2761**	949-428-5800
IMI Data Search Inc 275 E Hillcrest Dr Ste 102	Thousand Oaks	CA	91360	**800-860-7779**	805-495-1149
Information Management Systems Inc 114 W Main St Ste 211 PO Box 2924	New Britain	CT	06050	**888-403-8347**	860-229-1119
Kress Employment Screening 320 Westcott St Ste 108	Houston	TX	77007	**888-636-3693**	713-880-3693
Kroll Background America Inc 100 Centerview Dr Ste 300	Nashville	TN	37214	**800-697-7189**	615-320-9800
Laborchex Co, The 2506 Lakeland Dr Ste 200	Jackson	MS	39232	**800-880-0366**	601-664-6760
Legal Data Resources Inc 2816 W Summerdale Ave	Chicago	IL	60625	**844-732-2437**	773-561-2468
LegalEase Inc 211 E 43rd St Ste 2203	New York	NY	10017	**800-393-1277**	212-393-9070
MLQ Attorney Services 2000 River Edge Pkwy Ste 885	Atlanta	GA	30328	**800-446-8794**	770-984-7007
OPENonline 1650 Lk Shore Dr Ste 350	Columbus	OH	43204	**888-381-5656**	614-481-6999
Orange Tree Employment Screening 7275 Ohms Ln	Minneapolis	MN	55439	**800-886-4777**	952-941-9040
Parasec Inc 2804 Gateway Oaks Dr Ste 200 PO Box 160568 *General	Sacramento	CA	95833	**800-533-7272***	
Penncorp Servicegroup Inc 600 N Second St Ste 401	Harrisburg	PA	17101	**800-544-9050**	717-234-2300
Property Owners Exchange Inc 6630 Baltimore National Pk Ste 208	Catonsville	MD	21228	**800-869-3200**	410-719-0100
Questel Orbit 1725 Duke St Ste 625	Alexandria	VA	22314	**800-456-7248**	703-519-1820
Rental Research Services Inc 7525 Mitchell Rd Ste 301	Eden Prairie	MN	55344	**800-328-0333**	952-935-5700
Search Company International 1535 Grant St Ste 140	Denver	CO	80203	**800-727-2120**	303-863-1800
Search Network Ltd 1503 42nd St Ste 210	West Des Moines	IA	50266	**800-383-5050**	515-223-1153
Securitech Inc 8230 E Broadway Blvd	Tucson	AZ	85710	**888-792-4473**	520-721-0305
TABB Inc PO Box 10	Chester	NJ	07930	**800-887-8222**	
Thomson CompuMark 500 Victory Rd	North Quincy	MA	02171	**800-692-8833**	617-479-1600
Unisearch Inc 1780 Barnes Blvd SW	Tumwater	WA	98512	**800-722-0708**	360-956-9500
Verified Credentials Inc 20890 Kenbridge Ct	Lakeville	MN	55044	**800-473-4934**	952-985-7200
Westlaw Court Express 1100 13th St NW Ste 300	Washington	DC	20005	**877-362-7387**	202-423-2163

633 PUBLIC RELATIONS FIRMS

SEE ALSO Advertising Agencies

Name / Address	City	State	Zip	Toll-Free	Phone
Ackermann Public Relations & Marketing 1111 Northshore Dr Ste N-400 *General	Knoxville	TN	37919	**877-325-9453***	865-584-0550
Admarc Southwest Ltd 10 Desta Dr Ste 170LL	Midland	TX	79705	**888-823-6272**	432-687-1127
B & B Media Group 109 S Main St	Corsicana	TX	75110	**800-927-0517**	903-872-0517
Boardroom Communications Inc Bank Of America Plaza 1776 N Pine Island Rd Ste 320	Fort Lauderdale	FL	33322	**877-773-4761**	954-370-8999
Charles Ryan Assoc Inc 601 Morris St Ste 301	Charleston	WV	25301	**877-342-0161**	
Connect PR 1 Market St 36th Fl	San Francisco	CA	94105	**800-455-8855**	415-222-9691
Gulf Coast Tmc 7670 Hwy 10	Ethel	LA	70730	**866-683-6636**	225-683-6636
Hunter Public Relations 41 Madison Ave 5th Fl	New York	NY	10010	**866-395-7710**	212-679-6600
McNeely Pigott & Fox 611 Commerce St Ste 2800	Nashville	TN	37203	**800-818-6953**	615-259-4000
Montesquieu Winery 8221 Arjons Dr	San Diego	CA	92126	**800-860-2378**	
MSR Communications 832 Sansome St 2nd Fl	San Francisco	CA	94111	**866-247-6172**	415-989-9000
S&S Public Relations Inc 150 N Upper Wacker Dr Ste 2010	Chicago	IL	60606	**800-287-2279**	
Seyferth & Associates Inc 40 Monroe Ctr NW	Grand Rapids	MI	49503	**800-435-9539**	616-776-3511
SHIFT Communications LLC 275 Washington St Ste 410	Newton	MA	02458	**800-494-8477**	617-779-1800
Sitrick & Co 1840 Century Pk E Ste 800	Los Angeles	CA	90067	**800-288-8809**	310-788-2850
Thomson Safaris 14 Mt Auburn St	Watertown	MA	02472	**800-235-0289**	617-923-0426

PUBLICATIONS

SEE Magazines & Journals ; Newsletters ; Newspapers

634 PUBLISHING COMPANIES

SEE ALSO Magazines & Journals ; Newsletters ; Newspapers ; Book Producers

634-1 Atlas & Map Publishers

Name / Address	City	State	Zip	Toll-Free	Phone
DeLorme 2 DeLorme Dr PO Box 298 *Sales	Yarmouth	ME	04096	**800-452-5931***	207-846-7000
MARCOA Publishing Inc 9955 Black Mtn Rd	San Diego	CA	92126	**800-854-2935**	858-695-9600
Rand McNally 9855 Woods Dr PO Box 7600	Skokie	IL	60077	**800-275-7263**	
Simon & Schuster Interactive 1230 Ave of the Americas	New York	NY	10020	**800-223-2336**	212-698-7000

634-2 Book Publishers

Name / Address	City	State	Zip	Toll-Free	Phone
ABC-CLIO Inc 130 Cremona Dr	Goleta	CA	93117	**800-368-6868**	805-968-1911
American Printing House for the Blind 1839 Frankfort Ave PO Box 6085	Louisville	KY	40206	**800-223-1839**	502-895-2405
Antique Collectors Club 116 Pleasant St	EastHampton	MA	01027	**800-254-4100**	413-529-0861
Applewood Books Inc 1 River Rd *General	Carlisle	MA	01741	**800-277-5312***	978-369-4172
Atlantic Publishing Co 315 E Washington St	Starke	FL	32091	**800-814-1132**	
Author House 1663 Liberty Dr Ste 200	Bloomington	IN	47403	**888-728-8467**	812-339-6000
Aviation Supplies & Academics Inc 7005 132nd Pl Se	Newcastle	WA	98059	**800-272-2359**	425-235-1500
Barron's Educational Series Inc 250 Wireless Blvd	Hauppauge	NY	11788	**800-645-3476**	631-434-3311
BRB Publications Inc PO Box 27869	Tempe	AZ	85285	**800-929-3811**	480-829-7475
Brillacademic Publishers Inc 2 liberty Sq 11th Fl	Boston	MA	02109	**800-337-9255**	617-263-2323
Browntrout Publishers Inc 201 Continental Blvd	El Segundo	CA	90245	**800-777-7812**	310-607-9010
Bureau of National Affairs Inc 1801 S Bell St	Arlington	VA	22202	**800-372-1033**	703-341-3000
Carroll Publishing Co 4701 Sangamore Rd Ste S-155	Bethesda	MD	20816	**800-336-4240**	301-263-9800
Cengage Learning PO Box 6904	Florence	KY	41022	**800-354-9706**	
Charles C Thomas Publisher 2600 S First St *Sales	Springfield	IL	62704	**800-258-8980***	217-789-8980
Chronicle Books 680 Second St	San Francisco	CA	94107	**800-722-6657**	415-537-4200
Commemorative Brands Inc 7211 Cir S Rd	Austin	TX	78745	**800-225-3687**	
Corwin Press Inc 2455 Teller Rd *Orders	Thousand Oaks	CA	91320	**800-233-9936***	805-499-9734
CPP Inc 1055 Joaquin Rd Ste 200	Mountain View	CA	94043	**800-624-1765**	650-969-8901
CRC Press LLC 6000 Broken Sound Pkwy NW Ste 300 *Cust Svc	Boca Raton	FL	33487	**800-272-7737***	561-994-0555
Creative Communications For The Parish Inc 1564 Fencorp Dr	Fenton	MO	63026	**800-325-9414**	636-305-9777
Curriculum Assoc Inc 153 Rangeway Rd	North Billerica	MA	01862	**800-225-0248**	
D & B 103 JFK Pkwy *NYSE: DNB*	Short Hills	NJ	07078	**800-234-3867**	973-921-5500
Dalmation Press 113 Seaboard Ln Ste C-250	Franklin	TN	37067	**800-815-8696**	
Disney Consumer Products 500 S Buena Vista St *PR	Burbank	CA	91521	**855-553-4763***	818-560-1000
Donning Company Publishers 184 Business Pk Dr Ste 206	Virginia Beach	VA	23462	**800-296-8572**	
Dorling Kindersley Publishing 375 Hudson St *Cust Svc	New York	NY	10014	**800-631-8571***	646-674-4047
Educators Publishing Service Inc (EPS) 625 Mt Auburn St Third Fl PO Box 9031	Cambridge	MA	02139	**800-225-5750**	
EMC-Paradigm Publishing Co 875 Montreal Way	Saint Paul	MN	55102	**800-328-1452**	651-290-2800
Encyclopaedia Britannica Inc 331 N La Salle St	Chicago	IL	60654	**800-323-1229**	312-347-7159
FA Davis Co 1915 Arch St	Philadelphia	PA	19103	**800-323-3555**	215-568-2270
Financial Publishing Co PO Box 570 *Cust Svc	South Bend	IN	46624	**800-433-0090***	574-243-6040
Forbes Inc 60 Fifth Ave	New York	NY	10011	**800-295-0893**	212-620-2200
Free Spirit Publishing Inc 217 Fifth Ave N Ste 200	Minneapolis	MN	55401	**800-735-7323**	612-338-2068
Gale Cengage Learning 27500 Drake Rd *Cust Svc	Farmington Hills	MI	48331	**800-877-4253***	248-699-4253
Glencoe/McGraw-Hill 8787 Orion Pl	Columbus	OH	43240	**800-848-1567**	
Good Will Publishers Inc PO Box 269	Gastonia	NC	28052	**800-219-4663**	704-865-1256
Goodheart-Willcox Publisher 18604 W Creek Dr	Tinley Park	IL	60477	**800-323-0440**	708-687-5000
Government Research Service 1516 SW Boswell Ave	Topeka	KS	66604	**800-346-6898**	785-232-7720
Grade Finders Inc PO Box 944	Exton	PA	19341	**800-777-8074**	610-524-7070
Greenwood-Heinemann 361 Hanover St	Portsmouth	NH	03801	**800-541-2086**	603-431-7894
Grey House Publishing 4919 Rt 22 PO Box 56	Amenia	NY	12501	**800-562-2139**	518-789-8700
Hachette Book Group 237 Pk Ave	New York	NY	10017	**800-759-0190**	
Harlequin Enterprises Ltd 225 Duncan Mill Rd	Don Mills	ON	M3B3K9	**888-343-9777**	416-445-5860
Harlequin-Silhouette Books 233 Broadway Ste 1001	New York	NY	10279	**800-873-8635**	212-553-4200

Name / Address	City	State	Zip	Toll-Free	Phone
HarperCollins Publishers Inc 10 E 53rd St	New York	NY	10022	**800-242-7737**	212-207-7000
Harris Connect LLC 1511 Rt 22 Ste C-25	Brewster	NY	10509	**800-516-4915**	
Health Communications Inc (HCI) 3201 SW 15th St *Cust Svc	Deerfield Beach	FL	33442	**800-441-5569***	954-360-0909
Holtzbrinck Publishers 175 Fifth Ave	New York	NY	10010	**800-221-7945**	646-307-5151
Human Kinetics 1607 N Market St	Champaign	IL	61820	**800-747-4457**	217-351-5076
HW Wilson Co 10 Estes St	Ipswich	MA	01938	**800-653-2726**	978-356-6500
Inner Traditions International 1 Pk Row	Rochester	VT	05767	**800-246-8648**	802-767-3174
Island Press 2000 M St NW Ste 650	Washington	DC	20036	**800-621-2736**	202-232-7933
iUniverse 1663 Liberty Dr	Bloomington	IN	47403	**800-288-4677**	812-330-2909
Jane's Information Group 110 N Royal St Ste 200	Alexandria	VA	22314	**800-824-0768**	703-683-3700
Jeppesen Sanderson Inc 55 Inverness Dr E	Englewood	CO	80112	**800-621-5377**	303-799-9090
John Wiley & Sons Inc 111 River St *NYSE: JW/A* ■ *Sales	Hoboken	NJ	07030	**800-225-5945***	201-748-6000
Judaica Press Inc 123 Ditmas Ave	Brooklyn	NY	11218	**800-972-6201**	718-972-6200
Kendall/Hunt Publishing Co 4050 Westmark Dr PO Box 1840 *Cust Svc	Dubuque	IA	52002	**800-228-0810***	563-589-1000
Kensington Publishing Corp 119 W 40th St	New York	NY	10018	**800-221-2647**	212-407-1500
Key Curriculum Press 1150 65th St	Emeryville	CA	94608	**800-338-3987**	510-595-7000
Lawyers Diary & Manual 890 Mtn Ave Ste 300	New Providence	NJ	07974	**800-444-4041**	973-642-1440
Leadership Directories Inc 104 Fifth Ave 3rd Fl	New York	NY	10011	**800-627-0311**	212-627-4140
Lerner Publishing Group 1251 Washington Ave N	Minneapolis	MN	55401	**800-328-4929**	
LexisNexis Matthew Bender 744 Broad St	Newark	NJ	07102	**800-252-9257**	973-820-2000
Lightning Source 1246 Heil Quaker Blvd	La Vergne	TN	37086	**800-509-4156**	615-213-5815
Linden Publishing 2006 S Mary St *Sales	Fresno	CA	93721	**800-345-4447***	559-233-6633
Little Brown & Co 237 Pk Ave *Cust Svc	New York	NY	10017	**800-759-0190***	212-364-1100
Llewellyn Worldwide Inc 2143 Wooddale Dr	Woodbury	MN	55125	**800-843-6666**	651-291-1970
Lonely Planet Publications 50 Linden St	Oakland	CA	94607	**800-275-8555**	510-893-8555
LRP Publications 360 Hiatt Dr	Palm Beach Gardens	FL	33418	**800-621-5463**	561-622-6520
Marquis Who's Who 300 Connell Dr Ste 2000	Berkeley Heights	NJ	07922	**800-473-7020**	908-673-1000
McFarland & Company Inc 960 NC Hwy 88 W PO Box 611	Jefferson	NC	28640	**800-253-2187**	336-246-4460
McGraw-Hill Higher Education Group 1333 Burr Ridge Pkwy	Burr Ridge	IL	60527	**800-634-3963**	630-789-4000
McGraw-Hill Professional Publishing Group 2 Penn Plz 11th Fl	New York	NY	10121	**877-833-5524**	
Mel Bay Publications Inc 1734 Gilsinn Ln	Fenton	MO	63026	**800-863-5229**	636-257-3970
Midwest Plan Service 122 Davidson Hall ISU	Ames	IA	50011	**800-562-3618**	515-294-4337
Mike Murach & Assoc Inc 4340 N Knoll	Fresno	CA	93722	**800-221-5528**	559-440-9071
National Academy Press 500 Fifth St NW PO Box 285	Washington	DC	20055	**800-624-6242**	202-334-3313
National Braille Press Inc 88 St Stephen St	Boston	MA	02115	**888-965-8965**	617-266-6160
National Register Publishing Co 430 Mountain Ave Ste 400	New Providence	NJ	07974	**800-473-7020**	
National Underwriter Co 5081 Olympic Blvd	Erlanger	KY	41018	**800-543-0874**	
New Generation Research Inc 225 Friend St Ste 801	Boston	MA	02114	**800-468-3810**	617-573-9550
New Readers Press 104 Marcellus St	Syracuse	NY	13204	**800-448-8878**	315-422-9121
Newkirk Products Inc 15 Corporate Cir	Albany	NY	12203	**800-525-4237**	518-862-3200
Nightingale-Conant Corp 6245 W Howard St *Cust Svc	Niles	IL	60714	**800-557-1660***	
No Starch Press Inc 38 Ringold St	San Francisco	CA	94103	**800-420-7240**	415-863-9900
Nolo.com 950 Parker St	Berkeley	CA	94710	**800-728-3555**	
Omnigraphics Inc PO Box 31-1640	Detroit	MI	48231	**800-234-1340**	
Open Court Publishing Co 70 E Lake St Ste 800	Chicago	IL	60601	**800-815-2280**	
Overlook Press 141 Wooster St	New York	NY	10012	**800-527-9703**	212-673-2210
Oxford University Press 198 Madison Ave *Orders	New York	NY	10016	**800-445-9714***	212-726-6000
Pearson Education Inc 1 Lake St *Cust Svc	Upper Saddle River	NJ	07458	**800-922-0579***	201-236-6716
Pearson Education School Div 1900 E Lk Ave Ofc Ste B-110A	Glenview	IL	60025	**800-348-4474**	
Penguin Group (USA) Inc 375 Hudson St *Sales	New York	NY	10014	**800-847-5515***	212-366-2000
Penguin Random House 1745 Broadway	New York	NY	10019	**800-733-3000**	212-782-9000
Penguin Random House Inc *Bantam Dell Publishing Group* 1745 Broadway 10th Fl	New York	NY	10019	**888-523-9292**	212-782-9000
Perseus Books Group, The 210 American Dr	Jackson	TN	38301	**800-343-4499**	731-426-6061
Peter Lang Publishing Inc 29 Broadway	New York	NY	10006	**800-770-5264**	212-647-7706
Prentice-Hall Inc 1 Lake St	Upper Saddle River	NJ	07458	**800-328-5999**	
Price Books & Forms Inc 531 E Sierra Madre Ave	Glendora	CA	91741	**800-423-8961**	
Publications International Ltd 7373 N Cicero Ave *General	Lincolnwood	IL	60712	**800-777-5582***	847-676-3470
Rand McNally 9855 Woods Dr PO Box 7600	Skokie	IL	60077	**800-275-7263**	
Rosen Publishing Group Inc, The 29 E 21st St	New York	NY	10010	**800-237-9932**	
Rowman & Littlefield Publishers Inc 4501 Forbes Blvd Ste 200	Lanham	MD	20706	**800-462-6420**	301-459-3366
RR Bowker LLC 630 Central Ave	New Providence	NJ	07974	**888-269-5372**	908-286-1090
Sage Publications Inc 2455 Teller Rd	Thousand Oaks	CA	91320	**800-818-7243**	805-499-9774
Sams Technical Publishing 9850 E 30th St *Cust Svc	Indianapolis	IN	46229	**800-428-7267***	
Santillana USA Publishing Co 2023 NW 84th Ave	Doral	FL	33122	**800-245-8584**	305-591-9522
School Annual Publishing Co 2568 Park Ctr Blvd	State College	PA	16801	**800-436-6030**	
Slack Inc 6900 Grove Rd	Thorofare	NJ	08086	**800-257-8290**	856-848-1000
Sourcebooks Inc 1935 Brookdale Rd Ste 139	Naperville	IL	60563	**800-432-7444**	630-961-3900
SRDS 1700 Higgins Rd	Des Plaines	IL	60018	**800-851-7737**	
Standard & Poor's Corp 55 Water St	New York	NY	10041	**877-772-5436**	212-438-1000
Sterling Publishing Company Inc 387 Pk Ave S 5th Fl *Cust Svc	New York	NY	10016	**800-367-9692***	212-532-7160
Storey Publishing LLC 210 Mass Moca Way	North Adams	MA	01247	**800-827-7444**	413-346-2100
Sunset Publishing Corp 80 Willow Rd	Menlo Park	CA	94025	**800-227-7346**	650-321-3600
Taylor & Francis Group 6000 Broken Sound Pkwy NW Ste 300	Boca Raton	NY	33487	**877-622-5543**	207-017-6000
Technology Marketing Corp 1 Technology Plz *Cust Svc	Norwalk	CT	06854	**800-243-6002***	203-852-6800
Thomas Publishing Co 5 Penn Plaza	New York	NY	10001	**800-733-1127**	212-695-0500
Thorndike Press 10 Water St Ste 310	Waterville	ME	04901	**800-223-1244**	
Townsend Press 439 Kelley Dr	West Berlin	NJ	08091	**800-772-6410**	856-753-0554
Triumph Learning 136 Madison Ave	New York	NY	10016	**800-221-9372**	
Tuttle Publishing 364 Innovation Dr *Sales	North Clarendon	VT	05759	**800-526-2778***	802-773-8930
University Press of America 4501 Forbes Blvd Ste 200	Lanham	MD	20706	**800-462-6420**	301-459-3366
Walch Education 40 Walch Dr	Portland	ME	04103	**800-558-2846**	207-772-2846
Walsworth Publishing Co 306 N Kansas Ave	Marceline	MO	64658	**800-972-4968**	660-376-3543
West Group 610 Opperman Dr *Cust Svc	Eagan	MN	55123	**800-328-4880***	651-687-7000
Wheatmark Inc 1760 E River Rd Ste 145	Tucson	AZ	85718	**888-934-0888**	520-798-0888
Wilderness Press c/o Keen Communications 2204 First Ave S Ste 102	Birmingham	AL	35233	**800-443-7227**	
Wiley Publishing Inc 111 River St	Hoboken	NJ	07030	**800-225-5945**	201-748-6000
William H Sadlier Inc 9 Pine St *OTC: SADL*	New York	NY	10005	**800-221-5175**	
William Morrow & Co 10 E 53rd St	New York	NY	10022	**800-242-7737**	212-207-7000
William S Hein & Company Inc 1285 Main St	Buffalo	NY	14209	**800-828-7571**	716-882-2600
Workman Publishing 225 Varick St	New York	NY	10014	**800-722-7202**	212-254-5900
World Book Inc 233 N Michigan Ave Ste 2000	Chicago	IL	60601	**800-967-5325**	312-729-5800
WW Norton & Company Inc 500 Fifth Ave 6th Fl	New York	NY	10110	**800-233-4830**	212-354-5500
Zaner-Bloser Inc 1201 Dublin Rd	Columbus	OH	43215	**800-421-3018**	614-486-0221
Zebra Books *Kensington Publishing Corp* 119 W 40th St	New York	NY	10018	**800-221-2647**	212-407-1500

634-3 Book Publishers - Religious & Spiritual Books

Name / Address	City	State	Zip	Toll-Free	Phone
American Bible Society 1865 Broadway	New York	NY	10023	**800-322-4253**	212-408-1200
Augsburg Fortress Publishers 510 Marquette Ave Ste 800	Minneapolis	MN	55402	**800-426-0115**	612-330-3300
Baker Book House Company Inc 6030 E Fulton St *Orders	Ada	MI	49301	**800-877-2665***	616-676-9185
Baker Book House Company Inc Revell Div 6030 E Fulton St *Orders	Ada	MI	49301	**800-877-2665***	616-676-9185

Company / Address	City	State	Zip	Toll-Free	Phone
Bethany House Publishers 11400 Hampshire Ave S	Bloomington	MN	55438	**800-328-6109**	616-676-9185
Brethren Press 1451 Dundee Ave	Elgin	IL	60120	**800-441-3712**	
Broadman & Holman Publishers 127 Ninth Ave N MSN 114	Nashville	TN	37234	**800-448-8032**	
Concordia Publishing House Inc 3558 S Jefferson Ave *Cust Svc	Saint Louis	MO	63118	**800-325-3040***	314-268-1000
Cook Communications Ministries 4050 Lee Vance View	Colorado Springs	CO	80918	**800-708-5550**	719-536-0100
Deseret Book Co 57 W S Temple	Salt Lake City	UT	84111	**800-453-4532**	801-534-1515
Gospel Light Publications 1957 Eastman Ave	Ventura	CA	93003	**800-446-7735**	805-644-9721
Hay House Inc PO Box 5100	Carlsbad	CA	92018	**800-654-5126**	760-431-7695
Jewish Publication Society 2100 Arch St 2nd Fl	Philadelphia	PA	19103	**800-234-3151**	215-832-0600
NavPress 3820 N 30th St	Colorado Springs	CO	80904	**800-323-9400**	
New Leaf Publishing Group PO Box 726	Green Forest	AR	72638	**800-999-3777**	870-438-5288
New World Library 14 Pamaron Way	Novato	CA	94949	**800-972-6657**	415-884-2100
Northwestern Publishing House 1250 N 113th St *Orders	Milwaukee	WI	53226	**800-662-6022***	414-475-6600
Oregon Catholic Press (OCP) 5536 NE Hassalo St	Portland	OR	97213	**877-596-1653**	503-281-1191
Our Sunday Visitor Inc 200 Noll Plaza	Huntington	IN	46750	**800-348-2440**	260-356-8400
Pauline Books & Media 50 St Paul's Ave *Sales	Boston	MA	02130	**800-876-4463***	617-522-8911
Review & Herald Publishing Assn 55 W Oak Ridge Dr	Hagerstown	MD	21740	**800-456-3991**	301-393-3000
Standard Publishing Co 8805 Governors Hill Dr Ste 400 *Orders	Cincinnati	OH	45249	**800-543-1353***	513-931-4050
Standex International Corp Consumer Group 11 Keewaydin Dr *NYSE: SXI*	Salem	NH	03079	**800-514-5275**	603-893-9701
Thomas Nelson Inc 501 Nelson Pl PO Box 141000	Nashville	TN	37214	**800-251-4000**	615-889-9000
Tyndale House Publishers Inc 351 Executive Dr	Carol Stream	IL	60188	**800-323-9400**	
United Methodist Publishing House 201 Eigth Ave S	Nashville	TN	37203	**800-672-1789**	615-749-6000
Whitaker House/Anchor Distributors 1030 Hunt Vly Cir *General	New Kensington	PA	15068	**800-444-4484***	724-334-7000

634-4 Book Publishers - University Presses

Company / Address	City	State	Zip	Toll-Free	Phone
Catholic University of America Press 620 Michigan Ave NE 240 Leahy Hall	Washington	DC	20064	**800-537-5487**	202-319-5052
Columbia University Press 61 W 62nd St 3rd Fl	New York	NY	10023	**800-944-8648**	212-459-0600
Cornell University Press 750 Cascadilla St PO Box 6525 *Sales	Ithaca	NY	14850	**800-666-2211***	607-277-2338
Duke University Press 905 W Main St Ste 18-B *Cust Svc	Durham	NC	27701	**888-651-0122***	919-687-3600
Gallaudet University Press 800 Florida Ave NE	Washington	DC	20002	**800-621-2736**	202-651-5488
Harvard Business School Publishing 60 Harvard Way	Boston	MA	02163	**800-795-5200**	
Harvard University Press 79 Garden St	Cambridge	MA	02138	**800-405-1619**	617-495-2600
Indiana University Press 601 N Morton St	Bloomington	IN	47404	**800-842-6796**	812-855-8817
Johns Hopkins University Press 2715 N Charles St *Orders	Baltimore	MD	21218	**800-537-5487***	410-516-6900
Naval Institute Press 291 Wood Rd	Annapolis	MD	21402	**800-233-8764**	410-268-6110
Ohio University Press 19 Cir Dr The Ridges *Sales	Athens	OH	45701	**800-621-2736***	740-593-1154
Oregon State University Press 1500 Jefferson St *Orders	Corvallis	OR	97331	**800-426-3797***	541-737-3166
Pennsylvania State University Press 820 N University Dr USB1 Ste C	University Park	PA	16802	**800-326-9180**	814-865-1327
Princeton University Press 41 William St	Princeton	NJ	08540	**800-777-4726**	609-258-4900
Purdue University Press 504 W State St Stewart Ctr 370 *Orders	West Lafayette	IN	47907	**800-247-6553***	765-494-2038
Rutgers University Press 106 Somerset St 3rd Fl	New Brunswick	NJ	08901	**800-272-6817**	732-745-4935
Stanford University Press 1450 Page Mill Rd	Palo Alto	CA	94304	**800-621-2736**	650-723-9434
State University of New York Press (SUNY) 22 Corporate Woods Blvd 3rd Fl	Albany	NY	12211	**866-430-7869**	518-472-5000
Temple University Press 1852 N 10th St USB 305	Philadelphia	PA	19122	**800-621-2736**	215-926-2140
Texas A & M University Press John H Lindsey Bldg 4354 TAMU *Orders	College Station	TX	77843	**800-826-8911***	979-845-1436
Texas Tech University Press 2903 Fourth St	Lubbock	TX	79409	**800-832-4042**	806-742-2982
University of Alabama Press, The 200 Hackberry Ln Second Fl PO Box 870380 *Orders	Tuscaloosa	AL	35487	**800-621-2736***	205-348-5180
University of Alaska Press 1760 Wwood Wy Ste 220	Fairbanks	AK	99709	**888-252-6657**	907-474-5831
University of Arizona Press, The 1510 E University Blvd PO Box 210055	Tucson	AZ	85721	**800-426-3797**	520-621-1441
University of Arkansas Press McIlroy House 105 McIlroy	Fayetteville	AR	72701	**800-621-2736**	479-575-7258
University of California Press 2120 Berkeley Way	Berkeley	CA	94704	**800-343-4499**	
University of Chicago Press 1427 E 60th St *Sales	Chicago	IL	60637	**800-621-2736***	773-702-7700
University of Hawaii Press 2840 Kolowalu St	Honolulu	HI	96822	**888-847-7377**	808-956-8255
University of Illinois Press 1325 S Oak St	Champaign	IL	61820	**866-244-0626**	217-333-0950
University of Iowa Press 119 W Pk Rd 100 Kuhl House	Iowa City	IA	52242	**800-621-2736**	319-335-2000
University of Massachusetts Press PO Box 429	Amherst	MA	01004	**800-562-0112**	413-545-2217
University of Michigan Press 839 Greene St	Ann Arbor	MI	48104	**866-804-0002**	734-764-4388
University of Missouri Press 2910 LeMone Blvd	Columbia	MO	65201	**800-621-2736**	573-882-7641
University of Nebraska Press 1111 Lincoln Mall *Orders	Lincoln	NE	68508	**800-755-1105***	402-472-3581
University of North Carolina Press 116 S Boundary St	Chapel Hill	NC	27514	**800-848-6224**	919-966-3561
University of North Texas Press 1155 Union Cir Ste 311336	Denton	TX	76203	**800-826-8911**	940-565-2142
University of Pennsylvania Press 3902 Spruce St *Cust Svc	Philadelphia	PA	19104	**800-537-5487***	215-898-6261
University of Pittsburgh Press 3400 Forbes Ave 5th Fl *Sales	Pittsburgh	PA	15261	**800-621-2736***	412-383-2456
University of South Carolina Press 1600 Hampton St 5th Fl *Orders	Columbia	SC	29208	**800-768-2500***	803-777-5243
University of Texas Press 2100 Comal St *Sales	Austin	TX	78722	**800-252-3206***	512-471-7233
University of Utah Press 295 South 1500 East Ste 5400	Salt Lake City	UT	84112	**800-621-2736**	801-585-0082
University of Virginia Press 210 Sprigg Ln PO Box 400318 *Orders	Charlottesville	VA	22903	**800-831-3406***	434-924-3469
University of Washington Press 4333 Brooklyn Ave NE	Seattle	WA	98195	**800-537-5487**	206-543-4050
University Press of Colorado 5589 Arapahoe Ave Ste 206C	Boulder	CO	80303	**800-621-2736**	720-406-8849
University Press of Florida 15 NW 15th St *Sales	Gainesville	FL	32611	**800-226-3822***	352-392-1351
University Press of Kentucky 663 S Limestone St *Sales	Lexington	KY	40508	**800-537-5487***	859-257-8400
University Press of Mississippi 3825 Ridgewood Rd	Jackson	MS	39211	**800-737-7788**	601-432-6205
University Press of New England (UPNE) 1 Ct St Ste 250 *Orders	Lebanon	NH	03766	**800-421-1561***	603-448-1533
Vanderbilt University Press 2014 Broadway Ste 320	Nashville	TN	37203	**800-627-7377**	615-322-3585
Wesleyan University Press 215 Long Ln	Middletown	CT	06459	**800-421-1561**	860-685-7711
Yale University Press 302 Temple St *Sales	New Haven	CT	06511	**800-405-1619***	203-432-0960

634-5 Comic Book Publishers

Company / Address	City	State	Zip	Toll-Free	Phone
Dark Horse Comics Inc 10956 SE Main St	Milwaukie	OR	97222	**800-862-0052**	503-652-8815
Diamond Comic Distributors Inc 1966 Greenspring Dr Ste 300	Timonium	MD	21093	**800-452-6642**	410-560-7100
Fantagraphics Books 7563 Lk City Way NE	Seattle	WA	98115	**800-657-1100**	206-524-1967

634-6 Directory Publishers

Company / Address	City	State	Zip	Toll-Free	Phone
ASD Data Services LLC PO Box 1184	Manchester	TN	37349	**877-742-7297**	
Bresser's Cross Index Directory Co 684 W Baltimore St	Detroit	MI	48202	**800-995-0570**	313-874-0570
BurrellesLuce 30 B Vreeland Rd PO Box 674	Florham Park	NJ	07932	**800-631-1160**	973-992-6600
Chain Store Guide 10117 Princess Palm Ave Ste 375	Tampa	FL	33610	**800-927-9292**	
Cincinnati Bell Directory (CBD) 312 Plum St Ste 600	Cincinnati	OH	45202	**800-877-0475**	
Cole Information Services 3401 NW 39th St	Lincoln	NE	68524	**800-800-3271**	402-555-5678
Contractors Register Inc 800 E Main St PO Box 500	Jefferson Valley	NY	10535	**800-431-2584**	
DAG Media Inc 125-10 Queens Blvd Ste 14	Kew Gardens	NY	11415	**800-261-2799**	718-263-8454
Dickman Directories Inc 6145 Columbus Pk	Lewis Center	OH	43035	**877-836-4154**	740-548-6130

Company	Address	City	State	ZIP	Toll-Free	Phone
Genesis Publisher Services	3310 Eagle Pk Dr NE Ste 200	Grand Rapids	MI	49525	**800-828-1022**	616-831-2800
Haines & Company Inc	8050 Freedom Ave	North Canton	OH	44720	**800-843-8452**	
Hoover's Inc	5800 Airport Blvd	Austin	TX	78752	**800-486-8666**	512-374-4500
LexisNexis Martindale-Hubbell	121 Chanlon Rd	New Providence	NJ	07974	**800-526-4902**	
Marc Publishing Co	600 Germantown Pk	Lafayette Hill	PA	19444	**800-432-5478**	610-834-8585
Rasansky Law Firm	2525 McKinnon Ave Ste 625 *OTC: ATTY*	Dallas	TX	75201	**800-288-6763**	
Stewart Directories Inc	50314 Kings Point Dr PO Box 326	Frisco	NC	27936	**800-311-0786**	
Valley Yellow Pages	1850 N Gateway Blvd	Fresno	CA	93727	**800-350-8887**	559-251-8888
World Chamber of Commerce Directory Inc	446 E 29th St	Loveland	CO	80538	**888-883-3231**	970-663-3231
Yellow Book USA	398 RXR Plaza	Uniondale	NY	11556	**877-237-6120**	917-861-5858

634-7 Music Publishers

Company	Address	City	State	ZIP	Toll-Free	Phone
Carl Fischer Inc	48 Wall St 28th Fl	New York	NY	10005	**800-762-2328**	212-777-0900
Hal Leonard Corp	960 E Mark St	Winona	MN	55987	**800-321-3408**	507-454-2920
Lorenz Corp	501 E Third St	Dayton	OH	45402	**800-444-1144**	937-228-6118
Malaco Music Group Inc	3023 W Northside Dr *Cust Svc	Jackson	MS	39213	**800-272-7936***	601-982-4522
Mel Bay Publications Inc	1734 Gilsinn Ln	Fenton	MO	63026	**800-863-5229**	636-257-3970
Theodore Presser Co	588 N Gulph Rd	King of Prussia	PA	19406	**800-854-6764**	610-592-1222

634-8 Newspaper Publishers

Company	Address	City	State	ZIP	Toll-Free	Phone
Afro-American Newspapers Co	2519 N Charles St	Baltimore	MD	21218	**800-237-6892**	410-554-8200
Alameda Times-Star	7677 Oakport St Ste 950	Oakland	CA	94604	**866-225-5277**	510-208-6300
Albany Herald Publishing Company Inc	126 N Washington St	Albany	GA	31702	**800-234-3725**	229-888-9300
Albert Lea Tribune, The	808 W Front St	Albert Lea	MN	56007	**800-657-4996**	507-373-1411
Arizona Publishing Cos	PO Box 1950	Phoenix	AZ	85001	**800-331-9303**	602-444-8000
Auburn Publishers Inc	25 Dill St	Auburn	NY	13021	**800-878-5311**	315-253-5311
Bliss Communications Inc	PO Box 5001	Janesville	WI	53547	**800-422-7128**	608-754-3311
BMH Books	1104 Kings Hwy PO Box 544	Winona Lake	IN	46590	**800-348-2756**	
Burlington Hawk Eye Co	800 S Main St PO Box 10	Burlington	IA	52601	**800-397-1708**	319-754-8461
Capital Newspapers	1901 Fish Hatchery Rd	Madison	WI	53713	**888-798-4468**	920-887-0321
Casa Grande Valley Newspaper Inc	PO Box 15002	Casa Grande	AZ	85130	**800-352-3796**	520-836-7461
Casiano Communications Inc	1700 Fernandez Juncos Ave	San Juan	PR	00909	**844-723-2351**	787-728-3000
Cheyenne Newspaper Inc	702 W Lincolnway	Cheyenne	WY	82001	**800-561-6268**	307-634-3361
Christian Science Publishing Society	210 Massachusetts Ave P02-15	Boston	MA	02115	**800-456-2220**	617-450-2300
Community Newspaper Co Inc	72 Cherry Hill Dr	Beverly	MA	01915	**800-281-6498**	978-739-1300
Consolidated Publishing Co	PO Box 189	Anniston	AL	36202	**866-814-9253**	256-236-1551
Daily Globe, The	118 E McLeod Ave PO Box 548	Ironwood	MI	49938	**800-236-2887**	906-932-2211
Daily Progress	685 W Rio Rd	Charlottesville	VA	22902	**866-469-4866**	434-978-7200
Day Publishing Co	47 Eugene O'Neill Dr	New London	CT	06320	**800-542-3354**	860-442-2200
Delphos Herald Inc	405 N Main St	Delphos	OH	45833	**800-589-6950**	419-695-0015
Denver Newspaper Agency	101 W Colfax Ave	Denver	CO	80202	**800-336-7678**	303-954-1010
Derrick Publishing Co	1510 W First St	Oil City	PA	16301	**800-352-1002**	814-676-7444
Desert Sun Publishing Co	PO Box 2734 *Advertising	Palm Springs	CA	92263	**800-233-3741***	760-322-8889
Detroit Legal News Co	1409 Allen Rd Ste B	Troy	MI	48083	**800-875-5275**	248-577-6100
Diocese of Steubenville Catholic Charities	PO Box 969	Steubenville	OH	43952	**800-339-7890**	740-282-3631
Dispatch Printing Co	34 S Third St	Columbus	OH	43215	**800-282-0263**	614-461-5000
Eagle Publishing Co	75 S Church St	Pittsfield	MA	01201	**800-245-0254**	413-447-7311
East Hampton Star Inc, The	153 Main St PO Box 5002	East Hampton	NY	11937	**844-324-0777**	631-324-0002
Eau Claire Press Co	701 S Farwell St	Eau Claire	WI	54701	**800-236-8808**	715-833-9200
Edward A Sherman Publishing Co	101 Malbone Rd	Newport	RI	02840	**800-320-2378**	401-849-3300
EW Scripps Co	312 Walnut St Ste 2800 *NYSE: SSP*	Cincinnati	OH	45202	**800-888-3000**	513-977-3000
Express-News Corp	PO Box 2171	San Antonio	TX	78297	**800-555-1551**	210-250-3000
Finger Lakes Times	218 Genesse St PO Box 393	Geneva	NY	14456	**800-388-6652**	315-789-3333
Fort Wayne Newspapers Inc	600 W Main St	Fort Wayne	IN	46802	**800-444-3303**	260-461-8444
Freedom Communications Inc	17666 Fitch	Irvine	CA	92614	**855-862-7238**	949-253-2300
Galesburg Printing & Publishing Co	140 S Prairie St	Galesburg	IL	61401	**800-733-2767**	309-343-7181
Gazette Newspapers Inc	9030 Comprint Ct	Gaithersburg	MD	20877	**888-670-7100**	301-948-3120
George J Foster Co Inc	150 Venture Dr	Dover	NH	03820	**800-462-2265**	603-742-4455
Glastonbury Citizen Inc	PO Box 373	Glastonbury	CT	06033	**860-537-1772**	860-633-4691
Gray Television Inc	4370 Peachtree Rd NE *NYSE: GTN*	Atlanta	GA	30319	**888-835-2869**	404-504-9828
Guard Publishing Co	PO Box 10188	Eugene	OR	97440	**800-377-7428**	541-485-1234
Hastings & Sons Publishing	38 Exchange St	Lynn	MA	01901	**800-243-4636**	781-593-7700
Herald Publishing Co	PO Box 153	Houston	TX	77001	**888-421-1866**	713-630-0391
Herald-Mail Co, The	100 Summit Ave PO Box 439	Hagerstown	MD	21741	**800-626-6397**	301-733-5131
Herald-Star	401 Herald Sq	Steubenville	OH	43952	**800-526-7987**	740-283-4711
Hersam Acorn Newspapers	16 Bailey Ave	Ridgefield	CT	06877	**800-372-2790**	203-438-6544
High Plains Publishers Inc	1500 W Wyatt Earp Blvd	Dodge City	KS	67801	**800-452-7171**	620-227-7171
Home News Enterprises	333 Second St	Columbus	IN	47201	**800-876-7811**	
Hubbard Publishing Co	127 E Chillicothe Ave PO Box 40	Bellefontaine	OH	43311	**866-632-9992**	937-592-3060
Huse Publishing Co	525 Norfolk Ave PO Box 977	Norfolk	NE	68701	**877-371-1020**	402-371-1020
Independent Publishing Co	1000 Williamston Rd	Anderson	SC	29621	**800-859-6397**	864-224-4321
Indiana Printing & Publishing Co	899 Water St PO Box 10	Indiana	PA	15701	**800-262-3077**	724-465-5555
Journal Graphics Inc	2840 NW 35th Ave	Portland	OR	97210	**888-609-6051**	503-790-9100
Journal Publishing Co	1242 S Green St	Tupelo	MS	38804	**800-264-6397**	662-842-2611
Keene Publishing Corp	PO Box 546	Keene	NH	03431	**800-765-9994**	603-352-1234
Knight Publishing Co	600 S Tryon St	Charlotte	NC	28202	**800-332-0686**	704-358-5000
Lake Charles American Press Inc	PO Box 2893	Lake Charles	LA	70602	**800-737-2283**	337-433-3000
Lakeville Journal Co LLC	33 Bissell St PO Box 1688	Lakeville	CT	06039	**800-553-2234**	860-435-9873
Lancaster Newspapers Inc	8 W King St PO Box 1328	Lancaster	PA	17603	**800-809-4666**	717-291-8811
Landmark Community Newspapers Inc	601 Taylorsville Rd	Shelbyville	KY	40065	**800-939-9322**	502-633-4334
Lawrence Daily Journal-World Co	609 New Hampshire St PO Box 888	Lawrence	KS	66044	**800-578-8748**	785-843-1000
Livingston County Daily Press & Argus	323 E Grand River Ave	Howell	MI	48843	**888-999-1288**	517-548-2000
Lowell Sun Publishing Co	491 Dutton St *Cust Svc	Lowell	MA	01854	**800-359-1300***	978-458-7100
Madison Newspapers Inc	1901 Fish Hatchery Rd *Sales	Madison	WI	53713	**800-252-7723***	608-252-6200
Magic Valley Newspapers	132 Fairfield St W	Twin Falls	ID	83301	**800-658-3883**	208-733-0931
Marshall Independent	508 W Main St PO Box 411	Marshall	MN	56258	**877-276-6070**	507-537-1551
McClatchy Newspapers	2100 Q St	Sacramento	CA	95816	**866-807-2200**	916-321-1000
Memphis Publishing Co	495 Union Ave *Cust Svc	Memphis	TN	38103	**800-444-6397***	901-529-2666
Meridian Star Inc	814 22nd Ave *Cust Svc	Meridian	MS	39301	**800-232-2525***	601-693-1551
Mid-America Publishing Corp	9 Second St NW	Hampton	IA	50441	**800-558-1244**	641-456-2585
Milford Daily News Co	197 Main St	Milford	MA	01757	**800-281-6498**	508-634-7522
Missouri Lawyers Media	319 N Fourth St	Saint Louis	MO	63102	**800-635-5297**	314-421-1880
Missourian Publishing Co	14 W Main St	Washington	MO	63090	**888-239-7701**	636-239-7701
Moline Dispatch Publishing Co	1720 Fifth Ave	Moline	IL	61265	**800-660-2472**	309-764-4344
Morning Call Inc	101 N Sixth St	Allentown	PA	18101	**800-666-5492**	610-820-6500
Morris Communications Company LLC	725 Broad St	Augusta	GA	30901	**800-622-6358**	706-724-0851
Native American Times	PO Box 411	Tahlequah	OK	74465	**800-367-5390**	918-708-5838
Northwest Herald Inc	PO Box 250	Crystal Lake	IL	60039	**800-589-8910**	815-459-4040
Oakland Press	48 W Huron St	Pontiac	MI	48342	**888-977-3677**	248-332-8181
Observer & Eccentric Newspapers	615 W Lafayette Second Level	Detroit	MI	48226	**866-887-2737**	
Observer Publishing Co	122 S Main St	Washington	PA	15301	**800-222-6397**	724-222-2200
Oshkosh Northwestern Co	224 State St	Oshkosh	WI	54901	**800-924-6168**	920-235-7700
Our Sunday Visitor Inc	200 Noll Plaza	Huntington	IN	46750	**800-348-2440**	260-356-8400

Company / Address	City	State	Zip	Toll-Free	Phone
Palm Beach Newspapers Inc PO Box 24700	West Palm Beach	FL	33416	**800-432-7595**	561-820-4100
Papers Inc 206 S Main St	Milford	IN	46542	**800-733-4111**	574-658-4111
PG Publishing Co 34 Blvd of the Allies	Pittsburgh	PA	15222	**800-228-6397***	412-263-1100
*Cust Svc					
Phoenix Media Communications Group 126 Brookline Ave	Boston	MA	02215	**888-536-7464**	617-536-5390
Pipestone Publishing Co PO Box 277	Pipestone	MN	56164	**800-325-6440**	507-825-3333
Ponca City Publishing Inc PO Box 191	Ponca City	OK	74602	**866-765-3311**	580-765-3311
Press-Enterprise Co PO Box 792	Riverside	CA	92502	**800-794-6397**	951-684-1200
Press-Enterprise Inc 3185 Lackawanna Ave	Bloomsburg	PA	17815	**888-484-6345**	570-784-2121
Princeton Packet, The 300 Witherspoon St PO Box 350	Princeton	NJ	08542	**888-747-1122**	609-924-3244
Progressive Communications Corp 18 E Vine St PO Box 791	Mount Vernon	OH	43050	**800-772-5333**	740-397-5333
Quincy Newspapers Inc 130 S Fifth St	Quincy	IL	62301	**800-373-9444**	217-223-5100
Reminder Press Inc 130 Old Town Rd PO Box 27	Vernon	CT	06066	**888-456-2211**	860-875-3366
Republican Co 1860 Main St	Springfield	MA	01103	**800-828-5597**	413-788-1000
Republican-American Inc 389 Meadow St	Waterbury	CT	06702	**800-992-3232**	203-574-3636
Richmond Times-Dispatch PO Box 85333	Richmond	VA	23293	**800-468-3382**	804-649-6000
Rivertown Newspaper Group 2760 N Service Dr PO Box 15	Red Wing	MN	55066	**800-535-1660**	651-388-8235
Salisbury Post 131 W Innes St	Salisbury	NC	28144	**800-546-5664**	704-633-8950
San Angelo Standard Times Inc PO Box 5111	San Angelo	TX	76902	**800-588-1884**	325-653-1221
Santa Barbara News-Press Publishing Co 715 Anacapa St	Santa Barbara	CA	93101	**800-654-3292**	805-564-5200
Scripps Howard Inc PO Box 5380	Cincinnati	OH	45202	**800-888-3000**	513-977-3000
Stonebridge Press Inc 25 Elm St	Southbridge	MA	01550	**800-536-5836**	508-764-4325
Suburban Life Publications 1101 W 31st St Ste 100	Downers Grove	IL	60515	**800-397-9397**	630-368-1100
Sun Newspapers 1801 Superior Ave	Cleveland	OH	44114	**800-362-8008**	216-999-3900
TB Butler Publishing Co 410 W Erwin St	Tyler	TX	75702	**800-333-9141**	903-597-8111
Tennessee Valley Printing Company Inc PO Box 2213	Decatur	AL	35609	**888-353-4612**	256-353-4612
This Week Community Newspapers 7801 N Central Dr PO Box 608	Lewis Center	OH	43035	**800-860-1267**	740-888-6000
Times Herald Inc 410 Markley St PO Box 591	Norristown	PA	19404	**888-933-4233**	610-272-2500
Times News Publishing Co 707 S Main St	Burlington	NC	27215	**800-488-0085**	336-227-0131
Times-Citizen Communications Inc 406 Stevens St PO Box 640	Iowa Falls	IA	50126	**800-798-2691**	641-648-2521
Tribune Review Publishing Co 622 Cabin Hill Dr	Greensburg	PA	15601	**800-524-5700**	724-834-1151
Truth Publishing Company Inc 421 S Second St	Elkhart	IN	46516	**800-585-5416**	574-294-1661
Western States Weeklies Inc PO Box 600600	San Diego	CA	92160	**800-628-9466**	619-280-2985
William J Kline & Son Inc 1 Venner Rd	Amsterdam	NY	12010	**800-453-6397**	518-843-1100
Wooster Republican Printing Co 212 E Liberty St	Wooster	OH	44691	**800-686-2958**	330-264-1125
Worcester Telegram & Gazette Inc 20 Franklin St PO Box 15012	Worcester	MA	01615	**800-678-6680**	508-793-9100
World Publishing Co 315 S Boulder Ave	Tulsa	OK	74102	**800-444-6552**	918-583-2161
Yankton Press & Dakotan 319 Walnut St PO Box 56	Yankton	SD	57078	**800-743-2968**	605-665-7811
York Newspaper Co 1891 Loucks Rd	York	PA	17408	**800-559-3520**	717-767-6397

634-9 Periodicals Publishers

Company / Address	City	State	Zip	Toll-Free	Phone
Access Intelligence LLC 4 Choke Cherry Rd 2nd Fl	Rockville	MD	20850	**800-777-5006**	301-354-2000
Advertising Specialties Institute 4800 St Rd	Trevose	PA	19053	**800-546-1350**	215-942-8600
AHC Media LLC 3525 Piedmont Rd NE Bldg 6 Ste 400	Atlanta	GA	30305	**800-688-2421***	404-262-5476
*Cust Svc					
Alexander Communications Group Inc 712 Main St Ste 187-B	Boonton	NJ	07005	**800-232-4317**	973-265-2300
American Lawyer Media Inc (ALM) 120 Broadway 5th Fl	New York	NY	10271	**877-256-2472**	212-457-9400
American Psychiatric Publishing Inc 1000 Wilson Blvd Ste 1825	Arlington	VA	22209	**800-368-5777**	703-907-7322
Amos Press Inc 911 S Vandemark Rd	Sidney	OH	45365	**866-468-1622**	937-498-2111
Annual Reviews 4139 El Camino Way	Palo Alto	CA	94303	**800-523-8635**	650-493-4400
APN Media LLC PO Box 20113	New York	NY	10023	**800-470-7599**	212-581-3380
Atlantic Information Services Inc 1100 17th St NW Ste 300	Washington	DC	20036	**800-521-4323**	202-775-9008
Augsburg Fortress Publishers 510 Marquette Ave Ste 800	Minneapolis	MN	55402	**800-426-0115**	612-330-3300
BCC Research LLC 49 Walnut Pk Bldg 2	Wellesley	MA	02481	**866-285-7215**	781-489-7301
Boardroom Inc 281 Tresser Blvd 8th Fl	Stamford	CT	06901	**800-274-5611**	
Bobit Business Media 3520 Challenger St	Torrance	CA	90503	**888-239-2455**	310-533-2400
Bureau of National Affairs Inc 1801 S Bell St	Arlington	VA	22202	**800-372-1033**	703-341-3000
Business & Legal Reports Inc (BLR) 141 Mill Rock Rd E	Old Saybrook	CT	06475	**800-727-5257**	860-510-0100
Business News Publishing Co 2401 W Big Beaver Rd Ste 700	Troy	MI	48084	**800-837-7370**	248-362-3700
Cabot Heritage Corp 176 N St PO Box 2049	Salem	MA	01970	**800-326-8826**	978-745-5532
Challenge Publications Inc 9509 Vassar Ave Ste A	Chatsworth	CA	91311	**800-562-9182**	818-700-6868
Commodity Information Systems Inc 3030 NW Expy Ste 725	Oklahoma City	OK	73112	**800-231-0477**	405-604-8726
Consumers Union of US Inc 101 Truman Ave	Yonkers	NY	10703	**800-927-4357**	914-378-2000
Cook Communications Ministries 4050 Lee Vance View	Colorado Springs	CO	80918	**800-708-5550**	719-536-0100
Crain Communications Inc 1155 Gratiot Ave	Detroit	MI	48207	**888-288-6954**	313-446-6000
CRC Press LLC 6000 Broken Sound Pkwy NW Ste 300	Boca Raton	FL	33487	**800-272-7737***	561-994-0555
*Cust Svc					
Cutter Information Corp 37 Broadway Ste 1	Arlington	MA	02474	**800-964-5118**	781-648-8700
Deal LLC, The 20 Broad St	New York	NY	10005	**888-667-3325***	212-313-9325
*Cust Svc					
Disney Consumer Products 500 S Buena Vista St	Burbank	CA	91521	**855-553-4763***	818-560-1000
*PR					
Earl G Graves Ltd 130 Fifth Ave 10th Fl	New York	NY	10011	**800-727-7777***	212-242-8000
*Cust Svc					
EGW.com Inc 4075 Papazian Way	Fremont	CA	94538	**800-546-4754***	510-668-0268
*Cust Svc					
Elliott Wave International (EWI) PO Box 1618	Gainesville	GA	30503	**800-336-1618***	770-536-0309
*Cust Svc					
Elsevier Science Ltd 360 Pk Ave S	New York	NY	10010	**888-437-4636**	212-989-5800
Entrepreneur Media Inc 18061 Fitch	Irvine	CA	92614	**877-652-5295**	949-261-2325
Ernst Publishing Co LLC 1 Commerce Plaza 99 Washington Ave Ste 309	Albany	NY	12210	**800-345-3822**	
Essence Communications Inc 135 W 50th St 4th Fl	New York	NY	10020	**800-274-9398***	
*Sales					
F+W, A Content + eCommerce Co 10151 Carver Rd Ste 200	Cincinnati	OH	45236	**800-289-0963***	513-531-2690
*Sales					
Forbes Inc 60 Fifth Ave	New York	NY	10011	**800-295-0893**	212-620-2200
Forecast International 22 Commerce Rd	Newtown	CT	06470	**800-451-4975**	203-426-0800
Forum Publishing Co 383 E Main St	Centerport	NY	11721	**800-635-7654**	631-754-5000
Gardner Publications Inc 6915 Valley Ave	Cincinnati	OH	45244	**800-950-8020**	513-527-8800
Grace Communion International PO Box 5005	Glendora	CA	91740	**800-423-4444**	626-650-2300
Grand View Media Group Inc (GVMG) 200 Croft St Ste 1	Birmingham	AL	35242	**888-431-2877**	205-408-3700
Hanley-Wood LLC 1 Thomas Cir NW Ste 600	Washington	DC	20005	**800-227-8839**	202-452-0800
Hart Publications Inc 1616 S Voss Rd Ste 1000	Houston	TX	77057	**800-874-2544**	713-260-6400
Hatton Brown Publishers Inc PO Box 2268	Montgomery	AL	36102	**800-669-5613**	334-834-1170
Health Forum 155 North Wacker Drive Ste 400	Chicago	IL	60606	**800-621-6902**	312-893-6800
Healthy Directions LLC 7811 Montrose Rd	Potomac	MD	20854	**866-599-9491**	
Highlights for Children Inc 1800 Watermark Dr	Columbus	OH	43216	**800-255-9517***	614-486-0631
*Cust Svc					
Hli Properties Inc 1003 Central Ave	Fort Dodge	IA	50501	**800-247-2000**	515-955-1600
Hobsons CollegeView 50 E Business Way Ste 300	Cincinnati	OH	45241	**800-927-8439**	
Homes & Land Magazine Affiliates LLC 1830 E Pk Ave	Tallahassee	FL	32301	**800-277-7800**	850-575-0189
Honolulu Publishing Co Ltd 707 Richards St Ste PH3	Honolulu	HI	96813	**800-272-5245**	808-524-7400
IEEE Computer Society Press 10662 Los Vaqueros Cir PO Box 3014	Los Alamitos	CA	90720	**800-272-6657**	714-821-8380
Information Today Inc 143 Old Marlton Pike	Medford	NJ	08055	**800-300-9868**	609-654-6266
InfoWorld Media Group Inc 501 Second St 6 Fl	San Francisco	CA	94107	**800-227-8365**	415-243-0500
Inside Washington Publishers 1919 S Eads St Ste 201	Arlington	VA	22202	**800-424-9068**	703-416-8500
Institutional Investor Newsletters 225 Pk Ave S 8th Fl	New York	NY	10003	**800-437-9997**	212-224-3300
International Data Group Inc (IDG) 1 Exeter Plaza 15th Fl	Boston	MA	02116	**800-343-4952***	617-534-1200
*Orders					
Internet Business Network 303 Ross Dr	Mill Valley	CA	94941	**866-497-6747**	415-377-2255
JR O'Dwyer Co 271 Madison Ave 6th Fl	New York	NY	10016	**866-395-7710**	212-679-2471
Laurin Publishing Co Inc 100 West St	Pittsfield	MA	01202	**877-422-7300**	413-499-0514
Lawrence Ragan Communications Inc 111 E Wacker Dr Ste 500	Chicago	IL	60601	**800-878-5331**	800-493-4867
Lionheart Publishing Inc 506 Roswell St	Marietta	GA	30060	**888-303-5639**	

				Toll-Free	Phone
Liturgical Publications Inc 2875 S James Dr	New Berlin	WI	53151	800-876-4574	262-785-1188
LRP Publications 360 Hiatt Dr	Palm Beach Gardens	FL	33418	800-621-5463	561-622-6520
Mary Ann Liebert Publishers Inc 140 Huguenot St 3rd Fl	New Rochelle	NY	10801	800-654-3237	914-740-2100
McKnight's Long-Term Care News 1 Northfield Plz Ste 521	Northfield	IL	60093	800-558-1703	847-784-8706
Meister Media Worldwide 37733 Euclid Ave *Orders	Willoughby	OH	44094	800-572-7740*	440-942-2000
Mergent Inc 477 Madison Ave Ste 410	New York	NY	10022	800-937-1398	212-413-7700
Merion Publications Inc 2900 Horizon Dr	King of Prussia	PA	19406	800-355-1088	610-278-1400
Miles Media Group Inc 6751 Professional Pkwy W Ste 200	Sarasota	FL	34240	888-232-2499	941-342-2300
National Braille Press Inc 88 St Stephen St	Boston	MA	02115	888-965-8965	617-266-6160
National Catholic Reporter Publishing Co 115 E Armour Blvd	Kansas City	MO	64111	800-333-7373	816-531-0538
Nelson Publishing 2500 Tamiami Trl N	Nokomis	FL	34275	800-226-6113	941-966-9521
North American Publishing Co (NAPCO) 1500 Springarden St 12th Fl	Philadelphia	PA	19130	800-627-2689	215-238-5300
Our Sunday Visitor Inc 200 Noll Plaza	Huntington	IN	46750	800-348-2440	260-356-8400
Pacific Press 1350 N Kings Rd *Cust Svc	Nampa	ID	83687	800-765-6955*	208-465-2500
Paisano Publications LLC 28210 Dorothy Dr	Agoura Hills	CA	91301	800-323-3484	818-889-8740
Photosource International 1910 35th Rd	Osceola	WI	54020	800-786-6277	715-248-3800
Platts 2 Penn Plz 25th Fl	New York	NY	10121	800-752-8878	212-904-3070
Pohly Co 867 Boylston St 5th Fl	Boston	MA	02116	800-383-0888	617-451-1700
Progressive Impressions 1 Hardman Dr	Bloomington	IL	61701	800-644-0444	309-664-0444
Publications & Communications Inc 13552 Hwy 183 N Ste A	Austin	TX	78750	800-678-9724	512-250-9023
Publications International Ltd 7373 N Cicero Ave *General	Lincolnwood	IL	60712	800-777-5582*	847-676-3470
Putman Media Inc 555 W Pierce Rd	Itasca	IL	60143	866-666-6033	630-467-1301
Randall-Reilly Publishing Co 3200 Rice Mine Rd NE *Cust Svc	Tuscaloosa	AL	35406	800-633-5953*	
RentPath Inc 950 E Paces Ferry Rd NE Ste 2600	Norcross	GA	30092	800-216-1423	678-421-3000
RentPath, LLC 950 East Paces Ferry Rd NE Ste 2600	Atlanta	GA	30326	800-216-1423	678-421-3000
Review & Herald Publishing Assn 55 W Oak Ridge Dr	Hagerstown	MD	21740	800-456-3991	301-393-3000
Sage Publications Inc 2455 Teller Rd	Thousand Oaks	CA	91320	800-818-7243	805-499-9774
Saint Croix Press Inc 1185 S Knowles Ave	New Richmond	WI	54017	800-826-6622	715-246-5811
Sandhills Publishing 120 W Harvest Dr	Lincoln	NE	68521	800-331-1978	402-479-2181
Schaeffer's Investment Research Inc 5151 Pfeiffer Rd Ste 250	Cincinnati	OH	45242	800-448-2080	513-589-3800
Simba Information 60 Long Ridge Rd Ste 300	Stamford	CT	06902	888-297-4622	203-325-8193
Simmons-Boardman Publishing Corp 55 Broad St 26th fl 12th Fl	New York	NY	10004	800-895-4389	212-620-7200
Sky Publishing Corp 90 Sherman St	Cambridge	MA	02140	800-253-0245	617-864-7360
Slack Inc 6900 Grove Rd	Thorofare	NJ	08086	800-257-8290	856-848-1000
Smithsonian Institution Business Ventures Div 600 Maryland Ave SW Ste 6000	Washington	DC	20024	800-521-5330	202-633-6080
Source Media Inc 1 State St Plz 27th Fl	New York	NY	10004	800-221-1809	212-803-8200
Stamats Communications Inc 615 Fifth St SE	Cedar Rapids	IA	52401	800-553-8878	319-364-6167
Standard Publishing Co 8805 Governors Hill Dr Ste 400 *Orders	Cincinnati	OH	45249	800-543-1353*	513-931-4050
Strafford Publications Inc PO Box 13729	Atlanta	GA	30324	800-926-7926	404-881-1141
Sunset Publishing Corp 80 Willow Rd	Menlo Park	CA	94025	800-227-7346	650-321-3600
Tax Management Inc 1801 S Bell St	Arlington	VA	22202	800-372-1033	703-341-3000
Thompson Publishing Group Inc 805 15th St NW 3rd Fl *Cust Svc	Washington	DC	20005	800-677-3789*	202-872-4000
Transcontinental Inc 1100 Rene-Levesque Blvd W 24th Fl	Montreal	QC	H3B4X9	800-361-5479	514-392-9000
TransWorld Business 2052 Corte Del Nogal Ste 100 *General	Carlsbad	CA	92011	800-788-7072*	760-722-7777
United Methodist Publishing House 201 Eigth Ave S	Nashville	TN	37203	800-672-1789	615-749-6000
University of Chicago Press Journals Div PO Box 37005	Chicago	IL	60637	877-705-1878	773-702-7700
Vendome Group LLC 216 E 45th St 6th Fl	New York	NY	10017	800-519-3692	
Warren Communications News Inc 2115 Ward Ct NW	Washington	DC	20037	800-771-9202	202-872-9200
Wright's Media 2407 Timberloch Pl Ste B	The Woodlands	TX	77380	877-652-5295	281-419-5725
Yankee Publishing Inc PO Box 520	Dublin	NH	03444	800-729-9265	603-563-8111

634-10 Publishers (Misc)

				Toll-Free	Phone
AM Best Co Ambest Rd	Oldwick	NJ	08858	800-424-2378	908-439-2200
American Printing House for the Blind 1839 Frankfort Ave PO Box 6085	Louisville	KY	40206	800-223-1839	502-895-2405
Cathedral Press Inc 600 NE Sixth St *Cust Svc	Long Prairie	MN	56347	800-874-8332*	320-732-6143
Chalk & Vermilion Fine Arts Inc 55 Old Post Rd Ste 2	Greenwich	CT	06830	800-877-2250	203-869-9500
Channing Bete Co 1 Community Pl	South Deerfield	MA	01373	800-477-4776	413-665-7611
Clement Communications Inc 3 Creek Pkwy	Upper Chichester	PA	19061	800-253-6368	610-459-4200
Coastal Training Technologies Corp 500 Studio Dr	Virginia Beach	VA	23452	866-333-6888	757-498-9014
Drivers License Guide Co 1492 Oddstad Dr	Redwood City	CA	94063	800-227-8827	650-369-4849
EBSCO Publishing Inc 10 Estes St	Ipswich	MA	01938	800-653-2726	978-356-6500
Encyclopedia Britannica Inc 331 N La Salle St *Cust Svc	Chicago	IL	60654	800-323-1229*	312-347-7159
Flyer.Com 201 Kelsey Ln	Tampa	FL	33619	800-995-4433	813-626-9430
Forecast International 22 Commerce Rd	Newtown	CT	06470	800-451-4975	203-426-0800
Hadley House Co PO Box 219	Cokato	MN	55321	800-423-5390	
Interactive Data Corp 32 Crosby Dr	Bedford	MA	01730	800-228-9715	781-687-8500
Lifetouch Church Directories 1371 Portland Way N	Galion	OH	44833	800-521-4611	419-468-4739
Mergent FIS Inc 580 Kingsley Pk Dr	Fort Mill	SC	29715	800-342-5647	
New York Graphic Society Ltd 129 Glover Ave	Norwalk	CT	06850	800-221-1032	800-677-6947
OAG Worldwide 3025 Highland Pkwy Ste 200	Downers Grove	IL	60515	800-342-5624	630-515-3230
OneSource Information Services Inc 300 Baker Ave	Concord	MA	01742	800-433-0287	978-318-4300
Somerset Fine Arts PO Box 869 *Sales	Fulshear	TX	77441	800-444-2540*	
TechTarget 275 Grove St Ste 800	Newton	MA	02466	888-274-4111	617-431-9200
Thomson CenterWatch Inc 100 N Washington St Ste 301 *Cust Svc	Boston	MA	02114	800-765-9647*	617-948-5100
Wonderlic Inc 400 Lakeview Pkwy Ste 200	Vernon Hills	IL	60061	877-605-9496	847-680-4900

634-11 Technical Publishers

				Toll-Free	Phone
Aircraft Technical Publishers 101 S Hill Dr	Brisbane	CA	94005	800-227-4610	415-330-9500
Faulkner Information Services 7905 Browning Rd	Pennsauken	NJ	08109	800-843-0460	856-662-2070
Health Forum 155 North Wacker Drive Ste 400	Chicago	IL	60606	800-621-6902	312-893-6800
Information Gatekeepers Inc (IGI) 1340 Soldiers Field Rd Ste 2	Brighton	MA	02135	800-323-1088	617-782-5033
JJ Keller & Assoc Inc 3003 Breezewood Ln PO Box 368	Neenah	WI	54957	800-558-5011	920-722-2848
Mitchell 1 14145 Danielson St	Poway	CA	92064	888-724-6742	858-391-5000
Mitchell International Inc 6220 Greenwich Dr	San Diego	CA	92122	800-854-7030	858-368-7000
O'Reilly & Assoc Inc 1005 Gravenstein Hwy N	Sebastopol	CA	95472	800-998-9938	707-829-0515
Thompson Publishing Group Inc 805 15th St NW 3rd Fl *Cust Svc	Washington	DC	20005	800-677-3789*	202-872-4000

635 PULP MILLS

SEE ALSO Paper Mills ; Paperboard Mills

				Toll-Free	Phone
Alberta-Pacific Forest Industries Inc PO Box 8000	Boyle	AB	T0A0M0	800-661-5210	780-525-8000
International Paper Co 6400 Poplar Ave *NYSE: IP* ■ *Prod Info	Memphis	TN	38197	800-223-1268*	901-419-9000
Kimberly-Clark Corp 351 Phelps Dr *NYSE: KMB*	Irving	TX	75038	888-525-8388	972-281-1200
Omaha Paper Co 6936 L St	Omaha	NE	68117	800-288-7026	402-331-3243

636 PUMPS - MEASURING & DISPENSING

				Toll-Free	Phone
Assay Technology Inc 1382 Stealth St	Livermore	CA	94551	800-833-1258	925-461-8880
Bennett Pump Co 1218 Pontaluna Rd	Spring Lake	MI	49456	800-235-7618	231-798-1310
Brooks Utility Products Group 23847 Industrial Park Dr	Farmington Hills	MI	48335	888-687-3008	248-477-0250
Chen Instrument Design Inc 4845 NW Camas Meadows Dr	Camas	WA	98607	800-767-0119	360-833-8835
Controlled Access Inc 1515 W 130th St	Hinckley	OH	44233	800-942-0829	330-273-6185

Company / Address	City	State	ZIP	Toll-Free	Phone
DICKEY-John Corp 5200 Dickey-John Rd	Auburn	IL	62615	800-637-2952	217-438-3371
Electro Static Technology 31 Winterbrook Rd	Mechanic Falls	ME	04256	866-738-1857	207-998-5140
Gasboy International Inc 7300 W Friendly Ave *Sales	Greensboro	NC	27420	800-444-5579*	336-547-5000
Gerhart Systems & Controls Corp 754 Roble Rd Ste 140	Allentown	PA	18109	888-437-4278	610-264-2800
Medicomp Inc 7845 Ellis Rd	Melbourne	FL	32904	800-234-3278	321-794-3811
O'Day Equipment Inc 1301 40th St NW	Fargo	ND	58102	800-654-6329	701-282-9260
Rice Lake Weighing Systems Inc 230 W Coleman St	Rice Lake	WI	54868	800-472-6703	
Standard Imaging Inc 3120 Deming Way	Middleton	WI	53562	800-261-4446	608-831-0025
Tuthill Transfer Systems 8500 S Madison	Burr Ridge	IL	60527	800-825-6937	260-747-7529

637 PUMPS & MOTORS - FLUID POWER

Company / Address	City	State	ZIP	Toll-Free	Phone
Applied Energy Company Inc (AEC) 1205 Venture Ct Ste 100	Carrollton	TX	75006	800-580-1171	214-355-4200
Bosch Rexroth Corp 5150 Prairie Stone Pkwy	Hoffman Estates	IL	60192	800-860-1055	847-645-3600
Bosch Rexroth Corp Piston Pump Div 8 Southchase Ct	Fountain Inn	SC	29644	877-266-7811	864-967-2777
Fluid Metering Inc 5 Aerial Way Ste 500	Syosset	NY	11791	800-223-3388	516-922-6050
Jetstream of Houston LLP 4930 Cranswick	Houston	TX	77041	800-231-8192	713-462-7000
Permco Inc 1500 Frost Rd	Streetsboro	OH	44241	800-628-2801	330-626-2801
TII Network Technologies Inc 141 Rodeo Dr *NASDAQ: TIII*	Edgewood	NY	11717	888-844-4720	631-789-5000

638 PUMPS & PUMPING EQUIPMENT (GENERAL USE)

SEE ALSO Industrial Machinery, Equipment, & Supplies

Company / Address	City	State	ZIP	Toll-Free	Phone
Acme Dynamics Inc 3608 Sydney Rd PO Box 1780	Plant City	FL	33566	800-622-9355	813-752-3137
Aermotor Pumps Inc 293 Wright St	Delavan	WI	53115	800-230-1816	
Air Systems International Inc 829 Juniper Crescent	Chesapeake	VA	23320	800-866-8100	757-424-3967
American Machine & Tool Company Inc 400 Spring St	Royersford	PA	19468	888-268-7867	610-948-3800
Amico Corp 85 Fulton Way	Richmond Hill	ON	L4B2N4	877-462-6426	905-764-0800
Ampco Pumps Company Inc 2045 W Mill Rd	Glendale	WI	53209	800-737-8671	414-643-1852
AR Wilfley & Sons Inc 7350 E Progress Pl Ste 200	Englewood	CO	80111	800-525-9930	303-779-1777
Armstrong International Inc 2081 SE Ocean Blvd 4th Fl	Stuart	FL	34996	866-738-5125	772-286-7175
ASM Industries Inc Pacer Pumps Div 41 Industrial Cir *Cust Svc	Lancaster	PA	17601	800-233-3861*	717-656-2161
Barker Air & Hydraulics Inc 1308 Miller Rd	Greenville	SC	29607	800-922-3324	864-288-3537
Beckett Corp 3250 Skyway Cir N	Irving	TX	75038	888-232-5388	972-871-8000
Berkeley Pumps 293 Wright St	Delavan	WI	53115	866-582-2032	262-728-5551
Blackmer 1809 Century Ave	Grand Rapids	MI	49503	888-363-7886	616-241-1611
Busch Vacuum Technics Inc 1740 Lionel Bertrand	Boisbriand	QC	J7H1N7	800-363-6360	450-435-6899
CDS-John Blue Co 290 Pinehurst Dr	Huntsville	AL	35806	800-253-2583	256-721-9090
CLYDE UNION Pumps 4600 W Dickman Rd	Battle Creek	MI	49037	800-877-7867	269-966-4600
Coffin Turbo Pump Inc 326 S Dean St	Englewood	NJ	07631	800-568-9798	201-568-2826
Corken Inc 3805 NW 36th St	Oklahoma City	OK	73112	800-631-4929	405-946-5576
CS & P Technologies LP 18119 Telge Rd	Cypress	TX	77429	800-262-6103	713-467-0869
F E Myers 1101 Myers Pkwy	Ashland	OH	44805	855-274-8947	419-289-1144
Flint & Walling Inc 95 N Oak St *Sales	Kendallville	IN	46755	800-345-9422*	260-347-1600
Flowserve Corp 5215 N O'Connor Blvd Ste 2300 *NYSE: FLS*	Irving	TX	75039	800-350-1082	972-443-6500
FMG Enterprises Inc 1125 Memorex Dr	Santa Clara	CA	95050	800-327-6177	408-982-0110
GIW Industries Inc 5000 Wrightsboro Rd	Grovetown	GA	30813	888-832-4449	706-863-1011
Graco Inc 88 11th Ave NE PO Box 1441 *NYSE: GGG* ■ *Cust Svc	Minneapolis	MN	55413	800-328-0211*	612-623-6000
Graymills Corp 3705 N Lincoln Ave	Chicago	IL	60613	877-465-7867	773-477-4100
Great Plains Industries Inc 5252 E 36th St N *Sales	Wichita	KS	67220	800-835-0113*	316-686-7361
Hale Products Inc 700 Spring Mill Ave	Conshohocken	PA	19428	800-220-4253	610-825-6300
Hammelmann Corp 600 Progress Rd	Dayton	OH	45449	800-783-4935	937-859-8777
Harben Inc 2010 Ronald Regan Blvd	Cumming	GA	30041	800-327-5387	770-889-9535
Haskel International Inc 100 E Graham Pl	Burbank	CA	91502	800-743-2720	818-843-4000
Hydromatic Pump Co 740 E Ninth St	Ashland	OH	44805	888-957-8677	
HydroPressure Cleaning Inc 413 Dawson Dr	Camarillo	CA	93012	800-934-2399	
Hypro 375 Fifth Ave NW *Cust Svc	New Brighton	MN	55112	800-424-9776*	651-766-6300
Imo Pump 1710 Airport Rd	Monroe	NC	28110	888-478-6996	704-289-6511
Integrated Flow Solutions LLC 6461 Reynolds Rd	Tyler	TX	75708	800-859-7867	903-595-6511
Kerr Pump & Supply 12880 Cloverdale St	Oak Park	MI	48237	800-482-8259	248-543-3880
Koshin America Corp 1218 Remington Rd	Schaumburg	IL	60173	800-634-4092	847-310-0740
Kraft Fluid Systems Inc 14300 Foltz Pkwy	Strongsville	OH	44149	800-257-1155	440-238-5545
Lehigh Fluid Power Inc 1413 Rt 179	Lambertville	NJ	08530	800-257-9515	
Liberty Pumps Inc 7000 Apple Tree Ave	Bergen	NY	14416	800-543-2550	585-494-1817
Madden Manufacturing Inc PO Box 387	Elkhart	IN	46515	800-369-6233	574-295-4292
McNally Industries LLC 340 W Benson Ave	Grantsburg	WI	54840	800-366-1410	715-463-8300
Met-Pro Corp Fybroc Div 700 Emlen Way	Telford	PA	18969	800-392-7621	215-723-8155
Met-Pro Corp Sethco Div 800 Emlen Way	Telford	PA	18969	800-645-0500	215-799-2577
Micropump Inc 1402 NE 136th Ave *Sales	Vancouver	WA	98684	800-222-9565*	360-253-2008
Moyno Inc 1895 W Jefferson St	Springfield	OH	45506	877-486-6966	937-327-3111
MP Pumps Inc 34800 Bennett Dr	Fraser	MI	48026	800-563-8006	586-293-8240
National Pump Company LLC 7706 N 71st Ave	Glendale	AZ	85303	800-966-5240	623-979-3560
Neptune Chemical Pump Co PO Box 247	Lansdale	PA	19446	800-255-4017	215-699-8700
Neptune-Benson Inc 6 Jefferson Dr	Coventry	RI	02816	800-832-8002	401-821-2200
NH Yates & Company Inc 117 Church Ln # C	Cockeysville	MD	21030	800-878-8181	
PACO Pumps Inc 902 Koomey Rd	Brookshire	TX	77423	800-955-5847	281-994-2700
Peerless Pump Co 2005 ML King Jr St PO Box 7026	Indianapolis	IN	46207	800-879-0182	317-925-9661
Penn Air & Hydraulics Corp 1750 Industrial Hwy	York	PA	17402	888-631-7638	717-840-8100
Pentair Water Pool & Spa 1620 Hawkins Ave	Sanford	NC	27330	800-831-7133	
Roper Pump Co 3475 Old Maysville Rd *Sales	Commerce	GA	30529	800-944-6769*	706-335-5551
Roth Pump Co PO Box 4330	Rock Island	IL	61204	888-444-7684	309-787-1791
RS Corcoran Co 500 N Vine St	New Lenox	IL	60451	800-637-1067	815-485-2156
Scot Pump 6437 Pioneer Rd PO Box 286	Cedarburg	WI	53012	888-835-0600	262-377-7000
Serfilco Ltd 2900 MacArthur Blvd	Northbrook	IL	60062	800-323-5431	847-559-1777
SHURflo Pump Mfg Company Inc 5900 Katella Ave	Cypress	CA	90630	800-854-3218	562-795-5200
Simflo Pumps Inc 754 E Maley St PO Box 849	Willcox	AZ	85644	800-232-4142	520-384-2273
Standard Alloys & Mfg PO Box 969	Port Arthur	TX	77640	800-231-8240	409-983-3201
Thompson Pump & Mfg Company Inc 4620 City Ctr Dr PO Box 291370	Port Orange	FL	32129	800-767-7310	386-767-7310
Tuthill Corp 8500 S Madison St	Burr Ridge	IL	60527	800-634-2695	630-382-4900
Ultimate Washer Inc 711 Commerce Way Ste 1	Jupiter	FL	33458	866-858-4982	561-741-7022
Vaughan Company Inc 364 Monte-Elma Rd	Montesano	WA	98563	888-249-2467	360-249-4042
Vogelsang USA 7966 State Rt 44	Ravenna	OH	44266	800-984-9400	330-296-3820
Wastecorp Inc PO Box 70	Grand Island	NY	14072	888-829-2783	
Waterous Co 125 Hardman Ave	South Saint Paul	MN	55075	800-488-1228	651-450-5000
Waukesha Cherry-Burrell Corp (WCB) 611 Sugar Creek Rd	Delavan	WI	53115	800-252-5200	262-728-1900
Zoeller Co 3649 Kane Run Rd *OTC: ZOLR*	Louisville	KY	40211	800-928-7867	502-778-2731

639 RACING & RACETRACKS

SEE ALSO Motor Speedways

Company / Address	City	State	ZIP	Toll-Free	Phone
Alameda County Fair Assn (ACFA) 4501 Pleasanton Ave	Pleasanton	CA	94566	800-874-9253	925-426-7600
Brainerd International Raceway 5523 Birchdale Rd	Brainerd	MN	56401	866-444-4455	218-824-7223
Calder Casino & Race Course 21001 NW 27th Ave	Miami	FL	33056	800-522-4700	305-625-1311
Calgary Exhibition & Stampede Ltd 1410 Olympic Way S E	Calgary	AB	T2G2W1	888-883-3828	403-261-0101
Canterbury Park Holding Corp 1100 Canterbury Rd *NASDAQ: CPHC*	Shakopee	MN	55379	800-340-6361	952-445-7223

Classified Section

				Toll-Free	Phone
Charlotte Motor Speedway 5555 Concord Pkwy S	Concord	NC	28027	**800-455-3267**	704-455-3200
Churchill Downs Inc 700 Central Ave	Louisville	KY	40208	**800-994-9909**	502-636-4400
NASDAQ: CHDN					
Colonial Downs 10515 Colonial Downs Pkwy	New Kent	VA	23124	**888-482-8722**	804-966-7223
Delta Downs Racetrack 2717 Delta Downs Dr	Vinton	LA	70668	**800-589-7441**	
Dover Downs Hotel & Casino 1131 N DuPont Hwy	Dover	DE	19901	**800-711-5882**	302-674-4600
NYSE: DDE					
Dover International Speedway 1131 N DuPont Hwy PO Box 843	Dover	DE	19901	**800-441-7223**	302-883-6500
Fair Grounds Race Course 1751 Gentilly Blvd	New Orleans	LA	70119	**800-262-7983**	504-944-5515
Fair Meadows at Tulsa 4609 E 21st St	Tulsa	OK	74114	**877-781-2660**	918-743-7223
Finger Lakes Gaming & Race Track 5857 Rt 96	Farmington	NY	14425	**877-846-7369**	585-924-3232
Fort Erie Race Track 230 Catherine St PO Box 1130	Fort Erie	ON	L2A5N9	**800-295-3770**	905-871-3200
Fresno District Fair 1121 S Chance Ave	Fresno	CA	93702	**866-275-3772**	559-650-3247
Gillespie County Fairgrounds 530 Fair Dr PO Box 526	Fredericksburg	TX	78624	**800-280-9531**	830-997-2359
Grays Harbor Raceway 32 Elma McCleary Rd PO Box 911	Elma	WA	98541	**800-667-7711**	360-482-4374
Harrington Raceway 15 W Rider Rd	Harrington	DE	19952	**888-887-5687**	302-398-7223
Hazel Park Raceway 1650 E 10 Mile Rd	Hazel Park	MI	48030	**800-794-8001**	248-398-1000
Hollywood Casino at Charles Town Races 750 Hollywood Dr	Charles Town	WV	25414	**800-795-7001**	304-725-7001
Hoosier Park Racing & Casino 4500 Dan Patch Cir	Anderson	IN	46013	**800-526-7223**	765-642-7223
Josephine County Fairgrounds 1451 Fairgrounds Rd PO Box 672	Grants Pass	OR	97527	**800-773-1162**	541-476-3215
Laurel Park Rt 198 & Racetrack Rd PO Box 130	Laurel	MD	20724	**800-638-1859**	301-725-0400
MetraPark 308 6th Ave N	Billings	MT	59101	**800-366-8538**	406-256-2400
Mystique Casino 1855 Greyhound Pk Dr	Dubuque	IA	52001	**800-373-3647**	563-582-3647
Northville Downs 301 S Ctr St	Northville	MI	48167	**888-349-7100**	248-349-1000
Oaklawn Park 2705 Central Ave	Hot Springs	AR	71901	**800-625-5296***	501-623-4411
*General					
Ontario Lottery & Gaming Corp 70 Foster Dr Ste 800	Sault Sainte Marie	ON	P6A6V2	**800-563-5357**	705-946-6464
Penn National Gaming Inc 825 Berkshire Blvd Ste 200	Wyomissing	PA	19610	**877-565-2112**	
NASDAQ: PENN					
Pensacola Greyhound Track 951 Dog Track Rd	Pensacola	FL	32506	**800-345-3997**	850-455-8595
Pinnacle Entertainment Inc 3980 Howard Hughes Pkwy	Las Vegas	NV	89169	**877-764-8750**	702-541-7777
NYSE: PNK					
Ravalli County Fair 100 Old Corvallis Rd	Hamilton	MT	59840	**800-225-6779**	406-363-3411
Remington Park Race Track 1 Remington Pl	Oklahoma City	OK	73111	**866-456-9880**	405-424-1000
Scioto Downs Inc 6000 S High St	Columbus	OH	43207	**800-514-3849**	614-295-4700
Solano County Fair 900 Fairgrounds Dr	Vallejo	CA	94589	**800-700-2482**	707-551-2000
Sunland Park Racetrack & Casino 1200 Futurity Dr	Sunland Park	NM	88063	**800-572-1142**	575-874-5200
Tampa Bay Downs Inc 11225 Racetrack Rd	Tampa	FL	33626	**800-200-4434**	813-855-4401
Thistledown Racing Club Inc 21501 Emery Rd	Cleveland	OH	44128	**800-522-4700**	216-662-8600
TrackMaster 2083 Old Middlefield Way Ste 206	Mountain View	CA	94043	**800-334-3800**	650-316-1020
Turf Paradise Racetrack 1501 W Bell Rd	Phoenix	AZ	85023	**800-639-8783**	602-942-1101
Twin River Casino 100 Twin River Rd	Lincoln	RI	02865	**877-827-4837**	401-475-8505
Woodbine Entertainment Group Inc 555 Rexdale Blvd PO Box 156	Toronto	ON	M9W5L2	**888-675-7223**	416-675-7223

640 RADIO COMPANIES

				Toll-Free	Phone
Bible Broadcasting Network Inc 11530 Carmel Commons Blvd PO Box 7300	Charlotte	NC	28226	**800-888-7077**	704-523-5555
Bliss Communications Inc PO Box 5001	Janesville	WI	53547	**800-422-7128**	608-754-3311
Bott Radio Network 10550 Barkley St Ste 100	Overland Park	KS	66212	**800-875-1903**	913-642-7770
Eagle Communications Inc 2703 Hall St Ste 15 Ste 15	Hays	KS	67601	**877-613-2453**	785-625-5910
Eagle Radio Inc 2703 Hall St Ste 15	Hays	KS	67601	**877-613-2453**	
Educational Media Foundation 5700 W Oaks Blvd	Rocklin	CA	95765	**800-525-5683***	916-251-1600
*General					
Entercom Communications Corp 401 City Ave Ste 809	Bala Cynwyd	PA	19004	**800-776-9437**	610-660-5610
NYSE: ETM					
Family Radio 290 Hegenberger Rd	Oakland	CA	94621	**800-543-1495**	
Far East Broadcasting Co Inc 15700 Imperial Hwy PO Box 1	La Mirada	CA	90638	**800-523-3480**	
Midwest Communications Inc 904 Grand Ave	Wausau	WI	54403	**877-945-4236**	715-842-1437
Saga Communications Inc 73 Kercheval Ave	Grosse Pointe Farms	MI	48236	**800-777-3674**	313-886-7070
NYSE: SGA					
Shamrock Communications Inc 149 Penn Ave	Scranton	PA	18503	**800-228-4637**	570-348-9100
Telesouth Communications Inc 6311 Ridgewood Rd	Jackson	MS	39211	**888-808-8637**	601-957-1700
Zimmer Radio Group 3215 Lemone Industrial Blvd Ste 200	Columbia	MO	65201	**800-455-1099**	573-875-1099

641 RADIO NETWORKS

				Toll-Free	Phone
American Family Association PO Box 2440	Tupelo	MS	38803	**800-326-4543**	662-844-5036
Associated Press 1100 13th St NW Ste 700	Washington	DC	20005	**800-824-5498**	202-641-9000
Black Radio Network 166 Madison Ave	New York	NY	10016	**866-342-6892**	212-686-6850
Bott Radio Network 10550 Barkley St Ste 100	Overland Park	KS	66212	**800-875-1903**	913-642-7770
Family Life Communications Inc PO Box 35300	Tucson	AZ	85740	**800-776-1070**	
Far East Broadcasting Co Inc 15700 Imperial Hwy PO Box 1	La Mirada	CA	90638	**800-523-3480**	
Jones International Ltd 9697 E Mineral Ave	Centennial	CO	80112	**800-525-7002**	
Radio America 1100 N Glebe Rd Ste 900	Arlington	VA	22201	**800-807-4703**	703-302-1000
Relevant Radio 1496 Bellevue St Ste 202 PO Box 10707	Green Bay	WI	54311	**877-291-0123**	
Tiger Financial News Network 601 Cleveland St Ste 618	Clearwater	FL	33755	**877-518-9190**	727-467-9190
United Stations Radio Network 1065 Ave of the Americas 3rd Fl	New York	NY	10018	**866-989-1975**	212-869-1111
Yesterday USA Radio Networks, The 2001 Plymouth Rock Dr	Richardson	TX	75081	**800-624-2272**	972-889-9872

642 RADIO STATIONS

				Toll-Free	Phone
WICN-FM 90.5 (NPR) 50 Portland St	Worcester	MA	01608	**855-752-0700**	508-752-0700

642-1 Abilene, TX

				Toll-Free	Phone
KEAN-FM 105.1 (Ctry) 3911 S First St	Abilene	TX	79605	**800-588-5326**	325-676-5326
KGNZ-FM 88.1 (Rel) 542 Butternut St	Abilene	TX	79602	**800-588-8801**	325-673-3045

642-2 Akron, OH

				Toll-Free	Phone
Summit, The 65 Steiner Ave	Akron	OH	44301	**877-411-3662**	330-761-3099
WONE-FM 97.5 (Rock) 1795 W Market St	Akron	OH	44313	**888-588-8436**	330-869-9800

642-3 Albany, NY

				Toll-Free	Phone
WAMC-FM 90.3 (NPR) 318 Central Ave	Albany	NY	12206	**800-323-9262**	518-465-5233

642-4 Albuquerque, NM

				Toll-Free	Phone
KNML-AM 610 (Sports) 500 Fourth St NW 5th Fl	Albuquerque	NM	87102	**888-922-0610**	505-767-6700
KUNM-FM 89.9 (NPR) 1University of New Mexico MSC 06 3520	Albuquerque	NM	87131	**877-277-4806**	505-277-4806

642-5 Amarillo, TX

				Toll-Free	Phone
KACV-FM 90 (Alt) PO Box 447	Amarillo	TX	79178	**800-766-0176**	
KPRF-FM 98.7 (CHR) 6214 W 34th St	Amarillo	TX	79109	**866-930-5225**	806-355-9777

642-6 Anchorage, AK

				Toll-Free	Phone
KNBA-FM 90.3 (NPR) 3600 San Geronimo Dr Ste 480	Anchorage	AK	99508	**888-278-5622**	907-793-3500

642-7 Ann Arbor, MI

				Toll-Free	Phone
535 W William St Ste 110	Ann Arbor	MI	48103	**888-258-9866**	734-764-9210

642-8 Annapolis, MD

Name / Address	City	State	ZIP	Toll-Free	Phone
WRNR-FM 103.1 112 Main St 3rd Fl	Annapolis	MD	21401	**877-762-1031**	410-626-0103

642-9 Asheville, NC

Name / Address	City	State	ZIP	Toll-Free	Phone
WCQS-FM 88.1 (NPR) 73 Broadway	Asheville	NC	28801	**866-448-3881**	828-210-4800
WKJV-AM 1380 70 Adams Hill Rd	Asheville	NC	28806	**800-809-9558**	828-252-1380
WKSF-FM 99.9 (Ctry) 13 Summerlin Rd	Asheville	NC	28806	**800-303-5477**	828-257-2700

642-10 Atlanta, GA

Name / Address	City	State	ZIP	Toll-Free	Phone
Autonet Mobile Inc 3636 N Laughlin Rd Ste 150	Santa Rosa	CA	95403	**800-977-2107**	415-223-0316
WACG-FM 90.7 (NPR) 2500 Walton Way	Atlanta	GA	30904	**800-222-4788**	706-737-1661
WCLK-FM 91.9 (Jazz) 111 James P Brawley Dr SW	Atlanta	GA	30314	**888-448-3925**	404-880-8273

642-11 Baltimore, MD

Name / Address	City	State	ZIP	Toll-Free	Phone
102.7Jack FM 711 W 40th St	Baltimore	MD	21211	**888-410-1027**	410-366-7600
WPOC-FM 93.1 (Country) 711 W 40th St Ste 350	Baltimore	MD	21211	**866-962-5487**	410-366-7600
WRBS-FM 95.1 (Rel) 3500 Commerce Dr	Baltimore	MD	21227	**800-965-9324**	410-247-4100
WYPR-FM 88.1 (NPR) 2216 N Charles St	Baltimore	MD	21218	**866-789-8627**	410-235-1660

642-12 Bangor, ME

Name / Address	City	State	ZIP	Toll-Free	Phone
WHCF-FM 88.5 (Rel) PO Box 5000	Bangor	ME	04402	**800-947-2577**	207-947-2751
WMEH-FM 90.9 (NPR) 63 Texas Ave	Bangor	ME	04401	**800-884-1717**	207-941-1010
WVOM-FM 103.9 (N/T) 184 Target Industrial Cir	Bangor	ME	04401	**800-966-1039**	207-947-9100

642-13 Baton Rouge, LA

Name / Address	City	State	ZIP	Toll-Free	Phone
WBKL-FM 92.7 (Rel) PO Box 2098	Omaha	NE	68103	**800-525-5683**	
WRKF-FM 89.3 (NPR) 3050 Vly Creek Dr	Baton Rouge	LA	70808	**855-893-9753**	225-926-3050

642-14 Billings, MT

Name / Address	City	State	ZIP	Toll-Free	Phone
Yellowstone Public Radio 1500 University Dr	Billings	MT	59101	**800-441-2941**	406-657-2941

642-15 Birmingham, AL

Name / Address	City	State	ZIP	Toll-Free	Phone
WBHM-FM 90.3 (NPR) 650 11th St S	Birmingham	AL	35233	**800-444-9246**	205-934-2606
WDXB-FM 102.5 (Ctry) 600 Beacon Pkwy W Ste 400	Birmingham	AL	35209	**877-541-1966**	205-439-9600
WJSR-FM 91.1 (CR) Jefferson State Community College 2601 Carson Rd	Birmingham	AL	35215	**800-767-4984**	205-856-7702
WZZK-FM 104.7 (Ctry) 2700 Corporate Dr Ste 115	Birmingham	AL	35242	**866-998-1047**	205-916-1100

642-16 Bismarck, ND

Name / Address	City	State	ZIP	Toll-Free	Phone
KYYY-FM 92.9 (AC) 3500 E Rosser Ave	Bismarck	ND	58501	**866-929-9393**	701-224-9393

642-17 Boise, ID

Name / Address	City	State	ZIP	Toll-Free	Phone
KBXL-FM 94.1 (Rel) 1440 S Weideman Ave	Boise	ID	83709	**877-207-2276**	208-377-3790
KTIK-AM 1350 (Sports) 1419 W Bannock St	Boise	ID	83702	**866-296-1350**	208-336-3670

642-18 Boston, MA

Name / Address	City	State	ZIP	Toll-Free	Phone
WBUR-FM 90.9 (NPR) 890 Commonwealth Ave	Boston	MA	02215	**800-909-9287**	617-353-0909
WKLB-FM 102.5 (Ctry) 55 Morrissey Blvd	Boston	MA	02125	**888-819-1025**	617-822-9600
WUMB-FM 91.9 (Folk) 100 Morrissey Blvd	Boston	MA	02125	**800-573-2100**	617-287-6900

642-19 Branson, MO

Name / Address	City	State	ZIP	Toll-Free	Phone
KLFC-FM 88.1 (Rel) 205 W Atlantic St	Branson	MO	65616	**877-410-8592**	417-334-5532

642-20 Buffalo, NY

Name / Address	City	State	ZIP	Toll-Free	Phone
WDCX-FM 99.5 (Rel) 625 Delaware Ave Ste 308	Buffalo	NY	14202	**800-684-2848**	716-883-3010

642-21 Burlington, VT

Name / Address	City	State	ZIP	Toll-Free	Phone
WIZN-FM 106.7 (Rock) 255 S Champlain St	Burlington	VT	05401	**888-873-9496**	802-860-2440

642-22 Casper, WY

Name / Address	City	State	ZIP	Toll-Free	Phone
KRVK-FM 107.9 (Rock) 150 N Nichols Ave	Casper	WY	82601	**800-442-2256**	307-266-5252
KTRS-FM 104.7 (CHR) 150 N Nichols Ave	Casper	WY	82601	**800-442-2256**	307-266-5252
KWYY-FM 95.5 (Ctry) 150 N Nichols Ave	Casper	WY	82601	**800-339-4673**	307-266-5252

642-23 Cedar Rapids, IA

Name / Address	City	State	ZIP	Toll-Free	Phone
96.5 FM KISS Country 600 Old Marion Rd NE	Cedar Rapids	IA	52402	**800-258-0096**	319-395-0530

642-24 Champaign, IL

Name / Address	City	State	ZIP	Toll-Free	Phone
WBGL-FM 91.7 (Rel) 4101 Fieldstone Rd PO Box 111 *Cust Svc	Champaign	IL	61822	**800-475-9245***	217-359-8232
WDWS-AM 1400 (N/T) 2301 S Neil St	Champaign	IL	61820	**800-223-9397**	217-351-5300

642-45 Chattanooga, TN

Name / Address	City	State	ZIP	Toll-Free	Phone
WUTC-FM 88.1 (NPR) 615 McCallie Ave 104 Cadek Hall Dept 1151	Chattanooga	TN	37403	**800-272-3900**	423-425-4756

642-26 Charleston, WV

Name / Address	City	State	ZIP	Toll-Free	Phone
WQBE-FM 97.5 (Ctry) 817 Suncrest Pl	Charleston	WV	25303	**800-222-3697**	304-344-9700

642-27 Charlotte, NC

Name / Address	City	State	ZIP	Toll-Free	Phone
107.9 The Link 1 Julian Price Pl	Charlotte	NC	28208	**844-258-8477**	704-570-1079
WEND-FM 106.5 (Alt) 801 Wood Ridge Ctr Dr	Charlotte	NC	28217	**800-934-1065**	704-714-9444
WFAE-FM 90.7 (NPR) 8801 JM Keynes Dr Ste 91 *Cust Svc	Charlotte	NC	28262	**800-876-9323***	704-549-9323
WFNZ-AM 610 (Sports) 1520 S Blvd Ste 300	Charlotte	NC	28203	**866-570-9610**	704-319-9369

642-28 Chicago, IL

Name / Address	City	State	ZIP	Toll-Free	Phone
WMBI-FM 90.1 (Rel) 820 N LaSalle Blvd	Chicago	IL	60610	**877-376-2194**	312-329-4300

642-29 Cincinnati, OH

Name / Address	City	State	ZIP	Toll-Free	Phone
WAKW-FM 93.3 (Rel) 6275 Collegevue Pl PO Box 24126	Cincinnati	OH	45224	**888-542-9393**	513-542-9259
WIZF-FM 101.1 (Urban) 705 Central Ave	Cincinnati	OH	45202	**866-236-7588**	513-679-6000

642-30 Cleveland, OH

Name / Address	City	State	ZIP	Toll-Free	Phone
WENZ-FM 107.9 (Urban) 2510 St Clair Ave NE	Cleveland	OH	44114	**800-440-1079**	216-579-1111

642-31 Colorado Springs, CO

Station / Address	City	State	ZIP	Toll-Free	Phone
KILO-FM 94.3 (Rock) 1805 E Cheyenne Rd *General	Colorado Springs	CO	80905	**800-727-5456***	719-634-4896
KRCC-FM 91.5 (NPR) 912 N Weber St	Colorado Springs	CO	80903	**800-748-2727**	719-473-4801
KVOR-AM 740 (N/T) 6805 Corporate Dr Ste 130	Colorado Springs	CO	80919	**800-232-6459**	719-540-0740

642-32 Columbia, SC

Station / Address	City	State	ZIP	Toll-Free	Phone
WCOS-FM 97.5 (Ctry) 316 Greystone Blvd	Columbia	SC	29210	**800-570-9690**	803-343-1100

642-33 Columbus, GA

Station / Address	City	State	ZIP	Toll-Free	Phone
WRCG-AM 1420 (N/T) 1820 Wynnton Rd	Columbus	GA	31906	**844-706-7625**	706-327-1217

642-34 Columbus, OH

Station / Address	City	State	ZIP	Toll-Free	Phone
WBNS-FM 97.1 (AC) 605 S Front St Ste 300	Columbus	OH	43215	**888-691-9710**	614-460-3850
WCOL-FM 92.3 (Ctry) 2323 W Fifth Ave Ste 200	Columbus	OH	43204	**800-899-9265**	614-486-6101
WNND-FM 103.5 (NAC) 4401 Carriage Hill Ln	Columbus	OH	43220	**877-984-8786**	614-451-2191

642-35 Corpus Christi, TX

Station / Address	City	State	ZIP	Toll-Free	Phone
KEDT-FM 90.3 (NPR) 4455 S Padre Island Dr Ste 38	Corpus Christi	TX	78411	**800-307-5338**	361-855-2213

642-36 Dallas/Fort Worth, TX

Station / Address	City	State	ZIP	Toll-Free	Phone
KBFB-FM 97.9 (Urban) 13331 Preston Rd Ste 1180	Dallas	TX	75240	**888-362-8683**	972-331-5400
KERA-FM 90.1 (NPR) 3000 Harry Hines Blvd	Dallas	TX	75201	**800-456-5372**	214-871-1390
KLUV-FM 98.7 (Oldies) 4131 N Central Expy Ste 1000	Dallas	TX	75204	**855-987-5588**	214-525-7000
KRLD-AM 1080 (N/T) 4131 N Central Expy Ste 100	Dallas	TX	75204	**800-289-1080**	214-525-7000
KVIL-FM 103.7 (AC) 4131 N Central Expy Ste 1000	Dallas	TX	75204	**877-787-1037**	214-525-7000

642-37 Denver, CO

Station / Address	City	State	ZIP	Toll-Free	Phone
KUVO-FM 89.3 (Jazz) 2900 Welton St Ste 200	Denver	CO	80205	**800-574-5886**	303-480-9272

642-38 Des Moines, IA

Station / Address	City	State	ZIP	Toll-Free	Phone
KIOA-FM 93.3 (Oldies) 1416 Locust St	Des Moines	IA	50309	**877-984-8786**	515-280-1350

642-39 El Paso, TX

Station / Address	City	State	ZIP	Toll-Free	Phone
KELP-AM 1590 (Rel) 6900 Commerce St	El Paso	TX	79915	**800-658-6299**	915-779-0016
KINT-FM 93.9 (Span) 5426 N Mesa St	El Paso	TX	79912	**866-560-5673**	915-581-1126
KLAQ-FM 95.5 (Rock) 4180 N Mesa St	El Paso	TX	79902	**844-305-6210**	915-880-4955

642-40 Erie, PA

Station / Address	City	State	ZIP	Toll-Free	Phone
WQLN-FM 91.3 (NPR) 8425 Peach St	Erie	PA	16509	**800-727-8854**	814-864-3001

642-41 Eugene, OR

Station / Address	City	State	ZIP	Toll-Free	Phone
KLCC-FM 89.7 (NPR) 4000 E 30th Ave	Eugene	OR	97401	**800-922-3682**	541-463-6000

642-42 Evansville, IN

Station / Address	City	State	ZIP	Toll-Free	Phone
WDKS-FM 106.1 (CHR) 117 SE Fifth St	Evansville	IN	47708	**888-454-5477**	812-425-4226
WGBF-AM 1280 (N/T) 117 SE Fifth St	Evansville	IN	47708	**877-437-5995**	812-425-4226
WGBF-FM 103.1 (Rock) 117 SE Fifth St	Evansville	IN	47708	**888-900-9423**	812-425-4226
WIKY-FM 104.1 (AC) 1162 Mt Auburn Rd	Evansville	IN	47720	**800-866-5368**	812-424-8284
WNIN-FM 88.3 (NPR) 405 Carpenter St	Evansville	IN	47708	**855-888-9646**	812-423-2973
WSTO-FM 96.1 (CHR) 1162 Mt Auburn Rd	Evansville	IN	47720	**888-685-1961**	812-491-9468

642-43 Fairbanks, AK

Station / Address	City	State	ZIP	Toll-Free	Phone
KUAC-FM 89.9 (NPR) 312 Tanana Dr Ste 202 PO Box 755620	Fairbanks	AK	99775	**800-727-6543**	907-474-7491

642-44 Fargo, ND

Station / Address	City	State	ZIP	Toll-Free	Phone
KDSU-FM 91.9 (NPR) 207 Fifth St N	Fargo	ND	58102	**800-359-6900**	701-241-6900
WDAY-FM 93.7 (CHR) 1020 25th St S	Fargo	ND	58103	**877-478-5437**	701-237-5346

642-45 Flagstaff, AZ

Station / Address	City	State	ZIP	Toll-Free	Phone
KNAU-FM 88.7 (NPR) PO Box 5764 PO Box 5764	Flagstaff	AZ	86011	**800-523-5628**	928-523-5628

642-46 Fort Wayne, IN

Station / Address	City	State	ZIP	Toll-Free	Phone
89.1 WBOI 3204 Clairmont Ct *General	Fort Wayne	IN	46808	**800-471-9264***	260-452-1189
WLDE-FM 101.7 (Oldies) 347 W Berry St Ste 600	Fort Wayne	IN	46802	**888-450-1017**	260-423-3676
WOWO-AM 1190 (N/T) 2915 Maples Rd	Fort Wayne	IN	46816	**800-333-1190**	260-447-5511

642-47 Fort Smith, AR

Station / Address	City	State	ZIP	Toll-Free	Phone
B98-FM 97.9 311 Lexington Ave	Fort Smith	AR	72901	**866-503-1398**	479-782-8888

642-48 Fresno, CA

Station / Address	City	State	ZIP	Toll-Free	Phone
KMJ-AM 580 (N/T) 1071 W Shaw Ave	Fresno	CA	93711	**800-776-5858**	559-490-5800
KMJ-FM 105.9 1071 W Shaw Ave	Fresno	CA	93711	**800-491-1899**	559-490-5800
KPRX-FM 89.1 (NPR) 3437 W Shaw Ave Ste 101	Fresno	CA	93711	**800-275-0764**	559-275-0764
KSKS-FM 93.7 (Ctry) 1071 W Shaw Ave	Fresno	CA	93711	**800-767-5477**	559-490-5800
KVPR-FM 89.3 (NPR) 3437 W Shaw Ave Ste 101	Fresno	CA	93711	**800-275-0764**	559-275-0764
KWYE-FM 101.1 (CHR) 1071 W Shaw Ave	Fresno	CA	93711	**800-345-9101**	559-490-5800
Softrock-FM 98.9 (AC) 83 E Shaw Ave Ste 150	Fresno	CA	93710	**800-423-5870**	559-230-4300

642-49 Grand Forks, ND

Station / Address	City	State	ZIP	Toll-Free	Phone
KFJM-FM 90.7 (AAA) 207 N Fifth St	Fargo	ND	58102	**800-366-6888**	701-241-6900

642-50 Grand Rapids, MI

Station / Address	City	State	ZIP	Toll-Free	Phone
WBCT-FM 93.7 (Ctry) 77 Monroe Ctr St NW Ste 1000	Grand Rapids	MI	49503	**800-633-9393**	616-459-1919
WCSG-FM 91.3 (Rel) 1159 E Beltline Ave NE	Grand Rapids	MI	49525	**800-968-4543**	616-942-1500
WGRD-FM 97.9 (Rock) 50 Monroe Ave NW Ste 500	Grand Rapids	MI	49503	**800-947-3979**	616-451-4800
WGVU-FM 88.5 (NPR) 301 W Fulton St	Grand Rapids	MI	49504	**800-442-2771**	616-331-6666

642-51 Green Bay, WI

Station / Address	City	State	ZIP	Toll-Free	Phone
WDUZ-AM 1400 (Sports) 810 Victoria St	Green Bay	WI	54302	**855-724-1075**	920-468-4100
WNCY-FM 100.3 (Ctry) 1420 Bellevue St	Green Bay	WI	54311	**800-359-1003**	920-435-3771
WPNE-FM 89.3 (NPR) 2420 Nicolet Dr	Green Bay	WI	54311	**800-654-6228**	920-465-2444
WQLH-FM 98.5 (AC) 810 Victoria St	Green Bay	WI	54302	**855-782-7985**	920-468-4100

642-52 Greenville, SC

	City	State	Zip	Toll-Free	Phone
92.5 WESC-FM 101 N Main St PO Box 100	Greenville	SC	29601	**800-248-0863**	864-242-4660
WJMZ-FM 107.3 (Urban) 220 N Main St Ste 402	Greenville	SC	29601	**800-767-1073**	864-235-1073
WLFJ-FM 89.3 (Rel) 2420 Wade Hampton Blvd	Greenville	SC	29615	**800-447-7234**	864-292-6040
WROQ-FM 101.1 (CR) 25 Garlington Rd	Greenville	SC	29615	**888-257-0058**	864-271-9200
WTPT-FM 93.3 (Rock) 25 Garlington Rd	Greenville	SC	29615	**800-774-0093**	864-271-9200

642-53 Harrisburg, PA

	City	State	Zip	Toll-Free	Phone
BOB 94.9 WRBT 600 Corporate Cir	Harrisburg	PA	17110	**800-682-3047**	717-540-8800
WHP-AM 580 (N/T) 600 Corporate Cir	Harrisburg	PA	17110	**888-251-7797**	717-540-8800
WITF-FM 89.5 (NPR) 4801 Lindle Rd	Harrisburg	PA	17111	**800-366-9483**	717-704-3000

642-54 Honolulu, HI

	City	State	Zip	Toll-Free	Phone
JAMZ-FM 93.9 (CHR) 650 Iwilei Rd Ste 400	Honolulu	HI	96817	**800-745-3000**	808-550-9200
KHVH-AM 830 (N/T) 650 Iwilei Rd Ste 400	Honolulu	HI	96817	**888-565-8383**	808-550-9200

642-55 Hot Springs, AR

	City	State	Zip	Toll-Free	Phone
KHTO-FM 96.7 125 Corporate Terr	Hot Springs	AR	71913	**888-507-9538**	501-525-9700
KLAZ-FM 105.9 (CHR) 208 Buena Vista Rd	Hot Springs	AR	71913	**800-621-3362**	501-525-4600

642-56 Houston, TX

	City	State	Zip	Toll-Free	Phone
KBXX-FM 97.9 (Urban) 24 Greenway Plaza Ste 900	Houston	TX	77046	**888-407-4747**	713-623-2108
KKBQ-FM 92.9 (Ctry) 1990 Post Oak Blvd Ste 2300	Houston	TX	77056	**877-745-6591**	713-963-1200
KLAT-AM 1010 (Span N/T) 5100 SW Fwy	Houston	TX	77056	**800-646-6779**	713-407-1415
KRBE-FM 104.1 (CHR) 9801 Westheimer Rd Ste 700	Houston	TX	77042	**888-955-2993**	713-266-1000
KTHT-FM 1990 Post Oak Blvd Ste 2300	Houston	TX	77056	**877-745-6591**	713-963-1200
KUHF-FM 88.7 (Clas) 4343 Elgin St 3rd Fl	Houston	TX	77204	**877-252-0436**	713-743-0887
Rovi Corporation 1990 Post Oak Blvd Ste 2300	Houston	TX	77056	**877-745-6591**	713-963-1200

642-57 Huntsville, AL

	City	State	Zip	Toll-Free	Phone
WLRH-FM 89.3 (NPR) University of Alabama-Huntsville John Wright Dr	Huntsville	AL	35899	**800-239-9574**	256-895-9574

642-58 Indianapolis, IN

	City	State	Zip	Toll-Free	Phone
WIBC-FM 93.1 (N/T) 40 Monument Cir Ste 400	Indianapolis	IN	46204	**800-571-9422**	317-266-9422

642-59 Jackson, MS

	City	State	Zip	Toll-Free	Phone
WMAE-FM 89.5 (NPR) 3825 Ridgewood Rd	Jackson	MS	39211	**800-850-4406**	601-432-6565

642-60 Jacksonville, FL

	City	State	Zip	Toll-Free	Phone
WAPE-FM 95.1 (CHR) 8000 Belfort Pkwy Ste 100	Jacksonville	FL	32256	**800-475-9595**	904-245-8500
WJGL-FM 96.9 (CR) 8000 Belfort Pkwy	Jacksonville	FL	32256	**800-438-1601**	904-245-8500
WXXJ-FM 102.9 (AC) 8000 Belfort Pkwy	Jacksonville	FL	32256	**800-460-6394**	904-245-8500

642-61 Johnson City, TN

	City	State	Zip	Toll-Free	Phone
WETS-FM 89.5 (NPR) PO Box 70630	Johnson City	TN	37614	**888-895-9387**	423-439-6440

642-62 Kansas City, KS & MO

	City	State	Zip	Toll-Free	Phone
KCUR-FM 89.3 (NPR) 4825 Troost Ave Ste 202	Kansas City	MO	64110	**855-778-5437**	816-235-1551
KKFI-FM 90.1 (Var) 3901 Main St Ste 203	Kansas City	MO	64111	**888-931-0901**	816-931-3122
KPRS-FM 103.3 (Urban) 11131 Colorado Ave	Kansas City	MO	64137	**800-273-8255**	816-763-2040

642-63 Knoxville, TN

	City	State	Zip	Toll-Free	Phone
NEWS TALK 98.7 4711 Old Kingston Pike	Knoxville	TN	37919	**800-951-8255**	865-588-6511
WIVK-FM 107.7 (Ctry) 4711 Old Kingston Pike	Knoxville	TN	37919	**877-995-9961**	865-588-6511
WUOT-FM 91.9 (NPR) 209 Communications Bldg University of Tennessee	Knoxville	TN	37996	**888-266-9868**	865-974-5375

642-64 Lansing, MI

	City	State	Zip	Toll-Free	Phone
WITL-FM 100.7 (Ctry) 3420 Pine Tree Rd	Lansing	MI	48911	**800-968-9485**	517-394-7272

642-65 Las Vegas, NV

	City	State	Zip	Toll-Free	Phone
KDWN-AM 720 (N/T) 1455 E Tropicana Ave Ste 800	Las Vegas	NV	89119	**888-695-2664**	702-730-0300
KMXB-FM 94.1 (AC) 7255 S Tenaya Way Ste 100	Las Vegas	NV	89113	**866-438-0220**	702-257-9400
KNPR-FM 89.5 (NPR) 1289 S Torrey Pines Dr	Las Vegas	NV	89146	**888-258-9895**	702-258-9895

642-66 Lexington/Frankfort, KY

	City	State	Zip	Toll-Free	Phone
WKYL-FM 102.1 (NAC) 102 Perkins Bldg 521 Lancaster Ave	Richmond	KY	40475	**800-621-8890**	

642-67 Lincoln, NE

	City	State	Zip	Toll-Free	Phone
KFRX-FM 106.3 (CHR) 3800 Cornhusker Hwy	Lincoln	NE	68504	**800-523-9101**	402-466-1234

642-68 Little Rock, AR

	City	State	Zip	Toll-Free	Phone
KABZ-FM 103.7 (N/T) 2400 Cottondale Ln	Little Rock	AR	72202	**800-477-1037**	501-661-1037
KKPT-FM 94.1 (CR) 2400 Cottondale Ln	Little Rock	AR	72202	**800-844-0094**	501-664-9410

642-69 Los Angeles, CA

	City	State	Zip	Toll-Free	Phone
KABC-AM 790 (N/T) 3321 S La Cienega Blvd PO Box 790	Los Angeles	CA	90016	**800-222-5222**	310-840-4900
KLOS-FM 95.5 (CR) 3321 S La Cienega Blvd	Los Angeles	CA	90016	**800-955-5567**	310-840-4828
KROQ-FM 106.7 (Alt) 5901 Venice Blvd	Los Angeles	CA	90034	**800-520-1067**	323-930-1067
KRTH-FM 101.1 (Oldies) 5670 Wilshire Blvd Ste 200	Los Angeles	CA	90036	**800-232-5784**	323-936-5784
KSWD-FM 100.3 (Rock) 5900 Wilshire Blvd Ste 1900	Los Angeles	CA	90036	**888-696-1003**	323-634-1800
KUSC-FM 91.5 (Clas) 1149 S Hill St Ste H100 PO Box 7913	Los Angeles	CA	90015	**877-587-2227**	213-225-7400

642-70 Louisville, KY

	City	State	Zip	Toll-Free	Phone
WHAS-AM 840 (N/T) 4000 One Radio Dr	Louisville	KY	40218	**800-444-8484**	502-479-2222

642-71 Macon, GA

	City	State	Zip	Toll-Free	Phone
WIBB-FM 97.9 (Urban) 7080 Industrial Hwy	Macon	GA	31216	**800-813-8418**	478-781-1063

642-72 Madison, WI

	City	State	Zip	Toll-Free	Phone
WERN-FM 88.7 (NPR) 821 University Ave	Madison	WI	53706	**800-747-7444**	

				Toll-Free	Phone
WHA-AM 970 (NPR) 821 University Ave	Madison	WI	53706	800-747-7444	
WHIT-AM 1550 (Nost) 730 Rayovac Dr	Madison	WI	53711	800-422-7128	608-273-1000

642-73 Manchester, NH

				Toll-Free	Phone
WMLL-FM 96.5 (CR) 500 Commercial St	Manchester	NH	03101	800-666-0957	603-669-5777

642-74 Memphis, TN

				Toll-Free	Phone
600 WREC 2650 Thousand Oaks Blvd Ste 4100	Memphis	TN	38118	800-474-9732	901-259-1300
WDIA-AM 1070 (Urban) 2650 Thousand Oaks Blvd Ste 4100	Memphis	TN	38118	800-339-4673	901-259-1300
WHAL-FM 95.7 (Rel) 2650 Thousand Oaks Blvd Ste 4100	Memphis	TN	38118	888-302-6222	901-259-1300
WKNO-FM 91.1 (NPR) 900 Getwell Rd	Memphis	TN	38111	800-766-9566	901-325-6544

642-75 Miami/Fort Lauderdale, FL

				Toll-Free	Phone
WKIS-FM 99.9 (Ctry) 194 NW 187th St	Miami	FL	33169	866-978-0800	305-654-1700
WLYF-FM 101.5 (AC) 20450 NW Second Ave	Miami	FL	33169	877-790-1015	
WMBM-AM 1490 (Rel) 13242 NW Seventh Ave	North Miami	FL	33168	800-721-9626	305-769-1100
WMXJ-FM 102.7 (Oldies) 20450 NW Second Ave	Miami	FL	33169	800-924-1027	305-521-5240
WSUA-AM 1260 (Span) 2100 Coral Way Ste 201	Miami	FL	33145	877-453-5437	305-285-1260

642-76 Milwaukee, WI

				Toll-Free	Phone
WAUK-AM 540 (Sports) 310 W Wisconsin Ave Ste 100	Milwaukee	WI	53203	800-990-3776	414-273-3776
WHAD-FM 90.7 (NPR) 310 W Wisconsin Ave Ste 750-E	Milwaukee	WI	53203	800-486-8655	414-227-2040
WHQG-FM 102.9 (Rock) 5407 W McKinley Ave	Milwaukee	WI	53208	877-777-1029	414-978-9000

642-77 Minneapolis/Saint Paul, MN

				Toll-Free	Phone
KFAN-AM 1130 (Sports) 1600 Utica Ave S Ste 400	Minneapolis	MN	55416	800-320-5326	952-417-3000
KSTP-AM 1500 (N/T) 3415 University Ave	Saint Paul	MN	55114	877-615-1500	651-646-8255

642-78 Mobile, AL

				Toll-Free	Phone
WBHY-FM 88.5 (Rel) PO Box 1328	Mobile	AL	36633	888-473-8488	251-473-8488
WHIL-FM 91.3 (NPR) 166 Reese Phifer Hall PO Box 870150	Tuscaloosa	AL	35487	800-654-4262	205-348-6644

642-79 Monterey, CA

				Toll-Free	Phone
KCDU-FM 101.7 (AC) 60 Garden Ct Ste 300	Monterey	CA	93940	800-365-8630	831-658-5200
KHIP-FM 104.3 (CR) 60 Garden Ct Ste 300	Monterey	CA	93940	877-762-5104	831-658-5200

642-80 Naples, FL

				Toll-Free	Phone
WAVV-FM 101.1 (AC) 11800 Tamiami Trl E	Naples	FL	34113	866-310-9288	239-775-9288

642-81 Nashville, TN

				Toll-Free	Phone
SuperTalk 99.7 WTN 10 Music Cir E	Nashville	TN	37203	800-618-7445	615-321-1067
WLAC-AM 1510 (N/T) 55 Music Sq W	Nashville	TN	37203	800-688-9522	615-664-2400
WPLN-FM 90.3 (NPR) 630 Mainstream Dr	Nashville	TN	37228	877-760-2903	615-760-2903

642-82 New Orleans, LA

				Toll-Free	Phone
WWNO-FM 89.9 (NPR) University of New Orleans Lake Frnt Campus	New Orleans	LA	70148	800-286-7002	504-280-7000
WYLD-AM 940 (Rel) 929 Howard Ave	New Orleans	LA	70113	800-899-9265	504-679-7300

642-83 New York, NY

				Toll-Free	Phone
WAXQ-FM 104.3 (CR) 32 Ave of the Americas	New York	NY	10013	888-872-1043	212-377-7900
WHTZ-FM 100.3 (CHR) 32 Ave of the Americas	New York	NY	10013	800-242-0100	212-377-7900
WLTW-FM 106.7 (AC) 32 Ave of the Americas 2nd Fl	New York	NY	10013	800-222-1067	212-377-7900
WQHT-FM 97.1 (Urban) 395 Hudson St 7th Fl	New York	NY	10014	800-223-9797	212-229-9797
WWPR-FM 105.1 (Urban) 32 Ave of the Americas	New York	NY	10013	800-585-1051	212-377-7900

642-84 Omaha, NE

				Toll-Free	Phone
Z92 FM 10714 Mockingbird Dr	Omaha	NE	68127	800-955-9230	

642-85 Orlando, FL

				Toll-Free	Phone
WJHM-FM 102 (Urban) 1800 Pembrook Dr Ste 400	Orlando	FL	32810	866-438-0220	407-919-1000
WOCL-FM 105.9 (Rock) 1800 Pembrook Dr Ste 400	Orlando	FL	32810	877-919-1059	407-919-1000
WOMX-FM 105.1 (AC) 1800 Pembrook Dr Ste 400	Orlando	FL	32810	877-919-1051	407-919-1000
WWKA-FM 92.3 (Ctry) 4192 N John Young Pkwy	Orlando	FL	32804	866-438-0220	407-424-9236

642-86 Ottawa, ON

				Toll-Free	Phone
CFRA-AM 580 (N/T) 87 George St	Ottawa	ON	K1N9H7	800-580-2372	613-789-2486
Ottawa-AM 1200 (Sports) 87 George St	Ottawa	ON	K1N9H7	877-670-1200	613-789-2486

642-87 Pensacola, FL

				Toll-Free	Phone
WPCS-FM 89.5 (Rel) PO Box 18000	Pensacola	FL	32523	800-726-1191	850-479-6570
WUWF-FM 88.1 (NPR) 11000 University Pkwy	Pensacola	FL	32514	800-239-9893	850-474-2787

642-88 Peoria, IL

				Toll-Free	Phone
WCBU-FM 89.9 (NPR) 1501 W Bradley Ave	Peoria	IL	61625	888-488-9228	309-677-3690
WCIC-FM 91.5 (Rel) 3902 W Baring Trace	Peoria	IL	61615	877-692-9242	

642-89 Philadelphia, PA

				Toll-Free	Phone
WRTI-FM 90.1 (NPR) 1509 Cecil B Moore Ave 3rd Fl	Philadelphia	PA	19121	866-809-9784	215-204-8405

642-90 Phoenix, AZ

				Toll-Free	Phone
KOOL-FM 94.5 (Oldies) 840 N Central Ave	Phoenix	AZ	85004	800-222-4357	602-260-9494
KZZP-FM 104.7 (CHR) 4686 E Van Buren St Ste 300	Phoenix	AZ	85008	877-541-1966	602-374-6000

642-91 Pierre, SD

				Toll-Free	Phone
KMLO-FM 100.7 (Ctry) 214 W Pleasant Dr	Pierre	SD	57501	800-658-5439	605-224-8686
KPLO-FM 94.5 (Ctry) 214 W Pleasant Dr *General	Pierre	SD	57501	800-658-5439*	605-224-8686

642-92 Pittsburgh, PA

				Toll-Free	Phone
KQV-AM 1410 (N/T) 650 Smithfield St Ste 620 Ctr City Towers	Pittsburgh	PA	15222	888-272-7229	412-562-5900
WQED-FM 89.3 (Clas) 4802 Fifth Ave	Pittsburgh	PA	15213	800-876-1316	412-622-1436

642-93 Portland/Salem, OR

				Toll-Free	Phone
All Classical Portland 211 SE Caruthers St Ste 200	Portland	OR	97214	888-306-5277	503-943-5828

Station / Address	City	State	ZIP	Toll-Free	Phone
FM NEWS 101 KXL 1211 SW Fifth Ave Ste 6	Portland	OR	97204	**877-733-1011**	503-517-6000
KBNP-AM 1410 (N/T) 278 SW Arthur St	Portland	OR	97201	**888-214-9237**	503-223-6769
KEX-AM 1190 (N/T) 13333 SW 68th Parkway Ste 310	Tigard	OR	97223	**888-457-4838**	503-323-6400
KGON-FM 92.3 (CR) 0700 SW Bancroft St	Portland	OR	97239	**800-222-9236**	503-223-1441
KNRK-FM 94.7 (Alt) 0700 SW Bancroft St	Portland	OR	97239	**800-777-0947**	503-733-5470
KPDQ-FM 93.9 (Rel) 6400 SE Lake Rd Ste 350	Portland	OR	97222	**800-845-2162**	503-786-0600
KWJJ-FM 99.5 (Ctry) 0700 SW Bancroft St	Portland	OR	97239	**866-239-9653**	503-733-9653

642-94 Quebec City, QC

Station / Address	City	State	ZIP	Toll-Free	Phone
CBVE-FM 104.7 (CBC) PO Box 3220 Station C	Ottawa	ON	K1Y1E4	**866-306-4636**	

642-95 Raleigh/Durham, NC

Station / Address	City	State	ZIP	Toll-Free	Phone
Foxy 104.3 Fm 8001-101 Creedmoor Rd	Raleigh	NC	27613	**800-321-5975**	919-848-9736
Foxy 107.1 8001-101 Creedmoor Rd	Raleigh	NC	27613	**800-467-3699**	919-848-9736
WNNL-FM 103.9 (Rel) 8001-101 Creedmoor Rd	Raleigh	NC	27613	**877-310-9665**	919-848-9736
WPTF-AM 680 (N/T) 3012 Highwoods Blvd Ste 201	Raleigh	NC	27604	**800-662-7979**	919-790-9392
WRAL-FM 101.5 (AC) 3100 Highwoods Blvd Ste 140	Raleigh	NC	27604	**800-745-3000**	919-890-6101
WSHA-FM 88.9 (Jazz) 118 E S St	Raleigh	NC	27601	**800-241-0421**	919-546-8430

642-96 Reno/Carson City, NV

Station / Address	City	State	ZIP	Toll-Free	Phone
KDOT-FM 104.5 (Rock) 2900 Sutro St	Reno	NV	89512	**800-227-1885**	775-329-9261
KLCA-FM 96.5 (Alt) 961 Matley Ln Ste 120	Reno	NV	89502	**855-354-9111**	775-829-1964
KNIS-FM 91.3 (Rel) PO Box 21888	Carson City	NV	89721	**800-541-5647**	775-883-5647
KODS-FM 103.7 (Oldies) 961 Matley Ln Ste 120	Reno	NV	89502	**855-354-9111**	775-829-1964

642-97 Richmond, VA

Station / Address	City	State	ZIP	Toll-Free	Phone
WXGI-AM 950 (Sports) 701 German School Rd	Richmond	VA	23225	**877-994-4950**	804-233-7666

642-98 Riverside/San Bernardino, CA

Station / Address	City	State	ZIP	Toll-Free	Phone
KGGI-FM 99.1 (CHR) 2030 Iowa Ave Ste A	Riverside	CA	92507	**866-991-5444**	951-684-1991
KSGN-FM 89.7 (Rel) 2048 Orange Tree Ln Ste 200	Redlands	CA	92374	**888-897-5746**	909-583-2150
KVCR-FM 91.9 (NPR) 701 S Mt Vernon Ave	San Bernardino	CA	92410	**800-533-5827**	909-384-4444

642-99 Rochester, NY

Station / Address	City	State	ZIP	Toll-Free	Phone
WCMF-FM 96.5 (CR) 70 Commercial St	Rochester	NY	14614	**800-222-9196**	585-423-2900

642-100 Roanoke, VA

Station / Address	City	State	ZIP	Toll-Free	Phone
WFIR-AM 960 (N/T) 3934 Electric Rd SW	Roanoke	VA	24018	**800-367-7623**	540-345-1511
WSLQ-FM 99.1 (AC) 3934 Electric Rd SW	Roanoke	VA	24018	**800-410-9936**	540-387-0234
WVTF-FM 89.1 (NPR) 3520 Kingsbury Ln	Roanoke	VA	24014	**800-856-8900**	540-989-8900

642-101 Sacramento, CA

Station / Address	City	State	ZIP	Toll-Free	Phone
Capital Public Radio Inc 7055 Folsom Blvd	Sacramento	CA	95826	**877-480-5900**	916-278-8900
KHTK-AM 1140 (Sports) 5244 Madison Ave	Sacramento	CA	95841	**800-920-1140**	916-338-9200
KTKZ-AM 1380 (N/T) 1425 River Pk Dr Ste 520	Sacramento	CA	95815	**888-923-1380**	916-924-0710
KXPR-FM 88.9 (Clas) 7055 Folsom Blvd	Sacramento	CA	95826	**877-480-5900**	916-278-8900

642-102 Saint Louis, MO

Station / Address	City	State	ZIP	Toll-Free	Phone
KTRS-AM 550 (N/T) 638 Westport Plaza	Saint Louis	MO	63146	**888-550-5877**	314-453-5500

642-103 Salt Lake City, UT

Station / Address	City	State	ZIP	Toll-Free	Phone
KEGA-FM 101.5 (Ctry) 50 West Broadway Ste 200	Salt Lake City	UT	84101	**866-551-1015**	801-524-2600
KLO-AM 1430 (N/T) 257 East 200 South Ste 400	Salt Lake City	UT	84111	**866-627-1430**	801-364-9836
KZHT-FM 97.1 (CHR) 2801 S Decker Lake Dr	Salt Lake City	UT	84119	**800-888-8499**	801-908-1300

642-104 San Antonio, TX

Station / Address	City	State	ZIP	Toll-Free	Phone
930 AM The Answer 9601 McAllister Fwy Ste 1200	San Antonio	TX	78216	**866-308-8867**	210-344-8481
KISS-FM 99.5 (Rock) 8122 Datapoint Dr Ste 600	San Antonio	TX	78229	**855-787-2227**	210-615-5400
KSLR-AM 630 (Rel) 9601 McAllister Fwy Ste 1200	San Antonio	TX	78216	**800-247-4784**	210-344-8481
KSTX-FM 89.1 (NPR) 8401 Datapoint Dr Ste 800	San Antonio	TX	78229	**800-622-8977**	210-614-8977
WOAI-AM 1200 (N/T) 6222 NW IH-10	San Antonio	TX	78201	**800-707-5150**	210-736-9700

642-105 San Diego, CA

Station / Address	City	State	ZIP	Toll-Free	Phone
KFMB-AM 760 (N/T) 7677 Engineer Rd	San Diego	CA	92111	**800-760-5362**	858-292-7600
KLNV-FM 106.5 (Span) 600 W Broadway Ste 2150	San Diego	CA	92101	**800-879-4278**	619-235-0600
KPBS-FM 89.5 (NPR) San Diego State University 5200 Campanile Dr	San Diego	CA	92182	**888-399-5727**	619-265-6438
KSCF-FM 103.7 (N/T) 8033 Linda Vista Rd	San Diego	CA	92111	**888-388-1037**	858-571-7600
KYXY-FM 96.5 (AC) 8033 Linda Vista Rd	San Diego	CA	92111	**888-560-9650**	858-571-7600

642-106 San Francisco, CA

Station / Address	City	State	ZIP	Toll-Free	Phone
KITS-FM 105.3 (Alt) 865 Battery St	San Francisco	CA	94111	**800-696-1053**	
KMVQ-FM 99.7 (AC) 865 Battery St	San Francisco	CA	94111	**888-456-9970**	
KQED-FM 88.5 (NPR) 2601 Mariposa St	San Francisco	CA	94110	**800-723-3566**	415-864-2000
KSAN-FM 107.7 (Alt) 750 Battery St 3rd Fl	San Francisco	CA	94105	**888-303-2663**	415-995-6800
Wild 94.9 340 Townsend St Ste 5101	San Francisco	CA	94107	**888-333-9490**	415-975-5555

642-107 San Jose, CA

Station / Address	City	State	ZIP	Toll-Free	Phone
98.5 KFOX 201 Third St Ste 1200	San Francisco	CA	94103	**877-410-5369**	
KBAY-FM 94.5 (AC) 190 Pk Ctr Plz Ste 200	San Jose	CA	95113	**800-948-5229**	408-287-5775
KXSC-FM 104.9 (Alt) PO Box 6375	Artesia	CA	90702	**888-966-5332**	415-546-8710

642-108 Santa Fe, NM

Station / Address	City	State	ZIP	Toll-Free	Phone
KBAC-FM 98.1 (AAA) 2502 Camino Entrada Ste C	Santa Fe	NM	87507	**888-321-5123**	505-988-5222
KSWV-AM 810 (Span) 102 Taos St	Santa Fe	NM	87505	**800-873-3372**	505-983-3303
KTRC-AM 1260 (N/T) 2502 Camino Entrada Ste C	Santa Fe	NM	87507	**888-321-5123**	505-471-1067

642-109 Savannah, GA

Station / Address	City	State	ZIP	Toll-Free	Phone
97.3 Kiss Fm 245 Alfred St	Savannah	GA	31408	**800-543-3548**	912-964-7794
WSVH-FM 91.1 (NPR) 13040 Abercorn St Ste 8	Savannah	GA	31419	**877-472-1227**	912-344-3565
WTKS-AM 1290 (N/T) 245 Alfred St	Savannah	GA	31408	**877-263-7995**	912-964-7794

642-110 Scranton, PA

Station / Address	City	State	ZIP	Toll-Free	Phone
WEZX-FM 106.9 (Rock) 149 Penn Ave	Scranton	PA	18503	**800-228-4637**	570-346-6555

642-111 Seattle/Tacoma, WA

Station / Address	City	State	ZIP	Toll-Free	Phone
106.1 Kiss Fm 645 Elliott Ave W Ste 400	Seattle	WA	98119	**888-343-1061**	206-494-2000
KJAQ-FM 96.5 (Var) 1000 Dexter Ave N Ste 100	Seattle	WA	98109	**866-416-5225**	206-805-1100

				Toll-Free	Phone
KJR-AM 950 (Sports) 351 Elliott Ave W Ste 300	Seattle	WA	98119	800-829-0950	206-494-2000
KPLZ-FM 101.5 (AC) 140 Fourth Ave N Ste 340	Seattle	WA	98109	888-821-1015	206-404-4000
KUOW-FM 94.9 (NPR) 4518 University Way NE Ste 310	Seattle	WA	98105	800-289-5869	206-543-2710
KVI-AM 570 (N/T) 140 Fourth Ave N Ste 340	Seattle	WA	98109	888-312-5757	206-404-4000
KZOK-FM 102.5 (CR) 1000 Dexter Ave N	Seattle	WA	98109	800-252-1025	206-421-1025

642-112 Shreveport, LA

				Toll-Free	Phone
KDAQ-FM 89.9 (NPR) 1 University Pl PO Box 5250	Shreveport	LA	71115	800-552-8502	318-798-0102
KVKI-FM 96.5 (AC) 6341 W Port Ave	Shreveport	LA	71129	800-487-1840	318-688-1130

642-113 Sioux Falls, SD

				Toll-Free	Phone
KNWC-AM 96.5 (Rel) 6300 S Tallgrass Ave	Sioux Falls	SD	57108	888-569-5692	605-339-1270
KRRO-FM 103.7 (Rock) 500 S Phillips Ave	Sioux Falls	SD	57104	800-283-4867	605-331-5350
KTWB-FM 101.9 (Ctry) 500 S Phillips Ave	Sioux Falls	SD	57104	888-293-2832	605-331-5350
WNDV-FM 92.9 (CHR) 3371 Cleveland Rd Ste 300	South Bend	IN	46628	800-242-0100	574-273-9300

642-115 Spokane, WA

				Toll-Free	Phone
Spokane Public Radio 2319 N Monroe St	Spokane	WA	99205	800-328-5729	509-328-5729

642-116 Springfield, IL

				Toll-Free	Phone
WUIS-FM 91.9 (NPR) University of Illinois at Springfield 1 University Plz WUIS-130	Springfield	IL	62703	866-206-9847	217-206-9847

642-117 Springfield, MA

				Toll-Free	Phone
MIX 93.1 1331 Main St 4th Fl	Springfield	MA	01103	888-293-9310	413-781-1011
WSCB-FM 89.9 (Urban) 263 Alden St	Springfield	MA	01109	800-727-0504	413-748-3000

642-118 Springfield, MO

				Toll-Free	Phone
105.9 KGBX 1856 S Glenstone Ave	Springfield	MO	65804	800-445-1059	417-890-5555
KSMS-FM 90.5 (NPR) Missouri State University 901 S National Ave	Springfield	MO	65804	800-767-5768	417-836-5878
KSMU-FM 91.1 (NPR) Missouri State University 901 S National Ave	Springfield	MO	65897	800-767-5768	417-836-5878
KSWF-FM 100.5 (Ctry) 1856 S Glenstone Ave	Springfield	MO	65804	844-289-7234	417-890-5555
KTOZ-FM 95.5 (AC) 1856 S Glenstone Ave	Springfield	MO	65804	800-757-9550	417-890-5555
KTTS-FM 94.7 (Ctry) 2330 W Grand St	Springfield	MO	65802	800-621-3362	417-865-6614
KTXR-FM 101.3 (AC) 3000 E Chestnut Expy *General	Springfield	MO	65806	855-586-8852*	417-862-3751

642-119 Stamford/Bridgeport, CT

				Toll-Free	Phone
WEBE-FM 108 (AC) 2 Lafayette Sq	Bridgeport	CT	06604	800-932-3108	203-333-9108

642-120 Stockton, CA

				Toll-Free	Phone
KWIN-FM 97.7 (CHR) 3127 Transworld Dr Ste 270	Stockton	CA	95206	800-585-5946	209-507-8500
KYCC-FM 90.1 (Rel) 9019 W Ln	Stockton	CA	95210	800-654-5254	209-477-3690

642-121 Tallahassee, FL

				Toll-Free	Phone
WFSQ-FM 91.5 (Clas) 1600 Red Barber Plaza	Tallahassee	FL	32310	866-321-9378	850-487-3086
WFSU-FM 88.9 (NPR) 1600 Red Barber Plaza	Tallahassee	FL	32310	800-322-9378	850-487-3086

642-122 Tampa/Saint Petersburg, FL

				Toll-Free	Phone
Cox Media Group Tampa 11300 Fourth St N Ste 300	Saint Petersburg	FL	33716	888-723-9388	727-579-2000
WDAE-AM 620 (Sports) 4002 W Gandy Blvd	Tampa	FL	33611	888-546-4620	813-832-1000
WHPT-FM 102.5 (CR) 11300 Fourth St N Ste 300	Saint Petersburg	FL	33716	800-771-1025	727-579-2000
WSUN-FM 97.1 (Alt) 11300 Fourth St N Ste 300	Saint Petersburg	FL	33716	877-327-9797	727-579-2000
WUSF-FM 89.7 (NPR) 4202 E Fowler Ave TVB 100	Tampa	FL	33620	800-741-9090	813-974-8700
WXGL-FM 107.3 (AC) 11300 Fourth St N Ste 300	Saint Petersburg	FL	33716	800-242-1073	727-579-2000

642-123 Toledo, OH

				Toll-Free	Phone
WRQN-FM 93.5 (Oldies) 3225 Arlington Ave	Toledo	OH	43614	866-240-1935	419-725-5700
WSPD-AM 1370 (N/T) 125 S Superior St	Toledo	OH	43604	800-745-3000	419-244-8321
WXKR-FM 94.5 (CR) 3225 Arlington Ave	Toledo	OH	43614	866-240-9945	419-725-5700

642-124 Topeka, KS

				Toll-Free	Phone
KMAJ-AM 1440 (N/T) 825 S Kansas Ave Ste 100	Topeka	KS	66612	877-297-1077	785-272-2122
KMAJ-FM 107.7 (AC) 825 S Kansas Ave Ste 100	Topeka	KS	66612	877-297-1077	785-272-2122

642-125 Trenton, NJ

				Toll-Free	Phone
NJTV 825 Eighth Avenue	New York	NY	10019	800-882-6622	609-777-0031
WKXW-FM 101.5 (N/T) 109 Walters Ave	Trenton	NJ	08638	800-800-7822	609-359-5300

642-126 Tulsa, OK

				Toll-Free	Phone
KRMG-AM 740 (N/T) 7136 S Yale Ave Ste 500	Tulsa	OK	74136	855-297-9696	918-493-7400
Public Radio 89.5 800 Tucker Dr	Tulsa	OK	74104	888-594-5947	918-631-2577

642-127 Tuscaloosa, AL

				Toll-Free	Phone
WTBC-AM 1230 (N/T) 2110 McFarland Blvd E Ste C	Tuscaloosa	AL	35404	800-518-1977	205-758-5523
WUAL-FM 91.5 (NPR) 920 Paul W Bryant Dr Box 870370	Tuscaloosa	AL	35487	800-654-4262	205-348-6644

642-128 Washington, DC

				Toll-Free	Phone
WHUR-FM 96.3 (Urban AC) 529 Bryant St NW	Washington	DC	20059	855-787-2227	202-806-3500

642-129 West Palm Beach, FL

				Toll-Free	Phone
KOLL-FM 105.5 3071 Continental Dr	West Palm Beach	FL	33407	888-415-1055	561-616-6600
Sunny 107.9 Radio *Palm Beach Broadcasting* 701 Northpoint Pkwy Ste 500	West Palm Beach	FL	33407	800-919-1079	561-616-4777
WBZT-AM 1230 (N/T) 3071 Continental Dr	West Palm Beach	FL	33407	800-889-0267	
WMBX-FM 102.3 (Urban) 701 Northpoint Pkwy Ste 500	West Palm Beach	FL	33407	800-969-1023	
WXEL-FM 90.7 (NPR) 3401 S Congress Ave	West Palm Beach	FL	33426	800-915-9935	561-737-8000

642-130 Wilmington/Dover, DE

				Toll-Free	Phone
WDEL-AM 1150 (N/T) 2727 Shipley Rd	Wilmington	DE	19810	800-544-1150	302-478-2700
WSTW-FM 93.7 (CHR) 2727 Shipley Rd	Wilmington	DE	19810	800-544-9370	302-478-2700

642-131 Winston-Salem, NC

				Toll-Free	Phone
WFDD-FM 88.5 (NPR) 1834 Wake Forest Rd Ste 8850	Winston-Salem	NC	27109	800-262-8850	336-758-8850

643 RADIO STATIONS

SEE ALSO Internet Broadcasting

Station / Address	City	State	ZIP	Toll-Free	Phone
92.5 FM WVNN 1717 Hwy 72 E	Athens	AL	35611	**866-494-9866**	256-830-8300
99.5 The River 1203 Troy-Schenectady Rd Riverhill Ctr	Latham	NY	12110	**800-995-9783**	518-452-4800
99.5 WMAG 2-B PAI Pk	Greensboro	NC	27409	**866-415-4158**	336-822-2000
AM 570 LA Sports 3400 W Olive Ave Ste 550	Burbank	CA	91505	**866-987-2570**	818-559-2252
CBV-FM 106.3 (CBC) PO Box 500 Stn A	Toronto	ON	M5W1E6	**866-306-4636**	
CKLW-AM 800 (N/T) 1640 Ouellette Ave	Windsor	ON	N8X1L1	**800-263-2559**	519-258-8888
Family Stations Inc 290 Hegenberger Rd	Oakland	CA	94621	**800-543-1495**	
Freedom 95 Radio 645 Industrial Dr	Franklin	IN	46131	**800-278-9200**	317-736-4040
Fun 101.3 FM 1996 Auction Rd	Manheim	PA	17545	**877-870-5678**	717-653-0800
KABX-FM 97.5 (Oldies) 1020 W Main St	Merced	CA	95340	**800-350-3777**	209-723-2191
KANU-FM 91.5 (NPR) 1120 W 11th St Kansas Public Radio	Lawrence	KS	66044	**888-577-5268**	785-864-4530
KBBY-FM 95.1 (AC) 1376 Walter St	Ventura	CA	93003	**888-288-9242**	805-642-8595
KBHE-FM 89.3 (NPR) 555 N Dakota St PO Box 5000	Vermillion	SD	57069	**800-456-0766**	605-677-5861
KBIA-FM 91.3 (NPR) 409 Jesse Hall	Columbia	MO	65211	**800-292-9136**	573-882-3431
KBRG-FM 100.3 (Span AC) 750 Battery St Ste 200	San Francisco	CA	94111	**888-808-1003**	
KBYZ-FM 96.5 (CR) 4303 Memorial Hwy	Mandan	ND	58554	**888-663-9650**	701-663-9600
KCAQ-FM 104.7 (CHR) 2284 S Victoria Ave Ste 2G	Ventura	CA	93003	**877-440-1047**	805-289-1400
KCFR-FM 90.1 (NPR) 7409 S Alton Ct	Centennial	CO	80112	**800-722-4449**	303-871-9191
KCLR-FM 99.3 (Ctry) 3215 Lemone Industrial Blvd Ste 200	Columbia	MO	65201	**800-455-5257**	573-875-1099
KCMQ-FM 96.7 (CR) 3215 Lemone Industrial Blvd Ste 200	Columbia	MO	65201	**800-455-1967**	573-875-1099
KCRW-FM 89.9 (NPR) 1900 Pico Blvd	Santa Monica	CA	90405	**877-527-9227**	310-450-5183
KCSD-FM 90.9 (NPR) 555 N Dakota St PO Box 5000	Vermillion	SD	57069	**800-456-0766**	605-677-5861
KDON-FM 102.5 (CHR) 903 N Main St	Salinas	CA	93906	**888-558-5366**	831-755-8181
KFJM-FM 90.7 (AAA) 207 N Fifth St	Fargo	ND	58102	**800-366-6888**	701-241-6900
KFRG-FM 95.1 (Ctry) 900 E Washington St Ste 315	Colton	CA	92324	**888-431-3764**	909-825-9525
KGNU-FM 88.5 (Var) 4700 Walnut St	Boulder	CO	80301	**800-737-3030**	303-449-4885
KGOU-FM 106.3 (NPR) 860 Van Vleet Oval Rm 300	Norman	OK	73019	**866-533-2470**	405-325-3388
KIXI-AM 880 (Nost) 3650 131st Ave SE Ste 550	Bellevue	WA	98006	**866-880-5494**	425-562-8964
KNDR-FM 104.7 (Rel) 1400 NE Third St	Mandan	ND	58554	**800-767-5095**	701-663-2345
KNWI-FM 107.1 (Rel) 3737 Woodland Ave Ste 300	West Des Moines	IA	50266	**800-701-3123**	515-327-1071
KOPN-FM 89.5 (Var) 915 E Broadway	Columbia	MO	65201	**800-895-5676**	573-874-1139
KPLU-FM 88.5 (NPR) 12180 Pk Ave S	Tacoma	WA	98447	**800-677-5758**	253-535-7758
KPVU-FM 91.3 (NPR) Prairie View A & M University MS 1415	Prairie View	TX	77446	**877-241-1752**	936-261-3750
KROX-AM 1260 (Var) 208 S Main St	Crookston	MN	56716	**800-222-2537**	218-281-1140
KSME-FM 96.1 (CHR) 4270 Byrd Dr	Loveland	CO	80538	**877-498-9600**	970-461-2560
KTOM-FM 92.7 (Ctry) 903 N Main St *General	Salinas	CA	93906	**800-660-5866***	831-755-8181
KTSD-FM 91.1 (NPR) 555 N Dakota St PO Box 5000	Vermillion	SD	57069	**800-456-0766**	605-677-5861
KTXY-FM 106.9 (AC) 3215 Lemone Industrial Blvd Ste 200	Columbia	MO	65201	**800-500-9107**	573-875-1099
KUAD-FM 99.1 (Ctry) 600 Main St	Windsor	CO	80550	**800-500-2599**	
KUAF 91.3 Public Radio 9 S School Ave	Fayetteville	AR	72701	**800-522-5823**	479-575-2556
KUSP-FM 88.9 (NPR) 203 Eigth Ave	Santa Cruz	CA	95062	**800-655-5877**	831-476-2800
KUWJ-FM 90.3 (NPR) 1000 E University Ave	Laramie	WY	82071	**800-729-5897**	307-766-4240
KUWS-FM 91.3 (NPR) 1805 Catlin Ave	Superior	WI	54880	**800-300-8530**	715-394-8530
KVLC-FM 101.1 (Oldies) 101 Perkins Dr	Las Cruces	NM	88005	**877-527-1011**	575-527-1111
KWYR-FM 93.7 (AC) PO Box 491	Winner	SD	57580	**800-388-5997**	605-842-3333
KXFG-FM 92.9 (Ctry) 900 E Washington Ste 315	Colton	CA	92324	**888-431-3764**	909-825-9525
MEGA-FM 94.9 (Span CHR) 7601 Riviera Blvd	Miramar	FL	33023	**877-599-2946**	954-862-2000
Radio Kansas 815 N Walnut St Ste 300	Hutchinson	KS	67501	**800-723-4657**	620-662-6646
RadioU PO Box 1887	Westerville	OH	43086	**877-272-3468**	
Star 92.9 265 Hegeman Ave	Colchester	VT	05446	**866-865-7827**	802-655-0093
Super Talk 1270 4303 Memorial Hwy	Mandan	ND	58554	**844-255-7886**	701-663-1270

Station / Address	City	State	ZIP	Toll-Free	Phone
Triad's 105.7 Man Up, The 2-B PAI Pk	Greensboro	NC	27409	**800-950-2482**	336-822-2000
WALK-FM 97.5 (AC) 234 Airport Plz Ste 5	Farmingdale	NY	11735	**877-263-7995**	631-475-5200
WASH-FM 97.1 (AC) 1801 Rockville Pk Ste 601	Rockville	MD	20852	**866-927-4361**	240-747-2700
WAVA-AM 780 (Rel) 1901 N Moore St Ste 200	Arlington	VA	22209	**888-976-6924**	703-807-2266
WAVA-FM 105.1 (Rel) 1901 N Moore St Ste 200	Arlington	VA	22209	**888-293-9282**	703-807-2266
WAYV-FM 95.1 (CHR) 8025 Black Horse Pike	West Atlantic City	NJ	08232	**888-966-8146**	609-484-8444
WAYZ-FM 104.7 (Ctry) 10960 John Wayne Dr	Greencastle	PA	17225	**888-950-1047**	717-597-9200
WBEN-AM 930 (N/T) 500 Corporate Pkwy Ste 200	Amherst	NY	14226	**800-616-9236**	716-843-0600
WBIG-FM 100.3 (Oldies) 1801 Rockville Pk 6th fl	Rockville	MD	20852	**800-493-1003**	240-747-2700
WBRB-FM 101.3 (Ctry) 1065 Radio Pk Dr	Mount Clare	WV	26408	**877-232-7121**	304-623-6546
WCAT-FM 102.3 (Ctry) 728 N Hanover St	Carlisle	PA	17013	**888-513-5130**	717-243-1200
WCLT-FM 100.3 (Ctry) PO Box 5150	Newark	OH	43058	**800-837-9258**	740-345-4004
WCMR-AM 1270 (Rel) PO Box 307	Elkhart	IN	46515	**800-522-9376**	574-875-5166
WCNY-FM 91.3 (NPR) 506 Old Liverpool Rd	Liverpool	NY	13088	**800-451-9269**	315-453-2424
WCPV-FM 101.3 (CR) 265 Hegeman Ave	Colchester	VT	05446	**866-862-4267**	802-655-0093
WCQR-FM 88.3 (Rel) 2312 Oak St	Gray	TN	37615	**888-477-5676**	423-477-5676
WCTL-FM 106.3 (Rel) 10912 Peach St	Waterford	PA	16441	**800-568-8924**	814-796-6000
WDAS-FM 105.3 (Urban AC) 111 Presidential Blvd Ste 100	Bala Cynwyd	PA	19004	**800-745-3000**	610-784-3333
WDRM-FM 102.1 (Ctry) 26869 Peoples Rd	Madison	AL	35756	**866-302-0102**	256-309-2400
WEDR-FM 99.1 (Urban) 2741 N 29th Ave	Hollywood	FL	33020	**800-327-2323**	305-444-4404
WEEI-AM 850 (Sports) 20 Guest St 3rd Fl	Brighton	MA	02135	**888-525-0850**	617-779-3500
WEKU-FM 88.9 (Clas) 521 Lancaster Ave 102 Perkins Bldg-EKU	Richmond	KY	40475	**800-621-8890**	
WEMU-FM 89.1 (NPR) PO Box 980350	Ypsilanti	MI	48198	**888-299-8910**	734-487-2229
WERU-FM 89.9 (Var) 1186 Acadia Hwy	East Orland	ME	04431	**800-643-6273**	207-469-6600
WEVO-FM 89.1 (N/T) 2 Pillsbury St 6th Fl	Concord	NH	03301	**800-639-4131**	603-228-8910
WFCF-FM 88.5 (Var) Flagler College PO Box 1027	Saint Augustine	FL	32085	**800-304-4208**	904-819-6449
WFHN-FM 107.1 (CHR) 22 Sconticut Neck Rd	Fairhaven	MA	02719	**877-854-9467**	508-999-6690
WFIU-FM 103.7 Indiana University 1229 E Seventh St	Bloomington	IN	47405	**877-285-9348**	812-855-1357
WFPG-FM 96.9 (AC) 950 Tilton Rd Ste 200	Northfield	NJ	08225	**800-969-9374**	609-645-9797
WFUV-FM 90.7 (Var) 441 E Fordham Rd Fordham University	Bronx	NY	10458	**888-400-5520**	718-817-4550
WGAR-FM 99.5 (Ctry) 6200 Oak Tree Blvd S 4th Fl	Independence	OH	44131	**855-222-0995**	216-520-2600
WGGY-FM 101.3 (Ctry) 305 Hwy 315	Pittston	PA	18640	**800-570-1013**	570-883-1111
WGMD-FM 92.7 (N/T) PO Box 530	Rehoboth Beach	DE	19971	**800-518-9292**	302-945-2050
WGNE-FM 99.9 (Ctry) 6440 Atlantic Blvd	Jacksonville	FL	32211	**888-725-2345**	904-727-9696
WGTS-FM 91.9 (Rel) 7600 Flower Ave	Takoma Park	MD	20912	**800-700-1094**	301-891-4200
WGTY-FM 107.7 (Ctry) 1560 Fairfield Rd PO Box 3179	Gettysburg	PA	17325	**800-366-9489**	717-334-3101
WGY-AM 810 (N/T) 1203 Troy-Schenectady Rd	Latham	NY	12110	**800-825-5949**	518-452-4800
WIOQ-FM 102.1 (CHR) 111 Presidential Blvd Ste 100	Bala Cynwyd	PA	19004	**800-521-1021**	610-784-3333
WJQK-FM 99.3 (Rel) 425 Centerstone Ct	Zeeland	MI	49464	**866-931-9936**	616-931-9930
WKCQ-FM 98.1 (Ctry) 2000 Whittier St	Saginaw	MI	48601	**800-262-0098**	989-752-8161
WKDD-FM 98.1 (AC) 7755 Freedom Ave	North Canton	OH	44720	**888-533-4582**	330-836-4700
WKRR-FM 92.3 (CR) 192 E Lewis St	Greensboro	NC	27406	**800-762-5923**	336-274-8042
WKSU-FM 89.7 (NPR) 1613 E Summit St	Kent	OH	44242	**800-672-2132**	330-672-3114
WKVV-FM 101.7 PO Box 2098	Omaha	NE	68103	**800-525-5683**	
WKZL-FM 107.5 (CHR) 192 E Lewis St	Greensboro	NC	27406	**800-682-1075**	336-274-8042
WLLL-AM 930 (Rel) PO Box 11375 *Cust Svc	Lynchburg	VA	24506	**888-224-9809***	434-385-9555
WMIT-FM 106.9 (Rel) 3 Porters Cove Rd	Asheville	NC	28805	**800-330-9648**	828-285-8477
WMPI-FM 105.3 (Ctry) 22 E McClain Ave	Scottsburg	IN	47170	**800-441-1053**	812-752-3688
WMUM-FM 89.7 (NPR) 243 Carey Salem Rd	Cochran	GA	31014	**800-222-4788**	478-301-5760
WMZQ-FM 98.7 (Ctry) 1801 Rockville Pk 5th Fl	Rockville	MD	20852	**800-505-0098**	240-747-2700
WNCW-FM 88.7 (AAA) PO Box 804	Spindale	NC	28160	**800-245-8870**	828-287-8000
WNKU-FM 105.9 (Ctry) 301 Landrum Academic Ctr	Highland Heights	KY	41099	**855-897-7897**	859-572-6500
WNSN-FM 101.5 (AC) 1301 E Douglas Rd	Mishawaka	IN	46545	**855-757-1719**	574-233-3141

Name / Address	City	State	ZIP	Toll-Free	Phone
WODE-FM 99.9 107 Paxinosa Rd W	Easton	PA	18040	**800-733-2767**	610-258-6155
WOGG-FM 94.9 (Ctry) 123 Blaine Rd	Brownsville	PA	15417	**866-983-9898**	724-938-2000
WOGL-FM 98.1 (Oldies) 2 Bala Plz Ste 800	Bala Cynwyd	PA	19004	**800-942-8998**	610-668-5900
WOKO-FM 98.9 (Ctry) 70 Joy Dr	South Burlington	VT	05403	**800-354-9890**	802-862-9890
WOKQ-FM 97.5 (Ctry) 292 Middle Rd PO Box 576	Dover	NH	03821	**877-975-1037**	603-749-9750
Woodward Communications Inc 801 Bluff St	Dubuque	IA	52001	**800-553-4801**	
WPCV-FM 97.5 (Ctry) 404 W Lime St	Lakeland	FL	33815	**800-227-9797**	863-682-8184
WPGC-FM 95.5 (CHR) 4200 Parliament Pl Ste 300	Lanham	MD	20706	**877-955-5267**	
WPLM-FM 99.1 (AC) 17 Columbus Rd	Plymouth	MA	02360	**877-327-9991**	508-746-1390
WPRO-FM 92.3 (CHR) 1502 Wampanoag Trl	East Providence	RI	02915	**800-638-0092**	401-433-4200
WPST-FM 94.5 (AC) 619 Alexander Rd 3rd Fl	Princeton	NJ	08540	**800-248-9778**	609-419-0300
WQFL-FM 100.9 (Rel) PO Box 2118	Omaha	NE	68103	**888-937-2471**	
WQUN-AM 1220 (Nost) 3085 Whitney Ave	Hamden	CT	06518	**800-462-1944**	203-582-8984
WRCH-FM 100.5 (AC) 10 Executive Dr	Farmington	CT	06032	**800-530-1005**	860-677-6700
WRKO-AM 680 (N/T) 20 Guest St 3rd Fl	Brighton	MA	02135	**877-469-4322**	617-779-3400
WRVM-FM 102.7 (Rel) PO Box 212	Suring	WI	54174	**888-225-9786**	920-842-2900
WSHU-FM 91.1 (NPR) 5151 Pk Ave	Fairfield	CT	06825	**800-937-6045**	203-365-0425
WTFM-FM 98.5 (AC) 222 Commerce St	Kingsport	TN	37660	**888-633-5452**	423-246-9578
WTSU-FM 89.9 (NPR) Troy University Wallace Hall	Troy	AL	36082	**800-800-6616**	
WTTS-FM 92.3 (AAA) 400 One City Centre	Bloomington	IN	47404	**800-923-9887**	812-332-3366
WUMP-AM 730 (Sports) 3280 Peachtree Rd Ste 2300	Atlanta	GA	30305	**866-485-9867**	256-830-8300
WUNC-FM 91.5 (NPR) 120 Friday Center Dr	Chapel Hill	NC	27517	**800-962-9862**	919-445-9150
WVPE-FM 88.1 (NPR) 2424 California Rd	Elkhart	IN	46514	**888-399-9873**	574-674-9873
WVPS-FM 107.9 (NPR) 365 Troy Ave	Colchester	VT	05446	**800-639-2192**	802-655-9451
WWDC-FM 101.1 (Rock) 1801 Rockville Pk 5th Fl	Rockville	MD	20852	**866-913-2101**	240-747-2701
WWGR-FM 101.9 (Ctry) 10915 K-Nine Dr	Bonita Springs	FL	34135	**877-787-1019**	239-495-8383
WWKA-FM 92.3 (Ctry) 4192 N John Young Pkwy	Orlando	FL	32804	**866-438-0220**	407-424-9236
WXCY-FM 103.7 (Ctry) 707 Revolution St	Havre de Grace	MD	21078	**800-788-9929**	410-939-1100
WXRV-FM 92.5 (AAA) 30 How St	Haverhill	MA	01830	**800-352-9250**	978-374-4733
WZBT-FM 91.1 (Alt) 300 N Washington St Gettysburg College	Gettysburg	PA	17325	**800-431-0803**	717-337-6300

644 RADIO SYNDICATORS

Name / Address	City	State	ZIP	Toll-Free	Phone
American Urban Radio Networks 960 Penn Ave 4th Fl	Pittsburgh	PA	15222	**800-456-4211**	412-456-4000
Associated Press 1100 13th St NW Ste 700	Washington	DC	20005	**800-824-5498**	202-641-9000
Car Clinic Productions 5675 N Davis Hwy	Pensacola	FL	32503	**888-227-2546**	850-478-3139
Radio America 1100 N Glebe Rd Ste 900	Arlington	VA	22201	**800-807-4703**	703-302-1000
Syndication Networks Corp 8700 Waukegan Rd Ste 250	Morton Grove	IL	60053	**800-743-1988**	847-583-9000
Talk Radio Network (TRN) PO Box 3755	Central Point	OR	97502	**888-383-3733**	
Transmedia 719 Battery St	San Francisco	CA	94111	**800-229-7234**	415-956-3118
WCLV 1375 Euclid Ave Idea Ctr	Cleveland	OH	44115	**877-399-3307**	216-916-6301

645 RADIO & TELEVISION BROADCASTING & COMMUNICATIONS EQUIPMENT

SEE ALSO Telecommunications Equipment & Systems ; Audio & Video Equipment

Name / Address	City	State	ZIP	Toll-Free	Phone
AheadTek Inc 6410 Via Del Oro	San Jose	CA	95119	**800-971-9191**	408-226-9991
Airbiquity Inc 1011 Western Ave Ste 600	Seattle	WA	98104	**888-334-7741**	206-219-2700
Alien Technology Corp 18220 Butterfield Blvd	Morgan Hill	CA	95037	**866-734-3669**	408-782-3900
Andersen Manufacturing Inc 3125 N Yellowstone Hwy	Idaho Falls	ID	83401	**800-635-6106**	208-523-6460
Arris 60 Decibel Rd	State College	PA	16801	**800-233-2267**	814-238-2461
Arris Group Inc 3871 Lakefield Dr *NASDAQ: ARRS*	Suwanee	GA	30024	**866-362-7747**	678-473-2000
Artel Video Systems Corp 5B Lyberty Way	Westford	MA	01886	**800-225-0228**	978-263-5775
Atrex Inc 175 Industrial Loop S	Orange Park	FL	32073	**800-874-4505**	904-264-9086
ATX Networks Corp 1-501 Clements Rd W	Ajax	ON	L1S7H4	**800-565-7488**	905-428-6068
Avi Systems Inc 9675 W 76th St Ste 200	Eden Prairie	MN	55344	**800-488-4954**	952-949-3700
Axcera Corp 103 Freedom Dr	Lawrence	PA	15055	**800-215-2614**	724-873-8100
Beacon Wireless Solutions Inc 206 Laird Dr Ste 207	Toronto	ON	M4G3W5	**866-867-7770**	416-696-7555
Blonder Tongue Laboratories Inc 1 Jake Brown Rd *NYSE: BDR*	Old Bridge	NJ	08857	**877-407-8033**	732-679-4000
Coaxial Dynamics 6800 Lake Abrams Dr	Middleburg Heights	OH	44130	**800-262-9425**	440-243-1100
Cobalt Digital Inc 2506 Galen Dr	Urbana	IL	61802	**800-669-1691**	217-344-1243
Cohu Inc 12367 Crosthwaite Cir *NASDAQ: COHU*	Poway	CA	92064	**800-685-5050**	858-848-8100
COMARK Communications 104 Feeding Hills Rd	Southwick	MA	01077	**800-288-8364**	413-998-1100
Concurrent 4375 River Green Pkwy Ste 100 *NASDAQ: CCUR*	Duluth	GA	30096	**877-978-7363**	678-258-4000
Conolog Corp 5 Columbia Rd *OTC: CNLG*	Somerville	NJ	08876	**800-526-3984**	908-722-8081
Continental Electronics Corp 4212 S Buckner Blvd	Dallas	TX	75227	**800-733-5011**	214-381-7161
Destron Fearing 490 Villaume Ave	South Saint Paul	MN	55075	**800-328-0118**	651-455-1621
Eagle Comtronics Inc 7665 Henry Clay Blvd	Liverpool	NY	13088	**800-448-7474**	315-622-3402
EFJohnson Technologies 1440 Corporate Dr	Irving	TX	75038	**800-328-3911**	972-819-0700
GAI-Tronics Corp 400 E Wyomissing Ave	Mohnton	PA	19540	**800-492-1212**	610-777-1374
General Dynamics SATCOM Technologies 3111 Fujita St	Torrance	CA	90505	**888-874-7646**	828-464-4141
General Dynamics SATCOM Technologies 1500 Prodelin Dr	Newton	NC	28658	**888-874-7646**	828-464-4141
Globecomm Systems Inc 45 Oser Ave *NASDAQ: GCOM*	Hauppauge	NY	11788	**866-499-0223**	631-231-9800
Guardian Mobility Corp 43 Auriga Dr	Ottawa	ON	K2E7Y8	**888-817-8159**	613-225-8885
Harmonic Inc 4300 N First St *NASDAQ: HLIT*	San Jose	CA	95134	**800-322-2885**	408-542-2500
Harris Corp 1025 W NASA Blvd *NYSE: HRS*	Melbourne	FL	32919	**800-442-7747**	321-727-9100
Harris Corp RF Communications Div 1680 University Ave	Rochester	NY	14610	**866-264-8040**	585-244-5830
Hitachi Kokusai Electric America Ltd 150 Crossways Pk Dr	Woodbury	NY	11797	**855-490-5124**	516-921-7200
Honeywell International Inc 101 Columbia Rd PO Box M6/LM *NYSE: HON*	Morristown	NJ	07962	**877-841-2840**	480-353-3020
ICOM America Inc 2380 116th Ave NE	Bellevue	WA	98004	**800-872-4266**	425-454-8155
ID Systems Inc 123 Tice Blvd Ste 101 *NASDAQ: IDSY*	Woodcliff Lake	NJ	07677	**866-410-0152**	201-996-9000
Ikegami Electronics USA Inc 37 Brook Ave	Maywood	NJ	07607	**800-368-9171**	201-368-9171
Imagine GPS Inc 6847 S Ea Ste 104	Las Vegas	NV	89119	**866-477-2489**	702-990-5600
Iteris Inc 1700 Carnegie Ave Ste 100 *NYSE: ITI*	Santa Ana	CA	92705	**888-254-5487**	949-270-9400
Jem Engineering LLC 8683 Cherry Ln	Laurel	MD	20707	**877-317-1070**	301-317-1070
Kenwood USA Corp 2201 E Dominguez St	Long Beach	CA	90810	**800-536-9663**	310-639-9000
L-3 Communications Corp 600 Third Ave 34-35 Fl *NYSE: LLL*	New York	NY	10016	**800-351-8483**	212-697-1111
L-3 Communications ESSCO 90 Nemco Way	Ayer	MA	01432	**877-282-1168**	978-568-5100
L-3 Communications Telemetry East Div 1515 Grundy's Ln	Bristol	PA	19007	**800-351-8483**	267-545-7000
L-3 Communications Telemetry West Div 9020 Balboa Ave	San Diego	CA	92123	**800-351-8483**	858-694-7500
Lightspeed Aviation Inc 6135 Jean Rd	Lake Oswego	OR	97035	**800-332-2421**	503-968-3113
Logitek Electronic Systems Inc 5622 Edgemoor Dr	Houston	TX	77081	**877-231-5870**	713-664-4470
MCL Inc 501 S Woodcreek Rd *Support	Bolingbrook	IL	60440	**800-743-4625***	630-759-9500
MDI Security Systems Inc 12500 Network Dr Ste 303	San Antonio	TX	78249	**866-435-7634**	210-477-5400
MFJ Enterprises Inc 300 Industrial Pk Rd	Starkville	MS	39759	**800-647-1800**	662-323-5869
Minerva Networks Inc 2150 Gold St	Santa Clara	CA	95002	**800-806-9594**	408-567-9400
Nautel Ltd 10089 Peggy'S Cove Rd	Hackett'S Cove	NS	B3Z3J4	**877-662-8835**	902-823-3900
NSC Communications 6820 Power Line Dr	Florence	KY	41042	**800-543-1584**	859-727-6640
ParkerVision Inc 7915 Baymeadows Way *NASDAQ: PRKR*	Jacksonville	FL	32256	**800-532-8034**	904-737-1367
Pelco 3500 Pelco Way	Clovis	CA	93612	**800-289-9100**	559-292-1981
Pico Macom Inc 8880 Rehco Rd	San Diego	CA	92121	**800-421-6511**	858-546-5050
RA Miller Industries Inc 14500 168th Ave PO Box 858	Grand Haven	MI	49417	**888-845-9450**	616-842-9450

Company / Address	City	State	Zip	Toll-Free	Phone
RELM Wireless Corp 7100 Technology Dr *NYSE: RWC* ■ *Cust Svc	West Melbourne	FL	32904	**800-648-0947***	321-984-1414
RL Drake Co 9900 Springboro Pike	Miamisburg	OH	45342	**800-777-8876**	937-746-4556
Rockwell Collins Inc 400 Collins Rd NE *NYSE: COL*	Cedar Rapids	IA	52498	**888-721-3094**	319-295-1000
Shively Labs 188 Harrison Rd PO Box 389	Bridgton	ME	04009	**888-744-8359**	207-647-3327
Sonetics Corp 7340 Sw Durham Rd	Portland	OR	97224	**800-833-4558**	
Space Systems/Loral 3825 Fabian Way	Palo Alto	CA	94303	**800-332-6490**	650-852-4000
Synergy Broadcast Systems 16115 Dooley Rd	Addison	TX	75001	**800-601-6991**	
TCI International Inc 3541 Gateway Blvd	Fremont	CA	94538	**877-247-3797**	510-687-6100
Tecom Industries Inc 375 Conejo Ridge Ave	Thousand Oaks	CA	91361	**866-840-8550**	805-267-0100
Telepath Corp 49111 Milmont Dr	Fremont	CA	94538	**800-292-1700**	510-656-5600
Thales Communications Inc 22605 Gateway Ctr Dr	Clarksburg	MD	20871	**800-258-4420**	240-864-7000
TPL Communications 3825 Foothill Blvd Unit 206	La Crescenta	CA	91214	**800-447-6937**	323-256-3000
Ultra Electronics Flightline Systems Inc 7625 Omni Tech Pl	Victor	NY	14564	**888-959-9001**	585-924-4000
Ultra Electronics-DNE Technologies Inc 50 Barnes Industrial Pk N	Wallingford	CT	06492	**800-370-4485**	203-265-7151
Unique Broadband Systems Ltd 400 Spinnaker Way Unit 1 10	Vaughan	ON	L4K5Y9	**877-669-8533**	905-669-8533
VehSmart Inc 12180 Ridgecrest Rd Ste 412	Victorville	CA	92395	**855-834-7627**	
Vicon Industries Inc 89 Arkay Dr *NYSE: VII* ■ *Sales	Hauppauge	NY	11788	**800-645-9116***	631-952-2288
Wilcom Inc 73 Daniel Webster Hwy PO Box 508	Belmont	NH	03220	**800-222-1898**	603-524-2622
Winegard Co 3000 Kirkwood St *Cust Svc	Burlington	IA	52601	**800-288-8094***	319-754-0600
Xcitex Inc 25 First St Ste 105	Cambridge	MA	02141	**800-780-7836**	617-225-0080

646 RAIL TRANSPORT SERVICES

SEE ALSO Logistics Services (Transportation & Warehousing)

Company / Address	City	State	Zip	Toll-Free	Phone
Aberdeen & Rockfish Railroad Co 101 E Main St	Aberdeen	NC	28315	**800-849-8985**	910-944-2341
Buffalo & Pittsburgh Railroad Inc (BPRR) 1200-C Scottsville Rd Ste 200	Rochester	NY	14624	**800-603-3385**	585-463-3307
Burlington Northern & Santa Fe Railway (BNSF) 2650 Lou Menk Dr	Fort Worth	TX	76131	**800-795-2673**	
Canadian National Railway Co 935 Rue de la Gauchetiere O *TSE: CNR*	Montreal	QC	H3B2M9	**888-668-4626**	888-888-5909
Canadian Pacific Railway Co 401 9 Ave SW Ste 500	Calgary	AB	T2P4Z4	**888-333-6370**	403-319-7000
CHEP USA 8517 S Pk Cir *Cust Svc	Orlando	FL	32819	**866-855-2437***	407-370-2437
Chicago Southshore & South Bend Railroad 505 N Carroll Ave	Michigan City	IN	46360	**800-356-2079**	219-874-9000
Consolidated Rail Corp 1717 Arch St Ste 3210	Philadelphia	PA	19103	**800-272-0911**	215-209-2000
Dardanelle & Russellville Railroad Co 4416 S Arkansas Ave	Russellville	AR	72802	**888-877-7267**	479-968-6455
Georgetown Railroad Co 5300 S IH-35 PO Box 529	Georgetown	TX	78626	**888-456-6777**	512-863-2538
Iowa Interstate Railroad 5900 Sixth St SW	Cedar Rapids	IA	52404	**800-321-3884**	319-298-5400
Kansas City Southern Railway Co 427 W 12th St	Kansas City	MO	64105	**800-468-6527**	816-983-1303
Montana Rail Link Inc 101 International Way	Missoula	MT	59808	**800-338-4750**	406-523-1500
New York Susquehanna & Western Railway Corp (NYSW) 1 Railroad Ave *General	Cooperstown	NY	13326	**800-366-6979***	607-547-2555
Norfolk Southern Railway Co 3 Commercial Pl	Norfolk	VA	23510	**800-635-5768**	800-453-2530
Providence & Worcester Railroad Co 75 Hammond St *NASDAQ: PWX*	Worcester	MA	01610	**877-373-6374**	508-755-4000
Trans-Continental Systems Inc 10801 Evendale Dr	Cincinnati	OH	45241	**800-525-8726**	513-769-4774
Triple Crown Services 2720 Dupont Commerce Ct Ste 200	Fort Wayne	IN	46825	**800-325-6510**	260-416-3600
Union Pacific Railroad Co 1400 Douglas St	Omaha	NE	68179	**888-870-8777**	
Winston-Salem Southbound Railway Co 4550 Overdale Rd	Winston-Salem	NC	27107	**888-780-7245**	336-788-9407

647 RAIL TRAVEL

SEE ALSO Mass Transportation (Local & Suburban)

Company / Address	City	State	Zip	Toll-Free	Phone
Dew Distribution Services Inc 2201 Touhy Ave	Elk Grove Village	IL	60007	**800-837-3391**	
Indiana Rail Road Co, The 101 W Ohio St Ste 1600	Indianapolis	IN	46204	**888-596-2121**	317-262-5140
National Railroad Passenger Corp 60 Massachusetts Ave NE	Washington	DC	20002	**800-872-7245**	202-906-3741
Twin Cities & Western Railroad 2925 12th St E	Glencoe	MN	55336	**800-290-8297**	320-864-7200
VIA Rail Canada Inc 3 Pl Ville-Marie PO Box 8116	Montreal	QC	H3C3N3	**800-681-2561**	514-871-6000

648 RAILROAD EQUIPMENT - MFR

SEE ALSO Transportation Equipment & Supplies - Whol

Company / Address	City	State	Zip	Toll-Free	Phone
A Stucki Co 2600 Neville Rd	Pittsburgh	PA	15225	**888-266-6630**	412-771-7300
American Railcar Industries Inc 100 Clark St *NASDAQ: ARII*	Saint Charles	MO	63301	**800-489-9888**	636-940-6000
CANAC Inc 6505 Trans-Canada Hwy Ste 405	St Laurent	QC	H4T1S3	**800-588-4387**	514-734-4700
Cando Contracting Ltd 740 Rosser Ave Fl 4	Brandon	MB	R7A0K9	**866-989-5310**	204-725-2627
Dayton-Phoenix Group Inc 1619 Kuntz Rd	Dayton	OH	45404	**800-657-0707**	937-496-3974
Electro-Motive Diesel Inc 9301 W 55th St	La Grange	IL	60525	**800-255-5355**	708-387-6000
FreightCar America Inc 17 Johns St *NASDAQ: RAIL*	Johnstown	PA	15901	**800-458-2235**	
GE Transportation Rail 2901 E Lake Rd *Prod Info	Erie	PA	16531	**800-285-6545***	814-875-2234
Greenbrier Co 1 Centerpointe Dr Ste 200 *NYSE: GBX*	Lake Oswego	OR	97035	**800-343-7188**	503-684-7000
Interstate Transport Inc 324 First Ave N	St Petersburg	FL	33701	**866-281-1281**	727-822-9999
LB Foster Co 415 Holiday Dr *NASDAQ: FSTR*	Pittsburgh	PA	15220	**800-255-4500**	
Loram Maintenance of Way 3900 Arrowhead Dr PO Box 188	Hamel	MN	55340	**800-328-1466**	763-478-6014
Miner Enterprises Inc 1200 E State St	Geneva	IL	60134	**888-822-5334**	630-232-3000
National Railway Equipment Co (NREC) 14400 Robey St	Dixmoor	IL	60426	**800-253-2905**	708-388-6002
New York Air Brake Co 748 Starbuck Ave	Watertown	NY	13601	**888-836-6922**	315-786-5200
Nolan Co 1016 Ninth St SW	Canton	OH	44707	**800-297-1383**	330-453-7922
Pacific Coast Container Inc 432 Estudillo Ave	San Leandro	CA	94577	**800-458-4788**	510-346-6100
Rail Car Service Co 584 Fairground Rd	Mercer	PA	16137	**800-521-2151**	724-662-3660
Transco Railway Products Inc 820 Hopley Ave	Bucyrus	OH	44820	**800-472-4592**	419-562-1031
Trinity Mining Service 109 48th St	Pittsburgh	PA	15201	**800-264-2583**	412-682-4700
Trinity Rail Group LLC 2525 N Stemmons Fwy	Dallas	TX	75207	**800-631-4420**	214-631-4420
Union Tank Car Co 175 W Jackson Blvd	Chicago	IL	60604	**866-535-7685**	312-431-3111
Vapor Bus International 1010 Johnson Dr	Buffalo Grove	IL	60089	**866-375-4126**	847-777-6400
WABCO Locomotive Products 1001 Air Brake Ave *Cust Svc	Wilmerding	PA	15148	**877-922-2627***	412-825-1000
Wabtec Corp 1001 Air Brake Ave *NYSE: WAB* ■ *Cust Svc	Wilmerding	PA	15148	**877-922-2627***	412-825-1000
Watco Companies LLC 315 W Third St	Pittsburg	KS	66762	**866-386-9321**	620-231-2230

649 RAILROAD SWITCHING & TERMINAL SERVICES

Company / Address	City	State	Zip	Toll-Free	Phone
Belt Railway Co of Chicago 6900 S Central Ave	Bedford Park	IL	60638	**877-772-5772**	708-496-4000
Public Belt Railroad Commission 4822 Tchoupitulas St *Cust Svc	New Orleans	LA	70115	**800-524-3421***	504-896-7410
Rail Link Inc 13901 Sutton Pk Dr S Ste 125	Jacksonville	FL	32224	**877-777-4778**	904-223-1110
Railserve Inc 1691 Phoenix Blvd Ste 110	Atlanta	GA	30349	**800-345-7245**	770-996-6838
Rescar Inc 1101 31st St Ste 250	Downers Grove	IL	60515	**800-851-5196**	630-963-1114
Roadrunner Transportation Systems Inc 4900 S Pennsylvania Ave *NYSE: RRTS*	Cudahy	WI	53110	**800-831-4394**	414-615-1500

650 REAL ESTATE AGENTS & BROKERS

Company / Address	City	State	Zip	Toll-Free	Phone
Assist-2-Sell Inc 1610 Meadow Wood Ln	Reno	NV	89502	**800-528-7816**	775-688-6060
Bailey Properties 106 Aptos Beach Dr	Aptos	CA	95003	**800-347-6830**	831-688-7009
Baird & Warner Inc 120 S LaSalle St Ste 2000	Chicago	IL	60603	**888-661-1176**	312-368-1855
Beach Realty & Construction 4826 N Croatan Hwy	Kitty Hawk	NC	27949	**800-635-1559**	252-261-3815
Bosshardt Realty Services LLC 5542 NW 43rd St	Gainesville	FL	32653	**800-284-6110**	352-371-6100
Bray Real Estate 637 N Ave	Grand Junction	CO	81501	**888-760-4251**	970-242-8450
Brookfield Residential Services Ltd 3190 Steeles Ave E Ste 200	Markham	ON	L3R1G9	**800-949-0274**	416-510-8700
Brownstone Real Estate Co 1840 Fishburn Rd	Hershey	PA	17033	**877-533-6222**	717-533-6222

Company / Address	City	State	Zip	Toll-Free	Phone
Cambria Pines Realty Inc 746-A Main St	Cambria	CA	93428	**800-676-8616**	805-927-8616
Carolina Farms Real Estate 547 S Main St	King	NC	27021	**800-559-2113**	336-983-5263
Coldwell Banker Gundaker 2458 Old Dorsett Rd Ste 300	Maryland Heights	MO	63043	**800-325-1978**	314-298-5000
Coldwell Banker Residential Brokerage 600 Grant St Ste 925 *All	Denver	CO	80203	**800-552-6787***	303-409-1500
Coldwell Banker Residential Real Estate 5951 Cattleridge Ave	Sarasota	FL	34232	**888-937-6426**	941-487-1400
Conterra Ultra Broadband LLC 2101 Rexford Rd Ste 200E	Charlotte	NC	28211	**800-634-1374**	704-936-1800
Corcoran Group Inc, The 660 Madison Ave	New York	NY	10021	**800-544-4055**	212-355-3550
Crye-Leike Inc 6525 N Quail Hollow Rd	Memphis	TN	38120	**866-310-3102**	
Cutten Realty Inc 2120 Campton Rd Ste C	Eureka	CA	95503	**800-776-4458**	707-445-8811
Dart Appraisalcom 2600 W Big Beaver Rd Ste 540	Troy	MI	48084	**888-327-8123**	
DH Bader Management Services Inc 14435 Cherry Ln Ct Ste 210	Laurel	MD	20707	**888-953-1955**	301-953-1955
Equine Canada 2685 Queensview Dr	Ottawa	ON	K2B8K2	**866-282-8395**	613-248-3484
ERA Wilder Realty 120A Columbia Ave PO Box 610	Chapin	SC	29036	**866-593-7653**	803-345-6713
Fimc Commercial Realty 1619 S Tyler St	Amarillo	TX	79102	**800-658-2616**	806-358-7151
Gove Group Real Estate LLC 70 Portsmouth Ave	Stratham	NH	03885	**866-778-6400**	603-778-6400
H Pearce Real Estate Co 393 State St	North Haven	CT	06473	**800-373-3411**	203-281-3400
Hart Corp 900 Jaymor Rd	SoutHampton	PA	18966	**800-368-4278**	215-322-5100
Hoban & Assoc Dba Coast Real Estate Services 2829 Rucker Ave	Everett	WA	98201	**800-339-3634**	425-339-3638
HomeGain.com Inc 6001 Shellmound St Ste 550	Emeryville	CA	94608	**888-542-0800**	510-655-0800
HomeServices of America Inc 333 S Seventh St 27th Fl	Minneapolis	MN	55402	**888-485-0018**	
Hotpadscom PO Box 53104	Washington	DC	20009	**888-876-1992**	202-232-1581
Inland Group Inc 2901 Butterfield Rd	Oak Brook	IL	60523	**800-826-8228**	630-218-8000
Iowa Realty Company Inc 3501 Westown Pkwy	West Des Moines	IA	50266	**800-247-2430**	515-453-6222
Jack Conway 137 Washington St	Norwell	MA	02061	**800-283-1030**	781-871-0080
Janet Mcafee Real Estate 9889 Clayton Rd	Saint Louis	MO	63124	**888-991-4800**	314-997-4800
Jersey Cape Realty Inc 739 Washington St	Cape May	NJ	08204	**800-643-0043**	609-884-5800
John Daugherty Realtors 520 Post Oak Blvd 6th Fl	Houston	TX	77027	**800-231-2821**	713-626-3930
Joyner Fine Properties (JFP) 2727 Enterprise Pkwy	Richmond	VA	23294	**800-446-3858**	804-270-9440
JR Realty 101 E Horizon Dr	Henderson	NV	89015	**800-541-6780**	702-564-5142
Keefe Real Estate 1155 E Geneva St	Delavan	WI	53115	**800-690-2292**	262-728-8757
Keystone Property Group Inc 1 Presidential Blvd Ste 300	Bala Cynwyd	PA	19004	**866-980-1818**	610-980-7000
L b Property Management 4730 Woodman Ave Ste 200	Sherman Oaks	CA	91423	**888-400-7080**	
LG2 Environmental Solutions Inc 14785 Old St Augustine Rd Ste 4	Jacksonville	FL	32258	**800-435-0072**	904-288-8631
Long & Foster Realtors 14501 George Carter Way	Chantilly	VA	20151	**800-237-8800**	703-653-8500
Macdonald Realty 203 5188 Wminster Hwy	Richmond	BC	V7C5S7	**877-278-3888**	604-279-9822
MacPherson's Property Management Inc 18551 Aurora Ave N Ste 301	Shoreline	WA	98133	**800-962-6473**	206-542-6363
Mad Inc Dba Century 21 Salvadori Realty 3500 N G St	Merced	CA	95340	**800-557-6033**	209-383-6475
MCAP Service Corp 400-200 King St W	Toronto	ON	M5H3T4	**800-387-4405**	416-598-2665
Mcenearney Assoc Inc 109 S Pitt St	Alexandria	VA	22314	**877-624-9322**	703-549-9292
National Church Residences Inc 2335 N Bank Dr	Columbus	OH	43220	**800-388-2151**	
NP Dodge Real Estate 8701 W Dodge Rd Ste 300	Omaha	NE	68114	**800-642-5008**	402-397-4900
Ontario Real Estate Assn 99 Duncan Mill Rd	Don Mills	ON	M3B1Z2	**866-444-5557**	416-445-9910
Pacific Coast Valuations 740 Corporate Ctr Dr Ste 200	Pomona	CA	91768	**888-623-4001**	909-623-4001
Patterson-Schwartz & Assoc Inc 7234 Lancaster Pike Ste 100A	Hockessin	DE	19707	**877-456-4663**	302-234-5270
PMCS-ICAP 829 W Genesee St	Syracuse	NY	13204	**800-245-7627**	315-423-7962
Premier Realty Group 2 N Sewalls Point Rd	Stuart	FL	34996	**800-915-8517**	772-287-1777
Quad Cities Realty 1053 Ripon Ave	Lewiston	ID	83501	**877-798-7798**	208-798-7798
RE/MAX International Inc 5075 S Syracuse St *Cust Svc	Denver	CO	80237	**800-525-7452***	303-770-5531
RE/MAX of Western Canada Inc 1060 Manhattan Dr Ste 340	Kelowna	BC	V1Y9X9	**800-563-3622**	250-860-3628
RE/MAX Ontario-Atlantic 7101 Syntex Dr	Mississauga	ON	L5N6H5	**888-542-2499**	905-542-2400
RE/MAX Quebec Inc 1500 Cunard St	Laval	QC	H7S2B7	**800-361-9325**	450-668-7743
Real Estate Institute of Bc 1750 - 355 Burrard St	Vancouver	BC	V6C2G8	**800-667-2166**	604-685-3702
Real Estate One Inc 25800 NW Hwy Ste 100	Southfield	MI	48075	**800-521-0508**	248-304-6700
Real Living First Service Realty 13155 SW 42nd St Ste 200	Miami	FL	33175	**800-899-8477**	305-551-9400
Realestateexpresscom 12977 N 40 Dr Ste 108	Saint Louis	MO	63141	**866-739-7277**	
Realty Executives International Inc 7600 N 16th St Ste 100	Phoenix	AZ	85020	**800-252-3366**	602-957-0747
Relocation Center Inc, The 1042 E Juneau Ave	Milwaukee	WI	53202	**800-783-5337**	414-226-4200
RIS Media Inc 69 E Ave	Norwalk	CT	06851	**800-724-6000**	203-855-1234
Rose Assoc Inc 200 Madison Ave	New York	NY	10016	**888-475-8860**	212-210-6666
Ross Realty Investments Inc 3325 S University Dr Ste 210	Davie	FL	33328	**800-370-4202**	954-452-5000
Sam Hatfield Realty Inc 4470 Mansford Rd	Winchester	TN	37398	**866-959-7474**	931-968-0500
Semonin Realtors 4967 US Hwy 42 Ste 200	Louisville	KY	40222	**800-548-1650**	502-425-4760
Shorewest Realtors Inc 17450 W N Ave	Brookfield	WI	53008	**800-434-7350**	262-827-4200
Silicon Valley Assn of Realtors 19400 Stevens Creek Blvd Ste 100	Cupertino	CA	95014	**877-699-6787**	408-200-0100
Skyline Properties South Inc 50 116th Ave SE Ste 120	Bellevue	WA	98004	**800-753-6156**	425-455-2065
Sotheby's International Realty 38 E 61st St	New York	NY	10065	**866-899-4747**	212-606-7660
Stan White Realty & Construction Inc 812 Ocean Trl	Corolla	NC	27927	**800-753-6200**	252-453-6131
Strother Ventures II Inc 2929 Breezewood Ave Ste 200	Fayetteville	NC	28303	**855-753-6143**	910-864-2327
Sutton Alliance LLC 515 Rockaway Ave	Valley Stream	NY	11581	**866-435-6600**	516-837-6100
Themlsonline Com Inc 11150 Commerce Dr N	Champlin	MN	55316	**866-657-6654**	763-576-8286
Tri-Land Kansas City Investors LLC 1 Wbrook Corporate Ctr Ste 520	Westchester	IL	60154	**800-441-7032**	708-531-8210
United Country Real Estate Inc 2820 NW Barry Rd	Kansas City	MO	64154	**800-999-1020**	816-420-6200
Valuation Management Group LLC 1640 Powers Ferry Rd SE Bldg 15 Ste 100	Marietta	GA	30067	**866-799-7488**	678-483-4420
Walsh Property Management PO Box 2657	Castro Valley	CA	94546	**888-896-5510**	510-888-8965
Williams & Williams Real Estate Auction 7120 S Lewis Ave Ste 200	Tulsa	OK	74136	**800-801-8003**	918-250-2012
ZipRealty Inc 2000 Powell St Ste 300 *NASDAQ: ZIPR*	Emeryville	CA	94608	**800-225-5947**	510-735-2600

651 REAL ESTATE DEVELOPERS

SEE ALSO Construction - Building Contractors - Non-Residential ; Construction - Building Contractors - Residential

Company / Address	City	State	Zip	Toll-Free	Phone
Al Neyer Inc 302 W Third St Ste 800	Cincinnati	OH	45202	**877-271-6400**	513-271-6400
AV Homes Inc 8601 N Scottsdale Rd Ste 225 *NASDAQ: AVHI*	Scottsdale	AR	85283	**800-284-6637**	480-214-7400
Brooks Resources Corp 409 NW Franklin Ave	Bend	OR	97701	**877-475-9779**	541-382-1662
Cornerstone Group 2100 Hollywood Blvd	Hollywood	FL	33020	**800-809-4099**	305-443-8288
CountryTyme Inc 3451 Cincinnati-Zanesville Rd SW	Lancaster	OH	43130	**800-213-8365**	740-475-6001
David Weekley Homes Inc 1111 N Post Oak Rd	Houston	TX	77055	**800-390-6774**	713-963-0500
Deltona Corp 8014 SW 135th St Rd	Ocala	FL	34473	**800-333-5866**	352-347-2322
Double Diamond Co 5495 Belt Line Rd Ste 200	Dallas	TX	75254	**800-324-7438**	214-706-9801
DR Horton Inc 301 Commerce St Ste 500 *NYSE: DHI*	Fort Worth	TX	76102	**800-846-7866**	817-390-8200
Gilbane Inc 7 Jackson Walkway	Providence	RI	02903	**800-445-2263**	401-456-5890
Hines Interest LP 2800 Post Oak Blvd	Houston	TX	77056	**888-782-7937**	713-621-8000
Holiday Builders Inc 2293 W Eau Gallie Blvd	Melbourne	FL	32935	**866-431-2533**	321-610-5172
Hunt Midwest Enterprises Inc 8300 NE Underground Dr	Kansas City	MO	64161	**800-551-6877**	816-455-2500
Hunt Midwest Residential Development 8300 NE Underground Dr	Kansas City	MO	64161	**800-551-6877**	816-455-2500
Inland Real Estate Development Corp 2901 Butterfield Rd	Oak Brook	IL	60523	**866-954-5692**	630-218-8000
Intervest Construction Inc 2379 Beville Rd	Daytona Beach	FL	32119	**855-215-2974**	844-349-6401
Ivory Homes 970 E Woodoak Ln	Salt Lake City	UT	84117	**888-455-5561**	
JA Billipp Co 6925 Portwest Dr Ste 130	Houston	TX	77024	**800-216-9013**	713-426-5000
John F Buchan Homes 2821 Northup Way Ste 100	Bellevue	WA	98004	**866-528-2426**	425-827-2266
John Wieland Homes & Neighborhoods 4125 Atlanta Rd SE	Smyrna	GA	30080	**800-376-4663**	770-996-2400
KB Home 10990 Wilshire Blvd 7th Fl *NYSE: KBH*	Los Angeles	CA	90024	**800-304-0657**	310-231-4000
M/I Homes Inc 3 Easton Oval *NYSE: MHO*	Columbus	OH	43219	**888-644-4111**	614-418-8700
Richmond American Homes Inc 4350 S Monaco St	Denver	CO	80237	**888-402-4663**	303-773-1100
Robson Communities 9532 E Riggs Rd	Sun Lakes	AZ	85248	**800-732-9949**	
Schatten Properties Management Company Inc 1514 S St	Nashville	TN	37212	**800-892-1315**	615-329-3011
Sea Pines Resort, The 32 Greenwood Dr	Hilton Head Island	SC	29928	**866-561-8802**	843-785-3333

				Toll-Free	Phone
Sea Trail Corp 75A Clubhouse Rd	Sunset Beach	NC	28468	**888-321-9048**	910-287-1100
Silver Saddle Ranch & Club Inc 20751 Aristotle Dr	California City	CA	93505	**888-430-8728**	760-373-8617
Stanley Martin Cos 11111 Sunset Hills Rd Ste 200	Reston	VA	20190	**800-446-4807**	703-964-5000
Stratus Properties Inc 212 Lavaca St Ste 300 *NYSE: STRS*	Austin	TX	78701	**800-690-0315**	512-478-5788
Toll Bros Inc 250 Gibraltar Rd *NYSE: TOL*	Horsham	PA	19044	**855-897-8655**	215-938-8000
TransCon Builders Inc 25250 Rockside Rd	Cleveland	OH	44146	**800-451-2608**	440-439-2100
Village Green Cos 30833 NW Hwy	Farmington Hills	MI	48334	**800-521-2220**	248-851-9600
Villages of Lake Sumter Inc 1000 Lk Sumter Landing	The Villages	FL	32162	**800-245-1081**	352-753-2270
WCI Communities Inc 24301 Walden Ctr Dr	Bonita Springs	FL	34134	**800-924-4005**	239-498-8200
Weyerhaeuser Co 33663 Weyerhaeuser Way S *NYSE: WY*	Federal Way	WA	98003	**800-525-5440**	253-924-2345

652 REAL ESTATE INVESTMENT TRUSTS (REITS)

				Toll-Free	Phone
Alexandria Real Estate Equities Inc 385 E Colorado Blvd Ste 299 *NYSE: ARE*	Pasadena	CA	91101	**800-776-9437**	626-578-0777
Apartment Investment & Management Co 4582 S Ulster St Pkwy Ste 1100 *NYSE: AIV* ■ *General	Denver	CO	80237	**888-789-8600***	303-691-4350
Arbor Realty Trust Inc 333 Earle Ovington Blvd Ste 900 *NYSE: ABR*	Uniondale	NY	11553	**800-272-6710**	
AutoStar 114 Ave of the Americas Ste 39	New York	NY	10036	**800-288-6782**	212-930-9400
Benchmark Group 4053 Maple Rd	Amherst	NY	14226	**800-876-0160**	716-833-4986
BRT Realty Trust 60 Cutter Mill Rd Ste 303 *NYSE: BRT*	Great Neck	NY	11021	**800-450-5816**	516-466-3100
Camden Property Trust 11 Greenway Plz Ste 2400 *NYSE: CPT*	Houston	TX	77046	**800-922-6336**	713-354-2500
Capstead Mortgage Corp 8401 N Central Expy Ste 800 *NYSE: CMO*	Dallas	TX	75225	**800-358-2323**	214-874-2323
Chesapeake Lodging Trust (CLT) 1997 Annapolis Exchange Pkwy Ste 410 *NYSE: CHSP*	Annapolis	MD	21401	**800-698-2820**	
Colonial Properties Trust 6584 Poplar Ave *NYSE: CLP*	Memphis	TN	38138	**866-620-1130**	
Commercial Properties Realty Trust 402 N Fourth St	Baton Rouge	LA	70802	**800-648-9064**	225-924-7206
DiamondRock Hospitality Co (DRHC) 3 Bethesda Metro Ctr Ste 1500 *NYSE: DRH*	Bethesda	MD	20814	**888-246-5941**	240-744-1150
Dividend Capital Trust 518 17th St Ste 1700	Denver	CO	80202	**866-324-7348**	303-228-2200
Federal Realty Investment Trust 1626 E Jefferson St *NYSE: FRT*	Rockville	MD	20852	**800-658-8980**	301-998-8100
Franklin Street Properties Corp 401 Edgewater Pl Ste 200 *NYSE: FSP*	Wakefield	MA	01880	**877-686-9496**	781-557-1300
GE Capital Solutions Franchise Finance 8377 E Hartford Dr Ste 200	Scottsdale	AZ	85255	**866-438-4333**	
Health Care Property Investors Inc 1920 Main St Ste 1200	Irvine	CA	92614	**800-690-6903**	949-407-0700
Highwoods Properties Inc 3100 Smoketree Ct Ste 600 *NYSE: HIW*	Raleigh	NC	27604	**866-449-6637**	919-872-4924
Impac Mortgage Holdings Inc 19500 Jamboree Rd *NYSE: IMH*	Irvine	CA	92612	**800-597-4101**	949-475-3600
Inland Real Estate Corp 2901 Butterfield Rd *NYSE: IRC*	Oak Brook	IL	60523	**888-331-4732**	630-218-8000
InnSuites Hospitality Trust 1625 E Northern Ave Ste 105 *NYSE: IHT*	Phoenix	AZ	85020	**800-842-4242**	602-944-1500
iStar Financial Inc 1114 Ave of the Americas 39th Fl *NYSE: STAR*	New York	NY	10036	**888-603-5847**	212-930-9400
Kimco Realty Corp 3333 New Hyde Pk Rd *NYSE: KIM*	New Hyde Park	NY	11042	**800-645-6292**	516-869-9000
Kite Realty Group Trust 30 S Meridian St Ste 1100 *NYSE: KRG*	Indianapolis	IN	46204	**888-577-5600**	317-577-5600
Lexington Corporate Properties Trust 1 Penn Plz Ste 4015	New York	NY	10119	**800-850-3948**	212-692-7200
Mack-Cali Realty Corp 343 Thornall St *NYSE: CLI*	Edison	NJ	08837	**800-317-4445**	732-590-1000
New York Mortgage Trust Inc (NYMT) 52 Vanderbilt Ave Ste 403 *NASDAQ: NYMT*	New York	NY	10017	**800-937-5449**	212-792-0107
Novastar Financial Inc 2114 Central Ste 600	Kansas City	MO	64108	**800-591-1137**	816-237-7000
One Liberty Properties Inc 60 Cutter Mill Rd Ste 303 *NYSE: OLP*	Great Neck	NY	11021	**800-937-5449**	516-466-3100
Parkway Properties Inc 188 E Capitol St Ste 1000 *NYSE: PKY*	Jackson	MS	39201	**800-748-1667**	601-948-4091
Pennsylvania Real Estate Investment Trust 200 S Broad St 3rd Fl *NYSE: PEI*	Philadelphia	PA	19102	**866-875-0700**	215-875-0700
PMC Commercial Trust 17950 Preston Rd Ste 600 *NASDAQ: CMCT*	Dallas	TX	75252	**800-486-3223**	972-349-3200
ProLogis 4545 Airport Way *NYSE: PLD*	Denver	CO	80239	**800-566-2706**	303-375-9292
PS Business Parks Inc 701 Western Ave *NYSE: PSB* ■ *Cust Svc	Glendale	CA	91201	**888-782-6110***	818-244-8080
Public Storage Inc 701 Western Ave *NYSE: PSA* ■ *Cust Svc	Glendale	CA	91201	**800-567-0759***	818-244-8080
Regency Centers 1 Independent Dr Ste 114 *NYSE: REG*	Jacksonville	FL	32202	**800-950-6333**	904-598-7000
RioCan Real Estate Investment Trust 2300 Yonge St Ste 500 PO Box 2386 *TSE: REI.UN.CA*	Toronto	ON	M4P1E4	**800-465-2733**	416-866-3033
Starwood Hotels & Resorts Worldwide Inc 1111 Westchester Ave *NYSE: HOT* ■ *Cust Svc	White Plains	NY	10604	**888-625-5144***	914-640-8100
Tanger Factory Outlet Centers Inc 3200 Northline Ave Ste 360 *NYSE: SKT*	Greensboro	NC	27408	**800-720-6728**	336-292-3010
Taubman Centers Inc 200 E Long Lk Rd Ste 300 *NYSE: TCO*	Bloomfield Hills	MI	48303	**800-297-6003**	248-258-6800
Transcontinental Realty Investors Inc 1603 Lyndon B Johnson Fwy Ste 800 *NYSE: TCI*	Dallas	TX	75234	**800-400-6407**	469-522-4200
Vornado Realty Trust 888 Seventh Ave *NYSE: VNO*	New York	NY	10019	**800-294-1322**	212-894-7000
Washington Real Estate Investment Trust (WRIT) 1775 I St NW *NYSE: WRE*	Washington	DC	20006	**800-565-9748**	301-984-9400
Weingarten Realty Investors 2600 Citadel Plz Dr Ste 125 *NYSE: WRI*	Houston	TX	77008	**800-688-8865**	713-866-6000
Winthrop Realty Trust 7 Bulfinch Pl Ste 500 *NYSE: FUR*	Boston	MA	02114	**800-622-6757**	617-570-4614
WP Carey & Company LLC 50 Rockefeller Plz 2nd Fl *NYSE: WPC*	New York	NY	10020	**800-972-2739**	212-492-1100

653 REAL ESTATE MANAGERS & OPERATORS

SEE ALSO Retirement Communities ; Hotels & Hotel Companies

				Toll-Free	Phone
Alexandria Real Estate Equities Inc 385 E Colorado Blvd Ste 299 *NYSE: ARE*	Pasadena	CA	91101	**800-776-9437**	626-578-0777
American Golf Corp 2951 28th St	Santa Monica	CA	90405	**800-238-7267**	310-664-4000
American Motel Management 2200 Northlake Pkwy Ste 277	Tucker	GA	30084	**800-580-8258**	770-939-1801
American Realty Investors Inc 1800 Vly View Ln Ste 300 *NYSE: ARL*	Dallas	TX	75234	**800-400-6407**	469-522-4200
American Spectrum Realty Inc 2401 Fountain View 7th Fl *NYSE: AQQ*	Houston	TX	77057	**888-315-2776**	713-706-6200
Apartment Investment & Management Co 4582 S Ulster St Pkwy Ste 1100 *NYSE: AIV* ■ *General	Denver	CO	80237	**888-789-8600***	303-691-4350
Bozzuto Group 7850 Walker Dr Ste 400 *General	Greenbelt	MD	20770	**866-698-7513***	301-220-0100
Brandywine Realty Trust 555 E Lancaster Ave Ste 100 *NYSE: BDN*	Radnor	PA	19087	**866-426-5400**	610-325-5600
Brixmor Property Group 420 Lexington Ave 7th Fl	New York	NY	10170	**800-468-7526**	212-869-3000
Brookfield Properties Corp (BOP) 181 Bay St Ste 330 *NYSE: BPO*	Toronto	ON	M5J2T3	**800-387-0825**	416-369-2300
Calista Corp 301 Calista Ct Ste A	Anchorage	AK	99518	**800-277-5516**	907-279-5516
Camden Property Trust 11 Greenway Plz Ste 2400 *NYSE: CPT*	Houston	TX	77046	**800-922-6336**	713-354-2500
ClubCorp Inc 3030 Lyndon B Johnson Fwy Ste 600	Dallas	TX	75234	**800-433-5079**	972-243-6191
ClubLink Corp 15675 Dufferin St	King City	ON	L7B1K5	**800-661-1818**	905-841-3730
Colonial Properties Trust 6584 Poplar Ave *NYSE: CLP*	Memphis	TN	38138	**866-620-1130**	
Developers Diversified Realty Corp 3300 Enterprise Pkwy *NYSE: DDR*	Beachwood	OH	44122	**877-225-5337**	216-755-5500
Equity Lifestyle Properties Inc 2 N Riverside Plz Ste 800 *NYSE: ELS*	Chicago	IL	60606	**800-274-7314**	312-279-1400
Eugene Burger Management Corp 6600 Hunter Dr	Rohnert Park	CA	94928	**800-788-0233**	707-584-5123
Federal Realty Investment Trust 1626 E Jefferson St *NYSE: FRT*	Rockville	MD	20852	**800-658-8980**	301-998-8100
General Growth Properties Inc 110 N Wacker Dr *NYSE: GGP*	Chicago	IL	60606	**888-395-8037**	312-960-5000

Company	Address	City	State	ZIP	Toll-Free	Phone
Grady Management Inc	8630 Fenton St Ste 625	Silver Spring	MD	20910	**800-544-7239**	301-587-3330
Great American Group Inc *OTC: GAMR*	21860 Burbank Blvd Ste 300	Woodland Hills	CA	91367	**800-454-7328**	818-884-3737
Gundaker Property Management	2458 Old Dorsett Rd Ste 100	Maryland Heights	MO	63043	**800-325-1978**	314-298-5200
Health Care Property Investors Inc	1920 Main St Ste 1200	Irvine	CA	92614	**800-690-6903**	949-407-0700
Highwoods Properties Inc *NYSE: HIW*	3100 Smoketree Ct Ste 600	Raleigh	NC	27604	**866-449-6637**	919-872-4924
Holiday Retirement Corp	5885 Meadows Rd Ste 500	Lake Oswego	OR	97035	**800-322-0999**	503-370-7070
Hunt Midwest Enterprises Inc	8300 NE Underground Dr	Kansas City	MO	64161	**800-551-6877**	816-455-2500
Inland Group Inc	2901 Butterfield Rd	Oak Brook	IL	60523	**800-826-8228**	630-218-8000
Inland Real Estate Corp *NYSE: IRC*	2901 Butterfield Rd	Oak Brook	IL	60523	**888-331-4732**	630-218-8000
Kimco Realty Corp *NYSE: KIM*	3333 New Hyde Pk Rd	New Hyde Park	NY	11042	**800-645-6292**	516-869-9000
Lexington Corporate Properties Trust	1 Penn Plz Ste 4015	New York	NY	10119	**800-850-3948**	212-692-7200
Mack-Cali Realty Corp *NYSE: CLI*	343 Thornall St	Edison	NJ	08837	**800-317-4445**	732-590-1000
Mid-America Apartment Communities Inc (MAAC) *NYSE: MAA*	6584 Poplar Ave Ste 300	Memphis	TN	38138	**866-620-1130**	901-682-6600
Mid-Atlantic PenFed Realty Berkshire Hathaway HomeServices (PCR)	3050 Chain Bridge Rd	Fairfax	VA	22030	**866-225-5778**	703-691-7653
Miller Valentine Group	4000 Miller Valentine Ct	Dayton	OH	45439	**877-684-7687**	937-293-0900
Norfolk Southern Corp	800 Princeton Ave	Bluefield	WV	24701	**800-453-2530**	304-324-2400
Omega Healthcare Investors Inc *NYSE: OHI*	200 International Cir Ste 3500	Hunt Valley	MD	21030	**877-511-2891**	410-427-1700
One Liberty Properties Inc *NYSE: OLP*	60 Cutter Mill Rd Ste 303	Great Neck	NY	11021	**800-937-5449**	516-466-3100
Parkway Properties Inc *NYSE: PKY*	188 E Capitol St Ste 1000	Jackson	MS	39201	**800-748-1667**	601-948-4091
Pennsylvania Real Estate Investment Trust *NYSE: PEI*	200 S Broad St 3rd Fl	Philadelphia	PA	19102	**866-875-0700**	215-875-0700
Professional Community Management Inc	23726 Birtcher Dr	Lake Forest	CA	92630	**800-369-7260**	
ProLogis *NYSE: PLD*	4545 Airport Way	Denver	CO	80239	**800-566-2706**	303-375-9292
PS Business Parks Inc *NYSE: PSB* ■ *Cust Svc	701 Western Ave	Glendale	CA	91201	**888-782-6110***	818-244-8080
Realty Income Corp *NYSE: O*	11995 El Camino Real	San Diego	CA	92130	**877-924-6266**	858-284-5000
Regency Centers *NYSE: REG*	1 Independent Dr Ste 114	Jacksonville	FL	32202	**800-950-6333**	904-598-7000
Schatten Properties Management Company Inc	1514 S St	Nashville	TN	37212	**800-892-1315**	615-329-3011
Sea Island Co	PO Box 30351	Sea Island	GA	31561	**800-732-4752**	912-638-3611
Senior Housing Properties Trust *NYSE: SNH*	255 Washington St	Newton	MA	02458	**866-511-5038**	617-796-8350
Stirling Properties	109 Northpark Blvd Ste 300	Covington	LA	70433	**888-261-2022**	985-898-2022
Tanger Factory Outlet Centers Inc *NYSE: SKT*	3200 Northline Ave Ste 360	Greensboro	NC	27408	**800-720-6728**	336-292-3010
Taubman Centers Inc *NYSE: TCO*	200 E Long Lk Rd Ste 300	Bloomfield Hills	MI	48303	**800-297-6003**	248-258-6800
Transcontinental Realty Investors Inc *NYSE: TCI*	1603 Lyndon B Johnson Fwy Ste 800	Dallas	TX	75234	**800-400-6407**	469-522-4200
USAA Real Estate Co	9830 Colonnade Blvd Ste 600	San Antonio	TX	78230	**800-531-8182**	
Ventas Inc	111 S Wacker Dr Ste 4800	Chicago	IL	60606	**877-483-6827**	312-660-3800
Village Green Cos	30833 NW Hwy	Farmington Hills	MI	48334	**800-521-2220**	248-851-9600
Vornado Realty Trust *NYSE: VNO*	888 Seventh Ave	New York	NY	10019	**800-294-1322**	212-894-7000
Warren Properties Inc	PO Box 469114	Escondido	CA	92046	**800-831-0804**	
Washington Real Estate Investment Trust (WRIT) *NYSE: WRE*	1775 I St NW	Washington	DC	20006	**800-565-9748**	301-984-9400
Weingarten Realty Investors *NYSE: WRI*	2600 Citadel Plz Dr Ste 125	Houston	TX	77008	**800-688-8865**	713-866-6000
Winthrop Realty Trust *NYSE: FUR*	7 Bulfinch Pl Ste 500	Boston	MA	02114	**800-622-6757**	617-570-4614
WP Carey & Company LLC *NYSE: WPC*	50 Rockefeller Plz 2nd Fl	New York	NY	10020	**800-972-2739**	212-492-1100

654 REALTOR ASSOCIATIONS - STATE

SEE ALSO Real Estate Professionals Associations

Listed here are the state branches of the National Association of Realtors.

Association	Address	City	State	ZIP	Toll-Free	Phone
Alabama Assn of Realtors	522 Washington Ave PO Box 4070	Montgomery	AL	36104	**800-446-3808**	334-262-3808
Alaska Assn of Realtors	4205 Minnesota Dr	Anchorage	AK	99503	**800-478-3763**	907-563-7133
Arizona Assn of Realtors	255 E Osborne Rd Ste 200	Phoenix	AZ	85012	**800-426-7274**	602-248-7787
Arkansas Realtors Assn	11224 Executive Ctr Dr	Little Rock	AR	72211	**888-333-2206**	501-225-2020
Beach Properties of Hilton Head Inc	64 Arrow Rd PO Box 7408	Hilton Head Island	SC	29928	**800-671-5155**	843-671-5155
Carolina Designs Realty Inc	1197 Duck Rd	Kitty Hawk	NC	27949	**800-368-3825**	252-261-3934
Colorado Assn of Realtors	309 Inverness Way S	Englewood	CO	80112	**800-944-6550**	303-790-7099
Connecticut Assn of Realtors	111 Founders Plz Ste 1101	East Hartford	CT	06108	**800-335-4862**	860-290-6601
Delaware Assn of Realtors	134 E Water St	Dover	DE	19901	**800-305-4445**	302-734-4444
Florida Assn of Realtors	7025 Augusta National Dr	Orlando	FL	32822	**800-669-4327**	407-438-1400
Georgia Assn of Realtors	3200 Presidential Dr	Atlanta	GA	30340	**866-280-0576**	770-451-1831
Hawaii Assn of Realtors	1136 12th Ave Ste 220	Honolulu	HI	96816	**866-693-6767**	808-733-7060
Idaho Assn of Realtors	10116 W Overland Rd	Boise	ID	83702	**800-621-7553**	208-342-3585
Indiana Assn of Realtors	7301 N Shadeland Ave Ste A	Indianapolis	IN	46250	**800-284-0084**	317-842-0890
Iowa Assn of Realtors	1370 NW 114th St Ste 100	Clive	IA	50325	**800-532-1515**	515-453-1064
JEM Strapping Systems	116 Shaver St	Brantford	ON	N3T5M1	**877-536-6584**	519-754-5432
Kansas Assn of Realtors	3644 SW Burlingame Rd	Topeka	KS	66611	**800-366-0069**	785-267-3610
Kentucky Assn of Realtors	2801 Palumbo Dr Ste 202	Lexington	KY	40509	**800-264-2185**	859-263-7377
Maryland Assn of Realtors	2594 Riva Rd	Annapolis	MD	21401	**800-638-6425**	410-841-6080
Massachusetts Assn of Realtors	256 Second Ave	Waltham	MA	02451	**800-725-6272**	781-890-3700
Michigan Assn of Realtors	720 N Washington Ave	Lansing	MI	48906	**800-454-7842**	517-372-8890
Minnesota Assn of Realtors	5750 Lincoln Dr	Minneapolis	MN	55436	**800-862-6097**	952-935-8313
Mississippi Assn of Realtors	4274 Lakeland Dr PO Box 321000	Jackson	MS	39232	**800-747-1103**	601-932-9325
Missouri Assn of Realtors	2601 Bernadette Pl	Columbia	MO	65203	**800-403-0101**	573-445-8400
Montana Assn of Realtors	1 S Montana Ave Ste M1	Helena	MT	59601	**800-477-1864**	406-443-4032
Nebraska Realtors Assn	800 S 13th St Ste 200	Lincoln	NE	68508	**800-777-5231**	402-323-6500
Nevada Assn of Realtors	760 Margrave Dr Ste 200	Reno	NV	89502	**800-748-5526**	775-829-5911
New Hampshire Assn of Realtors	115A Airport Rd	Concord	NH	03301	**800-335-4862**	603-225-5549
New York State Assn of Realtors	130 Washington Ave	Albany	NY	12210	**800-462-7585**	518-463-0300
North Carolina Assn of Realtors Inc	4511 Weybridge Ln	Greensboro	NC	27407	**800-443-9956**	336-294-1415
North Dakota Assn of Realtors	318 W Apollo Ave	Bismarck	ND	58503	**800-279-2361**	701-355-1010
Oklahoma Assn of Realtors	9807 N Broadway	Oklahoma City	OK	73114	**800-375-9944**	405-848-9944
Oregon Assn of Realtors	2110 Mission St SE	Salem	OR	97308	**800-252-9115**	503-362-3645
Pennsylvania Assn of Realtors	500 N Twelfth St	Lemoyne	PA	17043	**800-555-3390**	717-561-1303
Rainier Group Investment Advisory LLC	500 108th Ave N E Ste 2000	Bellevue	WA	98004	**800-800-8974**	425-463-3000
Real Estate Institute of Canada, The	5407 Eglinton Ave W Ste 208	Toronto	ON	M9C5K6	**800-542-7342**	416-695-9000
Realtors Assn of New Mexico	2201 Bros Rd	Santa Fe	NM	87505	**800-224-2282**	505-982-2442
Rhode Island Assn of Realtors	100 Bignall St	Warwick	RI	02888	**866-438-8345**	401-785-9898
Signature Homes Inc	4670 Willow Rd Ste 200	Pleasanton	CA	94588	**888-673-0200**	925-463-1122
South Carolina Assn of Realtors	3780 Fernandina Rd	Columbia	SC	29210	**800-233-6381**	803-772-5206
South Dakota Assn of Realtors	204 N Euclid Ave	Pierre	SD	57501	**800-227-5877**	605-224-0554
Tennessee Assn of Realtors (TAR)	901 19th Ave S	Nashville	TN	37212	**877-321-1477**	615-321-1477
Texas Assn of Realtors	1115 San Jacinto Blvd Ste 200	Austin	TX	78701	**800-873-9155**	512-480-8200
Utah Assn of Realtors	230 W Towne Ridge Pkwy Ste 500	Sandy	UT	84070	**800-594-8933**	801-676-5200
Virginia Assn of Realtors	10231 Telegraph Rd	Glen Allen	VA	23059	**800-755-8271**	804-264-5033
Washington Assn of Realtors *General	504 14th Ave SE Ste 200	Olympia	WA	98501	**800-562-6024***	360-943-3100
West Virginia Assn of Realtors	2110 Kanawha Blvd E	Charleston	WV	25311	**800-445-7600**	304-342-7600
Wisconsin Realtors Assn	4801 Forest Run Rd Ste 201	Madison	WI	53704	**800-279-1972**	608-241-2047
Wyoming Assn of Realtors	777 Overland Trail Ste 220	Casper	WY	82601	**800-676-4085**	307-237-4085

655 RECORDING COMPANIES

Company	Address	City	State	Zip	Toll-Free	Phone
Alligator Records & Artist Management Inc	PO Box 60234	Chicago	IL	60660	**800-344-5609**	773-973-7736
American Gramaphone LLC	9130 Mormon Bridge Rd	Omaha	NE	68152	**800-348-3434**	402-457-4341
Integrity Music	4050 Lee Vance View	Colorado Springs	CO	80918	**888-888-4726**	719-536-0100
Malaco Music Group Inc	3023 W Northside Dr	Jackson	MS	39213	**800-272-7936*** *Cust Svc	601-982-4522
Naxos of America Inc	1810 Columbia Ave	Franklin	TN	37064	**877-629-6723**	615-771-9393
Nightingale-Conant Corp	6245 W Howard St	Niles	IL	60714	**800-557-1660*** *Cust Svc	
Rhino Records	3400 W Olive Ave	Burbank	CA	91505	**800-827-4466**	800-546-3670
Righteous Babe Records	341 Delaware Ave PO Box 95	Buffalo	NY	14202	**800-664-3769**	716-852-8020
Smithsonian Folkways Recordings	600 Maryland Ave SW Ste 200	Washington	DC	20024	**800-410-9815**	202-633-6450
Soar Corp (SOAR)	5200 Constitution Ave NE	Albuquerque	NM	87110	**866-616-4450**	505-268-6110

656 RECORDING MEDIA - MAGNETIC & OPTICAL

SEE ALSO Photographic Equipment & Supplies

Company	Address	City	State	Zip	Toll-Free	Phone
Allied Vaughn	7600 Parklawn Ste 300	Minneapolis	MN	55435	**800-323-0281**	952-832-3100
Ampex Corp	500 Broadway	Redwood City	CA	94063	**800-835-5095**	650-367-2011
Athana Inc	1624 W 240 St	Harbor City	CA	90710	**800-421-1591**	310-539-7280
Cine Magnetics Inc	100 Business Pk Dr	Armonk	NY	10504	**800-431-1102**	914-273-7500
Digital Excellence	300 York Ave	Saint Paul	MN	55101	**800-608-8008**	651-772-5100
Imation Corp	1 Imation Pl (*NYSE: IMN*)	Oakdale	MN	55128	**888-466-3456**	651-704-4000
Peripheral Manufacturing Inc	4775 Paris St	Denver	CO	80239	**800-468-6888**	303-371-8651
Verbatim Americas LLC	1200 W WT Harris Blvd	Charlotte	NC	28262	**800-538-8589**	704-547-6500

657 RECREATION FACILITY OPERATORS

SEE ALSO Bowling Centers

Company	Address	City	State	Zip	Toll-Free	Phone
Dave & Buster's Inc	2481 Manana Dr	Dallas	TX	75220	**800-842-5369**	214-357-9588

658 RECYCLABLE MATERIALS RECOVERY

Included here are companies that recycle post-consumer trash, tires, appliances, batteries, etc. as well as industrial recyclers of plastics, paper, wood, glass, solvents, and so on.

Company	Address	City	State	Zip	Toll-Free	Phone
American Paper Recycling Corp	87 Central St	Mansfield	MA	02048	**800-762-6790*** *Cust Svc	
Appliance Recycling Centers of America Inc	7400 Excelsior Blvd (*NASDAQ: ARCI*)	Minneapolis	MN	55426	**800-452-8680**	952-930-9000
Arrow Value Recovery	9101 Burnet Rd Ste 203	Austin	TX	78758	**800-393-7627**	
Better Management Corp (BMC)	41738 Esterly Dr	Columbiana	OH	44408	**877-293-4300**	330-482-7070
Clean Earth of North Jersey Inc	115 Jacobus Ave	South Kearny	NJ	07032	**877-445-3478**	973-344-4004
Giordano s Solid Waste Removal	110 N Mill Rd	Vineland	NJ	08360	**800-636-8625**	856-696-2068
GreenMan Technologies Inc	7 Kimball Ln Bldg A	Lynnfield	MA	01940	**866-994-7697**	781-224-2411
Greentec International Inc	95 Struck Ct	Cambridge	ON	N1R8L2	**888-858-1515**	519-624-3300
Jupiter Aluminum Corp	4825 Scott St	Schiller Park	IL	60176	**800-392-7265**	847-928-5930
Marborg Industries	728 E Yanonali St	Santa Barbara	CA	93103	**800-798-1852**	805-963-1852
MCF Systems Atlanta Inc	5353 Snapfinger Woods Dr	Decatur	GA	30035	**800-828-3240**	770-593-9434
Mervis Industries Inc	3295 E Main St	Danville	IL	61834	**800-637-3016**	217-442-5300
North Shore Recycled Fibers Inc	53 Jefferson Ave	Salem	MA	01970	**800-225-2369**	978-744-4330
Pall Corp	2200 Northern Blvd (*NYSE: PLL*)	East Hills	NY	11548	**800-645-6532**	516-484-5400
Paper Tigers, The	2201 Waukegan Rd Ste 180	Bannockburn	IL	60015	**800-621-1774**	847-919-6500
Pioneer Paper Stock	155 Irving Ave N	Minneapolis	MN	55405	**800-821-8512**	612-374-2280
Utah Metal Works Inc (UMW)	805 Everett Ave	Salt Lake City	UT	84116	**877-221-0099**	801-503-9153

659 RECYCLED PLASTICS PRODUCTS

SEE ALSO Flooring - Resilient

Company	Address	City	State	Zip	Toll-Free	Phone
Allen Ventures Inc	517 State Farm Rd	Deerfield	WI	53531	**877-423-9800**	608-423-9800
Amazing Recycled Products Inc	PO Box 312	Denver	CO	80201	**800-241-2174**	303-699-7693
American Recycled Plastic Inc	773 N. Union Grove Rd	Friendsville	TN	37737	**866-417-5821**	865-738-3439
Bedford Technology LLC	2424 Armour Rd PO Box 609	Worthington	MN	56187	**800-721-9037**	507-372-5558
Parkland Plastics Inc	104 Yoder Dr PO Box 339	Middlebury	IN	46540	**800-835-4110**	574-825-4336
Plastic Recycling of Iowa Falls Inc	10252 Hwy 65	Iowa Falls	IA	50126	**800-338-1438**	641-648-5073
Renew Plastics	PO Box 480 PO Box 480	Luxemburg	WI	54217	**800-666-5207**	920-845-2326
Resco Plastics Inc	93783 Newport Ln	Coos Bay	OR	97420	**800-266-5097**	541-269-5485
Witt Industries Inc	4600 Mason-Montgomery Rd	Mason	OH	45040	**800-543-7417**	

660 REFRACTORIES - CLAY

Company	Address	City	State	Zip	Toll-Free	Phone
BNZ Materials Inc	6901 S Pierce St Ste 260	Littleton	CO	80128	**800-999-0890**	303-978-1199
RENO Refractories Inc	601 Reno Dr	Morris	AL	35116	**800-741-7366**	205-647-0240
RENO Refractories Inc Reftech Div	601 Reno Dr	Morris	AL	35116	**800-741-7366*** *General	
Resco Products Inc	2 Penn Ctr W Ste 430	Pittsburgh	PA	15276	**888-283-5505**	412-494-4491
Riverside Refractories Inc	201 Truss Ferry Rd	Pell City	AL	35128	**800-924-0637**	205-338-3366
Whitacre Greer Fireproofing Inc	1400 S Mahoning Ave	Alliance	OH	44601	**800-947-2837*** *Cust Svc	330-823-1610

661 REFRACTORIES - NONCLAY

Company	Address	City	State	Zip	Toll-Free	Phone
Fedmet Resources Corp	PO Box 278	Montreal	QC	H3Z2T2	**800-609-5711**	514-931-5711
New Castle Refractories Co Inc	915 Industrial St	New Castle	PA	16102	**888-396-3566**	724-654-7711
Ransom & Randolph Co	3535 Briarfield Blvd	Maumee	OH	43537	**800-800-7496**	419-865-9497
RENO Refractories Inc	601 Reno Dr	Morris	AL	35116	**800-741-7366**	205-647-0240
RENO Refractories Inc Reftech Div	601 Reno Dr	Morris	AL	35116	**800-741-7366*** *General	
TYK America Inc	301 BrickyaRd Rd	Clairton	PA	15025	**800-569-9359**	412-384-4259
Wahl Refractory Solutions LLC	767 OH-19	Fremont	OH	43420	**800-837-9245**	419-334-2658

662 REFRIGERATION EQUIPMENT - MFR

SEE ALSO Air Conditioning & Heating Equipment - Commercial/Industrial

Company	Address	City	State	Zip	Toll-Free	Phone
Advance Energy Technologies Inc	1 Solar Dr	Clifton Park	NY	12065	**800-724-0198**	518-371-2140
American Panel Corp	5800 SE 78th St	Ocala	FL	34472	**800-327-3015**	352-245-7055
Applied Process Cooling Corp	555 Price Ave	Redwood City	CA	94063	**877-231-6406**	650-595-0665
Arctic Star Refrigeration Mfg Company Inc	3540 W Pioneer Pkwy	Arlington	TX	76013	**800-229-6562**	817-274-1396
Bessam-Aire Inc	10145 Philipp Pkwy Unit B	Streetsboro	OH	44146	**800-321-5992**	
Beverage-Air Corp	3779 Champion Blvd	Winston-Salem	NC	27105	**800-845-9800**	336-245-6400
CIMCO Refrigeration	65 Villiers St	Toronto	ON	M5A3S1	**800-267-1418**	416-465-7581
CrownTonka Inc	15600 37th Ave N Ste 100	Plymouth	MN	55446	**800-523-7337**	763-541-1410
Custom Coolers LLC	5609 Azle Ave	Fort Worth	TX	76114	**800-627-0488**	817-626-3737
Delfield Co	980 S Isabella Rd	Mount Pleasant	MI	48858	**800-733-8821**	989-773-7981
Dole Refrigerating Co	1420 Higgs Rd	Lewisburg	TN	37091	**800-251-8990**	931-359-6211
Eliason Corp	9229 Shaver Rd	Portage	MI	49024	**800-828-3655*** *Cust Svc	269-327-7003
Federal Industries Div Standex Corp	215 Federal Ave	Belleville	WI	53508	**800-356-4206**	
FRL Furniture	460 Grand Blvd	Westbury	NY	11590	**800-529-4375**	516-333-4400
Haws Corp	1455 Kleppe Ln	Sparks	NV	89431	**888-640-4297**	775-359-4712
Heatcraft Refrigeration Products	2175 W Pk Pl Blvd	Stone Mountain	GA	30087	**800-321-1881**	770-465-5600
Hill PHOENIX Inc	1003 Sigman Rd	Conyers	GA	30013	**800-518-6630**	770-285-3264
Hussmann Corp	12999 St Charles Rock Rd	Bridgeton	MO	63044	**800-592-2060**	314-291-2000
Ice-O-Matic	11100 E 45th Ave	Denver	CO	80239	**800-423-3367**	303-371-3737

Company	City	State	ZIP	Toll-Free	Phone
IMI Cornelius Inc 101 Broadway St W	Osseo	MN	55369	**800-238-3600**	763-488-8200
International Cold Storage Company Inc 215 E 13th St	Andover	KS	67002	**800-835-0001**	316-733-1385
KDIndustries 1525 E Lake Rd	Erie	PA	16511	**800-840-9577**	814-453-6761
Kloppenberg & Co 2627 W Oxford Ave	Englewood	CO	80110	**800-346-3246**	303-761-1615
Kolpak 2915 Tennessee Ave N	Parsons	TN	38363	**800-826-7036**	731-847-5328
Kysor Panel Systems 4201 N Beach St	Fort Worth	TX	76137	**800-633-3426**	817-281-5121
Lancer Corp 6655 Lancer Blvd	San Antonio	TX	78219	**800-729-1500**	210-310-7000
Leer LP 206 Leer St *Cust Svc	New Lisbon	WI	53950	**800-766-5337***	608-562-7100
Manitowoc Ice 2110 S 26th St	Manitowoc	WI	54220	**800-545-5720**	920-682-0161
McCann's Engineering & Manufacturing Co 4570 W Colorado Blvd	Los Angeles	CA	90039	**800-423-2429**	818-637-7200
Micro Matic USA Inc 10726 N Second St	Machesney Park	IL	61115	**866-291-5756**	815-968-7557
MicroMetl Corp 3035 N Shadeland Ave Ste 300	Indianapolis	IN	46226	**800-662-4822**	
Nance International Inc 2915 Milam St	Beaumont	TX	77701	**877-626-2322**	409-838-6127
Nor-Lake Inc 727 Second St PO Box 248	Hudson	WI	54016	**800-388-5253**	715-386-2323
Ontor Ltd 12 Leswyn Rd	Toronto	ON	M6A1K3	**800-567-1631**	416-781-5286
Perlick Corp 8300 W Good Hope Rd	Milwaukee	WI	53223	**800-558-5592**	414-353-7060
Scotsman Ice Systems 775 Corporate Woods Pkwy *Cust Svc	Vernon Hills	IL	60061	**800-726-8762***	847-215-4500
Silver King Refrigeration Inc 1600 Xenium Ln N	Minneapolis	MN	55441	**800-328-3329**	763-923-2441
True Manufacturing Co 2001 E Terra Ln	O'Fallon	MO	63366	**800-325-6152**	636-240-2400
Turbo Refrigerating 1000 W Ormsby Ave	Louisville	KY	40210	**800-853-8648**	502-635-3000
Victory Refrigeration Inc 110 Woodcrest Rd	Cherry Hill	NJ	08003	**800-523-5008**	856-428-4200
Vintage Air Inc 18865 Goll St	San Antonio	TX	78266	**800-862-6658**	210-654-7171
Vogt Ice 1000 W Ormsby Ave Ste 19	Louisville	KY	40210	**800-853-8648**	502-635-3000
WA Brown & Son Inc 209 Long Meadow Dr	Salisbury	NC	28147	**800-438-2316**	704-636-5131

663 REFRIGERATION EQUIPMENT - WHOL

SEE ALSO Plumbing, Heating, Air Conditioning Equipment & Supplies - Whol

Company	City	State	ZIP	Toll-Free	Phone
Allied Supply Company Inc 1100 E Monument Ave	Dayton	OH	45402	**800-589-5690**	937-224-9833
Baker Distributing Co 14610 Breakers Dr Ste 100	Jacksonville	FL	32258	**844-289-0033**	800-217-4698
Broich Enterprises Inc 6440 City W Pkwy	Eden Prairie	MN	55344	**800-853-3508**	952-941-2270
Cannon Marketing Inc 4684 US Hwy 70 W	Kinston	NC	28504	**800-952-5913**	252-527-3361
Dennis Supply Co PO Box 3376	Sioux City	IA	51102	**800-352-4618**	712-255-7637
Don Stevens Inc 980 Discovery Rd	Eagan	MN	55121	**800-444-2299**	651-452-0872
Ernest F Mariani Company Inc 573 West 2890 South	Salt Lake City	UT	84115	**800-453-2927**	
Gustave A Larson Co PO Box 910	Pewaukee	WI	53072	**800-829-9609**	262-542-0200
Hart & Price Corp PO Box 36368	Dallas	TX	75235	**800-777-9129**	214-521-9129
Insco Distributing Inc 12501 Network Blvd	San Antonio	TX	78249	**855-282-4295**	210-690-8400
ISI Commercial Refrigeration LP 640 W 6th St	Houston	TX	77007	**800-777-5070**	214-631-7980
Luce, Schwab & Kase Inc 9 Gloria Ln	Fairfield	NJ	07007	**800-458-7329**	973-227-4840
Minus Forty Technologies Corp 30 Armstrong Ave	Georgetown	ON	L7G4R9	**800-800-5706**	905-702-1441
Modern Ice Equipment & Supply Co 5709 Harrison Ave	Cincinnati	OH	45248	**800-543-1581**	513-367-2101
Norm's Refrigeration & Ice Equipment Inc 1175 N Knollwood Cir	Anaheim	CA	92801	**800-933-4423**	714-236-3600
RE Lewis Refrigeration Inc 803 S Lincoln St PO Box 92 *Cust Svc	Creston	IA	50801	**800-264-0767***	641-782-8183
Redico Inc 1850 S Lee Ct	Buford	GA	30518	**800-242-3920**	
Rogers Supply Company Inc PO Box 740	Champaign	IL	61824	**800-252-0406**	217-356-0166
Schroeder America 5620 Business Park	San Antonio	TX	78218	**877-404-2488**	210-662-8200
Southern Refrigeration Corp 3140 Shenandoah Ave	Roanoke	VA	24017	**800-763-4433**	540-342-3493
Stafford-Smith Inc 3414 S Burdick St	Kalamazoo	MI	49001	**800-968-2442**	269-343-1240
Supermarket Systems Inc 6419 Bannington Rd	Charlotte	NC	28226	**800-553-1905**	704-542-6000
SWH Supply Co 242 E Main St	Louisville	KY	40202	**800-321-3598**	502-589-9287
Taylor Freezer Sales Company Inc 2032 Atlantic Ave	Chesapeake	VA	23324	**800-768-6945**	
United Refrigeration Inc 11401 Roosevelt Blvd *General	Philadelphia	PA	19154	**888-578-9100***	215-698-9100

664 RELOCATION CONSULTING SERVICES

Company	City	State	ZIP	Toll-Free	Phone
Coldwell Banker Gundaker 2458 Old Dorsett Rd Ste 300	Maryland Heights	MO	63043	**800-325-1978**	314-298-5000
Crye-Leike Inc 6525 N Quail Hollow Rd	Memphis	TN	38120	**866-310-3102**	
RE/MAX LLC 5075 S Syracuse St	Denver	CO	80237	**800-525-7452**	
RELO Direct Inc 161 N Clark St Ste 1250	Chicago	IL	60601	**800-621-7356**	312-384-5900
Relocation America 25800 NW Hwy Ste 210	Southfield	MI	48075	**877-500-4466**	
Runzheimer International Runzheimer Pk	Rochester	WI	53167	**800-558-1702**	262-971-2200
SIRVA Inc 700 Oakmont Ln	Terrace	IL	60181	**888-444-4765**	630-570-8900
Windermere Relocation Inc 5424 Sand Point Way NE	Seattle	WA	98105	**866-740-9589**	206-527-3801

665 REMEDIATION SERVICES

SEE ALSO Waste Management ; Environmental Organizations ; Consulting Services - Environmental

Remediation services include clean-up, restorative, and corrective work to repair or minimize environmental damage caused by lead, asbestos, mining, petroleum, chemicals, and other pollutants.

Company	City	State	ZIP	Toll-Free	Phone
911 Restoration Enterprises Inc 7721 Densmore Ave	Van Nuys	CA	91406	**888-243-6653**	
Antea Group 5910 Rice Creek Pkwy Ste 100	Saint Paul	MN	55126	**800-477-7411**	651-639-9449
BELFOR (Canada) Inc 3300 Bridgeway St	Vancouver	BC	V5K1H9	**888-432-1123**	604-432-1123
Carylon Corp 2500 W Arthington St	Chicago	IL	60612	**800-621-4342**	312-666-7700
Central Insulation Systems Inc 300 Murray Rd	Cincinnati	OH	45217	**800-544-7502**	513-242-0600
Chemical Waste Management Inc 1001 Fannin St Ste 4000	Houston	TX	77002	**800-633-7871**	713-512-6200
Clean Harbors Inc 42 Longwater Dr PO Box 9149 *NYSE: CLH*	Norwell	MA	02061	**800-282-0058**	781-792-5000
Clean Venture/Cycle Chem Inc 201 S First St	Elizabeth	NJ	07206	**800-347-7672**	908-355-5800
Crosby & Overton Inc 1610 W 17th St	Long Beach	CA	90813	**800-827-6729**	562-432-5445
Custom Environmental Services Inc 8041 N I 70 Frontage Rd Unit 11	Arvada	CO	80002	**800-310-7445**	303-423-9949
Environmental Enterprises Inc (EEI) 10163 Cincinnati Dayton Rd	Cincinnati	OH	45241	**800-722-2818**	513-772-2818
Envirovantage Inc 629 Calef Hwy Ste 200	Epping	NH	03042	**800-640-5323**	603-679-9682
H Barber & Sons Inc 15 Raytkwich Rd	Naugatuck	CT	06770	**800-355-8318**	203-729-9000
IEP Technologies LLC 400 Main St	Ashland	MA	01721	**855-793-8407**	
Perma-Fix Environmental Services Inc 8302 Dunwoody Pl Ste 250 *NASDAQ: PESI*	Atlanta	GA	30350	**800-365-6066**	770-587-9898
PW Stephens Inc 15201 Pipeline Ln Unit B	Huntington Beach	CA	92649	**800-750-7733**	714-892-2028
Safety-Kleen Corp 2600 N Central Expwy Ste 400	Richardson	TX	75080	**800-669-5740**	800-323-5040
SEACOR Holdings Inc 2200 Eller Dr PO Box 13038 *NYSE: CKH*	Fort Lauderdale	FL	33316	**800-516-6203**	954-523-2200
US Ecology 300 E Mallard Dr Ste 300 *NASDAQ: ECOL*	Boise	ID	83706	**800-590-5220**	208-331-8400
WRR Environmental Services 5200 Ryder Rd	Eau Claire	WI	54701	**800-727-8760**	715-834-9624

666 RESEARCH CENTERS & INSTITUTIONS

SEE ALSO Testing Facilities ; Market Research Firms ; Public Policy Research Centers

Company	City	State	ZIP	Toll-Free	Phone
Aaron Diamond AIDS Research Ctr 455 First Ave 7th Fl	New York	NY	10016	**800-782-2737**	212-448-5000
ADA Technologies Inc 8100 Shaffer Pkwy Ste 130	Littleton	CO	80127	**800-232-0296**	303-792-5615
Advanced Cell Diagnostics Inc 3960 Point Eden Way	Hayward	CA	94545	**877-576-3636**	510-576-8800
Advion BioSciences Inc 19 Brown Rd	Ithaca	NY	14850	**877-523-8466**	607-266-0665
Air Force Research Laboratory (AFRL) AFRL/PA 1864 Fourth St Bldg 15 Rm 225	Wright-Patterson AFB	OH	45433	**800-222-0336**	
Albany International Research Co 216 Airport Dr	Rochester	NH	03867	**888-797-6735**	603-330-5850
American Institute for Cancer Research 1759 R St NW	Washington	DC	20009	**800-843-8114**	202-328-7744
American Institutes for Research 1000 Thomas Jefferson St NW	Washington	DC	20007	**877-334-3499**	202-403-5000
American Type Culture Collection (ATCC) 10801 University Blvd PO Box 1549 *Cust Svc	Manassas	VA	20108	**800-638-6597***	703-365-2700
Argonne National Laboratory (ANL) 9700 S Cass Ave	Argonne	IL	60439	**800-632-8990**	630-252-2000
Autism Research Institute (ARI) 4182 Adams Ave	San Diego	CA	92116	**866-366-3361**	619-281-7165

Name / Address	City	State	Zip	Toll-Free	Phone
Barbara Ann Karmanos Cancer Institute					
4100 John R St	Detroit	MI	48201	**800-527-6266**	
Battelle Memorial Institute Inc					
505 King Ave	Columbus	OH	43201	**800-201-2011**	614-424-6424
Berkeley Sensor & Actuator Ctr (BSAC)					
University of California					
403 Cory Hall MC Ste 1774	Berkeley	CA	94720	**800-549-1002**	510-643-6690
BioLegend Inc					
11080 Roselle St	San Diego	CA	92121	**877-246-5343**	858-455-9588
bioLytical Laboratories Inc					
1108 - 13351 Commerce Pkwy	Richmond	BC	V6V2X7	**866-674-6784**	604-204-6784
California Pacific Medical Ctr Research Institute					
475 Brannan St Ste 220	San Francisco	CA	94107	**855-354-2778**	415-600-1600
Center for Automation Research					
University of Maryland					
AV Williams Bldg 115 Rm 4413	College Park	MD	20742	**800-868-0094**	301-405-4526
Center for Grain & Animal Health Research					
1515 College Ave	Manhattan	KS	66502	**800-627-0388**	
Center for Research in Mathematics & Science Education					
San Diego State University					
6475 Alvarado Rd Ste 206	San Diego	CA	92120	**800-573-8804**	619-594-5090
Center for Space Plasma & Aeronomic Research					
University of Alabama Huntsville	Huntsville	AL	35899	**800-824-2255**	256-961-7403
Center on Education & Training for Employment					
Ohio State University 1900 Kenny Rd	Columbus	OH	43210	**800-848-4815**	614-292-6869
Center on Human Development & Disability					
University of Washington 1701 NE Columbia Rd					
PO Box 357920	Seattle	WA	98195	**800-636-1089**	206-543-2832
National Center for Environmental Health					
4770 Buford Hwy Bldg 101	Atlanta	GA	30341	**800-232-4636**	404-639-3311
National Institute for Occupational Safety & Health					
200 Independence Ave SW	Washington	DC	20201	**800-356-4674**	404-639-3286
Charles River Laboratories Inc					
251 Ballardvale St	Wilmington	MA	01887	**800-772-3271**	781-222-6000
NYSE: CRL					
Children's Research Institute					
Children's National Medical Ctr					
111 Michigan Ave NW Research Fl 5	Washington	DC	20010	**888-884-2327**	
CNA Corp					
4825 Mark Ctr Dr	Alexandria	VA	22311	**800-344-0007**	703-824-2000
Columbia Environmental Research Ctr (CERC)					
4200 New Haven Rd	Columbia	MO	65201	**888-283-7626**	573-875-5399
Coriell Institute for Medical Research					
403 Haddon Ave	Camden	NJ	08103	**800-752-3805**	856-966-7377
CRG Global Inc					
3 Signal Ave Ste A	Ormond Beach	FL	32174	**800-831-1718**	386-677-5644
CureSearch for Children's Cancer					
4600 East-West Hwy Ste 600	Bethesda	MD	20814	**800-458-6223**	301-718-0047
Dana-Farber Cancer Institute					
44 Binney St	Boston	MA	02115	**866-408-3324**	617-632-3000
Data Sciences International					
119 14th St NW Ste 100	St. Paul	MN	55112	**800-262-9687**	
Data Storage Systems Ctr (DSSC)					
Carnegie Mellon University ECE Dept					
5000 Forbes Ave	Pittsburgh	PA	15213	**800-864-8287**	412-268-6600
Diabetes Research Institute					
1450 NW Tenth Ave	Miami	FL	33136	**800-321-3437**	954-964-4040
Digital Monitoring Products Inc					
2500 N Partnership Blvd	Springfield	MO	65803	**800-641-4282**	417-831-9362
Digitec Inc					
2731 Van Dorn Rd	Milford	NE	68405	**888-761-3382**	402-761-3382
Dycor Technologies Ltd					
1851 94 St	Edmonton	AB	T6N1E6	**800-663-9267**	780-486-0091
Edison Biotechnology Institute					
Ohio University					
Konneker Research Laboratories The Ridges	Athens	OH	45701	**800-444-2420**	740-593-4713
Eikos Inc 2 Master Dr	Franklin	MA	02038	**888-345-6712**	508-528-0300
Environmental Management Inc					
5200 NE Hwy 33	Guthrie	OK	73044	**800-510-8510**	405-282-8510
EPIEN Medical Inc					
4225 White Bear Pkwy Ste 600	St Paul	MN	55110	**888-884-4675**	651-653-3380
Epitomics Inc					
863 Mitten Rd Ste 103	Burlingame	CA	94010	**888-772-2226**	650-583-6688
Evans Data Corp					
340 Soquel Ave	Santa Cruz	CA	95062	**800-831-3080**	831-425-8451
Exponent Inc					
149 Commonwealth Dr	Menlo Park	CA	94025	**888-656-3976**	650-326-9400
NASDAQ: EXPO					
Federal Aviation Administration					
Aviation Research Div					
800 Independence Ave SW Rm 528A	Washington	DC	20591	**866-835-5322**	202-267-9251
Florida Solar Energy Ctr					
1679 Clearlake Rd	Cocoa	FL	32922	**877-777-4778**	321-638-1000
Fox Chase Cancer Ctr					
333 Cottman Ave	Philadelphia	PA	19111	**888-369-2427**	215-728-6900
Framingham Heart Study					
73 Mt Wayte Ave Ste 2	Framingham	MA	01702	**800-854-7582**	508-935-3418
Friends Research Institute Inc					
1040 Pk Ave Ste 103	Baltimore	MD	21201	**800-822-3677**	410-823-5116
Social Research Ctr					
1040 Pk Ave Ste 103	Baltimore	MD	21201	**800-705-7757**	410-837-3977
Gatorade Sports Science Institute					
617 W Main St	Barrington	IL	60010	**800-616-4774**	
Genemed Biotechnologies Inc					
458 Carlton Ct S San Francisco	San Francisco	CA	94080	**877-436-3633**	650-952-0110
General Atomics					
3550 General Atomics Ct					
PO Box 85608	San Diego	CA	92121	**800-669-6820**	858-455-3000
Glen Research Corp					
22825 Davis Dr	Sterling	VA	20164	**800-327-4536**	703-437-6191
Goddard Institute for Space Studies					
2880 Broadway	New York	NY	10025	**888-661-1620**	212-678-5510
H Lee Moffitt Cancer Ctr & Research Institute					
University of S Florida					
12902 Magnolia Dr	Tampa	FL	33612	**800-456-3434**	888-663-3488
High Performance Computing Collaboratory					
PO Box 9627	Mississippi State	MS	39762	**800-521-4041**	662-325-8278
Idaho National Laboratory (INL)					
2525 Fremont Ave	Idaho Falls	ID	83402	**866-495-7440**	
Institute for Astronomy					
University of Hawaii					
2680 Woodlawn Dr	Honolulu	HI	96822	**800-351-1330**	808-956-8312
Institute for Research on Poverty					
University of Wisconsin Madison 1180 Observatory Dr					
3412 William H Sewell Social Sciences Bldg	Madison	WI	53706	**866-301-1753**	608-262-6358
Institute for Systems Research					
University of Maryland					
2173 AV Williams Bldg	College Park	MD	20742	**866-675-8967**	301-405-6615
Institute of Gerontology					
University of Michigan					
300 N Ingalls St	Ann Arbor	MI	48109	**877-865-2167**	734-936-2107
Institute of Materials Science					
University of Connecticut					
97 N Eagleville Rd	Storrs	CT	06269	**800-528-7411**	860-486-4623
Intelligent Mechatronic Systems Inc					
435 King St N	Waterloo	ON	N2J2Z5	**866-818-6637**	519-745-8887
Jackson Laboratory, The					
600 Main St	Bar Harbor	ME	04609	**800-422-6423**	207-288-6000
John F. Kennedy					
Space Ctr	Kennedy Space Center	FL	32899	**866-737-5235**	321-867-5000
Kendle International Inc					
441 Vine St 1200 Carew Twr	Cincinnati	OH	45202	**800-733-1572**	513-381-5550
Learning Research & Development Ctr (LRDC)					
University of Pittsburgh					
3939 O'Hara St	Pittsburgh	PA	15260	**800-397-0071**	412-624-7020
Lerner Research Institute					
9500 Euclid Ave	Cleveland	OH	44195	**800-223-2273**	216-444-3900
LIMRA International Inc					
300 Day Hill Rd	Windsor	CT	06095	**800-235-4672**	860-688-3358
Lincoln Laboratory					
Massachusetts Institute of Technology					
244 Wood St	Lexington	MA	02420	**800-445-8667**	781-981-5500
Lineagen Inc					
2677 E Parleys Way	Salt Lake City	UT	84109	**888-888-6736**	801-931-6200
Los Alamos National Laboratory (LANL)					
PO Box 1663	Los Alamos	NM	87545	**877-723-4101**	505-667-7000
Los Angeles Biomedical Research Institute					
1124 W Carson St	Torrance	CA	90502	**877-452-2674**	
Lovelace Respiratory Research Institute (LRRI)					
2425 Ridgecrest Dr SE	Albuquerque	NM	87108	**800-700-1016**	505-348-9400
Mailman Research Ctr					
McLean Hospital 115 Mill St	Belmont	MA	02478	**800-333-0338**	617-855-2000
Marine Biological Laboratory (MBL)					
7 MBL St	Woods Hole	MA	02543	**800-222-1222**	508-548-3705
Martec Group Inc, The					
105 W Adams St Ste 2125	Chicago	IL	60603	**888-811-5755**	312-606-9690
Massa Products Corp					
280 Lincoln St	Hingham	MA	02043	**800-962-7543**	781-749-4800
Massey Cancer Ctr					
Virginia Commonwealth University					
401 College St PO Box 980037	Richmond	VA	23298	**877-462-7739**	804-828-0450
MAX Technologies Inc					
2051 Victoria Ave 3rd Fl	Saint-Lambert	QC	J4S1H1	**800-361-1629**	450-443-3332
Mechanical Technology Inc					
325 Washington Sq Ste 3	Albany	NY	12205	**800-937-5449**	518-533-2200
NASDAQ: MKTY					
Memorial Sloan-Kettering Cancer Ctr					
1275 York Ave	New York	NY	10065	**800-525-2225**	212-639-2000
Miami Project to Cure Paralysis					
1095 NW 14th Terr Lois Pope LIFE Ctr	Miami	FL	33136	**800-782-6387***	305-243-6001
*General					
Michigan Mfg Technology Ctr					
47911 Halyard Dr	Plymouth	MI	48170	**888-414-6682**	
Monell Chemical Senses Ctr					
3500 Market St	Philadelphia	PA	19104	**800-732-0999**	267-519-4700
MSU-DOE Plant Research Laboratory					
612 Wilson Rd	East Lansing	MI	48824	**800-875-5090**	517-353-2270
NAHB Research Ctr					
400 Prince Georges Blvd	Upper Marlboro	MD	20774	**800-638-8556**	301-249-4000
Nanotechnology Research Ctr					
Georgia Institute of Technology					
791 Atlantic Dr	Atlanta	GA	30332	**800-424-9300**	404-894-5100
National Biodynamics Laboratory (NBDL)					
University of New Orleans College of Engineering					
2000 Lakeshore Dr	New Orleans	LA	70148	**888-514-4275**	
National Bureau of Economic Research					
1050 Massachusetts Ave	Cambridge	MA	02138	**800-621-8476**	617-868-3900
National Ctr for Genome Resources					
2935 Rodeo Pk Dr E	Santa Fe	NM	87505	**800-450-4854**	505-995-4400
National Ctr for Mfg Sciences (NCMS)					
3025 Boardwalk	Ann Arbor	MI	48108	**800-222-6267**	734-995-0300
National Energy Research Scientific Computing Ctr (NERSC)					
Lawrence Berkeley National Laboratory					
	Berkeley	CA	94720	**800-666-3772**	510-486-5849
National Energy Technology Laboratory (NETL)					
3610 Collins Ferry Rd	Morgantown	WV	26505	**800-432-8330**	304-285-4764
National Hansen's Disease Program (NHDP)					
1770 Physicians Pk Dr	Baton Rouge	LA	70816	**800-221-9393**	
National Homeland Security Research Ctr					
US Environmental Protection Agency					
26 W Martin Luther King Dr	Cincinnati	OH	45268	**888-372-7341**	513-569-7907
National Institute of Standards & Technology (NIST)					
100 Bureau Dr Sp 1070	Gaithersburg	MD	20899	**800-877-8339**	301-975-6478
National Institutes of Health					
National Cancer Institute					
Public Inquiries Office 6116 Executive Blvd					
Rm 3036A	Bethesda	MD	20892	**800-422-6237**	301-435-3848
National Institute of Mental Health					
6001 Executive Blvd Rm 8184 MSC 9663	Bethesda	MD	20892	**866-615-6464**	301-443-4513
National Institute of Neurological Disorders & Stroke					
PO Box 5801	Bethesda	MD	20824	**800-352-9424**	301-496-5751
National Institute on Deafness & Other Communication Disorders					
31 Ctr Dr Bldg 31 Rm 3C35	Bethesda	MD	20892	**800-241-1044**	301-496-7243
National Optical Astronomy Observatories					
950 N Cherry Ave	Tucson	AZ	85719	**888-809-4012**	520-318-8163
National Research Ctr for Coal & Energy (NRCCE)					
West Virginia University					
385 Evansdale Dr PO Box 6064	Morgantown	WV	26506	**800-624-8301**	304-293-2867

Classified Section

	City	State	Zip	Toll-Free	Phone
National Technical Information Service (NTIS) 5285 Port Royal Rd	Springfield	VA	22161	**800-553-6847***	703-605-6000
*Orders					
National Undersea Research Ctr for Hawaii & the Western Pacific University of Hawaii at Manoa 41-305 Kalanianaole Hwy	Waimanalo	HI	96795	**888-800-0460**	808-956-6335
National Undersea Research Ctr for the Mid-Atlantic Bight Institute of Marine & Coastal Sciences Rutgers University 71 Dudley Rd	New Brunswick	NJ	08901	**888-776-6537**	732-932-6555
National Wildlife Health Ctr 6006 Schroeder Rd	Madison	WI	53711	**800-232-4636**	608-270-2400
Natural Resources Research Institute (NRRI) *University of Minnesota Duluth* 5013 Miller Trunk Hwy	Duluth	MN	55811	**800-234-0054**	218-720-4294
Naval Surface Warfare Ctr *Dahlgren Div* 6149 Welsh Rd Ste 203	Dahlgren	VA	22448	**877-845-5656**	
North American Science Assoc Inc 6750 Wales Rd	Northwood	OH	43619	**866-666-9455**	419-666-9455
Northern Power Systems Inc 29 Pitman Rd	Barre	VT	05641	**877-906-6784**	802-461-2955
Ohio State University Police, The 1680 Madison Ave	Wooster	OH	44691	**800-358-4678**	330-287-0111
Oklahoma Medical Research Foundation (OMRF) 825 NE 13th St	Oklahoma City	OK	73104	**800-522-0211**	405-271-6673
Pacific Disaster Ctr 1305 N Holopono St Ste 2	Kihei	HI	96753	**888-808-6688**	808-891-0525
Pacific Island Ecosystems Research Ctr (PIERC) 12201 Sunrise Valley Dr Ste 615	Reston	VA	20192	**888-275-8747**	
Pacific Northwest National Laboratory (PNNL) 902 Battelle Blvd PO Box 999	Richland	WA	99352	**888-375-7665**	509-375-2121
PAREXEL International Corp 195 W St	Waltham	MA	02451	**800-301-5033**	781-487-9900
NASDAQ: PRXL					
Parks Assoc Inc 15950 N Dallas Pkwy Ste 575	Dallas	TX	75248	**800-727-5711**	972-490-1113
Peryam & Kroll Research Corp 6323 N Avondale Ave	Chicago	IL	60631	**800-747-5522**	800-281-3155
Pfenex Inc 10790 Roselle St	San Diego	CA	92121	**844-240-0005**	858-352-4400
Phantom Laboratory Inc, The 2727 SR- 29	Greenwich	NY	12834	**800-525-1190**	518-692-1190
Pittsburgh Supercomputing Ctr 300 S Craig St	Pittsburgh	PA	15213	**800-221-1641**	412-268-4960
Pleora Technologies Inc 340 Terry Fox Dr Ste 300	Kanata	ON	K2K3A2	**888-687-6877**	613-270-0625
Princeton Plasma Physics Laboratory (PPPL) James Forrestal Campus Princeton University PO Box 451	Princeton	NJ	08543	**800-772-2222**	609-243-2750
Providence Health & Services (JWCI) 2200 Santa Monica Blvd	Santa Monica	CA	90404	**800-262-6259**	310-582-7450
Quantiam Technologies Inc 1651 - 94 St NW	Edmonton	AB	T6N1E6	**877-461-0707**	780-462-0707
Quintiles Transnational Corp 4820 Emperor Blvd	Durham	NC	27703	**866-267-4479**	919-998-2000
Radiant Research Inc 11500 Northlake Dr Ste 320	Cincinnati	OH	45249	**855-427-8839**	513-247-5500
Research Triangle Institute 3040 Cornwallis Rd PO Box 12194	Research Triangle Park	NC	27709	**800-334-8571**	919-541-6000
Ricerca Biosciences LLC 7528 Auburn Rd	Concord	OH	44077	**888-742-3722**	440-357-3300
Robotics Institute Carnegie Mellon University 5000 Forbes Ave	Pittsburgh	PA	15213	**800-767-8483**	412-268-3818
Roswell Park Cancer Institute Elm and Carlton St	Buffalo	NY	14263	**877-275-7724**	716-845-2300
Roy J Carver Biotechnology Ctr 1206 W Gregory	Urbana	IL	61801	**800-550-3033**	217-333-1695
Sabrient Systems LLC 115 S La Cumbre Ln Ste 100	Santa Barbara	CA	93105	**888-502-3605**	805-730-7777
Safety Analysis & Forensic Engineering 5665 Hollister Ave	Goleta	CA	93117	**800-426-7866**	805-964-0676
Salk Institute for Biological Studies PO Box 85800	San Diego	CA	92186	**866-358-4354**	858-453-4100
Sandelman & Assoc Inc 257 La Paloma Ste 1	San Clemente	CA	92672	**888-897-7881**	949-388-5600
SEDL 4700 Mueller Blvd	Austin	TX	78723	**800-476-6861**	512-476-6861
SERVE 5900 Summit Ave Ste 201	Browns Summit	NC	27214	**800-755-3277**	336-315-7400
Siteman Cancer Ctr 4921 Parkview Pl	Saint Louis	MO	63110	**800-600-3606**	314-362-5196
Social & Economic Sciences Research Ctr (SESRC) *Washington State University* Wilson Hall Rm 133 PO Box 644014	Pullman	WA	99164	**800-932-5393**	509-335-1511
Socratic Technologies Inc 2505 Mariposa St	San Francisco	CA	94110	**800-576-2728**	415-430-2200
Software Engineering Institute (SEI) 4500 Fifth Ave	Pittsburgh	PA	15213	**888-201-4479**	412-268-5800
Software Engineering Services Corp 1311 Ft Crook Rd S	Bellevue	NE	68005	**800-244-1278**	402-292-8660
Southern Research Institute 2000 Ninth Ave S	Birmingham	AL	35205	**800-967-6774**	205-581-2000
Space Dynamics Laboratory 1695 N Research Pkwy	North Logan	UT	84341	**866-487-2365**	435-797-4600
Space Science & Engineering Ctr University of Wisconsin 1225 W Dayton St	Madison	WI	53706	**866-391-1753**	608-262-0544
Stanford Cancer Ctr 875 Lake Blake Wilbur Dr	Stanford	CA	94305	**800-422-6237**	650-498-6000
Synergy Co of Utah LLC, The 2279 S Resource Blvd	Moab	UT	84532	**800-723-0277**	
Syracuse Research Corp (SRC) 7502 Round Pond Rd	North Syracuse	NY	13212	**800-724-0451**	315-452-8000
Technology Service Corp 962 Wayne Ave Ste 800	Silver Spring	MD	20910	**800-324-7700**	301-565-2970
Transportation Research Ctr Inc (TRC Inc) 10820 State Rt 347 PO Box B-67	East Liberty	OH	43319	**800-837-7872**	937-666-2011
Trex Enterprises Corp 10455 Pacific Ctr Ct	San Diego	CA	92121	**800-626-5885**	858-646-5300
Turner-Fairbank Highway Research Ctr 6300 Georgetown Pike	McLean	VA	22101	**800-424-9071**	
UAB Comprehensive Cancer Ctr University of Alabama at Birmingham 1824 Sixth Ave S	Birmingham	AL	35294	**800-294-7780**	205-934-4011
UNC Neuroscience Ctr University of N Carolina 115 Mason Farm Rd CB 7250	Chapel Hill	NC	27599	**800-862-4938**	919-843-8536
University of Maryland Ctr for Environmental Science (UMCES) 2020 Horn Pt Rd	Cambridge	MD	21613	**866-842-2520**	410-228-9250
US Army Aeromedical Research Laboratory MCMR-UAC Bldg 6901	Fort Rucker	AL	36362	**888-386-7635**	334-255-6920
US Army Engineer Research & Development Ctr (ERDC) 3909 Halls Ferry Rd	Vicksburg	MS	39180	**800-522-6937**	601-634-3188
Vanderbilt Kennedy Ctr for Research on Human Development 21st Ave S	Nashville	TN	37203	**800-772-1213**	615-322-8240
Waisman Ctr University of Wisconsin 1500 Highland Ave	Madison	WI	53705	**888-428-8476**	608-263-5940
WestEd 730 Harrison St 5th Fl	San Francisco	CA	94107	**877-493-7833**	415-565-3000
Wisconsin National Primate Research Ctr 1220 Capitol Ct	Madison	WI	53715	**800-833-7050**	608-263-3500
Wistar Institute 3601 Spruce St	Philadelphia	PA	19104	**800-724-6633**	215-898-3700

667 RESORTS & RESORT COMPANIES

SEE ALSO Spas - Hotel & Resort ; Casinos ; Dude Ranches ; Hotels - Conference Center ; Hotels & Hotel Companies

Alabama

	City	State	Zip	Toll-Free	Phone
Joe Wheeler Resort Lodge & Convention Ctr 4401 McLean Dr	Rogersville	AL	35652	**800-544-5639**	256-247-5461
Perdido Beach Resort 27200 Perdido Beach Blvd	Orange Beach	AL	36561	**800-634-8001**	251-981-9811

Alaska

	City	State	Zip	Toll-Free	Phone
Alyeska Prince Hotel & Resort 1000 Arlberg Ave PO Box 249	Girdwood	AK	99587	**800-880-3880**	907-754-1111
Pybus Point Lodge PO Box 33497	Juneau	AK	99803	**800-947-9287**	907-790-4866

Alberta

	City	State	Zip	Toll-Free	Phone
Fairmont Banff Springs PO Box 960	Banff	AB	T1L1J4	**800-441-1414**	403-762-2211
Fairmont Chateau Lake Louise 111 Lk Louise Dr	Lake Louise	AB	T0L1E0	**800-441-1414**	403-522-3511
Rimrock Resort Hotel, The 300 Mountain Ave PO Box 1110	Banff	AB	T1L1J2	**888-746-7625**	403-762-3356
Waterton Lakes Lodge Resort 101 Clematis Ave PO Box 4	Waterton Park	AB	T0K2M0	**888-985-6343**	403-859-2150

Arizona

	City	State	Zip	Toll-Free	Phone
Arizona Biltmore Resort & Spa 2400 E Missouri	Phoenix	AZ	85016	**800-950-0086**	602-955-6600
Arizona Golf Resort & Conference Ctr 425 S Power Rd	Mesa	AZ	85206	**800-528-8282**	480-832-3202
Arizona Grand Resort 8000 S Arizona Grand Pkwy	Phoenix	AZ	85044	**866-267-1321**	602-438-9000
Boulders Resort & Golden Door Spa 34631 N Tom Darlington Dr PO Box 2090	Carefree	AZ	85377	**888-579-2631**	480-488-9009
Camelback Inn JW Marriott Resort Golf Club & Spa 5402 E Lincoln Dr	Scottsdale	AZ	85253	**800-242-2635**	480-948-1700
Canyon Ranch Tucson 8600 E Rockcliff Rd	Tucson	AZ	85750	**800-742-9000**	520-749-9000
Chaparral Suites Resort & Conference Ctr 5001 N Scottsdale Rd	Scottsdale	AZ	85250	**866-534-1797**	480-949-1414
CopperWynd Resort & Club 13225 N Eagle Ridge Dr	Fountain Hills	AZ	85268	**877-707-7760**	480-333-1900
Doubletree Paradise Valley Resort 5401 N Scottsdale Rd	Scottsdale	AZ	85250	**800-222-8733**	480-947-5400
Enchantment Resort 525 Boynton Canyon Rd	Sedona	AZ	86336	**800-826-4180**	
Esplendor Resort at Rio Rico 1069 Camino Caralampi	Rio Rico	AZ	85648	**800-288-4746**	520-281-1901
Fairmont Scottsdale Princess 7575 E Princess Dr	Scottsdale	AZ	85255	**800-257-7544**	480-585-4848
FireSky Resort & Spa 4925 N Scottsdale Rd	Scottsdale	AZ	85251	**800-528-7867**	480-945-7666
Four Seasons Resort Scottsdale at Troon North 10600 E Crescent Moon Dr	Scottsdale	AZ	85262	**800-332-3442**	480-515-5700
Francisco Grande Hotel & Golf Resort 26000 Gila Bend Hwy	Casa Grande	AZ	85222	**800-237-4238***	520-836-6444
*General					
Gold Canyon Golf Resort 6100 S Kings Ranch Rd	Gold Canyon	AZ	85118	**800-827-5281**	480-982-9090
Hacienda del Sol Guest Ranch Resort 5501 N Hacienda Del Sol Rd	Tucson	AZ	85718	**800-728-6514**	520-299-1501
Harrah's Ak-Chin Casino Resort 15406 Maricopa Rd	Maricopa	AZ	85139	**800-427-7247***	480-802-5000
*General					
Hilton Sedona Resort & Spa 90 Ridge Trl Dr	Sedona	AZ	86351	**877-273-3762***	928-284-4040
*General					

Classified Section

				Toll-Free	Phone
JW Marriott Desert Ridge Resort & Spa 5350 E Marriott Dr	Phoenix	AZ	85054	**800-845-5279**	480-293-5000
Lake Powell Resorts & Marinas 100 Lakeshore Dr	Page	AZ	86040	**800-622-6317**	888-896-3829
Legacy Golf Resort 6808 S 32nd St	Phoenix	AZ	85042	**888-828-3673**	602-305-5500
Lodge at Ventana Canyon - A Wyndham Luxury Resort 6200 N Clubhouse Ln	Tucson	AZ	85750	**800-828-5701**	520-577-1400
Loews Ventana Canyon Resort 7000 N Resort Dr	Tucson	AZ	85750	**800-234-5117**	520-299-2020
Los Abrigados Resort 160 Portal Ln	Sedona	AZ	86336	**877-374-2582**	928-282-1777
Millennium Resort Scottsdale McCormick Ranch 7401 N Scottsdale Rd	Scottsdale	AZ	85253	**800-243-1332**	716-681-2400
Orange Tree Golf & Conference Resort 10601 N 56th St	Scottsdale	AZ	85254	**866-729-7159**	480-948-6100
Phoenician, The 6000 E Camelback Rd	Scottsdale	AZ	85251	**800-888-8234**	480-941-8200
Pointe Hilton at Squaw Peak Resort 7677 N 16th St	Phoenix	AZ	85020	**800-685-0550**	602-997-2626
Pointe Hilton Resort at Tapatio Cliffs 11111 N Seventh St	Phoenix	AZ	85020	**800-947-9784**	602-866-7500
Rancho de los Caballeros 1551 S Vulture Mine Rd	Wickenburg	AZ	85390	**800-684-5030**	928-684-5484
Royal Palms Resort & Spa 5200 E Camelback Rd	Phoenix	AZ	85018	**800-672-6011**	602-840-3610
Sanctuary on Camelback Mountain 5700 E McDonald Dr	Paradise Valley	AZ	85253	**800-245-2051**	480-948-2100
Scottsdale Camelback Resort 6302 E Camelback Rd	Scottsdale	AZ	85251	**800-891-8585**	480-947-3300
Scottsdale Plaza Resort 7200 N Scottsdale Rd	Scottsdale	AZ	85253	**800-832-2025**	480-948-5000
Sheraton Wild Horse Pass Resort & Spa 5594 W Wild Horse Pass Blvd	Chandler	AZ	85226	**800-325-3535**	602-225-0100
Tanque Verde Guest Ranch 14301 E Speedway Blvd	Tucson	AZ	85748	**800-234-3833**	520-296-6275
Westward Look Resort 245 E Ina Rd	Tucson	AZ	85704	**800-722-2500**	520-297-1151
Wigwam Golf Resort & Spa 300 E Wigwam Blvd	Litchfield Park	AZ	85340	**800-327-0396**	623-935-3811

Arkansas

				Toll-Free	Phone
Arlington Resort Hotel & Spa 239 Central Ave	Hot Springs	AR	71901	**800-643-1502**	501-623-7771
Best Western Inn of the Ozarks 207 W Van Buren	Eureka Springs	AR	72632	**800-552-3785**	479-253-9768

British Columbia

				Toll-Free	Phone
Delta Whistler Village Suites 4308 Main St	Whistler	BC	V0N1B4	**888-299-3987**	604-905-3987
Fairmont Chateau Whistler 4599 Chateau Blvd	Whistler	BC	V0N1B4	**800-441-1414**	604-938-8000
Harrison Hot Springs Resort & Spa 100 Esplanade Ave	Harrison Hot Springs	BC	V0M1K0	**800-663-2266**	604-796-2244
Hilton Whistler Resort & Spa 4050 Whistler Way	Whistler	BC	V0N1B4	**800-515-4050**	604-932-1982
Holiday Trails Resorts (Western) Inc 53730 Bridal Falls Rd	Rosedale	BC	V0X1X1	**800-663-2265**	604-794-7876
Pan Pacific Whistler Mountainside 4320 Sundial Crescent	Whistler	BC	V0N1B4	**888-905-9995**	604-905-2999
River Rock Casino Resort 8811 River Rd	Richmond	BC	V6X3P8	**866-748-3718**	604-247-8900
Tantalus Resort Lodge 4200 Whistler Way	Whistler	BC	V0N1B4	**888-806-2299**	604-932-4146
Whistler Blackcomb Mountain Ski Resort 4545 Blackcomb Way	Whistler	BC	V0N1B4	**800-766-0449**	604-932-3434

California

				Toll-Free	Phone
Alisal Guest Ranch & Resort 1054 Alisal Rd	Solvang	CA	93463	**800-425-4725**	805-688-6411
Bacara Resort & Spa 8301 Hollister Ave	Santa Barbara	CA	93117	**855-968-0100**	805-968-0100
Bahia Resort Hotel 998 W Mission Bay Dr	San Diego	CA	92109	**800-576-4229**	858-488-0551
Barona Resort & Casino 1932 Wildcat Canyon Rd	Lakeside	CA	92040	**888-722-7662**	619-443-2300
Bear Mountain Golf Course 43101 Gold Mine Dr PO Box 77	Big Bear Lake	CA	92315	**844-462-2327**	909-866-5766
Calistoga Ranch 580 Lommel Rd	Calistoga	CA	94515	**800-942-4220**	707-254-2800
Carmel Valley Ranch Resort 1 Old Ranch Rd	Carmel	CA	93923	**866-405-5037**	831-625-9500
Casa Palmero 1518 Cypress Dr	Pebble Beach	CA	93953	**800-654-9300**	831-622-6650
Chaminade 1 Chaminade Ln	Santa Cruz	CA	95065	**800-283-6569**	831-475-5600
Claremont Resort & Spa 41 Tunnel Rd	Berkeley	CA	94705	**800-551-7266**	510-843-3000
Costanoa Coastal Lodge & Camp 2001 Rossi Rd	Pescadero	CA	94060	**877-262-7848**	650-879-1100
Desert Hot Springs Spa Hotel 10805 Palm Dr	Desert Hot Springs	CA	92240	**800-808-7727**	760-329-6000
Desert Springs Marriott Resort & Spa 74855 Country Club Dr	Palm Desert	CA	92260	**888-538-9459**	760-341-2211
Fairmont Sonoma Mission Inn & Spa, The PO Box 1447	Sonoma	CA	95476	**866-540-4499**	707-938-9000
Fess Parker's Doubletree Resort (FPDTR) 633 E Cabrillo Blvd	Santa Barbara	CA	93103	**800-879-2929**	805-564-4333
Flamingo Resort Hotel & Conference Ctr 2777 Fourth St	Santa Rosa	CA	95405	**800-848-8300**	707-545-8530
Four Seasons Resort Santa Barbara 1260 Ch Dr	Santa Barbara	CA	93108	**800-819-5053**	805-969-2261
Furnace Creek Inn & Ranch Resort Hwy 190	Death Valley	CA	92328	**800-236-7916**	760-786-2345
Grand Pacific Palisades Resort & Hotel 5805 Armada Dr	Carlsbad	CA	92008	**800-725-4723**	760-827-3200
Greenhorn Creek Resort 711 McCauley Ranch Rd	Angels Camp	CA	95222	**888-736-5900**	209-729-8111
Handlery Hotel & Resort 950 Hotel Cir N	San Diego	CA	92108	**800-676-6567**	619-298-0511
Harrah's Rincon Casino & Resort 777 Harrah's Rincon Way	Valley Center	CA	92082	**800-522-4700**	760-751-3100
Hilton San Diego Resort 1775 E Mission Bay Dr	San Diego	CA	92109	**800-445-8667**	619-276-4010
Hotel Del Coronado 1500 Orange Ave	Coronado	CA	92118	**800-468-3533**	619-435-6611
Indian Springs Resort & Spa 1712 Lincoln Ave	Calistoga	CA	94515	**800-877-3623**	707-942-4913
Indian Wells Resort Hotel 76-661 Hwy 111	Indian Wells	CA	92210	**800-248-3220**	760-345-6466
Inn at Rancho Santa Fe 5951 Linea Del Cielo PO Box 869	Rancho Santa Fe	CA	92067	**800-843-4661**	858-756-1131
Inn at Spanish Bay, The 2700 17-Mile Dr	Pebble Beach	CA	93953	**800-654-9300**	831-647-7500
Knott's Berry Farm Resort 7675 Crescent Ave	Buena Park	CA	90620	**866-752-2444**	714-995-1111
L'Auberge Del Mar 1540 Camino del Mar PO Box 2880	Del Mar	CA	92014	**800-245-9757**	858-259-1515
La Jolla Beach & Tennis Club 2000 Spindrift Dr	La Jolla	CA	92037	**888-828-0948**	858-454-7126
La Quinta Resort & Club 49-499 Eisenhower Dr	La Quinta	CA	92253	**800-598-3828**	760-564-4111
Laguna Cliffs Marriott Resort 25135 Pk Lantern	Dana Point	CA	92629	**800-545-7483**	949-661-5000
Lake Arrowhead Resort & Spa 27984 Hwy 189	Lake Arrowhead	CA	92352	**800-800-6792**	909-336-1511
Lakeland Village Beach & Mountain Resort 3535 Lake Tahoe Blvd	South Lake Tahoe	CA	96150	**888-484-7094**	530-544-1685
Leisure Sports Inc 7077 Koll Ctr Pkwy Ste 110	Pleasanton	CA	94566	**888-239-0930**	925-600-1966
Lodge at Pebble Beach 1700 17-Mile Dr	Pebble Beach	CA	93953	**800-654-9300**	831-624-3811
Lodge at Sonoma - A Renaissance Resort & Spa 1325 Broadway	Sonoma	CA	95476	**866-263-0758**	707-935-6600
Loews Coronado Bay Resort 4000 Coronado Bay Rd	Coronado	CA	92118	**800-815-6397**	619-424-4000
Mammoth Mountain Resort 10001 Minaret Rd	Mammoth Lakes	CA	93546	**800-626-6684**	760-934-2571
Meadowood Napa Valley 900 Meadowood Ln	Saint Helena	CA	94574	**800-458-8080**	707-963-3646
Miramonte Resort & Spa 45000 Indian Wells Ln	Indian Wells	CA	92210	**800-237-2926**	760-341-2200
Montage Resort & Spa 30801 S Coast Hwy	Laguna Beach	CA	92651	**866-271-6953**	949-715-6000
Morgan Run Resort & Club 5690 Cancha de Golf *Resv	Rancho Santa Fe	CA	92091	**800-378-4653***	858-756-2471
Morongo Casino Resort & Spa 49500 Seminole Dr	Cabazon	CA	92230	**800-252-4499**	951-849-3080
Mount Shasta Resort 1000 Siskiyou Lk Blvd	Mount Shasta	CA	96067	**800-958-3363**	530-926-3030
Northstar-at-Tahoe PO Box 129	Truckee	CA	96160	**800-466-6784**	
Ojai Valley Inn & Spa 905 Country Club Rd	Ojai	CA	93023	**800-422-6524**	805-640-2068
Pacific Palms Conference Resort 1 Industry Hills Pkwy *Cust Svc	City of Industry	CA	91744	**800-524-4557***	626-810-4455
Pala Casino Resort & Spa 35008 Pala-Temecula Rd	Pala	CA	92059	**877-946-7252**	760-510-5100
Pala Mesa Resort 2001 Old Hwy 395	Fallbrook	CA	92028	**800-722-4700**	760-728-5881
Palm Mountain Resort & Spa 155 S BelaRdo Rd	Palm Springs	CA	92262	**800-622-9451**	760-325-1301
Paradise Point Resort & Spa 1404 W Vacation Rd	San Diego	CA	92109	**800-344-2626**	858-274-4630
Pechanga Resort & Casino 45000 Pechanga Pkwy	Temecula	CA	92592	**877-711-2946**	951-693-1819
Quail Lodge Resort & Golf Club 8205 Valley Greens Dr	Carmel	CA	93923	**866-675-1101**	831-624-2888
Rancho Valencia Resort 5921 Valencia Cir PO Box 9126	Rancho Santa Fe	CA	92067	**800-548-3664**	858-756-1123
Renaissance Esmeralda Resort 44-400 Indian Wells Ln	Indian Wells	CA	92210	**888-236-2427**	760-773-4444
Resort at Squaw Creek 400 Squaw Creek Rd PO Box 3333	Olympic Valley	CA	96146	**800-327-3353**	530-583-6300
Ritz-Carlton Half Moon Bay 1 Miramontes Pt Rd *General	Half Moon Bay	CA	94019	**800-241-3333***	650-712-7000
Ritz-Carlton Laguna Niguel, The 1 Ritz Carlton Dr	Dana Point	CA	92629	**800-542-8680**	949-240-2000
Saint Regis Monarch Beach Resort & Spa 1 Monarch Beach Resort	Dana Point	CA	92629	**800-722-1543**	949-234-3200
San Vicente Inn & Golf Course 24157 San Vicente Rd	Ramona	CA	92065	**800-776-1289**	760-789-3788
Sea Venture Resort 100 Ocean View Ave	Pismo Beach	CA	93449	**800-443-7778**	805-773-4994
Shadow Mountain Resort & Club 45-750 San Luis Rey	Palm Desert	CA	92260	**800-472-3713**	760-346-6123
Silverado Resort & Spa 1600 Atlas Peak Rd	Napa	CA	94558	**800-532-0500**	707-257-0200
Snow Valley Mountain Resort 35100 State Hwy 18 PO Box 2337	Running Springs	CA	92382	**800-680-7669**	909-867-2751
Spa Resort, The 401 E Amado Rd	Palm Springs	CA	92262	**800-854-1279**	
Squaw Valley USA PO Box 2007	Olympic Valley	CA	96146	**800-403-0206**	

Classified Section

Name / Address	City	State	Zip	Toll-Free	Phone
Temecula Creek Inn 44501 Rainbow Canyon Rd	Temecula	CA	92592	**877-517-1823**	855-685-9299
Town & Country Resort Hotel 500 Hotel Cir N	San Diego	CA	92108	**800-772-8527**	619-291-7131
Two Bunch Palms Resort & Spa 67425 Two Bunch Palms Trl	Desert Hot Springs	CA	92240	**800-472-4334**	760-329-8791
Ventana Inn 48123 Hwy 1	Big Sur	CA	93920	**800-628-6500**	831-667-2331
Welk Resort Branson 8860 Lawrence Welk Dr	Escondido	CA	92026	**800-505-9355**	417-336-3575
Welk Resort San Diego 8860 Lawrence Welk Dr *Resv	Escondido	CA	92026	**800-932-9355***	760-749-3000
Winner's Cir Resort 550 Via de la Valle	Solana Beach	CA	92075	**800-874-8770**	858-755-6666

Colorado

Name / Address	City	State	Zip	Toll-Free	Phone
Aspen Meadows Resort 845 Meadows Rd	Aspen	CO	81611	**800-452-4240**	970-925-4240
Aspen Skiing Co 117 ABC	Aspen	CO	81611	**855-754-2863**	970-925-1220
Beaver Run Resort & Conference Ctr 620 Village Rd	Breckenridge	CO	80424	**800-525-2253**	970-453-6000
Broadmoor, The 1 Lake Ave	Colorado Springs	CO	80906	**866-837-9520**	719-577-5775
Copper Mountain Resort 209 Ten Mile Cir PO Box 3001	Copper Mountain	CO	80443	**888-219-2441**	970-968-2882
Crested Butte Mountain Resort (CBMR) 12 Snowmass Rd PO Box 5700	Crested Butte	CO	81225	**877-547-5143**	
Destination Hotels & Resorts Inc 10333 E Dry Creek Rd Ste 450	Englewood	CO	80112	**855-893-1011**	303-799-3830
Grand Lodge Crested Butte 6 Emmons Rd	Crested Butte	CO	81225	**877-547-5143**	970-349-8000
Hot Springs Lodge & Pool 415 E Sixth St PO Box 308	Glenwood Springs	CO	81602	**800-537-7946**	970-945-6571
Inverness Hotel & Golf Club 200 Inverness Dr W	Englewood	CO	80112	**800-346-4891**	303-799-5800
Keystone Resort 21996 Hwy 6 PO Box 38	Keystone	CO	80435	**877-625-1556**	970-496-2316
Manor Vail Lodge 595 E Vail Vly Dr	Vail	CO	81657	**800-950-8245**	970-476-5000
Mountain Lodge at Telluride 457 Mtn Village Blvd	Telluride	CO	81435	**866-368-6867**	970-369-5000
Omni Interlocken Resort 500 Interlocken Blvd	Broomfield	CO	80021	**800-843-6664**	303-438-6600
Park Hyatt Beaver Creek Resort & Spa 136 E Thomas Pl *Cust Svc	Avon	CO	81620	**800-233-1234***	970-949-1234
Peaks Resort & Golden Door Spa 136 Country Club Dr	Telluride	CO	81435	**800-789-2220**	
Ritz-Carlton Bachelor Gulch 0130 Daybreak Ridge	Avon	CO	81620	**800-241-3333**	970-748-6200
Saint Regis Resort Aspen 315 E Dean St	Aspen	CO	81611	**888-627-7198**	970-920-3300
Sonnenalp Resort of Vail 20 Vail Rd	Vail	CO	81657	**800-654-8312**	970-476-5656
Steamboat Grand Resort Hotel & Conference Ctr 2300 Mt Werner Cir	Steamboat Springs	CO	80487	**877-269-2628**	970-871-5500
Steamboat Ski & Resort Corp 2305 Mt Werner Cir	Steamboat Springs	CO	80487	**877-237-2628**	970-879-6111
Torian Plum Condo Resort 1855 Ski Time Sq Dr	Steamboat Springs	CO	80487	**800-228-2458**	970-879-8811
Vail Cascade Resort & Spa 1300 Westhaven Dr	Vail	CO	81657	**800-420-2424**	970-476-7111
Vail Resorts Management Co 390 Interlocken Crescent Ste 1000 *NYSE: MTN*	Broomfield	CO	80021	**800-842-8062**	303-404-1800
Wyndham Vacation Rentals 14 Sylvan Way	Vail	CO	81657	**800-467-3529**	973-753-6300

Connecticut

Name / Address	City	State	Zip	Toll-Free	Phone
Interlaken Inn 74 Interlaken Rd Rt 12	Lakeville	CT	06039	**800-222-2909**	860-435-9878
Mohegan Sun Resort & Casino 1 Mohegan Sun Blvd	Uncasville	CT	06382	**888-226-7711**	860-862-8150
Saybrook Point Inn & Spa 2 Bridge St	Old Saybrook	CT	06475	**800-243-0212**	860-395-2000
Water's Edge Resort & Spa 1525 Boston Post Rd PO Box 688	Westbrook	CT	06498	**800-222-5901**	860-399-5901

Florida

Name / Address	City	State	Zip	Toll-Free	Phone
Amelia Island Plantation 39 Beach Lagoon Rd	Amelia Island	FL	32034	**800-834-4900**	904-261-6161
Bahia Mar Beach Resort & Yachting Ctr 801 Seabreeze Blvd	Fort Lauderdale	FL	33316	**888-802-2442**	954-764-2233
Banyan Resort 323 Whitehead St	Key West	FL	33040	**866-371-9222**	305-296-7786
Bay Hill Golf Club & Lodge 9000 Bay Hill Blvd	Orlando	FL	32819	**888-422-9445**	407-876-2429
Beachcomber Resort Hotel & Villas 1200 S Ocean Blvd	Pompano Beach	FL	33062	**800-231-2423**	954-941-7830
Biltmore Hotel & Conference Ctr of the Americas 1200 Anastasia Ave *Cust Svc	Coral Gables	FL	33134	**800-727-1926***	305-445-1926
Bluewater Bay Resort 2000 Bluewater Blvd	Niceville	FL	32578	**800-874-2128**	850-897-3613
Boca Raton Resort & Club 501 E Camino Real	Boca Raton	FL	33432	**888-543-1224**	561-447-3000
Breakers, The 1 S County Rd	Palm Beach	FL	33480	**888-273-2537**	561-655-6611
Buena Vista Palace Hotel & Spa 1900 N Buena Vista Dr	Lake Buena Vista	FL	32830	**866-397-6516**	
Casa Ybel Resort 2255 W Gulf Dr	Sanibel Island	FL	33957	**800-276-4753**	239-472-3145
Club Med Sandpiper 4500 SE Pine Vly St	Port Saint Lucie	FL	34952	**888-932-2582**	772-398-5100
Deauville Beach Resort 6701 Collins Ave	Miami Beach	FL	33141	**800-327-6656**	305-865-8511
Don CeSar Beach Resort - A Loews Hotel 3400 Gulf Blvd	Saint Pete Beach	FL	33706	**888-430-4999**	727-360-1881
Doral Golf Resort & Spa 4400 NW 87th Ave	Miami	FL	33178	**800-713-6725**	305-592-2000
DoubleTree Resort by Hilton Hotel Grand Key (DGKR) 3990 S Roosevelt Blvd	Key West	FL	33040	**888-844-0454**	305-293-1818
Eden Roc - A Renaissance Beach Resort & Spa 4525 Collins Ave	Miami Beach	FL	33140	**855-433-3676**	305-531-0000
Fisher Island Club & Resort 1 Fisher Island Dr *Resv	Miami	FL	33109	**800-537-3708***	305-535-6000
Fontainebleau Miami Beach 4441 Collins Ave	Miami Beach	FL	33140	**800-548-8886**	305-538-2000
Four Seasons Resort Palm Beach 2800 S Ocean Blvd	Palm Beach	FL	33480	**800-432-2335**	561-582-2800
Galleon Resort & Marina 617 Front St	Key West	FL	33040	**800-544-3030**	305-296-7711
Grand Palms Hotel & Golf Resort 110 Grand Palms Dr	Pembroke Pines	FL	33027	**800-327-9246**	954-431-8800
Hammock Beach Resort 200 Ocean Crest Dr	Palm Coast	FL	32137	**866-841-0287**	386-246-5500
Harborside Suites At Little Harbor 611 Destiny Dr	Ruskin	FL	33570	**800-327-2773**	
Hard Rock Hotel at Universal Orlando Resort 5800 Universal Blvd	Orlando	FL	32819	**888-430-4999**	407-503-2000
Hawk's Cay Resort & Marina 61 Hawk's Cay Blvd	Duck Key	FL	33050	**888-395-5539**	305-743-7000
Hilton Sandestin Beach Golf Resort & Spa 4000 Sandestin Blvd S	Destin	FL	32550	**800-559-1805**	850-267-9500
Holiday Inn Express & Suites Oceanfront 3301 S Atlantic Ave	Daytona Beach Shores	FL	32118	**800-633-8464**	386-767-1711
Holiday Inn Resort Lake Buena Vista 13351 SR 535 *Sales	Orlando	FL	32821	**866-808-8833***	407-239-4500
Holiday Isle Beach Resort & Marina 84001 Overseas Hwy	Islamorada	FL	33036	**877-712-2842**	305-664-2321
Innisbrook Resort & Golf Club 36750 US Hwy 19 N	Palm Harbor	FL	34684	**800-492-6899**	727-942-2000
Jupiter Beach Resort 5 N A1A	Jupiter	FL	33477	**877-389-0571**	561-746-2511
JW Marriott Orlando Grande Lakes Resort 4040 Central Florida Pkwy	Orlando	FL	32837	**800-576-5750**	407-206-2300
Key Largo Grande Resort & Beach Club 97000 S Overseas Hwy *Resv	Key Largo	FL	33037	**888-871-3437***	305-852-5553
Key Largo Marriott Bay Resort 103800 Overseas Hwy *Resv	Key Largo	FL	33037	**888-731-9056***	305-453-0000
La Playa Beach & Golf Resort 9891 Gulf Shore Dr	Naples	FL	34108	**800-237-6883**	239-597-3123
Lago Mar Resort & Club 1700 S Ocean Ln	Fort Lauderdale	FL	33316	**855-209-5677**	954-678-3915
Little Palm Island Resort & Spa 28500 Overseas Hwy	Little Torch Key	FL	33042	**800-343-8567**	305-872-2524
Lodge & Club at Ponte Vedra Beach 607 Ponte Vedra Blvd	Ponte Vedra Beach	FL	32082	**800-243-4304**	888-839-9145
Longboat Key Club 220 Sands Point Rd	Longboat Key	FL	34228	**800-237-8821**	941-383-8821
Marco Beach Ocean Resort 480 S Collier Blvd	Marco Island	FL	34145	**800-715-8517**	239-393-1400
Miami Beach Resort & Spa 4833 Collins Ave	Miami Beach	FL	33140	**866-765-9090**	305-532-3600
Mission Inn Resort & Club 10400 County Rd 48	Howey in the Hills	FL	34737	**800-874-9053**	352-324-3101
Naples Bay Resort 1500 Fifth Ave S	Naples	FL	34102	**866-605-1199**	239-530-1199
Naples Beach Hotel & Golf Club 851 Gulf Shore Blvd N	Naples	FL	34102	**800-237-7600**	239-261-2222
Nickelodeon Family Suites by Holiday Inn 14500 Continental Gateway	Orlando	FL	32821	**877-642-5111**	407-387-5437
Ocean Key Resort & Spa 0 Duval St	Key West	FL	33040	**800-328-9815**	305-296-7701
Ocean Manor Resort 4040 Galt Ocean Dr	Fort Lauderdale	FL	33308	**800-955-0444**	954-566-7500
Ocean Sands Resort & Spa 1350 N Ocean Blvd	Pompano Beach	FL	33062	**800-721-7033**	954-590-1000
Omni Orlando Resort at Championsgate 1500 Masters Blvd	Champions Gate	FL	33896	**800-843-6664**	407-390-6664
Orange Lake Country Club Inc (OLCC) 8505 W Irlo Bronson Memorial Hwy	Kissimmee	FL	34747	**800-877-6522**	407-239-0000
Palms, The 3025 Collins Ave	Miami Beach	FL	33140	**800-550-0505**	305-534-0505
Park Shore Resort 600 Neapolitan Way	Naples	FL	34103	**800-548-2077**	239-263-2222
PGA National Resort & Spa 400 Ave of the Champions	Palm Beach Gardens	FL	33418	**800-633-9150**	561-627-2000
Pier House Resort Caribbean Spa 1 Duval St	Key West	FL	33040	**800-723-2791**	305-296-4600
Plantation Inn & Golf Resort 9301 W Ft Island Trl	Crystal River	FL	34429	**800-632-6262**	352-795-4211
Ponte Vedra Inn & Club 200 Ponte Vedra Blvd	Ponte Vedra Beach	FL	32082	**800-234-7842**	904-285-1111
Portofino Bay Hotel at Universal Orlando - A Loews Hotel 5601 Universal Blvd	Orlando	FL	32819	**800-235-6397**	407-503-1000
Quality Inn & Suites Naples Golf Resort 4100 Golden Gate Pkwy	Naples	FL	34116	**800-277-0017**	239-455-1010
Radisson Resort Parkway 2900 PkwyBlvd	Kissimmee	FL	34747	**800-333-3333**	407-396-7000
Reach Resort 1435 Simonton St	Key West	FL	33040	**888-318-4317**	305-296-5000
Renaissance Orlando Resort at SeaWorld 6677 Sea Harbor Dr	Orlando	FL	32821	**800-327-6677**	407-351-5555
Renaissance Resort at World Golf Village 500 S Legacy Trl	Saint Augustine	FL	32092	**888-740-7020**	904-940-8000

Classified Section

Name / Address	City	State	ZIP	Toll-Free	Phone
Renaissance Vinoy Resort & Golf Club 501 Fifth Ave NE	Saint Petersburg	FL	33701	**800-468-3571**	727-894-1000
Resort at Singer Island 3800 N Ocean Dr	Riviera Beach	FL	33404	**800-721-7033**	561-340-1700
Ritz-Carlton Amelia Island 4750 Amelia Island Pkwy	Amelia Island	FL	32034	**800-241-3333**	904-277-1100
Ritz-Carlton Key Biscayne 455 Grand Bay Dr	Key Biscayne	FL	33149	**800-241-3333**	305-365-4500
Ritz-Carlton Naples Golf Resort 2600 Tiburon Dr *Resv	Naples	FL	34109	**877-231-7916***	239-593-2000
Ritz-Carlton Orlando Grande Lakes 4012 Central Florida Pkwy	Orlando	FL	32837	**866-922-6882**	407-206-2400
Ritz-Carlton Sarasota 1111 Ritz-Carlton Dr	Sarasota	FL	34236	**800-241-3333**	941-309-2000
Rosen Hotels & Resorts Inc 9840 International Dr	Orlando	FL	32819	**800-204-7234**	407-996-9840
Royal Pacific Resort at Universal Orlando - A Loews Hotel 6300 Hollywood Way	Orlando	FL	32819	**800-235-6397**	407-503-3000
Safety Harbor Resort & Spa 105 N Bayshore Dr	Safety Harbor	FL	34695	**888-237-8772**	727-726-1161
Sandals Resorts International 4950 SW 72nd Ave	Miami	FL	33155	**888-726-3257**	305-284-1300
Sandestin Golf & Beach Resort 9300 Emerald Coast Pkwy W	Sandestin	FL	32550	**800-277-0800**	850-267-8000
Sanibel Harbour Marriott Resort & Spa 17260 Harbour Pt Dr	Fort Myers	FL	33908	**800-767-7777**	239-466-4000
Sawgrass Marriott Resort & Beach Club 1000 PGA Tour Blvd	Ponte Vedra Beach	FL	32082	**800-228-9290**	904-285-7777
Seminole Hard Rock Hotel & Casino Hollywood 1 Seminole Way	Hollywood	FL	33314	**888-236-4848**	866-502-7529
Sheraton Sand Key Resort 1160 Gulf Blvd	Clearwater Beach	FL	33767	**800-456-7263**	727-595-1611
South Seas Island Resort 5400 Plantation Rd	Captiva	FL	33924	**866-565-5089**	239-472-5111
Sundial Beach & Golf Resort 1451 Middle Gulf Dr	Sanibel	FL	33957	**866-717-2323**	239-472-4151
Sunset Beach Resort 3287 W Gulf Dr	Sanibel Island	FL	33957	**866-565-5091**	239-472-1700
Trump International Sonesta Beach Resort 18001 Collins Ave	Sunny Isles Beach	FL	33160	**800-766-3782**	305-692-5600
Vanderbilt Beach Resort 9225 Gulf Shore Dr N	Naples	FL	34108	**800-243-9076**	239-597-3144
Villas of Grand Cypress Golf Resort 1 N Jacaranda	Orlando	FL	32836	**800-835-7377**	407-239-4700
Walt Disney World Dolphin 1500 Epcot Resorts Blvd	Lake Buena Vista	FL	32830	**888-828-8850**	407-934-4000
Walt Disney World Swan 1200 Epcot Resorts Blvd	Lake Buena Vista	FL	32830	**888-828-8850**	407-934-4000
West Wind Inn 3345 W Gulf Dr	Sanibel	FL	33957	**800-824-0476**	239-472-1541
Westin Key West Resort & Marina 245 Front St	Key West	FL	33040	**866-837-4250**	305-294-4000

Georgia

Name / Address	City	State	ZIP	Toll-Free	Phone
Barnsley Gardens 597 Barnsley Gardens Rd	Adairsville	GA	30103	**877-773-2447**	770-773-7480
Brasstown Valley Resort 6321 US Hwy 76	Young Harris	GA	30582	**800-201-3205**	706-379-9900
Callaway Gardens 17800 Hwy 27	Pine Mountain	GA	31822	**800-225-5292**	706-663-2281
Chateau Elan Resort & Conference Ctr 100 Rue Charlemagne	Braselton	GA	30517	**800-233-9463**	678-425-0900
Forrest Hills Mountain Resort & Conference Ctr 135 Forrest Hills Rd	Dahlonega	GA	30533	**800-654-6313**	706-864-6456
Jekyll Island Club Hotel 371 Riverview Dr	Jekyll Island	GA	31527	**800-535-9547**	912-635-2600
King & Prince Beach & Golf Resort 201 Arnold Rd	Saint Simons Island	GA	31522	**800-342-0212**	912-638-3631
Lake Lanier Islands Resort 7000 Holiday Rd	Buford	GA	30518	**800-840-5253**	770-945-8787
Reynolds Plantation 100 Linger Longer Rd	Greensboro	GA	30642	**800-800-5250**	706-467-0600
Ritz-Carlton Lodge Reynolds Plantation 1 Lk Oc1e Trl	Greensboro	GA	30642	**877-231-7916**	706-467-0600
Sea Palms Golf & Tennis Resort 5445 Frederica Rd	Saint Simons Island	GA	31522	**800-841-6268**	912-638-3351
Villas by the Sea Resort 1175 N Beachview Dr	Jekyll Island	GA	31527	**800-841-6262**	912-635-2521

Hawaii

Name / Address	City	State	ZIP	Toll-Free	Phone
Fairmont Kea Lani 4100 Wailea Alanui Dr	Maui	HI	96753	**800-659-4100**	808-875-4100
Fairmont Orchid Hawaii 1 N Kaniku Dr	Kohala Coast	HI	96743	**800-845-9905**	808-885-2000
Four Seasons Resort Hualalai 100 Ka'upulehu Dr	Kailua-Kona	HI	96740	**888-340-5662**	808-325-8000
Four Seasons Resort Maui at Wailea 3900 Wailea Alanui Dr	Wailea	HI	96753	**800-334-6284**	808-874-8000
Grand Hyatt Kauai Resort & Spa 1571 Poipu Rd	Koloa	HI	96756	**800-233-1234**	808-742-1234
Grand Wailea Resort & Spa 3850 Wailea Alanui Dr	Wailea	HI	96753	**800-888-6100**	808-875-1234
Hanalei Bay Resort & Suites 5380 Honoiki Rd	Princeville	HI	96722	**877-344-0688**	808-826-6522
Hapuna Beach Prince Hotel 62-100 Kauna'oa Dr	Kamuela	HI	96743	**800-882-6060**	808-880-1111
Hawaii Prince Hotel Waikiki, The 100 Holomoana St	Honolulu	HI	96815	**888-977-4623**	
Hilton Hawaiian Village 2005 Kalia Rd	Honolulu	HI	96815	**800-445-8667**	808-949-4321
Hilton Waikoloa Village 425 Waikoloa Beach Dr	Waikoloa	HI	96738	**866-931-1679**	808-886-1234
Hyatt Regency Maui Resort & Spa 200 Nohea Kai Dr	Lahaina	HI	96761	**800-633-7313**	808-661-1234
Kapalua Villas, The 2000 Village Rd	Lahaina	HI	96761	**800-545-0018**	808-665-9170
Marriott Kaua'i Resort & Beach Club 3610 Rice St Kalapaki Beach	Lihue	HI	96766	**800-220-2925**	808-245-5050
Mauna Kea Beach Hotel 62-100 Maunakea Beach Dr	Island of Hawaii	HI	96743	**866-977-4589**	808-882-7222
Mauna Lani Bay Hotel & Bungalows 68-1400 Mauna Lani Dr	Kohala Coast	HI	96743	**800-367-2323**	808-885-6622
Napili Kai Beach Club 5900 Honoapiilani Rd	Lahaina	HI	96761	**800-367-5030**	808-669-6271
Outrigger Enterprises Group 2375 Kuhio Ave	Honolulu	HI	96815	**800-462-6262**	808-921-6941
Outrigger Hotels & Resorts 2375 Kuhio Ave	Honolulu	HI	96815	**800-688-7444**	808-921-6941
Outrigger Kanaloa at Kona 78-261 Manukai St	Kailua-Kona	HI	96740	**800-688-7444**	808-322-9625
Outrigger Reef on the Beach 2169 Kalia Rd	Honolulu	HI	96815	**800-688-7444**	808-923-3111
Prince Resorts Hawaii 100 Holomoana St	Honolulu	HI	96815	**888-977-4623**	808-956-1111
Ritz-Carlton Kapalua 1 Ritz-Carlton Dr Kapalua *Resv	Maui	HI	96761	**800-262-8440***	808-669-6200
Royal Lahaina Resort 2780 Kekaa Dr	Lahaina	HI	96761	**800-222-5642**	808-661-3611
Sheraton Kauai Resort 2440 Hoonani Rd *Resv	Koloa	HI	96756	**800-325-3535***	808-742-1661
Sheraton Maui Resort 2605 Kaanapali Pkwy	Lahaina	HI	96761	**866-716-8109**	808-661-0031
Sheraton Waikiki 2255 Kalakaua Ave	Honolulu	HI	96815	**800-325-3535**	808-922-4422
Travaasa Hana 5031 Hana Hwy	Hana	HI	96713	**855-868-7282**	808-248-8211
Turtle Bay Resort 57-091 Kamehameha Hwy	Kahuku	HI	96731	**866-475-2567**	808-293-6000
Wailea Beach Marriott Resort & Spa 3700 Wailea Alanui Dr	Wailea	HI	96753	**800-845-5279**	808-879-1922

Idaho

Name / Address	City	State	ZIP	Toll-Free	Phone
Aston Hotel & Resorts Sunvalley 333 S Main St	Ketchum	ID	83340	**877-997-6667**	208-622-6400
Coeur d'Alene Resort 115 S Second St	Coeur d'Alene	ID	83814	**800-688-5253**	208-765-4000
Red Lion Templin's Hotel on the River 414 E First Ave	Post Falls	ID	83854	**800-733-5466**	208-773-1611
Sun Valley Resort 1 Sun Valley Rd	Sun Valley	ID	83353	**800-786-8259**	208-622-4111

Illinois

Name / Address	City	State	ZIP	Toll-Free	Phone
Eagle Ridge Inn & Resort 444 Eagle Ridge Dr	Galena	IL	61036	**800-892-2269**	815-777-2444
Eaglewood Resort & Spa 1401 Nordic Rd	Itasca	IL	60143	**877-285-6150**	630-773-1400

Indiana

Name / Address	City	State	ZIP	Toll-Free	Phone
Belterra Casino Resort 777 Belterra Dr	Florence	IN	47020	**888-235-8377**	812-427-7777
Fourwinds Resort & Marina 9301 Fairfax Rd	Bloomington	IN	47401	**800-824-2628**	812-824-2628
French Lick Resort 8670 W State Rd 56	French Lick	IN	47432	**888-936-9360**	812-936-9300
Potawatomi Inn Pokagan State Pk 6 Ln 100A Lk James	Angola	IN	46703	**877-768-2928**	260-833-1077

Iowa

Name / Address	City	State	ZIP	Toll-Free	Phone
Grand Harbor Resort & Waterpark 350 Bell St	Dubuque	IA	52001	**866-690-4006**	563-690-4000

Kentucky

Name / Address	City	State	ZIP	Toll-Free	Phone
General Butler State Resort Park 1608 US Hwy 227	Carrollton	KY	41008	**866-462-8853**	502-732-4384
Griffin Gate Marriott Resort 1800 Newtown Pk	Lexington	KY	40511	**800-228-9290**	859-231-5100

Maine

Name / Address	City	State	ZIP	Toll-Free	Phone
Atlantic Oakes 119 Eden St	Bar Harbor	ME	04609	**800-356-3585**	207-288-5801
Bar Harbor Inn Oceanfront Resort Newport Dr	Bar Harbor	ME	04609	**800-248-3351**	207-288-3351
Bethel Inn & Country Club 21 Broad St PO Box 49	Bethel	ME	04217	**800-654-0125**	207-824-2175
Colony Hotel 140 Ocean Ave	Kennebunkport	ME	04046	**800-552-2363**	207-967-3331
Inn by the Sea 40 Bowery Beach Rd	Cape Elizabeth	ME	04107	**800-888-4287**	207-799-3134
Samoset Resort 220 Warrenton St	Rockport	ME	04856	**800-341-1650**	207-594-2511
Sebasco Harbor Resort 29 Keynon Rd	Phippsburg	ME	04562	**800-225-3819**	207-389-1161
Stage Neck Inn 8 Stage Neck Rd Rt 1A PO Box 70	York Harbor	ME	03911	**800-222-3238**	207-363-3850
Sugarloaf/USA 5092 Access Rd	Carrabassett Valley	ME	04947	**800-843-5623**	207-237-2000

	City	State	Zip	Toll-Free	Phone
Sunday River Ski Resort 15 S Ridge Rd PO Box 4500	Newry	ME	04261	**800-543-2754**	207-824-3500

Maryland

	City	State	Zip	Toll-Free	Phone
Coconut Malorie Resort 200 59th St	Ocean City	MD	21842	**855-826-6361**	410-723-6100
Francis Scott Key Family Resort 12806 Ocean Gateway	Ocean City	MD	21842	**800-213-0088**	410-213-0088
Harbourtowne Golf Resort & Conference Ctr 9784 Martingham Dr	Saint Michaels	MD	21663	**800-446-9066**	410-745-9066
Ritz-Carlton Hotel Co LLC, The 4445 Willard Ave Ste 800	Chevy Chase	MD	20815	**800-241-3333**	301-547-4700
Ritz-Carlton Huntington Hotel & Spa 4445 Willard Ave Ste 800	Chevy Chase	MD	20815	**800-241-3333**	301-547-4700
Turf Valley Resort & Conference Ctr 2700 Turf Vly Rd	Ellicott City	MD	21042	**888-833-8873**	410-465-1500

Massachusetts

	City	State	Zip	Toll-Free	Phone
Bayside Resort Hotel 225 Massachusetts 28	West Yarmouth	MA	02673	**800-243-1114**	508-775-5669
Blue Water Resort 291 S Shore Dr	South Yarmouth	MA	02664	**800-367-9393**	508-398-2288
Canyon Ranch 165 Kemble St *Resv	Lenox	MA	01240	**800-742-9000***	413-637-4100
Cape Codder Resort & Spa 1225 Iyanough Rd Rt 132 Bearse's Way	Hyannis	MA	02601	**888-297-2200**	508-771-3000
Chatham Bars Inn 297 Shore Rd	Chatham	MA	02633	**800-527-4884**	508-945-0096
Cranwell Resort Spa & Golf Club 55 Lee Rd	Lenox	MA	01240	**800-272-6935**	413-637-1364
New Seabury Resort 20 Red Brook Rd	Mashpee	MA	02649	**877-687-3228**	508-539-8200
Ocean Edge Resort & Golf Club 2907 Main St	Brewster	MA	02631	**800-343-6074**	508-896-9000
Ocean Mist Resort 97 S Shore Dr	South Yarmouth	MA	02664	**800-655-1972**	508-398-2633
Sea Crest Resort & Conference Ctr 350 Quaker Rd	North Falmouth	MA	02556	**800-225-3110**	508-540-9400

Michigan

	City	State	Zip	Toll-Free	Phone
Bay Valley Hotel & Resort 2470 Old Bridge Rd	Bay City	MI	48706	**888-241-4653**	989-686-3500
Boyne Highlands Resort 600 Highlands Dr	Harbor Springs	MI	49740	**800-462-6963**	231-526-3000
Boyne Mountain Resort 11521 Huffman Lake Rd	Boyne Falls	MI	49713	**800-462-6963**	231-549-6060
Crystal Mountain Resort 12500 Crystal Mtn Dr	Thompsonville	MI	49683	**800-968-7686**	231-378-2000
Evergreen Resort 7880 Mackinaw Trail	Cadillac	MI	49601	**800-634-7302**	
Garland Resort 4700 N Red Oak Rd	Lewiston	MI	49756	**877-442-7526**	989-786-2211
Grand Traverse Resort & Spa 100 Grand Traverse Blvd PO Box 404	Acme	MI	49610	**800-236-1577**	231-534-6000
Indianhead Mountain Resort 500 Indianhead Rd	Wakefield	MI	49968	**800-346-3426**	
Inn at Bay Harbor, The 3600 Village Harbor Dr	Bay Harbor	MI	49770	**800-462-6963**	231-439-4000
Lakewood Shores Resort 7751 Cedar Lake Rd	Oscoda	MI	48750	**800-882-2493**	989-739-2073
Mission Point Resort 6633 Main St	Mackinac Island	MI	49757	**800-833-7711**	
Otsego Club 696 M-32 E Main St PO Box 556	Gaylord	MI	49734	**800-752-5510**	989-732-5181
Shanty Creek Resort 5780 Shanty Creek Rd	Bellaire	MI	49615	**800-678-4111**	231-533-8621
Treetops Resort 3962 Wilkinson Rd	Gaylord	MI	49735	**866-348-5249**	989-732-6711

Minnesota

	City	State	Zip	Toll-Free	Phone
Arrowwood Resort & Conference Ctr 2100 Arrowwood Ln NW *Resv	Alexandria	MN	56308	**866-386-5263***	320-762-1124
Breezy Point Resort 9252 Breezy Pt Dr	Breezy Point	MN	56472	**800-432-3777**	218-562-7811
Caribou Highlands Lodge 371 Ski Hill Rd PO Box 99	Lutsen	MN	55612	**800-642-6036**	218-663-7241
Carlson *Radisson Hotels & Resorts* 701 Carlson Pkwy	Minnetonka	MN	55305	**800-333-3333**	763-212-5000
Cascade Lodge 3719 W Hwy 61	Lutsen	MN	55612	**800-322-9543**	218-387-1112
Cragun's Conference & Golf Resort 11000 Cragun's Dr	Brainerd	MN	56401	**800-272-4867**	
Fair Hills Resort 24270 County Hwy 20 *Resv	Detroit Lakes	MN	56501	**800-323-2849***	218-847-7638
Grand Casino Hinckley 777 Lady Luck Dr	Hinckley	MN	55037	**800-472-6321**	
Grand Casino Mille Lacs 777 Grand Ave PO Box 343	Onamia	MN	56359	**800-626-5825**	
Grand Portage Lodge & Casino PO Box 233	Grand Portage	MN	55605	**800-543-1384**	218-475-2401
Grand View Lodge 23521 Nokomis Ave	Nisswa	MN	56468	**866-801-2951**	218-963-2234
Lake Breeze Motel Resort 9000 Congdon Blvd	Duluth	MN	55804	**800-738-5884**	218-525-6808
Lutsen Resort 5700 W Hwy 61 PO Box 9	Lutsen	MN	55612	**800-258-8736**	218-663-7212
Madden's on Gull Lake 11266 Pine Beach Peninsula	Brainerd	MN	56401	**800-642-5363**	218-829-2811
Ruttger's Bay Lake Lodge 25039 Tame Fish Lk Rd PO Box 400	Deerwood	MN	56444	**800-450-4545**	218-678-2885
Superior Shores Resort 1521 Superior Shores Dr	Two Harbors	MN	55616	**800-242-1988**	218-834-5671

Mississippi

	City	State	Zip	Toll-Free	Phone
Beau Rivage Resort & Casino 875 Beach Blvd	Biloxi	MS	39530	**888-750-7111**	228-386-7111
Gulf Hills Hotel 13701 Paso Rd	Ocean Springs	MS	39564	**866-875-4211**	228-875-4211
IP Casino Resort & Spa 850 Bayview Ave *Resv	Biloxi	MS	39530	**888-946-2847***	228-436-3000
Treasure Bay Casino & Hotel 1980 Beach Blvd *General	Biloxi	MS	39531	**800-747-2839***	228-385-6000

Missouri

	City	State	Zip	Toll-Free	Phone
Dogwood Hills Golf Resort 1252 State Hwy KK	Osage Beach	MO	65065	**800-220-6571**	573-348-3153
Lilleys' Landing Resort 367 River Ln	Branson	MO	65616	**866-545-5397**	417-334-6380
Lodge of Four Seasons 315 Four Seasons Dr PO Box 215 *Resv	Lake Ozark	MO	65049	**888-265-5500***	573-365-3000
Resort at Port Arrowhead, The 3080 Bagnell Dam Blvd PO Box 1930	Lake Ozark	MO	65049	**800-532-3575**	573-365-2334
Tan-Tar-A Resort Golf Club & Spa 494 Tantara Dr PO Box 188TT *Resv	Osage Beach	MO	65065	**800-826-8272***	573-348-3131
Thousand Hills Golf Resort 245 S Wildwood Dr	Branson	MO	65616	**877-262-0430**	417-336-5873

Montana

	City	State	Zip	Toll-Free	Phone
Big Sky Resort 1 L1 Mtn Trl PO Box 160001	Big Sky	MT	59716	**800-548-4486**	406-995-5000
Fairmont Hot Springs Resort 1500 Fairmont Rd	Fairmont	MT	59711	**800-332-3272**	406-797-3241
Meadow Lake Resort 100 St Andrews Dr	Columbia Falls	MT	59912	**800-321-4653**	406-892-8700
Rock Creek Resort 6380 US Hwy 212	Red Lodge	MT	59068	**800-667-1119**	406-446-1111
Triple Creek Ranch 5551 W Fork Rd	Darby	MT	59829	**800-654-2943**	406-821-4600

Nebraska

	City	State	Zip	Toll-Free	Phone
Radisson Palm Beach Shores Resort & Vacation Villas 11340 Blondo S Ste 100	Omaha	NE	68164	**800-615-7253**	

Nevada

	City	State	Zip	Toll-Free	Phone
Alexis Park Resort 375 E Harmon Ave	Las Vegas	NV	89169	**800-582-2228**	702-796-3300
Aquarius Casino Resort 1900 S Casino Dr	Laughlin	NV	89029	**888-662-5825**	702-298-5111
Atlantis Casino Resort 3800 S Virginia St	Reno	NV	89502	**800-723-6500**	775-825-4700
Bellagio Hotel & Casino 3600 Las Vegas Blvd S	Las Vegas	NV	89109	**888-987-7111**	702-693-7111
Casablanca Resort 950 W Mesquite Blvd	Mesquite	NV	89027	**800-459-7529**	702-346-7529
Club Cal Neva Hotel Casino, The 38 E Second St PO Box 2071	Reno	NV	89501	**877-777-7303**	775-323-1046
Don Laughlin's Riverside Resort & Casino 1650 Casino Dr	Laughlin	NV	89029	**800-227-3849**	702-298-2535
Golden Nugget Hotel 129 E Fremont St	Las Vegas	NV	89101	**800-634-3454**	702-385-7111
Golden Nugget Laughlin 2300 S Casino Dr	Laughlin	NV	89029	**800-950-7700**	702-298-7111
Grand Sierra Resort & Casino 2500 E Second St	Reno	NV	89595	**800-501-2651**	775-789-2000
Hard Rock Hotel & Casino 4455 Paradise Rd	Las Vegas	NV	89169	**800-693-7625**	702-693-5000
JW Marriott Resort Las Vegas 221 N Rampart Blvd	Las Vegas	NV	89144	**877-869-8777**	702-869-7777
Mandalay Bay Resort & Casino 3950 Las Vegas Blvd S	Las Vegas	NV	89119	**877-632-7800**	702-632-7777
MGM Grand Hotel & Casino 3799 Las Vegas Blvd S	Las Vegas	NV	89109	**877-880-0880**	702-891-1111
Mirage, The 3400 Las Vegas Blvd S	Las Vegas	NV	89109	**800-627-6667**	702-791-7111
Monte Carlo Resort & Casino 3770 Las Vegas Blvd S	Las Vegas	NV	89109	**800-311-8999**	702-730-7777
Planet Hollywood Resort & Casino 3667 Las Vegas Blvd S	Las Vegas	NV	89109	**866-919-7472**	702-785-5555
Primm Valley Resort & Casino 31900 S Las Vegas Blvd	Primm	NV	89019	**800-926-4455**	
Ridge Tahoe 400 Ridge Club Dr PO Box 5790	Stateline	NV	89449	**800-334-1600**	775-588-3553
Treasure Island Hotel & Casino 3300 Las Vegas Blvd S	Las Vegas	NV	89109	**800-288-7206**	702-894-7111
Tropicana Resort & Casino 3801 Las Vegas Blvd S *Resv	Las Vegas	NV	89109	**800-462-8767***	702-739-2222
Venetian Resort Hotel & Casino 3355 Las Vegas Blvd S	Las Vegas	NV	89109	**866-659-9643**	702-414-1000

Classified Section

New Hampshire

Name / Address	City	State	Zip	Toll-Free	Phone
Cranmore Mountain Resort 1 Skimobile Rd PO Box 1640	North Conway	NH	03860	**800-786-6754**	603-356-5543
Mount Washington Hotel & Resort Rt 302	Bretton Woods	NH	03575	**800-314-1752**	603-278-1000
Waterville Valley Resort 1 Ski Area Rd PO Box 540	Waterville Valley	NH	03215	**800-468-2553**	603-236-8311
White Mountain Hotel & Resort 2560 W Side Rd PO Box 1828	North Conway	NH	03860	**800-533-6301**	603-356-7100

New Jersey

Name / Address	City	State	Zip	Toll-Free	Phone
Bally's Atlantic City 1900 Pacific Ave	Atlantic City	NJ	08401	**800-772-7777**	609-340-2000
Caesars Atlantic City Hotel Casino 2100 Pacific Ave	Atlantic City	NJ	08401	**800-522-4700**	609-348-4411
Montreal Inn Beach Dr & Madison Ave	Cape May	NJ	08204	**800-525-7011**	609-884-7011
Resorts Casino Hotel 1133 Boardwalk	Atlantic City	NJ	08401	**800-334-6378**	
Tropicana Entertainment 2831 Boardwalk *OTC: TPCA*	Atlantic City	NJ	08401	**800-843-8767**	
Trump Taj Mahal Casino Resort 1000 Boardwalk & Virginia Ave	Atlantic City	NJ	08401	**800-426-2537**	609-449-1000
Wyndham Vacation Rentals 14 Sylvan Way	Parsippany	NJ	07054	**800-467-3529**	973-753-6300

New Mexico

Name / Address	City	State	Zip	Toll-Free	Phone
Angel Fire Resort PO Box 130	Angel Fire	NM	87710	**800-633-7463**	575-377-6401
Inn of the Mountain Gods 287 Carrizo Canyon Rd	Mescalero	NM	88340	**800-545-9011**	
La Posada de Santa Fe Resort & Spa 330 E Palace Ave	Santa Fe	NM	87501	**866-280-3810**	505-986-0000
Lifts West Condominium Resort Hotel PO Box 330	Red River	NM	87558	**800-221-1859**	505-754-2778

New York

Name / Address	City	State	Zip	Toll-Free	Phone
Bonnie Castle Resort 31 Holland St	Alexandria Bay	NY	13607	**800-955-4511**	315-482-4511
Doral Arrowwood Conference Resort 975 Anderson Hill Rd	Rye Brook	NY	10573	**844-211-0512**	844-214-5500
High Peaks Resort 2384 Saranac Ave	Lake Placid	NY	12946	**800-755-5598**	518-523-4411
Holiday Valley Resort 6557 Holiday Valley Rd PO Box 370	Ellicottville	NY	14731	**800-323-0020**	716-699-2345
Mohonk Mountain House 1000 Mtn Rest Rd	New Paltz	NY	12561	**800-772-6646**	845-255-1000
Montauk Yacht Club Resort & Marina 32 Star Island Rd	Montauk	NY	11954	**888-692-8668**	631-668-3100
Otesaga, The 60 Lake St	Cooperstown	NY	13326	**800-348-6222**	607-547-9931
Point, The PO Box 1327	Saranac Lake	NY	12983	**800-255-3530**	518-891-5674
Roaring Brook Ranch & Tennis Resort Rte 9N S	Lake George	NY	12845	**800-882-7665**	518-668-5767
Rocking Horse Ranch Resort 600 Rt 44-55	Highland	NY	12528	**800-647-2624**	845-691-2927
Sagamore, The 110 Sagamore Rd	Bolton Landing	NY	12814	**866-384-1944**	518-644-9400
Starwood Hotels & Resorts Worldwide Inc 1111 Westchester Ave *NYSE: HOT* ■ *Cust Svc	White Plains	NY	10604	**888-625-5144***	914-640-8100
Saint Regis Hotels & Resorts 1111 Westchester Ave	White Plains	NY	10604	**888-625-4988**	914-640-8100
Villa Roma Resort & Conference Ctr 356 Villa Roma Rd	Callicoon	NY	12723	**800-533-6767**	845-887-4880
Woodcliff Hotel & Spa 199 Woodcliff Dr	Fairport	NY	14450	**800-365-3065**	585-381-4000

North Carolina

Name / Address	City	State	Zip	Toll-Free	Phone
Ballantyne Resort Hotel 10000 Ballantyne Commons Pkwy	Charlotte	NC	28277	**866-248-4824**	704-248-4000
Eseeola Lodge, The 175 Linville Ave PO Box 99	Linville	NC	28646	**800-742-6717**	828-733-4311
Fontana Village Resort 300 Woods Rd PO Box 68	Fontana Dam	NC	28733	**800-849-2258**	828-498-2211
Grove Park Inn Resort & Spa 290 Macon Ave	Asheville	NC	28804	**800-438-5800**	828-252-2711
High Hampton Inn & Country Club 1525 Hwy 107 S	Cashiers	NC	28717	**800-334-2551**	828-743-2450
Holiday Inn SunSpree Resort Wrightsville Beach 1706 N Lumina Ave	Wrightsville Beach	NC	28480	**888-211-9874**	910-256-2231
Maggie Valley Resort & Country Club 1819 Country Club Dr	Maggie Valley	NC	28751	**800-438-3861**	828-926-1616
Mid Pines Inn & Golf Club 1010 Midland Rd	Southern Pines	NC	28387	**800-747-7272**	910-692-2114
Pine Needles Lodge & Golf Club PO Box 88	Southern Pines	NC	28388	**800-747-7272**	910-692-7111
Pinehurst Resort & Country Club 80 Carolina Vista Dr	Pinehurst	NC	28374	**800-487-4653**	910-295-6811
Pinnacle Inn Resort 301 Pinnacle Inn Rd	Beech Mountain	NC	28604	**800-405-7888**	828-387-2231
Sanderling Resort & Spa 1461 Duck Rd	Duck	NC	27949	**800-701-4111**	252-261-4111
Waynesville Inn Golf & Country Club, The 176 Country Club Dr	Waynesville	NC	28786	**800-627-6250**	828-456-3551
Wolf Ridge Ski Resort 578 Vly View Cir	Mars Hill	NC	28754	**800-817-4111**	828-689-4111

Name / Address	City	State	Zip	Toll-Free	Phone
Prairie Knights Casino & Resort 7932 Hwy 24	Fort Yates	ND	58538	**800-425-8277**	701-854-7777

Nova Scotia

Name / Address	City	State	Zip	Toll-Free	Phone
Atlantica Hotel & Marina Oak Island 36 Treasure Dr PO Box 6	Western Shore	NS	B0J3M0	**800-565-5075**	902-627-2600
Pines Resort, The 103 Shore Rd	Digby	NS	B0V1A0	**800-667-4637**	902-245-2511

Ohio

Name / Address	City	State	Zip	Toll-Free	Phone
Sawmill Creek Resort 400 Sawmill Creek Dr	Huron	OH	44839	**800-729-6455**	419-433-3800

Oklahoma

Name / Address	City	State	Zip	Toll-Free	Phone
Lake Murray Resort Park 3323 Lodge Rd	Ardmore	OK	73401	**800-622-6317**	580-223-6600
Quartz Mountain Resort & Conference Ctr 22469 Lodge Rd	Lone Wolf	OK	73655	**877-999-5567**	580-563-2424

Ontario

Name / Address	City	State	Zip	Toll-Free	Phone
Deerhurst Resort 1235 Deerhurst Dr *Sales	Huntsville	ON	P1H2E8	**800-461-6522***	705-789-6411
Fallsview Casino Resort 6380 Fallsview Blvd	Niagara Falls	ON	L2G7X5	**888-325-5788**	
Pinestone Resort 4252 County Rd Ste 21	Haliburton	ON	K0M1S0	**800-461-0357**	705-457-1800

Oregon

Name / Address	City	State	Zip	Toll-Free	Phone
Black Butte Ranch 12930 Hawks BeaRd Rd PO Box 8000	Black Butte Ranch	OR	97759	**866-901-2961**	541-595-1252
Gearhart By the Sea 1157 N Marion Ave	Gearhart	OR	97138	**800-547-0115**	503-738-8331
Mount Bachelor Village Resort & Conference Ctr 19717 Mt Bachelor Dr	Bend	OR	97702	**800-547-5204**	541-389-5900
Salishan Lodge & Golf Resort PO Box 118	Gleneden Beach	OR	97388	**800-452-2300**	
Sunriver Resort 17600 Ctr Dr PO Box 3609	Sunriver	OR	97707	**800-547-3922**	541-593-1000
Timberline Lodge 27500 E Timberline Rd	Government Camp	OR	97028	**800-547-1406**	503-272-3311

Pennsylvania

Name / Address	City	State	Zip	Toll-Free	Phone
Allenberry Resort 1559 Boiling Springs Rd	Boiling Springs	PA	17007	**800-430-5468**	717-258-3211
Carroll Valley Golf Resort 78 Country Club Trail	Carroll Valley	PA	17320	**855-784-0330**	717-642-8282
Cove Haven Pocono Palace 5222 Milford Rd	East Stroudsburg	PA	18302	**877-822-3333**	800-432-9932
Fernwood Resort 5785 Milford Rd	East Stroudsburg	PA	18302	**888-337-6966**	
Heritage Hills Golf Resort & Conference Ctr 2700 Mt Rose Ave	York	PA	17402	**877-782-9752**	717-755-0123
Hidden Valley Resort & Conference Ctr 1 Craighead Dr PO Box 4420	Hidden Valley	PA	15502	**800-452-2223**	814-443-8000
Lancaster Host Resort 2300 Lincoln Hwy E *Resv	Lancaster	PA	17602	**800-233-0121***	717-299-5500
Mountain Laurel Resort & Spa Rt 940 PO Box 9	White Haven	PA	18661	**888-243-9300**	570-443-8411
Nemacolin Woodlands Resort & Spa 1001 Lafayette Dr	Farmington	PA	15437	**800-422-2736**	724-329-8555
Pocono Manor Golf Resort & Spa 1 Manor Dr Rt 314	Pocono Manor	PA	18349	**800-233-8150**	570-839-7111
Seven Springs Mountain Resort 777 Waterwheel Dr	Champion	PA	15622	**800-452-2223**	814-352-7777
Skytop Lodge 1 Skytop	Skytop	PA	18357	**800-345-7759**	570-595-7401
Split Rock Resort 100 Moseywood Rd	Lake Harmony	PA	18624	**800-255-7625**	570-722-9111
Tamiment Resort & Conference Ctr Bushkill Falls Rd	Tamiment	PA	18371	**800-233-8105**	570-588-6652
Woodlands Inn, The 1073 Hwy 315	Wilkes-Barre	PA	18702	**844-779-8472**	570-824-9831

Puerto Rico

Name / Address	City	State	Zip	Toll-Free	Phone
El Conquistador Resort & Golden Door Spa 1000 El Conquistador Ave *Resv	Fajardo	PR	00738	**888-543-1282***	787-863-1000
Ritz-Carlton San Juan, The 6961 Ave of the Governors Isla Verde	Carolina	PR	00979	**800-241-3333**	787-253-1700

Quebec

Name / Address	City	State	Zip	Toll-Free	Phone
Fairmont Le Chateau Montebello 392 Notre Dame St	Montebello	QC	J0V1L0	**800-441-1414**	819-423-6341
Hotel Cheribourg 2603 Ch du Parc	Orford	QC	J1X8C8	**877-845-5344**	819-843-3308

Name / Address	City	State	Zip	Toll-Free	Phone
Hotel du Lac 121 Rue Cuttle	Mont-Tremblant	QC	J8E1B9	**800-567-8341**	819-425-2731
Manoir du Lac Delage 40 Ave du Lac	Lac Delage	QC	G3C5C4	**888-202-3242**	418-848-2551

Rhode Island

Name / Address	City	State	Zip	Toll-Free	Phone
Castle Hill Inn & Resort 590 Ocean Dr	Newport	RI	02840	**888-466-1355**	401-849-3800

South Carolina

Name / Address	City	State	Zip	Toll-Free	Phone
Barefoot Resort & Golf 4980 Barefoot Resort Bridge Rd	North Myrtle Beach	SC	29582	**866-638-4818**	843-390-3200
Bay Watch Resort & Conference Ctr 2701 S Ocean Blvd	North Myrtle Beach	SC	29582	**866-270-2172**	843-272-4600
Beach Colony Resort 5308 N Ocean Blvd *General	Myrtle Beach	SC	29577	**800-222-2141***	843-449-4010
Bluewater Resort 2001 S Ocean Blvd	Myrtle Beach	SC	29577	**800-845-6994**	843-626-8345
Breakers Resort 3002 N Ocean Blvd	Myrtle Beach	SC	29577	**800-952-4507**	843-448-8082
Caravelle Resort Hotel & Villas 6900 N Ocean Blvd	Myrtle Beach	SC	29572	**800-507-9145**	843-918-8000
Caribbean Resort & Villas 3000 N Ocean Blvd	Myrtle Beach	SC	29577	**800-552-8509**	
Compass Cove Ocean Resort 2311 S Ocean Blvd	Myrtle Beach	SC	29577	**800-331-0934**	843-448-8373
Coral Beach Resort & Suites 1105 S Ocean Blvd	Myrtle Beach	SC	29577	**800-843-2684**	800-556-1754
Hilton Head Island Beach & Tennis Resort 40 Folly Field Rd *Resv	Hilton Head Island	SC	29928	**800-475-2631***	843-842-4402
Hilton Myrtle Beach Resort 10000 Beach Club Dr	Myrtle Beach	SC	29572	**800-445-8667**	843-449-5000
Kiawah Island Golf Resort 1 Sancturay Beach Dr *Resv	Kiawah Island	SC	29455	**800-654-2924***	843-768-2121
Litchfield Beach & Golf Resort 14276 Ocean Hwy	Pawleys Island	SC	29585	**888-766-4633**	843-237-3000
Myrtle Beach Resort Vacations 5905 S Kings Hwy PO Box 3936	Myrtle Beach	SC	29578	**888-627-3767**	843-238-1559
Mystic Sea Resort 2105 S Ocean Blvd	Myrtle Beach	SC	29577	**800-443-7050**	843-448-8446
Ocean Reef Resort 7100 N Ocean Blvd	Myrtle Beach	SC	29572	**888-322-6411**	843-449-4441
Palmetto Dunes Resort 4 Queen Folly Rd	Hilton Head Island	SC	29928	**866-380-1778**	
Palms Resort 2500 N Ocean Blvd	Myrtle Beach	SC	29577	**800-300-1198**	843-626-8334
Patricia Grand Resort 2710 N Ocean Blvd	Myrtle Beach	SC	29577	**800-255-4763**	843-448-8453
Pawleys Plantation 70 Tanglewood Dr	Pawleys Island	SC	29585	**800-367-9959**	843-237-6000
Player's Club Resort 35 Deallyon Ave	Hilton Head Island	SC	29928	**800-497-7529**	843-785-3355
Reef Resort 2101 S Ocean Blvd *Cust Svc	Myrtle Beach	SC	29577	**800-845-1212***	843-448-1765
Sand Dunes Resort Hotel 201 74th Ave N	Myrtle Beach	SC	29572	**800-726-3783**	
Sea Mist Resort 1200 S Ocean Blvd	Myrtle Beach	SC	29577	**800-793-6507**	843-448-1551
Seacrest Oceanfront Resort on the South Beach 803 S Ocean Blvd	Myrtle Beach	SC	29577	**888-889-8113**	
Wild Dunes Resort 5757 Palm Blvd	Isle of Palms	SC	29451	**800-845-8880**	843-886-6000
Wyndham Vacation Resorts King Cotton Villas 1 King Cotton Rd	Edisto Beach	SC	29438	**800-251-8736**	843-869-2561

South Dakota

Name / Address	City	State	Zip	Toll-Free	Phone
Spearfish Canyon Resort 10619 Roughlock Falls Rd	Lead	SD	57754	**877-975-6343**	605-584-3435

Tennessee

Name / Address	City	State	Zip	Toll-Free	Phone
Brookside Resort 463 E Pkwy	Gatlinburg	TN	37738	**800-251-9597**	865-436-5611

Texas

Name / Address	City	State	Zip	Toll-Free	Phone
Bahia Mar Resort & Conference Ctr 6300 Padre Blvd	South Padre Island	TX	78597	**800-926-6926**	
Four Seasons Resort & Club Dallas at Las Colinas 4150 N MacArthur Blvd	Irving	TX	75038	**800-332-3442**	972-717-0700
Hilton Galveston Island Resort 5400 Seawall Blvd	Galveston	TX	77551	**800-475-3386**	409-744-5000
Houstonian Hotel Club & Spa 111 N Post Oak Ln *Resv	Houston	TX	77024	**800-231-2759***	713-680-2626
Inn of the Hills River Resort 1001 Junction Hwy	Kerrville	TX	78028	**800-292-5690**	830-895-5000
Omni Barton Creek Resort & Spa 8212 Barton Club Dr	Austin	TX	78735	**800-336-6158**	512-329-4000
Rancho Viejo Resort & Country Club 1 Rancho Viejo Dr	Rancho Viejo	TX	78575	**800-531-7400**	956-350-4000
Rosewood Hotels & Resorts 500 Crescent Ct Ste 300	Dallas	TX	75201	**888-767-3966**	214-880-4200
San Luis Resort Spa & Conference Ctr 5222 Seawall Blvd *Cust Svc	Galveston Island	TX	77551	**800-445-0090***	409-744-1500
Silverleaf Resorts Inc 1221 Riverbend Dr Ste 120	Dallas	TX	75247	**800-613-0310**	214-631-1166
South Shore Harbour Resort & Conference Ctr 2500 S Shore Blvd *Resv	League City	TX	77573	**800-442-5005***	281-334-1000
Tanglewood Resort Hotel & Conference Ctr 290 Tanglewood Cir	Pottsboro	TX	75076	**800-833-6569**	903-786-2968
Tapatio Springs Golf Resort & Conference Ctr 1 Resort Way	Boerne	TX	78006	**800-999-3299**	855-627-2243

Utah

Name / Address	City	State	Zip	Toll-Free	Phone
Alta Lodge PO Box 8040 *Cust Svc	Alta	UT	84092	**800-707-2582***	801-742-3500
Deer Valley Resort Lodging PO Box 889	Park City	UT	84060	**800-558-3337**	435-645-6626
Homestead Resort 700 N Homestead Dr	Midway	UT	84049	**888-327-7220**	
Little America Hotels & Resorts 500 S Main St	Salt Lake City	UT	84101	**800-281-7899**	801-596-5700
Park City Mountain Resort (PCMR) 1345 Lowell Ave PO Box 39	Park City	UT	84060	**800-222-7275**	435-649-8111
Rustler Lodge 10380 East Hwy 210 PO Box 8030	Alta	UT	84092	**888-532-2582**	801-742-2200
Snowbasin Ski Resort 3925 E Snowbasin Rd	Huntsville	UT	84317	**888-437-5488**	801-620-1100
Snowbird Ski & Summer Resort Hwy 210 PO Box 929000	Snowbird	UT	84092	**800-453-3000**	801-742-2222
Solitude Ski Resort 12000 Big Cottonwood Canyon	Solitude	UT	84121	**800-748-4754**	801-534-1400
Stein Eriksen Lodge 7700 Stein Way	Park City	UT	84060	**800-453-1302**	435-649-3700

Vermont

Name / Address	City	State	Zip	Toll-Free	Phone
Basin Harbor Club 4800 Basin Harbor Rd	Vergennes	VT	05491	**800-622-4000**	802-475-2311
Equinox, The 3567 Main St	Manchester Village	VT	05254	**800-362-4747**	802-362-4700
Hawk Inn & Mountain Resort 75 Billings Rd	Plymouth	VT	05056	**800-685-4295**	802-672-3811
Inn at Stratton Mountain 5 Village Lodge Rd	Stratton Mountain	VT	05155	**800-787-2886**	802-297-2500
Jay Peak Resort 830 Jay Peak Rd	Jay	VT	05859	**800-451-4449**	802-988-2611
Killington Resort & Pico Mountain 4763 Killington Rd	Killington	VT	05751	**800-621-6867**	802-422-6200
Lake Morey Resort 1 Clubhouse Rd	Fairlee	VT	05045	**800-423-1211**	802-333-4311
Smugglers' Notch Resort 4323 Vermont Rt 108 S	Jeffersonville	VT	05464	**800-451-8752**	802-644-8851
Stowe Mountain Resort 5781 Mountain Rd	Stowe	VT	05672	**800-253-4754**	802-253-3000
Stoweflake Mountain Resort & Spa 1746 Mountain Rd PO Box 369	Stowe	VT	05672	**800-253-2232**	802-253-7355
Sugarbush Resort & Inn 1840 Sugarbush Access Rd	Warren	VT	05674	**800-537-8427**	802-583-6300
Topnotch at Stowe Resort & Spa 4000 Mountain Rd	Stowe	VT	05672	**800-451-8686**	
Trapp Family Lodge 700 Trapp Hill Rd PO Box 1428	Stowe	VT	05672	**800-826-7000**	802-253-8511
Woodstock Inn & Resort 14 The Green	Woodstock	VT	05091	**800-448-7900**	802-457-1100

Virginia

Name / Address	City	State	Zip	Toll-Free	Phone
Alamar Resort Inn 311 16th St	Virginia Beach	VA	23451	**800-346-5681**	757-428-7582
Boar's Head Inn 200 Ednam Dr	Charlottesville	VA	22903	**800-476-1988**	434-296-2181
Breakers Resort Inn 16th & Oceanfront	Virginia Beach	VA	23451	**800-237-7532**	757-428-1821
Great Wolf Lodge Williamsburg 549 E Rochambeau Dr	Williamsburg	VA	23188	**800-551-9653**	757-229-9700
Kingsmill Resort & Spa 1010 Kingsmill Rd	Williamsburg	VA	23185	**800-832-5665**	757-253-1703
Lansdowne Resort 44050 Woodridge Pkwy	Leesburg	VA	20176	**877-513-8400**	703-729-8400
Shenvalee Golf Resort 9660 Fairway Dr	New Market	VA	22844	**888-339-3181**	540-740-3181
Turtle Cay Resort 600 Atlantic Ave	Virginia Beach	VA	23451	**888-989-7788**	757-437-5565
Virginia Beach Resort Hotel & Conference Ctr 2800 Shore Dr	Virginia Beach	VA	23451	**800-468-2722**	757-481-9000
Virginia Crossings Resort 1000 Virginia Ctr Pkwy	Glen Allen	VA	23059	**888-444-6553**	804-727-1400
Williamsburg Inn 136 E Francis St	Williamsburg	VA	23185	**800-447-8679**	757-229-1000

Washington

Name / Address	City	State	Zip	Toll-Free	Phone
Alderbrook Resort & Spa 7101 E SR-106	Union	WA	98592	**800-622-9370**	360-898-2200
Campbell's Resort 104 W Woodin Ave PO Box 278	Chelan	WA	98816	**800-553-8225**	509-682-2561
Desert Canyon Golf Resort 1030 Desert Canyon Blvd	Orondo	WA	98843	**800-258-4173**	509-784-1111
Freestone Inn at Wilson Ranch 31 Early Winters Dr	Mazama	WA	98833	**800-639-3809**	509-996-3906
Lake Quinault Lodge 345 S Shore Rd	Quinault	WA	98575	**800-562-6672**	360-288-2900

	City	State	Zip	Toll-Free	Phone
Little Creek Casino Resort 91 W State Rt 108	Shelton	WA	98584	**800-667-7711**	360-427-7711
Polynesian Resort, The 615 Ocean Shores Blvd NW	Ocean Shores	WA	98569	**800-562-4836**	360-289-3361
Resort Semiahmoo 9565 Semiahmoo Pkwy	Blaine	WA	98230	**855-917-3767**	360-318-2000
Rosario Resort & Spa 1400 Rosario Rd	Eastsound	WA	98245	**800-562-8820**	360-376-2222
Salish Lodge & Spa 6501 Railroad Ave DE	Snoqualmie	WA	98065	**800-272-5474**	425-888-2556
Sun Mountain Lodge 604 Patterson Lk Rd PO Box 1000	Winthrop	WA	98862	**800-572-0493**	509-996-2211

West Virginia

	City	State	Zip	Toll-Free	Phone
Canaan Valley Resort & Conference Ctr 230 Main Lodge Rd	Davis	WV	26260	**800-622-4121**	304-866-4121
Glade Springs Resort 255 Resort Dr	Daniels	WV	25832	**866-562-8054**	
Greenbrier, The 300 W Main St	White Sulphur Springs	WV	24986	**800-453-4858**	304-536-1110
Lakeview Golf Resort & Spa 1 Lakeview Dr	Morgantown	WV	26508	**800-624-8300**	304-594-1111
Oglebay Resort & Conference Ctr 465 Lodge Dr Oglebay Pk	Wheeling	WV	26003	**800-624-6988**	304-243-4000
Pipestem Resort State Park PO Box 150	Pipestem	WV	25979	**800-225-5982**	304-466-1800
Snowshoe Mountain Resort 10 Snowshoe Dr	Snowshoe	WV	26209	**877-441-4386**	304-572-1000
Stonewall Resort 940 Resort Dr	Roanoke	WV	26447	**888-278-8150**	304-269-7400
Woods Resort & Conference Ctr Mountain Lk Rd PO Box 5	Hedgesville	WV	25427	**800-248-2222**	

Wisconsin

	City	State	Zip	Toll-Free	Phone
Abbey Resort & Fontana Spa 269 Fontana Blvd	Fontana	WI	53125	**800-709-1323**	262-275-9000
American Club, The 419 Highland Dr	Kohler	WI	53044	**800-344-2838**	920-457-8000
Chanticleer Inn 1458 E Dollar Lk Rd	Eagle River	WI	54521	**800-752-9193**	715-479-4486
Chula Vista Resort 2501 River Rd	Wisconsin Dells	WI	53965	**800-388-4782**	608-254-8366
Devil's Head Resort & Convention Ctr S 6330 Bluff Rd	Merrimac	WI	53561	**800-472-6670**	608-493-2251
Fox Hills Resort & Convention Ctr 250 W Church St	Mishicot	WI	54228	**800-950-7615**	920-755-2376
Grand Geneva Resort & Spa 7036 Grand Geneva Way	Lake Geneva	WI	53147	**800-558-3417**	262-248-8811
Heidel House Resort 643 Illinois Ave	Green Lake	WI	54941	**800-444-2812**	920-294-3344
Holiday Acres Resort 4060 S Shore Dr PO Box 460	Rhinelander	WI	54501	**800-261-1500**	715-369-1500
Lake Lawn Resort 2400 E Geneva St	Delavan	WI	53115	**800-338-5253**	262-728-7950
Landmark Resort 7643 Hillside Rd	Egg Harbor	WI	54209	**800-273-7877**	920-868-3205
Olympia Resort & Spa 1350 Royale Mile Rd	Oconomowoc	WI	53066	**800-558-9573**	262-369-4999
Osthoff Resort, The 101 Osthoff Ave PO Box 151	Elkhart Lake	WI	53020	**800-876-3399**	920-876-3366
Tundra Lodge Resort & Waterpark 865 Lombardi Ave	Green Bay	WI	54304	**877-886-3725**	920-405-8700

Wyoming

	City	State	Zip	Toll-Free	Phone
Amangani Resort 1535 NE Butte Rd	Jackson	WY	83001	**877-734-7333**	307-734-7333
Aramark Parks & Destinations 27655 Hwy 26 & 287	Moran	WY	83013	**866-278-4245**	307-543-2847
Four Seasons Resort Jackson Hole 7680 Granite Loop Rd PO Box 544	Teton Village	WY	83025	**800-914-5110**	307-732-5000
Grand Targhee Resort 3300 E Ski Hill Rd	Alta	WY	83414	**800-827-4433**	307-353-2300
Grand Teton Lodge Co 5 Miles N Hwy 89 PO Box 250 *Resv	Moran	WY	83013	**800-628-9988***	307-543-2811
Jackson Hole Mountain Resort 3395 Cody Ln PO Box 290	Teton Village	WY	83025	**800-450-0477**	307-733-2292
Jackson HoleResort Lodging 3200 W McCollister Dr PO Box 510	Teton Village	WY	83025	**800-443-8613**	307-733-3990
Jackson Lake Lodge PO Box 250	Moran	WY	83013	**800-628-9988**	307-543-2811
Rusty Parrot Lodge & Spa PO Box 1657	Jackson	WY	83001	**800-458-2004**	307-733-2000
Snow King Resort 400 E Snow King Ave Jackson Hole	Jackson	WY	83001	**800-522-5464**	307-733-5200

668 RESTAURANT COMPANIES

SEE ALSO Food Service ; Franchises ; Ice Cream & Dairy Stores ; Bakeries

	City	State	Zip	Toll-Free	Phone
Al Copeland Investments Inc 1001 Harimaw Ct S	Metairie	LA	70001	**800-401-0401**	504-830-1000
BAB Inc 500 Lk Cook Rd Ste 475 *OTC: BABB*	Deerfield	IL	60015	**800-251-6101**	
Beef O'Bradys Inc 5660 W Cypress St Ste A	Tampa	FL	33607	**800-728-8878**	813-226-2333
Bickford's Family Restaurants Inc 37 Oak St Ext	Brockton	MA	02301	**800-969-5653**	
Bill Miller Bar-B-Q Inc 2750 Bill Miller Ln PO Box 839925	San Antonio	TX	78223	**800-339-3111**	210-225-4461
Bob Evans Farms Inc 3776 S High St *NASDAQ: BOBE*	Columbus	OH	43207	**800-939-2338**	
Bojangles' Restaurants Inc 9432 Southern Pine Blvd	Charlotte	NC	28273	**800-366-9921**	704-335-1804
Boston Market Corp 14103 Denver W Pkwy *General	Golden	CO	80401	**866-977-9090***	303-278-9500
Boston Pizza Restaurants LP 1501 LBJ Fwy Ste 450	Dallas	TX	75234	**866-277-8721**	972-484-9022
BRAVO | BRIO Restaurant Group 777 Goodale Blvd Ste 100	Columbus	OH	43212	**888-452-7286**	614-326-7944
Brinker International Inc 6820 LBJ Fwy *NYSE: EAT*	Dallas	TX	75240	**800-983-4637**	972-980-9917
Brock & Company Inc 257 Great Vly Pkwy	Malvern	PA	19355	**866-468-2783**	610-647-5656
Bubba Gump Shrimp Co LLC 2501 Seawall Blvd	Galveston	TX	77550	**800-552-6379**	409-766-4952
Buck's Pizza Franchising Corp Inc PO Box 405	Du Bois	PA	15801	**800-310-8848**	
Burger King Corp 5505 Blue Lagoon Dr	Miami	FL	33126	**866-394-2493**	305-378-3000
Burgerville USA 109 W 17th St	Vancouver	WA	98660	**888-827-8369**	360-694-1521
Captain D's LLC 624 Grassmere Park Dr Ste 30	Nashville	TN	37211	**800-314-4819**	615-391-5461
Carlson Restaurants 4201 Marsh Ln	Carrollton	TX	75007	**800-374-3297**	972-662-5400
Cask 'n' Cleaver 8689 Ninth St	Rancho Cucamonga	CA	91730	**800-995-4452**	909-981-5771
CEC Entertainment Inc 3903 W Airport Frwy *NYSE: CEC*	Irving	TX	75062	**888-778-7193**	972-258-8507
Charley's Grilled Subs 2500 Farmers Dr Ste 140	Columbus	OH	43235	**800-437-8325**	614-923-4700
Checkers Drive-In Restaurants Inc 4300 W Cypress St Ste 600	Tampa	FL	33607	**800-800-8072**	813-283-7000
Cousins Submarines Inc N83 W13400 Leon Rd	Menomonee Falls	WI	53051	**800-238-9736**	262-253-7700
Cracker Barrel Old Country Store Inc PO Box 787 *NASDAQ: CBRL*	Lebanon	TN	37088	**800-333-9566**	615-444-5533
D'Angelo Sandwich Shops 600 Providence Hwy	Dedham	MA	02026	**800-727-2446**	781-461-1200
Del Taco Inc 25521 Commercentre Dr Ste 200 *Cust Svc	Lake Forest	CA	92630	**800-852-7204***	949-462-9300
Denny's Corp 203 E Main St *NASDAQ: DENN* ■ *Cust Svc	Spartanburg	SC	29319	**800-733-6697***	864-597-8000
Domino's Pizza Inc 30 Frank Lloyd Wright Dr *NYSE: DPZ*	Ann Arbor	MI	48106	**800-253-8182**	734-930-3030
Donatos Pizza 935 Taylor Stn Rd	Columbus	OH	43230	**800-366-2867**	
Eat'n Park Hospitality Group Inc 285 E Waterfront Dr PO Box 3000	Homestead	PA	15120	**800-947-4033**	412-461-2000
Edo Japan International Inc 32 St SE Ste 4838	Calgary	AB	T2B2S6	**888-336-9888**	403-215-8800
El Fenix Corp 11075 Harry Hines Blvd	Dallas	TX	75229	**877-591-1918**	972-241-2171
El Pollo Loco 3535 Harbor Blvd Ste 100	Costa Mesa	CA	92626	**877-375-4968**	714-599-5000
Famous Dave's of America Inc 12701 Whitewater Dr Ste 200 *NASDAQ: DAVE*	Minnetonka	MN	55343	**800-929-4040**	952-294-1300
Figaro's Italian Pizza Inc 1500 Liberty St SE Ste 160	Salem	OR	97302	**888-344-2767**	503-371-9318
Flamers Charbroiled Hamburgers 1515 International Pkwy Ste 2013	Heathrow	FL	32746	**866-749-4889**	407-574-8363
Fox's Pizza Den Inc 4425 Willaim Penn Hwy	Murrysville	PA	15668	**800-899-3697**	724-733-7888
Friendly Ice Cream Corp 1855 Boston Rd	Wilbraham	MA	01095	**800-966-9970**	413-731-4000
Frisch's Restaurants Inc 2800 Gilbert Ave *NYSE: FRS*	Cincinnati	OH	45206	**800-873-3633**	513-961-2660
Frullati Cafe & Bakery 9311 E Via de Ventura	Scottsdale	AZ	85258	**866-452-4252**	480-362-4800
Garden Fresh Restaurant Corp 15822 Bernardo Ctr Dr Ste A	San Diego	CA	92127	**800-874-1600**	858-675-1600
Gates Bar-B-Q 4621 Paseo Blvd	Kansas City	MO	64110	**800-662-7427**	816-923-0900
Gold Star Chili 650 Lunken Pk Dr	Cincinnati	OH	45226	**800-643-0465**	513-231-4541
Good Eats Inc 12200 Stemmons Fwy Ste 100	Dallas	TX	75234	**800-275-1337**	972-241-5500
Great Steak & Potato Co 9311 E Via de Ventura	Scottsdale	AZ	85258	**866-452-4252**	480-362-4800
Hacienda Mexican Restaurants 1501 N Ironwood Dr	South Bend	IN	46635	**800-541-3227**	
Hard Rock Cafe International Inc 6100 Old Pk Ln	Orlando	FL	32835	**888-519-6683**	407-445-7625
Hillstone Restaurant Group 147 S Beverly Dr	Beverly Hills	CA	90212	**800-230-9787**	310-385-7343
Hoss's Steak & Sea House 170 Patchway Rd	Duncansville	PA	16635	**800-992-4677**	814-695-7600
Hot Dog on a Stick 5942 Priestly Dr	Carlsbad	CA	92008	**877-639-2361**	760-930-0456
IHOP Corp 450 N Brand Blvd	Glendale	CA	91203	**866-444-5144**	818-240-6055
Il Fornaio America Corp 770 Tamalpais Dr Ste 400	Corte Madera	CA	94925	**888-454-6246**	415-945-0500
In-N-Out Burger Inc 4199 Campus Dr 9th Fl *Cust Svc	Irvine	CA	92612	**800-786-1000***	949-509-6200

Name / Address	City	State	Zip	Toll-Free	Phone
International Dairy Queen Corp 7505 Metro Blvd	Minneapolis	MN	55439	**866-793-7582**	952-830-0200
J Alexander's Corp 3401 W End Ave Ste 260 *NASDAQ: JAX*	Nashville	TN	37203	**888-528-1991**	615-269-1900
Jack in the Box Inc 9330 Balboa Ave *NASDAQ: JACK*	San Diego	CA	92123	**800-955-5225**	858-571-2121
Jack's Family Restaurants Inc 2831 19th St S	Homewood	AL	35209	**888-795-2707**	205-879-9321
Jan Cos 35 Sockanosset Cross Rd	Cranston	RI	02920	**888-693-6844**	401-946-4000
Jerry's Systems Inc 702 Russell Ave Ste 306	Gaithersburg	MD	20877	**800-990-9176**	
Jimmy John's Franchise Inc 2212 Fox Dr	Champaign	IL	61820	**800-546-6904**	217-356-9900
Joey's Only Seafood Franchising Corp 514-42nd Ave SE	Calgary	AB	T2G1Y6	**800-661-2123**	403-243-4584
K-Mac Enterprises Inc PO Box 6538	Fort Smith	AR	72906	**800-947-9277**	479-646-2053
KFC Corp 1441 Gardiner Ln	Louisville	KY	40213	**800-225-5532**	920-923-2321
Kimpton Hotel & Restaurant Group LLC 222 Kearny St Ste 200	San Francisco	CA	94108	**800-546-7866**	415-397-5572
Kona Grill Inc 7150 E Camelback Rd Ste 220 *NASDAQ: KONA*	Scottsdale	AZ	85251	**866-328-5662**	480-922-8100
La Salsa Fresh Mexican Grill 320 Commerce Ste 100	Irvine	CA	92602	**866-452-7257**	949-270-8900
Landry's Restaurants Inc 1510 W Loop S	Houston	TX	77027	**800-552-6379**	713-850-1010
Lawry's Restaurants Inc 234 E Colorado Blvd Ste 500	Pasadena	CA	91101	**888-552-9797**	626-440-5234
Little Caesars Inc 2211 Woodward Ave	Detroit	MI	48201	**800-722-3727**	313-983-6409
LongHorn Steakhouse 1000 Darden Ctr Dr	Orlando	FL	32837	**888-221-0642**	
Luby's Inc 13111 NW Fwy Ste 600 *NYSE: LUB*	Houston	TX	77040	**800-886-4600**	713-329-6800
Malnati Organization Inc 3685 Woodhead Dr	Northbrook	IL	60062	**800-568-8646**	847-562-1814
Marie Callender Restaurant & Bakery 27101 Puerta Real Ste 260	Mission Viejo	CA	92691	**800-776-7437**	
Maui Tacos International Inc 2001 Palmer Ave. Ste 105	Larchmont	NY	10538	**866-388-3758**	
McDonald's Corp 1 McDonald's Plz *NYSE: MCD*	Oak Brook	IL	60523	**800-244-6227**	630-623-3000
McDonald's Restaurants of Canada Ltd 1 McDonald's Pl	Toronto	ON	M3C3L4	**888-424-4622**	416-443-1000
Melting Pot Restaurants Inc 8810 Twin Lakes Blvd	Tampa	FL	33614	**800-783-0867**	813-881-0055
Monical Pizza Corp 530 N Kinzie Ave	Bradley	IL	60915	**800-929-3227**	815-937-1890
Mr Goodcents Franchise Systems Inc 8997 Commerce Dr	DeSoto	KS	66018	**800-648-2368**	
Mr Hero Restaurants 7010 Engle Rd Ste 100	Middleburg Heights	OH	44130	**888-860-5082**	440-625-3080
Mr Jim's Pizza Inc *Franchise Service Ctr* 2521 Pepperwood St	Farmers Branch	TX	75234	**800-583-5960**	972-267-5467
NPC International Inc 7300 W 129th St	Overland Park	KS	66213	**866-299-1148**	913-327-5555
Orange Julius of America 7505 Metro Blvd	Minneapolis	MN	55439	**866-793-7582**	952-830-0200
Palm Management Corp 1730 Rhode Island Ave NW Ste 900	Washington	DC	20036	**800-388-7256**	202-775-7256
Panda Express 1717 Walnut Grove Ave	Rosemead	CA	91770	**800-877-8988**	626-312-5401
Panda Restaurant Group Inc 1683 Walnut Grove Ave	Rosemead	CA	91770	**800-877-8988**	626-799-9898
Papa Gino's Inc 600 Providence Hwy	Dedham	MA	02026	**800-727-2446**	781-461-1200
Pappas Restaurants Inc 13939 NW Fwy	Houston	TX	77040	**877-277-2748**	713-869-0151
Pappas Seafood House 13939 NW Fwy	Houston	TX	77040	**877-277-2748**	713-869-0151
Pat O'Brien's International Inc 718 St Peter St	New Orleans	LA	70116	**800-597-4823**	504-525-4823
Patina Group 12700 Center Ct Dr S 9th Fl	Cerritos	CA	90703	**866-972-8462**	
Penguin Point Franchise Systems Inc 2691 E US 30	Warsaw	IN	46580	**800-577-5755**	574-267-3107
Perkins Restaurant & Bakery 6075 Poplar Ave Ste 800	Memphis	TN	38119	**800-877-7375**	901-766-6400
PF Chang's China Bistro Inc 7676 E Pinnacle Peak Rd *NASDAQ: PFCB*	Scottsdale	AZ	85255	**866-732-4264**	480-888-3000
Piccadilly Circus Pizza 1007 Okoboji Ave PO Box 188	Milford	IA	51351	**800-338-4340**	
Pizza Factory Inc 49430 Rd 426	Oakhurst	CA	93644	**800-654-4840**	559-683-3377
Pizza Inn Inc 3551 Plano Pkwy *NASDAQ: RAVE*	The Colony	TX	75056	**877-574-9924**	
Pizza Pro Inc 2107 N Second St PO Box 1285	Cabot	AR	72023	**800-777-7554**	501-605-1175
Pizza Ranch Inc 204 19th St SE	Orange City	IA	51041	**800-321-3401**	
Pretzelmaker 1346 Oakbrook Dr Ste 170	Norcross	GA	30093	**877-639-2361**	
Quality Dining Inc 4220 Edison Lakes Pkwy	Mishawaka	IN	46545	**800-589-3820**	574-271-4600
Quiznos Corp 7595 Technology Way Ste 200	Denver	CO	80237	**866-486-2783**	720-359-3300
Restaurant Developers Corp 7010 Engle Rd Ste 100	Cleveland	OH	44130	**888-860-5082**	440-625-3080
Restaurants Unlimited Inc 411 First Ave S Ste 200	Seattle	WA	98104	**877-855-6106**	206-634-0550
Rib Crib Corp 4535 S Harvard Ave	Tulsa	OK	74135	**800-275-9677**	918-712-7427
Rocky Rococo 105 E Wisconsin Ave	Oconomowoc	WI	53066	**800-888-7625**	262-569-5580
Rubio's Restaurants Inc 1902 Wright Pl Ste 300	Carlsbad	CA	92008	**800-354-4199**	760-929-8226
Russ' Restaurants Inc 390 E Eigth St	Holland	MI	49423	**800-521-1778**	616-396-6571
Ruth's Hospitality Group Inc 1030 W Canton Ave Ste 100 *NASDAQ: RUTH* ■ *Sales	Winter Park	FL	32789	**800-544-0808***	407-333-7440
Sagebrush Steakhouse 129 Fast Ln	Mooresville	NC	28117	**877-704-5939**	704-660-5939
Shari's Restaurant & Pies 9400 SW Gemini Dr	Beaverton	OR	97008	**800-433-5334**	503-605-4299
Shoney's Restaurants Inc 1717 Elm Hill Pk Ste B1	Nashville	TN	37210	**800-708-3558**	615-231-2333
Silver Diner Inc 12276 Rockville Pk	Rockville	MD	20852	**866-561-0518**	301-770-0333
Sizzler Restaurants 25910 Acero Rd Ste 350	Mission Viejo	CA	92691	**855-895-9703**	
Snappy Tomato Pizza Co 6111 A Burgundy Hill Dr	Burlington	KY	41005	**888-463-7627**	859-525-4680
Sonic Drive-in Restaurants 300 Johnny Bench Dr	Oklahoma City	OK	73104	**877-828-7868**	405-225-5000
Steak N Shake Co 3810 W Washington Holt Rd	Indianapolis	IN	46241	**877-785-6745**	317-241-0483
Stuckey's Corp 8555 16th St Ste 850	Silver Spring	MD	20910	**800-423-6171**	301-585-8222
Summerwood Corp 14 Balligomingo Rd	Conshohocken	PA	19428	**800-760-0950**	610-520-1000
Taco Cabana Inc 8918 Tesoro Dr Ste 200	San Antonio	TX	78217	**800-580-8668**	210-804-0990
Taco Time International Inc 9311 E Via de Venutra	Scottsdale	AZ	85258	**866-452-4252**	480-362-4800
Tacoma Inc 328 E Church St	Martinsville	VA	24112	**800-352-9417**	276-666-9417
Tavistock Restaurants LLC 4705 S Apopka Vineland Rd Ste 210	Orlando	FL	32819	**800-424-2753**	407-909-7101
Texas Roadhouse Inc 6040 Dutchmans Ln Ste 400 *NASDAQ: TXRH*	Louisville	KY	40205	**800-839-7623**	502-426-9984
Tim Hortons Inc 874 Sinclair Rd *NYSE: THI*	Oakville	ON	L6K2Y1	**888-601-1616**	905-845-6511
Tubbys Grilled Submarines 31920 Groesbeck Hwy	Fraser	MI	48026	**800-752-0644**	
Tumbleweed Inc 2301 River Rd	Louisville	KY	40206	**866-719-3892**	502-893-0323
Valentino's 2601 S 70th St	Lincoln	NE	68506	**888-289-8257**	402-434-9350
Village Inn 400 W 48th Ave	Denver	CO	80216	**800-800-3644**	303-296-2121
Ward's Food Systems Inc 5133 Lincoln Rd Ext	Hattiesburg	MS	39402	**800-748-9273**	601-268-9273
Weathervane Seafood Restaurant 306 US Rt 1	Kittery	ME	03904	**800-914-1774**	207-439-0330
Yoshinoya Beef Bowl 991 Knox St	Torrance	CA	90502	**800-576-8017**	310-527-6060
Yum! Brands Inc 1441 Gardiner Ln *NYSE: YUM*	Louisville	KY	40213	**800-225-5532**	502-874-8300
Zyng Inc RPO Atwater PO Box 72108	Montreal	QC	H3J2Z6	**888-328-9964**	514-288-8800

669 RESTAURANTS (INDIVIDUAL)

SEE ALSO Restaurant Companies ; Shopping/Dining/Entertainment Districts
Individual restaurants are organized by city names within state and province groupings. (Canadian provinces are interfiled among the US states, in alphabetical order.)

Alabama

Name / Address	City	State	Zip	Toll-Free	Phone
Dreamland BBQ 1427 14th Ave S	Birmingham	AL	35205	**800-752-0544**	205-933-2133

Alaska

Name / Address	City	State	Zip	Toll-Free	Phone
Best Western Grandma's Feather Bed 9300 Glacier Hwy	Juneau	AK	99801	**888-781-5005**	907-789-5005
Gold Room 127 N Franklin St	Juneau	AK	99801	**800-544-0970**	907-586-2660

Alberta

Name / Address	City	State	Zip	Toll-Free	Phone
Normand's 11639 A Jasper Ave	Edmonton	AB	T5K2S7	**866-308-4438**	780-482-2600

Arizona

Name / Address	City	State	Zip	Toll-Free	Phone
Grill at Hacienda del Sol 5501 N Hacienda del Sol Rd	Tucson	AZ	85718	**800-728-6514**	520-529-3500
Kiss the Cook Restaurant 72 Church St	Glendale	AZ	85301	**888-658-5477**	802-863-4226
L'Auberge de Sedona 301 L'Auberge Ln	Sedona	AZ	86336	**855-905-5745**	928-282-1661
T Cook's 5200 E Camelback Rd	Phoenix	AZ	85018	**800-672-6011**	602-808-0766

Arkansas

Name / Address	City	State	Zip	Toll-Free	Phone
McClard's Bar-B-Q 505 Albert Pike Rd	Hot Springs	AR	71901	**866-622-5273**	501-623-9665

California

Name / Address	City	State	ZIP	Toll-Free	Phone
Anaheim Marriott 700 W Convention Way	Anaheim	CA	92802	**800-845-5279**	714-750-8000
Baja Fresh 320 Commerce Ste 100	Irvine	CA	92602	**877-225-2373**	949-270-8900
Cafe Fina 47 Fisherman's Wharf Ste 1	Monterey	CA	93940	**800-843-3462**	831-372-5200
California Grill 11999 Harbor Blvd Hyatt Regency Orange County	Garden Grove	CA	92840	**800-233-1234**	714-740-6047
Chinois on Main 2709 Main St	Santa Monica	CA	90405	**888-646-3387**	310-392-9025
Duane's 3649 Mission Inn Ave	Riverside	CA	92501	**800-843-7755**	951-784-0300
Europa Restaurant 1620 S Indian Trl	Palm Springs	CA	92264	**800-245-2314**	760-327-2314
Hyatt Regency Huntington Beach Resort & Spa 21500 Pacific Coast Hwy	Huntington Beach	CA	92648	**800-633-7313**	714-698-1234
Lawry's the Prime Rib 100 N La Cienega Blvd	Beverly Hills	CA	90211	**877-529-7984**	310-652-2827
Marine Room, The 2000 Spindrift Dr	La Jolla	CA	92037	**866-644-2351**	858-459-7222
Marriott International Inc 11966 El Camino Real	San Diego	CA	92130	**888-236-2427**	
Silks 222 Sansome St	San Francisco	CA	94104	**800-526-6566**	415-986-2020
Sir Winston's Restaurant & Lounge 1126 Queens Hwy	Long Beach	CA	90802	**877-342-0738**	562-435-3511
Westgate Hotel, The 1055 Second Ave	San Diego	CA	92101	**800-522-1564**	619-238-1818

Colorado

Name / Address	City	State	ZIP	Toll-Free	Phone
Briarhurst Manor 404 Manitou Ave	Manitou Springs	CO	80829	**877-685-1448**	719-685-1864
Flying W Ranch Inc 3330 Chuckwagon Rd	Colorado Springs	CO	80919	**800-232-3599**	719-598-4000
Greenbriar Inn, The 8735 N Foothills Hwy	Boulder	CO	80302	**800-253-1474**	303-440-7979
Thyme on the Creek 1345 28th St	Boulder	CO	80302	**866-866-8086**	303-998-3835

Delaware

Name / Address	City	State	ZIP	Toll-Free	Phone
Green Room at the Hotel duPont 11th & Market St	Wilmington	DE	19801	**800-441-9019**	302-594-3100
Melting Pot, The 1601 Concord Pike Ste 43-47 Independence Mall	Wilmington	DE	19803	**800-783-0867**	302-652-6358

District Of Columbia

Name / Address	City	State	ZIP	Toll-Free	Phone
Charlie Palmer Steak 101 Constitution Ave NW	Washington	DC	20001	**877-632-7800**	202-547-8100
Loews Madison Hotel 1177 15th St NW	Washington	DC	20005	**888-825-2436**	202-862-1600

Florida

Name / Address	City	State	ZIP	Toll-Free	Phone
Angell & Phelps Chocolate Factory 154 S Beach St	Daytona Beach	FL	32114	**800-969-2634**	386-252-6531
Bahama Breeze 8849 International Dr	Orlando	FL	32819	**877-500-9715**	407-248-2499
Boheme, The 325 S Orange Ave	Orlando	FL	32801	**866-663-0024**	407-313-9000
Dave & Buster's 3000 Oakwood Blvd	Hollywood	FL	33020	**844-515-5157**	954-923-5505
Echo 230A Sunrise Ave	Palm Beach	FL	33480	**855-435-0061**	
Islamorada Fish Co 81532 Overseas Hwy PO Box 283	Islamorada	FL	33036	**800-258-2559**	
Joe's Stone Crab 11 Washington Ave	Miami Beach	FL	33139	**800-780-2722**	305-673-0365
Lombardi's 401 Biscayne Blvd	Miami	FL	33132	**888-286-3792**	
Melting Pot of Pensacola, The 418 Gregory St Ste 500	Pensacola	FL	32501	**800-783-0867**	850-438-4030
Melting Pot of Tampa, The 13164 N Dale Mabry Hwy	Tampa	FL	33618	**800-783-0867**	813-962-6936
Palm 5800 Universal Blvd Hard Rock Hotel	Orlando	FL	32819	**866-333-7256**	407-503-7256

Georgia

Name / Address	City	State	ZIP	Toll-Free	Phone
Cafe, The 3434 Peachtree Rd NE Ritz-Carlton Buckhead	Atlanta	GA	30326	**800-241-3333**	404-237-2700
Country's Barbecue 2016 12th Ave *General	Columbus	GA	31901	**800-285-4267***	706-327-7702
Olde Pink House 23 Abercorn St	Savannah	GA	31401	**800-554-1187**	912-232-4286

Hawaii

Name / Address	City	State	ZIP	Toll-Free	Phone
Bali Steak & Seafood 2005 Kalia Rd	Honolulu	HI	96815	**800-445-8667**	808-949-4321

Illinois

Name / Address	City	State	ZIP	Toll-Free	Phone
Giovanni's Restaurant & Convention Ctr 610 N Bell School Rd	Rockford	IL	61107	**877-926-8300**	815-398-6411

Indiana

Name / Address	City	State	ZIP	Toll-Free	Phone
Circle City Bar & Grille 350 W Maryland St	Indianapolis	IN	46225	**877-640-7666**	317-405-6100
LaSalle Grill 115 W Colfax Ave	South Bend	IN	46601	**800-382-9323**	574-288-1155
Marker, The 2544 Executive Dr	Indianapolis	IN	46241	**877-999-3223**	
Melting Pot of Indianapolis, The 5650 E 86th St Ste A	Indianapolis	IN	46250	**800-783-0867**	317-841-3601
Scholars Inn Gourmet Cafe 717 N College Ave	Bloomington	IN	47404	**800-765-3466**	812-332-1892

Kentucky

Name / Address	City	State	ZIP	Toll-Free	Phone
Gratz Park Inn 120 W Second St	Lexington	KY	40507	**800-752-4166**	859-231-1777

Louisiana

Name / Address	City	State	ZIP	Toll-Free	Phone
Arnaud's 813 Bienville St	New Orleans	LA	70112	**866-230-8895**	504-523-5433

Maryland

Name / Address	City	State	ZIP	Toll-Free	Phone
Coral Reef Restaurant 1701 Atlantic Ave	Ocean City	MD	21842	**866-627-8483**	410-289-2612
Fager's Island Restaurant 201 60th St	Ocean City	MD	21842	**855-432-4377**	410-524-5500
Famous Dave's Barbeque 181 Jennifer Rd	Annapolis	MD	21401	**877-833-9335**	410-224-2207
La Fontaine Bleue Inc 7514 S Ritchie Hwy	Glen Burnie	MD	21061	**877-778-6863**	410-760-4115
Melting Pot of Annapolis, The 2348 Solomons Island Rd	Annapolis	MD	21401	**800-783-0867**	410-266-8004
Ocean City Maryland Hotels 6600 Coastal Hwy	Ocean City	MD	21842	**800-837-3588**	410-524-5252
Red Hot & Blue Restaurants Inc 200 Old Mill Bottom Rd S	Annapolis	MD	21401	**888-509-7100**	410-626-7427

Massachusetts

Name / Address	City	State	ZIP	Toll-Free	Phone
Bristol, The 200 Boylston St	Boston	MA	02116	**800-819-5053**	617-338-4400
Capital Grille 900 Boylston St	Boston	MA	02115	**866-518-9113**	
Colonial House Inn 277 Main St Rt 6A	Yarmouth Port	MA	02675	**800-999-3416**	508-362-4348
KO Prime 90 Tremont St	Boston	MA	02108	**866-906-9090**	617-772-0202
Palm, The 200 Dartmouth St	Boston	MA	02116	**866-333-7256**	617-867-9292
Red Inn 15 Commercial St	Provincetown	MA	02657	**866-473-3466**	508-487-7334
Water Street 131 N Water St	Edgartown	MA	02539	**800-225-6005**	508-627-7000

Michigan

Name / Address	City	State	ZIP	Toll-Free	Phone
English Inn, The 677 S Michigan Rd	Eaton Rapids	MI	48827	**800-858-0598**	517-663-2500
Hard Rock Cafe 45 Monroe St	Detroit	MI	48226	**888-519-6683**	313-964-7625

Minnesota

Name / Address	City	State	ZIP	Toll-Free	Phone
Angie's Cantina 11 E Buchanan St	Duluth	MN	55802	**800-706-7672**	218-727-6117
Fitger's Brewery Complex 600 E Superior St	Duluth	MN	55802	**888-348-4377**	218-722-8826
Grandma's Saloon & Grill 522 Lake Ave S	Duluth	MN	55802	**800-706-7672**	218-727-4192
Lindey's Prime Steak House 3600 N Snelling Ave	Arden Hills	MN	55112	**866-491-0538**	651-633-9813

Mississippi

Name / Address	City	State	ZIP	Toll-Free	Phone
Eat With Us PO Box 1368	Columbus	MS	39703	**888-222-9550**	662-327-6982

Missouri

Name / Address	City	State	ZIP	Toll-Free	Phone
Buckingham's Restaurant & Oasis 2820 W Hwy 76	Branson	MO	65616	**800-725-2236**	417-337-7777
Capitol Plaza Hotel 415 W McCarty St	Jefferson City	MO	65101	**800-338-8088**	573-635-1234
Chateau Grille 415 N State Hwy 265	Branson	MO	65616	**888-333-5253**	417-334-1161
Plaza View 245 N Wildwood Dr	Branson	MO	65616	**800-850-6646**	417-335-2798

Nevada

Name / Address	City	State	ZIP	Toll-Free	Phone
Atlantis Seafood Steakhouse 3800 S Virginia St Atlantis Casino Resort	Reno	NV	89502	**800-723-6500**	
Caesar's Palace 3570 Las Vegas Blvd S Caesar's Palace	Las Vegas	NV	89109	**800-634-6001**	702-731-7110

	City	St	ZIP	Toll-Free	Phone
Canaletto 3355 Las Vegas Blvd S	Las Vegas	NV	89109	**866-659-9643**	702-414-1000
Grotto Ristorante 129 E Fremont St	Las Vegas	NV	89101	**800-634-3454**	702-385-7111
Le Cirque 3600 Las Vegas Blvd S	Las Vegas	NV	89109	**888-987-6667**	702-693-7111
Lillie's Asian Cuisine 129 E Fremont St	Las Vegas	NV	89101	**800-634-3454**	702-385-7111
Michael's 9777 Las Vegas Blvd S	Las Vegas	NV	89183	**866-796-7111**	702-796-7111
Nob Hill 3799 Las Vegas Blvd S MGM Grand Hotel *Resv	Las Vegas	NV	89109	**800-929-1111***	702-891-1111
Osteria Del Circo 3600 Las Vegas Blvd S	Las Vegas	NV	89109	**866-259-7111**	888-987-6667
Romanza 2707 S Virginia St Peppermill Hotel Casino	Reno	NV	89502	**866-821-9996**	775-826-2121
Second Street Grill 200 E Fremont St	Las Vegas	NV	89101	**800-634-6460**	702-385-3232
Spago 3500 Las Vegas Blvd S Ste G1	Las Vegas	NV	89109	**800-241-3333**	702-369-6300
SW Steakhouse 3131 Las Vegas Blvd S	Las Vegas	NV	89109	**888-320-7123**	702-770-7000
Trattoria Del Lupo 3950 Las Vegas Blvd S	Las Vegas	NV	89119	**800-275-8273**	702-740-5522
Willy & Jose's Mexican Cantina 5111 Boulder Hwy	Las Vegas	NV	89122	**800-897-8696**	702-456-7777
Bedford Village Inn 2 Olde Bedford Way	Bedford	NH	03110	**800-852-1166**	603-472-2001
Gaucho's Churrascaria 62 Lowell St	Manchester	NH	03101	**866-669-9460**	603-669-9460

New Jersey

	City	St	ZIP	Toll-Free	Phone
Sea Blue 1 Borgata Way *Cust Svc	Atlantic City	NJ	08401	**877-786-9900***	609-317-1000

New Mexico

	City	St	ZIP	Toll-Free	Phone
Fuego 330 E Palace Ave *Sales	Santa Fe	NM	87501	**855-811-0050***	505-986-0000
Old House 309 W San Francisco St	Santa Fe	NM	87501	**800-955-4455**	505-988-4455

New York

	City	St	ZIP	Toll-Free	Phone
Aureole 135 W 42nd St	New York	NY	10036	**800-889-7188**	212-319-1660
BLT Prime 111 E 22nd St	New York	NY	10010	**800-855-2880**	212-995-8500
Desmond Albany Hotel, The 660 Albany-Shaker Rd	Albany	NY	12211	**800-448-3500**	518-869-8100
Frank & Teressa's Anchor Bar & Restaurant 651 Delaware Ave	Buffalo	NY	14202	**866-248-9623**	716-883-1134
Kai 20 Jay St Ste 530	Brooklyn	NY	11201	**888-832-7832**	718-250-4000
Salvatore's Italian Gardens 6461 Transit Rd	Depew	NY	14043	**877-456-4097**	716-683-7990

North Carolina

	City	St	ZIP	Toll-Free	Phone
Angus Barn 9401 Glenwood Ave	Raleigh	NC	27617	**800-277-2270**	919-781-2444
McCormick & Schmick's 200 S Tryon St	Charlotte	NC	28202	**800-552-6379**	704-377-0201
Melting Pot of Charlotte, The 901 S Kings Dr Ste 140B	Charlotte	NC	28204	**800-783-0867**	704-334-4400
Alumni Center, The 1241 University Dr N	Fargo	ND	58102	**800-279-8971**	701-231-6800

Ohio

	City	St	ZIP	Toll-Free	Phone
M at Miranova 2 Miranova PL Ste 100	Columbus	OH	43215	**877-491-1267**	614-629-0000
Palace, The 601 Vine St	Cincinnati	OH	45202	**800-942-9000**	513-381-6006
Tony Packo's 1902 Front St	Toledo	OH	43605	**866-472-2567**	419-691-1953

Ontario

	City	St	ZIP	Toll-Free	Phone
Courtyard Cafe 18 St Thomas St *Cust Svc	Toronto	ON	M5S3E7	**877-999-2767***	416-921-2921
D'Arcy McGee's Irish Pub 199 Four Valley Dr	Vaughan	ON	L4K0B8	**888-854-4402**	613-230-4433
Hemispheres Restaurant & Bistro 108 Chestnut St	Toronto	ON	M5G1R3	**800-668-6600**	416-599-8000
Sante Restaurant 45 Rideau St 2nd Fl	Ottawa	ON	K1N5W8	**877-241-8889**	613-241-7113

Oregon

	City	St	ZIP	Toll-Free	Phone
Jake's Famous Crawfish 401 SW 12th Ave SW Stark	Portland	OR	97205	**800-552-6379**	503-226-1419
McCormick & Schmick's Harborside 0309 SW Montgomery *Resv	Portland	OR	97201	**888-262-4386***	503-220-1865

Pennsylvania

	City	St	ZIP	Toll-Free	Phone
Cashtown Inn Restaurant 1325 Old Rt 30 PO Box 103	Cashtown	PA	17310	**800-367-1797**	717-334-9722
Gettysburg Hotel 1 Lincoln Sq Best Western Gettysburg Hotel	Gettysburg	PA	17325	**866-378-1797**	717-337-2000
Herr Tavern & Public House 900 Chambersburg Rd	Gettysburg	PA	17325	**800-362-9849**	717-334-4332
Petra 3602 W Lake Rd	Erie	PA	16505	**866-906-2931**	814-838-7197

Quebec

	City	St	ZIP	Toll-Free	Phone
Auberge du Tresor 20 Rue Sainte-Anne	Quebec	QC	G1R3X2	**800-566-1876**	418-694-1876
Laurie Raphael 117 Dalhousie St	Quebec	QC	G1K9C8	**877-876-4555**	418-692-4555
LOEWS HOTELS 667 Madison Ave	New York	NY	10065	**800-235-6397**	615-340-2000

Rhode Island

	City	St	ZIP	Toll-Free	Phone
Hemenway's Seafood Grille 121 S Main St	Providence	RI	02903	**888-759-5557**	401-351-8570
Spiced Pear 117 Memorial Blvd	Newport	RI	02840	**866-793-5664**	401-847-2244

South Carolina

	City	St	ZIP	Toll-Free	Phone
82 Queen 82 Queen St	Charleston	SC	29401	**800-849-0082**	843-723-7591
Grill 225 225 E Bay St	Charleston	SC	29401	**877-440-2250**	843-266-4222
Melting Pot of Columbia, The 1410 Colonial Life Blvd	Columbia	SC	29210	**800-783-0867**	803-731-8500
Middleton Place 4300 Ashley River Rd	Charleston	SC	29414	**800-782-3608**	843-556-6020
Salty Dog Cafe, The 232 S Sea Pines Dr	Hilton Head Island	SC	29928	**877-725-8936**	843-671-5199
Signe's Bakery & Cafe 93 Arrow Rd	Hilton Head Island	SC	29928	**866-807-4463**	843-785-9118
Trotters Restaurant 2008 Savannah Hwy	Charleston	SC	29401	**800-334-6660**	843-571-1000

Tennessee

	City	St	ZIP	Toll-Free	Phone
Bar-B-Q Shop, The 1782 Madison Ave	Memphis	TN	38104	**877-372-8237**	901-272-1277
Morton's The Steakhouse 618 Church St	Nashville	TN	37219	**800-297-3276**	615-259-4558

Texas

	City	St	ZIP	Toll-Free	Phone
Anaqua Grill 555 S Alamo St	San Antonio	TX	78205	**800-845-5279**	210-229-1000
Cafe Modern 3200 Darnell St	Fort Worth	TX	76107	**866-824-5566**	817-738-9215
Genghis Grill 18900 Dallas Pkwy Ste 150	Dallas	TX	75244	**888-436-4447**	
Hudson's on the Bend 3509 Ranch Rd 620 N	Austin	TX	78734	**800-996-7655**	512-266-1369
Kam's 4500 Montrose Blvd	Houston	TX	77006	**800-510-3663**	713-529-5057
Melting Pot of San Antonio, The 14855 Blanco Rd Ste 110	San Antonio	TX	78216	**800-783-0867**	210-479-6358
Noe Restaurant & Bar 4 Riverway	Houston	TX	77056	**800-809-6664**	713-871-8181
Palm Restaurant 6100 Westheimer Rd	Houston	TX	77057	**866-333-7256**	713-977-2544
Rainbow Lodge 2011 Ella Blvd	Houston	TX	77008	**866-861-8666**	713-861-8666
Spring Creek Barbeque 2340 W I- 20 Ste 100	Arlington	TX	76017	**888-467-0505**	817-467-0505
Texas Land & Cattle Steak House 9911 W IH- 10	San Antonio	TX	78230	**855-685-1622**	210-699-8744

Vermont

	City	St	ZIP	Toll-Free	Phone
Trader Duke's 1117 Williston Rd	South Burlington	VT	05403	**800-445-8667**	802-660-7523

Virginia

	City	St	ZIP	Toll-Free	Phone
Morrison House 116 S Alfred St	Alexandria	VA	22314	**866-834-6628**	703-838-8000
North Beach Bar & Grill 3107 Atlantic Ave	Virginia Beach	VA	23451	**800-292-3297**	757-491-1800
Georgian, The 411 University St	Seattle	WA	98101	**888-363-5022**	206-621-7889
Sorrento Hotel 900 Madison St	Seattle	WA	98104	**800-426-1265**	206-622-6400

West Virginia

	City	St	ZIP	Toll-Free	Phone
Tidewater Grill 1060 Charleston Town Ctr	Charleston	WV	25389	**888-456-3463**	304-345-2620
Whitewater Grille 200 Lee St E	Charleston	WV	25301	**800-845-5279**	304-353-3636

Wisconsin

	City	St	ZIP	Toll-Free	Phone
Admiralty Room 666 Wisconsin Ave	Madison	WI	53703	**800-922-5512**	608-256-9071

Name / Address	City	State	ZIP	Toll-Free	Phone
Crawdaddy's 1025 S Moorland Rd Ste 400	Brookfield	WI	53005	**800-727-9477**	414-778-2228
Packing House 900 E Layton Ave	Milwaukee	WI	53207	**800-727-9477**	414-483-5054

Wyoming

Name / Address	City	State	ZIP	Toll-Free	Phone
Bar-T-5 Covered Wagon Cook Out & Wild West Show 812 Cache Creek Dr	Jackson	WY	83001	**800-772-5386**	307-733-5386

670 RETIREMENT COMMUNITIES

SEE ALSO Long-Term Care Facilities

Listed here are senior communities where the majority of residents live independently but where nursing care and/or other personal care is available on-site. The listings in this category are organized alphabetically by state names.

Name / Address	City	State	ZIP	Toll-Free	Phone
Abbey Delray 2000 Lowson Blvd	Delray Beach	FL	33445	**888-791-9363**	561-454-2000
Ability Center of Greater Toledo Inc 5605 Monroe St	Sylvania	OH	43560	**866-885-5733**	419-885-5733
Arbor Acres 1240 Arbor Rd	Winston-Salem	NC	27104	**866-658-2724**	336-724-7921
Armed Forces Retirement Home - Gulfport 1800 Beach Dr	Gulfport	MS	39507	**800-422-9988**	
Army Residence Community 7400 Crestway	San Antonio	TX	78239	**800-725-0083**	210-646-5316
Asbury Methodist Village 201 Russell Ave	Gaithersburg	MD	20877	**800-327-2879**	301-216-4100
Atherton Baptist Homes 214 S Atlantic Blvd	Alhambra	CA	91801	**800-340-4178**	626-863-1224
Bermuda Village 142 Bermuda Village Dr *Mktg	Advance	NC	27006	**800-843-5433***	
Bethea Baptist Retirement Community 157 Home Ave	Darlington	SC	29532	**877-393-2867**	843-393-2867
Brittany Pointe Estates 1001 S Valley Forge Rd	Lansdale	PA	19446	**800-504-2287**	215-855-4109
Brookdale Senior Living Inc 111 Westwood Pl Ste 400	Brentwood	TN	37027	**866-785-9025**	615-221-2250
Cadbury Retirement Community 2150 Rt 38	Cherry Hill	NJ	08002	**800-422-3287**	856-667-4550
Carmel Valley Manor 8545 Carmel Vly Rd	Carmel	CA	93923	**800-544-5546**	831-624-1281
Carol Woods Retirement Community 750 Weaver Dairy Rd	Chapel Hill	NC	27514	**800-518-9333**	919-968-4511
Carolina Meadows 100 Carolina Meadows	Chapel Hill	NC	27517	**800-458-6756**	919-942-4014
Carroll Lutheran Village 300 St Luke Cir	Westminster	MD	21158	**877-848-0095**	410-848-0090
Charlestown Retirement Community (CCI) 715 Maiden Choice Ln	Catonsville	MD	21228	**800-917-8649**	410-242-2880
Clark-Lindsey Village 101 W Windsor Rd	Urbana	IL	61802	**800-998-2581**	217-344-2144
Cokesbury Village 726 Loveville Rd	Hockessin	DE	19707	**800-530-2377**	302-235-6000
Collington Episcopal Community 10450 Lottsford Rd	Mitchellville	MD	20721	**888-257-9468**	
Cornwall Manor 1 Boyd St	Cornwall	PA	17016	**800-222-2476**	717-273-2647
Covenant Village of Golden Valley 5800 St Croix Ave	Minneapolis	MN	55422	**877-224-5051**	763-546-6125
Covenant Village of Turlock 2125 N Olive Ave	Turlock	CA	95382	**800-485-7844**	209-216-5610
Crestwood Manor 50 Lacey Rd *General	Whiting	NJ	08759	**877-467-1652***	732-849-4900
Cross Keys Village 2990 Carlisle Pk PO Box 128 *Mktg	New Oxford	PA	17350	**888-624-8242***	717-624-5350
Culpeper Baptist Retirement Community 12425 Village Loop	Culpeper	VA	22701	**800-894-2411**	540-825-2411
Deerfield Episcopal Retirement Community 1617 Hendersonville Rd	Asheville	NC	28803	**800-284-1531**	828-274-1531
Edgewater Pointe Estates 23315 Blue Water Cir *General	Boca Raton	FL	33433	**888-339-2287***	561-391-6305
Elim Park Place 140 Cook Hill Rd	Cheshire	CT	06410	**800-994-1776**	203-272-3547
Epoch Senior Living 51 Sawyer Rd Ste 500	Waltham	MA	02453	**877-376-2475**	781-891-0777
Eskaton Village 3939 Walnut Ave	Carmichael	CA	95608	**800-300-3929**	916-974-2000
Essex Meadows 30 Bokum Rd	Essex	CT	06426	**866-721-4838**	860-767-7201
Evergreen Woods 88 Notch Hill Rd *General	North Branford	CT	06471	**866-413-6378***	203-488-8000
Evergreens, The 309 Bridgeboro Rd	Moorestown	NJ	08057	**877-673-8234**	856-439-2000
Fairhaven 435 W Starin Rd	Whitewater	WI	53190	**877-624-2298**	262-473-2140
First Community Village 1800 Riverside Dr	Columbus	OH	43212	**877-364-2570**	614-324-4455
Fleet Landing Retirement Community 1 Fleet Landing Blvd *General	Atlantic Beach	FL	32233	**877-591-6547***	904-246-9900
Florida Presbyterian Homes 16 Lk Hunter Dr	Lakeland	FL	33803	**866-294-3352**	863-688-5521
Forest at Duke 2701 Pickett Rd	Durham	NC	27705	**800-474-0258**	919-490-8000
Foxdale Village 500 E Marylyn Ave	State College	PA	16801	**800-253-4951**	814-272-2117
Franciscan Oaks 19 Pocono Rd	Denville	NJ	07834	**800-237-3330**	973-586-6000
Freedom Village 23442 El Toro Rd	Lake Forest	CA	92630	**800-584-8084**	949-472-4700
Friendship Manor 1209 21st Ave	Rock Island	IL	61201	**888-382-1222**	309-786-9667
Friendship Village Kalamazoo 1400 N Drake Rd	Kalamazoo	MI	49006	**800-613-3984**	269-381-0560
Friendship Village of Tempe 2645 E Southern Ave	Tempe	AZ	85282	**800-824-1112**	480-831-5000
Friendsview Retirement Community 1301 E Fulton St	Newberg	OR	97132	**866-307-4371**	503-538-3144
Ginger Cove 4000 River Crescent Dr	Annapolis	MD	21401	**800-299-2683**	410-266-7300
Glen Meadows 11630 Glen Arm Rd	Glen Arm	MD	21057	**800-630-4689**	
Golden Oaks Village 5801 N Oakwood Rd	Enid	OK	73703	**800-259-0914**	580-249-2600
Grand Lake Gardens 401 Santa Clara Ave	Oakland	CA	94610	**800-416-6091**	
Granite Farms Estates 1343 W Baltimore Pike	Media	PA	19063	**888-499-2287**	610-358-3440
Harbour's Edge 401 E Linton Blvd	Delray Beach	FL	33483	**888-417-9281**	561-272-7979
Harrogate 400 Locust St	Lakewood	NJ	08701	**888-551-5531**	732-905-7070
Havenwood-Heritage Heights Havenwood Campus 33 Christian Ave	Concord	NH	03301	**800-457-6833**	603-224-5363
Heritage Club 2020 S Monroe St	Denver	CO	80210	**888-221-7317**	303-758-3017
Heron Point of Chestertown 501 E Campus Ave	Chestertown	MD	21620	**800-327-9138**	410-778-7300
Homewood at Williamsport 16505 Virginia Ave	Williamsport	MD	21795	**877-849-9244**	301-582-1750
Indian River Estates 2250 Indian Creek Blvd W *Mktg	Vero Beach	FL	32966	**800-544-0277***	772-562-7400
John Knox Village 651 SW Sixth St	Pompano Beach	FL	33060	**800-998-5669**	
Judson Park 23600 Marine View Dr S	Des Moines	WA	98198	**800-401-4113**	206-824-4000
Kendal at Ithaca 2230 N Triphammer Rd	Ithaca	NY	14850	**800-253-6325**	607-266-5300
Kendal at Longwood & Crosslands PO Box 100	Kennett Square	PA	19348	**800-216-1920**	610-388-1441
Kendal at Oberlin 600 Kendal Dr *Mktg	Oberlin	OH	44074	**800-548-9469***	
Kingswood Senior Living Community 10000 Wornall Rd *Sales	Kansas City	MO	64114	**888-942-2715***	816-942-0994
Knollwood 6200 Oregon Ave NW	Washington	DC	20015	**800-541-4255**	202-541-0400
La Vida Llena 10501 Lagrima de Oro NE	Albuquerque	NM	87111	**800-922-1344**	505-293-4001
Lake Park Retirement Residences 1850 Alice St	Oakland	CA	94612	**866-384-3130**	510-835-5511
Lake Seminole Square 8333 Seminole Blvd	Seminole	FL	33772	**866-785-9025**	727-228-7312
Lakewood Manor 1900 Lauderdale Dr	Richmond	VA	23238	**866-521-9100**	804-740-2900
Larksfield Place 7373 E 29th St N	Wichita	KS	67226	**866-232-8484**	316-858-3910
Laurel Lake Retirement Community 200 Laurel Lk Dr	Hudson	OH	44236	**866-650-2100**	
Lima Estates 411 N Middletown Rd	Media	PA	19063	**888-398-2287**	610-565-7020
Loomis Communities 246 N Main St	South Hadley	MA	01075	**800-865-7655**	413-532-5325
Lutheran Community at Telford 12 Lutheran Home Dr	Telford	PA	18969	**877-343-7518**	215-723-9819
Manor Park Inc 2208 N Loop 250 W	Midland	TX	79707	**800-523-9898**	432-689-9898
Maple Knoll Communities Inc 11100 Springfield Pk	Cincinnati	OH	45246	**800-272-3900**	513-782-2400
Mayflower Retirement Community 1620 Mayflower Ct	Winter Park	FL	32792	**800-228-6518**	407-672-1620
Medford Leas 1 Medford Leas Way	Medford	NJ	08055	**800-331-4302**	609-654-3000
Mennonite Village 5353 Columbus St SE	Albany	OR	97322	**866-453-4930**	541-928-7232
Methodist Country House 4830 Kennett Pk	Wilmington	DE	19807	**800-976-7610**	302-654-5101
Methodist ElderCare Services 5155 N High St	Columbus	OH	43214	**855-636-2225**	614-396-4990
Methodist Manor House 1001 Middleford Rd	Seaford	DE	19973	**800-775-4593**	302-629-4593
Moorings Park 120 Moorings Pk Dr	Naples	FL	34105	**866-802-4302**	239-643-9111
Morningside of Fullerton 800 Morningside Dr	Fullerton	CA	92835	**800-803-7597**	714-256-8000
O'Connor Woods 3400 Wagner Heights Rd	Stockton	CA	95209	**800-957-3308**	209-956-3400
Otterbein Retirement Living Communities 580 N SR 741	Lebanon	OH	45036	**888-513-9131**	513-933-5400
Panorama City 1751 Cir Ln SE	Lacey	WA	98503	**800-999-9807**	360-456-0111
Passavant Retirement Community 401 S Main St	Zelienople	PA	16063	**888-498-7753**	724-452-5400
Pennswood Village 1382 Newtown-Langhorne Rd	Newtown	PA	18940	**888-454-1122**	215-968-9110
Piedmont Gardens 110 41st St	Oakland	CA	94611	**800-496-8126**	510-596-2600
Pine Run Community 777 Ferry Rd	Doylestown	PA	18901	**888-992-8992**	215-345-9000
Pines at Davidson 400 Avinger Ln	Davidson	NC	28036	**877-574-8203**	704-896-1100
Plymouth Village 900 Salem Dr	Redlands	CA	92373	**800-391-4552**	909-793-9195
Pomperaug Woods 80 Heritage Rd	Southbury	CT	06488	**866-817-8935**	203-262-6555
Presbyterian Homes of SC 2817 Ashland Rd	Columbia	SC	29210	**888-842-4855**	803-772-5885

Name / Address	City	State	Zip	Toll-Free	Phone
Providence Life Services 18601 N Creek Dr	Tinley Park	IL	60477	**800-509-2800**	708-342-8100
Regents Point 19191 Harvard Ave	Irvine	CA	92612	**800-347-3735***	949-988-0849
*General					
RiverMead Retirement Community 150 RiverMead Rd	Peterborough	NH	03458	**800-200-5433**	603-924-0062
Rockwood Retirement Community 2903 E 25th Ave	Spokane	WA	99223	**800-727-6650**	509-536-6650
Rogue Valley Manor 1200 Mira Mar Ave	Medford	OR	97504	**800-848-7868**	541-857-7214
Rosewood Retirement Community 1301 New Stine Rd	Bakersfield	CA	93309	**800-984-4216**	661-834-0620
Saint Andrews Estates 6152 Verde Trail N	Boca Raton	FL	33433	**866-897-3490***	561-487-4728
*Mktg					
Seniorsplus 8 Falcon Rd	Lewiston	ME	04243	**800-427-1241**	207-795-4010
Shell Point Village 15101 Shell Pt Blvd	Fort Myers	FL	33908	**800-780-1131***	239-466-1131
*Mktg					
Shenandoah Valley Westminster-Canterbury 300 Westminster-Canterbury Dr	Winchester	VA	22603	**800-492-9463**	540-665-5914
Sherwood Oaks 100 Norman Dr	Cranberry Township	PA	16066	**800-642-2217**	724-776-8100
Smith Ranch Homes 400 Deer Vly Rd Ste L	San Rafael	CA	94903	**800-772-6264**	415-491-4918
Solheim Lutheran Home (SLH) 2236 Merton Ave	Los Angeles	CA	90041	**888-257-7518**	323-257-7518
Spanish Cove 11 Palm Ave	Yukon	OK	73099	**800-965-2683**	
Spring House Estates 728 Norristown Rd	Lower Gwynedd	PA	19002	**888-365-2287**	215-628-8110
Spring Lake Village 5555 Montgomery Dr	Santa Rosa	CA	95409	**800-795-1267**	707-538-8400
Stratford Court 45 Katherine Blvd	Palm Harbor	FL	34684	**888-434-4648**	727-787-1500
Temple Meridian 4312 S 31st St	Temple	TX	76502	**855-444-7658**	254-598-4019
Terraces at Phoenix, The 7550 N 16th St	Phoenix	AZ	85020	**800-836-4281**	602-906-4024
Terraces of Los Gatos 800 Blossom Hill Rd	Los Gatos	CA	95032	**800-673-1982**	408-356-1006
Valle Verde 900 Calle de los Amigos	Santa Barbara	CA	93105	**800-750-5089**	805-883-4000
Vi 71 S Wacker Dr	Chicago	IL	60606	**800-421-1442**	312-803-8800
Villa Gardens 842 E Villa St	Pasadena	CA	91101	**800-958-4552**	626-463-5330
Villa Marin 100 Thorndale Dr	San Rafael	CA	94903	**888-926-2030**	415-492-2408
Village on the Green 500 Village Pl	Longwood	FL	32779	**888-541-3443***	407-682-0230
*Mktg					
Village, The 2200 W Acacia Ave	Hemet	CA	92545	**800-257-7888**	951-658-3369
Vista del Monte 3775 Modoc Rd	Santa Barbara	CA	93105	**800-736-1333**	805-687-0793
Vista Grande Villa 2251 Springport Rd	Jackson	MI	49202	**800-889-8499**	517-787-0222
Waterford, The 601 Universe Blvd	Juno Beach	FL	33408	**888-335-1678**	561-627-3800
Wesley Homes 815 S 216th St	Des Moines	WA	98198	**866-937-5390**	206-824-5000
Wesley Towers 700 Monterey Pl	Hutchinson	KS	67502	**888-663-9175**	620-663-9175
Westlake Village 28550 Westlake Village Dr	Westlake	OH	44145	**855-308-2432**	
Westminster Bradenton Manor 1700 21st Ave W	Bradenton	FL	34205	**877-382-9036**	941-748-4161
Westminster Oaks 4449 Meandering Way	Tallahassee	FL	32308	**800-948-1881**	850-878-1136
Westminster Place 3200 Grant St	Evanston	IL	60201	**888-285-3233**	847-570-3422
Westminster Towers 1330 India Hook Rd	Rock Hill	SC	29732	**800-345-6026**	803-328-5000
Westminster Village 803 N Wahneta St	Allentown	PA	18109	**888-563-8147**	610-782-8300
Westminster-Canterbury of Lynchburg 501 VES Rd	Lynchburg	VA	24503	**800-962-3520**	434-386-3500
Westminster-Canterbury on Chesapeake Bay 3100 Shore Dr	Virginia Beach	VA	23451	**800-349-1722**	757-496-1785
Westminster-Canterbury Richmond 1600 Westbrook Ave	Richmond	VA	23227	**800-445-9904**	804-264-6000
White Oak Manor Inc 130 E Main St PO Box 3347	Spartanburg	SC	29304	**800-826-6762**	864-582-7503
White Sands of La Jolla 516 Burchett St	Glendale	CA	92037	**800-347-3735**	818-247-0420
Whitney Ctr 200 Leeder Hill Dr	Hamden	CT	06517	**800-237-3847**	203-848-2641
Willamette View 12705 SE River Rd	Portland	OR	97222	**800-446-0670**	503-654-6581
Williamsburg Landing 5700 Williamsburg Landing Dr	Williamsburg	VA	23185	**800-554-5517**	757-565-6505
Willow Valley Lakes Manor 300 Willow Vly Lakes Dr	Willow Street	PA	17584	**800-770-5445**	717-464-0800
Willows, The 1 Lyman St	Westborough	MA	01581	**800-464-8060**	508-366-4730

671 RETREATS - SPIRITUAL

The facilities listed here offer basic amenities and services such as bed linens, food preparation, maid service, etc. Although physical activity may play a role in the programs offered, the focus is on the spiritual.

Name / Address	City	State	Zip	Toll-Free	Phone
Chopra Ctr at La Costa Resort & Spa 2013 Costa del Mar Rd	Carlsbad	CA	92009	**888-424-6772**	760-494-1600
Elat Chayyim 116 Johnson Rd	Falls Village	CT	06031	**800-398-2630**	
Expanding Light 14618 Tyler Foote Rd	Nevada City	CA	95959	**800-346-5350**	530-478-7518
Harbin Hot Springs 18424 Harbin Springs Rd PO Box 782	Middletown	CA	95461	**800-622-2477**	707-987-2477
Hollyhock PO Box 127	Mansons Landing	BC	V0P1K0	**800-933-6339**	250-935-6576
Kalani Oceanside Retreat 12-6860 Kapoho Kalapana Rd	Pahoa	HI	96778	**800-800-6886**	808-965-7828
Kirkridge Retreat & Study Ctr 2495 Fox Gap Rd	Bangor	PA	18013	**800-231-2222**	610-588-1793
Laurelville Mennonite Church Ctr 941 Laurelville Ln	Mount Pleasant	PA	15666	**800-839-1021**	724-423-2056
Louhelen Baha'i School 3208 S State Rd	Davison	MI	48423	**800-894-9716**	810-653-5033
Omega Institute for Holistic Studies 150 Lake Dr	Rhinebeck	NY	12572	**800-944-1001**	845-266-4444
Our Lady of Fatima Retreat House 5353 E 56th St	Indianapolis	IN	46226	**800-382-9836**	317-545-7681
Pendle Hill 338 Plush Mill Rd	Wallingford	PA	19086	**800-742-3150**	610-566-4507
Saint Meinrad Archabbey 200 Hill Dr	Saint Meinrad	IN	47577	**800-682-0988**	812-357-6585
Satchidananda Ashram Yogaville (SAYVA) 108 Yogaville Way	Buckingham	VA	23921	**800-858-9642***	434-969-3121
*Resv					
Shambhala Mountain Ctr 151 Shambhala Wy	Red Feather Lakes	CO	80545	**888-788-7221**	970-881-2184
Spiritual Life Ctr 7100 E 45th St N	Wichita	KS	67226	**800-348-2440**	316-744-0167

672 ROLLING MILL MACHINERY

SEE ALSO Metalworking Machinery

Name / Address	City	State	Zip	Toll-Free	Phone
Bradbury Company Inc 1200 E Cole	Moundridge	KS	67107	**800-397-6394**	620-345-6394
Formtek Metal Forming Inc 4899 Commerce Pkwy	Cleveland	OH	44128	**800-631-0520**	216-292-4460
Magnum Integrated Technologies Inc 200 First Gulf Blvd	Brampton	ON	L6W4T5	**800-830-0642**	905-595-1998

673 ROYALTY TRUSTS

Name / Address	City	State	Zip	Toll-Free	Phone
ARC Resources Ltd 308 Fourth Ave SW Ste 1200	Calgary	AB	T2P0H7	**888-272-4900**	403-503-8600
TSE: ARX					
Great Northern Iron Ore Properties 332 Minnesota St Rm W1290	Saint Paul	MN	55101	**800-468-9716**	651-224-2385
NYSE: GNI					
Harvest Energy Trust 700 2nd St SW Ste 2100	Calgary	AB	T2P2W1	**866-666-1178**	403-265-1178
Hugoton Royalty Trust 2911 Turtle Creek Blvd, Ste 850 PO Box 962020	Dallas	TX	75219	**855-588-7839**	214-209-2400
NYSE: HGT					
Marine Petroleum Trust 2911 Turtle Creek Blvd Ste 850	Dallas	TX	75219	**800-758-4672**	
NASDAQ: MARPS					
North European Oil Royalty Trust 43 W Front St Ste 19A	Red Bank	NJ	07701	**800-368-5948**	732-741-4008
NYSE: NRT					
Pengrowth Energy Trust 222 Third Ave SW Ste 2100	Calgary	AB	T2P0B4	**800-223-4122**	403-233-0224
NYSE: PGH					
Penn West Energy Trust Penn W Plz 207 - 9th Ave SW Ste 200	Calgary	AB	T2P1K3	**866-693-2707**	403-777-2500
Texas Pacific Land Trust 1700 Pacific Ave Ste 2770	Dallas	TX	75201	**877-231-7500**	214-969-5530
NYSE: TPL					

674 RUBBER GOODS

Name / Address	City	State	Zip	Toll-Free	Phone
Aero Tec Labs Inc 45 Spear Rd Industrial Pk	Ramsey	NJ	07446	**800-526-5330**	201-825-1400
Alliance Rubber Co 210 Carpenter Dam Rd	Hot Springs	AR	71901	**800-626-5940**	
Biltrite Corp 51 Sawyer Rd	Waltham	MA	02454	**800-877-8775**	781-647-1700
BRP Manufacturing Co 637 N Jackson St	Lima	OH	45801	**800-858-0482**	419-228-4441
Durable Products Inc PO Box 826	Crossville	TN	38557	**800-373-3502**	931-484-3502
Flexsys America LP 260 Springside Dr	Akron	OH	44333	**800-455-5622**	330-666-4111
Griswold Corp 1 River St PO Box 638	Moosup	CT	06354	**800-472-8788**	860-564-3321
Hutchinson Aerospace & Industry Inc 82 S St	Hopkinton	MA	01748	**800-227-7962**	508-417-7000
Kent Elastomer Products Inc 1500 St Claire Ave	Kent	OH	44240	**800-331-4762***	330-673-1011
*Cust Svc					
Koneta Inc 1400 Lunar Dr	Wapakoneta	OH	45895	**800-331-0775**	419-739-4200
Ludlow Composites Corp 2100 Commerce Dr	Fremont	OH	43420	**800-628-5463**	
Mitchell Rubber Products Inc 10220 San Sevaine Way	Mira Loma	CA	91752	**800-453-7526**	
MSM Industries Inc 802 Swan Dr	Smyrna	TN	37167	**800-648-6648**	615-355-4355
Musson Rubber Company Inc 1320 E Archwood Ave	Akron	OH	44306	**800-321-2381***	330-773-7651
*Cust Svc					
National Rubber Technologies Corp 35 Cawthra Ave	Toronto	ON	M6N5B3	**800-387-8501**	416-657-1111

Company	Address	City	State	ZIP	Toll-Free	Phone
Pawling Corp	32 Nelson Hill Rd PO Box 200	Wassaic	NY	12592	**800-431-3456**	
Proco Products Inc	PO Box 590	Stockton	CA	95201	**800-344-3246**	209-943-6088
R & K Industrial Products Co	1945 Seventh St	Richmond	CA	94801	**800-842-7655**	510-234-7212
Regupol America	33 Keystone Dr	Lebanon	PA	17042	**800-537-8737**	
Shercon Inc	6262 Katella Ave	Cypress	CA	90630	**888-227-5847**	714-548-3999
SMR Technologies Inc	93 Nettie Fenwick Rd	Fenwick	WV	26202	**800-767-6899**	304-846-6636
Swarco Industries Inc	PO Box 89	Columbia	TN	38402	**800-216-8781**	931-388-5900
Teknor Apex Co	505 Central Ave	Pawtucket	RI	02861	**800-556-3864**	401-725-8000
Vulcan Corp	30 Garfield Pl Ste 1040 (*Sales)	Cincinnati	OH	45202	**800-447-1146***	513-621-2850

675 RUBBER GOODS - MECHANICAL

Mechanical rubber goods are rubber components used in machinery, such as o-rings, sprockets, sleeves, roller covers, etc.

Company	Address	City	State	ZIP	Toll-Free	Phone
American National Rubber Co	Main & High St (*Cust Svc)	Ceredo	WV	25507	**800-624-3410***	304-453-1311
Atlantic India Rubber Co	1437 Kentucky Rt 1428	Hagerhill	KY	41222	**800-476-6638**	606-789-9115
Fabreeka International Inc	1023 Tpke St (*Cust Svc)	Stoughton	MA	02072	**800-322-7352***	781-341-3655
Finzer Roller Co	129 Rawls Rd	Des Plaines	IL	60018	**888-486-1900**	847-390-6200
Griffith Rubber Mills	2625 NW Industrial St	Portland	OR	97210	**800-321-9677**	503-226-6971
Holz Rubber Company Inc	1129 S Sacramento St	Lodi	CA	95240	**800-285-1600**	209-368-7171
Jamak Fabrication Inc	1401 N Bowie Dr	Weatherford	TX	76086	**800-543-4747**	817-594-8771
Jasper Rubber Products Inc	1010 First Ave	Jasper	IN	47546	**800-457-7457**	812-482-3242
Lauren Mfg	2228 Reiser Ave SE	New Philadelphia	OH	44663	**800-683-0676**	330-339-3373
Lavelle Industries Inc	665 McHenry St	Burlington	WI	53105	**800-528-3553**	262-763-2434
Lord Corp	111 Lord Dr	Cary	NC	27511	**877-275-5673**	919-468-5979
Minor Rubber Company Inc	49 Ackerman St	Bloomfield	NJ	07003	**800-433-6886**	973-338-6800
MOCAP Inc	409 Parkway Dr	Park Hills	MO	63601	**800-633-6775**	314-543-4000
Pamarco	171 E Marquardt Dr (*Sales)	Wheeling	IL	60090	**800-323-7735***	847-459-6000
Precision Assoc Inc	3800 N Washington Ave	Minneapolis	MN	55412	**800-394-6590**	612-333-7464
Precix Inc	744 Bellville Ave	New Bedford	MA	02745	**800-225-8505**	508-998-4000
Thermodyn Corp	3550 Silica Rd	Sylvania	OH	43560	**800-654-6518**	419-841-7782

676 SAFETY EQUIPMENT - MFR

SEE ALSO Medical Supplies - Mfr ; Personal Protective Equipment & Clothing

Company	Address	City	State	ZIP	Toll-Free	Phone
ACR Electronics Inc	5757 Anglers Ave	Fort Lauderdale	FL	33312	**800-432-0227**	954-981-3333
Adams Elevator Equipment Co	6310 W Howard St	Niles	IL	60714	**800-929-9247**	847-581-2900
ALP Industries Inc	1229 W Lincoln Hwy	Coatesville	PA	19320	**800-220-2571**	610-384-1300
Ancra International LLC	4880 W Rosecrans Ave	Hawthorne	CA	90250	**800-973-5092**	310-973-5000
Bradley Corp	W 142 N 9101 Fountain Blvd	Menomonee Falls	WI	53051	**800-272-3539**	262-251-6000
Carsonite Composites LLC	19845 US Hwy 76	Newberry	SC	29108	**800-648-7916**	803-321-1185
CSE Corp	600 Seco Rd	Monroeville	PA	15146	**800-245-2224**	412-856-9200
Encon Safety Products Co	6825 W Sam Houston Pkwy N PO Box 3826	Houston	TX	77041	**800-283-6266**	713-466-1449
Gemtor Inc	1 Johnson Ave	Matawan	NJ	07747	**800-405-9048**	732-583-6200
Hawkins Traffic Safety Supply	1255 E Shore Hwy	Berkeley	CA	94710	**800-772-3995**	800-236-0112
Peerless Chain Co	1416 E Sanborn St	Winona	MN	55987	**800-533-8056**	507-457-9100
Peerless Industrial Group	PO Box 949	Clackamas	OR	97015	**800-547-6806**	800-873-1916
Plastic Safety Systems Inc	2444 Baldwin Rd	Cleveland	OH	44104	**800-662-6338**	
Potter-Roemer	17451 Hurley St	City of Industry	CA	91744	**800-366-3473**	626-855-4890
Reflexite North America	315 S St	New Britain	CT	06051	**800-654-7570**	860-223-9297
Rite-Hite Corp	8900 N Arbon Dr	Milwaukee	WI	53224	**800-456-0600**	414-355-2600
Rostra Precision Controls Inc	2519 Dana Dr (*Cust Svc)	Laurinburg	NC	28352	**800-782-3379***	910-276-4853
Safety Components International Inc	40 Emery St	Greenville	SC	29605	**800-896-6926**	864-240-2692

677 SAFETY EQUIPMENT - WHOL

Company	Address	City	State	ZIP	Toll-Free	Phone
Allstar Fire Equipment Inc	12328 Lower Azusa Rd	Arcadia	CA	91006	**800-425-5787**	626-652-0900
Arbill	PO Box 820542	Philadelphia	PA	19154	**800-523-5367**	
Brooks Equipment Company Inc	10926 David Taylor Dr Ste 300	Charlotte	NC	28269	**800-826-3473**	
Broward Fire Equipment & Service Inc	101 SW Sixth St	Fort Lauderdale	FL	33301	**800-866-3473**	954-467-6625
Calolympic Glove & Safety Company Inc	1720 Delilah St	Corona	CA	92879	**800-421-6630**	951-340-2229
Continental Safety Equipment	2935 Waters Rd Ste 140	Eagan	MN	55121	**800-844-7003**	651-454-7233
Empire Safety & Supply Inc	10624 Industrial Ave	Roseville	CA	95678	**800-995-1341**	916-781-3003
LaFrance Equipment Corp	516 Erie St	Elmira	NY	14904	**800-873-8808**	607-733-5511
LN Curtis & Sons	1800 Peralta St	Oakland	CA	94607	**800-443-3556**	510-839-5111
Mid-Continent Safety	8225 E 35th St N (*General)	Wichita	KS	67226	**800-776-0956***	316-522-0900
Nardini Fire Equipment Company Inc	405 County Rd E W	Saint Paul	MN	55126	**888-627-3464**	651-483-6631
Orr Safety Corp	11601 Interchange Dr	Louisville	KY	40229	**800-726-6789**	502-774-5791
PK Safety Supply	1829 Clement Ave Ste 200	Alameda	CA	94501	**800-829-9580**	510-337-8880
Saf-T-Gard International Inc	205 Huehl Rd	Northbrook	IL	60062	**800-548-4273**	847-291-1600
Safety Products Inc	3517 Craftsman Blvd	Lakeland	FL	33803	**800-248-6860**	863-665-3601
Safety Supply South Inc	100 Centrum Dr (*Cust Svc)	Irmo	SC	29063	**800-522-8344***	
Safeware Inc	3200 HubbaRd Rd (*Cust Svc)	Landover	MD	20785	**800-331-6707***	301-683-1234
Sun Devil Fire Equipment Inc	2929 W Clarendon Ave	Phoenix	AZ	85017	**800-536-3845**	623-245-0636
United Fire Equipment Co	335 N Fourth Ave	Tucson	AZ	85705	**800-362-0150**	520-622-3639
Wayest Safety Inc	3750 N I-44 Service Rd	Oklahoma City	OK	73112	**800-256-1003**	405-942-7101
Wenaas AGS Inc	12211 Parc Crest Dr Bldg Ste 100	Stafford	TX	77477	**888-576-2668**	281-931-4300

678 SALT

SEE ALSO Spices, Seasonings, Herbs

Companies listed here produce salt that may be used for a variety of purposes, including as a food ingredient or for deicing, water conditioning, or other chemical or industrial applications.

Company	Address	City	State	ZIP	Toll-Free	Phone
Cargill Salt Inc	PO Box 5621	Minneapolis	MN	55440	**888-385-7258**	
Compass Minerals International	9900 W 109th St Ste 100 (*NYSE: CMP* ■ *Cust Svc)	Overland Park	KS	66210	**866-755-1743***	913-344-9200
Morton Salt Inc	123 N Wacker Dr	Chicago	IL	60606	**800-725-8847**	312-807-2000
United Salt Corp	4800 San Felipe St	Houston	TX	77056	**800-554-8658**	713-877-2600

679 SATELLITE COMMUNICATIONS SERVICES

SEE ALSO Telecommunications Services ; Cable & Other Pay Television Services ; Internet Service Providers (ISPs)

Company	Address	City	State	ZIP	Toll-Free	Phone
ARINC Inc	2551 Riva Rd	Annapolis	MD	21401	**866-321-6060**	410-266-4000
CapRock Communications Inc	4400 S Sam Houston Pkwy E	Houston	TX	77048	**888-482-0289**	832-668-2300
Force10 Networks Inc	1415 N McDowell Blvd	Petaluma	CA	94954	**866-600-5100**	707-665-4400
Globalstar LP	3200 Zanker Rd Bldg 260	San Jose	CA	95134	**877-728-7466**	408-933-4000
Lightriver Technologies Inc	2150 John Glenn Dre Ste 200	Concord	CA	94520	**888-544-4825**	941-552-9410
Linkus Enterprises Inc	5595 W San Madele Ave	Fresno	CA	93722	**888-854-6587**	559-256-6600
MDU Communications International Inc	60 D Commerce Way (*OTC: MDTV*)	Totowa	NJ	07512	**866-286-9638**	973-237-9499
ORBCOMM	22970 Indian Creek Dr Ste 300 (*Cust Svc)	Sterling	VA	20166	**800-607-0088***	703-433-6300
Outerlink Corp	187 Ballardvale St Ste A260	Wilmington	MA	01887	**877-688-3770**	978-284-6070
SpaceNet Inc	1750 Old Meadow Rd	McLean	VA	22102	**800-237-3513**	703-848-1000
Star West Satellite Inc	580 Prong Horn Trl	Bozeman	MT	59718	**888-814-8402**	406-522-8402
Stratos Global Corp	6550 Rock Spring Dr Ste 650	Bethesda	MD	20817	**800-563-2255**	301-214-8800
ViaSat Inc	6155 El Camino Real (*NASDAQ: VSAT*)	Carlsbad	CA	92009	**855-463-9333**	760-476-2200

680 SAW BLADES & HANDSAWS

SEE ALSO Tools - Hand & Edge

Company	Address	City	State	ZIP	Toll-Free	Phone
California Saw & Knife Works	721 Brannan St	San Francisco	CA	94103	**888-729-6533**	415-861-0644
Contour Saws Inc	900 Graceland Ave	Des Plaines	IL	60016	**800-259-6834**	

Company / Address	City	State	ZIP	Toll-Free	Phone
Diamond Saw Works Inc 12290 Olean Rd	Chaffee	NY	14030	**800-828-1180**	716-496-7417
Disston Precision Inc 6795 State Rd *Cust Svc	Philadelphia	PA	19135	**800-238-1007***	215-338-1200
Great Neck Saw Manufacturing Inc 165 E Second St *Cust Svc	Mineola	NY	11501	**800-457-0600***	516-746-5352
ICS Blount Inc 4909 SE International Way	Portland	OR	97222	**800-321-1240**	
LS Starrett Co 121 Crescent St *NYSE: SCX*	Athol	MA	01331	**800-482-8710**	978-249-3551
Marvel Mfg Company Inc 3501 Marvel Dr	Oshkosh	WI	54902	**800-472-9464**	920-236-7200
MK Diamond Products Inc 1315 Storm Pkwy	Torrance	CA	90501	**800-421-5830**	310-539-5221
MK Morse Co 1101 11th St SE	Canton	OH	44707	**800-733-3377**	330-453-8187
Simonds International 135 Intervale Rd	Fitchburg	MA	01420	**800-343-1616**	

681 SAWMILLS & PLANING MILLS

Company / Address	City	State	ZIP	Toll-Free	Phone
Anthony Forest Products Co 309 N Washington Ave	El Dorado	AR	71730	**800-221-2326**	870-862-3414
Beadles Lumber Company Inc 900 Sixth St NE PO Box 3457	Moultrie	GA	31776	**800-763-2400**	229-985-6996
Buse Timber & Sales Inc 3812 28th Pl NE	Everett	WA	98201	**800-305-2577**	425-258-2577
Buskirk Lumber Co 319 Oak St	Freeport	MI	49325	**800-860-9663**	616-765-5103
Collins Cos 1618 SW First Ave Ste 500	Portland	OR	97201	**800-329-1219**	
Domtar Corp 395 de Maisonneuve W *NYSE: UFS*	Montreal	QC	H3A1L6	**877-848-4466**	514-848-5555
Fulghum Industries 317 S Main St	Wadley	GA	30477	**800-841-5980**	478-252-5223
Hampton Affiliates 9600 SW Barnes Rd Ste 200	Portland	OR	97225	**888-310-1464**	503-297-7691
Hardwoods of Michigan Inc 430 Div St	Clinton	MI	49236	**800-327-2812**	517-456-7431
Hunt Forest Products 401 E Reynolds Dr PO Box 1263	Ruston	LA	71273	**800-390-8589**	318-255-2245
Impact Guns 2710 South 1900 West	Ogden	UT	84401	**888-505-3086**	801-393-2474
Indiana Dimension Inc 1621 W Market St	Logansport	IN	46947	**888-875-4434**	
Industrial Timber & Lumber Corp (ITL) 23925 Commerce Pk Rd	Beachwood	OH	44122	**800-829-9663**	216-831-3140
Louisiana-Pacific Corp 414 Union St Ste 2000 *NYSE: LPX*	Nashville	TN	37219	**888-820-0325**	615-986-5600
Maibec Inc 1984, 5e Rue	Levis	QC	G6W5M6	**800-363-1930**	418-659-3323
Manke Lumber Company Inc 1717 Marine View Dr	Tacoma	WA	98422	**800-426-8488**	253-572-6252
Parton Lumber Company Inc 251 Parton Rd	Rutherfordton	NC	28139	**800-624-1501**	828-287-4257
Pike Lumber Company Inc PO Box 247	Akron	IN	46910	**800-356-4554**	574-893-4511
Robbins Inc 4777 Eastern Ave	Cincinnati	OH	45226	**800-543-1913**	513-871-8988
Roseburg Forest Products Co PO Box 1088	Roseburg	OR	97470	**800-245-1115**	541-679-3311
Rushmore Forest Products 23848 Hwy 385 PO Box 619	Hill City	SD	57745	**866-466-5254**	605-574-2512
Scotch Gulf Lumber 1850 Conception St Rd	Mobile	AL	36610	**800-496-3307**	251-457-6872
Scotch Lumber Co 119 W Main St PO Box 38	Fulton	AL	36446	**800-936-4424**	334-636-4424
Scott Industries Inc 1573 Hwy 136 W PO Box 7	Henderson	KY	42419	**800-951-9276**	270-831-2037
Stimson Lumber Co 520 SW Yamhill St Ste 700	Portland	OR	97204	**800-445-9758**	503-222-1676
Teal-Jones Group, The 17897 Triggs Rd	Surrey	BC	V4N4M8	**888-995-8325**	604-587-8700
Tembec Inc 800 Boul Rene Levesque O Bureau 1050 *TSE: TMB*	Montreal	QC	H3B1X9	**800-565-3021**	514-871-0137
TR Miller Mill Company Inc 215 Deer St PO Box 708	Brewton	AL	36427	**800-633-6740**	251-867-4331
Universal Forest Products Inc (UFPI) 2801 E Beltline Ave NE *NASDAQ: UFPI*	Grand Rapids	MI	49525	**800-598-9663**	616-364-6161
USNR 1981 Schurman Way PO Box 310	Woodland	WA	98674	**800-289-8767**	360-225-8267
Weyerhaeuser Co 33663 Weyerhaeuser Way S *NYSE: WY*	Federal Way	WA	98003	**800-525-5440**	253-924-2345

682 SCALES & BALANCES

SEE ALSO Laboratory Apparatus & Furniture

Company / Address	City	State	ZIP	Toll-Free	Phone
Advance Scale of MD LLC 2400 Egg Harbor Rd	Lindenwold	NJ	08021	**888-447-2253**	856-627-0700
Avery Weigh-Tronix Inc 1000 Armstrong Dr	Fairmont	MN	56031	**800-458-7062**	507-238-4461
BRK Brands Inc 3901 Liberty St Rd	Aurora	IL	60504	**800-323-9005**	630-851-7330
Cardinal Detecto Scale Manufacturing Co 203 E Daugherty St	Webb City	MO	64870	**800-441-4237**	417-673-4631
Detecto Scale Co 203 E Daugherty St PO Box 151	Webb City	MO	64870	**800-641-2008**	417-673-4631
Emery Winslow Scale Co 73 Cogwheel Ln	Seymour	CT	06483	**800-891-3952**	203-881-9333
Fairbanks Scales Inc 821 Locust St	Kansas City	MO	64106	**800-451-4107**	816-471-0231
Industrial Data Systems Inc 3822 E La Palma Ave	Anaheim	CA	92807	**800-854-3311**	714-921-9212
Intercomp Co 3839 County Rd 116	Medina	MN	55340	**800-328-3336**	763-476-2531
Jarden Consumer Solutions 2381 Executive Ctr Dr	Boca Raton	FL	33431	**800-777-5452**	561-912-4100
Johnson Scale Company Inc 36 Stiles Ln	Pine Brook	NJ	07058	**800-572-2531**	
Measurement Specialties Inc 1000 Lucas Way *NASDAQ: MEAS*	Hampton	VA	23666	**800-745-8008**	757-766-1500
Mettler-Toledo International Inc 5 Barr Rd	Ithaca	NY	14850	**800-836-0836**	
Ohaus Corp 19-A Chapin Rd PO Box 2033	Pine Brook	NJ	07058	**800-672-7722**	973-377-9000
Premier Tech Industrial Equipment Group 1 Premier Ave	Rivere-du-Loup	QC	G5R6C1	**866-571-7354**	418-867-8884
Schenck Trebel Corp 535 Acorn St	Deer Park	NY	11729	**800-873-2357**	631-242-4010
Scientech Inc 5649 Arapahoe Ave	Boulder	CO	80303	**800-525-0522**	303-444-1361
Setra Systems Inc 159 Swanson Rd	Boxborough	MA	01719	**800-257-3872**	978-263-1400
Tanita Corp of America Inc 2625 S Clearbrook Dr	Arlington Heights	IL	60005	**800-826-4828**	847-640-9241
TCI Scales Inc PO Box 1648	Snohomish	WA	98291	**800-522-2206**	425-353-4384
Thayer Scale Corp 91 Schoosett St	Pembroke	MA	02359	**855-784-2937**	781-826-8101
Yamato Corp 1775 S Murray Blvd	Colorado Springs	CO	80916	**800-538-1762**	719-591-1500

683 SCHOOL BOARDS (PUBLIC)

Company / Address	City	State	ZIP	Toll-Free	Phone
Alamance-Burlington School District 1712 Vaughn Rd	Burlington	NC	27217	**888-764-7001**	336-570-6060
Albuquerque Public Schools (APS) 6400 Uptown Blvd NE	Albuquerque	NM	87110	**866-563-9297**	505-880-3700
Alisal Union Elementary School District 1205 E Market St	Salinas	CA	93905	**800-782-7463**	831-753-5700
Allentown School District (ASD) 31 S Penn St	Allentown	PA	18105	**877-262-1492**	484-765-4000
Ames Community School District 415 Stanton Ave	Ames	IA	50014	**800-262-3867**	515-268-6600
Anchor Bay School District 5201 County Line Rd Ste 100	Casco Township	MI	48064	**800-285-4460**	586-725-2861
Anoka-Hennepin Independent School District 11 2727 N Ferry St	Anoka	MN	55303	**800-729-6164**	763-506-1000
Appling County Board of Education 249 Blackshear Hwy	Baxley	GA	31513	**866-632-9992**	912-367-8600
Arlington Central School District 144 Todd Hill Rd	LaGrangeville	NY	12540	**800-993-8982**	845-486-4460
Arlington School District 315 N French Ave	Arlington	WA	98223	**888-535-0747**	360-618-6200
Armstrong School District 410 Main St	Ford City	PA	16226	**888-573-5733**	724-763-5200
Ashland Independent School District PO Box 3000	Ashland	KY	41105	**800-752-6200**	606-327-2706
Atkinson County School System 98 Roberts Ave E	Pearson	GA	31642	**800-639-0850**	912-422-7373
Auburn City School District PO Box 3270	Auburn	AL	36831	**866-632-9992**	334-887-2100
Ave Intervision LLC 1840 W State St	Alliance	OH	44601	**800-448-9126**	
Barney Trucking Inc 235 State Rt 24	Salina	UT	84654	**800-524-7930**	
Bedford Public Schools 1623 W Sterns Rd	Temperance	MI	48182	**866-261-9184**	734-850-6000
Beemac Trucking 2747 Litionville Rd	Ambridge	PA	15003	**800-282-8781**	724-266-8781
Bellefonte Area School District 318 N Allegheny St	Bellefonte	PA	16823	**866-632-9992**	814-355-4814
Beverly Hills Unified School District 255 S Lasky Dr	Beverly Hills	CA	90212	**877-220-7229**	310-551-5100
Bexley City School District 348 S Cassingham Rd	Columbus	OH	43209	**800-282-1780**	614-231-7611
Big Spring Independent School District 708 E 11th Pl	Big Spring	TX	79720	**866-632-9992**	432-264-3600
Boarder to Boarder Trucking Inc PO Box 328	Edinburg	TX	78541	**800-678-8789**	956-316-4444
Breckinridge County School District 86 Airport Rd	Hardinsburg	KY	40143	**800-325-1713**	270-756-2186
Brookline College 2445 W Dunlap Ave Ste 100	Phoenix	AZ	85021	**800-793-2428**	602-242-6265
Brunswick County Board of Education 35 Referendum Dr	Bolivia	NC	28422	**800-662-7030**	910-253-2900
Buckingham Browne & Nichols School 46 Belmont St	Watertown	MA	02472	**800-233-6329**	617-547-6100
Bullock Creek Public Schools 1420 S Badour Rd	Midland	MI	48640	**877-706-2508**	989-631-9022
Butler Area School District 110 Campus Ln	Butler	PA	16001	**888-800-5583**	724-287-8720
Cache County School District 2063 N 1200 E	North Logan	UT	84341	**888-837-6437**	435-752-3925
Campbell County Board of Education 101 Orchard Ln	Alexandria	KY	41001	**800-942-3767**	859-635-2173
Canby School District 1130 S Ivy St	Canby	OR	97013	**800-475-7785**	503-266-7861
Charleston County School District (CCSD) 75 Calhoun St	Charleston	SC	29401	**800-255-7688**	843-937-6300
Charlotte-Mecklenburg Schools 701 E ML King Jr Blvd	Charlotte	NC	28202	**800-244-6224**	980-343-3000

Classified Section

Name / Address	City	State	ZIP	Toll-Free	Phone
Chignecto-central Regional 60 Lorne St	Truro	NS	B2N3K3	**800-770-0008**	902-897-8923
Christian County Public Schools 200 Glass Ave PO Box 609	Hopkinsville	KY	42240	**800-274-7374**	270-887-7000
Churchill County School District 545 E Richards St	Fallon	NV	89406	**800-232-6382**	775-423-5184
Circleville City School District 388 Clark Dr	Circleville	OH	43113	**800-418-6423**	740-474-4340
Clark County School District (CCSD) 5100 W Sahara Ave	Las Vegas	NV	89146	**866-799-8997**	702-799-5000
Clovis Unified School District 1450 Herndon Ave	Clovis	CA	93611	**800-498-9055**	559-327-9000
Clyde's Transfer Inc 8015 Industrial Pk Rd	Mechanicsville	VA	23116	**800-342-8758**	804-746-1135
Colorado Springs School District #11 1115 N El Paso St	Colorado Springs	CO	80903	**800-273-8255**	719-520-2000
Conestoga Valley School District 2110 Horseshoe Rd	Lancaster	PA	17601	**800-732-0025**	717-397-2421
Copperas Cove Independent School District 703 W Ave D	Copperas Cove	TX	76522	**866-632-9992**	254-547-1227
Corunna Public School District 124 N Shiawassee St	Corunna	MI	48817	**866-632-9992**	989-743-6338
Culver City Unified School District (CCUSD) 4034 Irving Pl	Culver City	CA	90232	**855-446-2673**	310-842-4220
D & T Trucking Inc 3686 140th St E PO Box 510	Rosemount	MN	55068	**800-624-8130**	651-480-7961
Dallas Independent School District 3700 Ross Ave	Dallas	TX	75204	**866-796-3682**	972-925-3700
Dallastown Area School District 700 New School Ln	Dallastown	PA	17313	**866-233-9796**	717-244-4021
Dawson County Board of Education, The 517 Allen St	Dawsonville	GA	30534	**866-632-9992**	706-265-3246
Delaware County Intermediate Unit 200 Yale Ave	Morton	PA	19070	**800-441-3215**	610-938-9000
Denver Public Schools 900 Grant St	Denver	CO	80203	**866-726-0033**	720-423-3200
Des Moines Independent School District 901 Walnut St	Des Moines	IA	50309	**800-452-1111**	515-242-7911
Desert Sands Charter High School 44130 20th St W	Lancaster	CA	93534	**877-360-5327**	
Desoto Parish School District 201 Crosby St	Mansfield	LA	71052	**888-741-0205**	318-872-2836
Detroit Public Schools 3031 W Grand Blvd	Detroit	MI	48202	**800-656-4673**	313-873-7927
Dickenson County School District PO Box 1127	Clintwood	VA	24228	**866-632-9992**	276-926-4643
Duarte Unified School District 1620 Huntington Dr	Duarte	CA	91010	**888-225-7377**	626-599-5000
Durham Academy Inc 3130 Pickett Rd	Durham	NC	27705	**888-904-9149**	919-489-9118
East Maine School District 63 (EMSD) 10150 Dee Rd	Des Plaines	IL	60016	**866-752-6850**	847-299-1900
Eastside Union School District 45006 30th St E	Lancaster	CA	93535	**877-263-7995**	661-952-1200
Ecampusalberta 1301 16 Ave Nw	Calgary	AB	T2M0L4	**877-284-7248**	403-284-8777
Elim Christian School 13020 S Central Ave	Palos Heights	IL	60463	**877-935-4627**	708-389-0555
Elzinga & Volkers 86 E Sixth St *General	Holland	MI	49423	**800-632-7734***	616-392-2383
Erie 2-Chautauqua Cattaraugus Boces (ECCB) 8685 Erie Rd	Angola	NY	14006	**800-228-1184**	716-549-4454
Etiwanda School District (ESD) 6061 E Ave	Etiwanda	CA	91739	**800-300-1506**	909-899-2451
Fannin County Board of Education 2290 E First St	Blue Ridge	GA	30513	**800-308-2145**	706-632-3771
Fayette County Board of Education 210 Stonewall Ave	Fayetteville	GA	30214	**800-550-5131**	770-460-3535
Fayette County Public Schools 701 E Main St	Lexington	KY	40502	**877-597-2331**	859-381-4100
First Bank Of Highland Park 1835 First St PO Box 546	Highland Park	IL	60035	**877-651-7800**	847-432-7800
First Farmers & Merchants National Bank 816 S Garden St PO Box 1148 *OTC: FIME*	Columbia	TN	38401	**800-882-8378**	931-388-3145
Floyd Blinsky Trucking Inc 210 Keys Rd	Yakima	WA	98901	**800-537-9599**	509-457-3484
Forest Lake Area School District 6100 210th St N	Forest Lake	MN	55025	**866-632-9992**	651-982-8100
Fort Bragg Unified School District 312 S Lincoln St	Fort Bragg	CA	95437	**800-734-7793**	707-961-2850
Franklin Local School District PO Box 428	Duncan Falls	OH	43734	**800-846-4976**	740-674-5203
Fredericksburg City Public Schools 817 Princess Anne St	Fredericksburg	VA	22401	**800-846-4464**	540-372-1130
Fremont Public Schools 220 W Pine St	Fremont	MI	49412	**800-822-9433**	231-924-2350
Fremont Unified School District PO Box 5008	Fremont	CA	94537	**800-544-5248**	510-657-2350
Fulton School District 58 2 Hornet Dr	Fulton	MO	65251	**800-456-2634**	573-590-8000
Gainesville City Schools 508 Oak St	Gainesville	GA	30501	**800-533-0682**	770-536-5275
Galveston Independent School District (GISD) 3904 Ave PO Box 660	Galveston	TX	77550	**877-262-1492**	409-766-5100
Garland Independent School District (GISD) 501 S Jupiter PO Box 469026	Garland	TX	75046	**800-252-5555**	972-494-8201
Gladstone School District 115 17789 Webster Rd	Gladstone	OR	97027	**800-328-0272**	503-655-2777
Granite Falls School District 307 N Alder Ave	Granite Falls	WA	98252	**888-651-8931**	360-691-7717
Gray Transportation Inc 2459 GT Dr	Waterloo	IA	50703	**800-234-3930**	319-234-3930
Greenwood School District 50 1855 Calhoun Rd PO Box 248	Greenwood	SC	29648	**888-260-9430**	864-941-5400
Guilford County Schools 617 W Market St	Greensboro	NC	27401	**866-286-7337**	336-370-8100
Gulf Coast Bank & Trust Co 200 St Charles Ave	New Orleans	LA	70130	**800-223-2060**	504-561-6100
Guy Shavender Trucking Inc PO Box 206	Pantego	NC	27860	**800-682-2447**	252-943-3379
Halifax County Public Schools 1030 Mary Bethune St PO Box 1849	Halifax	VA	24558	**800-253-2687**	434-476-2171
Hall County Schools 711 Green St NW Ste 100	Gainesville	GA	30501	**866-632-9992**	770-534-1080
Hamilton County Educational Service Ctr (HCESC) 11083 Hamilton Ave	Cincinnati	OH	45231	**800-964-8211**	513-674-4200
Harnett County Board of Education 1008 11th St PO Box 1029	Lillington	NC	27546	**800-942-3767**	910-893-8151
Hatboro-Horsham School District 229 Meetinghouse Rd	Horsham	PA	19044	**866-771-3170**	215-672-5660
Hawaii Dept of Education Honolulu District Office 4967 Kilauea Ave	Honolulu	HI	96816	**800-437-8641**	808-733-4950
Hillsborough County Public Schools 901 E Kennedy Blvd	Tampa	FL	33602	**800-962-2873**	813-272-4000
Hillsborough Township Board of Education 379 S Branch Rd	Hillsborough	NJ	08844	**800-272-1325**	908-431-6600
Holiday Express Corp 721 S 28th St	Estherville	IA	51334	**800-831-5078**	712-362-5812
Houston Independent School District 228 McCarty St	Houston	TX	77029	**800-446-2821**	713-556-6000
Hueneme Elementary School Dist 205 N Ventura Rd	Port Hueneme	CA	93041	**866-431-2478**	805-488-3588
Huntsville Board of Education 200 White St	Huntsville	AL	35801	**877-517-0020**	256-428-6800
Idaho Falls School District 91 Education Foundation Inc 690 John Adams Pkwy	Idaho Falls	ID	83401	**888-993-7120**	208-525-7500
Ilex Construction & Woodworking 3801 Northampton St NW Ste 3	Washington	DC	20015	**866-551-4539**	410-820-4393
J.M. Bozeman Enterprises Inc 166 Seltzer Ln *General	Malvern	AR	72104	**800-472-1836***	501-844-4060
Jackson County School District 6 300 Ash St	Central Point	OR	97502	**800-978-3040**	541-494-6200
Jackson County School System 1660 Winder Hwy	Jefferson	GA	30549	**800-760-3727**	706-367-5151
Jacksonville Independent School District PO Box 631	Jacksonville	TX	75766	**800-583-6908**	903-586-6511
Jennings County Schools 34 W Main St	North Vernon	IN	47265	**866-346-3724**	812-346-4483
John Carroll School, The 703 Churchville Rd	Bel Air	MD	21014	**800-422-0010**	410-879-2480
John Cooper School 1 John Cooper Dr	The Woodlands	TX	77381	**800-295-1162**	281-367-0900
Julian Charter School Inc 1704 Cape Horn	Julian	CA	92036	**866-853-0003**	760-765-3847
K12 Inc 2300 Corporate Pk Dr *NYSE: LRN*	Herndon	VA	20171	**866-512-2273**	703-483-7000
KBT Inc 3885 W Michigan St	Sidney	OH	45365	**800-860-9455**	
Klein Independent School District 7200 Spring Cypress Rd	Spring	TX	77379	**888-703-0083**	832-249-4000
Lake Superior Ind Sch Dist 381 1640 2 Hwy	Two Harbors	MN	55616	**888-878-0136**	218-834-8201
Lamesa Independent School District PO Box 261	Lamesa	TX	79331	**888-286-6700**	806-872-5461
Lancaster City School District 345 E Mulberry St	Lancaster	OH	43130	**888-647-4729**	740-687-7300
Las Cruces Public Schools 505 S Main St Ste 249	Las Cruces	NM	88001	**888-222-1498**	575-527-5800
Lawrence Public Schools 110 McDonald Dr	Lawrence	KS	66044	**800-772-1213**	785-832-5000
Lenoir County Public School (LCPS) 2017 W Vernon Ave PO Box 729	Kinston	NC	28504	**888-684-8404**	252-527-1109
Lewis S. Mills High School 24 Lyon Rd	Burlington	CT	06013	**800-673-2411**	860-673-0423
Longview School District 2715 Lilac St	Longview	WA	98632	**800-533-7881**	360-575-7000
Los Angeles Unified School District (LAUSD) 333 S Beaudry Ave	Los Angeles	CA	90017	**877-772-6273**	213-241-1000
Madera Unified School District 1902 HowaRd Rd	Madera	CA	93637	**800-322-6384**	559-675-4500
McLeod Express LLC 5002 Cundiff Ct *General	Decatur	IL	62526	**800-709-3936***	
Mecosta-Osceola Intermediate School District 15760 190th Ave	Big Rapids	MI	49307	**877-211-5253**	231-796-3543
Meramec Valley R-3 School District 126 N Payne St	Pacific	MO	63069	**866-632-9992**	636-271-1400
Metropolitan Nashville Public Schools (MNPS) 2601 Bransford Ave	Nashville	TN	37204	**800-848-0298**	615-259-8531
Michener Institute for Applied 222 Saint Patrick St	Toronto	ON	M5T1V4	**800-387-9066**	416-596-3101
Middlebury Community Schools 57853 Northridge Dr	Middlebury	IN	46540	**866-632-9992**	574-825-9425
Midland High School 615 W Missouri Ave	Midland	TX	79701	**866-632-9992**	989-923-5181
Midwestern Intermediate Unit Iv 453 Maple St	Grove City	PA	16127	**800-942-8035**	724-458-6700
Miken Builders Inc 32782 Cedar Dr Unit 1	Millville	DE	19967	**800-888-7501**	302-537-4444
Minneapolis Public Schools 3345 Chicago Ave	Minneapolis	MN	55407	**800-543-7709**	612-668-0000
Missouri School Boards Association 2100 I-70 Dr SW	Columbia	MO	65203	**800-221-6722**	573-445-9920
Mobile County Public Schools 1 Magnum Pass PO Box 180069	Mobile	AL	36618	**800-605-1033**	251-221-4000
Modesto City Schools 426 Locust St	Modesto	CA	95351	**800-942-3767**	209-576-4011
Mohawk Council of Akwesasne Stn Main Po Box 579	Cornwall	ON	K6H5T3	**888-632-6273**	613-575-2250
Monticello Central School District 237 Forestburgh Rd	Monticello	NY	12701	**866-805-0990**	845-794-7700
Mooresville Graded School District 305 N Main St	Mooresville	NC	28115	**800-222-1222**	704-658-2530

Name / Address	City	State	ZIP	Toll-Free	Phone
Mt. Lebanon School District 7 Horsman Dr	Pittsburgh	PA	15228	**800-222-3353**	412-344-2000
Murray Co 1215 Fern Ridge Pkwy Ste 213	Saint Louis	MO	63141	**888-323-5560**	314-576-2818
National Children's Ctr Inc 6200 Second St NW	Washington	DC	20011	**866-632-9992**	202-722-2300
National Outdoor Leadership School 284 Lincoln St	Lander	WY	82520	**800-710-6657**	307-332-5300
Nationwide Magazine & Book Distributors Inc 3000 E Grauwyler Rd PO Box 170427 *General	Irving	TX	75017	**800-777-9068***	972-438-7852
Niles Community School 111 Spruce St	Niles	MI	49120	**877-622-2321**	269-683-0732
Niskayuna Central School District (NCSD) 1239 Van Antwerp Rd	Schenectady	NY	12309	**866-893-6337**	518-377-4666
Norfolk Public Schools 800 E City Hall Ave	Norfolk	VA	23510	**800-846-4464**	757-628-3843
North Ridgeville City School District 5490 Mills Creek Ln	North Ridgeville	OH	44039	**877-644-6457**	440-327-4444
Northview Public School 4451 Hunsberger NE	Grand Rapids	MI	49525	**866-632-9992**	616-363-4857
Nye County School District Inc (NCSD) PO Box 113	Tonopah	NV	89049	**800-796-6273**	775-482-6258
Oakland Unified School District 1025 Second Ave	Oakland	CA	94606	**888-604-4636**	510-879-8582
Olympia School District 1113 Legion Way SE	Olympia	WA	98501	**855-846-8376**	360-596-6100
Orange County Public Schools 445 W Amelia St	Orlando	FL	32801	**800-378-9264**	407-317-3200
Ossining Union Free School District 190 Croton Ave	Ossining	NY	10562	**877-769-7447**	914-941-7700
Palm Beach County School District, The 3300 Forest Hill Blvd	West Palm Beach	FL	33406	**866-930-8402**	561-434-8000
Palmerton Area School District 680 Fourth St	Palmerton	PA	18071	**800-732-0999**	610-826-7101
Peach County School District Inc 523 Vineville St	Fort Valley	GA	31030	**866-632-9992**	478-825-5933
Penns Grove-Carneys Point Regional Board of Education 100 Iona Ave	Penns Grove	NJ	08069	**877-652-7624**	856-299-4250
Person County Public Schools 304 S Morgan St	Roxboro	NC	27573	**866-724-6650**	336-599-2191
Pittsylvania County School Board 39 Bank St SE PO Box 232	Chatham	VA	24531	**888-440-6520**	434-432-2761
Plaquemines Parish School Board 557 F Edward Hebert Blvd	Belle Chasse	LA	70037	**877-453-2721**	504-595-6400
Portland Public Schools 501 N Dixon St	Portland	OR	97227	**800-766-8206**	503-916-2000
Princeton Regional School District 25 Valley Rd Administration Bldg	Princeton	NJ	08540	**877-652-2873**	609-806-4200
Prior Lake-Savage Area Public School District 719 4540 Tower St SE	Prior Lake	MN	55372	**855-346-1650**	952-226-0000
Proteus Inc 1830 N Dinuba Blvd	Visalia	CA	93291	**888-776-9998**	559-733-5423
Provision Ministry Group PO Box 19700	Irvine	CA	92623	**800-233-3880**	
Puget Sound Educational Service District 800 Oakesdale Ave SW	Renton	WA	98057	**800-664-4549**	425-917-7600
Putnam Valley School District Inc 146 Peekskill Hollow Rd	Putnam Valley	NY	10579	**800-666-5327**	845-528-8143
Rabun County School District 963 Tiger Connector	Tiger	GA	30576	**866-632-9992**	706-212-4350
Robert e Webber Institute for Worship Studies, The 151 Kingsley Ave	Orange Park	FL	32073	**800-282-2977**	904-264-2172
Robstown High School 609 W Hwy 44	Robstown	TX	78380	**800-446-3142**	361-387-5999
Romeo Community School District 316 N Main St	Romeo	MI	48065	**888-427-6818**	586-752-0200
Rosetta Stone Ltd 1919 N Lynn St 7th Fl *NYSE: RST*	Arlington	VA	22209	**800-788-0822**	
Ross Valley School District 110 Shaw Dr	San Anselmo	CA	94960	**800-322-6384**	415-454-2162
Salem-Keizer Public Schools 2450 Lancaster Dr NE	Salem	OR	97305	**877-293-1090**	503-399-3000
Salin Bank 8455 Keystone Xing	Indianapolis	IN	46240	**800-320-7536**	317-452-8000
San Antonio Independent School District (SAISD) 141 Lavaca St	San Antonio	TX	78210	**866-632-9992**	210-554-2200
San Jose Unified School District 855 Lenzen Ave	San Jose	CA	95126	**800-433-3243**	408-535-6000
Saucon Valley School District 2097 Polk Vly Rd	Hellertown	PA	18055	**866-632-9992**	610-838-7026
Scarsdale Union Free School District 2 Brewster Rd	Scarsdale	NY	10583	**888-837-6437**	914-721-2410
School Board of Highlands County Florida PO Box 9300	Sebring	FL	33871	**877-357-7456**	863-471-5555
School District of The Chathams 58 Meyersville Rd	Chatham	NJ	07928	**800-225-5425**	973-457-2500
School Nurse Supply Co 1690 Wright Blvd	Schaumburg	IL	60193	**800-485-2737**	
Seguin Independent School District 1221 E Kingsbury St	Seguin	TX	78155	**866-632-9992**	830-372-5771
Sidney Transportation Services 777 W Russell Rd PO Box 946	Sidney	OH	45365	**800-743-6391**	937-498-2323
Solex Academy Inc 350 E Dundee Rd Ste 200	Wheeling	IL	60090	**866-797-6539**	847-229-9595
Southern Lehigh School District 5775 Main St	Center Valley	PA	18034	**800-360-8989**	610-282-3121
Southern Regional High School District Board of Education 600 North Main St	Manahawkin	NJ	08050	**866-850-0511**	609-597-9481
Southgate Community School District 14600 Dix Toledo Rd	Southgate	MI	48195	**888-263-5897**	734-246-4600
Springfield Public School District #186 1900 W Monroe St	Springfield	IL	62704	**877-632-7753**	217-525-3006
St Ignatius College Prep 2001 37th Ave	San Francisco	CA	94116	**888-225-5427**	312-421-5900
St. Clair County Regional Educational Service Agency 499 Range Rd	Marysville	MI	48040	**800-294-9229**	810-364-8990
Sumner School District 1202 Wood Ave	Sumner	WA	98390	**866-548-3847**	253-891-6000
Templeton Unified School District 960 Old County Rd	Templeton	CA	93465	**800-316-6142**	805-434-5800
Tforce Energy Services 6143 S Willow Ste 320	Greenwood Village	CO	80111	**877-234-1444**	
Thunderbird School of Global Management 1 Global Pl	Glendale	AZ	85306	**800-848-9084**	602-978-7000
Tomball Independent School District 310 S Cherry St	Tomball	TX	77375	**877-382-4357**	281-357-3100
Toppenish School District 202 306 Bolin Dr	Toppenish	WA	98948	**888-730-1101**	509-865-4455
Tulare Joint Union High School District 426 N Blackstone Ave	Tulare	CA	93274	**800-942-3767**	559-688-2021
Tulsa Public Schools 3027 S New Haven Ave	Tulsa	OK	74114	**866-632-9992**	918-746-6800
Twin Falls School District 411 201 Main Ave W	Twin Falls	ID	83301	**800-726-0003**	208-733-6900
Twin Rivers Unified School District 3222 Winona Way	North Highlands	CA	95660	**888-674-6854**	916-566-1628
Unified School District of Antigo 120 S Dorr St	Antigo	WI	54409	**800-795-3272**	715-627-4355
Upper Dauphin Area School District (UDASD) 5668 State Rt 209	Lykens	PA	17048	**866-632-9992**	717-362-8134
US Special Delivery Inc 821 E Blvd	Kingsford	MI	49802	**800-821-6389**	906-774-1931
Utica Community Schools (UCS) 11303 Greendale Dr	Sterling Heights	MI	48312	**800-877-8339**	586-797-1000
W. N. Morehouse Truck Line Inc 4010 Dahlman Ave	Omaha	NE	68107	**800-228-9378**	402-733-2200
Walker County Board of Education 1710 Alabama Ave PO Box 311	Jasper	AL	35501	**866-276-7735**	205-387-0555
Washington School District Inc 201 Allison Ave	Washington	PA	15301	**855-846-8376**	724-223-5085
Westfield Board of Education Inc 302 Elm St	Westfield	NJ	07090	**800-355-2583**	908-789-4401
Westminster School District 14121 Cedarwood St	Westminster	CA	92683	**800-678-9133**	714-894-7311
Wharton Independent School District 2100 N Fulton St	Wharton	TX	77488	**800-818-3453**	979-532-3612
William B Meyer Inc 255 Long Beach Blvd	Stratford	CT	06615	**800-727-5985**	203-375-5801
Williamsport Area School District 201 W Third St	Williamsport	PA	17701	**888-448-4642**	570-327-5500
Zanesville City School Board 160 N Fourth St	Zanesville	OH	43701	**866-280-7377**	740-454-9751

684 SCRAP METAL

SEE ALSO Recyclable Materials Recovery

Name / Address	City	State	ZIP	Toll-Free	Phone
Advantage Metals Recycling LLC 3005 Manchester Trfy	Kansas City	MO	64129	**866-527-4733**	816-861-2700
Alter Trading Corp 700 Office Pkwy	Saint Louis	MO	63141	**888-337-2727**	314-872-2400
AMG Resources Corp 2 Robinson Plaza # 350	Pittsburgh	PA	15205	**877-395-8338**	412-777-7300
Calbag Metals Co 2495 NW Nicolai St	Portland	OR	97210	**800-398-3441**	503-226-3441
Cleveland Corp 42810 N Green Bay Rd	Zion	IL	60099	**800-281-3464**	847-872-7200
Dimco Steel Inc 3901 S Lamar St	Dallas	TX	75215	**877-428-8336**	214-428-8336
Gachman Metals & Recycling Company Inc 2600 Shamrock Ave	Fort Worth	TX	76107	**800-749-0423**	817-334-0211
Grossman Iron & Steel 5 N Market St	Saint Louis	MO	63102	**800-969-9423**	314-231-9423
Iron & Metals Inc 5555 Franklin St	Denver	CO	80216	**800-776-7910**	303-292-5555
Lionetti Assoc 450 S Front St	Elizabeth	NJ	07202	**800-734-0910**	908-820-8800
Louis Padnos Iron & Metal Co PO Box 1979	Holland	MI	49422	**800-442-3509**	616-396-6521
Mervis Industries Inc 3295 E Main St	Danville	IL	61834	**800-637-3016**	217-442-5300
Metalico Annaco Inc 943 Hazel St	Akron	OH	44305	**800-966-1499**	330-376-1400
Metro Metals Northwest 5611 NE Columbia Blvd	Portland	OR	97218	**800-610-5680**	503-287-8861
OmniSource Corp 7575 W Jefferson Blvd	Fort Wayne	IN	46804	**800-666-4789**	260-422-5541
Progress Rail Services 1600 Progress Dr PO Box 1037	Albertville	AL	35950	**800-476-8769**	256-505-6600
PSC 5151 San Felipe Ste 1100	Houston	TX	77056	**800-726-1300**	
SA Recycling LLC 2411 N Glassell St	Orange	CA	92865	**800-468-7272**	714-632-2000
Sadoff & Rudoy Industries LLP 240 W Arndt St *General	Fond du Lac	WI	54936	**877-972-3633***	920-921-2070
Simon Metals LLC 2202 E River St	Tacoma	WA	98421	**800-562-8464**	253-272-9364
Sims Bros Inc 1011 S Prospect St PO Box 1170	Marion	OH	43301	**800-536-7465**	740-387-9041
Sugar Creek Scrap Inc 1201 W National Ave	West Terre Haute	IN	47885	**800-466-7462**	812-533-2147
Thermo Fluids Inc 4301 W Jefferson St	Phoenix	AZ	85043	**800-350-7565**	602-272-2400
Tri-State Iron & Metal Co 1725 E Ninth St	Texarkana	AR	71854	**800-773-8409**	870-773-8409
Tube City IMS Corp 1155 Business Ctr Dr Ste 200 *General	Horsham	PA	19044	**800-860-2442***	215-956-5500
Upstate Shredding LLC 1 Recycle Dr Tioga Industrial Pk	Owego	NY	13827	**800-245-3133**	607-687-7777
Yaffe Cos Inc, The 1200 S G St	Muskogee	OK	74403	**800-759-2333**	918-687-7543

685 SCREEN PRINTING

Company	City	State	ZIP	Toll-Free	Phone
Ares Sportswear Ltd 3704 Lacon Rd	Hilliard	OH	43026	**800-439-8614**	614-767-1950
Art Brands LLC 225 Business Ctr Dr	Blacklick	OH	43004	**877-755-4278**	614-755-4278
Designer Decal Inc 1120 E First Ave	Spokane	WA	99202	**800-622-6333**	509-535-0267
F&E Sportswear Corp 1230 Newell Pkwy	Montgomery	AL	36110	**800-523-7762**	334-244-6477
Flow-Eze Co 3209 Auburn St	Rockford	IL	61101	**800-435-4873**	815-965-1062
Gillespie Graphics 27676 SW Pkwy Ave	Wilsonville	OR	97070	**800-547-6841**	503-682-1122
Image Sport Inc 1115 SE Westbrooke Dr	Waukee	IA	50263	**800-919-0520**	515-987-7699
Kerusso Activewear Inc 402 Hwy 62 Spur	Berryville	AR	72616	**800-424-0943**	870-423-6242
M & M Designs Inc 1981 Quality Blvd	Huntsville	TX	77320	**800-627-0656**	
Mitographers Inc, The 4720 N Fourth Ave	Sioux Falls	SD	57104	**800-221-6486**	605-336-1818
Motson Graphics Inc 1717 Bethlehem Pk	Flourtown	PA	19031	**800-972-1986**	215-233-0500
Petra Manufacturing Co 6600 W Armitage Ave	Chicago	IL	60707	**800-888-7387**	773-622-1475
Primary Color Inc 9239 Premier Row	Dallas	TX	75247	**800-581-9555**	214-630-8800
Ram Graphics Inc 2408 S Pk Ave	Alexandria	IN	46001	**800-531-4656**	
Screen Graphics of Florida Inc 1801 N Andrews Ave	Pompano Beach	FL	33069	**800-346-4420**	
Service Graphics LLC 8350 Allison Ave	Indianapolis	IN	46268	**800-884-9876**	317-471-8246
Silkworm Inc 102 S Sezmore Dr	Murphysboro	IL	62966	**800-826-0577**	618-687-4077
Vincent Printing Company Inc 1512 Sholar Ave	Chattanooga	TN	37406	**800-251-7262**	

686 SCREENING - WOVEN WIRE

Company	City	State	ZIP	Toll-Free	Phone
ACS Industries Inc 1 New England Way	Lincoln	RI	02865	**866-783-4838**	401-769-4700
Belleville Wire Cloth Inc 18 Rutgers Ave	Cedar Grove	NJ	07009	**800-631-0490**	973-239-0074
Buffalo Wire Works Co 1165 Clinton St	Buffalo	NY	14206	**800-828-7028**	716-826-4666
Cleveland Wire Cloth & Manufacturing Co 3573 E 78th St	Cleveland	OH	44105	**800-321-3234**	216-341-1832
Edward J Darby & Son Inc 2200 N Eigth St PO Box 50049	Philadelphia	PA	19133	**800-875-6374**	215-236-2203
Gerard Daniel Worldwide 34 Barnhart Dr	Hanover	PA	17331	**800-232-3332**	717-637-5901
Jelliff Corp 354 Pequot Ave	Southport	CT	06890	**800-243-0052**	203-259-1615
TWP Inc 2831 Tenth St	Berkeley	CA	94710	**800-227-1570**	510-548-4434
Universal Wire Cloth Co 16 N Steel Rd	Morrisville	PA	19067	**800-523-0575**	215-736-8981

687 SEATING - VEHICULAR

Company	City	State	ZIP	Toll-Free	Phone
Freedman Seating Co 4545 W Augusta Blvd	Chicago	IL	60651	**800-443-4540**	773-524-2440
HO Bostrom Company Inc 818 Progress Ave	Waukesha	WI	53186	**800-332-5415**	262-542-0222
Milsco Mfg Co 9009 N 51st St	Milwaukee	WI	53223	**800-255-0337**	414-354-0500
Sears Manufacturing Co 1718 S Concord St PO Box 3667 *Cust Svc	Davenport	IA	52808	**800-553-3013***	563-383-2800
Seats Inc 1515 Industrial St	Reedsburg	WI	53959	**800-443-0615**	608-524-8261

688 SECURITIES BROKERS & DEALERS

SEE ALSO Commodity Contracts Brokers & Dealers ; Electronic Communications Networks (ECNs) ; Investment Advice & Management ; Mutual Funds

Company	City	State	ZIP	Toll-Free	Phone
1&1 Internet Inc 701 Lee Rd Ste 300	Chesterbrook	PA	19087	**877-461-2631**	
1st Discount Brokerage Inc 8927 Hypoluxo Rd Ste A-5	Lake Worth	FL	33467	**888-642-2811**	561-515-3200
AB Watley Direct Inc 50 Broad St Ste 1614	New York	NY	10004	**877-993-4886**	646-753-9301
Access Securities Inc 30 Buxton Farm Rd	Stamford	CT	06905	**800-331-6171**	203-322-3377
Allen & Co Inc 1401 South Florida Avenue	Lakeland	FL	33803	**800-950-2526**	863-688-9000
Ameriprise Brokerage 70400 Ameriprise Financial Ctr	Minneapolis	MN	55474	**800-535-2001**	
Avisen Securities Inc 3620 American River Dr Ste 145	Sacramento	CA	95864	**800-230-7704**	916-480-2747
Baird Patrick & Company Inc 305 Plz Ten	Jersey City	NJ	07311	**800-221-7747**	201-680-7300
Barclays Capital Inc 200 Pk Ave	New York	NY	10166	**888-227-2275**	212-412-4000
BaxterBoo 7025 S Fulton St Ste 150	Centennial	CO	80112	**888-887-0063**	
Bell Supply Inc 7221 Rt 130	Pennsauken	NJ	08110	**888-834-2371**	856-663-3900
Bernard L Madoff Investment Securities Co 885 Third Ave 18th Fl	New York	NY	10022	**800-334-1343**	212-230-2424
Berthel Fisher & Co 701 Tama St Bldg B PO Box 609	Marion	IA	52302	**800-356-5234**	319-447-5700
BHK Securities LLC 2200 Lakeshore Dr Ste 250	Birmingham	AL	35209	**888-529-2610**	205-322-2025
Blowfish Direct LLC 11130 Holder St	Cypress	CA	90630	**877-725-6934**	
Bourbon & Boots Inc 419 Main St	North Little Rock	AR	72114	**877-791-8079**	855-623-3562
Brighton Securities Corp 1703 Monroe Ave	Rochester	NY	14618	**800-388-1703**	585-473-3590
Brill Securities Inc 152 W 57th St 16th Fl	New York	NY	10019	**800-933-0800**	212-957-5700
Bull Wealth Management Group Inc 4100 Yonge St Ste 612	Toronto	ON	M2P2B5	**866-623-2053**	416-223-2053
Burgundy Asset Management Ltd Bay Wellington Tower Brookfield Pl 181 Bay St Ste 4510	Toronto	ON	M5J2T3	**888-480-1790**	416-869-3222
BUYandHOLD.com Securities Corp *c/o Freedom Investments, Inc* 375 Raritan Ctr Pkwy Ste D	Edison	NJ	08837	**800-646-8212**	
Caldwell Securities Ltd 150 King St W Ste 1710	Toronto	ON	M5H1J9	**800-387-0859**	416-862-7755
Calton & Assoc Inc 14497 N Dale Mabry Hwy	Tampa	FL	33618	**800-942-0262**	813-264-0440
Ceros Financial Services Inc 1445 Research Blvd Ste 530	Rockville	MD	20850	**866-842-3356**	
Cetera Financial Group Inc 200 N Sepulveda Blvd Ste 1200	El Segundo	CA	90245	**866-489-3100**	
Charles Schwab & Co Inc 211 Main St *Cust Svc	San Francisco	CA	94105	**800-648-5300***	415-667-1009
Chase Plastic Services Inc 6467 Waldon Ctr Dr	Clarkston	MI	48346	**800-232-4273**	248-620-2120
Cheevers & Company Inc 440 S LaSalle St Ste 710	Chicago	IL	60605	**866-928-7643**	312-224-7922
City Securities Corp 30 S Meridian St Ste 600	Indianapolis	IN	46204	**800-800-2489**	317-634-4400
CLS Investments LLC 17605 Wright St	Omaha	NE	68130	**888-455-4244**	402-493-3313
CNBS Inc 7200 W 132nd St Ste 240	Overland Park	KS	66213	**800-222-0978**	
Cobblestone Capital Advisors LLC 140 Allens Creek Rd	Rochester	NY	14618	**800-264-2769**	585-473-3333
Colorado West Investments Inc 1731 E Niagara Rd	Montrose	CO	81401	**888-249-9882**	970-249-9882
Conceptual Financial Planning Inc 3962 N Richmond St Ste B	Appleton	WI	54913	**800-300-9500**	920-731-9500
Convergex Holdings LLC 1633 Broadway 48th Fl	New York	NY	10019	**800-367-8998**	212-468-7713
Corinthian Partners LLC 850 Third Ave Ste 16C	New York	NY	10022	**800-899-8950**	212-287-1500
Credit Suisse 11 Madison Ave	New York	NY	10010	**800-222-8977**	212-325-2000
Crowell Weedon & Co 1 Wilshire Blvd 26th Fl	Los Angeles	CA	90017	**800-227-0319**	213-620-1850
DA Davidson & Company Inc 8 Third St N	Great Falls	MT	59401	**800-332-5915**	406-727-4200
Davenport & Co LLC 901 E Cary St 1 James Center Ste 1100	Richmond	VA	23219	**800-846-6666**	804-780-2000
Davidson Cos 8 Third St N PO Box 5015	Great Falls	MT	59401	**800-332-5915**	406-727-4200
DiscountMugs.com 12610 NW 115th Ave	Medley	FL	33178	**800-569-1980**	
Domestic Securities Inc 160 Summit Ave	Montvale	NJ	07645	**877-690-2274**	201-505-9855
Dot Com Holdings of Buffalo Inc 1460 Military Rd	Buffalo	NY	14217	**877-636-3673**	
Dougherty & Company LLC 90 S Seventh St Ste 4300	Minneapolis	MN	55402	**800-328-4000**	612-376-4000
E*Trade Financial Corp 1271 Ave of the Americas 14th Fl *NASDAQ: ETFC*	New York	NY	10020	**800-387-2331**	
eBX LLC 65 Franklin St Ste 201	Boston	MA	02110	**800-958-4813**	617-350-1600
ECMD Inc 2 Grandview St	North Wilkesboro	NC	28659	**888-222-3961**	336-667-5976
Ellie Fashion Group Inc 1447 Second St 3rd Fl	Santa Monica	CA	90401	**888-926-9615**	
Ema Brokerage LLC 1300 Rt 73 Ste 306	Mount Laurel	NJ	08054	**855-267-5867**	856-216-0211
Fastener Supply Co 13410 S Ridge Dr PO Box 7369	Charlotte	NC	28241	**800-888-9519**	704-596-7634
Fieldpoint Private Bank & Trust 100 Field Pt Rd	Greenwich	CT	06830	**877-438-4338**	203-413-9300
FIMAC Solutions LLC Denver Technological Ctr 5299 DTC Blvd Ste 950	Greenwood Village	CO	80111	**877-789-5905**	303-320-1900
Financial Service Corp 2300 Windy Ridge Pkwy Ste 1100	Atlanta	GA	30339	**800-547-2382**	
Fincantieri Marine Systems North America Inc 800-C Principal Ct	Chesapeake	VA	23320	**877-436-7643**	757-548-6000
Fisc Investment Services Corp 1849 Clairmont Rd	Decatur	GA	30033	**800-241-3203**	404-321-1212
Fisgard Capital Corp 3378 Douglas St	Victoria	BC	V8Z3L3	**866-382-9255**	250-382-9255
Franklin Templeton Investments 3344 Quality Dr	Rancho Cordova	CA	95670	**800-632-2350**	650-312-2000
Freedom Investments Inc 375 Raritan Ctr Pkwy	Edison	NJ	08837	**800-944-4033**	
Friedman Billings Ramsey Group Inc 1300 N 17th St Ste 1400	Arlington	VA	22209	**800-846-5050**	703-312-9500
FSB Warner Financial 1001 Peoples Sq	Waterloo	IA	50702	**800-747-9999**	319-235-6561

Name / Address	City	State	Zip	Toll-Free	Phone
Full Access Brokerage 1240 Charnelton St	Eugene	OR	97401	**866-890-5743**	541-284-5070
GE Richards Graphic Supplies Company Inc 928 Links Ave	Landisville	PA	17538	**800-233-0410**	717-898-3151
Geary Pacific Corp 1908 N Enterprise St	Orange	CA	92865	**800-444-3279**	714-279-2950
Geneos Wealth Management Inc 9055 E Mineral Cir Ste 200	Centennial	CO	80112	**888-812-5043**	303-785-8470
George K Baum & Co 4801 Main St Ste 500 Ste 500	Kansas City	MO	64112	**800-821-7195**	816-474-1100
Georgeson Securities Corp 480 Washington Blvd 27th Fl	Jersey City	NJ	07310	**800-428-0717**	
Global Maxfin Investments Inc 100 Mural St Ste 201	Richmond Hill	ON	L4B1J3	**866-666-5266**	416-741-1544
Great Pacific Fixed Income Securities Inc 151 Kalmus Dr Ste H-8	Costa Mesa	CA	92626	**800-284-4804**	714-619-3000
Hampton Securities Ltd 141 Adelaide St W Ste 1800	Toronto	ON	M5H3L5	**877-225-0229**	416-862-7800
Harris Financial Services Inc 940 Spokane Ave	Whitefish	MT	59937	**800-735-7895**	406-862-4400
Hogan-Knotts Financial Group, The 298 Broad St	Red Bank	NJ	07701	**800-801-3190**	732-842-7400
Huntleigh Securities Corp 7800 Forsyth Blvd 5th Fl	Saint Louis	MO	63105	**800-727-5405**	314-236-2400
Icor Technology Inc 935 Ages Dr	Ottawa	ON	K1G6L3	**877-483-7978**	613-745-3600
IDI Distributors Inc 8303 Audubon Rd	Chanhassen	MN	55317	**888-843-1318**	952-279-6400
Illinois Fair Plan Association 130 East Randolph PO Box 81469	Chicago	IL	60601	**800-972-4480**	312-861-0385
Impulse Technologies Ltd 920 Gana Crt	Mississauga	ON	L5S1Z4	**800-667-5475**	905-564-9266
Index Funds Advisors Inc 19200 Von Karman Ave Ste 150	Irvine	CA	92612	**888-643-3133**	949-502-0050
Industrial Tube & Steel Corp 4658 Crystal Pkwy	Kent	OH	44240	**800-662-9567**	330-474-5530
Investrade Discount Securities 950 N Milwaukee Ave Ste 102 *Cust Svc	Glenview	IL	60025	**800-498-7120***	847-375-6080
Isaak Bond Investments Inc 3900 S Wadsworth Blvd Ste 590	Lakewood	CO	80235	**800-279-4426**	303-623-7500
ITG Inc 1 Liberty Plz 165 Broadway	New York	NY	10006	**800-215-4484**	212-588-4000
Janney Montgomery Scott LLC 1801 Market St	Philadelphia	PA	19103	**800-526-6397**	215-665-6000
JD Ford & Company LLC 650 S Cherry St Ste 1200	Denver	CO	80246	**888-999-9495**	303-333-3673
JJB Hilliard WL Lyons Inc 500 W Jefferson St	Louisville	KY	40202	**800-444-1854**	502-588-8400
Kane Reid Securities Group Inc 13024 Ballantyne Corporate Pl Ste 500	Charlotte	NC	28277	**877-495-5464**	
Katalyst Surgical LLC 754 Goddard Ave	Chesterfield	MO	63005	**888-452-8259**	
Knight Capital Group Inc 545 Washington Blvd *NYSE: KCG*	Jersey City	NJ	07310	**800-544-7508**	201-222-9400
Kovack Securities Inc 6451 N Federal Hwy # 1201 Ste 1201	Fort Lauderdale	FL	33308	**800-711-4078**	954-782-4771
L B L Group 3631 S. Harbor Blvd Ste 200	Santa Ana	CA	92704	**800-451-8037**	657-232-0500
Ladenburg Thalmann Financial Services Inc 4400 Biscayne Blvd 12th Fl *NYSE: LTS*	Miami	FL	33137	**800-523-8425**	212-409-2000
Lazard 30 Rockefeller Plz *NYSE: LAZ*	New York	NY	10112	**866-867-4070**	212-632-6000
Leaders LLC 2 Portland Fish Pier Ste 214	Portland	ME	04101	**888-583-7770**	
Lebenthal Wealth Advisors 230 Park Ave Fl 32	New York	NY	10169	**877-425-6006**	212-425-6006
Legg Mason Inc (LMI) 100 International Dr *NYSE: LM*	Baltimore	MD	21202	**800-822-5544**	410-539-0000
Leigh Baldwin & Company LLC 1 Hopper St Ste 1	Utica	NY	13501	**800-659-8044**	315-734-1410
Lexington Investment Mortgage Company LLC 2365 Harrodsburg Rd Ste B375	Lexington	KY	40504	**800-264-7073**	859-224-7073
Loop Capital Markets LLC 111 W Jackson Blvd Ste 1901	Chicago	IL	60604	**888-294-8898**	312-913-4900
LPL Financial Services 75 State St 24th Fl	Boston	MA	02109	**800-877-7210**	
Mackie Research Capital Corp 110 Nineth Ave SW 9th Fl	Calgary	AB	T2P0T1	**888-292-0980**	403-218-6375
Mailender Inc 9500 Glades Dr	Hamilton	OH	45011	**800-998-5453**	513-942-5453
Mesirow Financial Inc 350 N Clark St	Chicago	IL	60610	**888-681-0082**	312-595-6000
Morgan Stanley 1585 Broadway *NYSE: MS* ■ *General	New York	NY	10036	**800-223-2440***	212-761-4000
Morgan Stanley Investment Management 1221 Ave of the Americas 5th Fl *General	New York	NY	10020	**800-223-2440***	212-296-6600
National Commerce Bank Services Inc 80 Monroe Ave Ste 250	Memphis	TN	38103	**800-264-2609**	
National Securities Corp 410 Park Ave 14th Fl	New York	NY	10022	**800-742-7730**	212-417-8000
Needham & Co Inc 445 Pk Ave 3rd Fl	New York	NY	10022	**800-903-3268**	212-371-8300
Newbridge Securities Corp 1451 W Cypress Creek Rd	Fort Lauderdale	FL	33309	**877-447-9625**	954-334-3450
Northern Industrial Sales Ltd 3526 Opie Cres	Prince George	BC	V2N2P9	**800-668-3317**	250-562-4435
Nuveen Investments Inc 333 W Wacker Dr	Chicago	IL	60606	**800-257-8787**	312-917-7700
NYLIFE Securities Inc 51 Madison Ave Rm 251	New York	NY	10010	**800-695-4785**	
Pacific Crest Securities Inc 111 SW Fifth Ave 42nd Fl	Portland	OR	97204	**800-314-9837**	503-248-0721
Patriot Flooring Supply Inc 110 Commerce Way	Woburn	MA	01801	**866-444-4433**	
PDI Financial Group 601 N Lynndale Dr	Appleton	WI	54914	**800-234-7341**	920-739-2303
Pennsylvania Trust Co 5 Radnor Corp Ctr Ste 450	Radnor	PA	19087	**800-975-4316**	610-975-4300
People's Securities Inc 850 Main St	Bridgeport	CT	06601	**800-772-4400**	203-338-0800
Phillips & Company Securities Inc 1300 Sw Fifth Ave Ste 2100	Portland	OR	97201	**800-572-4765**	503-224-0858
Piper Jaffray Cos 800 Nicollet Mall Ste 800 *NYSE: PJC*	Minneapolis	MN	55402	**800-333-6000**	612-303-6000
Planesmart! Aviation LLC Addison Airport 15841 Addison Rd	Addison	TX	75001	**888-228-4283**	972-380-8004
Precision IBC Inc 8054 Mcgowin Dr	Fairhope	AL	36532	**800-544-7069**	251-990-6789
Questar Capital Corp 5701 Golden Hills Dr	Minneapolis	MN	55416	**888-446-5872**	
R Seelaus & Company Inc 25 Deforest Ave Ste 304	Summit	NJ	07901	**800-922-0584**	
Raymond James Financial Inc 880 Carillon Pkwy *NYSE: RJF*	Saint Petersburg	FL	33716	**800-248-8863**	727-567-1000
RBC Capital Markets 1 Liberty Plaza	New York	NY	10006	**800-387-1122**	212-428-6200
RBC Dain Rauscher Inc 60 S Sixth St Dain Rauscher Plz	Minneapolis	MN	55402	**800-933-9946**	
Robert W Baird & Company Inc PO Box 672	Milwaukee	WI	53201	**800-792-2473**	414-765-3500
Roehl & Yi Investment Advisors LLC 450 Country Club Rd Ste 160	Eugene	OR	97401	**888-683-4343**	541-683-2085
Roosevelt & Cross Inc 1 Exchange Plz 55 Broadway 22nd Fl	New York	NY	10006	**800-348-3426**	212-344-2500
Royal Alliance Assoc Inc 1 World Financial Ctr 14th Fl	New York	NY	10281	**800-821-5100**	
Royal Securities Co 4095 Chicago Dr SW Ste 120	Grandville	MI	49418	**800-421-3518**	616-538-2550
SagePoint Financial Inc 2800 N Central Ave Ste 2100	Phoenix	AZ	85004	**800-552-3319**	
Samuel A Ramirez & Co Inc 61 Broadway Ste 2924	New York	NY	10006	**800-888-4086**	
Sandler O'Neill + Partners LP 1251 Avenue of the Americas 6th Fl	New York	NY	10020	**800-635-6851**	212-466-7800
Schroder Investment Management North America Inc (SIMNA) 875 Third Ave 22nd Fl	New York	NY	10022	**800-730-2932**	
Scotia Capital Markets 1 Liberty Plz	New York	NY	10006	**877-294-3435**	212-225-5000
Securities Center Inc, The 245 E St	Chula Vista	CA	91910	**800-244-1718**	619-426-3550
Securities Service Network Inc 9729 Cogdill Rd Ste 301	Knoxville	TN	37932	**866-843-4635**	
SFE Investment Counsel Inc 801 S Figueroa St Ste 2100	Los Angeles	CA	90017	**800-445-6320**	213-612-0220
Shank Wealth Management LLC 2627 Chestnut Ridge Dr Ste 110	Kingwood	TX	77339	**888-359-3133**	281-359-3133
Shore Morgan Young 300 W Wilson Bridge Rd	Worthington	OH	43085	**800-288-2117**	614-888-2117
Siebert Brandford Shank & Co LLC 100 Wall St 18th Fl	New York	NY	10005	**800-334-6800**	646-775-4850
Silver Legacy Capital Corp 407 N Virginia St	Reno	NV	89501	**800-687-8733**	
Stephens Inc 111 Ctr St	Little Rock	AR	72201	**800-643-9691**	501-377-2000
Sterne Agee & Leach Inc 800 Shades Creek Pkwy Ste 700	Birmingham	AL	35209	**800-240-1438**	205-949-3500
Stifel Financial Corp 501 N Broadway *NYSE: SF*	Saint Louis	MO	63102	**800-679-5446**	
Stifel Nicolaus & Co Inc 501 N Broadway	Saint Louis	MO	63102	**800-679-5446**	314-342-2000
Stonehenge Partners Inc 191 W Nationwide Blvd Ste 600	Columbus	OH	43215	**877-298-4409**	614-246-2500
SunTrust Robinson Humphrey Capital Markets 3333 Peachtree Rd NE	Atlanta	GA	30326	**800-634-7928**	404-926-5000
Tocco Financial Services Inc 6236 E Pima Ste 190	Tucson	AZ	85712	**877-881-1149**	520-881-1149
TradeStation Group Inc 8050 SW Tenth St Ste 2000	Plantation	FL	33324	**800-871-3577**	954-652-7000
Trading Direct 160 Broadway E Bldg 7th Fl	New York	NY	10038	**800-925-8566**	212-766-0230
Trumaker Inc 701 Sutter St Fl 5	San Francisco	CA	94109	**855-623-3878**	
UBS Financial Services Inc 1285 Ave of the Americas	New York	NY	10019	**800-221-3260**	212-713-2000
UBS Warburg LLC 677 Washington Blvd	Stamford	CT	06901	**800-221-3260**	203-719-3000
Vanguard Brokerage Services PO Box 1110	Valley Forge	PA	19482	**800-992-8327**	610-669-1000
Wayne Hummer Investments LLC 222 S Riverside Pz 28th Fl	Chicago	IL	60606	**800-621-4477**	866-943-4732
Western International Securities Inc 70 S Lake Ave Ste 700	Pasadena	CA	91101	**888-793-7717**	
William Blair & Company LLC 222 W Adams St	Chicago	IL	60606	**800-621-0687**	312-236-1600
Winetasting Network, The 578 Gateway Dr	Napa	CA	94558	**800-435-2225**	
Wolverton Securities Ltd 777 Dunsmuir St 17th Fl	Vancouver	BC	V7Y1J5	**877-390-7771**	604-622-1000
WR Hambrecht & Co 909 Montgomery St 3rd Fl *Cust Svc	San Francisco	CA	94133	**855-753-6484***	415-551-8600

689 SECURITIES & COMMODITIES EXCHANGES

Company / Address	City	State	Zip	Toll-Free	Phone
Axial Inc 45 E 20th St 12th Fl	New York	NY	10003	**800-860-4519**	
Border Gold Corp 15234 N Bluff Rd	White Rock	BC	V4B3E6	**888-312-2288**	604-535-3287
Chicago Board Options Exchange (CBOE) 400 S La Salle St	Chicago	IL	60605	**800-678-4667**	312-786-5600
CME Group Inc 20 S Wacker Dr *NASDAQ: CME*	Chicago	IL	60606	**866-716-7274**	312-930-1000
Convergent Wealth Advisors LLC 12505 Park Potomac Ave Ste 400	Potomac	MD	20854	**888-444-6347**	301-770-6300
IPC Securities Corp 2680 Skymark Ave Ste 700	Mississauga	ON	L4W5L6	**877-212-9799**	905-212-9788
MAS Capital Inc 2715 Coney Island Ave	Brooklyn	NY	11235	**866-553-7493**	
Minneapolis Grain Exchange 400 S Fourth St 130 Grain Exchange Bldg	Minneapolis	MN	55415	**800-827-4746**	612-321-7101
Montreal Exchange 800 Victoria Sq Third Fl PO Box 61	Montreal	QC	H4Z1A9	**800-361-5353**	514-871-2424
National Stock Exchange (NSX) 101 Hudson St Ste 1200	Jersey City	NJ	07302	**800-843-3924**	201-499-3700
NMS Capital Group LLC 433 N Camden Dr 4th Fl	Beverly Hills	CA	90210	**800-716-2080**	
NYSE Arce 115 Samsone St	San Francisco	CA	94104	**877-729-7291**	
NYSE Euronext 11 Wall St *NYSE: NYX*	New York	NY	10005	**866-873-7422**	212-656-3000
Pavilion Financial Corp 1001 Corydon Ave Ste 300	Winnipeg	MB	R3M0B6	**866-954-5101**	204-954-5101
Raymond James (USA) Ltd 2200 - 925 W Georgia St	Vancouver	BC	V6C3L2	**877-570-7558**	
Sprott Global Resource Investments Ltd 1910 Palomar Point Way Ste 200	Carlsbad	CA	92008	**800-477-7853**	
Toronto Stock Exchange 130 King St W	Toronto	ON	M5X1J2	**888-873-8392**	416-947-4670
World Currency USA Inc 16 W Main St	Marlton	NJ	08053	**888-593-7927**	

690 SECURITY PRODUCTS & SERVICES

SEE ALSO Signals & Sirens - Electric ; Fire Protection Systems ; Audio & Video Equipment

Company / Address	City	State	Zip	Toll-Free	Phone
ADS Security LP 3001 Armory Dr Ste 100	Nashville	TN	37204	**800-448-8652**	
ADT Security Services Inc 14200 E Exposition Ave	Aurora	CO	80012	**800-238-2455**	
Advantor Systems Corp 12612 Challenger Pkwy Ste 300	Orlando	FL	32809	**800-238-2686**	407-859-3350
Akal Security Inc 7 Infinity Loop	Espanola	NM	87532	**888-325-2527**	505-692-6600
Alken Inc 40 Hercules Dr	Colchester	VT	05446	**800-357-4777**	802-655-3159
Allied Fire & Security Inc 425 W Second Ave *Acctg	Spokane	WA	99201	**888-333-2632***	509-321-8778
AMAG Technology Inc 20701 Manhattan Pl	Torrance	CA	90501	**800-889-9138**	310-518-2380
American Locker Group Inc 815 S Main St *OTC: ALGI*	Grapevine	TX	76051	**800-828-9118**	817-329-1600
American Locker Security Systems Inc 608 Allen St *Sales	Jamestown	NY	14701	**800-828-9118***	
American Science & Engineering Inc 829 Middlesex Tpke *NASDAQ: ASEI*	Billerica	MA	01821	**800-225-1608**	978-262-8700
APi Systems Group Inc 10575 Vista Park Rd *General	Dallas	TX	75238	**877-828-1200***	214-291-1200
Authentix Inc 4355 Excel Pkwy Ste 100	Addison	TX	75001	**866-434-1402**	469-737-4400
BI Inc 6400 Lookout Rd	Boulder	CO	80301	**800-241-2911**	303-218-1000
Black Hat Inc 1932 First Ave Ste 204	Seattle	WA	98101	**866-203-8081**	206-443-5489
Bosch Security Systems 130 Perinton Pkwy	Fairport	NY	14450	**800-289-0096**	585-223-4060
Brivo Systems LLC 7700 Old Georgetown Rd Ste 300 *Tech Supp	Bethesda	MD	20814	**866-692-7486***	301-664-5242
BSM Wireless Inc 75 International Blvd Ste 100	Toronto	ON	M9W6L9	**866-768-4771**	416-675-1201
Carter Bros LLC 3015 RN Martin St	East Point	GA	30344	**888-818-0152**	
Central Signaling 2033 Hamilton Rd	Columbus	GA	31904	**800-554-1101**	706-322-3756
Checkpoint Systems Inc 101 Wolf Dr *NYSE: CKP*	Thorofare	NJ	08086	**800-257-5540**	856-848-1800
Corby Industries Inc 1501 E Pennsylvania St *Sales	Allentown	PA	18109	**800-652-6729***	610-433-1412
DEI Holdings Inc 1 Viper Way *OTC: DEIX*	Vista	CA	92081	**800-876-0800**	760-598-6200
Detex Corp 302 Detex Dr	New Braunfels	TX	78130	**800-729-3839**	830-629-2900
deView Electronics USA Inc 708 Vly Ridge Cir Ste 1	Lewisville	TX	75057	**877-433-8439**	214-222-3332
Diebold Inc 5995 Mayfair Rd *NYSE: DBD*	North Canton	OH	44720	**800-999-3600**	330-490-4000
Digital Security Controls (DSC) 3301 Langstaff Rd	Concord	ON	L4K4L2	**888-888-7838**	905-760-3000
Doyle Security Systems Inc 792 Calkins Rd	Rochester	NY	14623	**866-463-6953**	585-244-3400
eDist 97 McKee Dr	Mahwah	NJ	07430	**800-800-6624**	201-512-1400
ELK Products Inc 3266 Us 70 W	Connelly Springs	NC	28612	**800-797-9355**	828-397-4200
Federal APD Inc (FAPD) 28100 Cabot Dr Ste 200	Novi	MI	48377	**877-992-7749**	248-374-9600
Fiber SenSys LLC 2925 NW Aloclek Dr Ste 120	Hillsboro	OR	97124	**800-641-8150**	503-692-4430
FireKing Security Group 101 Security Pkwy	New Albany	IN	47150	**800-457-2424**	812-948-8400
First Action Security Security Team Inc 18702 Crestwood Dr *Cust Svc	Hagerstown	MD	21742	**800-372-7447***	301-797-2124
Fortress Technology Inc 51 Grand Marshall Dr	Toronto	ON	M1B5N6	**888-220-8737**	416-754-2898
GE Analytical Instruments Inc 6060 Spine Rd	Boulder	CO	80301	**800-255-6964**	303-444-2009
George Risk Industries Inc 802 S Elm St *OTC: RSKIA* ■ *Sales	Kimball	NE	69145	**800-523-1227***	308-235-4645
Guardian Alarm 20800 Southfield Rd	Southfield	MI	48075	**800-782-9688**	248-423-1000
Hanchett Entry Systems Inc (HES) 22630 N 17th Ave	Phoenix	AZ	85027	**800-626-7590**	623-582-4626
HandyTrac Systems LLC 510 Staghorn Ct	Alpharetta	GA	30004	**800-665-9994**	678-990-2305
Honeywell Security Group 2 Corporate Ctr Dr Ste 100	Melville	NY	11747	**800-467-5875**	516-577-2000
IDenticard Systems Inc 25 Race Ave FL 1	Lancaster	PA	17603	**800-233-0298**	717-569-5797
Integrated Biometrics Inc 121 Broadcast Dr	Spartanburg	SC	29303	**888-840-8034**	864-990-3711
Interface Security Systems LLC 6340 International Pkwy Ste 100	Plano	TX	75093	**866-593-3480**	972-996-2800
KWJ Engineering Inc 8430 Central Ave Ste C	Newark	CA	94560	**800-472-6626**	510-794-4296
Loomis Fargo & Co 2500 Citywest Blvd Ste 900	Houston	TX	77042	**866-383-5069**	713-435-6700
Matrix Systems Inc 1041 Byers Rd	Miamisburg	OH	45342	**800-562-8749**	937-438-9033
MDI Security Systems Inc 12500 Network Dr Ste 303	San Antonio	TX	78249	**866-435-7634**	210-477-5400
MMF Industries 1111 S Wheeling Rd	Wheeling	IL	60090	**800-323-8181**	
Monitronics International Inc 2350 Valley View Ln Ste 100 *Cust Svc	Dallas	TX	75234	**800-290-0709***	972-243-7443
MorphoTrust USA Inc 296 Concord Rd	Billerica	MA	01821	**888-245-1114**	978-215-2400
MSA Security 9 Murray St 2nd Fl	New York	NY	10007	**800-286-2000**	212-509-1336
NAPCO Security Systems Inc 333 Bayview Ave *NASDAQ: NSSC*	Amityville	NY	11701	**800-645-9445**	631-842-9400
National Fingerprint Inc 6999 Dolan Rd	Glouster	OH	45732	**888-823-7873**	740-767-3853
New England Security Inc 10 Industrial Dr	Westerly	RI	02891	**800-556-7395**	401-596-0660
Norment Security Group Inc 2511 Midpark Dr	Montgomery	AL	36109	**800-466-3007**	334-281-8440
Nortek Security & Control LLC 1950 Camino Vida Roble Ste 150 *Cust Svc	Carlsbad	CA	92008	**800-421-1587***	760-438-7000
Optex Inc 13661 Benson Ave Bldg C	Chino	CA	91710	**800-966-7839**	909-993-5770
Per Mar Security 1910 E Kimberly Rd	Davenport	IA	52807	**800-473-7627**	563-359-3200
protection One Alarm Monitoring 1035 N Third St Ste 101	Lawrence	KS	66044	**800-438-4357**	877-776-1911
Qualys Inc 1600 Bridge Pkwy	Redwood Shores	CA	94065	**866-801-6161**	650-801-6100
Seco-Larm USA Inc 16842 Millikan Ave	Irvine	CA	92606	**800-662-0800**	949-261-2999
Securitas Security Services USA Inc 2 Campus Dr	Parsippany	NJ	07054	**800-555-0906**	973-267-5300
Security Corp 22325 Roethel Dr	Novi	MI	48375	**877-374-5700**	
Security Defense Systems Corp 160 Pk Ave	Nutley	NJ	07110	**800-325-6339**	
Security Signal Devices Inc 1740 N Lemon St	Anaheim	CA	92801	**800-888-0444**	
Sensormatic Electronics Corp 6600 Congress Ave	Boca Raton	FL	33487	**800-327-1765**	561-912-6000
Sentry Group 900 Linden Ave *Cust Svc	Rochester	NY	14625	**800-828-1438***	585-381-4900
Sentry Technology Corp 1881 Lakeland Ave *OTC: SKVY*	Ronkonkoma	NY	11779	**800-645-4224**	
Sielox LLC 170 E Ninth Ave	Runnemede	NJ	08078	**800-424-2126**	856-939-9300
SIRCHIE Finger Print Laboratories Inc 100 Hunter Pl	Youngsville	NC	27596	**800-356-7311**	919-554-2244
Sizemore Inc 2116 Walton Way	Augusta	GA	30904	**800-445-1748**	706-736-1456
Slomin's Inc 125 Lauman Ln	Hicksville	NY	11801	**800-252-7663**	516-932-7000
Sofradir EC Inc 373 Rt 46W	Fairfield	NJ	07004	**800-759-9577**	973-882-0211
Southern Folger Detention Equipment Co 4634 S Presa St	San Antonio	TX	78223	**888-745-0530**	210-533-1231
Teletrac Inc 7391 Lincoln Way	Garden Grove	CA	92841	**800-500-6009**	714-897-0877
Tyco International Ltd 9 Roszel Rd *NYSE: TYC*	Princeton	NJ	08540	**800-685-4509**	609-720-4200

Company / Address	City	State	ZIP	Toll-Free	Phone
Unisec Inc 2555 Nicholson St	San Leandro	CA	94577	**800-982-4587**	
Universal Security Instruments Inc 11407 Cronhill Dr *TSE: UUU*	Owings Mills	MD	21117	**800-390-4321**	410-363-3000
Vector Security Inc 2000 Ericsson Dr	Warrendale	PA	15086	**800-832-8575**	
Verint Video Solutions 330 South Service Rd	Melville	NY	11747	**800-483-7468**	
Winner International LLC 32 W State St	Sharon	PA	16146	**800-258-2321**	724-981-1152

691 SECURITY & PROTECTIVE SERVICES

SEE ALSO Investigative Services

Company / Address	City	State	ZIP	Toll-Free	Phone
5 Alarm Fire & Safety Equipment LLC 350 Austin Cir	Delafield	WI	53018	**800-615-6789**	262-646-5911
Accuvant Inc 1125 17th St Ste 1700	Denver	CO	80202	**800-574-0896**	303-298-0600
Action Security Inc 243 E Fifth Ave	Anchorage	AK	99501	**800-478-3785**	907-279-7050
Advanced Alarm Systems Inc 101 Lindsey St	Fall River	MA	02720	**800-442-5276**	508-675-1937
Allegiance Security Group LLC 2900 Arendell St Ste 18	Morehead City	NC	28557	**866-747-2748**	252-247-1138
AlliedBarton Security Services 150 S Warner Rd	King of Prussia	PA	19406	**866-703-7666**	484-654-3800
Am-Gard Security Inc 600 Main St	Pittsburgh	PA	15215	**800-554-0412**	412-781-5800
American Services Inc 1300 Rutherford Rd	Greenville	SC	29609	**877-292-7450**	864-292-7450
Andy Frain Services Inc 761 Shoreline Dr	Aurora	IL	60504	**877-707-4771**	630-820-3820
APL Access & Security Inc 115 S William Dillard Dr	Gilbert	AZ	85233	**866-873-2288**	480-497-9471
ASP Inc 460 Brant St Ste 212	Burlington	ON	L7R4B6	**877-552-5535**	905-333-4242
AWP Inc 826 Overholt Rd	Kent	OH	44240	**800-343-2650**	
Bms Integrated Services Inc 1277 Georgia St E	Vancouver	BC	V6A2A9	**866-676-0136**	604-676-0136
Brink's Inc PO Box 619031	Dallas	TX	75261	**800-274-6575**	469-549-6000
Brokers International Financial Services LLC 102 Se 13th St	Panora	IA	50216	**877-886-1939**	641-755-4635
Cansec Systems Ltd 3105 Unity Dr Unit 9	Mississauga	ON	L5L4L2	**877-545-7755**	905-820-2404
Castlegarde Inc 4911 S W Shore Blvd	Tampa	FL	33611	**866-751-3203**	813-872-4844
Chubb Security Systems Inc 7700 Gulf Fwy	Houston	TX	77017	**800-513-3576**	
Counterforce Inc 2740 Matheson Blvd E Unit 2A	Mississauga	ON	L4W4X3	**800-591-7374**	905-282-6200
Criticom International Corp 715 W State Rd Ste 434	Longwood	FL	32750	**866-705-7705**	
Cypress Security LLC 478 Tehama St	San Francisco	CA	94103	**866-345-1277**	
Digistream Investigation 417 mace blvd	Davis	CA	95618	**800-747-4329**	
DSX Access Systems Inc 10731 Rockwall Rd	Dallas	TX	75238	**888-419-8353**	214-553-6140
East Coast Security Services Inc 68 Stiles Rd	Salem	NH	03079	**800-639-2086**	603-898-6823
Excelsior Defense Inc 2232 Central Ave	Saint Petersburg	FL	33712	**877-955-4636**	727-527-9600
Federal Protection Inc 2500 N Airport Commerce Ave	Springfield	MO	65803	**800-299-5400**	
First Alarm Security & Patrol Inc 1111 Estates Dr	Aptos	CA	95003	**800-684-1111**	831-476-1111
FJC Security Services Inc 275 Jericho Tpke	Floral Park	NY	11001	**888-832-6352**	516-328-6000
Fluent Home Ltd 7319 104 St NW	Edmonton	AB	T6E4B9	**855-238-4826**	
Garda World Security Corp 1390 Barre St *TSE: GW*	Montreal	QC	H3C1N4	**800-859-1599**	514-281-2811
GHS Interactive Security Inc 2081 Arena Blvd Ste 260	Sacramento	CA	95834	**855-208-2447**	
Gillmore Security Systems Inc 26165 Broadway Ave	Cleveland	OH	44146	**800-899-8995**	440-232-1000
Global Elite Group 825 E Gate Blvd Ste 301	Garden City	NY	11530	**877-425-0999**	516-414-0487
Guard Systems Inc 1190 Monterey Pass Rd	Monterey Park	CA	91754	**800-606-6711**	323-881-6711
Guardian Alarm 20800 Southfield Rd	Southfield	MI	48075	**800-782-9688**	248-423-1000
Guardian Protection Services Inc 174 Thorn Hill Rd *Cust Svc	Warrendale	PA	15086	**877-314-7092***	855-779-2001
guardNOW Inc 16209 Victory Blvd Ste 302	Van Nuys	CA	91406	**877-482-7366**	
Habitec Security Inc 2926 S Republic Blvd	Toledo	OH	43615	**888-422-4832**	419-537-6768
Hannon Security Services Inc 9036 Grand Ave S	Minneapolis	MN	55420	**800-328-3877**	952-881-5865
Hepaco Inc 2711 Burch Dr PO Box 26308	Charlotte	NC	28269	**800-888-7689**	704-598-9782
Houston Harris Div Patrol Inc 6420 Richmond Ave	Houston	TX	77057	**877-975-9922**	713-975-9922
Information Network Assoc Inc 5235 N Front St	Harrisburg	PA	17110	**800-443-0824**	717-599-5505
Innovative Industrial Solutions Inc 2830 Skyline Dr	Russellville	AR	72802	**888-684-8249**	479-968-4266
Intec Video Systems Inc 23301 Vista Grande Dr	Laguna Hills	CA	92653	**800-468-3254**	949-859-3800
Ipss Inc 150 Isabella St	Ottawa	ON	K1S1V7	**866-532-2207**	613-232-2228
isekurity Inc 24663 Mound Rd	Warren	MI	48091	**877-838-5734**	
Itech Digital LLC 4287 W 96th St	Indianapolis	IN	46268	**866-733-6673**	317-704-0440
J & J Security Services Corp 2922 Howland Blvd Ste 2	Deltona	FL	32725	**877-532-7233**	386-789-5555
JMG Security Systems Inc 17150 Newhope St Ste 109	Fountain Valley	CA	92708	**800-900-4564**	714-545-8882
Kent Security Services Inc 14600 Biscayne Blvd	North Miami Beach	FL	33181	**800-273-5368**	305-919-9400
Law Enforcement Assoc Corp (LEA) 120 Penmarc Dr Ste 125 *OTC: LAWEQ*	Raleigh	NC	27616	**800-354-9669**	919-872-6210
Loomis Armored US Inc 2500 Citywest Blvd Ste 900	Houston	TX	77042	**866-383-5069**	713-435-6700
Marlin Central Monitoring LLC 3600 Commerce Pl Ste 201	Kissimmee	FL	34742	**866-383-0333**	
McRoberts Protective Agency Inc 87 Nassau St	New York	NY	10038	**800-866-7233**	212-425-6500
Merchants Building Maintenance LLC 606 Monterey Pass Rd	Monterey Park	CA	91754	**800-560-6700**	
Mijac Alarm 9339 Charles Smith Ave Ste 100	Rancho Cucamonga	CA	91730	**800-982-7612**	909-982-7612
Mircom Technologies Ltd 25 Interchange Way	Vaughan	ON	L4K5W3	**888-660-4655**	905-660-4655
Monument Security Inc 5844 Price Ave	Sacramento	CA	95652	**877-506-1755**	916-564-4234
Murray Guard Inc 58 Murray Guard Dr	Jackson	TN	38305	**800-238-3830**	731-668-3400
My Alarm Center LLC 3803 W Chester Pike Ste 100	Newtown Square	PA	19073	**866-484-4800**	
National Monitoring Center 26800 Aliso Viejo Pkwy Ste 250	Aliso Viejo	CA	92656	**800-662-1711**	
Network Multi-Family Security Corp 4221 W John Carpenter Fwy	Irving	TX	75063	**800-541-3138**	214-277-7000
New York Merchants Protective Company Inc 75 W Merrick Rd	Freeport	NY	11520	**888-696-7911**	516-561-5210
Northwestern Ohio Security Systems Inc 121 E High St	Lima	OH	45801	**800-833-6416**	614-527-7037
OSI Security Devices Inc 1580 Jayken Way	Chula Vista	CA	91911	**800-711-6814**	619-628-1000
Pasek Corp 9 W Third St	South Boston	MA	02127	**800-628-2822**	617-269-7110
Pierce County Security Inc 2002 99th St E	Tacoma	WA	98445	**800-773-4432**	253-535-4433
Prestige Security 5721 W Slauson Ave Ste 120	Culver City	CA	90230	**800-482-7303**	310-670-5999
Pro Security Group 301B S Robinson Dr	Robinson	TX	76706	**855-753-7766**	254-753-7766
Prodco International Inc 9408 Boul du Golf	Montreal	QC	H1J3A1	**888-577-6326**	514-324-9796
Rancho Santa Fe Protective Services Inc 1991 Vlg Pk Way Ste 100	Encinitas	CA	92024	**800-303-8877**	760-942-0688
Rapid Focus Security LLC 253 Summer St Ste 303	Boston	MA	02210	**855-793-1337**	
Rapid Response Monitoring Services Inc 400 W Division St	Syracuse	NY	13204	**800-558-7767**	
RECON Dynamics LLC 2300 Carillon Point	Kirkland	WA	98033	**877-480-3551**	
Rodbat Security Services 8125 Somerset Blvd	Paramount	CA	90723	**877-676-3228**	562-806-9098
Safeguard Security & Communications Inc 8454 N 90th St	Scottsdale	AZ	85258	**800-426-6060**	480-609-6200
SDI Chicago 33 West Monroe Ste 400	Chicago	IL	60603	**888-968-7734**	312-580-7500
Security 101 LLC 2465 Mercer Ave Ste 101	West Palm Beach	FL	33401	**888-909-4101**	
Seico Security Systems 132 Court St	Pekin	IL	61554	**800-272-0316**	309-347-3200
Select Engineered Systems 7991 W 26th Ave	Hialeah	FL	33016	**800-342-5737**	305-823-5410
Sentry Alarm Systems of America Inc 8 Thomas Owens Way	Monterey	CA	93940	**800-424-7773**	831-375-2727
Sentry Security LLC 339 Egidi Dr	Wheeling	IL	60090	**888-272-7080**	847-353-7200
Sentry Watch Inc 1705 Holbrook St	Greensboro	NC	27403	**800-632-4961**	336-292-6468
St Moritz Security Services Inc 4600 Clairton Blvd	Pittsburgh	PA	15236	**800-218-9156**	412-885-3144
Stealth Monitoring Inc 15182 Marsh Lane	Dallas	TX	75001	**855-783-2584**	214-341-0123
Summit Security Services Inc 390 Rexcorp Plz W Tower - Lobby Level	Uniondale	NY	11556	**800-615-5888**	516-240-2400
Tyco International Ltd 9 Roszel Rd *NYSE: TYC*	Princeton	NJ	08540	**800-685-4509**	609-720-4200
UCIT Online Security 6441 Northam Dr	Mississauga	ON	L4V1J2	**866-756-7847**	905-405-9898
Universal Services of America Inc 1551 N Tustin Ave Ste 650	Santa Ana	CA	92705	**866-877-1965**	714-619-9700
US Security Assoc Inc 200 Mansell Ct 5th Fl	Roswell	GA	30076	**800-730-9599**	770-625-1500
US Security Inc 4544 NW 10th St	Oklahoma City	OK	73127	**877-917-5566**	405-947-3377
Vanguard Products Group Inc 720 Brooker Creek Blvd Ste 223	Oldsmar	FL	34677	**877-477-4874**	813-855-9639
Verant Identification Systems Inc 2496 Ridge Rd W Ste 203	Rochester	NY	14626	**866-257-4351**	585-214-2451
Vescom Corp 705 Main Rd N	Hampden	ME	04444	**800-841-1769**	207-945-5051
Vinson Guard Service Inc 955 Howard Ave	New Orleans	LA	70113	**800-441-7899**	504-529-2260
Whelan Security Co 1699 S Hanley Rd Ste 350	St Louis	MO	63144	**888-494-3526**	314-644-3227

692 SEED COMPANIES

SEE ALSO Farm Supplies

Seed production and development companies (horticultural and agricultural).

Company	Address	City	State	ZIP	Toll-Free	Phone
AgriGold Hybrids	5381 Akin Rd	Saint Francisville	IL	62460	**800-262-7333**	618-943-5776
Albert Lea Seed House	1414 W Main St	Albert Lea	MN	56007	**800-352-5247**	507-373-3161
Ampac Seed Co	32727 Hwy 99 E	Tangent	OR	97389	**800-547-3230**	541-928-1651
Foremostco Inc	8457 NW 66th St	Miami	FL	33166	**800-421-8986**	305-592-8986
Gries Seed Farms Inc	2348 N Fifth St	Fremont	OH	43420	**800-472-4797**	419-332-5571
Harris Moran Seed Co	PO Box 4938	Modesto	CA	95352	**800-808-7333**	800-320-4672
Johnny's Selected Seeds	955 Benton Ave	Winslow	ME	04901	**877-564-6697**	207-861-3900
JW Jung Seed Co	335 S High St	Randolph	WI	53956	**800-297-3123**	
Keithly-Williams Seeds Inc	420 Palm Ave	Holtville	CA	92250	**800-533-3465**	760-356-5533
Latham Seed Co	131 180th St	Alexander	IA	50420	**877-465-2842**	641-692-3258
Lebanon Seaboard Corp	1600 E Cumberland St	Lebanon	PA	17042	**800-233-0628**	717-273-1685
Nunhems USA Inc	1200 Anderson Corner Rd *Cust Svc	Parma	ID	83660	**800-733-9505***	208-674-4000
Park Seed Co	1 Parkton Ave *Orders	Greenwood	SC	29647	**800-845-3369***	
Red River Commodities Inc	501 42nd St N	Fargo	ND	58102	**800-437-5539**	701-282-2600
Renee's Garden Seeds Inc	7389 W Zayante Rd	Felton	CA	95018	**888-880-7228**	831-335-7228
Sand Seed Service Inc	4765 Hwy 143	Marcus	IA	51035	**800-352-2228**	712-376-4135
Schlessman Seed Co	11513 US Rt 250	Milan	OH	44846	**888-534-7333**	419-499-2572
Seedway LLC	1734 Railroad Pl	Hall	NY	14463	**800-836-3710**	585-526-6391
Sharp Bros Seed Co	1005 S Sycamore	Healy	KS	67850	**800-462-8483**	620-398-2231
Stock Seed Farms	28008 Mill Rd	Murdock	NE	68407	**800-759-1520**	402-867-3771
Stratton Seed Co	1530 Hwy 79 S	Stuttgart	AR	72160	**800-264-4433**	870-673-4433
W Atlee Burpee Co	300 Pk Ave *Cust Svc	Warminster	PA	18974	**800-333-5808***	215-674-4900
Weeks Seed Company Inc	1050 Moye Blvd	Greenville	NC	27834	**800-322-1234**	252-757-1234
Wetsel Inc	961 N Liberty St *Cust Svc	Harrisonburg	VA	22802	**800-572-4018***	540-434-6753

693 SEMICONDUCTOR MANUFACTURING SYSTEMS & EQUIPMENT

Company	Address	City	State	ZIP	Toll-Free	Phone
Advanced Energy Industries Inc	1625 Sharp Pt Dr *NASDAQ: AEIS*	Fort Collins	CO	80525	**800-446-9167**	970-221-4670
Aehr Test Systems	400 Kato Terr *NASDAQ: AEHR*	Fremont	CA	94539	**800-962-4284**	510-623-9400
Applied Materials Inc	3050 Bowers Ave PO Box 58039 *NASDAQ: AMAT*	Santa Clara	CA	95054	**877-356-9175**	408-727-5555
Applied Materials/Semitool	655 W Reserve Dr	Kalispell	MT	59901	**877-356-9175**	406-752-2107
Brooks Automation Inc	15 Elizabeth Dr *NASDAQ: BRKS*	Chelmsford	MA	01824	**800-698-6149**	978-262-2400
BTU International Inc	23 Esquire Rd *NASDAQ: BTUI*	North Billerica	MA	01862	**800-998-0666**	978-667-4111
Data I/O Corp	6464 185th Ave NE Ste 101 *NASDAQ: DAIO*	Redmond	WA	98052	**800-426-1045**	425-881-6444
Ebara Technologies Inc	51 Main Ave	Sacramento	CA	95838	**800-535-5376**	916-920-5451
Entegris Inc	129 Concord Rd Bldg 2 *NASDAQ: ENTG*	Billerica	MA	01821	**877-695-7654**	978-436-6500
Fortrend Corp	687 N Pastoria Ave	Sunnyvale	CA	94085	**888-937-3637**	408-734-9311
I.B.I.S. Inc	30 Technology Pkwy S Ste 400	Norcross	GA	30092	**866-714-8422**	770-368-4000
KLA-Tencor Corp	1 Technology Dr *NASDAQ: KLAC*	Milpitas	CA	95035	**800-600-2829**	408-875-3000
Kokusai Semiconductor Equipment Corp	2460 N First St Ste 290	San Jose	CA	95131	**800-800-5321**	408-456-2750
Lam Research Corp	4650 Cushing Pkwy *NASDAQ: LRCX*	Fremont	CA	94538	**800-526-7678**	510-572-0200
Mattson Technology Inc	47131 Bayside Pkwy *NASDAQ: MTSN*	Fremont	CA	94538	**800-315-6607**	510-657-5900
MaxLinear Inc	2051 Palomar Airport Rd Ste 100 *NYSE: MXL*	Carlsbad	CA	92011	**888-505-4369**	760-692-0711
N J R Corp	125 Nicholson Ln	San Jose	CA	95134	**800-800-5441**	408-321-0200
Rudolph Technologies Inc	1 Rudolph Rd PO Box 1000 *NASDAQ: RTEC*	Flanders	NJ	07836	**877-467-8365**	973-691-1300
Tokyo Electron America Inc	2400 Grove Blvd	Austin	TX	78741	**800-828-6596**	512-424-1000
Ultratech Inc	3050 Zanker Rd *NASDAQ: UTEK*	San Jose	CA	95134	**800-222-1213**	408-321-8835
Universal Instruments Corp (UIC)	33 Broome Corporate Pk	Conklin	NY	13748	**800-842-9732**	607-779-7522
Varian Semiconductor Equipment Assoc Inc	35 Dory Rd	Gloucester	MA	01930	**800-344-1111**	978-282-2000
Veeco Instruments Inc	1 Terminal Dr *NASDAQ: VECO*	Plainview	NY	11803	**888-724-9511**	516-677-0200

694 SEMICONDUCTORS & RELATED DEVICES

SEE ALSO Electronic Components & Accessories - Mfr ; Printed Circuit Boards

Company	Address	City	State	ZIP	Toll-Free	Phone
8x8 Inc	810 W Maude Ave *NASDAQ: EGHT*	Sunnyvale	CA	94085	**888-898-8733**	408-727-1885
Actel Corp	2061 Stierlin Ct	Mountain View	CA	94043	**800-262-1060**	650-318-4200
Advanced Micro Devices Inc (AMD)	1 AMD Pl PO Box 3453 *NYSE: AMD*	Sunnyvale	CA	94088	**800-538-8450**	408-749-4000
Advantage Electronic Product Development	34 Garden Ctr	Broomfield	CO	80020	**866-841-5581**	303-410-0292
Aeroflex Inc	35 S Service Rd PO Box 6022 *TSE: ARX*	Plainview	NY	11803	**800-843-1553**	516-694-6700
Altera Corp	101 Innovation Dr *NASDAQ: ALTR* ■ *Cust Svc	San Jose	CA	95134	**800-767-3753***	408-544-7000
Analog Devices Inc	3 Technology Way *NASDAQ: ADI*	Norwood	MA	02062	**800-262-5643**	781-329-4700
Axsun Technologies Inc	1 Fortune Dr	Billerica	MA	01821	**866-462-9786**	978-262-0049
B & B Electronics Manufacturing Co	PO Box 1040	Ottawa	IL	61350	**800-346-3119**	815-433-5100
Broadcom Corp	1320 Ridder Park Dr *NASDAQ: BRCM*	Irvine	CA	92617	**877-673-9442**	408-433-8000
Cirrus Logic Inc	2901 Via Fortuna *NASDAQ: CRUS*	Austin	TX	78746	**800-888-5016**	512-851-4000
Clare Inc	78 Cherry Hill Dr	Beverly	MA	01915	**800-272-5273**	978-524-6700
Conexant Systems Inc	1901 Main St Ste 300	Irvine	CA	92614	**888-855-4562**	949-483-4600
Cree Inc	4600 Silicon Dr *NASDAQ: CREE*	Durham	NC	27703	**800-533-2583**	919-313-5300
Cypress Semiconductor Corp	198 Champion Ct *NASDAQ: CY*	San Jose	CA	95134	**800-541-4736**	408-943-2600
Enphase Energy Inc	1420 N Mcdowell Blvd	Petaluma	CA	94954	**877-797-4743**	707-763-4784
Epson Electronics America Inc	150 River Oaks Pkwy	San Jose	CA	95134	**800-228-3964**	408-922-0200
Exar Corp	48720 Kato Rd *NYSE: EXAR*	Fremont	CA	94538	**855-755-1330**	510-668-7000
Fairchild Imaging Inc	1801 McCarthy Blvd	Milpitas	CA	95035	**800-325-6975**	408-433-2500
Fairchild Semiconductor Corp	82 Running Hill Rd *NASDAQ: FCS*	South Portland	ME	04106	**800-341-0392**	207-775-8100
Gel-Pak LLC	31398 Huntwood Ave	Hayward	CA	94544	**888-621-4147**	510-576-2220
Global Solar Energy Inc	8500 S Rita Rd	Tucson	AZ	85747	**866-999-8422**	520-546-6313
HEI Inc	1495 Steiger Lk Ln	Victoria	MN	55386	**866-720-2397**	952-443-2500
Hitachi Canada Ltd	5450 Explore Dr Ste 501	Mississauga	ON	L4W5N1	**877-248-4237**	905-629-9300
Integrated Device Technology Inc	6024 Silver Creek Vly Rd *NASDAQ: IDTI*	San Jose	CA	95138	**800-345-7015**	408-284-8200
Integrated Silicon Solution Inc (ISSI)	1940 Zanker Rd *NASDAQ: ISSI*	San Jose	CA	95112	**800-379-4774**	408-969-6600
Intel Corp	2200 Mission College Blvd *NASDAQ: INTC* ■ *Cust Svc	Santa Clara	CA	95052	**800-628-8686***	408-765-8080
Intermolecular Inc	3011 N First St	San Jose	CA	95134	**877-251-1860**	408-582-5700
Intersil Corp	1001 Murphy Ranch Rd *NASDAQ: ISIL*	Milpitas	CA	95035	**888-468-3774**	408-432-8888
Kyocera Solar Inc	7812 E Acoma Dr Ste 2	Scottsdale	AZ	85260	**800-544-6466**	480-948-8003
Lattice Semiconductor Corp	5555 NE Moore Ct *NASDAQ: LSCC*	Hillsboro	OR	97124	**800-528-8423**	503-268-8000
Linear Technology Corp	1630 McCarthy Blvd *NASDAQ: LLTC*	Milpitas	CA	95035	**888-500-6973**	408-432-1900
Logic Devices Inc	1375 Geneva Dr *OTC: LOGC*	Sunnyvale	CA	94089	**800-233-2518**	408-542-5400
M/A-COM Technology Solutions Inc	100 Chelmsford St	Lowell	MA	01851	**800-366-2266**	978-656-2500
Maxim Integrated Products Inc	120 San Gabriel Dr *NASDAQ: MXIM*	Sunnyvale	CA	94086	**888-629-4642**	408-737-7600
Micrel Inc	2180 Fortune Dr *NASDAQ: MCRL*	San Jose	CA	95131	**800-282-9855**	408-944-0800

Company / Address	City	State	Zip	Toll-Free	Phone
Microchip Technology Inc 2355 W Chandler Blvd *NASDAQ: MCHP*	Chandler	AZ	85224	**800-437-2767**	480-792-7200
Microsemi Corp 2381 Morse Ave *NASDAQ: MSCC*	Irvine	CA	92614	**800-713-4113**	949-221-7100
Mini-Circuits Laboratories Inc 13 Neptune Ave	Brooklyn	NY	11235	**800-654-7949**	718-934-4500
NVE Corp 11409 Vly View Rd *NASDAQ: NVEC*	Eden Prairie	MN	55344	**800-467-7141**	952-829-9217
ON Semiconductor Corp 5005 E McDowell Rd *NASDAQ: ON*	Phoenix	AZ	85008	**800-282-9855**	602-244-6600
Optek Technology Inc 1645 Wallace Dr	Carrollton	TX	75006	**800-341-4747**	972-323-2200
Pericom Semiconductor Corp 3545 N First St *NASDAQ: PSEM*	San Jose	CA	95134	**800-435-2336**	408-435-0800
Photronics Inc 15 Secor Rd *NASDAQ: PLAB*	Brookfield	CT	06804	**800-292-9396**	203-775-9000
Plascore Inc 615 N Fairview St	Zeeland	MI	49464	**800-630-9257**	616-772-1220
Powerex Inc 173 Pavilion Ln	Youngwood	PA	15697	**800-451-1415**	724-925-7272
Powerfilm Inc 2337 230th St	Ames	IA	50014	**888-354-7773**	515-292-7606
QLogic Corp 26650 Aliso Viejo Pkwy *NASDAQ: QLGC*	Aliso Viejo	CA	92656	**800-662-4471**	949-389-6000
Ramtron International Corp 1850 Ramtron Dr *NASDAQ: RMTR*	Colorado Springs	CO	80921	**800-541-4736**	719-481-7000
Raytek Inc 1201 Shaffer Rd	Santa Cruz	CA	95061	**800-227-8074**	831-458-3900
RF Micro Devices Inc 7628 Thorndike Rd *NASDAQ: RFMD*	Greensboro	NC	27409	**800-937-5449**	336-664-1233
Samsung Semiconductors Inc 3655 N First St *General	San Jose	CA	95134	**800-726-7864***	408-544-4000
Seiko Instruments USA Inc 21221 S Western Ave Ste 250 *Sales	Torrance	CA	90501	**800-688-0817***	310-517-7700
Sheldahl Inc 1150 Sheldahl Rd	Northfield	MN	55057	**800-927-3580**	507-663-8000
Silicon Laboratories Inc 400 W Cesar Chavez *NASDAQ: SLAB*	Austin	TX	78701	**877-444-3032**	512-416-8500
Solar Solutions & Distribution LLC 2500 W Fifth Ave	Denver	CO	80204	**855-765-3478**	303-948-6300
Solatube International Inc 2210 Oak Ridge Way	Vista	CA	92081	**888-765-2882**	760-477-1120
Spectrolab Inc 12500 Gladstone Ave	Sylmar	CA	91342	**800-936-4888**	818-365-4611
SRS Labs Inc 2909 Daimler St *NASDAQ: SRSL* ■ *General	Santa Ana	CA	92705	**800-322-2885***	949-442-1070
STMicroelectronics NV 134 Vintage Park Blvd Ste 192	Houston	TX	77070	**888-356-1766**	844-786-4276
Stretch Inc 1322 Orleans Dr	Sunnyvale	CA	94089	**800-468-6853**	408-543-2700
SunPower Corp 77 Rio Robles *NASDAQ: SPWR*	San Jose	CA	95134	**800-786-7693**	408-240-5500
Taiwan Semiconductor Mfg Company Ltd (TSMC) 2851 Junction Ave *NYSE: TSM*	San Jose	CA	95134	**877-248-4237**	408-382-8000
Tellurex Corp 1462 International Dr	Traverse City	MI	49686	**877-774-7468**	231-947-0110
Texas Instruments Inc 12500 TI Blvd *NASDAQ: TXN* ■ *Cust Svc	Dallas	TX	75243	**800-336-5236***	972-995-3773
Thorlabs Quantum Electronics Inc 10335 Guilford Rd	Jessup	MD	20794	**877-226-8342**	240-456-7100
TriQuint Semiconductor Inc 2300 NE Brookwood Pkwy *NASDAQ: TQNT*	Hillsboro	OR	97124	**855-367-8768**	503-615-9000
United Microelectronics Corp 488 De Guigne Dr *NYSE: UMC*	Sunnyvale	CA	94085	**800-990-1135**	408-523-7800
Veritec Inc 2445 Winnetka Ave N	Golden Valley	MN	55427	**866-546-1011**	763-253-2670
VIA Technologies Inc 940 Mission Ct	Fremont	CA	94539	**888-524-9382**	510-683-3300
Vishay Intertechnology Inc 63 Lancaster Ave *NYSE: VSH*	Malvern	PA	19355	**800-567-6098**	610-644-1300
Wabash Technologies 1375 Swan St PO Box 829	Huntington	IN	46750	**800-487-6865**	260-355-4100
Wallco Inc 53 E Jackson St # 55	Wilkes-Barre	PA	18701	**800-392-5526**	570-823-6181
Xilinx Inc 2100 Logic Dr *NASDAQ: XLNX*	San Jose	CA	95124	**800-594-5469**	408-559-7778

695 SHEET METAL WORK

SEE ALSO Plumbing, Heating, Air Conditioning Contractors ; Roofing, Siding, Sheet Metal Contractors

Company / Address	City	State	Zip	Toll-Free	Phone
Abalon Precision Mfg Corp 1040 Home St	Bronx	NY	10459	**800-888-2225**	718-589-5682
Accede Mold & Tool Company Inc 1125 Lexington Ave	Rochester	NY	14606	**888-236-2427**	585-254-6490
Air Comfort Corp 2550 Braga Dr	Broadview	IL	60155	**800-466-3779**	708-345-1900
Air Vent Inc 4117 Pinnacle Pnt Dr Ste 400	Dallas	TX	75211	**800-247-8368**	
Aircom Mfg Inc 6205 E 30th St	Indianapolis	IN	46219	**800-925-2426**	317-545-5383
Aluminum Line Products Co 24460 Sperry Cir	Westlake	OH	44145	**800-321-3154**	440-835-8880
Arizona Precision Sheet Metal 2140 W Pinnacle Peak Rd	Phoenix	AZ	85027	**800-443-7039**	623-516-3700
ASC Profiles Inc 2110 Enterprise Blvd *Cust Svc	West Sacramento	CA	95691	**800-360-2477***	916-372-0933
Associated Materials Inc 3773 State Rd	Cuyahoga Falls	OH	44223	**800-257-4335**	330-929-1811
ATS Systems Inc 30222 Esperanza	Rancho Santa Margarita	CA	92688	**800-321-1833**	949-888-1744
Automated Quality Technologies Inc 563 Shoreview Park Rd	St Paul	MN	55126	**800-250-9297**	651-484-6544
Ballew's Aluminum Products Inc 2 Shelter Dr	Greer	SC	29650	**800-231-6666**	864-272-4453
Berger Bldg Products Inc 805 Pennsylvania Blvd *Cust Svc	Feasterville	PA	19053	**800-523-8852***	215-355-1200
Captive-aire Systems Inc 4641 Paragon Pk Rd	Raleigh	NC	27616	**800-334-9256**	919-882-2410
CID Performance Tooling Inc 6 Willey Rd	Saco	ME	04072	**800-964-2331**	207-286-3319
Contech Construction Products Inc 9025 Centre Pt Dr Ste 400	West Chester	OH	45069	**800-338-1122**	513-645-7000
Crown Products Company Inc 6390 Phillips Hwy	Jacksonville	FL	32216	**800-683-7144**	904-737-7144
Data-Matique 2110 Sherwin St	Garland	TX	75041	**866-706-0981**	972-272-3446
Daviess County Metal Sales Inc 9929 E US Hwy 50	Cannelburg	IN	47519	**800-279-4299**	812-486-4299
Durand Forms Inc 6200 Equitable Rd	Kansas City	MO	64120	**800-545-6342**	
Edco & Arrowhead Products Inc 8700 Excelsior Blvd	Hopkins	MN	55343	**800-333-2580**	952-945-2680
EDM Zap Parts Inc 1108 Front St Ste 2	Lisle	IL	60532	**800-759-2839**	630-852-1699
Elixir Industries Inc 24800 Chrisanta Dr Ste 210	Mission Viejo	CA	92691	**800-421-1942**	949-860-5000
Epic Metals Corp 11 Talbot Ave	Rankin	PA	15104	**877-696-3742**	412-351-3913
Eze Lap Diamond Products 3572 Arrowhead Dr	Carson City	NV	89706	**800-843-4815**	775-888-9500
Flexbar Machine Corp 250 Gibbs Rd	Islandia	NY	11749	**800-879-7575**	631-582-8440
FS Tool Corp 71 Hobbs Gate	Markham	ON	L3R9T9	**800-387-9723**	905-475-1999
Gentek Bldg Products Inc 11 Craigwood Rd	Avenel	NJ	07001	**800-548-4542**	732-381-0900
H & H Industrial Corp 7612 Rt 130	Pennsauken	NJ	08110	**800-982-0341**	856-663-4444
Hi-Tech Fabrication Inc Leesville Industrial Park 8900 Midway W Rd	Raleigh	NC	27617	**800-359-7249**	919-781-2552
Hutchinson Manufacturing Inc 720 Hwy 7 W PO Box 487	Hutchinson	MN	55350	**800-795-1276**	320-587-4653
In-place Machining Company Inc 3811 N Holton St	Milwaukee	WI	53212	**800-833-3575**	414-562-2000
Industrial Louvers Inc 511 Seventh St S	Delano	MN	55328	**800-328-3421**	763-972-2981
Industrial Revolution Inc 9225 151st Ave NE	Redmond	WA	98052	**888-297-6062**	425-883-6600
Jones Metal Products Inc 3201 Third Ave	Mankato	MN	56001	**800-967-1750**	507-625-4436
LB Foster Co 415 Holiday Dr *NASDAQ: FSTR*	Pittsburgh	PA	15220	**800-255-4500**	
Link-Burns Mfg Company Inc 253 American Way	Voorhees	NJ	08043	**800-457-4358**	856-429-6844
Lippincott Marine 3420 Main St	Grasonville	MD	33701	**877-437-4193**	410-827-9300
M K Specialty Metal Fabricators 725 W Wintergreen Rd	Hutchins	TX	75141	**866-814-4617**	972-225-6562
M&M Manufacturing Co 4001 Mark IV Pkwy	Fort Worth	TX	76106	**866-706-3999**	817-336-2311
Mapes Panels LLC 2929 Cornhusker Hwy PO Box 80069	Lincoln	NE	68504	**800-228-2391**	
Mayco Industries LLC 18 W Oxmoor Rd	Birmingham	AL	35209	**800-749-6061**	205-942-4242
Mayville Products Corp 403 Degner Ave	Mayville	WI	53050	**800-558-7297**	920-387-3000
McCorvey Sheet Metal Works LP 8610 Wallisvile Rd	Houston	TX	77029	**800-580-7545**	713-672-7545
Menches Tool & Die Inc 30995 San Benito St	Hayward	CA	94544	**877-592-2328**	510-476-1160
Metal-Fab Inc 3025 May St	Wichita	KS	67213	**800-835-2830**	316-943-2351
Metcam Inc 305 Tidwell Cir	Alpharetta	GA	30004	**888-394-9633**	770-475-9633
Miller-Leaman 800 Orange Ave	Daytona Beach	FL	32114	**800-881-0320**	386-248-0500
Mitchell Metal Products Inc 19250 Hwy 12 E PO Box 789	Kosciusko	MS	39090	**800-258-6137**	662-289-7110
Morse Industries Inc 25811 74th Ave S	Kent	WA	98032	**800-325-7513**	
Murray Sheet Metal Co Inc 3112 Seventh St	Parkersburg	WV	26104	**800-464-8801**	304-422-5431
Napco Ply Gem Inc 5020 Weston Pkwy Ste 400	Cary	MO	27153	**800-786-2726**	888-975-9436
National Metal Fabricators 2395 Greenleaf Ave	Elk Grove Village	IL	60007	**800-323-8849**	847-439-5321
Newjac Inc 415 S Grant St	Lebanon	IN	46052	**800-827-3259**	765-483-2190
Nu-Way Industries Inc 555 Howard Ave	Des Plaines	IL	60018	**888-488-5631**	847-298-7710
OMAX Corp 21409 72nd Ave S	Kent	WA	98032	**800-838-0343**	253-872-2300
Panavise Products Inc 7540 Colbert Dr	Reno	NV	89511	**800-759-7535**	775-850-2900

Company / Address	City	State	ZIP	Toll-Free	Phone
Petersen Aluminum Corp 1005 Tonne Rd	Elk Grove Village	IL	60007	**800-323-1960**	847-228-7150
Platt & Labonia Co 70 Stoddard Ave	North Haven	CT	06473	**800-505-9099**	203-239-5681
Quality Metal Products Inc Orange Rd PO Box 273	Dallas	PA	18612	**888-251-2805**	570-333-4248
Rollex Corp 800 Chasa Ave *Cust Svc	Elk Grove Village	IL	60007	**800-251-3300***	847-437-3000
S & S X-Ray Products Inc 10625 Telge Rd	Houston	TX	77095	**800-231-1747**	281-815-1300
Saint Regis Culvert Inc 202 Morrell St	Charlotte	MI	48813	**800-527-4604**	517-543-3430
Simpson Dura-Vent Inc 877 Cotting Ct	Vacaville	CA	95688	**800-835-4429**	707-446-1786
SMT Inc 7300 ACC Blvd	Raleigh	NC	27617	**888-214-4804**	919-782-4804
Southwark Metal Mfg Company Inc 2800 Red Lion Rd	Philadelphia	PA	19114	**800-523-1052**	215-735-3401
Spencer Fabrications Inc 29511 County Rd 561	Tavares	FL	32778	**866-277-3623**	352-343-0014
Streimer Sheet Metal Works Inc 740 N Knott St	Portland	OR	97227	**888-288-3828**	503-288-9393
Structures Unlimited Inc 166 River Rd	Bow	NH	03304	**800-225-3895**	603-645-6539
T & C Industries Inc PO Box 629	Darien	WI	53114	**800-426-6447**	262-882-1227
TF System The Vertical ICF Inc 3030c Holmgren Way	Green Bay	WI	54304	**800-360-4634**	920-983-9960
Thybar Corp 913 S Kay Ave	Addison	IL	60101	**800-666-2872**	630-543-5300
Unist 4134 36th St SE	Grand Rapids	MI	49512	**800-253-5462**	616-949-0853
United Tool & Stamping Company of North Carolina Inc 2817 Enterprise Ave	Fayetteville	NC	28306	**800-883-6087**	910-323-8588
Valley Joist 3019 Gault Ave N	Fort Payne	AL	35967	**800-263-0324**	256-845-2330
Wilson Manufacturing Co 4725 Green Park Rd	Saint Louis	MO	63123	**800-634-5248**	314-416-8900
Wilson Tool International Inc 12912 Farnham Ave	White Bear Lake	MN	55110	**800-328-9646**	651-286-6001
Wisco Products Inc 109 Commercial St	Dayton	OH	45402	**800-367-6570**	937-228-2101
York Metal Fabricators Inc 27 Ne 26th St	Oklahoma City	OK	73105	**800-255-4703**	405-528-7495

696 SHIP BUILDING & REPAIRING

Company / Address	City	State	ZIP	Toll-Free	Phone
Colonna's Shipyard Inc 400 E Indian River Rd	Norfolk	VA	23523	**800-265-6627**	757-545-2414
Continental Maritime of San Diego Inc 1995 Bay Front St	San Diego	CA	92113	**877-631-0020**	619-234-8851
Earl Industries LLC 2 Harper Ave	Portsmouth	VA	23707	**800-433-8442**	757-215-2500
Elevating Boats LLC 201 Dean Ct	Houma	LA	70363	**800-843-2895**	985-868-9655
Greenbrier Co 1 Centerpointe Dr Ste 200 *NYSE: GBX*	Lake Oswego	OR	97035	**800-343-7188**	503-684-7000
Leevac Shipyards Inc 111 Bunge St	Jennings	LA	70546	**800-244-3262**	337-824-2210
MARCO Global 4259 22nd Ave W	Seattle	WA	98199	**866-966-2726**	206-285-3200
Northrop Grumman Newport News 13560 Jefferson Ave	Newport News	VA	23603	**888-493-7386**	757-886-7777
Pacific Fisherman Inc 5351 24th Ave NW	Seattle	WA	98107	**877-644-6148**	206-784-2562
Pocock Racing Shells 615 80Th St Sw	Everett	WA	98203	**888-762-6251**	425-438-9048
Robishaw Engineering Inc 10106 Mathewson Ln	Houston	TX	77043	**800-877-1706**	713-468-1706
Tecnico Corp 831 Industrial Ave *General	Chesapeake	VA	23324	**800-786-2207***	757-545-4013
Trinity Marine Products Inc 2525 N Stemmons Fwy	Dallas	TX	75207	**877-876-5463**	214-589-8446

697 SHUTTERS - WINDOW (ALL TYPES)

Company / Address	City	State	ZIP	Toll-Free	Phone
Atlantic Premium Shutters 29797 Beck Rd	Wixom	MI	48393	**866-288-2726**	248-668-6408
Champion Window Mfg Inc 12121 Champion Way	Cincinnati	OH	45241	**877-424-2674**	513-346-4600
Commonwealth Laminating & Coating Inc 345 Beaver Creek Dr *General	Martinsville	VA	24112	**888-321-5111***	276-632-4991
Perfect Shutters Inc 12213 Rte 173	Hebron	IL	60034	**800-548-3336**	815-648-2401
Roll Shutter Systems Inc 21633 N 14th Ave	Phoenix	AZ	85027	**800-551-7655**	623-869-7057
Roll-A-Way Inc 1661 Glenlake Ave	Itasca	IL	60143	**866-749-5424**	
Rolling Shield Inc 2500 NW 74th Ave	Miami	FL	33122	**800-474-9404**	
Shutter Mill Inc 8517 S Perkins Rd	Stillwater	OK	74074	**800-416-6455**	405-377-6455
Sunburst Shutters 6480 W Flamingo Rd Ste D	Las Vegas	NV	89103	**877-786-2877**	702-367-1600
Tapco Group 29797 Beck Rd	Wixom	MI	48393	**800-521-7567**	248-668-6400

698 SIGNALS & SIRENS - ELECTRIC

Company / Address	City	State	ZIP	Toll-Free	Phone
ADDCO LLC 240 Arlington Ave E	Saint Paul	MN	55117	**800-616-4408**	651-488-8600
ECCO 833 W Diamond St	Boise	ID	83705	**800-635-5900**	208-395-8000
Econolite Control Products Inc 3360 E La Palma Av	Anaheim	CA	92806	**800-225-6480**	714-630-3700
Federal Signal Corp Emergency Products Div 2645 Federal Signal Dr	University Park	IL	60466	**800-264-3578**	708-534-3400

699 SIGNS

SEE ALSO Signals & Sirens - Electric ; Displays - Exhibit & Trade Show ; Displays - Point-of-Purchase

Company / Address	City	State	ZIP	Toll-Free	Phone
Ad Art Co 3260 E 26th St	Los Angeles	CA	90058	**800-266-7522**	323-981-8941
Advance Corp Braille-Tac Div 8200 97th St S	Cottage Grove	MN	55016	**800-328-9451**	651-771-9297
Allen Industries Inc 6434 Burnt Poplar Rd	Greensboro	NC	27409	**800-967-2553**	336-668-2791
APCO Graphics Inc 388 Grant St SE	Atlanta	GA	30312	**877-988-2726**	404-688-9000
Apex Digital Imaging Inc 16057 Tampa Palms Blvd W	Tampa	FL	33647	**866-973-3034**	813-973-3034
ASL Services 3700 Commerce Blvd Ste 216	Kissimmee	FL	34741	**888-744-6275**	407-518-7900
Beyond Digital Imaging 36 Apple Creek Blvd	Markham	ON	L3R4Y4	**888-689-1888**	905-415-1888
Brady Corp 6555 W Good Hope Rd *NYSE: BRC* ■ *Cust Svc	Milwaukee	WI	53223	**800-541-1686***	414-358-6600
California Neon Products Inc 4530 Mission Gorge Pl	San Diego	CA	92120	**800-822-6366**	619-283-2191
Century Graphics & Metals Inc 550 S N Lake Blvd Ste 1000	Altamonte Springs	FL	32701	**800-327-5664**	
Colorado Time Systems 1551 E 11th St	Loveland	CO	80537	**800-279-0111**	970-667-1000
Couch & Philippi Inc 10680 Fern Ave PO Box A *Orders	Stanton	CA	90680	**800-854-3360***	714-527-2261
Cummings Signs Inc 15 Century Blvd Ste 200	Nashville	TN	37214	**800-489-7446**	
DiAZiT Company Inc 941 US 1 Hwy *Cust Svc	Youngsville	NC	27596	**800-334-6641***	919-556-5188
Dualite Sales & Service Inc 1 Dualite Ln	Williamsburg	OH	45176	**800-543-7271**	513-724-7100
Eastern Metal/USA-SIGN 1430 Sullivan St *Sales	Elmira	NY	14901	**800-872-7446***	607-734-2295
Everbrite Inc 4949 S 110th St PO Box 20020	Greenfield	WI	53220	**800-558-3888**	414-529-3500
FASTSIGNS International Inc 2542 Highlander Way	Carrollton	TX	75006	**800-327-8744**	972-447-0777
Formetco Inc 2963 Pleasant Hill Rd	Duluth	GA	30096	**800-367-6382**	770-476-7000
GableSigns Inc 7440 Ft Smallwood Rd	Baltimore	MD	21226	**800-854-0568**	410-255-6400
Gemini Inc 103 Mensing Way	Cannon Falls	MN	55009	**800-538-8377**	507-263-3957
George Patton Assoc Inc 55 Broadcommon Rd	Bristol	RI	02809	**800-572-2194**	401-247-0333
Gopher Sign Co 1310 Randolph Ave	Saint Paul	MN	55105	**800-383-3156**	651-698-5095
Grandwell Industries Inc 6109 S NC HWY 55 *Cust Svc	Fuquay Varina	NC	27526	**800-338-6554***	919-557-1221
Graphic Specialties Inc 3110 Washington Ave N	Minneapolis	MN	55411	**800-486-4605**	612-522-5287
Hall Signs Inc 4495 W Vernal Pk	Bloomington	IN	47404	**800-284-7446**	
Hallmark Nameplate Inc 1717 E Lincoln Ave	Mount Dora	FL	32757	**800-874-9063**	352-383-8142
Hawkins Traffic Safety Supply 1255 E Shore Hwy	Berkeley	CA	94710	**800-772-3995**	800-236-0112
Hy-Ko Products Co 60 Meadow Ln	Northfield	OH	44067	**800-292-0550**	330-467-7446
Icon Identity Solutions 1418 Elmhurst Rd	Elk Grove Village	IL	60007	**888-724-0380**	
Insignia Systems Inc 8799 Brooklyn Blvd *NASDAQ: ISIG*	Minneapolis	MN	55445	**800-874-4648**	763-392-6200
Kessler Sign Co 5804 Poe Ave	Dayton	OH	45414	**800-686-1870**	937-898-0633
Kieffer & Company Inc 3322 Washington Ave	Sheboygan	WI	53081	**800-458-4394**	
Lake Shore Industries Inc (LSI) 1817 Poplar St PO BOX 3427	Erie	PA	16508	**800-458-0463**	
LNI Custom Manufacturing Inc 12536 Chadron Ave	Hawthorne	CA	90250	**800-338-3387**	310-978-2000
M-R Sign Company Inc 1706 First Ave N	Fergus Falls	MN	56537	**800-231-5564**	218-736-5681
Magnetsigns Adv Inc 4225 38th St	Camrose	AB	T4V3Z3	**800-219-8977**	780-672-8720
MC Sign Company Inc 8959 Tyler Blvd	Mentor	OH	44060	**800-627-4460**	440-953-2280
McLoone 75 Sumner St	La Crosse	WI	54603	**800-624-6641**	608-784-1260
National Stock Sign Co 1040 El Dorado Ave	Santa Cruz	CA	95062	**800-462-7726**	831-476-2020
O'Ryan Group Inc 4010 Pilot Ste 108	Memphis	TN	38118	**800-253-0750**	901-794-4610
Pannier Graphics 345 Oak Rd	Gibsonia	PA	15044	**800-544-8428**	724-265-4900
Pattison Sign Group 555 Ellesmere Rd	Scarborough	ON	M1R4E8	**800-268-6536**	416-759-1111
Poblocki Sign Company LLC 922 S 70th St	West Allis	WI	53214	**800-776-7064**	414-453-4010
Precision Solar Controls Inc 2985 Market St	Garland	TX	75041	**800-686-7414**	972-278-0553
Protection Services Inc 635 Lucknow Rd	Harrisburg	PA	17110	**866-489-1234**	717-236-9307

Name / Address	City	State	Zip	Toll-Free	Phone
Quality Manufacturing Inc 969 Labore Industrial Ct	Saint Paul	MN	55110	**800-243-5473**	651-483-5473
Safeway Sign Co 9875 Yucca Rd	Adelanto	CA	92301	**800-637-7233**	760-246-7070
Scioto Sign Company Inc 6047 US Rt 68 N	Kenton	OH	43326	**800-572-4686**	419-673-1261
SFC Graphics 110 E Woodruff Ave	Toledo	OH	43604	**800-537-1130**	419-255-1283
Sign Builders Inc 4800 Jefferson Ave PO Box 28380	Birmingham	AL	35228	**800-222-7330**	
Sign Designs Inc 204 Campus Way	Modesto	CA	95352	**800-421-7446**	209-524-4484
Sign-A-Rama 2121 Vista Pkwy *All	West Palm Beach	FL	33411	**800-776-8105***	561-640-5570
Signs by Tomorrow USA Inc 8681 Robert Fulton Dr	Columbia	MD	21046	**800-765-7446**	410-312-3600
Signs Now 5368 Dixie Hwy Ste 1	Waterford	MI	48329	**800-356-3373**	248-596-8600
Signtech Electrical Adv Inc 4444 Federal Blvd	San Diego	CA	92102	**877-885-1135**	619-527-6100
Signtronix 1445 W Sepulveda Blvd	Torrance	CA	90501	**800-729-4853**	
Spectrum Corp 10048 Easthaven Blvd	Houston	TX	77075	**800-392-5050**	713-944-6200
Tube Art Group (TAG) 11715 SE Fifth St	Bellevue	WA	98005	**800-562-2854**	206-223-1122
U s Nameplate Company Inc Hwy 30 W	Mount Vernon	IA	52314	**800-553-8871**	319-895-8804
Vomela Co, The 274 E Fillmore Ave	Saint Paul	MN	55107	**800-645-1012**	651-228-2200
Walter Haas & Sons Inc 123 W 23rd St	Hialeah	FL	33010	**800-552-3845**	305-883-2257
World Wide Concessions Inc 1950 Old Cuthbert Rd Ste M	Cherry Hill	NJ	08034	**888-377-7666**	856-933-9900
Worldwide Sign Systems 446 N Cecil St	Bonduel	WI	54107	**800-874-3334**	
Young Electric Sign Co 2401 Foothill Dr	Salt Lake City	UT	84109	**866-779-8357**	801-464-4600
Zumar Industries Inc 9719 Santa Fe Springs Rd	Santa Fe Springs	CA	90670	**800-654-7446**	562-941-4633

700 SILVERWARE

SEE ALSO Cutlery ; Metal Stampings

Name / Address	City	State	Zip	Toll-Free	Phone
Old Newbury Crafters 36 Main St Ste 2	Amesbury	MA	01913	**800-343-1388**	
Olde Country Reproductions Inc 722 W Market St *Cust Svc	York	PA	17405	**800-358-3997***	717-848-1859
Pfaltzgraff Co PO Box 21769	York	PA	17402	**800-999-2811**	
Salisbury Inc 29085 Airpark Dr	Easton	MD	21601	**855-255-5309**	410-770-4901
Towle Silversmiths PO Box 21379	York	PA	17402	**800-264-0758**	
Woodbury Pewterers Inc 860 Main St S	Woodbury	CT	06798	**800-648-2014**	

701 SIMULATION & TRAINING SYSTEMS

Name / Address	City	State	Zip	Toll-Free	Phone
CAE Inc 8585 Cote de Liesse *NYSE: CAE*	Saint Laurent	QC	H4T1G6	**866-999-6223**	514-341-6780
Cubic Corp 9333 Balboa Ave PO Box 85587 *NYSE: CUB*	San Diego	CA	92186	**800-937-5449**	858-277-6780
Cubic Defense Systems 9333 Balboa Ave	San Diego	CA	92123	**800-937-5449**	858-277-6780
DRS C3 Systems LLC 400 Professional Dr	Gaithersburg	MD	20879	**800-694-5005**	301-921-8100
Energy Concepts Inc 404 Washington Blvd	Mundelein	IL	60060	**800-621-1247**	847-837-8191
Evans & Sutherland Computer Corp 770 Komas Dr *OTC: ESCC* ■ *Sales	Salt Lake City	UT	84108	**800-327-5707***	801-588-1000
Faac Inc 1229 Oak Valley Dr	Ann Arbor	MI	48108	**877-322-2387**	734-761-5836
Meggitt Training Systems Inc 296 Brogdon Rd	Suwanee	GA	30024	**800-813-9046**	678-288-1090
Nida Corp 300 S John Rodes Blvd	Melbourne	FL	32904	**800-327-6432**	321-727-2265

702 SMART CARDS

Name / Address	City	State	Zip	Toll-Free	Phone
CardLogix 16 Hughes Ste 100	Irvine	CA	92618	**866-392-8326**	949-380-1312
Clever Devices Ltd 300 Crossways Pk Dr	Woodbury	NY	11797	**800-872-6129**	516-433-6100
Credit Card Systems Inc 180 Shepard Ave	Wheeling	IL	60090	**800-747-1269**	847-459-8320
DataCard Corp 11111 Bren Rd W	Minnetonka	MN	55343	**800-328-8623**	952-933-1223
MDI Security Systems Inc 12500 Network Dr Ste 303	San Antonio	TX	78249	**866-435-7634**	210-477-5400

703 SNOWMOBILES

SEE ALSO Sporting Goods

Name / Address	City	State	Zip	Toll-Free	Phone
Yamaha Motor Corp USA 6555 Katella Ave *Cust Svc	Cypress	CA	90630	**800-656-7695***	

SOFTWARE

SEE Computer Software

704 SPAS - HEALTH & FITNESS

SEE ALSO Spas - Hotel & Resort ; Weight Loss Centers & Services ; Health & Fitness Centers

Facilities listed here provide multi-day programs designed to increase health and well-being. Types of programs offered include (but are not limited to) relaxation, smoking cessation, weight loss, and physical fitness.

Name / Address	City	State	Zip	Toll-Free	Phone
Amerispa 90 Rue de Stanstead St Ste 101	Bromont	QC	J2L1K6	**866-263-7477**	450-534-2717
Black Hills Health & Education Ctr PO Box 19 *Cust Svc	Hermosa	SD	57744	**866-757-0160***	605-255-4101
Cal-a-Vie Spa 29402 Spa Havens Way	Vista	CA	92084	**866-772-4283**	760-945-2055
Calistoga Spa Hot Springs 1006 Washington St	Calistoga	CA	94515	**866-822-5772**	707-942-6269
Cooper Wellness Program 12230 Preston Rd	Dallas	TX	75230	**800-444-5192**	972-386-4777
Deerfield Spa 650 Resica Falls Rd	East Stroudsburg	PA	18302	**800-852-4494**	570-223-0160
Duke Diet & Fitness Ctr (DFC) 501 Douglas St	Durham	NC	27705	**800-235-3853**	
Golden Door 777 Deer Springs Rd	San Marcos	CA	92069	**866-420-6414**	760-744-5777
Grand Wailea Resort & Spa 3850 Wailea Alanui Dr	Wailea	HI	96753	**800-888-6100**	808-875-1234
Green Mountain at Fox Run 262 Fox Ln PO Box 358	Ludlow	VT	05149	**800-448-8106**	802-228-8885
Green Valley Spa & Resort 1871 W Canyon View Dr	Saint George	UT	84770	**800-237-1068**	
Heartland Spa 1237 E 1600 N Rd	Gilman	IL	60938	**800-545-4853**	
Hilton Head Health Institute 14 Valencia Rd	Hilton Head Island	SC	29928	**800-292-2440**	843-785-3919
Hippocrates Health Institute Life-Change Ctr 1443 Palmdale Ct	West Palm Beach	FL	33411	**800-842-2125**	561-471-8876
Kripalu Ctr for Yoga & Health 57 Interlaken Rd	Stockbridge	MA	01262	**800-741-7353**	413-448-3400
Lodge & Spa at Cordillera 2205 Cordillera Way	Edwards	CO	81632	**800-877-3529**	970-926-2200
Miraval AZ Resort & Spa 5000 E Via Estancia Miraval	Tucson	AZ	85739	**800-232-3969**	
Oaks at Ojai 122 E Ojai Ave	Ojai	CA	93023	**800-753-6257**	805-646-5573
Ocean Waters Spa 600 N Atlantic Ave	Daytona Beach	FL	32118	**844-284-2685**	386-267-1660
Ojo Caliente Mineral Springs Resort 50 Los Banos Dr PO Box 68	Ojo Caliente	NM	87549	**800-222-9162**	505-583-2233
Optimum Health Institute 6970 Central Ave	Lemon Grove	CA	91945	**800-993-4325**	619-464-3346
Pritikin Longevity Ctr & Spa 8755 NW 36th St	Doral	FL	33178	**800-327-4914**	305-935-7131
Raj, The 1734 Jasmine Ave	Fairfield	IA	52556	**800-248-9050**	641-472-9580
Sagestone Spa & Salon *Red Mountain Resort* 1275 East Red Mtn Cir	Ivins	UT	84738	**877-246-4453**	435-673-4905
Spa at Coeur d'Alene 115 S Second St	Coeur d'Alene	ID	83814	**800-684-0514**	208-765-4000
Spa at Peninsula Beverly Hills 9882 S Santa Monica Blvd	Beverly Hills	CA	90212	**800-462-7899**	310-551-2888
Spa at The Setai 2001 Collins Ave	Miami Beach	FL	33139	**888-625-7500**	
Structure House 3017 Pickett Rd	Durham	NC	27705	**800-553-0052**	919-493-4205
Tennessee Fitness Spa 299 Natural Bridge Pk Rd	Waynesboro	TN	38485	**800-235-8365**	931-722-5589
Tracie Martyn Salon 59 Fifth Ave Ste 1	New York	NY	10003	**866-862-7896**	212-206-9333
Two Bunch Palms Resort & Spa 67425 Two Bunch Palms Trl	Desert Hot Springs	CA	92240	**800-472-4334**	760-329-8791
Uchee Pines Lifestyle Ctr 30 Uchee Pines Rd PO Box 75	Seale	AL	36875	**877-824-3374**	334-855-4764
Vail Cascade Resort & Spa 1300 Westhaven Dr	Vail	CO	81657	**800-420-2424**	970-476-7111

705 SPAS - HOTEL & RESORT

SEE ALSO Spas - Health & Fitness

Name / Address	City	State	Zip	Toll-Free	Phone
100 Fountain Spa at the Pillar & Post Inn 48 John St PO Box 48	Niagara-on-the-Lake	ON	L0S1J0	**888-669-5566**	905-468-2123
Abbey Resort & Fontana Spa 269 Fontana Blvd	Fontana	WI	53125	**800-709-1323**	262-275-9000
AdVantis Hospitality Alliance LLC 615 N Highland Ste 2A	Murfreesboro	TN	37130	**866-218-4782**	615-904-6133
Aloft Broomfield Denver 8300 Arista Pl	Broomfield	CO	80021	**866-716-8143**	303-635-2000
Aloft Chicago O'hare 9700 Balmoral Ave	Rosemont	IL	60018	**866-716-8143**	847-671-4444
Alpine Lodge 434 Indian Creek Cir	Branson	MO	65616	**888-563-4388**	417-338-2514
Amoray Dive Resort Inc 104250 Overseas Hwy	Key Largo	FL	33037	**800-426-6729**	305-451-3595
Ancient Cedars Spa at the Wickaninnish Inn 500 Osprey Ln PO Box 250	Tofino	BC	V0R2Z0	**800-333-4604**	250-725-3113
Aquae Sulis Spa at the JW Marriott Resort Las Vegas 221 N Rampart Blvd	Las Vegas	NV	89144	**877-869-8777**	702-869-7807
Aquaterra Spa at the Surf & Sand Resort 1555 S Coast Hwy	Laguna Beach	CA	92651	**877-741-5908**	949-376-2772

Classified Section

Listing	City	State	ZIP	Toll-Free	Phone
Aria Spa & Club at the Vail Cascade Resort 1300 Westhaven Dr	Vail	CO	81657	**888-824-5772**	970-479-5942
Arizona Biltmore Resort & Spa 2400 E Missouri	Phoenix	AZ	85016	**800-950-0086**	602-955-6600
Au Naturel Wellness & Medical Spa at the Brookstreet Hotel 525 Legget Dr	Ottawa	ON	K2K2W2	**888-826-2220**	613-271-1800
Auberge De La Fontaine b & b Inn 1301 Rue Rachel E	Montreal	QC	H2J2K1	**800-597-0597**	514-597-0166
Baccarat New York LLC 20 W 53rd St	New York	NY	10019	**866-957-5139**	212-790-8800
Battery Wharf Hotel & Spa, The 3 Battery Wharf	Boston	MA	02109	**877-794-6218**	617-994-9000
Best Western Tuscan Inn 425 N Point St	San Francisco	CA	94133	**800-648-4626**	415-561-1100
Boutique Spa at the Ritz-Carlton Georgetown 3100 S St NW	Washington	DC	20007	**800-241-3333**	202-912-4175
Canyon Ranch SpaClub at the Venetian 3355 Las Vegas Blvd S Ste 1159	Las Vegas	NV	89109	**877-220-2688**	702-414-3606
Cape Codder Resort & Spa 1225 Iyanough Rd Rt 132 Bearse's Way	Hyannis	MA	02601	**888-297-2200**	508-771-3000
Carefree Resort & Conference Ctr 37220 Mule Train Rd	Carefree	AZ	85377	**888-692-4343**	
Carneros Inn, The 4048 Sonoma Hwy	Napa	CA	94559	**888-400-9000**	707-299-4900
Centre for Well-Being at the Phoenician 6000 E Camelback Rd	Scottsdale	AZ	85251	**800-843-2392**	
CEPA Le Baluchon Inc 3550 chemin des Trembles	Saint-Paulin	QC	J0K3G0	**800-789-5968**	819-268-2555
Chateau Resort & Conference Center, The 300 Camelback Rd	Tannersville	PA	18372	**800-245-5900**	570-629-5900
Chateau Rouge 1505 S Broadway Ave	Red Lodge	MT	59068	**800-926-1601**	406-446-1601
Cheeca Lodge & Spa 81801 Overseas Hwy Mile Marker 82	Islamorada	FL	33036	**800-327-2888**	305-664-4651
Cliff Spa at Snowbird Hwy 210 PO Box 929000	Snowbird	UT	84092	**800-453-3000**	801-933-2225
Columbia Room Inc 1108 E Marina Way	Hood River	OR	97031	**800-828-7873**	541-386-2200
Coral Kay Resort 2300 Caravelle Cir	Kissimmee	FL	34746	**866-357-3682**	407-787-0718
Cranwell Resort Spa & Golf Club 55 Lee Rd	Lenox	MA	01240	**800-272-6935**	413-637-1364
Deer Lodge Hotels Ltd 106 Circle Dr	Saskatoon	SK	S7L4L6	**800-578-7878**	306-242-8881
Disney's Grand Floridian Spa 4401 Floridian Wy	Lake Buena Vista	FL	32830	**800-169-0730**	407-824-2332
El Caribe Resort 2125 S Atlantic Ave	Daytona Beach	FL	32118	**800-445-9889**	386-252-1558
Elizabeth Arden Red Door Spa at Mystic Marriott Hotel & Spa 625 N Rd	Groton	CT	06340	**866-449-7390**	860-446-2500
Emerson Resort & Spa 5340 Rt 28	Mount Tremper	NY	12457	**877-688-2828**	845-688-2828
EZ8 Motels Inc 2484 Hotel Cir Pl	San Diego	CA	92108	**855-413-1222**	619-291-4824
Festival Inn, The 1144 Ontario St	Stratford	ON	N5A6Z3	**800-463-3581**	519-273-1150
Ford Hotel Supply Company Inc 2204 N Broadway	Saint Louis	MO	63102	**800-472-3673**	314-231-8400
Four Seasons Spa at the Four Seasons Hotel Las Vegas 3960 Las Vegas Blvd S	Las Vegas	NV	89119	**800-332-3442**	702-632-5302
Four Seasons Spa at the Four Seasons Hotel Los Angeles at Beverly Hills 300 S Doheny Dr	Los Angeles	CA	90048	**800-819-5053**	310-786-2229
Four Seasons Spa at the Four Seasons Resort Jackson Hole 7680 Granite Loop Rd PO Box 544	Teton Village	WY	83025	**800-819-5053**	307-732-5120
Four Seasons Spa at the Four Seasons Resort Maui 3900 Wailea Alanui Dr	Wailea	HI	96753	**800-334-6284**	808-874-2925
Four Seasons Spa at the Four Seasons Resort Santa Barbara 1260 Ch Dr *General	Santa Barbara	CA	93108	**800-819-5053***	805-565-8250
Fox Harb'r Resort & Spa 1337 Fox Harbour Rd	Wallace	NS	B0K1Y0	**866-257-1801**	902-257-1801
Galvestonian Condominium Association 1401 E Beach Dr	Galveston	TX	77550	**888-526-6161**	409-765-6161
Garden Spa at MacArthur Place 29 E MacArthur St	Sonoma	CA	95476	**800-722-1866**	707-933-3193
Glacial Waters Spa at Grand View Lodge 23521 Nokomis Ave	Nisswa	MN	56468	**866-801-2951**	218-963-2234
Grand Hotel Marriott Resort Golf Club & Spa 1 Grand Blvd PO Box 639	Point Clear	AL	36564	**800-544-9933**	251-928-9201
Green Valley Ranch Resort Casino & Spa 2300 Paseo Verde Pkwy *Resv	Henderson	NV	89052	**866-782-9487***	702-617-7777
Greenbrier, The 300 W Main St	White Sulphur Springs	WV	24986	**800-453-4858**	304-536-1110
Groupe Riotel Hospitality Inc 250 Ave du Phare Est	Matane	QC	G4W3N4	**877-566-2651**	418-566-2651
Grove Park Inn Resort & Spa 290 Macon Ave	Asheville	NC	28804	**800-438-5800**	828-252-2711
Hilton Short Hills 41 JFK Pkwy	Short Hills	NJ	07078	**800-445-8667**	973-379-0100
Hilton Suites Toronto/Markham Conference Centre & Spa 8500 Warden Ave	Markham	ON	L6G1A5	**800-445-8667**	905-470-8500
Holly Shores Best Holiday 491 Route 9	Cape May	NJ	08204	**877-494-6559**	609-886-1234
Homestead Resort 700 N Homestead Dr	Midway	UT	84049	**888-327-7220**	
Hotel Mortagne 1228 Rue Nobel	Boucherville	QC	J4B5H1	**877-655-9966**	450-655-9966
Hotel Valencia Riverwalk 150 E Houston St	San Antonio	TX	78205	**855-596-3387**	210-227-9700
Hyatt Regency Scottsdale Resort at Gainey Ranch 7500 E Doubletree Ranch Rd	Scottsdale	AZ	85258	**800-233-1234**	480-483-5558
Indian Springs Resort & Spa 1712 Lincoln Ave	Calistoga	CA	94515	**800-877-3623**	707-942-4913
Jefferson Hotel Washington Dc, The 1200 16th St Nw	Washington	DC	20036	**877-313-9749**	202-448-2300
Jurlique Spa 4925 N Scottsdale Rd	Scottsdale	AZ	85251	**800-528-7867**	480-424-6072
JW Starr Pass Resort & Spa 3800 W Starr Pass Blvd	Tucson	AZ	85745	**800-845-5279**	520-792-3500
Kea Lani Spa at the Fairmont Kea Lani Maui 4100 Wailea Alanui Dr	Maui	HI	96753	**800-659-4100**	808-875-2229
Kohler Waters Spa 444 Highlands Dr	Kohler	WI	53044	**866-928-3777**	920-457-7777
Lafayette Park Hotel 3287 Mt Diablo Blvd	Lafayette	CA	94549	**855-382-8632**	925-283-3700
Lake Austin Spa Resort 1705 S Quinlan Pk Rd	Austin	TX	78732	**800-847-5637**	512-372-7380
Living Spa at El Monte Sagrado 317 Kit Carson Rd	Taos	NM	87571	**855-846-8267**	575-758-3502
Massage Ctr at Mohonk Mountain House 1000 Mtn Rest Rd	New Paltz	NY	12561	**800-772-6646**	845-255-1000
Mii Amo at Enchantment Resort 525 Boynton Canyon Rd	Sedona	AZ	86336	**888-749-2137**	928-203-8500
Mirbeau Inn & Spa 851 W Genesee St	Skaneateles	NY	13152	**877-647-2328**	315-685-5006
Mokara Hotel & Spa 212 W Crockett St	San Antonio	TX	78205	**866-605-1212**	210-396-5800
Montecito Inn Inc 1295 Coast Village Rd	Santa Barbara	CA	93108	**800-843-2017**	805-969-7854
Mountain Laurel Spa at Stonewall Resort 940 Resort Dr	Roanoke	WV	26447	**888-278-8150**	304-269-8881
Na Ho'ola Spa at Hyatt Regency Waikiki Resort 2424 Kalakaua Ave	Honolulu	HI	96815	**800-233-1234**	808-923-1234
Ohio House Motel 600 N La Salle Dr	Chicago	IL	60654	**866-601-6446**	312-943-6000
Omni Interlocken Resort 500 Interlocken Blvd	Broomfield	CO	80021	**800-843-6664**	303-438-6600
Omni Rancho Las Palmas Resort & Spa 41000 Bob Hope Dr	Rancho Mirage	CA	92270	**866-423-1195**	760-568-2727
Osprey Valley Resorts 18821 Main St	Alton	ON	L7K1R1	**800-833-1561**	519-927-9034
Pala Casino Resort & Spa 35008 Pala-Temecula Rd	Pala	CA	92059	**877-946-7252**	760-510-5100
Peaks Resort & Golden Door Spa 136 Country Club Dr	Telluride	CO	81435	**800-789-2220**	
Portofino Spa at Portofino Island Resort 10 Portofino Dr	Pensacola	FL	32561	**866-849-0223**	850-916-5000
Raindance Spa at the Lodge at Sonoma Renaissance Resort 1325 Broadway	Sonoma	CA	95476	**866-263-0758**	707-935-6600
Residence Inn Mystic 40 Whitehall Ave	Mystic	CT	06355	**888-268-7222**	860-536-5150
Resort at Squaw Creek 400 Squaw Creek Rd PO Box 3333	Olympic Valley	CA	96146	**800-327-3353**	530-583-6300
Revere Hotel Boston Common 200 Stuart St	Boston	MA	02116	**855-673-8373**	617-482-1800
Revive Spa at the JW Marriott Desert Ridge Resort Phoenix 5350 E Marriott Dr	Phoenix	AZ	85054	**800-845-5279**	480-293-3700
Ritz-Carlton Hotel Company, The 4445 Willard Ave Ste 800	Chevy Chase	MD	20815	**800-876-7280**	301-547-4700
Ritz-Carlton Tysons Corner, The 1700 Tysons Blvd	McLean	VA	22102	**800-241-3333**	703-506-4300
Safety Harbor Resort & Spa 105 N Bayshore Dr	Safety Harbor	FL	34695	**888-237-8772**	727-726-1161
Saint Regis Aspen 315 E Dean St *General	Aspen	CO	81611	**888-627-7198***	970-920-3300
Sanctuary Beach Resort Monterey Bay 3295 Dunes Rd	Marina	CA	93933	**855-693-6583**	831-883-9478
Sea Spa at Loews Coronado Bay Resort 4000 Loews Coronado Bay Rd	Coronado	CA	92118	**800-815-6397**	619-424-4000
Seasons Restaurant at Highland Lake Inn 86 Lilly Pad Ln	Flat Rock	NC	28731	**800-635-5101**	828-696-9094
Secret Garden Spa at the Prince of Wales Hotel 6 Picton St	Niagara-on-the-Lake	ON	L0S1J0	**888-669-5566**	905-468-3246
Senator Inn & Spa of Augusta 284 Western Ave	Augusta	ME	04330	**877-772-2224**	207-622-8800
Shell Island Ocean Front Suites 2700 N Lumina Ave	Wrightsville Beach	NC	28480	**800-689-6765**	910-256-8696
Sheraton Agoura Hills Hotel 30100 Agoura Rd	Agoura Hills	CA	91301	**866-716-8134**	818-707-1220
Sheraton Fishermans Wharf (San Francisco, CA) 2500 Mason St	San Francisco	CA	94133	**866-716-8134**	415-362-5500
Sheraton Gunter Hotel 205 E Houston St	San Antonio	TX	78205	**866-716-8134**	210-227-3241
Sheraton Phoenix Downtown Hotel 340 N Third St	Phoenix	AZ	85004	**866-716-8134**	602-262-2500
Sheraton Raleigh Hotel 421 S Salisbury St	Raleigh	NC	27601	**866-716-8134**	919-834-9900
Sheraton Safari Hotel & Suites 12205 S Apopka Vineland Rd	Orlando	FL	32836	**800-325-3535**	407-239-0444
Sheraton Washington North Hotel 4095 Powder Mill Rd	Beltsville	MD	20705	**866-716-8134**	301-937-4422
Shui Spa at Crowne Pointe Historic Inn 82 Bradford St	Provincetown	MA	02657	**877-276-9631**	508-487-6767
Sixty Hotels 54 Thompson St	New York	NY	10012	**877-431-0400**	
Spa & Fitness Club at the Four Seasons Hotel Washington 2800 Pennsylvania Ave NW	Washington	DC	20007	**800-819-5053**	202-944-2022
Spa at Big Cedar Lodge 612 Devil's Pool Rd	Ridgedale	MO	65739	**800-225-6343**	417-339-5201
Spa at Eagle Crest Resort 1522 Cline Falls Hwy	Redmond	OR	97756	**800-682-4786**	541-923-9647
Spa at Kingsmill Resort 1010 Kingsmill Rd	Williamsburg	VA	23185	**800-965-4772**	757-253-8230
Spa at Le Merigot JW Marriott Beach Hotel Santa Monica 1740 Ocean Ave	Santa Monica	CA	90401	**888-236-2427**	310-395-9700
Spa at Pebble Beach 1518 Cypress Dr	Pebble Beach	CA	93953	**800-654-9300**	831-649-7615
Spa at Pinehurst Resort 80 Carolina Vista Dr PO Box 4000	Pinehurst	NC	28374	**800-487-4653**	910-235-8320
Spa at the Beverly Wilshire, The 9500 Wilshire Blvd	Beverly Hills	CA	90212	**800-545-4000**	310-385-7023
Spa at the Bodega Bay Lodge 103 Coast Hwy 1	Bodega Bay	CA	94923	**888-875-2250**	707-875-3525

Name	Address	City	State	ZIP	Toll-Free	Phone
Spa at the Breakers	1 S County Rd	Palm Beach	FL	33480	**888-273-2537**	561-653-6656
Spa at the Broadmoor	1 Lake Ave	Colorado Springs	CO	80906	**800-634-7711**	719-634-7711
Spa at the Buena Vista Palace Resort in the Walt Disney World Resort	1900 Buena Vista Dr	Lake Buena Vista	FL	32830	**866-397-6516**	407-827-3200
Spa at the Camelback Inn JW Marriott Resort Golf Club & Spa	5402 E Lincoln Dr	Scottsdale	AZ	85253	**800-922-2635**	480-596-7040
Spa at the Chattanoogan	1201 S Broad St	Chattanooga	TN	37402	**800-619-0018**	423-756-3400
Spa at the Equinox Resort	3567 Main St	Manchester Village	VT	05254	**800-362-4747**	
Spa at the Fairmont Inn Sonoma Mission Inn	100 Boyes Blvd	Sonoma	CA	95476	**877-289-7354**	707-938-9000
Spa at the Hotel Hershey	100 Hotel Rd	Hershey	PA	17033	**877-772-9988**	717-520-5888
Spa at the JW Marriott Desert Springs Resort Palm Desert	74855 Country Club Dr	Palm Desert	CA	92260	**800-845-5279**	760-341-2211
Spa at the Norwich Inn	607 W Thames St	Norwich	CT	06360	**800-275-4772**	860-886-2401
Spa at the PGA National Resort	450 Ave of the Champions	Palm Beach Gardens	FL	33418	**800-633-9150**	561-627-3111
Spa at the Ritz-Carlton Amelia Island	4750 Amelia Island Pkwy	Amelia Island	FL	32034	**800-241-3333**	904-277-1087
Spa at the Ritz-Carlton Bachelor Gulch	0130 Daybreak Ridge	Avon	CO	81620	**800-241-3333**	970-748-6200
Spa at the Ritz-Carlton Half Moon Bay	1 Miramontes Pt Rd	Half Moon Bay	CA	94019	**800-241-3333**	650-712-7040
Spa at the Ritz-Carlton New Orleans	921 Canal St	New Orleans	LA	70112	**800-241-3333**	504-670-2929
Spa at the Saddlebrook Resort	5700 Saddlebrook Way	Wesley Chapel	FL	33543	**800-729-8383**	813-907-4419
Spa at the Sagamore	110 Sagamore Rd	Bolton Landing	NY	12814	**866-384-1944**	518-743-6081
Spa at the Sanderling Resort	1461 Duck Rd	Duck	NC	27949	**855-412-7866**	252-261-7744
Spa at the Vail Marriott Mountain Resort	715 W Lionshead Cir	Vail	CO	81657	**800-648-0720**	970-479-5004
Spa at the Villagio Inn	6481 Washington St	Yountville	CA	94599	**800-351-1133**	707-948-5050
Spa at White Oaks Conference Resort	253 Taylor Rd	Niagara-on-the-Lake	ON	L0S1J0	**800-263-5766**	905-641-2599
Spa Esmeralda at the Renaissance Esmeralda Resort	44400 Indian Wells Ln	Indian Wells	CA	92210	**800-845-5279**	760-836-1265
Spa Gaucin at the Saint Regis Monarch Beach	1 Monarch Beach Resort	Dana Point	CA	92629	**800-722-1543**	949-234-3367
Spa Grande at the Grand Wailea Resort Maui	3850 Wailea Alanui Dr	Wailea	HI	96753	**800-772-1933**	808-875-1234
Spa La Quinta at La Quinta Resort	49499 Eisenhower Dr	La Quinta	CA	92253	**877-527-7721**	760-777-4800
Spa Moana at the Hyatt Regency Maui Resort & Spa	200 Nohea Kai Dr	Lahaina	HI	96761	**800-233-1234**	808-667-4725
Spa Shiki at the Lodge of Four Seasons	315 Horseshoe Bend Pkwy	Lake Ozark	MO	65049	**800-843-5253**	573-365-8108
Spa Suites at Kahala Hotel & Resort	5000 Kahala Ave	Honolulu	HI	96816	**800-367-2525**	808-739-8938
Spa Terre at LaPlaya Beach & Golf Resort	9891 Gulf Shore Dr	Naples	FL	34108	**800-237-6883**	239-597-3123
Spa Terre at Paradise Point Resort	1404 Vacation Rd	San Diego	CA	92109	**800-344-2626**	858-581-5998
Spa Terre at the Hotel Viking	1 Bellevue Ave	Newport	RI	02840	**800-556-7126**	401-847-3300
Spa Terre at the Inn & Spa at Loretto	211 Old Santa Fe Trl	Santa Fe	NM	87501	**800-727-5531**	505-984-7997
Spa Toccare at Borgata Hotel Casino	1 Borgata Way	Atlantic City	NJ	08401	**877-448-5833**	609-317-7555
SpaHalekulani at the Halekulani Hotel	2199 Kalia Rd	Honolulu	HI	96815	**800-367-2343**	808-931-5322
Springmaid Beach Resort	3200 S Ocean Blvd	Myrtle Beach	SC	29577	**866-764-8501**	
Stillwater Spa at the Hyatt Regency Newport	1 Goat Island	Newport	RI	02840	**800-233-1234**	401-851-3225
Studio 6	PO Box 809092	Dallas	TX	75380	**855-249-0891**	614-601-4060
Taboo Resort Golf & Spa	1209 Muskoka Beach Rd	Gravenhurst	ON	P1P1R1	**800-461-0236**	705-687-2233
Tampa Marriott Waterside Hotel & Marina	700 S Florida Ave	Tampa	FL	33602	**888-268-1616**	813-204-6300
TMI Hospitality Inc	4850 32nd Ave South	Fargo	ND	58104	**800-210-8223**	701-235-1060
Trump Soho New York	246 Spring St	New York	NY	10013	**855-878-6700**	212-842-5500
Tulalip Resort Casino	10200 Quil Ceda Blvd	Tulalip	WA	98271	**888-272-1111**	
Vail Mountain Lodge & Spa, The	352 E Meadow Dr	Vail	CO	81657	**888-794-0410**	970-476-0700
Well Spa at Miramonte Resort	45000 Indian Wells Ln	Indian Wells	CA	92210	**800-237-2926**	760-837-1652
Westglow Resort & Spa	224 Westglow Cir	Blowing Rock	NC	28605	**800-562-0807**	828-295-4463
Westin Kierland Resort & Spa	6902 E Greenway Pkwy	Scottsdale	AZ	85254	**800-354-5892**	480-624-1000
Westin Maui Resort & Spa, The	2365 Kaanapali Pkwy	Lahaina	HI	96761	**866-716-8112**	808-667-2525
Westin Mission Hills Resort	71333 Dinah Shore Dr	Rancho Mirage	CA	92270	**866-716-8108**	760-328-5955
Westin Resort & Spa	4090 Whistler Way	Whistler	BC	V0N1B4	**888-627-8979**	604-905-5000
Willow Stream Spa at Fairmont Scottsdale Princess	7575 E Princess Dr	Scottsdale	AZ	85255	**800-908-9540**	480-585-2732
Willow Stream Spa at the Fairmont Banff Springs	405 Spray Ave	Banff	AB	T1L1J4	**800-404-1772**	403-762-1772
Willow Stream Spa at the Fairmont Empress	633 Humboldt St	Victoria	BC	V8W1A6	**866-854-7444**	250-995-4650
Wingate by Wyndham Calgary Hotel	400 Midpark Way SE	Calgary	AB	T2X3S4	**800-228-1000**	403-514-0099
Wintergreen Resort	Rt 664 PO Box 706	Wintergreen	VA	22958	**855-699-1858**	

706 SPEAKERS BUREAUS

Name	Address	City	State	ZIP	Toll-Free	Phone
AEI Speakers Bureau	214 Lincoln St Ste 113	Allston	MA	02134	**800-447-7325**	617-782-3111
Capitol City Speakers Bureau	1620 S Fifth St	Springfield	IL	62703	**800-397-3183**	217-544-8552
Elk Valley Rancheria	2332 Howland Hill Rd	Crescent City	CA	95531	**866-464-4680**	707-464-4680
Executive Speakers Bureau	8567 Cordes Cir	Germantown	TN	38139	**800-754-9404**	901-754-9404
Florexpo LLC	1960 Kellogg Ave	Carlsbad	CA	92008	**800-830-3567**	
Greater Talent Network Inc	437 Fifth Ave	New York	NY	10016	**800-326-4211**	212-645-4200
Justifacts Credential Verification Inc	5250 Logan Ferry Rd	Murrysville	PA	15668	**800-356-6885**	412-798-4790
Key Speakers Bureau Inc	3500 E Coast Hwy Ste 6	Corona del Mar	CA	92625	**800-675-1175**	949-675-7856
Leading Authorities Inc	1990 M St Ste 800	Washington	DC	20036	**800-773-2537**	202-783-0300
National Speakers Bureau	1177 W Bdwy Ste 300	Vancouver	BC	V6H1G3	**800-661-4110**	604-734-3663
National Speakers Bureau Inc	14047 W Petronalla Dr Ste 102	Libertyville	IL	60048	**800-323-9442**	847-295-1122
Solix Inc	30 Lanidex Plz W PO Box 685	Parsippany	NJ	07054	**800-200-0818**	973-581-6700
Speak Inc Speakers Bureau	10680 Treena St Ste 230	San Diego	CA	92131	**800-677-3324**	858-228-3771
Speakers Unlimited	PO Box 27225	Columbus	OH	43227	**888-333-6676**	614-864-3703
Steven Barclay Agency	12 Western Ave	Petaluma	CA	94952	**888-965-7323**	707-773-0654

707 SPEED CHANGERS, INDUSTRIAL HIGH SPEED DRIVES, GEARS

SEE ALSO Controls & Relays - Electrical ; Machine Shops ; Motors (Electric) & Generators ; Power Transmission Equipment - Mechanical ; Aircraft Parts & Auxiliary Equipment ; Automotive Parts & Supplies - Mfr

Name	Address	City	State	ZIP	Toll-Free	Phone
Bison Gear & Engineering Corp	3850 Ohio Ave	Saint Charles	IL	60174	**800-282-4766**	630-377-4327
Cleveland Gear Co	3249 E 80th St	Cleveland	OH	44104	**800-423-3169**	216-641-9000
Columbia Gear Corp	530 County Rd 50	Avon	MN	56310	**800-323-9838**	320-356-7301
Cone Drive Operations Inc - A Textron Co	240 E 12th St *Sales	Traverse City	MI	49685	**888-994-2663***	231-946-8410
Curtis Machine Company Inc	2500 E Trl St	Dodge City	KS	67801	**800-835-9166**	620-227-7164
Dalton Gear Co	212 Colfax Ave N	Minneapolis	MN	55405	**800-328-7485**	612-374-2150
Designatronics Inc	2101 Jericho Tpke *Orders	New Hyde Park	NY	11040	**800-345-1144***	516-328-3300
Emerson Industrial Automation	8000 W Florissant Ave PO Box 4100	St Louis	MO	63136	**888-213-0970**	952-995-8000
Fairchild Industrial Products Co	3920 Westpoint Blvd	Winston-Salem	NC	27103	**800-334-8422**	336-659-3400
Hub City Inc	2914 Industrial Ave	Aberdeen	SD	57401	**800-482-2489**	605-225-0360
Kurz Electric Solutions Inc	1325 McMahon Dr	Neenah	WI	54956	**800-776-3629**	920-886-8200
Lenze	630 Douglas St	Uxbridge	MA	01569	**800-217-9100**	508-278-9100
Nuttall Gear LLC	2221 Niagra Falls Blvd	Niagara Falls	NY	14304	**800-724-6710**	716-298-4100
Piller Inc	45 Turner Rd	Middletown	NY	10941	**800-597-6937**	
Regal-Beloit Corp	200 State St *NYSE: RBC*	Beloit	WI	53511	**800-672-6495**	608-364-8800
Regal-Beloit Corp Durst Div	PO Box 298	Beloit	WI	53512	**800-356-0775**	608-365-2563
Richmond Gear	PO Box 238 *Sales	Liberty	SC	29657	**800-934-2727***	864-843-9231
Rush Gears Inc	550 Virginia Dr	Fort Washington	PA	19034	**800-523-2576**	
Standard Machine Ltd	868-60th St E	Saskatoon	SK	S7K8G8	**800-329-4327**	306-931-3343
Sterling Electric Inc	7997 Allison Ave *Cust Svc	Indianapolis	IN	46268	**800-654-6220***	317-872-0471
Sumitomo Machinery Corp of America	4200 Holland Blvd	Chesapeake	VA	23323	**800-762-9256**	757-485-3355
Superior Gearbox Co	803 W Hwy 32	Stockton	MO	65785	**800-346-5745**	417-276-5191
TECO-Westinghouse Motor Co	5100 N IH-35	Round Rock	TX	78681	**800-451-8798**	512-255-4141

708 SPORTING GOODS

SEE ALSO Snowmobiles ; Swimming Pools ; Tarps, Tents, Covers ; Cord & Twine ; Exercise & Fitness Equipment ; Firearms & Ammunition (Non-Military) ; Gym & Playground Equipment ; Handbags, Totes, Backpacks ; Motor Vehicles - Commercial & Special Purpose ; Personal Protective Equipment & Clothing ; All-Terrain Vehicles ; Bicycles & Bicycle Parts & Accessories ; Boats - Recreational

Name	Address	City	State	ZIP	Toll-Free	Phone
Abel Automatics Inc	165 Aviador St	Camarillo	CA	93010	**866-511-7444**	805-484-8789
Acushnet Co	333 Bridge St	Fairhaven	MA	02719	**800-225-8500**	508-979-2000

Classified Section

Classified Section

Company / Address	City	State	ZIP	Toll-Free	Phone
AcuSport Corp 1 Hunter Pl	Bellefontaine	OH	43311	**800-543-3150**	937-593-7010
Adams USA Inc 610 S Jefferson Ave	Cookeville	TN	38501	**800-426-9784**	
Aldila Inc 14145 Danielson St Ste B; *OTC: ALDA*	Poway	CA	92064	**800-854-2786**	858-513-1801
American Sports 74 Albe Dr Ste 1	Newark	DE	19702	**866-207-3179**	302-369-9480
AMF Bowling Worldwide Inc 7313 Bell Creek Rd	Mechanicsville	VA	23111	**800-342-5263**	
Aqua-Leisure Industries Inc PO Box 239	Avon	MA	02322	**866-807-3998**	
Aqualung America Inc 2340 Cousteau Ct	Vista	CA	92083	**800-446-2671**	760-597-5000
Atomic USA 2030 Lincoln Ave	Ogden	UT	84401	**800-258-5020**	
Bankshot Sports Organization 330-U N Stonestreet Ave Ste 504	Rockville	MD	20852	**800-933-0140**	301-309-0260
Bauer Premium Fly Reels 585 Clover Ln Ste 1	Ashland	OR	97520	**888-484-4165**	541-488-8246
Bell Sports Corp 6225 N St Hwy 161 Ste 300	Irving	TX	75038	**866-525-2357**	469-417-6600
Big Rock Sports LLC 173 Hankison Dr	Newport	NC	28570	**800-334-2661**	252-808-3500
Biscayne Rod Manufacturing Inc 425 E Ninth St	Hialeah	FL	33010	**866-969-0808**	305-884-0808
Bison Inc 603 L St	Lincoln	NE	68508	**800-247-7668**	402-474-3353
Bravo Sports Corp 12801 Carmenita Rd; *Cust Svc	Santa Fe Springs	CA	90670	**800-234-9737***	562-484-5100
Bridgestone Golf Inc 15320 Industrial Pk Blvd NE	Covington	GA	30014	**800-358-6319**	770-787-7400
Brine Inc 32125 Hollingsworth Ave	Warren	MI	48092	**800-968-7845**	
Callaway Golf Co 2180 Rutherford Rd; *NYSE: ELY*	Carlsbad	CA	92008	**800-588-9836**	760-931-1771
Cascade Designs Inc 4000 First Ave S; *Cust Svc	Seattle	WA	98134	**800-531-9531***	206-505-9500
Century Sports Inc 1995 Rutgers University Blvd; *Sales	Lakewood	NJ	08701	**800-526-7548***	732-905-4422
Century Tool & Mfg 90 McMillen Rd	Antioch	IL	60002	**800-635-3831**	
Champion Shuffleboard Ltd 7216 Burns St	Richland Hills	TX	76118	**800-826-7856**	817-284-3499
Cleveland Golf Co 5601 Skylab Rd; *Cust Svc	Huntington Beach	CA	92647	**800-999-6263***	
Cobra Mfg Co Inc 7909 E 148th St S	Bixby	OK	74008	**800-352-6272**	918-366-7484
Coleman Co 1100 Stearns Dr	Sauk Rapids	MN	56379	**800-835-3278**	320-252-1642
Coleman Company Inc 3600 N Hydraulic; *Cust Svc	Wichita	KS	67219	**800-835-3278***	
Columbia Industries Inc PO Box 746	Hopkinsville	KY	42240	**800-531-5920**	270-881-1200
Confluence Watersports Co 575 Mauldin Rd Ste 200	Greenville	SC	29607	**800-595-2925**	
Coverstar LLC 1795 West 200 North	Lindon	UT	84042	**800-617-7283**	801-373-4777
Daisy Outdoor Products 400 W Stribling Dr	Rogers	AR	72756	**800-643-3458**	479-636-1200
Daiwa Corp 11137 Warland Dr	Cypress	CA	90630	**800-736-4653**	562-802-9589
Douglas Industries Co 3441 S 11th Ave	Eldridge	IA	52748	**800-553-8907**	563-285-4162
Dover Saddlery Inc 525 Great Rd PO Box 1100; *NASDAQ: DOVR*	Littleton	MA	01460	**800-406-8204**	978-952-8062
Eagle One Golf Products Inc 1340 N Jefferson St	Anaheim	CA	92807	**800-448-4409**	714-983-0050
Ebonite International Inc PO Box 746	Hopkinsville	KY	42241	**800-326-6483**	270-881-1200
Eppinger Manufacturing Co 6340 Schaefer Rd	Dearborn	MI	48126	**888-771-8277**	313-582-3205
Escalade Inc 817 Maxwell Ave; *NASDAQ: ESCA* ■ *Cust Svc	Evansville	IN	47711	**800-426-1421***	812-467-1200
Folbot Inc 4209 Pace St	Charleston	SC	29405	**800-533-5099**	843-744-3483
Franklin Sports Inc 17 Campanelli Pkwy PO Box 508	Stoughton	MA	02072	**800-225-8649**	781-344-1111
G & H Decoys Inc PO Box 1208; *Orders	Henryetta	OK	74437	**800-443-3269***	918-652-3314
Gamma Sports 200 Waterfront Dr	Pittsburgh	PA	15222	**800-333-0337**	412-323-0335
Gared Sports Inc 707 N Second St Ste 202	Saint Louis	MO	63102	**800-325-2682**	314-421-0044
Gill Athletics Inc 2808 Gemini Ct; *Cust Svc	Champaign	IL	61822	**800-637-3090***	217-367-8438
Goal Sporting Goods Inc 37 Industrial Pk Rd PO Box 236	Essex	CT	06426	**800-334-4625**	
Goals & Poles 7575 Jefferson Hwy	Baton Rouge	LA	70806	**800-275-0317**	225-923-0622
Goalsetter Systems Inc 1041 Cordova Ave	Lynnville	IA	50153	**800-362-4625**	
Golfsmith International Inc 11000 N IH-35; *Sales	Austin	TX	78753	**800-396-0099***	512-821-4050
GolfWorks, The 4820 Jacksontown Rd PO Box 3008	Newark	OH	43055	**800-848-8358**	740-328-4193
HEAD USA Inc 1 Selleck St	Norwalk	CT	06855	**800-874-3235**	
Hillerich & Bradsby Company Inc 800 W Main St	Louisville	KY	40202	**800-282-2287**	502-585-5226
Hireko Trading Company Inc 16185 Stephens St	City of Industry	CA	91745	**800-367-8912**	
Hobie Cat Co 4925 Oceanside Blvd	Oceanside	CA	92056	**800-462-4349**	760-758-9100
Hunter Company Inc 3300 W 71st Ave	Westminster	CO	80030	**800-676-4868**	303-427-4626
Intex Recreation Corp 1665 Hughes Way PO Box 1440; *Cust Svc	Long Beach	CA	90801	**800-234-6839***	
Jayhawk Bowling Supply Inc 355 N Iowa St PO Box 685	Lawrence	KS	66044	**800-255-6436**	785-842-3237
Jerry's Sport Ctr Inc 100 Capital Rd	Jenkins Township	PA	18640	**800-234-2612**	
Johnson Outdoors Inc 555 Main St; *NASDAQ: JOUT*	Racine	WI	53403	**800-468-9716**	262-631-6600
Jugs Sports 11885 SW Herman Rd	Tualatin	OR	97062	**800-547-6843**	
K2 Sports 4201 Sixth Ave S	Seattle	WA	98108	**800-426-1617**	206-805-4800
Kawasaki Motors Corp USA PO Box 25252	Santa Ana	CA	92799	**866-802-9381**	949-770-0400
KL Industries Inc 1790 Sun Dolphin Dr	Muskegon	MI	49444	**800-733-2727**	231-733-2725
Kolpin Powersports 9955 59th Ave N	Plymouth	MN	55442	**877-956-5746**	920-928-3118
Kwik Goal Ltd 140 Pacific Dr	Quakertown	PA	18951	**800-531-4252**	215-536-2200
Lamartek Inc 175 NW Washington St; *Orders	Lake City	FL	32055	**800-495-1046***	386-752-1087
Lifetime Products Inc Freeport Ctr Bldg D-11 PO Box 160010	Clearfield	UT	84016	**800-242-3865**	801-776-1532
Lobster Sports Inc 7340 Fulton Ave	North Hollywood	CA	91605	**800-210-5992**	818-764-6000
Louisville Golf Club Co 2320 Watterson Trail	Louisville	KY	40299	**800-456-1631**	502-491-5490
MacNeill Engineering Company Inc 140 Locke Dr PO Box 735	Marlborough	MA	01752	**800-652-4267**	508-481-8830
Manns Bait Co 1111 State Docks Rd	Eufaula	AL	36027	**800-841-8435**	
Maravia Corp of Idaho 602 E 45th St	Boise	ID	83714	**800-223-7238**	208-322-4949
Mares America Corp 1 Selleck St	Norwalk	CT	06855	**800-874-3236**	203-855-0631
Mizuno USA 4925 Avalon Ridge Pkwy	Norcross	GA	30071	**800-966-1211**	770-441-5553
Moultrie Feeders 150 Industrial Rd	Alabaster	AL	35007	**800-653-3334**	205-664-6700
Murrey International Inc 14150 S Figueroa St	Los Angeles	CA	90061	**800-421-1022**	310-532-6091
National Billiard Manufacturing Co 3315 Eugenia Ave	Covington	KY	41015	**800-543-0880**	859-431-4129
North Face, The 14450 Doolittle Dr	San Leandro	CA	94577	**855-500-8639**	877-992-0111
O'Brien International 14615 NE 91st St	Redmond	WA	98052	**800-662-7436**	425-202-2100
O'Neill Wetsuits USA 1071 41st Ave PO Box 6300	Santa Cruz	CA	95063	**800-538-0764**	
Ocean Kayak 125 Gilman Falls Ave Bldg B	Old Town	ME	04468	**800-852-9257**	
Oceanic USA 2002 Davis St	San Leandro	CA	94577	**800-435-3483**	510-562-0500
Old Town Canoe Co 125 Gilman Falls Ave Bldg B	Old Town	ME	04468	**800-343-1555**	207-827-5513
Orvis International Travel 178 Conservation Way	Sunderland	VT	05250	**800-547-4322**	802-362-8790
Penn Inc 306 S 45th Ave	Phoenix	AZ	85043	**800-289-7366**	
Pentair Ltd 1351 Rt 55	Lagrangeville	NY	12540	**888-711-7487**	845-463-7200
PIC Skate 22 Village Dr	Riverside	RI	02915	**800-882-3448**	401-490-9334
Ping Inc 2201 W Desert Cove Ave PO Box 82000	Phoenix	AZ	85071	**800-474-6434**	
Poolmaster Inc 770 Del Paso Rd	Sacramento	CA	95834	**800-854-1492**	916-567-9800
Powell Skate One Corp 30 S La Patera Ln	Santa Barbara	CA	93117	**800-288-7528**	805-964-1330
Precision Shooting Equipment Inc 2727 N Fairview Ave	Tucson	AZ	85705	**800-477-7789**	520-884-9065
Prince Global Sports LLC 1 Advantage Ct; *All	Bordentown	NJ	08505	**800-283-6647***	609-291-5800
Resilite Sports Products PO Box 764	Sunbury	PA	17801	**800-843-6287**	570-473-3529
Riedell Shoes Inc 122 Cannon River Ave	Red Wing	MN	55066	**800-698-6893**	651-388-8251
Rome Specialty Company Inc Rosco Div 501 W Embargo St	Rome	NY	13440	**800-794-8357**	315-337-8200
RSR Group Inc 4405 Metric Dr	Winter Park	FL	32792	**800-541-4867**	407-677-1000
Saunders Archery Co 1874 14th Ave PO Box 1707; *Cust Svc	Columbus	NE	68601	**800-228-1408***	402-564-7176
Scott Fly Rod Co 2355 Air Pk Way	Montrose	CO	81401	**800-728-7208**	
Scott USA Inc PO Box 2030	Sun Valley	ID	83353	**800-292-5874**	208-622-1000
Sea Eagle Boats Inc 19 N Columbia St Ste 1	Port Jefferson	NY	11777	**800-748-8066**	631-791-1799
Shakespeare Fishing Tackle Co 7 Science Ct; *Cust Svc	Columbia	SC	29203	**800-466-5643***	803-754-7000
Simms Fishing Products Corp 101 Evergreen Dr	Bozeman	MT	59715	**800-217-4667**	406-585-3557
Spalding PO Box 90015	Bowling Green	KY	42103	**855-253-4533**	
Storm Products Inc 165 South 800 West	Brigham City	UT	84302	**800-369-4402**	435-723-0403
TaylorMade - Adidas Golf 5545 Fermi Ct; *Cust Svc	Carlsbad	CA	92008	**800-555-1212***	760-918-6000

Company	Address	City	State	Zip	Toll-Free	Phone
Toobs Inc	347 Quintana Rd	Morro Bay	CA	93442	**800-795-8662**	
True Temper Sports	8275 Tournament Dr Ste 200	Memphis	TN	38125	**800-355-8783**	901-746-2000
Underwater Kinetics (UK)	13400 Danielson St	Poway	CA	92064	**800-852-7483**	858-513-9100
Weed USA Inc	5780 Harrow Glen Ct	Galena	OH	43021	**800-933-3758**	740-548-3881
West Coast Trends	17811 Jamestown Ln	Huntington Beach	CA	92647	**800-736-4568**	714-843-9288
Wiley Waterski and Wakeboard Pro Shop	1417 S Trenton	Seattle	WA	98108	**800-962-0785**	206-762-1300
Wilson Sporting Goods Co	8750 W Bryn Mawr Ave	Chicago	IL	60631	**800-874-5930**	773-714-6400
Wittek Golf Supply Co Inc	3865 N Commercial Ave	Northbrook	IL	60062	**800-869-1800**	847-943-2399
Worldwide Golf Shops Inc	1421 Village Wy	Santa Ana	CA	92705	**888-216-5252**	714-543-8284
Worth Co, The	214 Sherman Ave PO Box 88	Stevens Point	WI	54481	**800-944-1899**	715-344-6081
Yakima Bait Company Inc	PO Box 310	Granger	WA	98932	**800-527-2711**	509-854-1311
Yamaha Motor Corp USA	6555 Katella Ave *Cust Svc	Cypress	CA	90630	**800-656-7695***	
Yonex Corp	20140 S Western Ave	Torrance	CA	90501	**800-449-6639**	310-793-3800

709 SPORTING GOODS STORES

Company	Address	City	State	Zip	Toll-Free	Phone
3balls.com	319 Manley St Ste 1	West Bridgewater	MA	02379	**888-289-0300**	
Academy Sports & Outdoors	1800 N Mason Rd	Katy	TX	77449	**888-922-2336**	281-646-5200
Aero Tech Designs Cycling Apparel	1132 Fourth Ave	Coraopolis	PA	15108	**800-783-8326**	412-262-3255
Alabama Outdoors Inc	3054 Independence Dr	Birmingham	AL	35209	**800-870-0011**	205-870-1919
American Outfitters Ltd	3700 Sunset Ave	Waukegan	IL	60087	**800-397-6081**	847-623-3959
Apple Saddlery	1875 Innes Rd	Ottawa	ON	K1B4C6	**800-867-8225**	613-744-4040
Aspen Ski & Board Co	1170 E Powell Rd	Lewis Center	OH	43035	**877-861-0777**	614-848-6600
Athletic Supply Co	16101 NE 87th St	Redmond	WA	98052	**800-732-9259**	425-882-1456
Austad's Golf	2801 E 10th St *Cust Svc	Sioux Falls	SD	57103	**800-444-1234***	605-331-4653
Backcountry Gear LLC	1855 W Second Ave	Eugene	OR	97402	**800-953-5499**	541-485-4007
Barts Water Sports	7581 E 800 N	North Webster	IN	46555	**800-348-5016**	574-834-7666
Baseball Express Inc	5750 NW Pkwy Ste 100	San Antonio	TX	78249	**800-937-4824**	210-348-7000
Beads Galore International Inc	3320 S Priest Dr Ste 3	Tempe	AZ	85282	**800-424-9577**	480-921-3949
Bell Lifestyle Products Inc	3164 Pepper Mill Ct	Mississauga	ON	L5L4X4	**800-333-7995**	
Bent Gate Mountaineering	1313 Washington Ave	Golden	CO	80401	**877-236-8428**	303-271-9382
Berg's Ski & Snowboard Shop	367 W 13th Ave	Eugene	OR	97401	**800-800-1953**	541-683-1300
Bicycle Garage of Indy Inc	4340 E 82nd St	Indianapolis	IN	46250	**800-238-7389**	317-842-4140
Big 5 Sporting Goods Corp	2525 E El Segundo Blvd *NASDAQ: BGFV*	El Segundo	CA	90245	**800-898-2994**	310-536-0611
Birdie Golf Balls Golf Equipment	208 Margate Ct	Margate	FL	33063	**800-333-7271**	954-973-2741
Blade-Tech Industries Inc	5530 184th St East	Puyallup	WA	98375	**877-331-5793**	253-655-8059
Blue Sky Cycling Inc	2530 Randolph St	Huntington Park	CA	90255	**800-585-4137**	323-585-3934
Bob Reeves Brass Mouthpieces	25574 Rye Canyon Rd Ste D	Valencia	CA	91355	**800-837-0980**	661-775-8820
Bob Ward & Sons Inc	3015 Paxson St	Missoula	MT	59801	**800-800-5083**	406-728-3220
Boyne Country Sports	1200 Bay View Rd	Petoskey	MI	49770	**800-462-6963**	231-439-4906
Burghardt Sporting Goods	14660 W Capitol Dr	Brookfield	WI	53005	**866-790-6606**	262-790-1170
Busy Body Home Fitness	9990 Empire St	San Diego	CA	92126	**800-466-3348**	
C W I Inc	650 Three Springs Raod	Bowling Green	KY	42104	**888-626-7576**	
Cabela's Inc	1 Cabela Dr *NYSE: CAB*	Sidney	NE	69160	**800-237-8888**	308-254-5505
Cabela's Outdoor Adventures Inc	610 Glover Rd Ste A	Sidney	NE	69162	**800-346-8747**	
Capt Harrys Fishing Supply Company Inc	8501 Nw Seventh Ave	Miami	FL	33150	**800-327-4088**	305-374-4661
Carl's Golfland Inc	1976 S Telegraph Rd	Bloomfield Hills	MI	48302	**877-412-2757**	248-335-8095
Century Martial Art Supply Inc	1000 Century Blvd *Sales	Oklahoma City	OK	73110	**800-626-2787***	405-732-2226
Champs Sports	311 Manatee Ave W	Bradenton	FL	34205	**800-991-6813**	941-748-0577
Chick's	18011 S Dupont Hwy	Harrington	DE	19952	**800-444-2441**	302-398-4630
Coghlan's Ltd	121 Irene St	Winnipeg	MB	R3T4C7	**877-264-4526**	204-284-9550
Cole Sport Inc	1615 Park Ave	Park City	UT	84060	**800-345-2938**	435-649-4800
Condor Outdoor Products	5268 Rivergrade Rd	Irwindale	CA	91706	**800-552-2554**	
Coontail Corner	5466 Park St	Boulder Junction	WI	54512	**888-874-0885**	715-385-2582
Cycle-safe Inc	5211 Cascade Rd Se Ste 210	Grand Rapids	MI	49546	**888-950-6531**	616-954-9977
D & R Sports Ctr Inc	8178 W Main St	Kalamazoo	MI	49009	**800-992-1520**	269-372-2277
Dart World Inc	140 Linwood St	Lynn	MA	01905	**800-225-2558**	781-581-6035
Dharma Trading Co	1604 Fourth St	San Rafael	CA	94901	**800-542-5227**	415-456-1211
Direct Sports Inc	1720 Curve Rd	Pearisburg	VA	24134	**800-456-0072**	
Dixie Gun Works Inc	1412 W Reelfoot Ave PO Box 130 *Orders	Union City	TN	38281	**800-238-6785***	731-885-0700
Dolphin Swim School Inc	1530 El Camino Ave	Sacramento	CA	95815	**800-436-5744**	916-929-8188
Downtown Athletic Store Inc	1180 Seminole Trail Ste 210	Charlottesville	VA	22901	**800-348-2649**	434-975-3696
Duluth Pack	365 Canal Park Dr	Duluth	MN	55802	**800-777-4439**	218-722-1707
Eagle Grips Inc	460 Randy Rd	Carol Stream	IL	60188	**800-323-6144**	630-260-0400
Eastern Mountain Sports	1 Vose Farm Rd	Peterborough	NH	03458	**888-463-6367**	603-924-7231
Fanzz	2657 South 1030 West	Salt Lake City	UT	84119	**888-326-9946**	801-325-2700
Fibar Group LLC, The	80 Business Park Dr Suit 300	Armonk	NY	10504	**800-342-2721**	914-273-8770
Finlandia Sauna Products Inc	14010 Sw 72nd Ave Ste B	Portland	OR	97224	**800-354-3342**	503-684-8289
First to The Finish Inc	1325 N Broad St	Carlinville	IL	62626	**800-747-9013**	
Fitness Club Warehouse Inc	2210 S Sepulveda Blvd	Los Angeles	CA	90064	**800-348-4537**	310-235-2040
Fitness Zone	3439 Colonnade Pkwy Se 800	Birmingham	AL	35243	**800-875-9145**	
Fox Creek Leather Inc	2029 Elk Creek Pkwy	Independence	VA	24348	**800-766-4165**	276-773-3131
Gerry Cosby & Company Inc	11 Pennsylvania Plz	New York	NY	10001	**877-563-6464**	212-563-6464
Golf Etc of America Inc	2201 Commercial Ln	Granbury	TX	76048	**800-806-8633**	817-579-5263
Golf Shack Inc	1631 N Bell School Rd	Rockford	IL	61107	**888-446-5390**	815-397-3709
Golfsmith International Inc	11000 N IH-35 *Sales	Austin	TX	78753	**800-396-0099***	512-821-4050
Graf & Sons Whlse. Dept Inc	4050 S Clark St	Mexico	MO	65265	**800-531-2666**	573-581-2266
Great Skate Hockey Supl Co	3395 Sheridan Dr	Buffalo	NY	14226	**800-828-7496**	716-838-5100
Guildcraft Inc	100 Fire Tower Dr	Tonawanda	NY	14150	**800-345-5563**	
Gym Source	40 E 52nd St	New York	NY	10022	**800-496-3499**	212-688-4222
Half Hitch Tackle Company Inc	2206 Thomas Dr	Panama City	FL	32408	**888-668-9810**	850-234-2621
Hansen Surfboards	1105 S Coast Hwy 101	Encinitas	CA	92024	**800-480-4754**	760-753-6595
Heerema Co	200 Sixth Ave	Hawthorne	NJ	07506	**800-346-4729**	973-423-0505
Hoigaards Inc	5425 Excelsior Blvd	Minneapolis	MN	55416	**800-266-8157**	952-929-1351
Holabird Sports LLC	9220 Pulaski Hwy	Middle River	MD	21220	**866-860-1416**	410-687-6400
Holiday Diver Inc	180 Gulf Stream Way	Dania Beach	FL	33004	**800-348-3872**	954-925-7630
Hometown Sportswear Inc	3692 Us Rt 60 E	Barboursville	WV	25504	**888-770-7223**	304-736-4021
Hopkins Sporting Goods Inc	5485 NW Beaver Dr	Johnston	IA	50131	**800-362-2937**	515-270-0132
In The Swim Inc	320 Industrial Dr	West Chicago	IL	60185	**800-288-7946**	630-876-0040
Island Surf	1450 Miracle Strip Pkwy SE	Fort Walton Beach	FL	32548	**800-272-2065**	
Jan's Mountain Outfitters	1600 Pk Ave PO Box 280	Park City	UT	84060	**800-745-1020**	435-649-4949
Kirkham's Outdoor Products	3125 S State St	Salt Lake City	UT	84115	**800-453-7756**	801-486-4161
Kittery Trading Post	301 US 1	Kittery	ME	03904	**888-587-6246**	603-334-1157
Korney Board Aids Sporting	312 Harrison Ave	Roxton	TX	75477	**800-842-7772**	903-346-3269
Kreinik Manufacturing Company Inc	1708 Gihon Rd	Parkersburg	WV	26101	**800-537-2166**	304-422-8900
Leisure Pro	42 W 18th St	New York	NY	10011	**800-637-6880**	212-645-1234
Look Cycle Usa	6300 San Ignacio Ave Ste G	San Jose	CA	95119	**866-430-5665**	408-363-1406
MC Sports	3070 Shaffer Ave SE	Grand Rapids	MI	49512	**800-626-1762**	616-942-2600
Medallion Athletic Products Inc	150 River Park Rd	Mooresville	NC	28117	**888-600-3412**	704-660-3000
Midwest Sports Supply Inc	11613 Reading Rd	Cincinnati	OH	45241	**800-334-4580**	513-956-4900
Modell's Sporting Goods	498 Seventh Ave 20th Fl	New York	NY	10018	**888-645-8667**	800-275-6633
Mud Hole Custom Tackle Inc	400 Kane Ct	Oviedo	FL	32765	**866-790-7637**	407-447-7637
Nicros Inc	845 Phalen Blvd	Saint Paul	MN	55106	**800-699-1975**	651-778-1975
Nill Bros Sports	2814 S 44th St	Kansas City	KS	66106	**800-748-7221**	913-384-4242
No Fault Sports Products	2101 Briarglen Dr	Houston	TX	77027	**800-462-7766**	713-683-7101
Northern Wholesale Supply Inc	6800 Otter Lk Rd	Lino Lakes	MN	55038	**800-333-7777**	651-429-1515
Northland Fishing Tackle LLC	1001 Naylor Dr Se	Bemidji	MN	56601	**800-786-3474**	218-751-6723
Northwest Outlet	1814 Belknap St	Superior	WI	54880	**800-569-8142**	715-392-9838
Nova Fitness Equipment	4511 S 119th Cir	Omaha	NE	68137	**800-949-6682**	402-343-0552

Classified Section

Name	Address	City	State	Zip	Toll-Free	Phone
NRC Sports Inc	603 Pleasant St	Paxton	MA	01612	**800-243-5033**	
Out-fit	25 W Easy St Ste 304	Simi Valley	CA	93065	**800-376-3339**	805-584-1500
Outdoor Ventures	10579 S Main St	Hayward	WI	54843	**866-710-2846**	715-634-4447
Palos Sports Inc	11711 S Austin Ave	Alsip	IL	60803	**800-233-5484**	708-396-2555
Paragon Sporting Goods Corp	867 Broadway 18th St	New York	NY	10003	**800-961-3030**	212-255-8889
Performance Inc	1 Performance Way *Cust Svc	Chapel Hill	NC	27514	**800-727-2453***	
Peter Glenn Ski & Sports	2901 W Oakland Pk Blvd	Fort Lauderdale	FL	33311	**800-818-0946**	954-484-3606
Planet Bike	2402 Vondron Rd	Madison	WI	53718	**866-256-8510**	608-256-8510
Playwell Group, The	4743 Iberia Ave Ste C	Dallas	TX	75207	**800-726-1816**	
Price Point Mail Order Ltd	1490 W Walnut Pkwy	Rancho Dominguez	CA	90220	**800-774-2376**	
Pro Performance Sports LLC	2081 Faraday Ave	Carlsbad	CA	92008	**877-225-7275**	
Pro Sports Memorabilia Inc	725 Landwehr Rd	Northbrook	IL	60062	**888-950-5399**	
Proactive Sports Inc	1200 SE Second Ave	Canby	OR	97013	**800-369-8642**	503-263-8583
Protek Cargo	1568 Airport Blvd.	Napa	CA	94558	**800-439-1426**	707-254-9627
Recreational Equipment Inc (REI)	6750 S 228th St *Orders	Kent	WA	98032	**800-426-4840***	253-395-3780
Redden Marine Supply Inc	1411 Roeder Ave	Bellingham	WA	98225	**800-426-9284**	360-733-0250
Reeds Family Outdoor Outfitters	522 Minnesota Ave NW	Walker	MN	56484	**800-346-0019**	
Reliable Racing Supply Inc	643 Glen St	Queensbury	NY	12804	**800-223-4448**	518-793-5677
RJR Fashion Fabrics	2203 Dominguez Way	Torrance	CA	90501	**800-422-5426**	310-222-8782
Ron Jon Surf Shop	3850 S Banana River Blvd	Cocoa Beach	FL	32931	**888-757-8737**	321-799-8888
Royer Corp	805 East St	Madison	IN	47250	**800-457-8997**	812-265-3133
Rudolph Brothers	6550 Oley Speaks Way	Canal Winchester	OH	43110	**800-600-9508**	614-833-0707
Runner's Edge Inc, The	3195 N Federal Hwy	Boca Raton	FL	33431	**888-361-1950**	561-361-1950
Scuba Com Inc	1752 Langley Ave	Irvine	CA	92614	**800-347-2822**	949-221-9300
Sonoma Outfitters	2412 Magowan Dr	Santa Rosa	CA	95405	**800-290-1920**	707-528-1920
Sports Promotion Network	PO Box 200548	Arlington	TX	76006	**800-460-9989**	
Spot-Hogg Archery Products	125 Smith St	Harrisburg	OR	97446	**888-302-7768**	541-995-3702
Starline Inc	1300 W Henry St	Sedalia	MO	65301	**800-280-6660**	660-827-6640
Summit Hut	5045 E Speedway Blvd	Tucson	AZ	85712	**800-499-8696**	520-325-1554
Sun & Ski Sports	10560 Bissonnet St Ste 100	Houston	TX	77099	**866-786-3869**	281-340-5000
Sundance Beach	59 S La Patera Ln	Goleta	CA	93117	**877-968-0036**	
Tack Room Too Inc	201 Lee St Sw	Tumwater	WA	98501	**800-258-2581**	360-357-4268
Tahoe Mountain Sports	11200 Donner Pass Rd Ste 5e	Truckee	CA	96161	**866-891-9177**	
Texford Battery Co	2002 Milby St	Houston	TX	77003	**866-301-0125**	713-222-0125
Toledo Physical Education Supply Inc	5101 Advantage Dr	Toledo	OH	43612	**800-225-7749**	419-726-8122
Tri-State Pumps Inc	1162 Chastain Rd	Liberty	SC	29657	**800-868-4631**	864-843-8100
Triathlete Sports	186 Exchange St	Bangor	ME	04401	**800-635-0528**	207-990-2013
TriSports.com	4495 S Coach Dr	Tucson	AZ	85714	**888-293-3934**	
Turbo 2 n 1 Grip	46460 Continental Dr	Chesterfield	MI	48047	**800-530-9878**	586-598-3948
U.S. Kids Golf LLC	3040 Northwoods Pkwy	Norcross	GA	30071	**888-387-5437**	770-441-3077
Val Surf Inc	4810 Whitsett Ave	Valley Village	CA	91607	**888-825-7873**	818-769-6977
Warrior Custom Golf Inc	15 Mason Ste A	Irvine	CA	92618	**800-600-5113**	949-699-2499
Western Power Sports Inc	601 E Gowen Rd	Boise	ID	83716	**800-999-3388**	208-376-8400
Wheel & Sprocket Inc	5722 S 108th St	Hales Corners	WI	53130	**866-995-9918**	414-529-6600
Xs Sight Systems Inc	2401 Ludelle St	Fort Worth	TX	76105	**888-744-4880**	817-536-0136

710 SPORTS COMMISSIONS & REGULATORY AGENCIES - STATE

Name	Address	City	State	Zip	Toll-Free	Phone
New York Athletic Commission	123 William St 20th Fl	New York	NY	10038	**866-269-3769**	212-417-5700

SPORTS FACILITIES

SEE Stadiums & Arenas ; Motor Speedways ; Racing & Racetracks

711 SPORTS TEAMS

SEE ALSO Sports Organizations

Name	Address	City	State	Zip	Toll-Free	Phone
Atlanta Braves	PO Box 4064	Atlanta	GA	30302	**800-326-4000**	404-522-7630
Cincinnati Reds	100 Joe Nuxhall Way	Cincinnati	OH	45202	**877-647-7337**	513-381-7337
Detroit Tigers	Comerica Pk 2100 Woodward Ave	Detroit	MI	48201	**866-800-1275**	313-962-4000
Houston Astros	Minute Maid Pk 501 Crawford St	Houston	TX	77002	**800-771-2303**	713-259-8000
Kansas City Royals	Kauffman Stadium 1 Royal Way *Sales	Kansas City	MO	64129	**800-676-9257***	816-921-8000
Milwaukee Brewers	Miller Pk 1 Brewers Way	Milwaukee	WI	53214	**877-722-6458**	414-902-4452
Minnesota Twins	Metrodome 34 Kirby Puckett Pl	Minneapolis	MN	55415	**800-338-9467**	612-375-1366
New York Mets	Shea Stadium 123-01 Roosevelt Ave	Flushing	NY	11368	**888-652-7467**	718-507-6387
Pittsburgh Pirates	115 Federal St PO Box 7000	Pittsburgh	PA	15212	**800-289-2827**	412-321-2827
Seattle Mariners	Safeco Field 1250 First Ave S	Seattle	WA	98134	**800-255-7932**	206-346-4000
Texas Rangers	Rangers Ballpark in Arlington 1000 Ballpark Way	Arlington	TX	76011	**866-800-1275**	817-273-5222
Toronto Blue Jays	1 Blue Jays Way Ste 3200	Toronto	ON	M5V1J1	**888-654-6529**	416-341-1000

712 SPORTS TEAMS - BASKETBALL

SEE ALSO Sports Organizations

712-1 National Basketball Association (NBA)

Name	Address	City	State	Zip	Toll-Free	Phone
Cleveland Cavaliers	Quicken Loans Arena 1 Ctr Ct	Cleveland	OH	44115	**800-332-2287**	216-420-2000
Golden State Warriors	1011 Broadway	Oakland	CA	94607	**866-648-4668**	510-986-2200
Houston Rockets	1510 Polk St	Houston	TX	77002	**866-648-4668**	713-758-7200
Los Angeles Clippers	Staples Ctr 1111 S Figueroa St Ste 1100	Los Angeles	CA	90015	**855-895-0872**	213-742-7100
Los Angeles Lakers	555 N Nash St	El Segundo	CA	90245	**866-648-4668**	310-426-6000
Minnesota Timberwolves	Target Ctr 600 First Ave N	Minneapolis	MN	55403	**855-895-0872**	612-673-1600
New Jersey Nets	Nets Champion Ctr 390 Murray Hill Pkwy	East Rutherford	NJ	07073	**800-346-6387**	201-935-8888
Phoenix Suns	US Airways Ctr 201 E Jefferson St	Phoenix	AZ	85004	**866-648-4668**	602-379-7900
Sacramento Kings	ARCO Arena 1 Sports Pkwy	Sacramento	CA	95834	**866-746-7622**	916-928-0000
Seattle SuperSonics	1201 Third Ave Ste 1000	Seattle	WA	98101	**800-743-7021**	206-281-5800

712-2 Women's National Basketball Association (WNBA)

Name	Address	City	State	Zip	Toll-Free	Phone
Chicago Sky	20 W Kinzie St Ste 1000	Chicago	IL	60610	**877-329-9622**	312-828-9550
Indiana Fever	Conseco Fieldhouse 125 S Pennsylvania St	Indianapolis	IN	46204	**877-275-9007**	317-917-2500
Los Angeles Sparks	865 S Figueroa St Ste 104	Los Angeles	CA	90017	**888-694-3278**	213-929-1300
Mohegan Sun	1 Mohegan Sun Blvd	Uncasville	CT	06382	**877-962-2849**	860-862-4000
Washington Mystics	627 N Glebe Rd Ste 850	Arlington	VA	22203	**877-962-2849**	202-266-2200

713 SPORTS TEAMS - FOOTBALL

SEE ALSO Sports Organizations

713-1 Canadian Football League (CFL)

Name	Address	City	State	Zip	Toll-Free	Phone
Canadian Football League	50 Wellington St E 3rd Fl	Toronto	ON	M5E1C8	**855-264-4242**	416-322-9650
Saskatchewan Roughriders	1910 Piffles Taylor Way PO Box 1966	Regina	SK	S4P3E1	**888-474-3377**	306-569-2323

713-2 National Football League (NFL)

Name	Address	City	State	Zip	Toll-Free	Phone
Arizona Cardinals	8701 S Hardy Dr	Tempe	AZ	85284	**800-999-1402**	602-379-0101
Buffalo Bills	Ralph Wilson Stadium 1 Bills Dr	Orchard Park	NY	14127	**877-228-4257**	716-648-1800
Carolina Panthers	Bank of America Stadium 800 S Mint St	Charlotte	NC	28202	**888-297-8673**	704-358-7000
Cincinnati Bengals	1 Paul Brown Stadium	Cincinnati	OH	45202	**866-621-8383**	513-621-3550
Detroit Lions	222 Republic Dr	Allen Park	MI	48101	**800-745-3000**	313-216-4000
Indianapolis Colts	7001 W 56th St	Indianapolis	IN	46254	**800-805-2658**	317-297-2658
Kansas City Chiefs	Arrowhead Stadium 1 Arrowhead Dr	Kansas City	MO	64129	**800-332-6048**	816-920-9300
Minnesota Vikings	9520 Viking Dr	Eden Prairie	MN	55344	**877-722-6458**	952-828-6500

	City	State	Zip	Toll-Free	Phone
Oakland Raiders 1220 Harbor Bay Pkwy	Alameda	CA	94502	**800-724-3377**	510-864-5000
San Diego Chargers 4020 Murphy Canyon Rd	San Diego	CA	92123	**877-242-7437**	858-874-4500
Seattle Seahawks 12 Seahawks Way	Renton	WA	98056	**888-635-4295**	
Tennessee Titans 460 Great Cir Rd	Nashville	TN	37228	**800-334-4628**	615-565-4000

714 SPORTS TEAMS - HOCKEY

SEE ALSO Sports Organizations

	City	State	Zip	Toll-Free	Phone
Anaheim Ducks 2695 E Katella Ave	Anaheim	CA	92806	**877-945-3946**	
Buffalo Sabres HSBC Arena 1 Seymour H Knox III Plz	Buffalo	NY	14203	**888-467-2273**	716-855-4100
Carolina Hurricanes RBC Ctr 1400 EdwaRds Mill Rd	Raleigh	NC	27607	**800-521-7521**	919-467-7825
Edmonton Oilers 11230 110th St	Edmonton	AB	T5G3H7	**866-414-4625**	780-414-4000
Los Angeles Kings Staples Ctr 1111 S Figueroa St	Los Angeles	CA	90015	**888-546-4752**	213-742-7100
Minnesota Wild 317 Washington St	Saint Paul	MN	55102	**866-242-5006**	651-602-6000
Montreal Canadiens Bell Centre 1260 de la Gauchetiere St W	Montreal	QC	H3B5E8	**800-363-8162**	514-989-2841
Ottawa Senators 1000 Palladium Dr Scotia Bank Pl	Kanata	ON	K2V1A5	**800-444-7367**	613-599-0100
Phoenix Coyotes 6751 N Sunset Blvd Ste 200	Glendale	AZ	85305	**877-448-4483**	623-772-3200
Pittsburgh Penguins 1001 Fifth Avenue	Pittsburgh	PA	15219	**800-642-7367**	412-642-1300
San Jose Sharks HP Pavilion at San Jose 525 W Santa Clara St	San Jose	CA	95113	**800-755-5050**	408-287-7070
Tampa Bay Lightning St Pete Times Forum 401 Channelside Dr	Tampa	FL	33602	**800-745-3000**	813-301-6500
Vancouver Canucks 800 Griffiths Way	Vancouver	BC	V6B6G1	**877-788-3937**	604-899-7400

715 SPORTS TEAMS - SOCCER

SEE ALSO Sports Organizations

	City	State	Zip	Toll-Free	Phone
Chicago Fire 7000 S Harlem Ave	Bridgeview	IL	60455	**888-657-3473**	708-594-7200
Los Angeles Galaxy Home Depot Ctr 18400 Avalon Blvd Ste 200	Carson	CA	90746	**877-342-5299**	310-630-2200
Milwaukee Wave LLC 510 W Kilbourn Ave	Milwaukee	WI	53203	**800-745-3000**	414-224-9283
New England Revolution Gillette Stadium 1 Patriot Pl	Foxboro	MA	02035	**877-438-7387**	
New York Red Bulls 600 Cape May St	Harrison	NJ	07029	**877-727-6223**	

716 SPRINGS - HEAVY-GAUGE

	City	State	Zip	Toll-Free	Phone
General Wire Spring Co 1101 Thompson Ave	McKees Rocks	PA	15136	**800-245-6200**	412-771-6300
Service Spring Corp 4370 Moline Martin Rd	Millbury	OH	43447	**800-752-8522**	419-838-6081
Southern Spring & Stamping Inc 401 Sub Stn Rd	Venice	FL	34285	**800-450-5882**	941-488-2276

717 SPRINGS - LIGHT-GAUGE

	City	State	Zip	Toll-Free	Phone
Atlantic Spring PO Box 650	Flemington	NJ	08822	**877-231-6474**	908-788-5800
Century Spring Corp 222 E 16th St	Los Angeles	CA	90015	**800-237-5225**	213-749-1466
Economy Spring & Stamping Co 29 DePaolo Dr	Southington	CT	06489	**800-237-5225**	860-621-7358
General Wire Spring Co 1101 Thompson Ave	McKees Rocks	PA	15136	**800-245-6200**	412-771-6300
Hickory Springs Mfg Co 235 Second Ave NW	Hickory	NC	28601	**800-438-5341**	
Lee Spring Company Inc 140 58th St Unit 3C	Brooklyn	NY	11220	**800-110-2500**	718-236-2222
Leggett & Platt Inc Number 1 Leggett Rd PO Box 757 *NYSE: LEG*	Carthage	MO	64836	**800-888-4569**	417-358-8131
Mid-West Spring & Stamping Co 1404 Joliet Rd Unit C	Romeoville	IL	60446	**800-619-0909**	630-739-3800
Newcomb Spring Corp 235 Spring St	Southington	CT	06489	**888-579-3051**	860-621-0111
Southern Spring & Stamping Inc 401 Sub Stn Rd	Venice	FL	34285	**800-450-5882**	941-488-2276
Spring Dynamics Inc 7378 Research Dr	Almont	MI	48003	**888-274-8432**	810-798-2622
Spring Engineers Inc 9740 Tanner Rd	Houston	TX	77041	**800-899-9488**	713-690-9488

718 STADIUMS & ARENAS

SEE ALSO Convention Centers ; Performing Arts Facilities

	City	State	Zip	Toll-Free	Phone
Alamodome 100 Montana St	San Antonio	TX	78203	**800-884-3663**	210-207-3663
Allen County War Memorial Coliseum 4000 Parnell Ave	Fort Wayne	IN	46805	**800-745-3000**	260-482-9502
American Airlines Ctr 2500 Victory Ave	Dallas	TX	75219	**800-745-3000**	214-222-3687
Angel Stadium 2000 Gene Autry Way	Anaheim	CA	92806	**866-800-1275**	714-940-2000
AT&T Ctr 1 AT&T Ctr Pkwy *Resv	San Antonio	TX	78219	**800-745-3000***	210-444-5000
Canal Park Stadium 300 S Main St	Akron	OH	44308	**888-223-6000**	330-253-5151
Columbus Civic Ctr 400 Fourth St	Columbus	GA	31901	**800-745-3000**	706-653-4482
Cowtown Coliseum 121 E Exchange Ave	Fort Worth	TX	76164	**888-269-8696**	817-625-1025
FARGODOME 1800 N University Dr	Fargo	ND	58102	**855-694-6367**	701-241-9100
FedEx Forum 191 Beale St	Memphis	TN	38103	**866-648-4668**	901-205-1234
Fenway Park 4 Yawkey Way	Boston	MA	02215	**877-733-7699**	617-226-6000
Fiesta San Antonio Commission Inc, The 2611 Broadway St	San Antonio	TX	78215	**877-723-4378**	210-227-5191
First Niagara Ctr 1 Seymour Knox III Plz	Buffalo	NY	14203	**888-223-6000**	716-855-4100
Florida Repertory Theatre Inc 2267 Bay St	Fort Myers	FL	33901	**877-787-8053**	239-332-4665
Georgia Dome 1 Georgia Dome Dr NW	Atlanta	GA	30313	**888-333-4406**	404-223-9200
Honda Ctr 2695 E Katella Ave	Anaheim	CA	92806	**877-945-3946**	714-704-2400
i Wireless Ctr 1201 River Dr	Moline	IL	61265	**800-745-3000**	309-764-2001
Kauffman Stadium 1 Royal Way	Kansas City	MO	64129	**800-676-9257**	512-434-1542
Kemper Arena & American Royal Centers 1701 American Royal Ct	Kansas City	MO	64102	**800-767-7700**	816-221-5242
Lubbock Municipal Auditorium/Coliseum 1625 13th St	Lubbock	TX	79415	**800-735-2989**	806-775-2242
Macon Centreplex Coliseum 200 Coliseum Dr	Macon	GA	31217	**877-532-6144**	478-751-9152
MetraPark Arena 308 Sixth Ave N	Billings	MT	59101	**800-366-8538**	406-256-2400
Michigan Stadium 1201 S Main St University of Michigan	Ann Arbor	MI	48104	**866-296-6849**	734-647-2583
Minute Maid Park 501 Crawford St	Houston	TX	77002	**877-927-8767**	713-259-8000
Municipal Auditorium Arena 1321 Baltimore Ave	Kansas City	MO	64105	**800-767-7700**	816-691-3800
Nassau Veterans Memorial Coliseum 1255 Hempstead Tpke	Uniondale	NY	11553	**800-745-3000**	516-794-9300
Norfolk Scope Arena 201 E Brambleton Ave	Norfolk	VA	23510	**800-745-3000**	757-664-6464
Olympic Ctr Arena 2634 Main St	Lake Placid	NY	12946	**800-462-6236**	518-523-1655
Oriole Park at Camden Yards 333 Camden St	Baltimore	MD	21201	**888-848-2473**	410-547-6100
Paul Brown Stadium 1 Paul Brown Stadium	Cincinnati	OH	45202	**866-621-8383**	513-621-3550
Petco Park 100 Pk Blvd	San Diego	CA	92101	**866-800-1275**	619-795-5000
PNC Arena 1400 EdwaRds Mill Rd	Raleigh	NC	27607	**800-745-3000**	919-861-2300
PNC Park 115 Federal St	Pittsburgh	PA	15212	**866-800-1275**	412-321-2827
Qualcomm Stadium 9449 Friars Rd	San Diego	CA	92108	**800-400-7115**	619-641-3100
Quicken Loans Arena 1 Ctr Ct	Cleveland	OH	44115	**888-894-9424**	216-420-2000
Ralph Wilson Stadium 1 Bills Dr	Orchard Park	NY	14127	**877-228-4257**	716-648-1800
Richmond Coliseum 601 E Leigh St	Richmond	VA	23219	**800-228-9290**	804-780-4970
Rockford MetroCentre 300 Elm St	Rockford	IL	61101	**800-745-3000**	815-968-5600
Scottsdale Stadium 7408 E Osborn Rd	Scottsdale	AZ	85251	**877-229-5042**	480-312-2856
Seattle Theatre Group 911 Pine St	Seattle	WA	98101	**877-784-4849**	206-467-5510
Sioux Falls Arena 1201 NW Ave	Sioux Falls	SD	57104	**800-338-3177**	605-367-7288
Sky Sox Stadium 4385 Tutt Blvd Security Service Field	Colorado Springs	CO	80922	**866-698-4253**	719-597-1449
State Fair & Exposition 1001 Beulah Ave	Pueblo	CO	81004	**800-876-4567**	719-404-2018
Sun Devil Stadium 500 E Veterans Way Arizona State University	Tempe	AZ	85281	**888-786-3857**	480-965-3482
Times Union Ctr 51 S Pearl St	Albany	NY	12207	**866-308-3394**	518-487-2000
Toyota Ctr 1510 Polk St	Houston	TX	77002	**866-446-8849**	713-758-7200
Tropicana Field 1 Tropicana Dr	Saint Petersburg	FL	33705	**888-326-7297**	727-825-3137
US Cellular Ctr 370 First Ave E	Cedar Rapids	IA	52401	**800-745-3000**	319-398-5211
US Olympic Training Ctr 1750 E Boulder St	Colorado Springs	CO	80909	**800-775-8762**	719-866-4618
Valley View Casino Ctr 3500 Sports Arena Blvd	San Diego	CA	92110	**800-745-3000**	619-224-4171
Verizon Arena 1 Verizon Arena Way	North Little Rock	AR	72114	**800-745-3000**	501-340-5660
Webster Bank Arena 600 Main St	Bridgeport	CT	06604	**800-745-3000**	203-345-2300
Winnipeg Centennial Folk Festival Inc, The 211 Bannatyne Ave Ste 203	Winnipeg	MB	R3B3P2	**866-301-3823**	204-231-0096
Wrigley Field 1060 W Addison St	Chicago	IL	60613	**866-800-1275**	773-404-2827

719 STAFFING SERVICES

SEE ALSO Employment Offices - Government ; Employment Services - On-line ; Executive Recruiting Firms

Company / Address	City	State	Zip	Toll-Free	Phone
Accounting Principals 10151 Deerwood Park Blvd Ste 400	Jacksonville	FL	32256	**800-981-3849**	
Adecco Inc 175 Broad Hollow Rd *General	Melville	NY	11747	**800-978-3729***	631-844-7650
Advantage Resourcing 220 Norwood Pk S	Norwood	MA	02062	**800-343-4314**	781-251-8000
Aerotek Inc 7301 Pkwy Dr	Hanover	MD	21076	**800-237-6835**	410-694-5100
Allegis Group Inc 7301 Pkwy Dr	Hanover	MD	21076	**800-927-8090**	410-579-3000
Allied Health Group LLC 145 Technology Pkwy NW	Norcross	GA	30092	**800-355-6150**	800-741-4674
ALTRES Inc 967 Kapiolani Blvd	Honolulu	HI	96814	**888-425-8737**	808-591-4940
American Healthcare Services LLC 1000 John R Ste 250	Troy	MI	48083	**866-227-9998**	248-588-9700
AMN Healthcare Services Inc 12400 High Bluff Dr Ste 100 *NYSE: AHS*	San Diego	CA	92130	**866-871-8519**	
APEX Systems Inc 4400 Cox Rd Ste 100	Glen Allen	VA	23060	**800-452-7391**	804-254-2600
AppleOne Employment Services Inc 327 W Broadway	Glendale	CA	91204	**800-872-2677**	310-750-3400
Aquent LLC 711 Boylston St	Boston	MA	02116	**855-767-6333**	617-535-5000
ARC Industries Inc 2879 Johnstown Rd	Columbus	OH	43219	**800-734-7007**	
Area Temps Inc 1228 Euclid Ave	Cleveland	OH	44115	**866-995-5627**	440-646-1333
Artech Information Systems LLC 240 Cedar Knolls Rd Ste 100	Cedar Knolls	NJ	07927	**800-950-9496**	973-998-2500
Bartech Group 17199 N Laurel Pk Dr Ste 224	Livonia	MI	48152	**800-828-4410**	734-953-5050
Bay Area Anesthesia Inc PO Box 1547	Ukiah	CA	95482	**800-327-8427**	707-462-9420
Brooke Chase Associates Inc 1543 Second St Ste 201	Sarasota	FL	34236	**877-374-0039**	
C & A Industries Inc 13609 California St	Omaha	NE	68154	**800-574-9829**	402-891-0009
Calian Technology Ltd 340 Legget Dr Ste 101 *TSE: CTY*	Ottawa	ON	K2K1Y6	**877-225-4264**	613-599-8600
CareerStaff Unlimited Inc 6363 N State Hwy 161 Ste 525	Irving	TX	75038	**888-993-4599**	
Cejka Search Inc 4 Cityplace Dr Ste 300	Saint Louis	MO	63141	**800-678-7858**	314-726-1603
Command Ctr Inc 3609 S Wadsworth Blvd Ste 250 *OTC: CCNI*	Lakewood	ID	80235	**866-464-5844**	
CompHealth Inc 6440 S Millrock Dr Ste 175 Ste 175	Salt Lake City	UT	84121	**800-453-3030**	801-930-3000
Compunnel Software Group Inc 103 Morgan Ln Ste 102	Plainsboro	NJ	08536	**800-696-8128**	
Consultnet LLC 10813 S River Front Pkwy Ste 150	South Jordan	UT	84095	**888-215-9675**	801-208-3700
CPC Logistics Inc 14528 S Outer 40 Rd Ste 210	Chesterfield	MO	63017	**800-274-3746**	314-542-2266
Cross Country Healthcare Inc 6551 Pk of Commerce Blvd *NASDAQ: CCRN*	Boca Raton	FL	33487	**800-347-2264**	561-998-2232
Davis Cos 325 Donald J Lynch Blvd	Marlborough	MA	01752	**800-482-9494**	763-231-0700
Duran Human Capital Partners Inc 300 Orchard City Dr Ste 142	Campbell	CA	95008	**800-287-9682**	408-540-0070
Durham Cos Inc 6300 Transit Rd	Depew	NY	14043	**800-633-7724**	716-684-3333
Eagle Professional Resources Inc 67 Yonge St Ste 200	Toronto	ON	M5E1J8	**800-281-2339**	613-234-1810
Ensearch Management Consultants 905 E Cotati Ave	Cotati	CA	94931	**888-667-5627**	
Entegee Inc 70 BlanchaRd Rd Ste 102	Burlington	MA	01803	**800-368-3433**	781-221-5800
Express Employment Professionals 8516 NW Expy	Oklahoma City	OK	73162	**800-222-4057**	405-840-5000
G&A Partners 4801 Woodway Dr Ste 210W	Houston	TX	77056	**800-253-8562**	713-784-1181
Gibson Arnold & Assoc 5433 Westheimer Rd Ste 1016	Houston	TX	77056	**800-879-2007**	713-572-3000
Hire Image LLC 6 Alcazar Ave	Johnston	RI	02919	**888-433-0090**	401-490-2202
Integrity Staffing Solutions Inc 700 Prides Crossing Ste 300	Newark	DE	19713	**888-458-8367**	302-661-8776
Interim HealthCare Inc 1601 Sawgrass Corporate Pkwy	Sunrise	FL	33323	**800-338-7786**	954-858-6000
IPC Technologies Inc 7200 Glen Forest Dr Ste 100	Richmond	VA	23226	**877-947-2835**	804-622-7288
Joule Inc 1245 US Rt 1 S	Edison	NJ	08837	**800-341-0341**	732-548-5444
Judge Group Inc 300 Conshohocken State Rd Ste 300	West Conshohocken	PA	19428	**888-228-7162**	610-667-7700
Kforce Inc 1001 E Palm Ave *NASDAQ: KFRC*	Tampa	FL	33605	**877-453-6723**	813-552-5000
Kimco Staffing Services Inc 17872 Cowan Ave	Irvine	CA	92614	**800-649-5627**	949-752-6996
Labor Finders International Inc 11426 N Jog Rd	Palm Beach Gardens	FL	33418	**800-864-7749**	561-627-6507
LJ Gonzer Assoc Inc 14 Commerce Dr Ste 305	Cranford	NJ	07016	**866-692-4538**	908-709-9494
Lucas Assoc Inc 3384 Peachtree Rd Ste 900	Atlanta	GA	30326	**800-515-0819**	800-466-4489
Lumen Legal 1025 N Campbell Rd	Royal Oak	MI	48067	**877-933-1330**	248-597-0400
Medical Staffing Assoc Inc 6731 Whittier Ave 3rd Fl	McLean	VA	22101	**800-235-5105**	
Medical Staffing Network Holdings Inc 901 Yamato Rd Ste 110	Boca Raton	FL	33431	**800-676-8326**	
Medvantx Inc 5626 Oberlin Dr Ste 110	San Diego	CA	92121	**866-744-0621**	858-625-2990
Minute Men Staffing Services 3740 Carnegie Ave	Cleveland	OH	44115	**877-873-8856**	216-426-9675
National Engineering Service Corp 72 Mirona Rd	Portsmouth	NH	03801	**800-562-3463**	603-431-9740
Nursefinders Inc 12400 High Bluff Dr	San Diego	CA	92130	**800-445-0459**	877-214-4105
Orion International Consulting Group Inc 912 Capital of Texas Hwy S Ste 220	Austin	TX	78746	**800-336-7466**	512-327-7111
Oxford Global Resources Inc 100 Cummings Ctr Ste 206L	Beverly	MA	01915	**800-426-9196**	978-236-1182
Peak Technical Services Inc 583 Epsilon Dr	Pittsburgh	PA	15238	**888-888-7325**	412-696-1080
Principal Technical Services Inc 9960 Research Dr Ste 200	Irvine	CA	92618	**888-787-3711**	
Profiles International Inc 5205 Lk Shore Dr	Waco	TX	76710	**866-751-1644**	254-751-1644
RCM Technologies Inc 2500 McClellan Ave Ste 350 *NASDAQ: RCMT*	Pennsauken	NJ	08109	**800-322-2885**	856-356-4500
Remedy Temp Inc 3820 State St	Santa Barbara	CA	93105	**800-688-6162**	805-882-2200
Resources Global Professionals 17101 Armstrong Ave *NASDAQ: RECN*	Irvine	CA	92614	**800-900-1131**	714-430-6400
Right at Home Inc 6464 Crt St Ste 150	Omaha	NE	68106	**877-697-7537**	402-697-7537
Robert Half International Inc Accountemps Div 2884 Sand Hill Rd Ste 200	Menlo Park	CA	94025	**855-396-4598**	
Salem Group, The 2 TransAm Plz Dr Ste 170	Oakbrook Terrace	IL	60181	**877-768-7141**	630-932-7000
Select Staffing 3820 State St	Santa Barbara	CA	93105	**800-688-6162**	805-882-2200
Shimento 1350 Hayes St	Benicia	CA	94510	**877-211-8708**	
Silicon Valley Staffing 2336 Harrison St	Oakland	CA	94612	**877-660-6000**	510-923-9898
Softworld Inc 281 Winter St Ste 301	Waltham	MA	02451	**877-899-1166**	781-466-8882
Southwest Medical Assoc Inc 638 E Market St PO Box 2168	Rockport	TX	78382	**800-929-4854**	
Special Counsel Inc 10201 Centurion Pkwy N Ste 400	Jacksonville	FL	32256	**800-737-3436**	904-737-3436
Sterling Computer Corp 600 Stevens Port Dr Ste 200	Dakota Dunes	SD	57049	**877-242-4074**	605-242-4000
Superior Technical Resources Inc 250 International Dr	Williamsville	NY	14221	**800-568-8310**	716-929-1400
Surgical Staff Inc 120 St Matthews Ave	San Mateo	CA	94401	**800-339-9599**	650-558-3999
Sysazzle Inc 15815 S. 46th St Ste 116,	Phoenix	AZ	85048	**800-862-9545**	
TAJ Technologies Inc 1168 Northland Dr	Mendota Heights	MN	55120	**877-825-2801**	651-688-2801
Team Health Inc 265 Brookview Ctr Way Ste 400	Knoxville	TN	37919	**800-342-2898**	865-693-1000
TEKsystems Inc 7437 Race Rd	Hanover	MD	21076	**888-519-0776**	410-540-7700
Temporary Solutions Inc 10550 Linden Lk Plz Ste 200	Manassas	VA	20109	**888-222-0457**	703-361-2220
Thompson Technologies Inc 114 Townpark Dr Ste 100	Kennesaw	GA	30144	**888-794-7947**	770-794-8380
Transforce Inc 5520 Cherokee Ave Ste 200	Alexandria	VA	22150	**800-308-6989**	703-838-5580
True Blue Inc PO Box 2910 *NYSE: TBI*	Tacoma	WA	98401	**800-610-8920**	253-383-9101
UltraStaff 1818 Memorial Dr Ste 200	Houston	TX	77007	**800-522-7707**	713-522-7100
US Legal Support Inc 363 N Sam Houston Pkwy E Ste 900	Houston	TX	77060	**800-567-8757**	713-653-7100
VMC Consulting Corp 11611 Willows Rd NE	Redmond	WA	98052	**877-393-8622**	425-558-7700
White Glove Placement Inc 85 Bartlett St	Brooklyn	NY	11206	**866-387-8100**	718-387-8181
York Solutions LLC 1 Westbrook Corporate Ctr Ste 910	Westchester	IL	60154	**877-700-9675**	708-531-8362

720 STAGE EQUIPMENT & SERVICES

Company / Address	City	State	Zip	Toll-Free	Phone
Apollo Design Technology Inc 4130 Fourier Dr	Fort Wayne	IN	46818	**800-288-4626**	260-497-9191
Chapman/Leonard Studio Equipment Inc 12950 Raymer St	North Hollywood	CA	91605	**888-883-6559**	818-764-6726
Dreamworld Backdrops 6450 Lusk Blvd Ste E-106	San Diego	CA	92121	**800-737-9869**	
Grosh Scenic Rentals 4114 Sunset Blvd	Los Angeles	CA	90029	**877-363-7998**	
High End Systems Inc 2105 Gracy Farms Ln	Austin	TX	78758	**800-890-8989**	512-836-2242
Janson Industries 1200 Garfield Ave SW	Canton	OH	44706	**800-548-8982**	330-455-7029
Musson Theatrical Inc 890 Walsh Ave	Santa Clara	CA	95050	**800-843-2837**	408-986-0210
Rosco Laboratories Inc 52 Harbor View Ave	Stamford	CT	06902	**800-767-2669**	203-708-8900
Screen Works 2201 W Fulton St *Cust Svc	Chicago	IL	60612	**800-294-8111***	312-243-8265
Secoa Inc 8650 109th Ave N	Champlin	MN	55316	**800-328-5519**	763-506-8800
Syracuse Scenery & Stage Lighting Company Inc 101 Monarch Dr	Liverpool	NY	13088	**800-453-7775**	315-453-8096

721 STEEL - MFR

Company / Address	City	State	ZIP	Toll-Free	Phone
A Finkl & Sons Co 2011 N Southport Ave	Chicago	IL	60614	**800-343-2562**	773-975-2510
AK Steel Corp 9227 Centre Pt Dr *NYSE: AKS*	West Chester	OH	45069	**800-331-5050**	513-425-5000
Aleris International Inc 25825 Science Pk Dr Ste 400	Beachwood	OH	44122	**866-266-2586**	216-910-3400
Allegheny Technologies Inc 1000 Six PPG Pl *NYSE: ATI* *Sales	Pittsburgh	PA	15222	**800-258-3586***	412-394-2800
American Tank & Fabricating Co (AT&F) 12314 Elmwood Ave	Cleveland	OH	44111	**800-544-5316**	216-252-1500
ATI Allegheny Ludlum Corp 100 River Rd *Sales	Brackenridge	PA	15014	**800-258-3586***	724-224-1000
Bushwick Metals LLC 560 N Washington Ave	Bridgeport	CT	06604	**888-399-4070**	
Canam Group Inc 11535 First Ave Bureau 500 *TSE: CAM*	Saint-Georges	QC	G5Y7H5	**877-499-6049**	418-228-8031
Carpenter Specialty Alloys Operations 101 W Bern St	Reading	PA	19601	**800-654-6543**	610-208-2000
Carpenter Technology Corp PO Box 14662 *NYSE: CRS*	Reading	PA	19612	**800-654-6543**	610-208-2000
Cascade Steel Rolling Mills Inc (CSRM) 3200 N Hwy 99 W PO Box 687	McMinnville	OR	97128	**800-283-2776**	503-472-4181
Corey Steel Co 2800 S 61st Ct	Cicero	IL	60804	**800-323-2750**	708-735-8000
Creform Corp PO Box 830	Greer	SC	29652	**800-839-8823**	864-989-1700
Crucible Materials Corp 575 State Fair Blvd	Syracuse	NY	13209	**800-365-1180**	315-487-4111
Electralloy Corp 175 Main St	Oil City	PA	16301	**800-458-7273**	814-678-4100
Feroleto Steel Company Inc 300 Scofield Ave	Bridgeport	CT	06605	**800-243-2839**	203-366-3263
Gerdau AmeriSteel Corp 4221 W Boy Scout Blvd Ste 600 *Sales	Tampa	FL	33607	**800-876-7833***	813-286-8383
Gibraltar Industries Inc 3556 Lakeshore Rd *NASDAQ: ROCK*	Buffalo	NY	14219	**800-247-8368**	716-826-6500
GO Carlson Inc 350 Marshallton Thorndale Rd	Downingtown	PA	19335	**800-338-5622**	610-384-2800
Greer Steel Co 624 Blvd *Sales	Dover	OH	44622	**800-388-2868***	330-343-8811
Gulf Coast Machine & Supply Company Inc 6817 Industrial Rd	Beaumont	TX	77705	**800-231-3032**	409-842-1311
Intsel Steel Distributors LP 11310 W Little York	Houston	TX	77041	**800-762-3316**	713-937-9500
Jersey Shore Steel Co 70 Maryland Ave PO Box 5055	Jersey Shore	PA	17740	**800-833-0277**	570-753-3000
Kentucky Electric Steel LLC 2704 S Big Run Rd W	Ashland	KY	41102	**800-333-3012**	606-929-1200
LOKRING Technology LLC 38376 Apollo Pkwy	Willoughby	OH	44094	**800-876-2323**	440-942-0880
Metalex Corp 1530 Artaius Pkwy PO Box 399	Libertyville	IL	60048	**800-323-0792**	847-362-8300
Mill Steel Co 5116 36th St SE	Grand Rapids	MI	49512	**800-247-6455**	
Moore Erection LP 19921 Fm 2252	San Antonio	TX	78266	**800-656-6673**	210-648-7461
Niagara Corp 667 Madison Ave	New York	NY	10021	**877-289-2277**	212-317-1000
Nucor Corp 1915 Rexford Rd *NYSE: NUE*	Charlotte	NC	28211	**800-294-1322**	704-366-7000
Nucor Corp Cold Finish Div 2800 N Governor Williams Hwy	Darlington	SC	29540	**800-333-0590**	704-366-7000
Nucor-Yamato Steel Co 5929 E State Hwy 18	Blytheville	AR	72315	**800-289-6977**	870-762-5500
Sandmeyer Steel Co 1 Sandmeyer Ln	Philadelphia	PA	19116	**800-523-3663**	215-464-7100
Scion Steel Inc 21555 Mullin Ave	Warren	MI	48089	**800-288-2127**	586-755-4000
Steel Dynamics Inc 7575 W Jefferson Blvd Ste 200 *NASDAQ: STLD*	Fort Wayne	IN	46804	**866-740-8700**	260-969-3500
Steel of West Virginia Inc 17th St & Second Ave	Huntington	WV	25703	**800-624-3492**	304-696-8200
Ulbrich Stainless Steels & Special Metals Inc (USSM) 57 Dodge Ave	North Haven	CT	06473	**800-243-1676**	203-239-4481
United Performance Metals 3475 Symmes Rd	Hamilton	OH	45015	**888-282-3292**	513-860-6500
USS-POSCO Industries 900 Loveridge Rd	Pittsburg	CA	94565	**800-877-7672**	925-439-6000
Worthington Steel Co 200 W Old Wilson Bridge Rd	Columbus	OH	43085	**800-944-3733**	614-438-3210

722 STONE (CUT) & STONE PRODUCTS

Company / Address	City	State	ZIP	Toll-Free	Phone
Akdo Intertrade Inc 1435 State St	Bridgeport	CT	06605	**800-811-2536**	203-336-5199
AZ Countertops Inc 1445 S Hudson Ave	Ontario	CA	91762	**800-266-3524**	909-983-5386
Bristol Memorial Works Inc 797 King St	Bristol	CT	06010	**888-987-7821**	860-583-1654
Bybee Stone Company Inc 6293 N Matthews Dr	Ellettsville	IN	47429	**800-457-4530**	812-876-2215
Cold Spring Granite Inc 17482 Granite W Rd	Cold Spring	MN	56320	**800-328-5040**	320-685-3621
Coldspring 17482 Granite W Rd	Cold Spring	MN	56320	**800-328-5040**	
Columbus Marble Works Corp 2415 Hwy 45 N *Cust Svc	Columbus	MS	39705	**800-647-1055***	662-328-1477
Continental Cast Stone Manufacturing Inc 22001 W 83rd St	Shawnee	KS	66227	**800-989-7866**	
Dakota Granite Co 48391 150th St PO Box 1351	Milbank	SD	57252	**800-843-3333**	605-432-5580
Dakota Marble Inc 902 W 19th St	Yankton	SD	57078	**800-697-7241**	605-665-7241
Glenrock International Inc 985 E Linden Ave	Linden	NJ	07036	**800-453-6762**	908-862-3433
Keystone Retaining Wall Systems Inc 4444 W 78th St	Minneapolis	MN	55435	**800-642-3887**	952-897-1040
Little Falls Granite Works 10802 Hwy 10	Little Falls	MN	56345	**800-862-2417**	
Monumental Sales Inc 537 22nd Ave N PO Box 667	Saint Cloud	MN	56302	**800-442-1660**	320-251-6585
North Carolina Granite Corp 151 Granite Quarry Trl PO Box 151	Mount Airy	NC	27030	**800-227-6242**	336-786-5141
Northfield Block Co 1 Hunt Ct	Mundelein	IL	60060	**800-358-3003**	847-949-3600
RJ Marshall Co 26776 W 12-Mile Rd *Cust Svc	Southfield	MI	48034	**888-514-8600***	248-353-4100
Rock of Ages Corp 560 Graniteville Rd	Graniteville	VT	05654	**800-421-0166**	802-476-3119
Starrett Tru-Stone Technologies Div 1101 Prosper Dr PO Box 430	Waite Park	MN	56387	**800-959-0517**	320-251-7171
Vermont Structural Slate Company Inc 3 Prospect St PO Box 98	Fair Haven	VT	05743	**800-343-1900**	802-265-4933
Vetter Stone Co (VSC) 23894 Third Ave	Mankato	MN	56001	**800-878-2850**	507-345-4568
WS Hampshire Inc 365 Keyes Ave	Hampshire	IL	60140	**800-541-0251**	847-683-4400

723 STUDENT ASSISTANCE PROGRAMS

Company / Address	City	State	ZIP	Toll-Free	Phone
Alabama Prepaid Affordable College Tuition (PACT) Program 100 N Union St Ste 660	Montgomery	AL	36130	**800-252-7228**	334-242-7514
Alaska Commission on Postsecondary Education PO Box 110510	Juneau	AK	99811	**800-441-2962**	907-465-2962
Arkansas Financial Aid Office 114 Silas Hunt Hall	Fayetteville	AR	72701	**800-547-8839**	479-575-3806
California Student Aid Commission PO Box 419027	Rancho Cordova	CA	95741	**888-224-7268**	916-526-8999
Colorado CollegeInvest 1560 Broadway Ste 1700	Denver	CO	80202	**800-448-2424**	303-376-8800
DC Tuition Assistance Grant Program 810 First St NE	Washington	DC	20001	**877-485-6751**	202-727-2824
Dollars for Scholars Scholarship America 1 Scholarship Way	Saint Peter	MN	56082	**800-248-8080**	507-931-1682
EdVest PO Box 55244	Boston	MA	02205	**888-338-3789**	
FastWeb Inc 444 N Michigan Ave Ste 600	Chicago	IL	60611	**800-829-1040**	444-536-1212
FinAid Page LLC PO Box 2056	Cranberry Township	PA	16066	**800-433-3243**	724-538-4500
Florida Prepaid College Board PO Box 6567	Tallahassee	FL	32314	**800-552-4723**	
Florida Student Financial Assistance Office 1940 N Monroe St Ste 70	Tallahassee	FL	32303	**888-827-2004**	850-410-5200
Georgia Student Finance Commission 2082 E Exchange Pl Ste 200	Tucker	GA	30084	**800-505-4732**	770-724-9000
Hawaii Postsecondary Education Commission 2444 Dole St Bachman Hall Rm 209	Honolulu	HI	96822	**877-531-2333**	808-956-8213
Illinois Student Assistance Commission 1755 Lake Cook Rd	Deerfield	IL	60015	**800-899-4722**	847-948-8500
Indiana Students Assistance Commission 150 W Market St Ste 500	Indianapolis	IN	46204	**888-528-4719**	317-232-2350
Iowa College Student Aid Commission 603 E 12th St Fl 5th	Des Moines	IA	50319	**800-383-4222**	515-725-3400
Kentucky Higher Education Assistance Authority (KHEAA) 100 Airport Rd	Frankfort	KY	40602	**800-928-8926**	
Louisiana Office of Student Financial Assistance (LOSFA) 602 N Fifth St PO Box 91202	Baton Rouge	LA	70802	**800-259-5626**	225-219-1012
Maine Finance Authority of Maine (FAME) 5 Community Dr PO Box 949	Augusta	ME	04332	**800-228-3734**	207-623-3263
Maryland Student Financial Assistance Office 839 Bestgate Rd Ste 400	Annapolis	MD	21401	**800-974-0203**	410-260-4565
Michigan Education Trust (MET) PO Box 30198 *General	Lansing	MI	48909	**800-638-4543***	517-335-4767
Michigan Student Financial Services Bureau Austin Bldg 430 W Allegan *General	Lansing	MI	48922	**800-642-5626***	888-447-2687
Minnesota Office of Higher Education 1450 Energy Pk Dr Ste 350	Saint Paul	MN	55108	**800-657-3866**	651-642-0567
Mississippi Student Financial Aid Office 3825 Ridgewood Rd	Jackson	MS	39211	**800-327-2980**	601-432-6997
Montana Higher Education Board of Regents 2500 Broadway St PO Box 203201	Helena	MT	59620	**877-501-1722**	406-444-6570
New Hampshire Postsecondary Education Commission 64 South St Ste 300	Concord	NH	03301	**800-735-2964**	603-271-2555
New Jersey Higher Education Student Assistance Authority 4 Quakerbridge Plaza PO Box 540	Trenton	NJ	08625	**800-792-8670**	609-584-4480
New York Higher Education Services Corp 99 Washington Ave	Albany	NY	12255	**888-697-4372**	518-473-1574
North Carolina State Education Assistance Authority (NCSEAA) PO Box 14103	Research Triangle Park	NC	27709	**800-700-1775**	919-549-8614
Ohio Tuition Trust Authority 580 S High St Ste 208 *Cust Svc	Columbus	OH	43215	**800-233-6734***	614-752-9400
Pennsylvania Higher Education Assistance Agency 1200 N Seventh St	Harrisburg	PA	17102	**800-233-0557**	

Name / Address	City	State	Zip	Toll-Free	Phone
Scholarship America 1 Scholarship Way PO Box 297	Saint Peter	MN	56082	**800-537-4180**	507-931-1682
South Carolina Higher Education Tuition Grants Commission 115 Atrium Wy Ste 102	Columbia	SC	29203	**877-382-4357**	803-896-1120
Thurgood Marshall Scholarship Fund 901 F St NW Ste 300	Washington	DC	20004	**866-632-9992**	212-573-8888
Utah Higher Education Assistance Authority PO Box 145112	Salt Lake City	UT	84114	**877-336-7378**	801-321-7294
Vermont Student Assistance Corp (VSAC) PO Box 2000	Winooski	VT	05404	**800-642-3177**	802-655-9602
Virginia College Savings Plan 9001 Arboretum Pkwy	Richmond	VA	23236	**888-567-0540**	804-786-0719
West Virginia Higher Education Policy Commission 1018 Kanawha Blvd E Ste 700	Charleston	WV	25301	**888-825-5707**	304-558-2101

724 SUBSTANCE ABUSE TREATMENT CENTERS

SEE ALSO Self-Help Organizations ; General Hospitals - Canada ; General Hospitals - US ; Psychiatric Hospitals

Name / Address	City	State	Zip	Toll-Free	Phone
AdCare Hospital of Worcester 107 Lincoln St	Worcester	MA	01605	**800-252-6465**	508-799-9000
Anchor Hospital 5454 Yorktowne Dr	Atlanta	GA	30349	**866-667-8797**	770-991-6044
APT Foundation 1 Long Wharf Dr Ste 321	New Haven	CT	06511	**855-378-4373**	203-781-4600
AREBA Casriel Inc (ACI) 500 W 57th St	New York	NY	10019	**800-724-4444**	212-293-3000
Arms Acres 75 Seminary Hill Rd	Carmel	NY	10512	**800-989-2676**	845-225-3400
Baltimore Behavioral Health (BBH) 1101 W Pratt St	Baltimore	MD	21223	**800-789-2647**	410-962-7180
Bradford Health Services 2101 Magnolia Ave S Ste 518	Birmingham	AL	35205	**800-217-2849**	205-251-7753
Central Street Health Ctr 26 Central St	Somerville	MA	02143	**800-909-2677**	617-591-6033
Clear Brook Manor 1100 E Northampton St	Laurel Run	PA	18706	**800-582-6241**	
Coleman Professional Services 24 7 Emergency C 3920 Lovers Ln	Ravenna	OH	44266	**800-673-1347**	330-296-3555
Conifer Park 79 Glenridge Rd	Schenectady	NY	12302	**800-989-6446**	518-399-6446
Cornerstone Medical Arts Ctr Hospital 159-05 Union Tpke	Fresh Meadows	NY	11366	**800-233-9999**	718-906-6700
Daymark Recovery Services Inc Stanly Center 1000 N First St Ste 1	Albemarle	NC	28001	**866-275-9552**	704-983-2117
Dayton Rehabilitation Institute 1 Elizabeth Pl	Dayton	OH	45417	**800-765-4772**	937-424-8200
Eagleville Hospital 100 Eagleville Rd *General	Eagleville	PA	19408	**800-255-2019***	610-539-6000
Fairbanks Hospital 8102 Clearvista Pkwy	Indianapolis	IN	46256	**800-225-4673**	317-849-8222
Fellowship Hall Inc 5140 Dunstan Rd	Greensboro	NC	27405	**800-659-3381**	336-621-3381
Friary of Lakeview Ctr, The 4400 Hickory Shores Blvd	Gulf Breeze	FL	32563	**800-332-2271**	850-932-9375
Gateway Foundation Inc 1080 E Pk St	Carbondale	IL	62901	**877-505-4673**	
Glenbeigh Health Source 2863 SR 45	Rock Creek	OH	44084	**800-234-1001**	440-563-3400
Greenleaf Ctr 2209 Pineview Dr	Valdosta	GA	31602	**800-247-2747**	229-671-6700
Griffin Memorial Hospital 900 E Main St *General	Norman	OK	73071	**800-955-3468***	405-321-4880
Hampton Behavioral Health Center 650 Rancocas Rd	Westampton	NJ	08060	**800-603-6767**	
Harmony Foundation Inc 1600 Fish Hatchery Rd	Estes Park	CO	80517	**866-686-7867**	970-586-4491
Hazelden Chicago 867 N Dearborn St	Chicago	IL	60610	**800-257-7810**	312-943-3534
Hazelden Ctr for Youth & Families (HCYF) 11505 36th Ave N	Plymouth	MN	55441	**800-257-7810**	763-509-3800
Hazelden Foundation 15251 Pleasant Vly Rd	Center City	MN	55012	**800-257-7810**	651-213-4200
Hazelden New York 322 Eigth Ave 12th Fl	New York	NY	10001	**800-257-7800**	212-420-9520
Hazelden Springbrook 1901 Esther St	Newberg	OR	97132	**866-866-4662**	503-554-4300
HealthSource Saginaw 3340 Hospital Rd	Saginaw	MI	48603	**800-662-6848**	989-790-7700
Highland Ridge Hospital 7309 South 180 West	Midvale	UT	84047	**800-821-4357**	801-569-2153
Impact Drug & Alcohol Treatment Ctr 1680 N Fair Oaks Ave PO Box 93607	Pasadena	CA	91103	**866-734-4200**	626-798-0884
Keystone Ctr 2001 Providence Ave	Chester	PA	19013	**800-558-9600**	610-876-9000
La Hacienda Treatment Ctr 145 La Hacienda Way	Hunt	TX	78024	**800-749-6160**	830-238-4222
Livengrin Foundation 4833 Hulmeville Rd	Bensalem	PA	19020	**800-245-4746**	215-638-5200
Malvern Institute 940 W King Rd	Malvern	PA	19355	**888-643-3869**	610-647-0330
Mohave Mental Health Clinic Inc 3505 Western Ave	Kingman	AZ	86409	**888-757-8111**	928-757-8111
Mount Regis Ctr 405 Kimball Ave	Salem	VA	24153	**877-217-3447**	
Mountain Manor Treatment Ctr 9701 Keysville Rd	Emmitsburg	MD	21727	**800-537-3422**	301-447-2361
New Directions Inc 30800 Chagrin Blvd	Cleveland	OH	44124	**800-750-6709**	216-591-0324
Phoenix House Foundation Inc (PHF) 164 W 74th St 4th Fl	New York	NY	10023	**888-671-9392**	
Rimrock Foundation 1231 N 29th St	Billings	MT	59101	**800-227-3953**	406-248-3175
Rivervalley Behavioral Health Hospital 1100 Walnut St PO Box 1637	Owensboro	KY	42302	**800-755-8477**	270-689-6800
Samaritan Village 138-02 Queens Blvd	Briarwood	NY	11435	**800-532-4357**	718-206-2000
Schick Shadel Hospital 12101 Ambaum Blvd SW	Seattle	WA	98146	**800-500-6395**	
Serenity Lane 616 E 16th Ave	Eugene	OR	97401	**800-543-9905**	541-687-1110
Sierra Tucson Inc 39580 S Lago Del Oro Pkwy	Tucson	AZ	85739	**800-842-4487**	520-624-4000
Spencer Recovery Centers Inc 1316 S Coast Hwy	Laguna Beach	CA	92651	**800-334-0394**	
Talbott Recovery Campus 5448 Yorktowne Dr	Atlanta	GA	30349	**800-445-4232**	770-994-0185
Turning Point Hospital 3015 Veterans Pkwy PO Box 1177	Moultrie	GA	31776	**800-342-1075**	229-985-4815
Turning Point of Tampa 6227 Sheldon Rd	Tampa	FL	33615	**800-397-3006**	813-882-3003
Valley Forge Medical Ctr & Hospital 1033 W Germantown Pk	Norristown	PA	19403	**888-539-8500**	610-539-8500
Village South Inc 3050 Biscayne Blvd 9th Fl	Miami	FL	33137	**800-443-3784**	305-573-3784
Walter B Jones Alcohol & Drug Abuse Treatment Ctr 2577 W Fifth St	Greenville	NC	27834	**800-422-1884**	252-830-3426
Willingway Hospital 311 Jones Mill Rd	Statesboro	GA	30458	**800-242-9455**	912-764-6236
Wilmington Treatment Ctr 2520 Troy Dr	Wilmington	NC	28401	**877-762-3750**	
Youth Home Inc 20400 Colonel Glenn Rd	Little Rock	AR	72210	**800-728-6452**	501-821-5500

725 SURVEYING, MAPPING, RELATED SERVICES

SEE ALSO Engineering & Design

Name / Address	City	State	Zip	Toll-Free	Phone
Cochrane Technologies Inc PO Box 81276	Lafayette	LA	70598	**800-346-3745**	337-837-3334
Day & Zimmermann Group Inc 1818 Market St	Philadelphia	PA	19130	**877-319-0270**	215-299-8000
Geophysics GPR International Inc 100 - 2545 Delorimier Stree	Longueuil	QC	J4K3P7	**800-672-4774**	450-679-2400
H2 Engineering Surveying LLC 8880 N Hess St	Hayden	ID	83835	**877-700-9909**	208-772-6600
Huitt-Zollars Inc 1717 McKinney Ave Ste 1400	Dallas	TX	75202	**866-667-6572**	214-871-3311
KCI Technologies Inc 936 Ridgebrook Rd	Sparks	MD	21152	**800-572-7496**	410-316-7800
Landiscor 7310 N 16th St Ste 275	Phoenix	AZ	85020	**866-221-8578**	602-248-8989
Print-O-Stat Inc 1011 W Market St	York	PA	17404	**800-711-8014**	717-854-7821
Rouse-sirine Associates Ltd 333 Office Sq Ln	Virginia Beach	VA	23462	**800-276-2023**	757-490-2300
Sidwell Co Inc 675 Sidwell Ct	Saint Charles	IL	60174	**877-743-9355**	630-549-1000
Teletrac Inc 7391 Lincoln Way	Garden Grove	CA	92841	**800-500-6009**	714-897-0877
Wade-Trim Group Inc 500 Griswold Ave Ste 2500	Detroit	MI	48226	**800-482-2864**	313-961-3650

726 SWIMMING POOLS

Name / Address	City	State	Zip	Toll-Free	Phone
Anthony & Sylvan Pools Corp 3739 Easton Rd Rt 611	Doylestown	PA	18901	**800-366-7958**	215-489-5600
Delair Group LLC 8600 River Rd	Delair	NJ	08110	**800-235-0185**	215-676-4068
Fox Pool Corp 3490 BoaRd Rd	York	PA	17406	**800-723-1011**	717-764-8581
Hornerxpress Inc 5755 Powerline Rd	Fort Lauderdale	FL	33309	**800-432-6966**	954-772-6966
Imperial Pools Inc 33 Wade Rd	Latham	NY	12110	**800-444-9977**	518-786-1200
Morgan Bldg Systems Inc 2800 McCree Rd	Garland	TX	75041	**800-935-0321**	972-864-7300
Radiant Pools Div Trojan Leisure Products LLC 440 N Pearl St	Albany	NY	12207	**866-697-5870**	518-434-4161
Viking Pools Inc 121 Crawford Rd PO Box 96	Williams	CA	95987	**800-854-7665**	530-473-5319
Vogue Pool Products 7050 St Patrick St	LaSalle	QC	H8N1V2	**800-363-3232**	514-363-3232

727 SWITCHGEAR & SWITCHBOARD APPARATUS

SEE ALSO Transformers - Power, Distribution, Specialty ; Wiring Devices - Current-Carrying

Name / Address	City	State	Zip	Toll-Free	Phone
Bel Fuse Inc 206 Van Vorst St *NASDAQ: BELFA*	Jersey City	NJ	07302	**800-235-3873**	201-432-0463
Guardian Electric Mfg Company Inc 1425 Lake Ave	Woodstock	IL	60098	**800-762-0369**	815-334-3600
HVB AE Power Systems Inc 7250 Mcginnis Ferry Rd	Suwanee	GA	30024	**866-362-0798**	770-495-1755
ITW Switches 195 E Algonquin Rd	Des Plaines	IL	60016	**800-544-3354**	847-876-9400
Kasa Industrial Controls Inc 418 E Ave B	Salina	KS	67401	**800-755-5272**	785-825-7181
Littelfuse Inc 8755 W Higgins Rd Ste 500 *NASDAQ: LFUS* ■ *Sales	Chicago	IL	60631	**800-227-0029***	773-628-1000
Lumitex Inc 8443 Dow Cir	Strongsville	OH	44136	**800-969-5483**	440-243-8401
Norberg-ies 4237 S 74th E Ave	Tulsa	OK	74145	**800-739-9145**	918-665-6888

Classified Section

				Toll-Free	Phone
Otto Engineering Inc 2 E Main St	Carpentersville	IL	60110	**888-234-6886**	847-428-7171
Powell Industries Inc 8550 Mosely Dr *NASDAQ: POWL*	Houston	TX	77075	**800-480-7273**	713-944-6900
Power Distribution Inc 4200 Oakleys Ct	Richmond	VA	23223	**800-225-4838**	804-737-9880
Powercon Corp PO Box 477	Severn	MD	21144	**800-638-5055**	410-551-6500
Reliance Controls Corp 2001 Young Ct	Racine	WI	53404	**800-634-6155**	262-634-6155
Revere Control Systems Inc 2240 Rocky Ridge Rd	Birmingham	AL	35216	**800-536-2525**	205-824-0004
Russelectric Inc 99 Industrial Pk Rd	Hingham	MA	02043	**800-225-5250**	781-749-6000
S & C Electric Co 6601 N Ridge Blvd	Chicago	IL	60626	**800-621-5546**	773-338-1000
Satin American Corp 40 Oliver Terr	Shelton	CT	06484	**877-356-5050**	
Tapeswitch Corp 100 Schmitt Blvd	Farmingdale	NY	11735	**800-234-8273**	631-630-0442

728 TABLE & KITCHEN SUPPLIES - CHINA & EARTHENWARE

SEE ALSO

				Toll-Free	Phone
Heritage Mint Ltd PO Box 13750	Scottsdale	AZ	85267	**888-860-6245**	480-860-1300
Homer Laughlin China Co 672 Fiesta Dr	Newell	WV	26050	**800-452-4462**	304-387-1300
Lenox Corp PO Box 2006	Bristol	PA	19007	**800-223-4311**	
Lipper International Inc 235 Washington St	Wallingford	CT	06492	**800-243-3129**	203-269-8588
Luna Garcia 201 San Juan Ave	Venice	CA	90291	**800-905-9975**	310-396-8026
Pfaltzgraff Co PO Box 21769	York	PA	17402	**800-999-2811**	

TAPE - ADHESIVE

SEE Medical Supplies - Mfr

729 TAPE - CELLOPHANE, GUMMED, MASKING, PRESSURE SENSITIVE

SEE ALSO Medical Supplies - Mfr

				Toll-Free	Phone
3M Canada Co 300 Tartan Dr	London	ON	N5V4M9	**888-364-3577**	
American Biltrite Inc Tape Products Div (ABI) 105 Whittendale Dr	Moorestown	NJ	08057	**888-224-6325**	856-778-0700
Avery Dennison Corp 207 Goode Ave *NYSE: AVY* ■ *Cust Svc	Glendale	CA	91203	**888-567-4387***	626-304-2000
Avery Dennison Specialty Tapes Div 250 Chester St Bldg 5	Painesville	OH	44077	**866-462-8379**	626-304-2000
Brady Coated Products 6555 W Good Hope Rd	Milwaukee	WI	53223	**800-662-1191**	414-358-6600
Brite-Line LLC 10660 E 51st Ave	Denver	CO	80239	**888-201-6448**	
Decker Tape Products Inc 6 Stewart Pl	Fairfield	NJ	07004	**800-227-5252**	973-227-5350
DeWAL Industries Inc 15 Ray Trainor Dr	Narragansett	RI	02882	**800-366-8356**	401-789-9736
Eternabond 75 E Div St	Mundelein	IL	60060	**888-336-2663**	847-837-9400
Gaska-Tape Inc 1810 W Lusher Ave	Elkhart	IN	46517	**800-423-1571**	574-294-5431
Harris Industries Inc 5181 Argosy Ave	Huntington Beach	CA	92649	**800-222-6866**	714-898-8048
Holland Mfg Co Inc 15 Main St PO Box 404	Succasunna	NJ	07876	**800-345-0492**	973-584-8141
JHL Industries 10012 Nevada Ave	Chatsworth	CA	91311	**800-255-6636**	818-882-2233
Kruse Adhesive Tape Inc 1610 E McFadden Ave	Santa Ana	CA	92705	**800-992-7702**	714-640-2130
M & C Specialties Co 90 James Way *Cust Svc	SouthHampton	PA	18966	**800-441-6996***	215-322-1600
Neptco Inc 30 Hamlet St	Pawtucket	RI	02861	**800-354-5445**	401-722-5500
Presto Tape Inc 1626 Bridgewater Rd	Bensalem	PA	19020	**800-331-1373**	215-245-8555
Pro Tapes & Specialties PO Box 53026	Newark	NJ	07101	**800-345-0234**	732-346-0900
Shurtape Technologies LLC 1712 Eigth St Dr SE	Hickory	NC	28602	**888-442-8273**	828-322-2700
Tesa Tape Inc 5825 Carnegie Blvd	Charlotte	NC	28209	**800-426-2181**	704-554-0707
Tommy Tape 378 Four Rod Rd	Berlin	CT	06037	**888-866-8273**	860-378-0111
VIBAC Canada Inc 12250 Industrial Blvd	Montreal	QC	H1B5M5	**800-557-0192**	514-640-0250
WTP Inc PO Box 937	Coloma	MI	49038	**800-521-0731**	269-468-3399

730 TARPS, TENTS, COVERS

SEE ALSO Sporting Goods ; Bags - Textile

				Toll-Free	Phone
Aero Industries Inc 4243 W Bradbury Ave *Sales	Indianapolis	IN	46241	**800-535-9545***	317-244-2433
American Pavilion 1706 Warrington Ave	Danville	IL	61832	**800-424-9699**	217-443-0800
Anchor Industries Inc 1100 Burch Dr	Evansville	IN	47725	**800-544-4445**	812-867-2421
Canvas Products Co 274 S Waterman St	Detroit	MI	48209	**877-293-1669**	313-496-1000
Clamshell Structures Inc 1101 Maulhardt Ave	Oxnard	CA	93030	**800-360-8853**	805-988-1340
Commonwealth Canvas Inc 5 Perkins Way	Newburyport	MA	01950	**877-922-6827**	978-499-3900
CR Daniels Inc 3451 Ellicott Ctr Dr	Ellicott City	MD	21043	**800-933-2638**	410-461-2100
DC Humphrys Inc 5744 Woodland Ave *Sales	Philadelphia	PA	19143	**800-645-2059***	215-724-8181
Diamond Brand Canvas Products 145 Cane Creek Industrial Pk Rd Ste 1 *Sales	Fletcher	NC	28732	**800-459-6262***	828-684-9848
Eide Industries Inc 16215 Piuma Ave	Cerritos	CA	90703	**800-422-6827**	562-402-8335
Estex Mfg Co Inc 402 E Broad St PO Box 368	Fairburn	GA	30213	**800-749-1224**	
Fisher Canvas Products Inc 415 St Mary St	Burlington	NJ	08016	**800-892-6688**	
John Johnson Co 274 S Waterman St	Detroit	MI	48209	**800-991-1394**	313-496-0600
Johnson Outdoors Inc 555 Main St *NASDAQ: JOUT*	Racine	WI	53403	**800-468-9716**	262-631-6600
Loop-Loc Ltd 390 Motor Pkwy	Hauppauge	NY	11788	**800-562-5667**	631-582-2626
Rainier Industries Ltd 18375 Olympic Ave S	Tukwila	WA	98188	**800-869-7162**	425-251-1800
Robertson Manufacturing Inc 112 Woodland Ave	West Grove	PA	19390	**800-260-5423**	610-869-9600
Shur-Co Inc 2309 Shur-Lok St PO Box 713	Yankton	SD	57078	**800-474-8756**	605-665-6000
Steele Canvas Basket Corp 201 William St PO Box 6267 IMCN	Chelsea	MA	02150	**800-541-8929**	617-889-0202
Trimaco LLC 2300 Gateway Centre Blvd Ste 200	Morrisville	NC	27560	**800-325-7356**	919-674-3460
Troy Sunshade Co 607 Riffle Ave	Greenville	OH	45331	**800-833-8769**	937-548-2466
Universal Fabric Structures Inc 2200 Kumry Rd	Telford	PA	18969	**800-634-8368**	215-529-9921

731 TAX PREPARATION SERVICES

				Toll-Free	Phone
AccessPoint LLC 28800 Orchard Lake Rd	Farmington Hills	MI	48334	**866-513-3861**	
Active Professionals Inc 9647b Folsom Blvd	Sacramento	CA	95827	**888-838-5086**	
APA Services 4150 International Plz Tower I Ste 510	Fort Worth	TX	76109	**877-425-5023**	
Avitus Group PO Box 81590	Billings	MT	59108	**800-454-2446**	
Bayerkohler & Graff Ltd 11132 Zealand Ave N	Champlin	MN	55316	**866-315-2771**	763-427-2542
BDB Payroll Inc 768 Bedford Ave	Brooklyn	NY	11205	**800-729-7687**	718-522-2000
Defense Finance & Accounting Service 8899 E 56th St	Indianapolis	IN	46249	**888-332-7411**	
Eastridge Workforce Solutions 2375 Northside Dr Ste 360	San Diego	CA	92108	**877-862-2632**	619-296-8735
Employer Flexible 7850 N Sam Houston Parkway W Ste 100	Houston	TX	77064	**866-501-4942**	
Exactax Inc 2301 W Lincoln Ave Ste 100	Anaheim	CA	92801	**844-327-6740**	714-284-4802
Exerve Inc 2909 Langford Rd Ste 400B	Norcross	GA	30071	**800-364-0637**	770-447-1566
Farm Business Consultants Inc 150 3015 Fifth Ave Ne	Calgary	AB	T2A6T8	**800-265-1002**	403-735-6105
Fesnak & Associates LLP 1777 Sentry Pkwy W Ste 300	Blue Bell	PA	19422	**800-274-3978**	267-419-2200
Fiducial 1370 Ave of the Americas 31st Fl	New York	NY	10019	**866-343-8242**	212-207-4700
Fiducial 10100 Old Columbia Rd	Columbia	MD	21046	**800-323-9000**	410-290-8296
H & R Block Tax Services Inc 4400 Main St	Kansas City	MO	64111	**800-472-5625**	
Inova Payroll Inc 176 Thompson Ln Ste 204	Nashville	TN	37211	**888-244-6106**	615-921-0600
Jackson Hewitt Inc 3 Sylvan Way Ste 301 *OTC: JHTXQ*	Parsippany	NJ	07054	**800-234-1040**	
JG Tax Group 1430 S Federal Hwy	Deerfield Beach	FL	33441	**866-477-5291**	
Knight James E & Associates Pc 14825 Saint Marys Ln	Houston	TX	77079	**800-772-1213**	281-493-5080
Liberty Tax Service Inc 1716 Corporate Landing Pkwy *Cust Svc	Virginia Beach	VA	23454	**800-790-3863***	757-493-8855
Paycom 7501 W Memorial Rd	Oklahoma City	OK	73142	**800-580-4505**	
Payworks Inc 1565 Willson Pl	Winnipeg	MB	R3T4H1	**866-788-3500**	
PrO Unlimited Inc 301 Yamato Rd Ste3199	Boca Raton	FL	33431	**800-291-1099**	
Quantum Management Services Ltd 2000 McGill College Ave Ste 1800	Montreal	QC	H3A3H3	**800-978-2688**	514-842-5555
SALT Group, The 1845 Sidney Baker St	Kerrville	TX	78028	**888-257-1266**	830-257-1290
Silver Creek Financial ServicesInc 175 Hwy 82	Lostine	OR	97857	**866-569-0020**	541-569-2272
Verified Audit Circulation Inc 900 Larkspur Landing Cir	Larkspur	CA	94939	**800-775-3332**	415-461-6006

732 TELECOMMUNICATIONS EQUIPMENT & SYSTEMS

SEE ALSO Modems ; Radio & Television Broadcasting & Communications Equipment

Company / Address	City	State	Zip	Toll-Free	Phone
ADTRAN Inc 901 Explorer Blvd *NASDAQ: ADTN*	Huntsville	AL	35806	**800-923-8726**	256-963-8000
AltiGen Communications Inc 410 E Plumeria Dr *OTC: ATGN*	San Jose	CA	95134	**888-258-4436**	408-597-9000
Amtelco 4800 Curtin Dr	McFarland	WI	53558	**800-356-9148**	608-838-4194
AT & T Inc 175 E Houston St PO Box 2933 *NYSE: AT&T*	San Antonio	TX	78299	**800-351-7221**	210-821-4105
Atris Inc 1151 S Trooper Rd Ste E	Norristown	PA	19403	**800-724-3384**	
Audiovox Corp 180 Marcus Blvd *NASDAQ: VOXX*	Hauppauge	NY	11788	**800-645-4994**	631-231-7750
Aurora Networks Inc 5400 Betsy Ross Dr	Santa Clara	CA	95054	**888-287-6726**	408-235-7000
Call One Inc 400 Imperial Blvd PO Box 9002	Cape Canaveral	FL	32920	**800-749-3160**	321-783-2400
Charles Industries Ltd 5600 Apollo Dr	Rolling Meadows	IL	60008	**800-458-4747**	847-806-6300
CiDRA Corp 50 Barnes Pk N	Wallingford	CT	06492	**877-243-7277**	203-265-0035
CIENA Corp 1201 Winterson Rd *NASDAQ: CIEN*	Linthicum	MD	21090	**800-921-1144**	410-694-5700
ClearOne Communications Inc 5225 Wiley Post Way	Salt Lake City	UT	84116	**800-945-7730**	801-975-7200
Communication Technologies Inc 14151 Newbrook Dr Ste 400	Chantilly	VA	20151	**888-266-8358**	703-961-9080
Communications Test Design Inc 1339 Enterprise Dr	West Chester	PA	19380	**800-223-3910**	610-436-5203
Compunetix Inc 2420 Mosside Blvd	Monroeville	PA	15146	**800-879-4266**	412-373-8110
Digital Voice Corp 1201 S Beltline Rd Ste 150 *Cust Svc	Coppell	TX	75019	**800-777-8329***	469-635-6500
DynaMetric Inc 717 S Myrtle Ave	Monrovia	CA	91016	**800-525-6925**	626-358-2559
Ecessa Corp 13755 1st Ave N Ste 100	Plymouth	MN	55441	**800-669-6242**	763-694-9949
Electro Standards Laboratories Inc 36 Western Industrial Dr	Cranston	RI	02921	**877-943-1164**	401-943-1164
Electronic Tele-Communications Inc 1915 MacArthur Rd *OTC: ETCIA*	Waukesha	WI	53188	**888-746-4382**	262-542-5600
FleetBoss Global Positioning Solutions Inc 241 O'Brien Rd	Fern Park	FL	32730	**877-265-9559**	407-265-9559
Fujitsu America Inc 1250 E Arques Ave	Sunnyvale	CA	94085	**800-538-8460**	408-746-6200
GAI-Tronics Corp 400 E Wyomissing Ave	Mohnton	PA	19540	**800-492-1212**	610-777-1374
Genesys Telecommunications Laboratories Inc 2001 Junipero Serra Blvd	Daly City	CA	94014	**888-436-3797**	650-466-1100
GN US Inc 77 NE Blvd	Nashua	NH	03062	**800-327-2230**	603-598-1100
Harris Corp 1025 W NASA Blvd *NYSE: HRS*	Melbourne	FL	32919	**800-442-7747**	321-727-9100
Honeywell International Inc 101 Columbia Rd PO Box M6/LM *NYSE: HON*	Morristown	NJ	07962	**877-841-2840**	480-353-3020
Hughes Network Systems LLC 11717 Exploration Ln	Germantown	MD	20876	**800-461-9330**	301-428-5500
I Wireless 4135 NW Urbandale Dr *Cust Svc	Urbandale	IA	50322	**888-550-4497***	515-258-7000
iDirect Technologies Inc 13865 Sunrise Valley Dr Ste 100	Herndon	VA	20171	**888-362-5475**	703-648-8118
Infinera Corp 140 Caspian Ct *NASDAQ: INFN*	Sunnyvale	CA	94089	**877-742-3427**	408-572-5200
ISCO International LLC 1450 Arthur Ave Ste A	Elk Grove Village	IL	60007	**888-948-4726**	224-222-1666
JTech Communications Inc 6413 Congress Ave Ste 150	Boca Raton	FL	33487	**800-321-6221**	
L-3 Communications Corp 600 Third Ave 34-35 Fl *NYSE: LLL*	New York	NY	10016	**800-351-8483**	212-697-1111
Lantronix Inc 167 Technology Dr *NASDAQ: LTRX* ■ *Orders	Irvine	CA	92618	**800-526-8766***	949-453-3990
Metro-Tel Corp 290 NE 68 St	Miami	FL	33138	**888-998-8300**	402-498-2964
Mitel Networks Corp 350 Legget Dr PO Box 13089	Kanata	ON	K2K2W7	**800-722-1301**	613-592-2122
Molex Premise Networks 2222 Wellington Ct	Lisle	IL	60532	**866-733-6659**	630-969-4550
Motorola Inc IDEN Group 8000 W Sunrise Blvd	Plantation	FL	33322	**800-102-2344**	
NDS Americas 3500 Highland Ave	Costa Mesa	CA	92626	**866-398-8749**	714-434-2100
NEC America Inc 6555 N State Hwy 161 *Cust Svc	Irving	TX	75039	**866-632-3226***	214-262-2000
NICE Systems Inc 301 Rt 17 N 10th Fl	Rutherford	NJ	07070	**800-994-4498**	201-964-2600
Norsat International Inc 110-4020 Viking Way *TSE: NII*	Richmond	BC	V6V2N2	**800-644-4562**	604-821-2800
Numerex Corp 1600 Parkwood Cir 5th Fl *NASDAQ: NMRX*	Atlanta	GA	30339	**800-665-5686**	770-693-5950
Pics Telecom International Corp 1920 Lyell Ave	Rochester	NY	14606	**800-521-7427**	585-295-2000
Plantronics Inc 345 Encinal St *NYSE: PLT*	Santa Cruz	CA	95060	**800-544-4660**	831-426-5858
Polycom Inc 4750 Willow Rd	Pleasanton	CA	94588	**800-765-9266**	
Protel Inc 4150 Kidron Rd	Lakeland	FL	33811	**800-925-8882**	863-644-5558
Proxim Wireless Corp 1561 Buckeye Dr *OTC: PRXM*	Milpitas	CA	95035	**800-229-1630**	408-383-7600
Pulse Communications Inc 2900 Towerview Rd *Cust Svc	Herndon	VA	20171	**800-381-1997***	703-471-2900
RAD Data Communications Ltd 900 Corporate Dr	Mahwah	NJ	07430	**800-444-7234**	201-529-1100
Samsung Telecommunications America LLP 1301 E Lookout Dr	Richardson	TX	75082	**800-726-7864**	972-761-7000
Superior Essex Communications LP 6120 Powers Ferry Rd Ste 150	Atlanta	GA	30339	**800-551-8948**	770-657-6000
Suttle 1001 E Hwy 212	Hector	MN	55342	**800-852-8662**	320-848-6711
Symmetricom Inc 2300 Orchard Pkwy *NASDAQ: SYMM*	San Jose	CA	95131	**888-367-7966**	408-433-0910
System Engineering International Inc (SEI) 5115 Pegasus Ct Ste Q	Frederick	MD	21704	**800-765-4734**	301-694-9601
TAG Solutions LLC 12 Elmwood Rd	Albany	NY	12204	**800-724-0023**	518-292-6500
Technical Communications Corp 100 Domino Dr *NASDAQ: TCCO*	Concord	MA	01742	**800-952-4082**	978-287-5100
Tekelec 5200 Paramount Pkwy *NASDAQ: TKLC*	Morrisville	NC	27560	**800-633-0738**	919-460-5500
Tel Electronics Inc 313 S 740 E St Ste 1	American Fork	UT	84003	**800-748-5022**	801-756-9606
Telco Systems Inc 15 Berkshire Rd	Mansfield	MA	02048	**800-227-0937**	781-255-2120
Telect Inc 23321 E Knox Ave *Cust Svc	Liberty Lake	WA	99019	**800-551-4567***	509-926-6000
Teo Technologies Inc 11609 49th Pl W	Mukilteo	WA	98275	**800-524-0024**	425-349-1000
Tollgrade Communications Inc 3120 Unionville Rd Ste 400 *Cust Svc	Cranberry Township	PA	16066	**800-878-3399***	412-820-1400
Toshiba America Inc 1251 Ave of the Americas Ste 4100	New York	NY	10020	**800-457-7777**	212-596-0600
Tricomm Services Corp 1247 N Church St Ste 8	Moorestown	NJ	08057	**800-872-2401**	856-914-9001
TSI Global Cos 700 Fountain Lakes Blvd	Saint Charles	MO	63301	**800-875-5605**	636-949-8889
Uniden America Corp 4700 Amon Carter Blvd *Cust Svc	Fort Worth	TX	76155	**800-297-1023***	817-858-3300
UTStarcom Inc 1732 North First St Ste 220 *NASDAQ: UTSI*	San Jose	CA	95112	**877-547-6340**	408-453-4557
Valcom Inc 5614 Hollins Rd	Roanoke	VA	24019	**800-825-2661**	540-563-2000
Vbrick Systems Inc 12 Beaumont Rd	Wallingford	CT	06492	**866-827-4251**	203-265-0044
VTech Communications Inc 9590 SW Gemini Dr Ste 120	Beaverton	OR	97008	**800-595-9511**	503-596-1200
Westell Technologies Inc 750 N Commons Dr *NASDAQ: WSTL*	Aurora	IL	60504	**800-323-6883**	630-898-2500
Zhone Technologies Inc 7001 Oakport St *NASDAQ: ZHNE*	Oakland	CA	94621	**877-946-6320**	510-777-7000

733 TELECOMMUNICATIONS SERVICES

Company / Address	City	State	Zip	Toll-Free	Phone
Access Point Inc 1100 Crescent Green	Cary	NC	27518	**877-419-4274**	919-851-4838
ACT Conferencing 1526 Cole Blvd Bldg 3 Ste 300	Lakewood	CO	80401	**800-433-2900**	303-233-3500
AirIQ Inc 1845 Sandstone Manor Ste 10	Pickering	ON	L1W3W9	**888-606-6444**	905-831-6444
Airvoice Wireless LLC 2425 Franklin Rd	Bloomfield Hills	MI	48302	**888-944-2355**	
Alaska Communications Systems Group Inc 600 Telephone Ave *NASDAQ: ALSK*	Anchorage	AK	99503	**800-808-8083**	907-563-8000
Allstream Corp 200 Wellington St W *Cust Svc	Toronto	ON	M5V3G2	**888-288-2273***	416-345-2000
AmeriCom Inc PO Box 2146	Sandy	UT	84091	**800-820-6296**	801-571-2446
AT & T Inc 175 E Houston St PO Box 2933 *NYSE: AT&T*	San Antonio	TX	78299	**800-351-7221**	210-821-4105
Auragan LLC PO Box 1501	New Canaan	CT	06840	**866-644-2872**	
Bell Aliant Regional Communications 1505 Barrington St Maritime Ctr *TSE: BA*	Halifax	NS	B3J3K5	**800-555-1212**	800-267-1110
Bell Canada 1050 Beaver Hall Hill	Montreal	QC	H2Z1S4	**800-667-0123**	
Birch Communications Inc 2300 Main St 6th Fl	Kansas City	MO	64108	**866-424-5100**	816-300-3000
Bledsoe Telephone Co-op Corp (BTC) 338 Cumberland Ave PO Box 609	Pikeville	TN	37367	**888-382-1222**	423-447-2121
Bluegrass Cellular Inc 2902 Ring Rd	Elizabethtown	KY	42701	**800-928-2355**	270-769-0339
Broadview Networks Holdings Inc 800 Westchester Ave Ste N-501	Rye Brook	NY	10573	**800-260-8766**	914-922-7000
Cavalier Telephone LLC 2134 W Laburnum Ave	Richmond	VA	23227	**800-683-3944**	800-442-2410

				Toll-Free	Phone
Cellhire USA LLC					
3520 W Miller Rd Ste 100	Garland	TX	75041	**877-244-7242**	214-355-5200
Century Interactive LLC					
1505 Federal St Ste 200	Dallas	TX	75201	**877-921-7992**	817-713-2329
Cesium Telecom Inc					
5798 Ferrier	Montreal	QC	H4P1M7	**877-798-8686**	514-798-8686
Cincinnati Bell Inc					
221 E Fourth St	Cincinnati	OH	45202	**800-387-3638**	513-397-9900
NYSE: CBB					
Citizens Telephone Co-op					
PO Box 137	Floyd	VA	24091	**800-941-0426**	540-745-2111
Co-op Communciations Inc					
412 Washington Ave	Belleville	NJ	07079	**800-833-2700**	
Commenco Inc					
4901 Bristol Ave	Kansas City	MO	64129	**800-292-9725**	816-753-2166
Commonwealth Telephone Co					
1 Newbury St Ste 103	Peabody	MA	01960	**800-439-7170**	978-536-9500
Comporium Communications					
332 E Main St	Rock Hill	SC	29730	**866-922-5922**	888-403-2667
Corporate Telephone Services					
184 W Second St	Boston	MA	02127	**800-274-1211**	617-625-1200
Criticom Inc					
4211 Forbes Blvd	Lanham	MD	20706	**800-449-3384**	301-306-0600
Dakota Central Telecommunications Co-op					
630 Fifth St N	Carrington	ND	58421	**800-771-0974**	701-652-3184
Deltacom Inc					
7037 Old Madison Pike	Huntsville	AL	35806	**800-239-3000**	
deltathree Inc 75 Broad St	New York	NY	10004	**888-335-8230**	212-500-4850
PINK: DDDC					
Eastex Telephone Co-op Inc					
PO Box 150	Henderson	TX	75653	**800-232-7839**	903-854-1000
EATELCORP Inc					
913 S Burnside Ave	Gonzales	LA	70737	**800-621-4211**	225-621-4300
Empire Telephone Corp					
34 Main St PO Box 349	Prattsburgh	NY	14873	**800-338-3300**	607-522-3712
Excel Telecommunications					
433 Las Colinas Blvd Ste 400	Irving	TX	75039	**877-668-0808**	972-910-1900
FairPoint Communications Inc					
521 E Morehead St Ste 250	Charlotte	NC	28202	**866-740-2764**	704-344-8150
NASDAQ: FRP					
Farmers Telecommunications Co-op (FTC)					
144 McCurdy Ave N PO Box 217	Rainsville	AL	35986	**866-638-2144**	256-638-2144
Farmers Telephone Co-op Inc					
1101 E Main St	Kingstree	SC	29556	**888-218-5050**	843-382-2333
Faxaway 417 Second Ave W	Seattle	WA	98119	**800-906-4329**	206-301-7000
FaxBack Inc					
7007 SW Cardinal Ln Ste 105	Portland	OR	97224	**800-329-2225**	503-597-5350
Frontier Communications Corp					
3 High Ridge Pk	Stamford	CT	06905	**800-877-4390**	203-614-5600
NASDAQ: FTR					
Fusion Telecommunications International Inc					
420 Lexington Ave Ste 1718	New York	NY	10170	**888-301-1721**	212-201-2400
OTC: FSNN					
General Communication Inc					
2550 Denali St Ste 1000	Anchorage	AK	99503	**800-770-7886**	907-265-5600
NASDAQ: GNCMA					
Golden West Telecommunications					
415 Crown St PO Box 411	Wall	SD	57790	**866-279-2161**	605-279-2161
Granite Telecommunications LLC					
100 Newport Ave Ext	Quincy	MA	02171	**866-847-1500**	617-933-5500
Graphnet Inc					
40 Fultron St 28th Fl	New York	NY	10038	**800-327-1800**	212-994-1100
GTX Corp					
117 W Ninth St Ste 1214	Los Angeles	CA	90015	**877-489-3019**	213-489-3019
Guadalupe Valley Telephone Co-op (GVTC)					
36101 FM 3159	New Braunfels	TX	78132	**800-367-4882**	830-885-4411
Hargray Communications					
856 William Hilton Pkwy					
PO Box 5986	Hilton Head Island	SC	29938	**800-726-1266**	843-341-1501
Harrisonville Telephone Co					
213 S Main St PO Box 149	Waterloo	IL	62298	**888-482-8353**	618-939-6112
Horry Telephone Co-op Inc (HTC)					
3480 Hwy 701 N PO Box 1820	Conway	SC	29528	**800-824-6779**	843-365-2151
Integra Telecom Inc					
1201 NE Lloyd Blvd Ste 500	Portland	OR	97232	**866-468-3472***	503-453-8000
*General					
Inter-Community Telephone Co (ICTC)					
PO Box 8	Nome	ND	58062	**800-350-9137**	701-924-8815
InterCall					
8420 W Bryn Mawr Ste 1100	Chicago	IL	60631	**800-374-2441**	773-399-1600
Intrado Inc					
1601 Dry Creek Dr	Longmont	CO	80503	**877-262-3775**	720-494-5800
IVCi LLC					
601 Old Willets Path	Hauppauge	NY	11788	**800-224-7083**	631-273-5800
J2 Global Communications Inc					
6922 Hollywood Blvd 8th Fl	Los Angeles	CA	90028	**888-718-2000***	323-860-9200
*Sales					
Kaplan Telephone Company Inc (KTC)					
220 N Cushing Ave	Kaplan	LA	70548	**866-643-7171**	337-643-7171
Kennebec Telephone Company Inc					
220 S Main St	Kennebec	SD	57544	**888-868-3390**	605-869-2220
Lambeau Telecom					
1807 N Ctr St	Beaver Dam	WI	53916	**800-444-4014***	920-887-3148
*Cust Svc					
LICT Corp					
401 Theodore Fremd Ave	Rye	NY	10580	**800-690-6903**	914-921-8821
Lightower Fiber Networks					
80 Central St	Boxborough	MA	01719	**888-583-4237**	978-264-6000
Matanuska Telephone Assn Inc					
1740 S Chugach St	Palmer	AK	99645	**800-478-3211**	907-745-3211
Mercury Wireless LLC					
2825 se california ave	Topeka	KS	66605	**800-354-4915**	
Midcontinent Communications					
PO Box 5010	Sioux Falls	SD	57117	**800-888-1300**	605-274-9810
Molalla Communications Co					
211 Robbins St PO Box 360	Molalla	OR	97038	**800-332-2344**	503-829-1100
Net Access Corp					
2300 15th St Ste 300	Denver	CO	80202	**800-638-6336**	973-590-5000
Net2Phone Inc 520 Broad St	Newark	NJ	07102	**800-386-6438**	973-438-3111
Network Communications International Corp (NCIC)					
PO Box 551	Longview	TX	75601	**800-382-2887**	903-757-4455
New Ulm Telecom Inc					
27 N Minnesota St	New Ulm	MN	56073	**888-873-6853**	507-354-4111
OTC: NULM					
North Central Telephone Co-op Corp					
PO Box 70	Lafayette	TN	37083	**800-795-3272**	615-666-2151
NTELOS Holdings Corp					
1154 Shenandoah Village Dr	Waynesboro	VA	22980	**877-468-3567**	540-946-3500
NASDAQ: NTLS					
NTT DoCoMo USA Inc					
757 Third Ave 16th Fl	New York	NY	10017	**888-362-6661**	
01 Communications Inc					
4359 town ctr blvd Ste 217	El Dorado hills	CA	95762	**888-444-1111**	
Omnitracs LLC					
10290 Campus Point Dr	San Diego	CA	92121	**888-627-2716**	800-647-3325
Otelco Inc 505 Third Ave E	Oneonta	AL	35121	**866-471-7888**	205-625-3574
NASDAQ: OTT					
OTZ Telephone Co-op Inc					
PO Box 324	Kotzebue	AK	99752	**800-478-3111**	907-442-3114
Panhandle Telecommunication Systems Inc (PTSI)					
2222 NW Hwy	Guymon	OK	73942	**800-562-2556**	580-338-2556
Penasco Valley Telecommunications (PVT)					
4011 W Main St	Artesia	NM	88210	**800-505-4844**	
Pioneer Long Distance Inc					
PO Box 539	Kingfisher	OK	73750	**888-782-2667**	
Pioneer Telephone Assn Inc					
PO Box 707	Ulysses	KS	67880	**800-308-7536**	620-356-3211
Pratt Communications					
2913 Tech Ctr	Santa Ana	CA	92705	**800-980-2323***	714-540-6840
*General					
Primus Telecommunications (PTGi)					
7901 Jones Ranch Dr Ste 900	McLean	VA	22102	**866-385-3360**	703-902-2800
NYSE: PTGI					
PWR LLC 6402 Deere Rd	Syracuse	NY	13206	**800-342-0878**	315-701-0210
Questar InfoComm Inc					
180 East 100 South					
PO Box 45433	Salt Lake City	UT	84145	**800-729-6790**	801-324-5856
Reiko Wireless					
1218 flushing ave	Brooklyn	NY	11237	**888-797-3456**	212-213-1102
Reserve Telephone Company Inc					
PO Box T	Reserve	LA	70084	**888-611-6111**	985-536-1111
Rnk Inc 333 Elm St Ste 310	Dedham	MA	02026	**877-323-2486**	781-613-6000
Rogers Wireless Communications Inc					
333 Bloor St. E, 4th Fl	Toronto	ON	M4W1G9	**800-575-9090**	888-764-3771
Rural Telephone Service Company Inc					
PO Box 158	Lenora	KS	67645	**877-625-7872**	785-567-4281
Securus Technologies Inc					
14651 Dallas Pkwy	Dallas	TX	75254	**800-844-6591**	972-277-0300
Shawnee Telephone Co					
PO Box 69	Equality	IL	62934	**800-461-3956**	618-276-4211
Shenandoah Telecommunications Co					
500 Shentel Way	Edinburg	VA	22824	**800-743-6835**	540-984-5224
NASDAQ: SHEN					
SignalPoint Communications Corp					
433 Hackensack Ave					
Continental Plz 6th Fl	Hackensack	NJ	07601	**877-928-3292**	201-968-9797
Sirius Canada Inc					
135 Liberty St	Toronto	ON	M6K1A7	**888-539-7474**	
Skyline Telephone Membership Corp					
PO Box 759	West Jefferson	NC	28694	**877-475-9546**	336-877-3111
SkyTel Corp PO Box 2469	Jackson	MS	39225	**800-759-8737***	
*Cust Svc					
Smart City Networks					
5795 W Badura Ave Ste 110	Las Vegas	NV	89118	**888-446-6911**	702-943-6000
Solarus					
440 E Grand Ave	Wisconsin Rapids	WI	54494	**800-421-9282**	715-421-8111
SoundBite Communications Inc					
22 Crosby Dr	Bedford	MA	01730	**888-436-3797**	650-466-1100
NASDAQ: SDBT					
Southern Communications Services Inc					
5555 Glenridge Connector Ste 500	Atlanta	GA	30342	**800-818-5462**	
Spotwave Wireless Inc					
500 Van Buren St Box 550	Kemptville	ON	K0G1J0	**866-704-9750**	613-591-1662
Startec Global Communications Corp					
11300 Rockville Pike Ste 900	Rockville	MD	20852	**800-827-3374**	301-610-4300
T-Mobile USA Inc					
12920 SE 38th St	Bellevue	WA	98006	**800-318-9270**	425-383-4000
TDS Telecommunications Corp					
525 Junction Rd	Madison	WI	53717	**866-571-6662**	608-664-4000
TelAlaska Inc					
201 E 56th St	Anchorage	AK	99518	**888-570-1792**	907-563-2003
Telephone Service Co					
2 Willipie St	Wapakoneta	OH	45895	**800-743-5707**	419-739-2200
Teligent Inc 105 Lincoln Ave	Buena	NJ	08310	**800-656-0793**	
Thumb Cellular Ltd. Partnership					
82 S Main St	Pigeon	MI	48755	**800-443-5057**	989-453-4333
Total Telcom Inc					
540 1632 Dickson Ave	Kelowna	BC	V1Y7T2	**877-860-3762**	250-860-3762
TracFone Wireless Inc					
9700 NW 112th Ave	Miami	FL	33178	**800-876-5753**	305-640-2000
Trans National Communications International Inc (TNCI)					
2 Charlesgate W	Boston	MA	02215	**800-800-8400**	617-369-1000
Twin Lakes Telephone Co-op					
200 Telephone Ln	Gainesboro	TN	38562	**800-644-8582***	931-268-2151
*Cust Svc					
United Utilities Inc					
5450 A St	Anchorage	AK	99509	**800-478-2020**	907-561-1674
Unitel Inc PO Box 165	Unity	ME	04988	**888-760-1048**	207-948-3900
Universal Service Administrative Co (USAC)					
2000 L St NW Ste 200	Washington	DC	20036	**888-641-8722**	202-776-0200
Universal Service Administrative Company Schools & Libraries Div					
2000 L St NW Ste 200	Washington	DC	20036	**888-203-8100**	
Upper Peninsula Telephone Co					
PO Box 86	Carney	MI	49812	**800-950-8506**	906-639-2111
US Cellular Corp (USCC)					
8410 W Bryn Mawr Ave Ste 700	Chicago	IL	60631	**888-944-9400**	773-399-8900
NYSE: USM					

Company	Address	City	State	ZIP	Toll-Free	Phone
USA Datanet Corp	109 S Warren St Ste 602	Syracuse	NY	13202	**800-566-8655**	
USA Mobility Inc	6677 Richmond Hwy	Alexandria	VA	22306	**800-231-2556**	703-660-6677
Valley Telephone Co-op Inc	752 E Maley St	Willcox	AZ	85643	**800-421-5711**	520-384-2231
VeriSign Inc (*NASDAQ: VRSN* ■ *Sales)	350 Ellis St	Mountain View	CA	94043	**866-893-6565***	650-426-3100
Verizon Business (*Cust Svc)	1 Verizon Way	Basking Ridge	NJ	07920	**877-297-7816***	908-559-2000
Verizon Wireless	180 Washington Valley Rd	Bedminster	NJ	07921	**800-922-0204**	908-306-7000
Virgin Mobile USA Inc	10 Independence Blvd	Warren	NJ	07059	**888-322-1122**	908-607-4000
Voicecom	5900 Windward Pkwy Ste 500	Alpharetta	GA	30005	**888-468-3554**	
Vonage Holdings Corp (*NYSE: VG*)	23 Main St	Holmdel	NJ	07733	**877-862-2562**	732-528-2600
Wabash Telephone Co-op Inc	PO Box 299	Louisville	IL	62858	**800-228-9824**	618-665-3311
Warwick Valley Telephone Co (*NASDAQ: WWVY* ■ *Cust Svc)	47 Main St PO Box 592	Warwick	NY	10990	**800-952-7642***	845-986-8080
Wavedivision Holdings LLC	401 Kirkland Prk Pl Ste 500	Kirkland	WA	98033	**866-928-3123**	425-576-8200
West River Co-op Telephone Co (WRCTC)	801 Coleman Ave PO Box 39	Bison	SD	57620	**888-464-9513**	605-244-5213
West River Telecommunications Co-op	PO Box 467	Hazen	ND	58545	**800-748-7220**	701-748-2211
West Texas Rural TelephoneCo-op Inc	PO Box 1737	Hereford	TX	79045	**888-440-4331**	806-364-3331
WQN Inc (*OTC: WQNI*)	14911 Quorum Dr Ste 140	Dallas	TX	75254	**866-661-6176**	
XO Communications Inc	13865 Sunrise Vly Dr	Herndon	VA	20171	**866-349-0134**	703-547-2000
Yak Communications Corp	48 Yonge St Ste 1200	Toronto	ON	M5E1G6	**877-925-4925**	
York Telecom Corp	81 Corbett Way	Eatontown	NJ	07724	**866-836-8463**	732-413-6000

734 TELEMARKETING & OTHER TELE-SERVICES

Both inbound and outbound telephone marketing as well as other tele-services are included here.

Company	Address	City	State	ZIP	Toll-Free	Phone
Alta Resources	120 N Commercial St	Neenah	WI	54956	**877-464-2582**	
America's Call Center Inc	7901 Baymeadows Way Ste 14	Jacksonville	FL	32256	**800-598-2580**	904-224-2000
American Home Base (*General)	428 Childers St	Pensacola	FL	32534	**800-549-0595***	850-857-0860
Ameridial Inc	4535 Strausser St NW	North Canton	OH	44720	**800-445-7128**	
Aria Communications Corp	717 W Saint Germain St	St. Cloud	MN	56301	**800-955-9924**	
Calling Solutions By Phone Power Inc (*Cust Svc)	2200 McCullough Ave	San Antonio	TX	78212	**800-683-5500***	210-801-9630
Connection, The (*Sales)	11351 Rupp Dr	Burnsville	MN	55337	**800-883-5777***	952-948-5488
Convergys Corp (*NYSE: CVG*)	201 E Fourth St	Cincinnati	OH	45202	**888-284-9900**	513-723-7000
Harte-Hanks Response Management	2800 Wells Branch Pkwy	Austin	TX	78728	**800-456-9748**	512-434-1100
InfoCision Management Corp	325 Springside Dr	Akron	OH	44333	**800-210-6269**	330-668-1400
Integretel Inc	5883 Rue Ferrari	San Jose	CA	95138	**888-302-2750**	408-362-4000
iSky	1700 Pennsylvania Ave NW Ste 560	Washington	DC	20006	**855-475-4759**	
Julie Inc	3275 Executive Dr	Joliet	IL	60431	**800-892-0123**	815-741-5000
Lester Inc	19 Business Pk Dr	Branford	CT	06405	**800-999-5265**	203-488-5265
Mars Stout Inc	4500 Majestic Dr	Missoula	MT	59808	**800-451-6277**	406-721-6280
Meyer Assoc Inc	14 Seventh Ave N	Saint Cloud	MN	56303	**800-676-9233**	320-259-4000
Miratel Solutions Inc	2501 Steeles Ave W	North York	ON	M3J2P1	**866-647-2835**	416-650-7850
My Receptionist	800 Wisconsin St Ste 410	Eau Claire	WI	54703	**800-686-0162**	
ProCom Inc	28838 US Hwy 69 PO Box 27	Lamoni	IA	50140	**800-433-9893**	641-784-8841
SITEL Corp	2 American Ctr Ste 900	Nashville	TN	37203	**866-957-4835**	615-301-7100
Telax Voice Solutions	365 Evans Ave Ste 302	Toronto	ON	M8Z1K2	**888-808-3529**	416-207-0630
Tele Business USA	1945 Techny Rd Ste 3	Northbrook	IL	60062	**877-315-8353**	
Telerx	723 Dresher Rd	Horsham	PA	19044	**800-283-5379**	267-942-3300
TeleTech Holdings Inc (*NASDAQ: TTEC* ■ *General)	9197 S Peoria St	Englewood	CO	80112	**800-835-3832***	303-397-8100
Telexpertise Inc	7790 E Arapahoe Rd Ste 240	Centennial	CO	80112	**877-767-6762**	720-200-0590
USA 800 Inc	9808 E 66th Terr	Kansas City	MO	64133	**800-821-7539**	816-358-1303
VOX Data	1155 Metcalfe St 18th Fl	Montreal	QC	H3B2V6	**800-861-9599**	514-871-1920
West Corp (*Sales)	11808 Miracle Hills Dr	Omaha	NE	68154	**800-232-0900***	
Working Solutions	1820 Preston Pk Blvd Ste 2000	Plano	TX	75093	**866-857-4800**	972-964-4800
Young America Corp	10 S 5th St 7th Fl	Minneapolis	MN	55402	**800-533-4529**	
Your Selling Team	100 Spectrum Ctr Dr Ste 700	Irvine	CA	92618	**888-387-8002**	

TELEVISION - CABLE

SEE Television Networks ; Cable & Other Pay Television Services

735 TELEVISION COMPANIES

Company	Address	City	State	ZIP	Toll-Free	Phone
Ask Associates Inc	1201 Wakarusa Ste C-1	Lawrence	KS	66049	**800-315-4333**	785-841-8194
Capitol Broadcasting Co Inc	2619 Western Blvd	Raleigh	NC	27606	**800-234-4857**	919-890-6000
Christian Television Network Inc (CTN)	6922 142nd Ave N	Largo	FL	33771	**800-716-7729**	727-535-5622
EW Scripps Co (*NYSE: SSP*)	312 Walnut St Ste 2800	Cincinnati	OH	45202	**800-888-3000**	513-977-3000
Freedom Communications Inc	17666 Fitch	Irvine	CA	92614	**855-862-7238**	949-253-2300
Gray Television Inc (*NYSE: GTN*)	4370 Peachtree Rd NE	Atlanta	GA	30319	**888-835-2869**	404-504-9828
LeSea Broadcasting Corp	61300 S Ironwood Rd	South Bend	IN	46614	**800-365-3732**	574-291-8200
Media General Broadcast Group	333 E Franklin St	Richmond	VA	23219	**800-937-5449**	804-649-6000
On Event Services LLC	6550 McDonough Dr	Norcross	GA	30093	**800-967-2419**	770-457-0966
Quincy Newspapers Inc	130 S Fifth St	Quincy	IL	62301	**800-373-9444**	217-223-5100
Saga Communications Inc (*NYSE: SGA*)	73 Kercheval Ave	Grosse Pointe Farms	MI	48236	**800-777-3674**	313-886-7070
Univision Television Group Inc	5999 Ctr Dr	Los Angeles	CA	90045	**800-594-5387**	310-846-2800

736 TELEVISION NETWORKS

Company	Address	City	State	ZIP	Toll-Free	Phone
Accent Health	60 E 42nd St Ste 1543	New York	NY	10165	**800-235-4930**	
Business News Network (BNN)	299 Queen St W	Toronto	ON	M5V2Z5	**855-326-6266**	416-384-6600
Cable Public Affairs Ch (CPAC)	PO Box 81099	Ottawa	ON	K1P1B1	**877-287-2722**	
Christian Broadcasting Network (CBN)	977 Centerville Tpke	Virginia Beach	VA	23463	**800-759-0700**	757-226-7000
CRN Digital Talk Radio	10487 Sunland Blvd	Sunland	CA	91040	**866-554-7387**	818-352-7152
Cross TV	370 W Camino Gardens Blvd Ste 300	Boca Raton	FL	33432	**877-276-7788**	561-367-7454
Crown Media Holdings Inc (*NASDAQ: CRWN*)	12700 Ventura Blvd Ste 200	Studio City	CA	91604	**800-479-7328**	818-755-2400
Daystar Television Network	3901 Hwy 121 PO Box 610546	Bedford	TX	76021	**800-329-0029**	817-571-1229
Discovery Communications Inc (*NASDAQ: DISCA*)	1 Discovery Pl	Silver Spring	MD	20910	**877-324-5850**	240-662-2000
ESPN	545 Middle St	Bristol	CT	06010	**877-710-3776**	
ESPN Classic Inc	ESPN Plaza	Bristol	CT	06010	**877-710-3776**	
ESPN Deportes	2 Alhambra Plz 9th Fl	Coral Gables	FL	33134	**800-337-6783**	305-567-3797
EVINE Live Inc	6740 Shady Oak Rd	Eden Prairie	MN	55344	**800-676-5523**	
God's Learning Ch (GLC)	PO Box 61000	Midland	TX	79711	**800-707-0420**	432-563-0420
Hallmark Ch	12700 Ventura Blvd Ste 200	Studio City	CA	91604	**888-390-7474**	818-755-2400
History Ch — *A&E Television Networks LLC*	235 E 45th St 2nd Fl	New York	NY	10017	**888-371-5848**	212-210-1400
Ion Media Networks	601 Clearwater Pk Rd	West Palm Beach	FL	33401	**800-987-9936**	561-659-4122
Liberty Ch	1971 University Blvd	Lynchburg	VA	24506	**800-332-1883**	434-582-2000
MTV Networks On Campus Inc (MTVU)	1540 Broadway 33rd Fl	New York	NY	10036	**877-800-4483**	
NASA TV	300 E St SW	Washington	DC	20546	**877-546-1574**	202-358-0000
NFL Network	345 Park Avenue	New York	NY	10154	**800-724-3377**	212-450-2000
Outdoor Ch (*NASDAQ: OUTD*)	43445 Business Pk Dr Ste 103	Temecula	CA	92590	**800-770-5750**	951-699-6991
QVC Inc	1200 Wilson Dr	West Chester	PA	19380	**800-367-9444**	484-701-1000
Resort Sports Network — *Outside Television*	33 Riverside Ave 4th Fl	Westport	CT	06880	**888-795-9488**	203-221-9240
Shopping Ch, The — *Credit Card Dept*	59 Ambassador Dr	Mississauga	ON	L5T2P9	**888-202-0888**	
TCT Ministries Inc	11717 N Rt 37 PO Box 1010	Marion	IL	62959	**800-232-9855**	618-997-4700
Telelatino Network Inc (TLN)	5125 Steeles Ave W	Toronto	ON	M9L1R5	**800-551-8401**	416-744-8200

					Toll-Free	Phone
TFC USA 150 Shoreline Dr	Redwood City	CA	94065		**800-345-2465**	650-508-6000
Trinity Broadcasting Network (TBN) PO Box A	Santa Ana	CA	92711		**888-731-1000**	714-832-2950
Video Hits One (VH1) 1515 Broadway 20th Fl	New York	NY	10036		**800-745-1892**	
Weather Ch Inc, The 300 I N Pkwy Po Box 724554	Atlanta	GA	30339		**866-843-0392**	770-226-0000
Worship Network PO Box 428	Safety Harbor	FL	34695		**800-728-8723**	

737 TELEVISION NETWORKS - BROADCAST

	City	State	Zip	Toll-Free	Phone
Public Broadcasting Service (PBS) 2100 Crystal Dr	Arlington	VA	22202	**866-864-0828**	703-739-5000

738 TELEVISION STATIONS

SEE ALSO Internet Broadcasting

	City	State	Zip	Toll-Free	Phone
CKVR-TV Ch 3 (Ind) 299 Queen St W	Toronto	ON	M5V2Z5	**866-690-6179**	416-384-5000
Iowa Public Television 6450 Corporate Dr	Johnston	IA	50131	**800-532-1290**	515-242-3100
KAFT-TV Ch 13 (PBS) 350 S Donaghey Ave	Conway	AR	72034	**800-662-2386**	501-682-2386
KARE-TV Ch 11 (NBC) 8811 State Hwy 55	Golden Valley	MN	55427	**888-966-4532**	763-546-1111
KBHE-TV Ch 9 (PBS) 555 N Dakota St PO Box 5000	Vermillion	SD	57069	**800-333-0789**	
KBYU-TV Ch 11 (PBS) 2000 Ironton Blvd Brigham Young University	Provo	UT	84606	**800-298-5298**	801-422-8450
KCWC-TV Ch 4 (PBS) 2660 Peck Ave	Riverton	WY	82501	**800-495-9788**	307-856-6944
KESQ-TV Ch 3 (ABC) 42650 Melanie Pl	Palm Desert	CA	92211	**888-776-8538**	760-318-8528
KETG-TV Ch 9 (PBS) 350 S Donaghey Ave	Conway	AR	72034	**800-662-2386**	501-682-2386
KETS-TV Ch 2 (PBS) 350 S Donaghey Ave	Conway	AR	72034	**800-662-2386**	501-682-2386
KFBB-TV 3200 Old Havre Hwy	Black Eagle	MT	59414	**877-509-9785**	406-453-4377
KIMT-TV Ch 3 (CBS) 112 N Pennsylvania Ave	Mason City	IA	50401	**800-323-4883**	641-423-2540
KMAX-TV Ch 31 (CBS) 2713 Kovr Dr	West Sacramento	CA	95605	**800-374-8813**	916-374-1313
KMIZ-TV Ch 17 (ABC) 501 Business Loop 70 E	Columbia	MO	65201	**800-345-4109**	573-449-0917
KMOS-TV Ch 6 (PBS) University of Central Missouri	Warrensburg	MO	64093	**800-753-3436**	
KOMU-TV Ch 8 (NBC) 5550 Hwy 63 S	Columbia	MO	65201	**800-286-3932**	573-884-6397
KPDX-TV Ch 49 (MNT) 14975 NW Greenbrier Pkwy	Beaverton	OR	97006	**866-906-1249**	503-906-1249
KPLO-TV Ch 6 (CBS) 501 S Phillips Ave	Sioux Falls	SD	57104	**800-888-5356**	605-336-1100
KPTV-TV Ch 12 (Fox) 14975 NW Greenbrier Pkwy	Beaverton	OR	97006	**866-906-1249**	503-906-1249
KSMQ-TV Ch 15 (PBS) 2000 Eigth Ave NW	Austin	MN	55912	**800-658-2539**	507-433-0678
KSTW-TV Ch 11 (CW) 1000 Dexter Ave N Ste 205	Seattle	WA	98109	**866-313-5789**	206-441-1111
KTBN-TV Ch 40 (TBN) 2442 Michelle Dr	Tustin	CA	92780	**888-731-1000**	714-832-2950
KTSD-TV Ch 10 (PBS) 555 N Dakota St PO Box 5000	Vermillion	SD	57069	**800-333-0789**	
KTSF-TV Ch 26 (Ind) 100 Valley Dr	Brisbane	CA	94005	**800-772-1213**	415-468-2626
KUSD-TV Ch 2 (PBS) 555 N Dakota St PO Box 5000	Vermillion	SD	57069	**800-333-0789**	
KUSM-TV Ch 9 (PBS) Visual Communications Bldg Rm 183	Bozeman	MT	59717	**800-426-8243**	406-994-3437
KWPX-TV Ch 33 (I) 8112-C 304th Ave SE PO Box 426	Preston	WA	98050	**888-467-2988**	425-222-6010
KWWL-TV Ch 7 (NBC) 500 E Fourth St	Waterloo	IA	50703	**800-947-7746**	319-291-1200
UNC-TV Ch 4 (PBS) 10 TW Alexander Dr PO Box 14900	Research Triangle Park	NC	27709	**800-906-5050**	919-549-7000
WBNX-TV Ch 55 (CW) 2690 State Rd	Cuyahoga Falls	OH	44223	**800-282-0515**	330-922-5500
WBRE-TV Ch 28 (NBC) 62 S Franklin St	Wilkes-Barre	PA	18701	**800-367-9222**	570-823-2828
WCAU-TV Ch 10 (NBC) 10 Monument Rd	Bala Cynwyd	PA	19004	**800-847-9228**	610-668-5510
WCBB-TV Ch 10 (PBS) 1450 Lisbon St	Lewiston	ME	04240	**800-884-1717**	207-783-9101
WCIA-TV Ch 3 (CBS) PO Box 20	Champaign	IL	61824	**800-676-3382**	217-356-8333
WDAM-TV Ch 7 (NBC) PO Box 16269	Hattiesburg	MS	39404	**800-844-9326**	601-544-4730
WDSC-TV 1200 W International Speedway Blvd	Daytona Beach	FL	32114	**866-273-5825**	386-506-4415
WEAO-TV Ch 49 (PBS) 1750 Campus Ctr Dr	Kent	OH	44240	**800-544-4549**	330-677-4549
WEAR-TV Ch 3 (ABC) 4990 Mobile Hwy	Pensacola	FL	32506	**800-772-1213**	850-456-3333
WEHT-TV Ch 25 (ABC) 800 Marywood Dr	Henderson	KY	42420	**800-879-8542**	270-826-9566
WENH-TV Ch 11 (PBS) 268 Mast Rd	Durham	NH	03824	**800-639-8408**	603-868-1100
WFFF-TV Ch 44 (Fox) 298 Mountain View Dr	Colchester	VT	05446	**888-344-7233**	802-660-9333
WFMY-TV Ch 2 (CBS) 1615 Phillips Ave	Greensboro	NC	27405	**800-593-3692**	336-379-9369
WFXT-TV Ch 25 (Fox) 25 Fox Dr	Dedham	MA	02026	**877-369-2563**	781-467-2525
WGBH-TV Ch 2 (PBS) 1 Guest St	Brighton	MA	02135	**800-492-1111**	617-300-2000
WGGS-TV Ch 16 (Ind) 3409 Rutherford Rd Ext	Taylors	SC	29687	**800-849-3683***	864-244-1616
*General					
WGHP-TV Ch 8 (Fox) 2005 Francis St	High Point	NC	27263	**800-808-6397**	336-841-8888
WITV-TV Ch 7 (PBS) 1101 Geroge Rogers Blvd	Columbia	SC	29201	**800-277-3245**	803-737-3200
WKMJ-TV Ch 68 (PBS) 600 Cooper Dr	Lexington	KY	40502	**800-432-0951**	859-258-7000
WKNO-TV Ch 10 (PBS) 7151 Cherry Farms Rd	Cordova	TN	38016	**877-717-7822**	901-729-8765
WKPC-TV Ch 15 (PBS) 600 Cooper Dr	Lexington	KY	40502	**800-432-0951**	859-258-7000
WKPT-TV Ch 19 (ABC) 222 Commerce St	Kingsport	TN	37660	**855-646-1390**	423-246-9578
WLMB-TV Ch 40 (Ind) 825 Capital Commons Dr	Toledo	OH	43615	**800-218-5740**	419-720-9562
WMTW-TV Ch 8 (ABC) 99 Danville Corner Rd	Auburn	ME	04210	**800-248-6397**	207-782-1800
WMYD-TV Ch 20 (MNT) 2777 Franklin Rd Ste 1220	Southfield	MI	48034	**800-825-0770**	248-355-2020
WNEM-TV Ch 5 (CBS) 107 N Franklin St	Saginaw	MI	48607	**800-522-9636**	989-755-8191
WNEP-TV Ch 16 (ABC) 16 Montage Mtn Rd	Moosic	PA	18507	**800-982-4374**	570-346-7474
WNET PO Box 5776	Englewood	NJ	07631	**800-882-6622**	609-777-0031
WNJU-TV Ch 47 (Tele) 2200 Fletcher Ave 6th Fl	Fort Lee	NJ	07024	**877-478-3536**	
WOI-TV Ch 5 (ABC) 3903 Westown Pkwy	West Des Moines	IA	50266	**800-858-5555**	515-457-9645
WOUC-TV Ch 44 (PBS) 35 S College St	Athens	OH	45701	**800-456-2044**	740-593-1771
WOWK-TV Ch 13 (CBS) 555 Fifth Ave	Huntington	WV	25701	**800-333-7636**	304-525-1313
WPMT-TV Ch 43 (Fox) 2005 S Queen St	York	PA	17403	**866-976-8747**	717-843-0043
WPXD-TV Ch 31 (I) 3975 Varsity Dr	Ann Arbor	MI	48108	**888-467-2988**	734-973-7900
WSBT-TV Ch 22 (CBS) 1301 E Douglas Rd	Mishawaka	IN	46545	**877-634-7181**	574-232-6397
WSET-TV Ch 13 (ABC) 2320 Langhorne Rd	Lynchburg	VA	24501	**800-639-7847**	434-528-1313
WTIU-TV Ch 30 (PBS) 1229 E Seventh St	Bloomington	IN	47405	**800-662-3311**	812-855-5900
WVIT-TV Ch 30 (NBC) 1422 New Britain Ave	West Hartford	CT	06110	**800-523-9848**	860-521-3030
WWMT-TV Ch 3 (CBS) 590 W Maple St	Kalamazoo	MI	49008	**800-875-3333**	
WXYZ-TV Ch 7 (ABC) 20777 W 10-Mile Rd	Southfield	MI	48037	**800-825-0770**	248-827-7777
WYOU-TV Ch 22 (CBS) 62 S Franklin St	Wilkes-Barre	PA	18701	**855-241-5144**	570-961-2222

738-1 Albany, NY

	City	State	Zip	Toll-Free	Phone
WNYT-TV Ch 13 (NBC) 715 N Pearl St	Albany	NY	12204	**800-999-9698**	518-436-4791

738-2 Albuquerque/Santa Fe, NM

	City	State	Zip	Toll-Free	Phone
KNME-TV Ch 5 (PBS) 1130 University Blvd NE University of New Mexico	Albuquerque	NM	87102	**800-328-5663**	505-277-2121
KOAT-TV Ch 7 (ABC) 3801 Carlisle Blvd NE	Albuquerque	NM	87107	**877-871-0165**	505-884-7777
KRQE-TV Ch 13 (CBS) 13 Broadcast Plz SW	Albuquerque	NM	87104	**800-283-4227**	505-243-2285

738-3 Anchorage, AK

	City	State	Zip	Toll-Free	Phone
KTBY-TV Ch 4 (Fox) 2700 E Tudor Rd	Anchorage	AK	99507	**877-304-1313**	907-561-1313
KYUR-TV Ch 13 (ABC) 2700 E Tudor Rd	Anchorage	AK	99507	**877-304-1313**	907-561-1313

738-4 Asheville, NC/Greenville, SC/Spartanburg, SC

	City	State	Zip	Toll-Free	Phone
WLOS-TV Ch 13 (ABC) 110 Technology Dr	Asheville	NC	28803	**800-419-6356**	828-684-1340
WSPA-TV Ch 7 (CBS) 250 International Dr	Spartanburg	SC	29303	**866-946-6349**	864-576-7777
WYFF-TV Ch 4 (NBC) 505 Rutherford St	Greenville	SC	29609	**800-453-9933**	864-242-4404

738-5 Augusta, GA

	City	State	Zip	Toll-Free	Phone
WRDW-TV Ch 12 (CBS) PO Box 1212	Augusta	GA	30903	**866-591-2502**	803-278-1212

Classified Section

738-6 Austin, TX

				Toll-Free	Phone
KEYE-TV Ch 42 (CBS) 10700 Metric Blvd	Austin	TX	78758	**800-621-3362**	512-835-0042

738-7 Baltimore, MD

				Toll-Free	Phone
WBAL-TV Ch 11 (NBC) 3800 Hooper Ave	Baltimore	MD	21211	**800-622-4121**	410-467-3000

738-8 Bangor, ME

				Toll-Free	Phone
WLBZ-TV Ch 2 (NBC) 329 Mt Hope Ave	Bangor	ME	04401	**800-244-6306**	207-942-4821
WMEB-TV Ch 12 (PBS) 63 Texas Ave	Bangor	ME	04401	**800-884-1717**	207-941-1010
WVII-TV Ch 7 (ABC) 371 Target Industrial Cir *General	Bangor	ME	04401	**888-820-8458***	207-945-6457

738-9 Baton Rouge, LA

				Toll-Free	Phone
KLPB-TV Ch 24 (PBS) 7733 Perkins Rd	Baton Rouge	LA	70810	**800-272-8161**	225-767-5660
WAFB-TV Ch 9 (CBS) 844 Government St	Baton Rouge	LA	70802	**888-677-2900**	225-215-4700
WLPB-TV Ch 27 (PBS) 7733 Perkins Rd	Baton Rouge	LA	70810	**800-272-8161**	225-767-5660

738-10 Billings, MT

				Toll-Free	Phone
KTVQ-TV Ch 2 (CBS) 3203 Third Ave N	Billings	MT	59101	**800-908-4490**	406-252-5611

738-11 Birmingham, AL

				Toll-Free	Phone
WBIQ-TV Ch 10 (PBS) 2112 11th Ave S Ste 400	Birmingham	AL	35205	**800-239-5233**	205-328-8756
WCFT-TV Ch 33 (ABC) 800 Concourse Pkwy Ste 200	Birmingham	AL	35244	**800-784-8669**	205-403-3340
WEIQ-TV Ch 42 (PBS) 2112 11th Ave S Ste 400	Birmingham	AL	35205	**800-239-5233**	205-328-8756
WHIQ-TV Ch 24 (PBS) 2112 11th Ave S Ste 400	Birmingham	AL	35205	**800-239-5233**	205-328-8756
WVTM-TV Ch 13 (NBC) 1732 Valley View Dr	Birmingham	AL	35209	**844-248-7698**	205-933-1313

738-12 Boise, ID

				Toll-Free	Phone
KTVB-TV Ch 7 (NBC) 5407 Fairview	Boise	ID	83706	**800-537-8939**	208-375-7277

738-13 Buffalo, NY

				Toll-Free	Phone
WIVB-TV Ch 4 (CBS) 2077 Elmwood Ave	Buffalo	NY	14207	**800-794-3687**	716-874-4410
WKBW-TV Ch 7 (ABC) 7 Broadcast Plaza	Buffalo	NY	14202	**888-373-7888**	716-845-6100

738-14 Cedar Rapids, IA

				Toll-Free	Phone
KCRG-TV Ch 9 (ABC) 501 Second Ave SE	Cedar Rapids	IA	52401	**800-332-5443**	319-398-8393
KFXA-TV Ch 28 (Fox) 600 Old Marion Rd NE	Cedar Rapids	IA	52402	**800-222-5426**	800-462-8782
KGAN-TV Ch 2 (CBS) 600 Old Marion Rd NE	Cedar Rapids	IA	52402	**800-642-6140**	319-395-9060

738-15 Charleston, WV

				Toll-Free	Phone
WCHS-TV Ch 8 (ABC) 1301 Piedmont Rd	Charleston	WV	25301	**888-696-9247**	304-346-5358

738-16 Charlotte, NC

				Toll-Free	Phone
WAXN-TV Ch 64 (ABC) 1901 N Tryon St	Charlotte	NC	28206	**855-336-0360**	704-335-4786
WSOC-TV Ch 9 (ABC) 1901 N Tryon St	Charlotte	NC	28206	**855-336-0360**	704-338-9999

738-17 Cincinnati, OH

				Toll-Free	Phone
WKRC-TV Ch 12 (CBS) 1906 Highland Ave	Cincinnati	OH	45219	**877-889-5610**	513-763-5500

738-18 Cleveland/Akron, OH

				Toll-Free	Phone
WDLI-TV Ch 17 (TBN) PO Box A	Santa Ana	CA	92711	**888-731-1000**	714-832-2950
WKYC-TV Ch 3 (NBC) 1333 Lakeside Ave E	Cleveland	OH	44114	**877-790-7370**	216-344-3333

738-19 Columbia, SC

				Toll-Free	Phone
WRLK-TV Ch 35 (PBS) 1101 George Rogers Blvd	Columbia	SC	29201	**800-922-5437**	803-737-3200

738-20 Corpus Christi, TX

				Toll-Free	Phone
KEDT-TV Ch 16 (PBS) 4455 S Padre Island Dr Ste 38	Corpus Christi	TX	78411	**800-307-5338**	361-855-2213
KIII-TV Ch 3 (ABC) 5002 S Padre Island Dr	Corpus Christi	TX	78411	**800-882-9539**	361-986-8300

738-21 Dallas/Fort Worth, TX

				Toll-Free	Phone
KXTX-TV Ch 39 (Tele) 4805 Amon Carter Blvd	Fort Worth	TX	76155	**877-266-8365**	

738-22 Dayton, OH

				Toll-Free	Phone
WPTD-TV Ch 16 (PBS) 110 S Jefferson St	Dayton	OH	45402	**800-247-1614**	937-220-1600

738-23 Denver, CO

				Toll-Free	Phone
KDVR-TV Ch 31 (Fox) 100 E Speer Blvd	Denver	CO	80203	**888-397-3742**	303-595-3131
KRMA-TV Ch 6 (PBS) 1089 Bannock St	Denver	CO	80204	**800-274-6666**	303-892-6666

738-24 Des Moines, IA

				Toll-Free	Phone
WHO-TV Ch 13 (NBC) 1801 Grand Ave	Des Moines	IA	50309	**800-777-8398**	515-242-3500

738-25 Duluth, MN

				Toll-Free	Phone
WDIO-TV Ch 10 (ABC) 10 Observation Rd	Duluth	MN	55811	**800-477-1013**	218-727-6864
WDSE-TV Ch 8 (PBS) 632 Niagara Ct	Duluth	MN	55811	**888-563-9373**	218-788-2831

738-26 El Paso, TX

				Toll-Free	Phone
KVIA-TV Ch 7 (ABC) 4140 Rio Bravo St	El Paso	TX	79902	**800-433-7300**	915-496-7777

738-27 Erie, PA

				Toll-Free	Phone
WICU-TV Ch 12 (NBC) 3514 State St	Erie	PA	16508	**800-454-8812**	814-454-5201
WQLN-TV Ch 54 (PBS) 8425 Peach St	Erie	PA	16509	**800-727-8854**	814-864-3001
WSEE-TV Ch 35 (CBS) 3514 State St	Erie	PA	16508	**888-697-2217**	814-454-5201

738-28 Evansville, IN

				Toll-Free	Phone
WFIE-TV Ch 14 (NBC) 1115 Mt Auburn Rd	Evansville	IN	47720	**800-832-0014**	812-426-1414
WNIN-TV Ch 9 (PBS) 405 Carpenter St	Evansville	IN	47708	**855-888-9646**	812-423-2973

738-29 Fairbanks, AK

				Toll-Free	Phone
KTVF-TV Ch 11 (NBC) 3650 Braddock St	Fairbanks	AK	99701	**855-255-5975**	907-458-1800

				Toll-Free	Phone
KUAC-TV Ch 9 (PBS) University of Alaska PO Box 755620	Fairbanks	AK	99775	**800-727-6543**	907-474-7491

738-30 Fargo/Grand Forks, ND

				Toll-Free	Phone
KBME-TV Ch 3 (PBS) 207 N Fifth St	Fargo	ND	58102	**800-359-6900**	701-241-6900
KFME-TV Ch 13 (PBS) 207 N Fifth St	Fargo	ND	58102	**800-359-6900**	701-241-6900
KGFE-TV Ch 2 (PBS) 207 N Fifth St	Fargo	ND	58102	**800-359-6900**	701-241-6900
KVLY-TV Ch 11 (NBC) 1350 21st Ave S	Fargo	ND	58103	**800-450-5844**	701-237-5211
KXJB-TV Ch 4 (CBS) 1350 21st Ave S	Fargo	ND	58103	**877-571-0774**	701-237-5211
WDAZ-TV Ch 8 (ABC) 2220 S Washington St	Grand Forks	ND	58201	**877-382-4357**	701-775-2511

738-31 Fort Smith, AR

				Toll-Free	Phone
KHBS-TV Ch 40 (ABC) 2415 N Albert Pike *General	Fort Smith	AR	72904	**855-253-7122***	479-783-4040

738-32 Fort Wayne, IN

				Toll-Free	Phone
WFWA-TV Ch 39 (PBS) 2501 E Coliseum Blvd	Fort Wayne	IN	46805	**888-484-8839**	260-484-8839

738-33 Fresno, CA

				Toll-Free	Phone
KFTV-TV Ch 21 (Uni) 601 W Univision Plaza	Fresno	CA	93650	**866-783-2645**	559-222-2121
KMPH-TV Ch 26 (Fox) 5111 E McKinley Ave	Fresno	CA	93727	**800-101-2045**	559-453-8850

738-34 Grand Rapids, MI

				Toll-Free	Phone
WGVU-TV Ch 35 (PBS) 301 W Fulton St	Grand Rapids	MI	49504	**800-442-2771**	616-331-6666
WZPX-TV Ch 43 (I) 2610 Horizon Dr SE Ste E	Grand Rapids	MI	49546	**800-987-9936**	616-222-4343

738-35 Green Bay, WI

				Toll-Free	Phone
WBAY-TV Ch 2 (ABC) 115 S Jefferson St	Green Bay	WI	54301	**800-261-9229**	920-432-3331
WLUK-TV Ch 11 (Fox) 787 Lombardi Ave	Green Bay	WI	54304	**800-242-8067**	920-494-8711

738-36 Honolulu, HI

				Toll-Free	Phone
KHON-TV Ch 2 (Fox) 88 Piikoi St	Honolulu	HI	96814	**877-926-8300**	808-591-4278
KPXO-TV Ch 66 (I) 875 Waimanu St Ste 630	Honolulu	HI	96813	**800-987-9936**	808-591-1275
KWHE-TV Ch 14 (Ind) 1188 Bishop St Ste 502	Honolulu	HI	96813	**800-218-1414**	808-538-1414

738-37 Huntsville, AL

				Toll-Free	Phone
WAAY-TV Ch 31 (ABC) 1000 Monte Sano Blvd SE	Huntsville	AL	35801	**888-407-4747**	256-533-3131
WHNT-TV Ch 19 (CBS) PO Box 19	Huntsville	AL	35804	**800-533-8819**	256-533-1919

738-38 Indianapolis, IN

				Toll-Free	Phone
WRTV-TV Ch 6 (ABC) 1330 N Meridian St	Indianapolis	IN	46202	**877-667-4265**	317-635-9788

738-39 Johnson City, TN

				Toll-Free	Phone
WJHL-TV Ch 11 (CBS) 338 E Main St	Johnson City	TN	37601	**800-861-5255**	423-926-2151

738-40 Juneau, AK

				Toll-Free	Phone
KJUD-TV Ch 8 (ABC) 2700 E Tudor Rd	Anchorage	AK	99507	**877-304-1313**	907-561-1313

738-41 Kansas City, KS & MO

				Toll-Free	Phone
KSHB-TV Ch 41 (NBC) 4720 Oak St	Kansas City	MO	64112	**800-222-1222**	816-753-4141

738-42 Lansing, MI

				Toll-Free	Phone
WILX-TV Ch 10 (NBC) 500 American Rd	Lansing	MI	48911	**888-345-4124**	517-393-0110

738-43 Lexington, KY

				Toll-Free	Phone
WDKY-TV Ch 56 (Fox) 836 Euclid Ave Ste 201	Lexington	KY	40502	**888-404-5656**	859-269-5656

738-44 Lincoln, NE

				Toll-Free	Phone
KOLN-TV Ch 10 (CBS) 840 N 40th	Lincoln	NE	68503	**800-475-1011**	402-467-4321
NET Radio 1800 N 33rd St	Lincoln	NE	68503	**800-868-1868**	

738-45 Little Rock, AR

				Toll-Free	Phone
KTHV-TV Ch 11 (CBS) 720 S Izard St	Little Rock	AR	72201	**800-621-3362**	501-376-1111

738-46 Louisville, KY

				Toll-Free	Phone
WAVE-TV Ch 3 (NBC) 725 S Floyd St PO Box 32970	Louisville	KY	40203	**800-223-2579**	502-585-2201

738-47 Los Angeles, CA

				Toll-Free	Phone
KJLA-TV Ch 57 (Ind) 2323 Corinth Ave	Los Angeles	CA	90064	**800-588-5788**	310-943-5288

738-48 Miami/Fort Lauderdale, FL

				Toll-Free	Phone
WPBT-TV Ch 2 (PBS) 14901 NE 20th Ave	Miami	FL	33181	**800-222-9728**	305-949-8321

738-49 Milwaukee, WI

				Toll-Free	Phone
WVCY-TV Ch 30 (Ind) 3434 W Kilbourn Ave	Milwaukee	WI	53208	**800-729-9829**	414-935-3000

738-50 Montgomery, AL

				Toll-Free	Phone
WAIQ-TV Ch 26 (PBS) 1255 Madison Ave	Montgomery	AL	36107	**800-239-5239**	205-328-8756
WAKA-TV Ch 8 (CBS) 3020 Eastern Blvd	Montgomery	AL	36116	**800-467-0401**	334-271-8888
WNCF-TV Ch 32 (ABC) 3251 Harrison Rd	Montgomery	AL	36109	**800-467-0424**	334-270-2834

738-51 Naples/Fort Myers, FL

				Toll-Free	Phone
WZVN-TV Ch 26 (ABC) 3719 Central Ave	Fort Myers	FL	33901	**888-232-8635**	239-939-2020

738-52 Nashville, TN

				Toll-Free	Phone
WKRN-TV Ch 2 (ABC) 441 Murfreesboro Rd	Nashville	TN	37210	**800-222-5555**	615-369-7222

738-53 New Orleans, LA

				Toll-Free	Phone
WDSU-TV Ch 6 (NBC) 846 Howard Ave	New Orleans	LA	70113	**888-925-4127**	504-679-0600

738-54 New York, NY

				Toll-Free	Phone
WPXN-TV Ch 31 (I) 810 Seventh Ave 30th Fl	New York	NY	10019	**800-987-9936**	212-603-8419

738-55 Norfolk/Virginia Beach, VA

Station	Address	City	State	ZIP	Toll-Free	Phone
WTKR-TV Ch 3 (CBS)	720 Boush St	Norfolk	VA	23510	**866-347-2423**	757-446-1000

738-56 Oklahoma City, OK

Station	Address	City	State	ZIP	Toll-Free	Phone
KETA-TV Ch 13 (PBS)	PO Box 14190	Oklahoma City	OK	73113	**800-879-6382**	405-848-8501
KWTV-TV Ch 9 (CBS)	7401 N Kelley Ave	Oklahoma City	OK	73111	**888-550-5988**	405-843-6641

738-57 Omaha, NE

Station	Address	City	State	ZIP	Toll-Free	Phone
KETV-TV Ch 7 (ABC)	2665 Douglas St	Omaha	NE	68131	**800-279-5388**	402-345-7777
KMTV Action 3 News	10714 Mockingbird Dr	Omaha	NE	68127	**800-800-6619**	402-592-3333
WOWT-TV Ch 6 (NBC)	3501 Farnam St	Omaha	NE	68131	**866-434-8587**	402-346-6666

738-58 Orlando, FL

Station	Address	City	State	ZIP	Toll-Free	Phone
WKMG-TV Ch 6 (CBS)	4466 N John Young Pkwy	Orlando	FL	32804	**800-435-7352**	407-521-1200

738-59 Peoria, IL

Station	Address	City	State	ZIP	Toll-Free	Phone
WTVP-TV Ch 47 (PBS)	101 State St	Peoria	IL	61602	**800-837-4747**	309-677-4747

738-60 Phoenix, AZ

Station	Address	City	State	ZIP	Toll-Free	Phone
KNXV-TV Ch 15 (ABC)	515 N 44th St	Phoenix	AZ	85008	**800-222-4357**	602-273-1500
KSAZ-TV Ch 10 (Fox)	511 W Adams St	Phoenix	AZ	85003	**888-369-4762**	602-257-1234

738-61 Pittsburgh, PA

Station	Address	City	State	ZIP	Toll-Free	Phone
WQED-TV Ch 13 (PBS)	4802 Fifth Ave	Pittsburgh	PA	15213	**800-876-1316**	412-622-1370

738-62 Pocatello, ID

Station	Address	City	State	ZIP	Toll-Free	Phone
KISU-TV Ch 10 (PBS)	921 S Eighth Ave S-8111	Pocatello	ID	83209	**800-543-6868**	208-282-2857

738-63 Portland, ME

Station	Address	City	State	ZIP	Toll-Free	Phone
WCSH-TV Ch 6 (NBC)	1 Congress Sq	Portland	ME	04101	**800-464-1213**	207-828-6666

738-64 Portland, OR

Station	Address	City	State	ZIP	Toll-Free	Phone
KGW-TV Ch 8 (NBC)	1501 SW Jefferson St	Portland	OR	97201	**800-669-9777**	503-226-5000

738-65 Raleigh/Durham, NC

Station	Address	City	State	ZIP	Toll-Free	Phone
WRAL-TV Ch 5 (CBS)	2619 Western Blvd	Raleigh	NC	27606	**800-245-9725**	919-821-8555
WRAZ-TV Ch 50 (Fox)	512 S Mangum St	Durham	NC	27701	**877-369-5050**	919-595-5050

738-66 Rapid City, SD

Station	Address	City	State	ZIP	Toll-Free	Phone
KOTA-TV Ch 3 (ABC)	518 St Joseph St	Rapid City	SD	57701	**866-558-4554**	605-342-2000

738-67 Richmond, VA

Station	Address	City	State	ZIP	Toll-Free	Phone
WCVE-TV Ch 23 (PBS)	23 Sesame St	Richmond	VA	23235	**800-476-8440**	804-320-1301

738-68 Roanoke, VA

Station	Address	City	State	ZIP	Toll-Free	Phone
WSLS-TV Ch 10 (NBC)	PO Box 10	Roanoke	VA	24022	**855-447-7647**	540-981-9110

738-69 Rochester, MN

Station	Address	City	State	ZIP	Toll-Free	Phone
KTTC-TV Ch 10 (NBC)	6301 Bandel Rd NW	Rochester	MN	55901	**800-288-1656**	507-288-4444
KXLT-TV Ch 47 (Fox)	6301 Bandel Rd NW	Rochester	MN	55901	**800-452-4368**	507-252-4747

738-70 Sacramento, CA

Station	Address	City	State	ZIP	Toll-Free	Phone
KVIE-TV Ch 6 (PBS)	2030 W El Camino Ave	Sacramento	CA	95833	**800-347-5843**	916-929-5843

738-71 Saint Louis, MO

Station	Address	City	State	ZIP	Toll-Free	Phone
KETC-TV Ch 9 (PBS)	3655 Olive St	Saint Louis	MO	63108	**855-482-5382**	314-512-9000

738-72 Salt Lake City, UT

Station	Address	City	State	ZIP	Toll-Free	Phone
KSL-TV Ch 5 (NBC)	PO Box 1160	Salt Lake City	UT	84110	**800-862-9098**	801-575-5555
KUED-TV Ch 7 (PBS)	101 Wasatch Dr Rm 215	Salt Lake City	UT	84112	**800-477-5833**	801-581-7777
KUPX-TV Ch 16 (I)	466C Lawndale Dr	Salt Lake City	UT	84115	**888-467-2988**	801-474-0016
KUTV-TV Ch 2 (CBS)	299 S Main St Ste 150	Salt Lake City	UT	84111	**866-438-0220**	801-839-1234

738-73 San Antonio, TX

Station	Address	City	State	ZIP	Toll-Free	Phone
KABB-TV Ch 29 (Fox)	4335 NW Loop 410	San Antonio	TX	78229	**888-538-8541**	210-366-1129
KLRN-TV Ch 9 (PBS)	501 Broadway St	San Antonio	TX	78215	**800-627-8193**	210-270-9000

738-74 San Diego, CA

Station	Address	City	State	ZIP	Toll-Free	Phone
KPBS-TV Ch 15 (PBS)	5200 Campanile Dr	San Diego	CA	92182	**888-399-5727**	619-594-1515
XETV-TV Ch 6 (CW)	8253 Ronson Rd	San Diego	CA	92111	**866-700-6397**	858-279-6666

738-75 San Francisco, CA

Station	Address	City	State	ZIP	Toll-Free	Phone
KQED-TV Ch 9 (PBS)	2601 Mariposa St	San Francisco	CA	94110	**866-573-3123**	415-864-2000

738-76 Seattle/Tacoma, WA

Station	Address	City	State	ZIP	Toll-Free	Phone
KBTC-TV Ch 28 (PBS)	2320 S 19th St	Tacoma	WA	98405	**888-596-5282**	253-680-7700
KCTS-TV Ch 9 (PBS)	401 Mercer St	Seattle	WA	98109	**800-443-9991**	206-728-6463
KING 5 Television	333 Dexter Ave N	Seattle	WA	98109	**877-564-2261**	206-448-5555

738-77 Shreveport, LA

Station	Address	City	State	ZIP	Toll-Free	Phone
KSLA-TV Ch 12 (CBS)	1812 Fairfield Ave	Shreveport	LA	71101	**800-444-5752**	318-222-1212
KTAL-TV Ch 6 (NBC)	3150 N Market St	Shreveport	LA	71107	**800-259-4929**	318-629-6000
KTBS-TV Ch 3 (ABC)	312 E Kings Hwy	Shreveport	LA	71104	**866-543-3296**	318-861-5800

738-78 Sioux Falls, SD

Station	Address	City	State	ZIP	Toll-Free	Phone
KDLT-TV Ch 46 (NBC)	3600 S Westport Ave	Sioux Falls	SD	57106	**800-727-5358**	605-361-5555
KELO-TV Ch 11 (CBS)	501 S Phillips Ave	Sioux Falls	SD	57104	**800-888-5356**	605-336-1100

738-79 South Bend, IN

				Toll-Free	Phone
WNIT Public Television 300 W Jefferson Blvd PO Box 7034	South Bend	IN	46601	**877-411-3662**	574-675-9648
WSJV-TV Ch 28 (Fox) PO Box 28	South Bend	IN	46624	**800-435-3803**	574-679-9758

738-80 Spokane, WA

				Toll-Free	Phone
KREM-TV Ch 2 (CBS) 4103 S Regal St	Spokane	WA	99223	**888-404-3922**	509-448-2000
KSKN-TV Ch 22 (CW) 4103 S Regal St	Spokane	WA	99223	**888-404-3922**	509-448-2000
KSPS Public TV 3911 S Regal St	Spokane	WA	99223	**800-735-2377**	509-443-7800

738-81 Springfield, MA

				Toll-Free	Phone
WESTERN MASS NEWS 1300 Liberty St	Springfield	MA	01104	**877-872-2756**	413-733-4040

738-82 Springfield, MO

				Toll-Free	Phone
KOZK-TV Ch 21 (PBS) 901 S National Ave	Springfield	MO	65897	**866-684-5695**	417-836-3500
KSPR-TV Ch 33 (ABC) 1359 St Louis St	Springfield	MO	65802	**877-248-6922**	417-831-1333
KYTV-TV Ch 3 (NBC) PO Box 3500	Springfield	MO	65808	**888-476-6988**	417-268-3000

738-83 Syracuse, NY

				Toll-Free	Phone
WCNY-TV Ch 24 (PBS) 506 Old Liverpool Rd PO Box 2400	Syracuse	NY	13220	**800-638-5163**	315-453-2424

738-84 Tallahassee, FL

				Toll-Free	Phone
WCTV-TV Ch 6 (CBS) 1801 Halstead Blvd	Tallahassee	FL	32309	**888-297-9461**	850-893-6666
WFSU-TV Ch 11 (PBS) 1600 Red Barber Plz	Tallahassee	FL	32310	**800-322-9378**	850-487-3170

738-85 Tampa/Saint Petersburg, FL

				Toll-Free	Phone
WFLA-TV Ch 8 (NBC) PO Box 1410	Tampa	FL	33601	**800-338-0808**	813-228-8888
WFTS-TV Ch 28 (ABC) 4045 N Himes Ave	Tampa	FL	33607	**877-833-2828**	813-354-2828
WTSP-TV Ch 10 (CBS) 11450 Gandy Blvd N	Saint Petersburg	FL	33702	**877-248-6922**	727-577-1010
WUSF-TV Ch 16 (PBS) 4202 E Fowler Ave	Tampa	FL	33620	**800-654-3703**	813-974-4000

738-86 Topeka, KS

				Toll-Free	Phone
KSNT-TV Ch 27 (NBC) 6835 NW Hwy 24	Topeka	KS	66618	**800-222-8477**	785-582-4000
KTWU-TV Ch 11 (PBS) 1700 College	Topeka	KS	66621	**800-866-5898**	785-670-1111

738-87 Toronto, ON

				Toll-Free	Phone
CICA-TV Ch 19 (Ind) 2180 Yonge St Stn Q PO Box 200	Toronto	ON	M4T2T1	**800-613-0513**	416-484-2600
CITY-TV Ch 57 (Ind) 33 Dundas St E	Toronto	ON	M5B1B8	**888-336-9978**	416-764-3003

738-88 Tulsa, OK

				Toll-Free	Phone
KOTV-TV Ch 6 (CBS) PO Box 6	Tulsa	OK	74101	**888-434-8248**	918-732-6000

738-89 Washington, DC

				Toll-Free	Phone
WTTG-TV Ch 5 (Fox) 5151 Wisconsin Ave NW	Washington	DC	20016	**866-756-3587**	202-244-5151

738-90 West Palm Beach, FL

				Toll-Free	Phone
WFLX-TV Ch 29 (Fox) 4119 W Blue Heron Blvd	West Palm Beach	FL	33404	**844-555-1329**	561-845-2929
WXEL-TV Ch 42 (PBS) PO Box 6607	West Palm Beach	FL	33405	**800-915-9935**	561-737-8000

738-91 Wichita, KS

				Toll-Free	Phone
KPTS-TV Ch 8 (PBS) 320 W 21 St	Wichita	KS	67203	**800-794-8498**	316-838-3090
KSNW-TV 833 N Main St	Wichita	KS	67203	**800-432-3924**	316-265-3333
KWCH-TV Ch 12 (CBS) 2815 E 37th St N	Wichita	KS	67219	**888-512-6397**	316-838-1212

738-92 Winnipeg, MB

				Toll-Free	Phone
CTV-TV Ch 5 (CTV) 345 Graham Ave Ste 400	Winnipeg	MB	R3C5S6	**800-461-1542**	204-788-3300

738-93 Youngstown, OH

				Toll-Free	Phone
WFMJ-TV Ch 21 (NBC) 101 W Boardman St	Youngstown	OH	44503	**800-488-9365**	330-744-8611

739 TELEVISION SYNDICATORS

Television syndicators are companies that produce programming in-house and market and distribute the programs to networks on a national or regional basis.

				Toll-Free	Phone
Associated Press 1100 13th St NW Ste 700	Washington	DC	20005	**800-824-5498**	202-641-9000
Babe Winkelman Productions PO Box 407	Brainerd	MN	56401	**800-333-0471**	
Guthy-Renker Television Network 3340 Ocean Pk Blvd	Santa Monica	CA	90405	**888-651-6607**	310-581-6250
Independent Television Service (ITVS) 651 Brannan St Ste 410	San Francisco	CA	94107	**800-621-6196**	415-356-8383
K Rcr Tv News Channel 7 Tv 755 Auditorium Dr	Redding	CA	96001	**800-222-5727**	530-243-7777
National Educational Telecommunications Assn (NETA) 939 S Stadium Rd	Columbia	SC	29201	**866-270-5141**	803-799-5517

740 TESTING FACILITIES

				Toll-Free	Phone
Accusource Inc 1240 E Ontario Ave Ste 102-140	Corona	CA	92881	**888-649-6272**	951-734-8882
Acme Analytical Laboratories Ltd 1020 Cordova St E	Vancouver	BC	V6A4A3	**800-990-2263**	604-253-3158
Activation Laboratories Ltd 1336 Sandhill Dr	Ancaster	ON	L9G4V5	**888-228-5227**	905-648-9611
Akron Rubber Development Laboratory Inc 2887 Gilchrist Rd	Akron	OH	44305	**866-778-2735**	330-794-6600
ALine Inc 2206 E Gladwick St	Rancho Dominguez	CA	90220	**877-707-8575**	
Altran Solutions USA 2525 Rt 130 S	Cranbury	NJ	08512	**855-425-8726**	609-409-9790
Alturas Analytics Inc 1324 Alturas Dr	Moscow	ID	83843	**877-344-1279**	208-883-3400
Amplicon Express Inc 2345 Ne Hopkins Ct	Pullman	WA	99163	**877-332-8080**	509-332-8080
Analysts Inc 22750 Hawthorne Blvd Ste 220	Torrance	CA	90505	**800-336-3637**	
Analytics Corp 10329 Stony Run Ln	Ashland	VA	23005	**800-888-8061**	804-365-3000
Astro Pak Corp 270 E Baker St Ste 100	Costa Mesa	CA	92626	**888-278-7672**	866-492-7876
Bio-Research Products Inc 323 W Cherry St	North Liberty	IA	52317	**800-326-3511**	319-626-6707
BIOPAC Systems Inc 42 Aero Camino	Goleta	CA	93117	**877-524-6722**	805-685-0066
Biosan Laboratories Inc 1950 Tobsal Ct	Warren	MI	48091	**800-253-6800**	586-755-8970
bioTheranostics Inc 9640 Towne Centre Dr Ste 200	San Diego	CA	92121	**877-886-6739**	858-587-5870
Camin Cargo Control Inc 230 Marion Ave	Linden	NJ	07036	**800-756-8798**	908-862-1899
CanWest DHI 660 Speedvale Ave W	Guelph	ON	N1K1E5	**800-549-4373**	519-824-2320
Carrot Medical LLC 22122 20th Ave SE Ste H-166	Bothell	WA	98021	**866-492-3533**	425-318-8089
CTLGroup 5400 Old OrchaRd Rd	Skokie	IL	60077	**800-522-2285**	847-965-7500
Cyl-tec Inc 971 W Industrial Dr	Aurora	IL	60506	**888-429-5832**	630-844-8800
Dayton T Brown Inc 1175 Church St	Bohemia	NY	11716	**800-232-6300**	631-589-6300
E Pi Bio Analytical 9095 W Harristown Blvd	Niantic	IL	62551	**866-963-2143**	217-963-2143
Ellis & Associates Inc 7064 Davis Creek Rd	Jacksonville	FL	32256	**800-273-0960**	904-880-0960
Embryotech Laboratories Inc 140 Hale St	Haverhill	MA	01830	**800-673-7500**	978-373-7300
Endotronix Inc 1005 Internationale Pkwy Ste 104	Woodridge	IL	60517	**877-363-6879**	
EnviroLogix Inc 500 Riverside Industrial Pkwy	Portland	ME	04103	**866-408-4597**	207-797-0300
Environmental Enterprises Inc (EEI) 10163 Cincinnati Dayton Rd	Cincinnati	OH	45241	**800-722-2818**	513-772-2818
Everist Genomics Inc 709 W Ellsworth Rd	Ann Arbor	MI	48108	**855-383-7478**	

Name / Address	City	State	Zip	Toll-Free	Phone
Excalibre Engineering 9201 Irvine Blvd	Irvine	CA	92618	**877-922-5427**	949-454-6603
Forensic Fluids Laboratories Inc 225 Parsons St	Kalamazoo	MI	49007	**866-492-2517**	269-492-7700
Forensic It 57 E Southcrest Cir	Edwardsville	IL	62025	**877-483-3284**	314-677-3950
Glidewell Laboratories Inc 4141 MacArthur Blvd	Newport Beach	CA	92660	**800-854-7256**	
Huffman Laboratories Inc 4630 Indiana St	Golden	CO	80403	**877-886-6225**	303-278-4455
HyGreen Inc 3630 SW 47th Ave Ste 100	Gainesville	FL	32608	**877-574-9473**	
iHealth Lab Inc 719 N Shoreline Blvd	Mountain View	CA	94043	**855-816-7705**	
Ikonisys Inc 5 Science Park	New Haven	CT	06511	**866-456-6832**	203-776-0791
Immuno Concepts NA Ltd 9825 Goethe Rd Ste 350	Sacramento	CA	95827	**800-251-5115**	916-363-2649
Inovatia Laboratories LLC 120 E Davis St	Fayette	MO	65248	**800-280-1912**	660-248-1911
JM Test Systems Inc 7323 Tom Dr	Baton Rouge	LA	70806	**800-353-3411**	225-925-2029
Kett Engineering Corp 15500 Erwin St Ste 1029	Van Nuys	CA	91411	**877-372-6799**	818-908-5388
L&g Engineering Laboratory LLC 2100 W Expressway 83	Mercedes	TX	78570	**888-565-9813**	956-565-9813
Magna Chek Inc 32701 Edward Ave	Madison Heights	MI	48071	**800-582-8947**	248-597-0089
Metcut Research Inc 3980 Rosslyn Dr	Cincinnati	OH	45209	**877-847-1985**	513-271-5100
Micro-Clean Inc 177 N Commerce Way	Bethlehem	PA	18017	**800-523-9852**	610-867-5302
Mountain Research LLC 825 25th St	Altoona	PA	16601	**800-837-4674**	814-949-2034
National Technical Systems Inc 24007 Ventura Blvd Ste 200 *NASDAQ: NTSC*	Calabasas	CA	91302	**800-879-9225**	818-591-0776
Neuisys LLC 1500 Pinecroft Rd Ste 212	Greensboro	NC	27407	**877-299-9052**	
Newport Partners LLC 3760 Tanglewood Ln	Davidsonville	MD	21035	**866-302-0017**	301-889-0017
Norchem Drug Testing Laboratory 1760 E Route 66	Flagstaff	AZ	86004	**844-284-1843**	928-526-1011
NOVX Systems Inc 9133 Leslie St Ste 110	Richmond Hill	ON	L4B4N1	**877-879-6689**	905-474-5051
Nsl Analytical 4450 Cranwood Pkwy	Cleveland	OH	44128	**877-560-3943**	216-447-1550
NutriCorp International 4025 Rhodes Dr	Windsor	ON	N8W5B5	**888-446-8874**	
NuView Life Sciences Inc 1389 Center Dr Ste 250	Park City	UT	84098	**888-902-7779**	
Provista Diagnostics Inc 17301 N Perimeter Dr	Scottsdale	AZ	85255	**855-552-7439**	
Schneider Laboratories Inc 2512 W Cary St	Richmond	VA	23220	**800-785-5227**	804-353-6778
Scion Medical Technologies LLC 90 Oak St	Newton	MA	02464	**888-582-6211**	
SGS Canada Inc 6490 Vipond Dr *General	Mississauga	ON	L5T1W8	**877-747-7658***	905-364-3757
Simco Electronics 1178 Bordeaux Dr	Sunnyvale	CA	94089	**866-299-6029**	408-734-9750
Southern Petroleum Lab Inc 8850 Interchange Dr	Houston	TX	77054	**877-775-5227**	713-660-0901
Spectrum Analytical Inc 830 Silver St	Agawam	MA	01001	**800-789-9115**	413-789-9018
Speedie & Assoc Inc 3331 E Wood St	Phoenix	AZ	85040	**800-628-6221**	602-997-6391
Stimwave Technologies Inc 901 E Las Olas Blvd Ste 201	Fort Lauderdale	FL	33301	**800-965-5134**	786-565-3342
Syagen Technology Inc 1411 Warner Ave	Tustin	CA	92780	**877-258-8250**	714-258-4400
TestAmerica Laboratories Inc 4625 E Cotton Ctr Blvd Ste 189	Phoenix	AZ	85040	**866-785-5227**	602-437-3340
Testcountry 6310 Nancy Ridge Dr Ste 103	San Diego	CA	92121	**866-237-7976**	858-784-6904
Thought Technology Ltd 2180 Belgrave Ave	Montreal	QC	H4A2L8	**800-361-3651**	514-489-8251
Toxikon Corp 15 Wiggins Ave	Bedford	MA	01730	**800-458-4141**	781-275-3330
Transportation Research Ctr Inc (TRC Inc) 10820 State Rt 347 PO Box B-67	East Liberty	OH	43319	**800-837-7872**	937-666-2011
TriLink BioTechnologies Inc 9955 Mesa Rim Rd	San Diego	CA	92121	**800-863-6801**	858-546-0004
UL LLC (UL) 2600 NW Lk Rd	Camas	WA	98607	**877-854-3577**	
Verichem Laboratories Inc 90 Narragansett Ave	Providence	RI	02907	**800-552-5859**	401-461-0180
VJ Technologies Inc 89 Carlough Rd	Bohemia	NY	11716	**800-858-9729**	631-589-8800
Weecycle Environmental Consulting Inc 5375 Western Ave Ste B	Boulder	CO	80301	**800-875-7033**	303-413-0452

741 TEXTILE MACHINERY

Name / Address	City	State	Zip	Toll-Free	Phone
Bowman Hollis Manufacturing Inc 2925 Old Steele Creek Rd	Charlotte	NC	28208	**888-269-2358**	704-374-1500
Eastman Machine Co 779 Washington St	Buffalo	NY	14203	**800-872-5571**	716-856-2200
Gerber Technology Inc 24 Industrial Pk Rd W	Tolland	CT	06084	**800-826-3243**	860-871-8082
HH Arnold Co Inc 529 Liberty St	Rockland	MA	02370	**866-868-9603**	781-878-0346
Hix Corp 1201 E 27th Terr	Pittsburg	KS	66762	**800-835-0606**	620-231-8568
Ioline Corp 14140 NE 200th St	Woodinville	WA	98072	**800-598-0029**	425-398-8282
Lummus Corp 225 Bourne Blvd PO Box 929	Savannah	GA	31408	**800-458-6687**	912-447-9000
Thermopatch Corp 2204 Erie Blvd E	Syracuse	NY	13224	**800-252-6555**	315-446-8110
TrimMaster 4860 N Fifth St Hwy	Temple	PA	19560	**800-356-4237**	610-921-0203
Tuftco Corp 2318 S Holtzclaw Ave	Chattanooga	TN	37408	**800-288-3826**	423-698-8601
Tuftco Finishing Systems Inc 100 W Industrial Blvd	Dalton	GA	30720	**800-288-3826**	706-277-1110

742 TEXTILE MILLS

742-1 Broadwoven Fabric Mills

Name / Address	City	State	Zip	Toll-Free	Phone
American Cotton Growers Textile Div (ACG) PO Box 2827	Lubbock	TX	79408	**800-333-8011**	806-763-8011
DeRoyal Textiles 141 E York St	Camden	SC	29020	**800-845-1062**	803-432-2403
Garnet Hill Inc 231 Main St	Franconia	NH	03580	**800-870-3513**	603-823-5545
Hamrick Mills Inc 515 W Buford St PO Box 48	Gaffney	SC	29341	**800-600-4305**	864-489-4731
Henry Glass & Co 49 W 37th St	New York	NY	10018	**800-294-9495**	917-229-1080
JB Martin Co 645 Fifth Ave Ste 400	New York	NY	10022	**800-223-0525**	212-421-2020
KM Fabrics Inc 2 Waco St	Greenville	SC	29611	**800-873-7326**	864-295-2550
Kuraray America Inc 2625 Bay Area Blvd Ste 600	Houston	TX	77058	**800-423-9762**	281-909-5800
Lantal Textiles Inc 1300 Langenthal Dr PO Box 965	Rural Hall	NC	27045	**800-334-3309**	336-969-9551
Precision Fabrics Group Inc 301 N Elm St Ste 600	Greensboro	NC	27401	**800-284-8001**	336-510-8000
Scalamandre Silks Inc 350 Wireless Blvd	Hauppauge	NY	11788	**800-932-4361**	631-467-8800
Trelleborg Coated Systems US Inc 790 Reeves St	Spartanburg	SC	29301	**800-344-0714**	
Vectorply Corp 3500 Lakewood Dr	Phenix City	AL	36867	**800-577-4521**	334-291-7704
Warm Co 5529 186th Pl SW	Lynnwood	WA	98037	**800-234-9276**	425-248-2424

742-2 Coated Fabric

Name / Address	City	State	Zip	Toll-Free	Phone
Adell Plastics Inc 4530 Annapolis Rd	Baltimore	MD	21227	**800-638-5218**	410-789-7780
Alpha Assoc Inc 145 Lehigh Ave	Lakewood	NJ	08701	**800-631-5399**	732-634-5700
Bondcote Corp PO Box 729	Pulaski	VA	24301	**800-368-2160**	540-980-2640
Cooley Group 50 Esten Ave *Cust Svc	Pawtucket	RI	02860	**800-992-0072***	401-724-9000
Dazian Inc 18 Central Blvd	South Hackensack	NJ	07606	**877-232-9426**	
Deccofelt Corp 555 S Vermont Ave *Cust Svc	Glendora	CA	91741	**800-543-3226***	626-963-8511
Der-Tex Corp 1 Lehner Rd	Saco	ME	04072	**800-669-0364**	
Duracote Corp 350 N Diamond St	Ravenna	OH	44266	**800-321-2252**	330-296-3487
Herculite Products Inc 105 E Sinking Springs Ln *Cust Svc	Emigsville	PA	17318	**800-772-0036***	717-764-1192
ICG/Holliston 905 Holliston Mills Rd	Church Hill	TN	37642	**800-251-0451**	423-357-6141
Middlesex Research Mfg Company Inc 27 Apsley St	Hudson	MA	01749	**800-424-5188**	978-562-3697
Polyguard Products Inc PO Box 755	Ennis	TX	75120	**800-541-4994**	972-875-8421
Reflexite Corp 120 Darling Dr	Avon	CT	06001	**800-654-7570**	860-676-7100
Seaman Corp 1000 Venture Blvd	Wooster	OH	44691	**800-927-8578**	330-262-1111
Taconic 136 Coonbrook Rd PO Box 69	Petersburg	NY	12138	**800-833-1805**	518-658-3202
Twitchell Corp 4031 Ross Clark Cir *General	Dothan	AL	36303	**800-633-7550***	334-792-0002

742-3 Industrial Fabrics

Name / Address	City	State	Zip	Toll-Free	Phone
Albany International Corp 1373 Broadway PO Box 1907 *NYSE: AIN*	Albany	NY	12204	**888-797-6735**	518-445-2200
Amatex Corp 1032 Stambridge St	Norristown	PA	19404	**800-441-9680**	610-277-6100
AMETEK Inc Chemical Products Div 455 Corporate Blvd *Orders	Newark	DE	19702	**800-441-7777***	302-456-4400
AstenJohnson 4399 Corporate Rd	Charleston	SC	29405	**800-529-7990**	843-747-7800
Belton Industries Inc 1205 Hanby Rd PO Box 127	Belton	SC	29627	**800-845-8753**	864-338-5711
BGF Industries Inc 3802 Robert Porcher Way	Greensboro	NC	27410	**800-476-4845**	
Carthage Mills 4243 Hunt Rd *Sales	Cincinnati	OH	45242	**800-543-4430***	513-794-1600
Clear Edge Technical Fabrics 7160 Northland Cir N	Minneapolis	MN	55428	**800-328-3036**	763-535-3220
FH Bonn Co 4300 Gateway Blvd	Springfield	OH	45502	**800-323-0143**	937-323-7024
Firestone Fibers & Textiles Co 100 Firestone Ln PO Box 1369	Kings Mountain	NC	28086	**800-441-1336**	704-734-2132

				Toll-Free	Phone
Mutual Industries Inc 707 W Grange St	Philadelphia	PA	19120	**800-523-0888**	215-927-6000
Newtex Industries Inc 8050 Victor Mendon Rd	Victor	NY	14564	**800-836-1001**	585-924-9135
Sefar Printing Solutions Inc 111 Calumet St	Depew	NY	14043	**800-995-0531**	716-683-4050
TenCate Geosynthetics North America 365 S Holland Dr	Pendergrass	GA	30567	**888-795-0808**	706-693-2226
TenCate Protective Fabrics USA 6501 Mall Blvd	Union City	GA	30291	**800-241-8630**	
Ultrafabrics LLC 303 S Broadway	Tarrytown	NY	10591	**877-309-6648**	914-460-1730

742-4 Knitting Mills

				Toll-Free	Phone
Apex Mills Corp 168 Doughty Blvd	Inwood	NY	11096	**800-989-2739**	516-239-4400
Draper Knitting Co 28 Draper Ln	Canton	MA	02021	**800-808-7707**	781-828-0029
Lace For Less Inc 1500 Main Ave Ste 3	Clifton	NJ	07011	**800-533-5223**	973-478-2955
Monterey Mills Inc 1725 E Delavan Dr	Janesville	WI	53546	**800-255-9665**	608-754-2866

742-5 Narrow Fabric Mills

				Toll-Free	Phone
Avery Dennison 950 German St	Lenoir	NC	28645	**800-444-4947**	
Fulflex Inc 32 Justin Holden Dr	Brattleboro	VT	05301	**800-283-2500**	802-257-5256
Hickory Brands Inc (HBI) 429 27th St NW	Hickory	NC	28601	**800-438-5777**	
Hope Global Engineered Textile Solutions 50 Martin St	Cumberland	RI	02864	**800-854-7139***	401-333-8990
*General					
JRM Industries Inc 1 Mattimore St	Passaic	NJ	07055	**800-533-2697**	973-779-9340
Julius Koch USA Inc 387 Church St	New Bedford	MA	02745	**800-522-3652***	508-995-9565
*Sales					
Murdock Webbing Co 27 Foundry St	Central Falls	RI	02863	**800-375-2052**	401-724-3000
Name Maker Inc 4450 Commerce Cir PO Box 43821	Atlanta	GA	30336	**800-241-2890**	404-691-2237
Narrow Fabric Industries Corp 701 Reading Ave	Reading	PA	19611	**877-523-6373**	610-376-2891
Rhode Island Textile Co 211 Columbus Ave	Pawtucket	RI	02862	**800-556-6488**	401-722-3700
Ross Matthews Mills Inc 657 Quarry St	Fall River	MA	02723	**800-753-7677**	508-677-0601
Shelby Elastics Inc 639 N Post Rd PO Box 2405	Shelby	NC	28150	**800-562-4507**	704-487-4301
South Carolina Elastic Co 201 S Carolina Elastic Rd	Landrum	SC	29356	**800-845-6700**	864-457-3388
Southern Weaving Co 1005 W Bramlett Rd	Greenville	SC	29611	**800-849-8962**	864-233-1635
Tape Craft Corp 200 Tape Craft Dr	Oxford	AL	36203	**800-521-1783***	
*Cust Svc					
Wayne Mills Co Inc 130 W Berkley St	Philadelphia	PA	19144	**800-220-8053**	215-842-2134

742-6 Nonwoven Fabrics

				Toll-Free	Phone
Aetna Felt Corp 2401 W Emaus Ave	Allentown	PA	18103	**800-526-4451**	610-791-0900
Airtex Consumer Products a Div of Federal Foam Technologies 150 Industrial Pk Blvd	Cokato	MN	55321	**800-851-8887**	
Cerex Advanced Fabrics Inc 610 Chemstrand Rd	Cantonment	FL	32533	**800-572-3739**	850-968-0100
Fisher Textiles Inc 139 Business Pk Dr	Indian Trail	NC	28079	**800-554-8886**	704-821-8870
Foss Mfg Co LLC 11 Merrill Industrial Dr	Hampton	NH	03842	**800-343-3277**	603-929-6000
Hobbs Bonded Fibers Inc 200 Commerce Dr	Waco	TX	76710	**800-433-3357**	254-741-0040
National Nonwovens PO Box 150	EastHampton	MA	01027	**800-333-3469**	413-527-3445
Sellars 6565 N 60th St	Milwaukee	WI	53223	**800-237-8454**	414-353-5650
Tietex International 3010 N Blackstock Rd	Spartanburg	SC	29301	**800-843-8390**	864-574-0500

742-7 Textile Dyeing & Finishing

				Toll-Free	Phone
Aurora Textile Finishing Co 911 N Lake St PO Box 70	Aurora	IL	60507	**800-864-0303**	630-892-7651
Cranston Print Works Co 1381 Cranston St	Cranston	RI	02920	**800-876-2756**	401-943-4800
Westex Inc 122 W 22nd St	Oak Brook	IL	60523	**866-493-7839**	773-523-7000

742-8 Textile Fiber Processing Mills

				Toll-Free	Phone
Buffalo Industries Inc 99 S Spokane St	Seattle	WA	98134	**800-683-0052**	206-682-9900
Fabritech Inc 5740 Salmen St	New Orleans	LA	70123	**888-733-5009**	504-733-5009
JE Herndon Company Inc 1020 J E Herndon Access Rd	Kings Mountain	NC	28086	**800-277-0500**	704-739-4711

742-9 Yarn & Thread Mills

				Toll-Free	Phone
Charles Craft Inc 21381 Charles Craft Ln	Laurinburg	NC	28352	**800-275-4117**	910-844-3521
Coats North America 3430 Toringdon Way Ste 301	Charlotte	NC	28277	**800-631-0965**	704-329-5800
Eddington Thread Manufacturing Co PO Box 446	Bensalem	PA	19020	**800-220-8901**	215-639-8900
Interstock Premium Cabinets LLC 6300 Bristol Pike	Levittown	PA	19057	**800-896-9842**	267-288-1200
Lion Brand Yarn Co 135 Kero Rd	Carlstadt	NJ	07072	**800-795-5466**	212-243-8995
Parkdale Mills Inc 531 Cotton Blossom Cir	Gastonia	NC	28054	**800-331-1843**	704-874-5000
Supreme Corp 325 Spence Rd	Conover	NC	28613	**888-604-6975**	828-322-6975
Swift Spinning Inc 16 Corporate Ridge Pkwy	Columbus	GA	31907	**800-849-1252**	706-323-6303
Tuscarora Yarns Inc 8760 E Franklin St	Mount Pleasant	NC	28124	**800-849-6527**	704-436-6527

743 TEXTILE PRODUCTS - HOUSEHOLD

				Toll-Free	Phone
1888 Mills LLC 1520 Kensington Rd Ste 115	Oak Brook	IL	60523	**800-346-3660**	
American Textile Co 10 N Linden St	Duquesne	PA	15110	**800-289-2826***	412-948-1020
*Cust Svc					
Arden Cos 30400 Telegraph Rd Ste 200	Bingham Farms	MI	48025	**800-876-7336**	248-415-8500
Biddeford Blankets 300 Terr Dr	Mundelein	IL	60060	**800-789-6441**	
Carole Fabrics Inc PO Box 1436	Augusta	GA	30903	**800-241-0920**	706-863-4742
CHF Industries Inc 1 Pk Ave 9th Fl	New York	NY	10016	**800-243-7090***	212-951-7800
*Cust Svc					
Crown Crafts Inc 916 S Burnside	Gonzales	LA	70737	**800-433-9560**	225-647-9100
NASDAQ: CRWS					
Custom Drapery Blinds & Shutters 3402 E T C Jester	Houston	TX	77018	**800-929-9211**	713-225-9211
Echota Fabrics Inc 1394 US 41 N	Calhoun	GA	30701	**800-763-9750**	706-629-9750
Hollander Home Fashions Corp 6501 Congress Avenue Ste 300	Boca Raton	FL	33487	**800-233-7666**	561-997-6900
Kaslen Textiles 6099 Triangle Dr	Commerce	CA	90040	**800-777-5789**	323-588-7700
Kay Dee Designs Inc 177 Skunk Hill Rd	Hope Valley	RI	02832	**800-537-3433**	
Lafayette Venetian Blind Inc 3000 Klondike Rd. PO Box 2838	West Lafayette	IN	47996	**800-342-5523**	
Manual Woodworkers & Weavers Inc 3737 HowaRd Gap Rd	Hendersonville	NC	28792	**800-542-3139**	828-692-7333
Marietta Drapery & Window Coverings Company Inc 22 Trammel St PO Box 569	Marietta	GA	30064	**800-762-4774***	770-428-3335
*Mktg					
Pacific Coast Feather Co 1964 Fourth Ave S	Seattle	WA	98134	**888-297-1778**	206-624-1057
Pendleton Woolen Mills Inc 220 NW Broadway	Portland	OR	97209	**800-760-4844**	503-226-4801
Riegel Consumer Products 51 Riegel Rd	Johnston	SC	29832	**800-845-3251**	803-275-2541
Surefit Inc 6575 Snowdrift Rd Ste 101	Allentown	PA	18106	**888-796-0500**	
United Feather & Down Inc 414 E Golf Rd	Des Plaines	IL	60016	**888-297-1778**	847-296-6610
Wesco Fabrics Inc 4001 Forest St	Denver	CO	80216	**800-950-9372**	303-388-4101

744 THEATERS - BROADWAY

SEE ALSO Theaters - Resident ; Performing Arts Facilities ; Theater Companies

				Toll-Free	Phone
Al Hirschfeld Theatre 302 W 45th St	New York	NY	10036	**800-432-7780**	212-239-6262
Booth Theatre 222 W 45th St	New York	NY	10036	**800-432-7780**	212-239-6200
Broadhurst Theatre 235 W 44th St	New York	NY	10036	**800-447-7400**	212-239-6200
Helen Hayes Theatre 240 W 44th St	New York	NY	10036	**800-447-7400**	212-239-6200
Imperial Theatre 249 W 45th St	New York	NY	10036	**800-447-7400**	212-239-6200
Jacobs Theatre 242 W 45th St	New York	NY	10036	**800-447-7400**	212-239-6200
Longacre Theatre 220 W 48th St	New York	NY	10036	**800-447-7400**	212-239-6200
Lyceum Theatre 149 W 45th St	New York	NY	10036	**800-432-7780**	212-239-6200
Majestic Theatre 245 W 44th St	New York	NY	10036	**800-447-7400**	212-239-6200
Minskoff Theatre 200 W 45th St	New York	NY	10036	**800-714-8452**	212-869-0550
Richard Rodgers Theatre 226 W 46th St	New York	NY	10036	**866-755-3075**	212-221-1211

745 THEATERS - MOTION PICTURE

Name / Address	City	State	Zip	Toll-Free	Phone
AMC Star Theatres 25333 W 12-Mile Rd	Southfield	MI	48034	**888-262-4386**	248-368-1802
AMC Theatres 920 Main St	Kansas City	MO	64105	**877-341-6397**	816-221-4000
Cinemark USA Inc 3900 Dallas Pkwy Ste 500	Plano	TX	75093	**800-246-3627**	972-665-1000
Cineplex Entertainment LP 1303 Yonge St	Toronto	ON	M4T2Y9	**800-333-0061**	416-323-6600
Community Theater 100 S St	Morristown	NJ	07960	**888-278-7769**	973-455-1607
Landmark Theaters 2222 S Barrington Ave *Cust Svc	Los Angeles	CA	90064	**888-724-6362***	310-473-6701
Marcus Theatres Corp 100 E Wisconsin Ave Ste 2000 *Cust Svc	Milwaukee	WI	53202	**800-274-0099***	414-905-1000
Regal Entertainment Group 7132 Regal Ln *NYSE: RGC* ■ *Cust Svc	Knoxville	TN	37918	**877-835-5734***	865-922-1123

746 THEATERS - RESIDENT

SEE ALSO Theaters - Broadway ; Performing Arts Facilities ; Theater Companies

All of the theaters listed here are members of the League of Resident Theatres (LORT). In order to become a member of LORT, each theater must be incorporated as a non-profit, IRS-approved organization; must rehearse each self-produced production for a minimum of three weeks; must have a playing season of 12 weeks or more; and must operate under a LORT-Equity contract.

Name / Address	City	State	Zip	Toll-Free	Phone
A Contemporary Theatre (ACT) 700 Union St Kreielsheimer Pl	Seattle	WA	98101	**888-584-4849**	206-292-7660
Actors Theatre of Louisville 316 W Main St	Louisville	KY	40202	**800-428-5849**	502-584-1205
Alabama Shakespeare Festival 1 Festival Dr	Montgomery	AL	36117	**800-841-4273**	334-271-5300
Arkansas Repertory Theatre 601 Main St PO Box 110	Little Rock	AR	72201	**866-684-3737**	501-378-0445
Asolo Repertory Theatre 5555 N Tamiami Tr	Sarasota	FL	34243	**800-361-8388**	941-351-9010
Bb Riverboats Inc 101 Riverboat Row	Newport	KY	41071	**800-261-8586**	859-261-8500
Berkeley Repertory Theatre 2025 Addison St	Berkeley	CA	94704	**888-427-8849**	510-647-2949
Guthrie Theater 818 S Second St *Resv	Minneapolis	MN	55415	**877-447-8243***	612-377-2224
Lincoln Ctr Theater 150 W 65th St	New York	NY	10023	**800-432-7250**	
Maltz Jupiter Theatre 1001 E Indiantown Rd	Jupiter	FL	33477	**800-445-1666**	561-743-2666
Oregon Shakespeare Festival 15 S Pioneer St	Ashland	OR	97520	**800-219-8161**	541-482-2111
Pasadena Playhouse, The 39 S El Molino Ave	Pasadena	CA	91101	**800-733-2767**	626-356-7529
People's Light & Theatre Co 39 Conestoga Rd	Malvern	PA	19355	**800-732-0999**	610-647-1900
Pittsburgh Public Theater 621 Penn Ave	Pittsburgh	PA	15222	**800-732-0999**	412-316-8200
Seattle Repertory Theatre (SRT) 155 Mercer St PO Box 900923	Seattle	WA	98109	**877-900-9285**	206-443-2210
Shakespeare Theatre 516 Eigth St SE	Washington	DC	20003	**877-487-8849**	202-547-3230
Theatre For A New Audience 154 Christopher St Ste 3D	New York	NY	10014	**866-811-4111**	212-229-2819
Wilma Theater 265 S Broad St	Philadelphia	PA	19107	**800-732-0999**	215-893-9456
Yale Repertory Theatre 1120 Chapel St PO Box 1257	New Haven	CT	06505	**800-973-2837**	203-432-1234

747 THERMAL MANAGEMENT PRODUCTS - PERSONAL

Name / Address	City	State	Zip	Toll-Free	Phone
BRK Brands Inc 3901 Liberty St Rd	Aurora	IL	60504	**800-323-9005**	630-851-7330
Fike Corp 704 SW Tenth St	Blue Springs	MO	64015	**877-342-3453**	816-229-3405
Fire & Life Safety America 3017 Vernon Rd	Richmond	VA	23228	**800-252-5069**	804-222-1381
Firecom Inc 39-27 59th St	Woodside	NY	11377	**888-347-3269**	718-899-6100
First Alert Inc 3901 Liberty St Rd	Aurora	IL	60504	**800-323-9005**	630-851-7330
Gamewell FCI 12 Clintonville Rd	Northford	CT	06472	**800-606-1983**	203-484-7161
Honeywell Fire Solutions 1 Fire-Lite Pl	Northford	CT	06472	**800-627-3473**	203-484-7161
Potter Electric Signal Company Inc 5757 Phantom Dr Ste 125	Hazelwood	MO	63042	**800-325-3936**	314-878-4321
Siemens Bldg Technologies Inc Fire Safety Div 8 Fernwood Rd	Florham Park	NJ	07932	**888-303-3353**	973-593-2600
Silent Knight 7550 Meridian Cir Ste 100	Maple Grove	MN	55369	**800-328-0103**	763-493-6400
Task Force Tips Inc 3701 Innovation Way	Valparaiso	IN	46383	**800-348-2686**	219-462-6161
Tyco SimplexGrinnell 50 Technology Dr	Westminster	MA	01441	**800-746-7539**	978-731-2500
Viking Corp 210 N Industrial Pk Dr	Hastings	MI	49058	**800-968-9501**	269-945-9501

748 TICKET BROKERS

Name / Address	City	State	Zip	Toll-Free	Phone
All American Ticket Service 2616 Philadelphia Pike Ste E	Claymont	DE	19703	**800-669-0571**	
Americana Tickets NY 1535 Broadway	New York	NY	10036	**800-833-3121**	212-581-6660
Broadway.com 729 Seventh Ave	New York	NY	10019	**800-762-3929**	212-541-8457
Front Row USA Entertainment 900 N Federal Hwy Ste 200	Hallandale	FL	33009	**800-277-8499**	305-940-8499
Great Seats Inc 7338 Baltimore Ave Ste 108A	College Park	MD	20740	**800-664-5056**	301-985-6250
Select-A-Ticket Inc 25 Rt 23 S	Riverdale	NJ	07457	**800-735-3288**	973-839-6100
Theatre Development Fund 1501 Broadway 21st Fl	New York	NY	10036	**888-424-4685**	212-221-0885
Ticket Source Inc 5516 E Mockingbird Ln Ste 100	Dallas	TX	75206	**800-557-6872**	214-821-9011
Tickets.com Inc 555 Anton Blvd 11th Fl	Costa Mesa	CA	92626	**800-352-0212**	714-327-5400
TicketWeb Inc PO Box 77250 *Cust Svc	San Francisco	CA	94103	**866-777-8932***	
Western States Ticket Service 143 W McDowell Rd	Phoenix	AZ	85003	**800-326-0331**	602-254-3300

749 TILE - CERAMIC (WALL & FLOOR)

Name / Address	City	State	Zip	Toll-Free	Phone
American Marazzi Tile Inc 359 Clay Rd	Sunnyvale	TX	75182	**800-289-8453**	972-232-3801
Ann Sacks Tile & Stone Inc 8120 NE 33rd Dr	Portland	OR	97211	**800-278-8453**	503-281-7751
Armstrong World Industries Inc 2500 Columbia Ave *NYSE: AWI* ■ *Cust Svc	Lancaster	PA	17603	**800-233-3823***	717-397-0611
Crossville Porcelain Stone/USA PO Box 1168	Crossville	TN	38557	**800-221-9093**	931-484-2110
Dal-Tile International Inc 7834 Hawn Fwy	Dallas	TX	75217	**800-933-8453**	214-398-1411
Epro Tile Inc 10890 E CR 6	Bloomville	OH	44818	**866-818-3776**	
Florida Tile Industries Inc 998 Governors Ln Ste 300 *Cust Svc	Lexington	KY	40513	**800-352-8453***	859-219-5200
Interstyle Ceramics & Glass Ltd 3625 Brighton Ave	Burnaby	BC	V5A3H5	**800-667-1566**	604-421-7229
ME Tile 447 Atlas Dr	Nashville	TN	37211	**888-348-8453**	
Meredith Collection 1201 Millerton St SE	Canton	OH	44707	**888-325-3945**	330-484-1656
Metropolitan Ceramics 1201 Millerton St SE	Canton	OH	44707	**800-325-3945**	
Nudo Products Inc 1500 Taylor Ave	Springfield	IL	62703	**800-826-4132**	217-528-5636
Wood Pro Inc 421 Washington St PO Box 363	Auburn	MA	01501	**800-786-5577**	508-832-3291

750 TIMBER TRACTS

Name / Address	City	State	Zip	Toll-Free	Phone
Authentic Pine Floors Inc 4042 Hwy 42	Locust Grove	GA	30248	**800-283-6038**	
Federal Wage & Labor Institute 7001 W 43rd St	Houston	TX	77092	**800-767-9243**	713-690-5676
Haida Corp PO Box 89	Hydaburg	AK	99922	**800-478-3721**	907-285-3721
Holiday Tree Farms Inc 800 NW Cornell Ave	Corvallis	OR	97330	**800-289-3684**	541-753-3236
Industrial Timber & Lumber Corp (ITL) 23925 Commerce Pk Rd	Beachwood	OH	44122	**800-829-9663**	216-831-3140
JM Huber Corp 499 Thornall St 8th Fl	Edison	NJ	08837	**877-418-0038**	732-549-8600
Kohltech International Ltd 583 MacElmon Rd	Debert	NS	B0M1G0	**800-565-4396**	902-662-3100
McShan Lumber Company Inc PO Box 27	McShan	AL	35471	**800-882-3712**	205-375-6277
Moonworks 1137 Park E Dr	Woonsocket	RI	02895	**800-975-6666**	
Pike Lumber Company Inc PO Box 247	Akron	IN	46910	**800-356-4554**	574-893-4511
Pioneer Millworks 1180 Commercial Dr	Farmington	NY	14425	**800-951-9663**	585-924-9970
Weyerhaeuser Co 33663 Weyerhaeuser Way S *NYSE: WY*	Federal Way	WA	98003	**800-525-5440**	253-924-2345
Yule Tree Farms LLC 8804 S Heinz Rd	Canby	OR	97013	**888-970-8733**	503-651-2114

751 TIMESHARE COMPANIES

SEE ALSO Hotels & Hotel Companies

Name / Address	City	State	Zip	Toll-Free	Phone
Bluegreen Corp 4960 Conference Way N Ste 100 *NYSE: BXG*	Boca Raton	FL	33431	**800-456-2582**	561-912-8000
Disney Vacation Club 1390 Celebration Blvd	Celebration	FL	34747	**800-500-3990**	407-566-3100
Festiva Resorts 1 Vance Gap Rd *Resv	Asheville	NC	28805	**866-933-7848***	828-254-3378
Four Seasons Hotels & Resorts 1165 Leslie St	Toronto	ON	M3C2K8	**800-332-3442**	416-449-1750

Company	Address	City	State	ZIP	Toll-Free	Phone
Hilton Grand Vacations Company LLC	6355 Metro W Blvd Ste 180	Orlando	FL	32835	**800-230-7068**	407-722-3100
Hyatt Vacation Ownership Inc	140 Fountain Pkwy N Ste 570	Saint Petersburg	FL	33716	**800-926-4447**	727-803-9400
Interval International Inc	6262 Sunset Dr PO Box 431920	Miami	FL	33143	**800-828-8200**	305-666-1861
Marriott Vacation Club International	6649 Westwood Blvd Ste 500	Orlando	FL	32821	**800-307-7312**	407-206-6000
Resort Condominiums International (RCI)	9998 N Michigan Rd	Carmel	IN	46032	**800-338-7777**	317-805-8000
Royal Aloha Vacation Club	1505 Dillingham Blvd Ste 212	Honolulu	HI	96817	**800-367-5212**	808-847-8050
Silverleaf Resorts Inc	1221 Riverbend Dr Ste 120	Dallas	TX	75247	**800-613-0310**	214-631-1166
Sunchaser Vacation Villas	5129 Riverview Gate Rd *Resv	Fairmont Hot Springs	BC	V0B1L1	**877-451-1250***	250-345-4545
Tempus Resorts International	7380 Sand Lake Rd Ste 600	Orlando	FL	32819	**877-747-4747**	407-226-1000
Vacation Internationale	1417 116th Ave NE	Bellevue	WA	98004	**800-444-6633**	425-454-8429
WorldMark the Club	9805 Willows Rd NE	Redmond	WA	98052	**800-722-3487**	425-498-1950

752 TIRES - MFR

Company	Address	City	State	ZIP	Toll-Free	Phone
Bridgestone Americas Holding Inc	535 Marriott Dr *Cust Svc	Nashville	TN	37214	**877-201-2373***	615-937-1000
Continental Tire North America Inc	1800 Continental Blvd	Charlotte	NC	28273	**877-235-0102**	704-583-3900
Cooper Tire & Rubber Co	701 Lima Ave *NYSE: CTB*	Findlay	OH	45840	**800-854-6288**	419-423-1321
Dunlop Tires	3045 Sheridan Dr	Amherst	NY	14226	**800-845-8378**	800-522-7458
Goodyear Tire & Rubber Co	200 Innovation Way *NASDAQ: GT* ■ *Cust Svc	Akron	OH	44316	**800-321-2136***	330-796-2121
Hankook Tire America Corp	1450 Valley Rd	Wayne	NJ	07470	**800-426-8252**	973-633-9000
Hercules Tire & Rubber Co	16380 E US Rt 224 - 200	Findlay	OH	45840	**800-677-9535**	419-425-6400
K&M Tire Inc	965 Spencerville Rd PO Box 279	Delphos	OH	45833	**877-879-5407**	419-695-1061
La Cie Canada Tire Inc	21500 Transcanadienne	Baie-D'Urfe	QC	H9X4B7	**888-267-5097**	514-457-0155
Lyna Manufacturing Inc	1125 15th St W	North Vancouver	BC	V7P1M7	**800-993-4007**	604-990-0988
Martin Wheel Company Inc	342 W Ave	Tallmadge	OH	44278	**800-462-7846**	330-633-3278
Michelin North America Inc	1 PkwyS PO Box 19001 *Cust Svc	Greenville	SC	29602	**800-847-3435***	864-458-5000
Mickey Thompson Tires	4600 Prosper Dr	Stow	OH	44224	**800-222-9092**	330-928-9092
Mitchell Industrial Tire Co	2915 Eigth Ave PO Box 71839	Chattanooga	TN	37407	**800-251-7226**	423-698-4442
Robbins LLC	3415 Thompson St	Muscle Shoals	AL	35661	**800-633-3312**	256-383-5441
SolidBoss Worldwide Inc	200 Veterans Blvd	South Haven	MI	49090	**888-258-7252**	269-637-6356
Specialty Tires of America Inc	1600 Washington St	Indiana	PA	15701	**800-622-7327**	724-349-9010
Superior Tire & Rubber Corp	1818 Pennsylvania Ave W PO Box 308 *Cust Svc	Warren	PA	16365	**800-289-1456***	814-723-2370
Tech International	200 E Coshocton St	Johnstown	OH	43031	**800-336-8324**	740-967-9015
Titan Tire Co	2345 E Market St	Des Moines	IA	50317	**800-872-2327**	515-265-9200
Toyo Tire USA Corp	6261 Katella Ave Ste 2B	Cypress	CA	90630	**800-678-3250**	
Yokohama Tire Corp	601 S Acacia Ave	Fullerton	CA	92831	**800-423-4544**	714-870-3800

753 TIRES & TUBES - WHOL

Company	Address	City	State	ZIP	Toll-Free	Phone
Allied Oil & Supply Inc	2209 S 24th St	Omaha	NE	68108	**800-333-3717**	402-344-4343
American Tire Depot	1123 W Commonwealth Ave	Fullerton	CA	92833	**855-333-2823**	714-525-2306
Bauer Built Inc	PO Box 248	Durand	WI	54736	**800-268-5114**	715-672-4295
Ben Tire Distributors Ltd	203 E Madison St PO Box 158	Toledo	IL	62468	**800-252-8961**	
BFGoodrich Tires Inc	1 Pkwy S	Greenville	SC	29602	**877-788-8899**	
Dapper Tire Company Inc	4025 Lockridge St	San Diego	CA	92102	**800-266-7172**	619-266-1397
De Ronde Tire Supply Inc	95 Rapin Pl	Buffalo	NY	14211	**800-227-4647**	716-897-6690
East Bay Tire Co	2200 Huntington Dr Unit C	Fairfield	CA	94533	**800-831-8473**	707-437-4700
Free Service Tire Co Inc	PO Box 6187	Johnson City	TN	37602	**855-646-1423**	423-979-2250
Friend Tire Co	11 Industrial Dr	Monett	MO	65708	**800-950-8473**	
Ken Jones Tire Inc	73 Chandler St	Worcester	MA	01609	**800-225-9513**	508-755-5255
Kenda USA	7095 Americana Pkwy	Reynoldsburg	OH	43068	**866-536-3287**	614-866-9803
Kumho Tire USA Inc	10299 Sixth St	Rancho Cucamonga	CA	91730	**800-445-8646**	909-428-3999
Lakin Tire West Inc	15305 Spring Ave	Santa Fe Springs	CA	90670	**800-488-2752**	562-802-2752
Michelin North America Inc	1 PkwyS PO Box 19001 *Cust Svc	Greenville	SC	29602	**800-847-3435***	864-458-5000
Parrish Tire Company Inc	5130 Indiana Ave	Winston-Salem	NC	27106	**800-849-8473**	336-767-0202
Piedmont Truck Tires Inc	PO Box 18228	Greensboro	NC	27419	**800-274-8473**	336-668-0091
Pomps Tire Service Inc	1123 Cedar St	Green Bay	WI	54301	**800-236-8911**	920-435-8301
Reliable Tire Co	805 N Blackhorse Pk *All	Blackwood	NJ	08012	**800-342-3426***	
Snyder Tire	401 Cadiz Rd	Steubenville	OH	43953	**800-967-8473**	740-264-5543
Southeastern Wholesale Tire Co	4721 Trademark Dr *General	Raleigh	NC	27610	**800-849-9215***	919-832-3900
T BC Corp	4770 Hickory Hill Rd	Memphis	TN	38141	**866-822-4968**	
Terry's Tire Town Inc	2360 W Main St PO Box 2405	Alliance	OH	44601	**800-235-2921**	
Tire Centers LLC	310 Inglesby Pkwy	Duncan	SC	29334	**800-603-2430**	864-329-2700
Tire Rack	7101 Vorden Pkwy	South Bend	IN	46628	**888-541-1777**	574-287-2345
Tire Warehouse Inc	7500 NW 35 Terr	Miami	FL	33122	**877-235-0102**	305-696-0096
Tire's Warehouse Inc	240 Teller St	Corona	CA	92879	**800-655-8851**	951-808-0111
Tire-Rama Inc	1429 Grand Ave	Billings	MT	59102	**800-828-1642**	406-245-4006
TO Haas Tire Co Inc	2400 'O' St	Lincoln	NE	68510	**866-393-5204**	402-474-1525
Wheels Etc	17521 Mesa St	Hesperia	CA	92345	**800-758-4737**	909-350-8200

754 TOBACCO & TOBACCO PRODUCTS

Company	Address	City	State	ZIP	Toll-Free	Phone
Abel Reel, The	165 Aviador St	Camarillo	CA	93010	**866-511-7444**	805-484-8789
Albert H Notini & Sons Inc	225 Aiken St	Lowell	MA	01854	**800-366-8464**	978-459-7151
Alliance One International Inc	8001 Aerial Ctr Pkwy PO Box 2009 *NYSE: AOI*	Morrisville	NC	27560	**800-937-5449**	919-379-4300
AMCON Distributing Co	7405 Irvington Rd *NYSE: DIT*	Omaha	NE	68122	**888-201-5997**	402-331-3727
Burklund Distributors Inc	2500 N Main St Ste 3	East Peoria	IL	61611	**800-322-2876**	309-694-1900
Cigar.com Inc	1911 Spillman Dr	Bethlehem	PA	18015	**800-357-9800**	
Eby-Brown Co	280 W Shuman Blvd Ste 280	Naperville	IL	60563	**800-553-8249**	630-778-2800
Finck Cigar Co	414 Vera Cruz St *Orders	San Antonio	TX	78207	**800-221-0638***	210-226-4191
Holts Cigar Co	1522 Walnut St	Philadelphia	PA	19102	**800-523-1641**	215-732-8500
J Polep Distribution Services Inc	705 Meadow St	Chicopee	MA	01013	**800-447-6537**	413-592-4141
JC Newman Cigar Co	2701 16th St *Orders	Tampa	FL	33605	**800-477-1884***	813-248-2124
Keilson-Dayton Co	107 Commerce Pk Dr	Dayton	OH	45404	**800-759-3174**	937-236-1070
Klafter's Inc	216 N Beaver St	New Castle	PA	16101	**800-922-1233**	
Modern Distributors Inc	817 W Columbia St	Somerset	KY	42501	**800-880-5543**	606-679-1178
National Tobacco Company LP	5201 Interchange Way *Cust Svc	Louisville	KY	40229	**800-579-0975***	502-778-4421
Philip Morris USA	2325 Bells Rd	Richmond	VA	23234	**800-343-0975**	804-274-2000
Reynolds American Inc	401 N Main St PO Box 2990 *NYSE: LO*	Winston-Salem	NC	27101	**877-390-5533**	336-741-2000

755 TOOL & DIE SHOPS

Company	Address	City	State	ZIP	Toll-Free	Phone
A Finkl & Sons Co	2011 N Southport Ave	Chicago	IL	60614	**800-343-2562**	773-975-2510
Anchor Tool & Die Co	12200 Brookpark Rd	Cleveland	OH	44130	**888-341-8910**	216-362-1850
Bowden Manufacturing Corp	4590 Beidler Rd	Willoughby	OH	44094	**800-876-8970**	440-946-1770
Canadian Tool & Die Ltd	1331 Chevrier Blvd	Winnipeg	MB	R3T1Y4	**800-204-4150**	204-453-6833
Carlson Tool & Manufacturing Corp	W57 N14386 Doerr Way PO Box 85	Cedarburg	WI	53012	**800-532-2252**	262-377-2020
Cbw Automation	3939 automation way	Fort collins	CO	80525	**800-229-9500**	970-229-9500
Church Metal Spinning Co	5050 N 124th St	Milwaukee	WI	53225	**877-461-6460**	414-461-6460
Cleveland Punch & Die Co	666 Pratt St PO Box 769	Ravenna	OH	44266	**888-451-4342**	
Cole Tool & Die Co	241 Ashland Rd	Mansfield	OH	44905	**800-837-2653**	419-522-1272
Custom Mold Engineering Inc	9780 S Franklin Dr	Franklin	WI	53132	**800-448-2005**	414-421-5444
D & D Manufacturing Inc	500 Territorial Dr	Bolingbrook	IL	60440	**888-300-6869**	

Classified Section

Company / Address	City	State	ZIP	Toll-Free	Phone
D-M-E Co 29111 Stephenson Hwy	Madison Heights	MI	48071	**800-626-6653**	248-398-6000
Danly IEM 6779 Engle Rd Ste A-F	Cleveland	OH	44130	**800-652-6462**	
Del-Tech Manufacturing Inc 9703 Penn Rd	Prince George	BC	V2N5T6	**800-736-7733**	250-564-3585
Deluxe Stitcher Company Inc 3747 acorn ln	Franklin Park	IL	60131	**800-634-0810**	
Diamond Tool & Die Inc 508 29th Ave	Oakland	CA	94601	**800-227-1084**	510-534-7050
EF Precision Design Inc 2301 Computer Rd	Willow Grove	PA	19090	**800-536-3900**	215-784-0861
Ehrhardt Tool & Machine Co 25 Central Industrial Dr	Granite City	IL	62040	**877-386-7856**	314-436-6900
General Carbide Corp 1151 Garden St	Greensburg	PA	15601	**800-245-2465**	724-836-3000
General Tool Co 101 Landy Ln	Cincinnati	OH	45215	**800-314-9817**	513-733-5500
GlobalDie 1130 Minot Ave PO Box 1120	Auburn	ME	04211	**800-910-3747**	207-514-7252
Hydro Carbide 4439 State Rte 982	Latrobe	PA	15650	**800-245-2476**	724-539-9701
Hygrade Precision Technologies Inc 329 Cooke St	Plainville	CT	06062	**800-457-1666**	860-747-5773
Indian Creek Fabricators 1350 Commerce Pk Dr	Tipp City	OH	45371	**877-769-5880**	937-667-5818
Jones Metal Products Co 200 N Ctr St	West Lafayette	OH	43845	**888-868-6535**	740-545-6381
Lou-Rich Machine Tool Inc 505 W Front St	Albert Lea	MN	56007	**800-893-3235**	507-377-8910
Mahuta Tool Corp N118W19137 Bunsen Dr	Germantown	WI	53022	**888-686-4940**	262-502-4100
Mate Precision Tooling Inc 1295 Lund Blvd	Anoka	MN	55303	**800-328-4492**	763-421-0230
Mid-State Machine Products Inc 83 Verti Dr	Winslow	ME	04901	**800-341-4672**	207-873-6136
Moeller Mfg Company Inc Punch & Die Div 43938 Plymouth Oaks Blvd	Plymouth	MI	48170	**800-521-7613**	734-416-0000
Mold Base Industries Inc 7501 Derry St	Harrisburg	PA	17111	**800-241-6656**	
Mold-A-Matic Corp 147 River St	Oneonta	NY	13820	**866-886-2626**	607-433-2121
Northwestern Tools Inc 3130 Valleywood Dr	Dayton	OH	45429	**800-236-3956**	937-298-9994
Oberg Industries Inc 2301 Silverville Rd PO Box 368	Freeport	PA	16229	**866-487-2365**	724-295-2121
Panoramic Corp 4321 Goshen Rd	Fort Wayne	IN	46818	**800-654-2027**	
PCS Co 34488 Doreka Dr	Fraser	MI	48026	**800-521-0546**	586-294-7780
Peddinghaus Corp 300 N Washington Ave	Bradley	IL	60915	**800-786-2448**	815-937-3800
Penn United Technology Inc 799 N Pike Rd	Cabot	PA	16023	**866-572-7537**	724-352-1507
Pennsylvania Tool & Gages Inc PO Box 534	Meadville	PA	16335	**877-827-8285**	814-336-3136
Porter Precision Products Inc 2734 Banning Rd	Cincinnati	OH	45239	**800-543-7041**	513-923-3777
Precision Tool Die & Machine Co Inc 6901 Preston Hwy	Louisville	KY	40219	**877-511-9695**	
Producto Machine Co 800 Union Ave *Cust Svc	Bridgeport	CT	06607	**800-722-2606***	203-367-8675
Rome Tool & Die Company Inc 113 Hemlock St	Rome	GA	30161	**800-241-3369**	706-234-6743
RotoMetrics Group 800 Howerton Ln	Eureka	MO	63025	**800-325-3851**	636-587-3600
SB Whistler & Sons Inc PO Box 270	Medina	NY	14103	**800-828-1010**	585-318-4630
Serapid Inc 34100 Mound Rd	Sterling Heights	MI	48310	**800-663-4514**	586-274-0774
Specialty Design & Mfg Co PO Box 4039	Reading	PA	19606	**800-720-0867**	610-779-1357
SPX Corp OTC Div 655 Eisenhower Dr	Owatonna	MN	55060	**800-533-6127**	507-455-7000
Sterling Process Engineering & Services Inc 333 McCormick Blvd	Columbus	OH	43213	**800-783-7875**	614-868-5151
Superior Die Set Corp 900 W Drexel Ave	Oak Creek	WI	53154	**800-558-6040**	414-764-4900
Superior Die Tool & Machine Co 2301 Fairwood Ave	Columbus	OH	43207	**800-292-2181**	614-444-2181
Unipunch Products Inc 311 Fifth St NW	Clear Lake	WI	54005	**800-828-7061**	
Walker Tool & Die Inc 2411 Walker Ave NW	Grand Rapids	MI	49544	**877-925-5378**	616-453-5471
Weldangrind Ltd 10323 174 St NW	Edmonton	AB	T5S1H1	**866-226-2414**	780-484-3030
Westland Corp 1735 S Maize Rd	Wichita	KS	67209	**800-247-1144**	316-721-1144
Yarema Die & Engineering Co Inc 300 Minnesota Rd	Troy	MI	48083	**800-937-9311**	248-585-2830

756 TOOLS - HAND & EDGE

SEE ALSO Saw Blades & Handsaws ; Lawn & Garden Equipment ; Metalworking Devices & Accessories

Company / Address	City	State	ZIP	Toll-Free	Phone
Allway Tools Inc 1255 Seabury Ave	Bronx	NY	10462	**800-422-5592**	718-792-3636
Ames Taping Tools Inc 3350 Breckinridge Blvd Ste 100	Duluth	GA	30096	**800-408-2801**	800-303-1827
Ames True Temper Inc 465 Railroad Ave	Camp Hill	PA	17011	**800-393-1846**	
Arrow Fastener Co Inc 271 Mayhill St	Saddle Brook	NJ	07663	**800-776-2228**	201-843-6900
BARCO Industries Inc 1020 MacArthur Rd *Cust Svc	Reading	PA	19605	**800-234-8665***	
Bondhus Corp 1400 E Broadway St PO Box 660 *Cust Svc	Monticello	MN	55362	**800-328-8310***	763-295-2162
Cal-Van Tools 4300 Waterleaf Ct	Greensboro	NC	27410	**800-537-1077**	
Channellock Inc 1306 S Main St *Cust Svc	Meadville	PA	16335	**800-724-3018***	
Charles GG Schmidt & Company Inc 301 W Grand Ave	Montvale	NJ	07645	**800-724-6438**	201-391-5300
Consolidated Devices Inc (CDI) 19220 San Jose Ave	City of Industry	CA	91748	**800-525-6319**	626-965-0668
Cooper Industries 600 Travis St Ste 5400 *NYSE: ETN*	Houston	TX	77002	**866-853-4293**	713-209-8400
Cornwell Quality Tools 667 Seville Rd	Wadsworth	OH	44281	**800-321-8356**	330-336-3506
Danaher Corp 2200 Pennsylvania Ave NW Ste 800 *NYSE: DHR*	Washington	DC	20037	**800-833-9200**	202-828-0850
Dasco Pro Inc 340 Blackhawk Pk Ave	Rockford	IL	61104	**800-327-2690**	815-962-3727
Duo-Fast Corp 2400 Galvin Dr *Cust Svc	Elgin	IL	60123	**888-386-3278***	847-783-5500
Empire Level Manufacturing Corp 929 Empire Dr PO Box 800	Mukwonago	WI	53149	**800-558-0722**	
Enderes Tool Co 1103 Hershey St	Albert Lea	MN	56007	**800-874-7776**	
Everhard Products Inc 1016 Ninth St SW	Canton	OH	44707	**800-225-0984**	330-453-7786
Fiskars Brands Inc 2537 Daniels St	Madison	WI	53718	**866-348-5661**	
Fletcher-Terry Company Inc 65 Spring Ln *Cust Svc	Farmington	CT	06032	**800-843-3826***	860-677-7331
General Machine Products Company Inc 3111 Old Lincoln Hwy *Tech Supp	Trevose	PA	19053	**800-345-6009***	215-357-5500
General Tools Mfg Company LLC 80 White St	New York	NY	10013	**800-697-8665**	212-431-6100
Grobet File Company of America Inc 750 Washington Ave	Carlstadt	NJ	07072	**800-847-4188**	201-939-6700
Hyde Tools Co 54 Eastford Rd	Southbridge	MA	01550	**800-872-4933**	508-764-4344
Klein Tools Inc 450 Bond St *Cust Svc	Lincolnshire	IL	60069	**800-553-4676***	
Leatherman Tool Group Inc 12106 NE Ainsworth Cir	Portland	OR	97220	**800-847-8665**	503-253-7826
LS Starrett Co 121 Crescent St *NYSE: SCX*	Athol	MA	01331	**800-482-8710**	978-249-3551
Mac Tools Inc 505 N Cleveland Ave	Westerville	OH	43082	**800-622-8665**	614-755-7000
Malco Products Inc 14080 State Hwy 55 NW PO Box 400	Annandale	MN	55302	**800-328-3530**	320-274-8246
Marshalltown Co 104 S Eigth Ave	Marshalltown	IA	50158	**800-888-0127**	641-753-5999
Matco Tools 4403 Allen Rd	Stow	OH	44224	**866-289-8665**	330-926-5332
Mayhew Steel Products Inc 199 Industrial Blvd	Turners Falls	MA	01376	**800-872-0037**	413-863-4860
MIBRO Group 111 Sinnott Rd	Toronto	ON	M1L4S6	**866-941-9006**	416-285-9000
Newell Rubbermaid Inc Irwin Tools Div 8935 Northpointe Executive Dr	Huntersville	NC	28078	**800-866-5740**	704-987-4555
QEP Co Inc 1001 Broken Sound Pkwy NW Ste A *OTC: QEPC ■ *Sales	Boca Raton	FL	33487	**800-777-8665***	561-994-5550
Red Devil Inc 1437 S Boulder	Tulsa	OK	74119	**800-423-3845**	
Reed Manufacturing Co 1425 W Eigth St	Erie	PA	16502	**800-456-1697**	814-452-3691
Relton Corp 317 Rolyn Dr PO Box 60019 *Cust Svc	Arcadia	CA	91066	**800-423-1505***	323-681-2551
Ripley Co 46 Nooks Hill Rd	Cromwell	CT	06416	**800-528-8665**	860-635-2200
Seymour Mfg Co Inc PO Box 248	Seymour	IN	47274	**800-815-7253**	812-522-2900
Snap-on Inc 2801 80th St *NYSE: SNA*	Kenosha	WI	53143	**877-762-7664**	262-656-5200
Stabila Inc 332 Industrial Dr PO Box 402	South Elgin	IL	60177	**800-869-7460**	
Stanley Tools Inc 480 Myrtle St *Cust Svc	New Britain	CT	06053	**800-262-2161***	
Stride Tool Inc Imperial Div 30333 Emerald Vly Pkwy	Glenwillow	OH	44139	**888-467-8665**	440-247-4600
Superior Tool Co 100 Hayes Dr Unit C *Cust Svc	Cleveland	OH	44131	**800-533-3244***	216-398-8600
Tamco Inc 1466 Delberts Dr	Monongahela	PA	15063	**800-826-2672**	724-258-6622
Triumph Twist Drill Co Inc 1 SW 7th St	Chisholm	MN	55719	**800-942-1501**	218-263-3891
Ullman Devices Corp 664 Danbury Rd	Ridgefield	CT	06877	**800-784-7796**	203-438-6577
Vaughan & Bushnell Manufacturing Co 11414 Maple Ave	Hebron	IL	60034	**800-435-6000**	815-648-2446
Warner Manufacturing Co 13435 Industrial Pk Blvd	Plymouth	MN	55441	**800-444-0606**	763-559-4740
Wheeler-Rex Inc 3744 Jefferson Rd PO Box 688	Ashtabula	OH	44005	**800-321-7950**	440-998-2788
Zephyr Mfg Company Inc 201 Hindry Av	Inglewood	CA	90301	**800-624-3944**	310-410-4907

TOOLS - MACHINE

SEE Machine Tools - Metal Cutting Types ; Machine Tools - Metal Forming Types

757 TOOLS - POWER

SEE ALSO Lawn & Garden Equipment ; Metalworking Devices & Accessories

Name / Address	City	State	Zip	Toll-Free	Phone
Alpine Power Systems Inc 24355 Capitol	Redford	MI	48239	**877-769-3762**	313-531-6600
American Pneumatic Tool Inc 9949 Tabor Pl	Santa Fe Springs	CA	90670	**800-532-7402**	562-204-1555
Atlas Copco Tools & Assembly Systems 2998 Dutton Rd	Auburn Hills	MI	48326	**800-859-3746**	248-373-3000
Blackstone Industries Inc 16 Stoney Hill Rd	Bethel	CT	06801	**800-272-2885**	203-792-8622
Chicago Pneumatic Tool Co 1800 Overview Dr	Rock Hill	SC	29730	**800-624-4735**	803-817-7000
Cooper Industries 600 Travis St Ste 5400 *NYSE: ETN*	Houston	TX	77002	**866-853-4293**	713-209-8400
Dremel Inc 4915 21st St	Racine	WI	53406	**800-437-3635**	262-554-1390
Dynabrade Inc 8989 Sheridan Dr *Cust Svc	Clarence	NY	14031	**800-828-7333***	716-631-0100
Enerpac PO Box 3241 *Cust Svc	Milwaukee	WI	53201	**800-433-2766***	262-293-1600
Florida Pneumatic Manufacturing Corp 851 Jupiter Pk Ln	Jupiter	FL	33458	**800-327-9403**	561-744-9500
Greenlee Textron Inc 4455 Boeing Dr	Rockford	IL	61109	**800-435-0786**	
Hilti Inc 5400 S 122nd E Ave *Cust Svc	Tulsa	OK	74146	**800-879-8000***	918-252-6000
Hougen Manufacturing Inc 3001 Hougen Dr *Orders	Swartz Creek	MI	48473	**800-426-7818***	810-635-7111
Makita USA Inc 14930 Northam St	La Mirada	CA	90638	**800-462-5482**	714-522-8088
Master Appliance Corp 2420 18th St	Racine	WI	53403	**800-558-9413**	262-633-7791
Milwaukee Electric Tool Corp 13135 W Lisbon Rd	Brookfield	WI	53005	**800-729-3878**	262-781-3600
P & F Industries Inc 445 Broadhollow Rd *NASDAQ: PFIN*	Melville	NY	11747	**800-327-9403**	631-694-9800
Paslode 888 Forest Edge Dr *Cust Svc	Vernon Hills	IL	60061	**800-682-3428***	847-634-1900
Pioneer Tool & Forge Inc 101 Sixth St	New Kensington	PA	15068	**800-359-6408**	724-337-4700
Pneutek 17 Friars Dr	Hudson	NH	03051	**800-431-8665**	603-883-1660
Powernail Co 1300 Rose Rd	Lake Zurich	IL	60047	**800-323-1653**	847-634-3000
Robert Bosch Tool Corp 1800 W Central Rd	Mount Prospect	IL	60056	**877-267-2499**	224-232-2000
Ryobi Technologies Inc 1428 Pearman Dairy Rd	Anderson	SC	29625	**800-525-2579**	
SENCO Products Inc 4270 Ivy Pt Blvd *Tech Supp	Cincinnati	OH	45245	**800-543-4596***	
Shopsmith Inc 6530 Poe Ave *OTC: SSMH* ■ *Cust Svc	Dayton	OH	45414	**800-543-7586***	937-898-6070
Sioux Tools Inc 250 Snap-on Dr *Orders	Murphy	NC	28906	**800-722-7290***	828-835-9765
Stanley Assembly Technologies Div 5335 Avion Pk Dr	Cleveland	OH	44143	**877-787-7830**	440-461-5500
Stihl Inc 536 Viking Dr *Cust Svc	Virginia Beach	VA	23452	**800-467-8445***	757-486-9100
Thomas C Wilson Inc 21-11 44th Ave	Long Island	NY	11101	**800-230-2636**	718-729-3360

758 TOUR OPERATORS

SEE ALSO Travel Agencies ; Bus Services - Charter

Name / Address	City	State	Zip	Toll-Free	Phone
Academy Bus LLC 111 Paterson Ave	Hoboken	NJ	07030	**800-442-7272**	201-420-7000
Adventure Alaska Tours Inc PO Box 64	Hope	AK	99605	**800-365-7057**	907-782-3730
Adventure Connection PO Box 475	Coloma	CA	95613	**800-556-6060**	530-626-7385
Adventure Life South America 1655 S Third St W Ste 1	Missoula	MT	59801	**800-344-6118**	406-541-2677
Adventures Out West 1680 S 21st St	Colorado Springs	CO	80904	**800-755-0935**	
Africa Adventure Co, The 5353 N Federal Hwy Ste 300	Fort Lauderdale	FL	33308	**800-882-9453**	954-491-8877
African Travel Inc 330 N Brand Blvd Ste 950	Glendale	CA	91203	**800-421-8907**	818-507-7893
AHI International Corp 8550 W Bryn Mawr Ave Ste 600	Chicago	IL	60631	**800-323-7373**	
All Aboard Travel PO Box 90074	Chattanooga	TN	37412	**800-499-9877**	423-499-9977
Alpine Adventure Trails Tours Inc 7495 Lower Thomaston Rd	Macon	GA	31220	**888-478-4004**	
AmaWaterways 26010 Mureau Rd	Calabasas	CA	91302	**800-626-0126**	
American Trails West (ATW) 92 Middle Neck Rd	Great Neck	NY	11021	**800-645-6260**	516-487-2800
Anderson Coach & Travel 1 Anderson Plz	Greenville	PA	16125	**800-345-3435**	724-588-8310
ATS Tours 300 Continental Blvd Ste 350	El Segundo	CA	90245	**888-410-5770**	
Backroads 801 Cedar St	Berkeley	CA	94710	**800-462-2848**	510-527-1555
Badger Coaches Inc 5501 Femrite Dr	Madison	WI	53718	**800-442-8259**	608-255-1511
Banff Adventures Unlimited 211 Bear St Bison Courtyard	Banff	AB	T1L1A8	**800-644-8888**	403-762-4554
Beamers Hells Canyon Tours & Excursions PO Box 1243	Lewiston	ID	83501	**800-522-6966**	509-758-4800
Bestway Tours & Safaris 8678 Greenall Ave	Burnaby	BC	V5J3M6	**800-663-0844**	604-264-7378
Big Five Tours & Expeditions 1551 SE Palm Ct	Stuart	FL	34994	**800-244-3483**	772-287-7995
Bonaventure Tours 8 Boudreau Ln	Haute-Aboujagane	NB	E4P5N1	**800-561-1213**	506-532-3674
Boston Duck Tours Ltd 4 Copley Pl Ste 310	Boston	MA	02116	**800-226-7442**	617-450-0065
Breakaway Tours 3300 Bloor St Ste 1800	Toronto	ON	M8X2X2	**800-465-4257**	416-915-9880
Brendan Vacations 21625 Prairie St	Chatsworth	CA	91311	**800-687-1002**	
Brewster Travel Canada 100 Gopher St PO Box 1140	Banff	AB	T1L1J3	**866-606-6700**	403-762-6700
Burke International Tours Inc PO Box 890	Newton	NC	28658	**800-476-3900**	828-465-3900
California Parlor Car Tours 500 Sutter St Ste 401	San Francisco	CA	94102	**800-227-4250**	415-474-7500
Centennial Travelers 311 S College Ave	Fort Collins	CO	80524	**800-223-0675**	970-484-4988
Churchill Nature Tours PO Box 429	Erickson	MB	R0J0P0	**877-636-2968**	204-636-2968
Classic Student Tours 75 Rhoads Ctr Dr	Dayton	OH	45458	**800-860-0246**	937-439-0032
Club Europa 802 W Oregon St	Urbana	IL	61801	**800-331-1882**	217-344-5863
Coach Tours Ltd 475 Federal Rd	Brookfield	CT	06804	**800-822-6224**	203-740-1118
Contemporary Tours 1400 Old Country Rd Ste 100	Westbury	NY	11590	**800-627-8873**	516-484-5032
Contiki Holidays 801 E Katella Ave 3rd Fl	Anaheim	CA	92805	**800-944-5708**	714-935-0808
Cultural Experiences Abroad (CEA) 2999 N 44th St Ste 200	Phoenix	AZ	85018	**800-266-4441**	480-557-7900
Dash Tours 1024 Winnipeg St	Regina	SK	S4R8P8	**800-265-0000**	306-352-2222
Dipert Travel & Transportation Ltd PO Box 580	Arlington	TX	76004	**800-433-5335**	
Earthwatch Institute 114 Western Ave	Boston	MA	02134	**800-776-0188**	978-461-0081
Educational Tours 1123 Sterling Rd	Inverness	FL	34450	**800-343-9003**	
Educational Travel Consultants (ETC) PO Box 1580	Hendersonville	NC	28793	**800-247-7969**	828-693-0412
EF Tours 2 Education Cir	Cambridge	MA	02141	**800-872-8439**	877-205-9909
Esplanade Tours 160 Commonwealth Ave Ste U-1A	Boston	MA	02116	**800-628-4893**	617-266-7465
Explorica Inc 145 Tremont St	Boston	MA	02111	**888-310-7120**	
Fantastic Tours & Travel 6143 Jericho Tpke	Commack	NY	11725	**800-552-6262**	631-462-6262
Festive Holidays Inc 5501 New Jersey Ave	Wildwood Crest	NJ	08260	**800-257-8920**	609-522-6316
Friendly Excursions Inc PO Box 69	Sunland	CA	91041	**800-775-5018**	818-353-7726
Frontiers International Travel PO Box 959	Wexford	PA	15090	**800-245-1950**	724-935-1577
Gadabout Vacations 1801 E Tahquitz Canyon Way Ste 100	Palm Springs	CA	92262	**800-952-5068**	760-325-5556
General Tours 53 Summer St	Keene	NH	03431	**800-221-2216**	
Gerber Tours Inc 100 Crossways Park Dr W Ste 400	Woodbury	NY	11797	**800-645-9145**	516-826-5000
Globus 5301 S Federal Cir	Littleton	CO	80123	**866-755-8581**	
Go Next 8000 W 78th St Ste 345	Minneapolis	MN	55439	**800-842-9023**	952-918-8950
Go...With Jo! Tours & Travel Inc 910 Dixieland Rd	Harlingen	TX	78552	**800-999-1446**	956-423-1446
Good Time Tours 455 Corday St	Pensacola	FL	32503	**800-446-0886**	850-476-0046
Good Times Travel Inc 17132 Magnolia St	Fountain Valley	CA	92708	**888-488-2287**	714-848-1255
Grand European Tours 6000 Meadows Rd Ste 520	Lake Oswego	OR	97035	**877-622-9109**	503-718-2262
Gray Line Worldwide 1835 Gaylord St	Denver	CO	80206	**800-472-9546**	303-394-6920
Green Tortoise Adventure Travel & Hostels 494 Broadway	San Francisco	CA	94133	**800-867-8647**	415-834-1000
Gutsy Women Travel LLC 801 E Katella Ave	Anaheim	CA	92806	**866-464-8879**	
Hagey Coach & Tours Nrt 210 Schoolhouse Rd	Souderton	PA	18964	**800-544-2439**	215-723-4381
Hesselgrave International PO Box 30768	Bellingham	WA	98228	**800-457-5522**	360-734-3570
Historic Tours of America Inc 201 Front St Ste 224 *General	Key West	FL	33040	**800-844-7601***	305-296-3609
Hole in One International 6195 Ridgeview Ct Ste A	Reno	NV	89519	**800-827-2249**	775-828-4653
Holiday River Expeditions 544 East 3900 South	Salt Lake City	UT	84107	**800-624-6323**	801-266-2087
Isram World of Travel Inc 90 John St Ste 602	New York	NY	10038	**800-223-7460**	
Julian Tours 1721 Crestwood Dr	Alexandria	VA	22302	**800-541-7936**	703-379-2300
Katmai Coastal Bear Tours PO Box 1503	Homer	AK	99603	**800-532-8338**	907-235-8337
Ker & Downey Inc 6703 Hwy Blvd	Katy	TX	77494	**800-423-4236**	281-371-2500
Kincaid Coach Lines Inc 9207 Woodend Rd	Kansas City	KS	66111	**800-998-1901**	913-441-6200
Landmark Tours 1304 University Ave NE Ste 201	Minneapolis	MN	55413	**888-231-8735**	651-490-5408

Company	Address	City	State	ZIP	Toll-Free	Phone
Lindblad Expeditions	96 Morton St 9th Fl	New York	NY	10014	**800-397-3348**	212-765-7740
Macy's Travel	700 Nicollet Mall	Minneapolis	MN	55402	**800-316-6166**	
Maupintour Inc	2690 Weston Rd Ste 200	Weston	FL	33331	**800-255-4266**	954-653-3820
Mayflower Tours Inc	1225 Warren Ave PO Box 490	Downers Grove	IL	60515	**800-323-7604**	630-435-8500
Micato Safaris	15 W 26th St 11th Fl	New York	NY	10010	**800-642-2861**	212-545-7111
Mid-American Coaches Inc	4530 Hwy 47	Washington	MO	63090	**866-944-8687**	
Midnight Sun Adventure Travel	1027 Pandora Ave	Victoria	BC	V8V3P6	**800-255-5057**	250-480-9409
Monograms	5301 S Federal Cir	Littleton	CO	80123	**866-270-9841**	
Montana River Outfitters	923 Tenth Ave N	Great Falls	MT	59401	**800-800-8218**	406-761-1677
Moose Travel Network	192 Spadina Ave Unit 408	Toronto	ON	M5T2C2	**888-244-6673**	604-297-0255
Mountain Travel Sobek	1266 66th St Ste 4	Emeryville	CA	94608	**888-831-7526**	510-594-6000
Natural Habitat Adventures	PO Box 3065	Boulder	CO	80307	**800-543-8917**	303-449-3711
Networld Inc	300 Lanidex Plz Ste 1	Parsippany	NJ	07054	**800-992-3411**	973-884-7474
Off the Beaten Path	7 E Beall St	Bozeman	MT	59715	**800-445-2995**	406-586-1311
Olivia Cruises & Resorts	434 Brannan St	San Francisco	CA	94107	**800-631-6277**	415-962-5700
Onondaga Coach Corp	PO Box 277	Auburn	NY	13021	**800-451-1570**	315-255-2216
Orange Belt Stages	PO Box 949	Visalia	CA	93279	**800-266-7433**	559-733-4408
Overseas Adventure Travel	347 Congress St	Boston	MA	02210	**800-221-0814**	
Panorama Balloon Tours	2683 Via De La Valle 625G	Del Mar	CA	92014	**800-455-3592**	
Perillo Tours	577 Chestnut Ridge Rd	Woodcliff Lake	NJ	07677	**800-431-1515**	201-307-1234
Pilgrim Tours & Travel Inc	3071 Main St PO Box 268	Morgantown	PA	19543	**800-322-0788**	610-286-0788
Pink Jeep Tours Las Vegas Inc	3629 W Hacienda Ave	Las Vegas	NV	89118	**800-873-3662**	702-895-6777
Pioneer Golf Inc	609 Castle Ridge Rd. Ste 335	Austin	TX	78746	**800-262-5725**	512-327-2680
Pitmar Tours	7549 140th St Ste 9	Surrey	BC	V3W5J9	**877-596-9670**	604-596-9670
Polynesian Adventure Tours Inc	2880 Kilihau St	Honolulu	HI	96819	**800-622-3011**	808-833-3000
Premier Alaska Tours Inc	1900 Premier Ct	Anchorage	AK	99502	**888-486-8725**	907-279-0001
Premier Tours	21 S 12th St 9th Fl	Philadelphia	PA	19107	**800-545-1910**	
Presley Tours Inc	16 Presley Pk Dr PO Box 58	Makanda	IL	62958	**800-621-6100**	618-549-0704
REI Adventures	PO Box 1938	Sumner	WA	98390	**800-622-2236**	253-437-1100
Richmond Tours	1828 Hylan Blvd	Staten Island	NY	10305	**800-766-3868**	718-979-3111
Rivers Oceans & Mountains Adventures Inc (ROAM)	2485 Hwy 3A	Nelson	BC	V1L6K7	**888-639-1114**	
Roberts Hawaii Inc	680 Iwilei Rd Ste 700	Honolulu	HI	96817	**800-831-5541**	808-523-7750
Royal Coach Tours	630 Stockton Ave	San Jose	CA	95126	**800-927-6925**	408-279-4801
RSVP Vacations	2535 25th Ave S	Minneapolis	MN	55406	**800-328-7787**	310-432-2300
Scenic Airlines Inc	3900 Paradise Rd Ste 223	Las Vegas	NV	89169	**866-235-9422**	702-638-3300
Short Hills Tours	46 Chatham Rd Ste 1	Short Hills	NJ	07078	**800-348-6871**	973-467-2113
Silver Fox Tours & Motorcoaches	3 Silver Fox Dr	Millbury	MA	01527	**800-342-5998**	508-865-6000
Silverado Stages Inc	241 Prado Rd	San Luis Obispo	CA	93401	**888-383-8109**	805-545-8400
Sports Leisure Vacations	9812 Old Winery Pl	Sacramento	CA	95827	**800-951-5556**	916-361-2051
Sports Travel Inc	60 Main St PO Box 50	Hatfield	MA	01038	**800-662-4424**	413-247-7678
Straight A Tours & Travel	6881 Kingspointe Pkwy Ste 18	Orlando	FL	32819	**800-237-5440**	407-896-1242
Student Tours Inc	60 W Ave	Vineyard Haven	MA	02568	**800-331-7093**	508-693-5078
Student Travel Services Inc	1413 Madison Pk Dr	Glen Burnie	MD	21061	**800-648-4849**	
Sunny Land Tours Inc	21 Old Kings Rd N Ste B-212	Palm Coast	FL	32137	**800-783-7839**	386-449-0059
Super Holiday Tours	116 Gatlin Ave	Orlando	FL	32806	**800-327-2116**	
Tag-A-Long Expeditions	452 N Main St	Moab	UT	84532	**800-453-3292**	435-259-8946
Tauck World Discovery	10 Norden Pl	Norwalk	CT	06855	**800-468-2825**	203-899-6500
Timberwolf Tours Ltd	51404 RR 264 Ste 34	Spruce Grove	AB	T7Y1E4	**888-467-9697**	780-470-4966
Toto Tours Ltd	1326 W Albion Ave	Chicago	IL	60626	**800-565-1241**	773-274-8686
Travcoa	100 N Sepulveda Blvd Ste 1700	El Segundo	CA	90245	**800-992-2003**	310-649-7104
Tri-State Travel	4349 Industrial Pk Dr	Galena	IL	61036	**800-779-4869**	815-777-0820
Upstate Tours & Travel	207 Geyser Rd	Saratoga Springs	NY	12866	**800-237-5252**	518-584-5252
USA Student Travel	5080 Robert J Mathews Pkwy	El Dorado Hills	CA	95762	**800-448-4444**	916-939-6805
VBT Bicycling & Walking Vacations	614 Monkton Rd	Bristol	VT	05443	**800-245-3868**	802-453-4811
VentureOut	575 Pierce St Ste 604	San Francisco	CA	94117	**888-431-6789**	415-626-5678
VIP Tour & Charter Bus Co	129-137 Fox St *General	Portland	ME	04101	**800-231-2222***	207-772-4457
Wade Tours Inc	797 Burdeck St	Schenectady	NY	12306	**800-955-9233**	518-355-4500
Walking Adventures International	14612 NE Fourth Plain Rd Ste A	Vancouver	WA	98682	**800-779-0353**	
West Coast Connection	1725 Main St Ste 215	Weston	FL	33326	**800-767-0227**	954-888-9780
White Mountain Adventures	131 Eagle Crescent PO Box 4259	Banff	AB	T1L1A6	**800-408-0005**	403-760-4403
White Star Tours	26 E Lancaster Ave	Reading	PA	19607	**800-437-2323**	610-775-5000
Wilderness Travel	1102 Ninth St	Berkeley	CA	94710	**800-368-2794**	510-558-2488
Wildland Adventures Inc	3516 Ne 155th St	Lake Forest Park	WA	98155	**800-345-4453**	206-365-0686
Wings Tours Inc	11350 McCormick Rd Ste 703	Hunt Valley	MD	21031	**800-869-4647**	410-771-0925
WorldStrides	218 W Water St Ste 400 *General	Charlottesville	VA	22902	**800-999-7676***	

759 TOY STORES

Company	Address	City	State	ZIP	Toll-Free	Phone
Alabama Card Systems Inc	500 Gene Reed Dr Ste 102	Birmingham	AL	35215	**800-985-7507**	205-833-1116
Build-A-Bear Workshop Inc	1954 Innerbelt Business Ctr Dr *NYSE: BBW*	Saint Louis	MO	63114	**888-560-2327**	314-423-8000
Creative Kid Stuff	3939 E 46th St	Minneapolis	MN	55406	**800-353-0710**	612-929-2431
CRT Custom Products Inc	7532 Hickory Hills Ct	Whites Creek	TN	37189	**800-453-2533**	615-876-5490
Daron Worldwide Trading Inc	24 Stewart Pl Unit 4	Fairfield	NJ	07004	**800-776-2324**	973-882-0035
Digital Engineering Systems Corp	2450 Scott Blvd Ste 300	Santa Clara	CA	95050	**888-788-1898**	408-970-8551
Discount School Supplies	2 Lower Ragsdale Rd Ste 125	Monterey	CA	93940	**800-919-5238**	
Great Lakes Dart Manufacturing Inc	S84 W19093 Enterprise Dr	Muskego	WI	53150	**800-225-7593**	262-679-8730
Learning Express Inc	29 Buena Vista St	Devens	MA	01434	**888-725-8697**	978-889-1000
Mary Maxim Ltd	75 Scott Ave	Paris	ON	N3L3G5	**888-442-2266**	
MGA Entertainment Inc	16300 Roscoe Blvd Ste 150	Van Nuys	CA	91406	**800-222-4685**	818-894-2525
Trainworld Associates LLC	751 Mcdonald Ave	Brooklyn	NY	11218	**800-541-7010**	718-436-7072

760 TOYS, GAMES, HOBBIES

SEE ALSO Games & Entertainment Software ; Baby Products ; Bicycles & Bicycle Parts & Accessories

Company	Address	City	State	ZIP	Toll-Free	Phone
Airmate Co Inc	16280 County Rd D	Bryan	OH	43506	**800-544-3614**	419-636-3184
American Girl Inc	8400 Fairway Pl *Orders	Middleton	WI	53562	**800-845-0005***	608-836-4848
American Plastic Toys Inc	799 Ladd Rd	Walled Lake	MI	48390	**800-521-7080**	248-624-4881
Atlas Model Railroad Company Inc	378 Florence Ave *Orders	Hillside	NJ	07205	**800-872-2521***	908-687-0880
Bachmann Industries Inc	1400 E Erie Ave *Cust Svc	Philadelphia	PA	19124	**800-356-3910***	215-533-1600
Ball Bounce & Sport Inc/Hedstrom Plastics	1 Hedstrom Dr	Ashland	OH	44805	**800-765-9665**	419-289-9310
Bravo Sports Corp	12801 Carmenita Rd *Cust Svc	Santa Fe Springs	CA	90670	**800-234-9737***	562-484-5100
Buffalo Games Inc	220 James E Casey Dr	Buffalo	NY	14206	**855-895-4290**	
Cardinal Industries Inc	21-01 51st Ave	Long Island	NY	11101	**800-622-8339**	718-784-3000
Cepia LLC	121 Hunter Ave	Saint Louis	MO	63124	**800-225-9319**	314-725-4900
Creativity for Kids	9450 Allen Dr	Cleveland	OH	44125	**800-311-8684**	216-643-4660
Douglas Cuddle Toys Company Inc	69 Krif Rd PO Box D	Keene	NH	03431	**800-992-9002**	603-352-3414
Estes-Cox Corp	1295 H St	Penrose	CO	81240	**800-525-7561**	719-372-6565
Fisher-Price Inc	636 Girard Ave	East Aurora	NY	14052	**800-432-5437**	716-687-3000
Five Below Inc	1818 Market St Ste 2000	Philadelphia	PA	19103	**866-935-8852**	215-546-7909
Gayla Industries Inc	PO Box 920800	Houston	TX	77292	**800-231-7508**	
Great Planes Model Distributors	PO Box 9021	Champaign	IL	61826	**800-637-7660**	217-398-3630
Guidecraft USA	55508 Hwy 19 W	Winthrop	MN	55396	**800-524-3555**	507-647-5030
Gund Inc	1 Runyons Ln *Cust Svc	Edison	NJ	08817	**800-448-4863***	732-248-1500
Hasbro Inc	1027 Newport Ave *NASDAQ: HAS*	Pawtucket	RI	02861	**800-242-7276**	401-431-8697
International Playthings Inc	75D Lackawanna Ave	Parsippany	NJ	07054	**800-631-1272**	973-316-2500

Name / Address	City	State	ZIP	Toll-Free	Phone
JAKKS Pacific Inc 21749 Baker Pkwy *NASDAQ: JAKK*	Walnut	CA	91789	**877-875-2557**	909-594-7771
LeapFrog Enterprises Inc 6401 Hollis St Ste 100 *NYSE: LF*	Emeryville	CA	94608	**800-701-5327**	510-420-5000
Learning Resources 380 N Fairway Dr	Vernon Hills	IL	60061	**800-222-3909**	847-573-8400
LEGO Systems Inc 555 Taylor Rd	Enfield	CT	06082	**877-518-5346**	860-763-6731
Lionel .com LLC 26750 23 Mile Rd	Chesterfield	MI	48051	**800-454-6635**	586-949-4100
Little Tikes Co, The 2180 Barlow Rd *Cust Svc	Hudson	OH	44236	**800-321-0183***	
Losi 4710 E Guasti Rd	Ontario	CA	91761	**888-899-5674**	909-390-9595
Mag-Nif Inc 8820 E Ave	Mentor	OH	44060	**800-869-5463**	
Maple City Rubber Co 55 Newton St PO Box 587	Norwalk	OH	44857	**800-841-9434**	419-668-8261
Mattel Inc 333 Continental Blvd *NASDAQ: MAT*	El Segundo	CA	90245	**800-524-8697**	310-252-2000
Midwest Products Company Inc 400 S Indiana St *Orders	Hobart	IN	46342	**800-348-3497***	219-942-1134
Nintendo of America Inc 4820 150th Ave NE *Cust Svc	Redmond	WA	98052	**800-255-3700***	425-882-2040
Ohio Art Co 1 Toy St *OTC: OART*	Bryan	OH	43506	**800-800-3141**	419-636-3141
Pepperball Technologies Inc 6540 Lusk Blvd Ste C137	San Diego	CA	92121	**877-887-3773**	858-638-0236
Pioneer National Latex Co 5000 E 29th St N	Wichita	KS	67220	**800-386-4438**	316-685-2266
Plaid Enterprises Inc 3225 Westech Dr	Norcross	GA	30092	**800-842-4197**	678-291-8100
Pressman Toy Corp 121 New England Ave *Cust Svc	Piscataway	NJ	08854	**800-800-0298***	732-562-1590
Radio Flyer Inc 6515 W Grand Ave	Chicago	IL	60707	**800-621-7613**	773-637-7100
SIG Mfg Company Inc 401 S Front St *Sales	Montezuma	IA	50171	**800-247-5008***	641-623-5154
Spin Master Ltd 450 Front St W	Toronto	ON	M5V1B6	**800-622-8339**	416-364-6002
Steiff North America 24 Albion Rd Ste 220	Lincoln	RI	02865	**888-978-3433**	401-312-0080
Swibco Inc 4810 Venture Rd	Lisle	IL	60532	**877-794-2261**	630-968-8900
Testor Corp 440 Blackhawk Pk Ave	Rockford	IL	61104	**800-837-8677**	815-962-6654
TOMY International Inc 1111 W 22nd St Ste 320	Oak Brook	IL	60523	**800-704-8697**	
Tonner Doll Co 301 Wall St PO Box 4410	Kingston	NY	12402	**800-794-2107**	845-339-9537
Uncle Milton Industries Inc 29209 Canwood St Ste 120 *General	Agoura	CA	91301	**800-869-7555***	818-707-0800
Universal Mfg Co Inc 5030 Mackey S	Overland Park	KS	66203	**800-524-5860**	913-815-6230
University Games Corp 2030 Harrison St	San Francisco	CA	94110	**800-347-4818**	415-503-1600
Upper Deck Co LLC 5909 Sea Otter Pl *Cust Svc	Carlsbad	CA	92010	**800-873-7332***	
Vermont Teddy Bear Company Inc 6655 Shelburne Rd	Shelburne	VT	05482	**800-988-8277**	802-985-3001
VTech Electronics North America LLC 1155 W Dundee St Ste 130	Arlington Heights	IL	60004	**800-521-2010**	847-400-3600
Wham-O Inc 6301 Owensmouth Ave Ste 700	Woodland Hills	CA	91367	**888-942-6650**	
William K Walthers Inc 5601 W Florist Ave	Milwaukee	WI	53218	**800-877-7171**	414-527-0770
Wizards of the Coast Inc 1600 Lind Ave SW Ste 400	Renton	WA	98057	**800-324-6496**	425-226-6500

TRAILERS - TRUCK

SEE Truck Trailers

761 TRAILERS (TOWING) & TRAILER HITCHES

Name / Address	City	State	ZIP	Toll-Free	Phone
Bright Co-op Inc 803 W Seale St	Nacogdoches	TX	75964	**800-562-0730**	936-564-8378
Cequent Towing Products 47774 Anchor Ct W	Plymouth	MI	48170	**800-521-0510**	
Cequent Trailer Products 1050 Indianhead Dr	Mosinee	WI	54455	**800-604-9466**	715-693-1700
CM Trailers Inc 200 County Rd PO Box 680	Madill	OK	73446	**888-268-7577**	580-795-5536
Com-Fab Inc 4657 Price HilliaRds Rd	Plain City	OH	43064	**866-522-1794**	740-857-1107
Dethmers Manufacturing Co (DEMCO) 4010 320th St	Boyden	IA	51234	**800-543-3626**	712-725-2311
EZ Loader Boat Trailers Inc 717 N Hamilton St	Spokane	WA	99202	**800-398-5623**	509-489-0181
Gooseneck Trailer Mfg Co 4400 E Hwy 21 PO Box 832 *Cust Svc	Bryan	TX	77808	**800-688-5490***	979-778-0034
Load Rite Trailers Inc 265 Lincoln Hwy	Fairless Hills	PA	19030	**800-562-3783**	215-949-0500
Midwest Industries Inc 122 E State Hwy 175	Ida Grove	IA	51445	**800-859-3028**	712-364-3365
Rigid Hitch Inc 3301 W Burnsville Pkwy *Cust Svc	Burnsville	MN	55337	**800-624-7630***	952-895-5001
Sundowner Trailers Inc 9805 S State Hwy 48	Coleman	OK	73432	**800-654-3879**	580-937-4255
Take 3 Trailers Inc 1808 Hwy 105	Brenham	TX	77833	**800-428-2533**	979-337-9568
Unique Functional Products Corp 135 Sunshine Ln	San Marcos	CA	92069	**800-854-1905**	760-744-1610

762 TRAINING & CERTIFICATION PROGRAMS - COMPUTER & INTERNET

Name / Address	City	State	ZIP	Toll-Free	Phone
Animation Mentor 1400 65th St Ste 250	Emeryville	CA	94608	**877-326-4628**	
ASPE Inc 114 Edinburgh S Dr Ste 200	Cary	NC	27511	**877-800-5221**	
Computer Workshop Inc, The 5131 Post Rd Ste 102	Dublin	OH	43017	**800-639-3535**	614-798-9505
Coyne College Inc 330 N Green St	Chicago	IL	60607	**800-707-1922**	773-577-8100
Global Knowledge Training LLC 9000 Regency Pkwy Ste 500	Cary	NC	27518	**800-268-7737**	919-461-8600
Health & Safety Institute Inc 1450 Westec Dr	Eugene	OR	97402	**800-447-3177**	
It4ce Inc 1200 Aerowood Dr	Mississauga	ON	L4W2S7	**877-470-0008**	905-206-9947
Learning Tree International Inc 1831 Michael Faraday Dr *OTC: LTRE* ■ *Cust Svc	Reston	VA	20190	**800-843-8733***	703-709-9119
Metex Inc 789 Don Mills Rd Ste 218	North York	ON	M3C1T5	**866-817-8137**	416-203-8388
MindLeaders.com Inc 5500 Glendon Ct Ste 200	Dublin	OH	43016	**800-223-3732**	614-781-7300
My Service Depot 8774 Cotter St	Lewis Center	OH	43035	**888-518-0818**	
New Horizons Computer Learning Centers Inc 1900 S State College Blvd Ste 450	Anaheim	CA	92806	**888-236-3625**	714-940-8000
New Horizons Worldwide Inc 1900 S State College Blvd Ste 450	Anaheim	CA	92806	**888-236-3625**	
Optimum Talent Inc 25 York St Ste 1802	Toronto	ON	M5J2V5	**877-364-2605**	416-364-2605
Parker University 2540 Walnut Hill Ln	Dallas	TX	75229	**800-637-8337**	972-438-6932
PowerScore Inc 57 Hasell St	Charleston	SC	29401	**800-545-1750**	

763 TRAINING PROGRAMS - CORPORATE

Name / Address	City	State	ZIP	Toll-Free	Phone
AchieveGlobal Inc 8875 Hidden River Pkwy Ste 400	Tampa	FL	33637	**800-566-0630**	
ActionCOACH 5781 S Ft Apache Rd	Las Vegas	NV	89148	**888-483-2828**	702-795-3188
Baker Communications Inc 10101 SW Fwy #630	Houston	TX	77074	**877-253-8506**	713-627-7700
Christy Capital Management Inc 2939 Mcmanus Rd	Macon	GA	31220	**866-331-7749**	478-314-2160
ClickSafety.com Inc 2185 N California Blvd Ste 425	Walnut Creek	CA	94596	**800-971-1080**	
Creative Training Techniques International Inc 14530 Martin Dr	Eden Prairie	MN	55344	**800-383-9210**	952-829-1954
Dale Carnegie & Assoc Inc 290 Motor Pkwy	Hauppauge	NY	11788	**800-231-5800**	
Don Hutson Organization 516 Tennessee St Ste 219	Memphis	TN	38103	**800-647-9166**	901-767-0000
Elite Business Services PO Box 9630	Rancho Santa Fe	CA	92067	**800-204-3548**	
Executive Enterprises Institute 12 Skyline Dr	Hawthorne	NY	10532	**877-334-4273**	914-517-1122
Franklin Covey Co 2200 West PkwyBlvd *NYSE: FC*	Salt Lake City	UT	84119	**800-827-1776**	801-817-1776
Fred Pryor Seminars 9757 Metcalf Ave	Overland Park	KS	66212	**800-780-8476**	
Frontline Group of Texas LLC 15021 Katy Fwy Ste 575	Houston	TX	77094	**800-285-5512**	281-453-6000
HealthStream Inc 209 Tenth Ave S Ste 450 *NASDAQ: HSTM*	Nashville	TN	37203	**800-933-9293**	615-301-3100
Hinda Incentives Inc 2440 W 34th St	Chicago	IL	60608	**866-487-2365**	773-890-5900
Insight Information 214 King St W Ste 300	Toronto	ON	M5H3S6	**888-777-1707**	416-777-2020
Invitechange LLC 110 Third Ave N Ste 102	Edmonds	WA	98020	**877-228-2622**	425-778-3505
ITC Learning Corp 1616 Anderson Rd Ste 109	McLean	VA	22102	**800-638-3757**	
Leadership Management Inc 4567 Lk Shore Dr	Waco	TX	76710	**800-568-1241**	254-776-2060
Levinson Institute Inc 28 Main St Ste 100	Jaffrey	NH	03452	**800-290-5735**	603-532-4700
National Businesswomen's Leadership Assn PO Box 419107	Kansas City	MO	64141	**800-258-7246**	913-432-7755
National Seminars Training 6900 Squibb Rd	Shawnee Mission	KS	66202	**800-258-7246**	913-432-7755
Pacific Institute 1709 Harbor Ave SW	Seattle	WA	98126	**800-426-3660**	206-628-4800
Priority Management Systems Inc 11160 Silversmith Pl	Richmond	BC	V7A5E4	**800-437-1032**	604-214-7772
Productivity Inc 375 Bridgeport Ave 3rd Fl	Shelton	CT	06484	**800-966-5423**	203-225-0451
Rockhurst University Continuing Education Ctr Inc PO Box 419107	Kansas City	MO	64141	**800-258-7246**	913-432-7755
Safety Sam Inc 2626 S Roosevelt St Ste 2	Tempe	AZ	85282	**866-478-6980**	

				Toll-Free	Phone
SkillSoft PLC 107 NE Blvd	Nashua	NH	03062	**877-545-5763**	603-324-3000
US Learning Inc 516 Tennessee St Ste 219	Memphis	TN	38103	**800-647-9166**	901-767-0000
Veriforce LLC 19221 I-45 S Ste 200	Shenandoah	TX	77385	**800-426-1604**	
Voice Pro Inc 2055 Lee Rd Ste 101	Cleveland	OH	44118	**800-261-0104**	216-932-8040
Wilson Learning Corp 8000 W 78th St Ste 200	Edina	MN	55439	**800-328-7937**	952-944-2880

764 TRAINING PROGRAMS (MISC)

SEE ALSO Training & Certification Programs - Computer & Internet ; Training Programs - Corporate ; Children's Learning Centers

				Toll-Free	Phone
Academy for Guided Imagery Inc 10780 Santa Monica Blvd Ste 290	Los Angeles	CA	90025	**800-726-2070**	
Audio-Digest Foundation 1577 E Chevy Chase Dr	Glendale	CA	91206	**800-423-2308**	818-240-7500
Canter & Assoc LLC 12975 Coral Tree Pl *Cust Svc	Los Angeles	CA	90066	**800-669-9011***	310-578-4700
Ed Necco & Assoc 178 Private Dr	South Point	OH	45680	**866-996-3226**	513-771-9600
Executive Protection Institute 16 Penn Plz Ste 1570	New York	NY	10001	**800-947-5827**	212-268-4555
Global University 1211 S Glenstone Ave	Springfield	MO	65804	**800-443-1083**	417-862-9533
Mission Essential Personnel LLC 4343 Easton Commons Ste 100	Columbus	OH	43219	**888-542-3447**	614-416-2345
Outward Bound 910 Jackson St	Golden	CO	80401	**866-467-7651**	207-510-7533

765 TRANSFORMERS - POWER, DISTRIBUTION, SPECIALTY

				Toll-Free	Phone
Active Power Inc 2128 W Breaker Ln *NASDAQ: ACPW*	Austin	TX	78758	**800-625-1731**	512-836-6464
AFP Transformers Inc 206 Talmedge Rd	Edison	NJ	08817	**800-843-1215**	732-248-0305
Bodine Co PO Box 460	Collierville	TN	38027	**800-223-5728**	901-853-7211
Controlled Power Co 1955 Stephenson Hwy	Troy	MI	48083	**800-521-4792**	248-528-3700
DC Group Inc 1977 W River Rd N	Minneapolis	MN	55411	**800-838-7927**	
Delta Star Inc 270 Industrial Rd	San Carlos	CA	94070	**800-892-8673**	
Electric Research & Mfg Co-op Inc PO Box 1228	Dyersburg	TN	38025	**800-238-5587**	731-285-9121
Energy Transformation Systems Inc 43353 Osgood Rd	Fremont	CA	94539	**800-752-8208**	510-656-2012
Ensign Corp 201 Ensign Rd	Bellevue	IA	52031	**888-797-8658**	563-872-3900
Johnson Electric Coil Co 821 Watson St	Antigo	WI	54409	**800-826-9741**	715-627-4367
Legend Power Systems Inc 1480 Frances St	Vancouver	BC	V5L1Y9	**866-772-8797**	604-420-1500
Maruson Technology Corp 18557 Gale Ave	City Of Industry	CA	91748	**888-627-8766**	626-912-8388
Mesta Electronics Inc 11020 Parker Dr	North Huntingdon	PA	15642	**800-535-6798**	412-754-3000
MGM Transformer Co 5701 Smithway St	Commerce	CA	90040	**800-423-4366**	323-726-0888
Mirus International Inc 31 Sun Pac Blvd	Brampton	ON	L6S5P6	**888-866-4787**	905-494-1120
MTE Corp PO Box 9013	Menomonee Falls	WI	53051	**800-455-4683**	262-253-8200
Niagara Transformer Corp 1747 Dale Rd	Buffalo	NY	14225	**800-817-5652**	716-896-6500
Nova Power Solutions 23020 Eaglewood Ct Ste 100	Sterling	VA	20166	**800-999-6682**	
Olsun Electrics Corp 10901 Commercial St	Richmond	IL	60071	**800-336-5786**	
Philips Advance Light Elctro 10275 W Higgins Rd	Rosemont	IL	60018	**800-322-2086**	847-390-5000
Powersmiths International Corp 10 Devon Rd	Brampton	ON	L6T5B5	**800-747-9627**	905-791-1493
PWR LLC 6402 Deere Rd	Syracuse	NY	13206	**800-342-0878**	315-701-0210
Raf Technologies Inc 200 Lexington Ave	Deland	FL	32724	**888-876-6424**	386-736-1698
Shape LLC 2105 Corporate Dr	Addison	IL	60101	**800-367-5811**	630-620-8394
T & R Electric Supply Company Inc 308 SW Third St	Colman	SD	57017	**800-843-7994**	605-534-3555
Unique Lighting Systems Inc 1240 Simpson Way	Escondido	CA	92029	**800-955-4831**	
VanTran Industries Inc 7711 Imperial Dr	Waco	TX	76712	**800-433-3346**	254-772-9740
Virginia Transformer Corp 220 Glade View Dr	Roanoke	VA	24012	**800-882-3944**	540-345-9892
Waukesha Electric Systems Inc 400 S Prairie Ave	Waukesha	WI	53186	**800-835-2732**	262-547-0121

766 TRANSLATION SERVICES

SEE ALSO Language Schools

				Toll-Free	Phone
Argo Translation Inc 2420 Ravine Way Ste 200	Glenview	IL	60025	**888-961-9291**	847-901-4075
Birnbaum Interpreting Services 8730 Georgia Ave Ste 210	Silver Spring	MD	20910	**800-471-6441**	301-587-8885
Boston Language Institute Inc 648 Beacon St Kenmore Sq	Boston	MA	02215	**877-998-3500**	617-262-3500
Bridge-world Language Center Inc, The 110 Second St S Ste 213	Waite Park	MN	56387	**800-835-6870**	320-259-9239
Interpreters Unlimited Inc 11199 Sorrento Vly Rd Ste 203	San Diego	CA	92121	**800-726-9891**	
Kane Transport Inc 40925 403rd Ave	Sauk Centre	MN	56378	**800-892-8557**	320-352-2762
Language Line Services 1 Lower Ragsdale Dr Bldg 2	Monterey	CA	93940	**800-752-6096**	
Language Services Associates Inc 455 Business Ctr Dr - Ste 100	Horsham	PA	19044	**800-305-9673**	
Linguistics Systems Inc 201 Broadway	Cambridge	MA	02139	**877-654-5006**	
Masterword Services, International Inc 303 Stafford St	Houston	TX	77079	**866-716-4999**	281-589-0810
Merritt Interpreting Services 3626 N Hall St Ste 504	Dallas	TX	75219	**866-761-2585**	214-969-5585
Spanish-American Translating 330 Eagle Ave	West Hempstead	NY	11552	**800-870-5790**	516-481-3339
Vocalink Language Services 405 W First St Unit A	Dayton	OH	45402	**877-492-7754**	937-223-1415

767 TRANSPLANT CENTERS - BLOOD STEM CELL

				Toll-Free	Phone
Arthur G James Cancer Hospital & Richard J Solove Research Institute *Bone Marrow Transplant Program* 300 W Tenth Ave Ste 519	Columbus	OH	43210	**800-293-5066**	
Blood Donor Ctr at Presbyterian/St Luke's Medical Ctr 1719 E 19th Ave	Denver	CO	80218	**800-231-2222**	303-839-6000
Children's Hospital of New York-Presbyterian *Pediatric Blood & Marrow Transplantation Program* 3959 Broadway	New York	NY	10032	**866-463-2778**	212-305-5593
Children's Hospital of Orange County Blood & Donor Services 505 S Main St	Orange	CA	92868	**800-228-5234**	714-509-8339
Children's Hospital of Philadelphia Stem Cell Transplant Program 3401 Civic Ctr Blvd	Philadelphia	PA	19104	**800-879-2467**	
City of Hope National Medical Ctr Hematology & Hematopoietic Cell Transplantation Div 1500 E Duarte Rd	Duarte	CA	91010	**800-826-4673**	626-256-4673
Cleveland Clinic Bone Marrow Transplantation Program 9500 Euclid Ave	Cleveland	OH	44195	**800-223-2273**	216-444-0261
Dana-Farber Cancer Institute Stem Cell/Bone Marrow Transplant Program 450 Brookline Ave Dana 2	Boston	MA	02115	**866-408-3324**	617-632-3591
Fairfax PET Imaging Ctr 8503 Arlington Blvd Ste 120 Lowr Level	Fairfax	VA	22031	**800-358-8831**	703-698-4441
Froedtert Hospital Bone Marrow Transplant Program 9200 W Wisconsin Ave	Milwaukee	WI	53226	**800-272-3666**	414-805-3666
H Lee Moffitt Cancer Ctr & Research Institute Blood & Marrow Transplantation Program 12902 Magnolia Dr	Tampa	FL	33612	**888-663-3488**	
Helen DeVos Children's Hospital Pediatric Hematology/Oncology Program 100 Michigan NE	Grand Rapids	MI	49503	**866-989-7999**	616-391-9000
Indiana University Cancer Ctr Bone Marrow & Stem Cell Transplant Team 550 N University Blvd	Indianapolis	IN	46202	**888-600-4822**	317-948-6997
James Graham Brown Cancer Ctr 529 S Jackson St	Louisville	KY	40202	**866-530-5516**	502-562-4369
Karmanos Cancer Institute Bone Marrow/Stem Cell Transplant Program 4100 John R	Detroit	MI	48201	**800-527-6266**	
Mount Sinai Hospital Bone Marrow Transplant Program 19 E 98th St	New York	NY	10029	**866-682-9380**	212-241-6021
North Shore-Long Island Jewish Health System *Bone Marrow & Blood Cell Transplant Program* 300 Community Dr	Manhasset	NY	11030	**888-321-3627**	516-562-8973
Oregon Health & Science University *Bone Marrow Transplant Program (OHSU)* 3181 SW Sam Jackson Pk Rd	Portland	OR	97239	**800-222-1222**	503-494-1617
Penn State Milton S Hershey Medical Ctr Bone Marrow Transplantation Program 500 University Dr	Hershey	PA	17033	**800-243-1455**	717-531-1657
Roswell Park Cancer Institute Blood & Marrow Transplantation Program Elm & Carlton Sts	Buffalo	NY	14263	**800-685-6825**	716-845-3516
Saint Jude Children's Research Hospital Stem Cell Transplantation Div 262 Danny Thomas Pl	Memphis	TN	38105	**800-822-6344**	901-595-3300
Seattle Cancer Care Alliance 825 Eastlake Ave E PO Box 19023	Seattle	WA	98109	**800-804-8824**	206-288-1024
Stanford University School of Medicine Blood & Marrow Transplant Program 300 Pasteur Dr Rm H-3249 MC 5623	Stanford	CA	94305	**888-275-5724**	650-723-0822
Texas Transplant Institute 7700 Floyd Curl Dr	San Antonio	TX	78229	**800-298-7824**	210-575-3817
University Medical Ctr Blood & Marrow Transplantation Program 1400 Morreene Rd PO Box 24-5176	Durham	NC	27705	**800-524-5928**	520-694-0111
University of Maryland Greenebaum Cancer Ctr 22 S Greene St Ste N9E17	Baltimore	MD	21201	**800-888-8823**	410-328-7904
University of Miami Hospital & Clinics (UMHC) *Sylvester Comprehensive Cancer Ctr* 1475 NW 12th Ave	Miami	FL	33136	**800-545-2292**	305-243-1000
University of Nebraska Medical Ctr Bone Marrow & Stem Cell Transplantation Program (Adults) 987400 Nebraska Medical Ctr	Omaha	NE	68198	**800-922-0000**	402-559-2000
University of Pittsburgh Medical Ctr (UPMC) *Horizon* 110 N Main St	Greenville	PA	16125	**888-447-1122**	724-588-2100
University of Texas Southwestern Medical Ctr Dallas *Hematopoietic Cell Transplant Program* 2201 Inwood Rd 2nd Fl	Dallas	TX	75390	**866-645-6455**	214-645-4673
University of Utah Hospital & Clinics (UUHSC) *Blood & Marrow Transplant Program* 50 N Medical Dr *General	Salt Lake City	UT	84132	**800-824-2073***	801-581-2121
VA Puget Sound Health Care System - Seattle Div 1660 S Columbian Way	Seattle	WA	98108	**800-329-8387**	206-762-1010
Winship Cancer Institute of Emory University 1365 Clifton Rd NE	Atlanta	GA	30322	**888-946-7447**	404-778-1900

768 TRANSPORTATION EQUIPMENT & SUPPLIES - WHOL

				Toll-Free	Phone
A & K Railroad Materials Inc 1505 S Redwood Rd *Sales	Salt Lake City	UT	84104	**800-453-8812***	801-974-5484

Classified Section

Name / Address	City	State	ZIP	Toll-Free	Phone
AAR Aircraft Turbine Ctr 1100 N Wood Dale Rd 1 AAR Pl *General	Wood Dale	IL	60191	**800-422-2213***	630-227-2000
AAR Corp 1100 N Wood Dale Rd 1 AAR Pl *NYSE: AIR*	Wood Dale	IL	60191	**800-422-2213**	630-227-2000
AAR Defense Systems & Logistics 1100 N Wood Dale Rd 1 AAR Pl	Wood Dale	IL	60191	**877-227-9200**	630-227-2000
AAR Distribution 1100 N Wood Dale Rd 1 AAR Pl	Wood Dale	IL	60191	**800-422-2213**	630-227-2000
Airparts Company Inc 2310 NW 55th Ct	Fort Lauderdale	FL	33309	**800-392-4999**	954-739-3575
Argo International Corp 160 Chubb Ave	Lyndhurst	NJ	07071	**877-274-6468**	201-561-7010
Atlantic Track & Turnout Co 270 N Broad St	Bloomfield	NJ	07003	**800-631-1274**	973-748-5885
Birmingham Rail & Locomotive Company Inc PO Box 530157	Birmingham	AL	35253	**800-241-2260**	205-424-7245
Cargo Equipment Corp 640 Church Rd	Elgin	IL	60123	**888-557-8727**	847-741-7272
DAC International Inc 6702 McNeil Dr	Austin	TX	78729	**800-527-2531**	512-331-5323
Defender Industries Inc 42 Great Neck Rd	Waterford	CT	06385	**800-628-8225**	860-701-3400
Donovan Marine Inc 6316 Humphreys St	Harahan	LA	70123	**800-347-4464**	504-488-5731
Dreyfus-Cortney & Lowery Bros Rigging 4400 N Galvez St	New Orleans	LA	70117	**800-228-7660**	504-944-3366
E-Z-GO Division of Textron Inc 1451 Marvin Griffin Rd	Augusta	GA	30906	**800-241-5855**	706-798-4311
Edmo Distributors Inc 12830 E Mirabeau Pkwy	Spokane Valley	WA	99216	**800-235-3300**	509-535-8280
ERS Industries Inc 1005 Indian Church Rd	West Seneca	NY	14224	**800-993-6446**	716-675-2040
Fisheries Supply Co 1900 N Northlake Way	Seattle	WA	98103	**800-426-6930**	206-632-4462
Freundlich Supply Co Inc 2200 Arthur Kill Rd	Staten Island	NY	10309	**800-221-0260**	718-356-1500
Heli-Mart Inc 3184 Airway Ave Unit E	Costa Mesa	CA	92626	**800-826-6899**	714-755-2999
Helicopter Support Inc (HSI) 124 Quarry Rd	Trumbull	CT	06611	**800-795-6051**	203-416-4000
Heubel Material Handling Inc 6311 NE Equitable Rd	Kansas City	MO	64120	**800-283-4177**	
Industry-Railway Suppliers Inc 811 Golf Ln	Bensenville	IL	60106	**800-728-0029**	630-766-5708
Intermountain Air LLC 301 N 2370 W	Salt Lake City	UT	84116	**800-433-9617**	801-322-1645
Jerry's Marine Service 100 SW 16th St	Fort Lauderdale	FL	33315	**800-432-2231**	
JJ MacKay Canada Ltd 1342 Abercrombie Rd	New Glasgow	NS	B2H5C6	**888-462-2529**	902-752-5124
Kellogg Marine Supply Inc 5 Enterprise Dr	Old Lyme	CT	06371	**800-243-9303**	860-434-6002
Marine Depot 14271 Corporate Dr	Garden Grove	CA	92843	**800-566-3474**	
Markey Machinery Company Inc 7266 Eigth Ave S	Seattle	WA	98108	**800-637-3430**	206-622-4697
Material Handling Products Corp 6601 Joy Rd	East Syracuse	NY	13057	**866-980-4788**	315-437-2891
Norlift of Oregon Inc 7373 Se Milwaukie Expy	Portland	OR	97222	**888-716-2478**	503-659-5438
O'halloran International Inc 3311 Adventureland Dr	Altoona	IA	50009	**800-800-6503**	515-967-3300
Parker-Hannifin Corp 1160 Ctr Rd	Avon	OH	44011	**800-272-5464**	440-937-6211
PartsBase Inc 905 Clint Moore Rd *Cust Svc	Boca Raton	FL	33487	**888-322-6896***	561-953-0700
Paxton Co 1111 Ingleside Rd	Norfolk	VA	23502	**800-234-7290**	757-853-6781
Railhead Corp 12549 S Laramie Ave	Alsip	IL	60803	**800-235-1782**	708-844-5500
Rails Co 101 Newark Way	Maplewood	NJ	07040	**800-217-2457**	973-763-4320
Railtech Ltd 325 Lee Ave	Montreal	QC	H9X3S3	**877-759-3653**	514-457-4760
S-Line Cargo Control & Safety Products 11414 Mathis	Dallas	TX	75234	**800-687-9900**	
Sooner Lift Inc 3401 S Purdue St	Oklahoma City	OK	73179	**800-593-2830**	405-682-1400
Spencer Industries Inc 19308 68th Ave S	Kent	WA	98032	**800-367-5646**	253-796-1100
Standard Equipment Company Inc 75 Beauregard St	Mobile	AL	36602	**800-239-3442**	251-432-1705
Tanks-A-Lot Ltd 1810 Yellowhead Trail N.E.	Edmonton	AB	T6S1B4	**800-661-5667**	780-472-8265
Tornado Alley Turbo 300 Airport Rd	Ada	OK	74820	**877-359-8284**	580-332-3510
Valley Power Systems Inc 425 S Hacienda Blvd	City of Industry	CA	91745	**800-924-4265**	626-333-1243
Van Bortel Aircraft Inc 4912 S Collins	Arlington	TX	76018	**800-759-4295**	817-468-7788
Washington Chain & Supply Inc 2901 Utah Ave S PO Box 3645	Seattle	WA	98124	**800-851-3429**	206-623-8500
West Marine Inc 500 Westridge Dr *NASDAQ: WMAR*	Watsonville	CA	95076	**800-262-8464**	831-728-2700
Yingling Aircraft Inc 2010 Airport Rd	Wichita	KS	67209	**800-835-0083**	316-943-3246
ZAP 501 Fourth St *OTC: ZAAP* ■ *Orders	Santa Rosa	CA	95401	**800-251-4555***	707-525-8658

769 TRAVEL AGENCIES

SEE ALSO Tour Operators ; Travel Agency Networks

Name / Address	City	State	ZIP	Toll-Free	Phone
ABC Global Services 6400 Shafer Ct Ste 310	Rosemont	IL	60018	**800-722-5179**	
Adelman Travel Group 6980 N Port Washington Rd *Cust Svc	Milwaukee	WI	53217	**800-248-5562***	414-352-7600
ADTRAV Travel Management 4555 S Lake Pkwy	Birmingham	AL	35244	**800-476-2952**	205-444-4800
AESU Travel Inc 3922 Hickory Ave	Baltimore	MD	21211	**800-638-7640**	410-366-5494
Alamo Travel Group Inc 8930 Wurzbach Rd	San Antonio	TX	78240	**800-692-5266**	210-593-0084
Alaska Tour & Travel 9170 Jewel Lk Rd Ste 202 PO Box 221011	Anchorage	AK	99502	**800-208-0200**	907-245-0200
Alaska Travel Adventures Inc 9085 Glacier Hwy Ste 301	Juneau	AK	99801	**800-323-5757**	907-789-0052
All Aboard Cruises Inc 11114 SW 127th Ct	Miami	FL	33186	**800-883-8657**	305-385-8657
All Cruise Travel 1723 Hamilton Ave	San Jose	CA	95125	**800-227-8473**	408-295-1200
All-Inclusive Vacations Inc 1595 Iris St	Lakewood	CO	80215	**866-980-6483**	303-980-6483
Apple Vacations Inc 101 NW Pt Blvd	Elk Grove Village	IL	60007	**800-517-2000**	
Avanti Destinations Inc 1629 SW Salmon St	Portland	OR	97205	**800-422-5053**	503-295-1100
Balboa Travel Management Inc 5414 Oberlin Dr Ste 300	San Diego	CA	92121	**800-359-8773**	858-678-3300
Best Travel Inc 8600 W Bryn Mawr Ave	Chicago	IL	60631	**800-927-7357**	773-380-0150
Bon Voyage Travel 1640 E River Rd Ste 115	Tucson	AZ	85718	**800-439-7963**	520-797-1110
Brownell World Travel 216 Summit Blvd Ste 220	Birmingham	AL	35243	**800-999-3960**	205-802-6222
Burkhalter Travel Agency 6501 Mineral Pt Rd	Madison	WI	53705	**800-556-9286**	608-833-5200
Carefree Vacations Inc 11885 Carmel Mt Rd Ste 906	San Diego	CA	92128	**800-266-3476**	858-450-4060
Cass Tours 2621 Green River Rd Ste 105-222	Corona	CA	92882	**800-593-6510**	951-371-3511
Casto Travel Inc 2560 N First St Ste 150	San Jose	CA	95131	**800-832-3445**	408-984-7000
City Escape Holidays 13470 Washington Blvd Ste 101	Marina del Rey	CA	90292	**800-222-0022**	
Classic Custom Vacations 5893 Rue Ferrari	San Jose	CA	95138	**800-635-1333**	
Clipper Navigation Inc 2701 Alaskan Way Pier 69	Seattle	WA	98121	**800-888-2535**	206-443-2560
Conlin Travel Inc 3270 Washtenaw Ave	Ann Arbor	MI	48104	**800-426-6546**	734-677-0900
Corporate Travel Management Group 450 E 22nd St	Lombard	IL	60148	**866-545-6789**	630-691-8000
Covington International Travel 4401 Dominion Blvd	Glen Allen	VA	23060	**800-922-9238**	804-747-7077
Crown Travel & Cruises 240 Newton Rd Ste 106	Raleigh	NC	27615	**800-869-7447**	919-870-1986
Cruise Brokers 2803 W Busch Blvd Ste 100	Tampa	FL	33618	**800-409-1919**	813-288-9597
Cruise Concepts 1329 Eniswood Pkwy	Palm Harbor	FL	34683	**800-752-7963**	727-784-7245
Cruise Connection LLC 7932 N Oak Ste 210	Kansas City	MO	64118	**800-572-0004**	816-420-8688
Cruise Connections Inc 3411 Healy Dr Ste D	Winston-Salem	NC	27103	**800-248-7447**	
Cruise People Inc 10191 W Sample Rd Ste 215	Coral Springs	FL	33065	**800-642-2469**	954-753-0069
Cruise People Ltd 1252 Lawrence Ave E Ste 210	Don Mills	ON	M3A1C3	**800-268-6523**	416-444-2410
Cruise Shop, The 700 Pasquinelli Dr Ste C	Westmont	IL	60559	**800-622-6456**	630-325-7447
Cruise Vacation Ctr 2042 Central Pk Ave	Yonkers	NY	10710	**800-803-7245**	
Cruise Web Inc 3901 Calverton Blvd Ste 350	Calverton	MD	20705	**800-377-9383**	240-487-0155
CruiseOne Inc 1201 W Cypress Creek Rd Ste 100	Fort Lauderdale	FL	33309	**800-278-4731**	
Cruises Cruises 6604 Antoine Dr	Houston	TX	77091	**800-245-9806**	713-681-9866
Cruises Inc 1201 W Cypress Creek Rd Ste 100 *Cust Svc	Fort Lauderdale	FL	33309	**888-282-1249***	
Direct Travel 95 New Jersey 17	Paramus	NJ	07652	**800-831-1366**	201-847-9000
E Tour & Travel 3626 Quadrangle Blvd Ste 400 *Sales	Orlando	FL	32817	**800-339-5120***	407-515-2400
Elegant Voyages 1802 Keesling Ct	San Jose	CA	95125	**800-555-3534**	408-239-0300
Euro Lloyd Travel Inc 1640 Hempstead Tpke	East Meadow	NY	11554	**800-334-2724**	516-228-4970
Friendly Cruises 3081 S Sycamore Village Dr	Superstition Mountain	AZ	85118	**888-842-1786**	480-358-1496
Gant Travel Management 400 W Seventh St Ste 233 *Cust Svc	Bloomington	IN	47404	**800-742-4198***	
Gil Tours Travel Inc 1511 Walnut St 2nd Fl	Philadelphia	PA	19102	**800-223-3855**	215-568-6655
Giselle's Travel Inc 1300 Ethan Way Ste 100	Sacramento	CA	95825	**800-782-5545**	916-922-5500
Global Travel 900 W Jefferson St	Boise	ID	83702	**800-584-8888**	208-387-1000
GOGO WorldWide Vacations 69 Spring St	Ramsey	NJ	07446	**800-254-3477**	
Golden Sports Tours 301 W Parker Rd Ste 206	Plano	TX	75023	**800-966-8258**	
Gwin's Travel Planners Inc 212 N Kirkwood Rd	Saint Louis	MO	63122	**800-433-9211**	314-822-1957

Classified Section

Name / Address	City	State	Zip	Toll-Free	Phone
Islands in the Sun Cruises & Tours Inc 121 Bayview	Grasonville	MD	21638	**800-278-7786**	410-827-3812
Japan Travel Bureau USA Inc 156 W 56th St	New York	NY	10019	**800-235-3523**	212-698-4900
Lawyers' Travel Service 71 Fifth Ave *General	New York	NY	10003	**800-431-1112***	
Liberty Travel Inc 69 Spring St	Ramsey	NJ	07446	**888-271-1584**	201-934-3500
Lorraine Travel Bureau Inc 377 Alhambra Cir	Coral Gables	FL	33134	**800-666-8911**	305-446-4433
Maupin Travel Inc 2501 Blue Ridge Rd	Raleigh	NC	27607	**800-786-2738**	919-821-2146
MC & A Inc 615 Piikoi St Ste 1000 *General	Honolulu	HI	96814	**877-589-5589***	808-589-5500
Merit Travel Group Inc 111 Peter St Ste 200	Toronto	ON	M5V2H1	**800-268-5940**	416-364-3775
Miller Travel Services Inc 4380 W 12th St	Erie	PA	16505	**800-989-8747**	814-833-8888
Montrose Travel 2355 Honolulu Ave	Montrose	CA	91020	**800-766-4687**	
More Hawaii for Less Inc 11 Ash Tree Ln Ste 290	Irvine	CA	92660	**800-967-6687**	949-724-5050
National Discount Cruise Co 1401 N Cedar Crest Blvd Ste 110	Allentown	PA	18104	**800-788-8108**	610-439-4883
Northstar Cruises 80 Bloomfield Ave Ste 102	Caldwell	NJ	07006	**800-249-9360**	
Ocean One Cruise Outlet 3264 Marilynn St	Lancaster	CA	93536	**888-353-1922**	661-949-2873
Omega World Travel Inc 3102 Omega Office Pk Dr	Fairfax	VA	22031	**800-756-6342**	703-359-0200
Orvis International Travel 178 Conservation Way	Sunderland	VT	05250	**800-547-4322**	802-362-8790
Paradise Island Vacations 1000 S Pine Island Rd Ste 800 *Resv	Plantation	FL	33324	**888-877-7525***	954-809-2000
Pleasant Holidays LLC 2404 Townsgate Rd	Westlake Village	CA	91361	**800-742-9244**	818-991-3390
Premier Golf 4355 River Green Pkwy	Duluth	GA	30096	**866-260-4409**	770-291-4202
Prestige Travel & Cruises Inc 6175 Spring Mountain Rd	Las Vegas	NV	89146	**800-758-5693**	702-251-5552
Professional Travel Inc 25000 Great Northern Corporate Ctr Ste 170	Cleveland	OH	44070	**800-247-0060**	440-734-8800
Protravel International Inc 515 Madison Ave 10th Fl	New York	NY	10022	**800-227-1059**	212-755-4550
Regal Travel 615 Piikoi St Ste 104	Honolulu	HI	96814	**800-799-0865**	808-566-7620
Rich Worldwide Travel Inc 500 Mamaroneck Ave	Harrison	NY	10528	**800-431-1130**	914-835-7600
Roeder Travel Ltd 9805 York Rd	Cockeysville	MD	21030	**800-379-9887**	410-667-6090
Seaside Golf Vacations 218 Main St	North Myrtle Beach	SC	29582	**877-732-6999**	
SGH Golf Inc 6805 Mt Vernon Ave	Cincinnati	OH	45227	**800-284-8884**	513-984-0414
Sita World Travel Inc 16250 Ventura Blvd	Encino	CA	91436	**800-421-5643**	818-990-9530
Sports Empire PO Box 6169	Lakewood	CA	90714	**800-255-5258**	562-920-2350
Star Travel Services Inc 1025 Acuff Rd	Bloomington	IN	47404	**800-542-1687**	812-336-6811
Sterling Cruises & Travel 8700 W Flagler St	Miami	FL	33174	**800-435-7967**	305-592-2522
Stevens Travel Management Inc 119 W 40th St 14th Fl	New York	NY	10018	**800-275-7400**	212-696-4300
Studentcity.com Inc 8 Essex Ctr Dr	Peabody	MA	01960	**888-777-4642**	
SunQuest Vacations 77-6435 Kuakini Hwy	Kailua-Kona	HI	96740	**800-367-5168**	808-329-6438
Sunsational Cruises 2470 E Glen Canyon Rd	Green Valley	AZ	85614	**800-239-6252**	480-491-6248
Tenenbaum's Vacation Stores Inc 300 Market St	Kingston	PA	18704	**800-545-7099**	570-288-8747
Tower Travel Management 53 Ogden Ave	Clarendon Hills	IL	60514	**800-542-9700**	
Tramex Travel Inc 4505 Spicewood Springs Rd Ste 200	Austin	TX	78759	**800-527-3039**	512-343-2201
Transat AT Inc 300 Leo-Pariseau St Ste 600 *TSE: TRZ.B*	Montreal	QC	H2X4C2	**800-387-0825**	514-987-1616
Travel & Transport Inc 2120 S 72nd St	Omaha	NE	68124	**800-228-2545**	402-399-4500
Travel Destinations Management Group Inc 110 Painters Mill Rd	Owings Mills	MD	21117	**800-635-7307**	410-363-3111
Travel Impressions Ltd 465 Smith St	Farmingdale	NY	11735	**800-284-0044**	631-845-8000
Travel Inc 4355 River Green Pkwy	Duluth	GA	30096	**888-439-1831**	770-291-4100
Travel Team Inc 2495 Main St	Buffalo	NY	14214	**800-245-8326**	716-862-7600
Travelennium Inc 556 Colonial Rd	Memphis	TN	38117	**800-844-4924**	901-767-0761
Traveline Travel Agencies Inc 4074 Erie St	Willoughby	OH	44094	**888-700-8747**	440-602-8020
Travelong Inc 135 W 50th St Ste 500	New York	NY	10020	**800-537-6043**	212-736-2166
TravelStore Inc 11601 Wilshire Blvd	Los Angeles	CA	90025	**800-850-3224**	310-575-5540
Ultramar Travel Management International 14 E 47th St 5th Fl	New York	NY	10017	**888-856-2929**	
Valerie Wilson Travel Inc 475 Pk Ave S	New York	NY	10016	**800-776-1116**	212-532-3400
Virtuoso 505 Main St Ste 5	Fort Worth	TX	76102	**800-401-4274**	817-870-0300
World Travel Bureau Inc 618 N Main St	Santa Ana	CA	92701	**800-899-3370**	714-835-8111
World Travel Holdings (WTH) 100 Fordham Rd Bldg C Bldg C	Wilmington	MA	01887	**877-958-7447**	617-424-7990
World Travel Inc 1724 W Schuylkill Rd	Douglassville	PA	19518	**877-265-1881**	610-327-9000
Worldwide Holidays Inc 7800 Red Rd Ste 112	South Miami	FL	33143	**800-327-9854**	305-665-0841
Worldwide Travel & Cruise Assoc Inc 150 S University Dr Ste E	Plantation	FL	33324	**800-881-8484**	954-452-8800
Wright Travel Inc 2505 21st Ave S 5th Fl	Nashville	TN	37212	**800-577-0888**	615-783-1111

770 TRAVEL AGENCY NETWORKS

SEE ALSO Travel Agencies

A travel agency network is a consortium of travel agencies in which a host agency provides technology, marketing, distribution, customer support, and other services to the network member agencies in exchange for a percentage of the member agencies' profits.

Name / Address	City	State	Zip	Toll-Free	Phone
Alice Travel Luxury Cruises & Tour 277 Fairfield Rd Ste 218	Fairfield	NJ	07004	**800-229-2542**	
All Direct Travel Services Inc 19000 Macarthur Blvd Ste 625	Irvine	CA	92612	**800-862-1516**	949-474-8100
American Express Company Inc World Financial Ctr 200 Vesey St *NYSE: AXP*	New York	NY	10285	**800-528-4800**	212-640-2000
Berkeleys Northside Travel Inc 1824 Euclid Ave	Berkeley	CA	94709	**800-575-3411**	510-843-1000
Carlson Wagonlit Travel Inc 701 Carlson Pkwy	Minnetonka	MN	55305	**800-213-7295**	
Chartered Business Valuators 277 Wellington St W Ste 710	Toronto	ON	M5V3H2	**866-770-7315**	416-977-1117
Classic Travel Inc 4767 Okemos Rd	Okemos	MI	48864	**800-643-3449**	517-349-6200
CP Franchising LLC 3300 University Dr	Coral Springs	FL	33065	**800-683-0206**	954-344-8060
Cruise Brothers, The 950 Wellington Ave	Cranston	RI	02910	**800-827-7779**	
Cruise Deals.com 11111 Carmel Commons Blvd Ste 210	Charlotte	NC	28226	**800-668-6414**	704-542-6414
Cruisecheapcom 220 Congress Park Dr Ste 140	Delray Beach	FL	33445	**800-543-1915**	561-243-2100
CruiseOne Inc 1201 W Cypress Creek Rd Ste 100	Fort Lauderdale	FL	33309	**800-278-4731**	
D&F Travel Inc 338 Central Ave Ste 320	Dunkirk	NY	14048	**800-832-3516**	
Ensemble Travel 256 W 38th St 11th Fl	New York	NY	10018	**800-576-2378**	212-545-7460
Expedition Trips.com 6553 California Ave Sw	Seattle	WA	98136	**877-412-8527**	206-547-0700
Frosch International Travel Inc 1 Greenway Plz Ste 800	Houston	TX	77046	**800-866-1623**	
Gateway Travel Service Inc 28470 W 13 Mile Rd Ste 200	Farmington Hills	MI	48334	**800-423-4898**	248-432-8600
Georgia Hardy Tours 20 Eglinton Ave East	Toronto	ON	M4R1K8	**800-813-4509**	416-483-7533
Global Travel International 2600 Lk Lucien Dr Ste 201	Maitland	FL	32751	**800-715-4440**	407-660-7800
Goway Travel Ltd 3284 Yonge St Ste 300	Toronto	ON	M4N3M7	**800-665-4432**	416-322-1034
GTI Corporate Travel 111 Township Line Rd	Jenkintown	PA	19046	**800-223-3863**	215-379-6800
Happy Time Tours & Travel 1475 Walsh St W	Thunder Bay	ON	P7E4X6	**800-473-5955**	807-473-5955
HMJ Inc 212 W Colfax Ave	South Bend	IN	46601	**800-347-7986**	574-232-3061
Hume Travel Corp 401 WGeorgia St Ste 1680	Vancouver	BC	V6B5A1	**800-663-9787**	604-682-7581
Hunter Travel Managers 4683 Chabot Dr Ste 385	Pleasanton	CA	94588	**800-876-8785**	925-463-0560
Kahala Travel 3838 Camino Del Rio N Ste 300	San Diego	CA	92108	**800-852-8338**	619-282-8300
Luxury Link LLC 5200 W Century Blvd Ste 410	Los Angeles	CA	90045	**888-297-3299**	310-215-8060
MAST Vacation Partners Inc 635 Butterfield Rd Ste 150	Oakbrook Terrace	IL	60181	**855-824-9288**	630-889-9817
Music Celebrations International 1440 S Priest Dr Ste 102	Tempe	AZ	85281	**800-395-2036**	480-894-3330
New Wave Travel 1075 Bay St	Toronto	ON	M5S2B1	**800-463-1512**	416-928-3113
Nexion 6225 N State Hwy 161 Ste 450	Irving	TX	75038	**800-949-6410**	408-280-6410
Ohio Travel Association 130 E Chestnut St Ste 301	Columbus	OH	43215	**800-896-4682**	614-572-1931
Pan American Travel Services 320 East 900 South	Salt Lake City	UT	84111	**800-364-4359**	801-364-4300
Panda Travel 1017 Kapahulu Ave Fl 2	Honolulu	HI	96816	**800-303-6702**	808-734-1961
Premiere Travel Services Inc 7900 Westpark Dr Ste A60	Mclean	VA	22102	**800-458-8670**	703-893-2288
RADIUS 7700 Wisconsin Ave Ste 400	Bethesda	MD	20814	**800-989-3059**	301-718-9500
Raptim Humanitarian Travel 6420 Inducon Dr W Ste A	Sanborn	NY	14132	**800-272-7846**	716-754-9232
Red Label Vacations Inc 5450 Explorer Dr Ste 100	Mississauga	ON	L4W5N1	**866-573-3824**	905-283-6020
Results Travel 701 Carlson Pkwy	Minnetonka	MN	55305	**800-456-4000**	763-212-5000
Signal Travel & Tours Inc 219 E Main St	Niles	MI	49120	**800-811-1522**	269-684-2880
Strong Travel Services Inc 8214 Westche Ste 670	Dallas	TX	75225	**800-747-5670**	214-361-0027
Tangerine Travel Ltd 16017 Juanita Woodinville Way Ne Ste 201	Bothell	WA	98011	**800-678-8202**	425-822-2333
Thor Travel Services Inc 12202 Airport Way Ste 150	Broomfield	CO	80021	**800-825-1071**	303-439-4100

Name / Address	City	State	ZIP	Toll-Free	Phone
Tourism Richmond Inc South Tower 5811 Cooney Rd Ste 205	Richmond	BC	V6X3M1	**877-247-0777**	604-821-5474
Travel Berkley Springs 127 Fairfax St	Berkeley Springs	WV	25411	**800-447-8797**	304-258-9147
Travel One Inc 8009 34th Ave S 15th Fl	Minneapolis	MN	55425	**800-247-1311**	952-854-2551
Travelex International Inc 2061 N Barrington Rd	Hoffman Estates	IL	60169	**800-882-0499**	847-882-0400
UNIGLOBE Travel USA LLC 18662 MacArthur Blvd Ste 100	Irvine	CA	92612	**877-438-4338**	949-623-9000
Vacation.com Inc 1650 King St Ste 450	Alexandria	VA	22314	**800-843-0733**	
Virtuoso 505 Main St Ste 5	Fort Worth	TX	76102	**800-401-4274**	817-870-0300
WorldClass Travel Network 7831 Southtown Ctr Ste A	Bloomington	MN	55431	**800-234-3576**	952-835-8636
WorldTEK Event & Travel Management 1 Audubon Ste 400	New Haven	CT	06511	**800-233-5989**	203-772-0470

TRAVEL INFORMATION - CITY

SEE Convention & Visitors Bureaus

771 TRAVEL SERVICES - ONLINE

SEE ALSO Hotel Reservations Services

Name / Address	City	State	ZIP	Toll-Free	Phone
BedandBreakfast.com 700 Brazos St Ste B-700 *Sales	Austin	TX	78701	**800-462-2632***	512-322-2700
Cruises.com 100 Fordham Rd Bldg C	Wilmington	MA	01887	**800-288-6006**	
Hotwire.com 655 Montgomery St Ste 600 *Cust Svc	San Francisco	CA	94111	**866-468-9473***	415-343-8400
LastMinuteTravel.com Inc 220 E Central Pkwy Ste 4000	Altamonte Springs	FL	32701	**800-442-0568**	407-667-8700
Lonely Planet Online 150 Linden St	Oakland	CA	94607	**800-275-8555**	510-250-6400
National Recreation Reservation Service (NRRS) PO Box 140	Ballston Spa	NY	12020	**877-444-6777**	518-885-3639
Priceline.com LLC 800 Connecticut Ave *NASDAQ: PCLN*	Norwalk	CT	06854	**800-774-2354**	
ReserveAmerica Holdings Inc 2480 Meadowvale Blvd Ste 120	Mississauga	ON	L5N8M6	**877-444-6777**	
Vacation.com Inc 1650 King St Ste 450	Alexandria	VA	22314	**800-843-0733**	

772 TRAVEL & TOURISM INFORMATION - CANADIAN

Name / Address	City	State	ZIP	Toll-Free	Phone
Nova Scotia Dept of Tourism & Culture 1800 Argyle St PO Box 456	Halifax	NS	B3J2R5	**800-565-0000**	902-425-5781
NWT Tourism PO Box 610	Yellowknife	NT	X1A2N5	**800-661-0788**	867-873-7200
Ontario Tourism Marketing Partnership Corp 10 Dundas St E Ste 900	Toronto	ON	M7A2A1	**800-668-2746**	905-282-1721
Prince Edward Island Tourism PO Box 2000	Charlottetown	PE	C1A7N8	**800-463-4734**	902-368-4000
Tourism New Brunswick PO Box 6000	Fredericton	NB	E3B5H1	**800-561-0123**	
Tourism Saskatchewan 1621 Albert St	Regina	SK	S4P2S5	**877-237-2273**	306-787-9600
Tourism Yukon PO Box 2703	Whitehorse	YT	Y1A2C6	**800-661-0494**	
Travel Manitoba 155 Carlton St 7th Fl	Winnipeg	MB	R3C3H8	**800-665-0040**	204-927-7800

773 TRAVEL & TOURISM INFORMATION - FOREIGN TRAVEL

SEE ALSO Embassies & Consulates - Foreign, in the US

Name / Address	City	State	ZIP	Toll-Free	Phone
All World Travel Inc 314 Gilmer St	Sulphur Springs	TX	75482	**866-298-6067**	903-885-0896
Anguilla Tourist Marketing Office 246 Central Ave	White Plains	NY	10606	**800-553-4939**	914-287-2400
Antigua & Barbuda Dept of Tourism & Trade 305 E 47th St 6th Fl	New York	NY	10017	**888-268-4227**	212-541-4117
Aruba Tourism Authority 1750 Powder Springs St Ste 190	Marietta	GA	30064	**800-862-7822**	404-892-7822
Bahamas Tourism Office 1200 S Pine Island Rd Ste 750	Plantation	FL	33324	**800-327-7678**	954-236-9292
Bermuda Dept of Tourism 675 Third Ave 20th Fl	New York	NY	10017	**800-223-6106**	212-818-9800
Bike Friday Travel Systems 3364 W 11th Ave	Eugene	OR	97402	**800-777-0258**	541-687-0487
Blue Ribbon Travel-american 3601 W 76th St Ste 190	Minneapolis	MN	55435	**800-626-5309**	952-835-2724
Bonaire Government Tourist Office 80 Broad St Ste 3202 32nd Fl	New York	NY	10004	**877-267-2572**	212-956-5912
Caa Niagara 155 Main St E	Grimsby	ON	L3M1P2	**800-263-7272**	905-945-5555
Canyon Creek Travel Inc 333 W Campbell Rd Ste 440	Richardson	TX	75080	**800-952-1998**	972-238-1998
Cayman Islands Dept of Tourism 350 Fifth Ave	New York	NY	10118	**800-235-5888**	212-889-9009
China Travel Service Chicago Inc 2145b S China Pl	Chicago	IL	60616	**800-793-8856**	312-328-0688
Croatian National Tourist Office 350 Fifth Ave Ste 4003	New York	NY	10118	**800-829-4416**	212-279-8672
Duncan Hill Travel Ltd 2700 Beverly St	Duncan	BC	V9L5C7	**888-748-0391**	250-748-0391
Fiji Visitors Bureau 5777 W Century Blvd Ste 220	Los Angeles	CA	90045	**800-932-3454**	310-568-1616
Golden Anchor Travel 1909 Southwood St	Sarasota	FL	34231	**800-299-1125**	941-922-4070
Guided Tours of Trois-Rivieres 1457 Rue Notre Dame	Trois-Rivieres	QC	G9A4X4	**800-313-1123**	819-375-1122
Hong Kong Tourism Board 5670 Wilshire Blvd Ste 1230	Los Angeles	CA	90036	**800-282-4582**	323-938-4582
India Tourist Office 3550 Wilshire Blvd Ste 204 *General	Los Angeles	CA	90010	**800-425-1414***	213-380-8855
Israel Government Tourist Office 800 Second Ave 16th Fl	New York	NY	10017	**877-248-8687**	212-499-5660
Jamaica Tourist Board 5201 Blue Lagoon Dr Ste 670	Miami	FL	33126	**800-526-2422**	305-665-0557
Jordan Tourism Board (JTB) 1307 Dolley Madison Blvd Ste 2A	McLean	VA	22101	**877-733-5673**	703-243-7404
Kenya Tourism Board 6033 West Century Blvd Ste 900	Los Angeles	CA	90045	**800-223-6486**	310-649-7718
Korea National Tourism Organization 2 Executive Dr Ste 750	Fort Lee	NJ	07024	**800-868-7567**	201-585-0909
Mexico Tourism Board (CSTM) 225 N Michigan Ave Ste 1800 *General	Chicago	IL	60601	**800-446-3942***	
Ministry of Tourism of Dominican Republic 848 Brickell Ave	Miami	FL	33131	**888-358-9594**	305-358-2899
Monaco Government Tourist Office 565 Fifth Ave 23rd Fl	New York	NY	10017	**800-753-9696**	212-286-3330
Nova Tours & Travel Inc 504 Vine St	Liverpool	NY	13088	**800-543-6682**	315-451-0260
Plaza Travel 16530 Ventura Blvd Ste 106	Encino	CA	91436	**800-347-4447**	818-990-4053
Puerto Rico Tourism Co Paseo La Princesa	Old San Juan	PR	00902	**800-866-7827**	787-721-2400
Rail Europe Inc 44 S Broadway 11th Fl	White Plains	NY	10601	**800-361-7245**	914-682-2999
Russian National Tourist Office 224 W 30th St Ste 701	New York	NY	10001	**877-221-7120**	646-473-2233
Saint Lucia Tourist Board 800 Second Ave Ste 910	New York	NY	10017	**800-456-3984**	212-867-2950
Saint Vincent & the Grenadines Tourist Information Office 801 Second Ave 21st Fl	New York	NY	10017	**800-729-1726**	212-687-4981
Switzerland Tourism 608 Fifth Ave Ste 202	New York	NY	10020	**800-794-7795**	212-757-5944
Tourism Malaysia 818 W Seventh St Ste 970	Los Angeles	CA	90017	**800-336-6842**	213-689-9702
Tourism Saskatoon 202 Fourth Ave N	Saskatoon	SK	S7K0K1	**800-567-2444**	306-242-1206
Travel Network Corp, The 1920 Ave Rd	Toronto	ON	M5M4A1	**888-666-8747**	416-789-3271
Turks & Caicos Islands Tourism Office 225 W 35th St Ste 1200	New York	NY	10001	**800-241-0824**	646-375-8830
Voyages Groupe Ideal Inc 5415 Pare St Ste 1	Montreal	QC	H4P1P7	**800-342-9554**	514-342-9554

774 TREE SERVICES

SEE ALSO Landscape Design & Related Services

Name / Address	City	State	ZIP	Toll-Free	Phone
Arbor Tree Surgery Inc 802 Paso Robles St	Paso Robles	CA	93446	**800-247-8733**	805-239-1239
Asplundh Tree Expert Co 708 Blair Mill Rd	Willow Grove	PA	19090	**800-248-8733**	215-784-4200
Care of Trees Inc 2371 Foster Ave	Wheeling	IL	60090	**888-661-8268**	
Davey Tree Expert Co 1500 N Mantua St	Kent	OH	44240	**800-445-8733**	330-673-9511
FA Bartlett Tree Expert Co 1290 E Main St	Stamford	CT	06902	**877-227-8538**	203-323-1131
Lawn Dawg Inc 39 Simon St., Unit 14	Nashua	NH	03060	**888-993-3294**	
Lewis Tree Service Inc 300 Lucius Gordon Dr	West Henrietta	NY	14586	**800-333-1593**	585-436-3208
Nelson Tree Service Inc 3300 Office Pk Dr Ste 205	Dayton	OH	45439	**800-522-4311**	937-294-1313
Trees Inc 650 N Sam Houston Pkwy E Ste 205	Houston	TX	77060	**866-865-9617**	281-447-1327

775 TROPHIES, PLAQUES, AWARDS

Name / Address	City	State	ZIP	Toll-Free	Phone
Architectural Bronze Aluminum Corp 655 Deerfield Rd Ste 100	Deerfield	IL	60015	**800-339-6581**	
Au Sable Woodworking Co PO Box 108	Frederic	MI	49733	**800-248-9261**	989-348-7086
Classic Medallics Inc 520 S Fulton Ave	Mount Vernon	NY	10550	**800-221-1348**	914-530-6259
F & H Ribbon Co Inc 3010 S Pipeline Rd	Euless	TX	76040	**800-877-5775**	
Jostens Inc 3601 Minnesota Ave Ste 400	Minneapolis	MN	55435	**800-235-4774**	952-830-3300
Metallic Arts Inc 914 N Lake Rd	Spokane	WA	99212	**800-541-3200**	509-489-7173
Regalia Manufacturing Co 2018 Fourth Ave	Rock Island	IL	61201	**800-798-7471**	309-788-7471
Trophyland USA Inc 7001 W 20th Ave	Hialeah	FL	33014	**800-327-5820**	
US Bronze Sign Co 811 Second Ave	New Hyde Park	NY	11040	**800-872-5155**	516-352-5155
Wilson Trophy Co 1724 Frienza Ave	Sacramento	CA	95815	**800-635-5005**	916-927-9733

TRUCK BODIES

SEE Motor Vehicles - Commercial & Special Purpose

776 TRUCK RENTAL & LEASING

Company / Address	City	State	Zip	Toll-Free	Phone
Barco Rent a Truck 717 South 5600 West	Salt Lake City	UT	84104	**800-453-4761**	801-532-7777
Calmont Leasing Ltd 14610 Yellowhead Trail NW	Edmonton	AB	T5L3C5	**855-474-2568**	
Carco National Lease Inc 2905 N 32nd St	Fort Smith	AR	72904	**800-643-2596**	479-441-3200
DeCarolis Truck Rental Inc 333 Colfax St	Rochester	NY	14606	**800-666-1169**	585-254-1169
Idealease Inc 430 N Rand Rd	North Barrington	IL	60010	**800-435-3273**	847-304-6000
MHC Kenworth 1524 N Corrington Ave	Kansas City	MO	64120	**888-259-4826**	816-483-7035
National Truck Leasing System 450 S Summit Ave	Oakbrook	IL	60181	**800-729-6857**	630-953-8878
PACCAR Leasing Corp 777 106th Ave NE	Bellevue	WA	98004	**800-759-2979**	425-468-7877
Rush Enterprises Inc 555 IH 35 S Ste 500 *NASDAQ: RUSHA*	New Braunfels	TX	78130	**800-973-7874**	830-626-5200
Ryder System Inc 11690 NW 105th St *NYSE: R*	Miami	FL	33178	**800-297-9337**	305-500-3726
Star Leasing Co 4080 Business Pk Dr	Columbus	OH	43204	**888-771-1004**	614-278-9999
Star Truck Rentals Inc 3940 Eastern Ave SE	Grand Rapids	MI	49508	**800-748-0468**	616-243-7033
U-Haul International Inc 2727 N Central Ave	Phoenix	AZ	85004	**800-528-0361**	

777 TRUCK TRAILERS

SEE ALSO Motor Vehicles - Commercial & Special Purpose

Company / Address	City	State	Zip	Toll-Free	Phone
4-Star Trailers Inc 10000 NW Tenth St	Oklahoma City	OK	73127	**800-848-3095**	405-324-7827
Alta-Fab Structures Ltd 504-13 Ave	Nisku	AB	T9E7P6	**800-252-7990**	780-955-7733
American Carrier Equipment Trailer Sales LLC 2285 E Date Ave	Fresno	CA	93706	**800-344-2174**	559-442-1500
Arkansas Trailer Manufacturing Co 3200 S Elm St	Little Rock	AR	72204	**800-666-5417**	501-666-5417
Beall Corp 9200 N Ramsey Blvd	Portland	OR	97203	**855-219-5686**	
Bri-Mar Mfg LLC 1080 S Main St	Chambersburg	PA	17201	**800-732-5845**	717-263-6116
Circle J Trailers 312 W Simplot Blvd	Caldwell	ID	83605	**800-247-2535**	208-459-0842
Clement Industries Inc PO Box 914 *Cust Svc	Minden	LA	71058	**800-562-5948***	318-377-2776
CM Trailers Inc 200 County Rd PO Box 680	Madill	OK	73446	**888-268-7577**	580-795-5536
Cottrell Inc 2125 Candler Rd *Sales	Gainesville	GA	30507	**800-827-0132***	770-532-7251
Dakota Mfg Company Inc 1909 S Rowley St	Mitchell	SD	57301	**800-232-5682**	605-996-5571
East Mfg Corp 1871 State Rt 44 PO Box 277	Randolph	OH	44265	**888-405-3278**	330-325-9921
Featherlite Trailers Hwy 63 & 9 PO Box 320	Cresco	IA	52136	**800-800-1230**	563-547-6000
Fontaine Trailer Co 430 Letson Rd PO Box 619	Haleyville	AL	35565	**800-821-6535**	205-486-5251
Hesse Inc 6700 St John Ave	Kansas City	MO	64123	**800-821-5562**	816-483-7808
K-Dee Supply Inc 621 E Lake St	Lake Mills	WI	53551	**800-268-3681**	920-648-8202
Kentucky Trailer 7201 Logistics Dr	Louisville	KY	40258	**888-598-7245**	502-637-2551
Kentucky Trailer Technologies 1240 N Pontiac Trial	Walled Lake	MI	48390	**866-638-6080**	248-960-9700
LBT Inc 11502 "I" St	Omaha	NE	68137	**888-528-7278**	402-333-4900
Ledwell & Son Enterprises 3300 Waco St	Texarkana	TX	75501	**888-533-9355**	903-838-6531
Mac Trailer Mfg Inc 14599 Commerce St NE	Alliance	OH	44601	**800-795-8454**	330-823-9900
Maurer Mfg 1300 38th Ave W PO Box 160	Spencer	IA	51301	**888-274-6010**	712-262-2992
MCT Industries Inc 7451 Pan American Fwy	Albuquerque	NM	87109	**800-876-8651**	505-345-8651
Merritt Equipment Co 9339 Hwy 85	Henderson	CO	80640	**800-634-3036**	303-289-2286
Mickey Truck Bodies Inc 1305 Trinity Ave PO Box 2044	High Point	NC	27261	**800-334-9061**	336-882-6806
Midwest Systems 5911 Hall St	Saint Louis	MO	63147	**800-383-6281**	314-389-6280
Polar Service Centers 7600 E Sam Houston Pkwy N	Houston	TX	77049	**800-955-8558**	281-459-6400
Polar Tank Trailer Inc 12810 County Rd 17	Holdingford	MN	56340	**800-826-6589**	320-746-2255
Redneck Trailer Supplies 2100 NW By-Pass	Springfield	MO	65803	**877-973-3632**	417-864-5210
Rogers Bros Corp 100 Orchard St	Albion	PA	16401	**800-441-9880**	814-756-4121
Royal Camp Services Ltd 7111 - 67 St	Edmonton	AB	T6B3L7	**877-884-2267**	780-463-8000
Schwend Inc 28945 Johnston Rd	Dade City	FL	33523	**800-243-7757**	352-588-2220
Summit Trailer Sales Inc 1 Summit Plz	Summit Station	PA	17979	**800-437-3729**	570-754-3511
Timpte Inc 1827 Industrial Dr	David City	NE	68632	**888-256-4884**	402-367-3056
Towmaster Inc 61381 US Hwy 12	Litchfield	MN	55355	**800-462-4517**	320-693-7900
Trail King Industries Inc 147 Industrial Pk Rd	Brookville	PA	15825	**800-545-1549**	814-849-2342
Trailiner Corp PO Box 5270	Springfield	MO	65801	**800-833-8209**	417-866-7258
Travis Body & Trailer Inc 13955 FM529	Houston	TX	77041	**800-535-4372**	713-466-5888
Trinity Trailer Manufacturing Inc 8200 S Eisenman Rd	Boise	ID	83716	**800-235-6577**	208-336-3666
Truck Equipment Service Co 800 Oak St	Lincoln	NE	68521	**800-869-0363**	402-476-3225
Utility Trailer Mfg Co 17295 E Railroad St	City of Industry	CA	91748	**800-874-6807**	626-965-1541
Vantage Trailers Inc 29335 Hwy Blvd	Katy	TX	77494	**800-826-8245**	281-391-2664
Wabash National Corp 1000 Sagamore PkwyS PO Box 6129 *NYSE: WNC* ■ *Sales	Lafayette	IN	47903	**866-877-5062***	765-771-5300
Wells Cargo Inc 1503 W McNaughton St	Elkhart	IN	46514	**800-348-7553**	574-264-9661
Western Trailer Co 251 W Gowen Rd	Boise	ID	83716	**888-344-2539**	208-344-2539
Wilson Trailer Co 4400 S Lewis Blvd	Sioux City	IA	51106	**800-798-2002**	712-252-6500
Witzco Trailers Inc 6101 McIntosh Rd	Sarasota	FL	34238	**800-462-4123**	941-922-5301

778 TRUCKING COMPANIES

SEE ALSO Logistics Services (Transportation & Warehousing) ; Moving Companies

Company / Address	City	State	Zip	Toll-Free	Phone
A & A Express Inc PO Box 707	Brandon	SD	57005	**800-658-3549**	605-582-2402
AAA Cooper Transportation 1751 Kinsey Rd	Dothan	AL	36303	**800-633-7571**	334-793-2284
Aaa Moving & Storage Inc 747 E Ship Creek Ave	Anchorage	AK	99501	**866-641-4446**	888-927-3330
ABF Freight Systems Inc 3801 Old Greenwood Rd	Fort Smith	AR	72903	**800-610-5544**	479-785-8913
Ace Doran Hauling & Rigging Co Inc 1601 Blue Rock St	Cincinnati	OH	45223	**800-829-0929**	513-681-7900
Ace Relocation Systems Inc 5608 Eastgate Dr	San Diego	CA	92121	**800-453-0964**	858-677-5500
Acme Truck Line Inc 1180 Destrehan Ave	Harvey	LA	70058	**800-825-6246**	504-368-2510
Alabama Motor Express Inc 10720 E US Hwy 84 E	Ashford	AL	36312	**800-633-7590**	
Alan Ritchey Inc 740 S I-35 E Frontage Rd	Valley View	TX	76272	**800-877-0273**	940-726-3276
All American Moving Group LLC PO Box 271277	Memphis	TN	38167	**800-467-2900**	901-353-3900
Allegheny Design Management Inc 1154 Parks Industrial Dr	Vandergrift	PA	15690	**800-927-2611**	724-845-7336
Allied Automotive Group 2302 ParkLake Dr Bldg 15 Ste 600	Atlanta	GA	30345	**800-476-2058**	
Ameril-Co Carriers Inc 1702 E Overland	Scottsbluff	NE	69361	**800-445-5400**	308-635-3157
Amstan Logistics 101 Knightsbridge Dr	Hamilton	OH	45011	**800-322-5546**	513-863-4627
Anderson Trucking Service Inc 725 Opportunity St PO Box 1377	Saint Cloud	MN	56301	**800-328-2316**	320-255-7400
Ards Trucking Company Inc 4190 Alligator Rd	Timmonsville	SC	29161	**877-273-7297**	843-393-5101
ARG Trucking Corp 369 Bostwick Rd	Phelps	NY	14532	**800-334-1314**	315-789-8871
Arlo G. Lott Trucking Inc 257 S 100 E	Jerome	ID	83338	**800-443-5688**	208-324-5053
Armellini Express Lines Inc 3446 SW Armellini Ave	Palm City	FL	34990	**800-327-7887**	772-287-0575
Arnold Transportation Services Inc 9523 Florida Mining Blvd	Jacksonville	FL	32257	**800-846-4321**	972-986-3154
Associated Petroleum Carriers Inc PO Box 2808 *Cust Svc	Spartanburg	SC	29304	**800-573-9301***	864-573-9301
Averitt Express Inc 1415 Neal St	Cookeville	TN	38501	**800-283-7488**	
B-D-R Transport Inc 7994 US Rt 5	Westminster	VT	05158	**800-421-0126**	802-463-0606
Baggett Transportation Co 2 S 32nd St	Birmingham	AL	35233	**800-633-8982**	888-224-4388
Bailey's Express Inc 61 Industrial Pk Rd	Middletown	CT	06457	**800-523-3758**	860-632-0388
Barlow 1305 Grand Dd SE	Faucett	MO	64448	**800-688-1202**	816-238-3373
Bastian Trucking Inc 440 South Main	Aurora	UT	84620	**800-452-5126**	435-529-7453
Baylor Trucking Inc 9269 E State Rd 48	Milan	IN	47031	**800-322-9567**	812-623-2020
Bayshore Transportation System Inc 901 Dawson Dr	Newark	DE	19713	**800-523-3319**	302-366-0220
Beam Mack Sales & Service Inc 2674 W Henrietta Rd	Rochester	NY	14623	**877-650-8789**	585-424-4860
Beaver Express Service LLC 4310 Oklahoma Ave PO Box 1147	Woodward	OK	73802	**800-593-2328**	580-256-6460
Beelman Truck Co 1 Racehorse Dr *Sales	East Saint Louis	IL	62205	**800-541-5918***	618-646-5300
Benton Express Inc 1045 S River Industrial Blvd SE	Atlanta	GA	30315	**888-423-6866**	404-267-2200

Company / Address	City	State	ZIP	Toll-Free	Phone
Besl Transfer Co 5700 Este Ave	Cincinnati	OH	45232	**800-456-2375**	513-242-3456
Big G Express Inc PO Box 1650	Shelbyville	TN	37162	**800-955-9140**	800-684-9140
Bilkays Express Co 2400 Bedle Place	Linden	NJ	07036	**800-526-4006**	908-289-2400
Boyd Bros Transportation Inc 3275 Alabama 30	Clayton	AL	36016	**800-700-2693**	334-775-1400
Bryan Systems 14020 US 20A Hwy	Montpelier	OH	43543	**800-745-2796**	
Buchanan Hauling & Rigging 4625 Industrial Rd	Fort Wayne	IN	46825	**888-544-4285**	260-471-1877
Buddy Moore Trucking Inc PO Box 10047	Birmingham	AL	35202	**866-704-1598**	205-949-2260
Bulk Transit Corp 7177 Industrial Pkwy	Plain City	OH	43064	**800-345-2855**	614-873-4632
Bulkmatic Transport Co 2001 N Cline Ave	Griffith	IN	46319	**800-535-8505**	
Burns Motor Freight Inc 500 Seneca Trl N	Marlinton	WV	24954	**800-598-5674**	304-799-6106
Butler Transport Inc 347 N James St	Kansas City	KS	66118	**800-345-8158**	913-321-0047
Cal-ark Inc PO Box 990	Mabelvale	AR	72103	**888-422-5275**	501-455-3399
Calex Express Inc 58 Pittston Ave	Pittston	PA	18640	**800-292-2539**	570-603-0180
California Cartage Company Inc 2931 Redondo Ave	Long Beach	CA	90806	**888-537-1432**	
Cardinal Transport Inc 7180 E Reed Rd	Coal City	IL	60416	**800-435-9302**	815-634-4443
Cedar Rapids Truck Ctr Inc 9201 Sixth St SW	Cedar Rapids	IA	52404	**866-602-1597**	319-848-6230
Celadon Trucking Services Inc 9503 E 33rd St	Indianapolis	IN	46235	**800-235-2366**	317-972-7000
Central Freight Lines Inc PO Box 2638	Waco	TX	76702	**800-782-5036**	
Central Petroleum Transport Inc (CPT) 6115 Mitchell St	Sioux City	IA	51111	**800-798-6357**	712-258-6357
Central Refrigerated Service Inc 5175 W 2100 S	West Valley City	UT	84120	**800-777-0069**	801-924-7000
Chadderton Trucking Inc 40 Stewart Way	Sharon	PA	16146	**800-327-6868**	724-981-5050
Christenson Transportation Inc 2001 W Old Rt 66	Strafford	MO	65757	**800-980-2493**	417-866-5993
Coastal Transport Co Inc 1603 Ackerman Rd	San Antonio	TX	78219	**800-523-8612**	210-661-4287
Coleman American Moving Services Inc PO Box 960	Midland City	AL	36350	**877-693-7060**	866-929-1482
Colonial Freight Systems Inc 10924 McBride Ln	Knoxville	TN	37932	**800-826-1402**	865-966-9711
Colonial Truck Co 1833 Commerce Rd	Richmond	VA	23224	**800-234-8782**	804-232-3492
Combined Transport Inc 5656 Crater Lake Ave	Central Point	OR	97502	**800-547-2870**	541-734-7418
Comcar Industries Inc 502 E Bridgers Ave *Cust Svc	Auburndale	FL	33823	**800-524-1101***	863-967-1101
Con-Way Freight 2211 Old Earhart Rd	Ann Arbor	MI	48105	**800-755-2728**	734-994-6600
Cooke Trucking Co Inc 1759 S Andy Griffith Pkwy	Mount Airy	NC	27030	**800-888-9502**	336-786-5181
Covenant Transport Inc 400 Birmingham Hwy *NASDAQ: CVTI*	Chattanooga	TN	37419	**800-334-9686**	423-821-1212
Cox Transportation Services Inc 10448 Dow Gil Rd	Ashland	VA	23005	**800-288-8118**	804-798-1477
CR England & Sons Inc 4701 West 2100 South	Salt Lake City	UT	84120	**800-453-8826**	801-972-2712
Craig Transportation Co 26699 Eckel Rd	Perrysburg	OH	43551	**800-521-9119**	419-872-3333
Cresco Lines Inc 15220 S Halsted St	Harvey	IL	60426	**800-323-4476**	708-339-1186
Crete Carrier Corp 400 NW 56th St PO Box 81228 *Cust Svc	Lincoln	NE	68528	**800-998-4095***	402-475-9521
Crossett Inc 201 S Carver St *General	Warren	PA	16365	**800-876-2778***	
CRST International Inc 3930 16th Ave SW PO Box 68	Cedar Rapids	IA	52406	**800-736-2778**	
Crysteel Truck Equipment Inc 55248 Ember Rd *General	Lake Crystal	MN	56055	**800-722-0588***	507-726-6041
CTI Inc 11105 Norrth Casa Grande Hwy	Rillito	AZ	85654	**800-362-4952**	520-624-2348
CTL Distribution Inc 4201 Bonnie Mine Rd	Mulberry	FL	33860	**800-237-9088**	863-428-2373
D M Bowman Inc 10226 Governor Ln Blvd Ste 4009	Williamsport	MD	21795	**800-326-3274**	301-582-2784
D&D Sexton Inc PO Box 156	Carthage	MO	64836	**800-743-0265**	417-358-8727
D. P. Curtis Trucking Inc 1450 South Hwy 118	Richfield	UT	84701	**800-257-9151**	
Daggett Truck Line Inc 32717 County Rd 10	Frazee	MN	56544	**800-262-9393**	218-334-3711
Dahlsten Truck Line Inc 101 W Edgar PO Box 95	Clay Center	NE	68933	**800-228-4313**	402-762-3511
Daily Express Inc 1072 Harrisburg Pk	Carlisle	PA	17013	**800-735-3136**	717-243-5757
Dakota Line Inc PO Box 476	Vermillion	SD	57069	**800-532-5682**	605-624-5228
Dana Transport Inc 210 Essex Ave E	Avenel	NJ	07001	**800-733-3262**	732-750-9100
Davis Express Inc PO Box 1276	Starke	FL	32091	**800-874-4270**	
Daylight Transport 1501 Hughes Way Ste 200	Long Beach	CA	90810	**800-468-9999**	
Decker Truck Line Inc 4000 Fifth Ave S	Fort Dodge	IA	50501	**800-247-2537**	515-576-4141
Dejana Truck & Utility Equipment Company Inc 490 Pulaski Rd	Kings Park	NY	11754	**877-335-2621**	631-544-9000
Dick Lavy Trucking Inc 8848 State Rt 121	Bradford	OH	45308	**800-345-5289**	937-448-2104
Dilmar Oil Company Inc 1951 W Darlington St PO Box 5629	Florence	SC	29501	**800-922-5823**	
Dino's Trucking Inc 9615 Continental Indus Dr	Saint Louis	MO	63123	**800-771-7805**	314-631-3001
Dircks Moving Services Inc 4340 W Mohave St	Phoenix	AZ	85043	**800-523-5038**	602-267-9401
Don Hummer Trucking Corp 1486 Hwy 6 NW PO Box 310	Oxford	IA	52322	**866-248-6637**	319-828-2000
Dts Cos Inc 1640 Monad Rd	Billings	MT	59101	**800-755-5855**	406-245-4695
Duncan & Son Lines Inc 23860 W US Hwy 85	Buckeye	AZ	85326	**800-528-4283**	623-386-4511
Eagle Transport Corp 300 S Wesleyan Blvd Ste 202	Rocky Mount	NC	27804	**800-776-9937**	252-937-2464
Earl L Henderson Trucking Inc 206 W Main St	Salem	IL	62881	**800-447-8084**	618-548-4667
Epes Carriers Inc 3400 Edgefield Ct	Greensboro	NC	27409	**800-869-3737**	336-668-3358
Evans Dedicated Systems Inc PO Box 9	Maywood	CA	90270	**800-427-6387**	323-725-2928
EW Wylie Corp 1520 Second Ave NW *Cust Svc	West Fargo	ND	58078	**800-437-4132***	701-282-5550
Falcon Express Inc 2250 E Church St	Philadelphia	PA	19124	**800-544-6566**	215-992-3140
FFE Transportation Inc 1145 Empire Central Pl	Dallas	TX	75247	**800-569-9200**	214-630-8090
First Class Services Inc 9355 US Hwy 60 E *General	Lewisport	KY	42351	**800-467-8684***	270-295-3746
Firstexpress Inc 1135 Freightliner Dr	Nashville	TN	37210	**800-848-9203**	
Five Star Trucking Inc 4380 Glenbrook Rd	Willoughby	OH	44094	**800-321-3658**	440-953-9300
Fort Edward Express Company Inc 1402 Rt 9	Fort Edward	NY	12828	**800-342-1233**	518-792-6571
Forward Air Corp 430 Airport Rd PO Box 1058 *NASDAQ: FWRD*	Greeneville	TN	37744	**800-726-6654**	423-636-7100
Frank C. Alegre Trucking Inc PO Box 1508	Lodi	CA	95241	**800-769-2440**	209-334-2112
Fry-Wagner Moving & Storage Co 3700 Rider Trl S	Earth City	MO	63045	**800-899-4035**	314-291-4100
Godfrey Trucking Inc 6173 West 2100 South	West Valley City	UT	84128	**800-444-7669**	801-972-0660
Gordon Trucking Inc 151 Stewart Rd SW	Pacific	WA	98047	**800-426-8486**	253-863-7777
Grammer Industries Inc 6320 E State St	Columbus	IN	47201	**800-333-7410**	812-579-5655
Groendyke Transport Inc 2510 Rock Island Blvd	Enid	OK	73701	**800-843-2103**	580-234-4663
Guy M Turner Inc 4514 S Holden Rd PO Box 7776	Greensboro	NC	27406	**800-432-4859**	336-294-4660
H & M International Transportation Inc 485B Rt 1 S	Iselin	NJ	08830	**800-446-4685**	732-510-4640
H & W Trucking Company Inc 1772 N Andy Griffith Pkwy PO Box 1545	Mount Airy	NC	27030	**800-334-9181**	336-789-2188
H O Wolding Inc PO Box 217	Amherst	WI	54406	**800-950-0054**	715-824-5513
Hazen Transport Inc 27050 Wick Rd	Taylor	MI	48180	**800-251-2120**	313-292-2120
Heartland Express Inc 901 N Kansas Ave *NASDAQ: HTLD*	North Liberty	IA	52317	**800-654-1175**	
High Country Transportation Inc PO Box 700	Cortez	CO	81321	**800-635-7687**	
Hirschbach Motor Lines Inc 18355 US Hwy 20	East Dubuque	IL	61025	**800-554-2969**	402-494-5000
Holman Transportation Services Inc 1010 Holman Ct	Caldwell	ID	83605	**800-375-2416**	208-454-0779
Hot-Line Freight System Inc PO Box 205	West Salem	WI	54669	**800-468-4686**	608-486-1600
Houff Transfer Inc 46 Houff Rd	Weyers Cave	VA	24486	**800-476-4683**	540-234-9233
Howard F Baer Inc 1301 Foster Ave	Nashville	TN	37210	**800-447-7430**	615-255-7351
Howard Sheppard Inc PO Box 797	Sandersville	GA	31082	**800-846-1726**	478-552-5127
Howell's Motor Freight Inc PO Box 12308	Roanoke	VA	24024	**800-444-0585**	540-966-3200
HVH Transportation Inc 181 E 56th Ave Ste 200	Denver	CO	80216	**800-525-4844**	303-292-3656
Indian River Transport Co 2580 Executive Rd	Winter Haven	FL	33884	**800-877-2430**	863-324-2430
Interstate Distributor Co 11707 21st Ave S	Tacoma	WA	98444	**800-426-8560**	
J P Noonan Transportation Inc 415 W St	West Bridgewater	MA	02379	**800-922-8026**	508-583-2880
J-Mar Enterprises Inc PO Box 4143	Bismarck	ND	58502	**800-446-8283**	701-222-4518
Jack B Kelley Inc 801 S Fillmore St Ste 505	Amarillo	TX	79101	**800-225-5525**	806-353-3553
Jaro Transportation Services Inc 975 Post Rd	Warren	OH	44483	**800-451-3447**	330-393-5659
Jerry Lipps Inc 3888 Nash Rd	Cape Girardeau	MO	63702	**800-325-3331**	573-335-8204
Jet Star Inc 10825 Andrade Dr	Zionsville	IN	46077	**800-969-4222**	317-873-4222
JH Walker Trucking Company Inc 152 N Hollywood Rd	Houma	LA	70364	**800-535-5992**	985-868-8330
Jim Palmer Trucking Inc 9730 Derby Dr	Missoula	MT	59801	**888-698-3422**	406-721-5151
JNJ Express Inc 3935 Old Getwell Rd PO Box 30983	Memphis	TN	38130	**888-383-7157**	901-362-3444
Jones Motor Company Inc 900 W Bridge St PO Box 137	Spring City	PA	19475	**800-825-6637**	610-948-7900

Classified Section

Company	Address	City	State	ZIP	Toll-Free	Phone
KAG West	4076 Seaport Blvd	West Sacramento	CA	95691	**800-547-1587**	916-371-8241
Keim T S Inc	1249 N Ninth St PO Box 226	Sabetha	KS	66534	**800-255-2450**	
Keith Titus Corp	PO Box 920	Weedsport	NY	13166	**800-233-2126**	315-834-6681
Kenan Advantage Group Inc (KAG)	4366 Mt Pleasant St NW	North Canton	OH	44720	**800-969-5419**	330-491-0474
Kenan Transport Co	100 Europa Ctr Ste 320	Chapel Hill	NC	27517	**866-821-3444**	919-967-8221
Kenworth Sales Co	2125 Constitution Blvd *General	West Valley City	UT	84119	**800-222-7831***	801-487-4161
KLLM Inc	135 Riverview Dr	Richland	MS	39218	**800-925-5556**	800-925-1000
Knight Transportation Inc	5601 W Buckeye Rd *NYSE: KNX*	Phoenix	AZ	85043	**800-489-2000**	602-269-2000
Kruepke Trucking Inc	2881 Hwy P *Cust Svc	Jackson	WI	53037	**800-798-5000***	262-677-3155
Kuntzman Trucking Inc	13515 Oyster Rd	Alliance	OH	44601	**800-362-9779**	330-821-9160
La Rosa Del Monte Express Inc	1133-35 Tiffany St	Bronx	NY	10459	**800-452-7672**	718-991-3300
Landair Corp	1110 Myers St	Greeneville	TN	37743	**888-526-3247**	
Landmark International Trucks Inc	4550 Rutledge Pk	Knoxville	TN	37914	**800-968-9999**	865-637-4881
Landstar Express America Inc	13410 Sutton Pk Dr S	Jacksonville	FL	32224	**800-872-9400**	904-398-9400
Landstar Inway Inc	13410 Sutton Pk Dr S	Jacksonville	FL	61102	**800-435-7352**	800-872-9400
Lawrence Companies (LTS)	872 Lee Hwy PO Box 7667	Roanoke	VA	24019	**800-336-9626**	540-966-4000
Lightning Transportation Inc	16820 Blake Rd	Hagerstown	MD	21740	**800-233-0624**	301-582-5700
Linden Warehouse & Distribution Co Inc	1300 Lower Rd	Linden	NJ	07036	**800-333-2855**	908-862-1400
Liquid Transport Corp	8470 Allison Pt Blvd Ste 400	Indianapolis	IN	46250	**800-942-3175**	317-841-4200
Lisa Motor Lines	1145 Empire Central Pl PO Box 655888	Dallas	TX	75247	**800-569-9200**	214-630-8090
Lynden Transport Inc	3027 Rampart Dr	Anchorage	AK	99501	**800-327-9390**	
Market Transport Ltd	110 N Marine Dr	Portland	OR	97217	**800-547-0781**	503-283-2405
Marten Transport Ltd	129 Marten St *NASDAQ: MRTN*	Mondovi	WI	54755	**800-395-3000**	715-926-4216
Matheson Trucking Inc	9785 Goethe Rd	Sacramento	CA	95827	**800-455-7678**	916-685-2330
Maverick USA Inc	13301 Valentine Rd	North Little Rock	AR	72117	**800-289-6600**	501-955-1255
Mawson & Mawson Inc	1800 Old Lincoln Hwy PO Box 248	Langhorne	PA	19047	**800-262-9766**	215-750-1100
May Trucking Co	4185 Brooklake Rd PO Box 9039	Salem	OR	97305	**800-547-9169**	
Mayfield Transfer Company Inc	3200 W Lake St	Melrose Park	IL	60160	**800-222-2959**	708-681-4440
McKenzie Tank Lines Inc	1966 Commonwealth Ln	Tallahassee	FL	32303	**800-828-6495**	850-576-1221
MCT Transportation LLC	1600 E Benson Rd *Cust Svc	Sioux Falls	SD	57104	**800-843-9904***	605-339-8400
Mercer Transportation Co	1128 W Main St PO Box 35610	Louisville	KY	40232	**800-626-5375**	502-584-2301
Mergenthaler Transfer & Storage	1414 N Montana Ave *General	Helena	MT	59601	**800-826-5463***	406-442-9470
Midwest Motor Express Inc	5015 E Main Ave	Bismarck	ND	58502	**800-741-4097**	701-223-1880
Milan Express Company Inc	1091 Kefauver Dr	Milan	TN	38358	**800-231-7303**	731-686-7428
Miller Transporters Inc	5500 Hwy 80 W *Cust Svc	Jackson	MS	39209	**800-645-5378***	601-922-8331
Minuteman Trucks Inc	2181 Providence Hwy	Walpole	MA	02081	**800-231-8458**	508-668-3112
Murrows Transfer Inc	PO Box 4095 *Cust Svc	High Point	NC	27263	**800-669-2928***	336-475-6101
National Carriers Inc	1501 E Eigth St	Liberal	KS	67901	**800-835-9180**	620-624-1621
National Highway Express Co	971 Old Henderson St PO Box 20262	Columbus	OH	43220	**800-837-5700**	614-459-4900
Nationwide Truck Brokers Inc (NTB)	4203 Roger B Chaffee Memorial Blvd SE Ste 2	Grand Rapids	MI	49548	**800-446-0682**	616-878-5554
Navajo Express Inc	1400 W 64 Ave	Denver	CO	80221	**800-525-1969**	303-287-3800
New Penn Motor Express Inc	625 S Fifth Ave *Cust Svc	Lebanon	PA	17042	**800-285-5000***	717-274-2521
Newark School District	100 E Miller St 4th Fl	Newark	NY	14513	**877-789-2613**	315-332-3230
Nick Strimbu Inc	3500 PkwyRd	Brookfield	OH	44403	**800-446-8785**	330-448-4046
Northland Trucking Inc	1515 S 22nd Ave	Phoenix	AZ	85009	**800-214-5564**	602-254-0007
Nussbaum Trucking Inc	19336 N 1425 East Rd	Normal	IL	61748	**800-322-7305**	309-452-4426
O & S Trucking Inc	3769 E Evergreen St	Springfield	MO	65803	**855-861-9571**	417-864-4780
Old Dominion Freight Line Inc	500 Old Dominion Way *NASDAQ: ODFL*	Thomasville	NC	27360	**800-432-6335**	336-889-5000
Oliver Trucking Corp	1101 Harding Ct	Indianapolis	IN	46217	**888-561-4449**	317-787-1101
Online Transport System Inc	6311 W Stoner Dr	Greenfield	IN	46140	**866-543-1235**	317-894-2159
Osborn Transportation Inc	1245 West Grand Ave	Rainbow City	AL	35906	**866-215-3659**	256-442-2514
Overland Express Co	5539 Harvey Wilson PO Box 262322	Houston	TX	77207	**800-929-7402**	713-672-6161
Ozark Motor Lines Inc	3934 Homewood Rd	Memphis	TN	38118	**800-264-4100**	901-251-9711
Palmetto State Transportation Company Inc	1050 Pk W Blvd	Greenville	SC	29611	**800-269-0175**	864-672-3800
PAM Transportation Services Inc	297 W Henri De Tonti Blvd *NASDAQ: PTSI*	Tontitown	AR	72770	**800-879-7261**	479-361-9111
Paper Transport Inc	2701 Executive Dr	Green Bay	WI	54304	**800-317-3650**	
Patriot Transportation Holding Inc	501 Riverside Ave Ste 500 *NASDAQ: PATI*	Jacksonville	FL	32202	**877-704-1776**	904-396-5733
Peet Frate Line Inc	650 S Eastwood Dr PO Box 1129	Woodstock	IL	60098	**800-435-6909**	815-338-5500
Penn's Best Inc	PO Box 128	Meshoppen	PA	18630	**800-852-3243**	
Phoenix Transportation Services LLC	335 E Yusen Dr	Georgetown	KY	40324	**800-860-0889**	502-863-0108
Pitt Ohio Express	15 27th St *Cust Svc	Pittsburgh	PA	15222	**800-366-7488***	412-232-3015
Pleasant Trucking Inc	2250 Industrial Dr PO Box 778	Connellsville	PA	15425	**800-245-2402**	
Pozas Bros Trucking Company Inc	8130 Enterprise Dr	Newark	CA	94560	**800-874-8383**	510-742-9939
Predator Trucking Co	3181 Trumbull Ave	McDonald	OH	44437	**888-773-3875**	
Prestera Trucking	19129 US Rt 52	South Point	OH	45680	**855-761-7943**	740-894-4770
Pride Transport Inc	5499 W 2455 S	Salt Lake City	UT	84120	**800-877-1320**	801-972-8890
Prime Inc	PO Box 4208 *Cust Svc	Springfield	MO	65808	**800-848-4560***	417-866-0001
Pritchett Trucking Inc	1050 SE Sixth St PO Box 311	Lake Butler	FL	32054	**800-486-7504**	386-496-2630
Quality Distribution Inc	4041 Pk Oaks Blvd Ste 200 *NASDAQ: QLTY*	Tampa	FL	33610	**800-282-2031**	
Queensboro Co	113 E Broad St PO Box 467	Louisville	GA	30434	**800-236-2442**	478-625-2000
R & R Trucking Inc	302 Thunder Rd PO Box 545	Duenweg	MO	64841	**800-625-6885**	417-623-6885
Rbx Inc	PO Box 2118	Springfield	MO	65802	**877-450-2200**	800-245-5507
Refrigerated Food Express Inc	57 Littlefield St	Avon	MA	02322	**800-342-8822**	508-587-4600
Relco Systems Inc	7310 Chestnut Ridge Rd	Lockport	NY	14094	**800-262-1020**	716-434-8100
Riechmann Transport Inc	3328 W Chain of Rocks Rd	Granite City	IL	62040	**800-844-4225**	618-797-6700
Roadtex Transportation Corp	13 Jensen Dr	Somerset	NJ	08873	**800-762-3839**	
Robert Bearden Inc	2601 Industrial Pk Dr PO Box 870	Cairo	GA	39828	**888-298-6928**	229-377-6928
Roehl Transport Inc	1916 E 29th St PO Box 750	Marshfield	WI	54449	**800-826-8367**	715-591-3795
Roger Ward Inc	17275 Green Mtn Rd *General	San Antonio	TX	78247	**888-909-3147***	210-655-8623
Rountree Transport & Rigging Inc	2640 N Ln Ave	Jacksonville	FL	32254	**800-342-5036**	904-781-1033
Roy Bros Inc	764 Boston Rd *Cust Svc	Billerica	MA	01821	**800-225-0830***	978-667-1921
Royal Trucking Co	1323 Eshman Ave N PO Box 387	West Point	MS	39773	**800-321-1293**	662-494-1637
RWH Trucking Inc	2970 Old Oakwood Rd	Oakwood	GA	30566	**800-256-8119**	
S & S Transport Inc	PO Box 12579	Grand Forks	ND	58208	**800-726-8022**	
S T Bunn Construction	1904 University Blvd PO Box 20109	Tuscaloosa	AL	35401	**800-297-6302**	205-752-8195
S-j Transportation Co Inc	PO Box 169	Woodstown	NJ	08098	**800-524-2552**	856-769-2741
Sammons Trucking	3665 W Broadway	Missoula	MT	59808	**800-548-9276**	406-728-2600
Security Van Lines LLC	100 W Airline Dr	Kenner	LA	70062	**800-218-6915**	800-794-5961
Seward Motor Freight Inc	PO Box 126	Seward	NE	68434	**800-786-4468**	402-643-4503
Shaffer Trucking Inc	49 E Main St PO Box 418 *Cust Svc	New Kingstown	PA	17072	**800-742-3337***	402-475-9521
Sherman Bros Trucking	32921 Diamond Hill Dr PO Box 706	Harrisburg	OR	97446	**800-547-8980**	541-995-7751
Shetler Moving & Storage Inc	1253 E Diamond Ave	Evansville	IN	47711	**800-321-5069**	812-421-7750
Shippers Express Co	1651 Kerr Dr	Jackson	MS	39204	**800-647-2480**	601-948-4251
Short Freight Lines Inc	459 S River Rd PO Box 357	Bay City	MI	48707	**800-248-0625**	989-893-3505
Simons Trucking Inc	920 Simon Dr PO Box 8	Farley	IA	52046	**800-373-2580**	563-744-3304
Skinner Transfer Corp	PO Box 438	Reedsburg	WI	53959	**800-356-9350**	608-524-2326
South Shore Transportation Inc	4010 Columbus Ave	Sandusky	OH	44870	**888-428-0879**	419-626-6267
Southeastern Freight Lines Inc	420 Davega Rd	Lexington	SC	29073	**800-637-7335**	803-794-7300
Southwest Freightlines	11991 Transpark Dr *General	El Paso	TX	79927	**800-776-5799***	915-860-8592
Star Fleet Inc	915 South Main St	Middlebury	IN	46540	**877-805-9547**	888-281-8727

	City	State	Zip	Toll-Free	Phone
Star Transportation Inc PO Box 100925 *Cust Svc	Nashville	TN	37224	**800-333-3060***	615-256-4336
Steelman Transportation 2160 N Burton	Springfield	MO	65803	**800-488-6287**	417-831-6300
Stevens Transport PO Box 279010	Dallas	TX	75227	**800-233-9369**	866-551-0337
Styer Transportation Co 7870 215th St W	Lakeville	MN	55044	**800-548-9149**	952-469-4491
Summitt Trucking LLC 1800 Progress Way	Clarksville	IN	47129	**866-999-7799**	812-285-7777
Sunco Carriers Inc 1025 N Chestnut Rd	Lakeland	FL	33805	**800-237-8288**	863-688-1948
Superior Carriers Inc 711 Jory Blvd Ste 101-N	Oak Brook	IL	60523	**800-654-7707**	630-573-2555
Sweetwater County School District 1 (SCSD) 3550 Foothill Blvd PO Box 1089	Rock Springs	WY	82901	**888-503-7562**	307-352-3400
Swift Transportation Company Inc 2200 S 75th Ave *NYSE: SWFT*	Phoenix	AZ	85043	**800-800-2200**	602-269-9700
T & T Trucking Inc 11396 N Hwy 99 *Cust Svc	Lodi	CA	95240	**800-692-3457***	209-931-6000
T-w Transport Inc 7405 S Hayford Rd	Cheney	WA	99004	**800-356-4070**	509-623-4004
TanTara Transportation Corp 2420 Stewart Rd	Muscatine	IA	52761	**800-650-0292**	563-262-8621
Taylor Truck Line Inc 31485 Northfield Blvd	Northfield	MN	55057	**800-962-5994**	507-645-4531
Teal's Express Inc 22411 Teal Dr PO Box 6010	Watertown	NY	13601	**800-836-0369**	315-788-6437
Tennessee Steel Haulers Inc PO Box 78189	Nashville	TN	37207	**800-776-4004**	615-271-2400
Tiger Lines LLC Lodi 927 Black Diamond Way	Lodi	CA	95241	**800-967-8443**	209-334-4100
Total Package Express Inc 5871 Cheviot Rd	Cincinnati	OH	45247	**800-420-5505**	513-741-5500
TP Trucking LLC 5630 Table Rock Rd	Central Point	OR	97502	**800-292-4399**	
Trailer Bridge Inc 10405 New Berlin Rd E *OTC: TRBRQ*	Jacksonville	FL	32226	**800-554-1589**	904-751-7100
Trailer Transit Inc 1130 E US 20	Porter	IN	46304	**800-423-3647**	219-926-2111
Trans-Carriers Inc 5135 US Hwy 78	Memphis	TN	38118	**800-999-7383**	901-368-2900
Trans-Phos Inc PO Box 9004	Bartow	FL	33831	**800-940-1575**	863-534-1575
TransAm Trucking Inc 15910 S 169th Hwy	Olathe	KS	66062	**800-800-5945**	913-782-5300
Transport Corp of America Inc 1715 Yankee Doodle Rd	Eagan	MN	55121	**800-328-3927**	651-686-2500
Transport Distribution Co PO Box 306	Joplin	MO	64802	**800-866-7709**	417-624-3814
Transport Inc 2225 Main Ave SE	Moorhead	MN	56560	**800-598-7267**	218-236-6300
TransWood Carriers Inc PO Box 189	Omaha	NE	68101	**888-346-8092**	
Tri Star Freight System Inc 5407 Mesa Dr	Houston	TX	77028	**800-229-1095**	713-631-1095
Triple Crown Services 2720 Dupont Commerce Ct Ste 200	Fort Wayne	IN	46825	**800-325-6510**	260-416-3600
Truline Corp 9390 Redwood St	Las Vegas	NV	89139	**800-634-6489**	702-362-7495
Tryon Trucking Inc PO Box 68	Fairless Hills	PA	19030	**800-523-5254**	215-295-6622
Underwood Transfer Company LLC 940 W Troy Ave	Indianapolis	IN	46225	**800-428-2372**	317-783-9235
United Road Services Inc 10701 Middlebelt Rd	Romulus	MI	48174	**800-221-5127**	734-947-7900
Universal Truckload Services Inc 12755 E Nine Mile Rd *NASDAQ: UACL*	Warren	MI	48089	**800-233-9445**	586-920-0100
US Xpress Enterprises Inc 4080 Jenkins Rd	Chattanooga	TN	37421	**800-251-6291**	423-510-3000
USA Truck Inc 3200 Industrial Pk Rd *NASDAQ: USAK*	Van Buren	AR	72956	**800-643-9691**	479-471-2500
V & S Midwest Carriers Corp 2001 Hyland Ave PO Box 107	Kaukauna	WI	54130	**800-876-4330**	920-766-9696
Van Eerden Foodservice Co 650 Ionia Ave SW	Grand Rapids	MI	49503	**800-833-7374**	616-475-0900
Van Wyk Freight Lines Inc PO Box 70	Grinnell	IA	50112	**800-362-2595**	641-236-7551
Vitran Express Canada Inc 1201 Creditstone Rd *NASDAQ: VTNC*	Concord	ON	L4K0C2	**800-263-9588**	416-798-4965
Vitran Express Inc 1600 W Oliver Ave	Indianapolis	IN	46221	**800-366-0150**	317-803-4000
Volume Transportation Inc 6575 Marshall Blvd	Lithonia	GA	30058	**800-879-5565**	770-482-1400
Waggoners Trucking 5220 Midland Rd	Billings	MT	59101	**800-999-9097**	406-248-1919
Waller Truck Company Inc 400 S McCleary Rd	Excelsior Springs	MO	64024	**800-821-2196**	816-629-3400
Walpole Inc PO Box 1177	Okeechobee	FL	34973	**800-741-6500**	863-763-5593
Warren Transport Inc 210 Beck Ave *General	Waterloo	IA	50701	**800-553-2007***	319-233-6113
Watsontown Trucking Company Inc 60 Belford Blvd	Milton	PA	17847	**800-344-0313**	570-522-9820
WC McQuaide Inc 153 Macridge Rd	Johnstown	PA	15904	**800-456-0292**	814-269-6000
Wel Companies Inc 1625 S Broadway PO Box 5610	De Pere	WI	54115	**800-333-4415**	920-339-0110
Werner Enterprises Inc 14507 Frontier Rd *NASDAQ: WERN*	Omaha	NE	68138	**800-228-2240**	402-895-6640
Western Co-op Transport Assn 4501 72nd St SW	Montevideo	MN	56265	**800-992-8817**	320-269-5531
Western Express Inc 7135 Centennial Pl	Nashville	TN	37209	**800-316-7160**	615-259-9920
White Bros Trucking Co 4N793 School Rd	Wasco	IL	60183	**800-323-4762**	630-584-3810
Willis Shaw Express Inc 201 N Elm St	Elm Springs	AR	72728	**800-843-9904**	479-248-7261
Wilson Lines of Minnesota Inc 2131 Second Ave *General	Newport	MN	55055	**800-525-3333***	651-459-2384
Wilson Trucking Corp 137 Wilson Blvd	Fishersville	VA	22939	**866-645-7405**	540-949-3200
Wiseway Motor Freight Inc PO Box 838	Hudson	WI	54016	**800-876-1660**	
Woody Bogler Trucking Co PO Box 229	Rosebud	MO	63091	**800-899-4120**	573-764-3700
Wragtime Air Freight Inc 596 W 135th St	Gardena	CA	90248	**800-586-9701**	
Wright Transportation Inc 2333 Dauphin Island Pkwy	Mobile	AL	36605	**800-342-4598**	251-432-6390
Wyatt Transfer Inc 3035 Bells Rd PO Box 24326	Richmond	VA	23224	**800-552-5708**	804-743-3800
Wynne Transport Service Inc 2222 N 11th St	Omaha	NE	68108	**800-383-9330**	402-342-4001
Young's Commercial Transfer 2075 W Scranton Ave PO Box 871	Porterville	CA	93257	**800-289-1639**	559-784-6651
Yourga Trucking Inc 100 Shenango St	Wheatland	PA	16161	**800-245-1722**	724-981-3600

779 TYPESETTING & RELATED SERVICES

SEE ALSO Graphic Design ; Printing Companies - Commercial Printers

	City	State	Zip	Toll-Free	Phone
A A Blueprint Company Inc 2757 Gilchrist Rd	Akron	OH	44305	**800-821-3700**	330-794-8803
Auto-Graphics Inc 430 N Vineyard Ave	Ontario	CA	91764	**800-776-6939**	909-595-7004
Blanks Printing & Imaging Inc 2343 N Beckley Ave	Dallas	TX	75208	**800-325-7651**	214-741-3905
Boston Color Graphics LLC 755 Middlesex Tpke	Billerica	MA	01821	**800-767-0067**	
Carey Digital 1718 Central Pkwy	Cincinnati	OH	45214	**800-767-6071**	513-241-5210
Cohber Press PO Box 93100	Rochester	NY	14692	**800-724-3032**	585-475-9100
Color Communication Inc 4000 W Fillmore St	Chicago	IL	60624	**800-458-5743**	
Color House Graphics Inc 3505 Eastern Ave SE	Grand Rapids	MI	49508	**800-454-1916**	616-241-1916
GGS Technical Publications Services 3265 Farmtrail Rd	York	PA	17406	**800-927-4474**	717-764-2222
GotPrint 7651 N San Fernando Rd	Burbank	CA	91505	**877-922-7374**	818-252-3000
Imtech Graphics Inc 545 Dell Rd	Carlstadt	NJ	07072	**800-468-3240**	
Ligature, The 4909 Alcoa Ave	Los Angeles	CA	90058	**800-944-5440**	323-585-6000
Luminite Products Corp 148 Commerce Dr	Bradford	PA	16701	**888-545-2270**	814-817-1420
Para Plate 15910 Shoemaker Ave	Cerritos	CA	90703	**800-788-1556**	562-404-3434
Presstek Inc 55 Executive Dr *NASDAQ: PRST*	Hudson	NH	03051	**800-422-3616**	603-595-7000
Printing Prep Inc 12 E Tupper St	Buffalo	NY	14203	**877-878-7114**	716-852-5011
Quintessence Publishing Co 4350 Chandler Dr	Hanover Park	IL	60133	**800-621-0387**	630-736-3600
Regency Infographics Inc (SED) 2867 E Allegheny Ave	Philadelphia	PA	19134	**800-829-0020**	215-425-8800
Richards Graphic Communications Inc 2700 Van Buren St	Bellwood	IL	60104	**866-827-3686**	708-547-6000
Southern Graphic Systems Inc 502 N Willow Ave	Tampa	FL	33606	**800-777-6789**	813-253-3427
Southern Graphics Systems 7435 Empire Dr	Florence	KY	41042	**800-777-6789**	859-525-1190
State & Federal Communications Inc 80 S Summit St	Akron	OH	44308	**888-452-9669**	330-761-9960
West Essex Graphics Inc (WEG) 305 Fairfield Ave	Fairfield	NJ	07004	**800-221-5859**	

780 ULTRASONIC CLEANING EQUIPMENT

SEE ALSO Dental Equipment & Supplies - Mfr

	City	State	Zip	Toll-Free	Phone
Crest Ultrasonics Corp 10 Grumman Ave	Trenton	NJ	08628	**800-992-7378**	609-883-4000
Sonicor Inc 82 Otis St	West Babylon	NY	11704	**800-864-5022**	631-920-6555
Sonics & Materials Inc 53 Church Hill Rd *OTC: SIMA*	Newtown	CT	06470	**800-745-1105**	203-270-4600
Sterigenics 2015 Spring Rd Ste 650	Oak Brook	IL	60523	**800-472-4508**	630-928-1700

781 UNITED NATIONS AGENCIES, ORGANIZATIONS, PROGRAMS

	City	State	Zip	Toll-Free	Phone
Inter-American Development Bank 1300 New York Ave NW	Washington	DC	20577	**877-782-7432**	202-623-1000

782 UNITED NATIONS MISSIONS

	City	State	Zip	Toll-Free	Phone
Canada 885 Second Ave 14th Fl	New York	NY	10017	**800-267-8376**	212-848-1100

	City	State	Zip	Toll-Free	Phone
Cuba 315 Lexington Ave	New York	NY	10016	**800-553-3210***	212-689-7215
*General					
German Marshall Fund of the United States 1744 R St NW	Washington	DC	20009	**800-276-5680**	202-745-3950
Libyan Arab Jamahiriya 309-315 E 48th St	New York	NY	10017	**800-253-9646**	212-752-5775
Mexico 2 UN Plaza 28th Fl	New York	NY	10017	**800-553-3210**	212-752-0220
Micronesia 300 E 42nd St Ste 1600	New York	NY	10017	**800-469-4828**	212-697-8370

783 UNIVERSITIES - CANADIAN

	City	Prov	Postal Code	Toll-Free	Phone
Acadia University 15 University Ave	Wolfville	NS	B4P2R6	**877-585-1121**	902-542-2201
Alberta College of Art & Design 1407 14th Ave NW	Calgary	AB	T2N4R3	**800-251-8290**	403-284-7600
Athabasca University 1 University Dr	Athabasca	AB	T9S3A3	**800-788-9041**	780-675-6111
Bethany Bible College 26 Western St	Sussex	NB	E4E1E6	**888-432-4444**	506-432-4400
Campion College at the University of Regina 3737 Wascana Pkwy	Regina	SK	S4S0A2	**800-667-7282**	306-586-4242
Canadian College of Naturopathic Medicine 1255 Sheppard Ave E	Toronto	ON	M2K1E2	**866-241-2266**	416-498-1255
Canadian Memorial Chiropractic College 6100 Leslie St	Toronto	ON	M2H3J1	**800-463-2923**	416-482-2340
Cape Breton University 1250 Grand Lk Rd	Sydney	NS	B1P6L2	**888-959-9995**	902-539-5300
Carleton University 1125 Colonel By Dr	Ottawa	ON	K1S5B6	**888-354-4414**	613-520-7400
Columbia Bible College 2940 Clearbrook Rd	Abbotsford	BC	V2T2Z8	**800-283-0881**	604-853-3358
Concordia University 1455 de Maisonneuve Blvd W	Montreal	QC	H3G1M8	**866-333-2271**	514-848-2424
Concordia University College of Alberta 7128 Ada Blvd NW	Edmonton	AB	T5B4E4	**866-479-5200**	780-479-9220
Crandall University 333 Gorge Rd	Moncton	NB	E1G3H9	**888-968-6228**	506-858-8970
First Nations University of Canada *Northern* 1301 Central Ave	Prince Albert	SK	S6V4W1	**800-267-6303**	306-765-3333
Saskatoon 226 20th St E	Saskatoon	SK	S7K0A6	**800-267-6303**	306-931-1800
Heritage College & Seminary 175 Holiday Inn Dr	Cambridge	ON	N3C3T2	**800-465-1961**	519-651-2869
International Academy of Design & Technology *Chicago* 1 N State St Ste 500	Chicago	IL	60602	**888-318-6111**	312-386-7681
King's University College 9125 50th St	Edmonton	AB	T6B2H3	**800-661-8582**	780-465-3500
Laurentian University 935 Ramsey Lake Rd	Sudbury	ON	P3E2C6	**800-461-4030**	705-675-1151
Laval University 2325 Rue University	Quebec	QC	G1V0A6	**877-785-2825**	418-656-2131
Mount Royal College 4825 Mt Royal Gate SW	Calgary	AB	T3E6K6	**877-440-5001**	403-440-6111
Mount Saint Vincent University 166 Bedford Hwy	Halifax	NS	B3M2J6	**877-733-6788**	902-457-6117
Nipissing University 100 College Dr PO Box 5002	North Bay	ON	P1B8L7	**800-655-5154**	705-474-3450
Prairie Bible Institute 330 Fifth Ave NE PO Box 4000	Three Hills	AB	T0M2N0	**800-661-2425**	403-443-5511
Redeemer University College 777 Garner Rd E	Ancaster	ON	L9K1J4	**877-779-0913**	905-648-2131
Royal Roads University 2005 Sooke Rd	Victoria	BC	V9B5Y2	**800-788-8028**	250-391-2511
Ryerson University 350 Victoria St	Toronto	ON	M5B2K3	**866-592-8882**	416-979-5000
Saint Francis Xavier University PO Box 5000	Antigonish	NS	B2G2W5	**877-867-7839***	902-863-3300
*Admissions					
Saint Paul University 223 Main St	Ottawa	ON	K1S1C4	**800-637-6859**	613-236-1393
Saint Thomas University 51 Dineen Dr	Fredericton	NB	E3B5G3	**877-788-4443**	506-452-0640
Taylor University College & Seminary 11525 23rd Ave	Edmonton	AB	T6J4T3	**800-567-4988**	780-431-5200
Thompson Rivers University 900 McGill Rd PO Box 3010	Kamloops	BC	V2C5N3	**800-663-1663**	250-828-5000
Thorneloe University 935 Ramsey Lake Rd	Sudbury	ON	P3E2C6	**800-461-4030***	705-673-1730
*General					
Trent University 1600 W Bank Dr	Peterborough	ON	K9J7B8	**888-739-8885**	705-748-1011
Trinity Western University 7600 Glover Rd	Langley	BC	V2Y1Y1	**888-468-6898**	604-888-7511
Universite de Moncton *Campus Shippagan* 218 Blvd JD Gauthier	Shippagan	NB	E8S1P6	**800-363-8336**	506-336-3400
Edmundston 165 Blvd Hebert	Edmundston	NB	E3V2S8	**888-736-8623**	506-737-5051
Universite de Sherbrooke 2500 boul de l'Universite	Sherbrooke	QC	J1K2R1	**800-267-8337**	819-821-8000
Universite du Quebec a Trois-Rivieres 3351 Boul des Forges CP 500	Trois-Rivieres	QC	G9A5H7	**800-365-0922**	819-376-5011
Universite Sainte Anne 1695 Rt 1	Pointe-de-l'Eglise	NS	B0W1M0	**888-338-8337**	902-769-2114
University of Alberta *Augustana* 4901-46th Ave	Camrose	AB	T4V2R3	**800-661-8714**	780-679-1100
University of British Columbia 2016-1874 E Mall	Vancouver	BC	V6T1Z1	**877-272-1422**	604-822-9836
University of Guelph 50 Stone Rd E	Guelph	ON	N1G2W1	**877-674-1610**	519-824-4120
University of Manitoba 65 Chancellors Cir 424 University Ctr	Winnipeg	MB	R3T2N2	**800-224-7713***	204-474-8880
*Admissions					
University of Ottawa 550 Cumberland St	Ottawa	ON	K1N6N5	**877-868-8292**	613-562-5800
University of Regina 3737 Wascana Pkwy	Regina	SK	S4S0A2	**800-644-4756**	306-585-4111
Saint Thomas More College 1437 College Dr	Saskatoon	SK	S7N0W6	**800-667-2019**	306-966-8900
University of Western Ontario *King's University College* 266 Epworth Ave	London	ON	N6A2M3	**800-265-4406**	519-433-3491
York University 4700 Keele St	Toronto	ON	M3J1P3	**800-426-2255**	416-736-2100

784 UNIVERSITY SYSTEMS

Listings are organized by state names.

	City	State	Zip	Toll-Free	Phone
City University of New York (CUNY) 535 E 80th St	New York	NY	10075	**877-769-7441**	212-794-5555
Louisiana State University System 125 E Boyd Dr	Baton Rouge	LA	70803	**800-227-3002**	225-578-3357
New Mexico Higher Education Dept 2048 Galisteo St	Santa Fe	NM	87505	**800-279-9777**	505-476-8400
Pennsylvania State System of Higher Education 2986 N Second St	Harrisburg	PA	17110	**800-732-0999**	717-720-4000
State University of New York, The (SUNY) State University Plz	Albany	NY	12246	**800-342-3811**	518-320-1888
University of Alabama System 401 Queen City Ave	Tuscaloosa	AL	35401	**800-638-6420**	205-348-5861
University of California System 1111 Franklin St 12th Fl	Oakland	CA	94607	**800-888-8267**	510-987-9074
University of Missouri System 321 University Hall	Columbia	MO	65211	**800-225-6075**	573-882-2011
University of Nebraska System 3835 Holdrege St Varner Hall	Lincoln	NE	68583	**800-542-1602**	402-472-2111
University of South Dakota Foundation 1110 N Dakota St PO Box 5555	Vermillion	SD	57069	**800-521-3575**	605-677-6703
University of Texas System 601 Colorado St	Austin	TX	78701	**866-882-2034**	512-499-4200
University of Wisconsin System 1220 Linden Dr 1720 Van Hise Hall	Madison	WI	53706	**800-442-6461**	608-262-2321
Utah System of Higher Education 60 South 400 West	Salt Lake City	UT	84101	**800-418-8757**	801-321-7100
West Virginia Higher Education Policy Commission 1018 Kanawha Blvd E Ste 700	Charleston	WV	25301	**888-825-5707**	304-558-2101

785 UTILITY COMPANIES

SEE ALSO Electric Companies - Cooperatives (Rural) ; Gas Transmission - Natural Gas
Types of utilities included here are electric companies, water supply companies, and natural gas companies.

	City	State	Zip	Toll-Free	Phone
AGL Resources Inc 10 Peachtree Pl PO Box 4569	Atlanta	GA	30309	**866-977-4278***	404-584-4000
NYSE: GAS ■ *Cust Svc					
Alabama Gas Corp (Alagasco) 605 Richard Arrington Jr Blvd N	Birmingham	AL	35203	**800-292-4005**	205-326-8100
Alameda County Water District 43885 S Grimmer Blvd	Fremont	CA	94537	**866-275-3772**	510-668-4200
Alaska Power & Telephone Co 193 Otto St PO Box 3222	Port Townsend	WA	98368	**800-982-0136***	360-385-1733
OTC: APTL ■ *Cust Svc					
Allegheny Power 800 Cabin Hill Dr	Greensburg	PA	15601	**800-255-3443***	724-837-3000
*Cust Svc					
Alliant Energy Corp 4902 N Biltmore Ln Ste 1000	Madison	WI	53718	**800-255-4268**	
NYSE: LNT					
Alsco Inc 505 East South Temple	Salt Lake City	UT	84102	**800-408-0208**	801-328-8831
Ambit Energy LP 1801 N Lamar St Ste 200	Dallas	TX	75202	**877-282-6248**	
Aqua America Inc 762 W Lancaster Ave	Bryn Mawr	PA	19010	**877-987-2782**	
NYSE: WTR					
Aquarion Co 835 Main St	Bridgeport	CT	06604	**800-732-9678**	203-336-7662
Arizona Public Service Co (APS) 400 N Fifth St PO Box 53999	Phoenix	AZ	85004	**800-253-9405**	602-371-7171
ATCO Ltd 700 909 11th Ave SW	Calgary	AB	T2R1N6	**800-242-3447**	403-292-7500
TSE: ACO/X					
Avista Corp 1411 E Mission St	Spokane	WA	99202	**800-936-6629**	509-489-0500
NYSE: AVA					
Avista Utilities 1411 E Mission St	Spokane	WA	99252	**800-227-9187**	
Baltimore Gas & Electric Co 110 W Fayette St PO Box 1475	Baltimore	MD	21201	**800-685-0123**	410-470-7433
Bangor Hydro Electric Co PO Box 932	Bangor	ME	04402	**800-499-6600**	207-945-5621
Berkshire Gas Company Inc 115 Cheshire Rd	Pittsfield	MA	01201	**800-292-5012**	413-442-1511
Brownstown Electric Supply Company Inc 690 E State Rd 250 PO Box L	Brownstown	IN	47220	**800-742-8492**	812-358-4555
Cabot Oil & Gas Corp 840 Gessner Rd Ste 1200	Houston	TX	77024	**800-434-3985**	281-848-2799
NYSE: COG					
California ISO 151 Blue Ravine Rd PO Box 639014	Folsom	CA	95630	**800-220-4907**	916-351-4400
California Water Service Group 1720 N First St	San Jose	CA	95112	**800-750-8200**	408-367-8200
NYSE: CWT					
Calpine Corp 717 Texas Ave Ste 1000	Houston	TX	77002	**800-367-5690**	713-830-2000
NYSE: CPN					

	City	State	Zip	Toll-Free	Phone
Cascade Natural Gas Corp (CNGC)					
8113 W Grandridge Blvd	Kennewick	WA	99336	**888-522-1130**	206-624-3900
Central Hudson Gas & Electric Corp					
284 S Ave	Poughkeepsie	NY	12601	**800-527-2714**	845-452-2700
Central Maine Power Co					
83 Edison Dr	Augusta	ME	04336	**800-565-0121**	207-623-3521
Central Vermont Public Service Corp					
2154 Post Rd	Rutland	VT	05701	**800-649-2877**	888-835-4672
Citizens Gas & Coke Utility					
2020 N Meridian St	Indianapolis	IN	46202	**800-427-4217**	317-924-3311
City Public Service Board					
PO Box 1771	San Antonio	TX	78296	**800-870-1006**	210-353-2222
Cleco Corp					
2030 Donahue Ferry Rd	Pineville	LA	71361	**800-622-6537***	318-484-7400
*Cust Svc					
Colorado Springs Utilities					
111 S Cascade Ave PO Box 1103	Colorado Springs	CO	80903	**800-238-5434**	719-448-4800
Columbia Gas of Ohio Inc					
200 Civic Ctr Dr	Columbus	OH	43215	**800-807-9781**	614-460-6000
Columbia Gas of Virginia Inc					
1809 Coyote Dr	Chester	VA	23836	**800-543-8911***	
*Cust Svc					
Connecticut Light & Power Co					
107 Selden St	Berlin	CT	06037	**800-286-2000***	860-665-5000
*Cust Svc					
Consumers Energy Co					
1 Energy Plz	Jackson	MI	49201	**800-477-5050***	517-788-0550
*Cust Svc					
Covanta Energy Corp					
445 South St	Morristown	NJ	07960	**800-950-8749**	862-345-5000
NYSE: CVA					
Dakota Gasification Co					
PO Box 5540	Bismarck	ND	58506	**866-747-3546**	701-221-4400
Dayton Power & Light Co					
PO Box 1247	Dayton	OH	45401	**800-433-8500**	937-331-3900
Delmarva Power					
PO Box 231	Wilmington	DE	19899	**800-898-8042***	
*Cust Svc					
Delta Natural Gas Co Inc					
3617 Lexington Rd	Winchester	KY	40391	**800-262-2012**	859-744-6171
NASDAQ: DGAS					
Dominion East Ohio					
PO Box 26532	Richmond	VA	23261	**800-362-7557***	
*Cust Svc					
Dominion Hope					
701 E Cary St	Richmond	VA	23219	**866-366-4357**	888-366-8280
Dominion North Carolina Power					
701 E Cary St	Richmond	VA	23219	**888-667-3000**	757-857-2112
Dominion Virginia Power					
120 Tredegar St	Richmond	VA	23219	**800-688-4673**	
Duke Energy Corp					
550 S Tryon St Mail Drop WP 890	Charlotte	NC	28202	**800-521-2232**	713-627-5400
Eastern Shore Natural Gas Co					
1110 Forest Ave Ste 201	Dover	DE	19904	**877-650-1257**	302-734-6720
El Paso Electric Co					
100 N Stanton Stanton Tower	El Paso	TX	79901	**800-351-1621**	915-543-5711
NYSE: EE					
Elizabethtown Gas Co					
1 Elizabethtown Plz	Union	NJ	07083	**800-242-5830**	908-289-5000
Empire District Electric Co, The					
602 Joplin St PO Box 127	Joplin	MO	64802	**800-206-2300**	417-625-5100
NYSE: EDE					
Energy West Inc					
1 First Ave S	Great Falls	MT	59401	**800-570-5688**	406-791-7500
ENMAX Corp 141 50 Ave SE	Calgary	AB	T2G4S7	**877-571-7111**	403-514-3000
Entergy Arkansas Inc					
425 W Capitol Ave	Little Rock	AR	72201	**800-368-3749**	
Entergy Louisiana Inc					
639 Loyola Ave	New Orleans	LA	70113	**800-368-3749***	504-576-6116
*Cust Svc					
Entergy New Orleans Inc					
639 Loyola Ave	New Orleans	LA	70113	**800-368-3749***	
*Cust Svc					
Entergy Texas Inc					
350 Pine St	Beaumont	TX	77701	**800-368-3749**	409-981-3245
EQT Corp					
625 Liberty Ave Ste 1700	Pittsburgh	PA	15222	**800-242-1776**	412-553-5700
NYSE: EQT					
Equitable Gas Co					
PO Box 6766	Pittsburgh	PA	15212	**800-654-6335**	
Erie County Water Authority (ECWA)					
295 Main St Rm 350	Buffalo	NY	14203	**855-748-1076**	716-849-8484
Eversource					
1 Nstar Way NW200	Westwood	MA	02090	**800-592-2000***	781-441-8011
*Cust Svc					
Eversource					
1 Federal St Bldg 111-4	Springfield	MA	01105	**800-286-2000**	413-785-5871
Florida City Gas (FCG)					
955 E 25th St	Hialeah	FL	33013	**800-993-7546**	305-691-8710
Florida Public Utilities Co (FPUC)					
401 S Dixie Hwy	West Palm Beach	FL	33401	**800-427-7712**	
Gas Co, The					
515 Kamake'e St	Honolulu	HI	96814	**866-499-3941**	808-535-5933
Gatco Inc					
1550 Factor Ave	San Leandro	CA	94577	**800-227-5640**	510-352-8770
Georgia Power Co					
241 Ralph McGill Blvd NE	Atlanta	GA	30308	**866-506-5333***	404-506-5000
*Cust Svc					
GolfBC Holdings Inc					
1800-1030 W Georgia St	Vancouver	BC	V6E2Y3	**800-446-5322**	
Green Mountain Power Corp					
163 Acorn Ln	Colchester	VT	05446	**888-835-4672**	802-864-5731
Hawaiian Electric Industries Inc					
1001 Bishop St Ste 2900	Honolulu	HI	96813	**877-871-8461**	808-543-5662
Hydro One Inc					
483 Bay St 15th Fl	Toronto	ON	M5G2P5	**888-664-9376**	416-345-5000
Idaho Power Co					
1221 W Idaho St	Boise	ID	83702	**800-488-6151**	208-388-2200

	City	State	Zip	Toll-Free	Phone
Intermountain Gas Co Inc					
555 S Cole Rd	Boise	ID	83709	**800-548-3679***	208-377-6840
*Cust Svc					
Kansas City Power & Light Co					
1200 Main	Kansas City	MO	64141	**888-471-5275**	816-556-2200
Kansas Gas Service					
7421 W 129th St	Overland Park	KS	66213	**888-482-4950**	
Kinder Morgan Inc KN Energy Retail Div					
370 Van Gordon St	Lakewood	CO	80228	**800-232-1627**	303-989-1740
Kissimmee Utility Authority Inc (KUA)					
1701 W Carroll St	Kissimmee	FL	34741	**877-582-7700**	407-933-7777
Laclede Gas Co					
720 Olive St	Saint Louis	MO	63101	**800-887-4173**	314-342-0500
Lineage Power Corp					
601 Shiloh Rd	Plano	TX	75074	**877-546-3243**	972-244-9288
Long Island Power Authority					
333 Earle Ovington Blvd Ste 403	Uniondale	NY	11553	**877-275-5472***	516-222-7700
*Cust Svc					
Madison Gas & Electric Co					
133 S Blair St	Madison	WI	53703	**800-245-1125**	608-252-7000
Marts & Lundy Inc					
1200 Wall St W	Lyndhurst	NJ	07071	**800-526-9005**	201-460-1660
MEAG Power					
1470 Riveredge Pkwy NW	Atlanta	GA	30328	**800-333-6324**	770-563-0300
Merrithew Corp					
2200 Yonge St Ste 500	Toronto	ON	M4S2C6	**800-910-0001**	416-482-4050
Middle Tennessee Natural Gas Utility District (MTNG)					
1036 W Broad St PO Box 670	Smithville	TN	37166	**800-880-6373**	615-597-4300
Middlesex Water Co					
1500 Ronson Rd PO Box 1500	Iselin	NJ	08830	**800-549-3802**	732-634-1500
NASDAQ: MSEX					
Miller-Eads Company Inc					
4125 N Keystone Ave	Indianapolis	IN	46205	**800-530-0684**	317-545-7101
Minnesota Power					
30 W Superior St	Duluth	MN	55802	**800-228-4966**	218-722-2625
Missouri Gas Energy					
3420 Broadway	Kansas City	MO	64111	**800-582-1234**	816-756-5252
Monroe County Water Authority					
475 Norris Dr PO Box 10999	Rochester	NY	14610	**866-426-6292**	585-442-2000
Montana-Dakota Utilities Co (MDU)					
400 N Fourth St	Bismarck	ND	58501	**800-638-3278**	701-222-7900
Morris Products Inc					
53 Carey Rd	Queensbury	NY	12804	**888-777-6678**	518-743-0523
Mount Carmel Public Utility Co					
316 Market St PO Box 220	Mount Carmel	IL	62863	**877-262-7036**	618-262-5151
MRC Global Inc					
2 Houston Ctr	Houston	TX	77010	**877-294-7574**	
National Fuel Gas Supply Corp					
6363 Main St	Williamsville	NY	14221	**800-365-3234***	716-857-7000
*Cust Svc					
National Fuel Resources Inc					
165 Lawrence Bell Dr Ste 120	Williamsville	NY	14221	**800-839-9993**	716-630-6778
Nevada Irrigation District (NID)					
1036 W Main St	Grass Valley	CA	95945	**800-222-4102**	530-273-6185
Nevada Power Co					
6226 W Sahara Ave	Las Vegas	NV	89146	**800-331-3103***	702-402-5555
NYSE: NVE ■ *Cust Svc					
New York State Electric & Gas Corp					
Corporate Dr PO Box 5240	Binghamton	NY	13902	**800-572-1111**	
NextEra Energy Resources LLC					
NextEra Energy Resources LLC 700 Universe Blvd PO Box 14000	Juno Beach	FL	33408	**888-867-3050**	561-691-7171
Nicor Gas 1844 Ferry Rd	Naperville	IL	60563	**888-642-6748**	
Nippon Kodo Inc					
2771 Plz Del Amo Ste 805	Torrance	CA	90503	**888-775-5487**	310-320-8881
North Shore Gas Co					
3001 Grand Ave	Waukegan	IL	60085	**866-556-6004**	847-263-3200
Northern Electric Inc					
1275 W 124th Ave	Denver	CO	80234	**877-265-0794**	303-428-6969
Northern Kentucky Water District					
2835 Crescent Springs Rd	Erlanger	KY	41018	**800-772-4636**	859-578-9898
Northwest Natural Gas Co					
220 NW Second Ave	Portland	OR	97209	**800-422-4012**	503-226-4211
NYSE: NWN					
Nova Scotia Power Inc					
PO Box 910	Halifax	NS	B3J2W5	**800-428-6230**	902-428-6230
NSTAR Gas 1 N Star Way	Westwood	MA	02090	**800-592-2000**	
OG & E Electric Services					
PO Box 24990	Oklahoma City	OK	73124	**800-272-9741**	405-553-3000
Ohio Edison Co					
76 S Main St PO Box 3637	Akron	OH	44308	**800-736-3402**	
Oklahoma Natural Gas Co					
401 N Harvey PO Box 401	Oklahoma City	OK	73101	**800-664-5463**	
Olympia Financial Group Inc					
Ste 2300 125 - 9 Ave SE	Calgary	AB	T2G0P6	**888-668-8384**	403-261-0900
Oncor					
1616 Woodall Rodgers Fwy Ste 2M-012	Dallas	TX	75202	**888-313-6862**	214-486-2000
Orange & Rockland Utilities Inc					
390 W Rte 59	Spring Valley	NY	10977	**877-434-4100***	
*Cust Svc					
Otter Tail Power Co					
215 S Cascade St	Fergus Falls	MN	56537	**800-257-4044**	218-739-8200
Pacific Gas & Electric Co					
77 Beale St	San Francisco	CA	94105	**800-743-5000***	415-973-7000
*Cust Svc					
Pacific Power & Light					
825 NE Multnomah St	Portland	OR	97232	**888-221-7070***	503-813-6666
*Cust Svc					
PacifiCorp					
825 NE Multnomah St	Portland	OR	97232	**888-221-7070**	503-813-5000
Park Water Co					
9750 Washburn Rd	Downey	CA	90241	**800-727-5987**	562-923-0711
Parkway Electric Inc					
11952 James St	Holland	MI	49424	**800-574-9553**	616-392-2788
Passaic Valley Water Commission					
1525 Main Ave	Clifton	NJ	07011	**877-772-7077**	973-340-4300
Pennichuck Corp					
25 Manchester St	Merrimack	NH	03054	**800-553-5191**	603-882-5191
NASDAQ: PNNW					

Company / Address	City	State	Zip	Toll-Free	Phone
Peoples Gas Light & Coke Co 130 E Randolph Dr *Cust Svc	Chicago	IL	60601	**866-556-6001***	312-240-4000
Pepco Energy Services Inc 1300 N 17th St Ste 1600	Arlington	VA	22209	**800-424-8028**	703-253-1800
Piedmont Natural Gas 4720 Piedmont Row Dr PO Box 33068 *NYSE: PNY*	Charlotte	NC	28233	**800-752-7504**	704-364-3120
Portland General Electric 121 SW Salmon St *NYSE: POR*	Portland	OR	97204	**800-542-8818**	503-464-8000
Power Marketing Administrations *Bonneville Power Administration* 905 NE 11th Ave	Portland	OR	97232	**800-282-3713**	503-230-3000
PowerSecure International Inc 1609 Heritage Commerce Ct *NYSE: POWR*	Wake Forest	NC	27587	**866-347-5455**	919-556-3056
PPL Electric Utilities Corp 2 N Ninth St *Cust Svc	Allentown	PA	18101	**800-342-5775***	610-774-5151
PPL Global LLC 2 N Ninth St *NYSE: PPL*	Allentown	PA	18101	**800-345-3085**	610-774-5151
Pratt Communications 2913 Tech Ctr *General	Santa Ana	CA	92705	**800-980-2323***	714-540-6840
PS Energy Group Inc 2987 Clairmont Rd Ste 500	Atlanta	GA	30329	**800-334-7548**	404-321-5711
PSEG Power LLC 80 Pk Plz	Newark	NJ	07101	**800-436-7734**	973-430-7000
Public Service of New Hampshire 780 N Commercial St	Manchester	NH	03105	**800-662-7764**	603-669-4000
Public Works Commission of The City of Fayetteville North Carolina 955 Old Wilmington Rd PO Box 1089	Fayetteville	NC	28301	**877-687-7921**	910-483-1382
Puget Sound Energy Inc 10885 NE Fourth St	Bellevue	WA	98004	**888-225-5773**	425-452-1234
Questar Gas Co PO Box 45841	Salt Lake City	UT	84139	**800-323-5517**	801-324-5111
Reliant Energy Retail Services LLC 1201 Fannin St	Houston	TX	77002	**866-660-4900**	866-222-7100
Rochester Gas & Electric Corp 89 E Ave	Rochester	NY	14649	**800-743-2110**	
Roland's Electric Inc 307 Suburban Ave	Deer Park	NY	11729	**800-981-8010**	631-242-8080
Salt River Project (SRP) 1521 N Project Dr	Tempe	AZ	85281	**800-258-4777**	602-236-5900
San Diego Gas & Electric Co 101 Ash St	San Diego	CA	92101	**800-411-7343**	619-696-2000
SCANA Energy Marketing Inc 220 Operation Way	Cayce	SC	29033	**800-472-1051**	803-217-9000
SETEL UC 720 Cool Springs Blvd Ste 520	Franklin	TN	37067	**800-743-1340**	615-874-6000
SourceGas 655 E Millsap Dr	Fayetteville	AR	72703	**800-563-0012**	
South Carolina Electric & Gas Co PO Box 100255	Columbia	SC	29202	**800-251-7234**	803-635-4444
Southern California Edison Co 2244 Walnut Grove Ave	Rosemead	CA	91770	**800-655-4555**	626-302-1212
Southern California Gas Co 555 W Fifth St	Los Angeles	CA	90013	**800-427-2200**	909-305-8261
Southern Connecticut Gas (SCG) 60 Marsh Hill Rd	Orange	CT	06477	**866-268-2887**	
Southwest Gas Corp 5241 Spring Mtn Rd PO Box 98510 *NYSE: SWX*	Las Vegas	NV	89193	**877-860-6020**	702-876-7237
Southwest Gas Corp Northern Nevada Div 400 Eagle Stn Ln	Carson City	NV	89701	**877-860-6020**	
Southwest Gas Corp Southern Arizona Div PO Box 98512	Las Vegas	NV	89193	**877-860-6020**	
Southwest Gas Corp Southern California Div 13471 Mariposa Rd	Victorville	CA	92395	**877-860-6020**	
Southwest Gas Corp Southern Nevada Div 5241 Spring Mtn Rd	Las Vegas	NV	89150	**877-860-6020**	702-876-7011
Southwestern Energy Co 2350 N Sam Houston Pkwy E Ste 300 *NYSE: SWN*	Houston	TX	77032	**866-322-0801**	832-796-1000
Spectra Energy Corp 5400 Westheimer Ct	Houston	TX	77056	**800-700-8744**	713-627-5400
Stream Gas & Electric Ltd 1950 Stemmons Fwy Ste 3000	Dallas	TX	75207	**866-447-8732**	
Summer Infant Inc 1275 Park E Dr	Woonsocket	RI	02895	**800-268-6237**	
Superior Water Light & Power 2915 Hill Ave PO Box 519	Superior	WI	54880	**800-227-7957**	715-394-2200
Sweetwater Authority PO Box 2328	Chula Vista	CA	91912	**866-275-3772**	619-420-1413
SWEPCo 1 Riverside Plz 13th Fl	Columbus	OH	43215	**888-216-3523**	
System Engineering International Inc (SEI) 5115 Pegasus Ct Ste Q	Frederick	MD	21704	**800-765-4734**	301-694-9601
Texas-New Mexico Power Co (TNMP) 577 N Garden Ridge Blvd	Lewisville	TX	75067	**888-866-7456**	972-420-4189
Tile Shop Holdings Inc 14000 Carlson Pkwy	Plymouth	MN	55441	**888-398-6595**	
Toledo Edison Co PO Box 3687	Akron	OH	44309	**800-447-3333**	
Trans-Tel Central Inc (TTC) 2805 Broce Dr	Norman	OK	73072	**800-729-4636**	405-447-5025
TransAlta Corp 110 12th Ave SW PO Box 1900 Stn M *TSE: TA*	Calgary	AB	T2P2M1	**877-700-9288**	403-267-7110
Tricomm Services Corp 1247 N Church St Ste 8	Moorestown	NJ	08057	**800-872-2401**	856-914-9001
Tucson Electric Power Co 1 S Church Ave Ste 100	Tucson	AZ	85701	**800-430-4046**	520-571-4000
TXU Electric 1601 Bryan St	Dallas	TX	75201	**800-242-9113**	972-791-2888
United Electric Supply Inc 10 Bellecor Dr	New Castle	DE	19720	**800-322-3374**	302-322-3333
United Illuminating Co 157 Church St *Cust Svc	New Haven	CT	06510	**800-722-5584***	203-499-2000
United States Information Systems Inc (USIS) 35 W Jefferson Ave	Pearl River	NY	10965	**866-222-3778**	845-358-7755
Upland Software Inc Frost Tower 401 Congress Ave, Ste 2950	Austin	TX	78701	**855-944-7526**	
Virginia American Water Co (VAWC) 2223 Duke St	Alexandria	VA	22314	**800-452-6863**	703-706-3879
Virginia Natural Gas Inc AGL Resources Inc PO Box 4569	Atlanta	GA	30302	**800-633-4236**	404-584-4000
Wachter Inc 16001 W 99th St	Lenexa	KS	66219	**800-462-9638**	913-541-2500
Ward's Marine Electric Inc 617 SW Third Ave	Fort Lauderdale	FL	33315	**800-545-9273**	954-523-2815
Washington Gas & Light Co 6801 Industrial Rd	Springfield	VA	22151	**800-752-7520**	703-750-4440
We Energies 231 W Michigan St PO Box 2046	Milwaukee	WI	53203	**800-242-9137**	414-221-2345
Westar Energy PO Box 758500	Topeka	KS	66675	**800-544-4857**	785-575-6300
Wisconsin Power & Light Co 4902 N Biltmore Ln PO Box 77007	Madison	WI	53718	**800-255-4268**	
Wisconsin Public Service Corp PO Box 19001	Green Bay	WI	54307	**800-450-7260**	
Xcel Energy Inc 414 Nicollet Mall *NYSE: XEL*	Minneapolis	MN	55401	**800-328-8226**	612-330-5500
Yankee Gas Services Co 107 Selden St	Berlin	CT	06037	**800-989-0900**	
York Water Co, The 130 E Market St PO Box 15089 *NASDAQ: YORW*	York	PA	17405	**800-750-5561**	717-845-3601
Yucaipa Valley Water District PO Box 730	Yucaipa	CA	92399	**800-272-8869**	909-797-5117

786 VACUUM CLEANERS - HOUSEHOLD

SEE ALSO Appliances - Small - Mfr

Company / Address	City	State	Zip	Toll-Free	Phone
Beam Industries 1700 W Second St	Webster City	IA	50595	**800-369-2326**	515-832-4620
CentralVac International 23455 Hellman Ave PO Box 259	Dollar Bay	MI	49922	**800-666-3133**	
Electrolux Home Care Products Inc PO Box 3900 *Cust Svc	Peoria	IL	61612	**800-282-2886***	
Kirby Co 1920 W 114th St	Cleveland	OH	44102	**800-437-7170**	216-228-2400
Lindsay Manufacturing Inc PO Box 1708	Ponca City	OK	74602	**800-546-3729**	580-762-2457
Metropolitan Vacuum Cleaner Co Inc 1 Ramapo Ave PO Box 149	Suffern	NY	10901	**800-822-1602**	845-357-1600
Oreck Corp 1400 Salem Rd	Cookeville	TN	38506	**800-289-5888**	

787 VALVES - INDUSTRIAL

Company / Address	City	State	Zip	Toll-Free	Phone
American Cast Iron Pipe Co (ACIPCO) 1501 31st Ave N	Birmingham	AL	35207	**800-442-2347**	205-325-7701
Anderson Brass Co 1629 W Bobo Newsome Hwy	Hartsville	SC	29550	**800-476-9876**	843-332-4111
Armstrong International Inc 2081 SE Ocean Blvd 4th Fl	Stuart	FL	34996	**866-738-5125**	772-286-7175
Barksdale Inc 3211 Fruitland Ave	Los Angeles	CA	90058	**800-835-1060**	323-589-6181
Cash Acme Inc 2727 Paces Ferry Rd SE Ste 1800	Atlanta	GA	30339	**877-700-4242**	
Circle Seal Controls Inc 2301 Wardlow Cir	Corona	CA	92880	**800-991-2726**	951-270-6200
Clow Valve Co 902 S Second St	Oskaloosa	IA	52577	**800-829-2569**	641-673-8611
Crane Company Stockham Div 2129 Third Ave SE	Cullman	AL	35055	**800-786-2542**	256-775-3800
Engineered Controls International Inc (ECII) 100 Rego Dr PO Box 247	Elon	NC	27244	**800-650-0061**	336-449-7707
Fike Corp 704 SW Tenth St	Blue Springs	MO	64015	**877-342-3453**	816-229-3405
Flowserve Corp 5215 N O'Connor Blvd Ste 2300 *NYSE: FLS*	Irving	TX	75039	**800-350-1082**	972-443-6500
FMC Technologies Inc 1803 Gears Rd *NYSE: FTI*	Houston	TX	77067	**800-356-4898**	281-591-4000
Gemini Valve 2 Otter Ct	Raymond	NH	03077	**800-370-0936**	603-895-4761
Gonzales Inquirer, The 1000 Civic Ctr Loop	San Marcos	TX	78666	**800-210-5909**	830-672-2861
Goulds Pumps Inc Goulds Water Technologies Group 240 Fall St	Seneca Falls	NY	13148	**800-327-7700**	315-568-2811
Groth Corp 13650 N Promenade Blvd	Stafford	TX	77477	**800-354-7684**	281-295-6800
High Vacuum Apparatus LLC (HVA) 12880 Moya Blvd	Reno	NV	89506	**800-551-4422**	775-359-4442
Hudson Valve Company Inc 5301 Office Pk Dr Ste 330	Bakersfield	CA	93309	**800-748-6218**	661-869-1126
Humphrey Products Co 5070 E N Ave PO Box 2008	Kalamazoo	MI	49048	**800-477-8707**	269-381-5500
Hydroseal Valve Co Inc 1500 SE 89th St	Oklahoma City	OK	73149	**800-398-2493**	405-631-1533
ITT Goulds Pumps Industries/Goulds Industrial Pumps Group 240 Fall St	Seneca Falls	NY	13148	**800-327-7700**	315-568-2811
ITT Industries Inc Engineered Valves Div 33 Centerville Rd	Lancaster	PA	17603	**800-366-1111**	717-509-2200
Kennedy Valve 1021 E Water St	Elmira	NY	14902	**800-782-5831**	607-734-2211
KF Industries Inc 1500 SE 89th St	Oklahoma City	OK	73149	**800-398-2493**	405-631-1533

Classified Section

Company	Address	City	State	ZIP	Toll-Free	Phone
Kraft Fluid Systems Inc	14300 Foltz Pkwy	Strongsville	OH	44149	**800-257-1155**	440-238-5545
Leonard Valve Co	1360 Elmwood Ave	Cranston	RI	02910	**800-222-1208**	401-461-1200
Leslie Controls Inc	12501 Telecom Dr	Tampa	FL	33637	**800-323-8366**	813-978-1000
Mac Valves Inc	30569 Beck Rd	Wixom	MI	48393	**800-622-8587**	248-624-7700
Marotta Controls Inc	78 Boonton Ave PO Box 427	Montville	NJ	07045	**888-627-6882**	973-334-7800
Milwaukee Valve Company Inc	16550 W Stratton Dr	New Berlin	WI	53151	**800-348-6544**	262-432-2800
Mueller Co	500 W Eldorado St	Decatur	IL	62522	**800-423-1323**	217-423-4471
Mueller Refrigeration Co Inc	121 Rogers St *Cust Svc	Hartsville	TN	37074	**866-566-7233***	615-374-2124
Newdell Co, The	13750 Hollister Rd	Houston	TX	77086	**877-510-7853**	713-590-1312
Newport News Industrial Corp	182 Enterprise Dr	Newport News	VA	23603	**800-627-0353**	757-380-7053
NIBCO Inc	1516 Middlebury St	Elkhart	IN	46515	**800-234-0227**	574-295-3000
Ogontz Corp	2835 Terwood Rd	Willow Grove	PA	19090	**800-523-2478**	215-657-4770
Parker Hannifin Corp Hydraulic Valve Div	520 Ternes Ave	Elyria	OH	44035	**800-272-7537**	440-366-5200
Parker Instrumentation Group	6035 Parkland Blvd	Cleveland	OH	44124	**800-272-7537**	216-896-3000
Peter Paul Electronics Co Inc	480 John Downey Dr	New Britain	CT	06051	**800-825-8377**	860-229-4884
Plast-O-Matic Valves Inc	1384 Pompton Ave	Cedar Grove	NJ	07009	**800-323-2710**	973-256-3000
Plattco Corp	7 White St	Plattsburgh	NY	12901	**800-352-1731**	518-563-4640
Richards Industries Inc	3170 Wasson Rd *Cust Svc	Cincinnati	OH	45209	**800-543-7311***	513-533-5600
Robert H Wager Co	570 Montroyal Rd	Rural Hall	NC	27045	**800-562-7024**	336-969-6909
Sherwood	2200 North Main St	Washington	PA	15301	**888-508-2583**	724-225-8000
United Brass Works Inc	714 S Main St	Randleman	NC	27317	**800-334-3035**	336-498-2661

788 VALVES & HOSE FITTINGS - FLUID POWER

SEE ALSO Carburetors, Pistons, Piston Rings, Valves

Company	Address	City	State	ZIP	Toll-Free	Phone
Air-Way Manufacturing Co	586 N Main St *Cust Svc	Olivet	MI	49076	**800-253-1036***	269-749-2161
Arkwin Industries Inc	686 Main St	Westbury	NY	11590	**800-284-2551**	516-333-2640
Bosch Rexroth	PO Box 394	Wooster	OH	44691	**800-739-7684**	330-263-3300
Bosch Rexroth Corp	5150 Prairie Stone Pkwy	Hoffman Estates	IL	60192	**800-860-1055**	847-645-3600
Civacon	4304 N Mattox Rd *Sales	Kansas City	MO	64150	**888-526-5657***	816-741-6600
Clippard Instrument Lab	7390 Colerain Ave	Cincinnati	OH	45239	**877-245-6247**	513-521-4261
Control Flow Inc	9201 Fairbanks N Houston Rd	Houston	TX	77064	**800-231-9922**	281-890-8300
Daman Products Co Inc	1811 N Home St	Mishawaka	IN	46545	**800-959-7841**	574-259-7841
Deltrol Fluid Products	3001 Grant Ave	Bellwood	IL	60104	**800-477-9772**	708-547-0500
Dynaquip Controls	10 Harris Industrial Pk	Saint Clair	MO	63077	**800-545-3636**	636-629-3700
E H Lynn Industries Inc	524 Anderson Dr	Romeoville	IL	60446	**800-633-2948**	815-328-8800
Fresno Valves & Castings Inc	7736 E Springfield Ave PO Box 40	Selma	CA	93662	**800-333-1658**	559-834-2511
Hays Fluid Controls	114 Eason Rd	Dallas	NC	28034	**800-354-4297**	704-922-9565
Henry Pratt Co	401 S Highland Ave	Aurora	IL	60506	**877-436-7977**	630-844-4000
Hydraforce Inc	500 Barclay Blvd	Lincolnshire	IL	60069	**877-237-9101**	847-793-2300
Hyson Products	10367 Brecksville Rd	Brecksville	OH	44141	**800-876-4976**	440-526-5900
ITT Industries Inc	1133 Westchester Ave *NYSE: ITT*	White Plains	NY	10604	**800-254-2823**	914-641-2000
JD Gould Co Inc	4707 Massachusetts Ave	Indianapolis	IN	46218	**800-634-6853**	
Jetstream of Houston LLP	4930 Cranswick	Houston	TX	77041	**800-231-8192**	713-462-7000
Mead Fluid Dynamics Inc	4114 N Knox Ave *Cust Svc	Chicago	IL	60641	**877-632-3872***	773-685-6800
Morrison Bros Co	570 E Seventh St	Dubuque	IA	52001	**800-553-4840**	563-583-5701
Norgren	5400 S Delaware St	Littleton	CO	80120	**800-514-0129**	303-794-5000
Omega Flex Inc	451 Creamery Way *NASDAQ: OFLX*	Exton	PA	19341	**800-355-1039**	610-524-7272
Parker Fluid Connectors Group	6035 Parkland Blvd *General	Cleveland	OH	44124	**800-272-7537***	216-896-3000
Parker Hannifin Corp Brass Products Div	100 Parker Dr	Otsego	MI	49078	**800-272-7537**	269-694-9411
Parker Hannifin Corp General Valve Div	26 Clinton Dr Unit 103	Hollis	NH	03049	**800-272-7537**	
Parker Hannifin Corp Pneumatic Div	8676 E M 89	Richland	MI	49083	**877-321-4736**	269-629-5000
Parker Hannifin Corp Skinner Valve Div	95 Edgewood Ave	New Britain	CT	06051	**800-825-8305**	860-827-2300
PBM Inc	1070 Sandy Hill Rd	Irwin	PA	15642	**800-967-4726**	724-863-0550
Plattco Corp	7 White St	Plattsburgh	NY	12901	**800-352-1731**	518-563-4640
Rexarc Inc	PO Box 7	West Alexandria	OH	45381	**877-739-2721**	937-839-4604
Richards Industries Inc	3170 Wasson Rd *Cust Svc	Cincinnati	OH	45209	**800-543-7311***	513-533-5600
Ross Controls	1250 Stephenson Hwy	Troy	MI	48083	**800-438-7677**	248-764-1800
Rupe's Hydraulics Sales & Service	725 N Twin Oaks Vly Rd	San Marcos	CA	92069	**800-354-7873**	760-744-9350
Universal Valve Company Inc	478 Schiller St	Elizabeth	NJ	07206	**800-223-0741**	908-351-0606

789 VARIETY STORES

Company	Address	City	State	ZIP	Toll-Free	Phone
99 Cents Only Stores	4000 Union Pacific Ave	Commerce	CA	90023	**888-582-5999**	323-980-8145
AC Doctor LLC	2151 W Hillsboro Blvd Ste 400	Deerfield Beach	FL	33442	**866-264-1479**	
All Graphic Supplies	6691 Edwards Blvd	Mississauga	ON	L5T2H8	**800-501-4451**	905-795-2610
American Muscle	7 Lee Blvd	Malvern	PA	19355	**888-332-7930**	610-251-2397
Armature Dns 2000 Inc	11001 Jean Meunier	Montreal	QC	H1G4S7	**800-363-7996**	514-324-1141
AutoTruckToys.com	2814 W Wood St	Paris	TN	38242	**800-544-6194**	731-642-3535
Beere Precision Products Inc	4915 21st St	Racine	WI	53406	**800-348-0101**	262-632-0472
Big Lots Inc (BLI)	300 Phillipi Rd *NYSE: BIG*	Columbus	OH	43228	**877-998-1697**	614-278-6800
Black Forest Decor LLC	PO Box 297	Jenks	OK	74037	**800-605-0915**	
Camping World RV Sales	8155 Rivers Ave	Charleston	SC	29406	**888-586-5446**	
Clubfurniture.com	11535 Carmel Commons Blvd Ste 202	Charlotte	NC	28226	**888-378-8383**	
Coast Guard Exchange System	510 Independence Pkwy Ste 500	Chesapeake	VA	23320	**800-572-0230**	
Diamond Attachments LLC	2801A S Mississippi	Atoka	OK	74525	**800-445-1917**	580-889-6202
Dollar General Corp	100 Mission Ridge *NYSE: DG*	Goodlettsville	TN	37072	**800-777-1410**	615-855-4000
Dollar Tree Stores Inc	500 Volvo Pkwy *NASDAQ: DLTR*	Chesapeake	VA	23320	**877-530-8733**	
Easy Ice LLC	925 W Washington St Ste 100	Marquette	MI	49855	**866-327-9423**	
Exchange, The	3911 S Walton Walker Blvd	Dallas	TX	75236	**800-527-2345**	
Family Dollar Stores Inc	PO Box 1017 *NYSE: FDO*	Charlotte	NC	28201	**866-377-6420**	704-847-6961
Filtration Lab Inc	193 Rang De L Eglise	Saint Ligouri	QC	J0K2X0	**800-738-0168**	450-754-4222
Ghost Armor LLC	1470 N Horne St	Gilbert	AZ	85233	**888-960-2766**	480-921-3161
Great Canadian Dollar Store (1993) Ltd	2957 Jutland Rd Ste 101	Victoria	BC	V8T5J9	**877-388-0123**	250-388-0123
Home Furniture Mart	5301 Sheila St	Commerce	CA	90040	**888-936-6673**	909-627-5705
Howell Tractor & Equipment LLC	480 Blaine St	Gary	IN	46406	**800-852-8816**	
Kerley & Sears Inc	4331 Cement Vly Rd	Midlothian	TX	76065	**800-346-4381**	972-775-3902
Kryptonite Kollectibles	1441 Plainfield Ave	Janesville	WI	53545	**877-646-1728**	
Lynch Metals Inc	1075 Lousons Rd	Union	NJ	07083	**888-272-9464**	908-686-8401
McVean Trading & Investments LLC	850 Ridge Lk Blvd Ste One	Memphis	TN	38120	**800-374-1937**	901-761-8400
Navy Exchange Service Command (NEXCOM)	3280 Virginia Beach Blvd	Virginia Beach	VA	23452	**800-628-3924**	757-463-6200
New Vitality	260 Smith St	Farmingdale	NY	11735	**888-997-2941**	
Overstock.com Inc	6350 South 3000 East *NASDAQ: OSTK* ■ *Cust Svc	Salt Lake City	UT	84121	**800-843-2446***	801-947-3100
Peach Trader Inc	6286 Dawson Blvd	Norcross	GA	30093	**888-949-9613**	404-752-6715
Pet Supplies Inc	Customer Service Return Ctr 1 Maplewood Dr	Hazleton	PA	18202	**800-738-7877**	
Playscripts	7 Penn Plz Ste 904	New York	NY	10001	**866-639-7529**	
PLH Products Inc	6655 Knott Ave	Buena Park	CA	90620	**800-946-6001**	714-739-6600
Pride Products Corp	4333 Veterans Memorial Hwy	Ronkonkoma	NY	11779	**800-898-5550**	631-737-4444
R J Schinner Company Inc	16950 W Lincoln Ave	New Berlin	WI	53151	**800-234-1460**	262-797-7180
Rally House & Kansas Sampler	9750 Quivira Rd	Lenexa	KS	66215	**800-645-5394**	
Reliance Parts Corp	2535 Business Pkwy	Minden	NV	89423	**800-776-3113**	
Rennco LLC	300 Elm St	Homer	MI	49245	**800-409-5225**	
Scout Stuff	PO Box 7143	Charlotte	NC	28241	**800-323-0736**	
Shoplet.com	39 Broadway Ste 2030	New York	NY	10006	**800-757-3015**	212-619-3353
Speedway Motors	340 Victory Ln PO Box 81906	Lincoln	NE	68528	**800-736-3733**	402-323-3200
Stahl Peterbilt Inc	18020-118 Ave	Edmonton	AB	T5S2G2	**800-252-7981**	780-483-6666

Classified Section

Company	City	State	Zip	Toll-Free	Phone
Tiger Supplies Inc 27 Selvage St	Irvington	NJ	07111	**888-844-3765**	973-854-8636
Trydor Industries (Canada) Ltd 19275 - 25th Ave	Surrey	BC	V3S3X1	**800-567-8558**	604-542-4773
U-line Corp PO Box 245040	Milwaukee	WI	53224	**800-779-2547**	414-354-0300
Vermeer Mid Atlantic Inc 10900 Carpet St	Charlotte	NC	28273	**800-768-3444**	704-588-3238
West Springfield Auto Parts 92 Blandin Ave Ste C	Framingham	MA	01702	**800-615-2392**	508-879-6932

790 VENTURE CAPITAL FIRMS

Companies listed here are investors, not lenders.

Company	City	State	Zip	Toll-Free	Phone
Adobe Ventures LP 345 Pk Ave	San Jose	CA	95110	**877-722-7088**	408-536-6000
American Bullion Inc 12301 Wilshire Blvd Ste 650	Los Angeles	CA	90025	**800-326-9598**	310-689-7720
American Capital Group Inc 100 Spectrum Ctr Dr Ste 750	Irvine	CA	92618	**877-814-6871**	949-485-3005
Ampersand Capital Partners 55 William St Ste 240	Wellesley	MA	02481	**800-477-6834**	781-239-0700
BlackRock Inc 601 Union St 56th Fl *NYSE: BLK*	Seattle	WA	98101	**800-441-7450**	206-613-6700
Capital Resource Partners 31 State St 6th Fl	Boston	MA	02109	**800-623-2880**	617-478-9600
CIBC Wood Gundy Capital 425 Lexington Ave	New York	NY	10017	**800-999-6726**	212-856-4000
Code Hennessy & Simmons Inc 10 S Wacker Dr Ste 3175	Chicago	IL	60606	**888-603-5847**	312-876-1840
Connecticut Innovations Inc 865 Brook St 3rd Fl	Rocky Hill	CT	06067	**800-733-4763**	860-563-5851
Domain Assoc 1 Palmer Sq Ste 515	Princeton	NJ	08542	**866-803-9204**	609-683-5656
EQUUS Total Return Inc 700 Louisiana St 48th Fl	Houston	TX	77002	**888-323-4533**	
Harvest Partners 280 Pk Ave 25th Fl	New York	NY	10017	**866-771-1000**	212-599-6300
InterWest Partners 2710 Sand Hill Rd 2nd Fl	Menlo Park	CA	94025	**866-803-9204**	650-854-8585
INVESCO Private Capital Inc 1166 Ave of the Americas 26th Fl	New York	NY	10036	**800-959-4246**	212-278-9000
MDT Advisors Inc 125 High St Oliver St Tower Ste 2100	Boston	MA	02110	**800-685-4277**	617-235-7100
Mesirow Financial Private Equity 350 N Clark St	Chicago	IL	60610	**800-453-0600**	312-595-6000
Morgan Stanley Venture Partners 1585 Broadway 38th Fl	New York	NY	10036	**866-722-7310**	212-761-4000
MPM Capital Offices 200 Clarendon St 54th Fl	Boston	MA	02116	**888-286-8010**	617-425-9200
MRV Communications Inc 20415 Nordhoff St *OTC: MRVC* ■ *Sales	Chatsworth	CA	91311	**800-338-5316***	818-773-0900
MVC Capital Inc 287 Bowman Ave 2nd Fl *NYSE: MVC*	Purchase	NY	10577	**800-322-2885**	914-510-9400
Needham Capital Partners 445 Pk Ave	New York	NY	10022	**800-625-7071**	212-371-8300
Newtek Business Services Inc 1440 Broadway 17th Fl *NASDAQ: NEWT* ■ *Sales	New York	NY	10018	**866-820-8902***	212-356-9500
Northleaf Capital Partners 79 Wellington St W Sixth Fl PO Box 120	Toronto	ON	M5K1N9	**866-964-4141**	
Private Capital Management 8889 Pelican Bay Blvd Ste 500	Naples	FL	34108	**800-763-0337**	239-254-2500
Summit Partners 222 Berkeley St 18th Fl	Boston	MA	02116	**800-503-4611**	617-824-1000
Technology Funding Inc 460 St Michael's Dr Ste 1000	Santa Fe	NM	87505	**800-821-5323**	
Technology Partners 550 University Ave	Palo Alto	CA	94301	**800-747-3924**	650-289-9000
TEOCO Corp 12150 Monument Dr Ste 400	Fairfax	VA	22033	**888-868-3626**	703-322-9200
Thomas Weisel Partners Group LLC 1 Montgomery St	San Francisco	CA	94104	**888-267-3700**	415-364-2500
Tortoise Energy Capital Corp 11550 Ash St Ste 300 *NYSE: TYY*	Leawood	KS	66211	**866-362-9331**	913-981-1020
UPS Strategic Enterprise Fund 55 Glenlake Pkwy NE Bldg 1 4th Fl	Atlanta	GA	30328	**800-742-5877**	

791 VETERANS NURSING HOMES - STATE

SEE ALSO Veterans Hospitals

Company	City	State	Zip	Toll-Free	Phone
DJ Jacobetti Home for Veterans 425 Fisher St	Marquette	MI	49855	**800-433-6760**	906-226-3576
Floyd E Tut Fann State Veterans Home 2701 Meridian St	Huntsville	AL	35811	**855-212-8028**	256-851-2807
Grand Island Veterans' Home 2300 W Capital Ave	Grand Island	NE	68803	**800-358-8802**	308-385-6252
Hastings Veterans Home 1200 E 18th St	Hastings	MN	55033	**877-838-3803**	651-438-8500
Idaho State Veterans Home-Lewiston 821 21st Ave	Lewiston	ID	83501	**877-222-8387**	208-799-3422
Idaho State Veterans Home-Pocatello 1957 Alvin Ricken Dr	Pocatello	ID	83201	**877-222-8387**	208-236-6340
Illinois Veterans Home-Anna 792 N Main St	Anna	IL	62906	**888-261-3336**	618-833-6302
Iowa Veterans Home 1301 Summit St Bldg 3465	Marshalltown	IA	50131	**800-838-4692**	515-252-4698
Maine Veterans Home-Augusta 310 Cony Rd	Augusta	ME	04330	**888-684-4664**	
Maine Veterans Home-Bangor 44 Hogan Rd	Bangor	ME	04401	**888-684-4665**	207-942-2333
Maine Veterans Home-Caribou 163 Van Buren Rd Ste 2	Caribou	ME	04736	**888-684-4667**	207-498-6074
Maine Veterans Home-Scarborough 290 US Rt 1	Scarborough	ME	04074	**888-684-4666**	207-883-7184
Maine Veterans Home-South Paris 477 High St	South Paris	ME	04281	**888-684-4668**	207-743-6300
Minnesota Veterans Home-Minneapolis 5101 Minnehaha Ave S	Minneapolis	MN	55407	**877-838-6757**	612-721-0600
Minnesota Veterans Home-Silver Bay 45 Banks Blvd	Silver Bay	MN	55614	**877-729-8387**	218-226-6300
Mississippi State Veterans' Home Collins 3261 Hwy 49 S	Collins	MS	39428	**877-203-5632**	601-765-0403
Mississippi State Veterans' Home Kosciusko 310 Autumn Ridge Dr	Kosciusko	MS	39090	**877-203-5632**	662-289-7044
Missouri Veterans Home-Cape Girardeau 2400 Veterans Memorial Dr	Cape Girardeau	MO	63701	**800-392-0210**	573-290-5870
Montana Veterans Home 400 Veterans Dr	Columbia Falls	MT	59912	**888-279-7532**	406-892-3256
New Hampshire Veterans Home 139 Winter St	Tilton	NH	03276	**800-735-2964**	603-527-4400
New Mexico State Veterans Ctr 992 S Broadway St	Truth or Consequences	NM	87901	**800-964-3976**	575-894-4200
Ohio Veterans Home 3416 Columbus Ave *Admissions	Sandusky	OH	44870	**800-572-7934***	419-625-2454
Oklahoma Veterans Ctr Ardmore 1015 S Commerce	Ardmore	OK	73401	**800-941-2160**	580-223-2266
Oklahoma Veterans Ctr Norman 1776 E Robinson St	Norman	OK	73071	**800-782-5218**	405-360-5600
Oklahoma Veterans Ctr Talihina 10014 SE 1138th Ave PO Box 1168	Talihina	OK	74571	**800-941-2160**	918-567-2251
Oregon Veterans' Home 700 Veterans Dr	The Dalles	OR	97058	**800-846-8460**	541-296-7190
Thomson-Hood Veterans Ctr 100 Veterans Dr	Wilmore	KY	40390	**800-928-4838**	859-858-2814
Veterans Home of California-Barstow 100 E Veterans Pkwy	Barstow	CA	92311	**800-746-0606**	760-252-6200
Veterans Home of California-Chula Vista 700 E Naples Ct	Chula Vista	CA	91911	**800-952-5626**	
Veterans Home of California-Yountville 1227 O St	Sacramento	CA	95814	**800-952-5626**	916-653-2573
Wisconsin Veterans Home N2665 County Rd QQ	King	WI	54946	**877-944-6667**	715-258-5586

792 VETERINARY HOSPITALS

Company	City	State	Zip	Toll-Free	Phone
Banfield the Pet Hospital 18101 SE 6th Way	Vancouver	WA	98683	**866-894-7927**	
Imex Veterinary Inc 1001 Mckesson Dr	Longview	TX	75604	**800-828-4639**	903-295-2196
John Paul Pet Salon 32861 Camino Capistrano Ste F	San Juan Capistrano	CA	92675	**855-577-7669**	
National Veterinary Associates Inc 29229 Canwood St Ste 100	Agoura Hills	CA	91301	**888-767-7755**	805-777-7722
Penn Veterinary Supply Inc 53 Industrial Cir	Lancaster	PA	17601	**800-233-0210**	717-656-4121
Pipestone Veterinary Clinic LLC 1300 Hwy 75 S PO Box 188	Pipestone	MN	56164	**800-658-2523**	507-825-4211
Radiocat 32-A Mellor Ave	Baltimore	MD	21228	**800-323-9729**	
Summit Pet Product Distributors Inc 420 N Chimney Rock Rd	Greensboro	NC	27410	**800-323-2963**	336-294-3200
United Pet Care LLC 6232 N Seventh St Ste 202	Phoenix	AZ	85014	**877-872-8800**	602-266-5303
VDx Veterinary Diagnostics Inc 2019 Anderson Rd Ste C	Davis	CA	95616	**877-753-4285**	530-753-4285
VetSelect Animal Hospital 2150 Old Novi Rd	Novi	MI	48377	**800-462-8749**	248-624-1100
Western Veterinary Conference 2425 E Oquendo Rd	Las Vegas	NV	89120	**866-800-7326**	702-739-6698

793 VETERINARY MEDICAL ASSOCIATIONS - STATE

Company	City	State	Zip	Toll-Free	Phone
Colorado Veterinary Medical Assn 191 Yuma St	Denver	CO	80223	**800-228-5429**	303-318-0447
Georgia Veterinary Medical Assn 233 Peachtree St NE Ste 2205	Atlanta	GA	30303	**800-853-1625**	678-309-9800
Indiana Veterinary Medical Assn 201 S Capitol Ave Ste 405	Indianapolis	IN	46225	**800-270-0747**	317-974-0888
Iowa Veterinary Medical Assn 1605 N Ankeny Blvd Ste 110	Ankeny	IA	50023	**800-369-9564**	515-965-9237
Kansas Veterinary Medical Assn 816 SW Tyler St Ste 200	Topeka	KS	66612	**888-545-5862**	785-233-4141
Kentucky Veterinary Medical Assn 108 Consumer Ln	Frankfort	KY	40601	**800-552-5862**	502-226-5862
Louisiana Veterinary Medical Assn 8550 United Plz Blvd Ste 1001	Baton Rouge	LA	70809	**800-524-2996**	225-928-5862
Maine Veterinary Medical Assn (MVMA) 97A Exchange St Ste 305	Portland	ME	04101	**800-448-2772**	
Maryland Veterinary Medical Assn 8015 Corporate Dr Ste A	Baltimore	MD	21236	**888-884-6862**	410-931-3332
Minnesota Veterinary Medical Assn 101 Bridgepoint Way Ste 100	South Saint Paul	MN	55075	**888-933-5363**	651-645-7533
Missouri Veterinary Medical Assn 2500 Country Club Dr	Jefferson City	MO	65109	**800-632-6900**	573-636-8612
New York State Veterinary Medical Society 100 Great Oaks Blvd Ste 127	Albany	NY	12203	**800-876-9867**	518-869-7867
North Carolina Veterinary Medical Assn (NCVMA) 1611 Jones Franklin Rd Ste 108	Raleigh	NC	27606	**800-446-2862**	919-851-5850
Ohio Veterinary Medical Assn (OVMA) 3168 Riverside Dr	Columbus	OH	43221	**800-662-6862**	614-486-7253

Name / Address	City	State	ZIP	Toll-Free	Phone
Oklahoma Veterinary Medical Assn PO Box 14521	Oklahoma City	OK	73113	**800-248-2862**	405-478-1002
Oregon Veterinary Medical Assn 1880 Lancaster Dr NE Ste 118	Salem	OR	97305	**800-235-3502**	503-399-0311
South Carolina Assn of Veterinarians PO Box 11766	Columbia	SC	29211	**800-441-7228**	803-254-1027
Tennessee Veterinary Medical Assn PO Box 803	Fayetteville	TN	37334	**800-697-3587**	931-438-0070
Texas Veterinary Medical Assn 8104 Exchange Dr	Austin	TX	78754	**800-711-0023**	512-452-4224
Virginia Veterinary Medical Assn (VVMA) 3801 Westerre Pkwy Ste D	Henrico	VA	23233	**800-937-8862**	804-346-2611
Washington State Veterinary Medical Assn 8024 Bracken Pl SE	Snoqualmie	WA	98065	**800-399-7862**	425-396-3191
Wisconsin Veterinary Medical Assn (WVMA) 2801 Crossroads Dr Ste 1200	Madison	WI	53718	**888-254-5202**	608-257-3665
Wyoming Veterinary Medical Assn (WVMA) 1841 W Secluded Ct	Kuna	ID	83634	**800-272-1813**	208-922-9431

794 VIATICAL SETTLEMENT COMPANIES

A viatical settlement is the sale of an existing life insurance policy by a terminally ill person to a third party in return for a percentage of the face value of the policy paid immediately.

Name / Address	City	State	ZIP	Toll-Free	Phone
Coventry First LLC 7111 Vly Green Rd	Fort Washington	PA	19034	**877-836-8300**	
Crystal Wealth Management System Ltd 3385 Harvester Rd Ste 200	Burlington	ON	L7N3N2	**877-299-2854**	905-332-4414
Francis Investment Counsel LLC 21180 W Capitol Dr	Pewaukee	WI	53072	**866-232-6457**	
Habersham Funding LLC 3495 Piedmont Rd NE Ste 910	Atlanta	GA	30305	**888-874-2402**	404-233-8275
Indiana Trust & Investment Management Co 4045 Edison Lakes Pkwy Ste 100	Mishawaka	IN	46545	**800-362-7905**	574-271-0374
Legacy Benefits Corp 350 Fifth Ave Ste 4320	New York	NY	10118	**800-875-1000**	
Life Partners Inc (LPI) 204 Woodhew Dr	Waco	TX	76712	**800-368-5569**	254-751-7797
Life Settlement Solutions Inc 9201 Spectrum Ctr Blvd Ste 105	San Diego	CA	92123	**800-762-3387**	858-576-8067
Nicola Wealth Management Ltd 1508 W Broadway 5th Fl	Vancouver	BC	V6J1W8	**800-219-8032**	604-739-6450
Page & Assoc Inc 1979 Lakeside Pkwy Ste 200	Tucker	GA	30084	**800-252-5282**	
Pembroke Management Ltd 1002 Sherbrooke St W Ste 1700	Montreal	QC	H3A3S4	**800-667-0716**	514-848-1991
Senior Settlements LLC 1000 S Lenola Rd Bldg 1 Ste 202	Maple Shade	NJ	08052	**800-834-0628**	856-235-2133
Winfield Associates Inc 700 W St Clair Ave Ste 404	Cleveland	OH	44113	**888-322-2575**	216-241-2575

795 VIDEO STORES

SEE ALSO Book, Music, Video Clubs

Name / Address	City	State	ZIP	Toll-Free	Phone
Amazon.com Inc 1200 12th Ave S Ste 1200 *NASDAQ: AMZN* ■ *Cust Svc	Seattle	WA	98144	**800-201-7575***	206-266-1000
Best Buy Company Inc 7601 Penn Ave S *NYSE: BBY*	Minneapolis	MN	55423	**888-237-8289**	612-291-1000
DVD Empire 2140 Woodland Rd	Warrendale	PA	15086	**888-383-1880**	
Facets Multimedia Inc 1517 W Fullerton Ave *Cust Svc	Chicago	IL	60614	**800-331-6197***	773-281-9075
Family Video 2500 Lehigh Ave	Glenview	IL	60026	**888-332-6843**	847-904-9000
NetFlix Inc 100 Winchester Cir *NASDAQ: NFLX*	Los Gatos	CA	95032	**800-290-8191**	408-540-3700

796 VISION CORRECTION CENTERS

Name / Address	City	State	ZIP	Toll-Free	Phone
Barnet-Dulaney Eye Ctr 4800 N 22nd St	Phoenix	AZ	85016	**866-742-6581**	602-955-1000
Center for Lasik Ophthalmology Consultants, The 5800 Colonial Dr Ste 103	Margate	FL	33063	**800-448-8770**	954-969-0090
Eye Centers of Florida (ECOF) 4101 Evans Ave	Fort Myers	FL	33901	**888-393-2455**	239-939-3456
John-Kenyon Eye Ctr 1305 Wall St	Jeffersonville	IN	47130	**800-342-5393**	
Jones Eye Clinic 4405 Hamilton Blvd	Sioux City	IA	51104	**800-334-2015**	712-239-3937
LaserVue Eye Ctr 3540 Mendocino Ave Ste 200	Santa Rosa	CA	95403	**888-527-3745**	707-522-6200
LCA-Vision Inc 7840 Montgomery Rd *NASDAQ: LCAV*	Cincinnati	OH	45236	**800-688-4550**	513-792-9292
Minnesota Eye Consultants PA 710 E 24th St Ste 100	Minneapolis	MN	55404	**800-526-7632**	612-813-3600
Pacific Cataract & Laser Institute 2517 NE Kresky Ave	Chehalis	WA	98532	**800-888-9903**	360-748-8632
Southwestern Eye Ctr 2610 E University Dr *General	Mesa	AZ	85213	**800-224-3339***	480-892-8400
TLC Vision Corp 50 Burnhamthorpe Rd W Ste 101	Mississauga	ON	L5B3C2	**877-852-2020**	
Will Vision & Laser Centers 8100 NE Pkwy Dr Ste 125	Vancouver	WA	98662	**877-542-3937**	360-885-1327

797 VITAMINS & NUTRITIONAL SUPPLEMENTS

SEE ALSO Diet & Health Foods ; Medicinal Chemicals & Botanical Products ; Pharmaceutical Companies ; Pharmaceutical Companies - Generic Drugs

Name / Address	City	State	ZIP	Toll-Free	Phone
ADM Natural Health & Nutrition *Archer Daniels Midland Co* 4666 Faries Pkwy	Decatur	IL	62526	**800-637-5843**	217-451-7231
AST Sports Science Inc 120 Capitol Dr	Golden	CO	80401	**800-627-2788**	303-278-1420
Atkins Nutritionals Inc 1050 17th St Ste 1000	Denver	CO	80265	**800-628-5467**	303-633-2840
Beehive Botanicals Inc 16297 W Nursery Rd	Hayward	WI	54843	**800-233-4483**	715-634-4274
Cc Pollen Co 3627 E Indian School Rd Ste 209	Phoenix	AZ	85018	**800-875-0096**	
CytoSport Inc 4795 Industrial Way	Benicia	CA	94510	**888-313-1922**	707-751-3942
Douglas Laboratories Inc 600 Boyce Rd	Pittsburgh	PA	15205	**800-245-4440**	
Edom Laboratories Inc 100 E Jefryn Blvd Ste M	Deer Park	NY	11729	**800-723-3366**	631-586-2266
Enzymatic Therapy 825 Challenger Dr	Green Bay	WI	54311	**800-783-2286**	920-469-1313
Foodscience Corp 20 New England Dr Ste 10	Essex Junction	VT	05452	**800-451-5190**	802-878-5508
Futurebiotics LLC 70 Commerce Dr	Hauppauge	NY	11788	**800-367-5433**	631-273-6300
Garden of Life Inc 5500 Village Blvd Ste 102	West Palm Beach	FL	33407	**866-465-0051**	
GNC Inc 300 Sixth Ave 14th Fl *NYSE: GNC*	Pittsburgh	PA	15222	**877-462-4700**	
Hammer Nutrition Ltd 4952 Whitefish Stage Rd *Cust Svc	Whitefish	MT	59937	**800-336-1977***	406-862-1877
Herbalist, The 2106 NE 65th St	Seattle	WA	98115	**800-694-3727**	206-523-2600
Integrated BioPharma Inc 225 Long Ave *OTC: INBP*	Hillside	NJ	07205	**888-319-6962**	973-926-0816
Irwin Naturals 5310 Beethoven St	Los Angeles	CA	90066	**800-297-3273**	310-306-3636
Jarrow Formulas Inc 1824 S Robertson Blvd	Los Angeles	CA	90035	**800-726-0886**	310-204-6936
Labrada Nutrition 403 Century Plz Dr Ste 440	Houston	TX	77073	**800-832-9948**	
Maximum Human Performance Inc (MHP Inc) 21 Dwight Pl	Fairfield	NJ	07004	**888-783-8844**	973-785-9055
Mega-Pro International Inc 251 W Hilton Dr	Saint George	UT	84770	**800-541-9469**	435-673-1001
Natrol Inc 21411 Prairie St	Chatsworth	CA	91311	**800-262-8765**	818-739-6000
Naturade Products Inc 2030 Main St Ste 630	Irvine	CA	92614	**800-421-1830**	
Natural Alternatives International Inc 1185 Linda Vista Dr *NASDAQ: NAII*	San Marcos	CA	92078	**800-848-2646**	760-744-7340
Natural Factors Nutritional Products Ltd 1550 United Blvd	Coquitlam	BC	V3K6Y2	**800-663-8900**	604-777-1757
Natural Organics Inc 548 Broadhollow Rd	Melville	NY	11747	**800-645-9500**	
Naturally Vitamins 4404 E Elwood St	Phoenix	AZ	85040	**800-899-4499**	480-991-0200
Nature's Way Products Inc 3051 W Maple Loop Dr Ste 125	Lehi	UT	84043	**800-962-8873**	
Nickers International Ltd PO Box 50066	Staten Island	NY	10305	**800-642-5377**	718-448-6283
Nutraceutical International Corp 1400 Kearns Blvd *NASDAQ: NUTR*	Park City	UT	84060	**800-669-8877**	435-655-6000
Pacific Health Laboratories Inc 100 Matawan Rd Ste 150 *General	Matawan	NJ	07747	**877-363-8769***	732-739-2900
Paragon Laboratories 20433 Earl St	Torrance	CA	90503	**800-231-3670**	310-370-1563
Peak Nutrition Inc 1097 11th St PO Box 87 *Sales	Syracuse	NE	68446	**800-600-2069***	402-269-2825
Perrigo Co 515 Eastern Ave *NYSE: PRGO*	Allegan	MI	49010	**800-719-9260**	269-673-8451
Phibro Animal Health Corp 300 Frank W Burr Blvd Ste 21	Teaneck	NJ	07660	**800-223-0434**	201-329-7300
Power Organics 301 S Old Stage Rd	Mount Shasta	CA	96067	**877-769-3795**	530-926-6684
Prolab Nutrition 21411 Prairie St	Chatsworth	CA	91311	**800-776-5221**	818-739-6000
SportPharma Inc 3 Terminal Rd	New Brunswick	NJ	08901	**800-872-0101**	732-545-3130
Swanson Health Products Inc PO Box 2803	Fargo	ND	58108	**800-824-4491**	701-356-2700
Synutra International Inc 2275 Research Blvd Ste 500 *NASDAQ: SYUT*	Rockville	MD	20850	**866-405-2350**	301-840-3888
Thayers Natural Pharmaceuticals Inc PO Box 56	Westport	CT	06881	**888-842-9371**	
Tishcon Corp 50 Sylvester St	Westbury	NY	11590	**800-848-8442**	516-333-3050
Twinlab 600 E Quality Dr	American Fork	UT	84003	**800-645-5626**	801-763-0700
USANA Health Sciences Inc 3838 West PkwyBlvd *NYSE: USNA*	Salt Lake City	UT	84120	**888-950-9595**	801-954-7100
Wachters' Organic Sea Products Corp 550 Sylvan St	Daly City	CA	94014	**800-682-7100**	650-757-9851

				Toll-Free	Phone
Wakunaga of America Company Ltd					
23501 Madero	Mission Viejo	CA	92691	**800-421-2998**	949-855-2776
Windmill Health Products					
6 Henderson Dr	West Caldwell	NJ	07006	**800-822-4320**	973-575-6591
Young Living Essential Oils					
3125 Executive Pkwy	Lehi	UT	84043	**866-203-5666**	801-418-8900

798 VOCATIONAL & TECHNICAL SCHOOLS

SEE ALSO Universities - Canadian ; Children's Learning Centers ; Colleges - Community & Junior ; Colleges - Culinary Arts ; Colleges - Fine Arts ; Colleges & Universities - Four-Year ; Language Schools ; Military Service Academies

Listings in this category are organized alphabetically by states.

				Toll-Free	Phone
Enterprise-Ozark Community College					
1975 Ave C	Mobile	AL	36615	**877-701-0033**	251-438-2816
Herzing College Birmingham					
280 W Valley Ave	Birmingham	AL	35209	**800-425-9432**	205-916-2800
ITT Technical Institute Birmingham					
6270 Pk S Dr	Bessemer	AL	35022	**800-488-7033**	205-497-5700
JF Drake State Technical College					
3421 Meridian St N	Huntsville	AL	35811	**888-413-7253**	256-539-8161
Lawson State Community College					
Bessemer 1100 Ninth Ave SW	Bessemer	AL	35022	**800-373-4879**	205-925-2515
Lurleen B Wallace Community College					
Andalusia					
1000 Dannelly Blvd PO Box 1418	Andalusia	AL	36420	**877-382-4357**	334-222-6591
MacArthur					
1708 N Main St PO Box 910	Opp	AL	36467	**877-382-4357**	334-493-3573
Trenholm State Technical College					
1225 Air Base Blvd	Montgomery	AL	36108	**800-917-2081**	334-420-4200
Wallace Community College Selma					
3000 Earl Goodwin Pkwy	Selma	AL	36703	**855-428-8313**	334-876-9227
DeVry University					
Calgary 2700 Third Ave SE	Calgary	AB	T2A7W4	**800-363-5558***	403-235-3450
*General					
DeVry University Phoenix					
2149 W Dunlap Ave	Phoenix	AZ	85021	**800-528-0250***	602-870-9222
*Cust Svc					
ITT Technical Institute Tempe					
5005 S Wendler Dr	Tempe	AZ	85282	**800-879-4881**	602-437-7500
ITT Technical Institute Tucson					
1455 W River Rd	Tucson	AZ	85704	**800-870-9730**	520-408-7488
Southwest Institute of Healing Arts					
1100 E Apache Blvd	Tempe	AZ	85281	**888-504-9106**	480-994-9244
Remington College					
Little Rock					
10600 Colonel Glenn Rd Ste 100	Little Rock	AR	72204	**800-323-8122**	501-312-0007
Concorde Career Colleges Inc					
San Bernardino					
201 E Airport Dr	San Bernardino	CA	92408	**800-852-8434**	909-884-8891
San Diego					
4393 Imperial Ave Ste 100	San Diego	CA	92113	**800-693-7010**	619-688-0800
DeVry University Fremont					
6600 Dumbarton Cir	Fremont	CA	94555	**800-363-5558**	510-574-1200
DeVry University Long Beach					
3880 Kilroy Airport Way	Long Beach	CA	90806	**800-597-1333**	562-997-5300
DeVry University Pomona					
901 Corporate Ctr Dr	Pomona	CA	91768	**800-243-3660**	909-622-8866
DeVry University Sherman Oaks					
15301 Ventura Blvd Bldg D-100	Sherman Oaks	CA	91403	**888-610-0800**	818-713-8111
Everest College Alhambra					
2215 W Mission Rd	Alhambra	CA	91803	**888-223-8556**	626-979-4940
Everest College Anaheim					
511 N Brookhurst Ste 300	Anaheim	CA	92801	**888-224-6684**	714-953-6500
Everest College City of Industry					
12801 Crossroads Pkwy S	City of Industry	CA	91746	**888-224-6684**	562-908-2500
Everest College San Jose					
1245 S Winchester Blvd Ste 102	San Jose	CA	95128	**888-223-8556**	408-246-4171
Everest Institute Long Beach					
2161 Technology Pl	Long Beach	CA	90810	**888-223-8556**	562-624-9530
Golden Gate University					
Roseville					
7 Sierra Gate Plz Ste 101	Roseville	CA	95678	**800-448-4968**	916-648-1446
San Francisco					
536 Mission St	San Francisco	CA	94105	**800-448-4968**	415-442-7000
ITT Technical Institute					
Lathrop 16916 S Harlan Rd	Lathrop	CA	95330	**800-346-1786**	209-858-0077
Oxnard 2051 Solar Dr Ste 150	Oxnard	CA	93036	**800-530-1582**	805-988-0143
Rancho Cordova					
10863 Gold Ctr Dr	Rancho Cordova	CA	95670	**800-488-8466**	916-851-3900
San Bernardino					
670 Carnegie Dr	San Bernardino	CA	92408	**800-888-3801**	909-806-4600
San Dimas					
650 W Cienega Ave	San Dimas	CA	91773	**800-414-6522**	909-971-2300
Sylmar 12669 Encinitas Ave	Sylmar	CA	91342	**800-363-2086**	818-364-5151
Westwood College Inland Empire					
20 W Seventh St	Upland	CA	91786	**866-221-5632**	909-931-7550
Wyotech Sacramento					
980 Riverside Pkwy	West Sacramento	CA	95605	**888-308-7158**	916-376-8888
Bel-Rea Institute of Animal Technology					
1681 S Dayton St	Denver	CO	80247	**800-950-8001**	303-751-8700
Colorado Technical University Denver					
1865 W 121st Ave Bldg C Ste 100	Westminster	CO	80234	**877-250-9372**	303-362-2900
Denver Academy of Court Reporting					
9051 Harlan St Ste 20	Westminster	CO	80031	**866-712-2425**	303-427-5292
Colorado Springs					
1175 Kelly Johnson Blvd	Colorado Springs	CO	80920	**877-784-1997***	719-632-3000
*Help Line					
Everest College Aurora					
14280 E Jewell Ave Ste 100	Aurora	CO	80012	**888-223-8556**	303-745-6244
Everest College Thornton					
9065 Grant St	Thornton	CO	80229	**888-223-8556**	303-457-2757
Redstone College					
Denver 10851 W 120th Ave	Broomfield	CO	80021	**800-888-3995**	303-466-1714
Brown Mackie College Miami					
3700 Lakeside Dr	Miramar	FL	33027	**866-505-0335**	305-341-6600
Concorde Career Colleges inc Miramar					
10933 Marks Way	Miramar	FL	33025	**800-693-7010**	954-731-8880
DeVry University Orlando					
4000 Millenia Blvd	Orlando	FL	32839	**888-857-5757**	407-345-2800
Everest University					
Brandon 3924 Coconut Palm Dr	Tampa	FL	33619	**888-223-8556***	813-621-0041
*Cust Svc					
Jacksonville					
8226 Phillips Hwy	Jacksonville	FL	32256	**800-611-2101**	904-731-4949
Lakeland					
995 E Memorial Blvd Ste 110	Lakeland	FL	33801	**888-223-8556**	863-686-1444
Largo 1199 E Bay Dr	Largo	FL	33770	**888-223-8556**	727-725-2688
North Orlando					
5421 Diplomat Cir	Orlando	FL	32810	**888-223-8556**	407-628-5870
Orange Park					
805 Wells Rd	Orange Park	FL	32073	**888-223-8556**	904-264-9122
Pompano Beach					
225 N Federal Hwy	Pompano Beach	FL	33062	**888-223-8556**	954-783-7339
South Orlando					
9200 Southpark Ctr Loop	Orlando	FL	32819	**800-611-2101**	407-851-2525
Tampa 3319 W Hillsborough Ave	Tampa	FL	33614	**888-223-8556**	813-879-6000
Florida Technical College					
12900 Challenger Pkwy	Orlando	FL	32826	**888-678-2929***	407-447-7300
*General					
Full Sail University					
3300 University Blvd Ste 160	Winter Park	FL	32792	**800-226-7625**	407-679-6333
ITT Technical Institute Fort Lauderdale					
3401 S University Dr	Fort Lauderdale	FL	33328	**800-488-7797**	954-476-9300
ITT Technical Institute Jacksonville					
7011 AC Skinner Pkwy Ste 140	Jacksonville	FL	32256	**800-318-1264**	904-573-9100
ITT Technical Institute Tampa					
4809 Memorial Hwy	Tampa	FL	33634	**800-825-2831**	813-885-2244
Kaplan University					
6301 Kaplan University Ave	Fort Lauderdale	FL	33309	**866-527-5268**	
Keiser University					
Fort Lauderdale					
1500 W Commercial Blvd	Fort Lauderdale	FL	33309	**800-749-4456**	954-776-4456
Melbourne					
900 S Babcock St	Melbourne	FL	32901	**888-534-7379**	321-409-4800
Sarasota 6151 Lk Osprey Dr	Sarasota	FL	34240	**866-534-7372**	941-907-3900
Remington College Largo					
6302 E Dr Martin Luther King Jr Blvd Ste 400	Tampa	FL	33619	**800-323-8122**	
Remington College Tampa					
6302 E MLK Blvd Ste 400	Tampa	FL	33619	**800-323-8122***	813-935-5700
*General					
Stenotype Institute of Jacksonville					
3563 Phillips Hwy Bldg E Ste 501	Jacksonville	FL	32207	**800-273-5090**	904-398-4141
Brown College of Court Reporting & Medical Transcription (BCCR)					
1900 Emery St NW Ste 200	Atlanta	GA	30318	**800-849-0703**	404-876-1227
Brown Mackie College Atlanta					
4370 Peachtree Rd NE	Atlanta	GA	30319	**877-479-8419**	404-799-4500
Central Georgia Technical College					
3300 Macon Tech Dr	Macon	GA	31206	**866-430-0135**	478-757-3400
Gupton-Jones College of Funeral Service					
5141 Snapfinger Woods Dr	Decatur	GA	30035	**800-848-5352**	770-593-2257
Herzing College					
Atlanta					
3393 Peachtree Rd Ste 1003	Atlanta	GA	30326	**800-573-4533**	404-816-4533
Imedex Inc					
4325 Alexander Dr	Alpharetta	GA	30022	**800-243-6969**	770-751-7332
ITT Technical Institute Kennesaw					
2065 Baker Rd NW	Kennesaw	GA	30144	**800-564-9771**	770-426-2300
Savannah Technical College					
5717 White Bluff Rd	Savannah	GA	31405	**800-769-6362**	912-443-5700
Westwood College Atlanta Northlake					
2309 Parklake Dr NE	Atlanta	GA	30345	**800-227-5695**	770-743-3000
Argosy University Hawaii					
400 ASB Tower 1001 Bishop St	Honolulu	HI	96813	**888-323-2777**	808-536-5555
Eastern Idaho Technical College					
1600 S 25th E	Idaho Falls	ID	83404	**800-662-0261**	208-524-3000
ITT Technical Institute Boise					
12302 W Explorer Dr	Boise	ID	83713	**800-666-4888**	208-322-8844
DeVry University Addison					
1221 N Swift Rd	Addison	IL	60101	**800-346-5420**	630-953-1300
Midstate College					
411 W Northmoor Rd	Peoria	IL	61614	**800-251-4299**	309-692-4092
Northwestern College Chicago Campus					
4829 N Lipps Ave	Chicago	IL	60630	**888-205-2283**	773-777-4220
Westwood College O'Hare Airport					
8501 W Higgins Rd Ste 100	Chicago	IL	60631	**866-552-7536**	773-380-6800
Brown Mackie College					
Fort Wayne					
3000 E Coliseum Blvd	Fort Wayne	IN	46805	**866-433-2289***	260-484-4400
*General					
Merrillville					
1000 E 80th Pl Ste 205M	Merrillville	IN	46410	**800-258-3321**	219-769-3321
Michigan City					
1001 E US Hwy 20	Michigan City	IN	46360	**800-519-2416**	219-877-3100
South Bend					
3454 Douglas Rd	South Bend	IN	46635	**800-743-2447**	574-237-0774
College of Court Reporting Inc					
111 W Tenth St Ste 111	Hobart	IN	46342	**866-294-3974**	219-942-1459
International Business College					
5699 Coventry Ln	Fort Wayne	IN	46804	**800-589-6363**	260-459-4500
ITT Technical Institute Fort Wayne					
2810 Dupont Commerce Ct	Fort Wayne	IN	46825	**800-866-4488**	260-497-6200
ITT Technical Institute Indianapolis					
9511 Angola Ct	Indianapolis	IN	46268	**800-937-4488**	317-875-8640
ITT Technical Institute Newburgh					
10999 Stahl Rd	Newburgh	IN	47630	**800-832-4488**	812-858-1600
Ivy Tech Columbus College					
Columbus 4475 Central Ave	Columbus	IN	47203	**800-922-4838**	812-372-9925
Ivy Tech Community College					
Bloomington					
200 Daniels Way	Bloomington	IN	47404	**866-447-0700**	812-330-6137

	City	State	ZIP	Toll-Free	Phone
Central Indiana					
50 W Fall Creek Pkwy N Dr	Indianapolis	IN	46208	**888-489-5463**	317-921-4800
Kokomo 1815 E Morgan St	Kokomo	IN	46901	**800-459-0561**	765-459-0561
Muncie 4301 S Cowan Rd	Muncie	IN	47302	**800-589-8324**	765-289-2291
North Central					
220 Dean Johnson Blvd	South Bend	IN	46601	**888-489-3478**	574-289-7001
Northwest 1440 E 35th Ave	Gary	IN	46409	**888-489-5463**	219-981-1111
Richmond 2357 Chester Blvd	Richmond	IN	47374	**800-659-4562**	765-966-2656
Southeast 590 Ivy Tech Dr	Madison	IN	47250	**800-403-2190**	812-265-2580
Southern Indiana					
8204 old Indiana 311	Sellersburg	IN	47172	**800-321-9021**	812-246-3301
Wabash Valley					
8000 S Education Dr	Terre Haute	IN	47802	**888-489-5463**	812-298-2293
Lincoln College of Technology					
7225 Winton Dr Bldg 128	Indianapolis	IN	46268	**800-228-6232**	317-632-5553
Mid-America College of Funeral Science (MACFS)					
3111 Hamburg Pk	Jeffersonville	IN	47130	**800-221-6158**	812-288-8878
AIB College of Business					
2500 Fleur Dr	Des Moines	IA	50321	**800-444-1921**	515-244-4221
Brown Mackie College Bettendorf					
2119 E Kimberly Rd	Bettendorf	IA	52722	**888-420-1652**	563-344-1500
Western Iowa Tech Community College					
4647 Stone Ave	Sioux City	IA	51102	**800-352-4649**	712-274-6400
Brown Mackie College Lenexa					
9705 Lenexa Dr	Lenexa	KS	66215	**800-635-9101**	913-768-1900
Brown Mackie College Salina					
2106 S Ninth St	Salina	KS	67401	**800-365-0433**	785-825-5422
Concorde Career Colleges					
5800 Foxridge Dr Ste 500	Mission	KS	66202	**800-693-7010**	913-831-9977
Wichita Area Technical College					
301 S Grove St Bldg A	Wichita	KS	67211	**866-296-4031**	316-677-9400
Bowling Green Technical College					
1845 Loop Dr	Bowling Green	KY	42101	**866-590-9238**	270-901-1000
Brown Mackie College Hopkinsville					
4001 Ft Campbell Blvd	Hopkinsville	KY	42240	**800-359-4753**	270-886-1302
Brown Mackie College Louisville					
3605 Fern Vly Rd	Louisville	KY	40219	**800-999-7387**	502-968-7191
Brown Mackie College Northern Kentucky					
309 Buttermilk Pk	Fort Mitchell	KY	41017	**800-888-1445**	859-341-5627
Gateway Community & Technical College (GCTC)					
1025 Amsterdam Rd	Covington	KY	41011	**855-346-4282**	859-441-4500
ITT Technical Institute Louisville					
9500 Ormsby Stn Rd Ste 100	Louisville	KY	40223	**888-790-7427**	502-327-7424
Louisville Technical Institute					
Sullivan College of Technology & Design					
3901 Atkinson Sq Dr	Louisville	KY	40218	**800-844-6528**	502-456-6509
National College					
Lexington					
2376 Sir Barton Way	Lexington	KY	40509	**877-540-3494**	859-253-0621
National College of Business & Technology Florence					
8095 Connector Dr	Florence	KY	41042	**888-956-2732**	859-525-6510
National College of Business & Technology Pikeville					
50 National College Blvd	Pikeville	KY	41501	**800-664-1886**	606-478-7200
Owensboro Community & Technical College					
4800 New Hartford Rd	Owensboro	KY	42303	**866-755-6282**	270-686-4400
Andover College					
265 Western Ave	South Portland	ME	04106	**800-639-3110**	207-774-6126
Beal College 99 Farm Rd	Bangor	ME	04401	**800-660-7351**	207-947-4591
Central Maine Community College					
1250 Turner St	Auburn	ME	04210	**800-891-2002***	207-755-5100
*Admissions					
Eastern Maine Community College					
354 Hogan Rd	Bangor	ME	04401	**800-286-9357**	207-974-4600
Southern Maine Community College (SMCC)					
2 Ft Rd	South Portland	ME	04106	**877-282-2182**	207-741-5500
ITT Technical Institute Owings Mills					
11301 Red Run Blvd	Owings Mills	MD	21117	**877-411-6782**	443-394-7115
National Labor College					
10000 New Hampshire Ave	Silver Spring	MD	20903	**888-427-8100**	301-431-6400
Bay State College					
122 Commonwealth Ave	Boston	MA	02116	**800-815-3276**	617-217-9000
Benjamin Franklin Institute of Technology					
41 Berkeley St	Boston	MA	02116	**877-400-2348**	617-423-4630
Boston Architectural College					
320 Newbury St	Boston	MA	02115	**877-585-0100**	617-585-0100
Cambridge College Inc					
360 Merrimack St 4th fl	Lawrence	MA	01843	**800-829-4723**	617-868-1000
ITT Technical Institute Wilmington					
200 Ballardvale St Ste 200	Wilmington	MA	01887	**800-430-5097**	978-658-2636
National Aviation Academy					
150 Hanscom Dr	Bedford	MA	01730	**800-659-2080**	727-535-8727
New England College of Business & Finance					
10 High St Ste 204	Boston	MA	02110	**888-357-7332**	617-951-2350
Sanford-Brown College					
Boston 126 Newbury St	Boston	MA	02116	**877-809-2444**	617-578-7100
Academy of Court Reporting					
Clawson 1055 W Maple Rd	Clawson	MI	48017	**888-314-7780**	
Cleary University					
3601 Plymouth Rd	Ann Arbor	MI	48105	**800-686-1883**	734-332-4477
Livingston 3750 Cleary Dr	Howell	MI	48843	**800-686-1883**	517-548-3670
Everest Institute					
21107 Lahser Rd	Southfield	MI	48033	**800-611-2101***	248-799-9933
*General					
ITT Technical Institute Canton					
1905 S Haggerty Rd	Canton	MI	48188	**800-247-4477**	734-397-7800
ITT Technical Institute Grand Rapids					
1980 Metro Ct SW	Wyoming	MI	49519	**800-632-4676**	616-406-1200
ITT Technical Institute Troy					
1522 E Big Beaver Rd	Troy	MI	48083	**800-832-6817**	248-524-1800
Anoka Technical College					
1355 W Hwy 10	Anoka	MN	55303	**800-627-3529**	763-433-1100
Brown College					
1345 Mendota Heights Rd	Mendota Heights	MN	55120	**888-247-4238**	651-905-3400
Dakota County Technical College					
1300 E 145th St	Rosemount	MN	55068	**877-937-3282**	651-423-8301
Duluth Business University (DBU)					
4724 Mike Colalilo Dr	Duluth	MN	55807	**800-777-8406**	218-722-4000
Dunwoody College of Technology					
818 Dunwoody Blvd	Minneapolis	MN	55403	**800-292-4625**	612-374-5800
Hennepin Technical College					
9000 Brooklyn Blvd	Brooklyn Park	MN	55445	**800-345-4655**	952-995-1300
Ridgewater College					
Hutchinson					
2 Century Ave SE	Hutchinson	MN	55350	**800-722-1151**	320-234-8500
Willmar					
2101 15th Ave NW PO Box 1097	Willmar	MN	56201	**800-722-1151**	320-222-5200
Saint Cloud Technical & Community College					
1540 Northway Dr	Saint Cloud	MN	56303	**800-222-1009**	320-308-5089
Saint Paul College					
235 Marshall Ave	Saint Paul	MN	55102	**800-227-6029**	651-846-1600
DeVry University Kansas City					
1310 E 104th St 2nd Fl	Kansas City	MO	64131	**800-821-3766**	816-941-0430
Everest College					
1010 W Sunshine St	Springfield	MO	65807	**888-223-8556**	417-864-7220
ITT Technical Institute Arnold					
1930 Meyer Drury Dr	Arnold	MO	63010	**888-488-1082**	636-464-6600
ITT Technical Institute Earth City					
3640 Corporate Trl Dr	Earth City	MO	63045	**800-235-5488**	314-298-7800
ITT Technical Institute Kansas City					
9150 E 41st Terr	Kansas City	MO	64133	**877-488-1442**	816-276-1400
Vatterott College Berkeley					
8580 Evans Ave	Berkeley	MO	63134	**888-202-2636**	314-264-1000
Vatterott College Joplin					
809 Illinois Ave	Joplin	MO	64801	**866-200-1898**	417-781-5633
Vatterott College South County					
12900 Maurer Industrial Dr	Saint Louis	MO	63127	**866-312-8276**	314-843-4200
Vatterott College Springfield					
3850 S Campbell	Springfield	MO	65807	**844-244-3304**	417-831-8116
University of Montana					
32 Campus Dr	Missoula	MT	59812	**800-462-8636***	406-243-6266
*Admissions					
College of Technology					
909 S Ave W	Missoula	MT	59801	**800-542-6882**	406-243-7852
Helena College of Technology					
1115 N Roberts St	Helena	MT	59601	**800-827-1000**	406-444-6800
ITT Technical Institute Omaha					
1120 N 103rd Plz Ste 200	Omaha	NE	68114	**800-677-9260**	402-331-2900
Kaplan University Lincoln					
1821 K St	Lincoln	NE	68508	**800-987-7734**	
Kaplan University Omaha					
5425 N 103rd St	Omaha	NE	68134	**800-987-7734**	402-572-8500
Nebraska College of Technical Agriculture					
404 E 7th	Curtis	NE	69025	**800-328-7847**	308-367-4124
Southeast Community College					
Beatrice 4771 W Scott Rd	Beatrice	NE	68310	**800-233-5027**	402-228-3468
Milford 600 State St	Milford	NE	68405	**800-933-7223**	402-761-2131
ITT Technical Institute Henderson					
2300 Corporate Cir Ste 150	Henderson	NV	89074	**800-488-8459**	702-558-5404
Berkeley College					
Garrett Mountain					
44 Rifle Camp Rd	Woodland Park	NJ	07424	**800-446-5400**	973-278-5400
Paramus 64 E Midland Ave	Paramus	NJ	07652	**800-446-5400**	201-967-9667
Woodbridge					
430 Rahway Ave	Woodbridge	NJ	07095	**800-446-5400**	732-750-1800
DeVry University North Brunswick					
630 US Hwy 1	North Brunswick	NJ	08902	**800-333-3879**	
Divers Academy International					
1500 Liberty Pl	Erial	NJ	08081	**800-238-3483**	
Central New Mexico Community College					
10549 Universe Blvd NW	Albuquerque	NM	87114	**888-453-1304**	505-224-3000
ITT Technical Institute Albuquerque					
5100 Masthead St NE	Albuquerque	NM	87109	**800-636-1114**	505-828-1114
Southwestern Indian Polytechnic Institute					
9169 Coors Blvd NW PO Box 10146	Albuquerque	NM	87120	**800-586-7474**	505-346-2306
American Academy McAllister Institute of Funeral Service					
619 W 54th St 2nd Fl	New York	NY	10019	**866-932-2264**	212-757-1190
Berkeley College New York City					
3 E 43rd St	New York	NY	10017	**800-446-5400**	212-986-4343
Berkeley College White Plains					
99 Church St	White Plains	NY	10601	**800-446-5400**	914-694-1122
Bryant & Stratton College Syracuse North					
8687 Carling Rd	Liverpool	NY	13090	**800-836-5627**	315-652-6500
College of Westchester (CW)					
325 Central Ave	White Plains	NY	10606	**800-660-7093**	
Commercial Driver Training					
600 Patton Ave	West Babylon	NY	11704	**800-649-7447**	631-249-1330
DeVry University Long Island City					
3020 Thomson Ave	Long Island	NY	11101	**888-713-3879**	718-472-2728
ITT Technical Institute Albany					
13 Airline Dr	Albany	NY	12205	**800-489-1191**	518-452-9300
ITT Technical Institute Getzville					
2295 Millersport Hwy	Getzville	NY	14068	**800-469-7593**	716-689-2200
ITT Technical Institute Liverpool					
235 Greenfield Pkwy	Liverpool	NY	13088	**877-488-0011**	315-461-8000
Jamestown Business College					
7 Fairmount Ave PO Box 429	Jamestown	NY	14702	**877-557-2575**	716-664-5100
Monroe College					
2501 Jerome Ave	Bronx	NY	10468	**800-556-6676**	718-933-6700
TCI College of Technology					
320 W 31st St	New York	NY	10001	**800-878-8246**	212-594-4000
Utica School of Commerce					
201 Bleecker St	Utica	NY	13501	**800-321-4872**	315-733-2307
Wood Tobe-Coburn School					
8 E 40th St	New York	NY	10016	**800-394-9663**	212-686-9040
Forsyth Technical Community College					
2100 Silas Creek Pkwy	Winston-Salem	NC	27103	**800-870-3676**	336-723-0371
ITT Technical Institute High Point					
4050 Piedmont Pkwy	High Point	NC	27265	**877-536-5231**	336-819-5900
Stanly Community College					
141 College Dr	Albemarle	NC	28001	**877-275-4219**	704-982-0121
Academy of Court Reporting Cleveland					
2044 Euclid Ave	Cleveland	OH	44115	**888-314-7780**	
Academy of Court Reporting Columbus					
150 E Gay St	Columbus	OH	43215	**866-865-8067**	614-221-7770

Name / Address	City	State	ZIP	Toll-Free	Phone
Bradford School 2469 Stelzer Rd	Columbus	OH	43219	**800-678-7981**	614-416-6200
Brown Mackie College Findlay 1700 Fostoria Ave Ste 100	Findlay	OH	45840	**800-842-3687**	419-423-2211
Bryant & Stratton College *Cleveland* 3121 Euclid Ave	Cleveland	OH	44115	**866-948-0571**	216-771-1700
Cincinnati College of Mortuary Science 645 W N Bend Rd	Cincinnati	OH	45224	**888-377-8433**	513-761-2020
Cleveland Institute of Electronics 1776 E 17th St	Cleveland	OH	44114	**800-243-6446**	216-781-9400
Davis College 4747 Monroe St	Toledo	OH	43623	**800-477-7021**	419-473-2700
Eastern Gateway Community College 4000 Sunset Blvd	Steubenville	OH	43952	**800-682-6553**	740-264-5591
Hocking College 3301 Hocking Pkwy	Nelsonville	OH	45764	**877-462-5464**	740-753-3591
ITT Technical Institute Dayton 3325 S- Eight Rd	Dayton	OH	45414	**800-568-3241**	937-264-7700
ITT Technical Institute Norwood 4750 Wesley Ave	Norwood	OH	45212	**800-314-8324**	513-531-8300
ITT Technical Institute Strongsville 14955 Sprague Rd	Strongsville	OH	44136	**800-331-1488**	440-234-9091
ITT Technical Institute Warrensville Heights 4700 Richmond Rd	Warrensville Heights	OH	44128	**800-741-3494**	216-896-6500
ITT Technical Institute Youngstown 1030 N Meridian Rd	Youngstown	OH	44509	**800-832-5001**	330-270-1600
Marion Technical College 1467 Mt Vernon Ave	Marion	OH	43302	**800-772-1213**	740-389-4636
North Central State College 2441 Kenwood Cir	Mansfield	OH	44906	**888-755-4899**	419-755-4800
Stark State College of Technology 6200 Frank Ave NW	North Canton	OH	44720	**800-797-8275**	330-494-6170
Zane State College 1555 Newark Rd	Zanesville	OH	43701	**800-686-8324**	740-454-2501
Indian Capital Technology Ctr 2403 N 41st St E	Muskogee	OK	74403	**800-757-0877**	918-687-6383
Oklahoma State University 219 Student Union Bldg	Stillwater	OK	74078	**800-852-1255**	405-744-5000
Okmulgee 1801 E Fourth St	Okmulgee	OK	74447	**800-722-4471**	918-293-4678
Spartan College of Aeronautics & Technology 8820 E Pine St PO Box 582833 *Admissions	Tulsa	OK	74115	**800-331-1204***	918-836-6886
ITT Technical Institute Portland 9500 NE Cascades Pkwy	Portland	OR	97220	**800-234-5488**	503-255-6500
American College 270 S Bryn Mawr Ave	Bryn Mawr	PA	19010	**888-263-7265**	610-526-1000
Cambria-Rowe Business College (CRBC) 221 Central Ave	Johnstown	PA	15902	**800-639-2273**	814-536-5168
Central Pennsylvania College 600 Valley Rd PO Box 309	Summerdale	PA	17093	**800-759-2727**	717-732-0702
DuBois Business College 1 Beaver Dr	Du Bois	PA	15801	**800-692-6213**	814-371-6920
ITT Technical Institute Harrisburg 449 Eisenhower Blvd Ste 100	Harrisburg	PA	17111	**800-847-4756**	717-565-1700
Johnson College 3427 N Main Ave	Scranton	PA	18508	**800-293-9675**	570-342-6404
Lansdale School of Business 290 Wissahickon Ave	North Wales	PA	19454	**800-219-0486**	215-699-5700
Penn Commercial Inc 242 Oak Spring Rd	Washington	PA	15301	**888-309-7484**	724-222-5330
Penn Foster Career School 925 Oak St	Scranton	PA	18515	**800-275-4410**	570-342-7701
Pennco Tech 3815 Otter St *General	Bristol	PA	19007	**844-226-0975***	215-785-0111
Pennsylvania College of Technology 1 College Ave *Admissions	Williamsport	PA	17701	**800-367-9222***	570-326-3761
Pennsylvania Institute of Technology (PIT) 800 Manchester Ave *Admissions	Media	PA	19063	**800-422-0025***	610-892-1500
Philadelphia College of Osteopathic Medicine (PCOM) 4170 City Ave *Admissions	Philadelphia	PA	19131	**800-999-6998***	215-871-6100
Pittsburgh Institute of Aeronautics (PIA) 5 Allegheny County Airport	West Mifflin	PA	15122	**800-444-1440**	412-346-2100
Pittsburgh Institute of Mortuary Science Inc 5808 Baum Blvd	Pittsburgh	PA	15206	**800-933-5808**	412-362-8500
Pittsburgh Technical Institute (PTI) 1111 McKee Rd	Oakdale	PA	15071	**800-784-9675**	412-809-5100
Thaddeus Stevens College of Technology (TSCT) 750 E King St	Lancaster	PA	17602	**800-842-3832**	717-299-7701
Triangle Tech Inc *Du Bois* PO Box 551	Du Bois	PA	15801	**800-874-8324**	814-371-2090
Erie 2000 Liberty St	Erie	PA	16502	**800-874-8324**	814-453-6016
Greensburg 222 E Pittsburgh St	Greensburg	PA	15601	**800-874-8324**	724-832-1050
Welder Training & Testing Institute 1144 N Graham St	Allentown	PA	18109	**800-223-9884**	610-820-9551
Williamson Free School of Mechanical Trades, The 106 S New Middletown Rd	Media	PA	19063	**888-565-1095**	610-566-1776
New England Institute of Technology 2500 Post Rd	Warwick	RI	02886	**800-736-7744**	401-467-7744
Florence-Darlington Technical College 2715 W Lucas St	Florence	SC	29502	**800-228-5745**	843-661-8324
Horry-Georgetown Technical College 2050 E Hwy 501	Conway	SC	29526	**855-544-4482**	843-347-3186
Grand Strand Campus 743 Hemlock Ave	Myrtle Beach	SC	29577	**855-544-4482**	843-477-0808
ITT Technical Institute Greenville 6 Independence Pointe Independence Corporate Pk	Greenville	SC	29615	**800-932-4488**	864-288-0777
Piedmont Technical College 620 N Emerald Rd	Greenwood	SC	29646	**800-868-5528**	864-941-8324
Spartanburg Community College 800 Brisack Rd PO Box 4386	Spartanburg	SC	29305	**866-591-3700**	864-592-4800
Tri-County Technical College 7900 Hwy 76	Pendleton	SC	29670	**866-269-5677**	864-646-8361
Trident Technical College (TTC) 7000 Rivers Ave PO Box 118067	North Charleston	SC	29406	**877-349-7184**	843-574-6111
Southeast Technical Institute 2320 N Career Ave	Sioux Falls	SD	57107	**800-247-0789**	605-367-8355
Fountainhead College of Technology 3203 Tazewell Pk	Knoxville	TN	37918	**888-218-7335**	865-688-9422
ITT Technical Institute Cordova 7260 Goodlett Farms Pkwy	Cordova	TN	38016	**866-444-5141**	901-381-0200
ITT Technical Institute Nashville 2845 Elm Hill Pk	Nashville	TN	37214	**800-331-8386**	615-889-8700
Nashville State Community College (NSCC) 120 White Bridge Rd	Nashville	TN	37209	**800-272-7363**	615-353-3333
National College of Business & Technology Bristol 1328 Hwy 11 W	Bristol	TN	37620	**888-956-2732**	423-878-4440
National College of Business & Technology Nashville 1638 Bell Rd	Nashville	TN	37211	**855-800-1715**	615-333-3344
Northeast State Technical Community College 2425 Hwy 75 PO Box 246	Blountville	TN	37617	**800-836-7822**	423-323-3191
South College 3904 Lonas Dr	Knoxville	TN	37909	**877-557-2575**	865-251-1800
Aviation Institute of Maintenance Houston 7651 Airport Blvd	Houston	TX	77061	**888-349-5387**	713-644-7777
Court Reporting Institute of Dallas 1341 W Mockingbird Ln Ste 200-E	Dallas	TX	75247	**866-382-1284**	214-350-9722
Court Reporting Institute of Houston 13101 NW Fwy Ste 100	Houston	TX	77040	**866-996-8300**	713-996-8300
Dallas Institute of Funeral Service 3909 S Buckner Blvd	Dallas	TX	75227	**800-235-5444**	214-388-5466
DeVry University Houston 11125 Equity Dr	Houston	TX	77041	**866-338-7934**	713-973-3100
DeVry University Irving 4800 Regent Blvd Ste 200	Irving	TX	75063	**800-633-3879**	972-929-6777
ITT Technical Institute Arlington 551 Ryan Plz Dr	Arlington	TX	76011	**888-288-4950**	817-794-5100
ITT Technical Institute Austin 6330 Hwy 290 E Ste 150	Austin	TX	78723	**800-431-0677**	512-467-6800
ITT Technical Institute Houston 15651 N Fwy	Houston	TX	77090	**800-879-6486**	281-873-0512
ITT Technical Institute Richardson 2101 Waterview Pkwy	Richardson	TX	75080	**888-488-5761**	972-690-9100
ITT Technical Institute San Antonio 5700 NW Pkwy	San Antonio	TX	78249	**800-880-0570**	210-694-4612
Wade College 1950 N Stemmons Fwy LB 562 Ste 4080	Dallas	TX	75207	**800-624-4850**	214-637-3530
ITT Technical Institute Murray 920 Levoy Dr	Murray	UT	84123	**800-365-2136**	801-263-3313
Latter Day Saints Business College 95 North 300 West	Salt Lake City	UT	84101	**800-999-5767**	801-524-8100
Sterling College PO Box 72	Craftsbury Common	VT	05827	**800-648-3591**	802-586-7711
Vermont Technical College PO Box 500	Randolph Center	VT	05061	**800-442-8821**	802-728-1000
Bryant & Stratton College Richmond 8141 Hull St Rd	Richmond	VA	23235	**866-948-0571**	804-745-2444
ITT Technical Institute Norfolk 5425 Robin Hood Rd Ste 100	Norfolk	VA	23513	**888-253-8324**	757-466-1260
ITT Technical Institute Richmond 300 Gateway Centre Pkwy	Richmond	VA	23235	**888-330-4888**	804-330-4992
ITT Technical Institute Springfield 7300 Boston Blvd	Springfield	VA	22153	**866-817-8324**	703-440-9535
Jefferson College of Health Sciences 101 Elm Ave SE	Roanoke	VA	24031	**888-985-8483**	540-985-8483
National College of Business & Technology *Roanoke Valley* 1813 E Main St	Salem	VA	24153	**800-664-1886**	540-986-1800
DeVry University Federal Way 3600 S 344th Way	Federal Way	WA	98001	**877-923-3879**	253-943-2800
ITT Technical Institute Seattle 12720 Gateway Dr Ste 100	Seattle	WA	98168	**800-422-2029**	206-244-3300
Huntington Junior College 900 Fifth Ave	Huntington	WV	25701	**800-344-4522**	304-697-7550
West Virginia Junior College *Charleston* 1000 Virginia St E	Charleston	WV	25301	**800-924-5208**	304-345-2820
West Virginia Junior College - Bridgeport 176 Thompson Dr	Bridgeport	WV	26330	**800-470-5627**	304-842-4007
Blackhawk Technical College 6004 S County Rd G	Janesville	WI	53546	**800-498-1282**	608-758-6900
Bryant & Stratton College Milwaukee 310 W Wisconsin Ave Ste 500-E	Milwaukee	WI	53203	**866-948-0571**	414-276-5200
Chippewa Valley Technical College 620 W Clairemont Ave	Eau Claire	WI	54701	**800-547-2882**	715-833-6200
Fox Valley Technical College 1825 N Bluemound Dr PO Box 2277	Appleton	WI	54912	**800-735-3882**	920-735-5600
Gateway Technical College 3520 30th Ave	Kenosha	WI	53144	**800-247-7122**	262-564-2200
Herzing College Madison 5218 E Terr Dr	Madison	WI	53718	**800-582-1227**	608-249-6611
Lakeshore Technical College 1290 N Ave	Cleveland	WI	53015	**888-468-6582**	920-693-1000
Madison Area Technical College 1701 Wright St	Madison	WI	53704	**800-322-6282**	608-246-6100
Milwaukee Area Technical College 700 W State St	Milwaukee	WI	53233	**866-211-3380**	414-297-6600
Moraine Park Technical College 235 N National Ave	Fond du Lac	WI	54935	**800-472-4554**	920-922-8611
Northcentral Technical College 1000 W Campus Dr	Wausau	WI	54401	**888-682-7144**	715-675-3331
Northeast Wisconsin Technical College PO Box 19042	Green Bay	WI	54307	**800-422-6982**	920-498-5400
Southwest Wisconsin Technical College (SWTC) 1800 Bronson Blvd	Fennimore	WI	53809	**800-362-3322**	608-822-3262
Western Technical College 400 Seventh St N	La Crosse	WI	54601	**800-322-9982**	608-785-9200
Wisconsin Indianhead Technical College *New Richmond Campus* 1019 S Knowles Ave	New Richmond	WI	54017	**800-243-9482**	715-246-6561

	City	State	Zip	Toll-Free	Phone
Rice Lake Campus 1900 College Dr	Rice Lake	WI	54868	**800-243-9482**	715-234-7082
Superior Campus 600 N 21 St	Superior	WI	54880	**800-243-9482**	715-394-6677

799 VOTING SYSTEMS & SOFTWARE

	City	State	Zip	Toll-Free	Phone
Avante International Technology Inc (AIT) 70 Washington Rd	Princeton Junction	NJ	08550	**800-735-5040**	609-799-9388
Diebold Inc 5995 Mayfair Rd *NYSE: DBD*	North Canton	OH	44720	**800-999-3600**	330-490-4000
Dynapar 1675 Delany Rd *General	Gurnee	IL	60031	**800-873-8731***	
Election Systems & Software Inc 11208 John Galt Blvd *General	Omaha	NE	68137	**877-377-8683***	402-593-0101
Elections USA Inc 1927 E Saw Mill Rd	Quakertown	PA	18951	**800-789-8683**	215-538-0779
Hart InterCivic 15500 Wells Port Dr PO Box 80649	Austin	TX	78708	**800-223-4278**	512-252-6400
MicroVote General Corp 6366 Guilford Ave	Indianapolis	IN	46220	**800-257-4901**	317-257-4900
UniLect Corp PO Box 3026	Danville	CA	94526	**888-864-5328**	925-833-8660

800 WALLCOVERINGS

	City	State	Zip	Toll-Free	Phone
Fashion Wallcoverings 4005 Carnegie Ave *Orders	Cleveland	OH	44103	**800-362-9930***	216-432-1600
Goldcrest Wallcoverings PO Box 245	Slingerlands	NY	12159	**800-535-9513**	518-478-7214
Thibaut Inc 480 Frelinghuysen Ave	Newark	NJ	07114	**800-223-0704**	973-643-1118
York Wallcoverings Inc 750 Linden Ave PO Box 5166	York	PA	17405	**800-375-9675**	717-846-4456

801 WAREHOUSING & STORAGE

SEE ALSO Logistics Services (Transportation & Warehousing)

801-1 Commercial Warehousing

	City	State	Zip	Toll-Free	Phone
Acme Distribution Centers Inc 18101 E Colfax Ave	Aurora	CO	80011	**800-444-3614**	303-340-2100
All Source Security Container Mfg Corp 40 Mills Rd	Barrie	ON	L4N6H4	**866-526-4579**	705-726-6460
ASW Global LLC 3375 Gilchrist Rd	Mogadore	OH	44260	**888-826-5087**	330-733-6291
D & D Distribution Services Inc 789 Kings Mill Rd	York	PA	17403	**877-683-3358**	717-845-1646
DD Jones Transfer & Warehouse Co Inc 2121 Old Greenbrier Rd	Chesapeake	VA	23320	**800-335-4787**	757-494-0225
Derby Industries LLC 4451 Robards Ln	Louisville	KY	40218	**800-569-4812**	502-451-7373
Evans Distribution Systems 18765 Seaway Dr	Melvindale	MI	48122	**800-653-8267**	313-388-3200
Gulf Winds International Inc 411 Brisbane St	Houston	TX	77061	**866-238-4909**	713-747-4909
Habco Beverage Systems Inc 501 Gordon Baker Rd	Toronto	ON	M2H2S6	**800-448-0244**	416-491-6008
Iron Mountain 745 Atlantic Ave *NYSE: IRM*	Boston	MA	02111	**800-899-4766**	
Kenco Group Inc 2001 Riverside Dr	Chattanooga	TN	37406	**800-758-3289**	
Longistics Transportation Inc 10900 World Trade Blvd	Raleigh	NC	27617	**800-289-0082**	919-872-7626
Mackinnon Transport Inc 405 Laird Rd	Guelph	ON	N1G4P7	**800-265-9394**	519-821-2311
Monsoon Commerce Solutions Inc 1250 45th St Ste 100	Emeryville	CA	94608	**800-520-2294**	510-594-4500
Pacific Storage Co PO Box 334	Stockton	CA	95201	**888-823-5467**	209-320-6600
Security Storage Co 1701 Florida Ave NW	Washington	DC	20009	**888-903-7695**	202-234-5600
Tejas Logistics System PO Box 1339	Waco	TX	76703	**800-535-9786**	254-753-0301
Tri Union Express Inc 1939 N Lafayette Ct	Griffith	IN	46319	**800-228-9098**	219-838-5400
W O W Logistics Co 3040 W Wisconsin Ave	Appleton	WI	54914	**800-236-3565**	920-734-9924

801-2 Refrigerated Storage

	City	State	Zip	Toll-Free	Phone
Burris Logistics 501 SE Fifth St PO Box 219	Milford	DE	19963	**800-805-8135**	302-839-5157
Perley-Halladay Assn Inc 1037 Andrew Dr	West Chester	PA	19380	**800-248-5800**	610-296-5800
United Freezer & Storage Co 650 N Meridian Rd	Youngstown	OH	44509	**800-716-1416**	330-792-1739

801-3 Self-Storage Facilities

	City	State	Zip	Toll-Free	Phone
A-American Self Storage Management Co Inc 11560 Tennessee Ave	Los Angeles	CA	90064	**888-333-6479**	310-914-4022
Public Storage Inc 701 Western Ave *NYSE: PSA* ■ *Cust Svc	Glendale	CA	91201	**800-567-0759***	818-244-8080
Sovran Self Storage Inc 6467 Main St *NYSE: SSS*	Buffalo	NY	14221	**800-242-1715**	716-633-1850
Stor-All Storage 1375 W Hillsboro Blvd	Deerfield Beach	FL	33442	**877-786-7255**	954-421-7888

802 WASTE MANAGEMENT

SEE ALSO Recyclable Materials Recovery ; Remediation Services

	City	State	Zip	Toll-Free	Phone
Athens Services 14048 Valley Blvd	La Puente	CA	91746	**888-336-6100**	626-336-3636
Basin Disposal Inc 2021 N Commercial Ave	Pasco	WA	99301	**800-642-6447**	509-547-2476
Burrtec Waste Industries Inc 9890 Cherry Ave	Fontana	CA	92335	**888-287-7832**	909-429-4200
CalMet Services Inc 7202 Peterson Ln	Paramount	CA	90723	**800-990-6387**	562-259-1239
Casella Waste Systems Inc 25 Greens Hill Ln *NASDAQ: CWST*	Rutland	VT	05701	**800-227-3552**	802-775-0325
Consolidated Disposal Services Inc 12949 Telegraph Rd	Santa Fe Springs	CA	90670	**800-299-4898**	
Deffenbaugh Industries Inc 2601 Midwest Dr	Kansas City	KS	66111	**800-631-3301**	913-631-3300
Dolphins Plus Inc 31 Corrine Pl	Key Largo	FL	33037	**866-860-7946**	305-451-1993
Duncan Disposal Co *Arlington* 1212 Harrison Ave	Arlington	TX	76011	**800-766-1758**	817-317-2000
E J Harrison & Sons PO Box 4009	Ventura	CA	93007	**800-418-7274**	805-647-1414
EL Harvey & Sons Inc 68 Hopkinton Rd	Westborough	MA	01581	**800-321-3002**	508-836-3000
Exp Pharmaceutical Services Corp 48021 Warm Springs Blvd	Fremont	CA	94539	**800-350-0397**	510-476-0909
Health & Environment Dept 130 S Market St Ste 6050	Wichita	KS	67202	**800-842-0078**	316-337-6020
Modern Corp 4746 Model City Rd	Model City	NY	14107	**800-662-0012**	716-754-8226
N-Viro International Corp 2254 Centennial Rd *OTC: NVIC*	Toledo	OH	43606	**800-336-2225**	419-535-6374
National Serv-All Inc 6231 McBeth Rd	Fort Wayne	IN	46809	**800-876-9001**	260-747-4117
Oakleaf Waste Management LLC 415 Day Hill Rd	Windsor	CT	06095	**888-625-5323**	713-512-6200
Republic Services 1131 N Blue Gum St	Anaheim	CA	92806	**866-238-2444**	714-238-3300
Republic Services of Southern Nevada 770 E Sahara Ave	Las Vegas	NV	89193	**800-752-4092**	702-735-5151
Rumpke 10795 Hughes Rd	Cincinnati	OH	45251	**800-582-3107**	
Sanitary Services Co Inc 21 Bellwether Way Ste 404	Bellingham	WA	98225	**888-333-9882**	360-734-3490
Stericycle Inc 28161 N Keith Dr *NASDAQ: SRCL*	Lake Forest	IL	60045	**866-783-9816**	847-367-5910
Synagro Technologies Inc 435 Williams Ct Ste 100	Baltimore	MD	21220	**800-370-0035**	443-489-9017
Texas Disposal Systems Inc (TDS) 12200 Carl Rd	Creedmoor	TX	78610	**800-375-8375**	512-421-1300
Triumvirate Environmental 61 Innerbelt Rd	Somerville	MA	02143	**800-966-9282**	617-628-8098
Waste Industries USA Inc 3301 Benson Dr Ste 601	Raleigh	NC	27609	**800-647-9946**	919-325-3000
Waste Management Inc 1001 Fannin St Ste 4000 *NYSE: WM*	Houston	TX	77002	**800-633-7871**	713-512-6200
Wheelabrator Technologies Inc 4 Liberty Ln W	Hampton	NH	03842	**800-682-0026**	603-929-3000

803 WATER - BOTTLED

	City	State	Zip	Toll-Free	Phone
Absopure Water Co 8845 General Dr	Plymouth	MI	48170	**800-422-7678**	765-449-4892
Calistoga Beverage Co 865 Silverado Trl	Calistoga	CA	94515	**800-365-4446**	
Chester Water Authority PO Box 467	Chester	PA	19016	**800-793-2323**	610-876-8185
Culligan International Co 9399 W Higgins Rd Ste 1100	Rosemont	IL	60018	**800-285-5442**	847-430-2800
Distillata Co 1608 E 24th St *Cust Svc	Cleveland	OH	44114	**800-999-2906***	216-771-2900
DS Waters of America Inc 5660 New Northside Dr Ste 500 *Cust Svc	Atlanta	GA	30328	**800-201-6218***	
Glacier Clear Enterprises Inc 3291 Thomas St *Cust Svc	Innisfil	ON	L9S3W3	**800-668-5118***	705-436-6363
Polar Beverages Inc 1001 Southbridge St *Cust Svc	Worcester	MA	01610	**800-734-9800***	508-753-4300
Pure-Flo Water Co 7737 Mission Gorge Rd *Cust Svc	Santee	CA	92071	**800-787-3356***	619-448-5120

804 WATER TREATMENT & FILTRATION PRODUCTS & EQUIPMENT

	City	State	Zip	Toll-Free	Phone
Aqua-Aerobic Systems Inc 6306 N Alpine Rd	Loves Park	IL	61111	**800-940-5008**	815-654-2501

Classified Section

Company	Address	City	State	Zip	Toll-Free	Phone
Atlas Water Systems Inc	301 Second Ave	Waltham	MA	02451	**888-877-0561**	781-373-4700
Brita Products Co	1221 Broadway	Oakland	CA	94612	**800-242-7482**	510-271-7000
Bucks County Water & Sewer Authority (BCWSA)	1275 Almshouse Rd	Warrington	PA	18976	**800-222-2068**	215-343-2538
Carolina Filters Inc	109 E Newberry Ave	Sumter	SC	29150	**800-849-5646**	803-773-6842
Culligan International Co	9399 W Higgins Rd Ste 1100	Rosemont	IL	60018	**800-285-5442**	847-430-2800
Deepwater Chemicals Inc	1210 Airpark Rd	Woodward	OK	73801	**800-854-4064**	580-256-0500
Dow Liquid Separations	PO Box 1206	Midland	MI	48642	**800-447-4369**	989-636-1000
East Valley Water District	3654 E Highland Ave Ste 18	Highland	CA	92346	**866-275-3772**	909-889-9501
Energy Recovery Inc	1717 Doolittle Dr *NASDAQ: ERII*	San Leandro	CA	94577	**888-455-2263**	510-483-7370
Everpure LLC	1040 Muirfield Dr	Hanover Park	IL	60133	**800-323-7873**	630-307-3000
Filterspun	624 N Fairfield St	Amarillo	TX	79107	**800-323-5431**	806-383-3840
GE Water & Process Technologies	4636 Somerton Rd	Trevose	PA	19053	**866-439-2837**	215-355-3300
Graver Technologies LLC	200 Lake Dr	Newark	DE	19702	**800-249-1990**	302-731-1700
Graver Water Systems	675 Central Ave Ste 3	New Providence	NJ	07974	**877-472-8379**	908-516-1400
Kinetico Inc	10845 Kinsman Rd	Newbury	OH	44065	**800-944-9283**	
Lancaster Pump Co	1340 Manheim Pk	Lancaster	PA	17601	**800-442-0786**	717-397-3521
MSC Filtration Technologies	198 Freshwater Blvd *Cust Svc	Enfield	CT	06082	**800-237-7359***	860-745-7475
Pall Corp	2200 Northern Blvd *NYSE: PLL*	East Hills	NY	11548	**800-645-6532**	516-484-5400
PEP Filters Inc	322 Rolling Hill Rd	Mooresville	NC	28117	**800-243-4583**	704-662-3133
Polaris Pool Systems Inc	2620 Commerce Way	Vista	CA	92081	**800-822-7933**	760-599-9600
Pro Products LLC	7201 Engle Rd	Fort Wayne	IN	46804	**866-357-5063**	260-490-5970
Pure & Secure LLC	4120 NW 44th St *Cust Svc	Lincoln	NE	68524	**800-875-5915***	402-467-9300
Siemens Water Technologies	181 Thorn Hill Rd	Warrendale	PA	15086	**800-424-9300**	724-772-0044
Sydnor Hydro Inc	2111 Magnolia St PO Box 27186	Richmond	VA	23261	**800-552-7714**	804-643-2725
Taylor Technologies Inc	31 Loveton Cir *Cust Svc	Sparks	MD	21152	**800-837-8548***	410-472-4340
Tomco2 Equipment Co	3340 Rosebud Rd	Loganville	GA	30052	**800-832-4262**	770-979-8000
Walker Process Equipment	840 N Russell Ave	Aurora	IL	60506	**800-992-5537**	630-892-7921
Waterco USA Inc	1864 Tobacco Rd *General	Augusta	GA	30906	**800-277-4150***	706-793-7291
Zodiac Pool Systems Inc	2620 Commerce Way	Vista	CA	92081	**800-822-7933**	

805 WEAPONS & ORDNANCE (MILITARY)

SEE ALSO Simulation & Training Systems ; Firearms & Ammunition (Non-Military) ; Missiles, Space Vehicles, Parts

Company	Address	City	State	Zip	Toll-Free	Phone
North American Arms Inc	2150 South 950 East	Provo	UT	84606	**800-821-5783**	801-374-9990

806 WEB HOSTING SERVICES

SEE ALSO Internet Service Providers (ISPs)

Companies listed here are engaged primarily in hosting web sites for companies and individuals. Although many Internet Service Providers (ISPs) also provide web hosting services, they are not included among these listings.

Company	Address	City	State	Zip	Toll-Free	Phone
Baillio's Inc	5301 Menaul Blvd NE	Albuquerque	NM	87110	**800-540-7511**	505-883-7511
Catalog.com Inc	14000 Quail Springs Pkwy Ste 3600	Oklahoma City	OK	73134	**888-932-4376**	405-753-9300
DataPipe	10 Exchange Pl	Jersey City	NJ	07302	**877-773-3306**	201-792-4847
Datarealm Internet Services Inc	PO Box 1616	Hudson	WI	54016	**877-227-3783**	
Fortress Integrated Technologies	100 Delawanna Ave	Clifton	NJ	07014	**888-734-9320**	973-572-1070
Freeservers.com	1253 N Research Way Ste Q-2500	Orem	UT	84097	**800-396-1999**	
Global Knowledge Group Inc (GKG)	302 N Bryan Ave	Bryan	TX	77803	**866-776-7584**	
Homestead Technologies Inc	180 Jefferson Dr	Menlo Park	CA	94025	**800-797-2958**	650-944-3100
Host Depot Inc	4613 N University Dr Ste 227	Coral Springs	FL	33067	**888-340-3527**	954-340-3527
Hostcentric Inc	70 BlanchaRd Rd 3rd Fl *Tech Supp	Burlington	MA	01803	**866-897-5418***	602-716-5396
Hostedware Corp	16 Technology Dr Ste 116	Irvine	CA	92618	**800-211-6967**	949-585-1500
Hostway Corp	100 N Riverside Plaza 8th Fl	Chicago	IL	60606	**866-467-8929**	312-238-0125
INetU Inc	744 Roble Rd	Allentown	PA	18109	**888-664-6388**	610-266-7441
LightEdge Solutions Inc	215 10th St Ste 1000	Des Moines	IA	50309	**877-771-3343**	515-471-1000
Media3 Technologies LLC	33 Riverside Dr N River Commerce Pk	Pembroke	MA	02359	**800-903-9327**	781-826-1213
NetNation Communications Inc	550 Burrard St Ste 200	Vancouver	BC	V6C2B5	**888-277-0000**	604-688-8946
OLM LLC	4 Trefoil Dr	Trumbull	CT	06611	**877-265-6638**	203-445-7700
Opsource Inc	5201 Great America Pkwy Ste 120	Santa Clara	CA	95054	**800-664-9973**	408-567-2000
Pacific Internet	105 W Clay St	Ukiah	CA	95482	**888-722-8638**	707-468-1005
Radiant Communications Corp	1600-1050 W Pender St *CVE: RCN*	Vancouver	BC	V6E4T3	**888-219-2111**	
Superb Internet Corp	999 Bishop St Ste 1850	Honolulu	HI	96813	**888-354-6128**	808-544-0387
Telus	1000 Rue de Serigny	Longueuil	QC	J4K5B1	**888-709-8759**	450-928-6000
Verio Inc	8300 E Maplewood Ave Ste 400 *Sales	Greenwood Village	CO	80111	**800-438-8374***	561-912-2555
VPOP Technologies Inc	1772J Avenida de los Arboles Ste 374 *Sales	Thousand Oaks	CA	91362	**888-811-8767***	805-529-9374

807 WEB SITE DESIGN SERVICES

SEE ALSO Computer Systems Design Services ; Advertising Agencies ; Advertising Services - Online

Company	Address	City	State	Zip	Toll-Free	Phone
Acro Media Inc	2303 Leckie Rd Ste 103	Kelowna	BC	V1X6Y5	**877-763-8844**	250-763-8884
Armen Computing Ltd	286 Bethany Ct	Inman	SC	29349	**800-372-6078**	
Backupify Inc	17 Sellers St,	Cambridge	MA	02139	**800-571-4984**	
Boden Inc	P.O. Box 258	Helmetta	NJ	08828	**866-291-3363**	
bx.com Inc	1 W Exchange St	Providence	RI	02903	**800-262-8138**	401-274-8991
Champions Way Enterprises Inc	980 1st St W	North Vancouver	BC	V7P3N4	**877-774-5425**	
Fluid Innovation Inc	911 N RR 620 Ste 205	Austin	TX	78734	**866-934-7779**	
Litehaus Systems Inc	7445 132nd St Ste 2010	Surrey	BC	V3W1J8	**866-771-0044**	
Msights Inc	9935 Rea Rd Ste D-301	Charlotte	NC	28277	**877-267-4448**	
ProCare Pharmacy Benefit Manager Inc	1267 Professional Pkwy Ste 100	Gainesville	GA	30507	**888-821-5516**	
QuadriSpace Corp	705 N Greenville Ave Ste 800	Allen	TX	75002	**866-337-7223**	
Radianta Inc	2154 Michelson Dr Ste A	Irvine	CA	92612	**866-467-9695**	
Sapient Corp	131 Dartmouth St 3rd Fl *NASDAQ: SAPE*	Boston	MA	02116	**866-796-6860**	617-621-0200
Sigma Business Solutions Inc	55 York St	Toronto	ON	M5J1R7	**855-594-1991**	
SteelTorch Software Inc	423 Jamestown Rd	Belmont	NH	03220	**866-705-2730**	
Velaro Inc	8174 Lark Brown Rd Ste 201	Elkridge	MD	21075	**800-983-5276**	
Web.com	12808 Grand Bay Pkwy W	Jacksonville	FL	32258	**800-338-1771**	904-680-6600
Zen Ventures LLC	3939 S 6th St Ste 201	Klamath Falls	OR	97603	**888-936-2278**	

808 WEIGHT LOSS CENTERS & SERVICES

SEE ALSO Spas - Health & Fitness ; Health & Fitness Centers

Company	Address	City	State	Zip	Toll-Free	Phone
Barix Clinics	135 S Prospect St	Ypsilanti	MI	48198	**800-282-0066**	734-547-4700
Companions & Homemakers Inc	613 New Britain Ave	Farmington	CT	06032	**800-348-4663**	860-677-4948
Fit America MD	4864 Arthur Kill Rd	Staten Island	NY	10309	**800-940-7546**	718-227-4980
Greenpath Inc	36500 Corporate Dr	Farmington Hills	MI	48331	**800-550-1961**	248-553-5400
Jazzercise Inc	2460 Impala Dr *Cust Svc	Carlsbad	CA	92010	**800-348-4748***	760-476-1750
Jenny Craig International Inc	5770 Fleet St	Carlsbad	CA	92008	**800-443-2331**	760-696-4000
NutriSystem Inc	600 Office Center Dr Bldg 1 *NASDAQ: NTRI*	Fort Washington	PA	19034	**800-585-5483**	215-706-5300
Physicians Weight Loss Centers of America Inc	395 Springside Dr	Akron	OH	44333	**800-205-7887**	330-666-7952

809 WELDING & SOLDERING EQUIPMENT

Company	Address	City	State	Zip	Toll-Free	Phone
AGM Industries Inc	16 Jonathan Dr	Brockton	MA	02301	**800-225-9990**	508-587-3900
American Ultraviolet Co	40 Morristown Rd	Bernardsville	NJ	07924	**800-288-9288**	908-696-1130
Arcos Industries	1 Arcos Dr	Mount Carmel	PA	17851	**800-233-8460**	570-339-5200
BUG-O Systems Inc	161 Hillpointe Dr	Canonsburg	PA	15317	**800-245-3186**	412-331-1776

Company	Address	City	State	Zip	Toll-Free	Phone
CK Worldwide Inc	3501 C St NE	Auburn	WA	98002	**800-426-0877**	253-854-5820
Esab Welding & Cutting Products Inc	411 S Ebenezer Rd PO Box 100545	Florence	SC	29501	**800-372-2123**	843-669-4411
Eureka Welding Alloys Inc	2000 E Avis Dr	Madison Heights	MI	48071	**800-962-8560**	248-588-0001
Eutectic Corp	N 94 W 14355 Garwin Mace Dr	Menomonee Falls	WI	53051	**800-558-8524**	262-532-4677
Forney Industries Inc	1830 LaPorte Ave	Fort Collins	CO	80521	**800-521-6038**	
Goss Inc	1511 William Flynn Hwy	Glenshaw	PA	15116	**800-367-4677**	412-486-6100
Harris Products Group	4501 Quality Pl	Mason	OH	45040	**800-733-4043**	513-754-2000
Hobart Bros Co	101 Trade Sq E	Troy	OH	45373	**800-424-1543**	937-332-4000
Industrial Welders & Machinists Inc	610 Opperman Dr	Eagan	MN	55123	**800-455-4565**	
JWF Industries	84 Iron St PO Box 1286	Johnstown	PA	15907	**800-225-9359**	814-539-6922
Lincoln Electric Co	22801 St Clair Ave	Cleveland	OH	44117	**888-935-3878**	216-481-8100
M K Products Inc	16882 Armstrong Ave	Irvine	CA	92606	**800-787-9707**	949-863-1234
Maine Oxy	22 Albiston Way	Auburn	ME	04210	**800-639-1108**	207-784-5788
Merrill Mfg Corp	236 S Genesee St	Merrill	WI	54452	**888-662-9473**	715-536-5533
Miller Electric Mfg Co	1635 W Spencer St	Appleton	WI	54914	**888-843-7693**	920-734-9821
NLC Inc	319 W Main St *Sales	Jackson	MO	63755	**800-594-3958***	573-243-3141
Palomar Technologies	2728 Loker Ave W	Carlsbad	CA	92010	**800-854-3467**	760-931-3600
Smith Equipment Mfg Co	2601 Lockheed Ave *Cust Svc	Watertown	SD	57201	**866-931-9730***	605-882-3200
Sonobond Ultrasonics Inc	1191 McDermott Dr	West Chester	PA	19380	**800-323-1269**	610-696-4710
Systematics Inc	1025 Saunders Ln PO Box 2429	West Chester	PA	19380	**800-222-9353**	610-696-9040
Tuffaloy Products Inc	1400 S Batesville Rd	Greer	SC	29650	**800-521-3722**	864-879-0763
Uniweld Products Inc	2850 Ravenswood Rd	Fort Lauderdale	FL	33312	**800-323-2111**	954-584-2000
Weld Mold Co	750 Rickett Rd	Brighton	MI	48116	**800-521-9755**	810-229-9521
Western Enterprises Inc	875 Bassett Rd	Westlake	OH	44145	**800-783-7890**	

810 WHOLESALE CLUBS

Company	Address	City	State	Zip	Toll-Free	Phone
Costco Wholesale Corp	999 Lake Dr *NASDAQ: COST* ■ *Cust Svc	Issaquah	WA	98027	**800-774-2678***	425-313-8100

811 WIRE & CABLE

Company	Address	City	State	Zip	Toll-Free	Phone
Ace Wire & Cable Co Inc	7201 51st Ave	Woodside	NY	11377	**800-225-2354**	718-458-9200
AFC Cable Systems Inc	272 Duchaine Blvd	New Bedford	MA	02745	**800-757-6996**	508-998-1131
Allwire Inc	16395 Ave 24 1/2 PO Box 1000	Chowchilla	CA	93610	**800-255-3828**	559-665-4893
AmerCable Inc	350 Bailey Rd	El Dorado	AR	71730	**800-643-1516**	870-862-4919
Astro Industries Inc	4403 Dayton-Xenia Rd	Dayton	OH	45432	**800-543-5810**	937-429-5900
Cerro Wire & Cable Company Inc	1099 Thompson Rd SE	Hartselle	AL	35640	**800-523-3869**	256-773-2522
Charter Wire	3700 W Milwaukee Rd	Milwaukee	WI	53208	**800-436-9074**	414-390-3000
Elektrisola Inc	126 High St	Boscawen	NH	03303	**800-325-2022**	603-796-2114
Encore Wire Corp	1329 Millwood Rd *NASDAQ: WIRE*	McKinney	TX	75069	**800-962-9473**	972-562-9473
Eubanks Engineering Co	3022 Inland Empire Blvd	Ontario	CA	91764	**800-729-4208**	909-483-2456
Fiberwave Corp	140 58th St Bldg B Unit 6E	Brooklyn	NY	11220	**800-280-9011**	718-802-9011
Gehr Industries	7400 E Slauson Ave	Los Angeles	CA	90040	**800-688-6606**	323-728-5558
Insteel Industries Inc	1373 Boggs Dr *NASDAQ: IIIN*	Mount Airy	NC	27030	**800-334-9504**	336-786-2141
Kerite Co	49 Day St	Seymour	CT	06483	**800-777-7483**	203-888-2591
Keystone Consolidated Industries Inc	7000 SW Adams St *Sales	Peoria	IL	61641	**800-447-6444***	
Major Custom Cable Inc	281 Lotus Dr	Jackson	MO	63755	**800-455-6224**	
Mid-South Wire Company Inc	1070 Visco Dr	Nashville	TN	37210	**800-714-7800**	615-743-2850
Mount Joy Wire Corp	1000 E Main St	Mount Joy	PA	17552	**800-321-2305**	717-653-1461
Nichols Wire	1547 Helton Dr	Florence	AL	35630	**800-633-3156**	800-873-2011
Owl Wire & Cable Inc	3127 Seneca Tpke	Canastota	NY	13032	**800-765-9473**	315-697-2011
Rea Magnet Wire Company Inc	3600 E Pontiac St	Fort Wayne	IN	46803	**800-732-9473**	260-421-7321
Ribbon Technology Corp	825 Taylor Stn Rd	Gahanna	OH	43230	**800-848-0477**	614-864-5444
Sivaco Wire Group	800 Rue Ouellette	Marieville	QC	J3M1P5	**800-876-9473**	450-658-8741
Southwestern Wire Inc	PO Box CC	Norman	OK	73070	**800-348-9473**	405-447-6900
Southwire Co	1 Southwire Dr	Carrollton	GA	30119	**800-444-1700**	770-832-4242
Spotnails	1100 Hicks Rd	Rolling Meadows	IL	60008	**800-873-2239**	847-259-1620
Superior Essex Inc Magnet Wire/Winding Wire Div	1601 Wall St PO Box 1601	Fort Wayne	IN	46802	**800-551-8948**	260-461-4550
Techalloy Company Inc Baltimore Wire Div	2310 Chesapeake Ave	Baltimore	MD	21222	**800-638-1458**	410-633-9300
Times Fiber Communications Inc	358 Hall Ave PO Box 384	Wallingford	CT	06492	**800-677-2288**	203-265-8500
Tree Island Steel	12459 Arrow Rt	Rancho Cucamonga	CA	91739	**800-255-6974**	909-594-7511
Wirerope Works Inc	100 Maynard St *Cust Svc	Williamsport	PA	17701	**800-541-7673***	570-326-5146
Wrap-On Company Inc	5550 W 70th Pl	Chicago	IL	60638	**800-621-6947**	708-496-2150

812 WIRE & CABLE - ELECTRONIC

Company	Address	City	State	Zip	Toll-Free	Phone
Alpha Wire Co	711 Lidgerwood Ave	Elizabeth	NJ	07207	**800-522-5742**	908-925-8000
Belden Inc Americas Div	2200 US Hwy 27 S PO Box 1980	Richmond	IN	47375	**800-235-3362**	765-983-5200
Cables to Go Inc	3599 Dayton Pk Dr	Dayton	OH	45414	**800-826-7904**	937-224-8646
Champlain Cable Corp	175 Hercules Dr	Colchester	VT	05446	**800-451-5162**	
CommScope Inc	1100 Commscope Pl SE PO Box 339	Hickory	NC	28603	**800-982-1708**	828-324-2200
Compulink Inc	1205 Gandy Blvd N	Saint Petersburg	FL	33702	**800-231-6685**	727-579-1500
Consolidated Electronic Wire & Cable Co	11044 King St	Franklin Park	IL	60131	**800-621-4278**	847-455-8830
Corning Cable Systems	800 17th St NW	Hickory	NC	28603	**800-743-2671**	828-901-5000
CXtec	5404 S Bay Rd PO Box 4799 *Orders	Syracuse	NY	13212	**800-767-3282***	315-476-3000
General Cable Corp	4 Tesseneer Dr *NYSE: BGC*	Highland Heights	KY	41076	**800-572-8000**	859-572-8000
Harbour Industries Inc	4744 Shelburne Rd PO Box 188	Shelburne	VT	05482	**800-659-4733**	802-985-3311
Judd Wire Inc	124 Tpke Rd *Cust Svc	Turners Falls	MA	01376	**800-545-5833***	413-863-4357
Madison Cable Corp	125 Goddard Memorial Dr	Worcester	MA	01603	**877-623-4766**	508-752-2884
Nehring Electric Works Inc	1005 E Locust St	DeKalb	IL	60115	**800-435-4481**	815-756-2741
Oleco Inc	18683 Trimble Ct	Spring Lake	MI	49456	**800-575-3282**	616-842-6790
Optical Cable Corp (OCC)	5290 Concourse Dr *NASDAQ: OCC*	Roanoke	VA	24019	**800-622-7711**	540-265-0690
Prestolite Wire Corp	200 Galleria Officentre Ste 212	Southfield	MI	48034	**800-498-3132**	248-355-4422
Rockbestos-Surprenant Cable Corp	20 Bradley Pk Rd	East Granby	CT	06026	**800-327-7625**	860-653-8300
Siemon Co	101 Siemon Co Dr	Watertown	CT	06795	**866-548-5814**	860-945-4200
Superior Essex Inc	6120 Powers Ferry Rd Ste 150 *NASDAQ: SPSX*	Atlanta	GA	30339	**800-551-8948**	770-657-6000
Trilogy Communications Inc	2910 Hwy 80 E	Pearl	MS	39208	**888-713-1414**	601-932-4461

813 WIRING DEVICES - CURRENT-CARRYING

Company	Address	City	State	Zip	Toll-Free	Phone
Amphenol Corp	358 Hall Ave *NYSE: APH*	Wallingford	CT	06492	**877-267-4366**	203-265-8900
Bizlink Technology Inc	3400 Gateway Blvd	Fremont	CA	94538	**800-326-4193**	510-252-0786
Burndy LLC	47 E Industrial Park Dr	Manchester	NH	03109	**800-346-4175**	
Carling Technologies Inc	60 Johnson Ave	Plainville	CT	06062	**800-243-8556**	860-793-9281
Cherry Corp	11200 88th Ave	Pleasant Prairie	WI	53158	**800-510-1689**	262-942-6500
Cinch Connectors Inc	1700 Findley Rd	Lombard	IL	60148	**800-323-9612**	630-705-6000
Cole Hersee Co	20 Old Colony Ave	Boston	MA	02127	**800-365-2653**	617-268-2100
Component Enterprises Co Inc	235 E Penn St PO Box 189	Norristown	PA	19401	**877-232-7253**	
Cooper Bussmann Inc	114 Old State Rd	Ellisville	MO	63021	**855-287-7626**	636-394-2877
Cooper Crouse-Hinds	1201 Wolf St	Syracuse	NY	13208	**866-764-5454**	315-477-5531
Cooper Industries	600 Travis St Ste 5400 *NYSE: ETN*	Houston	TX	77002	**866-853-4293**	713-209-8400
Cooper Wiring Devices Inc	203 Cooper Cir *Cust Svc	Peachtree City	GA	30269	**866-853-4293***	770-631-2100
Cord Sets Inc	1015 Fifth St N	Minneapolis	MN	55411	**800-752-0580**	612-337-9700

Classified Section

Company	Address	City	State	Zip	Toll-Free	Phone
Cristek Interconnects Inc	5395 E Hunter Ave	Anaheim	CA	92807	**888-265-9162**	714-696-5200
Curtis Industries Inc	2400 S 43rd St PO Box 343925	Milwaukee	WI	53219	**800-657-0853**	414-649-4200
Edwin Gaynor Corp	200 Charles St	Stratford	CT	06615	**800-342-9667**	203-378-5545
EECO Switch	1240 Pioneer St Ste A	Brea	CA	92821	**800-854-3808**	714-835-6000
Electri-Cord Mfg Co Inc	312 E Main St	Westfield	PA	16950	**888-278-8253**	814-367-2265
Electroswitch	2010 Yonkers Rd	Raleigh	NC	27604	**888-768-2797**	919-833-0707
ERICO Products Inc	34600 Solon Rd	Solon	OH	44139	**800-248-2677**	440-248-0100
ETCO Inc	25 Bellows St	Warwick	RI	02888	**800-689-3826**	401-467-2400
Glenair Inc	1211 Air Way	Glendale	CA	91201	**888-465-4094**	818-247-6000
Group Dekko Services LLC	2505 Dekko Dr	Garrett	IN	46738	**800-829-3101**	260-357-3621
Hoffman Products	9600 Vly View Rd	Macedonia	OH	44056	**800-645-2014**	216-525-4320
Hubbell Premise Wiring Inc	23 Clara Dr	Mystic	CT	06355	**800-626-0005**	
Hubbell Wiring Device-Kellems	40 Waterview Dr	Shelton	CT	06484	**800-288-6000*** *Cust Svc	203-882-4800
ILSCO	4730 Madison Rd	Cincinnati	OH	45227	**800-776-9775*** *Sales	513-533-6200
Independent Protection Company Inc	1607 S Main St	Goshen	IN	46526	**800-860-8388**	574-533-4116
Lumens Light & Living	2028 K St	Sacramento	CA	95811	**877-445-4486**	916-444-5585
Marinco	2655 Napa Valley Corp Dr	Napa	CA	94558	**800-307-6702**	707-226-9600
McGill Electrical Product Group	9377 W Higgins Rd	Rosemont	IL	60018	**800-621-1506**	847-268-6000
Mill-Max Mfg Corp	190 Pine Hollow Rd	Oyster Bay	NY	11771	**800-333-4237**	516-922-6000
Minnesota Wire & Cable Co	1835 Energy Pk Dr	Saint Paul	MN	55108	**800-258-6922**	651-642-1800
Ohio Associated Enterprises LLC	1382 W Jackson St	Painesville	OH	44077	**888-637-4832**	440-354-3148
Omnetics Connector Corp	7260 Commerce Cir E	Minneapolis	MN	55432	**800-343-0025*** *Cust Svc	763-572-0656
Panduit Corp	17301 Ridgeland Ave	Tinley Park	IL	60477	**888-506-5400**	708-532-1800
Preformed Line Products	660 Beta Dr *NASDAQ: PLPC*	Cleveland	OH	44143	**800-622-6757**	440-461-5200
Shape LLC	2105 Corporate Dr	Addison	IL	60101	**800-367-5811**	630-620-8394
Veetronix Inc	1311 W Pacific Ave	Lexington	NE	68850	**800-445-0007*** *General	308-324-6661
Weidmuller Inc	821 Southlake Blvd	Richmond	VA	23236	**800-849-9343*** *Cust Svc	804-794-2877
Zierick Manufacturing Corp	131 Radio Cir	Mount Kisco	NY	10549	**800-882-8020**	914-666-2911

814 WIRING DEVICES - NONCURRENT-CARRYING

Company	Address	City	State	Zip	Toll-Free	Phone
Allied Moulded Products Inc	222 N Union St	Bryan	OH	43506	**800-722-2679**	419-636-4217
Bedford Materials Co Inc	7676 Allegheny Rd	Manns Choice	PA	15550	**800-773-4276**	
Chase & Sons Inc	295 University Ave	Westwood	MA	02090	**800-323-4182**	781-332-0700
Conduit Pipe Products Co	1501 W Main St	West Jefferson	OH	43162	**800-848-6125**	614-879-9114
Cooper B-Line Inc	509 W Monroe St	Highland	IL	62249	**800-851-7415**	618-654-2184
Cottrell Paper Company Inc	1135 Rock City Rd PO Box 35	Rock City Falls	NY	12863	**800-948-3559**	518-885-1702
EGS Electrical Group LLC	9377 W Higgins Rd	Rosemont	IL	60018	**800-621-1506**	847-268-6000
Electri-Flex Co	222 Central Ave	Roselle	IL	60172	**800-323-6174**	630-529-2920
Flex-Cable Inc	5822 N Henkel Rd	Howard City	MI	49329	**800-245-3539**	231-937-8000
Gaylord Manufacturing Co	1088 Montclaire Dr	Ceres	CA	95307	**800-375-0091**	209-538-3313
Hubbell Premise Wiring Inc	23 Clara Dr	Mystic	CT	06355	**800-626-0005**	
Hubbell RACO	3902 W Sample St	South Bend	IN	46619	**800-722-6437**	574-234-7151
Hughes Bros Inc	210 N 13th St PO Box 159	Seward	NE	68434	**800-869-0359**	402-643-2991
Ideal Industries Inc	1375 Pk Ave	Sycamore	IL	60178	**800-435-0705**	815-895-5181
Joslyn Sunbank Co LLC	1740 Commerce Way	Paso Robles	CA	93446	**800-523-0727**	805-238-2840
LoDan Electronics Inc	3311 N Kennicott Ave	Arlington Heights	IL	60004	**800-401-4995**	847-398-5311
MacLean Power Systems	11411 Addison St	Franklin Park	IL	60131	**855-677-7447**	847-455-0014
MP Husky Corp	204 Old Piedmont Hwy PO Box 16749	Greenville	SC	29605	**800-277-4810**	864-234-4800
O-Z/Gedney	9377 W Higgins Rd	Rosemont	IL	60018	**800-621-1506**	847-268-6000
Opti-Com Mfg Network Co Inc	259 Plauche St	New Orleans	LA	70123	**800-345-8774**	504-736-0331
Rittal Corp	1 Rittal Pl	Springfield	OH	45504	**800-477-4000**	937-399-0500
Saginaw Control & Engineering Inc	95 Midland Rd	Saginaw	MI	48638	**800-234-6871**	989-799-6871
TJ Cope Inc	11500 Norcom Rd	Philadelphia	PA	19154	**800-483-3473**	215-961-2570
Varflex Corp	512 W Ct St	Rome	NY	13440	**800-648-4014**	315-336-4400
Virginia Plastics Co Inc	3453 Aerial Way Dr PO Box 4577	Roanoke	VA	24018	**877-351-1699**	540-981-9700

WOMEN'S COLLEGES

SEE Colleges - Women's (Four-Year)

815 WOOD MEMBERS - STRUCTURAL

Company	Address	City	State	Zip	Toll-Free	Phone
Alpine Engineered Products Inc	1100 Pk Central Blvd S Ste 2400 & 3800	Pompano Beach	FL	33064	**800-786-6086*** *General	954-781-3333
Armstrong Lumber Co Inc	2709 Auburn Way N	Auburn	WA	98002	**800-868-9066**	253-833-6666
Automated Bldg Components Inc	2359 Grant Rd	North Baltimore	OH	45872	**800-837-2152**	419-257-2152
Enwood Structures Inc	5724 McCrimmon Pkwy PO Box 2002	Morrisville	NC	27560	**800-777-8648**	919-518-0464
Fullerton Bldg Systems Inc (FBS)	34620 250th St PO Box 308	Worthington	MN	56187	**800-450-9782**	507-376-3128
Goodfellow Inc	225 Goodfellow St	Delson	QC	J5B1V5	**800-361-6503**	450-635-6511
HM Stauffer & Sons Inc	33 Glenola Dr PO Box 567	Leola	PA	17540	**800-662-2226**	717-656-2811
Laminate Technologies Inc	161 Maule Rd	Tiffin	OH	44883	**800-231-2523**	
Laminated Wood Systems Inc (LWS)	1327 285th Rd PO Box 386	Seward	NE	68434	**800-949-3526**	
Laminators Inc	3255 Penn St	Hatfield	PA	19440	**877-663-4277**	215-723-8107
Molpus Co, The	502 Vly View Dr PO Box 59	Philadelphia	MS	39350	**800-535-5434**	601-656-3373
Montgomery Truss & Panel Inc	803 W Main St	Grove City	PA	16127	**800-942-8010**	724-458-7500
Robbins Mfg Co	13001 N Nebraska Ave	Tampa	FL	33612	**888-558-8199**	813-971-3030
Southern Components Inc	7360 Julie Frances Dr	Shreveport	LA	71129	**800-256-2144**	318-687-3330
Stow Co, The	3311 Windquest Dr	Holland	MI	49424	**800-562-4257**	616-399-3311
Structural Wood Corp	4000 Labore Rd	Saint Paul	MN	55110	**800-652-9058**	651-426-8111
Villaume Industries Inc	2926 Lone Oak Cir	Eagan	MN	55121	**800-488-3610*** *Cust Svc	651-454-3610

816 WOOD PRESERVING

Company	Address	City	State	Zip	Toll-Free	Phone
Bell Lumber & Pole Co	778 First St NW PO Box 120786	New Brighton	MN	55112	**877-633-4334**	651-633-4334
Brown Wood Preserving Company Inc	6201 Camp Ground Rd	Louisville	KY	40216	**800-537-1765**	502-448-2337
Building Products Plus	12317 Almeda Rd	Houston	TX	77045	**800-460-8627**	
Conrad Forest Products	68765 Wildwood Dr	North Bend	OR	97459	**800-356-7146**	
Cox Industries Inc	860 Cannon Bridge Rd PO Box 1124	Orangeburg	SC	29116	**800-476-4401**	803-534-7467
Elder Wood Preserving Co Inc	334 Elder Wood Rd	Mansura	LA	71350	**866-606-2470**	318-964-2196
Exterior Wood Inc	2685 Index St	Washougal	WA	98671	**800-222-1222**	360-835-8561
JH Baxter & Co	PO Box 5902	San Mateo	CA	94402	**800-556-1098**	650-349-0201
Koppers Inc	436 Seventh Ave *NYSE: KOP*	Pittsburgh	PA	15219	**800-385-4406**	412-227-2001
McFarland Cascade	1640 E Marc St PO Box 1496	Tacoma	WA	98421	**800-426-8430*** *Cust Svc	253-572-3033
Osmose Inc	980 Ellicott St	Buffalo	NY	14209	**800-877-7653**	716-882-5905
Professional Coaters Inc	100 Commerce Park Dr	Cabot	AR	72023	**800-962-0344**	501-843-7509
Robbins Mfg Co	13001 N Nebraska Ave	Tampa	FL	33612	**888-558-8199**	813-971-3030
Western Wood Preserving Co	1310 Zehnder St	Sumner	WA	98390	**800-472-7714**	253-863-8191
Wood Preservers Inc	15939 Historyland Hwy PO Box 158	Warsaw	VA	22572	**800-368-2536**	804-333-4022

817 WOOD PRODUCTS - RECONSTITUTED

Company	Address	City	State	Zip	Toll-Free	Phone
Aya Kitchens & Baths Ltd	1551 Caterpillar Rd	Mississauga	ON	L4X2Z6	**866-292-4968**	905-848-1999
Cabinet Tronix LLC	290 Trousdale Dr Ste A	Chula Vista	CA	91910	**866-876-6199**	
Geo Products LLC	8615 Golden Spike Ln	Houston	TX	77086	**800-434-4743**	281-820-5493
Homasote Co	932 Lower Ferry Rd PO Box 7240 *OTC: HMTC*	West Trenton	NJ	08628	**800-257-9491**	609-883-3300
Panel Processing Inc	120 N Industrial Hwy	Alpena	MI	49707	**800-433-7142**	989-356-9007
Panolam Industries International Inc	20 Progress Dr	Shelton	CT	06484	**877-391-4130**	203-925-1556
Rex Lumber Co	840 Main St	Acton	MA	01720	**800-343-0567**	978-263-0055
Tectum Inc	105 S Sixth St	Newark	OH	43055	**888-977-9691**	740-345-9691

818 WOOD PRODUCTS - SHAPED & TURNED

Name / Address	City	State	Zip	Toll-Free	Phone
A&M Supply Corp 6701 90th Ave N	Pinellas Park	FL	33782	**800-877-8551**	727-541-6631
Brown Wood Products Co 7040 N Lawndale Ave	Lincolnwood	IL	60712	**800-328-5858**	
Chicago Dowel Company Inc 4700 W Grand Ave	Chicago	IL	60639	**800-333-6935**	773-622-2000
Circular Technologies 3275 Prairie Ave	Boulder	CO	80301	**800-215-1831**	303-443-8512
Davidson Plyforms Inc 5505 33rd St SE	Grand Rapids	MI	49512	**800-505-4732**	616-956-0033
Frank Edmunds & Co 6111 S Sayre	Chicago	IL	60638	**800-447-3516**	773-586-2772
Jarden Home Brands 14611 W Commerce Rd *Cust Svc	Daleville	IN	47334	**800-240-3340***	765-557-3000
Wayne Kiltz Africa Imports 240 S Main St Unit A	South Hackensack	NJ	07606	**800-500-6120**	201-457-1995

819 WOODWORKING MACHINERY

Name / Address	City	State	Zip	Toll-Free	Phone
Baker Products 55480 Hwy 21 N PO Box 128	Ellington	MO	63638	**800-548-6914**	573-663-7711
James L. Taylor Manufacturing Co 108 Parker Ave	Poughkeepsie	NY	12601	**800-952-1320**	845-452-3780
Kimwood Corp 77684 Oregon 99	Cottage Grove	OR	97424	**800-942-4401**	541-942-4401
KVAL Inc 825 Petaluma Blvd S	Petaluma	CA	94952	**800-553-5825**	707-762-7367
Memphis Machinery & Supply Co Inc 2881 Directors Cove	Memphis	TN	38131	**800-932-8376**	901-527-4443
Mereen-Johnson Machine Co 4401 Lyndale Ave N	Minneapolis	MN	55412	**888-465-7297**	612-529-7791
Michael Weining Inc 124 Crosslake Pk Dr PO Box 3158	Mooresville	NC	28117	**877-548-0929**	704-799-0100
Oliver Machinery Co 6902 S 194th St	Kent	WA	98032	**800-559-5065**	253-867-0334
Pendu Manufacturing Inc 718 N Shirk Rd	New Holland	PA	17557	**800-233-0471**	717-354-4348
Safety Speed Cut Mfg Co Inc 13943 Lincoln St NE	Ham Lake	MN	55304	**800-772-2327**	763-755-1600
Thermwood Corp 904 Buffaloville Rd *OTC: TOOD* ■ *Mktg	Dale	IN	47523	**800-533-6901***	812-937-4476
USNR 1981 Schurman Way PO Box 310	Woodland	WA	98674	**800-289-8767**	360-225-8267
USNR Inc 558 Robinson Rd PO Box 310	Woodland	WA	98674	**800-289-8767**	360-225-8267
Viking Engineering & Development Inc 5750 Main St NE *Sales	Fridley	MN	55432	**800-328-2403***	763-571-2400
Voorwood Co 2350 Barney St	Anderson	CA	96007	**800-826-0089**	530-365-3311
Yates-American Machine Company Inc 2880 Kennedy Dr	Beloit	WI	53511	**800-752-6377**	608-364-6333

820 WORLD TRADE CENTERS

Name / Address	City	State	Zip	Toll-Free	Phone
Northern California World Trade Ctr 1 Capitol Mall Ste 300	Sacramento	CA	95814	**855-667-2259**	
Seaport World Trade Ctr Boston 200 Seaport Blvd	Boston	MA	02210	**800-440-3318**	617-385-4212

821 ZOOS & WILDLIFE PARKS

SEE ALSO Aquariums - Public ; Botanical Gardens & Arboreta

Name / Address	City	State	Zip	Toll-Free	Phone
African Lion Safari & Game Farm RR 1 Ste 1	Cambridge	ON	N1R5S2	**800-461-9453**	519-623-2620
African Safari Wildlife Park 267 S Lightner Rd	Port Clinton	OH	43452	**800-521-2660**	419-732-3606
Animal Ark Wildlife Sanctuary & Nature Ctr 1265 Deerlodge Rd	Reno	NV	89508	**866-366-5771**	775-970-3111
Assiniboine Park Zoo 55 Pavilion Crescent	Winnipeg	MB	R3P2N6	**877-927-6006**	204-927-8080
Audubon Nature Institute 6500 Magazine St	New Orleans	LA	70118	**800-774-7394**	504-581-4629
Brevard Zoo 8225 N Wickham Rd	Melbourne	FL	32940	**800-435-7352**	321-254-9453
Bronx Zoo 2300 Southern Blvd	Bronx	NY	10460	**800-433-4149**	718-220-5100
Busch Gardens Williamsburg 1 Busch Gardens Blvd	Williamsburg	VA	23185	**800-343-7946**	
Calgary Zoo Botanical Garden & Prehistoric Park 1300 Zoo Rd NE	Calgary	AB	T2E7V6	**800-588-9993**	403-232-9300
Caribbean Gardens 1590 Goodlette-Frank Rd	Naples	FL	34102	**888-520-3756**	239-262-5409
Central Florida Zoological Park 3755 NW Hwy 17-92 & I-4 PO Box 470309	Lake Monroe	FL	32747	**800-435-7352**	407-323-4450
Cincinnati Zoo & Botanical Garden 3400 Vine St	Cincinnati	OH	45220	**800-944-4776**	513-281-4700
Clyde Peeling's Reptiland 18628 US Rt 15	Allenwood	PA	17810	**800-737-8452**	
Columbian Park Zoo 1915 Scott St	Lafayette	IN	47904	**800-438-9926**	765-807-1540
Columbus Zoo & Aquarium 4850 W Powell Rd	Powell	OH	43065	**800-666-5397**	614-645-3400
Discovery Cove 6000 Discovery Cove Way	Orlando	FL	32821	**877-434-7268**	407-370-1280
Elmwood Park Zoo 1661 Harding Blvd	Norristown	PA	19401	**800-652-4143**	610-277-3825
Erie Zoo 423 W 38th St	Erie	PA	16508	**877-371-5422**	814-864-4091
Felix Neck Wildlife Sanctuary 100 Felix Neck Dr	Edgartown	MA	02539	**866-627-2267**	508-627-4850
Gator Park 24050 SW Eigth St	Miami	FL	33194	**800-559-2205**	305-559-2255
Gatorland 14501 S Orange Blossom Trl	Orlando	FL	32837	**800-393-5297**	407-855-5496
Good Zoo & Benedum Planetarium 465 Lodge Dr	Wheeling	WV	26003	**800-624-6988**	304-243-4030
Greenville Zoo 150 Cleveland Pk Dr	Greenville	SC	29601	**800-877-8339**	864-467-4300
Grizzly & Wolf Discovery Ctr 201 S Canyon St	West Yellowstone	MT	59758	**800-257-2570**	406-646-7001
Hutchinson Zoo 6 Emerson Loop E	Hutchinson	KS	67501	**800-362-3247**	620-694-2693
Jungle Adventures 26205 E Colonial Dr	Christmas	FL	32709	**877-424-2867**	407-568-2885
Kentucky Horse Park 4089 Iron Works Pkwy	Lexington	KY	40511	**800-678-8813**	859-233-4303
Louisville Zoo 1100 Trevilian Way	Louisville	KY	40213	**866-229-0502**	502-459-2181
Minnesota Zoo 13000 Zoo Blvd	Apple Valley	MN	55124	**800-366-7811**	952-431-9200
North Carolina Zoological Park 4401 Zoo Pkwy	Asheboro	NC	27205	**800-488-0444**	336-879-7000
Northeastern Wisconsin Zoo 305 E Walnut St Rm 102 PO Box 23600	Green Bay	WI	54301	**888-844-8070**	920-448-6242
Oklahoma City Zoological Park & Botanical Gardens 2101 NE 50th St	Oklahoma City	OK	73111	**800-891-2917**	405-424-3344
Pittsburgh Zoo & PPG Aquarium 1 Wild Pl	Pittsburgh	PA	15206	**800-732-0999**	412-665-3640
Rosamond Gifford Zoo at Burnet Park 1 Conservation Pl	Syracuse	NY	13204	**800-724-5006**	315-435-8511
Sacramento Zoo 3930 W Land Pk Dr	Sacramento	CA	95822	**866-570-7318**	916-808-5888
Safari West Wildlife Preserve & Tent Camp 3115 Porter Creek Rd	Santa Rosa	CA	95404	**800-616-2695**	707-579-2551
Saint Louis Zoological Park 1 Government Dr	Saint Louis	MO	63110	**800-966-8877**	314-781-0900
San Diego Zoo Safari Park 15500 San Pasqual Valley Rd *Cust Svc	Escondido	CA	92027	**877-363-6237***	760-747-8702
Sarasota Jungle Gardens 3701 Bay Shore Rd	Sarasota	FL	34234	**877-681-6547**	941-355-5305
Toledo Zoo 2700 Broadway	Toledo	OH	43609	**866-900-1146**	419-385-5721
Tupelo Buffalo Park & Zoo 2272 N Coley Rd	Tupelo	MS	38803	**866-272-4766**	662-844-8709
Wild Animal Safari 1300 Oak Grove Rd	Pine Mountain	GA	31822	**800-367-2751**	706-663-8744
Wildlife West Nature Park 87 N Frontage Rd	Edgewood	NM	87015	**877-981-9453**	505-281-7655
Wonders of Wildlife 500 W Sunshine St	Springfield	MO	65807	**877-245-9453**	417-890-9453

Index to Classified Headings

Citations provided in this index refer to the subject headings under which listings are organized in the Classified Section. The page number given for each citation refers to the page on which a particular subject category begins rather than to a specific company or organization name. "See" and "See also" references are included to help locate appropriate subject categories.

A

Abortion Rights
See Civil & Human Rights Organizations . . . 484
Abrasive Products . . . 465
Abstract Companies
See Title Insurance . . . 746
Accelerator Chips
See Semiconductors & Related Devices . . . 894
Accelerator Facilities
See Research Centers & Institutions . . . 871
Accelerators - Ion Beam
See Measuring, Testing, Controlling Instruments . . . 780
Accelerators/Processors - Graphics
See Multimedia Equipment & Supplies . . . 580
Access Control
See Security Products & Services . . . 892
Accessories - Automotive
See Automotive Parts & Supplies - Mfr . . . 507
Automotive Parts & Supplies - Whol . . . 508
Accessories - Fashion
See Clothing & Accessories - Mfr . . . 545
Clothing & Accessories - Whol . . . 547
Accessories - Hair (Bobby Pins, Clips, etc)
See Cosmetics, Skin Care, and Other Personal Care Products 620
Accessories - Leather (Personal)
See Leather Goods - Personal . . . 759
Accident Insurance
See Life & Accident Insurance . . . 740
Accounting Books
See Blankbooks & Binders . . . 520
Accounting Firms . . . 465
Accounting Software
See Business Software (General) . . . 586
Accounts Receivable Management Services
See Collection Agencies . . . 549
Acoustical Contractors
See Plastering, Drywall, Acoustical, Insulation Contractors . . . 600
Acoustical Products
See Insulation & Acoustical Products . . . 738
Acrylic
See Plastics - Laminated - Plate, Sheet, Profile Shapes . . . 835
Synthetic Resins & Plastics Materials . . . 837
Actuators - Hydraulic or Pneumatic
See Cylinders & Actuators - Fluid Power . . . 624
Addiction Treatment
See General Hospitals - US . . . 713
Psychiatric Hospitals . . . 718
Substance Abuse Treatment Centers . . . 906
Adhesive Tape
See Medical Supplies - Mfr . . . 784
Adhesives & Sealants . . . 466
Administration Software - System
See Systems & Utilities Software . . . 591
Administration Software - Web Site
See Internet & Communications Software . . . 588
Administrative Management Services
See Management Services . . . 776
Adoption Resources
See Children & Family Advocacy Organizations . . . 482
Adventure Tours
See Tour Operators . . . 921
Advertisers Associations
See Sales & Marketing Professional Associations . . . 499
Advertising Agencies . . . 466
See also Public Relations Firms 850
Advertising Displays
See Displays - Exhibit & Trade Show . . . 629
Displays - Point-of-Purchase . . . 629
Signs . . . 896
Advertising Services - Direct Mail . . . 467
Advertising Services - Media Buyers . . . 468
Advertising Services - Online . . . 468
Advertising Services - Outdoor Advertising . . . 469
Advertising Services - Telemarketing
See Telemarketing & Other Tele-Services . . . 910
Advertising Specialties . . . 469
See also Signs 896; Smart Cards 897; Trophies, Plaques, Awards 927
Advocacy Organizations - Children & Family
See Children & Family Advocacy Organizations . . . 482
Aerial Photography
See Surveying, Mapping, Related Services . . . 906
Aerial Platforms
See Construction Machinery & Equipment . . . 602
Aeronautical Systems & Instruments
See Navigation & Guidance Instruments & Systems . . . 805
Aerosol Products
See Chemicals - Specialty . . . 542
Aerosol Valves
See Metal Products (Misc) . . . 788
Aerospace & Avionics Communications Systems
See Radio & Television Broadcasting & Communications Equipment . . . 865
Aerospace Fastening Systems
See Fasteners & Fastening Systems . . . 654
Aggregate Mining
See Sand & Gravel Pits . . . 794
Stone Quarries - Crushed & Broken Stone . . . 794
Aging Services Agencies - State
See Government - State . . . 684
Agricultural Chemicals
See Fertilizers & Pesticides . . . 654
Agricultural Machinery & Equipment
See Farm Machinery & Equipment - Mfr . . . 652
Farm Machinery & Equipment - Whol . . . 653
Agricultural Products . . . 469
See also Fruit Growers 675; Horse Breeders 708; Horticultural Products Growers 708; Seed Companies 894
Cattle Ranches, Farms, Feedlots (Beef Cattle) . . . 469
Dairy Farms . . . 469
General Farms . . . 469
Grain Farms . . . 469
Hog Farms . . . 469
Mushroom Growers . . . 470
Poultry & Eggs Production . . . 470
Tree Nuts Growers . . . 470
Vegetable Farms . . . 470
Agricultural Project Management Services
See Management Services . . . 776
Agricultural Research
See Research Centers & Institutions . . . 871
Agricultural Services . . . 470
Crop Preparation Services . . . 470
Livestock Improvement Services . . . 470
Agriculture - US Department of
See US Department of Agriculture . . . 690
AIDS Test Kits
See Diagnostic Products . . . 628
Air Ambulance Services
See Ambulance Services . . . 475
Air Bags
See Safety Equipment - Mfr . . . 886
Air Cargo Carriers . . . 470
Air Charter Services . . . 471
See also Aviation - Fixed-Base Operations 509; Helicopter Transport Services 700
Air Cleaners
See Air Purification Equipment - Household . . . 472
Air Cleaners
See Air Purification Equipment - Industrial . . . 472
Air Conditioner Controls
See Controls - Temperature - Residential & Commercial . . . 612
Air Conditioning & Heating Equipment - Commercial/ Industrial . . . 471
See also Air Conditioning & Heating Equipment - Residential 472; Refrigeration Equipment - Mfr 870
Air Conditioning & Heating Equipment - Residential . . . 472
See also Air Conditioning & Heating Equipment - Commercial/ Industrial 471
Air Conditioning Contractors
See Plumbing, Heating, Air Conditioning Contractors . . . 601
Air Conditioning Equipment - Automotive
See Air Conditioning & Heating Equipment - Residential . . . 472
Air Conditioning Equipment - Whol
See Plumbing, Heating, Air Conditioning Equipment & Supplies - Whol . . . 840
Air Courier Services
See Freight Forwarders . . . 673
Package Delivery Services . . . 817
Air Fare Consolidators . . . 472
Air Freight
See Air Cargo Carriers . . . 470
Air Purification Equipment - Household . . . 472
See also Appliances - Small - Mfr 476
Air Purification Equipment - Industrial . . . 472
Air Quality Monitoring Instruments
See Controls - Industrial Process . . . 611
Air Rifles
See Firearms & Ammunition (Non-Military) . . . 655
Air Traffic Control Services . . . 473
Aircraft . . . 473
See also Airships 475
Aircraft & Parts - Whol
See Transportation Equipment & Supplies - Whol . . . 924
Aircraft Engines & Engine Parts . . . 473
Aircraft Instruments - Flight
See Navigation & Guidance Instruments & Systems . . . 805
Aircraft Instruments - Other Than Flight
See Measuring, Testing, Controlling Instruments . . . 780
Aircraft Lighting Equipment
See Lighting Equipment - Vehicular . . . 763
Aircraft Parts & Auxiliary Equipment . . . 473
See also Precision Machined Products 843
Aircraft Rental . . . 473
See also Aviation - Fixed-Base Operations 509
Aircraft Service & Repair . . . 474
Airline Magazines
See Travel & Regional Interest Magazines . . . 773
Airline Reservations Systems
See Global Distribution Systems (GDSs) . . . 682
Airlines - Commercial . . . 474
See also Air Cargo Carriers 470; Air Charter Services 471; Airlines - Frequent Flyer Programs 474
Airlines - Frequent Flyer Programs . . . 474
Airport Facilities Management Services
See Facilities Management Services . . . 652
Airports . . . 474
See also Ports & Port Authorities 842
Airships . . . 475
See also Aircraft 473
Alarms
See Fire Protection Systems . . . 655
Security Products & Services . . . 892
Albums - Photo
See Blankbooks & Binders . . . 520
Alcohol Testing Products
See Diagnostic Products . . . 628
Alcoholic Beverages
See Beer & Ale - Whol . . . 518
Breweries . . . 524
Liquor - Mfr . . . 518
Liquor Stores . . . 764
Wine & Liquor - Whol . . . 518
Wines - Mfr . . . 518

Alcoholism
See General Hospitals - US ... 713
Psychiatric Hospitals ... 718
Self-Help Organizations ... 490
Substance Abuse Treatment Centers ... 906
Ale
See Beer & Ale - Whol ... 518
Breweries ... 524
Alfalfa
See Grain Farms ... 469
All-Terrain Vehicles ... 475
See also Sporting Goods 899
Allergens
See Biotechnology Companies ... 519
Alloys
See Foundries - Nonferrous (Castings) ... 671
Almonds
See Tree Nuts Growers ... 470
Alternative Newsweeklies
See Weekly Newspapers - Alternative ... 812
Alternative Therapies
See Health & Health-Related Organizations ... 486
Alternators
See Electrical Equipment for Internal Combustion Engines ... 642
Aluminum
See Metal Industries (Misc) ... 788
Metal Tube & Pipe ... 789
Wire & Cable ... 943
Aluminum Cans
See Cans - Metal ... 530
Aluminum Castings
See Foundries - Nonferrous (Castings) ... 671
Aluminum Foil
See Metal Industries (Misc) ... 788
Aluminum Investment Castings
See Foundries - Investment ... 671
Ambulance Services ... 475
Ambulances - Mfr
See Motor Vehicles - Commercial & Special Purpose ... 797
Ambulatory Surgery Centers
See Health Care Providers - Ancillary ... 697
Ammeters
See Electrical Signals Measuring & Testing Instruments ... 642
Ammunition
See Firearms & Ammunition (Non-Military) ... 655
Weapons & Ordnance (Military) ... 942
Amphibious Vehicles
See Weapons & Ordnance (Military) ... 942
Amplifiers
See Audio & Video Equipment ... 502
Amplifiers - RF & IF
See Radio & Television Broadcasting & Communications Equipment ... 865
Amusement Park Companies ... 475
See also Circus, Carnival, Festival Operators 544
Amusement Parks ... 475
Analytical Instruments - Laboratory
See Laboratory Analytical Instruments ... 754
Analytical Testing
See Testing Facilities ... 915
Ancillary Health Care Providers
See Health Care Providers - Ancillary ... 697
Anesthetic Monitoring Systems
See Electromedical & Electrotherapeutic Equipment ... 642
Angiography Equipment
See Imaging Equipment & Systems - Medical ... 733
Animal Cages
See Baskets, Cages, Racks, etc - Wire ... 516
Pet Products ... 829
Animal Farming
See Cattle Ranches, Farms, Feedlots (Beef Cattle) ... 469
Dairy Farms ... 469
Hog Farms ... 469
Animal Fats
See Fats & Oils - Animal or Marine ... 660
Animal Foods
See Farm Supplies ... 653
Livestock & Poultry Feeds - Prepared ... 765
Pet Products ... 829
Animal Hospitals
See Veterinary Hospitals ... 936
Animal Rights
See Animals & Animal Welfare Organizations ... 480
Animation Companies ... 476
See also Motion Picture Production - Special Interest 796; Motion Picture & Television Production 796
Animation Software
See Multimedia & Design Software ... 589
Annealing - Metal
See Metal Heat Treating ... 787
Annuity Plans
See Life & Accident Insurance ... 740
Anodizing
See Metal Coating, Plating, Engraving ... 787
Antennas - Receiving
See Electronic Components & Accessories - Mfr ... 643
Antennas - Transmitting
See Radio & Television Broadcasting & Communications Equipment ... 865
Antifreeze Compounds
See Chemicals - Specialty ... 542
Antiserums
See Biotechnology Companies ... 519
Antivirus Software
See Internet & Communications Software ... 588
Apparel
See Clothing & Accessories - Mfr ... 545
Clothing & Accessories - Whol ... 547
Clothing Stores ... 547
Fashion Design Houses ... 654
Apples
See Deciduous Tree Fruit Growers ... 675
Appliance & Home Electronics Stores ... 476
See also Computer Stores 592; Department Stores 627; Furniture Stores 679; Home Improvement Centers 707
Appliance Controls
See Controls - Temperature - Residential & Commercial ... 612
Appliance Cords - Electrical
See Wiring Devices - Current-Carrying ... 943
Appliance Housings
See Electronic Enclosures ... 645
Appliances - Major - Mfr ... 476
See also Air Conditioning & Heating Equipment - Residential 472
Appliances - Small - Mfr ... 476
See also Air Purification Equipment - Household 472; Vacuum Cleaners - Household 934
Appliances - Whol ... 477
Appliances Rental
See Home & Office Equipment Rental (General) ... 650
Application Service Providers (ASPs) ... 477
Appointment Books
See Blankbooks & Binders ... 520
Appraisals - Real Estate
See Title Insurance ... 746
Appraisers Associations
See Real Estate Professionals Associations ... 498
Apricots
See Deciduous Tree Fruit Growers ... 675
Aquariums - Public ... 477
See also Botanical Gardens & Arboreta 523; Zoos & Wildlife Parks 945
Arbitration Services - Legal ... 478
Arboreta
See Botanical Gardens & Arboreta ... 523
Arbors (Machine Tool Accessories)
See Metalworking Devices & Accessories ... 791
Arcade Games
See Games & Gaming ... 680
Archery Equipment & Supplies
See Sporting Goods ... 899
Arches - Wood (Laminated)
See Wood Members - Structural ... 944
Architects
See Engineering & Design ... 647
Architects - Landscape
See Landscape Design & Related Services ... 756
Architectural Glass
See Glass - Flat, Plate, Tempered ... 681
Architectural Metal Work
See Metal Work - Architectural & Ornamental ... 789
Architecture Magazines
See Art & Architecture Magazines ... 768
Archival Storage Services
See Commercial Warehousing ... 941
Archiving Software
See Systems & Utilities Software ... 591
Arenas
See Stadiums & Arenas ... 903
Armament Systems
See Weapons & Ordnance (Military) ... 942
Armatures
See Electrical Equipment for Internal Combustion Engines ... 642
Armored Car Service
See Security & Protective Services ... 893
Army - US Department of the
See US Department of Defense - Department of the Army ... 690
Aromatic Chemicals - Whol
See Chemicals & Related Products - Whol ... 543
Art - Commercial
See Graphic Design ... 694
Art Dealers & Galleries ... 478
Art Materials & Supplies - Mfr ... 478
See also Pens, Pencils, Parts 826
Art Materials & Supplies - Whol ... 479
Art Publishers
See Publishers (Misc) ... 855
Art Schools
See Colleges - Fine Arts ... 557
Art Software - Clip Art
See Multimedia & Design Software ... 589
Art Supply Stores ... 479
Artificial Insemination
See Livestock Improvement Services ... 470
Artist Assistance Programs
See Arts & Artists Organizations ... 481
Government - State ... 684
Artists' Brushes
See Art Materials & Supplies - Mfr ... 478
Arts & Crafts
See Educational Materials & Supplies ... 632
Toys, Games, Hobbies ... 922
Arts Agencies - State
See Government - State ... 684
Arts Centers
See Cultural & Arts Centers ... 501
Arts Facilities - Performing
See Performing Arts Facilities ... 826
Arts Organizations - Performing Arts
See Performing Arts Organizations ... 827
Asbestos Abatement
See Remediation Services ... 871
Ascots
See Neckwear ... 546
Aspartame
See Sugar & Sweeteners ... 665
Asphalt Paving & Roofing Materials ... 479
ASPs
See Application Service Providers (ASPs) ... 477
Assembly Machines
See Metalworking Machinery ... 792
Association Management Companies ... 479
Associations & Organizations - General ... 480
See also Performing Arts Organizations 827; Political Action Committees 841; Political Parties (Major) 842
Accreditation & Certification Organizations ... 480
Agricultural Organizations ... 480
Animals & Animal Welfare Organizations ... 480
Arts & Artists Organizations ... 481
Charitable & Humanitarian Organizations ... 481
Children & Family Advocacy Organizations ... 482
Civic & Political Organizations ... 483
Civil & Human Rights Organizations ... 484
Computer & Internet Organizations ... 484
Consumer Interest Organizations ... 484
Educational Associations & Organizations ... 484
Energy & Natural Resources Organizations ... 484
Environmental Organizations ... 485
Ethnic & Nationality Organizations ... 485
Fraternal & Social Organizations ... 485
Greek Letter Societies ... 486
Health & Health-Related Organizations ... 486
Hobby Organizations ... 488
Military, Veterans, Patriotic Organizations ... 488
Religious Organizations ... 489
Self-Help Organizations ... 490
Sports Organizations ... 490
Travel & Recreation Organizations ... 491
Women's Organizations ... 491
Associations & Organizations - Professional & Trade ... 491

See also Bar Associations - State 516; Dental Associations - State 627; Labor Unions 753; Library Associations - State & Province 763; Medical Associations - State 781; Nurses Associations - State 812; Pharmacy Associations - State 832; Realtor Associations - State 869; Veterinary Medical Associations - State 936
Accountants Associations 491
Banking & Finance Professionals Associations 492
Construction Industry Associations 492
Consumer Sales & Service Professionals Associations 492
Education Professionals Associations 493
Food & Beverage Industries Professional Associations 494
Government & Public Administration Professional Associations 494
Health & Medical Professionals Associations 494
Insurance Industry Associations 496
Legal Professionals Associations 497
Library & Information Science Associations 497
Management & Business Professional Associations 497
Manufacturing Industry Professional & Trade Associations 497
Media Professionals Associations 498
Mental Health Professionals Associations 498
Publishing & Printing Professional Associations 498
Real Estate Professionals Associations 498
Sales & Marketing Professional Associations 499
Technology, Science, Engineering Professionals Associations 499
Telecommunications Professionals Associations 500
Transportation Industry Associations 500
Astrology Software
See Personal Software 589
Astronomy Research
See Research Centers & Institutions 871
Athletic Pads & Supporters
See Personal Protective Equipment & Clothing 828
Athletic Pads & Supporters
See Sporting Goods 899
Athletic Shoes
See Footwear 669
Athletics Commissions
See Sports Commissions & Regulatory Agencies - State 902
Athletics Organizations
See Sports Organizations 490
Sports Teams 902
Sports Teams - Basketball 902
Sports Teams - Football 902
Sports Teams - Hockey 903
Sports Teams - Soccer 903
ATM Networks
See Banking-Related Services 511
ATMs
See Automatic Teller Machines (ATMs) 504
Attorney Recruitment
See Executive Recruiting Firms 651
Attorneys
See Law Firms 756
Attractions 501
Cultural & Arts Centers 501
Historic Homes & Buildings 501
Monuments, Memorials, Landmarks 501
Nature Centers, Parks, Other Natural Areas 501
Shopping/Dining/Entertainment Districts 501
Wineries 502
ATVs
See All-Terrain Vehicles 475
Auctions 502
Audience Ratings
See Market Research Firms 778
Audio & Video Equipment 502
Audio Duplication
See Duplication & Replication Services 632
Audio Tapes - Blank
See Recording Media - Magnetic & Optical 870
Audio Tapes - Prerecorded
See Book, Music, Video Clubs 522
Music Stores 803
Recording Companies 870
Auditorium Seating
See Institutional & Other Public Buildings Furniture 678
Auditors - Freight Rate
See Freight Forwarders 673
Auditors Associations
See Accountants Associations 491
Auditory Testing & Treatment Services
See Health Care Providers - Ancillary 697
Auto Clubs 503
Auto Racing
See Motor Speedways 796
Auto Supply Stores 503
Automatic Merchandising Equipment & Systems 504
See also Food Service 669
Automatic Money Transactions Equipment
See Automatic Merchandising Equipment & Systems 504
Automatic Teller Machines (ATMs) 504
Automatic Teller Machines (ATMs) 504
Automation Software - Industrial
See Engineering Software 588
Professional Software (Industry-Specific) 589
Automobile Dealers & Groups 504
See also Automobile Sales & Related Services - Online 507
Automobile Insurance
See Property & Casualty Insurance 743
Automobile Leasing
See Credit & Financing - Commercial 621
Credit & Financing - Consumer 620
Fleet Leasing & Management 656
Automobile Sales & Related Services - Online 507
See also Automobile Dealers & Groups 504
Automobile Testing
See Testing Facilities 915
Automobiles - Mfr 507
See also All-Terrain Vehicles 475; Motor Vehicles - Commercial & Special Purpose 797; Motorcycles & Motorcycle Parts & Accessories 798; Snowmobiles 897
Automotive Accessories
See Automotive Parts & Supplies - Mfr 507
Automotive Parts & Supplies - Whol 508
Automotive Air Conditioning & Heating Systems
See Air Conditioning & Heating Equipment - Residential 472
Automotive Chemicals
See Chemicals - Specialty 542
Automotive Cleaning Products
See Cleaning Products 544
Automotive Fastening Systems
See Fasteners & Fastening Systems 654
Automotive Glass
See Glass - Flat, Plate, Tempered 681
Automotive Lighting Equipment
See Lighting Equipment - Vehicular 763
Automotive Paint
See Paints, Varnishes, Related Products 818
Automotive Parts & Supplies - Mfr 507
See also Carburetors, Pistons, Piston Rings, Valves 530; Electrical Equipment for Internal Combustion Engines 642; Engines & Turbines 649; Gaskets, Packing, Sealing Devices 681; Hose & Belting - Rubber or Plastics 709; Motors (Electric) & Generators 798
Automotive Parts & Supplies - Whol 508
Automotive Services 509
See also Gas Stations 680
Appearance Care - Automotive 509
Glass Replacement - Automotive 509
Mufflers & Exhaust Systems Repair - Automotive 509
Paint & Body Work - Automotive 509
Repair Service (General) - Automotive 509
Transmission Repair - Automotive 509
Van Conversions 509
Automotive Stampings
See Metal Stampings - Automotive 789
Automotive Tubing
See Pipe & Pipe Fittings - Metal (Fabricated) 834
Aviation - Fixed-Base Operations 509
See also Air Cargo Carriers 470; Air Charter Services 471; Aircraft Rental 473; Aircraft Service & Repair 474
Awards
See Trophies, Plaques, Awards 927
Awnings
See Metal Products (Misc) 788
Tarps, Tents, Covers 907

B

B2B Procurement
See Electronic Purchasing & Procurement Software 588
Baby Clothes
See Children's & Infants' Clothing 545
Baby Foods
See Fruits, Vegetables, Juices - Canned or Preserved 661
Specialty Foods 664
Baby Furniture
See Household Furniture 677
Baby Products 510
See also Children's & Infants' Clothing 545; Household Furniture 677; Paper Products - Sanitary 820; Toys, Games, Hobbies 922
Baby Shoes
See Footwear 669
Backpacks
See Handbags, Totes, Backpacks 695
Leather Goods - Personal 759
Luggage, Bags, Cases 767
Backpacks
See Sporting Goods 899
Bacon
See Meat Products - Prepared 663
Badges (Textile)
See Embroidery & Other Decorative Stitching 646
Badminton Equipment & Supplies
See Sporting Goods 899
Bagels
See Bakeries 511
Bakery Products - Fresh 658
Bakery Products - Frozen 659
Baggage Loss Insurance
See Travel Insurance 746
Bags - Coated Paper
See Bags - Plastics 510
Bags - Foil
See Bags - Plastics 510
Bags - Paper 510
Bags - Plastics 510
Bags - Textile 511
See also Handbags, Totes, Backpacks 695; Luggage, Bags, Cases 767
Bags - Travel
See Luggage, Bags, Cases 767
Bakeries 511
Bakeware
See Metal Products - Household 788
Balers
See Farm Machinery & Equipment - Mfr 652
Farm Machinery & Equipment - Whol 653
Ball Bearings
See Bearings - Ball & Roller 516
Ball Clay
See Clay, Ceramic, Refractory Minerals Mining 794
Ballasts (for Lighting Fixtures)
See Transformers - Power, Distribution, Specialty 924
Ballet Companies
See Dance Companies 827
Balloons
See Gifts & Novelties - Whol 681
Balloons - Hot Air
See Airships 475
Bananas
See Fruit Growers (Misc) 675
Bandwidth - Whol
See Internet Backbone Providers 747
Bankers - Mortgage
See Banks - Commercial & Savings 511
Mortgage Lenders & Loan Brokers 795
Banking Authorities - State
See Government - State 684
Banking Software
See Professional Software (Industry-Specific) 589
Banking-Related Services 511
Bankruptcy Courts - US
See US Bankruptcy Courts 693
Banks - Commercial & Savings 511
See also Credit & Financing - Consumer 620; Credit & Financing - Commercial 621; Credit Unions 622; Bank Holding Companies 700
Banks - Federal Reserve 515

Banners
See Flags, Banners, Pennants 656
Bar Associations - State 516
See also Legal Professionals Associations 497
Bar Code Printers
See Printers 580
Bar Code Readers
See Scanning Equipment 580
Bar Coding Software
See Systems & Utilities Software 591
Barbecue Grills
See Appliances - Major - Mfr 476
Barber Shop Equipment & Supplies
See Beauty Salon Equipment & Supplies 517
Barber Shops
See Beauty Salons 517
Barge Operators
See Freight Transport - Inland Waterways 674
Barge Services
See Marine Services 777
Barges - Building & Repairing
See Ship Building & Repairing 896
Barium
See Chemical & Fertilizer Minerals Mining 794
Barrels
See Containers - Metal (Barrels, Drums, Kegs) 610
Barware - Glass
See Glassware & Pottery - Household 682
Baseball Caps
See Hats & Caps 546
Baseball Equipment & Supplies
See Sporting Goods 899
Baseball Teams
See Sports Teams 902
Basketball Equipment & Supplies
See Sporting Goods 899
Basketball Teams
See Sports Teams - Basketball 902
Baskets, Cages, Racks, etc - Wire 516
See also Pet Products 829
Bath Robes
See Sleepwear 547
Bath Supplies
See Cosmetics, Skin Care, and Other Personal Care Products 620
Bathing Suits
See Swimwear 547
Bathroom Fixtures
See Plumbing Fixtures & Fittings - Metal 839
Plumbing Fixtures & Fittings - Vitreous China & Earthenware 840
Bathtubs
See Plumbing Fixtures & Fittings - Metal 839
Batteries 516
Batteries - Automotive
See Automotive Parts & Supplies - Mfr 507
Automotive Parts & Supplies - Whol 508
Batteries - Whol
See Electrical & Electronic Equipment & Parts - Whol 639
Batting
See Nonwoven Fabrics 917
Batting Ranges
See Recreation Facility Operators 870
BBBs
See Better Business Bureaus - Canada 517
Better Business Bureaus - US 517
BBS Software
See Internet & Communications Software 588
Bearings - Ball & Roller 516
Bearings - Journal
See Power Transmission Equipment - Mechanical 843
Beauty Salon Equipment & Supplies 517
Beauty Salons 517
Beauty Supplies
See Cosmetics, Skin Care, and Other Personal Care Products 620
Bed & Breakfasts
See Hotels & Hotel Companies 722
Bedding
See Home Furnishings - Whol 706
Textile Products - Household 917
Beds
See Furniture - Mfr 676
Furniture - Whol 678
Mattresses & Adjustable Beds 780
Beds - Convertible
See Household Furniture 677
Beds - Tanning
See Beauty Salon Equipment & Supplies 517
Bedspreads & Comforters
See Textile Products - Household 917
Beef Cattle
See Cattle Ranches, Farms, Feedlots (Beef Cattle) 469
Beepers
See Appliance & Home Electronics Stores 476
Telecommunications Equipment & Systems 908
Beer & Ale - Mfr
See Breweries 524
Behavioral Health Managed Care
See Managed Care - Behavioral Health 775
Behavioral Research
See Research Centers & Institutions 871
Belting - Rubber or Plastics
See Hose & Belting - Rubber or Plastics 709
Benefits Management Services - Employee
See Management Services 776
Benefits Management Services - Pharmacy
See Pharmacy Benefits Management Services 833
Better Business Bureaus - Canada 517
Better Business Bureaus - US 517
See also Consumer Interest Organizations 484
Beverage Carriers
See Boxes - Paperboard 524
Beverage Dispensers
See Automatic Merchandising Equipment & Systems 504
Beverage Distributors
See Beverages - Whol 518
Beverages - Mfr 518
See also Breweries 524; Water - Bottled 941
Liquor - Mfr 518
Soft Drinks - Mfr 518
Wines - Mfr 518
Beverages - Mfr - Powdered
See Fruits & Vegetables - Dried or Dehydrated 661
Beverages - Whol 518
Beer & Ale - Whol 518
Soft Drinks - Whol 518
Wine & Liquor - Whol 518
Bible Colleges
See Colleges - Bible 549
Bicycles & Bicycle Parts & Accessories 519
See also Sporting Goods 899; Toys, Games, Hobbies 922
Bicycles - Electric
See Bicycles & Bicycle Parts & Accessories 519
Bikinis
See Swimwear 547
Bilge Pumps
See Pumps & Pumping Equipment (General Use) 856
Bill Changers
See Automatic Merchandising Equipment & Systems 504
Bill Payment - Online
See Electronic Bill Presentment & Payment Services 643
Bill Status Hotlines
See Legislation Hotlines 759
Billboards
See Advertising Services - Outdoor Advertising 469
Billiard Centers
See Recreation Facility Operators 870
Billiard Equipment & Supplies
See Sporting Goods 899
Binderies
See Book Binding & Related Work 522
Binders - Looseleaf
See Blankbooks & Binders 520
Bingo Systems
See Games & Gaming 680
Bio-Recovery Services 519
Biohazard Suits
See Personal Protective Equipment & Clothing 828
Biohazardous Waste Disposal
See Waste Management 941
Biological Products
See Biotechnology Companies 519
Biological Research
See Research Centers & Institutions 871
Biomedicine
See Biotechnology Companies 519
Biometric Identification Equipment & Software 519
Biopharmaceuticals
See Biotechnology Companies 519
Biopsy Systems
See Imaging Equipment & Systems - Medical 733
Biotechnology Companies 519
See also Diagnostic Products 628; Medicinal Chemicals & Botanical Products 786; Pharmaceutical Companies 831; Pharmaceutical Companies - Generic Drugs 832
Bird Cages
See Pet Products 829
Bird Seed
See Pet Products 829
Birth Defects
See Health & Health-Related Organizations 486
Birthday Cards
See Cards - Greeting - Mfr 531
Biscuits - Mixes or Doughs
See Flour Mixes & Doughs 661
Biscuits - Packaged
See Cookies & Crackers 660
Bituminous Coal Mining
See Mining - Coal 793
Blankbooks & Binders 520
See also Checks - Personal & Business 541
Blankets
See Textile Products - Household 917
Bleachers
See Institutional & Other Public Buildings Furniture 678
Bleaching - Fabric
See Textile Dyeing & Finishing 917
Blenders - Electric
See Appliances - Small - Mfr 476
Blimps
See Airships 475
Blinds & Shades 520
Blister Packaging 520
Block - Concrete
See Concrete Products - Mfr 595
Blood Analyzing Equipment
See Laboratory Analytical Instruments 754
Blood Centers 520
See also Laboratories - Drug-Testing 754; Laboratories - Genetic Testing 754; Laboratories - Medical 754
Blood Testing
See Laboratories - Genetic Testing 754
Laboratories - Medical 754
Blue Printing
See Duplication & Replication Services 632
Blueberries
See Berry Growers 675
Boarding Schools
See Preparatory Schools - Boarding 844
Boards - Circuit (Printed)
See Printed Circuit Boards 845
Boat Lighting Equipment
See Lighting Equipment - Vehicular 763
Boat Trailers
See Trailers (Towing) & Trailer Hitches 923
Boats - Recreational 521
Boats - Whol
See Transportation Equipment & Supplies - Whol 924
Bobby Pins
See Cosmetics, Skin Care, and Other Personal Care Products 620
Body Warmers
See Thermal Management Products - Personal 918
Boiler Shops 521
Bologna
See Meat Products - Prepared 663
Bolts & Nuts
See Fasteners & Fastening Systems 654
Hardware - Whol 697
Bond Brokers
See Securities Brokers & Dealers 890
Bonded Fabrics
See Nonwoven Fabrics 917
Bonding Equipment
See Welding & Soldering Equipment 942
Bone Analyzer Systems
See Imaging Equipment & Systems - Medical 733
Bone Banks
See Organ & Tissue Banks 817
Bone Growth Stimulators
See Electromedical & Electrotherapeutic Equipment 642
Bone Marrow Analysis

See Laboratories - Genetic Testing 754
Laboratories - Medical 754
Bone Marrow Banks
See Organ & Tissue Banks 817
Book Binding & Related Work 522
See also Printing Companies - Book Printers 845
Book Distributors
See Books, Periodicals, Newspapers - Whol 522
Book Festivals
See Festivals - Book 655
Book Packagers
See Book Producers 522
Book Printers
See Printing Companies - Book Printers 845
Book Producers 522
Book Readers - Electronic
See Computers 578
Book Stores 523
Book, Music, Video Clubs 522
Bookkeepers Associations
See Accountants Associations 491
Bookmaking Operations
See Games & Gaming 680
Books, Periodicals, Newspapers - Whol 522
Boots
See Footwear 669
Botanical Gardens & Arboreta 523
See also Zoos & Wildlife Parks 945
Botanical Products
See Medicinal Chemicals & Botanical Products 786
Bottle Caps
See Closures - Metal or Plastics 545
Bottled Gas
See Fuel Dealers 675
Bottlers - Soft Drinks
See Soft Drinks - Mfr 518
Soft Drinks - Whol 518
Bottles - Plastics 524
Bow Ties
See Neckwear 546
Bowling Bags
See Luggage, Bags, Cases 767
Bowling Centers 524
Bowling Equipment & Supplies
See Sporting Goods 899
Bowling Shoes
See Footwear 669
Bows (Decorative)
See Packaging Materials & Products - Paper or Plastics 818
Boxes - Corrugated & Solid Fiber 524
Boxes - Paperboard 524
Boxes - Plastics
See Containers - Plastics (Drums, Cans, Crates, Boxes) 610
Boxes - Wood
See Containers - Wood 611
Boxing Equipment & Supplies
See Sporting Goods 899
Brake Repair - Automotive
See Mufflers & Exhaust Systems Repair - Automotive 509
Branding
See Advertising Agencies 466
Advertising Services - Online 468
Brass Plumbing Fittings
See Plumbing Fixtures & Fittings - Metal 839
Brazing - Metal
See Metal Heat Treating 787
Breads & Buns
See Bakeries 511
Bakery Products - Fresh 658
Bakery Products - Frozen 659
Breakfast Cereals
See Cereals (Breakfast) 659
Breast Biopsy Systems
See Imaging Equipment & Systems - Medical 733
Breeding Stock
See Livestock Improvement Services 470
Breweries 524
See also Malting Products 775
Brick
See Brick, Stone, Related Materials 602
Concrete Products - Mfr 595
Bridge Construction
See Highway, Street, Bridge, Tunnel Construction 598
Briefcases
See Luggage, Bags, Cases 767
Broaches (Machine Tool Accessories)
See Metalworking Devices & Accessories 791
Broaching Machines
See Machine Tools - Metal Cutting Types 767
Broadband Communications Services
See Internet Service Providers (ISPs) 748
Broadband Equipment
See Telecommunications Equipment & Systems 908
Broadcast Cases
See Luggage, Bags, Cases 767
Broadcast Networks
See Television Networks - Broadcast 911
Broadcasting - Internet
See Internet Broadcasting 747
Broadcasting Companies
See Radio Companies 857
Television Companies 910
Broadcasting Equipment
See Radio & Television Broadcasting & Communications Equipment 865
Broadcasting Organizations - Public
See Public Broadcasting Organizations 848
Broadcasting Stations
See Radio Stations 864
Television Stations 911
Broadway Theaters
See Theaters - Broadway 917
Brokers
See Commodity Contracts Brokers & Dealers 578
Electronic Communications Networks (ECNs) 643
Freight Forwarders 673
Insurance Agents, Brokers, Services 738
Mortgage Lenders & Loan Brokers 795
Real Estate Agents & Brokers 866
Securities Brokers & Dealers 890
Ticket Brokers 918
Bronze Castings
See Foundries - Nonferrous (Castings) 671
Brooms
See Brushes & Brooms 525
Browsers
See Internet & Communications Software 588
Brushes & Brooms 525
See also Art Materials & Supplies - Mfr 478
Brushes - Artists'
See Art Materials & Supplies - Mfr. 478
Brushing Machines (Metalworking Machinery)
See Machine Tools - Metal Cutting Types 767
Buckles
See Piece Goods & Notions 834
Buddhist Organizations
See Religious Organizations 489
Buffing & Polishing Machines (Machine Tools)
See Machine Tools - Metal Cutting Types 767
Buffing Wheels
See Abrasive Products 465
Builders
See Construction - Building Contractors - Non-Residential 597
Construction - Building Contractors - Residential 597
Construction - Heavy Construction Contractors 598
Builders Associations
See Construction Industry Associations 492
Building Components - Metal
See Buildings - Prefabricated - Metal 525
Building Components - Wood
See Buildings - Prefabricated - Wood 525
Building Maintenance Services 525
See also Cleaning Services 545
Building Services Monitoring Controls
See Controls - Temperature - Residential & Commercial 612
Building Supplies
See Construction Materials 602
Home Improvement Centers 707
Buildings - Portable
See Mobile Homes & Buildings 795
Buildings - Prefabricated - Metal 525
Buildings - Prefabricated - Wood 525
Bulbs - Electric
See Light Bulbs & Tubes 763
Bulk Storage Terminals - Petroleum
See Petroleum Storage Terminals 831
Bulldozers
See Construction Machinery & Equipment 602
Bulletin Boards
See Educational Materials & Supplies 632
Office & School Supplies 812
Bumper Stickers
See Gifts & Novelties - Whol 681
Buoys
See Plastics Foam Products 836
Burglar Alarms
See Security Products & Services 892
Burglary Insurance
See Property & Casualty Insurance 743
Burial Caskets
See Caskets & Vaults 533
Burial Services
See Mortuary, Crematory, Cemetery Products & Services 796
Burlap Bags
See Bags - Textile 511
Bus Conversions
See Van Conversions 509
Bus Services - Charter 526
Bus Services - Intercity & Rural 526
See also Bus Services - School 526; Mass Transportation (Local & Suburban) 779
Bus Services - School 526
Bus Tours
See Tour Operators 921
Buses - Mfr
See Motor Vehicles - Commercial & Special Purpose 797
Business & Professional Regulation Agencies - State
See Government - State 684
Business Cases
See Luggage, Bags, Cases 767
Business Checks
See Checks - Personal & Business 541
Business Colleges
See Vocational & Technical Schools 938
Business Credit Ratings
See Credit Reporting Services 622
Business Forms 526
See also Printing Companies - Commercial Printers 845
Business Machines - Mfr 527
See also Business Machines - Whol 527; Calculators - Electronic 529; Computer Equipment 578; Photocopying Equipment & Supplies 833
Business Machines - Whol 527
See also Business Machines - Mfr 527; Computer Equipment & Software - Whol 581; Photocopying Equipment & Supplies 833
Business Magazines
See General Interest Magazines 770
Business Management Services
See Management Services 776
Business Organizations
See Chambers of Commerce - Canadian 534
Chambers of Commerce - US - Local 534
Chambers of Commerce - US - State 540
Management & Business Professional Associations 497
Business Process Outsourcing
See Telemarketing & Other Tele-Services 910
Business Research
See Research Centers & Institutions 871
Business Service Centers 528
Business Travel
See Travel Agencies 925
Business-to-Business Procurement
See Electronic Purchasing & Procurement Software 588
Butter
See Butter (Creamery) 659
Dairy Products - Whol 666
Oils - Edible (Margarine, Shortening, Table Oils, etc) 664
Buttons
See Piece Goods & Notions 834
Buyer's Guides - Online 528
See also Investment Guides - Online 751

C

Cabinets - Metal
See Fixtures - Office & Store 656

Metal Products (Misc) 788
Cabinets - Wood 528
See also Carpentry & Flooring Contractors 599; Household Furniture 677
Cable
See Wire & Cable 943
Wire & Cable - Electronic 943
Cable & Other Pay Television Services 528
Cable - Coaxial
See Electronic Components & Accessories - Mfr 643
Wire & Cable - Electronic 943
Cable - Computer
See Wire & Cable - Electronic 943
Cable - Fiber Optic
See Wire & Cable - Electronic 943
Cable Harness Assemblies
See Electronic Components & Accessories - Mfr 643
Cable Reels 529
Cable Television Broadcasting Equipment
See Radio & Television Broadcasting & Communications Equipment 865
Cable Television Networks
See Television Networks 910
Cable Trays
See Boiler Shops 521
Wiring Devices - Noncurrent-Carrying 944
Cabs - Truck
See Motor Vehicles - Commercial & Special Purpose 797
CAD (Computer-Aided Design) Software
See Multimedia & Design Software 589
Cafeterias
See Restaurant Companies 880
Cages - Wire
See Baskets, Cages, Racks, etc - Wire 516
Pet Products 829
Cake Boxes
See Boxes - Paperboard 524
Cake Mixes
See Flour Mixes & Doughs 661
Cakes
See Bakeries 511
Bakery Products - Fresh 658
Bakery Products - Frozen 659
Calculators - Electronic 529
Calendar Publishers
See Publishers (Misc) 855
Calibration Services
See Testing Facilities 915
Call Centers
See Telemarketing & Other Tele-Services 910
CAM (Computer-Aided Manufacturing) Software
See Engineering Software 588
Professional Software (Industry-Specific) 589
Camcorders
See Audio & Video Equipment 502
Cameras & Related Supplies - Retail 529
Cameras - Mfr
See Photographic Equipment & Supplies 833
Campaign Disclosure
See Ethics Commissions 650
Campers, Travel Trailers, Motor Homes 529
Campground Operators 529
Camping Associations
See Travel & Recreation Organizations 491
Camping Gear
See Tarps, Tents, Covers 907
Camping Gear
See Sporting Goods 899
Can-Making Machines
See Machine Tools - Metal Forming Types 768
Canadian Better Business Bureaus
See Better Business Bureaus - Canada 517
Canadian Botanical Gardens
See Botanical Gardens & Arboreta 523
Canadian Chambers of Commerce
See Chambers of Commerce - Canadian 534
Canadian Hospitals
See General Hospitals - Canada 712
Canadian Hotels & Hotel Companies
See Hotels & Hotel Companies 722
Canadian Library Systems
See Library Systems - Regional - Canadian 763
Canadian Museums
See Museums 799
Canadian National Parks
See Parks - National - Canada 821
Canadian Newspapers
See Daily Newspapers - Canada 807
Canadian Radio Stations
See Radio Stations 864
Canadian Sports Teams
See Sports Teams 902
Sports Teams - Basketball 902
Sports Teams - Football 902
Sports Teams - Hockey 903
Canadian Stock Exchanges
See Securities & Commodities Exchanges 892
Canadian Television Stations
See Television Stations 911
Canadian Travel Information
See Travel & Tourism Information - Canadian 927
Canadian Universities
See Universities - Canadian 932
Canadian Zoos
See Zoos & Wildlife Parks 945
Cancer Hospitals
See Specialty Hospitals 719
Cancer Treatment Services
See Health Care Providers - Ancillary 697
Candles 529
See also Gift Shops 681
Candy
See Confectionery & Snack Foods - Whol 666
Confectionery Products 659
Candy Boxes
See Boxes - Paperboard 524
Candy Stores 530
Canning - Soft Drinks
See Soft Drinks - Mfr 518
Soft Drinks - Whol 518
Canoes
See Sporting Goods 899
Cans - Metal 530
See also Containers - Metal (Barrels, Drums, Kegs) 610
Cans, Tubes, Drums - Paper (Fiber) 530
Canvas Products
See Handbags, Totes, Backpacks 695
Tarps, Tents, Covers 907
Canvas Products
See Sporting Goods 899
Capacitors - Electronic
See Electronic Components & Accessories - Mfr 643
Caps
See Hats & Caps 546
Car Alarms
See Security Products & Services 892
Car Buying
See Automobile Dealers & Groups 504
Automobile Sales & Related Services - Online 507
Car Cleaning Products
See Cleaning Products 544
Car Clubs
See Auto Clubs 503
Car Dealers
See Automobile Dealers & Groups 504
Automobile Sales & Related Services - Online 507
Car Detailing
See Appearance Care - Automotive 509
Car Makers
See Automobiles - Mfr 507
Car Parts
See Automotive Parts & Supplies - Mfr 507
Automotive Parts & Supplies - Whol 508
Car Racing
See Motor Speedways 796
Car Rental Agencies 530
See also Fleet Leasing & Management 656; Truck Rental & Leasing 928
Car Repairs
See Automotive Services 509
Gas Stations 680
Repair Service (General) - Automotive 509
Car Washing & Polishing
See Appearance Care - Automotive 509
Car Window Replacement
See Glass Replacement - Automotive 509
Carbon & Graphite Products 530
Carbon Black
See Chemicals - Specialty 542
Carbon Paper
See Printing & Photocopying Supplies 847
Carbonated Beverages
See Soft Drinks - Mfr 518
Soft Drinks - Whol 518
Carburetors, Pistons, Piston Rings, Valves 530
See also Aircraft Engines & Engine Parts 473; Automotive Parts & Supplies - Mfr 507
Carburizing
See Metal Heat Treating 787
Card Shops 530
See also Gift Shops 681
Cardboard
See Boxes - Corrugated & Solid Fiber 524
Boxes - Paperboard 524
Paperboard & Cardboard - Die-Cut 821
Paperboard Mills 821
Cardiac Assist Devices
See Electromedical & Electrotherapeutic Equipment 642
Cardiorespiratory Systems
See Electromedical & Electrotherapeutic Equipment 642
Cards - Greeting - Mfr 531
Cards - Index
See Paperboard & Cardboard - Die-Cut 821
Cards - Playing
See Paperboard & Cardboard - Die-Cut 821
Cards - Smart
See Smart Cards 897
Cards - Trading
See Paperboard & Cardboard - Die-Cut 821
Cargo Carriers - Air
See Air Cargo Carriers 470
Cargo Container Rental
See Transport Equipment Rental 650
Cargo Containers
See Truck Trailers 928
Cargo Handling - Marine
See Marine Services 777
Cargo Restraint Systems
See Safety Equipment - Mfr 886
Cargo Screening Systems
See Security Products & Services 892
Cargo Vessels - Building & Repairing
See Ship Building & Repairing 896
Carnival Operators
See Circus, Carnival, Festival Operators 544
Carpet Backing
See Industrial Fabrics 916
Carpet Cleaning Services
See Cleaning Services 545
Carpets & Rugs 531
See also Flooring - Resilient 657; Tile - Ceramic (Wall & Floor) 918
Carpets & Rugs - Retail
See Floor Coverings Stores 657
Carpets & Rugs - Whol
See Home Furnishings - Whol 706
Carriers - Pet
See Pet Products 829
Carrying Cases
See Luggage, Bags, Cases 767
Cars - Passenger
See Automobile Dealers & Groups 504
Automobile Sales & Related Services - Online 507
Automobiles - Mfr 507
Car Rental Agencies 530
Cartoons
See Animation Companies 476
Cases
See Luggage, Bags, Cases 767
Cash Registers
See Business Machines - Whol 527
Casino Companies 531
See also Games & Gaming 680
Casinos 532
See also Games & Gaming 680
Caskets & Vaults 533
See also Mortuary, Crematory, Cemetery Products & Services 796
Cast Iron
See Foundries - Iron & Steel 671
Casters
See Metal Products (Misc) 788

Index

Castings - Investment
See Foundries - Investment 671
Castings - Nonferrous
See Foundries - Nonferrous (Castings) 671
Casualty Insurance
See Property & Casualty Insurance 743
Cat Carriers
See Pet Products 829
Cat Food
See Pet Products 829
Cat Insurance
See Animal Insurance 740
Cat Litter
See Pet Products 829
Catalog Publishers
See Publishers (Misc) 855
Catalog Sales
See Mail Order Houses 774
Cataract Surgery
See Vision Correction Centers 937
Caterers
See Food Service 669
Cathedrals
See Churches, Cathedrals, Synagogues, Temples 501
Catheters - Electromedical
See Electromedical & Electrotherapeutic Equipment 642
Cathode Ray Tube (CRT) Monitors
See Monitors & Displays 579
Cathode Ray Tubes
See Electronic Components & Accessories - Mfr 643
Catsup
See Fruits, Vegetables, Juices - Canned or Preserved 661
Cattle
See Cattle Ranches, Farms, Feedlots (Beef Cattle) 469
Dairy Farms 469
Livestock - Whol 765
Livestock Improvement Services 470
Cattle Insurance
See Animal Insurance 740
Caulking Compounds
See Adhesives & Sealants 466
CCTV (Closed Circuit Television) Systems
See Radio & Television Broadcasting & Communications Equipment 865
CD Players
See Audio & Video Equipment 502
CD Readers/Writers
See Storage Devices 580
CDs
See Book, Music, Video Clubs 522
Music Stores 803
Recording Media - Magnetic & Optical 870
Ceiling Tiles
See Insulation & Acoustical Products 738
Ceilings - Installation
See Plastering, Drywall, Acoustical, Insulation Contractors 600
Cell Phones
See Appliance & Home Electronics Stores 476
Telecommunications Equipment & Systems 908
Telecommunications Services 908
Cellophane Tape
See Tape - Cellophane, Gummed, Masking, Pressure Sensitive 907
Cellular Communications
See Telecommunications Services 908
Cellular Telephones
See Appliance & Home Electronics Stores 476
Telecommunications Equipment & Systems 908
Cellulose - Insulation
See Insulation & Acoustical Products 738
Cellulosic Fibers
See Synthetic Fibers & Filaments 837
Cement 533
Cement - Rubber
See Adhesives & Sealants 466
Cemeteries
See Mortuary, Crematory, Cemetery Products & Services 796
Cemeteries - National 533
See also Historic Homes & Buildings 501; Parks - National - US 821
Centrifugal Pumps
See Pumps & Pumping Equipment (General Use) 856
Ceramics
See Clay, Ceramic, Refractory Minerals Mining 794
Glassware & Pottery - Household 682
Tile - Ceramic (Wall & Floor) 918
Ceramics - Technical
See Electrical Supplies - Porcelain 642
Certification Organizations
See Accreditation & Certification Organizations 480
Certification Services - Maritime
See Marine Services 777
Certified Public Accountants
See Accountants Associations 491
Accounting Firms 465
Chain Hotels
See Hotels & Hotel Companies 722
Chain Link Fences
See Fences - Mfr 654
Chain Saws
See Tools - Power 921
Chairs
See Furniture - Mfr 676
Chalk Boards
See Educational Materials & Supplies 632
Chambers of Commerce 534
Chambers of Commerce - Canadian 534
Chambers of Commerce - US - Local 534
See also Civic & Political Organizations 483
Chambers of Commerce - US - State 540
Chamois
See Mops, Sponges, Wiping Cloths 795
Champagne
See Wine & Liquor - Whol 518
Wines - Mfr 518
Change Machines
See Automatic Merchandising Equipment & Systems 504
Channel Black
See Chemicals - Specialty 542
Charter School Management Services
See Educational Institution Operators & Managers 632
Charter Services - Air
See Air Charter Services 471
Charters - Bus
See Bus Services - Charter 526
Chassis Leasing
See Transport Equipment Rental 650
Check Cashing Services 541
Checkbooks
See Blankbooks & Binders 520
Checks - Personal & Business 541
Checks - Personal & Business 541
Cheese
See Cheeses - Natural, Processed, Imitation 659
Dairy Products - Whol 666
Chemical Dependency
See Self-Help Organizations 490
Substance Abuse Treatment Centers 906
Chemical Salt
See Salt 886
Chemicals & Related Products - Whol 543
Chemicals - Agricultural
See Fertilizers & Pesticides 654
Chemicals - Aromatic
See Chemicals - Industrial (Organic) 541
Chemicals - Automotive
See Chemicals - Specialty 542
Chemicals - Construction
See Chemicals - Specialty 542
Chemicals - Custom Blending
See Chemicals & Related Products - Whol 543
Chemicals - Deicing
See Chemicals - Specialty 542
Chemicals - Electroplating
See Chemicals - Specialty 542
Chemicals - Industrial (Inorganic) 541
Chemicals - Industrial (Organic) 541
Chemicals - Inorganic - Whol
See Chemicals & Related Products - Whol 543
Chemicals - Medicinal
See Medicinal Chemicals & Botanical Products 786
Chemicals - Organic - Whol
See Chemicals & Related Products - Whol 543
Chemicals - Specialty 542
Chemicals - Specialty - Whol
See Chemicals & Related Products - Whol 543
Chemicals - Textile Processing
See Chemicals - Specialty 542
Chemicals - Water Treatment
See Chemicals - Specialty 542
Cherries
See Deciduous Tree Fruit Growers 675
Chewing Tobacco
See Tobacco & Tobacco Products 919
Chicken Farms
See Poultry & Eggs Production 470
Child Abuse
See Children & Family Advocacy Organizations 482
Child Care Facilities Management Services
See Facilities Management Services 652
Child Care Monitoring Systems - Internet 543
Child Care Services
See Children's Learning Centers 543
Child Safety Products
See Safety Equipment - Mfr 886
Child Support Enforcement Agencies
See Government - State 684
Children - Missing
See Children & Family Advocacy Organizations 482
Children's Book Clubs
See Book, Music, Video Clubs 522
Children's Fitness Programs
See Health & Fitness Centers 698
Children's Furniture
See Baby Products 510
Household Furniture 677
Children's Learning Centers 543
Children's Museums
See Museums - Children's 802
Children's Shoes
See Footwear 669
Children's Vehicles
See Bicycles & Bicycle Parts & Accessories 519
Toy Stores 922
China
See Plumbing Fixtures & Fittings - Vitreous China & Earthenware 840
Table & Kitchen Supplies - China & Earthenware 907
Chiropractic Equipment
See Medical & Dental Equipment & Supplies - Whol 781
Chlorine
See Chemicals - Industrial (Inorganic) 541
Chocolate
See Confectionery & Snack Foods - Whol 666
Confectionery Products 659
Christian Book Stores
See Book Stores 523
Christian Colleges & Universities
See Colleges & Universities - Christian 558
Colleges & Universities - Jesuit 578
Colleges - Bible 549
Christian Organizations
See Religious Organizations 489
Christian Retreats
See Retreats - Spiritual 885
Christmas Cards
See Card Shops 530
Cards - Greeting - Mfr 531
Christmas Tree Growers
See Timber Tracts 918
Chucks - Drill or Lathe (Machine Tool Accessories)
See Metalworking Devices & Accessories 791
Church Furniture & Fixtures
See Institutional & Other Public Buildings Furniture 678
Church Organizations
See Religious Organizations 489
Cider
See Vinegar & Cider 665
Cigarettes
See Tobacco & Tobacco Products 919
Cigars
See Tobacco & Tobacco Products 919
Circuit Boards - Printed
See Printed Circuit Boards 845
Circuit Breakers
See Switchgear & Switchboard Apparatus 906
Circus, Carnival, Festival Operators 544
City Government
See Government - City 682

Civil Engineers
See Construction - Heavy Construction Contractors 598
Engineering & Design 647
Clay Products - Structural 544
See also Brick, Stone, Related Materials 602
Clay Quarrying
See Clay, Ceramic, Refractory Minerals Mining............794
Clay Refractories
See Refractories - Clay............................. 870
Clay Tile
See Clay Products - Structural........................ 544
Clean Room Construction
See Construction - Building Contractors - Non-Residential.. 597
Cleaners - Air
See Air Purification Equipment - Household 472
Cleaners - Air
See Air Purification Equipment - Industrial............... 472
Cleaning Products 544
See also Brushes & Brooms 525; Mops, Sponges, Wiping Cloths 795
Cleaning Services 545
See also Bio-Recovery Services 519; Building Maintenance Services 525
Cleaning Supplies - Whol
See Janitorial & Cleaning Supplies - Whol 751
Climate & Weather Research
See Research Centers & Institutions.................... 871
Climate Control Products - Dynamic
See Thermal Management Products - Personal 918
Clinical Laboratories
See Laboratories - Medical........................... 754
Clinical Research
See Research Centers & Institutions.................... 871
Clip Art Software
See Multimedia & Design Software 589
Clipping Services
See Press Clipping Services.......................... 844
Clocks, Watches, Related Devices, Parts 545
Cloning
See Livestock Improvement Services 470
Closed Circuit Television (CCTV) Systems
See Radio & Television Broadcasting & Communications Equipment.................................. 865
Closed-end Investment Companies
See Investment (Misc) 751
Closeout Stores
See Variety Stores 935
Closing Services - Real Estate
See Title Insurance.................................746
Closures - Metal or Plastics 545
Cloth Tape
See Tape - Cellophane, Gummed, Masking, Pressure Sensitive 907
Clothes Dryers
See Appliance & Home Electronics Stores 476
Appliances - Major - Mfr........................ 476
Appliances - Whol............................. 477
Clothing & Accessories - Mfr 545
See also Baby Products 510; Clothing & Accessories - Whol 547; Fashion Design Houses 654; Footwear 669; Leather Goods - Personal 759; Personal Protective Equipment & Clothing 828
Athletic Apparel................................ 545
Belts (Leather, Plastics, Fabric) 545
Casual Wear (Men's & Women's).................. 545
Children's & Infants' Clothing 545
Coats (Overcoats, Jackets, Raincoats, etc) 546
Costumes...................................... 546
Gloves & Mittens................................ 546
Hats & Caps 546
Hosiery & Socks................................. 546
Jeans 546
Men's Clothing.................................. 546
Neckwear....................................... 546
Robes (Ceremonial).............................. 546
Sleepwear 547
Sweaters (Knit).................................. 547
Swimwear 547
Undergarments.................................. 547
Uniforms & Work Clothes......................... 547
Western Wear (Except Hats & Boots) 547
Women's Clothing................................ 547
Clothing & Accessories - Whol...................... 547
Clothing Stores.................................... 547
See also Department Stores 627
Children's Clothing Stores........................ 547
Family Clothing Stores........................... 547
Men's & Women's Clothing Stores 548
Men's Clothing Stores 548
Specialty Clothing Stores 548
Women's Clothing Stores......................... 548
Clubs
See Fraternal & Social Organizations....................485
Greek Letter Societies 486
Hobby Organizations............................488
Sports Teams.................................. 902
Sports Teams - Basketball....................... 902
Sports Teams - Football 902
Sports Teams - Hockey 903
Sports Teams - Soccer 903
Clutches - Automotive
See Automotive Parts & Supplies - Mfr 507
Clutches - Industrial
See Power Transmission Equipment - Mechanical......... 843
CNC Machining
See Machine Shops 767
Coal Dealers
See Fuel Dealers.................................. 675
Coal Mining
See Mining - Coal 793
Coast Guard Installations.......................... 548
Coated Paper
See Bags - Plastics................................ 510
Coated & Laminated Paper 819
Coating - Metals
See Metal Coating, Plating, Engraving.................. 787
Coating - Paper
See Paper Finishers (Embossing, Coating, Gilding, Stamping) ... 820
Coaxial Cable
See Electronic Components & Accessories - Mfr.......... 643
Wire & Cable - Electronic 943
Cocoa & Cocoa Products - Mfr
See Confectionery Products 659
Coffee & Tea Stores 549
Coffee Makers
See Appliances - Small - Mfr......................... 476
Coffins
See Caskets & Vaults.............................. 533
Coilers
See Metalworking Machinery......................... 792
Coils - Electronic
See Electronic Components & Accessories - Mfr.......... 643
Coin Counting Machines
See Automatic Merchandising Equipment & Systems 504
Coin-Operated Games
See Games & Gaming 680
Coin-Operated Laundry Machines
See Laundry Equipment & Supplies - Commercial & Industrial.................................... 756
Colas
See Soft Drinks - Mfr...............................518
Soft Drinks - Whol.............................518
Cold Storage Facilities
See Refrigerated Storage 941
Collateral Insurance
See Surety Insurance 745
Collection Agencies 549
Collectors' Organizations
See Hobby Organizations............................488
College Loans & Scholarships
See Student Assistance Programs 905
College Preparation Services
See Educational Testing Services - Assessment & Preparation 633
College Preparation Software
See Educational & Reference Software...................587
College Savings Programs
See Student Assistance Programs 905
Colleges & Universities - Christian 558
See also Colleges - Bible 549; Colleges & Universities - Jesuit 578
Colleges & Universities - Four-Year 559
See also Colleges - Community & Junior 550; Colleges - Fine Arts 557; Colleges - Women's (Four-Year) 558; Colleges & Universities - Christian 558; Colleges & Universities - Graduate & Professional Schools 574; Colleges & Universities - Historically Black 577; Colleges & Universities - Jesuit 578; Military Service Academies 793; Universities - Canadian 932; Vocational & Technical Schools 938
Colleges & Universities - Graduate & Professional Schools.. 574
Law Schools 574
Medical Schools 575
Theological Schools............................. 575
Colleges & Universities - Historically Black 577
Colleges & Universities - Jesuit..................... 578
Colleges & Universities - Military
See Colleges & Universities - Four-Year 559
Military Service Academies 793
Colleges - Bible 549
See also Colleges & Universities - Christian 558
Colleges - Canadian
See Universities - Canadian.......................... 932
Colleges - Community & Junior...................... 550
See also Colleges - Fine Arts 557; Colleges - Tribal 557; Colleges & Universities - Four-Year 559; Vocational & Technical Schools 938
Colleges - Culinary Arts 557
Colleges - Fine Arts............................... 557
See also Colleges & Universities - Four-Year 559; Vocational & Technical Schools 938
Colleges - Tribal.................................. 557
See also Colleges - Community & Junior 550
Colleges - Women's (Four-Year)..................... 558
Collets (Machine Tool Accessories)
See Metalworking Devices & Accessories 791
Cologne
See Perfumes.................................... 828
Color Separations
See Typesetting & Related Services 931
Colostomy Appliances
See Medical Supplies - Mfr 784
Combat Simulation Systems
See Simulation & Training Systems.................... 897
Combat Vehicles
See Weapons & Ordnance (Military) 942
Combines
See Farm Machinery & Equipment - Mfr 652
Farm Machinery & Equipment - Whol............... 653
Commerce - US Department of
See US Department of Commerce 690
Commercial Air Conditioning & Heating Equipment
See Air Conditioning & Heating Equipment - Commercial/ Industrial 471
Commercial Airlines
See Airlines - Commercial........................... 474
Commercial Art
See Graphic Design 694
Commercial Cleaning Products
See Cleaning Products.............................. 544
Commercial Cleaning Services
See Cleaning Services 545
Commercial Credit
See Credit & Financing - Commercial 621
Commercial Fishing
See Fishing - Commercial 655
Commercial Laundry Equipment & Supplies
See Laundry Equipment & Supplies - Commercial & Industrial.................................... 756
Commercial Lighting Fixtures
See Lighting Fixtures & Equipment 763
Commercial Photography
See Photography - Commercial....................... 834
Commercial Printers
See Printing Companies - Commercial Printers........... 845
Commercials
See Motion Picture Production - Special Interest.......... 796
Commodity Contracts Brokers & Dealers............. 578
See also Investment Advice & Management 748; Securities Brokers & Dealers 890
Commodity Exchanges
See Securities & Commodities Exchanges............... 892
Communication Products - Visual
See Commercial & Industrial Furniture 676
Educational Materials & Supplies 632

Index

Communications Equipment
See Appliance & Home Electronics Stores 476
Fire Protection Systems 655
Intercom Equipment & Systems 746
Modems 579
Radio & Television Broadcasting & Communications Equipment 865
Security Products & Services 892
Signals & Sirens - Electric 896
Telecommunications Equipment & Systems 908
Communications Networks - Electronic
See Electronic Communications Networks (ECNs) 643
Communications Newsletters
See Media & Communications Newsletters 807
Communications Professionals Associations
See Media Professionals Associations 498
Telecommunications Professionals Associations 500
Communications Services
See Internet Service Providers (ISPs) 748
Satellite Communications Services 886
Telecommunications Services 908
Communications Software
See Internet & Communications Software 588
Communications Tower Operators 578
See also Communications Lines & Towers Construction 598
Communities - Online 578
See also Internet Service Providers (ISPs) 748
Community Colleges
See Colleges - Community & Junior 550
Compact Disc Players
See Audio & Video Equipment 502
Compact Discs
See Book, Music, Video Clubs 522
Music Stores 803
Recording Companies 870
Compilers (Software)
See Computer Languages & Development Tools 587
Compression Springs
See Springs - Light-Gauge 903
Compressors - Air & Gas 578
Compressors - Air Conditioning & Refrigeration
See Air Conditioning & Heating Equipment - Commercial/Industrial 471
Computed Tomography (CT) Equipment
See Imaging Equipment & Systems - Medical 733
Computer & Internet Training Programs
See Training & Certification Programs - Computer & Internet 923
Computer Cable
See Wire & Cable - Electronic 943
Computer Consultants
See Computer Systems Design Services 592
Computer Drives
See Storage Devices 580
Computer Equipment 578
See also Automatic Teller Machines (ATMs) 504; Business Machines - Mfr 527; Calculators - Electronic 529; Modems 579; Computer Networking Products & Systems 582; Flash Memory Devices 656; Point-of-Sale (POS) & Point-of-Information (POI) Systems 841
Computer Input Devices 579
Computers 578
Modems 579
Monitors & Displays 579
Multimedia Equipment & Supplies 580
Printers 580
Scanning Equipment 580
Storage Devices 580
Computer Equipment & Software - Whol 581
See also Business Machines - Whol 527; Electrical & Electronic Equipment & Parts - Whol 639
Computer Furniture
See Commercial & Industrial Furniture 676
Computer Games
See Games & Entertainment Software 588
Computer Integrators
See Computer Systems Design Services 592
Computer Logic Modules
See Semiconductors & Related Devices 894
Computer Maintenance & Repair 582
Computer Modems
See Modems 579
Computer Networking Products & Systems 582
See also Modems 579; Systems & Utilities Software 591; Telecommunications Equipment & Systems 908
Computer Programming Services - Custom 583
See also Computer Software 586; Computer Systems Design Services 592
Computer Resellers
See Computer Equipment & Software - Whol 581
Computer Reservations Systems
See Global Distribution Systems (GDSs) 682
Computer Science Research
See Research Centers & Institutions 871
Computer Security
See Systems & Utilities Software 591
Computer Software 586
See also Application Service Providers (ASPs) 477; Computer Equipment & Software - Whol 581; Computer Networking Products & Systems 582; Computer Programming Services - Custom 583; Computer Stores 592; Computer Systems Design Services 592; Educational Materials & Supplies 632
Business Software (General) 586
Computer Languages & Development Tools 587
Educational & Reference Software 587
Electronic Purchasing & Procurement Software 588
Engineering Software 588
Games & Entertainment Software 588
Internet & Communications Software 588
Multimedia & Design Software 589
Personal Software 589
Professional Software (Industry-Specific) 589
Service Software 590
Systems & Utilities Software 591
Computer Stores 592
See also Appliance & Home Electronics Stores 476
Computer Supplies
See Office & School Supplies 812
Printing & Photocopying Supplies 847
Computer Systems Design Services 592
See also Web Site Design Services 942
Computer Systems Management Services
See Management Services 776
Computer Training (General)
See Training Programs (Misc) 924
Computer-Aided Design Software
See Multimedia & Design Software 589
Computer-Aided Manufacturing Software
See Engineering Software 588
Professional Software (Industry-Specific) 589
Computing - Mobile
See Data Communications Services for Wireless Devices 624
Concert, Sports, Other Live Event Producers & Promoters 595
Concrete - Ready-Mixed 595
Concrete Admixtures
See Chemicals - Specialty 542
Concrete Products - Mfr 595
Concrete Products - Whol
See Brick, Stone, Related Materials 602
Condensed Milk
See Dairy Products - Dry, Condensed, Evaporated 660
Cones - Ice Cream
See Cookies & Crackers 660
Confectioner's Sugar
See Sugar & Sweeteners 665
Conference & Events Coordinators 596
Conference Center Facilities Management Services
See Facilities Management Services 652
Conference Centers
See Convention Centers 613
Hotels - Conference Center 721
Confetti
See Paper Converters 820
Conglomerates 596
See also Holding Companies 700
Congress - US
See Government - US - Legislative Branch 694
Congressional Committees
See US Congressional Committees 694
Congressional Representatives
See US Senators, Representatives, Delegates 694
Connectors - Electronic
See Electronic Components & Accessories - Mfr 643
Conservation Organizations
See Environmental Organizations 485
Consolidators - Air Fare
See Air Fare Consolidators 472
Construction - Building Contractors - Non-Residential 597
Construction - Building Contractors - Residential 597
Construction - Heavy Construction Contractors 598
Communications Lines & Towers Construction 598
Foundation Drilling & Pile Driving 598
Golf Course Construction 598
Highway, Street, Bridge, Tunnel Construction 598
Marine Construction 599
Mining Construction 599
Plant Construction 599
Railroad Construction 599
Refinery (Petroleum or Oil) Construction 599
Water & Sewer Lines, Pipelines, Power Lines Construction 599
Construction - Special Trade Contractors 599
See also Swimming Pools 906
Building Equipment Installation or Erection 599
Carpentry & Flooring Contractors 599
Concrete Contractors 599
Electrical Contractors 599
Excavation Contractors 600
Glass & Glazing Contractors 600
Masonry & Stone Contractors 600
Painting & Paperhanging Contractors 600
Plastering, Drywall, Acoustical, Insulation Contractors 600
Plumbing, Heating, Air Conditioning Contractors 601
Remodeling, Refinishing, Resurfacing Contractors 601
Roofing, Siding, Sheet Metal Contractors 601
Sprinkler System Installation (Fire Sprinklers) 602
Structural Steel Erection 602
Water Well Drilling 602
Wrecking & Demolition Contractors 602
Construction Chemicals
See Chemicals - Specialty 542
Construction Equipment
See Construction Machinery & Equipment 602
Heavy Equipment Distributors 699
Industrial & Heavy Equipment Rental 650
Construction Fasteners
See Fasteners & Fastening Systems 654
Construction Machinery & Equipment 602
See also Industrial Machinery, Equipment, & Supplies 735; Material Handling Equipment 779
Construction Management
See Construction - Building Contractors - Non-Residential 597
Construction - Building Contractors - Residential 597
Construction - Heavy Construction Contractors 598
Engineering & Design 647
Management Services 776
Construction Materials 602
See also Home Improvement Centers 707
Brick, Stone, Related Materials 602
Construction Materials (Misc) 603
Lumber & Building Supplies 603
Roofing, Siding, Insulation Materials 604
Consulates - Foreign, in the US
See Embassies & Consulates - Foreign, in the US 645
Consultants - Computer Systems
See Computer Systems Design Services 592
Consulting Services - Career
See Consulting Services - Human Resources 604
Consulting Services - Environmental 604
See also Recyclable Materials Recovery 870; Remediation Services 871; Waste Management 941
Consulting Services - Human Resources 604
Consulting Services - Management 605
See also Association Management Companies 479; Management Services 776
Consulting Services - Marketing 607
Consulting Services - Personnel
See Consulting Services - Human Resources 604
Consulting Services - Relocation
See Relocation Consulting Services 871
Consulting Services - Telecommunications 608
Consulting Services - Trial
See Litigation Support Services 764
Consumer Credit
See Credit & Financing - Consumer 620
Consumer Credit Ratings
See Credit Reporting Services 622
Consumer Electronics
See Appliance & Home Electronics Stores 476
Consumer Information Resources - Government 610

Consumer Magazines
See Art & Architecture Magazines 768
Automotive Magazines 769
Boating Magazines 769
Business & Finance Magazines 769
Computer & Internet Magazines 770
Entertainment & Music Magazines 770
General Interest Magazines 770
Health & Fitness Magazines 771
Hobby & Personal Interests Magazines 771
Political & Current Events Magazines 772
Science & Nature Magazines 772
Sports Magazines 773
Travel & Regional Interest Magazines 773
Consumer Product Studies
See Market Research Firms 778
Consumer Protection Agencies
See Government - State 684
Contact Lenses
See Ophthalmic Goods 816
Optical Goods Stores 816
Container Rental - Cargo & Freight
See Transport Equipment Rental 650
Containers - Metal (Barrels, Drums, Kegs) 610
Containers - Paper (Fiber)
See Cans, Tubes, Drums - Paper (Fiber) 530
Containers - Plastics (Drums, Cans, Crates, Boxes) 610
Containers - Plastics - Household
See Plastics Products - Household 838
Containers - Wood 611
See also Pallets & Skids 819
See Long-Term Care Facilities 766
Retirement Communities 884
Contract Warehousing
See Commercial Warehousing 941
Logistics Services (Transportation & Warehousing) 765
Controls & Relays - Electrical 612
Controls - Industrial Process 611
Controls - Temperature - Residential & Commercial 612
See Long-Term Care Facilities 766
Convenience Stores 613
See also Gas Stations 680; Grocery Stores 694
Convention & Visitors Bureaus 614
See also Travel & Tourism Information - Canadian 927; Travel & Tourism Information - Foreign Travel 927
Convention Centers 613
See also Performing Arts Facilities 826; Stadiums & Arenas 903
Converted Paper Products
See Paper Converters 820
Convertible Beds
See Household Furniture 677
Conveyors & Conveying Equipment 618
See also Material Handling Equipment 779
Cookies
See Baked Goods - Whol 665
Bakeries 511
Cookies & Crackers 660
Cooking Equipment - Commercial
See Food Service Equipment & Supplies 669
Cooking Equipment - Household
See Appliances - Major - Mfr 476
Appliances - Small - Mfr 476
Appliances - Whol 477
Cooking Schools
See Colleges - Culinary Arts 557
Cooking Utensils
See Metal Products - Household 788
Cooking Utensils - Cast Iron
See Foundries - Iron & Steel 671
Cooking/Recipes Software
See Personal Software 589
Cookware
See Home Furnishings - Whol 706
Metal Products - Household 788
Cooling Equipment - Industrial
See Air Conditioning & Heating Equipment - Commercial/Industrial 471
Cooling Systems - Automotive
See Air Conditioning & Heating Equipment - Residential 472
Cooling Systems - Residential
See Air Conditioning & Heating Equipment - Residential 472
Cooling Vests
See Thermal Management Products - Personal 918
Cooperatives - Electric (Rural)
See Electric Companies - Cooperatives (Rural) 633
Cooperatives - Travel
See Travel Agency Networks 926
Copper
See Metal Industries (Misc) 788
Metal Tube & Pipe 789
Wire & Cable 943
Copper Castings
See Foundries - Nonferrous (Castings) 671
Copper Foil
See Foil & Leaf - Metal 658
Copper Mining
See Mining - Metals 793
Copy Machines
See Business Machines - Whol 527
Photocopying Equipment & Supplies 833
Cord & Twine 619
Cork & Cork Products 619
See also Office & School Supplies 812
Corn
See Grain Farms 469
Corn Chips
See Snack Foods 664
Corn Milling
See Grain Mill Products 662
Corporate Housing 619
Corporate Training Programs
See Training Programs - Corporate 923
Corporate Travel
See Travel Agencies 925
Correctional & Detention Management (Privatized) 619
See also Correctional Facilities - State 619; Juvenile Detention Facilities 752
Correctional Facilities 619
Correctional Facilities - Juvenile
See Juvenile Detention Facilities 752
Correctional Facilities - State 619
See also Correctional & Detention Management (Privatized) 619; Juvenile Detention Facilities 752
Correspondence Schools
See Vocational & Technical Schools 938
Corrosion Inhibitors
See Chemicals - Specialty 542
Corrugated Boxes
See Boxes - Corrugated & Solid Fiber 524
Cosmetic Bags
See Handbags, Totes, Backpacks 695
Cosmetics Cases
See Leather Goods - Personal 759
Luggage, Bags, Cases 767
Cosmetics, Skin Care, and Other Personal Care Products 620
See also Perfumes 828
Costume Jewelry
See Jewelry - Costume 751
Cotton
See Broadwoven Fabric Mills 916
Cotton (Raw) - Whol
See Farm Product Raw Materials 653
Cotton Ginning Machinery
See Farm Machinery & Equipment - Mfr 652
Farm Machinery & Equipment - Whol 653
Cotton Pickers
See Farm Machinery & Equipment - Mfr 652
Farm Machinery & Equipment - Whol 653
Cottonseed Oil
See Oil Mills - Cottonseed, Soybean, Other Vegetable Oils 664
Counseling Services
See Managed Care - Behavioral Health 775
Counting Devices (Totalizing)
See Meters & Other Counting Devices 792
County Government
See Government - County 682
Couplings - Shaft
See Power Transmission Equipment - Mechanical 843
Courier Services - Air or Ground
See Freight Forwarders 673
Package Delivery Services 817
Court Filing Services
See Litigation Support Services 764
Court Reporting Services
See Litigation Support Services 764
Courts
See Government - US - Judicial Branch 693
Covers (Boats, Jet Skis, Motorcycles, etc)
See Tarps, Tents, Covers 907
Cowboy Boots
See Footwear 669
Cowboy Hats
See Hats & Caps 546
CPAs
See Accountants Associations 491
Accounting Firms 465
Crackers
See Cookies & Crackers 660
Crafts Magazines
See Hobby & Personal Interests Magazines 771
Crafts Software
See Personal Software 589
Crafts Supplies
See Art Materials & Supplies - Mfr. 478
Art Materials & Supplies - Whol 479
Art Supply Stores 479
Cranberries
See Berry Growers 675
Cranes - Construction
See Construction Machinery & Equipment 602
Cranes - Industrial
See Material Handling Equipment 779
Cream Products
See Milk & Cream Products 663
Credit & Financing - Commercial 621
See also Banks - Commercial & Savings 511; Credit & Financing - Consumer 620
Credit & Financing - Consumer 620
See also Banks - Commercial & Savings 511; Credit & Financing - Commercial 621; Credit Unions 622
Credit Bureaus
See Credit Reporting Services 622
Credit Card Providers & Related Services 621
Credit Insurance
See Surety Insurance 745
Credit Ratings
See Credit Reporting Services 622
Credit Reporting Services 622
See also
Credit Unions 622
Cremation Service
See Mortuary, Crematory, Cemetery Products & Services 796
Cremation Urns
See Caskets & Vaults 533
Creosoting
See Wood Preserving 944
Crime Scene Clean-up Services
See Bio-Recovery Services 519
Crime Victim Assistance Agencies
See Government - State 684
Crisis Counseling
See Managed Care - Behavioral Health 775
CRM (Customer Relationship Management) Services
See Management Services 776
Crops - Growing
See Agricultural Products 469
Cruise Lines 624
See also Casinos 532; Cruises - Riverboat 624; Ports & Port Authorities 842; Travel Agencies 925
Cruises - Riverboat 624
See also Casinos 532; Cruise Lines 624
Cryogenic Banks
See Organ & Tissue Banks 817
CT (Computed Tomography)
See Imaging Equipment & Systems - Medical 733
Culinary Arts Schools
See Colleges - Culinary Arts 557
Cups - Plastics
See Plastics Products - Household 838
Cups - Styrofoam
See Plastics Foam Products 836
Currency Conversion & Exchange
See Banking-Related Services 511
Curtains - Window or Shower
See Home Furnishings - Whol 706
Textile Products - Household 917
Custodial Services
See Building Maintenance Services 525

Customer Motivation Programs
See Incentive Program Management Services . . . 734
Customer Relationship Management (CRM) Services
See Management Services . . . 776
Customhouse Brokers
See Freight Forwarders . . . 673
Cutlery . . . 624
See also Silverware 897
Cutlery - Retail
See Home Furnishings Stores . . . 706
Cutlery - Whol
See Hardware - Whol . . . 697
Cutting Tools
See Metalworking Devices & Accessories . . . 791
Cylinders & Actuators - Fluid Power . . . 624
See also Automotive Parts & Supplies - Mfr 507
Cytology Diagnostic Products
See Diagnostic Products . . . 628

D

Dairy Products - Mfr
See Butter (Creamery) . . . 659
Cheeses - Natural, Processed, Imitation . . . 659
Dairy Products - Dry, Condensed, Evaporated . . . 660
Ice Cream & Frozen Desserts . . . 662
Milk & Cream Products . . . 663
Dance Shoes
See Footwear . . . 669
Dancewear
See Athletic Apparel . . . 545
Data - Wireless
See Data Communications Services for Wireless Devices . . . 624
Data Analysis Software
See Computer Languages & Development Tools . . . 587
Data Communications Services for Wireless Devices . . 624
Data Conversion Software
See Systems & Utilities Software . . . 591
Data Entry
See Data Processing & Related Services . . . 625
Data Processing & Related Services . . . 625
See also Electronic Transaction Processing 645; Payroll Services 825
Data Storage Software
See Systems & Utilities Software . . . 591
Dates
See Fruit Growers (Misc) . . . 675
Dating Services . . . 626
Day Care Services
See Children's Learning Centers . . . 543
Day Care Web Camera Companies
See Child Care Monitoring Systems - Internet . . . 543
Death (Accidental) & Dismemberment Insurance
See Life & Accident Insurance . . . 740
Death Services
See Bio-Recovery Services . . . 519
Mortuary, Crematory, Cemetery Products & Services . . . 796
Debit Card Services
See Banking-Related Services . . . 511
Debit Cards - Mfr
See Smart Cards . . . 897
Debt Recovery Services
See Collection Agencies . . . 549
Debugging Software
See Computer Languages & Development Tools . . . 587
Decals
See Labels - Other Than Fabric . . . 752
Decorative Glassware & Pottery
See Glassware & Pottery - Household . . . 682
Decorative Shutters
See Shutters - Window (All Types) . . . 896
Decorative Tile
See Tile - Ceramic (Wall & Floor) . . . 918
Defense - US Department of
See US Department of Defense . . . 690
Defense Communications Systems
See Radio & Television Broadcasting & Communications Equipment . . . 865
Defense Products & Systems
See Missiles, Space Vehicles, Parts . . . 794
Weapons & Ordnance (Military) . . . 942
Defense Research
See Research Centers & Institutions . . . 871
Defense Systems Testing
See Testing Facilities . . . 915
Defibrillators
See Electromedical & Electrotherapeutic Equipment . . . 642
Dehumidifiers
See Air Conditioning & Heating Equipment - Commercial/ Industrial . . . 471
Dehumidifiers - Portable
See Appliances - Small - Mfr . . . 476
Appliances - Whol . . . 477
Deicing Chemicals
See Chemicals - Specialty . . . 542
Deicing Equipment
See Aircraft Parts & Auxiliary Equipment . . . 473
Deicing Salt
See Salt . . . 886
Delegates - Territorial
See US Senators, Representatives, Delegates . . . 694
Demographics Analysis
See Market Research Firms . . . 778
Demolition Contractors
See Wrecking & Demolition Contractors . . . 602
Dental Associations - State . . . 627
See also Health & Medical Professionals Associations 494
Dental Care Products
See Cosmetics, Skin Care, and Other Personal Care Products 620
Dental Equipment & Supplies - Mfr . . . 627
Dental Equipment & Supplies - Whol
See Medical & Dental Equipment & Supplies - Whol . . . 781
Dental Insurance
See Medical & Hospitalization Insurance . . . 741
Dental Laboratories
See Laboratories - Dental . . . 753
Deodorants
See Cosmetics, Skin Care, and Other Personal Care Products 620
Department Stores . . . 627
Deposition Reporting Services
See Litigation Support Services . . . 764
Design Schools
See Colleges - Fine Arts . . . 557
Design Services
See Computer Systems Design Services . . . 592
Engineering & Design . . . 647
Fashion Design Houses . . . 654
Graphic Design . . . 694
Interior Design . . . 746
Landscape Design & Related Services . . . 756
Web Site Design Services . . . 942
Design Software
See Multimedia & Design Software . . . 589
Designers - Fashion
See Fashion Design Houses . . . 654
Desktop Computers
See Computers . . . 578
Desktop Publishing Software
See Business Software (General) . . . 586
Desserts - Frozen
See Dairy Products - Whol . . . 666
Ice Cream & Frozen Desserts . . . 662
Detection Systems
See Security Products & Services . . . 892
Detectives
See Investigative Services . . . 748
Detention Center Operators
See Correctional & Detention Management (Privatized) . . . 619
Detention Facilities - Juvenile
See Juvenile Detention Facilities . . . 752
Detergents
See Cleaning Products . . . 544
Detonators
See Explosives . . . 651
Developers - Property
See Real Estate Developers . . . 867
Developmental Centers . . . 628
Device Drivers
See Systems & Utilities Software . . . 591
Diabetes Treatment Services
See Health Care Providers - Ancillary . . . 697
Diagnostic Imaging Equipment & Systems
See Imaging Equipment & Systems - Medical . . . 733
Diagnostic Imaging Services
See Imaging Services - Diagnostic . . . 734
Diagnostic Instruments
See Medical Instruments & Apparatus - Mfr . . . 782
Diagnostic Laboratories
See Laboratories - Medical . . . 754
Diagnostic Products . . . 628
See also Biotechnology Companies 519; Medicinal Chemicals & Botanical Products 786; Pharmaceutical Companies 831; Pharmaceutical Companies - Generic Drugs 832
Diagnostic Products - Veterinary
See Pharmaceutical & Diagnostic Products - Veterinary . . . 831
Diamond Cutting
See Jewelers' Findings & Materials . . . 751
Diamond Cutting Tools
See Metalworking Devices & Accessories . . . 791
Diamond Dressing & Wheel Crushing Attachments
See Metalworking Devices & Accessories . . . 791
Diaper Services
See Laundry & Drycleaning Services . . . 756
Diapers - Disposable
See Paper Products - Sanitary . . . 820
Diaries & Journals
See Blankbooks & Binders . . . 520
Die Casting
See Foundries - Nonferrous (Castings) . . . 671
Die Makers
See Tool & Die Shops . . . 919
Die-Casting Machines
See Machine Tools - Metal Forming Types . . . 768
Dietary Supplements
See Vitamins & Nutritional Supplements . . . 937
Digital Subscriber Lines (DSL)
See Internet Service Providers (ISPs) . . . 748
Digital Video Disc (DVD) Players
See Audio & Video Equipment . . . 502
Digital Video Discs (DVDs)
See Book, Music, Video Clubs . . . 522
Video Stores . . . 937
Digital Video Servers
See Radio & Television Broadcasting & Communications Equipment . . . 865
Digitizing Software
See Systems & Utilities Software . . . 591
Dimension Stone
See Stone Quarries - Dimension Stone . . . 794
Dining
See Restaurant Companies . . . 880
Restaurants (Individual) . . . 881
Dinnerware
See Table & Kitchen Supplies - China & Earthenware . . . 907
Diodes
See Semiconductors & Related Devices . . . 894
Diplomatic Offices
See Embassies & Consulates - Foreign, in the US . . . 645
Direct Mail Advertising
See Advertising Services - Direct Mail . . . 467
Direct Selling
See Home Sales & Other Direct Selling . . . 708
Directories - Online
See Internet Search Engines, Portals, Directories . . . 748
Directories - Print
See Book Publishers . . . 850
Directory Publishers . . . 852
Dirigibles
See Airships . . . 475
Disability Insurance
See Life & Accident Insurance . . . 740
Disaster Management Simulation Systems
See Simulation & Training Systems . . . 897
Disaster Relief
See Charitable & Humanitarian Organizations . . . 481
Disc Jockey Services
See Concert, Sports, Other Live Event Producers & Promoters . . . 595
Disclosure - Campaign
See Ethics Commissions . . . 650
Discovery Centers
See Museums - Children's . . . 802
Dishes
See Table & Kitchen Supplies - China & Earthenware . . . 907
Dishwashers
See Appliance & Home Electronics Stores . . . 476
Appliances - Major - Mfr . . . 476
Appliances - Whol . . . 477

Dispensers
See Metal Products (Misc) ... 788
Display Cases & Racks
See Fixtures - Office & Store ... 656
Display Cases - Refrigerated
See Refrigeration Equipment - Whol ... 871
Display Forms
See Mannequins & Display Forms ... 777
Displays - Exhibit & Trade Show ... 629
Displays - Graphic
See Monitors & Displays ... 579
Displays - Point-of-Purchase ... 629
See also Signs 896
Disposable Briefs
See Paper Products - Sanitary ... 820
Disposable Clothing (Protective)
See Personal Protective Equipment & Clothing ... 828
Disposable Diapers
See Paper Products - Sanitary ... 820
Dissecting Tables
See Institutional & Other Public Buildings Furniture ... 678
Distilleries
See Liquor - Mfr ... 518
Distribution Centers
See Commercial Warehousing ... 941
Logistics Services (Transportation & Warehousing) ... 765
Distributors Associations
See Consumer Sales & Service Professionals Associations ... 492
Sales & Marketing Professional Associations ... 499
District Courts - US
See US District Courts ... 694
DNA Testing
See Diagnostic Products ... 628
Laboratories - Genetic Testing ... 754
Document Conversion
See Micrographics Products & Services ... 792
Documentaries
See Motion Picture Production - Special Interest ... 796
Documents Preparation - Shipping
See Freight Forwarders ... 673
Dog Carriers
See Pet Products ... 829
Dog Food
See Pet Products ... 829
Dog Insurance
See Animal Insurance ... 740
Dog Racing
See Racing & Racetracks ... 856
Dollar Stores
See Variety Stores ... 935
Dollies - Hand or Power
See Material Handling Equipment ... 779
Dolls & Stuffed Toys
See Toy Stores ... 922
Toys, Games, Hobbies ... 922
Dolomite
See Stone Quarries - Crushed & Broken Stone ... 794
Dolomitic Lime
See Lime ... 764
Domain Name Registrars
See Internet Domain Name Registrars ... 747
Dome Lights
See Lighting Equipment - Vehicular ... 763
Domestic Violence
See Children & Family Advocacy Organizations ... 482
Donor Services Facilities
See Organ & Tissue Banks ... 817
Donuts
See Bakeries ... 511
Bakery Products - Fresh ... 658
Door & Window Glass
See Glass - Flat, Plate, Tempered ... 681
Door-to-Door Sales
See Home Sales & Other Direct Selling ... 708
Doors & Windows - Metal ... 630
See also Shutters - Window (All Types) 896
Doors & Windows - Vinyl ... 630
Doors & Windows - Wood ... 630
See also Millwork 793; Shutters - Window (All Types) 896
Dosimeters
See Measuring, Testing, Controlling Instruments ... 780
Dot-Matrix Printers
See Printers ... 580
Doughnuts
See Bakeries ... 511
Bakery Products - Fresh ... 658
Dowels
See Wood Products - Shaped & Turned ... 945
Drafting Supplies
See Art Materials & Supplies - Mfr ... 478
Art Materials & Supplies - Whol ... 479
Art Supply Stores ... 479
Drama Schools
See Colleges - Fine Arts ... 557
Draperies
See Home Furnishings - Whol ... 706
Textile Products - Household ... 917
Dredging
See Marine Construction ... 599
Dresses
See Fashion Design Houses ... 654
Women's Clothing ... 547
Dressings - Salad
See Fruits & Vegetables - Pickled ... 661
Dressings - Surgical
See Medical Supplies - Mfr ... 784
Dressings - Window
See Blinds & Shades ... 520
Textile Products - Household ... 917
Dressmaking Forms
See Mannequins & Display Forms ... 777
Drilling Machine Tools (Metal Cutting)
See Machine Tools - Metal Cutting Types ... 767
Drills
See Tools - Power ... 921
Drinking Cups - Plastics
See Plastics Products - Household ... 838
Drinking Cups - Styrofoam
See Plastics Foam Products ... 836
Drinking Water
See Water - Bottled ... 941
Drives - Computer
See Storage Devices ... 580
Driving Simulation Systems
See Simulation & Training Systems ... 897
Drop Cloths
See Tarps, Tents, Covers ... 907
Drug Abuse
See General Hospitals - US ... 713
Psychiatric Hospitals ... 718
Self-Help Organizations ... 490
Substance Abuse Treatment Centers ... 906
Drug Delivery Systems
See Electromedical & Electrotherapeutic Equipment ... 642
Drug Stores ... 631
See also Health Food Stores 699
Drug-Testing Laboratories
See Laboratories - Drug-Testing ... 754
Druggists' Sundries
See Drugs & Personal Care Products - Whol ... 631
Drugs & Personal Care Products - Whol ... 631
Drugs - Mfr
See Biotechnology Companies ... 519
Diagnostic Products ... 628
Medicinal Chemicals & Botanical Products ... 786
Pharmaceutical & Diagnostic Products - Veterinary ... 831
Pharmaceutical Companies ... 831
Pharmaceutical Companies - Generic Drugs ... 832
Vitamins & Nutritional Supplements ... 937
Drums - Metal
See Containers - Metal (Barrels, Drums, Kegs) ... 610
Drums - Paper
See Cans, Tubes, Drums - Paper (Fiber) ... 530
Dry Erase Boards
See Commercial & Industrial Furniture ... 676
Office & School Supplies ... 812
Drycleaning
See Laundry & Drycleaning Services ... 756
Drycleaning Equipment
See Laundry Equipment & Supplies - Commercial & Industrial ... 756
Drydocks
See Ship Building & Repairing ... 896
Dryers - Clothes
See Appliances - Major - Mfr ... 476
Appliances - Whol ... 477
Dryers - Hair
See Appliances - Small - Mfr ... 476
Beauty Salon Equipment & Supplies ... 517
Drywall
See Gypsum Products ... 695
Plastering, Drywall, Acoustical, Insulation Contractors ... 600
DSL (Digital Subscriber Lines)
See Internet Service Providers (ISPs) ... 748
Duct Tape
See Tape - Cellophane, Gummed, Masking, Pressure Sensitive ... 907
Ductile Iron Castings
See Foundries - Iron & Steel ... 671
Dude Ranches ... 631
See also Resorts & Resort Companies 873
Duffel Bags
See Handbags, Totes, Backpacks ... 695
Luggage, Bags, Cases ... 767
Dumbwaiters
See Elevators, Escalators, Moving Walkways ... 645
Dump Trailers
See Truck Trailers ... 928
Dungarees
See Jeans ... 546
Duplication & Replication Services ... 632
Duty-Free Shops ... 632
See also Gift Shops 681
DVD Players
See Audio & Video Equipment ... 502
DVDs
See Book, Music, Video Clubs ... 522
Recording Media - Magnetic & Optical ... 870
Video Stores ... 937
Dyeing - Fabric
See Textile Dyeing & Finishing ... 917
Dyeing Machines
See Textile Machinery ... 916
Dynamic Climate Control Products
See Thermal Management Products - Personal ... 918
Dynamite
See Explosives ... 651

E

E-Commerce Management Services
See Management Services ... 776
E-Commerce Software
See Business Software (General) ... 586
Electronic Purchasing & Procurement Software ... 588
E-Mail Services
See Communities - Online ... 578
Internet Service Providers (ISPs) ... 748
E-Mail Software
See Internet & Communications Software ... 588
EAPs (Employee Assistance Programs)
See Managed Care - Behavioral Health ... 775
Ear Plugs
See Personal Protective Equipment & Clothing ... 828
Earth Sciences Research
See Research Centers & Institutions ... 871
Earth Stations
See Satellite Communications Services ... 886
Earthenware
See Plumbing Fixtures & Fittings - Vitreous China & Earthenware ... 840
Table & Kitchen Supplies - China & Earthenware ... 907
Eating Utensils - Plastics
See Plastics Products - Household ... 838
EBPP (Electronic Bill Presentment & Payment) Services
See Electronic Bill Presentment & Payment Services ... 643
EBPP (Electronic Bill Presentment & Payment) Software
See Business Software (General) ... 586
ECG (Electrocardiogram) Machines
See Electromedical & Electrotherapeutic Equipment ... 642
Echinacea
See Vitamins & Nutritional Supplements ... 937
ECNs (Electronic Communications Networks)
See Electronic Communications Networks (ECNs) ... 643
Economic Development Agencies - State
See Government - State ... 684
Education - US Department of
See US Department of Education ... 690

Index

Education Management Services
See Educational Institution Operators & Managers........ 632
Education Research
See Research Centers & Institutions.................... 871
Educational Facilities Management Services
See Facilities Management Services.................... 652
Educational Films
See Motion Picture Production - Special Interest.......... 796
Educational Institution Operators & Managers 632
Educational Institutions
See Children's Learning Centers 543
Colleges & Universities - Christian................. 558
Colleges & Universities - Four-Year 559
Colleges & Universities - Graduate & Professional Schools.. 574
Colleges & Universities - Historically Black 577
Colleges & Universities - Jesuit 578
Colleges - Bible................................ 549
Colleges - Community & Junior 550
Colleges - Culinary Arts 557
Colleges - Fine Arts............................. 557
Colleges - Tribal 557
Colleges - Women's (Four-Year).................. 558
Military Service Academies 793
Preparatory Schools - Boarding................... 844
Universities - Canadian.......................... 932
Vocational & Technical Schools 938
Educational Materials & Supplies 632
See also Educational & Reference Software 587; Office & School Supplies 812
Educational Testing Services - Assessment & Preparation 633
EFT (Electronic Funds Transfer Networks)
See Banking-Related Services 511
Egg Cartons
See Plastics Foam Products......................... 836
Eggs
See Poultry & Eggs Production 470
Poultry, Eggs, Poultry Products - Whol...............668
Elastic
See Narrow Fabric Mills.............................917
Elastic Fabrics
See Knitting Mills...................................917
Elastomers - Non-Vulcanizable
See Synthetic Resins & Plastics Materials................837
Elastomers - Vulcanizable
See Synthetic Rubber.................................838
Electric Appliances - Household
See Appliance & Home Electronics Stores............... 476
Appliances - Major - Mfr......................... 476
Appliances - Small - Mfr......................... 476
Appliances - Whol............................... 477
Vacuum Cleaners - Household 934
Electric Bicycles
See Bicycles & Bicycle Parts & Accessories 519
Electric Companies
See Utility Companies 932
Electric Companies - Cooperatives (Rural) 633
See also Utility Companies 932
Electric Fences
See Fences - Mfr 654
Electric Lighting Equipment
See Light Bulbs & Tubes 763
Lighting Equipment - Vehicular................... 763
Lighting Fixtures & Equipment 763
Electric Motors
See Motors (Electric) & Generators 798
Electric Razors
See Cosmetics, Skin Care, and Other Personal Care Products 620
Electric Signals
See Signals & Sirens - Electric....................... 896
Electric Signs
See Signs.. 896
Electric Tools
See Tools - Power 921
Electric Transmission & Distribution Equipment
See Switchgear & Switchboard Apparatus 906
Transformers - Power, Distribution, Specialty......... 924
Electric Vehicles
See Bicycles & Bicycle Parts & Accessories 519
Motor Vehicles - Commercial & Special Purpose...... 797
Electric Wiring Devices
See Wiring Devices - Current-Carrying 943
Wiring Devices - Noncurrent-Carrying 944

Electrical & Electronic Equipment & Parts - Whol..... 639
Electrical Discharge Machines
See Machine Tools - Metal Cutting Types 767
Electrical Equipment for Internal Combustion Engines 642
See also Automotive Parts & Supplies - Mfr 507; Motors (Electric) & Generators 798
Electrical Signals Measuring & Testing Instruments .. 642
Electrical Supplies - Porcelain..................... 642
Electrical Tape
See Tape - Cellophane, Gummed, Masking, Pressure Sensitive 907
Electricians
See Electrical Contractors............................599
Electrocardiogram Machines
See Electromedical & Electrotherapeutic Equipment 642
Electromedical & Electrotherapeutic Equipment...... 642
See also Medical Instruments & Apparatus - Mfr 782
Electron Microscopes
See Laboratory Analytical Instruments 754
Electron Tubes
See Electronic Components & Accessories - Mfr.......... 643
Electronic Bill Presentment & Payment Services 643
See also Application Service Providers (ASPs) 477
Electronic Bill Presentment & Payment Software
See Business Software (General) 586
Electronic Book Readers
See Computers.....................................578
Electronic Calculators
See Calculators - Electronic......................... 529
Electronic Communications Networks (ECNs)......... 643
See also Securities Brokers & Dealers 890; Securities & Commodities Exchanges 892
Electronic Components & Accessories - Mfr.......... 643
See also Printed Circuit Boards 845; Semiconductors & Related Devices 894
Electronic Enclosures............................. 645
Electronic Equipment & Parts - Whol
See Electrical & Electronic Equipment & Parts - Whol...... 639
Electronic Funds Transfer
See Banking-Related Services 511
Electronic Mail Software
See Internet & Communications Software 588
Electronic Publishing
See Book Publishers 850
Publishing Companies 850
Electronic Software Delivery
See Application Service Providers (ASPs) 477
Electronic Statement Presentment Software
See Business Software (General) 586
Electronic Transaction Processing 645
Electronic Warfare Simulators
See Simulation & Training Systems.................... 897
Electronics Fasteners
See Fasteners & Fastening Systems.................... 654
Electronics Stores - Home Electronics
See Appliance & Home Electronics Stores............... 476
Electroplating
See Metal Coating, Plating, Engraving.................. 787
Electroplating Chemicals
See Chemicals - Specialty 542
Electrosurgical Systems
See Electromedical & Electrotherapeutic Equipment 642
Electrotherapeutic Lamp Units
See Light Bulbs & Tubes 763
Elevator Installation
See Building Equipment Installation or Erection............599
Elevators - Grain
See Farm Product Raw Materials 653
Elevators, Escalators, Moving Walkways 645
Embassies & Consulates - Foreign, in the US......... 645
See also Travel & Tourism Information - Foreign Travel 927
Emblems & Insignia - Embroidered
See Embroidery & Other Decorative Stitching 646
Embossing - Paper
See Paper Finishers (Embossing, Coating, Gilding, Stamping) 820
Embossing Machines
See Business Machines - Mfr.......................... 527
Embroidering Machinery
See Textile Machinery 916
Embroidery & Other Decorative Stitching 646
Emergency Drench Showers
See Safety Equipment - Mfr 886

Emergency Response Systems
See Intercom Equipment & Systems.................... 746
Emergency Response Systems - Personal
See Personal Emergency Response Systems 828
Emergency Transport
See Ambulance Services 475
Emery Abrasives
See Abrasive Products 465
Employee Assistance Programs
See Managed Care - Behavioral Health 775
Employee Benefits Management Services
See Management Services........................... 776
Employee Motivation Programs
See Incentive Program Management Services 734
Employee Training
See Training Programs (Misc) 924
Employment Agencies
See Staffing Services 904
Employment Offices - Government................... 646
Employment Services - Online....................... 646
Emulsifiers - Food
See Food Emulsifiers.................................661
Enameled Steel Plumbing Fixtures
See Plumbing Fixtures & Fittings - Metal................ 839
Enclosures - Electronic
See Electronic Enclosures 645
Endoscopes
See Imaging Equipment & Systems - Medical 733
Energy - US Department of
See US Department of Energy..........................690
Energy Providers
See Electric Companies - Cooperatives (Rural) 633
Utility Companies 932
Energy Research
See Research Centers & Institutions.................... 871
Engine Electrical Equipment
See Electrical Equipment for Internal Combustion Engines .. 642
Engine Repair - Automotive
See Repair Service (General) - Automotive................509
Engineering & Design.............................. 647
See also Surveying, Mapping, Related Services 906
Engineering Professionals Associations
See Technology, Science, Engineering Professionals Associations 499
Engineering Research
See Research Centers & Institutions.................... 871
Engines & Turbines 649
See also Aircraft Engines & Engine Parts 473; Automotive Parts & Supplies - Mfr 507; Motors (Electric) & Generators 798
Engines - Aircraft
See Aircraft Engines & Engine Parts.................... 473
Engraving (on Metal)
See Metal Coating, Plating, Engraving.................. 787
Engraving (on Plates for Printing)
See Typesetting & Related Services 931
Entertainment Districts
See Shopping/Dining/Entertainment Districts 501
Entertainment News
See Weekly Newspapers - Alternative...................812
Entertainment Services
See Concert, Sports, Other Live Event Producers & Promoters 595
Entertainment Simulation Systems
See Simulation & Training Systems.................... 897
Entertainment Software
See Games & Entertainment Software...................588
Entertainment Systems
See Appliance & Home Electronics Stores............... 476
Audio & Video Equipment........................ 502
Envelopes.. 650
Environmental Consulting Services
See Consulting Services - Environmental................ 604
Environmental Engineering
See Engineering & Design 647
Environmental Newsletters
See Energy & Environmental Newsletters.................806
Environmental Sciences Research
See Research Centers & Institutions.................... 871
Environmental Test Equipment

See Simulation & Training Systems . . . 897
Environmental Testing
See Testing Facilities . . . 915
EPOs (Exclusive Provider Organizations)
See Medical & Hospitalization Insurance . . . 741
Epoxy
See Adhesives & Sealants . . . 466
Epoxy Resins
See Synthetic Resins & Plastics Materials . . . 837
Epsom Salt
See Salt . . . 886
Equine Insurance
See Animal Insurance . . . 740
Equipment Rental & Leasing . . . 650
See also Credit & Financing - Consumer 620; Credit & Financing - Commercial 621; Fleet Leasing & Management 656
Computer Equipment Leasing . . . 650
Home & Office Equipment Rental (General) . . . 650
Industrial & Heavy Equipment Rental . . . 650
Medical Equipment Rental . . . 650
Transport Equipment Rental . . . 650
Equipment Testing
See Testing Facilities . . . 915
Ergonomic Furniture
See Commercial & Industrial Furniture . . . 676
Escalators
See Elevators, Escalators, Moving Walkways . . . 645
Escrow Services
See Title Insurance . . . 746
ESP (Electronic Statement Presentment) Software
See Business Software (General) . . . 586
Essential Oils
See Chemicals - Specialty . . . 542
Essential Oils - Whol
See Chemicals & Related Products - Whol . . . 543
Etching (on Metal)
See Metal Coating, Plating, Engraving . . . 787
Etching (on Plates for Printing)
See Typesetting & Related Services . . . 931
Ethernet
See Computer Networking Products & Systems . . . 582
Ethics Commissions . . . 650
Ethnic Foods
See Restaurant Companies . . . 880
Restaurants (Individual) . . . 881
Specialty Foods . . . 664
Evangelical Organizations
See Religious Organizations . . . 489
Evaporated Milk
See Dairy Products - Dry, Condensed, Evaporated . . . 660
Events (Live) Producers & Promoters
See Concert, Sports, Other Live Event Producers & Promoters . . . 595
Events Coordinators
See Conference & Events Coordinators . . . 596
Exclusive Provider Organizations (EPOs)
See Medical & Hospitalization Insurance . . . 741
Executive Recruiting Firms . . . 651
Executive Seminars
See Training Programs - Corporate . . . 923
Exercise & Fitness Equipment . . . 651
See also Sporting Goods 899
Exercise Facilities
See Health & Fitness Centers . . . 698
Exercise Videos
See Motion Picture Production - Special Interest . . . 796
Exhaust Systems - Automotive
See Automotive Parts & Supplies - Mfr . . . 507
Exhaust Systems Repair - Automotive
See Mufflers & Exhaust Systems Repair - Automotive . . . 509
Exhibits - Trial
See Litigation Support Services . . . 764
Explosive Devices - Military
See Weapons & Ordnance (Military) . . . 942
Explosives . . . 651
Exports
See Embassies & Consulates - Foreign, in the US . . . 645
US Department of Commerce . . . 690
See Long-Term Care Facilities . . . 766
Extended Stay Hotels
See Hotels & Hotel Companies . . . 722
Extension Cords - Electrical
See Wiring Devices - Current-Carrying . . . 943
Extension Springs
See Springs - Light-Gauge . . . 903
Exterminators
See Pest Control Services . . . 829
Extracts - Flavoring
See Flavoring Extracts & Syrups . . . 661
Extruded Rubber Goods
See Rubber Goods - Mechanical . . . 886
Eye Banks . . . 651
See also Organ & Tissue Banks 817; Transplant Centers - Blood Stem Cell 924
Eye Protection Products
See Personal Protective Equipment & Clothing . . . 828
Eye Surgery
See Vision Correction Centers . . . 937
Eye Wash Stations
See Safety Equipment - Mfr . . . 886
Safety Equipment - Whol . . . 886
Eyewear
See Ophthalmic Goods . . . 816
Optical Goods Stores . . . 816

F

Fabric Finishing & Dyeing
See Textile Dyeing & Finishing . . . 917
Fabric Goods - Whol
See Piece Goods & Notions . . . 834
Fabric Stores . . . 651
See also Patterns - Sewing 825
Fabricated Plate Work
See Boiler Shops . . . 521
Fabricated Rubber Goods
See Rubber Goods . . . 885
Fabricators - Metal
See Boiler Shops . . . 521
Metal Fabricating - Custom . . . 787
Fabrics - Mfr
See Textile Mills . . . 916
Facilities Maintenance Services
See Building Maintenance Services . . . 525
Facilities Management Services . . . 652
See also Correctional & Detention Management (Privatized) 619
Facsimile Machines
See Photocopying Equipment & Supplies . . . 833
Facsimile Paper
See Coated & Laminated Paper . . . 819
Factors . . . 652
Factory Furniture & Fixtures
See Commercial & Industrial Furniture . . . 676
Fall Protection
See Safety Equipment - Mfr . . . 886
Family Advocacy Organizations
See Children & Family Advocacy Organizations . . . 482
Family Planning Organizations
See Children & Family Advocacy Organizations . . . 482
Family Services
See Children & Family Advocacy Organizations . . . 482
Fans - Household
See Appliances - Small - Mfr . . . 476
Fare Consolidators (Air Fares)
See Air Fare Consolidators . . . 472
Farm Machinery & Equipment - Mfr . . . 652
See also Lawn & Garden Equipment 758
Farm Machinery & Equipment - Whol . . . 653
Farm Product Raw Materials . . . 653
Farm Supplies . . . 653
Farming
See Agricultural Products . . . 469
Farming Magazines
See Agriculture & Farming Magazines . . . 768
Farming Organizations
See Agricultural Organizations . . . 480
Farms - Tree
See Timber Tracts . . . 918
Fashion Design Houses . . . 654
See also Clothing & Accessories - Mfr 545
Fashion Design Schools
See Colleges - Fine Arts . . . 557
Fast Food Chains
See Convenience Stores . . . 613
Franchises . . . 672
Restaurant Companies . . . 880
Fast Food Containers
See Plastics Foam Products . . . 836
Fasteners & Fastening Systems . . . 654
See also Hardware - Mfr 695; Precision Machined Products 843
Fasteners (Snaps, Zippers, Buttons)
See Piece Goods & Notions . . . 834
Fasteners - Metal (Bolts, Nuts, Screws, etc) - Whol
See Hardware - Whol . . . 697
Faucets
See Plumbing Fixtures & Fittings - Metal . . . 839
Plumbing Fixtures & Fittings - Vitreous China & Earthenware . . . 840
Fax Machines
See Photocopying Equipment & Supplies . . . 833
Fax Modems
See Modems . . . 579
Fax Paper
See Coated & Laminated Paper . . . 819
Fax Services
See Telecommunications Services . . . 908
Fax Transmission Software
See Internet & Communications Software . . . 588
FBOs (Fixed-Base Operations)
See Aviation - Fixed-Base Operations . . . 509
Feather Dusters
See Mops, Sponges, Wiping Cloths . . . 795
Federal Government
See Government - US - Executive Branch . . . 690
Government - US - Judicial Branch . . . 693
Government - US - Legislative Branch . . . 694
Federal Reserve Banks
See Banks - Federal Reserve . . . 515
Feed Supplements
See Livestock & Poultry Feeds - Prepared . . . 765
Feedlots
See Cattle Ranches, Farms, Feedlots (Beef Cattle) . . . 469
Feeds & Feed Ingredients
See Farm Supplies . . . 653
Livestock & Poultry Feeds - Prepared . . . 765
Felt
See Nonwoven Fabrics . . . 917
Fences - Mfr . . . 654
See also Recycled Plastics Products 870
Fertilizer Minerals Mining
See Chemical & Fertilizer Minerals Mining . . . 794
Fertilizers & Pesticides . . . 654
See also Farm Supplies 653
Festival Operators
See Circus, Carnival, Festival Operators . . . 544
Festivals - Book . . . 655
Festivals - Film . . . 655
Fiber Optic Cable
See Wire & Cable - Electronic . . . 943
Fiber Optic Materials
See Glass Fibers . . . 682
Fiber Optic Networks
See Telecommunications Equipment & Systems . . . 908
Fiber Waste Recovery
See Textile Fiber Processing Mills . . . 917
Fiberboard
See Wood Products - Reconstituted . . . 944
Fiberfill
See Nonwoven Fabrics . . . 917
Fiberglass Insulation
See Insulation & Acoustical Products . . . 738
Roofing, Siding, Insulation Materials . . . 604
Fibers - Manmade
See Broadwoven Fabric Mills . . . 916
Fibers - Synthetic
See Synthetic Fibers & Filaments . . . 837
Figs
See Fruit Growers (Misc) . . . 675
Figurines
See Glassware & Pottery - Household . . . 682
Filaments - Synthetic
See Synthetic Fibers & Filaments . . . 837
File Folders
See Paperboard & Cardboard - Die-Cut . . . 821
File Transfer Software
See Systems & Utilities Software . . . 591
Filing Boxes - Paperboard
See Boxes - Paperboard . . . 524
Filing Cabinets

See Commercial & Industrial Furniture 676
Filling Stations
See Gas Stations 680
Film - Plastics (for Packaging)
See Packaging Materials & Products - Paper or Plastics 818
Film - Plastics (Unsupported)
See Plastics - Unsupported - Film, Sheet, Profile Shapes 835
Film - Sensitized
See Photographic Equipment & Supplies 833
Film Developing
See Photo Processing & Storage 833
Film Festivals
See Festivals - Film 655
Films - Documentary
See Motion Picture Production - Special Interest 796
Films - Educational
See Motion Picture Production - Special Interest 796
Films - Industrial
See Motion Picture Production - Special Interest 796
Films - Motion Picture
See Motion Picture & Television Production 796
Motion Picture Distribution & Related Services 796
Motion Picture Pre- & Post-Production Services 796
Filters - Air
See Air Purification Equipment - Household 472
Automotive Parts & Supplies - Mfr 507
Automotive Parts & Supplies - Whol 508
Filters - Air
See Air Purification Equipment - Industrial 472
Filters - Fluid
See Industrial Machinery, Equipment, & Supplies 735
Filters - Fuel
See Automotive Parts & Supplies - Mfr 507
Automotive Parts & Supplies - Whol 508
Filters - Oil
See Automotive Parts & Supplies - Mfr 507
Automotive Parts & Supplies - Whol 508
Filters - Pipeline
See Industrial Machinery, Equipment, & Supplies 735
Filters - Water
See Water Treatment & Filtration Products & Equipment 941
Finance Companies
See Credit & Financing - Commercial 621
Credit & Financing - Consumer 620
Finance Magazines
See Business & Finance Magazines 769
Finance Newsletters
See Banking & Finance Newsletters 805
Finance Professionals' Associations
See Banking & Finance Professionals Associations 492
Financial Assistance Programs - Student
See Student Assistance Programs 905
Financial Institutions
See Banks - Commercial & Savings 511
Credit Unions 622
Financial Services
See Electronic Bill Presentment & Payment Services 643
Investment Advice & Management 748
Financial Services Software - Business
See Business Software (General) 586
Financial Services Software - Personal
See Personal Software 589
Fingerprinting Equipment
See Biometric Identification Equipment & Software 519
Finishing Agents
See Cleaning Products 544
Finishing Agents - Metal
See Chemicals - Specialty 542
Finishing Agents - Textile & Leather
See Chemicals - Specialty 542
Finishing Mills - Fabric (Printing, Bleaching, Dyeing)
See Textile Dyeing & Finishing 917
Fire Alarm Systems
See Security Products & Services 892
Fire Alarms
See Fire Protection Systems 655
Fire Clay
See Clay, Ceramic, Refractory Minerals Mining 794
Fire Extinguishers
See Safety Equipment - Mfr 886
Safety Equipment - Whol 886
Fire Fighting Services
See Helicopter Transport Services 700
Fire Hose
See Safety Equipment - Mfr 886
Safety Equipment - Whol 886
Fire Hydrant Valves
See Valves - Industrial 934
Fire Insurance
See Property & Casualty Insurance 743
Fire Protection Systems 655
See also Personal Protective Equipment & Clothing 828; Safety Equipment - Mfr 886; Security Products & Services 892
Fire Sprinklers
See Sprinkler System Installation (Fire Sprinklers) 602
Fire Trucks
See Motor Vehicles - Commercial & Special Purpose 797
Firearms & Ammunition (Non-Military) 655
See also Sporting Goods 899; Weapons & Ordnance (Military) 942
Firearms & Ammunition - Military
See Weapons & Ordnance (Military) 942
Firearms Training
See Simulation & Training Systems 897
Firefighter Gear
See Personal Protective Equipment & Clothing 828
Firefighting - Forest Fires
See Forestry Services 670
Firefighting Equipment
See Pumps & Pumping Equipment (General Use) 856
Safety Equipment - Mfr 886
Safety Equipment - Whol 886
Fireworks
See Explosives 651
First Aid Supplies
See Medical Supplies - Mfr 784
Fish Food (Aquarium Fish)
See Pet Products 829
Fish Oil
See Fats & Oils - Animal or Marine 660
Fisheries Research
See Research Centers & Institutions 871
Fishing - Commercial 655
Fishing Boats
See Boats - Recreational 521
Fishing Line
See Cord & Twine 619
Fishing Tackle
See Sporting Goods 899
Fitness Equipment
See Exercise & Fitness Equipment 651
Fitness Magazines
See Health & Fitness Magazines 771
Fitness Programs
See Health & Fitness Centers 698
Spas - Health & Fitness 897
Fitness Software
See Personal Software 589
Fitness Videos
See Motion Picture Production - Special Interest 796
Fixed-Base Operations (FBOs) - Aviation
See Aviation - Fixed-Base Operations 509
Fixtures - Office & Store 656
See also Commercial & Industrial Furniture 676
Flags, Banners, Pennants 656
Flanges
See Pipe & Pipe Fittings - Metal (Fabricated) 834
Flares
See Explosives 651
Flash Memory Devices 656
Flashlight Bulbs
See Light Bulbs & Tubes 763
Flatbed Forms Printers
See Printers 580
Flatbed Scanners
See Scanning Equipment 580
Flatware
See Silverware 897
Flavors & Fragrances - Whol
See Chemicals & Related Products - Whol 543
Flea & Tick Control Products
See Pet Products 829
Fleet Graphics
See Graphic Design 694
Fleet Leasing & Management 656
Flight Information Displays
See Monitors & Displays 579
Flight Insurance
See Travel Insurance 746
Flight Simulators & Training Systems
See Simulation & Training Systems 897
Flight Suits
See Personal Protective Equipment & Clothing 828
Flood Insurance
See Property & Casualty Insurance 743
Floor Coverings - Mfr
See Carpets & Rugs 531
Flooring - Resilient 657
Tile - Ceramic (Wall & Floor) 918
Floor Coverings - Whol
See Home Furnishings - Whol 706
Floor Coverings Stores 657
Flooring - Laminated
See Flooring - Resilient 657
Flooring - Plastics
See Flooring - Resilient 657
Flooring - Resilient 657
See also Recycled Plastics Products 870
Flooring Contractors
See Carpentry & Flooring Contractors 599
Flooring Mills
See Sawmills & Planing Mills 887
Floral Supplies - Whol
See Flowers & Nursery Stock - Whol 658
Florists 657
See also Garden Centers 680
Flour Milling
See Grain Mill Products 662
Flower Shops
See Florists 657
Flowers & Nursery Stock - Whol 658
See also Horticultural Products Growers 708
Fluid Meters
See Meters & Other Counting Devices 792
Fluid Power Equipment
See Cylinders & Actuators - Fluid Power 624
Pumps & Motors - Fluid Power 856
Valves & Hose Fittings - Fluid Power 935
Fluorescent & Vapor Lamps
See Light Bulbs & Tubes 763
Fluoroscopy Equipment
See Imaging Equipment & Systems - Medical 733
Fluxes - Brazing, Soldering, Welding
See Chemicals - Specialty 542
Flyers, Bulletins, etc
See Publishers (Misc) 855
Foam - Plastics
See Plastics Foam Products 836
Foggers
See Compressors - Air & Gas 578
Foil & Leaf - Metal 658
Foil - Aluminum
See Metal Industries (Misc) 788
Foil Bags
See Bags - Plastics 510
Foil Wrappers
See Foil & Leaf - Metal 658
Folders - Paperboard
See Paperboard & Cardboard - Die-Cut 821
Food & Beverage Dispensers
See Automatic Merchandising Equipment & Systems 504
Food Additives - Whol
See Chemicals & Related Products - Whol 543
Food Coloring
See Flavoring Extracts & Syrups 661
Food Containers - Paperboard
See Boxes - Paperboard 524
Food Packaging
See Bags - Plastics 510
Food Processors
See Appliances - Small - Mfr 476
Food Products - Mfr 658
See also Agricultural Products 469; Bakeries 511; Beverages - Mfr 517; Ice - Manufactured 733; Livestock & Poultry Feeds - Prepared 765; Meat Packing Plants 781; Pet Products 829; Poultry Processing 842; Salt 886
Bakery Products - Fresh 658
Bakery Products - Frozen 659
Butter (Creamery) 659
Cereals (Breakfast) 659
Cheeses - Natural, Processed, Imitation 659

Chewing Gum 659
Coffee - Roasted (Ground, Instant, Freeze-Dried) 659
Confectionery Products 659
Cookies & Crackers 660
Dairy Products - Dry, Condensed, Evaporated 660
Diet & Health Foods 660
Fats & Oils - Animal or Marine 660
Fish & Seafood - Canned 660
Fish & Seafood - Fresh or Frozen 660
Flavoring Extracts & Syrups 661
Flour Mixes & Doughs 661
Food Emulsifiers 661
Fruits & Vegetables - Dried or Dehydrated 661
Fruits & Vegetables - Pickled 661
Fruits, Vegetables, Juices - Canned or Preserved 661
Fruits, Vegetables, Juices - Frozen 662
Gelatin 662
Grain Mill Products 662
Honey 662
Ice Cream & Frozen Desserts 662
Meat Products - Prepared 663
Milk & Cream Products 663
Nuts - Edible 664
Oil Mills - Cottonseed, Soybean, Other Vegetable Oils 664
Oils - Edible (Margarine, Shortening, Table Oils, etc) 664
Pasta 664
Peanut Butter 664
Salads - Prepared 664
Sandwiches - Prepared 664
Snack Foods 664
Specialty Foods 664
Spices, Seasonings, Herbs 665
Sugar & Sweeteners 665
Syrup - Maple 665
Tea 665
Vinegar & Cider 665
Yeast 665
Food Products - Whol 665
See also Beverages - Whol 518
Baked Goods - Whol 665
Coffee & Tea - Whol 665
Confectionery & Snack Foods - Whol 666
Dairy Products - Whol 666
Fish & Seafood - Whol 666
Frozen Foods (Packaged) - Whol 666
Fruits & Vegetables - Fresh - Whol 666
Groceries - General Line 666
Meats & Meat Products - Whol 667
Poultry, Eggs, Poultry Products - Whol 668
Specialty Foods - Whol 668
Food Products Distributors
See Food Products - Whol 665
Food Products Machinery 668
See also Food Service Equipment & Supplies 669
Food Service 669
See also Restaurant Companies 880
Food Service Equipment & Supplies 669
See also Food Products Machinery 668
Food Service Facilities Management
See Facilities Management Services 652
Food Stores
See Bakeries 511
Coffee & Tea Stores 549
Convenience Stores 613
Gourmet Specialty Shops 682
Grocery Stores 694
Health Food Stores 699
Ice Cream & Dairy Stores 733
Food Supplements
See Diet & Health Foods 660
Health Food Stores 699
Vitamins & Nutritional Supplements 937
Food Testing
See Testing Facilities 915
Food Warming Equipment
See Food Service Equipment & Supplies 669
Foods Research
See Research Centers & Institutions 871
Foot Warmers
See Thermal Management Products - Personal 918
Football Equipment & Supplies
See Sporting Goods 899
Football Teams
See Sports Teams - Football 902
Footwear 669
Footwear - Protective
See Footwear 669
Footwear Components
See Footwear 669
Foreign Language Learning Software
See Educational & Reference Software 587
Foreign Languages
See Language Schools 756
Translation Services 924
Forensic Laboratories
See Laboratories - Medical 754
Forensic Testing
See Laboratories - Genetic Testing 754
Forestry Organizations
See Agricultural Organizations 480
Forestry Research
See Research Centers & Institutions 871
Forestry Services 670
See also Timber Tracts 918
Forging Machinery
See Machine Tools - Metal Forming Types 768
Forgings - Metal
See Metal Forgings 787
Forklifts
See Material Handling Equipment 779
Forming & Drawing Compounds
See Chemicals - Specialty 542
Forms
See Business Forms 526
Printing Companies - Commercial Printers 845
Forms - Dressmaking
See Mannequins & Display Forms 777
Formula One Racing
See Motor Speedways 796
Foundation Garments
See Undergarments 547
Foundations - Community 670
See also Charitable & Humanitarian Organizations 481
Foundations - Corporate 670
See also Charitable & Humanitarian Organizations 481
Foundations - Private 670
See also Charitable & Humanitarian Organizations 481
Foundries - Investment 671
Foundries - Iron & Steel 671
See also Foundries - Nonferrous (Castings) 671
Foundries - Nonferrous (Castings) 671
See also Foundries - Iron & Steel 671
Foundry Patterns
See Patterns - Industrial 825
Four-Wheelers
See All-Terrain Vehicles 475
Fractional Vacations
See Timeshare Companies 918
Fragrances
See Cosmetics, Skin Care, and Other Personal Care Products 620
Perfumes 828
Frames & Mouldings 672
Frames & Mouldings - Metal
See Doors & Windows - Metal 630
Franchises 672
See also Auto Supply Stores 503; Automotive Services 509; Bakeries 511; Beauty Salons 517; Business Service Centers 528; Candles 529; Car Rental Agencies 530; Children's Learning Centers 543; Cleaning Services 545; Remodeling, Refinishing, Resurfacing Contractors 601; Convenience Stores 613; Health Food Stores 699; Home Inspection Services 708; Hotels & Hotel Companies 722; Ice Cream & Dairy Stores 733; Laundry & Drycleaning Services 756; Optical Goods Stores 816; Pest Control Services 829; Printing Companies - Commercial Printers 845; Real Estate Agents & Brokers 866; Restaurant Companies 880; Staffing Services 904; Travel Agency Networks 926; Weight Loss Centers & Services 942
Fraternities
See Greek Letter Societies 486
Freezers - Household
See Appliance & Home Electronics Stores 476
Appliances - Major - Mfr 476
Appliances - Whol 477
Freight Cars & Equipment
See Railroad Equipment - Mfr 866
Freight Container Rental
See Transport Equipment Rental 650
Freight Forwarders 673
See also Logistics Services (Transportation & Warehousing) 765
Freight Rate Auditors
See Freight Forwarders 673
Freight Transport - Deep Sea (Domestic Ports) 674
Freight Transport - Deep Sea (Foreign Ports) 674
Freight Transport - Inland Waterways 674
Freight Transport - Rail
See Rail Transport Services 866
Freight Transport - Trucking
See Trucking Companies 928
Frequent Flyer Programs
See Airlines - Frequent Flyer Programs 474
Frequent Stay Programs
See Hotels - Frequent Stay Programs 721
Frozen Desserts
See Ice Cream & Frozen Desserts 662
Frozen Food Containers - Paperboard
See Boxes - Paperboard 524
Frozen Foods
See Food Products - Mfr 658
Food Products - Whol 665
Frozen Meals
See Specialty Foods 664
Fruit Drinks
See Soft Drinks - Mfr 518
Soft Drinks - Whol 518
Fruit Growers 675
See also Crop Preparation Services 470; Wines - Mfr 518
Berry Growers 675
Citrus Growers 675
Deciduous Tree Fruit Growers 675
Fruit Growers (Misc) 675
Grape Vineyards 675
Fruit Juice
See Fruits, Vegetables, Juices - Canned or Preserved 661
Fruits, Vegetables, Juices - Frozen 662
Fruit Packers & Shippers
See Crop Preparation Services 470
Fruit Growers 675
Fuel Dealers 675
Fuel Pumps
See Pumps - Measuring & Dispensing 855
Fuel Pumps - Automotive
See Automotive Parts & Supplies - Mfr 507
Automotive Parts & Supplies - Whol 508
Fuel Services - Aviation
See Aviation - Fixed-Base Operations 509
Fund-Raising Services 675
Funeral Insurance
See Life & Accident Insurance 740
Funeral Services
See Mortuary, Crematory, Cemetery Products & Services 796
Fur Goods - Retail
See Women's Clothing Stores 548
Furnace Black
See Chemicals - Specialty 542
Furnaces & Ovens - Industrial Process 676
Furnaces - Domestic
See Air Conditioning & Heating Equipment - Residential 472
Heating Equipment - Gas, Oil, Coal 699
Furnaces - Laboratory
See Laboratory Apparatus & Furniture 755
Furniture & Fixtures - Beauty Salons
See Beauty Salon Equipment & Supplies 517
Furniture & Fixtures - Laboratory
See Laboratory Apparatus & Furniture 755
Furniture - Mfr 676
See also Baby Products 510; Cabinets - Wood 528; Fixtures - Office & Store 656; Mattresses & Adjustable Beds 780; Recycled Plastics Products 870
Commercial & Industrial Furniture 676
Household Furniture 677
Institutional & Other Public Buildings Furniture 678
Outdoor Furniture 678
Furniture - Plastics
See Recycled Plastics Products 870
Furniture - Whol 678
Furniture Rental
See Home & Office Equipment Rental (General) 650

Index

Furniture Springs
See Springs - Light-Gauge 903
Furniture Stores 679
See also Department Stores 627
Futures Brokers & Dealers
See Commodity Contracts Brokers & Dealers 578

G

Galleries - Art
See Art Dealers & Galleries 478
Galoshes
See Footwear 669
Gambling
See Casino Companies 531
Casinos 532
Games & Entertainment Software 588
Games & Gaming 680
Games & Gaming 680
See also Casino Companies 531; Casinos 532; Lotteries, Games, Sweepstakes 767; Toys, Games, Hobbies 922
Games - Board
See Toy Stores 922
Toys, Games, Hobbies 922
Games - Coin-Operated
See Automatic Merchandising Equipment & Systems 504
Games & Gaming 680
Games - Online
See Lotteries, Games, Sweepstakes 767
Games - Video (Machines)
See Toy Stores 922
Toys, Games, Hobbies 922
Gaming Associations
See Travel & Recreation Organizations 491
Gaming Equipment & Supplies
See Games & Gaming 680
Garage Doors - Metal
See Doors & Windows - Metal 630
Garage Doors - Wood
See Doors & Windows - Wood 630
Garages
See Automotive Services 509
Gas Stations 680
Garages - Parking
See Parking Service 821
Garbage Bags
See Bags - Plastics 510
Garbage Cans - Metal
See Metal Stampings 789
Garbage Cans - Plastics
See Containers - Plastics (Drums, Cans, Crates, Boxes) 610
Garbage Collection
See Waste Management 941
Garbage Disposal Equipment - Commercial
See Industrial Machinery, Equipment, & Supplies 735
Garbage Disposals - Household
See Appliances - Major - Mfr 476
Appliances - Whol 477
Garden Centers 680
See also Horticultural Products Growers 708; Seed Companies 894
Gardening Equipment
See Lawn & Garden Equipment 758
Gardens
See Botanical Gardens & Arboreta 523
Zoos & Wildlife Parks 945
Garment Bags, Shoe Bags, etc
See Textile Products - Household 917
Garnet Abrasives
See Abrasive Products 465
Garnet Mining
See Minerals Mining (Misc) 794
Gas - Bottled
See Fuel Dealers 675
Gas - Natural
See Gas Transmission - Natural Gas 680
Oil & Gas Extraction 813
Gas Appliances - Household
See Appliances - Major - Mfr 476
Gas Companies
See Utility Companies 932
Gas Detection Products
See Fire Protection Systems 655
Gas Exploration
See Oil & Gas Field Exploration Services 814
Gas Extraction
See Oil & Gas Extraction 813
Gas Field Machinery & Equipment
See Oil & Gas Field Equipment 814
Gas Field Services
See Oil & Gas Field Services 814
Gas Heaters
See Heating Equipment - Gas, Oil, Coal 699
Gas Pumps
See Pumps - Measuring & Dispensing 855
Gas Stations 680
See also Convenience Stores 613
Gas Transmission - Natural Gas 680
Gas Well Drilling
See Oil & Gas Well Drilling 815
Gases - Industrial
See Chemicals - Industrial (Inorganic) 541
Gaskets, Packing, Sealing Devices 681
See also Automotive Parts & Supplies - Mfr 507
Gasoline
See Gas Stations 680
GDSs
See Global Distribution Systems (GDSs) 682
Gear Motors
See Motors (Electric) & Generators 798
Speed Changers, Industrial High Speed Drives, Gears 899
Gears - Aircraft (Power Transmission)
See Aircraft Parts & Auxiliary Equipment 473
Gears - Automotive (Power Transmission)
See Automotive Parts & Supplies - Mfr 507
Gems
See Jewelry - Precious Metal 751
Gems - Whol
See Jewelry, Watches, Gems - Whol 752
Gene Therapy
See Biotechnology Companies 519
Genealogy Software
See Personal Software 589
General Contractors
See Construction - Building Contractors - Non-Residential 597
Construction - Building Contractors - Residential 597
Construction - Heavy Construction Contractors 598
General Rental Services (Home & Office)
See Home & Office Equipment Rental (General) 650
General Stores
See Grocery Stores 694
Variety Stores 935
Generators & Generator Sets
See Motors (Electric) & Generators 798
Generators - Aircraft
See Electrical Equipment for Internal Combustion Engines 642
Generators - Automotive
See Electrical Equipment for Internal Combustion Engines 642
Generic Drugs - Mfr
See Pharmaceutical Companies - Generic Drugs 832
Genetic Testing Laboratories
See Laboratories - Genetic Testing 754
Genetics - Livestock
See Livestock Improvement Services 470
Geographic Information Systems
See Surveying, Mapping, Related Services 906
Geographic Information Systems Software
See Professional Software (Industry-Specific) 589
Geophysical Surveying
See Surveying, Mapping, Related Services 906
Geostationary Satellites
See Satellite Communications Services 886
Geotextiles
See Industrial Fabrics 916
Geriatric Health Care Services
See Health Care Providers - Ancillary 697
Gift Boxes
See Boxes - Paperboard 524
Gift Shops 681
See also Card Shops 530; Duty-Free Shops 632; Home Furnishings Stores 706
Gift Wrap
See Packaging Materials & Products - Paper or Plastics 818
Gifts & Novelties - Whol 681
Giftware
See Home Furnishings - Whol 706
Girdles
See Undergarments 547
GIS (Geographic Information Systems)
See Professional Software (Industry-Specific) 589
Surveying, Mapping, Related Services 906
Glass - Flat, Plate, Tempered 681
Glass - Ophthalmic
See Ophthalmic Goods 816
Glass Fibers 682
Glass Products - Industrial (Custom) 682
Glass Sand
See Sand & Gravel Pits 794
Glass Tubing
See Glass Products - Industrial (Custom) 682
Glass Wool
See Insulation & Acoustical Products 738
Glasses - Eye
See Ophthalmic Goods 816
Optical Goods Stores 816
Glassware & Pottery - Household 682
See also Table & Kitchen Supplies - China & Earthenware 907
Glassware - Decorative
See Glassware & Pottery - Household 682
Glassware - Laboratory & Scientific 682
Glazing Work
See Glass & Glazing Contractors 600
Gliders
See Aircraft 473
Global Distribution Systems (GDSs) 682
Globes
See Educational Materials & Supplies 632
Gloves
See Gloves & Mittens 546
Personal Protective Equipment & Clothing 828
Thermal Management Products - Personal 918
Gloves
See Sporting Goods 899
Glue
See Adhesives & Sealants 466
Goggles
See Ophthalmic Goods 816
Personal Protective Equipment & Clothing 828
Goggles
See Sporting Goods 899
Gold Foil
See Foil & Leaf - Metal 658
Gold Leaf
See Foil & Leaf - Metal 658
Gold Mining
See Mining - Metals 793
Gold Plating
See Metal Coating, Plating, Engraving 787
Golf Bags
See Luggage, Bags, Cases 767
Golf Cars
See Motor Vehicles - Commercial & Special Purpose 797
Golf Centers
See Recreation Facility Operators 870
Golf Equipment & Supplies
See Sporting Goods 899
Golf Shoes
See Footwear 669
Gourmet Specialty Shops 682
Government - City 682
Government - County 682
Government - Federal
See Government - US - Executive Branch 690
Government - US - Judicial Branch 693
Government - US - Legislative Branch 694
Government - State 684
See also Correctional Facilities - State 619; Employment Offices - Government 646; Ethics Commissions 650; Governors - State 694; Legislation Hotlines 759; Lotteries, Games, Sweepstakes 767; Parks - State 822; Sports Commissions & Regulatory Agencies - State 902; Student Assistance Programs 905; Veterans Nursing Homes - State 936
Alabama 684
Alaska 684
Arizona 684
Arkansas 684
California 684
Colorado 684
Connecticut 684
Delaware 684

Index

District of Columbia 685
Florida 685
Georgia 685
Hawaii 685
Idaho 685
Illinois 685
Indiana 685
Iowa 685
Kansas 685
Kentucky 685
Louisiana 686
Maine 686
Maryland 686
Massachusetts 686
Michigan 686
Minnesota 686
Mississippi 686
Missouri 687
Montana 687
Nebraska 687
Nevada 687
New Hampshire 687
New Jersey 687
New Mexico 687
New York 687
North Carolina 688
North Dakota 688
Ohio 688
Oklahoma 688
Oregon 688
Pennsylvania 688
Rhode Island 688
South Carolina 688
South Dakota 688
Tennessee 689
Texas 689
Utah 689
Virginia 689
Washington 689
West Virginia 689
Wisconsin 689
Wyoming 690
Government - US - Executive Branch 690
See also Cemeteries - National 533; Coast Guard Installations 548; Military Bases 792; Parks - National - US 821
US Department of Agriculture 690
US Department of Commerce 690
US Department of Defense 690
US Department of Defense - Department of the Army 690
US Department of Defense - Department of the Navy 690
US Department of Education 690
US Department of Energy 690
US Department of Health & Human Services 690
US Department of Homeland Security 691
US Department of Housing & Urban Development 691
US Department of Justice 691
US Department of Labor 691
US Department of State 692
US Department of the Interior 691
US Department of the Treasury 692
US Department of Transportation 692
US Department of Veterans Affairs 692
US Independent Agencies Government Corporations & Quasi-Official Agencies 692
Government - US - Judicial Branch 693
US Bankruptcy Courts 693
US District Courts 694
US Supreme Court 694
Government - US - Legislative Branch 694
See also Legislation Hotlines 759
US Congressional Committees 694
US Senators, Representatives, Delegates 694
Government Information Offices
See Government - State 684
Government Leaders
See Governors - State 694
US Senators, Representatives, Delegates 694
Governors - State 694
Governors - Territorial
See Governors - State 694
Gowns (Ceremonial)
See Robes (Ceremonial) 546
Graders
See Construction Machinery & Equipment 602
Graduate & Professional Schools
See Colleges & Universities - Graduate & Professional Schools 574
Grain Alcohol
See Liquor - Mfr 518
Grain Elevators
See Farm Product Raw Materials 653
Grain Marketing
See Farm Product Raw Materials 653
Granite
See Brick, Stone, Related Materials 602
Stone Quarries - Dimension Stone 794
Granite - Cutting & Finishing
See Stone (Cut) & Stone Products 905
Grapefruit
See Citrus Growers 675
Graph Paper (Ruled)
See Blankbooks & Binders 520
Graphic Design 694
See also Typesetting & Related Services 931
Graphic Displays
See Monitors & Displays 579
Graphics Accelerators/Processors
See Multimedia Equipment & Supplies 580
Graphics Services - Trial
See Litigation Support Services 764
Graphics Software
See Multimedia & Design Software 589
Graphite Products
See Carbon & Graphite Products 530
Grates - Metal
See Metal Work - Architectural & Ornamental 789
Gravel Pits
See Sand & Gravel Pits 794
Gravure Printing
See Printing Companies - Commercial Printers 845
Gray Iron Castings
See Foundries - Iron & Steel 671
Grease
See Oils & Greases - Lubricating 815
Greenhouses - Prefabricated
See Buildings - Prefabricated - Metal 525
Greeting Cards
See Card Shops 530
Cards - Greeting - Mfr 531
Grills - Barbecue
See Appliances - Major - Mfr 476
Grinders
See Tools - Power 921
Grinding Machines - Metalworking
See Machine Tools - Metal Cutting Types 767
Grinding Wheels
See Abrasive Products 465
Groceries
See Convenience Stores 613
Food Products - Mfr 658
Food Products - Whol 665
Grocery Stores 694
Grocery Bags
See Bags - Paper 510
Bags - Plastics 510
Grocery Carts
See Baskets, Cages, Racks, etc - Wire 516
Grocery Stores 694
See also Bakeries 511; Convenience Stores 613; Gourmet Specialty Shops 682; Health Food Stores 699; Ice Cream & Dairy Stores 733; Wholesale Clubs 943
Ground Support Equipment
See Material Handling Equipment 779
Grouting Equipment
See Construction Machinery & Equipment 602
Grouting Materials
See Chemicals - Specialty 542
Guard & Patrol Services
See Security & Protective Services 893
Guard Dogs
See Security & Protective Services 893
Guards - Wire
See Baskets, Cages, Racks, etc - Wire 516
Guest Ranches
See Dude Ranches 631
Guidance Systems
See Navigation & Guidance Instruments & Systems 805
Guided Missiles
See Missiles, Space Vehicles, Parts 794
Guitars
See Musical Instrument Stores 803
Musical Instruments 803
Gum - Chewing
See Chewing Gum 659
Gum Chemicals
See Chemicals - Industrial (Organic) 541
Gun Control
See Civic & Political Organizations 483
Gunbelts
See Leather Goods (Misc) 759
Gunpowder
See Explosives 651
Guns
See Firearms & Ammunition (Non-Military) 655
Weapons & Ordnance (Military) 942
Guyed Poles
See Communications Lines & Towers Construction 598
Gym & Playground Equipment 695
Gymnastics Mats
See Sporting Goods 899
Gyms
See Health & Fitness Centers 698
Gypsum Products 695

H

Hair Care Products
See Cosmetics, Skin Care, and Other Personal Care Products 620
Hair Dryers
See Appliances - Small - Mfr 476
Beauty Salon Equipment & Supplies 517
Hair Pins
See Cosmetics, Skin Care, and Other Personal Care Products 620
Hair Replacement
See Hairpieces, Wigs, Toupees 695
Hair Styling
See Beauty Salons 517
Hairpieces, Wigs, Toupees 695
Hall Effect Sensors
See Electronic Components & Accessories - Mfr 643
Halls of Fame
See Museums 799
Museums & Halls of Fame - Sports 802
Halogen Lamps
See Light Bulbs & Tubes 763
Ham (Cured)
See Meat Products - Prepared 663
Hammocks
See Outdoor Furniture 678
Hand Warmers
See Thermal Management Products - Personal 918
Handbags, Totes, Backpacks 695
See also Leather Goods - Personal 759; Luggage, Bags, Cases 767; Sporting Goods 899; Tarps, Tents, Covers 907
Handheld Computers
See Computers 578
Handheld Scanners
See Scanning Equipment 580
Handles - Wood
See Wood Products - Shaped & Turned 945
Handsaws
See Saw Blades & Handsaws 886
Handwriting Recognition Products
See Biometric Identification Equipment & Software 519
Handwriting Recognition Software
See Systems & Utilities Software 591
Hangers - Pipe
See Pipe & Pipe Fittings - Metal (Fabricated) 834
Harbor Commissions
See Ports & Port Authorities 842
Hard Hats
See Personal Protective Equipment & Clothing 828
Hardboard
See Wood Products - Reconstituted 944
Hardware - Mfr 695
Hardware - Whol 697
Hardware Stores
See Home Improvement Centers 707
Hardwood Dimension Lumber

See Sawmills & Planing Mills 887
Harness Assemblies - Wire & Cable
See Electronic Components & Accessories - Mfr........ 643
Harnesses
See Leather Goods (Misc) 759
Safety Equipment - Mfr 886
Harvesters
See Farm Machinery & Equipment - Mfr 652
Farm Machinery & Equipment - Whol........ 653
Hazardous Waste Remediation
See Remediation Services 871
Hazmat (Hazardous Materials) Gear
See Personal Protective Equipment & Clothing 828
HBCUs
See Colleges & Universities - Historically Black 577
Head Hunters
See Executive Recruiting Firms 651
Headsets - Computer
See Multimedia Equipment & Supplies 580
Health & Fitness Centers........ 698
See also Spas - Health & Fitness 897; Weight Loss Centers & Services 942
Health & Fitness Software
See Personal Software 589
Health & Human Services - US Department of
See US Department of Health & Human Services........690
Health & Medical Information - Online........ 699
Health Care Industry Associations
See Health & Medical Professionals Associations 494
Health Care Providers - Ancillary........ 697
See also Home Health Services 707; Hospices 709; Vision Correction Centers 937
Health Care Staffing Services
See Staffing Services 904
Health Care Systems........ 698
See also General Hospitals - US 713
Health Clubs
See Health & Fitness Centers........ 698
Health Food Stores........ 699
Health Foods - Mfr
See Diet & Health Foods 660
Health Insurance
See Medical & Hospitalization Insurance........741
Health Maintenance Organizations (HMOs)
See Medical & Hospitalization Insurance........741
Health Sciences Research
See Research Centers & Institutions........ 871
Health Services
See Health Care Providers - Ancillary........ 697
Home Health Services 707
Hospices........ 709
Hospitals........ 712
Imaging Services - Diagnostic........ 734
Substance Abuse Treatment Centers 906
Health Spas
See Spas - Health & Fitness........ 897
Hearing Aids
See Medical Supplies - Mfr 784
Heart Valves - Mechanical
See Electromedical & Electrotherapeutic Equipment 642
Heart-Lung Machines
See Electromedical & Electrotherapeutic Equipment 642
Heat Exchangers
See Boiler Shops 521
Heat Packs
See Personal Protective Equipment & Clothing 828
Thermal Management Products - Personal 918
Heat Pumps - Industrial
See Air Conditioning & Heating Equipment - Commercial/ Industrial 471
Heat Treating - Metal
See Metal Heat Treating........ 787
Heaters - Gloves & Boots
See Thermal Management Products - Personal 918
Heaters - Space
See Appliances - Small - Mfr........ 476
Heaters - Water
See Appliances - Major - Mfr........ 476
Appliances - Whol........ 477
Heating Contractors
See Plumbing, Heating, Air Conditioning Contractors 601
Heating Equipment - Electric
See Air Conditioning & Heating Equipment - Residential........ 472
Heating Equipment - Gas, Oil, Coal........ 699
See also Air Conditioning & Heating Equipment - Commercial/ Industrial 471; Air Conditioning & Heating Equipment - Residential 472; Boiler Shops 521; Furnaces & Ovens - Industrial Process 676
Heating Equipment - Warm Air
See Air Conditioning & Heating Equipment - Residential........ 472
Heating Equipment - Whol
See Plumbing, Heating, Air Conditioning Equipment & Supplies - Whol........ 840
Heating Systems - Automotive
See Air Conditioning & Heating Equipment - Residential........ 472
Heating Systems - Personal
See Thermal Management Products - Personal 918
Heating Valves
See Pipe & Pipe Fittings - Metal (Fabricated)........ 834
Heavy Construction Contractors
See Construction - Heavy Construction Contractors 598
Heavy Equipment
See Construction Machinery & Equipment........ 602
Heavy Equipment Distributors........ 699
See also Farm Machinery & Equipment - Whol 653; Industrial Equipment & Supplies (Misc) - Whol 734
Helicopter Transport Services........ 700
See also Air Charter Services 471; Ambulance Services 475
Helicopters
See Aircraft........ 473
Helmets - Safety
See Personal Protective Equipment & Clothing 828
Helmets - Safety
See Sporting Goods 899
Help Supply (Temporary or Continuing)
See Employment Offices - Government 646
Staffing Services 904
Hematology Diagnostic Reagents
See Diagnostic Products 628
Herbal Products
See Vitamins & Nutritional Supplements 937
Herbs
See Spices, Seasonings, Herbs 665
Hide-a-Beds
See Household Furniture 677
High Speed Drives - Industrial
See Speed Changers, Industrial High Speed Drives, Gears 899
Hiking Boots
See Footwear 669
Histology Diagnostic Products
See Diagnostic Products 628
Historic Hotels
See Hotels & Hotel Companies 722
Historic Preservation Agencies - State
See Government - State 684
Historic Sites - National - US
See Parks - National - US........ 821
Historically Black Colleges & Universities
See Colleges & Universities - Historically Black 577
Hitches - Trailer
See Trailers (Towing) & Trailer Hitches 923
HMOs (Health Maintenance Organizations)
See Medical & Hospitalization Insurance........741
Hobbies Software
See Personal Software 589
Hobby Supplies
See Art Materials & Supplies - Mfr........ 478
Art Materials & Supplies - Whol 479
Art Supply Stores........ 479
Toy Stores........ 922
Toys, Games, Hobbies........ 922
Hobs
See Metalworking Devices & Accessories 791
Hockey Equipment & Supplies
See Sporting Goods 899
Hockey Teams
See Sports Teams - Hockey 903
Hogs - Whol
See Livestock - Whol 765
Hoists
See Material Handling Equipment 779
Holding Companies 700
See also Conglomerates 596
Airlines Holding Companies 700
Bank Holding Companies........ 700
Holding Companies (General) 704
Insurance Holding Companies 704
Utilities Holding Companies........ 705
Holsters
See Leather Goods (Misc) 759
Home Appliances
See Appliance & Home Electronics Stores........ 476
Appliances - Major - Mfr........ 476
Appliances - Small - Mfr........ 476
Appliances - Whol........ 477
Vacuum Cleaners - Household 934
Home Builders
See Construction - Building Contractors - Residential........ 597
Home Cleaning Services
See Cleaning Services 545
Home Computers
See Computers........578
Home Electronics Equipment Rental
See Home & Office Equipment Rental (General)........650
Home Electronics Stores
See Appliance & Home Electronics Stores........ 476
Home Entertainment Systems
See Appliance & Home Electronics Stores........ 476
Audio & Video Equipment........ 502
Home Furnishings - Whol 706
Home Furnishings Rental
See Home & Office Equipment Rental (General)........650
Home Furnishings Stores 706
See also Department Stores 627; Furniture Stores 679
Home Health Equipment Rental
See Medical Equipment Rental........650
Home Health Services........ 707
See also Hospices 709
Home Heating & Cooling Systems
See Air Conditioning & Heating Equipment - Residential........ 472
Home Improvement Centers........ 707
See also Construction Materials 602
Home Inspection Services 708
Home Sales & Other Direct Selling........ 708
Home Security Systems
See Security Products & Services 892
Home Warranty Services........ 708
Homecare Services
See Home Health Services 707
Homeland Security - US Department of
See US Department of Homeland Security........691
Homeowners Insurance
See Property & Casualty Insurance 743
Homes - Mobile
See Mobile Homes & Buildings........ 795
Homicide Clean-up Services
See Bio-Recovery Services........ 519
Honor Societies
See Greek Letter Societies 486
Horse Breeders........ 708
See also Livestock Improvement Services 470
Horse Racing
See Racing & Racetracks 856
Horse Trailers
See Trailers (Towing) & Trailer Hitches 923
Horseradish - Prepared
See Fruits & Vegetables - Pickled 661
Horses Insurance
See Animal Insurance........740
Horticultural Products Growers 708
See also Garden Centers 680; Seed Companies 894
Hose & Belting - Rubber or Plastics 709
See also Automotive Parts & Supplies - Mfr 507
Hose - Fire
See Safety Equipment - Mfr 886
Safety Equipment - Whol........ 886
Hose Couplings
See Hardware - Mfr 695
Hose Fittings - Fluid Power
See Valves & Hose Fittings - Fluid Power 935
Hospices........ 709
See also Specialty Hospitals 719
Hospital Equipment & Supplies
See Medical & Dental Equipment & Supplies - Whol........ 781
Hospital Furniture
See Institutional & Other Public Buildings Furniture 678
Hospital Gowns
See Personal Protective Equipment & Clothing 828
Hospital Hospitality Houses........ 711
Hospital Hospitality Houses - Ronald McDonald House 712
Hospital Management Consultants

See Management Services 776
Hospital Staffing Services
See Staffing Services 904
Hospitality Management Services
See Facilities Management Services 652
Hotels & Hotel Companies 722
Hospitalization Insurance
See Medical & Hospitalization Insurance 741
Hospitals 712
See also Health Care Providers - Ancillary 697; Health Care Systems 698; Hospices 709; Veterans Nursing Homes - State 936
Children's Hospitals 712
General Hospitals - Canada 712
General Hospitals - US 713
Military Hospitals 682
Psychiatric Hospitals 718
Rehabilitation Hospitals 719
Specialty Hospitals 719
Veterans Hospitals 720
Hospitals - Developmental Disabilities
See Developmental Centers 628
Hospitals - Veterinary
See Veterinary Hospitals 936
Hosted Software
See Application Service Providers (ASPs) 477
Hot Air Balloons
See Airships 475
Hot Dogs
See Meat Products - Prepared 663
Hot Tubs, Spas, Whirlpool Baths 720
Hotel Franchises
See Hotels & Hotel Companies 722
Hotel Furniture
See Commercial & Industrial Furniture 676
Hotel Management Companies
See Hotels & Hotel Companies 722
Hotel Management Training
See Vocational & Technical Schools 938
Hotel Owners
See Hotels & Hotel Companies 722
Hotel Reservations Services 720
Hotel Spas
See Spas - Hotel & Resort 897
Hotels & Hotel Companies 722
See also Casino Companies 531; Corporate Housing 619; Hotel Reservations Services 720; Hotels - Conference Center 721; Hotels - Frequent Stay Programs 721; Resorts & Resort Companies 873
Hotels - Conference Center 721
Hotels - Extended Stay
See Hotels & Hotel Companies 722
Hotels - Frequent Stay Programs 721
Household Appliances
See Appliance & Home Electronics Stores 476
Appliances - Major - Mfr 476
Appliances - Small - Mfr 476
Appliances - Whol 477
Vacuum Cleaners - Household 934
Household Cleaning Products
See Cleaning Products 544
Household Cleaning Supplies
See Mops, Sponges, Wiping Cloths 795
Household Laundry Equipment
See Appliance & Home Electronics Stores 476
Appliances - Major - Mfr 476
Appliances - Whol 477
Household Products - Metal
See Metal Products - Household 788
Household Products - Paper
See Paper Products - Sanitary 820
Household Products - Plastics
See Plastics Products - Household 838
Household Products - Textile
See Textile Products - Household 917
Household Storage
See Self-Storage Facilities 941
Housewares
See Appliances - Small - Mfr 476
Glassware & Pottery - Household 682
Metal Products - Household 788
Plastics Products - Household 838
Table & Kitchen Supplies - China & Earthenware 907
Housewares & Other Home Furnishings - Retail
See Home Furnishings Stores 706
Housing & Urban Development - US Department of
See US Department of Housing & Urban Development 691
Housing - Corporate
See Corporate Housing 619
Housing - Mobile
See Mobile Homes & Buildings 795
Housing Assistance Agencies - State
See Government - State 684
Housings - Appliance
See Electronic Enclosures 645
HTML Software
See Internet & Communications Software 588
Human Resources Management Services
See Management Services 776
Human Resources Software
See Business Software (General) 586
Human Rights Organizations
See Civil & Human Rights Organizations 484
Human Services - US Department of Health &
See US Department of Health & Human Services 690
Humanitarian Organizations
See Charitable & Humanitarian Organizations 481
Humidifiers
See Air Conditioning & Heating Equipment - Residential 472
Humidifiers - Portable
See Appliances - Small - Mfr 476
Appliances - Whol 477
Hunting Accessories
See Sporting Goods 899
Hunting Rifles
See Firearms & Ammunition (Non-Military) 655
Hurricane Shutters
See Shutters - Window (All Types) 896
HVAC Equipment
See Air Conditioning & Heating Equipment - Residential 472
Hybrid Microcircuits
See Semiconductors & Related Devices 894
Hydrated Lime
See Lime 764
Hydraulic Cement
See Cement 533
Hydraulic Cylinders & Actuators
See Cylinders & Actuators - Fluid Power 624
Hydraulic Presses
See Machine Tools - Metal Forming Types 768
Hydraulic Pumps
See Pumps & Motors - Fluid Power 856
Hydraulic Tools
See Tools - Power 921
Hydraulic Valves
See Valves & Hose Fittings - Fluid Power 935
Hydrojet Systems
See Pumps & Pumping Equipment (General Use) 856

I

Ice - Manufactured 733
Ice Cream
See Dairy Products - Whol 666
Ice Cream & Dairy Stores 733
Ice Cream & Frozen Desserts 662
Ice Cream & Dairy Stores 733
Ice Cream Containers
See Boxes - Paperboard 524
Ice Hockey
See Sports Teams - Hockey 903
Identification Equipment
See Biometric Identification Equipment & Software 519
Illustrators
See Graphic Design 694
Imaging Equipment & Systems - Medical 733
See also Medical Instruments & Apparatus - Mfr 782
Imaging Services - Diagnostic 734
Imaging Software
See Multimedia & Design Software 589
Immunoassay
See Diagnostic Products 628
Import/Export Information
See Embassies & Consulates - Foreign, in the US 645
US Department of Commerce 690
Importers Associations
See Sales & Marketing Professional Associations 499
In Vitro & In Vivo Diagnostics
See Diagnostic Products 628
In-Flight Magazines
See Travel & Regional Interest Magazines 773
Incentive Program Management Services 734
See also Conference & Events Coordinators 596
Income Assistance Agencies - State
See Government - State 684
Incontinence Products
See Paper Products - Sanitary 820
Incubators
See Electromedical & Electrotherapeutic Equipment 642
Farm Machinery & Equipment - Mfr 652
Farm Machinery & Equipment - Whol 653
Venture Capital Firms 936
Indemnity Insurance
See Medical & Hospitalization Insurance 741
Index Cards
See Paperboard & Cardboard - Die-Cut 821
Indian Tribal Colleges
See Colleges - Tribal 557
Inductors - Electronic
See Electronic Components & Accessories - Mfr 643
Industrial Air Conditioning & Heating Equipment
See Air Conditioning & Heating Equipment - Commercial/Industrial 471
Industrial Automation Software
See Engineering Software 588
Professional Software (Industry-Specific) 589
Industrial Cases
See Luggage, Bags, Cases 767
Industrial Chemicals
See Chemicals - Industrial (Inorganic) 541
Chemicals - Industrial (Organic) 541
Industrial Cleaners
See Cleaning Products 544
Industrial Cleaning Services
See Cleaning Services 545
Industrial Controls
See Controls & Relays - Electrical 612
Industrial Design
See Engineering & Design 647
Industrial Drives (High Speed)
See Speed Changers, Industrial High Speed Drives, Gears 899
Industrial Equipment & Supplies (Misc) - Whol 734
Industrial Fasteners
See Fasteners & Fastening Systems 654
Industrial Films
See Motion Picture Production - Special Interest 796
Industrial Fluids
See Chemicals - Specialty 542
Industrial Gases
See Chemicals - Industrial (Inorganic) 541
Industrial Glass Products
See Glass Products - Industrial (Custom) 682
Industrial Lasers
See Lasers - Industrial 756
Industrial Launderers
See Linen & Uniform Supply 764
Industrial Laundry Equipment & Supplies
See Laundry Equipment & Supplies - Commercial & Industrial 756
Industrial Machinery - Whol
See Industrial Equipment & Supplies (Misc) - Whol 734
Industrial Machinery, Equipment, & Supplies 735
See also Conveyors & Conveying Equipment 618; Food Products Machinery 668; Furnaces & Ovens - Industrial Process 676; Machine Shops 767; Material Handling Equipment 779; Packaging Machinery & Equipment 817; Paper Industries Machinery 820; Printing & Publishing Equipment & Systems 848; Rolling Mill Machinery 885; Textile Machinery 916; Woodworking Machinery 945
Industrial Paper
See Paper Products - Whol 821
Industrial Patterns
See Patterns - Industrial 825
Industrial Process Controls
See Controls - Industrial Process 611
Industrial Process Furnaces & Ovens
See Furnaces & Ovens - Industrial Process 676
Industrial Pumps
See Pumps & Pumping Equipment (General Use) 856
Industrial Supplies - Whol
See Industrial Equipment & Supplies (Misc) - Whol 734

Industry Publications
See Trade & Industry Magazines .773
Trade & Industry Newsletters .807
Industry-Specific Software
See Professional Software (Industry-Specific) .589
Infants' Clothing
See Baby Products 510
Children's & Infants' Clothing .545
Children's Clothing Stores .547
Family Clothing Stores .547
Infomercials
See Motion Picture Production - Special Interest 796
Information - Health & Medical - Online
See Health & Medical Information - Online 699
Information Centers
See Libraries 759
Information Retrieval Services (General) 736
See also Investigative Services 748
Information Science Associations
See Library & Information Science Associations .497
Information Systems
See Computer Networking Products & Systems 582
Information Technology Management Services
See Management Services 776
Information Transaction Machines (ITMs)
See Point-of-Sale (POS) & Point-of-Information (POI) Systems 841
Infrared Lamps
See Light Bulbs & Tubes 763
Infusion Therapy Services
See Health Care Providers - Ancillary 697
Ink 738
Inked Ribbon
See Printing & Photocopying Supplies 847
Inkjet Printers
See Printers .580
Inorganic Chemicals - Industrial
See Chemicals - Industrial (Inorganic) 541
Insecticides
See Farm Supplies 653
Fertilizers & Pesticides 654
Inspection Services - Home
See Home Inspection Services 708
Instant Messaging Services
See Internet Service Providers (ISPs) 748
Instructional Videos
See Motion Picture Production - Special Interest 796
Instrument Cases
See Luggage, Bags, Cases 767
Instruments - Aeronautical & Nautical
See Navigation & Guidance Instruments & Systems 805
Instruments - Dental
See Dental Equipment & Supplies - Mfr 627
Instruments - Laboratory
See Laboratory Analytical Instruments 754
Instruments - Measuring, Testing, Controlling
See Electrical Signals Measuring & Testing Instruments 642
Measuring, Testing, Controlling Instruments 780
Instruments - Medical
See Electromedical & Electrotherapeutic Equipment 642
Imaging Equipment & Systems - Medical 733
Laser Equipment & Systems - Medical 756
Medical Instruments & Apparatus - Mfr 782
Instruments - Musical
See Musical Instrument Stores 803
Musical Instruments 803
Instruments - Navigation & Guidance
See Navigation & Guidance Instruments & Systems 805
Instruments - Optical
See Optical Instruments & Lenses 816
Instruments - Scanning
See Scanning Equipment .580
Instruments - Surgical
See Medical Instruments & Apparatus - Mfr 782
Insulation & Acoustical Products 738
Insulation Contractors
See Plastering, Drywall, Acoustical, Insulation Contractors .600
Insulation Materials
See Insulation & Acoustical Products 738
Roofing, Siding, Insulation Materials .604
Insurance Agents, Brokers, Services 738
Insurance Companies 740
See also Home Warranty Services 708; Viatical Settlement Companies 937
Animal Insurance 740
Life & Accident Insurance 740
Medical & Hospitalization Insurance 741
Property & Casualty Insurance 743
Surety Insurance 745
Title Insurance 746
Travel Insurance 746
Insurance Regulators - State
See Government - State 684
Integrated Circuits
See Semiconductors & Related Devices 894
Integrators - Computer
See Computer Systems Design Services 592
Interactive Billing Software
See Business Software (General) .586
Intercity Bus Services
See Bus Services - Intercity & Rural 526
Intercom Equipment & Systems 746
Interface Equipment
See Modems .579
Interior - US Department of the
See US Department of the Interior .691
Interior Design 746
Intermodal Transportation Equipment Rental
See Transport Equipment Rental .650
Internet Backbone Providers 747
Internet Broadcasting 747
Internet Child Care Monitoring Services
See Child Care Monitoring Systems - Internet 543
Internet Connectivity
See Internet Backbone Providers 747
Internet Directories
See Internet Search Engines, Portals, Directories 748
Internet Domain Name Registrars 747
Internet Magazines
See Computer & Internet Magazines .770
Internet Newsletters
See Computer & Internet Newsletters .806
Internet Organizations
See Computer & Internet Organizations .484
Internet Search Engines, Portals, Directories 748
Internet Service Providers (ISPs) 748
Internet Telephone & Voice Mail Services
See Telecommunications Services 908
Internet Telephony Software
See Internet & Communications Software .588
Interpreters
See Translation Services 924
Interval Vacations
See Timeshare Companies 918
Inventory Books
See Blankbooks & Binders 520
Inventory Services 748
Investigation Services - Credit
See Credit Reporting Services 622
Investigative Services 748
See also Information Retrieval Services (General) 736; Public Records Search Services 849; Security & Protective Services 893
Investment (Misc) 751
See also Banks - Commercial & Savings 511; Commodity Contracts Brokers & Dealers 578; Franchises 672; Investment Guides - Online 751; Mortgage Lenders & Loan Brokers 795; Mutual Funds 803; Investment Newsletters 807; Real Estate Investment Trusts (REITs) 868; Royalty Trusts 885; Securities Brokers & Dealers 890; Venture Capital Firms 936
Investment Advice & Management 748
See also Commodity Contracts Brokers & Dealers 578; Investment Guides - Online 751; Mutual Funds 803; Securities Brokers & Dealers 890
Investment Banks
See Securities Brokers & Dealers 890
Investment Companies - Small Business 750
Investment Companies - Specialized Small Business 751
Investment Companies - Venture Capital
See Venture Capital Firms 936
Investment Foundries
See Foundries - Investment 671
Investment Guides - Online 751
See also Buyer's Guides - Online 528
Investment Refractories
See Refractories - Nonclay 870
Investment Research
See Investment Guides - Online 751
Investment Software
See Professional Software (Industry-Specific) .589
Investment Trusts
See Real Estate Investment Trusts (REITs) 868
Royalty Trusts 885
Invitations
See Cards - Greeting - Mfr 531
Invoicing Software
See Business Software (General) .586
IPO Underwriters
See Securities Brokers & Dealers 890
Iron - Ornamental
See Metal Work - Architectural & Ornamental 789
Iron Foundries
See Foundries - Iron & Steel 671
Iron Ore Mining
See Mining - Metals 793
Irons - Electric
See Appliances - Small - Mfr 476
Irrigation Equipment
See Farm Machinery & Equipment - Mfr 652
Farm Machinery & Equipment - Whol 653
Lawn & Garden Equipment 758
Islamic Organizations
See Religious Organizations .489
Isoprene Rubbers
See Synthetic Rubber .838
ISPs (Internet Service Providers)
See Internet Service Providers (ISPs) 748
IT Training & Certification
See Training & Certification Programs - Computer & Internet 923
ITMs (Information Transaction Machines)
See Point-of-Sale (POS) & Point-of-Information (POI) Systems 841

J

Jackets
See Coats (Overcoats, Jackets, Raincoats, etc) .546
Men's Clothing .546
Women's Clothing .547
Jams & Jellies
See Fruits, Vegetables, Juices - Canned or Preserved .661
Janitorial & Cleaning Supplies - Whol 751
Janitorial Products
See Cleaning Products 544
Janitorial Services
See Cleaning Services 545
Java Software
See Computer Languages & Development Tools .587
Jazz Associations
See Arts & Artists Organizations .481
Jellies & Jams
See Fruits, Vegetables, Juices - Canned or Preserved .661
Jesuit Colleges & Universities
See Colleges & Universities - Jesuit 578
Jet Skis
See Sporting Goods 899
Jewelers' Findings & Materials 751
Jewelry - Costume 751
Jewelry - Precious Metal 751
Jewelry Boxes
See Boxes - Paperboard 524
Containers - Wood 611
Jewelry Stores 752
Jewelry, Watches, Gems - Whol 752
Jewish Organizations
See Religious Organizations .489
Jigs & Fixtures (Metalworking)
See Tool & Die Shops 919
Jobs
See Employment Offices - Government 646
Employment Services - Online 646
Executive Recruiting Firms 651
Staffing Services 904
Jokes Software
See Personal Software .589
Journal Bearings
See Power Transmission Equipment - Mechanical 843
Journals
See Magazines & Journals 768

Journals - Blank
See Blankbooks & Binders 520
Joysticks
See Computer Input Devices 579
Juices
See Fruits, Vegetables, Juices - Canned or Preserved 661
Fruits, Vegetables, Juices - Frozen 662
Jukeboxes
See Automatic Merchandising Equipment & Systems 504
Junior Colleges
See Colleges - Community & Junior 550
Justice - US Department of
See US Department of Justice 691
Juvenile Detention Facilities 752
See also Correctional & Detention Management (Privatized) 619; Correctional Facilities - State 619
Juvenile Furniture
See Household Furniture 677

K

Kaolin Clay
See Clay, Ceramic, Refractory Minerals Mining 794
Kayaks
See Sporting Goods 899
Keratotomy
See Vision Correction Centers 937
Ketchup
See Fruits, Vegetables, Juices - Canned or Preserved 661
Ketones - Whol
See Chemicals & Related Products - Whol 543
Keyboard Software
See Systems & Utilities Software 591
Keyboards - Computer
See Computer Input Devices 579
Keyboards - Musical
See Musical Instrument Stores 803
Musical Instruments 803
Kitchen Appliances
See Appliances - Major - Mfr 476
Appliances - Small - Mfr 476
Kitchen Cabinets
See Cabinets - Wood 528
Carpentry & Flooring Contractors 599
Kitchen Fixtures
See Plumbing Fixtures & Fittings - Metal 839
Plumbing Fixtures & Fittings - Vitreous China & Earthenware 840
Kitchen Gadgets
See Metal Products - Household 788
Plastics Products - Household 838
Kitchen Supplies
See Table & Kitchen Supplies - China & Earthenware 907
Kitchen Utensils - Metal
See Metal Products - Household 788
Metal Stampings 789
Silverware 897
Kitty Litter
See Pet Products 829
Knee Pads
See Personal Protective Equipment & Clothing 828
Knives
See Cutlery 624
Knives - Shear
See Metalworking Devices & Accessories 791

L

Labeling Machines
See Business Machines - Mfr 527
Labels - Fabric
See Narrow Fabric Mills 917
Labels - Other Than Fabric 752
Labor - US Department of
See US Department of Labor 691
Labor Providers
See Staffing Services 904
Labor Unions 753
Laboratories - Dental 753
See also Laboratories - Medical 754
Laboratories - Drug-Testing 754
See also Laboratories - Medical 754
Laboratories - Genetic Testing 754
See also Laboratories - Medical 754
Laboratories - Medical 754
See also Blood Centers 520; Laboratories - Dental 753; Laboratories - Drug-Testing 754; Laboratories - Genetic Testing 754; Organ & Tissue Banks 817
Laboratories - Photofinishing
See Photo Processing & Storage 833
Laboratories - Testing
See Laboratories - Drug-Testing 754
Laboratories - Genetic Testing 754
Testing Facilities 915
Laboratory Analytical Instruments 754
See also Glassware - Laboratory & Scientific 682; Laboratory Apparatus & Furniture 755
Laboratory Animal Cages
See Baskets, Cages, Racks, etc - Wire 516
Laboratory Apparatus & Furniture 755
See also Glassware - Laboratory & Scientific 682; Laboratory Analytical Instruments 754; Scales & Balances 887
Lace
See Knitting Mills 917
Lacquers
See Paints, Varnishes, Related Products 818
Ladders 756
Laminated Fabric
See Coated Fabric 916
Laminated Flooring
See Flooring - Resilient 657
Laminated Paper
See Coated & Laminated Paper 819
Packaging Materials & Products - Paper or Plastics 818
Laminated Paperboard/Cardboard
See Paperboard & Cardboard - Die-Cut 821
Laminated Plastics
See Packaging Materials & Products - Paper or Plastics 818
Plastics - Laminated - Plate, Sheet, Profile Shapes 835
Laminates - Metal
See Foil & Leaf - Metal 658
Lamp Black
See Chemicals - Industrial (Inorganic) 541
Lamps
See Light Bulbs & Tubes 763
Lamps - Marker
See Lighting Equipment - Vehicular 763
Land Developers
See Real Estate Developers 867
Landmarks
See Monuments, Memorials, Landmarks 501
Landscape Design & Related Services 756
Landscaping Products
See Lawn & Garden Equipment 758
Language Learning Software - Foreign Language
See Educational & Reference Software 587
Language Schools 756
See also Translation Services 924
LANs (Local Area Networks)
See Computer Networking Products & Systems 582
Lapidary Work
See Jewelers' Findings & Materials 751
Laptop Computers
See Computers 578
Laser Discs
See Book, Music, Video Clubs 522
Music Stores 803
Recording Companies 870
Laser Equipment & Systems - Medical 756
See also Medical Instruments & Apparatus - Mfr 782
Laser Printers
See Printers 580
Laser Surgery
See Vision Correction Centers 937
Lasers - Industrial 756
LASIK (Laser-Assisted Intrastomal Keratomileusis)
See Vision Correction Centers 937
Latex
See Synthetic Rubber 838
Latex Gloves
See Personal Protective Equipment & Clothing 828
Lathe-Cut Rubber Goods
See Rubber Goods - Mechanical 886
Launch Vehicles
See Missiles, Space Vehicles, Parts 794
Launderers - Industrial
See Linen & Uniform Supply 764
Laundromats
See Laundry & Drycleaning Services 756
Laundry & Drycleaning Services 756
See also Linen & Uniform Supply 764
Laundry Detergents & Soaps
See Cleaning Products 544
Laundry Equipment & Supplies - Commercial & Industrial 756
Laundry Equipment - Household
See Appliance & Home Electronics Stores 476
Appliances - Major - Mfr 476
Appliances - Whol 477
Lavatories
See Plumbing Fixtures & Fittings - Vitreous China & Earthenware 840
Law Enforcement Equipment
See Personal Protective Equipment & Clothing 828
Safety Equipment - Whol 886
Law Enforcement Training Facilities
See Simulation & Training Systems 897
Law Firms 756
See also Arbitration Services - Legal 478; Legal Professionals Associations 497; Bar Associations - State 516; Litigation Support Services 764
Law Newsletters
See Government & Law Newsletters 806
Lawn & Garden Equipment 758
See also Farm Machinery & Equipment - Mfr 652
Lawn Furniture
See Outdoor Furniture 678
Lawn Mowers
See Lawn & Garden Equipment 758
Lawn Ornaments - Plastics
See Plastics Products - Household 838
LCDs (Liquid Crystal Displays)
See Monitors & Displays 579
Lead Mining
See Mining - Metals 793
Learning Centers - Children's
See Children's Learning Centers 543
Lease Financing
See Credit & Financing - Commercial 621
Credit & Financing - Consumer 620
Leather Finishing Agents
See Chemicals - Specialty 542
Leather Goods (Misc) 759
Leather Goods - Personal 759
See also Clothing & Accessories - Mfr 545; Footwear 669; Handbags, Totes, Backpacks 695; Leather Goods (Misc) 759; Luggage, Bags, Cases 767
Leather Tanning & Finishing 759
Ledgers
See Blankbooks & Binders 520
Legal Malpractice Insurance
See Surety Insurance 745
Legal Pads
See Writing Paper 819
Legal Services
See Arbitration Services - Legal 478
Law Firms 756
Legal Staffing Services
See Staffing Services 904
Legal Videography
See Litigation Support Services 764
Legislation Hotlines 759
Legislatures
See Government - State 684
Government - US - Legislative Branch 694
Lemons
See Citrus Growers 675
Lenses
See Ophthalmic Goods 816
Optical Goods Stores 816
Optical Instruments & Lenses 816
LEO (Low Earth Orbit) Satellites
See Satellite Communications Services 886
Liability Insurance
See Surety Insurance 745
Librarians' Associations
See Library & Information Science Associations 497
Library Associations - State & Province 763

Index

Libraries 759
See also Library Systems - Regional - Canadian 763
Medical Libraries 759
Presidential Libraries 759
Public Libraries 759
Special Collections Libraries 761
State Libraries 761
University Libraries 761
Library Associations - State & Province 763
Library Furniture
See Institutional & Other Public Buildings Furniture 678
Library Systems - Regional - Canadian 763
Life Insurance
See Life & Accident Insurance 740
Travel Insurance 746
Life Preservers, Life Rafts, Lifeboats
See Safety Equipment - Mfr 886
Life Vests
See Personal Protective Equipment & Clothing 828
Lifelines
See Safety Equipment - Mfr 886
Lifts
See Material Handling Equipment 779
Light Bulbs & Tubes 763
Lighting Ballasts
See Transformers - Power, Distribution, Specialty 924
Lighting Equipment - Vehicular 763
Lighting Equipment - Whol
See Electrical & Electronic Equipment & Parts - Whol 639
Lighting Fixtures & Equipment 763
Lighting Services - Stage
See Stage Equipment & Services 904
Lignite Surface Mining
See Mining - Coal 793
Lime 764
Limestone - Crushed & Broken
See Stone Quarries - Crushed & Broken Stone 794
Limestone - Cutting & Finishing
See Stone (Cut) & Stone Products 905
Limousine Services 764
Linen & Uniform Supply 764
Linens
See Home Furnishings - Whol 706
Home Furnishings Stores 706
Textile Products - Household 917
Lingerie
See Sleepwear 547
Undergarments 547
Linoleum
See Flooring - Resilient 657
Liquefied Petroleum - Bottled
See Fuel Dealers 675
Liquid Crystal Displays (LCDs)
See Monitors & Displays 579
Liquor - Whol
See Wine & Liquor - Whol 518
Liquor Stores 764
Lithographic Printing
See Printing Companies - Commercial Printers 845
Lithotripsy Services
See Health Care Providers - Ancillary 697
Litigation Support Services 764
Livestock & Poultry Feeds - Prepared 765
Livestock - Whol 765
See also Cattle Ranches, Farms, Feedlots (Beef Cattle) 469; Hog Farms 469
Livestock Feeders
See Farm Machinery & Equipment - Mfr 652
Livestock Insurance
See Animal Insurance 740
Livestock Trailers
See Truck Trailers 928
Loan Brokers
See Mortgage Lenders & Loan Brokers 795
Loans - College
See Credit & Financing - Consumer 620
Student Assistance Programs 905
Local Area Networks
See Computer Networking Products & Systems 582
Lockers
See Commercial & Industrial Furniture 676
Fixtures - Office & Store 656
Institutional & Other Public Buildings Furniture 678
Security Products & Services 892
Locks
See Hardware - Mfr 695
Hardware - Whol 697
Locomotives (Frames & Parts)
See Railroad Equipment - Mfr 866
Log Homes - Prefabricated
See Buildings - Prefabricated - Wood 525
Logging 765
Logging Equipment
See Construction Machinery & Equipment 602
Logic Modules - Computer
See Semiconductors & Related Devices 894
Logistics Services (Transportation & Warehousing) 765
See also Freight Forwarders 673; Marine Services 777; Rail Transport Services 866; Trucking Companies 928; Commercial Warehousing 941
Long-Distance Telephone Service
See Telecommunications Services 908
Long-Term Care Facilities 766
See also Retirement Communities 884; Veterans Nursing Homes - State 936
Looseleaf Binders & Devices
See Blankbooks & Binders 520
Looseleaf Filler
See Writing Paper 819
Lotteries, Games, Sweepstakes 767
See also Games & Gaming 680
Lottery Software
See Games & Entertainment Software 588
Low Earth Orbit (LEO) Satellites
See Satellite Communications Services 886
LP Gas - Bottled
See Fuel Dealers 675
Lube & Oil Service
See Repair Service (General) - Automotive 509
Lubricants
See Oils & Greases - Lubricating 815
Luggage Racks
See Automotive Parts & Supplies - Mfr 507
Luggage, Bags, Cases 767
See also Handbags, Totes, Backpacks 695; Leather Goods - Personal 759
Lumber
See Home Improvement Centers 707
Lumber & Building Supplies 603
Sawmills & Planing Mills 887
Lunch Meats
See Meat Products - Prepared 663
Luxury Spas
See Spas - Hotel & Resort 897

M

Macadamia Nuts
See Tree Nuts Growers 470
Macaroni
See Pasta 664
Machine Shops 767
See also Precision Machined Products 843
Machine Tool Accessories
See Metalworking Devices & Accessories 791
Machine Tool Design
See Engineering & Design 647
Machine Tools - Metal Cutting Types 767
See also Machine Tools - Metal Forming Types 768; Metalworking Devices & Accessories 791
Machine Tools - Metal Forming Types 768
See also Machine Tools - Metal Cutting Types 767; Metalworking Devices & Accessories 791; Rolling Mill Machinery 885; Tool & Die Shops 919
Machined Products - Precision Machining
See Precision Machined Products 843
Machinists' Precision Measuring Devices
See Metalworking Devices & Accessories 791
Magazine Distributors
See Books, Periodicals, Newspapers - Whol 522
Magazines & Journals 768
See also Periodicals Publishers 854
Agriculture & Farming Magazines 768
Art & Architecture Magazines 768
Automotive Magazines 769
Boating Magazines 769
Business & Finance Magazines 769
Children's & Youth Magazines 769
Computer & Internet Magazines 770
Education Magazines & Journals 770
Entertainment & Music Magazines 770
Fraternal & Special Interest Magazines 770
General Interest Magazines 770
Government & Military Magazines 771
Health & Fitness Magazines 771
Hobby & Personal Interests Magazines 771
Law Magazines & Journals 772
Medical Magazines & Journals 772
Political & Current Events Magazines 772
Religious & Spiritual Magazines 772
Science & Nature Magazines 772
Sports Magazines 773
Trade & Industry Magazines 773
Travel & Regional Interest Magazines 773
Magazines - In-Flight
See Travel & Regional Interest Magazines 773
Magnetic Recording Media
See Recording Media - Magnetic & Optical 870
Magnetic Resonance Imaging (MRI) Equipment
See Imaging Equipment & Systems - Medical 733
Magnetic Resonance Imaging (MRI) Services
See Imaging Services - Diagnostic 734
Magnetic Shielding
See Metal Industries (Misc) 788
Magnets - Permanent 774
Magnets - Refrigerator
See Gifts & Novelties - Whol 681
Maid Services
See Cleaning Services 545
Mail Order Houses 774
See also Art Supply Stores 479; Book, Music, Video Clubs 522; Checks - Personal & Business 541; Computer Stores 592; Seed Companies 894
Mailing List Compilers
See Advertising Services - Direct Mail 467
Mailing Machines
See Business Machines - Mfr 527
Mailing Services
See Advertising Services - Direct Mail 467
Business Service Centers 528
Package Delivery Services 817
Mailing Software
See Internet & Communications Software 588
Mainframe Computers
See Computers 578
Maintenance Services
See Building Maintenance Services 525
Major League Baseball (MLB)
See Sports Teams 902
Makeup
See Cosmetics, Skin Care, and Other Personal Care Products 620
Malleable Iron Castings
See Foundries - Iron & Steel 671
Malls - Shopping 775
Malpractice Insurance
See Surety Insurance 745
Malt Beverages
See Beer & Ale - Whol 518
Breweries 524
Malting Products 775
See also Breweries 524
Mammography Services
See Imaging Services - Diagnostic 734
Mammography Systems
See Imaging Equipment & Systems - Medical 733
Managed Care
See Medical & Hospitalization Insurance 741
Managed Care - Behavioral Health 775
Management - Correctional & Detention (Privatized)
See Correctional & Detention Management (Privatized) 619
Management Seminars
See Training Programs - Corporate 923
Management Services 776
See also Association Management Companies 479; Educational Institution Operators & Managers 632; Facilities Management Services 652; Hotels & Hotel Companies 722; Incentive Program Management Services 734; Investment Advice & Management 748; Pharmacy Benefits Management Services 833

Index

Management Software
See Business Software (General) ... 586
Mangos
See Fruit Growers (Misc) ... 675
Manicure Tables
See Beauty Salon Equipment & Supplies ... 517
Manicurists
See Beauty Salons ... 517
Manifold Business Forms
See Business Forms ... 526
Manmade Fibers
See Broadwoven Fabric Mills ... 916
Synthetic Fibers & Filaments ... 837
Mannequins & Display Forms ... 777
Manufactured Housing
See Mobile Homes & Buildings ... 795
Manufactured Ice
See Ice - Manufactured ... 733
Manufacturers Associations
See Associations & Organizations - Professional & Trade ... 491
Manufacturing Software - Computer-Aided
See Professional Software (Industry-Specific) ... 589
Map Publishers
See Atlas & Map Publishers ... 850
Maple Syrup
See Syrup - Maple ... 665
Mapping Services
See Surveying, Mapping, Related Services ... 906
Mapping Software
See Multimedia & Design Software ... 589
Marble - Cutting & Finishing
See Stone (Cut) & Stone Products ... 905
Marble Quarrying
See Stone Quarries - Dimension Stone ... 794
Marble Refinishing
See Remodeling, Refinishing, Resurfacing Contractors ... 601
Margarine
See Oils - Edible (Margarine, Shortening, Table Oils, etc) ... 664
Marine Cargo Container Rental
See Transport Equipment Rental ... 650
Marine Cargo Handling
See Marine Services ... 777
Marine Insurance
See Property & Casualty Insurance ... 743
Marine Parts & Supplies
See Transportation Equipment & Supplies - Whol ... 924
Marine Pumps
See Pumps & Pumping Equipment (General Use) ... 856
Marine Salvage Services
See Marine Services ... 777
Marine Services ... 777
See also Freight Transport - Deep Sea (Domestic Ports) 674; Freight Transport - Deep Sea (Foreign Ports) 674; Freight Transport - Inland Waterways 674; Logistics Services (Transportation & Warehousing) 765
Marine Towing Services
See Marine Services ... 777
Market Makers
See Securities Brokers & Dealers ... 890
Market Research Firms ... 778
See also
Marketers Associations
See Sales & Marketing Professional Associations ... 499
Marketing - Direct Mail
See Advertising Services - Direct Mail ... 467
Marketing - Online
See Advertising Services - Online ... 468
Marketing - Telephone
See Telemarketing & Other Tele-Services ... 910
Marketing Consulting Services
See Consulting Services - Marketing ... 607
Marketing Software
See Business Software (General) ... 586
Marketing Support Services
See Advertising Agencies ... 466
Marking Devices ... 778
Masking Tape
See Tape - Cellophane, Gummed, Masking, Pressure Sensitive ... 907
Masks - Protective
See Personal Protective Equipment & Clothing ... 828
Masonry Cement
See Cement ... 533
Mass Transportation (Local & Suburban) ... 779
See also Bus Services - Intercity & Rural 526
Massage Tables
See Beauty Salon Equipment & Supplies ... 517
Medical & Dental Equipment & Supplies - Whol ... 781
Matches & Matchbooks ... 779
Matchmaking Services
See Dating Services ... 626
Material Handling Equipment ... 779
See also Conveyors & Conveying Equipment 618
Materials Testing
See Testing Facilities ... 915
Maternity Wear
See Women's Clothing ... 547
Mathematics Research
See Research Centers & Institutions ... 871
Mats
See Carpets & Rugs ... 531
Rubber Goods ... 885
Mattress Covers
See Textile Products - Household ... 917
Mattress Springs
See Springs - Light-Gauge ... 903
Mattresses & Adjustable Beds ... 780
See also Household Furniture 677
Mayonnaise
See Fruits & Vegetables - Pickled ... 661
Meal Replacement Powders
See Vitamins & Nutritional Supplements ... 937
Measuring Devices
See Measuring, Testing, Controlling Instruments ... 780
Metalworking Devices & Accessories ... 791
Measuring, Testing, Controlling Instruments ... 780
See also Electrical Signals Measuring & Testing Instruments 642
Meat Packing Plants ... 781
See also Poultry Processing 842
Mechanical Contractors
See Plumbing, Heating, Air Conditioning Contractors ... 601
Mechanical Engineers
See Engineering & Design ... 647
Mechanical Power Transmission Equipment
See Power Transmission Equipment - Mechanical ... 843
Mechanical Rubber Goods
See Rubber Goods - Mechanical ... 886
Medical & Dental Equipment & Supplies - Whol ... 781
Medical & Pharmaceutical Industry Software
See Professional Software (Industry-Specific) ... 589
Medical Associations - State ... 781
See also Health & Medical Professionals Associations 494
Medical Associations - Veterinary (State)
See Veterinary Medical Associations - State ... 936
Medical Centers - Veterans
See Veterans Hospitals ... 720
Medical Equipment - Mfr
See Electromedical & Electrotherapeutic Equipment ... 642
Imaging Equipment & Systems - Medical ... 733
Laser Equipment & Systems - Medical ... 756
Medical Instruments & Apparatus - Mfr ... 782
Medical Examiners - State
See Government - State ... 684
Medical Facilities
See Developmental Centers ... 628
Health Care Providers - Ancillary ... 697
Hospices ... 709
Hospitals ... 712
Imaging Services - Diagnostic ... 734
Substance Abuse Treatment Centers ... 906
Medical Information - Online
See Health & Medical Information - Online ... 699
Medical Instruments & Apparatus - Mfr ... 782
See also Imaging Equipment & Systems - Medical 733; Medical Supplies - Mfr 784
Medical Laboratories
See Laboratories - Medical ... 754
Medical Malpractice Insurance
See Surety Insurance ... 745
Medical Management Services
See Management Services ... 776
Medical Professionals Associations
See Health & Medical Professionals Associations ... 494
Medical Research
See Research Centers & Institutions ... 871
Medical Savings Accounts
See Medical & Hospitalization Insurance ... 741
Medical Staffing Services
See Staffing Services ... 904
Medical Supplies - Mfr ... 784
See also Personal Protective Equipment & Clothing 828
Medical Transcription Services ... 785
Medical Transport
See Ambulance Services ... 475
Medical Waste Disposal
See Waste Management ... 941
Medicinal Chemicals & Botanical Products ... 786
See also Biotechnology Companies 519; Diagnostic Products 628; Pharmaceutical Companies 831; Pharmaceutical Companies - Generic Drugs 832; Vitamins & Nutritional Supplements 937
Medium Earth Orbit (MEO) Satellites
See Satellite Communications Services ... 886
Meeting Planners
See Conference & Events Coordinators ... 596
Melons
See Fruit Growers (Misc) ... 675
Vegetable Farms ... 470
Memo Pads
See Writing Paper ... 819
Memorials - National
See Monuments, Memorials, Landmarks ... 501
Memory Devices - Flash
See Flash Memory Devices ... 656
Memory Management Software
See Systems & Utilities Software ... 591
Mental Health Facilities
See Developmental Centers ... 628
Psychiatric Hospitals ... 718
Mental Health Managed Care
See Managed Care - Behavioral Health ... 775
Mental Health Organizations
See Health & Health-Related Organizations ... 486
Mental Retardation Centers
See Developmental Centers ... 628
MEO (Medium Earth Orbit) Satellites
See Satellite Communications Services ... 886
Merchandise Bags
See Bags - Paper ... 510
Bags - Plastics ... 510
Merchandising Equipment - Automatic
See Automatic Merchandising Equipment & Systems ... 504
Merger & Acquisition Services
See Litigation Support Services ... 764
MESBICs (Minority Enterprise Small Business Investment Companies)
See Investment Companies - Specialized Small Business ... 751
Mesh - Wire
See Screening - Woven Wire ... 890
Message Boards
See Office & School Supplies ... 812
Messenger Services
See Package Delivery Services ... 817
Metal - Precious
See Jewelry - Precious Metal ... 751
Mining - Metals ... 793
Metal - Sheet
See Plumbing, Heating, Air Conditioning Contractors ... 601
Roofing, Siding, Sheet Metal Contractors ... 601
Sheet Metal Work ... 895
Metal - Structural (Fabricated) ... 786
Metal Alloys
See Foundries - Nonferrous (Castings) ... 671
Metal Buildings - Prefabricated
See Buildings - Prefabricated - Metal ... 525
Metal Cans
See Cans - Metal ... 530
Metal Castings
See Foundries - Investment ... 671
Foundries - Iron & Steel ... 671
Foundries - Nonferrous (Castings) ... 671
Metal Closures
See Closures - Metal or Plastics ... 545
Metal Coating, Plating, Engraving ... 787
Metal Conditioners
See Chemicals - Specialty ... 542
Metal Doors & Windows
See Doors & Windows - Metal ... 630
Metal Fabricating - Custom ... 787
Metal Fasteners
See Fasteners & Fastening Systems ... 654
Metal Finishing Agents

See Chemicals - Specialty ... 542
Metal Foil & Leaf
See Foil & Leaf - Metal ... 658
Metal Forgings ... 787
Metal Furniture
See Furniture - Mfr ... 676
Metal Heat Treating ... 787
Metal Industries (Misc) ... 788
See also Foundries - Investment 671; Foundries - Iron & Steel 671; Foundries - Nonferrous (Castings) 671; Metal Heat Treating 787; Metal Tube & Pipe 789; Steel - Mfr 905; Wire & Cable 943
Metal Laminates
See Foil & Leaf - Metal ... 658
Metal Mining
See Mining - Metals ... 793
Metal Plate Work - Fabricated
See Boiler Shops ... 521
Metal Plumbing Fixtures
See Plumbing Fixtures & Fittings - Metal ... 839
Metal Products (Misc) ... 788
Metal Products - Household ... 788
Metal Stampings ... 789
See also Closures - Metal or Plastics 545; Electronic Enclosures 645; Metal Stampings - Automotive 789
Metal Stampings - Automotive ... 789
See also Automotive Parts & Supplies - Mfr 507
Metal Stamps
See Marking Devices ... 778
Metal Tube & Pipe ... 789
Metal Work - Architectural & Ornamental ... 789
Metallized Fabric
See Coated Fabric ... 916
Metals - Recyclable
See Scrap Metal ... 889
Metals Marketing
See Metals Service Centers ... 790
Metals Mining
See Mining - Metals ... 793
Metals Service Centers ... 790
Metalworking Devices & Accessories ... 791
See also Machine Tools - Metal Cutting Types 767; Machine Tools - Metal Forming Types 768; Tool & Die Shops 919
Metalworking Equipment
See Machine Tools - Metal Cutting Types ... 767
Machine Tools - Metal Forming Types ... 768
Metalworking Devices & Accessories ... 791
Patterns - Industrial ... 825
Tool & Die Shops ... 919
Welding & Soldering Equipment ... 942
Metalworking Fluids
See Chemicals - Specialty ... 542
Metalworking Machinery ... 792
See also Rolling Mill Machinery 885
Meteorological Instruments
See Measuring, Testing, Controlling Instruments ... 780
Meters & Other Counting Devices ... 792
Mice - Computer
See Computer Input Devices ... 579
Microbiology Diagnostic Products
See Diagnostic Products ... 628
Microbreweries
See Breweries ... 524
Microcircuits
See Semiconductors & Related Devices ... 894
Microfilm & Microfiche
See Micrographics Products & Services ... 792
Micrographics Products & Services ... 792
Microphones
See Audio & Video Equipment ... 502
Computer Input Devices ... 579
Microprocessors
See Semiconductors & Related Devices ... 894
Microscopes
See Optical Instruments & Lenses ... 816
Microscopes - Electron & Proton
See Laboratory Analytical Instruments ... 754
Microwave Communications Equipment
See Radio & Television Broadcasting & Communications Equipment ... 865
Microwave Components - Electronic
See Electronic Components & Accessories - Mfr ... 643
Microwave Meals
See Specialty Foods ... 664
Microwave Ovens
See Appliances - Major - Mfr ... 476
Appliances - Whol ... 477
Microwave Test Equipment
See Electrical Signals Measuring & Testing Instruments ... 642
Military Bases ... 792
See also Coast Guard Installations 548
Air Force Bases ... 792
Army Bases ... 792
Naval Installations ... 793
Military Facilities Management Services
See Facilities Management Services ... 652
Military Hats
See Hats & Caps ... 546
Military Magazines
See Government & Military Magazines ... 771
Military Schools
See Preparatory Schools - Boarding ... 844
Military Service Academies ... 793
Military Service Insignia (Textile)
See Embroidery & Other Decorative Stitching ... 646
Military Weapons & Ordnance
See Weapons & Ordnance (Military) ... 942
Milk Cartons - Paperboard
See Boxes - Paperboard ... 524
Milk Products
See Dairy Products - Dry, Condensed, Evaporated ... 660
Dairy Products - Whol ... 666
Ice Cream & Dairy Stores ... 733
Ice Cream & Frozen Desserts ... 662
Milk & Cream Products ... 663
Milking Machinery
See Farm Machinery & Equipment - Mfr ... 652
Farm Machinery & Equipment - Whol ... 653
Millwork ... 793
See also Lumber & Building Supplies 603; Doors & Windows - Wood 630; Home Improvement Centers 707; Shutters - Window (All Types) 896
Mineral Products - Nonmetallic ... 793
See also Insulation & Acoustical Products 738
Mineral Water
See Water - Bottled ... 941
Mineral Wool
See Insulation & Acoustical Products ... 738
Minerals Mining
See Mining - Minerals ... 794
Miniblinds
See Blinds & Shades ... 520
Mining - Coal ... 793
Mining - Metals ... 793
Mining - Minerals ... 794
Chemical & Fertilizer Minerals Mining ... 794
Clay, Ceramic, Refractory Minerals Mining ... 794
Minerals Mining (Misc) ... 794
Sand & Gravel Pits ... 794
Stone Quarries - Crushed & Broken Stone ... 794
Stone Quarries - Dimension Stone ... 794
Mining Equipment - Mfr
See Construction Machinery & Equipment ... 602
Mining Equipment - Whol
See Heavy Equipment Distributors ... 699
Minivans
See Automobiles - Mfr ... 507
Minority Enterprise Small Business Investment Companies
See Investment Companies - Specialized Small Business ... 751
Minority Rights
See Civil & Human Rights Organizations ... 484
Mirrors
See Glass - Flat, Plate, Tempered ... 681
Glassware & Pottery - Household ... 682
Optical Instruments & Lenses ... 816
Missile Systems
See Missiles, Space Vehicles, Parts ... 794
Missile Tracking
See Navigation & Guidance Instruments & Systems ... 805
Missiles, Space Vehicles, Parts ... 794
See also Weapons & Ordnance (Military) 942
Missing Children
See Children & Family Advocacy Organizations ... 482
Mittens
See Gloves & Mittens ... 546
MLB (Major League Baseball)
See Sports Teams ... 902
MLS (Major League Soccer)
See Sports Teams - Soccer ... 903
Mobile Computing
See Computers ... 578
Data Communications Services for Wireless Devices ... 624
Mobile Home Insurance
See Property & Casualty Insurance ... 743
Mobile Homes & Buildings ... 795
Mobile Telephones
See Appliance & Home Electronics Stores ... 476
Telecommunications Equipment & Systems ... 908
Telecommunications Services ... 908
Model Kits
See Toy Stores ... 922
Toys, Games, Hobbies ... 922
Model Trains
See Toy Stores ... 922
Toys, Games, Hobbies ... 922
Modeling Schools ... 795
Modelling Agencies ... 795
Modern Dance Companies
See Dance Companies ... 827
Modular Buildings
See Buildings - Prefabricated - Wood ... 525
Modular Housing
See Construction - Building Contractors - Residential ... 597
Mold-Making
See Tool & Die Shops ... 919
Molded Rubber Goods
See Rubber Goods - Mechanical ... 886
Molding - Plastics
See Plastics Molding - Custom ... 837
Money Management
See Investment Advice & Management ... 748
Money Order Services
See Banking-Related Services ... 511
Money Transactions Equipment - Automatic
See Automatic Merchandising Equipment & Systems ... 504
Automatic Teller Machines (ATMs) ... 504
Monitoring & Tracking Systems Equipment
See Radio & Television Broadcasting & Communications Equipment ... 865
Monitoring Devices & Systems
See Security Products & Services ... 892
Monitoring Systems
See Child Care Monitoring Systems - Internet ... 543
Monitors - Computer
See Monitors & Displays ... 579
Monolithic Refractories
See Refractories - Nonclay ... 870
Monopoles
See Communications Lines & Towers Construction ... 598
Mops, Sponges, Wiping Cloths ... 795
See also Brushes & Brooms 525; Cleaning Products 544
Morphing Software
See Multimedia & Design Software ... 589
Mortgage Insurance
See Surety Insurance ... 745
Mortgage Lenders & Loan Brokers ... 795
See also Banks - Commercial & Savings 511
Mortuary, Crematory, Cemetery Products & Services . 796
Motion Detectors
See Security Products & Services ... 892
Motion Picture & Television Production ... 796
See also Animation Companies 476; Motion Picture Production - Special Interest 796
Motion Picture Distribution & Related Services ... 796
Motion Picture Pre- & Post-Production Services ... 796
Motion Picture Production - Special Interest ... 796
See also Animation Companies 476; Motion Picture & Television Production 796
Motion Picture Theaters
See Theaters - Motion Picture ... 918
Motor Coach Charters
See Bus Services - Charter ... 526
Motor Coach Tours
See Tour Operators ... 921
Motor Controllers - Electric
See Controls & Relays - Electrical ... 612
Motor Homes
See Campers, Travel Trailers, Motor Homes ... 529
Motor Oils
See Oils & Greases - Lubricating ... 815
Motor Speedways ... 796
Motor Vehicle Agencies - State

See Government - State 684
Motor Vehicle Dealers
See Automobile Dealers & Groups 504
Automobile Sales & Related Services - Online 507
Motor Vehicle Parts & Supplies
See Automotive Parts & Supplies - Mfr 507
Automotive Parts & Supplies - Whol 508
Motor Vehicle Testing
See Testing Facilities 915
Motor Vehicles - Amphibious & Combat
See Weapons & Ordnance (Military) 942
Motor Vehicles - Commercial & Special Purpose 797
See also All-Terrain Vehicles 475; Automobiles - Mfr 507; Campers, Travel Trailers, Motor Homes 529; Motorcycles & Motorcycle Parts & Accessories 798; Snowmobiles 897; Weapons & Ordnance (Military) 942
Motorboats
See Boats - Recreational 521
Motorcycles & Motorcycle Parts & Accessories 798
Motors (Electric) & Generators 798
See also Automotive Parts & Supplies - Mfr 507
Motors - Fluid Power
See Pumps & Motors - Fluid Power 856
Motors - Rocket
See Missiles, Space Vehicles, Parts 794
Mouldings - Metal
See Doors & Windows - Metal 630
Mouldings - Wood
See Frames & Mouldings 672
Millwork 793
Mouth Guards
See Personal Protective Equipment & Clothing 828
Movies
See Book, Music, Video Clubs 522
Motion Picture & Television Production 796
Motion Picture Distribution & Related Services 796
Motion Picture Pre- & Post-Production Services 796
Theaters - Motion Picture 918
Video Stores 937
Moving Companies 798
See also Trucking Companies 928
Moving Walkways
See Elevators, Escalators, Moving Walkways 645
Mowers - Agricultural
See Farm Machinery & Equipment - Mfr 652
Farm Machinery & Equipment - Whol 653
Mowers - Lawn
See Lawn & Garden Equipment 758
MRI Equipment
See Imaging Equipment & Systems - Medical 733
MRI Services
See Imaging Services - Diagnostic 734
Multiplexers
See Modems 579
Multiwall Bags
See Bags - Paper 510
Munitions
See Weapons & Ordnance (Military) 942
Museums 799
See also Museums - Children's 802; Museums & Halls of Fame - Sports 802
Museums & Halls of Fame - Sports 802
Museums - Children's 802
Music Clubs
See Book, Music, Video Clubs 522
Music Distributors 802
Music Programming Services 803
Music Publications
See Entertainment & Music Magazines 770
Music Recording
See Recording Companies 870
Music Software
See Multimedia & Design Software 589
Personal Software 589
Music Stores 803
See also Book, Music, Video Clubs 522
Music Videos
See Motion Picture Production - Special Interest 796
Musical Instrument Cases
See Luggage, Bags, Cases 767
Musical Instrument Stores 803
Musical Instruments 803
Mustard - Prepared
See Fruits & Vegetables - Pickled 661
Mutual Funds 803

N

Nail Care Products
See Cosmetics, Skin Care, and Other Personal Care Products 620
Nail Care Services
See Beauty Salons 517
Nameplates
See Signs 896
Napkins, Tissues, etc - Paper
See Paper Products - Sanitary 820
NASCAR Racing
See Motor Speedways 796
National Cemeteries
See Cemeteries - National 533
National Hockey League (NHL)
See Sports Teams - Hockey 903
National Memorials
See Monuments, Memorials, Landmarks 501
National Parks
See Parks - National - Canada 821
Parks - National - US 821
National Public Radio Stations
See Radio Stations 864
Native American Tribal Colleges
See Colleges - Tribal 557
Natural Gas
See Gas Transmission - Natural Gas 680
Oil & Gas Extraction 813
Utility Companies 932
Nature Magazines
See Science & Nature Magazines 772
Nature Organizations
See Environmental Organizations 485
Nautical Instruments & Systems
See Navigation & Guidance Instruments & Systems 805
Naval Stores (Gum & Wood)
See Chemicals - Industrial (Organic) 541
Navigation & Guidance Instruments & Systems 805
Navy - US Department of the
See US Department of Defense - Department of the Navy 690
NBA
See National Basketball Association (NBA) 902
Neck Ties
See Neckwear 546
Nectarines
See Deciduous Tree Fruit Growers 675
Needles & Pins
See Piece Goods & Notions 834
Needlework
See Embroidery & Other Decorative Stitching 646
Fabric Stores 651
Piece Goods & Notions 834
Neon Signs
See Signs 896
Neoprene
See Synthetic Rubber 838
Nets
See Cord & Twine 619
Networking Products & Systems - Computer
See Computer Networking Products & Systems 582
Networking Software
See Systems & Utilities Software 591
Networks - Broadcast Television
See Television Networks - Broadcast 911
Networks - Cable
See Television Networks 910
Networks - Electronic Communications
See Electronic Communications Networks (ECNs) 643
Networks - Fiber Optic
See Telecommunications Equipment & Systems 908
Networks - Local Area
See Computer Networking Products & Systems 582
Networks - Radio
See Radio Networks 857
Networks - Television
See Television Networks 910
Television Networks - Broadcast 911
Networks - Travel Agencies
See Travel Agency Networks 926
Networks - Wide Area
See Computer Networking Products & Systems 582
Newborn Monitoring Systems
See Electromedical & Electrotherapeutic Equipment 642
News Software
See Internet & Communications Software 588
News Syndicates, Services, Bureaus 805
Newsletters 805
Banking & Finance Newsletters 805
Business & Professional Newsletters 805
Computer & Internet Newsletters 806
Education Newsletters 806
Energy & Environmental Newsletters 806
General Interest Newsletters 806
Government & Law Newsletters 806
Health & Social Issues Newsletters 806
Investment Newsletters 807
Marketing & Sales Newsletters 807
Media & Communications Newsletters 807
Science & Technology Newsletters 807
Trade & Industry Newsletters 807
Newspaper Clipping Services
See Press Clipping Services 844
Newspaper Distributors
See Books, Periodicals, Newspapers - Whol 522
Newspapers 807
See also Newspaper Publishers 853
Daily Newspapers - Canada 807
Daily Newspapers - US 807
National Newspapers 811
Weekly Newspapers 811
Weekly Newspapers - Alternative 812
NHL (National Hockey League)
See Sports Teams - Hockey 903
Night Gowns
See Sleepwear 547
Nitriding - Metal
See Metal Heat Treating 787
Non-Cellulosic Fibers
See Synthetic Fibers & Filaments 837
Non-medical Home Care Services
See Home Health Services 707
Nonferrous Castings
See Foundries - Nonferrous (Castings) 671
Noodles
See Pasta 664
Note Cards
See Cards - Greeting - Mfr 531
Note Pads
See Writing Paper 819
Notebooks - Computer
See Computers 578
Notebooks - Looseleaf
See Blankbooks & Binders 520
Notions - Sewing
See Piece Goods & Notions 834
Novel Therapeutic Drugs
See Biotechnology Companies 519
Novelties
See Gift Shops 681
Gifts & Novelties - Whol 681
Jewelry - Costume 751
NPR (National Public Radio) Stations
See Radio Stations 864
Nuclear Valves
See Valves - Industrial 934
Nurse Call Systems
See Intercom Equipment & Systems 746
Nursery Products (Plants)
See Garden Centers 680
Horticultural Products Growers 708
Nursery Supplies - Whol
See Flowers & Nursery Stock - Whol 658
Nurses Associations - State 812
See also Health & Medical Professionals Associations 494
Nursing Homes
See Long-Term Care Facilities 766
Veterans Nursing Homes - State 936
Nursing Schools
See Colleges & Universities - Four-Year 559
Vocational & Technical Schools 938
Nutraceuticals
See Biotechnology Companies 519

Vitamins & Nutritional Supplements 937
Nutrition Centers
See Health Food Stores 699
Nutrition Research
See Research Centers & Institutions. 871
Nutritional Supplements - Mfr
See Vitamins & Nutritional Supplements 937
Nutritional Supplements - Retail
See Drug Stores 631
Health Food Stores 699
Nuts & Bolts
See Fasteners & Fastening Systems. 654
Hardware - Whol 697
Nuts - Edible
See Confectionery & Snack Foods - Whol 666
Nuts - Edible 664
Tree Nuts Growers 470
Nylon
See Broadwoven Fabric Mills 916
Nylon Fibers
See Synthetic Fibers & Filaments. 837

O

Observatories
See Planetariums 835
Occupational Therapy Services
See Health Care Providers - Ancillary. 697
Office & School Supplies 812
See also Office Supply Stores 813; Writing Paper 819; Pens, Pencils, Parts 826; Printing & Photocopying Supplies 847
Office Cleaning Services
See Cleaning Services 545
Office Clerical Service
See Staffing Services 904
Office Equipment Rental (Except Computers)
See Home & Office Equipment Rental (General). 650
Office Furniture
See Commercial & Industrial Furniture 676
Office Help
See Staffing Services 904
Office Machines
See Business Machines - Mfr. 527
Business Machines - Whol 527
Computer Equipment. 578
Office Management Services
See Management Services 776
Office Supply Stores 813
Offset Reproduction
See Printing Companies - Commercial Printers. 845
Oil & Gas Extraction 813
Oil & Gas Field Equipment 814
Oil & Gas Field Equipment Rental
See Industrial & Heavy Equipment Rental. 650
Oil & Gas Field Exploration Services. 814
Oil & Gas Field Services. 814
See also Oil & Gas Field Exploration Services 814
Oil & Gas Well Drilling. 815
Oil Dealers
See Fuel Dealers. 675
Oil Furnaces
See Heating Equipment - Gas, Oil, Coal. 699
Oil Refineries
See Petroleum Refineries 830
Oil Refinery Construction
See Refinery (Petroleum or Oil) Construction. 599
Oil-Spill Clean-Up Contractors
See Consulting Services - Environmental. 604
Oils & Greases - Lubricating 815
See also Chemicals - Specialty 542; Petroleum Refineries 830
Oils - Animal
See Fats & Oils - Animal or Marine 660
Oils - Essential
See Chemicals - Specialty 542
Olive Oil
See Oils - Edible (Margarine, Shortening, Table Oils, etc) 664
Olympic Sports Organizations
See Sports Organizations 490
Oncology Systems
See Imaging Equipment & Systems - Medical 733
Online Advertising Services
See Advertising Services - Online 468
Online Auctions
See Auctions 502
Online Bill Payment
See Electronic Bill Presentment & Payment Services 643
Online Book Stores
See Book Stores. 523
Online Broadcasting
See Internet Broadcasting. 747
Online Brokers
See Electronic Communications Networks (ECNs). 643
Securities Brokers & Dealers 890
Online Buyers Guides
See Buyer's Guides - Online. 528
Online Car Sales
See Automobile Sales & Related Services - Online 507
Online Communities
See Communities - Online 578
Online Employment Services
See Employment Services - Online. 646
Online Greeting Cards
See Cards - Greeting - Mfr. 531
Online Health & Medical Information
See Health & Medical Information - Online 699
Online Investment Guides
See Investment Guides - Online 751
Online Job Boards
See Employment Services - Online. 646
Online Marketing
See Advertising Services - Online 468
Online Music Stores
See Music Stores 803
Online Photo Storage
See Photo Processing & Storage 833
Online Searching
See Internet Search Engines, Portals, Directories 748
Online Shopping
See Malls - Shopping. 775
Online Telephone & Voice Mail Services
See Telecommunications Services 908
Online Trading Forums
See Electronic Communications Networks (ECNs). 643
Online Travel Services
See Travel Services - Online. 927
Online Video Stores
See Video Stores 937
Operating System Software
See Systems & Utilities Software 591
Ophthalmic Goods 816
See also Personal Protective Equipment & Clothing 828
Opinion Research
See Market Research Firms 778
Optical Goods Stores. 816
Optical Instruments & Lenses. 816
See also Laboratory Analytical Instruments 754
Optical Recording Media
See Recording Media - Magnetic & Optical 870
Optical Scanning Devices
See Scanning Equipment 580
Oranges
See Citrus Growers. 675
Ordnance - Military
See Weapons & Ordnance (Military) 942
Ore Mining (Misc Ores)
See Mining - Metals. 793
Organ & Tissue Banks. 817
See also Eye Banks 651
Organic Chemicals - Industrial
See Chemicals - Industrial (Organic) 541
Organic Fibers - Synthetic
See Synthetic Fibers & Filaments. 837
Organs
See Musical Instrument Stores. 803
Musical Instruments 803
Ornamental Iron
See Metal Work - Architectural & Ornamental 789
Orthopedic Shoes
See Footwear 669
Orthopedic Supplies
See Medical Supplies - Mfr 784
OS (Operating System) Software
See Systems & Utilities Software 591
Outplacement Counselors
See Consulting Services - Human Resources 604
Outsourcing Services
See Facilities Management Services. 652
Management Services 776
Oven Racks
See Baskets, Cages, Racks, etc - Wire 516
Ovens - Conventional
See Appliance & Home Electronics Stores 476
Appliances - Major - Mfr. 476
Appliances - Whol 477
Ovens - Industrial
See Furnaces & Ovens - Industrial Process 676
Ovens - Microwave
See Appliances - Major - Mfr. 476
Appliances - Whol. 477
Overshoes
See Footwear 669
Oxygen
See Medical Supplies - Mfr 784
Oxygen Systems
See Safety Equipment - Mfr 886
Oxygen Systems - Aircraft
See Aircraft Parts & Auxiliary Equipment 473

P

Pacemakers
See Electromedical & Electrotherapeutic Equipment 642
Package Delivery Services. 817
Package Filler
See Plastics Foam Products. 836
Package Stores
See Liquor Stores. 764
Packagers - Book
See Book Producers. 522
Packaging - Blister
See Blister Packaging. 520
Packaging - Paperboard
See Boxes - Corrugated & Solid Fiber 524
Boxes - Paperboard. 524
Packaging Machinery & Equipment. 817
Packaging Materials & Products - Paper or Plastics . . 818
See also Bags - Paper 510; Bags - Plastics 510; Blister Packaging 520; Coated & Laminated Paper 819; Paper Converters 820; Plastics Foam Products 836
Packaging Services (Contract)
See Packing & Crating 818
Packing & Crating 818
Packing & Shipping - Fruit
See Crop Preparation Services. 470
Fruit Growers. 675
Packing & Shipping Services
See Business Service Centers 528
Packings
See Gaskets, Packing, Sealing Devices 681
PACs
See Political Action Committees. 841
Pads - Paper
See Writing Paper. 819
Pagers
See Appliance & Home Electronics Stores 476
Telecommunications Equipment & Systems 908
Pain Management Devices
See Electromedical & Electrotherapeutic Equipment 642
Paint Brushes
See Art Materials & Supplies - Mfr. 478
Brushes & Brooms 525
Paint Dealers & Distributors
See Paints, Varnishes, Related Products 818
Paint Sprayers
See Compressors - Air & Gas 578
Paint Stores
See Home Improvement Centers 707
Paints, Varnishes, Related Products 818
Paint Sundries
See Paints, Varnishes, Related Products 818
Painting Software
See Multimedia & Design Software 589
Paints - Artists'
See Art Materials & Supplies - Mfr. 478
Paints, Varnishes, Related Products 818
Pajamas
See Sleepwear 547

Pallets & Skids 819
Palm Computers
See Computers 578
Paneling - Wood
See Home Improvement Centers 707
Lumber & Building Supplies 603
Plywood & Veneers 841
Sawmills & Planing Mills 887
Panels - Portable
See Fixtures - Office & Store 656
Papayas
See Fruit Growers (Misc) 675
Paper - Die-Cut
See Paperboard & Cardboard - Die-Cut 821
Paper - Graph (Ruled)
See Blankbooks & Binders 520
Paper - Mfr 819
See also Packaging Materials & Products - Paper or Plastics 818
Coated & Laminated Paper 819
Writing Paper 819
Paper - Printing
See Coated & Laminated Paper 819
Paper - Whol 819
Writing Paper 819
Paper - Specialty
See Coated & Laminated Paper 819
Paper - Whol 819
Paper Bags
See Bags - Paper 510
Paper Containers (Fiber)
See Cans, Tubes, Drums - Paper (Fiber) 530
Paper Converters 820
Paper Converting Machinery
See Paper Industries Machinery 820
Paper Cups
See Paper Converters 820
Paper Finishers (Embossing, Coating, Gilding, Stamping) 820
Paper Industries Machinery 820
Paper Mills 820
See also Paperboard Mills 821; Pulp Mills 855
Paper Plates
See Paper Converters 820
Paper Products - Pressed & Molded
See Paper Converters 820
Paper Products - Sanitary 820
Paper Products - Whol 821
Paper Recycling
See Paper Converters 820
Paper Recycling Equipment
See Paper Industries Machinery 820
Paper Shredders
See Business Machines - Mfr 527
Business Machines - Whol 527
Paper Supplies - Janitorial
See Paper Products - Whol 821
Paperboard & Cardboard - Die-Cut 821
Paperboard Boxes
See Boxes - Corrugated & Solid Fiber 524
Boxes - Paperboard 524
Paperboard Mills 821
See also Paper Mills 820; Pulp Mills 855
Paperhanging
See Painting & Paperhanging Contractors 600
Papermaking Machinery Fabrics
See Industrial Fabrics 916
Parachutes
See Safety Equipment - Mfr 886
Parentage Testing
See Laboratories - Genetic Testing 754
Park Benches
See Outdoor Furniture 678
Recycled Plastics Products 870
Parking Lots
See Parking Service 821
Parking Service 821
Parks - Amusement
See Amusement Park Companies 475
Amusement Parks 475
Parks - National - Canada 821
Parks - National - US 821
See also Nature Centers, Parks, Other Natural Areas 501; Cemeteries - National 533; Parks - State 822
Parks - State 822
See also Nature Centers, Parks, Other Natural Areas 501; Parks - National - Canada 821; Parks - National - US 821
Parks - Theme
See Amusement Parks 475
Parks - Wildlife
See Zoos & Wildlife Parks 945
Parks Agencies
See Government - State 684
US Department of the Interior 691
Particleboard
See Wood Products - Reconstituted 944
Partitions
See Commercial & Industrial Furniture 676
Fixtures - Office & Store 656
Party Favors
See Gifts & Novelties - Whol 681
Party Goods 825
Party Sales
See Home Sales & Other Direct Selling 708
Passenger Cars
See Automobile Dealers & Groups 504
Automobile Sales & Related Services - Online 507
Automobiles - Mfr 507
Paste - Adhesive
See Adhesives & Sealants 466
Pastries
See Bakeries 511
Bakery Products - Fresh 658
Bakery Products - Frozen 659
Patches - Embroidered
See Embroidery & Other Decorative Stitching 646
Patent Attorneys
See Law Firms 756
Paternity Testing
See Laboratories - Genetic Testing 754
Pathology Laboratories
See Laboratories - Medical 754
Patient Monitoring Equipment
See Electromedical & Electrotherapeutic Equipment 642
Patio Furniture
See Outdoor Furniture 678
Patriotic Organizations
See Military, Veterans, Patriotic Organizations 488
Patterns - Industrial 825
Patterns - Sewing 825
Pavers - Concrete
See Concrete Products - Mfr 595
Paving Contractors
See Concrete Contractors 599
Highway, Street, Bridge, Tunnel Construction 598
Paving Materials
See Asphalt Paving & Roofing Materials 479
Concrete Products - Mfr 595
Pawn Shops 825
Pay Television
See Cable & Other Pay Television Services 528
Payment Services - Online
See Electronic Bill Presentment & Payment Services 643
Payroll Services 825
See also Data Processing & Related Services 625
Payroll Software
See Business Software (General) 586
PBS (Public Broadcasting Service)
See Television Stations 911
PCS (Personal Communications Service)
See Telecommunications Services 908
PCS (Personal Communications Service) Devices
See Appliance & Home Electronics Stores 476
PCS (Personal Communications Systems)
See Telecommunications Equipment & Systems 908
PCs (Personal Computers)
See Computers 578
PDAs
See Computers 578
PDAs (Personal Digital Assistants)
See Telecommunications Equipment & Systems 908
Pea Gravel
See Sand & Gravel Pits 794
Peaches
See Deciduous Tree Fruit Growers 675
Peanut Shelling
See Crop Preparation Services 470
Peanuts
See Confectionery & Snack Foods - Whol 666
Nuts - Edible 664
Pears
See Deciduous Tree Fruit Growers 675
Pecans
See Tree Nuts Growers 470
Pegboard
See Wood Products - Reconstituted 944
Pencils
See Art Materials & Supplies - Mfr 478
Pens, Pencils, Parts 826
Penitentiaries
See Correctional Facilities - State 619
Pens, Pencils, Parts 826
See also Art Materials & Supplies - Mfr 478; Office & School Supplies 812
Pepper
See Spices, Seasonings, Herbs 665
Performance Testing
See Testing Facilities 915
Performing Arts Facilities 826
See also Convention Centers 613; Stadiums & Arenas 903; Theaters - Broadway 917; Theaters - Resident 918
Performing Arts Organizations 827
See also Arts & Artists Organizations 481
Dance Companies 827
Opera Companies 827
Orchestras 827
Theater Companies 828
Perfumes 828
See also Cosmetics, Skin Care, and Other Personal Care Products 620
Periodicals Distributors
See Books, Periodicals, Newspapers - Whol 522
Perlite Mining
See Minerals Mining (Misc) 794
Persimmons
See Deciduous Tree Fruit Growers 675
See Long-Term Care Facilities 766
Personal Care Products
See Cosmetics, Skin Care, and Other Personal Care Products 620
Personal Care Products - Whol
See Drugs & Personal Care Products - Whol 631
Personal Checks
See Checks - Personal & Business 541
Personal Communications Service (PCS) Devices
See Appliance & Home Electronics Stores 476
Personal Communications Systems
See Telecommunications Equipment & Systems 908
Personal Computers
See Computers 578
Personal Digital Assistants (PDAs)
See Telecommunications Equipment & Systems 908
Personal Emergency Response Systems 828
Personal Heating Systems
See Thermal Management Products - Personal 918
Personal Hygiene Products
See Cosmetics, Skin Care, and Other Personal Care Products 620
Personal Leather Goods
See Leather Goods - Personal 759
Personal Names
See Governors - State 694
US Senators, Representatives, Delegates 694
Personal Organizers
See Blankbooks & Binders 520
Computers 578
Personal Protective Equipment & Clothing 828
See also Medical Supplies - Mfr 784; Safety Equipment - Mfr 886; Safety Equipment - Whol 886; Sporting Goods 899
Personal Safety
See Fire Protection Systems 655
Personal Protective Equipment & Clothing 828
Safety Equipment - Mfr 886
Security Products & Services 892
Personal Thermal Management Products
See Thermal Management Products - Personal 918
Personal Watercraft
See Sporting Goods 899
Personnel Agencies
See Staffing Services 904
Personnel Consulting Services
See Consulting Services - Human Resources 604
Pest Control - Forests
See Forestry Services 670
Pest Control Services 829

Index

Pesticides
See Fertilizers & Pesticides 654
PET (Positron Emission Tomography)
See Imaging Equipment & Systems - Medical 733
Pet Cages & Carriers
See Pet Products 829
Pet Hospitals
See Veterinary Hospitals 936
Pet Insurance
See Animal Insurance 740
Pet Products 829
See also Leather Goods - Personal 759; Livestock & Poultry Feeds - Prepared 765
Pet Tagging Systems
See Pet Products 829
Petroleum & Petroleum Products - Whol 830
Petroleum - Crude
See Oil & Gas Extraction 813
Petroleum Refineries 830
Petroleum Refinery Construction
See Refinery (Petroleum or Oil) Construction 599
Petroleum Storage Terminals 831
Pharmaceutical & Diagnostic Products - Veterinary 831
Pharmaceutical Companies 831
See also Biotechnology Companies 519; Diagnostic Products 628; Medicinal Chemicals & Botanical Products 786; Pharmaceutical & Diagnostic Products - Veterinary 831; Pharmaceutical Companies - Generic Drugs 832; Vitamins & Nutritional Supplements 937
Pharmaceutical Companies - Generic Drugs 832
See also Biotechnology Companies 519; Diagnostic Products 628; Medicinal Chemicals & Botanical Products 786; Pharmaceutical & Diagnostic Products - Veterinary 831; Pharmaceutical Companies 831; Vitamins & Nutritional Supplements 937
Pharmaceutical Industry Software
See Professional Software (Industry-Specific) 589
Pharmaceutical Products - Retail
See Drug Stores 631
Health Food Stores 699
Pharmaceutical Products - Whol
See Drugs & Personal Care Products - Whol 631
Pharmaceutical Services
See Pharmacy Management Services 833
Pharmacies
See Drug Stores 631
Pharmacy Associations - State 832
See also Health & Medical Professionals Associations 494
Pharmacy Benefits Management Services 833
Pharmacy Management Services 833
Pharmacy Services - Specialty
See Pharmacy Management Services 833
Philanthropic Organizations
See Charitable & Humanitarian Organizations 481
Foundations - Community 670
Foundations - Corporate 670
Foundations - Private 670
Phone Cards - Mfr
See Smart Cards 897
Phosphate Rock
See Chemical & Fertilizer Minerals Mining 794
Photo Albums
See Blankbooks & Binders 520
Photo Processing & Storage 833
Photo Sharing
See Photo Processing & Storage 833
Photo Storage - Online
See Photo Processing & Storage 833
Photocomposition
See Typesetting & Related Services 931
Photocopying Equipment & Supplies 833
See also Business Machines - Whol 527
Photocopying Services
See Business Service Centers 528
Printing Companies - Commercial Printers 845
Photocopying Supplies
See Printing & Photocopying Supplies 847
Photofinishing Laboratories
See Photo Processing & Storage 833
Photoflash & Photoflood Lamps
See Light Bulbs & Tubes 763
Photograph Studios - Portrait 833
Photographic Equipment & Supplies 833
See also Cameras & Related Supplies - Retail 529
Photography - Aerial
See Surveying, Mapping, Related Services 906
Photography - Commercial 834
Photography - Stock 834
Photography Schools
See Colleges - Fine Arts 557
Photography Supplies
See Cameras & Related Supplies - Retail 529
Photovoltaic Devices
See Semiconductors & Related Devices 894
Physical Fitness Equipment
See Exercise & Fitness Equipment 651
Physical Fitness Software
See Personal Software 589
Physical Therapy Services
See Health Care Providers - Ancillary 697
Physician Recruitment
See Executive Recruiting Firms 651
Physician Staffing Services
See Staffing Services 904
Physics Research
See Research Centers & Institutions 871
Pianos
See Musical Instrument Stores 803
Musical Instruments 803
Pick-up Trucks
See Automobiles - Mfr 507
Pickles & Relishes
See Fruits & Vegetables - Pickled 661
Picnic Tables
See Outdoor Furniture 678
Recycled Plastics Products 870
Picture Framing
See Art Supply Stores 479
Piece Goods & Notions 834
See also Fabric Stores 651
Pies
See Bakeries 511
Bakery Products - Fresh 658
Bakery Products - Frozen 659
Piezoelectric Crystals
See Electronic Components & Accessories - Mfr 643
Pig Farms
See Hog Farms 469
Pigments - Inorganic
See Chemicals - Industrial (Inorganic) 541
Pigments - Organic
See Chemicals - Industrial (Organic) 541
Pigments - Whol
See Paints, Varnishes, Related Products 818
Pile Driving
See Foundation Drilling & Pile Driving 598
Pillows
See Textile Products - Household 917
Pinball Machines
See Games & Gaming 680
Pineapple
See Fruit Growers (Misc) 675
Pipe & Pipe Fittings - Metal (Fabricated) 834
See also Metal Tube & Pipe 789
Pipe & Pipe Fittings - Plastics 834
Pipe - Concrete
See Concrete Products - Mfr 595
Pipe - Metal - Mfr
See Metal Tube & Pipe 789
Pipe Tobacco
See Tobacco & Tobacco Products 919
Pipeline Construction
See Water & Sewer Lines, Pipelines, Power Lines Construction 599
Pipelines (Except Natural Gas) 835
Pipelines - Natural Gas
See Gas Transmission - Natural Gas 680
PIRGs
See Public Interest Research Groups (PIRGs) - State 848
Pistols
See Firearms & Ammunition (Non-Military) 655
Weapons & Ordnance (Military) 942
Pistons & Piston Rings
See Carburetors, Pistons, Piston Rings, Valves 530
Pizza
See Franchises 672
Restaurant Companies 880
Restaurants (Individual) 881
Specialty Foods 664
Pizza Boxes
See Boxes - Paperboard 524
Placement Services - Jobs
See Employment Offices - Government 646
Executive Recruiting Firms 651
Staffing Services 904
Planetariums 835
Planing Mills
See Sawmills & Planing Mills 887
Planners & Organizers
See Blankbooks & Binders 520
Planters (Agricultural)
See Farm Machinery & Equipment - Mfr 652
Farm Machinery & Equipment - Whol 653
Planters - Plastics
See Plastics Products - Household 838
Plants - Nursery
See Garden Centers 680
Horticultural Products Growers 708
Plaques
See Trophies, Plaques, Awards 927
Plaster & Plasterboard - Gypsum
See Gypsum Products 695
Plaster - Dental
See Dental Equipment & Supplies - Mfr 627
Plaster - Whol
See Brick, Stone, Related Materials 602
Plaster of Paris
See Gypsum Products 695
Plastic Lumber
See Flooring - Resilient 657
Recycled Plastics Products 870
Plastics & Other Synthetic Materials 837
Synthetic Fibers & Filaments 837
Synthetic Resins & Plastics Materials 837
Synthetic Rubber 838
Plastics - Laminated - Plate, Sheet, Profile Shapes 835
Plastics - Unsupported - Film, Sheet, Profile Shapes 835
See also Blister Packaging 520
Plastics Bags
See Bags - Plastics 510
Plastics Bottles
See Bottles - Plastics 524
Plastics Closures
See Closures - Metal or Plastics 545
Plastics Containers
See Containers - Plastics (Drums, Cans, Crates, Boxes) 610
Plastics Products - Household 838
Plastics Film (for Packaging)
See Packaging Materials & Products - Paper or Plastics 818
Plastics Flooring
See Flooring - Resilient 657
Plastics Foam Products 836
Plastics Hose & Belting
See Hose & Belting - Rubber or Plastics 709
Plastics Machining & Forming 836
See also Plastics Molding - Custom 837
Plastics Materials
See Synthetic Resins & Plastics Materials 837
Plastics Materials - Whol 836
Plastics Molding - Custom 837
Plastics Pipe
See Pipe & Pipe Fittings - Plastics 834
Plastics Plumbing Fixtures
See Plumbing Fixtures & Fittings - Plastics 839
Plastics Products (Misc) 838
Plastics Products - Fiberglass Reinforced 838
Plastics Products - Household 838
Plastics Products - Recycled Plastics
See Recycled Plastics Products 870
Plastics Resins - Custom Compounding
See Synthetic Resins & Plastics Materials 837
Plate Glass
See Glass - Flat, Plate, Tempered 681
Plate Work - Fabricated
See Boiler Shops 521
Plates & Cups - Plastics
See Plastics Products - Household 838
Plates & Cups - Styrofoam
See Plastics Foam Products 836
Platforms - Aerial
See Construction Machinery & Equipment 602

Playground Equipment
See Gym & Playground Equipment 695
Plotters
See Printers 580
Plows
See Farm Machinery & Equipment - Mfr 652
Farm Machinery & Equipment - Whol 653
Plumbing & Heating Valves
See Pipe & Pipe Fittings - Metal (Fabricated) 834
Plumbing Contractors
See Plumbing, Heating, Air Conditioning Contractors 601
Plumbing Fixtures & Fittings - Metal 839
Plumbing Fixtures & Fittings - Plastics 839
Plumbing Fixtures & Fittings - Vitreous China & Earthenware 840
Plumbing, Heating, Air Conditioning Equipment & Supplies - Whol 840
See also Refrigeration Equipment - Whol 871
Plums
See Deciduous Tree Fruit Growers 675
Plush Toys
See Toy Stores 922
Toys, Games, Hobbies 922
Plywood & Veneers 841
See also Lumber & Building Supplies 603; Home Improvement Centers 707
Pneumatic Cylinders & Actuators
See Cylinders & Actuators - Fluid Power 624
Pneumatic Pumps
See Pumps & Motors - Fluid Power 856
Pneumatic Tools
See Tools - Power 921
Pneumatic Valves
See Valves & Hose Fittings - Fluid Power 935
POI (Point-of-Information) Systems
See Point-of-Sale (POS) & Point-of-Information (POI) Systems 841
Point-of-Purchase Displays
See Displays - Point-of-Purchase 629
Point-of-Sale (POS) & Point-of-Information (POI) Systems 841
Point-of-Sale Appliances
See Scanning Equipment 580
Point-of-Sale Equipment
See Business Machines - Whol 527
Point-of-Sale Software
See Business Software (General) 586
Point-of-Service (POS) Insurance Plans
See Medical & Hospitalization Insurance 741
Police Equipment - Protective
See Personal Protective Equipment & Clothing 828
Police Products
See Firearms & Ammunition (Non-Military) 655
Police Training Facilities
See Simulation & Training Systems 897
Policy Research
See Public Policy Research Centers 849
Polishes & Waxes
See Cleaning Products 544
Polishing Cloths
See Mops, Sponges, Wiping Cloths 795
Political Action Committees 841
See also Civic & Political Organizations 483
Political Leaders
See Governors - State 694
US Senators, Representatives, Delegates 694
Political Organizations
See Civic & Political Organizations 483
Political Parties (Major) 842
See also Civic & Political Organizations 483
Democratic State Committees 842
Republican State Committees 842
Polling Services
See Market Research Firms 778
Pollution Control
See Consulting Services - Environmental 604
Polyesters
See Synthetic Resins & Plastics Materials 837
Polyethylene Bags
See Bags - Plastics 510
Polymers
See Synthetic Resins & Plastics Materials 837
Polystyrene Products
See Plastics Foam Products 836
Polyurethane Resins
See Synthetic Resins & Plastics Materials 837
Polyvinyl Resins
See Synthetic Resins & Plastics Materials 837
Pool Halls
See Recreation Facility Operators 870
Pools - Swimming
See Swimming Pools 906
POP (Point-of-Purchase) Displays
See Displays - Point-of-Purchase 629
Porcelain Electrical Supplies
See Electrical Supplies - Porcelain 642
Porcelain Refinishing
See Remodeling, Refinishing, Resurfacing Contractors 601
Porcelain-on-Steel Plumbing Fixtures
See Plumbing Fixtures & Fittings - Metal 839
Porch Furniture
See Outdoor Furniture 678
Portable Buildings
See Buildings - Prefabricated - Metal 525
Buildings - Prefabricated - Wood 525
Mobile Homes & Buildings 795
Portable Panels
See Fixtures - Office & Store 656
Portals
See Internet Search Engines, Portals, Directories 748
Portals - Voice 842
Portland Cement
See Cement 533
Portland Cement Concrete
See Concrete - Ready-Mixed 595
Ports & Port Authorities 842
See also Airports 474; Cruise Lines 624
POS (Point-of-Sale) Equipment
See Business Machines - Whol 527
POS (Point-of-Sale) Software
See Business Software (General) 586
POS (Point-of-Sale) Systems
See Point-of-Sale (POS) & Point-of-Information (POI) Systems 841
POS (Point-of-Service) Insurance Plans
See Medical & Hospitalization Insurance 741
Positron Emission Tomography (PET) Equipment
See Imaging Equipment & Systems - Medical 733
Post Exchange (PX) Stores
See Variety Stores 935
Posters
See Publishers (Misc) 855
Potash
See Chemical & Fertilizer Minerals Mining 794
Potato Chips
See Confectionery & Snack Foods - Whol 666
Snack Foods 664
Potato Growers
See Vegetable Farms 470
Pots & Pans
See Metal Products - Household 788
Pottery Products
See Glassware & Pottery - Household 682
Table & Kitchen Supplies - China & Earthenware 907
Poultry Feeds
See Livestock & Poultry Feeds - Prepared 765
Poultry Incubators
See Farm Machinery & Equipment - Mfr 652
Farm Machinery & Equipment - Whol 653
Poultry Pluckers
See Farm Machinery & Equipment - Mfr 652
Farm Machinery & Equipment - Whol 653
Poultry Processing 842
See also Meat Packing Plants 781
Power Companies
See Electric Companies - Cooperatives (Rural) 633
Utility Companies 932
Power Lines Construction
See Water & Sewer Lines, Pipelines, Power Lines Construction 599
Power Plant Construction
See Plant Construction 599
Power Pumps
See Pumps & Pumping Equipment (General Use) 856
Power Supplies - Electronic
See Electronic Components & Accessories - Mfr 643
Power Supply Cords
See Wiring Devices - Current-Carrying 943
Power Transmission Equipment
See Speed Changers, Industrial High Speed Drives, Gears .. 899
Switchgear & Switchboard Apparatus 906
Transformers - Power, Distribution, Specialty 924
Power Transmission Equipment - Mechanical 843
See also Bearings - Ball & Roller 516
Pozzolana Cement
See Cement 533
PPE (Personal Protective Equipment)
See Personal Protective Equipment & Clothing 828
PPOs (Preferred Provider Organizations)
See Medical & Hospitalization Insurance 741
Pre-Press Services
See Typesetting & Related Services 931
Pre-Trial Research Services
See Litigation Support Services 764
Precast Concrete
See Concrete Products - Mfr 595
Precision Machined Products 843
See also Aircraft Parts & Auxiliary Equipment 473; Machine Shops 767
Precision Tools - Machinists'
See Metalworking Devices & Accessories 791
Prefabricated Buildings
See Buildings - Prefabricated - Metal 525
Buildings - Prefabricated - Wood 525
Preferred Provider Organizations (PPOs)
See Medical & Hospitalization Insurance 741
Pregnancy Test Kits
See Diagnostic Products 628
Preparatory Schools - Boarding 844
See also
Preparatory Schools - Non-boarding 844
Prepared Meats
See Meat Products - Prepared 663
Prepared Salads
See Salads - Prepared 664
Prepared Sandwiches
See Sandwiches - Prepared 664
Prescription Benefit Management
See Pharmacy Benefits Management Services 833
Presentation Products
See Commercial & Industrial Furniture 676
Preserves, Jams, Jellies
See Fruits, Vegetables, Juices - Canned or Preserved 661
Presidents - US
See Government - US - Executive Branch 690
Press Clipping Services 844
Press Clubs
See Publishing & Printing Professional Associations 498
Press Services
See News Syndicates, Services, Bureaus 805
Presses - Hydraulic
See Machine Tools - Metal Forming Types 768
Pressure Cleaners
See Compressors - Air & Gas 578
Pressure Pumps
See Pumps & Pumping Equipment (General Use) 856
Pressure Sensitive Tape
See Tape - Cellophane, Gummed, Masking, Pressure Sensitive 907
Pretzels
See Baked Goods - Whol 665
Bakeries 511
Cookies & Crackers 660
Printed Circuit Boards 845
See also Electronic Components & Accessories - Mfr 643; Semiconductors & Related Devices 894
Printed Circuit Connectors
See Electronic Components & Accessories - Mfr 643
Printer Cartridges
See Printing & Photocopying Supplies 847
Printers - Screen Processing
See Screen Printing 890
Printing & Photocopying Supplies 847
Printing & Publishing Equipment & Systems 848
See also Printers 580
Printing - Fabric
See Textile Dyeing & Finishing 917
Printing Companies - Book Printers 845
Printing Companies - Commercial Printers 845
Printing Industry Associations
See Publishing & Printing Professional Associations 498
Printing Ink

Index

See Ink 738
Printing Paper
See Writing Paper 819
Prison Industries 848
See also Radio Networks 857; Television Networks - Broadcast 911
See also Radio Networks 857; Television Networks - Broadcast 911
Prisons - State
See Correctional Facilities - State 619
Prisons Operators
See Correctional & Detention Management (Privatized) 619
Process Serving & Court Filing Services
See Litigation Support Services 764
Produce - Fresh
See Vegetable Farms 470
Producers - Book
See Book Producers 522
Producers - Concerts, Sports, Other Live Events
See Concert, Sports, Other Live Event Producers & Promoters ... 595
Product Safety Testing
See Testing Facilities 915
Production Companies
See Motion Picture & Television Production 796
Motion Picture Production - Special Interest 796
Production Services
See Motion Picture Pre- & Post-Production Services 796
Professional & Trade Associations
See Associations & Organizations - Professional & Trade 491
Professional & Trade Magazines
See Art & Architecture Magazines 768
Boating Magazines 769
Business & Finance Magazines 769
Computer & Internet Magazines 770
Education Magazines & Journals 770
Entertainment & Music Magazines 770
Government & Military Magazines 771
Law Magazines & Journals 772
Medical Magazines & Journals 772
Science & Nature Magazines 772
Sports Magazines 773
Trade & Industry Magazines 773
Professional Newsletters
See Business & Professional Newsletters 805
Professional Sports Teams
See Sports Teams 902
Sports Teams - Basketball 902
Sports Teams - Football 902
Sports Teams - Hockey 903
Sports Teams - Soccer 903
Programming - Computer
See Computer Programming Services - Custom 583
Computer Systems Design Services 592
Programming Tutorials Software
See Computer Languages & Development Tools 587
Project Management Software
See Business Software (General) 586
Projectors
See Photographic Equipment & Supplies 833
Promoters & Producers - Concerts, Sports, Other Live Events
See Concert, Sports, Other Live Event Producers & Promoters 595
Promotional Products
See Advertising Specialties 469
Propane Gas - Bottled - Retail
See Fuel Dealers 675
Propane Production
See Oil & Gas Extraction 813
Property Development
See Real Estate Developers 867
Propulsion Systems
See Missiles, Space Vehicles, Parts 794
Prosthetic Devices
See Medical Supplies - Mfr 784
Protective Equipment & Clothing
See Personal Protective Equipment & Clothing 828
Protective Services
See Security & Protective Services 893
Protein Bars & Powders
See Vitamins & Nutritional Supplements 937
Public Address Systems
See Audio & Video Equipment 502
Public Administrators Associations
See Government & Public Administration Professional Associations 494
Public Aquariums
See Aquariums - Public 477
Public Broadcasting Organizations 848
See also Radio Networks 857; Television Networks - Broadcast 911
See also Radio Networks 857; Television Networks - Broadcast 911
Public Broadcasting Stations
See Television Stations 911
Public Disclosure
See Ethics Commissions 650
Public Figures
See Governors - State 694
US Senators, Representatives, Delegates 694
Public Interest Research Groups (PIRGs) - State 848
See also Consumer Interest Organizations 484
See also Consumer Interest Organizations 484
Public Policy Research Centers 849
Public Radio Stations
See Radio Stations 864
Public Records Search Services 849
See also Investigative Services 748
Public Relations Firms 850
See also Advertising Agencies 466
Public Television Stations
See Television Stations 911
Public Transportation
See Bus Services - Intercity & Rural 526
Mass Transportation (Local & Suburban) 779
Public Utilities
See Electric Companies - Cooperatives (Rural) 633
Utility Companies 932
Public Warehousing
See Commercial Warehousing 941
Logistics Services (Transportation & Warehousing) 765
Self-Storage Facilities 941
Publications
See Magazines & Journals 768
Newsletters 805
Newspapers 807
Publishers - Comic Books
See Comic Book Publishers 852
Publishing Companies 850
See also Book Producers 522; Magazines & Journals 768; Newsletters 805; Newspapers 807
Atlas & Map Publishers 850
Book Publishers 850
Book Publishers - Religious & Spiritual Books 851
Book Publishers - University Presses 852
Comic Book Publishers 852
Directory Publishers 852
Music Publishers 853
Newspaper Publishers 853
Periodicals Publishers 854
Publishers (Misc) 855
Technical Publishers 855
Publishing Equipment & Systems
See Printing & Publishing Equipment & Systems 848
Publishing Software - Desktop
See Business Software (General) 586
Pulp Mills 855
See also Paper Mills 820; Paperboard Mills 821
Pulp Processing Equipment
See Paper Industries Machinery 820
Pumice
See Abrasive Products 465
Pumps & Motors - Fluid Power 856
Pumps & Pumping Equipment (General Use) 856
See also Industrial Machinery, Equipment, & Supplies 735
Pumps - Gasoline
See Pumps - Measuring & Dispensing 855
Pumps - Hydraulic or Pneumatic
See Pumps & Motors - Fluid Power 856
Pumps - Industrial
See Pumps & Pumping Equipment (General Use) 856
Pumps - Measuring & Dispensing 855
Pumps - Vacuum
See Compressors - Air & Gas 578
Purification Equipment - Air
See Air Purification Equipment - Household 472
Air Purification Equipment - Industrial 472
Purses
See Handbags, Totes, Backpacks 695
Leather Goods - Personal 759
Puzzles
See Toy Stores 922
Toys, Games, Hobbies 922
PX (Post Exchange) Stores
See Variety Stores 935
Pyrotechnics
See Explosives 651

Q

Quality Rating Organizations
See Accreditation & Certification Organizations 480
Quarries
See Mining - Minerals 794
Quartz Crystals (Electronic Applications)
See Electronic Components & Accessories - Mfr 643
Quartzite
See Stone Quarries - Crushed & Broken Stone 794
Quicklime
See Lime 764
Quilting
See Embroidery & Other Decorative Stitching 646

R

Racetracks
See Motor Speedways 796
Racing & Racetracks 856
Racing & Racetracks 856
See also Motor Speedways 796
Rack & Panel Connectors
See Electronic Components & Accessories - Mfr 643
Racks - Storage
See Commercial & Industrial Furniture 676
Fixtures - Office & Store 656
Racks - Wire
See Baskets, Cages, Racks, etc - Wire 516
Racquet Sports Equipment & Supplies
See Sporting Goods 899
Racquet Strings
See Cord & Twine 619
Radar Instruments & Systems
See Navigation & Guidance Instruments & Systems 805
Radiation Therapy Services
See Health Care Providers - Ancillary 697
Radiators - Automotive
See Automotive Parts & Supplies - Mfr 507
Automotive Parts & Supplies - Whol 508
Radio & Television Broadcasting & Communications Equipment 865
See also Audio & Video Equipment 502; Telecommunications Equipment & Systems 908
Radio Broadcasting Equipment
See Radio & Television Broadcasting & Communications Equipment 865
Radio Companies 857
Radio Modems
See Modems 579
Radio Networks 857
Radio Program Transcription Services
See Information Retrieval Services (General) 736
Radio Stations 864
See also Internet Broadcasting 747
Abilene, TX 857
Akron, OH 857
Albany, NY 857
Albuquerque, NM 857
Amarillo, TX 857
Anchorage, AK 857
Ann Arbor, MI 857
Annapolis, MD 858
Asheville, NC 858
Atlanta, GA 858
Baltimore, MD 858
Bangor, ME 858
Baton Rouge, LA 858
Billings, MT 858

Birmingham, AL 858
Bismarck, ND 858
Boise, ID 858
Boston, MA 858
Branson, MO 858
Buffalo, NY 858
Burlington, VT 858
Casper, WY 858
Cedar Rapids, IA 858
Champaign, IL 858
Charleston, WV 858
Charlotte, NC 858
Chattanooga, TN 858
Chicago, IL 858
Cincinnati, OH 858
Cleveland, OH 858
Colorado Springs, CO 859
Columbia, SC 859
Columbus, GA 859
Columbus, OH 859
Corpus Christi, TX 859
Dallas/Fort Worth, TX 859
Denver, CO 859
Des Moines, IA 859
El Paso, TX 859
Erie, PA 859
Eugene, OR 859
Evansville, IN 859
Fairbanks, AK 859
Fargo, ND 859
Flagstaff, AZ 859
Fort Smith, AR 859
Fort Wayne, IN 859
Fresno, CA 859
Grand Forks, ND 859
Grand Rapids, MI 859
Green Bay, WI 859
Greenville, SC 860
Harrisburg, PA 860
Honolulu, HI 860
Hot Springs, AR 860
Houston, TX 860
Huntsville, AL 860
Indianapolis, IN 860
Jackson, MS 860
Jacksonville, FL 860
Johnson City, TN 860
Kansas City, KS & MO 860
Knoxville, TN 860
Lansing, MI 860
Las Vegas, NV 860
Lexington/Frankfort, KY 860
Lincoln, NE 860
Little Rock, AR 860
Los Angeles, CA 860
Louisville, KY 860
Macon, GA 860
Madison, WI 860
Manchester, NH 861
Memphis, TN 861
Miami/Fort Lauderdale, FL 861
Milwaukee, WI 861
Minneapolis/Saint Paul, MN 861
Mobile, AL 861
Monterey, CA 861
Naples, FL 861
Nashville, TN 861
New Orleans, LA 861
New York, NY 861
Omaha, NE 861
Orlando, FL 861
Ottawa, ON 861
Pensacola, FL 861
Peoria, IL 861
Philadelphia, PA 861
Phoenix, AZ 861
Pierre, SD 861
Pittsburgh, PA 861
Portland/Salem, OR 861
Quebec City, QC 862
Raleigh/Durham, NC 862
Reno/Carson City, NV 862
Richmond, VA 862
Riverside/San Bernardino, CA 862
Roanoke, VA 862
Rochester, NY 862
Sacramento, CA 862
Saint Louis, MO 862
Salt Lake City, UT 862
San Antonio, TX 862
San Diego, CA 862
San Francisco, CA 862
San Jose, CA 862
Santa Fe, NM 862
Savannah, GA 862
Scranton, PA 862
Seattle/Tacoma, WA 862
Shreveport, LA 863
Sioux Falls, SD 863
Spokane, WA 863
Springfield, IL 863
Springfield, MA 863
Springfield, MO 863
Stamford/Bridgeport, CT 863
Stockton, CA 863
Tallahassee, FL 863
Tampa/Saint Petersburg, FL 863
Toledo, OH 863
Topeka, KS 863
Trenton, NJ 863
Tulsa, OK 863
Tuscaloosa, AL 863
Washington, DC 863
West Palm Beach, FL 863
Wilmington/Dover, DE 863
Winston-Salem, NC 863

Radio Stations 857
Radio Stations - Public (National Public Radio)
See Radio Stations 864
Radio Syndicators 865
Radiological Equipment
See Imaging Equipment & Systems - Medical 733
Radiology Services
See Imaging Services - Diagnostic 734
Radiopharmaceuticals
See Diagnostic Products 628
Radios - Household & Automotive
See Appliance & Home Electronics Stores 476
Appliances - Whol 477
Audio & Video Equipment 502
Rags - Cleaning, Dusting, Polishing, etc
See Mops, Sponges, Wiping Cloths 795
Rail Transport Services 866
See also Logistics Services (Transportation & Warehousing) 765
Rail Travel 866
See also Mass Transportation (Local & Suburban) 779
Railings - Metal
See Metal Work - Architectural & Ornamental 789
Railings - Wood
See Millwork 793
Railroad Car Leasing
See Transport Equipment Rental 650
Railroad Equipment - Mfr 866
See also Transportation Equipment & Supplies - Whol 924
Railroad Equipment - Model
See Toy Stores 922
Toys, Games, Hobbies 922
Railroad Switching & Terminal Services 866
Railroads
See Logistics Services (Transportation & Warehousing) 765
Rail Transport Services 866
Rail Travel 866
Rain Gear
See Coats (Overcoats, Jackets, Raincoats, etc) 546
Rakes - Agricultural
See Farm Machinery & Equipment - Mfr 652
Farm Machinery & Equipment - Whol 653
Ranches
See Agricultural Products 469
Dude Ranches 631
Ranges & Ovens
See Appliance & Home Electronics Stores 476
Appliances - Major - Mfr 476
Appliances - Whol 477
Rapid Transit Cars & Equipment
See Railroad Equipment - Mfr 866
Rapid Transit Services
See Mass Transportation (Local & Suburban) 779
Raspberries
See Berry Growers 675
Rating Organizations - Quality
See Accreditation & Certification Organizations 480
Ratings Services
See Market Research Firms 778
Rattan Furniture
See Furniture - Mfr 676
Rayon
See Broadwoven Fabric Mills 916
Rayon Fibers
See Synthetic Fibers & Filaments 837
Razor Blades
See Cosmetics, Skin Care, and Other Personal Care Products 620
Cutlery 624
Razors - Safety, Straight, Electric
See Appliances - Small - Mfr 476
Cosmetics, Skin Care, and Other Personal Care Products 620
Real Estate Agents & Brokers 866
Real Estate Developers 867
See also Construction - Building Contractors - Non-Residential 597; Construction - Building Contractors - Residential 597
Real Estate Investment Trusts (REITs) 868
Real Estate Managers & Operators 868
See also Hotels & Hotel Companies 722; Retirement Communities 884
Real Estate Software
See Professional Software (Industry-Specific) 589
Realtor Associations - State 869
See also Real Estate Professionals Associations 498
Reamers - Machine Tool
See Metalworking Devices & Accessories 791
Reaming Machines
See Machine Tools - Metal Cutting Types 767
Receipt & Transaction Printers
See Printers 580
Receipt Books
See Blankbooks & Binders 520
Receivables Management Services
See Collection Agencies 549
Recipes (Cooking) Software
See Personal Software 589
Recognition Products
See Advertising Specialties 469
Trophies, Plaques, Awards 927
Record Labels
See Recording Companies 870
Recording Companies 870
Recording Equipment - Audio or Video
See Audio & Video Equipment 502
Recording Media - Magnetic & Optical 870
See also Photographic Equipment & Supplies 833
Records Storage
See Commercial Warehousing 941
Recovery Programs
See Self-Help Organizations 490
Substance Abuse Treatment Centers 906
Recreation Areas - Outdoor
See Nature Centers, Parks, Other Natural Areas 501
Recreation Associations
See Travel & Recreation Organizations 491
Recreation Facility Operators 870
See also Bowling Centers 524
Recreational Equipment & Supplies
See Sporting Goods Stores 901
Toy Stores 922
Toys, Games, Hobbies 922
Recreational Equipment & Supplies
See Sporting Goods 899
Recreational Vehicles
See Campers, Travel Trailers, Motor Homes 529
Recruiters
See Executive Recruiting Firms 651
Rectifiers
See Electronic Components & Accessories - Mfr 643
Semiconductors & Related Devices 894
Recyclable Materials Recovery 870
Recyclable Metals
See Scrap Metal 889
Recyclable Textiles
See Textile Fiber Processing Mills 917

Recycled Plastics Products ... 870
See also Flooring - Resilient 657
Recycling Companies
See Recyclable Materials Recovery ... 870
Recycling Equipment - Paper
See Paper Industries Machinery ... 820
Reels - Cable
See Cable Reels ... 529
Reference Software
See Educational & Reference Software ... 587
Refined Sugar
See Sugar & Sweeteners ... 665
Refineries - Petroleum or Oil
See Petroleum Refineries ... 830
Refinishing
See Remodeling, Refinishing, Resurfacing Contractors ... 601
Reflecting Tape
See Tape - Cellophane, Gummed, Masking, Pressure Sensitive ... 907
Reflectors
See Lighting Equipment - Vehicular ... 763
Reform School Operators
See Correctional & Detention Management (Privatized) ... 619
Reform Schools
See Juvenile Detention Facilities ... 752
Refractories - Clay ... 870
Refractories - Nonclay ... 870
Refractory Minerals Mining
See Clay, Ceramic, Refractory Minerals Mining ... 794
Refrigeration Equipment - Mfr ... 870
See also Air Conditioning & Heating Equipment - Commercial/Industrial 471
Refrigeration Equipment - Whol ... 871
See also Plumbing, Heating, Air Conditioning Equipment & Supplies - Whol 840
Refrigerators - Household
See Appliance & Home Electronics Stores ... 476
Appliances - Major - Mfr ... 476
Appliances - Whol ... 477
Refuse Systems
See Waste Management ... 941
Regional Interest Magazines
See Travel & Regional Interest Magazines ... 773
Regional Library Systems - Canadian
See Library Systems - Regional - Canadian ... 763
Regional Offices - Federal
See Government - US - Executive Branch ... 690
US Independent Agencies Government Corporations & Quasi-Official Agencies ... 692
Rehabilitation Facilities
See Substance Abuse Treatment Centers ... 906
Rehabilitation Services
See Health Care Providers - Ancillary ... 697
REITs
See Real Estate Investment Trusts (REITs) ... 868
Relays - Electrical
See Controls & Relays - Electrical ... 612
Relief Organizations
See Charitable & Humanitarian Organizations ... 481
Religious Publications
See Book Publishers - Religious & Spiritual Books ... 851
Religious & Spiritual Magazines ... 772
Religious Retreats
See Retreats - Spiritual ... 885
Relocation Consulting Services ... 871
Remediation Services ... 871
See also Environmental Organizations 485; Consulting Services - Environmental 604; Waste Management 941
Remodeling
See Construction - Building Contractors - Residential ... 597
Remodeling, Refinishing, Resurfacing Contractors ... 601
Rental & Leasing
See Aircraft Rental ... 473
Car Rental Agencies ... 530
Equipment Rental & Leasing ... 650
Fleet Leasing & Management ... 656
Stage Equipment & Services ... 904
Truck Rental & Leasing ... 928
Rental - Uniforms & Work Clothes
See Linen & Uniform Supply ... 764
Rental - Video
See Video Stores ... 937
Renters Insurance
See Property & Casualty Insurance ... 743
Repair Services
See Aircraft Service & Repair ... 474
Automotive Services ... 509
Replication Services
See Duplication & Replication Services ... 632
Report Writing Software
See Business Software (General) ... 586
Representatives - Congressional - US
See US Senators, Representatives, Delegates ... 694
Rescue Equipment
See Safety Equipment - Mfr ... 886
Research Centers & Institutions ... 871
See also Market Research Firms 778; Public Policy Research Centers 849; Testing Facilities 915
Reservations Services
See Hotel Reservations Services ... 720
Travel Services - Online ... 927
Reservations Systems - Computer
See Global Distribution Systems (GDSs) ... 682
Resident Theaters
See Theaters - Resident ... 918
Residential Air Conditioning & Heating Equipment
See Air Conditioning & Heating Equipment - Residential ... 472
Residential Building Construction
See Construction - Building Contractors - Residential ... 597
Residential Cleaning Services
See Cleaning Services ... 545
Residential Lighting Fixtures
See Lighting Fixtures & Equipment ... 763
Resilient Flooring
See Flooring - Resilient ... 657
Resins - Synthetic
See Synthetic Resins & Plastics Materials ... 837
Resistors - Electronic
See Electronic Components & Accessories - Mfr ... 643
Resort Conference Centers
See Hotels - Conference Center ... 721
Resort Operation & Management
See Resorts & Resort Companies ... 873
Resort Owners
See Resorts & Resort Companies ... 873
Resort Spas
See Spas - Hotel & Resort ... 897
Resorts & Resort Companies ... 873
See also Casinos 532; Dude Ranches 631; Hotels - Conference Center 721; Hotels & Hotel Companies 722; Spas - Hotel & Resort 897
Restaurant Companies ... 880
See also Bakeries 511; Food Service 669; Franchises 672; Ice Cream & Dairy Stores 733
Restaurant Furniture, Equipment, Supplies
See Commercial & Industrial Furniture ... 676
Food Service Equipment & Supplies ... 669
Restaurant Operators & Managers
See Restaurant Companies ... 880
Restaurants (Individual) ... 881
See also Shopping/Dining/Entertainment Districts 501; Restaurant Companies 880
Resume Banks - Internet
See Employment Services - Online ... 646
Retailers Associations
See Consumer Sales & Service Professionals Associations ... 492
Sales & Marketing Professional Associations ... 499
Retirement Communities ... 884
See also Long-Term Care Facilities 766
Retreats - Spiritual ... 885
Rice Milling
See Grain Mill Products ... 662
Rifles
See Firearms & Ammunition (Non-Military) ... 655
Weapons & Ordnance (Military) ... 942
Right-to-Die Organizations
See Civil & Human Rights Organizations ... 484
Riprap
See Stone Quarries - Crushed & Broken Stone ... 794
Risk Management Software
See Professional Software (Industry-Specific) ... 589
Riverboat Cruises
See Cruises - Riverboat ... 624
Riveting Machines
See Machine Tools - Metal Forming Types ... 768
Rivets
See Fasteners & Fastening Systems ... 654
Hardware - Whol ... 697
Road Building Contractors
See Highway, Street, Bridge, Tunnel Construction ... 598
Robes
See Robes (Ceremonial) ... 546
Sleepwear ... 547
Robot Systems
See Industrial Machinery, Equipment, & Supplies ... 735
Robotics Research
See Research Centers & Institutions ... 871
Rock Salt
See Chemical & Fertilizer Minerals Mining ... 794
Rocket Motors
See Missiles, Space Vehicles, Parts ... 794
Rockets & Rocket Systems
See Missiles, Space Vehicles, Parts ... 794
Roller Bearings
See Bearings - Ball & Roller ... 516
Rolling Mill Machinery ... 885
See also Metalworking Machinery 792
Rolling, Drawing, Extruding - Metals
See Metal Industries (Misc) ... 788
Wire & Cable ... 943
Ronald McDonald Houses
See Hospital Hospitality Houses - Ronald McDonald House ... 712
Roofing Contractors
See Roofing, Siding, Sheet Metal Contractors ... 601
Roofing Materials
See Asphalt Paving & Roofing Materials ... 479
Clay Products - Structural ... 544
Roofing, Siding, Insulation Materials ... 604
Roofing Tiles & Slabs - Concrete
See Concrete Products - Mfr ... 595
Rope
See Cord & Twine ... 619
Royalty Trusts ... 885
Rubber - Synthetic
See Synthetic Rubber ... 838
Rubber Cement
See Adhesives & Sealants ... 466
Rubber Compounding
See Synthetic Rubber ... 838
Rubber Goods ... 885
Rubber Goods - Mechanical ... 886
Rubber Goods - Synthetic Rubber
See Rubber Goods ... 885
Rubber Hose & Belting
See Hose & Belting - Rubber or Plastics ... 709
Rubber Stamps
See Marking Devices ... 778
Rug Cleaning Services
See Cleaning Services ... 545
Rugs
See Carpets & Rugs ... 531
Floor Coverings Stores ... 657
Runaways
See Children & Family Advocacy Organizations ... 482
Rural Bus Services
See Bus Services - Intercity & Rural ... 526
Bus Services - School ... 526
Rural Electric Cooperatives
See Electric Companies - Cooperatives (Rural) ... 633
Rust Preventatives
See Chemicals - Specialty ... 542
RV Conversions
See Van Conversions ... 509
RV Resort Operators
See Campground Operators ... 529
RVs
See Campers, Travel Trailers, Motor Homes ... 529

S

Saccharin
See Sugar & Sweeteners ... 665
Saddles & Tack
See Leather Goods (Misc) ... 759
Safaris
See Tour Operators ... 921
Safes
See Security Products & Services ... 892
Safes & Vaults - Whol
See Business Machines - Whol ... 527

Index

Safety Equipment - Mfr ... 886
See also Medical Supplies - Mfr 784; Personal Protective Equipment & Clothing 828
Safety Equipment - Whol ... 886
Safety Pins
See Piece Goods & Notions ... 834
Safety Razors
See Cosmetics, Skin Care, and Other Personal Care Products 620
Safety Restraints
See Safety Equipment - Mfr ... 886
Safety Tests
See Testing Facilities ... 915
Sailing Magazines
See Boating Magazines ... 769
Sails
See Tarps, Tents, Covers ... 907
Salad Dressings
See Fruits & Vegetables - Pickled ... 661
Salami
See Meat Products - Prepared ... 663
Salon Furniture & Fixtures
See Beauty Salon Equipment & Supplies ... 517
Salt ... 886
See also Spices, Seasonings, Herbs 665
Salt Mining
See Chemical & Fertilizer Minerals Mining ... 794
Saltines
See Cookies & Crackers ... 660
Salvage Services - Marine
See Marine Services ... 777
Sample Books
See Blankbooks & Binders ... 520
Sanctuaries - Wildlife
See Nature Centers, Parks, Other Natural Areas ... 501
Sand Bags
See Bags - Textile ... 511
Sandals
See Footwear ... 669
Sanders
See Tools - Power ... 921
Sandpaper
See Abrasive Products ... 465
SATCOM
See Satellite Communications Services ... 886
Satellite Communications Services ... 886
See also Cable & Other Pay Television Services 528; Internet Service Providers (ISPs) 748; Telecommunications Services 908
Satellite Dishes
See Radio & Television Broadcasting & Communications Equipment ... 865
Satellite Equipment & Systems
See Navigation & Guidance Instruments & Systems ... 805
Radio & Television Broadcasting & Communications Equipment ... 865
Satellite Television
See Cable & Other Pay Television Services ... 528
Sausage & Sausage Casings
See Meat Products - Prepared ... 663
Savings Accounts - Medical
See Medical & Hospitalization Insurance ... 741
Savings Banks
See Banks - Commercial & Savings ... 511
Savings Programs - College
See Student Assistance Programs ... 905
Saw Blades & Handsaws ... 886
See also Tools - Hand & Edge 920
Sawmill Machinery
See Woodworking Machinery ... 945
Sawmills & Planing Mills ... 887
Saws - Chain
See Tools - Power ... 921
Saws - Electric
See Tools - Power ... 921
Saws - Industrial
See Woodworking Machinery ... 945
SBICs (Small Business Investment Companies)
See Investment Companies - Small Business ... 750
Scaffolding - Metal - Mfr
See Metal Work - Architectural & Ornamental ... 789
Scales & Balances ... 887
See also Laboratory Apparatus & Furniture 755
Scanning Devices - Medical
See Imaging Equipment & Systems - Medical ... 733
Scanning Software
See Systems & Utilities Software ... 591
Scenery - Theater & Film
See Stage Equipment & Services ... 904
Schiffli Machine Embroideries
See Embroidery & Other Decorative Stitching ... 646
Scholarships - College
See Student Assistance Programs ... 905
School Boards (Public) ... 887
School Bus Services
See Bus Services - School ... 526
School Furniture
See Institutional & Other Public Buildings Furniture ... 678
School Supplies
See Office & School Supplies ... 812
Schools
See Children's Learning Centers ... 543
Colleges & Universities - Christian ... 558
Colleges & Universities - Four-Year ... 559
Colleges & Universities - Graduate & Professional Schools ... 574
Colleges & Universities - Historically Black ... 577
Colleges & Universities - Jesuit ... 578
Colleges - Bible ... 549
Colleges - Community & Junior ... 550
Colleges - Culinary Arts ... 557
Colleges - Fine Arts ... 557
Colleges - Tribal ... 557
Colleges - Women's (Four-Year) ... 558
Educational Institution Operators & Managers ... 632
Language Schools ... 756
Military Service Academies ... 793
Preparatory Schools - Boarding ... 844
School Boards (Public) ... 887
Training Programs (Misc) ... 924
Universities - Canadian ... 932
Vocational & Technical Schools ... 938
Science Professionals Associations
See Technology, Science, Engineering Professionals Associations ... 499
Scientific Journals
See Science & Nature Magazines ... 772
Scissors
See Cutlery ... 624
Scoreboards
See Signs ... 896
Scrap Metal ... 889
See also Recyclable Materials Recovery 870
Scrapbooks
See Blankbooks & Binders ... 520
Screen Printing ... 890
Screening - Woven Wire ... 890
Screening Equipment - X-Ray
See Security Products & Services ... 892
Screening Systems - Cargo
See Security Products & Services ... 892
Screw Machine Products
See Precision Machined Products ... 843
Screw Machines - Automatic
See Machine Tools - Metal Cutting Types ... 767
Screws
See Fasteners & Fastening Systems ... 654
Hardware - Whol ... 697
Sea Cruises
See Cruise Lines ... 624
Seafood - Canned - Mfr
See Fish & Seafood - Canned ... 660
Seafood - Fresh or Frozen - Mfr
See Fish & Seafood - Fresh or Frozen ... 660
Seafood - Fresh or Frozen - Whol
See Fish & Seafood - Whol ... 666
Sealants
See Adhesives & Sealants ... 466
Seals - Mechanical
See Gaskets, Packing, Sealing Devices ... 681
Seals - Notary, Corporate, etc
See Marking Devices ... 778
Search & Detection Equipment
See Navigation & Guidance Instruments & Systems ... 805
Search & Rescue Services
See Helicopter Transport Services ... 700
Search Engines
See Internet Search Engines, Portals, Directories ... 748
Seasoning Salt
See Salt ... 886
Seasonings
See Spices, Seasonings, Herbs ... 665
Seat Belts
See Safety Equipment - Mfr ... 886
Seat Frames - Automobile
See Metal Fabricating - Custom ... 787
Seating - Public Buildings
See Institutional & Other Public Buildings Furniture ... 678
Seating - Vehicular ... 890
Secretarial Schools
See Vocational & Technical Schools ... 938
Securities & Commodities Exchanges ... 892
Securities Administrators
See Government - State ... 684
Securities Brokers & Dealers ... 890
See also Commodity Contracts Brokers & Dealers 578; Electronic Communications Networks (ECNs) 643; Investment Advice & Management 748; Mutual Funds 803
Security & Protective Services ... 893
See also Investigative Services 748
Security Gates
See Fences - Mfr ... 654
Security Guards
See Security & Protective Services ... 893
Security Products & Services ... 892
See also Audio & Video Equipment 502; Fire Protection Systems 655; Signals & Sirens - Electric 896
Security Systems - Computer
See Systems & Utilities Software ... 591
Seed Companies ... 894
See also Farm Supplies 653
Seed Corn
See Grain Farms ... 469
Seltzer
See Soft Drinks - Mfr ... 518
Semiconductor Manufacturing Systems & Equipment . 894
Semiconductors & Related Devices ... 894
See also Electronic Components & Accessories - Mfr 643; Printed Circuit Boards 845
Seminars - Executive & Management
See Training Programs - Corporate ... 923
Semitrailers
See Truck Trailers ... 928
Senators - US
See US Senators, Representatives, Delegates ... 694
Senior Care
See Home Health Services ... 707
Senior Citizen Tours
See Tour Operators ... 921
Senior Citizens' Organizations
See Children & Family Advocacy Organizations ... 482
Senior Living Facilities
See Retirement Communities ... 884
Serigraphy
See Screen Printing ... 890
Serology Diagnostic Products
See Diagnostic Products ... 628
Serums
See Biotechnology Companies ... 519
Servers - Computer Networks
See Computer Networking Products & Systems ... 582
Service Bureaus - Computer
See Data Processing & Related Services ... 625
Typesetting & Related Services ... 931
Service Industries Associations
See Consumer Sales & Service Professionals Associations ... 492
Service Plazas
See Gas Stations ... 680
Service Providers - Internet
See Internet Service Providers (ISPs) ... 748
Service Stations
See Gas Stations ... 680
Servomotors
See Motors (Electric) & Generators ... 798
Settlement Services - Litigation
See Litigation Support Services ... 764
Sewage Plant Construction
See Plant Construction ... 599
Sewer Lines Construction
See Water & Sewer Lines, Pipelines, Power Lines Construction ... 599
Sewer Pumps
See Pumps & Pumping Equipment (General Use) ... 856
Sewing Machines

See Appliances - Small - Mfr 476
Sewing Patterns
See Patterns - Sewing 825
Sewing Supplies
See Fabric Stores 651
Piece Goods & Notions 834
Shades - Window
See Blinds & Shades 520
Shampoos
See Cosmetics, Skin Care, and Other Personal Care Products 620
Shear Knives
See Metalworking Devices & Accessories 791
Sheds & Outbuildings
See Buildings - Prefabricated - Metal 525
Buildings - Prefabricated - Wood 525
Sheep
See Livestock - Whol 765
Sheet Metal Work 895
See also Plumbing, Heating, Air Conditioning Contractors 601; Roofing, Siding, Sheet Metal Contractors 601
Sheet Metalworking Machines
See Machine Tools - Metal Forming Types 768
Sheet Music
See Music Publishers 853
Shelving
See Commercial & Industrial Furniture 676
Fixtures - Office & Store 656
Shims
See Metal Stampings 789
Shin Guards
See Personal Protective Equipment & Clothing 828
Ship Building & Repairing 896
Ship Certification Services
See Marine Services 777
Ship Lighting Equipment
See Lighting Equipment - Vehicular 763
Shipping
See Freight Transport - Deep Sea (Domestic Ports) 674
Freight Transport - Deep Sea (Foreign Ports) 674
Freight Transport - Inland Waterways 674
Logistics Services (Transportation & Warehousing) 765
Ports & Port Authorities 842
Shipping Agents
See Freight Forwarders 673
Shipping Cases
See Luggage, Bags, Cases 767
Shipping Container Rental - Cargo & Freight
See Transport Equipment Rental 650
Shipping Containers
See Containers - Metal (Barrels, Drums, Kegs) 610
Shipping Documents Preparation
See Freight Forwarders 673
Shipyards
See Ship Building & Repairing 896
Shoes
See Footwear 669
Shooting Sports
See Firearms & Ammunition (Non-Military) 655
Shopping Agents
See Buyer's Guides - Online 528
Shopping Bags
See Bags - Paper 510
Bags - Plastics 510
Shopping Malls
See Malls - Shopping 775
Shortening
See Oils - Edible (Margarine, Shortening, Table Oils, etc) 664
Shot Peening
See Metal Heat Treating 787
Shotguns
See Firearms & Ammunition (Non-Military) 655
Showcases
See Fixtures - Office & Store 656
Shower Curtains
See Textile Products - Household 917
Shower Heads
See Plumbing Fixtures & Fittings - Metal 839
Showers - Emergency
See Safety Equipment - Mfr 886
Shredders
See Business Machines - Mfr 527
Shredders - Agricultural
See Farm Machinery & Equipment - Mfr 652
Farm Machinery & Equipment - Whol 653
Shutters - Window (All Types) 896
Sidewalks - Moving
See Elevators, Escalators, Moving Walkways 645
Siding
See Roofing, Siding, Insulation Materials 604
Roofing, Siding, Sheet Metal Contractors 601
Signals & Sirens - Electric 896
Signals (Electrical) Testing Instruments
See Electrical Signals Measuring & Testing Instruments 642
Signs 896
See also Displays - Exhibit & Trade Show 629; Displays - Point-of-Purchase 629; Signals & Sirens - Electric 896
Silica Clay
See Clay, Ceramic, Refractory Minerals Mining 794
Silica Sand
See Sand & Gravel Pits 794
Silicon Wafers
See Semiconductors & Related Devices 894
Silicone Resins
See Synthetic Resins & Plastics Materials 837
Silicone Rubbers
See Synthetic Rubber 838
Silk
See Broadwoven Fabric Mills 916
Silk Screen Equipment
See Textile Machinery 916
Silk Screening
See Screen Printing 890
Silver Mining
See Mining - Metals 793
Silverware 897
See also Cutlery 624; Metal Stampings 789
Simulation & Training Systems 897
Simulation Software
See Games & Entertainment Software 588
Sinks
See Plumbing Fixtures & Fittings - Metal 839
Plumbing Fixtures & Fittings - Vitreous China & Earthenware 840
Sirens
See Signals & Sirens - Electric 896
Skating Centers
See Recreation Facility Operators 870
Skating Equipment & Supplies
See Sporting Goods 899
Skids & Pallets
See Pallets & Skids 819
Skiing Equipment & Supplies
See Sporting Goods 899
Skin Banks
See Organ & Tissue Banks 817
Skin Care Products
See Cosmetics, Skin Care, and Other Personal Care Products 620
Slag
See Stone Quarries - Crushed & Broken Stone 794
Slate - Cutting & Finishing
See Stone (Cut) & Stone Products 905
Sleeper Sofas
See Household Furniture 677
Sleeping Bag Warmers
See Thermal Management Products - Personal 918
Sleeping Bags
See Sporting Goods 899
Slippers
See Footwear 669
Sliprings
See Motors (Electric) & Generators 798
Slot Machines
See Automatic Merchandising Equipment & Systems 504
Games & Gaming 680
Small Business Investment Companies
See Investment Companies - Small Business 750
Investment Companies - Specialized Small Business 751
Smallwares
See Narrow Fabric Mills 917
Smart Card Readers
See Scanning Equipment 580
Smart Card Systems
See Point-of-Sale (POS) & Point-of-Information (POI) Systems 841
Smart Cards 897
Smoke Alarms
See Fire Protection Systems 655
Smokeless Tobacco
See Tobacco & Tobacco Products 919
Snack Foods
See Confectionery & Snack Foods - Whol 666
Snack Foods 664
Snaps
See Piece Goods & Notions 834
Snow Fences
See Fences - Mfr 654
Snowboarding Equipment & Supplies
See Sporting Goods 899
Snowmobiles 897
See also Sporting Goods 899
Snowplow Attachments
See Construction Machinery & Equipment 602
Snuff
See Tobacco & Tobacco Products 919
Soaps - Hand, Face, Body
See Cosmetics, Skin Care, and Other Personal Care Products 620
Soaps - Household Cleaning
See Cleaning Products 544
Soccer Equipment & Supplies
See Sporting Goods 899
Soccer Teams
See Sports Teams - Soccer 903
Social Issues Newsletters
See Health & Social Issues Newsletters 806
Social Organizations
See Fraternal & Social Organizations 485
Social Sciences Research
See Research Centers & Institutions 871
Social Welfare Organizations
See Charitable & Humanitarian Organizations 481
Children & Family Advocacy Organizations 482
Health & Health-Related Organizations 486
Socks
See Hosiery & Socks 546
Soda Ash
See Chemical & Fertilizer Minerals Mining 794
Soda Fountain Equipment
See Refrigeration Equipment - Whol 871
Software
See Computer Software 586
Software Services
See Application Service Providers (ASPs) 477
Solar Cells
See Semiconductors & Related Devices 894
Soldering Equipment
See Welding & Soldering Equipment 942
Soldering Fluxes
See Chemicals - Specialty 542
Solenoid Valves
See Valves & Hose Fittings - Fluid Power 935
Solvents
See Chemicals - Industrial (Organic) 541
Sonar Systems & Equipment
See Navigation & Guidance Instruments & Systems 805
Sororities
See Greek Letter Societies 486
Sound Cards
See Multimedia Equipment & Supplies 580
Sound Services - Concert, Stage, Theater, etc
See Stage Equipment & Services 904
Sound Systems
See Audio & Video Equipment 502
Soup Mixes
See Fruits & Vegetables - Dried or Dehydrated 661
Souvenir Products - Whol
See Gifts & Novelties - Whol 681
Soy Sauce
See Fruits & Vegetables - Pickled 661
Soybean Oil
See Oil Mills - Cottonseed, Soybean, Other Vegetable Oils 664
Soybeans
See Grain Farms 469
Spa Equipment & Supplies
See Beauty Salon Equipment & Supplies 517
Space Habitat Modules
See Missiles, Space Vehicles, Parts 794
Space Heaters
See Appliances - Small - Mfr 476
Space Helmets
See Personal Protective Equipment & Clothing 828
Space Operations Facilities Management Services

See Facilities Management Services. 652
Space Sciences Research
See Research Centers & Institutions. 871
Space Vehicles
See Missiles, Space Vehicles, Parts. 794
Spas - Health & Fitness 897
See also Health & Fitness Centers 698; Spas - Hotel & Resort 897; Weight Loss Centers & Services 942
Spas - Hotel & Resort 897
See also Spas - Health & Fitness 897
Spas - Luxury
See Spas - Hotel & Resort 897
Spas - Mfr
See Hot Tubs, Spas, Whirlpool Baths. 720
Speakers - Audio
See Audio & Video Equipment. 502
Speakers - Computer
See Multimedia Equipment & Supplies 580
Speakers Bureaus 899
Special Interest Groups
See Political Action Committees. 841
Special Interest Magazines
See Fraternal & Special Interest Magazines 770
Special Interest Motion Pictures
See Motion Picture Production - Special Interest. 796
Special Needs Facilities
See Developmental Centers 628
Special Trade Contractors
See Construction - Special Trade Contractors 599
Specialized Small Business Investment Companies
See Investment Companies - Specialized Small Business 751
Specialty Materials - Theatrical
See Stage Equipment & Services 904
Specialty Minerals Mining
See Minerals Mining (Misc). 794
Specialty Papers
See Coated & Laminated Paper 819
Specialty Pharmacy Services
See Pharmacy Management Services. 833
Specialty Tours
See Tour Operators. 921
Specialty Transformers
See Transformers - Power, Distribution, Specialty. 924
Speech Recognition Software
See Systems & Utilities Software 591
Speech Therapy Services
See Health Care Providers - Ancillary. 697
Speed Changers, Industrial High Speed Drives, Gears 899
See also Aircraft Parts & Auxiliary Equipment 473; Automotive Parts & Supplies - Mfr 507; Controls & Relays - Electrical 612; Machine Shops 767; Motors (Electric) & Generators 798; Power Transmission Equipment - Mechanical 843
Speedways - Motor
See Motor Speedways 796
Sperm Banks
See Organ & Tissue Banks. 817
Spinal Cord Stimulation Systems
See Electromedical & Electrotherapeutic Equipment 642
Spiritual Publications
See Book Publishers - Religious & Spiritual Books 851
Religious & Spiritual Magazines 772
Spiritual Retreats
See Retreats - Spiritual. 885
Spline Rolling Machines
See Machine Tools - Metal Forming Types 768
Sponges
See Mops, Sponges, Wiping Cloths. 795
Sport Utility Vehicles
See Automobiles - Mfr. 507
Sportfishing Boats
See Boats - Recreational. 521
Sporting Goods 899
See also All-Terrain Vehicles 475; Bicycles & Bicycle Parts & Accessories 519; Boats - Recreational 521; Cord & Twine 619; Exercise & Fitness Equipment 651; Firearms & Ammunition (Non-Military) 655; Gym & Playground Equipment 695; Handbags, Totes, Backpacks 695; Motor Vehicles - Commercial & Special Purpose 797; Personal Protective Equipment & Clothing 828; Snowmobiles 897; Swimming Pools 906; Tarps, Tents, Covers 907
Sporting Goods Stores 901
Sports Bags and Cases
See Luggage, Bags, Cases 767
Sports Cars
See Automobiles - Mfr. 507
Sports Clubs
See Sports Teams. 902
Sports Teams - Basketball 902
Sports Teams - Football 902
Sports Teams - Hockey 903
Sports Teams - Soccer 903
Sports Commissions & Regulatory Agencies - State 902
Sports Drinks
See Soft Drinks - Mfr 518
Soft Drinks - Whol. 518
Sports Drinks (Powdered)
See Diet & Health Foods 660
Sports Facilities
See Motor Speedways 796
Racing & Racetracks 856
Stadiums & Arenas 903
Sports Museums
See Museums & Halls of Fame - Sports. 802
Sports Promoters
See Concert, Sports, Other Live Event Producers & Promoters. 595
Sports Teams 902
See also Sports Organizations 490
Sports Teams - Basketball 902
See also Sports Organizations 490
National Basketball Association (NBA) 902
Women's National Basketball Association (WNBA) 902
Sports Teams - Football 902
See also Sports Organizations 490
Arena Football League (AFL) 902
Canadian Football League (CFL) 902
Sports Teams - Hockey 903
See also Sports Organizations 490
Sports Teams - Soccer 903
See also Sports Organizations 490
Sportswear
See Athletic Apparel 545
Casual Wear (Men's & Women's) 545
Swimwear 547
Sprayers
See Compressors - Air & Gas 578
Sprayers - Agricultural
See Farm Machinery & Equipment - Mfr 652
Farm Machinery & Equipment - Whol 653
Spreadsheet Software
See Business Software (General) 586
Spring Water
See Water - Bottled. 941
Springs - Automotive
See Springs - Heavy-Gauge 903
Springs - Heavy-Gauge 903
Springs - Light-Gauge 903
Springs - Steel
See Springs - Heavy-Gauge 903
Springs - Wire
See Springs - Light-Gauge. 903
Sprinklers & Sprinkler Systems - Lawn
See Lawn & Garden Equipment 758
Sprockets
See Power Transmission Equipment - Mechanical. 843
SSBICs (Specialized Small Business Investment Companies)
See Investment Companies - Specialized Small Business 751
SSPs (Storage Service Providers)
See Application Service Providers (ASPs) 477
Stadium Facilities Management Services
See Facilities Management Services. 652
Stadiums & Arenas 903
See also Convention Centers 613; Performing Arts Facilities 826
Staffing Services 904
See also Employment Offices - Government 646; Employment Services - Online 646; Executive Recruiting Firms 651
Stage Equipment & Services 904
Stage Rigging
See Stage Equipment & Services 904
Stainless Steel Plumbing Fixtures
See Plumbing Fixtures & Fittings - Metal. 839
Stainless Steel Ware
See Silverware 897
Stamping - Paper
See Paper Finishers (Embossing, Coating, Gilding, Stamping). 820
Stampings - Automotive
See Metal Stampings - Automotive 789
Stampings - Metal
See Metal Stampings 789
Stamps - Metal or Rubber (Hand Stamps)
See Marking Devices 778
Standards Development
See Research Centers & Institutions. 871
State - US Department of
See US Department of State 692
State Bar Associations
See Bar Associations - State. 516
State Chambers of Commerce
See Chambers of Commerce - US - State 540
State Correctional Facilities
See Correctional Facilities - State. 619
State Dental Associations
See Dental Associations - State 627
State Employment Offices
See Employment Offices - Government 646
State Ethics Commissions
See Ethics Commissions 650
State Government
See Government - State 684
State Governors
See Governors - State. 694
State Legislation Hotlines
See Legislation Hotlines. 759
State Library Associations
See Library Associations - State & Province 763
State Lotteries
See Lotteries, Games, Sweepstakes 767
State Medical Associations
See Medical Associations - State. 781
State Nurses Associations
See Nurses Associations - State. 812
State Parks
See Parks - State 822
State Pharmacy Associations
See Pharmacy Associations - State 832
State Prisons
See Correctional Facilities - State. 619
State Public Interest Research Groups
See Public Interest Research Groups (PIRGs) - State. 848
State Sports Commissions
See Sports Commissions & Regulatory Agencies - State. 902
State Student Aid Agencies
See Student Assistance Programs 905
State Veterans Nursing Homes
See Veterans Nursing Homes - State 936
State Veterinary Medical Associations
See Veterinary Medical Associations - State. 936
Stationery - Mfr
See Writing Paper. 819
Stationery Stores
See Card Shops 530
Office Supply Stores 813
Steel - Mfr 905
Steel Distributors & Warehouses
See Metals Service Centers 790
Steel Erectors
See Structural Steel Erection 602
Steel Fabricators
See Metal - Structural (Fabricated). 786
Steel Foundries
See Foundries - Iron & Steel 671
Steel Investment Castings
See Foundries - Investment 671
Steel Mills
See Steel - Mfr. 905
Steel Plumbing Fixtures (Stainless, Enameled, Porcelain-on-Steel)
See Plumbing Fixtures & Fittings - Metal. 839
Steel Springs
See Springs - Heavy-Gauge. 903
Steel Wool
See Abrasive Products 465
Stem Cell Transplant Centers
See Transplant Centers - Blood Stem Cell 924
Stencils
See Marking Devices 778
Stevedoring
See Marine Services. 777

Stickers
See Labels - Other Than Fabric 752
Stock Brokers
See Securities Brokers & Dealers 890
Stock Car Racing
See Motor Speedways 796
Stock Carts
See Fixtures - Office & Store 656
Stock Exchanges
See Securities & Commodities Exchanges 892
Stock Tickers Software
See Internet & Communications Software 588
Stockings
See Hosiery & Socks 546
Stocks Information
See Investment Guides - Online 751
Investment Newsletters 807
Stockyards
See Cattle Ranches, Farms, Feedlots (Beef Cattle) 469
Stone (Cut) & Stone Products 905
Stone - Whol
See Brick, Stone, Related Materials 602
Stone Fruits
See Deciduous Tree Fruit Growers 675
Stone Setting Contractors
See Masonry & Stone Contractors 600
Stoppers & Lids (Pharmaceutical Containers)
See Rubber Goods 885
Storage Batteries
See Batteries 516
Storage Containers
See Containers - Metal (Barrels, Drums, Kegs) 610
Plastics Products - Household 838
Storage Facilities
See Logistics Services (Transportation & Warehousing) 765
Petroleum Storage Terminals 831
Warehousing & Storage 941
Storage Racks
See Commercial & Industrial Furniture 676
Storage Service Providers (SSPs)
See Application Service Providers (ASPs) 477
Store Fixtures
See Fixtures - Office & Store 656
Storm Shutters
See Shutters - Window (All Types) 896
Stoves - Cooking
See Appliance & Home Electronics Stores 476
Appliances - Major - Mfr 476
Appliances - Whol 477
Strawberries
See Berry Growers 675
Streaming Media Services
See Internet Broadcasting 747
Streetcars & Equipment
See Railroad Equipment - Mfr 866
Stucco
See Brick, Stone, Related Materials 602
Stucco Contractors
See Concrete Contractors 599
Student Assistance Programs 905
Student Loans
See Credit & Financing - Consumer 620
Student Assistance Programs 905
Student Tours
See Tour Operators 921
Styrofoam
See Plastics Foam Products 836
Submersible Pumps
See Pumps & Pumping Equipment (General Use) 856
Substance Abuse Programs
See Self-Help Organizations 490
Substance Abuse Treatment Centers 906
See also Self-Help Organizations 490; General Hospitals - Canada 712; General Hospitals - US 713; Psychiatric Hospitals 718
Sugar - Granulated
See Sugar & Sweeteners 665
Sugar - Powdered
See Sugar & Sweeteners 665
Sugar Substitutes
See Sugar & Sweeteners 665
Suicide
See Bio-Recovery Services 519
Health & Health-Related Organizations 486
Suits
See Men's Clothing 546
Women's Clothing 547
Sulphur Mining
See Chemical & Fertilizer Minerals Mining 794
Sump Pumps
See Pumps & Pumping Equipment (General Use) 856
Sunglasses
See Ophthalmic Goods 816
Optical Goods Stores 816
Sunrooms - Prefabricated
See Buildings - Prefabricated - Metal 525
Supercomputers
See Research Centers & Institutions 871
Supermarkets
See Grocery Stores 694
Supply Chain Management Services
See Logistics Services (Transportation & Warehousing) 765
Support Groups
See Self-Help Organizations 490
Supreme Court - US
See US Supreme Court 694
Supreme Courts - State
See Government - State 684
Surface Active Agents
See Cleaning Products 544
Surface Mining
See Mining - Coal 793
Surfactants - Whol
See Chemicals & Related Products - Whol 543
Surfing Boards
See Sporting Goods 899
Surge Protectors
See Wiring Devices - Current-Carrying 943
Surgery Centers - Ambulatory
See Health Care Providers - Ancillary 697
Surgical Gowns
See Personal Protective Equipment & Clothing 828
Surgical Instruments & Apparatus
See Medical Instruments & Apparatus - Mfr 782
Surgical Monitoring Systems
See Electromedical & Electrotherapeutic Equipment 642
Surgical Supplies
See Medical Supplies - Mfr 784
Surplus Stores
See Variety Stores 935
Surveying Equipment
See Measuring, Testing, Controlling Instruments 780
Surveying, Mapping, Related Services 906
See also Engineering & Design 647
Suspenders
See Belts (Leather, Plastics, Fabric) 545
SUVs (Sport Utility Vehicles)
See Automobiles - Mfr 507
Sweepstakes
See Lotteries, Games, Sweepstakes 767
Sweet Corn
See Grain Farms 469
Sweeteners - Artificial
See Sugar & Sweeteners 665
Swimming Pool Facilities Management (Commercial Pools)
See Facilities Management Services 652
Swimming Pools 906
Swings
See Outdoor Furniture 678
Switchboard Apparatus
See Switchgear & Switchboard Apparatus 906
Switchgear & Switchboard Apparatus 906
See also Transformers - Power, Distribution, Specialty 924; Wiring Devices - Current-Carrying 943
Switching Services - Railroad
See Railroad Switching & Terminal Services 866
Synagogues
See Churches, Cathedrals, Synagogues, Temples 501
Syndicators - Radio
See Radio Syndicators 865
Syndicators -Television
See Television Syndicators 915
Synthetic Rubber Goods
See Rubber Goods 885
Syrup - Chocolate, Caramel, etc
See Flavoring Extracts & Syrups 661

T

T-Shirts
See Casual Wear (Men's & Women's) 545
Undergarments 547
Table & Kitchen Supplies - China & Earthenware 907
See also
Table Linens
See Home Furnishings - Whol 706
Textile Products - Household 917
Table Salt
See Salt 886
Tables
See Furniture - Mfr 676
Tablets - Writing
See Writing Paper 819
Tableware
See Glassware & Pottery - Household 682
Home Furnishings - Whol 706
Home Furnishings Stores 706
Table & Kitchen Supplies - China & Earthenware 907
Tableware - Plastics
See Plastics Foam Products 836
Plastics Products - Household 838
Tagging Systems - Pet
See Pet Products 829
Tags
See Labels - Other Than Fabric 752
Tail Lights
See Lighting Equipment - Vehicular 763
Talc Mining
See Minerals Mining (Misc) 794
Tank Suits
See Swimwear 547
Tank Trailers
See Truck Trailers 928
Tanks & Tank Components - Military
See Weapons & Ordnance (Military) 942
Tanning - Leather
See Leather Tanning & Finishing 759
Tanning Beds
See Beauty Salon Equipment & Supplies 517
Tape - Adhesive
See Medical Supplies - Mfr 784
Tape - Cellophane, Gummed, Masking, Pressure Sensitive 907
See also Medical Supplies - Mfr 784
Tape - Reflective
See Safety Equipment - Mfr 886
Tape - Cellophane, Gummed, Masking, Pressure Sensitive 907
Tape Duplication
See Duplication & Replication Services 632
Tape Measures
See Piece Goods & Notions 834
Tape Recorders/Players
See Audio & Video Equipment 502
Tapes - Audio
See Book, Music, Video Clubs 522
Music Stores 803
Recording Companies 870
Recording Media - Magnetic & Optical 870
Tapes - Video
See Book, Music, Video Clubs 522
Recording Media - Magnetic & Optical 870
Video Stores 937
Tarps, Tents, Covers 907
See also Bags - Textile 511; Sporting Goods 899
Tax Preparation Services 907
Tax Preparation Software
See Business Software (General) 586
Tea
See Coffee & Tea - Whol 665
Coffee & Tea Stores 549
Tea 665
Teachers Organizations
See Education Professionals Associations 493
Labor Unions 753
Technical Ceramics
See Electrical Supplies - Porcelain 642
Technical Schools

See Vocational & Technical Schools 938
Technological Testing
See Testing Facilities 915
Technology Development
See Research Centers & Institutions 871
Technology Newsletters
See Science & Technology Newsletters 807
Technology Transfer
See Research Centers & Institutions 871
Tedders
See Farm Machinery & Equipment - Mfr 652
Farm Machinery & Equipment - Whol 653
Tele-services
See Telemarketing & Other Tele-Services 910
Telecommunications Consulting Services
See Consulting Services - Telecommunications 608
Telecommunications Equipment & Systems 908
See also Modems 579; Radio & Television Broadcasting & Communications Equipment 865
Telecommunications Equipment - Retail
See Appliance & Home Electronics Stores 476
Telecommunications Equipment Distributors
See Electrical & Electronic Equipment & Parts - Whol 639
Telecommunications Services 908
Teleconferencing Systems & Services
See Telecommunications Services 908
Telegraph Equipment
See Electrical & Electronic Equipment & Parts - Whol 639
Telecommunications Equipment & Systems 908
Telemarketing & Other Tele-Services 910
Telemetry Equipment
See Radio & Television Broadcasting & Communications Equipment 865
Telephone Booths
See Fixtures - Office & Store 656
Telephone Equipment - Mfr
See Telecommunications Equipment & Systems 908
Telephone Sales
See Telemarketing & Other Tele-Services 910
Telephone Service
See Telecommunications Services 908
Telephones - Cellular
See Appliance & Home Electronics Stores 476
Telecommunications Equipment & Systems 908
Television "Set-Top Boxes"
See Radio & Television Broadcasting & Communications Equipment 865
Television - Cable
See Cable & Other Pay Television Services 528
Television Networks 910
Television - Satellite
See Cable & Other Pay Television Services 528
Television Broadcasting Equipment
See Radio & Television Broadcasting & Communications Equipment 865
Television Commercials
See Motion Picture Production - Special Interest 796
Television Communications Equipment
See Radio & Television Broadcasting & Communications Equipment 865
Television Companies 910
Television Dealers
See Appliance & Home Electronics Stores 476
Television Monitors - Closed Circuit
See Monitors & Displays 579
Television Networks 910
Television Networks - Broadcast 911
Television Production Companies
See Motion Picture & Television Production 796
Television Program Transcription Services
See Information Retrieval Services (General) 736
Television Sets
See Appliances - Whol 477
Audio & Video Equipment 502
Television Stations 911
See also Internet Broadcasting 747
Albany, NY 911
Albuquerque/Santa Fe, NM 911
Anchorage, AK 911
Asheville, NC/Greenville, SC/Spartanburg, SC 911
Augusta, GA 911
Austin, TX 912
Baltimore, MD 912
Bangor, ME 912
Baton Rouge, LA 912
Billings, MT 912
Birmingham, AL 912
Boise, ID 912
Buffalo, NY 912
Cedar Rapids, IA 912
Charleston, WV 912
Charlotte, NC 912
Cincinnati, OH 912
Cleveland/Akron, OH 912
Columbia, SC 912
Corpus Christi, TX 912
Dallas/Fort Worth, TX 912
Dayton, OH 912
Denver, CO 912
Des Moines, IA 912
Duluth, MN 912
El Paso, TX 912
Erie, PA 912
Evansville, IN 912
Fairbanks, AK 912
Fargo/Grand Forks, ND 913
Fort Smith, AR 913
Fort Wayne, IN 913
Fresno, CA 913
Grand Rapids, MI 913
Green Bay, WI 913
Honolulu, HI 913
Huntsville, AL 913
Indianapolis, IN 913
Johnson City, TN 913
Juneau, AK 913
Kansas City, KS & MO 913
Lansing, MI 913
Lexington, KY 913
Lincoln, NE 913
Little Rock, AR 913
Los Angeles, CA 913
Louisville, KY 913
Miami/Fort Lauderdale, FL 913
Milwaukee, WI 913
Montgomery, AL 913
Naples/Fort Myers, FL 913
Nashville, TN 913
New Orleans, LA 913
New York, NY 913
Norfolk/Virginia Beach, VA 914
Oklahoma City, OK 914
Omaha, NE 914
Orlando, FL 914
Peoria, IL 914
Phoenix, AZ 914
Pittsburgh, PA 914
Pocatello, ID 914
Portland, ME 914
Portland, OR 914
Raleigh/Durham, NC 914
Rapid City, SD 914
Richmond, VA 914
Roanoke, VA 914
Rochester, MN 914
Sacramento, CA 914
Saint Louis, MO 914
Salt Lake City, UT 914
San Antonio, TX 914
San Diego, CA 914
San Francisco, CA 914
Seattle/Tacoma, WA 914
Shreveport, LA 914
Sioux Falls, SD 914
South Bend, IN 915
Spokane, WA 915
Springfield, MA 915
Springfield, MO 915
Syracuse, NY 915
Tallahassee, FL 915
Tampa/Saint Petersburg, FL 915
Topeka, KS 915
Toronto, ON 915
Tulsa, OK 915
Washington, DC 915
Television Syndicators 915
Television Tubes
See Electronic Components & Accessories - Mfr 643
Temperature Controls & Sensing Instruments
See Controls - Temperature - Residential & Commercial 612
Tempering - Metal
See Metal Heat Treating 787
Temples
See Churches, Cathedrals, Synagogues, Temples 501
Temporary Help
See Staffing Services 904
Tennis Equipment & Supplies
See Sporting Goods 899
Tennis Shoes
See Footwear 669
Tents
See Tarps, Tents, Covers 907
Terminal Services - Railroad
See Railroad Switching & Terminal Services 866
Terminal Services - Shipping
See Marine Services 777
Termite Control
See Pest Control Services 829
Terrazzo Products (Precast)
See Concrete Products - Mfr 595
Territorial Governors
See Governors - State 694
Test Kits - Diagnostic
See Diagnostic Products 628
Test Preparation
See Educational Testing Services - Assessment & Preparation 633
Test Preparation Software
See Educational & Reference Software 587
Testing Facilities 915
Testing Instruments
See Electrical Signals Measuring & Testing Instruments 642
Measuring, Testing, Controlling Instruments 780
Testing Laboratories
See Laboratories - Drug-Testing 754
Laboratories - Genetic Testing 754
Laboratories - Medical 754
Testing Services - Educational
See Educational Testing Services - Assessment & Preparation 633
Textile Bags
See Bags - Textile 511
Textile Machinery 916
Textile Mills 916
Broadwoven Fabric Mills 916
Coated Fabric 916
Industrial Fabrics 916
Knitting Mills 917
Narrow Fabric Mills 917
Nonwoven Fabrics 917
Textile Dyeing & Finishing 917
Textile Fiber Processing Mills 917
Yarn & Thread Mills 917
Textile Processing Chemicals
See Chemicals - Specialty 542
Textile Products - Household 917
Textiles - Recyclable
See Textile Fiber Processing Mills 917
Theaters - Broadway 917
See also Performing Arts Facilities 826; Theater Companies 828; Theaters - Resident 918
Theaters - Motion Picture 918
Theaters - Resident 918
See also Performing Arts Facilities 826; Theater Companies 828; Theaters - Broadway 917
Theatrical Equipment & Services
See Stage Equipment & Services 904
Theft Insurance
See Property & Casualty Insurance 743
Theme Parks
See Amusement Park Companies 475
Amusement Parks 475
Therapeutic Drugs - Novel
See Biotechnology Companies 519
Thermal Management Products
See Nonwoven Fabrics 917
Personal Protective Equipment & Clothing 828
Thermal Management Products - Personal 918
Thermal Paper
See Coated & Laminated Paper 819
Thermal Printers

See Printers ... 580
Thermometers
See Controls - Industrial Process ... 611
Controls - Temperature - Residential & Commercial ... 612
Measuring, Testing, Controlling Instruments ... 780
Thermos Bottles
See Plastics Products - Household ... 838
Thermostats
See Controls - Temperature - Residential & Commercial ... 612
Thin Film Circuits
See Semiconductors & Related Devices ... 894
Think Tanks
See Public Policy Research Centers ... 849
Third-Party Logistics Services
See Logistics Services (Transportation & Warehousing) ... 765
Thread
See Fabric Stores ... 651
Piece Goods & Notions ... 834
Yarn & Thread Mills ... 917
Thread Rolling Machines
See Machine Tools - Metal Forming Types ... 768
Threading Tools (Machine Tool Accessories)
See Metalworking Devices & Accessories ... 791
Thrifts
See Banks - Commercial & Savings ... 511
Tick Control Products
See Pet Products ... 829
Ticket Brokers ... 918
Ties
See Neckwear ... 546
Tile - Ceiling
See Insulation & Acoustical Products ... 738
Tile - Ceramic (Wall & Floor) ... 918
Tile - Clay (Structural)
See Clay Products - Structural ... 544
Tile Repair
See Remodeling, Refinishing, Resurfacing Contractors ... 601
Tiles - Roofing (Concrete)
See Concrete Products - Mfr ... 595
Tillage Tools
See Farm Machinery & Equipment - Mfr ... 652
Farm Machinery & Equipment - Whol ... 653
Timber Grading
See Forestry Services ... 670
Timber Tracts ... 918
Timbers - Structural
See Wood Members - Structural ... 944
Timers
See Clocks, Watches, Related Devices, Parts ... 545
Timeshare Companies ... 918
See also Hotels & Hotel Companies 722
Timing Devices
See Controls & Relays - Electrical ... 612
Tin Cans
See Cans - Metal ... 530
Tire Chains
See Safety Equipment - Mfr ... 886
Tire Dealers
See Auto Supply Stores ... 503
Tire Fabrics
See Industrial Fabrics ... 916
Tire Sales & Service
See Repair Service (General) - Automotive ... 509
Tires & Tubes - Whol ... 919
Tires - Mfr ... 919
Tissue Banks
See Organ & Tissue Banks ... 817
Tissue Paper (Decorative)
See Packaging Materials & Products - Paper or Plastics ... 818
Toasters - Electric
See Appliances - Small - Mfr ... 476
Tobacco & Tobacco Products ... 919
Toilet Fixtures
See Plumbing Fixtures & Fittings - Metal ... 839
Plumbing Fixtures & Fittings - Vitreous China & Earthenware ... 840
Toilet Paper
See Paper Products - Sanitary ... 820
Toiletries
See Cosmetics, Skin Care, and Other Personal Care Products 620
Tombstones
See Stone (Cut) & Stone Products ... 905
Tomography Equipment
See Imaging Equipment & Systems - Medical ... 733
Toner Cartridges
See Printing & Photocopying Supplies ... 847
Tool & Die Shops ... 919
Tool Cases
See Luggage, Bags, Cases ... 767
Tools - Cutting
See Metalworking Devices & Accessories ... 791
Tools - Gardening
See Lawn & Garden Equipment ... 758
Tools - Hand & Edge ... 920
See also Lawn & Garden Equipment 758; Metalworking Devices & Accessories 791; Saw Blades & Handsaws 886
Tools - Hydraulic
See Tools - Power ... 921
Tools - Machine
See Machine Tools - Metal Cutting Types ... 767
Machine Tools - Metal Forming Types ... 768
Tools - Pneumatic
See Tools - Power ... 921
Tools - Power ... 921
See also Lawn & Garden Equipment 758; Metalworking Devices & Accessories 791
Tools - Whol
See Hardware - Whol ... 697
Toothbrushes
See Brushes & Brooms ... 525
Torque Converters - Industrial
See Speed Changers, Industrial High Speed Drives, Gears ... 899
Torque Motors
See Motors (Electric) & Generators ... 798
Torsion Springs
See Springs - Light-Gauge ... 903
Tortilla Chips
See Snack Foods ... 664
Tortillas
See Specialty Foods ... 664
Tote Bags
See Handbags, Totes, Backpacks ... 695
Luggage, Bags, Cases ... 767
Touchscreen Systems
See Point-of-Sale (POS) & Point-of-Information (POI) Systems ... 841
Touchscreens
See Computer Input Devices ... 579
Toupees
See Hairpieces, Wigs, Toupees ... 695
Tour Operators ... 921
See also Bus Services - Charter 526; Travel Agencies 925
Tourism Offices - Canadian
See Travel & Tourism Information - Canadian ... 927
Tourist Information
See Convention & Visitors Bureaus ... 614
Travel & Tourism Information - Foreign Travel ... 927
Tow Trucks
See Motor Vehicles - Commercial & Special Purpose ... 797
Towels
See Home Furnishings - Whol ... 706
Textile Products - Household ... 917
Towels - Paper
See Paper Products - Sanitary ... 820
Tower Operators - Communications Towers
See Communications Tower Operators ... 578
Towing Services - Marine
See Marine Services ... 777
Towing Trailers
See Trailers (Towing) & Trailer Hitches ... 923
Toy Stores ... 922
Toys - Pets'
See Pet Products ... 829
Toys, Games, Hobbies ... 922
See also Baby Products 510; Bicycles & Bicycle Parts & Accessories 519; Games & Entertainment Software 588
Trackballs
See Computer Input Devices ... 579
Tractors
See Farm Machinery & Equipment - Mfr ... 652
Farm Machinery & Equipment - Whol ... 653
Lawn & Garden Equipment ... 758
Tractors - Industrial
See Material Handling Equipment ... 779
Tractors - Truck
See Motor Vehicles - Commercial & Special Purpose ... 797
Trade Associations
See Associations & Organizations - Professional & Trade ... 491
Trade Centers
See World Trade Centers ... 945
Trade Schools
See Vocational & Technical Schools ... 938
Trade Show Displays
See Displays - Exhibit & Trade Show ... 629
Trade Show Managers
See Conference & Events Coordinators ... 596
Trade Unions
See Associations & Organizations - Professional & Trade ... 491
Labor Unions ... 753
Trading Cards
See Paperboard & Cardboard - Die-Cut ... 821
Trading Systems - Computerized
See Electronic Communications Networks (ECNs) ... 643
Traffic Signs & Signals
See Signals & Sirens - Electric ... 896
Trailer (Utility) Rental & Leasing
See Truck Rental & Leasing ... 928
Trailers (Towing) & Trailer Hitches ... 923
Trailers - Travel
See Campers, Travel Trailers, Motor Homes ... 529
Trailers - Truck
See Truck Trailers ... 928
Training & Certification Programs - Computer & Internet ... 923
Training Centers - Post-Secondary
See Training Programs (Misc) ... 924
Training Centers for the Developmentally Disabled
See Developmental Centers ... 628
Training Programs (Misc) ... 924
See also Children's Learning Centers 543; Training & Certification Programs - Computer & Internet 923; Training Programs - Corporate 923
Training Programs - Corporate ... 923
Training Programs - Employee
See Training Programs (Misc) ... 924
Training Seminars
See Training Programs - Corporate ... 923
Training Systems
See Simulation & Training Systems ... 897
Trains - Freight
See Rail Transport Services ... 866
Trains - Model
See Toy Stores ... 922
Toys, Games, Hobbies ... 922
Trains - Passenger
See Mass Transportation (Local & Suburban) ... 779
Rail Travel ... 866
Transaction Processing - Electronic
See Electronic Transaction Processing ... 645
Transcription Services (Radio & Television Programs)
See Information Retrieval Services (General) ... 736
Transcription Services - Medical
See Medical Transcription Services ... 785
Transducers
See Electronic Components & Accessories - Mfr ... 643
Transformers - Electronic
See Electronic Components & Accessories - Mfr ... 643
Transformers - Power, Distribution, Specialty ... 924
Transit Systems
See Mass Transportation (Local & Suburban) ... 779
Transit Systems Cars & Equipment
See Railroad Equipment - Mfr ... 866
Translation Services ... 924
See also Language Schools 756
Transmissions - Aircraft
See Aircraft Parts & Auxiliary Equipment ... 473
Transmissions - Automotive
See Automotive Parts & Supplies - Mfr ... 507
Transplant Centers - Blood Stem Cell ... 924
Transport Services - Ambulance (Air or Ground)
See Ambulance Services ... 475
Transport Services - Helicopter
See Helicopter Transport Services ... 700
Transportation - Local (Public Transportation)
See Bus Services - Intercity & Rural ... 526
Mass Transportation (Local & Suburban) ... 779
Transportation - US Department of
See US Department of Transportation ... 692
Transportation Equipment & Supplies - Whol ... 924
Transportation Logistics Services
See Logistics Services (Transportation & Warehousing) ... 765

Index

Transportation Research
See Research Centers & Institutions.... 871
Transportation Tests
See Testing Facilities.... 915
Trash Bags
See Bags - Plastics.... 510
Travel & Tourism Information - Canadian.... 927
Travel & Tourism Information - Foreign Travel.... 927
See also Embassies & Consulates - Foreign, in the US 645
Travel Accessories
See Leather Goods - Personal.... 759
Luggage, Bags, Cases.... 767
Travel Agencies.... 925
See also Tour Operators 921; Travel Agency Networks 926
Travel Agency Networks.... 926
See also Travel Agencies 925
Travel Associations
See Travel & Recreation Organizations.... 491
Travel Consortia
See Travel Agency Networks.... 926
Travel Information - City
See Convention & Visitors Bureaus.... 614
Travel Information - State
See Government - State.... 684
Travel Magazines
See Travel & Regional Interest Magazines.... 773
Travel Newsletters
See General Interest Newsletters.... 806
Travel Plazas
See Gas Stations.... 680
Travel Services - Incentive
See Incentive Program Management Services.... 734
Travel Services - Online.... 927
See also Hotel Reservations Services 720
Travel Trailers
See Campers, Travel Trailers, Motor Homes.... 529
Treasury - US Department of the
See US Department of the Treasury.... 692
Tree Fruits - Deciduous
See Deciduous Tree Fruit Growers.... 675
Tree Services.... 927
See also Landscape Design & Related Services 756
Trees
See Garden Centers.... 680
Horticultural Products Growers.... 708
Timber Tracts.... 918
Trees - Christmas
See Timber Tracts.... 918
Trial Consulting Services
See Litigation Support Services.... 764
Trial Exhibits
See Litigation Support Services.... 764
Trial Graphics Services
See Litigation Support Services.... 764
Tribal Colleges
See Colleges - Tribal.... 557
Tricycles
See Bicycles & Bicycle Parts & Accessories.... 519
Trolley Buses
See Railroad Equipment - Mfr.... 866
Trophies, Plaques, Awards.... 927
Truck Bodies
See Motor Vehicles - Commercial & Special Purpose.... 797
Truck Cabs
See Motor Vehicles - Commercial & Special Purpose.... 797
Truck Conversions
See Van Conversions.... 509
Truck Rental & Leasing.... 928
Truck Repairs
See Automotive Services.... 509
Truck Stops
See Gas Stations.... 680
Truck Trailers.... 928
See also Motor Vehicles - Commercial & Special Purpose 797
Truck Washing
See Appearance Care - Automotive.... 509
Trucking Companies.... 928
See also Logistics Services (Transportation & Warehousing) 765; Moving Companies 798
Trucks - Industrial
See Material Handling Equipment.... 779
Trucks - Pick-Up
See Automobiles - Mfr.... 507
Trunks - Travel
See Luggage, Bags, Cases.... 767
Trusses - Wood
See Wood Members - Structural.... 944
Tube - Metal - Mfr
See Metal Tube & Pipe.... 789
Tube Fittings
See Pipe & Pipe Fittings - Metal (Fabricated).... 834
Tube Mill Machinery
See Rolling Mill Machinery.... 885
Tubes - Electric
See Light Bulbs & Tubes.... 763
Tubes - Electron
See Electronic Components & Accessories - Mfr.... 643
Tubes - Paper
See Cans, Tubes, Drums - Paper (Fiber).... 530
Tugboat Services
See Marine Services.... 777
Tuition Assistance Programs
See Student Assistance Programs.... 905
Tung Oil
See Oil Mills - Cottonseed, Soybean, Other Vegetable Oils.... 664
Tunnel Construction
See Highway, Street, Bridge, Tunnel Construction.... 598
Turkey Farms
See Poultry & Eggs Production.... 470
Turntables
See Audio & Video Equipment.... 502
TV
See Motion Picture & Television Production.... 796
Television Companies.... 910
Television Networks.... 910
Television Networks - Broadcast.... 911
Television Stations.... 911
Television Syndicators.... 915
Twelve-Step Programs
See Self-Help Organizations.... 490
Twine
See Cord & Twine.... 619
Typesetting & Related Services.... 931
See also Graphic Design 694; Printing Companies - Commercial Printers 845
Typesetting Equipment
See Printing & Publishing Equipment & Systems.... 848
Typewriters
See Business Machines - Mfr.... 527
Business Machines - Whol.... 527

U

Ultrasonic Cleaning Equipment.... 931
See also Dental Equipment & Supplies - Mfr 627
Ultrasound Equipment
See Imaging Equipment & Systems - Medical.... 733
Ultraviolet Lamps
See Light Bulbs & Tubes.... 763
Underground Mining
See Mining - Coal.... 793
Undertakers
See Mortuary, Crematory, Cemetery Products & Services.... 796
Underwear
See Undergarments.... 547
Uniforms
See Linen & Uniform Supply.... 764
Uniforms & Work Clothes.... 547
Uninterruptible Power Supplies (UPS)
See Electronic Components & Accessories - Mfr.... 643
Unions
See Labor Unions.... 753
United Nations Agencies, Organizations, Programs.... 931
United Nations Missions.... 931
Universal Joints
See Power Transmission Equipment - Mechanical.... 843
Universities - Canadian.... 932
Universities - US
See Colleges & Universities - Christian.... 558
Colleges & Universities - Four-Year.... 559
Colleges & Universities - Graduate & Professional Schools.... 574
Colleges & Universities - Historically Black.... 577
Colleges & Universities - Jesuit.... 578
Military Service Academies.... 793
University Presses
See Book Publishers - University Presses.... 852
University Systems.... 932
Upholstered Furniture
See Furniture - Mfr.... 676
Upholstery Cleaning Services
See Cleaning Services.... 545
Upholstery Fabric
See Broadwoven Fabric Mills.... 916
Fabric Stores.... 651
Piece Goods & Notions.... 834
UPS (Uninterruptible Power Supplies)
See Electronic Components & Accessories - Mfr.... 643
Urban Development - US Department of Housing &
See US Department of Housing & Urban Development.... 691
Urethane Rubbers
See Synthetic Rubber.... 838
URL Registration
See Internet Domain Name Registrars.... 747
Urns - Cremation
See Caskets & Vaults.... 533
US Congress
See Government - US - Legislative Branch.... 694
US Government
See Government - US - Executive Branch.... 690
Government - US - Judicial Branch.... 693
Government - US - Legislative Branch.... 694
US National Parks
See Parks - National - US.... 821
US Presidents
See Government - US - Executive Branch.... 690
US State Parks
See Parks - State.... 822
US Vice Presidents
See Government - US - Executive Branch.... 690
Utilities Organizations
See Energy & Natural Resources Organizations.... 484
Utilities Software
See Systems & Utilities Software.... 591
Utility Buildings
See Buildings - Prefabricated - Metal.... 525
Utility Commissions
See Government - State.... 684
Utility Companies.... 932
See also Electric Companies - Cooperatives (Rural) 633; Gas Transmission - Natural Gas 680
Utility Trailer Rental & Leasing
See Truck Rental & Leasing.... 928
Utility Trailers
See Trailers (Towing) & Trailer Hitches.... 923
Utility Vehicles
See Motor Vehicles - Commercial & Special Purpose.... 797

V

Vacation Insurance
See Travel Insurance.... 746
Vacation Ownership
See Timeshare Companies.... 918
Vacation Travel
See Travel Agencies.... 925
Vaccines
See Biotechnology Companies.... 519
Vacuum Cleaners - Household.... 934
See also Appliances - Small - Mfr 476
Vacuum Pumps
See Compressors - Air & Gas.... 578
Valves & Hose Fittings - Fluid Power.... 935
See also Carburetors, Pistons, Piston Rings, Valves 530
Valves (Misc)
See Pipe & Pipe Fittings - Metal (Fabricated).... 834
Valves - Aerosol
See Metal Products (Misc).... 788
Valves - Engine
See Carburetors, Pistons, Piston Rings, Valves.... 530
Valves - Industrial.... 934
Valves - Plumbing & Heating
See Pipe & Pipe Fittings - Metal (Fabricated).... 834
Van Lines
See Moving Companies.... 798
Vans - Mfr
See Automobiles - Mfr.... 507

Motor Vehicles - Commercial & Special Purpose 797
Van Conversions 509
Variety Stores 935
Varnishes
See Paints, Varnishes, Related Products 818
Vaults
See Security Products & Services 892
Vaults - Burial
See Caskets & Vaults 533
Vegetable Oils
See Oil Mills - Cottonseed, Soybean, Other Vegetable Oils ...664
Oils - Edible (Margarine, Shortening, Table Oils, etc) 664
Vegetables
See Fruits & Vegetables - Dried or Dehydrated 661
Fruits & Vegetables - Fresh - Whol 666
Fruits & Vegetables - Pickled 661
Fruits, Vegetables, Juices - Canned or Preserved 661
Fruits, Vegetables, Juices - Frozen 662
Vegetable Farms 470
Vehicle Parts & Supplies
See Automotive Parts & Supplies - Mfr 507
Automotive Parts & Supplies - Whol 508
Vehicle Testing
See Testing Facilities 915
Vehicles - Amphibious & Combat
See Weapons & Ordnance (Military) 942
Vehicles - Motor
See All-Terrain Vehicles 475
Automobiles - Mfr 507
Motor Vehicles - Commercial & Special Purpose 797
Motorcycles & Motorcycle Parts & Accessories 798
Snowmobiles 897
Vehicular Lighting Equipment
See Lighting Equipment - Vehicular 763
Velour
See Broadwoven Fabric Mills 916
Velvet
See Broadwoven Fabric Mills 916
Vending Machines
See Automatic Merchandising Equipment & Systems 504
Food Service 669
Veneers - Wood
See Plywood & Veneers 841
Ventilation Equipment
See Air Conditioning & Heating Equipment - Commercial/ Industrial 471
Air Conditioning & Heating Equipment - Residential 472
Venture Capital Firms 936
Vestments
See Robes (Ceremonial) 546
Veterans Affairs - US Department of
See US Department of Veterans Affairs 692
Veterans Agencies - State
See Government - State 684
Veterans Associations
See Military, Veterans, Patriotic Organizations 488
Veterans Nursing Homes - State 936
See also Veterans Hospitals 720
Veterinary Hospitals 936
Veterinary Insurance
See Animal Insurance 740
Veterinary Medical Associations - State 936
Veterinary Pharmaceutical & Diagnostic Products
See Pharmaceutical & Diagnostic Products - Veterinary 831
Veterinary Sciences Research
See Research Centers & Institutions 871
Viatical Settlement Companies 937
Vibration Monitors
See Measuring, Testing, Controlling Instruments 780
Vice Presidents - US
See Government - US - Executive Branch 690
Video Arcades
See Recreation Facility Operators 870
Video Cards & Boards
See Multimedia Equipment & Supplies 580
Video Clubs
See Book, Music, Video Clubs 522
Video Distributors
See Motion Picture Distribution & Related Services 796
Video Duplication
See Duplication & Replication Services 632
Video Editing Equipment
See Multimedia Equipment & Supplies 580
Video Equipment
See Audio & Video Equipment 502
Video Games & Players
See Toy Stores 922
Video Stores 937
Video Production Companies
See Motion Picture & Television Production 796
Motion Picture Production - Special Interest 796
Video Recorders
See Audio & Video Equipment 502
Video Rental
See Video Stores 937
Video Stores 937
See also Book, Music, Video Clubs 522
Video Walls
See Monitors & Displays 579
Videoconferencing Systems & Services
See Telecommunications Services 908
Videography - Legal
See Litigation Support Services 764
Vineyards
See Grape Vineyards 675
Wines - Mfr 518
Vinyl Doors & Windows
See Doors & Windows - Vinyl 630
Vinyl Flooring
See Flooring - Resilient 657
Vinyl Repair - Automotive
See Appearance Care - Automotive 509
Vinyl Resins
See Synthetic Resins & Plastics Materials 837
Vinyl-Coated Fabric
See Coated Fabric 916
Virology Diagnostic Products
See Diagnostic Products 628
Virtual Communities
See Communities - Online 578
Vision Correction Centers 937
Vision Insurance
See Medical & Hospitalization Insurance 741
Vision Products
See Ophthalmic Goods 816
Optical Goods Stores 816
Visitor Information
See Convention & Visitors Bureaus 614
Visual Basic Software
See Computer Languages & Development Tools 587
Vital Records Offices
See Government - State 684
Vitamins & Nutritional Supplements 937
See also Diet & Health Foods 660; Medicinal Chemicals & Botanical Products 786; Pharmaceutical Companies 831; Pharmaceutical Companies - Generic Drugs 832
Vitamins & Nutritional Supplements - Retail
See Drug Stores 631
Health Food Stores 699
Vitreous China
See Plumbing Fixtures & Fittings - Vitreous China & Earthenware 840
Vocational & Technical Schools 938
See also Children's Learning Centers 543; Colleges - Community & Junior 550; Colleges - Culinary Arts 557; Colleges - Fine Arts 557; Colleges & Universities - Four-Year 559; Language Schools 756; Military Service Academies 793; Universities - Canadian 932
Vocational Rehabilitation Agencies
See Government - State 684
Voice Identification Equipment
See Biometric Identification Equipment & Software 519
Voice Mail Services
See Telecommunications Services 908
Voice Mail Systems
See Telecommunications Equipment & Systems 908
Voice Portals
See Portals - Voice 842
Voice Recognition Software
See Internet & Communications Software 588
Systems & Utilities Software 591
Voting Systems & Software 941
Vulcanization
See Synthetic Rubber 838

W

Wafers - Silicon
See Semiconductors & Related Devices 894
Wagering Facilities
See Casinos 532
Games & Gaming 680
Walkways - Moving
See Elevators, Escalators, Moving Walkways 645
Wallboard
See Gypsum Products 695
Wood Products - Reconstituted 944
Wallcoverings 941
Wallets
See Leather Goods - Personal 759
Wallpaper Hangers & Removers
See Painting & Paperhanging Contractors 600
Wallpapering Supplies
See Home Improvement Centers 707
Walnuts
See Tree Nuts Growers 470
WANs (Wide Area Networks)
See Computer Networking Products & Systems 582
Warehouse Logistics Services
See Logistics Services (Transportation & Warehousing) 765
Warehouse Stores
See Wholesale Clubs 943
Warehousing & Storage 941
See also Logistics Services (Transportation & Warehousing) 765
Commercial Warehousing 941
Refrigerated Storage 941
Self-Storage Facilities 941
Warehousing & Storage - Petroleum
See Petroleum Storage Terminals 831
Warfare Simulators
See Simulation & Training Systems 897
Warmers - Hand, Foot, Body
See Thermal Management Products - Personal 918
Warp Knit Fabrics
See Knitting Mills 917
Washed Sand
See Sand & Gravel Pits 794
Washers
See Fasteners & Fastening Systems 654
Hardware - Whol 697
Washing Machines - Commercial
See Laundry Equipment & Supplies - Commercial & Industrial 756
Washing Machines - Household
See Appliance & Home Electronics Stores 476
Appliances - Major - Mfr 476
Appliances - Whol 477
Waste Baskets - Metal
See Metal Products (Misc) 788
Waste Disposal
See Consulting Services - Environmental 604
Recyclable Materials Recovery 870
Waste Management 941
Waste Disposal Trailers
See Truck Trailers 928
Waste Management 941
See also Recyclable Materials Recovery 870; Remediation Services 871
Waste Materials
See Scrap Metal 889
Waste Recovery - Fiber
See Textile Fiber Processing Mills 917
Wastewater Plant Construction
See Plant Construction 599
Watchbands - Leather
See Leather Goods - Personal 759
Watches - Mfr
See Clocks, Watches, Related Devices, Parts 545
Watches - Retail
See Jewelry Stores 752
Watches - Whol
See Jewelry, Watches, Gems - Whol 752
Water - Bottled 941
Water - Carbonated
See Soft Drinks - Mfr 518
Water Heaters
See Appliances - Major - Mfr 476
Appliances - Whol 477

Index

Water Lines Construction
See Water & Sewer Lines, Pipelines, Power Lines Construction....599
Water Pumps
See Pumps & Pumping Equipment (General Use).... 856
Water Sports Equipment & Supplies
See Sporting Goods.... 899
Water Supply
See Utility Companies.... 932
Water Treatment & Filtration Products & Equipment.. 941
Water Treatment Plants
See Plant Construction....599
Water Treatment Products
See Chemicals - Specialty.... 542
Wax - Sealing
See Adhesives & Sealants.... 466
Weapons & Ordnance (Military).... 942
See also Firearms & Ammunition (Non-Military) 655; Missiles, Space Vehicles, Parts 794; Simulation & Training Systems 897
Weapons Testing
See Testing Facilities.... 915
Weapons Training
See Simulation & Training Systems.... 897
Weather Instruments
See Measuring, Testing, Controlling Instruments.... 780
Weather Stripping - Metal
See Doors & Windows - Metal.... 630
Weather Stripping - Wood
See Millwork.... 793
Web Authoring Tools
See Internet & Communications Software....588
Web Hosting Services.... 942
See also Internet Service Providers (ISPs) 748
Web Site Administration Software
See Internet & Communications Software....588
Web Site Design Services.... 942
See also Advertising Agencies 466; Advertising Services - Online 468; Computer Systems Design Services 592
Web Site Development Software
See Internet & Communications Software....588
Web TV Systems
See Radio & Television Broadcasting & Communications Equipment.... 865
Webcam Companies
See Child Care Monitoring Systems - Internet.... 543
Weft Knit Fabrics
See Knitting Mills....917
Weight Lifting Equipment
See Exercise & Fitness Equipment.... 651
Weight Loss Centers & Services.... 942
See also Health & Fitness Centers 698; Spas - Health & Fitness 897
Weights & Measures Offices
See Government - State.... 684
Welding & Soldering Equipment.... 942
Welding Repair
See Machine Shops.... 767
Well Drilling
See Oil & Gas Well Drilling.... 815
Water Well Drilling....602
Western Boots
See Footwear.... 669
Western Hats
See Hats & Caps....546
Wet Corn Milling
See Grain Mill Products....662
Wheat
See Grain Farms....469
Wheelchairs
See Medical Supplies - Mfr.... 784
Whirlpool Baths
See Hot Tubs, Spas, Whirlpool Baths.... 720
Wholesale Clubs.... 943
Wholesalers Associations
See Consumer Sales & Service Professionals Associations...492
Sales & Marketing Professional Associations....499
Wicker Furniture
See Furniture - Mfr.... 676
Wide Area Networks
See Computer Networking Products & Systems.... 582
Wigs
See Hairpieces, Wigs, Toupees.... 695
Wildlife Parks
See Zoos & Wildlife Parks.... 945
Wildlife Sanctuaries
See Nature Centers, Parks, Other Natural Areas....501
Winches
See Construction Machinery & Equipment.... 602
Wind Machines
See Farm Machinery & Equipment - Mfr.... 652
Farm Machinery & Equipment - Whol.... 653
Window Blinds & Shades
See Blinds & Shades.... 520
Window Dressings
See Blinds & Shades.... 520
Textile Products - Household.... 917
Window Frames & Sash - Metal
See Doors & Windows - Metal.... 630
Window Frames & Sash - Vinyl
See Doors & Windows - Vinyl.... 630
Window Frames & Sash - Wood
See Doors & Windows - Wood.... 630
Window Glass
See Glass - Flat, Plate, Tempered.... 681
Window Replacement - Vehicular
See Glass Replacement - Automotive....509
Window Screens
See Screening - Woven Wire.... 890
Window Shutters
See Shutters - Window (All Types).... 896
Windshield Repair - Automotive
See Glass Replacement - Automotive....509
Wine Stores
See Liquor Stores.... 764
Winter Traction Products
See Safety Equipment - Mfr.... 886
Wiping Cloths
See Mops, Sponges, Wiping Cloths.... 795
Wire & Cable.... 943
Wire & Cable - Electronic.... 943
Wire & Cable Harness Assemblies
See Electronic Components & Accessories - Mfr.... 643
Wire Baskets
See Baskets, Cages, Racks, etc - Wire.... 516
Wire Cages
See Baskets, Cages, Racks, etc - Wire.... 516
Wire Cloth
See Screening - Woven Wire.... 890
Wire Guards
See Baskets, Cages, Racks, etc - Wire.... 516
Wire Mesh
See Screening - Woven Wire.... 890
Wire Racks
See Baskets, Cages, Racks, etc - Wire.... 516
Wire Screens
See Screening - Woven Wire.... 890
Wire Services
See News Syndicates, Services, Bureaus.... 805
Wire Springs
See Springs - Light-Gauge.... 903
Wireless Cable Television Systems
See Cable & Other Pay Television Services.... 528
Wireless Communications Equipment
See Appliance & Home Electronics Stores.... 476
Telecommunications Equipment & Systems.... 908
Wireless Communications Services
See Telecommunications Services.... 908
Wireless Communications Towers
See Communications Tower Operators.... 578
Wireless Data
See Data Communications Services for Wireless Devices... 624
Wireless Devices - Data Communications Services for
See Data Communications Services for Wireless Devices... 624
Wireless Modems
See Modems....579
Wiring Devices - Current-Carrying.... 943
Wiring Devices - Noncurrent-Carrying.... 944
WNBA
See Women's National Basketball Association (WNBA)......902
Women's Colleges
See Colleges - Women's (Four-Year).... 558
Wood Boxes
See Containers - Wood.... 611
Wood Buildings - Prefabricated
See Buildings - Prefabricated - Wood.... 525
Wood Chemicals
See Chemicals - Industrial (Organic).... 541
Wood Containers
See Containers - Wood.... 611
Wood Doors & Windows
See Doors & Windows - Wood.... 630
Wood Fences
See Fences - Mfr.... 654
Wood Flooring
See Sawmills & Planing Mills.... 887
Wood Furniture
See Cabinets - Wood.... 528
Furniture - Mfr.... 676
Wood Members - Structural.... 944
Wood Paneling
See Home Improvement Centers.... 707
Lumber & Building Supplies....603
Plywood & Veneers.... 841
Sawmills & Planing Mills.... 887
Wood Preserving.... 944
Wood Products - Reconstituted.... 944
Wood Products - Shaped & Turned.... 945
Wood Stains
See Paints, Varnishes, Related Products.... 818
Wood Veneers
See Plywood & Veneers.... 841
Woodwork (Interior)
See Millwork.... 793
Woodworking Machinery.... 945
Wool
See Broadwoven Fabric Mills....916
Wool Scouring
See Textile Fiber Processing Mills....917
Worcestershire Sauce
See Fruits & Vegetables - Pickled....661
Work Clothes
See Linen & Uniform Supply.... 764
Uniforms & Work Clothes....547
Worker's Compensation Insurance
See Property & Casualty Insurance....743
World Trade Centers.... 945
Wound Care Centers
See Health Care Providers - Ancillary.... 697
Wrapping Paper
See Coated & Laminated Paper....819

X

X-Ray Film & Plates
See Imaging Equipment & Systems - Medical.... 733

Y

Yachting Magazines
See Boating Magazines....769
Yachts
See Boats - Recreational.... 521
Yard Goods
See Fabric Stores.... 651
Piece Goods & Notions.... 834
Yard Tools
See Lawn & Garden Equipment.... 758
Yarn
See Fabric Stores.... 651
Piece Goods & Notions.... 834
Yarn & Thread Mills....917
Yogurt
See Dairy Products - Whol....666
Milk & Cream Products....663
Yogurt - Frozen
See Ice Cream & Frozen Desserts....662
Youth Magazines
See Children's & Youth Magazines....769
Youth Tours
See Tour Operators.... 921

Z

Zinc Castings
See Foundries - Nonferrous (Castings).... 671

Zinc Mining
See Mining - Metals 793
Zippers
See Piece Goods & Notions 834
Zoos & Wildlife Parks 945
See also Aquariums - Public 477; Botanical Gardens & Arboreta 523